BRB's Guide to

County
Court
Records

A National Resource to
Criminal, Civil, and Probate Records
Found at the Nation's
County, Parish, and Municipal Courts

Complied by BRB Publications, Inc.

Edited by Michael Sankey

Facts ON DEMAND PRESS

BRB's Guide to County Court Records
A National Resource to Criminal, Civil, and Probate Records Found at the Nation's County, Parish, and Municipal Courts

Edited by Michael Sankey
Cover by Robin Fox & Associates
First Edition

©2011 by Facts on Demand Press *and* BRB Publications, Inc.
PO Box 27869
Tempe, AZ 85285
800-929-3811   Fax 800-929-4981

www.brbpublications.com

Publisher's Cataloging-in-Publication
(Provided by Quality Books, Inc.)

> BRB's guide to county court records : a national resource
> to criminal, civil, and probate records found at the
> nation's county, parish, and municipal courts / compiled
> by BRB Publications, Inc. ; edited by Michael Sankey. --
> 1st ed.
>   p. cm.
>   ISBN-13: 978-1-889150-57-4
>   ISBN-10: 1-889150-57-6
>
>   1. Public records--United States--States--
> Directories. 2. Court records--United States--States--
> Directories. 3. Cities and towns--United States--
> Directories.   I. Sankey, Michael L., 1949- II. BRB
> Publications.
>
> JK468.P76B73 2011   352.3'87'02573
>   QBI11-600158

Contents

Introduction

What This Guide is About

The purpose of this publication is to provide quick yet detailed access information to more than 8,300 courts that have jurisdiction over significant criminal and civil cases under state or local law.

We have included every state felony court, larger claim civil courts, and probate court in the US. Since most courts have jurisdiction over a number of categories of cases, there are also thousands of courts profiled herein that hear misdemeanors, evictions, small claims cases, etc. In addition, the **State Introductions** summarize where other major categories-DUI, preliminary hearings, and juvenile cases-can be found.

The term County Courts, as used in this book, refers to those courts within each state's court system that handle:

• Felonies	Generally defined as crimes punishable by one year or more of jail time
• Civil Action	For money damages or judgments greater than $3,000
• Probate	Estate matters
• Misdemeanors	Generally defined as minor infractions with a fine or minimal jail time
• Evictions	Landlord tenant actions
• Small Claims	Actions for small damages generally under $3,000
• Domestic	Often referred to as *Domestic Relations or Family Law*, can include family matters, divorce, abuse, etc.
• Juvenile	Actions of youth, usually under 18.
• Ordinance	Violations of local city, town, or village laws

Applications

The Guide to County Court Records is especially useful for four kinds of applications-

1. General litigation searching/background investigations.
2. Pre-employment background screening...Included is full coverage of local criminal courts at the felony level, and many misdemeanor courts as well.
3. Tenant background screening...Courts where landlord/tenant cases are filed are shown in the state introduction charts, and most of the courts are profiled herein.
4. Asset/Lien searching...Civil court cases often lead to liens recorded on assets, probate courts that have records of wills and estate matters that can be used to determine assets, related parties, and even addresses.

We are proud to present, at your fingertips, the results of many man hours of research and compilations. With the acquired facts in this book, you are on your way to becoming an expert in County Court Records!

The Research Staff at Facts on Demand Press/BRB Publications

Lynn Beshara, Kenna Garinger, Annette Jackson,
Peter Weber, William White, and Michael Sankey
September 2011

This Book is
Dedicated to the Memory of
Carl Ernst

How to Use This Book

First - Let's Define What We Mean by County

In Louisiana the word Parish is equivalent to what is a county in another state. Alaska is organized by Boroughs. In Colorado, Missouri, and Virginia a city may have the same jurisdictional authority of a county. Rather than continually restate these facts, **assume when the text is speaking of county courts that these other courts are included**.

How to Read the State Summary Pages

The beginning of each state section has a unique series of tables and information charts that together provide condensed overview of the court structure, jurisdiction, fees, record searching procedures and online access suggestions. The upper portion indicates basic information such as the state's web page, number of counties (or parishes or boroughs).

Court Administration and the Appellate Courts

Every state has an administrator of courts that manages the state court systems. Usually known as the Office of Court Administration or similar, this agency is an excellent resource for questions regarding court procedures in the state. Contact and web information is provided.

There is also a review of the state's Appellate Courts with the necessary web links to view opinions or appellate cases. All states have a upper appellate court, usually called the Supreme Court, and 40 states have an intermediate appellate division as well.

Court Structure

This portion provides information what types of cases each court hears. Where more than one court has jurisdiction for a particular kind of civil case, the minimum and maximum claim fields clarify whether there is overlapping jurisdiction in the state.

Although these charts admittedly oversimplify complex sets of state statues, their purpose is to provide you with a practical starting point to help you decide where to search for case records. When you cannot make a determination to your satisfaction where to search, we suggest you contact the administrator of courts for that state.

Do not assume that the structure of the court system in the nearest state to yours is anything like your home state. In one state, the Circuit Court maybe the highest trial court and in another it is a limited jurisdiction court.

Search Tips and Fees

This is a very useful section - do not overlook the many helpful searching tips presented here. In this section one can learn when certain statewide court record search programs for the public are in place, see New York, South Dakota and Mississippi for example.

This section indicates when a state has pre-set fees for copies, record certification, and record searches OR gives guidance when there are statewide characteristics for fees or procedures in a state.

Overview of Online Access

The court administrator's office in 30 states provides an online search system for court records. You will learn that the type of service varies greatly from state to state. Some online systems are statewide, some are only civil or only criminal, some are free, and some work on a subscription or pay basis. The level of identifiers shown in the resulting index or record will vary as well.

This section provides cautionary suggestions when these online searches should only be used as supplemental searches for those users who require extreme due diligence.

How to Read the Court Profiles

3,155 counties (parishes, town, cities, etc., where applicable) are headlined in alphabetical order within each state. If a county has more than one court profiled, the courts appear in order from court of general jurisdiction down to more limited jurisdictions. Civil courts are listed before criminal courts if a level of court has divisions. Where more than one court of the same type is located in a county, they are listed in order of the name of the city where they are located. The first line shows the types of records held by the court.

All city/Zip Code combinations have been verified against our County Court Locator for accuracy. In addition to the address and telephone, the time zone is indicated. Fax numbers are given for most courts, as are hours of operation and the home web page.

There are three sections for each court profile.

1. General Information

The General Information includes comments on the following court characteristics—

- If the court covers a certain geographic region or helpful historical facts, such as if courts have been combined or closed, or other special notes pertaining only to a specific court.
- When records that are restricted from access.
- If the identifiers on public access computer terminals are the same as shown online if available.
- Fees for copies by court or if self serve, certification, and for faxing documents.
- Type of funds accepted (personal or business checks); if credit cards accepted and if surcharges are imposed; and who the Payee is.
- If mail requests require a self-addressed stamped envelope (SASE).

2. Civil Name Search

The first item noted are the access methods (phone fax, mail, in-person, online) that a court accepts for name searches and required fees. **If noted that the court does not perform an in-person search (and visitors must do their own search), then a search fee is not applicable.**

Other information shown, when applicable includes—

- If the court offers a public access computer terminal **(PAT)** that the public can use to look-up a name to find a case number. In the event that in-person searching is offered, we indicate when only court personnel do name look-up and when the court permits the public to do its own lookup.
- The year when the computer indexing starts and how the records are organized (books, microfilm, etc.) prior to computerization or if not computerized at all.
- The fee a court charges to do a name search, if at all.
- The turnaround time for mail requests (not including the mailing time).
- Detail on online access if offered, or a referral statement to the front of the state for a full explanation.
- **SASE** = Self Addressed, Stamped Envelope required.

3. Criminal Name Search

The profile for the criminal name search is nearly identical as described above for civil searches. The profile will show if additional information is needed if there are any name search requirements beyond merely supplying the name – such as if the date of birth (DOB) is needed.

About The Smaller Limited Courts: Probate, Local, and Minor Specialty Courts

There are a number of small, limited jurisdiction courts and specialty courts listed that are not frequently searched. These include City, Municipal, Town, County, and Village courts. Also, if probate is handled by a separate court clerk, this agency also has a separate listing. If the need arises to call one of these courts, be sure to make note of the hours and days open, as they can vary dramatically.

Court Record Searching Primer

Court records are perhaps the most widely sought public record in the U.S. However researching court records can be very complicated because of the extensive diversity of the courts and their record keeping systems. Courts exist at four levels: federal, state, county (or parish), and local municipalities. All four levels can be found within the same county.

Before searching an index of court records you should first familiarize yourself with basic court structures and procedures. And an important first step in determining where a court case is located is to know how the structure of the court system operates in that particular state.

How the States' Courts Operate

Each state has its own court system, created by statutes or constitution to enforce state civil and criminal laws. Sometimes the terms "state court" and "county court" can be a source of confusion because state trial courts are located at county courthouses. In this book we refer to state courts as the courts belonging to the state court systems, and county courts as those administered by county authority. Local municipal courts can be managed by the local city, town or village government whose laws they enforce. Some lower level courts are called justice courts.

The general structure of all state court systems has four tiers:

1. Appellate Courts
2. Intermediate Appellate Courts
3. General Jurisdiction Trial Courts
4. Limited Jurisdiction Trial Courts

The two highest levels, **appellate** and **intermediate appellate** courts, only hear cases on appeal from the trial courts. "Opinions" of these appellate courts are of particular interest to attorneys seeking legal precedents for newer cases. However, opinions can be useful to record searchers because they summarize facts about the case that will not show on an index or docket.

General jurisdiction trial courts oversee a full range of civil and criminal litigation, usually handling felonies and higher dollar civil cases. The general jurisdiction courts often serve as the appellate courts for cases appealed from limited jurisdiction courts and even from the local courts. Court researchers often refer to general jurisdiction courts as upper courts.

Limited jurisdiction trial courts come in several varieties. Many limited jurisdiction courts handle smaller civil claims (usually no higher than $10,000), misdemeanors, and pretrial hearings for felonies. Localized municipal courts are also referred to as courts of limited jurisdiction. Many court researchers refer to limited jurisdiction courts as lower courts.

A number of states, Iowa for instance, have consolidated their general and limited court structure into one combined court system.

Some courts – sometimes called *special jurisdiction courts* – have general jurisdiction but are limited to one type of litigation. An example is the Court of Claims in New York which only processes liability cases against the state.

▶ Searching Tip: Watch for Divisions and Name Variations

The structure of the court system and the names used for courts often vary widely from state-to-state. Civil and criminal records may be handled by different divisions within a court or sometimes by completely different courts with different names. For example, in Tennessee the Chancery Court oversees civil cases but criminal cases are tried in Circuit Courts, except in districts with separate Criminal Courts as established by the state legislature. Also, in one state, the Circuit Court may be the highest trial court whereas in another it is a limited jurisdiction court. In New York, the Supreme Court is not very "supreme" and the downstate court structure varies from counties upstate.

The Localized Courts: County, Municipal, Town, and Village

Localized courts preside over misdemeanors, infractions, and city ordinance violations at the county, city, town or township level. Sometimes these courts are known as *Justice Courts*. While state courts are operated at the county level, many states have lower jurisdiction county-based courts that are funded and managed by the county, not the state. The term *county courts* may be confusing in this context. A key point to keep in mind is the records from the local courts may not appear on the state's case management system. So, if your record searching needs call for a search of all civil or criminal records in a county you will have to search the local courts separately.

The Types of Court Records That Can be Searched

Below is a list of types of court cases and records found at the state or local level. Note that bankruptcies are not found on this list because bankruptcy cases are filed at the federal level.

- **Civil Actions** – For money damages usually greater than $5,000. Also, some states have designated dollar amount thresholds for upper or lower (limited) civil courts. Most civil litigation involves torts or contracts.

- **Small Claims** – Actions for minor money damages, generally at $5,000 or less, no juries involved.

- **Criminal Felonies** – Generally defined as crimes punishable by one year or more of jail time. There can be multiple levels or classes.

- **Criminal Misdemeanors** – Generally defined as minor infractions with a fine and less than one year of jail time. Misdemeanors also have multiple levels or classes.

- **Probate** – Estate matters, settling the estate of a deceased person, resolving claims and distributing the decedent's property. Sometimes if a probate action is contested, the case is moved from the Probate Court to a Civil Court.

- **Eviction Actions** – Landlord/tenant actions, can also known as an unlawful detainer, forcible detainer, summary possession, or repossession.

- **Domestic Relations** – Sometimes known as Family Law, with authority over family disputes, divorces, dissolutions, child support or custody cases.

- **Juvenile** – Authority over cases involving individuals under a specified age, usually 18 years but sometimes 21.

- **Traffic** – May also have authority over municipal ordinances.

- **Specialty Courts** – Water, equity in fiduciary questions, tort, contracts, tax, etc.

More about Civil Court Cases

A **civil case** usually commences when a plaintiff files a complaint with a court against defendants. The defendants respond to the complaint with an answer. After this initial round, there may be literally hundreds of activities before the court issues a judgment. These activities can include revised complaints and their answers, motions of various kinds, discovery proceedings (including depositions) to establish the documentation and facts involved in the case. All of these activities are listed on a *docket sheet*, which may be a piece of paper or a computerized index.

Once a civil court issues a judgment, either party may appeal the ruling to an appellate division or court. In the case of a money judgment, the winning side can usually file it as a judgment lien with the county recorder. Appellate divisions usually deal only with legal issues and not the facts of the case.

About Judgments

When a judgment is rendered in court, the winning party usually files and records a lien notice (called an Abstract of Judgment in many states) against real estate owned by the defendant or party against whom the judgment is given. Sometimes judgments can be used to garnish wages or can be placed on bank accounts.

Judgments can be searched at the local or county level usually in the same index as real estate records. Many times judgments are bought and sold as commodities. An Assignment of Judgment is the transfer of the title and interest in a judgment from one person to another person.

One common problem when searching civil records is that they often show very few, if any, personal identifiers on the index or case files. Sometimes extensive research is required to properly determine the identity of a person subject of a search. See *The Use of Identifiers and Redaction* later in this chapter.

▶ **Searching Tip: Watch for Overlapping Jurisdictions.** In some states, the general jurisdiction court and the limited jurisdiction court have overlapping dollar amounts for civil cases. That means a case could be filed in either court. Check both courts; never assume.

More about Criminal Court Cases

In a **criminal case**, the plaintiff is a government jurisdiction. The government brings the action against the defendant for violation of one or more of its statutes. The term **disposition** is frequently used when discussing or searching criminal records. A disposition is the final outcome of a criminal court case. A disposition is an important piece of information on a criminal record or record index, along with the defendant's name, some type of personal identifier, the charge, and the case number. This is also a key term when legal use of records is governed by state laws and the federal FCRA (Fair Credit Reporting Act). The information that *could be* disclosed on a criminal record includes the arrest record, criminal charges, fines, sentencing and incarceration information.

Criminal court records are eventually submitted to a central repository controlled by a state agency such as the State Police or Department of Public Safety. See **Other Resources: State Criminal Record Repositories** later in this chapter.

There is a huge difference on the record access procedures between the state repositories and the courts. Records maintained by the court are generally open to the public, but not all state criminal record repositories open their criminal records to the public.

The Record Searching Paradox

Adding to the mystique of court records is the searching paradox. For example, in some states or counties the methods of access or types of records may be severely restricted, while the same records may be easy to view and obtain in the next county or state. For example, some Justice Courts in Arizona charge $24 to first determine if a person/subject has a case file and then charge another $24 to allow the public to view the file. The Justice Court in the next town or county may provide a public access terminal to first determine if a file exists, and if provided with a case file number will provide the file to view for no charge.

The allowable record searching access methods can vary greatly as well. One court may offer searching by phone, fax and mail, while a court in the next county may provide search services only to those who physically visit the court house. Perhaps one of the most inconsistencies among counties is if the court records or indices are searchable online. With the widespread use of the web, one would think all records are online. But in reality, just over 62% of the courts holding felony records provide online.

The text in the box printed below is significant. We are not trying to fill up space. As your court record searching takes you from county-to-county or from state-to-state, this is the one important truth to keep in mind.

> "Just because court records are accessed in a certain way in your state or county, do not assume that any other county or state does things the same way."

How Courts Maintain Records

Understanding Case Numbering and Indexing is Important

When a case is filed, a case number is assigned. Using a case number is the primary indexing method in every court. Therefore, to search specific case file documents, you will need to first know – or find – the applicable case number.

Be aware that case numbering procedures are not necessarily consistent throughout a state court system. One district may assign numbers by district while another may assign numbers by location (division) within the district, or by judge. Remember: case numbers appearing in legal text citations may not be adequate for searching unless they appear in the proper form for the particular court in which you are searching.

If you are searching an index of court records, then you are searching what is called the *docket*.

The Docket Sheet – A Key Information Resource

Information from cover sheets and from documents filed as a case goes forward is recorded on the docket sheet. Thus the docket sheet is a running summary of a case history from initial filing to its current status. While docket sheets differ somewhat in format from court to court, the basic information contained on a docket sheet is consistent. All docket sheets contain:

- Name of court, including location (division) and the judge assigned;
- Case number and case name;
- Names of all plaintiffs and defendants/debtors;
- Names and addresses of attorneys for the plaintiff or debtor;
- Nature and cause (e.g., statute) of action.

When a case is decided, a decision or disposition is rendered and entered onto the docket index. Most courts enter the docket data into a computer system. Within a state or judicial district, the courts may be linked together via a single computer system. A record index can be organized in a variety of ways – by name, by year, by case or file number, or by name and year. Depending on the type of public record, an alpha index could be by plaintiff and/or defendant, by grantor and/or grantee, by address, etc.

But docket sheets from cases closed before the advent of computerization may not be in the computer system. And in some locations all docket information is non-computerized. Other media formats include microfilm, microfiche, index cards, and paper that may even be hand-written.

▶ **Searching Tip: Know what you are searching.** The primary search that courts provide is a search of the docket index. When someone tells you *I can view xxx county court records online* this person is most likely talking about searching an index summary of records and not about the all documents and pages maintained within a case history file.

Dispositions, Expungments, and Sealed Records

There are some cases where decisions were rendered, but the results are not recorded or the case file number is removed from the index. In certain situations, a judge can order the case file sealed or removed – expunged – from the public repository. Examples include if a defendant enters a diversion program (drug or family counseling), or a defendant makes restitution as part of a plea bargain; these cases may not be searchable. The only way to gain direct access to these types of case filings is through a subpoena. However, savvy researchers and investigators will sometimes search news media sources if need be.

The Difference Between a Name Search and a Document Request

There is a significant difference between searching an index to determine if a public record exists versus viewing an image or obtaining copies of documents in the record file.

Name Searching

Let us say you wish to determine if an individual has a criminal record or if an individual has collateralized certain assets such as a real estate holding or ownership of equipment used in a business.

The best way to perform this research is to do a "name search" – also known as an "alpha search" – of an index at the government agency that holds the records.

However, name searching is not always an easy task. An index may or may not contain helpful identifiers such as a middle initial or a date of birth to distinguish the subject or person of your search versus other people who have the same name. Due to privacy concerns, most indices no longer show the full or even a partial Social Security Number. Since many agencies withhold personal identifiers from appearing on the web, using their Internet site to perform a name search has lesser value overall and is often merely a supplemental or 'verifying' search.

Another consideration when performing name searches is to watch for the incorrect spelling or variation of the name. There can be typos in the index. Records could be filed under a variation of a first name – Ted vs. Theodore, Robert vs. Bob, Deborah vs. Debra vs. Debbie, etc. Knowing how to maneuver through an agency's index, be it on-site or online, is quite important and an aid to the serious investigator.

Requesting a Specific Document

When you know the "document number" or exact location of a record you are able to request a specific case file. It now becomes much easier to view or obtain a copy. When you provide the exact document number, then a 'search' per se is not part of the record retrieval process and you usually save a search fee charge. If you are requesting a specific document in person or by mail, the government personnel are much more apt to help compared to asking them to do a name search first.

When using a government web page to search for a specific document it is often easier when you have the document number or an identifier, like the court docket number.

The Use of Identifiers and Redaction

As mentioned, identifiers are important to record searching. They serve two different although related purposes.

1. *First*, the identifiers of the subject must be used to analyze a public record for the purpose of determining if the record is about that subject. Perhaps the records are indexed by the last name and also by either the DOB or part of a SSN. If so, a searcher with a DOB or SSN will have a more accurate search result.

2. *Second*, the identifiers act as an important safeguard for both the requesting party and the subject of the search. There is always the chance that the "Harold Johnson" on whom a given repository has a record is not the same "Harold Johnson" on whom a check has been requested. The possibility of a misidentification can be decreased substantially if other identifiers can match the individual to the record. Providing an identifier as simple as just the middle initial is likely to help identify the correct Harold Johnson.

The federal, state, and local agencies that maintain court record systems make substantial efforts to protect the public and limit the disclosure of certain personal information such as Social Security Numbers, phone numbers, and addresses. Many agencies are now also taking this a step farther and *redacting* the records. Redaction is simply removing or hiding certain elements within a record itself or the record index.

Almost daily news stories appear related to ongoing privacy debates and efforts to remove personal identifiers from public records. One of the latest states to make this an issue is Wyoming. Effective January 1, 2011, all court documents filed and viewable by the public must have the Day and Month of the Birthdate redacted. In those cases where the SSN still appears the only portion of a SSN that can be shown on documents filed after that date are the last four digits.

The lack of identifiers displayed when searching the court docket is a real problem for employers or pre-employment screening companies who require a certain high level of accuracy in their due diligence. The existence of any possible adverse information must be checked by a hands-on search to insure the proper identity of the subject. Even then identifiers may be removed.

Government agencies who offer online access on a fee or subscription basis – usually to pre-approved requesters – are more apt to disclose personal identifiers such as the date of birth than the free access sites. Very few give a partial Social Security Numbers where the first five digits are cloaked or masked. Some now even cloak the month and day of the birth and only release the year. For example, most U.S. District Court and Bankruptcy Court PACER search systems give little if any personal identifiers at all on search results, thus making a reliable "name search" nearly impossible.

► **Searching Tip: What If the Index Doesn't Have Matching Identifiers?**

You will often find that an online index of records or the local docket terminal at the courthouse does not contain a personal identifier. In that situation, one must search within in the record file itself or in associated paperwork.

For example, let us say you are searching for a record on Joe B. Cool with a DOB of 01/01/1985. And let us say the index gives you an index showing a possible record match of J Cool with no DOB, and another possible match with a Joseph Cool with a partial DOB match. The next step is to examine the two files. The file content may contain the matching personal identifiers you seek. If you are a professional and the highest form of accuracy is vital, then you may have times where a common name requires you to view dozens of files.

Another way to identify the correct subject of a records try is to call an attorney involved in a case and ask for assistance. If the case is a criminal matter call the jail or find the agency managing the incarceration records. Also a search of news stories is another way to determine proper identification.

The balance of privacy interests versus public jeopardy goes beyond the purposes of this book. However, the key point here is to be aware of change and know that redactions can and will alter court record searching procedures.

The Common Methods Used to Search Court Records

The following is a look at the various methods available to access public records.

Visit in Person

This is easy if you live close by. As mentioned, many courthouses and recorders offices have free access terminals open to the public. Throughout this book you will find reference to those courts who provide these terminals which are often referred to as **PATs** which stands for public access terminals.

Mail, Fax, or Telephone

Although some agencies permit phone or fax requests, the majority of agencies prefer mail requests. Some courts consider fax requesting to be an expedited service that incurs higher fees. Agencies that permit telephone requests may merely answer "Yes" or "No" to questions such as "Does John Doe have a civil court case in his name?" We have indicated when telephone and fax requesting is available, as well as the extent of the service. Most courts will not fax results of search requests, but many will fax specific documents if the case file or docket number is given.

A worthy piece of advice is to always include a **SASE** (the acronym for a self-addressed stamped envelope) or a prepaid express delivery return envelope. Providing either one insures the court is not going to reject your request because you did not include postage. You may even go to the top of the request pile!

Online

The Internet may serve as a free means to access certain court records, or the Internet may serve as the conduit to a subscription or commercial site. Also, a few private dial systems (non-Internet) still exist for some subscription services. When searching online, there is a significant difference between viewing an image of a record versus looking at an index of available records. Keep in mind that most Internet access sites permit the latter, not the former. Usually the searchable and viewable information is limited to name indexes and summary data rather than document images.

Many courts may not offer access to historical records, but will provide access to the current court calendar.

Also, the Internet is a good place to find general information about a court. Many sites contain detailed descriptions of case filing and regulations. If records or indices are not searchable on the web, some sites enable one to download or print record request forms.

Later in this chapter is a section about searching records online.

Hire Someone Else

As mentioned previously, one method to search court records is through a vendor. There are a variety of companies that can be hired to perform record searches.

To find an onsite record searcher who can visit a local court, go to **www.prrn.us.** This site contains a searchable list of the members of the **Public Record Research Network**. Also, refer to the back of this book for the article **A Checklist To Use Before Placing an Order With a Record Retriever**.

If you are looking for database vendors, an excellent, quick resource is the Resource Center at **www.brbpublications.com**.

About Record Fees and Charges

Although court records may be free of charge to view, they are not necessarily free of charge when obtaining file copies. Fees may be expected if government personnel must perform searches on-site.

The common charges found at courts – whether searching is performed online or on site – include copy fees (to make copies of documents), search fees (for clerical personnel to search for the record), certification fees (to certify a document as being accurate and coming from that particular agency), and expedite fees (to place you at the "front of the line").

Fees can and do vary widely from jurisdiction to jurisdiction for the same record type. Copy fees vary from $.03 to $10.00 per page, search fees range from under a dollar to as much as $65.00. Certification can be free or as high as $14.00. Where specified, we indicate whether the court requires a self-addressed stamped envelope (SASE) to accompany a written search request. Even where it is not indicated, we recommend including a SASE to make sure the results are returned to you.

Searching the State Court Administrator's Records

Every state has an Administration Office of the Courts (AOC) that oversees the state's trial and appellate court system. All offer online access to the appellate court records.

A Valuable Resource

In 32 states this agency offers a program for a public search of state or county court docket information. Most of these systems are online, but Mississippi, South Dakota and Tennessee also offer unique, non-online programs. The summary page at the outset of each state chapter explains each of these state systems, including how to access, fees, if a subscription is required, if personal identifiers are redacted, etc.

A search from one of these court systems can be a particularly useful tool in states – such as New York, North Carolina, or Utah – that do not permit a state criminal records repository search.

Another value to using these AOC record systems is there may be a higher likelihood that the current disposition records are presented. Thus, these databases may be very current when compared to the state repository databases.

Be Aware of the State-by-State Variations

Online researchers must be aware that there are many nuances to these searches. The value of a "statewide" court search varies by state. All counties may not be included. There may be no uniformity with respect to the length of time criminal activity is archived. For example, one county may have cases dating back for seven years, while another county may have only two years of history. Another concern is the lack of identifiers to properly identify a subject as part of the search; this may vary widely from state-to-state. This is especially true with free access search systems.

Subscription or Pay Accounts

Be aware that not all is for free. The use of subscription accounts is more common than some people may be aware. Some state AOC agencies only provide online record access to registered or even pre-approved, high-volume, ongoing accounts. Typically, this contractual access involves fees and a specified, minimum amount of usage.

A growing trend is to offer online access to information on a pay-as-you-go basis, usually requiring a credit card payment online. Some agencies will give you a glimpse of the index or docket, but will charge a fee for the record copy. Some allow the record to be printed on the spot; others may only mail a document.

Overall, only a little of over 62% of the courts holding felony records provide online. This fact makes you wonder about the legitimacy of the so-called instant national background checks sold on the web.

Tip Sheet for Searching Court Records

Below are a series of tips that should be keep in mind as you perform your record searching at the courts.

1. Learn the Index & Record Systems

Most civil courts index records by both plaintiffs and defendants, but some only index by the defendant name. A plaintiff search is useful, for example, to determine if someone is especially litigious.

2. Understand the Search Requirements

There is a strong tendency for courts to overstate their search requirements. For civil cases, the usual reasonable requirement is a defendant (or plaintiff) name – full name if it is a common name – and the time frame to search – e.g., 1993-2002. For criminal cases, the court may require more identification, such as date of birth (DOB), to ascertain the correct individual.

3. Be Aware of Restricted Records

Courts have types of case records, such as juvenile and adoptions, which are not released without a court order. Records may also be sealed from view or expunged. The presiding judge often makes a determination of whether a particular record type is available to the public. Some criminal court records include the arresting officer's report. In some locations this information is regarded as public record, while in other locations the police report may be sealed.

4. Watch for Multiple Courts at Same Location

When the general jurisdiction and limited jurisdiction courts are in the same building and use the same support staff, chances are the record databases are combined as well. But that does not necessarily mean you will receive a search of both databases and pay for one search unless you ask for it. Do not assume.

5. Watch for Overlapping Jurisdictions

In some states, the general jurisdiction court and the limited jurisdiction court have overlapping dollar amounts for civil cases. That means a case could be filed in either court. Check both courts; never assume.

6. Online Searching is Generally Limited to Docket Sheets

Most courts that offer online access limit the search to the docket sheet data. But checking a courthouse's computer online docket index is the quickest way to find if case records exist online. Just be sure to check all name variations and spelling variations.

Case document images are not generally available online because courts are still experimenting and developing electronic filing and imaging. Generally, copies of case documents are only on-site.

6. The Less you Pay for Online Searching the Less Useful the Data Is

Look closely for a disclaimer. As you will read in the book, there are certain states or counties that provide free record searching on the web. Look closely for a disclaimer. Is this the official record? Are you doing the search for employment or litigation purposes and need the official record? Does the site provide any personal identifiers beyond the name? This can be a problem when researching a common name.

Other Resources: Court Records of Native Americans

Tribal Courts represent a unique legal system that works within the separate sovereignty of the Indian nations within the United States. The impact on using these courts in business investigations is considerable within the gaming industry. The key point here is that case information in tribal courts is NOT found in any level within the rest of the courts in the U.S.

Depending on the nature of the search need, searching tribal courts is a must for any obvious Native American name. Also this is a good resource on cases which may be brought against any gambling facilities or casinos on Reservation land. These court systems encapsulate criminal, civil, summary judgments and similar cases. Below are several excellent sources to find tribal courts.

In this book we have included the contact information for a number of Tribal Courts. Below are two excellent resources of Tribal court locations and information.

Tribal Court Clearinghouse - www.tribal-institute.org/index.htm

Sponsored by the Tribal Institute, the Tribal Court Clearinghouse is a comprehensive website resource for American Indian and Alaska Native Nations, tribal justice systems, victim services providers, tribal service providers, and others involved in the improvement of justice in Indian country. The Tribal Law tab provides direct links to many resources including Tribal Courts, Tribal Court Decisions, and Law Enforcement resources. The Tribal Institute also does a great job of listing and describing the many federal government agencies and native organizations involved with Native Americans.

The National Indian Justice Center - www.nijc.org/index.html

Per their web page at The National Indian Justice Center, Inc. (NIJC) is an Indian owned and operated non-profit corporation with principal offices in Santa Rosa, California. The National Indian Justice Center was established in 1983 through the collective efforts of the National American Indian Court Judges Association, the American Indian Lawyer Training Program, and the Bureau of Indian Affairs in order to establish an independent national resource for Native communities and tribal governments.

Other Resources: State Criminal Record Repositories

As mentioned, all states have a central repository of criminal records of those individuals who have been subject to that state's criminal justice system. The database is managed by a law enforcement agency typically called the State Police or Department of Public Safety. The information at the state repository is submitted by state, county, parish, and municipal courts as well as from local law enforcement. Information forwarded to the state includes notations of arrests and charges, sometimes the disposition, and a set of fingerprints.

In general, the criminal records are public when at the courts, but when the records are forwarded to the state repositories there are often restrictions placed on access. For example, only 23 states release criminal records (name search) to the general public without consent of the subject, 18 states require a signed release from the subject, and 9 states require submission of fingerprints.

As you might expect, online access to these records varies widely. For example, while at least 24 states offer online access to these records, 19 states offer access only via paid subscription, and at least 4 states provide both free and pay access.

When using state criminal record repositories as the sole source for performing a criminal record search there are certain factors that search professionals must take into consideration. These include:

- Level of Automation
- Level of Quality Control
- Timeliness of Receiving Arrest and Disposition Data
- Timeliness of Entering Arrest and Disposition Data into the Repository

So how widespread is the disposition problem? As of December, 31 2008, per the most recent statistics released by the U.S. Department of Justice, there was a backlog of 1.6 million unprocessed or partially processed court dispositions not entered into the states' criminal history databases. [1]

Please don't misunderstand the message here – there are certainly good reasons for performing a search of a state repository record database. A statewide search covers a wider geographic range than a county search. And a state search is certainly less expensive than a separate search of each county. Many states do have strong database systems. But for proper due diligence for performing a criminal record search, using a state search AND a county search of criminal records AND even a search from a database vendor should be considered. This is extremely critical for employers making hiring decisions in states with legislative limitations on using criminal records without dispositions or using misdemeanor records.

---

[1] The statistics here are taken from U.S. Department of Justice, Bureau of Justice Statistic's *Survey of State Criminal History* Information Systems, 2008 (released October 2009) found at http://bjs.ojp.usdoj.gov/index.cfm?ty=pbse&sid=52.

About Web-Based Criminal Record Background Checks

Perhaps the most over-hyped type of record promoted on the web is a criminal record search. Some consumer sites offering background checks sound very inviting. Look at those low prices and fast turnaround. These sites often advertise that you can do an instant, national background check to learn about anyone's past.

But this is not necessarily true. Some of these sites are misleading. Some try to disguise themselves as sites used by professionals, or they tout unrealistic features. Also keep in mind the figure mentioned earlier that just over 62% of courts holding felony records provide an online access mode.

If you find a site using any of the marketing schemes listed below, then a giant red flag should pop up in your mind. Take a closer look—

Charging membership fees for unlimited access to national background data

The most common type of site is charging a $29 to $35 fee for a one- to five-year membership term. Sites even offer an affiliate program where you set up your own site to sell memberships to others. But there is some benefit. These sites provide the ability to simultaneously search hundreds of free government sites at once; but there are no magic or special databases used. The membership fee essentially is paying for a sophisticated search of multiple free sites or to be linked to a series of free search pages belonging to others. Problems are currency of the data and how national is "national?"

Show endorsement by a phony or suspect trade association

Several of the suspect public records membership sites tout an endorsement from a national association of private investigators. Do a Google search on that association's name. Read the results. Some are phony.

Promote non-FCRA compliant employment screening

Any public record professional will tell you that you cannot purchase a "background check" on a new hire for $15 and you will be truly protected from a negligent hiring lawsuit nor will you be in compliance with the Federal Fair Credit Reporting Act (FCRA). You may be able to do quick record search from a couple web pages or court repository, or from a supplementary database vendor, but that does not equate to fulfilling the due diligence necessary in a professional pre-employment background check. Be cautious.

Database limitations

Compiled data typically comes from a mix of state repositories, correctional institutions, courts and any number of other counties agencies. Inherent issues of searching a private database are the limitations about completeness, name variations, timeliness, and lack of identifiers.

The Bottom Line

Most Consumer Reporting Agencies who conduct background checks concur that the most effective and FCRA compliant method of criminal record research is: a County Court Criminal record search conducted in each county of residency and employment during the past 7 years, supplemented by Statewide Criminal Record searches or a Multi-State Criminal Database search. County court searches generally require a visit to the courthouse or use of a statewide database IF the content shown online is identical to what is shown at the courthouse. If a record is identified by one of the instant database searches and you plan to use it in making an employment decision, it should be verified via a County Court search.

Alabama

Time Zone:	CST
Capital:	**Montgomery, Montgomery County**
# of Counties:	67
State Web:	**www.alabama.gov**
Court Web:	**http://judicial.alabama.gov**

Administration

Administrative Director of Courts, 300 Dexter Ave, Montgomery, AL, 36104; 334-954-5000.

The Supreme and Appellate Courts

The Supreme Court is the court of last resort. Alabama has both a Court of Civil Appeals and a Court of Criminal Appeals. One may view Civil Appeals, Criminal Appeals, and Reporter Decisions at http://judicial.alabama.gov/supreme.cfm. Attorneys may subscribe to the Appellate Court's Online Information Service at https://acis.alabama.gov.

The Alabama Courts

Court	Type	How Organized	Jurisdiction Highpoints
Circuit*	General	67 Courts in 41 Districts	Felony, Misdemeanor, Civil, Small Claims, Juvenile, Traffic, Eviction, Domestic Relations, Estate
District*	Limited	67 Courts in 67 Districts (often combined with Circuit Courts)	Misdemeanors, Small Claims, Civil Matters under $10,000
Probate*	Special	68 Courts	Probate, Guardianship, Estates
Municipal	Limited	273 Courts	Municipal ordinances

* = profiled in this book

Details on the Court Structure

Circuit Courts are the courts of general jurisdiction and exclusive jurisdiction on civil matters over $10,000. **District Courts** are the limited jurisdiction in civil matters. Civil cases between $3,000 and $10,000 may be concurrent and heard at either court, depending on local practice.

Circuit and District courts are combined in all but eight larger counties. Barbour, Coffee, Jefferson, St. Clair, Talladega, and Tallapoosa Counties have two court locations within the county. Jefferson County (Birmingham), Madison (Huntsville), Marshall, and Tuscaloosa Counties have separate criminal divisions for Circuit Courts and/or District Courts.

All counties have separate **Probate Courts**.

A misdemeanor committed with a felony is tried with the felony. The Circuit Courts hear appeals for misdemeanors from the District Courts. District Courts can receive guilty pleas in felony cases.

Record Searching Facts You Need to Know

Fees and Record Searching Tips

Although in most counties Circuit Courts and District Courts are combined, each index could be separate. Therefore, when you request a search of both courts, a good idea is to ask the search to cover "both the Circuit and District Court records." A number of courts do not perform searches, you must hire a retriever. Many courts offer public access computer terminals. A Directive from 2007 set mandatory fees for record copies at a flat rate of $5.00

for the first 20 copies then $.50 per copy. The certification fee was set at $5.00. Also the Directive indicates courts MAY charge $10.00 for a computerized case history check, $20.00 for a search of paper records, and $25.00 for a search of archival records.

Online Access is Statewide for State Trial Courts

ON-DEMAND Access to Alabama State Trial Court Records is a subscription service that provides access to criminal, civil, small claims, state traffic, domestic relations and child support case information. A name search is $9.99 which includes details on one case; each additional case is $9.99. A case number search is $9.99. Images are $5.00 for the first 20 pages and $.50 per page each add'l. There is a case monitoring service offered as well; $29.99 for a Circuit Court case and $19.99 for a District Court case.

To sign up visit https://pa.alacourt.com/default.aspx

Autauga County

Circuit & District Court 134 N Court St, #114, Courthouse, Prattville, AL 36067; 334-358-6800; fax: 334-361-4830; 8AM-N, 1PM-5PM (CST). *Felony, Misdemeanor, Civil, Eviction, Small Claims.*

General Information: No sealed, adoptions, youthful offenders or juvenile records released. Will not fax documents. Court makes copy: $5.00 for 1st 20 pages then $.50 each add'l. Certification fee: $5.00 plus copy fee. Payee: Circuit Court. Cashiers checks and money orders accepted. Major credit cards accepted. Prepayment required.

Civil Name Search: Access: Mail, in person, online. Only the court performs in person name searches; visitors may not. Search fee: depends on age of case, usually $25.00. Civil cases indexed by defendant, plaintiff. Civil records on computer since 1977 and in books from 1950. Mail turnaround time 1-2 weeks. **See details of online access in the description at the front and rear of this chapter.**

Criminal Name Search: Access: Mail, online, in person. Only the court performs in person name searches; visitors may not. Search fee: Depends on age of case, usually $25.00. Required to search: name, years to search; also helpful: DOB, SSN. Criminal records on computer since 1977 and in books from 1950. Mail turnaround time 1-2 weeks. **See details of online access in the description at the front and rear of this chapter.**

Probate Court 176 W 5th, Prattville, AL 36067; probate phone: 334-361-3728/4842; fax: 334-361-3740; 8:30AM-5PM (CST). *Probate.* www.autaugaprobate.com/

Baldwin County

Circuit & District Court 312 Courthouse Sq #10, Bay Minette, AL 36507; 251-937-0370; criminal phone: 251-937-0280; civil phone: 251-937-0299; probate phone: 251-937-0230;; 8AM-4:30PM (CST). *Felony, Misdemeanor, Civil, Eviction, Small Claims, Traffic.* http://28jc.alacourt.gov/clerk.htm

General Information: Court will not do name searches. Court has satellite offices in Fairhope 251-990-4624 and Foley 251-972-6818. Probate is a separate office at 220 Courthouse Sq, with satellite offices in Baldwinville, Fairhope and Foley. No sealed, youthful offenders or juvenile records released. Will not fax documents. Court makes copy: $5.00 for 1st 20 pages then $.50 each add'l. Self serve copy: $.50 per page. Certification fee: $5.00 per cert. Payee: Circuit Court Clerk. Only cashiers checks and money orders accepted. Major credit cards accepted. Prepayment required.

Civil Name Search: Access: Online, in person. Visitors must perform in person searches themselves. Civil cases indexed by defendant, plaintiff. Civil records indexed on computer from 1977, index books by case # to early 1900s. Note: Court will not do name searches. If record known fee is $10.00 for computerized or paper record or $25.00 for archived record. Civil PAT goes back to 1990 for records; 1977 for indices. **See details of online access in the description at the front and rear of this chapter.** Probate records are accessible at www.deltacomputersystems.com/al/al05/probatea.html.

Criminal Name Search: Access: Online, in person. Visitors must perform in person searches themselves. Required to search: name, years to search, DOB. Criminal records indexed on computer from 1977, index books by case # to early 1900s. Note: Court will not do name searches. If record known fee is $10.00 for computerized or paper record or $25.00 for archived record. **See details of online access in the description at the front and rear of this chapter.** Online results show name, DOB.

Probate Court PO Box 459, 220 Courthouse Sq, Bay Minette, AL 36507; probate phone: 251-937-9561; fax: 251-937-0252; 8AM-4:30PM (CST). *Probate.*

General Information: Online access to probate record index is free at www.deltacomputersystems.com/al/al05/probatea.html.

Barbour County

Circuit & District Court - Clayton Division PO Box 219, 1 Court Sq, Clayton, AL 36016; 334-687-1500; fax: 334-687-1599; 8AM-4:30PM (CST). *Felony, Misdemeanor, Civil, Eviction, Small Claims, Probate.*

General Information: Ask that your search include both Circuit and District Courts; fee is the same for both or one. District Ct clerk phone- 334-775-8366. No sealed, adoptions, youthful offenders records released. Fee to fax document $.50 per page. Court makes copy: $5.00 for 1st 20 pages then $.50 each add'l. Self serve copy: same. Certification fee: $5.00 per cert. Payee: David S Nix. Business checks accepted. No credit cards accepted. Prepayment required. Mail requests: SASE required.

Civil Name Search: Access: Mail, in person, online. Only the court performs in person name searches; visitors may not. Search fee: $10.00 for computerized case history check; $20.00 for background check; $25.00 per case record search. Required to search: name, years to search; a release of liability is requested. Civil cases indexed by defendant. Civil records on computer back to 1993; books from 1977; archives back to 1920. Mail turnaround time 2-3 days. **See details of online access in the description at the front and rear of this chapter.**

Criminal Name Search: Access: Mail, online, in person. Only the court performs in person name searches; visitors may not. Search fee: $10.00 for computerized case history check; $20.00 for background check; $25.00 per case record search. Required to search: name, years to search, DOB; also helpful: SSN. Criminal records computerized from 1993, books from 1977; archives back to 1920. Mail turnaround time 2-3 days. **See details of online access in the description at the front and rear of this chapter.**

Circuit & District Court - Eufaula Division 303 E Broad St, Rm 201, Eufaula, AL 36027; 334-687-1515/16; fax: 334-687-1599; 8AM-4:30PM, closed N-1PM (CST). *Misdemeanor, Civil, Eviction, Small Claims, Probate.*

General Information: No sealed, adoptions, youthful offenders or juvenile records released. Will fax out documents. Court makes copy: $5.00 for 1st 20 pages then $.50 each add'l. Certification fee: $5.00. Payee: Clerk of Courts. No personal checks or credit cards accepted. Prepayment required.

Civil Name Search: Access: Online, in person. Visitors must perform in person searches themselves. Civil cases indexed by defendant, plaintiff. Civil records on computer from 1993. Index from 1977 to present; prior to 1977 difficult to search. Note: If case number is known, court will provide copies within 2 days. Civil PAT goes back to 1977. **See details of online access in the description at the front and rear of this chapter.**

Criminal Name Search: Access: Online, in person. Visitors must perform in person searches themselves. Required to search: name, years to search; also helpful: DOB, SSN. Criminal records computerized from 1993. Index from 1977 to present; prior to 1977 difficult to search. Note: If case number is known, will provide copies within 2 days. Criminal PAT goes back to same as civil. **See details of online access in the description at the front and rear of this chapter.**

Probate Court - Clayton Division PO Box 158, 201 Court Sq, Clayton, AL 36016; probate phone: 334-775-8371; fax: 334-775-1126; 8AM-N, 1-4:30PM (CST). *Probate.*

Probate Court - Eufaula Division PO Box 758, 303 E Broad St, Rm 101 (36027), Eufaula, AL 36072; probate phone: 334-687-1530; fax: 334-687-0921; 8AM-4:30PM (EST). *Probate.*

Bibb County

Circuit & District Court PO Box 185, Bibb County Courthouse, 35 Court Sq East, Centreville, AL 35042; 205-926-3103 Civil (Circuit); criminal phone: 205-926-3107; civil phone: 205-926-3100 (Dist); fax: 205-926-3132; 8AM-5:00PM (CST). *Felony, Misdemeanor, Civil, Eviction, Small Claims, Probate.*

General Information: No sealed, adoptions, youthful offenders or juvenile records released. Will fax 1-2 documents to local or toll-free number. Court makes copy: $5.00 for 1st 20 pages then $.50 each add'l. Self serve copy: same. Certification fee: $5.00 plus copy fee. Payee: Gayle S Bearden, Clerk. Business checks accepted; no personal checks. Prepayment required. Mail requests: SASE required.

Civil Name Search: Access: Mail, in person, online. Both court and visitors may perform in person name searches. No search fee. Civil cases indexed by defendant. Civil records on index book back to 1940s. Mail turnaround time 3-4 days. **See details of online access in the description at the front and rear of this chapter.**

Criminal Name Search: Access: Mail, online, in person. Both court and visitors may perform in person name searches. Search fee: $10.00. Required to search: name, years to search, DOB; also helpful: SSN. Criminal records computerized from 1995, on index books back to 1940s. Mail turnaround time 1-2 days. **See details of online access in the description at the front and rear of this chapter.**

Probate Court 8 Court Sq W, #A, Centerville, AL 35042; probate phone: 205-926-3104; fax: 205-926-3131; 8AM-5PM (EST). *Probate.*

Blount County

Circuit & District Court 220 2nd Ave East Rm 208, Oneonta, AL 35121; 205-625-4153; criminal phone: 205-625-4153;; 8AM-5PM (CST). *Felony, Misdemeanor, Civil, Eviction, Small Claims.*

General Information: Small claims court phone: x4. No sealed, adoptions, youthful offenders or juvenile records released. Will not fax documents. Court makes copy: $5.00 for 1st 20 pages then $.50 each add'l. Self serve copy: same. Certification fee: $5.00 per cert plus copy fee. Payee: Mike Criswell. No personal checks accepted. Prepayment required. Mail requests: SASE required.

Civil Name Search: Access: Mail, in person, online. Only the court performs in person name searches; visitors may not. Search fee: $10.00 for computerized case history check; $20.00 for background check; $25.00 per case record search. Civil cases indexed by defendant, plaintiff. Civil records on computer from 3/1994, on index books from 1977. Mail turnaround time 7-10 days. **See details of online access in the description at the front and rear of this chapter.**

Criminal Name Search: Access: Mail, online, in person. Only the court performs in person name searches; visitors may not. Search fee: $10.00 for computerized case history check; $20.00 for background check; $25.00 per case record search. Required to search: name, years to search, DOB; also helpful: SSN. Criminal records computerized from 1998, on index books from 1977. Mail turnaround time 7-10 days. **See details of online access in the description at the front and rear of this chapter.**

Probate Court 220 2nd Ave E, Oneonta, AL 35121; 205-625-4191; fax: 205-625-4206; 8AM-5PM (CST). *Probate.*

Bullock County

Circuit & District Court PO Box 230, 217 Prairie St, Union Springs, AL 36089; 334-738-2280; fax: 334-738-2282; 8AM-4:30PM (CST). *Felony, Misdemeanor, Civil, Eviction, Small Claims, Probate.*

General Information: Ask that your search include both court indexes, all one fee. An add'l $10 fee is added if the search includes the older archives. No sealed, adoptions, youthful offenders or juvenile records released. Will not fax out documents. Court makes copy: $5.00 for 1st 20 pages then $.50 each add'l. Certification fee: $5.00 per doc. No personal checks accepted, business and local checks accepted. No credit cards accepted. Prepayment required. Mail requests: SASE required.

Civil Name Search: Access: Phone, fax, mail, online, in person. Both court and visitors may perform in person name searches. Search fee: $25.00 per name. Civil cases indexed by defendant, plaintiff. Civil index on docket books back to 1930s; on computer back to 1996. Mail turnaround time depends on clerk availability. **See details of online access in the description at the front and rear of this chapter.**

Criminal Name Search: Access: Phone, fax, mail, online, in person. Both court and visitors may perform in person name searches. Search fee: $25.00 per name. Required to search: name, years to search, DOB; also helpful: SSN, signed release. Criminal records indexed in books back to 1930s; on computer back to 1996. Mail turnaround time depends on clerk availability. **See details of online access in the description at the front and rear of this chapter.**

Probate Court PO Box 71, 217 N Prairie St, Union Springs, AL 36089; probate phone: 334-738-2250; fax: 334-738-2240; 8AM-4PM (EST). *Probate.*

Butler County

Circuit & District Court PO Box 236, 700 Court Sq, Greenville, AL 36037; 334-382-3521; fax: 334-382-7488; 7:30AM-4:30PM (CST). *Felony, Misdemeanor, Civil, Eviction, Small Claims, Probate, Domestic, Traffic.*

General Information: Online identifiers in results same as on public terminal. No sealed, adoptions, youthful offenders or juvenile records released. Fee to fax out file $1.00 per page. Court makes copy: $5.00 for 1st 20 pages then $.50 each add'l. Self serve copy: same. Certification fee: $5.00 per cert. Payee: Butler County District Court. Business checks accepted. No credit cards accepted. Prepayment required. Mail requests: SASE requested.

Civil Name Search: Access: Mail, in person, online. Both court and visitors may perform in person name searches. Search fee: $5.00 per name. Civil cases indexed by defendant, plaintiff. Civil records on computer from 1992, books to 1979. Mail turnaround time 1-2 weeks. Civil PAT goes

back to 1994. **See details of online access in the description at the front and rear of this chapter.**

Criminal Name Search: Access: Mail, online, in person. Both court and visitors may perform in person name searches. Search fee: $5.00 per name. Fee for first 2-3 years. Required to search: name, years to search; also helpful: SSN, DOB. Criminal records computerized from 1992, books to 1979. Mail turnaround time 1-2 weeks. Criminal PAT goes back to 1992. **See details of online access in the description at the front and rear of this chapter.**

Probate Court PO Box 756, 700 Court Sq, Greenville, AL 36037; probate phone: 334-382-3512; fax: 334-382-5489; 8AM-4PM M,T,TH,F; 8AM-N W (EST). *Probate.*

Calhoun County

Circuit Court 25 W 11th St, #300, Anniston, AL 36201; 256-231-1750; fax: 256-231-1826; 8AM-4:30PM (CST). *Felony, Civil Actions over $10,000.*

www.alacourt.gov

General Information: No sealed, adoptions, youthful offenders or juvenile records released. Will not fax documents. Court makes copy: $5.00 for 1st 20 pages then $.50 each add'l. Certification fee: $5.00 per document plus copy fee. Payee: Circuit/District Clerk. No personal checks or credit cards accepted. Prepayment required.

Civil Name Search: Access: Mail, online, in person. Visitors must perform in person searches themselves. Search fee: $10.00 per name, add $25.00 if pre-2000. Civil cases indexed by defendant, plaintiff. Civil records indexed on computer from 1970s, prior in books. Civil PAT goes back to 1970. **See details of online access in the description at the front and rear of this chapter.**

Criminal Name Search: Access: Mail, online person. Visitors must perform in person searches themselves. Search fee: $10.00 per name, add $25.00 if pre-2000. Required to search: name, years to search, DOB; also helpful: SSN. Criminal records indexed on computer from 1970s, prior on books. Criminal PAT goes back to same as civil. **See details of online access in the description at the front and rear of this chapter.** The County sex offender registry is online at www.calhouncountysheriff.org/sex_offenders.cfm.

District Court 25 W 11th St, #260, Anniston, AL 36201; 256-231-1850; civil phone: 256-231-1750; fax: 256-231-1863; 8AM-4:30PM (CST). *Misdemeanor, Civil Actions under $10,000, Eviction, Small Claims.*

General Information: No sealed, adoptions, youthful offenders or juvenile records released. Will not fax documents. Court makes copy: $5.00 for 1st 20 pages then $.50 each add'l. Self serve copy: same. Certification fee: $5.00 per doc plus copy fee. Payee: District Court. No personal checks. No credit cards accepted. Prepayment required.

Civil Name Search: Access: Mail, in person, online. Visitors must perform in person searches themselves. Search fee: $10.00 per name; if pre-1990 then add add'l $25.00 to $10.00 search fee. Civil cases indexed by defendant, plaintiff. Civil records on computer from 1989, books from 1977 to 1989. Civil PAT goes back to 1977. Public terminal located in District Court. **See details of online access in the description at the front and rear of this chapter.**

Criminal Name Search: Access: Mail, online, in person. Visitors must perform in person searches themselves. Search fee: $10.00 per name; if pre-2000 then add add'l $25.00 to $10.00 search fee. Required to search: name, years to search; also helpful: SSN. Criminal records computerized from 1989, books from 1977 to 1989. Criminal PAT goes back to same as civil. Public terminal located in District Court. **See details of online access in the description at the front and rear of this chapter.**

Probate Court 1702 Noble St, #102, Anniston, AL 36201; 256-241-2825; fax: 256-231-1728; 8AM-4:30PM (CST). *Probate.*

www.calhouncounty.org/probate/index.html

General Information: Email questions to probate@calhouncounty.org.

Chambers County

Circuit & District Court Chambers County Courthouse, Clerks Office, #2, Lafayette St South, Lafayette, AL 36862; 334-864-4348; fax: 334-864-4368; 8AM-N, 1-4:30PM (CST). *Felony, Misdemeanor, Civil, Eviction, Small Claims, Probate.*

General Information: Court will search both indexes if asked, one fee. No sealed, adoptions, youthful offenders or juvenile records released. Will not fax out documents. Court makes copy: $5.00 for 1st 20 pages then $.50 each add'l. Self serve copy: same. Certification fee: $5.00 per cert. Business checks accepted. No personal checks. Visa/MC accepted in person only. Prepayment required. Mail requests: SASE required.

Civil Name Search: Access: Mail, in person, online. Only the court performs in person name searches; visitors may not. Search fee: $10.00 per name. Civil cases indexed by defendant, plaintiff. Civil records on computer from 4/93, on index books to early 1900s. Mail turnaround time 1 week. **See details of online access in the description at the front and rear of this chapter.**

Criminal Name Search: Access: Mail, online, in person. Only the court performs in person name searches; visitors may not. Search fee: $10.00 per name. Required to search: name, years to search; also helpful: DOB, SSN. Criminal records are computerized since 1993. Mail turnaround time 1 week. **See details of online access in the description at the front and rear of this chapter.**

Probate Court #2 Lafayette St S, Lafayette, AL 36862; 334-864-4380; fax: 334-864-4394; 8AM-4:30PM (EST). *Probate.*

Cherokee County

Circuit & District Court 100 Main St, Rm 203, Centre, AL 35960-1532; 256-927-3337; fax: 256-927-3444; 8AM-4PM (CST). *Felony, Misdemeanor, Civil, Eviction, Small Claims.* http://9jc.alacourt.gov/cherokee/

General Information: No sealed, adoptions, youthful offenders or juvenile records released. Court makes copy: $5.00 for 1st 20 pages then $.50 each add'l. Self serve copy: same. Certification fee: $5.00 per cert plus copy fee. Payee: Circuit Clerk. Business checks accepted; no personal checks. No credit cards accepted. Prepayment required.

Civil Name Search: Access: In person, online. Visitors must perform in person searches themselves. Civil cases indexed by defendant, plaintiff. Civil records on books from 1977. Civil PAT goes back to 8/1995. **See details of online access in the description at the front and rear of this chapter.**

Criminal Name Search: Access: Online, in person. Visitors must perform in person searches themselves. Required to search: name, years to search; also helpful: DOB, SSN. Criminal docket on books from 1977. Criminal PAT goes back to same as civil. **See details of online access in the description at the front and rear of this chapter.**

Probate Court 260 Cedar Bluff Rd, #101, Centre, AL 35960; probate phone: 256-927-3363; fax: 256-927-9218; 8AM-4PM (CST). *Probate.*

Chilton County

Circuit & District Court PO Box 1946, 500 2nd Ave N, Clanton, AL 35046; 205-755-4275 Dist; 280-1844 Dist.; civil phone: 205-280-1844; fax: 205-755-1387; 8AM-Noon, 1PM-5PM (CST). *Felony, Misdemeanor, Civil, Eviction, Small Claims, Probate.*

General Information: Search fee includes both civil and criminal indexes. No sealed, adoptions, youthful offenders or juvenile records released. Will not fax out documents. Court makes copy: $5.00 for 1st 20 pages then $.50 each add'l. Self serve copy: same. Certification fee: $5.00 per cert. Payee: Clerk. Business checks accepted. No personal checks. No credit cards accepted. Prepayment required.

Civil Name Search: Access: Mail, in person, online. Visitors must perform in person searches themselves. Search fee: $10.00 per name. Civil cases indexed by defendant, plaintiff. Civil records on computer from 9/93, on books from 1950s. Civil PAT goes back to 1993. **See details of online access in the description at the front and rear of this chapter.**

Criminal Name Search: Access: Mail, online, in person. Visitors must perform in person searches themselves. Search fee: $10.00 per name. Required to search: name, years to search; also helpful: DOB, SSN. Criminal records on computer since 1993. Criminal PAT goes back to same as civil. T **See details of online access in the description at the front and rear of this chapter.**

Probate Court PO Box 270, 500 2nd Ave N (35045, Clanton, AL 35046; probate phone: 205-755-1555; fax: 205-280-7219; 8AM-4PM (EST). *Probate.*

Choctaw County

Circuit & District Court Choctaw County Courthouse, #10, PO Box 428, Butler, AL 36904; 205-459-2155; fax: 205-459-3218; 8AM-4:30PM (CST). *Felony, Misdemeanor, Civil, Eviction, Small Claims.*

General Information: No sealed, adoptions, youthful offenders or juvenile records released. Court makes copy: $5.00 for 1st 20 pages then $.50 each add'l. Certification fee: $5.00 per cert. Payee: Circuit Clerk. Business checks accepted. Visa/MC accepted. Prepayment required.

Civil Name Search: Access: Online, in person. Both court and visitors may perform in person name searches. No search fee. Civil cases indexed by defendant, plaintiff. Civil index on docket books from 1940. Putting records on computer from 9/1994. Civil PAT goes back to 1994. **See details of online access in the description at the front and rear of this chapter.**

Criminal Name Search: Access: Online, in person. Visitors must perform in person searches themselves. Required to search: name, years to search; also helpful: DOB, SSN. Criminal records indexed in books from 1940. Putting records on computer from 9/1994. Criminal PAT goes back to same as civil. **See details of online access in the description at the front and rear of this chapter.**

Probate Court 117 S Mulberry, Courthouse, Butler, AL 36904; probate phone: 205-459-2417; fax: 205-459-4248; 8AM-4:30PM (EST). *Probate.*

Clarke County

Circuit & District Court PO Box 921, Grove Hill, AL 36451; 251-275-3363; fax: 251-275-3271; 8AM-5PM (CST). *Felony, Misdemeanor, Civil, Eviction, Small Claims.*

General Information: No sealed, adoptions, youthful offenders or juvenile records released. Will not fax documents. Court makes copy: $5.00 for 1st 20 pages then $.50 each add'l. Self serve copy: same. Certification fee: $5.00. Payee: Circuit Clerk. Business checks accepted. Prepayment required.

Civil Name Search: Access: Mail, in person, online. Both court and visitors may perform in person name searches. Search fee: $5.00 per name. Civil cases indexed by defendant, plaintiff. Civil index on cards from 1977. Mail turnaround time 1 week. Civil PAT goes back to 1993. **See details of online access in the description at the front and rear of this chapter.**

Criminal Name Search: Access: Mail, online, in person. Both court and visitors may perform in person name searches. Search fee: $5.00 per name. Required to search: name, years to search; also helpful: DOB, SSN. Criminal records indexed by cards from 1977. Mail turnaround time 1 week. Criminal PAT goes back to same as civil. **See details of online access in the description at the front and rear of this chapter.**

Probate Court PO Box 10, 114 Court St, Courthouse, Grove Hill, AL 36451; probate phone: 251-275-3251; fax: 251-275-8427; 8AM-5PM (CST). *Probate.* www.clarkecountyal.com/probate/index.htm

Clay County

Circuit & District Court PO Box 816, Ashland, AL 36251; 256-354-7926; fax: 256-354-2249; 8AM-4:30PM (CST). *Felony, Misdemeanor, Civil, Eviction, Small Claims, Probate.*

General Information: Online identifiers in results same as on public terminal. No sealed, adoptions, youthful offenders or juvenile records released. Fee to fax out file $1.00 per page. Court makes copy: $5.00 for 1st 20 pages then $.50 each add'l. Certification fee: $5.00 per doc. Payee: Circuit Clerk. Business checks accepted. No credit cards accepted. Prepayment required. Mail requests: SASE required.

Civil Name Search: Access: Mail, in person, online. Visitors must perform in person searches themselves. Search fee: $10.00 per name, computer index only. Civil cases indexed by defendant, plaintiff. Overall records go back to 1977; computerized records go back to 1994. Mail turnaround time 10-14 days. Civil PAT goes back to 1994. Terminal results include SSN. **See details of online access in the description at the front and rear of this chapter.**

Criminal Name Search: Access: Mail, online, in person. Visitors must perform in person searches themselves. Search fee: $10.00 per name, computer index only. Required to search: name, years to search; also helpful: SSN, DOB, signed release. Overall records go back to 1977; computerized records go back to 1994. Mail turnaround time 10-14 days. Criminal PAT goes back to same as civil. Terminal results include SSN. **See details of online access in the description at the front and rear of this chapter.**

Probate Court PO Box 1120, 25 Courthouse Sq, Ashland, AL 36251; 256-354-2198; probate phone: 256-354-3006; fax: 256-354-4778; 8AM-4:30PM . *Probate.* www.claycountyprobate.com/

Cleburne County

Circuit & District Court 120 Vickery St, Rm 202, Heflin, AL 36264; 256-463-2651; fax: 256-463-2257; 8AM-4:30PM (CST). *Felony, Misdemeanor, Civil, Eviction, Small Claims.*

General Information: No sealed, adoptions, youthful offenders or juvenile records released. Will fax documents for no fee. Court makes copy: $5.00 for 1st 20 pages then $.50 each add'l. Self serve copy: same. Certification fee: $5.00 plus copy fee. Payee: Clerk. Only cashiers checks and money orders accepted. Prepayment required. Mail requests: SASE required.

Civil Name Search: Access: Phone, mail, online, in person. Both court and visitors may perform in person name searches. No search fee. Civil cases indexed by defendant, plaintiff. Civil records on computer from 1993, on books and cards from 1900. Mail turnaround time 1-2 days. **See details of online access in the description at the front and rear of this chapter.**

Criminal Name Search: Access: Mail, online, in person. Only the court performs in person name searches; visitors may not. No search fee. Required to search: name, years to search, DOB; also helpful: SSN. Criminal records computerized from 1995, on books and cards from 1900. Mail turnaround time 1-2 days. **See details of online access in the description at the front and rear of this chapter.**

Probate Court 120 Vickery St, Rm 101, Heflin, AL 36264; probate phone: 256-463-5655; fax: 256-463-1044; 8AM-5PM (EST). *Probate.*

Coffee County

Circuit & District Court - Elba Division 230 M Court Ave, Elba, AL 36323; 334-897-2954; fax: 334-897-3224; 8:30AM-5PM (CST). *Felony, Misdemeanor, Civil, Eviction, Small Claims, Probate.*

General Information: The court shares the same computer system as Enterprise, so a clerk's electronic search at either should include both, but this may be up to the clerk's discretion. This Elba Div does not appear to charge a search fee on mail requests, just mailing charge No sealed, adoptions, youthful offenders or juvenile records released. Court makes copy: $5.00 for 1st 20 pages then $.50 each add'l. Self serve copy: same. Certification fee: $5.00 per cert includes copy, but fee is up to clerk's kind discretion. Payee: Circuit Clerk. Business checks accepted but must be pre-approved. Mail requests: SASE required.

Civil Name Search: Access: Mail, in person, online. Both court and visitors may perform in person name searches. No search fee. Civil cases indexed by defendant. Civil records on computer back to 8/1993. Mail turnaround time 3-4 days. **See details of online access in the description at the front and rear of this chapter.**

Criminal Name Search: Access: Mail, online, in person. Only the court performs in person name searches; visitors may not. No search fee. Required to search: name, years to search; also helpful: DOB. Criminal records computerized from 8/1993. Mail turnaround time varies, usually 3-4 days. **See details of online access in the description at the front and rear of this chapter.**

Circuit & District Court - Enterprise Division PO Box 311284, 101 S Edwards St, Enterprise, AL 36331; 334-347-2519; fax: 334-393-2047; 8AM-5PM (CST). *Felony, Misdemeanor, Civil, Eviction, Small Claims.*

General Information: The court shares the same computer system as Elba. A search here includes both Enterprise Courts, for a single fee. No sealed, adoptions, youthful offenders or juvenile records released. Will fax back docs no fee. Court makes copy: $5.00 for 1st 20 pages then $.50 each add'l. Certification fee: $5.00 per cert. Payee: Clerk of Courts. Only cashiers checks and money orders accepted. No credit cards accepted. Prepayment required. Mail requests: SASE required.

Civil Name Search: Access: Mail, fax, online, in person. Visitors must perform in person searches themselves. Search fee: $25.00 per name. Civil cases indexed by defendant, plaintiff. Civil records on computer since 8/1993. Civil PAT goes back to 1980. **See details of online access in the description at the front and rear of this chapter.**

Criminal Name Search: Access: Mail, online, in person. Visitors must perform in person searches themselves. No search fee. Required to search: name, years to search; DOB; also helpful: SSN. Criminal records on computer since 8/1993. Mail turnaround time up to 1 week. Criminal PAT goes back to same as civil. **See details of online access in the description at the front and rear of this chapter.**

Probate Court - Elba Division 230 N Court Ave, Elba, AL 36323; 334-897-2211 or 2212; fax: 334-897-2028; 8AM-4:30PM (EST). *Probate.* www.probateoffice.info

Probate Court - Enterprise Division PO Box 311247, 101 S Edwards St, Enterprise, AL 36331-1247; probate phone: 334-347-2688; fax: 334-347-2095; 8AM-4:30PM (CST). *Probate.* www.probateoffice.info/

General Information: Presided by the same judge, there is also a Probate office in Elba, 334-897-2211, fax-334-897-2028, 230 N Court St, Elba, Al 36330. To subscribe contact Syscon at 205-758-2000 x8112.

Colbert County

Circuit and District Court - Criminal PO Box 740370, 201 N Main St, Courthouse, Criminal Office, Tuscumbia, AL 35674; 256-386-8517; fax: 256-386-7633; 8AM-4:30PM (CST). *Felony, Misdemeanor, Traffic.*

General Information: For practical purposes, Circuit and District Court are virtually combined, then divided into a Civil section and a Criminal section. No sealed, adoptions, youthful offenders or juvenile records released. Will not fax documents. Court makes copy: $5.00 for 1st 20 pages then $.50 each add'l. Certification fee: $5.00 per doc. Payee: Court Clerk. No personal checks or credit cards accepted. Prepayment required.

Criminal Name Search: Access: Online, in person. Visitors must perform in person searches themselves. Required to search: name, years to search; also helpful: SSN. Criminal records computerized from 1993, prior on books. Public use terminal has crim records back to 1977. The types of personal identifiers on index and records varies. **See details of online access in the description at the front and rear of this chapter.**

Circuit and District Court - Civil Colbert County Courthouse, 201 N Main St, Civil Office, Tuscumbia, AL 35674; 256-386-8511; civil phone: 256-386-8513; probate phone: 256-386-8542; fax: 256-386-8505; 8AM-4:30PM (CST). *Civil Actions, Small Claims, Family, Eviction, Probate.*

General Information: For practical purposes, Circuit and District Court are virtually combined, then divided into a Civil section and a Criminal section. Probate court is separate from this court but at same address; probate phone number above. No sealed, youthful offenders or juvenile records released. Will not fax documents. Court makes copy: $5.00 for 1st 20 pages then $.50 each add'l. Self serve copy: same. Certification fee: $5.00 per doc. Payee: Circuit Court Clerk. Business checks accepted, personal checks are not. No credit cards accepted. Prepayment required.

Civil Name Search: Access: Online, in person. Both court and visitors may perform in person name searches. Search fee: $20.00. Civil cases indexed by defendant, plaintiff. Civil records on computer from 1993, books from 1959. Public use terminal has civil records back to 1993. **See details of online access in the description at the front and rear of this chapter.**

Probate Court PO Box 47, 201 N Main St, Tuscumbia, AL 35674; 246-314-5900; fax: 256-386-8547; 8AM-4:30PM (EST). *Probate.* www.colbertprobatejudge.org/

Conecuh County

Circuit & District Court 111 Court St Rm 203, Evergreen, AL 36401; 251-578-2066; fax: 251-578-7013; 8AM-4:30PM (CST). *Felony, Misdemeanor, Civil, Eviction, Small Claims, Probate.*

General Information: No sealed, adoptions, youthful offenders or juvenile records released. Will fax out specific case files for $5.00. Court makes copy: $5.00 for 1st 20 pages then $.50 each add'l. Certification fee: $5.00. Payee: Circuit Clerk, David Jackson. Business checks accepted upon prior approval. No credit cards accepted. Prepayment required.

Civil Name Search: Access: In person, online. Both court and visitors may perform in person name searches. Search fee: $25.00. Civil cases indexed by defendant, plaintiff. Civil index on cards from 1977, on computer back to 12/1994. Civil PAT goes back to 12/1994. **See details of online access in the description at the front and rear of this chapter.**

Criminal Name Search: Access: In person, online. Both court and visitors may perform in person name searches. Search fee: $25.00. Required to search: name, years to search, DOB; also helpful: SSN. Criminal records indexed on cards from 1977, on computer back to 1994. Criminal PAT goes back to same as civil. **See details of online access in the description at the front and rear of this chapter.**

Probate Court PO Box 149, 111 Court Square, Rm 104, Evergreen, AL 36401; probate phone: 251-578-1221; fax: 251-578-7034; 8AM-4:30PM (CST). *Probate.*

Coosa County

Circuit & District Court PO Box 98, 1 Main St, Rockford, AL 35136; 256-377-4988; criminal phone: x2; fax: 256-377-1599; 8AM-4:30PM (CST). *Felony, Misdemeanor, Civil, Eviction, Small Claims, Probate.*

General Information: Computer indexes all on one system, so a search can be requested to include all. No sealed, adoptions, youthful offenders or juvenile records released. Will not fax documents. Court makes copy: $5.00 for 1st 20 pages then $.50 each add'l. Certification fee: $5.00 per cert. Payee: Clerk of Court. Business checks accepted. Visa/MC accepted at traffic court only. Prepayment required.

Civil Name Search: Access: Online, in person. Visitors must perform in person searches themselves. Civil cases indexed by plaintiff. Civil records on books from the late 1800s, computerized records go back to 7/1994. Public use terminal has civil records back to 10 years. **See details of online access in the description at the front and rear of this chapter.**

Criminal Name Search: Access: Online, in person, fax, mail. Visitors must perform in person searches themselves. Search fee: $5.00. Required to search: name, years to search; also helpful: DOB, SSN. Criminal docket on books from the late 1800s, computerized records go back to 7/1994. Mail turnaround time 2-3 days. **See details of online access in the description at the front and rear of this chapter.**

Probate Court PO Box 218, 100 Main St, Courthouse, Rockford, AL 35136; probate phone: 256-377-4919; fax: 256-377-1549; 8AM-4PM (EST). *Probate.*

Covington County

Circuit & District Court Covington County Courthouse, Andalusia, AL 36420; 334-428-2520; probate phone: 334-428-2513; fax: 334-428-2531; 8AM-5PM (CST). *Felony, Misdemeanor, Civil, Eviction, Small Claims, Probate.*

General Information: For subscription service contact Administrative Office of Courts at 866-954-9411. Probate mailing address- PO Box 789. No sealed, youthful offenders or juvenile records released. Will not fax documents. Court makes copy: $5.00 for 1st 20 pages then $.50 each add'l. per case. Certification fee: $5.00 per cert plus copy fee. Payee: Circuit Clerk. Business checks accepted. No credit cards accepted. Prepayment required.

Civil Name Search: Access: Online, in person. Both court and visitors may perform in person name searches. Search fee: Search fees may apply up to $25.00. Civil cases indexed by defendant, plaintiff. Civil records on computer from 3/94; prior on books to 1920. Civil PAT goes back to 1994. **See details of online access in the description at the front and rear of this chapter.**

Criminal Name Search: Access: Online, in person. Visitors must perform in person searches themselves. Required to search: name, years to search, DOB; also helpful: SSN. Criminal records computerized from 3/94; prior on books to 1920. Criminal PAT goes back to same as civil. **See details of online access in the description at the front and rear of this chapter.**

Probate Court PO Box 789, 1 Court Sq, Andalusia, AL 36420; probate phone: 334-428-2512/2513; fax: 334-428-2563; 8AM-5PM (EST). *Probate.*

Crenshaw County

Circuit & District Court PO Box 167, Luverne, AL 36049; 334-335-6575; fax: 334-335-2076; 8AM-4:30PM (CST). *Felony, Misdemeanor, Civil, Eviction, Small Claims, Probate.*

General Information: No sealed, adoptions, youthful offenders or juvenile records released. Will fax documents. Court makes copy: $5.00 for 1st 20 pages then $.50 each add'l. Self serve copy: same. Certification fee: No fee if copy fee paid, otherwise is $5.00. Payee: Circuit Clerk. Only cashiers checks and money orders accepted. No credit cards accepted. Prepayment required. Mail requests: SASE requested.

Civil Name Search: Access: Mail, in person, online. Only the court performs in person name searches; visitors may not. No search fee. Civil cases indexed by defendant, plaintiff. Civil records on computer from 1993, on book from 1977. Mail turnaround time 2-3 days. **See details of online access in the description at the front and rear of this chapter.**

Criminal Name Search: Access: Mail, online, in person. Only the court performs in person name searches; visitors may not. No search fee. Required to search: name, years to search, DOB; also helpful: SSN. Criminal records computerized from 1993, on book from 1977. Mail turnaround time 2-3 days. **See details of online access in the description at the front and rear of this chapter.**

Probate Court PO Box 328, 29 S Glenwood Ave, Luverne, AL 36049; 334-335-6568; fax: 334-335-3616; 8AM-4:30PM (EST). *Probate.*

Cullman County

Circuit Court Cullman County Courthouse, Rm 303, 500 2nd Ave SW, Cullman, AL 35055; 256-775-4654; criminal phone: 256-775-4799; civil phone: 256-775-4800; probate phone: 256-775-4652;; 8AM-4:30PM (CST). *Felony, Civil Actions over $10,000, Probate.*

www.co.cullman.al.us/courts.htm

General Information: No sealed, adoptions, youthful offenders or juvenile records released. Will not fax documents. Court makes copy: $5.00 for 1st 20 pages then $.50 each add'l. Self serve copy: same. Certification fee: $5.00 per doc plus copy fee. Payee: Robert Bates, Circuit Clerk. Business checks accepted. No credit cards accepted. Prepayment required. Mail requests: SASE required.

Civil Name Search: Access: Phone, mail, online, in person. Both court and visitors may perform in person name searches. Search fee for computerized search-$10.00; paper record search-$20.00; archived record search-$25.00. Civil cases indexed by defendant, plaintiff. Civil records on computer back to 1993, index back to 1977; books from 1900s. Mail turnaround time 10 days. Civil PAT goes back to 1977. Public terminal has indices only. **See details of online access in the description at the front and rear of this chapter.**

Criminal Name Search: Access: Mail, online, in person. Both court and visitors may perform in person name searches. Search fee: Search fee for computerized search-$10.00; paper record search-$20.00; archived record search-$25.00. Required to search: name, years to search, DOB; also helpful: SSN. Criminal records computerized from 1993; index back to 1977; prior in books. Mail turnaround time 10 days. Criminal PAT goes back to same as civil. Public terminal has indices only. **See details of online access in the description at the front and rear of this chapter.**

District Court 500 2nd Ave SW, Courthouse Rm 211, Cullman, AL 35055-4197; 256-775-4660; 8AM-4:30PM (CST). *Misdemeanor, Civil Actions under $10,000, Eviction, Small Claims.*

www.co.cullman.al.us/courts.htm#District

General Information: No sealed, adoptions, youthful offenders or juvenile records released. Will not fax documents. Court makes copy: $5.00 for 1st 20 pages then $.50 each add'l. Self serve copy: $.50 per page. Certification fee: $5.00 per cert. Payee: District Clerk. Only cashiers checks and money orders accepted. Credit cards not accepted for records or copies. Prepayment required. Mail requests: SASE required.

Civil Name Search: Access: Mail, in person, online. Both court and visitors may perform in person name searches. Search fee: $10.00 for computer search; $20.00 paper search; $25.00 to search archives. Civil cases indexed by defendant. Civil records on computer from 11/92, on books 10 yrs back. Mail turnaround time 1 week. Civil PAT goes back to 1992. **See details of online access in the description at the front and rear of this chapter.**

Criminal Name Search: Access: Mail, online, in person. Both court and visitors may perform in person name searches. Search fee: $10.00 for computer search; $20.00 paper search; $25.00 to search archives. Required to search: name, years to search, DOB; also helpful: SSN. Criminal records computerized from 11/92, on books 10 yrs back. Mail turnaround time 1 week. Criminal PAT goes back to same as civil. **See details of online access in the description at the front and rear of this chapter.**

Probate Court PO Box 970, 500 2nd Ave SW, Courthouse, Cullman, AL 35056; 256-775-4665 or 4805; fax: 256-775-4813; 8AM-4:30PM (EST). *Probate.*

www.co.cullman.al.us/serv03.htm

Dale County

Circuit & District Court PO Box 1350, Ozark, AL 36361; 334-774-5003;; 8AM-4:30PM (CST). *Felony, Misdemeanor, Civil, Eviction, Small Claims, Probate.*

General Information: No sealed, adoptions, youthful offenders or juvenile records released. Will not fax documents. Court makes copy: $5.00 for 1st 20 pages then $.50 each add'l. Certification fee: $5.00 per page. Payee: Dale County Circuit Clerk. Only cashiers checks and money orders accepted. No credit cards accepted. Prepayment required.

Civil Name Search: Access: Online, in person. Visitors must perform in person searches themselves. Civil cases indexed by defendant, plaintiff. Civil records on computer from 8/92, on books and index cards from the 1920s. Civil PAT goes back to 1994. **See details of online access in the description at the front and rear of this chapter.**

Criminal Name Search: Access: Online, in person. Visitors must perform in person searches themselves. Required to search: name, years to search, DOB; also helpful: SSN. Criminal records computerized from 8/92, on books and index cards from the 1920s. Criminal PAT goes back to same as civil. **See details of online access in the description at the front and rear of this chapter.**

Probate Court PO Box 580, 1 Court Sq (36360), Ozark, AL 36361-0580; probate phone: 334-774-2754; fax: 334-774-0468; 8AM-5PM (EST). *Probate.*

Dallas County

Circuit Court PO Box 1148, Selma, AL 36702; 334-874-2523; criminal phone: x3; civil phone: x6; fax: 334-877-0637; 8AM-4:30PM (CST). *Felony, Civil Actions over $10,000, Probate.*

General Information: Probate court is separate from this court. No sealed, youthful offenders or juvenile records released. Will fax documents to local or toll-free number if not a lot of pages. Court makes copy: $5.00 for 1st 20 pages then $.50 each add'l. Self serve copy: $.10 per page. Certification fee: $5.00 per file. Payee: Dallas County Circuit Court. Personal checks not accepted. No credit cards accepted for record requests. Prepayment required. Mail requests: SASE required.

Civil Name Search: Access: Mail, in person, online. Both court and visitors may perform in person name searches. No search fee. Civil cases indexed by defendant, plaintiff. Civil records on computer from 1992, on microfiche from the late 1970s, index books prior. Mail turnaround time less than 1 week for civil cases. Civil PAT goes back to 1992. Public terminal may not include recent activity. **See details of online access in the description at the front and rear of this chapter.**

Criminal Name Search: Access: Phone, mail, online, in person. Both court and visitors may perform in person name searches. No search fee. Required to search: name, years to search, DOB; also helpful: SSN. Criminal records computerized from 1992, on microfiche from the late 1970s, index books prior. Mail turnaround time less than 1 week. Criminal PAT goes back to same as civil. Public terminal may not include recent activity. **See details of online access in the description at the front and rear of this chapter.**

District Court PO Box 1148, 105 Lauderdale, Selma, AL 36702; 334-874-2523; fax: 334-877-0637; 8AM-4:30PM (CST). *Misdemeanor, Civil Actions under $10,000, Eviction, Small Claims.*

General Information: No sealed, adoptions, youthful offenders or juvenile records released. Will fax documents to local or toll-free number. Court makes copy: $5.00 for 1st 20 pages then $.50 each add'l. Self serve copy: same. Certification fee: $5.00 per cert plus copy fee. Payee: Circuit Clerk. Cashiers checks and money orders only. No credit cards accepted. Prepayment required. Mail requests: SASE required.

Civil Name Search: Access: Phone, mail, online, in person. Visitors must perform in person searches themselves. No search fee. Civil cases indexed by defendant. Civil records on books from 1967, on computer since 1993. Civil PAT goes back to 1993. **See details of online access in the description at the front and rear of this chapter.**

Criminal Name Search: Access: Mail, online, in person. Visitors must perform in person searches themselves. No search fee. Required to search: name, years to search; also helpful: DOB, SSN. Criminal docket on books from 1967, on computer since 1992. Mail turnaround time- varies . Criminal PAT goes back to same as civil. **See details of online access in the description at the front and rear of this chapter.**

Probate Court PO Box 987, 105 Lauderdale St, Selma, AL 36702; 334-874-2513; fax: 334-874-2553; 8:30AM-4:30PM (EST). *Probate.*

De Kalb County

Circuit & District Court PO Box 681149, 300 Grand Ave South, Fort Payne, AL 35968; 256-845-8525; fax: 256-845-8535; 8AM-4PM (CST). *Felony, Misdemeanor, Civil, Eviction, Small Claims, Probate.*
General Information: Search fee includes copy fee. Search fee includes both indexes if you request both. No sealed, adoptions, youthful offenders or juvenile records released. Court makes copy: $5.00 for 1st 20 pages then $.50 each add'l. Certification fee: $5.00 per doc. Payee: Circuit Clerk. Business checks accepted. No credit cards accepted. Prepayment required.
Civil Name Search: Access: Mail, in person, online. Both court and visitors may perform in person name searches. Search fee: $10.00 for a computer search, $20.00 for a paper search, and $25.00 if archival. Civil cases indexed by defendant. Civil records on computer from 8/1993, on books from 1959. Mail turnaround time 1 week. Civil PAT goes back to 1993. **See details of online access in the description at the front and rear of this chapter.**
Criminal Name Search: Access: Mail, online, in person. Both court and visitors may perform in person name searches. Search fee: $10.00 for a computer search, $20.00 for a paper search, and $25.00 if archival. Required to search: name, years to search; also helpful: DOB, SSN. Criminal records computerized from 8/1993, on books from 1959. Mail turnaround time 1 week. Criminal PAT goes back to same as civil. **See details of online access in the description at the front and rear of this chapter.**

Probate Court 300 Grand Ave SW, #100, Courthouse, Fort Payne, AL 35967; 256-845-8510; fax: 256-845-8514; 8AM-4PM (EST). *Probate.*
http://judgeronnieosborn.com/

Elmore County

Circuit & District Court - Civil Division PO Box 310, 8935 Hwy 231, Judicial Complex, Wetumpka, AL 36092; 334-514-3116; fax: 334-567-5957; 8AM-4:30PM (CST). *Civil, Probate.*
General Information: No sealed, adoptions, youthful offenders or juvenile records released. Will not fax out documents. Court makes copy: $5.00 for 1st 20 pages then $.50 each add'l. Self serve copy: same. Certification fee: $5.00 per doc plus copy fee. Payee: Circuit Court Clerk. Business checks accepted. Prepayment required.
Civil Name Search: Access: Mail, in person, online. Visitors must perform in person searches themselves. Search fee: $10.00 per name for computer search; $25.00 per name if archives search is required. Civil cases indexed by defendant, plaintiff. Civil records on computer from 1991, books from 1930. Mail turnaround time varies. Public use terminal has civil records back to 1991. **See details of online access in the description at the front and rear of this chapter.**

Circuit Court - Criminal Division PO Box 310, 8935 US Hwy 231, Wetumpka, AL 36092; 334-514-4221; fax: 334-567-5957; 8AM-4:30PM (CST). *Felony, Misdemeanor.*
General Information: No sealed, adoptions, youthful offenders or juvenile records released. Will not fax documents. Court makes copy: $5.00 for 1st 20 pages then $.50 each add'l. Self serve copy: same. Certification fee: $5.00 per cert plus copy fee. Payee: Circuit Court Clerk. Only cashiers checks and money orders accepted. Prepayment required. Mail requests: SASE required; use their form.
Criminal Name Search: Access: In person, Fax, online. Both court and visitors may perform in person name searches. Search fee: $20.00 each; archives search $30.00. Required to search: name, years to search, DOB, SSN. Criminal records computerized from mid-1991, books from 1960-1992. Note: Fax requests must be set-up in advance; telephone to get rate sheet and approval to fax. Public use terminal has crim records back to 1991. **See details of online access in the description at the front and rear of this chapter.**

Probate Court PO Box 280, 200 Commerce St, Wetumpka, AL 36092; probate phone: 334-567-1143; fax: 334-567-1144; 8AM-4:30PM (EST). *Probate.*

Escambia County

Circuit & District Court PO Box 856, Brewton, AL 36427; 251-867-0305; criminal phone: 251-867-0220; civil phone: 251-867-0285; fax: 251-867-0365; 8AM-4PM (CST). *Felony, Misdemeanor, Civil, Eviction, Small Claims, Probate.*
General Information: No sealed, adoptions, youthful offenders or juvenile records released. Fee to fax document $1.00 each plus $.25 per page. Court makes copy: $5.00 for 1st 20 pages then $.50 each add'l. Self serve copy: same. Certification fee: $5.00 per doc plus copy fee. Payee: Escambia County Circuit Court. Business checks accepted. No credit cards accepted. Prepayment required. Mail requests: SASE required.
Civil Name Search: Access: Mail, fax, online, in person. Both court and visitors may perform in person name searches. Search fee: $10.00 per name. Civil cases indexed by defendant, plaintiff. Civil records on computer from 1993, books and cards back to 1990. Mail turnaround time 10-14 days. Civil PAT goes back to 10/1993. **See details of online access in the description at the front and rear of this chapter.**
Criminal Name Search: Access: Mail, fax, online, in person. Both court and visitors may perform in person name searches. Search fee: $10.00 per name. Required to search: name, years to search, DOB. Criminal records computerized from 10/93, books and cards back to 1950. Mail turnaround time 10-14 days. Criminal PAT goes back to same as civil. **See details of online access in the description at the front and rear of this chapter.**

Probate Court PO Box 557, 314 Belleville Ave, Rm 205 (36426), Brewton, AL 36427; 251-867-0301; fax: 251-867-0284; 8AM-4PM (EST). *Probate.*
www.co.escambia.al.us

Etowah County

Circuit & District Court 801 Forrest Ave, Ste 202, Gadsden, AL 35901; 256-549-2150; criminal phone: 256-549-5437;; 8:30AM-5PM (CST). *Felony, Misdemeanor, Civil, Eviction, Small Claims.*
http://16jc.alacourt.gov/clerk/
General Information: No sealed, adoptions, youthful offenders or juvenile records released. Will not fax documents. Court makes copy: $5.00 for 1st 20 pages then $.50 each add'l. Self serve copy: $.15 per page. Certification fee: $5.00 per doc. Payee: Clerk of Court. Only cashiers checks and money orders accepted. Visa/MC accepted. Prepayment required. Mail requests: SASE requested.
Civil Name Search: Access: Mail, in person, online. Both court and visitors may perform in person name searches. Search fee: $10.00 for computerized records; $20.00 for paper records; $25.00 for archived/microfilmed records. Civil cases indexed by defendant, plaintiff. Civil records on computer from 1984, index on computer since 1977, books prior to 1977. Mail turnaround time 4-6 weeks. Civil PAT goes back to 1984. **See details of online access in the description at the front and rear of this chapter.**
Criminal Name Search: Access: Mail, online, in person. Both court and visitors may perform in person name searches. Search fee: $10.00 for computerized records; $20.00 for paper records; $25.00 for archived/microfilmed records. Required to search: name, years to search; also helpful: DOB, SSN. Criminal records computerized from 1984, index on computer since 1977, books prior to 1977. Mail turnaround time 4-6 weeks. Criminal PAT goes back to 1984. **See details of online access in the description at the front and rear of this chapter.**

Probate Court 800 Forest Ave, #122, PO Box 187, Gadsden, AL 35901; probate phone: 256-549-5341/5342; fax: 256-546-1149; 8AM-5PM . *Probate.*
www.etowahcounty.org/#

Fayette County

Circuit & District Court PO Box 906, 113 N Temple Ave, Fayette, AL 35555; 205-932-4617; fax: 205-932-2697; 8AM-4:30PM (CST). *Felony, Misdemeanor, Civil, Eviction, Small Claims, Probate.*
www.alacourt.gov
General Information: No sealed, youthful offenders or juvenile records released. Will fax documents $.25 per page. Court makes copy: $5.00 for 1st 20 pages then $.50 each add'l. Self serve copy: same. Certification fee: $5.00 per doc plus copy fee. Payee: Circuit Clerk. Business checks accepted. No credit cards accepted. Prepayment required.
Civil Name Search: Access: Online, mail, fax, in person. Visitors must perform in person searches themselves. Search fee: $20.00 per name. Civil cases indexed by defendant. Civil records on computer from 3/94, on books and cards from 1977. Civil PAT goes back to 1994. **See details of online access in the description at the front and rear of this chapter.**
Criminal Name Search: Access: Online, mail, fax, in person. Visitors must perform in person searches themselves. Search fee: $20.00 per name. Required to search: name, years to search, DOB; also helpful: SSN. Criminal records computerized from 3/94, on books and cards from 1977. Criminal PAT goes back to same as civil. Terminal results include SSN. **See details of online access in the description at the front and rear of this chapter.**

Probate Court PO Box 509, 113 Temple Ave N, Courthouse, Fayette, AL 35555; 205-932-5916; fax: 205-932-7600; 8AM-5PM M; 8AM04PM T-F (EST). *Probate.*

Franklin County

Circuit & District Court PO Box 160, 410 N Jackson Ave, Russellville, AL 35653; 256-332-8861;; 8AM-5PM (CST). *Felony, Misdemeanor, Civil, Eviction, Small Claims, Probate.*
General Information: No sealed, youthful offenders or juvenile released. Court makes copy: $5.00 for 1st 20 pages then $.50 each add'l. Self serve copy: same. Certification fee: $5.00 plus copy fee. Payee: Circuit Court Clerk. Business checks accepted. No credit cards accepted. Prepayment required. Mail requests: SASE required.

Civil Name Search: Access: Mail, in person, online. Both court and visitors may perform in person name searches. Search fee: $10.00 per name per index. Required to search: name, years to search; also helpful: address. Civil cases indexed by defendant, plaintiff. Civil records on computer from 1993, on index books prior. SSN and DOB helpful, but records are not indexed by SSN. Mail turnaround time 5-7 days. Civil PAT goes back to 1993. **See details of online access in the description at the front and rear of this chapter.**

Criminal Name Search: Access: Mail, online, in person. Both court and visitors may perform in person name searches. Search fee: $10.00 per name per index. Required to search: name, years to search, DOB; also helpful: SSN. Criminal records computerized from 1993, on index books prior. SSN and DOB helpful, but records are not indexed by SSN. Mail turnaround time 5-7 days. Criminal PAT goes back to same as civil. **See details of online access in the description at the front and rear of this chapter.**

Probate Court PO Box 70, 410 N Jackson St, Russellville, AL 35653; 256-332-8801; fax: 256-332-8423; 8AM-5PM (EST). *Probate.*

Geneva County

Circuit & District Court PO Box 86, Geneva, AL 36340; 334-684-5620; fax: 334-684-5605; 8AM-5PM (CST). *Felony, Misdemeanor, Civil, Eviction, Small Claims, Probate.*

General Information: Online identifiers in results same as on public terminal. No sealed, adoptions, youthful offenders or juvenile records released. Will not fax documents. Court makes copy: $5.00 for 1st 20 pages then $.50 each add'l. Self serve copy: same. Certification fee: $5.00 per case plus copy fee. Payee: Circuit Clerk. Business checks accepted. Out of state personal checks not accepted. No credit cards accepted. Prepayment required.

Civil Name Search: Access: Online, in person. Visitors must perform in person searches themselves. Required to search: name, years to search; also helpful: address. Civil cases indexed by defendant, plaintiff. Civil records on computer from 1992. Civil PAT goes back to 1992. **See details of online access in the description at the front and rear of this chapter.**

Criminal Name Search: Access: Online, in person. Visitors must perform in person searches themselves. Required to search: name, years to search, DOB; also helpful: SSN. Criminal records computerized from 1992. Criminal PAT goes back to same as civil. Terminal results include SSN. **See details of online access in the description at the front and rear of this chapter.**

Probate Court PO Box 430, 200 N Commerce St, Courthouse, Geneva, AL 36340; probate phone: 334-684-5647; fax: 334-684-5723; 8AM-5PM (EST). *Probate.*

Greene County

Circuit & District Court PO Box 307, Eutaw, AL 35462; 205-372-3598; fax: 205-372-1510; 8AM-N. 1-4:30PM (CST). *Felony, Misdemeanor, Civil, Eviction, Small Claims, Probate.*

General Information: Online identifiers in results same as on public terminal. No sealed, adoptions, youthful offenders or juvenile records released. Will fax documents. Court makes copy: $5.00 for 1st 20 pages then $.50 each add'l. Self serve copy: same. Certification fee: $5.00 per page plus copy fee. Payee: Circuit Clerk. Business checks accepted. No credit cards accepted. Prepayment required. Mail requests: SASE required.

Civil Name Search: Access: Mail, in person, online. Both court and visitors may perform in person name searches. Search fee: $25.00 per name; $10.00 if computer only search. Required to search: name, years to search; also helpful: DOB, SSN and signed release. Civil cases indexed by defendant, plaintiff. Civil records on books from 1984. Mail turnaround time 1 week. Civil PAT goes back to 1993. Terminal results also show SSNs. **See details of online access in the description at the front and rear of this chapter.**

Criminal Name Search: Access: Mail, online, in person. Visitors must perform in person searches themselves. Search fee: $25.00 per name; $10.00 if computer only search. Required to search: name, years to search; also helpful: DOB, SSN and signed release. Criminal docket on books from 1984. Mail turnaround time 1 week. Criminal PAT goes back to same as civil. Terminal results include SSN. **See details of online access in the description at the front and rear of this chapter.**

Probate Court PO Box 790, 400 Morrow Ave, Courthouse, Eutaw, AL 35462; probate phone: 205-372-3340; fax: 205-372-3323; 8AM-4PM (EST). *Probate.*

Probate Court PO Box 665, 65 N Alabama Ave (36460), Monroeville, AL 36461-0665; probate phone: 251-743-4107; fax: 251-575-4756; 8AM-5PM M,T,W,F; 8AM-N TH (EST). *Probate.*

Hale County

Circuit & District Court County Courthouse, Rm 8, PO Drawer 99, Greensboro, AL 36744; 334-624-4334; fax: 334-624-8064; 8AM-4:30PM (CST). *Felony, Misdemeanor, Civil, Eviction, Small Claims, Probate.*

General Information: Search fee includes both civil and criminal indexes. No sealed, adoptions, youthful offenders or juvenile records released. Will fax documents to local and toll free numbers. Court makes copy: $5.00 for 1st 20 pages then $.50 each add'l. Certification fee: $5.00 per cert. Payee: Clerk of the Court. Business checks accepted but not personal checks. No credit cards accepted for search requests. Prepayment required. Mail requests: SASE required.

Civil Name Search: Access: Mail, in person, online. Both court and visitors may perform in person name searches. Search fee: $10.00 per name. Civil cases indexed by defendant, plaintiff. Civil records on books from 1985. Mail turnaround time 1 week. **See details of online access in the description at the front and rear of this chapter.**

Criminal Name Search: Access: Mail, online, in person. Both court and visitors may perform in person name searches. Search fee: $10.00 per name. Required to search: name, years to search; also helpful: DOB, SSN. Criminal docket on books from 1985. Mail turnaround time 1 week. **See details of online access in the description at the front and rear of this chapter.**

Probate Court 1001 Main St, Courthouse, Greensboro, AL 36744; 334-624-7391; fax: 334-624-8725; 8AM-4PM (EST). *Probate.*

Henry County

Circuit & District Court 101 Court Square, Ste. J, Abbeville, AL 36310-2135; 334-585-2753; fax: 334-585-5006; 8AM-4:30PM (CST). *Felony, Misdemeanor, Civil, Eviction, Small Claims, Probate.*

General Information: No sealed, adoptions, youthful offenders or juvenile records released. Court makes copy: $5.00 for 1st 20 pages then $.50 each add'l. Self serve copy: same. Certification fee: $5.00 per cert plus copy fee. Payee: Circuit Clerk. No personal checks accepted. No credit cards accepted expect online. Prepayment required. Mail requests: SASE required.

Civil Name Search: Access: Mail, in person, online. Only the court performs in person name searches; visitors may not. Search fee: $10.00 per name. There is a 30 minute or 5 name limit per order. Civil cases indexed by defendant. Civil records on computer from 1994, index cards 10 yrs back. Mail turnaround time 2-3 days. **See details of online access in the description at the front and rear of this chapter.**

Criminal Name Search: Access: Mail, online, in person. Only the court performs in person name searches; visitors may not. Search fee: $10.00 per name. There is a 30 minute or 5 name limit per order. Required to search: name, years to search, DOB; also helpful: SSN. Criminal records computerized from 5/93, index cards 10 yrs back. Mail turnaround time 2-3 days. **See details of online access in the description at the front and rear of this chapter.**

Probate Court 101 Court Sq, #A, Abbeville, AL 36310; probate phone: 334-585-3257; fax: 334-585-3610; 8AM-4:30PM (EST). *Probate.*
http://probate.henrycountyalabama.org/default.htm

Houston County

Circuit & District Court PO Drawer 6406, Dothan, AL 36302; 334-677-4800; criminal phone: Circ-334-677-4858; Dist-334-677-4870; civil phone: Circ-334-677-4859; Dist-334-677-4868;; 8AM-4:30PM (CST). *Felony, Misdemeanor, Civil, Eviction, Small Claims, Probate.*

General Information: No sealed, adoptions, youthful offenders or juvenile records released. Will not fax documents. Court makes copy: $5.00 for 1st 20 pages then $.50 each add'l. Certification fee: $5.00. Payee: Carla Woodall. No personal checks or credit cards accepted. Prepayment required.

Civil Name Search: Access: Mail, in person, online. Both court and visitors may perform in person name searches. No search fee. Civil cases indexed by defendant. Civil records on computer from 1977, index books from 1950s. Civil PAT goes back to 1978. **See details of online access in the description at the front and rear of this chapter.**

Criminal Name Search: Access: Mail, online, in person. Both court and visitors may perform in person name searches. No search fee. Required to search: name, years to search; also helpful: DOB, SSN. Criminal records computerized from 1977, index books from 1950s. Criminal PAT goes back to 1977. **See details of online access in the description at the front and rear of this chapter.**

Probate Court 462 N Oates St, Dothan, AL 36302; 334-677-4792; fax: 334-677-4724; 7AM-5:30PM M-TH (EST). *Probate.*
www.houstoncounty.org/dept.php?id=10

Jackson County

Circuit & District Court PO Box 397, 102 E Laurel St, Courthouse, Scottsboro, AL 35768; 256-574-9320; criminal phone: 256-574-9320; civil phone: 256-574-9320; fax: 256-259-9981; 8AM-4:30PM (CST). *Felony, Misdemeanor, Civil, Eviction, Small Claims, Probate.*

General Information: Search fee includes both civil and criminal indexes. No sealed, adoptions, youthful offenders or juvenile records released. Will fax documents only if situation urgent enough to require quick return. Court makes copy: $5.00 for 1st 20 pages then $.50 each add'l. Self serve copy: $.50 per page. Certification fee: $5.00 per case plus copy fee. Payee: Circuit

Court Clerk. In-state personal checks accepted. No credit cards accepted. Prepayment required. Mail requests: SASE required.

Civil Name Search: Access: Mail, fax, online, in person. Both court and visitors may perform in person name searches. Search fee: $10.00 database search; $15.00 if manual index or archives. Add'l fees if search exceeds 30 minutes. Civil cases indexed by defendant. Civil records on computer from 5/1993, on cards from 1977. Mail turnaround time 1-3 weeks. Civil PAT goes back to 1993. **See details of online access in the description at the front and rear of this chapter.**

Criminal Name Search: Access: Mail, fax, online, in person. Both court and visitors may perform in person name searches. Search fee: $10.00 database search; $15.00 if manual index or archives. Add'l fees is search exceeds 30 minutes. Required to search: name, years to search, DOB; also helpful: SSN. Criminal records computerized from 5/1993, on cards from 1977. Mail turnaround time 1-2 weeks. Criminal PAT goes back to 1993. **See details of online access in the description at the front and rear of this chapter.**

Probate Court PO Box 128, 102 E Laurel St, #11, Scottsboro, AL 35768; probate phone: 256-574-9290; fax: 256-574-9318; 8AM-4:30PM T-F; 8AM-6PM M (EST). *Probate.*

www.deltacomputersystems.com/al/al39/index.html

Jefferson County

Circuit Court - Bessemer Division 1852 2nd Ave N, #130, Bessemer, AL 35020; 205-497-8510;; 8AM-5PM (CST). *Felony, Civil Actions over $10,000.*

General Information: Online identifiers in results same as on public terminal. No sealed, adoptions, youthful offenders or juvenile records released. Will not fax documents. Court makes copy: $5.00 for 1st 20 pages then $.50 each add'l. Self serve copy: $.10 per page. Certification fee: $5.00 per cert plus copy fee. Payee: Clerk of Circuit Court. Only cashiers checks and money orders accepted. No credit cards accepted. Prepayment required.

Civil Name Search: Access: Mail, online, in person. Visitors must perform in person searches themselves. Search fee: Computerized record is $10.00, paper record is $20.00, archived/microfilmed record is $25.00, but no fee to search. Civil cases indexed by defendant, plaintiff. Civil records on computer from 1988, on index books from 1930s to 1977. Mail turnaround time is 7-10 days. Civil PAT goes back to 1985. **See details of online access in the description at the front and rear of this chapter.**

Criminal Name Search: Access: Mail, online, in person. Visitors must perform in person searches themselves. Search fee: Computerized record is $10.00, paper record is $20.00, archived/microfilmed record is $25.00, but no fee to search. Required to search: name, years to search, DOB; also helpful: SSN. Criminal records computerized from 1988, on index books from 1930s to 1977. Mail turnaround time is 7-10 days. Criminal PAT goes back to same as civil. **See details of online access in the description at the front and rear of this chapter.**

Circuit Court - Birmingham Civil Division 716 Richard Arrington Blvd N, Rm 400, Birmingham, AL 35263; 205-325-5355; 8AM-5PM (CST). *Civil Actions over $10,000.*

General Information: SM & DV- 325-5331. No sealed, adoptions, youthful offenders or juvenile records released. Will not fax documents. Court makes copy: $5.00 for 1st 20 pages then $.50 each add'l. Certification fee: $5.00 per doc plus copy fee. Payee: Clerk of Circuit Court. Business checks accepted. No credit cards accepted. Prepayment required.

Civil Name Search: Access: Mail, online, in person. Both court and visitors may perform in person name searches. Search fee: $25.00 per search. Civil cases indexed by defendant, plaintiff. Civil records on computer from 1976, on index books from 1976 to 1986, prior to 1976 archived. Mail turnaround time 1-2 weeks. Public use terminal has civil records back to 1976. Not all results show address or DOB. **See details of online access in the description at the front and rear of this chapter.**

Circuit Court - Birmingham Criminal Division 801 Richard Arrington Blvd, Rm 901, Birmingham, AL 35203; 205-325-5285; 8AM-4:55PM (CST). *Felony.*

General Information: No sealed, adoptions, youthful offenders, sex offender cases or juvenile records released. Will not fax documents. Court makes copy: $5.00 for 1st 20 pages then $.50 each add'l. Certification fee: $5.00 per case plus copy fee. Payee: Clerk of Court. Only cashiers checks and money orders accepted. No credit cards accepted. Prepayment required.

Criminal Name Search: Access: Online, in person. Visitors must perform in person searches themselves. Required to search: name, years to search, DOB, signed release; also helpful: address, SSN. Criminal records computerized from 1970, index books prior. Public use terminal has crim records back to 1971. The terminal is in the courthouse and at the CJC Bldg. **See details of online access in the description at the front and rear of this chapter.** Online results show name, DOB, address.

District Court - Bessemer Division 1852 2nd Ave N, #130, Bessemer, AL 35020; 205-497-8620; civil phone: 205-497-8510;; 8AM-5PM (CST). *Felony, Misdemeanor, Civil Actions under $10,000, Eviction, Small Claims, Traffic.*

www.alacourt.gov

General Information: No sealed, adoptions, youthful offenders or juvenile records released. Will not fax documents. Court makes copy: $5.00 for 1st 20 pages then $.50 each add'l. Self serve copy: same. Certification fee: $5.00 per cert plus copy fee. Payee: Bessemer District Court. Business checks accepted; no personal checks. No credit cards accepted. Prepayment required.

Civil Name Search: Access: Online, in person. Visitors must perform in person searches themselves. Civil cases indexed by defendant, plaintiff. Civil records on computer from 1986, on index cards from 1977, prior on docket books. **See details of online access in the description at the front and rear of this chapter.**

Criminal Name Search: Access: Online, in person, mail. Visitors must perform in person searches themselves. Search fee: $25.00 per name. Required to search: name, years to search, DOB; also helpful: SSN. Criminal records computerized from 1986, on index cards from 1977, prior on docket books. Mail turnaround time varies. **See details of online access in the description at the front and rear of this chapter.**

District Court - Birmingham Civil Division 716 Richard Arrington Blvd N, Rm 500, Birmingham, AL 35203; 205-325-5331; 8AM-5PM (CST). *Civil Actions under $10,000, Eviction, Small Claims.*

General Information: No sealed, adoptions, youthful offenders or juvenile records released. Will not fax documents. Court makes copy: $5.00 for 1st 20 pages then $.50 each add'l. Certification fee: $5.00 per case plus copy fee. Payee: District Court. No personal checks or credit cards accepted. Prepayment required.

Civil Name Search: Access: Online, in person. Both court and visitors may perform in person name searches. No search fee. Civil cases indexed by defendant, plaintiff. Civil records on computer from 1977, index books stored in warehouse. Public use terminal has civil records back to 1977; also some criminal records. **See details of online access in the description at the front and rear of this chapter.**

District Court - Birmingham Criminal Division 801 Richard Arrington Blvd N, Rm 207, Birmingham, AL 35203; 205-325-5309;; 8AM-5PM (CST). *Misdemeanor.*

General Information: No sealed, sexual abuse, adoptions, youthful offenders or juvenile records released. Will not fax documents. Court makes copy: $5.00 for 1st 20 pages then $.50 each add'l.For microfilm copy fee is $30.00. Certification fee: $5.00 per case plus copy fee. Payee: District Court. Only cashiers checks and money orders accepted. No credit cards accepted. Prepayment required. Mail requests: SASE required.

Criminal Name Search: Access: Mail, online, in person. Both court and visitors may perform in person name searches. No search fee. Required to search: name, DOB; also helpful: years to search, SSN, sex, date of arrest. Criminal records computerized from 1986. To search for records prior to 1987, require arrest date. Mail turnaround time 5-10 days. Public use terminal has crim records back to 1986. **See details of online access in the description at the front and rear of this chapter.**

Probate Court 716 Richard Arrington Jr Blvd N., Birmingham, AL 35203; 205-325-5411; fax: 205-325-4885; 8AM-4:45PM (CST). *Probate.*

http://jeffconline.jccal.org/

Probate Court - Bessemer Division 1801 3rd Ave N, Rm 101, Bessemer, AL 35020; 205-481-4100; probate phone: 205-481-4100;; 8AM-4:30PM (EST). *Probate.*

Lamar County

Circuit & District Court PO Box 434, Vernon, AL 35592; 205-695-7193; fax: 205-695-0046; 8AM-4:30PM (CST). *Felony, Misdemeanor, Civil, Eviction, Small Claims, Probate.*

General Information: Online identifiers in results same as on public terminal. No sealed, adoptions, youthful offenders or juvenile records released. Will not fax documents. Court makes copy: $5.00 for 1st 20 pages then $.50 each add'l. Certification fee: $5.00. Payee: Circuit Clerk. Only cashiers checks and money orders accepted. Major credit cards accepted. Prepayment required.

Civil Name Search: Access: Online, in person. Visitors must perform in person searches themselves. Required to search: name, years to search; also helpful: address. Civil cases indexed by defendant, plaintiff. Civil records on books from 1900; computerized records go back to 1995. Civil PAT goes back to 1995. Terminal results include SSN. **See details of online access in the description at the front and rear of this chapter.**

Criminal Name Search: Access: Online, in person. Visitors must perform in person searches themselves. Required to search: name, years to search, DOB, signed release; also helpful: SSN. Criminal docket on books from 1900; computerized records go back to 1995. Criminal PAT goes back to 1995. Terminal results include SSN. T **See details of online access in**

the description at the front and rear of this chapter. Online results show name, DOB.

Probate Court PO Box 338, 44690 Hwy 17, Vernon, AL 35592; probate phone: 205-695-9119; fax: 205-695-9253; 8AM-5PM M,T,TH,F; 8AM-N W,Sat (EST). *Probate.*

Lauderdale County

Circuit Court PO Box 795, Florence, AL 35631; 256-760-5710; criminal phone: 256-760-5713; fax: 256-760-5727; 8AM-5PM (CST). *Felony, Civil Actions over $10,000, Probate.*

www.alacourt.gov

General Information: No sealed, adoptions, youthful offenders or juvenile records released. Will fax documents to local or toll-free number. Court makes copy: $5.00 for 1st 20 pages then $.50 each add'l. Self serve copy: same. Certification fee: $5.00. Payee: Circuit Court Clerk. Personal checks accepted. No credit cards accepted. Prepayment required.

Civil Name Search: Access: Online, in person. Visitors must perform in person searches themselves. Civil cases indexed by defendant, plaintiff. Civil records on computer from 1977, index books from the 1930s. Civil PAT goes back to 1985. **See details of online access in the description at the front and rear of this chapter.**

Criminal Name Search: Access: Online, in person. Visitors must perform in person searches themselves. Required to search: name, years to search, DOB; also helpful: SSN. Criminal records computerized from 1977, index books from the 1930s. Criminal PAT goes back to same as civil. **See details of online access in the description at the front and rear of this chapter.**

District Court PO Box 776, Florence, AL 35631; 256-760-5726; criminal phone: 256-760-5724; civil phone: 256-760-5722; fax: 256-760-5727; 8AM-N, 1-5PM (CST). *Misdemeanor, Civil Actions under $10,000, Eviction, Small Claims.*

www.alacourt.gov

General Information: No sealed, adoptions, youthful offenders or juvenile records released. No fee to fax documents. Court makes copy: $5.00 for 1st 20 pages then $.50 each add'l. Certification fee: $5.00. Payee: District Clerk. Personal checks accepted. No credit cards accepted. Prepayment required. Mail requests: SASE required.

Civil Name Search: Access: Mail, fax, online, in person. Visitors must perform in person searches themselves. No search fee. Civil cases indexed by defendant, plaintiff. Civil records on computer from 1986, books from the 1930s. Civil PAT goes back to 1985. **See details of online access in the description at the front and rear of this chapter.**

Criminal Name Search: Access: Mail, fax, online, in person. Visitors must perform in person searches themselves. No search fee. Required to search: name, years to search, DOB; also helpful: SSN. Criminal records computerized from 1986, books from the 1930s. Mail turnaround time 1 week. Criminal PAT goes back to same as civil. **See details of online access in the description at the front and rear of this chapter.**

Probate Court PO Box 1059, 200 S Court St (35630), Florence, AL 35631; probate phone: 256-760-5800; fax: 256-760-5807; 8AM-5PM (EST). *Probate.*

www.lauderdalecountyonline.com

Lawrence County

Circuit & District Court PO Box 249, 14330 Court St #103, Moulton, AL 35650; 256-974-2432; criminal phone: 256-974-2436. Mis'd/&/Traffic-974-2434/2379; civil phone: 256-974-2433/; fax: 256-974-1118; 8AM-N, 1-4PM MTWF, 8AM-N Thurs (CST). *Felony, Misdemeanor, Civil, Eviction, Small Claims, Probate.*

General Information: Search includes both indexes. An add'l search fee is charged if the archives is accessed. No sealed, adoption, youthful offender, juvenile records released. Will not fax documents. Court makes copy: $5.00 for 1st 20 pages then $.50 each add'l. Certification fee: $5.00 per cert plus copy fee. Payee: Court clerk. No personal checks or credit cards accepted. Prepayment required.

Civil Name Search: Access: Online, in person. Visitors must perform in person searches themselves. Civil cases indexed by defendant. Civil records on computer from mid-1994, on books and index cards from 1920s. Civil PAT goes back to 1994. **See details of online access in the description at the front and rear of this chapter.**

Criminal Name Search: Access: Online, in person. Visitors must perform in person searches themselves. Required to search: name, years to search; also helpful: DOB, SSN. Criminal records computerized from mid-1994, on books and index cards from 1920s. Criminal PAT goes back to same as civil. **See details of online access in the description at the front and rear of this chapter.**

Probate Court PO Box 310, 14330 Court St, #102, Moulton, AL 35650; probate phone: 256-974-2440; fax: 256-974-3188; 8AM-4PM (CST). *Probate.*

Lee County

Circuit & District Court 2311 Gateway Dr, Rm 104, Opelika, AL 36801; 334-737-3526; fax: 334-737-3520; 8:30AM-4:30PM; no phone svc N-2PM (CST). *Felony, Misdemeanor, Civil, Eviction, Small Claims.*

General Information: No sealed, adoptions, youthful offenders or juvenile records released. Court makes copy: $5.00 for 1st 20 pages then $.50 each add'l. Certification fee: $5.00 per page. Payee: Clerk's Office. Only cashiers checks and money orders accepted. No credit cards accepted. Prepayment required. Mail requests: SASE required.

Civil Name Search: Access: Mail, online, in person. Only the court performs in person name searches; visitors may not. Search fee: $10.00 for computerized check; $20.00 for search of paper records; $25.00 for search of closed cases or otherwise archived records. Civil cases indexed by defendant, plaintiff. Civil records on computer from 1980s, on index cards from 1988. Mail turnaround time 1 week. **See details of online access in the description at the front and rear of this chapter.**

Criminal Name Search: Access: Mail, online, in person. Only the court performs in person name searches; visitors may not. Search fee: $10.00 for computerized check; $20.00 for search of paper records; $25.00 for search of closed cases or otherwise archived records. Required to search: name, years, DOB to search; also helpful: SSN. Criminal records computerized from 1980s, on index cards from 1988. Mail turnaround time 1 week. **See details of online access in the description at the front and rear of this chapter.**

Probate Court PO Drawer 2266, 215 S 9th St, Opelika, AL 36803; 334-745-9761; fax: 334-705-5082; 8:30AM-4:30PM (EST). *Probate.*

Limestone County

Circuit & District Court 200 Washington St West, Athens, AL 35611; 256-233-6406;; 8AM-3:30PM (CST). *Felony, Misdemeanor, Civil, Eviction, Small Claims, Probate.*

General Information: No juvenile, youthful offender records released. Will not fax documents. Court makes copy: $5.00 for 1st 20 pages then $.50 each add'l. Self serve copy: $.25 per page. Certification fee: $5.00. Payee: Clerk of Court. Personal checks accepted. No credit cards accepted. Prepayment required.

Civil Name Search: Access: In person, online. Visitors must perform in person searches themselves. No search fee. Civil cases indexed by defendant, plaintiff. Civil records on computer since 1993; prior in docket books. Civil PAT goes back to 1993. **See details of online access in the description at the front and rear of this chapter.**

Criminal Name Search: Access: In person, online. Visitors must perform in person searches themselves. No search fee. Required to search: name, years to search, DOB. Criminal records on computer since 1993, prior in docket books. Note: Office is not staffed to perform criminal background checks. Criminal PAT goes back to 1993. **See details of online access in the description at the front and rear of this chapter.**

Probate Court 100 S Clinton St, #D, 2nd Fl, Clinton St Annex, Athens, AL 35611; probate phone: 256-233-6427; fax: 256-233-6474; 8AM-4:30PM (EST). *Probate.*

www.probate.limestonecounty.net/

Lowndes County

Circuit & District Court PO Box 876, 1 Washington St, Hayneville, AL 36040; 334-548-2252; 8AM-4:30PM (CST). *Felony, Misdemeanor, Civil, Eviction, Small Claims, Probate.*

General Information: No sealed, adoptions, youthful offenders or juvenile records released. Will fax documents to local or toll free line. Court makes copy: $5.00 for 1st 20 pages then $.50 each add'l. Self serve copy: same. Certification fee: $5.00 per cert plus copy fee. Payee: District Court Clerk. Business checks accepted. Credit cards accepted for criminal searches only. Prepayment required. Mail requests: SASE required.

Civil Name Search: Access: Mail, in person, online. Both court and visitors may perform in person name searches. Search fee: $10.00 per name. Civil cases indexed by defendant, plaintiff. Civil index on cards from 1977; computerized since 1996. Mail turnaround time up to 1 week. Civil PAT goes back to 1995. **See details of online access in the description at the front and rear of this chapter.**

Criminal Name Search: Access: Mail, online, in person. Both court and visitors may perform in person name searches. Search fee: $10.00 per name. Required to search: name, years to search; also helpful: DOB, SSN. Criminal records indexed on cards from 1977; computerized since 1996. Mail turnaround time up to 1 week. Criminal PAT goes back to same as civil. **See details of online access in the description at the front and rear of this chapter.**

Probate Court PO Box 5, 1 Washington St, Courthouse, Hayneville, AL 36040; probate phone: 334-548-2365; fax: 334-548-5399; 8AM-4:30PM (EST). *Probate.*

Macon County

Circuit & District Court PO Box 830723, Tuskegee, AL 36083; 334-724-2614; fax: 334-727-6483; 8AM-N, 1-4:30PM (CST). *Felony, Misdemeanor, Civil, Eviction, Small Claims, Probate.*

General Information: No sealed, adoption, youthful offender, juvenile records released. Will fax documents to local or toll free line. Court makes copy: $5.00 for 1st 20 pages then $.50 each add'l. Certification fee: $2.50 per page includes copy fee. Payee: Office of Circuit Clerk. Business checks accepted. Major credit cards accepted. Prepayment required.

Civil Name Search: Access: Mail, in person, online. Both court and visitors may perform in person name searches. Search fee: $10.00 per name. Civil cases indexed by defendant, plaintiff. Civil index on docket books from 1977; on computer back to 1993. Mail turnaround time 30 days. **See details of online access in the description at the front and rear of this chapter.**

Criminal Name Search: Access: Mail, online, in person. Only the court performs in person name searches; visitors may not. Search fee: $10.00 per name. Required to search: name, years to search; also helpful: DOB, SSN. Criminal records go back to 1977; on computer back to 1993. Mail turnaround time 30 days. **See details of online access in the description at the front and rear of this chapter.**

Probate Court 101 E Rosa Parks Ave, #101, Tuskegee, AL 36083-1731; probate phone: 334-724-2611; fax: 334-724-2512; 8:30AM-4:30PM (CST). *Probate.*

Madison County

Circuit Court - Civil 100 N Side Square, Courthouse, Records Search, Circuit Court Div, Huntsville, AL 35801; 256-532-3381; 8:30AM-5PM (CST). *Civil Actions over $10,000, Probate.*

www.madisoncountycircuitclerk.org

General Information: No sealed, adoptions, youthful offenders or juvenile records released. Will not fax documents. Court makes copy: $5.00 for 1st 20 pages then $.50 each add'l. Self serve copy: same. Certification fee: $5.00 per cert. No personal checks or credit cards accepted. Prepayment required.

Civil Name Search: Access: Mail, online, in person. Visitors must perform in person searches themselves. Search fee: $25.00 per name. Required to search: name, years to search; also helpful: address. Civil cases indexed by defendant, plaintiff. Civil records on computer from 1977, index books from 1937. Mail turnaround time 1-5 days. Public use terminal has civil records back to 1977. **See details of online access in the description at the front and rear of this chapter.**

Circuit Court - Criminal 100 N Side Square, Courthouse, Huntsville, AL 35801-4820; criminal phone: 256-532-3386; fax: 256-532-3768; 8:30AM-5PM (CST). *Felony.*

www.madisoncountyal.gov/probate/home.shtml

General Information: No sealed, adoptions, youthful offenders or juvenile records released. Court makes copy: $.50 per page. Self serve copy: same. Certification fee: $5.00 per cert plus copy fee. Payee: Circuit Court Clerk. No personal checks or credit cards accepted. Prepayment required.

Criminal Name Search: Access: Mail, online, in person. Visitors must perform in person searches themselves. Search fee: $10.00 per name. Required to search: name, years to search; also helpful: DOB, SSN. Criminal records computerized from 1977, books from 1937-1977 (at the Huntsville Public Library, 3rd fl archives, only). Public use terminal has crim records back to 1977. SSNs appear less frequently the older the case is. 2 PATs. **See details of online access in the description at the front and rear of this chapter.**

District Court 100 N Side Square, Rm 821 Courthouse, Huntsville, AL 35801; criminal phone: 256-532-3373; civil phone: 256-532-3622; fax: 256-532-6972; 8:30AM-5PM (CST). *Misdemeanor, Civil Actions under $10,000, Eviction, Small Claims.*

www.madisoncountycircuitclerk.org/

General Information: No sealed, adoptions, youthful offenders or juvenile records released. Will not fax out documents. Court makes copy: $5.00 for 1st 20 pages then $.50 each add'l. Certification fee: $5.50 per cert plus copy fee. Payee: District Court. Only cashiers checks, cash or money orders accepted. No credit cards accepted. Prepayment required.

Civil Name Search: Access: Online, in person. Visitors must perform in person searches themselves. Civil cases indexed by defendant, plaintiff. Civil records on computer from 1982, index books prior. Civil PAT goes back to 1980. **See details of online access in the description at the front and rear of this chapter.**

Criminal Name Search: Access: Online, in person. Visitors must perform in person searches themselves. Required to search: name, years to search; also helpful: DOB, SSN. Criminal records computerized from 1982, index books prior since 1979. Criminal PAT goes back to 1977. **See details of online access in the description at the front and rear of this chapter.**

Probate Court 100 Northside Sq, Rm 101, Huntsville, AL 35801-4820; 256-532-3330; probate phone: 256-532-3339; fax: 256-532-3338; 8:30AM-4:30PM (EST). *Probate.*

www.co.madison.al.us/probate/home.shtml

Marengo County

Circuit & District Court PO Box 480566, 101 E Coats Ave #104, Linden, AL 36748; 334-295-2220; criminal phone: 334-295-2222; civil phone: 334-295-2219; probate phone: 334-289-4852; fax: 334-295-2092; 8AM-4:30PM (CST). *Felony, Misdemeanor, Civil, Eviction, Small Claims, Probate.*

General Information: No sealed, adoptions, youthful offenders or juvenile records released. Court makes copy: $5.00 for 1st 20 pages then $.50 each add'l. Self serve copy: none. Certification fee: $5.00. Payee: Circuit Clerk. Business checks accepted. No personal checks. No credit cards accepted. Prepayment required.

Civil Name Search: Access: Mail, in person, online. Both court and visitors may perform in person name searches. No search fee. Civil cases indexed by defendant, plaintiff. Civil records on computer from 6/94, on books and index cards from 1965. Mail turnaround time 1 week. Civil PAT goes back to 1994. **See details of online access in the description at the front and rear of this chapter.**

Criminal Name Search: Access: Mail, online, in person. Both court and visitors may perform in person name searches. No search fee. Required to search: name, years to search; also helpful: DOB, SSN. Criminal records computerized from 6/94, on books and index cards from 1965. Mail turnaround time 1 week. Criminal PAT goes back to same as civil. **See details of online access in the description at the front and rear of this chapter.**

Probate Court PO Box 480668, 101 E Coats Ave, Courthouse, Linden, AL 36748; probate phone: 334-295-2210; fax: 334-295-2081; '8AM-4:30PM (EST). *Probate.*

Marion County

Circuit & District Court PO Box 1595, 132 Military St, Hamilton, AL 35570; 205-921-7451; fax: 205-952-9851; 8AM-4:30PM (CST). *Felony, Misdemeanor, Civil, Eviction, Small Claims, Probate.*

General Information: No sealed, adoptions, youthful offenders or juvenile records released. Will fax documents for no fee. Court makes copy: $5.00 for 1st 20 pages then $.50 each add'l. Self serve copy: $.25 per page. Certification fee: $1.50. Payee: Circuit Clerk. Only cashiers checks and money orders accepted. No credit cards accepted. Prepayment required. Mail requests: SASE required.

Civil Name Search: Access: Mail, in person, online. Both court and visitors may perform in person name searches. No search fee. Civil cases indexed by defendant, plaintiff. Civil records on computer from 5/94, on books from 1950s. Mail turnaround time 7-10 days. Civil PAT goes back to 1994. **See details of online access in the description at the front and rear of this chapter.**

Criminal Name Search: Access: Mail, online, in person. Both court and visitors may perform in person name searches. No search fee. Required to search: name, years to search; also helpful: DOB, SSN. Criminal records computerized from 5/94, on books from 1950s. Mail turnaround time 7-10 days. Criminal PAT goes back to same as civil. **See details of online access in the description at the front and rear of this chapter.**

Probate Court PO Box 1687, 132 Military St S, Hamilton, AL 35570; 205-921-2471; fax: 205-921-5109; 8AM-N 1PM-5PM (EST). *Probate.*

Marshall County

Circuit Court - Guntersville Criminal Division 424 Blount Ave #201, Guntersville, AL 35976; 256-571-7791; 8AM-4:30PM (CST). *Felony, Misdemeanor.*

General Information: No sealed, adoptions, youthful offenders or juvenile records released. Court makes copy: $5.00 for 1st 20 pages then $.50 each add'l. Certification fee: $5.00 per cert. Payee: Circuit Clerk. Business checks not accepted, suggest money order or cashier's check. No credit cards accepted. Prepayment required.

Criminal Name Search: Access: Online, in person. Visitors must perform in person searches themselves. Search fee: There is a $25 "retrieval fee.". Required to search: name, years to search; also helpful: DOB, SSN. Criminal records computerized from 1992, on index books from 1984, prior back to 1930s. Public use terminal has crim records back to 1992. **See details of online access in the description at the front and rear of this chapter.**

Circuit & District Court - Albertville Division 133 S Emmet St, Albertville, AL 35950; 256-878-4515; criminal phone: 256-878-4522; civil phone: 256-878-4521;; 8AM-4:30PM (CST). *Misdemeanor, Civil, Eviction, Small Claims, Domestic.*

General Information: No sealed, adoptions, youthful offenders or juvenile records released. Will not fax documents. Court makes copy: $5.00 for 1st 20 pages then $.50 each add'l for pending cases only. Certification fee: $5.00 per cert plus court copy fee. Payee: Clerk of Courts. Business checks accepted. No credit cards accepted. Prepayment required.

Civil Name Search: Access: Mail, in person, online. Both court and visitors may perform in person name searches. Search fee: There is a $25.00 retrieval fee on disposed cases, includes copies. Civil cases indexed by defendant. Civil records on computer from 8/92, on index books from 1974. Public use terminal has civil records back to 8/1992. **See details of online access in the description at the front and rear of this chapter.**

Criminal Name Search: Access: In person, online. Both court and visitors may perform in person name searches. Search fee: There is a $25.00 retrieval fee on disposed cases, includes copies. Required to search: name, years to search, DOB; also helpful: SSN. Criminal records computerized from 8/92, on index books from 1974. **See details of online access in the description at the front and rear of this chapter.**

Circuit Court - Guntersville Civil Division 424 Blount Ave, Ste 201, Guntersville, AL 35976; 256-571-7788; civil phone: 256-571-7785;; 8AM-4:30PM (CST). *Civil Actions over $10,000, Small Claims, Probate.*

General Information: No sealed, adoptions, youthful offenders or juvenile records released. Court makes copy: $5.00 for 1st 20 pages then $.50 each add'l. Self serve copy: same. Certification fee: $5.00 per cert. Payee: Circuit Clerk. Business checks not accepted, money order or cashier's check preferred. No credit cards accepted. Prepayment required.

Civil Name Search: Access: In person, online. Visitors must perform in person searches themselves. Search fee: There is a $25.00 retrieval fee. Civil cases indexed by defendant, plaintiff. Civil records on computer for past 10 years, on index books early 1900s. Public use terminal has civil records back to 1992. **See details of online access in the description at the front and rear of this chapter.**

Probate Court 425 Gunter Ave, #110, Guntersville, AL 35976; probate phone: 256-571-7764 x4; fax: 256-571-7732; 8AM-4:30PM (EST). *Probate.*
www.marshallco.org/index.php

Mobile County

Circuit Court 205 Government Plaza #913, Mobile, AL 36644-2936; 251-574-8786; criminal phone: 251-574-8430; civil phone: 251-574-8420; 8AM-5PM (CST). *Felony, Civil Actions over $10,000.*

General Information: Courthouse information line is 251-574-4636. No sealed, adoptions, youthful offenders or juvenile records released. Will not fax documents. Court makes copy: $5.00 for 1st 20 pages then $.50 each add'l. Certification fee: $5.00 per cert. Payee: Circuit Clerk. Cashiers checks and money orders accepted. Exact change for payment is required. Major credit cards accepted for criminal searches. Prepayment required. Exact change for payments is required.

Civil Name Search: Access: Online, in person, mail. Visitors must perform in person searches themselves. Search fee: $10.00 per name. Civil cases indexed by defendant. Civil records on computer from 1977, microfiche from early 1900s. Civil PAT goes back to 1977. **See details of online access in the description at the front and rear of this chapter.**

Criminal Name Search: Access: Online, in person, mail. Visitors must perform in person searches themselves. Search fee: $25.00 per name. Required to search: name, years to search; also helpful: DOB, SSN. Criminal records computerized from 1977, microfiche from early 1900s. Criminal PAT available. **See details of online access in the description at the front and rear of this chapter.**

District Court 205 Government St, Mobile, AL 36644; 251-574-8511; criminal phone: 251-574-8511; civil phone: 251-574-8425; fax: 251-574-4840; 8AM-5PM (CST). *Misdemeanor, Civil Actions under $10,000, Eviction, Small Claims, Probate.*

General Information: No sealed, youthful offenders, protected files or juvenile records released. Will fax back documents for $5.00 fee. Court makes copy: $5.00 for 1st 20 pages then $.50 each add'l. Certification fee: $5.00 per cert. Payee: Clerk, District Court. Business checks accepted if pre-approved. No credit cards accepted. Prepayment required. Mail requests: SASE required.

Civil Name Search: Access: Phone, fax, mail, online, in person. Both court and visitors may perform in person name searches. Search fee: $10.00. Civil cases indexed by defendant, plaintiff. Civil records on computer from 1977, index books from 1950s. Mail turnaround time 7 days. Civil PAT goes back to 2001. **See details of online access in the description at the front and rear of this chapter.**

Criminal Name Search: Access: Phone, mail, online, in person. Both court and visitors may perform in person name searches. Search fee: $10.00. Required to search: name, years to search, DOB; also helpful: SSN. Criminal records computerized from 1977, index cards from 1950s. Mail turnaround time 7 days. Criminal PAT goes back to 2001. **See details of online access in the description at the front and rear of this chapter.** Search City of Mobile Municipal court records at www.cityofmobile.org/mcourts/index.php.

Probate Court PO Box 7, 151 Government St (36602), Mobile, AL 36601; 251-574-6070; fax: 251-574-6072; 8AM-5PM (EST). *Probate.* www.probate.mobilecountyal.gov/

General Information: Online access to the probate record index is free at http://probate.mobilecountyal.gov/.

Monroe County

Circuit & District Court County Courthouse, 65 N Alabama Ave, Monroeville, AL 36460; 251-743-2283; probate phone: 251-743-4107; fax: 251-575-5933; 8AM-5PM (CST). *Felony, Misdemeanor, Civil, Eviction, Small Claims, Probate.*

General Information: Search includes civil and criminal. No sealed, adoptions, youthful offenders or juvenile records released. Will not fax documents. Court makes copy: $5.00 for 1st 20 pages then $.50 each add'l. Self serve copy: same. Certification fee: $5.00 per cert. Cert fee includes copies. Payee: WR McMillen, Circuit Clerk. Business checks accepted. No credit cards accepted. Prepayment required. Mail requests: SASE required.

Civil Name Search: Access: Mail, in person, online. Both court and visitors may perform in person name searches. Search fee: $10.00 per name, $20.00 if by hand. Civil cases indexed by defendant. Civil index on cards from 1977 and on computer since 7/1994. Mail turnaround time 1 week. Civil PAT goes back to 1977. **See details of online access in the description at the front and rear of this chapter.**

Criminal Name Search: Access: Mail, online, in person. Both court and visitors may perform in person name searches. Search fee: $10.00 per name, $20.00 if by hand. Required to search: name, years to search; also helpful: DOB, SSN. Criminal records indexed on cards from 1977 and on computer since 7/1994. Mail turnaround time 1 week. Criminal PAT goes back to same as civil. **See details of online access in the description at the front and rear of this chapter.**

Probate Court PO Box 665, 65 N Alabama Ave (36460), Monroeville, AL 36461-0665; probate phone: 251-743-4107; fax: 251-575-4756; 8AM-5PM M,T,W,F; 8AM-N TH (EST). *Probate.*

Montgomery County

Circuit Court PO Box 1667, 251 S Lawrence, Montgomery, AL 36102-1667; criminal phone: 334-832-1289; civil phone: 334-832-1266; probate phone: 334-832-1240;; 8AM-5PM (CST). *Felony, Civil Actions over $10,000, Probate.*

General Information: Probate is a separate office at 101 S Lawrence St, and separate search page and includes marriages; see civil section. No sealed, youthful offenders or juvenile records released. Will not fax documents. Court makes copy: $5.00 for 1st 20 pages then $.50 each add'l. Self serve copy: same. Certification fee: $5.00 per page. Payee: Circuit Clerk. Business checks accepted. No credit cards accepted. Prepayment required. Mail requests: SASE required.

Civil Name Search: Access: Mail, in person, online. Both court and visitors may perform in person name searches. Search fee: $20.00; $25.00 if archives also be searched. Required to search: name, years to search, DOB; also helpful: SSN. Civil cases indexed by defendant, plaintiff. Civil records on computer from 1982, microfiche from 1976. Note: Search includes both civil and criminal but not probate. Mail turnaround time 3-4 days. Civil PAT goes back to 1985. **See details of online access in the description at the front and rear of this chapter.** Search probate and marriages at www.mc-ala.org/ElectedOfficials/ProbateJudge/ProbateResources/Pages/ProbateRecordsSearch.aspx.

Criminal Name Search: Access: Mail, online, in person. Both court and visitors may perform in person name searches. Search fee: $20.00; $25.00 if archives also to be searched. Required to search: name, years to search, DOB; also helpful: SSN. Criminal records computerized from 1982, microfiche from 1976. Note: Search includes both civil and criminal but not probate. Mail turnaround time 3-4 days. Criminal PAT goes back to same as civil. **See details of online access in the description at the front and rear of this chapter.**

District Court PO Box 1667, 251 S Lawrence, Montgomery, AL 36102; 334-832-4950 x2; criminal phone: x4; civil phone: x3;; 8AM-N, 1-5PM (CST). *Misdemeanor, Civil Actions under $10,000, Eviction, Small Claims.*

General Information: No sealed, youthful offender, juvenile records released. Will not fax documents. Court makes copy: $5.00 for 1st 20 pages then $.50 each add'l. Certification fee: $5.00 per doc. Payee: District Court. Only cashiers checks and money orders accepted. No credit cards accepted.

Civil Name Search: Access: Mail, in person, online. Both court and visitors may perform in person name searches. No search fee. Civil cases indexed by defendant. Civil records on computer from the 1980s, index books from 1977. Mail turnaround time 2 weeks. Civil PAT goes back to 1995. **See details of online access in the description at the front and rear of this chapter.**

Criminal Name Search: Access: Mail, online, in person. Both court and visitors may perform in person name searches. No search fee. Required to search: name, years to search; also helpful: DOB, SSN. Criminal records computerized from the 1980s, index books from 1977. Mail turnaround time 2 weeks. Criminal PAT goes back to same as civil. **See details of online access in the description at the front and rear of this chapter.**

Probate Court PO Box 223, 100 S Lawrence St, 3rd Fl (36104), Montgomery, AL 36101; probate phone: 334-832-1244; fax: 334-832-7137; 8AM-5PM (EST). *Probate.*

www.mc-ala.org/ElectedOfficials/ProbateJudge/ProbateDivisions/ProbateCourt/Pages/Default.aspx

Morgan County

Circuit Court PO Box 668, 302 Lee St, Decatur, AL 35602; 256-351-4790; criminal phone: 256-351-4792; civil phone: 256-351-4796; fax: 256-351-4880; 8AM-4:30PM (CST). *Felony, Civil Actions over $10,000, Probate.*

www.morgancountycircuitclerk.org/

General Information: No sealed, adoption, youthful offender, juvenile records released. Court makes copy: $5.00 for 1st 20 pages then $.50 each add'l. Certification fee: $5.00 per page. Payee: John Pat Orr, Circuit Clerk. Only cashiers checks and money orders accepted. No credit cards accepted. Prepayment required. Mail requests: SASE required.

Civil Name Search: Access: Mail, in person, online. Visitors must perform in person searches themselves. Search fee: $10.00 per name. Civil cases indexed by defendant, plaintiff. Civil records on computer from 1994, on microfiche from 1950s, books from 1965. Public use terminal available. T **See details of online access in the description at the front and rear of this chapter.** Search probate records for this county at http://morgancountyprobate.com/DesktopDefault.aspx?tabindex=5&tabid=99.

Criminal Name Search: Access: Mail, online, in person. Visitors must perform in person searches themselves. Search fee: $10.00 per name. Required to search: name, years to search; also helpful: DOB, SSN. Criminal records computerized from 1992. Public use terminal available. **See details of online access in the description at the front and rear of this chapter.**

District Court PO Box 668, Decatur, AL 35602; 256-351-4649; fax: 256-351-4880; 8:30AM-4:30PM (CST). *Misdemeanor, Civil Actions under $10,000, Eviction, Small Claims.*

www.morgancountycircuitclerk.org/

General Information: No sealed, adoption, youthful offender, juvenile records released. Will fax documents to local or toll-free number. Court makes copy: $5.00 for 1st 20 pages then $.50 each add'l. Self serve copy: $.25 per page. Certification fee: $5.00. Payee: District Court. Only cashiers checks and money orders accepted. No credit cards accepted. Prepayment required.

Civil Name Search: Access: Mail, in person, online. Visitors must perform in person searches themselves. Search fee: $10.00 per name. Civil cases indexed by defendant. Civil records on computer from 1992, books from 1960. Civil PAT goes back to 1992. **See details of online access in the description at the front and rear of this chapter.**

Criminal Name Search: Access: Mail, online, in person. Visitors must perform in person searches themselves. Search fee: $10.00 per name. $25.00 for full case record. Required to search: name, years to search; also helpful: DOB, SSN. Criminal records computerized from 1992, books from 1960. Mail turnaround time varies. Criminal PAT goes back to 1992. **See details of online access in the description at the front and rear of this chapter.**

Probate Court PO Box 848, 302 Lee St NE #2 (35601), Decatur, AL 35602; probate phone: 256-351-4680; fax: 256-351-4884; 8AM-4:30PM (EST). *Probate.*

www.morgancountyprobate.com/DesktopDefault.aspx

Perry County

Circuit & District Court 300 Washington St, Marion, AL 36756; 334-683-6106; 8AM-4:30PM (CST). *Felony, Misdemeanor, Civil, Eviction, Small Claims, Probate.*

General Information: Mailing address is PO Box 505, same ZIP. No sealed, adoption, youthful offender, juvenile records released. Will not fax documents. Court makes copy: $5.00 for 1st 20 pages then $.50 each add'l. Certification fee: $5.00 per page. Payee: District Court Clerk. Business checks accepted. No credit cards accepted. Prepayment required. Mail requests: SASE required.

Civil Name Search: Access: Mail, in person, online. Both court and visitors may perform in person name searches. Search fee: $10.00 for computer search, $20.00 for paper check, and $25.00 to check archives. Civil cases indexed by defendant, plaintiff. Civil records on books from 1900's, on computer back to 1990. Mail turnaround time 2-3 days. Civil PAT goes back to 1990. **See details of online access in the description at the front and rear of this chapter.**

Criminal Name Search: Access: Mail, online, in person. Both court and visitors may perform in person name searches. Search fee: $10.00 for computer search, $20.00 for paper check, and $25.00 to check archives. Required to search: name, years to search; also helpful: DOB, SSN. Criminal records indexed on cards back to 1900, computerized back to 1980. Mail turnaround time 2-3 days. Criminal PAT goes back to same as civil. **See details of online access in the description at the front and rear of this chapter.**

Probate Court PO Box 478, 300 Washington St, Courthouse, Marion, AL 36756; probate phone: 334-683-2210; fax: 334-683-2211; 8AM-4:30PM (EST). *Probate.*

Pickens County

Circuit & District Court PO Box 418, Carrollton, AL 35447; 205-367-2050 dist ct; fax: 205-367-2054; 8AM-4:30PM (CST). *Felony, Misdemeanor, Civil, Eviction, Small Claims.*

General Information: No sealed, adoption, youthful offender, juvenile records released. Will not fax documents. Court makes copy: $.50 per page. Self serve copy: same. Certification fee: $5.00 plus copy fee. Payee: District Court. Business checks accepted. No credit cards accepted. Prepayment required. Mail requests: SASE required.

Civil Name Search: Access: Mail, in person, online. Only the court performs in person name searches; visitors may not. Search fee: $10.00 up to $20.00. Archived records $25.00. Civil cases indexed by defendant, plaintiff. Civil records on computer from 10/93, on books and index cards from 1840s. Mail turnaround time 1-2 weeks. **See details of online access in the description at the front and rear of this chapter.**

Criminal Name Search: Access: Mail, online, in person. Only the court performs in person name searches; visitors may not. Search fee: $10.00 up to $20.00. Archived records $25.00. Required to search: name, years to search; also helpful: DOB, SSN. Criminal records on computer, on books and index cards from 1840s. Mail turnaround time 1-2 weeks. **See details of online access in the description at the front and rear of this chapter.**

Probate Court PO Box 370, 50 Courthouse Sq, Rm 106, Carrollton, AL 35447; probate phone: 205-367-2010; fax: 205-367-2011; 8AM-4PM (CST). *Probate.*

Pike County

Circuit & District Court 120 W Church St, Troy, AL 36081; 334-566-4622/5113; 8AM-5PM (CST). *Felony, Misdemeanor, Civil, Eviction, Small Claims, Probate.*

General Information: No sealed, youthful offender, juvenile records released. Will not fax documents. Court makes copy: $5.00 for 1st 20 pages then $.50 each add'l. Self serve copy: same. Certification fee: $5.00 per page plus copy fee. Payee: Pike County Circuit/District Court. Only cashiers checks and money orders accepted. Prepayment required. Mail requests: SASE required.

Civil Name Search: Access: Mail, in person, online. Both court and visitors may perform in person name searches. Search fee: $10.00 for computer search, $20.00 for paper check, and $25.00 to check archives. Civil cases indexed by defendant, plaintiff. Civil records on computer from 1977, on books from 1938. Mail turnaround time same day. Civil PAT goes back to 1993. The public terminal index goes far back but there is very little case info. **See details of online access in the description at the front and rear of this chapter.**

Criminal Name Search: Access: Mail, online, in person. Both court and visitors may perform in person name searches. Search fee: $10.00 for computer search, $20.00 for paper check, and $25.00 to check archives. Required to search: name, years to search, DOB, SSN. Criminal records computerized from 1977, on books from 1938. Mail turnaround time same day. Criminal PAT goes back to same as civil. The public terminal index goes far back but there is very little case info. **See details of online access in the description at the front and rear of this chapter.**

Probate Court 120 W Church St, Pike County Courthouse, Troy, AL 36081; probate phone: 334-566-1246; fax: 334-566-8585; 8AM-5PM (CST). *Probate.*

www.alabama.gov/portal/secondary.jsp?id=countiesRiver&countyID=pike

Randolph County

Circuit & District Court PO Box 328, 1 Main St, Wedowee, AL 36278; 256-357-4551; fax: 256-357-9012; 8AM-5PM (CST). *Felony, Misdemeanor, Civil, Eviction, Small Claims, Probate.*

General Information: No sealed, adoption, youthful offender, juvenile records released. Will fax documents $.25 per page. Court makes copy: $5.00 for 1st 20 pages then $.50 each add'l. Self serve copy: same. Certification fee: $1.50 per page plus made-by-office-copy fee. Business checks accepted. No credit cards accepted. Prepayment required.

Civil Name Search: Access: Online, in person. Visitors must perform in person searches themselves. Civil cases indexed by defendant, plaintiff. Civil records on computer from 1994. **See details of online access in the description at the front and rear of this chapter.**

Criminal Name Search: Access: Online, in person. Visitors must perform in person searches themselves. Required to search: name, years to search; also helpful: DOB, SSN. Criminal records index on computer from 1977. **See details of online access in the description at the front and rear of this chapter.**

Probate Court PO Box 249, 1 Main St, Courthouse, Wedowee, AL 36278; 256-357-4933; fax: 256-357-9053; 8AM-5PM (CST). *Probate.* www.randolphcountyalabama.gov/Probate_office.htm

Russell County

Circuit & District Court 501 14th St, Phenix City, AL 36868; 334-298-0516; fax: 334-297-6250; 8:30AM-5PM (EST). *Felony, Misdemeanor, Civil, Eviction, Small Claims.*

www.russellcountycircuitclerk.com/Home.aspx

General Information: The physical address is 1206 7th Ave. Above is mailing address. No sealed, adoption, youthful offender, juvenile records released. Will not fax documents. Court makes copy: $5.00 for 1st 20 pages then $.50 each add'l. Certification fee: $5.00 per cert. Payee: Clerk of Circuit Court. Business checks accepted. No credit cards accepted. Prepayment required.

Civil Name Search: Access: Mail, in person, online. Only the court performs in person name searches; visitors may not. Search fee: $10.00 per name search back to 1/2005 on computer, plus copy fee. Fee is $25.00 per name if any part of search is before 1/2005, plus copy fee. Required to search: name, years to search; also helpful DOB, last 4 digits of SSN. Civil cases indexed by defendant, plaintiff. Civil records on computer from 1988, books from 1800s (prior to 1940 extremely difficult to find). Note: Make search requests on the court's request form only; call for form. Mail turnaround time 2 weeks. **See details of online access in the description at the front and rear of this chapter.**

Criminal Name Search: Access: Mail, in person, online. Only the court performs in person name searches; visitors may not. Search fee: $10.00 per name search back to 1/2005 on computer, plus copy fee. Fee is $25.00 per name if any part of search is before 1/2005, plus copy fee. Required to search: name, years to search, DOB, alias; also helpful: last 4 digits of SSN. Criminal records computerized from 1988, books from 1800s (prior to 1940 extremely difficult to find). Note: Make search requests on the court's request form only; call for form. Mail turnaround time 2 weeks. Cases prior to 1977 take add'l time to research. **See details of online access in the description at the front and rear of this chapter.**

Probate Court PO Box 700, Broad St (36867), Phenix City, AL 36868-0700; probate phone: 334-298-7979; fax: 334-298-7979; 8:30AM-4:45PM (EST). *Probate.* www.russellcountyprobate.us/

Shelby County

Circuit & District Court PO Box 1810, 112 N Main St #128, Columbiana, AL 35051; 205-669-3760; criminal phone: 205-669-3773; civil phone: 205-669-3783; probate phone: 205-669-3710; fax: 205-669-3786; 8AM-4:30PM (CST). *Felony, Misdemeanor, Civil, Eviction, Small Claims, Probate.* http://18jc.alacourt.gov

General Information: Fax number here is for criminal search requests only. No sealed, adoption, youthful offender, juvenile records released. Will not fax documents. Court makes copy: $5.00 for 1st 20 pages then $.50 each add'l. Self serve copy: same. Certification fee: $5.00 per cert. Payee: Mary Harris, Circuit Clerk. Only cashiers checks and money orders accepted. No credit cards accepted. Prepayment required.

Civil Name Search: Access: Mail, fax, online, in person. Visitors must perform in person searches themselves. Search fee: $10.00 per name for computer search; $20.00 to search paper records; $25.00 to search archives. Civil cases indexed by defendant, plaintiff. Civil records on computer from 1993, on index books from 1820s. Mail turnaround time approximately 2 weeks. Civil PAT goes back to 1993. **See details of online access in the description at the front and rear of this chapter.**

Criminal Name Search: Access: Mail, fax, online, in person. Visitors must perform in person searches themselves. Search fee: $10.00 per name for computer search; $20.00 to search paper records; $25.00 to search archives. Required to search: name, years to search, DOB; also helpful: SSN. Criminal records computerized from 1993, on index books from 1820s. Mail turnaround time approx. 2 weeks. Criminal PAT goes back to same as civil. **See details of online access in the description at the front and rear of this chapter.**

Probate Court PO Box 825, 112 N Main St, Columbiana, AL 35051; probate phone: 205-669-3720; fax: 205-669-3884; 8AM-4:30PM (CST). *Probate.* www.shelbyal.com/probate/default.htm

St. Clair County

Circuit & District Court - Ashville Division 100 6th Ave #400, Ashville, AL 35953; 205-594-2184; fax: 205-594-2196; 8AM-5PM (CST). *Felony, Misdemeanor, Civil, Eviction, Small Claims, Probate.* www.stclairco.com/

General Information: No sealed, adoption, youthful offender, juvenile records released. Court makes copy: $5.00 for 1st 20 pages then $.50 each add'l. Self serve copy: same. Certification fee: $5.00 per doc. Payee: Jeff Wyatt Circuit Clerk. Business checks accepted. No credit cards accepted. Prepayment required. Mail requests: SASE required.

Civil Name Search: Access: Mail, Fax, in person, online. Both court and visitors may perform in person name searches. Search fee: $25.00 per name; search includes copy fee. Civil cases indexed by defendant, plaintiff. Civil records on computer from 1/94, in books from 1800s, no index before 1940. Mail turnaround time 10 days. Civil PAT goes back to 1993. **See details of online access in the description at the front and rear of this chapter.**

Criminal Name Search: Access: Mail, Fax, online, in person. Both court and visitors may perform in person name searches. Search fee: $25.00 per name; search includes copy fee. Required to search: name, years to search, DOB. Criminal records computerized from 1/94, in books from 1800s, no index before 1940. Mail turnaround time 10 days. Criminal PAT goes back to same as civil. **See details of online access in the description at the front and rear of this chapter.**

Circuit & District Court - Pell City Division 1815 Cogswell Ave, #217, Pell City, AL 35125; 205-338-2511; Circuit: 205-338-7224 District; fax: 205-884-2196; 8AM-5PM (CST). *Felony, Misdemeanor, Civil, Eviction, Small Claims, Probate.* www.stclairco.com/

General Information: No sealed, adoption, youthful offender, juvenile records released. Will not fax documents. Court makes copy: $5.00 for 1st 20 pages then $.50 each add'l. Self serve copy: $.25 per page. Certification fee: $5.00 per cert. Payee: Clerk of Courts. Business checks accepted w/ phone number. No credit cards accepted. Prepayment required. Mail requests: SASE required.

Civil Name Search: Access: Mail, in person, online. Both court and visitors may perform in person name searches. No search fee, but $25 fee to search archived records. Civil cases indexed by defendant, plaintiff. Civil records on computer from 11/93, on books from 1950s. Mail turnaround time 7-14 days. Civil PAT goes back to 1993. **See details of online access in the description at the front and rear of this chapter.**

Criminal Name Search: Access: Mail, online, in person. Both court and visitors may perform in person name searches. No search fee, but $25 fee to search archived records. Required to search: name, years to search, DOB; also helpful: SSN, signed release. Criminal records computerized from 11/93, on books from 1950s. Mail turnaround time 7-14 days. Criminal PAT goes back to same as civil. **See details of online access in the description at the front and rear of this chapter.**

Probate Court (Northern Congressional District) PO Box 220, 165 5th Ave, Ashville, AL 35953; probate phone: 205-594-2434 or 205-2120; fax: 205-594-2125; 8AM-5PM (CST). *Probate.* www.stclairco.com/index.php

Probate Court (Southern Congressional District) 1815 Cogswell Ave, #212, Courthouse, Pell City, AL 35125; probate phone: 205-338-9449; fax: 205-884-1182; 8AM-5PM (CST). *Probate.* www.stclairco.com/

Sumter County

Circuit & District Court PO Box 936, 115 Franklin St, Livingston, AL 35470; 205-652-2291; fax: 205-652-1010; 8AM-4:30PM (CST). *Felony, Misdemeanor, Civil, Eviction, Small Claims, Probate.*

General Information: No sealed, adoption, youthful offender, juvenile records released. Will not fax documents. Court makes copy: $5.00 for 1st 20 pages then $.50 each add'l. Self serve copy: same. Certification fee: $5.00 per cert. Payee: Circuit Court Clerk. No personal checks or credit cards accepted. Prepayment required. Mail requests: SASE required.

Civil Name Search: Access: Mail, in person, online. Both court and visitors may perform in person name searches. Search fee: $10.00 per name for computer search; $20.00 to search paper records; $25.00 to search archives. Civil cases indexed by defendant, plaintiff. Civil records on computer from early 1995, on index books from 1962. Mail turnaround time 2 weeks. Civil PAT goes back to mid-1990s. T **See details of online access in the description at the front and rear of this chapter.**

Criminal Name Search: Access: Mail, online, in person. Both court and visitors may perform in person name searches. Search fee: $10.00 per name for computer search; $20.00 to search paper records; $25.00 to search archives. Required to search: name, years to search; also helpful: DOB, SSN. Criminal records computerized from early 1995, on index books from 1962. Mail turnaround time 2 weeks. Criminal PAT goes back to mid 1990s. **See details of online access in the description at the front and rear of this chapter.**

Probate Court PO Drawer 1040, 115 Marshall St, Livingston, AL 35470; probate phone: 205-652-7281; fax: 205-652-6206; 8AM-4PM (CST). *Probate.*

Talladega County

Circuit & District Court - Northern Division PO 6137, 148 E St N, Talladega, AL 35161; 256-761-2102 Circ Ct; fax: 256-480-5291; 8AM-5PM (CST). *Felony, Misdemeanor, Civil, Eviction, Small Claims, Probate.*

General Information: District Court Clerk phone- 256-761-2104; Sm Claims and Dist. Civil phone- x1210 or x1213. Talladega County Southern 5th Division phone- 256-245-4352. No sealed, adoption, youthful offender, juvenile records released. Will not fax out documents. Court makes copy: $5.00 for 1st 20 pages then $.50 each add'l. Self serve copy: same. Certification fee: $5.00 per cert plus copy fee, $10.00 for divorce cert. Payee: Circuit Court Clerk. Business checks accepted; no personal checks. No credit cards accepted. Prepayment required.

Civil Name Search: Access: Online, in person. Visitors must perform in person searches themselves. Civil cases indexed by defendant, plaintiff. Civil records on computer from 1989, index books from 1970s. Civil PAT goes back to 1989. T **See details of online access in the description at the front and rear of this chapter.**

Criminal Name Search: Access: Online, in person. Visitors must perform in person searches themselves. Required to search: name, years to search; also helpful: DOB, SSN. Criminal records computerized from 1989, index books from 1970s. Criminal PAT goes back to 1985. The state court system offers various pay subscription plans for criminal and traffic case information at https://pa.alacourt.com/Default.aspx. A name search or case search is $9.99. Images are $5.00 for first 20 pages and $.50 ea add'l page.

District Court - Southern Division PO Box 183, Sylacauga, AL 35150; 256-245-4352; fax: 256-249-1013; 7:30AM-4:30AM (CST). *Misdemeanor, Civil Actions under $10,000, Eviction, Small Claims.*

General Information: No juvenile, youthful offender records released. Will fax documents to local or toll free line. Court makes copy: $5.00 for 1st 20 pages then $.50 each add'l. Self serve copy: same. Certification fee: $5.00 per page includes copy fee. Payee: Clerk of District Court. Business checks accepted, no personal checks. No credit cards accepted. Prepayment required. Mail requests: SASE required.

Civil Name Search: Access: Mail, in person, online. Visitors must perform in person searches themselves. No search fee. Civil cases indexed by defendant. Civil records on computer from 1977, on index books and cards prior to 1982 at the Northern Division District Court. Civil PAT goes back to 1989. **See details of online access in the description at the front and rear of this chapter.**

Criminal Name Search: Access: Mail, online, in person. Visitors must perform in person searches themselves. No search fee. Required to search: name, years to search; also helpful: DOB, SSN. Criminal records computerized from 1977, on index books and cards prior to 1982 at the Northern Division District Court. Mail turnaround time up to 7-10 days. Criminal PAT goes back to same as civil. Terminal results include SSN. **See details of online access in the description at the front and rear of this chapter.**

Probate Court PO Box 737, Talladega, AL 35161; probate phone: 256-362-4175; fax: 256-761-2128; 8AM-5PM (CST). *Probate.*

General Information: Physical Address: #1 Court Sq, Talladega, AL 35160

Tallapoosa County

Circuit & District Court - Eastern Division Tallapoosa County Courthouse, 125 N Broadnax, Dadeville, AL 36853; 256-825-1098; x1-Dist; x2-Circ; 8AM-5PM (CST). *Felony, Misdemeanor, Civil, Eviction, Small Claims, Probate.*

General Information: No sealed, adoption, youthful offender, juvenile records released. Will fax documents for no fee. Court makes copy: $5.00 for 1st 20 pages then $.50 each add'l. Certification fee: $5.00. Payee: Circuit Clerk. No credit cards accepted. Prepayment required. Mail requests: SASE required.

Civil Name Search: Access: Mail, in person, online. Only the court performs in person name searches; visitors may not. Search fee: $3.00 per name. Civil cases indexed by defendant, plaintiff. Civil records on computer from 1993, on index books from 1977. Mail turnaround time 1-2 weeks. **See details of online access in the description at the front and rear of this chapter.**

Criminal Name Search: Access: Mail, online, in person. Only the court performs in person name searches; visitors may not. Search fee: $3.00 per name. Required to search: name, years to search, DOB; also helpful: SSN. Criminal records computerized from 1993, on index books from 1977. Mail turnaround time 1-2 weeks. **See details of online access in the description at the front and rear of this chapter.**

Circuit & District Court - Western Division 82 Court Sq, Alexander City, AL 35010; 256-234-3264; 8AM-5PM T, W, TH (CST). *Felony, Misdemeanor, Civil, Eviction, Small Claims.*

General Information: No sealed, adoption, youthful offender, juvenile records released. Will fax documents to local or toll free line. Court makes

copy: $5.00 for 1st 20 pages then $.50 each add'l. Self serve copy: same. Certification fee: $5.00 per cert plus copy fee. Payee: Clerk of Courts. Business checks accepted. No credit cards accepted. Prepayment required. Mail requests: SASE requested.

Civil Name Search: Access: Mail, in person, online. Both court and visitors may perform in person name searches. Search fee: $3.00 per name. Civil cases indexed by defendant, plaintiff. Civil index on docket books from 1977, prior in docket books; on computer back to 1994. Mail turnaround time up to 2 weeks. **See details of online access in the description at the front and rear of this chapter.**

Criminal Name Search: Access: Mail, online, in person. Both court and visitors may perform in person name searches. Search fee: $3.00 per name. Required to search: name, years to search, DOB; also helpful: SSN, signed release. Criminal records indexed in books from 1977, prior in docket books; on computer back to 1994. Mail turnaround time up to 2 weeks. **See details of online access in the description at the front and rear of this chapter.**

Probate Court 125 N Broadnax St, Rm 126, Courthouse, Dadeville, AL 36853; probate phone: 256-825-1090; fax: 256-825-1604; 8AM-5PM (CST). *Probate.*
www.tallaco.com

Tuscaloosa County

Circuit Court - Civil 714 Greensboro Ave, 2nd Fl, #214, Tuscaloosa, AL 35401; 205-349-3870; civil phone: Circuit: 205-349-3870 X260; District: x357; fax: 205-469-6590; 8:30AM-5PM (CST). *Civil Actions over $10,000.*

General Information: No sealed, adoption, youthful offender, juvenile records released. Will not fax documents. Court makes copy: $5.00 for 1st 20 pages then $.50 each add'l. Self serve copy: $.25 per page; use copier in Law Library.Self serve copier in law library. Certification fee: $5.00. Payee: Circuit Clerk. Business checks accepted. No credit cards accepted. Prepayment required.

Civil Name Search: Access: Online, in person. Visitors must perform in person searches themselves. Civil cases indexed by defendant, plaintiff. Civil records on computer from 1977, index books early 1900s. Public use terminal has civil records back to 1977. Public terminal search requires name, other names used, and DOB. **See details of online access in the description at the front and rear of this chapter.**

Circuit Court - Criminal 714 Greensboro Ave, 3rd Fl, Tuscaloosa, AL 35401; 205-349-3870 X326; 8AM-5PM (CST). *Felony.*

General Information: Online identifiers in results same as on public terminal. No sealed, adoption, youthful offender, juvenile records released. Will not fax documents. Court makes copy: $5.00 for 1st 20 pages then $.50 each add'l. Self serve copy: same. Certification fee: $5.00 per cert plus copy fee. Payee: Circuit Clerk. Business checks accepted. No credit cards accepted. Prepayment required. Mail requests: SASE required.

Criminal Name Search: Access: Mail, online, in person. Both court and visitors may perform in person name searches. Search fee: $10.00. Required to search: name, years to search, DOB; also helpful: SSN. Criminal records on computer and index books back to 1977. Mail turnaround time 1-2 days. Public use terminal has crim records back to 1977. Terminal results include SSN. **See details of online access in the description at the front and rear of this chapter.**

District Courts - Civil PO Box 2883, 714 Greensboro Ave, 6th Fl, Tuscaloosa, AL 35401; 205-349-3870; civil phone: 205-349-3870 x355;; 8:30AM-5PM (CST). *Civil Actions under $10,000, Probate.*

General Information: No sealed records released. Court makes copy: $5.00 for 1st 20 pages then $.50 each add'l. Certification fee: $5.00 per cert. Payee: District Clerk. Business checks accepted. Visa/MC accepted. Prepayment required.

Civil Name Search: Access: Online, in person. Visitors must perform in person searches themselves. Civil cases indexed by defendant, plaintiff. Civil records on computer from 1977, index books early 1965. Note: The fee is $25.00 if a file must be pulled form the archives. Public use terminal has civil records back to 1977. **See details of online access in the description at the front and rear of this chapter.**

District Court - Criminal Division PO Box 1687, 714 Greensboro Ave, 6th Fl, Tuscaloosa, AL 35403; 205-349-3870 x357; 8AM-5PM (CST). *Misdemeanor.*

General Information: No sealed, youthful offender records released. Will fax documents to local or toll free line. Court makes copy: $5.00 for 1st 20 pages then $.50 each add'l. Certification fee: $5.00 per doc plus copy fee. Payee: District Court Clerk. Business checks accepted. Visa/MC accepted; a 4% usage fee will be added. Prepayment required. Mail requests: SASE preferred.

Criminal Name Search: Access: Mail, online, in person. Both court and visitors may perform in person name searches. Search fee: $10.00 per name. Required to search: name, years to search, signed release; also helpful: DOB, SSN. Criminal records computerized from mid-90s, books in storage from early 1965. Mail turnaround time 5 days. Public use terminal has crim records back to 1997. Public terminals are usually very busy. See details of online access in the description at the front and rear of this chapter.

Probate Court PO Box 20067, 714 Greensboro Ave (35401), Tuscaloosa, AL 35402-0067; 05-349-3870 x205/6; 8:30AM-5PM (CST). *Probate.* www.tuscco.com

Walker County

Circuit & District Court 1801 3rd Ave #205, Jasper, AL 35501; 205-384-7268; fax: 205-384-7271; 8AM-4:30PM (CST). *Felony, Misdemeanor, Civil, Eviction, Small Claims, Probate.*
General Information: Will search all indexes in one search, if asked, though there is a fee for records or searches in the older archives. No sealed, adoption, youthful offender, juvenile records released. Will not fax documents. Court makes copy: $5.00 for 1st 20 pages then $.50 each add'l. Certification fee: $5.00 per page plus copy fee. Payee: Vinita Thompson, Circuit Clerk. No personal or business checks accepted. No credit cards accepted. Prepayment required.
Civil Name Search: Access: Mail, online, in person. Visitors must perform in person searches themselves. No search fee. Civil cases indexed by defendant, plaintiff. Civil records on computer from 3/93, on index books from 1920s. Civil PAT goes back to 1993. **See details of online access in the description at the front and rear of this chapter.**
Criminal Name Search: Access: Mail, online, in person. Visitors must perform in person searches themselves. No search fee. Criminal records computerized from 3/93, on index books from 1920s. Criminal PAT goes back to same as civil. **See details of online access in the description at the front and rear of this chapter.**

Probate Court PO Box 502, 1900 3rd Ave, Annex 2 (35501), Jasper, AL 35502-0502; probate phone: 205-384-7282; fax: 205-384-7005; 8:30AM-4PM (CST). *Probate.* www.walkercounty.com

Washington County

Circuit & District Court PO Box 548, 45 Court St, Chatom, AL 36518; 251-847-2239; 8AM-4:30PM (CST). *Felony, Misdemeanor, Civil, Eviction, Small Claims, Probate.*
General Information: No sealed, adoption, youthful offender, juvenile records released. Court makes copy: $5.00 for 1st 20 pages then $.50 each add'l. Certification fee: $5.00. Payee: Circuit Clerk. Only cashiers checks and money orders accepted. Visa/MC accepted. Prepayment required.
Civil Name Search: Access: Online, in person. Visitors must perform in person searches themselves. Civil cases indexed by defendant. Civil records on computer since 9/1994; prior 7 years on index cards. Civil PAT goes back to 1994. **See details of online access in the description at the front and rear of this chapter.**
Criminal Name Search: Access: Online, in person. Visitors must perform in person searches themselves. Required to search: name, years to search, DOB; also helpful: SSN. Criminal records on computer since 9/1994; prior 7 years on index cards. Criminal PAT goes back to same as civil. **See details of online access in the description at the front and rear of this chapter.**

Probate Court 1 Court St, Chatom, AL 36518; 251-847-3899; fax: 251-847-6450; 8AM-4:30PM (CST). *Probate.*

Wilcox County

Circuit & District Court PO Box 608, 12 Water St, Camden, AL 36726; 334-682-4126; fax: 334-682-4025; 8AM-N, 1-4:30PM (CST). *Felony, Misdemeanor, Civil, Eviction, Small Claims, Probate.*
General Information: No sealed, adoption, youthful offender, juvenile records released. Will not fax documents. Court makes copy: $5.00 for 1st 20 pages then $.50 each add'l. Self serve copy: same. Certification fee: $5.00. Payee: Clerk. Business checks accepted. No credit cards accepted. Prepayment required.
Civil Name Search: Access: Online, in person. Only the court performs in person name searches; visitors may not. No search fee. Required to search: name, years to search, address. Civil cases indexed by defendant, plaintiff. Civil records on computer since 1995; prior records on index books from 1970s, prior to 1970s in vault. **See details of online access in the description at the front and rear of this chapter.**
Criminal Name Search: Access: Online, in person. Only the court performs in person name searches; visitors may not. No search fee. Required to search: name, years to search; also helpful: DOB. Criminal records on computer since 1995; prior records on index books from 1970s, prior to 1970s in vault. **See details of online access in the description at the front and rear of this chapter.**

Probate Court PO Box 668, 100 Broad St, Courthouse, Camden, AL 36726; probate phone: 334-682-4883; fax: 334-682-9484; 8AM-4:30PM (CST). *Probate.*

Winston County

Circuit & District Court PO Box 309, 11 Blake Dr, Double Springs, AL 35553; 205-489-5533; fax: 205-489-5140; 8AM-4:30PM (CST). *Felony, Misdemeanor, Civil, Eviction, Small Claims, Probate.*
General Information: No sealed, adoption, youthful offender, juvenile records released. Will fax back documents for legitimate purpose, but prefer not to. Court makes copy: $.50 per page; copy fee is $25.00 for older docs retrieved from archives. Self serve copy: $.50 per page. Certification fee: $5.00 per cert plus copy fee. Payee: Circuit Clerk. Business checks, money orders accepted; no personal checks. No credit cards accepted. Prepayment required. Mail requests: SASE requested.
Civil Name Search: Access: Mail, fax, online, in person. Visitors must perform in person searches themselves. Search fee: $10.00. Civil cases indexed by defendant, plaintiff. Civil index on docket books from 1977, on computer since 6/1994 including pending cases. **See details of online access in the description at the front and rear of this chapter.**
Criminal Name Search: Access: Mail, fax, online, in person. Visitors must perform in person searches themselves. Search fee: $10.00. Required to search: name, years to search, DOB; also helpful: SSN. Criminal records indexed in books from 1977, on computer since 6/1994 including pending cases. **See details of online access in the description at the front and rear of this chapter.**

Probate Court PO Box 27, 25125 Hwy 195, Rm 1, Double Springs, AL 35553; probate phone: 205-489-5219; fax: 205-489-5135; 8AM-4:30PM (8AM-N 1st Sat of every month) (CST). *Probate.*

About Access Online Statewide

ON-DEMAND Access to Alabama State Trial Court Records is a subscription service that provides access to criminal, civil, small claims, state traffic, domestic relations and child support case information.

A name search is $9.99 which includes details on one case; each additional case is $9.99. A case number search is $9.99. Images are $5.00 for the first 20 pages and $.50 per page each add'l. There is a case monitoring service offered as well; $29.99 for a Circuit Court case and $19.99 for a District Court case.

To sign up visit:

https://pa.alacourt.com/default.aspx

Alaska

Time Zone:	**AK** (Alaska Standard Time)
	Parts of Alaska's Aleutian Islands are HT (Hawaii Standard Time)
Capital:	**Juneau, Juneau Borough**
# of Boroughs:	**19** (includes home Rule Cities)
State's Web:	**www.alaska.gov**
Courts' Web:	**www.courts.alaska.gov**

Administration

Office of the Administrative Director, 820 W 4th Ave, Anchorage, AK, 99501; Telephone: 907-264-8232; Records: 907-264-0491, Fax: 907-264-8291.

Supreme and Appellate Courts

The Alaska Supreme Court is the highest level of state court in Alaska. It hears appeals from lower state courts and also administers the state's judicial system. The Court of Appeals has jurisdiction to hear appeals in cases involving criminal prosecutions, post-conviction relief, juvenile delinquency, extradition, habeas corpus, probation and parole, bail, and the excessiveness or leniency of a sentence.

The home web page gives access to Appellate opinions. Also, the site at http://government.westlaw.com/akcases/ provides access to opinions of the Alaska Supreme Court and Alaska Court of Appeals.

The Alaska Courts

Court	Type	How Organized	Jurisdiction Highpoints
Superior	General	42 Courts in 4 Districts	Felony, Civil, Juvenile, Domestic
District	Limited	58 Courts in 4 Districts	Misdemeanor, Civil under $100,000, Small Claims, Domestic, Ordinance, Traffic
Magistrate	Limited	Part of District Courts	Ordinance, Traffic, Small Claims, Civil

Details on the Court Structure

Alaska has a unified, centrally administered, and totally state-funded judicial system with 4 Judicial Districts. Municipal governments do not maintain separate court systems. Alaska has 19 boroughs or home rule cities or combination borough and home rule cities. Also 12 home rule cities do not directly coincide with the 4 Judicial Districts. In other words, judicial boundaries cross borough boundaries.

The **Superior Court** is the trial court of general jurisdiction. The Superior Court hears felony and civil cases, generally involving $100,000 or more. The court also hears cases that involve children and cases about domestic relations matters.

The **District Court** hears cases that involve hear state misdemeanors and violations of city and borough ordinances, first appearances and preliminary hearings in felony cases, record vital statistics (in some areas of the state), civil cases valued up to $100,000, small claims cases at $10,000 maximum, cases involving children on an emergency basis, and domestic violence cases.

Magistrates are judicial officers of the District Courts and preside in areas of the state where a fulltime district judge is not required and in metropolitan areas to help the workload of the District Court. Small claims cases are $10,000 maximum for most cases; but can be $20,000 for wage claims brought by the Department of Labor.

Courts are listed herein by their borough or home rule city for a convenient alphabetical format. Search by the city court location names to determine the correct court for your search

Searching Tips and Fees

The fees established by court rules for Alaska courts are: search fee- $15.00 per hour or fraction thereof; certification fee- $5.00 per document and $2.00 per additional copy of the document. Copy fee- $.25 per page. Magistrate Courts vary widely in how records are maintained and in the hours of operation – some are open only a few hours per week.

Online Access is Statewide

The case summary and docket information for Alaska trial courts is found on Courtview at www.courtrecords.alaska.gov/pa/pa.urd/pamw6500.display. Records available include civil criminal, traffic and wills. One may search by name, case number or ticket number. Although all courts participate, the dates of the earliest available cases vary by court. There are other cautionary facts to consider. The use of identifiers is limited on the initial search index. For example a recent search for Michael Smith pulled 789 cases and only slightly more than 50% showed a DOB on the index.

Aleutian Islands Borough

Unalaska District Court (3rd District) PO Box 245, Unalaska, AK 99685-0245; 907-581-1266; fax: 907-581-2809; 8AM-4:30PM (AK). *Felony, Misdemeanor, Civil.*
www.courts.alaska.gov/
General Information: For more about the area, visit www.aleutianseast.org/. Online identifiers in results same as on public terminal. No juvenile, needy children, probate records released. Will fax documents to local or toll free line. Court makes copy: $.25 per page. Certification fee: $5.00 per doc; $2.00 for add'l cert of same doc. Payee: State of Alaska. Personal checks accepted. No credit cards accepted. Prepayment required.
Civil Name Search: Access: In person, online. Visitors must perform in person searches themselves. Required to search: name, DOB. Civil records on computer back to 1992. Civil PAT goes back to 1992. **Note: For a complete description of online access see the *Online Access is Statewide* section at the front or back of this chapter.**
Criminal Name Search: Access: In person, online. Visitors must perform in person searches themselves. Required to search: name, years to search, DOB. Criminal records computerized from 1992. Criminal PAT goes back to 1992. **Note: For a complete description of online access see the Online Access is Statewide section at the front or back of this chapter.**

Sand Point Magistrate Court (3rd District) *Felony, Misdemeanor, Civil Actions under $10,000, Small Claims.*
General Information: Court closed; records at Cordova Court in Valdez-Cordova District.

St Paul Island Magistrate Court (3rd District) *Misdemeanor, Civil Actions under $10,000, Small Claims.*
www.aleutianseast.org/
General Information: Court closed. See Seward Magistrate Court in Kenai Peninsula Borough.

Anchorage Borough

Superior & District Court (3rd District) 825 W 4th Ave, Anchorage, AK 99501-2004; 907-264-0491; probate phone: 907-264-0433; fax: 907-264-0873; 8AM-4:30PM (AK). *Felony, Misdemeanor, Civil, Eviction, Small Claims, Probate.*
www.courts.alaska.gov
General Information: Probate fax- 907-264-0598. Online identifiers in results same as on public terminal. No adoption, juvenile, sealed or mental records released. Will fax non-certified documents to local or toll-free number, or can email. Court makes copy: $.25 per page. Self serve copy: $.20 per page. Certification fee: $5.00 per document; exemplification is $10.00. Cert fee includes copies. Payee: Alaska Court System. Personal checks accepted. Credit cards accepted in person or for FedEx expediting. However large requests will require prepayment.
Civil Name Search: Access: Fax, mail, in person, online. Both court and visitors may perform in person name searches. Search fee: $15.00 per hour. Required to search: name, years to search; also helpful: address. Civil records on computer from 1990, on microfiche and archived from 1977 to 1989, on roll index from 1950s. Mail turnaround time 1-4 weeks. Civil PAT goes back to 1990. Terminal results can include address, SSN, and DOB; most have middle initial. **Note: For a complete description of online access see the *Online Access is Statewide* section at the front or back of this chapter.**
Criminal Name Search: Access: Fax, mail, in person, online. Both court and visitors may perform in person name searches. Search fee: $15.00 per hour. Required to search: name, years to search; also helpful: address, DOB, SSN. Criminal records computerized from 1990, on microfiche and archived from 1977 to 1989, on roll index from 1950s. Mail turnaround time 1-4 weeks. Criminal PAT goes back to 1990. Terminal results can include

address, SSN, and DOB; most have middle initial. **Note: For a complete description of online access see the *Online Access is Statewide* section at the front or back of this chapter** .

Bethel District

Superior & District Court (4th District) PO Box 130, 204 Chief Eddie Hoffman Hiway, Bethel, AK 99559-0130; 907-543-2298; fax: 907-543-4419; 8AM-4:30PM; 9AM-4:30 W (AK). *Felony, Misdemeanor, Civil, Eviction, Small Claims, Probate.*
www.courts.alaska.gov/
General Information: No adoption, juvenile, guardianship or mental records released. Fee to fax document $.25 per page. Court makes copy: $.25 per page. Certification fee: $5.00 plus $2.00 per page after first. Payee: Clerk of Court. Personal checks accepted. No credit cards accepted. Prepayment required. Mail requests: SASE required.
Civil Name Search: Access: Fax, mail, in person, online. Both court and visitors may perform in person name searches. Search fee: $15.00 per name. Civil records on computer back to 1983, on microfiche, archived and on index from 1977. Mail turnaround time 2 weeks. Public use terminal available. **Note: For a complete description of online access see the *Online Access is Statewide* section at the front or back of this chapter.**
Criminal Name Search: Access: Fax, mail, in person, online. Both court and visitors may perform in person name searches. Search fee: $15.00 per name. Required to search: name, years to search, DOB; also helpful- case number. Criminal records computerized from 1983, on microfiche, archived and on index from 1977. Mail turnaround time 2 weeks. Public use terminal available. **Note: For a complete description of online access see the *Online Access is Statewide* section at the front or back of this chapter** .

Aniak District Court (4th District) PO Box 147, Riverroad, Aniak, AK 99557-0147; 907-675-4325; fax: 907-675-4278; 8AM-4:30PM (AK). *Misdemeanor, Civil Actions under $10,000, Small Claims.*
www.courts.alaska.gov
General Information: This court also holds records for McGrath. Will fax documents. Court makes copy: $.25 per page. Certification fee: $5.00 per document, $2.00 per add'l copy. Payee: Aniak District Court. Personal checks accepted. No credit cards accepted. Prepayment required.
Civil Name Search: Access: Phone, mail, fax, in person, online. Both court and visitors may perform in person name searches. Search fee: $15.00 per search. Required to search: name plus DOB, SSN, years to search. Civil records go back to 1960; on computer back to 1998. Mail turnaround time 1-2 weeks. **Note: For a complete description of online access see the *Online Access is Statewide* section at the front or back of this chapter.**
Criminal Name Search: Access: Phone, mail, fax, in person, online. Both court and visitors may perform in person name searches. Search fee: $15.00 per search. Required to search: name, years to search, DOB. Criminal records go back to 1960-2004 in microfilm; 2005-present in court. Mail turnaround time 1-2 weeks. **Note: For a complete description of online access see the *Online Access is Statewide* section at the front or back of this chapter** .

Quinhagak Magistrate Court (Bethel Area)
General Information: Court is closed. Old records at Bethel Clerk of Courts.

Bristol Bay Borough

Naknek District Court (3rd District) PO Box 229, #1 Main St (basement in Borough Bldg), Naknek, AK 99633-0229; 907-246-4240/4224; fax: 907-246-7418; 8AM-4:30PM (AK). *Felony, Misdemeanor, Civil Actions under $10,000, Small Claims.*
www.courts.alaska.gov/
General Information: Naknek is 3NA on the state court record numbers. Some Lake and Peninsula cases heard here. Will not fax documents. Court

makes copy: $.25 per page. Certification fee: $10.00 per cert. Payee: Alaska Court System. Personal checks accepted. No credit cards accepted. Prepayment required. Mail requests: SASE requested.

Civil Name Search: Access: Mail, in person, online. Only the court performs in person name searches; visitors may not. Search fee: $15.00 per hour. Required to search: name. Records go back to 1970's; computerized from 1993. Mail turnaround time same day. **Note: For a complete description of online access see the *Online Access is Statewide* section at the front or back of this chapter.**

Criminal Name Search: Access: Mail, in person, online. Only the court performs in person name searches; visitors may not. Search fee: $15.00 per hour. Records go back to 1970's; computerized from 1993. Mail turnaround time same day. **Note: For a complete description of online access see the *Online Access is Statewide* section at the front or back of this chapter .**

Denali Borough

Healy Magistrate Court (4th District) *Misdemeanor, Civil Actions under $10,000, Small Claims.*

General Information: Served by the court in Nenana. See that profile. Felony cases are at Fairbanks Superior & District Court.

Dillingham

Dillingham Superior Court (3rd District) PO Box 909, Dillingham, AK 99576-0909; 907-842-5215; fax: 907-842-5746; 8AM-4:30PM (AK). *Felony, Misdemeanor, Civil, Small Claims.*
www.courts.alaska.gov/

General Information: Physical location is 715 Seward Street. Will not fax documents. Court makes copy: $.25 per page. Certification fee: $3.00 per doc. Payee: State of Alaska. Cashiers checks, money orders, personal checks accepted. No credit cards accepted. Prepayment required. Mail requests: SASE required.

Civil Name Search: Access: In person, mail, online. Only the court performs in person name searches; visitors may not. Search fee: $15.00. Civil records go back 7 years. Mail turnaround time 1-2 weeks. **Note: For a complete description of online access see the *Online Access is Statewide* section at the front or back of this chapter.**

Criminal Name Search: Access: In person, mail, online. Only the court performs in person name searches; visitors may not. Search fee: $15.00 per name. Required to search: name, years to search, DOB. Mail turnaround time 1-2 weeks. **Note: For a complete description of online access see the Online Access is Statewide section at the front or back of this chapter .**

Fairbanks North Star Borough

Superior & District Court (4th District) 101 Lacey St, Fairbanks, AK 99701-4761; 907-452-9277; criminal phone: 907-452-9289; civil phone: 907-452-9267; probate phone: 907-452-9256; fax: 907-452-9330; 8AM-4:30PM (AK). *Felony, Misdemeanor, Civil, Eviction, Small Claims, Probate.*
www.courts.alaska.gov/

General Information: Online identifiers in results same as on public terminal. No adoption, juvenile, guardianship or mental records released. Will not fax documents. Court makes copy: $.25 per page. Self serve copy: same. Certification fee: $5.00 per doc, $2.00 per add'l doc. Payee: Clerk of Court. Personal checks accepted. Credit cards accepted in person only. Prepayment required.

Civil Name Search: Access: In person, online. Both court and visitors may perform in person name searches. Search fee: $15.00 per hour. Civil records on computer from 1988, on microfiche, archived and on index from 1900s. Note: Access to closed civil cases goes back 6 months. The court will do limited research on names if case number not known, as time permits. Civil PAT goes back to 1988. Terminal results can include DOB; most have middle initial. **Note: For a complete description of online access see the *Online Access is Statewide* section at the front or back of this chapter.**

Criminal Name Search: Access: In person, online. Both court and visitors may perform in person name searches. Search fee: $15.00 per hour. Required to search: name, years to search, DOB. Criminal records computerized from 1988, on microfiche, archived and on index from 1900s. Note: The court will do limited research on names if case number not known, as time permits. Criminal PAT goes back to same as civil. **Note: For a complete description of online access see the *Online Access is Statewide* section at the front or back of this chapter .**

Haines Borough

District Court (1st District) PO Box 169, Haines, AK 99827-0169; 907-766-2801; fax: 907-766-3148; 8AM-N, 1-4:30PM (AK). *Misdemeanor, Civil Actions under $50,000, Small Claims.*
www.courts.alaska.gov/

General Information: Felony cases are at Juneau Superior & District Court. No juvenile records released. Will fax documents to local or toll-free number. Court makes copy: $.25 per page. Certification fee: $5.00 plus $2.00 per each add'l document requested at same time. Payee: Alaska Court System. Personal checks accepted. No credit cards accepted. Prepayment required. Mail requests: SASE required.

Civil Name Search: Access: Phone, fax, mail, in person, online. Only the court performs in person name searches; visitors may not. Search fee: $15.00 per hour if time consuming. Required to search: name, years to search; also helpful: address. Civil records on computer since 1993, index from 1960s. Note: Limited information is available by phone. Mail turnaround time 1-2 days. **Note: For a complete description of online access see the *Online Access is Statewide* section at the front or back of this chapter.**

Criminal Name Search: Access: Phone, fax, mail, in person, online. Only the court performs in person name searches; visitors may not. Search fee: $15.00 per hour if time consuming. Required to search: name, years to search; also helpful: address, DOB, SSN. Criminal records on computer since 1993, index from 1960s. Mail turnaround time 1-2 days. **Note: For a complete description of online access see the *Online Access is Statewide* section at the front or back of this chapter .**

Juneau Borough & City

Superior & District Court (1st District) Dimond Courthouse, PO Box 114100, Juneau, AK 99811-4100; 907-463-4700; fax: 907-463-3788; 8AM-4:30PM (AK). *Felony, Misdemeanor, Civil, Eviction, Small Claims, Probate.*
www.courts.alaska.gov/

General Information: No adoption, juvenile, guardianship or mental records released. Will not fax documents. Court makes copy: $.25 per page. Certification fee: $5.00 plus $2.00 per additional certifications after first. Payee: Juneau Trial Court. Personal checks accepted. No credit cards accepted. Prepayment required. Mail requests: SASE required.

Civil Name Search: Access: Fax, mail, in person, online. Both court and visitors may perform in person name searches. Search fee: $15.00 per hour. Civil cases indexed by defendant. Civil records on computer back to 1987, on microfiche from 1960 to 1986, on index from 1959 to 1987. Mail turnaround time 2-5 days. Results include full name. **Note: For a complete description of online access see the *Online Access is Statewide* section at the front or back of this chapter.**

Criminal Name Search: Access: Fax, mail, in person, online. Both court and visitors may perform in person name searches. Search fee: $15.00 per hour. Criminal records computerized from 1987, on microfiche from 1960 to 1986, on index from 1959 to 1987. Mail turnaround time 2-5 days. Results include full name. **Note: For a complete description of online access see the *Online Access is Statewide* section at the front or back of this chapter .**

Kenai Peninsula Borough

Superior & District Court (3rd District) 125 Trading Bay Dr, #100, Kenai, AK 99611; 907-283-3110; fax: 907-283-8535; 8AM-4:30PM (AK). *Felony, Misdemeanor, Civil, Eviction, Small Claims, Probate.*
www.courts.alaska.gov/

General Information: Closed 8-9AM on Thursdays. No adoption, guardianship, children's, conservatorship or coroner records released. Will fax documents to local or toll-free number. Court makes copy: $.25 per page. Certification fee: $5.00 plus $2.00 per page after first. Payee: Clerk of Court. Personal checks accepted. Visa/MC accepted. Prepayment required.

Civil Name Search: Access: Mail, Fax, in person, online. Both court and visitors may perform in person name searches. No search fee. Civil records on computer from 1982, on microfiche, archived and on index from 1959. Mail turnaround time 1 week. Civil PAT goes back to 1982. **Note: For a complete description of online access see the *Online Access is Statewide* section at the front or back of this chapter.**

Criminal Name Search: Access: Mail, Fax, in person, online. Both court and visitors may perform in person name searches. Search fee: $15.00 per hour. Required to search: name, years to search, DOB. Criminal records computerized from 1982, on microfiche, archived and on index from 1959. Mail turnaround time 1 week. Criminal PAT goes back to same as civil. **Note: For a complete description of online access see the Online Access is Statewide section at the front or back of this chapter .**

Homer District Court (3rd District) 3670 Lake St, Building A, Homer, AK 99603-9647; 907-235-8171; fax: 907-235-4257; 8AM-4:30PM (AK). *Felony, Misdemeanor, Civil, Small Claims.*
www.courts.alaska.gov/

General Information: Old felony cases could be here or at the Kenai District Court. Online identifiers in results same as on public terminal. No confidential or sealed records released. Will not fax out documents. Court makes copy: $.25 per page. Certification fee: $5.00. Cert fee includes copies. Payee: Alaska Court System. Personal checks accepted. Major credit cards accepted in person only. Prepayment required.

Civil Name Search: Access: Phone, fax, mail, in person, online. Visitors must perform in person searches themselves. Search fee: $15.00 per hour. Civil records on computer back to 1984. Mail turnaround time 7-10 days. Public use terminal available. **Note: For a complete description of online access see the *Online Access is Statewide* section at the front or back of this chapter.**

Criminal Name Search: Access: Phone, fax, mail, in person, online. Visitors must perform in person searches themselves. Search fee: $15.00 per hour. Criminal records computerized from 1984. Mail turnaround time 7-10 days. Public use terminal available. **Note: For a complete description of online access see the *Online Access is Statewide* section at the front or back of this chapter** .

Seward District Court (3rd District) PO Box 1929, 5th and Adams Strs, Seward, AK 99664-1929; 907-224-3075; fax: 907-224-7192; 8AM-4:30PM (AK). *Misdemeanor, Civil Actions under $10,000, Small Claims.*
www.courts.alaska.gov/

General Information: Handles cases for St. Paul Island. Civil actions can also be Superior Court Filings. Online identifiers in results same as on public terminal. Will fax documents to local or toll-free number. Court makes copy: $.25 per page. Certification fee: $5.00 by mail, $7.00 if in person and on demand. Payee: State of Alaska. Personal checks accepted. No credit cards accepted. Prepayment required. Mail requests: SASE helpful.

Civil Name Search: Access: In person, mail, online. Both court and visitors may perform in person name searches. Search fee: $15.00 per name. Required to search: DOB, years to search. Civil records on computer since 1983. Mail turnaround time 1-2 weeks. Civil PAT goes back to 1983. **Note: For a complete description of online access see the *Online Access is Statewide* section at the front or back of this chapter.**

Criminal Name Search: Access: In person, mail, online. Both court and visitors may perform in person name searches. Search fee: $15.00 per name. Required to search: name, years to search, DOB. Criminal records on computer since 1983. Mail turnaround time 1-2 weeks. Criminal PAT goes back to same as civil. **Note: For a complete description of online access see the *Online Access is Statewide* section at the front or back of this chapter** .

Ketchikan Gateway Borough

Superior & District Court (1st District) 415 Main, Rm 400, Ketchikan, AK 99901-6399; 907-225-3195; fax: 907-225-7849; 8AM-4:30PM M-TH, 9AM-4:30PM F (AK). *Felony, Misdemeanor, Civil, Eviction, Small Claims, Probate.*
www.courts.alaska.gov/

General Information: Online identifiers in results same as on public terminal. No confidential probate or children's records released. No fee to fax documents if toll-free. Court makes copy: $.25 per page. Certification fee: $5.00. Payee: Alaska Court System. Personal checks accepted. No credit cards accepted. Prepayment required. Mail requests: SASE required.

Civil Name Search: Access: Mail, in person, online. Both court and visitors may perform in person name searches. Search fee: $15.00 per hour. Civil records on computer from 1983, on microfiche from 1972 to 1989, index from 1972. Mail turnaround time 2 weeks. Civil PAT goes back to 1983. **Note: For a complete description of online access see the *Online Access is Statewide* section at the front or back of this chapter.**

Criminal Name Search: Access: Mail, in person, online. Both court and visitors may perform in person name searches. Search fee: $15.00 per hour. Required to search: name, years to search, DOB. Criminal records computerized from 1983, on microfiche from 1972 to 1989, index from 1972. Mail turnaround time 2 weeks. Criminal PAT goes back to same as civil. **Note: For a complete description of online access see the *Online Access is Statewide* section at the front or back of this chapter** .

Kodiak Island Borough

Superior & District Court (3rd District) 204 Mission Rd, Rm 124, Kodiak, AK 99615-7312; 907-486-1600; fax: 907-486-1660; 8AM-4:30PM M,T,TH,F; 9AM-4:30PM W (AK). *Felony, Misdemeanor, Civil, Eviction, Small Claims, Probate.*
www.courts.alaska.gov/

General Information: No adoption, juvenile, guardianship or mental records released. Will not fax documents. Court makes copy: $.25 per page. Certification fee: $5.00 plus $2.00 per add'l copy. If party to action there is no fee. Payee: Clerk of Court. Personal checks or cash accepted. No credit cards accepted. Prepayment required. Mail requests: SASE required.

Civil Name Search: Access: Mail, fax, in person, online. Both court and visitors may perform in person name searches. Search fee: $15.00.

Required to search: name, years to search; also helpful: address. Civil records on computer from 1982, on microfiche, index and archived from 1959. Mail turnaround time 10 days. Civil PAT goes back to 1983. **Note: For a complete description of online access see the *Online Access is Statewide* section at the front or back of this chapter.**

Criminal Name Search: Access: Mail, fax, in person, online. Both court and visitors may perform in person name searches. Search fee: $15.00. Required to search: name, years to search; also helpful: address, DOB, SSN. Criminal records computerized from 1982, on microfiche, index and archived from 1959. Mail turnaround time 10 business days. Criminal PAT goes back to same as civil. **Note: For a complete description of online access see the Online Access is Statewide section at the front or back of this chapter** .

Matanuska-Susitna Borough

Superior & District Court (3rd District) 435 S Denali St, Palmer, AK 99645-6437; 907-746-8181; criminal phone: x4; fax: 907-746-4151; 8AM-4:30PM M-F; 9AM-N Sat (AK). *Felony, Misdemeanor, Civil, Eviction, Small Claims, Probate.*
www.courts.alaska.gov/

General Information: Online identifiers in results same as on public terminal. No adoption, juvenile, guardianship or mental records released. Will fax documents to local or toll-free number. Court makes copy: $.25 per page. Self serve copy: $.25 per page. Certification fee: $5.00 1st doc; add'l docs are $2.00, includes copy fee. Payee: State of Alaska. Personal checks accepted. Visa/MC accepted in person only. Prepayment required. Mail requests: SASE required.

Civil Name Search: Access: Mail, Fax, in person, online. Both court and visitors may perform in person name searches. Search fee: $15.00 per hour. Required to search: name, years to search; also helpful: address. Civil records on computer from 1988, on microfiche, archived and index from 1974. Mail turnaround time 1-3 weeks. Civil PAT goes back to 1988. Terminal results can include DOB; most have middle initial. **Note: For a complete description of online access see the *Online Access is Statewide* section at the front or back of this chapter.**

Criminal Name Search: Access: Mail, Fax, in person, online. Both court and visitors may perform in person name searches. Search fee: $15.00 per hour. Required to search: name, years to search; also helpful: address, DOB, SSN. Criminal records computerized from 1988, on microfiche, archived and index from 1974. Mail turnaround time 1-3 weeks. Criminal PAT goes back to same as civil. **Note: For a complete description of online access see the *Online Access is Statewide* section at the front or back of this chapter** .

Nome

Superior & District Court (2nd District) PO Box 1110, 113 Front St, 2nd Fl, Nome, AK 99762-1110; 907-443-5216; fax: 907-443-2192; 8AM-4:30PM M,T,TH,F; 9AM-4:30 W (AK). *Felony, Misdemeanor, Civil, Eviction, Small Claims, Probate.*
www.courts.alaska.gov/courtdir.htm

General Information: Probate fax is same as main fax number. Online identifiers in results same as on public terminal. No adoption, juvenile, guardianship or mental records released. Will fax documents to toll-free number. Court makes copy: $.25 per page. Self serve copy: same. Certification fee: $5.00 plus $2.00 per copy after first. Payee: Nome Trial Courts. Personal checks accepted. Visa/MC accepted. Prepayment required. Mail requests: SASE required.

Civil Name Search: Access: Fax, mail, in person, online. Both court and visitors may perform in person name searches. Search fee: $15.00 per hour or fraction of. Required to search: name, years to search; also helpful: DOB. Civil records on computer from 1983, on microfiche from 1960 to 1983, on index and archived from 1960. Mail turnaround time 5 days. Civil PAT goes back to 1983. Terminal results can include DOB; most have middle initial. **Note: For a complete description of online access see the *Online Access is Statewide* section at the front or back of this chapter.**

Criminal Name Search: Access: Fax, mail, in person, online. Both court and visitors may perform in person name searches. Search fee: $15.00 per hour or fraction of. Required to search: name, years to search; also helpful: DOB, SSN. Criminal records computerized from 1983, on microfiche from 1960 to 1983, on index and archived from 1960. Mail turnaround time 5 days. Criminal PAT goes back to same as civil. **Note: For a complete description of online access see the *Online Access is Statewide* section at the front or back of this chapter** .

Unalakleet Magistrate Court (2nd District) PO Box 250, Unalakleet, AK 99684-0250; 907-624-3015; fax: 907-624-3118; 8AM-4PM (irregular hours & days) (AK). *Misdemeanor, Civil Actions under $10,000, Small Claims.*
www.courts.alaska.gov/

General Information: This is a one-person court and very quiet. Will fax documents for free. Court makes copy: $.25 per page. Certification fee: $5.00

per doc plus copy fee. Payee: Alaska Court System. Personal checks accepted. No credit cards accepted. Prepayment required.

Civil Name Search: Access: In person, mail, fax, online. Only the court performs in person name searches; visitors may not. Search fee: $15.00 per hour. Civil records indexed by defendant, plaintiff. Civil records go back to 1998. Mail turnaround time 1-2 weeks. **Note: For a complete description of online access see the *Online Access is Statewide* section at the front or back of this chapter.**

Criminal Name Search: Access: In person, mail, fax, online. Only the court performs in person name searches; visitors may not. Search fee: $15.00 per hour. Criminal records go back to 1998. Mail turnaround time 1-2 weeks. **Note: For a complete description of online access see the *Online Access is Statewide* section at the front or back of this chapter**.

Gambell Magistrate Court (2nd District) - See Nome
Misdemeanor, Civil Actions under $10,000, Small Claims.
www.courts.alaska.gov/
General Information: Court is vacant; records at Superior Court in Nome.

North Slope Borough

Superior & District Court (2nd District) PO Box 270, 1250 Agvik St, 2nd Fl, Barrow, AK 99723-0270; 907-852-4800; fax: 907-852-4804; 8AM-4:30PM except Weds 9AM-4:30PM (AK). *Felony, Misdemeanor, Civil, Eviction, Small Claims, Probate.*
www.courts.alaska.gov/
General Information: Online identifiers in results same as on public terminal. No confidential records released. Will fax documents to local or toll-free number. Court makes copy: $.25 per page. Certification fee: $5.00 1st doc; add'l docs are $2.00. Payee: Alaska Court System. Personal checks accepted. Visa/MC accepted in person only. Prepayment required. Mail requests: SASE required.
Civil Name Search: Access: Fax, mail, in person, online. Both court and visitors may perform in person name searches. Search fee: $15.00 per hour. Required to search: name, years to search; also helpful: address. Civil records on computer from 1983, prior on microfiche. Hard copies go back only 5 years. Mail turnaround time 3 weeks. Civil PAT goes back to 1983. Terminal results can include DOB; most have middle initial. **Note: For a complete description of online access see the *Online Access is Statewide* section at the front or back of this chapter.**
Criminal Name Search: Access: Fax, mail, in person, online. Both court and visitors may perform in person name searches. Search fee: $15.00 per hour. Required to search: name, years to search; also helpful: address, DOB, SSN. Criminal records computerized from 1983, prior on microfiche. Hard copies go back only 5 years. Mail turnaround time 3 weeks. Criminal PAT goes back to same as civil. **Note: For a complete description of online access see the *Online Access is Statewide* section at the front or back of this chapter.**

Northwest Arctic Borough

Superior & District Court (2nd District) PO Box 317, 605 3rd Ave, Kotzebue, AK 99752-0317; 907-442-3208; fax: 907-442-3974; 8AM-4:30PM (AK). *Felony, Misdemeanor, Civil, Eviction, Small Claims, Probate.*
www.courts.alaska.gov/
General Information: This court holds records for the closed Magistrate Court formerly in Ambler, Kiana, Pt. Hope, Selawick and Noorvik. Online identifiers in results same as on public terminal. No adoption, juvenile, guardianship or mental records released. Will fax documents to local or toll-free number. Court makes copy: $.25 per page. Self serve copy: same. Certification fee: $5.00 plus $2.00 per page after first; $15.00 for exemplification. Notary fee is $3.00. Payee: Alaska Court System. Personal checks accepted. Visa/MC in person only accepted. Prepayment required.
Civil Name Search: Access: Phone, fax, mail, in person, online. Both court and visitors may perform in person name searches. Search fee: $15.00. Civil records on computer from 1993, prior records on microfiche archived and index from 1966 on microfilm. Note: Copy of check required before faxed requests are processed. Mail turnaround time 2 day to 3 weeks. Civil PAT goes back to 1983. Terminal results can include DOB; most have middle initial. **Note: For a complete description of online access see the *Online Access is Statewide* section at the front or back of this chapter.**
Criminal Name Search: Access: Mail, fax, in person, online. Both court and visitors may perform in person name searches. Search fee: $15.00. Required to search: name, years to search, DOB; also helpful: SSN. Criminal records computerized from 1983, prior records on microfiche, archived and index from 1966 on microfilm. Mail turnaround time 2 days to 3 weeks. Criminal PAT goes back to same as civil. **Note: For a complete description of online access see the *Online Access is Statewide* section at the front or back of this chapter**.
Kiana Magistrate Court (2nd District) - See Kotzebue

General Information: Court is temporarily vacant; contact the Kotzebue Court for record information.

Selawik Magistrate Court (2nd District) *Misdemeanor, Civil Actions under $10,000, Small Claims.*
General Information: Selawik court closed. Contact the Kotzebue Court for record information

Prince of Wales Island - Outer Ketchikan

Craig Trial Court (1st District) PO Box 646, 1305 Craig-Klawock Hwy, Craig, AK 99921-0646; 907-826-3316/3306; fax: 907-826-3904; 8AM-4:30PM M-TH; 9AM-4:30PM F (AK). *Felony, Misdemeanor, Civil Actions, Small Claims, Probate.*
www.courts.alaska.gov/
General Information: Court also holds minor offenses. Felony cases prior to 7/1/2007 are at Ketchikan Superior & District Court. Will fax documents for free. Court makes copy: $.25 per page. Certification fee: $5.00 per doc, $2.00 per add'l copy. Payee: Alaska Court System. Personal checks accepted. No credit cards accepted. Prepayment required. Mail requests: SASE requested.
Civil Name Search: Access: In person, phone, fax, mail, online. Only the court performs in person name searches; visitors may not. Search fee: $15.00 per hour. No fee to call for the court to check index for a name and case number. Required to search: name, years to search; also helpful: DOB. Civil records go back to 1960s; on computer back to 1993. Mail turnaround time 2 weeks. **Note: For a complete description of online access see the *Online Access is Statewide* section at the front or back of this chapter.**
Criminal Name Search: Access: In person, phone, fax, mail, online. Only the court performs in person name searches; visitors may not. Search fee: $15.00 per hour. No fee to call for the court to check index for a name and case number. Required to search: name, years to search; also helpful: DOB. Misdemeanor records go back to 1960s; on computer back to 1993. Mail turnaround time 2 weeks. **Note: For a complete description of online access see the *Online Access is Statewide* section at the front or back of this chapter**.

Sitka Borough

Superior & District Court (1st District) 304 Lake St, Rm 203, Sitka, AK 99835-7759; 907-747-3291; fax: 907-747-6690; 8AM-4:30PM M-TH; 9AM-4:30 F (AK). *Felony, Misdemeanor, Civil, Eviction, Small Claims, Probate.*
www.courts.alaska.gov/
General Information: Probate is in a separate index at this address. Probate fax is same as main fax number. Former Pelican Magistrate Court (closed) records located here. No adoption, juvenile, guardianship or mental records released. No fee to fax document to toll-free number. Court makes copy: $.25 per page. Self serve copy: $.10 per page. Certification fee: $5.00 per doc; exemplifications- $10.00. Payee: Alaska Court System. Personal checks accepted. No credit cards accepted. Prepayment required. Mail requests: SASE required.
Civil Name Search: Access: Phone, fax, mail, in person, online. Both court and visitors may perform in person name searches. Search fee: $15.00 per hour. No fee for info given out over the phone. Required to search: name. Civil records on computer from 1983, on microfilm and archived from 1970 to 1987, on index from 1960. Mail turnaround time 1 week. Civil PAT goes back to 1980s. **Note: For a complete description of online access see the *Online Access is Statewide* section at the front or back of this chapter.**
Criminal Name Search: Access: Phone, fax, mail, in person, online. Both court and visitors may perform in person name searches. Search fee: $15.00 per hour. No fee for info given out over the phone. Required to search: name. Criminal records computerized from 1983, on microfilm and archived from 1970 to 1987, on index from 1960. Mail turnaround time 1 week. Criminal PAT goes back to same as civil. **Note: For a complete description of online access see the *Online Access is Statewide* section at the front or back of this chapter**.

Skagway-Yakutat-Angoon

Hoonah District Court (1st District) PO Box 430, Hoonah, AK 99829-0430; 907-945-3668; fax: 907-945-3637; 8AM-N, 1-4:30PM (AK). *Misdemeanor, Civil Actions under $100,000, Small Claims.*
www.courts.alaska.gov/
General Information: Felony cases are at Juneau Superior & District Court. No confidential, juvenile or sex related records released. Will fax documents to toll-free number. Court makes copy: $.25 per page. Certification fee: $5.00 plus $2.00 per page after first. Payee: Alaska Court System. Personal checks accepted. No credit cards accepted. Prepayment required. Mail requests: SASE required.
Civil Name Search: Access: Mail, in person, online. Only the court performs in person name searches; visitors may not. No search fee. Required to search: name, years to search, case number. Civil docket indexed from 1971 to present. Mail turnaround time 2-3 days. **Note: For a**

complete description of online access see the *Online Access is Statewide* section at the front or back of this chapter.

Criminal Name Search: Access: Mail, in person, online. Only the court performs in person name searches; visitors may not. Search fee: $15.00. Required to search: name, DOB, case number. Criminal records indexed from 1996 to present. Note: Older criminal records on microfilm in Juneau; research time is $15.00 per hour. Mail turnaround time 2-3 days. **Note: For a complete description of online access see the *Online Access is Statewide* section at the front or back of this chapter.**

Angoon Magistrate Court (1st District) PO Box 250, 700 Ondanaog St, Angoon, AK 99820-0250; 907-788-3229; fax: 907-788-3108; 8AM-1PM Tu-F; Closed M (AK). *Misdemeanor, Civil Actions under $10,000, Small Claims.*

www.courts.alaska.gov/

General Information: Felony cases are at Sitka Superior & District Court. Will fax to toll-free numbers no charge. Court makes copy: $.25 per page. Certification fee: $5.00 per doc. Payee: Alaska Court System. Personal checks accepted. No credit cards accepted. Prepayment required. Mail requests: SASE helpful.

Civil Name Search: Access: Phone, mail, fax, in person. Only the court performs in person name searches; visitors may not. Search fee: $15.00 per hour. Records go back to 1994. Mail turnaround time 1 week.

Criminal Name Search: Access: Phone, mail, fax, in person. Only the court performs in person name searches; visitors may not. Search fee: $15.00 per hour. Required to search: name, years to search, date of birth. Records go back to 1994. Mail turnaround time 1 week.

Skagway District Magistrate Court PO Box 495, 7th & Spring, McCabe Bldg, Skagway, AK 99840-0495; 907-983-2368; fax: 907-983-3801; 9AM-3PM T,W; 9AM-2:30PM Th; closed M & F (AK). *Misdemeanor, Civil Actions under $10,000, Small Claims.*

www.courts.alaska.gov/

General Information: Felony cases are at Juneau Superior & District Court. Will fax to toll-free numbers no charge. Court makes copy: $.25 per page. Certification fee: $5.00 per doc. Payee: State of Alaska. Personal checks accepted. No credit cards accepted. Prepayment required.

Civil Name Search: Access: Mail, fax, in person, online. Only the court performs in person name searches; visitors may not. Search fee: $15.00 per hour. Required to search: DOB, SSN, years to search. Civil records go back to 1970 on microfilm in Anchorage; on computer back to 1998. Mail turnaround time 1-2 weeks. **Note: For a complete description of online access see the *Online Access is Statewide* section at the front or back of this chapter.**

Criminal Name Search: Access: In person, fax, mail, online. Only the court performs in person name searches; visitors may not. Search fee: $15.00 per hour. Required to search: name, years to search, DOB. Criminal records go back to 1970; on computer back to 1996. No charge for a simple name search. Mail turnaround time 1-2 weeks. **Note: For a complete description of online access see the *Online Access is Statewide* section at the front or back of this chapter.**

Yakutat Magistrate Court (1st District) PO Box 426, 508 Max Italio Dr, Yakutat, AK 99689-0426; 907-784-3274; fax: 907-784-3257; 8:30AM-N, 1-4:30PM M-TH, 8:30AM-10:30AM F (AK). *Misdemeanor, Civil Actions under $10,000, Small Claims.*

www.courts.alaska.gov/

General Information: Felony cases are at Juneau Superior & District Court. Will fax documents to local or toll-free number. Court makes copy: $.25 per page. Certification fee: $5.00 per doc. Payee: Alaska Court System. Personal checks accepted. No credit cards accepted. Prepayment required. Mail requests: SASE required.

Civil Name Search: Access: Phone, mail, fax, in person, online. Only the court performs in person name searches; visitors may not. Search fee: $15.00 per name. Required to search: name. Civil records go back to 1998; on computer back to 1976. Mail turnaround time 7-12 days. **Note: For a complete description of online access see the *Online Access is Statewide* section at the front or back of this chapter.**

Criminal Name Search: Access: Mail, fax, in person, email, online. Only the court performs in person name searches; visitors may not. Search fee: $15.00 per name. Required to search: name and DOB or SSN. Criminal records go back to 1959; on computer back to 1998. Mail turnaround time 7-12 days. **Note: For a complete description of online access see the *Online Access is Statewide* section at the front or back of this chapter.**

Pelican Magistrate Court - See Sitka Court

www.courts.alaska.gov/

General Information: This Pelican court closed permanently on 12/31/99. All records are at the Sitka court, address and phone given here.

Southeast Fairbanks

Delta Junction District Court (4th District) PO Box 401, Mile 266 Richardson Hiway, Delta Junction, AK 99737-0401; 907-895-4211; fax: 907-895-4204; 8AM-N, 1-4:30PM (AK). *Misdemeanor, Civil Actions under $10,000, Small Claims, Eviction, Traffic.*

www.courts.alaska.gov/

General Information: Felony cases are at Fairbanks Superior & District Court. Will fax documents if fees paid upfront. Court makes copy: $.25 per page. Certification fee: $5.00 per doc. Payee: District Court. Personal checks accepted. Major credit cards accepted for traffic only. Prepayment required. Mail requests: SASE helpful.

Civil Name Search: Access: In person, mail, online. Only the court performs in person name searches; visitors may not. Search fee: $15.00. Civil records go back to 2000, hard copies to 2004. Mail turnaround time 1 week or more. **Note: For a complete description of online access see the *Online Access is Statewide* section at the front or back of this chapter.**

Criminal Name Search: Access: Phone, mail, fax, in person, online. Only the court performs in person name searches; visitors may not. Search fee: $15.00. Criminal records computerized go back to 1980; prior records go back to mid-70's on fiche. Mail turnaround time 1 week or more. **Note: For a complete description of online access see the Online Access is Statewide section at the front or back of this chapter.**

Tok Magistrate Court (4th District) PO Box 187, 1313.5 Alaska Hwy, Tok, AK 99780-0187; 907-883-5171; fax: 907-883-4367; 8AM-N; 1PM-4:30PM (AK). *Misdemeanor, Civil Actions under $10,000, Small Claims.*

www.courts.alaska.gov/

General Information: Felony cases are at Fairbanks Superior & District Court. Online identifiers in results same as on public terminal. Will fax documents. Court makes copy: $.25 per page. Certification fee: $5.00 per doc, $2.00 per add'l copy. Payee: Court. Personal checks accepted. Major credit cards accepted in person only. Prepayment required. Mail requests: SASE required.

Civil Name Search: Access: In person, phone, mail, online. Visitors must perform in person searches themselves. Search fee: $15.00. Required to search: Name, DOB, SSN. Civil records computerized since 1994. Mail turnaround time 5 days. Civil PAT goes back to 1994. Terminal results can include DOB; most have middle initial. **Note: For a complete description of online access see the *Online Access is Statewide* section at the front or back of this chapter.**

Criminal Name Search: Access: In person, phone, mail, online. Visitors must perform in person searches themselves. No search fee. Required to search: name, years to search, DOB. Criminal records computerized since 1994. Mail turnaround time 5 days. Criminal PAT goes back to same as civil. **Note: For a complete description of online access see the *Online Access is Statewide* section at the front or back of this chapter.**

Valdez-Cordova

District Court (3rd District) PO Box 127, 213 Meals Ave, Valdez, AK 99686-0127; 907-835-2266; fax: 907-835-3764; 8AM-4:30PM (AK). *Felony, Misdemeanor, Civil, Eviction, Small Claims, Probate.*

www.courts.alaska.gov/

General Information: In rare instances, some of the older Valdez felony records may be found at Cordova. No adoption, juvenile, guardianship or mental records released. Will fax documents $15.00 fee. Court makes copy: $.25 per page. Certification fee: $5.00 per doc. Payee: Valdez Trial Court of Alaska. Personal checks accepted. No credit cards accepted. Prepayment required. Mail requests: SASE required.

Civil Name Search: Access: Fax, mail, in person, online. Both court and visitors may perform in person name searches. No search fee. Required to search: name, years to search; also helpful: address. Civil records on computer from 1989, on microfiche, archived and index from 1960. Mail turnaround time 1-3 weeks. Civil PAT goes back to 1974. **Note: For a complete description of online access see the *Online Access is Statewide* section at the front or back of this chapter.**

Criminal Name Search: Access: Fax, mail, in person, online. Both court and visitors may perform in person name searches. No search fee. Required to search: name, years to search; also helpful: address, DOB. Criminal records computerized from 1984, on microfiche, archived and index from 1960. Mail turnaround time 1-3 weeks. Criminal PAT goes back to 1980s. **Note: For a complete description of online access see the *Online Access is Statewide* section at the front or back of this chapter.**

Cordova District Court (3rd District) PO Box 898, 500 Water St, Cordova, AK 99574-0898; 907-424-3378; fax: 907-424-7581; 8AM-4:30PM (AK). *Felony, Misdemeanor, Civil, Small Claims, Probate.*

www.courts.alaska.gov/

General Information: Some very old Valdez court records may also reside here. Although some felony cases may be assigned to a Valdez judge or a

Anchorage judge, the actual case records will be found here in Cordova. Online identifiers in results same as on public terminal. Will not fax documents. Court makes copy: $.25 per page. Self serve copy: $.25 per page. Certification fee: $5.00 per doc. Payee: State of Alaska. Personal checks accepted. No credit cards accepted. Prepayment required.

Civil Name Search: Access: Phone, mail, fax, in person, online. Both court and visitors may perform in person name searches. Search fee: $15.00 per name. Required to search: DOB, years to search. Civil records on computer back to 1993; other records back to 1975. Note: Access by phone if time allows. Mail turnaround time 1 week. Civil PAT goes back to 7-10 years. Terminal results can include DOB; most have middle initial. **Note: For a complete description of online access see the** *Online Access is Statewide* **section at the front or back of this chapter** .

Criminal Name Search: Access: Phone, mail, fax, in person, online. Both court and visitors may perform in person name searches. Search fee: $15.00 per name. Required to search: name, years to search, DOB. Criminal records computerized from 1993; other records back to 1975. Note: Will take phone requests if time allows. Results include name and address. Mail turnaround time 1 week. Criminal PAT goes back to same as civil. **Note: For a complete description of online access see the** *Online Access is Statewide* **section at the front or back of this chapter** .

Glennallen District Court (3rd District) PO Box 86, Mile 115 Richardson Hiway, Glennallen, AK 99588-0086; 907-822-3405; ; 8AM-4:30PM (AK). *Felony, Misdemeanor, Civil, Small Claims, Probate.*
www.courts.alaska.gov/

General Information: Will not fax documents. Court makes copy: $.25 per page. Certification fee: $5.00 per doc, $2.00 per add'l copy. Payee: Alaska Court System. Personal checks accepted. No credit cards accepted. Prepayment required.

Civil Name Search: Access: Mail, in person, online. Only the court performs in person name searches; visitors may not. Search fee: $15.00 per hour. Required to search: DOB, years to search. Records go back to 1960; on computer back to 1992. Mail turnaround time 1-2 weeks. **Note: For a complete description of online access see the** *Online Access is Statewide* **section at the front or back of this chapter**.

Criminal Name Search: Access: Mail, in person, online. Only the court performs in person name searches; visitors may not. Search fee: $15.00 per hour. Required to search: name, years to search, DOB. Records go back to 1960; on computer back to 1992. Mail turnaround time 1-2 weeks. **Note: For a complete description of online access see the** *Online Access is Statewide* **section at the front or back of this chapter** .

Whittier Magistrate Court (3rd District). *Court closed; records available in Anchorage.*
www.courts.alaska.gov/

Wade Hampton

Chevak Magistrate Court (Bethel Area) PO Box 238, Chevak, AK 99563-0238; 907-858-7231; fax: 907-858-7230; 8AM-4:30PM (AK). *Misdemeanor, Civil Actions under $10,000, Small Claims.*
www.courts.alaska.gov/

General Information: Felony cases at Bethel Trial Court. Will fax documents. Court makes copy: $.25 per page. Self serve copy: same. Certification fee: $3.00 per document includes copy fee. Payee: Alaska Court System. Personal checks accepted. No credit cards accepted. Prepayment required. Mail requests: SASE helpful.

Civil Name Search: Access: Mail, fax, in person, online. Both court and visitors may perform in person name searches. Search fee: $15.00. Civil records go back to 1993; on computer back to 1997. Mail turnaround time 1-2 weeks. Public use terminal available, records go back to 2004. **Note: For a complete description of online access see the** *Online Access is Statewide* **section at the front or back of this chapter**.

Criminal Name Search: Access: Mail, fax, in person, online. Both court and visitors may perform in person name searches. Search fee: $15.00 per hour. Required to search: name, years to search, address, DOB, SSN, signed release. Criminal records go back to 1993; on computer back to 1997. Mail turnaround time 1-2 weeks. Public use terminal available, crim records go back to same. **Note: For a complete description of online access see the** *Online Access is Statewide* **section at the front or back of this chapter** .

Emmonak Magistrate Court (Bethel Area) PO Box 176, Emmonak, AK 99581-0176; 907-949-1748; fax: 907-949-1535; 8AM-4:30PM (AK). *Misdemeanor, Civil Actions under $15,000, Small Claims.*
www.courts.alaska.gov/

General Information: Felony cases are at Bethel Superior & District Court. Will fax out documents. Court makes copy: $.25 per page. Certification fee: $5.00 includes copy fee. Payee: State of Alaska, Alaska Court System. Personal checks accepted. No credit cards accepted. Prepayment required. Mail requests: SASE required.

Civil Name Search: Access: Mail, in person, online. Only the court performs in person name searches; visitors may not. Search fee: $15.00

per hour. Required to search: name, years to search, DOB, signed release. Civil records indexed by defendant, plaintiff. Overall records go back to 1995. Computerized records go back to 2000. Mail turnaround time 1-2 weeks. **Note: For a complete description of online access see the** *Online Access is Statewide* **section at the front or back of this chapter**.

Criminal Name Search: Access: Mail, in person, online. Only the court performs in person name searches; visitors may not. Search fee: $15.00 per hour. Required to search: name, years to search, address, DOB, signed release. Overall records go back to 1995. Computerized records go back to 2000. Mail turnaround time 1-2 weeks. **Note: For a complete description of online access see the** *Online Access is Statewide* **section at the front or back of this chapter** .

St Mary's Magistrate Court (Bethel Area) PO Box 269, St Mary's, AK 99658-0183; 907-438-2912; criminal fax: 907-438-2819; civil fax: 8AM-4:30PM; 8AM-4:30PM (AK). *Misdemeanor, Civil Actions under $10,000, Small Claims.*
www.courtrecords.alaska.gov/pa/pa.urd/pamw6500.display

General Information: Felony cases are at Bethel Superior & District Court. Will fax documents. Court makes copy: $.25 per page. Self serve copy: same. Certification fee: $5.00 per doc + $.25 per page copy fee, $2.00 per add'l doc. Payee: District Court. Checks accepted. No credit cards accepted. Prepayment required.

Civil Name Search: Access: Mail, in person, online. Only the court performs in person name searches; visitors may not. Search fee: $15.00 per hour. Required to search: Name, DOB, SSN, years to search 2001-2006, prior years must be requested from Bethel Court 907-543-2298. Civil records computerized go back to 1996. Mail turnaround time 3 weeks. **Note: For a complete description of online access see the** *Online Access is Statewide* **section at the front or back of this chapter**.

Criminal Name Search: Access: Mail, in person, online. Only the court performs in person name searches; visitors may not. Search fee: $15.00 per hour. Required to search: name, years to search; also helpful: DOB. Criminal records computerized go back to 1996. Mail turnaround time 3 weeks. **Note: For a complete description of online access see the** *Online Access is Statewide* **section at the front or back of this chapter**

.

Wrangell

Wrangell Superior & District Court (1st District) PO Box 869, Wrangell, AK 99929-0869; 907-874-2311; fax: 907-874-3509; 8AM-4:30PM (AK). *Felony, Misdemeanor, Civil, Eviction, Small Claims, Probate.*
www.courts.alaska.gov/

General Information: The TDD office can be reached at 800-770-8255. No adoption, juvenile, guardianship or mental records released. Will not fax out documents. Court makes copy: $.25 per page. Certification fee: $5.00 plus $2.00 per copy after first. Exemplification- $10.00. Payee: Alaska Court System or State of Alaska. Personal checks accepted. Major credit cards accepted in person only. Prepayment required.

Civil Name Search: Access: Phone, fax, mail, in person, online. Both court and visitors may perform in person name searches. Search fee: $15.00 per hour. Search fee is charged for all written responses. Civil records on computer from 1988, on microfiche and card files from 1959. Mail turnaround time 7 days. Civil PAT goes back to 1989. **Note: For a complete description of online access see the** *Online Access is Statewide* **section at the front or back of this chapter**.

Criminal Name Search: Access: Phone, fax, mail, in person, online. Both court and visitors may perform in person name searches. Search fee: $15.00 per hour. Required to search: name, years to search, DOB. Criminal records computerized from 1988, on microfiche and card files from 1959. Mail turnaround time 7 days. Criminal PAT goes back to 1989. **Note: For a complete description of online access see the Online Access is Statewide section at the front or back of this chapter** .

Wrangell-Petersburg

Petersburg Superior & District Court (1st District) PO Box 1009, Petersburg, AK 99833-1009; 907-772-3824; fax: 907-772-3018; 8AM-4:30PM (AK). *Felony, Misdemeanor, Civil, Eviction, Small Claims, Probate.*
www.courts.alaska.gov/

General Information: Note that Wrangell records are not mixed within this court, Wrangell is a separate entity. No adoption, juvenile, guardianship or mental records released. Will not fax out documents. Court makes copy: $.25 per page. Certification fee: $5.00 for 1st document, $2.00 each add'l document. Payee: Alaska Court System. Personal checks accepted. No credit cards accepted. Prepayment required. Mail requests: SASE required.

Civil Name Search: Access: Phone, fax, mail, in person, online. Only the court performs in person name searches; visitors may not. No search fee unless on microfilm- $15.00 per hour. Required to search: name, years to search; also helpful: address. Civil records on computer from 1988, on microfiche and index from 1960s, archived from 1920s. Mail turnaround time 1 week. **Note: For a complete description of online access see the** *Online Access is Statewide* **section at the front or back of this chapter**.

Criminal Name Search: Access: Phone, fax, mail, in person, online. Only the court performs in person name searches; visitors may not. Search fee: $15.00 per hour fee on archive cases. Required to search: name, years to search; also helpful: address, DOB. Criminal records computerized from 1988, on microfiche and index from 1960s, archived from 1920s. Mail turnaround time 1 week. **Note: For a complete description of online access see the** *Online Access is Statewide* **section at the front or back of this chapter**.

Kake Magistrate Court (1st District) PO Box 100, Kake, AK 99830-0100; 907-785-3651; fax: 907-785-3152; 9AM-N (AK). *Misdemeanor, Civil Actions under $10,000, Small Claims.*
www.courts.alaska.gov/courtdir.htm

General Information: Located at 200 Third Ave. Felonies committed in the Kake area should be searched at the Petersburg court (not Wrangell). Will not fax documents. Court makes copy: $.25 per page. Certification fee: $5.00 per doc, $2.00 per add'l copy. Payee: Alaska Court System. Personal checks accepted. No credit cards accepted. Prepayment required.

Civil Name Search: Access: Fax, mail, in person, online. Only the court performs in person name searches; visitors may not. Search fee: $15.00 per name. Required to search: name. Civil records go back to 1990. Mail turnaround time 1-2 weeks. **Note: For a complete description of online access see the** *Online Access is Statewide* **section at the front or back of this chapter**.

Criminal Name Search: Access: Fax, mail, in person, online. Only the court performs in person name searches; visitors may not. Search fee: $15.00 per name. Required to search: name, years to search, DOB, SSN, signed release. Criminal records go back to 1990. Mail turnaround time 1-2 weeks. **Note: For a complete description of online access see the** *Online Access is Statewide* **section at the front or back of this chapter.**

Yukon-Koyukuk

Fort Yukon Magistrate Court (4th District) PO Box 211, Fort Yukon, AK 99740-0211; 907-662-2336; ; 9AM-1:30PM, 3:30PM-4:30PM (AK). *Misdemeanor, Civil Actions under $10,000, Small Claims.*
www.courts.alaska.gov/

General Information: Felony cases are at Fairbanks Superior & District Court. Will fax documents to local or toll free line. Court makes copy: $.25 per page. Certification fee: $5.00 per doc, $2.00 per add'l copy. Payee: District Court. . Prepayment required.

Civil Name Search: Access: Fax, mail, in person, online. Only the court performs in person name searches; visitors may not. Search fee: $15.00 per name. Required to search: name, DOB. Records go back to 1960s. Mail turnaround time 1-2 weeks. **Note: For a complete description of online access see the** *Online Access is Statewide* **section at the front or back of this chapter**.

Criminal Name Search: Access: Fax, mail, in person, online. Only the court performs in person name searches; visitors may not. Search fee: $15.00 per hour. Required to search: name, years to search, DOB. Records go back to 1960s. Mail turnaround time 1-2 weeks. **Note: For a complete description of online access see the Online Access is Statewide section at the front or back of this chapter** .

Galena Magistrate Court (4th District) PO Box 167, Galena, AK 99741-0167; 907-656-1322; fax: 907-656-1546; 8AM-4:30PM, closed N-1PM (AK). *Misdemeanor, Civil Actions under $10,000, Small Claims.*
www.courts.alaska.gov/

General Information: Felony cases are at Fairbanks Superior & District Court. Will not fax documents. Court makes copy: $.25 per page. Certification fee: $5.00 per doc, $2.00 per add'l copy. Payee: Magistrate Court. No credit cards accepted. Prepayment required.

Civil Name Search: Access: Mail, in person, online. Only the court performs in person name searches; visitors may not. Search fee: $15.00 per name. Required to search: name. Civil record computerized since 1995. Mail turnaround time 1-2 weeks. **Note: For a complete description of online access see the** *Online Access is Statewide* **section at the front or back of this chapter**.

Criminal Name Search: Access: Mail, in person, online. Only the court performs in person name searches; visitors may not. Search fee: $15.00 per hour. Criminal records computerized since 1995. Mail turnaround time 1-2 weeks. **Note: For a complete description of online access see the** *Online Access is Statewide* **section at the front or back of this chapter**

Nenana District Court (4th District) PO Box 449, Nenana, AK 99760-0449; 907-832-5430; fax: 907-832-5841; 8AM-N, 1-4:30PM (AK). *Misdemeanor, Civil Actions under $10,000, Small Claims.*
www.courts.alaska.gov/

General Information: Felony cases are at Fairbanks Superior & District Court. Will fax back docs but only a few pages free. Court makes copy: $.25

per page. Certification fee: $5.00 per doc, $2.00 per add'l copy. Personal checks accepted. No credit cards accepted.

Civil Name Search: Access: Fax, mail, in person, online. Both court and visitors may perform in person name searches. Search fee: $15.00 per name. Required to search: name, years to search, DOB. Civil records on file for five years, online index goes back much farther. **Note: For a complete description of online access see the** *Online Access is Statewide* **section at the front or back of this chapter.**

Criminal Name Search: Access: Phone, fax, mail, in person, online. Only the court performs in person name searches; visitors may not. No search fee. Required to search: name, years to search, DOB. Criminal records computerized from 1995. **Note: For a complete description of online access see the** *Online Access is Statewide* **section at the front or back of this chapter** .

Tanana Magistrate Court (4th District) PO Box 167, Galena, AK 99741; 907-656-1322; fax: 907-656-1546; 8AM-4:30PM M-F (AK). *Misdemeanor, Civil Actions under $10,000, Small Claims.*
www.courts.alaska.gov/

General Information: Magistrate may also be contacted by phone at 907-832-5430. Felony cases are at Fairbanks Superior & District Court. All case record files moved to Galena Court 6/2005. Will not fax documents. Court makes copy: $.25 per page. Certification fee: $5.00 per doc plus copy fee. Payee: Magistrate Court. Personal checks accepted. No credit cards accepted. Prepayment required.

Civil Name Search: Access: In person, phone, fax, mail, online. Both court and visitors may perform in person name searches. Search fee: $15.00 per name. Paper records kept 4 years. Mail turnaround time 1-2 weeks. **Note: For a complete description of online access see the** *Online Access is Statewide* **section at the front or back of this chapter.**

Criminal Name Search: Access: In person, phone, mail, online. Both court and visitors may perform in person name searches. Search fee: $15.00 per name. Required to search: name, years to search, DOB, signed release. Paper records kept 4 years. Mail turnaround time 1-2 weeks. Public use terminal has crim records. **Note: For a complete description of online access see the** *Online Access is Statewide* **section at the front or back of this chapter.**

McGrath Magistrate Court (4th District) PO Box 167, Galena, AK 99741-0167; 907-656-1322; fax: 907-656-1546; 8AM-4:30PM (AK). *Misdemeanor, Civil Actions under $10,000, Small Claims.*
www.courts.alaska.gov/

General Information: McGrath Court is vacant. Court records at Galena Magistrate Court, address and phone given here.

About Statewide Online Access

The case summary and docket information for Alaska trial courts for civil criminal, traffic and wills is found on Courtview at:

www.courtrecords.alaska.gov/pa/pa.urd/pamw6500.display.

One may search by name, case number or ticket number.

Although all courts participate, the dates of the earliest available cases vary by court. There are other cautionary facts to consider. The use of identifiers is limited on the initial search index. For example a recent search for Michael Smith pulled 789 cases and only slightly more than 50% showed a DOB on the index.

Arizona

Time Zone:	**MST***

*Note that Arizona does not go on Daylight Savings Time

Capital:	**Phoenix, Maricopa County**
# of Counties:	**15**
State Web:	**http://az.gov**
Court Web:	**www.azcourts.gov**

Administration

Administrative Office of the Courts (AOC) , Arizona Supreme Court Bldg, 1501 W Washington, Phoenix, AZ, 85007; 602-452-3300.

The Supreme and Appellate Courts

The Supreme Court is Arizona's highest court and the court of last resort. The Court of Appeals is the intermediate appellate court and is the first appeal level for the Superior Court. The Court of Appeals, Division One, hears appeals from the Industrial Commission, unemployment compensation rulings of the Department of Economic Security, and rulings by the Tax Court.

View opinions and summaries from the home page above.

The Arizona Trial Courts

Court	Type	How Organized	Jurisdiction Highpoints
Superior*	General	15 Courts in 15 counties	Felony, Misdemeanor, Civil, Small Claims, Juvenile, Traffic, Eviction, Domestic Relations, Estate
Justice of the Peace*	Limited	79 courts in 79 precincts	Misdemeanor, Limited Civil, Small Claims, Eviction, Traffic
Municipal	Municipal	85	Traffic, Ordinance

* = profiled in this book

Details on the Court Structure

The **Superior Court** is the court of general jurisdiction and acts as an appellate court for Justice and Municipal courts. The Superior Court hears felony, misdemeanor (if not heard elsewhere), civil, property cases of $1,000 or more, eviction, probate, estate, divorce and naturalization issues.

Justice Courts oversee civil lawsuits where the amount in dispute is $10,000 or less, landlord and tenant controversies, small claims cases and a full range of civil and criminal traffic offenses, including DUIs. Justices of the peace also resolve other types of misdemeanor allegations (e.g. shoplifting, writing bad checks, violating restraining orders)

Municipal Courts may also be known as City or Magistrate Courts. These courts hear misdemeanor or civil traffic cases where no serious injuries occur as well as violations of city ordinances. They do not hear civil lawsuits between citizens.

Civil cases between $5,000 and $10,000 may be filed at either Justice Courts or Superior Courts. Preliminary felonies can be heard at either the Superior Court of Justice Courts, but not at the Municipal Courts. Justice Courts and Municipal Courts generally have separate jurisdiction based on case types as indicated in the text herein.

Record Searching Facts You Need to Know

Fees and Record Searching Tips

Fees across all jurisdictions as established by the Arizona Supreme Court and state legislature are as follows: Superior Courts $26.00 per name search, $26.00 per certification; Justice of the Peace Courts $24.00 per name search, $24.00 per certification; Municipal Courts $17.00 per name search and $17.00 per record duplication. Of course there is no fee in the Superior Court if a researcher does his/her own onsite name search there is no. fee. The copy fee for all courts is $.50 per page.

Be aware that some Justice Courts will charge a "search fee" to pull a file even if the case file is already known and given. Also, some courts will charge a separate search fee for each case found under the same name. Useful advice from AZ private investigators and record researchers is to bring a copy of the law in hand when visiting certain courts.

Generally a misdemeanor action occurring within the city on a city street will be heard in the city's Municipal Court, and a misdemeanor action occurring on a county maintained roadway will be heard at a Justice of the Peace Court. Thus Municipal Courts may hold more records than just low level ordinance violations and traffic. It is important to note that not all Municipal Courts report misdemeanors to the AOC online database (see below). Thus a high level of due diligence is required for background checks, research is often necessary to be performed at the Municipal Court level. This can be problematic as access is limited and statutory court fees are relatively high (compared to other states).

Public access to all Maricopa County court case indexes is available at a central location - One W. Madison Ave in downtown Phoenix. However, file copies must be obtained from the court where the case is heard.

Online Access is Nearly for All Courts – But Not From One System

The Public Access to Court Case Information online system provided by Administrative Office of the Courts (AOC) contains information about court cases for nearly all courts in Arizona. Courts not covered include Pima County and certain parts of Yavapai and Maricopa counties. Information provided includes detailed case information (i.e., case type, charges, filing and disposition dates), the parties in the case (not including victims and witnesses), and the court mailing address and location. For more information go to http://apps.supremecourt.az.gov/publicaccess/. Please note this site has a strong disclaimer which states in part "...not all cases from a participating court may be included....information should not be used as a substitute for a thorough background search of official public records..." Use caution if this site is accessed for pre-employment screening or high due diligence needs, as it is merely supplemental.

Maricopa County (Phoenix metro area) provides search site for free Superior Court criminal, civil, probate, and family case records, and for Justice Court case docket data is at www.superiorcourt.maricopa.gov/Docket/. See Maricopa County for further details.

Pima County (Tucson metro area) provides online access for civil Superior Court records, but not criminal. There are three Justice Courts in Pima. Two are on the state system, one is on its one online system

Apache County

Superior Court PO Box 365, St Johns, AZ 85936; 928-337-7550; fax: 928-337-2771; 8AM-5PM (MST). *Felony, Civil Actions over $10,000, Probate.* www.co.apache.az.us/Departments/Superior/Superior.htm
General Information: No juvenile dependencies, mental health, victims, sealed or adoption records released. Will fax out docs $7.00 each. Court makes copy: $.50 per page. Self serve copy: same. Certification fee: $26.00 per doc. Payee: Clerk of the Court. Business checks accepted. Credit cards accepted. Prepayment required. Mail requests: SASE required.
Civil Name Search: Access: Mail, in person, online. Both court and visitors may perform in person name searches. Search fee: $26.00 per name. Required to search: name, years to search; also helpful: address. Civil records on computer and docket books. Mail turnaround time 3 days. Civil PAT goes back to 1995. Online access to records from 1995 forward is free at http://apps.supremecourt.az.gov/publicaccess/.
Criminal Name Search: Access: Mail, in person, online. Both court and visitors may perform in person name searches. Search fee: $26.00 per name. Add $7.00 if no SASE. Required to search: name, years to search, DOB; also helpful: address, SSN. Criminal records on computer and docket books. Mail turnaround time 3 days. Criminal PAT goes back to same as civil. Online access to records from 1995 forward is free at www.supreme.state.az.us/publicaccess/. Online results show middle initial, DOB.

Chinle Justice Court PO Box 888, US Hwy 191 MP 447, Chinle, AZ 86503; 928-674-5922; fax: 928-674-5926; 8AM-5PM (MST). *Misdemeanor, Civil Actions under $10,000, Eviction, Small Claims.* www.co.apache.az.us/Departments/Justice/Chinle/ChinleJP.htm
General Information: No juvenile, mental health, victims, sealed or adoption records released. Fee to fax out file $1.25 per page. Court makes copy: $.50 per page. Self serve copy: same. Certification fee: $24.00 per doc. Payee: Chinle Justice Court. Business checks accepted. No credit cards accepted. Prepayment required. Mail requests: SASE required.
Civil Name Search: Access: Fax, mail, in person, online. Both court and visitors may perform in person name searches. Search fee: $24.00 per name. Required to search: name, years to search; also helpful: address. Civil cases indexed by defendant. Civil index in docket books from 1977, computerized back to 2002. Mail turnaround time 1-2 days. Civil PAT goes back to 2002. Access to the docket is free at http://apps.supremecourt.az.gov/publicaccess/.
Criminal Name Search: Access: Fax, mail, in person, online. Both court and visitors may perform in person name searches. Search fee: $24.00 per name. Required to search: name, years to search; also helpful: address, DOB, SSN. Criminal docket on books from 1977, computerized back to 2002. Note: Phone access is discouraged. Mail turnaround time 1-2 days. Criminal PAT goes back to same as civil. Access to the docket is free at http://apps.supremecourt.az.gov/publicaccess/.

Puerco Justice Court PO Box 610, Sanders, AZ 86512; 928-688-2954; fax: 928-688-2244; 8AM-N, 1-5PM (MST). *Misdemeanor, Civil Actions under $10,000, Eviction, Small Claims.*

General Information: When a case number is given, the court also charges a $24 fee to pull a record, but this could change. This interpretation is not per guidelines of the Administrative Offices of the Courts and is not the procedure followed in the Superior Court. No juvenile, mental health, victims, sealed or adoption records released. Court makes copy: $.50 per page. Certification fee: $24.00 per doc. Payee: Puerco Justice Court. Only cashiers checks and money orders accepted. No credit cards accepted. Prepayment required. Mail requests: SASE required.

Civil Name Search: Access: Mail, in person, online. Only the court performs in person name searches; visitors may not. Search fee: $24.00 per name. Required to search: name, years to search; also helpful: address, case number. Civil cases indexed by defendant. Civil index on docket books prior to 3/1996. Mail turnaround time ASAP. Access to the docket is free at http://apps.supremecourt.az.gov/publicaccess/.

Criminal Name Search: Access: Mail, in person, online. Only the court performs in person name searches; visitors may not. Search fee: $24.00 per name. Required to search: name, years to search, DOB; also helpful: address, SSN, case number. Criminal docket on books prior to 3/1996. Mail turnaround time ASAP. Access to the docket is free at http://apps.supremecourt.az.gov/publicaccess/.

Round Valley Justice Court PO Box 1356, Springerville, AZ 85938; 928-333-4613; fax: 928-333-4205; 8AM-N, 1-5PM (MST). *Misdemeanor, Civil Actions under $10,000, Eviction, Small Claims.*
www.co.apache.az.us/Departments/Justice/RoundValley/RoundValleyJP.htm
General Information: When a case number is given, the court also charges a $24 fee to pull a record, but this could change. This interpretation is not per guidelines of the Administrative Offices of the Courts and is not the procedure followed in the Superior Court. No juvenile, mental health, victims, sealed or adoption records released. Will not fax documents. Court makes copy: $.50 per page. Self serve copy: same. Certification fee: $24.00 per doc. Payee: Round Valley Justice Court. Only cashiers checks and money orders accepted. Major credit cards accepted, $6.00 transaction fee added. Prepayment required. Mail requests: SASE required.

Civil Name Search: Access: Phone, fax, mail, in person, online. Both court and visitors may perform in person name searches. Search fee: $24.00 per name. Required to search: name, years to search; also helpful: address. Civil index in docket books from 1990, computerized since 2/96, record file copies purged from 2005 back. Mail turnaround time 5 working days. Access to the docket is free at http://apps.supremecourt.az.gov/publicaccess/.

Criminal Name Search: Access: Phone, fax, mail, in person, online. Both court and visitors may perform in person name searches. Search fee: $24.00 per name. Required to search: name, years to search; also helpful: address, DOB, SSN. Criminal docket on books from 1990, computerized since 2/96, record file copies purged from 2005 back. Mail turnaround time 5 working days. Access to the docket is free at http://apps.supremecourt.az.gov/publicaccess/.

St Johns Justice Court PO Box 308, St Johns, AZ 85936; 928-337-7558; fax: 928-337-2683; 8AM-5PM (MST). *Misdemeanor, Civil Actions under $10,000, Eviction, Small Claims.*
www.co.apache.az.us/Departments/Justice/StJohns/STJOHNSJP.htm
General Information: No juvenile, mental health, victims, sealed or adoption records released. Will fax documents. Court makes copy: $.50 per page. Certification fee: $24.00 per doc. Only cashiers checks and money orders accepted. Major credit cards accepted, $6.00 fee applies. Prepayment required. Mail requests: SASE required.

Civil Name Search: Access: Mail, in person, online. Only the court performs in person name searches; visitors may not. Search fee: $24.00 per name. Required to search: name, years to search; also helpful: address. Civil cases indexed by defendant. Civil records on computer since 1996. Mail turnaround time 48 hours. Access to the docket is free at http://apps.supremecourt.az.gov/publicaccess/.

Criminal Name Search: Access: Mail, in person, online. Only the court performs in person name searches; visitors may not. Search fee: $24.00 per name. Required to search: name, years to search, DOB; also helpful: address, SSN. Criminal records on computer since 1996. Mail turnaround time 48 hours. Access to the docket is free at http://apps.supremecourt.az.gov/publicaccess/. Online results show middle initial, DOB.

Cochise County

Superior Court PO Drawer CK, 100 Quality Hill St, Bisbee, AZ 85603; 520-432-8604; fax: 520-432-4850; 8AM-5PM (MST). *Felony, Civil Actions over $5,000, Probate.*
http://cochise.az.gov/cochise_clerk_court.aspx?id=194

General Information: A court records request form is available at www.co.cochise.az.us/E_Forms/Court/CourtRecordRequest.aspx. Search fee includes both civil and criminal indexes. No juvenile, mental health, victims, sealed or adoption records released. Fee to fax document $.50 per page. Court makes copy: $.50 per page. Certification fee: $26.00 per doc. Payee: Clerk of Superior Court. No personal checks accepted. Visa/MC accepted in person only. Prepayment required. Mail requests: SASE required.

Civil Name Search: Access: Fax, mail, in person, online. Both court and visitors may perform in person name searches. Search fee: $26.00 per name per year, add $7.00 to mail search results. Civil records on computer since 1996 and on index books from 1881 to present. Mail turnaround time 7-14 days. Public access at http://apps.supremecourt.az.gov/publicaccess/.

Criminal Name Search: Access: Fax, mail, in person, online. Both court and visitors may perform in person name searches. Search fee: $26.00 per name. Per every 5 years. Add $7.00 to return results by mail. Required to search: name, years to search; also helpful: DOB, SSN. Criminal records on computer since 1996; prior records on index books. Mail turnaround time 7-14 days. Public access at http://apps.supremecourt.az.gov/publicaccess. Access the current inmate list at http://cochise.az.gov/content/sheriff/inmate%20list.pdf. Online results show middle initial, DOB.

Benson Justice Court 126 W 5th St, #1, Benson, AZ 85602; 520-586-8100; criminal phone: 520-586-8106; civil phone: 520-586-8102; fax: 520-586-9647; 8AM-5PM (MST). *Misdemeanor, Civil Actions under $10,000, Eviction, Small Claims.*
http://cochise.az.gov/cochise_court_administration.aspx?id=230

General Information: There is no fee to access if case number is given and in person, for up to 3 cases per day. Otherwise, when a case number is given, the court also charges a $24 fee to pull a record. No juvenile, mental health, victims, sealed records released. No fee to fax documents. Court makes copy: $.50 per page. Certification fee: $24.00 per doc. Payee: Benson Justice Court. No personal checks accepted without DR ID. Major credit cards accepted. Prepayment required. Mail requests: SASE required.

Civil Name Search: Access: Fax, mail, in person, online. Only the court performs in person name searches; visitors may not. Search fee: $24.00 per name. Required to search: name, years to search; also helpful: address. Civil records go back to 1997. Mail turnaround time 7-10 days. Public access at http://apps.supremecourt.az.gov/publicaccess/.

Criminal Name Search: Access: Fax, mail, in person, online. Only the court performs in person name searches; visitors may not. Search fee: $24.00 per name. Required to search: name, years to search; also helpful: address, DOB, SSN. Criminal records go back to 1997. Mail turnaround time 1-3 days. Public access at http://apps.supremecourt.az.gov/publicaccess/. Online results show middle initial, DOB.

Bisbee Justice Court 207 N Judd Dr, Bisbee, AZ 85603; 520-432-9542; criminal phone: 520-432-9540; fax: 520-432-5271; 8AM-5PM (MST). *Misdemeanor, Civil Actions under $10,000, Eviction, Small Claims.*
http://cochise.az.gov/cochise_court_administration.aspx?id=230

General Information: No juvenile, mental health, victims, sealed or adoption records released. No fee to fax documents. Court makes copy: $.50 per page. Certification fee: $24.00 per doc. Payee: Bisbee Justice Court #1. No personal checks accepted. Visa/MC accepted. Prepayment required. Mail requests: SASE required.

Civil Name Search: Access: Fax, mail, in person, online. Only the court performs in person name searches; visitors may not. Search fee: $24.00 per name. Required to search: name, years to search; also helpful: address. Civil records on computer from 1992. Some records on dockets. Mail turnaround time 1-7 days. Public access at http://apps.supremecourt.az.gov/publicaccess/, but sometime records are not updated frequently.

Criminal Name Search: Access: Fax, mail, in person, online. Only the court performs in person name searches; visitors may not. Search fee: $24.00 per name. Required to search: name, years to search; also helpful: address, DOB, SSN. Criminal records computerized from 7/92. Some records on dockets; computerized records since 1992. Note: Note that this court will charge a "search fee" when a specific case number is requested and a name search is not requested. Mail turnaround time 1-7 days. Public access at http://apps.supremecourt.az.gov/publicaccess/, but sometime records are not updated frequently.

Bowie Justice Court PO Box 317, Bowie, AZ 85605; 520-847-2303; fax: 520-847-2242; 8AM-5PM (MST). *Misdemeanor, Civil Actions under $10,000, Eviction, Small Claims.*
http://cochise.az.gov/cochise_court_administration.aspx?id=230

General Information: No juvenile, mental health, victims, sealed or adoption records released. Will fax documents $2.00 per page. Court makes copy: $.50 per page. Certification fee: $24.00 per doc. Payee: Bowie Justice

Court. Cashiers checks and money orders accepted. No credit cards accepted. Prepayment required. Mail requests: SASE required.

Civil Name Search: Access: Phone, fax, mail, in person, online. Only the court performs in person name searches; visitors may not. Search fee: $24.00 per case (not name). Required to search: name, years to search; also helpful: address. Civil cases indexed by defendant. Civil records on computer from 7/85, some from 1994. Files maintained for 5 years after closure. Mail turnaround time 10 days. Public access at http://apps.supremecourt.az.gov/publicaccess/, but sometime records are not updated frequently.

Criminal Name Search: Access: Phone, fax, mail, in person, online. Only the court performs in person name searches; visitors may not. Search fee: $24.00 per case #. Required to search: name, years to search, DOB; also helpful: address, SSN. Criminal records computerized from 1989. Files maintained for 5 years after closure. Mail turnaround time 10 days. Public access at http://apps.supremecourt.az.gov/publicaccess/, but sometime records are not updated frequently.

Douglas Justice Court 661 G Ave, Douglas, AZ 85607; 520-805-5640; fax: 520-364-3684; 8AM-5PM (MST). *Misdemeanor, Civil Actions under $10,000, Eviction, Small Claims.*
http://cochise.az.gov/cochise_court_administration.aspx?id=230
General Information: No juvenile, mental health, victims, sealed or adoption records released. Fee to fax out certified document is $.50 per page. Court makes copy: $.50 per page. Certification fee: $24.00 per doc. Payee: Douglas Justice Court. Personal checks accepted with valid AZ DL. Credit cards accepted. Prepayment required.

Civil Name Search: Access: Fax, mail, in person, online. Both court and visitors may perform in person name searches. Search fee: $24.00 per name. Required to search: name, years to search; also helpful: address. Civil records on computer from 1991. Some records on dockets. Mail turnaround time 7-10 days. Civil PAT available. Public access at http://apps.supremecourt.az.gov/publicaccess/, but sometime records are not updated frequently.

Criminal Name Search: Access: Fax, mail, in person, online. Both court and visitors may perform in person name searches. Search fee: $24.00 per name. Required to search: name, years to search, DOB; also helpful: address, SSN. Criminal records computerized from 1990. Some records on dockets. Mail turnaround time 7-10 days. Criminal PAT goes back to 5 years, then file destroyed. Public access at http://apps.supremecourt.az.gov/publicaccess/, but sometime records are not updated frequently. Online results show middle initial, DOB.

Sierra Vista Justice Court 100 Colonia de Salud #108, Sierra Vista, AZ 85635; 520-803-3800/3801; fax: 520-439-9106; 8AM-5PM (MST). *Misdemeanor, Civil Actions under $10,000, Eviction, Small Claims.*
http://cochise.az.gov/cochise_court_administration.aspx?id=230
General Information: When a case number is given, the court also charges a $24 fee to pull a record, but this could change. This interpretation is not per guidelines of the Administrative Offices of the Courts and is not the procedure followed in the Superior Court. No juvenile, mental health, victims, sealed, financial, or adoption records released. Will fax documents to local or toll free line. Court makes copy: $.50 per page. Certification fee: $24.00 per doc. Payee: Cochise County Treasurer. Personal checks accepted. Major credit cards except. Prepayment required. Mail requests: SASE required.

Civil Name Search: Access: Fax, mail, in person, online. Only the court performs in person name searches; visitors may not. Search fee: $24.00 per name. Required to search: name, years to search; also helpful: address. Civil cases indexed by plaintiff and defendant. Civil records on computer since 8/96. Note: In person access requires a written request. Mail turnaround time 3-7 days. Public access at http://apps.supremecourt.az.gov/publicaccess/, but sometime records are not updated frequently.

Criminal Name Search: Access: Fax, mail, in person, online. Only the court performs in person name searches; visitors may not. Search fee: $24.00 per name. Required to search: name, years to search; also helpful: address, DOB, SSN. Criminal records by case number, on computer back to 8/1996. Note: In person access requires a written request. Mail turnaround time 3-7 days. Public access at http://apps.supremecourt.az.gov/publicaccess/, but sometime records are not updated frequently. Online results show name, DOB.

Willcox Justice Court 450 S Haskell, Willcox, AZ 85643; 520-384-7000; fax: 520-384-7101; 8AM-5PM (MST). *Misdemeanor, Civil Actions under $10,000, Eviction, Small Claims.*
http://cochise.az.gov/cochise_court_administration.aspx?id=230
General Information: When a case number is given, the court also charges a $24 fee to pull a record, but this could change. This interpretation is not per guidelines of the Administrative Offices of the Courts and is not the procedure followed in the Superior Court. No juvenile, mental health, victims, sealed or adoption records released. No fee to fax documents. Court

makes copy: $.50 per page. Certification fee: $24.00 per doc. Payee: Willcox Justice Court. Only cashiers checks and money orders accepted. Visa/MC/Discover accepted. Prepayment required. Mail requests: SASE required.

Civil Name Search: Access: Phone, fax, mail, in person, online. Both court and visitors may perform in person name searches. Search fee: $24.00 per name per three cases. Required to search: name; also helpful: years to search, address. Civil records index on computer from 1996. Physical records back to 2004. Mail turnaround time usually 1-5 days. Public access at http://apps.supremecourt.az.gov/publicaccess/, but sometime records are not updated frequently.

Criminal Name Search: Access: Phone, fax, mail, in person, online. Both court and visitors may perform in person name searches. Search fee: $24.00 per each three cases. Required to search: name, DOB; also helpful: years to search, address, SSN. Criminal records computerized from 1996. Physical records back to 2004. Mail turnaround time usually 1-3 days. Public access at http://apps.supremecourt.az.gov/publicaccess/, but sometime records are not updated frequently. Online results show middle initial, DOB, address.

Coconino County

Superior Court 200 N San Francisco St, Courthouse, Flagstaff, AZ 86001; 928-679-7600; ; 8AM-5PM (MST). *Felony, Civil Actions over $5,000, Probate.*
www.coconino.az.gov/courts.aspx?id=242
General Information: No mental health, victims, sealed or adoption records released. Will not fax documents. Court makes copy: $.50 per page. Certification fee: $26.00 per doc. Payee: Clerk of Superior Court. Business checks accepted. No credit cards accepted. Prepayment required. Mail requests: SASE required.

Civil Name Search: Access: Mail, in person, online. Both court and visitors may perform in person name searches. Search fee: $26.00 per name per year. Required to search: name, years to search; also helpful: address. Civil cases indexed by defendant. Civil records on handwritten ledger books from 1890. Some records on microfiche and dockets; computer from 1994. Mail turnaround time 2 weeks. Access to the docket is free at http://apps.supremecourt.az.gov/publicaccess/.

Criminal Name Search: Access: Mail, in person, online. Both court and visitors may perform in person name searches. Search fee: $26.00 per name per year. Required to search: name, years to search, DOB; also helpful: address, SSN. Criminal records on handwritten ledger books from 1890. Some records on microfiche and dockets; computer from 1994. Mail turnaround time 2 weeks. Access to the docket is free at http://apps.supremecourt.az.gov/publicaccess/. Online results show middle initial, DOB.

Flagstaff Justice Court 200 N San Francisco St., Courthouse, 1st Fl, Flagstaff, AZ 86001; 928-679-7650; ; 8AM-5PM (MST). *Misdemeanor, Civil Actions under $10,000, Eviction, Small Claims.*
General Information: When a case number is given, the court may charge a $24 fee to pull a record, but this could change. This interpretation is not per guidelines of the Administrative Offices of the Courts and is not the procedure followed in the Superior Court. No juvenile, mental health, victims, sealed or adoption records released. Will not fax out documents. Court makes copy: $.50 per page. Certification fee: $24.00 per doc. Payee: Flagstaff Justice Court. No Personal checks and credit cards accepted. Prepayment required. Mail requests: SASE required.

Civil Name Search: Access: Mail, fax, in person, online. Only the court performs in person name searches; visitors may not. Search fee: $24.00 per name. Required to search: name, years to search; also helpful: address. Civil index on docket books. Will only maintain records for 5 years. Mail turnaround time 14-20 days. Access to the docket is free at http://apps.supremecourt.az.gov/publicaccess/.

Criminal Name Search: Access: Mail, fax, in person, online. Only the court performs in person name searches; visitors may not. Search fee: $24.00 per name per year. Required to search: name, years to search, DOB; also helpful: address, SSN. Criminal records on computer since 1987. Will only maintain records for 5 years. Mail turnaround time 14-20 days. Access to the docket is free at http://apps.supremecourt.az.gov/publicaccess/.

Fredonia Justice Court PO Box 559, 112 N Main, Fredonia, AZ 86022-0559; 928-643-7472; fax: 928-643-7491; 8AM-5PM (closed noon hr) (MST). *Misdemeanor, Civil Actions under $10,000, Eviction, Small Claims, Traffic.*
www.coconino.az.gov/courts.aspx?id=303
General Information: No juvenile, mental health, victims, sealed or adoption records released. Will fax documents $1.00 per page. Court makes copy: $.50 per page. Certification fee: $24.00 per doc. Payee: Fredonia Justice Court. Only cashiers checks and money orders accepted. Major credit cards accepted with convenience fee of $4.95 per $250.00. Prepayment required. Mail requests: SASE required.

Civil Name Search: Access: Mail, in person, online. Only the court performs in person name searches; visitors may not. Search fee: $24.00 per name. Required to search: name, years to search; also helpful: address. Civil cases indexed by number. Civil index on docket books. Will only maintain records for 5 years. Mail turnaround time 5 business days. Access to the docket is free at http://apps.supremecourt.az.gov/publicaccess/.

Criminal Name Search: Access: Mail, in person, online. Only the court performs in person name searches; visitors may not. Search fee: $24.00 per name. Required to search: name, years to search, DOB; also helpful: address, SSN. Criminal records for misdemeanors on computer from 1992, all others on docket books. Note: Public access terminal is located in the local library adjacent to the court. Mail turnaround time 5 days from date received. Access to the docket is free at http://apps.supremecourt.az.gov/publicaccess/. Online results show name, DOB.

Page Justice Court PO Box 1565, 547 Vista Ave, Page, AZ 86040; 928-645-8871; fax: 928-645-1869; 8AM-5PM (MST). *Misdemeanor, Civil Actions under $10,000, Eviction, Small Claims.*

www.coconino.az.gov/courts.aspx?id=298

General Information: When a case number is given, the court also charges a $24 fee to pull a record and a judge reviews request, but this could change. This interpretation is not per guidelines of the AOC and is not the procedure followed in the Superior Court. No juvenile, mental health, victims, sealed or adoption records released. Will fax documents. Court makes copy: $.50 per page. Certification fee: $24.00 per doc. Payee: Page Justice Court. Cashiers checks and money orders accepted. Visa/MC accepted. Prepayment required. Mail requests: SASE required.

Civil Name Search: Access: Mail, in person, online. Only the court performs in person name searches; visitors may not. Search fee: $24.00 per name. Required to search: name, years to search; also helpful: address. Civil cases indexed by defendant. Civil records on computer since 9/96; prior on docket books. Will only maintain records for 5 years (DUIs for 7). Mail turnaround time 5 days. Access to the docket is free at http://apps.supremecourt.az.gov/publicaccess/.

Criminal Name Search: Access: Mail, in person, online. Only the court performs in person name searches; visitors may not. Search fee: $24.00 per name. Required to search: name, years to search, DOB; also helpful: address, SSN. Criminal records for misdemeanors on computer from 1987, felony since 1991, all others on docket books. Mail turnaround time 5 days. Access to the docket is free at http://apps.supremecourt.az.gov/publicaccess/.

Williams Justice Court 700 W Railroad Ave, Williams, AZ 86046; 928-635-2691; fax: 928-635-4463; 8AM-N; 1-5PM (MST). *Misdemeanor, Civil Actions under $10,000, Eviction, Small Claims.*

www.coconino.az.gov/courts.aspx?id=311

General Information: When a case number is given, the court also charges a $24 fee to pull a record, but this could change. This interpretation is not per guidelines of the Administrative Offices of the Courts and is not the procedure followed in the Superior Court. No juvenile, mental health, victims, sealed or adoption records released. Will not fax documents. Court makes copy: $.50per page. Certification fee: $24.00 per doc. Payee: Williams Justice Court. Only cashiers checks and money orders accepted. No credit cards accepted. Prepayment required. Mail requests: SASE required.

Civil Name Search: Access: Mail, in person, online. Both court and visitors may perform in person name searches. Search fee: $24.00 per name. Required to search: name, years to search; also helpful: address. Civil index on docket books. Will only maintain records for 5 years. Mail turnaround time 2-3 weeks. Access to the docket is free at http://apps.supremecourt.az.gov/publicaccess/.

Criminal Name Search: Access: Mail, in person, online. Both court and visitors may perform in person name searches. Search fee: $24.00 per name. Required to search: name, years to search, DOB; also helpful: address, SSN. Criminal docket on books. Mail turnaround time 2-3 weeks. Access to the docket is free at http://apps.supremecourt.az.gov/publicaccess/.

Gila County

Superior Court 1400 E Ash, Globe, AZ 85501; 928-425-3231 X8553; fax: 928-425-7802; 8AM-5PM (MST). *Felony, Civil Actions over $5,000, Probate.*

www.supreme.state.az.us/gilasc/

General Information: No juvenile prior to June 1996, mental health, victims, sealed or adoption records released. Will not fax documents. Court makes copy: $.50 per page. Certification fee: $26.00 per doc. Exemplification- $52.00, Authentication- $78.00. Payee: Clerk of Superior Court. Personal checks accepted. No credit cards accepted. Prepayment required. Mail requests: SASE required.

Civil Name Search: Access: Mail, in person, online. Both court and visitors may perform in person name searches. Search fee: $26.00 per name per year. Required to search: name, years to search; also helpful: address. Civil records indexed on computer from 1982. On microfiche from 1913 to 1982. Some records on docket books and index cards. Mail turnaround time 10 days to 2 weeks. Access to the docket is free at http://apps.supremecourt.az.gov/publicaccess/.

Criminal Name Search: Access: Mail, in person, online. Both court and visitors may perform in person name searches. Search fee: $26.00 per name. Required to search: name, years to search, DOB; also helpful: address, SSN. Criminal records computerized from 1913. Mail turnaround time 10 days to 2 weeks. Access to the docket is free at http://apps.supremecourt.az.gov/publicaccess/. Online results show middle initial, DOB.

Globe Regional Justice Court Globe/Miami Magistrate Court, 1400 E Ash, Globe, AZ 85501; 928-425-3231 x8545; fax: 928-425-4773; 8AM-5PM (MST). *Misdemeanor, Civil Actions under $10,000, Eviction, Small Claims.*

General Information: This courts holds the records for the justice courts formerly located in Miami and Hayden/Winkelman. No juvenile, mental health, victims, sealed or adoption records released. Will fax documents to local or toll free line. Court makes copy: $.50 per page. Certification fee: $24.00 per doc plus copy fee. Payee: Globe Regional Justice Court. Business checks accepted. No credit cards accepted. Prepayment required. Mail requests: SASE required.

Civil Name Search: Access: Mail, fax, in person, online. Both court and visitors may perform in person name searches. Search fee: $24.00 per name. Civil records on computer from 2000. Some records on dockets. Will retain for 5 years. Mail turnaround time 2-4 days. Civil PAT goes back to 1997. Public access terminal in Law Library on 1st fl. Access to the docket is free at http://apps.supremecourt.az.gov/publicaccess/.

Criminal Name Search: Access: Mail, fax, in person, online. Both court and visitors may perform in person name searches. Search fee: $24.00 per name. Required to search: name, years to search; also helpful: SSN, DOB, signed release. Criminal records computerized from 1997. Some records on dockets. Will retain for 5 years, 7 for DUIs. Mail turnaround time 2-4 days. Criminal PAT goes back to 1997. Public access terminal in Law Library on 1st Fl. Access to the docket is free at http://apps.supremecourt.az.gov/publicaccess/.

Northern Regional Justice Court 714 S Beeline Hwy, #103, Payson, AZ 85541; 928-474-5267; fax: 928-474-6214; 8AM-5PM (MST). *Misdemeanor, Civil Actions under $10,000, Eviction, Small Claims.*

General Information: This court also holds the records for the closed Pine Justice Court. No juvenile, mental health, victims, sealed or adoption records released. Will fax documents to local or toll-free number. Court makes copy: $.50 per page. Certification fee: $24.00 per doc. Payee: Payson Justice Court. No Personal checks and credit cards accepted. Prepayment required. Mail requests: SASE required.

Civil Name Search: Access: Fax, mail, in person, online. Both court and visitors may perform in person name searches. Search fee: $24.00 per name. Required to search: name, years to search; also helpful: address. Civil cases indexed by party names; defendant and plaintiff. Civil records on computer since 1992. Records on dockets. Will retain for 5 years. Mail turnaround time 10 days. Civil PAT goes back to 1992. Access to the docket is free at http://apps.supremecourt.az.gov/publicaccess/.

Criminal Name Search: Access: Fax, mail, in person, online. Both court and visitors may perform in person name searches. Search fee: $24.00 per name. Required to search: name, years to search, DOB; also helpful: address, SSN. Criminal records on computer since 1992. Records on dockets. Will retain for 5 years. Mail turnaround time 10 days. Criminal PAT goes back to 1992. Access to the docket is free at http://apps.supremecourt.az.gov/publicaccess/. Online results show middle initial, DOB, address.

Winkleman Justice Court - See Globe.
General Information: Now part of the Globe Regional Justice Court.

Graham County

Superior Court 800 Main St, Safford, AZ 85546-3803; 928-428-3803; fax: 928-428-0061; 8AM-5PM (MST). *Felony, Civil Actions over $5,000, Probate.*

www.graham.az.gov/Graham_CMS/Clerk.aspx?id=420

General Information: Probate fax is same as main fax number. Online identifiers in results same as on public terminal. No mental health, victims, sealed or adoption records released. Will fax documents $7.00 fee. Court makes copy: $.50 per page. Self serve copy: same. Certification fee: $.50 per doc. Payee: Clerk of Superior Court. No personal checks. Visa/MC accepted. Prepayment required. Mail requests: SASE required.

Civil Name Search: Access: Fax, mail, in person, online. Both court and visitors may perform in person name searches. Search fee: $26.00 per name. Civil records on dockets. Mail turnaround time 3 days minimum. Civil PAT goes back to 9/1995. Access to the docket is free at http://apps.supremecourt.az.gov/publicaccess/.

Criminal Name Search: Access: Phone, fax, mail, in person, online. Both court and visitors may perform in person name searches. Search fee:

$26.00 per name. Criminal records on dockets. Mail turnaround time 3 days minimum. Criminal PAT goes back to same as civil. Access to the docket is free at http://apps.supremecourt.az.gov/publicaccess/. Online results show middle initial, DOB.

Justice Court Precinct #1 800 W Main St, Safford, AZ 85546; 928-428-1210; fax: 928-428-3523; 8AM-5PM (MST). *Misdemeanor, Civil Actions under $10,000, Eviction.*

www.graham.az.gov/Graham_CMS/Judicial.aspx?id=424

General Information: No juvenile, mental health, victims, sealed or adoption records released. Will fax documents to local or toll free line. Court makes copy: $.50 per page. Certification fee: $24.00 per doc. Payee: Safford Justice Court. Cashiers checks and money orders accepted. Major credit cards accepted. Prepayment required. Mail requests: SASE required.

Civil Name Search: Access: Mail, in person, online. Both court and visitors may perform in person name searches. Search fee: $24.00 per name. Required to search: name, years to search; also helpful: address. Civil cases indexed by case number. Civil records on computer from 1995, on dockets prior. Mail turnaround time 3-4 days. Access to the docket is free at http://apps.supremecourt.az.gov/publicaccess/.

Criminal Name Search: Access: Mail, in person, online. Both court and visitors may perform in person name searches. Search fee: $24.00 per name. Required to search: name, years to search, DOB; also helpful: address, SSN. Criminal records computerized from 1995, on dockets prior. Mail turnaround time 2-3 days. Access to the docket is free at http://apps.supremecourt.az.gov/publicaccess/.

Pima Justice Court Precinct #2 PO Box 1159, 136 W Center St, Pima, AZ 85543; 928-485-2771; fax: 928-485-9961; 8AM-5PM (MST). *Misdemeanor, Civil Actions under $10,000, Eviction, Small Claims.*

www.graham.az.gov/Graham_CMS/Judicial.aspx?id=426

General Information: This court also handles criminal traffic. No juvenile, mental health, victims, sealed or adoption records released. Will fax documents $17.00 per doc. Court makes copy: $.50 per page. Self serve copy: same. Certification fee: $24.00 per doc. Payee: Graham Justice Court. Cashiers checks and money orders accepted. Major credit cards accepted. Prepayment required. Mail requests: SASE required.

Civil Name Search: Access: Fax, mail, in person, online. Both court and visitors may perform in person name searches. Search fee: $24.00 per name. Required to search: name, years to search; also helpful: address, docket number. Civil cases indexed by defendant. Civil records on dockets back to 1985; on computer back to 1995. Retained for 5 years. Mail turnaround time 2 weeks. Access to the docket is free at http://apps.supremecourt.az.gov/publicaccess/.

Criminal Name Search: Access: Fax, mail, in person, online. Both court and visitors may perform in person name searches. Search fee: $24.00 per name. Required to search: name, years to search, DOB; also helpful: address, SSN, docket number. Criminal records on dockets back to 1985; on computer back to 1995. Retained for 5 years. Mail turnaround time 2 weeks. Access to the docket is free at http://apps.supremecourt.az.gov/publicaccess/.

Greenlee County

Superior Court PO Box 1027, 223 Fifth St, Clifton, AZ 85533; 928-865-4242; fax: 928-865-5358; 8AM-5PM (MST). *Felony, Civil Actions over $5,000, Probate.*

General Information: Search fee includes both civil and criminal index. No adoption released. Will fax documents to local or toll free line. Court makes copy: $.50 per page. Certification fee: $26.00 per doc. Payee: Clerk of Superior Court. Personal checks accepted. No credit cards accepted. Prepayment required. Mail requests: SASE required.

Civil Name Search: Access: Mail, in person, online. Both court and visitors may perform in person name searches. Search fee: $26.00 per name per year. Civil records in docket books from 1911; on computer from 12/97. Mail turnaround time 3 days. Access to the docket is free at http://apps.supremecourt.az.gov/publicaccess/.

Criminal Name Search: Access: Mail, in person, online. Both court and visitors may perform in person name searches. Search fee: $26.00 per name per year. Criminal records on computer since 12/97; on books from 1911. Mail turnaround time 7 days. Access to the docket is free at http://apps.supremecourt.az.gov/publicaccess/. Online results show middle initial, DOB.

Justice Court Precinct #1 PO Box 517, Clifton, AZ 85533; 928-865-4312; fax: 928-865-5644; 8AM-5PM (MST). *Misdemeanor, Civil Actions under $10,000, Eviction, Small Claims.*

www.co.greenlee.az.us/courts/

General Information: No juvenile, sealed, victims, mental health or adoption records released. Will fax documents to local or toll-free number. Court makes copy: $.50 per page. Certification fee: $24.00 per doc. Payee: Justice of the Peace. Only cashiers checks and money orders accepted. No credit cards accepted. Prepayment required.

Civil Name Search: Access: Mail, in person, online. Only the court performs in person name searches; visitors may not. Search fee: $24.00 per case. Civil records on computer Aztec System. Mail turnaround time 1 week. Access to the docket is free at http://apps.supremecourt.az.gov/publicaccess/.

Criminal Name Search: Access: Mail, in person, online. Only the court performs in person name searches; visitors may not. Search fee: $24.00 per case. Required to search: name, years to search; also helpful: DOB, SSN. Criminal records on computer Aztec System. Mail turnaround time 1 week. Access to the docket is free at http://apps.supremecourt.az.gov/publicaccess/.

Justice Court Precinct #2 PO Box 208, Duncan, AZ 85534; 928-359-2536; fax: 928-359-1936; 8AM-5PM (MST). *Misdemeanor, Civil Actions under $10,000, Eviction, Small Claims.*

www.co.greenlee.az.us/courts/

General Information: No juvenile, victims, sealed, mental health or adoption records released. Will fax documents for no fee. Court makes copy: $.50 per page. Self serve copy: same. Certification fee: $24.00 per doc. Payee: Justice Court. No personal checks. No credit cards accepted. Prepayment required. Mail requests: SASE required.

Civil Name Search: Access: Mail, in person, online. Both court and visitors may perform in person name searches. Search fee: $24.00 per case. Civil records on computer since 1996. Documents retained for 5 years. Mail turnaround time 2 days. Access to the docket is free at http://apps.supremecourt.az.gov/publicaccess/.

Criminal Name Search: Access: Mail, in person, online. Both court and visitors may perform in person name searches. Search fee: $24.00 per case. Criminal Records computerized since 1996. Mail turnaround time 2 days. Access to the docket is free at http://apps.supremecourt.az.gov/publicaccess/.

La Paz County

Superior Court 1316 Kofa Ave, #607, Parker, AZ 85344; 928-669-6131; fax: 928-669-2186; 8AM-5PM (MST). *Felony, Civil Actions over $5,000, Probate.*

www.co.la-paz.az.us/

General Information: Online identifiers in results same as on public terminal. No dependency or adoption records released. Will fax documents for certification fee. Court makes copy: $.50 per page. Certification fee: $26.00 per doc. Payee: Clerk of Superior Court. Business checks accepted, but no personal. Major credit cards accepted. Prepayment required. Mail requests: SASE required.

Civil Name Search: Access: Mail, in person, online. Both court and visitors may perform in person name searches. Search fee: $26.00 per name per year. Required to search: name, years to search; also helpful: address. Civil records computerized since 1996, to 1983 on docket books. For records prior to 1983, check with Yuma County Superior Court. Mail turnaround time 2-3 days. Civil PAT goes back to 1996. Public access at http://apps.supremecourt.az.gov/publicaccess/.

Criminal Name Search: Access: Mail, in person, online. Both court and visitors may perform in person name searches. Search fee: $26.00 per name per year. Required to search: name, years to search; also helpful: address, DOB, SSN. Criminal records computerized since 1996, to 1983 on docket books. For records prior to 1983, check with Yuma County Superior Court. Mail turnaround time 2-3 days. Criminal PAT goes back to same as civil. Public access at http://apps.supremecourt.az.gov/publicaccess/. Online results show middle initial, DOB.

Parker Justice Court 1105 Arizona Ave, Parker, AZ 85344; 928-669-2504; fax: 928-669-2915; 8AM-5PM (MST). *Misdemeanor, Civil Actions under $10,000, Eviction, Small Claims.*

www.co.la-paz.az.us/

General Information: When a case number is given, the court also charges $24 per case to pull a record, but this could change. This interpretation is not per guidelines of the Administrative Offices of the Courts and is not the procedure followed in the Superior Court. No juvenile, mental health, victims or sealed records released. Will fax documents out. Court makes copy: $.50 per page. Certification fee: $24.00 per doc. Payee: Clerk of Justice Court. Only cashiers checks and money orders accepted. No credit cards accepted. Prepayment required. Mail requests: SASE required.

Civil Name Search: Access: Mail, in person, online. Only the court performs in person name searches; visitors may not. Search fee: $24.00 per name/per case. Required to search: name, years to search; also helpful: address. Civil cases indexed by defendant. Civil records on dockets back to 1800s, computerized since 1996. Mail turnaround time 1 week. Public access at http://apps.supremecourt.az.gov/publicaccess/, but sometime records are not updated frequently.

Criminal Name Search: Access: Mail, in person, online. Only the court performs in person name searches; visitors may not. Search fee: $24.00 per name/per case. Required to search: name, years to search, DOB; also helpful: address, SSN. Criminal records on dockets back to 1800s, computerized since 1996. Mail turnaround time 1 week. Public access at http://apps.supremecourt.az.gov/publicaccess/, but sometime records are not updated frequently.

Quartzsite Justice Court PO Box 580, Quartzsite, AZ 85346; 928-927-6313; fax: 928-927-4842; 8AM-5PM (MST). *Misdemeanor, Civil Actions under $10,000, Eviction, Small Claims.*
www.co.la-paz.az.us/
General Information: No juvenile, mental health, victims, sealed or adoption records released. Will fax documents to local or toll-free number. Court makes copy: $.50 per page. Certification fee: $24.00 per doc. Payee: Quartsite Justice Court. Cashiers checks and money orders accepted. Visa/MC accepted. Prepayment required. Mail requests: SASE required.
Civil Name Search: Access: Fax, mail, in person, online. Both court and visitors may perform in person name searches. Search fee: $24.00 per name/year. Civil records computerized since 7/96. Files retained for 5 yrs after final disposition. Mail turnaround time within 3 weeks. Public access at http://apps.supremecourt.az.gov/publicaccess/.
Criminal Name Search: Access: Fax, mail, in person, online. Both court and visitors may perform in person name searches. Search fee: $24.00 per name. Required to search: name, years to search, date of offense; also helpful: DOB, SSN, offense. Criminal records computerized since 7/96. Files retained for 5 yrs after final disposition. Mail turnaround time within 3 weeks. Public access at http://apps.supremecourt.az.gov/publicaccess/.

Salome Justice Court PO Box 661, Salome, AZ 85348; 928-859-3871;; 8AM-5PM (MST). *Misdemeanor, Civil Actions under $10,000, Eviction, Small Claims.*
www.co.la-paz.az.us/
General Information: When a case number is given, the court charges a $24 fee to pull a record, but this could change. This interpretation is not per guidelines of the Administrative Offices of the Courts and is not the procedure followed in the Superior Court. No juvenile, mental health, victims, sealed or adoption records released. Will fax documents after payment received. Court makes copy: $.50 per page. Certification fee: $24.00 per request. Payee: Salome Justice Court. Only cashiers checks and money orders accepted. No business or personal checks. Visa/MC/Discover accepted. Prepayment required.
Civil Name Search: Access: Mail, in person, online. Only the court performs in person name searches; visitors may not. Search fee: $24.00 per name. Required to search: name, years to search; also helpful: address. Civil cases indexed by defendant. Civil records on dockets from mid-1980s. Records destroyed after 5 years. Computerized back to 1996. Note: Civil traffic records destroyed after 1 year. Mail turnaround time 2-3 days. Public access at http://apps.supremecourt.az.gov/publicaccess/.
Criminal Name Search: Access: Mail, in person, online. Only the court performs in person name searches; visitors may not. Search fee: $24.00 per case (not name). Required to search: name, years to search, DOB; also helpful: address, SSN. Criminal docket index from mid-1980s. Records destroyed after 5 years. Computerized back to 1996. Mail turnaround time 2-3 days. Public access at http://apps.supremecourt.az.gov/publicaccess/.

Maricopa County

Note: Maricopa County Superior Cases can only be located and retrieved from the Clerk of Court Customer Service Center at 601W. Jackson, Phoenix. County Justice cases can only be found at each of the individual 23 courts around the county. There are 4 regional centers which have terminal access for limited information as well. Currently, at print time only one is in service in North Phoenix. Municipal information and files can only be located at the individual Municipal Court.

Superior Court 601 W Jackson St., Phoenix, AZ 85003; 602-506-3360; fax: 602-506-7619; 8AM-5PM (MST). *Felony, Civil Actions over $5,000, Probate.*
www.clerkofcourt.maricopa.gov/
General Information: Online identifiers in results same as on public terminal. No mental health, victims, sealed or adoption records released. Will fax documents for $7.00 plus $.50 per page. Court makes copy: $.50 per page. Certification fee: $26.00 per doc. Payee: Clerk of Superior Court. Personal checks accepted. Visa/MC, AMEX accepted. Prepayment required. Mail requests: SASE not required, but if not, include $5.00 shipping & handling.
Civil Name Search: Access: Fax, mail, online, in person. Both court and visitors may perform in person name searches. Search fee: $26.00 per name. Civil records on computer from 7/87, on microfiche from 1969 to present. Some records on docket books. Note: DOB not provided on civil search results. Mail turnaround time 2 weeks. Civil PAT goes back to 7/1987. Access to civil, probate, and family case dockets is free at www.superiorcourt.maricopa.gov/docket/index.asp. Case file docket can

be printed. Search by first and last name or by business name or by case number. DOB not shown. Access is now also available at the Public Access system at http://apps.supremecourt.az.gov/publicaccess/. Due to name variations and aliases, online search result dockets are easily misinterpreted.
Criminal Name Search: Access: Fax, mail, online, in person. Both court and visitors may perform in person name searches. Search fee: $26.00 per name. Required to search: name, years to search; also helpful: DOB. Criminal records computerized from 7/87, on microfiche from 1969 to present. Some records on docket books. Mail turnaround time 2 weeks. Criminal PAT goes back to same as civil. Public access to court information is at http://apps.supremecourt.az.gov/publicaccess/caselookup.aspx. Access to current only criminal case dockets is free at www.superiorcourt.maricopa.gov/docket/index.asp. Online results show middle initial, DOB.

Agua Fria (Tolleson) Justice Court 9550 W Van Buren, #6, Tolleson, AZ 85353; 623-936-1449; fax: 623-936-4859; 8AM-5PM (MST). *Misdemeanor, Civil Actions under $10,000, Eviction, Small Claims.*
www.superiorcourt.maricopa.gov/justiceCourts/
General Information: Countywide Justice Court docket information is sold on disk. Data on disks and countywide terminals may be several months old. No juvenile, mental health, victims, sealed or adoption records released. Will not fax documents. Court makes copy: $.50 per page. Certification fee: $24.00 per doc. Payee: Agua Fria Justice Court. Personal checks accepted. Credit cards accepted. Prepayment required. Mail requests: SASE required.
Civil Name Search: Access: Mail, in person, online. Only the court performs in person name searches; visitors may not. Search fee: $24.00 per name. Required to search: name, years to search; also helpful: address. Civil records on computer since 1993. Note: The court requires a signed form to release information in case file to a person not involved with case. Mail turnaround time 1-2 weeks. Access court index free on countywide site at www.superiorcourt.maricopa.gov/docket/JusticeCourtCases/caseSearch.asp. Incomplete dockets, also expired data online.
Criminal Name Search: Access: Mail, in person, online. Only the court performs in person name searches; visitors may not. Search fee: $24.00 per name. Required to search: name, years to search, DOB; also helpful: address, SSN. Criminal records on computer since 1993. Mail turnaround time 1-2 weeks. Online access same as civil. Some DOBs shown, addresses are not. Online results show middle initial, DOB.

Arcadia Biltmore (East Phoenix #2) Justice Court 620 W Jackson St, Phoenix, AZ 85003; 602-372-6300; fax: 602-372-6412; 8AM-5PM (MST). *Misdemeanor, Civil Actions under $10,000, Eviction, Small Claims.*
www.superiorcourt.maricopa.gov/justiceCourts/
General Information: Countywide Justice Court docket information is sold on disk. Data on disks and countywide terminals may be several months old. No juvenile, mental health, victims, sealed or adoption records released. Will not fax documents. Court makes copy: $.50 per page. Self serve copy: is available. Certification fee: $24.00 per doc. Payee: Arcadia Biltmore Justice Court. Personal checks accepted. Credit cards accepted. Prepayment required. Mail requests: SASE required.
Civil Name Search: Access: Mail, in person, online. Both court and visitors may perform in person name searches. Search fee: $24.00 per name. Civil records on computer since 1981. Mail turnaround time 1-2 weeks. Civil PAT available. Countywide dockets on iCIS system; no print outs. Access court index free on countywide site at www.superiorcourt.maricopa.gov/docket/JusticeCourtCases/caseSearch.asp. The DOB does not always show on online results. Incomplete dockets, also expired data online.
Criminal Name Search: Access: Mail, in person, online. Both court and visitors may perform in person name searches. Search fee: $24.00 per name. Required to search: name, years to search, DOB. Criminal records computerized since 1991. Mail turnaround time 1-2 weeks. Criminal PAT available. Countywide dockets on iCIS system; no print outs. Access court index free on countywide site at www.superiorcourt.maricopa.gov/docket/JusticeCourtCases/caseSearch.asp. Some DOBs shown, addresses are not. Online results show middle initial.

Arrowhead Justice Court 14264 W Tierra Buena Ln, Surprise, AZ 85374; 602-372-2000; fax: 602-372-2620; 8AM-5PM (MST). *Misdemeanor, Civil Actions under $10,000, Eviction, Small Claims.*
www.superiorcourt.maricopa.gov/justiceCourts/
General Information: Countywide Justice Court docket information is sold on disk. Data on disks and countywide terminals may be several months old. No juvenile, mental health, victims, sealed or adoption records released. Will fax documents to 602, 480, 623 area codes only- $1.25 per page. Court makes copy: $.50 per page. Certification fee: $24.00 per doc. Payee: Peoria

Justice Court. Personal checks accepted. Credit cards accepted. Prepayment required. Mail requests: SASE required.

Civil Name Search: Access: Phone, mail, in person, online. Only the court performs in person name searches; visitors may not. Search fee: $24.00 per name. Civil records on computer by case number. Mail turnaround time 1-2 weeks. Access court index free on countywide site at www.superiorcourt.maricopa.gov/docket/JusticeCourtCases/caseSearch.asp. Incomplete dockets, also expired data online.

Criminal Name Search: Access: Phone, mail, in person, online. Only the court performs in person name searches; visitors may not. Search fee: $24.00 per name. Required to search: name, years to search; also helpful: DOB. Criminal records on computer by case number. Mail turnaround time 1-2 weeks. Online access same as civil. Some DOBs shown, addresses are not. Online results show middle initial.

Desert Ridge Justice Court 18380 N 40th St, Phoenix, AZ 85032; 602-372-7000; fax: 602-372-7912; 8AM-5PM (MST). *Misdemeanor, Civil Actions under $10,000, Eviction, Small Claims.*
www.superiorcourt.maricopa.gov/justiceCourts/

General Information: Now co-located with the Moon Valley, McDowell Mountain (Scottsdale), and Dreamy Draw. Countywide Justice Court docket information is sold on disk. Data on disks and countywide terminals may be 2-3 months old. No juvenile, mental health, victims, sealed or adoption records released. Will not fax documents. Court makes copy: $.50 per page. Certification fee: $24.00 per doc. Payee: Clerk of Justice Court. Personal checks accepted; cashier's check or money orders only for traffic. Visa/MC accepted only from person named on card. Prepayment required. Mail requests: SASE required.

Civil Name Search: Access: Mail, in person, online. Only the court performs in person name searches; visitors may not. Search fee: $24.00 per name. Required to search: name, years to search; also helpful: address. Civil records on computer since 1993. Records on dockets by name and case number. Mail turnaround time 1-2 weeks. Access court index free at www.superiorcourt.maricopa.gov/docket/JusticeCourtCases/caseSearch.asp. Incomplete dockets, also expired data online.

Criminal Name Search: Access: Mail, in person, online. Only the court performs in person name searches; visitors may not. Search fee: $24.00 per name. Required to search: name, years to search, DOB; also helpful: address, SSN. Criminal dockets by name and case number. Mail turnaround time 1-2 weeks. Online access same as civil. Some DOBs shown, addresses are not. Online results show middle initial, DOB.

Downtown (East Phoenix #1) Justice Court 620 W Jackson St, Phoenix, AZ 85003; 602-372-6300; fax: 602-372-6406; 8AM-5PM (MST). *Misdemeanor, Civil Actions under $10,000, Eviction, Small Claims.*
www.superiorcourt.maricopa.gov/justiceCourts/

General Information: Countywide Justice Court docket information is sold on disk. Data on disks and countywide terminals may be several months old. No mental health, victims, or sealed records released. Will not fax documents. Court makes copy: $.50 per page. Certification fee: $24.00 per doc. Payee: East Phoenix #1 Justice Court. Personal checks accepted. Credit cards accepted in person only. Prepayment required. Mail requests: SASE required.

Civil Name Search: Access: Mail, in person, online. Visitors must perform in person searches themselves. Search fee: $24.00 per name. Civil records on dockets by number; computerized records since 1990's. Mail turnaround time 1-2 weeks. Civil PAT available. Countywide dockets on iCIS system; no print outs. Access court index free on countywide site at www.superiorcourt.maricopa.gov/docket/JusticeCourtCases/caseSearch.asp. Incomplete dockets, also expired data online.

Criminal Name Search: Access: Mail, in person, online. Visitors must perform in person searches themselves. Search fee: $24.00 per name. Required to search: name, years to search, DOB. Criminal dockets by number; computerized records since 1990's. Mail turnaround time 1-2 weeks. Criminal PAT available. Countywide dockets on iCIS system; no print outs. Online access same as civil. Some DOBs shown, addresses are not. Online results show middle initial, DOB.

Dreamy Draw (Northeast Phoenix) Justice Court 18380 N 40th St, Phoenix, AZ 85032; 602-372-7000; fax: 602-372-7911; 8AM-5PM (MST). *Misdemeanor, Civil Actions under $10,000, Eviction, Small Claims.*
www.superiorcourt.maricopa.gov/justiceCourts/

General Information: Now co-located with the Moon Valley, Desert Ridge, and McDowell Mountain (Scottsdale), but records are separate. Countywide Justice Court docket information is sold on disk. Data on disks and countywide terminals may be 2-3 months old. No juvenile, mental health, victims, sealed or adoption records released. Will not fax documents. Court makes copy: $.50 per page. Certification fee: $24.00 per doc. Payee: Clerk of Justice Court. Personal checks accepted; cashier's check or money orders

only for traffic. Visa/MC accepted only from person named on card. Prepayment required. Mail requests: SASE required.

Civil Name Search: Access: Mail, in person, online. Only the court performs in person name searches; visitors may not. Search fee: $24.00 per name. Required to search: name, years to search; also helpful: address. Civil records on computer since 1985. Records kept for 5 years on closed cases. Mail turnaround time 1-2 weeks. Access court index free on countywide site at www.superiorcourt.maricopa.gov/docket/JusticeCourtCases/caseSearch.asp. Incomplete dockets, also expired data online.

Criminal Name Search: Access: Mail, in person, online. Only the court performs in person name searches; visitors may not. Search fee: $24.00 per name. Required to search: name, years to search, DOB; also helpful: address, SSN. Criminal records on computer since 1985. Records kept for 5 years on closed cases. Mail turnaround time 1-2 weeks. Online access same as civil. Some DOBs shown, addresses are not. Online results show middle initial, DOB.

East Mesa Justice Court 4811 E Julep, #128, Mesa, AZ 85205; 480-985-0188; fax: 480-396-6327; 8AM-5PM (MST). *Misdemeanor, Civil Actions under $10,000, Eviction, Small Claims.*
www.superiorcourt.maricopa.gov/justiceCourts/

General Information: Countywide Justice Court docket information is sold on disk. Data on disks and countywide terminals may be several months old. No juvenile, mental health, victims, sealed or adoption records released. Will not fax documents. Court makes copy: $.50 per page. Certification fee: $24.00 per doc. Payee: East Mesa Justice Court. Business checks accepted. Credit cards accepted in person. Prepayment required. Mail requests: SASE required.

Civil Name Search: Access: Mail, in person, online. Only the court performs in person name searches; visitors may not. Search fee: $24.00 per name. Required to search: name, years to search; also helpful: address. Civil records on computer since 1990. Prior records in docket books by number. Mail turnaround time 1-2 weeks. Nearest public terminal located at San Tan JC, 201 E Chicago in Chandler. Access court index free at www.superiorcourt.maricopa.gov/docket/JusticeCourtCases/caseSearch.asp. Incomplete dockets, also expired data online.

Criminal Name Search: Access: Mail, in person, online. Only the court performs in person name searches; visitors may not. Search fee: $24.00 per name. Required to search: name, years to search, DOB; also helpful: address, SSN. Criminal records on computer since 1990. Prior records in docket books by number. Mail turnaround time 1-2 weeks. Nearest public terminal located at San Tan JC, 201 E Chicago in Chandler. Online access same as civil. Some DOBs shown, addresses are not. Online results show middle initial, DOB.

Encanto (Central Phoenix) Justice Court 620 W Jackson St, Phoenix, AZ 85003; 602-372-6300; fax: 602-372-6414; 8AM-5PM (MST). *Misdemeanor, Civil Actions under $10,000, Eviction, Small Claims.*
www.superiorcourt.maricopa.gov/justiceCourts/

General Information: Countywide Justice Court docket information is sold on disk. Data on disks and countywide terminals may be several months old. No sealed records released. Will not fax out documents. Court makes copy: $.50 per page. Certification fee: $24.00 per doc. Payee: Encanto Justice Court. Personal checks accepted with DL. Visa/MC accepted. Prepayment required. Mail requests: SASE required.

Civil Name Search: Access: Phone, fax, mail, in person, online. Only the court performs in person name searches; visitors may not. Search fee: $24.00 per name. Civil records on computer since 1985, but will vary with type of record. Note: Court personnel will only do look-ups for the walk-in public if not busy. Mail turnaround time 1-2 weeks. Access court index free on countywide site at www.superiorcourt.maricopa.gov/docket/JusticeCourtCases/caseSearch.asp. Incomplete dockets, also expired data online.

Criminal Name Search: Access: Mail, fax, in person, online. Only the court performs in person name searches; visitors may not. Search fee: $24.00 per name. Required to search: name, years to search, DOB, SSN. Criminal records on computer since 1985. Note: Court personnel will only do look-ups for the walk-in public if not busy. Mail turnaround time 1-2 weeks. Online access same as civil. Some DOBs shown, addresses are not. Online results show middle initial, DOB.

Estrella Mountain (Buckeye Precinct) Justice Court 21749 W Yuma Rd Ste B-101, Buckeye, AZ 85326; 623-386-4822; fax: 623-386-5796; 8AM-5PM (MST). *Misdemeanor, Civil Actions under $10,000, Eviction, Small Claims.*
www.superiorcourt.maricopa.gov/justiceCourts/

General Information: Countywide Justice Court docket information is sold on disk. Data on disks and countywide terminals may be several months old. No juvenile, mental health, victims, sealed or adoption records released. Will fax documents to local or toll free line. Court makes copy: $.50 per page. Certification fee: $24.00 per doc. Payee: Estrella Mountain Justice

Court. Personal checks accepted. Visa/MC accepted. Prepayment required. Mail requests: SASE required.

Civil Name Search: Access: Mail, in person, online. Only the court performs in person name searches; visitors may not. Search fee: $24.00 per name. Civil records on dockets by number, computerized since 1990. Mail turnaround time 1-2 weeks. Countywide dockets on iCIS system; no print outs. Access court index free on countywide site at www.superiorcourt.maricopa.gov/docket/JusticeCourtCases/caseSearch.asp. Incomplete dockets, also expired data online.

Criminal Name Search: Access: Mail, in person, online. Only the court performs in person name searches; visitors may not. Search fee: $24.00 per name. Required to search: name, years to search, DOB. Criminal dockets by number, computerized since 1990. Mail turnaround time 1-2 weeks. Countywide dockets on iCIS system; no print outs. Online access same as civil. Some DOBs shown, addresses are not. Online results show middle initial, DOB.

Hassayampa (Wickenburg) Justice Court 14264 W Tierra Buena Ln, Surprise, AZ 85374; 602-372-2000; fax: 602-372-2620; 8AM-5PM (MST). *Misdemeanor, Civil Actions under $10,000, Eviction, Small Claims.*
www.superiorcourt.maricopa.gov/justiceCourts/

General Information: Wickenburg Town Court phone is 928-684-5451. Countywide Justice Court docket info is sold on disk. Data on disks and countywide terminals may be 5-6 months old. No juvenile, mental health, victims, sealed records released. Will not fax out documents. Court makes copy: $.50 per page. Certification fee: $24.00 per doc. Payee: Wickenburg Justice Court. Personal checks accepted. Credit cards accepted. Prepayment required. Mail requests: SASE required.

Civil Name Search: Access: Mail, in person, online. Only the court performs in person name searches; visitors may not. Search fee: $24.00 per name. Required to search: name, years to search; also helpful: address. Civil records on computer since 1994. Mail turnaround time 1-2 weeks. Access court index free on countywide site at www.superiorcourt.maricopa.gov/docket/JusticeCourtCases/caseSearch.asp. Incomplete dockets, also expired data online.

Criminal Name Search: Access: Mail, in person, online. Only the court performs in person name searches; visitors may not. Search fee: $24.00 per name. Required to search: name, years to search, DOB; also helpful: SSN. Criminal records on computer by name and case number. Mail turnaround time 1-2 weeks. Online access same as civil. Some DOBs shown, addresses are not. Online results show middle initial, DOB.

Highland Regional Justice Court 55 E Civic Center Dr, Ste 55, Phoenix, AZ 85032; 602-372-8300; fax: 602-372-8301; 8AM-5PM (MST). *Misdemeanor, Civil Actions under $10,000, Eviction, Small Claims.*
www.superiorcourt.maricopa.gov/justiceCourts/

General Information: This court is relatively new as it started in 2009. Some case files here from San Tan 2008 are here. No juvenile, mental health, victims, sealed or adoption records released. Will not fax documents. Court makes copy: $.50 per page. Certification fee: $24.00 per doc. Payee: Clerk of Justice Court. Personal checks accepted; cashier's check or money orders only for traffic. Visa/MC accepted only from person named on card. Prepayment required. Mail requests: SASE required.

Civil Name Search: Access: Mail, in person, online. Only the court performs in person name searches; visitors may not. Search fee: $24.00 per name. Required to search: name, years to search; also helpful: address. Civil records on computer since 2008. Note: Countywide Justice Court docket information is sold on disk. Data on disks and countywide terminals may be 2-3 months old. Mail turnaround time 1-2 weeks. Access court index free on countywide site at www.superiorcourt.maricopa.gov/docket/JusticeCourtCases/caseSearch.asp.

Criminal Name Search: Access: Mail, in person, online. Only the court performs in person name searches; visitors may not. Search fee: $24.00 per name. Required to search: name, years to search, DOB; also helpful: address, SSN. Civil records on computer since 2008. Note: Countywide Justice Court docket information is sold on disk. Data on disks and countywide terminals may be 2-3 months old. Mail turnaround time 1-2 weeks. Online access same as civil. Some DOBs shown, addresses are not. Online results show middle initial, DOB.

Ironwood (Gila Bend) Justice Court 209 E Pima St, Gila Bend, AZ 85337; 928-683-2651; fax: 928-683-6412; 8AM-5PM (MST). *Misdemeanor, Civil Actions under $10,000, Eviction, Small Claims.*
www.superiorcourt.maricopa.gov/justiceCourts/

General Information: Countywide Justice Court docket information is sold on disk. Data on disks and countywide terminals may be several months old. No juvenile, mental health, victims, sealed or adoption records released. Will fax documents to local or toll-free number. Court makes copy: $.50 per page. Payee: Gila Bend or Ironwood Justice Court. Personal checks accepted. Visa/MC accepted. Prepayment required. Mail requests: SASE required.

Civil Name Search: Access: Mail, in person, online. Only the court performs in person name searches; visitors may not. Search fee: $24.00 per name. Civil records on computer since 1987. Mail turnaround time 1-2 weeks. Access court index free on countywide site at www.superiorcourt.maricopa.gov/docket/JusticeCourtCases/caseSearch.asp. Incomplete dockets, also expired data online.

Criminal Name Search: Access: Mail, in person, online. Only the court performs in person name searches; visitors may not. Search fee: $24.00 per name. Required to search: name, years to search; also helpful: DOB. Criminal records on computer since 1987. Mail turnaround time 1-2 weeks. Online access same as civil. Some DOBs shown, addresses are not. Online results show middle initial, DOB.

Kyrene (West Tempe) Justice Court 201 E Chicago St, #104, Chandler, AZ 85225; 602-372-3400; fax: 602-372-3494; 8AM-5PM (MST). *Misdemeanor, Civil Actions under $10,000, Eviction, Small Claims, Traffic.*
www.superiorcourt.maricopa.gov/justiceCourts/

General Information: Formerly known as the West Tempe Justice Court. Countywide Justice Court docket information is sold on disk. Data on disks and countywide terminals may be 2-3 months old. No juvenile, mental health, victims, sealed records released. Will not fax documents. Court makes copy: $.50 per page. Certification fee: $24.00 per doc. Payee: Kyrene Justice Court. Personal checks accepted. Credit cards accepted. Prepayment required. Mail requests: SASE required.

Civil Name Search: Access: Mail, in person, online. Both court and visitors may perform in person name searches. Search fee: $24.00 per name. Civil records on computer by case number. Mail turnaround time 5 days Civil PAT available. Countywide dockets on iCIS system; no print outs. Access court index free on countywide site at www.superiorcourt.maricopa.gov/docket/JusticeCourtCases/caseSearch.asp. Incomplete dockets, also expired data online.

Criminal Name Search: Access: Mail, in person, online. Both court and visitors may perform in person name searches. Search fee: $24.00 per name. Required to search: name, years to search, DOB. Criminal records on computer by case number. Mail turnaround time 5 days. Criminal PAT available. Countywide dockets on iCIS system; no print outs. Online access same as civil. Some DOBs shown, addresses are not. Online results show middle initial, DOB.

Manistee (Glendale) Justice Court 14264 W Tierra Buena Ln, Surprise, AZ 85374; 602-372-2000; fax: 602-372-2620; 8AM-5PM (MST). *Misdemeanor, Civil Actions under $10,000, Eviction, Small Claims.*
www.superiorcourt.maricopa.gov/justiceCourts/

General Information: Countywide Justice Court docket information is sold on disk. Data on disks and countywide terminals may be several months old. No juvenile, mental health, victims, sealed or adoption records released. Will not fax documents. Court makes copy: $.50 per page. Certification fee: $24.00 per doc. Payee: Glendale Justice Court. Personal checks accepted. Visa/MC accepted. Prepayment required. Mail requests: SASE required.

Civil Name Search: Access: Mail, in person, online. Only the court performs in person name searches; visitors may not. Search fee: $24.00 per name. Civil records on dockets by case number, computerized since 1993. Mail turnaround time 1-2 weeks. Access court index free on countywide site at www.superiorcourt.maricopa.gov/docket/JusticeCourtCases/caseSearch.asp. Incomplete dockets, also expired data online.

Criminal Name Search: Access: Mail, in person, online. Only the court performs in person name searches; visitors may not. Search fee: $24.00 per name. Required to search: name, years to search, DOB; also helpful: SSN. Criminal dockets by case number, computerized since 1992. Note: The DOB shows approx 50% of the time on search results. Mail turnaround time 1-2 weeks. Online access same as civil. The DOB shows approx 50% of the time on search results. Online results show middle initial, DOB.

Maryvale Justice Court 4622 W Indian School Rd, Bldg D10, Phoenix, AZ 85031; 623-245-0432; fax: 623-245-1216; 8AM-5PM (MST). *Misdemeanor, Civil Actions under $10,000, Eviction, Small Claims.*
www.superiorcourt.maricopa.gov/justiceCourts/

General Information: Countywide Justice Court docket information is sold on disk. Data on disks and countywide terminals may be several months old. No juvenile, mental health, victims, sealed or adoption records released. Will not fax documents. Court makes copy: $.50 per page. Certification fee: $24.00 per doc. Payee: Maryvale Justice Court. Personal checks accepted if preprinted. Major credit cards accepted. Prepayment required. Mail requests: SASE required.

Civil Name Search: Access: Mail, in person, online. Only the court performs in person name searches; visitors may not. Search fee: $24.00 per name. Required to search: name, years to search, address. Civil records on dockets by number. Mail turnaround time 1-2 weeks. Nearest public

terminal located downtown Phoenix. Access court index free on countywide site at www.superiorcourt.maricopa.gov/docket/JusticeCourtCases/caseSearch.asp. Incomplete dockets, also expired data online.
Criminal Name Search: Access: Mail, in person, online. Only the court performs in person name searches; visitors may not. Search fee: $24.00 per name. Required to search: name, years to search, address, DOB; also helpful: SSN, aliases. Criminal dockets by number. Mail turnaround time 1-2 weeks. Nearest public terminal located downtown Phoenix. Online access same as civil, however chance of DOB appearing is greater. Online results show middle initial, DOB.

McDowell Mountain (Scottsdale) Justice Court 18380 N 40th St, Phoenix, AZ 85032; 602-372-7000; fax: 602-372-7910; 8AM-5PM (MST). *Misdemeanor, Civil Actions under $10,000, Eviction, Small Claims.*
www.superiorcourt.maricopa.gov/justiceCourts/
General Information: Now co-located with the Moon Valley, Desert Ridge, and Dreamy Draw. Countywide Justice Court docket information is sold on disk. Data on disks and countywide terminals may be 2-3 months old. No juvenile, mental health, victims, sealed or adoption records released. Will not fax documents. Court makes copy: $.50 per page. Certification fee: $24.00 per doc. Payee: Clerk of Justice Court. Personal checks accepted; cashier's check or money orders only for traffic. Visa/MC accepted only from person named on card. Prepayment required. Mail requests: SASE required.
Civil Name Search: Access: Mail, in person, online. Only the court performs in person name searches; visitors may not. Search fee: $24.00 per name. Required to search: name, years to search; also helpful: address. Civil records on computer since 1993. Records on dockets by name and case number. Mail turnaround time 1-2 weeks. Access court index free on countywide site at www.superiorcourt.maricopa.gov/docket/JusticeCourtCases/caseSearch.asp. Incomplete dockets, also expired data online.
Criminal Name Search: Access: Mail, in person, online. Only the court performs in person name searches; visitors may not. Search fee: $24.00 per name. Required to search: name, years to search, DOB; also helpful: address, SSN. Criminal dockets by name and case number. Mail turnaround time 1-2 weeks. Online access same as civil. Some DOBs shown, addresses are not. Online results show middle initial, DOB.

Moon Valley (Northwest Phoenix) Justice Court 18380 N 40th St, Phoenix, AZ 85032; 602-372-7000; fax: 602-372-7910; 8AM-5PM (MST). *Misdemeanor, Civil Actions under $10,000, Eviction, Small Claims.*
www.superiorcourt.maricopa.gov/justiceCourts/
General Information: Now co-located with the McDowell Mountain (Scottsdale) Desert Ridge, and Dreamy Draw. But records are separate. Countywide Justice Court docket information is sold on disk. Data on disks and countywide terminals may be 2-3 months old. No juvenile, mental health, victims, sealed or adoption records released. Will not fax documents. Court makes copy: $.50 per page. Certification fee: $24.00 per doc. Payee: Northwest Phoenix Justice Court. Personal checks accepted. Visa/MC accepted only from person named on card. Prepayment required. Mail requests: SASE required.
Civil Name Search: Access: Mail, in person, online. Only the court performs in person name searches; visitors may not. Search fee: $24.00 per name. Required to search: name, years to search; also helpful: address. Civil records on dockets. Will retain for 5 years, computerized records since 1987. Mail turnaround time 1-2 weeks. Access court index free on countywide site at www.superiorcourt.maricopa.gov/docket/JusticeCourtCases/caseSearch.asp.
Criminal Name Search: Access: Mail, in person, online. Only the court performs in person name searches; visitors may not. Search fee: $24.00 per name. Required to search: name, years to search, DOB; also helpful: address, SSN. Criminal dockets by name and case number. Mail turnaround time 1-2 weeks. Online access same as civil. Some DOBs shown, addresses are not. Online results show middle initial, DOB.

North Mesa Justice Court 1837 S Mesa Dr, #B-103, Mesa, AZ 85210; 480-926-9731; fax: 480-926-7763; 8AM-5PM (MST). *Misdemeanor, Civil Actions under $10,000, Eviction, Small Claims.*
www.superiorcourt.maricopa.gov/justiceCourts/
General Information: Countywide Justice Court docket information is sold on disk. Data on disks and countywide terminals may be several months old. No juvenile, mental health, victims or sealed records released. Will not fax documents. Court makes copy: $.50 per page. Certification fee: $24.00 per doc. Payee: North Mesa Justice Court. Personal checks accepted. Credit cards accepted. Prepayment required. Mail requests: SASE required.
Civil Name Search: Access: Mail, in person, online. Only the court performs in person name searches; visitors may not. Search fee: $24.00 per name, limit 3 names. Civil records on computer by case number. Mail turnaround time 1-2 weeks. Nearest public terminal located at San Tan

JC, 201 E Chicago in Chandler. Access index free on countywide site at www.superiorcourt.maricopa.gov/docket/JusticeCourtCases/caseSearch.asp. Incomplete dockets, also expired data online.
Criminal Name Search: Access: Mail, in person, online
Mail, in person. Only the court performs in person name searches; visitors may not. Search fee: $24.00 per name, limit 3 names. Required to search: name, years to search, offense; also helpful: DOB. Criminal records on computer by case number. Mail turnaround time 1-2 weeks. Nearest public terminal located at San Tan JC, 201 E Chicago in Chandler. Online access same as civil. Some DOBs shown, addresses are not. Online results show middle initial, DOB.

North Valley Justice Court 14264 W Tierra Buena Ln, Surprise, AZ 85374; 602-372-2000 x4; fax: 602-372-2620; 8AM-5PM (MST). *Misdemeanor, Civil Actions under $10,000, Eviction, Small Claims.*
www.superiorcourt.maricopa.gov/justiceCourts/
General Information: Countywide Justice Court docket information is sold on disk. Data on disks and countywide terminals may be several months old. No juvenile, mental health, victims, sealed or adoption records released. Will not fax documents. Court makes copy: $.50 per page. Certification fee: $24.00 per doc. Payee: North Valley Justice Court. Personal checks accepted. Credit cards accepted. Prepayment required. Mail requests: SASE required.
Civil Name Search: Access: Mail, in person, online. Both court and visitors may perform in person name searches. Search fee: $24.00 per name. Civil records on dockets by case number; on computer back to 1999. Mail turnaround time 1-2 weeks. Civil PAT available. Countywide dockets on iCIS system. Access court index free on countywide site at www.superiorcourt.maricopa.gov/docket/JusticeCourtCases/caseSearch.asp. Incomplete dockets, also expired data online.
Criminal Name Search: Access: Mail, in person, online. Both court and visitors may perform in person name searches. Search fee: $24.00 per name. Required to search: name, years to search, DOB; also helpful: SSN. Criminal dockets by case number; on computer back to 1999. Mail turnaround time 1-2 weeks. Criminal PAT available. Countywide dockets on iCIS system; no print outs. Online access same as civil. Some DOBs shown, addresses are not. Online results show middle initial, DOB.

San Marcos (Chandler) Justice Court 201 E Chicago St, #103, Chandler, AZ 85225-8502; 602-372-3400 x3; fax: 602-372-3468; 8AM-5PM (MST). *Misdemeanor, Civil Actions under $10,000, Eviction, Small Claims.*
www.superiorcourt.maricopa.gov/justiceCourts/
General Information: Formerly known as Chandler Justice Court. There are 3 other Justice Courts co-located at this address, separate phones. Countywide Justice Court docket information is sold on disk. No juvenile, mental health, victims, sealed or adoption records released. Will not fax documents. Court makes copy: $.50 per page. Certification fee: $24.00 per doc. Payee: San Marcos Justice Court. Personal checks accepted. Credit cards accepted. Prepayment required. Mail requests: SASE required.
Civil Name Search: Access: Mail, in person, online. Only the court performs in person name searches; visitors may not. Search fee: $24.00 per name. Required to search: name, years to search; also helpful: address. Civil records on dockets by number; records go back 5 years; on computer back to 1991. Mail turnaround time 1-2 weeks. Access court index free on countywide site at www.superiorcourt.maricopa.gov/docket/JusticeCourtCases/caseSearch.asp. Incomplete dockets, also expired data online.
Criminal Name Search: Access: Mail, in person, online. Only the court performs in person name searches; visitors may not. Search fee: $24.00 per name. Required to search: name, years to search, DOB; also helpful: address, SSN. Criminal docket by number; records on computer go back to 1991. Note: The court will not conduct any criminal record checks, Mail turnaround time 1-2 weeks. Online access same as civil. Some DOBs shown, addresses are not. Online results show middle initial, DOB.

San Tan (South Mesa/Gilbert) Justice Court 201 E Chicago St, #102, Chandler, AZ 85225-8502; 602-372-3400; fax: 602-372-3441; 8AM-5PM (MST). *Misdemeanor, Civil Actions under $10,000, Eviction, Small Claims.*
www.superiorcourt.maricopa.gov/justiceCourts/
General Information: Formerly known as South Mesa./Gilbert Justice Court. Countywide Justice Court docket information is sold on disk. Data on disks and countywide terminals may be 2-3 months old. No juvenile, mental health, victims, sealed or adoption records released. Will not fax documents. Court makes copy: $.50 per page. Certification fee: $24.00 per doc. Payee: San Tan Justice Court. Cashiers checks and money orders accepted. Visa/MC accepted. Prepayment required. Mail requests: SASE required.
Civil Name Search: Access: Mail, in person, online. Both court and visitors may perform in person name searches. Search fee: $24.00 per name. Required to search: name, years to search, DOB, SSN, signed release. Civil records on computer by case number back to 1994. Mail turnaround

time 1-2 weeks. Civil PAT available. Countywide dockets on iCIS system; no print outs. Access court index free on countywide site at www.superiorcourt.maricopa.gov/docket/JusticeCourtCases/caseSearch.asp. Incomplete dockets, also expired data online.

Criminal Name Search: Access: Mail, in person, online. Both court and visitors may perform in person name searches. Search fee: $24.00 per name. Required to search: name, years to search, DOB, SSN, signed release. Criminal records on computer by case number; computerized back to 1994. Mail turnaround time 1-2 weeks. Criminal PAT available. Countywide dockets on iCIS system; no print outs. Online access same as civil. Some DOBs shown, addresses are not. Online results show middle initial, DOB.

South Mountain (South Phoenix) Justice Court 620 W Jackson St, M/S 1044, Phoenix, AZ 85003; 602-372-6300; fax: 602-372-6410; 8AM-5PM (MST). *Misdemeanor, Civil Actions under $10,000, Eviction, Small Claims.*

www.superiorcourt.maricopa.gov/justiceCourts/

General Information: Countywide Justice Court docket information is sold on disk. Data on disks and countywide terminals may be several months old. No juvenile, mental health, victims, sealed or adoption records released. Will not fax documents. Court makes copy: $.50 per page. Certification fee: $24.00 per doc. Payee: South Mountain Justice Court. Personal checks accepted. Credit cards accepted. Prepayment required. Mail requests: SASE required.

Civil Name Search: Access: Mail, in person, online. Visitors must perform in person searches themselves. Search fee: $24.00 per name. Required to search: name, years to search; also helpful: address. Civil records on computer since 1990, on dockets by number. Mail turnaround time 1-2 weeks. Access court index free on countywide site at www.superiorcourt.maricopa.gov/docket/JusticeCourtCases/caseSearch.asp. Incomplete dockets, also expired data online.

Criminal Name Search: Access: Mail, in person, online. Visitors must perform in person searches themselves. Search fee: $24.00 per name. Required to search: name, years to search; also helpful: DOB. Criminal dockets by number. Mail turnaround time 1-2 weeks. Online access same as civil. Some DOBs shown, addresses are not. Online results show middle initial, DOB.

University Lakes (East Tempe) Justice Court 201 E Chicago St, #101, Chandler, AZ 85225-8502; 602-372-3400; fax: 602-372-3414; 8AM-5PM (MST). *Misdemeanor, Civil Actions under $10,000, Eviction, Small Claims.*

www.superiorcourt.maricopa.gov/justiceCourts/

General Information: Formerly known as East Tempe Justice Court. Countywide Justice Court docket information is sold on disk. Data on disks and countywide terminals may be 2-3 months old. No juvenile, mental health, victims, sealed records released. Will not fax documents. Court makes copy: $.50 per page. Certification fee: $24.00 per doc. Payee: University Lakes Justice Court. Personal checks accepted. Visa/MC accepted. Prepayment required. Mail requests: SASE required.

Civil Name Search: Access: Mail, in person, online. Both court and visitors may perform in person name searches. Search fee: $24.00 per name. Civil records on computer by case number. Mail turnaround time 1-2 weeks Civil PAT available. Countywide dockets on iCIS system; no print outs. Access court index free on countywide site at www.superiorcourt.maricopa.gov/docket/JusticeCourtCases/caseSearch.asp. Incomplete dockets, also expired data online.

Criminal Name Search: Access: Mail, in person, online. Both court and visitors may perform in person name searches. Search fee: $24.00 per name. Required to search: name, years to search, DOB. Criminal records on computer by case number. Mail turnaround time is 1-2 weeks . Criminal PAT available. Countywide dockets on iCIS system; no print outs. Online access same as civil. Some DOBs shown, addresses are not. Online results show middle initial, DOB.

West McDowell (West Phoenix) Justice Court 620 W Jackson St, #1038, Courtroom 200, Phoenix, AZ 85003; 602-372-6300; fax: 602-372-6408; 8AM-5PM (MST). *Misdemeanor, Civil Actions under $10,000, Eviction, Small Claims.*

www.superiorcourt.maricopa.gov/justiceCourts/

General Information: Countywide Justice Court docket information is sold on disk. Data on disks and countywide terminals may be several months old. No juvenile, mental health, victims, sealed or adoption records released. Will not fax documents. Court makes copy: $.50 per page. Certification fee: $24.00 per doc. Payee: West McDowell Justice Court. Personal checks and credit cards accepted. Prepayment required. Mail requests: SASE required for civil.

Civil Name Search: Access: Mail, in person, online. Both court and visitors may perform in person name searches. Search fee: $24.00 per name. Some but not all civil records on computer since 1993. Note: Also, records 8/31/2005 forward are not on public access system. Mail

turnaround time varies. Civil PAT available. Countywide dockets on iCIS system; no print outs. Access court index free on countywide site at www.superiorcourt.maricopa.gov/docket/JusticeCourtCases/caseSearch.asp. Incomplete dockets, also expired data online.

Criminal Name Search: Access: In person, online. Both court and visitors may perform in person name searches. Search fee: $24.00 per name. Required to search: name, years to search, DOB. Some but not all criminal records on computer since 1993 by case number. Note: Records 8/31/2005 forward are not on public access system. Criminal PAT available. Countywide dockets on iCIS system; no print outs. Online access same as civil. Some DOBs shown, addresses are not. Online results show middle initial, DOB.

West Mesa Justice Court 2050 W University Dr, Mesa, AZ 85201; 480-964-2958; fax: 480-969-1098; 8AM-5PM (MST). *Misdemeanor, Civil Actions under $10,000, Eviction, Small Claims.*

www.superiorcourt.maricopa.gov/justiceCourts/

General Information: Countywide Justice Court docket information is sold on disk. Data on disks and countywide terminals may be several months old. No juvenile, mental health, victims, sealed or adoption records released. Will not fax documents. Court makes copy: $.50 per page. Certification fee: $24.00 per doc. Payee: West Mesa Justice Court. Personal checks accepted. Credit cards accepted. Prepayment required. Mail requests: SASE required.

Civil Name Search: Access: Mail, in person, online. Only the court performs in person name searches; visitors may not. Search fee: $24.00 per name. Civil records on computer since 1990 by case number. Mail turnaround time 1-2 weeks Nearest public terminal located at San Tan JC, 201 E Chicago in Chandler, or downtown Phoenix. Access court index free on countywide site at www.superiorcourt.maricopa.gov/docket/JusticeCourtCases/caseSearch.asp. Incomplete dockets, also expired data online.

Criminal Name Search: Access: Mail, in person, online. Only the court performs in person name searches; visitors may not. Search fee: $24.00 per name. Required to search: name, years to search, DOB; also helpful: SSN. Criminal records on computer since 1990 by case number. Mail turnaround time is 1-2 weeks . Nearest public terminal located at San Tan JC, 201 E Chicago in Chandler, or downtown Phoenix. Online access same as civil. Some DOBs shown, addresses are not. Online results show middle initial, DOB.

Mohave County

Superior Court PO Box 7000, Kingman, AZ 86402-7000; 928-753-0713; fax: 928-753-0781; 8AM-5PM (MST). *Felony, Civil Actions over $5,000, Probate.*

www.mohavecourts.az.gov

General Information: No mental health, victims, sealed or adoption records released. Will fax documents for $26.00. Court makes copy: $.50 per page. Self serve copy: same. Certification fee: $26.00 per doc. Payee: Clerk of Superior Court. Business checks accepted. Major credit cards accepted. Prepayment required. Mail requests: SASE required.

Civil Name Search: Access: Phone, fax, mail, in person, online. Both court and visitors may perform in person name searches. Search fee: $26.00 per name per year per index. Civil records on computer since 11/95; prior records on microfiche and index books. Mail turnaround time 5 days. Civil PAT goes back to 1995. Public access at http://apps.supremecourt.az.gov/publicaccess/ but sometime records are not updated frequently.

Criminal Name Search: Access: Phone, fax, mail, in person, online. Both court and visitors may perform in person name searches. Search fee: $26.00 per name. Required to search: name, years to search; also helpful: DOB, SSN. Criminal records on computer since 11/95; prior records on microfiche and index books. Mail turnaround time 5 days. Criminal PAT goes back to same as civil. Online access to criminal is the same as civil. Access county list of registered sex offenders at www.ctaz.com/~mcso/page19.html. Online results show middle initial, DOB.

Bullhead City Justice Court 2225 Trane Rd, Bullhead City, AZ 86442; 928-758-0709; fax: 928-758-2644; 8AM-5PM (MST). *Misdemeanor, Civil Actions under $10,000, Eviction, Small Claims.*

www.mohavecourts.com

General Information: When a case number is given, the court does charge $24 to pull a record. This interpretation is not per guidelines of the Administrative Offices of the Courts and is not the procedure followed in the Superior Court. No juvenile, mental health, victims, sealed or adoption records released. Will fax documents to local or toll-free number; long distance faxing depends on shortness of document. Court makes copy: $.50 per page. Certification fee: $24.00 per doc. Payee: Bullhead City Justice Court. Personal checks accepted. Major credit cards accepted if $50.00 minimum charge. Prepayment required. Mail requests: SASE requested.

Civil Name Search: Access: Phone, fax, mail, in person, online. Both court and visitors may perform in person name searches. Search fee:

$24.00 per name. Civil records on computer from 1988. Some records on docket books. Records retained for 5 years. Will only search back to 1988 unless w/docket number. Note: Visitors may search record files if prior arrangements made, request must be on company letterhead. Mail turnaround time 2-3 days. Public access at http://apps.supremecourt.az.gov/publicaccess/, but sometime records are not updated frequently.
Criminal Name Search: Access: Mail, in person, online. Only the court performs in person name searches; visitors may not. Search fee: $24.00 per 10 cases. Required to search: name, years to search; also helpful: DOB, SSN. Criminal records computerized from 1988. Some records on docket books. Records retained for 5 years. Will only search back to 1988 unless w/docket numb. Mail turnaround time 2-3 days. Public access at http://apps.supremecourt.az.gov/publicaccess/, but sometime records are not updated frequently. Online results show middle initial, DOB.

Kingman/Cerbat Justice Court 524 W Beale St, PO Box 29, Kingman, AZ 86401-0029; 928-753-0710; fax: 928-753-7840; 8AM-5PM (MST). *Misdemeanor, Civil Actions under $10,000, Eviction, Small Claims.*
www.mohavecourts.com
General Information: No juvenile, mental health, victims, sealed or adoption records released. Will not fax out documents. Court makes copy: $.50 per page. Certification fee: $24.00 per doc. Payee: Kingman/Cerbat Justice Court. Personal checks accepted. Credit cards accepted. Prepayment required. Mail requests: SASE required.
Civil Name Search: Access: Phone, fax, mail, in person, online. Only the court performs in person name searches; visitors may not. Search fee: $24.00 per name. Civil records on computer from 1988. Paper records retained for 5 years. Mail turnaround time 2-3 days. Public access at http://apps.supremecourt.az.gov/publicaccess/.
Criminal Name Search: Access: Phone, fax, mail, in person, online. Only the court performs in person name searches; visitors may not. Search fee: $24.00 per name. Required to search: name, years to search; also helpful: DOB, SSN. Criminal records computerized from 1988. Paper records retained for 5 years. Mail turnaround time 2-3 days. Public access at http://apps.supremecourt.az.gov/publicaccess/. Online results show middle initial, DOB.

Lake Havasu Consolidated Court 2001 College Dr, #148, Lake Havasu City, AZ 86403; 928-453-0705; fax: 928-680-0193; 8AM-5PM (MST). *Misdemeanor, Civil Actions under $10,000, Eviction, Small Claims.* www.mohavecourts.com
General Information: When a case number is given, the court also charges $24 per 10 cases per day. No juvenile or victims records released. Will fax non-certified documents. Court makes copy: $.50 per page. Certification fee: $41 for Municipal documents, $48 for Justice Court documents. Payee: Lake Havasu Consolidated Court. Personal checks and credit cards accepted. Prepayment required. Mail requests: SASE required.
Civil Name Search: Access: Mail, fax, in person, online. Only the court performs in person name searches; visitors may not. Search fee: $24.00 per name. Civil records on computer from 1983. Some records on docket books. Records retained for 5 years after closed/satisfied. Mail turnaround time 3 days. Public access at http://apps.supremecourt.az.gov/publicaccess/, but sometime records are not updated frequently.
Criminal Name Search: Access: Fax, mail, in person, online. Both court and visitors may perform in person name searches. Search fee: $24.00 per name. Required to search: name, years to search; also helpful: DOB. Criminal records computerized from 1983. Records retained for 5 years after closed/satisfied. Mail turnaround time 3 days. Public use terminal has crim records. Public access at http://apps.supremecourt.az.gov/publicaccess/, but sometime records are not updated frequently.

Moccasin Justice Court HC-65, Box 90, 123 S Main, Moccasin, AZ 86022; 928-643-7104; fax: 928-643-6206; 8AM-5PM (MST). *Misdemeanor, Civil Actions under $10,000, Eviction, Small Claims.*
www.mohavecourts.com
General Information: This court is also the Magistrate Court for Colorado City. No juvenile, mental health, victims, sealed or adoption records released. Will fax documents $24.00. Court makes copy: $.50 per page. Certification fee: $24.00 per doc. Payee: Moccasin Justice Court. Personal checks accepted. Visa/MC accepted. Prepayment required.
Civil Name Search: Access: Mail, in person, online. Only the court performs in person name searches; visitors may not. Search fee: $24.00 per name. Civil index on docket books. Records retained for 5 years. Mail turnaround time 7-30 days. Public access at http://apps.supremecourt.az.gov/publicaccess/, but sometime records are not updated frequently.
Criminal Name Search: Access: Mail, in person, online. Only the court performs in person name searches; visitors may not. Search fee: $24.00

per name. Criminal docket on books. Records retained for 5 years. Mail turnaround time 14-30 days. Public access at http://http://apps.supremecourt.az.gov/publicaccess/, but sometime records are not updated frequently.

Navajo County

Superior Court PO Box 668, Holbrook, AZ 86025; 928-524-4188; fax: 928-524-4261; 8AM-5PM (MST). *Felony, Civil Actions over $5,000, Probate.*
General Information: Online identifiers in results same as on public terminal. No mental health, victims, sealed or adoption records released. Fee to fax out doc $26.00. Court makes copy: $.50 per page. Self serve copy: same. Certification fee: $26.00 per doc. Payee: Clerk of Superior Court. Only cashiers checks and money orders accepted. Visa/MC accepted. Prepayment required. Mail requests: SASE required.
Civil Name Search: Access: Phone, fax, mail, in person, online. Both court and visitors may perform in person name searches. Search fee: $26.00 per name. Civil index on docket books, index cards and microfiche back to 1890; computerized back to 1994. Mail turnaround time ASAP. Civil PAT goes back to 1994. Access to the docket is free at http://apps.supremecourt.az.gov/publicaccess/.
Criminal Name Search: Access: Phone, fax, mail, in person, online. Both court and visitors may perform in person name searches. Search fee: $26.00 per name. Required to search: name, years to search; also helpful: DOB, SSN. Criminal docket on books, index cards and microfiche back to 1890; computerized back to 1994. Mail turnaround time ASAP. Criminal PAT goes back to same as civil. Access to the docket is free at http://apps.supremecourt.az.gov/publicaccess/. Online results show middle initial, DOB.

Holbrook Justice and Magistrate Court PO Box 366, 121 W Buffalo, Holbrook, AZ 86025; 928-524-4720; fax: 928-524-4725; 8AM-5PM (MST). *Misdemeanor, Civil Actions under $10,000, Eviction, Small Claims, Traffic.*
www.town-court.com/getTownCourt.php?courtID=9486
General Information: No victim names or sealed records released. Will not fax documents. Court makes copy: $.50 per page. Certification fee: $24.00 per doc. Payee: Holbrook Justice Court. Business checks accepted. No personal checks accepted. MC and AmEx accepted. Prepayment required. Mail requests: SASE required.
Civil Name Search: Access: Mail, in person, online. Both court and visitors may perform in person name searches. Search fee: $24.00 per name. Civil records on computer since 1994. Records on dockets and index cards back for 5 years. Mail turnaround time 1 week. Civil PAT goes back to 1996. Access to the docket is free at http://apps.supremecourt.az.gov/publicaccess/.
Criminal Name Search: Access: Mail, in person, online. Both court and visitors may perform in person name searches. Search fee: $24.00 per name. Criminal records on computer since 1992. Records on dockets and stat books back for 5 years. Mail turnaround time 1 week. Criminal PAT goes back to 1996. Access to the docket is free at http://apps.supremecourt.az.gov/publicaccess/.

Kayenta Justice Court PO Box 38, (Courthouse is east of Jct Hiways 160 and 163), Kayenta, AZ 86033; 928-697-3522; fax: 928-697-3528; 8AM-N,1-5PM (MST). *Misdemeanor, Civil Actions under $10,000, Eviction, Small Claims.*
www.town-court.com/getTownCourt.php?courtID=9487
General Information: When a case number is given, the court also charges $24 per case to pull a record, but this could change. This interpretation is not per guidelines of the Administrative Offices of the Courts and is not the procedure followed in the Superior Court. No victim's names released. Will not fax documents. Court makes copy: $.50 per page. Certification fee: $24.00 per doc. Payee: Kayenta Justice Court. Only cashiers checks and money orders accepted. No credit cards accepted. Prepayment required. Mail requests: SASE required.
Civil Name Search: Access: Mail, in person, online. Only the court performs in person name searches; visitors may not. Search fee: $24.00 per name. Required to search: name, years to search, address. Civil index on docket books and index cards; on computer back to 1994. Note: If planning to make an in-person search, call to make an appointment. Mail turnaround time 1 week. Access to the docket is free at http://apps.supremecourt.az.gov/publicaccess/.
Criminal Name Search: Access: Mail, in person, online. Only the court performs in person name searches; visitors may not. Search fee: $24.00 per name. Required to search: name, years to search, address, DOB, SSN, signed release. Criminal docket on books and index cards; on computer back to 1994. Note: If planning to make an in-person search, call to make an appointment. Mail turnaround time 1 week. Access to the docket is free at http://apps.supremecourt.az.gov/publicaccess/.

Pinetop-Lakeside Justice Court PO Box 2020, 1360 Neils Hansen Dr, Lakeside, AZ 85929; 928-368-6200; fax: 928-368-8674; 8AM-5PM

(MST). *Misdemeanor, Civil Actions under $10,000, Eviction, Small Claims, Traffic.*

General Information: When a case number is given, the court also charges $24 per name to pull a record, but this could change. This interpretation is not per guidelines of the Administrative Offices of the Courts and is not the procedure followed in the Superior Court. No victim's names released, orders of protection or harassment. No fee to fax documents. Court makes copy: $.50 per page. Certification fee: $24.00 per doc. Payee: Pinetop-Lakeside Justice Court. No personal checks accepted. Major credit cards accepted only in person. Prepayment required. Mail requests: SASE requested.

Civil Name Search: Access: Fax, mail, in person, online. Only the court performs in person name searches; visitors may not. Search fee: $24.00 per name per year. Civil cases indexed by case number. Civil records on electronic dockets by case number and case files by numeric. Mail turnaround time 7-10 days. Access to the docket is free at http://apps.supremecourt.az.gov/publicaccess/.

Criminal Name Search: Access: Fax, mail, in person, online. Only the court performs in person name searches; visitors may not. Search fee: $24.00 per name per year. Criminal records on electronic dockets by case number and case files by alpha back to 1996. Computerized back to 1970. Mail turnaround time 7-10 days. Access to the docket is free at http://apps.supremecourt.az.gov/publicaccess/.

Show Low Justice Court 620 E Mcneil, Show Low, AZ 85901; 928-532-6030; fax: 928-532-6035; 8AM-5PM (MST). *Misdemeanor, Civil Actions under $10,000, Eviction, Small Claims.*

General Information: No victim's names released. Will fax documents if fees prepaid. Court makes copy: $.50 per page. Certification fee: $24.00 per doc. Payee: Show Low Justice Court. Personal checks accepted. No credit cards accepted. Prepayment required. Mail requests: SASE required.

Civil Name Search: Access: Mail, in person, online. Only the court performs in person name searches; visitors may not. Search fee: $24.00 per name per year. Civil cases indexed by plaintiff. Civil records on computer. Note: In person access requires a written request. Mail turnaround time 48 hours. Access to the docket is free at http://apps.supremecourt.az.gov/publicaccess/.

Criminal Name Search: Access: Mail, in person, online. Only the court performs in person name searches; visitors may not. Search fee: $24.00 per name per year. Required to search: name, years to search; also helpful: DOB, SSN. Criminal records on computer for five years. Note: In person access requires a written request. Mail turnaround time up to 10 days. Access to the docket is free at http://apps.supremecourt.az.gov/publicaccess/.

Snowflake Justice Court 145 S Main St #D, Snowflake, AZ 85937; 928-536-4141; fax: 928-536-3511; 8AM-5PM (MST). *Misdemeanor, Civil Actions under $10,000, Eviction, Small Claims.*
www.ci.snowflake.az.us/res-court.htm

General Information: When a case number is given, the court also charges $24 per case to pull a record, but this could change. This interpretation is not per guidelines of the Administrative Offices of the Courts and is not the procedure followed in the Superior Court. No victim's names or search warrants released, no juvenile records released. Will not fax out documents. Court makes copy: $.50 per page. Certification fee: $24.00 per doc. Payee: Snowflake Justice Court. Only cashiers checks and money orders accepted. Prepayment required. Mail requests: SASE required.

Civil Name Search: Access: Phone, fax, mail, in person, online. Only the court performs in person name searches; visitors may not. Search fee: $24.00 per case. Civil records on computer back to 6/96, prior on docket books and index cards. Misdemeanors, DUI's and traffic records kept for 3 years, others held f. Mail turnaround time 2 weeks. Access to the docket is free at http://apps.supremecourt.az.gov/publicaccess/.

Criminal Name Search: Access: Fax, mail, in person, online. Only the court performs in person name searches; visitors may not. Search fee: $24.00 per case. Required to search: name, years to search; also helpful: DOB, SSN. Criminal records computerized from 6/96, prior on docket books and index cards. Misdemeanors, DUI's and traffic records kept for 3 years, others held. Mail turnaround time 2 weeks. Access to the docket is free at http://apps.supremecourt.az.gov/publicaccess/.

Winslow Justice Court Box 808, 605 E 3rd St, Winslow, AZ 86047; 928-289-6840; fax: 928-289-6847; 8AM-5PM (MST). *Misdemeanor, Civil Actions under $10,000, Eviction, Small Claims.*
www.town-court.com/getTownCourt.php?courtID=9491

General Information: When a case number is given, the court also charges $24 per case to pull a record, but this could change. This interpretation is not per guidelines of the Administrative Offices of the Courts and is not the procedure followed in the Superior Court. No victim's names released. Will fax documents to local or toll free line. Court makes copy: $.50 per page. Certification fee: $24.00 per doc. Payee: Winslow Courts. Only cash or money order accepted. Major credit cards accepted. Prepayment required. Mail requests: SASE required.

Civil Name Search: Access: Fax, mail, in person, online. Only the court performs in person name searches; visitors may not. Search fee: $24.00 per name. Civil index on docket books; on computer since 1994. Mail turnaround time 1 week. Access to the docket is free at http://apps.supremecourt.az.gov/publicaccess/.

Criminal Name Search: Access: Fax, mail, in person, online. Only the court performs in person name searches; visitors may not. Search fee: $24.00 per name. Required to search: name, years to search; also helpful: DOB, SSN. Criminal docket on books; on computer since 1995. Mail turnaround time 1 week. Access to the docket is free at http://apps.supremecourt.az.gov/publicaccess/.

Pima County

Superior Court Legal Records, 110 W Congress, Rm 241, Tucson, AZ 85701; 520-740-3240; criminal phone: 520-740-3228; civil phone: 520-740-3210; fax: 520-798-3531; 8AM-5PM (MST). *Felony, Civil Actions over $5,000, Probate.*
www.cosc.co.pima.az.us

General Information: Address correspondence to attention of civil or criminal section. Superior Court general phone 520-740-4200. Online identifiers in results same as on public terminal. No juvenile, mental health, adoption, victims or sealed records released. Fee to fax out file $5.00 plus $.50 per page. Court makes copy: $.50 per page. Certification fee: $26.00 per doc. Payee: Clerk of Superior Court. Cashiers checks and money orders accepted. Visa/MC accepted in person only. Prepayment required.

Civil Name Search: Access: Phone, mail, in person, online. Both court and visitors may perform in person name searches. Search fee: $26.00 per name. Required to search: name, years to search, DOB. Civil records on computer since 1980s, on microfilm since late 1800s. Mail turnaround time 14 days; include $5.00 mailing fee. Civil PAT goes back to 1970s. Online access to superior court records is free at www.agave.cosc.pima.gov/PublicDocs/. Search by name, business name, or by case number.

Criminal Name Search: Access: Mail, in person. Both court and visitors may perform in person name searches. Search fee: $26.00 per name. Add $5.00 for postage and handling. Required to search: name, years to search, DOB. Criminal records on computer since 1980s, on microfilm since late 1800s. Mail turnaround time 14 days; include $5.00 mailing fee. Criminal PAT goes back to 1983. Online results show middle initial, DOB.

Ajo Justice Court 111 La Mina Ave, Ajo, AZ 85321; 520-387-7684; fax: 520-387-6028; 8AM-5PM (MST). *Misdemeanor, Civil Actions under $10,000, Eviction, Small Claims.*

General Information: When a case number is given, the court also charges $24 per name to pull a record, but this could change. This interpretation is not per guidelines of the Administrative Offices of the Courts and is not the procedure followed in the Superior Court. No juvenile, sealed, victim records released. Will fax documents to local or toll-free number. Court makes copy: $.50 per page. Certification fee: $24.00 per doc. Payee: Ajo Justice Court. Personal checks accepted. No credit cards accepted. Prepayment required.

Civil Name Search: Access: Mail, in person, online. Only the court performs in person name searches; visitors may not. Search fee: $24.00 per name. Civil records on computer since 1997, prior in docket books. Mail turnaround time 2 weeks. Access to the docket is free at http://apps.supremecourt.az.gov/publicaccess/.

Criminal Name Search: Access: Mail, in person, online, fax. Only the court performs in person name searches; visitors may not. Search fee: $24.00 per name. Criminal records on computer since 1987, prior in docket books. Mail turnaround time 2 weeks. Access to the docket is free at http://apps.supremecourt.az.gov/publicaccess/.

Green Valley Justice Court 601 N LaCanada, Green Valley, AZ 85614; 520-648-0658; fax: 520-648-2235; 8AM-4:30PM (MST). *Misdemeanor, Civil Actions under $10,000, Eviction, Small Claims.*
www.jp.pima.gov/

General Information: When a case number is given, the court also charges $24 per name to pull a record, but this could change. This interpretation is not per guidelines of the Administrative Offices of the Courts and is not the procedure followed in the Superior Court. No juvenile, mental health, victims, sealed or adoption records released. Will not fax documents. Court makes copy: $.50 per page. Certification fee: $24.00 per doc. Payee: Green Valley Justice Court. Personal checks accepted. Visa/MC accepted. Prepayment required. Mail requests: SASE required.

Civil Name Search: Access: Mail, in person, online. Only the court performs in person name searches; visitors may not. Search fee: $24.00 per name. Civil records on computer back to 1996; card files prior. Note: Clerk will only search computerized records. Mail turnaround time 2 weeks. Access to the docket is free at http://apps.supremecourt.az.gov/publicaccess/.

Criminal Name Search: Access: Mail, in person, online. Only the court performs in person name searches; visitors may not. Search fee: $24.00 per name. Required to search: name, years to search, DOB. Criminal records computerized from 1996; card files prior. Note: Clerk will only search computerized records. Mail turnaround time 14 days. Access to the docket is free at http://apps.supremecourt.az.gov/publicaccess/.

Pima County Consolidated Justice Court 115 N Church Ave, Tucson, AZ 85701; 520-740-3171; fax: 520-884-0346; 8AM-5PM (MST). *Misdemeanor, Civil Actions under $10,000, Eviction, Small Claims, Traffic.*

www.jp.pima.gov/

General Information: Note that this court serves the city of Tucson. There are two other Justice Courts in this county. No information about set-aside judgments, unserved search warrants or felony warrants released. Will not fax documents. Court makes copy: $.50 per page. Certification fee: $24.00 per doc. Payee: Pima County Consolidated Justice Court. Personal checks accepted. Credit cards accepted. Prepayment required. Mail requests: SASE required.

Civil Name Search: Access: Fax, mail, in person, online. Both court and visitors may perform in person name searches. Search fee: $24.00 per name. Required to search: name, years to search, DOB and/or SSN. Civil records on computer since 1988, on docket books prior. Mail turnaround time 2 days. Public use terminal available. Online access is free http://jp.co.pima.az.us/casesearch/CaseSearch.aspx. You can search docket information for civil, criminal or traffic cases by name, docket or citation number. This site does not include the other Justice Courts in this county.

Criminal Name Search: Access: Fax, mail, online, in person. Both court and visitors may perform in person name searches. Search fee: $24.00 per name. Required to search: name, years to search, DOB, SSN. Criminal records on computer since 1988, on docket books prior. Mail turnaround time 2 days. Public use terminal available. Online access is free http://jp.co.pima.az.us/casesearch/CaseSearch.aspx. You can search docket information for civil, criminal or traffic cases by name, docket or citation number. This site does not include the other Justice Courts in this county. Online results show middle initial, DOB.

Pinal County

Superior Court PO Box 2730, 971 Jason Lopez Cir Bldg A, Florence, AZ 85132-2730; 520-866-5300; fax: 520-866-5320; 8AM-5PM (MST). *Felony, Civil Actions over $5,000, Probate.*

http://pinalcountyaz.gov/Departments/JudicialBranch/SuperiorCourt/Pages/Home.aspx

General Information: Probate fax is same as main fax number. Online identifiers in results same as on public terminal. No victim names, adoption records released. Fee to fax document $.50 per page. Court makes copy: $.50 per page. Certification fee: $26.00 per doc. Payee: Clerk of Superior Court. Business checks accepted. No credit cards accepted. Prepayment required. Mail requests: SASE required.

Civil Name Search: Access: Phone, mail, in person, online. Both court and visitors may perform in person name searches. Search fee: $26.00 per name. Civil records on computer from 1993. Some records on docket books back to 1775. Mail turnaround time 7 days. Civil PAT goes back to 1993. Access to the docket is free at http://apps.supremecourt.az.gov/publicaccess/.

Criminal Name Search: Access: Phone, mail, in person, online. Both court and visitors may perform in person name searches. Search fee: $26.00 per name. Criminal records computerized from 1987. Some records on docket books back to 1875. Mail turnaround time 7 days. Criminal PAT goes back to 1987. Access to the docket is free at http://apps.supremecourt.az.gov/publicaccess/. Online results show middle initial, DOB.

Apache Junction Justice Court 575 N Idaho Rd, #200, Apache Junction, AZ 85219; 480-982-2921; fax: 520-866-6153; 8AM-5PM (MST). *Misdemeanor, Civil Actions under $10,000, Eviction, Small Claims.*

http://pinalcountyaz.gov/Departments/JudicialBranch/JusticeCourts/Pages/Precinct7.aspx

General Information: Yes, the area code for the fax number is different than the voice number. Will fax documents $1.25 per page. Court makes copy: $.50 per page. Certification fee: $24.00 per doc. Payee: Apache Junction Justice Court. No personal checks or credit cards accepted. Prepayment required. Mail requests: SASE required.

Civil Name Search: Access: Fax, mail, in person, online. Both court and visitors may perform in person name searches. Search fee: $24.00 per name. Civil records on computer since 1999. Records retained for 5 years. Mail turnaround time varies. Access to the docket is free at http://apps.supremecourt.az.gov/publicaccess/.

Criminal Name Search: Access: Fax, mail, in person, online. Only the court performs in person name searches; visitors may not. Search fee: $24.00 per name. Criminal records on computer since 1999, older cases 1993-1998 are on if case was open in 1999. Records retained for 5 years.

Mail turnaround time varies. Access to the docket is free at http://apps.supremecourt.az.gov/publicaccess/.

Casa Grande Justice Court 820 E Cottonwood Ln, Bldg B, Casa Grande, AZ 85222; 520-836-5471; fax: 520-866-7404; 8AM-5PM (MST). *Misdemeanor, Civil Actions under $10,000, Eviction, Small Claims.*

General Information: No juvenile, mental health, victims, sealed or adoption records released. Will fax documents. Court makes copy: $.50 per page. Certification fee: $24.00 per doc. Payee: Casa Grande Justice Court. Business checks must be pre-approved. Visa/MC by phone at Official Payments 877-309-4917. Prepayment required. Mail requests: SASE required.

Civil Name Search: Access: Mail, in person, online. Only the court performs in person name searches; visitors may not. Search fee: $24.00 per name. Civil records on computer since 1999, index back to 1999. Mail turnaround time 1 day. Public access at http://apps.supremecourt.az.gov/publicaccess/, but sometime records are not updated frequently.

Criminal Name Search: Access: Mail, in person, online. Only the court performs in person name searches; visitors may not. Search fee: $24.00 per name. Required to search: name, years to search, DOB; also helpful: SSN. Criminal records on computer since 1999, index back to 2000. Mail turnaround time 1 day. Public access at http://apps.supremecourt.az.gov/publicaccess/, but sometime records are not updated frequently.

Eloy Justice Court PO Box 586, Eloy, AZ 85231; 520-866-7983; fax: 520-466-4473; 8AM-N, 1-5PM (MST). *Misdemeanor, Civil Actions under $10,000, Eviction, Small Claims.*

General Information: No juvenile, mental health, victims, sealed or adoption records released. Will not fax documents. Court makes copy: $.50 per page. Certification fee: $24.00 per doc. Payee: Eloy Justice Court. No personal checks accepted. Visa/MC accepted. Prepayment required. Mail requests: SASE required.

Civil Name Search: Access: Mail, in person, online. Only the court performs in person name searches; visitors may not. Search fee: $24.00 per name. Civil records on computer since 8/92. On docket books and index cards from 1981. Mail turnaround time 1-2 weeks. Public access at http://apps.supremecourt.az.gov/publicaccess/, but sometime records are not updated frequently.

Criminal Name Search: Access: Mail, in person, online. Only the court performs in person name searches; visitors may not. Search fee: $24.00 per name. Required to search: name, years to search, DOB. Criminal records on computer since 8/92. On docket books and index cards from 1981. Mail turnaround time 1-2 weeks. Public access at http://apps.supremecourt.az.gov/publicaccess/, but sometime records are not updated frequently.

Florence Justice Court PO Box 1818, Florence, AZ 85132; 520-866-7194; civil phone: 520-866-7193; fax: 520-866-7190; 8AM-5PM (MST). *Misdemeanor, Civil Actions under $10,000, Eviction, Small Claims.*

General Information: When a case number is given, the court also charges $24 to pull a record, but this could change. This interpretation is not per guidelines of the Administrative Offices of the Courts and is not the procedure followed in the Superior Court. No juvenile, mental health, victims, sealed or adoption records released. Will fax documents no fee. Court makes copy: $.50 per page. Certification fee: $24.00 per doc. Payee: Florence Justice Court. Only cashiers checks and money orders accepted. No credit cards accepted. Prepayment required. Mail requests: SASE required.

Civil Name Search: Access: Mail, in person, online. Only the court performs in person name searches; visitors may not. Search fee: $24.00 per name. Civil records are on computer since 1/1999. Mail turnaround time 1 week. Access to the docket is free at http://apps.supremecourt.az.gov/publicaccess/.

Criminal Name Search: Access: Mail, in person, online. Only the court performs in person name searches; visitors may not. Search fee: $24.00 per name. Criminal records are on computer since 1/1999. Mail turnaround time 1 week. Access to the docket is free at http://apps.supremecourt.az.gov/publicaccess/. Online results show middle initial, DOB.

Mammoth Justice Court PO Box 777, Mammoth, AZ 85618; 520-487-2262; fax: 520-866-7839; 8AM-5PM (MST). *Misdemeanor, Civil Actions under $10,000, Eviction, Small Claims.*

General Information: No juvenile, mental health, victims, sealed or adoption records released. Will fax documents to local or toll free line. Court makes copy: $.50 per page. Certification fee: $24.00 per doc. Cert fee includes copies. Payee: Mammoth Justice Court. Personal checks accepted. No credit cards accepted. Prepayment required. Mail requests: SASE required.

Civil Name Search: Access: Mail, fax, in person, online. Both court and visitors may perform in person name searches. Search fee: $24.00 per name. Civil index on docket books. Civil records retained for 7 years; on computer back 5 years. Mail turnaround time 2 days. Access to the docket is free at http://apps.supremecourt.az.gov/publicaccess/.

Criminal Name Search: Access: Mail, in person, online. Both court and visitors may perform in person name searches. Search fee: $24.00 per name. Required to search: name, years to search, DOB. Criminal docket on books. Misdemeanor records retained for 7 years; on computer back 5 years. Mail turnaround time 2 days. Access to the docket is free at http://apps.supremecourt.az.gov/publicaccess/.

Maricopa Justice Court PO Box 201, 19955 N Wilson Ave, Maricopa, AZ 85139; 520-866-3999; fax: 520-866-3990; 8AM-5PM (MST). *Misdemeanor, Civil Actions under $10,000, Eviction, Small Claims.*

General Information: When a case number is given, the court also charges $24 per case to pull a record, but this could change. This interpretation is not per guidelines of the Administrative Offices of the Courts and is not the procedure followed in the Superior Court. No juvenile, mental health, victims, sealed or adoption records released. Will fax documents to local or toll-free number. Court makes copy: $.50 per page. Certification fee: $24.00 per doc. Payee: Maricopa Justice Court. Personal checks accepted. No credit cards accepted. Prepayment required. Mail requests: SASE required.

Civil Name Search: Access: Fax, mail, in person, online. Only the court performs in person name searches; visitors may not. Search fee: $24.00 per name. Civil cases indexed by defendant. Civil records on computer since 1999; on dockets to 1993. Mail turnaround time 7 days. Access to the docket is free at http://apps.supremecourt.az.gov/publicaccess/.

Criminal Name Search: Access: Fax, mail, in person, online. Only the court performs in person name searches; visitors may not. Search fee: $24.00 per name. Criminal records on computer since 1999; on dockets to 1993. Mail turnaround time 7 days. Access to the docket is free at http://apps.supremecourt.az.gov/publicaccess/.

Oracle Justice Court 1470 Justice Dr, Oracle, AZ 85623; 520-896-9250; fax: 520-866-7812; 8AM-5PM (MST). *Misdemeanor, Civil Actions under $10,000, Eviction, Small Claims, Traffic.*

General Information: No juvenile, mental health, victims, sealed, adoption records released. Fee to fax out file $1.00 per page. Court makes copy: $.50 per page. Self serve copy: same. Certification fee: $24.00 per doc. Payee: Oracle Justice Court. No personal checks; money orders, cashier's checks or cash only. Prepayment required. Mail requests: SASE required.

Civil Name Search: Access: Mail, in person, online. Both court and visitors may perform in person name searches. Search fee: $24.00 per name. Required to search: name, years to search; also helpful: address. Civil cases indexed by defendant. Civil index on docket books and computer back to 1999 per state 's suggested retention schedule. Mail turnaround time 5 days Access to the docket is free at http://apps.supremecourt.az.gov/publicaccess/.

Criminal Name Search: Access: Mail, in person, online. Both court and visitors may perform in person name searches. Search fee: $24.00 per name. Required to search: name, years to search, DOB; also helpful: address, SSN. Criminal docket on books and computer back to 1999. Mail turnaround time 5 days. Access to the docket is free at http://apps.supremecourt.az.gov/publicaccess/.

Superior/Kearny Justice Court 60 E Main St, Superior, AZ 85173; 520-689-5871; fax: 520-689-2369; 8AM-N, 1-5PM (MST). *Misdemeanor, Civil Actions under $10,000, Eviction, Small Claims.*

General Information: No juvenile, mental health, victims, sealed or adoption records released. Will not fax out documents. Court makes copy: $.50 per page. Certification fee: $26.00 per doc; $24 for Justice Court. Payee: Superior/Kearny Justice Court. No personal checks accepted. Cash, money order or cashier's check accepted only. Prepayment required. Mail requests: SASE required.

Civil Name Search: Access: Fax, mail, in person, online. Only the court performs in person name searches; visitors may not. Search fee: $24.00 per name. Civil computerized records go back to 2002. Mail turnaround time 3 days. Public access at http://apps.supremecourt.az.gov/publicaccess/, but sometime records are not updated frequently.

Criminal Name Search: Access: Fax, mail, in person, online. Only the court performs in person name searches; visitors may not. Search fee: Justice- $24.00 per name Superior - $18.00 per name (increases to $26 effective 09/26/08). Required to search: name, years to search, DOB; also helpful: SSN. Criminal records computerized records go back to 2002. Mail turnaround time 3 days. Public access at http://apps.supremecourt.az.gov/publicaccess/, but sometime records are not updated frequently.

Santa Cruz County

Superior Court PO Box 1265, 2150 N Congress Dr, Nogales, AZ 85628; 520-375-7700; criminal phone: 6711; civil phone: 6705; fax: 520-375-7703; 8AM-5PM (MST). *Felony, Civil Actions over $5,000, Probate.* http://sccazcourts.org

General Information: Direct record search requests to Mr Garcia. Online identifiers in results same as on public terminal. No mental health, victims, sealed or adoption records released. Fee to fax document $.50 per page. Court makes copy: $.50 per page. Certification fee: $26.00 per doc. Payee: Clerk of Superior Court. Personal checks accepted. Visa/MC accepted. Prepayment required. Mail requests: SASE required.

Civil Name Search: Access: Mail, fax, in person, online. Both court and visitors may perform in person name searches. Search fee: $26.00 per name per year per index. Civil records on microfiche from 1898 to 1950. Records on docket books from 1950 to 1996; on computer after 1996. Mail turnaround time 10 days. Civil PAT goes back to 1996. Public access at http://apps.supremecourt.az.gov/publicaccess/, but sometime records are not updated frequently.

Criminal Name Search: Access: Mail, fax, in person, online. Both court and visitors may perform in person name searches. Search fee: $26.00 per name. Required to search: name, years to search, DOB; also helpful: SSN. Criminal records archived on microfiche from 1898 to 1995. Records on docket books from 1977 to 1996; on computer after 1996. Mail turnaround time 1 1/2 weeks. Criminal PAT goes back to same as civil. Public access at http://http://apps.supremecourt.az.gov/publicaccess/, but sometime records are not updated frequently. Online results show middle initial, DOB.

East Santa Cruz County Justice Court - Precinct #2 PO Box 1330, 3147 State Rte 83, #103, Sonoita, AZ 85637-1330; 520-455-5796; fax: 520-455-5133; 8:30AM-5PM (MST). *Misdemeanor, Civil Actions under $10,000, Eviction, Small Claims.*

General Information: Send fax requests to Attention: Justice Court. No juvenile, mental health, victims, sealed or adoption records released. Will fax documents to local or toll free line. Court makes copy: $.50 per page. Certification fee: $24.00 per doc. Payee: East Santa Cruz County Justice Court. Personal checks and credit cards accepted. Prepayment required.

Civil Name Search: Access: Mail, fax, in person, online. Only the court performs in person name searches; visitors may not. Search fee: $24.00 per name. Required to search: name, years to search; also helpful: address. Civil cases indexed by plaintiff. Civil index on docket books. Mail turnaround time 3-5 days. Public access at http://apps.supremecourt.az.gov/publicaccess/, but sometime records are not updated frequently.

Criminal Name Search: Access: Mail, fax, in person, online. Only the court performs in person name searches; visitors may not. Search fee: $24.00 per name. Required to search: name, years to search, DOB, SSN, signed release; also helpful: address. Criminal docket on books. Mail turnaround time 3-5 days. Public access at http://apps.supremecourt.az.gov/publicaccess/, but sometime records are not updated frequently. Online results show middle initial, DOB.

Santa Cruz Justice Court PO Box 1150, Nogales, AZ 85628; 520-375-7762; fax: 520-375-7759; 8AM-5PM (MST). *Misdemeanor, Civil Actions under $10,000, Eviction, Small Claims.* www.sccazcourts.org

General Information: No juvenile, mental health, victims, sealed or adoption records released. Will fax documents. Court makes copy: $.50 per page. Self serve copy: same. Certification fee: $24.00 per doc. Payee: Santa Cruz Justice Court. Personal checks accepted. Credit cards accepted. Prepayment required. Mail requests: SASE required.

Civil Name Search: Access: Fax, mail, in person, online. Both court and visitors may perform in person name searches. Search fee: $24.00 per name. Required to search: name, years to search; also helpful: address. Civil records go back to 1975; on computer back to 2/96. Mail turnaround time 1-3 weeks. Civil PAT goes back to 1996. Public access at http://apps.supremecourt.az.gov/publicaccess/, but sometime records are not updated frequently. Also, weekly court calendars are at www.sccazcourts.org/court_calendars.htm.

Criminal Name Search: Access: Fax, mail, in person, online. Both court and visitors may perform in person name searches. Search fee: $24.00 per name. Required to search: name, years to search, DOB; also helpful: address, SSN. Criminal records go back to 1975; on computer back to 2/96. Mail turnaround time 1-3 weeks. Criminal PAT goes back to same as civil. Public access at http://apps.supremecourt.az.gov/publicaccess/, but sometime records are not updated frequently. Also, weekly court calendars are at www.sccazcourts.org/court_calendars.htm.

Yavapai County

Superior Court Yavapai County Courthouse, Court Clerk, 120 S Cortez, Prescott, AZ 86303; 928-771-3312, 928-777-7934; fax: 928-771-3111; 8AM-5PM (MST). *Felony, Civil Actions over $10,000, Probate.* www.co.yavapai.az.us/supct.aspx

General Information: Direct search requests to the record room. No juvenile, mental health, victims, sealed or adoption records released. Will fax documents $7.00 per doc plus copy fee. Court makes copy: $.50 per page. Certification fee: $26.00 per doc. Authentication of all pages- $78.00 plus copy fee. Exemplification is $52.00. Payee: Clerk of Superior Court. Personal checks and credit cards accepted. Prepayment required. Mail requests: SASE required.

Civil Name Search: Access: Fax, mail, in person, online. Both court and visitors may perform in person name searches. Search fee: $26.00 per name and source searched. Civil records archived from 1900s. Some records on handwritten index book. Mail turnaround time 10 days. Civil PAT goes back to 1992. PAT has images, online system does not. Access to Superior Court records is free at http://apps.supremecourt.az.gov/publicaccess/.

Criminal Name Search: Access: Fax, mail, in person, online. Both court and visitors may perform in person name searches. Search fee: $26.00 per name and source searched. Required to search: name, years to search, offense. Criminal records archived from 1900s. Some records on handwritten index book. Mail turnaround time 10 days. Criminal PAT goes back to 1992. DOB, middle initial and/or address may appear on crim results, but not always on newer records. PAT has images, online system does not. Free access to Superior Court records at http://apps.supremecourt.az.gov/publicaccess. Online results show middle initial, DOB.

Bagdad Justice Court PO Box 243, Bagdad, AZ 86321; 928-633-2141; fax: 928-633-4451; 8AM-5PM M; 8:00AM-4:00PM T-TH (MST). *Misdemeanor, Civil Actions under $10,000, Eviction, Small Claims.* www.co.yavapai.az.us/LawandJustice.aspx

General Information: When a case number is given, the court also charges $24 to pull a record, but this could change. This interpretation is not per guidelines of the Administrative Offices of the Courts and is not the procedure followed in the Superior Court. No juvenile, mental health, victims, sealed or adoption records released. Will not fax documents. Court makes copy: $.50 per page. Certification fee: $24.00 per doc. Payee: Bagdad Justice Court. Only cashiers checks and money orders accepted. Visa/MC accepted. Prepayment required. Mail requests: SASE required.

Civil Name Search: Access: Mail, in person, online. Only the court performs in person name searches; visitors may not. Search fee: $24.00 per name. Required to search: name, years to search; also helpful: address. Records indexed by plaintiff name. Civil records on computer since 3/94. Records on docket books and index cards. Records purged after 10 years. Mail turnaround time 2 days. Access to the docket is free at http://apps.supremecourt.az.gov/publicaccess/.

Criminal Name Search: Access: Mail, in person, online. Only the court performs in person name searches; visitors may not. Search fee: $24.00 per name. Required to search: name, years to search, DOB; also helpful: address, SSN. Criminal records on computer since 3/94. Records on docket books and index cards. Records purged after 5 years. Mail turnaround time 2 days. Access to the docket is free at http://apps.supremecourt.az.gov/publicaccess/.

Mayer Justice Court PO Box 245, 12840 Central Ave, Mayer, AZ 86333; 928-771-3355; fax: 928-771-3356; 8AM-5PM (MST). *Misdemeanor, Civil Actions under $10,000, Eviction, Small Claims.* www.co.yavapai.az.us/LawandJustice.aspx

General Information: Search fee includes both civil and criminal indexes. No juvenile, mental health, victims, sealed or adoption records released. Will not fax documents. Court makes copy: $.50 per page. Certification fee: $24.00 per doc. Payee: Mayer Justice Court. Only cashiers checks and money orders accepted. No credit cards accepted. Prepayment required. Mail requests: SASE required.

Civil Name Search: Access: Mail, in person, online. Only the court performs in person name searches; visitors may not. Search fee: $24.00 per name. Civil records on computer back to 1989. Records purged after 5 years. Mail turnaround time 4 days. Access to the docket is free at http://apps.supremecourt.az.gov/publicaccess/.

Criminal Name Search: Access: Mail, in person, online. Only the court performs in person name searches; visitors may not. Search fee: $24.00 per name. Required to search: name, years to search; also helpful: DOB. Criminal records computerized from 1989. Records purged after 5 years. Mail turnaround time 4 days. Access to the docket is free at http://apps.supremecourt.az.gov/publicaccess/.

Prescott Justice Court Yavapai County Courthouse, 120 S Cortez, Rm 103, Prescott, AZ 86303-4747; 928-771-3300; fax: 928-771-3302; 8AM-5PM (MST). *Misdemeanor, Civil Actions under $10,000, Eviction, Small Claims.* www.prescottjpcourt.com

General Information: No juvenile, victims or sealed records released. Will not fax out documents. Court makes copy: $.50 per page. Certification fee: $24.00 per doc. Payee: City of Prescott. No 2-party checks accepted. Visa/MC accepted. Prepayment required. Mail requests: SASE required.

Civil Name Search: Access: Fax, mail, in person, online. Both court and visitors may perform in person name searches. Search fee: $24.00 per name. Required to search: name, years to search; also helpful: address. Civil

records are indexed on computer then purged after 5 years. Note: Court only provides searches for past 5 years. Mail turnaround time 2 days. Access to City and Justice court records is free at www.prescottjpcourt.com/csp/pcc/csp1.csp.

Criminal Name Search: Access: Fax, mail, in person, online. Both court and visitors may perform in person name searches. Search fee: $24.00. Required to search: name, years to search, DOB; also helpful: address, SSN. Criminal records are indexed on computer then purged after 5 years. Note: Court only provides searches for past 5 years. Mail turnaround time 2 days. Access to City Court and Justice Court records is free at www.prescottjpcourt.com/csp/pcc/csp1.csp. Online results show middle initial, DOB.

Seligman Justice Court PO Box 56, 54150 N Floyd St, Seligman, AZ 86337-0056; 928-422-3281; fax: 928-442-5982; 8AM-5PM (MST). *Misdemeanor, Civil Actions under $10,000, Eviction, Small Claims.* www.co.yavapai.az.us/LawandJustice.aspx

General Information: No juvenile or victims records released. Will fax back documents no add'l fee. Court makes copy: $.10 per page. Certification fee: $24.00 per doc. Payee: Seligman Justice Court. Business checks accepted. Visa/MC and other cards accepted. Prepayment required. Mail requests: SASE required.

Civil Name Search: Access: Phone, fax, mail, in person, online. Both court and visitors may perform in person name searches. No search fee. Required to search: name, years to search; also helpful: address. Civil records on computer. Records purged after 5 years. Mail turnaround time 2 days. Access to the docket is free at http://apps.supremecourt.az.gov/publicaccess/.

Criminal Name Search: Access: Phone, fax, mail, in person, online. Both court and visitors may perform in person name searches. No search fee. Required to search: name, years to search, DOB; also helpful: address, SSN. Criminal records on computer. Records purged after 5 years. Mail turnaround time 2 days. Access to the docket is free at http://apps.supremecourt.az.gov/publicaccess/.

Verde Valley Justice Court 10 S 6th St, Cottonwood, AZ 86326; 928-639-5820; fax: 928-639-5828; 8AM-5PM (MST). *Misdemeanor, Civil Actions under $10,000, Eviction, Small Claims.* www.co.yavapai.az.us/VVJC.aspx

General Information: When a case number is given, the court also charges $24 per name to pull a record, but this could change. This interpretation is not per guidelines of the Administrative Offices of the Courts and is not the procedure followed in the Superior Court. No juvenile, mental health, victims, sealed records released. Will not fax documents. Court makes copy: $.50 per page. Certification fee: $24.00 per doc. Payee: Verde Valley Justice Court. Personal checks accepted. Credit cards accepted. Prepayment required. Mail requests: SASE required.

Civil Name Search: Access: Mail, in person, online. Only the court performs in person name searches; visitors may not. Search fee: $24.00 per name; up to 10 searches per person. Required to search: name, years to search; also helpful: DOB. Civil cases indexed by plaintiff. Civil records on computer from 6/99. Records purged after 5 years. Mail turnaround time 2 days. Access to the docket is free at http://apps.supremecourt.az.gov/publicaccess/.

Criminal Name Search: Access: Mail, in person, online. Only the court performs in person name searches; visitors may not. Search fee: $24.00 per search; up to 10 searches per person. Required to search: name, years to search, DOB; also helpful: address, SSN. Criminal records computerized since 6/99. Records purged after 5 years. Mail turnaround time 2 days. Access to the docket is free at http://apps.supremecourt.az.gov/publicaccess/.

Yarnell Justice Court PO Box 65, Justice Court Bldg, Yarnell, AZ 85362; 928-427-3318; fax: 928-771-3362; 8AM-5PM (MST). *Misdemeanor, Civil Actions under $10,000, Eviction, Small Claims.* www.co.yavapai.az.us/LawandJustice.aspx

General Information: No juvenile, mental health, victims, sealed or adoption records released. Will fax out documents $.50 per page. Court makes copy: $.50 per page. Certification fee: $24.00 per doc. Payee: Yarnell Justice Court. Only cashiers checks and money orders accepted. Visa/MC accepted. Prepayment required. Mail requests: SASE required.

Civil Name Search: Access: Mail, in person, online. Only the court performs in person name searches; visitors may not. Search fee: $24.00 per name. Civil records on computer from 1989. Prior records on docket books. Records purged after 10 years. Mail turnaround time 5 days. Access to the docket is free at http://apps.supremecourt.az.gov/publicaccess/.

Criminal Name Search: Access: Mail, in person, online. Only the court performs in person name searches; visitors may not. Search fee: $24.00 per name. Criminal records computerized from 1989, prior on docket books. Records purged after 5 years. Mail turnaround time 5 days. Access to the docket is free at http://apps.supremecourt.az.gov/publicaccess/. Also, view current warrants, sentencing's and felony complaints at www.co.yavapai.az.us/VVJC.aspx. Online results show middle initial, DOB.

Yuma County

Superior Court 250 W 2nd St, #B, Yuma, AZ 85364; 928-817-4210; fax: 928-817-4211; 8AM-5PM (MST). *Felony, Civil Actions over $5,000, Probate.*

www.yumacountyaz.gov/index.aspx?page=125

General Information: No adoption, mental health records released. Will fax documents for $26.00 per doc. Court makes copy: $.50 per page. Certification fee: $26.00 per doc. Payee: Clerk of Superior Court. Business checks and money orders accepted. Visa/MC accepted. Prepayment required. Mail requests: SASE not required, but $5.00 shipping & handling fee.

Civil Name Search: Access: Fax, mail, in person, online. Both court and visitors may perform in person name searches. Search fee: $26.00 per name per year. Civil index in docket books from 1900s, new and pending cases from 11/1994 on computer. Mail turnaround time 7-10 days. Civil PAT goes back to 1995. Results include name (first, last) and case number. Access to the docket is free at http://apps.supremecourt.az.gov/publicaccess/.

Criminal Name Search: Access: Fax, mail, in person, online. Both court and visitors may perform in person name searches. Search fee: $26.00 per name. Criminal docket on books from 1900s, new and pending cases from 11/1994 on computer. Mail turnaround time 1 week to 10 days . Criminal PAT goes back to same as civil. Results include name (first, last) and case number. Access to the docket is free at http://apps.supremecourt.az.gov/publicaccess/. Online results show middle initial, DOB.

Somerton-San Luis Justice Court PO Box 7650, 1358 E Liberty St, San Luis, AZ 85349; 928-314-5100; fax: 928-314-5105; 8AM-5PM (MST). *Misdemeanor, Civil Actions under $10,000, Eviction, Small Claims.*

www.yumacountyaz.gov/index.aspx?page=588

General Information: No set aside judgment records released. Will fax documents $.50 per page. Court makes copy: $.50 per page. Certification fee: $24.00 per doc. Payee: Somerton Justice Court. Business checks accepted. Visa/MC accepted. Prepayment required. Mail requests: SASE required.

Civil Name Search: Access: Phone, fax, mail, in person, online. Both court and visitors may perform in person name searches. Search fee: $24.00 per name. Civil cases indexed by defendant. Civil records on computer. Mail turnaround time 7-10 days. Online access to records is free the website above as well as at http://apps.supremecourt.az.gov/publicaccess/.

Criminal Name Search: Access: Phone, fax, mail, in person, online. Only the court performs in person name searches; visitors may not. Search fee: $24.00 per name. Required to search: name, years to search, DOB, SSN, offense, date of offense. Criminal records on computer. Mail turnaround time 2-4 days. Access records free at the website above as well at www.supreme.state.az.us/publicaccess/.

Wellton Justice Court PO Box 384, Wellton, AZ 85356; 928-785-3321; fax: 928-785-4933; 8AM-5PM (MST). *Misdemeanor, Civil Actions under $10,000, Eviction, Small Claims.*

www.yumacountyaz.gov/index.aspx?page=588

General Information: When a case number is given, the court may charge $24 to pull a record depending on clerk, but could change. This interpretation is not per guidelines of the Administrative Offices of the Courts and is not the procedure followed in the Superior Court. No set aside judgment records released. Will fax documents to local or toll free line. Court makes copy: $.50 per page. Certification fee: $24.00 per doc. Payee: Wellton Justice Court. Personal checks accepted. All major credit cards accepted. Prepayment required.

Civil Name Search: Access: Phone, fax, mail, in person, online. Only the court performs in person name searches; visitors may not. No search fee. Civil records on computer to 1992. Mail turnaround time same day. Access to the docket is free at http://apps.supremecourt.az.gov/publicaccess/.

Criminal Name Search: Access: Phone, fax, mail, in person, online. Only the court performs in person name searches; visitors may not. No search fee. Required to search: name, years to search, offense, date of offense. Criminal records on computer to 1992. Mail turnaround time same day. Access to the docket is free at http://apps.supremecourt.az.gov/publicaccess/.

Yuma Justice Court 250 W 2nd St, #A, Yuma, AZ 85364; 928-817-4100; fax: 928-817-4101; 8AM-5PM (MST). *Misdemeanor, Civil Actions under $10,000, Eviction, Small Claims.*

www.yumacountyaz.gov/index.aspx?page=588

General Information: When a case number is given, the court also charges a $24 fee to pull a record, but this could change. This interpretation is not per guidelines of the Administrative Offices of the Courts and is not the procedure followed in the Superior Court. Court will not release victim's names. Will not fax documents. Court makes copy: $.50 per page. Certification fee: $24.00 per doc. Payee: Justice Court #1. Personal checks accepted. No credit cards accepted. Prepayment required. Mail requests: SASE required.

Civil Name Search: Access: Mail, in person, online. Both court and visitors may perform in person name searches. Search fee: $24.00 per name. Civil cases indexed by defendant. Civil records on computer. Purged after 5 years. Info available only for cases after 9/01/97; computerized records since 1997. Mail turnaround time 2-4 days. Civil PAT goes back to 1994. Access to the docket is free at http://apps.supremecourt.az.gov/publicaccess/.

Criminal Name Search: Access: Mail, in person, online. Both court and visitors may perform in person name searches. Search fee: $24.00 per name. Criminal records on computer. Purged after 5 years. Info available only for cases after 9/01/97; computerized records since 1997. Mail turnaround time 2-4 days. Criminal PAT available. Access to the docket is free at http://apps.supremecourt.az.gov/publicaccess/

Common Abbreviations Found in Text

- **DL**   Driver's license
- **PAT**   Public use access terminal
- **SASE**   Self-addressed, stamped envelope
- **SSN**   Social Security Number

Arkansas

Time Zone:	**CST**
Capital:	**Little Rock, Pulaski County**
# of Counties:	**75**
State Web:	**www.arkansas.gov**
Court Web:	**www.courts.state.ar.us**

Administration	Administrative Office of Courts, 625 Marshall St, Ste 1100, Little Rock, AR, 72201; 501-682-9400, 501-682-6849, Fax: 501-682-9410.
The Supreme and Appellate Courts	The Arkansas Supreme Court has general superintending control over all courts of the state. The Court of Appeals has 7 districts. Opinions from 2009 forward are available online at the home page.

The Arkansas Courts

Court	Type	How Organized	Jurisdiction Highpoints
Circuit*	General	85 Courts in 28 Circuits	Felony, Misdemeanor, Civil, Small Claims, Juvenile, Traffic, Eviction, Domestic Relations, Estates
State District*	Limited	29 Court locations profiled	Misdemeanor, Civil to $25,000, Small Claims
Local District*	Limited	127 Court locations profiled	Misdemeanor, Civil to $5,000, Small Claims
City	Limited	91 Locations – Will be closing and converted	Ordinance

* = profiled in this book

Details on the Court Structure	**Circuit Courts** are the courts of general jurisdiction and are arranged in 28 circuits. Note that circuits number only to 23, but some numeric circuits have multiple circuits – such as 11W and 11E. Circuit Courts consist of five subject matter divisions: criminal, civil, probate, domestic relations, and juvenile. The Circuit clerks who are the keepers of records of Circuit Court also serve as the country recorder of deeds and other instruments; however some counties have a County Clerk that handles probate.

District Courts, formerly known as Municipal Courts, exercise countywide jurisdiction over misdemeanor cases, preliminary felony cases, and civil cases in matters of less than $5,000, including small claims.

The state is in the midst of a major transition. There are **State District Courts** and **Local District Courts**, depending on which agency pays the judge (state or local). Local District courts hear civil cases with a limit of $5,000. State District Courts hear civil cases with a limit of $25,000.

The **City Courts** exercise citywide jurisdiction and operate in smaller communities where District Courts do not exist.

About The Transition – All City Courts will be closed or combined with Local District Courts by January 1, 2012. Also, over time some Local District Courts will be closed or combined with State District Courts. This event will be accomplished by 2017. To view details, see Act 1219 at www.arkleg.state.ar.us/assembly/2011/2011R/Acts/Act1219.pdf.

Record Searching Facts You Need to Know

Fees and Record Searching Tips

Many courts that allow written search requests require an SASE. Fees vary widely across jurisdictions as do prepayment requirements. Less than half of the courts charge a search fee, which can vary from $1.00 to $10.00. Both the Circuit and District Courts in the participating counties (indicated in the individual court's profile) should be searched if a true countywide search is needed.

Online Access is Limited

A handful of counties offer online access. One new system offered by the AOC has Circuit Courts in with six counties participating, with plans to add more over time. See https://arep2.aoc.arkansas.gov/cconnect/PROD/public/ck_public_qry_main.cp_main_idx.

Arkansas County

Circuit Court - Northern District 302 S College St, Stuttgart, AR 72160; 870-673-2056; probate phone: 870-673-7311; fax: 870-673-3869; 8AM-4:30PM (CST). *Felony, Civil Actions, Probate.* www.arcocircuitclerk.com/

General Information: The court is not bonded to search Civil or Chancery records. Probate has a different Clerk. No juvenile records released. Will fax documents $1.00 fee per page. Will email return $1.00 per page. Court makes copy: $.50 per page. Self serve copy: same. Certification fee: $5.00 per doc plus copy fee. Payee: Arkansas Circuit Clerk. Personal checks accepted. No credit cards accepted. Prepayment required.

Civil Name Search: Access: In person, online. Visitors must perform in person searches themselves. Civil records in files from 1913. Civil PAT goes back to 2004. Click on document search from the home page. Although this service leads to Title Searcher, the court has placed court records on this system. There is a monthly fee of $70.00 for unlimited searching and a $3.00 fee to view an image. Images are available from 2005, the docket index goes back to 1996. Includes both Districts in this county.

Criminal Name Search: Access: In person, online. Visitors must perform in person searches themselves. Required to search: name, years to search, DOB. Criminal records in files from 1913, earlier records located in DeWitt. Criminal PAT goes back to same as civil. Click on document search from the home page. Although this service leads to Title Searcher, the court has placed court records on this system. There is a monthly fee of $70.00 for unlimited searching and a $3.00 fee to view an image. Images are available from 2005, the docket index goes back to 1996. Includes both Districts in this county.

Circuit Court - Southern District 101 Courthouse Sq, De Witt, AR 72042; 870-946-4219; fax: 870-946-1394; 8AM-4:30PM (CST). *Felony, Civil Actions over $5,000.* www.arcocircuitclerk.com/

General Information: No longer performs current records searches. Court will honor written requests to do searches for genealogy purposes for $10.00 base rate per search. No juvenile, expunged records released. Will not fax documents. Court makes copy: $.50 per page. Self serve copy: same. Certification fee: $5.00 per doc plus copy fee. Payee: Arkansas County Circuit Clerk. Personal checks accepted. No credit cards accepted. Prepayment required.

Civil Name Search: Access: In person only. Visitors must perform in person searches themselves. Civil records in files from 1923, computerized since 1995, prior records (the two other courts in this county also) located at this court. Civil PAT goes back to 1996. Click on document search from the home page. Although this service leads to Title Searcher, the court has placed court records on this system. There is a monthly fee of $70.00 for unlimited searching and a $3.00 fee to view an image. Images are available from 2005, the docket index goes back to 1996. Includes both Districts in this county.

Criminal Name Search: Access: In person, online. Visitors must perform in person searches themselves. Required to search: name, DOB; also helpful: SSN. Criminal records in files from 1923, computerized since 1995, prior records (the two other courts in this county also) located at this court. Criminal PAT goes back to same as civil. Results include name and case number. Click on document search from the home page. Although this service leads to Title Searcher, the court has placed court records on this system. There is a monthly fee of $70.00 for unlimited searching and a $3.00 fee to view an image. Images are available from 2005, the docket index goes back to 1996. Includes both Districts in this county.

DeWitt Local District Court 120 Court Square, DeWitt, AR 72042; 870-946-2503; fax: 870-946-1005; 8AM-4:30PM (CST). *Misdemeanor, Civil Actions under $5,000, Eviction, Small Claims.*

Stuttgart Local District Court 304 S Maple, Stuttgart, AR 72160; 870-673-7951; fax: 870-673-6522; 8AM-4:30PM (CST). *Misdemeanor, Civil Actions under $5,000, Eviction, Small Claims.*

General Information: Court clerk location is 514 S Main. Will fax documents to local or toll-free number. Court makes copy: None. No certification fee . Personal checks accepted. No credit cards accepted. Mail requests: SASE required.

Ashley County

Circuit Court Ashley County Courthouse, 205 E Jefferson, Hamburg, AR 71646; 870-853-2030; probate phone: 870-853-2020; fax: 870-853-2034; 8AM-4:30PM (CST). *Felony, Civil Actions over $5,000, Probate.*

General Information: Probate records managed by the county clerk office. No juvenile records released. Fee to fax out file $1.00 per page. Court makes copy: $.50 per page. Self serve copy: same. Certification fee: $2.50 per doc plus copy fee per page. Payee: Circuit Clerk's Office. Personal checks accepted. No credit cards accepted. Prepayment required. Mail requests: SASE required.

Civil Name Search: Access: Mail, in person. Visitors must perform in person searches themselves. Search fee: $5.00 per name. Civil records on files and index cards from 1950s. Mail turnaround time 2 days. Civil PAT available.

Criminal Name Search: Access: Mail, in person. Visitors must perform in person searches themselves. Search fee: $5.00 per name. Required to search: name, years to search; also helpful: DOB, SSN. Criminal records on files and index cards from 1950s. Mail turnaround time 2 days. Criminal PAT available.

Crossett Local District Court PO Box 459, 307 Main St, Crossett, AR 71635; 870-364-7620; fax: 870-364-6144; 8AM-4:30PM (CST). *Misdemeanor, Civil Actions under $5,000, Small Claims, Traffic.*

Hamburg Local District Court PO Box 72, 305 W Adams, Hamburg, AR 71646; 870-853-8326; fax: 870-853-5433; 8AM-4:30PM (CST). *Misdemeanor, Civil Actions under $5,000, Eviction, Small Claims, Traffic.*

General Information: Will not fax documents. Court makes copy: $.50 per page. Self serve copy: same. Certification fee: $10.00 per doc. Payee: District Court. No personal checks or credit cards accepted. Prepayment required.

Baxter County

Circuit Court One E 7th St, Rm 103, Courthouse Square, Mountain Home, AR 72653; 870-425-3475; fax: 870-424-5105; 8AM-4:30PM (CST). *Felony, Civil Actions over $25,000, Probate.*

General Information: Probate records managed by the county clerk office. No adoption or juvenile records released. Will fax documents $5.00 per page. Court makes copy: $.25 per page. Certification fee: $5.00 per doc. Payee: Baxter County Clerk. Personal checks accepted. No credit cards accepted. Prepayment required.

Civil Name Search: Access: In person. Both court and visitors may perform in person name searches. No search fee. Civil records on computer from 1982. Civil PAT goes back to 1982.

Criminal Name Search: Access: In person. Both court and visitors may perform in person name searches. No search fee. Required to search: name, years to search, SSN. Criminal records computerized from 1982, on criminal fee book from early 1900s. Criminal PAT goes back to same as civil. Results include case number.

BriarCliff City Court 945 Scenic Drive, Briarcliff, AR 72653; 870-491-5762; fax: 870-491-5772; 8AM-4:30PM (CST). *Misdemeanor, Ordinances.*

Lakeview District Court 14 Skyles Lane, Lakeview, AR 72642; 870-431-8744; fax: 870-431-8800; 9AM-12 M-TH (CST). *Misdemeanor.*

Norfork State District Court PO Box 239, Norfork, AR 72658; 870-499-5225; fax: 870-499-5224; 8AM-4:30PM (CST). *Misdemeanor, Civil Actions under $25,000, Eviction, Small Claims.*

General Information: The case limit on civil records was raised to $25,000 as of 01/01/2008.

Mountain Home State District Court 301 E 6th St #130, Mountain Home, AR 72653; 870-425-3140; criminal phone: 870-425-3140; civil phone: 870-425-8910; fax: 870-425-8470; 8AM-4:30PM (CST). *Misdemeanor, Civil Actions under $25,000, Eviction, Small Claims.*

General Information: Will not fax documents. Court makes copy: $.25 per page. Certification fee: $5.00 per doc. Payee: Baxter County District Court. Personal checks accepted. No credit cards accepted. Prepayment required.

Cotter State District Court PO Box 9, Cotter, AR 72626-0009; 870-435-2122; fax: 870-435-2438; 8AM-4:30PM (CST). *Misdemeanor, Civil Actions under $25,000, Eviction.*

General Information: The case limit on civil records was raised to $25,000 as of 01/01/2008.

Gassville State District Court PO Box 28, Gassville, AR 72635; 870-435-6439; fax: 870-435-6276; 8AM-4:30PM (CST). *Misdemeanor, Civil Actions under $25,000, Eviction, Small Claims.*

General Information: The case limit on civil records was raised to $25,000 as of 01/01/2008.

Benton County

Circuit Court 102 NE "A" St, Bentonville, AR 72712; 479-271-1015; probate phone: 479-271-5727; fax: 479-271-5719; 8AM-4:30PM (CST). *Felony, Civil Actions over $25,000, Probate.*

www.co.benton.ar.us/CircuitClerk/Default.aspx

General Information: Probate records managed by the County Clerk at 215 E Central St, Rm 206, phone # 479-271-5727. The case limit on civil records was raised to $25,000 as of 01/01/2008. Online identifiers in results same as on public terminal. No juvenile records released. Will fax documents to local or toll free line. Court makes copy: $.25 per page. Self serve copy: same. Certification fee: $5.00 plus copy fee. Payee: Benton County Circuit Clerk. Personal checks accepted. No credit cards accepted. Prepayment required. Mail requests: SASE required.

Civil Name Search: Access: Mail, in person, online. Visitors must perform in person searches themselves. No search fee. Civil records on computer from 1991, on dockets from 1880s. Civil PAT goes back to 1987. Shows only index from this court. Search civil court docket information free at http://records.co.benton.ar.us:5061/

Criminal Name Search: Access: Mail, online, in person. Visitors must perform in person searches themselves. No search fee. Required to search: name, years to search. Criminal records computerized from 1991, on dockets from 1880s. Note: This court suggests to direct search requests to AR State Police. Mail turnaround time 24 hours. Criminal PAT goes back to same as civil. Shows only index from this court. Search criminal court docket information free at http://records.co.benton.ar.us:5061/ Online results show middle initial, DOB.

Bentonville State District Court 2706 S Walton Blvd, Bentonville, AR 72712; criminal phone: 479-271-3120; civil phone: 479-271-3121; fax: 479-271-3134; 8AM-4:30PM (CST). *Misdemeanor, Civil Actions under $25,000, Small Claims.*

www.bentonvillear.com/district_court_main.html

General Information: Small claims limit is $5000. No sealed or expunged records released. Will fax documents to local or toll free line. Court makes copy: $.25 per page non-certified. Certification fee: $5.00 per doc includes copy fee. Payee: Bentonville District Court. Personal checks accepted. No out of state checks accepted. No credit cards accepted. Prepayment required. Mail requests: SASE required.

Civil Name Search: Access: Mail, in person. Only the court performs in person name searches; visitors may not. No search fee. Required to search: name, address, DOB, SSN. Civil records on computer back to 1995; paper/microfilm records go back to 1989. Mail turnaround time 5 days.

Criminal Name Search: Access: Mail, in person. Only the court performs in person name searches; visitors may not. No search fee. Required to search: name, years to search, DOB. Criminal records computerized from 1992; other records go back to 1982. Mail turnaround time 5 days.

Bethel Heights State District Court 530 Sunrise Dr, Bethel Heights, AR 72764; 479-751-7481 x20; fax: 479-750-1698; 8AM-4:30PM (CST). *Misdemeanor, Traffic.*

Cave Springs State District Court PO Box 36, Cave Springs, AR 72718; 479-248-1040: 8AM-5PM (CST). *Misdemeanor.*

General Information: Will fax documents to local or toll free line. Court makes copy: $.25 per page non-certified. Self serve copy: same. Certification fee: $5.00 per doc includes copy fee. Payee: Cave Springs District Court. Personal checks accepted. No out of state checks accepted. Major credit cards accepted. Prepayment required. Mail requests: SASE required.

Centerton State District Court PO Box 100, 753 W Centerton Blvd, Centerton, AR 72719; 479-795-4431; fax: 479-795-2545; 8AM-5PM (CST). *Misdemeanor, Civil Actions under $25,000, Small Claims.*

www.centertonar.us/page_display.asp?pid=3

General Information: The case limit on civil records was raised to $25,000 as of 01/01/2008. Court Clerk can be reached at centertoncourt@cox-internet.com.

Gentry State District Court PO Box 459, Gentry, AR 72734; 479-736-8579; fax: 479-736-8743; 8AM-4:30PM, closed N-1PM (CST). *Misdemeanor, Civil Actions under $25,000, Small Claims.*

General Information: Will fax documents to local or toll free line. Court makes copy: $.25 per page non-certified. Self serve copy: same. Certification fee: $3.00 per doc includes copy fee. Payee: Bentonville District Court. Personal checks accepted. No out of state checks accepted. No credit cards accepted. Prepayment required. Mail requests: SASE required.

Gravette State District Court 604 1st Ave, Gravette, AR 72736; 479-787-5757; fax: 479-787-5018; 8AM-4:30PM (CST). *Misdemeanor, Civil Actions under $25,000, Small Claims.*

General Information: The case limit on civil records was raised to $25,000 as of 01/01/2008.

Little Flock State District Court 1500 Little Flock DR, Rogers, AR 72756; 479-636-2081; fax: 479-636-2318; 8AM-4:30PM (CST). *Misdemeanor.*

General Information: The case limit on civil records was raised to $25,000 as of 01/01/2008.

Lowell State District Court 214 N Lincoln, Lowell, AR 72745; 479-770-0166 ext 2; fax: 479-659-0894; 8AM-4:30PM (CST). *Misdemeanor, Civil Actions under $25,000, Small Claims.*

www.lowellarkansas.gov/departments/city-court/

General Information: The case limit on civil records was raised to $25,000 as of 01/01/2008 (as were all the lower District Courts listed below).

Pea Ridge State District Court PO Box 10, Pea Ridge, AR 72751; 479-451-1101; fax: 479-451-1681; 8AM-4:30PM (CST). *Misdemeanor, Civil Actions under $25,000, Small Claims.*

Rogers State District Court 1901 S Dixieland, Rogers, AR 72758; 479-621-1132; fax: 479-621-1136; 8AM-4:30PM (CST). *Misdemeanor, Civil Actions under $25,000, Small Claims.*

Siloam Springs State District Court PO Box 80, Siloam Springs, AR 72761; 479-524-4947; fax: 479-238-0995; 8AM-4:30PM (CST). *Misdemeanor, Civil Actions under $25,000, Small Claims.*

www.siloamsprings.com/departments/court/index.php

Sulphur Springs State District Court PO Box 145, Sulphur Springs, AR 72768; 479-298-3103; fax: 479-298-3515; 8AM-4:30PM (CST). *Misdemeanor, Civil Actions under $25,000, Small Claims.*

Boone County

Circuit Court 100 N Main St #200, Harrison, AR 72601; 870-741-5560; fax: 870-741-4335; 8AM-4:30PM (CST). *Felony, Civil Actions over $25,000.*

https://gov.propertyinfo.com/ar-boone/

General Information: Probate records are in the County Clerk's office, 870-741-8428. The case limit on civil records was raised to $25,000 as of 01/01/2008. No indictments or juvenile records released. Fee to fax out file $5.00 each. Court makes copy: $.25 per page. Self serve copy: same. Certification fee: $5.00. Payee: Circuit Clerk. Personal checks accepted. No credit cards accepted. Prepayment required. Mail requests: SASE required for mail return of any copies.

Civil Name Search: Access: In person. Visitors must perform in person searches themselves. Civil records archived from 1940, index from 1977, computerized from 1990. Civil PAT goes back to 1997.

Criminal Name Search: Access: In person. Both court and visitors may perform in person name searches. No search fee. Required to search: name, years to search. Criminal records archived from 1940, index from 1977, computerized from 1990. Criminal PAT goes back to same as civil. Online results show name only.

Alpena State District Court PO Box 500, Alpena, AR 72611; 870-437-2272; fax: 870-437-5437; 8AM-4:30PM (CST). *Misdemeanor, Traffic, Criminal.*

General Information: The case limit on civil records was raised to $25,000 as of 01/01/2008.

Harrison State District Court PO Box 968, Harrison, AR 72602; 870-741-2788; fax: 870-741-4329; 8AM-4:30PM (CST). *Misdemeanor, Civil Actions under $25,000, Eviction, Small Claims.*

General Information: Will fax documents $1.00 per page. Court makes copy: $.25 per page. Self serve copy: $.25 per copy. Certification fee: $5.00 per doc. Payee: Boone County District Court. No personal checks accepted.

No credit cards accepted for copies or record searches. Prepayment required. Mail requests: SASE required.

Civil Name Search: Access: Mail, in person. Both court and visitors may perform in person name searches. No search fee. Required to search: name and years to search. Civil cases indexed by Defendant, Plaintiff. Records indexed since 1997. Mail turnaround time 2 weeks.

Criminal Name Search: Access: Mail, fax, in person. Both court and visitors may perform in person name searches. No search fee. Required to search: name, years to search; also helpful: DOB. Records indexed since 1997 on computer. Mail turnaround time 2 weeks.

Alpena State District Court PO Box 500, Alpena, AR 72611; 870-437-2272; fax: 870-437-5437; 8AM-4:30PM (CST). *Misdemeanor, Traffic, Criminal.*

General Information: The case limit on civil records was raised to $25,000 as of 01/01/2008.

Bradley County

Circuit Court Bradley County Courthouse - Records, 101 E Cedar, Warren, AR 71671; 870-226-2272; probate phone: 870-226-3464; fax: 870-226-8404; 8AM-4:30PM (CST). *Felony, Civil Actions over $5,000, Probate.*

General Information: Probate records are handled by the County Clerk, who can be reached thru the number above. No juvenile released. Will not fax documents. Court makes copy: $.50 per page. Self serve copy: $.50 per page. Certification fee: $5.00. Payee: Circuit Court. Personal checks accepted. No credit cards accepted.

Civil Name Search: Access: In person only. Visitors must perform in person searches themselves. Civil records (active cases) on dockets, retired cases on indexes from 1880, no computerization.

Criminal Name Search: Access: In person only. Visitors must perform in person searches themselves. Required to search: name, years to search; also helpful: DOB, SSN. Criminal records (active cases) on dockets, retired cases on indexes from 1880, no computerization.

Local District Court PO Box 352, 101 Myrtle, City Hall, Warren, AR 71671; 870-226-2567; fax: 870-226-8305; 8AM-4:30PM (CST). *Misdemeanor, Civil Actions under $5,000, Eviction, Small Claims.*

General Information: Search fee includes both the civil and criminal indexes. Will fax back documents for no fee. Court makes copy: included in search fee. Certification fee: Search fee includes certification. Payee: Bradley County District Court. No personal checks or credit cards accepted. Prepayment required. Mail requests: SASE required.

Civil Name Search: Access: Mail, in person. Both court and visitors may perform in person name searches. Search fee: $6.00 per name. Required to search: name; also helpful address, other names used, case number. Computerized records since 1993. Note: Only the court may search on computer; visitors may hand-search indexed records indexed by case number only. Mail turnaround time 2-3 days.

Criminal Name Search: Access: Mail, in person. Only the court performs in person name searches; visitors may not. Search fee: $6.00 per name. Required to search: name, years to search, DOB; searcher may be required to provide DR number. Computerized records since 1993, on paper since 1964. Mail turnaround time 3-5 days.

Calhoun County

Circuit Court PO Box 1175, Hampton, AR 71744; 870-798-2517; fax: 870-798-2428; 8AM-4:30PM (CST). *Felony, Civil Actions over $5,000, Probate.*

General Information: Probate records are handled by the County Clerk, who can be reached thru the number above. No juvenile or adoption released. Will fax documents $2.00. Court makes copy: $.25 per page. Self serve copy: same. Certification fee: $5.00. Payee: Calhoun County Clerk. Personal checks accepted. No credit cards accepted. Prepayment required. Mail requests: SASE required.

Civil Name Search: Access: Mail, in person. Only the court performs in person name searches; visitors may not. Search fee: $6.00. Civil records on dockets from 1851. Mail turnaround time 1-3 days.

Criminal Name Search: Access: Mail, in person. Only the court performs in person name searches; visitors may not. Search fee: $6.00. Required to search: name, years to search, DOB; also helpful: SSN. Criminal docket index from 1851. Mail turnaround time 1-3 days.

Local District Court PO Box 783, 121 N 2nd St, Courthouse, Hampton, AR 71744; 870-798-2753; criminal phone: 870-798-4610; civil phone: 870-798-2165; fax: 870-798-3201; 8AM-4:30PM (CST). *Misdemeanor, Civil Actions under $5,000, Eviction, Small Claims.*

General Information: Separate PO Box for civil court - PO Box 864. Archives located across street. Phone city's Municipal Clerk at 870-798-3201. Will fax documents. Court makes copy: $10.00 per document. Certification fee: $5.00 per doc. Payee: Hampton Police Dept. No personal checks or credit cards accepted. Mail requests: SASE requested.

Civil Name Search: Access: Mail, in person. Both court and visitors may perform in person name searches. Search fee: $5.00 per name. Required to search: name, years to search; SSN helpful. Records on computer back to 1998. Mail turnaround time 2 days.

Criminal Name Search: Access: Mail, in person. Both court and visitors may perform in person name searches. Search fee: $5.00 per name. Required to search: name, years to search; SSN helpful. Records on computer back to 1998. Mail turnaround time 2 days.

Carroll County

Berryville Circuit Court - Eastern District Carroll County Circuit Court, PO Box 71, Berryville, AR 72616; 870-423-2422; probate phone: 870-423-2022; fax: 870-423-4796; 8:30AM-4:30PM (CST). *Felony, Civil Actions over $5,000, Eviction, Probate.*

General Information: Probate handled by county clerk at 210 W Church Ave. Probate fax- 870-423-7400. No juvenile records released. Fee to fax out file $1.00 per page for either receiving or sending. Court makes copy: $.25 per page; $.50 per page if mailed. Self serve copy: $.25 per page. Certification fee: $5.00 per doc. Payee: Circuit Clerk of Carroll County. Personal checks accepted. No credit cards accepted. Prepayment required. Mail requests: SASE required.

Civil Name Search: Access: Mail, in person. Both court and visitors may perform in person name searches. Search fee: $6.00 per name. Civil records on computer from 1997, on index books since 1869. Mail turnaround time same or next day. Civil PAT goes back to 1997.

Criminal Name Search: Access: Fax, mail, in person. Both court and visitors may perform in person name searches. Search fee: $6.00 per name. Required to search: name, years to search, DOB, SSN. Criminal records computerized from 1997, on index books since 1869. Mail turnaround time 1-2 days. Criminal PAT goes back to same as civil. Online results show name only.

Eureka Springs Circuit Court - Western District 44 S Main, PO Box 109, Eureka Springs, AR 72632; 479-253-8646; fax: 479-253-6013; 8:30AM-4:30PM (CST). *Felony, Civil Actions over $5,000, Eviction, Probate.*

General Information: Probate records are handled by the County Clerk, who can be reached thru the number above. No expunged criminal records released. Fee to fax out file $1.00 per page. Court makes copy: $.50 per page. Self serve copy: $.25 per page. Certification fee: $5.00 per doc. Payee: Circuit Clerk of Carroll County or County Clerk. Personal checks accepted. No credit cards accepted. Prepayment required. Mail requests: SASE required for criminal.

Civil Name Search: Access: In person only. Visitors must perform in person searches themselves. Required to search: name, years to search. Civil records on indexes from 1883.

Criminal Name Search: Access: Phone, mail, in person. Both court and visitors may perform in person name searches. Search fee: $6.00 per name. Required to search: name, years to search; also helpful: DOB. Criminal records on indexes from 1883, computerized since 2/21/02. Mail turnaround time varies. Public use terminal has crim records. Public terminal has recent criminal cases only.

Berryville Eastern Local District Court 103 S Springs, Berryville, AR 72616; 870-423-6247; fax: 870-423-7069; 8AM-4:30PM (CST). *Misdemeanor, Civil Actions under $5,000, Small Claims.*

General Information: Will fax documents to local or toll-free number. Court makes copy: $.25 per page. No personal checks or credit cards accepted.

Civil Name Search: Access: Mail, fax, in person. Only the court performs in person name searches; visitors may not. No search fee. Required to search: name, DOB. Records computerized since 1987. Mail turnaround time 1-2 days.

Criminal Name Search: Access: Mail, in person. Only the court performs in person name searches; visitors may not. No search fee. Required to search: name, years to search; also helpful: DOB. Records computerized since 1987. Mail turnaround time 1-2 days.

Eureka Springs Western Local District Court Courthouse, 44 S Main, Eureka Springs, AR 72632; 479-253-8574; fax: 479-253-6887; 8AM-5PM (CST). *Misdemeanor, Civil Actions under $5,000, Small Claims.*

www.cityofeurekasprings.org

General Information: Will fax documents to local or toll-free number. Court made copy fee: none. Self serve copy: Civil $1.00 each. No certification fee. Payee: District Court. Personal checks accepted. No credit cards accepted. Mail requests: SASE required.

Civil Name Search: Access: Phone, mail, in person. Both court and visitors may perform in person name searches. No search fee. Required to search: name. Civil cases indexed by defendant, plaintiff. Records on computer back to 1992. Mail turnaround time 1 week.

Criminal Name Search: Access: Phone, mail, in person. Both court and visitors may perform in person name searches. No search fee. Required to search: name, years to search. Criminal records computerized from 1990. Mail turnaround time 1 week.

Chicot County

Circuit Court 108 Main St, County Courthouse, Lake Village, AR 71653; 870-265-8010; probate phone: 870-265-8000: 8AM-4:30PM (CST). *Felony, Civil Actions over $5,000, Probate.*

General Information: Probate records managed by the county clerk, here in a separate office. No juvenile records released. Will fax out docs $1.00 per page. Court makes copy: $.50 per page. Self serve copy: same. Certification fee: $2.00 per doc plus copy fee. Payee: Circuit Clerk. Personal checks accepted. No credit cards accepted. Prepayment required.

Civil Name Search: Access: In person only. Both court and visitors may perform in person name searches. No search fee. Civil records on dockets and files from 1900s.

Criminal Name Search: Access: In person only. Both court and visitors may perform in person name searches. No search fee. Required to search: name, years to search. Criminal records on dockets and files from 1900s. Note: Court suggest to search at the State Police.

Lake Village Local District Court PO Box 832, Lake Village, AR 71653; 870-265-3283; fax: 870-265-5668; 9AM-4:30PM (CST). *Misdemeanor, Civil Actions under $5,000, Eviction, Small Claims.*

General Information: Will fax documents. Court makes copy: none. Certification fee: $5.00 per doc. Payee: Lake Village District Court. No personal checks or credit cards accepted. Prepayment required. Mail requests: SASE required.

Civil Name Search: Access: Mail, fax, in person. Both court and visitors may perform in person name searches. Search fee: $5.00 per name. Required to search: name, years to search, other names used; also helpful-DOB, SSN, address, signed release. Civil cases indexed by Defendant, Plaintiff. Civil records on computer go back to 10/02; other records go back to 1977. Mail turnaround time ASAP.

Criminal Name Search: Access: Mail, in person. Both court and visitors may perform in person name searches. Search fee: $5.00 per name. Required to search: name, years to search; also helpful: DOB, SSN. Criminal records on computer go back to 8/2000; other records go back to 1977. Mail turnaround time ASAP.

Dermott Department Local District Court PO Box 217, Dermott, AR 71638; 870-538-3476; fax: 870-538-3476; 9AM-4PM (CST). *Misdemeanor, Civil Actions under $5,000, Eviction, Small Claims.*

Eudora Department Local District Court 111 N Archer, Eudora, AR 71640; 870-355-2878; fax: 870-355-4914; 9AM-4:30PM (CST). *Misdemeanor, Civil Actions under $5,000, Eviction, Small Claims.*

General Information: Will fax documents. Court makes copy: $.25 per page. Certification fee: $5.00 per doc. Payee: Eudora District Court. No personal checks or credit cards accepted. Prepayment required. Mail requests: SASE required.

Civil Name Search: Access: Mail, fax, in person. Both court and visitors may perform in person name searches. Search fee: $5.00 per name. Required to search: name, years to search, other names used; also helpful-DOB, SSN, address, signed release. Civil cases indexed by Defendant, Plaintiff. Civil records on computer go back to 10/02; other records go back to 1977. Mail turnaround time ASAP.

Criminal Name Search: Access: Mail, in person. Both court and visitors may perform in person name searches. Search fee: $5.00 per name. Required to search: name, years to search; also helpful: DOB, SSN. Criminal records on computer go back to 8/2000; other records go back to 1977. Mail turnaround time ASAP.

Clark County

Circuit Court PO Box 576, Arkadelphia, AR 71923; 870-246-4281; probate phone: 870-246-4491; fax: 870-246-1419; 8:30AM-4:30PM (CST). *Felony, Civil Actions over $5,000, Probate.*

General Information: Probate records managed by the county clerk office, is a separate index, separate address. No juvenile records released. Will fax documents $1.00 per page. Court makes copy: $1.00 per page. Self serve copy: same. Certification fee: $5.00 per document plus copy fee. Payee: Martha J Smith Circuit Clerk. Personal checks accepted. No credit cards accepted. Prepayment required. Mail requests: SASE required.

Civil Name Search: Access: Mail, in person. Both court and visitors may perform in person name searches. Search fee: $5.00 per name. Civil records on computer back to 2004. Mail turnaround time 1-2 days. Civil PAT goes back to 2004.

Criminal Name Search: Access: Mail, in person. Both court and visitors may perform in person name searches. Search fee: $5.00 per name. Required to search: name, years to search. Criminal records on computer since 2004. Mail turnaround time 1-2 days. Criminal PAT goes back to same as civil.

Local District Court PO Box 449, 412 Crittenden St, Arkadelphia, AR 71923; 870-246-9552; fax: 870-246-1415; 8:30AM-4:30PM (CST). *Misdemeanor, Civil Actions under $5,000, Eviction, Small Claims.*

General Information: Will fax documents to local or toll-free number. Court makes copy: none. No certification fee . No personal checks or credit cards accepted.

Civil Name Search: Access: In person only. Both court and visitors may perform in person name searches. No search fee. Required to search: name, DOB, SSN, signed release, other names used; also helpful-DL number. Civil cases indexed by defendant, plaintiff. Records go back to 1980; on computer since 1990.

Criminal Name Search: Access: In person. Both court and visitors may perform in person name searches. No search fee. Required to search: name, years to search; also helpful: DOB. Records go back to 1980; on computer since 1990.

Clay County

Corning Circuit Court 800 SW 2nd St, Corning, AR 72422-2715; 870-857-3221; probate phone: 870-857-3480; fax: 870-857-9201; 8AM-4:30PM (CST). *Felony, Civil Actions over $5,000, Probate.*

General Information: Probate records managed by the county clerk office, is a separate index at this address. No juvenile records released. Will not fax out case files. Court makes copy: $1.00 per page if mailed, $.50 if in person. Self serve copy: $.50 per page. Certification fee: $5.00 per document. Payee: Circuit Clerk. Personal checks accepted. No credit cards accepted. Prepayment required.

Civil Name Search: Access: In person only. Visitors must perform in person searches themselves. Civil records on books from 1893. Public use terminal available, records go back to 2005-06 only.

Criminal Name Search: Access: In person only. Visitors must perform in person searches themselves. Required to search: name, years to search. Criminal docket on books from 1893. Note: Court personnel will not do a name search, but will pull specific case data if docket number given. Public use terminal available, crim records go back to 2005-06 only.

Piggott Circuit Court 151 S 2nd Street, Piggott, AR 72454; 870-598-2524; probate phone: 870-598-2813; fax: 870-598-1107; 8AM-4:30PM (CST). *Felony, Civil Actions over $5,000.*

General Information: No expunged criminal records released. Will fax documents $5.00 per doc. Court makes copy: $.25 per page. Self serve copy: same. Certification fee: $5.00 per doc plus copy fee. Payee: Circuit Clerk. Personal checks accepted. No credit cards accepted. Prepayment required.

Civil Name Search: Access: In person only. Visitors must perform in person searches themselves. Civil records on books from 1893.

Criminal Name Search: Access: In person only. Visitors must perform in person searches themselves. Required to search: name, years to search, DOB, SSN. Criminal docket on books from 1893.

Piggott Local District Court 151 S 2nd Ave, Piggott, AR 72454; 870-598-2265; fax: 870-598-2229; 8AM-4:30PM (CST). *Misdemeanor, Civil Actions under $5,000, Eviction, Small Claims.*

General Information: Office is only open 20 hours per week only. For eviction information the court says to contact Clay County Sheriff, 151 S 2nd St, Piggott, AR 72454, 870-598-2266. Will fax documents to local or toll free line. Court makes copy: $.25 per page. Certification fee: $5.00 per docket. Payee: District Court. No personal checks or credit cards accepted. Prepayment required. Mail requests: SASE required.

Civil Name Search: Access: Mail, in person. Only the court performs in person name searches; visitors may not. Search fee: $8.00. Required to search: name, DOB, years. Civil cases indexed by Defendant, Plaintiff. Records on computer back to 1998. Mail turnaround time 3-4 days.

Criminal Name Search: Access: Mail, in person. Only the court performs in person name searches; visitors may not. Search fee: $8.00. Required to search: name, years, SSN; also helpful: DOB. Records on computer back to 1998. Mail turnaround time 3-4 days.

Corning Local District Court 800 SW 2nd St, Corning, AR 72422; 870-857-0115; fax: 870-857-3271; 8AM-4:30PM (CST). *Misdemeanor, Civil Actions under $5,000, Eviction, Small Claims.*

General Information: For eviction information the court says to contact Clay County Sheriff, 151 S 2nd St, Piggott, AR 72454, 870-598-2266.

Rector Local District Court 407 S Stewart, Rector, AR 72461; 870-595-9805; 8AM-3PM M-W (CST). *Misdemeanor, Civil Actions under $5,000, Eviction, Small Claims.*

General Information: For eviction information the court says to contact Clay County Sheriff, 151 S 2nd St, Piggott, AR 72454, 870-598-2266. Will fax documents to local or toll free line. Court makes copy: $.25 per page. Certification fee: $5.00 per docket. Payee: District Court. No personal checks or credit cards accepted. Prepayment required. Mail requests: SASE required.

Civil Name Search: Access: Mail, in person. Only the court performs in person name searches; visitors may not. Search fee: $8.00. Required to search: name, DOB, years. Civil cases indexed by Defendant, Plaintiff. Records on computer back to 1998. Mail turnaround time 3-4 days.

Criminal Name Search: Access: Mail, in person. Only the court performs in person name searches; visitors may not. Search fee: $8.00. Required to search: name, years to search, SSN; also helpful: DOB. Records on computer back to 1998. Mail turnaround time 3-4 days.

Cleburne County

Circuit Court PO Box 543, 301 W Main St, Heber Springs, AR 72543; 501-362-8149; fax: 501-362-4681; 8AM-6PM M-TH, 8:30AM-4:30PM Fri (CST). *Felony, Civil Actions over $25,000, Probate.*

General Information: Probate is on a separate index at this address. Probate fax is same as main fax number. The case limit on civil records increased from $5,000 to $25,000 as of 07/01/2009. No juvenile records released. Will fax documents $4.00 1st page; $1.00 each add'l page. Court makes copy: $.50 per page. Self serve copy: same. Certification fee: $1.00 per document. Payee: Circuit Clerk. Personal checks accepted. No credit cards accepted. Prepayment required. Mail requests: SASE required.

Civil Name Search: Access: Fax, mail, in person. Both court and visitors may perform in person name searches. Search fee: $6.00 per name. Civil records on dockets from 1883. Mail turnaround time 1-2 days. Civil PAT goes back to 1997.

Criminal Name Search: Access: Phone, mail, in person. Both court and visitors may perform in person name searches. Search fee: $6.00 per name. Required to search: name, years to search. Criminal docket index from 1883. Mail turnaround time 1-2 days. Criminal PAT goes back to 1997.

Quitman District Court PO Box 159, Quitman, AR 72131; 501-589-3512; fax: 501-589-3022; 8AM-6PM M-Th (CST). *Misdemeanor, Traffic.*

Greers Ferry District Court PO Box 1355, Greers Ferry, AR 72067; 501-825-7172; fax: 501-825-8029. *Misdemeanor Traffic.*

General Information: This court only handles misdemeanor traffic for the city of Greers Ferry.

Heber Springs State District Court 102 E Main, Heber Springs, AR 72543; 501-362-6585; fax: 501-362-4661; 8AM-6PM M-Th (CST). *Misdemeanor, Civil Actions under $25,000, Small Claims, Eviction.*

General Information: Court makes copy: none. No certification fee . No personal checks or credit cards accepted. Mail requests: SASE required.

Civil Name Search: Access: Phone, mail, fax, in person. Both court and visitors may perform in person name searches. No search fee. Civil records on computer back to 2002. Mail turnaround time 10 working days.

Criminal Name Search: Access: Phone, mail, fax, in person. Both court and visitors may perform in person name searches. No search fee. Required to search: name, years to search, offense, DOB. Criminal records computerized from 1989. Mail turnaround time 10 working days.

Concord State District Court PO Box 273, Concord, AR 72523; 870-668-3315; fax: same - call first; 8:30AM-3PM TH & F only (CST). *Misdemeanor, Civil Actions under $25,000, Small Claims, Eviction.*

Cleveland County

Circuit Court PO Box 368, Rison, AR 71665; 870-325-6902; fax: 870-325-6144; 8AM-4:30PM (CST). *Felony, Civil Actions over $5,000, Probate.*

General Information: Probate is a separate office (county clerk) and separate index at this same address. Probate fax is same as main fax number. No juvenile or adoption records released. Fee to fax out file $1.00 per page. Court makes copy: $.50 per page. Self serve copy: same. Certification fee: $5.00 per document. Payee: Clerk of Circuit Court. Personal checks accepted. No credit cards accepted. Prepayment required.

Civil Name Search: Access: Mail, in person. Visitors must perform in person searches themselves. No search fee. Civil PAT goes back to 01/2009.

Criminal Name Search: Access: Mail, in person. Both court and visitors may perform in person name searches. No search fee. Required to search: name, years to search, DOB. Mail turnaround time same day, if possible. Criminal PAT goes back to 01/2009.

Local District Court PO Box 405, City Hall, 405 Main St, Rison, AR 71665; 870-325-7382; fax: 870-325-6152; 8AM-4PM (CST). *Misdemeanor, Civil Actions under $5,000, Eviction, Small Claims.*

General Information: Will not fax documents. Court makes no copies. No certification fee. No personal checks or credit cards accepted.

Civil Name Search: Access: In person only. Both court and visitors may perform in person name searches. No search fee; court will charge for multiple records. Computerized records go back 5 years.

Criminal Name Search: Access: In person only. Both court and visitors may perform in person name searches. No search fee, but court will charge for multiple records. Required to search: name, years to search, SSN. Computerized records go back 5 years.

Columbia County

Circuit Court 1 Court Sq #3, PO Box 327, Magnolia, AR 71753-3595; 870-235-3700; probate phone: 870-235-3774; fax: 870-235-3786; 8AM-4:30PM (CST). *Felony, Civil Actions over $5,000, Probate.*
www.countyofcolumbia.net/circuit-clerk/

General Information: Probate is handled by County Clerk with a separate record index at this same address. No juvenile or adoption. Will fax documents. Court makes copy: $1.00 per page. Self serve copy: $.50 per page. Certification fee: $5.00 per document. Payee: Circuit Clerk. Personal checks accepted. No credit cards accepted. Prepayment required.

Civil Name Search: Access: In person. Visitors must perform in person searches themselves. Civil records on dockets and index cards; computerized records since 8/97. Civil PAT available.

Criminal Name Search: Access: In person. Visitors must perform in person searches themselves. Required to search: name, years to search, DOB, SSN. Criminal records on dockets and index cards; computerized records since 8/97. Criminal PAT available.

Magnolia Local District Court 216 S Washington, Magnolia, AR 71753; 870-234-7312; ; 8AM-5PM (CST). *Misdemeanor, Civil Actions under $5,000, Eviction, Small Claims.*

General Information: Will fax documents to local or toll-free number. Court makes copy: No charge. Certification fee: $10.00. Payee: District Court Clerk. No credit cards accepted. Prepayment required.

Civil Name Search: Access: In person only. Visitors must perform in person searches themselves. Required to search: Name, plus DOB or SSN. Civil cases indexed by case number. Civil records available since 1993. Civil PAT goes back to 2003.

Criminal Name Search: Access: In person only. Visitors must perform in person searches themselves. Required to search: name, DOB and SSN, years to search; also helpful: address. Criminal records available since 1987. Note: Court does not do criminal searches except for Law Enforcement Agencies. Criminal PAT goes back to 1987.

Conway County

Circuit Court Conway County Courthouse, Rm 206, 115 S Moose, Morrilton, AR 72110; 501-354-9617; probate phone: 501-354-9621; fax: 501-354-9612; 8AM-5PM (CST). *Felony, Civil Actions over $5,000, Probate.*

General Information: Probate is handled by County Clerk with a separate record index at this same address. No juvenile records released. Fee to fax out file $1.00 per page. Court makes copy: $1.00 per page. Self serve copy: same. Certification fee: $5.00 per doc includes copies. Payee: Circuit Clerk. Personal checks accepted. No credit cards accepted. Prepayment required.

Civil Name Search: Access: In person only. Visitors must perform in person searches themselves. Civil records indexed by dockets back to 1900's.

Criminal Name Search: Access: In person only. Both court and visitors may perform in person name searches. No search fee. Required to search: name, years to search, DOB; also helpful: sex, SSN. Criminal records indexed in books back to 1900's.

Local District Court PO Box 127, Conway County Courthouse, Morrilton, AR 72110; 501-354-9615; fax: 501-354-9633; 8AM-4:30PM (CST). *Misdemeanor, Civil Actions under $5,000, Eviction, Small Claims.*

General Information: Will fax documents. Court makes copy: $1.00 per page. Self serve copy: same. Certification fee: $5.00. Payee: District Court Clerk. No personal checks or credit cards accepted. Prepayment required. Mail requests: SASE required.

Civil Name Search: Access: Mail, in person. Both court and visitors may perform in person name searches. No search fee. Computerized records since 1994. Mail turnaround time 1-2 days. Civil PAT available. Terminal results include driver's license number.

Criminal Name Search: Access: Mail, in person. Both court and visitors may perform in person name searches. No search fee. Required to search: name, years to search; also helpful: DOB. Computerized records since 1994. Mail turnaround time 1-2 days. Criminal PAT available.

Craighead County

Jonesboro Circuit Court PO Box 120, 511 S Main, Jonesboro, AR 72403; 870-933-4530; probate phone: 870-933-4520; fax: 870-933-4534; 8AM-5PM (CST). *Felony, Civil Actions over $5,000, Probate.*
www.craigheadcounty.org

General Information: Probate is handled by County Clerk with a separate record index at this same address. Probate fax- 870-933-4514 No juvenile records released. Will fax documents $1.00 per page. Court makes copy: $.25 per page. Self serve copy: same. Certification fee: $3.00 per document plus copy fee. Payee: Circuit Clerk. Personal checks accepted. No credit cards accepted. Prepayment required. Mail requests: SASE required.

Civil Name Search: Access: Fax, mail, in person. Both court and visitors may perform in person name searches. Search fee: $6.00 per name. Civil records on computer from 1972, on microfiche from 1800s. Mail turnaround time 1-2 days. Civil PAT goes back to 1997.

Criminal Name Search: Access: Fax, mail, in person. Both court and visitors may perform in person name searches. Search fee: $6.00 per name. Required to search: name, years to search, DOB; also helpful: address, SSN. Criminal records computerized from 1972, on microfiche from 1800s. Mail turnaround time 1-2 days. Criminal PAT goes back to 1997.

Lake City Circuit Court - Eastern District PO Box 537, 107 Cobean Blvd, Lake City, AR 72437; 870-237-4342; fax: 870-237-8174; 8AM-5PM (CST). *Felony, Civil Actions over $5,000, Probate.*

General Information: No adoption records released. Will fax documents for $1.00 per doc. Court makes copy: $.25 per page. Certification fee: $5.00 per doc. Payee: Circuit Clerk. Business checks accepted. No credit cards accepted, except MC Debit cards. Prepayment required. Mail requests: SASE required.

Civil Name Search: Access: In person. Both court and visitors may perform in person name searches. Required to search: name, years to search, address. Civil cases indexed by defendant, plaintiff. Civil records on computer from 1976. Civil PAT goes back to 1976.

Criminal Name Search: Access: Mail, fax, in person. Both court and visitors may perform in person name searches. No search fee. Required to search: name, years to search, address, DOB; also helpful: SSN. Criminal records computerized from 1976. Criminal PAT goes back to same as civil.

Jonesboro Local District Court 410 W Washington, Jonesboro, AR 72401; 870-933-4508; criminal phone: x1; fax: 870-933-4582; 8AM-5PM (CST). *Misdemeanor, Civil Actions under $5,000, Eviction, Small Claims.* www.craigheadcounty.org/

General Information: Will fax documents to local or toll-free number; fee may apply otherwise. Court makes copy: $.20 per page. Certification fee: $2.00 each usually includes copy fee. Payee: District Court. Personal checks accepted. No credit cards accepted. Prepayment required. Mail requests: SASE required.

Civil Name Search: Access: Mail, in person. Only the court performs in person name searches; visitors may not. Search fee: $4.00 per name. Required to search: name, DOB. Civil cases indexed by defendant, plaintiff. Computerized records go back 10 years. Mail turnaround time 1-2 days.

Criminal Name Search: Access: Mail, in person. Only the court performs in person name searches; visitors may not. Search fee: $4.00 per name. Required to search: name, years to search, SSN. Computerized records go back 10 years. Mail turnaround time 1-2 days.

Local District Court PO Box 537, Lake City, AR 72437; 870-237-4142; fax: 870-237-8174; 8AM-5PM (CST). *Misdemeanor, Civil Actions under $5,000, Eviction, Small Claims.* www.craigheadcounty.org/

Crawford County

Circuit Court 300 Main St, Rm 22, Van Buren, AR 72956; 479-474-1821; probate phone: 479-474-1312; fax: 479-471-0622; 8AM-5PM (CST). *Felony, Civil Actions over $5,000, Probate.* www.crawford-county.org/circuit_clerk.html

General Information: Probate is handled by County Clerk with a separate record index at this same address in Room 7. No juvenile records released. Will fax documents to toll-free number. Court makes copy: $1.00 per page if mailed, otherwise $.50. Self serve copy: $.50 per page. Certification fee: $5.00. Payee: Circuit Clerk. Personal checks accepted. No credit cards accepted. Prepayment required. Mail requests: SASE required.

Civil Name Search: Access: Mail, in person. Both court and visitors may perform in person name searches. Search fee: $6.00 per name, if written response needed. Civil records on computer from 1992, on dockets from 1877. Mail turnaround time same day. Civil PAT goes back to 1992.

Criminal Name Search: Access: Mail, in person. Visitors must perform in person searches themselves. Search fee: $6.00 per name, if written response needed. Required to search: name, years to search. Criminal records computerized from 1992, on dockets from 1877. Note: Will not do name searches. Mail turnaround time 1-2 days. Criminal PAT goes back to same as civil. Online results show middle initial.

Local District Court 1003 Broadway, Van Buren, AR 72956; 479-474-1671; fax: 479-471-5005; 8:30AM-4:30PM (CST). *Misdemeanor, Civil Actions under $5,000, Eviction, Small Claims.*

General Information: Will fax documents to local or toll-free number. Court makes copy: $.50 per page. Certification fee: $10.00 per document. Payee: Crawford County District Court. Personal checks accepted. No credit cards accepted. Prepayment required. Mail requests: SASE required.

Civil Name Search: Access: Mail, in person. Both court and visitors may perform in person name searches. No search fee. Civil cases indexed by defendant, plaintiff. Records available from 1975, computerized from 2000. Mail turnaround time 2-3 days. Civil PAT goes back to 2000. Public terminal only available Fridays.

Criminal Name Search: Access: Mail, in person. Both court and visitors may perform in person name searches. No search fee. Required to search: name, years to search; also helpful: DOB, SSN. Specific court cases prior to 2000 need the conviction date. Records available from 1975, computerized from 2000. Mail turnaround time 2-3 days. Criminal PAT goes back to same as civil. Public terminal only available Fridays.

Crittenden County

Circuit Court 100 Court St, Marion, AR 72364; 870-739-3248; probate phone: 870-739-4434; fax: 870-739-3287; 8AM-4:30PM (CST). *Felony, Civil Actions over $5,000, Probate.*

General Information: Probate is not in the Circuit Clerk's office and is managed by the County Clerk office. The phone number is given above. No juvenile records released. Fee to fax out file $4.50 per document. Court makes copy: $.25 per page. Self serve copy: same. Certification fee: $5.00. Payee: Circuit Court. Personal checks accepted. No credit or debit cards accepted. Prepayment required. Mail requests: SASE required for civil.

Civil Name Search: Access: Mail, in person. Both court and visitors may perform in person name searches. Search fee: $6.00 per name. Required to search: name, years to search. Civil cases indexed by plaintiff only. Civil records on dockets from 1930s; manual lookups by plaintiff only.

Criminal Name Search: Access: In person only. Visitors must perform in person searches themselves. Required to search: name, case number. Criminal docket index from 1930s; manual lookups. Note: The court suggests to send criminal record inquiries to Ark. State Police, 501-681-8100.

Marion District Court PO Box 717, Marion, AR 72364; 870-739-5411; fax: 870-739-3150; 8AM-4:30PM (CST). *Misdemeanor.*

West Memphis Local District Court PO Box 766, West Memphis, AR 72303; 870-732-7560; fax: 870-732-7566; 8AM-4:30PM (CST). *Misdemeanor, Civil Actions under $5,000, Eviction, Small Claims.*

General Information: No fee to fax documents in very special circumstances only. Court makes copy: $.25 per page. Self serve copy: no copy fee. No certification fee . Payee: District Court. Personal checks accepted. Visa/MC/Discover accepted. Prepayment required.

Civil Name Search: Access: Phone, fax, mail, in person. Both court and visitors may perform in person name searches. No search fee. Required to search: name, years to search, DOB or SSN. Civil records on computer back to 1989; other records go back to 1945. Mail turnaround time 2-3 days.

Criminal Name Search: Access: Phone, mail, in person. Both court and visitors may perform in person name searches. No search fee. Required to search: name, years to search; also helpful: SSN, race, sex, DOB. Criminal records computerized from 1989; other records go back to 1945. Mail turnaround time 2-3 days.

Cross County

Circuit Court County Courthouse, 705 E Union, Rm 9, Wynne, AR 72396; 870-238-5720; probate phone: 870-238-5735; fax: 870-238-5722; 8AM-4PM (CST). *Felony, Civil Actions over $5,000, Probate.* www.crosscountyar.org/page_viewd708.html?id=3

General Information: Child Support records found in Domestic Relations records. Probate is handled by County Clerk, Rm 8, with a separate record index at this same address. Phone #-870-238-5735, Fax 870-238-5739. No juvenile records released. Will fax documents for $1.00 per page. Court makes copy: $.50 per page. Self serve copy: $.50 per page. Certification fee: $5.00 per doc. Payee: Cross County Circuit Court. Personal checks accepted. No credit cards accepted. Prepayment required.

Civil Name Search: Access: In person only. Visitors must perform in person searches themselves. Required to search: name, years to search. Civil cases indexed by defendant and plaintiff. Civil records (child support) on computer. All on dockets from 1800s. Civil PAT goes back to 2001.

Criminal Name Search: Access: In person only. Visitors must perform in person searches themselves. Required to search: name, years to search; SSN helpful. Criminal records (child support) on computer. All on dockets from 1800s. Criminal PAT goes back to same as civil.

Local District Court 205 Mississippi St, Wynne, AR 72396; 870-238-9171; fax: 870-238-3930; 8AM-4PM (CST). *Misdemeanor, Civil Actions under $5,000, Eviction, Small Claims.*

General Information: Will fax documents to local or toll-free number. Court makes copy: none. Certification fee: $5.00 per doc. Payee: Cross County Court. Personal checks accepted. No credit cards accepted. Prepayment required. Mail requests: SASE required.

Civil Name Search: Access: Mail, in person. Only the court performs in person name searches; visitors may not. Search fee: $10.00. Required to search: name, years to search. Records on computer back to 1986. Mail turnaround time 5-7 days.

Criminal Name Search: Access: Mail, in person. Only the court performs in person name searches; visitors may not. Search fee: $10.00. Required to search: name, years to search, signed release; also helpful: SSN. Records on computer back to 1986. Mail turnaround time 5-7 days.

Dallas County

Circuit Court Dallas County Courthouse, Fordyce, AR 71742; 870-352-2307; fax: 870-352-7179; 8:30AM-4:30PM (CST). *Felony, Civil Actions over $5,000, Probate.*

General Information: Probate records are handled by the County Clerk, who can be reached thru the number above. No juvenile records released. Will fax documents $1.00 per page. Court makes copy: $.50 per page. Self serve copy: same. Certification fee: $5.00. Payee: Circuit Clerk. Business checks, money orders or cashiers checks accepted; Law firm accounts allowed. No credit cards accepted. Prepayment required. Mail requests: SASE required for civil.

Civil Name Search: Access: Phone, fax, mail, in person. Visitors must perform in person searches themselves. No search fee. Civil records go back to 1863; on computer back to 8/1997. Civil PAT goes back to 8/1997.

Criminal Name Search: Access: In person only. Visitors must perform in person searches themselves. Required to search: name, years to search, DOB; SSN helpful. Criminal records go back to 1863; on computer back to 8/1997. Criminal PAT goes back to same as civil.

Local District Court 206 W 3rd St, 2nd Fl, Fordyce, AR 71742; 870-352-2332; fax: 870-352-3414; 9AM-4PM (CST). *Misdemeanor, Civil Actions under $5,000, Eviction, Small Claims.*

General Information: Will fax documents. Court makes copy: $1.00 per page. Self serve copy: same. Certification fee: $5.00. Payee: Dallas County District Court. Checks or cash accepted. No credit cards accepted. Prepayment required.

Civil Name Search: Access: In person, mail. Only the court performs in person name searches; visitors may not. No search fee. Required to search: name. Computerized records since 1997. Mail turnaround time 1-2 days. Civil PAT goes back to 1997.

Criminal Name Search: Access: In person, mail. Visitors must perform in person searches themselves. No search fee. Required to search: name, years to search; also helpful: DOB. Computerized records since 1997. Criminal PAT goes back to 1997.

Desha County

Circuit Court PO Box 309, 604 President St, Arkansas City, AR 71630; 870-877-2411; probate phone: 870-877-2323; fax: 870-877-3407; 8AM-4PM (CST). *Felony, Civil Actions over $5,000, Probate.*

General Information: Probate records are handled by the County Clerk, who can be reached thru the number above. No juvenile records released. No fee to fax documents. Court makes copy: $.50 per page. Self serve copy: $.25 per page. Certification fee: $3.00 per doc plus copy fee. Payee: Skippy Leek, Circuit Court Clerk. Personal checks accepted. No credit cards accepted. Prepayment required. Mail requests: SASE required.

Civil Name Search: Access: Fax, mail, in person. Both court and visitors may perform in person name searches. No search fee. Civil records on dockets from 1920s; on computer back to 1990. Mail turnaround time 1-2 days. Public use terminal has civil records back to 1990. Public terminal may only have deeds, mortgages, judgments.

Criminal Name Search: Access: Fax, mail, in person. Both court and visitors may perform in person name searches. No search fee. Required to search: name, years to search, SSN. Criminal docket index from 1920s, on computer back to 1997. Mail turnaround time 1-2 days.

Dumas Local District Court PO Box 157, 149 E Waterman, Dumas, AR 71639-2226; 870-382-6972; criminal phone: 870-382-6862; civil phone: 870-382-6972; fax: 870-382-1106; 8AM-4:30PM (CST). *Misdemeanor, Civil Actions under $5,000, Eviction, Small Claims.*

General Information: Will fax documents for no fee. Court makes copy: search fee includes copy fee if record found. Certification fee: $5.00 per record includes copy fee. Payee: Dumas District Court. Personal checks accepted. No credit cards accepted. Prepayment required. Mail requests: SASE required.

Civil Name Search: Access: Mail, in person. Only the court performs in person name searches; visitors may not. Search fee: $5.00 per name. Required to search: name, years to search, signed release; also helpful: address. Civil records go back to 1988, computerized since 2003. Note: search fee includes copy fee if record found Mail turnaround time 1-2 days.

Criminal Name Search: Access: Mail, in person. Only the court performs in person name searches; visitors may not. Search fee: $5.00 per name. Required to search: name, years to search, signed release; also helpful: address. Criminal records go back to 1988. Mail turnaround time 1-2 days.

McGehee Dept Local District Court. PO Box 11, McGehee, AR 71654; 870-222-3859; fax: 870-222-6659; 8AM-4:30PM (CST). *Misdemeanor, Civil Actions under $5,000, Eviction, Small Claims.*

Drew County

Circuit Court 210 S Main, Monticello, AR 71655; 870-460-6250; probate phone: 870-460-6260; fax: 870-460-6255; 8AM-4:30PM (CST). *Felony, Civil Actions over $5,000, Probate.*

General Information: Probate records are handled by the County Clerk, who can be reached thru the number above. No juvenile or expunged records released. Will fax documents $1.25 1st page, $1.00 each add'l. Court makes copy: $.75 per page. Self serve copy: $.50 per page. Certification fee: $2.50 per doc. Payee: Drew County Circuit Clerk. Personal checks accepted. No credit cards accepted. Prepayment required.

Civil Name Search: Access: In person only. Both court and visitors may perform in person name searches. No search fee. Civil records on dockets from 1846; on computer back to 1996 approx. Civil PAT goes back to 1996.

Criminal Name Search: Access: In person only. Visitors must perform in person searches themselves. Required to search: name, years to search. Criminal docket index from 1846; on computer back to 1997 approx. Criminal PAT goes back to 1997.

Local District Court PO Box 505, Railroad St, Monticello, AR 71657; 870-367-4420; fax: 870-460-9056; 8AM-4:30PM (CST). *Misdemeanor, Civil Actions under $5,000, Eviction, Small Claims.*

General Information: Will fax documents to local or toll free line. Court makes copy: none. No certification fee . Payee: Drew County District Court. No personal checks or credit cards accepted. Mail requests: SASE required.

Civil Name Search: Access: Mail, fax, in person. Both court and visitors may perform in person name searches. No search fee. Required to search: name, years to search, DOB, SSN, signed release. Name or case number. Records overall since 1980, on computer since 1987. Mail turnaround time 1-2 days.

Criminal Name Search: Access: Mail, fax, in person. Only the court performs in person name searches; visitors may not. No search fee. Required to search: name, years to search, DOB; also helpful: SSN. DL#, sex, signed release. Records overall since 1980, on computer since 1987. Mail turnaround time 1-2 days.

Faulkner County

Circuit Court Circuit Clerk, PO Box 9, Conway, AR 72033; 501-450-4911; probate phone: 501-450-4909; fax: 501-450-4948; 8AM-4:30PM (CST). *Felony, Civil Actions over $5,000, Domestic Relations, Probate.* www.faulknercounty.org/

General Information: Probate handled at the county clerk's office, number above. No juvenile records released. Will fax documents $1.00 if local, $3.50 plus $.25 per page if long distance. Court makes copy: $.25 per page. Self serve copy: same. Certification fee: $3.00 per doc. Payee: Faulkner County Circuit Clerk. Personal checks accepted. No credit cards accepted. Mail requests: SASE required.

Civil Name Search: Access: In person, online. Visitors must perform in person searches themselves. Civil records on computer back to 1987; on docket from 1800s. Note: Court will not do name searches. Mail turnaround time 1-2 days. Civil PAT goes back to 1987. Not all cases will show DOB, SSN, full name. Search by name or case number at https://arep2.aoc.arkansas.gov/cconnect/PROD/public/ck_public_qry_main.cp_main_idx. For a name search, one may submit the DOB, but the DOB is not shown in results.

Criminal Name Search: Access: In person, online. Both court and visitors may perform in person name searches. Required to search: name, years to search. Criminal records computerized from 1987; on docket from 1800s. Note: Court will not do name searches. Mail turnaround time 1-2 days. Criminal PAT goes back to 1987. Not all cases will show DOB, SSN, full name. Online access same as described for civil. Online results show name only.

Local District Court 810 Parkway, Conway, AR 72034; 501-450-6112; criminal phone: ext 302; civil phone: ext 304; fax: 501-450-6184; 8AM-12; 1PM--4:30PM (CST). *Misdemeanor, Civil Actions under $5,000, Small Claims, Traffic.* www.cityofconway.org/departments/district_court/district_court.html

General Information: The District Court Building is locked from 11:30am-12:30pm. Sealed records are not open to the public. Will fax documents to local or toll free number. Court makes copy: $.03 per page. Certification fee: $5.00 per doc. Payee: Conway District Court. Personal checks accepted. Visa/MC accepted. Prepayment required. Mail requests: SASE required.

Civil Name Search: Access: Mail, fax, in person. Both court and visitors may perform in person name searches. No search fee. Required to search: name, years to search, DOB, signed release; also helpful: address. Computerized records go back to 2005. Mail turnaround time 2 days.

Criminal Name Search: Access: Mail, fax, in person. Both court and visitors may perform in person name searches. No search fee. Required to search: name, years to search, DOB, signed release; also helpful: address. Computerized records go back to 1993. Mail turnaround time 2 days. Terminal results include SSN.

Franklin County

Charleston Circuit Court 607 E main, Charleston, AR 72933; 479-965-7332; probate phone: 479-965-2129; fax: 479-965-9322; 8AM-4:30PM (CST). *Felony, Civil Actions over $5,000, Probate.*

General Information: This court will not perform name searches. Probate is filed in County Clerk's office. No juvenile records released. Will fax documents $1.00 per page. Court makes copy: $.25 per page. Self serve copy: same. Certification fee: $5.00. Payee: Franklin County. Personal checks accepted. No credit cards accepted. Prepayment required. Mail requests: SASE required.

Civil Name Search: Access: In person. Both court and visitors may perform in person name searches. Required to search: name, years to search, DOB. Civil cases indexed by defendant, plaintiff. Civil records on dockets from 1900s. Mail turnaround time 1-2 days.

Criminal Name Search: Access: In person. Both court and visitors may perform in person name searches. Required to search: name, years to search, DOB. Criminal docket index from 1900s.

Ozark Circuit Court PO Box 1112, 211 W Commercial, Ozark, AR 72949; 479-667-3818; probate phone: 479-667-3607; fax: 479-667-5174; 8AM-4:30PM (CST). *Felony, Civil Actions over $5,000, Probate.*

General Information: Probate is maintained at the County Clerk's Office. Court personnel will NOT perform name searches. No juvenile records released. Will fax documents $1.00 per page. Court makes copy: $.25 per page. Self serve copy: same. Certification fee: $5.00. Payee: Circuit Clerk. Personal checks accepted. No credit cards accepted. Prepayment required.

Civil Name Search: Access: In person only. Visitors must perform in person searches themselves. Required to search: name, years to search. Civil cases indexed by plaintiff. Civil records on dockets from 1900s.

Criminal Name Search: Access: In person only. Visitors must perform in person searches themselves. Required to search: name, years to search. Criminal docket index from 1900s.

Charleston Local District Court PO Box 426, 1418 E Main St, Charleston, AR 72933; 479-965-7455; fax: 479-965-9980; 8AM-11:30AM, 12:30PM-5PM (CST). *Misdemeanor, Civil Actions under $5,000, Small Claims.*

General Information: Will fax back documents. Court makes copy: none. No certification fee . Personal checks accepted. No credit cards accepted.

Civil Name Search: Access: Mail, fax, in person. Both court and visitors may perform in person name searches. No search fee. Civil cases indexed by defendant, plaintiff. Civil records are not computerized, records index in docket books. Mail turnaround time 3-4 days.

Criminal Name Search: Access: Mail, fax, in person. Only the court performs in person name searches; visitors may not. No search fee. Required to search: name, years to search, DOB; also helpful-SSN, signed release. Criminal records computerized from 1/2000. Mail turnaround time 3-4 days.

Ozark Local District Court PO Box 403, 116 S 2nd St, Ozark, AR 72949; 479-667-4808; fax: 479-667-4599; 8AM-5PM (CST). *Misdemeanor, Civil Actions under $5,000, Small Claims.*

Fulton County

Circuit Court PO Box 219, Salem, AR 72576; 870-895-3310; fax: 870-895-3383; 8AM-4:30PM (CST). *Felony, Civil Actions over $5,000, Probate.*

General Information: Probate is handled by County Clerk with a separate record index at this same address. No juvenile records released. Will fax documents. Court makes copy: $.25 per page. Self serve copy: same. Certification fee: $5.00 per doc. Payee: Fulton County Clerks. Personal checks accepted. No credit cards accepted. Prepayment required. Mail requests: SASE required.

Civil Name Search: Access: Mail, in person. Both court and visitors may perform in person name searches. Search fee: $6.00 per name. Civil records on dockets from 1900s; on computer back to 2000. Mail turnaround time 1-2 days.

Criminal Name Search: Access: Mail, in person. Both court and visitors may perform in person name searches. Search fee: $6.00 per name. Required to search: name, years to search. Criminal docket index from 1900s; on computer back to 2000. Note: Only the court can search on the computer terminal. Mail turnaround time 1-2 days.

Local District Court PO Box 928, Salem, AR 72576; 870-895-4136; fax: 870-895-4137; 8AM-4:30PM (CST). *Misdemeanor, Civil Actions under $5,000, Eviction, Small Claims.*

General Information: Will fax documents to local or toll-free number. Court makes copy: none. No certification fee . Payee: Fulton County District Court. Personal checks accepted. No credit cards accepted. Mail requests: SASE required.

Civil Name Search: Access: Mail, in person. Only the court performs in person name searches; visitors may not. No search fee. Required to search: name. Computerized records since 1995. Mail turnaround time 1 week.

Criminal Name Search: Access: Phone, mail, in person. Both court and visitors may perform in person name searches. No search fee. Required to search: name, years to search, DOB. Computerized records since 1995. Mail turnaround time 1 week.

Garland County

Circuit Court Garland County Courthouse, 501 Ouachita Ave, Rm 207, Hot Springs, AR 71901; 501-622-3630; probate phone: 501-622-3610; fax: 501-609-9043; 8AM-5PM (CST). *Felony, Civil Actions over $5,000, Domestic Relations, Probate.*

www.garlandcounty.org/

General Information: Criminal searches performed by the court for Law enforcement personnel only. Probate records are handled by the County Clerk, phone number above. No expunged, sealed records released. Fee to fax out file $2.00 plus $.25 per page. Court makes copy: $.25 per page. Self serve copy: same. Certification fee: $.50 per doc plus copy fee. Payee: Garland County Circuit Clerk. Personal checks accepted. No credit cards accepted. Prepayment required.

Civil Name Search: Access: In person, online. Visitors must perform in person searches themselves. Required to search: name; also helpful: years to search. Civil cases indexed by defendant, plaintiff. Civil records on microfiche and docket from 1900s; on computer back to 1989. Note: Index is in book form for the public. Computer index for Court Orders available to public. Search the index at https://arep2.aoc.arkansas.gov/cconnect/PROD/public/ck_public_qry_main.cp_main_idx.

Criminal Name Search: Access: In person, online. Visitors must perform in person searches themselves. Required to search: name, years to search; also helpful: DOB, SSN, maiden name, race, aliases, sex. Criminal records on microfiche and docket from 1900s; on computer back to 1989. Note: Index is in book form for the public. Computer index for Court Orders available to public. Search the index at https://arep2.aoc.arkansas.gov/cconnect/PROD/public/ck_public_qry_main.cp_main_idx.

Local District Court 607 Ouachita, Rm 150, Hot Springs, AR 71901; 501-321-6765; fax: 501-321-6764; 8AM-4:30PM (CST). *Misdemeanor, Civil Actions under $5,000, Eviction, Small Claims.*

General Information: Will not fax documents. Court makes copy: $.25 per page. Certification fee: $5.00 per doc. Payee: HSDC. No personal checks or credit cards accepted. Prepayment required.

Civil Name Search: Access: In person only. Both court and visitors may perform in person name searches. No search fee. Required to search: name, DOB, SSN, years to search. Civil cases indexed by both defendant/plaintiff. Civil record on computer back to 2000.

Criminal Name Search: Access: In person only. Only the court performs in person name searches; visitors may not. Required to search: name, years to search, offense. Criminal records computerized from 1990.

Grant County

Circuit Court Grant County Courthouse, 101 W Center, Rm 106, Sheridan, AR 72150; 870-942-2631; fax: 870-942-3564; 8AM-4:30PM (CST). *Felony, Civil Actions over $5,000, Probate.*

General Information: Probate is handled by County Clerk with a separate record index at this same address. Probate fax is same as main fax number. No juvenile, probate or adoption records released. Will fax specific case docs for $3.00 fee. Court makes copy: $.50 per page. Self serve copy: same. Certification fee: $5.00 per cert plus copy fee. Payee: Circuit Clerk. Personal checks accepted. No credit cards accepted. Prepayment required.

Civil Name Search: Access: In person only. Visitors must perform in person searches themselves. Civil records on dockets and index from 1877.

Criminal Name Search: Access: In person only. Visitors must perform in person searches themselves. Required to search: name, years to search. Criminal records on dockets and index from 1897.

Local District Court PO Box 603, 125 S Oak St, Sheridan, AR 72150; 870-942-3464; fax: 870-942-8885; 8AM-N, 1-4:15PM (CST). *Misdemeanor, Civil Actions under $5,000, Small Claims, Eviction.*

General Information: Probate is a separate index, separate court Will fax documents $3.00 per fax. Court makes copy: $.25 per page. Self serve copy: same. Certification fee: $5.00. Payee: Grant County District Court. Personal checks accepted. No credit cards accepted. Prepayment required. Mail requests: SASE required.

Civil Name Search: Access: Mail, in person. Only the court performs in person name searches; visitors may not. No search fee. Required to search: name. Computerized records since 1992. Mail turnaround time 3 days.

Criminal Name Search: Access: Mail, in person. Only the court performs in person name searches; visitors may not. No search fee. Required to search: name, years to search, DOB, also DL# or SSN. Computerized records since 1992. Mail turnaround time 3 days.

Greene County

Circuit Court 320 W Court #124, Paragould, AR 72450; 870-239-6330; fax: 870-239-3550; 8AM-4:30PM (CST). *Felony, Civil Actions over $25,000, Probate.*

General Information: Probate records are held by county clerk (Linda Heritage) at 870-239-6311. The case limit on civil records was raised to $25,000 as of 01/01/2008. No juvenile records released. For fax return, $1.00 each for first 3 pages then $.25 per page. Court makes copy: $.20 per page. Self serve copy: same. Certification fee: $5.00 per doc. Payee: Greene County Circuit Clerk. Personal checks accepted. No credit cards accepted. Prepayment required. Mail requests: SASE required.

Civil Name Search: Access: Fax, mail, in person. Both court and visitors may perform in person name searches. Search fee: $6.00 per name. Required to search: name, years to search. Civil cases indexed by plaintiff. Civil docket indexed from 1830. Note: Searching is done by viewing the printouts. Mail turnaround time 1-2 days.

Criminal Name Search: Access: Fax, mail, in person. Both court and visitors may perform in person name searches. Search fee: $6.00 per name. Required to search: name, years to search; also helpful: DOB, SSN. Criminal records indexed since 1876. Note: Searching is done by viewing the printouts. Mail turnaround time 1-2 days.

Marmaduke District Court PO Box 208, Marmaduke, AR 72443; 870-597-7507; fax: 870-597-2754; 8AM-4:30PM (CST). *Misdemeanor.* www.gccourt.com

General Information: The case limit on civil records was raised to $25,000 as of 01/01/2008.

Paragould State District Court 320 W Court, Rm 227, Paragould, AR 72450; 870-239-7507; fax: 870-239-7506; 8AM-4:30PM (CST). *Misdemeanor, Civil Actions under $25,000, Eviction, Small Claims.* www.gccourt.com

General Information: Will fax documents to local or toll-free number. Court makes copy: $.50 per page. Certification fee: $5.00 per doc. Payee: District Clerk. Only cashiers checks and money orders accepted. No credit cards accepted. Prepayment required. Mail requests: SASE required.

Civil Name Search: Access: Mail, in person. Only the court performs in person name searches; visitors may not. Search fee: $5.00. Required to search: name, years to search, DOB or SSN. Civil cases indexed by Defendant/Plaintiff. Records on computer back to 1989. Mail turnaround time 2 days.

Criminal Name Search: Access: Mail, in person. Only the court performs in person name searches; visitors may not. Search fee: $5.00 per name. Required to search: name, years to search, DOB or SSN. Records on computer back to 1989. Mail turnaround time 2 days.

Hempstead County

Circuit Court PO Box 1420, 400 S Washington, Hope, AR 71802; 870-777-2384; probate phone: 870-777-2241; fax: 870-777-7827; 8AM-4PM (CST). *Felony, Civil Actions over $5,000, Probate.* http://hempsteadcountyar.com/circuitclerk.html

General Information: Probate is handled by the County Clerk at same address. No juvenile records released. Will fax documents $.50 per page. Court makes copy: $.50 per page. Self serve copy: $.25 per page. Certification fee: $5.00. Payee: Circuit Clerk. Personal checks accepted. No credit cards accepted. Prepayment required. Mail requests: SASE required.

Civil Name Search: Access: Phone, fax, mail, in person. Both court and visitors may perform in person name searches. Search fee: $6.00 per name. Civil records on dockets from 1910, computerized since 1977. Mail turnaround time 1-2 days.

Criminal Name Search: Access: Phone, fax, mail, in person. Both court and visitors may perform in person name searches. Search fee: $6.00 per name. Required to search: name, years to search, DOB, SSN. Criminal docket index from 1910; computerized since 1977. Mail turnaround time 1-2 days.

Local District Court PO Box 1420, Hope, AR 71802-1420; 870-777-2525; fax: 870-777-7830; 8AM-4PM (CST). *Misdemeanor, Civil Actions under $5,000, Small Claims.*

General Information: Will not fax documents. Court makes copy: n/a. Certification fee: $5.00 per doc includes copies. Payee: District Court. Personal checks accepted. No credit cards accepted. Prepayment required. Mail requests: SASE required.

Civil Name Search: Access: Mail, in person. Both court and visitors may perform in person name searches. Search fee: $5.00 per name includes copies. Civil records are computerized since 2009. Mail turnaround time less than 1 week.

Criminal Name Search: Access: Mail, in person. Both court and visitors may perform in person name searches. Search fee: $5.00 per name includes copies. Required to search: name, years to search, SSN, DOB. Criminal records computerized from 1987. Mail turnaround time less than 1 week.

Hot Spring County

Circuit Court PO Box 1220, 210 Locust St, Malvern, AR 72104; 501-332-2281; probate phone: 501-332-2291; fax: 501-332-2221; 8AM-4:30PM (CST). *Felony, Civil Actions over $5,000.*

General Information: No juvenile records released. Will not fax documents. Court makes copy: $.50 per page. Self serve copy: $.25 per page. Certification fee: $5.00 per doc. Payee: Circuit Clerk. Personal checks accepted only if local. No credit cards accepted. Prepayment required. Mail requests: SASE required.

Civil Name Search: Access: Mail, in person, online. Both court and visitors may perform in person name searches. Search fee: $5.00. Required to search: name, years to search, plaintiff's name. Civil cases indexed by plaintiff. Civil records on dockets from 1980. Mail turnaround time 1-2 days. Search the index at https://arep2.aoc.arkansas.gov/cconnect/PROD/public/ck_public_qry_main.cp_main_idx.

Criminal Name Search: Access: Mail, in person, online. Both court and visitors may perform in person name searches. Search fee: $5.00. Required to search: name, years to search, DOB or SSN. Criminal docket index from 1980. Mail turnaround time 1-2 days. Search the index at https://arep2.aoc.arkansas.gov/cconnect/PROD/public/ck_public_qry_main.cp_main_idx. Online results show name only.

Malvern Local District Court 305 Locust St, Rm 201, Malvern, AR 72104; 501-332-7604; criminal phone: 501-332-7606; fax: 501-332-3144; 8AM-4:30PM (CST). *Misdemeanor, Civil Actions under $5,000, Eviction, Small Claims.*

General Information: Formerly known as Malvern Municipal Court before 7/1/01. Sealed records. Will fax documents $.25 per record. Court makes copy: $.25 per page. No certification fee . No personal checks or credit cards accepted. Prepayment required. Mail requests: SASE required.

Civil Name Search: Access: Mail, fax, in person. Visitors must perform in person searches themselves. No search fee. Required to search: name, years to search and DOB or SSN, case number. Civil cases indexed by Defendant, Plaintiff. Records computerized from 2008.

Criminal Name Search: Access: Mail, fax, in person. Visitors must perform in person searches themselves. No search fee. Required to search: name, years to search, DOB; also helpful: address, SSN. Records computerized back to 1994. Mail turnaround time 3 days.

Howard County

Circuit Court 421 N Main, Rm 7, Nashville, AR 71852; 870-845-7506; probate phone: 870-845-7503; ; 8AM-4:30PM (CST). *Felony, Civil Actions over $5,000, Probate.*

General Information: Fax is 870-845-7505, but call first so they can set up line. Probate is handled by the County Clerk at this address in Room 10. No juvenile or sealed records released. Will fax documents $1.00 per page; incoming fax also $1.00. Court makes copy: $.25 per page. Self serve copy: same. Certification fee: $5.00 plus $.50 per page for copies. Payee: Circuit Clerk. Personal checks accepted. No credit cards accepted. Prepayment required. Mail requests: SASE required for civil.

Civil Name Search: Access: Phone, mail, in person. Both court and visitors may perform in person name searches. Search fee: $6.00. Civil records on dockets from 1873. Mail turnaround time 2 days. Civil PAT goes back to 7/2003.

Criminal Name Search: Access: In person only. Visitors must perform in person searches themselves. Required to search: name, years to search, DOB. Criminal docket index from 1873. Criminal PAT goes back to same as civil. Online results show name only.

Local District Court 426 N Main, #7, Nashville, AR 71852-2009; 870-845-7522; fax: 870-845-3705; 8AM-4:30PM (CST). *Misdemeanor, Civil Actions under $5,000, Eviction, Small Claims.*

General Information: No SSN or bank account info released. Will fax documents to local or toll free line. Court makes copy: none. Certification fee: $5.00 per doc plus copy fee. Payee: Howard County District Court. Personal checks accepted. No credit cards accepted. Prepayment required. Mail requests: SASE required.

Civil Name Search: Access: Mail, in person. Visitors must perform in person searches themselves. No search fee. Civil records viewable back to 1989.

Criminal Name Search: Access: Mail, in person. Both court and visitors may perform in person name searches. No search fee. Required to search: name, years to search, DOB; also helpful: address, SSN. Criminal records viewable past 7 years. Mail turnaround time 1-3 days.

Independence County

Circuit Court PO Box 2155, 192 E Main at Broad St, Batesville, AR 72503; 870-793-8833; fax: 870-793-8888; 8AM-4:30PM (CST). *Felony, Civil Actions over $25,000.* www.independencecircuitclerk.com/

General Information: No juvenile records released. Will fax documents $3.50 1st page; $.25 ea add'l. Court makes copy: $.25 per page. Self serve copy: same. Certification fee: $5.00 per page. Payee: Circuit Clerk. Personal checks accepted. No credit cards accepted. Prepayment required.

Civil Name Search: Access: In person, online. Visitors must perform in person searches themselves. Required to search: name, years to search; also helpful: address. Civil cases indexed by defendant, plaintiff. Civil judgments on computer from 1980, all others on index books from 1970s. Civil PAT available. Online access to judgments and some civil records to be available by subscription in 2011; see website for details.

Criminal Name Search: Access: In person only. Visitors must perform in person searches themselves. Required to search: name, years to search, DOB; also helpful: address. Criminal records indexed in books from 1970s. Criminal PAT available.

State District Court 549 W Main, Batesville, AR 72501; 870-793-8804; fax: 870-793-8875; 8AM-4:30PM (CST). *Misdemeanor, Civil Actions under $25,000, Eviction, Small Claims.*

General Information: Will fax documents. Court makes copy: none. No certification fee . Payee: District Court. Only cashiers checks and money orders accepted. Major credit cards accepted online only. Prepayment required. Mail requests: SASE required.

Civil Name Search: Access: Mail, in person. Both court and visitors may perform in person name searches. No search fee. Civil cases indexed by Defendant, Plaintiff. Civil records go back to 1975. Mail turnaround time 1-2 days.

Criminal Name Search: Access: Mail, in person. Both court and visitors may perform in person name searches. No search fee. Required to search: name, years to search. Criminal records go back to 1975. Mail turnaround time 1-2 days.

Izard County

Circuit Court PO Box 95, Main St, Courthouse, Melbourne, AR 72556; 870-368-4316; fax: 870-368-4748; 8:30AM-4:30PM (CST). *Felony, Civil Actions over $5,000, Probate.*

General Information: Probate records are handled by the County Clerk, who can be reached thru the number above. No juvenile records released. No fee to fax documents locally; is $1.00 per page if long distance. Court makes copy: $.20 per page. Self serve copy: same. Certification fee: $5.00 per document. Payee: Izard County and Circuit Clerk. Personal checks accepted. No credit cards accepted. Prepayment required. Mail requests: SASE required.

Civil Name Search: Access: Fax, mail, in person. Visitors must perform in person searches themselves. No search fee. Required to search: name, years to search. Civil cases indexed by plaintiff. Civil records on judgment books from 1889. Mail turnaround time 2 weeks.

Criminal Name Search: Access: Phone, In person. Both court and visitors may perform in person name searches. No search fee. Required to search: name, years to search, DOB; also helpful: address. Criminal records on judgment books from 1889. Note: Phone search will only verify if a case record exists. Mail turnaround time 2 weeks.

Local District Court PO Box 337, Melbourne, AR 72556; 870-368-4390; fax: 870-368-2267; 8AM-4PM (CST). *Misdemeanor, Civil Actions under $5,000, Small Claims.*

General Information: Court located at the Jail annex west end of town. Will fax documents $1.00 per page. Court makes copy: $.25 per page. Self serve copy: same. Certification fee: $6.00 per doc. Payee: District Court. Personal checks accepted. No credit cards accepted. Prepayment required. Mail requests: SASE required.

Civil Name Search: Access: Mail, fax, in person. Only the court performs in person name searches; visitors may not. Search fee: $6.00. Required to search: name, years to search, Case #. Civil cases indexed by Defendant, Plaintiff. Civil records go back to 1977. Mail turnaround time varies.

Criminal Name Search: Access: Mail, fax, in person. Only the court performs in person name searches; visitors may not. Search fee: $6.00. Required to search: name, years to search, DOB. Criminal records go back to 1977; on computer back to 1997. Mail turnaround time varies.

Jackson County

Circuit Court Jackson County Courthouse, 208 Main St, Newport, AR 72112; 870-523-7423; fax: 870-523-3682; 8AM-4:30PM (CST). *Felony, Civil Actions over $5,000, Probate.*

General Information: Probate records are handled by the County Clerk, who can be reached at 870-523-7420. No juvenile records released. Will fax back $1.00 per page. Court makes copy: $.25 per page. Self serve copy: same. Certification fee: $5.00 per doc. Payee: Circuit Clerk. Personal checks accepted. No credit cards accepted. Prepayment required.

Civil Name Search: Access: In person only. Visitors must perform in person searches themselves. Civil records on dockets from 1800s. Civil PAT goes back to 1997.

Criminal Name Search: Access: In person only. Visitors must perform in person searches themselves. Required to search: name, years to search. Criminal docket index from 1800s, computerized back to 1997. Criminal PAT goes back to 1997. Public terminal has name index.

Local District Court 615 Third St, Newport, AR 72112; 870-523-9555; criminal phone: x119; civil phone: Ext 120; fax: 870-217-0397; 8AM-4:30PM (CST). *Misdemeanor, Civil Actions under $5,000, Eviction, Small Claims.*

General Information: Will fax documents to local or toll free line. Court makes copy: $5.00 for 10+ pages. No certification fee . Payee: Newport District Court. No personal checks or credit cards accepted. Prepayment required. Mail requests: SASE required.

Civil Name Search: Access: Phone, mail, fax, in person. Both court and visitors may perform in person name searches. No search fee. Records indexed by defendant only. Civil records go back to 1987. Mail turnaround time 5-7 days.

Criminal Name Search: Access: Mail, fax, in person. Both court and visitors may perform in person name searches. No search fee. Required to search: name, years to search, DOB. Criminal records go back to 1993 on computer, searchable to 1950. Mail turnaround time 5-7 days.

Jefferson County

Circuit Court PO Box 7433, 101 W Baraaque St, Pine Bluff, AR 71611; 870-541-5311; criminal phone: 870-541-5307; civil phone: 870-541-5306; fax: 870-541-5453; 8:30AM-5PM (CST). *Felony, Civil Actions over $5,000, Probate.*

General Information: Probate records are handled by the County Clerk, who can be reached thru the number above. No juvenile records released. Court makes copy: $.50 per page. Self serve copy: same. Certification fee: $.50 per page plus copy fee. Payee: Circuit Clerk. Only cashiers checks and money orders accepted. No credit cards accepted. Prepayment required.

Civil Name Search: Access: In person only. Visitors must perform in person searches themselves. Civil records on dockets from 1950. Civil PAT goes back to 1991. Results include name and case number.

Criminal Name Search: Access: In person only. Visitors must perform in person searches themselves. Required to search: name, years to search, DOB. Criminal docket index from 1950. Criminal PAT goes back to same as civil. Results include name and case number.

Local District Court 200 E 8th Ave, Pine Bluff, AR 71601; 870-543-1860 Div.I; 850-7584 Div. II; fax: 870-850-2440; 8AM-5PM (CST). *Misdemeanor, Civil Actions under $5,000, Eviction, Small Claims.*

General Information: There are two Divisions of the District Court Houses here. Both court's databases are searched when a record search is done. Will fax documents for fee, takes 3 days for return. Court makes copy: $1.00 per page. Certification fee: none. Payee: District Court. Cashiers checks money orders, and Visa/MC accepted. Mail requests: SASE required.

Civil Name Search: Access: Mail, in person. Both court and visitors may perform in person name searches. Search fee: $5.00 per name. Required to search: name. Civil records go back to 1994. Mail turnaround time 3 days.

Criminal Name Search: Access: Mail, in person. Both court and visitors may perform in person name searches. Search fee: $5.00 per name. Required to search: name, years to search; also helpful: DOB, SSN. Criminal records go back to 1989; computerized records since 1997. Mail turnaround time 3 days.

Johnson County

Circuit Court PO Box 189, 215 Main St, Clarksville, AR 72830-0189; 479-754-2977; probate phone: 479-754-3967; fax: 479-754-4235; 8AM-4:30PM (CST). *Felony, Civil Actions over $5,000, Probate.*

General Information: Probate records handled by County Clerk, PO Box 57, 479-754-3967. No juvenile records released. Will fax to 800 numbers only. Court makes copy: $.50 per page. Self serve copy: $.50 per page. Certification fee: $1.00 per cert. Personal checks accepted. No credit cards accepted. Prepayment required. Mail requests: SASE required.

Civil Name Search: Access: Fax, mail, in person. Both court and visitors may perform in person name searches. No search fee. Civil docket indexed from 1900s. Mail turnaround time 1-2 days.

Criminal Name Search: Access: Mail, in person. Both court and visitors may perform in person name searches. No search fee. Required to search: name, years to search, DOB; also helpful: SSN. Criminal records indexed from 1900s. Mail turnaround time 1-2 days.

Clarksville Local District Court PO Box 581, 301 Porter Industrial Rd, Clarksville, AR 72830; 479-754-8533; fax: 479-754-6014; 8AM-4:30PM (CST). *Misdemeanor, Civil Actions under $5,000, Eviction, Small Claims, Traffic.*

General Information: Will fax documents if only a page or 2. Court makes copy: no charge for 1st 10 pages. Self serve copy: same. No certification fee . Payee: Dist Ct of Johnson County. Will accept checks, but prefer not to. No credit cards accepted. Prepayment required. Mail requests: SASE required.

Civil Name Search: Access: Mail, in person. Both court and visitors may perform in person name searches. No search fee. Civil records go back 10 years. Mail turnaround time 2-3 days.

Criminal Name Search: Access: Mail, in person. Both court and visitors may perform in person name searches. No search fee. Required to search: name, years to search; also helpful: DOB, SSN. Records not computerized. Mail turnaround time 2-3 days.

Lamar Local District Court PO Box 700, 437 W Main St, Lamar, AR 72846; 479-885-3865; fax: 479-885-6171; 8AM-4:30PM (CST). *Misdemeanor, Civil Actions under $5,000, Eviction, Small Claims.*

Lafayette County

Circuit Court #3 Courthouse Square, Lewisville, AR 71845; 870-921-4878; probate phone: 870-921-4633; fax: 870-921-4879; 8AM-4:30PM (CST). *Felony, Civil Actions over $5,000, Probate.*

General Information: Probate is handled by County Clerk with a separate record index at #2 Courthouse Square. No juvenile records released without written order from the judge. Will fax documents to local or toll-free number. Court makes copy: $.50 per page. Self serve copy: same. Certification fee: $5.00 per doc. Payee: Circuit Clerk. Personal checks accepted. No credit cards accepted. Prepayment required. Mail requests: SASE required.

Civil Name Search: Access: Phone, mail, in person. Both court and visitors may perform in person name searches. No search fee. Civil records on dockets since 1950s. Mail turnaround time 3 days.

Criminal Name Search: Access: Mail, in person. Visitors must perform in person searches themselves. No search fee. Required to search: name, years to search. Criminal docket index from 1950s. Mail turnaround time 3 days.

Local District Court 110 E Fourth, #1, Lewisville, AR 71845; 870-921-5555; fax: 870-921-6666; 8AM-4:30PM (CST). *Misdemeanor, Civil Actions under $5,000, Eviction, Small Claims.*

General Information: Will fax docs no add'l fee. Court makes copy: $.25 per page. Self serve copy: same. Certification fee: $5.00 per doc plus copy fee. Payee: District Court. No credit cards accepted. Prepayment required.

Civil Name Search: Access: In person only. Visitors must perform in person searches themselves. Required to search: name; helpful- SSN.

Criminal Name Search: Access: Phone, In person. Both court and visitors may perform in person name searches. No search fee. Required to search: name, years to search, DOB; helpful- SSN. Records on computer back to 1994. Note: Office may do a name lookup via phone, but only back to 4/1996. Public use terminal has crim records back to 1996.

Lawrence County

Circuit Court PO Box 581, 315 W Main St, Rm 7, Walnut Ridge, AR 72476; 870-886-1112; probate phone: 870-886-1111; fax: 870-886-1128; 8AM-4:30PM (CST). *Felony, Civil Actions over $5,000, Probate.*

General Information: Probate is handled by County Clerk with a separate record index. No juvenile records released. Will fax documents $1.00 per page. Court makes copy: $.25 per page. Self serve copy: same. Certification fee: $5.00 per document plus copy fee. Payee: Circuit Clerk. Personal checks accepted. No credit cards accepted. Prepayment required.

Civil Name Search: Access: In person only. Visitors must perform in person searches themselves. Civil docket indexed from 1981, on docket sheets from 1960s.

Criminal Name Search: Access: In person only. Visitors must perform in person searches themselves. Required to search: name, years to search. Criminal records indexed from 1981, on docket sheets from 1960s.

Walnut Ridge Local District Court 116 NW 3rd, Walnut Ridge, AR 72476; 870-886-1140; fax: 870-886-3905; 8AM-4:30PM (CST). *Misdemeanor, Civil Actions under $5,000, Small Claims.*

General Information: Will fax documents to local or toll free line. Court makes copy: None. Self serve copy: same. No certification fee . No credit cards accepted.

Civil Name Search: Access: Mail, in person. Both court and visitors may perform in person name searches. No search fee. Civil cases indexed by Defendant, Plaintiff, Case #. Computerized records since 1992. Mail turnaround time 2-3 days.

Criminal Name Search: Access: Mail, in person. Both court and visitors may perform in person name searches. No search fee. Required to search: name, years to search, offense. Computerized records since 1992. Mail turnaround time 2-3 days.

Lee County

Circuit Court 15 E Chestnut, Marianna, AR 72360; 870-295-7710; probate phone: 870-295-7715; fax: 870-295-7712; 8:30AM-4:30PM (CST). *Felony, Civil Actions over $5,000, Probate.*

General Information: Probate is handled by County Clerk with a separate record index at this same address. Probate fax- 870-295-7766 No juvenile records released. Will fax documents $1.00 per page. Court makes copy: $.25 per page. Self serve copy: same. Certification fee: $5.00. Payee: Circuit

Court. Personal checks accepted. No credit cards accepted. Prepayment required.

Civil Name Search: Access: In person only. Visitors must perform in person searches themselves. Civil index on docket books from 1873; computerized records since 1/2002. Civil PAT goes back to 2002.

Criminal Name Search: Access: In person only. Visitors must perform in person searches themselves. Required to search: name, years to search, DOB. Criminal records indexed in books from 1873; computerized records since 1/2002. Criminal PAT goes back to same as civil.

Local District Court 15 E Chestnut, Rm 9, Marianna, AR 72360; 870-295-7730; fax: 870-295-7788; 8:30AM-4:30PM (CST). *Misdemeanor, Civil Actions under $5,000, Eviction, Small Claims.*

General Information: Court makes copy: $.25 per page. Certification fee: $5.00 per doc. Payee: Lee County District Court. Personal checks accepted. No credit cards accepted. Mail requests: SASE requested.

Civil Name Search: Access: Mail, in person. Only the court performs in person name searches; visitors may not. Search fee: $5.00. Civil records go back to 1995; on computer back to 1995 except some small claims only back to 2006. Mail turnaround time 5 days.

Criminal Name Search: Access: Mail, in person. Only the court performs in person name searches; visitors may not. Search fee: $5.00. Required to search: name, years to search. Computerized records since 1994. Mail turnaround time 5 days.

Lincoln County

Circuit Court Courthouse, 300 S Drew, Star City, AR 71667; 870-628-3154; probate phone: 870-628-5114; fax: 870-628-5546; 8AM-4:30PM (CST). *Felony, Civil Actions over $5,000, Probate.*

General Information: Probate is handled by County Clerk with a separate record index at this same address. No sealed records released. Will fax documents $1.00 per page. Court makes copy: $.50 per page. Self serve copy: same. Certification fee: $5.00 per document. Payee: Lincoln County Circuit Court. Personal checks accepted. No credit cards accepted. Prepayment required.

Civil Name Search: Access: In person only. Both court and visitors may perform in person name searches. No search fee. Civil docket indexed from 1920, archived from 1920. Public use terminal has civil records. Only judgments are available, and only on the Recorder's Office index.

Criminal Name Search: Access: In person only. Visitors must perform in person searches themselves. Required to search: name, years to search. Criminal records indexed from 1920, archived from 1920.

Star City Lincoln County District Court 300 S Drew St, Rm 201, Star City, AR 71667; 870-628-4904; civil phone: 870-628-4244; fax: 870-628-6442; 8AM-4:30PM (CST). *Misdemeanor.*

General Information: No fee to fax 5 pages or less. Court makes copy: $.50 per page. No certification fee . Payee: District Court of Star City. .

Criminal Name Search: Access: Mail, in person. Both court and visitors may perform in person name searches. No search fee. Required to search: name, years to search, DOB, signed release; also helpful: address, SSN, DL#. Criminal records go back to 1980; on computer back to 1991. Mail turnaround time 3-5 days.

Gould Local District Court PO Box 536, Gould, AR 71643; 870-263-4475; ; 8AM-4:30PM (CST). *Misdemeanor, Traffic.*

Star City Local District Court PO Box 219, Star City, AR 71667; 870-628-4166; fax: 870-628-4055; 8AM-4:30PM (CST). *Civil Actions under $5,000, Eviction, Small Claims.*

Little River County

Circuit Court PO Box 575, Ashdown, AR 71822; 870-898-7212; probate phone: 870-898-7210; fax: 870-898-5783; 8AM-4:30PM (CST). *Felony, Civil Actions over $5,000, Probate.*

General Information: Probate is handled by County Clerk with a separate record index at this same address. Probate fax is same as main fax number. No juvenile records released. Will not fax documents. Court makes copy: $.50 per page. Self serve copy: same. Certification fee: $5.00 per document plus copy fee. Payee: Circuit Clerk. Personal checks accepted. No credit cards accepted. Prepayment required.

Civil Name Search: Access: in person only. Both court and visitors may perform in person name searches. No search fee. Required to search: name, years to search. Civil cases indexed by plaintiff. Civil records docket books back to 1868.

Criminal Name Search: Access: In person only. Visitors must perform in person searches themselves. Required to search: name. Criminal docket on books back to 1893. Note: Direct criminal records searches to AR state police; 870-777-4641 .

Local District Court 351 N 2nd St, #8, Ashdown, AR 71822; 870-898-7230; fax: 870-898-7262; 8AM-4:30PM (CST). *Misdemeanor, Civil Actions under $5,000, Eviction, Small Claims.*

General Information: Will fax documents. Court makes copy: $.50 per page. Certification fee: $5.00 per doc. Payee: District Court. Only cashiers checks and money orders accepted. No credit cards accepted. Mail requests: SASE required.

Civil Name Search: Access: Mail, in person. Both court and visitors may perform in person name searches. Search fee: $5.00. Civil records on computer since 1987. Mail turnaround time 1 week.

Criminal Name Search: Access: Mail, in person. Both court and visitors may perform in person name searches. Search fee: $5.00. Required to search: name, years to search; also helpful: DOB, SSN. Criminal records on computer since 1987. Mail turnaround time 1 week. Public use terminal has crim records back to 10 years. Results include driver's license number.

Logan County

Circuit Court Courthouse, 25 W Walnut, Paris, AR 72855; 479-963-2164; probate phone: 479-963-2618; fax: 479-963-3304; 8AM-4:30PM (CST). *Felony, Civil Actions over $5,000, Probate.*

General Information: Probate is handled by the county clerk in Rm #25. Probate fax- 479-963-9017. There is another Circuit Court in Booneville, at 479-675-2894. Will fax documents for $1.00 per page fee. Court makes copy: $.25 per page in person, $.50 mail. Self serve copy: same. Certification fee: $5.00. Payee: Circuit Clerk. Personal checks accepted. No credit cards accepted. Prepayment required.

Civil Name Search: Access: In person only. Visitors must perform in person searches themselves. Civil records on index from 1901, on computer back to 1991-92.

Criminal Name Search: Access: In person only. Visitors must perform in person searches themselves. Required to search: name, years to search. Criminal records on index from 1901.

Booneville Local District Court 461 East 5th Street, Booneville, AR 72927; 479-675-4929; fax: 479-675-0133; 8:30AM-4:30PM (CST). *Misdemeanor, Civil Actions under $5,000, Eviction, Small Claims.*

General Information: Will fax documents to local or toll free line. Court makes copy: none. No certification fee . Payee: District Court. No credit cards accepted. Mail requests: SASE required.

Civil Name Search: Access: Mail, in person. Both court and visitors may perform in person name searches. No search fee. Civil records go back to the 1970's; computerized records since 1994. Mail turnaround time 1-2 days.

Criminal Name Search: Access: Mail, in person. Both court and visitors may perform in person name searches. No search fee. Required to search: name, years to search; also helpful: DOB. Criminal records go back to 1970's; computerized records since 1994. Mail turnaround time 1-2 days.

Paris Local District Court Paris Courthouse, 25 W Walnut, Paris, AR 72855; 479-963-3792; fax: 479-963-2762; 8:30AM-4:30PM (CST). *Misdemeanor, Civil Actions under $5,000, Eviction, Small Claims.*

General Information: Will fax documents to local or toll free line. Court makes copy: none. No certification fee . Payee: District Court. No credit cards accepted. Mail requests: SASE required.

Civil Name Search: Access: Mail, in person. Both court and visitors may perform in person name searches. No search fee. Civil records go back to the 1970's; computerized records since 1994. Mail turnaround time 1-2 days.

Criminal Name Search: Access: Mail, in person. Both court and visitors may perform in person name searches. No search fee. Required to search: name, years to search; also helpful: DOB. Criminal records go back to 1970's; computerized records since 1994. Mail turnaround time 1-2 days.

Lonoke County

Circuit Court PO Box 219, Attn: Circuit Clerk, 301 N Center St, Lonoke, AR 72086; 501-676-2316; probate phone: 501-676-2368; fax: 501-676-3014; 8AM-4:30PM (CST). *Felony, Civil Actions over $5,000, Probate.* www.lonokecountycircuitclerk.com/

General Information: Probate is in the County Clerks' office. No juvenile records released. Will fax documents $1.00 per page. Court makes copy: $.25 per page. Self serve copy: same. Certification fee: $6.00. Payee: Circuit Clerk. Personal checks accepted. Major credit cards accepted in person, there is a fee. Prepayment required. Mail requests: SASE required for criminal.

Civil Name Search: Access: in person only. Visitors must perform in person searches themselves. Required to search: name, years to search. Civil cases indexed by defendant. Civil records on computer from 1989, on dockets from 1918's. Civil PAT available.

Criminal Name Search: Access: In person. Visitors must perform in person searches themselves. Required to search: name, years to search, SSN. Criminal records computerized from 1989, on dockets from 1918's (not for public use). Mail turnaround time 1-2 days. Criminal PAT available.

Cabot Northern Local District Court 208 N 1st St, Cabot, AR 72023; 501-843-8908; fax: 501-843-8168; 8AM-4:30PM (CST). *Misdemeanor, Civil Actions under $5,000, Eviction, Small Claims.* www.cabotar.gov/department/?fDD=17-0

Carlisle Southern Local District Court PO Box 49, 100 W Main St, Carlisle, AR 72024; 870-552-3436; fax: 870-552-1188; 8AM-4:30PM (CST). *Misdemeanor, Civil Actions under $5,000, Eviction, Small Claims.* www.carlislear.org/Court/District%20Court.htm

England Southern Local District Court PO Box 249, England, AR 72046; 501-842-3904; fax: 501-842-8200; 8:30AM-4:30PM (CST). *Misdemeanor, Civil Actions under $5,000, Eviction, Small Claims.*

Lonoke Local District Court 107 W 2nd St, Lonoke, AR 72086-2701; 501-676-3585; fax: 501-676-4316; 8AM-4:30PM (CST). *Misdemeanor, Civil Actions under $5,000, Eviction, Small Claims.*

Ward Northern Local District Court PO Box 237, Ward, AR 72176; 501-605-0339; fax: 501-941-4699; 8AM-4:30PM (CST). *Misdemeanor, Civil Actions under $5,000, Eviction, Small Claims.*

Madison County

Circuit Court PO Box 626, Courthouse, Huntsville, AR 72740; 479-738-2215; probate phone: 479-738-2747; fax: 479-738-1544; 8AM-4:30PM (CST). *Felony, Civil Actions over $5,000, Probate.*

General Information: Probate is in the County Clerk's office, PO Box 37. Probate fax- 479-738-2735 No juvenile records released. Will fax specific doc for $1.00 per page. Court makes copy: $.25 per page. Self serve copy: same. Certification fee: $5.00 per doc. Payee: Circuit Clerk. Personal checks accepted. No credit cards accepted. Prepayment required.

Civil Name Search: Access: In person only. Visitors must perform in person searches themselves. Required to search: name, years to search; also helpful: address. Civil cases indexed by defendant, plaintiff. Civil records on dockets back to 1892. Civil PAT goes back to 1994. PAT index includes only court orders and judgments.

Criminal Name Search: Access: In person only. Visitors must perform in person searches themselves. Required to search: name, years to search; also helpful: DOB, SSN. Criminal records on dockets back to 1906. Criminal PAT goes back to 1994. PAT index includes only court orders and judgments.

Local District Court PO Box 549, 208 E War Eagle, Huntsville, AR 72740; 479-738-2911; fax: 479-738-6846; 8AM-4:30PM (CST). *Misdemeanor, Civil Actions under $5,000, Eviction, Small Claims.*

General Information: Will not fax documents. Court makes copy: $.25 per page. Self serve copy: $.25 per page.If citation is in Madison County payments are sent to: The Madison County Sheriff's Dept, PO Box 476, Huntsville, AR 72740. Certification fee: $5.00 per doc. Payee: District Court. No personal checks or credit cards accepted. Mail requests: SASE required.

Civil Name Search: Access: Mail, fax, in person. Both court and visitors may perform in person name searches. No search fee. Records go back 10 years. Note: Court will search only if time permits. Mail turnaround time 1 week. Civil PAT goes back to 1999.

Criminal Name Search: Access: In person only. Visitors must perform in person searches themselves. Required to search: name, years to search, DOB, SSN. Criminal records go back to 1991; on computer seven years. Note: This court will not perform background checks. Mail turnaround time 1 week. Criminal PAT goes back to same as civil.

Marion County

Circuit Court PO Box 385, Yellville, AR 72687; 870-449-6226; fax: 870-449-4979; 8AM-4:30PM (CST). *Felony, Civil Actions over $5,000, Probate.*

General Information: Probate is handled by County Clerk with a separate record index at this same address. The fax number listed above is not in this office. Please call ahead if faxing. No juvenile or adoption records released. Will fax specifically-requested case file for $1.00 per page. Court makes copy: $.25 per page. Self serve copy: same. Certification fee: $5.00 per document includes copies. Payee: Marion County Circuit Clerk. Personal checks accepted. No credit cards accepted. Prepayment required.

Civil Name Search: Access: In person only. Visitors must perform in person searches themselves. Required to search: name, years to search. Civil cases indexed by plaintiff. Civil records on dockets from 1956, records are not computerized.

Criminal Name Search: Access: In person only. Visitors must perform in person searches themselves. Required to search: name, years to search. Criminal docket index from 1956, records are not computerized. Note: The court recommends to use the State Police for criminal record checks.

Local District Court PO Box 301, 105 S Berry St, Yellville, AR 72687; 870-449-6030; fax: 870-449-1177; 8AM-N, 1PM-4:30PM (CST). *Misdemeanor, Civil Actions under $5,000, Small Claims.*

General Information: This court will absolutely not do name searches for the public. Will fax documents to local or toll free line. Court makes copy:

$.25 per page. Self serve copy: same. Certification fee: $5.00 per doc. Payee: Marion County Court. Personal checks accepted. No credit cards accepted. Prepayment required.

Civil Name Search: Access: In person only. Visitors must perform in person searches themselves. Required to search: name. Civil records go back to 1985. Mail turnaround time 1-2 days.

Criminal Name Search: Access: In person only. Visitors must perform in person searches themselves. Required to search: name, years to search, DOB. Criminal records go back to 1985; on computer back to 1996. Mail turnaround time 1-2 days.

Miller County

Circuit Court 412 Laurel St, Rm 109, Texarkana, AR 71854; 870-774-4501; probate phone: 870-774-1501; fax: 870-772-5293; 8AM-4:30PM (CST). *Felony, Civil Actions over $25,000, Probate.*

General Information: Probate is at the County Clerk's office and not part of the Circuit Court. The case limit on civil records was raised to $25,000 as of 01/01/2008. No expunged records released. Will fax documents to local or toll free line. Court makes copy: $1.00 per page. Self serve copy: same. Certification fee: $5.00 per doc plus copy fee. Payee: Miller County Circuit Clerk. Personal checks not accepted. No credit cards accepted. Prepayment required. Mail requests: SASE required.

Civil Name Search: Access: Phone, mail, in person, online. Both court and visitors may perform in person name searches. Search fee: $8.00 per name. Civil docket indexed from 1850s. Note: If court to perform name search, approximate date needed. Mail turnaround time 1-3 days. Civil PAT goes back to 2003. Online access to circuit court dockets by subscription through RecordsUSA.com. Credit card, username and password is required; choose either monthly or per-use plan. Visit the website for sign-up or call Rob at 888-633-4748 x17 for information.

Criminal Name Search: Access: Mail, in person, online. Both court and visitors may perform in person name searches. Search fee: $8.00 per name. Required to search: name, years to search. Criminal records indexed from 1850s; computerized records since 2000. Note: Clerk will only perform your criminal search if you have a case number; clerk will certify the disposition on that case. Or, direct search to AR State Police or the ACIC. Mail turnaround time 1-2 days. Criminal PAT goes back to same as civil. Online access to criminal dockets is the same as civil. Online results show name only.

Miller County District Court 2300 East St, Texarkana, AR 71854; 870-772-2780; fax: 870-773-3595; 8AM-4:30PM (CST). *Misdemeanor, Eviction.*

General Information: Will fax documents to local or toll free line. Court makes copy: none. Certification fee: $5.00. No credit cards accepted. Prepayment required. Mail requests: SASE required.

Criminal Name Search: Access: Mail, in person. Only the court performs in person name searches; visitors may not. Search fee: $5.00 per name. Required to search: name, years to search, DOB. Criminal records on computer back to 1997. Mail turnaround time 2 days.

Texarkana State District Court 100 N Stateline #2, Texarkana, AR 75501; 903-798-3016; fax: 903-798-3588; 8AM-5PM (CST). *Misdemeanor, Civil Actions under $25,000, Small Claims, Eviction.* www.txkusa.org/

General Information: Restrictions apply to some records. Will fax documents to local or toll free line. Court makes copy: $1.00 each from computer screen. Certification fee: $10.00 per transcript. Payee: Miller District Court. Only cashiers checks and money orders accepted. No credit cards accepted. Prepayment required. Mail requests: SASE required.

Civil Name Search: Access: Mail, in person. Both court and visitors may perform in person name searches. Search fee: $6.00 per name. Required to search: name, DOB. Civil cases indexed by defendant, plaintiff. Civil records on docket index, year not given. Mail turnaround time 2 days.

Criminal Name Search: Access: Mail, in person. Only the court performs in person name searches; visitors may not. No search fee, unless extensive searching involved. Required to search: name, years to search, DOB. Criminal records on computer back to 1997. Mail turnaround time 2 days.

Mississippi County

Blytheville Circuit Court PO Box 1498, 200 W Walnut St, Blytheville, AR 72316; 870-762-2332; fax: 870-762-8148; 9AM-4:30PM (CST). *Felony, Civil Actions over $25,000.*

General Information: No juvenile records released. Will fax specific case file $1.00 per page. Court makes copy: $.50 per page. Self serve copy: same. Certification fee: $5.00 includes copy fee. Court may add add'l copy fee is document is lengthy. Payee: Circuit Clerk. No personal checks or credit cards accepted. Prepayment required.

Civil Name Search: Access: In person only. Visitors must perform in person searches themselves. Required to search: name, years to search. Civil cases indexed by plaintiff. Civil records prior on index from 1940; court orders on imaging computer back to 1/2003.

Criminal Name Search: Access: In person only. Visitors must perform in person searches themselves. Required to search: name, years to search, DOB, SSN. Criminal records prior on index for 7 years, in storage from 1940; court orders on imaging computer back to 1/2003. Note: The court refers all criminal record name searches to AR State Police.

Osceola Circuit Court PO Box 466, 200 W Hale, County Courthouse, Osceola, AR 72370; 870-563-6471; fax: 870-563-5063; 9AM-4:30PM (CST). *Felony, Civil Actions over $5,000, Probate.*

General Information: Probate records are handled by the County Clerk, who can be reached thru the number above. No juvenile records released. Will fax documents $1.00 per page. Court makes copy: $.50 per page. Self serve copy: same. Certification fee: $5.00 per document. Payee: Circuit Clerk. Personal checks accepted. No credit cards accepted. Prepayment required.

Civil Name Search: Access: In person only. Visitors must perform in person searches themselves. Required to search: name, years to search. Civil cases indexed by plaintiff. Civil records computerized since 1992, on index from 1940. Civil PAT goes back to 1992. Results include plaintiff's name.

Criminal Name Search: Access: In person only. Both court and visitors may perform in person name searches. No search fee. Required to search: name, years to search, DOB, charge; also helpful: SSN. Criminal records on computer since 1992. Note: Court directs criminal search requests to the AR State Police. Criminal PAT goes back to 1988. Results include plaintiff's name.

Blytheville State District Court 121 N 2nd St, #104, Blytheville, AR 72315; 870-763-7513; fax: 870-762-0433; 8AM-5PM (CST). *Misdemeanor, Civil Actions under $25,000, Small Claims.*

General Information: Will fax documents to local or toll free line. Court makes copy: $.50 per page. Self serve copy: $.25 per page. Certification fee: $5.00. Payee: City of Blytheville. Personal checks accepted. No credit cards accepted. Prepayment required. Mail requests: SASE required.

Civil Name Search: Access: Mail, fax, in person. Only the court performs in person name searches; visitors may not. Search fee: $4.00 per name. Civil cases indexed by Defendant, Plaintiff. Civil records go back to 1960; on computer back to 1987. Mail turnaround time 1-2 days.

Criminal Name Search: Access: Mail, fax, in person. Only the court performs in person name searches; visitors may not. Search fee: $4.00 per name. Required to search: name, years to search; also helpful: DOB, SSN. Criminal records go back to 1960; on computer back to 1987. Mail turnaround time 1-2 days.

Dell State District Court PO Box 206, Dell, AR 72426; 870-564-2659; fax: 870-564-2811; 8AM-5PM (CST). *Misdemeanor, Civil Actions under $25,000, Small Claims.*

General Information: The case limit on civil records was raised to $25,000 as of 01/01/2008.

Gosnell State District Court 201 S Airbase Hwy, Gosnell, AR 72315; 870-532-8544; fax: 870-532-5958; 8AM-5PM (CST). *Misdemeanor, Civil Actions under $25,000, Small Claims.*

General Information: The case limit on civil records was raised to $25,000 as of 01/01/2008.

Leachville State District Court PO Box 67, Leachville, AR 72438; 870-539-6604; fax: 870-539-2490; 8AM-4:30PM (CST). *Misdemeanor, Civil Actions under $25,000, Small Claims.*

General Information: The case limit on civil records was raised to $25,000 as of 01/01/2008.

Manilla State District Court PO Box 895, Manilla, AR 72442; 870-561-3554; fax: 870-561-4438; 8AM-5PM (CST). *Misdemeanor, Civil Actions under $25,000, Small Claims.*

General Information: The case limit on civil records was raised to $25,000 as of 01/01/2008.

Osceola State District Court 397 W Keiser, Osceola, AR 72370; 870-563-1303; fax: 870-563-8439; 8AM-4PM (CST). *Misdemeanor, Civil Actions under $25,000, Small Claims.*

General Information: Will fax documents to local or toll free line. Court makes copy: $1.00 per page. Self serve copy: same. Certification fee: $2.00 per page plus copy fee. Payee: Osceola District Court. Personal checks accepted. No credit cards accepted. Prepayment required. Mail requests: SASE required.

Civil Name Search: Access: Mail, in person, fax. Only the court performs in person name searches; visitors may not. Search fee: $10.00. Required to search: name, DOB and SSN. Records computerized for at least 7 years. Mail turnaround time 1-2 days.

Criminal Name Search: Access: Mail, in person. Only the court performs in person name searches; visitors may not. Search fee: $10.00. Required to search: name, years to search; also helpful: address, DOB, SSN. Records computerized for at least 7 years. Mail turnaround time 1-2 days.

Monroe County

Circuit Court 123 Madison St, Courthouse, Clarendon, AR 72029; 870-747-3615; probate phone: 870-747-3632; fax: 870-747-3710; 8AM-4:30PM (CST). *Felony, Civil Actions over $5,000, Probate.*

General Information: Probate is managed by the County Clerk office. No juvenile records released. Will fax documents $2.50 per page and $2.50 per doc. Add $.50 per page if more than 4. Court makes copy: $.25 per page. Self serve copy: same. Certification fee: $5.00. Payee: Monroe County Circuit Clerk. Personal checks accepted. No credit cards accepted. Prepayment required. Mail requests: SASE required for civil.

Civil Name Search: Access: Fax, mail, in person. Both court and visitors may perform in person name searches. No search fee. Civil index on docket books from 1931.

Criminal Name Search: Access: In person only. Visitors must perform in person searches themselves. Required to search: name, years to search. Criminal records indexed in books from 1933.

Clarendon Local District Court City Hall, 270 Madison St, Clarendon, AR 72029; 870-747-5200; fax: 870-747-3903; 8AM-5PM (CST). *Misdemeanor, Civil Actions under $5,000, Small Claims, Traffic.*

General Information: Will fax documents to local or toll free line. Court makes copy: $.25 per page. Self serve copy: same. Certification fee: $5.00 per doc includes copy fee. Payee: Clarendon District Court. Personal checks accepted. No credit cards accepted. Prepayment required.

Civil Name Search: Access: Mail, in person. Both court and visitors may perform in person name searches. No search fee. Required to search: name, years to search, DOB. Records go back to 1988, on computer since 1993. Mail turnaround time 1-2 days.

Criminal Name Search: Access: Mail, in person. Both court and visitors may perform in person name searches. No search fee. Required to search: name, years to search, DOB, SSN. Records go back to 1988, on computer since 1998. Mail turnaround time 1-2 days.

Brinkley Local District Court City Hall, 233 W Cedar, Brinkley, AR 72021; 870-734-2520; fax: 870-734-3163; 8AM-5PM (CST). *Misdemeanor, Civil Actions under $5,000, Small Claims, Traffic.*

General Information: Will fax documents to local or toll free line. Court makes copy: $1.00 per page. Self serve copy: same. Certification fee: $5.00 per doc includes copy fee. Payee: Brinkley District Court. Personal checks accepted. No credit cards accepted. Prepayment required.

Civil Name Search: Access: Mail, in person. Both court and visitors may perform in person name searches. No search fee. Required to search: name, years to search, DOB. Records go back to 1988, on computer since 1993. Mail turnaround time 1-2 days.

Criminal Name Search: Access: Mail, in person. Both court and visitors may perform in person name searches. No search fee. Required to search: name, years to search, DOB, SSN. Records go back to 1988, on computer since 1998. Mail turnaround time 1-2 days.

Montgomery County

Circuit Court 105 Hwy 270 E, #10, Courthouse, Mount Ida, AR 71957; 870-867-3521; fax: 870-867-2177; 8AM-4:30PM (CST). *Felony, Civil Actions over $5,000, Probate.*

General Information: Probate is handled by County Clerk with a separate record index at this same address. No juvenile or adoption records released. Will fax out docs for $3.00 per each 5 pages; call office to confirm. Court makes copy: $.50 per page. Self serve copy: $.25 per page. Certification fee: $5.00. Payee: Circuit Clerk. Personal checks accepted. No credit cards accepted. Prepayment required. Mail requests: SASE required for civil.

Civil Name Search: Access: Phone, fax, mail, in person. Both court and visitors may perform in person name searches. Search fee: $6.00 per name. Required to search: name, years to search; also helpful: address. Civil cases indexed by defendant, plaintiff. Civil records on card files from 1960s. Mail turnaround time same day. Civil PAT goes back to 6/2006.

Criminal Name Search: Access: In person only. Visitors must perform in person searches themselves. Required to search: name, years to search; also helpful: DOB, SSN. Criminal records on card files from 1960s. Criminal PAT goes back to 6/2006.

Local District Court 105 Hwy 270 E #2, Mount Ida, AR 71957; 870-867-2221; fax: 870-867-3695; 8AM-4:30PM (CST). *Misdemeanor, Civil Actions under $5,000, Eviction, Small Claims.*

General Information: No fee to fax documents. Court makes copy: none. Self serve copy: none. No certification fee . Payee: Montgomery County Sheriff Office. Personal checks accepted. No credit cards accepted. Prepayment required. Mail requests: SASE required.

Civil Name Search: Access: Mail, in person. Both court and visitors may perform in person name searches. No search fee. Required to search: name, years to search, DOB, SSN. Records indexed by plaintiff and defendant. Records go back to 1973; computerized records go back to 1993. Mail turnaround time 1-2 days.

Criminal Name Search: Access: Mail, in person. Both court and visitors may perform in person name searches. No search fee. Required to search: name, years to search, DOB, SSN. Records go back to 1973; computerized records go back to 1993. Mail turnaround time 1-2 days.

Nevada County

Circuit Court 215 E 2nd S., Prescott, AR 71857; 870-887-2511; fax: 870-887-1911; 8AM-4:30PM (CST). *Felony, Civil Actions over $5,000.*

General Information: No juvenile records released. Will fax documents $1.00 per page. Court makes copy: $1.00 per page. Self serve copy: same. Certification fee: $2.00 plus copy fee. Payee: Nevada County Circuit Clerk. Personal checks accepted. No credit cards accepted. Prepayment required. Mail requests: SASE required.

Civil Name Search: Access: Phone, fax, mail, in person. Both court and visitors may perform in person name searches. Search fee: $6.00 per name. Civil records on index since 1871. Mail turnaround time 1-2 days.

Criminal Name Search: Access: In person only. Visitors must perform in person searches themselves. Required to search: name, years to search, DOB. Criminal records on index since 1871.

Local District Court 215 E 2nd St S, #104, Prescott, AR 71857; 870-887-6016; fax: 870-887-5795; 8:30AM-4:30PM (CST). *Misdemeanor, Civil Actions under $5,000, Small Claims.*

General Information: Will fax documents to local or toll free line. Court makes copy: $6.00 per page. Certification fee: $6.00. Will only certify civil records, not criminal. Payee: District Court. No personal checks or credit cards accepted. Prepayment required. Mail requests: SASE requested.

Civil Name Search: Access: Phone, mail, fax, in person. Only the court performs in person name searches; visitors may not. Search fee: $6.00 per name. Records on computer go back to 1997. Mail turnaround time 2-5 days.

Criminal Name Search: Access: Phone, mail, fax, in person. Only the court performs in person name searches; visitors may not. Search fee: $6.00 per name. Required to search: name, years to search, DOB, SSN. Records on computer go back to 1997. Mail turnaround time 2-5 days.

Newton County

Circuit Court PO Box 410, Jasper, AR 72641; 870-446-5125; fax: 870-446-5755; 8AM-4:30PM (CST). *Felony, Civil Actions over $5,000, Probate.*

General Information: Probate records are handled by the County Clerk, who can be reached thru the number above. No juvenile records released. Will fax documents $2.50 1st page, $.50 each add'l. Court makes copy: $.25 per page. Self serve copy: same. Certification fee: $5.00. Payee: Circuit Clerk. Personal checks accepted. No credit cards accepted. Prepayment required. Mail requests: SASE required.

Civil Name Search: Access: Fax, mail, in person. Both court and visitors may perform in person name searches. Search fee: $6.00 per name. Civil records on dockets from 1800s. Mail turnaround time varies.

Criminal Name Search: Access: Fax, mail, in person. Both court and visitors may perform in person name searches. Search fee: $6.00 per name. Required to search: name, years to search, DOB. Criminal docket index from 1800s. Mail turnaround time varies.

Local District Court PO Box 550, 100 E Court St, 2nd Fl, Jasper, AR 72641; 870-446-5335; fax: 870-446-2234; 8AM-4:30PM (CST). *Misdemeanor, Civil Actions under $5,000, Eviction, Small Claims.*

General Information: Will fax documents to local or toll free line. Court makes copy: $.25 per page. Self serve copy: same. Certification fee: $10.00. Payee: Newton County District Court. Personal checks accepted. No credit cards accepted. Prepayment required.

Civil Name Search: Access: Mail, fax, in person. Only the court performs in person name searches; visitors may not. No search fee. Required to search: name plus years to search, and DOB or SSN. Civil cases indexed by defendant, plaintiff. Records go back to 1984, civil records not computerized. Mail turnaround time 24 hours.

Criminal Name Search: Access: Mail, fax, in person. Only the court performs in person name searches; visitors may not. Search fee: $10.00 per name. Required to search: name plus years to search, and DOB or SSN. Records go back to 1972, on computer back to 1997. Mail turnaround time 24 hours.

Ouachita County

Circuit Court PO Box 667, Camden, AR 71701; 870-837-2230 (Circuit); probate phone: 870-837-2220; fax: 870-837-2252; 8AM-4:30PM (CST). *Felony, Civil Actions over $5,000, Probate.*

General Information: Probate is a separate index c/o County Clerk, PO Box 1041. Probate fax- 870-837-2251. No juvenile records released. Will fax specific case file $3.00 per fax plus copy fee. Court makes copy: $.50 per page. Self serve copy: same. Certification fee: $5.00 per cert plus copy fee. Payee: Circuit Clerk of Ouachita County. Personal checks accepted. No credit cards accepted. Prepayment required.

Civil Name Search: Access: In person only. Visitors must perform in person searches themselves. Civil records archived from 1950s; on computer back to 3/1999. Civil PAT goes back to 1999.

Criminal Name Search: Access: In person only. Visitors must perform in person searches themselves. Required to search: name, years to search; also helpful: DOB, SSN. Criminal records archived from 1950s; on computer back to 3/1999. Criminal PAT goes back to same as civil.

Camden Local District Court 213 Madison St, Camden, AR 71701; 870-836-0331; fax: 870-837-5530; 8AM-4:30PM (CST). *Misdemeanor, Civil Actions under $5,000, Eviction, Small Claims.*

General Information: Will fax documents to local or toll free line. Court makes copy: $.25 per page. Self serve copy: same. Certification fee: $5.00 per document plus copy fee. Payee: District Court. No personal checks accepted. Business check and money orders accepted. No credit cards accepted. Prepayment required.

Civil Name Search: Access: Mail, fax, in person. Both court and visitors may perform in person name searches. Search fee: $5.00 per name. Required to search: name, years to search, also helpful Case #. Civil records are indexed by Plaintiff, Defendant. Records go back to 1950; computerized since 1987. Mail turnaround time 1-2 days.

Criminal Name Search: Access: Mail, fax, in person. Both court and visitors may perform in person name searches. Search fee: $5.00 per name. Required to search: name, years to search, DOB; also helpful: SSN. Records go back to 1950; computerized since 1987. Note: Access to traffic records also provided. Mail turnaround time 1-2 days.

East Camden Local District Court PO Box 3046, East Camden, AR 71701; 870-574-2900; fax: 870-574-2905; 8AM-4:30PM (CST). *Misdemeanor, Civil Actions under $5,000, Eviction, Small Claims.*

Perry County

Circuit Court PO Box 358, Perryville, AR 72126; 501-889-5126; fax: 501-889-5759; 8AM-4:30PM (CST). *Felony, Civil Actions over $5,000, Probate.*

General Information: Probate records are handled by the County Clerk, who can be reached thru the number above. No juvenile or adoption records released. Will fax specific case file $1.00 per page. Court makes copy: $.50 first page, $.25 each add'l. Self serve copy: same. Certification fee: $5.00 per document. Payee: Circuit Clerk. Personal checks accepted. No credit cards accepted. Prepayment required. Mail requests: SASE required for criminal.

Civil Name Search: Access: In person only. Both court and visitors may perform in person name searches. No search fee. Civil records on computer from 1997, on dockets from 1916. Civil PAT goes back to 1997.

Criminal Name Search: Access: Phone, mail, in person. Both court and visitors may perform in person name searches. No search fee. Required to search: name, years to search, DOB. Criminal records computerized from 1997, on dockets from 1916. Note: The court's phone search is a quick index search. Criminal PAT goes back to same as civil.

Local District Court PO Box 186, Perryville, AR 72126; 501-889-5296; fax: 501-889-5835; 8AM-4:30PM (CST). *Misdemeanor, Civil Actions under $5,000, Small Claims, Traffic.*

General Information: Will fax documents. Court makes copy: $.25 per page. Certification fee: $5.00 per doc. Payee: District Court. Personal checks accepted. No credit cards accepted. Prepayment required.

Civil Name Search: Access: Mail, fax, in person. Only the court performs in person name searches; visitors may not. Search fee: $2.00 per name. Required to search: name. Records back to 1993. Mail turnaround time 3-5 days.

Criminal Name Search: Access: Fax, mail, in person. Only the court performs in person name searches; visitors may not. Search fee: $2.00 per name. Required to search: name, years to search, DOB, SSN. Computerized records back to 1997, prior on hard copy back to 1993. Mail turnaround time 3-5 days.

Phillips County

Circuit Court 620 Cherry St #206, Courthouse, Helena, AR 72342; 870-338-5515; probate phone: 870-338-5505; fax: 870-338-5513; 8AM-4:30PM (CST). *Felony, Civil Actions over $5,000, Probate.*

General Information: Probate records located in the County Clerk office. No juvenile records released. Fee to fax document $1.00 each. Court makes copy: $.25 per page. Self serve copy: same. Certification fee: $3.00 per cert plus copy fee. Payee: Circuit Clerk. Personal checks accepted. No credit cards accepted. Prepayment required.

Civil Name Search: Access: In person. Visitors must perform in person searches themselves. Required to search: name, years to search, DOB. Civil cases indexed by plaintiff. Civil records on fee books from 1970; on computer back to 1998. Civil PAT goes back to 2000 (judgments and only).

Criminal Name Search: Access: In person. Visitors must perform in person searches themselves. Required to search: name, years to search; also helpful-DOB. Criminal records on fee books from 1970. Note: Court

suggests Arkansas State Police or ACIC for criminal search. Criminal PAT available.

Local District Court 226 Perry St, City Hall, Helena, AR 72342; 870-817-7450; fax: 870-338-9832; 8AM-5PM (CST). *Misdemeanor, Civil Actions under $5,000, Eviction, Small Claims.*

General Information: Will fax documents if prepaid. Court makes copy: $.25 per page. Certification fee: $5.00 per doc plus copy fee. Payee: City of Helena District Court. No personal checks or credit cards accepted. Prepayment required. Mail requests: SASE helpful.

Civil Name Search: Access: Mail, fax, in person. Both court and visitors may perform in person name searches. Search fee: $5.00. Civil cases indexed by case number. Computerized from 1993-2000. Mail turnaround time 3 days.

Criminal Name Search: Access: Mail, fax, in person. Both court and visitors may perform in person name searches. Search fee: $5.00 per name. Required to search: name, years to search, address, DOB, SSN. Computerized back to 1993. Mail turnaround time 3 days.

Pike County

Circuit Court PO Box 219, Murfreesboro, AR 71958; 870-285-2231; fax: 870-285-3281; 8AM-4:30PM (CST). *Felony, Civil Actions over $5,000, Probate.*

General Information: Probate is at the County Clerk's office at 870-285-2743. No juvenile or adoption records released. Will fax documents $1.50 1st 3 pages, $.50 ea add'l. Court makes copy: $.50 per page. Self serve copy: same. Certification fee: $5.00 per doc. Payee: Pike County Clerk. Personal checks accepted. No credit cards accepted. Prepayment required.

Civil Name Search: Access: In person only. Visitors must perform in person searches themselves. Required to search: name, years to search. Civil cases indexed by defendant. Civil records archived from 1895. Some records on dockets books, computerized since 1989. Civil PAT goes back to 2008.

Criminal Name Search: Access: In person only. Visitors must perform in person searches themselves. Required to search: name, years to search, DOB. Criminal records archived from 1895. Some records on dockets, fee books. Computerized records from 1992. Criminal PAT goes back to 2008.

Local District Court PO Box 197, 114 N Washington, Ste A, Murfreesboro, AR 71958; 870-285-3865; fax: 870-285-3540; 8AM-4:30PM (CST). *Misdemeanor, Civil Actions under $5,000, Eviction, Small Claims.*

General Information: Sealed cases restricted. Will fax documents. Court makes copy: $.50 per page if extensive copies needed. No certification fee . Payee: Pike County District Court. . Prepayment required. Mail requests: SASE helpful.

Civil Name Search: Access: Phone, fax, mail, in person. Both court and visitors may perform in person name searches. No search fee. Required to search: name, years to search. Civil records are not computerized, dockets on index books. Mail turnaround time 2-3 days.

Criminal Name Search: Access: Phone, fax, mail, in person. Both court and visitors may perform in person name searches. No search fee. Required to search: name, years to search, offense. Criminal records computerized from 1997; prior on index books. Mail turnaround time 2-3 days.

Poinsett County

Circuit Court PO Box 46, Harrisburg, AR 72432; 870-578-4420; fax: 870-578-4427; 8:30AM-4:30PM (CST). *Felony, Civil Actions over $5,000, Probate.*

General Information: Probate records are handled by the County Clerk, who can be reached at 870-578-4410. No juvenile records released. Will fax documents to toll-free number for no fee. Court makes copy: $.50 per page. Self serve copy: same. Certification fee: $5.00 per doc, includes all copy fees. Payee: Circuit Clerk. Personal checks accepted. No credit cards accepted. Prepayment required. Mail requests: SASE required.

Civil Name Search: Access: Mail, in person. Only the court performs in person name searches; visitors may not. Search fee: $6.00 per name. Civil records on computer from 1985. Some records on dockets. Note: All requests must be in writing. Mail turnaround time 1-2 days.

Criminal Name Search: Access: Mail, in person. Only the court performs in person name searches; visitors may not. Search fee: $6.00 per name. Required to search: name, years to search, DOB. Criminal records computerized from 1985. Some records on dockets. Note: All requests must be in writing. Mail turnaround time 1-2 days.

Harrisburg State District Court 202 N East St, Harrisburg, AR 72432; 870-578-4110; fax: 870-578-4123; 7:30AM-4:30PM (CST). *Misdemeanor, Civil Actions under $25,000, Eviction, Small Claims.*

General Information: No record released until court appearance. Will not fax documents. Court makes copy: $.25 per page. Certification fee: $5.00. Payee: Harrisburg District Court. Attorney checks accepted. No credit cards accepted. Prepayment required. Mail requests: SASE required.

Civil Name Search: Access: Mail, in person. Only the court performs in person name searches; visitors may not. Search fee: $2.00. Required to search: name, DOB, SSN, signed release. Civil records go back to 1978. Note: Mail requests must include SASE. Mail turnaround time 1 day.

Criminal Name Search: Access: Mail, in person. Only the court performs in person name searches; visitors may not. Search fee: $2.00. Required to search: name, years to search; also helpful: DOB, SSN, signed release. Criminal records computerized from 1987. Mail turnaround time 1 day.

Lepanto State District Court PO Box 610, 117 Greenwood, Lepanto, AR 72354; 870-475-2415; fax: 870-475-3161; 8AM-4PM (CST). *Misdemeanor, Civil Actions under $25,000, Eviction, Small Claims.*

General Information: Will not fax documents. Court makes copy: $.25 per page. Certification fee: $5.00 per doc. Payee: District Court. No personal checks or credit cards accepted. Prepayment required.

Civil Name Search: Access: Mail, in person. Both court and visitors may perform in person name searches. Search fee: $2.00. Required to search: name, DOB, SSN, signed release. Civil cases indexed by Defendant. Civil records go back to 1978. Mail turnaround time 1-2 days.

Criminal Name Search: Access: Mail, in person. Both court and visitors may perform in person name searches. Search fee: $2.00. Required to search: name, years to search; also helpful: DOB, SSN, signed release. Criminal records computerized from 2003. Note: All requests must be in writing. Mail turnaround time 1-2 days.

Marked Tree State District Court #1 Elm St, Marked Tree, AR 72365; 870-358-2024; fax: 870-358-7867; 8AM-4:30PM (CST). *Misdemeanor, Civil Actions under $25,000, Eviction, Small Claims.*

General Information: Will fax documents for fee. Court makes copy: $.25 per page. Certification fee: $5.00 per doc. Payee: District Court. No personal checks or credit cards accepted. Prepayment required. Mail requests: SASE required.

Civil Name Search: Access: Mail, in person. Both court and visitors may perform in person name searches. No search fee. Required to search: name, DOB, SSN, signed release. Civil records go back to 1978. Mail turnaround time 1-2 days.

Criminal Name Search: Access: Mail, in person. Only the court performs in person name searches; visitors may not. No search fee. Required to search: name, years to search; also helpful: DOB, SSN, signed release. Criminal records computerized from 1998. Mail turnaround time 1-2 days.

Trumann District Court 221 S Melton, Trumann, AR 72472; 870-483-7771; fax: 870-483-2620; 8AM-4:30PM (CST). *Misdemeanor, Civil Actions under $25,000, Eviction, Small Claims.*

General Information: Will fax documents. Court makes copy: $.25 per page. Self serve copy: same. Certification fee: $5.00 per doc. Payee: District Court. No personal checks or credit cards accepted. Prepayment required. Mail requests: SASE required.

Civil Name Search: Access: Mail, in person. Only the court performs in person name searches; visitors may not. Required to search: name, DOB, SSN, signed release. Civil cases indexed by defendant, plaintiff. Civil records go back to 1978. Mail turnaround time 3 days.

Criminal Name Search: Access: Mail, in person. Only the court performs in person name searches; visitors may not. No search fee. Required to search: name, years to search; also helpful: DOB, SSN, signed release. Criminal records computerized from 1999. Mail turnaround time 3 days.

Tyronza District Court PO Box 275, 143 S Main, Tyronza, AR 72386; 870-487-2168; fax: 870-487-2729; 8AM-5PM (CST). *Misdemeanor, Civil Actions under $25,000, Eviction, Small Claims.*

General Information: Will fax documents. Court makes copy: $.25 per page. Certification fee: $10.00 per doc includes copy fee. Payee: District Court. Personal checks (in-state) accepted. No credit cards accepted. Prepayment required.

Civil Name Search: Access: Mail, in person. Both court and visitors may perform in person name searches. Search fee: $2.00. Required to search: name, DOB, SSN, signed release. Civil records go back to 1994.

Criminal Name Search: Access: Mail, in person. Both court and visitors may perform in person name searches. Search fee: $2.00. Required to search: name, years to search; also helpful: DOB, SSN, signed release. Criminal records computerized from 1994. Note: All requests must be in writing. Mail turnaround time is 2 days.

Weiner District Court 123 W 2nd St, Weiner, AR 72479; 870-684-2284; fax: 870-684-7649; 8AM-4:30PM (CST). *Misdemeanor, Civil Actions under $25,000, Eviction, Small Claims.*

General Information: The case limit on civil records was raised to $25,000 as of 01/01/2008.

Polk County

Circuit Court 507 Church St, Mena, AR 71953; 479-394-8100; probate phone: 479-394-8123; fax: 479-394-8170; 8AM-4:30PM (CST). *Felony, Civil Actions over $5,000, Probate, Domestic Relations.*

General Information: Probate is handled separately from the court by the County Clerk's Office. Probate fax- 479-394-8115 Online identifiers in results same as on public terminal. No juvenile records released. Will fax documents to local or toll free line. Court makes copy: $.25 per page; $.50 legal size. Self serve copy: same. Certification fee: $5.00. Payee: Circuit Clerk. Personal checks accepted. No credit cards accepted. Prepayment required. Mail requests: SASE required.

Civil Name Search: Access: Mail, in person, online. Both court and visitors may perform in person name searches. No search fee. Civil records on dockets and index from late 1800s. Mail turnaround time 1-2 days. Civil PAT goes back to 7/03. Online access to circuit court dockets by subscription through RecordsUSA.com. Credit card, username and password is required; choose either monthly or per-use plan. Visit the website for sign-up or call Rob at 888-633-4748 x17 for information.

Criminal Name Search: Access: Mail, in person, online. Both court and visitors may perform in person name searches. No search fee. Required to search: name, years to search, DOB. Criminal records on dockets and index from late 1800s. Mail turnaround time 1-2 days. Criminal PAT goes back to same as civil. Online access to criminal dockets is the same as civil.

Local District Court 507 Church Ave, Courthouse, Mena, AR 71953; 479-394-8140; fax: 479-394-6199; 8AM-4:30PM (CST). *Misdemeanor, Civil Actions under $5,000, Eviction, Small Claims.*

General Information: Will not fax documents. Court makes copy: none. No certification fee . No credit cards accepted.

Civil Name Search: Access: In person only. Both court and visitors may perform in person name searches. No search fee. Civil cases indexed by Defendant, Plaintiff. Civil records go back 10 years; computerized records go back 10 years. Note: Court will assist visitors with search.

Criminal Name Search: Access: In person only. Both court and visitors may perform in person name searches. No search fee. Required to search: name, years to search, DOB; SSN helpful. Criminal records go back 10 years; computerized records go back 10 years. Note: Court will assist visitors with search.

Pope County

Circuit Court 100 W Main, Russellville, AR 72801; 479-968-7499; probate phone: 479-968-6064; fax: 479-880-8463; 8AM-5PM (CST). *Felony, Civil Actions over $25,000.*

General Information: Probate is a separate office at this same address. The case limit on civil records was raised to $25,000 as of 01/01/2008. No juvenile records released. Will not fax documents. Court makes copy: $1.00 per page. Self serve copy: $.25 per page. Certification fee: $5.00. Payee: Pope County Circuit Clerk. Personal checks accepted. No credit cards accepted. Prepayment required.

Civil Name Search: Access: In person. Both court and visitors may perform in person name searches. Civil records on dockets from early 1900s; on computer back to 1998. Civil PAT goes back to 1998.

Criminal Name Search: Access: In person. Both court and visitors may perform in person name searches. Required to search: name, years to search, DOB; also helpful: SSN. Criminal docket index from early 1900s; on computer back to 1998. Criminal PAT goes back to same as civil.

Atkins State District Court 305 E Main Street, Atkins, AR 72823; 479-641-1811; fax: 479-641-1861; 8AM-5PM (CST). *Misdemeanor, Civil Actions under $25,000, Small Claims.*

Dover State District Court PO Box 258, Dover, AR 72837; 479-331-4238; fax: 479-331-3388; 8:30AM-5:30PM (CST). *Misdemeanor, Civil Actions under $25,000, Small Claims.*

London District Court PO Box 130, London, AR 72847; 479-293-4115; fax: 479-293-4127; 8AM-4:30PM (CST). *Traffic.*

Pottsville Local District Court Pottsville Department, 173 E Ash Street, Pottsville, AR 72858; 479-968-3029; fax: 479-890-3570; 7:30AM-4PM (CST). *Misdemeanor, Traffic.*

Russellville State District Court 210 N Shamrock Blvd, Russellville, AR 72802; 479-968-1393; fax: 479-968-4166; 8AM-5PM (CST). *Misdemeanor, Civil Actions under $25,000, Small Claims.*

General Information: City Hall is being renovated and this is new address.

Prairie County

Circuit Court - Southern District PO Box 283, De Valls Bluff, AR 72041; 870-998-2314; fax: 870-998-2314; 8AM-4:30PM (CST). *Felony, Civil Actions over $5,000, Probate.*

General Information: Probate records are handled by the County Clerk, who can be reached thru the number above. No juvenile or adoption records released. Will fax documents $1.00 per page. Court makes copy: $.50 per page. Self serve copy: same. Certification fee: $5.00 per doc plus copy fee.

Payee: Circuit Clerk. Personal checks accepted. No credit cards accepted. Prepayment required. Mail requests: SASE required.

Civil Name Search: Access: Phone, fax, mail, in person. Both court and visitors may perform in person name searches. Search fee: $6.00. Civil records on dockets from 1885. Mail turnaround time 1 day. Civil PAT goes back to 1885.

Criminal Name Search: Access: Phone, fax, mail, in person. Both court and visitors may perform in person name searches. Search fee: $6.00. Required to search: name, years to search, DOB, SSN. Criminal docket index from 1885. Mail turnaround time 1 day. Criminal PAT goes back to 1885.

Circuit Court - Northern District 200 Courthouse Sq, #104, Des Arc, AR 72040; 870-256-4434; fax: 870-256-4434; 8AM-4:30PM (CST). *Felony, Civil Actions over $5,000, Probate.*

General Information: Probate is handled by County Clerk with a separate record index at this same address. No juvenile, adoption records released. Fee to fax out file $1.00 per page. Court makes copy: $1.00 per page. Self serve copy: $.50 per page. Certification fee: $5.00 per cert. Payee: Circuit Clerk. Personal checks accepted. No credit cards accepted. Prepayment required. Mail requests: SASE required.

Civil Name Search: Access: Mail, in person. Both court and visitors may perform in person name searches. Search fee: $6.00 per name. Civil records on dockets from 1800s. Mail turnaround time 1 day.

Criminal Name Search: Access: Mail, in person. Both court and visitors may perform in person name searches. Search fee: $6.00 per name. Required to search: name, years to search. Criminal docket index from 1800s. Mail turnaround time 1 day.

Biscoe Local District Court PO Box 187, Biscoe, AR 72017; 870-998-2226; fax: 870-998-2449; 8AM-4:30PM (CST). *Misdemeanor, Civil Actions under $5,000, Small Claims.*

Des Arc Local District Court PO Box 389, 107 S 3rd St, Des Arc, AR 72040; 870-256-3011; fax: 870-256-4612; 8AM-4:30PM (CST). *Misdemeanor, Civil Actions under $5,000, Small Claims.*

DeValls Bluff District Court PO Box 297, DeValls Bluff, AR 72041; 870-998-2301; fax: 870-998-7252; 8AM-5PM (CST). *Misdemeanor.*

Hazen Local District Court PO Box 564, Hazen, AR 72064; 870-255-4514; fax: 870-255-3637; 8AM-4:30PM (CST). *Misdemeanor, Civil Actions under $5,000, Small Claims.*

Pulaski County

Circuit Court 401 W Markham St, #100, Little Rock, AR 72201; 501-340-8500; fax: 501-340-8884; 8AM-4:30PM (CST). *Felony, Civil Actions over $25,000, Probate.*
www.pulaskiclerk.com/

General Information: Probate handled by County Clerk. No expunged records released. Will fax documents to local or toll-free number. Court makes copy: $.50 1st page; $.25 per each add'l page. Self serve copy: same. Certification fee: $5.00 per cert plus copy fee. Payee: Circuit Clerk. Personal checks accepted. No credit cards accepted. Prepayment required. Mail requests: SASE required for mail return of any copies.

Civil Name Search: Access: In person, online. Visitors must perform in person searches themselves. Civil records on computer from 1982, on microfiche from 1974 to 1982, archived from 1900. Civil PAT goes back to early 1990s. The web page directs online searchers to the state site at https://aprod3.aoc.arkansas.gov/cconnect/PROD/public/ck_public_qry_main.cp_main_idx.

Criminal Name Search: Access: In person, online. Visitors must perform in person searches themselves. Required to search: name, years to search, DOB, SSN. Criminal records computerized from 1982, on microfiche from 1974 to 1982, archived from 1900. Criminal PAT goes back to mid-1980s. PAT results include alias. Online access same as civil. Online results show name only.

Pulaski County State District Court 3001 W Roosevelt, Little Rock, AR 72204; 501-340-6824; fax: 501-340-6899; 7AM-5:30PM (CST). *Misdemeanor, Civil Actions under $25,000, Eviction, Small Claims.*
www.co.pulaski.ar.us/districtcourt.shtml

General Information: The case limit on civil records increased to $25,000 on 07/01/2009. Will fax documents to local or toll-free number only if time permits. Court makes copy: $.50 per page. Certification fee: $1.00 per page plus copy fee. Payee: County District Court. Personal checks accepted. No credit cards accepted.

Civil Name Search: Access: Phone, mail, in person. Both court and visitors may perform in person name searches. No search fee. Required to search: DOB, SSN, case number. Overall records and computerized records go to 1988. Mail turnaround time 2-3 days.

Criminal Name Search: Access: Phone, mail, in person. Both court and visitors may perform in person name searches. No search fee. Required to search: name, years to search; also helpful: SSN. Overall records and computerized records go to 1988. Mail turnaround time 2-3 days.

Jacksonville State District Court 1414 W Main, Jacksonville, AR 72076; 501-982-9531; fax: 501-985-1100; 8AM-5PM (CST). *Misdemeanor, Civil Actions under $25,000, Eviction, Small Claims.*

General Information: The case limit on civil records increased to $25,000 on 07/01/2009. There is no centralized location of District Court civil records. Each court must be searched. Will fax documents to local or toll-free number only if time permits. Court makes copy: $.50 per page. Certification fee: $5.00. Payee: Jacksonville District Court. Personal checks and credit cards accepted.

Civil Name Search: Access: Phone, mail, in person. Only the court performs in person name searches; visitors may not. Search fee: $5.00. Required to search: DOB, SSN, case number. Overall records and computerized records go back 10 years. Mail turnaround time 2-3 days.

Criminal Name Search: Access: Phone, mail, in person. Only the court performs in person name searches; visitors may not. Search fee: $5.00. Required to search: name, years to search; also helpful: SSN. Overall records and computerized records go back 10 years. Mail turnaround time 2-3 days.

Maumelle Local District Court 100 Millwood Circle, Maumelle, AR 72113; 501-851-7800; fax: 501-851-7427; 8AM-5PM (CST). *Misdemeanor, Traffic, Civil Actions under $5,000, Small Claims.*

North Little Rock State District Court 200 West Pershing Blvd, North Little Rock, AR 72114; 501-791-8559; fax: 501-791-8599; 8:30AM-4:30PM (CST). *Misdemeanor, Civil Actions under $25,000, Small Claims.*
www.northlr.org/government/courts.asp

General Information: The case limit on civil records increased to $25,000 on 07/01/2009. There is no centralized location of District Court civil records. Each court must be searched. Will fax documents to local or toll-free number only if time permits. Court makes copy: $.25 per page. Certification fee: $5.00 per page plus copy fee. Payee: North Little Rock District Court. Personal checks accepted. No credit cards accepted.

Civil Name Search: Access: Mail, in person. Both court and visitors may perform in person name searches. No search fee. Required to search: Name and DOB. Mail turnaround time 2-3 days.

Criminal Name Search: Access: Mail, in person. Both court and visitors may perform in person name searches. No search fee. Required to search: name, years to search. Note: This court refers requesters doing a background check to the Police Dept. in North Little Rock. Will look up files if case number given. Mail turnaround time 2-3 days.

Sherwood State District Court PO Box 6256, Sherwood, AR 72124; 501-835-3693; fax: 501-835-8918; 8AM-4:30PM (CST). *Misdemeanor, Civil Actions under $25,000, Small Claims.*
General Information: The case limit on civil records increased to $25,000 as of 07/01/2009.

Wrightsville Local District Court PO Box 237, Wrightsville, AR 72183; 501-897-4547; fax: 501-897-5647; 8AM-4:30PM (CST). *Misdemeanor/Traffic, Civil Actions under $5,000, Small Claims.*

City of Little Rock District Court Little Rock City hall, 600 W Markham, Little Rock, AR 72201; 501-371-4739; fax: 501-371-4515; 8AM-4:30PM (CST). *Misdemeanor, Civil Actions under $25,000, Small Claims, Traffic.*
www.littlerock.org
General Information: There are three Departments at this location. Traffic can be reached at 501-371-4733

Randolph County

Circuit Court 107 W Broadway, Pocahontas, AR 72455; 870-892-5522 or 0239; probate phone: 870-892-5822; fax: 870-892-8794; 8AM-4:30PM (CST). *Felony, Civil Actions over $5,000, Probate.*
General Information: Probate records are located at the same address, right down the hall. No juvenile records released. Will not fax documents. Court makes copy: $.25 per page. Self serve copy: $.20 per page. Certification fee: $5.00. Payee: Circuit Clerk. Personal checks accepted. No credit cards accepted. Prepayment required. Mail requests: SASE required for mail return of any copies.

Civil Name Search: Access: In person. Visitors must perform in person searches themselves. Civil records on index from 1836. Mail turnaround time same day.

Criminal Name Search: Access: In person. Visitors must perform in person searches themselves. Required to search: name, years to search, DOB. Criminal records on index from 1836.

Local District Court 1510 Pace Rd, Pocahontas, AR 72455; 870-892-4033; fax: 870-892-4392; 8AM-4:30PM (CST). *Misdemeanor, Civil Actions under $5,000, Eviction, Small Claims.*
General Information: Will fax documents to local or toll free line. Court makes copy: none. Certification fee: $5.00 per cert includes copies. Payee: District Court. No personal checks or credit cards accepted. Prepayment required. Mail requests: SASE required.

Civil Name Search: Access: Mail, in person. Both court and visitors may perform in person name searches. Search fee: $6.00. Required to search: name, years to search, DOB, SSN. Records maintained since 1983, computerized since 2004. Mail turnaround time 1-2 days.

Criminal Name Search: Access: Mail, in person. Both court and visitors may perform in person name searches. Search fee: $6.00. Required to search: name, years to search, DOB, SSN. Records maintained since 1986. Mail turnaround time 1 day.

Saline County

Circuit Court 200 N Main St, Benton, AR 72015; 501-303-5615; probate phone: 501-303-5630; 8AM-4:30PM (CST). *Felony, Civil Actions over $25,000, Domestic Relations, Probate.*

General Information: Probate records located at 215 N Main St. at County Court. Probate fax- 501-303-5684. The case limit on civil records was raised to $25,000 as of 01/01/2008. No juvenile records released. Will not fax documents. Court makes copy: $.25 per page. Self serve copy: same. Certification fee: $5.00 plus copy fee. Payee: Circuit Court. Personal checks accepted. No credit cards accepted. Prepayment required.

Civil Name Search: Access: In person, online. Visitors must perform in person searches themselves. Civil records on computer since 1990, prior on docket books. Civil PAT goes back to 1991. A court records index search is free at https://www.ark.org/grs/app/saline but fees are changed for record copies. Annual subscription account is $75.00 and the cost per record is $1.00.

Criminal Name Search: Access: In person, online. Visitors must perform in person searches themselves. Required to search: name, years to search. Criminal records on computer since 1991, prior on docket books. Criminal PAT goes back to same as civil. Online access to criminal is same as civil. Online results show name only.

Alexander District Court PO Box 610, Alexander, AR 72002; 501-455-2585; fax: 501-455-5531; 8AM-4:30PM (CST). *Misdemeanor.*

Bauxite Division State District Court 6055 Stanley Circle, Bauxite, AR 72011; 501-557-5184; fax: 501-557-5291; 8AM-4:30PM (CST). *Misdemeanor, Civil Actions under $25,000, Eviction, Small Claims.*

General Information: Search fee includes both civil and criminal index. The case limit on civil records was raised to $25,000 as of 01/01/2008.

Benton State District Court 1605 Edison Ave #19, Benton, AR 72015; 501-303-5670/1; fax: 501-303-5696; 8AM-4:30PM (CST). *Misdemeanor, Civil Actions under $25,000, Eviction, Small Claims.*

General Information: Search fee includes both civil and criminal index. The case limit on civil records was raised to $25,000 as of 01/01/2008. Will fax back documents for no fee. Court makes copy: $.50 per page. Certification fee: $5.00 per doc. Payee: Benton District Court. No Personal checks and credit cards accepted. Prepayment required.

Civil Name Search: Access: Mail, in person. Only the court performs in person name searches; visitors may not. Search fee: $5.00 per name. Required to search: name. Civil cases indexed by Defendant, Plaintiff. Civil records go back to 1982. Mail turnaround time 72 hours.

Criminal Name Search: Access: Mail, in person. Only the court performs in person name searches; visitors may not. Search fee: $5.00 per name. Required to search: name, years to search, DOB; also helpful: DOB, SSN, DL. Criminal records go back to 1994 on computer. Mail turnaround time 72 hours.

Bryant State District Court 208 South West 3rd, Bryant, AR 72022; 501-847-5223; fax: 501-847-1154; 8AM-4:30PM (CST). *Misdemeanor, Civil Actions under $25,000, Eviction, Small Claims.*

General Information: Search fee includes both civil and criminal index. The case limit on civil records was raised to $25,000 as of 01/01/2008.

Haskell State District Court 2520 Highway 229, Haskell, AR 72015; 501-776-2666; fax: 501-776-1201; 8AM-4:30PM (CST). *Misdemeanor, Civil Actions under $25,000, Eviction, Small Claims.*

General Information: Search fee includes both civil and criminal index. The case limit on civil records was raised to $25,000 as of 01/01/2008.

Shannon Hills State District Court 10401 High Road East, Shannon Hills, AR 72103; 501-455-4391; fax: 501-455-3103; 10AM-4PM (CST). *Misdemeanor, Civil Actions under $25,000, Eviction, Small Claims.*

General Information: Search fee includes both civil and criminal index. The case limit on civil records was raised to $25,000 as of 01/01/2008. Will fax back documents for no fee. Court makes copy: $.50 per page. Certification fee: $5.00 per doc. Payee: Shannon Hills District Court. No Personal checks and credit cards accepted. Prepayment required.

Civil Name Search: Access: Mail, in person. Only the court performs in person name searches; visitors may not. Search fee: $5.00 per name. Required to search: name and year. Civil cases indexed by Defendant, Plaintiff. Civil records go back to 2004. Mail turnaround time 7 business days.

Criminal Name Search: Access: Mail, in person. Only the court performs in person name searches; visitors may not. Search fee: $5.00 per name. Required to search: name, years to search, DOB; also helpful: DOB, SSN, DL. Criminal records go back to 2004 on computer. Mail turnaround time 7 working days.

Scott County

Circuit Court PO Box 2165, 190 W First St Box 10, Waldron, AR 72958; 479-637-2642; fax: 479-637-0124; 8AM-4:30PM (CST). *Felony, Civil Actions over $5,000, Probate.*

General Information: Probate is handled by County Clerk with a separate record index at this same address. No juvenile or adoption records released. Will fax documents for $1.00 per page. Court makes copy: $.50 per page. Self serve copy: $.50 per page. Certification fee: $5.00 per cert includes copies. Payee: Scott County Clerk. Personal checks accepted. No credit cards accepted. Prepayment required. Mail requests: SASE required.

Civil Name Search: Access: Phone, mail, fax, in person. Both court and visitors may perform in person name searches. No search fee. Civil index on docket books from 1882. Mail turnaround time 1 week.

Criminal Name Search: Access: Mail, fax, in person. Both court and visitors may perform in person name searches. No search fee. Required to search: name, years to search, DOB, SSN. Criminal records indexed in books from 1882. Mail turnaround time 1 week.

Local District Court 190 W 1st St, Box 15, Waldron, AR 72958; 479-637-4694; fax: 479-637-4712; 8AM-4:30PM (CST). *Misdemeanor, Civil Actions under $5,000, Eviction, Small Claims.*

General Information: Will fax documents to local or toll-free number. Court makes copy: none. No certification fee . Payee: District Court of Scott County. No personal checks accepted. Money order and cash accepted. No credit cards accepted. Mail requests: SASE required.

Civil Name Search: Access: Mail, in person. Both court and visitors may perform in person name searches. No search fee. Required to search: name, years to search, DOB; also helpful-other names used, SSN. Records on computer go back to 1998. Mail turnaround time 1-2 days.

Criminal Name Search: Access: Mail, in person. Both court and visitors may perform in person name searches. No search fee. Required to search: name, years to search. Records go back to 1998; on computer back to 10/1998. Mail turnaround time 1-2 days.

Searcy County

Circuit Court PO Box 998, 200 Highway 27 S, Marshall, AR 72650; 870-448-3807; fax: 870-448-5005; 8AM-4:30PM (CST). *Felony, Civil Actions over $5,000, Probate.*

General Information: Probate records are handled by the County Clerk, who can be reached thru the number above. No juvenile or adoption records released. Will fax documents $1.00 per page. Court makes copy: $.25 per page. Self serve copy: same. Certification fee: $5.00 per document. Payee: Searcy County Clerk. Personal checks accepted. No credit cards accepted. Prepayment required. Mail requests: SASE required.

Civil Name Search: Access: In person, online. Visitors must perform in person searches themselves. Required to search: name, years to search, written request. Civil records archived from 1881. Some records on dockets. Mail turnaround time 1 day. Search the index at https://arep2.aoc.arkansas.gov/cconnect/PROD/public/ck_public_qry_main_idx.

Criminal Name Search: Access: In person, online. Visitors must perform in person searches themselves. Required to search: name, years to search, offense; also helpful: DOB, SSN. Criminal records archived from 1881. Some records on dockets. Note: Court may try to direct you to the state police. Search the index at https://arep2.aoc.arkansas.gov/cconnect/PROD/public/ck_public_qry_main.cp_main_idx.

Local District Court PO Box 885, 108 College St, Marshall, AR 72650; 870-448-5411; fax: 870-448-5927; 8AM-430PM (CST). *Misdemeanor, Civil Actions under $5,000, Eviction, Small Claims.*

General Information: Will fax documents to local or toll-free number; fee if out-of-state. Court makes copy: $.25 per page. Certification fee: $5.00 per doc. Payee: Court. No personal checks or credit cards accepted. Prepayment required. Mail requests: SASE helpful.

Civil Name Search: Access: Mail, fax, in person. Both court and visitors may perform in person name searches. Search fee: $6.00 per name. Required to search: name. Civil records go back to 1992. Mail turnaround time 1 week.

Criminal Name Search: Access: Mail, fax, in person. Both court and visitors may perform in person name searches. No search fee. Required to search: name, years to search, DOB, SSN. Criminal records go back to 1992. Mail turnaround time 1 week.

Sebastian County

Circuit Court - Greenwood Division PO Box 310, County Courthouse, 11 Town Sq, Rm 103, Greenwood, AR 72936; 479-996-4175; fax: 479-996-6885; 8AM-5PM (CST). *Felony, Civil Actions over $25,000, Probate.*

www.sebastiancountyonline.com

General Information: Record index from both Circuit Courts - Fort Smith and Greenwood Division - are on the same computer system, but copies of case files must be pulled from individual courts. The case limit on civil records was raised to $25,000 as of 01/01/2008. No juvenile records released. Will fax documents $1.00 per page. Court makes copy: $1.00 per page by mail; $.50 in person. Self serve copy: $.50 per page. Certification fee: $5.00 per cert. Payee: Circuit Clerk. Personal checks accepted. No credit cards accepted. Prepayment required. Mail requests: SASE required for civil.

Civil Name Search: Access: Mail, in person. Both court and visitors may perform in person name searches. Search fee: $6.00 per name. Civil records on computer from 10/87, on dockets from 1900. Mail turnaround time 1-2 weeks. Civil PAT goes back to 1988. An index search to civil records, domestic relations, and probate from 1998 forward is at www.sebastiancountyonline.com/. This is tricky to find. Click on the 'site map' and choose 'Circuit Clerk.' The public access password and user is shown. Only attorneys may view the DOBs, they must secure a special password before access.

Criminal Name Search: Access: In person, online. Both court and visitors may perform in person name searches. No search fee. Required to search: name, years to search; also helpful: SSN. Criminal records computerized from 10/87, on dockets from 1900. Criminal PAT goes back to same as civil. Terminal results include SSN. The criminal record index from 1998 forward is at www.sebastiancountyonline.com/. This is tricky to find. Click on the 'site map' and choose 'Circuit Clerk.' The public access password and user is shown. Only attorneys may view the DOBs, they must secure a special password before access.

Circuit Court - Fort Smith 901 South B St, #205, PO Box 1179, Fort Smith, AR 72902; 479-782-1046; fax: 479-784-1580; 8AM-5PM (CST). *Felony, Civil Actions over $5,000, Probate.*
www.sebastiancountyonline.com

General Information: Records from Circuit Courts-Ft Smith & Greenwood Districts-on the same computer system, copies must be pulled from individual Districts. Closed files in this Circuit are maintained in Ft Smith & Greenwood. Probate records are handled by the County Clerk. No juvenile records released. Will fax documents $1.00 per page. Court makes copy: $1.00 per page if mailed, otherwise $.50. Self serve copy: $.50 per page. Certification fee: $5.00. Payee: Circuit Clerk. Personal checks accepted. No credit cards accepted. Prepayment required. Mail requests: SASE required.

Civil Name Search: Access: Mail, in person, online. Visitors must perform in person searches themselves. Search fee: $6.00 per name. Required to search: name, years to search; also helpful: address. Civil cases indexed by defendant, plaintiff. Civil records computerized from 1988, on dockets from 1900. Mail turnaround time 1-2 days. Civil PAT goes back to 1988. An index search to civil records, domestic relations, and probate from 1998 forward is at www.sebastiancountyonline.com/. This is tricky to find. Click on the 'site map' and choose 'Circuit Clerk.' The public access password and user is shown. Only attorneys may view the DOBs, they must secure a special password before access.

Criminal Name Search: Access: Mail, in person, online. Visitors must perform in person searches themselves. Search fee: $6.00 per name. Required to search: name, years to search; also helpful: address, DOB, SSN. Criminal records computerized from 1988, on dockets from 1900. Note: Court will only perform searches for criminal justice purposes. Mail turnaround time 1-2 days. Criminal PAT goes back to same as civil. An index search to civil records, domestic relations, and probate from 1998 forward is at www.sebastiancountyonline.com/. This is tricky to find. Click on the 'site map' and choose 'Circuit Clerk.' The public access password and user is shown. Only attorneys may view the DOBs, they must secure a special password before access.

Barling-Greenwood State District Court PO Box 23039, Barling, AR 72923; 479-452-1568; fax: 479-452-5568; 8:30AM-5PM (CST). *Misdemeanor, Civil Actions under $25,000, Traffic, Small Claims.*
General Information: Fee to fax document $.25 per page. Court makes copy: $.25 per page. Certification fee: $5.00 per doc. Payee: Sebastian District Court. Personal checks accepted. Major credit cards accepted in person only, by person named. Prepayment required. Mail requests: SASE required for mail return of any copies.

Civil Name Search: Access: Phone, fax, mail, in person. Both court and visitors may perform in person name searches. No search fee. Required to search: full name, years to search. Record stored from 1984. Note: If copies are required, then your request must be in writing. Mail turnaround time 1-2 days. Civil PAT goes back to 1993.

Criminal Name Search: Access: Phone, fax, mail, in person. Both court and visitors may perform in person name searches. No search fee. Required to search: name, years to search, DOB; also helpful: SSN. Records are computerized since 1993. Note: If copies are required, then your request must be in writing. Mail turnaround time 1-2 days. Criminal PAT goes back to same as civil.

Central City District Court 1101 Highway 255, Central City, AR 72941; 479-452-6680; ; 8:30AM-5PM (CST). *Misdemeanor, Traffic, Small Claims.*

Fort Smith State District Court 901 South B Street, #103, Fort Smith, AR 72901; 479-784-2420; fax: 479-784-2438; 8:30AM-5PM (CST). *Misdemeanor, Civil Actions under $25,000, Traffic, Small Claims.*
www.districtcourtfortsmith.org

General Information: Sealed records and SSNs are restricted from public view. Fee to fax document $.25 per page. Court makes copy: $.25 per page. Certification fee: $5.00 per doc. Payee: Fort Smith District Court. Personal checks accepted. Major credit cards accepted in person only, by person named. Prepayment required. Mail requests: SASE required for mail return of any copies.

Civil Name Search: Access: Phone, fax, mail, in person, online. Both court and visitors may perform in person name searches. No search fee. Required to search: full name, years to search. Record stored from 1984. Note: If copies are required, then your request must be in writing. Mail turnaround time 1-2 days. Civil PAT goes back to 1993. Access court records free at www.districtcourtfortsmith.org/ and click on Online Records Search. The site will provide user password and ID. Type of identifiers found online not always consistent.

Criminal Name Search: Access: Phone, fax, mail, in person, online. Both court and visitors may perform in person name searches. No search fee. Required to search: name, years to search, DOB. Records are computerized since 1993. Note: If copies are required, then your request must be in writing. Mail turnaround time 1-2 days. Criminal PAT goes back to same as civil. Access court records free at www.districtcourtfortsmith.org/ and click on Online Records Search. The site will provide user password and ID. Type of identifiers found online not always consistent. Online results show middle initial, DOB, address.

Greenwood State District Court PO Box 925, Greenwood, AR 72936; 479-996-6501; fax: 479-996-1175; 8:30AM-5PM (CST). *Misdemeanor, Civil Actions under $25,000, Traffic, Small Claims.*
www.sebastiancountyonline.com

General Information: Fee to fax document $.25 per page. Court makes copy: $.50 per page. Certification fee: $5.00 per doc. Payee: Greenwood District Court. No personal checks accepted. Major credit cards accepted in person only, by person named. Prepayment required. Mail requests: SASE required for mail return of any copies.

Civil Name Search: Access: Mail, in person, online. Both court and visitors may perform in person name searches. Search fee: $5.00. Required to search: full name, years to search. Records stored from 1984. Note: If copies are required, then your request must be in writing. Mail turnaround time 3-5 days. The index to civil records, domestic relations, and probate from 1998 forward is at www.sebastiancountyonline.com/. Click on Greenwood District Court.

Criminal Name Search: Access: Mail, in person, online. Both court and visitors may perform in person name searches. Search fee: $5.00. Required to search: name, years to search, DOB; also helpful: SSN. Records are computerized since 1985. Note: If copies are required, then your request must be in writing. Mail turnaround time 3-5 days. Online access is same as civil.

Sevier County

Circuit Court 115 N 3rd St., Courthouse, DeQueen, AR 71832; 870-584-3055; probate phone: 870-642-2852; fax: 870-642-3119; 8AM-4:30PM (CST). *Felony, Civil Actions over $5,000, Probate.*
General Information: Probate index in the same building at County Clerk. No juvenile records released. Fee to fax out file $5.00 each; free if to a toll-free number. Court makes copy: $.25 per page. Self serve copy: same. Certification fee: $5.00 per document plus copy fee. Payee: Circuit Clerk. Personal checks accepted. No credit cards accepted. Prepayment required.

Civil Name Search: Access: In person only. Visitors must perform in person searches themselves. Civil records archived from 1900. Civil PAT goes back to 2003.

Criminal Name Search: Access: In person only. Visitors must perform in person searches themselves. Required to search: name, years to search. Criminal records index goes back to 1961, prior back to 1912. Criminal PAT goes back to same as civil.

Local District Court 115 N 3rd St, Rm 215, De Queen, AR 71832; 870-584-7311; fax: 870-642-6651; 8AM-4:30PM (CST). *Misdemeanor, Civil Actions under $5,000, Eviction, Small Claims.*
General Information: No fee to fax back documents. Court makes copy: none but that may change. No certification fee . Payee: District Court. Personal checks accepted. No credit cards accepted. Mail requests: SASE required.

Civil Name Search: Access: Mail, fax, in person. Both court and visitors may perform in person name searches. No search fee. Required to search: name, DOB, SSN, address. Records available since 1991. Mail turnaround time 1-2 weeks.

Criminal Name Search: Access: Mail, fax, in person. Both court and visitors may perform in person name searches. No search fee. Required to search: name, years to search, DOB. Records available since 1991. Mail turnaround time 1-2 weeks.

Sharp County

Circuit Court PO Box 307, Ash Flat, AR 72513; 870-994-7361; fax: 870-994-7712; 8AM-4PM (CST). *Felony, Civil Actions over $5,000, Probate.*

General Information: Probate records are handled by the County Clerk, who can be reached thru the number above. No juvenile or expunged records released. No fee to fax documents to toll free numbers only. Court makes copy: $.25 per page. Certification fee: $5.00 per doc. Payee: Sharp County Clerk. Personal checks accepted. No credit cards accepted. Prepayment required. Mail requests: SASE required for civil.

Civil Name Search: Access: Fax, mail, in person, online. Both court and visitors may perform in person name searches. Search fee: $6.00 per name. Civil records on card files from 1970s. Some records on dockets, computerized since 1986. Mail turnaround time 1 week Civil PAT goes back to 1986. Court has outsourced online access to probate and court orders to www.etitlesearch.com/. The data is mostly recorded documents, fees are involved.

Criminal Name Search: Access: In person. Visitors must perform in person searches themselves. Required to search: name, years to search; also helpful: DOB, SSN. Criminal records on card files from 1970s. Some records on dockets, computerized since 1986. Criminal PAT goes back to same as civil.

Cherokee Village District Court PO Box 129, Cherokee Village, AR 72525; 870-257-5522; fax: 870-257-5524; 8AM-4PM (CST). *Misdemeanor.*

Ash Flat Local District Court PO Box 2, Ash Flat, AR 72513; 870-994-2745; fax: 870-994-7901; 8AM-4PM (CST). *Misdemeanor, Civil Actions under $5,000, Eviction, Small Claims.*

General Information: Will fax documents to local or toll-free number. Court makes copy: $.50 per page. Self serve copy: same. Certification fee: $2.00 per page. Payee: Sharp County District Court. Personal checks accepted. No credit cards accepted. Prepayment required. Mail requests: SASE required.

St. Francis County

Circuit Court 313 S Izard #8, Forrest City, AR 72335; 870-261-1715; fax: 870-261-1723; 8AM-4:30PM (CST). *Felony, Civil Actions over $25,000, Probate.*

General Information: Probate is a separate index at this same address. Probate fax- 870-630-1210. The case limit on civil records increased from $5,000 to $25,000 as of 07/01/2009. No juvenile records released. Will fax documents $5.00 fee. Court makes copy: $.25 per page. Self serve copy: same. Certification fee: $5.00 per cert includes copy fee. Payee: Circuit Clerk. Personal checks accepted. No credit cards accepted. Prepayment required. Mail requests: SASE required for civil.

Civil Name Search: Access: Fax, mail, in person. Both court and visitors may perform in person name searches. Search fee: $5.00 per name. Civil docket indexed from 1982, archived from 1920s. Mail turnaround time same day. Civil PAT available.

Criminal Name Search: Access: In person only. Visitors must perform in person searches themselves. Required to search: name, years to search, DOB, SSN. Criminal records indexed from 1982, archived from 1920s. Note: Court directs criminal searches to AR State Police, phone 501-618-8500. Criminal PAT available.

Forrest City State District Court 615 E Cross, Forrest City, AR 72335; 870-261-1410; fax: 870-261-1411; 8AM-4:30PM (CST). *Misdemeanor, Civil Actions under $25,000, Eviction, Small Claims.*

General Information: The case limit on civil records increased from $5,000 to $25,000 on 07/01/2009. Will fax documents. Court makes copy: $.25 per page. Certification fee: $5.00 per doc. Payee: District Court. No Personal checks and credit cards accepted. $10.00 transaction fee. Prepayment required. Mail requests: SASE required.

Civil Name Search: Access: Mail, in person. Only the court performs in person name searches; visitors may not. Search fee: $5.00 per name. Required to search: Name, DOB, also helpful- SSN. Civil cases indexed by defendant, plaintiff. Civil records on computer since 1994. Mail turnaround time 5 days.

Criminal Name Search: Access: Mail, in person. Only the court performs in person name searches; visitors may not. Search fee: $5.00 per name. Required to search: name, years to search. Criminal records on computer since 1990. Mail turnaround time 5 days.

Madison State District Court PO Box 109, Madison, AR 72359; 870-633-2172; fax: 870-630-0935; 8AM-4:30PM (CST). *Misdemeanor, Civil Actions under $25,000, Eviction, Small Claims.*

General Information: The case limit on civil records increased from $5,000 to $25,000 as of 07/01/2009.

Palestine State District Court PO Box 124, Palestine, AR 72372; 870-581-2489; fax: 870-581-4434; 8AM-4:30PM (CST). *Misdemeanor, Civil Actions under $25,000, Eviction, Small Claims.*

General Information: The case limit on civil records increased from $5,000 to $25,000 as of 07/01/2009.

Stone County

Circuit Court 107 W Mail #D, Mountain View, AR 72560; 870-269-3271; fax: 870-269-2303; 8AM-4:30PM (CST). *Felony, Civil Actions over $5,000, Probate.*

www.16thdistrictark.org

General Information: Probate records are handled by the County Clerk, who can be reached thru the number above. No juvenile or adoption records released. Court makes copy: $.25 per page. Self serve copy: same. Certification fee: $5.00 per document. Payee: Stone County Clerk. Personal checks accepted. No credit cards accepted. Prepayment required.

Civil Name Search: Access: In person only. Visitors must perform in person searches themselves. Civil records on dockets from 1960s; computerized records since 1992. Note: Mountain View Abstract Corp does searches by mail. Call 870-269-3470. Civil PAT goes back to 1992.

Criminal Name Search: Access: In person only. Visitors must perform in person searches themselves. Required to search: name, years to search, DOB; SSN helpful. Criminal docket index from 1960s; computerized records since 1992. Criminal PAT goes back to same as civil.

Local District Court 107 W Main, #H, Mountain View, AR 72560; 870-269-3465; ; 8AM-4:30PM (CST). *Misdemeanor, Civil Actions under $5,000, Eviction, Small Claims.*

General Information: Fax number is same as voice, call first before trying to fax. Will fax documents to local or toll-free number. Court makes copy: $.25 per page. Self serve copy: same. Certification fee: $5.00 per doc. Payee: District Court. No personal checks or credit cards accepted. Prepayment required.

Civil Name Search: Access: Phone, fax, mail, in person. Both court and visitors may perform in person name searches. No search fee. Required to search: names used, years to search. Civil cases indexed by case number. Records available since 1984, not computerized. Mail turnaround time varies.

Criminal Name Search: Access: Phone, fax, mail, in person. Both court and visitors may perform in person name searches. No search fee. Required to search: name, years to search; also helpful: DOB, SSN. Records on computer since 1990. Mail turnaround time varies.

Union County

Circuit Court 101 N Washington, El Dorado, AR 71730; 870-864-1940; probate phone: 870-864-1910; fax: 870-864-1994; 8:30AM-5PM (CST). *Felony, Civil Actions over $25,000, Probate.*

General Information: Probate records are handled by the County Clerk, who can be reached thru the number above. Online identifiers in results same as on public terminal. No juvenile records released. Will fax out specific case files for $1.00 per page. Court makes copy: $.50 per page. Self serve copy: same. Certification fee: $3.00. Payee: Circuit Clerk. Personal checks accepted. No credit cards accepted. Prepayment required.

Civil Name Search: Access: In person, online. Visitors must perform in person searches themselves. Civil records on computer back to 1996 on dockets from 1800s. Civil PAT goes back to 1999. Online access to circuit court dockets by subscription through RecordsUSA.com. Credit card, username and password is required; choose either monthly or per-use plan. Visit the website for sign-up or call Rob at 888-633-4748 x17 for information.

Criminal Name Search: Access: In person, online. Visitors must perform in person searches themselves. Required to search: name, years to search, DOB; also helpful: SSN. Criminal records computerized from 1996 on dockets from 1800s. Criminal PAT goes back to same as civil. Online access to criminal dockets is the same as civil. Online results show name only.

State District Court 250 American #A, El Dorado, AR 71730; 870-864-1950; fax: 870-864-1955; 8:30AM-5PM (CST). *Misdemeanor, Civil Actions under $25,000, Eviction, Small Claims.*

General Information: Will fax back documents. Court makes copy: none. No certification fee . No personal checks or credit cards accepted.

Civil Name Search: Access: In person, fax, mail. Both court and visitors may perform in person name searches. No search fee. Required to search: name. Computerized records since 1987. Mail turnaround time 1-2 days. Civil PAT goes back to 1987.

Criminal Name Search: Access: In person, fax, mail. Both court and visitors may perform in person name searches. No search fee. Required to search: name, years to search, DOB; also helpful: SSN. Computerized records since 1987. Mail turnaround time 1-2 days. Criminal PAT goes back to same as civil.

Van Buren County

Circuit Court 273 Main St, Ste 2, Clinton, AR 72031; 501-745-4140; fax: 501-745-7400; 8AM-4:30PM F-F (5PM M) (CST). *Felony, Civil Actions over $5,000, Probate.*
www.vanburencountycircuitclerk.com/
General Information: Probate records are handled by the County Clerk, who can be reached thru the number above. No juvenile or adoption records released. Will fax documents to local or toll free line, $1.00 per page. Court makes copy: $.50 per page. Self serve copy: same. Certification fee: $5.00. Payee: Van Buren County Clerk's Office. Personal checks accepted. No credit cards accepted. Prepayment required. Mail requests: SASE required.
Civil Name Search: Access: In person, online. Visitors must perform in person searches themselves. Required to search: name, years to search; also helpful: address. Civil cases indexed by defendant, plaintiff. Civil records on computer from 1987, archived from 1900s. Mail turnaround time 7-10 days. Civil PAT goes back to 1987. Search by name or case number at https://arep2.aoc.arkansas.gov/cconnect/PROD/public/ck_public_qry_ma in.cp_main_idx. For a name search, one may submit the DOB, but the DOB is not shown in results.
Criminal Name Search: Access: In person, online. Both court and visitors may perform in person name searches. Required to search: name, years to search; also helpful: address, DOB, SSN. Criminal records computerized from 1987, archived from 1900s. Mail turnaround time 7-10 days. Criminal PAT goes back to 1987. Online access is same as described for civil.

Local District Court 339 South Boykin St, Clinton, AR 72031; 501-745-8894; fax: 501-745-5810; 8AM-4:30PM (CST). *Misdemeanor, Civil Actions under $5,000, Small Claims.*
General Information: Will fax documents. Certification fee: $5.00 per doc. Payee: Clinton District Court. Personal checks accepted. No credit cards accepted. Prepayment required.
Civil Name Search: Access: Phone, mail, fax, in person. Visitors must perform in person searches themselves. No search fee. Required to search: name, years to search, DOB. Civil records on computer back to 1992; in books back to 1992.
Criminal Name Search: Access: Phone, mail, fax, in person. Both court and visitors may perform in person name searches. No search fee. Required to search: name, years to search, DOB, SSN; also helpful-docket or ticket number. Criminal records computerized from 1992; in books back to 1992; computerized since 1992. Mail turnaround time is 1 week .

Washington County

Circuit Court 280 N College, #302, Fayetteville, AR 72701; 479-444-1538; probate phone: 479-444-1711; fax: 479-444-1537; 8AM-4:30PM (CST). *Felony, Civil Actions over $5,000, Probate.*
www.co.washington.ar.us
General Information: Probate is a separate index in the County Clerk's office. No juvenile records released. Will fax documents $5.00 per doc. Court makes copy: $.05 per page. Self serve copy: same. Certification fee: $5.00 per document includes copy fee. Payee: Circuit Clerk. Personal checks accepted. No credit cards accepted. Prepayment required. Mail requests: SASE required.
Civil Name Search: Access: Fax, mail, in person, online. Visitors must perform in person searches themselves. No search fee. Civil records on computer from 1992, on index from 1950. Civil PAT goes back to 1992. Search case index online from the home page. Includes probate records. There is a guest sign-in, but detailed information is via a commercial system, fee is $50.00 per month prepaid. Civil cases indexed from 1992 forward. Search pre-1973 court indices free at www.co.washington.ar.us/ArchiveSearch/CourtRecordSearch.asp.
Criminal Name Search: Access: In person, online. Visitors must perform in person searches themselves. Required to search: name, years to search. Criminal records computerized from 1992, on index from 1950. Note: This court will not do criminal record name searches and refers requests to the state police. Criminal PAT goes back to 1992. For online access - see as described for civil. Pre-1933 criminal court indices free at www.co.washington.ar.us/ArchiveSearch/CourtRecordSearch.asp. Note that these cases are very old.

Elkins Local District Court 1874 Stokenbury Rd, Elkins, AR 72727; 479-643-4170; fax: 479-643-3368; 7:30AM-4:30PM (CST). *Misdemeanor, Civil Actions under $5,000, Small Claims.*
www.co.washington.ar.us

Fayetteville Local District Court 176 S Church Ste 1, Fayetteville, AR 72701; 479-587-3596; fax: 479-444-3480; 7:30AM-4:30PM (CST). *Misdemeanor, Civil Actions under $5,000, Small Claims.*
www.co.washington.ar.us

General Information: Will fax documents no charge. Court makes copy: $5.00 per document. No certification fee . Payee: City of Fayetteville. Personal checks accepted. Prepayment required.
Civil Name Search: Access: Phone, mail, fax, in person. Both court and visitors may perform in person name searches. No search fee. Required to search: name, years to search. Civil records on computer go back to 1984. Mail turnaround time 1 week.
Criminal Name Search: Access: Mail, in person. Only the court performs in person name searches; visitors may not. Search fee: $5.00 per name. Required to search: name, years to search, DOB, SSN, signed release; also helpful: address. Criminal records on computer go back to 1984. Mail turnaround time 1 week.

Prairie Grove Local District Court 151 E Buchanan Street, Prairie Grove, AR 72753; 479-846-3467: 7:30AM-4:30PM (CST). *Misdemeanor, Civil Actions under $5,000, Small Claims.*
www.prairiegrovearkansas.org/

Springdale Local District Court 201 N Spring Street, Springdale, AR 72764; 479-750-8143; fax: 479-750-8564; 8AM-4PM (CST). *Misdemeanor, Civil Actions under $5,000, Small Claims.*
www.co.washington.ar.us

West Fork Local District Court PO Box 339, West Fork, AR 72774; 479-839-3249; fax: 479-839-3335; 8AM-5PM (CST). *Misdemeanor, Civil Actions under $5,000, Small Claims.*
General Information: This court's jurisdiction is Southern Washington county. No expunged, sealed case or current trial case files released. Will fax documents no charge. Court makes copy: $5.00 per document. No certification fee . Payee: West Fork District Court. Personal checks accepted. Prepayment required.
Civil Name Search: Access: Phone, mail, fax, in person. Both court and visitors may perform in person name searches. Search fee: $5.00 per name. Required to search: name, years to search. Civil records on computer go back to 2001. Mail turnaround time 1 week.
Criminal Name Search: Access: Mail, in person. Only the court performs in person name searches; visitors may not. Search fee: $5.00 per name. Required to search: name, years to search, DOB, SSN, signed release; also helpful: address. Criminal records on computer go back to 1996. Mail turnaround time 1 week.

White County

Circuit Court 301 W Arch, Searcy, AR 72143; 501-279-6223; probate phone: 501-279-6204: 8AM-4:30PM (CST). *Felony, Civil Actions over $5,000, Probate.*
General Information: Records in this court are not computerized. Probate is a separate office, address is Courthouse Sq, Searcy, AR 72143. No juvenile records released. Will fax documents $1.00 per page. Court makes copy: $.50 per page. Self serve copy: same. Certification fee: $2.50 per certification. Payee: Circuit Clerk. Personal checks accepted. No credit cards accepted. Prepayment required. Mail requests: SASE required.
Civil Name Search: Access: Mail, in person. Both court and visitors may perform in person name searches. Search fee: $6.00 per name. Required to search: name, years to search; also helpful: address. Civil cases indexed by plaintiff and defendant. Records book indexed back to 2000. Mail turnaround time 1 day.
Criminal Name Search: Access: Mail, in person. Both court and visitors may perform in person name searches. Search fee: $6.00 per name. Required to search: name, years to search, DOB, SSN; also helpful: address. Criminal docket on books back to 1982. Note: All requests must be in writing, even if in person. Mail turnaround time 1 day.

Beebe Local District Court 201 W Illinois St, Beebe, AR 72012; 501-882-8110; fax: 501-882-8113; 8AM-4:30PM (CST). *Misdemeanor, Civil Actions under $5,000, Small Claims.*

Searcy Local District Court PO Box 958, 1600 E Booth Rd, Searcy, AR 72145; 501-279-1040, 268-7622; fax: 501-305-4638; 8AM-4:30PM (CST). *Misdemeanor, Civil Actions under $5,000, Small Claims.*
www.searcy.com/city/courts-probation/home-page
General Information: On 1/27/05 the courthouse burned down and a significant amount of records were lost. Clerk now located in White County Law Enforcement Center Bldg. Will fax documents. Court makes copy: $.50 per page. No certification fee . Payee: Searcy District Court for civil; City of Searcy for criminal. Instate personal checks accepted. No credit cards accepted. Prepayment required. Mail requests: SASE requested.
Civil Name Search: Access: Mail, fax, phone, in person. Only the court performs in person name searches; visitors may not. Search fee: $6.00 per name. Required to search: name plus SSN, years to search. Records on computer back to 6/1995; older records destroyed by fire. Mail turnaround time 5 days.
Criminal Name Search: Access: In person, phone, fax, mail. Only the court performs in person name searches; visitors may not. Search fee: $6.00 per name. Required to search: name, years to search, DOB, SSN.

Records on computer back to 6/1995; older records destroyed by fire. Mail turnaround time 5 days.

Woodruff County

Circuit Court PO Box 492, 500 N 3rd St, Augusta, AR 72006; 870-347-2391; probate phone: 870-347-2871; fax: 870-347-8703; 8AM-4PM (CST). *Felony, Civil Actions over $5,000.*

General Information: Probate is handled by the County Clerk. No juvenile records released. Will fax documents $1.00 per page. Court makes copy: $1.00 per page. Self serve copy: $.50 per page. Certification fee: $5.00. Payee: Circuit Court. Personal checks accepted. No credit cards accepted. Prepayment required.

Civil Name Search: Access: In person only. Both court and visitors may perform in person name searches. No search fee. Civil records on dockets from 1982. Note: There is no public access terminal, index must be looked on docket.

Criminal Name Search: Access: In person only. Both court and visitors may perform in person name searches. No search fee. Required to search: name, years to search, DOB. Criminal docket index from 1980. Note: There is no public access terminal, index must be looked on docket.

Augusta Local District Court PO Box 381, Augusta, AR 72006; 870-347-2790; fax: 870-347-2436; 7:30AM-5PM (CST). *Misdemeanor, Civil Actions under $5,000, Eviction, Small Claims.*

General Information: No fee to fax documents. Court makes copy: $.25 per page. No certification fee . Payee: Woodruff District Court. Personal checks accepted. No credit cards accepted for record copies. Prepayment required. Mail requests: SASE required.

McCrory Local District Court PO Box 897, McCrory, AR 72101; 870-731-2041; fax: 870-731-5159; 7:30AM-5PM (CST). *Misdemeanor, Civil Actions under $5,000, Eviction, Small Claims.*

Yell County

Danville Circuit Court PO Box 219, Danville, AR 72833; 479-495-4850; fax: 479-495-4875; 8AM-4PM (CST). *Felony, Civil Actions over $5,000, Probate.*

General Information: Probate is handled by County Clerk with a separate record index at this same address. No juvenile or adoption records released. Will fax documents $3.00 if file is lengthy. Court makes copy: $.25 per page. Self serve copy: same. Certification fee: $5.00 per document plus copy fee. Payee: Circuit Clerk of Yell County. Personal checks accepted. No credit cards accepted. Prepayment required. Mail requests: SASE required.

Civil Name Search: Access: Mail, fax, in person. Both court and visitors may perform in person name searches. Search fee: $6.00 per name. Required to search: name, years to search; also helpful: address. Civil cases indexed by defendant. Civil records on dockets from 1900s. Mail turnaround time 1 day. Civil PAT goes back to 1946.

Criminal Name Search: Access: Mail, fax, in person. Both court and visitors may perform in person name searches. Search fee: $6.00 per name. Required to search: name, years to search, DOB; also helpful: address. Criminal docket index from 1900s. Mail turnaround time 1 day. Criminal PAT goes back to 1918.

Dardanelle Circuit Court County Courthouse, 108 Union St, #105, Dardanelle, AR 72834; 479-229-4404; fax: 479-229-5634; 8AM-4PM (CST). *Felony, Civil Actions over $5,000, Probate.*

General Information: Probate records are handled by the County Clerk, who can be reached thru the number above. No adoption or juvenile records released. Will fax documents $3.00 each plus $1.00 per page. Court makes copy: $.25 per page. Self serve copy: same. Certification fee: $5.00 per doc. Payee: Circuit Clerk of Yell County. Personal checks accepted. No credit cards accepted. Prepayment required. Mail requests: SASE required.

Civil Name Search: Access: Mail, in person. Both court and visitors may perform in person name searches. Search fee: $6.00 per name. Required to search: name, years to search. Civil cases indexed by defendant. Civil records on dockets from 1800s. Mail turnaround time 1 day. Civil PAT goes back to - cases currently being scanned; incomplete.

Criminal Name Search: Access: Mail, in person. Both court and visitors may perform in person name searches. Search fee: $6.00 per name. Required to search: name, years to search; also helpful: DOB. Criminal docket index from 1800s. Mail turnaround time 1 day. Criminal PAT goes back to - cases currently being scanned; incomplete. Can also search by date filed.

Local District Court County Courthouse, Dardanelle, AR 72834; 479-229-1389; fax: 479-229-5740; 8AM-4PM (CST). *Misdemeanor, Civil Actions under $5,000, Eviction, Small Claims.*

General Information: Will fax documents to local or toll free line. Court makes copy: $.25 per page. No certification fee . Payee: District Court. No credit cards accepted. Prepayment required.

Civil Name Search: Access: Mail, in person. Both court and visitors may perform in person name searches. Search fee: $3.00 per name. Civil records on computer back to 2001. Mail turnaround time 2-4 days.

Criminal Name Search: Access: Mail, in person. Both court and visitors may perform in person name searches. Search fee: $3.00 per name. Required to search: name, years to search, signed release; also helpful: address, DOB, SSN. Criminal records go back to 1982, on computer back to 2001. Mail turnaround time 2-4 days.

California

Time Zone:	**PST**
Capital:	**Sacramento, Sacramento County**
# of Counties:	**58**
State Web:	**www.ca.gov**
Court Web:	**www.courts.ca.gov**

Administration

Administrative Office of Courts, 455 Golden Gate Ave, San Francisco, CA, 94102; 415-865-4200 or 865-7740, Fax: 415-865-4334.

The Supreme and Appellate Courts

The Supreme Court is the court of last resort. The Courts of Appeal are organized into six districts. The website above provides access to all opinions from the Supreme Court and Appeals Courts from 1850 to present. Click on *Case Information*.

The California Courts

Court	Type	How Organized	Jurisdiction Highpoints
Superior*	General	58 trial courts – one per county – with 450 + locations	Felony, Misdemeanor, Civil, Small Claims, Family, Probate, Juvenile, Traffic, Eviction, Domestic Relations
Limited Superior*	Limited	See above	Misdemeanor, Civil Actions Under $25,000 (tort, contract, real property rights)

* = profiled in this book

Details on Court Structure

Superior Courts have jurisdiction over all felonies, misdemeanors, traffic matters, and all civil cases including family law, probate, juvenile, and general civil matters.

Between 1998 and 2000 individual counties unified the Superior Courts and Municipal Courts within their respective counties. Some courts that were formerly Municipal Courts became **Limited Jurisdiction Superior Courts**. They generally hear civil cases under $25,000. Appeals in limited civil cases (where $25,000 or less is at issue) and misdemeanors are heard by the appellate division of the Superior Court. When a small claims case is appealed, a Superior Court judge decides the case.

If there is more than one court of a type within a county, then where the case is tried and where the record is held depends on how a citation is written, or where the infraction occurred, or where the filer chose to file the case.

It is important to note that Limited Courts may try minor felonies.

Record Searching Facts You Need to Know

Fees and Record Searching Tips

Fees are set by statute, the last change was in early 2006. There is no search fee unless the search takes more than 10 minutes, in which case the fee is $15.00. Certification is $25.00 per document plus copy fee; copies are $.50 per page. Most courts follow these guidelines, but not all do - some courts charge the fee regardless of the time involved.

Some courts require a signed release from the subject in order to perform criminal searches and will no longer allow the public to conduct such searches. Personal checks are accepted per state law.

Due to its large number of courts, the Los Angeles County section is arranged uniquely herein. Each branch or "Division" of the Los Angeles Superior Court is given by name, which usually indicates a court's general jurisdictional and geographic boundary. The court name is followed by the District it is located in — South Central, West, Northeast, Central, etc. Also, a court name may mention whether its jurisdiction is "Civil only" or "Criminal only."

Online Access is on a County Basis

There is no statewide online access available for the trial court record index. However, a number of counties have their own online access systems, some provide web access at no fee. Of note, the Los Angeles County has an extensive free and fee-based online system at www.lasuperiorcourt.org.

Alameda County

Superior Court - Criminal 1225 Fallon St, Rm 107, Rene C Davidson Courthouse, Oakland, CA 94612; 510-891-6009; 8:30AM-4PM (PST). *Felony.*
www.alameda.courts.ca.gov/
General Information: No probation, medical, adoption, juvenile or sealed records released. Will fax documents. Court makes copy: $.50 per page. Certification fee: $25 per doc plus copy fee. Payee: Clerk of Superior Court. Personal checks accepted. No credit cards accepted. Prepayment required. Mail requests: SASE required.
Criminal Name Search: Access: Mail, in person. Both court and visitors may perform in person name searches. Search fee: $15.00 per name if search exceeds 10 minutes. Required to search: name, years to search, signed release; also helpful: DOB, SSN. Criminal records on computer back 10 years; on microfiche from 1940, archived and indexed from 1880. Mail turnaround time 1 week. Public use terminal has crim records back to 1998. At the website, search "Find Your Court Date" to determine if a name has an upcoming court date.

Hayward Superior Court 24405 Amador St, Hayward, CA 94544; 510-690-2700; fax: 510-690-2773; 8:30AM-4PM (PST). *Felony, Misdemeanor.*
www.alameda.courts.ca.gov/
General Information: Includes the cities of San Leandro, Hayward and adjoining unincorporated areas of Castro Valley and San Lorenzo. Located at the Hayward Hall of Justice. No sealed or confidential records released. No fee to fax documents. Court makes copy: $.50 per page. Certification fee: $25 per doc plus copy fee. Payee: Clerk of the Court. Local personal checks accepted. ATM and credit cards accepted in person. Prepayment required. Mail requests: SASE required.
Criminal Name Search: Access: Mail, in person. Both court and visitors may perform in person name searches. Search fee: $15.00 per name if search exceeds 10 minutes. Will only search back 7 years. Required to search: name, years to search, DOB. Signed release is required if court does name search. Criminal records on computer back at least 20 years; also on paper index. Mail turnaround time 2-3 days. At the website, search "Find Your Court Date" to determine if a name has an upcoming court date. Online results show middle initial.

South Branch/Hayward Superior Court 24405 Amador St, Rm 108, Hayward, CA 94544; 510-690-2705; fax: 510-690-2773; 8:30AM-4PM (PST). *Civil, Small Claims, Probate.*
www.alameda.courts.ca.gov/
General Information: Located at the Hayward Hall of Justice. No sealed files, paternity or adoption records released. Will not fax out documents. Court makes copy: $.50 per page. Certification fee: $25 per doc plus copy fee. Payee: Clerk of Superior Court. Personal checks accepted. Credit cards accepted. Prepayment required. Mail requests: SASE required.
Civil Name Search: Access: Mail, in person, online. Visitors must perform in person searches themselves. Search fee: $15.00 per name if search exceeds 10 minutes. Civil records on computer from 1974, on microfiche and archived from 1900s (see Oakland court house). Mail turnaround time 2-3 weeks. Public use terminal has civil records back to 1974. Online access to calendars, limited civil case summaries, probate and complex litigations are free from Register of Actions/Domain Web at the website. Search limited cases by number; litigations by case number. No name searching. At the website, search "Find Your Court Date" to determine if a name has an upcoming court date.

Oakland Superior Court - Admin. Bldg Records Management, Ste 16, 1221 Oak St, Oakland, CA 94612; 510-891-6005; 8:30AM-4PM (PST). *Civil Actions under $25,000, Eviction, Small Claims.*
www.alameda.courts.ca.gov/
General Information: Comprises the cities of Oakland, Piedmont and Emeryville. Formerly at the Broussard Justice Complex, now abandoned. Records Mgmt has online records from 2004 forward. No sealed or confidential records released. Will not fax out documents. Court makes copy: $.50 per page. Certification fee: $25.00 per doc. Payee: Clerk of Court, Alameda Superior Court. Personal checks accepted. Visa/MC accepted. Prepayment required. Mail requests: SASE required.

Civil Name Search: Access: Mail, in person, online. Both court and visitors may perform in person name searches. Search fee: $15.00 per name if search exceeds 10 minutes. Add $10 retrieval fee if you are not a party. Civil records on computer from 1990. Note: To find case numbers and locations, visit Records Mgmt. Mail turnaround time 2-3 weeks. Public use terminal has civil records back to 15 years. Online access to calendars, limited civil case summaries and complex litigations are free from Domain Web at the website. Search limited cases by number; litigations by case name or number. At the website, search "Find Your Court Date" to determine if a name has an upcoming court date.

Alameda Branch Superior Court 2233 Shoreline Dr, George E McDonald Hall of Justice, Alameda, CA 94501; 510-263-4300; civil phone: 510-263-4305; fax: 510-263-4330; 8:30AM-4:00PM; phones- 8:30AM-5PM (PST). *Civil Actions under $25,000, Family Law.*
www.alameda.courts.ca.gov/
General Information: Co-extensive with the city limits of Alameda only. The fax number is not for public use. Family Law can be reached at 510-263-4305. No confidential records released. Will not fax documents. Court makes copy: $.50 per page. Certification fee: $25 per doc plus copy fee. Payee: Alameda Superior Court. Personal checks accepted. Accepts credit cards in person only. Prepayment required. Mail requests: SASE required.
Civil Name Search: Access: Mail, in person, online. Both court and visitors may perform in person name searches. Search fee: $15.00 per name if search exceeds 10 minutes. Civil records on computer since 1987. Mail turnaround time 3 days to 1 week. Public use terminal has civil records back to at least 7 years, some 10. Online access to calendars, limited civil case summaries and complex litigations are free from Domain Web at the website. Search limited cases by number; litigations by case number.

Fremont Superior Court 39439 Paseo Padre Pky, Fremont Hall of Justice, Fremont, CA 94538; criminal phone: 510-818-7501; civil phone: 510-818-7503; criminal fax: 8:30AM-4PM; civil fax: 8:30AM-4PM (PST). *Felony, Misdemeanor, Civil Actions under $25,000, Eviction, Small Claims, Traffic.*
www.alameda.courts.ca.gov/
General Information: Jurisdiction includes Fremont, Newark, and Union City. Located at the Fremont Hall of Justice. No sealed or confidential records released. Will fax civil documents only, $1.00 per page. Court makes copy: $.50 per page. Certification fee: $25 per doc plus copy fee. Payee: Fremont Superior Court. Personal checks accepted. No credit cards accepted. Prepayment required. Mail requests: SASE required.
Civil Name Search: Access: Fax, mail, in person, online. Both court and visitors may perform in person name searches. Search fee: $15.00 per name if search exceeds 10 minutes. Civil records on computer from 1990. Note: 3 file limit at counter. Mail turnaround time 1 week. Civil PAT goes back to 15 years. Online access to calendars, limited civil case summaries, probate and complex litigations are free at the DomainWeb section at the website. Search limited cases by number; litigations by case name or number.
Criminal Name Search: Access: Mail, in person. Both court and visitors may perform in person name searches. Search fee: $15.00 per name if search exceeds 10 minutes. Required to search: name, years to search, DOB, signed release. Criminal records on computer only go back 7 years. Note: 5 file limit at counter. Mail turnaround time 1 week. Criminal PAT goes back to 7 years. At the website, search "Find Your Court Date" to determine if a name has an upcoming court date.

Oakland - Wiley W. Manuel Superior Court 661 Washington St, 2nd Fl, Wiley W Manuel Courthouse, Oakland, CA 94607; 510-627-4700; criminal phone: 510-891-6005; fax: 510-627-4909; 8:30AM-4PM (PST). *Misdemeanor (also Felony Welfare Fraud and H&S Violations), Civil, Small Claims, Traffic.*
www.alameda.courts.ca.gov/
General Information: Comprises the cities of Oakland, Piedmont and Emeryville, Albany and Berkeley. No sealed or confidential records released. Will not fax documents. Court makes copy: $.50 per page. Certification fee: $25 per doc plus copy fee. Payee: Clerk of Superior Court. Personal checks

accepted. Visa/MC accepted in person only. Prepayment required. Mail requests: SASE required.

Civil Name Search: Access: Mail, in person, online. Both court and visitors may perform in person name searches. Search fee: $15.00 per name if search exceeds 10 minutes. Add $10 retrieval fee if you are not a party. Civil records on computer from 1990. Note: To find case numbers and locations, visit Records Mgmt. Mail turnaround time 2-3 weeks. Civil PAT goes back to 15 years. Online access to calendars, limited civil case summaries and complex litigations are free from Domain Web at the website. Search limited cases by number; litigations by case name or number. At the website, search "Find Your Court Date" to determine if a name has an upcoming court date.

Criminal Name Search: Access: Mail, in person. Both court and visitors may perform in person name searches. Search fee: $15.00 per name if search exceeds 10 minutes. Required to search: name, years to search. Criminal records computerized from 1994, maintained since 1972. Mail turnaround time 1 week. Criminal PAT goes back to 1998. At the website, search "Find Your Court Date" to determine if a name has an upcoming court date.

Pleasanton Superior Court 5672 Stoneridge Dr, Gale/Schenone Hall of Justice, Pleasanton, CA 94588; criminal phone: 925-227-6750; civil phone: 925-227-6787; fax: 925-227-6772; 8:30AM-4PM (PST). *Misdemeanor, Civil Actions over $25,000, Eviction, Small Claims, Family.*
www.alameda.courts.ca.gov/

General Information: Includes the cities of Livermore, Dublin, Sunol and Pleasanton and all areas east to San Joaquin County line, north of Highway 580 to Contra Costa line. Online identifiers in results same as on public terminal. No records older than 10 years are released. Will not fax documents. Court makes copy: $.50 per page. Certification fee: $25 per doc plus copy fee. Payee: Alameda County Superior Court. Personal checks accepted. Credit card accepted in person only. Prepayment required. Mail requests: SASE required.

Civil Name Search: Access: Mail, in person, online. Both court and visitors may perform in person name searches. Search fee: $15.00 per name if search exceeds 10 minutes. Civil records on computer from 1990. Mail turnaround time 4-6 weeks. Civil PAT goes back to 1998. Online access to calendars, civil case summaries, probate, family law, and complex litigations are free from Domain Web at the website. Search all cases by case number.

Criminal Name Search: Access: Mail, in person. Both court and visitors may perform in person name searches. Search fee: $15.00 per name if search exceeds 10 minutes. Required to search: name, years to search; also helpful: address, DOB. Criminal records computerized from 1990. Note: Court prefers that you use their "consent form." Mail turnaround time 4-6 weeks. Criminal PAT goes back to same as civil. At the website, search "Find Your Court Date" to determine if a name has an upcoming court date within five days.

Berkeley Superior Court - Civil 2120 Martin Luther King Jr Way, Berkeley Courthouse, Berkeley, CA 94704; 510-647-4439; probate phone: 510-647-4429; fax: 510-883-9359; 8:30AM-4:00PM (PST). *Civil, Eviction, Small Claims, Probate.*
www.alameda.courts.ca.gov/

General Information: Co-extensive with the city limits of Berkeley and Albany.

Civil Name Search: Access: Mail, in person, online. Both court and visitors may perform in person name searches. Search fee: $15.00 per name if search exceeds 10 minutes. Civil records on computer since 1986. Mail turnaround time 1 week. Public use terminal has civil records back to 1986. Online access to calendars, limited civil case summaries and complex litigations are free from Domain Web at the website. Search limited cases by number; litigations by case number.

Alpine County

Superior Court PO Box 518, Markleeville, CA 96120; 530-694-2113; fax: 530-694-2119; 8AM-4:30PM (PST). *Felony, Misdemeanor, Civil, Eviction, Small Claims, Probate.*
www.alpine.courts.ca.gov

General Information: No juvenile, paternity, adoption or sealed released. Fee to fax out file $1.00 per page. Court makes copy: $.50 per page. Self serve copy: same. Certification fee: $25 per doc plus copy fee. Payee: Alpine County Superior Court. Personal checks and credit cards accepted. Prepayment required. Mail requests: SASE required.

Civil Name Search: Access: Mail, in person. Both court and visitors may perform in person name searches. Search fee: $15.00 per name if search exceeds 10 minutes. Civil records on index file from 1981, closed files archived from 1800s to 1998. Computer records go back 10 years. Mail turnaround time 2-3 days.

Criminal Name Search: Access: Mail, in person. Only the court performs in person name searches; visitors may not. Search fee: $15.00 per name if search exceeds 10 minutes. Required to search: name, years to

search; also helpful-SSN. Criminal records on index file from 1981, archived from 1800s. Computer records go back 10 years. Mail turnaround time 1-3 days.

Amador County

Superior Court 500 Argonaut Ln, Jackson, CA 95642-9534; criminal phone: 209-257-2604; civil phone: 209-257-2603; fax: 209-257-2676; 9:30AM-4PM (PST). *Felony, Misdemeanor, Civil, Eviction, Small Claims, Probate.*
www.amadorcourt.org

General Information: No adoption, juvenile or paternity records released. Unlawful detainee released after 60 days of filing. Will not fax documents. Court makes copy: $.50 per page. Certification fee: $25 per doc plus copy fee. Payee: Amador Superior Court. Personal checks accepted for correct amount only. No credit cards accepted. Prepayment required. Mail requests: SASE required for private agencies.

Civil Name Search: Access: Mail, in person. Only the court performs in person name searches; visitors may not. Search fee: $15.00 per name if search exceeds 10 minutes. Civil records on computer back to 1989. Archived and indexed in books from 1800s. Mail turnaround time 7-14 days. Court calendars are by date up to 7 days ahead at www.amadorcourt.org/courtcal/courtcal.html. Personal identifiers are name and case number.

Criminal Name Search: Access: Mail, in person. Only the court performs in person name searches; visitors may not. Search fee: $15.00 per name if search exceeds 10 minutes. Names searches go back to 1989 only. Required to search: name, years to search. Criminal records computerized from 1989. Felonies are archived and indexed in books from 1800s; misdemeanors retained 2-10 years depending on offense. Mail turnaround time 2-4 weeks. Court calendars are by date up to 10 days ahead at www.amadorcourt.org/courtcal/courtcal.html. Personal identifiers are name and case number.

Butte County

Superior Court One Court St, Oroville, CA 95965; 530-532-7002 Admin; criminal phone: 530-532-7011; civil phone: 530-532-7009; probate phone: 530-532-7017;; 8:30AM-4PM (PST). *Felony, Misdemeanor, Small Claims, Eviction, Traffic, Probate, Family.*
www.buttecourt.ca.gov

General Information: Courthouse physically holds most criminal court files for the county, including Gridley, Chico, Paradise Branches; however, search countywide computer index at any court. Civil cases were transferred to the Chico court in 2003. No juvenile, paternity, confidential, adoption records released. Will fax documents $5.00 1st page, $1.00 each add'l. Court makes copy: $.50 per page. Certification fee: $25 per doc plus copy fee; exemplification fee is $20 plus copy fee. Payee: Butte County Superior Court. Personal checks accepted. Visa/MC accepted. Prepayment required. Mail requests: SASE required.

Civil Name Search: Access: Mail, in person, online. Both court and visitors may perform in person name searches. Search fee: $15.00 per name if search exceeds 10 minutes. Required to search: name, years to search; also helpful: address. Civil cases indexed by defendant, plaintiff. Civil records on computer from 1988, on microfiche from 1983 thru 1988. Mail turnaround time 2-5 days. Civil PAT goes back to 1990. Limited case index searching by name is free at www.buttecourt.ca.gov/online_index/cmssearch.cfm. There is also a calendar lookup at www.buttecourt.ca.gov/calendarlookup/cmscalendarlookup.cfm.

Criminal Name Search: Access: Mail, in person, online. Both court and visitors may perform in person name searches. Search fee: $15.00 per name if search exceeds 10 minutes. Required to search: name, years to search; also helpful: DOB. Criminal records computerized from 1988, on microfiche from 1983 thru 1988. Mail turnaround time 1-2 weeks. Criminal PAT goes back to same as civil. 2 terminals available. Limited case index searching by name is free online at www.buttecourt.ca.gov/online_index/cmssearch.cfm. There is also a calendar lookup, see above. Online results show name only.

Chico Branch - Superior Court 655 Oleander Ave, Chico, CA 95926; 530-532-7005 (Traffic); civil phone: 530-532-7009; probate phone: 530-532-7017; fax: 530-892-8516; 8:30AM-4PM (PST). *Civil Actions, Eviction, Small Claims, Probate, Traffic.*
www.buttecourt.ca.gov

General Information: Traffic phone- 530-892-9407. This court handles civil cases previously handled by Oroville court. All misdemeanor cases now at Oroville. Active probate case records located here at Chico; closed cases archived in basement of the main Court in Oroville. No sealed records released. Will not fax documents. Court makes copy: $.50 per page. Certification fee: $25 per doc plus copy fee. Payee: Superior Court. Personal checks accepted. No credit cards accepted. Prepayment required. Mail requests: SASE required.

Civil Name Search: Access: Mail, in person, online. Both court and visitors may perform in person name searches. Search fee: $15.00 per name if search exceeds 10 minutes. Civil records in index files. Records destroyed after 10 years. Mail turnaround time 4 weeks. Public use terminal has civil records back to 1986. Limited index name searching is free at www.buttecourt.ca.gov/online_index/cmssearch.cfm. There is also a calendar lookup at www.buttecourt.ca.gov/calendarlookup/cmscalendarlookup.cfm.

Gridley Branch - Superior Court , , CA; . *Court closed. Closed cases must be searched at Oroville court.*

Paradise Branch - Superior Court One Court St, Oroville, CA 95965; 530-532-7002; civil phone: 530-532-7009; probate phone: 530-532-7017; fax: 530-538-8567; 8:30AM-4PM (PST). *Small Claims, Eviction, Misdemeanor Traffic, Infraction.*

www.buttecourt.ca.gov

General Information: 530-532-7018 Sm Clms. Probate fax- 530-538-8516. This Paradise Branch at 747 Elliott Rd now largely a data center. See the Oroville Court -address/phone here - for Paradise court's old misdemeanor records. Most copy work done at main branch in Oroville. No sealed records released. Court makes copy: $.50 per page. Certification fee: $25 per doc plus copy fee. Payee: Superior Court. Personal checks accepted. Visa/MC accepted. Prepayment required. Mail requests: SASE required for civil.

Civil Name Search: Access: Mail, in person, online. Only the court performs in person name searches; visitors may not. Search fee: $15.00 per name if search exceeds 10 minutes. Required to search: name; also helpful: years to search. Civil cases indexed by defendant, plaintiff. Civil records are located in The Chico Superior Court. Records go back to 1980; on computer back to 1997. Limited case index searching by name is free at www.buttecourt.ca.gov/online_index/cmssearch.cfm. A calendar lookup is at www.buttecourt.ca.gov/calendarlookup/cmscalendarlookup.cfm.

Calaveras County

Superior Court 891 Mt Ranch Rd, San Andreas, CA 95249; 209-754-9800 info; 8:15AM-4PM (PST). *Felony, Misdemeanor, Civil, Small Claims, Probate, Infractions.*

www.calaveras.courts.ca.gov

General Information: No juvenile or confidential records released. Will not fax documents. Court makes copy: $.50 per page. Certification fee: $25 per doc plus copy fee. Payee: Calaveras Superior Court. Personal checks accepted. No credit cards accepted. Prepayment required. Mail requests: SASE required.

Civil Name Search: Access: Mail, in person. Both court and visitors may perform in person name searches. Search fee: $15.00 per name if search exceeds 10 minutes. Civil records on computer since 6/96; in index books and microfiche from 1975. Mail turnaround time 1-2 weeks.

Criminal Name Search: Access: Mail, in person. Both court and visitors may perform in person name searches. Search fee: $15.00 per name if search exceeds 10 minutes. Required to search: name, years to search, DOB; also helpful: aliases. Criminal records on computer since 6/96; in index books and microfiche from 1975. Mail turnaround time 1-2 weeks.

Colusa County

Superior Court - Dept 1 547 Market, Colusa, CA 95932; 530-458-5149; fax: 530-458-2230; 8:30AM-5PM (PST). *Felony, Civil Actions over $25,000, Probate.*

www.colusa.courts.ca.gov

General Information: Since 1994, the records have been combined for both courts in this county. No juvenile, paternity (except Judgment) or adoption records released. Will not fax documents. Court makes copy: $.50 per page. Certification fee: $25.50 per doc plus $.50 ea add'l page. Payee: Colusa County Superior Court. Personal checks accepted. No credit cards accepted for fees. Prepayment required. Mail requests: SASE required.

Civil Name Search: Access: Mail, in person, online. Both court and visitors may perform in person name searches. Search fee: $15.00 per name if search exceeds 10 minutes. Civil records on computer from 1994, in index files from 1800s. Mail turnaround time 7 days. Civil PAT goes back to 1994. The actual web search site is http://cms.colusa.courts.ca.gov/ for a civil or family case index search. Can search by name or case number.

Criminal Name Search: Access: Mail, in person, online. Both court and visitors may perform in person name searches. Search fee: $15.00 per name if search exceeds 10 minutes. Required to search: name, years to search. Criminal records computerized from 1994, in index files from 1800s. Mail turnaround time 7 days. Criminal PAT goes back to same as civil. The actual web search site is http://cms.colusa.courts.ca.gov/ for a criminal or traffic case index search. Can search by name or case number.

Superior Court - Dept 2 Clerk's Office, 532 Oak St, Colusa, CA 95932; 530-458-5149; fax: 530-458-2230; 8:30AM-11:30AM, 12:30PM-5PM (PST). *Felony, Misdemeanor, Civil, Eviction, Small Claims.*

www.colusa.courts.ca.gov

General Information: Since 1995, the records have been combined for both courts in this county; prior records must be searched at the individual courts. Dept. 1's courtroom is at 547 Market St. No sealed records released. Will not fax documents. Court makes copy: $.50 per page. Self serve copy: same. Certification fee: $25 per doc plus copy fee. Payee: Colusa Superior Court. Personal checks accepted. No credit cards accepted. Prepayment required. Mail requests: SASE required.

Civil Name Search: Access: Mail, in person, online. Both court and visitors may perform in person name searches. Search fee: $15.00 per name if search exceeds 10 minutes. Civil records on computer from 1994, index books prior. Mail turnaround time up to 2 weeks. Civil PAT goes back to 1995. Visit http://cms.colusa.courts.ca.gov/ for a civil or family case index search. Can search by name or case number.

Criminal Name Search: Access: Mail, in person, online. Both court and visitors may perform in person name searches. Search fee: $15.00 per name if search exceeds 10 minutes. Required to search: name, years to search, DOB. Criminal records computerized from 1994, index books prior. Mail turnaround time up to 2 weeks. Criminal PAT goes back to same as civil. Visit http://cms.colusa.courts.ca.gov/ for a criminal or traffic case index search. Can search by name or case number.

Contra Costa County

Superior Court PO Box 991, 725 Court St, Wafefield Taylor Courthouse, Rm 103, Martinez, CA 94553; 925-646-2950; criminal phone: 925-646-2440; civil phone: 925-646-2951;; 8AM-2PM (PST). *Felony, Civil Actions over $25,000, Probate.*

www.cc-courts.org

General Information: Make records requests at 1111 Ward St, Health Dept Bldg. Civil and Probate cases heard at the Wakefield Taylor Courthouse (address above); Criminal at AF Bray Bldg.,1020 Ward St. Traffic and Small Claims cases from this area heard in the Concord Court. No adoption, juvenile or sealed records released. Will not fax documents. Court makes copy: $.50 per page per side. Certification fee: $25 per doc plus copy fee, exemplification fee $20.00 plus copy fee. Payee: Clerk of the Superior Court. Business checks accepted. No credit cards accepted. Prepayment required. Mail requests: SASE required.

Civil Name Search: Access: Mail, in person, online. Both court and visitors may perform in person name searches. Search fee: $15.00 per name if search exceeds 10 minutes. Civil records on computer from 1987, on microfiche from 1900s. Note: Court visitors can view microfiche. Mail turnaround time 7-10 days With registration, use Open Access to view Civil, Probate, Family and Small Claims information is free at http://icms.cc-courts.org/iotw/. Also, lookup your court case info free at http://icms.cc-courts.org/tellme/. Online civil search results include month/year of birth.

Criminal Name Search: Access: Mail, in person. Both court and visitors may perform in person name searches. Search fee: $15.00 per name if search exceeds 10 minutes. There is a $.50 fee for a computer printout page. Required to search: name, DOB. Criminal records computerized from 1987, on microfiche from 1900s. Note: Send written requests to Room 127. Visitors can view microfiche. Mail turnaround time 7-10 days.

Walnut Creek Branch - Superior Court 640 Ygnacio Valley Rd, Walnut Creek, CA 94596-3820; criminal phone: 925-646-6572; civil phone: 925-646-6578; 8AM-2PM (PST). *Felony, Misdemeanor, Eviction, Small Claims, Traffic.*

www.cc-courts.org

General Information: Includes Alamo, Canyon, Danville, Lafayette, Moraga, Orinda, Rheem, San Ramon, St Mary's College, Walnut Creek and Ygnacio Valley. Effective 01/01/99, this court has all civil records formerly at the municipal court in Concord. No probation reports or sealed case records released. Will not fax documents. Court makes copy: $.50 per page. Certification fee: $25 per doc plus copy fee. Payee: Walnut Creek Superior Court. Personal checks accepted. No credit cards accepted. Prepayment required. Mail requests: SASE required.

Civil Name Search: Access: Phone, mail, online, in person. Both court and visitors may perform in person name searches. Search fee: $5.00 per name if search exceeds 10 minutes. Add $5.00 archive retrieval fee for older cases. In person searching of microfiche is free. Required to search: name; also helpful: years to search. Civil cases indexed by defendant, plaintiff. Civil records on computer from 1991. Records are destroyed after 10 years. Mail turnaround time 1 week. Civil PAT available. With registration, use Open Access to view Civil case, Probate, Family and Small Claims information is free at http://icms.cc-courts.org/iotw/. Also, lookup your court case info free at http://icms.cc-courts.org/tellme/. Online civil search results include month/year of birth.

Criminal Name Search: Access: Mail, in person. Both court and visitors may perform in person name searches. Search fee: $15.00 per name. Add $5.00 archive retrieval fee for older cases. A surcharge of $15 is added for lists of 51 or more. There is a $.50 fee for a computer printout. Required to search: name, years to search, DOB. Criminal records go back 10 years. Mail turnaround time 1 week. Criminal PAT available.

Concord Branch - Superior Court 2970 Willow Pass Rd, Concord, CA 94519; 925-646-5410; 8AM-2PM (PST). *Eviction, Small Claims, Traffic.*
www.cc-courts.org
General Information: Includes Avon, Clayton, Clyde, Concord, Martinez, Pacheco, Pleasant Hill. This court serves as the lowest court for the Main Court in Martinez. Probate, Family and Small Claims information free at www.cc-courts.org/index.cfm.

Pittsburg Branch - Superior Court 45 Civic Ave, Pittsburg, CA 94565-0431; criminal phone: 925-427-8173; civil phone: 925-427-8158 or 9; 8AM-2PM (PST). *Felony, Misdemeanor, Eviction, Small Claims, Traffic.*
www.cc-courts.org
General Information: Includes Antioch, Bay Pt., Bethel Is, Bradford Is, Brentwood, Byron, Holland Tract, Jersey Is, Knightsen, Oakley, Pittsburg, Quimby Is, Shore Acres, Webb Tract and parts of Clayton. No probation reports released. Will not fax documents. Court makes copy: $.50 per page. Certification fee: $25 per doc plus copy fee. Payee: Superior Court. Personal checks accepted. No credit cards accepted. Prepayment required. Mail requests: SASE required.
Civil Name Search: Access: Mail, in person, online. Both court and visitors may perform in person name searches. Search fee: $5.00 per name if search exceeds 15 minutes. Civil records on computer from 1991. Records are destroyed after 10 years. Mail turnaround time 1 week. Civil PAT goes back to 1989. With registration, use Open Access to view Civil case, Probate, Family and Small Claims information is free at http://icms.cc-courts.org/iotw/. Also, lookup your court case info free at http://icms.cc-courts.org/tellme/. Online civil search results include month/year of birth.
Criminal Name Search: Access: Mail, in person. Both court and visitors may perform in person name searches. Search fee: $15.00 per name. A surcharge of $15 is added for lists of 51 or more. There is a $.50 fee for a computer printout. Required to search: name, years to search, DOB. Criminal records computerized from 1991, index files for 10 years. Records are destroyed after 10 years. Note: Visitor may search microfiche only. Mail turnaround time 1 week. Criminal PAT goes back to 1994.

Richmond Superior Court 100 - 37th St, Richmond, CA 94805; 510-374-3138; criminal phone: 510-374-3156; civil phone: 510-374-3137; 8AM-2PM (PST). *Felony, Misdemeanor, Eviction, Small Claims, Traffic.*
www.cc-courts.org
General Information: Includes Crockett, El Cerrito, El Sobrante, Hercules, Kensington, North Richmond, Pinole, Point Richmond, Port Costa, Richmond, Rodeo, Rollingwood, San Pablo, Tilden North Pk. Traffic phone-510-374-3171. No probation reports released. Will not fax documents. Court makes copy: $.50 per page. Certification fee: $25 per doc plus copy fee. Payee: Richmond Superior Court. Personal checks accepted. No credit cards accepted in person; cards accepted for full payment on internet. Prepayment required. Mail requests: SASE required.
Civil Name Search: Access: Mail, in person, online. Both court and visitors may perform in person name searches. Search fee: $5.00 per name if search exceeds 10 minutes. Required to search: name. Civil cases indexed by defendant, plaintiff. Civil records on computer from 1991. Records are destroyed after 10 years unless renewal of judgment filed. Mail turnaround time 5 days. With registration, use Open Access to view Civil case, Probate, Family and Small Claims information is free at http://icms.cc-courts.org/iotw/. Also, lookup your court case info free at http://icms.cc-courts.org/tellme/. Online civil search results include month/year of birth.
Criminal Name Search: Access: Mail, in person. Only the court performs in person name searches; visitors may not. Search fee: $15.00 per name. There is an additional fee for retrieval of archive files. A surcharge of $15 is added for lists of 51 or more. There is a $.50 fee for a computer printout. Required to search: name, years to search; also helpful: address, DOB, SSN. Criminal records maintained for 10 years, but can be destroyed after 2 years depending on violation code. Mail turnaround time 5 days.

Del Norte County
Superior Court 450 "H" St, Rm 209, Crescent City, CA 95531; 707-464-8115; criminal phone: x4; civil phone: x4; criminal fax: 707-465-4005; civil fax: 8AM-5PM; 8AM-5PM (PST). *Felony, Misdemeanor, Civil, Eviction, Small Claims, Probate.*
www.delnorte.courts.ca.gov
General Information: No adoption, juvenile, LPS conservatorship or confidential files released. Will not fax documents. Court makes copy: $.50

per page. Certification fee: $25 per doc plus copy fee. Payee: Superior Court. Personal checks accepted. No credit cards accepted. Prepayment required. Mail requests: SASE required.
Civil Name Search: Access: Fax, mail, in person. Only the court performs in person name searches; visitors may not. Search fee: $15.00 per name if search exceeds 10 minutes. Required to search: name, years to search, DOB. Civil cases indexed by defendant, plaintiff. Civil records in index files and on microfiche back to 1800s. Mail turnaround time 1 week.
Criminal Name Search: Access: Mail, fax, in person. Only the court performs in person name searches; visitors may not. Search fee: $15.00 per name if search exceeds 10 minutes. Required to search: name, years to search, DOB, middle name; also helpful-SSN. Criminal records in index files and microfiche back to 1800s. Mail turnaround time 1 week.

El Dorado County
Placerville Branch - Superior Court 495 Main St, Placerville, CA 95667; 530-621-6426; criminal phone: 530-621-6716; fax: 530-622-9774; 8AM-4PM (PST). *Felony, Misdemeanor.*
www.eldoradocourt.org/
General Information: Family Law and Juvenile cases also located here. No adoption, juvenile, mental or confidential released. Will not fax documents. Court makes copy: $.50 per page. Certification fee: $25 per doc plus copy fee. Payee: Superior Court. Personal checks accepted. No credit cards accepted. Prepayment required. Mail requests: SASE required.
Criminal Name Search: Access: Mail, in person, online. Both court and visitors may perform in person name searches. Search fee: $15.00 per name if search exceeds 10 minutes. Fee is $4.00 to request a file from archives. Required to search: name, years to search. Criminal records computerized from 2000, in hardbound books from 1979 to 1999, prior archived in Placerville. Mail turnaround time 2 weeks. Access alpha Case Index lists back to year 2000 free at www.eldoradocourt.org/caseindex/case_index.aspx. Search monthly calendars free at http://eldocourtweb.eldoradocourt.org/calendar.aspx. Online results show name only.

South Lake Tahoe Branch - Superior Court - Civil 1354 Johnson Blvd, South Lake Tahoe, CA 96150; 530-573-3075; fax: 530-544-6532; 8AM-4PM (PST). *Civil, Eviction, Probate, Family Law.*
www.eldoradocourt.org/
General Information: No adoption, juvenile, mental or confidential released. Court makes copy: $.50 per page. Certification fee: $25 per doc plus copy fee. Payee: Superior Court. Personal checks accepted. No credit cards accepted. Prepayment required. Generally, submit a 'not to exceed' $30.00 check. Mail requests: SASE required for civil.
Civil Name Search: Access: Mail, in person, online. Both court and visitors may perform in person name searches. Search fee: $15.00 per name if search exceeds 10 minutes. Required to search: name, years to search; also helpful-case number. Civil cases indexed by defendant, plaintiff. Civil records on computer from 1990, in hardbound books from 1979 to 1989, prior archived in Placerville. Mail turnaround time 2 weeks. Access alpha Case Index lists back to year 2000 free at www.eldoradocourt.org/caseindex/case_index.aspx. Judge's weekly tentative rulings may be free at the website. Search monthly calendars free at http://eldocourtweb.eldoradocourt.org/calendar.aspx.

South Lake Tahoe Branch - Superior Court - Criminal 1354 Johnson Blvd, South Lake Tahoe, CA 96150; 530-573-3044; fax: 530-542-9102; 8AM-4PM (PST). *Felony, Misdemeanor.*
www.eldoradocourt.org/
General Information: No probation reports released. Faxed record request must be prepaid. Court makes copy: $.50 per page. Certification fee: $25 per doc plus copy fee. Payee: El Dorado Superior Court. Personal checks accepted. Credit cards only accepted at www.paybill.com/eldoradocourt. Prepayment required. Mail requests: SASE required.
Criminal Name Search: Access: Mail, in person, online. Both court and visitors may perform in person name searches. Search fee: $15.00 per name if search exceeds 10 minutes. Required to search: name, years to search; also helpful: DOB. Criminal records computerized from 2000, index files from 1983. Mail turnaround time 2 weeks. Public use terminal has crim records. Access alpha Case Index lists back to year 2000 free at www.eldoradocourt.org/caseindex/case_index.aspx. Search monthly calendars free at http://eldocourtweb.eldoradocourt.org/calendar.aspx. Online results show name only.

Cameron Park Branch - Superior Court 3321 Cameron Park Dr, Cameron Park, CA 95682; 530-621-5867; fax: 530-672-2413; 8AM-4PM (PST). *Civil, Probate, Small Calims, Evictions.*
www.eldoradocourt.org/
General Information: Small Claims and Eviction housed here since 2010. Older records (circa1999) may be available at the Placerville Branch Superior Court OR at record storage location in Sacramento. Will not fax documents. Court makes copy: $.50 per page. Certification fee: $25 per doc plus copy fee; Exemplification fee $20.00. Payee: Superior Court. Personal checks

accepted. No credit cards accepted. Prepayment required. Mail requests: SASE required.

Civil Name Search: Access: Mail, in person, online. Both court and visitors may perform in person name searches. Search fee: $15.00 per name if search exceeds 10 minutes. Required to search: name, years to search. Civil records on computer from 2000, index cards prior. Paper records are destroyed or shipped after 3 years. Mail turnaround time 10 days. Access alpha Case Index lists back to year 2000 free at www.eldoradocourt.org/caseindex/case_index.aspx. Judge's weekly tentative rulings may be free at the website. Search monthly calendars free at http://eldocourtweb.eldoradocourt.org/calendar.aspx.

Fairlane Branch - Superior Court 2850 Fairlane Ct, Bldg C, Placerville, CA 95667; criminal phone: 530-621-7464; civil phone: 530-621-7470; criminal fax: 530-626-0656; civil fax: 8AM-4PM; 8AM-4PM (PST). *Misdemeanor, Evictions, Traffic.*
www.eldoradocourt.org/
General Information: Also known as the West Slope Branch, has three facilities. Building C houses criminal, traffic. Civil and Small Claims cases were moved to the Cameron Park Branch. However, some older case files are still here. No probation reports released. Will not fax documents. Court makes copy: $.50 per page. Certification fee: $25 per doc plus copy fee. Payee: El Dorado County Superior Courts. Personal checks accepted. No credit cards accepted. Prepayment required. Mail requests: SASE required.
Criminal Name Search: Access: Mail, in person, online. Both court and visitors may perform in person name searches. Search fee: $15.00 per name if search takes 10 minutes or more. $4.00 retrieval fee for records in storage. Required to search: name, years to search; also helpful: DOB. Criminal records computerized from 2000, prior index on paper. Note: Address search requests to Dept 7. In-person searchers can look up paper indices: no computer terminal. Mail turnaround time 2 weeks. Access alpha Case Index lists back to year 2000 free at www.eldoradocourt.org/caseindex/case_index.aspx. Use Court Form M6. Search monthly calendars free at http://eldocourtweb.eldoradocourt.org/calendar.aspx. Online results show name only.

Fresno County

Superior Court - Criminal 1100 Van Ness Ave, Fresno, CA 93724; 559-457-1801; fax: 559-457-1820; 8AM-4PM (PST). *Felony, Misdemeanor, Traffic, Family.*
www.fresnosuperiorcourt.org
General Information: Felony address is Rm 200; Misdemeanor address is Rm 402; Phone # for misdemeanors is 599-457-1802; Fax; 599-457-1810. Civil court main office is at 2317 Tuolumne St. No confidential, adoption or juvenile records released. Will not fax documents. Court makes copy: $.50 per page. Certification fee: $25 per doc plus copy fee. Payee: Superior Court Clerk's Office. Personal checks accepted. Visa/MC accepted. Prepayment required. Mail requests: SASE required.
Criminal Name Search: Access: Phone, fax, mail, in person, online. Both court and visitors may perform in person name searches. Search fee: $15.00 per name if search exceeds 10 minutes. Required to search: name, years to search. Criminal records computerized from 1976; microfiche, index files and archived from 1800s. Mail turnaround time 3-5 days. Public use terminal has crim records back to 1976. Access court index free at www.fresnosuperiorcourt.org/case_info/.
Superior Court - Civil 1130 O St, Fresno, CA 93721-2220; 559-457-1900; fax: 559-457-1624; 8AM-4PM (PST). *Civil, Small Claims, Eviction.*
General Information: The civil court was separated from the criminal court location in 2007. Holds records for closed court in Kerman. No confidential, adoption or juvenile records released. Will not fax documents. Court makes copy: $.50 per page. Certification fee: $25 per doc plus copy fee. Payee: Superior Court Clerk's Office. Personal checks accepted. Visa/MC accepted. Prepayment required. Mail requests: SASE required.
Civil Name Search: Access: Phone, fax, mail, in person, online. Only the court performs in person name searches; visitors may not. Search fee: $15.00 per name if search exceeds 10 minutes. Civil records on computer back to 1976; on microfiche, index files and archived from 1800s. Mail turnaround time 3-5 days. Public use terminal has civil records back to 1976. Access to civil, probate, family, small claims cases is free at www.fresnosuperiorcourt.org/case_info/.

Clovis Division - Superior Court 1011 5th St, Clovis, CA 93612; 559-457-6392; 8AM-4PM (PST). *Misdemeanor, Civil Actions under $25,000, Eviction, Small Claims, Traffic.*
www.fresnosuperiorcourt.org
General Information: Includes Alder Springs, Auberry, Big Creek, Burroughs Valley, Clovis, Friant, Huntington Lake, Millerton Lake, Pine Ridge, Prather, Shaver, Tollhouse, and Watts. Does felony welfare fraud cases only. No probation reports released. Will not fax documents. Court makes copy: $.50 per page. Certification fee: $25 per doc plus copy fee.

Payee: Clovis Superior Court. Personal checks accepted. Visa/MC accepted in person only. Prepayment required. Mail requests: SASE required.
Civil Name Search: Access: Mail, in person, online. Only the court performs in person name searches; visitors may not. Search fee: $15.00 per name if search exceeds 10 minutes. Civil records on computer and index files from 1983. Records destroyed after 10 years. Mail turnaround time 2 weeks. Access to civil, probate, family, small claims cases is free at www.fresnosuperiorcourt.org/case_info/.
Criminal Name Search: Access: Mail, in person, online. Only the court performs in person name searches; visitors may not. Search fee: $15.00 per name if search exceeds 10 minutes. Required to search: name, years to search, DOB. Criminal records on computer and index files from 1983. Records destroyed after 10 years. Mail turnaround time 2 weeks.

Coalinga Division - Superior Court 160 W Elm St, Coalinga, CA 93210; 559-457-6398; 8AM-4PM (PST). *Misdemeanor, Civil Actions under $25,000, Eviction, Small Claims, Traffic.*
www.fresnosuperiorcourt.org
General Information: Includes Coalinga and Huron. No confidential records or cases not finished released. Will not fax documents. Court makes copy: $.50 per page. Certification fee: $25 per doc plus copy fee. Payee: Superior Court. Personal checks accepted. Credit cards accepted at the counter, but not over on phone. Prepayment required. Mail requests: SASE required.
Civil Name Search: Access: Mail, in person, online. Only the court performs in person name searches; visitors may not. Search fee: $15.00 per name if search exceeds 10 minutes. Required to search: name, years to search; also helpful: address. Civil cases indexed by defendant, plaintiff. Civil index on cards and are computerized since 1990. Will only search back 10 years. Mail turnaround time 1 week. Access to civil, probate, family, small claims cases is free at www.fresnosuperiorcourt.org/case_info/.
Criminal Name Search: Access: Mail, in person, online. Only the court performs in person name searches; visitors may not. Search fee: $15.00 per name if search exceeds 10 minutes. Required to search: name, years to search, DOB; also helpful: address. Criminal records computerized from 1990, on index cards prior. Will only search back 10 years, Traffic 10 years. Mail turnaround time 1 week.

Firebaugh Division - Superior Court 1325 "O" St, Firebaugh, CA 93622; 559-457-6397; fax: 559-457-1620; 8AM-4PM (PST). *Misdemeanor, Civil Actions under $25,000, Eviction, Small Claims.*
www.fresnosuperiorcourt.org
General Information: Includes Firebaugh and Mendota. Now also houses Kernan Division. Public terminal available at the Fresno main Superior Court. No confidential records released. Will not fax documents. Court makes copy: $.50 per page. Certification fee: $25 per doc plus copy fee. Payee: Firebaugh Superior Court. Personal checks accepted. Visa/MC accepted over-the-counter only. Prepayment required. Mail requests: SASE required.
Civil Name Search: Access: Phone, fax, mail, in person, online. Only the court performs in person name searches; visitors may not. Search fee: $25.00 per search per name. Civil records on computer from 1990, index cards prior. Will only search back 7 years. Note: 5 name limit at counter. Mail turnaround time 1 week. Access to civil, probate, family, small claims cases is free at www.fresnosuperiorcourt.org/case_info/.
Criminal Name Search: Access: Phone, fax, mail, in person, online. Only the court performs in person name searches; visitors may not. Search fee: $25.00 per search per name. Required to search: name, years to search, DOB. Criminal records computerized from 1990. Will only search back 7 years. Note: 5 name limit at counter. Mail turnaround time 1 week.

Kingsburg Division - Superior Court 1600 California St, Kingsburg, CA 93631; 559-457-6395; fax: 559-457-6324; 8AM-4PM (PST). *Felony, Misdemeanor, Civil (Limited), Traffic.*
www.fresnosuperiorcourt.org
General Information: This court includes criminal case records from the branch courts closed in Riverdale, Selma/Parlier/Fowler, and cases from the cities of Burrel, Camden, Kingsburg, Lanare, Laton, and Riverdale. Civil records kept at Selma Division location. No confidential records released. Will not fax documents. Court makes copy: $.50 per page. Certification fee: $25 per doc plus copy fee. Payee: Superior Court. Personal checks accepted. Visa/MC accepted. Prepayment required. Mail requests: SASE required.
Civil Name Search: Access: Mail, in person, online. Only the court performs in person name searches; visitors may not. Search fee: $15.00 per name if search exceeds 10 minutes. Required to search: name, years to search. Hard copies stored from 2006 for this court's jurisdiction. Mail turnaround time 1 week. Access to civil, probate, family, small claims cases is free at www.fresnosuperiorcourt.org/case_info/.
Criminal Name Search: Access: Mail, in person, online. Only the court performs in person name searches; visitors may not. Search fee: $15.00 per name if search exceeds 10 minutes. Required to search: name, years to search, DOB. Criminal records computerized from 4/1994, index cards prior.

Mail turnaround time 1 week. Access court index free at www.fresnosuperiorcourt.org/case_info/.

Reedley Division - Superior Court 815 "G" St, Reedley, CA 93654; 559-457-6396; 8AM-4PM (PST). *Misdemeanor, Civil Actions under $25,000, Eviction, Small Claims.*
www.fresnosuperiorcourt.org
General Information: Includes Badger, Cedarbrook, Cedar Pines, Dunlap, Hume, Kings River Canyon, Navalencia, Minkler, Miramonte, Orange Cove, Piedra, Reedley, Sanger (only criminal cases), Squaw Valley, Trimmer Springs and Wahtoke. No confidential records released. Will not fax documents. Court makes copy: $.50 per page. Certification fee: $25 per doc plus copy fee. Payee: Reedley Superior Court. Personal checks accepted. Visa/MC accepted. Prepayment required. Mail requests: SASE required.
Civil Name Search: Access: Mail, in person, online. Only the court performs in person name searches; visitors may not. Search fee: $15.00 per name if search exceeds 10 minutes. Civil records on computer back 10 years. Will only search back 10 years. Mail turnaround time 1 week. Access to civil, probate, family, small claims cases is free at www.fresnosuperiorcourt.org/case_info/.
Criminal Name Search: Access: Mail, in person, online. Only the court performs in person name searches; visitors may not. Search fee: $15.00 per name if search exceeds 10 minutes. Required to search: name, years to search, DOB. Criminal records on computer back 18 years. Note: The record index is not available online, but the docket calendar is. Mail turnaround time 1 week. Access court index free at www.fresnosuperiorcourt.org/case_info/.

Sanger Division - Superior Court 619 N St, Sanger, CA 93657; 559-457-6393; fax: 559-457-6312; 8AM-4PM (PST). *Civil Actions under $25,000, Eviction, Small Claims, Traffic, Ordinance.*
www.fresnosuperiorcourt.org
General Information: This court closed in 2003 then later re-opened for civil cases only. Misdemeanor cases files are still in Reedley for Centerville and Sanger.

Selma Division - Superior Court 2424 McCall Ave, Selma, CA 93662; 559-457-6399; 8AM-4PM (PST). *Civil Actions under $25,000, Eviction, Small Claims, Traffic.*
www.fresnosuperiorcourt.org
General Information: This court holds the records for the closed courts in Fowler (4-30-2010), Caruthers, Parlier, as well as cases from the cities of Bowles, Del Rey, Fowler, Kingsburg, Monmouth, and Raisin City. Kingsburg traffic cases held here since 2/1/2008. No confidential records released. Will not fax documents. Court makes copy: $.50 per page. Certification fee: $25 per doc plus copy fee. Payee: Fresno Superior Court. Personal checks accepted. Prepayment required. Mail requests: SASE required.
Civil Name Search: Access: Mail, in person, online. Only the court performs in person name searches; visitors may not. Search fee: $15.00 per name if search exceeds 10 minutes. Civil index on cards. Note: Court will only search back 7 years. Mail turnaround time 1 week. Access to civil, probate, family, small claims cases is free at www.fresnosuperiorcourt.org/case_info/.

Fowler Division - Superior Court , , CA; . *Civil Actions under $25,000, Eviction, Small Claims.*
www.fresnosuperiorcourt.org
General Information: Closed April 30, 2010. Cases moved to Selma. Case files older than 2008 are stored in archives in Fresno.

Kerman Division - Superior Court , , CA; . *Misdemeanor, Civil Actions under $25,000, Eviction, Small Claims.*
www.fresnosuperiorcourt.org
General Information: Court was closed in early 2009, case files moved to Fresno. Jurisdiction included Biola, Biola Junction, Cantua, Five Points, Helm, Kerman, Rolinda, San Joaquin, and Tranquillity.

Probate Court 1130 O Street, Fresno, CA 93721-2220; 559-457-1888; fax: 559-457-1835; 8AM-4PM (PST). *Probate.*
www.fresnosuperiorcourt.org/probate/
General Information: Access to probate case information is free at www.fresnosuperiorcourt.org/case_info/.

Glenn County

Superior Court 526 W Sycamore, Willows, CA 95988; 530-934-6446; fax: 530-934-6728; 8AM-5PM (PST). *Felony, Misdemeanor, Civil, Small Claims, Probate, Family.*
www.glenncourt.ca.gov
General Information: Records from the municipal court were combined with this court when the courts were consolidated. Records-530-934-6446. No adoption, juvenile or paternity released. Will not fax documents. Court makes copy: $.50 per page. Self serve copy: same. Certification fee: $25 per

doc plus copy fee. Payee: Superior Court. Personal checks accepted. No credit cards accepted. Prepayment required. Mail requests: SASE required.
Civil Name Search: Access: Mail, in person, online. Both court and visitors may perform in person name searches. Search fee: $15.00 per name if search exceeds 10 minutes. Civil records on computer back to 1996, on microfiche, archived and in index file from 1894. Mail turnaround time 1 day. Civil PAT goes back to 1996. Search case index at www.glenncourt.ca.gov/online_index/.
Criminal Name Search: Access: Mail, in person, online. Both court and visitors may perform in person name searches. Search fee: $15.00 per name if search exceeds 10 minutes. Required to search: name, years to search; also helpful: DOB. Criminal records computerized from 1996, on microfiche, archived and in index file from 1894. Mail turnaround time 1 day. Criminal PAT goes back to same as civil. Search case index at www.glenncourt.ca.gov/online_index/.

Humboldt County

Superior Court 825 5th St, Eureka, CA 95501; 707-445-7256; fax: 707-445-7041; 9AM-4PM (PST). *Felony, Civil, Small Claims, Eviction, Probate, Traffic.*
www.humboldt.courts.ca.gov/
General Information: Address for civil window is 421 I St. Do countywide search from this court, records computerized back 10 years. Former Eureka, Eel River, and N Humboldt Muni Court Divisions part of this court. Hoopa Tribal & Garberville Branches court held here. No probation, medical, adoption, juvenile or sealed records released. Will not fax documents. Court makes copy: $.50 per page. Certification fee: $25 per doc plus copy fee. Payee: Humboldt Superior Court. Personal checks accepted. No credit cards accepted. Prepayment required. Mail requests: SASE required.
Civil Name Search: Access: Mail, in person. Both court and visitors may perform in person name searches. Search fee: $15.00 per name if search exceeds 10 minutes. Civil records on computer back to 1993; on microfiche and archived from 1964. Note: Phone requests are limited to 3 names only. Mail turnaround time 2 weeks. Public use terminal available.
Criminal Name Search: Access: Mail, in person, phone. Both court and visitors may perform in person name searches. Search fee: $15.00 per name if search exceeds 10 minutes. Required to search: name, years to search; also helpful: DOB. Criminal records computerized from 1985; on microfiche and archived from 1964. Note: Phone requests are limited to 2 names only. Mail turnaround time 2 weeks. Public use terminal available.

Klamath/Trinity Branch - Superior Court - See Eureka. *Misdemeanor, Civil Actions under $25,000, Eviction, Small Claims.*
General Information: Records for this branch are housed at the main court in Eureka, address given here.

Garberville Branch - Superior Court - See Eureka *Misdemeanor, Eviction, Small Claims.*
www.humboldt.courts.ca.gov/
General Information: All mail inquires or research are directed to the Superior Court in Eureka. Garberville fax number for Fridays only is 707-923-3133.

Imperial County

Imperial Branch - Superior Court 939 W Main St, El Centro, CA 92243; 760-482-4374; criminal phone: 760-482-4256; civil phone: 760-482-4217; criminal fax: 760-482-4219; civil fax: 8AM-4PM; 8AM-4PM (PST). *Felony, Misdemeanor, Civil, Eviction, Small Claims, Probate.*
www.imperial.courts.ca.gov/
General Information: All in person record searching for Imperial county must be done at each location. Only court can use the countywide system. However, if case is 10 years or older, it can be found on the books here. No adoption, juvenile, medical, probation or sealed records released. Court makes copy: $.50 per page. Certification fee: $25 per doc plus copy fee. Payee: Imperial County Superior Court. Personal checks accepted. Prepayment required. Mail requests: SASE required.
Civil Name Search: Access: Mail, in person. Only the court performs in person name searches; visitors may not. Search fee: $15.00 per name if search exceeds 10 minutes. Civil records on microfiche from 1972, in index file from 1917. Mail turnaround time 2-4 days.
Criminal Name Search: Access: Mail, in person. Only the court performs in person name searches; visitors may not. Search fee: $15.00 per name if search exceeds 10 minutes. Required to search: name, years to search, year action filed. Criminal records on microfiche from 1972, index file from 1917. Mail turnaround time 2-4 days.

Brawley Branch - Superior Court 220 Main St., Brawley, CA 92227; 760-336-3550; fax: 760-351-7703; 8AM-4PM (PST). *Misdemeanor, Civil Actions under $25,000, Eviction, Small Claims, Traffic.*
www.imperial.courts.ca.gov/
General Information: Traffic phone- ext1. There is no countywide public access database in this county. However, if case is 10 years or older, it can be

found on the books at the main court in El Centro. No probation reports released. Will not fax documents. Court makes copy: $.50 per page. Certification fee: $25 per doc plus copy fee. Payee: Brawley Superior Court. Personal checks accepted. Visa/MC accepted. Prepayment required. Mail requests: SASE required.

Civil Name Search: Access: Fax, mail, in person. Both court and visitors may perform in person name searches. Search fee: $25.00 per name if search exceeds 10 minutes. Civil records on computer from 09/93 (traffic from 1991), in index files from 1983. Records destroyed after 10 years. Mail turnaround time 1 week.

Criminal Name Search: Access: Fax, mail, in person. Only the court performs in person name searches; visitors may not. Search fee: $25.00 per name if search exceeds 10 minutes. Required to search: name, years to search, DOB. Criminal records on computer back about 5 years (traffic only from 1991), in index files from 1983. Records destroyed after 10 years. Mail turnaround time 1 week.

Calexico Branch - Superior Court 415 E 4th St, Calexico, CA 92231; 760-336-3565; fax: 760-357-6571; 8AM-4PM (PST). *Misdemeanor, Civil Actions under $25,000, Eviction, Small Claims, Traffic.*
www.imperial.courts.ca.gov/

General Information: Traffic phone- x3. There is no countywide public access database in this county. Only court can use the countywide system. However, if case is 10 years or older, it can be found on the books at the main court in El Centro. No probation reports released. Will fax documents for $1.00 per page fee. Court makes copy: $1.00 1st page, $.50 each add'l. Certification fee: $25 per doc plus copy fee. Payee: Superior Court. Business and some personal checks accepted. Write case number on check; write 'not-to-exceed amount' in memo field. Visa/MC accepted in person or by phone only. Prepayment required. Mail requests: SASE required.

Civil Name Search: Access: Fax, mail, in person. Both court and visitors may perform in person name searches. Search fee: $15.00 per name. Civil records on computer from 1991, index files from 1983. Records destroyed after 10 years. Note: Civil search fee is separate from the criminal search fee. Mail turnaround time 1-2 weeks. Civil PAT goes back to 1998.

Criminal Name Search: Access: Fax, mail, in person. Both court and visitors may perform in person name searches. Search fee: $15.00 per name. Required to search: name, years to search. Criminal records computerized from 1991, index files from 1983. Records destroyed after 10 years. Mail turnaround time 1-2 weeks. Criminal PAT goes back to 1998.

Winterhaven Branch - Superior Court PO Box 1087, 2124 Winterhaven Dr, Winterhaven, CA 92283-1087; 760-336-3500; fax: 760-572-2683; 8AM-11AM; 12-4PM (PST). *Small Claims, Infraction.*
www.imperial.courts.ca.gov/

General Information: Misdemeanor and civil records have been moved to the Calexico Branch. Only small claims and traffic records remain here.

Inyo County

Superior Court PO Drawer U, 168 N Edwards St, Independence, CA 93526; 760-872-3038; fax: 760-873-5213; 8AM-4PM (PST). *Felony, Civil Actions over $25,000, Probate.*
www.inyocourt.ca.gov

General Information: At this Superior court, there is a Independence Dept. and a Bishop Dept. In name search requests, specify to search both. There is a countywide searchable database; but had copies must be obtained at the branch courts. No adoption, juvenile, medical, probation or sealed records released. Will fax to 800 number no fee; otherwise $1.00 per page. Court makes copy: $.50 per page. Certification fee: $25 per doc plus copy fee. Payee: Inyo Superior Court. Personal checks accepted. No credit cards accepted. Prepayment required. Mail requests: SASE required.

Civil Name Search: Access: Mail, in person. Both court and visitors may perform in person name searches. Search fee: $15.00 per name if search exceeds 10 minutes. Civil records on computer to mid-1999, on microfiche and in index files from 1800s. Mail turnaround time 1 week.

Criminal Name Search: Access: Mail, in person. Both court and visitors may perform in person name searches. Search fee: $15.00 per name if search exceeds 10 minutes. Required to search: name, years to search. Criminal records computerized from 1993, on microfiche and in index files from 1800s. Mail turnaround time 1 week.

Bishop Branch - Superior Court 301 W Line St, Bishop, CA 93514; 760-872-3038; fax: 760-872-4984; 8AM-4PM (PST). *Misdemeanor, Civil Actions under $25,000, Eviction, Small Claims, Traffic.*
www.inyocourt.ca.gov

General Information: There is no countywide database, each branch court must be searched. The phones are answered 8:30 AM-4PM. No confidential records released. Will fax to 800 number no fee; otherwise $1.00 per page. Court makes copy: $.50 per page. Certification fee: $25 per doc plus copy fee. Payee: Superior Court. Personal checks accepted. No credit cards accepted for copies or record searches. Prepayment required. Mail requests: SASE required.

Civil Name Search: Access: Mail, in person. Only the court performs in person name searches; visitors may not. Search fee: $15.00 per name if search exceeds 10 minutes. Civil index on cards. Will only search back 7 years. Mail turnaround time 1 week.

Criminal Name Search: Access: Mail, in person. Only the court performs in person name searches; visitors may not. Search fee: $15.00 per name if search exceeds 10 minutes. Required to search: name, years to search. Criminal records computerized from 1993, index cards prior. Mail turnaround time 1 week.

Kern County

Superior Court 1415 Truxtun Ave, Bakersfield, CA 93301; 661-868-5393; criminal fax: 661-868-4883; civil fax: 8AM-4PM; 8AM-4PM (PST). *Felony, Civil Actions, Eviction, Small Claims, Probate.*
www.kern.courts.ca.gov

General Information: Has electronic access to all divisions. Felonies in Rm 111. Misdemeanors at separate address - see separate listing. No faxing to criminal record section. Probate at #100, 1st Fl. Online identifiers in results same as on public terminal. No adoption, juvenile, medical, probation or sealed records released. Will not fax out docs. Court makes copy: $.50 per page. Certification fee: $25 per doc plus copy fee. Exemplification- $20.00 plus copy fee. Payee: Kern Superior Court. Personal checks accepted. No credit cards accepted. Prepayment required. Mail requests: SASE required.

Civil Name Search: Access: Mail, fax, in person, online. Both court and visitors may perform in person name searches. Search fee: $15.00 per name if search exceeds 10 minutes. Civil records on microfiche from 1964, archived and in index file from 1800s. Mail turnaround time 1 day to 1 week. Civil PAT available. Terminal in 3rd Fl law library Terminal results show year of birth only. Search civil records free at www.kern.courts.ca.gov/home.aspx. Civil case info and calendars on special kiosk computers located at every court location and at website.

Criminal Name Search: Access: Mail, in person, online. Both court and visitors may perform in person name searches. Search fee: $15.00 per name if search exceeds 10 minutes. Required to search: name, years to search, DOB. Criminal records computerized from 1989, also microfiche, archived, and in index files. Note: Visitors may search court counter index which excludes identifiers; court searches electronically with identifiers. Mail turnaround time up to 2 weeks. Criminal PAT goes back to 1989. Terminal in 3rd Floor law library. Terminal results show year of birth only. Access defendant database free at www.co.kern.ca.us/courts/crimcal/crim_index_def.asp; Results show year of birth only; old records being added. Current court calendars free at www.co.kern.ca.us/courts/crim_index_case_info_cal.asp. Access defendant hearings schedule at www.co.kern.ca.us/courts/crimcal/crim_hearing_srch.asp. Also, search sheriff inmate list at www.kern.courts.ca.gov/case-menu-main.asp. Click on "inmate search." Online results show middle initial, DOB.

Delano/McFarland Branch Superior Court - North Division 1122 Jefferson St, Delano, CA 93215; 661-720-5800; criminal phone: x3; civil phone: x4; fax: 661-721-1237; 8AM-4PM (PST). *Misdemeanor, Civil Actions under $25,000, Eviction, Small Claims.*
www.kern.courts.ca.gov/

General Information: Access all recent court division criminal defendant records from this division computer. No probation reports released. Will not fax documents. Court makes copy: $.50 per page. Certification fee: $25 per doc plus copy fee. Payee: Superior Court Kern County-Delano/McFarland Branch. Personal checks and credit cards accepted. Prepayment required. Mail requests: SASE required.

Civil Name Search: Access: Fax, mail, in person, online. Both court and visitors may perform in person name searches. Search fee: $15.00 per name if search exceeds 10 minutes. Civil records in index files from 1983. Records destroyed after 10 years. Mail turnaround time 2 days. Civil PAT goes back to 1988. Terminal results show year of birth only. Search civil records free at www.kern.courts.ca.gov/home.aspx. Civil case info and calendars on special kiosk computers located at every court location and at website.

Criminal Name Search: Access: Mail, in person, online. Both court and visitors may perform in person name searches. Search fee: $15.00 per name if search exceeds 10 minutes. Required to search: name, years to search; also helpful: DOB. Criminal records computerized from 1988, in index files from 1983. Records destroyed after 10 years. Note: Visitors may search counter index which excludes identifiers; court searches electronically with identifiers. Mail turnaround time 2 days. Criminal PAT goes back to 1988. Terminal results show year of birth only. Access defendant search database free at www.co.kern.ca.us/courts/crimcal/crim_index_def.asp; new system with old records being added. Current court calendars are free at www.co.kern.ca.us/courts/crim_index_case_info_cal.asp. Also, access court defendant hearings schedule by name at www.co.kern.ca.us/courts/crimcal/crim_hearing_srch.asp. Also, search county sheriff inmate list at www.kern.courts.ca.gov/case-menu-main.asp. Click on "inmate search." Online results show middle initial, DOB.

Kern River Branch Superior Court - East Division 7046 Lake Isabella Blvd, Lake Isabella, CA 93240; 760-549-2000; fax: 760-549-2120; 8AM-4PM (PST). *Misdemeanor, Civil Actions under $25,000, Eviction, Small Claims.*
www.kern.courts.ca.gov/
General Information: Includes the communities of Lake Isabella, Kern River, Weldon, Onyx, and Mt Mesa. You should be able to access all recent court division criminal defendant records from this division computer. No probation reports released. Will fax documents for $.50 per page if pre-paid. Court makes copy: $.50 per page. Certification fee: $25 per doc plus copy fee. Payee: East Kern Superior Court. Personal checks accepted. Visa, AmEx accepted. Prepayment required. Mail requests: SASE required.
Civil Name Search: Access: Phone, fax, mail, in person, online. Only the court performs in person name searches; visitors may not. Search fee: $15.00 per name if search exceeds 10 minutes. Required to search: name, DOB, years to search. Civil cases indexed by defendant, plaintiff. Civil records on computer from 1991, in index files from 1983. Records destroyed after 10 years. Mail turnaround time 10 days or less. Search civil records free at www.kern.courts.ca.gov/home.aspx. Civil case info and calendars on special kiosk computers located at every court location and at website.
Criminal Name Search: Access: Phone, mail, in person, online. Both court and visitors may perform in person name searches. Search fee: $15.00 per name if search exceeds 10 minutes. Required to search: name, years to search. Criminal records computerized from 1991, in index files from 1983. Records destroyed after 10 years. Note: H&S violations and PC codes go back 5 years. Some VC codes and Fish and game go back three years. Mail turnaround time 10 days or less. Public use terminal has crim records back to 1987. Terminal results show year of birth only. Access defendant search database free at www.co.kern.ca.us/courts/crimcal/crim_index_def.asp; new system with old records being added. Current court calendars are free at www.co.kern.ca.us/courts/crim_index_case_info_cal.asp. Also, access court defendant hearings schedule by name at www.co.kern.ca.us/courts/crimcal/crim_hearing_srch.asp. Also, search county sheriff inmate list at www.kern.courts.ca.gov/case-menu-main.asp. Click on "inmate search." Online results show middle initial, DOB.

Lamont/Arvin Branch Superior Court - South Division 12022 Main St, Lamont, CA 93241; 661-868-5800; fax: 661-845-9142; 8AM-4PM (PST). *Misdemeanor, Civil Actions under $25,000, Eviction, Small Claims.*
www.kern.courts.ca.gov/
General Information: Access all recent court division criminal defendant records from this division computer. No probation reports released. Will fax documents for fee, call. Court makes copy: $.50 per page. Certification fee: $25 per doc plus copy fee. Payee: Superior Court Lamont Branch. Personal checks accepted. Visa/MC, AmEx accepted. Prepayment required. Mail requests: SASE required.
Civil Name Search: Access: Mail, in person, online. Both court and visitors may perform in person name searches. Search fee: $15.00 per name if search exceeds 10 minutes. Civil records on computer from 1989. Records destroyed after 10 years. Mail turnaround time 2 days. Civil PAT goes back to 1989. Terminal results show year of birth only. Search civil records free at www.kern.courts.ca.gov/home.aspx. Civil case info and calendars on special kiosk computers located at every court location and at website.
Criminal Name Search: Access: Fax, mail, in person, online. Both court and visitors may perform in person name searches. Search fee: $15.00 per name if search exceeds 10 minutes. Required to search: name, years to search, DOB; also helpful CA DL#, SSN, signed release. Criminal records computerized from 1989. Records destroyed after 10 years. Note: Visitors may search court counter index which excludes identifiers; court searches electronically with identifiers. Results include name, entity name, case number and calendar. Mail turnaround time 2 days. Criminal PAT goes back to same as civil. Results include year of DOB, filing date and arrest date. Access defendant search database free at www.co.kern.ca.us/courts/crimcal/crim_index_def.asp; new system with old records being added. Current court calendars are free at www.co.kern.ca.us/courts/crim_index_case_info_cal.asp. Also, access court defendant hearings schedule by name at www.co.kern.ca.us/courts/crimcal/crim_hearing_srch.asp. Also, search county sheriff inmate list at www.kern.courts.ca.gov/case-menu-main.asp. Click on "inmate search." Online results show middle initial, DOB.

Mojave Branch Superior Court - East Division 1773 Hwy 58, Mojave, CA 93501; 661-824-7100; criminal phone: x3; civil phone: x4; criminal fax: 661-824-7089; civil fax: 8AM-3PM; 8AM-3PM (PST). *Misdemeanor, Civil Actions under $25,000, Eviction, Small Claims.*
www.kern.courts.ca.gov/
General Information: Includes California City, Edwards AFB, Mojave, Boron, Rosemond, Cantil, and Tehachapi. You should be able to access all recent court division criminal defendant records from this division computer. Online identifiers in results same as on public terminal. No probation reports released. Will not fax documents. Court makes copy: $.50 per page. Certification fee: $25 per doc plus copy fee. Payee: East Kern Superior Court. Personal checks accepted. Visa, AmEx accepted; there is a $7.50 credit card charge. Prepayment required. Mail requests: SASE required.
Civil Name Search: Access: Mail, fax, in person, online. Both court and visitors may perform in person name searches. Search fee: $15.00 per name if search exceeds 10 minutes. Civil records on computer from 1991, in index files from 1983. Records destroyed after 10 years. Mail turnaround time up to 1 week. Civil PAT goes back to 1991. Terminal results show year of birth only. Search civil records free at www.kern.courts.ca.gov/home.aspx. Civil case info and calendars on special kiosk computers located at every court location and at website.
Criminal Name Search: Access: Mail, fax, in person, online. Both court and visitors may perform in person name searches. Search fee: $15.00 per name if search exceeds 10 minutes. Required to search: name, years to search, DOB. Criminal records computerized from 1991, in index files from 1983. Mail turnaround time up to 10 days. Criminal PAT goes back to same as civil. Terminal results show year of birth only. Access defendant search database free at www.co.kern.ca.us/courts/crimcal/crim_index_def.asp; new system with old records being added. Current court calendars are free at www.co.kern.ca.us/courts/crim_index_case_info_cal.asp. Also, access court defendant hearings schedule by name at www.co.kern.ca.us/courts/crimcal/crim_hearing_srch.asp. Also, search county sheriff inmate list at www.kern.courts.ca.gov/case-menu-main.asp. Click on "inmate search." Online results show middle initial, DOB.

Ridgecrest Branch Superior Court - East Division 132 E Coso St, Ridgecrest, CA 93555; 760-384-5900; civil phone: 760-384-5986; fax: 760-384-5899; 8AM-4PM (PST). *Misdemeanor, Civil Actions under $25,000, Eviction, Small Claims.*
www.kern.courts.ca.gov/
General Information: Includes the communities of Ridgecrest, Inyokern, China Lake, Johannesburg, and Randsburg. You should be able to access all recent court division criminal defendant records from this division computer. No probation reports released. Will not fax documents. Court makes copy: $.50 per page. Certification fee: $25 per doc plus copy fee. Payee: Kern County Superior Court. Personal checks accepted. Visa, AmEx accepted. Prepayment required. Mail requests: SASE required.
Civil Name Search: Access: Mail, in person, online. Both court and visitors may perform in person name searches. Search fee: $15.00 per name if search exceeds 10 minutes. Civil records on computer from 1990, in index files from 1983. Records destroyed after 10 years. Mail turnaround time 2 days. Civil PAT goes back to 1990. Terminal results show year of birth only. Search civil records free at www.kern.courts.ca.gov/home.aspx. Civil case info and calendars on special kiosk computers located at every court location and at website.
Criminal Name Search: Access: Phone, fax, mail, in person, online. Both court and visitors may perform in person name searches. Search fee: $15.00 per name if search exceeds 10 minutes. Required to search: name, years to search; also helpful: DOB, SSN. Criminal records computerized from 1990, in index files from 1983. Records destroyed after 5 years. Mail turnaround time 2 days. Criminal PAT goes back to same as civil. Terminal results show year of birth only. Access defendant search database free at www.co.kern.ca.us/courts/crimcal/crim_index_def.asp; new system with old records being added. Current court calendars are free at www.co.kern.ca.us/courts/crim_index_case_info_cal.asp. Also, access court defendant hearings schedule by name at www.co.kern.ca.us/courts/crimcal/crim_hearing_srch.asp. Also, search county sheriff inmate list at www.kern.courts.ca.gov/case-menu-main.asp. Click on "inmate search." Online results show middle initial, DOB.

Shafter/Wasco Branch Superior Court - North Division 325 Central Valley Hwy, Shafter, CA 93263; 661-746-7500; fax: 661-746-0545; 8AM-4PM (PST). *Misdemeanor, Civil Actions under $25,000, Eviction, Small Claims.*
www.kern.courts.ca.gov/
General Information: Access all recent court division criminal defendant records from this division computer. No probation reports released. No fee to fax documents. Court makes copy: $.50 per page. Certification fee: $25 per doc plus copy fee. Payee: Superior Court North Division. Personal checks

accepted. Visa/Amex/Discover accepted. Prepayment required. Mail requests: SASE required.

Civil Name Search: Access: Phone, fax, mail, in person, online. Both court and visitors may perform in person name searches. Search fee: $15.00 per name if search exceeds 10 minutes. Required to search: name, years to search; also helpful: address. Civil cases indexed by defendant, plaintiff. Civil records go back to 1994. Note: Visitors may search counter index that excludes identifiers; court searches electronically with identifiers. Mail turnaround time 2 days. Civil PAT available. Terminal results show year of birth only. Search civil records free at www.kern.courts.ca.gov/home.aspx. Civil case info and calendars on special kiosk computers located at every court location and at website.

Criminal Name Search: Access: Mail, in person, online. Both court and visitors may perform in person name searches. Search fee: $15.00 per name if search exceeds 10 minutes. Required to search: name, years to search, DOB; also helpful: address, SSN. Criminal records on computer since 1988, traffic since 1991. Note: Visitors may search court counter index which excludes identifiers; court searches electronically with identifiers. Phone searches limited to a few names only. Mail turnaround time 2 days. Criminal PAT goes back to 1988. Terminal results show year of birth only. Access defendant search database free at www.co.kern.ca.us/courts/crimcal/crim_index_def.asp; new system with old records being added. Current court calendars are free at www.co.kern.ca.us/case-menu-main.aspx. Also, search county sheriff inmate list at same site. Online results show middle initial, DOB.

Superior Court Metropolitan Division 1215 Truxtun Ave, Bakersfield, CA 93301; 661-868-2482; criminal phone: x4; fax: 661-868-2695; 8AM-4PM (PST). *Misdemeanor, Traffic.*
www.kern.courts.ca.gov/
General Information: Formerly Bakersfield Municipal Court. Includes Bakersfield, Oildale, Edison, Glenville, Woody. Access all recent court division criminal defendant records from this division computer. Online identifiers in results same as on public terminal. No probation reports, rap sheets, medical or financial released. No fee to fax document. Will only fax one or two pages due to time constraints. Court makes copy: $.50 per page. Certification fee: $25 per doc plus copy fee. Payee: Superior Court of California. Personal checks accepted. No credit cards accepted. Prepayment required. Mail requests: SASE helpful.
Criminal Name Search: Access: Mail, in person, online. Both court and visitors may perform in person name searches. Search fee: $15.00 per name if search exceeds 10 minutes. Required to search: name, years to search. Criminal records on computer since 1988, microfilm since 1988. Note: Visitors may search court counter index which excludes identifiers; court searches electronically with identifiers. Mail turnaround time 10 days. Public use terminal has crim records back to 1988. Results include birth year. Access defendant search database free at www.co.kern.ca.us/courts/crimcal/crim_index_def.asp; new system with old records being added. Current court calendars are free at www.co.kern.ca.us/courts/crim_index_case_info_cal.asp. Also, access court defendant hearings schedule by name at www.co.kern.ca.us/courts/crimcal/crim_hearing_srch.asp. Also, search county sheriff inmate list at www.co.kern.ca.us/apps/detentions/display_inmate/inmate_srch.asp. Online results show middle initial, DOB.

Taft Branch Superior Court - South Division 311 N Lincoln St, Taft, CA 93268; 661-763-8531; fax: 661-763-2439; 8AM-4PM (PST). *Misdemeanor, Civil Actions under $25,000, Eviction, Small Claims.*
www.kern.courts.ca.gov/
General Information: Access all recent court division criminal defendant records from this division's computer. No probation reports released. Will fax documents to local or toll-free number. Court makes copy: $.50 per page. Certification fee: $25 per doc plus copy fee. Payee: Superior Court Taft Branch. Personal checks accepted. Credit cards accepted. Prepayment required. Mail requests: SASE required.
Civil Name Search: Access: Phone, mail, in person, online. Both court and visitors may perform in person name searches. No search fee. Required to search: name, years to search; also helpful: address. Civil cases indexed by defendant, plaintiff. Civil records on computer from 1988, in index files from 1983. Records destroyed after 10 years. Mail turnaround time 2 days. Civil PAT goes back to 1988. Terminal results show year of birth only. Search civil records free at www.kern.courts.ca.gov/home.aspx. Civil case info and calendars on special kiosk computers located at every court location and at website.
Criminal Name Search: Access: Phone, mail, in person, online. Both court and visitors may perform in person name searches. No search fee. Required to search: name, years to search, DOB; also helpful: address, SSN. Criminal records computerized from 1988, in index files from 1983. Records destroyed after 10 years. Mail turnaround time 2 days. Criminal PAT goes back to same as civil. Terminal results show year of birth only. Access defendant search database free at www.co.kern.ca.us/courts/crimcal/crim_index_def.asp; new system with

old records being added. Current court calendars are free at www.co.kern.ca.us/courts/crim_index_case_info_cal.asp. Also, access court defendant hearings schedule by name at www.co.kern.ca.us/courts/crimcal/crim_hearing_srch.asp. Also, search county sheriff inmate list at www.co.kern.ca.us/courts/caseinfo_menu.asp. Click on "inmate search." Online results show middle initial, DOB.

Kings County

Superior Court - Criminal 1426 South Dr, Hanford, CA 93230; 559-582-1010 x3042; fax: 559-585-3267; 8AM-4PM (PST). *Felony, Misdemeanor.* www.kings.courts.ca.gov
General Information: No probation or police reports released. Will not fax documents. Court makes copy: $.50 per page. Certification fee: $25 per doc plus copy fee. Payee: Kings County Superior Court. Personal checks accepted. No credit cards accepted. Prepayment required. Mail requests: SASE required.
Criminal Name Search: Access: Mail, in person. Both court and visitors may perform in person name searches. Search fee: $15.00 per name if search exceeds 10 minutes. Required to search: name, years to search, DOB. Criminal records computerized from 1991, in index files from 1983. Records destroyed after 10 years. Mail turnaround time 10 days. Public use terminal has crim records back to 1991.

Superior Court - Civil 1426 South Dr, Hanford, CA 93230; 559-582-1010; probate phone: x3083; fax: 559-585-3242; 8AM-4PM (PST). *Civil Actions, Eviction, Small Claims, Probate.* www.kings.courts.ca.gov
General Information: No adoption, juvenile, medical, probation or sealed records released. Will not fax documents. Court makes copy: $.50 per page. Certification fee: $25 per doc plus copy fee. Payee: Superior Court of the State of California. Business checks accepted with proper identification. No credit cards accepted. Prepayment required. Mail requests: SASE required.
Civil Name Search: Access: Mail, in person. Both court and visitors may perform in person name searches. Search fee: $15.00 per name if search exceeds 10 minutes. Civil records on computer from 1989, on microfiche and archived from 1970s, in index file from 1914. Mail turnaround time 4 weeks. Public terminal civil records back to 1989. Access case information at www.kings.courts.ca.gov:7777/courtconnect/ck_public_qry_main.cp_main_idx.

Avenal Division Superior Court 501 E Kings St, Avenal, CA 93204; 559-582-1010 x4094; 559-386-5225; fax: 559-585-3269; 8AM-5PM (PST). *Misdemeanor, Civil Actions under $25,000, Eviction, Small Claims.*
www.kings.courts.ca.gov
General Information: No juvenile or adoption records released. Court makes copy: $.50 per page. Certification fee: $25 per doc plus copy fee. Payee: Superior Court. Personal checks accepted. No credit cards accepted. Prepayment required. Mail requests: SASE required.
Civil Name Search: Access: Mail, in person, online. Both court and visitors may perform in person name searches. Search fee: $15.00 per name if search exceeds 10 minutes. Required to search: name, years to search. Civil index on cards, computerized. Mail turnaround time 10 working days Public use terminal has civil records back to 1990. Search by name or case type, including judgments at www.kings.courts.ca.gov:7777/courtconnect/ck_public_qry_main.cp_main_idx.
Criminal Name Search: Access: Fax, mail, in person. Both court and visitors may perform in person name searches. Search fee: $15.00 per name if search exceeds 10 minutes. Required to search: name, years to search, DOB. Criminal records computerized from 1991, index cards prior. Mail turnaround time 10 working days.

Corcoran Division Superior Court 1000 Chittenden Ave, Corcoran, CA 93212; 559-582-1010 x3004; 559-992-5193; fax: 559-585-3270; 8AM-5PM (PST). *Misdemeanor, Civil Actions under $25,000, Eviction, Small Claims.*
www.kings.courts.ca.gov
General Information: No juvenile or adoption records released. Will not fax documents. Court makes copy: $.50 per page. Certification fee: $25 per doc plus copy fee. Payee: Superior Court of California. Personal checks accepted. Prepayment required. Mail requests: SASE required.
Civil Name Search: Access: Mail, in person, online
Mail, in person. Only the court performs in person name searches; visitors may not. Search fee: $15.00 per name if search exceeds 10 minutes. Required to search: name, years to search; also helpful: address. Civil cases indexed by defendant, plaintiff. Civil records on computer from 1990, index cards to 1974. Will only search back 7 years. Mail turnaround time 10 days. Search by name or case type, including judgments at www.kings.courts.ca.gov:7777/courtconnect/ck_public_qry_main.cp_main_idx.

Criminal Name Search: Access: Mail, in person. Both court and visitors may perform in person name searches. Search fee: $15.00 per name if search exceeds 10 minutes. Required to search: name, years to search, DOB; also helpful: address, AKA's. Criminal records computerized from 1990, index cards to 1974. Will only search back 7 years. Mail turnaround time 1 week.

Lemoore Division Superior Court 449 "C" St, Lemoore, CA 93245; 559-582-1010 x3014; 559-924-7757; criminal phone: x3034; civil phone: x3075;; 8AM-4PM (PST). *Civil Actions under $25,000, Eviction, Small Claims.*

www.kings.courts.ca.gov

General Information: Court says to search records at Hanford court; 1426 South Dr, Hanford, CA 93230, Ph-559-582-1010 x3034 Criminal; x2075 Civil. Will not fax documents. Court makes copy: $.50 per page. Certification fee: $25 per doc plus copy fee; exemplification fee is $20. Payee: Kings County Superior Court. Personal checks accepted. No credit cards accepted. Prepayment required. Mail requests: SASE required.

Civil Name Search: Access: Fax, mail, in person, online. Both court and visitors may perform in person name searches. Search fee: $15.00 per name if search exceeds 10 minutes. Civil records computerized since 1990, on index cards back to 1982. Note: In person access limited. Fax requests are accepted, though the court will recommend a fax processing service; add'l charge for fax requests. Mail turnaround time 10 days. Public use terminal has civil records back to 1990. Search by name or case type, including judgments at www.kings.courts.ca.gov:7777/courtconnect/ck_public_qry_main.cp_main_idx.

Lake County

Superior Court - Lakeport Division 255 N Forbes St, 4th Fl, Rm 417, Lakeport, CA 95453; 707-263-2374; fax: 707-262-1327; 8AM-2:30PM (PST). *Felony, Misdemeanor, Civil, Eviction, Small Claims, Probate.*

www.lake.courts.ca.gov/gi/lakeport.htm

General Information: This court holds the records for the former Northlake Municipal Court. Please note that there are also felony records at the South Lake Division, and both courts should be checked when doing a criminal record search. No adoption, juvenile, medical, probation or sealed records released. Will not fax documents. Court makes copy: $.50 per page. Certification fee: $25 per doc plus copy fee. Payee: Lake County Superior Court. Personal checks accepted. No credit cards accepted. Prepayment required. Mail requests: SASE required.

Civil Name Search: Access: Mail, in person. Both court and visitors may perform in person name searches. Search fee: $15.00 per name if search exceeds 10 minutes. Civil records on computer from 1991, on microfiche, archived, and in index files from 1800s. Mail turnaround time 1-3 weeks. Civil PAT goes back to 1991. Public access terminal is at the Lake Port Courthouse.

Criminal Name Search: Access: Mail, in person. Both court and visitors may perform in person name searches. Search fee: $15.00 per name if search exceeds 10 minutes. Required to search: name, years to search, DOB. Criminal records computerized from 1991, on microfiche, archived, and in index files from 1800s. Mail turnaround time 1-3 weeks. Criminal PAT goes back to same as civil. Public access terminal is at the Lake Port Courthouse.

Superior Court - Clearlake Division 7000A S Center Dr, Clearlake, CA 95422; 707-994-6598; fax: 707-994-1625; 8AM-2:30PM (PST). *Felony, Misdemeanor, Eviction, Small Claims, Traffic.*

www.lake.courts.ca.gov/gi/clearlake.htm

General Information: For record searches call 707-994-6598. Some felony cases will not be on the computer index. No police reports or sealed records released. Will not fax documents. Court makes copy: $.50 per page. Certification fee: $25 per doc plus copy fee. Payee: Lake County Superior Court. Personal checks accepted. No credit cards accepted. Prepayment required. Mail requests: SASE required.

Civil Name Search: Access: Mail, in person, phone. Both court and visitors may perform in person name searches. Search fee: $15.00 per name if search exceeds 10 minutes. Civil index on docket books. Mail turnaround time 1-2 weeks. Civil PAT goes back to 1990.

Criminal Name Search: Access: Mail, in person, phone. Both court and visitors may perform in person name searches. Search fee: $15.00 per name if search exceeds 10 minutes. Required to search: name, years to search, DOB. Criminal records computerized from 1990, index books prior. Mail turnaround time 1-2 weeks for criminal. Criminal PAT goes back to 1990. Some records prior to 1990 also available on public terminal.

Lassen County

Superior Court 220 S Lassen St, #2, Susanville, CA 96130; 530-251-8205; fax: 530-257-9061; 8AM-Noon, 1-5PM (PST). *Felony, Misdemeanor, Civil, Eviction, Small Claims, Probate.*

www.lassencourt.ca.gov

General Information: Probate fax is same as main fax number. No adoption, juvenile, medical, probation or sealed records released. Will fax documents if all fees prepaid. Court makes copy: $.50 per page. Self serve copy: same. Certification fee: $25 per doc plus copy fee. Payee: Lassen County Superior Court. Business checks accepted. Major credit cards accepted. Prepayment required. Pay via the Official Payments at 800-272-9829 using jurisdiction code 1506. Or, pay online at www.officialpayments.com. Mail requests: SASE required.

Civil Name Search: Access: Mail, in person. Only the court performs in person name searches; visitors may not. Search fee: $15.00 per request if search exceeds 10 minutes. A request can have multiple names but may not exceed five. Civil records on computer from 11/89, archived and in index files from 1900s. Mail turnaround time 5-10 days.

Criminal Name Search: Access: Mail, in person. Only the court performs in person name searches; visitors may not. Search fee: $15.00 per request if search exceeds 10 minutes. A request can have multiple names, but not exceed five. No hit, no fee. Required to search: name, years to search. Criminal records computerized from 11/89, archived and in index files from 1900s. Mail turnaround time 5-10 days.

Los Angeles County

Los Angeles County provides online access to all courts as follows:

Civil: There are two searches at https://www.lasuperiorcourt.org/onlineservices/LAECourtOnlineIndex.htm. One may do a free civil party name search. One may also purchase civil case document images. A name search is $4.75. The flat fee for each case file is $7.50 for first 10 pages, then $.07 each add'l page. Records back to 1991 (92 is Small Claims).

Criminal: Search felony & misdemeanor defendant index at https://www.lasuperiorcourt.org/OnlineServices/criminalindex/index.asp. Search fee is $4 to $4.75 based on volume. If available, counts, current charges, disposition and disposition dates are shown.

Los Angeles Superior Court - Central District - Civil Stanley Mosk Courthouse, Civic Ctr, 111 N Hill St, Rm 106, Civil Indexing, Los Angeles, CA 90012; 213-974-5171; probate phone: 213-974-5471; fax: 213-625-3244; 8:30AM-4:30PM (PST). *Civil Actions, Eviction, Small Claims, Probate.*

www.lasuperiorcourt.org

General Information: Any civil cases here under $25,000 are co-extensive with the city limits of Los Angeles and includes the City of San Fernando and sections designated as San Pedro, West Los Angeles, Van Nuys, Venice and the unincorporated county area known as Florence. No probation reports released. Will not fax documents. Court makes copy: $.50 per page. Certification fee: $20 per doc plus copy fee; Exemplification fee- $10.00. Payee: Los Angeles Superior Court. Personal checks accepted. Visa/MC accepted. Prepayment required. Mail requests: SASE required.

Civil Name Search: Access: Phone, mail, online, in person. Both court and visitors may perform in person name searches. Search fee: $15.00 per name if search exceeds 10 minutes. Civil records on computer from 1991, index files from 1983. Records destroyed after 10 years. Note: Small Claims (213-974-6350) and Probate and Family Law are located at 110 N Grand Ave. Mail turnaround time 24 hours, more if busy. Public use terminal has civil records back to 1991. 4 PA terminals in 106, 1 add'l in Rm118. **See the Online Accesss Note at the start of this county.**

Los Angeles Superior Court - Central District - Felony Clara Shortridge Foltz Criminal Justice Center, 210 W Temple St, Rm M-6, Los Angeles, CA 90012; 213-974-6141; criminal phone: 213-974--6141/42; Felon Recs- 213-974-6147; fax: 213-617-1224; 8:30AM-4:30PM (PST). *Felony, Misdemeanor.*

www.lasuperiorcourt.org

General Information: This court now handles felonies and misdemeanors; they can do misdemeanor searches for the Central District area of downtown LA, East LA, and Hollywood. Fax number above is for government agencies only. Clerk's office on 5th Fl, records on 2nd. No adoption, juvenile, medical, probation or sealed records released. Will not fax out docs. Court makes copy: $.50 per page. Certification fee: $25 per doc plus copy fee. Certification clerk phone- 213-974-6141. Payee: Los Angeles Superior Court. Personal checks accepted. Major credit cards accepted but no AmEx. Prepayment required. Mail requests: SASE required.

Criminal Name Search: Access: Mail, in person, online. Only the court performs in person name searches; visitors may not. Search fee: $15.00 per name if search exceeds 10 minutes. Required to search: name, years to search, DOB, sex. Criminal records on microfiche and index files since 1956, computerized misdemeanors since 1988; felonies since 1996. Note: In requests, court suggests to include full spelling of middle name. 5 name limit at counter. Mail turnaround time 24 hours; up to 3 weeks if busy. **See the Online Accesss Note at the start of this county.**

Airport Superior Court - West District 11701 S La Cienega Blvd, Los Angeles, CA 90045; 310-727-6020- Misdemeanors; criminal phone: 310-727-6100- Felony; fax: 310-727-0591; 8:30AM-4:30PM (PST). *Felony, Misdemeanor.*
www.lasuperiorcourt.org/locations/ui/location.aspx?loc=LAX&
General Information: New court in 2000; includes the areas of Palms, Mar Vista, Rancho Park, Marina del Rey, Venice, Playa del Rey, Sawtelle. Holds records for the former West LA Court covering Culver, El Segundo. No probation reports released. Will not fax documents. Court makes copy: $.50 per page. Certification fee: $25 per doc plus copy fee. Payee: Los Angeles Superior Court. Personal checks accepted. Visa/MC accepted. Prepayment required. Mail requests: SASE required.
Criminal Name Search: Access: Mail, in person, online. Only the court performs in person name searches; visitors may not. Search fee: $15.00 per name if search exceeds 10 minutes. Required to search: name, years to search; helpful: DOB, address. Criminal records computerized from 1991, index files from 1983. Records destroyed after 10 years. Note: Will do search if you have a case number. **See the Online Accesss Note at the start of this county.**

Alhambra Superior Court - Northeast District 150 W Commonwealth Ave, 2nd Fl, Rm 200, Alhambra, CA 91801; criminal phone: 626-308-5525; civil phone: 626-308-5521; fax: 626-570-4667; 8:30AM-4:30PM (phone:8:30AM-10:30AM; 1:30PM-3:30PM) (PST). *Misdemeanor, Civil Actions under $25,000, Eviction, Small Claims.*
www.lasuperiorcourt.org
General Information: Includes cities of Alhambra, Monterey Park, San Gabriel, Temple City, Monrovia, Arcadia, Duarte, Bradbury and the unincorporated County area including South San Gabriel. No probation records released. Will not fax documents. Court makes copy: $.50 per page. Certification fee: $25 per doc plus copy fee. Payee: Los Angeles Superior Court. Personal checks accepted. Credit cards accepted. Prepayment required. Mail requests: SASE required.
Civil Name Search: Access: Mail, in person, online. Only the court performs in person name searches; visitors may not. Search fee: $15.00 per name if search exceeds 10 minutes. Civil records on computer back to 1991, index files from 1983. Records destroyed after 10 years. Note: Address the specific division (criminal, civil, small claims) in correspondence. Mail turnaround time 2 days. **See the Online Accesss Note at the start of this county.**

Beverly Hills Superior Court - West District 9355 Burton Way, Beverly Hills, CA 90210; criminal phone: 310-288-1309; civil phone: 310-288-1308; fax: 310-275-5224; 8:30AM-4:30PM (phone:8:30AM-10:30AM; 1:30PM-3:30PM) (PST). *Misdemeanor, Civil Actions under $25,000, Eviction, Small Claims.*
www.lasuperiorcourt.org
General Information: Includes cities of Beverly Hills and West Hollywood. Small Claims phone- 310-288-1305. Traffic phone- 213-742-6648. The fax number is used for filing only. No probation, arrest records released. Will not fax documents. Court makes copy: $.50 per page. Certification fee: $25 per doc plus copy fee. Payee: Los Angeles Superior Court. Personal checks accepted. Credit cards accepted. Prepayment required. Mail requests: SASE required.
Civil Name Search: Access: Phone, mail, online, in person. Both court and visitors may perform in person name searches. Search fee: $15.00 per name if search exceeds 10 minutes. Fee is per data bank per year. Required to search: name, years to search; also helpful: address. Civil cases indexed by defendant, plaintiff. Civil records on computer from 1991, index files from 1983. Records destroyed after 10 years. Note: 5 name limit at counter. Mail turnaround time 2 days. **See the Online Accesss Note at the start of this county.**
Criminal Name Search: Access: Phone, mail, in person, online. Only the court performs in person name searches; visitors may not. Search fee: $15.00 per name if search exceeds 10 minutes. Fee is per database per year. Required to search: name, years to search, DOB; also helpful: address, sex, signed release. Criminal records computerized from 1991, index files from 1983. Records destroyed after 10 years. Note: 5 name limit at counter. Mail turnaround time 2 days. **See the Online Accesss Note at the start of this county.**

Burbank Superior Court - North Central District 300 E Olive Ave, Burbank, CA 91502-1215; criminal phone: 818-557-3466; civil phone: 818-557-3482; 818-557-3461 Sm Claims; criminal fax: 818-569-7413; civil fax: 8:30AM-4:30PM; 8:30AM-4:30PM (PST). *Felony, Misdemeanor, Civil Actions, Eviction, Small Claims, Older Probate.*
www.lasuperiorcourt.org
General Information: Small Claims now heard in Glendale Court. No probation reports released. Will fax documents $3.37 per page. Court makes copy: $.50 per page. Certification fee: $25 per doc plus copy fee, Exemplification fee $20.00 & copy fee. Payee: Los Angeles Superior Court.

Personal checks accepted. Visa/MC accepted. Prepayment required. Mail requests: SASE required.
Civil Name Search: Access: Mail, in person, online. Both court and visitors may perform in person name searches. Search fee: $15.00 per name if search exceeds 10 minutes. Civil records on computer from 1991. Limited hard copy civil records, destroyed 10 years after judgment. Mail turnaround time 3-5 days. Public use terminal has civil records back to 1977. Public terminal has Courtney; includes probate records. **See the Online Accesss Note at the start of this county.**
Criminal Name Search: Access: Mail, in person, online, phone. Only the court performs in person name searches; visitors may not. Search fee: $15.00 per name if search exceeds 10 minutes. Required to search: name, years to search, DOB. Criminal records computerized from 1991, index files from 1983. Records destroyed after 10 years. Note: Supply case number and they give case info over phone. 5 name limit at counter. Mail turnaround time 3-5 days. **See the Online Accesss Note at the start of this county.**
Criminal Name Search: Access: Mail, in person, online. Only the court performs in person name searches; visitors may not. Search fee: $15.00 per name if search exceeds 10 minutes. Required to search: name, years to search, DOB; also helpful: CDL. Criminal records computerized from 1996, index files from 1991. Records destroyed after 10 years. Note: Address the specific division (criminal, civil, small claims) in correspondence. Traffic phone- 213-742-1928. Mail turnaround time 2 days. Search felony & misdemeanor defendant index for a fee at https://www.lasuperiorcourt.org/OnlineServices/criminalindex/index.asp. Search fee is $4 to $4.75 based on volume. If available, counts, current charges, disposition and disposition dates are shown.

Chatsworth Courthouse 9425 Penfield Avenue, Chatsworth, CA 91311; 818-576-8595- Civil Unlimited; 576-8575- Limited; fax: 818-576-8687; 8:30AM-4:30PM (PST). *Civil, Small Claims, Traffic.*
www.lasuperiorcourt.org
General Information: Phone for small claims- 818-576-8586. No probation reports released. Will not fax documents. Court makes copy: $.50 per page. Certification fee: $25 per doc plus copy fee. Payee: Los Angeles Superior Court. Major credit cards accepted. Prepayment required. Mail requests: SASE requested.
Civil Name Search: Access: Mail, in person, online. Both court and visitors may perform in person name searches. Search fee: $15.00 per name if search exceeds 10 minutes. Civil cases indexed by defendant, plaintiff. Civil records on computer from 1991, index files from 1983. Records destroyed after 10 years. Mail turnaround time 1-3 days. **See the Online Accesss Note at the start of this county.**

Compton Superior Court - South Central District 200 W Compton Blvd, Compton, CA 90220; 310-762-9100; criminal phone: 310-603-7112; civil phone: 310-603-7842; criminal fax: 310-223-5941; civil fax: 8:30AM-4:30PM; clerks- 9-11AM, 2-4PM; 8:30AM-4:30PM; clerks-9-11AM, 2-4PM (PST). *Felony, Misdemeanor, Civil Actions, Eviction, Small Claims.* www.lasuperiorcourt.org
General Information: Includes cities of Carson, Compton, Lynwood, Paramount and unincorporated county areas around them. Civil Div- 9th Fl; Criminal in Rm 403. Probate was moved to the court in Norwalk. No complaint records released. Will not fax documents. Court makes copy: $.50 per page. Certification fee: $25 per doc plus copy fee. Payee: Los Angeles Superior Court-Compton. Personal checks accepted. Credit cards accepted. Prepayment required. Mail requests: SASE required.
Civil Name Search: Access: Mail, in person, online. Both court and visitors may perform in person name searches. Search fee: $15.00 per name if search exceeds 10 minutes. Civil records on computer from 1991, index files from 1983. Records destroyed after 10 years. Mail turnaround time 7 days. Public use terminal has civil records back to 1991. **See the Online Accesss Note at the start of this county.**
Criminal Name Search: Access: Mail, in person, online. Only the court performs in person name searches; visitors may not. Search fee: $15.00 per name if search exceeds 10 minutes. Required to search: name, years to search, DOB. Criminal records computerized from 1991, index files from 1983. Records destroyed after 10 years. Mail turnaround time 2 weeks. **See the Online Accesss Note at the start of this county.**

Culver City Superior Court - See Santa Monica
General Information: Now combined with Santa Monica. Culver City did include Angelus Vista, portions of Marina del Rey, View Park and Windsor Hills, all surrounded by City of LA, on south bounded by Inglewood.

Downey Superior Court - Southeast District 7500 E Imperial Hwy, Downey, CA 90242; criminal phone: 562-803-7049; civil phone: 562-803-7044; fax: 562-803-6392; 8:30AM-4:30PM (PST). *Misdemeanor, Civil Actions under $25,000, Eviction, Small Claims.*
www.lasuperiorcourt.org

General Information: Comprised of the cities of Downey, Norwalk, La Mirada. Sm Claims phone- 562-803-7054. No adoption, juvenile, medical, probation or sealed records released. Will not fax documents. Court makes copy: $.50 per page. Certification fee: $25 per doc plus copy fee. Payee: Los Angeles Superior Court. Personal checks accepted. Visa/MC accepted. Prepayment required. Mail requests: SASE required.

Civil Name Search: Access: Mail, in person, online. Both court and visitors may perform in person name searches. Search fee: $15.00 per name if search exceeds 10 minutes. Civil records on computer from 1991, index files from 1983. Records destroyed after 10 years. Mail turnaround time 5 days. **See the Online Accesss Note at the start of this county.**

Criminal Name Search: Access: Mail, in person, online. Only the court performs in person name searches; visitors may not. Search fee: $15.00 per name if search exceeds 10 minutes. Required to search: name, years to search; also helpful: DOB. Criminal records computerized from 1989, on microfiche, archived, and index files. Note: Mail or in person - court may choose not to run lists of names. Mail turnaround time 5 days. **See the Online Accesss Note at the start of this county.**

East Los Angeles Superior Court - Central District 4848 E Civic Center Way, Los Angeles, CA 90022; criminal phone: 323-780-2025 (2-4PM only); civil phone: 323-780-2017 (2-4 PM only); fax: 323-780-3538; 8AM-4:30PM (PST). *Misdemeanor, Eviction, Small Claims, Traffic.*
www.lasuperiorcourt.org
General Information: Includes cities of Montebello, Commerce, and adjacent unincorporated area bordering Monterey Park to north and Los Angeles to the west. Civil actions discontinued as of 5/2003. Court offers night court 2nd & 4th Monday each month. Traffic- 323-780-2086 No probation reports released. Will not fax documents. Court makes copy: $.50 per page. Certification fee: $25 per doc plus copy fee. Payee: Superior Court of East Los Angeles. Personal checks accepted. Accepts Visa/MC/Discover cards. Prepayment required. Mail requests: SASE required.

Civil Name Search: Access: Mail, in person, online. No in-person civil name searches permitted at this court. Search fee: $15.00 per name if search exceeds 10 minutes. Civil records on computer from 1991, index files from 1983. Records destroyed after 10 years. Note: No civil actions since 5/03, however, there are eviction and small claims records. **See the Online Accesss Note at the start of this county.**

Criminal Name Search: Access: Mail, in person, online. Only the court performs in person name searches; visitors may not. Search fee: $15.00 per name if search exceeds 10 minutes. Required to search: name, years to search; also helpful: DOB. Criminal records computerized from 1991, index files from 1983. Records destroyed after 10 years. Mail turnaround time 2 days. **See the Online Accesss Note at the start of this county.**

El Monte Superior Court - East District 11234 E Valley Blvd, El Monte, CA 91731; criminal phone: 626-575-4121; civil phone: 626-575-4117; fax: 626-444-9029; 8AM-4:30PM (PST). *Misdemeanor, Civil Actions under $25,000, Eviction, Small Claims.*
www.lasuperiorcourt.org
General Information: Includes cities of El Monte, South El Monte, La Puente, Rosemead and adjacent unincorporated county area. Will not release unlawful detainer for 60 days. No probation reports, med records, search warrants, rap sheet, CLETS's, transcripts or sealed records released. Will fax docs for fee. Court makes copy: $.50 per page. Certification fee: $25 per doc plus copy fee. Payee: Los Angeles Superior Court. 2-party checks not accepted. Write "not to exceed $x.xx" on check. Major credit cards accepted. Prepayment required. Mail requests: SASE required.

Civil Name Search: Access: Mail, in person, online. Only the court performs in person name searches; visitors may not. Search fee: $15.00 per name if search exceeds 10 minutes. Civil records on computer since 1989, microfiche since 1980. Records destroyed after 10 years. Mail turnaround time 5 days. **See the Online Accesss Note at the start of this county.**

Criminal Name Search: Access: Mail, in person, online. Only the court performs in person name searches; visitors may not. Search fee: $15.00 per name if search exceeds 10 minutes. Required to search: name, years to search; also helpful: DOB. Criminal records computerized from 1985, microfiche to 1980. Mail turnaround time 5 days. **See the Online Accesss Note at the start of this county.**

Glendale Superior Court - North Central District 600 E Broadway, Glendale, CA 91206; criminal phone: 818-500-3530; civil phone: 818-500-3551;; 8:15AM-4:30PM (PST). *Misdemeanor, Civil Actions under $25,000, Eviction, Small Claims.*
www.lasuperiorcourt.org
General Information: Includes cities of Glendale, LaCanada-Flintridge and county areas known as Montrose, La Crescenta, Verdugo City, Highway Highlands, Kogel Canyon. No probation, police, CII reports released. Will not fax out docs. Court makes copy: $.50 per page. Certification fee: $25 per doc plus copy fee. Payee: Los Angeles Superior Court. Personal checks accepted. Visa/MC accepted. Prepayment required. Mail requests: SASE required.

Civil Name Search: Access: Mail, in person, online. Both court and visitors may perform in person name searches. Search fee: $15.00 per name if search exceeds 10 minutes. On computer from 1990, small claims from 7/92, index files from 1983. Paper records destroyed per state law. Note: 5 name limit at counter. Public use terminal has civil records back to 1970. **See the Online Accesss Note at the start of this county.**

Criminal Name Search: Access: Mail, in person, online. Only the court performs in person name searches; visitors may not. Search fee: $15.00 per name if search exceeds 10 minutes. Required to search: name, years to search. On computer from 1990, microfilm past 10 years. Note: 5 name limit at counter. Mail turnaround time based on staffing. **See the Online Accesss Note at the start of this county.**

Hollywood Superior Court - Central District 5925 Hollywood Blvd, Los Angeles, CA 90028; 323-856-5747; fax: 323-962-6157; 8:30AM-4:30PM (PST). *Misdemeanor.*
www.lasuperiorcourt.org
General Information: Handles high-grade and low-grade Misdemeanors for the Hollywood area. Fax number used strictly for business. No probation, driver's license, medical, arrest report or confidential reports released. Will not fax documents. Court makes copy: $.50 per page. Self serve copy: same. Certification fee: $25 per doc plus copy fee. Payee: Los Angeles Superior Court. Personal checks accepted. Credit cards accepted except AMEX. Prepayment required. Mail requests: SASE required.

Criminal Name Search: Access: In person only. Only the court performs in person name searches; visitors may not. Required to search: name, years to search, DOB. Criminal records on computer go back 10 years, prior on microfiche. Mail turnaround time 2-3 days. **See the Online Accesss Note at the start of this county.**

Huntington Park Superior - Southeast District 6548 Miles Ave, Huntington Park, CA 90255; 323-586-6365; civil phone: Sm Claims- 323-586-6359; fax: 323-589-6769; 8AM-4:30PM (PST). *Civil Actions under $25,000, Eviction, Small Claims, Traffic Pre-8/2004 Misdemeanor.*
www.lasuperiorcourt.org
General Information: Includes Bell, Bell Gardens, Cudahy, Huntington Park, Maywood, Vernon. Also includes South Gate, Hollydale and unincorporated area of Walnut Park from closed court at South Gate. Court no longer handles criminal cases as 8/2004. No probation reports released. Will not fax out docs. Court makes copy: $.50 per page. Certification fee: $25 per doc plus copy fee. Payee: LA Superior Court. Personal checks accepted. Credit cards accepted. Prepayment required. Mail requests: SASE required.

Civil Name Search: Access: Mail, in person, online. Only the court performs in person name searches; visitors may not. Search fee: $15.00 per name if search exceeds 10 minutes. Civil on computer from 1991, index files from 1983. Records destroyed after 10 years. Mail turnaround time 2-5 days. **See the Online Accesss Note at the start of this county.**

Inglewood Superior Court - Southwest District 1 Regent St, Inglewood, CA 90301; 310-419-5132; criminal fax: 310-680-7053; civil fax: 8:15AM-4:30PM; 8:15AM-4:30PM (PST). *Felony, Misdemeanor, Civil Actions under $25,000, Eviction, Small Claims, Traffic.*
www.lasuperiorcourt.org
General Information: Includes cities of Inglewood, Lennox and adjoining unincorporated areas. Felony cases are only from these areas. Administration "clarification" fax-310-674-4862. No probation reports released. Will not fax out docs. Court makes copy: $.50 per page. Self serve copy: same. Certification fee: $25 per doc plus copy fee. Payee: Los Angeles Superior Court. Personal checks accepted. Credit cards accepted. Prepayment required. Mail requests: SASE required.

Civil Name Search: Access: Mail, in person, online. Only the court performs in person name searches; visitors may not. Search fee: $15.00 per name if search exceeds 10 minutes. Civil records on computer from 1991, index files from 1983. Records destroyed after 10 years. Mail turnaround time 2 days. **See the Online Accesss Note at the start of this county.**

Criminal Name Search: Access: Mail, in person, online. Only the court performs in person name searches; visitors may not. Search fee: $15.00 per name if search exceeds 10 minutes. Required to search: name, years to search; also helpful: DOB. Criminal records computerized from 1991, index files from 1983. Records destroyed after 10 years. Mail turnaround time 2 days. **See the Online Accesss Note at the start of this county.**

Lancaster Superior Court - North District Michael D Antonovich Antelope Valley Courthouse, 42011 4th St West, Lancaster, CA 93534; 661-974-7200; criminal phone: x3; civil phone: x4; probate phone: 661-974-7200;; 8AM-4:30PM (PST). *Felony, Misdemeanor, Civil, Small Claims, Probate, Family, Traffic.*
www.lasuperiorcourt.org
General Information: Formerly Antelope; includes Lancaster, City of Palmdale, and unincorporated County territory including Acton, Agua Dulce, Fairmont, Lake Hughes, Llano, Leona Valley, Littlerock, Pearblossom, Quartz Hill, Roosevelt, Green Valley, Big Pines, Lake Elizabeth No

probation reports released. Will not fax documents. Court makes copy: $.50 per page. Certification fee: $25 per doc plus copy fee. Payee: Los Angeles Superior Court. Personal checks accepted; must be pre-imprinted. Prepayment required. Mail requests: SASE required.

Civil Name Search: Access: Phone, mail, online, in person. Only the court performs in person name searches; visitors may not. Search fee: $15.00 per name if search exceeds 10 minutes. Civil records on computer since 1989, index books since 1983. Records destroyed after 10 years. Mail turnaround time 2 days. Public use terminal has civil records. **See the Online Accesss Note at the start of this county.**

Criminal Name Search: Access: Mail, in person, online. Only the court performs in person name searches; visitors may not. Search fee: $15.00 per name if search exceeds 10 minutes. Required to search: name, years to search; also helpful: case number. Criminal records on computer since 1989, index books since 1983. Records destroyed after 10 years. Mail turnaround time 2 days. **See the Online Accesss Note at the start of this county.**

Long Beach Superior Court - South District 415 W Ocean Blvd, Long Beach, CA 90802; 562-491-6201; criminal phone: 562-491-6226; civil phone: 562-491-6234 Limited; 562-491-5925- unlimited; 562-491-6235 Sm Claims; probate phone: 562-491-6235;; 8:30AM-4:30PM; phones- 8:30-10:30AM & 1:30-3:30PM (PST). *Felony, Misdemeanor, Civil Actions under $25,000, Eviction, Small Claims, Probate.*
www.lasuperiorcourt.org
General Information: Includes cities of Long Beach and Signal Hill and adjoining unincorporated area. Address requests to civil or criminal division. Criminal on 4th Fl; Civil on 2nd Fl. No probation reports released. Will fax documents for fee. Court makes copy: $.50 per page. Self serve copy: same. Certification fee: $25 per doc plus copy fee. Payee: Los Angeles Superior Court. Personal checks accepted. Visa/MC, Discover accepted, in person only. Prepayment required. Mail requests: SASE required.
Civil Name Search: Access: Mail, in person, online. Both court and visitors may perform in person name searches. Search fee: $15.00 per name if search exceeds 10 minutes. Civil records on computer from 1991, index files from 1983. Records destroyed after 10 years. Note: Traffic division phone is 562-491-6284. Civil PAT goes back to 1991; index files back to 1983. Public terminals on 1st Fl as well as rooms #207 and #401. **See the Online Accesss Note at the start of this county.**
Criminal Name Search: Access: Mail, in person, online. Both court and visitors may perform in person name searches. Search fee: $15.00 per name if search exceeds 10 minutes. Required to search: name, years to search, DOB. Criminal records computerized from 1991, index files from 1983. Records destroyed after 10 years. Mail turnaround time 2 days. Criminal PAT goes back to same as civil. Public terminals on 1st Fl as well as Rms #207 and #401. **See the Online Accesss Note at the start of this county.**

Malibu Superior Court - West District 23525 W Civic Center Way, Malibu, CA 90265; criminal phone: 310-317-1335; civil phone: 310-317-1331; fax: 310-456-0194; 8:30AM-4:30PM (PST). *Misdemeanor, Civil Actions under $25,000, Eviction, Small Claims.*
www.lasuperiorcourt.org
General Information: Includes Malibu, Agoura Hills, Calabasas, Westlake Village, Hidden Hills and unincorporated areas known as Topanga and Chatsworth Lake, bounded by Ventura County on the west and north, Pacific Ocean on the south and City of Los Angeles on the east. No probation reports released. Will not fax out docs. Court makes copy: $.50 per page. Certification fee: $25 per doc plus copy fee. Payee: Los Angeles Superior Court. Personal checks and credit cards accepted. Prepayment required. Mail requests: SASE required.
Civil Name Search: Access: Mail, in person, online. Only the court performs in person name searches; visitors may not. Search fee: $15.00 per name if search exceeds 10 minutes. Civil records on computer from 1991, index files from 1983. Records destroyed after 10 years. Mail turnaround time 1-5 days. **See the Online Accesss Note at the start of this county.**
Criminal Name Search: Access: Mail, in person, online. Only the court performs in person name searches; visitors may not. Search fee: $15.00 per name if search exceeds 10 minutes. Required to search: name, years to search; also helpful: DOB. Criminal records computerized from 1991, index files from 1983. Records destroyed after 10 years. Mail turnaround time 1-5 days. **See the Online Accesss Note at the start of this county.**

Metropolitan Branch Superior Court - Central District 1945 S Hill St, Rm 200, Los Angeles, CA 90007; 213-744-4023/4022; fax: 213-744-1879; 8:30AM-4:30PM (PST). *Misdemeanor, Traffic.*
www.lasuperiorcourt.org
General Information: Vehicle Code misdemeanor and traffic citations for the incorporated City of Los Angeles excluding the areas known as San Pedro, W. Los Angeles and communities of San Fernando Valley and the unincorporated County area more commonly known as Florence. No probation, driver's license, medical, arrest report or confidential reports

released. Will not fax documents. Court makes copy: $.50 per page. Certification fee: $25 per doc plus copy fee. Payee: Los Angeles Superior Court. Personal checks and credit cards accepted. Prepayment required. Mail requests: SASE requested.
Criminal Name Search: Access: Mail, in person, online. Only the court performs in person name searches; visitors may not. Search fee: $15.00 per name. Required to search: name, years to search, DOB. Criminal records computerized from 1991. Records destroyed after 10 years. Mail turnaround time 2-3 days. **See the Online Accesss Note at the start of this county.**

Norwalk Superior Court - Southeast District 12720 Norwalk Blvd, Norwalk, CA 90650; 562-807-7266; probate phone: 562-807-7263; fax: 562-863-8757; 8:30AM-4:30PM (PST). *Felony, Civil Actions over $25,000, Probate.*
www.lasuperiorcourt.org
General Information: The probate cases formerly held in Compton are now held here. No probation reports released. Will not fax out docs. Court makes copy: $.50 per page. Certification fee: $25 per doc plus copy fee. Payee: Los Angeles Superior Court. Personal checks and credit cards accepted. Prepayment required. Mail requests: SASE required.
Civil Name Search: Access: Mail, in person, online. Both court and visitors may perform in person name searches. Search fee: $15.00 per name if search exceeds 10 minutes. Civil records on computer from 1991, index files from 1983. Mail turnaround time 2-10 days. Civil PAT available. Use public terminal to find case number only. **See the Online Accesss Note at the start of this county.**
Criminal Name Search: Access: Mail, in person, online. Both court and visitors may perform in person name searches. Search fee: $15.00 per name if search exceeds 10 minutes. Required to search: name, years to search, DOB; also helpful: sex. Criminal records computerized from 1991, index files from 1983. Mail turnaround time 2-10 days. Criminal PAT available. Use public terminal to find case number only. **See the Online Accesss Note at the start of this county.**

Pasadena Superior Court - Northeast District 300 E Walnut Ave, Pasadena, CA 91101; 626-356-5689; criminal phone: 626-356-5254 (Misd); civil phone: 626-356-5547; fax: 626-568-3903; 8:30AM-4:30PM (PST). *Felony, Misdemeanor, Civil Actions under $25,000, Civil Actions over $25,000, Eviction, Small Claims, Probate.*
www.lasuperiorcourt.org
General Information: Includes cities of Pasadena, South Pasadena, San Marino, Sierra Madre and the area of Altadena. Traffic phone- 213-742-1928. Some older probate records may be found in the Burbank Court. No probation reports released. Will fax out docs to local or toll-free number. Court makes copy: $.50 per page. Certification fee: $15.00; exemplification fee- $20.00. Payee: Los Angeles Superior Court. Personal checks and credit cards accepted. Prepayment required. Mail requests: SASE required.
Civil Name Search: Access: Mail, in person, online. Both court and visitors may perform in person name searches. Search fee: $15.00 per name if search exceeds 10 minutes. Civil records on computer from 1991, index files from 1983. Limited Juris records destroyed after 10 years; General Juris are not. Mail turnaround time 2 days. Public use terminal has civil records. **See the Online Accesss Note at the start of this county.**
Criminal Name Search: Access: Mail, in person, online. Only the court performs in person name searches; visitors may not. Search fee: $15.00 per name if search exceeds 10 minutes. Required to search: name, years to search. Criminal records computerized from 1991, index files from 1983. Mail turnaround time 2 days. **See the Online Accesss Note at the start of this county.**

Pomona Superior Court - North 350 W Mission Blvd, Pomona, CA 91766; 909-802-9944; probate phone: 909-620-3023; criminal fax: 909-865-6767; civil fax: 8AM-4:30PM; 8AM-4:30PM (PST). *Misdemeanor, Civil Actions under $25,000, Eviction, Small Claims, Probate.*
www.lasuperiorcourt.org
General Information: Includes cities of West Covina, Covina, Baldwin Park There is another court in Pomona at 400 Civic Center that deals with criminal, civil, and probate matters. No probation, mental health or police reports released. Will not fax documents. Court makes copy: $.50 per page. Certification fee: $25 per doc plus copy fee. Payee: Los Angeles Superior Court. Personal checks accepted. Visa/MC accepted. Prepayment required. Mail requests: SASE required.
Civil Name Search: Access: Fax, mail, online, in person. Only the court performs in person name searches; visitors may not. Search fee: $15.00 per name if search exceeds 10 minutes. Civil records on computer from 1990, index files from 1983. Records destroyed after 10 years. Mail turnaround time 1-2 days. **See the Online Accesss Note at the start of this county.**
Criminal Name Search: Access: Mail, in person, online. Only the court performs in person name searches; visitors may not. Search fee: $15.00 per name if search exceeds 10 minutes. Required to search: name, years to search, DOB. Criminal records computerized from 1990, index files from 1983. Records destroyed after 10 years. Note: Drop box available. Mail

turnaround time 2-4 days. **See the Online Accesss Note at the start of this county.**

Pomona Superior Court - South 350 W Mission Blvd, Pomona, CA 91766; 909-620-3002; fax: 909-865-6547; 8AM-4:30PM (PST). *Felony, Misdemeanor, Civil Actions under $25,000, Eviction, Small Claims, Probate.*
www.lasuperiorcourt.org
General Information: Includes cities of Pomona, Claremont, La Verne, Walnut, San Dimas and unincorporated area including Diamond Bar. There is another court in Pomona at 400 350 W Mission that deals with Civil, Small Claims and Traffic matters. No probation, mental health or police reports released. Will not fax documents. Court makes copy: $.50 per page. Certification fee: $25 per doc plus copy fee. Payee: Los Angeles Superior Court. Personal checks accepted. Visa/MC accepted. Prepayment required. Mail requests: SASE required.
Civil Name Search: Access: Fax, mail, online, in person. Only the court performs in person name searches; visitors may not. Search fee: $15.00 per name if search exceeds 10 minutes. Civil records on computer from 1990, index files from 1983. Records destroyed after 10 years. Mail turnaround time 1-2 days. **See the Online Accesss Note at the start of this county.**
Criminal Name Search: Access: Mail, in person, online. Only the court performs in person name searches; visitors may not. Search fee: $15.00 per name if search exceeds 10 minutes. Required to search: name, years to search, DOB. Criminal records computerized from 1990, index files from 1983. Records destroyed after 10 years. Note: Drop box available. Mail turnaround time 2-4 days. **See the Online Accesss Note at the start of this county.**

San Fernando Superior Court - North Valley District 900 3rd St, #1135 or #1137, San Fernando, CA 91340; 818-898-2401 Admin.; criminal phone: 818-898-2407; civil phone: Sm Claims- 818-898-2425; fax: 818-837-7297; 8:30AM-4:30PM (PST). *Felony, Misdemeanor, Small Claims.*
www.lasuperiorcourt.org
General Information: Includes Granada Hills, Northridge, Chatsworth, Sunland, Tujunga, Pacoima, Mission Hills, Sylmar, Arleta, Lake View Terrace, Sun Valley, San Fernando. Court merged with Newhall Court to become North Valley Court. Traffic ph- 818-898-2405. No probation reports or arrest reports released. Will not fax out docs. Court makes copy: $.50 per page. Certification fee: $25 per doc plus copy fee. Payee: Los Angeles Superior Court. Personal checks and credit cards accepted. Prepayment required. Mail requests: SASE required.
Civil Name Search: Access: Mail, in person, online. Only the court performs in person name searches; visitors may not. Search fee: $15.00 per name if search exceeds 10 minutes. Civil records on computer from 1991, index files from 1983. Records destroyed after 10 years. Note: Probate is at Van Nuys Courthouse. **See the Online Accesss Note at the start of this county.**
Criminal Name Search: Access: Mail, online, in person. Both court and visitors may perform in person name searches. Search fee: $15.00 per name if search exceeds 10 minutes. Required to search: name, years to search; also helpful: DOB. Criminal records computerized from 1988. Records destroyed after 10 yrs. Note: Misdemeanor clerk's office is Rm 1137. Sheriff's Department (Court Services)- 818-898-2436. Mail turnaround time 2 days. Public use terminal has crim records back to 1996. **See the Online Accesss Note at the start of this county.**

San Pedro Superior Court - South District 505 S Centre St, Rm 202, San Pedro, CA 90731; 310-519-6018- general civil; civil phone: 310-519-6015 Limited Civil; 310-519-6014- Sm Claims; fax: 310-514-0314; 8:30AM-4:30PM; Traffic- 8AM-4:30PM (PST). *Civil Actions, Eviction, Small Claims, Traffic.*
www.lasuperiorcourt.org
General Information: Includes San Pedro, Wilmington, and a county strip in Torrance extending up to Western Ave. Traffic phone- 213-742-1884. The San Pedro Courthouse Annex is located at 638 S. Beacon St, phone-310-519-6018 for clerk's office. No probation, arrest, records released. Will not fax out documents. Court makes copy: $.50 per page. Certification fee: $25 per doc plus copy fee. Payee: Los Angeles Superior Court. Personal checks accepted. Visa/MC accepted. Prepayment required. Mail requests: SASE required.
Civil Name Search: Access: Mail, in person, online. Only the court performs in person name searches; visitors may not. Search fee: $15.00 per name if search exceeds 10 minutes. Civil records on computer go back 10 years; on index files from 1984. Records destroyed after 10 years. Mail turnaround time 2 days. **See the Online Accesss Note at the start of this county.**

Santa Anita Superior Court - Northeast District
Court closed - merged with Alhambra Court. See that court.

Santa Clarita Superior Court - North Valley District 23747 W Valencia Blvd, Santa Clarita, CA 91355; 661-253-7316; criminal phone: 661-253-7384; civil phone: 661-253-7309, 253-7313; criminal fax: 661-254-4107; civil fax: 8:30AM-4:30PM; 8:30AM-4:30PM (PST). *Misdemeanor, Civil Actions under $25,000, Eviction, Small Claims.*
www.lasuperiorcourt.org
General Information: Formerly Newhall Sup. Ct. Includes Saugus, Canyon Country, Valencia, Santa Clarita and open area bound by Ventura County, Kern County line, Agua Dulce, and Glendale/Los Angeles city limits (south). Sm Claims phone- 661-253-7311/12. Traffic- 213-742-6648. No probation, or police reports w/out court approval released. Will fax civil docs for $.75 per page and $4.50 per verification. Court makes copy: $.50 per page. Certification fee: $25 per doc plus copy fee. Payee: Los Angeles Superior Court. Personal checks accepted. Credit cards accepted. Prepayment required. Mail requests: SASE required.
Civil Name Search: Access: Mail, in person, online. Both court and visitors may perform in person name searches. Search fee: $15.00 per name if search exceeds 10 minutes. Civil records on computer from 1991. Records destroyed after 10 years; Many records on microfiche. Mail turnaround time 7-10 days. **See the Online Accesss Note at the start of this county.**
Criminal Name Search: Access: Mail, in person, online. Only the court performs in person name searches; visitors may not. Search fee: $15.00 per name if search exceeds 10 minutes. Required to search: name, years to search; also helpful: DOB. Records on computer from 1991, indices from 1983. Records destroyed after 10 years, many records on microfiche. Mail turnaround time 7-10 days. **See the Online Accesss Note at the start of this county.**

Santa Monica Superior Court - West District 1725 Main St, Rm 224, Santa Monica, CA 90401; 310-260-1876; probate phone: 310-260-3521; fax: 310-576-1399; 8:30AM-4:30PM (PST). *Civil Actions under $25,000, Eviction, Small Claims.*
www.lasuperiorcourt.org
General Information: Includes Santa Monica City and unincorporated area of Veteran's Admin. facilities in West LA. Now has Culver City records. Small claims-310-260-1886. Criminal section moved to LAX-Airport Courthouse, 2004, 310-727-6020. No probation reports or unlawful detainer records released. Will not fax out docs. Court makes copy: $.50 per page. Certification fee: $25 per doc plus copy fee. Payee: Los Angeles Superior Court. Personal checks and credit cards accepted. Prepayment required. Mail requests: SASE required.
Civil Name Search: Access: Mail, in person, online. Both court and visitors may perform in person name searches. Search fee: $15.00 per name if search exceeds 10 minutes. Civil records on computer from 1991, files from 1983. Records destroyed after 10 yrs. Mail turnaround time 1-2 days. **See the Online Accesss Note at the start of this county.**

Southeast District Superior Court Bellflower Courthouse, 10025 E Flower St, Bellflower, CA 90706; 562-804-8025; criminal phone: 562-804-8017; civil phone: 562-804-8010;; 8AM-4:30PM (PST). *Misdemeanor, Civil Actions under $25,000, Eviction, Small Claims.*
www.lasuperiorcourt.org/locations/ui/location.aspx?loc=LC&
General Information: Includes Artesia, Bellflower, Hawaiian Gardens, Lakewood, Cerritos. Also includes Norwalk for criminal cases only. Sm claims phone- 562-804-8011. No probation reports released. Will not fax documents. Court makes copy: $.50 per page. Certification fee: $25 per doc plus copy fee. Payee: Los Angeles Superior Court. Personal checks accepted. Credit cards accepted. Prepayment required. Mail requests: SASE required.
Civil Name Search: Access: Mail, in person, online. Both court and visitors may perform in person name searches. Search fee: $15.00 per name if search exceeds 10 minutes. Civil records on computer from 1991, index files from 1983. Records destroyed after 10 years. Note: Specify it is a "civil records" search request. Mail turnaround time 2-3 days. Public use terminal has civil records back to 10 years. PAT also shows company name and case number in a date range. **See the Online Accesss Note at the start of this county.**
Criminal Name Search: Access: Mail, in person, online. Only the court performs in person name searches; visitors may not. Search fee: $15.00 per name if search exceeds 10 minutes. Required to search: name, years to search, DOB. Criminal records computerized from 1991, index files from 1983. Records destroyed after 10 years. Note: Specify it is a "criminal records" search request. Mail turnaround time 2-3 days. **See the Online Accesss Note at the start of this county.**

Torrance Superior Court - Southwest District 825 Maple Ave, Torrance, CA 90503-5058; 310-222-6505, 222-6501 Admin.; criminal phone: 310-222-6506; civil phone: 310-222-8801/09; 222-6400 Sm Claims; probate phone: 310-222-8802/8809; fax: 310-783-5108; 8:15AM-4:30PM (PST). *Misdemeanor, Civil, Traffic, Eviction, Small Claims, Probate.*
www.lasuperiorcourt.org

General Information: Includes cities of Torrance, Gardena, Rolling Hills/Estates, Manhattan Beach, Lomita, Redondo Beach, Hermosa Beach, Palos Verdes Estates, Rancho Palos Verdes & Lawndale. No probation reports, medical or psychiatric reports, criminal history rap sheets released. Will not fax out docs. Court makes copy: $.50 per page. Certification fee: $25 per doc plus copy fee. Payee: LA Superior Court. Personal checks and credit cards accepted. Prepayment required. Mail requests: SASE required.

Civil Name Search: Access: Mail, in person, online. Both court and visitors may perform in person name searches. Search fee: $15.00 per name if search exceeds 10 minutes. Required to search: name. Civil cases indexed by defendant, plaintiff. Civil records on computer from 1991, index files from 1983. Records destroyed after 10 yrs. Mail turnaround time 5 days. Public use terminal has civil records. Public terminal in Rm 100. **See the Online Accesss Note at the start of this county.**

Criminal Name Search: Access: Mail, in person, online. Only the court performs in person name searches; visitors may not. Search fee: $15.00 per name if search exceeds 10 minutes. Required to search: name, years to search, DOB. Criminal records computerized from 1991, index files from 1983. Records destroyed after 10 yrs. Mail turnaround time 5 days. **See the Online Accesss Note at the start of this county.**

Van Nuys Superior Court - East - Civil 6230 Sylmar St, Van Nuys, CA 91401; 818-374-2208; fax: 818-779-7713; 8:30AM-4:30PM (PST). *Civil Actions, Eviction, Small Claims, Family Law, Probate, Unlawful Detainer.* www.lasuperiorcourt.org

General Information: Includes Sherman Oaks, Van Nuys, Reseda, North Hollywood, Woodland Hills, Canoga Park, Tarzana, Porter Ranch, Winnetka and Panorama City. Civil jurisdiction depends if limited or general. See filing court locator on the web. No probation reports or arrest reports released. Will not fax documents. Court makes copy: $.50 per page. Certification fee: $25 per doc; exemplification- $20.00 plus copies. Payee: Los Angeles Superior Court or LASC. Personal checks accepted; write 'not to exceed" and the amount on the check. Major credit cards accepted. Prepayment required. Mail requests: SASE required.

Civil Name Search: Access: Mail, in person, online. Both court and visitors may perform in person name searches. Search fee: $15.00 per name if search exceeds 10 minutes. Civil records on computer from 1991, index files from 1983. Records destroyed after 10 years. Mail turnaround time 2-3 days. Public use terminal has civil records back to 1991. **See the Online Accesss Note at the start of this county.**

Van Nuys Superior Court - West - Criminal 14400 Erwin St Mall, Rm 200, Van Nuys, CA 91401; 818-374-2903; fax: 818-904-0534; 7:30AM-4:30PM (PST). *Felony, Misdemeanor.*
www.lasuperiorcourt.org

General Information: Misdemeanors for that part of city known as Sherman Oaks, Van Nuys, Reseda, North Hollywood, Woodland Hills, Canoga Park, Tarzana, Porter Ranch, Winnetka and Panorama City. No probation reports or arrest reports released. Will not fax documents. Court makes copy: $.50 per page. Certification fee: $25 per doc plus copy fee. Payee: Los Angeles Superior Court. Personal checks and credit cards accepted. Prepayment required. Mail requests: SASE required.

Criminal Name Search: Access: Phone, mail, in person, online. Only the court performs in person name searches; visitors may not. Search fee: $15.00 per name if search exceeds 10 minutes. Required to search: name, years to search, sex; also helpful: DOB. Criminal records computerized from 1991, index files from 1983. Mail turnaround time 2-3 days. **See the Online Accesss Note at the start of this county.**

West Covina Superior Court - East District 1427 W Covina Pky, West Covina, CA 91790; criminal phone: 626-813-3239; civil phone: 626-813-3236 Civil; 626-813-3226 Sm Claims; fax: 626-338-7364; 8:30AM-4:30PM (PST). *Misdemeanor, Civil Actions under $25,000, Eviction, Small Claims.*
www.lasuperiorcourt.org

General Information: Formerly known as Citrus Court. Includes cities of Azusa, Baldwin Pk, Covina, Glendora, Industry, Irwindale, Valinda, West Covina and surrounding unincorporated county area. Traffic phone- 213-742-1928. No probation reports released. Will not fax out docs. Court makes copy: $.50 per page. Certification fee: $25 per doc plus copy fee. Payee: Los Angeles Superior Court. Personal checks accepted. Credit cards accepted. Prepayment required. Mail requests: SASE required.

Civil Name Search: Access: Mail, in person, online. Both court and visitors may perform in person name searches. Search fee: $15.00 per name if search exceeds 10 minutes. Civil records on computer from 1991, index files from 1983. Records destroyed after 10 years. Mail turnaround time 2 weeks Public use terminal has civil records back to 1996. **See the Online Accesss Note at the start of this county.**

Criminal Name Search: Access: Mail, in person, online. Only the court performs in person name searches; visitors may not. Search fee: $15.00 per name if search exceeds 10 minutes. Required to search: name, years to search; also helpful: DOB. Criminal records computerized from 1991, index

files from 1983. Records destroyed after 10 years. Note: Direct criminal searches to; LA County Court, Felony; phone-213-974-6145, address-210 W Temple St, LA, CA. Mail turnaround time is 2 weeks. **See the Online Accesss Note at the start of this county.**

West Los Angeles Superior Court - West District 1633 Purdue Ave, Los Angeles, CA 90025; 310-312-6545; civil phone: 310-312-6550 Sm Claims; fax: 310-478-1275; 8:30AM-4:30PM (PST). *Civil Actions under $25,000, Eviction, Small Claims.*
www.lasuperiorcourt.org

General Information: Includes the areas of Palms, Mar Vista, Rancho Park, Marina del Rey, Venice, Playa del Rey and Sawtelle. Holds records for the former Robertson branch. Criminal felony and misdemeanors are at the new Airport Court. No probation records released. Will not fax documents. Court makes copy: $.50 per page. Certification fee: $25 per doc plus copy fee. Payee: Los Angeles Superior Court. Personal checks and credit cards accepted. Prepayment required. Mail requests: SASE required.

Civil Name Search: Access: Phone, mail, online, in person. Both court and visitors may perform in person name searches. Search fee: $15.00 per name if search exceeds 10 minutes. Civil records on computer from 1991, index files from 1983. Records destroyed after 10 years. Mail turnaround time 1-5 days. Public use terminal has civil records. **See the Online Accesss Note at the start of this county.**

Whittier Superior Court - Southeast District 7339 S Painter Ave, Whittier, CA 90602; criminal phone: 562-907-3113; civil phone: 562-907-3127; criminal fax: 562-696-9285; civil fax: 8AM-4:30PM; 8AM-4:30PM (PST). *Misdemeanor, Civil Actions under $25,000, Eviction, Small Claims.*
www.lasuperiorcourt.org

General Information: Includes cities of Whittier, Santa Fe Springs, Pico Rivera, La Habra Heights plus unincorporated territory in the Whittier area including areas designated as Los Nietos and South Whittier. No probation reports released. Will not fax documents. Court makes copy: $.50 per page. Certification fee: $25 per doc plus copy fee. Payee: Los Angeles Superior Court. Personal checks accepted. Credit cards accepted. Prepayment required. Mail requests: SASE required.

Civil Name Search: Access: Mail, in person, online. Both court and visitors may perform in person name searches. Search fee: $15.00 per name if search exceeds 10 minutes. Civil records on computer from 1991, index files from 1983. Records destroyed after 10 years. Note: Civil and small claims in basement. Mail turnaround time 2 days. **See the Online Accesss Note at the start of this county.**

Criminal Name Search: Access: Mail, in person, online. Only the court performs in person name searches; visitors may not. Search fee: $15.00 per name if search exceeds 10 minutes. Required to search: name, years to search; also helpful: DOB. Criminal records computerized since 1987. Note: Criminal in Rm 100. Mail turnaround time 2 days. **See the Online Accesss Note at the start of this county.**

Los Angeles Superior Court - Probate Department 111 N Hill St, Rm 258, Los Angeles, CA 90012; 213-974-5471; 8:15AM-4:30PM (PST). *Probate.*
www.lasuperiorcourt.org/probate/

General Information: Case summaries-notes available free at website; search by case number. Also, probate for current cases in Central Dist. including Burbank, Compton, Glendale, Lancaster, Long Beach, Pasadena, Pomona, San Fernando, Santa Monica, Torrance District Courts.

Catalina Courthouse 215 Summer Ave, Avalon, CA 90712; 310-510-0026; fax: 310-514-0314; 8:15AM-4:30PM (PST). *Traffic Juvenile.*
www.lasuperiorcourt.org

General Information: Juvenile matters are confidential. Court will give out information or to even verify that a case exists because it is a misdemeanor to do so.

Los Angeles County provides online access to all courts as follows:

Civil: There are two searches at https://www.lasuperiorcourt.org/onlineservices/LAECourtOnlineIndex.htm. One may do a free civil party name search. One may also purchase civil case document images. A name search is $4.75. The flat fee for each case file is $7.50 for first 10 pages, then $.07 each add'l page. Records back to 1991 (92 is Small Claims).

Criminal: Search felony & misdemeanor defendant index at https://www.lasuperiorcourt.org/OnlineServices/criminalindex/index.asp. Search fee is $4 to $4.75 based on volume. If available, counts, current charges, disposition and disposition dates are shown.

Madera County

Superior Court 209 W Yosemite Ave, Madera, CA 93637; 559-675-7944; criminal phone: 559-675-7734; civil phone: 559-675-7995; probate phone: 559-675-7795; criminal fax: 559-675-7618; civil fax: 8AM-4PM; 8AM-4PM (PST). *Felony, Civil, Probate, Eviction, Small Claims.* www.madera.courts.ca.gov

General Information: The Superior and Municipal courts located in the City of Madera have combined into a consolidated court. There is a countywide index of criminal records. No adoption, juvenile, medical, probation or sealed records released. Will not fax documents. Court makes copy: $.50 per page. Certification fee: $25 per doc plus copy fee. Payee: Madera Superior Court. Only business checks accepted. No credit cards accepted. Prepayment required. Mail requests: SASE required.

Civil Name Search: Access: Mail, fax, in person. Both court and visitors may perform in person name searches. Search fee: $15.00 per name if search exceeds 10 minutes. Civil records on microfiche, archived and index file from 1893. Mail turnaround time 2-3 weeks. Civil PAT goes back to 2003.

Criminal Name Search: Access: Mail, fax, in person. Both court and visitors may perform in person name searches. Search fee: $15.00 per name if search exceeds 10 minutes. Required to search: name, years to search, DOB, signed release. Criminal records on microfiche, archived and index file from 1980. Note: The card index, which goes back further than 2003, is viewable by "professionals" - such as public record researchers and attorneys. Mail turnaround time 2-3 weeks. Criminal PAT goes back to 2003.

Sierra Division - Superior Court 40601 Road 274, Bass Lake, CA 93604; 559-642-3235; fax: 559-642-3445; 8AM-4PM (PST). *Felony, Misdemeanor, Civil Actions, Eviction, Small Claims, Probate, Family.* www.madera.courts.ca.gov

General Information: There is a countywide index database of court records. No adoption, juvenile, medical, probation or sealed records released. Will not fax documents. Court makes copy: $.50 per page. Certification fee: $25 per doc plus copy fee. Payee: Madera Superior Court. Personal checks accepted. No credit cards accepted. Prepayment required. Mail requests: SASE required.

Civil Name Search: Access: Mail, in person. Both court and visitors may perform in person name searches. Search fee: $15.00 per name if search exceeds 10 minutes. Civil records on computer back to 3/30/03 prior on index cards. Will only search back 7 years. Mail turnaround time 1-2 weeks. Public use terminal available.

Criminal Name Search: Access: Mail, in person. Both court and visitors may perform in person name searches. Search fee: $15.00 per name if search exceeds 10 minutes. Required to search: name, years to search; also helpful: DOB. Criminal records computerized from 3/30/03 prior on index cards for criminal. Mail turnaround time 1-2 weeks. Public use terminal available.

Traffic Division - Superior Court 209 W. Yosemite Ave, Madera, CA 93637; 559-673-2662; fax: 559-675-7618; 8AM-4PM (PST). *Misdemeanor Traffic, Infraction Traffic.* www.madera.courts.ca.gov

General Information: Formerly located at 141 S 2nd. St. in Chowchilla. Now at the main courthouse in Madera.

Marin County

Superior Court PO Box 4988, San Rafael, CA 94913-4988; 415-444-7080; criminal phone: 415-444-7070; civil phone: 415-444-7040;; 8:30AM-3:30PM (PST). *Felony, Misdemeanor, Civil, Eviction/Family, Small Claims, Probate.* www.marincourt.org/

General Information: No adoption, paternity, sole custody, juvenile, medical, probation or sealed records released. Will not fax documents. Court makes copy: $.50 per page. Certification fee: $25 per doc plus copy fee. Payee: Marin County Superior Court. Personal checks accepted. Out-of-state checks not accepted. Write "not to exceed $x.xx" on check. Call first. Major credit cards accepted. Prepayment required. Mail requests: SASE required.

Civil Name Search: Access: Mail, in person, online. Both court and visitors may perform in person name searches. Search fee: $15.00 per name if search exceeds 10 minutes. Required to search: name, years to search, case number if known. Civil cases indexed by defendant, plaintiff. Civil records on computer from 1986, on microfiche from 1973 to 1985, archived from 1900 to 1972, on reel from 1900. Mail turnaround time 3 weeks. Civil PAT goes back to 1980. Access to the court index back to the 1970s is free at www.marincourt.org/PublicIndex/Default.aspx or http://public.marincourt.org/publicindex/default.aspx.

Criminal Name Search: Access: Mail, in person, online. Both court and visitors may perform in person name searches. Search fee: $15.00 per name if search exceeds 10 minutes. Required to search: name, years to search, case number if known. Criminal records computerized from 1986, on microfiche from 1973 to 1985, archived from 1900 to 1972, on reel from

1900. Mail turnaround time 3 weeks. Criminal PAT goes back to 1976. Online access to the criminal index is the same as civil.

Mariposa County

Superior Court PO Box 28, 5088 Bullion St, Mariposa, CA 95338; 209-966-2005; criminal phone: 209-966-2005; civil phone: 209-966-6599; probate phone: 209-966-6599; fax: 209-742-6860; 8:30AM-3PM (PST). *Felony, Misdemeanor, Civil, Small Claims, Eviction, Probate.* www.mariposacourt.org/

General Information: Public access terminals are offsite at Self Help Ctr. But the case number is needed to access the index, one may not do a name search. No adoption, juvenile, medical, probation or sealed records released. Will fax documents for no add'l fee. Court makes copy: $.50 per page. Certification fee: $25 per doc plus copy fee' exemplification- $20.00. Payee: Mariposa Superior Court. Personal checks accepted. No credit cards accepted. Prepayment required. Mail requests: SASE required.

Civil Name Search: Access: Mail, fax, in person. Only the court performs in person name searches; visitors may not. Search fee: $15.00 per name if search exceeds 10 minutes. Include fax return number with any faxed requests. Required to search: name, DOB, years to search. Civil cases indexed by defendant, plaintiff. Civil records on computer from 1999, on microfiche and index files from 1800s. Note: 5 name limit at counter. Mail turnaround time 5 days.

Criminal Name Search: Access: Mail, fax, in person. Only the court performs in person name searches; visitors may not. Search fee: $15.00 per name if search exceeds 10 minutes. Required to search: name, DOB, years to search. Note: 5 name limit at counter. Mail turnaround time 5 days.

Mendocino County

Superior Court 100 N State St, Ukiah, CA 95482; 707-468-2000; criminal phone: 707-463-4661; civil phone: 707-463-4481; probate phone: 707-468-2005; criminal fax: 707-463-4655; civil fax: 8:30AM-4PM; 8:30AM-4PM (PST). *Felony, Civil Actions over $25,000, Probate.* www.mendocino.courts.ca.gov

General Information: Anderson Branch/Boonville closed permanently 6/26/2003. The Willits Branch closed 0/01/2010 and case files are here. Most of Anderson Judicial District merged into Ukiah. MP marker 13.6 on Highway 128 is the new western district boundary. No adoption, juvenile, medical, probation or sealed records released. Will not fax documents. Court makes copy: $.50 per page. Certification fee: $25 per doc plus copy fee. Payee: Mendocino Superior Court. Personal checks accepted. Prepayment required. Mail requests: SASE required.

Civil Name Search: Access: Mail, in person, online. Both court and visitors may perform in person name searches. Search fee: $15.00 per name if search exceeds 10 minutes. Civil records on computer from 1990s, on microfilm from 1800 to 1997. Mail turnaround time 1-2 weeks. Public use terminal available. Search index at www.mendocino.courts.ca.gov/caseindex.html. Online index may be up to 2 months behind.

Criminal Name Search: Access: Mail, in person, online. Search fee: $15.00 per name if search exceeds 10 minutes. Required to search: name, years to search. Criminal records computerized from 1990s, on microfilm from 1800 to 1997. Mail turnaround time -12 weeks. Public use terminal available, crim records go back to same as civil. Search index at www.mendocino.courts.ca.gov/caseindex.html. Online index may be up to 2 months behind. Online results show middle initial.

Ten Mile Branch - Superior Court 700 S Franklin St, Fort Bragg, CA 95437; 707-964-3192; fax: 707-961-2611; 8:30AM-4PM (PST). *Felony, Misdemeanor, Civil Actions, Eviction, Small Claims.* www.mendocino.courts.ca.gov/fortbragg.html

General Information: Records of the Port Arena Branch are now located here at Ft Bragg. No juvenile or probation records released. Will not fax documents. Court makes copy: $.50 per page. Certification fee: $25 per doc plus copy fee. Payee: Superior Court. Personal checks accepted. No credit cards accepted. Prepayment required. Mail requests: SASE required.

Civil Name Search: Access: Mail, in person, online. Only the court performs in person name searches; visitors may not. Search fee: $15.00 per case if search exceeds 10 minutes. Will only search back 10 years. Paper record s maintained on to 1989, computerized since. Mail turnaround time 2 weeks. Search index at www.mendocino.courts.ca.gov/caseindex.html. Not all indices are online.

Criminal Name Search: Access: Mail, in person, online. Only the court performs in person name searches; visitors may not. Search fee: $15.00 per case if search exceeds 10 minutes. Will only search back 10 years. Required to search: name, years to search, DOB. Criminal records go back to 1990; on computer back 1995. Mail turnaround time 2 weeks. Search index at www.mendocino.courts.ca.gov/caseindex.html. A separate search must be performed for records prior to 2000. Online results show middle initial.

Anderson Branch in Boonville - Superior Cour,
Closed: This court is closed. Records transferred to Ukiah. Everything east of Mile Post marker 13.6 on Highway 128 is now in Ukiah; everything west is in Ft Bragg.

rena Branch - Superior Court.
Merged Effective June 30, 2003, operations for the Arena Branch of the Superior Court was merged with the Ten Mile Court in Fort Bragg.

Willits Branch - Superior Court
Closed: Court closed 01/01/2010. Case files at main court in Ukiah.

Merced County

Superior Court 2260 N St, Merced, CA 95340; criminal phone: 209-725-4113; civil phone: 209-725-4111; probate phone: 209-725-4117; criminal fax: 209-725-4114; civil fax: 8AM-4PM; 8AM-4PM (PST). *Felony, Misdemenaor, Civil Actions over $25,000, Probate.*
www.merced.courts.ca.gov/
General Information: No juvenile nor adoption records released. Court makes copy: $.50 per page. Certification fee: $25.00 per doc plus copy fee. Payee: Merced County Superior Court. Business checks and money orders accepted. No credit cards accepted. Prepayment required. Mail requests: SASE required.
Civil Name Search: Access: Mail, in person. Both court and visitors may perform in person name searches. Search fee: $15.00 per name if search exceeds 10 minutes. Mail turnaround time 3-4 weeks. Civil PAT goes back to 1979.
Criminal Name Search: Access: Mail, in person. Both court and visitors may perform in person name searches. Search fee: $15.00 per name if search exceeds 10 minutes. Required to search: name, years to search. Felony cases prior to 1998 are on microfiche. Mail turnaround time 3 weeks. Criminal PAT goes back to 1986.

Los Banos Division - Superior Court 445 "I" St, Los Banos, CA 93635; 209-725-4124; fax: 209-725-4125; 8AM-4PM (PST). *Misdemeanor, Civil Actions under $25,000, Eviction, Small Claims.*
www.merced.courts.ca.gov/
General Information: This court was combined with the old Dos Palos and Gustine Superior Courts. No juvenile or probation records released. Will fax documents to local or toll free line. Court makes copy: $.50 per page. Certification fee: $25.00 per doc plus copy fee; exemplification is $20.00. Payee: Merced Superior Court. Personal checks accepted. No credit cards accepted. Prepayment required. Mail requests: SASE required.
Civil Name Search: Access: Mail, in person. Only the court performs in person name searches; visitors may not. Search fee: $15.00 per name if search exceeds 10 minutes. Civil records on microfiche. Mail turnaround time 2-3 days.
Criminal Name Search: Access: Mail, in person. Only the court performs in person name searches; visitors may not. Search fee: $15.00 per name if search exceeds 10 minutes. Required to search: name, years to search; also helpful: DOB. Criminal records on microfiche. Mail turnaround time 2-3 days.

Merced Superior Court Civil Limited 627 W 21st St, Merced, CA 95340; 209-725-4109; fax: 209-725-4110; 8AM-4PM (PST). *Civil Actions under $25,000, Eviction, Small Claims.*
www.merced.courts.ca.gov/
General Information: Deliveries to 670 W 22nd St, Rm 15. Court makes copy: $.50 per page. Certification fee: $25 per doc plus copy fee. Payee: Merced Superior Court. No credit cards accepted. Prepayment required. Mail requests: SASE required.
Civil Name Search: Access: Mail, in person. No in-person civil name searches permitted at this court. Search fee: $15.00 per name if search exceeds 10 minutes. Civil records on microfiche, computer. Mail turnaround time 2-3 days.

Modoc County

Superior Court 205 S East St, Alturas, CA 96101; criminal phone: 530-233-6515; civil phone: 530-233-6516; fax: 530-233-6500; 8:30AM-5PM (PST). *Felony, Misdemeanor, Civil, Small Claims, Eviction, Probate.*
www.modocsuperiorcourt.ca.gov/
General Information: No adoption, juvenile, medical, probation or sealed records released. Will fax documents to local or toll-free number. Court makes copy: $.50 per page. Self serve copy: $.25 per page. Certification fee: $25 per doc plus copy fee. Payee: Modoc Superior Courts. Personal checks accepted. Visa/MC accepted. Prepayment required. Mail requests: SASE required.
Civil Name Search: Access: Mail, in person. Only the court performs in person name searches; visitors may not. Search fee: $15.00 per name if search exceeds 10 minutes. Required to search: name, years to search, DOB. Civil cases indexed by plaintiff. Civil records in index file from 1874, computerized since 7/25/95. Mail turnaround time 1-2 weeks.

Criminal Name Search: Access: Fax, mail, in person. Only the court performs in person name searches; visitors may not. Search fee: $15.00 per name if search exceeds 10 minutes. Required to search: name, years to search, DOB. Criminal records computerized since 1991. Mail turnaround time 1-2 weeks.

Mono County

Mammoth Lakes Division - Superior Court PO Box 1037, Mammoth Lakes, CA 93546; 760-924-5444; fax: 760-924-5419; 8:30AM-4PM (PST). *Felony, Misdemeanor, Civil, Eviction, Small Claims.*
www.monocourt.org/
General Information: This court performs all record searches for the Bridgeport Branch. No juvenile or probation records released. Will fax documents to local or toll-free number. Court makes copy: $.50 per page. Certification fee: $25 per doc plus $1.00 per page copy fee. Payee: Mono Superior Court. Personal checks accepted. No credit cards accepted. Prepayment required. Mail requests: SASE required.
Civil Name Search: Access: Mail, in person. Only the court performs in person name searches; visitors may not. Search fee: $15.00 per name if search exceeds 10 minutes. Civil index on cards. Will only search back 10 years. Mail turnaround time 1 week.
Criminal Name Search: Access: Mail, in person. Only the court performs in person name searches; visitors may not. Search fee: $15.00 per name if search exceeds 10 minutes. Required to search: name, years to search, DOB. Criminal records computerized from 1989, index cards prior. Will search back 20 years, but case file may not be available after 7 years,. Mail turnaround time 1 week.

Superior Court - Bridgeport Branch PO Box 537, St Highway 395 & School St, Bridgeport, CA 93517; 760-932-5239; fax: 760-932-7520; 8:30AM-5PM (PST). *Felony, Misdemeanor, Civil, Small Claims, Probate.*
www.monocourt.org/
General Information: All record searches are directed to the court in Mammoth Lakes. There is only 1 staff person at this court. Older records are stored in another building which is hard to access.

Monterey County

Superior Court - Monterey Division 1200 Aguajito Rd, 2nd Fl, Monterey, CA 93940; 831-647-5800; criminal phone: x3002; civil phone: x3008;; 8AM-4PM; make file requests before 3:30PM (PST). *Civil Limited/Unlimited, Probate, Small Claims, Family Law.*
www.monterey.courts.ca.gov
General Information: This court holds the civil records from the city of Salinas. Criminal records for Monterey are held in Salinas. No juvenile or probation records released. Will not fax documents. Court makes copy: $.50 per page. Certification fee: $25 per doc plus copy fee; exemplification fee is $20. Payee: Superior Court. Personal checks accepted. No credit cards accepted. Prepayment required. Mail requests: SASE required.
Civil Name Search: Access: Mail, in person. Visitors must perform in person searches themselves. Search fee: $15.00 per name. Some civil records computerized since 7/03, on microfiche from 1973, index books prior. Mail turnaround time 2-3 weeks. Public use terminal has civil records back to 1992. Terminal results may also show SSN. Terminals in the Public Viewing Room. Access court data free at https://www.justicepartners.monterey.courts.ca.gov/Public/JPPublicIndex.aspx, Search calendars at https://www.justicepartners.monterey.courts.ca.gov/Public/JPPublicCalendarSearch.aspx, When searching court record index online there could be missing identifiers, and computer systems are not always up-to-date, and do not have as wide a date range as when searching onsite.

Superior Court - Salinas Division 240 Church St, Rm 318, Salinas, CA 93901; 831-775-5400; criminal phone: 831-775-5400 x302;; 8AM-4PM (PST). *Felony, Misdemeanor.*
www.monterey.courts.ca.gov
General Information: All criminal records are filed at the Salinas courthouse; main court administration is here. All civil, probate, and family law cases are files at the Monterey courthouse. No adoption, juvenile, medical, probation or sealed records released. Will not fax documents. Court makes copy: $.50 per page. Certification fee: $25 per doc plus copy fee. Payee: Monterey Superior Court. Personal checks and credit cards accepted. Add'l fees apply to credit card payments. Prepayment required. Mail requests: SASE required.
Criminal Name Search: Access: Mail, in person, online. Both court and visitors may perform in person name searches. Search fee: $15.00 per name if search exceeds 10 minutes. Required to search: name, years to search; also helpful: DOB. Felony records computerized since 1998, on microfiche to 1940s. Misdemeanor records computerized since 1992, on microfiche since 1986. Mail turnaround time 2 weeks. Public use terminal has crim records back to 1990. Access court data free at https://www.justicepartners.monterey.courts.ca.gov/Public/JPPublicIndex.aspx, Search calendars at https://www.justicepartners.monterey.courts.ca.gov/Public/JPPublicCale

ndarSearch.aspx. When searching court record index online there could be missing identifiers, and computer systems are not always up-to-date, and do not have as wide a date range as when searching onsite. Online results show middle initial, DOB.

Superior Court - King City Division PO Box 647, 250 Franciscan Way, King City, CA 93930; 831-386-5200;; 9:30AM-4PM (PST). *Felony, Misdemeanor, Eviction, Small Claims Limited, Traffic.*
www.monterey.courts.ca.gov
General Information: Encompasses the cities of King City, Greenfield, Soledad, areas south of King City to the San Luis Obispo County line. For Civil and add'l small claims, contact Monterey Div. No probation reports released. Will not fax documents. Court makes copy: $.50 per page. Certification fee: $25 per doc plus copy fee. Payee: Monterey County Courts. Personal checks accepted. Visa, AmEx cards accepted; add'l fee charged for credit card. Prepayment required. Mail requests: SASE required.
Civil Name Search: Access: Mail, in person, online. Both court and visitors may perform in person name searches. Search fee: $15.00 per name if search exceeds 10 minutes. Civil records on computer from 1992, index files from 1983. Records destroyed after 10 years. Mail turnaround time 2-4 weeks. Access court data free at https://www.justicepartners.monterey.courts.ca.gov/Public/JPPublicIndex.aspx, Search calendars at https://www.justicepartners.monterey.courts.ca.gov/Public/JPPublicCalendarSearch.aspx,
Criminal Name Search: Access: Mail, in person, online. Both court and visitors may perform in person name searches. Search fee: $15.00 per name if search exceeds 10 minutes. Required to search: name, years to search; also helpful: DOB. Criminal records computerized from 1992, index files from 1983. Records destroyed after 10 years. Mail turnaround time 2-4 week. Access court data free at https://www.justicepartners.monterey.courts.ca.gov/Public/JPPublicIndex.aspx, Calendar search- same as civil, above. When searching court record index online there could be missing identifiers, and computer systems are not always up-to-date, and do not have as wide a date range as when searching onsite. Online results show middle initial.

Superior Court - Marina Division 3180 Del Monte Blvd, Marina, CA 93933; 831-883-5300; fax: 831-883-5306; 8AM-4PM (PST). *Traffic.*
www.monterey.courts.ca.gov
General Information: Access court data free at https://www.justicepartners.monterey.courts.ca.gov/Public/JPPublicIndex.aspx,

Napa County

Superior Court - Civil 825 Brown St, Napa, CA 94559; 707-299-1140-records; civil phone: 707-299-1130; probate phone: 707-299-1130; fax: 707-253-4229; 8AM-5PM (PST). *Civil, Eviction, Small Claims, Probate.*
www.napa.courts.ca.gov
General Information: No adoption, juvenile, medical, probation or sealed records released. Will not fax documents. Court makes copy: $.50 per page. Certification fee: $25 per doc plus copy fee. Payee: Napa Superior Court. Personal checks and credit cards accepted. Prepayment required. Mail requests: SASE required.
Civil Name Search: Access: Mail, in person. Both court and visitors may perform in person name searches. Search fee: $15.00 per name if search exceeds 10 minutes. Civil records on computer since 1989; prior records on index books or microfilm back to 1800s. Mail turnaround time 2 weeks. Public use terminal has civil records back to 1989. Access to tentative rulings is online free at www.napa.courts.ca.gov/Civil/civil_tentative.asp. These only go back about 1 week. Civil calendars are also online.

Superior Court - Criminal 1111 3rd St, Napa, CA 94559; 707-299-1180; fax: 707-253-4673; 8AM-5PM (PST). *Felony, Misdemeanor.*
www.napa.courts.ca.gov
General Information: Small Claims phone- 707-299-1130. No adoption, juvenile, medical, probation or sealed records released. Court makes copy: $.50 per page. Self serve copy: same. Certification fee: $25 per doc plus copy fee. Payee: Napa Superior Court. Personal checks accepted. Visa/MC accepted - requested for mail requests. Prepayment required. Mail requests: SASE required for all mail requests.
Criminal Name Search: Access: Mail, fax, in person, online. Both court and visitors may perform in person name searches. Search fee: $15.00 per name if search exceeds 10 minutes. Required to search: name, years to search, DOB; also helpful: address. Records on computer back to 1990. Mail turnaround time 2 weeks. Public use terminal has crim records back to 1990. Online access (BUT no name search) to criminal and traffic index is at https://secure.napa.courts.ca.gov/UnifiedLookup/UnifiedCaseLookup.html. Results return name and case number.

Nevada County

Superior Court - Civil 201 Church St, #5, Nevada City, CA 95959; 530-265-1294; probate phone: 530-265-1293; fax: 530-478-5627; 8AM-4PM (PST). *Civil, Eviction, Small Claims, Family.*
www.nevadacountycourts.com/
General Information: Phone number for Family Law is 530-265-1293. No probation reports released. Will not fax documents. Court makes copy: $.50 per page. Certification fee: $25 per doc plus copy fee. Payee: Nevada County Superior Court. Personal checks accepted. No credit cards accepted. Prepayment required. Mail requests: SASE required.
Civil Name Search: Access: Mail, in person, online. Both court and visitors may perform in person name searches. Search fee: $15.00 per name if search exceeds 10 minutes. Required to search: name or case number. Civil cases indexed by defendant, plaintiff. Civil records on computer back to 1990. Cases with dispositions available on microfilm in most cases, also some Limited Civil, Small Claims. Mail turnaround time 5 days. Public use terminal has civil records back to 1990. Access to case calendar is free at www.court.co.nevada.ca.us/cgi/dba/casecal/db.cgi.

Superior Court - Criminal 201 Church St, #7, Nevada City, CA 95959; 530-265-1311; fax: 530-478-1938; 8AM-4PM (PST). *Felony, Misdemeanor.*
www.nevadacountycourts.com/
General Information: No adoption, paternity, juvenile, medical, probation or sealed records released. Will fax documents to local or toll free line. Court makes copy: $.50 per page. Certification fee: $25.00 per doc plus copy fee. Payee: Nevada County Superior Courts. Personal checks accepted. No credit cards accepted. Prepayment required. Mail requests: SASE required.
Criminal Name Search: Access: Phone, mail, in person, online. Only the court performs in person name searches; visitors may not. Search fee: $15.00 per name if search exceeds 10 minutes. Required to search: name, years to search; also helpful: DOB. Criminal records computerized from 1987, felony only prior to 1987; felony in books back to 1800s. Mail turnaround time 2 weeks. Access to case calendar is free at www.court.co.nevada.ca.us/cgi/dba/casecal/db.cgi.

Truckee Branch - Superior Court 10075 Levon Ave, #301, Truckee, CA 96161; criminal phone: 530-582-7835; civil phone: 530-582-7835; fax: 530-582-7875; 8AM-4PM (PST). *Misdemeanor, Civil, Eviction, Small Claims.* www.nevadacountycourts.com/
General Information: No probation reports released. Will not fax documents. Court makes copy: $.50 per page. Certification fee: $25 per doc plus copy fee. Payee: Superior Court. Personal checks accepted. No credit cards accepted. Prepayment required. Mail requests: SASE required.
Civil Name Search: Access: Mail, in person, online. Both court and visitors may perform in person name searches. Search fee: $15.00 per name if search exceeds 10 minutes. Civil records on computer from 1991, index files from 1983. Records destroyed after 10 years. Mail turnaround time 1 week. Civil PAT goes back to 1989. Access to case calendar is free at http://nevadacountycourts.com/cgi/dba/casecal/db.cgi.
Criminal Name Search: Access: Mail, in person, online. Both court and visitors may perform in person name searches. Search fee: $15.00 per name if search exceeds 10 minutes. Required to search: name, years to search. Criminal records computerized from 1991, index files from 1983. Records destroyed after 10 years. Mail turnaround time 1 week. Criminal PAT goes back to 1992. Access to case calendar is free at http://nevadacountycourts.com/cgi/dba/casecal/db.cgi.

Orange County

Superior Court - Civil 700 Civic Center Dr W, Santa Ana, CA 92701; 657-622-5300; fax: 714-834-5589; 8AM-4PM (PST). *Civil Actions, Small Claims.*
www.occourts.org
General Information: This court handles civil actions over $25,000 countywide, but holds only limited civil and small claims cases for this central jurisdiction venue (Santa Ana area). No adoption, juvenile, medical, probation or sealed records released. Will not fax out documents. Court makes copy: $.50 per page. Certification fee: $25 per doc plus copy fee. Payee: Clerk of the Court. Personal checks accepted. Visa/MC accepted. Prepayment required. Mail requests: SASE required.
Civil Name Search: Access: Mail, in person, online. Both court and visitors may perform in person name searches. Search fee: $15.00 per name if search exceeds 10 minutes. Civil records on computer from mid 1980s, partial prior to 1986, microfiche and index file from 1900s. Note: This court's fax back service fee is $1.00 per page. Mail turnaround time 1-2 weeks. Public use terminal has civil records back to 9/2003. Access civil case index and calendars free at www.occourts.org/online-services/case-access/. Family court calendars also shown. Civil, small claims, probate cases index for the county can be purchased on CD; index goes back to 12/31/01 or can be purchased on monthly basis.

Superior Court - Criminal Operations 700 Civic Center Dr W, Santa Ana, CA 92702; 657-622-6878; criminal phone: 877-872-2122;; 7:30AM-5PM (PST). *Felony, Misdemeanor.*
www.occourts.org

General Information: No adoption, juvenile, medical, probation or sealed records released. Will not fax documents. Court makes copy: $.50 per page. Certification fee: $25 per doc plus copy fee. Payee: Clerk of the Court. Personal checks accepted. Visa/MC accepted. Prepayment required. Mail requests: SASE required.

Criminal Name Search: Access: Mail, in person, online. Both court and visitors may perform in person name searches. Search fee: $15.00 per name if search exceeds 10 minutes. Required to search: name, years to search, DOB. Criminal records computerized from 1988, on microfiche and archived from 1966. Note: Dockets in storage may take add'l 5-6 days to retrieve. Mail turnaround time 1-2 weeks. Public use terminal has crim records back to 1995. 8 public access terminals available. Online access to criminal, traffic and calendars free at www.occourts.org/online-services/case-access/. Search results include dispositions, dismissals, sentences, and participants, but no DOB. Index rarely goes back beyond 2002. Also shows names, aliases, and Court True name. The case index can be purchased on CD; index goes back to 12/31/01 or can be purchased on monthly basis.

Central Orange County Superior Court - Limited Jurisdiction 700 Civic Ctr Dr West, Santa Ana, CA 92701; 657-622-7513; fax: 714-834-5589; 7:30AM-5PM (PST). *Misdemeanor, Civil Actions under $25,000, Eviction, Small Claims, Traffic.*
www.occourts.org

General Information: Includes cities of Santa Ana, Orange, Tustin and surrounding unincorporated territories including Cowan Heights, El Modena, Tustin Marine Air Base, Lemon Heights, Modjeska, Orange Park Acres, Silverado Canyon and Villa Park. No probation reports released. Will not fax documents. Court makes copy: $.50 per page. Certification fee: $15 per case number plus copy fee. Payee: Clerk of Court. Personal checks accepted. Credit cards accepted. Prepayment required. Mail requests: SASE required.

Civil Name Search: Access: Mail, in person, online. Both court and visitors may perform in person name searches. Search fee: $15.00 per name if search exceeds 10 minutes. Required to search: name, years to search, DOB. Civil cases indexed by defendant, plaintiff. Civil records on index files and microfiche from 1985. Records destroyed after 10 years. Mail turnaround time 2-4 days. Civil PAT goes back to 1995. Public access terminal is in Rm K107. Access civil case index and calendars free at www.occourts.org/online-services/case-access/. Family court calendars also shown. Civil, small claims, probate cases index for the county can be purchased on CD; index goes back to 12/31/01 or can be purchased on monthly basis.

Criminal Name Search: Access: Mail, in person, online. Both court and visitors may perform in person name searches. Search fee: $15.00 per name if search exceeds 10 minutes. Required to search: name, years to search, DOB. Criminal records on index files and microfiche from 1986; on computer since 1995. Records destroyed after 10 years. Mail turnaround time 2-4 days. Criminal PAT available. Public access terminal is in Rm K107. Online access to criminal, traffic and calendars free at www.occourts.org/online-services/case-access/. Search result includes dispositions, dismissals, sentences, and participants, but no DOB. Index rarely goes back beyond 2002. Also shows names, aliases, and Court True name. The case index can be purchased on CD; index goes back to 12/31/01 or can be purchased on monthly basis. Online results show middle initial.

Harbor - Laguna Hills Superior Court - Civil Division 23141 Moulton Pky, Laguna Hills, CA 92653; 657-622-8670; 7:30AM-5PM (PST). *Civil Actions under $25,000, Eviction, Small Claims.*
www.occourts.org/

General Information: Formerly known as South Orange, this includes Aliso Viejo, Capistrano Bch, Coto De Caza, Dana Pt, Laguna (various), Lake Forest, Mission Viejo, Rancho St. Margarita, San Clemente, San Juan Capistrano, Trabuco Canyon. No unlawful detainer records released for 60 days. Will not fax documents. Court makes copy: $.50 per page. Certification fee: $25 per doc plus copy fee. Payee: Clerk of Court. Personal checks accepted. Credit cards accepted. Prepayment required. Mail requests: SASE required.

Civil Name Search: Access: Mail, in person, online. Both court and visitors may perform in person name searches. Search fee: $15.00 per name if search exceeds 10 minutes. Civil records in index files and on microfiche back to 1987; on computer back to 2000. Mail turnaround time 2-3 days. Public use terminal has civil records back to 12/1989. Access civil case index and calendars free at www.occourts.org/online-services/case-access/. Family court calendars also shown. Civil, small claims, probate cases index for the county can be purchased on CD; index goes back to 12/31/01 or can be purchased on monthly basis.

Harbor - Newport Beach Superior Court Justice Center, 4601 Jamboree Rd, Newport Beach, CA 92660-2595; 657-622-5400; civil phone: 9657-622-8640; fax: 714-647-4850; 7:30AM-5PM (PST). *Misdemeanor, Civil Actions under $25,000, Eviction, Small Claims.*
www.occourts.org

General Information: Includes Balboa Island, Corona Del Mar, Costa Mesa, Newport Beach, Irvine, Santa Ana Heights, John Wayne/Orange Co Airport, Lido Isle and surrounding unincorporated areas. Mention issues about criminal division phone service to 714-834-7413. No probation reports nor police reports released. Court makes copy: $.50 per page. Certification fee: $25 per doc plus copy fee. Payee: Clerk of Court. Personal checks accepted; checks must be in-state and be imprinted with name and address. Major credit cards accepted. Prepayment required. Mail requests: SASE required.

Civil Name Search: Access: Mail, in person, online. Both court and visitors may perform in person name searches. Search fee: $15.00 per name if search exceeds 10 minutes. Required to search: name, years to search, DOB. Civil cases indexed by defendant, plaintiff. Civil records go back 10 years. Note: Court is closed third Wed of each month. Mail turnaround time 5-10 days. Civil PAT goes back to 1999. Access civil case index and calendars free at www.occourts.org/online-services/case-access/. Family court calendars also shown. Civil, small claims, probate cases can be purchased on CD; index goes back to 12/31/01 or can be purchased on monthly basis.

Criminal Name Search: Access: Mail, in person, online. Both court and visitors may perform in person name searches. Search fee: $15.00 per name if search exceeds 10 minutes. Required to search: name, years to search, DOB. Criminal records on computer go back 10 years; on microfiche -- felonies kept as long as 75 years, misdemeanors 5 years or more per Code 68152. Note: Court is closed third Wed of each month. Mail turnaround time 5-10 days. Criminal PAT goes back to 1999. Online access to criminal, traffic and calendars free at www.occourts.org/online-services/case-access/. Search results include dispositions, dismissals, sentences, and participants, but no DOB. Index rarely goes back beyond 2002. Also shows names, aliases, and Court True name. The case index can be purchased on CD; index goes back to 12/31/01 or can be purchased on monthly basis. Online results show middle initial.

Harbor Justice Center - Criminal Division 23141 Moulton Pkwy, Laguna Hills, CA 92653; 877-872-2122; fax: 714-647-4851; 7:30AM-5PM (PST). *Felony, Misdemeanor.*
www.occourts.org

General Information: Includes Capistrano Bch, Coto De Caza, Dana Pt, Laguna Hills, Laguna Niguel, Mission Viejo, Rancho St. Margarita, San Clemente, San Juan Capistrano, Trabuco Canyon. No probation report, unlawful detainer records released. Will fax out documents. Court makes copy: $.50 per page. Certification fee: $25 per doc plus copy fee. Payee: Clerk of Court. Personal checks accepted. Credit cards accepted. Prepayment required. Mail requests: SASE required.

Criminal Name Search: Access: Mail, in person, online. Both court and visitors may perform in person name searches. Search fee: $15.00 per name if search exceeds 10 minutes. Required to search: name, DOB. Criminal records on computer since 1987; prior records on books. Mail turnaround time 2-3 days. Online access to criminal, traffic and calendars free at www.occourts.org/online-services/case-access/. Search results include dispositions, dismissals, sentences, and participants, but no DOB. Index rarely goes back beyond 2002. Also shows names, aliases, and Court True name. The case index can be purchased on CD; index goes back to 12/31/01 or can be purchased on monthly basis. Online results show middle initial.

North Orange County Superior Court North Justice Court, 1275 N Berkeley Ave, PO Box 5000, Fullerton, CA 92832-0500; 657-622-5600; criminal phone: 877-872-2122; civil phone: 657-622-6641;; 7:30AM-5PM (PST). *Felony, Misdemeanor, Civil Actions under $25,000, Eviction, Small Claims.*
www.occourts.org/

General Information: Traffic phone- 877-872-2122. Includes the cities of Anaheim, Brea, Buena Park, Fullerton, La Habra, La Palma, Placentia, Yorba Linda and surrounding unincorporated area including Anaheim Hills. No probation reports or UD's for 60 days released. Will not fax documents. Court makes copy: $.50 per page. Certification fee: $25 per doc plus copy fee. Payee: Clerk of Court. Personal checks accepted with proper ID. Major credit cards accepted. Prepayment required. Mail requests: SASE required.

Civil Name Search: Access: Mail, in person, online. Both court and visitors may perform in person name searches. Search fee: $15.00 per name if search exceeds 10 minutes. Required to search: name, also helpful: years to search. Civil cases indexed by defendant, plaintiff. Records destroyed after 10 years. Mail turnaround time 5 days. Civil PAT available. Access the PAT at kiosk out front. Access civil case index and calendars free at www.occourts.org/online-services/case-access/. Family court calendars also shown. Civil, small claims, probate cases index for the county can be purchased on CD; index goes back to 12/31/01 or can be purchased on monthly basis.

Criminal Name Search: Access: Mail, in person, online. Both court and visitors may perform in person name searches. Search fee: $15.00 per name if search exceeds 10 minutes. Required to search: name, years to search, DOB. Misdemeanor records are destroyed after 5-7 years from date of conviction. Most felony records are retained for 75 years. Mail turnaround time 1-10 working days. Criminal PAT available. Access the PAT at kiosk out front. Online access to criminal, traffic and calendars free at www.occourts.org/online-services/case-access/. Search results include dispositions, dismissals, sentences, and participants, but no DOB. Index rarely goes back beyond 2002. Also shows names, aliases, and Court True name. The case index can be purchased on CD; index goes back to 12/31/01 or can be purchased on monthly basis. Online results show middle initial.

West Orange County Superior Court 8141 13th St, Westminster, CA 92683; 657-622-5900; civil phone: 657-622-8690; criminal fax: 714-647-4843; civil fax: 8AM-5PM; 8AM-5PM (PST). *Misdemeanor, Civil Actions under $25,000, Eviction, Small Claims.*

www.occourts.org

General Information: Includes the cities of Cypress, Fountain Valley, Garden Grove, Huntington Beach, Los Alamitos, Rossmore, Seal Beach, Stanton, Sunset Beach, Surfside, Westminster and adjoining and unincorporated territory. No probation reports, unlawful detainer (under 60 days old) records released. Will not fax documents. Court makes copy: $.50 per page. Certification fee: $25 per doc plus copy fee. Payee: Clerk of Court. Personal checks accepted. Credit cards accepted. Prepayment required. Mail requests: SASE required.

Civil Name Search: Access: Mail, in person, online. Both court and visitors may perform in person name searches. Search fee: $15.00 per name if search exceeds 10 minutes. Civil records on computer back to 1992, microfiche from 1983. Records destroyed after 10 years. Mail turnaround time 2 days. Public use terminal has civil records. Not all civil data on terminal; some restrictions. Access civil case index and calendars free at www.occourts.org/online-services/case-access/. Family court calendars also shown. Civil, small claims, probate cases index for the county can be purchased on CD; index goes back to 12/31/01 or can be purchased on monthly basis.

Criminal Name Search: Access: Mail, in person, online. Both court and visitors may perform in person name searches. Search fee: $15.00 per name if search exceeds 10 minutes. Required to search: name, years to search, DOB. Criminal records computerized from 1996, microfiche from 1983. Most misdemeanor records destroyed after 5 years. Mail turnaround time approx. 4 days. Online access to criminal, traffic and calendars free atwww.occourts.org/online-services/case-access/. Search results include dispositions, dismissals, sentences, and participants, but no DOB. Index rarely goes back beyond 2002. Also shows names, aliases, and Court True name. The case index can be purchased on CD; index goes back to 12/31/01 or can be purchased on monthly basis.

Orange County Probate Court 341 The City Dr, Lamoreaux Justice Center, Orange, CA 92868; 657-622-5500; 8AM-5PM (PST). *Probate.*

www.occourts.org/directory/probate/

General Information: Jurisdiction includes juvenile, family law, and mental health filings. Search free at www.occourts.org/online-services/case-access/.

Placer County

Superior Court - Civil PO Box 619072, Roseville, CA 95661-9072; 530-745-2210-info; 916-408-6000;; 8AM-3PM (9AM on some W) (PST). *Civil, Eviction, Small Claims, Probate.*

www.placer.courts.ca.gov/

General Information: The $5.00 computer search by mail request at this office gives access to all county court record types including criminal. Physical address is 10820 Justice Center Dr. No adoption, juvenile, medical, paternity, probation or sealed records released. Will fax documents for fee. Court makes copy: $.50 per page. Certification fee: $25 per doc plus copy fee. Payee: Clerk of the Court. Personal checks accepted. Major credit cards accepted in person only. Prepayment required. Mail requests: SASE required.

Civil Name Search: Access: Mail, in person, online. Both court and visitors may perform in person name searches. Search fee: $15.00 per name if search exceeds 10 minutes. Civil records on computer from 1992, on microfiche from 1974, archived and index file from 1800s. Note: Records filed at the Auburn court are either at this court or in Tahoe City. Mail turnaround time 4-6 weeks. Public use terminal has civil records back to 1992. An online index search is available at www.placer.courts.ca.gov/case-search.html for cases back to 1999. Data is updated once a week.

Superior Court - Criminal 10820 Justice Center Dr, P.O. Box 619072, Roseville, CA 95678; 916-408-6000; 8AM-3PM (PST). *Felony, Misdemeanor.*

www.placer.courts.ca.gov/

General Information: Includes Auburn, Penryn, Newcastle, Bowman, Colfax, Weimar, Alta, Dutch Flat, Loomis -- Roseville, Rocklin, Lincoln criminal as of 12/8/97. Has most all county criminal records except Tahoe Department 14. No probation reports or copies of warrants released. Will not fax documents. Court makes copy: $.50 per page. Self serve copy: same. Certification fee: $25 per doc plus copy fee. Payee: Clerk of the Court. Personal checks accepted. Prepayment required. Mail requests: SASE required.

Criminal Name Search: Access: Mail, in person, online. Both court and visitors may perform in person name searches. Search fee: $15.00 per name if search exceeds 10 minutes. Required to search: name, years to search, DOB. Criminal Records indexed on computer back to 1992; felonies back to 1999; records go back 10 years. Note: A felony name search here includes all of Placer County computer system records, including the Tahoe Court felony cases. Mail turnaround time 2 weeks. Public use terminal has crim records back to mid-1999. An online index search is available at www.placer.courts.ca.gov/case-search.html for cases back to 1999. Data is updated once a week.

Tahoe Division - Superior Court PO Box 5669, 2501 N Lake Blvd, Tahoe City, CA 96145; 530-584-3460; criminal phone: 530-584-3463; civil phone: 530-584-3464; fax: 530-584-3471; 8AM-3PM (PST). *Felony (Limited), Misdemeanor, Civil, Eviction, Small Claims, Traffic, Probate.*

www.placer.courts.ca.gov/

General Information: This court does all areas of law (including felony prelims and guilty pleas, adoptions and out-of-custody). No probation reports released. Will not fax documents. Court makes copy: $.50 per page. Certification fee: $25 per doc plus copy fee. Payee: Clerk of Court. Personal checks accepted. Write "not to exceed $x.xx" on check. Major credit cards accepted if in person. Prepayment required. Mail requests: SASE required.

Civil Name Search: Access: Mail, in person, online. Only the court performs in person name searches; visitors may not. Search fee: $15.00 per name. Required to search: name, years to search, DOB. Civil cases indexed by defendant, plaintiff. Civil records computerized since 1999, previous on index cards. Note: Will accept fax search requests under agreement. Records filed at the Auburn court are either here or in Roseville. Mail turnaround time 1 week. Public access terminal only available in Roseville court. An online index search is available at www.placer.courts.ca.gov/case-search.html for cases back to 1999.

Criminal Name Search: Access: Mail, in person, online. Only the court performs in person name searches; visitors may not. Search fee: $15.00 per name. Required to search: name, years to search, DOB. Criminal records indexed on cards. Will only search back 10 years; computerized records since 1999. Note: Will accept fax search requests under agreement. A felony name search here includes all of Placer County computer system records. Mail turnaround time 1 week. Public access terminal only available in Roseville court. An online index search is available at www.placer.courts.ca.gov/case-search.html for cases back to 1999. Data is updated once a week.

Lincoln Division - Superior Court

General Information: This Lincoln Division is now fully consolidated with the Roseville Court. All traffic cases have been transferred to Roseville custody.

Roseville Division - Superior Court PO Box 619072, 10820 Justice Center Dr (95678), Roseville, CA 95661-9072; 916-408-6000; 8AM-3PM (PST). *Traffic.* www.placer.courts.ca.gov/

General Information: This court holds the records for the Foresthill Division Court which has closed, also Lincoln Court Traffic only.

Plumas County

Superior Court 520 Main St, Rm 104, Quincy, CA 95971; 530-283-6232; civil phone: 530-283-6305; fax: 530-283-6415; 8AM-4PM (PST). *Felony, Misdemeanor, Civil, Small Claims, Probate.*

http://plumascourt.ca.gov

General Information: Telephone hours are 8:30 AM to 4PM. This is the county seat. No probation reports, financial statements or juvenile released. Will fax documents, turnaround is 3-4 days. Court makes copy: $.50 per page. Certification fee: $25 per doc plus copy fee. Payee: Plumas Superior Court. Personal checks accepted. No credit cards accepted. Prepayment required. Mail requests: SASE required.

Civil Name Search: Access: Phone, fax, mail, in person. Only the court performs in person name searches; visitors may not. Search fee: $15.00 per name if search exceeds 10 minutes. Civil records on computer from 1993, archived from 1980, index file from 1850. Mail turnaround time 3-4 days.

Criminal Name Search: Access: Mail, fax, in person. Only the court performs in person name searches; visitors may not. Search fee: $15.00 per name if search exceeds 10 minutes. Required to search: name, years to search, DOB; also, signed release if juvenile. Criminal records indexed on computer back to 1989. Mail turnaround time 3-4 days.

Chester Branch - Superior Court PO Box 722, 222 First Ave, Chester, CA 96020; 530-258-2646; fax: 530-258-2652; 8AM-4PM (PST). *Civil Actions under $25,000, Eviction, Small Claims.*
www.plumascourt.ca.gov
General Information: No probation reports released. Fee to fax out file $5.00 each. Court makes copy: $1.00 per page. Certification fee: $25 per doc plus copy fee. Payee: Superior Court. Personal checks accepted. No credit cards accepted. Prepayment required. Mail requests: SASE required.
Civil Name Search: Access: Fax, phone, mail, in person. Only the court performs in person name searches; visitors may not. Search fee: $15.00 per name if search exceeds 10 minutes. Traffic on computer, index cards for civil records. Records on computer back 13 years. Note: Will only search back 7 years. Mail turnaround time 1-2 days.

Portola Branch - Superior Court 600 S Gulling, Portola, CA 96122; 530-832-4286; fax: 530-832-5838; 8:30AM-4PM phone hours (PST). *Civil Actions under $25,000, Eviction, Small Claims, Traffic.*
www.plumascourt.ca.gov
General Information: No probation reports released. Will not fax documents. Court makes copy: $1.00 per page. Certification fee: $25 per doc plus copy fee. Payee: Superior Court. Personal checks accepted. No credit cards accepted. Prepayment required. Mail requests: SASE required.
Civil Name Search: Access: Phone, fax, mail, in person. Only the court performs in person name searches; visitors may not. Search fee: $15.00 per name if search exceeds 10 minutes. Traffic on computer, computer for civil records. Note: Court will only search back 10 years Mail turnaround time ASAP.
Criminal Name Search: Access: Phone, mail, in person. Only the court performs in person name searches; visitors may not. Search fee: $15.00 per name if search exceeds 10 minutes. Required to search: name, years to search. Traffic on computer, computer for criminal records. Court will only search back 10 years. Mail turnaround time ASAP.

Greenville Branch - Superior Court PO Box 722, 115 State Hiway 89, Greenville, CA 95947; 530-284-7213; fax: 530-284-0857; 8AM-4PM (PST). *Misdemeanor, Small Claims, Eviction, Ordinance.*
www.plumascourt.ca.gov
General Information: Phone hours are 8:30AM-4PM.

Riverside County

Superior Court - Civil 4050 Main St, Historic Courthouse, Riverside, CA 92501; 951-955-4600; probate phone: 951-955-1970; fax: 951-955-1751; 8AM-4PM (PST). *Civil Actions, Probate. Eviction.*
www.riverside.courts.ca.gov/
General Information: Has Superior Court and Limited Jurisdiction files except for those cases filed within Mt. San Jacinto Judicial Dist. and Three Lakes Judicial Dist. Includes case records from closed branch in Lake Elsinore, Moreno Valley, Perris, Hemet, Corona. Online identifiers in results same as on public terminal. No adoption, juvenile, medical, probation, unlawful detainers for 60 days or sealed records released. Will not fax out documents except to attorneys; $100 admin fee for unlimited fax filing. Court makes copy: $.50 per page. Self serve copy: same. Certification fee: $25 per doc plus copy fee. Payee: Riverside County Superior Court. Personal checks accepted. Credit cards accepted. Prepayment required. Mail requests: SASE required.
Civil Name Search: Access: Phone, fax, mail, online, in person. Both court and visitors may perform in person name searches. Search fee: $15.00 per name if search exceeds 10 minutes. Civil records on computer and microfiche from 1970, index file from 1956, archived from 1900s. Mail turnaround time 3 days. Public use terminal has civil records back to 1991. The fee for a name search from http://public-access.riverside.courts.ca.gov/OpenAccess/ is $1 for 1 search, $3.50 for 2-5 searches, or $5 for 6-10 searches. A flat fee of $250 per month provides an unlimited number of online searches. To view or print civil court documents, the fee is $1.00 per page 1st 5 pages, then $.40 ea add'l with cap of $40. If a civil case number is provided, the register of actions for that case may be viewed free of charge.

Superior Court - Criminal 4100 Main St, Riverside Hall of Justice, Riverside, CA 92501; 951-955-4600; fax: 951-955-4007; 7:30AM-4PM (PST). *Felony, Misdemeanor.*
www.riverside.courts.ca.gov/
General Information: Criminal indexes available on CD-Rom, but no DOBs. Overall index goes back to 6/90. Online identifiers in results same as on public terminal. No adoption, juvenile, medical, probation, unlawful detainers for 60 days or sealed records released. Will not fax out documents. Court makes copy: $.50 per page. Certification fee: $25 per doc plus copy fee. Payee: Clerk of the Court. Personal checks and credit cards accepted. Prepayment required. Mail requests: SASE required.

Criminal Name Search: Access: Phone, fax, mail, online, in person. Both court and visitors may perform in person name searches. Search fee: $15.00 per name if search exceeds 10 minutes. Required to search: name, years to search, DOB; also helpful: SSN. Criminal records on microfiche and computer since 1970, index file from 1956. Note: For phone requests, clerk will do a name lookup only. Mail turnaround time 1-4 weeks. Public use terminal has crim records back to 1989. PAT located in basement of civil court bldg. PAT search is countywide. The fee for a name search from http://public-access.riverside.courts.ca.gov/OpenAccess/ is $1 for 1 search, $3.50 for 2-5 searches, or $5 for 6-10 searches. A flat fee of $250 per month provides an unlimited number of online searches. Criminal case images are not provided. Email courtweb1@riverside.courts.ca.gov or contact the Executive Office at 951-955-5536 to establish an account. Online results show name only.

Banning Division - Superior Court 135 N Alessandro Rd, Banning, CA 92220; 951-922-7140; fax: 951-922-7150; 7:30AM-4PM (PST). *Felony, Misdemeanor, Civil Actions under $25,000, Eviction, Small Claims, Traffic.*
www.riverside.courts.ca.gov/
General Information: Includes Banning, Cabazon, Highland Springs, Poppet Flatt, Silent Valley, Beaumont, Calimesa, Cherry Valley and Whitewater. No probation reports released. Will not fax out documents. Court makes copy: $.50 per page. Certification fee: $25 per doc plus copy fee. Payee: Clerk of the Court. Personal checks accepted. Visa/MC accepted. Prepayment required. Mail requests: SASE required.
Civil Name Search: Access: Phone, mail, online, in person. Both court and visitors may perform in person name searches. Search fee: $15.00 per name if search exceeds 10 minutes. Required to search: name, years to search; also helpful-case number. Civil cases indexed by defendant, plaintiff. Civil records on computer from 1991, index files from 1983. Records destroyed after 10 years. Note: Phone access limited to short searches. Mail turnaround time 2 days. Public use terminal has civil records back to 1997. The fee for a name search from http://public-access.riverside.courts.ca.gov/OpenAccess/ is $1 for 1 search, $3.50 for 2-5 searches, or $5 for 6-10 searches. A flat fee of $250 per month provides an unlimited number of online searches. To view or print civil court documents, the fee is $1.00 per page 1st 5 pages, then $.40 ea add'l with cap of $40. If a civil case number is provided, the register of actions for that case may be viewed free of charge.
Criminal Name Search: Access: Phone, mail, online, in person. Only the court performs in person name searches; visitors may not. Search fee: $15.00 per name if search exceeds 10 minutes. Required to search: name, years to search; also helpful-case number. Criminal records computerized from 1992, index files from 1983. Records destroyed after 10 years. Note: Will perform phone searches for one or two names only. Mail turnaround time 2 days. The fee for a name search from http://public-access.riverside.courts.ca.gov/OpenAccess/ is $1 for 1 search, $3.50 for 2-5 searches, or $5 for 6-10 searches. A flat fee of $250 per month provides an unlimited number of online searches. Criminal case images are not provided. Email courtweb1@riverside.courts.ca.gov or contact the Executive Office at 951-955-5536 to establish an account.

Blythe Division - Superior Court 265 N Broadway, Blythe, CA 92225; 760-921-5902; criminal phone: 760-921-7828; civil phone: 760-921-7981;; 7:30AM-4PM (PST). *Felony, Misdemeanor, Civil Actions, Eviction, Small Claims, Traffic.*
www.riverside.courts.ca.gov/
General Information: Includes Blythe, Ripley. Phone for Family Law is 760-921-7982. Traffic phone is 760-921-7828. No probation reports released. $1.00 per page to fax in or fax out. Court makes copy: $.50 per page. Certification fee: $25 per doc plus copy fee. Payee: Clerk of the Court. Personal checks accepted. Visa/MC accepted. Prepayment required. Mail requests: SASE required.
Civil Name Search: Access: Phone, fax, mail, online, in person. Both court and visitors may perform in person name searches. Search fee: $15.00 per name if search exceeds 10 minutes. Civil records on computer from 1991, index files from 1983. Records destroyed after 10 years. Mail turnaround time 2 days. Civil PAT goes back to 1994. The fee for a name search from http://public-access.riverside.courts.ca.gov/OpenAccess/ is $1 for 1 search, $3.50 for 2-5 searches, or $5 for 6-10 searches. A flat fee of $250 per month provides an unlimited number of online searches. To view or print civil court documents, the fee is $1.00 per page 1st 5 pages, then $.40 ea add'l with cap of $40. If a civil case number is provided, the register of actions for that case may be viewed free of charge.
Criminal Name Search: Access: Phone, fax, mail, online, in person. Both court and visitors may perform in person name searches. Search fee: $15.00 per name if search exceeds 10 minutes. Required to search: name, years to search; also helpful: DOB, sex. Criminal records computerized from 1991, index files from 1983. Records destroyed after 10 years. Mail turnaround time 2 days. Criminal PAT goes back to 11/1992. The fee for

a name search from http://public-access.riverside.courts.ca.gov/OpenAccess/ is $1 for 1 search, $3.50 for 2-5 searches, or $5 for 6-10 searches. A flat fee of $250 per month provides an unlimited number of online searches. Criminal case images are not provided. Email courtweb1@riverside.courts.ca.gov or contact the Executive Office at 951-955-5536 to establish an account.

Southwest Justice Center - Superior Court 30755-D Auld Rd, #1226, Murrieta, CA 92563; 951-704-7634; fax: 951-704-7638; 7:30AM-4PM (PST). *Felony, Misdemeanor, Family Law.*
www.riverside.courts.ca.gov/
General Information: This is a relatively new court that as of 1/21/03 took in the criminal court cases from the closed Superior Courts in Hemet and Perris. No adoption, juvenile, medical, probation or sealed records released. Will not fax out documents. Court makes copy: $.50 per page. Certification fee: $25 per doc plus copy fee. Payee: Clerk of the Court. Personal checks accepted. Visa/MC/AMEX accepted. Prepayment required. Mail requests: SASE required.
Criminal Name Search: Access: Mail, fax, online, in person. Both court and visitors may perform in person name searches. Search fee: $15.00 per name if search exceeds 10 minutes. Required to search: name, years to search. Criminal records on computer since 1992; prior records on fiche. Mail turnaround time 1 week. Public use terminal has crim records. The fee for a name search from http://public-access.riverside.courts.ca.gov/OpenAccess/ is $1 for 1 search, $3.50 for 2-5 searches, or $5 for 6-10 searches. A flat fee of $250 per month provides an unlimited number of online searches. Criminal case images are not provided. Email courtweb1@riverside.courts.ca.gov or contact the Executive Office at 951-955-5536 to establish an account.

Hemet Division - Superior Court 880 N State St, Hemet, CA 92543; 951-766-2310; civil phone: 951-766-2321; fax: 951-766-2317; 7:30AM-4PM (PST). *Civil Actions under $25,000, Eviction, Small Claims, Traffic.*
www.riverside.courts.ca.gov/
General Information: Includes Aguanga, Anza, Gilman Hot Springs, Hemet, Idyllwild, Mountain Center, Pine Cove, Redec, Sage, San Jacinto, Sobba Hot Spring, Valle Vista and Winchester. Online identifiers in results same as on public terminal. Will not fax out documents. Court makes copy: $.50 per page. Certification fee: $25 per doc plus copy fee. Payee: Clerk of the Court. Personal checks accepted. Visa/MC accepted. Prepayment required. Mail requests: SASE required.
Civil Name Search: Access: Mail, in person, online. Both court and visitors may perform in person name searches. Search fee: $15.00 per name if search exceeds 10 minutes. Civil records on computer from 1996, index files from 1983. Records destroyed after 10 years. Public use terminal has civil records. The fee for a name search from http://public-access.riverside.courts.ca.gov/OpenAccess/ is $1 for 1 search, $3.50 for 2-5 searches, or $5 for 6-10 searches. A flat fee of $250 per month provides an unlimited number of online searches. To view or print civil court documents, the fee is $1.00 per page 1st 5 pages, then $.40 ea add'l with cap of $40. If a civil case number is provided, the register of actions for that case may be viewed free of charge.

Indio Division - Superior Court 46200 Oasis St, Larson Justice Center, Indio, CA 92201; 760-393-2426; criminal phone: 760-393-2196; civil phone: 760-393-2682; probate phone: 760-778-2207;; 7:30AM-4PM (PST). *Misdemeanor, Civil Actions under $25,000, Eviction, Small Claims, Probate, Traffic.*
www.riverside.courts.ca.gov/
General Information: Includes Bermuda Dunes, Coachella, Desert Center, Eagle Mountain, Indian Wells, Indio, La Quinta, Mecca, North Shore, Pinyon Pines, Palm Springs, Rancho Mirage, Salton Sea, Oasis, Thermal, Thousand Palms,. Most Palm Springs records here. Online identifiers in results same as on public terminal. No probation reports released. Will fax documents $1.00 per page. Court makes copy: $.50 per page. Self serve copy: same. Certification fee: $25 per doc plus copy fee. Payee: Clerk of the Court. Personal checks accepted. Credit cards accepted. Prepayment required. Mail requests: SASE required.
Civil Name Search: Access: Phone, fax, mail, online, in person. Visitors must perform in person searches themselves. Search fee: $15.00 per name if search exceeds 10 minutes. Civil records on computer from 1993, index files from 1983. Records destroyed after 10 years. Note: Phone and fax access limited to short searches. Civil PAT goes back to 1993. The fee for a name search from http://public-access.riverside.courts.ca.gov/OpenAccess/ is $1 for 1 search, $3.50 for 2-5 searches, or $5 for 6-10 searches. A flat fee of $250 per month provides an unlimited number of online searches. To view or print civil court documents, the fee is $1.00 per page 1st 5 pages, then $.40 ea add'l with cap of $40. If a civil case number is provided, the register of actions for that case may be viewed free of charge.
Criminal Name Search: Access: Phone, fax, mail, online, in person. Visitors must perform in person searches themselves. Search fee: $15.00 per name if search exceeds 10 minutes. Required to search: name, years to

search, signed release. Criminal records computerized from 1993, index files from 1983. Records destroyed after 10 years. Mail turnaround time 2 days. Criminal PAT goes back to same as civil. The fee for a name search from http://public-access.riverside.courts.ca.gov/OpenAccess/ is $1 for 1 search, $3.50 for 2-5 searches, or $5 for 6-10 searches. A flat fee of $250 per month provides an unlimited number of online searches. Criminal case images are not provided. Email courtweb1@riverside.courts.ca.gov or contact the Executive Office at 951-955-5536 to establish an account.

Temecula Branch - Superior Court 41002 County Center Dr, Temecula, CA 92591; 951-600-6400; fax: 951-600-6423; 7:30AM-4PM (PST). *Civil Actions under $25,000, Small Claims, Traffic.*
www.riverside.courts.ca.gov/
General Information: Includes Alberhill, Canyon Lk, Perris, Lake Elsinore, Lakeland Village, Sun City, Romoland, Homeland, Lakeview, Glenn Valley, Mead Valley, Murrieta Hot Spgs, Menifee, Meadowbrook, Sedco Hills, Quail Valley, Nuevo, Temecula, Wildonar, Vail Lk. Online identifiers in results same as on public terminal. No confidential, adoption or sealed records released. Unlawful detainers not released for 60 days. Will not fax documents. Court makes copy: $.50 per page. Certification fee: $25 per doc plus copy fee. Payee: Riverside Superior Court. Personal checks accepted. Credit cards accepted. Prepayment required. Mail requests: SASE required.
Civil Name Search: Access: Phone, mail, online, in person. Both court and visitors may perform in person name searches. Search fee: $15.00 per name if search exceeds 10 minutes. Required to search: name, years to search, DOB. Civil cases indexed by defendant, plaintiff. Civil records on computer go back 10-12 years; records held for 10 years. Note: Visitors may search on terminal, but court recommends to ask the clerk to do the search. Mail turnaround time 7 days. The fee for a name search from http://public-access.riverside.courts.ca.gov/OpenAccess/ is $1 for 1 search, $3.50 for 2-5 searches, or $5 for 6-10 searches. A flat fee of $250 per month provides an unlimited number of online searches. To view or print civil court documents, the fee is $1.00 per page 1st 5 pages, then $.40 ea add'l with cap of $40. If a civil case number is provided, the register of actions for that case may be viewed free of charge.

Palm Springs Superior Court 3255 E. Tahquitz Canyon Way, Palm Springs, CA 92262; 760-778-2252; fax: 760-778-2269; 7;30AM-4PM (PST). *Probate.*
www.riverside.courts.ca.gov/
General Information: Since 2003, only Probate cases are heard here.

Corona Branch - Superior Court 505 S Buena Vista, Corona, CA 92882; 909-272-5620; *Felony, Misdemeanor, Civil Actions under $25,000, Eviction, Small Claims.*
General Information: This court has criminal and traffic trials only. No documents are filed at this location. See Riverside for record files and online access.

Lake Elsinore Division - Superior Court
General Information: This court closed 01/01/03. See the Riverside Superior Court for case files and online access.

Perris Branch - Superior Court
General Information: This court closed 01/01/03. See Riverside Superior Court for case files and online access.

Sacramento County

Superior Court 720 9th St, #102/#101, Gordon D Schaber Sacramento County Courthouse, Sacramento, CA 95814; criminal phone: 916-874-5744; civil phone: 916-874-5522; fax: 916-874-5620; 8:30AM-4:00PM (PST). *Felony, Misdemeanor, Civil Limited/Unlimited.*
www.saccourt.ca.gov/
General Information: Galt, Elk Grove, and Walnut Grove branches are closed; this court now holds their Misd. records. Probate, Family Law, Juvenile at Family Relations Courthouse. Small Claims and Unlawful Detainers at Carol Miller Justice Ctr. Online identifiers in results same as on public terminal. No adoption, juvenile, medical, probation or sealed records released. Will not fax out documents. Court makes copy: $.50 per page. Self serve copy: $.15 per page. Certification fee: $25 per doc. Payee: Superior Court. Personal checks accepted. Visa/Amex accepted. Prepayment required. Mail requests: SASE required.
Civil Name Search: Access: Phone, mail, online, in person. Both court and visitors may perform in person name searches. Search fee: $15.00 per name if search exceeds 10 minutes. Required to search: name, years to search; also helpful: address, add'l parties to the action. Civil cases indexed by defendant, plaintiff. Civil records on microfiche and archived from 1937, index books from 1800s. Mail turnaround time 2-4 weeks. Public use terminal available. Access court records back to 1993 free at https://services.saccourt.com/indexsearchnew/. Includes civil, probate, small claims, unlawful detainer, family as well as criminal.
Criminal Name Search: Access: Phone, mail, online, in person. Both court and visitors may perform in person name searches. Search fee:

$15.00 per name if search exceeds 10 minutes. Required to search: name, DOB; also helpful: address, years to search, SSN, OLN. Criminal records on computer since 1989 (Superior & Muni), on microfiche and archived from 1962 (Superior only). Mail turnaround time 2-4 weeks. Public use terminal available. Access criminal records back to 1989 free at https://services.saccourt.com/indexsearchnew/. May also search using DOB. Online results show middle initial.

Carol Miller Justice Center 301 Bicentennial Circle, Carol Miller Justice Ctr, Sacramento, CA 95826; 916-875-7514-Small Claims; 875-7800-Traffic; 8:30AM-4PM (PST). *Small Claims, Evictions, Traffic.*
www.saccourt.ca.gov/locations/cmjc.aspx
General Information: Access court records back to 1993 free at https://services.saccourt.com/indexsearchnew/. Online includes civil, probate, small claims, unlawful detainer, family as well as criminal.

Family Relations Courthouse 3341 Power Inn Rd, William R Ridgeway Family Relations Courthouse, Sacramento, CA 95826; 916-875-3400; 8:30AM-4PM (phone hrs-8:30AM-N) (PST). *Probate, Family, Juvenile.*
www.saccourt.ca.gov/
General Information: Access records back to 1993 free at https://services.saccourt.com/indexsearchnew/. Includes civil, probate, sm claims, unlawful detainer, family. Search also at https://services.saccourt.com/publicdms2/DefaultDMS.aspx.

Galt Division - Superior Court. *Misdemeanor, Small Claims.*
General Information: This court is closed as of 03/03. Misdemeanor records and files are now housed at the Sacramento Superior Court. Traffic records were sent to the Carol Miller Justice Center, 916-875-7354/7800.

South Sacramento Superior Court - Elk Grove Branch
Misdemeanor, Civil Actions under $25,000, Eviction, Small Claims.
General Information: This court has been closed. All records are located at the Superior Court in Sacramento.

Walnut Grove Branch - Superior Court
General Information: This court was closed, records are now at the Superior Court in Sacramento.

San Benito County

Superior Court 440 Fifth St, Courthouse Rm 205, Hollister, CA 95023; 831-636-4057; fax: 831-636-4195; 8AM-4PM (PST). *Felony, Misdemeanor, Civil, Small Claims, Eviction, Probate.*
www.sanbenito.courts.ca.gov
General Information: Court calendar for the week at the website. Family Court located at 390 Fifth St. No adoption, juvenile, medical, probation or sealed records released. Will not fax documents. Court makes copy: $.50 per page. Certification fee: $25 per doc plus copy fee. Payee: Superior Court. Personal checks accepted. No credit cards accepted. Prepayment required. Mail requests: SASE required.
Civil Name Search: Access: Mail, in person. Both court and visitors may perform in person name searches. Search fee: $15.00 per name if search exceeds 10 minutes. Civil records on computer since 1990, index books and archived from 1873. Mail turnaround time 1-2 weeks. Civil PAT goes back to 1990.
Criminal Name Search: Access: Mail, in person. Both court and visitors may perform in person name searches. Search fee: $15.00 per name if search exceeds 10 minutes. Required to search: name, years to search. Criminal records on computer since 1989, index books and archived from 1900. Mail turnaround time 1-2 weeks. Criminal PAT goes back to same as civil.

San Bernardino County

Central District - Superior Court 351 N Arrowhead Ave, San Bernardino, CA 92415; 909-885-0139; criminal phone: 909-384-1888; civil phone: 909-387-3922; criminal fax: 909-387-4993; civil fax: 8AM-4PM; 8AM-4PM (PST). *Felony, Misdemeanor, Civil Actions, Small Claims, Eviction.*
www.sb-court.org/
General Information: Civil Division is at 303 W Third ST. Small claims phone- 909-885-0139. Probate cases for this jurisdiction are handled by the Redlands District Superior Court. Online identifiers in results same as on public terminal. No adoption, juvenile, medical, probation or sealed records released. Will not fax documents. Court makes copy: $.50 per page. Certification fee: $25 per doc plus copy fee. Payee: Superior Court. Business and personal checks accepted. Visa/MC accepted. Prepayment required. Mail requests: SASE required.
Civil Name Search: Access: Mail, fax, in person, online. Both court and visitors may perform in person name searches. Search fee: $15.00 per name if search exceeds 10 minutes. Civil records on computer from 1992, microfiche from 1972, archived and index file from approx 1856. Note: Address mail search access requests to Research Dept. Mail turnaround time 7-14 days. Civil PAT goes back to 1998. Online access to civil cases is free at www.sb-court.org/Divisions/Civil/CaseInformationOnline.aspx. Access to limited Probate Notes is free at www.sb-court.org/Divisions/Probate/ProbateNotes.aspx. Online results show DOB month and year only.
Criminal Name Search: Access: Mail, in person, online. Both court and visitors may perform in person name searches. Search fee: $15.00 per name if search exceeds 10 minutes. Required to search: name, years to search, DOB, SSN. Criminal records computerized from 1996, microfiche from 1972, index files from 1983, archived back to 1856. Mail turnaround time 7-14 days. Criminal PAT goes back to same as civil. Access to criminal cases and traffic is free at http://206.169.61.205/openaccess/CRIMINAL/. Includes calendars. Note that this Internet service is provided "as is", with no warranties, express or implied, including the implied warranty of fitness for a particular purpose, the court does not guarantee or warrant the completeness. Caution.

Barstow District - Superior Court 235 E Mountain View Ave, Barstow, CA 92311; 760-256-4814; 8AM-4PM (PST). *Felony, Misdemeanor, Civil, Eviction, Small Claims.*
www.sb-court.org/Locations/Barstow.aspx
General Information: Includes the City of Barstow and the unincorporated areas of Yermo, Lenwood, Daggett, Hinkley and Baker. Probate filings after 10/23/2006 can be found at San Bernardino District. Includes criminal cases from Needles since 09/08/2009. No probation or confidential reports released. Will not fax documents. Court makes copy: $.50 per page per side. Certification fee: $25 per doc plus copy fee. Payee: Clerk of the Court. Cashiers checks and money orders accepted. Major credit cards accepted. Prepayment required. Mail requests: SASE required.
Civil Name Search: Access: Mail, in person, online. Both court and visitors may perform in person name searches. Search fee: $15.00 per name if search exceeds 10 minutes. Civil records on computer from 1991, index books and microfilm. Microfilm is 3 to 4 weeks current. Records destroyed after 10 years. Mail turnaround time 2-5 days. Civil PAT goes back to 1999. Online access to civil cases is free at www.sb-court.org/Divisions/Civil/CaseInformationOnline.aspx. Access to limited Probate Notes is free at www.sb-court.org/Divisions/Probate/ProbateNotes.aspx. Online results show DOB month and year only.
Criminal Name Search: Access: Mail, in person, online. Both court and visitors may perform in person name searches. Search fee: $15.00 per name if search exceeds 10 minutes. Required to search: name, years to search. Criminal records computerized from 1999, index books and microfilm. Microfilm is 3 to 4 weeks current. Records destroyed after 10 years. Mail turnaround time 2-5 days. Criminal PAT goes back to same as civil. Access to criminal cases and traffic is free at http://206.169.61.205/openaccess/CRIMINAL/. Includes calendars. Note that this Internet service is provided "as is", with no warranties, express or implied, including the implied warranty of fitness for a particular purpose, the court does not guarantee or warrant the completeness. Caution.

Joshua Tree District - Superior Court 6527 White Feather Rd, Joshua Tree, CA 92252; 760-366-5770; criminal phone: 760-366-5775; civil phone: 760-366-5770; fax: 760-366-4156; 8AM-4PM (PST). *Felony, Misdemeanor, Civil, Eviction, Small Claims, Family Law.*
www.sb-court.org/
General Information: Includes the incorporated area of City of Twenty-Nine Palms, Town of Yucca Valley and unincorporated areas of Morongo Valley, Pioneertown, Landers, Johnson Valley, Joshua Tree, and Wonder Valley. Probate now at Redlands. No probation reports, confidential records released. Will not fax documents. Court makes copy: $.50 per page. Certification fee: $25 per doc plus copy fee. Payee: Joshua Tree Superior Court. Personal checks accepted. Visa/MC accepted. Prepayment required. Mail requests: SASE required.
Civil Name Search: Access: Mail, in person, online. Both court and visitors may perform in person name searches. Search fee: $15.00 per name if search exceeds 10 minutes. Civil records on computer from 1991, index books from 1983. Records destroyed after 10 years. Note: Note that all probate cases within this geographic area are handled at the San Bernardino location. Mail turnaround time 1 week. Civil PAT goes back to 1998. Online access to civil cases is free at www.sb-court.org/Divisions/Civil/CaseInformationOnline.aspx. Access to limited Probate Notes is free at www.sb-court.org/Divisions/Probate/ProbateNotes.aspx. Online results show DOB month and year only.
Criminal Name Search: Access: Mail, in person, online. Both court and visitors may perform in person name searches. Search fee: $15.00 per name if search exceeds 10 minutes. Required to search: name, years to search, DOB. Criminal records computerized from 1991, index books from 1983. Records destroyed after 10 years. Mail turnaround time 1 week.

Criminal PAT goes back to same as civil. Access to criminal cases and traffic is free at http://206.169.61.205/openaccess/CRIMINAL/. Includes calendars. Note that this Internet service is provided "as is", with no warranties, express or implied, including the implied warranty of fitness for a particular purpose, the court does not guarantee or warrant the completeness. Caution.

Rancho Cucamonga District - Superior Court
8303 N Haven Ave, Rancho Cucamonga, CA 91730; criminal phone: 909-350-9764; civil phone: 909-285-3558; fax: 909-285-3529; 8AM-4PM (PST). *Felony, Misdemeanor, Civil, Eviction, Small Claims, Probate, Traffic.*
www.sb-court.org/Locations/RanchoCucamonga.aspx

General Information: Formerly West District Superior Ct. Effective 2/28/11, probate & conservatorships filings shall be filed in the San Bernardino Historic Courthouse, 351 N Arrowhead, 1st Fl, San Bernardino, CA 92415. No probation reports released. Will not fax out docs. Court makes copy: $.50 per page. Certification fee: $25 per doc plus copy fee. Payee: Superior Court. Personal checks not accepted for criminal records. Visa/MC accepted for civil records. Prepayment required. Mail requests: SASE required.

Civil Name Search: Access: Phone, fax, mail, in person, online. Both court and visitors may perform in person name searches. Search fee: $15.00 per name if search exceeds 10 minutes; $5.00 if less then 10. Civil records on computer since 4/1994, index cards prior. Records destroyed after 10 years. Note: Effective July 6, 2010, all small claims cases are heard at the Fontana location. Mail turnaround time 1 week. Online access to civil cases is free at www.sb-court.org/Divisions/Civil/CaseInformationOnline.aspx. Access to limited Probate Notes is free at www.sb-court.org/Divisions/Probate/ProbateNotes.aspx.

Criminal Name Search: Access: Phone, mail, in person, online. Both court and visitors may perform in person name searches. Search fee: $15.00 per name if search exceeds 10 minutes. Required to search: name, years to search; also helpful: DOB. Criminal records computerized since 1994, prior on index cards and microfiche. Mail turnaround time 2-4 weeks. DOB on public terminal results shows year of birth only. Access to criminal cases and traffic is free at http://206.169.61.205/openaccess/CRIMINAL/. Includes calendars. Note that this Internet service is provided "as is", with no warranties, express or implied, including the implied warranty of fitness for a particular purpose, the court does not guarantee or warrant the completeness. Caution.

Victorville District - Superior Court
14455 Civic Dr, Victorville, CA 92392; 760-245-6215; 8AM-4PM (PST). *Felony, Misdemeanor, Civil, Eviction, Small Claims, Probate.*
www.sb-court.org/Locations/Victorville.aspx

General Information: Includes the cities of Victorville, Adelanto Hesperia and the areas of Apple Valley, El Mirage, Helendale, Lucerne Valley, Oro Grande, Phelan, Pinon Hill, Oakhills and Wrightwood. Probate filings after 2/28/2011 are in San Bernardino. Online identifiers in results same as on public terminal. No probation reports released. Will not fax documents. Court makes copy: $.50 per page. Payee: Superior Court. Personal checks accepted. $5.00 minimum for credit card payment. Prepayment required. Mail requests: SASE required.

Civil Name Search: Access: Mail, in person, online. Both court and visitors may perform in person name searches. Search fee: $15.00 per name if search exceeds 10 minutes. Civil records on microfiche from 1982 to 7/1999, on computer from 1989 to present, index books prior. Records destroyed after 10 years. Mail turnaround time 2-3 weeks. Civil PAT goes back to 1984. Online access to civil cases is free at www.sb-court.org/Divisions/Civil/CaseInformationOnline.aspx. Access to limited Probate Notes is free at www.sb-court.org/Divisions/Probate/ProbateNotes.aspx.

Criminal Name Search: Access: Mail, in person, online. Both court and visitors may perform in person name searches. Search fee: $15.00 per name if search exceeds 10 minutes. Required to search: name, years to search; also helpful: DOB, date of offense. Criminal index books by defendant 1984 to present; older cases on microfilm. Mail turnaround time 2-3weeks. Criminal PAT goes back to 1998. Access to criminal cases and traffic is free at http://206.169.61.205/openaccess/CRIMINAL/. Includes calendars. Note that this Internet service is provided "as is", with no warranties, express or implied, including the implied warranty of fitness for a particular purpose, the court does not guarantee or warrant the completeness. Caution.

Chino Division - Superior Court
13260 Central Ave, Chino, CA 91710; 909-356-5337; 8AM-4PM (PST). *Felony, Misdemeanor, Eviction.*
www.sb-court.org/Locations/Chino.aspx

General Information: Includes city of Chino, Chino Hills, and surrounding unincorporated area. Rancho Cucamonga Courts handles all civil cases since 01/01/99. Effective July 6, 2010, all small claims cases are heard at the Fontana location. Online identifiers in results same as on public terminal. No probation reports released. Will not fax documents. Court makes copy: $.50 per page. Certification fee: $25 per doc plus copy fee. Payee: Chino Superior Court. Personal checks and credit cards accepted. Prepayment required. Mail requests: SASE required.

Criminal Name Search: Access: Mail, in person, online. Both court and visitors may perform in person name searches. Search fee: $15.00 per name. Required to search: name, years to search, DOB; also helpful: address. Criminal records computerized from 1991, index books from 1983. Records destroyed after 10 years. Mail turnaround time 2 weeks. Access to criminal cases and traffic is free at http://206.169.61.205/openaccess/CRIMINAL/. Includes calendars. Note that this Internet service is provided "as is", with no warranties, express or implied, including the implied warranty of fitness for a particular purpose, the court does not guarantee or warrant the completeness. Caution.

Fontana District - Superior Court
17780 Arrow Blvd, Fontana, CA 92335; 909-350-9322; 7:30AM-4PM (PST). *Felony, Misdemeanor, Small Claims.*
www.sb-court.org/

General Information: Includes the Cities of Fontana, Rialto, Crestmore and the unincorporated areas of Lytle Creek Canyon and Bloomington. Includes small claims cases form Chino and Rancho Cucamonga since July 6, 2010. No probation reports or police records released. Will not fax documents. Court makes copy: $.50 per page. Certification fee: $25 per doc plus copy fee. Payee: Fontana Courts. Personal checks accepted. Prepayment required. Mail requests: SASE required.

Criminal Name Search: Access: Mail, in person, online. Both court and visitors may perform in person name searches. Search fee: $15.00 per name if search exceeds 10 minutes. Required to search: name, years to search; also helpful: DOB. Criminal records computerized from 1987, microfilm prior. Mail turnaround time 2-5 days. Access to criminal cases and traffic is free at http://206.169.61.205/openaccess/CRIMINAL/. Includes calendars. Note that this Internet service is provided "as is", with no warranties, express or implied, including the implied warranty of fitness for a particular purpose, the court does not guarantee or warrant the completeness. Caution.

Needles District - Superior Court
1111 Bailey Ave, Needles, CA 92363; 760-326-4355; fax: 760-326-9254; 8AM-4:30PM when court in session; 8AM-1PM otherwise (PST). *Civil Actions under $25,000, Eviction, Small Claims.*
www.sb-court.org/Locations/Needles.aspx

General Information: No criminal records here since 09-08-09, cases now in Barstow. No probation reports released. Will not fax documents. Court makes copy: $.50 per page. Certification fee: $25 per doc plus copy fee. Payee: Superior Court. Personal checks accepted. Visa/MC cards accepted but not over phone. Prepayment required. Mail requests: SASE required.

Civil Name Search: Access: Mail, in person, online. Only the court performs in person name searches; visitors may not. Search fee: $15.00 per name if search exceeds 10 minutes. Required to search: name, years to search. Civil cases indexed by plaintiff. Civil records in index books. Will only search back 7 years. Mail turnaround time 1-2 weeks. Public use terminal has civil records. Online access to civil cases is free at www.sb-court.org/Divisions/Civil/CaseInformationOnline.aspx. Access to limited Probate Notes is free at www.sb-court.org/Divisions/Probate/ProbateNotes.aspx. Online results show DOB month and year only.

Big Bear District - Superior Court
477 Summit Blvd, Big Bear Lake, CA 92315; 909-866-0150; 8AM-4PM (PST). *Civil Actions under $25,000, Eviction, Small Claims.*
www.sbcounty.gov/courts/index.asp

General Information: This court is only open the first full week of the month. All mail should be sent C/O the Victorville District at 14455 Civic Dr Ste 200, Victorville, CA 92392-2397. Probate within this district is handled at San Bernardino location.

Redlands District - Superior Court. *Traffic Infractions, Probate.*
www.sb-court.org/

General Information: This court is closed. Most case files were moved to the court in San Bernardino.

Twin Peaks District - Superior Court. *Traffic Misdemeanor, Civil under $25,000, Eviction, Small Claims.*
www.sb-court.org/

General Information: Court Closed 10/2/2006; cases now heard at the San Bernardino District Courthouse, 351 N Arrowhead Ave, San Bernardino, 909-885-0139. For traffic- 909-384-1888; Civil- 909-387-3922; Small Claims- 909-387-3170.

San Diego County

Superior Court - Civil PO Box 120128, 330 W Broadway Rm 225, San Diego, CA 92112-0128; 619-450-7275; probate phone: 619-450-7676;; 8:30AM-3:30PM; records- 9AM-4PM (PST). *Civil, Probate, Eviction, Small Claims, Probate.* www.sdcourt.ca.gov

General Information: Has Central Div. Ltd Jurisdiction civil cases. For any San Diego County request, always specify which division - Central, East, North or South. Central Records is in the basement, phone- 619-450-7361. Probate located at Madge Bradley Bldg, 1409 4th Ave. Will not fax documents. Court makes copy: $.50 per copy. Certification fee: $25 per doc plus copy fee. Payee: San Diego Superior Court. Personal checks accepted. Major credit cards accepted, in person only. Prepayment required. Mail requests: SASE required.

Civil Name Search: Access: Mail, in person, online. Both court and visitors may perform in person name searches. Search fee: $15.00 per name if search exceeds 10 minutes. Civil records index on computer from 1974 to present. Mail turnaround time 1 day. Public use terminal has civil records back to 1974. Online search for case information for civil and probate cases initiated after 01/01/2008 is free at www.sdcourt.ca.gov/. Also lists calendars and new filings. Also, the court sells a county-wide CD-ROM of civil, domestic, mental health, and probate indices, generally from 1974 to 1999, for $25.00.

Superior Court - Criminal PO Box 120128, 220 W Broadway, Rm 2005, San Diego, CA 92101; 619-450-5400 or 5700;; 8:30AM-3:30PM (PST). *Felony, Misdemeanor.* www.sdcourt.ca.gov/portal/page?_pageid=55,1&_dad=portal&_schema=PORTAL

General Information: Both General and Limited Criminal records are located here. Central Records is in the basement, phone is 619-450-7361. No adoption, juvenile, medical, probation or sealed records released. Will not fax documents. Court makes copy: $.50 per page. Certification fee: $25 per doc plus copy fee. Payee: San Diego Superior Court. No out of state personal checks. Major credit cards accepted in person only. Prepayment required. Mail requests: SASE required.

Criminal Name Search: Access: Mail, in person, online. Both court and visitors may perform in person name searches. Search fee: $15.00 per name if search exceeds 10 minutes. Required to search: name, years to search, DOB. Felony records on index from 1974 to present, paper ledgers from 1880s. Mail turnaround time 1-2 weeks. Public use terminal has crim records back to 25 yrs for felony, 10 for misd. Online search for case information, calendars, and new filings is free at www.sdcourt.ca.gov/. See Quick Links. The CD-ROM of county criminal records is no longer available for purchase. Online results show name only.

East County Division - Superior Court 250 E Main St, El Cajon, CA 92020; 619-456-4100; 8AM-3:30PM crim; 8:30AM-3:30PM civil (PST). *Felony, Misdemeanor, Civil, Small Claims, Eviction, Traffic.* www.sdcourt.ca.gov

General Information: Court now houses the former municipal court records. Includes El Cajon, La Mesa, Lemon Grove, Santee and unincorporated towns of Alpine, Boulevard, Campo, Dulzura, Grossmont, Jacumba, Jamul, Julian, Lakeside, Mesa Grande, Ramona, Spring Valley, Tecate. No confidential or sealed records released. Will not fax documents. Court makes copy: $.50 per page. Certification fee: $25 per doc plus copy fee. Payee: Clerk of Superior Court. Personal checks accepted. Law firm and Calif. checks with preprinted name and address accepted only. Major credit cards accepted. Prepayment required. Mail requests: SASE required.

Civil Name Search: Access: Mail, in person, online. Both court and visitors may perform in person name searches. Search fee: $15.00 per name if search exceeds 10 minutes. Civil records on computer since 1974; microfilm prior. Mail turnaround time 3-5 days. Civil PAT goes back to 1974. Online search for case information for civil and probate cases initiated after 01/01/2008 is free at www.sdcourt.ca.gov/. Also lists calendars and new filings.

Criminal Name Search: Access: Mail, in person, online. Both court and visitors may perform in person name searches. Search fee: $15.00 per name if search exceeds 10 minutes. Required to search: name, years to search; also helpful: DOB. Criminal records on computer since 1974; microfilm prior. Mail turnaround time 3-5 days. Criminal PAT goes back to 1974. Terminal results may or may not include middle initial. Online search for case information, calendars, and new filings is free at www.sdcourt.ca.gov/. See Quick Links. Online results show name only.

North County Branch - Superior Court 325 S Melrose Dr, Vista, CA 92081; 760-201-8600; criminal phone: x160; civil phone: x150; probate phone: x1823;; 8:30AM-3:30PM (PST). *Felony, Misdemeanor, Civil Actions, Eviction, Small Claims, Probate, Traffic.* www.sdcourt.ca.gov/portal/page?_pageid=55,1058990&_dad=portal&_schema=PORTAL

General Information: Includes cities of Oceanside, Del Mar, Carlsbad, Solana Beach, Encinitas, Escondido, San Marcos, Vista and unincorporated towns of Del Dios, Olivehain, San Luis Rey, San Pasqual, Rancho Santa Fe, Valley Ctr., Bonsall, Palomar Mt., Borrego Spr., Pala, etc. No sealed or confidential documents released. Will not fax documents. Court makes copy: $.50 per page. Certification fee: $25 per doc plus copy fee. Payee: Clerk of the Superior Court. Personal checks accepted. Out of state checks not accepted. Major credit cards accepted. Prepayment required. Mail requests: SASE required.

Civil Name Search: Access: Mail, in person, online. Both court and visitors may perform in person name searches. Search fee: $15.00 per name if search exceeds 10 minutes. Off site retrieval of documents is an additional $10.00. Civil records on computer back to 1993; prior on microfiche and index books. Mail turnaround time 2-3 days. Civil PAT goes back to 10 years. Online search for case information for civil and probate cases initiated after 01/01/2008 is free at www.sdcourt.ca.gov/portal/page?_pageid=55,1056871&_dad=portal&_schema=PORTAL. Also lists calendars and new filings.

Criminal Name Search: Access: Mail, in person, online. Both court and visitors may perform in person name searches. Search fee: $15.00 per name if search exceeds 10 minutes. Off site retrieval of documents is an additional $10.00. Required to search: name, years to search. Criminal records computerized from 1993; prior on microfiche and index books. Mail turnaround time 2-3 days. Criminal PAT goes back to same as civil. Online search for case information, calendars, and new filings is free at www.sdcourt.ca.gov/portal/page?_pageid=55,1&_dad=portal&_schema=PORTAL. Online results show name only.

South County Branch - Superior Court 500 3rd Ave, Chula Vista, CA 91910; 619-746-6200; 8:30AM-3:30PM civil; 7:30AM-3:30PM crim (PST). *Felony, Misdemeanor, Civil Actions, Eviction, Small Claims.* www.sdcourt.ca.gov

General Information: Includes National City, Chula Vista, Coronado, Imperial Beach and that portion of the City of San Diego lying south of the City of Chula Vista and contiguous unincorporated areas. No confidential or sealed records released. Will fax documents to local or toll-free number. Court makes copy: $.50 per page. Certification fee: $25 per doc plus copy fee. Payee: Superior Court (Civil)-Clerk of the Court (Criminal). Personal checks and credit cards accepted. Prepayment required. Mail requests: SASE required.

Civil Name Search: Access: Mail, in person, online. Both court and visitors may perform in person name searches. Search fee: $15.00 per name per year. No fee for small claims searches. Civil records on computer; for case files prior to 1991, contact Superior Court's Main Records Division, Downtown. Mail turnaround time up to 1 week. Civil PAT goes back to 10 years. Online search for case information for civil and probate cases initiated after 01/01/2008 is free at www.sdcourt.ca.gov/. Also lists calendars and new filings.

Criminal Name Search: Access: Phone, fax, mail, in person, online. Both court and visitors may perform in person name searches. Search fee: $15.00 per name if search exceeds 10 minutes. Off site retrieval of documents is an additional $10.00. Required to search: name, years to search, DOB. Criminal records on computer, cases files prior to 1987 on microfiche. Mail turnaround time depends on clerk availability. Criminal PAT goes back to same as civil. Online search for case information, calendars, and new filings is free at www.sdcourt.ca.gov/. See Quick Links. Online results show name only.

Kearny Mesa Branch - Central Division 8950 Clairemont Mesa Blvd, San Diego, CA 92123; 858-634-1919 Small Claims; 8:30AM-3:30PM (PST). *Small Claims, Traffic, Infractions.* www.sdcourt.ca.gov/portal/page?_pageid=55,1&_dad=portal&_schema=PORTAL

General Information: Traffic phone is 858-634-1800. Some minor infractions are heard at this court.

Ramona Branch - East Division 1428 Montecito Rd, Ramona, CA 92065; 760-738-2435, 760-738-2400; 8:30AM-N, 1-3:30PM (PST). *Civil Actions under $25,000, Eviction, Small Claims, Traffic.* www.sdcourt.ca.gov

General Information: Jurisdiction over the northeast area of the county. Criminal cases and Unlimited civil cases and searches at El Cajon Branch. No probation reports or DMV records released. Will not fax documents. Court makes copy: $.50 per page. Certification fee: $25 per doc plus copy fee. Payee: Clerk of the Court. Personal checks accepted. Visa/MC accepted. Prepayment required. Mail requests: SASE required.

Civil Name Search: Access: Mail, in person, online. Only the court performs in person name searches; visitors may not. Search fee: $15.00 per name if search exceeds 10 minutes. Civil records on computer from 1991, index files since 1983. Files destroyed after 10 years. Mail turnaround time 2-3 days. Online search for case information for civil and probate cases initiated after 01/01/2008 is free at www.sdcourt.ca.gov/. Also lists calendars and new filings.

San Marcos Branch - North Division *Misdemeanor, Traffic.*
General Information: On July 14, 2003, they moved into the North County Branch in Vista at 325 S Melrose Dr, #350, Annex Bldg, 92081.

San Francisco County

Superior Court - Criminal 850 Bryant St, Rm 101, Hall of Justice, San Francisco, CA 94103; 415-551-0651; criminal phone: x2; fax: 415-551-8044; 8AM-4:30PM M-TH; 1AM-12 F (PST). *Felony, Misdemeanor.*
www.sfsuperiorcourt.org/
General Information: No medical, probation or sealed records released. No fee to fax documents if prepaid. Court makes copy: $.50 per page. Certification fee: $25.00 per doc plus copy fee. Payee: SF Superior Court. Personal checks accepted with ID. Cashier checks and money orders accepted. Visa/MC cards accepted in person only. Prepayment required. Mail requests: SASE required.
Criminal Name Search: Access: Mail, in person. Both court and visitors may perform in person name searches. Search fee: $15.00 per name if search exceeds 10 minutes. Required to search: name, years to search, DOB. Criminal records go back to the beginning. Note: If searching by mail, direct your request to "Prior Convictions" Mail turnaround time 1 week.
Superior Court - Civil 400 McAllister St, #103, San Francisco, CA 94102; 415-551-4000 (general info); 415-551-3802 records section; civil phone: 415-551-3888; probate phone: 415-551-3892/3891/3893; fax: 415-551-3801; 8AM-4PM M-TH; 8AM-12 Fri (PST). *Civil, Small Claims, Eviction, Probate.*
www.sfsuperiorcourt.org/
General Information: Civil Limited and Civil Unlimited sections are combined. Includes all of San Francisco County, including former municipal court on Folsom St. Small Claims phone- 415-551-3955. Online identifiers in results same as on public terminal. No medical, probation or sealed records released without court order. Will not fax documents. Court makes copy: $.50 per page.If doc is 5 pages or less, it is copied same day. If over 5, it is sent out to be copies and is delayed. Certification fee: $25 per doc plus copy fee. Payee: San Francisco Superior Court. Personal checks accepted. Visa/MC accepted in person only. Prepayment required. Mail requests: SASE required.
Civil Name Search: Access: Mail, in person, online. Both court and visitors may perform in person name searches. Search fee: $15.00 per name if search exceeds 10 minutes. No charge if easily pulled from computer after 1987. Civil records on computer since 1987 for limited and unlimited jurisdiction; indexes on microfilm and microfiche for prior years. Mail turnaround time 7 business days; in person turnaround is 3-5 days. Public use terminal has civil records back to 1987. Public terminal available starting at 8AM. Older records may contain DOB. The San Francisco Superior Court offers online queries by case number, name search, and tentative rulings to the Register of Actions. Documents included for cases in the following departments: Civil, Family Law, Probate, and Small Claims. Visit www.sfsuperiorcourt.org/index.aspx?page=467

San Joaquin County

Superior Court - Criminal 222 E Weber Ave, Rm 101, Stockton, CA 95202; 209-468-2935; fax: 209-468-8577; 8AM-3PM (phones til 4PM) (PST). *Felony, Misdemeanor.*
www.stocktoncourt.org/courts/
General Information: This is a county central mail criminal request processing unit. No juvenile, medical, probation, sealed records released. Will not fax back to the public. Court makes copy: $.50 per page. Certification fee: $25 per doc plus copy fee. Payee: San Joaquin Superior Court. Personal checks and money orders accepted. No credit cards accepted. Prepayment required. Mail requests: SASE required.
Criminal Name Search: Access: Mail, in person, online. Both court and visitors may perform in person name searches. Search fee: $15.00 per name if search exceeds 10 minutes. Required to search: name, years to search; also helpful: DOB, SSN. Criminal Records on computer since 1990, on microfiche since 1973, older records archived to 1880s. Mail turnaround time 1-2 weeks. Public use terminal has crim records back to 1991. Data is countywide. Access calendars free at www.stocktoncourt.org/courts/caseinquiry.htm. Effective 04/01/2011 access to historical records was removed.

Superior Court - Civil 222 E Weber Ave, Rm 303, Stockton, CA 95202-2709; 209-468-2355; civil phone: 209-468-2933; probate phone: 209-468-2843; fax: 209-468-0539; 8AM-3PM (phones til 4PM) (PST). *Civil Actions, Eviction, Small Claims, Probate.*
www.stocktoncourt.org/courts/
General Information: Includes city of Stockton and suburban areas Farmington and Linden, Delta area and surrounding unincorporated areas. Small claims phone is 209-468-2949. Family Court is now located at 540 E Main St. Courthouse. Online identifiers in results same as on public

terminal. No probation, confidential records released. Will not fax documents. Court makes copy: $.50 per page. Certification fee: $25 per doc plus copy fee; Exemplification- $20.00. Payee: Superior Court. Personal checks accepted. Major credit cards accepted in person only. Prepayment required. Mail requests: SASE required.
Civil Name Search: Access: Mail, in person, online. Both court and visitors may perform in person name searches. Search fee: $15.00 per name if search exceeds 10 minutes. Civil records on computer from 1996; indices/books from 1850-1977; Microfiche to 1973. Note: Case inquiry phone numbers when online access is down are- Civil tentative rulings- 209-468-2827; Probate Tentative- 209-468-2866; Probate Notes- 209-468-9895. Mail turnaround time 7-10 days. Public use terminal has civil records back to 1996. Free access to civil and family case summaries countywide, with name searching, at www.stocktoncourt.org/courts/caseinquiry.htm.

Lodi Division - Superior Court - Civil 315 W Elm St, Lodi, CA 95240; 209-331-2101; fax: 209-331-2133; 8AM-3PM (phones til 4PM) (PST). *Misdemeanor Traffic, Civil Actions under $25,000, Eviction, Small Claims.*
www.stocktoncourt.org/courts/
General Information: Includes city of Lodi, eight mile road to Sacramento County line, towns of Acampo, Clements, Lockeford, Terminous, Thornton, Woodbridge. No probation reports released. Will not fax documents. Court makes copy: $.50 per page. Certification fee: $25 per doc plus copy fee. Payee: Superior Court. Personal checks and credit cards accepted. Prepayment required. Mail requests: SASE required.
Civil Name Search: Access: Phone, mail, fax, in person, online. Both court and visitors may perform in person name searches. Search fee: $15.00 per name if search exceeds 10 minutes. Civil records on computer from 1994, index files from 1989. Records destroyed after 10 years. Note: Case inquiry phone numbers when online access is down are- Civil tentative rulings- 209-468-2827; Probate Tentative- 209-468-2866; Probate Notes- 209-468-9895. Mail turnaround time 5 days. Free access to civil case summaries countywide, with name searching, at www.stocktoncourt.org/courts/caseinfo.htm. Also, access court calendars.

Lodi Division - Superior Court - Criminal 217 W Elm St, Lodi, CA 95240; 209-331-2121; fax: 209-331-2135; 8AM-3PM (phones til 4PM) (PST). *Felony, Misdemeanor.*
www.stocktoncourt.org/courts/
General Information: Includes city of Lodi, eight mile road to Sacramento County line, towns of Acampo, Clements, Lockeford, Terminous, Thornton, Woodbridge. No probation reports released. Will not fax documents. Court makes copy: $.50 per page. Certification fee: $25 per doc plus copy fee. Payee: Superior Court. Personal checks accepted only for payments above $10.00. Visa/MC accepted. Prepayment required. Mail requests: SASE required.
Criminal Name Search: Access: Phone, mail, fax, in person. Both court and visitors may perform in person name searches. Search fee: $15.00 per name if search exceeds 10 minutes. Required to search: name, years to search, DOB; also helpful: address, SSN, sex. Criminal records computerized from 1991, index files from 1983. Records destroyed after 10 years. Mail turnaround time 5 days. Public use terminal has crim records back to 1991. Data is countywide. Access court case record index countywide and calendars free at www.stocktoncourt.org/courts/caseinquiry.htm.

Manteca Branch - Superior Court 315 E Center St, Manteca, CA 95336; criminal phone: 209-239-1316; civil phone: 209-239-9188;; 8AM-3PM (PST). *Felony, Misdemeanor, Civil Actions under $25,000, Eviction, Small Claims.*
www.stocktoncourt.org/courts/
General Information: Includes cities of Manteca, Ripon, Escalon, French Camp, Lathrop and surrounding unincorporated areas. No judge's notes, probation or police reports released. Will not fax documents. Court makes copy: $.50 per page. Certification fee: $25 per doc plus copy fee. Payee: Superior Court. Personal checks accepted. Visa/MC accepted. Prepayment required. Mail requests: SASE required.
Civil Name Search: Access: Mail, in person, online. Only the court performs in person name searches; visitors may not. Search fee: $15.00 per name if search exceeds 10 minutes. Records on microfiche since 1986, index files from 1983, computerized docket since 1996. Paper records destroyed after 10 years. Note: Case inquiry phone numbers when online access is down are- Civil tentative rulings- 209-468-2827; Probate Tentative- 209-468-2866; Probate Notes- 209-468-9895. Mail turnaround time 1-2 weeks. Free access to civil and family case summaries countywide, with name searching, at www.stocktoncourt.org/courts/caseinquiry.htm. Also, access court calendars.
Criminal Name Search: Access: Mail, in person, online. Only the court performs in person name searches; visitors may not. Search fee: $15.00

per name if search exceeds 10 minutes. Required to search: name, years to search; also helpful: DOB. Criminal records on computer since 1990, microfiche since 1986, index files from 1983. Note: Use of special request form required to view files in person. Mail turnaround time 1-2 weeks. Access court case record index countywide and calendars free at www.stocktoncourt.org/courts/caseinquiry.htm. Online results show name only.

Tracy Branch - Superior Court 475 E 10th St, Tracy, CA 95376; 209-831-5909; criminal phone: 209-831-5900; civil phone: 209-831-5902; fax: 209-831-5919; 8AM-3PM (phones til 4PM) (PST). *Felony, Misdemeanor, Civil Actions under $25,000, Eviction, Small Claims.* www.stocktoncourt.org/courts/

General Information: All closed cases are located at the Manteca court; search there. This Tracy Court includes Cities of Tracy, Banta, portion of Vernalis and surrounding unincorporated area. No probation reports, DMV history and criminal history records released. Will not fax documents. Court makes copy: $.50 per page. Certification fee: $25 per doc plus copy fee. Payee: Tracy Superior Court. Personal checks accepted. Visa/MC accepted. Prepayment required. Mail requests: SASE required.

Civil Name Search: Access: Phone, mail, in person, online. Only the court performs in person name searches; visitors may not. Search fee: $15.00 per name if search exceeds 10 minutes. Civil records on computer since 3/95; on index files from 1983. Records destroyed after 10 years. Note: Case inquiry phone numbers when online access is down are- Civil tentative rulings- 209-468-2827; Probate Tentative- 209-468-2866; Probate Notes- 209-468-9895. Mail turnaround time 5-10 days. Free access to civil and family case summaries countywide, with name searching, at www.stocktoncourt.org/courts/caseinquiry.htm. Also, access court calendars.

Criminal Name Search: Access: Mail, in person, online. Only the court performs in person name searches; visitors may not. Search fee: $15.00 per name if search exceeds 10 minutes. Required to search: name, years to search, DOB. Criminal records computerized from 1991; on index files from 1983. Records destroyed after 10 years. Mail turnaround time 5-10 days. Access court case record index countywide and calendars free at www.stocktoncourt.org/courts/caseinquiry.htm. Online results show name only.

San Luis Obispo County

Superior Court - Civil 1035 Palm St, Rm 385, Government Ctr, San Luis Obispo, CA 93408; 805-781-5677; probate phone: 805-781-5242;; 8:30AM-4PM (PST). *Civil Actions, Small Claims, Eviction, Probate, Family Law.* http://slocourts.net/

General Information: This Court has jurisdiction over all of San Luis Obispo County for Civil actions over $25,000, and also the current and former "limited jurisdiction" (under $25,000) civil cases and small claims in the immediate area. No probation reports released. Will not fax documents. Court makes copy: $.50 per page. Certification fee: $25 per doc plus copy fee. Payee: Superior Court. Personal checks and credit cards accepted. Prepayment required. Mail requests: SASE required.

Civil Name Search: Access: Mail, in person. Both court and visitors may perform in person name searches. Search fee: $15.00 per name if search exceeds 10 minutes. Civil records on computer from 1975, index files from 1865. Records destroyed after 10 years. Mail turnaround time 2-5 days. Public use terminal has civil records back to 1975. Access daily calendars from the website.

Superior Court - Criminal Government Center, Rm 220, 1050 Monterey St., San Luis Obispo, CA 93408; 805-781-5143; criminal phone: 805-781-5670;; 8:30AM-4PM (PST). *Felony, Misdemeanor, Traffic.* http://slocourts.net/

General Information: No adoption, juvenile, medical, probation or sealed records released. Will not fax documents. Court makes copy: $.50 per page. Certification fee: $25 per doc plus copy fee. Payee: Superior Court Criminal Court Operations. Personal checks and credit cards accepted. Prepayment required. Mail requests: SASE required.

Criminal Name Search: Access: Mail, in person. Both court and visitors may perform in person name searches. Search fee: $15.00 if search exceeds 10 minutes; limit 5 names per contact. Matters stored off-site will also carry a $15.00 file retrieval fee. Required to search: name and date of birth, case number, years to search. Criminal records on computer and microfiche from 1975, archived and index felony files from late 1800s. Note: A "11 search" is for 1985 to present for misd., felonies, and non-traffic infractions; a name search of 1975-1985 misd. Records is a "10 search,' or a electronic felony index 1975-1995. Mail turnaround time 7-10 days. Public use terminal has crim records back to 1975-felony; 1985-misdemeanors. Access daily calendar from their website.

Paso Robles Branch - Superior Court 901 Park Street, Paso Robles, CA 93446-2593; 805-237-3079; 8:30AM-4PM (PST). *Civil Actions, Eviction, Small Claims, Traffic.* http://slocourts.net/

General Information: Includes Atascadero, Templeton, Paso Robles, San Miguel, Shandon, Cholame, areas north and east of the Cuesta Grade. No driving histories, rap sheets, sealed or probation reports released. Will not fax documents. Court makes copy: $.50 per page. Certification fee: $25 per doc plus copy fee. Payee: Superior Court. Personal checks and credit cards accepted. Prepayment required. Mail requests: SASE required.

Civil Name Search: Access: Phone, mail, in person. Both court and visitors may perform in person name searches. Search fee: $15.00 per name if search exceeds 10 minutes. Civil records on computer from 1975, index files from 1983. Records destroyed after 10 years. Note: Mail requests limited to 5 at a time. Mail turnaround time 1-7 days. Public use terminal has civil records back to 10 years. Access daily calendar from the website.

Grover Beach Branch - Superior Court 214 S 16th St, Grover Beach, CA 93433-2299; criminal phone: 805-473-7072; civil phone: 805-473-7077; 8:30AM-4PM (PST). *Misdemeanor, Civil Actions under $25,000, Eviction, Small Claims.* http://slocourts.net/

General Information: Includes Nipomo, Grover Beach, Arroyo Grande, Pismo Beach, Oceano, South Coast unincorporated areas. No probation reports released. Will not fax documents. Court makes copy: $.50 per page. Certification fee: $25 per doc plus copy fee. Payee: Superior Court. Personal checks and credit cards accepted. Prepayment required. Mail requests: SASE required.

Civil Name Search: Access: Phone, mail, in person. Both court and visitors may perform in person name searches. Search fee: $15.00 per name if search exceeds 10 minutes. Civil index on cards to 1976; on computer back to 1998 Records destroyed after 10 years. Mail turnaround time 2-3 weeks. Civil PAT goes back to 10 years. Access daily calendar from the website.

Criminal Name Search: Access: Phone, mail, in person. Both court and visitors may perform in person name searches. Search fee: $15.00 per name if search exceeds 10 minutes. Required to search: name, years to search. Criminal records indexed on cards to 1976; on computer back to 1986. Records destroyed after 10 years. Mail turnaround time 1 week. Criminal PAT goes back to same as civil. Access daily calendar from their website.

San Mateo County

Superior Court 400 County Center, Redwood City, CA 94063; 650-363-4711; criminal phone: x1; civil phone: 650-363-4576; fax: 650-363-4914; 8AM-4PM (PST). *Felony, Civil Actions over $25,000, Probate.* www.sanmateocourt.org

General Information: Southern Area Limited Criminal, lower-value civil actions, evictions and small claims also located here, but shown in a separate listing. No confidential jackets on conservatorships & guardianships, adoptions, juvenile, medical, probation or sealed records released. Will not fax out documents. Court makes copy: $.50 per page. Certification fee: $25 per doc plus copy fee. Payee: Superior Court. Personal checks accepted. Visa/MC accepted. Prepayment required. Mail requests: SASE required.

Civil Name Search: Access: Mail, in person, online. Both court and visitors may perform in person name searches. Search fee: $15.00 per name if search exceeds 10 minutes. Civil records and Family Law on computer from 1978; index books prior. Mail turnaround time 1 week. Civil PAT goes back to 1978. Public terminal has probate records back to 1972. Online access is free at www.sanmateocourt.org/midx/. Includes probate and small claims.

Criminal Name Search: Access: Mail, in person, online. Both court and visitors may perform in person name searches. Search fee: $15.00 per name if search exceeds 10 minutes. Required to search: name, DOB, SSN, CADL#. Criminal records on computer since 1964; prior on books. Note: Criminal matters only filed by Belmont, Foster City, Half Moon Bay, San Carlos, Menlo Pk, East Palo Alto and unincorporated areas are heard at the Southern Branch. Mail turnaround time 1 week. Criminal PAT goes back to 1964. Search all county case records including criminal for free at www.sanmateocourt.org/midx/. Online results show middle initial.

Superior Court - Southern Branch Limited 400 County Center, Redwood City, CA 94063; criminal phone: 650-363-4302; civil phone: 650-363-4576; fax: 650-363-4976; 8AM-4PM (PST). *Misdemeanor, Civil, Eviction, Small Claims.* www.sanmateocourt.org

General Information: Limited Criminal/Civil (former Muni Ct). Small Claims Divisions for San Mateo and South San Francisco divisions have been relocated here in Rm A on the 1st Floor of the Hall of Justice. No probation reports or confidential information records released. Court makes copy: $.50 per side. Certification fee: $25 per doc plus copy fee. Payee: Superior Court. Personal checks accepted. Write "not to exceed $x.xx" on check. Visa/MC accepted in person only. Prepayment required. Mail requests: SASE required.

Civil Name Search: Access: Mail, fax, in person, online. Both court and visitors may perform in person name searches. Search fee: $15.00 per name if search exceeds 10 minutes. Civil Records on computer back to 1959. Mail turnaround time 1-2 weeks. Civil PAT goes back to 1959. Online access is free at www.sanmateocourt.org/midx/.

Criminal Name Search: Access: Mail, fax, in person, online. Both court and visitors may perform in person name searches. Search fee: $15.00 per name if search exceeds 10 minutes. Required to search: name, years to search. Limited Criminal records computerized from 1991, index files from 1983. Records destroyed after 10 years. Note: Only limited criminal cases for the Southern District can be found at this location. Mail turnaround time 1-2 weeks. Criminal PAT goes back to 1991. Search all county case records including criminal for free at www.sanmateocourt.org/midx/. Also, search traffic citations at https://www.sanmateocourt.org/traffic/.

San Mateo Central Branch 800 N Humboldt St, San Mateo, CA 94401; 650-573-2617 Traf.; fax: 650-342-5438; 7:30AM-4PM M-TH; 8AM-4PM F (PST). *Small Claims, Traffic, Infractions.*
www.sanmateocourt.org/court_divisions/traffic/

General Information: Small Claims Division has been relocated in Redwood City. Consolidated with the Civil Division in Redwood City. New location for the consolidated Small Claims Clerk's office will be in Rm A in the 1st Fl, Hall of Justice, 400 County Center, Redwood City.

Superior Court - Northern Branch 1050 Mission Rd, South San Francisco, CA 94080; 650-877-5773; criminal phone: 650-877-5771; civil phone: 650-877-5705; criminal fax: 650-877-5703; civil fax: 8AM-4PM; 8AM-4PM (PST). *Misdemeanor, Traffic.*
www.sanmateocourt.org

General Information: Includes Brisbane, Daly City (including Westlake), Pacifica, San Bruno, South San Francisco, the northern coastal towns and all unincorporated areas in the north end of the county including Colma, Bart and Broadmoor. Online identifiers in results same as on public terminal. No probation reports or confidential information records released. Will fax documents to local or toll free line, limit 3-5 pages. Court makes copy: $.50 per page. Certification fee: $25 per doc plus copy fee. Payee: Superior Court. Personal checks and credit cards accepted. Prepayment required. Mail requests: SASE required for civil.

Civil Name Search: Access: Mail, in person, online. Both court and visitors may perform in person name searches. Search fee: $15.00 per name if search exceeds 10 minutes. Civil records go back to 1959 by name index. Note: Probate filings are accepted here, but there are no probate records to search here. Mail turnaround time 2 days to 2 weeks. Civil PAT goes back to 1978. Online access is free at www.sanmateocourt.org/midx/. Includes probate and small claims.

Criminal Name Search: Access: In person, online. Both court and visitors may perform in person name searches. Search fee: $15.00 per name if search exceeds 10 minutes. Required to search: name, years to search; also helpful: DOB. Criminal records computerized from 1991, index files from 1983. Records destroyed after 10 years. Criminal PAT goes back to 1964. Search all county case records including criminal for free at www.sanmateocourt.org/midx/. Also, search traffic citations at https://www.sanmateocourt.org/traffic/. Online results show middle initial.

Santa Barbara County

Superior Court - Civil - Anacapa Division Box 21107, 1100 Anacapa St, Santa Barbara, CA 93121; 805-882-4520; civil phone: 805-882-4550; probate phone: 805-882-4520; fax: 805-882-4519; 8AM-3PM (PST). *Civil Actions, Eviction, Small Claims, Probate.*
www.sbcourts.org/index.asp

General Information: Also known as the Anacapa Division. Includes the City of Santa Barbara, Goleta, and adjacent unincorporated areas, Carpenteria and Montecito. Daily calendars free at www.sbcourts.org/pubcal/. Online identifiers in results same as on public terminal. No adoption, juvenile, medical, probation or sealed records released. Will not fax documents. Court makes copy: $.50 per page. Certification fee: $25 per doc plus copy fee. Payee: Superior Court. Personal checks accepted. Visa/MC accepted. Prepayment required. Mail requests: SASE required.

Civil Name Search: Access: Fax, mail, in person, online. Both court and visitors may perform in person name searches. Search fee: $15.00 per name if search exceeds 10 minutes. Civil records on computer and microfiche from 1975, archived and index file from 1900s. Mail turnaround time 1 week. Public use terminal has civil records back to 1977. Search general civil index 1975 to present or limited civil back to 1977 free at www.sbcourts.org/pubindex/.

Superior Court - Criminal - Figueroa Division 118 E Figueroa St, Santa Barbara, CA 93101; 805-568-3959; 802-882-4735; criminal phone: 805-882-4778-records; fax: 805-882-4607; 7:45AM-3PM; phones- 9AM-N, 1:30PM-3PM (PST). *Felony, Misdemeanor, Small Claims.*
www.sbcourts.org/

General Information: Includes the City of Santa Barbara, Goleta and adjacent unincorporated areas, Carpenteria, Montecito. For civil cases call Anacapa Division at 805-882-4520. Daily calendars free at www.sbcourts.org/pubcal/. No probation reports released. Will not fax documents. Court makes copy: $.50 per page. Certification fee: $25 per doc plus copy fee. Payee: Clerk of the Court. Personal checks and credit cards accepted. Prepayment required. Mail requests: SASE required.

Criminal Name Search: Access: Mail, in person. Both court and visitors may perform in person name searches. Search fee: $15.00 per name if search exceeds 10 minutes. Add $15 fee if records in storage. Required to search: name, years to search; also helpful: DOB. Criminal records computerized from 1991, index files from 1983, microfiche from 1975. Records destroyed after 10 years. Note: Will accept fax requests from gov't agencies only. A CD-Rom of monthly court indices from all divisions is $40.00. Mail turnaround time 3-5 days. Public use terminal has crim records back to 1991.

Santa Maria Cook Division - Superior Court PO Box 5369, 312-C E Cook St Ste C, Santa Maria, CA 93454-5369; 805-614-6414; fax: 805-614-6616; 8AM-3PM (PST). *Civil Actions, Probate, Eviction, Small Claims.*
www.sbcourts.org/index.asp

General Information: The Cook Division handles Civil; its sister court (Miller Division) handles Criminal. Cook includes Betteravia, Casmalia, Cuyama, Guadalupe, Gary, Los Alamos, New Cuyama, Orcutt, Santa Maria, Sisquoc, Tepusquet and sections of Vandenburg Air Force Base. No probation reports, financial, judges notes, confidential or sealed records released. Will fax documents $1.00 per page fee. Court makes copy: $.50 per page. Certification fee: $25 per doc plus copy fee. Payee: Clerk of Court. Personal checks accepted. Visa/MC accepted; include name address of card holder. Prepayment required. Mail requests: SASE required.

Civil Name Search: Access: Mail, in person, online. Both court and visitors may perform in person name searches. Search fee: $15.00 per name if search exceeds 10 minutes. Civil records in index files from 1964. Records destroyed after 10 years. Note: Also, a CD-Rom of monthly court indices from all divisions is for $40.00. Mail turnaround time 5 days. Public use terminal has civil records back to 2000. Search general civil index 1975 to present or limited civil back to 1977 free at www.sbcourts.org/pubindex/. Daily calendars free at www.sbcourts.org/pubcal/.

Santa Maria Miller Division - Superior Court 312 E Cook St, Bldg E, Santa Maria, CA 93454-5165; 805-614-6590; fax: 805-614-6591; 8AM-3PM (PST). *Felony, Misdemeanor, Traffic.*
www.sbcourts.org/index.asp

General Information: Miller Division is in the same building complex as the Cook Division, which handles civil, small claims, family cases. Miller includes the same jurisdictional area as Cook Division. A CD-Rom of monthly court indices from all divisions is for $40.00. No probation reports, financial, judges notes, confidential or sealed records released. Will fax documents $1.00 per page. Court makes copy: $.50 per page. Certification fee: $25 per doc plus copy fee. Payee: Clerk of Court. Personal checks accepted. Visa/MC accepted if you provide name and mailing address. Prepayment required. Mail requests: SASE required.

Criminal Name Search: Access: Mail, fax, in person. Both court and visitors may perform in person name searches. Search fee: $15.00 per name per birthdate if search exceeds 10 minutes. Required to search: complete name and alias, years to search, DOB; also helpful- driver license number. Criminal records in index files from 7/1964. Note: A CD-Rom of monthly court indices from all divisions is $40.00. Mail turnaround time 5 days. Public use terminal has crim records back to 1990, some back to 1980. Public record terminal has index only.

Lompoc Division - Superior Court 115 Civic Center Plz, Lompoc, CA 93436; 805-737-7789; criminal phone: 805-737-5390; civil phone: 805-737-5452; fax: 805-737-5440; 8AM-4PM (PST). *Felony. Misdemeanor, Civil Actions under $25,000, Eviction, Small Claims.*
www.sbcourts.org/

General Information: Includes Lompoc and adjacent unincorporated areas including sections of Vandenburg Air Force Base. Daily calendars free at www.sbcourts.org/pubcal/. A CD-Rom of monthly court indices from all divisions is $40.00. No probation reports released. Will fax documents $1.00 per page. Court makes copy: $.50 per page. Certification fee: $25 per doc plus copy fee. Payee: Clerk of the Superior Court. Personal checks accepted. Prepayment required. Mail requests: SASE required.

Civil Name Search: Access: Mail, in person, online. Both court and visitors may perform in person name searches. Search fee: $15.00 per name if search exceeds 10 minutes. Civil records on computer from 1991, index files from 1983. Records destroyed after 10 years. Mail turnaround time 1 week. Public use terminal available. Search general civil index 1975 to present or limited civil back to 1977 free at www.sbcourts.org/pubindex/.

Criminal Name Search: Access: Mail, in person. Both court and visitors may perform in person name searches. Search fee: $25.00 per name if search exceeds 10 minutes. Required to search: name, years to search, DOB; also helpful: address. Criminal records computerized from 1991, index files from 1983. Records destroyed after 10 years. Note: Includes Solvang jurisdiction filings from 1997 to present. Mail turnaround time 1 week. Public use terminal available. A CD-Rom of monthly court indices from all divisions is $40.00. Online results show name only.

Solvang Division - Superior Court 1745 Mission Dr, #C, Solvang, CA 93463; 805-686-5040; criminal phone: 805-686-7483; civil phone: 805-686-7482; fax: 805-686-7491; 8AM-3PM (PST). *Civil, Small Claims, Traffic.* www.sbcourts.org/index.asp

General Information: Includes the City of Solvang, Buellton, and adjacent unincorporated areas, Los Olivos and Santa Ynez. Daily calendars free at www.sbcourts.org/pubcal/. A CD-ROM of monthly court indices from all divisions is $40.00. Online identifiers in results same as on public terminal. No sealed or confidential records released. Will not fax documents. Court makes copy: $.50 per page. Self serve copy: Self-serve copier across the hall. Certification fee: $25 per doc plus copy fee. Payee: Superior Court. Personal checks accepted. Visa/MC only accepted at the counter and by phone. Prepayment required. Mail requests: SASE required.

Civil Name Search: Access: Phone, mail, in person, online. Both court and visitors may perform in person name searches. Search fee: $15.00 per name if search exceeds 10 minutes. Civil records on computer from 1997 to present, index lists prior. Mail turnaround time 1 week. Public use terminal has civil records back to 1976. Search general civil index 1975 to present or limited civil from 1997 free at www.sbcourts.org/pubindex/. Also, a CD-Rom of monthly court indices from all divisions is for $40.00.

Santa Clara County

Superior Court - Civil 191 N 1st St, San Jose, CA 95113; 408-882-2100; probate phone: 408-882-2100;; 8:30AM-4PM (PST). *Civil, Eviction, Probate.*
www.scscourt.org/

General Information: Handles cases for San Jose, Milpitas, Santa Clara, Los Gatos and Campbell areas. Santa Clara Courthouse at 1095 Homestead Rd, Santa Clara, but records here, ditto for Family Court, 170 Park Center Plaza (408-481-3500). No probation reports or confidential records released. Will not fax documents. Court makes copy: $.50 per page. Certification fee: $25 per doc plus copy fee. Payee: Clerk of Superior Court. Personal checks and credit cards accepted. Prepayment required. Mail requests: SASE required.

Civil Name Search: Access: Mail, in person, online. Both court and visitors may perform in person name searches. Search fee: $15.00 per name if search exceeds 10 minutes. Civil records on computer 1993 to present; prior on books to 1800s. Mail turnaround time 2 weeks. Public use terminal has civil records back to 1993. Civil, Family, Probate, and Small Claims case records and court calendars are free online at www.sccaseinfo.org/. CD-ROM is also available, fee-$150.00.

Superior Court - Criminal 191 N 1st St, Hall of Justice, San Jose, CA 95113; 408-808-6600; 8:30AM-4PM (PST). *Felony, Misdemeanor.*
www.scscourt.org/

General Information: Handles criminal matters for San Jose, Milpitas, Los Gatos, Saratoga, Monte Sereno, and Santa Clara. Terraine Courthouse Drug Court, 115 Terraine St (408-491-4700), records also here. No probation, confidential or sealed records released. Will not fax documents. Court makes copy: $.50 per page plus postage charge based on number of copies. Certification fee: $25 per doc plus copy fee. Payee: Santa Clara Superior Court. Personal checks accepted. Visa/MC/Discover/AmEx accepted with $12.95 usage fee. Prepayment required. Mail requests: SASE required.

Criminal Name Search: Access: Mail, in person. Both court and visitors may perform in person name searches. Search fee: $15.00 per name if search exceeds 10 minutes. Required to search: name, years to search, DOB. Criminal indexes on microfiche from 1975-present. Old files are kept in archives or on microfilm to 1954. Note: 5 name limit for counter service. Above address is mailing address. Street address is 190-200 W Hedding St, ZIP- 95110. Mail turnaround time 3-7 days. Public use terminal has crim records. Access to the criminal case index is at www.scscourt.org/court_divisions/criminal/index_search.asp. Traffic and Local Ordinance case information is at www.sccaseinfo.org.

South County Courthouse - Superior Court 301 Diana Ave, Morgan Hill, CA 95037-4403; 408-695-5000/882-2777; criminal phone: 408-695-5014; civil phone: 408-695-5012;; 8:30AM-4PM (PST). *Felony, Misdemeanor, Civil Actions under $25,000, Eviction, Small Claims, Family, Traffic.* www.scscourt.org/

General Information: Jurisdiction includes the Cities of Gilroy, Morgan Hill, San Martin and surrounding unincorporated areas. Traffic case phone number is 408-695-5011. No adoption, juvenile, medical, probation or sealed records released. Will not fax documents. Court makes copy: $.50 per page.

Certification fee: $25 per doc plus copy fee. Payee: Superior Court. Personal checks accepted. Credit cards accepted. Prepayment required. Mail requests: SASE required.

Civil Name Search: Access: Mail, in person, online. Both court and visitors may perform in person name searches. Search fee: $5.00 per name if search exceeds 10 minutes. Civil records on microfiche. Mail turnaround time 1 week. Civil, Family, Probate, and Small Claims case records and court calendars are free online at www.sccaseinfo.org/. CD-Rom is also available, fee-$150.00.

Criminal Name Search: Access: Mail, in person, online. Both court and visitors may perform in person name searches. Search fee: $5.00 per name if search exceeds 10 minutes. Required to search: name, years to search; also helpful: DOB. Same record keeping as civil. Mail turnaround time 1 week. Access to the criminal case index is at www.scscourt.org/court_divisions/criminal/index_search.asp. Traffic and Local Ordinance case information is at www.sccaseinfo.org. Online results show middle initial.

Palo Alto Facility - Superior Court 270 Grant Ave, Palo Alto, CA 94306; 650-462-3800; 8:30AM-4PM (PST). *Felony, Misdemeanor, Small Claims, Traffic.*
www.scscourt.org/

General Information: Handles criminal matters for Cupertino, Mountain View, Palo Alto, and Sunnyvale. No probation, doctor report, pretrial report records released. Will not fax documents. Court makes copy: $.50 per page. Certification fee: $25 per doc plus copy fee. Payee: Superior Court. Personal checks accepted. Credit cards accepted. Prepayment required. Mail requests: SASE required.

Civil Name Search: Access: Mail, in person, online. Both court and visitors may perform in person name searches. Search fee: $15.00 per name if search exceeds 10 minutes. Required to search: name, years to search. Note: Note only Small Claims civil cases here. Mail turnaround time 1 week. Civil PAT available. Civil, Family, Probate, and Small Claims case records and court calendars are free online at www.sccaseinfo.org/.

Criminal Name Search: Access: Mail, in person, online. Both court and visitors may perform in person name searches. Search fee: $15.00 per name if search exceeds 10 minutes. Required to search: name, years to search; also helpful: DOB. Criminal records on microfiche. Mail turnaround time 1 week. Criminal PAT available. Access to the criminal case index is at www.scscourt.org/court_divisions/criminal/index_search.asp. Traffic and Local Ordinance case information is at www.sccaseinfo.org.

Notre Dame Superior Court 99 Notre Dame Ave, San Jose, CA 95113; 408-882-2912; 8:30AM-4PM (PST). *Family Law.*
www.scscourt.org/

General Information: Includes Los Gatos, Monte Sereno towns; Campbell, Saratoga cities; surrounding unincorporated areas; also San Jose, Milpitas, Santa Clara. This is also the mailing address for Los Gatos (14205 Capri Dr) and Sunnyvale Courthouses (605 W El Camino Real).

Santa Cruz County

Superior Court - Civil 701 Ocean St, Rm 110, Santa Cruz, CA 95060; 831-420-2200; 8AM-3PM (PST). *Civil, Probate.*
www.santacruzcourt.org

General Information: Family Law is handled by the Watsonville courthouse. No adoption, juvenile, medical, probation or sealed records released. Will not fax documents. Court makes copy: $.50 per page. Certification fee: $25 per doc. Payee: Superior Court. Personal checks accepted. Visa/Amex/Discover accepted for add'l fee. Prepayment required. Mail requests: SASE required.

Civil Name Search: Access: Phone, mail, in person, online. Both court and visitors may perform in person name searches. Search fee: $15.00 per name if search exceeds 10 minutes. Civil records on computer back to 6/1985; microfiche, archived and index books from 1880. Mail turnaround time 10-15 days. Public use terminal has civil records back to 1985. Access civil records free at www.santacruzcourt.org/Case%20Info/index.htm. Includes civil, small claims, family law, probate. Access using case number or party name. When searching online court record there could be missing identifiers, and computer systems are not always up-to-date, and do not have as wide a date range as when searching onsite.

Superior Court - Criminal 701 Ocean St, Rm 120, Santa Cruz, CA 95060; 831-420-2200 x2; criminal phone: x2; fax: 831-420-2265; 8AM-3PM (PST). *Felony, Misdemeanor, Traffic.*
www.santacruzcourt.org

General Information: Phone is only answered 8AM to noon. No juvenile, probation or sealed records released. Will fax documents to local or toll free line if 25 pages or . Court makes copy: $.50 per page. Certification fee: $26.00 per doc includes copies. Payee: Superior Court. Personal checks accepted. No credit cards accepted. Prepayment required. Mail requests: SASE required.

Criminal Name Search: Access: Fax, mail, in person. Both court and visitors may perform in person name searches. Search fee: If found on computer no charge, unless "Certified Record Search Letter" required, then $15.00, fee includes search of archives. Required to search: name; also helpful: years to search, DOB. Criminal records on computer since mid-1994; older records on microfiche index by party name back to 1972. Note: may request a countywide index search. Mail turnaround time 1-2 weeks, longer if archives.

Watsonville Division - Superior Court 1 2nd St #300, Watsonville, CA 95076; 831-786-7200; 8AM-3PM (PST). *Misdemeanor, Civil Actions under $25,000, Eviction, Small Claims, Traffic.*
www.santacruzcourt.org
General Information: Includes all of Santa Cruz County. Wireless internet available at courthouse for fee. No probation or juvenile records released. Will not fax documents. Court makes copy: $.50 per page. Self serve copy: $.15 per page. Certification fee: $16 per doc includes copies. Payee: Superior Court. Personal checks accepted. Visa/Amex/Discover accepted for add'l fee. Prepayment required. Mail requests: SASE required.
Civil Name Search: Access: Mail, in person, online. Both court and visitors may perform in person name searches. Search fee: $15.00 per name if search exceeds 10 minutes. Civil records on computer from 1992, index books prior. Records destroyed after 10 years. Mail turnaround time 2-5 days. Civil PAT goes back to 2004. Search the index at www.santacruzcourt.org/Case%20Info/index.htm. Includes small claims, family law, probate. When searching online court record index there could be missing identifiers, and computer systems are not always up-to-date, and do not have as wide a date range as when searching onsite.
Criminal Name Search: Access: Mail, in person. Both court and visitors may perform in person name searches. Search fee: $15.00 per name if search exceeds 10 minutes. Required to search: name, years to search; also helpful: DOB. Criminal records computerized from 1994, microfilm to 1993, index books prior. Records destroyed after 10 years. Note: In person searchers may use microfilm - records back to 1993. Mail turnaround time 2-5 days. Criminal PAT goes back to 1993-2002. Online results show name only.

Shasta County

Superior Court 1500 Court St, Redding, CA 96001; 530-245-6761; fax: 530-225-5339; 8:30AM-4:30PM (PST). *Felony, Misdemeanor, Civil, Small Claims, Eviction, Probate.*
www.shastacourts.com
General Information: Address #319 for civil division and #219 for criminal division. No probation or confidential records released. Will fax documents to local or toll free line. Court makes copy: $.50 per page. Certification fee: $25 per doc plus copy fee. If for a Family law Judgment, then fee is $15 plus copy fee. Payee: Superior Court. Personal checks accepted. Cash only accepted in person. Credit cards accepted. Prepayment required. Mail requests: SASE required.
Civil Name Search: Access: Phone, mail, in person, online. Both court and visitors may perform in person name searches. Search fee: $15.00 per name if search exceeds 10 minutes. Civil records on computer from 1992, index books prior. Mail turnaround time 2-7 days. Civil PAT goes back to 1992. Access to civil division index free back to 1993 at http://caselookup.shastacourts.com:8080/cgi-bin/webcase01r. Search by case, name, or date. Also, the county offers access to the Integrated Justice System (IJS), this is meant for attorneys and requires a password. And registration.
Criminal Name Search: Access: Mail, in person, online. Both court and visitors may perform in person name searches. Search fee: $15.00 per name if search exceeds 10 minutes. Required to search: name, years to search. Criminal records computerized from 1992, index books prior. Mail turnaround time 2-7 days. Criminal PAT goes back to same as civil. Access is the same as described for civil. Online results show name only.

Burney Branch - Superior Court 20509 Shasta St, Burney, CA 96013; 530-335-3571; fax: 530-225-5684; 8AM-N, 1-4:30PM (PST). *Misdemeanor, Eviction, Small Claims.*
www.shastacourts.com
General Information: Civil actions handled by Redding Branch since 1992. Prior civil limited jurisdiction records maintained here. While there is no public access terminal at this court, there is access at the office next door. No probation, juvenile, or DMV reports released. Will not fax documents. Court makes copy: $.50 per page. Certification fee: $25 per doc plus copy fee. Payee: Superior Court. Personal checks accepted. Write 'not to exceed' a dollar amount on checks. No credit cards accepted at this branch. Prepayment required. Mail requests: SASE required.
Civil Name Search: Access: Mail, in person, online. Only the court performs in person name searches; visitors may not. Search fee: $15.00 per name if search exceeds 10 minutes. Civil records on computer from 1992, index books prior. Mail turnaround time 2-14 days. Access to civil division index free back to 1993 at

http://caselookup.shastacourts.com:8080/cgi-bin/webcase01r. Search by case, name, or date. Also, the county offers access to the Integrated Justice System (IJS), this is meant for attorneys and requires a password.
Criminal Name Search: Access: Mail, in person, online. Only the court performs in person name searches; visitors may not. Search fee: $15.00 per name if search exceeds 10 minutes. Required to search: name, years to search, DOB. Criminal records computerized from 1993, index books prior. Mail turnaround time 2-14 days. Online access same as civil. While there is no public access terminal at this court, there is access at the office next door. Online results show name only.

Sierra County

Superior Court PO Box 476, 100 Courthouse Sq, 2nd Fl, Downieville, CA 95936; 530-289-3698; fax: 530-289-0205; 8AM-N, 1-5PM (PST). *Felony, Misdemeanor, Civil, Eviction, Small Claims, Probate.*
www.sierracourt.org
General Information: Probate is a separate index at this same address. Probate fax is same as main fax number. There is no court in Loyalton. No adoption, juvenile, medical, probation or sealed records released. Will fax documents $.50 per page. Court makes copy: $.50 per page. Certification fee: $25 per doc plus copy fee. Payee: Superior Court. Personal checks and credit cards accepted. Prepayment required. Mail requests: SASE required.
Civil Name Search: Access: Phone, fax, mail, in person. Only the court performs in person name searches; visitors may not. Search fee: $15.00 per name if search exceeds 10 minutes. Civil records on computer from 1985, index books from 1852. Mail turnaround time 2-4 days.
Criminal Name Search: Access: Phone, fax, mail, in person. Only the court performs in person name searches; visitors may not. Search fee: $15.00 per name if search exceeds 10 minutes. Required to search: name, years to search. Criminal records computerized from 1985, index books from 1852. Mail turnaround time 2-4 days.

Siskiyou County

Superior Court PO Box 1026, 311 4th St, Yreka, CA 96097; criminal phone: 530-842-8195; civil phone: 530-842-8238; criminal fax: 530-842-8339; civil fax: 8AM-4PM; 8AM-4PM (PST). *Felony, Misdemeanor, Civil, Probate.*
www.siskiyou.courts.ca.gov
General Information: The phone number for research is 530-842-8390. Most branch electronic records indexed here, but branches can be searched manually for paper records, except Happy Camp court which is temporarily closed and records are here. No adoption, juvenile, medical, probation or sealed records released. Will fax documents to local or toll free line. Court makes copy: $.50 per page. Certification fee: $25 per doc plus copy fee. Payee: Siskiyou Superior Court. Personal checks accepted. No credit cards accepted. Prepayment required. Mail requests: SASE required.
Civil Name Search: Access: Phone, mail, in person, online. Both court and visitors may perform in person name searches. Search fee: $15.00 per name if search exceeds 10 minutes. Civil records on computer since 1991, archived and index book from 1900 for felonies. Mail turnaround time 1 week. Civil PAT goes back to 1998. Public terminal here includes case indexes from all four courts. Access to county superior court records is free at www.siskiyou.courts.ca.gov/CaseHistory.asp. Includes traffic but not juvenile or confidential cases.
Criminal Name Search: Access: Mail, in person, online. Both court and visitors may perform in person name searches. Search fee: $15.00 per name if search exceeds 10 minutes. Required to search: name, years to search. Criminal records on computer since 1991, archived and index book from 1900. Mail turnaround time 1 week. Criminal PAT goes back to same as civil. Online access to criminal records is same as civil

Weed Branch - Superior Court 550 Main St, Weed, CA 96094; 530-938-2483; civil phone: 530-842-0107; fax: 530-842-0109; 8AM-4PM (PST). *Misdemeanor, Small Claims, Traffic Infractions.*
www.siskiyou.courts.ca.gov
General Information: Fee to fax out file $1.00 per page. Court makes copy: $.50 per page. Certification fee: $25 per doc plus copy fee. Payee: Siskiyou Superior Court. Personal checks accepted only from party to the case. No credit cards accepted. Prepayment required. Mail requests: SASE required.
Civil Name Search: Access: Mail, fax, in person, online. Only the court performs in person name searches; visitors may not. Search fee: $15.00 per name if search exceeds 10 minutes. Required to search: full name, years to search. Civil cases indexed by defendant, plaintiff. Civil records go back to 1980; on computer since 1995. Mail turnaround time 10 days. Access to county superior court records is free at www.siskiyou.courts.ca.gov/CaseHistory.asp. Includes traffic but not juvenile.
Criminal Name Search: Access: Mail, fax, in person, online. Only the court performs in person name searches; visitors may not. Search fee: $15.00 per name if search exceeds 10 minutes. Required to search: full name, years to search, DOB, SSN. Criminal records go back to 1994; computerized

records back 7 years. Mail turnaround time 10 days. Online access to criminal records is same as civil. Online results show middle initial, DOB.

Dorris/Tulelake Branch - Superior Court 324 N Pine St, Dorris, CA 96023; 530-397-3161; fax: 530-397-3169; 8-10:30AM, 12-4PM (PST). *Civil Actions under $25,000, Eviction, Small Claims.*
www.siskiyou.courts.ca.gov
General Information: This court only maintains a few misdemeanor records for a year. Most new misdemeanor cases are referred to Weed, CA Branch. This Dorris branch jurisdiction includes the Tulelake court sessions at 591 Main St., Tulelake. No probation reports released. Will not fax documents. Court makes copy: $.50 per page. Certification fee: $25 per doc plus copy fee. Payee: Siskiyou Superior Court. Personal checks accepted. Visa/MC accepted, but not for search fee. Prepayment required. Mail requests: SASE required.
Civil Name Search: Access: Mail, in person, online. Only the court performs in person name searches; visitors may not. Search fee: $15.00 per name. Required to search: name, years to search. Civil records on computer back to 1998; prior on books back to 1992. Note: Public access terminal available at the Yreka Main court only. Mail turnaround time 1 week. Access to county superior court records is free at www.siskiyou.courts.ca.gov/CaseHistory.asp. Includes traffic but not juvenile.

Happy Camp Branch - Superior Court
Closed until further notice; cases now managed by Yreka court.

Solano County

Superior Court - Civil 600 Union Ave, Hall of Justice, Fairfield, CA 94533; 707-207-7330; probate phone: 707-207-7341; fax: 707-525-4996; 8AM-4PM (PST). *Civil, Eviction, Probate.*
www.solano.courts.ca.gov/
General Information: Includes Bencia, Fairfield, Suisun, Vacaville, Dixon, Rio Vista, and surrounding area. Northern Solano Muni. Ct. has been combined with this Court. Probate is a separate office at this address. Small claims phone-707-207-7335 in Fairfield. No sealed records released. Will not fax documents. Court makes copy: $.50 per page. Certification fee: $25 per doc plus copy fee. Payee: Solano County Courts. Personal checks accepted. Visa/MC accepted; add'l usage fee applies. Prepayment required. Mail requests: SASE required.
Civil Name Search: Access: Mail, in person, online. Both court and visitors may perform in person name searches. Search fee: $15.00 per name if search exceeds 10 minutes. Civil records on computer since 1992, microfiche since 1971, archived and index files since 1800s. Note: Phone access limited to short searches. Mail turnaround time 2-3 days. Public use terminal has civil records back to 1992. Online access to countywide civil record index is free online. Click on Court Connect from the home page. Also, civil tentative rulings and probate notes are available. Online search provides a case number and limited docket entry information, no personal identifiers except name. Online search request does not allow for add'l identifiers. Missing records can be avoided with an in person search.

Vallejo Branch - Superior Court 321 Tuolumne St, Solano Justice Bldg, Vallejo, CA 94590; 707-561-7800; criminal phone: 707-561-7880; civil phone: 707-561-7830; fax: 707-648-8101; 8AM-4PM (PST). *Felony, Misdemeanor, Civil, Eviction, Small Claims, Probate.*
www.solano.courts.ca.gov/
General Information: Includes cities of Vallejo and Benicia and the adjacent unincorporated areas. No probation reports released. Will fax documents for fee. Court makes copy: $.50 per page. Certification fee: $25 per doc plus copy fee. Payee: Superior Court. Personal checks accepted. Visa, AmEx accepted, add'l usage fee applies. Prepayment required. Mail requests: SASE required.
Civil Name Search: Access: Mail, in person, online. Only the court performs in person name searches; visitors may not. Search fee: $15.00 per name if search exceeds 10 minutes. Civil records on computer from 1/1992, index files from 1983 for Fairfield only. Records destroyed after 10 years. Mail turnaround time 2 days. Public use terminal has civil records back to 1991. Online access to countywide civil record index is free online. Click on Court Connect from the home page. Also, civil tentative rulings and probate notes are available. Online search provides a case number and limited docket entry information, no personal identifiers except name. Online search request does not allow for add'l identifiers. Missing records can be avoided with an in person search.
Criminal Name Search: Access: Mail, in person, online. Only the court performs in person name searches; visitors may not. Search fee: $15.00 per name if search exceeds 10 minutes. Required to search: name, years to search. Criminal records computerized from 1996; index files from 1998. Records destroyed after 5 years. Mail turnaround time 2 days. Online access to countywide record index (back to 2000 generally) is free at

http://courtconnect.solanocourts.com/courtconnect/ck_public_qry_main. cp_main_idx. Online search provides a case number and limited docket entry information, no personal identifiers except name. Online search request does not allow for add'l identifiers. Missing records, often older felonies, can be avoided with an in person search.

Superior Court - Criminal 600 Union Ave, #151, Hall of Justice, Fairfield, CA 94533; 707-207-7380; fax: 707-436-2291; 8AM-3PM (PST). *Felony, Misdemeanor.*
www.solano.courts.ca.gov/
General Information: The Northern Solano Municipal Court has been combined with the Superior Court. This court includes Fairfield, Suisun City, Vacaville, Dixon, Rio Vista Village and adjacent unincorporated areas. Online identifiers in results same as on public terminal. No probation reports released. Will fax out docs to gov't agencies only. Court makes copy: $.50 per page. Certification fee: $25 per doc plus copy fee. Payee: Solano Superior Court. Personal checks accepted. Major credit cards accepted, add'l usage fee applies. Prepayment required. Mail requests: SASE required.
Criminal Name Search: Access: Mail, in person, online. Visitors must perform in person searches themselves. Search fee: $15.00 per name if search exceeds 10 minutes. Required to search: name, years to search; also helpful: DOB, SSN. Superior Court records on computer since 1992, microfiche since 1971; Felonies maintained 75 years, misdemeanors 2-7 years depending on offense. Municipal Court records on computer for past 10 years. Note: Records from this court found here only, not at other divisions. 5 name limit at counter. Fax requests discouraged.- Mail turnaround time 1 week. Public use terminal has crim records back to 1999. Access to countywide record index (to 2000 generally) is free at http://courtconnect.solanocourts.com/courtconnect/ck_public_qry_main. cp_main_idx. Online search provides a case number and limited docket entry information, no personal identifiers except name. Online search request does not allow for add'l identifiers. Missing records, often older felonies, can be avoided with an in person search. Online results show middle initial.

Sonoma County

Superior Court - Criminal 600 Administration Dr, Rm 105J, Hall of Justice, Santa Rosa, CA 95403; 707-521-6500; fax: 707-521-6755; 8AM-4:30PM; phones- 8AM-N (PST). *Felony, Misdemeanor.*
http://sonoma.courts.ca.gov/divisions/criminal
General Information: Archived/older records are located here in Rm 110J. Archived record request form at www.sonomasuperiorcourt.com/index.php. No adoption, juvenile, medical, probation or sealed records released. Will not fax documents. Court makes copy: $.50 per page.Copy fee $2.25 minimum if copies to be mailed back. Certification fee: $25 per doc plus copy fee; exemplification- $20.00. Payee: Superior Court. No out of state personal checks accepted. No credit cards accepted. Prepayment required. Mail requests: SASE required.
Criminal Name Search: Access: Phone, mail, fax, in person. Both court and visitors may perform in person name searches. Search fee: $15.00 per name if search exceeds 10 minutes. Required to search: name, years to search, DOB. Criminal records computerized from 1985, microfiche and index books 1850 to 1984. Note: Misdemeanor record hard copies can be destroyed after 10 years. Mail turnaround time 2-3 weeks. Public use terminal has crim records back to 10/1984. Search free calendars directly at www.sonomasuperiorcourt.com/index.php. Online index does not provide register of actions, just case number and parties. Goes back 3 months.

Superior Court - Civil 600 Administration Dr, Hall of Justice, Santa Rosa, CA 95403; 707-521-6500;; 8AM-4:30PM (PST). *Civil, Eviction, Small Claims, Probate.*
http://sonoma.courts.ca.gov/
General Information: Archived/older records are located here in Rm 110J. No probation reports or sealed records released. Will not fax documents. Court makes copy: $.50 per page.Copy fee $2.25 minimum if mailed. Certification fee: $25 per doc plus copy fee; exemplification- $20.00. Payee: Superior Court. Personal checks accepted. Write 'not to exceed' or 'NTE' and the estimated amount for copy cost and search cost. No credit cards accepted. Prepayment required. Mail requests: SASE required.
Civil Name Search: Access: Mail, in person, online. Both court and visitors may perform in person name searches. Search fee: $15.00 per name per each 10 minutes. Civil records on computer to 10/84, index files prior. Judgment records destroyed after 10 years, dismissals after 1. Computer index include criminal data. Mail turnaround time 3 days to 2 weeks. Public use terminal has civil records back to 1984. Public access terminal includes probate records. If terminal search exceeds 10 minutes, court may charge you $15.00. Limited search free at www.sonomasuperiorcourt.com/index.php for court calendars, cases recently filed, tentative rulings.

Stanislaus County

Superior Court - Criminal PO Box 1098, 800 11 St, Rm 140, Modesto, CA 95353; 209-530-3100; fax: 209-236-7746; 8AM-3PM (PST). *Felony, Misdemeanor.*
www.stanct.org/

General Information: No adoption, juvenile, medical, probation or sealed records released. Court makes copy: $.50 per page. Certification fee: $25 per doc plus copy fee. Payee: Superior Court Clerk. Personal checks accepted. Visa/MC accepted. Prepayment required. Mail requests: SASE required.

Criminal Name Search: Access: Phone, mail, in person, online. Both court and visitors may perform in person name searches. Search fee: $15.00 per name if search exceeds 10 minutes. Required to search: name, years to search, DOB; also helpful- charges, felony/or/misd. Criminal records on microfiche since 1974, archived back to 1800s. Mail turnaround time 6-8 weeks. Public use terminal has crim records back to 1995. Index and case numbers only on public terminal; some records go back further than 1995. Access the yearly case indices free at http://caseindex.stanct.org/.l Superior Court Case Index is available alphabetically in a 2-CD set. Case Index is updated quarterly and includes cases filed 1900-1999, and 2000-present day. Cost is $15.00 per each 2-CD set, which includes S&H. Online results show name only.

Superior Court - Civil 801 Tenth St, 4th Fl, Modesto, CA 95354; 209-530-3102; probate phone: 209-525-4432;; 8AM-5PM (PST). *Civil, Eviction, Small Claims, Probate.*
www.stanct.org/

General Information: Ceres Branch is operational, but all filings are here. Small Claims is located at 2260 Floyd Ave. No probation or juvenile records released. Will not fax documents. Court makes copy: $.50 per side. Certification fee: $25 per doc plus copy fee. Payee: Superior Court. Personal checks accepted. Visa/MC accepted. Prepayment required. Mail requests: SASE required.

Civil Name Search: Access: Mail, in person, online. Both court and visitors may perform in person name searches. Search fee: $15.00 per name if search exceeds 10 minutes. Civil records on computer from 1991, in index files from 1983, microfilm to 1974. Records destroyed after 10 years. Mail turnaround time varies. Public use terminal has civil records. Results include year case was filed. Search yearly case index by name and year at http://caseindex.stanct.org/. Also, Superior Court Case Index is available alphabetically in a 2-CD set. Case Index is updated quarterly and includes cases filed 1900-1999, and 2000-present day. Cost is $15.00 per each 2-CD set, which includes S&H.

Turlock Division - Superior Court 800 11th St, Modesto, CA 95354; 209-530-3101; 8AM-3PM (PST). *Small Claims, Traffic, Ordinances, Infractions.*
www.stanct.org/
General Information: Traffic phone is open until 4PM.

Sutter County

Superior Court - Civil 463 2nd St, Rm 211, Courthouse East, 2nd Fl, Yuba City, CA 95991; 530-822-3304; fax: 530-822-3504; 8AM-5PM (PST). *Civil, Eviction, Small Claims, Probate, Family Law.*
www.suttercourts.com

General Information: No adoption, juvenile, medical, probation or sealed records released. Will not fax documents. Court makes copy: $.50 per page. Certification fee: $25 per doc plus copy fee. Payee: Superior Court. Personal checks accepted. Visa/MC accepted and 5% usage fee applies. Prepayment required. Mail requests: SASE required.

Civil Name Search: Access: Mail, in person. Both court and visitors may perform in person name searches. No search fee, unless case prior to 1994 then $15.00 per name. Required to search: name, years to search, type of case. Civil cases indexed by defendant, plaintiff. Civil records in index books and archived from 1800s, on computer back to 1/94. Mail turnaround time 2 weeks. Public use terminal has civil records back to 1994. Access calendars free at www.suttercourts.com/unprotected/Calendar/themed.asp.

Superior Court - Criminal 446 2nd St, Yuba City, CA 95991; 530-822-3306; fax: 530-822-3506; 8AM-5PM (PST). *Felony, Misdemeanor.*
www.suttercourts.com
General Information: Walk-in hours are 8:30AM-4:30PM. No police reports or probation records released. Will fax out documents if requested. Court makes copy: $.50 per page. Certification fee: $25 per doc includes copies, usually. Payee: Sutter County Superior Court. Personal checks accepted. Visa/MC accepted and 5% usage fee applies. Prepayment required. Mail requests: SASE required.

Criminal Name Search: Access: Fax, mail, in person. Both court and visitors may perform in person name searches. Search fee: $15.00 per name if search exceeds 15 minutes, or the case is pre-1994. Criminal docket on books and archived from 1800s, computerized since 1992. Mail turnaround time 1 week. Public use terminal has crim records back to

1992, index shown is countywide. Calendars free at www.suttercourts.com/unprotected/Calendar/themed.asp.

Tehama County

Superior Court - Civil PO Box 310, 633 Washington St, Rm 17, Red Bluff, CA 96080; 530-527-6441; fax: 530-527-0984; 8AM-4PM M-TH; till 3PM F (PST). *Civil, Small Claims, Eviction, Probate, Family Law.*
www.tehamacourt.ca.gov

General Information: No adoption, juvenile, mental, probation or sealed records released. Will not fax documents. Court makes copy: $.50 per page. Certification fee: $25 per doc plus copy fee; $20.00 for exemplification. Payee: Tehama County Superior Court. Personal checks accepted. Visa/MC accepted. Prepayment required. Mail requests: SASE required.

Civil Name Search: Access: Mail, in person, online. Only the court performs in person name searches; visitors may not. Search fee: $15.00 per name if search exceeds 10 minutes. Civil records on computer back to 1991, archived and index books from 1900s. Mail turnaround time same day. Search by name or case number at http://cms.tehamacourt.ca.gov/. Daily calendars also online. Cases online starting with NT or NCR are at Red Bluff; ST or SCR are at Corning.

Superior Court - Criminal PO Box 1170, 445 Pine St, Red Bluff, CA 96080; 530-527-3563; fax: 530-527-0956; 8AM-4PM M-TH; till 3PM F (PST). *Felony, Misdemeanor.*
www.tehamacourt.ca.gov
General Information: No probation reports released. Will not fax documents. Court makes copy: $.50 per page. Certification fee: $25 per doc plus copy fee. Payee: Superior Court. Personal checks accepted. Credit cards accepted in person only. Prepayment required. Mail requests: SASE required.

Criminal Name Search: Access: Mail, in person, online. Both court and visitors may perform in person name searches. Search fee: $15.00 per name if search exceeds 10 minutes. Required to search: name, years to search; also helpful: DOB. Criminal records computerized from 1991, index cards prior. Will only search back 7 years. Mail turnaround time within 1 week. Search by name or case number at http://cms.tehamacourt.ca.gov/. Daily calendars also online. Cases online starting with NT or NCR are at Red Bluff; St or SCR are at Corning. Online results show middle initial.

Corning Branch - Superior Court 720 Hoag St, Corning, CA 96021; 530-824-4601; fax: 530-824-6457; 8AM-4PM M-TH; till 3PM F (PST). *Misdemeanor, Civil Actions under $25,000, Eviction, Small Claims.*
www.tehamacourt.ca.gov/

General Information: No probation reports released. Will fax documents to local or toll free line, if other fees paid. Court makes copy: $.50 per page. Certification fee: $25 per doc plus copy fee. Payee: Tehama Superior Court. Personal checks accepted. Visa/MC accepted. Prepayment required. Mail requests: SASE required.

Civil Name Search: Access: Mail, in person, online. Both court and visitors may perform in person name searches. Search fee: $15.00 per name if search exceeds 10 minutes. Civil index on cards. Will only search back 7 years; records on computer since 1990. Note: Requests must be in writing. Mail turnaround time 1 week. Search by name or case number at http://cms.tehamacourt.ca.gov/. Daily calendars also online. Cases online starting with NT or NCR are at Red Bluff; St or SCR are at Corning.

Criminal Name Search: Access: Mail, in person, online. Only the court performs in person name searches; visitors may not. Search fee: $15.00 per name if search exceeds 10 minutes. Required to search: name, years to search; also helpful: DOB. Criminal records computerized from 1990, index cards prior. Will only search back 7 years. Note: Requests must be in writing. Mail turnaround time 1 week. Search by name or case number at http://cms.tehamacourt.ca.gov/. Daily calendars also online. Cases online starting with NT or NCR are at Red Bluff; St or SCR are at Corning. Online results show middle initial.

Trinity County

Superior Court PO Box 1258, 11 Court St, Weaverville, CA 96093; 530-623-1208; fax: 530-623-3762; 8AM-5PM (PST). *Felony, Misdemeanor, Civil, Eviction, Small Claims, Probate.*
www.trinity.courts.ca.gov/
General Information: Probate fax is same as main fax number. No adoption, juvenile, medical, probation or sealed records released. Will not fax documents. Court makes copy: $.50 per page. Certification fee: $25 per doc plus copy fee. Payee: Superior Court. Personal checks accepted. No credit cards accepted. Prepayment required. Mail requests: SASE required.

Civil Name Search: Access: Mail, in person. Only the court performs in person name searches; visitors may not. Search fee: $15.00 per name if search exceeds 10 minutes. Civil records on microfiche, archived and index files from 1900s. Note: 1-2 names only counter service. Mail turnaround time 1-5 days.

Criminal Name Search: Access: Mail, in person. Only the court performs in person name searches; visitors may not. Search fee: $15.00 per name if search exceeds 10 minutes. Required to search: name, years to search. Criminal records on microfiche, archived and index files from 1900s. Note: 1-2 names only counter service. Mail turnaround time 1-5 days.

Tulare County

Superior Court Courthouse, 221 S Mooney Blvd, Visalia, CA 93291; 559-730-5000,; fax: 559-737-4547; 8AM-4PM (PST). *Felony, Civil, Eviction, Small Claims, Probate.*
www.tularesuperiorcourt.ca.gov
General Information: This court has records from Exeter, Woodlake, Farmersville, Goshen and Three Rivers. Also holds records from closed court in Dinuba for Dinuba, Cutler, Orosi, Selville, Traver, London, Delf, and Orange Cove. No adoption, juvenile, mental, probation reports or sealed records released. Will not fax documents. Court makes copy: $.50 per page. Certification fee: $25 per doc plus copy fee. Payee: Tulare County Superior Court. Personal checks accepted. Prepayment required. Mail requests: SASE required.
Civil Name Search: Access: Mail, in person. Both court and visitors may perform in person name searches. Search fee: $15.00 per name if search exceeds 10 minutes. Civil records on computer back to 2/1986; microfiche and index books from 1800s. Note: Address civil record requests to Rm. 201. Mail turnaround time 3 weeks. Civil PAT goes back to 1986. Daily calendar and civil tentative rulings and probate recommendations at www.tularesuperiorcourt.ca.gov.
Criminal Name Search: Access: Mail, in person. Both court and visitors may perform in person name searches. Search fee: $15.00 per name if search exceeds 10 minutes. Required to search: name, years to search, DOB or SSN. Criminal records computerized from 2/1986; microfiche and index books from 1800s. Note: Address criminal record requests to Rm. 124. Mail turnaround time 1 week. Criminal PAT goes back to same as civil. Daily calendar at www.tularesuperiorcourt.ca.gov.

Porterville Division - Superior Court 87 E Morton Ave, Porterville, CA 93257; 559-782-3700; fax: 559-782-4805; 8AM-4PM (PST). *Felony, Misdemeanor, Civil Actions under $25,000, Eviction, Small Claims.*
www.tularesuperiorcourt.ca.gov
General Information: Includes Porterville, Springville, Camp Nelson, Johnsondale, Lindsay, Terra Bella, Ducor, Richgrove, Poplar, Strathmore and surrounding areas. No probation reports released. Court makes copy: $.50 per page. Certification fee: $25 per doc plus copy fee. Payee: Porterville Superior Court. Personal checks accepted. Major credit cards accepted, at 3.5% surcharge is added. Prepayment required. Mail requests: SASE required.
Civil Name Search: Access: Mail, in person. Both court and visitors may perform in person name searches. Search fee: $15.00 per name if search exceeds 10 minutes. Required to search: name, years to search, DOB, SSN, case #. Civil cases indexed by defendant, plaintiff. Civil records on computer from 2/1992, index book prior. Records destroyed after 10 years. Mail turnaround time 3-5 days. Civil PAT goes back to 2/1992. Daily calendar and civil tentative rulings and probate recommendations at www.tularesuperiorcourt.ca.gov.
Criminal Name Search: Access: Mail, in person. Both court and visitors may perform in person name searches. Search fee: $15.00 per name if search exceeds 10 minutes. Required to search: name, years to search; also helpful: DOB, SSN, case #. Criminal records computerized from 2/1992, index book prior. Records destroyed after 10 years. Mail turnaround time 3-5 days. Criminal PAT goes back to same as civil. Daily calendar at www.tularesuperiorcourt.ca.gov.

Tulare/Pixley Division - Superior Court PO Box 1136, 425 E Kern St, Tulare, CA 93275; 559-685-5500; 559-685-2556; criminal phone: x1; civil phone: x3; fax: 559-685-2663; 8AM-5PM (Lobby hours til 4PM) (PST). *Misdemeanor, Civil Actions under $25,000, Eviction, Small Claims.*
www.tularesuperiorcourt.ca.gov
General Information: Includes Tulare, Pixley, Tipton, Earlimart, Alpaugh, Allensworth, Woodville, Waukena and surrounding areas. No probation reports released. Will not fax documents. Court makes copy: $.50 per page. Certification fee: $25 per doc plus copy fee. Payee: Superior Court. Personal checks accepted. Visa/MC accepted. Prepayment required. Mail requests: SASE required.
Civil Name Search: Access: Mail, fax, in person. Both court and visitors may perform in person name searches. Search fee: $15.00 per name if search exceeds 10 minutes. Civil records in index books. Records destroyed after 10 years; on computer back to 1992. Mail turnaround time 2 days. Civil PAT goes back to 1992. Daily calendar and civil tentative rulings and probate recommendations at www.tularesuperiorcourt.ca.gov.
Criminal Name Search: Access: Mail, fax, in person. Both court and visitors may perform in person name searches. Search fee: $15.00 per name if search exceeds 10 minutes. Required to search: name, years to search, DOB; also helpful: address, SSN. Criminal index in books. Records destroyed after 10 years; on computer back to 1992. Mail turnaround time 2 days. Criminal PAT goes back to same as civil. Daily calendar at www.tularesuperiorcourt.ca.gov.

Dinuba Division - Superior Court.
www.tularesuperiorcourt.ca.gov
General Information: Criminal and Civil Records no longer available in Dinuba. All business was re-allocated to Visalia.

Tuolumne County

Superior Court - Civil 41 W Yaney Ave, Sonora, CA 95370; 209-533-5555; fax: 209-533-6616; 8AM-4PM (PST). *Civil, Eviction, Small Claims, Probate.*
www.tuolumne.courts.ca.gov
General Information: Departments 1, 2, and 5. The small claims court can be reached at 209-533-6509. Unlawful detainer clerk- 209-533-5555. No adoption, juvenile, medical, probation or sealed records released. Will not fax documents. Court makes copy: $.50 per page. Certification fee: $25 per doc plus copy fee. Payee: Superior Court. Personal checks accepted but not out of state checks. Major credit cards accepted, in person only. Prepayment required. Mail requests: SASE required.
Civil Name Search: Access: Mail, in person. Both court and visitors may perform in person name searches. Search fee: $15.00 per name if search exceeds 10 minutes. Civil records on computer back to 1994, microfiche and archived from 1900, index files from 1800s. Mail turnaround time 1 week. Public use terminal has civil records back to 1994.

Superior Court - Criminal 60 N Washington St, Sonora, CA 95370; 209-533-5563; fax: 209-533-5581; 8AM-4PM (PST). *Felony, Misdemeanor, Traffic.*
www.tuolumne.courts.ca.gov
General Information: Add'l court office location at 41 W Yaney St; public searching also available there. Traffic court phone is 209-533-5671. No sealed records released. Most records are public. Will only fax to public agencies. Court makes copy: $.50 per page. Certification fee: $25 per doc plus copy fee. Payee: Tuolumne County Superior Court. Personal checks accepted. Visa/MC accepted plus $10.00 usage fee, in person only,. Prepayment required. Mail requests: SASE required.
Criminal Name Search: Access: Mail, fax, in person, online. Both court and visitors may perform in person name searches. Search fee: $15.00 per name if search exceeds 10 minutes. Required to search: name, years to search, DOB. Felony records on computer from 1993; misdemeanors from 1999; index files prior. Will only search back 7 years. Mail turnaround time 10-14 days. Public use terminal has crim records back to 1993. Access criminal records by case number of DR# at www.tuolumne.courts.ca.gov; click on "Criminal Division." Online results show middle initial.

Ventura County

Ventura Superior Court PO Box 6489, 800 S Victoria Ave, #218, Ventura, CA 93006-6489; criminal phone: 805-654-2611; civil phone: 805-654-2609; probate phone: 805-654-2264; fax: 805-650-4032; 8AM-11:30AM; 1:30PM-4PM (PST). *Felony, Misdemeanor, Civil, Eviction, Small Claims, Probate.*
www.ventura.courts.ca.gov
General Information: Records Division phone- 805-654-2880. Sm Claims- 805-654-2610. Search request can include civil and criminal if you specify. Court record indexes also available in bulk format. No adoption, mental health, paternity actions, juvenile, medical, probation or sealed records released. Will not fax out documents. Court makes copy: $.50 per page. Certification fee: $25 per doc plus copy fee. Payee: Superior Court. Personal checks accepted. Credit cards accepted; a surcharge is added. Prepayment required. Mail requests: SASE required.
Civil Name Search: Access: Phone, mail, online, in person. Both court and visitors may perform in person name searches. Search fee: $15.00 per name if search exceeds 10 minutes. Civil records prior to 10/93 are on microfiche, after are on computer. Mail turnaround time 5-10 days; archived records require longer. Civil PAT goes back to 1993. Access to case information, calendars and dockets is free at www.ventura.courts.ca.gov/via/CaseSearch.aspx. Search by defendant or plaintiff name, case number, or date. Search probate at www.venturacogensoc.org/Probate.html. Also, search family cases but case number required at www.ventura.courts.ca.gov/civcase/case_home.asp.
Criminal Name Search: Access: Phone, mail, online, in person. Both court and visitors may perform in person name searches. Search fee: $15.00 per name if search exceeds 10 minutes. Required to search: name, years to search, DOB, case type. Criminal records go back to 1893; Criminal records computerized from 1989, prior on microfiche. Mail turnaround time 5-10 days; records from archives require longer. Criminal PAT goes back to same as civil. Access to case information back to 1995, calendars and dockets is free at https://secured.countyofventura.org/courtservices/CourtServiceHome.aspx. Online results show name only.

East County Superior Court PO Box 1200, 3855F Alamo St, Simi Valley, CA 93062; 805-582-8086; criminal phone: 805-654-2611;; 8AM-11:30AM; 1:30PM-4PM (PST). *Civil, Eviction, Small Claims, Family Law, Misdemeanor Traffic.*
www.ventura.courts.ca.gov

General Information: Other phones- Eviction 582-8086; Small Claims 582-8078; Family Law 582-8086; Traffic 582-8080. Online identifiers in results same as on public terminal. No adoption, mental health, paternity actions, juvenile, medical, probation or sealed records released. Court makes copy: $.50 per page. Self serve copy: $.15 per page. Certification fee: $25 per doc plus copy fee. Payee: Ventura County Superior Courts. Personal checks accepted. All major credit cards accepted; add'l transaction fee for credit card. Prepayment required. Mail requests: SASE required.

Civil Name Search: Access: Phone, mail, online, in person. Both court and visitors may perform in person name searches. Search fee: $15.00 per name if search exceeds 10 minutes. Civil records go back to 4/92. Mail turnaround time 5 days. Civil PAT goes back to 10/1993. Access to civil court records 10/93-present is free at the www.ventura.courts.ca.gov/via/CaseSearch.aspx. Search by defendant or plaintiff name, case number, or date. Search probate at www.venturacogensoc.org/Probate.html. Also, search family cases but case number required at www.ventura.courts.ca.gov/civcase/case_home.asp.

Criminal Name Search: Access: Phone, mail, in person, online. Both court and visitors may perform in person name searches. Search fee: $15.00 per name if search exceeds 10 minutes. Required to search: name, years to search, DOB, case type. Same record keeping as civil. Mail turnaround time 5 days. Criminal PAT available. Access to case information back to 1995, calendars and dockets is free at https://secured.countyofventura.org/courtservices/CourtServiceHome.aspx. Online results show name only.

Yolo County

Superior Court 725 Court St, Woodland, CA 95695; 530-406-6700; criminal phone: 530-406-6705; civil phone: 530-406-6704; criminal fax: 530-406-6763; civil fax: 8:30AM-4PM; 8:30AM-4PM (PST). *Felony, Misdemeanor, Civil, Eviction, Small Claims, Probate.*
www.yolo.courts.ca.gov/

General Information: Identify specific dept room number when mailing requests. Address: civil requests #103 and criminal #111. Small claims phone is 530-406-6706. No adoption, juvenile, medical, probation or sealed records released. Will not fax documents. Court makes copy: $.50 per page. Self serve copy: $.25 per page. Certification fee: $25 per doc. Payee: Yolo Superior Court. Personal checks accepted. No credit cards accepted. Prepayment required. Mail requests: SASE required.

Civil Name Search: Access: Phone, mail, in person. Both court and visitors may perform in person name searches. Search fee: $15.00 per name if search exceeds 10 minutes. Civil records on computer from 1995, microfiche, archived and index files from 1800s. Note: Court will do only a few names in a phone search request. Mail turnaround time 2 weeks. Public use terminal has civil records back to 3/1995. Some not all cases will show address. Calendars are online free at www.yolocourts.com/calendar_daily.html. Search Probate Notes at www.yolocourts.com/probate_notes.html.

Criminal Name Search: Access: Mail, in person, online. Both court and visitors may perform in person name searches. Search fee: $15.00 per name if search exceeds 10 minutes. Required to search: name, years to search; also helpful: DOB. Criminal records computerized from 1995, microfiche, archived and index files from 1800s. Mail turnaround time 2 weeks. Access criminal and traffic records free at http://secure.yolo.courts.ca.gov:80/GetWeb/YoloCrimTrafStart.html but no name searching; search by case number or DL only, DOB requested. Also, calendars are free at www.yolocourts.com/calendar_daily.html. Online results show name, DOB.

Yuba County

Superior Court 215 Fifth St, Ste 200, Marysville, CA 95901; 530-749-7600; criminal phone: x3; fax: 530-749-7351; 8:30AM-4:30PM (PST). *Felony, Misdemeanor, Civil, Small Claims, Probate.*
www.yubacourts.org

General Information: No adoption, paternity, juvenile, medical, probation or sealed records released. Will not fax out documents. Court makes copy: $.50 per page. Certification fee: $25 per doc plus copy fee. Payee: Yuba County Superior Court. Personal checks accepted. No credit cards accepted. Prepayment required. Mail requests: SASE required.

Civil Name Search: Access: Mail, in person. Both court and visitors may perform in person name searches. Search fee: $15.00 per name if search exceeds 10 minutes. Civil records on computer from 1992, index books through 1962, archives and index files from 1854. Note: The Court Calendar is viewable online. Mail turnaround time 1-2 weeks. Civil PAT goes back to 1993. Results may include DOB.

Criminal Name Search: Access: Mail, in person. Both court and visitors may perform in person name searches. Search fee: $15.00 per name if search exceeds 10 minutes. Required to search: name, years to search. Criminal records computerized from 1992, index books through 1962, archives and index files from 1854. Note: Court calendars are found online. Mail turnaround time 1-2 weeks. Criminal PAT goes back to same as civil.

Yuba County Superior Court 215 5th St, #200, Marysville, CA 95901; 530-749-7600; fax: 530-749-7351; 8:30AM-4:30PM (PST). *Civil Actions under $25,000, Eviction, Small Claims.*
www.yubacourts.org

General Information: All record requests must be directed to H. Stephen Konishi, Court Executive Officer. No labor commissioner judgment, juvenile, or judge's records released. Will not fax documents. Court makes copy: $.50 per page. Certification fee: $25 per doc plus copy fee. Payee: Yuba County Superior Court. Personal checks accepted. No credit cards accepted. Prepayment required. Mail requests: SASE required.

Civil Name Search: Access: Mail, in person. Both court and visitors may perform in person name searches. Search fee: $15.00 per name if search exceeds 10 minutes. Required to search: name, years to search, DOB. Civil cases indexed by defendant, plaintiff. Civil records on computer through 1992, index books prior back to 1850's. Note: Court calendars are found online. Mail turnaround time 1-2 weeks. Public use terminal has civil records back to 1993. Probate Notes arranged by session back 4 months are available free at www.yubacourts.org/probate.html

Colorado

Time Zone:	MST
Capital:	**Denver, Denver County**
# of Counties:	**64**
State Web:	**www.colorado.gov**
Court Web:	**www.courts.state.co.us**

Administration

State Court Administrator, 101 W Colfax, Ste 500, Denver, CO, 80202; 303-861-1111, Fax: 303-837-2340.

The Supreme and Appellate Court

The Supreme Court is the court of last resort. The Colorado Court of Appeals is usually the first court of appeals for decisions from the district courts, Denver Probate Court, and Denver Juvenile Court. The Court of Appeals also reviews decisions of several state administrative agencies. Opinions are online found on the home page.

The Colorado Courts

Court	Type	How Organized	Jurisdiction Highpoints
District*	General	64 Courts in 22 Districts	Felony, Misdemeanor, Civil, Probate, Juvenile, Domestic Relations
County*	Limited	See above	Misdemeanor, Civil Actions Under $15,000, Small Claims, Eviction
Municipal	Limited	Approx 100	Ordinances
Water	Special	7 in 7 Districts	Water Rights
Denver County*, Probate and Juvenile	General and Limited	Denver County	Misdemeanor, Civil Actions Under $15,000, Small Claims, Probate, Juvenile

* = profiled in this book

Details on the Trial Court Structure

District Courts hear civil cases in any amount (District and County Courts have overlapping jurisdiction over civil cases involving less than $15,000), as well as domestic relations, criminal, juvenile, probate, and mental health cases. District court decisions may be appealed to the Colorado Court of Appeals and in some cases directly to the Colorado Supreme Court).

County Courts handle civil cases under $15,000, misdemeanors, traffic infractions, felony complaints (which may be sent to District Court), protection orders, and small claims. County court decisions may be appealed to the District Court.

Water Courts have exclusive jurisdiction over cases relating to the determination of water rights, use and administration of water, and all other water matters. There are seven Water Courts - one per major river basins - located in Weld, Pueblo, Alamosa, Montrose, Garfield, Routt, and La Plata counties.

The **Denver Court System** differs from those in the rest of the state, in part because Denver is both a city and a county. The Denver County Court functions as a municipal and a county court and is paid for entirely by Denver taxes, rather than by state taxes. The Denver County Court is not part of the state court system; the District Court is.

Municipal Courts only have jurisdiction over traffic, parking, and ordinance violations. Denver is the only county where the **Probate Court** and **Juvenile Court** is separate from the District Court.

Record Searching Facts You Need to Know

Fees and Record Searching Tips

Most courts charge $5.00 per name for a name search and the copy fee is $.75, $.25 if self serve. Some courts charge $25.00 per hour. Certification is set at $20.00 per document. See fees at www.courts.state.co.us/userfiles/File/Self_Help/fees.pdf. Almost all courts require a self-addressed, stamped envelope (SASE) for return of information.

Water Court records are maintained by the Water Clerk and fees are similar to those for other court records. To retrieve a Water Court record, one must furnish the case number or the legal description (section, township, and range) or the full name of the respondent (case number or legal description are preferred).

Online Access is Statewide via Designated Vendors

Online access to the dockets is not available directly through the Colorado Judicial Branch website, but there are 2 designated vendors who provide a statewide search for the state. Fees vary. See www.courts.state.co.us/Administration/Program.cfm/Program/11.

Denver County data is not in the statewide system, but has its own separate free online access system at www.denvergov.org/apps/newcourt/court_select.aspx. Current dockets free; includes case, party and action information, possibly DOB. Note that the designated vendors providing above mentioned statewide access by subscription also include a search of Denver as part of their services. Document image copies are not available from any of the websites; file copies may only be obtained from the local court of record.

Adams County

17th District Court 1100 Judicial Center Dr, Brighton, CO 80601; 303-659-1161; criminal phone: 303-654-3314; civil phone: 303-654-3237; probate phone: 303-654-3237; fax: 303-654-3216; 8AM-5PM (MST). *Felony, Civil Actions over $10,000, Probate, Domestic.*
www.17thjudicialdistrict.com
General Information: District and County courts have combined but records are searched separately unless you ask the court to search both courts for no extra fee). Probate is in a separate index. Probate fax is same as main fax number. No adoption, sealed, juvenile, paternity, mental health or expunged cases released. Will not fax documents. Court makes copy: $.75 per page. Self serve copy: $.25 per page. Certification fee: $20.00 per doc. Payee: Clerk of Court. Personal checks accepted. Accepts credit cards in person only. Prepayment required. Mail requests: SASE required.
Civil Name Search: Access: Mail, in person, online. Both court and visitors may perform in person name searches. Search fee: $5.00 per name. Fee is $10.00 for cases before 1990. There is no fee if search done by party of case. Civil records on computer from 1990, index books back to early 1900s. Mail turnaround time 3 days. Pay service to civil case look-up at www.courts.state.co.us; click on Court Records Search.
Criminal Name Search: Access: Mail, in person, online. Both court and visitors may perform in person name searches. Search fee: $5.00 per name. Fee is $10.00 for cases before 1990. Required to search: name, years to search, DOB. Criminal records computerized from 1990, index books back to early 1900s. Mail turnaround time 3 days. Criminal case index at www.courts.state.co.us. Current dockets free, records not- click on Court Records Search.

County Court 1100 Judicial Center Dr, Brighton, CO 80601; 303-659-1161; criminal phone: 303-654-3314; civil phone: 303-654-3335; fax: 303-654-3216; 8AM-5PM; Lunch hour- slow. File Rm open till 4PM (MST). *Misdemeanor, Civil Actions under $15,000, Eviction, Small Claims, Traffic.*
www.courts.state.co.us
General Information: The District and County courts have combined, but records are searched separately unless you specifically ask the court to search both courts for no add'l fee. Public use terminals are in development. No adoption, sealed, juvenile, paternity, mental health or expunged cases released. Will not fax documents. Court makes copy: $.75 per page. Self serve copy: $.25 per page. Certification fee: $20.00 per doc. Payee: Adams County Combined Court. Personal checks accepted. Credit cards accepted. Prepayment required. Mail requests: SASE required.
Civil Name Search: Access: Mail, in person, online. Both court and visitors may perform in person name searches. Search fee: $5.00 per name. $10.00 per name for pre-computer records. Civil records on computer from 1/1990, index books back to 1965. Mail turnaround time 3 working days. Pay service to civil case look-up at www.courts.state.co.us; click on Court Records Search.
Criminal Name Search: Access: Mail, in person, online. Both court and visitors may perform in person name searches. Search fee: $5.00 per name. $10.00 per name for pre-computer records. Required to search: name, years to search, DOB. Criminal records computerized from 1/1990, index books

back to 1965. Mail turnaround time 3 working days. Still in development, the public terminals are not recommended as reliable or complete. Criminal case index at www.courts.state.co.us. Current dockets free, records not- click on Court Records Search.

Alamosa County

Alamosa Combined Court 702 4th St, Alamosa, CO 81101; 719-589-4996; 8AM-12: 1PM-4PM (MST). *Felony, Misdemeanor, Civil, Eviction, Small Claims, Probate, Traffic.*
www.courts.state.co.us/Courts/County/Choose.cfm
General Information: Email to alamosaclerk@judicial.state.co.us. No adoption, juvenile, mental health, sealed or expunged cases released. Will not fax documents. Court makes copy: $.75 per page. Certification fee: $20.00 plus copy fee. Payee: Clerk, Combined Court. Personal checks and credit cards accepted. Prepayment required. Mail requests: SASE required.
Civil Name Search: Access: Phone, mail, in person, online. Both court and visitors may perform in person name searches. Search fee: $5.00 per name. $25.00 per hour if extensive research is needed. Civil records on computer from 1993, index cards from 5/1978, index books back to 1913. Mail turnaround time 10 days. Public use terminal has civil records back to 2001. Pay service to civil case look-up at www.courts.state.co.us; click on Court Records Search. Also, use the site at www.courts.state.co.us/Courts/County/Dockets.cfm/County_ID/32 for a county docket search going back one week only.
Criminal Name Search: Access: Phone, mail, in person, online. Both court and visitors may perform in person name searches. Search fee: $5.00 per name. $25.00 per hour if extensive research is needed. Required to search: name, years to search, DOB. Criminal records computerized from 1993, index cards from 5/1978, index books back to 1913. Mail turnaround time 10 days. Criminal case index at www.courts.state.co.us. Current dockets free, records not- click on Court Records Search. Also, use the site at www.courts.state.co.us/Courts/County/Dockets.cfm/County_ID/32 for a county docket search. - only goes back one week however. Online results show middle initial, DOB.

Arapahoe County

Combined Court 7325 S Potomac St, Centennial, CO 80112; 303-649-6355; civil phone: x5;; 8AM-4PM (MST). *Felony, Civil Actions over $15,000, Probate.*
www.courts.state.co.us/Courts/County/Index.cfm?County_ID=57
General Information: Since August 2010, this main county courthouse has Aurora court's cases (except Small Claims which are in the Littleton Court) from 2008 forward, plus all Aurora electronic records, and maintains access to Aurora's hard-copy case files. No adoption, sealed, juvenile, mental health or expunged cases released. Will not fax documents. Court makes copy: $.75 per page. Self serve copy: $.25 per page. Certification fee: $20.00 per doc. Payee: Clerk of District Court. Personal checks accepted - write 'not to exceed 'and amount on check. Credit cards accepted in person. Prepayment required. Mail requests: SASE required.
Civil Name Search: Access: Phone, mail, in person, online. Both court and visitors may perform in person name searches. Search fee: $5.00 per

name. $25.00 per hour if extensive research is needed. Civil records on computer from 1985, microfiche back to 1903. Note: Hard-copies of Pre-2008 records from Aurora may require an additional two day turnaround. Mail turnaround time 10 working days, usually 48 hours for newer records. Pay service to civil case look-up at www.courts.state.co.us and click on Court Records Search.

Criminal Name Search: Access: Phone, mail, in person, online. Both court and visitors may perform in person name searches. Search fee: $5.00 per name. $25.00 per hour if extensive research is needed. Required to search: name, years to search, DOB. Criminal records computerized from 1985, microfiche back to 1903. Note: Hard-copies of Pre-2008 records from Aurora may require an additional two day turnaround. Mail turnaround time 48 hours, though older records may require 7-10 days. Public use terminal has crim records back to 1990 and some not all order cases 1986-1989. Criminal case index at www.courts.state.co.us. Current dockets free, records not- click on Court Records Search. Will perform computer terminal searches in answer to phone name search requests.

Arapahoe County Court Division A 1790 W Littleton Blvd, Littleton, CO 80120-2060; 720-798-4591; fax: 720-688-4888; 8AM-N-1:15-4PM (MST). *Misdemeanor, Civil Actions under $15,000, Eviction, Small Claims, Traffic.*
www.courts.state.co.us/Courts/County/Choose.cfm

General Information: Since August 2010, this Littleton courthouse hears Aurora court's area Small Claims only cases. No adoption, sealed, juvenile, mental health or expunged cases released. Will not fax documents. Court makes copy: $.75 per page. Self serve copy: $.25 per page. Certification fee: $20.00 per doc plus copy fee. Payee: Clerk of County Court. Personal checks accepted. Credit cards accepted. Prepayment required. Mail requests: SASE required.

Civil Name Search: Access: Mail, in person, online. Only the court performs in person name searches; visitors may not. Search fee: $5.00 per name. $25.00 per hour if extensive research is needed. Civil records on computer from 1986, index cards from 1965, microfiche from 1861 in District Court. Note: Only court performs searches of files prior to March 1986. Mail turnaround time 5-10 business days. Pay service to civil case look-up at www.courts.state.co.us; click on Court Records Search.

Criminal Name Search: Access: Mail, in person, online. Only the court performs in person name searches; visitors may not. Search fee: $5.00 per name. $25.00 per hour if extensive research is needed. Required to search: name, years to search, DOB. Criminal records computerized from 1986, index cards from 1965, microfiche from 1861 in District Court. Note: Only court performs searches prior to March 1986. Mail turnaround time 5-10 business days. Criminal case index at www.courts.state.co.us. Current dockets free, records not- click on Court Records Search.

Arapahoe County Court Division B 15400 E 14th Pl, Closed to public, no staff present, Aurora, CO 80011; 303-649-6355; . *Misdemeanor, Civil Actions under $15,000, Eviction.*
www.courts.state.co.us/Courts/County/Choose.cfm

General Information: Court closed. Since 8/2010, main county courthouse (Centennial) has heard Aurora cases. Centennial clerk has all Div B Aurora records from 2008 forward; older records still stored in Aurora, not publicly assessable. Small Claims cases now at Littleton.

Archuleta County

Combined Courts PO Box 148, Pagosa Springs, CO 81147; 970-264-5932; fax: 970-264-2407; 8AM-4PM (MST), *Felony, Misdemeanor, Civil, Eviction, Small Claims, Probate.*
www.courts.state.co.us/Courts/County/Choose.cfm

General Information: No adoption, sealed, juvenile, mental health or expunged cases released. Will fax documents to local or toll free line, otherwise $1.00 per page. Must be prepaid. Court makes copy: $.75 per page. Certification fee: $20.00 per doc. Payee: Archuleta Combined Court. Personal checks accepted. Major credit cards accepted in person only. Prepayment required. Mail requests: SASE required.

Civil Name Search: Access: Mail, in person, online. Only the court performs in person name searches; visitors may not. Search fee: $5.00 per name, $10.00 if name not on computer. Specific case information $5.00 per file after 1st file. Civil index on cards from 1976, index books back to 1885, on computer since 1996. Mail turnaround time 1-2 week, maybe. Pay service to civil case look-up at www.courts.state.co.us; click on Court Records Search.

Criminal Name Search: Access: Mail, in person, online. Only the court performs in person name searches; visitors may not. Search fee: $5.00 per name, $10.00 if name not on computer. Specific case information $5.00 per file after 1st file. Required to search: name, years to search, DOB. Criminal records indexed on cards from 1976, index books back to 1885, on computer since 1996. Mail turnaround time 1-2 weeks, maybe. Criminal case index at www.courts.state.co.us. Current dockets free, records not- click on Court Records Search.

Baca County

Baca County District & County Courts 741 Main St, Springfield, CO 81073; 719-523-4555; fax: 719-523-4552; 8AM-5PM (MST). *Felony, Misdemeanor, Civil, Eviction, Small Claims, Probate.*
www.courts.state.co.us/Courts/County/Choose.cfm

General Information: No adoption, sealed, juvenile, mental health or expunged cases released. Will fax documents $1.00 per page only two pages. Will not fax back lengthy docs. Court makes copy: $.75 per page. Certification fee: $20.00 per doc. Payee: Baca County Combined Courts. Personal checks accepted. No credit cards accepted. Prepayment required. Mail requests: SASE required.

Civil Name Search: Access: Mail, in person, online. Only the court performs in person name searches; visitors may not. Search fee: $5.00 per name. $25.00 per hour if extensive research is needed. Civil index on cards from 1945, index books back to 1910, computerized since 1995. Mail turnaround time 1-2 days. Pay service to civil case look-up at www.courts.state.co.us; click on Court Records Search.

Criminal Name Search: Access: Mail, in person, online. Only the court performs in person name searches; visitors may not. Search fee: $5.00 per name. $25.00 per hour if extensive research is needed. Required to search: name, years to search, DOB. Criminal records indexed on cards from 1945, index books back to 1910, computerized since 1995. Mail turnaround time 1-2 days. Criminal case index at www.courts.state.co.us. Current dockets free, records not- click on Court Records Search.

Bent County

16th District Court Bent County Courthouse, 725 Bent, Las Animas, CO 81054; 719-456-1353; fax: 719-456-0040; 8AM-N, 1-5PM (MST). *Felony, Misdemeanor, Civil, Eviction, Small Claims, Probate.*
www.courts.state.co.us/Courts/County/Choose.cfm

General Information: Free access to daily dockets at the web. No adoption, sealed, juvenile, mental health or expunged cases released. Will fax documents to local or toll free line. Court makes copy: $.75 per page; off-site copies may be more. Certification fee: $20.00. Payee: Clerk of Combined Court. Personal checks accepted. No credit cards accepted. Prepayment required. Mail requests: SASE required.

Civil Name Search: Access: Mail, in person, online. Only the court performs in person name searches; visitors may not. Search fee: $5.00 per name. $25.00 per hour if extensive research is needed, or off-site. Civil index on cards to 1976, some on microfilm, on computer from 11/95 forward- all indexes available at this office. Mail turnaround time 4-5 days. Pay service to civil case look-up at www.courts.state.co.us; click on Court Records Search. Free access to daily dockets at the web.

Criminal Name Search: Access: Mail, in person, online. Only the court performs in person name searches; visitors may not. Search fee: $5.00 per name. $25.00 per hour if extensive research is needed, or off-site. Required to search: name, years to search, DOB. Criminal records indexed on cards to 1976, some on microfilm, on computer from 11/95 forward- all indexes available at this office. Mail turnaround time 4-5 days. Criminal case index at www.courts.state.co.us. Current dockets free, records not- click on Court Records Search.

Boulder County

20th District & County Courts 6th & Canyon, 1777 6th St, Boulder, CO 80306; 303-441-3750; probate phone: 303-441-4740; fax: 303-441-3737; 9AM-5PM (MST). *Felony, Misdemeanor, Civil, Eviction, Small Claims, Probate.*
www.courts.state.co.us/Courts/County/Choose.cfm

General Information: Research Dept. phone- 303-441-4860. Probate fax- 303-441-3737. No adoption, sealed, juvenile, mental health or expunged cases released. Will fax documents to local or toll-free number for $1.00 per page. Court makes copy: $.75 per page. Self serve copy: $.25 per page. Certification fee: $20.00. Payee: 20th Judicial District. Business checks or attorney checks accepted. Visa/MC/Discover accepted. Prepayment required. Mail requests: SASE required.

Civil Name Search: Access: Mail, in person, online. Only the court performs in person name searches; visitors may not. Search fee: $5.00 per name. $20.00 per hour if extensive research is needed. Civil records on computer from 1983, microfiche prior from 1977, all prior records in books. Mail turnaround time 3-10days. Pay service to civil case look-up at www.courts.state.co.us; click on Court Records Search.

Criminal Name Search: Access: Mail, in person, online. Only the court performs in person name searches; visitors may not. Search fee: $5.00 per name. $20.00 per hour if extensive research is needed. Required to search: name, years to search, DOB, signed release. Criminal records computerized from 1983, microfiche prior from 1977, all prior records in books. Mail turnaround time 3-10 days. Criminal case index at www.courts.state.co.us. Current dockets free, records not- click on Court Records Search.

Broomfield County

Broomfield Combined Court District, County & Municipal, 17 DesCombes Dr, Broomfield, CO 80020; 720-887-2100; fax: 720-887-2122; 8AM-5PM (MST). *Felony, Misdemeanor, Civil, Eviction, Small Claims, Probate.*
www.broomfield.org/courts/
General Information: County created on Nov. 15, 2001. Older records should be searched in Adams, Boulder, Jefferson or Weld counties. This court holds Municipal court records also. No Juvenile or protective custody records released. Will not fax documents. Court makes copy: $.75 per page. Self serve copy: $.25 per page. Certification fee: $20.00. Payee: Broomfield Combined Courts. Will accept checks. Major credit cards accepted. Prepayment required. Mail requests: SASE required.
Civil Name Search: Access: Mail, in person, online. Only the court performs in person name searches; visitors may not. Search fee: $5.00 per name. $25.00 per hour if extensive research is needed. Required to search: DOD, years to search; address helpful. Civil records on computer since 11/15/01. Mail turnaround time 3 days. Pay service to civil case look-up at www.courts.state.co.us; click on Court Records Search.
Criminal Name Search: Access: Mail, in person, online. Only the court performs in person name searches; visitors may not. Search fee: $5.00 per name. $25.00 per hour if extensive research is needed. Required to search: name, also helpful: address, DOB. Criminal records computerized from 11/15/01. Mail turnaround time 3 days. Criminal case index at www.courts.state.co.us. Current dockets free, records not- click on Court Records Search.

Chaffee County

11th District & County Courts PO Box 279, 142 Crestone Ave, Salida, CO 81201; 719-539-2561/6031; fax: 719-539-6281; 8AM-5PM (MST). *Felony, Misdemeanor, Civil, Eviction, Small Claims, Probate.*
www.courts.state.co.us/Courts/County/Index.cfm?County_ID=28
General Information: This court combined in 2002; formerly two courts: one county court, one district court. Probate fax is same as main fax number. No adoption, sealed, juvenile, mental health or expunged cases released. Fee to fax document $1.00 per page. Court makes copy: $.75 per page. Certification fee: $20.00 per certification plus copy fee. Payee: Clerk of District Court. Personal checks accepted. No credit cards accepted. Prepayment required. Mail requests: SASE required.
Civil Name Search: Access: Phone, mail, in person, online. Only the court performs in person name searches; visitors may not. Search fee: $5.00 per name. $25.00 per hour if extensive research is needed. Civil records on computer back to 1995; index cards from 4/1976, index books back to late 1800s. Mail turnaround time ASAP. Pay service to civil case look-up at www.courts.state.co.us; click on Court Records Search.
Criminal Name Search: Access: Phone, mail, in person, online. Only the court performs in person name searches; visitors may not. Search fee: $5.00 per name. Fee applies if 3 or more files involved. Required to search: name, years to search, DOB. Criminal records computerized from 1995; index cards back to 4/1976, index books back to late 1800s. Mail turnaround time 2-3 days. Criminal case index at www.courts.state.co.us. Current dockets free, records not- click on Court Records Search.

Cheyenne County

District & County Courts PO Box 696, 51 S First St, Cheyenne Wells, CO 80810; 719-767-5649; fax: 719-767-5671; 8AM-4PM M-TH; till noon F (MST). *Felony, Misdemeanor, Civil, Eviction, Small Claims, Probate.*
www.courts.state.co.us/Courts/County/Choose.cfm
General Information: No adoption, sealed, juvenile, mental health or expunged cases released. Will fax documents $1.00 per page. Court makes copy: $.75 per page. Certification fee: $20.00 per document. Payee: Cheyenne County Combined Court. Business checks accepted. No credit cards accepted. Prepayment required. Mail requests: SASE required.
Civil Name Search: Access: Mail, in person, online. Only the court performs in person name searches; visitors may not. Search fee: $5.00 per name. $25.00 per hour if extensive research is needed. Civil records on computer since 11/1/95, index cards from 1960, index books back to early 1900s. Mail turnaround time 5-7 days. Pay service to civil case look-up at www.courts.state.co.us; click on Court Records Search.
Criminal Name Search: Access: Mail, in person, online. Only the court performs in person name searches; visitors may not. Search fee: $5.00 per name. $25.00 per hour if extensive research is needed. Required to search: name, years to search, DOB, notarized signed release. Criminal records on computer since 11/1/95, index cards from 1960, index books back to early 1900s. Mail turnaround time 5-7 days. Criminal case index at www.courts.state.co.us. Obtain current dockets free, records require payment- click on Court Records Search.

Clear Creek County

Clear Creek Combined Courts PO Box 367, 405 Argentine St, Georgetown, CO 80444; 303-679-4220; fax: 303-569-3274; 8AM-5PM (MST). *Felony, Misdemeanor, Civil, Eviction, Small Claims, Probate.*
www.courts.state.co.us/Courts/County/Choose.cfm
General Information: No searches done on records prior to 1976. No adoption, sealed, juvenile, mental health or expunged cases released. Will not fax documents. Court makes copy: $.75 per page. Certification fee: $20.00 per doc does not include copies. Payee: Clerk of Combined Court. Personal checks accepted. Visa/MC accepted. Prepayment required. Mail requests: SASE required.
Civil Name Search: Access: Mail, in person, online. Both court and visitors may perform in person name searches. Search fee: $5.00 per name. $25.00 per hour if extensive research is needed. Civil index on cards from 1976, ledger books back to late 1800. Mail turnaround time 1 week. Pay service to civil case look-up at www.courts.state.co.us; click on Court Records Search.
Criminal Name Search: Access: Mail, in person, online. Both court and visitors may perform in person name searches. Search fee: $5.00 per name. $25.00 per hour if extensive research is needed. Required to search: name, years to search, DOB. Criminal records indexed on cards from 1976, ledger books back to late 1800, computerized since 9/95. Mail turnaround time 1 week. Criminal case index at www.courts.state.co.us. Current dockets free, records not- click on Court Records Search. Online results show middle initial, DOB.

Conejos County

12th District & County Courts PO Box 128, 6683 County Road 13, Conejos, CO 81129; 719-376-5466; probate phone: 719-376-5465;; 8AM-4PM (MST). *Felony, Misdemeanor, Civil, Eviction, Small Claims, Probate.*
www.courts.state.co.us/Courts/County/Choose.cfm
General Information: No adoption, sealed, juvenile, mental health or expunged cases released. Will not fax documents. Court makes copy: $.75 per page. Certification fee: $20.00. Payee: Conejos Combined Court. Personal checks and credit cards accepted. Prepayment required. Mail requests: SASE required.
Civil Name Search: Access: Mail, in person, online. Only the court performs in person name searches; visitors may not. Search fee: $5.00 per name. $25.00 per hour if extensive research is needed. Civil records on computer since 6/94, on index cards from 1980. Mail turnaround time 2 weeks. Pay service to civil case look-up at www.courts.state.co.us; click on Court Records Search.
Criminal Name Search: Access: Mail, in person, online. Only the court performs in person name searches; visitors may not. Search fee: $5.00 per name. $25.00 per hour if extensive research is needed. Required to search: name, years to search, DOB. Criminal records on computer since 6/94, on index cards from 1980. Mail turnaround time 2 weeks. Criminal case index at www.courts.state.co.us. Current dockets free, records not- click on Court Records Search.

Costilla County

12th District & County Courts Costilla Combined Courts, 304 Main Street, San Luis, CO 81152; 719-672-3681; 8AM-N, 1-4PM (MST). *Felony, Misdemeanor, Civil, Eviction, Small Claims, Probate.*
www.courts.state.co.us/Courts/County/Choose.cfm
General Information: They no longer accept faxes. No adoption, sealed, juvenile, mental health, certain criminal cases or expunged cases released. Court makes copy: $.75 per page. Self serve copy: $.25 per page. Certification fee: $20.00 per document. Payee: Costilla Combined Courts. Personal checks and credit cards accepted. Prepayment required. Mail requests: SASE required.
Civil Name Search: Access: Mail, in person, online. Both court and visitors may perform in person name searches. Search fee: $5.00 per name. Records prior to 1994 are $25.00 per hour. Required to search: name, years to search; also helpful: address. Civil index on cards from 1970, index books back to 1865, indexed on computer since 1994. In CO state archives prior to 1970. Mail turnaround time 1-2 weeks. Pay service to civil case look-up at www.courts.state.co.us; click on Court Records Search.
Criminal Name Search: Access: Mail, in person, online. Only the court performs in person name searches; visitors may not. Search fee: $5.00 per name, records prior to 1994 are $25.00 per hour. Required to search: name, years to search, DOB; also helpful: address, SSN. Criminal records indexed on cards from 1970, index books back to 1865, indexed on computer since 1994. In CO state archived prior to 1970. Mail turnaround time 1-2 weeks. Criminal case index at www.courts.state.co.us. Current dockets free, records not- click on Court Records Search. Online results show middle initial, DOB.

Crowley County

Combined Courts 110 E 6th St, #303, Ordway, CO 81063; 719-267-4468; fax: 719-267-3753; 8AM-N, 1-5PM (MST). *Felony, Misdemeanor, Civil, Eviction, Small Claims, Probate.*
www.courts.state.co.us/Courts/County/Choose.cfm
General Information: Search fee includes both civil and criminal indexes. No adoption, sealed, juvenile, mental health or expunged cases released. Will fax documents for $1.00 per page fee. Court makes copy: $.75 per page. Certification fee: $20.00 per doc plus copy fee. Payee: Crowley Combined Court. Personal checks accepted. No credit cards accepted. Prepayment required. Mail requests: SASE required.
Civil Name Search: Access: Phone, mail, fax, in person, online. Only the court performs in person name searches; visitors may not. Search fee: $5.00 per name. $25.00 per hour if extensive research is needed. Civil records on computer back to 1993, fiche since 1980s, index books back to 1925. Mail turnaround time 3-5 days. Pay service to civil case look-up at www.courts.state.co.us; click on Court Records Search.
Criminal Name Search: Access: Mail, fax, in person, online. Only the court performs in person name searches; visitors may not. Search fee: $5.00 per name. $25.00 per hour if extensive research is needed. Required to search: name, years to search, DOB, SSN. Criminal records computerized from 1993, fiche since 1980's, index books back to 1925. Mail turnaround time 3-5 days. Criminal case index at www.courts.state.co.us. Current dockets free, records not- click on Court Records Search.

Custer County

11th District & County Courts PO Box 60, 205 S 6th St, Westcliffe, CO 81252; 719-783-2274; fax: 719-783-2995; 8AM-4PM (MST). *Felony, Misdemeanor, Civil, Eviction, Small Claims, Probate, Traffic.*
www.courts.state.co.us/Courts/County/Index.cfm?County_ID=29
General Information: No adoption, sealed, juvenile, mental health or expunged cases released. Will fax documents $1.00 per page. This fee applies to incoming faxes too. Court makes copy: $.75 per page. Certification fee: $20.00. Payee: Custer Combined Court. Personal checks and credit cards accepted. Prepayment required. Mail requests: SASE required.
Civil Name Search: Access: Mail, in person, online. Only the court performs in person name searches; visitors may not. Search fee: $5.00 per name. $25.00 per hour if extensive research is needed. Civil index on cards from 1973, ledger books back to 1965, on computer since 1993, archived from 1879-1972. Mail turnaround time 3-4 days. Pay service to civil case look-up at www.courts.state.co.us; click on Court Records Search.
Criminal Name Search: Access: Mail, in person, online. Only the court performs in person name searches; visitors may not. Search fee: $5.00 per name. $25.00 per hour if extensive research is needed. Required to search: name, years to search, DOB. Criminal records indexed on cards from 1973, ledger books back to 1965, on computer since 1993, archived from 1879-1972. Mail turnaround time 3-4 days. Criminal case index at www.courts.state.co.us. Current dockets free, records not- click on Court Records Search.

Delta County

Combined Courts 501 Palmer St, Rm 338, Delta, CO 81416; 970-874-6280; fax: 970-874-4306; 8AM-4PM (MST). *Felony, Misdemeanor, Civil, Eviction, Small Claims, Probate, Traffic.*
www.courts.state.co.us/Courts/County/Choose.cfm
General Information: No adoption, sealed, juvenile, mental health or expunged cases released. Will fax documents $1.00 per page, but only if authorized by Clerk or Judge. Court makes copy: $.75 per page. Certification fee: $20.00 per cert plus copy fee. Payee: Clerk of Court. Personal and business checks accepted. Visa/MC accepted. Prepayment required. Mail requests: SASE required.
Civil Name Search: Access: Mail, fax, in person, online. Only the court performs in person name searches; visitors may not. Search fee: $5.00 per name. $25.00 per hour if extensive research is needed. Civil records on computer back to 10/1994, index cards from 1972, index books back to 1900. Mail turnaround time 10 days. Pay service to civil case look-up at www.courts.state.co.us; click on Court Records Search. Also, weekly dockets are at www.courts.state.co.us/.
Criminal Name Search: Access: Mail, fax, in person, online. Only the court performs in person name searches; visitors may not. Search fee: $5.00 per name. $25.00 per hour if extensive research is needed. Required to search: name, years to search, DOB, signed release. Criminal records computerized from 10/1994, index cards from 1972, index books back to 1900. Mail turnaround time 10 days. Criminal case index at www.courts.state.co.us. Current dockets free, records not- click on Court Records Search. Also, weekly dockets are available, see civil, above.

Denver County

2nd District Court - Civil, Pre-2007 Felony 1437 Bannock, Rm 256, Office of the Court Clerk, Denver, CO 80202; 720-865-8301; 7:30AM-4:30PM (MST). *Felony (Pre-2007), Civil Actions over $15,000, Domestic.*
www.courts.state.co.us/Courts/County/Index.cfm?County_ID=3
General Information: This court will not process written requests for information. You must use the Internet or hire a retriever, or visit in person. Case files located in Rm 38, but note that newer felony case records are at the new criminal courthouse on Colfax St. No sealed or expunged cases released. Will not fax documents. Court makes copy: $.75 per page. Self serve copy: $.25 per page. Certification fee: $20.00 per cert. Payee: Denver District Court. Personal checks accepted. Visa/MC accepted. Prepayment required.
Civil Name Search: Access: In person, online. Both court and visitors may perform in person name searches. No search fee. Civil records on computer from 1974, index books back to the late 1800s. Online search of Denver County Civil Division court cases is at www.denvergov.org/apps/newcourt/court_select.aspx. Search by name, business name, or case number. DOBs do not always appear on Denver online results. A subscription account is also available via www.courts.state.co.us where daily trial court dockets can be searched free. Also, week of dockets available free at www.courts.state.co.us/Courts/County/Dockets.cfm?County_ID=3.
Criminal Name Search: Access: In person, online. Both court and visitors may perform in person name searches. No search fee. Required to search: name, years to search, DOB. Criminal records computerized from 1974, index books back to the late 1800s if convicted of criminal charges. Note: Mailing address for 2007-forward criminal matters is Lindsey-Flanigan Courthouse, 520 West Colfax Ave, Rm 135, Denver, CO 80204, 720-865-8301. Criminal case index at www.denvergov.org/apps/newcourt/court_select.aspx where Denver case histories go back at least 5 years; results include case, party and action information. DOBs do not always appear on Denver online results. A subscription account is also available via www.courts.state.co.us where daily trial court dockets can be searched free. Also, week of dockets available free at www.courts.state.co.us/Courts/County/Index.cfm?County_ID=3. Online results show middle initial.

2nd District Court - Felony 520 W Colfax Ave, Rm 135, Denver, CO 80204; 720-865-8301;; 8AM-4PM (MST). *Felony (2007-Present).*
www.courts.state.co.us/Courts/County/Index.cfm/County_ID/3
General Information: This criminal courthouse has case records for felonies from 2007 to present only. Older records are located at the old courthouse on Bannock St, although all electronic felony records appear on court clerk's terminals. No sealed or expunged cases released. Will not fax out documents. Court makes copy: $.75 per page. Self serve copy: $.25 per page. Certification fee: $20.00 per cert. Payee: Denver District Court. Personal checks accepted. Visa/MC accepted. Prepayment required.
Criminal Name Search: Access: In person, Online. Both court and visitors may perform in person name searches. No search fee. Required to search: name, years to search, DOB. Criminal records computerized from 1976. Hard-copies of felonies from 2007-forward only. Note: Mailing address for pre-2007 felony matters is 1437 Bannock, Rm 256, Denver, CO 80202. Criminal case index at www.denvergov.org/apps/newcourt/court_select.aspx where Denver case histories go back at least 5 years; results include case, party and action information. DOBs do not always appear on Denver online results. A subscription account is also available via www.courts.state.co.us where daily trial court dockets can be searched free. Also, weekly dockets free at www.courts.state.co.us/Courts/County/Dockets.cfm/County_ID/3. Online results show middle initial.

County Court - Civil Division 1515 Cleveland Pl, 4th Fl, Denver, CO 80202; 303-865-7840; fax: 303-865-8259; 8AM-5PM (MST). *Civil Actions under $15,000, Eviction, Small Claims.*
www.courts.state.co.us/Courts/County/Choose.cfm
General Information: Week of dockets available free at www.courts.state.co.us/Courts/County/Dockets.cfm/County_ID/3. No adoption, sealed, juvenile, mental health or expunged cases released. Will not fax documents. Court makes copy: $.75 per page. Self serve copy: $.25 per page. Certification fee: $20.00. Payee: Denver County Court. Personal checks accepted. No credit cards accepted. Prepayment required. Mail requests: SASE required.
Civil Name Search: Access: Mail, in person, online. Only the court performs in person name searches; visitors may not. No search fee. Civil records on computer from 1987. Will hold paper on lawsuits 4 years. Mail turnaround time 1 week. Online search of Denver County Civil Division court cases is at www.denvergov.org/apps/newcourt/court_select.aspx. Search by name, business name, or case number. DOBs do not always appear on Denver online results. A subscription account is also available via www.courts.state.co.us where daily trial court dockets can be searched free.

County Court - Criminal Division 520 W Colfax, Rm 160, Denver, CO 80202; 720-337-0410; fax: 720-337-0807; 7:30AM-5PM (MST). *Misdemeanor.*

www.courts.state.co.us/Courts/County/Choose.cfm

General Information: Week of dockets available free at www.courts.state.co.us/Courts/County/Dockets.cfm?County_ID=3. No adoption, sealed, juvenile, mental health or expunged cases released. Will fax documents $5.00 per name plus $.75 per page. Court makes copy: $.25 per page. Certification fee: $20.00 per doc. Payee: Denver County Court. Personal checks and credit cards accepted. Prepayment required. Mail requests: SASE required.

Criminal Name Search: Access: Mail, in person, online. Only the court performs in person name searches; visitors may not. No search fee, until after 2nd request by the person of record, then $5.00. Required to search: name, years to search, DOB; also helpful: address. Criminal records computerized since 1978. Note: Only the person of record can make search requests to the office. Office suggests the online search for background checks. Mail turnaround time 1 week. Criminal case index and dockets at www.denvergov.org/apps/newcourt/court_select.aspx where Denver case histories go back at least 10 years; results include case, party and action information. A subscription account is also available via www.courts.state.co.us where daily trial court dockets can be searched free but DOBs do not always appear on Denver online results.

Probate Court 1437 Bannock St, Rm 230, Denver, CO 80202; 720-865-8310; fax: 720-865-8329; 8AM-12; 1PM-4PM (MST). *Probate.*

www.denverprobatecourt.org

General Information: There is an online record request form at www.denverprobatecourt.org/recordsrequest.htm. Online access to selected opinions is available free at www.denverprobatecourt.org/selectedopinions.htm.

Dolores County

22nd District & County Courts PO Box 511, Dove Creek, CO 81324; 970-677-2258; fax: 970-677-4156; 8AM-5PM M, T; 8AM-N F (MST). *Felony, Misdemeanor, Civil, Eviction, Small Claims, Probate.*

www.courts.state.co.us/Courts/County/Choose.cfm

General Information: Office is closed on Wednesday & Thursday. No adoption, sealed, juvenile, mental health or expunged cases released. Will not fax documents. Court makes copy: $.75 per page. Certification fee: $20.00. Payee: Dolores County Combined. Only cashiers checks and money orders accepted. No credit cards accepted. Prepayment required. Mail requests: SASE required.

Civil Name Search: Access: Phone, mail, in person, online. Only the court performs in person name searches; visitors may not. No search fee. Civil index on cards from 1972, index books back to 1895, on computer from 6/95 to present. Mail turnaround time 1 week. Pay service to civil case look-up at www.courts.state.co.us; click on Court Records Search.

Criminal Name Search: Access: Phone, mail, in person, online. Only the court performs in person name searches; visitors may not. No search fee. Required to search: name, years to search, DOB. Criminal records indexed on cards from 1972, index books back to 1895, on computer from 6/95 to present. Mail turnaround time 1 week. Criminal case index at www.courts.state.co.us. Current dockets free, records not- click on Court Records Search.

Douglas County

Douglas County Combined Court 4000 Justice Way, #2009, Castle Rock, CO 80109; 303-663-7200; fax: 303-688-1962; 8AM-4PM (MST). *Felony, Misdemeanor, Civil, Eviction, Small Claims, Probate.*

www.courts.state.co.us/Courts/County/Choose.cfm

General Information: Probate fax is same as main fax number. No adoption, sealed, juvenile, mental health or expunged cases released. Will not fax documents. Court makes copy: $.75 per page. Self serve copy: $.25 per page. Certification fee: $20.00 per cert. Payee: Clerk of Court. Credit cards accepted in person. Prepayment required. Mail requests: SASE required.

Civil Name Search: Access: Mail, in person, online. Only the court performs in person name searches; visitors may not. Search fee: $5.00 per name. $25.00 per hour for extensive search for records pre-2000. Required to search: name, years to search, case number if available. Civil records on computer back to 1/1988, index cards from 1975, index books to 1880s. Note: Only the court personnel may search microfilm and CDs. Mail turnaround time 1-2 weeks. Pay service to civil case look-up at www.courts.state.co.us; click on Court Records Search.

Criminal Name Search: Access: Mail, in person, online. Only the court performs in person name searches; visitors may not. Search fee: $5.00 per name. $25.00 per hour for extensive search for records pre-2000. Required to search: name, years to search, case number if available. Criminal records computerized from 1/1994 (in fee cases to 1988 with limited data), index cards from 1975, index books to 1880s. Note: Only the court personnel may search microfilm and CDs. Mail turnaround time 1-2 weeks.

Criminal case index at www.courts.state.co.us. Current dockets free, records not- click on Court Records Search.

Eagle County

Eagle Combined Court PO Box 597, 0885 Chambers Ave, Eagle, CO 81631; 970-328-6373; fax: 970-328-6328; 8AM-N; 1-4PM (MST). *Felony, Misdemeanor, Civil, Eviction, Small Claims, Probate.*

www.courts.state.co.us/Courts/County/Choose.cfm

General Information: No adoption, sealed, juvenile, mental health or expunged cases released. Will fax documents $1.00 per page; pay fax fee with credit card. Court makes copy: $.75 per page. Certification fee: $20.00 per doc. Payee: Eagle Combined Courts. Personal checks accepted. Visa/MC accepted. Prepayment required. Mail requests: SASE required.

Civil Name Search: Access: Fax, mail, in person, online. Both court and visitors may perform in person name searches. Search fee: $5.00 per name. $25.00 per hour if extensive research is needed. Civil records on computer since 9/95; prior on fiche to 1970, books to 1930. Mail turnaround time 5-7 days. Pay service to civil case look-up at www.courts.state.co.us; click on Court Records Search.

Criminal Name Search: Access: Fax, mail, in person, online. Both court and visitors may perform in person name searches. Search fee: $5.00 per name. $25.00 per hour if extensive research is needed. Required to search: name, years to search, DOB. Criminal records on computer since 9/95; prior on fiche to 1970, books to 1930. Mail turnaround time 5-7 days. Criminal case index at www.courts.state.co.us. Current dockets free, records not- click on Court Records Search.

El Paso County

El Paso Combined Court PO Box 2980, 270 S Tejon, Colorado Springs, CO 80901-2980; 719-448-7599, record search- 448-7700; fax: 719-448-7695; 8AM-N, 1PM-4PM (MST). *Felony, Misdemeanor, Civil Actions, Probate.*

www.elpasocountycourts.com/

General Information: Request form available at website. Records Center is located in the basement. No adoption, sealed, juvenile, mental health, expunged cases or other access restricted cases released. Added fee to fax document is $1.00 per page. Court makes copy: $.75 per page. Certification fee: $20.00 per doc. Payee: Clerk of District Court. Personal checks and credit cards accepted. Prepayment required. Mail requests: SASE required.

Civil Name Search: Access: Fax, mail, in person, online. Both court and visitors may perform in person name searches. Search fee: $5.00 per name. Retrieval of file/document from off-site facility is $15.00 per file. Civil records on computer from 1/1975, index cards to 1975, index books to 1861. Mail turnaround time 5-7 days. Pay service to civil case look-up at www.courts.state.co.us; click on Court Records Search. One may also order record copies from the home page at same fees mentioned here. See www.elpasocountycourts.com/public_data_request_form.htm.

Criminal Name Search: Access: Fax, mail, in person, online. Both court and visitors may perform in person name searches. Search fee: $5.00 per name; if pre-1988, fee is $25.00 per hour. Required to search: name, years to search, DOB; also helpful: SSN. Criminal records computerized from 1/1975, index cards to 1975, index books to 1861. Mail turnaround time 5-7 days. Criminal case index at www.courts.state.co.us. Current dockets free, records not- click on Court Records Search. One may also order record copies from the home page at same fees mentioned here. See www.elpasocountycourts.com/public_data_request_form.htm. Online results show middle initial, DOB.

Elbert County

Elbert District & County Courts 751 Ute Ave, Kiowa, CO 80117; 303-621-2131/2137; fax: 303-621-9489; 8AM-5PM M-F (MST). *Felony, Misdemeanor, Civil, Eviction, Small Claims, Probate.*

www.courts.state.co.us/Courts/County/Choose.cfm

General Information: No adoption, sealed, juvenile, mental health or expunged cases released. Will not fax documents. Court makes copy: $.75 per page. Certification fee: $20.00. Payee: Elbert Combined Courts. Business checks accepted. Visa/MC accepted in person only. Prepayment required. Mail requests: SASE required.

Civil Name Search: Access: Mail, in person, online. Only the court performs in person name searches; visitors may not. Search fee: $5.00 per name. $25.00 per hour if extensive research is needed. Required to search: full name, years to search. Civil records on computer back to 1995, index cards from 1978-1994, index books from 1920s, archived prior to 1920. Mail turnaround time 1-2 weeks. Pay service to civil case look-up at www.courts.state.co.us; click on Court Records Search.

Criminal Name Search: Access: Mail, in person, online. Only the court performs in person name searches; visitors may not. Search fee: $5.00 per name. $25.00 per hour if extensive research is needed. Required to search: full name, years to search, DOB, signed release. Criminal records computerized from 1995, index cards from 1978, index books from 1920s. Mail turnaround time 1-2 weeks. Criminal case index at www.courts.state.co.us. Current dockets free, records not- click on Court Records Search.

Fremont County

District & County Courts 136 Justice Center Rd, Rm 103, Canon City, CO 81212; 719-269-0100; fax: 719-269-0134; 8AM-4PM (MST). *Felony, Misdemeanor, Civil, Eviction, Small Claims, Probate, Traffic.*
www.courts.state.co.us/Courts/County/Index.cfm?County_ID=30
General Information: No adoption, sealed, juvenile, mental health or expunged cases released. Will not fax documents. Court makes copy: $.75 per page. Certification fee: $20.00. Payee: Clerk of the Combined Courts. Personal checks accepted. Visa/MC accepted. Prepayment required. Mail requests: SASE required.
Civil Name Search: Access: Mail, fax, in person, online. Only the court performs in person name searches; visitors may not. Search fee: $5.00 per name. $25.00 per hour if extensive research is needed. Required to search: name, years to search; also helpful: address. Civil records computerized since 1995, on index cards from 1978, index books at archives in Denver back to 1861. Mail turnaround time up to 14 working days. Pay service to civil case look-up at www.courts.state.co.us; click on Court Records Search.
Criminal Name Search: Access: Mail, in person, online. Only the court performs in person name searches; visitors may not. Search fee: $5.00 per name. $25.00 per hour if extensive research is needed. Required to search: name, years to search; also helpful: address, DOB. Criminal records computerized since 1995, on index cards from 1978. Mail turnaround time up to 14 working days. Criminal case index at www.courts.state.co.us. Current dockets free, records not- click on Court Records Search. Online results show middle initial, DOB.

Garfield County

9th District & County Courts 109 8th St, #104, Glenwood Springs, CO 81601; 970-945-5075; fax: 970-945-8756; 8AM-4:55PM (MST). *Felony, Misdemeanor, Civil, Eviction, Small Claims, Probate.*
www.courts.state.co.us/Courts/County/Choose.cfm
General Information: No adoption, sealed, juvenile, mental health or expunged cases released. Will fax back documents $1.00 per page. Court makes copy: $.75 per page. Self serve copy: $.25 per page. Certification fee: $20.00 per doc includes copy fee. Payee: Garfield Combined Courts. Personal checks accepted. Visa/MC accepted. Prepayment required. Mail requests: SASE required.
Civil Name Search: Access: Mail, in person, online. Only the court performs in person name searches; visitors may not. Search fee: $5.00 per name. $25.00 per hour if extensive research is needed. Civil records on computer from 1992, on fiche from 1970, index books back to late 1800s. Mail turnaround time 1-2 weeks. Pay service to civil case look-up at www.courts.state.co.us; click on Court Records Search.
Criminal Name Search: Access: Mail, in person, online. Only the court performs in person name searches; visitors may not. Search fee: $5.00 per name. $25.00 per hour if extensive research is needed. Criminal records computerized from 1992, on fiche from 1970, index books back to late 1800s. Mail turnaround time 1-2 weeks. Criminal case index at www.courts.state.co.us. Current dockets free, records not- click on Court Records Search.

County Court - Rifle 200 E 18th St, Ste. 103, Rifle, CO 81650; 970-625-5100; fax: 970-625-1125; 8AM-5PM (MST). *Misdemeanor, Civil Actions under $15,000, Eviction, Small Claims, Traffic.*
www.courts.state.co.us/Courts/County/Choose.cfm
General Information: This court handles cases in the county for the area from New Castle to the west. No adoption, sealed, juvenile, mental health or expunged cases released. Will fax documents $1.00 per page to send or receive. Court makes copy: $.75 per page. Certification fee: $20.00 per page. Payee: Associate County Court. Personal checks accepted. Credit cards accepted. Prepayment required. Mail requests: SASE required.
Civil Name Search: Access: Phone, fax, mail, in person, online. Only the court performs in person name searches; visitors may not. No search fee. Civil index on cards from 1965, computerized since 1994. Mail turnaround time 1 week. Results include name and case number. Pay service to civil case look-up at www.courts.state.co.us; click on Court Records Search.
Criminal Name Search: Access: Phone, fax, mail, in person, online. Only the court performs in person name searches; visitors may not. No search fee. Required to search: name, years to search, DOB. Criminal records indexed on cards from 1965, computerized since 1994. Mail turnaround time 1 week. Criminal case index at www.courts.state.co.us. Current dockets free, records not- click on Court Records Search.

Gilpin County

1st District & County Courts 2960 Dory Hill Rd, #200, Black Hawk, CO 80422; 303-582-5522; fax: 303-582-3112; 9AM-4PM (MST). *Felony, Misdemeanor, Civil, Eviction, Small Claims, Probate.*
www.courts.state.co.us/Courts/County/Choose.cfm

General Information: No adoption, sealed, juvenile, mental health or expunged cases released. Will fax documents to local or toll free line. Court makes copy: $.75 per page. Certification fee: $20.00 per doc. Payee: Clerk of the Combined Courts. Personal checks and credit cards accepted. Prepayment required. Mail requests: SASE required.
Civil Name Search: Access: Mail, in person, online. Only the court performs in person name searches; visitors may not. Search fee: $5.00 per name. Fee for more than a 7 year search is $20.00. Civil records on computer (County-1993, District-1994), on index cards from 1970s, index books from 1950s. Mail turnaround time 5 days. Pay service to civil case look-up at www.courts.state.co.us; click on Court Records Search.
Criminal Name Search: Access: Mail, in person, online. Only the court performs in person name searches; visitors may not. Search fee: $10.00 per name. Fee for more than a 7 year search is $20.00. Required to search: name, years to search, DOB. Criminal records on computer (County-1993, District-1994), on index cards from 1970s, index books from 1950s. Mail turnaround time 5 days. Criminal case index at www.courts.state.co.us. Current dockets free, records not- click on Court Records Search.

Grand County

14th District & County Courts PO Box 192, Hot Sulphur Springs, CO 80451; 970-725-3357; 8AM-5PM (MST). *Felony, Misdemeanor, Civil, Eviction, Small Claims, Probate.*
www.courts.state.co.us/Courts/County/Choose.cfm
General Information: No adoption, sealed, juvenile, mental health or expunged cases released. Will not fax documents. Court makes copy: $.75 per page. Certification fee: $20.00. Payee: Grand County Combined Court. Personal checks and credit cards accepted. Prepayment required. Mail requests: SASE required.
Civil Name Search: Access: Phone, mail, in person, online. Both court and visitors may perform in person name searches. Search fee: $5.00 per name if 1976-1991; $20.00 if pre-1976; No fee 1992-present. Civil records on computer from 7/1991, fiche from 1970, index books from 1900. Note: Phone requests accepted only if no fees involved. Mail turnaround time 1 week. Public use terminal has civil records. Pay service to civil case look-up at www.courts.state.co.us; click on Court Records Search.
Criminal Name Search: Access: Phone, mail, in person, online. Only the court performs in person name searches; visitors may not. Search fee: No fee 1992-present, $5.00 per name if 1976-1991; $20.00 if pre-1976. Required to search: name, years to search, DOB. Criminal records computerized from 7/1991, fiche from 1970, index books from 1900. Note: Phone requests accepted only if no fees involved. Mail turnaround time 1 week. Criminal case index at www.courts.state.co.us. Current dockets free, records not- click on Court Records Search.

Gunnison County

7th District & County Courts 200 E Virginia Ave, Gunnison, CO 81230; 970-641-3500; fax: 970-641-6876; 8AM-5PM (MST). *Felony, Misdemeanor, Civil, Eviction, Small Claims, Probate.*
www.courts.state.co.us/Courts/County/Choose.cfm
General Information: Search fee includes civil and criminal indexes of both courts. Fax requests should include credit card for payment. Phone requests are usually limited to those with a need to know. No adoption, sealed, juvenile, mental health or expunged cases released. Will fax documents $1.00 per page. Court makes copy: $.75 per page. Certification fee: $20.00 per doc. Payee: Gunnison Combined Courts. Personal checks accepted to pay fines only. Visa/MC accepted. Prepayment required. Payments may be made online via www.courts.state.co.us. Mail requests: SASE required.
Civil Name Search: Access: Phone, fax, mail, in person, online. Only the court performs in person name searches; visitors may not. Search fee: $5.00 per name. $25.00 per hour if extensive research is needed. Civil cases indexed by defendant. Civil records on computer from 1994, index cards from 1977, index books back to 1877. Mail turnaround time 1-2 days. Pay service to civil case look-up at www.courts.state.co.us; click on Court Records Search.
Criminal Name Search: Access: Phone, fax, mail, in person, online. Only the court performs in person name searches; visitors may not. Search fee: $5.00 per name. $25.00 per hour if extensive research is needed. Required to search: name, years to search, DOB. Criminal records computerized from 1994, index cards from 1977, index books back to 1877. Mail turnaround time 1-2 days. Criminal case index at www.courts.state.co.us. Current dockets free, records not- click on Court Records Search. Online results show middle initial, DOB.

Hinsdale County

7th District & County Courts PO Box 245, Lake City, CO 81235; 970-944-2227; fax: 970-944-2289; 8:30AM-1:30PM W,F (MST). *Felony, Misdemeanor, Civil, Eviction, Small Claims, Probate.*
www.courts.state.co.us/Courts/County/Choose.cfm

General Information: Probate fax is same as main fax number. No adoption, sealed, juvenile, mental health or expunged cases released. Will fax out docs $1.00 per page. Incoming faxes are 1-10 pgs-$10; 6-10 pgs-$20; 11-15 pgs $30; 16-20 pgs - $40. Court makes copy: $.75 per page. Certification fee: $20.00 per cert plus copy fee. Payee: Clerk of the Combined Courts. Personal checks accepted. No credit cards accepted. Prepayment required. Mail requests: SASE required.

Civil Name Search: Access: Phone, fax, mail, in person, online. Only the court performs in person name searches; visitors may not. Search fee: Fee depends on time required for search. Civil index on cards from 1975, index books back to 1900. Mail turnaround time 2-4 weeks. Pay service to civil case look-up at www.courts.state.co.us; click on Court Records Search.

Criminal Name Search: Access: Phone, fax, mail, in person, online. Only the court performs in person name searches; visitors may not. Search fee: Fee depends on time required for search. Required to search: name, years to search, DOB. Criminal records indexed on cards from 1975, index books back to 1900. Mail turnaround time 2-4 weeks. Criminal case index at www.courts.state.co.us. Current dockets free, records not- click on Court Records Search.

Huerfano County

3rd District & County Courts 401 Main St, #304, Walsenburg, CO 81089; 719-738-1040; fax: 719-738-1267; 8AM-12; 1PM-4PM (MST). *Felony, Misdemeanor, Civil, Eviction, Small Claims, Probate.*
www.courts.state.co.us/Courts/County/Choose.cfm

General Information: No adoption, sealed, juvenile, mental health or expunged cases released. Will fax documents $1.00 per page. Court makes copy: $.75 per page. Certification fee: $20.00 plus copy fee. Payee: Huerfano County Combined Courts. No personal checks accepted. Visa/MC accepted. Prepayment required. Mail requests: SASE required.

Civil Name Search: Access: Mail, in person, online. Only the court performs in person name searches; visitors may not. Search fee: $5.00 per name. $25.00 per hour if extensive research is needed. Civil records on computer from 1995 (county court only), index cards from 1978, index books from 1861. Mail turnaround time 2 weeks. Pay service to civil case look-up at www.courts.state.co.us; click on Court Records Search.

Criminal Name Search: Access: Mail, in person, online. Only the court performs in person name searches; visitors may not. Search fee: $5.00 per name. $25.00 per hour if extensive research is needed. Required to search: name, years to search, DOB. Criminal records computerized from 1995 (county court only), index cards from 1978, index books from 1861. Mail turnaround time 2 weeks. Criminal case index at www.courts.state.co.us. Current dockets free, records not- click on Court Records Search. Online results show middle initial, DOB.

Jackson County

8th District & County Courts PO Box 308, Walden, CO 80480; 970-723-4363; fax: 970-723-4337; 9AM-1PM (MST). *Felony, Misdemeanor, Civil, Eviction, Small Claims, Probate.*
www.courts.state.co.us/Courts/County/Choose.cfm

General Information: No adoption, sealed, juvenile, mental health or expunged cases released. Will not fax documents. Court makes copy: $.75 per page. Self serve copy: same. Certification fee: $20.00. Payee: Clerk of the Combined Courts. Personal checks accepted. No credit cards accepted. Prepayment required. Mail requests: SASE required.

Civil Name Search: Access: Mail, in person, online. Both court and visitors may perform in person name searches. Search fee: $5.00 per name. Civil records on computer since 1994; prior on index cards from 1974, index books from the 1900s. Mail turnaround time 2 weeks. Pay service to civil case look-up at www.courts.state.co.us; click on Court Records Search.

Criminal Name Search: Access: Mail, in person, online. Both court and visitors may perform in person name searches. Search fee: $5.00 per name. Required to search: name, years to search, DOB. Criminal records on computer since 1994; prior on index cards from 1974, index books from the 1900s. Mail turnaround time 2 weeks. Criminal case index at www.courts.state.co.us. Current dockets free, records not- click on Court Records Search.

Jefferson County

1st District & County Courts 100 Jefferson County Pky, Golden, CO 80401-6002; 303-271-6215; criminal phone: 303-271-6237; civil phone: 303-271-6228; probate phone: 303-271-6135; fax: 303-271-6188; 8AM-4PM (MST). *Felony, Misdemeanor, Civil, Eviction, Small Claims, Probate, Traffic.*
www.courts.state.co.us/Courts/County/Choose.cfm

General Information: Probate fax is 303-271-6268. No adoption, sealed, juvenile, mental health or expunged cases released. Will not fax documents. Court makes copy: $.75 per page. Self serve copy: $.25 per page. Certification fee: $20.00 per document. Payee: Clerk of Combined Courts. Personal checks accepted. Visa/MC accepted in person only. Prepayment required. Mail requests: SASE required.

Civil Name Search: Access: Mail, in person, online. Both court and visitors may perform in person name searches. Search fee: $5.00 per name. Fee is per case. Add $5.00 if search includes microfilm records. Required to search: name, years to search; also helpful: DOB. Civil records on computer from 1985, microfiche from 1975, index books from 1963-1974, archived prior to 1963. Mail turnaround time 1 week. Pay service to civil case look-up at www.courts.state.co.us; click on Court Records Search.

Criminal Name Search: Access: Mail, in person, online. Both court and visitors may perform in person name searches. Search fee: $5.00 per name. Fee varies depending on number of years searched. Add $5.00 if search includes microfilm records. Required to search: name, years to search, DOB; also helpful: address. Criminal records computerized from 1985, microfiche from 1975, index books from 1963-1974, archived prior to 1963. Mail turnaround time 1 week. Criminal case index at www.courts.state.co.us. Current dockets free, records not- click on Court Records Search. Online results show middle initial, DOB.

Kiowa County

15th District & County Courts PO Box 353, Eads, CO 81036; 719-438-5558; fax: 719-438-5300; 9AM-4PM (MST). *Felony, Misdemeanor, Civil, Eviction, Small Claims, Probate.*
www.courts.state.co.us/Courts/County/Choose.cfm

General Information: No adoption, sealed, juvenile, mental health or expunged cases released. Will fax documents $1.00 each. Court makes copy: $.75 per page. Certification fee: $20.00 per doc. Payee: Kiowa County Court. Business checks accepted. No credit cards accepted. Prepayment required. Mail requests: SASE required.

Civil Name Search: Access: Phone, fax, mail, in person, online. Only the court performs in person name searches; visitors may not. Search fee: $5.00 per name. $25.00 per hour if extensive research is needed. Civil index on cards from the 1960s, index books from 1889. Recent records are computerized. Mail turnaround time 1 week. Pay service to civil case look-up at www.courts.state.co.us; click on Court Records Search.

Criminal Name Search: Access: Phone, fax, mail, in person, online. Only the court performs in person name searches; visitors may not. Search fee: $5.00 per name. $25.00 per hour if extensive research is needed. Required to search: name, years to search, DOB. Criminal records indexed on cards from the 1960s, index books from 1889. Recent records are computerized. Mail turnaround time 1 week. Criminal case index at www.courts.state.co.us. Current dockets free, records not- click on Court Records Search.

Kit Carson County

Kit Carson Combined Court 251 16th St, #301, Burlington, CO 80807; 719-346-5524 x303; fax: 719-346-7805; 8AM-4PM (MST). *Felony, Misdemeanor, Civil, Eviction, Small Claims, Probate.*
www.courts.state.co.us/Courts/County/Choose.cfm

General Information: No adoption, sealed, juvenile, mental health or expunged cases released. Will fax documents $1.00 per page. Court makes copy: $.75 per page. Certification fee: $20.00. Payee: Combined Courts. No personal checks accepted. Major credit cards accepted except Amex. Prepayment required. Mail requests: SASE required.

Civil Name Search: Access: Mail, in person, online. Only the court performs in person name searches; visitors may not. Search fee: $5.00 per name. $25.00 per hour if extensive research is needed. Civil index on cards from 1910, index books from 1889. Mail turnaround time 1 week. Pay service to civil case look-up at www.courts.state.co.us; click on Court Records Search.

Criminal Name Search: Access: Mail, in person, online. Only the court performs in person name searches; visitors may not. Search fee: $5.00 per name. $25.00 per hour if extensive research is needed. Required to search: name, years to search, DOB. Criminal records indexed on cards from 1910, index books from 1889. Mail turnaround time 1 week. Criminal case index at www.courts.state.co.us. Current dockets free, records not- click on Court Records Search.

La Plata County

La Plata Combined Courts 1060 E 2nd Ave #106, Durango, CO 81301; 970-247-2304; criminal fax: 970-247-4348; civil fax: 8AM-4PM; 8AM-4PM (MST). *Felony, Misdemeanor, Civil, Small Claims, Probate.*
www.courts.state.co.us/Courts/County/Choose.cfm

General Information: No adoption, sealed, juvenile, mental health or expunged cases released. Fee to fax out file $1.00 per page. Court makes copy: $.75 per page. Certification fee: $20.00. Payee: Clerk of the Combined Courts. Personal checks and credit cards accepted. Prepayment required. Mail requests: SASE required.

Civil Name Search: Access: Mail, in person, online. Only the court performs in person name searches; visitors may not. Search fee: $5.00 to $20 .00 per name, depending on year of the case. Civil records on computer from 1990, index cards from 1976, index books from 1874. Mail turnaround time 3-7 days. Pay service to civil case look-up at www.courts.state.co.us; click on Court Records Search.

Criminal Name Search: Access: Mail, in person, online. Only the court performs in person name searches; visitors may not. Search fee: $5.00 to $20 .00 per name, depending on year of the case. Extensive research is 425.00 per hour. Required to search: name, years to search, DOB. Criminal records computerized from 1996, index cards from 1976, index books from 1874. Mail turnaround time 3-7 days. Criminal case index at www.courts.state.co.us. Current dockets free, records not- click on Court Records Search.

Lake County

Lake County Combined Courts PO Box 55, 505 Harrison St, Leadville, CO 80461; 719-486-0535; fax: 719-486-5006; 8AM-N, 1-4PM (MST). *Felony, Misdemeanor, Civil, Eviction, Small Claims, Probate.* www.courts.state.co.us/Courts/County/Choose.cfm

General Information: No adoption, sealed, juvenile, mental health or expunged cases released. Will fax documents $1.00 per page. Court makes copy: $.75 per page. Certification fee: $20.00 per cert plus copy fee. Payee: Lake County Court. Business checks accepted. Visa/MC accepted. Prepayment required. Mail requests: SASE required.

Civil Name Search: Access: Phone, mail, in person, online. Only the court performs in person name searches; visitors may not. Search fee: $20.00 per name. Civil index on cards from 1988 (District), 1970 (County), index books from 1865. Note: Court may do a phone search for no fee if the request is simple - for a recent record. Mail turnaround time 7 days. Pay service to civil case look-up at www.courts.state.co.us; click on Court Records Search.

Criminal Name Search: Access: Phone, mail, in person, online. Only the court performs in person name searches; visitors may not. Search fee: $20.00 per name. Required to search: name, years to search, DOB. Criminal records indexed on cards from 1988 (District), 1970 (County), index books from 1865. Note: Court may do a phone search for no fee if the request is simple - for a recent record. Mail turnaround time 7 days. Criminal case index at www.courts.state.co.us. Current dockets free, records not- click on Court Records Search.

Larimer County

8th District Court 201 La Porte Ave, #100, Ft Collins, CO 80521; 970-498-6100; probate phone: 970-498-6111; fax: 970-498-6110; 7:30AM-4:30PM (MST). *Felony, Civil Actions over $10,000, Probate.* www.courts.state.co.us/Courts/County/Choose.cfm

General Information: No adoption, sealed, juvenile, mental health or expunged cases released. Will not fax documents. Court makes copy: $.75 per page. Self serve copy: $.25 per page. Certification fee: $20.00. Payee: Clerk of District Court. Personal checks accepted. Visa/MC accepted. Prepayment required. Mail requests: SASE required.

Civil Name Search: Access: Phone, mail, in person, online. Both court and visitors may perform in person name searches. Search fee: $5.00 per name. $25.00 per hour if extensive research is needed. Required to search: name; also helpful: years to search. Civil records on computer from 1976, index books back to 1861. Mail turnaround time 1-2 weeks. Public use terminal has civil records. The terminal shows E-filings only. Pay service to civil case look-up at www.courts.state.co.us; click on Court Records Search.

Criminal Name Search: Access: Mail, in person, online. Only the court performs in person name searches; visitors may not. Search fee: $5.00 per name. $25.00 per hour if extensive research is needed. Required to search: name; also helpful: years to search, DOB, SSN. Criminal records computerized from 1976, index books back to 1861. Mail turnaround time 7-10 days. Criminal case index at www.courts.state.co.us. Current dockets free, records not- click on Court Records Search.

County Court 201 La Porte Ave, #100, Ft Collins, CO 80521; 970-498-6100; fax: 970-498-6110; 7:30AM-4:30PM (MST). *Misdemeanor, Civil Actions under $15,000, Eviction, Small Claims.* www.courts.state.co.us/Courts/County/Choose.cfm

General Information: No sealed cases released. Will not fax documents. Court makes copy: $.75 per page. Self serve copy: $.25 per page. Certification fee: $20.00. Payee: Larimer County Combined Court. Personal checks accepted. Visa/MC accepted. Prepayment required. Mail requests: SASE required.

Civil Name Search: Access: Mail, in person, online. Both court and visitors may perform in person name searches. Search fee: $5.00 per name. $25.00 per hour if extensive research is needed. Required to search: name, years to search; also helpful: address. Some records on computer from 1986, index cards from 1965. Note: Daily dockets found online by link at court main website. Mail turnaround time 1-2 weeks. Public use terminal has civil records. The terminal shows E-filings only. Pay service to civil case look-up at www.courts.state.co.us; click on Court Records Search.

Criminal Name Search: Access: Mail, in person, online. Only the court performs in person name searches; visitors may not. Search fee: $5.00 per name. $25.00 per hour if extensive research is needed. Required to search: name, years to search, DOB, signed release, offense; also helpful: address.

Some records on computer from 1986, index cards from 1965. Note: Daily dockets found online by link at court main website. Mail turnaround time 1-2 weeks. Criminal case index at www.courts.state.co.us. Current dockets free, records not- click on Court Records Search.

Las Animas County

3rd District Court 200 E 1st St, Rm 304, Trinidad, CO 81082; 719-846-3316; probate phone: 719-846-3316 x25; fax: 719-846-9367; 8AM-N; 1-4PM (MST). *Felony, Misdemeanor, Civil, Eviction, Small Claims, Probate.* www.courts.state.co.us/Courts/County/Choose.cfm

General Information: No adoption, sealed, juvenile, mental health or expunged cases released. Fee to fax out file $1.00 per page. Court makes copy: $.75 per page. Certification fee: $20.00. Payee: Combined Courts. Personal checks and credit cards accepted. Prepayment required. Mail requests: SASE required.

Civil Name Search: Access: Mail, in person, online. Only the court performs in person name searches; visitors may not. Search fee: $5.00 per name. $25.00 per hour if extensive research is needed. Civil index on cards from 1976, index books to 1890s. Mail turnaround time 1 week. Pay service to civil case look-up at www.courts.state.co.us; click on Court Records Search.

Criminal Name Search: Access: Mail, in person, online. Only the court performs in person name searches; visitors may not. Search fee: $5.00 per name. $25.00 per hour if extensive research is needed. Required to search: name, years to search, DOB; also helpful: SSN. Criminal records indexed on cards from 1976, index books to 1890s. Mail turnaround time 1 week. Criminal case index at www.courts.state.co.us. Current dockets free, records not- click on Court Records Search.

Lincoln County

18th District & County Courts PO Box 128, Hugo, CO 80821; 719-743-2455; 8AM-4PM (MST). *Felony, Misdemeanor, Civil, Eviction, Small Claims, Probate, Traffic.* www.courts.state.co.us/Courts/County/Choose.cfm

General Information: No adoption, sealed, juvenile, mental health or expunged cases released. Will not fax documents. Court makes copy: $.75 per page. Certification fee: $20.00 per document plus copy fee. Payee: Lincoln County Combined Courts. Personal checks and credit cards accepted. Prepayment required. Mail requests: SASE required.

Civil Name Search: Access: Mail, in person, online. Only the court performs in person name searches; visitors may not. Search fee: $5.00 per name. $25.00 per hour if extensive research is needed. Civil records on computer since 12/94, index cards from 1977, index books back to 1889, archived 10 years back. Mail turnaround time within 10 days. Pay service to civil case look-up at www.courts.state.co.us; click on Court Records Search.

Criminal Name Search: Access: Mail, in person, online. Only the court performs in person name searches; visitors may not. Search fee: $5.00 per name. $25.00 per hour if extensive research is needed. Required to search: name, years to search, DOB. Criminal records on computer since 12/94, index cards from 1977, index books back to 1889, archived 10 years back. Mail turnaround time within 10 days. Criminal case index at www.courts.state.co.us. Current dockets free, records not- click on Court Records Search.

Logan County

Combined Court 110 N Riverview Rd, Rm 205, Sterling, CO 80751; 970-522-6565 District; 970-522-1572 County Ct; fax: 970-522-6566; 8AM-4PM (MST). *Felony, Misdemeanor, Civil Actions, Eviction, Small Claims, Probate.* www.courts.state.co.us/Courts/County/Choose.cfm

General Information: County Court Fax is 970-526-5359. In search request, specify to search both court indexes; fee is $5.00 for the combined search. Access to Domestic Relations and Probate cases are limited to those involved unless petitioned in writing. No adoption, sealed, juvenile, mental health or expunged cases released. Fee to fax out file $1.00 per page local; $2.00 per page long-distance. Court makes copy: $.75 per page. Certification fee: $20.00 per doc plus copy fee. Payee: Logan District Court. Personal checks accepted. Visa/MC accepted. Prepayment required. Mail requests: SASE required.

Civil Name Search: Access: Mail, fax, in person, online. Only the court performs in person name searches; visitors may not. Search fee: $5.00 per name. $25.00 per hour if extensive research is needed. Civil records computerized since 8/95, on index cards from 1973, index books back to 1887. Mail turnaround time 1 week. Pay service to civil case look-up at www.courts.state.co.us; click on Court Records Search. Public can only view redacted information.

Criminal Name Search: Access: Mail, fax, in person, online. Only the court performs in person name searches; visitors may not. Search fee: $5.00 per name. $25.00 per hour if extensive research is needed. Required to search: name, years to search, DOB. Criminal records computerized since

8/95, on index cards from 1973, index books back to 1887. Mail turnaround time 1 week. Criminal case index at www.courts.state.co.us. Current dockets free, records not- click on Court Records Search. Public can only view redacted information.

Mesa County

Mesa County Combined Court PO Box 20000-5030, 125 N Spruce, County District Court, Grand Junction, CO 81502; 970-257-3640; probate phone: 970-257-3640; fax: 970-257-8776; 8AM-4PM (MST). *Felony, Civil Actions over $10,000, Small Claims, Probate, Traffic.*
www.mesacourt.org/
General Information: Domestic and Probate records open to the public minus redactable information. No adoption, sealed, juvenile, mental health or expunged cases released. Will not fax documents. Court makes copy: $.75 per page. Certification fee: $20.00 per doc plus copy fee. Payee: Mesa County Combined Court. Business checks accepted. Visa/MC accepted. Prepayment required. Mail requests: SASE required.
Civil Name Search: Access: Mail, in person, online. Only the court performs in person name searches; visitors may not. Search fee: $5.00 per name. $10.00 per hour if extensive research is needed. Required to search: name, years to search, DOB. Civil records on computer since 1989, on microfiche to 1970s. Mail turnaround time 2-4 days. Pay service to civil case look-up at www.courts.state.co.us; click on Court Records Search.
Criminal Name Search: Access: Mail, in person, online. Only the court performs in person name searches; visitors may not. Search fee: $5.00 per name. $10.00 per hour if extensive research is needed. Required to search: name, years to search, DOB. Criminal records on computer since 1989, on microfiche to 1970s. Mail turnaround time 2-4 days. Criminal case index at www.courts.state.co.us. Current dockets free, records not- click on Court Records Search. Online results show name, DOB.

Mineral County

12th District & County Courts PO Box 337, Creede, CO 81130; 719-658-2575; 9AM-4PM M & F only (MST). *Felony, Misdemeanor, Civil, Eviction, Small Claims, Probate.*
www.courts.state.co.us/Courts/County/Choose.cfm
General Information: No adoption, sealed, juvenile, mental health or expunged cases released. Will not fax documents. Court makes copy: $.75 per page. Certification fee: $20.00 per doc. Payee: Mineral Combined Courts. Personal checks accepted. No credit cards accepted. Prepayment required. Mail requests: SASE required.
Civil Name Search: Access: Mail, in person, online. Only the court performs in person name searches; visitors may not. Search fee: $5.00 per name. $25.00 per hour if extensive research is needed. Civil records on computer since 7/1993, on index cards from 1977, index books back to 1893. Mail turnaround time 2-3 days. Pay service to civil case look-up at www.courts.state.co.us; click on Court Records Search.
Criminal Name Search: Access: Mail, in person, online. Only the court performs in person name searches; visitors may not. Search fee: $5.00 per name. $25.00 per hour if extensive research is needed. Required to search: name, years to search, DOB. Criminal records on computer since 7/1993, on index cards from 1977, index books back to 1893. Mail turnaround time 2-3 days. Criminal case index at www.courts.state.co.us. Current dockets free, records not- click on Court Records Search.

Moffat County

Moffat County Combined Court 221 W Victory Wy, #300, Craig, CO 81625; 970-824-8254; 8AM-5PM (MST). *Felony, Misdemeanor, Civil, Eviction, Small Claims, Probate, Traffic, Domestic.*
www.courts.state.co.us/Courts/County/Choose.cfm
General Information: No adoption, sealed, juvenile, mental health or expunged cases released. Will not fax documents. Court makes copy: $.75 per page. Certification fee: $20.00 per document plus copy fee. Payee: Moffat County Combined Courts. Personal checks and credit cards accepted. Prepayment required. Mail requests: SASE required.
Civil Name Search: Access: Phone, mail, in person, online. Only the court performs in person name searches; visitors may not. Search fee: $5.00 for records 1976-91; $20.00 prior to 1976. $25.00 per hour search fee for lengthy search projects. Civil records on computer from 1992, index cards from 1976, either microfilmed or archived back to 1911. Mail turnaround time 1-2 weeks. Pay service to civil case look-up at www.courts.state.co.us; click on Court Records Search.
Criminal Name Search: Access: Mail, in person, online. Only the court performs in person name searches; visitors may not. Search fee: $5.00 1976-1991; $20.00 prior to 1976. $25.00 per hour search fee for lengthy search projects. Required to search: name, years to search, DOB. Criminal records computerized from 1992, index cards from 1976, either microfilmed or archived back to 1911. Mail turnaround time 1-2 weeks. Criminal case index at www.courts.state.co.us. Current dockets free, records not- click on Court Records Search. Access the sheriff's sex offender list at www.moffatcountysheriff.com/offender_login.htm.

Montezuma County

22nd District Court 109 W Main St, #210, Cortez, CO 81321; 970-565-1111; fax: 970-565-8516; 8AM-4PM (MST). *Felony, Civil Actions over $15,000, Probate.*
www.courts.state.co.us/Courts/County/Choose.cfm
General Information: No adoption, sealed, juvenile, mental health or expunged cases released. Will not fax documents. Court makes copy: $.75 per page. Certification fee: $20.00 per doc. Payee: Montezuma District Court. Personal checks accepted. No credit cards accepted. Prepayment required. Will bill mailing and copy costs. Mail requests: SASE required.
Civil Name Search: Access: Mail, in person, online, fax. Only the court performs in person name searches; visitors may not. Search fee: $5.00 per name or case number, or $20.00 per hour to search. Civil records on computer back to 6/95, index cards from 1975, State Archives has index books back to late 1890s. Note: Fax requests must be pre-approved. Search fee includes civil and criminal indexes. Mail turnaround time 1-2 weeks. Pay service to civil case look-up at www.courts.state.co.us; click on Court Records Search.
Criminal Name Search: Access: Mail, in person, online, fax. Only the court performs in person name searches; visitors may not. Search fee: $5.00 per name or case number, or $20.00 per hour to search. Required to search: name, years to search, DOB. Criminal computer back to 6/95, index cards from 1975, State Archives has index books back to late 1890s. Note: Fax requests must be pre-approved. Search fee includes civil and criminal indexes. Mail turnaround time 1-2 weeks. Criminal case index at www.courts.state.co.us. Current dockets free, records not- click on Court Records Search.

County Court 601 N Mildred Rd, Cortez, CO 81321; 970-565-7580; fax: 970-565-8798; 8AM-4PM (MST). *Misdemeanor, Civil Actions under $15,000, Eviction, Small Claims, Traffic.*
www.courts.state.co.us/Courts/County/Index.cfm?County_ID=66
General Information: No adoption, sealed, juvenile, mental health or expunged cases released. Will fax documents for $1.00 per page fee, prepaid only. Court makes copy: $.75 per page. Certification fee: $20.00 per doc plus copy fee. Payee: Montezuma County Court. Personal checks accepted. No credit cards accepted. Prepayment required. Mail requests: SASE required.
Civil Name Search: Access: Mail, in person, online. Only the court performs in person name searches; visitors may not. Search fee: $5.00 per name/per case. $25.00 per hour if extensive research is needed. Civil records on computer since 1993. Note: All requests must be in writing. Mail turnaround time 5-7 days. Pay service to civil case look-up at www.courts.state.co.us, click on Court Records Search.
Criminal Name Search: Access: Mail, in person, online. Only the court performs in person name searches; visitors may not. Search fee: $5.00 per name/per case. $25.00 per hour if extensive research is needed. Required to search: name, years to search, DOB. Criminal records indexed on computer from 1993 forward, previous records sent to state archives. Note: Search requests must be in writing. Mail turnaround time 5-7 days. Criminal case index at www.courts.state.co.us. Current dockets free, records not- click on Court Records Search.

Montrose County

Montrose County Combined Court 1200 N Grand Ave, Bin A, Montrose, CO 81401-3164; 970-252-4300; fax: 970-252-4309; 9AM-4PM (MST). *Felony, Misdemeanor, Civil, Eviction, Small Claims, Probate, Domestic, Traffic.*
www.courts.state.co.us/Courts/County/Choose.cfm
General Information: No adoption, sealed, juvenile, mental health or expunged cases released. Will fax documents $1.00 per page only if pre-approved by clerk and prepayment of fees. Court makes copy: $.75 per page. Certification fee: $20.00 per doc. Payee: Montrose Combined Courts. Personal checks and credit cards accepted. Prepayment required. Mail requests: SASE required.
Civil Name Search: Access: Mail, in person, online. Only the court performs in person name searches; visitors may not. Search fee: $5.00 per name plus $25.00 per hour. Required to search: name, DOB, years to search. Civil index on cards from 1975, index books back to 1890. Mail turnaround time 10 days. Pay service to civil case look-up at www.courts.state.co.us/; click on Court Records Search. Also, weekly dockets available free at www.7thjudicialdistrictco.org/programs/dockets.html.
Criminal Name Search: Access: Mail, fax, in person, online. Only the court performs in person name searches; visitors may not. Search fee: $5.00 per name plus $25.00 per hour. Required to search: name, years to search, DOB. Criminal records indexed on cards from 1975, index books back to 1890. Mail turnaround time 10 days. Criminal case index at www.courts.state.co.us/. Current dockets free, click on Am I Due In a Court this Week?, Access to records for a fee go to www.courts.state.co.us/Administration/Program.cfm?Program=11.

Morgan County

13 Judicial District Combined Court 400 Warner St, Ft Morgan, CO 80701; 970-542-3435 Dist; 970-542-3414 County; fax: 970-542-3436; 8AM-4PM (MST). *Felony, Misdemeanor, Civil, Probate, Eviction, Small Claims, Traffic, Domestic.*
www.courts.state.co.us/Courts/County/Choose.cfm
General Information: District and County Court combined in 2006. Fax for County Court Division (Misdemeanor, Civil Actions Under $15,000, Eviction, Small Claims, Traffic) is 970-542-3416. District Court is 970-542-3486. No adoption, sealed records, juvenile, mental health or expunged cases released. Will fax documents if less than 5 pages for $1.00 per page if local or toll-free call. Court makes copy: $.75 per page. Certification fee: $20.00. Payee: Morgan District Court. Personal checks accepted. Credit cards accepted. Prepayment required. Will bill copy fees to attorneys. Mail requests: SASE required.
Civil Name Search: Access: Fax, mail, in person, online. Only the court performs in person name searches; visitors may not. Search fee: $5.00 per name. $25.00 per hour if extensive research is needed. Civil index on cards from 1967 for District Court (County court back to 1980), index books back to 1906; computerized since 8/95. Mail turnaround time 1 week. Public use terminal has civil records. Terminal shows civil e-file cases. Pay service to civil case look-up at www.courts.state.co.us; click on Court Records Search. In person searching must look at both indices, the District and County Court records are not commingled.
Criminal Name Search: Access: Fax, mail, in person, online. Only the court performs in person name searches; visitors may not. Search fee: $5.00 per name. $25.00 per hour if extensive research is needed. Required to search: name, years to search, DOB, SSN; also helpful: signed release. Criminal records indexed on cards from 1967 for District Court (County court back to 1980), index books back to 1906, computerized since 8/95. Mail turnaround time 1 week. Criminal case index at www.courts.state.co.us. Current dockets free, records not- click on Court Records Search. In person searching must look at both indices, the District and County Court records are not commingled.

Otero County

District & County Courts Courthouse, Rm 207, 13 W 3rd St, La Junta, CO 81050; 719-384-4951 district; -4721 County; fax: 719-384-4991; 8AM-5PM (MST). *Felony, Misdemeanor, Civil, Eviction, Small Claims, Probate.*
www.courts.state.co.us/Courts/County/Choose.cfm
General Information: While these courts have been "combined" for certain practical purposes, there are separate offices and record databases, although the search fee covers both courts. But Probate is also a separate index; Probate fax is same as main fax number. No adoption, sealed, juvenile, mental health or expunged cases released. Will fax documents $1.00 per page. Court makes copy: $.75 per page. Self serve copy: same. Certification fee: $20.00 per document plus copy fee. Payee: Otero County Combined Courts. Personal checks accepted. No credit cards accepted. Prepayment required. Mail requests: SASE required.
Civil Name Search: Access: Mail, in person, online. Only the court performs in person name searches; visitors may not. Search fee: $5.00 per name. $25.00 per hour if extensive research is needed. Civil index on cards from 1978, index books back to 1889, microfiche from 1889-1992. Mail turnaround time 5-8 days. Pay service to civil case look-up at www.courts.state.co.us; click on Court Records Search.
Criminal Name Search: Access: Mail, in person, online. Only the court performs in person name searches; visitors may not. Search fee: $5.00 per name. $25.00 per hour if extensive research is needed. Required to search: name, years to search, DOB. Criminal records indexed on cards from 1978, index books back to 1889, microfiche from 1889-1992. Mail turnaround time 5-8 days. Criminal case index at www.courts.state.co.us. Current dockets free, records not- click on Court Records Search.

Ouray County

7th District & County Courts PO Box 643, Ouray, CO 81427; 970-325-4405; fax: 970-325-7364; 9AM-N, 1-4PM M-F (MST). *Felony, Misdemeanor, Civil, Eviction, Small Claims, Probate.*
www.courts.state.co.us/Courts/County/Choose.cfm
General Information: Probate fax is same as main fax number. No adoption, sealed, juvenile, financial, drug/alcohol evaluations, mental health or expunged cases released. Fee to fax out file $1.00 per page. Court makes copy: $.75 per page. Self serve copy: $.25 per page. Certification fee: $20.00. Payee: Ouray Combined Courts. Personal checks accepted. Visa/MC accepted. Prepayment required. Mail requests: SASE requested.
Civil Name Search: Access: Mail, in person, online. Only the court performs in person name searches; visitors may not. Search fee: $5.00 per name. $25.00 per hour if extensive research is needed. Required to search: name, years to search, case type if known. Civil records on computer since 1994, index cards from 1976, index books back to 1876, archived prior to

1925. Mail turnaround time 1 week. Pay service to civil case look-up at www.courts.state.co.us; click on Court Records Search.
Criminal Name Search: Access: Mail, in person, online. Only the court performs in person name searches; visitors may not. Search fee: $5.00 per name. $25.00 per hour if extensive research is needed. Required to search: name, years to search, DOB, case type if known. Criminal records on computer since 1994, index cards from 1976, index books back to 1876, archived prior to 1925. Mail turnaround time 1 week. Criminal case index at www.courts.state.co.us. Current dockets free, records not- click on Court Records Search.

Park County

Park County Combined Courts PO Box 190, 300 4th St, Fairplay, CO 80440; 719-836-2940; fax: 719-836-2892; 7:30AM-4:30PM (MST). *Felony, Misdemeanor, Civil, Eviction, Small Claims, Probate.*
www.courts.state.co.us/Courts/County/Index.cfm?County_ID=31
General Information: No adoption, sealed, juvenile, mental health or expunged cases released. Will not fax documents. Court makes copy: $.75 per page. Certification fee: $20.00. Payee: Park County Combined Court. Personal checks accepted. No credit cards accepted. Prepayment required. Mail requests: SASE required.
Civil Name Search: Access: Mail, online, in person. Only the court performs in person name searches; visitors may not. Search fee: $5.00 per name. $25.00 per hour if extensive research is needed. Civil records computerized since 1995, on index cards from 1978, index books back to 1950, archived prior to 1950. Mail turnaround time within 1 week. Pay service to civil case look-up at www.courts.state.co.us; click on Court Records Search.
Criminal Name Search: Access: Mail, online, in person. Only the court performs in person name searches; visitors may not. Search fee: $5.00 per name. $25.00 per hour if extensive research is needed. Required to search: name, years to search, DOB, signed release. Criminal records computerized since 1995, on index cards from 1978, index books back to 1950, archived prior to 1950. Mail turnaround time within 1 week. Criminal case index at www.courts.state.co.us. Current dockets free, records not- click on Court Records Search.

Phillips County

13th District & County Combined Court 221 S Interocean, Holyoke, CO 80734; 970-854-3279; fax: 970-854-3179; 8AM-1PM (MST). *Felony, Misdemeanor, Civil, Eviction, Small Claims, Probate.*
www.courts.state.co.us/Courts/County/Choose.cfm
General Information: No adoption, sealed, juvenile, mental health or expunged cases released. Will fax documents $1.00 per page, prepaid. Court makes copy: $.75 per page. Certification fee: $20.00 per document. Payee: Phillips County Combined Court. Personal checks accepted. No credit cards accepted. Prepayment required. Mail requests: SASE required.
Civil Name Search: Access: Phone, fax, mail, in person, online. Only the court performs in person name searches; visitors may not. Search fee: $5.00 per name. $25.00 per hour if extensive research is needed. Civil records on computer since 1995; records go back to 1880. Mail turnaround time 1-3 days. Pay service to civil case look-up at www.courts.state.co.us; click on Court Records Search.
Criminal Name Search: Access: Phone, fax, mail, in person, online. Only the court performs in person name searches; visitors may not. Search fee: $5.00 per name. $25.00 per hour if extensive research is needed. Required to search: name, years to search, DOB. Criminal records on computer since 1995; records go back to 1880. Mail turnaround time 1-3 days. Criminal case index at www.courts.state.co.us. Current dockets free, records not- click on Court Records Search.

Pitkin County

9th District & County Courts 506 E Main St, #300, Aspen, CO 81611; 970-925-7635; probate phone: x2; fax: 970-925-6349; 8AM-N, 1-5PM (MST). *Felony, Misdemeanor, Civil, Eviction, Small Claims, Probate.*
www.courts.state.co.us/Courts/County/Choose.cfm
General Information: No adoption, sealed, juvenile, mental health or expunged cases released. Fee to fax out file $1.00 per page. Court makes copy: $.75 per page. Certification fee: $20.00 per doc. Payee: Pitkin County Combined Court. Cashiers checks and money orders accepted. Visa/MC accepted. Prepayment required.
Civil Name Search: Access: Phone, mail, fax, in person, online. Both court and visitors may perform in person name searches. Search fee: No fee for computer search. Civil cases indexed by defendant. Civil records on computer back to 1990, microfiche from 1940-1970, index cards from 1975. Note: The court will charge $25.00 an hour if extensive researched is needed. Mail turnaround time 1 week. Pay service to civil case look-up at www.courts.state.co.us; click on Court Records Search. Search probate 1881-1953 at www.colorado.gov/dpa/doit/archives/probate/pitkin_probate.htm.
Criminal Name Search: Access: Mail, fax, in person, online. Both court and visitors may perform in person name searches. Search fee: There is no

fee for searching computer, otherwise rate determined by time and volume. Required to search: name, years to search, DOB, SSN. Criminal records computerized from 1990, microfiche from 1940-1970, index cards from 1975. Note: The court will charge $25.00 an hour if extensive researched is needed. Mail turnaround time 1 week. Criminal case index at www.courts.state.co.us. Current dockets free, records not- click on Court Records Search.

Prowers County

15th District and County Court 301 S Main St, #300, Lamar, CO 81052-2834; 719-336-7424; fax: 719-336-9757; 8AM-5PM (MST). *Felony, Misdemeanor, Civil Actions, Eviction, Small Claims, Traffic, Probate.*

www.courts.state.co.us/Courts/County/Choose.cfm

General Information: Search fee includes both civil and criminal indexes, and includes both courts. County court phone-719-336-7416. No adoption, sealed, juvenile, mental health or expunged cases released. Will fax documents $1.00 per page. Court makes copy: $.75 per page. Certification fee: $20.00 per doc. Payee: Clerk of District Court. Business checks accepted. No credit cards accepted. Prepayment required. Mail requests: SASE required.

Civil Name Search: Access: Fax, mail, in person, online. Only the court performs in person name searches; visitors may not. Search fee: $5.00 per name. $25.00 per hour if extensive research is needed. Civil records computerized since 1995, on microfiche from 1920, index books from the late 1800s. Mail turnaround time 1 week. Pay service to civil case look-up at www.courts.state.co.us; click on Court Records Search.

Criminal Name Search: Access: Fax, mail, in person, online. Only the court performs in person name searches; visitors may not. Search fee: $5.00 per name. $25.00 per hour if extensive research is needed. Required to search: name, years to search, DOB. Criminal records computerized since 1995, on microfiche from 1920, index books from the late 1800s. Mail turnaround time 1 week. Criminal case index at www.courts.state.co.us. Current dockets free, records not- click on Court Records Search.

Pueblo County

Combined Courts 320 W 10th St, Pueblo, CO 81003; 719-583-7000; probate phone: 719-583-7030;; 8AM-4PM (MST). *Felony, Misdemeanor, Civil, Eviction, Small Claims, Probate.*

www.courts.state.co.us/Courts/County/Choose.cfm

General Information: No adoption, sealed, juvenile, mental health or expunged cases released. Will fax documents $1.00 per page. Court makes copy: $.75 per page. Certification fee: $20.00 per doc. Payee: Pueblo Combined Courts. Personal checks accepted. Visa/MC accepted in person only. Prepayment required. Mail requests: SASE required.

Civil Name Search: Access: Mail, in person, online. Only the court performs in person name searches; visitors may not. Search fee: $5.00 per name. $25.00 per hour if extensive research is needed. Required to search: name, years to search; also helpful: address. Civil records on computer from 1976, index books back to the 1890s. Mail turnaround time 3-5 days. Pay service to civil case look-up at www.courts.state.co.us; click on Court Records Search.

Criminal Name Search: Access: Mail, in person, online. Only the court performs in person name searches; visitors may not. Search fee: $5.00 per name. $25.00 per hour if extensive research is needed. Required to search: name, years to search, DOB; also helpful: address. Criminal records computerized from 1976, index books back to the 1890s. Mail turnaround time 3-5 days, longer if archived. Criminal case index at www.courts.state.co.us. Current dockets free, records not- click on Court Records Search.

Rio Blanco County

9th District & County Courts PO Box 1150, 555 Main St, Rm 303, Meeker, CO 81641; 970-878-5622; fax: 970-878-4295; 8AM-N, 1-5PM (MST). *Felony, Misdemeanor, Civil, Eviction, Small Claims, Probate.*

www.courts.state.co.us/Courts/County/Choose.cfm

General Information: You may fax in after agreeing to $1.00 per page fax fee. The search fee includes both civil and criminal indexes. Phoned-in search requests may or may not be acceptable - depends on clerk availability and your friendly demeanor. No adoption, sealed, juvenile, mental health or expunged cases released. Fee to fax out file $1.00 per page. Court makes copy: $.75 per page. Certification fee: $20.00 per doc. Payee: Clerk of the Combined Courts. Business checks accepted, no personal. Visa/MC accepted. Prepayment required. Mail requests: SASE required.

Civil Name Search: Access: Phone, fax, mail, in person, online. Only the court performs in person name searches; visitors may not. Search fee: $5.00 per name. May charge for lengthy in-person search request. Required to search: name; also helpful: years to search. Civil records on computer since 8/1994, on index cards from 4/1976, index books back to 1889. Mail turnaround time 4 days. Pay service to civil case look-up at www.courts.state.co.us; click on Court Records Search.

Criminal Name Search: Access: Phone, fax, mail, in person, online. Only the court performs in person name searches; visitors may not. Search fee: $5.00 per name. Required to search: name, years to search; also helpful: DOB. Criminal records on computer since 8/1994, on index cards from 4/1976, index books back to 1889. Mail turnaround time 4 days. Criminal case index at www.courts.state.co.us. Current dockets free, records not- click on Court Records Search.

Rio Grande County

12th District & County Courts PO Box 427, 925 6th St, RM 204, Del Norte, CO 81132; 719-657-3394; 8AM-N, 1PM-4PM (MST). *Felony, Misdemeanor, Civil, Eviction, Small Claims, Probate.*

www.courts.state.co.us/Courts/County/Choose.cfm

General Information: No adoption, sealed, juvenile, mental health or expunged cases released. Will fax documents $1.00 per page. Court makes copy: $.75 per page. Certification fee: $20.00. Payee: Rio Grande Combined Court. Personal and business checks accepted. Visa/MC accepted. Prepayment required. Mail requests: SASE required.

Civil Name Search: Access: Mail, in person, online. Only the court performs in person name searches; visitors may not. Search fee: $5.00 per name, additional $25.00 to search archived records. Civil records on computer from 5/95, County on index cards from 1950s, District from 1977. All on index books from the 1800s. Mail turnaround time 2-4 days. Pay service to civil case look-up at www.courts.state.co.us; click on Court Records Search.

Criminal Name Search: Access: Mail, in person, online. Only the court performs in person name searches; visitors may not. Search fee: $5.00 per name, additional $25.00 to search archived records. Required to search: name, DOB; also helpful: years to search. Criminal records computerized from 5/95, County on index cards from 1950s, District from 1977. All on index books from the 1800s. Mail turnaround time 2-4 days. Criminal case index at www.courts.state.co.us. Current dockets free, records not- click on Court Records Search.

Routt County

Routt Combined Courts PO Box 773117, 1955 Shield Dr, Justice Center, Steamboat Springs, CO 80477; 970-879-5020 x7; fax: 970-879-3531; 8AM-5PM (MST). *Felony, Misdemeanor, Civil, Eviction, Small Claims, Probate.*

www.courts.state.co.us/Courts/County/Choose.cfm

General Information: No adoption, sealed, juvenile, mental health or expunged cases released. Will not fax documents. Court makes copy: $.75 per page. Certification fee: $20.00 per doc. Payee: Routt Combined Court. Personal checks accepted. Visa/MC accepted. Prepayment required. Mail requests: SASE required.

Civil Name Search: Access: Mail, in person, online. Both court and visitors may perform in person name searches. Search fee: $5.00 for 1976-1991; prior to 1976 $20.00. There is no fee to search computerized records,. Civil cases indexed by defendant. Civil records on computer back to 1994, on index cards from 1977, microfiche from 1/1977 to 12/1990, archived from 1877. Mail turnaround time 7-10 days. Pay service to civil case look-up at www.courts.state.co.us; click on Court Records Search.

Criminal Name Search: Access: Mail, in person, online. Both court and visitors may perform in person name searches. Search fee: $5.00 for 1976-1991; prior to 1976 $20.00. There is no fee to search computerized records,. Required to search: name, years to search, DOB, maiden name, aliases. Criminal records computerized from 1994, on index cards from 1977, microfiche from 1/1977 to 12/1990, archived from 1877. Mail turnaround time 7-10 days. Criminal case index at www.courts.state.co.us. Current dockets free, records not- click on Court Records Search.

Saguache County

12th District & County Courts PO Box 197, 4th and Christy Sts, Courthouse, Saguache, CO 81149; 719-655-2522; 8AM-N, 1-4PM, phones til 5PM (MST). *Felony, Misdemeanor, Civil, Eviction, Small Claims, Probate.*

www.courts.state.co.us/Courts/County/Choose.cfm

General Information: Probate fax is same as main fax number. No adoption, sealed, juvenile, mental health or expunged cases released. Will not fax documents. Court makes copy: $.75 per page. Certification fee: $20.00 per doc plus copy fee. Payee: Saguache Combined Courts. Personal checks accepted. Visa/MC accepted. Prepayment required. Mail requests: SASE required.

Civil Name Search: Access: Mail, in person, online. Only the court performs in person name searches; visitors may not. Search fee: $5.00 per name or $25.00 per hour if extensive research is needed. Civil records on computer since 6/94, on index cards from 1980s, index books back to 1866. Note: Civil records containing financial information are not available by mail. Mail turnaround time 1 week. Pay service to civil case look-up at www.courts.state.co.us; click on Court Records Search.

Criminal Name Search: Access: Mail, in person, online. Only the court performs in person name searches; visitors may not. Search fee: $5.00 per name or $25.00 per hour if extensive research is needed. Required to search: name, years to search, DOB. Criminal records on computer since 6/94, on index cards from 1980s, index books back to 1866. Note: Generally criminal record search at this office will reveal dispositions only, Mail turnaround time 1 week. Criminal case index at www.courts.state.co.us. Current dockets free, records not- click on Court Records Search.

San Juan County

6th District & County Courts PO Box 900, 1557 Greene St, Silverton, CO 81433; 970-387-5790; fax: 970-387-0295; 8AM-4PM T & TH (MST). *Felony, Misdemeanor, Civil, Eviction, Small Claims, Probate.*
www.courts.state.co.us/Courts/County/Choose.cfm
General Information: No adoption, sealed, juvenile, mental health, open domestic, probate or expunged cases released. Will fax documents to local numbers only. Court makes copy: $.75 per page. Certification fee: $20.00 per doc. Payee: San Juan County Court. Business checks accepted. No credit cards accepted. Prepayment required. Mail requests: SASE required.
Civil Name Search: Access: Phone, fax, mail, in person, online. Only the court performs in person name searches; visitors may not. Search fee: $9.00 per name. Fee is $20.00 for lengthy search. Civil records on computer since 1995; prior on index cards from 1975, index books back to 1876. Mail turnaround time 1 week. Pay service to civil case look-up at www.courts.state.co.us; click on Court Records Search.
Criminal Name Search: Access: Mail, fax, in person, online. Only the court performs in person name searches; visitors may not. Search fee: $9.00 per name. Required to search: name, years to search, DOB, signed release. Criminal records on computer since 1995; prior on index cards from 1975, index books back to 1876. Mail turnaround time 1 week. Criminal case index at www.courts.state.co.us. Current dockets free, records not-click on Court Records Search.

San Miguel County

7th District & County Courts PO Box 919, 305 W Colorado St, Telluride, CO 81435; 970-728-3891; fax: 970-728-6216; 8:30AM-4:45PM (MST). *Felony, Misdemeanor, Civil, Eviction, Small Claims, Probate.*
www.7thjudicialdistrictco.org
General Information: No adoption, sealed, juvenile, mental health or expunged cases released. Will fax documents if prepaid. Court makes copy: $.75 per page. Certification fee: $20.00 per doc. Payee: Combined Courts. Personal checks accepted. Visa/MC accepted. Prepayment required. Mail requests: SASE required.
Civil Name Search: Access: Phone, mail, in person, online. Only the court performs in person name searches; visitors may not. Search fee: $5.00 per name if after 1994. Civil index on cards from 1970, index books back to 1861, archived back to 1880; on computer back to 1994. Note: Will do very limited phone searches back to 1994 - computer lookup no charge Mail turnaround time 30 days. Pay service to civil case look-up at www.courts.state.co.us; click on Court Records Search.
Criminal Name Search: Access: Phone, mail, in person, online. Only the court performs in person name searches; visitors may not. Search fee: $5.00 per name if after 1994. Required to search: name, years to search, DOB. Criminal records indexed on cards from 1970, index books back to 1861, archived back to 1880; on computer back to 1994. Note: Will do very limited phone searches back to 1994 - computer lookup no charge. Mail turnaround time 30 days. Criminal case index at www.courts.state.co.us. Current dockets free, records not- click on Court Records Search.

Sedgwick County

13th District & County Courts 3rd & Pine, Julesburg, CO 80737; 970-474-3627; fax: 970-474-2026; 8AM-1PM (MST). *Felony, Misdemeanor, Civil, Eviction, Small Claims, Probate.*
www.courts.state.co.us/Courts/County/Choose.cfm
General Information: Probate fax is same as main fax number. No adoption, sealed, juvenile, mental health or expunged cases released. Fee to fax out file $2.00 each. Court makes copy: $.75 per page. Certification fee: $20.00 per doc plus copy fee. Payee: Sedgwick County Combined Court. Personal checks accepted. No credit cards accepted. Prepayment required. Mail requests: SASE required.
Civil Name Search: Access: Fax, mail, in person, online. Only the court performs in person name searches; visitors may not. Search fee: The court reserves the right to charge if an extensive search is required. Required to search: name; also helpful: years to search. Civil index on cards from early 1970s, index books back to 1889; on computer back to 8/1995. Mail turnaround time 1-2 days. Pay service to civil case look-up at www.courts.state.co.us; click on Court Records Search.
Criminal Name Search: Access: Fax, mail, in person, online. Only the court performs in person name searches; visitors may not. Search fee: The court reserves the right to charge if an extensive search is required. Required to search: name, DOB; also helpful: years to search. Criminal records indexed on cards from early 1970s, index books back to 1889; on computer back to 8/1995. Mail turnaround time 1-3 days. Criminal case index at

www.courts.state.co.us. Current dockets free, records not- click on Court Records Search.

Summit County

Summit Combined Courts PO Box 185, Breckenridge, CO 80424; 970-453-2241; District; 970-453-2272 County; fax: 970-453-1134; 8AM-4PM (MST). *Felony, Misdemeanor, Civil, Eviction, Small Claims, Probate.*
www.courts.state.co.us/Courts/County/Choose.cfm
General Information: District Court uses PO Box 269. No adoption, sealed, juvenile, mental health or expunged cases released. Will not fax documents. Court makes copy: $.75 per page. Certification fee: $20.00. Payee: Summit Combined Court. Only cashiers checks and money orders accepted; cash accepted in person. Visa/MC accepted. Prepayment required.
Civil Name Search: Access: In person, online. Only the court performs in person name searches; visitors may not. Search fee: $5.00 per name. $25.00 per hour if extensive research is needed. Required to search: name. Civil records on computer back to 1995, index cards from the early 1970s, index books back to 1861, archived from 1980 and prior. Note: Records prior to 2003 in storage; request must be in writing and fee paid prior to court providing record. Pay service to civil case look-up at www.courts.state.co.us; click on Court Records Search.
Criminal Name Search: Access: Mail, in person, online. Only the court performs in person name searches; visitors may not. Search fee: $5.00 per name. $25.00 per hour if extensive research is needed. Required to search: name, DOB, signed release. Criminal records name index on computer as of 9/95. Note: Records prior to 2003 in storage; request must be in writing and fee paid prior to court providing record. Criminal case index at www.courts.state.co.us. Current dockets free, records not- click on Court Records Search.

Teller County

Teller Combined Courts PO Box 997, Cripple Creek, CO 80813; 719-689-2574; fax: 719-686-8000; 8AM-4:30PM (MST). *Felony, Misdemeanor, Civil, Eviction, Small Claims, Probate.*
www.courts.state.co.us/
General Information: No adoption, sealed, juvenile, mental health or expunged cases released. Will fax documents $1.00 per page. Court makes copy: $.75 per page. Certification fee: $20.00 per document. Payee: Teller County Combined Courts. Personal and business checks accepted. Credit cards accepted. Prepayment required. Mail requests: SASE required.
Civil Name Search: Access: Mail, in person, online. Only the court performs in person name searches; visitors may not. Search fee: $5.00 per name. If not on computer, fee is $15.00 to retrieve file from offsite. Civil records computerized back to 1988, on index cards from 1960, index books back to 1899. Note: Download a record request form at https://33.securedata.net/gofourth/pub_data_req_form.htm. Mail turnaround time 5-7 days; 7-10 days if not on computer. Pay service to civil case look-up at www.courts.state.co.us; click on Court Records Search. One may also record copies from the home page at same fees mentioned here.
Criminal Name Search: Access: Mail, in person, online. Only the court performs in person name searches; visitors may not. Search fee: $5.00 per name. If not on computer, fee is $15.00 to retrieve file from offsite. Required to search: name, years to search, DOB; also helpful: address, SSN. Criminal records computerized back to 1988, on index cards from 1960, index books back to 1899. Mail turnaround time 5-7 days; 7-10 days if file not on computer. Criminal case index at www.courts.state.co.us. Current dockets free, records not- click on Court Records Search. One may also record copies from the home page at same fees mentioned here.

Washington County

Washington County Combined Court 26861 Hwy 34, PO Box 455, Akron, CO 80720; 970-345-2756; fax: 970-345-2829; 8AM-4PM (MST). *Felony, Misdemeanor, Civil, Eviction, Small Claims, Probate.*
www.courts.state.co.us/Courts/County/Index.cfm?County_ID=43
General Information: No adoption, sealed, juvenile, mental health or expunged cases released. Will fax documents $5.00 fee. Court makes copy: $.75 per page. Certification fee: $20.00 per document. Payee: Washington County Combined Court. Personal checks and credit cards accepted. Prepayment required. Mail requests: SASE required.
Civil Name Search: Access: Phone, mail, in person, online. Only the court performs in person name searches; visitors may not. No search fee. Civil cases indexed by defendant. Civil index on cards from 1970, index books back to 1887; computerized since 1995. Mail turnaround time 5-7 days. Pay service to civil case look-up at www.courts.state.co.us; click on Court Records Search.
Criminal Name Search: Access: Phone, mail, in person, online. Only the court performs in person name searches; visitors may not. No search fee. Required to search: name, years to search, DOB. Criminal records indexed on cards from 1970, index books back to 1887; computerized since 1995. Note: Criminal case index available for a fee via a choice of 3 private

providers. Mail turnaround time 5-7 days. Criminal case index at www.courts.state.co.us. Current dockets free, records not- click on Court Records Search.

Weld County

19th District & County Courts PO Box 2038, 901 9th Ave, Centennial Bldg (80631), Greeley, CO 80632; 970-351-7300; criminal phone: x5597; civil phone: x5596; probate phone: x5400; fax: 970-336-7245; 7:30AM-4:30PM (MST). *Felony, Misdemeanor, Civil, Eviction, Small Claims, Probate.*
www.courts.state.co.us/Courts/County/Index.cfm?County_ID=61
General Information: The court will not accept fax requests. No adoption, sealed, juvenile, mental health or expunged cases released. Will not fax out documents. Court makes copy: $.75 per page. Certification fee: $20.00 per doc. Payee: Clerk of Combined Court. Personal checks and credit cards accepted. Prepayment required. Mail requests: SASE required.
Civil Name Search: Access: Mail, in person, online. Only the court performs in person name searches; visitors may not. Search fee: $5.00 per name. $25.00 per hour if extensive research is needed. Required to search: name, years to search, DOB. Civil cases indexed by defendant, plaintiff, and case #. Civil records on computer from 1975 (District), 1990 (County), index cards from 1958, index books back to 1876. Mail turnaround time ASAP. Pay service to civil case look-up at www.courts.state.co.us; click on Court Records Search.
Criminal Name Search: Access: Mail, in person, online. Only the court performs in person name searches; visitors may not. Search fee: $5.00 per name. $25.00 per hour if extensive research is needed. Required to search: name, years to search; also helpful: DOB. Criminal records computerized from 1975 (District), 1990 (County), index cards from 1958, index books back to 1876. Mail turnaround time ASAP. Online access same as described for civil records. Search the sheriff's list of sex offender and most wanted at www.weldsheriff.com/.

Yuma County

13th District & County Courts 310 Ash St, Ste L, Wray, CO 80758; 970-332-4118; fax: 970-332-4119; 8AM-4PM (MST). *Felony, Misdemeanor, Civil, Eviction, Small Claims, Probate.*
www.courts.state.co.us/Courts/County/Choose.cfm
General Information: No adoption, sealed, juvenile, mental health or expunged cases released. Will fax documents $1.00 per page. Fee applies incoming fax as well. Court makes copy: $.75 per page. Certification fee: $20.00 per cert. Payee: Yuma County Combined Court. Personal checks accepted. No credit cards accepted. Prepayment required. Mail requests: SASE required.
Civil Name Search: Access: Mail, in person, online. Only the court performs in person name searches; visitors may not. Search fee: $5.00 per name. $25.00 per hour if extensive research is needed. Civil cases indexed by defendant. Civil records on computer back to 3/1996; on index cards from 1982, index books back to 1889. Mail turnaround time 2-5 days. Pay service to civil case look-up at www.courts.state.co.us; click on Court Records Search.
Criminal Name Search: Access: Mail, in person, online. Only the court performs in person name searches; visitors may not. Search fee: $5.00 per name. May be no charge if it is an in person search and for only a couple years. Required to search: name. Criminal records computerized from 3/1996; on index cards from 1982, index books back to 1889. Mail turnaround time 2-5 days. Criminal case index at www.courts.state.co.us. Current dockets free, records not- click on Court Records Search.

Connecticut

Time Zone:	EST
Capital:	Hartford, Hartford County
# of Counties:	8
State Web:	www.ct.gov
Court Web:	www.jud.ct.gov

Administration Chief Court Administrator, 231 Capitol Av, Hartford, CT, 06106; 860-757-2100, Fax: 860-757-2130

The Supreme and Appellate Courts The Supreme Court is the court of last resort. The Courts of Appeal hears appeals from the Superior Courts. The website above provides access to all opinions; click on *Case Look-up.*

The Connecticut Courts

Court	Type	How Organized	Jurisdiction Highpoints
Superior Courts* Shown By District	General	15 courts in 13 Districts	Felony, Misdemeanor, Civil, Small Claims, Family, Probate, Juvenile, Traffic, Eviction, Domestic Relations
Geographic Area*	Limited	20 courts in 20 Districts	Misdemeanor, Civil Actions Under $25,000 (tort, contract, real property rights)
Centralized Small Claims*	Special	1 court	Small Claims
Probate*	Special	54 courts	Probate

* = profiled in this book

Details on the Court Structure The **Superior Court** is the sole court of original jurisdiction for all causes of action, except for matters over which the Probate Courts have jurisdiction as provided by statute. Overall, the courts are divided into 13 Judicial Districts, 20 Geographic Area Courts, and 13 Juvenile Districts. The Superior Court - comprised primarily of the **Judicial District Courts** and the **Geographical Area Courts** – has 5 divisions: Criminal, Civil, Family, Juvenile, and Administrative Appeals. The Civil Division hears Landlord-Tenant and Small Claims. When not combined, the Judicial District Courts handle felony and civil cases while the Geographic Area Courts handle misdemeanors and limited civil cases. Divorce records are maintained by the Chief Clerk of the Judicial District Courts.

Probate is handled by city Probate Courts which are not part of the Judicial District Court system. In January 2011, the state judiciary consolidated and reduced the number of probate courts from 117 to 54 locations.

In May, 2006 the state centralized all small claims cases to the **Centralized Small Claims Office**. This location holds all records since that date. Older case files must be searched at the Geographic Area Courts – except all Manchester cases small claims files were forwarded to the Centralized Office. Small claims matters may be filed at the Centralized Office or at a local Geographic Court; however if filed at the Geographic Office the case is immediately sent to the Centralized Office.

Record Searching Facts You Need to Know

Fees and Record Searching Tips The following fees are set by statute; $1.00 for a copy and $2.00 to certify a copy page. A certified copy of a judgment file is $25.00.

Probate information request requirements are consistent across the state – requesters must provide full name of decedent, year and place of death, and SASE. There is no search fee. The certification fee is $5.00 for 1st 2 pages and $2.00 for each additional page. The probate copy fee is $5.00 for each five pages or fraction thereof. Fees are set by statute.

The Superior Court Record Center

The Superior Court Record Center in Enfield, CT is the repository for criminal and some civil records and is open 9AM-5PM. Case records are sent to the Enfield Record Center from 3 months to 5 years after disposition by the courts. Records are maintained 10 years for misdemeanors and 20+ years for felonies. If a requester is certain that the record is at the Record Center, it is quicker to direct the request here rather than to the original court of record. Only written requests are accepted. Enfield does not do name searches. Search requirements– full defendant name, docket number, disposition date, and court action. Fee is $3.00 for each docket, $5.00 if certified. Fee payee is Treasurer, State of Connecticut. Direct Requests to: Connecticut Record Center, 111 Phoenix Avenue, Enfield, CT 06082, telephone 860-741-3714.

Personal checks must have name and address printed on the check. If requesting in person, your check must have same address as your drivers' license.

Online Access is on a County Basis

The Judicial Branch offers web look-up to case docket information at www.jud.ct.gov/jud2.htm. Case look-ups are segregated into five types; civil/family, criminal/motor vehicle, housing, juvenile, and small claims. For civil/family and small claims cases statewide are available within 10 years after the disposition date, depending on location. Search statewide or by location. The criminal and motor vehicle case docket data is available on cases up to ten years after a disposition or bond forfeiture occurred.

Youthful Offender cases are not shown on the criminal/motor vehicle look-ups. To search statewide, leave the location field blank. For housing (landlord/tenant) cases, search by name, address, or docket number.

The Housing case record search is available only for Hartford, New Haven, New Britain, Bridgeport, Norwalk and Waterbury districts. However, Case records for summary process matters in Tolland and Meriden Judicial Districts can be found using the Civil/Family look-up.

Fairfield County

Danbury Judicial District Court 146 White St, Danbury, CT 06810; 203-207-8600; criminal phone: x1; civil phone: x3; criminal fax: 203-207-8666; civil fax: 9AM-5PM; 9AM-5PM (EST). *Felony, Misdemeanor, Civil Actions, Eviction, Small Claims, Divorce.*
www.jud.ct.gov/directory/directory/directions/24.htm
General Information: No sealed records released. Will not fax documents. Court makes copy: $1.00 per page. Certification fee: $2.00 per cert plus copy fee. The fee for a certified copy of a judgment is always $25.00. Will not certify unless copies are made by the court personnel. Payee: Clerk of Superior Court. ID required with personal check. Visa/MC accepted in person only. Prepayment required.
Civil Name Search: Access: Mail, in person, online. Only the court performs in person name searches; visitors may not. No search fee. Civil cases indexed by plaintiff and defendant. Civil records on microfilm from 11-87, prior on index cards. Mail turnaround time 2-4 days. Access civil/family case index free at http://civilinquiry.jud.ct.gov/. Search by name or case number. From this site there is also access to Housing and Small Claims.
Criminal Name Search: Access: Mail, in person, online. Only the court performs in person name searches; visitors may not. No search fee. Required to search: name, years to search, DOB. Criminal records on microfilm from 11-87, prior on index cards but only list docket number and disposal date. Mail turnaround time 3-4 days. Pending, current and disposed criminal and motor vehicle dockets back to 2000 free at www.jud.ct.gov/jud2.htm. Online criminal results also show year of birth. Online criminal/traffic record search requests allow you to include the birth year; in person searching allows use of add'l personal identifiers. Online results show name only.

Fairfield Judicial District - Bridgeport 1061 Main St, Attn: criminal or civil, Bridgeport, CT 06604; 203-579-6527; fax: 203-382-8406; 9AM-5PM (EST). *Felony, Civil Actions, Divorce.*
www.jud.ct.gov/external/super/default.htm
General Information: Online identifiers in results same as on public terminal. No sealed, adoption records released. Court makes copy: $1.00 per page. Certification fee: $2.00 per cert; Exemplification fee- $20.00; judgment copy- $15.00, $25 if certified. Payee: Clerk Superior Court. Personal checks accepted; proper ID required. Visa/MC accepted. Prepayment required. Mail requests: SASE requested.

Civil Name Search: Access: Mail, in person, online. Both court and visitors may perform in person name searches. No search fee. Civil records on computer from 1990, on microfiche from 1975 to 1990, prior on index cards. After 5 years sent to Records Center at Enfield, CT. Mail turnaround time 2-3 weeks. Access civil/family case index free at http://civilinquiry.jud.ct.gov/. Search by name or case number. From this site there is also access to Housing and Small Claims.
Criminal Name Search: Access: Mail, in person, online. Only the court performs in person name searches; visitors may not. No search fee. Required to search: name, years to search, DOB. Criminal records on computer since 1997, on microfiche from 1975 to 1996,. Mail turnaround time 4 weeks. Pending, current and disposed criminal and motor vehicle dockets back to 2000 free at www.jud.ct.gov. Online criminal results also show year of birth. Online criminal/traffic record search requests allow you to include the birth year; in person searching allows use of add'l personal identifiers. Online results show name only.

Stamford-Norwalk Judicial District & GA Court #1 123 Hoyt St, #100, Criminal Court Clerk, Stamford, CT 06905; criminal phone: 203-965-5208; civil phone: 203-965-5307; criminal fax: 203-965-5355; civil fax: 9AM-5PM; 9AM-5PM (EST). *Felony, Misdemeanors, Civil Actions, Divorce, Eviction, Small Claims.*
www.jud.ct.gov/external/super/default.htm
General Information: This court also includes Geographical Area Court #1. Family court- 203-965-0368. Civil clerk on 2nd Fl, #123 - public access civil terminal on 4th Fl. Online identifiers in results same as on public terminal. No sealed records released. Will not fax documents. Court makes copy: $1.00 per page. Certification fee: $3.00 per doc plus copy fee. Payee: Clerk of Superior Court. Personal checks accepted. Visa/MC accepted in person only. Prepayment required.
Civil Name Search: Access: Mail, in person, online. Both court and visitors may perform in person name searches. No search fee. Only pending civil cases on computer, on microfiche from 1970s, on index cards from 1958. Note: Small Claims cases from May 2006 forward are kept with the Centralized Small Claims Office in Hartford - 860-756-7800. Public use terminal has civil records. Public terminal has pending cases only. Access civil/family case index free at http://civilinquiry.jud.ct.gov/. Search by name or case number. From this site there is also access to Housing and Small Claims.
Criminal Name Search: Access: Mail, in person, online. Both court and visitors may perform in person name searches. No search fee. Required to search: name, years to search, DOB. Only pending cases on computer, on

microfiche from 1970s, on index cards from 1962. Pending, current and disposed criminal and motor vehicle dockets back to 2000 free at www.jud.ct.gov/jud2.htm. Online criminal results also show year of birth. Online criminal/traffic record search requests allow you to include the birth year; in person searching allows use of add'l personal identifiers.

Geographical Area Court #2 172 Golden Hill St, 1st Fl, Bridgeport, CT 06604; 203-579-6560; criminal phone: x2; civil phone: 203-579-6527; fax: 203-382-8408; 9AM-5PM (EST). *Misdemeanor, Eviction, Small Claims.*
www.jud.ct.gov/external/super/default.htm
General Information: Serves the towns of Bridgeport, Easton, Fairfield, Monroe, Stratford and Trumbull. Civil Division is located at 1051 Main St, phone- 203-579-7240. Online identifiers in results same as on public terminal. No sealed records released. Court makes copy: $1.00 per page. Certification fee: $3.00 per doc plus copy fee. Payee: Clerk of Superior Court. In-state personal checks accepted - names must match DL name. Visa/MC accepted. Prepayment required.
Civil Name Search: Access: In person, online. Both court and visitors may perform in person name searches. No search fee. Civil cases indexed by defendant. Civil records pending and from 1990 on computer, on microfiche from 1982 to 1990, prior on index cards. After are microfilmed and entered on index cards. Note: Small Claims cases from May 2006 forward are kept with the Centralized Small Claims Office in Hartford - 860-756-7800. Civil PAT goes back to 2001. Access small claims and housing case index free at http://civilinquiry.jud.ct.gov/.
Criminal Name Search: Access: In person, online. Visitors must perform in person searches themselves. Criminal records pending and from 1990 on computer, on microfiche from 1982. Note: Refer mail requests to the state criminal records agency, PO Box 2794, Middletown CT 06457. For access via the state Dept of Public Safety system, see www.ct.gov/dps and click on *Reports And Records*. Criminal PAT goes back to 2001. Pending, current and disposed criminal and motor vehicle dockets back to 2000 free at www.jud.ct.gov/jud2.htm. Online criminal results also show year of birth. Online criminal/traffic record search requests allow you to include the birth year; in person searching allows use of add'l personal identifiers. Online results show name only.

Geographical Area Court #20 17 Belden Ave, Norwalk, CT 06850; 203-846-3237; criminal phone: 203-846-3237; civil phone: 203-846-4206; fax: 203-847-8710; 9AM-5PM (EST). *Misdemeanor, Eviction, Small Claims.*
www.jud.ct.gov/external/super/default.htm
General Information: Serving the towns of New Canaan, Norwalk, Weston, Westport, and Wilton. Will fax back doc for no fee. Court makes copy: $1.00 per page. Certification fee: $2.00 per cert. Payee: Superior Court GA #20. Only cashiers checks and money orders accepted. Visa/MC accepted. Prepayment required.
Civil Name Search: Access: Mail, online, in person. Visitors must perform in person searches themselves. Search fee: $25.00. Civil records on computer from 1986. Note: Small Claims cases from May 2006 forward are kept with the Centralized Small Claims Office in Hartford - 860-756-7800. Access housing case index free at http://civilinquiry.jud.ct.gov/.
Criminal Name Search: Access: In person, online. Visitors must perform in person searches themselves. Required to search: name, years to search; also helpful: DOB. Criminal records computerized from 1986, prior records on index cards for 25 years. Pending, current and disposed criminal and motor vehicle dockets back to 2000 free at www.jud.ct.gov/jud2.htm. Online criminal results also show year of birth. Online criminal/traffic record search requests allow you to include the birth year; in person searching allows use of add'l personal identifiers. Online results show name only.

Geographical Area Court #3 146 White St, Danbury, CT 06810; 203-207-8600; fax: 203-207-8642; 9AM-5PM (EST). *Misdemeanor, Eviction, Small Claims.* www.jud.ct.gov/external/super/default.htm
General Information: Serving the towns of Bethel, Brookfield, Danbury, New Fairfield, Newtown, Redding, Ridgefield, Sherman. No youthful offender or dispositions by dismissal after 20 days from date of judgment records released. Court makes copy: $1.00 per page. Certification fee: $2.00 per cert. Payee: Clerk of Superior Court. Personal checks accepted. Visa/MC accepted. Prepayment required. Mail requests: SASE required for civil.
Civil Name Search: Access: Mail, in person, online. Only the court performs in person name searches; visitors may not. No search fee. Civil cases indexed by defendant. Civil records on microfilm from 11-87, prior on index cards, but only list docket number and disposal date, then referred to Records Center at Enfield. Note: In person searches are returned by mail. Small Claims cases from May 2006 forward are kept with the Centralized Small Claims Office in Hartford - 860-756-7800. Access small claims case index free at http://civilinquiry.jud.ct.gov/.

Criminal Name Search: Access: In person, online. Visitors must perform in person searches themselves. Required to search: name, years to search; also helpful: DOB. Criminal records computerized from 11/9/87. Pending, current and disposed criminal and motor vehicle dockets back to 2000 free at www.jud.ct.gov/jud2.htm. Online criminal results also show year of birth. Online criminal/traffic record search requests allow you to include the birth year; in person searching allows use of add'l personal identifiers. Online results show name only.

Bridgeport Probate District 48 202 State St, McLevy Hall, 3rd Fl, Bridgeport, CT 06604; 203-576-3945; fax: 203-576-7898; 8:30AM-5PM M-TH; 8:30AM-4PM F (EST). *Probate.* www.jud.ct.gov/probate/

Danbury Probate District 43 155 Deer Hill Ave, City Hall Building, Danbury, CT 06810; 203-797-4521; fax: 203-796-1563; 7:30AM-5:30PM M-TH (EST). *Probate.* www.jud.ct.gov/probate/

Darien-New Canaan Probate District 52 Town Hall, 2 Renshaw Rd, Darien, CT 06820; 203-656-7342; fax: 203-656-0774; 8:30AM-4:30PM (EST). *Probate.* www.jud.ct.gov/probate/
General Information: Formerly Darien Probate Court. Also open Fridays 8:30AM-12:30PM in Summer.

Fairfield Probate District 49 Independence Hall, 725 Old Post Rd, Fairfield, CT 06824; 203-256-3041; fax: 203-256-3044; 8:30AM-4:30PM (EST). *Probate.* www.jud.ct.gov/probate/

Greenwich Probate District 54 101 Field Point Rd, Greenwich, CT 06836; 203-622-7879; fax: 203-622-6451; 8AM-4PM M-F (EST). *Probate.* www.jud.ct.gov/probate/

Northern Fairfield County Probate District 45 1 School St, PO Box 144, Bethel, CT 06801; 203-794-8508; fax: 203-778-7517; 8:30AM-4:30PM (EST). *Probate.* www.jud.ct.gov/probate/
General Information: Formerly Bethel Probate Court. District includes Bethel, Newtown, Redding, Ridgefield. Fax is located in City Hall.

Norwalk Probate District 51 125 East Ave, PO Box 2009, Norwalk, CT 06852-2009; 203-854-7737; fax: 203-854-7825; 8:30AM-4:30PM (EST). *Probate.* www.jud.ct.gov/probate/
General Information: District includes Towns of Norwalk, Wilton.

Shelton Probate District 42 40 White St, PO Box 127, Shelton, CT 06484; 203-924-8462; fax: 203-924-8943; 9AM-5PM (EST). *Probate.* www.jud.ct.gov/probate/

Stamford Probate District 53 888 Washington Blvd, 8th Fl, PO Box 10152, Stamford, CT 06904-2152; 203-323-2149; fax: 203-964-1830; 8:30AM-4:30PM (EST). *Probate.* www.jud.ct.gov/probate/

Stratford Probate District 47 468 Birdseye St, 2nd Fl, Stratford, CT 06615; 203-385-4023; fax: 203-375-6253; 9:30AM-4:30PM (EST). *Probate.* www.jud.ct.gov/probate/

Trumbull Probate District 46 Town Hall, 5866 Main St, Trumbull, CT 06611-5416; 203-452-5068; fax: 203-452-5092; 8:30AM-4:30PM (EST). *Probate.* www.jud.ct.gov/probate/
General Information: District includes Town of Easton, Monroe, Trumbull.

Westport Probate District 50 Town Hall, 110 Myrtle Ave, Westport, CT 06880; 203-341-1100; fax: 203-341-1102; 8:30AM-4:30PM (EST). *Probate.* www.jud.ct.gov/probate/
General Information: District includes Weston, Westport.

Hartford County

Hartford Judicial District Court - Civil 95 Washington St, Hartford, CT 06106; 860-548-2700; fax: 860-548-2711; 9AM-5PM (EST). *Civil Actions.* www.jud.ct.gov
General Information: Hartford Family Court located at 90 Washington St, 860-706-5100. Online identifiers in results same as on public terminal. Will not fax documents. Court makes copy: $1.00 per page. Certification fee: $2.00 per doc plus copy fee. Payee: Clerk of Superior Court. Personal checks accepted. Credit cards accepted in person only. Prepayment required. Mail requests: SASE required.
Civil Name Search: Access: Mail, in person, online. Both court and visitors may perform in person name searches. No search fee. Civil records on computer if active, older on microfiche, older records at Enfield Records Center. Mail turnaround time 7-10 days. Public use terminal has civil records. Access civil/family case index free at http://civilinquiry.jud.ct.gov/. Search by name or case number. From this site there is also access to Housing and Small Claims.

Hartford Judicial District Court - Criminal 101 LaFayette St, Hartford, CT 06106; 860-566-1630; criminal phone: x5; fax: 860-566-1983; 9AM-5PM (EST). *Felony.*
www.jud.ct.gov/external/super/default.htm

General Information: This court shares phone line and address with Geographical Court #14. No youthful offender records or dismissals released. Will fax documents. Court makes copy: $1.00 per page. Certification fee: $3.00 per doc plus copy fee. Payee: Clerk of Superior Court. Personal checks accepted. Visa/MC accepted, $10.00 minimum. Prepayment required. Mail requests: SASE required.

Criminal Name Search: Access: In person, online. Only the court performs in person name searches; visitors may not. Required to search: name, years to search; also helpful: DOB. Criminal records computerized from 1989. Note: This court will only search to provide you with a docket number, then search at records center. Mail turnaround time 7-10 days. Pending, current and disposed criminal and motor vehicle dockets back to 2000 free at www.jud.ct.gov/jud2.htm. Online criminal results also show year of birth. Online criminal/traffic record search requests allow you to include the birth year or a range of years; in person searching allows use of add'l personal identifiers. Online results show name only.

New Britain Judicial District Court 20 Franklin Square, #123, New Britain, CT 06051; criminal phone: 860-515-5080; civil phone: 860-515-5180; fax: 860-515-5185; 9AM-5PM (EST). *Felony, Civil Actions, Small Claims, Divorce.* www.jud.ct.gov/external/super/default.htm

General Information: Civil is on 2nd Fl, #212. Small Claims- best to use centralized system, 860-756-7800 in Hartford. Online identifiers in results same as on public terminal. Certain paternity, family case studies and sealed records not released. Will not fax out documents. Court makes copy: $1.00 per page. Self serve copy: Court Srvs lets you have 1st 10 pages free, then $.10 per page. Certification fee: $2.00 per cert plus copy fee. Payee: Clerk of Superior Court. No personal checks accepted. Visa/MC accepted; $10 minimum. Prepayment required. Mail requests: SASE required.

Civil Name Search: Access: Phone, mail, online, in person. Both court and visitors may perform in person name searches. No search fee. Civil cases indexed by plaintiff. Civil records on computer up to one year after closing, index cards back to 1989, prior in Hartford. Mail turnaround time 1-3 days. Civil PAT available. Civil public access terminal in Rm 210 across hallway from civil. Access civil/family case index free at http://civilinquiry.jud.ct.gov/. Search by name or case number. From this site there is also access to Housing and Small Claims.

Criminal Name Search: Access: Mail, in person, online. Both court and visitors may perform in person name searches. No search fee. Criminal records on computer for 2 years, then purged when cases sent to State Record Center. Note: This court prefers that you search at Enfield Mail turnaround time 3 days. Criminal PAT available. Crim public access terminal upstairs, may be re-located elsewhere. Pending, current and disposed criminal and motor vehicle dockets back to 2000 free at www.jud.ct.gov/jud2.htm. Online criminal results also show year of birth. Online criminal/traffic record search requests allow you to include the birth year; in person searching allows use of add'l personal identifiers. Online results show name only.

Geographical Area Court #12 410 Center St, Manchester, CT 06040; 860-647-1091; fax: 860-645-7540; 9AM-5PM; Phone Hours 9AM-4PM (EST). *Misdemeanor, Eviction.* www.jud.ct.gov/external/super/default.htm

General Information: Serving the towns of East Hartford, Glastonbury, Manchester, Marlborough and South Windsor. Evictions are handled by a special Housing Court, 80 Washington St, Hartford, CT, 860-756-7920. No non discloseable records released. Will not fax documents. Court makes copy: $1.00 per page. Certification fee: $2.00 per doc plus copy fee. Payee: Clerk of Superior Court. Personal checks accepted. Visa/MC accepted; $10.00 minimum. Prepayment required. Mail requests: SASE required.

Civil Name Search: Access: Mail, in person. Both court and visitors may perform in person name searches. No search fee. Civil cases indexed by defendant. Civil records on computer for 3 years. Note: Small Claims cases from this area are filed with the Centralized Small Claims Office in Hartford - 860-756-7800. Mail turnaround time 1-2 weeks.

Criminal Name Search: Access: Mail, in person, online. Only the court performs in person name searches; visitors may not. No search fee. Required to search: name, years to search, DOB. Criminal records on computer since 2002, available since 1979. Note: In person search results returned by mail only. The court urges requesters to go to the State Police for criminal record searches. Mail turnaround time 1-2 weeks. Pending, current and disposed criminal and motor vehicle dockets back to 2000 free at www.jud.ct.gov/jud2.htm. Online criminal results also show year of birth. Online criminal/traffic record search requests allow you to include the birth year; in person searching allows use of add'l personal identifiers. Online results show name only.

Geographical Area Court #13 111 Phoenix Ave, Enfield, CT 06082; 860-741-3727 x2; fax: 860-741-3474; 9AM-5PM (EST). *Misdemeanor.* www.jud.ct.gov/external/super/default.htm

General Information: Serving the towns of East Granby, East Windsor, Enfield, Granby, Simsbury, Suffield, Windsor and Windsor Locks. Eviction

cases are handled by Hartford Housing, 860-756-7920. Will not fax out documents. Court makes copy: $1.00 per page. Certification fee: $2.00 per doc plus copy fee. Payee: Clerk of Superior Court. Will take personal check with ID. Visa/MC accepted; only in person. Prepayment required.

Criminal Name Search: Access: Mail, in person, online. Visitors must perform in person searches themselves. No search fee. Required to search: name, years to search, DOB. Criminal records on computer for 15 years; earlier archived at Record Center which is also here in Enfield. Note: Generally, this court will perform an index search to provide you with docket numbers, etc, then you can visit the statewide records center also located in this building. Mail turnaround time 1-2 weeks. Pending, current and disposed criminal and motor vehicle cases back to 2000 free at www.jud.ct.gov/jud2.htm. Online criminal results also show year of birth. Online criminal/traffic record search requests allow you to include the birth year; in person searching allows use of add'l personal identifiers. Online results show name only.

Geographical Area Court #15 20 Franklin Square, New Britain, CT 06051; criminal phone: 860-515-5080; civil phone: 860-515-5180; criminal fax: 860-515-5103; civil fax: 9AM-5PM; 9AM-5PM (EST). *Misdemeanor, Eviction, Small Claims.* www.jud.ct.gov/external/super/default.htm

General Information: Serving the towns of Berlin, New Britain, Newington, Rocky Hill and Wethersfield. No sealed records released. Court makes copy: $1.00 per page. Certification fee: $2.00 per cert plus copy fee. Payee: Clerk of Superior Court. No out-of-state checks accepted. Major credit cards accepted with proper ID; $10.00 minimum. Prepayment required. Mail requests: SASE required.

Civil Name Search: Access: Mail, in person, online. Both court and visitors may perform in person name searches. No search fee. Civil records on computer for 3 years, then on microfiche. All info in archives at Record Center at Enfield, CT. Note: Small Claims cases from May 2006 forward are kept with the Centralized Small Claims Office in Hartford - 860-756-7800. Mail turnaround time 1 month. Civil PAT available. Access small claims and housing case index free at http://civilinquiry.jud.ct.gov/.

Criminal Name Search: Access: Mail, in person, online. Both court and visitors may perform in person name searches. No search fee. Required to search: name, years to search, DOB. Data is purged every two years. Criminal records computerized from 1985, then on microfiche. All info in archives at Enfield Record Center. Mail turnaround time 1 month. Criminal PAT available. Pending, current and disposed criminal and motor vehicle dockets back to 2000 free at www.jud.ct.gov/jud2.htm. Online criminal results also show year of birth. Online criminal/traffic record search requests allow you to include the birth year; in person searching allows use of add'l personal identifiers. Online results show name only.

Geographical Area Court #17 131 N Main St, Bristol, CT 06010; 860-582-8111 x1; fax: 860-585-8799; 9AM-5PM (EST). *Misdemeanor, Some Felony.* www.jud.ct.gov

General Information: Serving the towns of Bristol, Burlington, Plainville, Plymouth, Southington. No dismissals, not guilty, youthful offender or NOLLE records released. Will fax documents. Court makes copy: $1.00 per page. Certification fee: $2.00; exemplification fee is $20.00. Payee: Clerk of Superior Court. Personal checks accepted with ID. Visa/MC accepted; $10.00 minimum. Prepayment required. Mail requests: SASE required.

Criminal Name Search: Access: Mail, Fax, in person, online. Only the court performs in person name searches; visitors may not. No search fee. Required to search: name, years to search, DOB, date of arrest and/or disposition. Criminal records computerized from 1986, prior on index cards from 1979-1992, microfiche 1988-1996 and docket books. Note: Most convictions and older records are stored off-site. No personal information provided over the phone. Mail turnaround time 1-2 days. Pending, current and disposed criminal and motor vehicle dockets back to 2000 free at www.jud.ct.gov/jud2.htm. Online criminal results also show year of birth. Online criminal/traffic record search requests allow you to include the birth year; in person searching allows use of add'l personal identifiers. Online results show name only.

Centralized Small Claims Court 80 Washington St, Hartford, CT 06106; 860756-7800; fax: 860-756-7805; 9AM-5PM (EST). *Small Claims Statewide.* www.jud.ct.gov/directory/directory/directions/smallclaims.htm

General Information: This court holds all small claims cases since May 2006, plus all of Manchester's small claims cases. Cases filed here or if a case is filed at a Geographic Court, the case is immediately and automatically forwarded here. Court makes copy: $1.00 per page. Certification fee: $2.00 per doc plus copy fee. Payee: Centralized Small Claims Court. . Prepayment required. Mail requests: SASE required.

Civil Name Search: Access: Mail, in person, online. Both court and visitors may perform in person name searches. No search fee. All cases file are here since May 2006. Access the small claims case index free at http://civilinquiry.jud.ct.gov/. Online record search requests allow you to include only the name; in person searching allows use of add'l personal identifiers.

Geographical Area Court #14 101 LaFayette St, Hartford, CT 06106; 860-566-1630; criminal phone: x5; fax: 860-566-1983; 9AM-5PM (EST). *Misdemeanor.*
www.jud.ct.gov/external/super/default.htm
General Information: Serving the towns of Avon, Bloomfield, Canton, Farmington, Hartford and West Hartford. Will fax documents. Court makes copy: $1.00 per page. Certification fee: $2.00 per doc plus copy fee. Payee: Clerk of Superior Court. Only cashiers checks and money orders accepted. No credit cards accepted. Prepayment required. Mail requests: SASE required.
Criminal Name Search: Access: In person, online. Only the court performs in person name searches; visitors may not. Required to search: name, years to search, DOB. Criminal records on computer for 3 years, microfiche by year. Archived at Record Center which is also here in Enfield, CT. Note: This court can only search to provide you with a docket number, then search at records center. Pending, current and disposed criminal and motor vehicle dockets back to 2000 free at www.jud.ct.gov/jud2.htm. Online criminal results also show year of birth. Online criminal/traffic record search requests allow you to include the birth year; in person searching allows use of add'l personal identifiers. Online results show name only.

Berlin Probate District 8 1 Liberty Square, PO Box 400, New Britain, CT 06050-0400; 860-826-2696; fax: 860-826-2695; 8:30AM-4:30PM (EST). *Probate.*
www.jud.ct.gov/probate/
General Information: District includes New Britain, Kennsington, East Berlin.

East Hartford Probate District 5 Town Hall, 740 Main St, East Hartford, CT 06108; 860-291-7278; fax: 860-291-7211; 8:30AM-4:30PM (EST). *Probate.* www.jud.ct.gov/probate/

Farmington-Burlington Probate District 10 One Monteith Dr, Farmington, CT 06032; 860-675-2360; fax: 860-673-8262; 8:30-4:30AM (EST). *Probate.* www.jud.ct.gov/probate/
General Information: Formerly Farmington Probate Court.

Glastonbury-Hebron Probate District 6 PO Box 6523, 2155 Main St, Glastonbury, CT 06033-6523; 860-652-7629; fax: 860-368-2520; 8:30AM-4:30PM (7PM on T) (EST). *Probate.*
www.jud.ct.gov/probate/
General Information: Formerly Glastonbury Probate Court.

Greater Manchester Probate District 13 66 Center St, Manchester, CT 06040; 860-647-3227; fax: 860-647-3236; 8:30AM-4:30PM (EST). *Probate.* www.jud.ct.gov/probate/
General Information: Formerly Manchester Probate Court. Includes Andover, Bolton, Columbia, Manchester.

Greater Windsor Probate District 4 1540 Sullivan Ave, Town Hall, South Windsor, CT 06074; 860-644-2511 X371; fax: 860-648-5047; 8AM-4PM (EST). *Probate.* www.jud.ct.gov/probate/
General Information: Formerly East Windsor Probate Court. District includes East Windsor, South Windsor, Windsor.

Hartford Probate District 1 250 Constitution Plaza, 3rd Fl, Hartford, CT 06103; 860-757-9150; fax: 860-724-1503; 8:30AM-4:30PM (EST). *Probate.* www.jud.ct.gov/probate/

Newington Probate District 7 66 Cedar St, Newington, CT 06111; 860-665-1285; fax: 860-665-1331; 8:30AM -4:30 PM M,W,Th, til 5PMTu, till 4PM F (EST). *Probate.* www.jud.ct.gov/probate/
General Information: District includes Newington, Rocky Hill, Wethersfield.

North Central CT Probate District 11 820 Enfield St, Enfield, CT 06082; 860-253-6305; fax: 860-253-6388; 9AM-4:30PM (EST). *Probate.* www.jud.ct.gov/probate/
General Information: Formerly Enfield Probate Court. District includes Enfield, Somers, Stafford, Union.

Region 14 Probate District 9 Austin Dr, S-211, PO Box 29, Marlborough, CT 06447; 860-295-6239; fax: 860-295-6122; 8-11AM M,F; 10AM-N Wed; 8AM-3:00PM T,T (EST). *Probate.* www.jud.ct.gov/probate/
General Information: Formerly Marlborough Probate Court. District includes East Haddam, East Hampton, Marlborough, Portland.

Region 19 Probate District 111 N Main St, City Hall, 3rd Fl, Bristol, CT 06010; 860-584-6230; fax: 860-584-3818; 8:30AM-5PM (EST). *Probate.* www.jud.ct.gov/probate/
General Information: Formerly Bristol Probate Court. District includes Bristol, Plainville, Plymouth.

Simsbury Regional Probate District 9 933 Hopmeadow St, PO Box 495, Simsbury, CT 06070; 860-658-3277; fax: 860-658-3204; 8:30AM-4:30PM (EST). *Probate.* www.jud.ct.gov/probate/
General Information: District includes Avon, Canton, Granby, Simsbury.

Tobacco Valley Probate-District PDO3 50 Church St, Town Office Bldg, Windsor Locks, CT 06096; 860-627-1450; fax: 860-654-8919; 8AM-4PM M-W; 8AM-6PM TH; 8AM-1PMF (EST). *Probate.* www.jud.ct.gov/probate/
General Information: Formerly Windsor Locks Probate Court. District includes Bloomfield, East Granby, Suffield, Windsor Locks. Another good web page is www.windsorlocksct.org/.

West Hartford Probate District 2 50 S Main St, West Hartford, CT 06107; 860-561-7940; fax: 860-561-7591; 8:30AM-4:30PM (EST). *Probate.* www.jud.ct.gov/probate/

Litchfield County

Litchfield Judicial District Court PO Box 247, Litchfield, CT 06759; 860-567-0885; fax: 860-567-4779; 9AM-5PM (EST). *Felony, Civil Actions, Divorce.*
www.jud.ct.gov/external/super/default.htm
General Information: No sealed files released. No fee to fax documents. Court makes copy: $1.00 per page. Certification fee: $2.00 per cert. Payee: Clerk of Superior Court. Personal checks accepted. Visa/MC accepted in person only. Prepayment required. Mail requests: SASE required.
Civil Name Search: Access: Fax, mail, online, in person. Only the court performs in person name searches; visitors may not. No search fee. Pending cases only on computer, on index cards from 1972. Note: Must make search request in writing. Mail turnaround time 3-4 weeks. Public use terminal has civil records back to 2010 paperless files. Access civil/family case index free at http://civilinquiry.jud.ct.gov/. Search by name or case number. From this site there is also access to Housing and Small Claims.
Criminal Name Search: Access: Fax, mail, in person, online. Only the court performs in person name searches; visitors may not. No search fee. Required to search: name, years to search; also helpful: DOB. Pending cases only on computer, on index cards from 1972. Note: Must make requests in writing. Mail turnaround time 3-4 weeks. Pending, current and disposed criminal and motor vehicle dockets back to 2000 free at www.jud.ct.gov/jud2.htm. Online criminal results also show year of birth. Online criminal/traffic record search requests allow you to include the birth year; in person searching allows use of add'l personal identifiers. Online results show name only.

Geographical Area Court #18 PO Box 667, 80 Doyle Rd, Bantam, CT 06750; 860-567-3942; fax: 860-567-3934; 9AM-5PM (EST). *Misdemeanor, Eviction, Small Claims.*
www.jud.ct.gov
General Information: Serving Barkhamsted, Bethlehem, Bridgewater, Canaan, Colebrook, Cornwall, Goshen, Hartland, Harwinton, Kent,Litchfield, Morris, New Hartford, New Milford, Norfolk, N Canaan, Roxbury, Salisbury, Sharon, Thomaston, Torrington, Warren, Wash Dep. & Winchester No youthful offender or non-discloseable records released. Court makes copy: $1.00 per page. Certification fee: $2.00 per doc plus copy fee. Payee: Clerk of Superior Court. Personal checks accepted. Visa/MC accepted. Prepayment required. Mail requests: SASE required.
Civil Name Search: Access: Mail, in person, online. Both court and visitors may perform in person name searches. No search fee. Civil cases indexed by defendant. Civil records on computer for 2 years, on microfiche from 1986. Note: Small Claims cases from May 2006 forward are kept with the Centralized Small Claims Office in Hartford - 860-756-7800. Mail turnaround time 1 week. Access small claims case index free at http://civilinquiry.jud.ct.gov/.
Criminal Name Search: Access: Mail, in person, online. Only the court performs in person name searches; visitors may not. No search fee. Required to search: name, years to search, DOB; also helpful: address. Criminal records on computer for 1 year, microfiche from 1986, on index cards for 40 years. Archived at Records Center at Enfield, CT. Mail turnaround time 1 week. Pending, current and disposed criminal and motor vehicle dockets back to 2000 free at www.jud.ct.gov/jud2.htm. Online criminal results also show year of birth. Online criminal/traffic record search requests allow you to include the birth year; in person searching allows use of add'l personal identifiers. Online results show name only.

Housatonic Probate District 44 10 Main St, Town Hall, New Milford, CT 06776; 860-355-6029; fax: 860-355-6024; 8:30AM-5PM M-F (EST). *Probate.* www.newmilford.org/content/240/
General Information: Formerly New Milford Probate Court. District includes Bridgewater, Brookfield, New Fairfield, New Milford, Sherman.

Litchfield Hills Probate District 24 PO Box 505, 74 West St, Litchfield, CT 06759-0505; 860-567-8065; fax: 860-567-2538; 9AM-4PM and by app't (EST). *Probate.* www.jud.ct.gov/probate/
General Information: District includes Canaan, Cornwall, Harwinton, Kent, Litchfield, Morris, Norfolk, N. Canaan, Salisbury, Sharon, Thomaston, Warren

Torrington Area Probate District 23 140 Main St, Municipal Bldg, Torrington, CT 06790; 860-489-2215; fax: 860-496-5910; 8AM-4:30PM, M-W; 8AM-6:30PM T; 8AM-12:30PM F (EST). *Probate.* www.jud.ct.gov/probate/
General Information: District includes Barkhamsted, Colebrook, Goshen, Hartland, New Hartford, Torrington, Winchester.

Middlesex County

Middlesex District Court - Criminal & GA Court #9 1 Court St, 1st Fl, Middletown, CT 06457-3348; 860-343-6445; fax: 860-343-6566; 9AM-5PM (EST). *Felony, Misdemeanor.*
www.jud.ct.gov/external/super/default.htm
General Information: Serving the towns of Chester, Clinton, Cromwell, Deep River, Durham, East Haddam, East Hampton, Essex, Haddam, Killingworth, Middlefield, Middletown, Old Saybrook, Portland and Westbrook. No youthful offender records or dismissals released. Will not fax documents. Court makes copy: $1.00 per page. Certification fee: No charge, cert fee not impose. Payee: Clerk, Superior Court. Personal checks accepted. Visa/MC accepted in person only. Prepayment required. Mail requests: SASE required.
Criminal Name Search: Access: Mail, in person, online. Only the court performs in person name searches; visitors may not. No search fee. Required to search: name, years to search, DOB, signed release; also helpful: address, SSN. Criminal records on computer for 1 year from disposition or sentence, on microfiche prior to 1984, prior on index cards to 1961. Mail turnaround time 3-4 days. Closed cases sent to Enfield after 1 month. Online- pending, current and disposed criminal and motor vehicle dockets back to 2000 free at www.jud.ct.gov/jud2.htm. Online criminal results also show year of birth. Online criminal/traffic record search requests allow you to include the birth year; in person searching allows use of add'l personal identifiers. Online results show name only.

Middlesex Judicial District Court - Civil 1 Court St, 2nd Fl, Middletown, CT 06457-3374; 860-343-6400; fax: 860-343-6423; 9AM-5PM (EST). *Civil Actions, Divorce, Eviction, Small Claims.*
www.jud.ct.gov/external/super/default.htm
General Information: Online identifiers in results same as on public terminal. No sealed records released. Will not fax documents. Court makes copy: $1.00 per page. Self serve copy: $.10 per page, but you cannot copy court papers. Certification fee: $2.00; judgment file copy-$15.00 ($25 if certified); Cert. Judgment in Foreclosure action-$25.00. Exemplification copies-$20.00. Payee: Clerk, Superior Court. Personal checks accepted; name and address must be on pre-printed check. Credit cards accepted if payment over $10.00. Prepayment required. Mail requests: SASE required.
Civil Name Search: Access: Mail, in person, online. Only the court performs in person name searches; visitors may not. No search fee. Required to search: name, years to search; also helpful: type of case, docket number. Civil records on computer 1 year post-judgment; on index card back 15 years, prior on docket books, microfiche. Note: Small Claims cases from May 2006 forward are kept with the Centralized Small Claims Office in Hartford - 860-756-7800. Mail turnaround time 1 week. Public use terminal has civil records back to 1997. Access civil/family case index free at http://civilinquiry.jud.ct.gov/. Search by name or case number. From this site there is also access to Housing and Small Claims.

Middletown Probate District 15 94 Court St, Middletown, CT 06457; 860-347-7424; fax: 860-346-1520; 8:30AM-4:30PM (EST). *Probate.* www.jud.ct.gov/probate/ **General Information:** District includes towns of Cromwell, Durham, Middlefield, Middletown.

Saybrook Probate District 33 302 Main St 2nd Fl, Old Saybrook, CT 06475; 860-510-5028; fax: 860-388-3734; 8:30AM-4:30PM (EST). *Probate.* www.jud.ct.gov/probate/
General Information: District includes Chester, Clinton, Deep River, Essex, Haddam, Killingworth, Lyme, Old Saybrook, Westbrook.

New Haven County

Ansonia-Milford Judicial District Court PO Box 210, 14 W River St, 1st Fl, Milford, CT 06460; 203-877-4293; fax: 203-876-8640; 9AM-5PM (EST). *Felony (higher), Civil Actions, Divorce, Eviction.*
www.jud.ct.gov/directory/directory/directions/23.htm
General Information: Sealed records. Will fax documents only to toll-free or local numbers. Court makes copy: $1.00 per page. Certification fee: $2.00 per cert plus copy fee; Exemplification is $20.00 add'l. Judgment file- $25.00. Payee: Clerk of Superior Court. Personal checks accepted if proper ID

provided. Visa/MC accepted. Prepayment required. Mail requests: SASE required.
Civil Name Search: Access: Mail, fax, online, in person. Only the court performs in person name searches; visitors may not. No search fee. Civil records on computer back to 1993, on index cards from 1978. Purged computer records are on microfilm. Maintained 75 years at Records Center at E. Mail turnaround time 1-2 days. Access civil/family case index free at http://civilinquiry.jud.ct.gov/. Search by name or case number. From this site there is also access to Housing and Small Claims.
Criminal Name Search: Access: Mail, in person, online. Only the court performs in person name searches; visitors may not. No search fee. Required to search: name, years to search, DOB; also helpful-SSN. Criminal records computerized from 1993, on index cards from 1978. Purged computer records are on microfilm. Maintained 75 years at Records Center. Mail turnaround time 1-2 days. Pending, current and disposed criminal and motor vehicle dockets back to 2000 free at www.jud.ct.gov/jud2.htm. Online criminal results also show year of birth. Online criminal/traffic record search requests allow you to include the birth year; in person searching allows use of add'l personal identifiers. Online results show name only.

Meriden Judicial District Court 54 W Main St, Meriden, CT 06451; 203-238-6666; fax: 203-238-6322; 9AM-5PM (EST). *Civil Actions, Divorce, Eviction, Housing, Small Claims.*
www.jud.ct.gov/external/super/default.htm
General Information: Online identifiers in results same as on public terminal. No acknowledgments of paternity, agreements to support prior to 10/01/95 records released. Will not fax documents. Court makes copy: $1.00 per page. Certification fee: $2.00 per doc plus copy fee. Payee: Clerk of Superior Court. In state personal checks accepted. Visa/MC accepted. Prepayment required. Mail requests: SASE required.
Civil Name Search: Access: Mail, in person, online. Only the court performs in person name searches; visitors may not. No search fee. Pending and 1 yr after disposed cases on computer, on microfiche from 1984, prior on index cards. Note: Small Claims cases from May 2006 forward are kept with the Centralized Small Claims Office in Hartford - 860-756-7800. Mail turnaround time 1-2 days. Public use terminal has civil records. Access civil/family case index free at http://civilinquiry.jud.ct.gov/. Search by name or case number. From this site there is also access to Housing and Small Claims. However, Meriden housing matters must be looked up in the civil/family case index.

New Haven Judicial District Court 235 Church St, New Haven, CT 06510; 203-503-6800; criminal phone: x2; civil phone: x1; fax: 203-789-6424; 9AM-5PM (EST). *Felony, Civil Actions, Family, Divorce, Eviction, Small Claims.* www.jud.ct.gov/external/super/default.htm
General Information: Will search both civil and criminal indexes at once if requested. Small Claims and Eviction phone - x7. Online identifiers in results same as on public terminal. No sealed records released. Will not fax documents. Court makes copy: $1.00 per page.No pro se personal checks for copies. Certification fee: $2.00 per doc plus copy fee. Payee: Clerk of Superior Court. This office limits personal checks accepted - should be local CT and include DR number. Visa/MC accepted. Prepayment required. Mail requests: SASE required.
Civil Name Search: Access: Mail, in person, online. Only the court performs in person name searches; visitors may not. No search fee. Pending cases on computer, disposed cases deleted after 1 year, on microfiche from 1972, prior on index cards. Note: Small Claims cases from May 2006 forward are kept with the Centralized Small Claims Office in Hartford - 860-756-7800. Mail turnaround time 2-5 weeks. Public use terminal has civil records back to 1991. Access civil/family case index free at http://civilinquiry.jud.ct.gov/. Search by name or case number. From this site there is also access to Housing and Small Claims.
Criminal Name Search: Access: Mail, in person, online. Only the court performs in person name searches; visitors may not. No search fee. Required to search: name, years to search, DOB. Pending criminal cases on computer, disposed deleted after 1 year, prior on index cards. Mail turnaround time 2-5 weeks. Pending, current and disposed criminal and motor vehicle dockets back to 2000 free at www.jud.ct.gov/jud2.htm. Online criminal results also show year of birth. Online criminal/traffic record search requests allow you to include the birth year; in person searching allows use of add'l personal identifiers.

Waterbury Judicial District Court 300 Grand St, Waterbury, CT 06702; 203-591-3300; fax: 203-596-4032; 9AM-5PM (EST). *Civil Actions, Small Claims, Divorce, Eviction.*
www.jud.ct.gov/external/super/default.htm
General Information: Address mail requests for Misdemeanor searches to 400 Grand St. (Geographical Area Court #4). Online identifiers in results same as on public terminal. Will not fax documents. Court makes copy: $1.00 per page. Certification fee: $2.00 per page. Payee: Clerk of Superior

Court. Personal checks accepted. Major credit cards accepted, in person only. Prepayment required. Mail requests: SASE requested.

Civil Name Search: Access: Fax, mail, online, in person. Only the court performs in person name searches; visitors may not. No search fee. Civil cases indexed by defendant. Civil records on computer back to 1990; non-computer records go back to 1900. Note: Phone access limited to one search. Mail turnaround time 1-2 weeks. Public use terminal has civil records back to about 10 years. Access civil/family case index free at http://civilinquiry.jud.ct.gov/. Search by name or case number. From this site there is also access to Housing and Small Claims.

Geographical Area Court #22 14 W River St, 2nd Fl, Milford, CT 06460; criminal phone: 203-874-1116; civil phone: 203-877-4293; fax: 203-874-5233; 9AM-5PM (EST). *Felony (lower), Misdemeanor, Small Claims, Traffic.*
www.jud.ct.gov/external/super/default.htm
General Information: Serving the towns of Milford and West Haven. This court handles lower-grade felonies; see the Judicial district court for other felonies. Will fax out documents in emergency situations only. Court makes copy: $1.00 per page. Certification fee: $2.00 per cert plus copy fee. Payee: Clerk of Superior Court. Personal checks accepted if address shown on check. Visa/MC accepted. Prepayment required. Mail requests: SASE required.
Civil Name Search: Access: Mail, in person, online. No in-person civil name searches permitted at this court. No search fee. Access small claims case index free at http://civilinquiry.jud.ct.gov/. Search by name or case number.
Criminal Name Search: Access: Mail, in person, online. Only the court performs in person name searches; visitors may not. No search fee. Required to search: name, years to search; also helpful: DOB, town where offense occurred. Criminal records on computer for 6 months, after disposal, on microfiche from 1989, prior on docket books and cards only. Mail turnaround time 1 week. Pending, current and disposed criminal and motor vehicle dockets back to 2000 free at www.jud.ct.gov/jud2.htm. Online criminal results also show year of birth. Online criminal/traffic record search requests allow you to include the birth year; in person searching allows use of add'l personal identifiers. Online results show name only.

Geographical Area Court #23 121 Elm St, New Haven, CT 06510; 203-789-7461; fax: 203-789-7492; 9AM-5PM (EST). *Misdemeanor.*
www.jud.ct.gov/external/super/default.htm
General Information: Serving towns of Bethany, Branford, E Haven, Guilford, Madison, New Haven, North Branford, Woodbridge. Small claims is located at 235 Church St, Clerk's Office, New Haven, CT 06510, 860-503-6800, instate-866-383-5927; Evictions phone- 203-789-7937. Online identifiers in results same as on public terminal. No dismissals, juvenile records released. Will not fax documents. Court makes copy: $1.00 per page. Self serve copy: $1.00 per page. Certification fee: $2.00 per cert plus copy fee. Payee: Superior Court. Personal checks accepted. Visa/MC accepted. Prepayment required. Mail requests: SASE required.
Criminal Name Search: Access: Mail, in person, online. Both court and visitors may perform in person name searches. No search fee. Required to search: name, years to search, DOB. Criminal records on computer back to 1996, microfiche from 1986, prior archived. Note: In person search results can be mailed back. Mail turnaround time 2-3 weeks. Public use terminal has crim records back to 2004. Public terminal located at information desk in building. Pending, current and disposed criminal and motor vehicle dockets back to 2000 free at www.jud.ct.gov/jud2.htm. Online criminal results show year of birth only. Online criminal/traffic record search requests allow you to include the birth year; in person searching allows use of add'l personal identifiers. Online results show name, DOB.

Geographical Area Court #4 400 Grand St, Waterbury, CT 06702; 203-236-8100; fax: 203-236-8099; 9AM-5PM (EST). *Felony, Misdemeanor, Traffic.*
www.jud.ct.gov/external/super/default.htm
General Information: Serving the towns of Middlebury, Naugatuck, Prospect, Southbury, Waterbury, Watertown, Wolcott and Woodbury. No dismissals, juvenile records released. Will not fax documents. Court makes copy: $1.00 per page. Certification fee: $2.00; certifications made at the record center. Payee: Clerk of Superior Court. Personal checks accepted. Visa/MC accepted. Prepayment required. Mail requests: SASE required.
Criminal Name Search: Access: Mail, in person, online fax. Only the court performs in person name searches; visitors may not. No search fee. Required to search: name, years to search; also helpful: DOB. Criminal records on computer since 1985. Mail turnaround time 1-2 weeks. Pending, current and disposed criminal and motor vehicle dockets back to 2000 free at www.jud.ct.gov/jud2.htm. Online criminal results also show year of birth. Online criminal/traffic record search requests allow you to include the birth year; in person searching allows use of add'l personal identifiers. Online results show name only.

Geographical Area Court #5 106 Elizabeth St, Derby, CT 06418; 203-735-7438; criminal phone: x1; fax: 203-735-2047; 9AM-5PM (EST). *Misdemeanor, Eviction, Small Claims.*
www.jud.ct.gov/external/super/default.htm
General Information: Serving the towns of Ansonia, Beacon Falls, Derby, Orange, Oxford, Seymour and Shelton. No sealed records released. Will not fax documents. Court makes copy: $1.00 per page. Certification fee: $2.00 per cert. Payee: Clerk of Superior Court. Personal checks accepted. Visa/MC accepted in person only. Prepayment required.
Civil Name Search: Access: Mail, in person, online. Only the court performs in person name searches; visitors may not. No search fee. Pending and records for 1 yr after disposal on computer, prior on index cards. Note: Small Claims cases from May 2006 forward are kept with the Centralized Small Claims Office in Hartford - 860-756-7800. Mail turnaround time 1-2 weeks. Access small claims and housing case index free at http://civilinquiry.jud.ct.gov/.
Criminal Name Search: Access: Mail, in person, online. Only the court performs in person name searches; visitors may not. No search fee. Required to search: name, years to search, DOB. Pending and records for 1 yr after disposal on computer, on microfiche from 1986, prior on index cards. Note: In person search results returned by mail only. Mail turnaround time 1-2 weeks. Pending, current and disposed criminal and motor vehicle dockets back to 2000 free at www.jud.ct.gov/jud2.htm. Online criminal results also show year of birth. Online criminal/traffic record search requests allow you to include the birth year; in person searching allows use of add'l personal identifiers. Online results show name only.

Geographical Area Court #7 54 W Main St, Meriden, CT 06451; 203-238-6130; fax: 203-238-6016; 9AM-5PM (EST). *Misdemeanor, Small Claims, Eviction.* www.jud.ct.gov/external/super/default.htm
General Information: Serving the towns of Cheshire, Hamden, Meriden, North Haven and Wallingford. Online identifiers in results same as on public terminal. No sealed records released. Will not fax documents. Court makes copy: $1.00 per page. Certification fee: $2.00 per cert plus copy fee. Payee: Clerk of Superior Court. Personal checks accepted. Visa/MC accepted. Prepayment required. Mail requests: SASE required.
Civil Name Search: Access: Mail, in person, online. Both court and visitors may perform in person name searches. No search fee. Pending and 1 yr after disposed cases on computer, on microfiche from 1985, prior on index cards. All manual records by docket number. Note: Small Claims cases from May 2006 forward are kept with the Centralized Small Claims Office in Hartford - 860-756-7800. Mail turnaround time 1-2 days. Civil PAT available. Access small claims and housing case index free at http://civilinquiry.jud.ct.gov/.
Criminal Name Search: Access: Phone, mail, in person, online. Both court and visitors may perform in person name searches. No search fee. Required to search: name, years to search, DOB. Criminal records on computer since 1986, purged every 6 months and maintained in Enfield, CT. Mail turnaround time 1-2 days. Criminal PAT available. Pending, current and disposed criminal and motor vehicle dockets back to 2000 free at www.jud.ct.gov/jud2.htm. Online criminal results also show year of birth. Online criminal/traffic record search requests allow you to include the birth year; in person searching allows use of add'l personal identifiers. Online results show name only.

Branford-N. Branford Probate District 35 PO Box 638, 1019 Main St, Branford, CT 06405-0638; 203-488-0318; fax: 203-315-4715; 8:30AM-4:30PM (EST). *Probate.* www.branford-ct.gov/Probate%20Court.htm
General Information: Formerly Branford Probate Court. District includes North Branford.

Cheshire-Southington Probate District 18 84 S Main St, Cheshire, CT 06410; 203-271-6608; fax: 203-271-3735; 8:15AM-4:15 PM (EST). *Probate.* www.jud.ct.gov/probate/
General Information: Formerly Cheshire Probate Court. District includes Cheshire, Southington, Prospect.

Derby Probate District 41 253 Main St, 2nd Fl, Ansonia, CT 06401; 203-734-1277; fax: 203-736-1434; 8;30AM-5:30PM M-TH; 8:30AM-2:30PM F (EST). *Probate.* www.jud.ct.gov/probate/
General Information: District includes Ansonia, Derby, Seymour, Woodbridge.

East Haven--North Haven Probate District 36 250 Main St, Town Hall, East Haven, CT 06512; 203-468-3895; fax: 203-468-5155; 9:30AM-4:30PM (EST). *Probate.* www.jud.ct.gov/probate/
General Information: Formerly East Haven Probate Court.

Hamden-Bethany Probate District 37 2750 Dixwell Ave, Gov't Center, Hamden, CT 06518; 203-287-7082; fax: 203-287-7087; 8:30AM-4:30PM (EST). *Probate.* www.jud.ct.gov/probate/
General Information: Formerly Hamden Probate Court.

Madison-Guilford Probate District 34 8 meetinghouse Lane, Madison, CT 06443; 203-245-5661; fax: 203-245-5653; 9AM-4PM and by app't (EST). *Probate.* www.jud.ct.gov/probate/
General Information: Formerly Madison Probate Court.

Meriden Probate District 16 City Hall, 142 E Main St, Rm 113, Meriden, CT 06450; 203-630-4150; fax: 203-630-4043; 8:30AM-4:30 (EST). *Probate.* www.jud.ct.gov/probate/

Milford-Orange Probate District 40 PO Box 414, 70 W River St, Parsons Government Office Complex, Milford, CT 06460; 203-783-3205; fax: 203-783-3364; 8:30AM-4:30PM (EST). *Probate.* www.jud.ct.gov/probate/
General Information: Formerly Milford Probate Court.

Naugatuck Probate District 21 Town Hall, 229 Church St, Naugatuck, CT 06770; 203-720-7046; fax: 203-720-5476; 8AM-5PM (EST). *Probate.* www.jud.ct.gov/probate/
General Information: District includes Beacon Falls, Middlebury, Naugatuck, Prospect.

New Haven Probate District 38 200 Orange St, 1st Fl, PO Box 905, New Haven, CT 06504; 203-946-4880; fax: 203-946-5962; 9AM-5PM (EST). *Probate.* www.jud.ct.gov/probate/

Region 22 Probate District 501 Main St South, Southbury, CT 06488; 203-262-0641; fax: 203-264-9310; 9AM-4:30PM (EST). *Probate.* www.jud.ct.gov/probate/
General Information: Formerly Southbury Probate Court. District includes Bethlehem, Oxford, Roxbury, Southbury, Washington, Watertown, Woodbury.

Wallingford Probate District 17 Town Hall, 45 S Main St, Rm 114, Wallingford, CT 06492; 203-294-2100; fax: 203-294-2109; 9AM-5PM (EST). *Probate.* www.jud.ct.gov/probate/

Waterbury Probate District 20 49 Leavenworth St, Waterbury, CT 06702; 203-755-1127; fax: 203-597-0824; 8:45AM-4:45PM (EST). *Probate.* www.jud.ct.gov/probate/
General Information: District includes towns of Middlebury, Wolcott, Waterbury.

West Haven Probate District 39 355 Main St, PO Box 127, West Haven, CT 06516; 203-937-3552; fax: 203-937-3556; 8:30AM-5PM (EST). *Probate.* www.jud.ct.gov/probate/

New London County

New London Judicial District Court 70 Huntington St, New London, CT 06320; 860-443-5363; criminal phone: 860-443-6016; fax: 860-442-7703; 9AM-5PM (EST). *Felony, Civil Actions, Divorce.* www.jud.ct.gov
General Information: Online identifiers in results same as on public terminal. No sealed or youthful offender records released. Will fax documents for fee, call first. Court makes copy: $1.00 per page. Certification fee: $2.00. Payee: Clerk of Superior Court. Personal checks accepted. Visa/MC accepted. Prepayment required. Mail requests: SASE required.
Civil Name Search: Access: Mail, in person, online. No search fee. Required to search: exact name of both parties, years to search. Civil records pending and 1 yr after disposed on computer, on microfiche from mid-70s. Mail turnaround time 2 weeks. Public use terminal has civil records. Access civil/family case index free at http://civilinquiry.jud.ct.gov/. Search by name or case number. From this site there is also access to Housing and Small Claims.
Criminal Name Search: Access: Mail, in person, online. Both court and visitors may perform in person name searches. No search fee. Required to search: name, years to search; also helpful: DOB. Criminal records computerized from 1991, prior on index cards. Note: Results include name and address. Mail turnaround time 2 weeks. Pending, current and disposed criminal and motor vehicle dockets back to 2000 free at www.jud.ct.gov/jud2.htm. Online criminal results also show year of birth. Online criminal/traffic record search requests allow you to include the birth year; in person searching allows use of add'l personal identifiers.

Norwich Judicial District Court 1 Courthouse Sq, Norwich, CT 06360; 860-887-3515; fax: 860-887-8643; 9AM-5PM (EST). *Civil Actions, Family* .www.jud.ct.gov
General Information: Online identifiers in results same as on public terminal. No criminal search warrant, acknowledgment of paternity prior to 1995, sealed records released. Will fax documents $1.00 per page. Court makes copy: $1.00 per page. Judgment copies $15.00. Certification fee: $2.00 per doc plus copy fee. Certified copy of Judgment $25.00. Payee: Clerk of Superior Court. Personal checks accepted; checks must have imprinted name and address and match valid CT driver license or picture ID. Visa/MC accepted in person only. Prepayment required.

Civil Name Search: Access: Phone, mail, fax, online, in person. Both court and visitors may perform in person name searches. No search fee. Pending and disposed cases on computer from 1992, on microfiche from 1975, prior on index cards. Mail turnaround time up to 4 weeks. Public use terminal has civil records back to 1992. Shows list of pleadings as well. Access civil/family case index free at http://civilinquiry.jud.ct.gov/. Search by name or case number. From this site there is also access to Housing and Small Claims.

Geographical Area Court #10 112 Broad St, New London, CT 06320; 860-443-8343; civil phone: 860-443-8346;; 9AM-5PM (EST). *Misdemeanor, Eviction, Small Claims.* www.jud.ct.gov/external/super/default.htm
General Information: Serving the towns of East Lyme, Groton, Ledyard, Lyme, New London, North Stonington, Old Lyme, Stonington and Waterford. No sealed, dismissed, youth or program records released. Court makes copy: $1.00 per page. Certification fee: $2.00 per page. Payee: Clerk, Superior Court. Personal checks accepted. Visa/MC accepted. Prepayment required. Mail requests: SASE required.
Civil Name Search: Access: Mail, in person, online. Both court and visitors may perform in person name searches. No search fee. Civil cases indexed by defendant. Civil index on cards and docket books. Note: Small Claims cases from May 2006 forward are kept with the Centralized Small Claims Office in Hartford - 860-756-7800. Mail turnaround time up to 2 months. Access small claims case index free at http://civilinquiry.jud.ct.gov/.
Criminal Name Search: Access: Mail, in person, online. Only the court performs in person name searches; visitors may not. No search fee. Required to search: name, years to search, DOB. Criminal records on computer for 2 years; on microfiche back to 1962. Mail turnaround time up to 2 months. Pending, current and disposed criminal and motor vehicle dockets back to 2000 free at www.jud.ct.gov/jud2.htm. Online criminal results also show year of birth. Online criminal/traffic record search requests allow you to include the birth year; in person searching allows use of add'l personal identifiers. Online results show name only.

Geographical Area Court #21 1 Courthouse Sq, Rm 145, Norwich, CT 06360; 860-889-7338; fax: 860-885-0509; 9AM-5PM (EST). *Misdemeanor, Eviction.* www.jud.ct.gov/external/super/default.htm
General Information: Serving the towns of Bozrah, Colchester, Franklin, Griswold, Lebanon, Lisbon, Montville, Norwich, Preston, Salem, Sprague and Voluntown. Online identifiers in results same as on public terminal. No youthful offender or dismissed/erased records released. Court makes copy: $1.00 per page. Certification fee: $2.00 per cert plus copy fee. Payee: Superior Court GA #21. Personal checks accepted. Visa/MC accepted. Prepayment required.
Civil Name Search: Access: Online, in person. Visitors must perform in person searches themselves. Civil cases indexed by defendant. Pending and 2-4 years history of disposed on computer, on microfiche from 1986, prior on index cards and docket books. Small claims, evictions not on. Note: Small Claims cases from May 2006 forward are kept with the Centralized Small Claims Office in Hartford - 860-756-7800. Civil PAT available. Access small claims case index free at http://civilinquiry.jud.ct.gov/.
Criminal Name Search: Access: In person, online. Visitors must perform in person searches themselves. Required to search: name, years to search, DOB. Pending and 2-4 years history of disposed on computer, on microfiche from 1986, prior on index cards and docket books. Small claims, evictions not on. Note: Mail requests are referred to the Judicial Records Center in Enfield. Criminal PAT available. Pending, current and disposed criminal and motor vehicle dockets back to 2000 free at www.jud.ct.gov/jud2.htm. Online criminal results also show year of birth. Online criminal/traffic record search requests allow you to include the birth year; in person searching allows use of add'l personal identifiers, but may not year of birth. Online results show name only.

New London Probate District 31 PO Box 148, 181 State St, Municipal Bldg, New London, CT 06320; 860-443-7121; fax: 860-437-8155; 8:30AM-4PM (EST). *Probate.* www.jud.ct.gov/probate/
General Information: District includes City of New London, Town of Waterford.

Niantic Regional Probate District 32 PO Box 519, 118 Pennsylvania Ave, Niantic, CT 06357; 860-739-6052; fax: 860-739-6738; 8:30AM-4:30PM (EST). *Probate.* www.jud.ct.gov/probate/
General Information: District includes Lyme, Montville, Old Lyme, Salem.

Norwich Probate District 29 PO Box 38, 100 Broadway, Rm 122, Norwich, CT 06360; 860-887-2160; fax: 860-887-2401; 9AM-4:30PM (EST). *Probate.* www.jud.ct.gov/probate/
General Information: District includes Bozrah, Franklin, Griswold, Lisbon, Norwich, Preston, Sprague, Voluntown.

Southeastern Corner Region Probate District 30 45 Fort Hill Rd, Town Hall, Groton, CT 06340; 860-441-6655; fax: 860-441-6657; . *Probate.* www.jud.ct.gov/probate/
General Information: District includes Groton, Ledyard, North Stonington, Stonington.

Tolland County

Tolland Judicial District Court - Civil 69 Brooklyn St, Rockville, CT 06066; 860-896-4920; civil phone: x2; fax: 860-875-0777; 9AM-5PM (EST). *Civil Actions, Family.*
www.jud.ct.gov/directory/JudDir.pdf#page=100
General Information: No youthful offender, dismissed or not guilty verdict records released. Will not fax documents. Court makes copy: $1.00 per page; Copy of Judgment- $15.00. Exemplification fee- $20.00 plus copy fee. Certification fee: $2.00 plus copy fee. A full Certified Copy of Judgment is $25.00 including copy fee. Payee: Clerk of Superior Court. Personal checks accepted. Visa/MC accepted. Prepayment required. Mail requests: SASE required.
Civil Name Search: Access: Mail, in person, online. Only the court performs in person name searches; visitors may not. No search fee. Civil records on computer from 2003, on microfiche from 1980, all prior on index cards. Mail turnaround time 1-2 weeks. Access civil/family case index free at http://civilinquiry.jud.ct.gov/. Search by name or case number. From this site there is also access to Housing and Small Claims.

Tolland Judicial District Court - Criminal 20 Park St, Rockville, CT 06066; 860-870-3200; fax: 860-870-3290; 9AM-5PM (EST). *Felony.*
www.jud.ct.gov/external/super/default.htm
General Information: The address can use either Rockville or Vernon. No youthful offender, dismissed or not guilty verdict records released. Will not fax documents. Court makes copy: $1.00 per page. Certification fee: $2.00 plus copy fee. Payee: Clerk of Superior Court. Personal checks accepted. Visa/MC accepted. Prepayment required.
Criminal Name Search: Access: Mail, online. Only the court performs in person name searches; visitors may not. No search fee. Required to search: name, years to search; also helpful: DOB. Criminal records on computer approx. 10 yrs from disposition, on microfiche from 1985, prior on index cards,. Note: Criminal records are for active cases generally; completed cases should be searched State Police. Mail turnaround time 7-14 days. This court holds court records on computer approx 2 years; mail requests for older records may result in only limited information. Online- pending, current and disposed criminal and motor vehicle dockets back to 2000 free at www.jud.ct.gov/jud2.htm. Online criminal results also show year of birth. Online criminal/traffic record search requests allow you to include the birth year; in person searching allows use of add'l personal identifiers. Online results show name only.

Geographical Area Court #19 20 Park St, Rockville, CT 06066-0980; 860-870-3200; fax: 860-870-3290; 9AM-5PM (EST). *Misdemeanor.*
www.jud.ct.gov/external/super/default.htm
General Information: Serving the towns of Andover, Bolton, Columbia, Coventry, Ellington, Hebron, Mansfield, Somers, Stafford, Tolland, Union, Vernon and Willington. No youthful offender records released. Will not fax documents. Court makes copy: $1.00 per page. Certification fee: $2.00. Payee: Clerk of Superior Court. Personal checks accepted. Visa/MC accepted. Prepayment required. Mail requests: SASE required.
Criminal Name Search: Access: Mail, online. Only the court performs in person name searches; visitors may not. No search fee. Required to search: name, years to search, DOB. Criminal records on computer approx. 2 yrs from disposition, on microfiche from 1985, prior on index cards,. Mail turnaround time 7-14 days. This court holds court records on computer approx 2 years; mail requests for older records may result in only limited information. Online- pending, current and disposed criminal and motor vehicle dockets back to 2000 free at www.jud.ct.gov/jud2.htm. Online criminal results also show year of birth. Online criminal/traffic record search requests allow you to include the birth year; in person searching allows use of add'l personal identifiers. Online results show name only.

Hebron Probate Court 15 Gilead St, Hebron, CT 06248; 860-228-5971 x127; fax: 860-228-4859; 8:30AM-12:30PM and by app't (EST). *Probate.* www.jud.ct.gov/probate/

Ellington Probate District 12 PO Box 268, 14 Park Pl, Rockville, CT 06066; 860-872-0519; fax: 860-870-5140; 8:15AM-4:30PM M-W; 8:15AM-7PM TH; 8:30AM-1PM F (EST). *Probate.*
www.jud.ct.gov/probate/
General Information: District includes Ellington. Vernon.

Tolland-Mansfield Probate District 25 21 Tolland Green, Tolland, CT 06084; 860-871-3640; fax: 860-871-3641; 8AM-12PM 1-4:30PM M,T; 1-4:30PM W; 1-6:30PM TH; 8AM-N M (EST). *Probate.*
www.jud.ct.gov/scripts/protest.asp
General Information: Formerly Mansfield Probate Court. Consolidated with Tolland. District includes Coventry, Mansfield, Tolland, Willington.

Windham County

Windham Judicial District Court 155 Church St, Putnam, CT 06260; 860-928-7749; civil phone: 860-756-7800-small claims; fax: 860-928-7076; 9AM-5PM (EST). *Civil Actions, Divorce.*
www.jud.ct.gov/external/super/default.htm
General Information: Online identifiers in results same as on public terminal. No sealed, dismissed records released. Will not fax documents. Court makes copy: $1.00 per page. Certification fee: $2.00 per cert plus copy fee. Payee: Clerk of Superior Court. Personal checks accepted. Visa/MC accepted. Prepayment required. Mail requests: SASE required for civil.
Civil Name Search: Access: Phone, mail, online, in person. Only the court performs in person name searches; visitors may not. No search fee. Civil records on computer for 1 year, prior on index cards, prior to 70s archived. Note: The court must look up records for searches of records over 1 year old. Mail turnaround time 1-2 days. Public use terminal has civil records back to 1 year only. Access civil/family case index free at http://civilinquiry.jud.ct.gov/. Search by name or case number. From this site there is also access to Housing and Small Claims.

Geographical Area Court #11 120 School St, #110, Danielson, CT 06239-3024; 860-779-8480; fax: 860-779-8488; 9AM-5PM (EST). *Felony, Misdemeanor, Eviction.* www.jud.ct.gov
General Information: Serving the towns of Ashford, Brooklyn, Canterbury, Chaplin, Eastford, Hampton, Killingly, Plainfield, Pomfret, Putnam, Scotland, Sterling, Thompson, Windham and Woodstock. Online identifiers in results same as on public terminal. No sealed records released. Will not fax documents. Court makes copy: $1.00 per page. Certification fee: $2.00 per page plus copy fee. Payee: Clerk of Superior Court. Personal checks and credit cards accepted. Prepayment required. Mail requests: SASE required.
Civil Name Search: Access: Phone, mail, in person. Both court and visitors may perform in person name searches. No search fee. Civil cases indexed by defendant. Small claims records on computer since 8/96; 2006 forward centralized Small Claims. Mail turnaround time 1-2 weeks. Public use terminal has civil records back to 8/1996. Terminal results include hearing date, charges and bond information.
Criminal Name Search: Access: Mail, in person, online. Only the court performs in person name searches; visitors may not. No search fee. Required to search: name, years to search, DOB, dates of disposition. Pending criminal and 1 year after disposed on computer, on microfiche from 1986, prior on index cards. Note: Requests must be in writing. Mail turnaround time 1-2 weeks. Pending, current and disposed criminal and motor vehicle dockets back to 2000 free at www.jud.ct.gov/jud2.htm. Online criminal/traffic record search requests allow you to include the birth year; in person searching allows use of add'l personal identifiers.

Northeast Probate District 26 815 Riverside Dr, Town Hall, PO Box 40, North Grosvenordale, CT 06255; 860-923-2203; fax: 860-923-1971; 8:30AM-4:30PM M-W; 8:30AM-6PM TH; 8:30AM-3PM F (EST). *Probate.*
www.jud.ct.gov/probate/
General Information: Formerly Thompson Probate Court. District includes Ashford, Brooklyn, Eastford, Pomfret, Putnam, Thompson, Woodstock.

Plainfield-Killingly Regional Probate District 27 Town Hall, 8 Community-Ave, Plainfield, CT 06374; 860-230-3031; fax: 860-564-0126; 8:30AM-4:30PM (EST). *Probate.* www.jud.ct.gov/probate/
General Information: Formerly Plainfield Probate Court. District includes Canterbury, Killingly, Plainfield, Sterling.

Windham-Colchester Probate District 28 979 Main St, Town Hall, PO Box 34, Willimantic, CT 06226; 860-465-3049; fax: 860-465-2162; 8AM-5PM M-W; 8AM-7:30PM Th; 8AM-12 F (EST). *Probate.*
www.jud.ct.gov/probate/
General Information: Formerly Hampton Probate Court. District includes Chaplin, Colchester, Hampton, Lebanon, Scotland, Windham.

Delaware

Time Zone:	**EST**
Capital:	**Dover, Kent County**
# of Counties:	**3**
State Web:	**http://delaware.gov**
Court Web:	**http://courts.delaware.gov**

Administration

Administrative Office of the Courts, Supreme Court of Delaware, 500 N King St, #11600, Wilmington, DE, 19801; 302-255-0090, Fax: 302-255-2217. 8:30AM-5PM.

The Supreme Court

The Delaware Supreme Court is the highest court in the State of Delaware. The Court has final appellate jurisdiction in criminal cases in which the sentence exceeds certain minimums, in civil cases as to final judgments and for certain other orders of the Court of Chancery, the Superior Court, and the Family Court. The Supreme Court has discretionary jurisdiction to issue writs of prohibition, quo warranto, certiorari, mandamus or to accept appeals of certain non-final orders or certified questions. See below about access to opinions.

The Delaware Courts

Court	Type	How Organized	Jurisdiction Highpoints
Superior*	General	3 courts, one per county	Felony, Civil
Chancery*	General	3 courts, one per county	Equity Matters and Causes
Court of Common Pleas*		3 courts, one per county	Misdemeanor, Civil Actions under $50,000,
Justice of the Peace		15 courts, per district	Misdemeanor, Civil Actions under $15,000, Eviction, Traffic
Alderman's Court		7 courts	Traffic, Local Ordinances
Family	Special	3 courts, one per county	Domestic Relations, juvenile

* = profiled in this book

Details on the Court Structure

The **Superior Court** has original jurisdiction over criminal and civil cases except equity cases. The Superior Court has exclusive jurisdiction over felonies and drug offenses, except drug offenses involving minors, and offenses involving possession of marijuana.

The **Court of Common Pleas** has jurisdiction in civil cases where the amount in controversy, exclusive of interest, does not exceed $50,000. In criminal cases, the Court of Common Pleas handles all misdemeanors occurring in the state except certain drug-related offenses and traffic offenses. Appeals may be taken to the Superior Court.

Court of Chancery cases consist largely of corporate matters, trusts, estates, and other fiduciary matters, disputes involving the purchase and sale of land, questions of title to real estate, and commercial and contractual matters in general.

The **Family Court** has jurisdiction over juvenile, child neglect, custody, guardianship, adoptions, divorces and annulments, property divisions, and separation agreements.

The **Justice of the Peace Court** jurisdiction will vary by court – not all courts have the same jurisdiction. Depending of the court, it may handle civil cases in which the disputed amount is less than $15,000, landlord/tenant proceedings, certain misdemeanors including DUIs and Truancy, and most motor vehicle cases (excluding felonies). The Court may act as Committing magistrates for all crimes.

Alderman's Courts usually have jurisdiction over misdemeanors, municipal ordinances, and traffic offenses that occur within their town limits.

Record Searching Facts You Need to Know

Fees and Record Searching Tips

Search fees and copy fees vary widely by court or type of court. The Superior Courts will not perform criminal namem checks, but do offer public access terminals for onsite research.

Statewide Online Access is Offered for Certain Record Types

There is a free site to search trial court civil case information and judgments. Go to http://courtconnect.courts.delaware.gov/public/ck_public_qry_main.cp_main_idx. Note the site states *Any commercial use of data obtained through the use of this site is strictly prohibited.*

Chancery, Superior, Common Pleas, and Supreme Courts opinions and orders are available free online at http://courts.delaware.gov/opinions/?ag=all_courts. Supreme, Superior. Common Pleas Courts calendars are available free at http://courts.delaware.gov/calendars. Probate records are found at http://archives.delaware.gov/collections/probate.shtml.

In the Superior Court in each county there is a Prothonotary which is where the registration of Business, Trade and Fictitious Names must be filed. There is a free online access page to this data, go to http://courts.delaware.gov/Superior/trade_names.stm.

Also subscription-based filing service (eFlex or eFiling system) for Common Pleas and Justice Courts is at http://courts.delaware.gov/efiling/index.stm, note this is vendor operated.

Kent County

Superior Court Office of Prothonotary, 38 The Green, Dover, DE 19901; 302-739-3184; criminal phone: x6; civil phone: x7; fax: 302-739-6717; 8AM-4:30PM (EST). *Felony, Misdemeanor, Civil Actions over $50,000.*
http://courts.delaware.gov/Superior/
General Information: Access to e-filed records is available online by subscription through LexisNexis eFlex system for filing. See http://courts.delaware.gov/efiling/index.stm. Court refers records request to State Agency-302-739-5961. No sealed or psychological evaluation records released. Will not fax documents. Court makes copy: $1.50 per page; same for copies off the computer. Self serve copy: same. Certification fee: $6.00 fee for 3 pages; add copy fee for add'l pages. Exemplification fee- $10.00. Payee: Prothonotary. Personal checks accepted. No credit cards accepted. Prepayment required.
Civil Name Search: Access: In person, online. Visitors must perform in person searches themselves. Judgments on computer from 1996, on books from 1918. Civil PAT goes back to 7/1996. Search civil case and judgment information at http://courtconnect.courts.delaware.gov/public/ck_public_qry_main.cp_main_idx. Although not a court record, Trade, Business and Fictitious Names can be searched at a court location at http://courts.delaware.gov/Courts/Superior%20Court/?trade_names.htm.
Criminal Name Search: Access: In person only. Both court and visitors may perform in person name searches. No search fee, but $25.00 search fee for retrieval of closed cases. Required to search: name, years to search, DOB. Judgments on computer from 1996, on microfiche from 1918. Can contact Dept of Records for search assistance. Criminal PAT goes back to 1987.
Chancery Court 38 The Green, Dover, DE 19901; 302-736-2242; probate: 302-744-2330; fax: 302-736-2240; 8AM-4:30PM (EST). *Civil, Probate.*
http://courts.delaware.gov/Chancery/
General Information: This is an Equity Court only. No juvenile, sealed or mental health records released. Fee to fax out file $10.00 1st page, $2.00 each add'l. Court makes copy: $1.50 per page. Certification fee: $25.00 per doc plus copy fee. Payee: Register in Chancery. Personal checks accepted. No credit cards accepted. Prepayment required.
Civil Name Search: Access: In person, online. Visitors must perform in person searches themselves. Search fee: Archival retrieval fee is $25. Civil index on docket books. The Court of Chancery oversees corporate and equity matters and guardianship. The Register of Wills oversees estate, and. Public use terminal has civil records back to 1997. Access to e-filed records is available online by subscription through LexisNexis eFlex system for filing. See http://courts.delaware.gov/efiling/index.stm.
Dover Justice of the Peace #7 480 Bank Ln, Dover, DE 19903; 302-739-4554; fax: 302-739-6797; Open 24 hours (EST). *Misdemeanor.*
http://courts.delaware.gov/Locations/jp07.stm
General Information: Search requests must include charge/or/disposition; name searches without charge are referred to the State Bureau of Investigation. Will fax most documents. Court makes copy: $.25 per page.

Certification fee: $7.00 per charge. Payee: State of Delaware. Personal checks and credit cards accepted. Prepayment required.
Criminal Name Search: Access: Mail, fax, in person. Only the court performs in person name searches; visitors may not. Required to search: name, charge info, DOB, signed release, offense, date of offense; also helpful: address. Record computerized since 1992, manually searched 1967-1992 (30 years retention). Note: Technically, this court does not do 'name searches' so, in requests, it is necessary to provide as much case info and identifiers as possible.
Harrington Justice of the Peace #6 35 Cams Fortune Way, Harrington, DE 19952; 302-422-5922; fax: 302-422-1527; 8AM-4PM (EST). *Misdemeanor.*
http://courts.delaware.gov/Locations/jp06.stm
General Information: Also holds records for JP #5 which has been closed. Will fax out documents no fee. Court makes copy: $1.00 per page. Certification fee: $7.00 per doc includes copies. Payee: State of Delaware. Personal checks accepted. Visa/MC/Discover accepted. Prepayment required.
Criminal Name Search: Access: Mail, fax, In person. Only the court performs in person name searches; visitors may not. No search fee. Required to search: name, years to search, DOB. Criminal records go back to 2004. Note: Best to use court form for search requests.
Smyrna Justice of the Peace #8 100 Monrovia Ave, Smyrna, DE 19977; 302-653-7083; fax: 302-653-2888; 8AM-4PM, closed Tues (EST). *Misdemeanor.*
http://courts.delaware.gov/Locations/jp08.stm
General Information: Will fax documents to local or toll-free number. Court makes copy: $.25 per page. Certification fee: $7.00 per doc includes copies. Payee: State of Delaware. Personal checks accepted. Visa/MC accepted. Prepayment required.
Criminal Name Search: Access: Mail, in person. Only the court performs in person name searches; visitors may not. No search fee. Required to search: name, years to search; also helpful: DOB. Criminal records go back to 1992. Note: Search requests must be on court's form. Mail turnaround time is 1 week .
Court of Common Pleas 38 The Green, Dover, DE 19901; 302-735-3900; criminal phone: x3; civil phone: x4; criminal fax: 302-739-4501; civil fax: 8AM-4:30PM; 8AM-4:30PM (EST). *Misdemeanor, Civil Actions under $50,000.*
http://courts.delaware.gov/CommonPleas/
General Information: Superior Court has most of the records. No sealed records released. Will fax documents to local or toll free line. Court makes copy: $1.00 per page for docket copy. Certification fee: $10.00. Payee: Court of Common Pleas. Personal checks accepted. No credit cards accepted. Prepayment required.
Civil Name Search: Access: In person, online. Visitors must perform in person searches themselves. Civil records on computer from 1992, on microfiche from 10/85, archived prior. Civil PAT goes back to 1992. Access to e-filed records is available online by subscription through LexisNexis eFlex system for filing. See http://courts.delaware.gov/efiling/index.stm.

Criminal Name Search: Access: In person. Visitors must perform in person searches themselves. Required to search: name, years to search, DOB, offense, date of offense. Criminal records computerized from 1980, on microfiche from 10/85, archived prior. Criminal PAT goes back to 1980.

Dover Justice of the Peace #16 480 Bank Ln, Dover, DE 19904; 302-739-4316; fax: 302-739-6797; 8AM-4PM (EST). *Civil Actions under $15,000, Eviction, Small Claims.*

http://courts.delaware.gov/Locations/jp16.stm

General Information: Access to e-filed records is available online by subscription through LexisNexis eFlex system for filing. See http://courts.delaware.gov/efiling/index.stm, Will not fax documents. Court makes copy: $.25 per page. Certification fee: $10.00 per doc. Payee: JCP Court 16. Personal checks and credit cards accepted. Prepayment required. Mail requests: SASE requested for civil.

Civil Name Search: Access: Mail, in person, Online. Only the court performs in person name searches; visitors may not. No search fee. Civil records computerized since 10/98. Mail turnaround time varies. Access to e-filed records is available online by subscription through LexisNexis eFlex system for filing. See http://courts.delaware.gov/efiling/index.stm. Access to Delaware State CourtConnect for records for free go to http://courtconnect.courts.delaware.gov.

New Castle County

Superior Court Office of the Prothonotary, 500 N King St, #500, Wilmington, DE 19801; 302-255-0800; fax: 302-255-2264; 8:30AM-5PM (EST). *Felony, Misdemeanor, Civil Actions over $50,000.*

http://courts.delaware.gov/Superior/

General Information: Access to e-filed records is available online by subscription through LexisNexis eFlex system for filing. See http://courts.delaware.gov/efiling/index.stm, No psychological evaluation, sealed records released. Will fax documents $6.00 for 1st 3 pages, $1.50 each add'l page. Court makes copy: $1.50 per page. Certification fee: $10.00 for 1st 3 pages; $1.50 each add'l. Exemplification fee- $25.00 for 1st 3 pages; $1.50 each add'l. Payee: Prothonotary's Office. Personal checks accepted. No credit cards accepted. Prepayment required.

Civil Name Search: Access: In person, online. Visitors must perform in person searches themselves. Civil records on computer from 1991, prior in docket books or on microfilm. Civil PAT goes back to 1991. Search civil case and judgment information at http://courtconnect.courts.delaware.gov/public/ck_public_qry_main.cp_main_idx. Although not a court record, Trade, Business and Fictitious Names can be searched at a court location at http://courts.delaware.gov/Courts/Superior%20Court/?trade_names.htm.

Criminal Name Search: Access: In person only. Visitors must perform in person searches themselves. Criminal records computerized from 4/80, prior on microfilm. Criminal PAT goes back to 1980.

Chancery Court 500 N King St, #1551, Attn: Register in Chancery, Wilmington, DE 19801; 302-255-0544; probate phone: 302-395-7800; fax: 302-255-2213; 8:30AM-5PM (EST). *Civil, Probate, Guardianship.*

http://courts.delaware.gov/Chancery/

General Information: Probate records in a separate index in separate office. Probate fax- 302-395-7801. No guardianship records released. Will fax documents $10.00 1st page, $2.00 each add'l. Court makes copy: $1.50 per page. $2.00 if from microfilm. Self serve copy: same. Certification fee: $25.00; if exemplification then $50.00. Payee: Register in Chancery (Register of Wills for Probate). Personal checks accepted. No credit cards accepted. Prepayment required. Will bill fax requests.

Civil Name Search: Access: Phone, fax, mail, in person, online. Both court and visitors may perform in person name searches. No search fee. Required to search: name; also helpful: years to search. Civil records indexed on computer since 1963, in books prior to 1963. The civil records for the Court of Chancery deal with corporate and equity matters. Mail turnaround time 2 days. Public use terminal has civil records back to 1963. Access to e-filed records is available online by subscription through LexisNexis eFlex system for filing. See http://courts.delaware.gov/efiling/index.stm.

New Castle Justice of the Peace #11 2 Penns Way #100-A, New Castle, DE 19720; 302-323-4450; fax: 302-323-4452; Open 24 hours (EST). *Misdemeanor, DUI.*

http://courts.delaware.gov/Locations/jp11.stm

General Information: In December 2009, Court #11 consolidated with the closed Court #15 from Claymont. Claymont case files are located here. Court makes copy: $.25 per page. Certification fee: $7.00 per doc. Cert fee includes copies. Payee: State of Delaware. Cashiers checks and money orders accepted. Credit cards accepted.

Criminal Name Search: Access: In person only. Visitors must perform in person searches themselves. Records indexed on computer to 1966, older records hand written in log book.

Wilmington Justice of the Peace #20 Public Safety Bldg, 300 N Walnut St, Wilmington, DE 19801; 302-577-7234; fax: 302-577-7237/7238; 24 hours (EST). *Misdemeanor.*

http://courts.delaware.gov/Locations/jp20.stm

General Information: This court also maintains the case records from the former JP Court #18. Records department phone is 302-255-0000. Search requests may also be directed to Dover - 800-464-4557 for information. Will not fax documents. Court makes copy: $7.00 per disposition. Certification fee included with copy. Payee: Justice of the Peace Court #13. Only cashiers checks and money orders accepted. Major credit cards accepted. Prepayment required.

Criminal Name Search: Access: In person only. Visitors must perform in person searches themselves.

Court of Common Pleas 500 N King St, Wilmington, DE 19801-3704; 302-255-0900; criminal phone: x3; civil phone: x4; criminal fax: 302-255-2244; civil fax: 8:30AM-4:30PM; 8:30AM-4:30PM (EST). *Misdemeanor, Civil Actions under $50,000, Traffic.*

http://courts.delaware.gov/CommonPleas/

General Information: No closed records released. Will fax documents $1.00 per page. Court makes copy: $1.00 per page. Certification fee: $10.00. Payee: Court of Common Pleas. No personal checks accepted for record searches. Prepayment required. Mail requests: SASE required for civil.

Civil Name Search: Access: Phone, fax, mail, in person, online. Both court and visitors may perform in person name searches. No search fee. Civil records on computer from 1989; prior records on docket books. Mail turnaround time up to 3 weeks. Civil PAT goes back to 1974. Access to e-filed records is available online by subscription through LexisNexis eFlex system for filing. See http://courts.delaware.gov/efiling/index.stm,

Criminal Name Search: Access: In person only. Visitors must perform in person name searches - Court does not do name searches; you must know the charge or arrest date for court response. No search fee, unless need to pull from storage or microfilm then $10.00. Required to search: name, charge year of offense; also helpful: DOB. Criminal records computerized from 1993; prior records on docket books. Criminal PAT goes back to 1988.

Middletown Justice of the Peace #9 757 N Broad St, Middletown, DE 19709; 302-378-5221; fax: 302-378-5220; 8AM-4PM M,T,TH,F, N-8PM W (EST). *Civil Actions under $15,000, Misdemeanor, Eviction, Small Claims.*

http://courts.delaware.gov/Locations/jp09.stm

General Information: Due to a court fire, criminal cases 7/24/2000 to 5/1/2001 were held at New Castle JP Court 11, 323-4450. Civil cases were held at Prices Corner JP Court 12, 995-8646. Now, all new cases are back here at Middletown. Will fax documents to local or toll-free number. Court makes copy: $.25 per page. Certification fee: $10.00 per Civil doc includes copies; $7.00 per criminal doc. Payee: State of Delaware. Personal checks and credit cards accepted. Prepayment required.

Civil Name Search: Access: In person, online. Both court and visitors may perform in person name searches. No search fee. Civil cases indexed by defendant. Due to fire, records on computer only back to mid-1990s. Note: The Court said they will not do name searches, but will search if a civil action # is presented. Online access is not available for all records, but the E-Flex filing system does give access to those records. Access to e-filed records is available online by subscription through LexisNexis eFlex system for filing. See http://courts.delaware.gov/efiling/index.stm.

Criminal Name Search: Access: In person only. Both court and visitors may perform in person name searches. No search fee. Required to search: name, years to search, DOB. Due to fire, records on computer only back to mid-1990s. Note: This office prefers that you search through the state agency, though this office did not say they would refuse all search requests.

Wilmington Justice of the Peace #13 1010 Concord Ave, Concord Professional Ctr, Wilmington, DE 19802; 302-577-2550; fax: 302-577-2526; 8AM-4PM (EST). *Civil Actions under $15,000, Eviction, Small Claims.*

http://courts.delaware.gov/Locations/jp13.stm

General Information: Justice of the Peace Court #12 is now located here. No sealed, juvenile, adoption or mental health records released. Will not fax out documents. Court makes copy: $.25 per page. Certification fee: $10.00 per case includes copies. Payee: Justice of the Peace Court #13. Personal checks accepted. Visa/MC/Discover accepted. Prepayment required.

Civil Name Search: Access: In person, online. Visitors must perform in person searches themselves. Civil records are computerized since 9/01/99. Note: The court will pull specific case data if CA# given, if and when time permitting. Access to e-filed records is available online by subscription through LexisNexis eFlex system for filing. See http://courts.delaware.gov/efiling/index.stm,

Justice of the Peace #10 210 Greenbank Rd, Wilmington, DE 19808; 302-995-8640; fax: 302-995-8642; 8AM-4PM M,T,TH,F: 8AM-10PM W (EST). *Misdemeanor Traffic.*
http://courts.delaware.gov/Locations/jp10.stm
General Information: Court refers records request to State Agency-302-739-5961.
Prices Corner Justice of the Peace #12 - Prices Corner (Closed) This court and records is now located at Justice of the Peace Court #13.
Wilmington Justice of the Peace #15 - Claymont (Closed), This court closed in December 2009 and case files were moved to the new Consolidated Court #11 location in New Castle.

Sussex County

Superior Court 1 The Circle #2, Georgetown, DE 19947; criminal phone: 302-856-5741; civil phone: 302-856-5742; criminal fax: 302-856-5739; civil fax: 8:30AM-4:30PM; 8:30AM-4:30PM (EST). *Felony, Misdemeanor, Civil Actions.*
http://courts.delaware.gov/Superior/
General Information: Access to e-filed records is available online by subscription through LexisNexis eFlex system for filing. See http://courts.delaware.gov/efiling/index.stm, No divorce, victim info, sealed records, expungments, or CCDW permit records released. Will fax documents for $3.00 plus $1.00 per page. Court makes copy: $.50 per page. Self serve copy: same. Certification fee: $6.00 plus $1.00 per page after 1st three. Payee: Prothonotary. Personal checks accepted. No credit cards accepted. Prepayment required.
Civil Name Search: Access: In person, online. Visitors must perform in person searches themselves. Civil records on computer from 6/91 or as far back as 1980 if case was pending in 1991; microfiche prior. Civil PAT goes back to 1980s. Search civil case and judgment information at http://courtconnect.courts.delaware.gov/public/ck_public_qry_main.cp_main_idx. Although not a court record, Trade, Business and Fictitious Names can be searched at a court location at http://courts.delaware.gov/Courts/Superior%20Court/?trade_names.htm.
Criminal Name Search: Access: In person only. Visitors must perform in person searches themselves. Required to search: name, years to search, DOB. Criminal records on manual index; computerized records since 1983. Criminal PAT goes back to 1983.
Chancery Court Register in Chancery, 34 The Circle, Georgetown, DE 19947; 302-856-5775; probate phone: 302-855-7875; fax: 302-856-5778; 8:30AM-4:30PM (EST). *Civil, Probate.*
http://courts.delaware.gov/Chancery/
General Information: Fees charged by Register of Wills for Probate are separate. All records public. Will fax documents $10.00 plus $2.00 each add'l page. Court makes copy: $1.50 per page. Self serve copy: same. Certification fee: $25.00 per cert plus copy fee. Exemplifications fee- $50.00 per doc. Payee: Register in Chancery (or Register of Wills for Probate). Personal checks accepted. No credit cards accepted. Prepayment required. Mail requests: SASE required.
Civil Name Search: Access: In person, online. Visitors must perform in person searches themselves. Search fee: $25.00 or more to retrieve a file from the archives, depending on size of file, otherwise n/a. Civil index on docket books; on computer back to 1999. Note: Court personnel will not perform a name search. Mail turnaround time 1-3 days. Public use terminal has civil records back to 1999. Access to e-filed records is available online by subscription through LexisNexis eFlex system for filing. See http://courts.delaware.gov/efiling/index.stm,

Georgetown Justice of the Peace #3 23730 Shortly Rd, Georgetown, DE 19947; 302-856-1445; fax: 302-856-5844; 24 hours daily (EST). *Misdemeanor, Traffic.*
http://courts.delaware.gov/Locations/jp03.stm
General Information: Will fax documents to local or toll-free number. Court makes copy: $.25 per page. Certification fee: $7.00 per case. Payee: State of Delaware. Personal checks accepted. Debit cards accepted in person only. Visa/MC, Discover accepted. Prepayment required. Mail requests: SASE requested.
Criminal Name Search: Access: Mail, in person. Only the court performs in person name searches; visitors may not. Search fee: $7.00 per case. Search fee includes certification. Required to search: name, years to search, DOB; also helpful: SSN. Records are here from 2005 to present. On microfilm 1966-1983. From 1984-2004 records archived. Mail turnaround time 3-10 days.

Justice of the Peace #1 9 Main St, Frankford, DE 19945; 302-732-9580; fax: 302-732-9586; 8AM-4PM (EST). *Misdemeanor.*
http://courts.state.de.us/Locations/jp01.stm
General Information: This court also handles traffic. Will fax documents to local or toll-free number only if an emergency situation. Court makes copy: $.25 per page. Certification fee: $7.00 per case. Payee: State of Delaware. Personal checks accepted. Credit cards accepted. Prepayment required.
Criminal Name Search: Access: Mail, in person. Only the court performs in person name searches; visitors may not. No search fee. Required to search: name, years to search, DOB. Records available from 1983, computerized since 1990. Mail turnaround time same day.
Rehoboth Beach Justice of the Peace #2 35252 Hudson Way, #1, Rehoboth Beach, DE 19971-9738; 302-645-6163; fax: 302-645-8842; 8AM-Midnight (EST). *Misdemeanor, Traffic.*
http://courts.delaware.gov/Locations/jp02.stm
General Information: Will fax documents to local or toll-free number. Court makes copy: $1.00 per page. Certification fee: $7.00. Payee: State of Delaware. Personal checks and credit cards accepted. Prepayment required. Mail requests: SASE required.
Criminal Name Search: Access: Mail, in person. Both court and visitors may perform in person name searches. No search fee. Required to search: name, years to search, DOB. Records available since 1990, computerized since 1992. Mail turnaround time 3 weeks .
Seaford Justice of the Peace #4 408 Stein Hwy, Seaford, DE 19973; 302-628-2036; fax: 302-628-2049; 8AM-4PM (EST). *Misdemeanor.*
http://courts.delaware.gov/Locations/jp04.stm
General Information: Court refers records request to State Agency-302-739-5961. This court considers the records non-public. One may not obtain a record on someone else. Will not fax documents. Court makes copy: $.25 per page. Certification fee: $7.00 per cert plus copy fee. Payee: JP Court 4. . Prepayment required.
Criminal Name Search: Access: In person only. Visitors must perform in person searches themselves. Criminal records go back to 2000. Note: This court considers their records non-public. One may not obtain a record on someone else.
Court of Common Pleas 1 The Circle #1, Georgetown, DE 19947; 302-856-5333; criminal phone: x2; fax: 302-856-5056; 8:30AM-4:30PM (EST). *Misdemeanor, Civil Actions under $50,000.*
http://courts.delaware.gov/CommonPleas/
General Information: Fees for archive or closed file retrieval is $25.00. No closed case records released. No fee to fax documents. Court makes copy: $.25 per page. Certification fee: $10.00. Payee: Court of Common Pleas. Personal checks accepted. Visa/MC, Discover accepted. Prepayment required. Mail requests: SASE required.
Civil Name Search: Access: Phone, fax, mail, in person, online. Both court and visitors may perform in person name searches. No search fee. Civil cases indexed by defendant. Civil records on computer from 1993, on microfiche from 9/53, archived prior. Mail turnaround time 1-2 weeks. Civil PAT goes back to 1993. Access to e-filed records is available online by subscription through LexisNexis eFlex system for filing. See http://courts.delaware.gov/efiling/index.stm.
Criminal Name Search: Access: Phone, fax, mail, in person. Both court and visitors may perform in person name searches. No search fee. Required to search: name, years to search, DOB, offense, date of offense. Criminal records computerized from 1994, on microfiche from 10/65, archived prior. Mail turnaround time 1-2 weeks. Criminal PAT goes back to 1994. Criminal PAT results include name and case number only.
Georgetown Justice of the Peace #17 23730 Shortly Rd, Georgetown, DE 19947; 302-856-1447; fax: 302-856-4654; 8AM-4PM (EST). *Civil Actions under $15,000, Eviction, Small Claims.*
http://courts.delaware.gov/Locations/jp17.stm
General Information: See also Court 19 in Seaford. Will fax documents to local or toll-free number. Court makes copy: $.25 per page. Certification fee: $10.00. Payee: State of Delaware. Personal checks accepted. No credit cards accepted. Prepayment required. Mail requests: SASE requested.
Civil Name Search: Access: Mail, in person, online. Only the court performs in person name searches; visitors may not. No search fee. Required to search: name, years to search, parties in case. Civil index on docket books from 1966 to present. Mail turnaround time 1-2 days. Access to e-filed records is available online by subscription through LexisNexis eFlex system for filing. See http://courts.delaware.gov/efiling/index.stm.
Seaford Justice of the Peace #19 Court closed, records now at Georgetown JP court #17, address and phones given here.

District of Columbia

Time Zone:	**EST**
State Web:	**www.dc.gov**
Court Web:	**www.dccourts.gov/dccourts/index.jsp**

Administration

Executive Office, 500 Indiana Av NW, Room 1500, Washington, DC, 20001; 202-879-1700, Fax: 202-879-4829. The D.C. Courts are funded by the Federal government; the Courts' budget request is submitted to the Office of Management and Budget for presidential recommendation and then to the U.S. Congress. The Courts also submit their budget to the Mayor and the Council of the District of Columbia.

The Court of Appeal

The Court of Appeals, the highest court of the District, reviews decisions of the Superior Court and the District of Columbia government's administrative agencies. The decisions of the Court of Appeals are reviewable by the Supreme Court of the United States. The court home page above provides online access to opinions from the Court of Appeals.

The DC Courts

Court	Type	How Organized	Jurisdiction Highpoints
Superior*	General	4 Branches	Felony, Misdemeanor, Civil, Small Claims, Family, Probate, Juvenile, Traffic, Eviction, Domestic Relations

* = profiled in this book

Details on the Court Structure

The **Superior Court** handles all local trial matters and consists of five divisions: Civil, Criminal, Family, Probate, and Domestic Violence.

The **Civil Division** is divided into four branches: the Civil Actions Branch, the Quality Review Branch, the Landlord and Tenant Branch and the Small Claims Branch. The Criminal Division hears all local criminal matters including felony, misdemeanor, and serious traffic cases.

The **Family Court** (part of the Superior Court) is divided into six branches: the Domestic Relations Branch, the Juvenile and Neglect Branch, the Paternity and Child Support Branch, the Marriage Bureau Branch, the Mental Health and Mental Retardation Branch, and the Counsel for Child Abuse and Neglect Branch. The Probate Division has jurisdiction over estates guardianships of minors and of incapacitated adults.

Note the District of Columbia Courts have two community courts: the D.C. Misdemeanor and Traffic Community Court and the East of the River Community Court.

Record Searching Facts You Need to Know

Online Access

The Court Cases Online system at https://www.dccourts.gov/cco provides public information of docket entries in civil, criminal, criminal domestic violence and tax cases, probate cases for large estates and small estates, disclaimers of interest, major litigation, wills and foreign estate proceedings. The results are returned by name match only; there is no DOB provided online. While dockets are continually updated throughout the day, there is a disclaimer that states the *District cannot make assurances that the latest information will be recorded and viewable.*

Request copies of transcripts of court proceedings from the web page at www.dccourts.gov/dccourts/courtsystem/reporting.jsp.

District of Columbia

Superior Court - Criminal 500 Indiana Ave NW, 4th Fl, W, Washington, DC 20001; 202-879-1373; fax: 202-638-5352; 8:30AM-5PM (EST). *Felony, Misdemeanor.*

www.dccourts.gov/dccourts/index.jsp

General Information: The court is selective of the type of document they will make copies of. No sealed records released. Will not fax documents. Court makes copy: $.25 per page. Self serve copy: $.25 per page. No certification fee . Payee: DC Superior Court. Personal checks accepted. No credit cards accepted.

Criminal Name Search: Access: Mail, fax, in person, online. Visitors must perform in person searches themselves. Search fee: $10.00 per name. Required to search: name, years to search, DOB. Criminal records computerized from 1978, on microfiche from 1974, on index from 1970, archived from 1962. Note: This court recommends that you contact the Metro DC Police to perform a "police clearance" record check for $7.00. ID and signed release is required. Metro Police is at 202-727-4245, ID & Records Sec, Mail Correspondence Sec., 300 Indiana Ave NW 20001. Mail turnaround time depends on case involved. Public use terminal has crim records back to 1978. Three public access terminals available, includes Traffic cases index. Access criminal case information free at https://www.dccourts.gov/cco/ but records do not contain DOBs; some sentencing and dockets are incorrect compared to court records. The public information on the Remote Access to Case Dockets (RACD) System reflects the docket entries in civil, criminal, domestic violence and tax cases, probate, disclaimers of interest, major litigation, wills and foreign estate proceedings.

Superior Court - Civil 500 Indiana Ave NW, Rm 5000, Washington, DC 20001; 202-879-1133; fax: 202-879-8335; 8:30AM-5PM M-F; 9AM-12 Sat (EST). *Civil Actions.*

www.dccourts.gov/dccourts/superior/civil/index.jsp

General Information: Since 2005 Small Claims is a separate branch that handles claims of $5,000 or less. Online identifiers in results same as on public terminal. No sealed records released. Will not fax documents. Court makes copy: $.50 per page. Self serve copy: $.25 per page. Certification fee: $5.00. Payee: Clerk-Superior Court of DC. Only cashiers checks and money orders accepted. No credit cards accepted. Prepayment required. Mail requests: SASE required.

Civil Name Search: Access: Mail, in person, online. Both court and visitors may perform in person name searches. Search fee: $10.00 per name. Required to search: name. Civil records on computer from 1983, on microfiche, archived and on index from 1976. Note: Attorneys and legal professionals participating in the e-Filing Project must register for the CaseFileXpress eFile service either by logging onto www.lexisnexis.com/courtlink/online/ or calling 1-877-433-4533. Mail turnaround time depends on case involved. Public use terminal has civil records back to 1983. Access civil records free at https://www.dccourts.gov/pa/. The public information on the Remote Access to Case Dockets (RACD) System reflects the docket entries in civil, criminal, domestic violence and tax cases, probate, disclaimers of interest, major litigation, wills and foreign estate proceedings.

Civil Division - Small Claims and Conciliation Branch 510 Fourth St NW, #120, Washington, DC 20001; 202-879-1120; fax: 202-508-1696; 8:30AM-5PM M-F; 9AM-12 Sat (EST). *Small Claims - $5,000 or less.*

www.dccourts.gov/dccourts/superior/civil/index.jsp

General Information: Will not fax documents. Court makes copy: $.50 per page. Certification fee: $5.00 per doc includes copy fee. Payee: The Clerk of DC Superior Court. No personal checks accepted. Will accept checks from members of the DC Bar. No credit cards accepted. Prepayment required.

Civil Name Search: Access: Mail, in person, online. Both court and visitors may perform in person name searches. Search fee: $10.00. Required to search: name. Small Claims records on computer back to 1986; non-computer records go back to 1976; 1987-97 some, not all, records in archives. Public use terminal has civil records back to 2002, but some prior cases are held. Access civil records free at https://www.dccourts.gov/cco/.

Superior Court - Civil Division - Landlord & Tenant Branch 510 4th Street NW Rm110, Building B, Washington, DC 20001; 202-879-4879; fax: 202-508-1621; 8:30AM-5PM; 9AM-N Sat (EST). *Eviction.*

www.dccourts.gov/dccourts/index.jsp

General Information: This information applies to the Landlord & Tenant Branch only. Will fax documents to local or toll-free number. Court makes copy: $.50 per page. Certification fee: $5.00. Payee: Clerk-Superior Court of DC. No personal checks or credit cards accepted. Prepayment required.

Civil Name Search: Access: Mail, In person, online. Both court and visitors may perform in person name searches. Search fee: $10.00. Required to search: name, years to search; also helpful-case number. Civil records go back to 1994; computerized records go back 5 years. Note: No out of district inquires taken by phone. Mail turnaround time depends on case involved. Public use terminal has civil records back to 2002. Access civil records free at https://www.dccourts.gov/cco/.

Superior Court - Family Court Division 500 Indiana Ave NW, John Marshall Level, East Wing, JM 520, Washington, DC 20001; 202-879-1212; 8:30AM-5PM (EST). *Domestic Relations.*

www.dccourts.gov/dccourts/superior/family/index.jsp

Superior Court - Probate Division 515 5th Street BW, 3rd Fl, Washington, DC 20001; 202-879-1499; fax: 202-879-9466; 8:30AM-5PM (EST). *Probate.*

www.dccourts.gov/dccourts/superior/probate/index.jsp

Florida

Time Zone:	**EST & CST***

> *Florida's ten western-most counties are CST: They are: Bay, Calhoun, Escambia, Gulf, Holmes, Jackson, Okaloosa, Santa Rosa, Walton, Washington.

Capital:	**Tallahassee, Leon County**
# of Counties:	**67**
State Web:	**www.myflorida.com**
Court Web:	**www.flcourts.org**

Administration

Office of State Courts Administrator, Supreme Court Bldg, 500 S Duval, Tallahassee, FL, 32399-1900; 850-922-5081, Fax: 850-488-0156.

The Supreme and District Appellate Courts

The Supreme Court is the court of last resort. It's web page provides opinions and dockets from www.floridasupremecourt.org/ . However, most appeals are heard by the five District Courts of Appeal. See www.flcourts.org/courts/dca/dca.shtml.

The Florida Courts

Court	Type	How Organized	Jurisdiction Highpoints
Circuit*	General	67 courts in 20 circuits	Felony, Civil over $15,000, Juvenile, Domestic Relations, Estates
County*	Limited	67 courts in 67 Districts	Misdemeanor, Civil Actions Under $15,000, Small Claims, Eviction, DWI/DUI

* = profiled in this book

Details on the Court Structure

The trial jurisdiction of **Circuit Courts** includes, among other matters, original jurisdiction over felonies, civil disputes involving more than $15,000, estates, minors and persons adjudicated as incapacitated, juveniles tax disputes; title and boundaries of real property; suits for declaratory judgments. Circuit Courts also have general trial jurisdiction over matters not assigned by statute to the county courts and also hear appeals from county court cases.

The trial jurisdiction of **County Courts** includes civil disputes involving $15,000 or less, misdemeanors, traffic and small claims.

Record Searching Facts You Need to Know

Fees and Record Searching Tips

All courts have one address and switchboard in that the clerk of courts serves both the County and the Circuit Courts. Requesters should specify which court and which division – e.g., Circuit Civil, County Civil, etc. – to direct the request. Most courts have very lengthy phone recording systems.

The profiles of a County and Circuit Court in a county are often combined by record types (criminal or civil) herein. This is because the record searching and indexing are the same – a search includes both court indices.

Fees are set by statute and are as follows as of July 1, 2008: search fee of $2.00 per name per year; certification fee of $1.50 per document plus copy fee; copy fee of $1.00 per page. Most but not all courts follow this schedule.

Online Access is on a County Basis

There is no statewide access to trial court data, but many counties offer access. Also a number of courts offer online access of recorded civil judgment liens via www.myfloridacountycom. Fees are involved when ordering copies; save $1.50 per record by becoming a subscriber.

Visit www.flcourts.org/gen_public/stratplan/privacy.shtml for information regarding the electronic release and privacy of court records in Florida.

Alachua County

Circuit & County Courts - Criminal 220 S Main St, Gainesville, FL 32602; 352-374-3681; fax: 352-381-0144; 8AM-5PM (EST). *Felony, Misdemeanor.*
www.alachuacounty.us/Depts/Clerk/Pages/Clerk.aspx/
General Information: Criminal Divisions are now in a separate building from the civil; county Official Records court records and recorder. etc., are located at Civil Court Clerk Office, 201 E University Ave. Telephone for ancient (older, pre-1950s) records- 352-384-3174. No juvenile, child abuse or sexual battery records released. Will fax documents $1.00 per page. Court makes copy: $1.00 per page. Certification fee: $2.00 per doc plus copy fee. Payee: Clerk of Circuit Court. Personal checks accepted. Visa/MC accepted; a $2.50 usage fee may apply. Prepayment required.
Criminal Name Search: Access: Fax, mail, in person, online. Both court and visitors may perform in person name searches. Search fee: $2.00 per name per year. Required to search: name, years to search, DOB; also helpful-address, SSN, race, sex. Criminal records on computer since 1990. Mail turnaround time 1-3 days. Public use terminal has crim records back to 1990. Search limited criminal and traffic citations at https://www.alachuaclerk.org/court_records/.

Circuit & County Courts - Civil PO Box 600, 201 E University Ave, Gainesville, FL 32602; 352-374-3636; criminal phone: 352-337-6250; civil phone: 352-374-3618; criminal fax: 352-381-0144; civil fax: 8:15AM-5PM; 8:15AM-5PM (EST). *Civil, Eviction, Small Claims, Probate, Civil Traffic.* www.alachuacounty.us/Depts/Clerk/Pages/Clerk.aspx
General Information: The county's Official Records court records and recorder. etc., are located at this address. There is a separate phone for ancient (older, pre-1950s) records- 352-384-3174. No juvenile records released. Will fax documents $1.00 per 5 pages. Court makes copy: $1.00 per page.Computer printouts of civil records are $1.00 per page Certification fee: $2.00 per doc plus copy fee. Payee: Clerk of Circuit Court. Personal checks accepted. Major credit cards accepted; a $5.00 usage fee may apply. Prepayment required.
Civil Name Search: Access: Fax, mail, in person, online. Both court and visitors may perform in person name searches. Search fee: $2.00 per name per year. Required to search: name, years to search; also helpful: address. Civil records on computer from 1979, images to 2001, some records on docket books. Mail turnaround time 24 hours. Public use terminal has civil records back to 2001. Results that show index may or may not have DOB, address; usually, records do show DOB, address, DL number, and other identifiers. Search civil records free at https://www.alachuaclerk.org/court_records/. Also, access to an index of judgments & recorded documents at www.myfloridacounty.com. Fees involved to order copies; Also, search the probate index (no images) and other ancient records free at www.alachuaclerk.org/Archive/default.cfm. Court accepts record requests by email llr@alachuacounty.org.

Baker County

Circuit & County Courts - Civil 339 E Macclenny Ave, Macclenny, FL 32063; civil phone: 904-259-0209; probate phone: 904-259-8449; fax: 904-259-4176; 8:30AM-5PM (EST). *Civil, Eviction, Small Claims, Probate.* http://208.75.175.18/clerk/
General Information: Recorder: 904-259-0208 No juvenile, child abuse or sexual battery records released. Will fax documents $3.00 each. Court makes copy: $1.00 per page. Self serve copy: same. Certification fee: $2.00. Payee: Clerk of Circuit Court. Business checks accepted. No credit cards accepted. Prepayment required. Mail requests: SASE preferred.
Civil Name Search: Access: Mail, in person, online. Both court and visitors may perform in person name searches. Search fee: $2.00 per name per year. Required to search: name, years to search; also helpful: address. Civil records on computer back to 2000; prior on index cards and docket books. Mail turnaround time 2 days. Public use terminal has civil records back to 2000. The court does not provide online access, but there is an index of judgments (not dockets) at www.myfloridacounty.com. Fees involved to order copies; save $1.50 per record by becoming a subscriber.

Circuit & County Courts - Criminal 339 E Macclenny Ave, Macclenny, FL 32063; 904-259-0206/0274; fax: 904-259-4176; 8:30AM-5PM (EST). *Felony, Misdemeanor.* http://208.75.175.18/clerk/
General Information: County Court Misdemeanor phone number is 904-259-0204 and 0212. No juvenile or guardianship records released. Court

makes copy: $1.00 per page. Self serve copy: same. Certification fee: $2.00 per doc plus copy fee. Payee: Clerk of Circuit Court. Business checks accepted. No credit cards accepted. Prepayment required. Mail requests: SASE required.
Criminal Name Search: Access: Mail, in person, online. Both court and visitors may perform in person name searches. Search fee: $2.00 per name per year. Required to search: name, years to search, DOB. Criminal records on computer since 1989. Some records on docket books. Mail turnaround time 1-2 days. Public use terminal has crim records back to 1989. Access the circuit-wide criminal quick lookup at http://circuit8.org. Account and password is required; restricted usage. Call the court for details. Online results show name only.

Bay County

Circuit Court - Criminal 300 E 4th St, Rm 111, Panama City, FL 32401; 850-763-9061; fax: 850-747-5263; 8AM-4:30PM (CST). *Felony, Misdemeanor.* www.baycoclerk.com
General Information: Online identifiers in results same as on public terminal. No sealed, juvenile or expunged records released. Will fax documents for $1.00 per page local, $2.50 if long distance. Court makes copy: $1.00 per page. Certification fee: $2.00 per cert plus copy fee. Payee: Clerk of Circuit Court. No personal checks accepted. Visa/MC accepted, a usage fee is added. Prepayment required. Mail requests: SASE requested.
Criminal Name Search: Access: Mail, fax, in person, online. Both court and visitors may perform in person name searches. Search fee: $2.00 per name per year. Required to search: name, years to search, DOB; also helpful: SSN, signed release. Criminal records computerized from 1986, on microfilm from 1938 to 1982, prior archived. Mail turnaround time 7-10 days. Public use terminal has crim records. Terminal located in room 110. Search court cases free at www.baycoclerk.com/courts/case-search/. Online results show middle initial, DOB.

Circuit Court - Civil 300 E 4th St, Room 105, Panama City, FL 32401; 850-763-9061; civil phone: 850-747-5141; probate phone: 850-747-5118; fax: 850-747-5249; 8AM-4:30PM (CST). *Civil Actions over $15,000, Probate.* www.baycoclerk.com
General Information: No juvenile, adoption, child abuse or sexual battery records released. Will not fax documents. Court makes copy: $1.00 per page. Certification fee: $2.00 per doc plus copy fee. Payee: Clerk of Circuit Court. No personal checks. Credit cards accepted in person only, $5.00 surcharge. Prepayment required. Mail requests: SASE required.
Civil Name Search: Access: Fax, mail, in person, online. Both court and visitors may perform in person name searches. Search fee: $2.00 per name per year. Civil records on computer from 1984, on microfiche and books from 1950 to 1980, archived from 1913 to 1949. Some records on dockets. Mail turnaround time 1-2 days. Public use terminal has civil records back to 1984. PATs located in Rm 101 or in 3rd Fl law library. Sometimes DOB shows on PAT. Search the court cases, including traffic and probate, for free at www.baycoclerk.com/courts/case-search/. Also, access an index of judgments, liens, recorded documents at www.myfloridacounty.com. Fees involved to order copies; save $1.50 per record by becoming a subscriber.

County Court - Civil 300 E 4th St, Rm 105, Panama City, FL 32401; 850-763-9061; fax: 850-747-5141; 8AM-4:30PM (CST). *Civil Actions under $15,000, Eviction, Small Claims.*
www.baycoclerk.com
General Information: No juvenile, child abuse or sexual battery records released. Will fax documents $1.25 per page local, $1.50 per page long distance, must be prepaid. Court makes copy: $1.00 per page. Self serve copy: same. Certification fee: $2.00 per page. Payee: Clerk of Circuit Court. No personal checks. Credit cards accepted in person, $3.5% surcharge. Prepayment required. Mail requests: SASE requested.
Civil Name Search: Access: Phone, fax, mail, in person, online. Both court and visitors may perform in person name searches. Search fee: $2.00 per name per year. Civil records on computer from 1986, on microfiche from 1950 to 1980, archived from 1913 to 1979. Some records on docket books. Mail turnaround time 2 days. Public use terminal has civil records. Terminals is in Rooms 203 and 101 and will show personal identifiers if on index. Search the court cases, including traffic and probate, for free at www.baycoclerk.com/courts/case-search/. Also, access an index of judgments, liens, recorded documents at www.myfloridacounty.com. Fees involved to order copies; save $1.50 per record by becoming a subscriber.

County Court - Misdemeanor PO Box 2269, 300 E 4th St, Rm 109, Panama City, FL 32402; 850-763-9061; fax: 850-747-5163; 8AM-4:30PM (CST). *Misdemeanor.*

www.baycoclerk.com

General Information: No sealed or expunged records released. Will fax documents $2.00 each. Court makes copy: $1.00 per page. Self serve copy: same. Certification fee: $2.00 per doc plus copy fee. Payee: Clerk of Circuit Court. No personal checks accepted. Visa/MC accepted; usage fee is 3.5% of total. Prepayment required. Mail requests: SASE requested.

Criminal Name Search: Access: Fax, mail, in person, online. Both court and visitors may perform in person name searches. Search fee: $2.00 per name per year. Required to search: name, years to search; also helpful: DOB, SSN. Criminal records computerized from 1984, felonies on microfilm from 1950 to 1987, archived from 1913. Misdemeanors from 1996-present; pending cases back. Mail turnaround time 7-10 days. Search the courts case database free at www.baycoclerk.com/courts/case-search/. Online results show middle initial, DOB.

Circuit Court - Probate Division 300 E 4th St, Rm 205, Panama City, FL 32401; 850-763-9061; fax: 850-747-5260; 8AM-4:30PM (CST). *Probate.*

www.baycoclerk.com/courts/probate/

General Information: Search probate records free at www.baycoclerk.com/courts/case-search/. •Probate cases end in CP or GA.

Bradford County

Circuit Court PO Drawer B, 945 N Temple Ave, Starke, FL 32091; criminal phone: 904-966-6255; civil phone: 904-966-6282; probate phone: 904-966-6297; fax: 904-964-4454; 8AM-5PM (EST). *Felony, Civil Actions over $15,000, Probate.*

http://circuit8.org

General Information: No juvenile, child abuse or sexual battery records released. Court makes copy: $1.00 per page. Self serve copy: same. Certification fee: $2.00 per document. Payee: Clerk at Circuit Court. Business checks accepted; personal checks in person with ID accepted. Visa/MC accepted in person with ID, there is a surcharge. Prepayment required. Mail requests: SASE required.

Civil Name Search: Access: Mail, fax, in person, online. Only the court performs in person name searches; visitors may not. Search fee: $2.00 per name per year. Civil records on computer since late 1987, others on index books. Mail turnaround time 1 week. Access an index of judgments (not dockets) is at www.myfloridacounty.com. Fees involved to order copies; save $1.50 per record by becoming a subscriber.

Criminal Name Search: Access: Mail, fax, in person, online. Only the court performs in person name searches; visitors may not. Search fee: $2.00 per name per year. Required to search: name, years to search, DOB, SSN. Criminal records on computer since 1989, others on index books. Mail turnaround time 1 week. Access to the circuit-wide criminal quick lookup is at http://circuit8.org. Account and password is required; restricted usage.

County Court PO Drawer B, 945 N Temple Ave, Starke, FL 32091; 904-966-6280; criminal phone: 904-966-2264; civil phone: 904-966-6297; fax: 904-964-4454; 8AM-5PM (EST). *Misdemeanor, Civil Actions under $15,000, Eviction, Small Claims.*

www.bradford-co-fla.org

General Information: Send mail requests to "Attention Records" and mention the case type: civil, sm claims, Misd., etc. No juvenile records released. Will not fax documents. Court makes copy: $1.00 per page. Self serve copy: same. Certification fee: $2.00 per doc; exemplification- $7.00. Payee: Clerk of Court. Personal checks accepted with valid driver's license for ID. Credit cards accepted in person only, with valid driver's license for ID. Prepayment required. Mail requests: SASE required.

Civil Name Search: Access: Mail, in person, online. Only the court performs in person name searches; visitors may not. Search fee: $2.00 per name per year. Civil records on computer back to 1989. Some records on docket books, some microfilm. Mail turnaround time up to 1 week. Access an index of judgments (not dockets) is at www.myfloridacounty.com. Fees involved to order copies; save $1.50 per record by becoming a subscriber.

Criminal Name Search: Access: Mail, in person. Only the court performs in person name searches; visitors may not. Search fee: $2.00 per name per year. Required to search: name, years to search, DOB, SSN. Criminal records computerized from 1988. Records back to 1970's on docket books. Mail turnaround time up to 1 week. Online results show name only.

Brevard County

Circuit Court - Civil PO Box 2767, Official Records Copy Desk, Titusville, FL 32781-2767; 321-637-2004; fax: 321-264-5246; 8AM-5PM (EST). *Civil, Eviction, Small Claims, Probate, Family.*

http://199.241.8.125/

General Information: No juvenile, child abuse or sexual battery victim records released. Will fax documents $2.00 per page, no fee if local. Court makes copy: $1.00 per page. Certification fee: $2.00 per doc, exemplification is $7.00 plus $1.00 per page. Payee: Circuit Clerk. Personal checks and credit cards accepted. Visa credit/debit not accepted in person. There is 2.95% surcharge, with $2.00 minimum surcharge. Prepayment required. Mail requests: SASE required or else send postage amt.

Civil Name Search: Access: Phone, fax, mail, online, in person. Both court and visitors may perform in person name searches. Search fee: $2.00 per name per year. A written confirmation of search is $7.00 plus $1.00 per page. Civil records on computer since 1987, on microfiche since early 1900s. Some records on docket books. Note: For an additional $10.00, request will be expedited within 48 hours. Mail turnaround time 5-10 days. Public use terminal has civil records back to 1987. Access records index free at http://199.241.8.125/index.cfm?FuseAction=PublicRecords.Home. Online records back to 1988 can be searched by name, case number or citation number.

Circuit Court - Felony PO Box 2767, Titusville, FL 32781-2767; 321-637-2004; fax: 321-264-5246; 8AM-5PM (EST). *Felony.*

http://199.241.8.125/

General Information: Online identifiers in results same as on public terminal. No juvenile, child abuse, sexual battery or adoption records released. Will fax documents $2.00 per order if long distance. Court makes copy: $1.00 per page. Self serve copy: same. Certification fee: $2.00 per doc, exemplification is $7.00 plus $1.00 per page. Payee: Circuit Clerk. Personal checks and credit cards accepted. Visa credit/debit not accepted in person. There is 2.95% surcharge, with $2.00 minimum surcharge. Prepayment required. Mail requests: SASE required or else send postage amt.

Criminal Name Search: Access: Phone, fax, mail, online, in person. Both court and visitors may perform in person name searches. Search fee: $2.00 per name per year. A written confirmation of search is $7.00 plus $1.00 per page. Required to search: name, DOB. Criminal records on computer since 1989, on microfiche from early 1900s. Some records on docket books. Note: For an additional $10.00, request will be expedited within 48 hours. Mail turnaround time 5-10 days. Public use terminal has crim records back to 1989. Access index free at http://199.241.8.125/index.cfm?FuseAction=PublicRecords.Home. Online records back to 1989 can be searched by name, case number or citation number. Online results show middle initial, DOB.

County Court - Misdemeanor PO Box 2767, 700 S Park Ave, Bldg B, Titusville, FL 32781; 321-637-5413; fax: 321-264-5246; 8AM-5PM (EST). *Misdemeanor.*

http://199.241.8.125/

General Information: Online identifiers in results same as on public terminal. No juvenile, child abuse, sexual battery or adoption records released. Will fax documents $2.00 per doc long distance; no charge to fax out to 321 local area code. Court makes copy: $1.00 per page. Certification fee: $2.00 per doc, exemplification is $7.00 plus $1.00 per page. Payee: Brevard County Clerk. Personal checks and credit cards accepted. Visa credit/debit not accepted in person. There is 2.95% surcharge, with $2.00 minimum surcharge. Prepayment required. Mail requests: SASE required or else send postage amt.

Criminal Name Search: Access: Phone, fax, mail, online, in person. Both court and visitors may perform in person name searches. Search fee: $2.00 per name per year. A written confirmation of search is $7.00 plus $1.00 per page. Required to search: name, years to search, DOB. Criminal records on computer since 1991, on microfiche from early 1900s. Note: For an additional $10.00, request will be expedited within 48 hours. Mail turnaround time up to 10 days; phone turnaround 1-10 days. Public use terminal has crim records back to 1989. Access records index free at http://webinfo4.brevardclerk.us/facts/facts_search.cfm. Online records back to 1989 can be searched by name, case number or citation number. Online results show middle initial, DOB.

Broward County

Circuit & County Courts 201 SE 6th St, Ft Lauderdale, FL 33301; 954-831-6565; criminal phone: 954-831-6565; civil phone: 954-831-7196 Circuit CT; County civil- 831-5622; probate phone: 954-831-7154; criminal fax: 954-831-5661; civil fax: 954-831-6565; 8AM-4:30PM (EST). *Felony, Misdemeanor, Civil, Eviction, Small Claims, Probate.*

www.clerk-17th-flcourts.org/ClerkWebsite/welcome2.aspx

General Information: Civil circuit- Rm 230; civil- Rm 120; Misd Dept- Rm 130; Probate- Rm 252. The Correspondence Clerk handles searches. There is a free dial-up case records system (Chips) for phone access to case files; case # or name required- 954-712-7899. Court makes copy: $1.00 per page. Certification fee: $2.00; Exemplification is- $7.00 each. Payee: Clerk of the Court. Only cashiers checks and money orders accepted. No credit cards accepted. Prepayment required.

Civil Name Search: Access: Phone, mail, online, in person. Both court and visitors may perform in person name searches. Search fee: $2.00 per

name per year. Add $4.00 for written response (affidavit). Written requests may be submitted to Rm 230 for Circuit Civil; use Rm 120 for County Ct Civil Div searches. Civil records on computer from 1986. Will search back 10 years. Note: Chips free dial-up system is 954-712-7899; civil- x5; probate- x4. Mail turnaround time 1-14 days. Civil PAT goes back to 2003. Address sometimes appears on results. Basic information is free at www.clerk-17th-flcourts.org/BCCOC2/Pubsearch/CaseSearch.aspx.
Search by name, case number or case type. There is also a premium case subscription service available to registered users and free to one-time users. Direct email record requests to eclerk@browardclerk.org.
Criminal Name Search: Access: Mail, online, in person, email. Both court and visitors may perform in person name searches. Search fee: $2.00 per name per year. Add $4.00 for written response (affidavit). Required to search: name, years to search, DOB. Criminal records on computer since 1980. Note: Requests can be made in writing at #160 Central Courthouse. Mail turnaround time 1-14 days. Criminal PAT goes back to 2003. 3 public terminals available in Rm 230. Address sometimes appears on results. Basic information free at www.clerk-17th-flcourts.org/BCCOC2/Pubsearch/CaseSearch.aspx. Search by name, case number or case type. Also, there is a "Premium Access" for detailed case information; requires a fee, registration and password. Call 954-831-5654 for information or visit the website. Also, direct email record requests to eclerk@browardclerk.org. Online results show middle initial, DOB.

Calhoun County

Circuit & County Court 20859 E Central Ave, #130, Blountstown, FL 32424; 850-674-4545; fax: 850-674-5553; 8AM-4PM (CST). *Felony, Misdemeanor, Civil, Eviction, Small Claims, Probate.*
https://www.myfloridacounty.com/ori/index.do
General Information: No juvenile, child abuse or sexual battery records released. Will not fax documents. Court makes copy: $.15 per page. Certification fee: $3.00. Cert fee includes copy fee. Payee: Clerk of Court. Personal checks and credit cards accepted. Prepayment required. Mail requests: SASE required.
Civil Name Search: Access: Phone, mail, in person, online. Both court and visitors may perform in person name searches. Search fee: $7.00 per name. Civil records on computer back to 1986, books from 1970s. Mail turnaround time 2 days. Access an index of judgments (not dockets) is at www.myfloridacounty.com. Fees involved to order copies; save $1.50 per record by becoming a subscriber.
Criminal Name Search: Access: Phone, mail, in person. Both court and visitors may perform in person name searches. Search fee: $7.00 per name. Criminal records computerized from 1986, on docket books from 1970s. Mail turnaround time 2 days.

Charlotte County

Circuit & County Courts - Civil Division 350 E Marion Ave, Justice Center, Civil Dept., Punta Gorda, FL 33950; 941-505-4751 rec ctr; 941-639-3111; civil phone: 941-637-2113; probate phone: 941-637-2210; fax: 941-637-2159; 8AM-5PM (EST). *Civil, Eviction, Small Claims, Probate.*
http://co.charlotte.fl.us/clrkinfo/clerk_default.htm
General Information: County Court phone- 941-637-2261. There is also a Murdock Annex in Port Charlotte. No juvenile, child abuse, sexual battery, adoption records released. Will fax documents for $2.00 fee, 15 page limit. Court makes copy: $1.00 per page. Certification fee: $2.00 per doc plus copy fee; Exemplification fee $6.00. Payee: Clerk of Circuit Court. Personal checks accepted. Visa/MC accepted; 3.5% transaction fee added. Prepayment required. Mail requests: SASE requested.
Civil Name Search: Access: Phone, fax, mail, in person, online. Both court and visitors may perform in person name searches. Search fee: $2.00 per name per year. Civil records on computer back to 1982, on microfiche since 1987. Mail turnaround time 1-2 days. Public use terminal has civil records back to 1982 countywide. Public terminals located on 1st Fl and in Murdock Ofc. Not all terminal results show a DOB or an address. Access civil court records free at https://courts.co.charlotte.fl.us/benchmarkweb/default.aspx. Also, access an index of judgments, liens, recorded documents at www.myfloridacounty.com fees for copies.

Circuit & County Courts - Criminal Division 350 E Marion Ave, Punta Gorda, FL 33951-1687; 941-637-2269; fax: 941-637-2159; 8AM-5PM (EST). *Felony, Misdemeanor, Traffic.*
http://co.charlotte.fl.us/clrkinfo/clerk_default.htm
General Information: No juvenile, child abuse or sexual battery records released. Fee to fax out file $2.00 per page. Court makes copy: $1.00 per page. Self serve copy: same. Certification fee: $2.00 plus copy fee. Payee: Clerk of Circuit Court. Personal checks accepted. Visa/MC accepted. Prepayment required.
Criminal Name Search: Access: Phone, mail, in person, online. Both court and visitors may perform in person name searches. Search fee: $2.00

per name per year. Required to search: name, years to search, DOB; also helpful: address, SSN, race, sex. Criminal records on computer since 1985, misdemeanors on index cards, felonies on judgment books, imaging on disc from 1993. Mail turnaround time 1 week. Public use terminal has crim records back to 1985. Terminal results include SSN. Access index free at https://www.co.charlotte.fl.us/scripts/mgrqispi.dll?appname=MPI%20Criminal&prgname=PUBSEARCHF. Name only required to search. Online results show name, DOB.

Citrus County

Circuit Court 110 N Apopka, Rm 101, Inverness, FL 34450-4299; 352-341-6400; fax: 352-341-6413; 8AM-5PM (EST). *Felony, Civil Actions over $15,000, Probate.*
www.clerk.citrus.fl.us/nws/home.jsp?section=1&item=1
General Information: Marriage license data is found online at the website. Online identifiers in results same as on public terminal. No juvenile, adoption, child abuse or sexual battery records released. Will fax documents $1.00 per page if local; $2.00 per page long distance. Court makes copy: $1.00 per page. Certification fee: $2.00 plus copy fee. Payee: Clerk of Circuit Court. Personal checks and credit cards accepted. Prepayment required. Mail requests: SASE required.
Civil Name Search: Access: Phone, fax, mail, in person, online. Both court and visitors may perform in person name searches. Search fee: $2.00 per name per year. Required to search: name, years to search; also helpful: address. Indicate on search request type of cases to search. Civil records on computer from 1989, archived from 1940 to 1991. Some records on docket books. By phone only back to 1989. Mail turnaround time 1-2 days. Civil PAT goes back to 1989. View court record index (no images) free at http://search.clerk.citrus.fl.us/courts/login.asp; Subscription system giving full identifiers also available. Also there is an index of judgments, liens, recorded documents at www.myfloridacounty.com. Fees involved to order copies; save $2.00 per record by becoming a subscriber.
Criminal Name Search: Access: Phone, fax, mail, in person, online. Both court and visitors may perform in person name searches. Search fee: $2.00 per name per year; $7.00 if for exemplification. Required to search: name, years to search, DOB; also helpful: address, SSN, race, sex. Criminal records computerized from 1989, on microfiche from 1948 to 1987, archived from 1940-1991. Note: By phone only back to 1989. Mail turnaround time 1 week. Criminal PAT goes back to same as civil. View court record index (no images) free at www.clerk.citrus.fl.us/courts/search. Also, see www.clerk.citrus.fl.us/nws/home.jsp?section=1&item=17 for a subscription system giving full address and DOB identifiers also available.

County Court 110 N Apopka, Rm 101, Inverness, FL 34450; 352-341-6400; fax: 352-341-6413; 8AM-5PM (EST). *Misdemeanor, Civil Actions under $15,000, Eviction, Small Claims.*
www.clerk.citrus.fl.us/nws/home.jsp?section=1&item=1
General Information: Online identifiers in results same as on public terminal. No juvenile, child abuse or sexual battery records released. Will fax documents $1.00 per page; $2.00 per page for long distance. Court makes copy: $1.00 per page. Certification fee: $2.00 per cert. Payee: Clerk of Circuit Court. Personal checks and credit cards accepted. Prepayment required. Mail requests: SASE required.
Civil Name Search: Access: Phone, fax, mail, in person, online. Both court and visitors may perform in person name searches. Search fee: $2.00 per name per year. Required to search: name, years to search; also helpful: address. Civil records on computer from 1990, prior records on docket books. Mail turnaround time 1-3 days. Civil PAT goes back to 1990. View court record index (no images) free at http://search.clerk.citrus.fl.us/courts/login.asp; Subscription system with identifiers also available. Free index search does not give DOB or full address, subscription system does. Access an index of judgments, liens, recorded documents at www.myfloridacounty.com/services/officialrecords_intro.shtml; Fees involved to order copies; save $1.50 per record by becoming a subscriber.
Criminal Name Search: Access: Phone, fax, mail, in person, online. Both court and visitors may perform in person name searches. Search fee: $2.00 per name per year. Required to search: name, years to search, DOB; also helpful: address, SSN, race, sex. Criminal records computerized from 1990, prior records on docket books. Mail turnaround time 1-3 days. Criminal PAT goes back to same as civil. Results may include address. View court record index (no images) free at www.clerk.citrus.fl.us/home.jsp; Subscription system with identifiers also available. Free index search does not give DOB or full address, subscription system does.

Clay County

Circuit Court PO Box 698, Green Cove Springs, FL 32043; 904-284-6302; probate phone: ext 6516; fax: 904-284-6390; 8:30AM-4:30PM (EST). *Felony, Civil Actions over $15,000, Probate.*
www.clayclerk.com/

General Information: Online identifiers in results same as on public terminal. No juvenile, child abuse or sexual battery records released. Will fax documents upon payment. Court makes copy: $1.00 per page. Certification fee: $2.00; exemplification is $7.00 plus $1.00 ea add'l page. Payee: Clerk of Circuit Court. Cash, cashiers checks and money orders accepted. Major credit cards accepted. Prepayment required. Mail requests: SASE required.

Civil Name Search: Access: Mail, in person, online. Both court and visitors may perform in person name searches. Search fee: $2.00 per name per year. Required to search: name, years to search; also helpful: address. Civil records on computer from 6/5/1958, prior records on docket books. Mail turnaround time 1-3 days. Public use terminal available, records go back to 1983. Clerk of the circuit court provides free access to record index of civil actions and judgments at http://clayclerk.com/OdysseyPA/default.aspx. Also, from an approved vendor, access an index of judgments, liens, recorded documents at www.myfloridacounty.com. Fees involved to order copies; save $1.50 per record by becoming a subscriber.

Criminal Name Search: Access: Mail, in person, online. Both court and visitors may perform in person name searches. Search fee: $1.00 per name per year. $6.00 for clerk certification. Required to search: name, years to search, DOB; also helpful: address, SSN, race, sex. Criminal records (felony) on microfilm in recording department from 1958, 1970-1985 case files, prior records on docket books. Mail turnaround time 1-2 days. Public use terminal available. Access to criminal record index is free at www.clayclerk.com/Search/default.html. There is a separate search for the index of microfilm records of misdemeanor and felony cases between 1978 and 1998.

County Court PO Box 698, 825 N Orange, Green Cove Springs, FL 32043; 904-284-6316; criminal phone: 904-284-6302 x6699; civil phone: 904-278-3695; criminal fax: 904-278-3670; civil fax: 8:30AM-4:30PM; 8:30AM-4:30PM (EST). *Misdemeanor, Civil Actions under $15,000, Eviction, Small Claims.*

http://clayclerk.com/default.html

General Information: Online identifiers in results same as on public terminal. No juvenile, child abuse or sexual battery records released. Fee to fax out file $1.00 per page. Court makes copy: $1.00 per page. Certification fee: $2.00 per cert plus copy fee. Payee: Clerk of Circuit Court. No personal checks accepted. Credit cards accepted; $2.50 convenience fee applies. Prepayment required. Mail requests: SASE required.

Civil Name Search: Access: Mail, in person, online. Both court and visitors may perform in person name searches. Search fee: $2.00 per name per year. $6.00 for 3 years if search is pre-1986. Required to search: name, years to search; also helpful: address. Civil records on computer back to 1986, prior records on docket books. Mail turnaround time 1-2 days. Civil PAT goes back to 1980s. Access civil records back to 1992 free at http://clayclerk.com/OdysseyPA/default.aspx. Also, access an index of judgments, liens, recorded documents at www.myfloridacounty.com. Fees involved to order copies; save $1.50 per record by becoming a subscriber.

Criminal Name Search: Access: Mail, in person, online. Both court and visitors may perform in person name searches. Search fee: $7.00 per name per three years searched and $2.00 for additional years. Required to search: name, years to search, DOB, SSN; also helpful: address, race, sex. Criminal records computerized from 1992, prior records on docket books. Mail turnaround time 1 week. Criminal PAT goes back to same as civil. Access criminal records free at http://clayclerk.com/OdysseyPA/default.aspx. Online results show middle initial, DOB.

Collier County

Circuit & County Court 3301 Tamiami Trail East, Courthouse Annex, Naples, FL 34112; 239-252-2646; 8AM-5PM (EST). *Felony, Misdemenaor, Civil, Probate, Eviction, Small Claims.*
www.collierclerk.com/

General Information: Civil on 3rd Fl in annex; criminal on 4th Fl in annex. No sealed by court or statute records released. Will not fax out documents. Court makes copy: $1.00 per page. Certification fee: $2.00 per doc. Payee: Clerk of Circuit Court. Personal checks accepted. No credit cards accepted. Prepayment required. Mail requests: SASE required.

Civil Name Search: Access: Mail, in person, online. Both court and visitors may perform in person name searches. Search fee: $2.00 per name per year. Civil records on computer from 1990, on microfiche 1922 to 2006. Mail turnaround time within 1 week. Civil PAT goes back to 1988. Public access terminal is on the 1st Fl of courthouse. Some records may show SSN. Online access is free at www.collierclerk.com/RecordsSearch/CourtRecords. Records include probate, traffic and domestic. Search dockets at www.collierclerk.com/RecordsSearch/Dockets. Data is viewable only, no printing. Access an index of judgments, liens, recorded documents at www.myfloridacounty.com. Fees involved to order copies; save $1.50 per record by becoming a subscriber.

Criminal Name Search: Access: Phone, mail, online, in person. Both court and visitors may perform in person name searches. Search fee: $2.00 per name per year. Required to search: name, years to search, DOB; also helpful: SSN, add your phone number. Criminal records computerized from 1988, microfiche from 1922 to 2003 (2004 for misdemeanor), archived from 1922. Note: Clerk often refers full background check requests to the County Sheriff's Ofc. Mail turnaround time within 1 week. Criminal PAT goes back to same as civil. Public access terminal is on the 1st Fl of courthouse and 1st Fl of annex. Search the criminal record index at http://apps.collierclerk.com/public_inquiry/Search.aspx. Data is viewable only, no printing. Online results show name only.

Columbia County

Circuit & County Courts PO Drawer 2069, Lake City, FL 32056; 386-719-7403; criminal phone: 386-758-1164; civil phone: 386-758-1036; probate phone: 386-758-1054; fax: 386-719-7539; 8AM-5PM (EST). *Felony, Misdemeanor, Civil, Eviction, Small Claims, Probate.*
www.columbiaclerk.com/

General Information: Online identifiers in results same as on public terminal. No names of victims of sex related offenses, juveniles, incompetence or mental health records released. Fee to fax out file $3.00 per page. Court makes copy: $1.00 per page. Self serve copy: same. Certification fee: $2.00 per cert; $700 for exemplification. Payee: Clerk of Circuit Court. Cashiers check or money order only. Major credit cards accepted. Prepayment required. Mail requests: SASE required for civil.

Civil Name Search: Access: Mail, in person, online. Both court and visitors may perform in person name searches. Search fee: $2.00 per name per year per department. Civil records on computer from 1990, archived from 1800s. DOB and SSN also helpful for searching. Mail turnaround time 48 hours. Civil PAT goes back to 1990. Access to County Clerk of Circuit Court records is at https://www2.myfloridacounty.com/ccm/?county=12

Criminal Name Search: Access: In person, online. Both court and visitors may perform in person name searches. Search fee: $2.00 per name per year per department. Required to search: name, years to search, DOB; SSN helpful. Criminal records computerized from 1989, archived from 1800s. Criminal PAT goes back to 1989. Access to County Clerk of Circuit Court felony, misdemeanor, and traffic records is at https://www2.myfloridacounty.com/ccm/?county=12

Dade County - See Miami-Dade County

De Soto County

Circuit & County Courts 115 E Oak St, Arcadia, FL 34266; criminal phone: 863-993-4876; civil phone: 863-993-4878; probate phone: 863-993-4878; fax: 863-993-4669; 8:30AM-4:30PM (EST). *Felony, Misdemeanor, Civil, Eviction, Small Claims, Probate.*
www.desotoclerk.com

General Information: For misdemeanor record call 863-993-4880. County Court & Evictions 863-993-4880. Probate fax is same as main fax number. Online identifiers in results same as on public terminal. No juvenile or sex related records released. Will fax documents $1.00 per page. Court makes copy: $1.00 per page. Self serve copy: same. Certification fee: $2.00 per cert. Payee: Clerk of the Court. Personal checks accepted. Visa/MC/AmEx accepted. Prepayment required. Mail requests: SASE requested.

Civil Name Search: Access: Mail, in person, online. Both court and visitors may perform in person name searches. Search fee: $2.00 per name per year. Civil records on computer from 1986, on microfiche from 1974, archived from 1887. Note: The County Civil Court settles disputes for cases that exceed $5,000 but do not exceed $15,000. Mail turnaround time 2 days. Civil PAT goes back to 1984. Free access to civil information, marriage/divorce, small claims, traffic/parking, Muni ordinances, domestic relations, name changes, foreclosures from 1980 to present at www.desotoclerk.com. Also, access an index of judgments, liens, recorded documents at www.myfloridacounty.com. Fees involved to order copies; save $1.50 per record by becoming a subscriber.

Criminal Name Search: Access: Mail, in person, online. Both court and visitors may perform in person name searches. Search fee: $2.00 per name per year. Required to search: name, years to search, DOB; also helpful: SSN, aliases. Criminal records on computer since 1986, archived since 1887. Mail turnaround time 2 days. Criminal PAT goes back to same as civil. Terminal results include SSN. Traffic Criminal cases are free at www.desotoclerk.com/dpa/cvweb.asp. Online results show middle initial, DOB.

Dixie County

Circuit & County Courts PO Drawer 1206, Cross City, FL 32628-1206; 352-498-1200; fax: 352-498-1201; 8:30AM-5:30PM (EST). *Felony, Misdemeanor, Civil, Eviction, Small Claims, Probate.*
https://www.myfloridacounty.com/ori/index.do

General Information: No juvenile, child abuse or sexual battery records released. Fee to fax out file $1.00 per page. Court makes copy: $1.00 per page. Certification fee: $1.50 per doc. Payee: Clerk of Circuit Court. Personal checks accepted. No credit cards accepted at present time. Prepayment required. Mail requests: SASE required.

Civil Name Search: Access: Mail, in person, online. Only the court performs in person name searches; visitors may not. Search fee: $1.50 per name per year. Required to search: name, years to search; also helpful: address. Civil records on computer since 1987, archived to 1920's. Mail turnaround time 1 week. Access to County Clerk of Circuit Court records is at https://www2.myfloridacounty.com/ccm/?county=15

Criminal Name Search: Access: Mail, in person, online. Only the court performs in person name searches; visitors may not. Search fee: $1.50 per name per year. Required to search: name, years to search, DOB; also helpful: address, SSN, race, sex. Criminal records on computer since 1989, archived to 1920's. Mail turnaround time 1 week. Access to index of felony, misdemeanor and traffic records is at https://www2.myfloridacounty.com/ccm/?county=12.

Duval County

Circuit & County Courts - Civil Division 330 E Bay St, 2nd Fl Copy Center, M103, Jacksonville, FL 32202; 904-630-1276; civil phone: 904-630-2031; probate phone: 904-630-2053; fax: 904-630-7506; 8AM-5PM (EST). *Civil, Eviction, Small Claims, Probate.* www.duvalclerk.com/ccWebsite/

General Information: Direct search requests to the Copy Center; phone number given above. Separate search fee for each court, and for each division. County civil clerk phone- 904-630-2045. Fax is for Circuit Court Clerk. Probate is Rm #101, probate fax- 904-630-0493. Online identifiers in results same as on public terminal. No juvenile, child abuse or sexual battery records released. Will fax documents for $1.00 per page fee. Court makes copy: $1.00 per page. Certification fee: $2.00 per doc plus copy fee. Payee: Clerk of Circuit Court. Business checks accepted. Major credit cards except AmEx accepted; a 3.5% transaction fee applies. Prepayment required. Mail requests: SASE required.

Civil Name Search: Access: Mail, online, in person. Both court and visitors may perform in person name searches. Search fee: $2.00 per name per year. Required to search: name, years to search; also helpful: address. Civil records (Circuit) on computer from 1968, county from 1984. County civil on index books from 1975 to 1986, prior on docket books. Circuit civil o. Mail turnaround time 2-4 days. Public use terminal has civil records back to 1968. Two sources are available. Access records to 1986 free at https://showcase.duvalclerk.com/Login.aspx?ReturnUrl=%2fDefault.aspx. Login is Public, password is Public. Also, access an index of judgments, liens, recorded documents at https://www.myfloridacounty.com/. Fees involved to order copies; save $1.50 per record by becoming a subscriber.

Circuit & County Courts - Criminal Division Attn: Copy Center, 330 E Bay St, Rm M101, Jacksonville, FL 32202; 904-630-1276 Copy Ctr; 904-630-2065 felony; fax: 904-630-1115; 8AM-5PM (EST). *Felony, Misdemeanor.* www.duvalclerk.com/ccWebsite/

General Information: Direct search requests to the Copy Center, or alternatively make a search request to the County Sheriff Office (JSO) Records Dept at 501 E Bay St, or phone 904-630-2209; search fee is $5.00. Online identifiers in results same as on public terminal. No juvenile, child abuse or sexual battery records released. Will not fax documents. Court makes copy: $1.00 per page. Certification fee: $2.00 per doc. Payee: Clerk of the Court. Business checks accepted. Major credit cards except AmEx accepted; a $2.50 courtesy fee applies. Prepayment required. Mail requests: SASE helpful.

Criminal Name Search: Access: Mail, in person, online. Visitors must perform in person searches themselves. Search fee: $2.00 per name, per year, per court. Required to search: name, years to search, DOB; also helpful: address, SSN, race, sex. Criminal records computerized from 1986, prior records must be searched manually. Note: Search request must be in writing. Court sometimes recommends to contact JSO Records. Mail turnaround time 2-3 days. Public use terminal has crim records back to 1988. Not all court records have correct names or DOBs. Access court records free at https://showcase.duvalclerk.com/Login.aspx?ReturnUrl=%2fDefault.aspx. Login is Public, password is Public. Online results show name, DOB.

Escambia County

Circuit & County Courts - Civil Division PO Box 333, 190 Governmental Ctr, Pensacola, FL 32591-0333; 850-595-4170; civil phone: 850-595-4130 (Circ Ct. Civil); probate phone: 850-595-4300; fax: 850-595-4176; 8AM-5PM (CST). *Civil, Eviction, Small Claims, Probate.* www.escambiaclerk.com/clerk/index.aspx

General Information: Archive Dept. performs searches. No juvenile, child abuse, adoption, mental health or sexual battery records released. Will fax documents $1.10 per page if local, $1.25 per page long distance. Court makes copy: $1.00 per page. Certification fee: $2.00 per page. Payee: Clerk of

Circuit Court. Personal checks accepted. Credit cards accepted. Prepayment required. Mail requests: SASE requested for civil.

Civil Name Search: Access: Phone, fax, mail, in person, online. Both court and visitors may perform in person name searches. Search fee: $1.50 per year per name. $6.00 for cover letter response (no record found, etc.). Required to search: name, years to search; also helpful: address. County civil records on computer from mid 1986; Circuit Court civil on computer from mid 1987. Prior on index books. Judgments/small claims on microfilm. Mail turnaround time 1-5 days. Public use terminal has civil records back to 1986. Online access to county clerk records is free at http://public.escambiaclerk.com/xml/xml_web_1a.asp. Search by name, citation, or case number. Small claims, traffic, and marriage data also available. Access an index of judgments, liens, recorded documents at www.myfloridacounty.com. Fees involved to order copies; save $1.50 per record by becoming a subscriber.

Circuit & County Courts - Criminal Division 190 Governmental Ctr, Pensacola, FL 32501; 850-595-4150; criminal phone: 850-595-4185 County; fax: 850-595-4198; 8AM-5PM (CST). *Felony, Misdemeanor.* www.escambiaclerk.com/clerk/index.aspx

General Information: Misdemeanor records phone is 850-595-4185. Online identifiers in results same as on public terminal. No juvenile, child abuse, mental health, adoption or sexual battery records released. Will fax documents $1.00 per page plus $1.25 phone charge. Court makes copy: $1.00 per page. Self serve copy: same. Certification fee: $2.00; Exemplification fee- $7.00. Payee: Clerk of Circuit Court. Personal checks accepted. Credit cards accepted by phone. Prepayment required.

Criminal Name Search: Access: Fax, mail, in person, online. Both court and visitors may perform in person name searches. Search fee: $2.00 per name per year. Required to search: name, years to search, DOB; also helpful: address, SSN, race, sex. Criminal records on computer and microfiche from 1973, archived from 1940 to 1972. Note: Court will provide documents by email if requested. Mail turnaround time within 1 week. Public use terminal has crim records back to 1984. Online access to felony, criminal traffic and municipal ordinance records is free at http://public.escambiaclerk.com/xml/xml_web_1a.asp. Search by name, citation, or case number. Online results show middle initial, DOB.

Flagler County

Circuit & County Courts Attn: Records Management, 1769 E Moody Blvd., Bldg. 1, Bunnell, FL 32110; 386-313-4380; criminal phone: 386-313-4472; civil phone: 386-313-4495 (Circ), 386-313-4483 (Cty); probate phone: 386-313-4486; criminal fax: 8:30AM-5PM; civil fax: 8:30AM-5PM; 8:30AM-5PM (EST). *Felony, Misdemeanor, Civil, Eviction, Small Claims, Probate.* www.flaglerclerk.com/

General Information: Direct search requests to Records Management; Records Mgmt fax is above. The criminal court department fax is-386-437-2681. Misdemeanor phone- 386-313-4476. No juvenile, adoption, child abuse or sexual battery records released. Will fax documents $1.00 per page plus a fax usage fee. Court makes copy: $1.00 per page. Certification fee: $2.00 per doc. Payee: Clerk of Court. Local business checks, money orders, or cashiers checks accepted. Major credit cards accepted with form; 3.5% courtesy fee applies. Prepayment required. Mail requests: SASE required.

Civil Name Search: Access: Mail, in person, email. Both court and visitors may perform in person name searches. Search fee: $2.00 per name per year. Required to search: name, years to search; also helpful: address. Civil records on computer from 1990. All archived from 1917, some on index books. Mail turnaround time 2-7 days. Civil PAT goes back to 1990. Terminal results show year of birth. Access clerk's civil records free at www.flaglerclerk.com/courtrecords.htm. Also, access an index of judgments, liens, recorded documents at www.myfloridacounty.com. Fees involved to order copies. Also, you may email record requests to rmlo@flaglerclerk.com.

Criminal Name Search: Access: ail, in person, email. Both court and visitors may perform in person name searches. Search fee: $2.00 per name per year. Required to search: name, years to search, DOB; also helpful: address, SSN, race, sex. Felony records on computer back to 1999; misdemeanors back to 1988. All archived from 1917, some on index books. Note: Email record requests to rmld@flaglerclerk.com Mail turnaround time 2-7 days. Criminal PAT goes back to 1999 felony; 1988 misdemeanor. Terminal results show year of birth. Access clerk's criminal records free at www.flaglerclerk.com/courtrecords.htm. Also, you may email record requests to rmlo@flaglerclerk.com. Online results show middle initial, DOB.

Franklin County

Circuit & County Courts 33 Market St, #203, Apalachicola, FL 32320; 850-653-8861; criminal phone: x166 or x107; civil phone: x106 or x149; probate phone: x106; fax: 850-653-2261; 8:30AM-4:30PM (EST). *Felony, Misdemeanor, Civil, Eviction, Small Claims, Probate.* www.franklinclerk.com

General Information: Probate is a separate index at this courthouse. Probate fax is same as main fax number. No juvenile, child abuse or sexual battery records released. Will fax documents if prepaid. Court makes copy: $1.00 per page. Self serve copy: same. Certification fee: $2.00 plus copy fee. Payee: Clerk of Circuit Court. In county personal checks accepted. No credit cards accepted. Prepayment required. Mail requests: SASE requested.

Civil Name Search: Access: Mail, in person, online. Both court and visitors may perform in person name searches. Search fee: $2.00 per name per year. Required to search: name, years to search; also helpful: address. Civil records on computer from 3/92. Mail turnaround time 2-5 days. Civil PAT goes back to 1992. Access index and records free at https://www2.myfloridacounty.com/ccm/?county=19. Circuit goes back to 3/1997; County to 10/1998; Probate back to 2/1982. Also, access an index of judgments with other recorded documents at https://www3.myfloridacounty.com/official_records/index.html. Fees involved to order copies; save $1.50 per record by becoming a subscriber.

Criminal Name Search: Access: Mail, in person, online. Both court and visitors may perform in person name searches. Search fee: $2.00 per name per year. Required to search: name, years to search, DOB; also helpful: address, race, sex. Criminal records on computer since 1989. Mail turnaround time 2-5 days. Criminal PAT goes back to 1989. Access index and records free at https://www2.myfloridacounty.com/ccm/?county=19. Felony goes back to 3/4/1984; Misdemeanors back to 8/18/1978. Also, access criminal records by subscription at https://www.myfloridacounty.com/subscription/. Fees are involved.

Gadsden County

Circuit & County Courts - Criminal Division 10 E Jefferson, Quincy, FL 32351; 850-875-8601; fax: 850-875-7265; 8:30AM-5PM (EST). *Felony, Misdemeanor.*
www.leoncountyfl.gov/2ndCircuit/
General Information: Requests may be sent to PO Box 1649, ZIP is 32353. Email addresses are Felony@gadsdenclerk.com and Misdemeanor@gadsdenclerk.com. The misdemeanor department fax is 850-875-4083 No juvenile or sex offender records released. Will fax documents $1.00 per page. Court makes copy: $.25 per page. Certification fee: $2.00 per doc. Payee: Clerk of Circuit Court. Personal checks accepted. Visa/MC, Discover accepted. Prepayment required.
Criminal Name Search: Access: Mail, in person, online. Both court and visitors may perform in person name searches. Search fee: $2.00 per name per year. Required to search: name, years to search, DOB; also helpful: SSN. Criminal records computerized from 1984, some on index books and cards. Mail turnaround time 3-5 days. Public use terminal has crim records back to 2000. The index of criminal and traffic case files is free to view at www.gadsdenclerk.com/unifiedcourtweb/.

Circuit & County Courts - Civil Division PO Box 1649, 10 E Jefferson St, Quincy, FL 32353; 850-875-8601; civil phone: x231; probate phone: 850-875-8601 x232; fax: 850-627-6925; 8:30AM-5PM (EST). *Civil, Eviction, Small Claims, Probate.*
www.gadsdenclerk.com/
General Information: Extension 246 is County Civil Clerk- Marsha Moore; fax-850-875-3253. No juvenile, child abuse or sexual battery records released. Will fax documents $1.00 per page. Court makes copy: $1.00 per page for official. Self serve copy: same. Certification fee: $2.00 per certification. Payee: Clerk of Circuit Court. Only cashiers checks and money orders accepted. Major credit cards accepted; photo ID required. Prepayment required. Mail requests: SASE required.
Civil Name Search: Access: Phone, fax, mail, in person, online, email. Both court and visitors may perform in person name searches. Search fee: $2.00 per name, per yr. Civil records on computer since 1985. Mail turnaround time 1 week. Public use terminal has civil records back to 1985. Search for judgments only on the Official Records Index. The index of civil court judgments is free to view from the County Clerk at www.gadsdenclerk.com/unifiedcourtweb/. Also, subscription access an index of judgments, liens, recorded documents at www.myfloridacounty.com. Fees involved to order copies; save $1.50 per record by becoming a subscriber.

Gilchrist County

Circuit & County Courts PO Box 37, Trenton, FL 32693; 352-463-3170; fax: 352-463-3166; 8:30AM-5PM (EST). *Felony, Misdemeanor, Civil, Eviction, Small Claims, Probate.*
www.gilchristclerk.com/
General Information: No juvenile, child abuse or sexual battery records released. Will fax documents $1.00 per page; available for civil only. Court makes copy: $1.00 per page. Self serve copy: same. Certification fee: $2.00. Payee: Clerk of Circuit Court. Personal checks and credit cards accepted. Prepayment required. Mail requests: SASE required.

Civil Name Search: Access: Mail, in person, online. Only the court performs in person name searches; visitors may not. Search fee: $2.00 per name per year. Required to search: name, years to search; also helpful: address. Civil records on computer from 1987, prior on index books. Mail turnaround time 2-3 days. Search judgments and liens online at http://records.gilchrist.fl.us/oncoreweb/. Access to County Clerk of Circuit Court records is at https://www2.myfloridacounty.com/ccm/?county=21
Criminal Name Search: Access: Mail, in person, online. Only the court performs in person name searches; visitors may not. Search fee: $2.00 per name per year. Required to search: name, years to search, DOB; also helpful: address, SSN, race, sex. Criminal records on computer since 1989, prior on index books. Mail turnaround time 2-3 days. Access to County Clerk of Circuit Court records is at https://www2.myfloridacounty.com/ccm/?county=12

Glades County

Circuit & County Courts PO Box 10, 500 Avenue J, Moore Haven, FL 33471; 863-946-6011; fax: 863-946-0560; 8AM-5PM (EST). *Felony, Misdemeanor, Civil, Eviction, Small Claims, Probate.*
www.gladesclerk.com/
General Information: Probate is separate index at this same address. Probate fax is same as main fax number. No juvenile, child abuse or sexual battery records released. Will fax documents $3.00 per page. Court makes copy: $1.00 per page. Self serve copy: same. Certification fee: $2.00 per doc plus copy fee. Payee: Clerk of Circuit Court. Personal checks and credit cards accepted. Prepayment required. Mail requests: SASE required.
Civil Name Search: Access: Mail, in person, online. Only the court performs in person name searches; visitors may not. Search fee: $2.00 per name per year. Required to search: name, years to search; also helpful: address. Civil records on computer from 1991. Mail turnaround time 2-3 days. Access an index of judgments only available at www.myfloridacounty.com. Fees involved to order copies; save $1.50 per record by becoming a subscriber.
Criminal Name Search: Access: Mail, in person. Only the court performs in person name searches; visitors may not. Search fee: $2.00 per name per year. Required to search: name, years to search, DOB; also helpful: address, SSN, race, sex. Criminal records computerized from 1991. Mail turnaround time 2-3 days.

Gulf County

Circuit & County Courts 1000 Cecil Costin Blvd, Port St Joe, FL 32456; 850-229-6112; fax: 850-229-6174; 9AM-5PM (EST). *Felony, Misdemeanor, Civil, Eviction, Small Claims, Probate.*
www.gulfclerk.com
General Information: No juvenile, adoption, child abuse or sexual battery records released. Will fax documents $1.50 per page. Court makes copy: $1.00 per page. Certification fee: $2.00 per cert. Payee: Clerk of Circuit Court. Personal checks and credit cards accepted. Prepayment required. Mail requests: SASE requested.
Civil Name Search: Access: Fax, mail, in person, online. Only the court performs in person name searches; visitors may not. Search fee: $2.00 per name per year. Civil records on computer from 1990; archived to 1925. Mail turnaround time 1-3 days. Access an index of judgments (not dockets) is at www.myfloridacounty.com. Fees involved to order copies; save $1.50 per record by becoming a subscriber.
Criminal Name Search: Access: Fax, mail, in person. Only the court performs in person name searches; visitors may not. Search fee: $2.00 per name per year. Required to search: name, years to search, DOB; also helpful: SSN. Criminal records computerized from 1990; archived to 1925. Mail turnaround time 1-3 days.

Hamilton County

Circuit & County Courts 207 NE 1st St, #106, Jasper, FL 32052; 386-792-1288; fax: 386-792-3524; 8:30AM-4:30PM (EST). *Felony, Misdemeanor, Civil, Eviction, Small Claims, Probate.*
General Information: No juvenile, child abuse or sexual battery records released. Will fax documents $2.00 per page. Court makes copy: $1.00 per page. Self serve copy: same. Certification fee: $2.00 per cert. Payee: Clerk of Circuit Court. No personal checks. Major credit cards accepted, but only in person. Prepayment required. Mail requests: SASE requested.
Civil Name Search: Access: Mail, in person, online. Both court and visitors may perform in person name searches. Search fee: $2.00 per name per year. Required to search: name, years to search; also helpful: address. Civil records on computer from 1/91, county civil from 3/91. Mail turnaround time 2-3 days. Access an index of judgments (not dockets) is at www.myfloridacounty.com. Fees involved to order copies; save $1.50 per record by becoming a subscriber.
Criminal Name Search: Access: Mail, in person. Both court and visitors may perform in person name searches. Search fee: $2.00 per name per year. Required to search: name, years to search, DOB; also helpful: address,

SSN, race, sex. Criminal records on computer since 1/89. Mail turnaround time 2-3 days.

Hardee County

Circuit & County Courts PO Drawer 1749, Wauchula, FL 33873-1749; 863-773-4174; fax: 863-773-4422; 8AM-12; 1PM-5PM (EST). *Felony, Misdemeanor, Civil, Eviction, Small Claims, Probate.*
www.hardeeclerk.com/

General Information: No juvenile, child abuse or sexual battery records released. Fee to fax out file $1.00 per page. Court makes copy: $1.00 per page. Certification fee: $2.00 per instrument. Exemplification fee is $7.00. Payee: B Hugh Bradley, Clerk of Court. Business checks accepted. Cash, money orders, cashier checks. Visa/MC accepted. Prepayment required. Mail requests: SASE requested.

Civil Name Search: Access: Mail, in person, online. Both court and visitors may perform in person name searches. Search fee: $2.00 per name per year per department. Required to search: name, years to search; also helpful: address. Civil records on computer from 1984. Note: Will accept email requests. Mail turnaround time 2 days. Access an index of judgments (not dockets) is at www.myfloridacounty.com. Fees involved to order copies; save $1.50 per record by becoming a subscriber.

Criminal Name Search: Access: Mail, in person. Only the court performs in person name searches; visitors may not. Search fee: $2.00 per name per year per department. Required to search: name, years to search, DOB; also helpful: address, race, sex. Criminal records computerized from 1984. Note: Will accept email requests. Mail turnaround time 3 days. same as civil.

Hendry County

Circuit & County Courts PO Box 1760, 25 E Hickpoochee Ave, LaBelle, FL 33975; 863-675-5369; criminal phone: 863-675-5214; civil phone: 863-675-5206; criminal fax: 863-612-4748; civil fax: 8:30AM-5PM; 8:30AM-5PM (EST). *Felony, Misdemeanor, Civil, Eviction, Small Claims, Probate.*
www.hendryclerk.org/

General Information: No juvenile, child abuse or sexual battery records released. Will fax documents to local or toll-free number. Court makes copy: $1.00 per page. Certification fee: $2.00 per cert. Payee: Clerk of Circuit Court. Cashiers checks and money orders accepted. Visa/MC accepted. Prepayment required. Pay as you go plan. Mail requests: SASE requested.

Civil Name Search: Access: Mail, fax, in person, online. Both court and visitors may perform in person name searches. Search fee: $2.00 per name per year plus cert fee. Required to search: name, years to search, DOB, SSN or DL, specify index to search; also helpful: address. Civil records on computer since 5/2000; on microfiche prior to 1989 if filed. Note: Fax search requests must include credit card payment. Mail turnaround time varies. Access an index of judgments (not dockets) is at www.myfloridacounty.com. Fees involved to order copies; save $1.50 per record by becoming a subscriber.

Criminal Name Search: Access: Mail, in person. Both court and visitors may perform in person name searches. Search fee: $2.00 per name per year plus cert fee. Required to search: name, years to search, DOB, SSN or DL, specify index to search; also helpful: address, race, sex. Misdemeanor records on computer since 1989, felony back to 1986; prior on microfiche. Mail turnaround time varies.

Hernando County

Circuit & County Courts 20 N Main St, Brooksville, FL 34601; 352-754-4201; criminal phone: 352-540-6444; civil phone: 352-540-6377; probate phone: 352-540-6366; fax: 352-754-4247; 8AM-5PM (EST). *Felony, Misdemeanor, Civil, Eviction, Small Claims, Probate.*
http://hernandoclerk.com/

General Information: Online identifiers in results same as on public terminal. No juvenile, child abuse or sexual battery records released. Will fax documents $1.25 per page, $1.00 if local. Court makes copy: $1.00 per page; public record copy printouts for criminal are $.15. Self serve copy: same. Certification fee: $2.00; an exemplification certificate is $7.00. Payee: Clerk of Circuit Court. Personal checks and credit cards accepted. Prepayment required.

Civil Name Search: Access: Mail, in person, online. Both court and visitors may perform in person name searches. Search fee: $2.00 per name per year. Civil records on computer from 1982, archived from late 1800s. Mail turnaround time approx. 5 days. Civil PAT goes back to 1983. Online access to court records is free at https://www2.myfloridacounty.com/ccm/do/personSearch?county=27. Online records may go as far back as 1/1983. Searchable online record index for court records often does not provide identifiers and addresses. Fees involved to order copies; save $1.50 per record by becoming a subscriber.

Criminal Name Search: Access: Mail, online, in person. Both court and visitors may perform in person name searches. Search fee: $2.00 per name

per year. Required to search: name, years to search, DOB; also helpful: SSN. Criminal records computerized from 1982, archived from late 1800s. Index and docket information is available for felony and misdemeanor records. Mail turnaround time approx. 5 days. Criminal PAT goes back to same as civil. Online access to court records is free at https://www2.myfloridacounty.com/ccm/do/personSearch?county=27. Online records may go as far back as 1/1983. Searchable online record index for court records often does not provide identifiers and addresses.

Highlands County

Circuit & County Courts 430 S Commerce Ave, Sebring, FL 33870-3867; 863-402-6595; criminal phone: 863-402-6594; civil phone: 863-402-6591; fax: 863-402-6575; 8AM-5PM (EST). *Felony, Misdemeanor, Civil, Eviction, Small Claims, Probate.*
www.hcclerk.org/Home.aspx

General Information: Probate fax- 863-402-6903. No juvenile, child abuse or sexual battery records released. Will fax documents $1.00 per page. Court makes copy: $1.00 per page. Certification fee: $2.00 plus copy fee. Payee: Clerk of Courts. Personal checks and credit cards accepted. Prepayment required.

Civil Name Search: Access: Mail, in person, online. Only the court performs in person name searches; visitors may not. Search fee: $2.00 per name per year. Civil records on computer since 1992, prior on microfiche and film. Mail turnaround time 1 week. Access to county clerk civil and probate records is free at www.hcclerk.org/Home/Search-Court-Records.aspx back to 1991. Also includes small claims, probate, and tax deeds. Access an index of judgments, liens, recorded documents at www.myfloridacounty.com. Fees involved to order copies; save $1.50 per record by becoming a subscriber.

Criminal Name Search: Access: Mail, in person, online. Only the court performs in person name searches; visitors may not. Search fee: $2.00 per name per year. Required to search: name, years to search; also helpful: SSN. Criminal records on computer since 1991, prior on microfiche and film. Mail turnaround time 1 week. Subscribe for access to court records at http://courts.hcclerk.org/iquery/. Online results show name, DOB.

Hillsborough County

Circuit & County Courts 800 E Twiggs, 1st Fl, Tampa, FL 33602; 813-276-8100; criminal phone: 813-276-8100 x4368; civil phone: 813-276-8100 x4382; fax: 813-276-8639; 8AM-5PM (EST). *Felony, Misdemeanor, Civil, Eviction, Small Claims, Probate.*
www.hillsclerk.com/publicweb/home.aspx

General Information: Fax number is for felony records department only. Direct extension to Felony (only) records clerk is x3986. No juvenile, child abuse or sexual battery records released. No fee to fax documents from felony Div. - others: fax account required. Court makes copy: $1.00 per page. Certification fee: $2.00 per cert. Payee: Clerk of Circuit Court. Local personal checks accepted. Visa/MC accepted. Prepayment required.

Civil Name Search: Access: Fax, mail, in person, online. Both court and visitors may perform in person name searches. Search fee: $2.00 per name per year. Required to search: name, years to search; also helpful: address. Civil records on computer since 5/85, prior on microfiche. Mail turnaround time 1-2 days. Civil PAT available. Online access to records at http://publicrecord.hillsclerk.com/. Searchable online record index for court records often does not provide identifiers and addresses. Also Progress Dockets free at http://publicrecord.hillsclerk.com/oridev/criminal_pack.ins. A subscription service is also available for records; visit home page for details/fees. Also, access index of judgments, liens, recorded documents at www.myfloridacounty.com. Fees involved to order copies; save $1.50 per record by becoming a subscriber.

Criminal Name Search: Access: Fax, mail, online, in person. Both court and visitors may perform in person name searches. Search fee: $2.00 per name per year. Required to search: name, years to search, DOB, SSN. Criminal records on computer since 1989, prior on microfiche to 1975, archived 1953 to 1974. Note: Felony records requests may be faxed or mailed to Donna Johnson, PO Box 1119, Tampa 33601, or visit felony recs office #202, 601 E Kennedy, County Center. Mail turnaround time 1-2 days. Criminal PAT available. Online access to Criminal Court Progress Dockets Search is same as civil.

Holmes County

Circuit & County Courts PO Box 397, 201 N Oklahoma St, Bonifay, FL 32425; 850-547-1100; criminal phone: x3; fax: 850-547-6630; 8AM-4PM (CST). *Felony, Misdemeanor, Civil, Eviction, Small Claims, Probate.*
https://www.myfloridacounty.com/ori/index.do

General Information: Online identifiers in results same as on public terminal. No juvenile, child abuse or sexual battery records released. Will fax documents $2.00 1st page, $1.00 each add'l. Court makes copy: $1.00 per page. Certification fee: $2.00 plus copy fee. Payee: Holmes County Clerk of Court. Personal checks accepted. Visa/MC accepted, a 3.5% processing fee is added. Prepayment required. Mail requests: SASE required.

Civil Name Search: Access: Mail, in person, online. Both court and visitors may perform in person name searches. Search fee: $2.00 per name per year. Required to search: name, years to search; also helpful: address. Civil records on computer from 10/91, archived from early 1900s. Mail turnaround time 1 week. Civil PAT goes back to 1983. Access to County Clerk of Circuit Court records is at https://www2.myfloridacounty.com/ccm/?county=30 Note that there is a disclaimer that states this search should not be used as an authoritative public record.

Criminal Name Search: Access: Mail, in person, online. Both court and visitors may perform in person name searches. Search fee: $2.00 per name per year. Required to search: name, years to search, DOB, aliases. Criminal records on computer since 1989, prior archived since early 1900s. Mail turnaround time 1 week. Criminal PAT goes back to same as civil. Online access to criminal is the same as civil, see above.

Indian River County

Circuit & County Courts PO Box 1028, Vero Beach, FL 32961; 772-770-5185; fax: 772-770-5008; 8:30AM-5PM (EST). *Felony, Misdemeanor, Civil, Eviction, Small Claims, Probate.*
www.clerk.indian-river.org

General Information: No juvenile, child abuse or sexual battery records released. Will not fax documents. Court makes copy: $1.00 per page. Certification fee: $2.00. Payee: Clerk of Circuit Court. Cashiers checks and money orders accepted. Credit cards accepted in person. Prepayment required. Mail requests: SASE helpful.

Civil Name Search: Access: Mail, in person, online. Both court and visitors may perform in person name searches. Search fee: $2.00 per name per year. Required to search: name, years to search; also helpful: address. Civil records on computer since 1984, prior on microfiche. Mail turnaround time 2 days. Civil PAT goes back to 1983. Free access to the index for civil, family, and probate is at http://public.indian-river.org/. Full access to court records is via the clerk's subscription service. Fee is $25.00 per month. For information about the fee access, call Gary at 772-567-8000 x1216.

Criminal Name Search: Access: Mail, in person, online. Both court and visitors may perform in person name searches. Search fee: $2.00 per name per year. Required to search: name, years to search, DOB; also helpful: address, SSN, race, sex. Criminal records on computer (Felony since 1986, Misdemeanor since 1983), both archived since 1925. Mail turnaround time 2 days. Criminal PAT goes back to same as civil. Free access to the index for criminal and traffic is at http://public.indian-river.org/. Full access to court records is via the clerk's subscription service. Fee is $25.00 per month For information about the fee access, call Gary at 772-567-8000 x1216. Online results show middle initial, DOB.

Jackson County

Circuit & County Courts PO Drawer 510, Marianna, FL 32447; 850-482-9552; fax: 850-482-7849; 8AM-4:30PM (CST). *Felony, Misdemeanor, Civil, Eviction, Small Claims, Probate.*
https://www.myfloridacounty.com/ori/index.do

General Information: Online identifiers in results same as on public terminal. No juvenile, child abuse or sexual battery records released. Will fax documents $3.00 1st page, $1.00 each add'l. Court makes copy: $1.00 per page. Self serve copy: same. Certification fee: $2.00. Payee: Clerk of Circuit Court. Personal checks accepted only if it is a local bank in Marianna. Credit cards accepted. Prepayment required. Mail requests: SASE helpful.

Civil Name Search: Access: Fax, mail, in person, online. Both court and visitors may perform in person name searches. Search fee: $2.00 per name per year. Required to search: name, years to search; also helpful: address. Civil records go back to 1900; computerized records go back to 1992. Mail turnaround time 1-5 days. Civil PAT goes back to 1992. Access an index of judgments (not dockets) is at www.myfloridacounty.com. Fees involved to order copies; save $1.50 per record by becoming a subscriber.

Criminal Name Search: Access: Fax, mail, in person. Both court and visitors may perform in person name searches. Search fee: $2.00 per name per year. Required to search: name, years to search, DOB; also helpful: address, SSN, race, sex. Criminal records go back to 1900; computerized records since 1989. Mail turnaround time 1-5 days. Criminal PAT goes back to same as civil.

Jefferson County

Circuit & County Courts ! Courthouse Circle, Monticello, FL 32344; 850-342-0218; criminal phone: x283; civil phone: x228; fax: 850-342-0222; 8AM-5PM (EST). *Felony, Misdemeanor, Civil, Eviction, Small Claims, Probate.*
www.jeffersonclerk.com/

General Information: No juvenile, child abuse or sexual battery records released. Fee to fax out file $2.00 per page. Court makes copy: $1.00 per page. Certification fee: $2.00. Payee: Clerk of Circuit Court. Personal checks

accepted. Visa/MC cards accepted in person, surcharges apply. Prepayment required.

Civil Name Search: Access: Mail, in person, online. Only the court performs in person name searches; visitors may not. Search fee: $2.00 per name per year. Required to search: name, years to search; also helpful: address. Civil records on computer since 7/90, prior on dockets. Mail turnaround time 1 week. Access to County Clerk of Circuit Court records is at https://www2.myfloridacounty.com/ccm/?county=33

Criminal Name Search: Access: Fax, mail, in person, online. Only the court performs in person name searches; visitors may not. Search fee: $2.00 per name per year. Required to search: name, years to search, DOB; also helpful: address, SSN, race, sex. Criminal records on computer since 1989, prior on microfiche from 1969 to 1980, archived since 1950s, prior to 1950 on dockets. Mail turnaround time 1 week. Online access to criminal same as civil.

Lafayette County

Circuit & County Courts PO Box 88, 120 W Main St, Mayo, FL 32066; 386-294-1600; fax: 386-294-4231; 8AM-5PM (EST). *Felony, Misdemeanor, Civil, Eviction, Small Claims, Probate.*
https://www.myfloridacounty.com/ori/index.do

General Information: No juvenile, child abuse or sexual battery records released. Court makes copy: $1.00 per page. Self serve copy: same. Certification fee: $2.00. Payee: Clerk of Circuit Court. Personal checks accepted. No credit cards accepted. Prepayment required. Mail requests: SASE required.

Civil Name Search: Access: Phone, mail, fax, in person, online. Both court and visitors may perform in person name searches. No search fee. Required to search: name, years to search; also helpful: address. Civil records on computer since 1997, on books back to early 1900s. Mail turnaround time 5-7 days. Public use terminal has civil records back to 11 years. Access an index of judgments (not dockets) is at www.myfloridacounty.com. Fees involved to order copies; save $1.50 per record by becoming a subscriber.

Criminal Name Search: Access: Phone, mail, fax, in person. Both court and visitors may perform in person name searches. Search fee: $2.00 per name per yr. Required to search: name, years to search, DOB; also helpful: address, SSN, race, sex. Criminal records computerized since 1989. Mail turnaround time 5-7 days. Online results show name, DOB.

Lake County

Circuit & County Courts PO Box 7800, 550 W Main St, Tavares, FL 32778; 352-742-4100; criminal phone: 352-742-4126(Felony) 352-742-4128(Misdemeanor); civil phone: 352-742-4148 County; 352-742-4145 Circuit; probate phone: 352-742-4122; fax: 352-742-4166; 8:30AM-5PM (EST). *Felony, Misdemeanor, Civil, Eviction, Small Claims, Probate.*
www.lakecountyclerk.org/

General Information: Expunged or sealed records not released. No mental health, juvenile, child abuse or sexual battery records released. Will fax documents $1.00 per page. Court makes copy: $1.00 per page. Certification fee: $2.00. Payee: Clerk of Circuit Court. Personal checks accepted. No credit cards accepted. Prepayment required. Mail requests: SASE helpful.

Civil Name Search: Access: Fax, mail, in person, online. Both court and visitors may perform in person name searches. Search fee: $2.00 per name per year. Civil records on computer since 1984, county civil on index books since 11/51, circuit civil since 1888. Mail turnaround time 7-10 days. Civil PAT goes back to 1985. Online access to court records free at web page. Civil records back to 1985; Circuit records back to 9/84. Also, previous 2-weeks civil records and divorces on a private site at http://extra.orlandosentinel.com/publicrecords/search.asp.

Criminal Name Search: Access: Fax, mail, in person, online. Both court and visitors may perform in person name searches. Search fee: $2.00 per name per year. Required to search: name, years to search, DOB; also helpful: SSN, sex. Criminal records on computer since 1989, archived since 1888. Some on index books. Mail turnaround time 7-10 days. Criminal PAT goes back to 01/01/1989. Online access is the same as civil, see above. Online results show middle initial.

Lee County

Circuit & County Courts PO Box 2507, Justice Ctr, 2nd Fl, Monroe & 2nd Sts, Ft Myers, FL 33902; 239-533-5000; criminal phone: x7 then x0; civil phone: x5;; 7:45AM-5PM (EST). *Felony, Misdemeanor, Civil, Eviction, Small Claims, Probate, Traffic.*
www.leeclerk.org

General Information: Mailing address for Civil Div is PO Box 310. A 2nd office is at Cape Coral Branch Office (Lee County Gov't Ctr): 1039 SE 9th Pl, Cape Coral, FL 33990, near Cape Coral City Hall. No juvenile, child abuse or sexual offense records released. Will not fax documents. Court makes copy: $1.00 per page. Certification fee: $2.00 per doc. Payee: Clerk of Circuit Court. Personal checks accepted. Credit cards accepted; $2.50 transaction fee added. Prepayment required. Mail requests: SASE required.

Civil Name Search: Access: Mail, in person, online. Both court and visitors may perform in person name searches. Search fee: $2.00 per name per year. Civil records on computer since 1988, prior on microfilm and dockets. Note: Civil Div mailing address is PO Box 310. Mail turnaround time 5 days. Civil PAT goes back to 1990. Access records free at www.leeclerk.org/court_inquiry_disclaimer.htm. Online records go back to 1988. Includes traffic, felony, misdemeanor, civil, small claims and probate. Access an index of judgments, liens, recorded documents at www.leeclerk.org or www.myfloridacounty.com. Search free but fees involved to order certified copies; save the per-record copy fee by becoming a subscriber; sub fee is $25.00 per month.

Criminal Name Search: Access: Mail, online, in person. Both court and visitors may perform in person name searches. Search fee: $2.00 per name per year. Required to search: name, years to search, DOB; also helpful: address, SSN, race, sex. Criminal records on computer-(Felony since 1978, Misdemeanor since 1986), prior on microfilm. Mail turnaround time 5 days. Criminal PAT goes back to same as civil. Access records free at www.leeclerk.org/court_inquiry_disclaimer.htm. Online records go back to 1988. Includes traffic, felony, misdemeanor, civil, small claims and probate. Online results show middle initial, DOB.

Leon County

Circuit & County Courts PO Box 726, Tallahassee, FL 32302; 850-577-4000; criminal phone: 850-577-4070; civil phone: 850-577-4170; probate phone: 850-577-4180; criminal fax: 850-577-8016; civil fax: 8AM-5PM; 8AM-5PM (EST). *Felony, Misdemeanor, Civil, Eviction, Small Claims, Probate.*
www.clerk.leon.fl.us

General Information: Address above is for felony cases. Misdemeanor at PO Box 105; Probate at PO Box 1024, both use 32302. No juvenile, child abuse or sexual battery records released. Will not fax documents. Court makes copy: $1.00 per page. Certification fee: $2.00 per doc. Payee: Clerk of Circuit Court. Personal checks and credit cards accepted. Prepayment required. Mail requests: SASE helpful.

Civil Name Search: Access: Mail, fax, online, in person. Both court and visitors may perform in person name searches. Search fee: $2.00 per name per year. Required to search: full name, years to search; also helpful: address, other identifiers. Civil records on computer since 8/86, prior on docket books. Note: All request must be in writing. Mail turnaround time 5 days. Public use terminal has civil records back to 1944. Includes traffic cases. No images shown. Search all types of civil and traffic cases free at http://cvweb.clerk.leon.fl.us/index.asp. Access an index of judgments, liens, recorded documents at www.myfloridacounty.com. Fees involved to order copies; save $1.50 per record by becoming a subscriber.

Criminal Name Search: Access: Mail, fax, in person. Both court and visitors may perform in person name searches. Search fee: $2.00 per name per year. Required to search: full name, years to search, DOB; also helpful: address, SSN, race, sex. Criminal records on computer since 1976, on microfiche since 1937, archived since late 1800s/early 1900s. Mail turnaround time 5 days. Terminal results may include add'l identifiers but no images. Traffic shown from 1944. Search traffic infraction cases free at http://cvweb.clerk.leon.fl.us/index.asp. Also access an inmate search at http://lcso.leonfl.org/jailinfo/inmate_search.asp. Criminal searching online is not available at publication time.

Levy County

Circuit & County Courts 355 S Courtstreet, Bronson, FL 32621; 352-486-5266; criminal phone: x256; civil phone: x238; probate phone: x241;; 8AM-5PM (EST). *Felony, Misdemeanor, Civil, Eviction, Small Claims, Probate.*
www.levyclerk.com

General Information: No juvenile, child abuse or sexual battery records released. Court makes copy: $1.00 per page. Self serve copy: same. Certification fee: $2.00. Payee: Clerk of Circuit Court. Business checks accepted. Credit cards accepted, there is a 3.5% service fee. Prepayment required. Mail requests: SASE required.

Civil Name Search: Access: Mail, in person, online. Both court and visitors may perform in person name searches. Search fee: $2.00 per name per year. Required to search: name, years to search; also helpful: address. Civil records on computer from 1986, microfiche to 1981 (in process), prior on docket books. Mail turnaround time 2-3 days. Public use terminal has civil records back to 1986. Judgments available on the Clerk of the Circuit Court Official Records Index free at http://oncore.levyclerk.com/oncoreweb/.

Criminal Name Search: Access: Mail, in person. Only the court performs in person name searches; visitors may not. Search fee: $2.00 per name per year. Required to search: name, years to search, DOB, signed release; also helpful: address, SSN, race, sex. Criminal records computerized from 1986 to present, prior on docket books. Mail turnaround time 2-3 days.

Liberty County

Circuit & County Courts PO Box 399, Bristol, FL 32321; 850-643-2215; fax: 850-643-2866; 8AM-5PM (EST). *Felony, Misdemeanor, Civil, Eviction, Small Claims, Probate.*
www.libertyclerk.com/

General Information: No juvenile, child abuse or sexual battery records released. Will fax documents to local or toll-free number. Court makes copy: $1.00 per page. Certification fee: $2.00. Payee: Clerk of Circuit Court. Business checks accepted. Major credit cards accepted. Prepayment required. Mail requests: SASE required.

Civil Name Search: Access: Mail, in person, online. Both court and visitors may perform in person name searches. Search fee: $2.00 per name per year. Required to search: name, years to search; also helpful: address. Civil index on docket books. Mail turnaround time 1 week. Civil PAT goes back to 2002. The docket index is available at https://www2.myfloridacounty.com/ccm/?county=39. Also, access an index of judgments with other recorded documents at https://www3.myfloridacounty.com/official_records/index.html. Fees involved to order copies; save $1.50 per record by becoming a subscriber.

Criminal Name Search: Access: Mail, in person, online. Both court and visitors may perform in person name searches. Search fee: $2.00 per name per year. Required to search: name, years to search, DOB; also helpful: address, SSN, race, sex. Criminal docket on books. Mail turnaround time 1 week. Criminal PAT goes back to 1998. The docket index is available at https://www2.myfloridacounty.com/ccm/?county=39.

Madison County

Circuit & County Courts PO Box 237, Madison, FL 32341; 850-973-1500; fax: 850-973-2059; 8AM-5PM (EST). *Felony, Misdemeanor, Civil, Eviction, Small Claims, Probate.*
www.madisonclerk.com/

General Information: No juvenile, child abuse or sexual battery records released. Will fax documents for $1.00 per page or flat rate of $2.00 for toll free calls. Court makes copy: $1.00 per page. Self serve copy: same. Certification fee: $2.00. Payee: Clerk of Circuit Court. Personal checks and credit cards accepted. Prepayment required. Mail requests: SASE requested.

Civil Name Search: Access: Phone, mail, in person, online. Both court and visitors may perform in person name searches. Search fee: $2.00 per name per year. Required to search: name, years to search; also helpful: address. Civil records on computer since 1990, prior on docket books. Mail turnaround time 1-3 days. Access an index of judgments (not dockets) is at www.myfloridacounty.com. Fees involved to order copies; save $1.50 per record by becoming a subscriber.

Criminal Name Search: Access: Phone, mail, in person. Both court and visitors may perform in person name searches. Search fee: $2.00 per name per year. Required to search: name, years to search, DOB; also helpful: address, SSN, race, sex. Criminal records on computer since 1988, prior on docket books. Mail turnaround time 1-3 days.

Miami-Dade County

Circuit & County Courts - Civil 73 W Flagler St, Miami, FL 33130; 305-275-1155; 9AM-4PM (EST). *Civil, Eviction, Small Claims, Probate.*
www.miami-dadeclerk.com/dadecoc/

General Information: Actual name is Dade County, but is better known as Miami-Dade County. No juvenile, adoption, mental health records releases. Will not fax documents. Court makes copy: $1.00 per page. Certification fee: $2.00 per cert. Payee: Clerk of Circuit & County Courts. Personal checks and money orders accepted. Credit cards accepted. Prepayment required. Mail requests: SASE requested.

Civil Name Search: Access: Mail, in person, online. Both court and visitors may perform in person name searches. Search fee: $2.00 per name per year. Civil and domestic relations cases indexed by plaintiff/petitioner, defendant/respondent. Civil and domestic relations records on computer back to 1984; archives from 1836; microfilm in county recorder office. Note: Order certified copies of court records from the web page. Mail turnaround time 10 days. Public use terminal has civil records back to 1984. Clerk of Court's online services- choose between Standard (free) and Premier fee-based services. Subscribers to the Premier service may access 3 advanced options: Civil/Family/Probate, Public Records, Traffic. Fees based on # of units purchased; minimum $5.00 in advance. Also, though limited, search felony, misdemeanor, civil and county ordinance violations free at www2.miami-dadeclerk.com/CJIS/CaseSearch.aspx.. Search Civil/Family/Probate free at www.miami-dadeclerk.com/dadecoc/.

Circuit & County Courts - Criminal 1351 NW 12th St, #9000, Miami, FL 33125; 305-275-1155; fax: 305-548-5526; 9AM-4PM (EST). *Felony, Misdemeanor.*
www.miami-dadeclerk.com/dadecoc/

General Information: Better known as Miami-Dade County. Although located in the same building, the records of the felony and the misdemeanor courts are not co-mingled. Search the Circuit Court for felony and the County Court for misdemeanor records. No juvenile, child abuse or sexual battery records released. Will not fax documents. Court makes copy: $1.00 per page. Certification fee: $7.00 per doc plus copy fee. Payee: Clerk of Circuit and County Court. Personal checks accepted. Credit cards accepted in person only. Prepayment required. Mail requests: SASE required.

Criminal Name Search: Access: Mail, online, in person. Both court and visitors may perform in person name searches. Search fee: $2.00 per year, per name. Required to search: name, years to search, DOB; also helpful: address, SSN, race, sex. Criminal records computerized from 1971, on microfiche from 1975, archived from 1836. Mail turnaround time 10-15 days. Public use terminal has crim records back to 1970. Race and sex also appear on terminal search results. Free and Premier fee-based online services available. Though limited, search felony, misdemeanor, civil and county ordinance violations free at www2.miami-dadeclerk.com/CJIS/CaseSearch.aspx. Subscribers to the Clerk's Premier Services may Access advanced options in 3 of the Clerk's internet-based systems: Civil/Family/Probate, Public Records, Traffic. Fee is $.25 per search, in advance. Also, search traffic cases free at www.miami-dadeclerk.com/spirit/publicsearch/defnamesearch.asp.

Manatee County

Circuit & County Courts PO Box 25400, Bradenton, FL 34206; 941-749-1800; criminal phone: 941-741-4019; civil phone: 941-741-4025; probate phone: 941-741-4021; criminal fax: 941-741-4082; civil fax: 8:30AM-5PM; 8:30AM-5PM (EST). *Felony, Misdemeanor, Civil, Eviction, Small Claims, Probate.*
www.manateeclerk.com

General Information: Probate fax- 941-741-4093. No juvenile, adoption, child abuse or sexual battery victim records released. Will fax documents $1.00 per page. Court makes copy: $1.00 per page. Self serve copy: same. Certification fee: $2.00. Payee: Clerk of Circuit Court. Personal checks accepted. Credit cards accepted. Prepayment required. Mail requests: SASE helpful.

Civil Name Search: Access: Phone, fax, mail, online, in person, email. Both court and visitors may perform in person name searches. Search fee: $2.00 per name per year. Required to search: name, years to search; also helpful: address. Civil records on computer since 9/80, prior on microfilm back to 1972. Mail turnaround time 2 days. Civil PAT goes back to 9/1980. Access public court record index at clerk's office free at www.manateeclerk.org. Pre-3/1/04 unavailable. Searchable online record index often does not provide identifiers, nor access to recent scanned images as hands-on does. Also, you may direct email record requests to lori.tolksdorf@manateeclerk.com. Access an index of judgments, liens, recorded documents at www.myfloridacounty.com. Fees involved to order copies; save $1.50 per record by becoming a subscriber.

Criminal Name Search: Access: Phone, fax, mail, online, in person, email. Both court and visitors may perform in person name searches. Search fee: $2.00 per name per year. Required to search: name, years to search, DOB; also helpful: address, charge, race, sex. Criminal records on computer since 1981, prior on docket books back to 1972. Mail turnaround time 2 days. Criminal PAT goes back to 1981. Access public court record index at clerk's office at www.manateeclerk.org. Pre-3/1/04 unavailable. Searchable online record index often does not provide identifiers, nor access to recent scanned images as hands-on does. Online results show name, DOB.

Marion County

Circuit & County Courts PO Box 1030, Ocala, FL 34478-1030; 352-671-5604; criminal phone: 352-671-5674; civil phone: 352-671-5610 (Circ); probate phone: 352-671-5658; fax: 352-671-5600; 8AM-5PM (EST). *Felony, Misdemeanor, Civil, Eviction, Small Claims, Probate, Traffic.*
www.marioncountyclerk.org/public/

General Information: No juvenile records released. Will fax documents to local or toll free line, otherwise fee involved. Court makes copy: $1.00 per page. Certification fee: $2.00 per cert; exemplification- $7.00. Payee: Clerk of Court. Personal checks accepted. In person or phone requester may use credit card, surcharge applies. Prepayment required. Mail requests: SASE requested.

Civil Name Search: Access: Fax, mail, in person, online. Both court and visitors may perform in person name searches. Search fee: $2.00 per name per year. Required to search: name, years to search; also helpful: address. Civil records on computer since 1983, on microfiche since 1958. Mail turnaround time 1-2 weeks. Civil PAT goes back to 1983. Online access to county clerk records is free at www.marioncountyclerk.org/public/index.cfm?Pg=casesearch. Click on 'Search Records Now.". Also, access an index of judgments, liens, recorded documents at www.myfloridacounty.com. Fees involved to order copies; save $1.50 per record by becoming a subscriber.

Criminal Name Search: Access: Fax, mail, in person, online. Both court and visitors may perform in person name searches. Search fee: $2.00 per name per year. Required to search: name, years to search, DOB; also helpful: address, SSN, race, sex. Criminal records since 1984, on microfiche from 1950 to 1979, prior on index cards. Misdemeanors since 1983, on microfiche from. Mail turnaround time 1-2 weeks. Criminal PAT goes back to same as civil. Online access to criminal same as civil. Felony, misdemeanor and traffic case information available since 1991. Online results show name, DOB.

Martin County

Circuit & County Courts 100 E Ocean Blvd, Stuart, FL 34994; 772-288-5576; criminal phone: 772-288-5536; civil phone: 772-288-5717; probate phone: 772-288-5540; criminal fax: 772-288-5548; civil fax: 8AM-5PM; 8AM-5PM (EST). *Felony, Misdemeanor, Civil, Eviction, Small Claims, Probate, Family, Domestic.*
http://clerk-web.martin.fl.us/ClerkWeb/

General Information: Probate fax- 772-221-2388 No juvenile, child abuse or sexual battery records released. Will fax documents $1.25 per page. Court makes copy: $1.00 per page. Certification fee: $2.00. Payee: Clerk of Circuit Court. Personal checks and credit cards accepted. Prepayment required. Mail requests: SASE required.

Civil Name Search: Access: Phone, fax, mail, online, in person. Both court and visitors may perform in person name searches. Search fee: $2.00 per name per year. Required to search: name, years to search; also helpful: address. Civil records on computer since 10/86, prior on microfiche, microfilm and archived. Mail turnaround time 1 week. Civil PAT goes back to 1984. Search all court records free at http://clerk-web.martin.fl.us/ClerkWeb/ccis_disclaimer.htm. Also includes small claims, recordings, other document types. Search online by name or SSN.

Criminal Name Search: Access: Phone, fax, mail, in person, online. Both court and visitors may perform in person name searches. Search fee: $2.00 per name per year prior to 1990. Required to search: name, years to search, DOB; also helpful: address, SSN. Criminal records on computer, felonies to 1986 (misdemeanors since 1985), on microfiche since 1956, prior on index cards/docket books. Mail turnaround time 1 week. Criminal PAT goes back to 1989. Search all court records free at http://clerk-web.martin.fl.us/ClerkWeb/ccis_disclaimer.htm. Search online by name or SSN. Online results include partial address, sex, race, alias. Online results show name only.

Monroe County

Circuit & County Courts Clerk of the Court, 500 Whitehead St, Key West, FL 33040; 305-294-4641 x2; criminal phone: 305-294-4641 x3512; civil phone: 305-294-3507; criminal fax: 305-295-3610; civil fax: 8:30AM-5PM; 8:30AM-5PM (EST). *Felony, Misdemeanor, Civil, Eviction, Small Claims, Probate.*
www.clerk-of-the-court.com/

General Information: Felony, misdemeanor, or civil are all separate searches. Felony clerk- Debbie Niles, phone- x3321; direct felony searches to Deb at main court address. Misdemeanor clerk fax-305-295-3610. Direct civil mail requests- Civil Div.- POB 1980, zip-33041. No juvenile, child abuse or sexual battery records released. Fee to fax out file $1.00 per page; not all departments will do so,. Court makes copy: $1.00 per page. Certification fee: $2.00 per doc. Payee: Clerk of Circuit Court. Personal checks accepted. No credit cards accepted. Prepayment required. Mail requests: SASE helpful.

Civil Name Search: Access: Mail, fax, in person, online. Both court and visitors may perform in person name searches. Search fee: $2.00 per name per year. Civil records on computer since 1983, on microfiche since 1972, prior on docket books. Some records purged after 2 years. Probate from 1972. Mail turnaround time 1-2 weeks. Civil PAT goes back to 1982. Online access to civil cases is free at www.clerk-of-the-court.com/searchCivilCases.asp. Subscription is required for viewing full document library. Also, search probate cases free at www.clerk-of-the-court.com/searchProbateCases.asp.

Criminal Name Search: Access: Mail, fax, in person, online. Both court and visitors may perform in person name searches. Search fee: $2.00 per name per year. Required to search: name, years to search, DOB, aliases; also helpful in felony search request: address, SSN last 4, sex. Criminal records (pending felony and misdemeanors) on computer, others since 1992, non-pending on microfiche since 1945. Mail turnaround time 1-2 weeks. Criminal PAT goes back to same as civil. Online access to criminal records is free at www.clerk-of-the-court.com/searchTrafficCriminalCases.asp. Includes traffic cases online. Subscription is required for viewing full document library. Online results show name, DOB.

Nassau County

Circuit & County Courts 76347 Veterans Way, Yulee, FL 32097; criminal phone: 904-548-4613; civil phone: 904-548-4606; probate phone: 904-548-4606; criminal fax: 904-548-4529; civil fax: 8:30AM-5PM; 8:30AM-5PM (EST). *Felony, Misdemeanor, Civil, Eviction, Small Claims, Probate, Family.*
www.nassauclerk.com
General Information: No juvenile, child abuse or sexual battery records released. Will fax documents to local or toll-free number. Court makes copy: $1.00 per page. Certification fee: $2.00. Payee: Clerk of Circuit Court. Personal checks accepted in person only with proper ID. Major credit cards accepted. Prepayment required. Mail requests: SASE required.
Civil Name Search: Access: Phone, fax, mail, in person, online. Only the court performs in person name searches; visitors may not. Search fee: $2.00 per name per year. Required to search: name, years to search; also helpful: address. Civil records on computer since 1989, on microfiche since 1984, prior on docket books. Mail turnaround time 1 week. Public use terminal has civil records. Civil judgments, etc. on the recording office PA terminal. Search civil cases free back to 1989 and perhaps earlier at www.nassauclerk.com/cocoa/cocoa.index.cfm. Access an index of judgments, sentences, county commitments, uniform state commitments, disposition notices and nolle prosequi only at www.myfloridacounty.com. Fees involved to order copies; save $1.50 per record by becoming a subscriber.
Criminal Name Search: Access: Phone, fax, mail, in person, online. Only the court performs in person name searches; visitors may not. Search fee: $2.00 per name per year. Required to search: name, years to search, DOB; also helpful: address, SSN, race, sex. Criminal records on computer since 1987, on microfiche since 1984, prior on docket books. Note: Past 10 years only can be done on the phone. Mail turnaround time 1 week. Search criminal and traffic cases free at www.nassauclerk.com/cocoa/cocoa.index.cfm

Okaloosa County

Circuit & County Courts 1250 N Eglin Pky, Shalimar, FL 32579; 850-651-7200; fax: 850-651-7230; 8AM-5PM (CST). *Felony, Misdemeanor, Civil, Eviction, Small Claims, Probate.*
www.clerkofcourts.cc
General Information: No juvenile, child abuse or sexual battery records released. Will fax documents $2.00 per page. Court makes copy: $1.00 per page. Certification fee: $2.00 per doc; exemplification is $7.00. Payee: Clerk of Circuit Court. Personal checks and credit cards accepted. Prepayment required. Mail requests: SASE required.
Civil Name Search: Access: Mail, in person, online. Both court and visitors may perform in person name searches. Search fee: $2.00 per year per name. Required to search: name, years to search; also helpful: address. Civil records on computer from 1/86; archives from 1915; prior on microfilm. Mail turnaround time 1 day. Civil PAT goes back to 6/1986. Civil record index search is free at http://benchmark.clerkofcourts.cc/Search.aspx. Records go back to 1/83. Search civil index by defendant or plaintiff, date, or file type. Also, access an index of judgments, liens, recorded documents back to 11/1986 at www.myfloridacounty.com. Fees involved to order copies; save $1.50 per record by becoming a subscriber.
Criminal Name Search: Access: Mail, online, in person. Both court and visitors may perform in person name searches. Search fee: $2.00 per year per name. Required to search: name, years to search, DOB; also helpful: address, SSN, race, sex. Criminal records computerized from 1/89; archives from 1915; prior on microfilm. Mail turnaround time 1 day to 1 week. Criminal PAT goes back to 1/1989. Personal identifiers can be shown, if on file. Limited criminal record docket is at http://benchmark.clerkofcourts.cc/Search.aspx. Online results show name only.

Okeechobee County

Circuit & County Courts Okeechobee County Judicial Center, 312 NW Third Street, Okeechobee, FL 34972; 863-763-2131; fax: 863-763-1258; 8:30AM-5PM (EST). *Felony, Misdemeanor, Civil, Eviction, Small Claims, Probate.*
www.clerk.co.okeechobee.fl.us/
General Information: No confidential, adoption, records released. Will fax documents for fee varying on number of pages sent, basically $.25 per page. Court makes copy: $1.00 per page. Certification fee: $2.00, if exemplified then $7.00. Payee: Sharon Roberson, Clerk of Circuit Court. Personal checks and credit cards accepted. Prepayment required. Mail requests: SASE required.
Civil Name Search: Access: Mail, in person, online. Both court and visitors may perform in person name searches. Search fee: $2.00 per name per year. Required to search: name, years to search; also helpful: address. Civil records on computer since 1990, on index cards from 1983 to 1989. Mail turnaround time 1 week. Civil PAT goes back to 1990. Index of judgments and recorded documents can be searched at

http://204.215.37.218/wb_or1/. Also, access to County Clerk of Circuit Court records is at https://www2.myfloridacounty.com/ccm/?county=47
Criminal Name Search: Access: Mail, in person, online. Both court and visitors may perform in person name searches. Search fee: $2.00 per name per year. Required to search: name, years to search, DOB; also helpful: address, SSN, race, sex. Criminal records on computer since 1989, on index cards from 1983 to 1988; docket books 1932 to 1982. Mail turnaround time 1 week. Criminal PAT goes back to 1989. Online access to criminal is same as civil.

Orange County

Circuit & County Courts PO Box 4994, 425 N Orange Ave, Rm 310, Orlando, FL 32801-1544; 407-836-2000; fax: 407-836-2225; 8AM-5PM (EST). *Felony, Misdemeanor, Civil, Eviction, Small Claims, Probate.*
http://myorangeclerk.com/enu/Pages/orange-county-clerk-of-court-home.aspx
General Information: Mail requests should use room numbers; civil circuit-310; civil county-350; crim circuit-210; crim county-250. No sex-related or adoption records released. Court makes copy: $1.00 per page. Certification fee: $2.00. Payee: Orange County Clerk of Courts. Personal checks accepted from Orange County only. No credit cards accepted. Prepayment required. Mail requests: SASE helpful.
Civil Name Search: Access: In person, online. Both court and visitors may perform in person name searches. Search fee: $2.00 per name per year. Civil records are on computer as follows: Circuit civil-1992; Domestic civil-1992; Probate-1993; Traffic-1980. Mail turnaround time 2 days. Civil PAT goes back to 2000. Public terminal available in Records Management Division. The free Myclerk Case Inquiry System is at http://myclerk.myorangeclerk.com/default.aspx. Civil and Probate records available. Also, only previous 2-weeks civil records on a private site at http://extra.orlandosentinel.com/publicrecords/search.asp.
Criminal Name Search: Access: Online, in person. Both court and visitors may perform in person name searches. Search fee: $2.00 per name per year. Required to search: name, years to search, DOB. Criminal records on computer go back to 1990; prior records go back to 1987. Mail turnaround time 2 days. Criminal PAT goes back to same as civil. Public terminal available in Records Management Division. Access criminal records free on the Myclerk Case Inquiry System at http://myclerk.myorangeclerk.com/default.aspx. Online results show name, DOB.

County Court #3 Clerk of Courts, 475 W Story Rd, Ocoee, FL 34761; 407-836-2007; criminal phone: 407-836-2066; civil phone: 407-836-2065; fax: 407-254-6841; 8AM-5PM (EST). *Misdemeanor, Civil Actions under $15,000, Eviction, Small Claims.*
http://myorangeclerk.com/
General Information: Incoming calls are handled by the Branch Call Center, which is very helpful. No sex related or adoption records released. Will not fax documents. Court makes copy: $1.00 per page. Certification fee: $2.00 per cert. Payee: Clerk of County Court. Personal checks accepted. No credit cards accepted. Prepayment required. Mail requests: SASE helpful.
Civil Name Search: Access: Mail, fax, online, in person. Both court and visitors may perform in person name searches. Search fee: $2.00 per name per year. Civil records go back to 1890; on computer back to 1990. All dockets are on microfilm or microfiche. Mail turnaround time 2 days depending on file availability. The free Myclerk Case Inquiry System is at http://myorangeclerk.com/criminal/iclerk_disclaimer.shtml. Civil and Probate records available. Also, previous 2-weeks civil records on a private site at http://extra.orlandosentinel.com/publicrecords/search.asp.
Criminal Name Search: Access: Mail, fax, online, in person. Both court and visitors may perform in person name searches. Search fee: $2.00 per name per year. Required to search: name, years to search, DOB; also helpful: SSN. Criminal records go back to 1890; on computer back to 1990. All dockets are on microfilm or microfiche. Mail turnaround time 2 days depending on file. Access criminal records free at http://myorangeclerk.com/criminal/iclerk_disclaimer.shtml. Online results show name, DOB.

County Court - Apopka Branch 1111 N Rock Springs Rd, Apopka, FL 32712; 407-836-2007; criminal phone: 407-836-2056; civil phone: 407-836-2065; fax: 407-254-1031; 8AM-5PM (EST). *Misdemeanor, Civil Actions under $15,000, Eviction, Small Claims.*
http://myorangeclerk.com/
General Information: No sex related or adoption records released. Court makes copy: $1.00 per page. Certification fee: $2.00. Payee: Clerk of County Court. Personal checks accepted for traffic only. Visa/MC accepted in person only. Prepayment required. Mail requests: SASE helpful.
Civil Name Search: Access: Mail, in person, online. Only the court performs in person name searches; visitors may not. Search fee: $2.00 per name per year. Pending civil records on computer. All dockets on microfilm or microfiche; some records on index cards. Mail turnaround time 2 days. The free Myclerk Case Inquiry System is at

http://myorangeclerk.com/criminal/iclerk_disclaimer.shtml. Civil and Probate records available. Also, previous 2-weeks civil records on a private site at http://extra.orlandosentinel.com/publicrecords/search.asp.

Criminal Name Search: Access: Mail, online, in person. Only the court performs in person name searches; visitors may not. Search fee: $2.00 per name per year. Required to search: name, years to search, DOB; also helpful: SSN. Criminal records (Pending) on computer. All dockets on microfilm or microfiche. Some records on index cards. Mail turnaround time 2 days. Access criminal records free on the Myclerk Case Inquiry System at http://myorangeclerk.com/criminal/iclerk_disclaimer.shtml. Online results show name, DOB.

County Court - Winter Park Branch 450 N Lakemont Ave, Winter Park, FL 32792; 407-836-2007; criminal phone: 407-836-2056; civil phone: 407-836-2065; fax: 407-836-0558; 8AM-5:30PM (EST). *Misdemeanor, Civil Actions under $15,000, Eviction, Small Claims.*
http://myorangeclerk.com/

General Information: No sex related or adoption records released. Will fax documents to local or toll-free number. Court makes copy: $1.00 per page. Certification fee: $2.00. Payee: Clerk of County Court. Only cashiers checks and money orders accepted. Major credit cards accepted in person only. Prepayment required. Mail requests: SASE helpful.

Civil Name Search: Access: Phone, mail, online, in person. Only the court performs in person name searches; visitors may not. Search fee: $2.00 per name per year. Civil records (Pending) on computer. All dockets on microfilm or microfiche. Mail turnaround time 2 days. The free Myclerk Case Inquiry System is at http://myorangeclerk.com/criminal/iclerk_disclaimer.shtml. Civil and Probate records available. Also, previous 2-weeks civil records on a private site at http://extra.orlandosentinel.com/publicrecords/search.asp.

Criminal Name Search: Access: Phone, mail, online, in person. Only the court performs in person name searches; visitors may not. Search fee: $2.00 per name per year. Required to search: name, years to search, DOB; also helpful: SSN. Criminal records (Pending) on computer. All dockets on microfilm or microfiche. Note: Results include address. Mail turnaround time 2 days. Access criminal records free on the Myclerk Case Inquiry System at http://myorangeclerk.com/criminal/iclerk_disclaimer.shtml. Online results show name, DOB.

Osceola County

Circuit Court - Civil 2 Courthouse Sq, Ste 2000, Kissimmee, FL 34741; 407-742-3500; 8:30AM-5PM (EST). *Civil Actions over $15,000, Probate.*
www.osceolaclerk.com/

General Information: Probate is at www.osceolaclerk.com/Probate.htm. No appeal records released. Will fax documents for $.50 per page. Court makes copy: $1.00 per page. Certification fee: $2.00 per cert; $7.00 if exemplified. Payee: Clerk of Court. Business checks accepted. Visa/MC accepted. Prepayment required. Mail requests: SASE required.

Civil Name Search: Access: Mail, in person, online. Both court and visitors may perform in person name searches. Search fee: $2.00 per name per year per division. Civil records on computer from 1990, on docket books from 1800s to 1990. Mail turnaround time 1-2 days. Public use terminal has civil records back to 1990. Online access to court records on the Clerk of Circuit Court database are free at http://198.140.240.34/pa/. Also, access an index of judgments, liens, recorded documents at www.myfloridacounty.com. Fees involved to order copies; save $1.50 per record by becoming a subscriber. Also, previous 2-weeks civil records on a private site at http://extra.orlandosentinel.com/publicrecords/search.asp.

Circuit & County Courts - Criminal Division 2 Courthouse Square, #2000, Kissimmee, FL 34741; 407-742-3566, 407-742-3500; fax: 407-742-3552; 8AM-5PM (EST). *Felony, Misdemeanor, Traffic.*
www.osceolaclerk.com

General Information: Misdemeanors fax 407-742-3563. No juvenile or sealed records released. Will fax documents for $.50 per page. Court makes copy: $1.00 per page. Certification fee: $2.00 per doc. Payee: Clerk of the Court. Business checks accepted. Credit cards except VISA accepted; a surcharge is added. Prepayment required. Mail requests: SASE requested.

Criminal Name Search: Access: Mail, in person, online. Both court and visitors may perform in person name searches. Search fee: $2.00 per name per year. Required to search: name, years to search, DOB, SSN. Criminal records computerized from 1990, on index since 1978, prior on docket books 1800s to 1978. Note: Both the court and visitors may perform in person searches as long as the case occurred 1990 or after. Mail turnaround time 1 week. Public use terminal has crim records back to 1990. The most reliable public terminal is in the Public Information Room, #2200. Online access to criminal records is free at www.osceolaclerkcourt.org/. Includes party index and case summary searching. Online results show name only.

County Court - Civil 2 Courthouse Sq, #2000, Kissimmee, FL 34741; 407-742-3500; civil phone: x3; fax: 407-742-3652; 8AM-5PM (EST). *Civil Actions under $5,000, Eviction, Small Claims, Family.*
www.osceolaclerk.com

General Information: No juvenile records released. Will fax documents back if payments complete. Court makes copy: $1.00 per page. Certification fee: $2.00 per doc plus copy fee. Payee: Clerk of Court. Local business checks accepted. No personal checks. Credit cards accepted in the office only, no mail or phone use. Prepayment required. Mail requests: SASE helpful.

Civil Name Search: Access: Mail, in person, online. Both court and visitors may perform in person name searches. Search fee: $2.00 per name per year per division. Civil records on computer from 1991, on index cards from 1972 to 1991, on docket books from 1800s to 1972. Mail turnaround time 1 week. Public use terminal has civil records back to 1990. Terminal is located on 2nd floor. Online access to court records on the Clerk of Circuit Court database are free at http://198.140.240.34/pa/ or www.osceolaclerkcourt.org.

Palm Beach County

Circuit Court - Civil Division PO Box 4667, 205 N Dixie Highway, Rm 3.2300, West Palm Beach, FL 33402; 561-355-2986; fax: 561-355-4643; 8AM-5PM (EST). *Civil Actions over $15,000.*
www.mypalmbeachclerk.com/

General Information: No juvenile, child abuse or sexual battery records released. Court makes copy: $1.00 per page. Certification fee: $2.00 per doc. Payee: Clerk and Comptroller. Personal checks accepted. Prepayment required. Mail requests: SASE required.

Civil Name Search: Access: Mail, in person, online. Both court and visitors may perform in person name searches. Search fee: $2.00 per exact name per year (mail requests accepted on at the Official Records Serv Section). Required to search: name, years to search; also helpful: address. Civil records (Circuit) on computer from 1982, prior records on microfiche and dockets. County on computer from 1987, prior on microfilm. Mail turnaround time 1 week. Public use terminal has civil records back to 2000. Access to the countywide online remote system is free. Civil index goes back to '88. Records also include probate, traffic and domestic. Also, civil records are free at http://courtcon.co.palm-beach.fl.us/pls/jiwp/ck_public_qry_main.cp_main_idx. Records include criminal and traffic.

Circuit & County Courts - Criminal Division PO Box 2906, 205 N Dixie Hwy, 3rd Fl, Rm 3.24, West Palm Beach, FL 33401; 561-355-2519; local toll free- 888-760-9167; fax: 561-355-3802; 8AM-5PM (EST). *Felony, Misdemeanor.*
www.mypalmbeachclerk.com/

General Information: Faxes can only be received from state agencies. Misdemeanor are in County Court, 2nd Fl, Rm 2.23. Mail address for Circuit Felony Division is PO Box 2906, 33402. County Court Misdemeanor mailing address is PO Box 3544. No juvenile, child abuse or sexual battery records released. Will not fax documents. Court makes copy: $1.00 per page. Certification fee: $2.00 per doc. Payee: Clerk and Comptroller. Personal checks accepted. Visa/MC accepted. Prepayment required. Mail requests: SASE required.

Criminal Name Search: Access: Phone, fax, mail, online, in person. Both court and visitors may perform in person name searches. Search fee: $2.00 per exact name per year. Required to search: name, years to search, DOB, aliases. Criminal records on computer & microfiche (some files) from 1970s, archived from 1920s. Mail turnaround time 5-7 days . Public use terminal has crim records back to varies by type. Includes microfiche and on-demand access. Access to the countywide criminal online system is available at www.mypalmbeachclerk.com/courtrecords.aspx. Record index available also includes civil, probate, traffic and domestic. Online results show middle initial, DOB.

County Court - Civil Division 205 N Dixie Hwy, West Palm Beach, FL 33402; 561-355-2500, records- 561-355-2932; fax: 561-355-6211; 8AM-5PM (EST). *Civil Actions under $15,000, Eviction, Small Claims.*
www.mypalmbeachclerk.com/

General Information: Direct mail requests to the Official Records Svcs Section, Rm 425 - for judgments and court paper searches. No juvenile, child abuse or sexual battery records released. Will not fax out documents. Records Services will expedite doc return by Fed Ex if prepaid. Court makes copy: $1.00 per page. Certification fee: $2.00 per doc. Payee: Clerk and Comptroller. Personal checks accepted. No credit cards accepted. Prepayment required. Mail requests: SASE required.

Civil Name Search: Access: Mail, in person, online. Both court and visitors may perform in person name searches. Search fee: $2.00 per exact name per year (mail requests accepted online). Required to search: name, years to search; also helpful: address. Civil records (Circuit) on computer from 1982, prior records on microfiche and dockets. County on computer from 1987, prior on microfilm. Mail turnaround time 1 week. Public use terminal has civil records back to 2000. Access to the civil record index back to 1988 is free at http://courtcon.co.palm-beach.fl.us/pls/jiwp/ck_public_qry_main.cp_main_idx. Records also include probate, traffic and domestic. Also the court offers a more detailed record, there is no fee per record, but a one-time registration fee is charged. Also downloadable civil and criminal reports are available for purchase.

Circuit Court - Probate Division PO Box 4667, 205 N Dixie Hwy, 3rd Fl, Rm 3.23, West Palm Beach, FL 33402; 561-355-2986; fax: 561-355-4643; 8AM-5PM (EST). *Probate.*
www.mypalmbeachclerk.com/probate.aspx
General Information: Access to the countywide court online system at http://courtcon.co.palm-beach.fl.us/pls/jiwp/ck_public_qry_main.cp_main_idx. Public access terminals in Rm 2.22 and File Rm 3.23 - probate records on terminal go back to 1990.

Pasco County

Circuit & County Courts - Civil Division 38053 Live Oak Ave, Dade City, FL 33523; 352-523-2411 x2211; probate phone: 352-523-2411 x2216; 8:30AM-5PM (EST). *Civil, Eviction, Small Claims, Probate.*
www.pascoclerk.com/
General Information: A branch court at West Pasco Judicial Ctr, 7530 Little Rd, New Port Richey, 34654. No adoption records released. Will not fax documents. Court makes copy: $1.00 per page. Certification fee: $2.00. Payee: Clerk of Court. Personal Florida checks and Attorney's offices personal checks accepted only. Major credit cards accepted; small fee added if you use credit card. Prepayment required.
Civil Name Search: Access: Mail, in person, online. Both court and visitors may perform in person name searches. Search fee: $2.00 per name per year. Civil records on computer from 1985, on docket cards and docket books from 1900s. Mail turnaround time 2-4 days. Public use terminal has civil records back to 3/1985. Results include aliases. Access court records free at www.pascoclerk.com/public-courts-svcs-info.asp. Also, access to County Clerk of Circuit Court records is at https://www2.myfloridacounty.com/ccm/?county=51

Circuit & County Courts - Criminal Division 38053 Live Oak Ave, Dade City, FL 33523-3894; 352-523-2411 x2200;; 8:30AM-5PM (EST). *Felony, Misdemeanor.*
www.pascoclerk.com/
General Information: Circuit Court at 727-847-2411 x 2200. A branch court at West Pasco Judicial Ctr, 7530 Little Rd, New Port Richey, 34654. No confidential, sealed or juvenile records released. Court makes copy: $1.00 per page. Certification fee: $2.00. Payee: Clerk of Courts. No out of state personal checks accepted. Major credit cards accepted, small surcharge is added. Prepayment required.
Criminal Name Search: Access: Mail, online, in person. Both court and visitors may perform in person name searches. Search fee: $2.00 per name per year. Required to search: name, years to search, address, DOB; also helpful: SSN. Criminal records on computer since 1979. Mail turnaround time 2-4 days. Public use terminal has crim records back to 1979. Access court records free at Access the criminal docket index at www.pascoclerk.com/public-courts-svcs-info.asp.
This online record index often does not provide identifiers or case info may be restricted, i.e. sexual offenses. Watch for insufficient case numbers. Also, access to County Clerk of Circuit Court records is at https://www2.myfloridacounty.com/ccm/?county=51 Online results show middle initial, DOB, address.

Pinellas County

Circuit Court - Criminal Criminal Justice Center, Circuit Court, 14250 49th St N, Clearwater, FL 34722; 727-464-7000 x3; fax: 727-464-7040; 8AM-5PM (EST). *Felony.* www.pinellasclerk.org
General Information: Online identifiers in results same as on public terminal. Will fax documents $1.00 per page. Court makes copy: $1.00 per page. Certification fee: $2.00 per doc plus copy fee. Payee: Clerk of Circuit Court. Personal checks accepted. Major credit cards accepted; $5 convenience fee is added. Prepayment required.
Criminal Name Search: Access: Fax, mail, online, in person. Both court and visitors may perform in person name searches. Search fee: $2.00 per name per year. Required to search: name, years to search, DOB. Criminal records computerized from 1977, on microfilm from 1912 to 1976, on docket books from 1912. Mail turnaround time 2 weeks. Public use terminal has crim records back to 1977. Access the clerk's criminal and other data free at https://pubtitles.co.pinellas.fl.us/login/loginx.jsp. Criminal index goes back to 1972. Subscription required for full access.

Circuit & County Courts - Civil Division 315 Court St, Rm170, Clearwater, FL 33756; 727-464-3267; probate phone: 727-464-3321; fax: 727-464-4070; 8AM-5PM (EST). *Civil, Eviction, Small Claims, Probate, Traffic.*
www.pinellasclerk.org

General Information: There are also branches in St Petersburg, 545 1st Ave N, and North County, 29582 US Hiway 19 N, Clearwater. Probate Court located at 315 Court St, Clearwater No adoption or juvenile records released. Will fax documents $1.00 per page. Court makes copy: $1.00 per page. Certification fee: $2.00 per doc plus copy fee. Payee: Clerk of the Court. Personal checks accepted. Major credit cards accepted; $5 convenience fee is added. Prepayment required. Mail requests: SASE helpful.
Civil Name Search: Access: Fax, mail, online, in person. Both court and visitors may perform in person name searches. Search fee: $2.00 per name per year. Civil records on computer from 1980, on microfiche from 1900s to 1982, older data in warehouse. Mail turnaround time 1 week. Public use terminal has civil records back to 1972. Access to the countywide civil system requires $60 fee plus $5.00 a month & $.05 per screen over 100. Index back to 1972. Includes probate & traffic records. Contact Sue Maskeny-727-464-3779. Also, access clerk's criminal & other data as a non-subscriber at https://pubtitles.co.pinellas.fl.us/login/loginx.jsp. Also, access index of judgments and recorded docs at www.myfloridacounty.com. Fees to order copies; subscribers save $1.50 per record.

County Court - Criminal Division 14250 49th St N, Clearwater, FL 34762; 727-464-7000 x3; fax: 727-464-7040; 8AM-5PM (EST). *Misdemeanor, Ordinances, Citations.*
www.pinellasclerk.org/aspInclude2/ASPInclude.asp?pageName=index.htm
General Information: Online identifiers in results same as on public terminal. No sealed or non-arrested case records released. Court makes copy: $1.00 per page. Certification fee: $2.00 per doc plus copy fee. Payee: Clerk of Courts. Personal checks accepted. Major credit cards accepted except Discover. Prepayment required.
Criminal Name Search: Access: Mail, online, in person. Both court and visitors may perform in person name searches. Search fee: $2.00 per name per year. Required to search: name, years to search; also helpful: address, DOB, SSN. Criminal records on computer since 10/77, prior on index books. Prior to 1993 on microfilm. Mail turnaround time 3-5 days. Public use terminal has crim records back to 1980. Access to the countywide criminal online system requires $60 fee plus $5.00 a month and $.05 per screen over 100. Criminal index goes back to 1972. Contact Sue Maskeny at 727-464-3779 for information. Also, you can access the clerk's criminal and other data as a free non-subscriber at https://pubtitles.co.pinellas.fl.us/login/loginx.jsp. Online results show middle initial, DOB.

Polk County

Circuit & County Courts - Felony Division PO Box 9000, Drawer CC-9, 255 N Broadway Ave, Bartow, FL 33830; 863-534-4462; fax: 863-534-4457; 8AM-5PM (EST). *Felony.*
www.polkcountyclerk.net/
General Information: No sex related cases, victims or child abuse released. Will not fax documents. Court makes copy: $1.00 per page. Self serve copy: same. Certification fee: $2.00 per page; Exemplified cert fee-$7.00. Payee: Clerk of Circuit Court. Personal checks accepted. Visa/MC accepted. Prepayment required. Mail requests: SASE required.
Criminal Name Search: Access: Phone, mail, in person, online. Both court and visitors may perform in person name searches. Search fee: $2.00 per name. Required to search: name, years to search, DOB. Criminal records on computer-felonies since 1977, misdemeanors purged periodically. Both on microfiche and archived since 1800s. Mail turnaround time varies. Indicate date on request when record is needed. Public use terminal has crim records back to 1977. Access to County Clerk of Circuit Court records is free at www.polkcountyclerk.net/. Criminal index goes back to 1991; Online record index may not provide addresses; in-person search at court only provides most recent address. Online results show middle initial.

Circuit Court - Civil Division PO Box 9000, Drawer CC-12, 255 N Broadway Ave, Bartow, FL 33831-9000; 863-534-4556; probate phone: 863-534-4478; fax: 863-534-4045; 8AM-5PM (EST). *Civil Actions over $15,000, Probate.*
www.polkcountyclerk.net/
General Information: No sex related cases, adoption, confidential, victims or child abuse records released. Will not fax out documents. Court makes copy: $1.00 per page. Certification fee: $2.00 per cert. Payee: Clerk of Court. Personal checks accepted. Major credit cards accepted in person only. Prepayment required. Mail requests: SASE required.
Civil Name Search: Access: Mail, Fax, online, in person. Both court and visitors may perform in person name searches. Search fee: $2.00 per name per year. Required to search: name, years to search; also helpful: DOB, SSN, address. Civil Records on computer since 1978; on microfiche from 1800s to 1978. Mail turnaround time 2-3 days. Public use terminal has civil records back to 1978, but not complete. Free online access to dockets at https://ori2.polk-county.net/ct_web1/search.asp. Searchable online record index does not provide addresses; in-person search at court will only provide most recent address. Also, access to County Clerk of

Circuit Court records is free at https://www2.myfloridacounty.com/ccm/?county=53.

Circuit & County Courts - Misdemeanor Division PO Box 9000, Drawer CC10, Bartow, FL 33831-9000; 863-534-4446; fax: 863-534-4137; 8AM-4:30PM (EST). *Misdemeanor, Traffic.*
www.polkcountyclerk.net
General Information: No sex related cases, victims or child abuse released. Will not fax documents. Court makes copy: $1.00 per page. Certification fee: $2.00 per cert. Payee: Clerk of Circuit Court. Personal checks accepted. Visa/MC accepted. Prepayment required. Mail requests: SASE required.
Criminal Name Search: Access: Mail, in person, online. Both court and visitors may perform in person name searches. Search fee: $7.00 per search. Required to search: name, years to search, DOB; also helpful: SSN. Criminal records on computer; felonies since 1977, misdemeanors purged periodically. Both on microfiche and archived since 1800s. Mail turnaround time varies. Indicate date on request when record is needed. Public use terminal has crim records back to 1977. Misdemeanor, traffic, and ordinance record indices are free at www.polkcountyclerk.net/RecordsSearch/CriminalRecords.aspx. Online record index may not provide addresses; in-person search at court only provides most recent address. Also, access is also available via a third party at https://www2.myfloridacounty.com/ccm/?county=53. Online results show middle initial, DOB.

County Court - Civil Division PO Box 9000, Drawer CC12, 255 N Broadway Ave, Bartow, FL 33830-9000; 863-534-4556; fax: 863-534-4045; 8AM-5PM (EST). *Civil Actions under $15,000, Eviction, Small Claims.*
www.polkcountyclerk.net
General Information: Online identifiers in results same as on public terminal. Will fax documents if you have an escrow account. Court makes copy: $1.00 per page. Certification fee: $2.00 per doc. Payee: Clerk of Court. Checks, cash, cashiers checks and money orders accepted. Visa/MC/Discover/AmEx accepted; add 3.5% to cover transaction cost. Prepayment required. Mail requests: SASE required.
Civil Name Search: Access: Fax, mail, online, in person. Both court and visitors may perform in person name searches. Search fee: $2.00 per name per year. Civil records on computer from 1983, on microfiche from 1961 to 1995. Mail turnaround time 2-3 days. Public use terminal has civil records back to 1983. Terminal located in Official records office. Access to County Clerk of Circuit Court records is at https://ori2.polk-county.net/ct_web1/search.asp.

Putnam County

Circuit & County Courts - Civil Division PO Box 758, 410 St Johns Ave (32177), Palatka, FL 32178; 386-329-7690 (Ccounty); 386-326-7620 (Circuit); civil phone: 386-329-0251; probate phone: 386-329-0251; fax: 386-329-0888; 8:30AM-5PM (EST). *Civil, Eviction, Small Claims, Probate.*
www.putnam-fl.com/coc/
General Information: No juvenile or incompetency records released. Fee to fax out file $1.00 1st page per page, $1.25 ea addl. Court makes copy: $.15 per page. Self serve copy: $.15 per page. Certification fee: $1.00 per certified copy. Payee: Putnam County Clerk of Court. Personal checks and credit cards accepted. Prepayment required. Mail requests: SASE requested.
Civil Name Search: Access: Mail, fax, in person, email, online. Both court and visitors may perform in person name searches. Search fee: $2.00 per name per year. Civil records on computer from 1984, on microfiche from 1973 to 1984, on index cards and docket books from 1900s to 1973. Mail turnaround time 2-3 days. Public use terminal has civil records back to 1984. Access to the countywide remote online system requires $400 setup fee and $40. monthly charge plus $.05 per minute over 20 hours. Civil records go back to 1984. System includes criminal and real property records. Contact Putnam County IT Dept at 386-329-0390 to register. Also, access a free index of dockets at https://www.putnam-fl.com/secure/public_menu.php

Circuit & County Courts - Criminal Division PO Box 758, Palatka, FL 32178; 386-326-7630; fax: 386-329-1223; 8:30AM-5PM (EST). *Felony, Misdemeanor.*
www.putnam-fl.com/coc/
General Information: Online identifiers in results same as on public terminal. No juvenile records released. Fee to fax out file $2.25 per page. Court makes copy: $1.00 per page. Self serve copy: $.15 per page. Certification fee: $2.50 per doc plus copy fee. Payee: Clerk of Circuit Court. Personal checks and credit cards accepted. Prepayment required. Mail requests: SASE required.
Criminal Name Search: Access: Mail, fax, in person, email, online. Both court and visitors may perform in person name searches. Search fee: $2.00 per name per year. Required to search: name, years to search; also helpful: DOB. Criminal records computerized from 1988, in files from 1930s to 1988.

Mail turnaround time 5-7 days. Public use terminal has crim records back to 1972. Access to the countywide criminal online system requires $400 setup fee and $40. monthly charge plus $.05 per minute over 20 hours. Criminal records go back to 1972. System includes civil and real property records. Contact 386-329-0390 to register. Access a free index of dockets at https://www.putnam-fl.com/secure/public_menu.php. Also, you may direct email criminal record requests to gailwillis@putnam-fl.us. Online results show name only.

Santa Rosa County

Circuit & County Courts - Civil Division PO Box 472, Milton, FL 32572; 850-981-5676 (Circuit); 981-5667 (County Civil); probate phone: 850-981-5584; fax: 850-983-1991; 8AM-4:30PM (CST). *Civil, Eviction, Small Claims, Probate.*
https://www.myfloridacounty.com/ori/index.do
General Information: Small claims at 850-981-5667, fax - 850-983.4627. No adoption records released. Will fax documents $2.00 per page. Court makes copy: $1.00 per page. Certification fee: $2.00 per instrument. Payee: Clerk of Courts. Personal checks accepted. Credit cards accepted. Prepayment required. Mail requests: SASE required.
Civil Name Search: Access: Fax, mail, in person, online. Both court and visitors may perform in person name searches. Search fee: $2.00 per name per year. Civil records (Circuit) on computer from 1990, archived and on docket books from 1900s. County on computer from 1989, on microfiche from 1900s, on doc. Mail turnaround time ASAP. Public use terminal has civil records back to 1991. Access to County Clerk of Circuit Court records is at https://www2.myfloridacounty.com/ccm/?county=57

Circuit & County Courts - Criminal Division PO Box 472, 6865 Caroline St (32570), Milton, FL 32572; 850-981-5577/5579; fax: 850-626-0346; 8AM-4:30PM (CST). *Felony, Misdemeanor.*
www.santarosaclerk.com
General Information: Misdemeanor phone number is 850-981-5561. No records released before sentencing. Fee to fax out file $2.00 per page. Court makes copy: $1.00 per page. Certification fee: $2.00 per page. Payee: Clerk's Office (include Division/Department name). Personal checks accepted. Credit cards accepted. Prepayment required. Mail requests: SASE required.
Criminal Name Search: Access: Mail, fax, in person, online. Both court and visitors may perform in person name searches. Search fee: $2.00 per name per year. Required to search: name, years to search, DOB. Criminal records computerized from 1989; felonies on index cards from 1925, misdemeanors on docket books from 1900s. Mail turnaround time 1 week. Public use terminal has crim records back to 1989. Also, access to County Clerk of Circuit Court records is at www2.myfloridacounty.com/ccm/?county=57. Online results show name only.

Sarasota County

Circuit & County Courts - Civil PO Box 3079, Attn: Clerk of the Circuit Court, Public Access, 2000 Main St, Historic Courthouse, Sarasota, FL 34230; 941-861-7400; civil phone: 861-861-7770; fax: 941-861-7738; 8:30AM-5PM (EST). *Civil, Eviction, Small Claims, Probate.*
www.sarasotaclerk.com
General Information: No adoption, mental health, or sealed records released. Will fax out documents no fee. Court makes copy: $1.00 per page. Certification fee: $2.00 per instrument; Exemplification fee- $7.00. Payee: Clerk of Circuit Court. Personal checks and credit cards accepted. 3.5% transaction fee added. Prepayment required. Mail requests: SASE helpful.
Civil Name Search: Access: Phone, Mail, in person, online. Both court and visitors may perform in person name searches. Search fee: $2.00 per name per year. Civil records on computer from 1983, circuit & county on docket books from 1900s to 1983. Note: Make phone search requests at 941-861-7425. Mail turnaround time 2 days Public use terminal has civil records back to 1984. Civil and DV case dockets from the Clerk of Circuit Court database are free at www.clerk.co.sarasota.fl.us/srqapp/civilinq.asp. Probate court dockets are at www.clerk.co.sarasota.fl.us/srqapp/probinq.asp. Also see the clerk's judgment/official document search for images back 10 years. Also, access an index of judgments, liens, recorded documents at www.myfloridacounty.com. Fees involved to order copies; save $1.50 per record by becoming a subscriber.

Circuit & County Courts - Criminal PO Box 3079, 2000 Main St, Sarasota, FL 34230; 941-861-7400; 8:30AM-5PM (EST). *Felony, Misdemeanor.*
www.sarasotaclerk.com
General Information: There is also a branch in Venice. Online identifiers in results same as on public terminal. No juvenile records released. Will fax out documents no fee. Court makes copy: $1.00 per page. Certification fee: $2.00 per instrument; Exemplification fee- $7.00. Payee: Clerk of Circuit Court. Personal checks and credit cards accepted. 3.5% transaction fee added. Prepayment required. Mail requests: SASE helpful.

Criminal Name Search: Access: Phone, mail, online, in person. Both court and visitors may perform in person name searches. Search fee: $2.00 per name per year. Required to search: name, years to search, DOB, SSN. Criminal records on computer since 1983, (circuit) on docket books from 1900s to 1983, (county) on docket books from 1960s to 1983. Mail turnaround time 48 hours. Public use terminal has crim records back to 1995. Criminal and traffic case dockets from the Clerk of the Circuit Court database are free online at http://clerk.co.sarasota.fl.us/cvdisclaim.htm. Civil, probate and domestic dockets are also available. Missing records can be avoided with an in person search. Not all document images are online. Online results show middle initial, DOB.

Seminole County

Circuit & County Courts - Civil Division PO Box 8099, 301 N Park Ave, Sanford, FL 32771; 407-665-4330; civil phone: 407-665-4378 Circ; 665-4361 Count Civil; Sm Claims 665-4362; probate phone: 407-665-4328; fax: 407-330-7193; 8AM-4:30PM (EST). *Civil, Eviction, Small Claims, Probate.*
www.seminoleclerk.org
General Information: No confidential files pursuant to law or sealed records released. Will fax documents $1.00 per page local or $2.00 per page long-distance. Court makes copy: $1.00 per page. Certification fee: $2.00 per doc; Exemplification certificate $7.00 (includes signing and sealing). Payee: Clerk of the Circuit Court. Personal checks accepted. No credit cards accepted. Prepayment required. Mail requests: SASE required.
Civil Name Search: Access: Mail, in person, online. Both court and visitors may perform in person name searches. Search fee: $2.00 per name per year. Civil records on computer since 1987, on microfiche since 1913. Note: The court does not provide a DOB on name search results. Mail turnaround time 1 week. Public use terminal has civil records back to 1987. Access to judgment records is free at http://officialrecords.seminoleclerk.org/. Images related to probate cases are not available on the Clerk's website. The court does not provide a DOB on name search results either online or on the public terminal.

Circuit & County Courts - Criminal Division 101 Bush Blvd, 1st Fl, Sanford, FL 32773; 407-665-4450; fax: 407-665-4545; 8AM-4:30PM (EST). *Felony, Misdemeanor.*
www.seminoleclerk.org
General Information: No records of investigations which have not resulted in an arrest released. Local faxes $1.00 per page; out of state faxes $2.00 per page. Court makes copy: $1.00 per page. Certification fee: $2.00 per doc; $7.00 to sign and seal (Exemplification certificate). Payee: Clerk of Courts. Local personal and company checks accepted. Major credit cards accepted. Prepayment required.
Criminal Name Search: Access: Mail, in person, online. Both court and visitors may perform in person name searches. Search fee: $2.00 per name per year. Required to search: name, years to search, DOB; also helpful: race, sex. Criminal records computerized from 1986; prior on microfiche. Mail turnaround time 2-4 days for felonies, no set time for misdemeanors. Public use terminal has crim records back to 1986. Partial DOB in results only. Access criminal dockets free at www.seminoleclerk.org click on Criminal Dockets Search. Partial DOB shown.

St. Johns County

Circuit & County Courts - Civil Division 4010 Lewis Speedway, St Augustine, FL 32084; 904-819-3600; civil phone: 904-819-3652/51; probate phone: 904-819-3654; fax: 904-819-3661; 8AM-5PM (EST). *Civil, Eviction, Small Claims, Probate.*
www.clk.co.st-johns.fl.us/
General Information: No confidential or sealed records released. Will not fax out documents. Court makes copy: $1.00 per page. Certification fee: $2.00. Payee: Clerk of Circuit Court. Personal checks accepted. Visa/MC accepted. Prepayment required. Mail requests: SASE required.
Civil Name Search: Access: Fax, mail, online, in person. Both court and visitors may perform in person name searches. Search fee: $2.00 per name per year. Civil records on computer from 1984, on microfiche from 1976 to 1986, on docket books from 1820 to 1983. County on computer from 1991, microfiche from. Mail turnaround time 4-5 days. Public use terminal has civil records back to 1986. Also, data free at http://doris.clk.co.st-johns.fl.us/uc_web_live/default.aspx. Access an index of judgments, liens, recorded documents at www.myfloridacounty.com. Fees involved to order copies; save $1.50 per record by becoming a subscriber at $25.00 per month.

Circuit & County Courts - Criminal Division 4010 Lewis Speedway, St Augustine, FL 32084; 904-819-3615; criminal phone: 904-819-3625; fax: 904-819-3666; 8AM-5PM (EST). *Felony, Misdemeanor.*
www.clk.co.st-johns.fl.us/
General Information: Online identifiers in results same as on public terminal. No juvenile or sexual offense records released. Will fax documents for $2.00 flat rate. Court makes copy: $1.00 per page. Certification fee: $2.00

per doc. Payee: Clerk of Circuit Court. Personal checks accepted. Credit cards accepted. Prepayment required. Escrow/billing accounts available to government agencies. Mail requests: SASE required.
Criminal Name Search: Access: Fax, mail, online, in person. Both court and visitors may perform in person name searches. Search fee: $2.00 per name per year. Required to search: name, years to search, DOB; also helpful: address, SSN. Criminal Records on computer. Felony since 1986, Misdemeanor since 12000. Felony on log books from 1950 to 1985. Mail turnaround time 4-5 days. Public use terminal has crim records back to Felony 1986; Misd.-2000. Search docket index free at http://doris.clk.co.st-johns.fl.us/benchmarkweb/. Search by name or case number.

St. Lucie County

Circuit & County Courts - Civil Division PO Box 700, 201 S Indian River Dr (34950), Ft Pierce, FL 34954; 772-462-6978 (Circuit); civil phone: 772-785-5884 (County); criminal fax: 772-462-1998; civil fax: 8AM-5PM; 8AM-5PM (EST). *Civil, Eviction, Small Claims.*
www.stlucieclerk.com/circuitcivil/circuitcivil.htm
General Information: Small claims phone is 772-785-5880; Small Claims and County Civil files and microfiche are located at the Courthouse Annex, 250 NW County Club Dr, Rm 115, Pt St. Lucie, FL 34986. No sealed cases or adoption records released. Will fax documents to local or toll free line. Court makes copy: $1.00 per page. Self serve copy: same. Certification fee: $2.00 per doc. Payee: Clerk of Court. No personal checks accepted. Visa/MC accepted. Prepayment required.
Civil Name Search: Access: Mail, in person, online. Both court and visitors may perform in person name searches. Search fee: $2.00 per name per year. Circuit records on computer back to 1992. Circuit on microfiche from 1981 to 1992, County from 1981 to 1992. Circuit on docket books from 1900s to 198. Mail turnaround time 1 day. Public use terminal has civil records back to 10 years. Online access to index is free at http://casesearch.slcclerkofcourt.com/PublicSearch/. Online records go back to 7/6/1992. For added search capability download of public access mail merge data, call 772-462-6997 to sign up for a business account. Also, access an index of judgments, liens, recorded documents at www.myfloridacounty.com. Fees involved to order copies; save $1.50 per record by becoming a subscriber.

Circuit & County Courts - Criminal Division PO Drawer 700, 201 S Indian River Dr (34950), Ft Pierce, FL 34954; 772-462-6900; criminal phone: 772-462-3228; fax: 772-462-2833; 8AM-5PM (EST). *Felony, Misdemeanor.*
www.stlucieclerk.com/Criminal/Criminal.htm
General Information: County Misdemeanor and criminal traffic phone is 772-462-6943 or 772-462-6930; fax number is 772)-462-6868. No sealed or expunged records released. Fee to fax out file $1.25 per page. Court makes copy: $1.00 per page. Certification fee: $2.00. Payee: Clerk of Court. Cashiers checks and money orders accepted. Credit cards accepted; 3.5% surcharge. Prepayment required.
Criminal Name Search: Access: Fax, mail, in person, online. Both court and visitors may perform in person name searches. Search fee: $2.00 per name per year. Required to search: name, years to search, DOB, signed release; also helpful: SSN, race, sex. Criminal records computerized from 1982, on microfiche to 1960, on books prior to 1900s. Mail turnaround time 1-2 weeks; fax turnaround time 1-5 days. Public use terminal has crim records back to 1983. You may print docs off the PAT. Online access to bonds, traffic and misdemeanor index is free at http://casesearch.slcclerkofcourt.com/PublicSearch/. Online records go back to 7/6/1992. For added search capability and ability to download public access mail merge data, call 772-462-6997 to sign up for a business account. Online results show middle initial, DOB.

Probate Court Clerk of Circuit. Ct; Attn: Probate Dept, PO Box 700, Ft Pierce, FL 34954; 772-462-6920; fax: 772-462-6984; 8AM-5PM (EST). *Probate, Guardianship.*
www.stlucieclerk.com/probate/probate.htm
General Information: Physical Address: 201 S Indian River Dr, Fort Pierce, Fl, 34950.

Sumter County

Circuit & County Courts - Civil Division 209 N Florida St, Bushnell, FL 33513; 352-793-0211; fax: 352-568-6608; 8:30AM-5PM (EST). *Civil, Eviction, Small Claims, Probate.*
www.sumterclerk.com/public/
General Information: No juvenile or adoption records released. Will fax documents $1.00 per page. Court makes copy: $1.00 per page. Certification fee: $2.00 per doc. Payee: Clerk of Circuit Court. No personal checks accepted. Visa/MC accepted in person. Prepayment required. Mail requests: SASE required.
Civil Name Search: Access: Fax, mail, in person, online. Both court and visitors may perform in person name searches. Search fee: $2.00 per name per year. Civil records go back to 1800s; on computer go back to 12/1999; in

docket books from 1986 to 11/30/99 (circuit only). Note: Faxes accepted if only pre-paid. Mail turnaround time 1 week. Access an index of civil, probate and domestic relationship records at https://www2.myfloridacounty.com/ccm/?county=60.F

Circuit & County Courts - Criminal Division 209 N Florida St, Bushnell, FL 33513; 352-793-0211; fax: 352-568-6608; 8:30AM-5PM (EST). *Felony, Misdemeanor.*
www.sumterclerk.com/public/
General Information: No juvenile records released. Fee to fax out file $1.00 per page. Court makes copy: $1.00 per page. Certification fee: $2.00 per doc plus copy fees. Payee: Clerk of Court. Only cashiers checks and money orders accepted. Major credit cards accepted. Prepayment required. Mail requests: SASE requested.
Criminal Name Search: Access: Mail, in person, online. Both court and visitors may perform in person name searches. Search fee: $2.00 per name per year. Required to search: name, years to search, DOB. Criminal records (circuit) on computer since 2000, on index books from 1965 to 1999, prior in vaults. County on computer since 1982. Mail turnaround time 1 week. Access an index of felony, criminal traffic and misdemeanor records at https://www2.myfloridacounty.com/ccm/?county=60. Race, sex, city and ZIP Shown.

Suwannee County

Circuit & County Courts 200 S Ohio Ave, Live Oak, FL 32064; 386-362-0500; civil phone: 386-362-0517; fax: 386-362-0577; 8AM-4:30PM (EST). *Felony, Misdemeanor, Civil, Eviction, Small Claims, Probate.*
www.suwclerk.org/mambo/
General Information: No juvenile or adoption records released. Will fax documents $3.00 1st page, $.50 each add'l. Court makes copy: $1.00 per page. Self serve copy: same. Certification fee: $2.00. Payee: Suwannee Court Clerk. Personal checks and credit cards accepted. Prepayment required. Mail requests: SASE required.
Civil Name Search: Access: Mail, in person, online. Both court and visitors may perform in person name searches. Search fee: $2.00 per name per year. Fee is per index. Required to search: name, years to search; also helpful: address. Civil records on computer from 1983, archived from 1859 to 1983. Note: Written requests require prepayment. Mail turnaround time 1 week. Access to civil judgment records is available by subscription at https://www.myfloridacounty.com/official_records/index.html.
Criminal Name Search: Access: Mail, in person. Both court and visitors may perform in person name searches. Search fee: $2.00 per name per year. Fee is per index. Required to search: name, years to search, DOB, signed release; also helpful: address. Criminal records computerized from 1983, archived from 1859 to 1983. Note: Written requests require prepayment. Mail turnaround time 1 week.

Taylor County

Circuit & County Courts PO Box 620, Perry, FL 32348; 850-838-3506; probate phone: x 110; fax: 850-838-3549; 8AM-5PM (EST). *Felony, Misdemeanor, Civil, Eviction, Small Claims, Probate.*
https://www.myfloridacounty.com/ori/index.do
General Information: No juvenile records released. Will fax documents $1.00 per fax. Court makes copy: n/a. Self serve copy: $1.00 per page. Certification fee: $2.00. Payee: Taylor County Clerk of Court. Business checks accepted. No credit cards accepted. Prepayment required. Mail requests: SASE helpful.
Civil Name Search: Access: Mail, in person, online. Only the court performs in person name searches; visitors may not. Search fee: $2.00 per name per year. Civil records on computer back to 1982; on index from 1973 to 1991, prior on index books to 1856. Mail turnaround time 1 week. Access an index of judgments (not docket) is at www.myfloridacounty.com. Fees involved to order copies; save $1.50 per record by becoming a subscriber.
Criminal Name Search: Access: Mail, in person. Only the court performs in person name searches; visitors may not. Search fee: $2.00 per name per year. Required to search: name, years to search, DOB; also helpful: SSN, race, sex. Criminal records computerized from 1982; on index from 1973 to 1991, prior on index books to 1950. Mail turnaround time 1 week.

Union County

Circuit & County Courts 55 W Main, Rm 103, Lake Butler, FL 32054; 386-496-3711; fax: 386-496-1718; 8AM-5PM (EST). *Felony, Misdemeanor, Civil, Eviction, Small Claims, Probate.*
http://circuit8.org
General Information: No juvenile records released. Will fax documents $1.00 per page. Court makes copy: $1.00 per page. Self serve copy: same. Certification fee: $2.00. Payee: Clerk of Court. Personal checks accepted. Visa/MC accepted. Prepayment required. Mail requests: SASE preferred.
Civil Name Search: Access: Fax, mail, in person, online. Only the court performs in person name searches; visitors may not. Search fee: $2.00 per name per year. Civil index in docket books from 1921. Mail turnaround

time 2-3 days. Public use terminal has civil records. Civil PAT includes judgments, liens and other recorded documents generally. Access an index of judgments (not dockets) is at www.myfloridacounty.com. Fees involved to order copies; save $1.50 per record by becoming a subscriber. A free search is offered at https://www2.myfloridacounty.com/ccm/?county=63.
Criminal Name Search: Access: Fax, mail, in person, online. Only the court performs in person name searches; visitors may not. Search fee: $2.00 per name per year. Required to search: name, years to search, DOB; also helpful: SSN. Criminal docket on books from 1921. Mail turnaround time 2-3 days. Access the circuit-wide criminal quick lookup at http://circuit8.org. Account and password is required; restricted usage. Also, limited free search is at https://www2.myfloridacounty.com/ccm/?county=63.

Volusia County

Circuit & County Courts - Civil Division PO Box 6043, 101 N Alabama Ave., De Land, FL 32721; 386-736-5907; probate phone: 386-736-5914; fax: 386-740-5254; 8AM-4:30PM (EST). *Civil, Eviction, Small Claims, Probate.*
www.clerk.org
General Information: Family law can be reached at 386-736-5908. Online identifiers in results same as on public terminal. No sealed records released. Fee to fax out file $1.00 per page. Court makes copy: $1.00 per page. Certification fee: $2.00 per doc plus copy fee. Payee: Clerk of Circuit Court. Personal checks accepted. Major credit cards accepted in person only; service fee applies, fee depends on size of doc. Prepayment required. Mail requests: SASE requested.
Civil Name Search: Access: Fax, mail, online, in person. Both court and visitors may perform in person name searches. Search fee: $2.00 per name per year. Civil records on computer from 1986, on docket books prior. Note: This office is prohibited from providing electronic access to a party's address or full date of birth contained in a court record or progress docket. Mail turnaround time 1 week. Public use terminal has civil records back to 1986. There is both a free and pay site. Access to the countywide Clerk of Circuit Court record index for 1982 to present is free at www.clerk.org/cm/publicrecords/publicrecords.jsp. Also, access an index of judgments, liens, recorded documents at www.myfloridacounty.com with fees for copies.

Circuit & County Courts - Criminal Division PO Box 6043, De Land, FL 32721-6043; 386-736-5909/5910; fax: 386-740-5711; 8AM-4:30PM (EST). *Felony, Misdemeanor.*
www.clerk.org
General Information: No confidential, sexual battery and juvenile records released. Will not fax out documents. Court makes copy: $1.00 per page. Certification fee: $2.00. Payee: Clerk of Court. Personal and out of state checks accepted with proper ID. No credit cards accepted. Prepayment required. Mail requests: SASE required.
Criminal Name Search: Access: Mail, online, in person. Both court and visitors may perform in person name searches. Search fee: $2.00 per name per year. Required to search: name, years to search, DOB; also helpful: SSN, race, sex. Criminal records 1982 to present on computer, on microfiche from 1856 to 1988, on docket books prior to 1983. Note: This office is prohibited from providing electronic access to a party's address or full date of birth contained in a court record or progress docket. Mail turnaround time up to 1 week. Public use terminal has crim records back to 2000. There is both a free and pay site. Access to the countywide Clerk of Circuit Court record index for 1982 to present is free at www.clerk.org/cm/publicrecords/publicrecords.jsp. Access to restricted data is $100 setup fee. Access to the database of Citation Violations and 24-hour Arrest Reports for 1990 forward is free at www.clerk.org/index.html. Online results show middle initial.

Wakulla County

Circuit & County Courts 3056 Crawfordville Hwy, Crawfordville, FL 32327; 850-926-0905; fax: 850-926-0936; 8AM-5PM (EST). *Felony, Misdemeanor, Civil, Eviction, Small Claims, Probate.*
www.wakullaclerk.com
General Information: Felony/Misdemeanor court can be reached at 850-926-0327, for records searches. No juvenile, adoption records released. Will fax prepaid documents to toll-free number. Court makes copy: $1.00 per page. Certification fee: $2.00. Payee: Clerk of Court. Personal checks and credit cards accepted. Prepayment required. Mail requests: SASE required.
Civil Name Search: Access: Phone, fax, mail, in person, online. Both court and visitors may perform in person name searches. Search fee: $2.00 per name per year. Civil records on computer since 1990, on docket books from 1800s. Note: Fax requests must be pre-paid. Mail turnaround time 3-4 days. Access to County Clerk of Circuit Court records is at https://www2.myfloridacounty.com/ccm/?county=65
Criminal Name Search: Access: Fax, mail, in person, online. Only the court performs in person name searches; visitors may not. Search fee:

$2.00 per name per year. Required to search: name, years to search, DOB; also helpful: SSN. Criminal records on computer since 1990, on docket books from 1800s. Note: Court performs name searches. Faxes must be pre-paid. Mail turnaround time 3-4 days. Online access to criminal is same as civil.

Walton County

Circuit & County Courts PO Box 1260, De Funiak Springs, FL 32435; 850-892-8115; criminal fax: 850-892-8017; civil fax: 8AM-4:30PM; 8AM-4:30PM (CST). *Felony, Misdemeanor, Civil, Eviction, Small Claims, Probate.*

http://clerkofcourts.co.walton.fl.us

General Information: Probate is a separate index at this same address. Probate fax- 850-892-7551 No sealed, expunged, or pre-sentence investigation records released. Will fax documents $1.00 per page. Court makes copy: $1.00 per page. Self serve copy: same. Certification fee: $2.00 per instrument. Payee: Clerk of Courts. Personal checks accepted. Major credit cards accepted, $5.00 minimum. Prepayment required. Mail requests: SASE helpful.

Civil Name Search: Access: Fax, mail, online, in person. Only the court performs in person name searches; visitors may not. Search fee: $2.00 per name per year. Civil records on computer from 1988, on dockets from 1900s. Note: You may deposit money into an escrow account for future record searches. Contact any of the personnel for add'l information. Mail turnaround time 24 hours. Access final judgments or orders on closed cases at http://orsearch.clerkofcourts.co.walton.fl.us/ORSearch/. Also, access to County Clerk of Circuit Court records is at https://www2.myfloridacounty.com/ccm/?county=66.

Criminal Name Search: Access: Fax, mail, online, in person. Only the court performs in person name searches; visitors may not. Search fee: $2.00 per name per year. Required to search: name, years to search, DOB. Criminal records computerized from 1988, on dockets from 1900s. Note: You may deposit money into an escrow account for future record searches. Contact any of the personnel for add'l information. Mail turnaround time 24 hours. Access felony judgments of guilt only at http://clerkofcourts.co.walton.fl.us/ORSearch/. Also, access to County Clerk of Circuit Court records is at https://www2.myfloridacounty.com/ccm/?county=66.

Washington County

Circuit & County Courts PO Box 647, 1293 Jackson Ave, #100, Chipley, FL 32428-0647; 850-638-6285; criminal phone: x229; civil phone: x226; probate phone: x225; fax: 850-638-6297; 8AM-4PM (CST). *Felony, Misdemeanor, Civil, Eviction, Small Claims, Probate.*

https://www.myfloridacounty.com/ori/index.do

General Information: Small Claims phone- x246. Online identifiers in results same as on public terminal. No adoption or juvenile records released. Will fax documents for $5.00 first page, $1.00 ea add'l. Court makes copy: $1.00 per page. Self serve copy: same. Certification fee: $2.00 per document certified. Payee: Clerk of Court. Business checks accepted. Local personal checks accepted. No credit cards accepted. Prepayment required. Mail requests: SASE required for mail return of any copies.

Civil Name Search: Access: Phone, fax, mail, in person, online. Both court and visitors may perform in person name searches. Search fee: $2.00 per name per year. Civil records on computer from 1990; on docket books from 1940. Mail turnaround time 1 day. Public use terminal has civil records back to 1990. Access an index of judgments (not dockets) is at www.myfloridacounty.com. Fees involved to order copies; save $1.50 per record by becoming a subscriber.

Criminal Name Search: Access: Phone, fax, mail, in person. Only the court performs in person name searches; visitors may not. Search fee: $2.00 per name per year. Criminal records computerized from 1990, felonies on docket books from 1900. Mail turnaround time 1 day.

Georgia

Time Zone:	**EST**
Capital:	**Atlanta, Fulton County**
# of Counties:	**67**
State Web:	**www.georgia.com**
Court Web:	**www.georgiacourts.gov**

Administration

Court Administrator, 244 Washington St SW, Suite 300, Atlanta, GA, 30334; 404-656-5171, Fax: 404-651-6449.

The Supreme and Appellate Courts

The Supreme Court is the court of last resort. Opinions and summaries are available from the web page at www.gasupreme.us.

The Court of Appeals has statewide appellate jurisdiction of all cases except those involving constitutional questions, land title disputes, the construction of wills, murder, election contests, habeas corpus, extraordinary remedies, divorce and alimony and cases where original appellate jurisdiction lies with the Superior Courts. See the web page at www.gaappeals.us.

The Georgia Courts

Court	Type	How Organized	Jurisdiction Highpoints
Superior*	General	159 courts in 49 circuits in 10 Districts	Felony, Civil over $15,000, Juvenile, Domestic Relations, Estate
State* - Can be combined with Superior	Limited	70 courts in 70 counties	Misdemeanor, Civil Actions Under $15,000, Small Claims, Eviction, DWI/DUI
Magistrate*	Limited	159 Courts	Misdemeanor, Civil Actions Under $15,000
Civil*	Limited	2 in Bibb, Richmond	Civil Actions
Municipal	Limited	370 Courts	Ordinances
Juvenile	Special	159 Courts	Juvenile
Probate	Special	159 Courts	Probate

* = profiled in this book

Details on the Court Structure

The Superior Court is Georgia's general jurisdiction trial court. It has exclusive, constitutional authority over felony cases, divorce, equity and cases regarding title to land.

State Courts exercise limited jurisdiction within one county. These judges hear misdemeanors including traffic violations, issue search and arrest warrants, hold preliminary hearings in criminal cases and try civil matters not reserved exclusively for the Superior Courts. The Superior Court will also assume the role of a State Court if the county does not have one.

Magistrate Courts have jurisdiction for bad checks, arrest warrants, preliminary hearings, and county ordinance violations and can also issue arrest warrants and set bond on all felonies. The Magistrate Court has jurisdiction over civil actions under $15,000, also one type of misdemeanor related to passing bad checks. Two counties (Bibb and Richmond) have Civil/Magistrate courts with varied civil limits.

Municipal Courts try municipal ordinance violations, issue criminal warrants, conduct preliminary hearings, and may have concurrent jurisdiction over shoplifting cases and cases involving possession of one ounce or less of marijuana.

The jurisdiction of **Juvenile Courts** extends to delinquent children under the age of 17 and deprived or unruly children under the age of 18. Juvenile courts have concurrent jurisdiction with Superior Courts in cases involving capital felonies, custody and child support cases, and in proceedings to terminate parental rights. The Juvenile Court also has jurisdiction over minors committing traffic violations or enlisting in the military services, consent to marriage for minors, and cases involving the Interstate Compact on Juveniles. Note the Superior Courts have original jurisdiction over those juveniles who commit certain serious felonies.

Probate Courts can, in certain jurisdictions, issue search and arrest warrants, and hear miscellaneous misdemeanors, or local ordinance violations.

Record Searching Facts You Need to Know

Fees and Record Searching Tips

The copy fee is usually $.50 per page, but a number of courts will charge $1.00 if their personnel make the copy. The certification fee is usually $2.50 for the first page and $.50 each add'l page. Many Georgia county trial courts will not perform criminal record searches and, in many cases, will not do civil record searches. Hiring a local record retriever is advised, if no retriever is available ask a local law firm for assistance.

Online Access is Limited

There is no statewide online access available. Less than 15% of the trial courts offer online access to court docket data.

Appling County

Superior & State Court PO Box 269, 69 Tippins St #103, Baxley, GA 31513; 912-367-8126; fax: 912-367-8180; 8AM-5PM (EST). *Felony, Misdemeanor, Civil.*
www.baxley.org/
General Information: No juvenile, adoption, sealed, sexual, mental health or expunged records released. Will fax back documents. Court makes copy: $.50 per page. Self serve copy: same. Certification fee: $2.50 plus $.50 per page after first. Payee: Court Clerk. Personal checks accepted. No credit cards accepted.
Civil Name Search: Access: In person only. Visitors must perform in person searches themselves. Civil index on docket books back to 1960s, archived to 1800s.
Criminal Name Search: Access: In person only. Visitors must perform in person searches themselves. Required to search: name, years to search, DOB; SSN helpful. Criminal index on docket books back to 1960s, archived to 1800s.

Magistrate Court PO Box 366, 72 Tippins St, Baxley, GA 31515; 912-367-8116, 367-8117; fax: 912-367-8182; 8:30AM-5PM (EST). *Misdemeanor, Civil Actions under $15,000, Eviction, Small Claims.*
/www.georgiacourts.org/
General Information: Court also has jurisdiction for bad checks, arrest warrants, preliminary hearings, and county ordinance violations.

Probate Court 36 S Main St, Baxley, GA 31513; 912-367-8114; fax: 912-367-8166; 8:30AM-5PM (EST). *Probate.*

Atkinson County

Superior Court PO Box 6, 305 S Main, Courthouse Square, Pearson, GA 31642; 912-422-3343; fax: 912-422-7025; 8AM-5PM (EST). *Felony, Misdemeanor, Civil.*
www.atkinson-ga.org/5.html
General Information: No juvenile, adoption, sealed, sexual, mental health or expunged records released. Will fax documents $1.00 per page. Court makes copy: $1.00 per page. Self serve copy: $.50 per page. Certification fee: $2.50 plus $.50 per page after first. Payee: Clerk of Superior Court. Personal checks accepted. Prepayment required.
Civil Name Search: Access: In person only. Visitors must perform in person searches themselves. Civil cases indexed by defendant. Civil records in docket books back to 1919. Public use terminal has civil records back to 1/2005.
Criminal Name Search: Access: In person only. Visitors must perform in person searches themselves. Criminal records in docket books back to 1919.

Magistrate Court PO Box 674, 19 Roberts Ave W, Pearson, GA 31642; 912-422-7158; fax: 912-422-7989; 8AM-5PM (EST). *Civil Actions under $15,000, Eviction, Small Claims.*
General Information: Court also has jurisdiction for bad checks, arrest warrants, preliminary hearings, and county ordinance violations.

Probate Court PO Box 855, 19 Roberts Ave W, Pearson, GA 31642; 912-422-3552; fax: 912-422-7842; 8AM-5PM (EST). *Probate.*
General Information: Traffic and Vital Records at this court also.

Bacon County

Superior & State Court PO Box 376, Alma, GA 31510; 912-632-4915; probate phone: 912-632-7661; fax: 912-632-6545; 9AM-5PM (EST). *Felony, Misdemeanor, Civil.*
General Information: No juvenile, adoption, sealed, sexual, mental health, expunged or first offender records released. Will fax documents. Court makes copy: $1.00 per page. Self serve copy: $.50 per page. Certification fee: $2.50 plus $.50 per page after first. Payee: Clerk of Superior Court. Personal checks accepted. No credit cards accepted. Prepayment required. Mail requests: SASE required.
Civil Name Search: Access: Mail, in person. Both court and visitors may perform in person name searches. No search fee. Civil docket indexed from 1970, archived to 1918, computerized since 2000. Mail turnaround time 1 day. Civil PAT goes back to 2000.
Criminal Name Search: Access: In person only. Visitors must perform in person searches themselves. Required to search: name, years to search, DOB; also helpful: SSN, race, sex. Criminal records indexed from 1970, archived to 1918, computerized since 2000. Criminal PAT goes back to same as civil.

Magistrate Court Box 389, 502 W 12th St, Rm 100, Alma, GA 31510; 912-632-5961; civil phone: 912-632-7661; probate phone: 912-632-7661; fax: 912-632-7662; 9AM-5PM (EST). *Civil Actions under $15,000, Eviction, Small Claims.*
www.georgiacourts.org/
General Information: Court also has jurisdiction for bad checks, arrest warrants and preliminary hearings.

Probate Court PO Box 389, 502 W 12th St, Rm 100, Alma, GA 31510; 912-632-7661; fax: 912-632-7662; 9AM-5PM (EST). *Probate.*

Baker County

Superior Court PO Box 10, 167 Baker Pl, Courthouse, Newton, GA 39870; 229-734-3004; fax: 229-734-7670; 9AM-N, 1-5PM (EST). *Felony, Misdemeanor, Civil.*
General Information: No juvenile, adoption, sealed, sexual or expunged records released. Will not fax documents. Court makes copy: $1.00 per page. Self serve copy: $.50 per page. Certification fee: $2.50 plus $.50 per page after first. Payee: Court Clerk. No personal checks or credit cards accepted. Prepayment required.
Civil Name Search: Access: In person only. Visitors must perform in person searches themselves. Civil cases indexed by defendant. Civil docket indexed from 1850. Public use terminal has civil records back to 1998. Results include name and case number.
Criminal Name Search: Access: In person only. Visitors must perform in person searches themselves. Required to search: name, years to search, DOB; SSN helpful. Criminal records indexed from 1850.

Magistrate & Probate Court PO Box 548, 167 Baker Pl, Newton, GA 39870; 229-734-3009; fax: 229-734-3200; 9AM-5PM (EST). *Civil Actions under $15,000, Eviction, Small Claims, Probate.*
General Information: Court also has jurisdiction for bad checks, arrest warrants, preliminary hearings, and county ordinance violations. Probate fax is same as main fax number.

Baldwin County

Superior & State Court PO Drawer 987, Milledgeville, GA 31059-0987; 478-445-4007; criminal phone: 478-445-6949; civil phone: 478-445-6328; fax: 478-445-6039; 8:30AM-5PM (EST). *Felony, Misdemeanor, Civil.* www.baldwincountyga.com/clerk.htm

General Information: Numbers above are for Superior Court. State Court criminal is 478-445-1799, civil is 478-445-4698, clerk is at 478-445-6324. No juvenile, adoption, sealed, sexual, mental health or expunged records released. Court makes copy: $.50 per page. Certification fee: $2.50 plus $.50 per page after first. Payee: Clerk of Courts. Personal checks accepted. No credit cards accepted. Prepayment required.

Civil Name Search: Access: In person only. Visitors must perform in person searches themselves. Civil records on docket from 1861; on computer back to 1996. Civil PAT goes back to 1998.

Criminal Name Search: Access: In person only. Visitors must perform in person searches themselves. Criminal records on docket from 1861; on computer back to 1996. Criminal PAT goes back to same as civil.

Magistrate Court 121 N Wilkinson St, #107, Milledgeville, GA 31061; 478-445-4446; fax: 478-445-5918; 8AM-5PM (EST). *Civil Actions under $15,000, Eviction, Small Claims.* www.baldwincountyga.com/magistrate.htm

General Information: Court also has jurisdiction for bad checks, arrest warrants, preliminary hearings, and county ordinance violations.

Probate Court 121 N Wilkinson St, #109, Milledgeville, GA 31061; 478-445-4807; fax: 478-445-5178; 8:30AM-5PM (EST). *Probate.*

Banks County

Superior Court PO Box 337, 144 Yonah Homer Rd #8, Homer, GA 30547; 706-677-6243; fax: 706-677-6294; 8AM-5PM (EST). *Felony, Misdemeanor, Civil.*

General Information: No juvenile, adoption, sealed, sexual, mental health or expunged records released. Will fax documents for $1.00 per page. Court makes copy: $.50 per page. Certification fee: $2.60 per doc plus copy fee. Payee: Clerk of Superior Court. Personal checks accepted. Visa/MC and debit cards accepted. Prepayment required.

Civil Name Search: Access: In person only. Visitors must perform in person searches themselves. Civil records on docket from 1960. Civil PAT goes back to 2000.

Criminal Name Search: Access: In person only. Visitors must perform in person searches themselves. Required to search: name, years to search, DOB. Criminal records on docket from 1960. Criminal PAT goes back to same as civil.

Magistrate Court 144 Yonah Homer Rd #10, Homer, GA 30547-2614; 706-677-6270; fax: 706-677-6215; 8:30AM-5PM (EST). *Civil Actions under $15,000, Eviction, Small Claims.*

General Information: Court also has jurisdiction for bad checks, arrest warrants, preliminary hearings, and county ordinance violations.

Probate Court 144 Yonah Homer Rd,#7, Homer, GA 30547; 706-677-6250; fax: 706-677-2337; 8AM-5PM (EST). *Probate, Misdemeanor Traffic.*

General Information: This court also hold the vital records.

Barrow County

Superior Court 652 Barrow Park Dr, First Floor, Ste B, Winder, GA 30680; 770-307-3035; fax: 770-867-4800; 8AM-5PM (EST). *Felony, Misdemeanor, Civil.*

General Information: No juvenile, adoption, sealed, sexual, mental health or expunged records released. Will fax documents $2.50 1st page, $1.00 each add'l page. Court makes copy: $.50 per page. Self serve copy: same. Certification fee: $2.50 1st page plus $.50 each add'l. Payee: Clerk of Superior Court. Business checks accepted. No credit cards accepted. Prepayment required.

Civil Name Search: Access: In person only. Visitors must perform in person searches themselves. Civil records on computer from 1990, docket from 1915. Civil PAT goes back to 1990.

Criminal Name Search: Access: In person only. Visitors must perform in person searches themselves. Required to search: name, years to search, DOB. Criminal records computerized from 1990, docket from 1915. Criminal PAT goes back to 1992.

Magistrate Court 652 Barrow Park Dr, Ste F, Winder, GA 30680; 770-307-3050; fax: 770-868-1440; 8AM-5PM (EST). *Civil Actions under $15,000, Eviction, Small Claims.* www.barrowga.org/magistrate/

General Information: Court also has jurisdiction for bad checks, arrest warrants, preliminary hearings, and county ordinance violations.

Probate Court 652 Barrow Park Dr, Ste D, Barrow County Courthouse, Winder, GA 30680; 770-307-3045; fax: 770-307-4470; 8AM-5PM (EST). *Probate, Misdemeanor.* www.barrowga.org/probate/

Bartow County

Superior Court 135 W Cherokee Ave, #233, Cartersville, GA 30120; 770-387-5025; criminal phone: x2; fax: 770-387-5611; 8AM-5PM (EST). *Felony, Misdemeanor, Civil.*

General Information: No juvenile, adoptions or sealed records released. Will not fax documents. Court makes copy: $.50 per page. Certification fee: $2.50 1st page plus $.25 each add'l page. Payee: Clerk of Superior Court. Personal checks accepted. No credit cards accepted. Prepayment required.

Civil Name Search: Access: In person only. Visitors must perform in person searches themselves. Civil records on computer from 9/92, on books from 1900s.

Criminal Name Search: Access: In person only. Visitors must perform in person searches themselves. Required to search: name, years to search, DOB, SSN, signed release. Criminal records on computer for 10 years, prior on books. Public use terminal has crim records back to 1992.

Magistrate Court 112 W Cherokee Ave, #101, Cartersville, GA 30120; 770-387-5070; fax: 770-387-5073; 7AM-5:30PM (EST). *Civil Actions under $15,000, Eviction, Small Claims, Misdemeanors.* www.georgiacourts.org/councils/magistrate/county.asp

General Information: Court also has jurisdiction for bad checks, arrest warrants, preliminary hearings, and county ordinance violations.

Probate Court 135 W Cherokee Ave, #243A, Cartersville, GA 30120; 770-387-5075; fax: 770-387-5074; 8AM-5PM (EST). *Probate, Traffic.* www.bartowga.org/index.php?option=com_content&view=article&id=183&Itemid=111

Ben Hill County

Superior Court PO Box 1104, 115 S Sheridan, Fitzgerald, GA 31750; 229-426-5135; civil phone: 229-426-5272; fax: 229-426-5487; 8:30AM-5PM (EST). *Felony, Misdemeanor, Civil.*

General Information: No juvenile, adoption, sealed, sexual, mental health or expunged records released. Will fax documents for $2.50 1st page and $1.00 ea addl. Court makes copy: $1.00 per page. Self serve copy: $.50 per page. Certification fee: $2.00 plus $.50 per page. Payee: Clerk. Personal checks accepted. No credit cards accepted. Prepayment required.

Civil Name Search: Access: In person only. Visitors must perform in person searches themselves. Civil cases indexed by defendant. Civil records computerized since 1994, archived from 1907, docket 1907.

Criminal Name Search: Access: In person only. Visitors must perform in person searches themselves. Required to search: name, years to search, signed release; also helpful: DOB, SSN. Criminal records computerized since 1994, archived from 1907, docket 1907.

Magistrate Court Box 1163, 255 Appomattox Rd, Fitzgerald, GA 31750; 229-426-5141; fax: 229-426-5123; 8:30AM-4:30PM (EST). *Misdemeanor, Civil Actions under $15,000, Eviction, Small Claims.* https://www.ncourt.com/forms/GA/navigation.aspx?Juris=GABenHill

General Information: Court also has jurisdiction for bad checks, arrest warrants, preliminary hearings, and county ordinance violations.

Probate Court 111 S Sheridan St, Fitzgerald, GA 31750; 229-426-5137; fax: 229-426-5486; 8:30AM-4:30PM (EST). *Probate, Misdemeanor.* www.benhillcounty.com/probate.htm

Berrien County

Superior Court PO Box 504, 201 N Davis St, Room 230, Nashville, GA 31639; 229-686-5506; fax: 229-543-1032; 8AM-4:30PM (EST). *Felony, Misdemeanor, Civil.*

General Information: No juvenile, adoption, sealed, sexual, mental health or expunged records released. Court makes copy: $.50 per page. Self serve copy: $.50 per page. Certification fee: $2.50. Payee: Court Clerk. Personal checks accepted. No credit cards accepted. Prepayment required.

Civil Name Search: Access: In person only. Both court and visitors may perform in person name searches. No search fee. Civil records on docket back to 1800.

Criminal Name Search: Access: In person only. Both court and visitors may perform in person name searches. No search fee. Required to search: name, years to search, DOB; also helpful: SSN, race, sex. Criminal records on docket back to 1800.

Magistrate Court 201 N Davis St #250, Nashville, GA 31639; 229-686-7019; fax: 229-686-6328; 8:30AM-4:30PM (EST). *Civil Actions under $15,000, Eviction, Small Claims.*

General Information: Court also has jurisdiction for bad checks, arrest warrants, preliminary hearings, and county ordinance violations.

Probate Court 201 N Davis St, Rm 175, Nashville, GA 31639; 229-686-5213; fax: 229-686-9495; 8AM-4:30PM (EST). *Probate.*

Bibb County

Superior Court PO Box 1015, 275 2nd St, Rm 216, Macon, GA 31202; 478-621-6527; fax: 478-621-6033; 8:30AM-5PM (EST). *Felony, Civil.* www.co.bibb.ga.us/

General Information: This court suggests to hire a local retriever for record name searches. No adoption or sealed records released. Will not fax documents. Court makes copy: $1.00 per page. Self serve copy: $.50 per page. Certification fee: $2.50 plus $.50 per page after first. Payee: Superior Court Clerk. Only cashiers checks and money orders accepted. No credit cards accepted. Prepayment required.

Civil Name Search: Access: In person, online. Both court and visitors may perform in person name searches. Search fee: $10.00. Civil records on computer from 1993, on books from 1823. Civil PAT goes back to 1995. Terminal results also show SSNs. Court calendars online at www.co.bibb.ga.us/CalendarDirectory/CalendarDirectory.asp. Also, a subscription service is offered for limited civil records. However you must click on the "Deeds Online - Superior Court" to find information. Also, a subscription service is offered for limited civil & other records at https://bibbclerkindexsearch.com/external/User/Login.aspx?ReturnUrl=%2fexternal%2findex.aspx. Fee is $24.95 for one month.

Criminal Name Search: Access: In person, online. Both court and visitors may perform in person name searches. Search fee: $10.00. Required to search: name, years to search, DOB, signed release; also helpful: SSN. Criminal records on computer since 1989. Criminal PAT goes back to 1993. Terminal results include SSN. Search the District Attorney's criminal case index at www.co.bibb.ga.us/da/criminalcases/. The Superior court calendars are at www.co.bibb.ga.us/CalendarDirectory/CalendarDirectory.asp. Also, a subscription service is offered for limited criminal and other records at https://bibbclerkindexsearch.com/external/User/Login.aspx?ReturnUrl=%2fexternal%2findex.aspx. Fee is $39.95.for one month.

State Court PO Box 5086, 601 Mulberry St Rm 500, Macon, GA 31213-7199; 478-621-6676; fax: 478-621-6326; 8AM-5PM (EST). *Misdemeanor, Civil.*
www.co.bibb.ga.us/StateCourt/StateCourt.aspx

General Information: No juvenile, adoption, sealed, sexual, mental health or expunged records released. Will fax to toll-free line if 5 pages or less, otherwise documents mailed. Court makes copy: $1.00 per page. Self serve copy: $.50 per page. Certification fee: $2.50 per page. Exemplification is an add'l $5.00 per page. Payee: Bibb State Court Clerk. Business checks accepted, personal check are not. No credit cards accepted. Prepayment required. Mail requests: SASE required.

Civil Name Search: Access: Mail, in person, online. Both court and visitors may perform in person name searches. Search fee: $10.00. Civil records on computer from 1990, docket from 1952. Mail turnaround time 1 day usually. Civil PAT goes back to 1990. Search civil court calendars online at www.co.bibb.ga.us/StateCourtClerk/Civil/Default.htm. Website will have access to full court record indexes in the future.

Criminal Name Search: Access: Mail, in person, online. Both court and visitors may perform in person name searches. Search fee: $10.00. Required to search: name, years to search, DOB; also helpful: SSN, race, sex. Criminal records computerized from 1990, docket from 1945. Mail turnaround time usually 1 day. Criminal PAT goes back to 1990. Search the State Court criminal docket at www.co.bibb.ga.us/StateCourt/StateCourt.aspx. Also, search the District Attorney's criminal case index at www.co.bibb.ga.us/da/criminalcases/.

Civil & Magistrate Court 601 Mulberry, Rm 101, Bibb County Courthouse, Macon, GA 31201; 478-621-6495; fax: 478-621-6861; 8AM-5PM (EST). *Civil Actions under $25,000, Eviction, Small Claims under $15,000.* www.co.bibb.ga.us/magcourtcivil/Default.aspx

General Information: Searchable database not yet available for this jurisdiction. No juvenile, adoption, sealed, sexual, mental health or expunged records released. Court makes copy: $.50 per page. Certification fee: $2.50 plus $.50 per page after first. Payee: Civil & Magistrate Court. Business checks accepted. Prepayment required.

Civil Name Search: Access: In person, online. Visitors must perform in person searches themselves. Civil cases indexed by defendant. Civil records on computer from 1992, index from 1945. Access the index at www.co.bibb.ga.us/magcourtcivil/cmcasesearch.aspx. Search by name or case number.

Probate Court PO Box 6518, 601 Mulberry St, 207 County Courthouse, Macon, GA 31208-6518; 478-621-6494; fax: 478-621-6686; 8AM-5PM (EST). *Probate.* www.co.bibb.ga.us/ProbateCourt/ProbateCourt.aspx

General Information: The Probate Court exercises jurisdiction over estates of deceased persons, the appointment of guardians or conservators for incapacitated adults and minors, and involuntary treatment of persons suffering from mental illness or abusing drugs or alcohol.

Bleckley County

Superior Court PO Box 272, 112 N 2nd St, Cochran, GA 31014; 478-934-3210; fax: 478-934-6671; 8:30AM-5PM (EST). *Felony, Misdemeanor, Civil.* www.gsccca.org/clerks/displayclerk.asp

General Information: No juvenile, adoption, sealed, sexual, mental health or expunged records released. Will not fax documents. Court makes copy:

$.50 per page. Self serve copy: same. Certification fee: $2.50 plus $.50 per page after first. Payee: Clerk of the Superior Court. No personal checks. No credit cards accepted. Prepayment required.

Civil Name Search: Access: In person only. Visitors must perform in person searches themselves. Civil records archived from 1913, docket from 1913. Public use terminal has civil records back to 1995.

Criminal Name Search: Access: In person only. Visitors must perform in person searches themselves. Required to search: name, years to search, DOB; SSN helpful. Criminal records archived from 1913, docket from 1913.

Magistrate Court 112 N 2nd St, Cochran, GA 31014; 478-934-3202; fax: 478-934-7826; 8:30AM-5PM (EST). *Civil Actions under $15,000, Eviction, Small Claims.*

General Information: Court also has jurisdiction for bad checks, arrest warrants, preliminary hearings, and county ordinance violations.

Probate Court 306 SE 2nd St, Cochran, GA 31014; 478-934-3204; fax: 478-934-3205; 8:30AM-5PM (EST). *Probate, Misdemeanor.*
www.georgiacourts.org/councils/state/index_test.asp?county=1256&Submit=GO

Brantley County

Superior Court PO Box 1067, 234 Brantley St, Ste 200, Nahunta, GA 31553; 912-462-5635; fax: 912-462-6247; 8AM-5PM (EST). *Felony, Misdemeanor, Civil.*

General Information: No juvenile, adoption, sealed, 1st offenders, expunged or confidential records released. Will fax documents for $2.50 plus $1.00 per page after first. Court makes copy: $.50 per page. Certification fee: $2.50 plus $.50 per page after first. Payee: Superior Court Clerk. Personal checks accepted. No credit cards accepted. Prepayment required.

Civil Name Search: Access: In person only. Visitors must perform in person searches themselves. Civil records on dockets from 1920; computerized records go back 2004. Note: Civil books can be viewed, data back to 1920s.

Criminal Name Search: Access: In person only. Both court and visitors may perform in person name searches. Search fee: No search fee, but assistance with copies is $1.00 per page. Required to search: name, years to search, DOB, SSN, signed release. Criminal docket index from 1920, computerized since 2004. Note: Criminal books open to public to view, data back to 1920's.

Magistrate Court PO Box 1150, 234 Brantley St, #300, Nahunta, GA 31553; 912-462-6780; criminal phone: 912-462-6730; fax: 912-462-6897; 8AM-4:30PM (EST). *Civil Actions under $15,000, Eviction, Small Claims.*
www.georgiacourts.org/councils/state/index_testmagistarte.asp?county=1416&Submit=GO

General Information: Court also has jurisdiction for bad checks, arrest warrants, preliminary hearings and county ordinance violations.

Probate Court PO Box 207, 234 Brantley St, Ste 100, Nahunta, GA 31553; 912-462-5192/5882; fax: 912-462-8360; 8AM-5PM (EST). *Probate.*

Brooks County

Superior & State Court PO Box 630, 100 Schevens, Quitman, GA 31643; 229-263-4747/5150; civil phone: 229-263-8054; fax: 229-263-5050; 8AM-5PM (EST). *Felony, Misdemeanor, Civil.*
http://southernjudicialcircuit.com

General Information: Fax in a search request and the clerk says she will post it on the bulletin board and someone may perform the search for you. No juvenile, adoption, sealed, sexual, mental health or expunged records released. Will fax documents to local or toll free line. Court makes copy: $.50 per page. Self serve copy: same. Certification fee: $2.50 plus $.50 per page after first. Payee: Clerk Superior Court. Business checks accepted. No credit cards accepted. Prepayment required.

Civil Name Search: Access: In person only. Visitors must perform in person searches themselves. Civil records in books back to 1857. Note: Will accept phone requests for specific documents. Public use terminal has civil records back to 2007.

Criminal Name Search: Access: In person only. Visitors must perform in person searches themselves. Required to search: name, years to search, DOB; SSN helpful. Criminal records in books back to 1857. Note: Searchers must look thru docket books.

Magistrate Court PO Box 387, 400 E Courtland Ave, Quitman, GA 31643; 229-263-9989; fax: 229-263-7847; 8AM-5PM (EST). *Civil Actions under $15,000, Eviction, Small Claims, Ordinance.*
www.georgiacourts.org/councils/magistrate/county.asp

General Information: Court also has jurisdiction for bad checks, arrest warrants, preliminary hearings, garnishments.

Probate Court PO Box 665, 100 Screven St, Quitman, GA 31643; 229-263-5567; fax: 229-263-5058; 8AM-5PM (EST). *Probate.*

Bryan County

Superior & State Court PO Box 670, 151 S College St, Pembroke, GA 31321; 912-653-3872; criminal phone: 912-653-3872 x3; civil phone: 912-

653-3874; criminal fax: 912-653-3870; civil fax: 8AM-5PM; 8AM-5PM (EST). *Felony, Misdemeanor, Civil.*

General Information: No juvenile, adoption, sealed, sexual, mental health or expunged records released. Will fax specific case file $2.00 1st page, $1.00 each add'l, if prepaid. Court makes copy: $1.00 per page. Self serve copy: $.50 per page. Certification fee: $2.50 1st page, $.50 ea addl. Payee: Clerk of Superior & State Court. Personal checks accepted. No credit cards accepted. Prepayment required.

Civil Name Search: Access: In person only. Visitors must perform in person searches themselves. Civil records on dockets from 1960, recent records are computerized since 9/93. Civil PAT goes back to 1993.

Criminal Name Search: Access: In person only. Visitors must perform in person searches themselves. Required to search: name, years to search, DOB; SSN helpful. Criminal docket index from 1960, recent records are computerized since 9/93. Criminal PAT goes back to same as civil.

Magistrate Court Box 670, 151 S College St, Pembroke, GA 31321; 912-653-3860; fax: 912-653-5254; 8AM-5PM (EST). *Civil Actions under $15,000, Eviction, Small Claims.*
www.bryancountyga.org
General Information: Court also has jurisdiction for bad checks, arrest warrants, initial appearance, and county ordinance violations.

Probate Court PO Box 418, 151 S College, #106, Pembroke, GA 31321; 912-653-3856; fax: 912-653-3845; 8:30AM-N, 1-5PM (EST). *Probate.*
www.georgiacourts.org/councils/state/index_test.asp?county=1259&Submit=GO

Bulloch County

Superior & State Court Judicial Annex Bldg, 20 Siebald St, Statesboro, GA 30458; 912-764-9009; fax: 912-764-5953; 8AM-5PM (EST). *Felony, Misdemeanor, Civil.*

General Information: No juvenile, adoption, sexual, mental health or expunged records released. Will not fax documents. Court makes copy: $.50 per page. Self serve copy: same. Certification fee: $2.50 plus cert plus copy fee. Payee: Court Clerk. Personal checks accepted. No credit cards accepted. Prepayment required.

Civil Name Search: Access: In person only. Both court and visitors may perform in person name searches. No search fee. Civil cases indexed by defendant. Civil records on computer from 1991, dockets back to 1796. Civil PAT goes back to 1991.

Criminal Name Search: Access: In person only. Both court and visitors may perform in person name searches. No search fee. Criminal records computerized from 1991, dockets back to 1796. Criminal PAT goes back to 1991.

Magistrate Court Box 1004, 101 Oak St, 30458, Statesboro, GA 30459-1004; 912-764-6458, 912-764-5050; fax: 912-489-6731; 8AM-5PM (EST). *Civil Actions under $15,000, Eviction, Small Claims.*

General Information: Court also has jurisdiction for bad checks, arrest warrants, preliminary hearings, and county ordinance violations.

Probate Court PO Box 1005, 2 N Main St #103, Statesboro, GA 30459; 912-489-8749; fax: 912-764-8740; 8AM-5PM (EST). *Probate.*
www.bullochcounty.net/departments/probate.htm
General Information: Located in the Bulloch County Courthouse.

Burke County

Superior & State Court PO Box 803, 111 E 6th St, Rm 107, Waynesboro, GA 30830; 706-554-2279; fax: 706-554-7887; 9AM-5PM (EST). *Felony, Misdemeanor, Civil.*

General Information: No juvenile, adoption, sexual, mental health or expunged records released. Will not fax documents. Court makes copy: $1.00 per page. Self serve copy: $.50 per page. Certification fee: $2.50 plus $.50 per page after first. Payee: Clerk of Superior Court. Personal checks accepted. No credit cards accepted. Prepayment required.

Civil Name Search: Access: In person only. Visitors must perform in person searches themselves. Civil cases indexed by defendant. Civil records on minute books back to 1856, indexed on computer since 1996. Public use terminal has civil records back to 1996.

Criminal Name Search: Access: In person only. Visitors must perform in person searches themselves. Required to search: name, years to search, DOB; SSN helpful. Criminal records on minute books back to 1856, indexed on computer since 1996.

Magistrate Court Box 401, 602 N Liberty St, Waynesboro, GA 30830; 706-554-4281; fax: 706-554-8772; 8AM-5PM (EST). *Civil Actions under $15,000, Eviction, Small Claims.*

General Information: Court also has jurisdiction for bad checks, arrest warrants, preliminary hearings, county ordinance violations.

Probate Court PO Box 322, 111 E 6th St, Waynesboro, GA 30830; 706-554-3000; fax: 706-554-6693; 9AM-5PM (EST). *Probate.*

Butts County

Superior Court PO Box 320, 26 3rd St, Jackson, GA 30233; 770-775-8215; fax: 770-504-1359; 8AM-5PM (EST). *Felony, Misdemeanor, Civil.*

General Information: No juvenile, adoption, sexual, mental health or expunged records released. Will not fax documents. Court makes copy: n/a. Self serve copy: $.50 per page. Certification fee: $2.50 plus $.50 per page. Payee: Clerk of Superior Court. Personal checks accepted. No credit cards accepted. Prepayment required.

Civil Name Search: Access: In person. Visitors must perform in person searches themselves. Civil records on dockets from 1966, computerized since 1998. Civil PAT goes back to 1998.

Criminal Name Search: Access: In person. Visitors must perform in person searches themselves. Required to search: name, years to search, signed release; also helpful: DOB, SSN, race, sex. Criminal docket index from 1966, computerized since 1998. Criminal PAT goes back to 1998.

Magistrate Court Box 457, Jackson, GA 30233; 770-775-8220; fax: 770-775-1954; 8:30AM-4:30PM (EST). *Civil Actions under $15,000, Eviction, Small Claims, Misdemeanor Fraud, Ordinance.*

General Information: Court also has jurisdiction for bad checks, arrest warrants, preliminary hearings, and county ordinance violations. Street address is 835 Ernest Biles Dr.

Probate Court 25 3rd St, #7, Jackson, GA 30233; 770-775-8204; fax: 770-775-8004; 8AM-5PM (EST). *Misdemeanor, Traffic, Probate.*

Calhoun County

Superior Court PO Box 69, Morgan, GA 39866; 229-849-2715; fax: 229-849-0072; 8AM-12; 1PM-5PM (EST). *Felony, Misdemeanor, Civil.* www.calhouncourtclerk.com/

General Information: No juvenile, adoption, mental health or expunged records released. Will fax $1.50 per page;. Court makes copy: $1.00 per page. Self serve copy: $.50 per page. Certification fee: $3.00. Payee: Superior Court Clerk. Personal checks accepted. No credit cards accepted. Prepayment required. Mail requests: SASE required.

Civil Name Search: Access: Fax, in person. Both court and visitors may perform in person name searches. Search fee: $5.00 per name. Required to search: name, years to search, proof of payment, i.e. copy of check. Civil records on dockets back to 1854. Civil PAT available. Only dockets available. Court civil calendars by month available at the website.

Criminal Name Search: Access: Mail, fax, in person. Both court and visitors may perform in person name searches. Search fee: $5.00 per name. Required to search: name, years to search, DOB, proof of payment, i.e. copy of check. Criminal records on dockets back to 1854. Criminal PAT available. Only dockets available.

Magistrate & Probate Court PO Box 87, 31 Court St Ste C, Morgan, GA 39866; 229-849-2115, 849-2116; fax: 229-849-2117; 8AM-5PM (EST). *Civil Actions under $15,000, Eviction, Small Claims, Probate.*

General Information: Court also has jurisdiction for wills, garnishments, traffic, vital records, bad checks, arrest warrants, preliminary hearings, and county ordinance violations.

Camden County

Superior Court PO Box 550, 210 E 4th St, Woodbine, GA 31569; 912-576-5631; fax: 912-576-5648; 9AM-5PM (EST). *Felony, Misdemeanor, Civil.*

General Information: No juvenile, adoption, sexual or expunged records released. Will not fax out case files. Court makes copy: $1.00 per page. Self serve copy: $.50 per page. Certification fee: $2.50 plus $.50 per page. Payee: Clerk of Superior Court. Personal checks accepted. No credit cards accepted. Prepayment required.

Civil Name Search: Access: In person only. Visitors must perform in person searches themselves. Civil records on computer from 1989, on dockets from 1776. Civil PAT goes back to 1991.

Criminal Name Search: Access: In person only. Visitors must perform in person searches themselves. Required to search: name, years to search, signed release; also helpful: DOB, SSN. Criminal records computerized from 1989, on dockets from 1776. Criminal PAT goes back to 1989.

Magistrate Court PO Box 386, 210 E 4th Street, Woodbine, GA 31569; 912-576-5658; fax: 912-576-7955; 9AM-5PM (EST). *Civil Actions under $15,000, Eviction, Small Claims.*
https://www.ncourt.com/forms/GA/navigation.aspx?Juris=GACamden
General Information: Court also has jurisdiction for bad checks, arrest warrants, preliminary hearings, and county ordinance violations.

Probate Court PO Box 818, 210 E 4th St, Woodbine, GA 31569; 912-576-3785; fax: 912-576-5484; 9AM-5PM (EST). *Probate, Misdemeanor Drug, Traffic.*
www.co.camden.ga.us/index.aspx?nid=246
General Information: Probate fax- 912-576-7145. Record search fee is $15.00. This court also hold records for Dept Natural Resources (DNR).

Candler County

Superior & State Court PO Drawer 830, 355 Broad St, Metter, GA 30439; 912-685-5257; probate phone: 912-685-2357; fax: 912-685-2946; 8:30AM-5PM (EST). *Felony, Misdemeanor, Civil.*

General Information: No juvenile, adoption, mental health, expunged or sealed records released. Will fax documents to local or toll free line. Court makes copy: $.50 per page. Self serve copy: $.50 per page. Certification fee: $2.00 plus $.50 per page. Payee: Clerk of Superior & State Court. Personal checks accepted. No credit cards accepted. Prepayment required.

Civil Name Search: Access: In person. Visitors must perform in person searches themselves. Civil records on dockets from 1914. Civil PAT goes back to 1995.

Criminal Name Search: Access: In person. Visitors must perform in person searches themselves. Criminal docket index from 1914. Criminal PAT goes back to same as civil.

Magistrate Court 35 SW Broad St #5, Metter, GA 30439; 912-685-2888; fax: 912-685-3995; 8:30AM-N, 1-5PM (EST). *Civil Actions under $15,000, Eviction, Small Claims.*

www.georgiacourts.org/councils/state/index_testmagistarte.asp?county=1424&Submit=GO

General Information: Court also has jurisdiction for bad checks, arrest warrants, preliminary hearings, and county ordinance violations.

Probate Court 35 Southwest Broad St, Ste B, Metter, GA 30439; 912-685-2357; fax: 912-685-5130; 8:30AM-5PM (EST). *Probate.*

www.georgiacourts.org/councils/state/index_test.asp?county=1265&Submit=GO

Carroll County

Superior & State Court PO Box 1620, Carrollton, GA 30112; 770-214-3125; criminal phone: 770-830-5835 x2247/2239; civil phone: 770-830-5835 x2245/2246; probate phone: 770-830-5840; fax: 770-214-3125; 8AM-5PM (EST). *Felony, Misdemeanor, Civil.* www.carrollcountyclerk.com/

General Information: No juvenile, adoption, sexual, mental health or expunged records released. Court makes copy: $1.00 per page. Self serve copy: $.50 per page. Certification fee: $2.50 plus $.50 per page after first. Payee: Clerk of Superior & State Court. Personal checks accepted. No credit cards accepted. Prepayment required. Mail requests: SASE required.

Civil Name Search: Access: Mail, in person. Both court and visitors may perform in person name searches. Search fee: $5.00 per name. Civil records on computer from 1993, docket. Mail turnaround time 2 weeks. Civil PAT goes back to 9/00.

Criminal Name Search: Access: Mail, in person. Both court and visitors may perform in person name searches. Search fee: $5.00 per name. Required to search: name, years to search, DOB; also helpful: SSN, race, sex. Criminal records computerized from 1986 for State Court, Superior Court records are computerized from 9/00 to present. Mail turnaround time 2 weeks. Criminal PAT goes back to same as civil.

Magistrate Court 166 Independence Dr #A, Carrollton, GA 30117; 770-830-5874; fax: 770-830-5851; 8AM-5PM (EST). *Misdemeanors, Civil Actions under $15,000, Eviction, Small Claims.*

www.carrollcountyga.com/section/magistrate_court/

General Information: Court also has jurisdiction for bad checks, arrest warrants, preliminary hearings, abandonment hearings (child), personal property, foreclosures, abandoned motor vehicles, garnishments, mechanic liens and county ordinance violations.

Probate Court PO Box 338, 323 Newnan St, Rm 204, Carrollton, GA 30112; 770-830-5840; fax: 770-830-5995; 8AM-4:30PM (EST). *Probate.*

www.carrollcountyga.com/section/probate_court/

Catoosa County

Superior Court 875 Lafayette St, Ringgold, GA 30736; 706-935-4231; fax: 706-965-7431; 8:30AM-5PM (EST). *Felony, Misdemeanor, Civil,.*

General Information: As a courtesy, clerk may do single name lookup for you via phone or mail. No juvenile, adoption, sexual, mental health or expunged records released. Will not fax documents. Court makes copy: $1.00 per page. Self serve copy: $.50 per page. Certification fee: $2.50 plus $.50 per page after first. Payee: Superior Court Clerk. Personal checks accepted. No credit cards accepted. Prepayment required.

Civil Name Search: Access: In person only. Visitors must perform in person searches themselves. Civil records on dockets from 1800. Civil PAT goes back to 1996.

Criminal Name Search: Access: In person only. Visitors must perform in person searches themselves. Required to search: name, years to search, DOB. Criminal docket index from 1800. Criminal PAT goes back to 1997.

Magistrate Court 877 Lafayette St, Ringgold, GA 30736; 706-935-3114; fax: 706-965-9036; 9AM-N, 1-5PM (EST). *Misdemeanor, Civil Actions under $15,000, Eviction, Small Claims, Ordinance.*

www.catoosa.com/

Probate Court 875 Lafayette St, Justice Bldg, Ringgold, GA 30736; 706-935-3511; fax: 706-935-3519; 8:30AM-5PM (EST). *Probate.*

www.catoosa.com/probate%20court/probate-index.htm

General Information: This court will not perform mail searches.

Charlton County

Superior & State Court PO Box 760, Courthouse, 1520 Third St, Ste A, Folkston, GA 31537; 912-496-2354; fax: 912-496-3882; 8:30AM-5PM (EST). *Felony, Misdemeanor, Civil.*

General Information: No juvenile, adoption, sexual, mental health or expunged records released. Will fax documents for fee $2.50 first page and $1.00 ea addl. Court makes copy: $1.00 per page. Self serve copy: $.50 per page. Certification fee: $2.50 plus $.50 per page after first. Payee: Court Clerk. Personal checks accepted. No credit cards accepted. Prepayment required.

Civil Name Search: Access: In person only. Visitors must perform in person searches themselves. Civil cases indexed by defendant. Civil docket indexed from 1954.

Criminal Name Search: Access: In person. Visitors must perform in person searches themselves. Required to search: name, years to search, DOB, SSN. Criminal records indexed from 1954.

Magistrate Court 1520 3rd St #D, Folkston, GA 31537; 912-496-2617; fax: 912-496-2560; 9AM-4:30PM (EST). *Civil Actions under $15,000, Eviction, Small Claims.*

General Information: Court also has jurisdiction for bad checks, arrest warrants, preliminary hearings.

Probate Court 1520 Third Street, Ste B, Folkston, GA 31537; 912-496-2230; fax: 912-496-7045; 8AM-5PM (EST). *Probate.*

www.georgiacourts.org/councils/state/index_test.asp?county=1268&Submit=GO

Chatham County

Superior Court PO Box 10227, 133 MontgomerySt, #304, Savannah, GA 31412-0427; 912-652-7197; criminal phone: 912-652-7209; civil phone: 912-652-7200; fax: 912-652-7380; 8AM-5PM (EST). *Felony, Civil.*

www.chathamcounty.org/chatcourts.html

General Information: Online identifiers in results same as on public terminal. No adoption records released. Will not fax documents. Court makes copy: $.50 per page. Certification fee: $2.00 plus $.50 per page. Payee: Court Clerk. Personal checks accepted. No credit cards accepted. Prepayment required. Mail requests: SASE requested.

Civil Name Search: Access: Mail, in person, online. Both court and visitors may perform in person name searches. No search fee. Civil records on computer from 1984, archived back to 1900, dockets back to 1900. Mail turnaround time 1 week. Civil PAT goes back to 1984. Search county civil dockets and cases free at www.chathamcounty.org/jims/. Two systems are offered.

Criminal Name Search: Access: Mail, in person, online. Both court and visitors may perform in person name searches. No search fee. Required to search: name, years to search, signed release; also helpful: DOB, SSN. Criminal records computerized from 1984, archived back to 1900, dockets back to 1900s. Mail turnaround time 1 week. Criminal PAT goes back to same as civil. Search county criminal dockets and cases free at www.chathamcounty.org/jims/. Two systems are offered. Online results show middle initial, DOB.

State Court PO Box 9927, 133 Montgomery St #308, Courthouse, Savannah, GA 31412; 912-652-7224; criminal phone: x1; fax: 912-652-7229; 8AM-5PM (EST). *Misdemeanor, Civil.*

www.chathamcourts.org/StateCourt.aspx

General Information: Search fines, tickets, and restitution records free at www.chathamcounty.org/jims/fines/default.asp. No first time criminal offender or sealed civil records released. Will fax documents $1.00 per page. Court makes copy: $1.00 per page. Self serve copy: $.50 per page. Certification fee: $2.50 plus $.50 per page. Payee: Clerk of State Court. Only cashiers checks and money orders accepted. Visa/MC accepted. Prepayment required. Mail requests: SASE required.

Civil Name Search: Access: Mail, fax, in person, online. Both court and visitors may perform in person name searches. Search fee: $3.00 per name per index. Required to search: name, years to search, address. Civil records on computer from 1983, prior on books. Mail turnaround time 2 days. Civil PAT goes back to 1983. Search county civil dockets and cases free at www.chathamcounty.org/jims/. Two systems are offered.

Criminal Name Search: Access: Mail, fax, in person, online. Both court and visitors may perform in person name searches. Search fee: $3.00 per name per index. Criminal records computerized from 1983, prior on books. Note: Results include name and address. Mail turnaround time 2 days. Criminal PAT goes back to 1983. Search county criminal dockets and cases free at www.chathamcounty.org/jims/. Two systems are offered. Online results show name, DOB.

Magistrate Court 133 Montgomery St, Rm 303, 3rd Fl, Savannah, GA 31401; 912-652-7181; fax: 912-652-7550; 8AM-5PM (EST). *Civil Actions under $15,000, Eviction, Small Claims.*

www.chathamcounty.org/magcourt.html

General Information: The Magistrate Court serves the area of Chatham County which encompasses the City of Savannah and other municipalities including Bloomingdale, Garden City, Pooler, Port Wentworth, Thunderbolt and Tybee Island.

Probate Court 133 Montgomery St, Rm 509, Savannah, GA 31401; 912-652-7265; fax: 912-652-7262; 8AM-5PM (EST). *Probate.*
www.chathamcounty.org/probatecourt.html

Chattahoochee County

Superior & Magistrate Court PO Box 120, Cusseta, GA 31805; 706-989-3643- Mag Ct; 706-989-3424- Superior Ct; fax: 706-989-1508; 8AM-5PM (EST). *Felony, Misdemeanor, Civil, Eviction, Small Claims.*

General Information: Magistrate Court is 706-989-3643. No juvenile, adoption, sexual, mental health or expunged records released. Will not fax documents. Court makes copy: $1.00 per page. Self serve copy: $.50 per page. Certification fee: $2.50 plus $.50 per page after first. Payee: Court Clerk. Business checks accepted. No credit cards accepted. Prepayment required.

Civil Name Search: Access: In person only. Visitors must perform in person searches themselves. Civil records on dockets from 1854; on computer back to 1990. Civil PAT goes back to 1998 Magistrate.

Criminal Name Search: Access: In person only. Visitors must perform in person searches themselves. Required to search: name, years to search, DOB; SSN helpful. Criminal docket index from 1854. Criminal PAT available.

Probate Court PO Box 119, 379 Broad Street, Cusseta, GA 31805; 706-989-3603; fax: 706-989-2015; 8AM-N, 1-5PM (EST). *Probate.*

Chattooga County

Superior & State Court PO Box 159, 10035 Commerce St, Summerville, GA 30747; 706-857-0706; fax: 706-857-0686; 8:30AM-5PM (EST). *Felony, Misdemeanor, Civil, Eviction, Small Claims.*

General Information: No juvenile, adoption, sexual, mental health or expunged records released. Will not fax documents. Court makes copy: $.50 per page. Self serve copy: same. Certification fee: $2.50 plus $.50 per page after first. Payee: Clerk of Court. Personal checks accepted. No credit cards accepted. Prepayment required.

Civil Name Search: Access: In person, mail. Both court and visitors may perform in person name searches. No search fee. Civil records on dockets from 1960. Civil PAT goes back to 2000.

Criminal Name Search: Access: In person, mail. Both court and visitors may perform in person name searches. No search fee. Required to search: name, years to search, DOB; SSN helpful. Criminal docket index from 1960. Criminal PAT available.

Magistrate Court 120 Cox St, Summerville, GA 30747; 706-857-0711; fax: 706-857-0675; 9AM-5PM (EST). *Civil Actions under $15,000, Eviction, Small Claims, Ordinance.*

General Information: Court also has jurisdiction for bad checks, arrest warrants, preliminary hearings, and county ordinance violations.

Probate Court PO Box 467, 10035 Commerce St, Summerville, GA 30747; 706-857-0709; fax: 706-857-0877; 8:30AM-N, 1-5PM (EST). *Probate.*

Cherokee County

Superior & State Court 90 North St, #G170, Canton, GA 30114; 678-493-6511; fax: 770-479-0467; 8:30AM-5PM (EST). *Felony, Misdemeanor, Civil.* www.cherokeega.com/

General Information: This court location also handles juvenile records. No juvenile, adoption, sexual, mental health, expunged or confidential records released. Will not fax documents. Court makes copy: $1.00 per page. Self serve copy: $.50 per page. Certification fee: $2.50 plus $.50 per add'l page. Payee: Clerk of Court. Only cashiers checks, cash and money orders accepted. Major credit cards accepted with 3% surcharge. Prepayment required. Mail requests: SASE required for criminal.

Civil Name Search: Access: In person only. Visitors must perform in person searches themselves. Required to search: name. Civil records on computer from 1970s, archived 1900-1991, on dockets back to 1900. Civil PAT goes back to 1970's.

Criminal Name Search: Access: Phone, mail, In person. Both court and visitors may perform in person name searches. No search fee. Criminal records computerized from 1970s, archived 1900-1990, on dockets back to 1900. Note: There is a Criminal history Request Form available from the web. Criminal PAT goes back to same as civil.

Magistrate Court 90 North St, #150, Canton, GA 30114; 678-493-6431; fax: 678-493-6440; 8:30AM-5PM (EST). *Civil Actions under $15,000, Eviction, Small Claims.*

General Information: Court also has jurisdiction for bad checks, arrest warrants, preliminary hearings, and county ordinance violations.

Probate Court 90 North St, Ste 340, Canton, GA 30114; 678-493-6160; fax: 678-493-6170; 8AM-5PM (EST). *Probate.*

Clarke County

Superior & State Court 325 E Washington, Rm 450, Athens, GA 30601; 706-613-3190; fax: 706-613-3189; 8:30AM-5PM (EST). *Felony, Misdemeanor, Civil.*
www.athensclarkecounty.com/index.aspx?nid=324

General Information: This court will perform no name searches for the public. No juvenile, adoptions, sealed, sexual, mental health or expunged records released. Will fax out documents $1.00 per page if prepaid. Court makes copy: $.50 each; by mail copy fee is $1.00 per page. Self serve copy: $.50 per page. Certification fee: $2.50 plus $.50 per page after 1st. Payee: County Clerk. Local personal checks accepted. Visa/MC accepted but in person only. Prepayment required.

Civil Name Search: Access: In person, online. Visitors must perform in person searches themselves. Civil records on computer from 1993, docket books from 1801. Civil PAT goes back to 1993. Public access available to the docket from the home page.

Criminal Name Search: Access: In person, online. Visitors must perform in person searches themselves. Required to search: name, years to search, DOB. Criminal records computerized from 1993, docket books from 1801. Criminal PAT goes back to same as civil. Public access available to the docket from the home page.

Magistrate Court PO Box 1868, 325 E Washington St, #230, Athens, GA 30603; 706-613-3310; fax: 706-613-3314; 8AM-5PM (EST). *Civil Actions under $15,000, Eviction, Small Claims.*

General Information: Court also has jurisdiction for bad checks, arrest warrants, and preliminary hearings, also foreclosures, garnishments, abandoned vehicles.

Probate Court 325 E Washington St, #215, Athens, GA 30601; 706-613-3320; fax: 706-613-3323; 8AM-5PM (EST). *Probate.*
www.athensclarkecounty.com/index.aspx?NID=228

Clay County

Superior Court PO Box 550, Ft Gaines, GA 39851; 229-768-2631; fax: 229-768-3047; 8AM-4:30PM (EST). *Felony, Misdemeanor, Civil, Eviction.*

General Information: No juvenile, adoption, sexual, mental health or expunged records released. Court makes copy: $1.00 per page. Self serve copy: $.50 per page. Certification fee: $3.00. Payee: Superior Court Clerk. Personal checks accepted. No credit cards accepted. Prepayment required.

Civil Name Search: Access: In person only. Visitors must perform in person searches themselves. Civil records on computer from 1990, on dockets from 1854. Civil PAT goes back to 1990.

Criminal Name Search: Access: In person only. Visitors must perform in person searches themselves. Criminal records computerized from 1990, on dockets from 1854. Criminal PAT goes back to same as civil.

Magistrate Court PO Box 73, 210 S Washington St, Ft Gaines, GA 39851; 229-768-2841; fax: 229-768-3047; 8AM-4:30PM (EST). *Civil Actions under $15,000, Eviction, Small Claims.*

General Information: Court also has jurisdiction for bad checks, arrest warrants, preliminary hearings, and county ordinance violations.

Probate Court PO Box 448, 210 S Washington, Ft Gaines, GA 39851; 229-768-2445; fax: 229-768-3028; 8AM-4:30PM (EST). *Probate, Misdemeanor.* www.claycountyga.org/probate-judge.php

Clayton County

Superior Court 9151 Tara Blvd, #ICL19, Jonesboro, GA 30236-4912; 770-477-3405; fax: 678-479-5009; 8AM-5PM (EST). *Felony, Civil.*
www.claytoncountyga.gov/courts/clerk-of-superior-court.aspx

General Information: The Clerk's Office is divided into divisions: Civil, Criminal, and Microfilm. No adoption, sexual, mental health or expunged records released. Will not fax documents. Court makes copy: $1.00 per page, or if court assists. Self serve copy: $.50 per page. Certification fee: $2.50 plus $.50 per page. Payee: Clerk of Superior Court. Only cashiers checks, money orders and attorney checks accepted. Major credit cards accepted. Prepayment required.

Civil Name Search: Access: Mail, in person, online. Visitors must perform in person searches themselves. No search fee. Civil cases indexed by defendant. Civil index on docket books for all records, on computer from 1991, on microfilm from 1990, archived from 1858-1982, dockets to 1858. Civil PAT goes back to 1991. Online access is the same as criminal, see below.

Criminal Name Search: Access: Mail, in person, online. Visitors must perform in person searches themselves. No search fee. Required to search: name, years to search, DOB; also helpful: race, sex. Criminal record keeping same as civil. Mail turnaround time 1 week. Criminal PAT goes back to 1985. Search records free at www.claytoncountyga.gov/courts/court-case-inquiry.aspx. Court calendars at www.claytoncountyga.gov/courts/court-calendars.aspx. Searches and records also available on the statewide system.

Magistrate Court 9151 Tara Blvd, #2TC08, Jonesboro, GA 30236-4912; 770-477-3443; fax: 770-473-5750; 8AM-5PM (EST). *Civil Actions under $15,000, Eviction, Small Claims. Ordinance.*
www.claytoncountyga.gov/courts/magistrate-court.aspx
General Information: Online access free at http://weba.co.clayton.ga.us/casinqsvr/htdocs/index.shtml. Court also has jurisdiction for felony prelims, bad checks, arrest warrants, and county ordinance violations.

State Court 9151 Tara Blvd, #1CL181, Harold R Banke Justice Ctr, Jonesboro, GA 30236; 770-477-3388; fax: 770-472-8159; 8AM-5PM (EST). *Misdemeanor.*
www.claytoncountyga.gov/courts/clerk-of-state-court.aspx
General Information: The Clerk's Office is divided into divisions: Civil, Criminal, Traffic, and Microfilm. No juvenile, adoption, sexual, mental health or expunged records released. Will not fax documents. Court makes copy: $.50 per page. Certification fee: $2.50 plus $.50 per page after first. Payee: State Court Clerk. Business checks or money orders accepted via mail. No credit cards accepted. Prepayment required. Mail requests: SASE required for mail return of any copies.
Criminal Name Search: Access: In person, online. Visitors must perform in person searches themselves. Criminal records computerized from 1984. Public use terminal has crim records back to 1990. Results include full name and birth year. Search criminal database by name or case at http://weba.co.clayton.ga.us/casinqsvr/htdocs/index.shtml. Results shows year of birth. Index goes back to 1999.

Probate Court 121 S McDonough St, Annex Bldg 3, Jonesboro, GA 30236-3694; 770-477-3299; fax: 770-477-3306; 8AM-4:30PM (EST). *Probate.*
www.claytoncountyga.gov/courts/probate-court.aspx

Clinch County

Superior & State Court PO Box 433, 25 Court Sq #C, Homerville, GA 31634; 912-487-5854; fax: 912-487-2316; 8AM-5PM (EST). *Felony, Misdemeanor, Civil.*
General Information: No juvenile, adoption, sexual, mental health or expunged records released. Will fax documents $1.00 per page. Court makes copy: $.50 per page. Self serve copy: same. Certification fee: $2.50 plus $.50 per page after first. Payee: Court Clerk. Personal checks accepted. No credit cards accepted. Prepayment required. Mail requests: SASE requested.
Civil Name Search: Access: In person only. Both court and visitors may perform in person name searches. Civil records on dockets from 1900. Civil PAT goes back to 1998.
Criminal Name Search: Access: In person only. Both court and visitors may perform in person name searches. Required to search: name, years to search, DOB; also helpful: SSN, race, sex. Criminal docket index from 1900. Criminal PAT goes back to same as civil.

Magistrate Court 110 Court Sq, PO Box 364, Homerville, GA 31634; 912-487-2514; fax: 912-487-5507; 9AM-N, 1-5PM (EST). *Civil Actions under $15,000, Eviction, Small Claims.*
General Information: Court also has jurisdiction for bad checks, arrest warrants, preliminary hearings, and county ordinance violations.

Probate Court PO Box 364, 110 Court Sq, Homerville, GA 31634; 912-487-5523; fax: 912-487-5507; 9AM-N, 1-5PM (EST). *Probate, Traffic, Magistrate.*

Cobb County

Superior Court PO Box 3370, 32 Wadell St, Murietta Sq, 5th Fl, Marietta, GA 30061; 770-528-1300, 770-528-1344; 8AM-5PM (EST). *Felony, Misdemeanor, Civil.*
www.cobbsuperiorcourtclerk.com
General Information: Court calendars available at www.cobbsuperiorcourtclerk.org/courts/Calendars.htm. No juvenile, adoption, sexual, mental health or expunged records released. Will not fax out documents. Court makes copy: $1.00 per page. Self serve copy: $.50 per page. Certification fee: $2.00 plus $.50 per page. Payee: Clerk of Superior Court. Personal checks accepted. No credit cards accepted. Prepayment required. Mail requests: SASE required for criminal.
Civil Name Search: Access: Mail, online, in person. Visitors must perform in person searches themselves. No search fee. Civil records on computer from 1982, records on dockets from 1958. Mail turnaround time 3-5 days Civil PAT goes back to 1982. Civil indexes and images from Clerk of Superior Court are free at www.cobbsuperiorcourtclerk.org/courts/Civil.htm. Search by name, type or case number. Data updated Fridays. Images go back thru 2004.
Criminal Name Search: Access: Mail, online, in person. Both court and visitors may perform in person name searches. No search fee. Criminal records computerized from 1982, Records on dockets from 1958. Mail turnaround time 1-3 days. Criminal PAT goes back to same as civil. Criminal indexes and images from Clerk of Superior Court are free at www.cobbsuperiorcourtclerk.org/courts/Criminal.htm. Search by name, type or case number. Data updated Fridays but indexing can be nearly a month behind.

State Court - Civil & Criminal Divisions 12 E Park Sq, Marietta, GA 30090-9630; criminal phone: 770-528-1262; civil phone: 770-528-1203; criminal fax: 770-528-1268; civil fax: 8AM-5PM; 8AM-5PM (EST). *Misdemeanor, Civil, Eviction, Traffic.*
www.cobbstatecourtclerk.com
General Information: No sealed records released. Will fax documents to local or toll-free number. Court makes copy: $.25 per page. Certification fee: $3.00 plus copy costs; $5.00 for exemplification. Payee: State Court Clerk. No personal checks accepted. Money orders accepted. Major credit cards accepted in person only. Prepayment required.
Civil Name Search: Access: Phone, in person. Both court and visitors may perform in person name searches. No search fee unless record is offsite, then $7.00 per case retrieval fee. Civil records on computer since 3/10/97, docket books from 1965, and microfilm up to 1998. Note: Court will do a simple lookup over the phone to determine if a name exists in the index. Civil PAT goes back to 3/10/97.
Criminal Name Search: Access: In person only. Visitors must perform in person searches themselves. Required to search: name, years to search, offense; also helpful: DOB. Criminal records on computer since 1981, docket books from 1965. Criminal PAT goes back to 1981.

Magistrate Court 32 Waddell St, 3rd Fl, Marietta, GA 30090-9656; 770-528-8900; 8AM-5PM (EST). *Civil Actions under $15,000, Small Claims.*
www.cobbcountyga.gov/judicial/#magistrate
General Information: Court also has jurisdiction for bad checks, arrest warrants, preliminary hearings, and county ordinance violations.

Probate Court 32 Waddell St, Marietta, GA 30060; 770-528-1990; fax: 770-528-1996; 8AM-4:30PM (EST). *Probate.*
www.cobbcounty.org/judicial/index.htm#pro

Coffee County

Superior & State Court 101 S Peterson Ave #218B, Douglas, GA 31533; 912-384-2865; fax: 912-393-3252; 8:30AM-5PM (EST). *Felony, Misdemeanor, Civil.*
General Information: No juvenile, adoption, sexual, mental health or expunged records released. Will not fax documents. Court makes copy: $1.00 per page. Certification fee: $3.00 per cert. Payee: Clerk Superior Court. Business checks accepted. No credit cards accepted.
Civil Name Search: Access: In person only. Visitors must perform in person searches themselves. Required to search: name. Civil records on dockets, on computer after 1999. Civil PAT goes back to 2000.
Criminal Name Search: Access: In person only. Visitors must perform in person searches themselves. Criminal records on dockets, on computer after 1999. Criminal PAT available.

Magistrate Court 825 Thompson Drive, Douglas, GA 31535; 912-384-1381; fax: 912-383-0800; 8:30AM-5PM (EST). *Civil Actions under $15,000, Eviction, Small Claims.*
www.georgiacourts.org/councils/state/index_testmagistarte.asp?county=1437&Submit=GO
General Information: Court also has jurisdiction for bad checks, arrest warrants, preliminary hearings, and county ordinance violations.

Probate Court 101 S Peterson Ave, Ste A-20, Douglas, GA 31533; 912-384-5213; fax: 912-383-8116; 8:30AM-5PM (EST). *Probate, Marriage.*
www.coffeecountygov.com/index-pc.html

Colquitt County

Superior & State Court PO Box 2827, Moultrie, GA 31776; 229-616-7420; criminal phone: 229-616-7423 Sup; 616-7064 state; civil phone: 229-616-7066 Sup; 616-7420 state; fax: 229-616-7029; 8AM-5PM (EST). *Felony, Misdemeanor, Civil.*
http://southernjudicialcircuit.com
General Information: No juvenile, adoption, sexual, mental health or expunged records released. Will not fax documents. Court makes copy: $1.00 per page. Self serve copy: $.50 per page. Certification fee: $2.50. Payee: Court Clerk. Personal checks accepted. No credit cards accepted. Prepayment required.
Civil Name Search: Access: In person only. Visitors must perform in person searches themselves. Civil records go back to 1800s, civil records on dockets books, computerized records go back to 1999. Civil PAT goes back to 1999.
Criminal Name Search: Access: In person only. Visitors must perform in person searches themselves. Criminal docket on books; computerized records go back to 1999. Criminal PAT goes back to same as civil.

Magistrate Court PO Box 70, 101 E Central Ave, Rm 175, Moultrie, GA 31768; 229-616-7450; fax: 229-616-7494; 8AM-5PM (EST). *Civil Actions under $15,000, Eviction, Small Claims.*
General Information: Court also has jurisdiction for bad checks, arrest warrants, and county ordinance violations.

Probate Court PO Box 264, 9 South Main St, 1st Fl, Rm 108, Moultrie, GA 31776-0264; 229-616-7415; fax: 229-616-7489; 8AM-5PM (EST). *Probate.* www.ccboc.com/Dept/probate.htm

Columbia County

Superior Court PO Box 2930, 640 Ronald Reagan Dr, Evans, GA 30809; 706-312-7139; fax: 706-312-7152; 8AM-5PM (EST). *Felony, Misdemeanor, Civil.*
www.columbiaclerkofcourt.com
General Information: No juvenile, adoption, sexual, mental health or expunged records released. Will fax documents $2.50 1st page; $1.00 each add'l page. Court makes copy: $.50 per page. Certification fee: $2.00 plus $.50 per page. Payee: Clerk of Superior Court. No personal checks. No credit cards accepted. Prepayment required.
Civil Name Search: Access: In person, online. Visitors must perform in person searches themselves. Civil cases indexed by plaintiff. Civil records on computer from 1987, prior on docket books. Civil PAT goes back to 1987. Terminal results also show SSNs. Online search to docket from web page. Search by case number or name. Use last name, first name.
Criminal Name Search: Access: In person, online. Visitors must perform in person searches themselves. Required to search: name, years to search, DOB; SSN helpful. Criminal records computerized from 1987, prior on docket books. Criminal PAT goes back to 1987. Online access same as civil. Online results show middle initial.

Magistrate Court PO Box 777, 640 Ronald Reagan Dr, Evans, GA 30809; 706-868-3316; fax: 706-868-3314; 8AM-5PM (EST). *Civil Actions under $15,000, Eviction, Small Claims.*
www.columbiacountyga.gov/Index.aspx?page=2861
General Information: Court also has jurisdiction for bad checks, arrest warrants, preliminary hearings, and county ordinance violations.

Probate Court PO Box 525, 1956 Appling Harlem Hwy, Appling, GA 30802; 706-541-1254; fax: 706-541-4001; 8AM-4:30PM (EST). *Probate.* www.georgiacourts.org/councils/state/index_test.asp?county=1280&Submit= GO

Cook County

Superior Court 212 N Hutchinson Ave, Adel, GA 31620; 229-896-7717; fax: 229-896-7589; 8AM-5PM (EST). *Felony, Misdemeanor, Civil.*
www.gsccca.org/
General Information: No juvenile, adoption, sexual, 1st offenders, mental health or expunged records released. Will fax documents for fee $2.50 1st page and $.50 ea add'l. Court makes copy: $1.00 per page. Self serve copy: $.50 per page. Certification fee: $2.50 plus $.50 per page after first. Payee: Superior Court Clerk. Business checks accepted. No credit cards accepted. Prepayment required.
Civil Name Search: Access: Phone, mail, in person. Both court and visitors may perform in person name searches. Search fee: $10.00 per name, per 7 year period. Civil cases indexed by defendant. Civil records on dockets books, microfilm. Mail turnaround time same day. Civil PAT goes back to 1992.
Criminal Name Search: Access: Mail, in person. Both court and visitors may perform in person name searches. Search fee: $10.00 per name per 7 year period. Required to search: name, years to search, DOB, signed release; also helpful: SSN, race, sex. Criminal docket on books, microfilm. Mail turnaround time same day. Criminal PAT goes back to 2009.

Magistrate Court 1000 County Farm Rd, Adel, GA 31620; 229-896-3151; fax: 229-896-5186; 8AM-4:30PM (EST). *Civil Actions under $15,000, Eviction, Small Claims.*
https://www.ncourt.com/forms/GA/navigation.aspx?Juris=GACook
General Information: Court also has jurisdiction for bad checks, arrest warrants, preliminary hearings, and county ordinance violations.

Probate Court 212 N Hutchinson Ave, Adel, GA 31620; 229-896-3941; fax: 229-896-6083; 8:30AM-4:30PM (EST). *Probate, Misdemeanor Traffic.*
www.cookcountyga.us/probate/probate.html
General Information: This court also holds vital records.

Coweta County

Superior Court PO Box 943, 72 Greenville St, Newnan, GA 30264; 770-254-2693/2695; fax: 770-254-3700; 8AM-5PM (EST). *Felony, Civil.*
www.coweta.ga.us/Index.aspx?page=199
General Information: No juvenile, adoption, sexual, mental health or expunged records released. Will fax documents $1.00 per page. Court makes copy: $1.00 per page. Self serve copy: $.50 per page. Certification fee: $2.50 plus $.50 per page after first. Payee: Clerk of Superior Court. Business checks accepted. No credit cards accepted. Prepayment required.
Civil Name Search: Access: Mail, in person, online. Both court and visitors may perform in person name searches. Search fee: $5.00 per name. Civil records on computer from 1990, dockets books to 1970. Civil PAT

goes back to 1990. Access court records free online at http://sccweb.coweta.ga.us/cmwebsearchppp/.
Criminal Name Search: Access: In person, online. Both court and visitors may perform in person name searches. Search fee: $5.00 per name. Required to search: name, years to search, DOB. Criminal docket on books back to 1919. Note: Court can only conduct felony searches from 1990 to present. Court says they will not do crim searches for private agencies. Criminal PAT goes back to same as civil. Access court records free online at http://sccweb.coweta.ga.us/cmwebsearchppp/.
State Court PO Box 884, 72 Greenville St, Newnan, GA 30264-0884; 770-254-2699; fax: 770-252-6422; 8AM-5PM (EST). *Misdemeanor, Civil, Traffic.*
www.coweta.ga.us/Index.aspx?page=197
General Information: No juvenile, adoption, sexual, mental health or expunged records released. Will fax documents $2.50 1st page, $1.00 ea addl. Court makes copy: $1.00 per page. Self serve copy: $.50 per page. Certification fee: $2.50 plus $.50 per page after first. Payee: Clerk of State Court. Only cashiers checks and money orders accepted. Visa/MC accepted for fine payments only. Prepayment required.
Civil Name Search: Access: In person, online. Visitors must perform in person searches themselves. No search fee, but a $5.00 fee applies to retrieval of an older record not onsite. Civil records on computer from 1990, dockets books to 1970. Civil PAT goes back to 1990. Online access to index provided at www.cowetastatecourt.com/webFormFrame.aspx?page=main.
Criminal Name Search: Access: In person, online. Visitors must perform in person searches themselves. No search fee, but a $5.00 fee applies to retrieval of an older record not onsite. Required to search: name, years to search, DOB. Criminal docket on books back to 1919; on computer from 1990. Note: Court can only retrieve records if given a case number. Criminal PAT goes back to 1990. Online access, including traffic at www.cowetastatecourt.com/webFormFrame.aspx?page=main.

Magistrate Court 72 Greenville St #1200, Newnan, GA 30263; 770-254-2610; fax: 770-254-2614; 8AM-5PM (EST). *Civil Actions under $15,000, Eviction, Small Claims.*
General Information: Court also has jurisdiction for bad checks, arrest warrants, preliminary hearings, and county ordinance violations.

Probate Court 200 Court Square, Newnan, GA 30263; 770-254-2640; fax: 770-254-2648; 8AM-4:30PM (EST). *Probate.*
www.coweta.ga.us/Index.aspx?page=184

Crawford County

Superior Court 100 GA Hwy 42 South, Roberta, GA 31050; 478-836-3328; probate phone: 478-836-3313; fax: 478-836-9170; 8AM-5PM (EST). *Felony, Misdemeanor, Civil.*
General Information: No juvenile, adoption, sexual, mental health or expunged records released. Will fax documents $2.50 1st page, $1.00 each add'l page, prepaid. Court makes copy: $1.00 per page. Self serve copy: $.50 per page. Certification fee: $2.50 first page, $.50 ea add'l. Payee: Clerk of Superior Court. Local personal checks accepted. No credit cards accepted. Prepayment required.
Civil Name Search: Access: In person only. Visitors must perform in person searches themselves. Civil records on dockets books to 1830, records computerized since 1998. Civil PAT goes back to 1998.
Criminal Name Search: Access: In person only. Visitors must perform in person searches themselves. Required to search: name, years to search, DOB; also helpful: SSN, race, sex. Criminal docket on books to 1830, records computerized since 1998. Criminal PAT goes back to same as civil.

Probate Court PO Box 1028, GA Hwy 42 South, Knoxville, Roberta, GA 31078; 478-836-3313; fax: 478-836-4111; 8AM-5PM (EST). *Probate, Misdemeanor, Ordinance.*
General Information: Traffic records here also.

Magistrate Court PO Box 568, 100 US Hwy 42, Roberta, GA 31078; 478-836-5804; fax: 478-836-4340; 9AM-5PM (EST). *Misdemeanor, Eviction, Small Claims.*
General Information: Court also has jurisdiction for bad checks, arrest warrants, preliminary hearings, and county ordinance violations.

Crisp County

Superior & Juvenile Court PO Box 747, 510 N 7th Street, Suite 202, Cordele, GA 31010-0747; 229-271-4726; fax: 229-271-4737; 8:30AM-5PM (EST). *Felony, Misdemeanor, Civil Actions over $15,000.*
General Information: No juvenile, adoption, sexual, mental health or expunged records released. Fee to fax out file $2.50 1st page, $1.00 each add'l. Court makes copy: $1.00 per page. Self serve copy: $.50 per page. Certification fee: $2.00 plus $.50 per page. Cert fee includes copies. Payee: Clerk of Superior Court. Personal checks accepted. No credit cards accepted. Prepayment required. Mail requests: SASE required.

Civil Name Search: Access: Mail, in person. Visitors must perform in person searches themselves. No search fee. Civil cases indexed by defendant. Civil index on docket books to 1905, computerized since 1994. Civil PAT goes back to 1994.

Criminal Name Search: Access: Mail, in person. Visitors must perform in person searches themselves. No search fee. Required to search: name, years to search; also helpful: SSN. Criminal docket on books to 1905, computerized since 1994. Mail turnaround time 1-2 days. Criminal PAT goes back to same as civil.

Magistrate Court 510 N 7th St, Rm 105, Cordele, GA 31015; 229-271-4728; fax: 229-271-4715; 8:30AM-5PM (EST). *Civil Actions under $15,000, Eviction, Small Claims.*
www.crispcounty.com/departments/index.html#magistrate
General Information: Court also has jurisdiction for bad checks, arrest warrants, preliminary hearings, and county ordinance violations.

Probate Court PO Box 26, Cordele, GA 31010; 229-271-4731; fax: 229-271-4716; 9AM-5PM (EST). *Probate, Misdemeanor, Traffic.*

Dade County

Superior Court PO Box 417, 255 W Crabtree St, #203, Trenton, GA 30752; 706-657-4778; probate phone: 706-657-4414; fax: 706-657-8284; 8:30AM-5PM (EST). *Felony, Misdemeanor, Civil, Eviction, Small Claims.*
www.dadegaclerkofcourt.com/
General Information: This office will not perform civil or criminal record name searches. No juvenile, adoption, sexual, mental health or expunged records released. Fee to fax out file $1.00 per page. Court makes copy: $.50 per page. Self serve copy: $.50 per page. Certification fee: $2.50 certification plus $.50 per page. Payee: Superior Court. Personal checks accepted. Prepayment required.

Civil Name Search: Access: In person, online. Both court and visitors may perform in person name searches. No search fee. Civil records on computer back to 1/1994; prior on docket books. Civil PAT goes back to 1994. The court provides access to docket information at www.dadesuperiorcourt.com/webFormFrame.aspx?page=main. Also, the home page provides case calendars.

Criminal Name Search: Access: In person, online. Both court and visitors may perform in person name searches. No search fee. Required to search: name, years to search, DOB. Criminal records computerized from 1/1994; prior on docket books to 1900's. Criminal PAT goes back to 1994. The court provides access to docket information at www.dadesuperiorcourt.com/webFormFrame.aspx?page=main. Also, the home page provides case calendars.

Magistrate Court PO Box 605, 75 Case Ave, Trenton, GA 30752; 706-657-4113; fax: 706-657-8618; 8AM-5PM (EST). *Civil Actions under $15,000, Eviction, Small Claims.*
www.dadecounty-ga.gov/**Magistrate Court**.cfm?lid=1130
General Information: Court also has jurisdiction for bad checks, arrest warrants, preliminary hearings and county ordinance violations.

Probate Court PO Box 605, 255 W Crabtree St, Trenton, GA 30752; 706-657-4414; fax: 706-657-4305; 8:30AM-N,1-5PM (EST). *Probate, Misdemeanor Traffic.*
General Information: This court also holds vital records, firearm licenses and marriage licenses.

Dawson County

Superior Court 25 Tucker Ave, #106, Dawsonville, GA 30534; 706-344-3510; criminal phone: x262; civil phone: x273; fax: 706-344-3511; 8AM-5PM (EST). *Felony, Misdemeanor, Civil.*
General Information: No juvenile, adoption, sexual, mental health or expunged records released. Will fax documents $1.00 per page. Court makes copy: $.50 per page. Self serve copy: same. Certification fee: $2.50. Payee: Superior Court. Personal checks accepted. No credit cards accepted. Prepayment required.

Civil Name Search: Access: Phone, mail, fax, in person. Visitors must perform in person searches themselves. No search fee. Civil cases indexed by plaintiff. Civil records on computer back to 1994, prior in dockets books. Note: The court search only searches the computer index. Civil PAT goes back to 1994.

Criminal Name Search: Access: mail, fax, in person. No search fee. Required to search: name, years to search, DOB; also helpful: SSN, race, sex. Criminal records computerized from 1994, prior in dockets books. Note: The court only searches the computer index. Mail turnaround time 1 week. Criminal PAT goes back to same as civil.

Magistrate Court 59 Justice Way, Dawsonville, GA 30534; 706-344-3730; fax: 706-265-8480; 8AM-5PM (EST). *Civil Actions under $15,000, Eviction, Small Claims.*
General Information: Court also has jurisdiction for bad checks, arrest warrants, preliminary hearings and county ordinance violations.

Probate Court 25 Tucker Ave, #102, Dawsonville, GA 30534; 706-344-3580; fax: 706-265-6155; 8AM-5PM (EST). *Probate, Traffic.*
www.dawsoncounty.org/page.php?id=176

De Kalb County

Superior Court 556 N McDonough St, Decatur, GA 30030; 404-371-2836; criminal phone: 404-687-3875; civil phone: 404-687-3854; fax: 404-371-2635; 8:30AM-5PM (EST). *Felony, Misdemeanor, Civil.*
www.co.dekalb.ga.us/superior/index.htm
General Information: No juvenile, adoption, sexual, mental health or expunged records released. Will not fax documents. Court makes copy: $1.00 per page. Self serve copy: $.50 per page. Certification fee: $2.50 plus $.50 per page after first. Payee: Clerk of Superior Court. No personal checks or credit cards accepted. Prepayment required.

Civil Name Search: Access: Mail, in person, online. Visitors must perform in person searches themselves. Civil records on computer back 10 years, prior archived. Public use terminal available. Online access is free at www.ojs.dekalbga.org.

Criminal Name Search: Access: Mail, in person, online. Visitors must perform in person searches themselves. Search fee: $20.00 per name. Required to search: name, years to search, DOB; also helpful: SSN, race, sex. Criminal records on computer back 10 years, on microfilm from 1947. Public use terminal available. Results include case number. Online access is free at www.ojs.dekalbga.org. Jail and inmate records are also available.

State Court 556 N McDonough St, 2nd Floor Administration Tower, Decatur, GA 30030; 404-371-2261; fax: 404-371-3064; 8:30AM-5PM (EST). *Misdemeanor, Civil.*
http://web.co.dekalb.ga.us/StateCourt/index.html
General Information: Civil located on the 2nd floor, Administrative Tower. The fax is not available for public use. Online identifiers in results same as on public terminal. Will not fax documents. Court makes copy: $.50 per page for civil. Certification fee: $5.00 per page. Payee: Court Clerk. Only attorney checks, cashiers checks, cash and money orders accepted. Prepayment required. Mail requests: SASE requested.

Civil Name Search: Access: Mail, in person, online. Visitors must perform in person searches themselves. No search fee. Civil records on computer from 1988, back records on docket books. Note: The court will perform limited searches. Public use terminal has civil records. Online access is free at www.ojs.dekalbga.org. Also, current court calendars free at www.dekalbstatecourt.net.

Criminal Name Search: Access: In person, online, mail. No search fee. Required to search: name. Criminal records readily available from 2005, otherwise searching is generally via docket books. Mail turnaround time 7 days if prior to 2005. Online access is free at www.ojs.dekalbga.org. Jail and inmate records also available. Also, current court calendars free at www.dekalbstatecourt.net. Online results show name, DOB.

Magistrate Court 556 N McDonough St, Rm 270, Decatur, GA 30030; 404-371-4766; 8:30AM-5PM (EST). *Civil Actions under $15,000, Eviction, Small Claims.*
http://web.co.dekalb.ga.us/StateCourt/index.html
General Information: Online access is available free at www.ojs.dekalbga.org. Court also has jurisdiction for bad checks, arrest warrants, preliminary hearings, and county ordinance violations.

Probate Court Courthouse Annex, Rm 1100, 556 N McDonough St, Decatur, GA 30030; 404-371-2718; fax: 404-371-7055; 8:30AM-4:00PM (EST). *Probate.*
http://web.co.dekalb.ga.us/probate_court/index.html

Decatur County

Superior & State Court PO Box 336, 112 W Water St, Bainbridge, GA 39818; 229-248-3025; fax: 229-248-3029; 8AM-5PM (EST). *Felony, Misdemeanor, Civil.*
General Information: No juvenile, adoption, sexual, mental health or expunged records released. Will not fax documents. Court makes copy: $.50 per page. Certification fee: $2.50 plus $.50 per page. Payee: Court Clerk. Personal checks accepted. No credit cards accepted. Prepayment required.

Civil Name Search: Access: In person only. Visitors must perform in person searches themselves. Civil index in docket books from 1823; computerized from 1996. Civil PAT goes back to 1997.

Criminal Name Search: Access: In person only. Visitors must perform in person searches themselves. Required to search: name, years to search, DOB; SSN helpful. Criminal docket on books from 1823; computerized from 1996. Criminal PAT goes back to 1996.

Magistrate Court 912 Spring Creek Rd, Box #3, Bainbridge, GA 39817; 229-248-3014; fax: 229-248-3863; 9AM-5PM (EST). *Civil Actions under $15,000, Eviction, Small Claims.*
General Information: Court also has jurisdiction for bad checks, arrest warrants, preliminary hearings, and county ordinance violations.

Probate Court PO Box 234, 112 W Water St, Bainbridge, GA 39818; 229-248-3016; fax: 229-248-3858; 9AM-5PM (EST). *Probate.*

Dodge County

Superior Court PO Drawer 4276, 5401 Anson Ave, Eastman, GA 31023; 478-374-2871; fax: 478-374-3035; 9AM-5PM (EST). *Felony, Misdemeanor, Civil.*
www.dodgeclerkofcourt.com/
General Information: No juvenile, adoption, sexual, mental health or expunged records released. Will fax documents $2.00 1st page, $1.00 each add'l page. Court makes copy: $.50 per page. Self serve copy: $.50 per page. Certification fee: $2.00 plus $.50 per page after first. Payee: Court Clerk. Personal checks accepted. No credit cards accepted. Prepayment required.
Civil Name Search: Access: In person only. Visitors must perform in person searches themselves. Civil cases indexed by defendant. Civil index on docket books.
Criminal Name Search: Access: In person, online. Visitors must perform in person searches themselves. Required to search: name, years to search, DOB, signed release; SSN helpful. Criminal docket on books and computer. There is a subscription service offered for online access, however this is only made available to attorneys. The fee is 3140 per year. Please call the Clerk's office for details.

Magistrate Court 5018 Courthouse Cir, #202, Eastman, GA 31023; 478-374-7243/8144; fax: 478-374-5716; 8:30AM-N; 1-4:30PM (EST). *Civil Actions under $15,000, Eviction, Small Claims.*
General Information: Court also has jurisdiction for bad checks, pre-warrants, warrants, preliminary hearings, and county ordinance violations.

Probate Court PO Box 514, 5401 Anson Ave, Rm 100, Eastman, GA 31023; 478-374-3775/478-374-8152; fax: 478-374-9197; 9AM-5PM (EST). *Probate.*

Dooly County

Superior Court PO Box 326, 104 Second St, Vienna, GA 31092-0326; 229-268-4234; fax: 229-268-1427; 8:30AM-5PM (EST). *Felony, Misdemeanor, Civil.*
General Information: No juvenile, adoption, sexual, mental health or expunged records released. Will fax documents $2.50 1st page, 41.00 ea add'l. Court makes copy: $1.00 per page. Self serve copy: $.50 per page. Certification fee: $2.50 + copy fee. Payee: Dooly County Superior Court Clerk. Personal checks accepted. No credit cards accepted. Prepayment required.
Civil Name Search: Access: In person only. Visitors must perform in person searches themselves. Civil records on computer since 1995. Public use terminal has civil records back to 1995.
Criminal Name Search: Access: In person only. Prefer to have public to perform searches. Required to search: name, years to search, DOB; also helpful: SSN, race, sex. Criminal records on computer since 1995, docket books prior to 1857.

Magistrate Court 113 N 3rd Street, Room 2, Vienna, GA 31092; 229-268-4324; fax: 229-268-4230; 8AM-N, 1-5PM (EST). *Civil Actions under $15,000, Eviction, Small Claims.*
www.georgiacourts.org/councils/magistrate/county.asp
General Information: Court also has jurisdiction for bad checks, arrest warrants, preliminary hearings, and ordinance violations.

Probate Court PO Box 304, 104 2nd St S, Rm 11, Vienna, GA 31092; 229-268-4217 x1; fax: 229-268-6142; 8AM-5PM (EST). *Probate, Misdemeanor, Traffic.*
www.doolycountyprobate.com

Dougherty County

Superior & State Court PO Box 1827, 225 Pine Ave, #126, Albany, GA 31702; 229-431-2198; criminal fax: 229-878-3155; civil fax: 8:30AM-5PM; 8:30AM-5PM (EST). *Felony, Misdemeanor, Civil.*
www.albany.ga.us/content/1800/2887/2985/default.aspx
General Information: Online identifiers in results same as on public terminal. No juvenile, adoption, sexual, mental health or expunged records released. Will fax documents to local or toll-free number. Court makes copy: $1.00 per page. Self serve copy: $.50 per page. Certification fee: $3.00 for 1st page. Copy fee for add'l pages. Payee: Court Clerk. Personal checks accepted. No credit cards accepted. Prepayment required.
Civil Name Search: Access: In person. Visitors must perform in person searches themselves. Civil records on computer from 1992, overall records go back to 1854. Civil PAT goes back to 1992.
Criminal Name Search: Access: In person. Visitors must perform in person searches themselves. Required to search: name, years to search SSN. Criminal records computerized from 1992, overall records go back to 1854. Criminal PAT goes back to same as civil.

Magistrate Court PO Box 1827, 225 Pine Ave, Rm 308, Albany, GA 31702; 229-431-3216; fax: 229-434-2692; 8:30AM-5PM (EST). *Civil Actions under $15,000, Eviction, Small Claims.*
www.dougherty.ga.us/

General Information: Court also has jurisdiction for bad checks, arrest warrants, preliminary hearings, and county ordinance violations.
Probate Court PO Box 1827, 225 Pine Ave, #123, Albany, GA 31702; 229-431-2102; fax: 229-434-2694; 8:30AM-5PM (EST). *Probate.*
General Information: Search the probate court index free at www.albany.ga.us/court_system/court_clerk.htm.

Douglas County

Superior & State Court Douglas County Courthouse, 8700 Hospital Dr, Douglasville, GA 30134; 770-920-7252;; 8AM-5PM (EST). *Felony, Misdemeanor, Civil.*
www.celebratedouglascounty.com
General Information: Records from both courts can be searched at once. No juvenile, adoption, sexual, mental health or expunged records released. Will not fax documents. Court makes copy: $1.00 per page. Self serve copy: $.50 per page. Certification fee: $2.50 plus $.50 per page. Payee: Clerk of Superior Court. Personal checks accepted from local bank only. No credit cards accepted. Prepayment required.
Civil Name Search: Access: In person only. Visitors must perform in person searches themselves. Civil records on computer from 1994, prior on docket books to 1871. Civil PAT goes back to 1994.
Criminal Name Search: Access: In person only. Visitors must perform in person searches themselves. Required to search: name, years to search, DOB, signed release; SSN helpful. Criminal records computerized from 1994, prior on docket books to 1871. Criminal PAT goes back to same as civil.

Magistrate Court 8700 Hospital Dr, Douglasville, GA 30134; 770-920-7215; 8AM-5PM (EST). *Civil Actions under $15,000, Eviction, Small Claims.*
www.celebratedouglascounty.com/view/departments/view_dept/&cdept=187&department=Magistrate%20Court
General Information: Court also has jurisdiction for bad checks, arrest warrants, preliminary hearings and county ordinance violations.

Probate Court 8700 Hospital Dr, Douglasville, GA 30134; 770-920-7249; fax: 770-920-7381; 8AM-5PM (EST). *Probate.*
www.celebratedouglascounty.com/view/departments/view_dept/&cdept=146&department=Probate%20Court

Early County

Superior & State Court PO Box 849, Blakely, GA 39823; 229-723-3033; fax: 229-723-4411; 8AM-5PM (EST). *Felony, Misdemeanor, Civil.*
http://earlycounty.georgia.gov/03/home/0,2230,8867984,00.html
General Information: No juvenile, adoption, sexual, mental health or expunged records released. Will fax documents $2.50 1st page, $1.00 each add'l page. Court makes copy: $1.00 per page. Self serve copy: $.50 per page. Certification fee: $2.50 plus $.50 per page after first. Payee: Court Clerk. Personal checks accepted. No credit cards accepted. Prepayment required.
Civil Name Search: Access: In person only. Visitors must perform in person searches themselves. Civil records on dockets.
Criminal Name Search: Access: In person only. Visitors must perform in person searches themselves. Required to search: name, years to search, DOB; SSN helpful. Criminal records on dockets.

Magistrate Court Early County Courthouse, 111 Court Sq, Ste D, Blakely, GA 39823; 229-723-3454 and 229-723-5492; fax: 229-723-5246; 8AM-5PM (EST). *Civil Actions under $15,000, Eviction, Small Claims, Probate, Ordinance.*
General Information: Court also has jurisdiction for bad checks, arrest warrants, preliminary hearings, and county ordinance violations.

Echols County

Superior Court PO Box 213, Statenville, GA 31648; 229-559-5642; fax: 229-559-5792; 8AM-N, 1-4:30PM (EST). *Felony, Misdemeanor, Civil.*
http://southernjudicialcircuit.com
General Information: No juvenile, adoption, sexual, mental health or expunged records released. Will fax out documents $2.50 1st page, $.50 each add'l. Court makes copy: $1.00 per page. Self serve copy: same. Certification fee: $2.00 1st page, $.50 each add'l page. Payee: Court Clerk. Personal checks accepted. No credit cards accepted. Prepayment required.
Civil Name Search: Access: In person only. Both court and visitors may perform in person name searches. Search fee: $5.00. Civil records on dockets books, computerized since 1995.
Criminal Name Search: Access: In person only. Both court and visitors may perform in person name searches. Search fee: $5.00. Criminal docket on books, computerized since 1995.

Magistrate & Probate Court PO Box 118, 110 Hwy 94 East, Statenville, GA 31648; 229-559-7526; fax: 229-559-8128; 8AM-4:30PM (EST). *Civil Actions under $15,000, Eviction, Small Claims, Probate.*

General Information: Court also has jurisdiction for bad checks, arrest warrants, preliminary hearings, and county ordinance violations. Name search for citations free at https://www.ncourt.com/courtpayment/Default.aspx.

Effingham County

Superior & State Court 700 N Pine St #110, Springfield, GA 31329-5079; 912-754-2146; civil phone: x3104; probate phone: 912-754-2112; 8:30AM-5PM (EST). *Felony, Misdemeanor, Civil.* www.effinghamcounty.org/

General Information: No juvenile, adoption, sexual, mental health or expunged records released. Will not fax documents. Court makes copy: $.50 per page. Self serve copy: same. Certification fee: $2.50 plus $.50 per add'l page, plus copy fee. Payee: Court Clerk. Business checks accepted. No credit cards accepted. Prepayment required. Mail requests: SASE required.

Civil Name Search: Access: Mail, in person. Both court and visitors may perform in person name searches. Search fee: $20.00 per name. Civil records on computer from 1991, dockets books. Mail turnaround time 3-5 days. Civil PAT goes back to 1991.

Criminal Name Search: Access: Mail, in person. Both court and visitors may perform in person name searches. Search fee: $20.00 per name. Required to search: name, years to search, DOB; also helpful: SSN, race, sex. Criminal records computerized from 1991, dockets books. Mail turnaround time 3-5 days. Criminal PAT goes back to same as civil.

Magistrate Court PO Box 819, 700 N Pine St, Springfield, GA 31329; 912-754-2124; fax: 912-754-4893; 8AM-5PM (EST). *Civil Actions under $15,000, Eviction, Small Claims, Ordinance.* www.effinghamcounty.org/

General Information: Court also has jurisdiction for bad checks, arrest warrants, preliminary hearings, and county ordinance violations.

Probate Court 700 N Pine St, #146, Springfield, GA 31329; 912-754-2112; fax: 912-754-3894; 8:30AM-5PM (EST). *Probate.* www.effinghamcounty.org/

Elbert County

Superior & State Court PO Box 619, 12 S Olive St, Elberton, GA 30635; 706-283-2005; fax: 706-213-7286; 8AM-5PM (EST). *Felony, Misdemeanor, Civil.*

General Information: No juvenile, adoption, sexual, mental health or expunged records released. Will fax documents $2.50 1st page, $1.00 each add'l. Court makes copy: $.50 per page. Self serve copy: same. Certification fee: $2.00 per cert plus $.50 per page. Payee: Clerk of Court. No personal checks or credit cards accepted. Prepayment required.

Civil Name Search: Access: Mail, in person. Visitors must perform in person searches themselves. No search fee. Civil records on computer from 1996 excluding felonies; docket books prior. Civil PAT goes back to 1996.

Criminal Name Search: Access: Mail, in person. Visitors must perform in person searches themselves. No search fee. Criminal records computerized from 1996 excluding felonies; docket books prior. Mail turnaround time 1 week. Criminal PAT goes back to same as civil.

Magistrate Court 12 S Oliver St, Elberton, GA 30635; 706-283-2027; fax: 706-283-2004; 8AM-5PM (EST). *Civil Actions under $15,000, Eviction, Small Claims.*

General Information: Court also has jurisdiction for bad checks, arrest warrants, preliminary hearings, and county ordinance violations.

Probate Court 45 Forest Ave, Suite 41, Elberton, GA 30635; 706-283-2016; fax: 706-283-9668; 8AM-5PM (EST). *Probate.*

General Information: There is a $5.00 search fee.

Emanuel County

Superior & State Court PO Box 627, 125 S Main, Swainsboro, GA 30401; 478-237-8911; fax: 478-237-1220; 8AM-5PM (EST). *Felony, Misdemeanor, Civil.*

General Information: No juvenile, adoption, sexual, mental health or expunged records released. Will not fax documents. Court makes copy: $1.00 per page. Self serve copy: $.50 per page. Certification fee: $2.50 per doc. Payee: Court Clerk. Personal checks accepted. No credit cards accepted. Prepayment required.

Civil Name Search: Access: In person only. Visitors must perform in person searches themselves. Civil records computerized since 1999, earlier on dockets books. Civil PAT available.

Criminal Name Search: Access: In person only. Visitors must perform in person searches themselves. Required to search: name, years to search, DOB; SSN helpful. Criminal records computerized since 1999, earlier on dockets books. Note: Because there is no court record retrievers in this county, this office will accept a fax request but it must be on official company letterhead. They will review the request and are likely to perform the search. Criminal PAT available.

Magistrate Court 107 N Main St, Swainsboro, GA 30401; 478-237-7278; fax: 478-237-9154; 8AM-5PM F-7:30-4:30 (EST). *Civil Actions up to $15,000, Eviction, Small Claims.*

General Information: Court also has jurisdiction for bad checks, arrest warrants, preliminary hearings, and county ordinance violations.

Probate Court PO Box 70, 125 S Main St, Swainsboro, GA 30401; 478-237-7091; fax: 478-237-2633; 8AM-5PM (EST). *Probate.* www.emanuelprobate.com/

Evans County

Superior & State Court PO Box 845, Claxton, GA 30417; 912-739-3868; fax: 912-739-2504; 8AM-5PM (EST). *Felony, Misdemeanor, Civil.*

General Information: No juvenile, adoption, sexual, mental health or expunged records released. Will not fax documents. Court makes copy: $1.00 per page. Self serve copy: $.50 per page. Certification fee: $2.50 plus $.50 per page after first. Payee: Court Clerk. Personal checks accepted. No credit cards accepted. Prepayment required. Mail requests: SASE required.

Civil Name Search: Access: Mail, in person. Visitors must perform in person searches themselves. No search fee. Civil records on computer from 1989, dockets bookstore 1915. Note: Mail requests must include case number. Civil PAT goes back to 1989.

Criminal Name Search: Access: Mail, in person. Visitors must perform in person searches themselves. No search fee. Required to search: name, years to search, DOB; SSN helpful. Criminal records computerized from 1989, dockets books to 1915. Note: Mail requests must include case number. Criminal PAT goes back to same as civil.

Magistrate Court Courthouse Annex, 7 Freeman St, Claxton, GA 30417; 912-739-3745; fax: 912-739-8856; 8AM-5PM (EST). *Civil Actions under $15,000, Eviction, Small Claims.*

General Information: Court also has jurisdiction for bad checks, arrest warrants, preliminary hearings, garnishments and county ordinance violations.

Probate Court PO Box 852, 201 Freeman St, Ste 9, Claxton, GA 30417; 912-739-4080; fax: 912-739-4077; 8AM-N, 1-5PM (EST). *Probate.*

Fannin County

Superior Court PO Box 1300, 400 W Main St, Blue Ridge, GA 30513; 706-632-2039; probate phone: 706-632-3011; 9AM-5PM (EST). *Felony, Misdemeanor, Civil.* www.fannincountyga.org/index.php?option=com_content&view=article&id=51:clerk-of-court&catid=57:county-departments&Itemid=64

General Information: No juvenile, adoption, or DD214 records released. Will not fax documents. Court makes copy: $1.00 per page. Self serve copy: $.50 per page. Certification fee: $2.50 plus $.50 per page after first. Payee: Fannin County Court Clerk. Personal checks accepted. No credit cards accepted. Prepayment required.

Civil Name Search: Access: In person only. Visitors must perform in person searches themselves. Civil index on docket books back to the early 1900's.

Criminal Name Search: Access: In person only. Visitors must perform in person searches themselves. Required to search: name, years to search, DOB, signed release; SSN helpful. Criminal docket on books back to the early 1900's.

Magistrate Court 400 W Main St #202, Fannin County Courthouse, Blue Ridge, GA 30513; 706-632-5558; fax: 706-632-8236; 9AM-5PM (EST). *Civil Actions under $15,000, Eviction, Small Claims, Misdemeanor.* www.fannincountyga.org

General Information: Court also has jurisdiction for bad checks, arrest warrants, preliminary hearings, and county ordinance violations.

Probate Court 400 W Main St #204, Blue Ridge, GA 30513; 706-632-3011; fax: 706-632-7167; 8AM-5PM (EST). *Probate, Misdemeanor.*

Fayette County

Superior & State Court PO Box 130, 1 Center Dr, Justice Center, Fayetteville, GA 30214; 770-716-4290; criminal phone: 770-716-4293; civil phone: 770-716-4294; fax: 770-716-4868; 8AM-5PM (EST). *Felony, Misdemeanor, Civil.* www.fayetteclerk.com/

General Information: The court will copy and mail specific documents for $1.00 per page. No juvenile, adoption, sexual, mental health or expunged records released. Will not fax documents. Court makes copy: $1.00 per page. Self serve copy: $.50 each on vault copier. Certification fee: $2.50 plus $.50 per copy page. Payee: Court Clerk. Only cashiers checks and money orders accepted. No credit cards accepted. Prepayment required.

Civil Name Search: Access: In person, online. Visitors must perform in person searches themselves. Civil records on computer since 1989; prior records on dockets books (found at the vault). Civil PAT goes back to 1989. Index by last name, alpha. Search dockets free at www.fayetteclerkofcourt.com/webFormFrame.aspx?page=main.

Criminal Name Search: Access: In person, online. Visitors must perform in person searches themselves. Required to search: name, years to search, DOB; SSN helpful. Criminal records on computer since 1991; prior records on dockets books. Criminal PAT goes back to 1991. Search dockets free at www.fayetteclerkofcourt.com/webFormFrame.aspx?page=main.

Magistrate Court 1 Center Dr, Fayetteville, GA 30214-8401; 770-716-4230; fax: 770-716-4855; 8AM-5PM (EST). *Civil Actions under $15,000, Eviction, Small Claims.*
www.fayetteclerk.com/
General Information: Court also has jurisdiction for bad checks, arrest warrants, and preliminary hearings. Free docket search at www.fayetteclerkofcourt.com/webFormFrame.aspx?page=main.

Probate Court 1 Center Dr, Fayetteville, GA 30214; 770-716-4220; fax: 770-716-4854; 8AM-4PM (EST). *Probate.*
www.fayettecountyga.gov/courts/probate_court/index.asp
General Information: This court also hold vital records.

Floyd County

Superior Court PO Box 1110, #3 Government Plaza, #101, Rome, GA 30163; 706-291-5190; probate phone: 706-291-5136; fax: 706-233-0035; 8AM-5PM (EST). *Felony, Misdemeanor, Civil.*
www.romefloyd.com/CitizenSafety/Courts/FloydCounty/SuperiorCourt/tabid/200/Default.aspx
General Information: No juvenile, adoption, sexual, mental health or expunged records released. Will fax out file for $1.00 per page. Court makes copy: $.50 per page. Self serve copy: same. Certification fee: $2.00. Payee: Court Clerk. No personal checks. No credit cards accepted. Prepayment required.
Civil Name Search: Access: Phone, in person. Visitors must perform in person searches themselves. No search fee. Civil records on computer since 11/95; prior on docket books to 1833. Note: The court will only do a name search to determine if a case exists, then provides a case number. Civil PAT goes back to 11/1995.
Criminal Name Search: Access: In person only. Both court and visitors may perform in person name searches. No search fee. Required to search: name, years to search, signed release. Criminal records on computer since 1/96; prior on docket books back to 1833. Note: Court will only do a name search to determine if a case exists, then provides a case number. Criminal PAT goes back to 1/1996.

Magistrate Court 3 Government Plaza, Rm 227, Rome, GA 30161; 706-291-5250; fax: 706-291-5269; 8:15AM-4:45PM (EST). *Civil Actions under $15,000, Eviction, Small Claims, Garnishments.*
General Information: Copy fee is $.25 a page; certification is $2.50; will fax results. Court also has jurisdiction for bad checks, arrest warrants, preliminary hearings, county ordinance violations, civil actions up to $15,000, dispossessories and garnishments.

Probate Court 3 Government Plaza, Ste 201, County Administrative Offices, Rome, GA 30161; 706-291-5136/8; fax: 706-291-5189; 8:15AM-5:00PM (EST). *Probate, Traffic.*

Forsyth County

Superior & State Court 100 Courthouse Square, Rm 010, Cumming, GA 30040; 770-781-2120; fax: 770-886-2858; 8:30AM-5PM (EST). *Felony, Misdemeanor, Civil, Eviction.*
www.forsythclerk.com/
General Information: No juvenile, adoption, sexual, mental health or expunged records released. Will fax documents $3.00 per page. Court makes copy: $.50 per page. Self serve copy: same. Certification fee: $2.50 plus $.50 per page after first. Payee: Clerk of Court. Personal checks accepted. No credit cards accepted. Prepayment required.
Civil Name Search: Access: Mail, fax, in person. Both court and visitors may perform in person name searches. No search fee. Civil cases indexed by defendant. Civil records on computer since 1999; prior records on docket books back to 1832. Note: Will search computer index back to 1999 only. Civil PAT goes back to 1999.
Criminal Name Search: Access: Mail, fax, in person. Both court and visitors may perform in person name searches. No search fee. Required to search: name, years to search; SSN helpful. Criminal records on computer since late 1989. Note: Court will search computer index back to 1999 only. Searches of older records must be performed in person. Criminal PAT goes back to 1999.

Magistrate Court 1090 Tribble Gap Rd, Cumming, GA 30040; 770-781-2211; fax: 770-844-7581; 8AM-4:30PM (EST). *Misdemeanor, Civil Actions under $15,000, Eviction, Small Claims.*
www.forsythco.com/department.asp?DeptID=12
General Information: Court also has jurisdiction for bad checks, arrest warrants, preliminary hearings, and county ordinance violations.

Probate Court 112 W Maple St, Cumming, GA 30040; 770-781-2140; fax: 770-886-2839; 8:30AM-5PM (EST). *Probate.*
www.forsythco.com/department.asp?DeptID=16

Franklin County

Superior Court PO Box 70, 9592 Lavonia Rd, Carnesville, GA 30521; 706-384-2514;; 8AM-5PM (EST). *Felony, Misdemeanor, Civil.*
General Information: No juvenile, adoption, sexual, mental health or expunged records released. Will not fax documents. Court makes copy: $1.00 per page. Self serve copy: $.50 per page. Certification fee: $2.50 for 1st page, $.50 each add'l. Payee: Court Clerk. No personal checks or credit cards accepted. Prepayment required.
Civil Name Search: Access: In person only. Visitors must perform in person searches themselves. Civil records on computer since 2002; prior records on docket books. Civil PAT goes back to 2002.
Criminal Name Search: Access: In person only. Visitors must perform in person searches themselves. Required to search: name, years to search, DOB; SSN helpful. Criminal records on computer since 2002; prior records on docket books. Criminal PAT goes back to same as civil.

Magistrate Court 7085 Hwy 145, Ste B, Carnesville, GA 30521; 706-384-7473; 8AM-5PM (EST). *Civil Actions under $15,000, Eviction, Small Claims.*
General Information: Court also has jurisdiction for bad checks, arrest warrants, preliminary hearings, and county ordinance violations.

Probate Court 7085 Highway 145, #A, Carnesville, GA 30521; 706-384-2403; fax: 706-384-2636; 8AM-5PM (EST). *Probate, Misdemeanor.*
www.franklincountyga.com/Departments/Probate.html
General Information: This location also holds traffic misdemeanors and vital records.

Fulton County

Superior Court - Civil 136 Pryor St SW, Rm C-155, Superior Court Clerk, Atlanta, GA 30303; 404-613-5313; criminal phone: 404-612-5174; 8:30AM-5PM (EST). *Civil.*
www.fcclk.org
General Information: Phone for the Closed File Rm- 404-730-6872. No juvenile, adoption, sexual, mental health, sealed or expunged records released. Will fax documents for $2.00 per page, pre-paid. Court makes copy: $.50 per page. Certification fee: $2.50 for 1st page; $.50 each add'l, includes copy fee. Payee: Clerk of Fulton Superior Court. In-state personal checks accepted. No credit cards accepted. Prepayment required. Mail requests: SASE requested.
Civil Name Search: Access: Mail, in person, online. Both court and visitors may perform in person name searches. Search fee: $15.00 per name. Civil records on computer since 1972. Mail turnaround time 2-5 days. Public use terminal has civil records back to 1972. Access Clerk of Superior Court Judicial civil records free at www.fcclkjudicialsearch.org/CivilSearch/civfrmd.htm. Search by either party name, case number, and date range. Search includes status, attorney. Images provided. Also a Hearing Search free at www.fcclkjudicialsearch.org/CVHearSearch/cvhearfrmd.htm.

Superior Court - Criminal 136 Pryor St SW, Rm 106, Atlanta, GA 30303; 404-613-5313 info; 404-612-6872 rec; 8:30AM-5PM (EST). *Felony, Misdemeanor, Eviction.*
www.fcclk.org
General Information: Closed files- 404-612-8430, 404-612-5375. No sealed or expunged records released. Will not fax out case files. Court makes copy: $.50 per page. Certification fee: $2.50 for 1st page; $.50 each add'l, includes copies. Cert Dept. phone- 404-730-6872. Payee: Clerk of Superior Court. Personal checks accepted. No credit cards accepted. Prepayment required.
Criminal Name Search: Access: In person only. Visitors must perform in person searches themselves. Required to search: name, years to search, DOB; charges helpful. Criminal records computerized from 1973. Note: Criminal record room, who process criminal record requests, will accept requests for specific cases only, but will not do name searches per se, perhaps one via phone. Public use terminal has crim records back to 1974.

State Court TG100 Justice Center Bldg, 185 Central Ave SW, Atlanta, GA 30303; 404-730-5002; criminal phone: x7; civil phone: x1; fax: 404-730-8141; 8:30AM-5PM (EST). *Misdemeanor, Civil, Small Claims, Traffic.*
www.georgiacourts.org/courts/fulton/
General Information: For online case docket info from present back 365 days, search at New State Court Case Numbers at website, then use case number at the separate 'online access to court records' tab, but this is not always functional. No juvenile, adoption, sexual, mental health or expunged records released. Will not fax documents. Court makes copy: $.50 per page. Certification fee: $2.50 per page. Payee: Court Clerk. Cashier check or

money order accepted for criminal. Visa/MC accepted at cashier office. Prepayment required. Mail requests: SASE required.

Civil Name Search: Access: Mail, in person. Both court and visitors may perform in person name searches. Search fee: $15.00 per name per index. Civil records on computer from 1984, books back to 1982. Civil PAT goes back to 1984.

Criminal Name Search: Access: Mail, in person. Both court and visitors may perform in person name searches. Search fee: $15.00 per name per index. Required to search: name, years to search, DOB; also helpful, race, aliases, date of offense, sex, approximate arrest date. Criminal records computerized from 1984, books back to 1982. Mail 2-7 days . Criminal PAT goes back to same as civil.

Magistrate Court 185 Central Ave SW, TG-700, Justice Ctr Tower, Atlanta, GA 30303; 404-613-5045; criminal phone: 404-613-4752; fax: 404-332-0352; 8:30AM-5PM (EST). *Civil Actions under $15,000, Eviction, Small Claims, Criminal Preliminaries.* www.georgiacourts.org/courts/fulton/magistrate.html

General Information: Court also has jurisdiction for bad checks, arrest warrants, and county ordinance violations. The criminal warrants division (does no record checks) is located at 160 Prior St SW, J-135, phone above.

Probate Court 136 Pryor St, # 230, Atlanta, GA 30303; 404-612-4693; fax: 404-893-6576; 8:30AM-4:45PM (EST). *Probate.*

Gilmer County

Superior Court 1 Broad St, Ste 102, Ellijay, GA 30540; 706-635-4462; fax: 706-635-1462; 8:30AM-5PM (EST). *Felony, Misdemeanor, Civil.* www.georgiacourts.org/councils/state/index_testmagistarte.asp?county=1463&Submit=GO

General Information: No juvenile, adoption, sealed, sexual, mental health, expunged or sealed records released. Will not fax documents. Court makes copy: $.50 per page. Self serve copy: same. Certification fee: $2.50 plus $.50 per page after first. Payee: Superior Court Clerk. Personal checks accepted. No credit cards accepted. Prepayment required.

Civil Name Search: Access: In person only. Visitors must perform in person searches themselves. Civil index on docket books computerized records since 1994. Public use terminal has civil records back to 1994.

Criminal Name Search: Access: In person only. Only the court performs in person name searches; visitors may not. Required to search: name, years to search, signed release; also helpful: DOB, SSN. Criminal docket on books; computerized since 1994.

Magistrate Court 1 Broad St, Ste 203, Ellijay, GA 30540; 706-635-2515; fax: 706-635-7756; 8:30AM-5PM (EST). *Civil Actions under $15,000, Eviction, Small Claims.* www.gilmercounty-ga.gov

General Information: Court also has jurisdiction for bad checks, arrest warrants, preliminary hearings, first appearance hearings, extradition hearings and county ordinance violations.

Probate Court 1 Broad St. Ste 204, Ellijay, GA 30540; 706-635-4763; fax: 706-635-4761; 8:30AM-5PM (EST). *Probate.*

Glascock County

Superior Court PO Box 231, 62 E Main St, Gibson, GA 30810; 706-598-2084; fax: 706-598-2577; 8AM-5PM M,Tu,TH,F; Wed 8AM-N (EST). *Felony, Misdemeanor, Civil.*

General Information: No juvenile, adoption, sexual, mental health or expunged records released. Will fax specific case file $1.00 per page. Court makes copy: $1.00 per page. Self serve copy: $.50 per page. Certification fee: $2.50 plus $.50 per page copy fee after first. Payee: Court Clerk. Personal checks accepted. No credit cards accepted. Prepayment required.

Civil Name Search: Access: In person only. Visitors must perform in person searches themselves. Civil records on computer from 1991, records go back to 1990. Civil PAT goes back to 1991. Public access terminal has county cases only.

Criminal Name Search: Access: In person only. Visitors must perform in person searches themselves. Required to search: name, years to search, DOB; SSN helpful. Criminal records computerized from 1991 records go back to 1990. Criminal PAT goes back to same as civil. Public access terminal has county cases only.

Magistrate Court PO Box 277, 62 E Main St, Gibson, GA 30810; 706-598-3241; fax: 706-598-2471; 8AM-5PM (EST). *Misdemeanor, Civil Actions under $15,000, Eviction, Small Claims.*

General Information: Court also has jurisdiction for bad checks, arrest warrants, preliminary hearings, and county ordinance violations.

Probate Court 62 E Main St, 370 W Main St, Gibson, GA 30810; 706-598-3241; fax: 706-598-2471; 8AM-N, 1-5PM-M (EST). *Probate.*

Glynn County

Superior Court PO Box 1355, Brunswick, GA 31521; 912-554-7272; fax: 912-267-5625; 8AM-5PM (EST). *Felony, Civil.*

General Information: No juvenile, adoption, sexual, mental health or expunged records released. Fee to fax out file $5.00 each. Court makes copy:

$.50 per page. Self serve copy: $.50 per page. Certification fee: $2.50 plus $.50 per copy. Payee: Court Clerk. Personal checks accepted. No credit cards accepted. Prepayment required. Will bill copy and cert fees. Mail requests: SASE requested.

Civil Name Search: Access: Phone, fax, mail, in person. Both court and visitors may perform in person name searches. No search fee. Civil records on computer back to 1987, archived and in docket books from 1800s. Mail turnaround time 1-3 days. Civil PAT goes back to 1987.

Criminal Name Search: Access: Phone, fax, mail, in person. Both court and visitors may perform in person name searches. No search fee. Required to search: name, years to search, DOB, signed release; also helpful: SSN, race, sex. Criminal records computerized from 1987, index back to 1800s. Mail turnaround time 1-3 days. Criminal PAT goes back to same as civil.

State Court 701 "H" St, #104, Brunswick, GA 31520; 912-554-7325; fax: 912-261-3849; 8AM-5PM (EST). *Misdemeanor, Civil.* www.glynncounty.org/index.aspx?nid=296

General Information: No juvenile, adoption, sexual, mental health or expunged records released. Will not fax documents. Court makes copy: $1.00 per page. Certification fee: $2.50 plus $.50 per page. Payee: Clerk of State Court. Only cashiers checks and money orders accepted. No credit cards accepted. Prepayment required.

Civil Name Search: Access: In person only. Visitors must perform in person searches themselves. Civil cases indexed by defendant. Civil records on dockets books to 1980; on computer back to 1994. Civil PAT goes back to 1994. Results include name and case number.

Criminal Name Search: Access: In person only. Visitors must perform in person searches themselves. Criminal docket on books to 1979; on computer back to 1994. Criminal PAT goes back to same as civil. Results include name and case number.

Magistrate Court PO Box 1355, 701 H St, Brunswick, GA 31521; 912-554-7250; fax: 912-267-5677; 8AM-5PM (EST). *Civil Actions under $15,000, Eviction, Small Claims.* www.georgiacourts.org/councils/state/index_testmagistarte.asp?county=1466&Submit=GO

General Information: Court also has jurisdiction for bad checks, arrest warrants, preliminary hearings, and county ordinance violations.

Probate Court 11 Judicial Ln, #275, Brunswick, GA 31520; 912-554-7231; fax: 912-466-8001; 8AM-5PM (EST). *Probate.* www.glynncounty.org/index.aspx?nid=138

Gordon County

Superior Court 100 Wall St, #102, Calhoun, GA 30701; 706-629-9533; fax: 706-629-2139; 8:30AM-5PM (EST). *Felony, Misdemeanor, Civil.* www.gordoncounty.org/

General Information: No sealed records released. Will fax back documents $2.50 1st pg. $1.00 ea add'l. Court makes copy: $1.00 per page. Self serve copy: $.50 per page. Certification fee: $2.50. Payee: Superior Court Clerk. Personal checks accepted. No credit cards accepted. Prepayment required. Mail requests: SASE required.

Civil Name Search: Access: Mail, fax, in person. Both court and visitors may perform in person name searches. No search fee. Civil records on computer since 3/97; prior records on docket books. Mail turnaround time 1-2 days. Civil PAT goes back to 1997.

Criminal Name Search: Access: Mail, fax, in person. Both court and visitors may perform in person name searches. No search fee. Criminal records on computer since 3/97; prior records on docket books. Mail turnaround time 1-2 days. Criminal PAT goes back to same as civil.

Magistrate Court 100 S Wall St, 1st Fl, Courthouse, Calhoun, GA 30701; 706-629-6818 x2270, x2271; criminal phone: 706-879-2272; civil phone: 706-879-2271; fax: 706-602-1751; 8:30AM-5PM (EST). *Misdemeanors, Civil Actions under $15,000, Eviction, Small Claims.* www.gordoncounty.org/Departments/JudicialOffices/**Magistrate Court**.aspx

General Information: Court also has jurisdiction for bad checks, arrest warrants, preliminary hearings, and county ordinance violations.

Probate Court PO Box 669, 30703, 100 S Wall St, Calhoun, GA 30701; 706-629-7314; fax: 706-629-4698; 8:30AM-5PM (EST). *Probate, Misdemeanor.*

Grady County

Superior & State Court 250 N Broad St, Box 8, Cairo, GA 39828; 229-377-2912; fax: 229-377-7078; 8AM-5PM (EST). *Felony, Misdemeanor, Civil.*

General Information: No juvenile or adoption records released. Will not fax documents. Court makes copy: n/a. Self serve copy: $.50 per page. Certification fee: $2.00 per cert plus $.50 per page. Payee: Superior Court Clerk. Personal checks accepted. No credit cards accepted. Prepayment required.

Civil Name Search: Access: In person only. Both court and visitors may perform in person name searches. No search fee. Civil cases indexed by defendant, plaintiff on computer. Civil records on computer since 1993; prior records on docket books from 1906. Civil PAT goes back to 1993. Identifiers will show if existing on docket; address if available.

Criminal Name Search: Access: In person only. Visitors must perform in person searches themselves. Criminal records on computer since 1993; prior records on docket books from 1906. Criminal PAT goes back to 1993. Identifiers will show if existing on docket.

Magistrate Court 250 N Broad St, Box 2, Cairo, GA 39828; 229-377-4132; fax: 229-377-4127; 8AM-5PM (EST). *Civil Actions under $15,000, Eviction, Small Claims.*

General Information: Court also has jurisdiction for bad checks, arrest warrants, preliminary hearings, and county ordinance violations.

Probate Court 250 N Broad St, Box #1, Courthouse, Cairo, GA 39828; 229-377-4621; fax: 229-378-8052; 8AM-5PM (EST). *Probate.*

Greene County

Superior & Juvenile Court 113 N Main St, #109, Greensboro, GA 30642; 706-453-3340; fax: 706-453-9179; 8AM-5PM (EST). *Felony, Misdemeanor, Civil, Eviction, Small Claims.*

General Information: As a courtesy, court may do a single name search via phone or mail, but not background record checks per se. No juvenile or adoption records released. Will not fax out documents. Court makes copy: $.50 per page. Certification fee: $2.50 plus $.50 per page after first. Payee: Superior Court Clerk. Personal checks accepted. No credit cards accepted. Prepayment required.

Civil Name Search: Access: In person only. Visitors must perform in person searches themselves. Overall records go back to 1700. Computerized records go back to 2000. Civil PAT goes back to 2000.

Criminal Name Search: Access: In person only. Visitors must perform in person searches themselves. Required to search: name, years to search; SSN helpful. Overall records go back to 1700. Computerized records go back to 2000. Criminal PAT goes back to 2000.

Magistrate & Probate Court 113 N Main St, #113, Greensboro, GA 30642; 706-453-3346; fax: 706-453-7649; 8AM-5PM (EST). *Civil Actions under $15,000, Eviction, Small Claims, Probate.*
https://www.gaprobate.org/find_court.asp

General Information: Court also has jurisdiction for bad checks, arrest warrants, preliminary hearings, and county ordinance violations.

Gwinnett County

Superior & State Court PO Box 880, 75 Langley Dr, Lawrenceville, GA 30046; 770-822-8100;; 8AM-5PM (EST). *Felony, Misdemeanor, Civil, Eviction, Small Claims.* www.gwinnettcourts.com/

General Information: No sealed records released. Will not fax out documents. Court makes copy: $.50 per page. Certification fee: $2.50 plus $.50 per page includes copy fee. Payee: Superior Court Clerk. No personal checks or credit cards accepted. Prepayment required.

Civil Name Search: Access: Online, in person. Visitors must perform in person searches themselves. Civil records on computer from 1990, prior records on card index. Civil PAT goes back to 1990. Public terminal has Superior court records back to 1980. Online access to court case party index is free at www.gwinnettcourts.com/home.asp#partycasesearch/. Search by name or case number.

Criminal Name Search: Access: Online, in person. Visitors must perform in person searches themselves. Criminal records computerized from 1990, prior records on card index. Criminal PAT goes back to same as civil. Public terminal 90% of info available to public, other 10% can only be searched by staff. Online access to court case party index is free at www.gwinnettcourts.com/home.asp#partycasesearch/. Search by name or case number.

Magistrate Court 75 Langley Dr, Justice & Admin. Ctr, PO Box 246, Lawrenceville, GA 30045-6900; 770-822-8100; criminal phone: 770-619-6720; civil phone: 770-822-8100; fax: 770-822-8075; 8AM-5PM (EST). *Civil Actions under $15,000, Eviction, Small Claims.*
www.gwinnettcourts.com/#courtsjudges_magistrate/

General Information: Court also has jurisdiction for bad checks, arrest warrants, preliminary hearings, and county ordinance violations. Search cases and calendars countywide free at www.gwinnettcourts.com/#home/

Probate Court Justice & Admin Ctr, 75 Langley Dr, Lawrenceville, GA 30045; 770-822-8250; fax: 770-822-8217; 8AM-4:30PM (EST). *Probate.*
www.gwinnettcourts.com/

General Information: Probate records may be available online free at www.gwinnettcourts.com/#home.

Habersham County

Superior & State Court 555 Monroe St, Unit 35, PO Box 2320, Clarkesville, GA 30523; 706-754-2923; probate phone: 706-754-2013; fax: 706-839-6351; 8AM-5PM (EST). *Felony, Misdemeanor, Civil.*

www.co.habersham.ga.us

General Information: The Probate Court uses PO Box 876 for mail. No juvenile, sexual, mental health or expunged records released. Will fax documents to local or toll free line. Court makes copy: $1.00 per page. Self serve copy: $.50 per page. Certification fee: $2.50 per document. Payee: Court Clerk. No personal checks or credit cards accepted. Prepayment required.

Civil Name Search: Access: Mail, in person. Visitors must perform in person searches themselves. No search fee. Civil index on docket books from 1819. Civil PAT goes back to 1992.

Criminal Name Search: Access: Mail, in person. Visitors must perform in person searches themselves. No search fee. Criminal records indexed in books from 1819. Mail turnaround time 1-2 days. Criminal PAT goes back to same as civil. Pre-2008 cases may not show SSN or DOB.

Magistrate Court PO Box 580, 226 Grant St, Clarkesville, GA 30523; 706-754-4871; fax: 706-839-7093; 8:30AM-5PM (EST). *Misdemeanor, Civil Actions under $15,000, Ordinance.*
www.co.habersham.ga.us

General Information: Court also has jurisdiction for bad checks, arrest warrants, preliminary hearings, and county ordinance violations.

Probate Court PO Box 876, 555 Monroe St, County Courthouse, Clarkesville, GA 30523; 706-754-2013; fax: 706-754-5093; 8AM-5PM (EST). *Probate.* www.habershamga.com/probatecourt.cfm

Hall County

Superior & State Court PO Box 1336, 225 Green St, SE, Gainesville, GA 30503; 770-531-7025; criminal phone: 770-531-7025; fax: 770-531-7070; 8AM-5PM (EST). *Felony, Misdemeanor, Civil.*
www.hallcounty.org/judicial/

General Information: Clerk and records located in the basement. No juvenile, adoption, sexual, mental health or expunged records released. Will fax documents $2.50 1st page, $1.00 ea add'l. Court makes copy: $.50 per page. Certification fee: $2.00 plus $.50 per page. Payee: Hall County Clerk of Court. No personal checks accepted. Prepayment required.

Civil Name Search: Access: In person only. Visitors must perform in person searches themselves. Civil records on computer back to 1989, dockets books from early 1900s in storage. Civil PAT goes back to 7/1989. Results include plaintiffs and defendants.

Criminal Name Search: Access: In person only. Visitors must perform in person searches themselves. Criminal records computerized from 1989, dockets books from early 1900s in storage. Criminal PAT goes back to same as civil.

Magistrate Court PO Box 1435, 225 Green St, 2nd Fl, Gainesville, GA 30503; 770-531-6912; fax: 770-531-6917; 8AM-5PM (EST). *Civil Actions under $15,000, Eviction, Small Claims, Misdemeanors.*
www.hallcounty.org/judicial/#majistrate

General Information: Court also has jurisdiction for bad checks, arrest warrants, preliminary hearings, and county ordinance violations.

Probate Court Hall County Courthouse, Rm 1000, 225 Green St, Gainesville, GA 30501; 770-531-6923; fax: 770-531-4946; 8:30AM-4:30PM (EST). *Probate.* www.hallcounty.org/judicial/#probate

General Information: The search fee is $4.00 per record

Hancock County

Superior Court PO Box 451, Courthouse Sq, Sparta, GA 31087; 706-444-6644; fax: 706-444-5685; 9AM-5PM (EST). *Felony, Misdemeanor, Civil.*

General Information: No juvenile, adoptions, sealed, sexual, mental health or expunged records released. Will not fax documents. Court makes copy: $1.00 per page. Self serve copy: same. Certification fee: $2.50 1st page, $.50 each add'l page. Payee: Clerk of Superior Court. Personal checks accepted. No credit cards accepted. Prepayment required. Mail requests: SASE required.

Civil Name Search: Access: In person. Visitors must perform in person searches themselves. Civil index in docket books from 1991. Mail turnaround time 1 week.

Criminal Name Search: Access: In person. Visitors must perform in person searches themselves. Required to search: name, years to search, DOB. Criminal docket on books since 1991.

Magistrate Court 40 Courthouse Square, Sparta, GA 31087; 706-444-6234; fax: 706-444-6178; 9AM-5PM (EST). *Civil Actions under $15,000, Eviction, Small Claims.*
www.georgiacourts.org/councils/state/index_testmagistarte.asp?county=1473&Submit=GO

General Information: Court also has jurisdiction for bad checks, arrest warrants, preliminary hearings, and county ordinance violations.

Probate Court 12630 Broad St, Sparta, GA 31087; 706-444-5343; fax: 706-444-8024; 8AM-5PM (EST). *Probate.*
www.hancockprobatecourtga.com/

Haralson County

Superior Court Drawer 849, 4485 Georgia Hwy 120, Buchanan, GA 30113; 770-646-2005; probate phone: 770-646-2008; fax: 770-646-8827; 8:30AM-5PM (EST). *Felony, Misdemeanor, Civil.*

General Information: No juvenile, adoption, sexual, mental health or expunged records released. Will not fax documents. Court makes copy: $.50 per page. Self serve copy: same. Certification fee: $2.50 plus $.50 per page after first. Payee: Clerk of Superior Court. Personal checks accepted. No credit cards accepted. Prepayment required. Mail requests: SASE required.

Civil Name Search: Access: Mail, in person. Both court and visitors may perform in person name searches. No search fee. Civil index in docket books from the 1864. Mail turnaround time 1 week. Civil PAT goes back to 2005.

Criminal Name Search: Access: In person. Both court and visitors may perform in person name searches. No search fee. Required to search: name, years to search, signed release. Criminal docket on books from the 1864. Mail turnaround time 1 week. Criminal PAT goes back to 2005.

Magistrate Court PO Box 1040, 4485 Hwy 120, Buchanan, GA 30113; 770-646-2015; fax: 770-646-6627; 8:30AM-5PM (EST). *Civil Actions under $15,000, Eviction, Small Claims.*

General Information: Court also has jurisdiction for bad checks, arrest warrants, preliminary hearings, and county ordinance violations.

Probate Court PO Box 620, 4485 Georgia Hwy 120, Buchanan, GA 30113; 770-646-2008; fax: 770-646-3419; 8:30AM-5PM (EST). *Probate.*

Harris County

Superior Court PO Box 528, 102 N College St, Hamilton, GA 31811; 706-628-4944; fax: 706-628-7039; 8AM-5PM (EST). *Felony, Misdemeanor, Civil.*
www.harrisclerkofcourt.com/

General Information: Juvenile, adoption, sexual, mental health or expunged records are only released with a signed release. Will not fax documents. Court makes copy: $.50 per page. Self serve copy: same. Certification fee: $2.50 plus $.50 per page after first. Payee: Court Clerk. No personal checks or credit cards accepted. Prepayment required.

Civil Name Search: Access: In person, online. Visitors must perform in person searches themselves. Civil index in docket books from 1900; on computer back to 1999. Civil PAT goes back to 1999. Access court records by subscription; for information and signup contact Lisa Culpeper at 706-628-4944.

Criminal Name Search: Access: In person, online. Visitors must perform in person searches themselves. Required to search: name, years to search, DOB; also helpful: race, sex. Criminal docket on books from 1900; on computer back to 1999. Criminal PAT goes back to same as civil. Access court records by subscription; for information and signup contact Lisa Culpeper at 706-628-4944.

Magistrate Court PO Box 347, 102 N College St, Hamilton, GA 31811; 706-628-4977; fax: 706-628-5416; 8AM-5PM (EST). *Civil Actions under $15,000, Eviction, Small Claims.*
www.harriscountyga.gov/departments/court-magistrate.php

General Information: Court also has jurisdiction for bad checks, arrest warrants, preliminary hearings, and county ordinance violations. Website may soon have court records available.

Probate Court PO Box 569, 102 N College St #116, Hamilton, GA 31811; 706-628-5038; fax: 706-628-7322; 8AM-5PM (EST). *Probate, Misdemeanor Traffic.*
http://harriscountyga.gov/departments/court-probate.php

Hart County

Superior Court PO Box 386, Hartwell, GA 30643; 706-376-7189; fax: 706-376-1277; 8:30AM-5PM (EST). *Felony, Misdemeanor, Civil.*
http://hartcountyga.gov/clerkcourt.html

General Information: No juvenile, adoption, sexual, mental health or expunged records released. Will fax documents for $1.00 per page. Court makes copy: $1.00 per page. Self serve copy: $.50 per page. Certification fee: $2.50 first page plus $.50 ea add'l. Payee: Clerk of Court. Personal checks accepted. No credit cards accepted. Prepayment required.

Civil Name Search: Access: In person only. Visitors must perform in person searches themselves. Civil records on computer back to 1997, dockets books from 1853. Civil PAT goes back to 1997.

Criminal Name Search: Access: In person only. Visitors must perform in person searches themselves. Required to search: name, years to search, DOB. Criminal records computerized from 1997, dockets books from 1853. Criminal PAT goes back to same as civil.

Magistrate Court PO Box 698, 165 W Franklin, Hartwell, GA 30643; 706-376-6817; fax: 706-376-6821; 8:30AM-5PM (EST). *Civil Actions under $15,000, Eviction, Small Claims.*
http://hartcountyga.gov/magistrate.html

General Information: Court also has jurisdiction for bad checks, arrest warrants, preliminary hearings, and county ordinance violations.

Probate Court PO Box 1159, 185 W Franklin St, Hartwell, GA 30643; 706-376-2565; fax: 706-376-9032; 8:30AM-5PM (EST). *Probate, Misdemeanor Traffic.*

General Information: Also handles births, deaths, marriages, firearm permits, passports, elections

Heard County

Superior Court PO Box 249, 215 Court St, Franklin, GA 30217; 706-675-3301; fax: 706-675-6138; 8:30AM-5PM (EST). *Felony, Misdemeanor, Civil.*

General Information: No juvenile, adoptions, sealed, sexual, mental health or expunged records released. Will fax specific case file $1.00 per page. Court makes copy: $.50 per page. Certification fee: $2.50 plus $.50 per page after first. Payee: Court Clerk. No personal checks or credit cards accepted. Prepayment required.

Civil Name Search: Access: In person only. Visitors must perform in person searches themselves. Civil index in docket books from 1894. Civil PAT goes back to 1996.

Criminal Name Search: Access: In person only. Visitors must perform in person searches themselves. Required to search: name, years to search, DOB, signed release; SSN helpful. Criminal docket on books from 1894. Criminal PAT goes back to same as civil.

Magistrate Court PO Box 395, 215 E Court Square, Rm 11, Franklin, GA 30217; 706-675-3002; fax: 706-675-6059; 8:30AM-5PM (EST). *Misdemeanor, Civil Actions under $15,000, Eviction, Small Claims.*
www.heardcountyga.com/magistrate.htm

General Information: Court also has jurisdiction for bad checks, arrest warrants, preliminary hearings, and county ordinance violations.

Probate Court PO Box 478, 215 E Court Sq, Rm 3, Franklin, GA 30217; 706-675-3353; fax: 706-675-0819; 8:30AM-5PM (EST). *Probate, Misdemeanor.*

Henry County

Superior Court One Courthouse Square, McDonough, GA 30253; 770-288-8022; fax: 770-288-8105; 8AM-5PM (EST). *Felony, Civil.*
www.co.henry.ga.us/SuperiorCourt/index.shtml

General Information: Misdemeanor records will show here only if filed with a felony on same subject. No juvenile, adoption, sexual, mental health or expunged records released. Will fax documents for $2.50 1st page and $1.00 ea addl. Court makes copy: $1.00 per page. Self serve copy: $.50 per page. Certification fee: $2.50 plus $.50 per add'l page. Payee: Clerk of Superior Court. Personal checks accepted. No credit cards accepted. Prepayment required.

Civil Name Search: Access: Phone, mail, in person, online. Visitors must perform in person searches themselves. No search fee. Civil index in docket books from 1800s. Note: The court will assist the public and will help with a name search time permitting. Civil PAT goes back to 1993. The court provides a free docket search at https://hcwebb.boca.co.henry.ga.us/SuperiorCMWebSearch/. Search by name or case number, or associated party. The DOB is not shown, it is hard to identify common names if used for a specific name search.

Criminal Name Search: Access: In person, online. Visitors must perform in person searches themselves. Required to search: name, years to search, DOB, signed release; SSN helpful. Criminal docket on books from 1800s. Criminal PAT available. The court provides a free docket search at https://hcwebb.boca.co.henry.ga.us/SuperiorCMWebSearch/. Search by name or case number.

State Court One Judicial Center, Ste120, McDonough, GA 30253; 770-288-7800; fax: 770-288-7801; 8AM-5PM (EST). *Misdemeanor, Civil.*

General Information: This court was formed in 1999. No juvenile, adoption, sexual, mental health or expunged records released. No fee to fax documents. Court makes copy: $.50 per page. Certification fee: $2.50 plus $.25 per add'l page. Payee: Clerk of State Court. Personal checks accepted. No credit cards accepted. Prepayment required.

Civil Name Search: Access: In person. Visitors must perform in person searches themselves. Record file copies searchable since 1999. Civil PAT goes back to 01/1999.

Criminal Name Search: Access: In person. Visitors must perform in person searches themselves. Required to search: name, years to search, DOB, signed release; SSN helpful. Criminal docket on books from 1999. Criminal PAT available.

Magistrate Court One Judicial Ctr, #260, McDonough, GA 30253; 770-288-7700; fax: 770-288-7722; 8AM-5PM (EST). *Misdemeanor, Civil Actions under $15,000, Eviction, Small Claims.*
www.co.henry.ga.us/**Magistrate Court**/

General Information: Court also has jurisdiction for bad checks, arrest warrants, preliminary hearings, and county ordinance violations.

Probate Court 99 Sims St., McDonough, GA 30253; 770-288-7600; fax: 770-288-7616; 8AM-4:30PM (EST). *Probate.*
www.co.henry.ga.us/Probate/

Houston County

Superior Court 201 Perry Pky, Perry, GA 31069; 478-218-4720; criminal phone: 478-218-4730; civil phone: 478-218-4740; fax: 478-218-4745; 8:30AM-5PM (EST). *Felony, Civil.*
www.houstoncountyga.org/index.htm
General Information: Misdemeanor records will show here only if filed with a felony on same subject. No juvenile, adoption, mental health or expunged records released. Will fax documents. Court makes copy: $1.00 per page. Self serve copy: same. Certification fee: $2.50 plus $.50 per page after first. Payee: Court Clerk. No personal checks or credit cards accepted. Prepayment required. Mail requests: SASE required.
Civil Name Search: Access: Phone, fax, mail, in person. Only the court performs in person name searches; visitors may not. No search fee. Civil records on computer from 1984, dockets books back to 1823. Mail turnaround time 1-2 days.
Criminal Name Search: Access: In person. Visitors must perform in person searches themselves. Required to search: name, years to search, DOB; also helpful: SSN, race, sex. Criminal records computerized from 1984, dockets books back to 1823. Mail turnaround time 1-2 days. Public use terminal has crim records back to 1984.
State Court 202 Carl Vinson Pky, Warner Robins, GA 31088; 478-542-2105; fax: 478-542-2077; 8AM-5PM (EST). *Misdemeanor, Civil.*
www.houstoncountyga.org/index.htm
General Information: No juvenile, adoption, sexual, mental health or expunged records released. Court makes copy: $1.00 per page. Self serve copy: $.50 per page. Certification fee: $2.50 plus $.50 per page after first. Payee: Court Clerk. Only cashiers checks and money orders accepted. No credit cards accepted. Prepayment required. Mail requests: SASE required.
Civil Name Search: Access: Mail, fax, in person. Both court and visitors may perform in person name searches. No search fee. Civil cases indexed by defendant. Civil records on computer from 20037, dockets books from 1965. Mail turnaround time 3 days. Civil PAT goes back to 2003.
Criminal Name Search: Access: In person only. Visitors must perform in person searches themselves. Required to search: name, years to search, DOB; SSN helpful. Criminal records computerized from 1987, dockets books from 1965. Criminal PAT goes back to same as civil. Terminal results include SSN.
Magistrate Court 89 Cohen Walker Dr, Warner Robins, GA 31088; 478-987-4695; fax: 478-987-5249; 8AM-5PM (EST). *Civil Actions under $15,000, Eviction, Small Claims.*
www.houstoncountyga.com/government/houston-county-magistrate-court.aspx
General Information: Court also has jurisdiction for bad checks, arrest warrants, preliminary hearings and county ordinance violations.
Probate Court PO Box 1801, 201 N Perry Pky, Perry, GA 31069; 478-218-4710; fax: 478-218-4715; 8:30AM-4:30PM (EST). *Probate.*
www.houstoncountyga.com/government/probate-court/

Irwin County

Superior Court 301 S Irwin Ave #103, Ocilla, GA 31774; 229-468-5356; fax: 229-468-9753; 8AM-5PM (EST). *Felony, Misdemeanor, Civil.*
General Information: No juvenile, adoption, sexual, mental health or expunged records released. Will fax documents $2.50 1st page, $1.00 each add'l page. Court makes copy: $1.00 per page. Self serve copy: $.50 per page. Certification fee: $2.50 plus $.50 per page after first. Payee: Court Clerk. No personal checks or credit cards accepted. Prepayment required.
Civil Name Search: Access: Phone, mail, in person. Visitors must perform in person searches themselves. No search fee. Civil index in docket books from 1870s, records are not computerized. Note: Court will not do general record searches; the specific case file must be given. Civil PAT goes back to 2003.
Criminal Name Search: Access: Phone, mail, in person. Visitors must perform in person searches themselves. No search fee. Required to search: name, years to search, DOB, signed release; also helpful: SSN, race, sex. Criminal docket on books from 1900, records are not computerized. Note: Court will not do general record searches, the specific case file must be given. Mail turnaround time 2-3 days. Criminal PAT goes back to same as civil.
Magistrate Court 301 S Irwin Ave, #102, Ocilla, GA 31774; 229-468-7671; fax: 229-468-8444; 8AM-5PM, M-TH, 8AM-N, F (EST). *Civil Actions under $15,000, Eviction, Small Claims.*
www.georgiacourts.org/councils/state/index_testmagistarte.asp?county=1480&Submit=GO
General Information: Court also has jurisdiction for bad checks, arrest warrants, preliminary hearings, and county ordinance violations.

Probate Court 301 S Irwin Ave., Ocilla, GA 31774; 229-468-5138; fax: 229-468-5702; 8AM-N,1-5PM (EST). *Probate.*

Jackson County

Superior & State Court PO Box 7, 5000 Jackson Pkwy, #150, Jefferson, GA 30549; 706-387-6246; criminal phone: 707-387-6254; civil phone: 707-387-6248; fax: 706-387-6273; 8AM-5PM (EST). *Felony, Misdemeanor, Civil.* www.jacksoncountygov.com/Index.aspx?page=81
General Information: No juvenile, adoption, sexual, mental health or expunged records released. Will not fax out documents. Court makes copy: $.50 per page. Self serve copy: $.50 per page. Certification fee: $2.50 plus $.50 per page after first. Payee: Court Clerk. No personal checks accepted. Prepayment required.
Civil Name Search: Access: In person only. Visitors must perform in person searches themselves. Civil records on computer from 1992, on dockets books from 1800s. Civil PAT goes back to 1992.
Criminal Name Search: Access: Mail, in person. Visitors must perform in person searches themselves. Search fee: $25.00 per name. Required to search: name, years to search, DOB; SSN helpful. Criminal records computerized from 1992, on dockets books from 1800s. Criminal PAT goes back to same as civil.
Magistrate Court 5000 Jackson Parkway #230, Jefferson, GA 30549; 706-387-6356; fax: 706-387-6369; 8AM-5PM (EST). *Civil Actions under $15,000, Eviction, Small Claims.*
www.jacksoncountygov.com/Index.aspx?page=99
General Information: Court also has jurisdiction for bad checks, arrest warrants, preliminary hearings, and county ordinance violations.
Probate Court 5000 Jackson Pky, Ste 140, Jefferson, GA 30549; 706-387-6275; fax: 706-387-6285; 8AM-5PM (EST). *Probate.*
www.jacksoncountygov.com/Index.aspx?page=103

Jasper County

Superior Court 126 W Green St, #110, Monticello, GA 31064; 706-468-4901; fax: 706-468-4946; 8AM-5PM (EST). *Felony, Misdemeanor, Civil.*
General Information: No juvenile, adoption, sexual, mental health or expunged records released. Will not fax out documents. Court makes copy: $1.00 per page. Self serve copy: $.50 per page. Certification fee: $2.50 plus $.50 per page after first. Payee: Court Clerk. Personal checks accepted. No credit cards accepted. Prepayment required.
Civil Name Search: Access: In person only. Visitors must perform in person searches themselves. Civil records on computer from 1990, dockets books from 1807. Civil PAT goes back to 1990.
Criminal Name Search: Access: In person only. Visitors must perform in person searches themselves. Required to search: name, years to search, DOB; SSN helpful. Criminal records computerized from 1990, dockets books from 1807. Criminal PAT goes back to 1992.
Magistrate Court 126 W Green St, #110, Monticello, GA 31064; 706-468-4909; fax: 706-468-4928; 8AM-5PM (EST). *Civil Actions under $15,000, Eviction, Small Claims.*
www.georgiacourts.org/councils/state/index_testmagistarte.asp?county=1482&Submit=GO
General Information: Court also has jurisdiction for bad checks, arrest warrants, preliminary hearings, garnishments, trovers and county ordinance violations.
Probate Court Jasper County Courthouse, 126 W Green St, #111, Monticello, GA 31064; 706-468-4903; fax: 706-468-4926; 8AM-4:30PM (EST). *Probate.*

Jeff Davis County

Superior & State Court PO Box 429, 14 Jeff Davis St, #105, Hazlehurst, GA 31539; 912-375-6615; fax: 912-375-6637; 8AM-5PM (EST). *Felony, Misdemeanor, Civil.*
General Information: No juvenile, confidential, adoption or sealed records released. Fee to fax out file $2.00 1st page, $1.00 each add'l. Court makes copy: $1.00 per page. Self serve copy: $.50 per page. Certification fee: $3.00 plus $1.00 per page after first. Payee: Clerk of Court. No personal checks accepted. Money orders only. No credit cards accepted. Prepayment required. Mail requests: SASE helpful.
Civil Name Search: Access: Mail, in person. Both court and visitors may perform in person name searches. Search fee: $3.00 per name. Civil cases indexed by defendant. Civil records on dockets books. Mail turnaround time 1 week.
Criminal Name Search: Access: Mail, in person. Both court and visitors may perform in person name searches. Search fee: $3.00 per name. Required to search: name, years to search; also helpful- offense. Criminal docket on books. Mail turnaround time 1 week.

Magistrate Court PO Box 568, 14 Jeff Davis St, Hazlehurst, GA 31539; 912-375-6630; fax: 912-375-6629; 8AM-5PM (EST). *Civil Actions under $15,000, Eviction, Small Claims.*
www.georgiacourts.org/councils/state/index_testmagistarte.asp?county=1483&Submit=GO

General Information: Court also has jurisdiction for bad checks, arrest warrants, preliminary hearings and county ordinance violations.

Probate Court PO Box 446, 14 Jeff Davis St, Hazlehurst, GA 31539; 912-375-6626; fax: 912-375-0502; 9AM-5PM (EST). *Probate.*

Jefferson County

Superior & State Court PO Box 151, 202 E Broad St, Louisville, GA 30434; 478-625-7922; fax: 478-625-4037; 9AM-5PM (EST). *Felony, Misdemeanor, Civil.*

General Information: No juvenile, adoption, sexual, mental health or expunged records released. Will fax documents to local or toll-free number. Court makes copy: $1.00 per page. Self serve copy: $.50 per page. Certification fee: $2.50 plus $1.00 per add'l page. Payee: Court Clerk. Personal checks accepted. No credit cards accepted. Prepayment required.

Civil Name Search: Access: In person only. Both court and visitors may perform in person name searches. No search fee. Civil index in docket books from 1865; on computer back to 1995. Civil PAT goes back to 1995. Results include drivers license number and SSN.

Criminal Name Search: Access: In person only. Both court and visitors may perform in person name searches. No search fee. Required to search: name, years to search, DOB or SSN. Criminal docket on books from 1865; on computer back to 1995. Criminal PAT goes back to same as civil. Results include name, SSN, drivers license.

Magistrate Court PO Box 749, 911 Clarks Mill Rd, Louisville, GA 30434; 478-625-8834; fax: 478-625-4039; 8:30AM-4;30PM (EST). *Civil Actions under $15,000, Eviction, Small Claims.*
www.georgiacourts.org/councils/state/index_testmagistarte.asp?county=1484&Submit=GO

General Information: Court also has jurisdiction for bad checks, arrest warrants, preliminary hearings, and county ordinance violations.

Probate Court PO Box 505, 202 E Broad St, Louisville, GA 30434; 478-625-3258; fax: 478-625-0245; 8AM-N, 1-5PM (EST). *Probate.*

Jenkins County

Superior & State Court PO Box 659, 611 Winthrop Ave, Millen, GA 30442; 478-982-4683; fax: 478-982-1274; 8:30AM-5PM (EST). *Felony, Misdemeanor, Civil.*

General Information: No juvenile, adoption, sexual, mental health or expunged records released. Will fax documents $.50 per page. Court makes copy: $.50 per page. Self serve copy: same. Certification fee: $2.50 plus $.50 per page after first. Payee: Clerk of Court. Personal checks accepted. No credit cards accepted. Prepayment required.

Civil Name Search: Access: In person only. Visitors must perform in person searches themselves. Civil cases indexed by defendant. Civil records on dockets books. Civil PAT goes back to 1990.

Criminal Name Search: Access: In person only. Visitors must perform in person searches themselves. Required to search: name, years to search, DOB; SSN helpful. Criminal docket on books. Criminal PAT goes back to same as civil.

Magistrate Court PO Box 892, 611 Winthrop Ave, Millen, GA 30442; 478-982-5580; fax: 478-982-4911; 8:30AM-5PM (EST). *Civil Actions under $15,000, Eviction, Small Claims, Misdemeanor, Ordinance.*
https://www.ncourt.com/forms/GA/navigation.aspx?Juris=GAJenkins

General Information: Court also has jurisdiction for bad checks, arrest warrants, preliminary hearings, and county ordinance violations.

Probate Court PO Box 904, 611 E Winthrope Ave, Millen, GA 30442; 478-982-5581; fax: 478-982-2829; 8:30AM-5PM (EST). *Probate.*

Johnson County

Superior & Magistrate Court PO Box 321, 2557 E Elm St, Wrightsville, GA 31096; 478-864-3484; fax: 478-864-1343; 9AM-5PM (EST). *Felony, Misdemeanor, Civil, Eviction, Small Claims.*
http://johnsonco.org/clerk-of-superior-court/

General Information: No juvenile, adoption, sexual, mental health or expunged records released. Will fax documents $2.00 per fax. Court makes copy: $.50 per page. Self serve copy: same. Certification fee: $3.00 per cert. Payee: Court Clerk. Personal checks accepted. Prepayment required.

Civil Name Search: Access: In person only. Visitors must perform in person searches themselves. Civil records on computer from 1991, dockets books from 1859.

Criminal Name Search: Access: In person only. Visitors must perform in person searches themselves. Required to search: name, years to search, DOB; SSN helpful. Criminal records computerized from 1991, dockets books from 1859.

Probate Court PO Box 264, 2557 E Elm St, Wrightsville, GA 31096; 478-864-3316; fax: 478-864-0528; 9AM-5PM (EST). *Probate.*
http://johnsonco.org/probate-court/

Jones County

Superior Court PO Box 39, 110 S Jefferson St, Gray, GA 31032; 478-986-6671/6674; fax: 478-986-2030; 9AM-5PM (EST). *Felony, Misdemeanor, Civil over $15,000.*
www.jonescounty.org/

General Information: No juvenile, adoption, sexual, mental health or expunged records released. Will fax out results $.50 per page, $5.00 minimum prepaid. Court makes copy: $1.00 per page. Self serve copy: $.50 per page. Certification fee: $2.50 plus $.50 per page after first. Payee: Superior Court. Personal checks accepted. No credit cards accepted. Prepayment required.

Civil Name Search: Access: In person only. Visitors must perform in person searches themselves. Civil records on computer since 1989, dockets books from 1800s. Note: The court will fax records not requiring a search, $5.00 minimum. Civil PAT goes back to 1995.

Criminal Name Search: Access: In person only. Visitors must perform in person searches themselves. Required to search: name, years to search, signed release. Criminal docket on books, computerized since 1995. Criminal PAT goes back to same as civil.

Magistrate Court PO Box 88, 110 S Jefferson St, Gray, GA 31032; 478-986-5113; fax: 478-986-6536; 8AM-5PM (EST). *Civil under $15,000, Small Claims, Eviction.*

Probate Court PO Box 1090, 110 S Jefferson St, Gray, GA 31032; 478-986-6668; fax: 478-986-1715; 8AM-5PM (EST). *Probate, Traffic, Vital Records.*
www.georgiacourts.org/

Lamar County

Superior Court 326 Thomaston St, Box 7, Barnesville, GA 30204; 770-358-5145; fax: 770-358-5814; 8AM-5PM (EST). *Felony, Misdemeanor, Civil.*

General Information: No juvenile, adoption, sexual, mental health or expunged records released. Will not fax out case files. Court makes copy: $1.00 first page. Self serve copy: $.50 per page. Certification fee: $2.50 for 1st page, $.50 each add'l page. Payee: Court Clerk. Personal checks accepted. No credit cards accepted. Prepayment required. Will bill copy fees if you have an account.

Civil Name Search: Access: In person only. Visitors must perform in person searches themselves. Civil cases indexed by defendant. Civil index in docket books from 1921; on computer back to 9/2000. Civil PAT goes back to 2000.

Criminal Name Search: Access: In person only. Visitors must perform in person searches themselves. Required to search: name, years to search, DOB, date of offense; SSN helpful. Criminal docket on books from 1921; on computer back to 9/2000. Criminal PAT goes back to 2000.

Magistrate Court 121 Roberta Dr, Barnesville, GA 30204; 770-358-5154; fax: 770-358-5214; 8AM-N, 1-5PM (EST). *Civil Actions under $15,000, Eviction, Small Claims.*

General Information: Court also has jurisdiction for bad checks, arrest warrants, preliminary hearings, and county ordinance violations.

Probate Court 326 Thomaston St, #6, Barnesville, GA 30204; 770-358-5155; fax: 770-358-5348; 8AM-5PM (EST). *Probate, Misdemeanor, Traffic.*
www.georgiacourts.org/councils/state/index_test.asp?county=1329&Submit=GO

Lanier County

Superior Court County Courthouse, 100 Main St, Ste 5, Lakeland, GA 31635; 229-482-3594; fax: 229-482-8333; 8AM-N, 1-5PM (EST). *Felony, Misdemeanor, Civil.*

General Information: No juvenile, adoption, sexual, mental health or expunged records released. Will not fax documents. Court makes copy: $.50 per page. Self serve copy: $.50 per page. Certification fee: $3.00. Payee: Court Clerk. Personal checks accepted. No credit cards accepted. Prepayment required.

Civil Name Search: Access: In person only. Visitors must perform in person searches themselves. Civil index in docket books from 1921; on computer back to 1995.

Criminal Name Search: Access: In person only. Visitors must perform in person searches themselves. Required to search: name, years to search, DOB, signed release. Criminal docket on books from 1921; on computer back to 1995.

Magistrate Court 56 W Main St, #10, County Courthouse, Lakeland, GA 31635; 229-482-2207; fax: 229-482-8358; 8AM-N; 1PM-5PM (EST). *Civil Actions under $15,000, Eviction, Small Claims.*
www.georgiacourts.org/councils/magistrate/county.asp

General Information: Court also has jurisdiction for bad checks, arrest warrants, preliminary hearings, and county ordinance violations.

Probate Court County Courthouse, 56 W Main, Ste #10, Lakeland, GA 31635; 229-482-3668; fax: 229-482-3680; 8AM-N, 1-5PM (EST). *Probate.*

General Information: This location also holds traffic, marriage, and other vital records.

Laurens County

Superior & Magistrate Court PO Box 2028, 101 N Jefferson, Dublin, GA 31021; 478-272-3210; fax: 478-275-2595; 8:30AM-5:30PM (EST). *Felony, Misdemeanor, Civil, Eviction, Small Claims.*
www.laurenscoga.org/

General Information: No juvenile, adoption, sexual, mental health or expunged records released. Will fax documents $2.50 flat fee. Court makes copy: $.50 per page. Self serve copy: same. Certification fee: $2.50 plus $.50 per page after first. Payee: Court Clerk. Personal checks accepted. No credit cards accepted. Prepayment required.

Civil Name Search: Access: In person only. Visitors must perform in person searches themselves. Civil records on computer from 1992, dockets books from 1800s. Civil PAT goes back to 1992.

Criminal Name Search: Access: In person only. Visitors must perform in person searches themselves. Criminal records computerized from 1992, dockets books from 1800s. Criminal PAT goes back to same as civil. Results include name and address - docket sheets show DOB.

Probate Court PO Box 2098, 101 N Jefferson St, Courthouse, Dublin, GA 31040; 478-272-2566; fax: 478-277-2932; 8:30AM-5:30PM (EST). *Probate, Traffic.*

General Information: This court also holds the traffic records.

Lee County

Superior Court PO Box 49, 100 Leslie Hwy, Leesburg, GA 31763; 229-759-6018; fax: 229-438-6049; 8AM-5PM (EST). *Felony, Misdemeanor, Civil.*

General Information: No juvenile, adoption, sexual, mental health or expunged records released. Will fax documents to local or toll free line. Court makes copy: $1.00 per page. Self serve copy: $.50 per page. Certification fee: $2.50 per cert. Payee: Court Clerk. Personal checks accepted. No credit cards accepted. Prepayment required. Mail requests: SASE required.

Civil Name Search: Access: In person. Both court and visitors may perform in person name searches. Civil index in docket books from 1850.

Criminal Name Search: Access: Mail, in person. Both court and visitors may perform in person name searches. Search fee: $5.00. Required to search: name, years to search, DOB; also helpful: SSN, race, sex. Criminal docket on books from 1850, computerized since 1997. Mail turnaround time 1 week.

Magistrate Court PO Box 522, 104 Leslie Hwy, Leesburg, GA 31763-0522; 229-759-6016; fax: 229-759-3303; 8AM-5PM (EST). *Civil Actions under $15,000, Eviction, Small Claims.*
www.lee.ga.us/departments/e_magistrate.html

General Information: Court also has jurisdiction for bad checks, arrest warrants, preliminary hearings, and county ordinance violations.

Probate Court 100 Leslie Hwy, Leesburg, GA 31763; 229-759-6005; fax: 229-759-3345; 8AM-5PM (EST). *Probate, Misdemeanor Traffic.*

Liberty County

Superior & State Court 201 S Main St, Ste 1200, Hinesville, GA 31313-0050; 912-876-3625; criminal phone: 912-876-7340; civil phone: 912-876-7365; fax: 912-876-7394; 8:30AM-4:30PM (EST). *Felony, Misdemeanor, Civil.*
www.libertyco.com

General Information: No juvenile, adoption, sexual, mental health or expunged records released. Will fax documents $5.00 1st 5 pages, $1.00 each add'l pg. Court makes copy: $1.00 per page. Self serve copy: $.50 per page. Certification fee: $2.50 plus $.50 per page after first. Payee: Court Clerk. Business checks accepted. Visa/MC accepted; small usage charge is added. Prepayment required.

Civil Name Search: Access: Fax, mail, in person, online. Both court and visitors may perform in person name searches. Search fee: $12.81 per hour if over 15 minutes. Required to search: name, years to search, signed release. Civil records on computer from 1986, dockets books from 1700s. Mail turnaround time 1-3 days. Civil PAT goes back to 1986. Terminal results also show SSNs. The docket index is available for no charges, includes magistrate records as well. Go the home page and click on Docket Search. Record available from 1986 forward. Search by case number or party name.

Criminal Name Search: Access: In person, online. Both court and visitors may perform in person name searches. No search fee. Required to search: name, years to search, DOB, signed release; also helpful: SSN, race, sex. Criminal records computerized from 1986, dockets books from 1700s. Criminal PAT goes back to same as civil. Terminal results include SSN.

Online access same as described for criminal. Some entries have DOB, usually are traffic. Most online results show name only.

Magistrate Court PO Box 912, 201 S Main St, #253, Hinesville, GA 31310; 912-368-2063; fax: 912-876-2474; 8AM-Noon,1-5PM (EST). *Civil Actions under $15,000, Eviction, Small Claims.*
www.libertyco.com

General Information: Court also has jurisdiction for bad checks, arrest warrants, preliminary hearings, Foreclosures, Garnishments, and county ordinance violations.

Probate Court PO Box 28, 201 S. Main Ste 220, Hinesville, GA 31310; 912-876-3635; fax: 912-876-3589; 8AM-5PM (EST). *Probate.*

Lincoln County

Superior Court PO Box 340, Lincolnton, GA 30817; 706-359-5505; fax: 706-359-5027; 9AM-5PM (EST). *Felony, Misdemeanor, Civil.*
www.lincolncountyga.com/

General Information: No adoption or juvenile records released. Will not fax documents. Court makes copy: $1.00 per page. Self serve copy: $.50 per page. Certification fee: $2.50. Payee: Superior Court Clerk. Personal checks accepted. No credit cards accepted. Prepayment required.

Civil Name Search: Access: In person only. Visitors must perform in person searches themselves. Civil index on docket books from 1796, computerized since 1992. Civil PAT goes back to 1990. Daily calendars online at the website.

Criminal Name Search: Access: In person only. Visitors must perform in person searches themselves. Criminal records indexed in books from 1796, records computerized since 2000. Criminal PAT goes back to same as civil. Daily calendars online at the website.

Magistrate & Probate Court PO Box 205, 210 Humphrey St, Lincolnton, GA 30817; 706-359-5519; probate phone: 706-359-5528; fax: 706-359-5520; 8AM-5PM (EST). *Civil Actions under $15,000, Eviction, Small Claims, Probate.*

General Information: Court also has jurisdiction for bad checks, arrest warrants, preliminary hearings, and county ordinance violations.

Long County

Superior & State Court PO Box 458, 459 S McDonald Ave, Ludowici, GA 31316; 912-545-2123; fax: 912-545-2020; 8:30AM-5PM (EST). *Felony, Misdemeanor, Civil.*

General Information: No juvenile, adoption, sealed, sexual, mental health, expunged or confidential records released. Will not fax documents. Court makes copy: $1.00 per page. Self serve copy: $.50 per page. Certification fee: $2.50 for 1st page, $.50 each add'l. Cert fee includes copies. Payee: Court Clerk. Business checks accepted. No credit cards accepted. Prepayment required. Mail requests: SASE required.

Civil Name Search: Access: Mail, fax, in person. Both court and visitors may perform in person name searches. Search fee: $5.00 per name. Civil index on docket books, archived from 1921. Mail turnaround time 1 week. Civil PAT goes back to 1993.

Criminal Name Search: Access: Mail, fax, in person. Both court and visitors may perform in person name searches. Search fee: $5.00 per name. Required to search: name, years to search, DOB; also helpful: SSN, race, sex. Criminal docket on books, archived from 1921. Mail turnaround time 1 week. Criminal PAT goes back to same as civil.

Magistrate & Probate Court PO Box 426, 447 S McDonald St, Ludowici, GA 31316; 912-545-2131; probate phone: 912-545-2131; fax: 912-545-2029; 8:30AM-4:30PM (EST). *Civil Actions under $15,000, Eviction, Small Claims, Probate.*

General Information: Court also has jurisdiction for bad checks, arrest warrants, preliminary hearings, and county ordinance violations. Use PO Box 87 for Magistrate Court.

Lowndes County

Superior & State Court PO Box 1349, 327 Ashley St, Valdosta, GA 31603; 229-333-5127; fax: 229-333-7637; 8AM-5PM (EST). *Felony, Misdemeanor, Civil.*
http://georgiainfo.galileo.usg.edu/courthouses/lowndesCH.htm

General Information: No juvenile, adoption, sexual, mental health or expunged records released. Fee to fax document $.25 per page. Court makes copy: $.50 per page. Self serve copy: same. Certification fee: $2.50 plus $.50 per page after 1st. Payee: Court Clerk. No personal checks or credit cards accepted. Prepayment required.

Civil Name Search: Access: Mail, in person. Visitors must perform in person searches themselves. Search fee: $3.00 per name for mail requests. Civil records on computer from 1990, prior on dockets books. Civil PAT goes back to 1990.

Criminal Name Search: Access: Mail, in person. Visitors must perform in person searches themselves. Search fee: $3.00 per name for mail requests. Required to search: name, years to search, DOB. Criminal records computerized from 1984; prior records on docket books. Criminal PAT goes back to 1984.

Magistrate Court PO Box 1349, Valdosta, GA 31603; 229-671-2610; fax: 229-671-3442; 8AM-5PM (EST). *Civil Actions under $15,000, Eviction, Small Claims.*
www.lowndescounty.com/default.asp
General Information: Court also has jurisdiction for bad checks, arrest warrants, preliminary hearings, and county ordinance violations. Physical address is 327 N. Ashley Street, Valdosta, GA 3160

Probate Court 327 N. Ashley Street, Valdosta, GA 31601; 229-671-2650; fax: 229-333-7646; 8AM-5PM (EST). *Probate.*
www.lowndescounty.com/content.asp?pid=24&id=126

Lumpkin County

Superior, Juvenile & Magistrate Court 235 Riley Rd, Rm 108, Dahlonega, GA 30533-0820; 706-864-3736; fax: 706-864-5298; 8AM-5PM (EST). *Felony, Misdemeanor, Civil, Eviction, Small Claims.*
www.lumpkincounty.gov/index.php?go=departments&dept=clerkCourt
General Information: For Magistrate Court criminal records info, call 706-864-7760. No juvenile, adoption, sealed records released. Will fax specific case file documents if copies prepaid. Court makes copy: $1.00 per page; if 11x17 then $2.00 per page. Self serve copy: $.50 per page. Certification fee: $2.50 plus $.50 per page after first. Payee: Clerk of Courts. Personal checks accepted. No credit or debit cards accepted. Prepayment required.
Civil Name Search: Access: In person only. Visitors must perform in person searches themselves. Required to search: name, years to search; also helpful: address. Civil records on computer from 1988, prior on dockets books to 1833. Civil PAT goes back to 1998.
Criminal Name Search: Access: In person only. Visitors must perform in person searches themselves. Required to search: name, years to search, DOB; SSN helpful. Criminal records computerized from 1988, prior on dockets books to 1833. Criminal PAT goes back to 1998.
Probate Court 325 Riley Rd, #122, Dahlonega, GA 30533; 706-864-3847; fax: 706-864-9271; 8AM-5PM (EST). *Probate, Traffic, Vital Records.*

Macon County

Superior Court PO Box 337, Oglethorpe, GA 31068; 478-472-7661; fax: 478-472-4775; 8AM-5PM (EST). *Felony, Misdemeanor, Civil.*
General Information: This court will not perform name searches. The public access terminal has only real estate records available, everything else is in docket books. No juvenile, adoption, sexual, mental health or expunged records released. Will fax documents $2.00 copy fee. Court makes copy: $1.00 per page. Self serve copy: $.50 per page. Certification fee: $2.50 1st page; $.50 each add'l. Payee: Court Clerk. Business checks accepted. No credit cards accepted. Prepayment required.
Civil Name Search: Access: In person. Visitors must perform in person searches themselves. Civil index in docket books from 1800s. Civil PAT goes back to 2002.
Criminal Name Search: Access: In person only. Visitors must perform in person searches themselves. Criminal docket on books from 1800s. Criminal PAT goes back to 2002.
Magistrate Court PO Box 605, Oglethorpe, GA 31068; 478-472-8509; fax: 478-472-8510; 8AM-N, 1-5PM (EST). *Civil Actions under $15,000, Eviction, Small Claims.*
www.georgiacourts.org/councils/magistrate/county.asp
General Information: Physical Address: 103 S Sumter St, Oglethorpe, GA 31069. Court also has jurisdiction for bad checks, arrest warrants, preliminary hearings, and county ordinance violations.
Probate Court PO Box 216, 121 S. Sumter St, Oglethorpe, GA 31068; 478-472-7685; fax: 478-472-5643; 8AM-N, 1-5PM (EST). *Probate.*

Madison County

Superior Court PO Box 247, Danielsville, GA 30633; 706-795-6310; fax: 706-795-2209; 8AM-5PM (EST). *Felony, Misdemeanor, Civil.*
www.madisonclerkofcourt.com/
General Information: No juvenile, adoption, sexual, mental health or expunged records released. Will fax documents $2.50 1st page, $1.00 each add'l page. Court makes copy: $1.00 per page. Self serve copy: $.50 per page. Certification fee: $2.50 plus $.50 per page after first. Payee: Court Clerk. No personal checks or credit cards accepted. Prepayment required.
Civil Name Search: Access: In person, online. Visitors must perform in person searches themselves. Civil cases indexed by defendant. Civil records on computer since 7/96, archived since 1811. Civil PAT goes back to 7/1997. Search the docket index at www.madisonsuperiorcourt.com/webFormFrame.aspx?page=main, records go to 1998.
Criminal Name Search: Access: In person, online. Visitors must perform in person searches themselves. Required to search: name, years to search, DOB; SSN helpful. Criminal records on computer since 7/96, archived since 1811. Criminal PAT goes back to 7/1996. Search at

www.madisonsuperiorcourt.com/webFormFrame.aspx?page=main for docket index, records go to 1998.
Magistrate Court PO Box 6, 91 Albany Ave, Danielsville, GA 30633; 706-795-6375; fax: 706-795-2222; 8AM-5PM (EST). *Civil Actions under $15,000, Eviction, Small Claims.*
General Information: Court also has jurisdiction for bad checks, arrest warrants, preliminary hearings, and county ordinance violations.
Probate Court PO Box 207, 91 Albany Ave, Danielsville, GA 30633; 706-795-6365; fax: 706-795-5933; 8AM-5PM (EST). *Probate.*

Marion County

Superior Court PO Box 41, 100 N Broad St, Buena Vista, GA 31803; 229-649-7321; fax: 229-649-7931; 8AM-5PM (EST). *Felony, Misdemeanor, Civil.*
General Information: No juvenile, adoption, sexual, mental health or expunged records released. Will fax documents $1.00 per page. Court makes copy: $1.00 first page then $.50 per page. Self serve copy: $.50 per page. Certification fee: $2.50 plus $.50 per page after first. Payee: Court Clerk. Personal checks accepted. No credit cards accepted. Prepayment required.
Civil Name Search: Access: In person only. Visitors must perform in person searches themselves. Civil records on books, computerized 10 years.
Criminal Name Search: Access: In person only. Visitors must perform in person searches themselves. Required to search: name, years to search; SSN helpful. Criminal docket on books, computerized 10 years.
Magistrate & Probate Court PO Box 196, 100 N Broad St, Buena Vista, GA 31803; 229-649-5542; fax: 229-649-7931; 8:30AM-5PM (EST). *Civil under $15,000, Eviction, Small Claims, Probate.*
General Information: Court also has jurisdiction for bad checks, arrest warrants, preliminary hearings, and county ordinance violations.

McDuffie County

Superior Court PO Box 158, 337 Main St, Rm 101, Thomson, GA 30824; 706-595-2134; criminal phone: 706-595-2139; civil phone: 706-595-2138; probate phone: 706-595-2124; fax: 706-595-9150; 8AM-5PM (EST). *Felony, Misdemeanor, Civil.*
General Information: No juvenile or adoption records released. Will fax documents for $2.50 plus $1.00 per page after first page. Court makes copy: $1.00 per page. Self serve copy: $.50 per page. Certification fee: $2.50 plus $.50 per page after first. Payee: Clerk Superior Court. Personal checks accepted. No credit cards accepted. Prepayment required.
Civil Name Search: Access: In person only. Visitors must perform in person searches themselves. Civil records on computer from 1991, dockets books from 1871. Civil PAT goes back to 1991.
Criminal Name Search: Access: In person only. Visitors must perform in person searches themselves. Required to search: name, years to search, signed release; also helpful: DOB. Criminal records computerized from 1991, dockets books from 1800s. Criminal PAT goes back to same as civil.
Magistrate Court PO Box 252, 337 Main St, Thomson, GA 30824; 706-597-2618; fax: 706-595-2041; 8AM-5PM (EST). *Civil Actions under $15,000, Eviction, Small Claims.*
www.georgiacourts.org/councils/state/index_testmagistarte.asp?county=1500&Submit=GO
General Information: Court also has jurisdiction for bad checks, arrest warrants, preliminary hearings, and county ordinance violations.
Probate Court PO Box 2028, 337 Main St, Rm 108, Thomson, GA 30824; 706-595-2124; fax: 706-595-4710; 8AM-5PM (EST). *Probate.*
www.thomson-mcduffie.com/index-mc-probate.shtml

McIntosh County

Superior & State Court PO Box 1661, 310 North Way, Darien, GA 31305; 912-437-6641; fax: 912-437-6673; 8AM-5PM (EST). *Felony, Misdemeanor, Civil.*
www.mcintoshclerkofcourts.com/
General Information: No juvenile, adoption, sexual, or expunged records released. Court makes copy: $1.00 per page. Self serve copy: $.50 per page. Certification fee: $2.50. Payee: Court Clerk. Personal checks accepted. No credit cards accepted. Prepayment required.
Civil Name Search: Access: In person only. Visitors must perform in person searches themselves. Civil records on computer from 1991. Civil PAT goes back to 1990.
Criminal Name Search: Access: Mail, in person. Both court and visitors may perform in person name searches. Search fee: $5.00. Required to search: name, years to search, DOB; SSN helpful. Criminal records computerized from 1991. Criminal PAT goes back to same as civil.
Magistrate Court PO Drawer 459, 310 Northway, Darien, GA 31305; 912-437-4888; fax: 912-437-6635; 8AM-4:30PM (EST). *Civil Actions under $15,000, Eviction, Small Claims.*
www.georgiacourts.org/councils/state/index_testmagistarte.asp?county=1501&Submit=GO

General Information: Court also has jurisdiction for bad checks, arrest warrants, preliminary hearings, and county ordinance violations.

Probate/Magistrate Court PO Drawer 459, 310 Northway Hwy 17, Darien, GA 31305; 912-437-4888; fax: 912-437-6635; 8AM-4:30PM (EST). *Probate.*

www.georgiacourts.org/councils/state/index_test.asp?county=1342&Submit=GO

Meriwether County

Superior Court PO Box 160, Greenville, GA 30222; 706-672-4416; fax: 706-672-9465; 8:30AM-5PM (EST). *Felony, Misdemeanor, Civil.*

General Information: This court will not do name searches. No juvenile, adoption, sexual, mental health or expunged records released. Will fax documents $2.50 1st page, $1.00 each add'l page. Court makes copy: $1.00 per page. Self serve copy: $.50 per page. Certification fee: $2.50 plus $.50 per page after first. Payee: Court Clerk. Business checks accepted. No credit cards accepted. Prepayment required.

Civil Name Search: Access: In person only. Visitors must perform in person searches themselves. Civil records on microfilm and computer from 1990, prior on writ and minute books to 1827. Civil PAT goes back to 1990.

Criminal Name Search: Access: In person only. Visitors must perform in person searches themselves. Required to search: name, years to search, DOB, SSN. Criminal records go back to 1827; on computer back to 1991. Criminal PAT goes back to 1991.

Magistrate Court PO Box 702, 100 Courtsquare, Greenville, GA 30222; 706-672-1247; fax: 706-672-1172; 8:30AM-4:30PM (EST). *Civil Actions under $15,000, Eviction, Small Claims.*

General Information: Court also has jurisdiction for bad checks, arrest warrants, preliminary hearings, and county ordinance violations.

Probate Court PO Box 608, 100 N Court Sq, Greenville, GA 30222; 706-672-4952; probate phone: 706-672-1817; fax: 706-672-6660; 8:30AM-5PM (EST). *Probate.*

www.georgiacourts.org/councils/state/index_test.asp?county=1343&Submit=GO

Miller County

Superior & State Court PO Box 66, Colquitt, GA 39837; 229-758-4102; fax: 229-758-6585; 9AM-5PM (EST). *Felony, Misdemeanor, Civil.*

General Information: No juvenile or adoption records released. Will not fax documents. Court makes copy: $1.00 per page. Self serve copy: $.50 per page. Certification fee: $2.50 plus $1.00 per page after first. Payee: Court Clerk. Business checks accepted. No credit cards accepted. Prepayment required.

Civil Name Search: Access: In person only. Visitors must perform in person searches themselves. Civil index in docket books from 1800s, computerized from 1995. Civil PAT goes back to 1995.

Criminal Name Search: Access: In person only. Visitors must perform in person searches themselves. Criminal docket on books from 1800s, computerized from 1995. Criminal PAT goes back to same as civil.

Magistrate & Probate Court 155 S 1st St, #110, Colquitt, GA 39837; 229-758-4110; fax: 229-758-8133; 9AM-5PM (EST). *Civil Actions under $15,000, Small Claims, Probate.*

www.georgiacourts.org/councils/state/index_testmagistarte.asp?county=1503&Submit=GO

General Information: Court also has jurisdiction for bad checks, arrest warrants, preliminary hearings and county ordinance violations.

Mitchell County

Superior & State Court PO Box 427, 11 W Broad St, Camilla, GA 31730; 229-336-2022; fax: 229-336-9866; 8:30AM-5PM (EST). *Felony, Misdemeanor, Civil.*

General Information: No juvenile, adoption, sexual, mental health or expunged records released. Will fax documents $1.00 per page. Court makes copy: $.50 per page. Self serve copy: same. Certification fee: $2.50 first page, $.50 ea add'l. Payee: Court Clerk. Personal checks accepted. No credit cards accepted. Prepayment required.

Civil Name Search: Access: In person only. Visitors must perform in person searches themselves. Civil cases indexed by defendant. Civil index in docket books from 1800s. Civil PAT goes back to 1997.

Criminal Name Search: Access: In person only. Visitors must perform in person searches themselves. Required to search: name, years to search, DOB; SSN helpful. Criminal docket on books from 1800s. Criminal PAT goes back to 2006.

Magistrate Court PO Box 626, 22 N Court St, Camilla, GA 31730-0626; 229-336-2076/7; fax: 229-336-2039; 8:30AM-5PM (EST). *Civil Actions under $15,000, Eviction, Small Claims.*

General Information: Court also has jurisdiction for bad checks, arrest warrants, preliminary hearings, and county ordinance violations.

Probate Court PO Box 229, 11 W Broad St #102, Camilla, GA 31730; 229-336-2016; fax: 229-336-2354; 8:30AM-5PM (EST). *Probate.*

www.georgiacourts.org/

Monroe County

Superior Court PO Box 450, 15 W Main St, #1 Courthouse Sq, Forsyth, GA 31029; 478-994-7022; fax: 478-994-7053; 8AM-5PM (EST). *Felony, Misdemeanor, Civil.*

General Information: No juvenile, adoption, sexual, mental health or expunged records released. Will not fax documents. Court makes copy: $1.00 per page. Self serve copy: $.50 per page. Certification fee: $2.50 plus $.50 per page after first. Payee: Court Clerk. Personal checks accepted. No credit cards accepted. Prepayment required. Mail requests: SASE required.

Civil Name Search: Access: Mail, in person. Visitors must perform in person searches themselves. No search fee. Civil records on name index 1986 forward. Civil PAT goes back to 1989.

Criminal Name Search: Access: Mail, in person. Both court and visitors may perform in person name searches. No search fee. Criminal records on name index from 1989. Note: Mail request must have signed release. Mail turnaround time 3 days. Criminal PAT goes back to 1989.

Magistrate Court PO Box 974, 145 L Cary Bittick Dr, Justice Center, Forsyth, GA 31029; 478-994-7018; fax: 478-994-7284; 9:00AM-5:00PM (EST). *Civil Actions under $15,000, Eviction, Small Claims.*

www.monroecountygeorgia.com/pages.php?s=64&p=62

General Information: Court also has jurisdiction for bad checks, arrest warrants, preliminary hearings, and county ordinance violations.

Probate Court PO Box 187, Courthouse, Rm 2, Forsyth, GA 31029; 478-994-7036; fax: 478-994-7054; 8AM-4:30PM (EST). *Probate, Misdemeanor Traffic.*

Montgomery County

Superior Court PO Box 311, Mt Vernon, GA 30445; 912-583-4401; fax: 912-583-4343; 8:30AM-4:30 PM (EST). *Felony, Misdemeanor, Civil.*

General Information: No juvenile or adoption records released. Will fax documents $2.50 1st page and $1.00 ea addl. Court makes copy: $1.00 per page. Self serve copy: $.50 per page. Certification fee: $2.50 per page. Payee: Superior Court Clerk. Personal checks accepted. No credit cards accepted. Prepayment required.

Civil Name Search: Access: In person only. Visitors must perform in person searches themselves. Civil records on computer from 1993, on dockets from 1793. Civil PAT goes back to 1993.

Criminal Name Search: Access: In person only. Visitors must perform in person searches themselves. Required to search: name, years to search, DOB; SSN helpful. Criminal records computerized from 1993, on dockets from 1793. Criminal PAT goes back to same as civil. Terminal results include SSN.

Magistrate Court PO Box 174, 400 Railroad Ave, Mt Vernon, GA 30445; 912-583-2170; fax: 912-583-4343; 8:30AM-4:30PM (EST). *Civil Actions under $15,000, Eviction, Small Claims.*

General Information: Court also has jurisdiction for bad checks, arrest warrants, preliminary hearings, and county ordinance violations.

Probate Court PO Box 444, 400 Railroad Ave, Mt Vernon, GA 30445; 912-583-2681; fax: 912-583-4343; 8:30AM-4:30PM (EST). *Probate, Misdemeanor-Traffic.* www.montgomerycountyga.gov

Morgan County

Superior Court PO Drawer 551, 384 Hancock St, Madison, GA 30650; 706-342-3605; fax: 706-343-6462; 9AM-5PM (EST). *Felony, Misdemeanor, Civil.* www.morganga.org/

General Information: No juvenile, adoption, sexual, mental health or expunged records released. Will fax documents $2.50 1st page, $1.00 each add'l page. Court makes copy: $.50 per page. Self serve copy: same. Certification fee: $2.50 plus $.50 per page after first. Payee: Superior Court Clerk. Personal checks accepted. No credit cards accepted. Prepayment required.

Civil Name Search: Access: In person only. Visitors must perform in person searches themselves. Civil records on computer from 1986, on dockets from 1900s. Public use terminal available, records go back to 1986.

Criminal Name Search: Access: In person only. Visitors must perform in person searches themselves. Required to search: name, years to search, signed release. Criminal records computerized from 1986, on dockets from 1900s. Public use terminal available, crim records go back to 1986.

Magistrate Court PO Box 589, 149 E Jefferson St, Madison, GA 30650; 706-342-3088; fax: 706-343-6364; 9AM-5PM (EST). *Civil Actions under $15,000, Eviction, Small Claims.*

www.morganga.org

General Information: Court also has jurisdiction for certain misdemeanors including bad checks, arrest warrants, preliminary hearings, and county ordinance violations.

Probate Court PO Box 857, 149 E Jefferson St, Madison, GA 30650; 706-343-6500; fax: 706-343-6465; 9AM-5PM (EST). *Probate.*

www.morganga.org/CourtsServices/ProbateCourt/tabid/81/Default.aspx

General Information: This court also has Misdemeanor and Traffic cases.

Murray County

Superior Court PO Box 1000, 121 N Third Ave, Chatsworth, GA 30705; 706-695-2932; fax: 706-517-9672; 8:30AM-5PM (EST). *Felony, Misdemeanor, Civil.*
www.murrayclerk.com/
General Information: No juvenile, adoption, sexual, mental health or expunged records released. Will not fax out documents. Court makes copy: $.50 per page. Self serve copy: same. Certification fee: $2.50 plus $.50 per page after first. Payee: Superior Court Clerk. Personal checks accepted. No credit cards accepted. Prepayment required.
Civil Name Search: Access: In person only. Visitors must perform in person searches themselves. Civil records on dockets from 1940, prior to 1940 archived; computerized records since 2000. Civil PAT goes back to 2000. Calendar free to view at the website.
Criminal Name Search: Access: In person only. Visitors must perform in person searches themselves. Required to search: name, years to search, signed release. Criminal docket index from 1940, prior to 1940 archived; computerized records since 2000. Criminal PAT goes back to same as civil. Calendar free to view at the website.
Magistrate Court 121 N 4th Ave, Chatsworth, GA 30705; 706-517-1400 x4; fax: 706-695-7525; 8AM-4:30PM (EST). *Civil Actions under $15,000, Eviction, Small Claims.*
www.murraycountyga.org/index.aspx?nid=89
General Information: Court also has jurisdiction for bad checks, arrest warrants, preliminary hearings and county ordinance violations.
Probate Court 115 Fort St, Chatsworth, GA 30705; 706-695-3812; fax: 706-517-1340; 8:30AM-5PM (EST). *Misdemeanor, Probate.*

Muscogee County

Superior & State Court PO Box 2145, 100 10th St, Columbus, GA 31902; 706-653-4351; fax: 706-653-4359; 8:30AM-5PM (EST). *Felony, Misdemeanor, Civil.*
www.muscogeecourts.com
General Information: No adoption, sealed or first offender records released. Will fax documents $5.00 per fax. Court makes copy: $.50 per page. Self serve copy: same. Certification fee: $2.50 plus $.50 per add'l page. Payee: Superior Court Clerk. Business checks accepted. No credit cards accepted. Prepayment required. Mail requests: SASE requested.
Civil Name Search: Access: Mail, in person, online. Both court and visitors may perform in person name searches. Search fee: $5.00 per name. Civil records on computer from 1989, on dockets from 1919 to 1989. Mail turnaround time 1 week. Civil PAT goes back to 1989. Current dockets in pdf format are free at www.muscogeecourts.com. There is no historical data available online.
Criminal Name Search: Access: Mail, in person, online. Both court and visitors may perform in person name searches. Search fee: $5.00 per name. Required to search: name, years to search, DOB; also helpful: SSN. Criminal records on computer since 1989, on dockets from 1989 to 1957. Note: For a mail request, they ask for a minimum of $10.00 in advance to cover search and copy fees. Mail turnaround time 1 week. Criminal PAT goes back to same as civil. Online access to criminal is the same as civil; see above.
Magistrate Court PO Box 1340, 100 Tenth St, Columbus, GA 31902; 706-653-4390; fax: 706-653-4559; 9AM-N, 1-5PM (EST). *Civil Actions under $15,000, Eviction, Small Claims.*
www.columbusga.org/statecourt/
General Information: Court also has jurisdiction for bad checks, arrest warrants, preliminary hearings, and county ordinance violations.
Probate Court PO Box 1340, Columbus, GA 31902; 706-653-4333; 8:30AM-4PM (EST). *Probate.*
www.georgiacourts.org/councils/state/index_test.asp?county=1350&Submit=GO

Newton County

Superior Court 1132 Usher St, Rm 338, Covington, GA 30014; 770-784-2035; probate phone: 770-784-2045; fax: 770-385-8930; 8AM-5PM (EST). *Felony, Misdemeanor, Civil.*
General Information: No adoption, sexual, mental health or expunged records released. Will not fax documents. Court makes copy: $1.00 per page. Self serve copy: $.50 per page. Certification fee: $2.50 plus $.50 per page after first. Payee: Superior Court Clerk. No personal checks or credit cards accepted. Prepayment required.
Civil Name Search: Access: In person only. Visitors must perform in person searches themselves. Civil records on computer from 1991, on dockets from 1900s. Civil PAT goes back to 1991.
Criminal Name Search: Access: In person only. Visitors must perform in person searches themselves. Required to search: name, years to search, signed release. Criminal records computerized from 1991, on dockets from 1900s. Criminal PAT goes back to same as civil.

Magistrate Court 1132 Usher St, Rm 148, Covington, GA 30014; 770-784-2050; probate phone: 770-784-2045; fax: 770-784-2145; 8AM-5PM (EST). *Civil Actions under $15,000, Eviction, Small Claims, Probate.*
General Information: Court also has jurisdiction for bad checks, arrest warrants, preliminary hearings, and county ordinance violations.

Oconee County

Superior & Magistrate Courts PO Box 1099, 23 N Main, Rm 208, Watkinsville, GA 30677; 706-769-3940; probate phone: 706-769-3936; fax: 706-769-3948; 8AM-5PM (EST). *Felony, Misdemeanor, Civil, Eviction, Small Claims.*
www.oconeecounty.com/OCWeb2009/ClerkofCourts/ClerkofCourts.htm
General Information: No juvenile, adoption, sexual, mental health or expunged records released. Will fax documents $2.50 1st page, $1.00 each add'l page. Court makes copy: $.50 per page. Self serve copy: same. Certification fee: $2.50 plus $.50 per page after first. Payee: Superior Court Clerk. Personal checks accepted. No credit cards accepted. Prepayment required.
Civil Name Search: Access: In person only. Visitors must perform in person searches themselves. Civil records on computer from 1989, on dockets from 1875. Civil PAT goes back to 1989.
Criminal Name Search: Access: In person, fax, mail. Visitors must perform in person searches themselves. No search fee. Required to search: name, years to search; also helpful: DOB, SSN. Criminal records computerized from 1989, on dockets from 1875. Mail turnaround time 1-3 days. Criminal PAT goes back to same as civil.
Probate Court PO Box 54, 23 N Main St, #304, Watkinsville, GA 30677; 706-769-3936; fax: 706-769-3934; 8AM-5PM (EST). *Probate.*
www.oconeecounty.com/OCWeb2009/Probate/Probate.htm
General Information: Direct questions to probate@oconee.ga.us.

Oglethorpe County

Superior Court PO Box 68, Lexington, GA 30648; 706-743-5731; fax: 706-743-5335; 8AM-5PM (EST). *Felony, Misdemeanor, Civil.*
www.gsccca.org/Clerks/default.asp
General Information: No juvenile or adoption records released. Will fax documents $2.50 per page. Court makes copy: $1.00 per page. Self serve copy: $.50 per page. Certification fee: $2.00 per cert plus $.50 per page copy fee. Payee: Superior Court Clerk. Personal checks accepted. No credit cards accepted. Prepayment required. Mail requests: SASE required for mail return of any copies.
Civil Name Search: Access: Mail, in person. Visitors must perform in person searches themselves. Search fee: $25.00. Civil cases indexed by defendant. Civil records on computer from 1992, on dockets from 1900s. Mail turnaround time 1-5 days. Civil PAT available.
Criminal Name Search: Access: In person only. Visitors must perform in person searches themselves. Required to search: name, years to search, DOB; SSN helpful. Criminal records computerized from 1992, on dockets from 1900s. Note: The court will not perform a name search. But the court provides index books for the public to search in-person. Criminal PAT goes back to same as civil.
Magistrate Court PO Box 356, 339 W Main St, Lexington, GA 30648; 706-743-8321; fax: 706-743-3177; 8AM-N, 1-5PM (EST). *Civil Actions under $15,000, Eviction, Small Claims.*
www.onlineoglethorpe.com
General Information: Court also has jurisdiction for bad checks, arrest warrants, preliminary hearings, and county ordinance violations.
Probate Court PO Box 70, 111 W Main St, Lexington, GA 30648; 706-743-5350; fax: 706-743-3514; 7:30AM-5PM, closed N-1PM on F (EST). *Probate.*
www.onlineoglethorpe.com/Probate-Court-v-29.html

Paulding County

Superior Court 280 Constitution Blvd, Rm 1023, Dallas, GA 30132; 770-443-7527; criminal phone: x2; civil phone: x1; fax: 770-505-3863; 8AM-5PM (EST). *Felony, Misdemeanor, Civil.*
www.paulding.gov/index.aspx?NID=92
General Information: No juvenile, adoption, sexual, mental health or expunged records released. Will not fax documents. Court makes copy: $1.00 per page. Self serve copy: $.50 per page. Certification fee: $2.50 plus $.50 per page after first. Payee: Court Clerk. Personal checks accepted. No credit cards accepted. Prepayment required.
Civil Name Search: Access: In person only. Visitors must perform in person searches themselves. Civil records on computer from 1990, archived from 1850. Civil PAT goes back to 2001.
Criminal Name Search: Access: In person only. Visitors must perform in person searches themselves. Required to search: name, years to search, DOB; SSN helpful. Criminal docket on books. Criminal PAT goes back to 2001.

Magistrate Court 280 Constitution Blvd., Dallas, GA 30132; 770-443-7506; fax: 678-443-8980; 8AM-12; 1PM-5PM (EST). *Civil Actions under $15,000, Eviction, Small Claims.*
www.paulding.gov/index.aspx?nid=167
General Information: Court also has jurisdiction for bad checks, arrest warrants, preliminary hearings, garnishments and county ordinance violations.

Probate Court 280 Constitution Blvd, Rm 2009, Dallas, GA 304132; 770-443-7541; fax: 770-443-7631; 8AM-N, 1PM-5PM (EST). *Probate.*
www.paulding.gov/index.aspx?NID=182

Peach County

Superior Court PO Box 389, Ft Valley, GA 31030; 478-825-5331; fax: 478-825-8662; 8:30AM-5PM (EST). *Felony, Misdemeanor, Civil.*
General Information: No juvenile, adoption, sexual, mental health or expunged records released. Will not fax documents. Court makes copy: $.50 per page. Self serve copy: same. Certification fee: $3.00. Payee: Court Clerk. Personal checks accepted. No credit cards accepted. Prepayment required. Mail requests: SASE required.
Civil Name Search: Access: Mail, in person. Both court and visitors may perform in person name searches. No search fee. Civil records on computer back to 1997; on dockets from 1925. Mail turnaround time 1 week.
Criminal Name Search: Access: Mail, in person. Both court and visitors may perform in person name searches. No search fee. Required to search: name, years to search, DOB; also helpful: SSN, race, sex. Criminal records computerized from 1997; on dockets from 1925. Mail turnaround time 1 week.

Magistrate Court 700 Spruce St, Wing A, Ft Valley, GA 31030; 478-825-2060; fax: 478-825-1893; 8AM-5PM (EST). *Civil Actions under $15,000, Eviction, Small Claims.*
www.peachcounty.net/magistrate.cfm
General Information: Court also has jurisdiction for bad checks, arrest warrants, preliminary hearings, and county ordinance violations.

Probate Court PO Box 327, 205 W Church St, Ft Valley, GA 31030; 478-825-2313; fax: 478-825-3083; 8AM-5PM (EST). *Probate.*

Pickens County

Superior Court 52 N Main St, #102, Jasper, GA 30143; criminal phone: 706-253-8764/8772; civil phone: 706-253-8766/8771; fax: 706-253-8825; 8AM-5PM (EST). *Felony, Misdemeanor, Civil.*
http://9thjudicialdistrict-ga.org/dca9apphp.shtml
General Information: No juvenile, adoption, sexual, mental health or expunged records released. Court makes copy: $1.00 per page. Self serve copy: $.50 per page. Certification fee: $2.50 plus $.50 per page after first. Cert fee includes copies. Payee: Pickens Court Clerk. Personal checks accepted. No credit cards accepted. Prepayment required.
Civil Name Search: Access: In person only. Visitors must perform in person searches themselves. Civil records on computer from 1998, dockets from 1854. Civil PAT goes back to 1999.
Criminal Name Search: Access: In person only. Visitors must perform in person searches themselves. Required to search: name, years to search, DOB, signed release; SSN helpful. Criminal records computerized from 1998, dockets from 1854. Criminal PAT goes back to same as civil. Sometimes the address is shown.

Magistrate Court 50 N Main St, #105, Jasper, GA 30143; 706-253-8747; fax: 706-253-8750; 8AM-5PM (EST). *Civil Actions under $15,000, Eviction, Small Claims, Warrants.*
General Information: Court also has jurisdiction for bad checks, arrest warrants, preliminary hearings, and county ordinance violations.

Probate Court 50 N Main St, #203, Jasper, GA 30143; 706-253-8756; criminal phone: 706-253-8755; probate phone: 706-253-8757; fax: 706-253-8760; 8AM-N, 1-5PM (EST). *Probate, Misdemeanor, Traffic.*
General Information: Misdemeanors are limited to traffic and DNRs. Probate fax is same as main fax number.

Pierce County

Superior & State Court PO Box 588, 3550 Hwy 84, Blackshear, GA 31516; 912-449-2020; fax: 912-449-2106; 9AM-5PM (EST). *Felony, Misdemeanor, Civil.*
General Information: Court will provide assistance with your search, but will not name search for you. Will fax documents $1.00 per page. Court makes copy: $.50 per page. Self serve copy: same. Certification fee: $5.00 for 1st page, $.50 each add'l. Payee: Superior Court Clerk. Personal checks accepted. No credit cards accepted. Prepayment required.
Civil Name Search: Access: In person only. Visitors must perform in person searches themselves. Civil cases indexed by defendant. Civil records on computer from 1991, on index from 1800s. Civil PAT goes back to 1991.

Criminal Name Search: Access: In person only. Visitors must perform in person searches themselves. Criminal records computerized from 1991, on index from 1800s. Criminal PAT goes back to same as civil.

Magistrate Court 3550 US Hwy 84, Blackshear, GA 31516-1926; 912-449-2027; fax: 912-449-2103; 9AM-5PM (EST). *Civil Actions under $15,000, Eviction, Small Claims.*
www.piercecountyga.org/judicialcourts/**Magistrate Court**.html
General Information: Court also has jurisdiction for bad checks, arrest warrants, preliminary hearings, and county ordinance violations.

Probate Court PO Box 406, 3550 W Highway 84, Blackshear, GA 31516; 912-449-2029; fax: 912-449-1417; 9AM-5PM (EST). *Probate.*

Pike County

Superior Court PO Box 10, 16001 Barnesville St, Zebulon, GA 30295; 770-567-2000; fax: 770-567-2017; 8AM-5PM (EST). *Felony, Misdemeanor, Civil.*
General Information: No juvenile, adoption, sexual, mental health or expunged records released. Will not fax documents. Court makes copy: $1.00 per page. Self serve copy: $.50 per page. Certification fee: $2.50 plus $.50 per page after first. Payee: Court Clerk. Personal checks accepted. No credit cards accepted. Prepayment required.
Civil Name Search: Access: In person only. Visitors must perform in person searches themselves. Civil index in docket books from 1823. Civil PAT goes back to 2001. Terminal results may sometimes show SSN.
Criminal Name Search: Access: In person only. Visitors must perform in person searches themselves. Criminal docket on books from 1823. Criminal PAT goes back to 2001.

Magistrate Court PO Box 466, 331 Thomaston St, Zebulon, GA 30295; 770-567-2004; fax: 770-567-2023; 8AM-N, 1PM-5PM (EST). *Civil Actions under $15,000, Eviction, Small Claims.*
General Information: Court also has jurisdiction for bad checks, arrest warrants, preliminary hearings, and county ordinance violations.

Probate Court PO Box 324, 16001 Barnesville St, Zebulon, GA 30295; 770-567-8734; fax: 770-567-2019; 8:30AM-N; 1PM-5PM (EST). *Probate, Traffic.*

Polk County

Superior Court PO Box 948, 100 Proir St, Rm 106, Cedartown, GA 30125; 770-749-2114; fax: 770-749-2148; 9AM-5PM (EST). *Felony, Misdemeanor, Civil.*
General Information: No adoption, sexual, mental health or expunged records released. Fee to fax out file $1.00 per page. Court makes copy: $.50 per page. Self serve copy: same. Certification fee: $2.50 plus $.50 per page after first. Payee: Court Clerk. Personal checks accepted. Make sure phone number is on check. No credit cards accepted. Prepayment required. Mail requests: SASE required.
Civil Name Search: Access: Mail, in person. Visitors must perform in person searches themselves. Search fee: $5.00 per name. Civil records on computer from 1991 to present, alpha indexes from 1930. Public use terminal available, records go back to 1991.
Criminal Name Search: Access: Mail, in person. Visitors must perform in person searches themselves. Search fee: $5.00 per name. Required to search: name, years to search, DOB, signed release; also helpful: race, sex. Criminal records computerized from 1991, alpha indexes from 1930. Public use terminal available, crim records go back to same. Results include charges.

Magistrate Court 102 Prior St, Rm 203, Cedartown, GA 30125; criminal phone: 770-749-2130; civil phone: 770-749-2187; fax: 770-749-2186; 9AM-5PM (EST). *Misdemeanor, Civil Actions under $15,000, Eviction, Small Claims, Ordinance.*
General Information: Court also has jurisdiction for bad checks, arrest warrants, preliminary hearings, and county ordinance violations.

Probate Court County Courthouse #1, 100 Prior St, Rm 102, Cedartown, GA 30125; 770-749-2128/ 2129; fax: 770-749-2150; 9AM-5PM (EST). *Probate.*
www.polkcountygeorgia.us/courts.php
General Information: This location also holds traffic and vital records.

Pulaski County

Superior Court PO Box 60, Hawkinsville, GA 31036; 478-783-1911; fax: 478-892-3308; 8AM-5PM (EST). *Felony, Misdemeanor, Civil.*
General Information: No juvenile or adoption records released. Will not fax documents. Court makes copy: $1.00 per page. Self serve copy: $.50 per page. Certification fee: $2.00 plus $.50 per page. Payee: Court Clerk. Personal checks accepted. No credit cards accepted. Prepayment required.
Civil Name Search: Access: in person only. Visitors must perform in person searches themselves. Civil records on computer from 1986, alpha index from early 1800s. Civil PAT goes back to 1989.
Criminal Name Search: Access: In person only. Visitors must perform in person searches themselves. Required to search: name, years to search,

signed release; also helpful: DOB, SSN. Criminal records computerized from 1986, alpha index from early 1800s. Criminal PAT goes back to 1986.

Magistrate Court PO Box 667, #105 Courthouse Annex, Lumpkin St, Hawkinsville, GA 31036; 478-783-1357; fax: 478-783-9209; 8AM-5PM (EST). *Civil Actions under $15,000, Eviction, Small Claims.*
General Information: Court also has jurisdiction for bad checks, arrest warrants, preliminary hearings, and county ordinance violations.

Probate Court PO Box 156, 141 Commerce St, County Courthouse, Hawkinsville, GA 31036; 478-783-2061; fax: 478-783-9219; 8AM-5PM (EST). *Probate, Traffic.*

Putnam County

Superior & State Court County Courthouse, 100 Jefferson Ave #236, Eatonton, GA 31024; 706-485-4501 superior ct; 706-485-4056 state ct; criminal phone: x140; civil phone: x142; fax: 706-485-2875; 8AM-5PM (EST). *Felony, Misdemeanor, Civil.*
www.putnamcourtclerk.org/
General Information: No juvenile, adoption, sexual, mental health or expunged records released. Will not fax out case files. Court makes copy: $1.00 per page. Self serve copy: $.50 per page. Certification fee: $2.50 plus $.50 per add'l page. Payee: Court Clerk. Personal checks accepted. Prepayment required.
Civil Name Search: Access: In person only. Visitors must perform in person searches themselves. Civil records on computer since 1997; prior records on dockets to early 1900s. Civil PAT goes back to 1997.
Criminal Name Search: Access: In person only. Visitors must perform in person searches themselves. Required to search: name, years to search, DOB. Criminal records on computer since 1997; prior records on dockets to early 1930s. Criminal PAT goes back to same as civil.

Magistrate Court 100 S Jefferson Ave, Rm 306, Eatonton, GA 31024; 706-485-4306; fax: 706-484-1814; 8AM-5PM (EST). *Civil Actions under $15,000, Eviction, Small Claims.*
http://putnamcountymagistrate.com/
General Information: Court also has jurisdiction for bad checks, arrest warrants, preliminary hearings, and county ordinance violations.

Probate Court County Courthouse, 100 S Jefferson Ave #318, Eatonton, GA 31024; 706-485-5476; fax: 706-485-2515; 8AM-5PM (EST). *Probate, Estate.*
www.putnamprobate.com/

Quitman County

Superior Court PO Box 307, Georgetown, GA 39854; 229-334-2578; fax: 229-334-3991; 8AM-N, 1-5PM (EST). *Felony, Misdemeanor, Civil.*
General Information: No juvenile, adoption, sexual, mental health or expunged records released. Will fax documents $2.50 1st page, $1.00 each add'l page. Court makes copy: $1.00 per page. Self serve copy: $.50 per page. Certification fee: $2.50 for 1st page, $.50 each add'l. Payee: Clerk of Superior Court. No credit cards accepted. Prepayment required.
Civil Name Search: Access: In person only. Visitors must perform in person searches themselves. Records indexed by plaintiff and defendant. Civil records go back to 1920s. Civil PAT goes back to 2002.
Criminal Name Search: Access: In person only. Visitors must perform in person searches themselves. Required to search: name, years to search, DOB; SSN helpful. Records go back to 1930s. Criminal PAT goes back to 2002.

Magistrate & Probate Court PO Box 7, 115 Main St, Georgetown, GA 39854; 229-334-2224; fax: 229-334-6826; 8AM-5PM (EST). *Civil Actions under $15,000, Small Claims, Probate.*
General Information: Court also has jurisdiction for bad checks, arrest warrants, preliminary hearings, and county ordinance violations.

Rabun County

Superior Court 25 Courthouse Sq, #105, Clayton, GA 30525; 706-782-3615; fax: 706-782-1391; 8:30AM-5PM (EST). *Felony, Misdemeanor, Civil.*
General Information: No juvenile, adoption, sexual, mental health or expunged records released. Will fax documents $.25 per copy, prepaid. Court makes copy: $1.00 per page. Self serve copy: same. Certification fee: $2.50 for 1st page, $.50 each add'l. Payee: Court Clerk. Personal checks and credit cards accepted. Prepayment required.
Civil Name Search: Access: Mail, in person. Visitors must perform in person searches themselves. No search fee. Civil records on dockets from 1949; on computer since. Civil PAT goes back to 1993.
Criminal Name Search: Access: Mail, in person. Visitors must perform in person searches themselves. No search fee. Required to search: name, years to search, DOB, signed release; also helpful: SSN, race, sex. Criminal docket index from 1949; on computer since. Mail turnaround time is 1 week. Criminal PAT goes back to 1991.

Magistrate Court 25 Courthouse Sq, #105, Clayton, GA 30525; 706-782-3615; fax: 706-782-1391; 8:30AM-5PM (EST). *Civil Actions under $15,000, Eviction, Small Claims.*
General Information: Court also has jurisdiction for bad checks, arrest warrants, preliminary hearings, and county ordinance violations.

Probate Court 25 Courthouse Square, #215, Clayton, GA 30525; 706-782-3614; fax: 706-782-9278; 8AM-5PM (EST). *Probate.*
www.rabuncountygov.com/probatejudge.html

Randolph County

Superior Court PO Box 98, Cuthbert, GA 39840; 229-732-2216; fax: 229-732-5881; 8AM-5PM (EST). *Felony, Misdemeanor, Civil.*
General Information: No juvenile, adoption, sexual, mental health or expunged records released. Will fax documents for fee. Court makes copy: $1.00 per page. Self serve copy: $.50 per page. Certification fee: $2.00 plus $.50 per page after first. Payee: Court Clerk. Personal checks accepted. No credit cards accepted. Prepayment required.
Civil Name Search: Access: In person only. Visitors must perform in person searches themselves. Civil cases indexed by defendant. Civil docket indexed from 1835. Civil PAT goes back to 2005.
Criminal Name Search: Access: In person only. Visitors must perform in person searches themselves. Required to search: name, years to search, DOB; SSN helpful. Criminal records indexed from 1835. Criminal PAT goes back to same as civil.

Magistrate Court PO Box 6, 76 W Pearl St, Cuthbert, GA 39840; 229-732-6182; fax: 229-732-5635; 8AM-5PM; W 8AM-N (EST). *Civil Actions under $15,000, Eviction, Small Claims.*
General Information: Court also has jurisdiction for bad checks, arrest warrants, preliminary hearings, and county ordinance violations.

Probate Court PO Box 424, 93 Front St., Cuthbert, GA 39840; 229-732-2671; fax: 229-732-5781; 8AM-5PM (EST). *Probate.*
General Information: This court also holds guardianship records.

Richmond County

Superior Court 735 James Brown Blvd, #1500, Augusta, GA 30901; 706-821-2460; fax: 706-821-2448; 8:30AM-5PM (EST). *Felony, Misdemeanor, Civil.* www.augustaga.gov/index.aspx?nid=804
General Information: No juvenile, adoption, sexual, mental health or expunged records released. Will not fax documents. Court makes copy: $.50 per page. Self serve copy: $.50 per page. Certification fee: $2.50 plus $.50 per page after first. Payee: Superior Court Clerk. No personal or business checks accepted. No credit cards accepted. Prepayment required. Mail requests: SASE requested.
Civil Name Search: Access: Mail, in person, online. Visitors must perform in person searches themselves. No search fee. Civil index on docket books and microfilm from 1940s; 1986 forward on computer. Civil PAT goes back to 1999. Access court index free at www.augustaga.gov/index.aspx?NID=421 for records 2001 forward.
Criminal Name Search: Access: Mail, in person, online. Visitors must perform in person searches themselves. No search fee. Criminal records on docket books and microfilm from 1940s; 1986 forward on computer. Mail turnaround time 1 week. Criminal PAT available. Access court index free at www.augustaga.gov/index.aspx?NID=421 for records 2001 forward.

State Court 401 Walton Way, #218A, Augusta, GA 30911; 706-821-1233; fax: 706-821-1218; 8:30AM-5PM (EST). *Misdemeanor, Civil.*
www.augustaga.gov/index.aspx?nid=818
General Information: No juvenile, adoption, sexual, mental health or expunged records released. Court makes copy: $.50 per page. Certification fee: $2.50 plus $.50 per page after first. Payee: Court Clerk. Only cashiers checks and money orders accepted. No credit cards accepted. Prepayment required.
Civil Name Search: Access: In person, online. Visitors must perform in person searches themselves. Civil index on docket books and microfilm from 1940s, prior archived; computerized records since 2001. Civil PAT goes back to 1999. Name search civil dockets free at www.augustaga.gov/index.aspx?NID=421.
Criminal Name Search: Access: In person, online. Visitors must perform in person searches themselves. Required to search: name, years to search, DOB. Criminal docket on books and microfilm from 1940s, prior archived; computerized records since 2001. Criminal PAT goes back to 1/2001. Name search of misdemeanor cases is free at www.augustaga.gov/index.aspx?NID=421. Online results show middle initial, DOB.

Civil & Magistrate Court 530 Greene St, Rm 705, Augusta, GA 30911; 706-821-2370; fax: 706-821-2381; 8:30AM-5PM (EST). *Civil Actions under $45,000, Eviction, Small Claims.*
www.augustaga.gov/index.aspx?nid=67
General Information: Court does have some misdemeanor records that are city ordinance violations. Will fax documents to local or toll-free number.

Court makes copy: $.50 per page. Certification fee: $5.00. Payee: Magistrate Court. Business checks accepted. No credit cards accepted. Prepayment required. Mail requests: SASE requested for civil.

Civil Name Search: Access: Phone, mail, in person. Both court and visitors may perform in person name searches. No search fee. Civil records on dockets back to 1982. Mail turnaround time 1-7 day. Due to heavy case loads the court suggests to search in person for best results.

Probate Court 735 James Brown Blvd, Ste 1000, Augusta, GA 30911; 706-821-2434; fax: 706-821-2442; 8:30AM-5PM (EST). *Probate.* www.augustaga.gov/index.aspx?nid=197

Rockdale County

Superior Court PO Box 937, 922 Court St, Conyers, GA 30012; 770-929-4021;; 8:15AM-4:45PM (EST). *Felony, Civil.* http://rockdaleclerk.com/

General Information: No juvenile, adoption, sexual, mental health or expunged records released. Will not fax documents. Court makes copy: $1.00 per page. Self serve copy: $.50 per page. Certification fee: $2.50 plus $.50 per page after first. Payee: Clerk Superior Court. No personal checks or credit cards accepted. Prepayment required.

Civil Name Search: Access: In person only. Visitors must perform in person searches themselves. Civil records on computer back to 1993, in books from 1900. Civil PAT goes back to 1993.

Criminal Name Search: Access: In person only. Visitors must perform in person searches themselves. Required to search: name, case number. Criminal records computerized from 1990, in books from 1900. Criminal PAT goes back to 1990.

State Court PO Box 938, Conyers, GA 30012; 770-278-7900; fax: 770-278-7921; 8AM-4:45PM (EST). *Misdemeanor, Civil.* http://rockdaleclerk.com/

General Information: No juvenile, adoption, sexual, mental health or expunged records released. Will not fax documents. Court makes copy: $1.00 per page. Self serve copy: $.50 per page. Certification fee: $2.50 plus $.50 per page after first. Payee: Rockdale State Court. Business checks accepted. Prepayment required.

Civil Name Search: Access: In person only. Visitors must perform in person searches themselves. Civil records on computer from 1994, on dockets to 1994. Civil PAT goes back to 1993.

Criminal Name Search: Access: In person only. Visitors must perform in person searches themselves. Criminal records computerized from 1990, on dockets to 1990. Criminal PAT goes back to same as civil.

Magistrate Court PO Box 289, 945 Court St, Conyers, GA 30012; 770-278-7800; fax: 770-278-8915; 8:30AM-4:30PM (EST). *Civil Actions under $15,000, Eviction, Small Claims.* www.rockdalecounty.org/main.cfm?id=2259

General Information: Court also has jurisdiction for bad checks, arrest warrants, preliminary hearings, bond hearings, garnishments, abandoned motor vehicles and county ordinance violations.

Probate Court 922 Court St NE, Rm 107, Conyers, GA 30012; 770-278-7700; fax: 770-918-6502; 8:30AM-4:30PM (EST). *Probate.* www.rockdalecounty.org/main.cfm?id=2265

Schley County

Superior Court PO Box 7, 14 S Broad St., Ellaville, GA 31806; 229-937-5581; fax: 229-937-5588; 8AM-N,1-5PM (EST). *Felony, Misdemeanor, Civil.*

General Information: No adoption records released. Will not fax out case files. Court makes copy: $.50 per page. Self serve copy: same. Certification fee: $2.50 per document includes copies. Payee: Clerk Superior Court. Personal checks accepted. No credit cards accepted. Prepayment required.

Civil Name Search: Access: In person only. Visitors must perform in person searches themselves. Civil cases indexed by defendant. Civil records in docket books from 1885.

Criminal Name Search: Access: In person only. Visitors must perform in person searches themselves. Required to search: name, years to search, DOB, signed release; SSN helpful. Criminal records in docket books from 1934.

Magistrate Court PO Box 372, 14 Broad St, Ellaville, GA 31806; 229-937-5110; fax: 229-937-5010; 9AM-5PM (closed at noon) (EST). *Misdemeanor, Civil Actions under $15,000, Eviction, Small Claims.*

General Information: Court also has jurisdiction for bad checks, arrest warrants, preliminary hearings, and county ordinance violations.

Probate Court PO Box 385, 14 S Broad St, Ellaville, GA 31806; 229-937-2905; fax: 229-937-5588; 8:30AM-N, 1-5PM (EST). *Probate, Misdemeanor, Traffic.*

Screven County

Superior Court PO Box 156, 216 Mims Rd, Sylvania, GA 30467; 912-564-2614; fax: 912-564-2622; 8AM-5PM (EST). *Felony, Misdemeanor, Civil.*

General Information: No juvenile or adoption records released. Will fax documents $1.00 per page. Court makes copy: $1.00 per page. Self serve copy: $.50 per page. Certification fee: $3.00 first page, $1.50 ea add'l. Payee: Court Clerk. Personal checks accepted. No credit cards accepted. Prepayment required.

Civil Name Search: Access: In person only. Visitors must perform in person searches themselves. Civil records on dockets. Civil PAT goes back to 1991.

Criminal Name Search: Access: In person only. Visitors must perform in person searches themselves. Required to search: name, years to search, DOB; SSN helpful. Criminal records on dockets to 1991 (misdemeanors to 2001). Criminal PAT goes back to same as civil.

State Court PO Box 156, 216 Mims Rd, Sylvania, GA 30467; 912-564-2614; fax: 912-564-2622; 8AM-5PM (EST). *Misdemeanor, Civil.*

General Information: No juvenile, adoption, sexual, mental health or expunged records released. Will fax documents $1.00 per page. Court makes copy: $1.00 per page. Self serve copy: $.50 per page. Certification fee: $3.00 per cert. Payee: Court Clerk. Personal checks accepted. No credit cards accepted. Prepayment required.

Civil Name Search: Access: In person only. Visitors must perform in person searches themselves. Civil records on dockets from 1793; computerized records since 1991. Civil PAT goes back to 1991.

Criminal Name Search: Access: In person only. Visitors must perform in person searches themselves. Required to search: name, years to search, DOB; SSN helpful. Criminal docket index from 1793; computerized records since 1991. Criminal PAT goes back to same as civil.

Magistrate Court PO Box 64, 216 Mims Rd, Sylvania, GA 30467; 912-564-7375; fax: 912-564-5618; 8AM-5PM (EST). *Civil Actions under $15,000, Eviction, Small Claims.* www.georgiacourts.org/councils/magistrate/courts_county.asp?county=1527&Submit=GO

General Information: Court also has jurisdiction for bad checks, arrest warrants, preliminary hearings, and county ordinance violations.

Probate Court 216 Mims Rd, #107, Sylvania, GA 30467; 912-564-2783; fax: 912-564-9139; 8AM-5PM (EST). *Probate.*

Seminole County

Superior Court PO Box 672, 200 S Knox Ave, Donalsonville, GA 39845; 229-524-2525; fax: 229-524-8883; 9AM-5PM (EST). *Felony, Misdemeanor, Civil.*

General Information: No juvenile, adoption, sexual, mental health or expunged records released. Will fax documents $2.50 per page. Court makes copy: $1.00 per page. Self serve copy: $.50 per page. Certification fee: $2.50 per page. Payee: Court Clerk. Personal checks accepted. No credit cards accepted. Prepayment required. Mail requests: SASE required.

Civil Name Search: Access: Fax, in person. Visitors must perform in person searches themselves. Civil records on computer from 1994, on dockets from 1921.

Criminal Name Search: Access: In person. Visitors must perform in person searches themselves. Criminal records computerized from 1994, on dockets from 1921. Mail turnaround time 3 days.

Magistrate & Probate Court Seminole County Courthouse, 200 S Knox Ave, Donallsonville, GA 39845; 229-524-5256; fax: 229-524-8644; 8:30AM-5PM (EST). *Civil Actions under $15,000, Eviction, Small Claims.* www.georgiacourts.org/councils/state/index_test.asp?county=1369&Submit=GO

General Information: Court also has jurisdiction for bad checks, arrest warrants, preliminary hearings and county ordinance violations.

Spalding County

Superior Court PO Box 1046, Griffin, GA 30224; criminal phone: 770-467-4745; civil phone: 770-467-4746;; 8AM-5PM (EST). *Felony, Misdemeanor, Civil.* www.spaldingcounty.com/officials.htm

General Information: No juvenile, adoption, sexual, mental health or expunged records released. Will not fax documents. Court makes copy: $.50 per page. Self serve copy: same. Certification fee: $2.50 per document; $.50 per page. Payee: Court Clerk. Business checks accepted. No personal checks accepted. Prepayment required.

Civil Name Search: Access: In person. Visitors must perform in person searches themselves. Civil records on computer from 1995; on dockets from 1852. Note: Mail for specific case info only, the court will not do name searches. Civil PAT goes back to 1995.

Criminal Name Search: Access: In person. Visitors must perform in person searches themselves. Required to search: name, years to search; also helpful: DOB, SSN, race, sex. Criminal records computerized from 1995; dockets from 1852. Note: Court will not do name searches; will only process specific case files. Criminal PAT goes back to 1995.

State Court PO Box 1046, Griffin, GA 30224; 770-467-4356; criminal phone: 770-467-4745; civil phone: 770-467-4746;; 8AM-5PM (EST). *Misdemeanor, Civil.*

General Information: No juvenile, adoption, sexual, mental health or expunged records released. Will not fax documents. Court makes copy: $1.00 per page. Self serve copy: $.50 per page. Certification fee: $2.50 per cert plus $.50 each add'l page. Payee: Court Clerk. Business checks accepted. No personal checks accepted. Prepayment required. Mail requests: SASE required.

Civil Name Search: Access: In person. Visitors must perform in person searches themselves. Civil records on computer back to 1995; prior records on dockets from 1852. Note: No name searching by the court. Docket books are viewable.

Criminal Name Search: Access: In person. Visitors must perform in person searches themselves. Required to search: name, years to search, DOB; also helpful: SSN, race, sex. Records on dockets from 1852. Note: No name searching by the court. Docket books are viewable. Mail turnaround time 2 days.

Magistrate Court 132 E Solomon St, Griffin, GA 30223; 770-467-4320; fax: 770-467-0081; 8AM-5PM (EST). *Civil Actions under $15,000, Eviction, Small Claims.*

General Information: Court also has jurisdiction for bad checks, arrest warrants, preliminary hearings, and county ordinance violations.

Probate Court 132 E Solomon St, Griffin, GA 30223; 770-467-4340; fax: 770-467-4243; 8AM-N, 1-5PM (EST). *Probate.*

General Information: This court also holds estate and marriage records.

Stephens County

Superior Court 70 N Alexander St, #202, Toccoa, GA 30577; 706-886-9496; fax: 706-886-5710; 8AM-5PM (EST). *Felony, Misdemeanor, Civil.*

www.stephenscountyga.com/

General Information: No name searches performed by court personnel; case number needed. No juvenile, adoption, sexual, mental health or expunged records released. Fee to fax out documents prepaid: $2.00 1st page, $1.00 each add'l. Court makes copy: $1.00 per page. Self serve copy: $.50 per page. Certification fee: $2.50 plus $.50 per page after first. Payee: Court Clerk. Personal checks accepted. Major credit and debit cards accepted. Prepayment required.

Civil Name Search: Access: In person only. Visitors must perform in person searches themselves. Civil records on computer back to 1988, on dockets from 1906. Civil PAT goes back to 1988.

Criminal Name Search: Access: In person only. Visitors must perform in person searches themselves. Required to search: name, years to search, DOB, signed release; SSN helpful. Criminal records computerized from 1988, on dockets from 1906. Criminal PAT goes back to 1990.

State Court 70 N Alexander St, Rm 202, Stephens County Government Bldg, Toccoa, GA 30577; 706-886-3598/9496; fax: 706-886-5710; 8AM-5PM (EST). *Misdemeanor, Civil.*

www.stephenscountyga.com/

General Information: This agency will not perform name searches. No juvenile, adoption, sexual, mental health or expunged records released. Will not fax out case files. Court makes copy: $1.00 per page. Self serve copy: $.50 per page. Certification fee: $2.50 plus $.50 per page after first. Payee: Court Clerk. Personal checks accepted. No credit cards accepted. Prepayment required.

Civil Name Search: Access: In person only. Visitors must perform in person searches themselves. Civil records on computer back to 1991, on dockets from 1906. Civil PAT goes back to 1991. Personal identifiers on terminal results vary case to case.

Criminal Name Search: Access: In person only. Visitors must perform in person searches themselves. Required to search: name, years to search, DOB. Criminal records computerized from 1990, on dockets from 1906. Criminal PAT goes back to 1990. Personal identifiers on terminal results vary case to case.

Magistrate Court 70 N Alexander St, Ste 107, Toccoa, GA 30577; 706-886-6205; fax: 706-886-5569; 8:30AM-5PM (EST). *Civil Actions under $15,000, Eviction, Small Claims.*

General Information: Court also has jurisdiction for bad checks, arrest warrants, preliminary hearings, and county ordinance violations.

Probate Court 70 N Alexander, Rm 108, Toccoa, GA 30577; 706-886-2828; fax: 706-886-0335; 8AM-5PM, closed for lunch hour (EST). *Probate.*

Stewart County

Superior Court PO Box 910, Main St, Lumpkin, GA 31815; 229-838-6220; fax: 229-838-4505; 8AM-4:30PM (EST). *Felony, Misdemeanor, Civil.*

General Information: No juvenile, adoption, sexual, mental health or sealed records are released. Will not fax documents. Court makes copy: $1.00 per page. Self serve copy: $.50 per page. Certification fee: $2.50 plus $.50

per page after first. Payee: Clerk of Superior Court. Personal checks accepted. No credit cards accepted. Prepayment required.

Civil Name Search: Access: In person only. Visitors must perform in person searches themselves. Required to search: name, years to search; also helpful: address. Civil cases indexed by defendant. Civil index in books.

Criminal Name Search: Access: In person only. Visitors must perform in person searches themselves. Required to search: name, years to search; also helpful: address, DOB, SSN. Criminal docket on book to 1840s.

Magistrate Court PO Box 712, 1813 Broad St, Lumpkin, GA 31815; 229-838-0505; fax: 229-838-0015; 8AM-5PM (EST). *Civil Actions under $15,000, Eviction, Small Claims.*

www.georgiacourts.org/councils/state/index_testmagistarte.asp?county=1531&Submit=GO

General Information: Court also has jurisdiction for bad checks, arrest warrants, preliminary hearings, and county ordinance violations.

Probate Court PO Box 876, 1765 Main St, Lumpkin, GA 31815; 229-838-4394; fax: 229-838-9084; 8AM-N, 1-4:30PM (EST). *Probate, Traffic.*

Sumter County

State Court PO Box 333, Americus, GA 31709; 229-928-4537;; 9AM-5PM (EST). *Felony, Misdemeanor, Civil.*

General Information: No juvenile, adoption, sealed, sexual, mental health or expunged records released. Will not fax documents. Court makes copy: $1.00 per page (assisted). Self serve copy: $.50 per page. Certification fee: $2.50 plus $.50 per page. Certification only done if court performs makes the copy. Payee: Court Clerk. No out-of-county personal checks accepted. No credit cards accepted. Prepayment required.

Civil Name Search: Access: In person only. Visitors must perform in person searches themselves. Civil records on dockets from late 1800s.

Criminal Name Search: Access: In person only. Visitors must perform in person searches themselves. Required to search: name, years to search, DOB. Criminal docket index from late 1800s.

Magistrate Court PO Box 563, 500 W Lamar St, Americus, GA 31709; 229-928-4524; fax: 229-928-4527; 9AM-5PM (EST). *Civil Actions under $15,000, Eviction, Small Claims.*

General Information: Court also has jurisdiction for bad checks, arrest warrants, preliminary hearings, and county ordinance violations.

Probate Court PO Box 246, 500 W Lamar St, Rm 208, Americus, GA 31709; 229-928-4551; fax: 229-928-4723; 8AM-5PM (EST). *Probate.*

http://ga-sumtercounty.civicplus.com/index.asp?NID=102

Talbot County

Superior Court PO Box 325, 25 W Monroe St, Courthouse, Talbotton, GA 31827; 706-665-3239; fax: 706-665-8637; 8AM-5PM (EST). *Felony, Misdemeanor, Civil.*

General Information: No juvenile, adoption, sexual, mental health or expunged records released. Will fax documents $2.00 per page. Court makes copy: $1.00 per page. Self serve copy: $.50 per page. Certification fee: $2.00 plus $.50 per page after first. Payee: Superior Court. Business checks accepted. No credit cards accepted. Prepayment required.

Civil Name Search: Access: In person only. Visitors must perform in person searches themselves. Civil records on dockets from 1827. Civil PAT available.

Criminal Name Search: Access: In person only. Visitors must perform in person searches themselves. Criminal records are computerized. Historical documents are indexed in docket books. Criminal PAT available.

Magistrate & Probate Court PO Box 157, 26 S Washington St, Talbotton, GA 31827; 706-665-8866; fax: 706-665-8240; 8AM-5PM (EST). *Civil Actions under $15,000, Eviction, Small Claims, Probate.*

https://www.gaprobate.org/find_court.asp

General Information: Court also has jurisdiction for bad checks, arrest warrants, preliminary hearings, and county ordinance violations.

Taliaferro County

Superior Court PO Box 182, Crawfordville, GA 30631; 706-456-2123; fax: 706-456-2749; 9AM-5PM (EST). *Felony, Misdemeanor, Civil.*

General Information: No juvenile, adoption, sexual, mental health or expunged records released. Court makes copy: $1.00 per page. Self serve copy: $.50 per page. Certification fee: $2.00. Payee: Court Clerk. Personal checks accepted. No credit cards accepted. Prepayment required.

Civil Name Search: Access: In person only. Visitors must perform in person searches themselves. Civil records on dockets from 1825.

Criminal Name Search: Access: In person only. Visitors must perform in person searches themselves. Required to search: name, years to search, DOB; SSN helpful. Criminal docket index from 1825.

Magistrate & Probate Court PO Box 264, 113 Monument St, Courthouse, Crawfordville, GA 30631; 706-456-2253; fax: 706-456-3550; 9AM-5PM (EST). *Civil Actions under $15,000, Eviction, Small Claims, Probate, Misdemeanor Traffic.*

General Information: Court also has jurisdiction for bad checks, arrest warrants, preliminary hearings, and county ordinance violations.

Tattnall County

Superior & State Court PO Box 39, 111 N Main St, Reidsville, GA 30453; 912-557-6716; fax: 912-557-4861; 8AM-5PM (EST). *Felony, Misdemeanor, Civil.*

General Information: No juvenile, adoption, sexual, mental health or expunged records released. Will fax documents $2.50 per page. Court makes copy: $1.00 per page. Self serve copy: $.50 per page. Certification fee: $2.50 1st page plus $.50 each add'l. Payee: Court Clerk. Business checks accepted. No credit cards accepted. Prepayment required.

Civil Name Search: Access: In person only. Visitors must perform in person searches themselves. Required to search: name, years to search; also helpful: address. Civil records on computer back to 2000; on dockets from 1800s. Civil PAT goes back to 2000.

Criminal Name Search: Access: In person only. Visitors must perform in person searches themselves. Required to search: name, years to search, DOB; SSN helpful. Criminal records computerized from 2000; on dockets from 1800s. Criminal PAT goes back to same as civil.

Magistrate Court PO Box 513, 111 N Main St Courthouse Sq, Reidsville, GA 30453; 912-557-4372; fax: 912-557-3136; 8AM-5PM (EST). *Civil Actions under $15,000, Eviction, Small Claims.*

General Information: Court also has jurisdiction for bad checks, arrest warrants, preliminary hearings, and county ordinance violations, dispossery, writ of possessions, civil claims.

Probate Court PO Box 699, 111 N Main St, Reidsville, GA 30453; 912-557-6719; fax: 912-557-3976; 8AM-5PM (EST). *Probate.*

Taylor County

Superior Court PO Box 248, Courthouse Sq, Butler, GA 31006; 478-862-5594; fax: 478-862-5334; 8AM-5PM (EST). *Felony, Misdemeanor, Civil.*

General Information: No juvenile, adoption, sexual, mental health or expunged records released. Will fax specific case file $2.50 per page. Court makes copy: $1.00 per page. Self serve copy: $.50 per page. Certification fee: $2.50 1st page, $1.00 ea add'l. Payee: Court Clerk. Personal checks accepted. No credit cards accepted. Prepayment required.

Civil Name Search: Access: In person only. Visitors must perform in person searches themselves. Civil records on computer from 1991, dockets from 1852. Public use terminal has civil records back to 1995.

Criminal Name Search: Access: In person only. Visitors must perform in person searches themselves. Required to search: name, years to search, DOB; SSN helpful. Criminal records computerized from 1991, dockets from 1852.

Magistrate & Probate Court PO Box 536, 2 N Broad St, Butler, GA 31006; 478-862-3357; fax: 478-862-9447; 8AM-5PM (EST). *Civil Actions under $15,000, Eviction, Small Claims, Probate, Traffic.*

https://www.gaprobate.org/find_court.asp

General Information: Court also has jurisdiction for bad checks, arrest warrants, preliminary hearings, and county ordinance violations.

Telfair County

Superior Court Courthouse, 19 E Oak St, #C, McRae, GA 31055; 229-868-6525; fax: 229-868-7956; 8:30AM-4:30PM (EST). *Felony, Misdemeanor, Civil.*

www.telfairclerkofcourt.com/

General Information: No juvenile, adoption, sexual, mental health or expunged records released. Will fax documents $2.00 per page. Court makes copy: $.50 per page. Self serve copy: same. Certification fee: $2.50 1st page and $.50 ea addl. Payee: Court Clerk. Personal checks accepted. No credit cards accepted. Prepayment required.

Civil Name Search: Access: In person only. Visitors must perform in person searches themselves. Civil cases indexed by defendant. Civil records on dockets from early 1900s. Civil PAT goes back to 2001.

Criminal Name Search: Access: In person only. Visitors must perform in person searches themselves. Required to search: name, years to search, DOB, signed release; also helpful: SSN, race, sex. Criminal docket index from early 1900s. Criminal PAT goes back to 2001.

Magistrate Court 19 E Oak #D, McRae, GA 31055; 229-868-6772; fax: 229-868-6902; 8AM-4:30PM (EST). *Civil Actions under $15,000, Eviction, Small Claims.*

General Information: Court also has jurisdiction for bad checks, arrest warrants, preliminary hearings, and county ordinance violations.

Probate Court 19 E Oak St, Suite A, McRae, GA 31055; 229-868-6038; probate phone: 229-868-7987; fax: 229-868-7620; 8:30AM-N, 1-4:30PM (EST). *Probate, Misdemeanor, Traffic.*

http://telfaircounty.georgia.gov/03/home/0,2230,8477407,00.html

Terrell County

Superior Court PO Box 189, 235 E Lee St, Dawson, GA 39842; 229-995-2631;; 8:30AM-5PM (EST). *Felony, Misdemeanor, Civil.*

General Information: No juvenile, adoption, sexual, mental health or expunged records released. Will not fax documents. Court makes copy: $1.00 per page. Self serve copy: $.50 per page. Certification fee: $2.50 plus $.50 per page after first; $1.00 per seal. Payee: Court Clerk. Business checks accepted. No credit cards accepted. Prepayment required.

Civil Name Search: Access: In person only. Visitors must perform in person searches themselves. Civil cases indexed by defendant. Civil records on computer from 1988, dockets books from 1900s. Civil PAT goes back to 1989.

Criminal Name Search: Access: In person only. Visitors must perform in person searches themselves. Required to search: name, years to search, DOB, signed release; SSN helpful. Criminal records computerized from 1988, dockets books from 1900s. Criminal PAT goes back to same as civil.

Magistrate Court PO Box 793, 513 S Main St, Dawson, GA 39842; 229-995-3757; fax: 229-995-4496; 8AM-5PM (EST). *Civil Actions under $15,000, Eviction, Small Claims, Misdemeanors.*

General Information: Court also has jurisdiction for bad checks, arrest warrants, preliminary hearings, and county ordinance violations.

Probate Court PO Box 67, 513 S Main St, Dawson, GA 39842; 229-995-5515; fax: 229-995-5574; 8AM-5PM (EST). *Probate, Traffic.*

Thomas County

Superior & State Court PO Box 1995, 325 N Madison St, Thomasville, GA 31799; 229-225-4108; fax: 229-225-4110; 8AM-5PM (EST). *Felony, Misdemeanor, Civil.*

www.thomascoclerkofcourt.org

General Information: No juvenile or adoption records released. Will fax specific case file $2.50 per fax, plus $1.00 per copy. Court makes copy: $1.00 per page. Self serve copy: $.50 per page. Certification fee: $2.00. Payee: Court Clerk. Personal checks accepted. No credit cards accepted. Prepayment required.

Civil Name Search: Access: In person only. Visitors must perform in person searches themselves. Civil records on computer from 1989, archived from 1826. Civil PAT goes back to 1989.

Criminal Name Search: Access: In person only. Visitors must perform in person searches themselves. Required to search: name, years to search, DOB; SSN helpful. Criminal records computerized since 1989. Criminal PAT goes back to same as civil.

Magistrate Court PO Box 879, 921 Smith Ave, Bobby Hines Jail/Justice Center, Thomasville, GA 31799; 229-225-3330; fax: 229-225-3342; 8AM-5PM (EST). *Civil Actions under $15,000, Eviction, Small Claims.*

General Information: Court also has jurisdiction for bad checks, arrest warrants, preliminary hearings, and county ordinance violations.

Probate Court PO Box 1582, Thomasville, GA 31799; 229-225-4116; fax: 229-227-1698; 8AM-5PM (EST). *Probate.*

General Information: Physical Address: 225 N Broad St, Thomasville, GA 31792.

Tift County

Superior & State Court PO Box 354, 237 E 2nd St, Tifton, GA 31793; 229-386-7815; fax: 229-386-7813; 8AM-N, 1-5PM (EST). *Felony, Misdemeanor, Civil.*

http://tiftoncircuit.com/

General Information: Court calendars available online at court website. No juvenile, adoption, sexual, mental health or expunged records released. Will fax documents to local or toll-free number. Court makes copy: $.50 per page. Self serve copy: same. Certification fee: $2.50 plus $.50 per page after first. Payee: Court Clerk. Personal checks accepted. No credit cards accepted. Prepayment required.

Civil Name Search: Access: In person only. Visitors must perform in person searches themselves. Civil cases indexed by defendant. Civil index in docket books from 1905. Civil PAT goes back to 2002. Some results may show SSN.

Criminal Name Search: Access: Phone, Mail, in person. Visitors must perform in person searches themselves. No search fee. Criminal docket on books from 1905. Note: As a courtesy, the clerk will do one name search only, not lists. Criminal PAT goes back to same as civil.

Magistrate Court PO Box 214, 225 N Tift Ave, Tifton, GA 31793; 229-386-7907; fax: 229-386-7978; 8AM-5PM (EST). *Civil Actions under $15,000, Eviction, Small Claims.*

General Information: Court also has jurisdiction for bad checks, arrest warrants, preliminary hearings, and county ordinance violations.

Probate Court PO Box 792, Tifton, GA 31793; 229-386-7914; fax: 229-386-7926; 8AM-5PM (EST). *Probate.*

http://georgiacourts.org/councils/state/tift.html

General Information: Physical Address: 225 Tift Ave, Rm 117, Tifton, GA 31794

Toombs County

Superior & State Court PO Drawer 530, Lyons, GA 30436; 912-526-3501; fax: 912-526-1004; 8:30AM-5PM (EST). *Felony, Misdemeanor, Civil.*

General Information: No juvenile, adoption, sexual, mental health records released. Will not fax documents. Court makes copy: $1.00 per page. Self serve copy: $.50 per page. Certification fee: $2.50 plus $.50 per page after first. Payee: Court Clerk. No personal checks or credit cards accepted. Prepayment required.

Civil Name Search: Access: In person only. Visitors must perform in person searches themselves. Civil index in docket books from 1985, archived to 1908, on computer since 1995. Civil PAT goes back to 1995.

Criminal Name Search: Access: In person only. Visitors must perform in person searches themselves. Required to search: name, years to search, DOB; SSN helpful. Criminal docket books from 1985, archived to 1908, on computer since 1995. Criminal PAT goes back to same as civil.

Magistrate Court PO Box 1460, 100 Courthouse Sq, Lyons, GA 30436; 912-526-8984; fax: 912-526-8985; 8:30AM-5PM (EST). *Civil Actions under $15,000, Eviction, Small Claims.*

General Information: Court also has jurisdiction for bad checks, arrest warrants, preliminary hearings, county ordinance violations.

Probate Court 100 Courthouse Square, Lyons, GA 30436; 912-526-8696; fax: 912-526-1008; 8:30AM-5PM (EST). *Probate.*

Towns County

Superior Court 48 River St, #E, Hiawassee, GA 30546; 706-896-2130; fax: 706-896-1772; 8:30AM-4:30PM (EST). *Felony, Misdemeanor, Civil.* www.townscountyga.com/County_offices.php

General Information: No juvenile, adoption, sexual, mental health or expunged records released. Will not fax documents. Court makes copy: $1.00 per page. Self serve copy: $.50 per page. Certification fee: $2.50 per page first page, $.50 ea addl. Payee: Court Clerk. Personal checks accepted. No credit cards accepted. Prepayment required.

Civil Name Search: Access: In person only. Visitors must perform in person searches themselves. Civil cases indexed by defendant. Civil index in docket books from 1923, records computerized 2002 forward. Public use terminal has civil records.

Criminal Name Search: Access: In person only. Visitors must perform in person searches themselves. Required to search: name, years to search, DOB, signed release; SSN helpful. Criminal docket on books to 1945, indexed by defendant; records computerized 2002 forward.

Magistrate & Probate Court 48 River St, #C, Hiawassee, GA 30546; 706-896-3467; fax: 706-896-1772; 8:30AM-4:30PM (EST). *Civil Actions under $15,000, Eviction, Small Claims, Probate, Traffic.*

General Information: Court also has jurisdiction for arrest warrants, preliminary hearings, garnishments, traffic, and county ordinance violations.

Treutlen County

Superior & State Court 639 2nd St South, #301, Soperton, GA 30457; 912-529-4215; probate phone: 912-529-3342; fax: 912-529-6737; 8AM-5PM (EST). *Felony, Misdemeanor, Civil.*

General Information: The probate court is not in this office. No juvenile, adoption, sexual, mental health or expunged records released. Will not fax documents. Court makes copy: $1.00 per page. Self serve copy: $.50 per page. Certification fee: $2.50 plus $.50 per page after first. Payee: Court Clerk. Personal checks accepted. No credit cards accepted. Prepayment required. Mail requests: SASE required.

Civil Name Search: Access: Mail, in person. Both court and visitors may perform in person name searches. No search fee. Civil records on computer from 1991, dockets books from 1919. Mail turnaround time 1-2 days. Civil PAT goes back to 1990.

Criminal Name Search: Access: Mail, in person. Both court and visitors may perform in person name searches. No search fee. Required to search: name, years to search, DOB; also helpful: SSN, race, sex. Criminal records computerized from 1991, dockets books from 1919. Mail turnaround time 1-2 days. Criminal PAT goes back to same as civil.

Magistrate & Probate Court 650 2nd St South, #101, Soperton, GA 30457; 912-529-3342; probate phone: 912-529-4320; fax: 912-529-6838; 8AM-4:30PM (EST). *Civil Actions under $15,000, Eviction, Small Claims, Probate.*

General Information: Court also has jurisdiction for bad checks, arrest warrants, preliminary hearings, and county ordinance violations.

Troup County

Superior & State Court PO Box 866, 100 Ridley Ave, LaGrange, GA 30241; 706-883-1740 x6; criminal phone: x4 Superior, x5 State; civil phone: x2; fax: 706-883-1724; 8AM-5PM (EST). *Felony, Misdemeanor, Civil.* www.troupclerkofcourt.com

General Information: Calendars available at the website. No juvenile, adoption, sexual, mental health or expunged records released. Will not fax documents. Court makes copy: $.50 per page. Certification fee: $2.50 plus $.50 per page after first. Cert fee includes copies. Payee: Court Clerk. Personal checks accepted if local. No credit cards accepted. Prepayment required.

Civil Name Search: Access: In person only. Visitors must perform in person searches themselves. Civil records on computer from 1996, on docket books from 1940s. Civil PAT goes back to 1996.

Criminal Name Search: Access: In person only. Visitors must perform in person searches themselves. Required to search: name, years to search, DOB; SSN helpful. Criminal records computerized from 1996, on docket books from 1940s. Criminal PAT goes back to same as civil.

Magistrate Court 100 Ridley Ave, LaGrange, GA 30240; 706-883-1695; fax: 706-883-1632; 8AM-5PM (EST). *Civil Actions under $15,000, Eviction, Small Claims.*

General Information: Court also has jurisdiction for bad checks, arrest warrants, preliminary hearings, and county ordinance violations.

Probate Court 100 Ridley, Troup County Government Center, LaGrange, GA 30240; 706-883-1690; fax: 706-812-7933; 8AM-5PM (EST). *Probate.*

General Information: Includes guardianship, administrations, custodial accounts, marriages, pistol licenses, passports, elections, and mental or substance abuse affidavits.

Turner County

Superior Court PO Box 106, 219 E College Ave, Rm 3, Ashburn, GA 31714; 229-567-2011; fax: 229-567-0450; 8AM-5PM (EST). *Felony, Civil.*

General Information: Misdemeanor records will only show here if filed with a felony on same subject. No juvenile, adoption, sexual, mental health or expunged records released. Will not fax out documents. Court makes copy: $.50 per page. Self serve copy: $.50 per page. Certification fee: $2.50 plus $1.00 per page after first. Payee: Court Clerk. No personal checks. No credit cards accepted. Prepayment required.

Civil Name Search: Access: In person only. Visitors must perform in person searches themselves. Civil index on docket books, archived from 1905.

Criminal Name Search: Access: In person only. Visitors must perform in person searches themselves. Required to search: name, years to search, DOB, signed release; SSN helpful. Criminal docket on books, archived from 1905.

State Court PO Box 532, 219 E College, Rm #1, Ashburn, GA 31714; 229-567-0490; fax: 229-567-0496; 8AM-5PM (EST). *Misdemeanor, Civil.*

General Information: No juvenile, adoption, sexual, mental health or expunged records released. Will fax documents $2.50. Court makes copy: $1.00 per page. Self serve copy: $.50 per page. Certification fee: $2.50 plus $1.00 per page after first. Payee: Court Clerk. No personal checks. Prepayment required.

Civil Name Search: Access: In person only. Visitors must perform in person searches themselves. Civil index on docket books, archived from 1905.

Criminal Name Search: Access: In person only. Visitors must perform in person searches themselves. Required to search: name, years to search, DOB, signed release; SSN helpful. Criminal docket on books, archived from 1905.

Magistrate Court 219 E College, #2, Ashburn, GA 31714; 229-567-3155; 9AM-5PM (EST). *Civil Actions under $15,000, Eviction, Small Claims.*

General Information: Court also has jurisdiction for bad checks, arrest warrants, preliminary hearings, and county ordinance violations.

Probate Court PO Box 2506, 219 E College Ave, Rm 4, Ashburn, GA 31714-2506; 229-567-2151; fax: 229-567-0358; 8AM-5PM, closed for lunch (EST). *Probate, Misdemeanor.*

General Information: Misdemeanors prior to 7/1/2002 only. Currently no new misdemeanor cases.

Twiggs County

Superior Court PO Box 234, 425 Railroad St North, Jeffersonville, GA 31044; 478-945-3350; fax: 478-945-6751; 8AM-5PM (EST). *Felony, Misdemeanor, Civil.*

General Information: No juvenile, adoption, sexual, mental health or expunged records released. Will fax documents to local or toll-free number. Court makes copy: $1.00 per page. Certification fee: $2.50 plus $.50 per page after first. Payee: Court Clerk. Personal checks accepted. No credit cards accepted. Prepayment required.

Civil Name Search: Access: In person only. Visitors must perform in person searches themselves. Civil records on computer from 1991, dockets books to 1901. Note: Can print the index back to 1901.

Criminal Name Search: Access: In person only. Visitors must perform in person searches themselves. Required to search: name, years to search,

DOB, signed release; SSN helpful. Criminal records computerized from 1991, dockets books to 1901. Note: Can print the index back to 1901.

Magistrate Court PO Box 146, 425 N Railroad St #212, Jeffersonville, GA 31044; 478-945-3428; fax: 478-945-2083; 9AM-5PM (EST). *Civil Actions under $25,000, Eviction, Small Claims.*

General Information: Court also has jurisdiction for bad checks, arrest warrants, preliminary hearings, and county ordinance violations.

Probate Court PO Box 186, 425 Railroad St N, Jeffersonville, GA 31044; 478-945-3390/3252; fax: 478-945-6070; 9AM-5PM (EST). *Probate, Misdemeanor Traffic.*

www.georgiacourts.org/councils/state/index_test.asp?county=1387&Submit= GO

Union County

Superior Court 114 Courthouse St, #5, Blairsville, GA 30512; 706-439-6022; fax: 706-439-6026; 8AM-5PM (EST). *Felony, Misdemeanor, Civil.*

General Information: No juvenile, adoption, sexual, mental health or expunged records released. Will not fax documents. Court makes copy: $1.00 per page. Self serve copy: $.50 per page. Certification fee: $2.50 plus $.25 per page after first. Payee: Court Clerk. Personal checks accepted. No credit cards accepted. Prepayment required.

Civil Name Search: Access: In person only. Both court and visitors may perform in person name searches. No search fee. Civil records on computer from 1993, on dockets from 1936. Civil PAT goes back to 1993.

Criminal Name Search: Access: In person only. Both court and visitors may perform in person name searches. No search fee. Required to search: name, years to search, DOB, signed release; SSN helpful. Criminal docket on books from 1930; computerized back to 1997. Criminal PAT goes back to 1997.

Magistrate Court 65 Courthouse St, #10, Blairsville, GA 30512; 706-439-6008; fax: 706-439-6104; 8AM-4:30PM (EST). *Civil Actions under $15,000, Eviction, Small Claims.*

General Information: Court also has jurisdiction for bad checks, arrest warrants, preliminary hearings, county ordinance violations, civil suits, foreclosures, abandonments and dispossessions.

Probate Court 65 Courthouse St, #8, Blairsville, GA 30512; 706-439-6006; fax: 706-439-6009; 8AM-4:30PM (EST). *Probate.*

Upson County

Superior Court PO Box 469, Thomaston, GA 30286; 706-647-7835; probate phone: 706-647-7015; fax: 706-647-8999; 8AM-5PM (EST). *Felony, Misdemeanor, Civil.*

www.upsoncountyga.org/departments/clerk_court.htm

General Information: No juvenile, adoption, sexual, mental health or expunged records released. Will fax documents to local or toll-free number. Court makes copy: $1.00 per page. Self serve copy: $.50 per page. Certification fee: $2.50 plus $.50 per page after first. Payee: Court Clerk. No personal checks or credit cards accepted. Prepayment required.

Civil Name Search: Access: In person. Visitors must perform in person searches themselves. Search fee: $5.00. Civil index in docket books from 1927; on computer back to 1990. Note: The court personnel will not perform name searches for the public. The docket index is not online, but calendar data is provided. Mail turnaround time 15 days. Civil PAT goes back to 1990.

Criminal Name Search: Access: In person. Visitors must perform in person searches themselves. Required to search: name, years to search, DOB; also helpful: SSN, race, sex. Criminal docket on books from 1937; on computer back to 1990. Note: The court personnel will not perform name searches for the public. The docket index is not online, but pleas going back 5 or 6 months and calendar data is provided. Mail turnaround time 15 days. Criminal PAT goes back to same as civil.

Magistrate Court PO Box 890, 305 S Hightower, D120, Thomaston, GA 30286; 706-647-6891; fax: 706-647-1248; 8AM-4:45PM (EST). *Civil Actions under $15,000, Eviction, Small Claims.*

General Information: Court also has jurisdiction for bad checks, arrest warrants, preliminary hearings, and county ordinance violations.

Probate Court PO Box 906, 106 E Lee St #210, Thomaston, GA 30286; 706-647-7015; fax: 706-646-3341; 8AM-5PM (EST). *Probate, Misdemeanor Traffic.*

Walker County

Superior & State Court PO Box 1125, 303 S Duke St, LaFayette, GA 30728; 706-638-1742; fax: 706-638-1779; 8AM-5PM (EST). *Felony, Misdemeanor, Civil.*

General Information: No juvenile, adoption, sexual, mental health or expunged records released. Will fax documents for $2.50 fee. Court makes copy: $1.00 per page. Self serve copy: $.50 per page. Certification fee: $2.50 plus $.50 per page after first. Payee: Court Clerk. Personal checks accepted. No credit cards accepted. Prepayment required.

Civil Name Search: Access: In person only. Visitors must perform in person searches themselves. Civil index in docket books from 1883; computerized since 2000. Civil PAT goes back to 10 years.

Criminal Name Search: Access: In person only. Visitors must perform in person searches themselves. Required to search: name, years to search, DOB; SSN helpful. Criminal docket on books from 1883. Criminal PAT goes back to same as civil.

Magistrate Court 102 Napier St, LaFayette, GA 30728; 706-638-1217; fax: 706-638-1218; 8AM-5PM (EST). *Civil Actions under $15,000, Eviction, Small Claims.*

General Information: Court also has jurisdiction for bad checks, arrest warrants, search warrants, preliminary hearings (15K Civil), and county ordinance violations.

Probate Court PO Box 436, 103 S Duke St, Rm 101, LaFayette, GA 30728; 706-638-2852; fax: 706-638-2869; 8AM-5PM (EST). *Probate.*

Walton County

Superior Court 303 S Hammond Dr, Ste 335, Monroe, GA 30655; 770-267-1307; fax: 770-267-1441; 8:30AM-5PM (EST). *Felony, Misdemeanor, Civil.*

www.waltoncountyga.gov/CoCt/ClkSupCt.html

General Information: No juvenile, adoption, sexual, mental health or expunged records released. Will not fax documents. Court makes copy: $1.00 per page. Self serve copy: same. Certification fee: $2.50 per doc plus $/50 per page per doc. Payee: Court Clerk. Local personal checks with ID accepted. No credit cards accepted. Prepayment required.

Civil Name Search: Access: In person only. Visitors must perform in person searches themselves. Civil records on computer from 1990, dockets books from 1900s. Civil PAT goes back to 1990.

Criminal Name Search: Access: In person only. Visitors must perform in person searches themselves. Required to search: name, years to search; also helpful: DOB, race, sex. Criminal records computerized from 1990, dockets books from 1900s. Criminal PAT goes back to 1990.

Magistrate Court 303 S Hammond Dr #116, Monroe, GA 30655; 770-267-1349; fax: 770-266-1512; 8AM-5PM (EST). *Civil Actions under $15,000, Eviction, Small Claims, Criminal warrants, Ordinance.*

www.waltoncountyga.gov/MagCt/MagCt.html

General Information: Court also has jurisdiction for bad checks, arrest warrants, preliminary hearings, pre-warrant hearings, personal property foreclosure, and county ordinance violations.

Probate Court 303 S Hammond Dr, Suite 118, Monroe, GA 30655; 770-267-1345, 266-1751; fax: 770-267-1417; 8:30AM-5PM (EST). *Probate, Misdemeanor.*

www.alcovycircuit.com/web/index.php?option=com_content&task=category &sectionid=6&id=19&Itemid=47

General Information: This location also has traffic records.

Ware County

Superior & State Court PO Box 776, 800 Church St #124, Waycross, GA 31502; 912-287-4340; fax: 912-287-2498; 9AM-5PM (EST). *Felony, Misdemeanor, Civil.*

General Information: Court will copy and return docs if case number provided; in some circumstances they may do a name search if your mail request specifies which court index to search. No juvenile, adoption, sexual, mental health or expunged records released. Will not fax documents. Court makes copy: $1.00 per page. Self serve copy: $.50 per page. Certification fee: $2.50 plus $.50 per page after first. Payee: Court Clerk. In-state personal checks accepted. No credit cards accepted. Prepayment required.

Civil Name Search: Access: In person only. Visitors must perform in person searches themselves. Civil cases indexed by defendant. Civil records on computer since 1995; prior records on dockets books from 1874.

Criminal Name Search: Access: In person only. Visitors must perform in person searches themselves. Required to search: name, years to search, DOB; SSN helpful. Criminal records on computer since 1995; prior records on dockets books from 1874.

Magistrate Court PO Box 17, 301 Albany Ave, Waycross, GA 31501; 912-287-4375; criminal phone: 912-287-4373; civil phone: 912-287-4375; criminal fax: 912-287-4377; civil fax: 9AM-5PM; 9AM-5PM (EST). *Civil Actions under $15,000, Eviction, Small Claims, Foreclosure, Garnishment.*

www.warecounty.com/MagistrateCourt.aspx

General Information: Court also has jurisdiction for bad checks, arrest warrants, preliminary hearings, county ordinance and good behavior violations.

Probate Court Ware County Courthouse, 800 Church St, #123, Waycross, GA 31501; 912-287-4315/6; fax: 912-287-4317; 9AM-5PM (EST). *Probate.*

www.georgiacourts.org/courts/probate/ware/index.shtm

General Information: This court holds marriage license, firearms permits, order to apprehend, estates, guardianship of adult wards & minors.

Warren County

Superior Court PO Box 227, 100 Main St, Ste 201, Warrenton, GA 30828; 706-465-2262; fax: 706-465-0232; 8AM-5PM (EST). *Felony, Misdemeanor, Civil.*

General Information: Court personnel will not perform name searches for the public. You must do yourself or hire a record researcher. No juvenile, adoption, sexual, mental health or expunged records released. Will fax documents $2.50 1st page, $1.00 each add'l. Court makes copy: $1.00 per page. Self serve copy: $.50 per page. Certification fee: $2.50 for 1st page, $.50 each add'l. Payee: Court Clerk. Personal checks accepted. No credit cards accepted. Prepayment required.

Civil Name Search: Access: In person. Visitors must perform in person searches themselves. Civil index on docket books to 1950. Civil PAT goes back to 1994.

Criminal Name Search: Access: In person. Visitors must perform in person searches themselves. Required to search: name, years to search, DOB, signed release; also helpful: SSN, race, sex. Criminal docket on books to 1950, computerized since 2000. Criminal PAT goes back to 1994.

Magistrate Court 521 Main St, #104, Warrenton, GA 30828; 706-465-2227; fax: 706-465-1347; 8AM-N, 1-5PM (EST). *Civil Actions under $15,000, Eviction, Small Claims.*

www.georgiacourts.org/councils/state/index_testmagistarte.asp?county=1552&Submit=GO

General Information: Court also has jurisdiction for bad checks, arrest warrants, preliminary hearings, and county ordinance violations.

Probate Court 521 main St, Ste 104, Warrenton, GA 30828; 706-465-2227; fax: 706-465-1347; 8AM-5PM (EST). *Probate, Magisatrate, Traffic.*
General Information: Also holds municipal traffic.

Washington County

Superior & State Court PO Box 231, 132 W Haynes St, Sandersville, GA 31082; 478-552-3186; fax: 478-553-9969; 9AM-5PM (EST). *Felony, Misdemeanor, Civil.*

General Information: As a courtesy, this court may do single name searches and ask for a small fee. No juvenile, adoption, sexual, mental health or expunged records released. Will fax documents to local or toll free line, if copy prepaid. Court makes copy: $1.00 per page. Self serve copy: $.50 per page. Certification fee: $2.50 plus $.50 per page after first. Payee: Court Clerk. No personal checks. No credit cards accepted. Prepayment required.

Civil Name Search: Access: In person only. Visitors must perform in person searches themselves. Civil records on dockets books to 1869. Civil PAT goes back to 1995.

Criminal Name Search: Access: In person only. Visitors must perform in person searches themselves. Criminal docket on books to 1869. Criminal PAT goes back to same as civil.

Magistrate Court PO Box 1053, 132 W Haynes St, Ste 110, Sandersville, GA 31082; 478-552-3591; fax: 478-552-4010; 9AM-5PM (EST). *Civil Actions under $15,000, Eviction, Small Claims.*

General Information: Court also has jurisdiction for bad checks, arrest warrants, preliminary hearings, and county ordinance violations.

Probate Court PO Box 669, 132 W Haynes ST #106, Sandersville, GA 31082; 478-552-3304; fax: 478-552-3304; 9AM-5PM (EST). *Probate.*

Wayne County

Superior & State Court PO Box 920, Jesup, GA 31598; 912-427-5930; fax: 912-427-5939; 8:30AM-5PM (EST). *Felony, Misdemeanor, Civil.*

General Information: No juvenile, adoption, sexual, mental health or expunged records released. Will fax documents $.50 per page. Court makes copy: $.50 per page. Self serve copy: same. Certification fee: $2.50 plus $.50 per page after first. Payee: Superior Court Clerk. Personal checks accepted. No credit cards accepted. Prepayment required.

Civil Name Search: Access: In person only. Visitors must perform in person searches themselves. Civil records on computer, on docket books from 1810. Civil PAT goes back to 1994. Terminal results also show SSNs.

Criminal Name Search: Access: In person only. Visitors must perform in person searches themselves. Required to search: name, years to search, DOB. Criminal records on computer, on docket books from 1810. Criminal PAT goes back to same as civil. Terminal results include SSN.

Magistrate Court PO Box 27, 174 N Brunswick St, Jesup, GA 31598; 912-427-5960; fax: 912-427-5962; 8:30AM-N; 1-5PM (EST). *Civil Actions under $15,000, Eviction, Small Claims.*

General Information: Court also has jurisdiction for bad checks, arrest warrants, preliminary hearings, bond hearings and county ordinance violations.

Probate Court 174 N Brunswick St, Jesup, GA 31546; 912-427-5940; fax: 912-427-5944; 8:30AM-5PM (EST). *Probate.*

Webster County

Superior Court PO Box 117, 6330 Hamilton St, Rm 102, Preston, GA 31824; 229-828-3525; fax: 229-828-6961; 9AM-5PM (EST). *Felony, Misdemeanor, Civil.*

General Information: No juvenile, adoption, sexual, mental health or expunged records released. Will fax documents $2.50 first page, $1.00 each add'l page. Court makes copy: $.50 per page, Legal size $2.00 per page. Self serve copy: same. Certification fee: $2.50 plus $.50 per page after 1st page. Payee: Clerk Superior Court. Personal checks accepted. No credit cards accepted. Prepayment required.

Civil Name Search: Access: In person only. Visitors must perform in person searches themselves. Civil index in docket books from 1860; computerized records since 2000. Civil PAT goes back to 2000.

Criminal Name Search: Access: In person only. Visitors must perform in person searches themselves. Required to search: name, years to search, signed release. Criminal docket on books from 1860; computerized records since 2000. Criminal PAT goes back to same as civil.

Magistrate & Probate Court PO Box 18, Preston, GA 31824; 229-828-3615; fax: 229-828-3616; 8AM-4:30PM (EST). *Civil Actions under $15,000, Eviction, Small Claims, Traffic, Probate.*

General Information: This court will not give out SSNs. Court also has jurisdiction for bad checks, arrest warrants, preliminary hearings, and county ordinance violations

Wheeler County

Superior Court PO Box 38, Alamo, GA 30411; 912-568-7137; fax: 912-568-7453; 8AM-4PM (EST). *Felony, Misdemeanor, Civil.*

General Information: No juvenile or adoption records released. Will not fax documents. Court makes copy: $1.00 per page plus hourly fee if it takes more than 15 minutes. Self serve copy: $.50 per page. Certification fee: $2.50 plus $.50 per add'l page. Payee: Superior Court Clerk. Personal checks accepted. No credit cards accepted. Prepayment required.

Civil Name Search: Access: In person only. Visitors must perform in person searches themselves. Civil cases indexed by defendant. Civil index in docket books from 1913. Note: Public must view docket books.

Criminal Name Search: Access: In person only. Visitors must perform in person searches themselves. Criminal docket on books from 1913. Note: Public must view docket books.

Magistrate & Probate Court PO Box 477, 16 W Pearl St, Alamo, GA 30411; 912-568-7133; fax: 912-568-1743; 8AM-4PM (EST). *Civil Actions under $15,000, Eviction, Small Claims, Probate, Traffic, Garnishments.*

General Information: Court also has jurisdiction for bad checks, arrest warrants, preliminary hearings, and county ordinance violations. Probate fax is same as main fax number.

White County

Superior Court 59 S Main St, #B, Cleveland, GA 30528; 706-865-2613; criminal phone: ext 222; civil phone: ext 218; fax: 706-865-2613; 8:30AM-5PM (EST). *Felony, Misdemeanor, Civil.*

www.whitecounty.net/clerk/clerk.htm

General Information: No juvenile, adoption, sexual, mental health or expunged records released. Will fax specific case file $2.50 1st page and $1.00 ea add'l, prepaid. Court makes copy: $1.00 per page. Self serve copy: $.50per page. Certification fee: $2.50 plus $.50 per page after first. Payee: Superior Court Clerk. Business checks accepted. No credit cards accepted. Prepayment required. Mail requests: SASE required.

Civil Name Search: Access: Mail, in person. Visitors must perform in person searches themselves. No search fee. Civil records on computer from 1996, on docket books from 1857. Note: Will accept mail requests if prepaid and specific case info provided. Civil PAT goes back to 1996.

Criminal Name Search: Access: Mail, In person. Visitors must perform in person searches themselves. No search fee. Criminal records computerized from 1996, on docket books from 1857. Note: Will accept mail requests if prepaid and specific case info provided. Mail turnaround time 10 days; search performed as time permits. Criminal PAT goes back to same as civil.

Magistrate Court 59 S Main St, #D, Cleveland, GA 30528; 706-865-6636; criminal phone: 706-865-6636; civil phone: 706-865-2613; criminal fax: 706-865-7738; civil fax: 8:30AM-5PM; 8:30AM-5PM (EST). *Civil Actions under $15,000, Misdemeanor, Eviction, Small Claims.*

www.whitecounty.net/magistrate/mag.htm

General Information: Court also has jurisdiction for bad checks, arrest warrants, preliminary hearings, and county ordinance violations.

Probate Court 59 S Main St, Ste H, Cleveland, GA 30528; 706-865-4141; fax: 706-219-1512; 8:30AM-5PM (EST). *Probate, Misdemeanor.*

www.whitecounty.net/probate/pro.htm

Whitfield County

Superior Court PO Box 868, Dalton, GA 30722; 706-275-7450; criminal phone: 706-275-7483; civil phone: 706-275-7480; fax: 706-275-7456; 8AM-5PM (EST). *Felony, Misdemeanor, Civil.*

General Information: Street address is 205 N Selvidge St. No juvenile, adoption, sexual, mental health or expunged records released. Will not fax documents. Court makes copy: $.50 per page. Self serve copy: $.50 per page. Certification fee: $3.00 per cert. Payee: Superior Court Clerk. Business checks accepted. No credit cards accepted. Prepayment required.

Civil Name Search: Access: In person only. Visitors must perform in person searches themselves. Civil records on computer from 1988, on docket books from 1852. Civil PAT goes back to 8/1988.

Criminal Name Search: Access: In person only. Visitors must perform in person searches themselves. Required to search: name, years to search, offense, date of offense. Criminal records computerized from 1988, on docket books from 1852. Criminal PAT goes back to same as civil.

Magistrate Court PO Box 386, 205 N Selvidge St, Ground Fl, Dalton, GA 30722-0386; 706-278-5052; fax: 706-278-8810; 8AM-5PM (EST). *Civil Actions under $15,000, Eviction, Small Claims, Misdemeanor, Ordinance.*

www.whitfieldcountyga.com/MagistrateCourt/magistrate_court.htm

General Information: Court also has jurisdiction for bad checks, arrest warrants, preliminary hearings, and county ordinance violations.

Probate Court 205 N Selvidge St, Ste G, Dalton, GA 30720; 706-275-7400; fax: 706-281-1735; 8AM-4:45PM (EST). *Probate.*

www.whitfieldcountyga.com/probatecourt/probate_court.htm

General Information: Court handles marriage, traffic and estates. Access these records by subscription at probate court webpage listed above.

Wilcox County

Superior & Magistrate Courts 103 N Broad St, Abbeville, GA 31001; 229-467-2442; probate phone: 229-467-2220; fax: 229-467-2886; 9AM-5PM (EST). *Felony, Misdemeanor, Civil, Eviction, Small Claims.*

General Information: Magistrate: 229-467-2458 No juvenile, adoption, sexual, mental health or expunged records released. Will not fax out documents. Court makes copy: $1.00 per page. Self serve copy: $.50 per page. Certification fee: $2.50 plus $.50 per page after first. Payee: Superior Court Clerk. Personal checks accepted. No credit cards accepted. Prepayment required.

Civil Name Search: Access: In person only. Both court and visitors may perform in person name searches. Civil records on computer since 1995; prior records on docket books from 1950s. Civil PAT available.

Criminal Name Search: Access: In person only. Both court and visitors may perform in person name searches. Required to search: name, years to search, DOB; also helpful: SSN. Criminal records on computer since 1995; prior records on docket books from 1950s. Criminal PAT available.

Probate Court 103 N Broad St, Abbeville, GA 31001; 229-467-2220; fax: 229-467-2067; 9AM-5PM (EST). *Probate.*

Wilkes County

Superior Court 23 Court St, Rm 205, Washington, GA 30673; 706-678-2423; fax: 706-678-2115; 9AM-5PM (EST). *Felony, Misdemeanor, Civil.*

General Information: No juvenile or adoption records released. Will fax specific documents $2.50 1st page, $1.00 ea add'l. Court makes copy: $.50 per page. Self serve copy: $.50 per page. Certification fee: $2.50 plus $.50 per page after 1st. Payee: Superior Court Clerk. Personal checks accepted. No credit cards accepted. Prepayment required.

Civil Name Search: Access: In person only. Visitors must perform in person searches themselves. Civil index in docket books from 1700s, computerized from 1998. Civil PAT goes back to 1998.

Criminal Name Search: Access: In person only. Visitors must perform in person searches themselves. Criminal docket on books from 1700s, computerized from 1998. Criminal PAT goes back to same as civil.

Magistrate Court 23 E Court St, Rm 427, Washington, GA 30673; 706-678-1881; fax: 706-678-1865; 8:30AM-5PM (EST). *Civil Actions up to $15,000, Eviction, Small Claims.*

www.washingtonwilkes.org/blog/

General Information: Court also has jurisdiction for bad checks, arrest warrants, preliminary hearings, and county ordinance violations.

Probate Court 23 Court St, Rm 422, Washington, GA 30673; 706-678-2523; fax: 706-678-4854; 8AM-5PM (EST). *Probate.*

Wilkinson County

Superior Court PO Box 250, Irwinton, GA 31042; 478-946-2221; fax: 478-946-1497; 8AM-5PM (EST). *Felony, Misdemeanor, Civil.*

www.gsccca.org/clerks/

General Information: This court will not provide name searches. No juvenile, adoption, sexual, mental health or expunged records released. Will fax documents $2.50 first page plus $1.00 ea addl. Court makes copy: $1.00

per page. Self serve copy: $.50 per page. Certification fee: $2.50 per doc plus $.50 per page after 1st. Payee: Superior Court Clerk. Personal checks accepted. No credit cards accepted. Prepayment required.

Civil Name Search: Access: In person only. Visitors must perform in person searches themselves. Civil records on computer from 1991, on docket PAT goes back to 1991.

Criminal Name Search: Access: In person only. Visitors must perform in person searches themselves. Required to search: name, years to search, DOB. Criminal records computerized from 1991, on docket books from 1900s. Criminal PAT goes back to 1991.

Magistrate & Probate Court PO Box 201, 100 Bacon St, Irwinton, GA 31042; 478-946-2222; fax: 478-946-3810; 8AM-5PM (EST). *Civil Actions under $15,000, Eviction, Small Claims, Probate.*

www.wilkinsoncounty.net/Probate.htm

General Information: Court also has jurisdiction for bad checks, arrest warrants, preliminary hearings, and county ordinance violations. Magistrate Court website at www.wilkinsoncounty.net/Magistrate.htm.

Worth County

Superior & State Court 201 N Main St, Rm 13, Sylvester, GA 31791; 229-776-8205; fax: 229-776-8237; 8AM-5PM (EST). *Felony, Misdemeanor, Civil.*

General Information: Small Claims is in Magistrate Court. No juvenile, adoption, sexual, mental health or expunged records released. Will not fax out case files. Court makes copy: $1.00 per page. Self serve copy: $.50 per page. Certification fee: $2.50 1st page, $.50 each add'l. Payee: Superior Court Clerk. No personal checks. No credit cards accepted. Prepayment required.

Civil Name Search: Access: In person only. Visitors must perform in person searches themselves. Civil records computerized since 1995, on books since 1880, real estate records from 9/93. Civil PAT goes back to 1995.

Criminal Name Search: Access: In person only. Visitors must perform in person searches themselves. Required to search: name, years to search; SSN helpful. Criminal records computerized since 1995. Criminal PAT goes back to same as civil.

Magistrate Court 201 N Main St, Rm 21, Courthouse, Sylvester, GA 31791; 229-776-8210; fax: 229-776-8245; 9AM-5PM (EST). *Civil Actions under $15,000, Eviction, Small Claims.*

www.worthcountyboc.com/magistrate-court.html

Probate Court 201 N Main St, Rm 12, Courthouse, Sylvester, GA 31791; 229-776-8207; fax: 229-776-1540; 8AM-5PM (EST). *Probate, Marriage.*

General Information: This court also holds firearms, birth and death records.

Hawaii

Time Zone:	HT
Capital:	**Honolulu, Honolulu County**
# of Counties:	4
Court Web:	**www.courts.state.hi.us**
State Web:	**www.ehawaii.gov**

Administration

Administrative Director of Courts, Judicial Branch, 417 S King St, Honolulu, HI, 96813; 808-539-4900, Fax: 808-539-4855.

The Supreme and Appellate Courts

The Supreme Court of Hawaii is the state's court of last resort. The Supreme Court hears appeals from the Intermediate Court of Appeals and reserved questions of law from the Circuit Courts, the Land Court, and the Tax Appeal court. The Intermediate Court of Appeals (ICA) is the court that hears nearly all appeals from trial courts and some state agencies in the State of Hawaii. There is also a Tax Appeal Court that hears appeals regarding real estate taxation and this is a court of record.

Opinions and decisions from the Supreme and Appeals courts are on the home page above.

The Hawaii Courts

Court	Type	How Organized	Jurisdiction Highpoints
Circuit*	General	4 courts in 4 circuits	Felony, Civil over $15,000, Juvenile, Domestic Relations, Estate
District*	Limited	4 courts in 4 circuits	Misdemeanor, Civil Actions Under $15,000, Small Claims, Eviction, DWI/DUI
Family	Special	4 courts in 4 circuits	Juvenile, Guardianship, Domestic Relations, Domestic Violence
Land	Special	1 court	Land matters

* = profiled in this book

Details on the Court Structure

Hawaii's trial level is comprised of Circuit Courts (includes Family Courts) and District Courts. These trial courts function in four judicial circuits: First (Oahu), Second (Maui-Molokai-Lanai), Third (Hawaii County), and Fifth (Kauai-Niihau). The Fourth Circuit was merged with the Third in 1943.

Circuit Courts are general jurisdiction and handle all jury trials, felony cases, and civil cases over $25,000, also probate and guardianship. There is **concurrent jurisdiction** with District Courts in **civil** non-jury cases that specify amounts between **$10,000-$25,000**. Other cases heard by the Circuit Courts include mechanics' liens and misdemeanor violations transferred from the District Courts for jury trials

The **District Court** handles criminal cases punishable by a fine and/or less than one year imprisonment, landlord/tenant, traffic, DUI cases, civil cases up to $25,000, and small claims ($5,000 limit).

The **Family Court** rules in all legal matters involving children, such as delinquency, waiver, status offenses, abuse and neglect, termination of parental rights, adoption, guardianships and detention. Also hears traditional domestic-relations cases, including divorce, nonsupport, paternity, uniform child custody jurisdiction cases, miscellaneous custody matters, as well as guardianships of adults, and adult abuse cases.

The **Land Court** has exclusive original jurisdiction over all applications and questions for the registration of title to land easements or rights in land held and possessed in fee simple.

Record Searching Facts You Need to Know

Fees and Record Searching Tips

Most Hawaii courts offer a public access terminal to search records at the courthouse. Most courts charge $5.00 per name for a name search and $1.00 for the first copy and $.50 each add'l.

Hawaii is unique in that it does not have a central agency that manages and regulates motor vehicle and driver functions. In Hawaii, the State Judiciary is responsible for Traffic Abstracts and Traffic Court Reports. Therefore each county has a Traffic Violation Bureau, part of the State Judiciary, which manages the county's driving record convictions. The Traffic Violations Bureau in Honolulu is the centralized agency that processes most of the manual record requests. Electronic access to driving records is through the Hawaii Information Consortium (HIC).

Online Access is Nearly Statewide on As-Is Basis

There are two free online access systems available from the home page. Click on *Ho'Ohiki* This page offers civil and criminal case information from the Circuit and Family Courts and certain civil information in the District Courts. Search by name or case number. Most courts offer access back to mid 1980s.

Traffic records are available online, click on *eCourt Kokua* at the home page.

Case information provided by the Judiciary through this website is made available "as is," as a public service with no warranties, express or implied, including any implied warranties of merchantability, accuracy, non-infringement or fitness for a particular purpose.

Hawaii County

3rd Circuit Court Legal Document Section 777 Kilauea Ave, Hilo, HI 96720; 808-961-7404; fax: 808-961-7493; 8AM-4PM (HT). *Felony, Misdemeanor, Civil Actions over $10,000, Probate.* www.courts.state.hi.us/
General Information: Records are indexed for this county as 3 = Big Island. Online identifiers in results same as on public terminal. No adoption, juvenile, dependencies, confidential records released without court's approval. Will fax documents to local or toll free line. Court makes copy: $1.00 first page, $.50 each add'l. Microfilm copy is $1.00 per page. Certification fee: $2.00; $4.00 for exemplification and certification together. Payee: Clerk, 3rd Circuit Court. Personal checks accepted. No credit cards accepted. Prepayment required. Mail requests: SASE required.
Civil Name Search: Access: Mail, fax, in person, online. Both court and visitors may perform in person name searches. Search fee: $5.00 per name. Civil records on computer from 1988, index card system prior to 1988. Mail turnaround time 2 days depending on staff coverage. Civil PAT goes back to 1987. Free record searching at http://hoohiki2.courts.state.hi.us/jud/Hoohiki/main.htm or click on "Search Court Records" at www.courts.state.hi.us/. Search back to 1983 by name, case number, or circuit.
Criminal Name Search: Access: Mail, fax, in person, online. Both court and visitors may perform in person name searches. Search fee: $5.00 per name. Criminal records computerized from 1988, index card system prior to 1988. Mail turnaround time 2 days depending upon staff coverage. Criminal PAT goes back to 1987. Results may sometimes include other identifiers. Online access to criminal records is same as civil.

District Court 777 Kilauea Ave, Hilo, HI 96720-4212; 808-961-7470; criminal phone: 808-961-7470; civil phone: 808-961-7515; fax: 808-961-7447; 7:45AM-4:30PM (HT). *Misdemeanor, Civil Actions under $25,000, Eviction, Small Claims.* www.courts.state.hi.us/
General Information: No family court records released. Will fax documents $2.00 1st page, $1.00 each add'l. Extra fee for out of state faxing. Court makes copy: $1.00 first page, $.50 each add'l. Off-site storage- usual copy fees plus $5.00. Certification fee: $2.00 plus copy fee. Payee: Clerk of the District Court. Personal checks accepted. Credit cards accepted. Prepayment required. Mail requests: SASE requested.
Civil Name Search: Access: Phone, fax, mail, in person, online. Only the court performs in person name searches; visitors may not. Search fee: $5.00 per name. Required to search: name, years to search, case number; also helpful: address. Civil cases indexed by defendant. Civil records on ledgers from statehood. Mail turnaround time 1 week. Free record searching at http://hoohiki2.courts.state.hi.us/jud/Hoohiki/main.htm or click on "Search Court Records" at www.courts.state.hi.us/. Search by name or case number.
Criminal Name Search: Access: Phone, fax, mail. Only the court performs in person name searches; visitors may not. Search fee: $5.00 per name. Required to search: name, years to search, case number; also helpful:

address, DOB, SSN. Criminal records on computer since 3/1996. Mail turnaround time 1 week. Online results show middle initial.

Honolulu County

1st Circuit Court Legal Documents Branch, 777 Punchbowl St, 1st Fl, Honolulu, HI 96813; 808-539-4300; fax: 808-539-4314; 7:45AM-4:30PM (9AM-4PM files) (HT). *Felony, Civil Actions over $10,000, Probate, Family.* www.courts.state.hi.us/
General Information: Records are indexed for this county as 1 = Honolulu. Online identifiers in results same as on public terminal. No adoption, paternity or sealed records released. Will fax documents within US for $5.00 1st page, $2 each add'l; Foreign- $10.00 1st page and $5.00 each add'l. Court makes copy: $1.00 first page, $.50 each add'l. Microfilm service fee $5.00; cost of copies $1.00 per page. Self serve copy: $.15 per page. Certification fee: $2.00 per cert. Payee: 1st Circuit Court. No personal checks or credit cards accepted. Prepayment required. Mail requests: SASE required.
Civil Name Search: Access: Mail, in person, online. Both court and visitors may perform in person name searches. Search fee: $5.00 per name. Civil records on computer back to 1984, on microfiche and archived from 1900. Mail turnaround time same day. Civil PAT available. Free record searching at http://hoohiki2.courts.state.hi.us/jud/Hoohiki/main.htm or click on "Search Court Records" at www.courts.state.hi.us/. Search back to 1983 by name, case number, or circuit.
Criminal Name Search: Access: Mail, in person, online. Both court and visitors may perform in person name searches. Search fee: $5.00 per name. Required to search: name, years to search, DOB; also helpful: SSN. Criminal records computerized from 1984, on microfiche and archived from 1900. Mail turnaround time same day. Criminal PAT available. Online access to criminal is the same as civil. Online results show middle initial.

District Court - Criminal Division 1111 Alakea St, 3rd Fl, Files/Services, Attn: Certification Clerk, Honolulu, HI 96813; 808-538-5100; 808-538-5767- info; criminal phone: 808-538-5149; fax: 808-538-5111; 8AM-4:15PM (HT). *Misdemeanor, Traffic.* www.courts.state.hi.us/
General Information: No sealed records released. Will not fax documents. Court makes copy: $1.00 1st pg, $.50 each add'l. Certification fee: $2.00 per cert. Payee: District Court of the 1st Judicial Circuit. No out-of-state checks accepted. Visa/MC accepted for traffic only. Prepayment required. Mail requests: SASE required.
Criminal Name Search: Access: Mail, in person. Only the court performs in person name searches; visitors may not. Required to search: name, years to search, SSN, signed release, aliases; also helpful: address, DOB. Criminal records on computer go back to 1999. Mail turnaround time 1 week. Misdemeanor records are not online, but free searches of traffic records at www.courts.state.hi.us. Click on "Search Court Records." Choose JIMS CourtConnect.

District Court - Civil Division 1111 Alakea St, 3rd Fl, Attn: Certification Clerk, Honolulu, HI 96813; 808-538-5151; fax: 808-538-5444; 7:45AM-4PM (HT). *Civil Actions under $25,000, Eviction, Small Claims.* www.courts.state.hi.us/

General Information: Online identifiers in results same as on public terminal. No sealed records released. Will not fax documents. Court makes copy: $1.00 1st page; $.50 each add'l. Certification fee: $2.00 per doc. Payee: District Court of the 1st Circuit. No personal checks accepted. Visa/MC accepted. Prepayment required. Mail requests: SASE required.

Civil Name Search: Access: Mail, in person, online. Both court and visitors may perform in person name searches. Search fee: $5.00 per name. Civil cases indexed by defendant. Civil records on computer from 1990; plaintiff index only on computer records. Mail turnaround time 1 week. Public use terminal has civil records back to 1990. Free record searching at http://hoohiki2.courts.state.hi.us/jud/Hoohiki/main.htm or click on "Search Court Records" at www.courts.state.hi.us/. Search by name or case number.

Kauai County

5th Circuit Court 3970 Kaana St #207, Lihue, HI 96766; 808)-482-2300- info; Docs- 808-482-2330; fax: 808-482-2553; 7:45AM-4:30PM (HT). *Felony, Misdemeanor, Civil Actions over $10,000, Probate.* www.courts.state.hi.us/

General Information: Customer service window open 8AM-4PM. Online identifiers in results same as on public terminal. No juvenile, dependencies records released. Will fax out documents, $2.00 1st page, $1.00 add'l within Hawaii; $5.00 1st page, $2.00 add'l in U.S.; $10.00 1st page, $5.00 add'l outside the U.S. Court makes copy: $1.00 first page, $.50 each add'l. Certification fee: $2.00. Payee: 5th Circuit Court. Only cashiers checks, money orders or cash accepted. No credit cards accepted. Prepayment required. Mail requests: SASE required.

Civil Name Search: Access: Mail, in person, online. Both court and visitors may perform in person name searches. Search fee: $5.00 per name. Civil cases indexed by plaintiff & defendant. Civil records on computer from 1987, microfiche from 1960. Mail turnaround time approx. 1 week. Civil PAT available. Free record searching at http://hoohiki2.courts.state.hi.us/jud/Hoohiki/main.htm or click on "Search Court Records" at www.courts.state.hi.us/p. Search back to 1983 by name, case number, or circuit.

Criminal Name Search: Access: Mail, in person, online. Both court and visitors may perform in person name searches. Search fee: $5.00 per name. Required to search: name, years to search, DOB; also helpful: SSN. Criminal records computerized from 1987, microfiche from 1960. Mail turnaround time approx. 1 week. Criminal PAT available. Online access to criminal records is same as civil. Online results show middle initial.

District Court of the 5th Circuit - Civil 3970 Ka'ana St #207, Lihue, HI 96766; 808-482-2303; fax: 808-482-2553; 7:45AM-4:30PM (HT). *Civil Actions under $25,000, Eviction, Small Claims.* www.courts.state.hi.us/

General Information: Customer service window open 8AM-4PM. Online identifiers in results same as on public terminal. No juvenile records released. Will fax out documents, $2.00 1st page, $1.00 add'l within Hawaii; $5.00 1st page, $2.00 add'l in U.S.; $10.00 1st page, $5.00 add'l outside the U.S. Court makes copy: $1.00 first page, $.50 each add'l. Self serve copy: $.15 per page. Certification fee: $2.00. Payee: District Court of the Fifth Judicial Circuit. Personal in-state checks accepted; no third party checks. No credit cards accepted. Prepayment required. Mail requests: SASE required for civil.

Civil Name Search: Access: Phone, fax, mail, in person, online. Both court and visitors may perform in person name searches. Search fee: $5.00 per case. Civil index on cards. Mail turnaround time 1-7 days. Public use terminal has civil records back to 2003. Free record searching at http://hoohiki2.courts.state.hi.us/jud/Hoohiki/main.htm or click on "Search Court Records" at www.courts.state.hi.us/. Search back to 1983 by name, case number, or circuit.

Maui County

2nd Circuit Court 2145 Main St, #106, Wailuku, HI 96793; 808-244-2969; fax: 808-244-2932; 8AM-4PM (HT). *Felony, Misdemeanor, Civil Actions over $10,000, Probate.* www.courts.state.hi.us/

General Information: This court also covers Lanai and Molokai. Records are indexed for this county as 2 = Maui. Provide your toll-free number and they'll give you court costs. Online identifiers in results same as on public terminal. No juvenile or paternity records released. Fee to fax out file $5.00 1st page, $2.00 each add'l in USA; $2.00 for first and $1.00 each add'l in Hawaii. Court makes copy: Microfilm, file marked copy- $1.00 per page; non-file marked- $1.00 1st page, $.50 each add'l. Certification fee: $2.00 per doc plus copy fee. Payee: Clerk, 2nd Circuit Court. Personal checks accepted. No credit cards accepted. Prepayment required. Mail requests: SASE required.

Civil Name Search: Access: Mail, fax, in person, online. Both court and visitors may perform in person name searches. Search fee: $5.00 per name. Civil records on computer from 10/85, some prior on microfiche; claims and

small claims on computer back to 10/23/2003. Mail turnaround time 1 week. Civil PAT goes back to 1985. Terminal results may include address. Free record searching at http://hoohiki2.courts.state.hi.us/jud/Hoohiki/main.htm or click on "Search Court Records" at www.courts.state.hi.us/. Search back to 1983 by name, case number, or circuit.

Criminal Name Search: Access: Mail, fax, in person, online. Both court and visitors may perform in person name searches. Search fee: $5.00 per name. Required to search: name, years to search; also helpful: DOB, SSN. Criminal records computerized from 10/85, some prior on microfiche. Mail turnaround time 1 week. Criminal PAT goes back to 1985. Online access to criminal records is same as civil. Online results show middle initial.

Lanai District Court PO Box 631376, Lanai City, HI 96763; 808-565-6447; fax: 808-565-7543; 7:45AM-4:30PM; counter- 8AM-4PM (HT). *Misdemeanor, Civil Actions under $25,000, Eviction, Small Claims.* www.courts.state.hi.us/

General Information: Search all Maui District Courts by one request to the Wailuku address and fax. Will fax documents $5.00 1st page, $2.00 each add'l. Within HI; $2.00 1st page, $1.00 each add'l. Court makes copy: $1.00 first page, $.50 each add'l. Certification fee: $2.00 per doc plus copy fee. Payee: Lanai District Court. Personal checks accepted, address and phone proof required. No credit cards accepted. Prepayment required. Mail requests: SASE required.

Civil Name Search: Access: Mail, in person, online. Only the court performs in person name searches; visitors may not. Search fee: $5.00 per search. Civil index and docket books back to statehood. Mail turnaround time 2-3 weeks. Free searching at http://hoohiki2.courts.state.hi.us/jud/Hoohiki/main.htm or click on "Search Court Records" at www.courts.state.hi.us/. Search by name or case number. Records go back to 12/03.

Criminal Name Search: Access: Mail, in person. Only the court performs in person name searches; visitors may not. Search fee: $5.00 per search. Required to search: name, years to search; also helpful: DOB, SSN. Criminal records on computer since 1997. Mail turnaround time 2-3 weeks.

Molokai District Court PO Box 284, Kaunakakai, HI 96748; 808-553-1100; fax: 808-553-3374; 8AM-4PM (HT). *Misdemeanor, Civil Actions under $25,000, Eviction, Small Claims.* www.courts.state.hi.us/

General Information: Search all Maui District Courts by one request to the Wailuku address and fax. No juvenile or paternity records released. Will fax documents $5.00 1st page, $2.00 each add'l. Within HI; $2.00 1st page, $1.00 each add'l. Court makes copy: $1.00 first page, $.50 each add'l. Certification fee: $2.00 per doc plus copy fee. Payee: Molokai District Court. Personal checks accepted, address and phone proof required. No credit cards accepted. Prepayment required.

Civil Name Search: Access: Mail, online., in person Only the court performs in person name searches; visitors may not. Search fee: $5.00 per name. Required to search: name, years to search, DOB, SSN. Civil index and docket books back to statehood. Mail turnaround time 3 days Free record searching at http://hoohiki2.courts.state.hi.us/jud/Hoohiki/main.htm or click on "Search Court Records" at www.courts.state.hi.us/. Search by name or case number.

Criminal Name Search: Access: Mail, in person. Only the court performs in person name searches; visitors may not. Search fee: $5.00 per name. Required to search: name, years to search, DOB, SSN. Criminal records on computer since 1980. Mail turnaround time is 3 days.

Wailuku District Court 2145 Main St, #106, Wailuku, HI 96793; 808-244-2969; fax: 808-244-2932; 7:45AM-4:30PM (HT). *Misdemeanor, Civil Actions under $25,000, Eviction, Small Claims, Traffic.* www.co.maui.hi.us/index.aspx?NID=1063

General Information: Traffic phone- 808-244-2800. You may search all Maui District Courts by one request to this court. Will fax documents $5.00 1st page, $2.00 each add'l. Within HI; $2.00 1st page, $1.00 each add'l. Court makes copy: $1.00 first page, $.50 each add'l. Certification fee: $2.00 per doc plus copy fee. Payee: District Court 2nd Circuit. Personal checks accepted, address and phone proof required. No credit cards accepted. Prepayment required. Mail requests: SASE required.

Civil Name Search: Access: Mail, fax, in person, online. Only the court performs in person name searches; visitors may not. Search fee: $5.00 per name per court. Required to search: name, years to search; also helpful: address. Civil index and docket books. Mail turnaround time 2-3 weeks. Free record searching at http://hoohiki2.courts.state.hi.us/jud/Hoohiki/main.htm or click on "Search Court Records" at www.courts.state.hi.us/. Search by name or case number.

Criminal Name Search: Access: Mail, fax, in person. Only the court performs in person name searches; visitors may not. Search fee: $5.00 per name per court. Required to search: name, years to search, DOB, SSN. Criminal records on computer since 1980. Mail turnaround time 2-3 weeks.

Idaho

Time Zone: MST*

> * Idaho's ten northwestern-most counties are PST:
> They are: Benewah, Bonner, Boundary, Clearwater,
> Idaho, Kootenai, Latah, Lewis, Nez Perce, Shoshone

Capital: Boise, Ida County

# of Counties: 44

State Web: www.idaho.gov

Court Web: www.isc.idaho.gov

Administration	Administrative Director of Courts, Supreme Court Building, PO Box 83720, Boise, ID, 83720-0101; 208-334-2246, Fax: 208-334-2146 or 2616.
The Supreme and Appellate Courts	The Supreme Court is the court of last resort. The Court of Appeals has limited jurisdiction to appeals from the District Courts which are assigned by the Supreme Court. Appellate and supreme court opinions are available at www.isc.idaho.gov/opinions/.

The Idaho Courts

Court	Type	How Organized	Jurisdiction Highpoints
District *	General	106 Courts in 7 Districts	Felony, Civil cases involving $10,000 or more, property Disputes, Contracts
Magistrate*	Limited	45 Courts, often combined with District Courts	Misdemeanor, Limited Civil, Small Claims, Juvenile, Traffic, Eviction, Domestic Relations, Estate,
Tribal Courts*	Special	4 Courts, 1 per Tribe	Incidents on Tribal Land

* = profiled in this book

Details on the Court Structure	**District Courts** have original jurisdiction over felony criminal cases and civil actions if the amount involved is more than $10,000, and hear appeals of decisions of the Magistrate Division. District judges may also hear domestic relation cases, such as divorces and child custody matters, but in most counties, such cases are handled by Magistrate judges.
	The **Magistrate Courts** hears probate matters, divorce proceedings, juvenile proceedings, initial felony proceedings through the preliminary hearing, criminal misdemeanors, infractions, civil cases when the amount in dispute does not exceed $10,000. Magistrates also hear Small Claims cases, established for disputes of $4,000 or less.
	An excellent overview is found at www.isc.idaho.gov/overview.pdf .

Record Searching Facts You Need to Know

Fees and Record Searching Tips	All courts provide public access terminals onsite. District and Magistrate Courts are often combined, making it easier for onsite searching. These fees are mandated statewide and usually but not always followed: search fee- none (eight courts will charge $5.00 per name search); certification - $1.00 (can be $1.50) per document plus copy fee; copy fee- $1.00 per page. Many courts require a signed release for employment record searches.
Online Access is Statewide for Trial Courts	Free access to trial court record index is at https://www.idcourts.us/repository/start.do. Records are searchable by name statewide or by individual county, and by case number. Results date back to 1995 or further depending on the county. Online results include identifiers year of birth and middle initial. The following personal information is not released: DL, address, and first 6 characters of the SSN.

Ada County

Ada County Criminal Court 200 W Front St, Rm 1190, Boise, ID 83702-5931; 208-287-6900; criminal phone: x2; fax: 208-287-6919; 8AM-5PM (MST). *Felony, Misdemeanor, Traffic.*
www2.state.id.us/fourthjudicial/
General Information: No alcohol level or confidential evaluation records released. Will fax documents to local or toll free line. Court makes copy: $1.00 per page. Certification fee: $1.00 per page plus copy fee. Payee: Ada County. No personal checks accepted; business checks must be okayed. Visa/MC accepted if in person. Prepayment required. Mail requests: SASE required.
Criminal Name Search: Access: Mail, fax, in person, online. Both court and visitors may perform in person name searches. No search fee. Required to search: name, years to search; also helpful: address, DOB, SSN. Criminal records computerized from 1985, microfiche from 1983, docket books back to statehood. Mail turnaround time up to 1-7 days. Public use terminal has crim records back to 1990. Search trial court index back to 1995 and calendars free at https://www.idcourts.us. Search by name and DOB or case number. Results show year of birth.

County District & Magistrate Courts - Civil 200 W Front, Rm 1155, Boise, ID 83702-5931; 208-287-6900; fax: 208-287-6919; 8AM-5PM (MST). *Civil, Eviction, Small Claims, Probate.*
www2.state.id.us/fourthjudicial/
General Information: No juvenile, adoption, child protection records released. Will not fax out documents. Court makes copy: $1.00 per page. Certification fee: $1.00 per certification. Payee: Ada County. No personal checks accepted. Major credit cards accepted in person only. Prepayment required. Mail requests: SASE required.
Civil Name Search: Access: Mail, in person, online. Both court and visitors may perform in person name searches. No search fee. Required to search: name, years to search; also helpful: address. Civil records on computer since 1994, microfiche and docket books from 1860s. Mail turnaround time 7-10 days. Public use terminal has civil records back to 1994. Search trial court records back to 1995 and calendars free at https://www.idcourts.us. Online results include identifiers year of birth and middle initial. The following personal information is not released: DL, address, and first 6 characters of the SSN.

Adams County

District & Magistrate Courts PO Box 48, Council, ID 83612; 208-253-4561/4233; fax: 208-253-4880; 8AM-5PM (MST). *Felony, Misdemeanor, Civil, Eviction, Small Claims, Probate.*
www.co.adams.id.us
General Information: Probate fax is same as main fax number. No juvenile, sealed cases records released. Will fax documents $2.00 per page. Court makes copy: $1.00 per page. Self serve copy: same. Certification fee: $1.00. Payee: Adams County. Personal checks and credit cards accepted. Prepayment required. Mail requests: SASE requested.
Civil Name Search: Access: Fax, mail, in person, online. Both court and visitors may perform in person name searches. No search fee. Civil records on computer back to 1993, docket books from 1911. Mail turnaround time 2 days. Civil PAT goes back to 1993. Search trial court records back to 1995 and calendars free at https://www.idcourts.us. Online results include identifiers year of birth and middle initial. The following personal information is not released: DL, address, and first 6 characters of the SSN.
Criminal Name Search: Access: Fax, mail, in person, online. Both court and visitors may perform in person name searches. No search fee. Required to search: name, years to search, signed release, DOB or SSN. Criminal records computerized from 1993, docket books from 1911. Mail turnaround time 2 days. Criminal PAT goes back to same as civil. Search trial court index back to 1995 and calendars free at https://www.idcourts.us. Online access is same as described for civil.

Bannock County

District & Magistrate Courts 624 E Center, Rm 220, Pocatello, ID 83201; 208-236-7351; criminal phone: 208-236-7273; civil phone: 208-236-7350; probate phone: 208-236-7351; criminal fax: 208-236-7293; civil fax: 8AM-5PM; 8AM-5PM (MST). *Felony, Misdemeanor, Civil, Eviction, Small Claims, Probate, Infractions.*
www.bannockcounty.us/courts/
General Information: Phone number for Misdemeanors- 208-236-7272. No adoption, mental, juvenile, termination, domestic violence records released. Will fax documents $1.00 per page. Court makes copy: $1.00 per page. Certification fee: $1.50 per page. Payee: Bannock County District Court. Personal checks accepted. Credit cards accepted for searches or copies. Prepayment required. Mail requests: SASE required.
Civil Name Search: Access: Fax, mail, in person, online. Both court and visitors may perform in person name searches. No search fee, unless extensive research involved. Civil records on computer from 1986, on docket

books from 1970s. Mail turnaround time 1 day to 2 weeks. Civil PAT goes back to 1995. Search trial court records back to 1995 and calendars free at https://www.idcourts.us. Online results include identifiers year of birth and middle initial. The following personal information is not released: DL, address, and first 6 characters of the SSN.
Criminal Name Search: Access: Fax, mail, in person, online. Both court and visitors may perform in person name searches. No search fee, unless extensive research involved. Required to search: name, years to search; also helpful: DOB, SSN. Criminal records computerized from 1986, on docket books from 1970s. Mail turnaround time 1 day to 2 weeks. Criminal PAT goes back to same as civil. Search trial court index back to 1995 and calendars free at https://www.idcourts.us. Search by name and DOB or case number. Results show year of birth. The DL, address, and all 6 characters of the SSN are not released. Results shows year of birth only. Online results show middle initial.

Bear Lake County

District & Magistrate Courts PO Box 190, Paris, ID 83261; 208-945-2208 x6; fax: 208-945-2780; 8:30AM-5PM (MST). *Felony, Misdemeanor, Civil, Eviction, Small Claims, Probate.*
General Information: No juvenile, CPA, divorce records released. Will fax documents $1.00 per page. Court makes copy: $1.00 per page. Self serve copy: same. Certification fee: $2.50 per document plus copy fee. Payee: Clerk of Court. Business checks accepted. Visa/MC accepted; $3.00 technology fee added. Prepayment required. Mail requests: SASE required.
Civil Name Search: Access: Fax, mail, online. Only the court performs in person name searches; visitors may not. No search fee. Civil records on computer back to 1991, docket books from early 1900s. Mail turnaround time 2-3 days. Court prefers written search requests be made by fax. Search trial court records back to 1995 and calendars free at https://www.idcourts.us. Online results include identifiers year of birth and middle initial. The following personal information is not released: DL, address, and first 6 characters of the SSN.
Criminal Name Search: Access: Fax, mail, online. Only the court performs in person name searches; visitors may not. No search fee. Required to search: name, years to search, DOB; also helpful: SSN, signed release. Criminal records computerized from 1991, docket books from early 1900s. Mail turnaround time 2-3 days. Court prefers written search requests be made by fax. Search trial court index back to 1995 and calendars free at https://www.idcourts.us. Search by name and DOB or case number. Results show year of birth and middle initial.

Benewah County

District & Magistrate Courts Courthouse, 701 W College Ave, #203, St Maries, ID 83861; 208-245-3241; fax: 208-245-3046; 9AM-5PM (PST). *Felony, Misdemeanor, Civil, Eviction, Small Claims, Probate.*
General Information: No juvenile, adoptions, mental commitments or sealed records released. No fee to fax documents if search fee paid. Court makes copy: $1.00 per page. Certification fee: $1.00 per seal plus copy fee. Payee: Clerk of Court. Personal checks accepted. Major credit cards accepted with a $3.00 additional fee. Prepayment required. Mail requests: SASE required.
Civil Name Search: Access: Fax, mail, in person, online. Both court and visitors may perform in person name searches. Search fee: $5.00 per name. Civil records on computer from 1991, index cards and docket books from early 1900s. Note: Fax requests must include copy of fees check. Mail turnaround time 3 days. Civil PAT goes back to 1991. Search trial court records back to 1992 and calendars free at https://www.idcourts.us. Online results include identifiers year of birth and middle initial. The following personal information is not released: DL, address, and first 6 characters of the SSN.
Criminal Name Search: Access: Mail, fax, in person, online. Both court and visitors may perform in person name searches. Search fee: $5.00 per name. If printout required $.10 per page. Criminal records computerized from 1991, index cards and docket books from early 1900s. Note: Fax requests must include copy of fees check. Mail turnaround time 3-5 days. Criminal PAT goes back to 1991. Search trial court index back to 1995 and calendars free at https://www.idcourts.us. Search by name and DOB or case number. Results show year of birth and middle initial.

Coeur d'Alene Tribal Court Courthouse, RR PO Box 11CDA, Plummer, ID 83851; 208-686-1777; fax: 208-686-1289; 9AM-5PM (PST). *Jurisdiction on Tribal Land.* www.isc.idaho.gov/coeurdal.htm

Bingham County

District & Magistrate Courts 501 N Maple St, #402, Blackfoot, ID 83221-1700; 208-785-8040 X3121-Dist, X3121-Magis; criminal phone: X3118, X3117; civil phone: X3123 or X3124; probate phone: X3123 or X3124; fax: 208-782-3167; 8AM-N, 1-5PM (MST). *Felony, Misdemeanor, Civil, Eviction, Small Claims, Probate, Traffic.*
www.co.bingham.id.us/
General Information: Direct phone for District Ct is 208-782-3145. Small Claims phone X3120. Probate fax is same as main fax number. No juvenile,

adoption, mental records released. Will fax documents for $2.00 per page. Court makes copy: $1.00 per page. Certification fee: $1.00 per page plus copy fee. Payee: Clerk of Court. Personal checks accepted. Visa/MC accepted. Prepayment required. Mail requests: SASE required.

Civil Name Search: Access: Phone, fax, mail, in person, online. Both court and visitors may perform in person name searches. No search fee. Required to search: name, years to search; also helpful: address. Civil records on computer from 1989, from microfiche from 1865. Mail turnaround time 1-2 weeks. Civil PAT goes back to 1995. Search trial court records back to 1995 and calendars free at https://www.idcourts.us. Online results include identifiers year of birth and middle initial. The following personal information is not released: DL, address, and first 5 characters of the SSN.

Criminal Name Search: Access: Phone, fax, mail, in person, online. Both court and visitors may perform in person name searches. No search fee. Required to search: name, years to search, signed release; also helpful: address, DOB, SSN. Criminal records computerized from 1989, from microfiche from 1865. Mail turnaround time 1-2 weeks. Criminal PAT goes back to 1995. Search trial court index back to 1995 and calendars free at https://www.idcourts.us. Online access is same as described for civil.

Shoshone-Bannock Tribal Court PO Box 306, Fort Hall, ID 83203; 208-7238-4078; fax: 208-238-4061; 8AM-N, 1-5PM (MST). *Jurisdiction on Tribal Land.*
www.isc.idaho.gov/shobann.htm

Blaine County

District & Magistrate Courts 201 2nd Ave S, #106, Hailey, ID 83333; 208-788-5521; fax: 208-788-5512; 9AM-5PM (MST). *Felony, Misdemeanor, Civil, Eviction, Small Claims, Probate.*

General Information: The Magistrate Court (Misdemeanor, Small Claims, Eviction, Probate) are also in #106. No sealed juvenile records released; unsealed juvenile records are on court's database. Will fax documents $1.00 per page. Court makes copy: $1.00 per page. Certification fee: $1.00 per document. Payee: Clerk of Court. Personal checks accepted. Visa/MC accepted with surcharge of $3.00. Prepayment required. Mail requests: SASE required for mail return of any copies.

Civil Name Search: Access: In person, online. Visitors must perform in person searches themselves. Civil records on computer from 11/1992. Civil PAT goes back to 11/1992. Search trial court records back to 1995 and calendars free at https://www.idcourts.us. Online results include identifiers year of birth and middle initial. The following personal information is not released: DL, address, and first 6 characters of the SSN.

Criminal Name Search: Access: In person, online. Visitors must perform in person searches themselves. Required to search: name, years to search, DOB, SSN. Criminal records on computer since 1992. Criminal PAT goes back to same as civil. Search trial court index back to 1992 and calendars free at https://www.idcourts.us. Search by name and DOB or case number. Results show year of birth and middle initial.

Boise County

District & Magistrate Courts PO Box 126, Idaho City, ID 83631; 208-392-4452; fax: 208-392-6712; 8AM-5PM (MST). *Felony, Misdemeanor, Civil, Eviction, Small Claims, Probate.*
www.boisecounty.us/Courts_Justice.aspx

General Information: Court recommends document retriever Heidi at 208-392-6709. No juvenile, adoption records released. Will fax documents $5.00 1st page, $1.00 each add'l page. Court makes copy: $1.25 per page. Certification fee: $1.00 per page. Payee: Boise County. Personal checks accepted. Visa/MC and debit cards accepted, with $3.00 technology fee. Prepayment required.

Civil Name Search: Access: In person, online. Visitors must perform in person searches themselves. Civil records on computer from 6/90, on docket books from 1863. Civil PAT goes back to 1989. Search trial court records back to 1995 and calendars free at https://www.idcourts.us. Online results include identifiers year of birth and middle initial. The following personal information is not released: DL, address, and first 6 characters of the SSN.

Criminal Name Search: Access: In person, online. Visitors must perform in person searches themselves. Required to search: name, years to search; also helpful: DOB. Criminal records computerized from 6/90, on docket books from 1863. Criminal PAT goes back to same as civil. Search trial court index back to 1995 and calendars free at https://www.idcourts.us. Search by name and DOB or case number. Results show year of birth and middle initial.

Bonner County

District & Magistrate Courts 215 S 1st Ave, Courthouse, Sandpoint, ID 83864; 208-265-1432; criminal phone: x3; civil phone: x2; fax: 208-265-1447; 9AM-5PM (PST). *Felony, Misdemeanor, Civil, Eviction, Small Claims, Probate.*

General Information: No juvenile records released. Will fax documents for $3.00 1st page, $1.00 each add'l. Court makes copy: $1.00 per page. Self serve copy: same. Certification fee: $1.00 per doc. Payee: Bonner County Clerk. Personal checks accepted. Visa/MC accepted and $3.00 usage fee added. Prepayment required.

Civil Name Search: Access: In person, online. Visitors must perform in person searches themselves. Required to search: name, years to search; also helpful: address. Civil records on computer from 1990, index and docket books from 1907. Civil PAT goes back to 1990. Search trial court records back to 1995 and calendars free at https://www.idcourts.us. Online results include identifiers year of birth and middle initial. The following personal information is not released: DL, address, and first 6 characters of the SSN.

Criminal Name Search: Access: In person, online. Visitors must perform in person searches themselves. Required to search: name, years to search; also helpful: address, DOB, SSN. Criminal records computerized from 1990, index and docket books from 1907. Criminal PAT goes back to same as civil. Search trial court index back to 1995 and calendars free at https://www.idcourts.us. Search by name and DOB or case number. Results show year of birth and middle initial.

Bonneville County

District & Magistrate Courts 605 N Capital, Idaho Falls, ID 83402; 208-529-1350 x1379; fax: 208-529-1300; 8AM-5PM (MST). *Felony, Misdemeanor, Civil, Eviction, Small Claims, Probate.*
www.co.bonneville.id.us

General Information: No child protective, protection orders, juvenile, sanity, adoption or termination records released. Will fax documents $2.00 per page, 10 page limit. Court makes copy: $1.00 per page. Certification fee: $1.00 per document plus copy fee. Payee: Bonneville County. No personal checks accepted. Visa/MC and debit cards accepted. Prepayment required.

Civil Name Search: Access: Mail, in person, online. Visitors must perform in person searches themselves. No search fee. Required to search: name, years to search, case type. Civil records on computer from civil from 1991. Docket books by case number ongoing. Actual case records are archived before 10/91. Civil PAT goes back to 1991. Search trial court records back to 1995 and calendars free at https://www.idcourts.us. Online results include identifiers year of birth and middle initial. The following personal information is not released: DL, address, and first 6 characters of the SSN.

Criminal Name Search: Access: Mail, in person, online. Visitors must perform in person searches themselves. No search fee. Required to search: name, years to search, DOB, signed release; also helpful: SSN, offense. Criminal misdemeanor records on computer from 1983, felony on computer from 1991. Criminal on microfiche from 1977. Docket books by case number ongoing. Criminal PAT goes back to same as civil. Search trial court index back to 1995 and calendars free at https://www.idcourts.us. Search by name and DOB or case number. Results show year of birth and middle initial.

Boundary County

District & Magistrate Courts Boundary County Courthouse, PO Box 419, Bonners Ferry, ID 83805; 208-267-5504; fax: 208-267-7814; 9AM-5PM (PST). *Felony, Misdemeanor, Civil, Eviction, Small Claims, Probate.*
www.boundarycountyid.org/court/index.htm

General Information: No sealed records released. Will fax documents for fee; long distance- $3.00 1st page, $1.00 each add'l; local fax- $2.00 1st page, $.50 each add'l. Court makes copy: $1.00 per page. Certification fee: $1.00 per document. Payee: Clerk of Court. Personal checks and credit cards accepted. Prepayment required.

Civil Name Search: Access: In person, online. Both court and visitors may perform in person name searches. No search fee. Required to search: name, years to search; also helpful: address. Civil records on computer from 1989; by case number, index books, cards or microfiche by name from early 1900s. Civil PAT goes back to 1989. Results include name and DOB. Search trial court records back to 1995 and calendars free at https://www.idcourts.us. Online results include identifiers year of birth and middle initial. The following personal information is not released: DL, address, and first 6 characters of the SSN.

Criminal Name Search: Access: In person, online. Visitors must perform in person searches themselves. Required to search: name, years to search, SSN; also helpful: DOB. Criminal records computerized from 1989; by case number, index books, cards or microfiche by name from early 1900s. Criminal PAT goes back to same as civil. Results include name and DOB. Online access is same as described for civil.

Tribal Court of the Kootenai Tribe of Idaho PO Box 1269, Bonners Ferry, ID 83805; 208-267-3519; fax: 208-267-2960; 9AM-5PM (PST). *Jurisdiction on Tribal Land.*
www.isc.idaho.gov/kootenai.htm

Butte County

District & Magistrate Courts 326 W Grand Ave, Arco, ID 83213; 208-527-8259; fax: 208-527-3448; 9AM-N; 1PM-5PM (MST). *Felony, Misdemeanor, Civil, Eviction, Small Claims, Probate.*

General Information: Most juvenile records not released. Fee to fax out file $1.00 per page. Court makes copy: $1.00 per page. Self serve copy: $.10 per page. Certification fee: $1.00 per page. Payee: Butte County Magistrate Court. Personal checks accepted. No credit cards accepted. Prepayment required. Mail requests: SASE required.

Civil Name Search: Access: Phone, fax, mail, in person, online. Both court and visitors may perform in person name searches. No search fee. Required to search: name, years to search; also helpful: address. Civil records on computer from 1993, archives prior. Docket books by case number from early 1910s. Mail turnaround time 1 week. Civil PAT goes back to 1993. Search trial court records back to 1995 and calendars free at https://www.idcourts.us. Online results include identifiers year of birth and middle initial. The following personal information is not released: DL, address, and first 6 characters of the SSN.

Criminal Name Search: Access: Phone, fax, mail, in person, online. Both court and visitors may perform in person name searches. No search fee. Required to search: name, years to search; also helpful: address, DOB, SSN. Criminal records computerized from 1993 archives prior. Docket books by case number from early 1910s. Mail turnaround time 1 week. Criminal PAT goes back to 1993. Search trial court index back to 1995 and calendars free at https://www.idcourts.us. Search by name and DOB or case number. Results show year of birth and middle initial.

Camas County

District & Magistrate Courts PO Box 430, 501 Soldier Rd, Fairfield, ID 83327; 208-764-2238; fax: 208-764-2349; 8:30AM-N, 1-5PM (MST). *Felony, Misdemeanor, Civil, Eviction, Small Claims, Probate.*

General Information: Probate fax is same as main fax number. No juvenile or domestic violence records released. Will fax documents for $1.50 per page. Court makes copy: $1.00 per page. Self serve copy: same. Certification fee: $1.00 plus copy fee. Payee: Camas County Courthouse. Personal checks accepted. No credit cards accepted. Prepayment required. Mail requests: SASE required.

Civil Name Search: Access: Mail, in person, online. Both court and visitors may perform in person name searches. No search fee. Required to search: name, years to search; also helpful: address. Civil records from archives from 1917. Register of actions by case number. Mail turnaround time same day. Civil PAT goes back to 1994. Search trial court records back to 1995 and calendars free at https://www.idcourts.us. Online results include identifiers year of birth and middle initial. The following personal information is not released: DL, address, and first 6 characters of the SSN.

Criminal Name Search: Access: Mail, in person, online. Both court and visitors may perform in person name searches. No search fee. Required to search: name, years to search; also helpful: address, DOB, SSN. Criminal records from archives from 1917. Register of actions by case number. Mail turnaround time 1 day. Criminal PAT goes back to 1994. Online access is same as described for civil.

Canyon County

District & Magistrate Courts 1115 Albany, Caldwell, ID 83605; 208-454-7575; criminal phone: 208-454-7571; civil phone: 208-454-7570; fax: 208-454-7525; 8AM-5PM (MST). *Felony, Misdemeanor, Civil, Eviction, Small Claims, Probate.*
www.the3rdjudicialdistrict.com

General Information: Small claims phone is 208-454-7577. No adoption, mental, domestic violence records not released. Will not fax documents. Court makes copy: $1.00 per page. Self serve copy: $.30 per page, coin-operated machine and court will not provide change. Certification fee: $1.00 per page. Payee: Clerk of Court. Only cashiers checks and money orders accepted. Visa/MC accepted plus $3.00 technology fee. Prepayment required. Mail requests: SASE required for mail return of any copies.

Civil Name Search: Access: In person, online. Both court and visitors may perform in person name searches. No search fee. Required to search: name, years to search, or case number. Civil records on computer from 1989, microfiche from 1800s, and docket books. Public use terminal has civil records back to 1989. Search trial court records back to 1995 and calendars free at https://www.idcourts.us. Access the daily court calendar at www.the3rdjudicialdistrict.com. Online results include identifiers year of birth and middle initial. The following personal information is not released: DL, address, and first 6 characters of the SSN.

Criminal Name Search: Access: In person, online. Both court and visitors may perform in person name searches. No search fee. Required to search: name, years to search; also helpful: DOB, case number. Criminal records computerized from 1989, microfiche from 1800s, and docket books. Search trial court index back to 1995 and calendars free at https://www.idcourts.us. Access daily court calendar at www.the3rdjudicialdistrict.com. Results shows year of birth only.

Caribou County

District & Magistrate Courts 159 S Main, Soda Springs, ID 83276; 208-547-4342; fax: 208-547-4759; 9AM-5PM (MST). *Felony, Misdemeanor, Civil, Eviction, Small Claims, Probate.*

General Information: No adoption, guardianship records released. Will fax documents $2.00 1st page, $1.00 each add'l. Court makes copy: $1.00 per page. Self serve copy: same. Certification fee: $1.50. Payee: Clerk of Court. Business checks accepted. Out of state checks not accepted. Major credit cards accepted with $3.00 handling fee. Prepayment required. Mail requests: SASE required.

Civil Name Search: Access: Phone, fax, mail, in person, online. Both court and visitors may perform in person name searches. No search fee. Civil records on computer from 1989, from 1930 archived in vault. Mail turnaround time up to 1 week. Civil PAT goes back to 1989. Search trial court records back to 1995 and calendars free at https://www.idcourts.us. Online results include identifiers year of birth and middle initial. The following personal information is not released: DL, address, and first 6 characters of the SSN.

Criminal Name Search: Access: Phone, fax, mail, in person, online. Both court and visitors may perform in person name searches. No search fee. Required to search: name, years to search, DOB, SSN; also helpful: address. Criminal records computerized from 1989, from 1930 archived in vault. Mail turnaround time up to 1 week. Criminal PAT goes back to same as civil. Search trial court index back to 1995 and calendars free at https://www.idcourts.us. Search by name and DOB or case number. Results show year of birth and middle initial.

Cassia County

District & Magistrate Courts 1459 Overland, Burley, ID 83318; 208-878-5231; fax: 208-878-5344; 8:30AM-5PM (MST). *Felony, Misdemeanor, Civil, Eviction, Small Claims, Probate.*
http://cassiacounty.org/judicial/index.htm

General Information: Probate is a separate index at this same address. Probate fax is same as main fax number. No juvenile, adoption, mental commitment, child protection records released. Will fax documents $2.50 per page. Court makes copy: $1.00 per page. Self serve copy: $1.00 per page if court's document; $.15 in not. Certification fee: $1.50 per page plus copy fee. Payee: Clerk of Court. Personal checks and credit cards accepted. Prepayment required. Mail requests: SASE required.

Civil Name Search: Access: Phone, fax, mail, in person, online. Both court and visitors may perform in person name searches. No search fee. Required to search: name, years to search; also helpful: address. Civil records on computer from 1990, archives from 1900s. Mail turnaround time 1-2 days. Civil PAT goes back to 1990. Search trial court records back to 1995 and calendars free at https://www.idcourts.us. Online results include identifiers year of birth and middle initial. The following personal information is not released: DL, address, and first 6 characters of the SSN.

Criminal Name Search: Access: Fax, mail, in person, online. Both court and visitors may perform in person name searches. No search fee. Required to search: name, years to search; also helpful: address, DOB, SSN. Criminal records computerized from 1990, archives from 1900s. Mail turnaround time 1-2 days. Criminal PAT goes back to same as civil. Search trial court index back to 1995 and calendars free at https://www.idcourts.us. Search by name and DOB or case number. Results show year of birth and middle initial.

Clark County

District & Magistrate Courts PO Box 205, Dubois, ID 83423; 208-374-5402; fax: 208-374-5609; 9AM-5PM (MST). *Felony, Misdemeanor, Civil, Eviction, Small Claims, Probate.*

General Information: This court does not normally perform name searches, however they also say that there is no one locally who will perform them either; the court may perform record searches under these limiting circumstances. No juvenile, adoption records released. Will not fax documents. Court makes copy: n/a. Self serve copy: $1.00 per page. Certification fee: $1.00 per page. Payee: Clerk of Court. Personal checks accepted. No credit cards accepted. Prepayment required. Mail requests: SASE required.

Civil Name Search: Access: Mail, fax, in person, online. Both court and visitors may perform in person name searches. No search fee. Required to search: name, years to search; also helpful: address. Civil records on computer from 1985, on microfiche for civil judgments and from archives from 1919. Civil PAT goes back to 10 years countywide. Search trial court records back to 1995 and calendars free at https://www.idcourts.us. Online results include identifiers year of birth and middle initial. The following personal information is not released: DL, address, and first 6 characters of the SSN.

Criminal Name Search: Access: Mail, fax, in person, online. Visitors must perform in person searches themselves. No search fee. Required to search: name, years to search; also helpful: address, DOB, SSN. Criminal records computerized from 1985. Criminal PAT goes back to same as civil. Search trial court index back to 1995 and calendars free at https://www.idcourts.us. Search by name and DOB or case number. Results show year of birth and middle initial.

Clearwater County

District & Magistrate Courts PO Box 586, 150 Michigan Ave, Orofino, ID 83544; 208-476-5596; 8:00AM-5PM (PST). *Felony, Misdemeanor, Civil, Eviction, Small Claims, Probate.*
www.clearwatercounty.org/
General Information: No juvenile, domestic violence, adoption, social records released. Will fax documents $1.00 per page. Court makes copy: $1.00 per page. Certification fee: $1.00 per cert. Payee: Clerk of Court. Business checks accepted. Visa/MC accepted. Prepayment required. Mail requests: SASE requested.
Civil Name Search: Access: Phone, fax, mail, in person, online. Only the court performs in person name searches; visitors may not. No search fee. Civil records on computer from 8/91, in docket books prior to 1911. Mail turnaround time 7 days. Search trial court records back to 1995 and calendars free at https://www.idcourts.us. Online results include identifiers year of birth and middle initial. The following personal information is not released: DL, address, and first 6 characters of the SSN.
Criminal Name Search: Access: Phone, fax, mail, in person, online. Only the court performs in person name searches; visitors may not. No search fee. Required to search: name or case number, years to search. Criminal records computerized from 8/91, in docket books prior to 1911. Mail turnaround time 7 days. Search trial court index back to 1995 and calendars free at https://www.idcourts.us. Search by name and DOB or case number. Results show year of birth and middle initial.

Custer County

District & Magistrate Courts PO Box 385, Challis, ID 83226; 208-879-2359; fax: 208-879-6412; 8AM-5PM (MST). *Felony, Misdemeanor, Civil, Eviction, Small Claims, Probate.*
www.co.custer.id.us
General Information: Probate fax is same as main fax number. No juvenile, adoption records released. Will fax out documents for $1.00 per page. Court makes copy: $1.00 per page. Certification fee: $1.00 per page. Payee: Custer County. Personal checks and credit cards accepted. Prepayment required.
Civil Name Search: Access: Phone, mail, in person, online. Both court and visitors may perform in person name searches. Search fee: $5.00 per name. Civil cases indexed by defendant. Civil records on computer from 1990, archived from early 1900s. Mail turnaround time 1 week. Civil PAT goes back to 1990. Search trial court records back to 1995 and calendars free at https://www.idcourts.us. Online results include identifiers year of birth and middle initial. The following personal information is not released: DL, address, and first 6 characters of the SSN.
Criminal Name Search: Access: Phone, mail, in person, online. Both court and visitors may perform in person name searches. Search fee: $5.00 per name. Required to search: name, years to search, DOB, signed release; also helpful: SSN. Criminal records computerized from 1990, archived from early 1900s. Mail turnaround time 1 week. Criminal PAT goes back to same as civil. Search trial court index back to 1995 and calendars free at https://www.idcourts.us. Search by name and DOB or case number. Results show year of birth and middle initial.

Elmore County

District & Magistrate Courts 150 S 4th E, #5, Mountain Home, ID 83647; 208-587-2133 x208; fax: 208-587-2134; 9AM-5PM (MST). *Felony, Misdemeanor, Civil, Eviction, Small Claims, Probate.*
www.elmorecounty.org/
General Information: No juvenile, adoption, domestic violence, mental commitment records released. Will fax specific case file for $7.00 plus $1.00 per page. Court makes copy: $1.00 per page. Certification fee: $1.00 per page. Payee: Elmore County. Personal checks and credit cards accepted. Prepayment required.
Civil Name Search: Access: In person, online. Visitors must perform in person searches themselves. Required to search: name; also helpful: years to search. Civil records on computer from 1992, on microfiche from 1972, archived from early 1900s. Civil PAT goes back to 1992. Search trial court records back to 1995 and calendars free at https://www.idcourts.us. Online results include identifiers year of birth and middle initial. The following personal information is not released: DL, address, and first 6 characters of the SSN.
Criminal Name Search: Access: In person, online. Visitors must perform in person searches themselves. Required to search: name, DOB, signed release; also helpful: years to search, SSN. Criminal records

computerized from 1992, on microfiche from 1972, archived from early 1900s. Criminal PAT goes back to same as civil. Search trial court index back to 1995 and calendars free at https://www.idcourts.us. Search by name and DOB or case number. Results show year of birth and middle initial.

Franklin County

District & Magistrate Courts 39 W Oneida, Preston, ID 83263; 208-852-0877; fax: 208-852-2926; 9AM-5PM (MST). *Felony, Misdemeanor, Civil, Eviction, Small Claims, Probate.*
General Information: No adoption records released. Will not fax out documents. Court makes copy: $1.00 per page. Certification fee: $1.00 per cert. Payee: Clerk of Court. Personal checks not accepted for records or copies. Major credit cards accepted. Prepayment required. Mail requests: SASE required.
Civil Name Search: Access: Phone, fax, mail, in person, online. Both court and visitors may perform in person name searches. Search fee: $10.00 per name. Civil records on computer from 1987, microfiche from 1983, archived from 1920. Mail turnaround time 2-3 days. Civil PAT goes back to 1984. Search trial court records back to 1995 and calendars free at https://www.idcourts.us. Online results include identifiers year of birth and middle initial. The following personal information is not released: DL, address, and first 6 characters of the SSN.
Criminal Name Search: Access: Phone, fax, mail, in person, online. Both court and visitors may perform in person name searches. Search fee: $5.00 per name for a report history. Required to search: name, years to search; also helpful: DOB, SSN. Criminal records computerized from 1987, microfiche from 1977, archived from 1920. Mail turnaround time 2-3 days. Criminal PAT goes back to same as civil. Terminal results include driver license number. Search trial court index back to 1995 and calendars free at https://www.idcourts.us. Search by name and DOB or case number. Results show year of birth and middle initial.

Fremont County

District & Magistrate Courts 151 W 1st N, Rm 15, St Anthony, ID 83445; 208-624-7401; fax: 208-624-4607; 9AM-5PM (MST). *Felony, Misdemeanor, Civil, Eviction, Small Claims, Probate.*
www.co.fremont.id.us/
General Information: Address search requests to attention of Miriam. Thursday is the best day for in person searches. Probate fax is same as main fax number. No adoption or juvenile records released. Fee to fax out file $2.00 per page or free to toll-free line. Court makes copy: $1.00 per page. Certification fee: $1.00 per page plus copy fee. Payee: Clerk of Court. Personal checks accepted. Visa/MC accepted but with a $3.00 Tech Fee added. Prepayment required. Mail requests: SASE required.
Civil Name Search: Access: Phone, fax, mail, in person, online. Both court and visitors may perform in person name searches. Search fee: $4.00 if search request is mailed or faxed in. Required to search: name, years to search; also helpful: address. Civil records on computer back to 1990, microfiche for last 20 years, prior archives. Mail turnaround time 1 week. Civil PAT goes back to 1990. Search trial court records back to 1995 and calendars free at https://www.idcourts.us. Online results include identifiers year of birth and middle initial. The following personal information is not released: DL, address, and first 6 characters of the SSN.
Criminal Name Search: Access: Fax, mail, in person, online. Both court and visitors may perform in person name searches. No search fee; add $4.00 if search request is mailed or faxed in. Required to search: name, years to search, DOB; also helpful: SSN. Criminal records computerized from 1990, microfiche for last 20 years, prior archives. Mail turnaround time 1 week. Criminal PAT goes back to same as civil. Search trial court index back to 1995 and calendars free at https://www.idcourts.us. Search by name and DOB or case number. Results show year of birth and middle initial.

Gem County

District & Magistrate Courts 415 E Main St, Emmett, ID 83617; 208-365-5621-District Court 208-365-4221-Magistrate Court; fax: 208-365-6172; 8AM-5PM (MST). *Felony, Misdemeanor, Civil, Eviction, Small Claims, Probate.*
www.co.gem.id.us/judicial/default.htm
General Information: No juvenile, adoption records or domestic violence released. Will fax documents to local or toll free line. Court makes copy: $1.00 per page. Certification fee: $1.00 plus copy fee. Payee: Gem County. Personal checks and credit cards accepted. Prepayment required. Mail requests: SASE required.
Civil Name Search: Access: Mail, in person, online. Only the court performs in person name searches; visitors may not. Search fee: $5.00 per name. Required to search: name, years to search; also helpful: address. Civil records on computer from 1990, on microfiche and archived from 1916. Mail turnaround time 5 days. Search trial court records back to 1990 and calendars free at https://www.idcourts.us. Online results include

identifiers year of birth and middle initial. The following personal information is not released: DL, address, and first 6 characters of the SSN.

Criminal Name Search: Access: Mail, in person, online. Only the court performs in person name searches; visitors may not. Search fee: $5.00 per name per court. Required to search: name, years to search, DOB, SSN; also helpful: address. Criminal records computerized from 1990, on microfiche and archived from 1972. Mail turnaround time 5 days. Search trial court index back to 1990 and calendars free at https://www.idcourts.us. Search by name and DOB or case number. Results show year of birth and middle initial.

Gooding County

District & Magistrate Courts PO Box 27, Gooding, ID 83330; criminal phone: 208-934-4861; fax: 208-934-4408; 9AM-5PM (MST). *Felony, Misdemeanor, Civil, Eviction, Small Claims, Probate.*

General Information: Magistrate Court can be reached at 208-934-4261. Magistrate Court address is PO Box 477. Only felony records are available at District Court. No juvenile, adoption, domestic violence records released. Fee to fax out file $1.00 per page. Court makes copy: $1.00 per page. Certification fee: $1.00. Payee: Gooding County Clerk. Personal checks accepted. Prepayment required.

Civil Name Search: Access: In person, online. Visitors must perform in person searches themselves. Civil records on computer from 1994, on microfiche, docket books from 1860s. Public use terminal available, records go back to 8/94. Search trial court records back to 1995 and calendars free at https://www.idcourts.us. Online results include identifiers year of birth and middle initial. The following personal information is not released: DL, address, and first 6 characters of the SSN.

Criminal Name Search: Access: In person, online. Visitors must perform in person searches themselves. Required to search: name, years to search, DOB, SSN. Criminal records computerized from 1994, on microfiche, docket books from 1860s. Public use terminal available, crim records go back to same. Search trial court index back to 1995 and calendars free at https://www.idcourts.us. Search by name and DOB or case number. Results show year of birth. Results shows year of birth only. Online results show middle initial, DOB.

Idaho County

District & Magistrate Courts 320 W Main, Grangeville, ID 83530; 208-983-2776; fax: 208-983-2376; 8:30AM-5PM (PST). *Felony, Misdemeanor, Civil, Eviction, Small Claims, Probate.*

General Information: Probate fax is same as main fax number. No domestic violence, juvenile, hospitalization, adoption, termination records released. Will fax documents $1.00 per page. Court makes copy: $1.00 per page. Certification fee: $1.00 per cert. Payee: Idaho County. Personal checks accepted. No credit cards accepted. Prepayment required.

Civil Name Search: Access: Phone, fax, mail, in person, online. Both court and visitors may perform in person name searches. No search fee. Civil records on computer from 1989, on microfiche and archived from late 1800s. Mail turnaround time same week. Civil PAT goes back to 1989. Search trial court records back to 1995 and calendars free at https://www.idcourts.us. Online results include identifiers year of birth and middle initial. The following personal information is not released: DL, address, and first 6 characters of the SSN.

Criminal Name Search: Access: Phone, fax, mail, in person, online. Both court and visitors may perform in person name searches. No search fee. Criminal records computerized from 1989, on microfiche and archived from late 1800s. Mail turnaround time same week. Criminal PAT available. Search trial court index back to 1995 and calendars free at https://www.idcourts.us. Search by name and DOB or case number. Results show year of birth and middle initial.

Jefferson County

District & Magistrate Courts 210 Courthouse Way #120, Rigby, ID 83442; 208-745-7736; fax: 208-745-6636; 9AM-5PM (MST). *Felony, Misdemeanor, Civil, Eviction, Small Claims, Probate.*

www.co.jefferson.id.us/courts.php

General Information: Information is on the public access computer; please use this before requesting the clerks' assistance. No juvenile, adoption, some domestic records released. Will fax back $1.00 per page. Court makes copy: $1.00 per page. Certification fee: $1.00 per page plus copy fee. Payee: Clerk of Court. Personal checks accepted. No credit cards accepted. Prepayment required.

Civil Name Search: Access: In person, online. Both court and visitors may perform in person name searches. No search fee. Civil records archived from early 1900s; on computer back to 8/1992. Civil PAT goes back to 8/1992. Search trial court records back to 1995 and calendars free at https://www.idcourts.us. Online results include identifiers year of birth and middle initial. The following personal information is not released: DL, address, and first 6 characters of the SSN.

Criminal Name Search: Access: In person, online. Both court and visitors may perform in person name searches. No search fee. Required to search: name, years to search, DOB. Criminal records archived from early 1900s; on computer back to 8/1992. Criminal records archived from early 1900s; on computer back to 8/1992. Criminal PAT goes back to same as civil. Search trial court index back to 1995 and calendars free at https://www.idcourts.us. Search by name and DOB or case number. Results show year of birth and middle initial.

Jerome County

District & Magistrate Courts 233 W Main St, Jerome, ID 83338; 208-644-2600; fax: 208-644-2609; 8:30AM-5PM (MST). *Felony, Misdemeanor, Civil, Eviction, Small Claims, Probate.*

General Information: No juvenile records released without court approval. Will fax documents $3.00 per page. Court makes copy: $1.00 per page. Certification fee: $1.50 per page. Payee: Clerk of Court. Personal checks accepted. No credit cards accepted. Prepayment required. Mail requests: SASE required.

Civil Name Search: Access: Fax, mail, in person, online. Visitors must perform in person searches themselves. No search fee. Civil records on computer back to 1991, prior on microfiche back to 1919. Note: Court will perform civil search only for requests with dates prior to 1991. Civil PAT goes back to 1991. Search trial court records back to 1995 and calendars free at https://www.idcourts.us. Online results include identifiers year of birth and middle initial. The following personal information is not released: DL, address, and first 6 characters of the SSN.

Criminal Name Search: Access: Fax, mail, in person, online. Visitors must perform in person searches themselves. No search fee. Required to search: name, years to search, address, DOB, SSN. Criminal records computerized from 1991, prior on microfiche back to 1919. Note: Will not do background searches. Mail turnaround time 7-10 business days. Criminal PAT goes back to 1991. Search trial court index back to 1995 and calendars free at https://www.idcourts.us. Search by name and DOB or case number. Results show year of birth and middle initial.

Kootenai County

District & Magistrate Court PO Box 9000, 324 W Garden Ave, Coeur d'Alene, ID 83816-9000; 208-446-1180; criminal phone: 208-446-1170; civil phone: 208-446-1160; probate phone: 208-446-1160; fax: 208-446-1188; 9AM-5PM (PST). *Felony, Misdemeanor, Civil, Eviction, Small Claims, Probate.*

www.kcgov.us/departments/districtcourt/

General Information: No sealed, adoption, parental termination, mentally incapacitated records released. Will fax documents to local or toll free line. Court makes copy: $1.00 per page. Certification fee: $1.00; exemplification: $4.00; plus copy fee. Payee: Clerk of Court. Personal checks accepted. Credit cards accepted through Official Payments 800-533-0743. Prepayment required. Mail requests: SASE required.

Civil Name Search: Access: Mail, in person, online. Visitors must perform in person searches themselves. Search fee: $.10 a page found. Civil records on computer from 1989, on microfiche from 1881, archived from 1819. Mail turnaround time 2 days. Civil PAT goes back to 1989. Search trial court records back to 1995 and calendars free at https://www.idcourts.us. Online results include identifiers year of birth and middle initial. The following personal information is not released: DL, address, and first 6 characters of the SSN.

Criminal Name Search: Access: Mail, in person, online. Visitors must perform in person searches themselves. Search fee: $.10 a page found. Required to search: name, years to search; also helpful: DOB, SSN. Criminal records computerized from 1989, on microfiche from 1881, archived from 1819. Mail turnaround time in 2 days. Criminal PAT goes back to same as civil. Search trial court index back to 1995 and calendars free at https://www.idcourts.us. Search by name and DOB or case number. Results show year of birth and middle initial.

Latah County

District & Magistrate Courts PO Box 8068, Moscow, ID 83843; 208-883-2255; fax: 208-883-2259; 8:30AM-5PM M,W; 8AM-5PM T,TH,F (PST). *Felony, Misdemeanor, Civil, Eviction, Small Claims, Probate, Traffic.*

www.latah.id.us

General Information: this court also handles adoptions and hospitalizations. No adoption, sealed juvenile, or hospitalization records released. Will fax documents to local or toll free line. Court makes copy: $1.00 per page. Certification fee: $1.00 per page plus copy fee if the court makes copy. If copy is provided to be certified, $.50 per page plus $1.00 for the cert. Payee: Latah County District Court. Personal checks accepted. No credit cards accepted. Prepayment required.

Civil Name Search: Access: Phone, fax, mail, in person, online. Both court and visitors may perform in person name searches. Search fee: $4.00 per name. Required to search: name, years to search; also helpful: address. Civil records on computer from 1986, archived from 5/1888. Mail turnaround time 1-2 days. Civil PAT goes back to 1992. Search trial court records back to 1995 and calendars free at https://www.idcourts.us. Online results include identifiers year of birth and middle initial. The following personal information is not released: DL, address, and first 6 characters of the SSN.

Criminal Name Search: Access: Phone, fax, mail, in person, online. Both court and visitors may perform in person name searches. Search fee: $4.00 per name. Required to search: name, years to search; also helpful: address, DOB, SSN. Criminal records computerized from 1986, archived from 5/1888. Mail turnaround time 1-2 days. Criminal PAT goes back to same as civil. Search trial court index back to 1995 and calendars free at https://www.idcourts.us. Search by name and DOB or case number. Results show year of birth and middle initial.

Lemhi County

District & Magistrate Courts 206 Courthouse Dr, Salmon, ID 83467; 208-756-2815; criminal phone: x225; civil phone: x225; probate phone: x242; criminal fax: 208-756-8424; civil fax: 8AM-5PM; 8AM-5PM (MST). *Felony, Misdemeanor, Civil, Eviction, Small Claims, Probate.*

General Information: Probate fax- 208-756-4673 No PSI, sealed records released. Fee to fax out file $1.00 per page. Court makes copy: $1.00 per page. Self serve copy: same. Certification fee: $1.00 per document and $.50 per page. Payee: Lemhi County Clerk. Personal checks and credit cards accepted. Prepayment required. Mail requests: SASE requested.

Civil Name Search: Access: Phone, fax, mail, in person, online. Both court and visitors may perform in person name searches. Search fee: $5.00 per name. Required to search: name, years to search; also helpful: address. Civil records on computer from 1991, on microfiche from 1964, archives from 1869. Mail turnaround time 1-3 days. Civil PAT goes back to 1991. Search trial court records back to 1995 and calendars free at https://www.idcourts.us. Note this is not the official record, data should be verified locally. Online results include identifiers year of birth and middle initial. The following personal information is not released: DL, address, and first 6 characters of the SSN.

Criminal Name Search: Access: Phone, fax, mail, in person, online. Both court and visitors may perform in person name searches. Search fee: $5.00 per name. Required to search: name, years to search; also helpful: address, DOB, SSN. Criminal records computerized from 1991, on microfiche from 1964, archives from 1869. Mail turnaround time 1 day. Criminal PAT goes back to same as civil. Search trial court index back to 1995 and calendars free at https://www.idcourts.us. Search by name and DOB or case number. Results show year of birth. The following personal information is not released: DL, address, and first 6 characters of the SSN. Results shows year of birth only. Online results show middle initial.

Lewis County

District & Magistrate Courts 510 Oak St, Rm 1, Nezperce, ID 83543-5065; 208-937-2251; fax: 208-937-9233; 9AM-5PM (PST). *Felony, Misdemeanor, Civil, Eviction, Small Claims, Probate.*

General Information: No juvenile, adoption records released. Will fax documents $1.00 per page. Court makes copy: $1.00 per page. Certification fee: $1.00; exemplification fee is $3.00. Payee: Clerk of Court. Two-party checks not accepted. Major credit cards accepted. Prepayment required. Mail requests: SASE required.

Civil Name Search: Access: Phone, fax, mail, in person, online. Only the court performs in person name searches; visitors may not. No search fee. Civil records on computer from 1991, archived from late 1911. Mail turnaround time 1 week. Search trial court records back to 1991 and calendars free at https://www.idcourts.us. Online results include identifiers year of birth and middle initial. The following personal information is not released: DL, address, and first 6 characters of the SSN.

Criminal Name Search: Access: Phone, fax, mail, in person, online. Only the court performs in person name searches; visitors may not. No search fee. Required to search: name, years to search; also helpful: DOB, SSN. Criminal records computerized from 1991, archived from late 1911. Mail turnaround time 1 week. Search trial court index back to 1991 and calendars free at https://www.idcourts.us. Search by name and DOB or case number. Results show year of birth. The following personal information is not released: DL, address, and first 6 characters of the SSN. Results shows year of birth only. Online results show middle initial.

Lincoln County

District & Magistrate Courts 111 W B St, Shoshone, ID 83352; 208-886-2173; fax: 208-886-2458; 8:30AM-5PM (MST). *Felony, Misdemeanor, Civil, Eviction, Small Claims, Probate.*

General Information: No juvenile, domestic violence, sealed records released. Will not fax documents. Court makes copy: $1.00 per page. Certification fee: $2.50 plus copy fee. Payee: Lincoln County Courts. Personal checks accepted. No credit cards accepted. Prepayment required. Mail requests: SASE required.

Civil Name Search: Access: In person, mail, fax, online. Both court and visitors may perform in person name searches. No search fee. Civil records on computer from 1992, archives from 1800s. Mail turnaround time 5 days. Civil PAT goes back to 1995. Search trial court records back to 1995 and calendars free at https://www.idcourts.us. Online results include identifiers year of birth and middle initial. The following personal information is not released: DL, address, and first 6 characters of the SSN.

Criminal Name Search: Access: In person, mail, fax, online. Both court and visitors may perform in person name searches. No search fee. Required to search: name, years to search; also helpful: DOB, SSN. Criminal records computerized from 1992, archives from 1800s. Mail turnaround time 5 days. Criminal PAT goes back to same as civil. Search trial court index back to 1995 and calendars free at https://www.idcourts.us. Search by name and DOB or case number. Results show year of birth. The following personal information is not released: DL, address, and first 6 characters of the SSN. Results shows year of birth only. Online results show middle initial.

Madison County

District & Magistrate Courts PO Box 389, 159 E main, Rexburg, ID 83440; 208-356-9383; fax: 208-356-5425; 9AM-5PM (MST). *Felony, Misdemeanor, Civil, Eviction, Small Claims, Probate.*

General Information: No juvenile records released. Will fax documents for $3.00 per page. Court makes copy: $1.00 per page. Certification fee: $1.00 plus copy fee. Payee: Clerk of Court. Personal checks accepted. Prepayment required.

Civil Name Search: Access: In person, online. Visitors must perform in person searches themselves. No search fee. Required to search: name, years to search; also helpful: address. Civil records on computer from 1991, microfilm and archives from early 1900s. Civil PAT goes back to 1991. Search trial court records back to 1995 and calendars free at https://www.idcourts.us. Online results include identifiers year of birth and middle initial. The following personal information is not released: DL, address, and first 6 characters of the SSN.

Criminal Name Search: Access: In person, online. Visitors must perform in person searches themselves. Required to search: name, years to search; also helpful: address, DOB, SSN. Criminal records computerized from 1991, microfilm and archives from early 1900s. Criminal PAT goes back to same as civil. Online access is same as described for civil.

Minidoka County

District & Magistrate Courts PO Box 368, Rupert, ID 83350; 208-436-9041 (Dist) 436-7186 (Magis); fax: 208-436-5857; 8:30AM-5PM (MST). *Felony, Misdemeanor, Civil, Eviction, Small Claims, Probate.* www.minidoka.id.us/judicial/default.htm

General Information: Probate fax is same as main fax number. District wide fax number is 208-436-5272. Juvenile records released with a signed release. Will fax documents $.50 per page. Court makes copy: $1.00 per page. Certification fee: $1.00 per document plus copy fee. Payee: Clerk of Court. Personal checks accepted. No credit cards accepted. Prepayment required. Mail requests: SASE required for mail return of any copies.

Civil Name Search: Access: In person, online. Visitors must perform in person searches themselves. Civil records on computer from 1989, archives from early 1900s. Civil PAT goes back to 1989. Search trial court records back to 1995 and calendars free at https://www.idcourts.us. Online results include identifiers year of birth and middle initial. The following personal information is not released: DL, address, and first 6 characters of the SSN.

Criminal Name Search: Access: In person, online. Visitors must perform in person searches themselves. Required to search: name, years to search, DOB, SSN, signed release. Criminal records computerized from 1989, archives from early 1900s. Criminal PAT goes back to same as civil. Terminal may also be searched by address and DR number. Search trial court index back to 1995 and calendars free at https://www.idcourts.us. Search by name and DOB or case number. Results show year of birth and middle initial.

Nez Perce County

District & Magistrate Court PO Box 896, 1230 Main St, Lewiston, ID 83501; 208-799-3040; fax: 208-799-3058; 8AM-5PM (PST). *Felony, Misdemeanor, Civil, Eviction, Small Claims, Probate.* www.co.nezperce.id.us/clerk/clerk.htm

General Information: Sealed information includes, but is not limited to, adoptions, child protection actions, and partners of civil protection orders. Will fax documents $1.00 per doc, $1.00 1st page, If long-distance, add $.50 each add'l minute. Court makes copy: $1.00 per page. Certification fee: $1.00 per doc. Payee: Clerk of Court. Personal checks accepted. Visa/MC accepted. Prepayment required. Mail requests: SASE required.

Civil Name Search: Access: Phone, fax, mail, in person, online. Both court and visitors may perform in person name searches. No search fee. Required to search: name; also helpful: years to search. Civil records on computer from 1990, microfiche from 1970 and archives from late 1800s. Mail turnaround time- 10 day waiting period. Civil PAT goes back to 1983. Search trial court records back to 1995 and calendars free at https://www.idcourts.us. Online results include identifiers year of birth and middle initial. The following personal information is not released: DL, address, and first 6 characters of the SSN.

Criminal Name Search: Access: Phone, fax, mail, in person, online. Both court and visitors may perform in person name searches. No search fee. Required to search: name, DOB; also helpful: years to search, aliases, SSN. Criminal records computerized from 1990, microfiche from 1970 and archives from late 1800s. Mail turnaround time 10 day waiting period. Criminal PAT goes back to same as civil. Search trial court index back to 1995 and calendars free at https://www.idcourts.us. Search by name and DOB or case number. Results show year of birth and middle initial.

Nez Perce Tribal Court PO Box 365, Lapwai, ID 83540; 208-843-7338; fax: 208-843-7337; 8AM-5PM (PST). *Jurisdiction on Tribal Land.* www.isc.idaho.gov/nezperce.htm

Oneida County
District & Magistrate Courts 10 Court St, Malad City, ID 83252; 208-766-4116; fax: 208-766-2990; 9AM-5PM (MST). *Felony, Misdemeanor, Civil, Eviction, Small Claims, Probate.*

General Information: Probate is a separate index at the same address. Probate fax is same as main fax number. No juvenile, adoption records released. Will fax documents $1.00 per page. Court makes copy: $1.00 per page. Self serve copy: same. Certification fee: $1.00 per page. Payee: Clerk of Court. Personal checks and credit cards accepted. Prepayment required. Mail requests: SASE requested.

Civil Name Search: Access: Phone, fax, mail, in person, online. Both court and visitors may perform in person name searches. No search fee. Required to search: name, years to search; also helpful: address. Civil cases indexed by case number, defendant, plaintiff. Civil records on computer from 7/90, archives from 1886. Mail turnaround time 1-2 days. Civil PAT goes back to 1990. Search trial court records back to 1995 and calendars free at https://www.idcourts.us. Online results include identifiers year of birth and middle initial. The following personal information is not released: DL, address, and first 6 characters of the SSN.

Criminal Name Search: Access: Phone, fax, mail, in person, online. Both court and visitors may perform in person name searches. No search fee. Required to search: name, years to search; also helpful: address, DOB, SSN. Criminal records computerized from 7/90, archives from 1886. Mail turnaround time 1-2 days. Criminal PAT goes back to 7/1990. Search trial court index back to 1995 and calendars free at https://www.idcourts.us. Search by name and DOB or case number. Results show year of birth and middle initial.

Owyhee County
District & Magistrate Courts-I PO Box 128, 20381 State Hwy 78, Courthouse, Murphy, ID 83650; 208-495-2806; fax: 208-495-1226; 8:30AM-12; 1PM-5PM (MST). *Felony, Misdemeanor, Civil, Eviction, Small Claims, Probate.*
www.owyheecounty.net/index1.php?court

General Information: No adoption, juvenile (except for some that are open), domestic violence records released. Fee to fax out file $5.00 each plus copy fee. Court makes copy: $1.00 per page. Certification fee: $1.00 per page. Payee: Owyhee County. Major credit cards accepted. Prepayment required. Mail requests: Include $.44 for return postage, or SASE.

Civil Name Search: Access: Mail, fax, in person, online. Only the court performs in person name searches; visitors may not. Search fee: $5.00 per name found. Civil records on computer from 1992, archives from 1800s. Mail turnaround time 5-10 days; archived records require longer. Search trial court records back to 1992 and calendars free at https://www.idcourts.us. Online results include identifiers year of birth and middle initial. The following personal information is not released: DL, address, and first 6 characters of the SSN.

Criminal Name Search: Access: Fax, mail, in person, online. Only the court performs in person name searches; visitors may not. Search fee: $5.00 per name found. Required to search: name, years to search; also helpful: DOB. Criminal records computerized from 1992, archives from 1800s. Note: Signed release required for search of juvenile records. Mail turnaround time 5-10 days, longer if records archived. Search trial court index back to 1992 and calendars free at https://www.idcourts.us. Search by name and DOB or case number. Results show year of birth and middle initial.

Homedale Magistrate Court 31 W Wyoming, Homedale, ID 83628-3402; 208-337-4540; fax: 208-337-3035; 8:30AM-5PM T,W,TH (MST). *Misdemeanor, Civil Actions under $10,000, Eviction, Small Claims.*
www.owyheecounty.net/index1.php?court

General Information: No juvenile or mental records released. Will fax documents $5.00 each 1st 2 pages, $2.00 pages 3-10; $.75 each add'l. Court makes copy: $1.00 per page. Certification fee: $1.00 per page. Payee: Clerk

of Court. Personal checks accepted. No credit cards accepted. Prepayment required. Mail requests: SASE required.

Civil Name Search: Access: Mail, in person, online. Only the court performs in person name searches; visitors may not. No search fee. Required to search: name, years to search; also helpful: address. Civil cases indexed by defendant. Civil records on computer from 1992, archives from 1975. Mail turnaround time 2 days. Search trial court records back to 1995 and calendars free at https://www.idcourts.us. Online results include identifiers year of birth and middle initial. The following personal information is not released: DL, address, and first 6 characters of the SSN.

Criminal Name Search: Access: Mail, in person, online. Only the court performs in person name searches; visitors may not. No search fee. Required to search: name, years to search; also helpful: address, DOB, SSN. Criminal records computerized from 1992, archives from 1975. Mail turnaround time 2 days. Search trial court index back to 1995 and calendars free at https://www.idcourts.us. Search by name and DOB or case number. Results show year of birth and middle initial.

Payette County
District & Magistrate Courts 1130 3rd Ave N, #104, Payette, ID 83661; 208-642-6000 (Dist) 642-6010(Magis); fax: 208-642-6011; 9AM-5PM (MST). *Felony, Misdemeanor, Civil, Eviction, Small Claims, Probate.*
www.payettecounty.org/

General Information: District Court is Rm 104; Magistrate Court is Rm 106. Probate fax is same as main fax number. No juvenile, adoption records released. Will fax documents after payment. Court makes copy: $1.00 per page. Self serve copy: same. Certification fee: $1.00 per doc. Payee: Clerk of Court. Personal checks accepted. Major credit cards accepted for fine payments only. Prepayment required. Mail requests: SASE required.

Civil Name Search: Access: Fax, mail, in person, online. Both court and visitors may perform in person name searches. Search fee: $5.00 per name. Required to search: name, years to search; also helpful: address. Civil records on computer back to 1992, prior on microfiche or archived from 1917. Mail turnaround time 1 day. Civil PAT goes back to 1992, countywide. Search trial court records back to 1995 and calendars free at https://www.idcourts.us. Online results include identifiers year of birth and middle initial. The following personal information is not released: DL, address, and first 6 characters of the SSN.

Criminal Name Search: Access: Fax, mail, in person, online. Both court and visitors may perform in person name searches. Search fee: $5.00 per name. Required to search: name, years to search, signed release; also helpful: address, DOB, SSN. Criminal records computerized from 1992, prior microfiche or archived from 1917. Mail turnaround time 1 day. Criminal PAT goes back to same as civil. Search trial court index back to 1995 and calendars free at https://www.idcourts.us. Search by name and DOB or case number. Results show year of birth and middle initial.

Power County
District & Magistrate Courts 543 Bannock Ave, American Falls, ID 83211; 208-226-7611 (Dist) 226-7618(Magistrate); fax: 208-226-7612; 9AM-5PM (MST). *Felony, Misdemeanor, Civil, Eviction, Small Claims, Probate.*
www.co.power.id.us/

General Information: No juvenile, mental commitment records released. Fee to fax out file $1.00 per page. Court makes copy: $1.00 per page. Self serve copy: same. Certification fee: $1.50 per cert. Payee: Power County Magistrate Court. Cashiers check or money order accepted. Visa/MC accepted. Prepayment required. Mail requests: SASE required.

Civil Name Search: Access: Phone, fax, mail, in person, online. Both court and visitors may perform in person name searches. Search fee: $5.00 per name found. Civil records on computer from 1994, prior archived from 1913. Note: Will respond to email requests for $1.00 per page - csteinlicht@co.power.id.us. Mail turnaround time 3-10 days. Civil PAT goes back to 1994. Search trial court records back to 1995 and calendars free at https://www.idcourts.us. Online results include identifiers year of birth and middle initial. The following personal information is not released: DL, address, and first 6 characters of the SSN.

Criminal Name Search: Access: Phone, fax, mail, in person, online. Both court and visitors may perform in person name searches. Search fee: $5.00 per name found. Required to search: name, years to search, DOB, SSN, signed release. Criminal records computerized from 1988, prior archived from 1913. Note: Will respond to email requests for $1.00 per page - csteinlicht@co.power.id.us. Mail turnaround time 10 days. Criminal PAT goes back to 1988. Search trial court index back to 1995 and calendars free at https://www.idcourts.us. Search by name and DOB or case number. Results show year of birth and middle initial.

Shoshone County
District & Magistrate Courts 700 Bank St, Wallace, ID 83873; 208-752-1266; fax: 208-753-0921; 9AM-5PM (PST). *Felony, Misdemeanor, Civil, Eviction, Small Claims, Probate.*

General Information: Probate fax is same as main fax number. No special proceeding, juvenile records released. Will fax documents $2.00 1st page, $1.00 each add'l. Add $1.00 1st page if long distance. Court makes copy: $1.00 per page. Certification fee: $1.00 plus copy fee. Payee: Clerk of Court. Personal checks accepted. Will accept debit cards in person only; credit cards in person and over phone. Prepayment required. Mail requests: SASE required.

Civil Name Search: Access: Phone, fax, mail, in person, online. Both court and visitors may perform in person name searches. No search fee. Required to search: name, years to search; also helpful: address. Civil records on computer from 1988, archived from late 1880s. Note: Juvenile case information not available by fax. Mail turnaround time 1-2 days. Civil PAT goes back to 10/1995. Search trial court records back to 1995 and calendars free at https://www.idcourts.us. Online results include identifiers year of birth and middle initial. The following personal information is not released: DL, address, and first 6 characters of the SSN.

Criminal Name Search: Access: Phone, mail, in person, online. Both court and visitors may perform in person name searches. No search fee. Required to search: name, years to search; also helpful: address, DOB, SSN. Criminal records computerized from 1988, archived from late 1880s. Mail turnaround time 1-2 days. Criminal PAT goes back to same as civil. Search trial court index back to 1995 and calendars free at https://www.idcourts.us. Search by name and DOB or case number. Results show year of birth and middle initial.

Teton County

District & Magistrate Courts 150 Courthouse Dr, #307, Driggs, ID 83422; 208-354-2239; fax: 208-354-8496; 9AM-5PM (MST). *Felony, Misdemeanor, Civil, Eviction, Small Claims, Probate.*

General Information: Address and telephone given above are for District Court. If you wish to access only the Magistrate Court and call 208-354-2239. No juvenile, DV records released. Will fax documents $2.00 per page. Court makes copy: $1.00 per page. Self serve copy: same. Certification fee: $1.00. Payee: Clerk of Court. Personal checks accepted. Visa/MC accepted. Prepayment required. Mail requests: SASE required.

Civil Name Search: Access: Phone, fax, mail, in person, online. Both court and visitors may perform in person name searches. Search fee: $5.00 per name. Required to search: name, years to search; also helpful: address. Civil records on computer from 1992, archives from 1974, I-Star since 1992. Mail turnaround time 3 days. Civil PAT goes back to 1992. Search trial court records back to 1995 and calendars free at https://www.idcourts.us. Online results include identifiers year of birth and middle initial. The following personal information is not released: DL, address, and first 6 characters of the SSN.

Criminal Name Search: Access: Phone, fax, mail, in person, online. Both court and visitors may perform in person name searches. Search fee: $5.00 per name. Required to search: name, years to search; also helpful: address, DOB, SSN. Criminal records computerized from 1992, archives from 1974, I-Star since 1993. Note: The court only performs research on Fridays. Mail turnaround time 1-7 days. Criminal PAT goes back to same as civil. Online access is same as described for civil.

Twin Falls County

District & Magistrate Courts PO Box 126, Twin Falls, ID 83303-0126; 208-736-4013; fax: 208-736-4155; 8AM-5PM (MST). *Felony, Misdemeanor, Civil, Eviction, Small Claims, Probate.*

General Information: No adoption, termination, juvenile records released. Will fax out document $2.50 each plus copy fee with 25 page limit. Court makes copy: $1.00 per page. Certification fee: $1.00 per doc plus copy fee. Payee: Court Services. Personal checks accepted. Visa/MC accepted; add $3.00 technology cost. Prepayment required.

Civil Name Search: Access: In person, online. Visitors must perform in person searches themselves. Required to search: name, years to search; also helpful: address. Civil records on computer from 12/1989, archives from early 1900s. Civil PAT goes back to 12/1989. Printouts on terminal are free for first 100 pages, then $.10 per page. Search trial court records back to 1995 and calendars free at https://www.idcourts.us. Online results include identifiers year of birth and middle initial. The following personal information is not released: DL, address, and first 6 characters of the SSN.

Criminal Name Search: Access: In person, online. Visitors must perform in person searches themselves. Required to search: name, years to search; also helpful: address, DOB, SSN. Criminal records computerized from 12/1989, archives from 1951 felonies, 1970 for misdemeanors. Criminal PAT goes back to same as civil. Printouts on terminal are free for first 100 pages, then $.10 per page. Online access is same as described for civil.

Valley County

District & Magistrate Courts PO Box 1350, Cascade, ID 83611; 208-382-7178; fax: 208-382-7184; 8AM-5PM (MST). *Felony, Misdemeanor, Civil, Eviction, Small Claims, Probate.*

General Information: A Courthouse Annex in McCall handles Juvenile. However, the McCall Court does not do background checks nor does the court in Cascade. No juvenile records released. Will fax documents $1.00 per page. Court makes copy: $1.00 per page. Self serve copy: is available. Certification fee: $1.00 per page plus copy fee. Payee: Valley County. Two-party or out-of-country (w/o printed-stamped US Funds) checks not accepted. Visa/MC accepted. Prepayment required. Mail requests: SASE required for mail return of any copies.

Civil Name Search: Access: In person, online. Both court and visitors may perform in person name searches. No search fee. Required to search: name, case number, years to search; also helpful: address. Civil records on computer from 1990, microfiche and archives from early 1900s. Civil PAT goes back to 1990. Search trial court records back to 1995 and calendars free at https://www.idcourts.us. Online results include identifiers year of birth and middle initial. The following personal information is not released: DL, address, and first 6 characters of the SSN.

Criminal Name Search: Access: In person, online. Both court and visitors may perform in person name searches. No search fee. Required to search: name, case number, years to search; also helpful: address, DOB, SSN. Criminal records computerized from 1990, microfiche and archives from early 1900s. Criminal PAT goes back to same as civil. Search trial court index back to 1995 and calendars free at https://www.idcourts.us. Search by name and DOB or case number. Results show year of birth and middle initial.

Washington County

District & Magistrate Courts PO Box 670, Weiser, ID 83672; 208-414-2092; fax: 208-414-3925; 8:30AM-5PM (MST). *Felony, Misdemeanor, Civil, Eviction, Small Claims, Probate.* www.the3rdjudicialdistrict.com

General Information: This court will only perform searches for probate records; these requests must be in writing. Turnaround time on probate records is 3-10 days. No juvenile, adoption, hospitalization, child protection-termination of parental rights records released. Will not fax documents. Court makes copy: $1.00 per page. Self serve copy: same. Certification fee: $1.00. Payee: Washington County. Business checks accepted if local. Major credit cards accepted. Prepayment required.

Civil Name Search: Access: In person, online. Visitors must perform in person searches themselves. Required to search: name. Civil records on computer from 2/90, archives from late 1800s. Civil PAT goes back to 2/1990. Search trial court records back to 1990 and calendars free at https://www.idcourts.us. Online results include identifiers year of birth and middle initial. The following personal information is not released: DL, address, and first 6 characters of the SSN.

Criminal Name Search: Access: In person, online. Visitors must perform in person searches themselves. Required to search: name. Criminal records computerized from 2/90, archives from late 1800s. Criminal PAT goes back to same as civil. Online access is same as described for civil.

Illinois

Time Zone:	**CST**
Capital:	**Springfield, Sangamon County**
# of Counties:	**102**
State Web:	**www.illinois.gov**
Court Web:	**www.state.il.us/court**

Administration

Administrative Office of Courts, 3101 Old Jacksonville Road, Springfield, IL 62704; 217-558-4490.

The Supreme and Appellate Courts

The Supreme Court is the highest court in the state. There are five Appellate Court Districts. Opinions and dockets for the Supreme and Appellate Courts are available from the home page shown above.

The Illinois Trial Courts

Court	Type	How Organized	Jurisdiction Highpoints
Circuit*	General	106 Courts in 23 Circuits	Felony, Misdemeanor, Civil, Small Claims, Juvenile, Traffic, Eviction, Domestic, Probate, Estate

* = profiled in this book

Details on the Court Structure

The **Circuit Court** is the Unified Trail Court in Illinois and has jurisdiction for all matters properly brought before it and shares jurisdiction with the Supreme Court to hear cases relating to revenue, mandamus, prohibition, and habeas corpus. Illinois is divided into twenty-three circuits. Five are single county circuits (Cook, Will, DuPage, Lake, and McHenry) and the remaining eighteen circuits comprise as few as two and as many as twelve counties each. There are two types of judges in the Circuit Court: circuit judges and associate judges. Circuit judges, elected for six years, can hear any kind of case. An associate judge can hear any case, except criminal cases punishable by a prison term of one year or more (felonies).

Probate is handled by the Circuit Court in all counties.

Record Searching Facts You Need to Know

Fees and Record Searching Tips

The search fee is set by the Clerk of Courts Act (705 ILCS 105). The statute sets different pricing court filings and services based on county population tiers (under 500,000, between 500,000 and 3,000,000, and over 3,000,000). The higher the population, the higher the fee. For record searching fees, the statute also gives a minimum and maximum that that can be charged with rules how to reach the maximum. Searching is supposed to be calculated at a per year searched basis. In general, search fees range from $4.00 to $9.00 per name per year. Copy fees are generally $1.00 or $2.00 for the first page then $.50 per page for the next 19, then $.25 per page. Usually. The bottom line is you will find pricing all over the board.

In most courts, both civil and criminal data is on computer from the same starting date. At least 90% of the courts offer public access terminals to look-up docket data.

Online Access is by County and Limited

There is no statewide public online system available to trial courts. However at least 64 counties endorse and are participating with a vendor. The site at www.judici.com provides a free index search and a premium subscription service with more detailed information. Visit the site to find the participating counties; they are shown by map and with a drop-down box. More counties will be added.

Adams County

Circuit Court 521 Vermony St, Quincy, IL 62301; 217-277-2100; fax: 217-277-2116; 8:15AM-4:30PM (CST). *Felony, Misdemeanor, Civil, Eviction, Small Claims, Probate.*
www.co.adams.il.us
General Information: Online identifiers in results same as on public terminal. No juvenile or adoption records released. Will not fax documents. Court makes copy: $.50 per page. Certification fee: $6.00. Payee: Clerk of Circuit Court. Personal checks accepted. No credit cards accepted. Prepayment required. Mail requests: SASE required.
Civil Name Search: Access: Phone, mail, fax, in person, online, email. Both court and visitors may perform in person name searches. Search fee: $6.00 per name. Fee is $10.00 for years prior to 1987. Civil records on computer from 1987, books and index cards from 1920. Mail turnaround time 2-3 days. Civil PAT goes back to 1987. Results include name and case number. Online access is same as described under criminal records. Direct email search requests to rfrese@co.adams.il.us.
Criminal Name Search: Access: Phone, mail, fax, in person, online, email. Both court and visitors may perform in person name searches. Search fee: $6.00 per name. Fee is $10.00 for years prior to 1987. Required to search: name, years to search, DOB. Criminal records computerized from 1987, books and index cards from 1920. Mail turnaround time 2-3 days. Criminal PAT goes back to same as civil. Online access is free at www.judici.com/. A premium fee service is also available with multi-county search capabilities and other features. Case files are available from 1987. Direct email search requests to rfrese@co.adams.il.us. The county inmate list and warrant list is at the home page.

Alexander County

Circuit Court 2000 Washington Ave, Cairo, IL 62914; 618-734-0107; 8AM-N 1PM-4PM (CST). *Felony, Misdemeanor, Civil, Eviction, Small Claims, Probate.*
www.state.il.us/court/CircuitCourt/CircuitMap/1st.asp#Alexander
General Information: No juvenile or adoption records released. Will fax documents to local or toll free line. Court makes copy: $2.00 1st page; $.50 each for 2-19 pages; then $.25 each add'l. Certification fee: $6.00 per cert plus copy fees. Payee: Clerk of Circuit Court. Business checks accepted; no personal checks. No credit cards accepted. Prepayment required. Mail requests: SASE required.
Civil Name Search: Access: Fax, mail, in person, online. Only the court performs in person name searches; visitors may not. Search fee: $6.00 per name per year. Civil records on computer from 1987, books and index cards from 1800s. Mail turnaround time 1 day. Online access is same as described under criminal records.
Criminal Name Search: Access: Fax, mail, in person, online. Only the court performs in person name searches; visitors may not. Search fee: $6.00 per name per year. Required to search: name. Criminal records computerized from 1987, books and index cards from 1800s. Mail turnaround time 1 day. Online access is free at www.judici.com/. A premium fee service is also available with multi-county search capabilities and other features. Case files are available from 1986.

Bond County

Circuit Court 200 W College Ave, Greenville, IL 62246; 618-664-3208; fax: 618-664-2257; 8AM-4:30PM (CST). *Felony, Misdemeanor, Civil, Small Claims, Probate.*
www.bondcountyil.com/circuitclerk/
General Information: Probate fax is same as main fax number. No juvenile or adoption records released. Will fax documents to local or toll-free number. Court makes copy: $.50 per page. Self serve copy: same. Certification fee: $5.00 plus copy fee. Payee: Clerk of Circuit Court. No personal checks accepted. MasterCard and Discover accepted in person only. Prepayment required. Mail requests: SASE required.
Civil Name Search: Access: Mail, in person, online. Both court and visitors may perform in person name searches. Search fee: $5.00 per name per year. Civil records on computer back to 1/87 (and are limited); in index books from 1900s. Mail turnaround time 1-2 weeks. Civil PAT goes back to 1987. Online access is same as criminal, see below.
Criminal Name Search: Access: Mail, in person, online. Both court and visitors may perform in person name searches. Search fee: $5.00 per name per year. Required to search: name, years to search, DOB. Criminal records computerized from 1964; index books from 1900s. Mail turnaround time 1-

2 weeks. Criminal PAT goes back to 1964. Online access is free at www.judici.com/. A premium fee service is also available with multi-county search capabilities and other features. Case files are available from 1987. Online results show middle initial, DOB.

Boone County

Circuit Court 601 N Main, #303, Belvidere, IL 61008; 815-544-0371; criminal phone: x2; civil phone: x1; probate phone: x6911; fax: 815-547-8129; 8:30AM-5PM (CST). *Felony, Misdemeanor, Civil, Eviction, Small Claims, Probate.*
www.boonecountyil.org
General Information: Search fee includes both civil and criminal index. Fax search requests must be on letterhead. No juvenile or adoption records released. Will not fax documents. Court makes copy: $2.00 1st page, $.50 each add'l, beyond 19 $.25 each. Certification fee: $6.00 per document plus copy fee. Payee: Clerk of Circuit Court. Personal checks accepted. Prepayment required. Mail requests: SASE required.
Civil Name Search: Access: Mail, fax, in person, online. Both court and visitors may perform in person name searches. Search fee: $6.00 per name per year. Civil records on computer since 8/1993, on index books from 1800s. Mail turnaround time 1-2 days. Civil PAT goes back to 9/1993. Online access is same as described under criminal records.
Criminal Name Search: Access: Mail, in person, online. Both court and visitors may perform in person name searches. Search fee: $6.00 per name per year. Required to search: name, years to search, DOB. Records on computer since 8/1993, on index books from 1800s. Mail turnaround time 1-2 days. Criminal PAT goes back to 9/1993. Search cases since 08/23/1993 free online at www.judici.com/courts/cases/case_search.jsp?court=IL004015J. Also, a premium fee service is available. Online results show middle initial.

Brown County

Circuit Court Brown County Courthouse, 200 Court St, Rm 5, Mt Sterling, IL 62353; 217-773-2713 X2; fax: 217-773-3648; 8:30AM-4:30PM (CST). *Felony, Misdemeanor, Civil, Eviction, Small Claims, Probate.*
General Information: No juvenile or adoption records released. Will fax documents $3.00 per page. Court makes copy: $.35 per page. Certification fee: $3.00. Payee: Clerk of Circuit Court. Only cashiers checks and money orders accepted. No credit cards accepted. Prepayment required. Mail requests: SASE required.
Civil Name Search: Access: Phone, fax, mail, in person. Both court and visitors may perform in person name searches. Search fee: $4.00 per name per year. Civil records on computer since 1994, on index books from 1830s. Mail turnaround time 1 week. Civil PAT goes back to 1994.
Criminal Name Search: Access: Phone, fax, mail, in person. Both court and visitors may perform in person name searches. Search fee: $4.00 per name. Required to search: name, years to search, DOB, signed release. Criminal records on computer since 1994, on index books from 1830s. Mail turnaround time 1 week. Criminal PAT goes back to 1994.

Bureau County

Circuit Court 702 S Main St, Princeton, IL 61356; 815-872-2001; fax: 815-872-0027; 8AM-4PM (CST). *Felony, Misdemeanor, Civil, Eviction, Small Claims, Probate.*
www.bccirclk.gov/
General Information: No juvenile or adoption records released. Fee to fax out file $2.00 1st pg; $1.00 each add'l. Court makes copy: $.50 for pages 1-19, $.25 for page 20 and over. Self serve copy: same. Certification fee: $6.00. Payee: Bureau County Circuit Clerk. No personal checks accepted. Money orders accepted. No credit cards accepted. Prepayment required. Mail requests: SASE required for criminal.
Civil Name Search: Access: In person, online. Both court and visitors may perform in person name searches. No search fee. Civil records on computer from 8/1988, prior on index books. Civil PAT goes back to 8/1988. Online access to Judicial Circuit records is free at http://75.149.91.99/bureau/caseinfo.htm. Index includes dates, defendants, record sheets and dispositions and goes back to 8/1988.
Criminal Name Search: Access: Mail, in person, online. Both court and visitors may perform in person name searches. No search fee. Required to search: name, years to search, DOB. Criminal records computerized from 8/1988, prior on index books. Mail turnaround time 1 week. Criminal PAT goes back to same as civil. Online access to criminal records is the same

as civil. The year of birth shows, but that is the only part of the DOB. Online results show middle initial.

Calhoun County

Circuit Court PO Box 486 (101 N County Rd, Hardin, IL 62047; 618-576-2451; fax: 618-576-9541; 8:30AM-4:30PM (CST). *Felony, Misdemeanor, Civil, Eviction, Small Claims, Probate.*

General Information: Probate is a separate index at this same address. Probate fax is same as main fax number. No juvenile or adoption records released. No fee to fax documents; there is a limit on quantity before a fee applies. Court makes copy: $2.00 first page; $.50 each for 2-19 pages; then $.25 each add'l. Self serve copy: same. Certification fee: $2.00 plus copy fee. Payee: Clerk of Circuit Court. Only cashiers checks and money orders accepted. No credit cards accepted. Prepayment required. Mail requests: SASE required or include postage.

Civil Name Search: Access: Phone, fax, mail, in person. Both court and visitors may perform in person name searches. Search fee: $6.00 per name for search back to 1998 on computer; separate search fee to search ledger books. Civil index on docket books from 1800s, computerized since 7/98. Mail turnaround time 1 day.

Criminal Name Search: Access: Phone, fax, mail, in person. Both court and visitors may perform in person name searches. Search fee: $6.00 per name for search back to 1998 on computer; separate search fee to search ledger books. Required to search: name, years to search, DOB. Criminal records indexed in books from 1800s, computerized since 7/98. Mail turnaround time 1 day.

Carroll County

Circuit Court 301 N Main St, PO Box 32, Mt Carroll, IL 61053; 815-244-0230; fax: 815-244-3869; 8:30AM-4:30PM (CST). *Felony, Misdemeanor, Civil, Eviction, Small Claims, Probate.*
www.15thjudicialcircuit.com

General Information: No juvenile, mental health or adoption records released. Will fax documents for $2.00. Court makes copy: $2.00 1st page, $.50 ea add'l next 19 then $.25 ea add'l. Certification fee: $10.00 per doc plus copy fee. Payee: Clerk of Circuit Court. Local personal checks accepted. Credit cards accepted for in-person research, fees involved using online card vendor. Prepayment required. Mail requests: SASE required.

Civil Name Search: Access: Mail, in person, online. Both court and visitors may perform in person name searches. Search fee: $6.00 per name per year. Civil cases indexed by defendant. Civil records on computer from 1988, prior on index books. Mail turnaround time 2-3 days. Civil PAT goes back to 1988. Access is free to civil, small claims, probate and traffic records at www.judici.com/courts/index.jsp?court=IL008015J. Records go back to 1988. A premium fee service is also available.

Criminal Name Search: Access: Mail, in person, online. Both court and visitors may perform in person name searches. Search fee: $6.00 per name per year. Required to search: name, years to search, DOB. Criminal records computerized from 1988, prior on index books. Mail turnaround time 2-3 days. Criminal PAT goes back to same as civil. Criminal records access is free at www.judici.com/courts/index.jsp?court=IL008015J. Records go back to 1988.

Cass County

Circuit Court PO Box 203, Virginia, IL 62691; 217-452-7225; 8:30AM-4:30PM (CST). *Felony, Misdemeanor, Civil, Eviction, Small Claims, Probate.*

General Information: No juvenile or adoption records released. Will not fax documents. Court makes copy: $1.00 1st page, $.50 each add'l. Certification fee: $5.00 per document. Payee: Cass County Circuit Clerk. Personal checks accepted. No credit cards accepted. Prepayment required. Mail requests: SASE required.

Civil Name Search: Access: Mail, in person. Visitors must perform in person searches themselves. Search fee: $6.00 per name per year, for search conducted by staff. Civil index on docket books from 1800s. Mail turnaround time 1-2 weeks. Civil PAT goes back to 8/8/1998.

Criminal Name Search: Access: Mail, in person. Visitors must perform in person searches themselves. Search fee: $6.00 per name per year, for search performed by staff. Required to search: name, years to search, DOB; also helpful: SSN. Criminal records indexed in books from 1800s, on computer back 1998 to present. Mail turnaround time 1-2 weeks. Criminal PAT goes back to same as civil. The DOB will appear only if available.

Champaign County

Circuit Court 101 E Main, Urbana, IL 61801; criminal phone: 217-384-3727; civil phone: 217-384-3725; fax: 217-384-3879; 8AM-4:30PM (CST). *Felony, Misdemeanor, Civil, Eviction, Small Claims, Probate.*
www.cccircuitclerk.com

General Information: Online identifiers in results same as on public terminal. No juvenile or adoption records released. Will fax documents $1.50 1st page, $.50 ea add'l. Court makes copy: $1.00 1st page, $.50 add'l page. Certification fee: $2.00. Payee: Clerk of Circuit Court. Personal checks

accepted for a $1.25 surcharge. Visa/MC accepted; usage fee $5.00 per transaction. Prepayment required. Mail requests: SASE required.

Civil Name Search: Access: Mail, in person, online. Both court and visitors may perform in person name searches. Search fee: $6.00 per name per year. Civil records on computer from 1986, index books from 1800s. Mail turnaround time 1-2 weeks. Civil PAT goes back to 1992. Access to the circuit clerk's case query online system called PASS is now free at https://secure.jtsmith.com/clerk/clerk.asp. Online case records go back to '92. A vendor provides online access via subscription is a $59 setup fee plus annual subscription of $240 for this county, or $300/yr for all 7 counties - Champaign, DeKalb, Kendall, LaSalle, Madison, Sangamon, and Will. Visit www.clericusmagnus.com/.

Criminal Name Search: Access: Mail, online, in person. Both court and visitors may perform in person name searches. Search fee: $6.00 per name per year. Required to search: name, years to search; also helpful: DOB, SSN. Criminal records computerized from 1988, index books from 1800s. Mail turnaround time 1-2 weeks. Criminal PAT goes back to 1992. Access to the circuit clerk's case query online system called PASS is now free at https://secure.jtsmith.com/clerk/clerk.asp. Online case records go back to '92. Online results show name, DOB.

Christian County

Circuit Court PO Box 617, Taylorville, IL 62568; 217-824-4966; fax: 217-824-5030; 8AM-4PM (CST). *Felony, Misdemeanor, Civil, Eviction, Small Claims, Probate.*
www.christiancountyil.com/

General Information: No juvenile or adoption records released. Will not fax out documents. Court makes copy: $1.00 1st page, $.50 each add'l. Certification fee: $6.00. Payee: Clerk of Circuit Court. Business checks accepted. No credit cards accepted. Prepayment required. Mail requests: SASE required.

Civil Name Search: Access: Phone, mail, in person, online. Both court and visitors may perform in person name searches. Search fee: $5.00 per name per year. Required to search: name; also helpful: years to search. Civil records on computer from 1988, index books from 1840. Mail turnaround time 1-2 days. Civil PAT goes back to 1988. Online access is same as described under criminal records.

Criminal Name Search: Access: Phone, mail, in person, online. Both court and visitors may perform in person name searches. Search fee: $5.00 per name per year. Required to search: name; also helpful: years to search, DOB. Criminal records computerized from 1988, index books from 1840. Mail turnaround time 1-2 days. Criminal PAT goes back to same as civil. Online access is free at www.judici.com/. A premium fee service is also available with multi-county search capabilities and other features. Case files are available from 1987.

Clark County

Circuit Court PO Box 187, 501 Archer Ave, Marshall, IL 62441; 217-826-2811; criminal phone: 217-826-2811; fax: 217-826-1391; 8AM-4PM (CST). *Felony, Misdemeanor, Civil, Eviction, Small Claims, Probate.*
www.clarkcountyil.org/circuit_clerk.htm

General Information: No juvenile, maternity, or adoption records released. Will not fax documents. Court makes copy: $2.00 1st page, $.50 each add'l. $.25 per page after 20. Certification fee: $6.00. Payee: Clerk of Circuit Court. Only cashiers checks and money orders accepted. No credit cards accepted. Prepayment required. Mail requests: SASE required.

Civil Name Search: Access: Mail, in person, online. Both court and visitors may perform in person name searches. Search fee: $6.00 per name per year. Required to search: name, years to search; also helpful: address. Civil records on computer from 1989, index books from 1800s. Mail turnaround time 1 week. Civil PAT goes back to 8/1989. Results include name and case number. Access court index free from 1989 forward at www.judici.com/courts/cases/case_search.jsp?court=IL012015J.

Criminal Name Search: Access: Mail, in person, online. Both court and visitors may perform in person name searches. Search fee: $6.00 per name per year. Required to search: name, years to search, DOB, signed release; also helpful: address, SSN. Criminal records computerized from 1989, index books from 1800s. Mail turnaround time 1 week. Criminal PAT goes back to same as civil. Results include name and DOB. Access to criminal records online is same as civil, see above.

Clay County

Circuit Court PO Box 100, 111 Chestnut St, Louisville, IL 62858; 618-665-3523; fax: 618-665-3543; 8AM-4PM (CST). *Felony, Misdemeanor, Civil, Eviction, Small Claims, Probate.*
www.claycountyillinois.org/index.aspx?page=14

General Information: Also, use www.fourthcircuitil.com. Probate fax is same as main fax number. No juvenile or adoption records released. Will fax documents $1.00 1st page, $.50 each add'l. Court makes copy: $1.00 1st page, $.50 each add'l; After 20 pages $.25 each. Certification fee: $6.00 plus copy fee. Payee: Clerk of Circuit Court. No personal checks accepted. Credit card accepted through Government Payment Service at 888-604-7888. Prepayment required. Mail requests: SASE required.

Civil Name Search: Access: Fax, mail, in person, online. Both court and visitors may perform in person name searches. Search fee: $5.00 per name. Fee is $5.00 per year prior to 1988. Civil cases indexed by defendant. Civil records on computer from 1988, index books from 1850s. Mail turnaround time 2-3 days. Civil PAT goes back to 1988. Search cases free online at www.judici.com/courts/cases/case_search.jsp?court=IL013015J. Also, a premium fee service is available.

Criminal Name Search: Access: Fax, mail, in person, online. Both court and visitors may perform in person name searches. Search fee: $5.00 per name. Fee is $5.00 per year prior to 1988. Required to search: name, years to search; also helpful: DOB. Criminal records computerized from 1988, index books from 1850s. Mail turnaround time 2-3 days. Criminal PAT goes back to same as civil. Online access to criminal same as civil, see above.

Clinton County

Circuit Court County Courthouse, PO Box 407, Carlyle, IL 62231; 618-594-2464; 8AM-4PM (CST). *Felony, Misdemeanor, Civil, Eviction, Small Claims, Probate.*

www.fourthcircuitil.com/

General Information: No juvenile or adoption records released. Will not fax documents. Court makes copy: $.50 per page. Certification fee: $10.00 per document plus copy fee. Payee: Clerk of Circuit Court. Personal checks accepted. No credit cards accepted. Prepayment required. Mail requests: SASE required.

Civil Name Search: Access: Mail, in person, online. Both court and visitors may perform in person name searches. Search fee: $10.00 per name. Fee is for 10 year search. Civil records on computer from 1988, index books from 1825. Mail turnaround time 2-4 days. Civil PAT goes back to 1988. Search cases free online at www.judici.com/courts/cases/index.jsp?court=IL014015J. Also, a premium fee service is available.

Criminal Name Search: Access: Mail, in person, online. Both court and visitors may perform in person name searches. Search fee: $10.00 per name. Flat fee for 10 year search. Required to search: name, years to search, DOB. Criminal records computerized from 1988, index books from 1825. Mail turnaround time 2-4 days. Criminal PAT goes back to same as civil. Online access to criminal same as civil, see above.

Coles County

Circuit Court PO Box 48, 651 Jackson, Charleston, IL 61920; 217-348-0516; fax: 217-348-7324; 8:30AM-4:30PM (CST). *Felony, Misdemeanor, Civil, Eviction, Small Claims, Probate.*

www.judici.com/courts/index.jsp?court=IL015025J

General Information: No juvenile or adoption records released. Will fax documents to local or toll free line. Court makes copy: $2.00 1st page; $.50 each add'l. Certification fee: $10.00. Payee: Clerk of Circuit Court. Personal checks accepted if Illinois, with driver license number. No credit cards accepted. Prepayment required. Mail requests: SASE required.

Civil Name Search: Access: Fax, mail, in person, online. Both court and visitors may perform in person name searches. Search fee: $6.00 per year. Civil records on computer from 1989, index books from 1800s. Mail turnaround time 1 day or same day. Civil PAT goes back to 1989. Results include name and case number. Access civil, small claims, probate and traffic records for free at www.judici.com/courts/index.jsp?court=IL015025J, to 1989. A premium fee service is also available.

Criminal Name Search: Access: Fax, mail, in person, online. Both court and visitors may perform in person name searches. Search fee: $6.00 per name per year. Required to search: name, years to search, DOB; also helpful: SSN. Criminal records computerized from 1989, index books from 1800s. Note: Results include name, address and case number. Mail turnaround time 1-2 days. Criminal PAT goes back to 1989. Criminal records access is free at www.judici.com/courts/index.jsp?court=IL015025J Online results show name, DOB.

Cook County

Circuit Court - Criminal Division 2650 S California Ave, #526, Chicago, IL 60608; 773-674-3147; criminal phone: 773-674-3147; fax: 773-674-4444; 8:30AM-4:30PM (CST). *Felony.*

www.cookcountyclerkofcourt.org

General Information: Records Dept on 5th Fl. Cases are heard in six district courts within the county and each court also has a central index. This location houses felony records only, but both felony and misdemeanor are on this division's computer system. No juvenile or adoption records released. Will not fax documents. Court makes copy: $2.00 1st page, $.50 each add'l. but only $.25 per page after 20. Certification fee: $9.00 per doc plus copy fee. Payee: Clerk of Circuit Court. Personal checks accepted with drivers license number. Major credit cards accepted. Prepayment required. Mail requests: SASE required.

Criminal Name Search: Access: Mail, in person. Both court and visitors may perform in person name searches. Search fee: $9.00 per name per year per division. Required to search: name, years to search, DOB. Criminal records on computer since 1964; prior records on microfiche from 1800s. Note: No hard copies of misdemeanors here; you must get them from the branch where they were heard. Mail turnaround time 7-10 days. Pre-2003 archived records may take add'l 2-3 processing days. Public use terminal has crim records back to 1985. Multiple public terminals in the lobby - includes felony and all misdemeanors from branches. A record request form is at http://198.173.15.31/forms/pdf_files/CriminalForm.pdf.

Bridgeview District 5 10220 S 76th Ave, Rm 121, Bridgeview Court Bldg, Bridgeview, IL 60453; 708-974-6500; criminal phone: 708-974-6387; civil phone: 708-974-6599; fax: 708-974-6384; 8:30AM-4:30PM (CST). *Felony, Misdemeanor, Civil Action under $100,000, Eviction, Small Claims.*

www.cookcountyclerkofcourt.org

General Information: Alsip, Bedford Pk, Bridgeview, Burbank, Countryside, Evergreen Pk, Forest View, Hickory Hills, Hinsdale, Hodgkins, Hometown, Justice, Lagrange, Lemont, Lyons, McCook, Oak Forest, Oak Lawn, Orland Hills, Palos Pk, Stickney, Summit, Tinley Pk, West Haven, Willow Springs, Worth. Will not fax documents. Court makes copy: $2.00 1st page, $.50 each add'l. Self serve copy: same. Certification fee: $9.00 per doc plus copy fee. Payee: Clerk of Circuit Court. On personal checks write your SSN and driver's license numbers. Major credit cards accepted for traffic court only. Prepayment required. Mail requests: SASE required.

Civil Name Search: Access: Mail, in person, online. Visitors must perform in person searches themselves. Search fee: $9.00 per name per year and district or division. Civil records computerized since 1985, microfiche to early 1970s. Note: An online search request form is at http://198.173.15.31/forms/pdf_files/CivilForm.pdf. Mail turnaround time 1-2 days. Civil PAT goes back to 1985. Online case information is available at www.cookcountyclerkofcourt.org. Click on Online Case Info.

Criminal Name Search: Access: Mail, in person. Visitors must perform in person searches themselves. Search fee: $9.00 per name per year per district. Required to search: name. Criminal records computerized since 1985, prior on microfiche to early 1970s. Note: Misdemeanor records (countywide) are also located at Circuit Court - Chicago Dist 1, Richard J. Daley Ctr, 50 W. Washington Ave, Rm 1006, Chicago, IL 60602. Mail turnaround time varies. Criminal PAT goes back to same as civil. Felony mail requests- download criminal search request form at http://198.173.15.31/forms/pdf_files/CriminalForm.pdf; mail to Clerk of Circuit Court, Criminal Div - Records, 2650 S California, Chicago, IL 60608, 773-869-3147. Online results show middle initial.

Circuit Court - Chicago District 1 50 W Washington, Rm 601, Richard J Daley Center, Chicago, IL 60602; 312-603-5030 general; criminal phone: 312-603-4641; civil phone: 312-603-5145; probate phone: 312-603-6441; fax: 312-603-3330; 8:30AM-4:30PM (CST). *Misdemeanor, Civil Action under $100,000, Eviction, Small Claims, Probate.*

www.cookcountyclerkofcourt.org

General Information: Cases heard in 6 district courts within the county. Each court has a central index, but all case files wind up here. Probate is a separate division in Rm 1202. No juvenile or adoption records released. Will not fax documents. Court makes copy: $2.00 1st page, $.50 each add'l. Self serve copy: $.50 per page. Certification fee: $9.00 per doc. Payee: Clerk of Circuit Court. On personal checks write your SSN and driver's license numbers. Visa/MC accepted for traffic court only. Prepayment required. Mail requests: SASE required.

Civil Name Search: Access: Phone, mail, online, in person. Both court and visitors may perform in person name searches. Search fee: $9.00 per name per year and district or division. Civil records on computer from 1983, index books from 1800s. Note: An online search request form is at http://198.173.15.31/forms/pdf_files/CivilForm.pdf. Mail turnaround time 1 week. Civil PAT goes back to 1985. Search full case dockets free at www.cookcountyclerkofcourt.org and click on Online Case Info. Among the choices are dockets, case snapshots, probate and traffic. Search by name, number, or date. Data includes attorneys, case type, filing date, the amount of damages sought, division/district, and most current court date.

Criminal Name Search: Access: Phone, mail, in person. Visitors must perform in person searches themselves. Search fee: $9.00 per name per year per district. Required to search: name, years to search, DOB. Note: Search misdemeanors in person in Rm 1006. Phone inquiries are to check case status only. Download criminal records search request form at http://198.173.15.31/forms/pdf_files/CriminalForm.pdf. Mail turnaround time 1 week. Criminal PAT goes back to same as civil. Online results show middle initial.

Maywood District 4 1500 S Maybrook Dr, Rm 236, Maywood, IL 60153-2410; 708-865-6040; criminal phone: 708-865-5517; civil phone: 708-865-5187; fax: 708-865-4881; 8:30AM-4:30PM (CST). *Felony, Misdemeanor, Civil Action under $100,000, Eviction, Small Claims.*
www.cookcountyclerkofcourt.org
General Information: Bellwood, Berkeley, Berwyn, Broadview, Brookfield, Cicero, Elmwood Park, Forest Park, Franklin Park, Hillside, La Grange Park, Maywood, Melrose Park, Northlake, North Riverside, Oak Park, River Forest, River Grove, Riverside, Stone Park, Westchester. Will not fax documents. Court makes copy: $2.00 1st page, $.50 each add'l. Certification fee: $9.00 per doc. Payee: Clerk of Circuit Court. On personal checks write your driver's license number. Major credit cards accepted for traffic and criminal fines. Prepayment required. Mail requests: SASE required.
Civil Name Search: Access: Mail, in person, online. Both court and visitors may perform in person name searches. Search fee: $9.00 per name per year and district or division. Required to search: name; also helpful: years to search. Civil records computerized since 1982, docket books to 1970s, prior archived. Note: An online search request form is at http://198.173.15.31/forms/pdf_files/CivilForm.pdf. Mail turnaround time 1-2 days. Civil PAT goes back to 1988. Online case information is available at www.cookcountyclerkofcourt.org. Click on Online Case Info.
Criminal Name Search: Access: Mail, in person. Both court and visitors may perform in person name searches. Search fee: $9.00 per name per year per district. Required to search: name, years to search, DOB. Note: Misdemeanor records (countywide) are also located at Circuit Court - Chicago Dist 1, Richard J. Daley Ctr, 50 W. Washington Ave, Rm 1006, Chicago, IL 60602. Mail turnaround time varies. Criminal PAT goes back to 1989. Felony mail requests- download criminal search request form at http://198.173.15.31/forms/pdf_files/CriminalForm.pdf; mail to Clerk of Circuit Court, Criminal Div - Records, 2650 S California, Chicago, IL 60608, 773-869-3147. Online results show middle initial.

Rolling Meadows District 3 2121 Euclid Ave, Rm 121, Rolling Meadows, IL 60008-1566; 847-818-2850/818-3000; criminal phone: 847-818-3000; civil phone: 847-818-2300; fax: 847-818-2706; 8:30AM-4:30PM (CST). *Felony, Misdemeanor, Civil Action under $100,000, Eviction, Small Claims.*
www.cookcountyclerkofcourt.org/
General Information: See list of cities and villages of this geographic area at http://198.173.15.34/?section=DDPage&DDPage=2900. Will not fax documents. Court makes copy: $2.00 1st page, $.50 each add'l. Certification fee: $9.00 per doc plus copy fee. Payee: Clerk of Circuit Court. On personal checks write your SSN and driver's license number. Visa/MC accepted for traffic court only. Prepayment required. Mail requests: SASE required.
Civil Name Search: Access: Mail, in person, online. Visitors must perform in person searches themselves. Search fee: First search is free, then $9.00 per name per year and district or division. Required to search: name; also helpful: years to search. Civil records are computerized since 1986. Note: An online search request form is at http://198.173.15.31/forms/pdf_files/CivilForm.pdf. Mail turnaround time 1-2 days. Civil PAT goes back to 1985. Online case information is available at www.cookcountyclerkofcourt.org. Click on Online Case Info. Search by case number or name.
Criminal Name Search: Access: Mail, in person. Visitors must perform in person searches themselves. Search fee: $9.00 per name per year and district or division. Required to search: name; also helpful: DOB, SSN. Criminal records on computer, also plaintiff/defendant index on microfilm back to 1871. Note: Misdemeanor records (countywide) are also located at Circuit Court - Chicago Dist 1, Richard J. Daley Ctr, 50 W. Washington Ave, Rm 1006, Chicago, IL 60602. Mail turnaround time varies. Criminal PAT goes back to 10 years. Felony mail requests- download criminal search request form at http://198.173.15.31/forms/pdf_files/CriminalForm.pdf; mail to Clerk of Circuit Court, Crim Div - Records, 2650 S California, Chicago, 773-869-3147. Online results show middle initial.

Skokie District 2 Skokie Court Bldg, Rm 136, 5600 Old Orchard Rd, Skokie, IL 60076-1023; 847-470-7250; fax: 847-470-5049; 8:30AM-4:30PM (CST). *Felony, Misdemeanor, Civil Action under $100,000, Eviction, Small Claims.*
www.cookcountyclerkofcourt.org
General Information: Deerfield, Des Plaines, Evanston, Glencoe, Glenview, Golf, Kenilworth, Lincolnwood, Morton Grove, Niles, Northbrook, Northfield, Park Ridge, Prospect Heights, Skokie, Wilmette, Winnetka. All records are public. Will not fax documents. Court makes copy: $2.00 1st page, $.50 each add'l. Self serve copy: $.50 per page. Certification fee: $9.00 per doc. Payee: Clerk of Circuit Court. On personal checks write your SSN and driver's license numbers. Visa/MC accepted for traffic court only. Prepayment required.

Civil Name Search: Access: Phone, mail, online, in person. Visitors must perform in person searches themselves. Search fee: $9.00 per name per year and district or division. No fee if only one or two to search. Civil records computerized since 1983. Note: An online search request form is at http://198.173.15.31/forms/pdf_files/CivilForm.pdf. Mail turnaround time 1-3 weeks. Civil PAT goes back to 1988. 2 public access terminals are in the Info booth and 2 in Rm 136. Results include some addresses. Online case information is available at www.cookcountyclerkofcourt.org. Click on Online Case Info.
Criminal Name Search: Access: Mail, in person. Both court and visitors may perform in person name searches. Search fee: $9.00 per name per year per district; will only do 1 or 2 names per request. Required to search: name, years to search; also helpful: DOB, SSN. Note: Misdemeanor records (countywide) are also located at Circuit Court - Chicago Dist 1, Richard J. Daley Ctr, 50 W. Washington Ave, Rm 1006, Chicago, IL 60602. Mail turnaround time 1 week to 1 month. Criminal PAT goes back to same as civil. 2 public access terminals are in the Info booth and 2 in Rm 136. Felony mail requests- download criminal search request form at http://198.173.15.31/forms/pdf_files/CriminalForm.pdf; mail to Clerk of Circuit Court, Criminal Div - Records, 2650 S California, Chicago, IL 60608, 773-869-3147. Online results show middle initial.

Markham District 6 16501 S Kedzie Pkwy, Rm 119, Markham, IL 60428; 708-232-4551; fax: 708-232-4441; 8:30AM-4:30PM (CST). *Felony, Misdemeanor, Civil Action under $30,000, Eviction, Small Claims, Traffic, Domestic.*
www.cookcountyclerkofcourt.org
General Information: Will not fax documents. Court makes copy: $2.00 1st page, $.50 each add'l. Self serve copy: $.25 per page. Certification fee: $9.00 per doc. Payee: Clerk of Circuit Court. On personal checks write your SSN and driver's license numbers. No credit cards accepted for record searches. Prepayment required. Mail requests: SASE required.
Civil Name Search: Access: Mail, in person, online. Visitors must perform in person searches themselves. Search fee: $9.00 per name per year if assistance needed. Required to search: name. Civil records computerized since 1989. Note: An online search request form is at http://198.173.15.31/forms/pdf_files/CivilForm.pdf. Mail turnaround time 2 weeks. Civil PAT goes back to 1985. Results include name and case number. Online case information is available at www.cookcountyclerkofcourt.org. Click on Online Case Info.
Criminal Name Search: Access: Mail, in person. Visitors must perform in person searches themselves. Search fee: $9.00 per name per year if assistance needed. Misdemeanor records go back 10 years. Note: Misdemeanor records (county-wide) are also located at Circuit Court - Chicago Dist 1, Richard J. Daley Ctr, 50 W. Washington Ave, Rm 1006, Chicago, IL 60602. Mail turnaround time 2 weeks. Criminal PAT goes back to 1985. Felony mail requests- download criminal search request form at http://198.173.15.31/forms/pdf_files/CriminalForm.pdf; mail to Clerk of Circuit Court, Criminal Div - Records, 2650 S California, Chicago, IL 60608, 773-869-3147. Online results show middle initial.

Crawford County

Circuit Court PO Box 655, Robinson, IL 62454-0655; 618-544-3512; fax: 618-546-5628; 8AM-4PM (CST). *Felony, Misdemeanor, Civil, Eviction, Small Claims, Probate.*
www.crawfordcountycentral.com/circuitclerk/index.htm
General Information: No juvenile or adoption records released. Will fax documents $2.00 1st page, $.25 each add'l. Court makes copy: $1.00 1st page, $.50 second, then $.25 each add'l. Self serve copy: same. Certification fee: $5.00. Payee: Circuit Clerk. Personal checks accepted. No credit cards accepted. Prepayment required. Mail requests: SASE required.
Civil Name Search: Access: Fax, mail, in person, online. Both court and visitors may perform in person name searches. Search fee: $4.00 per name per year. Civil records on computer from 1992, index books from 1800s. Mail turnaround time 2-4 days. Civil PAT goes back to 1992. Access is free to civil, small claims, probate and traffic records at www.judici.com/courts/cases/index.jsp?court=IL017015J. Premium fee service also available.
Criminal Name Search: Access: Fax, mail, in person, online. Both court and visitors may perform in person name searches. Search fee: $4.00 per name per year. Required to search: name, years to search, DOB. Criminal records computerized from 1992, index books from 1800s. Mail turnaround time up to 1 week. Criminal PAT goes back to same as civil. Criminal access free at www.judici.com/courts/cases/index.jsp?court=IL017015J. Online results show middle initial, DOB.

Cumberland County

Circuit Court PO Box 145, 1 Courthouse Square, Toledo, IL 62468; 217-849-3601; fax: 217-849-2655; 8AM-4PM (CST). *Felony, Misdemeanor, Civil, Eviction, Small Claims, Probate.*
General Information: No juvenile or adoption records released. Will fax documents for $5.00 fee, paid in advance. Court makes copy: $2.00 1st page,

$.50 each next 19, then $.25 per add'l. Certification fee: $10.00. Payee: Clerk of Circuit Court. Only cashiers checks and money orders accepted. No credit cards accepted. Prepayment required. Mail requests: SASE required.

Civil Name Search: Access: Fax, mail, in person, online. Both court and visitors may perform in person name searches. Search fee: $6.00 per name per year. Civil records on computer from 1990, index books from 1885. Mail turnaround time up to 1 week. Civil PAT goes back to 1990. Online access free at www.judici.com/courts/cases/index.jsp?court=IL003015J. Premium/fee service is also available.

Criminal Name Search: Access: Fax, mail, in person, online. Both court and visitors may perform in person name searches. Search fee: $6.00 per name per year. Required to search: name, years to search; also helpful: DOB. Criminal records computerized from 1990, index books from 1885. Mail turnaround time up to 1 week. Criminal PAT goes back to 1990. Online access free at www.judici.com/courts/cases/index.jsp?court=IL003015J. Premium/fee service is also available.

De Kalb County

Circuit Court 133 W State St, Sycamore, IL 60178; criminal phone: 815-895-7138; civil phone: 815-895-7131; fax: 815-895-7140; 8:30AM-4:30PM (CST). *Felony, Misdemeanor, Civil, Eviction, Small Claims, Probate.* www.circuitclerk.org/

General Information: Online identifiers in results same as on public terminal. No juvenile or adoption records released. Will fax documents for $2.00,. Court makes copy: $1.00 1st page, $.50 each add'l. After 20 pages $.25 each. Certification fee: $5.00 plus copy fee. Payee: DeKalb County Circuit Clerk. Personal checks accepted. Visa/MC accepted via phone only. Prepayment required. Mail requests: SASE required.

Civil Name Search: Access: Mail, in person, online. Both court and visitors may perform in person name searches. Search fee: $4.00 per name per year. Required to search: name, years to search; also helpful: address. Civil records on computer since 1987, records go back to 1858. Mail turnaround time 2 weeks. Civil PAT goes back to 1987. Online access to civil court records is the same as criminal, see below.

Criminal Name Search: Access: Mail, in person, online. Both court and visitors may perform in person name searches. Search fee: $4.00 per name per year. Required to search: name, years to search, signed release; also helpful: address, DOB. Criminal records on computer since 9/91, on index books back 60 years. Mail turnaround time 2 weeks. Criminal PAT goes back to 1991. Online access via subscription requires a setup fee plus annual subscription of $240 for this county, or $300/yr for all participating IL counties - Champaign, DeKalb, Kendall, LaSalle, Madison, Sangamon, Will. Visit www.clericusmagnus.com or www.janojustice.com or call 800-250-9884 for details ands signup. Online results show middle initial, DOB.

De Witt County

Circuit Court 201 Washington St, Clinton, IL 61727; 217-935-7750; fax: 217-935-7759; 8:30AM-12; 1PM-4:30PM (CST). *Felony, Misdemeanor, Civil, Eviction, Small Claims, Probate.* www.dewittcountyill.com/clerk.htm

General Information: No juvenile or adoption records released. Will fax documents to local or toll free line. Court makes copy: $2.00 1st page, $.50 each add'l, after 20 $.25 each. Self serve copy: same. Certification fee: $10.00 per document plus copy fee. Payee: Clerk of Circuit Court. Only cashiers checks and money orders accepted. No credit cards accepted for record purchases. Prepayment required. Mail requests: SASE required.

Civil Name Search: Access: Mail, fax, in person, online. Both court and visitors may perform in person name searches. Search fee: $6.00 per name per year. Civil cases indexed by defendant. Civil records on computer from 1989, index books from 1839. Mail turnaround time 1-2 weeks. Civil PAT goes back to 1989. Online access is same as described under criminal records.

Criminal Name Search: Access: Mail, fax, in person, online. Both court and visitors may perform in person name searches. Search fee: $6.00 per name per year. Required to search: name, years to search, DOB. Criminal records computerized from 1989, index books from 1839. Mail turnaround time 1-2 weeks. Criminal PAT goes back to same as civil. Online access is free at www.judici.com/. A premium fee service is also available with multi-county search capabilities and other features. Case files are available from 1989.

Douglas County

Circuit Court PO Box 50, Tuscola, IL 61953; 217-253-2352; fax: 217-253-9006; 8:30AM-4:30PM (CST). *Felony, Misdemeanor, Civil, Eviction, Small Claims, Probate.*

General Information: No juvenile or adoption records released. Will fax documents $5.00 for 1st 4 pages; $1.00 each add'l. Court makes copy: $2.00 1st page, $.50 each add'l. After 20 pages $.25 each. Certification fee: $5.00 per doc. Payee: Douglas County Circuit Clerk. Only local personal checks accepted. No credit cards accepted. Prepayment required. Mail requests: SASE required.

Civil Name Search: Access: Phone, mail, in person, online. Both court and visitors may perform in person name searches. Search fee: $5.00 per name per year per computer search. Civil records on computer from 1989, index books from 1859. Mail turnaround time 1 week. Civil PAT goes back to 1989. Online access is same as described under criminal records.

Criminal Name Search: Access: Mail, in person, online. Both court and visitors may perform in person name searches. Search fee: $5.00 per name per year per computer search. Required to search: name, years to search: also helpful: DOB, SSN. Criminal records computerized from 1989, index books from 1859. Mail turnaround time 1 week. Criminal PAT goes back to same as civil. Terminal results also may show sex, height, weight, eyes. Online access is free at www.judici.com/. A premium fee service is also available with multi-county search capabilities and other features. Case files are available from 1989.

Du Page County

Circuit Court 505 N County Farm Rd, Wheaton, IL 60187; 630-407-8700; fax: 630-407-8575; 8:30AM-4:30PM (CST). *Felony, Misdemeanor, Civil, Eviction, Small Claims, Probate.* www.co.dupage.il.us/courtclerk/

General Information: No juvenile or adoption records released. Will not fax documents. Court makes copy: $2.00 1st page, $.50 each add'l. Certification fee: $6.00 per doc. Payee: Clerk of Circuit Court. Personal checks accepted. Visa/MC accepted. Prepayment required. Mail requests: SASE required.

Civil Name Search: Access: Mail, in person. Both court and visitors may perform in person name searches. Search fee: $6.00 per name per year. Civil records online from 1976, microfilm records back to 1939, index records back to 1839. All document files after 1/92 are on optical disk. Mail turnaround time 1 week. Civil PAT goes back to 1976.

Criminal Name Search: Access: Mail, in person. Both court and visitors may perform in person name searches. Search fee: $6.00 per name per year. Required to search: name, years to search, DOB. Criminal records online from 1976, microfilm records back to 1939, index records back to 1839. All document files after 1/01/92 are on optical disk. Mail turnaround time 1 week. Criminal PAT goes back to same as civil. Online results show name, DOB. Online results show birth year.

Edgar County

Circuit Court County Courthouse, 115 W Court, Paris, IL 61944; 217-466-7447; fax: 217-466-7443; 8AM-4PM (CST). *Felony, Misdemeanor, Civil, Eviction, Small Claims, Probate.*

General Information: No juvenile or adoption records released. Will not fax documents. Court makes copy: $2.00 1st page; $1.00 each add'l. Self serve copy: $.50 per page. Certification fee: $10.00 per cert. Payee: Circuit Clerk. Personal checks accepted. No credit cards accepted. Prepayment required. Mail requests: SASE required for civil.

Civil Name Search: Access: Phone, mail, in person, online. Both court and visitors may perform in person name searches. Search fee: $6.00 per page. Civil records on computer from 1992, index books from 1823. Mail turnaround time 2-3 days. Civil PAT goes back to 1992-3. Terminal results also show SSNs. Access is free to civil, small claims, probate and traffic records from 1992 forward at www.judici.com/courts/cases/case_search.jsp?court=IL023015J. A premium fee service also available.

Criminal Name Search: Access: In person, online. Both court and visitors may perform in person name searches. Search fee: $6.00 per page. Required to search: Name, years to search, DOB. Criminal records computerized from 1992, index books from 1880. Criminal PAT goes back to same as civil. Terminal results include SSN. Online access to criminal is the same as civil, above. Online results show middle initial, DOB, address.

Edwards County

Circuit Court County Courthouse, Albion, IL 62806; 618-445-2016; fax: 618-445-4943; 8AM-4PM (CST). *Felony, Misdemeanor, Civil, Eviction, Small Claims, Probate.*

General Information: No juvenile or adoption records released. Will fax documents to local or toll-free number $2.00 per page. Court makes copy: $.50 per page. Self serve copy: same. Certification fee: $5.00. Payee: Clerk of Circuit Court. Only cashiers checks and money orders accepted. No credit cards accepted. Prepayment required. Mail requests: SASE required.

Civil Name Search: Access: Mail, in person, online. Both court and visitors may perform in person name searches. Search fee: $4.00 per name per year. Civil cases indexed by defendant. Civil records on computer from 1988, books and index cards from 1815. Mail turnaround time 1 week. Civil PAT goes back to 1988. Online access is same as described under criminal records.

Criminal Name Search: Access: Mail, in person, online. Both court and visitors may perform in person name searches. Search fee: $4.00 per name per year. Required to search: name, years to search, DOB. Criminal records computerized from 1988, index books from 1815. Mail turnaround time 1

week. Criminal PAT goes back to same as civil. Online access is free at www.judici.com/. A premium fee service is also available with multi-county search capabilities and other features. Case files are available from 2000.

Effingham County

Circuit Court PO Box 586, 120 W Jefferson #101, Effingham, IL 62401; 217-342-4065; fax: 217-342-6183; 8AM-4PM (CST). *Felony, Misdemeanor, Civil, Small Claims, Probate.*

www.fourthcircuitil.com/

General Information: Probate fax is same as main fax number. Online identifiers in results same as on public terminal. No juvenile or adoption records released. Will not fax documents. Court makes copy: $1.00 1st page, $.50 each add'l. $.25 per page after 20. Certification fee: $6.00 per document. Payee: Effingham County Circuit Clerk. Pre-approved business checks accepted; no personal checks. Major credit cards accepted. Prepayment required. Mail requests: SASE required.

Civil Name Search: Access: Mail, in person, online. Both court and visitors may perform in person name searches. Search fee: $5.00 per name; also $5.00 per year if prior to 1988; $5.00 per page for computer generated info. Required to search: name, years to search; also helpful: address. Civil records on computer from 1988, index books from 1800s. Mail turnaround time 1 week. Civil PAT goes back to 1988. Access is free to civil, small claims, probate and traffic records from 1987 forward at www.judici.com/courts/cases/index.jsp?court=IL025015J. A premium fee service also available.

Criminal Name Search: Access: Mail, in person, online. Both court and visitors may perform in person name searches. Search fee: $5.00 per name; also $5.00 per year if prior to 1988; $5.00 per page for computer generated info. Required to search: name, years to search, DOB; also helpful: address. Criminal records computerized from 1988, index books from 1800s. Mail turnaround time 1 week. Criminal PAT goes back to same as civil. Criminal records access is free at www.judici.com/courts/cases/index.jsp?court=IL025015J.

Fayette County

Circuit Court 221 S 7th St, Vandalia, IL 62471; 618-283-5009; fax: 618-283-4490; 8AM-4PM (CST). *Felony, Misdemeanor, Civil, Eviction, Small Claims, Probate.*

www.fourthcircuitil.com/

General Information: No juvenile, impounded or adoption records released. Will fax documents. Court makes copy: $1.00 1st page, $.50 each add'l. Self serve copy: $.25 per page. Certification fee: $2.00. Payee: Clerk of Circuit Court. Business checks accepted. No credit cards accepted. Prepayment required. Mail requests: SASE required.

Civil Name Search: Access: Phone, mail, fax, in person, online. Both court and visitors may perform in person name searches. Search fee: $5.00 per name per year. Civil cases indexed by defendant. Civil records on computer from 1988, index books from 1800s. Mail turnaround time 1 month. Civil PAT goes back to 1989. Access court index and records from 1988 forward free at www.judici.com/courts/cases/case_search.jsp?court=IL026015J.

Criminal Name Search: Access: Phone, mail, fax, in person, online. Both court and visitors may perform in person name searches. Search fee: $5.00 per name per year. Required to search: name, years to search, DOB. Criminal records computerized from 1988, index books from 1800s. Mail turnaround time 1 month. Criminal PAT goes back to 1989. Access to criminal records is same as civil, see above. Online results show middle initial, DOB, address.

Ford County

Circuit Court 200 W State St, Paxton, IL 60957; 217-379-9420; fax: 217-379-9429; 8:30AM-4:30PM (CST). *Felony, Misdemeanor, Civil, Eviction, Small Claims, Probate.*

General Information: Probate fax is same as main fax number. No juvenile or adoption records released. Will fax documents to local or toll free line. Court makes copy: $1.00 1st page, $.50 each add'l; after 20- $.25 each add'l. Self serve copy: same. Certification fee: $5.00 per certification. Payee: Clerk of Circuit Court. Personal checks accepted. No credit cards accepted. Prepayment required. Mail requests: SASE required.

Civil Name Search: Access: Mail, fax, in person, online. Both court and visitors may perform in person name searches. Search fee: $4.00 per name per year. Civil cases indexed by defendant. Civil index on docket books from 1800s; on computer back to 3/2000. Mail turnaround time 2 days. Civil PAT goes back to 3/2000. Records back to 1980s may be available. Online access is same as described under criminal records.

Criminal Name Search: Access: Mail, fax, in person, online. Both court and visitors may perform in person name searches. Search fee: $4.00 per name per year. Required to search: name, years to search, DOB (signed release if for juvenile). Criminal records indexed in books from 1800s; on computer back to 3/2000. Mail turnaround time 2 days. Criminal PAT goes back to same as civil. Some records back to 1980s may be

available. Online access is free at www.judici.com/. A premium fee service is also available with multi-county search capabilities and other features. Criminal and civil case files are available from March 2000, traffic records form 1989.

Franklin County

Circuit Court County Courthouse, PO Box 485, Benton, IL 62812; 618-439-2011; fax: 618-439-4119; 8AM-4PM (CST). *Felony, Misdemeanor, Civil, Small Claims, Probate, Eviction, Traffic.*

General Information: Traffic 618-438-6731. Online identifiers in results same as on public terminal. No juvenile or adoption records released. Will fax non-certified documents to local or toll-free number. Court makes copy: $1.00 1st page, $.50 each add'l. Self serve copy: same. Certification fee: $5.00 per cert. Payee: Franklin County Circuit Clerk. Only cashiers checks and money orders accepted. No credit cards accepted. Prepayment required. Mail requests: SASE required.

Civil Name Search: Access: Fax, mail, in person, online. Both court and visitors may perform in person name searches. Search fee: $5.00 per name per year. Civil records on computer from 1987, index books from 1843. Civil PAT goes back to 1987. Access is free to civil, small claims, probate and traffic at www.judici.com/courts/cases/index.jsp?court=IL028015J. A premium fee service also available.

Criminal Name Search: Access: Fax, mail, in person, online. Both court and visitors may perform in person name searches. Search fee: $5.00 per name per year. Required to search: name, years to search, DOB. Criminal records computerized from 1987, index books from 1843. Note: Results also include address. Criminal PAT goes back to same as civil. Index access free at www.judici.com/courts/cases/index.jsp?court=IL028015J. Online results show middle initial, DOB.

Fulton County

Circuit Court PO Box 152, Lewistown, IL 61542; 309-547-3041; fax: 309-547-3674; 8AM-4PM (CST). *Felony, Misdemeanor, Civil, Eviction, Small Claims, Probate.*

www.9thjudicial.org/Fulton/indexFulton.htm

General Information: Probate fax is same as main fax number. No juvenile, impounded or adoption records released. Court makes copy: $2.00 1st page, $.50 each add'l; $.25 each after 19 pgs. Certification fee: $3.00. Payee: Fulton County Circuit Clerk. Business checks accepted. Visa/MC accepted. Prepayment required. Mail requests: SASE required.

Civil Name Search: Access: Phone, mail, fax, in person. Both court and visitors may perform in person name searches. Search fee: $5.00 per name per year. Civil records on computer back to 1990, index books from 1900. Mail turnaround time 2-3 days. Civil PAT goes back to 1992.

Criminal Name Search: Access: Mail, in person. Both court and visitors may perform in person name searches. Search fee: $5.00 per name per year. Required to search: name, years to search; also helpful: DOB. Criminal records computerized from 1990, index books from 1879. Mail turnaround time 1-2 days; older, archived records require add'l 2-3 days. Criminal PAT goes back to 1992.

Gallatin County

Circuit Court County Courthouse, PO Box 249, Shawneetown, IL 62984; 618-269-3140; fax: 618-269-4324; 8AM-N, 1-4PM (CST). *Felony, Misdemeanor, Civil, Eviction, Small Claims, Probate.*

General Information: Because of a "computer crash" the electronic index was rebuilt and only goes back to 2009. No juvenile or adoption records released. Will fax documents $2.00 1st page, $1.00 ea. add'l page. Court makes copy: $.25 per page. Self serve copy: same. Certification fee: $3.00 per cert plus copy fee. Payee: Clerk of Circuit Court. Business checks accepted. No credit cards accepted. Prepayment required. Mail requests: SASE required.

Civil Name Search: Access: Fax, mail, in person. Both court and visitors may perform in person name searches. Search fee: $6.00 per name, per year. Civil index on docket books from 1800s; computerized records since 2009. Mail turnaround time 1 week. Civil PAT goes back to 2009.

Criminal Name Search: Access: Fax, mail, in person. Both court and visitors may perform in person name searches. Search fee: $6.00 per name, per year. Required to search: name, years to search, DOB, signed release. Criminal records indexed in books from 1800s; computerized records since 2009. Mail turnaround time 1 week. Criminal PAT goes back to 2009.

Greene County

Circuit Court 519 N Main, County Courthouse, Carrollton, IL 62016; 217-942-3421; fax: 217-942-5431; 8AM-4PM (CST). *Felony, Misdemeanor, Civil, Eviction, Small Claims, Probate.*

General Information: No juvenile or adoption records released. Will fax documents $.25 per page. Court makes copy: $.25 per page. Self serve copy: $.10 per page. Certification fee: $5.00. Payee: Clerk of Circuit Court. Personal checks accepted. No credit cards accepted. Prepayment required. Mail requests: SASE required.

Civil Name Search: Access: Phone, mail, in person. Both court and visitors may perform in person name searches. Search fee: $5.00 per name. Civil index on docket books from 1830s; computerized since 2000. Mail turnaround time 1-2 days. Civil PAT goes back to 2000.

Criminal Name Search: Access: Phone, fax, mail, in person. Both court and visitors may perform in person name searches. Search fee: $5.00 per name. Required to search: name, years to search, DOB. Criminal records indexed in books from 1875; computerized since 2000. Note: No felony searches by phone. Include signed release with felony search requests. Mail turnaround time 1-2 days. Criminal PAT goes back to same as civil.

Grundy County

Circuit Court PO Box 707, Morris, IL 60450; 815-941-3256; fax: 815-941-3265; 8AM-4:30PM (CST). *Felony, Misdemeanor, Civil, Eviction, Small Claims, Probate.*

General Information: Probate fax is same as main fax number. No juvenile or adoption records released. Will not fax documents. Court makes copy: $2.00 1st page; $.50 each add'l. Certification fee: $4.00 per document. Payee: Clerk of Circuit Court. Personal checks accepted. Major credit cards accepted; add $5.00 transaction fee. Prepayment required. Mail requests: SASE required.

Civil Name Search: Access: Mail, in person, online. Both court and visitors may perform in person name searches. Search fee: $5.00 per name per year. Civil records on computer back to 1988. Mail turnaround time 1-2 days. Civil PAT goes back to 1988. Access is free online to civil, small claims, probate and traffic records at www.judici.com/courts/cases/case_search.jsp?court=IL004015J. Premium fee service also available.

Criminal Name Search: Access: Mail, in person, online. Both court and visitors may perform in person name searches. Search fee: $5.00 per name per year. Required to search: name, years to search, DOB, signed release. Criminal records computerized from 1988. Mail turnaround time 1-2 days. Criminal PAT goes back to 1988. Online access same as civil records.

Hamilton County

Circuit Court 100 S Jackson, Courthouse, McLeansboro, IL 62859; 618-643-3224; fax: 618-643-3455; 8AM-4:30PM (CST). *Felony, Misdemeanor, Civil, Eviction, Small Claims, Probate.*

General Information: Probate is a separate index at this address. Probate fax is same as main fax number. Online identifiers in results same as on public terminal. No juvenile or adoption records released. Will fax documents. Court makes copy: $2.00 first page, $.50 ea for next 19, then $.25 remaining pages. Self serve copy: same. Certification fee: $10.00 plus copy fee. Payee: Clerk of Circuit Court. No personal checks or credit cards accepted. Prepayment required. Mail requests: SASE required.

Civil Name Search: Access: Mail, in person, online. Both court and visitors may perform in person name searches. Search fee: $6.00 per name per year. Civil index on docket books from 1800s; computer records go back to 1990. Mail turnaround time 1-2 days. Civil PAT goes back to 1//2002. Online access is same as described under criminal records.

Criminal Name Search: Access: Mail, in person, online. Both court and visitors may perform in person name searches. Search fee: $6.00 per name per year. Required to search: name, years to search, DOB. Criminal records indexed in books from 1800s; computer records go back to 1990. Mail turnaround time 1-2 days. Criminal PAT goes back to same as civil. Online access is free at www.judici.com/. A premium fee service is also available with multi-county search capabilities and other features. Case files are available from 2000. Online results show middle initial, DOB.

Hancock County

Circuit Court PO Box 189, 500 Main St, #8, Carthage, IL 62321; 217-357-2616; fax: 217-357-2231; 8AM-4PM (CST). *Felony, Misdemeanor, Civil, Eviction, Small Claims, Probate.*

www.hancockcountycourthouse.org/

General Information: No juvenile or adoption records released. Will fax documents no fee. Court makes copy: $2.00 1st page, $.50 each add'l. Certification fee: $3.00. Payee: Clerk of Circuit Court. Personal checks accepted, if local bank. Prepayment required. Mail requests: SASE required.

Civil Name Search: Access: Fax, mail, in person. Both court and visitors may perform in person name searches. Search fee: $5.00 per name per year. Civil records on computer from 1992, index books from 1800s. Note: For fax searches, they will only search to determine if a record exists. Mail turnaround time 1 week. Civil PAT available.

Criminal Name Search: Access: Fax, mail, in person. Both court and visitors may perform in person name searches. Search fee: $5.00 per name. Required to search: name, years to search, DOB. Criminal records computerized from 1992, index books from 1970, archived to 1800s. Note: For phone and fax searches, they will only search to determine if a record exists. Mail turnaround time 1 week. Criminal PAT available.

Hardin County

Circuit Court PO Box 308, Main & Market Sts, County Courthouse, Elizabethtown, IL 62931; 618-287-2735; fax: 618-287-2713; 8AM-4PM (CST). *Felony, Misdemeanor, Civil, Eviction, Small Claims, Probate.*

General Information: Probate fax is same as main fax number. No juvenile or adoption records released. Fee to fax out file $2.00 for 1st 2 pages; $.50 each add'l page. Court makes copy: $1.00 1st page; $.50 each add'l. Certification fee: $6.00 per document plus copy fee; certified judgment is $10.00 plus copy fee. Payee: Circuit Clerk. Business check, cashiers check or money order accepted. No credit cards accepted. Prepayment required. Mail requests: SASE required.

Civil Name Search: Access: Mail, fax, in person. Both court and visitors may perform in person name searches. Search fee: $6.00 per name per year. Civil records on computer back to 2000/2002; on index books from 1800s. Mail turnaround time 1 week.

Criminal Name Search: Access: Mail, fax, in person. Both court and visitors may perform in person name searches. Search fee: $6.00 per name per year. Required to search: name, years to search, DOB. Criminal records computerized from 2000/2002; on index books from 1800s. Mail turnaround time 1 week.

Henderson County

Circuit Court County Courthouse, PO Box 546, Oquawka, IL 61469; 309-867-3121; fax: 309-867-3207; 8AM-4PM (CST). *Felony, Misdemeanor, Civil, Eviction, Small Claims, Probate.*

General Information: No juvenile or adoption records released. Will not fax documents. Court makes copy: $2.00 1st page; $.50 each for 2-19 pages; then $.25 per page. Certification fee: $3.00 1st page plus $.50 each add'l. Payee: Clerk of Circuit Court. Personal checks accepted. No credit cards accepted. Prepayment required. Mail requests: SASE required.

Civil Name Search: Access: Phone, mail, in person. Both court and visitors may perform in person name searches. Search fee: $5.00 per name per year. Civil records on computer from 1991, index books from 1800s. Note: Any search information given over the phone must be pre-paid with a money order. Mail turnaround time 1 day to 1 week. Civil PAT goes back to 1991.

Criminal Name Search: Access: Phone, mail, in person. Both court and visitors may perform in person name searches. Search fee: $5.00 per name per year. Required to search: name, years to search, DOB; also helpful: SSN. Criminal records computerized from 1991, index books from 1800s. Note: Any search information given over the phone must be pre-paid with a money order. Mail turnaround time 1 day to 1 week. Criminal PAT goes back to same as civil.

Henry County

Circuit Court 307 W Center St, Henry County Courthouse, Cambridge, IL 61238; 309-937-3572; fax: 309-937-3990; 8AM-4:30PM (CST). *Felony, Misdemeanor, Civil, Eviction, Small Claims, Probate.*

www.henrycty.com/codepartments/CircuitClerk/index.html

General Information: Probate is a separate index at this same address. Probate fax is same as main fax number. Online identifiers in results same as on public terminal. No juvenile or adoption records released. Will fax documents to local or toll free line. Court makes copy: $2.00 1st page, $.50 each add'l. Document hard copy from automated system- $6.00. Certification fee: $6.00 per page plus copy fee; Exemplifications are $6.00. Payee: Clerk of Circuit Court. Only cashiers checks and money orders accepted. No credit cards accepted. Prepayment required. Mail requests: SASE required.

Civil Name Search: Access: Mail, in person. Both court and visitors may perform in person name searches. Search fee: $6.00 per name per year. Civil cases indexed by defendant. Civil records on computer from 1989, index books from 1800s. Mail turnaround time 2 weeks. Civil PAT goes back to 1989. Terminal results may include address.

Criminal Name Search: Access: Mail, in person, online. Both court and visitors may perform in person name searches. Search fee: $6.00 per name per year. Required to search: name, middle initial, years to search, DOB; also helpful-last known address. Criminal records computerized from 1989, index books from 1800s. Mail turnaround time 2 weeks. Criminal PAT goes back to same as civil. Online access is free at www.judici.com/. A premium fee service is also available with multi-county search capabilities and other features. Case files are available from 1989.

Iroquois County

Circuit Court 550 S 10th St, Watseka, IL 60970; 815-432-6950; fax: 815-432-9333; 8:30AM-4:30PM (CST). *Felony, Misdemeanor, Civil, Eviction, Small Claims, Probate.*

www.judici.com/courts/index.jsp?court=IL038025J

General Information: No juvenile or adoption records released. Fee to fax out file $6.00 per document. Court makes copy: $1.00 first page, $.50 ea add'l. Certification fee: $2.00. Payee: Clerk of Circuit Court. Local personal checks accepted. Visa/MC, Discover, debit cards accepted; add $5.00 usage surcharge. Prepayment required. Mail requests: SASE required.

Civil Name Search: Access: Fax, mail, in person, online. Both court and visitors may perform in person name searches. Search fee: $6.00 per name per year. Civil cases indexed by defendant. Civil index on docket books from 1900, computerized since 1993. Mail turnaround time 1-2 days. Civil PAT goes back to 1993. Search cases free online at www.judici.com/courts/cases/index.jsp?court=IL038025J. A premium fee service is also available.

Criminal Name Search: Access: Fax, mail, in person, online. Both court and visitors may perform in person name searches. Search fee: $6.00 per name per year. Required to search: name, years to search, DOB. Criminal records indexed in books from 1820, computerized since 1993. Mail turnaround time 1-2 days. Criminal PAT goes back to 1988. Results includes disposition if available. Access criminal records free at www.judici.com/courts/cases/index.jsp?court=IL038025J. Online results show name, DOB.

Jackson County

Circuit Court PO Drawer 730, 1001 Walnut, County Courthouse, Murphysboro, IL 62966; 618-687-7300; 8AM-4PM, til 6PM Tues (CST). *Felony, Misdemeanor, Civil, Eviction, Small Claims, Probate.* www.circuitclerk.co.jackson.il.us/index-2.html

General Information: Online identifiers in results same as on public terminal. No juvenile or adoption records released. May fax documents if not busy. Court makes copy: $1.00 1st page, $.50 each add'l. Certification fee: $10.00 per doc. Payee: Circuit Clerk. Personal checks accepted. No credit cards accepted. Prepayment required. Mail requests: SASE required.

Civil Name Search: Access: Mail, in person, online. Both court and visitors may perform in person name searches. Search fee: $4.00 per name per year. Civil records on computer from 1986, index books from 1860. Mail turnaround time 1-2 weeks. Civil PAT goes back to 1970. Online access is same as described under criminal records.

Criminal Name Search: Access: Mail, in person, online. Both court and visitors may perform in person name searches. Search fee: $4.00 per name per year. Criminal records computerized from 1986, index books from 1860. Mail turnaround time 1-2 weeks. Criminal PAT goes back to same as civil. Online access is free at www.judici.com/. A premium fee service is also available with multi-county search capabilities and other features. Case files are available from 1985. Online results show middle initial, DOB.

Jasper County

Circuit Court 100 W Jourdan St, Newton, IL 62448; 618-783-2524; fax: 618-783-8626; 8AM-4PM (CST). *Felony, Misdemeanor, Civil, Eviction, Small Claims, Probate.* www.fourthcircuitil.com/

General Information: Probate is a separate index at this same address. Probate fax is same as main fax number. No juvenile or adoption records released. Fee to fax out file $2.00 each. Court makes copy: $1.00 1st page; $.50 each add'l. Certification fee: $6.00 per cert plus copy fee. Payee: Clerk of Circuit Court. Personal checks accepted. No credit cards accepted. Prepayment required. Mail requests: SASE required.

Civil Name Search: Access: Mail, in person. Both court and visitors may perform in person name searches. Search fee: $5.00 per name. Required to search: name, years to search; also helpful: address. Civil records on computer from 1988, index books from 1835. Mail turnaround time 1 week.

Criminal Name Search: Access: Mail, in person. Both court and visitors may perform in person name searches. Search fee: $5.00 per name. Required to search: name, years to search, DOB, sex, signed release. Criminal records computerized from 1988, index books from 1835. Mail turnaround time 1 week.

Jefferson County

Circuit Court PO Box 1266, 100 10th St, Mt Vernon, IL 62864; 618-244-8008; fax: 618-244-8029; 8AM-4PM (CST). *Felony, Misdemeanor, Civil, Eviction, Small Claims, Probate.*

General Information: Sealed records not released. Will fax documents $.25 per page plus phone charge. Court makes copy: $.50 per page, up to 100, then $.25 per page over 100. No certification fee . Payee: Clerk of Circuit Court. Only cashiers checks and money orders accepted. No credit cards accepted. Prepayment required. Mail requests: SASE required.

Civil Name Search: Access: Phone, fax, mail, in person, online. Both court and visitors may perform in person name searches. Search fee: $8.00. Civil cases indexed by defendant. Civil records on computer back to 1988, index books from 1800s. Note: Fax requests must be followed by original by mail before being processed. Mail turnaround time 1-2 weeks. Civil PAT goes back to 1988. Online access is same as described under criminal records.

Criminal Name Search: Access: Phone, fax, mail, in person, online. Both court and visitors may perform in person name searches. Search fee: $8.00. Required to search: name, years to search, DOB, SSN. Criminal records computerized from 1988, index books from 1800s. Mail turnaround time 1-2 weeks. Criminal PAT goes back to same as civil. Online access is free at www.judici.com/. A premium fee service is also available with multi-county search capabilities and other features. Case files are available from 1987.

Jersey County

Circuit Court 201 W Pearl St, Jerseyville, IL 62052; 618-498-5571; fax: 618-498-6128; 8AM-4PM (CST). *Felony, Misdemeanor, Civil, Eviction, Small Claims, Probate.* www.jerseycounty-il.us

General Information: No juvenile or adoption records released. Will fax documents for fee, depends on number of pages. Call to make arrangements. Court makes copy: $.50 per page. Self serve copy: $.25 per page. Certification fee: $2 for 1st 2 pages; $.50 each add'l. Payee: Clerk of Circuit Court. Personal checks accepted. No credit cards accepted. Prepayment required. Mail requests: SASE required.

Civil Name Search: Access: Fax, mail, in person, online. Both court and visitors may perform in person name searches. Search fee: $6.00 per name. Civil cases indexed by defendant. Civil records on computer from 1991, index books from 1800s. Mail turnaround time 1 week. Public use terminal available, records go back to 1990. Court records may be accessed free at www.jerseycounty-il.us by clicking on Court Record Search. Also, online access is free at www.judici.com/. A premium fee service is also available with multi-county search capabilities and other features. Case files are available from 1990.

Criminal Name Search: Access: Fax, mail, in person, online. Both court and visitors may perform in person name searches. Search fee: $6.00 per name. Required to search: name, years to search, DOB. Criminal records computerized from 1991, index books from 1800s. Mail turnaround time 1 week. Public use terminal available, crim records go back to same. Online access to criminal is the same as civil - both systems are operational. Online results show middle initial.

Jo Daviess County

Circuit Court 330 N Bench St, Galena, IL 61036; 815-777-2295/0037; criminal phone: 815-777-2295; civil phone: 815-777-0037; probate phone: 815-777-0037; fax: 815-776-9146; 8AM-4PM (CST). *Felony, Misdemeanor, Civil, Eviction, Small Claims, Probate.* www.jodaviess.org/

General Information: Online identifiers in results same as on public terminal. No juvenile or adoption records released. Will fax documents; fee is same as copy fee; to toll- free number only. Court makes copy: $.25 per page. Self serve copy: same. Certification fee: $10.00 per cert includes copies. Payee: Circuit Clerk. Business checks accepted. Major credit cards accepted. Prepayment required. Mail requests: SASE required.

Civil Name Search: Access: Mail, in person, online. Visitors must perform in person searches themselves. No search fee. Civil records on computer since 1992, on index books from 1960; will and probate back to 1850. Note: Clerk accepts mail requests to perform a probate search for $6.00, paid in advance. Civil PAT goes back to 1992. Online access is same as described under criminal records.

Criminal Name Search: Access: Mail, in person, online. Both court and visitors may perform in person name searches. Search fee: $6.00 per name. Fee is for 1992 to present. Prior to 1992 $6.00 per name per year. Required to search: name, years to search, DOB. Criminal records on computer since 1992, on index books from 1960. Mail turnaround time 1 week. Criminal PAT goes back to same as civil. Online access is free at www.judici.com/. A premium fee service is also available with multi-county search capabilities and other features. Case files are available from 1992. Online results show middle initial.

Johnson County

Circuit Court PO Box 517, Vienna, IL 62995; 618-658-4751; fax: 618-658-2908; 8AM-4PM (CST). *Felony, Misdemeanor, Civil, Eviction, Small Claims, Probate.*

General Information: Probate fax is same as main fax number. No juvenile or adoption records released. Will fax documents if prepaid. Court makes copy: $.50 per page. Self serve copy: same. Certification fee: $10.00 per certification. Payee: Circuit Clerk. Business checks accepted. No credit cards accepted. Prepayment required. Mail requests: SASE required.

Civil Name Search: Access: Mail, in person, online. Both court and visitors may perform in person name searches. Search fee: $6.00 per name per year. Civil records on computer from 1987, index books from 1930s. Mail turnaround time 1 week. Civil PAT goes back to 1987. Online access is same as described under criminal records.

Criminal Name Search: Access: Mail, in person, online. Both court and visitors may perform in person name searches. Search fee: $6.00 per case per year. Required to search: name, years to search, DOB. Criminal records computerized from 1987, index books from 1930s. Mail turnaround time 1 week. Criminal PAT goes back to same as civil. Online access is free at www.judici.com/. A premium fee service is also available with multi-county search capabilities and other features. Case files are available from April 1987.

Kane County

Circuit Court PO Box 112, 540 S Randall Rd, Geneva, IL 60134; 630-232-3413; fax: 630-208-2172; 8:30AM-4:30PM M,T,TH,F; open til 7PM W (CST). *Felony, Misdemeanor, Civil, Eviction, Small Claims, Probate.*
www.cic.co.kane.il.us

General Information: Court physical location is in St Charles. No juvenile, mental health or adoption records released. Will fax documents $2.00 1st page, $.50 each add'l. Court makes copy: $2.00 1st page, $.50 each next 19, then $.25 per add'l. Certification fee: $4.00. Judgment orders certification fee $10.00. Payee: Clerk of Circuit Court. Personal checks accepted. Credit cards accepted. Prepayment required. Mail requests: SASE required.

Civil Name Search: Access: Phone, fax, mail, in person, online. Both court and visitors may perform in person name searches. Search fee: $6.00 per name per year. Civil records on computer from 1984, index books from 1800s. Mail turnaround time 2 days. Civil PAT goes back to 1984. Multiple public access terminals are available. Online access to civil court records is the same as criminal, see below. Electronic results may include DL number

Criminal Name Search: Access: Phone, fax, mail, in person, online. Both court and visitors may perform in person name searches. Search fee: $6.00 per name per year. Required to search: name, years to search, DOB. Criminal records computerized from 1986, index books from 1800s. Mail turnaround time 2 days. Criminal PAT goes back to same as civil. Multiple public access terminals are available. Results may include DL number. Online access at www.cic.co.kane.il.us/OnlineCourtInformation.php. User name and password is PUBLIC. Visit www.clericusmagnus.com for details and signup. Online results show middle initial, DOB.

Kankakee County

Circuit Court 450 E Court St, County Courthouse, Kankakee, IL 60901; 815-937-2905; fax: 815-939-8830; 8:30AM-4:30PM (CST). *Felony, Misdemeanor, Civil, Eviction, Small Claims, Probate.*
www.co.kankakee.il.us/circuitclerk.html

General Information: No juvenile, impounded, mental health, expunged or adoption records released. Will not fax documents. Court makes copy: $2.00 1st page, $.50 each add'l. Certification fee: $10.00 per certification. Payee: Kankakee Circuit Court. No personal checks or credit cards accepted. Prepayment required. Mail requests: SASE required.

Civil Name Search: Access: Mail, in person. Both court and visitors may perform in person name searches. Search fee: $5.00 per name per year. Civil records on computer from 1990, index books from 1800s. Mail turnaround time 1-2 weeks. Civil PAT goes back to 1990.

Criminal Name Search: Access: Mail, in person. Both court and visitors may perform in person name searches. Search fee: $5.00 per name per year. Required to search: name, years to search, DOB. Criminal records computerized from 1990, index books from 1800s. Mail turnaround time 1-2 weeks. Criminal PAT goes back to same as civil.

Kendall County

Circuit Court Kendall County Courthouse, 807 W John St, Yorkville, IL 60560; criminal phone: 630-553-4184; civil phone: 630-553-4183; fax: 630-553-4964; 8AM-4:30PM (CST). *Felony, Misdemeanor, Civil, Eviction, Small Claims, Probate.*

General Information: Traffic/DUI at 630-553-4185. No juvenile or adoption records released. Will not fax out documents. Court makes copy: $2.00 1st page, $.50 each add'l. $4.00 per page when hard copy printouts are maintained on an automated medium. Certification fee: $4.00 per doc. Payee: Clerk of Circuit Court. Personal checks accepted. No credit cards accepted. Prepayment required. Mail requests: SASE required.

Civil Name Search: Access: Mail, in person, online. Both court and visitors may perform in person name searches. Search fee: $4.00 per name per year. Civil records on computer since 1992, on index books from 1800s. Mail turnaround time 2-3 days. Civil PAT goes back to 1992. Results include name and case number. Online access to civil court records is the same as criminal, see below.

Criminal Name Search: Access: Mail, in person, online. Both court and visitors may perform in person name searches. Search fee: $4.00 per name per year. Required to search: name, years to search, DOB. Criminal records on computer since 1992, on index books from 1800s. Mail turnaround time 2-3 days. Criminal PAT goes back to same as civil. Online access via subscription requires a setup fee plus annual subscription of $240 for this county, or $300/yr for all participating IL counties - Champaign, DeKalb, Kendall, LaSalle, Madison, Sangamon, Will. Visit www.clericusmagnus.com or www.janojustice.com or call 800-250-9884 for details ands signup.

Knox County

Circuit Court 200 S Cherry St, Galesburg, IL 61401; 309-343-3121, 345-3817-Clerk; fax: 309-345-0098; 8:30AM-4:30PM (CST). *Felony, Misdemeanor, Civil, Eviction, Small Claims, Probate.*

General Information: Search fee includes civil and criminal indexes. Court plans to offer online access soon. No juvenile or adoption records released. Will fax back documents no add'l fee. Court makes copy: $2.00 1st page, $.50 each add'l.A self-serve copier is located in the basement. Certification fee: $3.00 per page plus copy fee. Payee: Clerk of Circuit Court. Personal checks accepted. No credit cards accepted. Prepayment required.

Civil Name Search: Access: Fax, mail, in person. Both court and visitors may perform in person name searches. Search fee: $5.00 per year per name. Civil index on docket books from 1800s. Mail turnaround time 1 week. Civil PAT goes back to 2000. Public terminal in Law Library in basement.

Criminal Name Search: Access: Fax, mail, in person. Both court and visitors may perform in person name searches. Search fee: $5.00 per year per name. Required to search: name, years to search, DOB, sex. Criminal records indexed in books from 1800s. Mail turnaround time 1 week. Criminal PAT goes back to same as civil. Address does not appear on all terminal results.

La Salle County

Circuit Court - Civil Division 119 W Madison St, #201, Ottawa, IL 61350-0617; 815-434-8671; fax: 815-433-9198; 8AM-4:30PM (CST). *Civil, Eviction, Small Claims, Probate.*
www.lasallecounty.com

General Information: Online identifiers in results same as on public terminal. No juvenile or adoption records released. Will not fax documents. Court makes copy: $2.00 1st page, $.50 each add'l. Certification fee: $6.00 per doc. Payee: Clerk of Circuit Court. In-state personal checks accepted; out-of-state checks held 10 days. Visa/MC accepted, 4% transaction fee added. Prepayment required. Mail requests: SASE required.

Civil Name Search: Access: Mail, online, in person. Both court and visitors may perform in person name searches. Search fee: $6.00 per name per year. Some records on computer since late 1980s; prior records on index books from 1800s. Public use terminal has civil records back to 1989. Results include name and case number. A vendor provides online access via subscription is a $59 setup fee plus annual subscription of $240 for this county, or $300/yr for all participating counties - Champaign, Dekalb, Kendall, Madison, Sangamon, Will and Winnebago. Visit www.clericusmagnus.com/.

Circuit Court - Criminal Division 707 Etna Rd, #141, Ottawa, IL 61360; 815-434-8271; fax: 815-434-8299; 8AM-4:30PM (CST). *Felony, Misdemeanor.*
www.lasallecounty.com

General Information: Online identifiers in results same as on public terminal. No juvenile or adoption records released. Will not fax out documents. Court makes copy: $2.00 1st page, $.50 each add'l. Certification fee: $6.00 per doc. Payee: Clerk of Circuit Court. Personal checks accepted. Credit cards accepted; $3.00 usage fee added or 4% if over $100 in a transaction. Prepayment required. Mail requests: SASE required.

Criminal Name Search: Access: In person, online. Visitors must perform in person searches themselves. Required to search: name, years to search; also helpful: DOB. Criminal records go back to 1985. Public use terminal has crim records back to 1984. Online access via subscription requires a setup fee plus annual subscription of $240 for this county, or $300/yr for all participating IL counties - Champaign, DeKalb, Kendall, LaSalle, Madison, Sangamon, Will. Visit www.clericusmagnus.com or www.janojustice.com or call 800-250-9884 for details and signup. Online results show middle initial, DOB.

Lake County

Circuit Court 18 N County St, Waukegan, IL 60085; 847-377-3380; criminal phone: 847-377-3278; civil phone: 847-377-3209; 8:30AM-5PM (CST). *Felony, Misdemeanor, Civil, Eviction, Small Claims, Probate.*
www.lakecountyil.gov/CircuitClerk/Pages/Default.aspx

General Information: No juvenile or adoption records released. Will not fax documents. Court makes copy: $2.00 1st pg, $.50 each add'l to 19, then $.25 ea. Self serve copy: same. Certification fee: $6.00 per doc plus copy fee. Payee: Clerk of the Circuit Court. No personal checks accepted. Discover cards accepted in person only. Prepayment required. Mail requests: SASE required.

Civil Name Search: Access: Mail, in person. Both court and visitors may perform in person name searches. Search fee: $6.00 per name per year. Civil records on computer or microfiche from 1968, microfiche 2003 back, and index books from 1800s. Mail turnaround time 1-2 days. Civil PAT goes back to 1985.

Criminal Name Search: Access: Mail, in person. Both court and visitors may perform in person name searches. Search fee: $6.00 per name per year. Required to search: name, years to search, DOB. Criminal records on computer or microfiche from 1968, index books from 1800s. Mail turnaround time 1-2 days. Criminal PAT goes back to same as civil.

Lawrence County

Circuit Court County Courthouse, 1100 State St, Lawrenceville, IL 62439; 618-943-2815; fax: 618-943-5205; 8AM-4PM (CST). *Felony, Misdemeanor, Civil, Eviction, Small Claims, Probate.*

General Information: Probate is a separate index at this same address. No juvenile or adoption records released. Will fax documents $1.00 1st page, $.50 each add'l; after 20 pages, will copy for $.25 per page. Court makes copy: $1.00 1st page, $.50 each add'l; after 20- $.25 each add'l. Certification fee: $5.00 plus copy fee (if only one or two pages, no copy charge). Payee: Clerk of Circuit Court. Only cashiers checks and money orders accepted. No credit cards accepted. Prepayment required. Mail requests: SASE required.

Civil Name Search: Access: Mail, in person, online. Both court and visitors may perform in person name searches. Search fee: $4.00 per name per year. Required to search: name, years to search, address. Civil records on computer from 10/99, index books from 1800s. Mail turnaround time 2-3 days. Online access is same as described under criminal records.

Criminal Name Search: Access: Mail, in person, online. Both court and visitors may perform in person name searches. Search fee: $4.00 per name per year. Required to search: name, years to search, address, DOB, SSN, signed release. Criminal records computerized from 10/99, index books from 1800s. Mail turnaround time 2-3 days. Online access is free at www.judici.com/. A premium fee service is also available with multi-county search capabilities and other features. Case files are available from 1999.

Lee County

Circuit Court 309 S Galena, #320, Dixon, IL 61021; 815-284-5234; fax: 815-288-5615; 8:30AM-4:30PM (CST). *Felony, Misdemeanor, Civil, Eviction, Small Claims, Probate.*

General Information: Online identifiers in results same as on public terminal. No juvenile, impounded or adoption records released. Will not fax documents. Court makes copy: $.50 per page. Certification fee: $2.00 per cert. Payee: Clerk of Circuit Court. Personal checks accepted. Prepayment required. Mail requests: SASE required.

Civil Name Search: Access: Mail, in person, online. Both court and visitors may perform in person name searches. Search fee: $6.00 per name per year. Civil records on computer from 1989, index books from 1800s. Mail turnaround time 1 week. Civil PAT goes back to 8/1989. Online access is same as described under criminal records.

Criminal Name Search: Access: Mail, in person, online. Both court and visitors may perform in person name searches. Search fee: $6.00 per name per year. Required to search: name, years to search, DOB; also helpful: SSN. Criminal records computerized from 1989, index books from 1800s. Mail turnaround time 1 week. Criminal PAT goes back to same as civil. Online access is free at www.judici.com/. A premium fee service is also available with multi-county search capabilities and other features. Case files are available from 1987. Online results show middle initial.

Livingston County

Circuit Court Circuit Clerk, 112 W Madison St, Pontiac, IL 61764; 815-844-2602; criminal phone: x1; civil phone: x2; probate phone: x3 (also Juvenile); fax: 815-844-2322; 8AM-4:30PM (CST). *Felony, Misdemeanor, Civil, Eviction, Small Claims, Probate.*

www.livingstoncountyil.gov/circuitclerk.shtml

General Information: Small claims phone is x4, and tax deeds phone is x5. Probate fax is same as main fax number. No juvenile, impound, forcible entry & detainer, or adoption records released. Fee to fax out file $3.00 per fax. Court makes copy: $1.00 1st page; $.50 each add'l; after 19 pages $.25 each. Self serve copy: $.25 per page. Certification fee: $2.00 per document. Payee: Livingston County Circuit Clerk. Checks or cash only accepted in civil division. Major credit cards accepted in traffic division only. Prepayment required. Mail requests: SASE required.

Civil Name Search: Access: Mail, in person, online. Both court and visitors may perform in person name searches. Search fee: $4.00 per name per year. Required to search: name, years to search; also helpful: address. Civil records on computer from 1989 (child support since 1988), index books from 1837. Mail turnaround time 3-5 days. Civil PAT goes back to 1989. Probate along with divorce, traffic, miscellaneous remedy cases, law, all in separate indexes at this same address. Search probate index 1837-1958 at www.cyberdriveillinois.com/departments/archives/pontiac.html. Search cases free online at www.judici.com/courts/cases/case_search.jsp?court=IL053015J. Also, a premium fee service is available. Records back to 2000.

Criminal Name Search: Access: Mail, in person, online. Both court and visitors may perform in person name searches. Search fee: $4.00 per name per year. Required to search: name, years to search, DOB, SSN; also helpful: address. Criminal records computerized from 1989, index books from 1837. Note: Signed release by juvenile required for juvenile cases for military recruiters. Mail turnaround time 3-5 days. Criminal PAT goes back to same as civil. Search cases free online at www.judici.com/courts/cases/case_search.jsp?court=IL053015J. Also, a premium fee service is available. Records back to 2000.

Logan County

Circuit Court County Courthouse, PO Box 158, Lincoln, IL 62656; 217-735-2376; criminal phone: 217-735-2376; civil phone: 217-732-1163; criminal fax: 217-732-1231; civil fax: 8:30AM-4:30PM; 8:30AM-4:30PM (CST). *Felony, Misdemeanor, Civil, Eviction, Small Claims, Probate.*

www.co.logan.il.us/circuit_clerk/

General Information: Online identifiers in results same as on public terminal. No juvenile or adoption records released. Will not fax documents. Court makes copy: $2.00 1st page, $.50 each add'l. $.25 per page after 19. Certification fee: $5.00 per doc. Payee: Carla Bender, Circuit Clerk. Business or personal checks accepted. Visa/MC accepted. Prepayment required.

Civil Name Search: Access: Mail, fax, in person, online. Both court and visitors may perform in person name searches. Search fee: $5.00 per name per year. Civil records on computer back to 1990, index books from 1857. Mail turnaround time 1 week. Civil PAT goes back to 1989. Online access is same as described under criminal records.

Criminal Name Search: Access: Mail, fax, in person, online. Both court and visitors may perform in person name searches. Search fee: $5.00 per name per year. Required to search: name, years to search, DOB; also helpful: sex. Criminal records computerized from 1990, index books from 1857. Mail turnaround time 1 week. Criminal PAT goes back to same as civil. Online access is free at www.judici.com/. A premium fee service is also available with multi-county search capabilities and other features. Case files are available from 1987. Online results show middle initial, DOB.

Macon County

Circuit Court 253 E Wood St, Decatur, IL 62523; criminal phone: 217-421-0272; civil phone: 217-424-1454; probate phone: 217-424-1455; fax: 217-424-1350; 8AM-4:30PM (CST). *Felony, Misdemeanor, Civil, Eviction, Small Claims, Probate.*

www.court.co.macon.il.us

General Information: No juvenile or adoption records released. Will fax documents to local or toll free line, if not certified copy. Court makes copy: $2.00 1st page, $.50 each add'l. Certification fee: $2.00 per cert. Payee: Macon County Circuit Clerk. No personal checks accepted. Money orders, certified checks, or cash only. No credit cards accepted. Prepayment required. Mail requests: SASE required.

Civil Name Search: Access: Phone, fax, mail, online, in person. Both court and visitors may perform in person name searches. Search fee: $6.00 per name per year. Civil records on computer from 1989, index books from 1800s. Mail turnaround time 1 week. Civil PAT goes back to 1989. Access to court records is free at www.court.co.macon.il.us/Templates/SearchCaseInfo.htm. Search docket information back to 04/96. Includes traffic, probate, family, small claims.

Criminal Name Search: Access: Fax, mail, online, in person. Both court and visitors may perform in person name searches. Search fee: $6.00 per name per year. Required to search: name, years to search; also helpful: DOB. Criminal records computerized from 1989, index books from 1800s. Mail turnaround time 1 week. Criminal PAT goes back to same as civil. Access to court records is free online at www.court.co.macon.il.us/Templates/SearchCaseInfo.htm. Search docket information back to 04/96.

Macoupin County

Circuit Court PO Box 197, Carlinville, IL 62626; 217-854-3211; fax: 217-854-7361; 8:30AM-4:30PM (CST). *Felony, Misdemeanor, Civil, Eviction, Small Claims, Probate.*

www.macoupincountyil.gov/circuit_clerk.htm

General Information: No juvenile or adoption records released. Will fax documents; fee is same as copy fees. Court makes copy: $2.00 1st page, $.50 each add'l. $.25 per page after 19. Certification fee: $6.00. Payee: Mike Mathis Circuit Clerk. Personal checks and credit cards accepted. Prepayment required. Mail requests: SASE required.

Civil Name Search: Access: Mail, in person. Both court and visitors may perform in person name searches. Search fee: $6.00 per name per year. Civil records on computer from 1994, index books from 1837. Mail turnaround time 1 month to 6 weeks. Civil PAT goes back to 1994.

Criminal Name Search: Access: Mail, in person, online. Both court and visitors may perform in person name searches. Search fee: $6.00 per name per year. Required to search: name, years to search; also helpful: DOB. Criminal records computerized from 1994, index books from 1837. Mail turnaround time 1 month to 6 weeks. Criminal PAT goes back to same as civil. Online access is free at www.judici.com/. A premium fee service is also available with multi-county search capabilities and other features. Case files are available from 1994.

Madison County

Circuit Court - Civil/Misdemeanor Division 155 N Main St, Edwardsville, IL 62025; 618-692-6240; civil phone: 618-296-4464; fax: 618-692-0676; 8:30AM-4:30PM (CST). *Misdemeanor, Civil, Eviction, Small Claims, Probate.*

www.co.madison.il.us

General Information: There are three add'l court locations (Collinsville, Alton, Granite City) but all can be searched on the same system located at this Edwardsville courthouse. No juvenile, mental health, adoption records released. Will fax documents to local or toll free line. Court makes copy: $2.00 1st page; $.50 each for pgs 2-19; $.25 ea add'l pg. Certification fee: $6.00. Payee: Circuit Clerk. Personal checks accepted (there is a $25 NSF charge). Major credit cards accepted via GovPay. Prepayment required. Mail requests: SASE required.

Civil Name Search: Access: Mail, in person, online. Both court and visitors may perform in person name searches. Search fee: $6.00 per name per year. Civil records on computer from 1990, index books from 1800s. Note: Images from 2006 forward can be emailed, contact eabechel@co.madison.il.us. Mail turnaround time 5-10 days. Civil PAT goes back to 1995. Results may include middle initial. other personal identifiers may appear on pleadings, which can be viewed at the public access terminals. A vendor provides online access via subscription is a $59 setup fee plus annual subscription of $240 for this county, or $300/yr for all 7 counties - Champaign, Dekalb, Kendall, Madison, Sangamon, Will and Winnebago. Visit www.clericusmagnus.com/.

Criminal Name Search: Access: Mail, in person, online. Both court and visitors may perform in person name searches. Search fee: $6.00 per name per year. Required to search: name, years to search, DOB. Criminal records computerized from 1990, index books from 1800s. Note: Images from 2006 forward can be emailed, contact prcarach@co.madison.il.us or jlnelson@co.madison.il.us. Mail turnaround time 10-15 days. Criminal PAT goes back to 1995. Results may include middle initial. Traffic cases and pleadings may show DOB. Online access to misdemeanor records is the same as civil, see above. Online results show name, DOB.

Circuit Court - Felony Division 509 Ramey St, Edwardsville, IL 62025; 618-692-6240; fax: 618-655-2006; 8:30AM-4:30PM (CST). *Felony.*

http://madisoncountycircuitcourt.org/courts/criminal/

General Information: For felony questions, email prcarach@co.madison.il.us or jlnelson@co.madison.il.us. For traffic or misdemeanor email cmhale@co.madison.il.us or kbardill@co.madison.il.us. Online identifiers in results same as on public terminal. No juvenile, mental health, adoption records released. Will fax documents to local or toll free line. Court makes copy: $2.00 1st page; $.50 each for pgs 2-19; $.25 ea add'l pg. Certification fee: $6.00 per doc plus copy fee. Payee: Clerk of Circuit Court. Personal checks accepted. Major credit cards accepted via GovPay. Prepayment required. Mail requests: SASE required.

Criminal Name Search: Access: Mail, in person, online. Both court and visitors may perform in person name searches. Search fee: $6.00 per name per year. Required to search: name, years to search, DOB. Criminal records computerized from 1995, index books from 1958. Note: Will email scanned documents if requested. Mail turnaround time 2-10 days. Public use terminal has crim records back to 1994. Cases are being scanned and images are being added. Online access via subscription requires a setup fee plus annual subscription of $240 for this county, or $300/yr for all participating IL counties - Champaign, DeKalb, Kendall, LaSalle, Madison, Sangamon, Will. Visit www.clericusmagnus.com or www.janojustice.com or call 800-250-9884 for details ands signup. Online results show name, DOB.

Marion County

Circuit Court PO Box 130, 100 E Main, Salem, IL 62881; 618-548-3856; fax: 618-740-0118; 8AM-4PM (CST). *Felony, Misdemeanor, Civil, Eviction, Small Claims, Probate.*

www.fourthcircuitil.com/

General Information: Online identifiers in results same as on public terminal. No juvenile or adoption records released. Will not fax documents. Court makes copy: $1.00 1st page, $.50 each add'l. Certification fee: $6.00 per doc. Payee: Clerk of Circuit Court. Only cashiers checks and money orders accepted. No credit cards accepted. Prepayment required.

Civil Name Search: Access: Mail, in person, online. Visitors must perform in person searches themselves. Search fee: $5.00 per name. Civil records on computer from 1988, index books from 1800s. Mail turnaround time 2-3 days. Civil PAT goes back to 1988. Online access is same as described under criminal records.

Criminal Name Search: Access: Mail, in person, online. Visitors must perform in person searches themselves. Search fee: $5.00 per name. Required to search: name, years to search; also helpful: DOB, SSN. Criminal records computerized from 1988, index books from 1800s. Note: Results include address, driver license number and case number. Mail turnaround time 2-3 days. Criminal PAT goes back to same as civil. Results include

driver license number and case number. Online access is free at www.judici.com/. A premium fee service is also available with multi-county search capabilities and other features. Case files are available from 1988. Online results show middle initial, DOB.

Marshall County

Circuit Court PO Box 328, 122 N Prairie St, Lacon, IL 61540-0328; 309-246-6435; fax: 309-246-2173; 8:30AM-N, 1-4:30PM (CST). *Felony, Misdemeanor, Civil, Eviction, Small Claims, Probate.*

www.marshallcountyillinois.com/home/ElectedOfficials/CircuitClerk.aspx

General Information: No juvenile or adoption records released. Will fax documents to local or toll free line. Court makes copy: $2.50 1st pg; $.50 ea add'l. Certification fee: $5.00. Payee: Clerk of Circuit Court. Personal checks and credit cards accepted. Prepayment required. Mail requests: SASE required.

Civil Name Search: Access: Mail, in person, online. Both court and visitors may perform in person name searches. Search fee: $6.00 per name per year. Civil records on computer from 1988, microfiche since 1964, index books from 1800s. Mail turnaround time 1 week. Civil PAT goes back to 1988. Online access is same as described under criminal records.

Criminal Name Search: Access: Mail, in person, online. Both court and visitors may perform in person name searches. Search fee: $6.00 per name per year. Required to search: name, years to search, DOB. Criminal records computerized from 1988, microfiche since 1964, index books from 1800s. Mail turnaround time 1 week. Criminal PAT goes back to same as civil. Online access is free at www.judici.com/. A premium fee service is also available with multi-county search capabilities and other features. Case files are available from 1987.

Mason County

Circuit Court 125 N Plum, Havana, IL 62644; 309-543-6619; fax: 309-543-4214; 8AM-4PM (CST). *Felony, Misdemeanor, Civil, Eviction, Small Claims, Probate.*

www.masoncountyil.org

General Information: Probate fax is same as main fax number. No juvenile or adoption records released. Will fax documents $5.00 per fax. Court makes copy: $1.00 1st page, $.50 each add'l. Self serve copy: $.25 per page. Certification fee: $2.50 per cert. Payee: Clerk of Circuit Court. Only cashiers checks and money orders accepted. No credit cards accepted. Prepayment required. Mail requests: SASE required.

Civil Name Search: Access: Mail, in person, online. Both court and visitors may perform in person name searches. Search fee: $5.00 per name per year. Civil records on computer from 1989, index books from 1800s. Mail turnaround time 1-2 weeks. Civil PAT goes back to 1989. Online access is free at www.judici.com/. A premium fee service is also available with multi-county search capabilities and other features. Case files are available from 1987.

Criminal Name Search: Access: Mail, in person, online. Both court and visitors may perform in person name searches. Search fee: $5.00 per name per year. Required to search: name, years to search, DOB. Criminal records computerized from 1989, index books from 1800s. Mail turnaround time 1-2 weeks. Criminal PAT goes back to same as civil. Online access is free at www.judici.com/. A premium fee service is also available with multi-county search capabilities and other features. Case files are available from 1987.

Massac County

Circuit Court PO Box 152, Courthouse Sq, Metropolis, IL 62960; 618-524-9359; fax: 618-524-4850; 8AM-N, 1-4PM (CST). *Felony, Misdemeanor, Civil, Eviction, Small Claims, Probate.*

General Information: No juvenile or adoption records released. Will not fax documents. Court makes copy: $.25 per page. Certification fee: $3.00. Payee: Clerk of Circuit Court. Only cashiers checks and money orders accepted. No credit cards accepted. Prepayment required. Mail requests: SASE required.

Civil Name Search: Access: Mail, in person. Both court and visitors may perform in person name searches. Search fee: $6.00 per name. Civil cases indexed by defendant. Civil records on computer from 1986, index books from 1800s. Mail turnaround time 5 business days. Civil PAT goes back to 1986.

Criminal Name Search: Access: Mail, in person. Both court and visitors may perform in person name searches. Search fee: $6.00 per name. Required to search: name, years to search, DOB, signed release. Criminal records computerized from 1986, index books from 1800s. Mail turnaround time 5 business days. Criminal PAT goes back to same as civil.

McDonough County

Circuit Court County Courthouse, #1 Courthouse Sq, Macomb, IL 61455; 309-837-4889; probate phone: 309-837-4889; fax: 309-833-4493; 8AM-4PM (CST). *Felony, Misdemeanor, Civil, Eviction, Small Claims, Probate.*

www.9thjudicial.org/

General Information: Traffic cases can be reached at 309-836-2777. No juvenile or adoption records released. Fee to fax out file $2.00 per page. Court makes copy: $2.00 1st page; $.50 each add'l 19 pages; $.25 each add'l. Certification fee: $6.00. Payee: Clerk of Circuit Court. Personal checks accepted for civil; not for criminal. Major credit cards accepted via GovPay. Prepayment required. Mail requests: SASE required.

Civil Name Search: Access: Phone, fax, mail, in person. Both court and visitors may perform in person name searches. Search fee: $6.00 per name per year. Civil records on computer from 1991, index books from 1800s. Mail turnaround time 1 week. Civil PAT goes back to 1990.

Criminal Name Search: Access: Phone, fax, mail, in person. Both court and visitors may perform in person name searches. Search fee: $6.00 per name per year. Required to search: name, years to search; also helpful: SSN. Criminal records computerized from 1991, index books from 1800s. Mail turnaround time 1 week. Criminal PAT goes back to 1985.

McHenry County

Circuit Court 2200 N Seminary Ave, Rte 47, Woodstock, IL 60098; criminal phone: 815-334-4313; civil phone: 815-334-4310; fax: 815-338-8583; 8AM-4:30PM (CST). *Felony, Misdemeanor, Civil, Eviction, Small Claims, Probate, Traffic.*

www.co.mchenry.il.us/departments/circuitclerk/Pages/index.aspx

General Information: Felony Dept is Rm 353. Traffic, 136, Civil 356. Online identifiers in results same as on public terminal. No juvenile or adoption records released. Will not fax documents. Court makes copy: $2.00 1st page, $.50 each pages 2-19; after 19 pages $.25 each. Certification fee: $6.00 per doc. Payee: Clerk of Circuit Court. Personal checks and credit cards accepted. Prepayment required. Mail requests: SASE required.

Civil Name Search: Access: Phone, fax, mail, online, in person. Both court and visitors may perform in person name searches. Search fee: $6.00 per name per year. Civil records on computer from 1991, index books from 1800s. Mail turnaround time 1 week. Civil PAT goes back to 1991. Access to civil, traffic and domestic records is the same as criminal, see below. One may order copies online from the home page, same copy and search fees apply.

Criminal Name Search: Access: Phone, fax, mail, online, in person. Both court and visitors may perform in person name searches. Search fee: $6.00 per name per year. Required to search: name, years to search, DOB. Criminal records computerized from 1990, index books from 1800s. Note: Phone searches are limited to one only. One may order copies online from the home page, same copy and search fees apply. Mail turnaround time 1 week; criminal requests processed same day. Criminal PAT goes back to 1991. Free docket search is at http://68.21.116.46/wow65/runApp?id=0. For complete case file information, access to records on the subscription system requires $750 license fee and $92.50 set-up fee, plus $50 per month. Records date back to 1990 with civil, criminal, probate, traffic, and domestic records. For more info, call 815-334-4193. Online results show middle initial, DOB.

McLean County

Circuit Court Circuit Clerk, 104 W. Front St, #404, Bloomington, IL 61702-2420; 309-888-5301; criminal phone: 309-888-5320; civil phone: 309-888-5341; 8:30AM-4:30PM (CST). *Felony, Misdemeanor, Civil, Eviction, Small Claims, Probate.*

www.mcleancountyil.gov

General Information: No juvenile or adoption records released. Will not fax documents. Court makes copy: $2.00 1st page, $.50 each add'l. Certification fee: $6.00. Payee: McLean County Circuit Clerk. Personal checks accepted. No credit cards accepted. Prepayment required. Mail requests: SASE required.

Civil Name Search: Access: Mail, in person. Both court and visitors may perform in person name searches. Search fee: $6.00 per name per year. Civil records on computer from 1991, index books from 1800s. Mail turnaround time 10 days.

Criminal Name Search: Access: Mail, in person, online. Both court and visitors may perform in person name searches. Search fee: $6.00 per name per year. Required to search: name, years to search, DOB; also helpful: address, SSN. Criminal records computerized from 1991, index books from 1800s. Mail turnaround time 10 days. Public use terminal has crim records back to 1991. Free public access at http://webapp.mcleancountyil.gov/webapps/PublicAccess/pubac_main.htm. System has traffic as well as criminal index.

Menard County

Circuit Court PO Box 466, Petersburg, IL 62675; 217-632-2615; fax: 217-632-4124; 8:30AM-4:30PM (CST). *Felony, Misdemeanor, Civil, Eviction, Small Claims, Probate.*

General Information: No juvenile or adoption records released. Will not fax documents. Court makes copy: $1.00 1st page, $.50 each add'l. Certification fee: $2.00. Payee: Clerk of Circuit Court. Only cashiers checks and money orders accepted. No credit cards accepted. Prepayment required. Mail requests: SASE required.

Civil Name Search: Access: Mail, in person. Both court and visitors may perform in person name searches. Search fee: $6.00 per name per year. Civil cases indexed by defendant. Civil records on computer from 3/1994, on index books from 1839. Mail turnaround time 2 days.

Criminal Name Search: Access: Mail, in person. Both court and visitors may perform in person name searches. Search fee: $6.00 per name per year. Required to search: name, years to search, DOB. Criminal records computerized from 3/1994, on index books from 1839. Mail turnaround time 2 days.

Mercer County

Circuit Court PO Box 175, 100 SE 3rd St, Aledo, IL 61231; 309-582-7122; fax: 309-582-7121; 8AM-4PM (CST). *Felony, Misdemeanor, Civil, Eviction, Small Claims, Probate.*

www.mercercountyil.org/

General Information: Probate fax is same as main fax number. Online identifiers in results same as on public terminal. No juvenile or adoption records released. Fee to fax out file $1.00 per page. Court makes copy: $.50 per page. Self serve copy: same. Certification fee: $5.00 per cert, includes copies. Payee: Clerk of Circuit Court. Business checks accepted. No credit cards accepted. Prepayment required. Mail requests: SASE required.

Civil Name Search: Access: Fax, mail, in person, online. Both court and visitors may perform in person name searches. No search fee. Civil records on computer from 1989, index books from 1800s. Mail turnaround time 2-3 days. Civil PAT goes back to 1988. Online access is same as described under criminal records.

Criminal Name Search: Access: Phone, fax, mail, in person, online. Both court and visitors may perform in person name searches. Search fee: $5.00 per name per year. Required to search: name, years to search, DOB. Criminal records computerized from 1989, index books from 1800s. Mail turnaround time 2-3 days. Criminal PAT goes back to same as civil. Online access is free at www.judici.com/. A premium fee service is also available with multi-county search capabilities and other features. Case files are available from 1988.

Monroe County

Circuit Court 100 S Main St, Waterloo, IL 62298; 618-939-8681; criminal phone: x273; civil phone: x274; probate phone: x274; fax: 618-939-1929; 8AM-4:30PM (CST). *Felony, Misdemeanor, Civil, Eviction, Small Claims, Probate.*

General Information: Probate fax is same as main fax number. No juvenile or adoption records released. No fee to fax documents. Court makes copy: $1.00 1st page, $.50 each add'l. After 20 pages $.25 each. Self serve copy: $.20 per page. Certification fee: $5.00 per cert. Payee: Circuit Clerk. Business checks accepted. No credit cards accepted. Mail requests: SASE required.

Civil Name Search: Access: Mail, fax, in person. Both court and visitors may perform in person name searches. Search fee: $6.00 per name per year. Required to search: name, years to search, DOB. Civil records on computer from 1992, index books from 1818. Mail turnaround time 1 week. Civil PAT goes back to 1992.

Criminal Name Search: Access: Mail, fax, in person. Both court and visitors may perform in person name searches. Search fee: $6.00 per name per year. Required to search: name, years to search, DOB. Criminal records computerized from 1992, index books from 1818. Mail turnaround time 1 week. Criminal PAT goes back to same as civil.

Montgomery County

Circuit Court 120 N Main, PO Box C, Hillsboro, IL 62049; 217-532-9546; criminal phone: 217-532-9547; civil phone: 217-532-9546; probate phone: 217-532-9546; fax: 217-532-9614; 8AM-4PM (CST). *Felony, Misdemeanor, Civil, Eviction, Small Claims, Probate.*

www.montgomeryco.com/news/7_1.html

General Information: Also use www.fourthcircuitil.com/. No juvenile or adoption records released. Will not fax documents. Court makes copy: $1.00 1st pg, then $.50 ea next 19 pgs, then $.25 ea add'l. Certification fee: $10.00 per doc. Payee: Clerk of Circuit Court. Only cashiers checks and money orders accepted. Credit cards accepted, service fees through outside venders (e-pay & GPS). They do not swipe cards at counter. Prepayment required. Mail requests: SASE required.

Civil Name Search: Access: Mail, in person, online. Both court and visitors may perform in person name searches. Search fee: $5.00 per name per year. Civil records on computer from 1988, index books from 1821, microfiche (probate only) since 1939. Mail turnaround time 1 week. Civil PAT goes back to 1988. Online access is same as described under criminal records.

Criminal Name Search: Access: Mail, online, in person. Both court and visitors may perform in person name searches. Search fee: $5.00 per name per year. Required to search: name, years to search, DOB. Criminal records computerized from 1988, index books from 1821, microfiche (probate only) since 1939. Mail turnaround time 1 week. Criminal PAT goes back to same as civil. Online access is free at www.judici.com/. A premium fee service is also available with multi-county search capabilities and other features. Case files are available from 1992.

Morgan County

Circuit Court PO Box 1120, 300 W State St, Jacksonville, IL 62651; 217-243-5419; fax: 217-243-2009; 8:30AM-4:30PM (CST). *Felony, Misdemeanor, Civil, Eviction, Small Claims, Probate.*

General Information: Probate is a separate index at this same address. Probate fax is same as main fax number. No juvenile or adoption records released. Will fax documents $1.50 1st page, $.50 ea add'l. Court makes copy: $1.50 1st page, $.50 each add'l. Self serve copy: same. Certification fee: $4.00 per document plus copy fee. Payee: Clerk of Circuit Court. Cashiers checks and money orders accepted, no personal checks. No credit cards accepted for record searching. Prepayment required. Mail requests: SASE required.

Civil Name Search: Access: Mail, in person, online. Both court and visitors may perform in person name searches. Search fee: $5.00 per name per year. Civil records on computer from 1990, index books from mid 1800s. Mail turnaround time 1 week. Civil PAT goes back to 1990. Online access is same as described under criminal records.

Criminal Name Search: Access: Mail, in person, online. Both court and visitors may perform in person name searches. Search fee: $5.00 per name per year. Required to search: name, years to search, DOB. Criminal records computerized from 1990, index books from mid 1800s. Mail turnaround time 1 week. Criminal PAT goes back to 1990. Online access is free at www.judici.com/. A premium fee service is also available with multi-county search capabilities and other features. Case files are available from 1990. Online results show middle initial, DOB, address.

Moultrie County

Circuit Court 10 S Main, #7, Moultrie County Courthouse, Sullivan, IL 61951; 217-728-4622; fax: 217-728-7833; 8:30AM-12; 1PM-4:30PM (CST). *Felony, Misdemeanor, Civil, Eviction, Small Claims, Probate.* www.circuit-clerk.moultrie.il.us

General Information: Probate fax is same as main fax number. No juvenile or adoption records released. If necessary, Will fax documents $2.00 per page fax fee, up to 10 pages. Court makes copy: $.50 per page. Certification fee: $3.00 per cert plus copy fee. Payee: Clerk of Circuit Court. Business checks accepted. No credit cards accepted. Prepayment required. Mail requests: SASE required.

Civil Name Search: Access: Mail, in person, online. Both court and visitors may perform in person name searches. Search fee: $4.00 per name per year. Civil cases indexed by defendant. Civil records on computer from 1990, index books from 1850. Mail turnaround time 1 week. Public use terminal available. Online access is same as described under criminal records.

Criminal Name Search: Access: Mail, in person, online. Both court and visitors may perform in person name searches. Search fee: $4.00 per name per year. Required to search: name, years to search, DOB. Criminal records computerized from 1990, index books from 1850. Mail turnaround time 1 week. Public use terminal available. Online access is free at www.judici.com/. A premium fee service is also available with multi-county search capabilities and other features. Case files are available from June 1990. Online results show middle initial, DOB.

Ogle County

Circuit Court 106 S Fifth St #300, Oregon, IL 61061; 815-732-1130; criminal phone: 815-732-1140; civil phone: 815-732-1130; fax: 815-732-9093; 8:30AM-4:30PM (CST). *Felony, Misdemeanor, Civil, Eviction, Small Claims, Probate.* www.oglecircuitclerk.org/

General Information: No juvenile or adoption records released. Will not fax documents. Court makes copy: $2.00 1st page, $.50 each add'l. $.25 per page after 19. Certification fee: $10.00 per document plus copy fee. Payee: Clerk of Circuit Court. Only cashiers checks and money orders accepted. No credit cards accepted. Prepayment required. Mail requests: SASE required.

Civil Name Search: Access: Mail, in person, online. Both court and visitors may perform in person name searches. Search fee: $6.00 per name per year. Civil records on computer back to 1994; prior records on microfiche last 10 years, index books from 1836. Mail turnaround time 2-3 weeks. Civil PAT goes back to 1994. DOB is listed on the complaint, not on the docket index. Online access is free at www.judici.com/. A premium fee service is also available with multi-county search capabilities and other features. Case files are available from 1994.

Criminal Name Search: Access: Mail, online, in person. Both court and visitors may perform in person name searches. Search fee: $6.00 per name per year. Required to search: name, years to search, DOB. Criminal records computerized from 1989; prior records on microfiche last 10 years, index books from 1836. Mail turnaround time 2-3 weeks. Criminal PAT goes back to 1989. Online access is free at www.judici.com/. A premium fee

service is also available with multi-county search capabilities and other features. Case files are available from 1989.

Peoria County

Circuit Court 324 Main St, Rm G22, Peoria, IL 61602; 309-672-6953; fax: 309-677-6228; 8:30AM-5PM (CST). *Felony, Misdemeanor, Civil, Eviction, Small Claims, Probate.*

General Information: No juvenile or adoption records released. Will not fax documents. Court makes copy: $2.00 1st page, $.50 each add'l. Certification fee: $6.00 per doc. Payee: Clerk of Circuit Court. Personal checks accepted. Credit cards accepted. Prepayment required. Mail requests: SASE required.

Civil Name Search: Access: Phone, mail, in person. Both court and visitors may perform in person name searches. Search fee: $6.00 per name per year. Civil records on computer from 1986 (traffic), from 1987 (civil), archived from 1800s. Mail turnaround time 1 week. Civil PAT goes back to 1979.

Criminal Name Search: Access: Phone, mail, in person. Both court and visitors may perform in person name searches. Search fee: $6.00 per name per year, Add'l $10.00 to mail. Required to search: name, years to search, DOB; also helpful: SSN. Criminal records computerized from 1978, archived from 1800s. Mail turnaround time 1 week. Criminal PAT goes back to same as civil. Results include name and case number.

Perry County

Circuit Court PO Box 219, Pinckneyville, IL 62274; 618-357-6726; fax: 618-357-8336; 8AM-4PM (CST). *Felony, Misdemeanor, Civil, Eviction, Small Claims, Probate.*

General Information: Probate is a separate index at this same address. No juvenile or adoption records released. Will not fax documents. Court makes copy: $1.00 1st page; $.50 each add'l; after 19 pages $.25 each. Certification fee: $2.00 plus copy fee. Payee: Clerk of Circuit Court. Only cashiers checks and money orders accepted. No credit cards accepted. Prepayment required. Mail requests: SASE required.

Civil Name Search: Access: Mail, in person. Both court and visitors may perform in person name searches. Search fee: $5.00 per name per year. Civil records on computer from 1990, index books from 1800s. Mail turnaround time up to 1 week. Civil PAT goes back to 1990.

Criminal Name Search: Access: Mail, in person. Both court and visitors may perform in person name searches. Search fee: $5.00 per name per year. Required to search: name, years to search; also helpful: DOB. Criminal records computerized from 1990, index books from 1800s. Mail turnaround time up to 1 week. Criminal PAT goes back to same as civil.

Piatt County

Circuit Court PO Box 288, 101 W Washington, Monticello, IL 61856; 217-762-4966; fax: 217-762-5906; 8:30AM-4:30PM (CST). *Felony, Misdemeanor, Civil, Eviction, Small Claims, Probate.* www.piattcounty.org/

General Information: Probate fax is same as main fax number. No juvenile or adoption records released. Will fax documents $2.00 1st page, $1.00 each add'l. Court makes copy: $1.00 1st page, $.50 each add'l. No certification fee . Payee: Clerk of Circuit Court. Business checks accepted. No Visa credit cards accepted. Prepayment required.

Civil Name Search: Access: Phone, fax, mail, in person, online. Both court and visitors may perform in person name searches. No search fee. Civil records on computer since 1988, index books from 1800s. Mail turnaround time 2-3 days. Civil PAT available. Online access is free at www.judici.com/. A premium fee service is also available with multi-county search capabilities and other features. Case files are available from 1999.

Criminal Name Search: Access: Phone, fax, mail, in person, online. Both court and visitors may perform in person name searches. No search fee. Required to search: name, years to search, DOB; also helpful: SSN. Criminal records on computer since 1988, index books from 1800s. Mail turnaround time 2-3 days. Criminal PAT available. Online access is free at www.judici.com/. A premium fee service is also available with multi-county search capabilities and other features. Case files are available from 1999.

Pike County

Circuit Court Pike County Courthouse, 100 E Washington St, Pittsfield, IL 62363; 217-285-6612; fax: 217-285-4726; 8:30AM-4:30PM (CST). *Felony, Misdemeanor, Civil, Eviction, Small Claims, Probate.*

General Information: No juvenile or adoption records released. Will fax out civil documents only. Court makes copy: $2.00 1st page, $.50 each add'l. $.25 per page after 19. Self serve copy: $.25 per page. Certification fee: $6.00 per document includes copies; $10.00 for judgment. Payee: Circuit Clerk. No personal checks accepted; money order or cash only. No credit cards accepted. Prepayment required. Mail requests: SASE required.

Civil Name Search: Access: Mail, in person, online. Both court and visitors may perform in person name searches. Search fee: $6.00 per name per year. Civil records on computer since 1992, index books from 1800s. Mail turnaround time ASAP. Public use terminal has civil records back to 1992. Online access is free at www.judici.com/. A premium fee service is also available with multi-county search capabilities and other features. Case files are available from 1991.

Criminal Name Search: Access: Mail, in person, online. Both court and visitors may perform in person name searches. Search fee: $6.00 per name per year. Required to search: name, years to search; also helpful: SSN. Criminal records on computer since 1992, index books from 1800s. Mail turnaround time ASAP. Online access is free at www.judici.com/. A premium fee service is also available with multi-county search capabilities and other features. Case files are available from 1991.

Pope County

Circuit Court PO Box 438, Golconda, IL 62938; 618-683-3941; fax: 618-683-3018; 8AM-4PM (CST). *Felony, Misdemeanor, Civil, Eviction, Small Claims, Probate.*

General Information: No juvenile or adoption records released. Will fax documents $.50 per page. Court makes copy: $.25 per page. Self serve copy: same. Certification fee: $6.00. Payee: Circuit Clerk. Business checks accepted. No credit cards accepted. Prepayment required. Mail requests: SASE required.

Civil Name Search: Access: Phone, fax, mail, in person, online. Both court and visitors may perform in person name searches. Search fee: $6.00 per name per year. Civil cases indexed by defendant. Civil records on computer from 1989, index books from 1800s. Mail turnaround time 2-3 days. Civil PAT goes back to 1989. Online access is free at www.judici.com/. A premium fee service is also available with multi-county search capabilities and other features. Case files are available from 1989.

Criminal Name Search: Access: Phone, fax, mail, in person, online. Both court and visitors may perform in person name searches. Search fee: $6.00 per name per year. Required to search: name, years to search, DOB. Criminal records computerized from 1989, index books from 1800s. Mail turnaround time 2-3 days. Criminal PAT goes back to same as civil. Online access is free at www.judici.com/. A premium fee service is also available with multi-county search capabilities and other features. Case files are available from 1987.

Pulaski County

Circuit Court 500 Illinois Ave, Rm C, PO Box 88, Mound City, IL 62963; 618-748-9300; fax: 618-748-9329; 8AM-N, 1-4PM (CST). *Felony, Misdemeanor, Civil, Eviction, Small Claims, Probate.*

General Information: No juvenile, adoption records released. Will fax documents to local or toll-free number. Court makes copy: $2.00 1st page, $.50 each add'l. After 20 pages $.25 each. Certification fee: $6.00 per doc. Payee: Clerk of Circuit Court. Only cashiers checks and money orders accepted. No credit cards accepted. Prepayment required. Mail requests: SASE required.

Civil Name Search: Access: Mail, fax, in person, online. Both court and visitors may perform in person name searches. Search fee: $6.00 per name. Civil records on computer since 1989, on books prior. Mail turnaround time 1 week. Online access is free at www.judici.com/. A premium fee service is also available with multi-county search capabilities and other features. Case files are available from 1986.

Criminal Name Search: Access: Mail, fax, in person, online. Both court and visitors may perform in person name searches. Search fee: $6.00 per name per year. Required to search: name, years to search, signed release; also helpful: DOB, SSN. Criminal records on computer since 1989, on books prior. Mail turnaround time 1 week. Online access is free at www.judici.com/. A premium fee service is also available with multi-county search capabilities and other features. Case files are available from 1986.

Putnam County

Circuit Court 120 N 4th St, Hennepin, IL 61327; 815-925-7016; fax: 815-925-7492; 9AM-4PM (CST). *Felony, Misdemeanor, Civil, Eviction, Small Claims, Probate.*

General Information: No juvenile or adoption records released. Will fax documents $.50 per page. Court makes copy: $.50 per page. $.25 per page after 20. Certification fee: $2.00. Payee: Clerk of Circuit Court. Only cashiers checks and money orders accepted. No credit cards accepted. Prepayment required. Mail requests: SASE required.

Civil Name Search: Access: Mail, in person, online. Both court and visitors may perform in person name searches. Search fee: $5.00 per name. Fee is per 5 years searched. Civil cases indexed by defendant. Civil records on computer from 1991, index books from 1836. Mail turnaround time 3 days. Civil PAT goes back to 1991. Online access is free at www.judici.com/. A premium fee service is also available with multi-county search capabilities and other features. Case files are available from 1990.

Criminal Name Search: Access: Mail, in person, online. Both court and visitors may perform in person name searches. Search fee: $5.00 per name. Fee is per 5 years searched. Required to search: name, years to search, DOB. Criminal records computerized from 1991, index books from 1836. Note: No criminal searches performed on Thursdays. Mail turnaround time 3 days. Criminal PAT goes back to same as civil. Online access is free at www.judici.com/. A premium fee service is also available with multi-county search capabilities and other features. Case files are available from 1990.

Randolph County

Circuit Court County Courthouse, Rm 302, #1 Taylor St, Chester, IL 62233; 618-826-5000 X194; fax: 618-826-3761; 8AM-4PM (CST). *Felony, Misdemeanor, Civil, Eviction, Small Claims, Probate.* www.randolphco.org/gov/judicial/index.cfm

General Information: Any electronic output is $1.00 per page. No juvenile or adoption records released. Will fax documents to local or toll-free number. Court makes copy: $.50 per page. Certification fee: $4.00 for seal and $1.00 1st page and $.50 each add'l page. Payee: Clerk of Circuit Court. Business checks accepted. No credit cards accepted. Prepayment required. Mail requests: SASE required.

Civil Name Search: Access: Mail, in person. Both court and visitors may perform in person name searches. Search fee: $4.00 per name per year. Civil records on computer from 1992, index books from 1800s. Visitors can search both. Mail turnaround time 1-2 days. Civil PAT goes back to 1992.

Criminal Name Search: Access: Mail, in person. Both court and visitors may perform in person name searches. Search fee: $4.00 per name per year. Required to search: name, years to search, DOB. Criminal records computerized from 1992, index books from 1800s. Visitors can search both. Mail turnaround time 1-2 days. Criminal PAT goes back to same as civil.

Richland County

Circuit Court 103 W Main, #21, Olney, IL 62450; 618-392-2151; fax: 618-392-5041; 8AM-4PM (CST). *Felony, Misdemeanor, Civil, Eviction, Small Claims, Probate.*

General Information: Probate fax is same as main fax number. No juvenile or adoption records released. Will fax documents $.25 per page. Court makes copy: $1.00 per page; ea add'l page to 19- $.50. $.25 ea add'l . Certification fee: $5.00 per certification plus copy fee. Payee: Clerk of Circuit Court. Only cashiers checks and money orders accepted. No credit cards accepted. Prepayment required. Mail requests: SASE required.

Civil Name Search: Access: Phone, mail, fax, in person, online. Both court and visitors may perform in person name searches. Search fee: $4.00 per name per year. $25.00 maximum. Civil cases indexed by defendant. Civil index on docket books from 1867; on computer back to 1999. Mail turnaround time 1-2 weeks. Civil PAT goes back to 1999. Online access is free at www.judici.com/. A premium fee service is also available with multi-county search capabilities and other features. Case files are available from 1999.

Criminal Name Search: Access: Mail, in person, online. Both court and visitors may perform in person name searches. Search fee: $4.00 per name per year. $25.00 maximum. Required to search: name, years to search, DOB. Criminal records indexed in books from 1867; on computer back to 1986. Mail turnaround time 1-2 weeks. Criminal PAT goes back to same as civil. Online access is free at www.judici.com/. A premium fee service is also available with multi-county search capabilities and other features. Case files are available from 1999. Online results show middle initial, DOB.

Rock Island County

Circuit Court PO Box 5230, 210 15th St, Rock Island, IL 61204-5230; 309-786-4451; fax: 309-786-3029; 8AM-4:30PM (CST). *Felony, Misdemeanor, Civil, Eviction, Small Claims, Probate.* www.rockislandcounty.org/CircuitClerk/CivilDiv/Home/

General Information: Search fee includes both the civil and criminal indexes. No juvenile or adoption records released. Will not fax documents. Court makes copy: $2.00 1st page, $.50 each next 19, then $.25 per add'l. Certification fee: $6.00 per doc. Payee: Circuit Clerks Office. Money orders accepted. Visa/MC accepted; there is a 3.5% usage fee and $3.50 minimum. Prepayment required. Mail requests: SASE required.

Civil Name Search: Access: Mail, in person, online. Both court and visitors may perform in person name searches. Search fee: $6.00 per name per year. Civil records on computer from 1989, index books from 1950s. Mail turnaround time 1 week. Civil PAT goes back to 5/1989. Full access to court records on the remote online system requires contract and fees. Civil, criminal, probate, traffic, and domestic records can be accessed by name or case number. Online access is free at www.judici.com/. A premium fee service is also available with multi-county search capabilities and other features. Case files are available from 1989.

Criminal Name Search: Access: Mail, in person, online. Both court and visitors may perform in person name searches. Search fee: $6.00 per name per year. Required to search: name, years to search, DOB. Criminal records computerized from 1989, index books from 1950s. Mail turnaround time 1 week. Criminal PAT goes back to 5/1989. Not all records include DOBs. Online access to criminal records is the same as civil - there are two methods. Online results show middle initial, DOB.

Saline County

Circuit Court County Courthouse, Harrisburg, IL 62946; 618-253-5096; fax: 618-253-3904; 8AM-4PM (CST). *Felony, Misdemeanor, Civil, Eviction, Small Claims, Probate.*

General Information: No juvenile or adoption records released. Fee to fax out file $2.00 1st page, $1.00 each add'l. Court makes copy: $1.00 1st page, $.50 each add'l. Self serve copy: $.10 per page. Certification fee: $5.00. Payee: Clerk of Circuit Court. Business checks accepted. Credit cards accepted in person, $5.00 fee extra. Prepayment required. Mail requests: SASE required.

Civil Name Search: Access: Fax, mail, in person, phone, online. Both court and visitors may perform in person name searches. Search fee: $5.00 per name per year. Civil records on computer back to 1986, index books archived from 1886. Mail turnaround time 1 week. Civil PAT goes back to 1986. Online access is free at www.judici.com/. A premium fee service is also available with multi-county search capabilities and other features. Case files are available from 1986.

Criminal Name Search: Access: Fax, mail, in person, phone, online. Both court and visitors may perform in person name searches. Search fee: $5.00 per name per year. Required to search: name, years to search, DOB. Criminal records computerized from 1986, index books archived from 1800s. Mail turnaround time 1-2 weeks. Criminal PAT goes back to same as civil. Online access is free at www.judici.com/. A premium fee service is also available with multi-county search capabilities and other features. Case files are available from 1986.

Sangamon County

Circuit Court 200 S 9th St, Rm 405, Springfield, IL 62701; 217-753-6674; fax: 217-753-6665; 8:30AM-4:30PM (CST). *Felony, Misdemeanor, Civil, Eviction, Small Claims, Probate.*
www.sangamoncountycircuitclerk.org

General Information: No juvenile, mental health, adoption records released. No fee to fax documents. Court makes copy: $2.00 1st page, $.50 each add'l. $.25 per page after 21. Certification fee: $6.00 if a copy, $8.00 if computer generated. Payee: Circuit Clerk. Personal checks accepted. No credit cards accepted for copies. Prepayment required. Mail requests: SASE required.

Civil Name Search: Access: Fax, mail, in person, online. Both court and visitors may perform in person name searches. Search fee: $6.00 per name per year. Civil records on computer from 1990, index books from 1800s. Mail turnaround time 1-2 weeks. Civil PAT goes back to 1990. Online access to civil records is the same as criminal, see below.

Criminal Name Search: Access: Fax, mail, in person, online. Both court and visitors may perform in person name searches. Search fee: $6.00 per name per year. Required to search: name, years to search, DOB. Criminal records computerized from 1993, index books from 1800s. Mail turnaround time 1-2 weeks. Criminal PAT goes back to 1993. Online access via subscription requires a setup fee plus annual subscription of $240 for this county, or $300/yr for all participating IL counties - Champaign, DeKalb, Kendall, LaSalle, Madison, Sangamon, Will. Visit www.clericusmagnus.com or www.janojustice.com or call 800-250-9884 for details and signup. A free search is also offered at http://67.128.239.91/sccc/Home.sc, but this is a limited search and not official. Online results show middle initial, DOB.

Schuyler County

Circuit Court PO Box 80, Rushville, IL 62681; 217-322-4633; fax: 217-322-6164; 8AM-4PM (CST). *Felony, Misdemeanor, Civil, Eviction, Small Claims, Probate.*

General Information: No juvenile or adoption records released. Fee to fax out file $1.00 per page. Court makes copy: $2.00 1st page, $.50 each add'l. $.25 per page after 19. Certification fee: $10.00. Payee: Clerk of Circuit Court. Only cashiers checks and money orders accepted. No credit cards accepted. Prepayment required. Mail requests: SASE required.

Civil Name Search: Access: Mail, in person, online. Both court and visitors may perform in person name searches. Search fee: $6.00 per name. Civil cases indexed by defendant. Civil records on computer from 1988, index books from 1800s. Mail turnaround time 1 week. Civil PAT available. Online access is free at www.judici.com/. A premium fee service is also available with multi-county search capabilities and other features. Case files are available from 1988.

Criminal Name Search: Access: Mail, in person, online. Both court and visitors may perform in person name searches. Search fee: $6.00 per name. Required to search: name, years to search, DOB. Criminal records computerized from 1988, index books from 1800s. Mail turnaround time 1 week. Criminal PAT available. Online access is free at www.judici.com/.

A premium fee service is also available with multi-county search capabilities and other features. Case files are available from 1988.

Scott County

Circuit Court 35 E Market St, Winchester, IL 62694; 217-742-5217; fax: 217-742-5853; 8AM-N, 1-4PM (CST). *Felony, Misdemeanor, Civil, Eviction, Small Claims, Probate.*

General Information: No juvenile or adoption records released. Will not fax documents. Court makes copy: $1.00 1st page, $.50 each add'l. After 20 pages $.25 each. Self serve copy: same. Certification fee: $2.00. Payee: Clerk of Circuit Court. Only cashiers checks and money orders accepted. Call 888-604-7888 to use credit card. Prepayment required. Mail requests: SASE required.

Civil Name Search: Access: Mail, in person. Both court and visitors may perform in person name searches. Search fee: $6.00 per name per year. Civil index on docket books from 1800s. Mail turnaround time 1 week.

Criminal Name Search: Access: Mail, in person. Both court and visitors may perform in person name searches. Search fee: $6.00 per name per year. Required to search: name, years to search, DOB. Criminal records indexed in books from 1800s. Mail turnaround time 1 week.

Shelby County

Circuit Court County Courthouse, PO Box 469, Shelbyville, IL 62565; 217-774-4212; fax: 217-774-4109; 8AM-4PM (CST). *Felony, Misdemeanor, Civil, Eviction, Small Claims, Probate.*
www.fourthcircuitil.com/

General Information: Probate fax is same as main fax number. Online identifiers in results same as on public terminal. No juvenile or adoption records released. Will fax documents to local or toll-free number. Court makes copy: $.25 per page. Self serve copy: $.25 per page. Certification fee: $10.00 per document plus copy fee for add'l pages. Payee: Circuit Clerk. Personal checks accepted. No credit cards accepted. Prepayment required. Mail requests: SASE required.

Civil Name Search: Access: Fax, mail, in person, online. Both court and visitors may perform in person name searches. Search fee: $5.00 per name per year. Civil records on computer from 1988, index books from 1848. Mail turnaround time 1-2 weeks. Civil PAT goes back to 1988. Sometimes DOB will show on docket. Online access is free at www.judici.com/. A premium fee service is also available with multi-county search capabilities and other features. Case files are available from 1988.

Criminal Name Search: Access: Fax, mail, in person, online. Both court and visitors may perform in person name searches. Search fee: $5.00 per name per year. Required to search: name, years to search, DOB. Criminal records computerized from 1988, index books from 1848. Mail turnaround time 1-2 weeks. Criminal PAT goes back to same as civil. Online access is free at www.judici.com/. A premium fee service is also available with multi-county search capabilities and other features. Case files are available from 1988. Online results show name, DOB.

St. Clair County

Circuit Court 10 Public Square, Belleville, IL 62220-1623; 618-277-6832; criminal phone: x4 for felony; probate phone: x2307; fax: 618-825-2742; 8AM-4:30PM (CST). *Felony, Misdemeanor, Civil, Eviction, Small Claims, Probate.*
www.circuitclerk.co.st-clair.il.us/

General Information: No juvenile or adoption records released. Will not fax documents. Court makes copy: $2.00 1st page, $.50 each add'l. $.25 per page after 19. Certification fee: $6.00. Payee: Clerk of Circuit Court. Personal checks not excepted. No credit cards accepted. Prepayment required. Mail requests: SASE required.

Civil Name Search: Access: Mail, in person. Both court and visitors may perform in person name searches. Search fee: $6.00 per name. Required to search: name, years to search; also helpful: address. Civil records on computer from 1990, microfiche from 1800s. Mail turnaround time 1-2 days. Civil PAT goes back to 1990.

Criminal Name Search: Access: Mail, in person. Both court and visitors may perform in person name searches. Search fee: $6.00 per name. Required to search: name, years to search, DOB. Criminal records computerized from 1990 (with some info available back to 1980) microfiche from 1800s. Cases prior to 1995 archived in basement. Mail turnaround time 1-2 days. Criminal PAT goes back to same as civil. Results also give charges, disposition, key dates.

Stark County

Circuit Court 130 W Main St, Toulon, IL 61483; 309-286-5941; fax: 309-286-4039; 8:30AM-4:30PM (CST). *Felony, Misdemeanor, Civil, Eviction, Small Claims, Probate.*

General Information: No juvenile or adoption records released. Will not fax documents. Court makes copy: $1.00 1st page, $.50 each add'l. Self serve copy: same. Certification fee: $5.00. Payee: Clerk of Circuit Court. Personal checks accepted. No credit cards accepted. Prepayment required. Mail requests: SASE required.

Civil Name Search: Access: Mail, in person, online. Both court and visitors may perform in person name searches. Search fee: $6.00 per name per year. Civil cases indexed by defendant. Civil index on docket books from 1800s. Mail turnaround time 2-3 days. Civil PAT goes back to 2001. Online access is free at www.judici.com/. A premium fee service is also available with multi-county search capabilities and other features. Case files are available from 2000.

Criminal Name Search: Access: Mail, in person, online. Both court and visitors may perform in person name searches. Search fee: $6.00 per name per year. Required to search: name, years to search, DOB. Criminal records indexed in books from 1800s. Mail turnaround time 2-3 days. Criminal PAT goes back to same as civil. Online access is free at www.judici.com/. A premium fee service is also available with multi-county search capabilities and other features. Case files are available from 2000.

Stephenson County

Circuit Court 15 N Galena Ave, 2nd Fl, Freeport, IL 61032; 815-235-8266; criminal fax: 815-233-1576; civil fax: 8:30AM-4:30PM; 8:30AM-4:30PM (CST). *Felony, Misdemeanor, Civil, Eviction, Small Claims, Probate.*

www.co.stephenson.il.us/circuitclerk/

General Information: Online identifiers in results same as on public terminal. No juvenile or adoption records released. Will not fax documents. Court makes copy: $2.00 1st page, $.50 each add'l to 20, $.25 after 20. Self serve copy: same. Certification fee: $10.00 plus copy fee. Payee: Clerk of Circuit Court. Business checks accepted. Visa/MC/Discover accepted via Illinoisepay.com. Prepayment required. Mail requests: SASE required.

Civil Name Search: Access: Mail, in person, online. Both court and visitors may perform in person name searches. Search fee: $6.00 per name per year. Civil records on computer from 8/1989, index books from 1875. Mail turnaround time 5-15 days. Civil PAT goes back to 1989. Online access is free at www.judici.com/. A premium fee service is also available with multi-county search capabilities and other features. Case files are available from 1989.

Criminal Name Search: Access: Mail, in person, online. Both court and visitors may perform in person name searches. Search fee: $6.00 per name per year. Required to search: name, years to search, DOB. Criminal records computerized from 8/1989, index books from 1875. Mail turnaround time 5-15 days. Criminal PAT goes back to 1989. Online access is free at www.judici.com/. A premium fee service is also available with multi-county search capabilities and other features. Case files are available from 1989. Online results show middle initial, DOB, address.

Tazewell County

Circuit Court Courthouse, 243 Court St, Pekin, IL 61554; 309-477-2214; criminal phone: 309-477-2775; probate phone: 309-477-2217; fax: 309-353-7801; 8:30AM-5PM (CST). *Felony, Misdemeanor, Civil, Small Claims, Probate, Traffic.*

www.tazewell.com/

General Information: Traffic Phone: 309-477-2218. No juvenile or adoption records released. Court makes copy: $2.00 1st page, $.50 each add'l. $.25 per page after 19. Self serve copy: same. Certification fee: $6.00. Payee: Clerk of Circuit Court. Cashiers checks and money orders accepted; personal checks accepted for add'l $2.00 fee. Credit cards accepted in person only. A convenience fee of $5.00 added on charge up to $100.00; add $5.00 more if over $100.00. Prepayment required. Mail requests: SASE required.

Civil Name Search: Access: Mail, in person, online. Both court and visitors may perform in person name searches. Search fee: $6.00 per name per year. Civil records on computer from 2/89 index books from 1800s. Mail turnaround time 3-4 days. Civil PAT goes back to 2/1989. Online access is free at www.judici.com/. A premium fee service is also available with multi-county search capabilities and other features. Case files are available from Feb. 1989.

Criminal Name Search: Access: Mail, in person, online. Both court and visitors may perform in person name searches. Search fee: $6.00 per name per year. Required to search: name, years to search, DOB, signed release. Criminal records computerized from 2/89 index books from 1800s. Mail turnaround time 3-4 days. Criminal PAT goes back to same as civil. Online access is free at www.judici.com/. A premium fee service is also available with multi-county search capabilities and other features. Case files are available from Feb. 1989.

Union County

Circuit Court Union County Courthouse, 309 W Market, Rm 101, Jonesboro, IL 62952; 618-833-5913; fax: 618-833-5223; 8AM-N,1-4PM (CST). *Felony, Misdemeanor, Civil, Eviction, Small Claims, Probate.*

General Information: No juvenile or adoption records released. Fee to fax out file $5.00. Court makes copy: $2.00 1st page, $.50 each add'l 19 pages; $.25 each add'l. Certification fee: $6.00 per doc. Payee: Lorraine Moreland, Circuit Clerk. Business checks accepted. No personal checks. No credit cards accepted. Prepayment required. Mail requests: SASE required.

Civil Name Search: Access: Fax, mail, in person, online. Both court and visitors may perform in person name searches. Search fee: $6.00 per name per year. Civil records on computer from 1986, index books from 1800s. Note: Public can only search paper records up to 1986. Only court personnel have access to computer records. Mail turnaround time 1 week. Civil PAT available. Online access is free at www.judici.com/. A premium fee service is also available with multi-county search capabilities and other features. Case files are available from 1986.

Criminal Name Search: Access: Fax, mail, in person, online. Both court and visitors may perform in person name searches. Search fee: $6.00 per name per year. Required to search: name, years to search; also helpful: DOB. Criminal records computerized from 1986, index books from 1800s. Note: In person criminal record search procedures are the same as civil. Mail turnaround time 1 week. Criminal PAT available. Online access is free at www.judici.com/. A premium fee service is also available with multi-county search capabilities and other features. Case files are available from 1986.

Vermilion County

Circuit Court 7 N Vermilion, Danville, IL 61832; 217-554-7700; probate phone: 217-554-7734; fax: 217-554-7728; 8:30AM-4:30PM (CST). *Felony, Misdemeanor, Civil, Eviction, Small Claims, Probate.*

www.co.vermilion.il.us

General Information: No juvenile, impounded, mental health or adoption records released. Will not fax documents. Court makes copy: $2.00 1st page, $.50 each add'l. Self serve copy: $.10 per page. Certification fee: $5.00 per doc. Payee: Clerk of Circuit Court. Business checks accepted. No credit cards accepted. Prepayment required. Mail requests: SASE required.

Civil Name Search: Access: Phone, mail, in person, online. Both court and visitors may perform in person name searches. Search fee: $6.00 per name per year. Civil records on computer from 1989; microfilm from 3/1949 to 5/1989; index books from 1800s. Mail turnaround time 1-2 weeks. Civil PAT goes back to 1989. Search the index at www.judici.com/courts/cases/case_search.jsp?court=IL092015J. Records are current to 1989. Premium fee service also available.

Criminal Name Search: Access: Phone, mail, in person, online. Both court and visitors may perform in person name searches. Search fee: $6.00 per name per year. Required to search: name, years to search, DOB; also helpful: SSN. Criminal records computerized from 1989; microfilm from 3/1949 to 5/1989; index books from 1800s. Mail turnaround time 1-2 weeks. Criminal PAT goes back to 1989. Search the index at www.judici.com/courts/cases/case_search.jsp?court=IL092015J. Records are current to 1989.

Wabash County

Circuit Court PO Box 997, 401 Market St, Mt Carmel, IL 62863; 618-262-5362; fax: 618-263-4441; 8AM-5PM (CST). *Felony, Misdemeanor, Civil, Eviction, Small Claims, Probate.*

General Information: Probate fax is same as main fax number. Online identifiers in results same as on public terminal. No juvenile or adoption records released. Will fax documents for $2.50 per page pre-paid. Court makes copy: $.50 each 1st 20 pages; $.25 each add'l. Self serve copy: $.25 per page. Certification fee: $5.00 per seal plus copy fee if over 1-2 pages. Payee: Clerk of Circuit Court. Only cashiers checks and money orders accepted. No credit cards accepted. Prepayment required. Mail requests: SASE required.

Civil Name Search: Access: Mail, in person, online. Both court and visitors may perform in person name searches. Search fee: $4.00 per name per year. Civil records on computer from 1988, index books from 1800s. Mail turnaround time 5 days. Civil PAT goes back to 1988. Online access is free at www.judici.com/. A premium fee service is also available with multi-county search capabilities and other features. Case files are available from 2000.

Criminal Name Search: Access: Mail, in person, online. Both court and visitors may perform in person name searches. Search fee: $4.00 per name per year. Required to search: name, years to search, DOB. Criminal records computerized from 1988, index books from 1800s. Note: Results include name and case number. Mail turnaround time 5 days. Criminal PAT goes back to same as civil. Online access is free at www.judici.com/. A premium fee service is also available with multi-county search capabilities and other features. Case files are available from 2000. Online results show name, DOB.

Warren County

Circuit Court 100 W Broadway, Monmouth, IL 61462; 309-734-5179; criminal phone: x302; civil phone: x304; probate phone: x306; fax: 309-734-4151; 8AM-4:30PM (CST). *Felony, Misdemeanor, Civil, Eviction, Small Claims, Probate.*

General Information: No juvenile or adoption records released. Will fax documents uncertified. Court makes copy: $2.00 1st page; $.50 each add'l. Certification fee: $3.00 plus copy fee. Payee: Clerk of Circuit Court. Only cashiers checks and money orders accepted. Major credit cards accepted. Prepayment required. Mail requests: SASE required.

Civil Name Search: Access: Mail, in person. Both court and visitors may perform in person name searches. Search fee: $5.00 per name per year. Civil cases indexed by defendant. Civil records on computer from 2000, index books from 1800s. Mail turnaround time 7-10 days. Civil PAT goes back to 1999.

Criminal Name Search: Access: Mail, in person. Both court and visitors may perform in person name searches. Search fee: $5.00 per name per year. Required to search: name, years to search, DOB. Criminal records computerized from 2000, index books from 1800s. Mail turnaround time 7-10 days. Criminal PAT goes back to same as civil.

Washington County

Circuit Court 101 E St Louis St, Nashville, IL 62263; 618-327-4800 X305; fax: 618-327-3583; 8AM-4PM (CST). *Felony, Misdemeanor, Civil, Eviction, Small Claims, Probate.*

General Information: Probate fax is same as main fax number. No juvenile or adoption records released. Will fax documents to local or toll free line. Court makes copy: $1.00 per page. Self serve copy: $.50 per page. Certification fee: $3.00 per document. Payee: Washington County Circuit Clerk. No personal checks accepted. Prepayment required. Will bill to attorneys. Mail requests: SASE required.

Civil Name Search: Access: Mail, in person, online. Both court and visitors may perform in person name searches. Search fee: $5.00 per name per year. Civil records on computer since 1998; 1988 for child support; prior records on index books from 1800s. Mail turnaround time 3-5 days. Civil PAT goes back to 1997. Online access is free at www.judici.com/. A premium fee service is also available with multi-county search capabilities and other features. Case files are available from 1997.

Criminal Name Search: Access: Mail, in person, online. Both court and visitors may perform in person name searches. Search fee: $5.00 per name per year. Required to search: name, years to search; also helpful: DOB. Criminal records on computer since 1998; 1988 for child support; prior records on index books from 1800s. Mail turnaround time 3-5 days. Criminal PAT goes back to same as civil. Online access is free at www.judici.com/. A premium fee service is also available with multi-county search capabilities and other features. Case files are available from 1997. Online results show middle initial, DOB.

Wayne County

Circuit Court County Courthouse, 307 E Main St, Fairfield, IL 62837; 618-842-7684; fax: 618-842-2556; 8AM-4:30PM (CST). *Felony, Misdemeanor, Civil, Small Claims, Probate.*
www.illinoissecondcircuit.info/county_wayne.html

General Information: Probate fax is same as main fax number. Online identifiers in results same as on public terminal. No juvenile or adoption records released. Will fax documents. Court makes copy: $1.00 1st page, $.50 each add'l. Self serve copy: same. Certification fee: $5.00 per certification. Payee: Clerk of Circuit Court. Only cashiers checks and money orders accepted. Visa/MC/AmEx cards accepted through Illinoispay.com. Prepayment required. Mail requests: SASE required.

Civil Name Search: Access: Mail, fax, in person, online. Both court and visitors may perform in person name searches. Search fee: $4.00 per name per year. Civil records on computer back to 11/88, index books from 1800s. Mail turnaround time 1 week. Civil PAT goes back to 1988. Online access is free at www.judici.com/. A premium fee service is also available with multi-county search capabilities and other features. Case files are available from 1988.

Criminal Name Search: Access: Mail, fax, in person, online. Both court and visitors may perform in person name searches. Search fee: $4.00 per name per year. Required to search: name, years to search, DOB. Criminal records computerized back 1/1990. Mail turnaround time 1 week. Criminal PAT goes back to same as civil. Online access is free at www.judici.com/. A premium fee service is also available with multi-county search capabilities and other features. Case files are available from 1988. Online results show middle initial.

White County

Circuit Court PO Box 310, 301 E Main, County Courthouse, Carmi, IL 62821; 618-382-2321 x4; fax: 618-382-2322; 8AM-4PM (CST). *Felony, Misdemeanor, Civil, Small Claims, Probate.*
www.whitecounty-il.gov/

General Information: Probate fax is same as main fax number. Online identifiers in results same as on public terminal. No juvenile or adoption records released. Will fax documents $2.00 per page. Court makes copy: $.50 per page. Self serve copy: same. Certification fee: $5.00 1st page plus copy fee for 2nd or add'l pages. Payee: Clerk of Circuit Court. Only cashier's checks or money orders accepted. No credit cards accepted. Prepayment required. Mail requests: SASE required.

Civil Name Search: Access: Fax, mail, in person, online. Both court and visitors may perform in person name searches. Search fee: $4.00 per name

per year. Civil records on computer from 1992, index books from 1800s. Mail turnaround time 1-2 weeks. Civil PAT goes back to 1992. Results include name and case number. Online access is free at www.judici.com/. A premium fee service is also available with multi-county search capabilities and other features. Case files are available from 1992.

Criminal Name Search: Access: Fax, mail, in person, online. Both court and visitors may perform in person name searches. Search fee: $4.00 per name per year. Required to search: name, years to search; also helpful: DOB. Criminal records computerized from 1992, index books from 1800s. Mail turnaround time 1-2 weeks. Criminal PAT goes back to same as civil. Results include name and DOB. Online access is free at www.judici.com/. A premium fee service is also available with multi-county search capabilities and other features. Case files are available from 1992.

Whiteside County

Circuit Court 200 E Knox St, Morrison, IL 61270-2698; 815-772-5188; fax: 815-772-5187; 8:30AM-4:30PM (CST). *Felony, Misdemeanor, Civil, Eviction, Small Claims, Probate.*
www.whiteside.org/circuit-clerk/

General Information: Online identifiers in results same as on public terminal. No juvenile or adoption records released. No fee to fax documents locally only. Court makes copy: $1.50 1st page, $.50 each add'l up to 20, $.25 each add'l. $3.00 if microfilmed. Certification fee: $4.00. Payee: Clerk of Circuit Court. Personal checks accepted for search/copy-related fees. No credit cards accepted. Prepayment required. Mail requests: SASE required.

Civil Name Search: Access: Phone, fax, mail, in person, online. Both court and visitors may perform in person name searches. Search fee: $6.00 per name. Civil cases indexed by defendant. Civil records on computer from 1989, index books from 1800s. Mail turnaround time 1 month. Civil PAT goes back to 1989. Online access is free at www.judici.com/. A premium fee service is also available with multi-county search capabilities and other features. Case files are available from 1989.

Criminal Name Search: Access: Phone, fax, mail, in person, online. Both court and visitors may perform in person name searches. Search fee: $6.00 per name. Required to search: name, years to search, DOB. Criminal records computerized from 1989, index books from 1800s. Mail turnaround time 1-3 weeks. Criminal PAT goes back to same as civil. Access to criminal records is the same as civil. Online results show middle initial, DOB.

Will County

Circuit Court 14 W Jefferson St, #212, Joliet, IL 60432; 815-727-8592; probate phone: 815-730-7155; fax: 815-727-8896; 8:30AM-4:30PM (CST). *Felony, Misdemeanor, Civil, Eviction, Small Claims, Probate.*
www.willcountycircuitcourt.com

General Information: Probate fax- 815-730-7160 No juvenile, adoption, mental health records released. Will not fax documents. Court makes copy: $2.00 1st page; $.50 each for 2-19 pages; then $.25 each add'l per case. Certification fee: $6.00 per certification. Payee: Pamela J McGuire Clerk of Circuit Court. Cash, cashiers checks and money orders accepted. No personal checks. Major credit cards accepted. Prepayment required. Mail requests: SASE required.

Civil Name Search: Access: Fax, mail, in person, online. Both court and visitors may perform in person name searches. Search fee: $6.00 per name per year. Civil records on computer from 1989, index books from 1800s. Mail turnaround time 48 hours. Civil PAT goes back to 10 years. Online access to civil court records is the same as criminal, see below.

Criminal Name Search: Access: Fax, mail, in person, online. Both court and visitors may perform in person name searches. Search fee: $6.00 per name per year. Required to search: name, years to search, DOB. Criminal records computerized from 1989, index books from 1800s. Mail turnaround time 48 hours. Criminal PAT goes back to same as civil. A free online name search of the docket is at http://66.158.72.242/pa/cms/SearchPrompt.php. Also a subscription service with an annual fee of $240 for this county, or $300/yr for all participating IL counties is offered. Counties are: Champaign, DeKalb, Kendall, LaSalle, Madison, Sangamon, Will. Visit www.clericusmagnus.com or www.janojustice.com or call 800-250-9884 for details and signup. Online results show middle initial, DOB.

Williamson County

Circuit Court 200 W Jefferson St, Marion, IL 62959; 618-997-1301; 8AM-4PM (CST). *Felony, Misdemeanor, Civil, Eviction, Small Claims, Probate.*
www.state.il.us/court/CircuitCourt/default.asp

General Information: Online identifiers in results same as on public terminal. No juvenile or adoption records released. Will not fax documents. Court makes copy: $1.00 1st page, $.50 each add'l. Certification fee: $2.00. Payee: Clerk of Circuit Court. Business checks accepted. No credit cards accepted. Prepayment required. Mail requests: SASE required.

Civil Name Search: Access: Mail, in person, online. Both court and visitors may perform in person name searches. Search fee: $4.00 per name per year. Civil records on computer from 7/86, index books from 1800s. Mail turnaround time 1 week. Civil PAT goes back to 7/1986. Online access is free at www.judici.com/. A premium fee service is also available with multi-county search capabilities and other features. Case files are available from 1986. Also, court calendars available free at http://williamsoncountycourthouse.com/p/calendars.php.

Criminal Name Search: Access: Mail, in person, online. Both court and visitors may perform in person name searches. Search fee: $4.00 per name per year. Required to search: name, years to search, DOB. Criminal records computerized from 7/86, index books from 1800s. Mail turnaround time 1 week. Criminal PAT goes back to same as civil. Online access to criminal same as civil, see above. Online results show name, DOB.

Winnebago County

Circuit Court 400 W State St, Rockford, IL 61101; 815-319-4500; fax: 815-319-4571; 8AM-5PM (CST). *Felony, Misdemeanor, Civil, Eviction, Small Claims, Probate.*
www.cc.co.winnebago.il.us

General Information: Criminal records is in Rm 108. Civil is Rm 104. No juvenile, mental or adoption records released. Will fax documents to local or toll-free number. Court makes copy: $2.00 1st page, $.50 each add'l. $.25 per page after 19. Certification fee: $6.00 per doc. Payee: Clerk of Circuit Court. Personal checks accepted. Prepayment required. Mail requests: SASE required.

Civil Name Search: Access: Phone, mail, in person, online. Both court and visitors may perform in person name searches. Search fee: $6.00 per name per year. Civil records on computer back to 1983; prior records on index books from 1800s. Mail turnaround time 1 week. Civil PAT goes back to 1980. Online access to civil court records is the same as describe for criminal - see that section. Cases are available from 1988.

Criminal Name Search: Access: Phone, mail, in person, online. Both court and visitors may perform in person name searches. Search fee: $6.00 per name per year. Required to search: name, years to search, DOB. Criminal records computerized from 1983; prior records on index books from 1800s. Mail turnaround time 1 week. Criminal PAT goes back to 1985. Online access is at www.cc.co.winnebago.il.us/caseinfo.asp?P=I. Complete case files are available from 1980. Traffic citations, DUIs, and ordinance violations are available from 1996. The web page offers an excellent User's Guide that explains how to fully use the system. Court calendars are also available.

Woodford County

Circuit Court PO Box 284, 115 N Main, County Courthouse #201, Eureka, IL 61530; 309-467-3312; 8AM-5PM (CST). *Felony, Misdemeanor, Civil, Eviction, Small Claims, Probate.*

General Information: No juvenile or adoption records released. Will not fax documents. Court makes copy: $.50 per page. Certification fee: $4.00. Cert fee includes copies. Payee: Woodford County Circuit Clerk. Personal checks accepted. Major credit cards accepted in person. Prepayment required. Mail requests: SASE required.

Civil Name Search: Access: Mail, in person, online. Both court and visitors may perform in person name searches. Search fee: $5.00 per name per year. Civil records on computer from 1990, index books from 1800s. Mail turnaround time 2-3 days. Civil PAT goes back to 1990. Online access to civil cases same as criminal, see below.

Criminal Name Search: Access: Mail, in person, online. Both court and visitors may perform in person name searches. Search fee: $5.00 per name per year. Required to search: name, years to search, DOB. Criminal records computerized from 1990, index books from 1800s. Mail turnaround time 2-3 days. Criminal PAT goes back to same as civil. Online access is free at www.judici.com/. A premium fee service is also available with multi-county search capabilities and other features. Case files are available from 2000.

Common Abbreviations Found in Text

- DL   Driver's license number
- PAT   Public use access terminal
- SASE   Self-addressed, stamped envelope
- SSN   Social Security Number

Indiana

Time Zone: **EST & CST***

*12 Western Indiana counties are CST. They are: Gibson, Jasper, La Porte, Lake, Newton, Perry, Porter, Posey, Spencer, Starke, Vanderburgh, Warrick. The remainder are in the EST. All IN counties now observe daylight savings time.

Capital: **Indianapolis, Marion County**

# of Counties: **92**

State Web: **www.in.gov**

Court Web: **www.in.gov/judiciary**

Administration

Division of State Court Administrator, 30 South Meridian St, Suite 500, Indianapolis, IN, 46204; 317-232-2542, Fax 317-233-6586.

The Supreme and Appellate Courts

The Supreme Court is the court of last resort. The Court of Appeals of Indiana is an intermediate appellate court and Indiana's second-highest court. Decisions and case records from the Supreme and Appellate Courts are viewable online from the home page mentioned above.

The Indiana Courts

Court	Type	How Organized	Jurisdiction Highpoints
Circuit*	General	92 Courts in 90 Circuits	Felony, Misdemeanor, Civil, Small Claims, Juvenile, Traffic, Eviction, Domestic Relations, Estate
Superior*	General	72 Courts	Felony, Misdemeanor, Civil, Small Claims, Juvenile, Traffic, Eviction, Domestic Relations, Estate
City/Town	Limited	75	Misdemeanors, Ordinances, Traffic
Probate	Special	1	Probate
Small Claims - Marion	Special	9 Courts in Townships	Small Claims

* = profiled in this book

Details on the Court Structure

Indiana has 92 counties, and 90 of these counties comprise their own circuit, with their own **Circuit Court**. The remaining two small counties (Ohio and Dearborn counties) have combined to form one circuit. Circuit courts traditionally heard all civil and criminal cases and have unlimited trial jurisdiction, except when exclusive or concurrent (shared) jurisdiction is conferred upon other courts. Circuit Courts also have appellate jurisdiction over appeals from City and Town Courts.

The majority of Indiana trial court cases are held in the **Superior Courts** and almost all Indiana counties have Superior Courts in addition to their Circuit Court. For the most part Superiors Courts also have general jurisdiction but their trial jurisdiction and organization varies from county to county. They can hear all civil and criminal cases, and small claims and minor offense cases.

In counties without Superior Courts, the Circuit Courts in addition to all other cases, also handle small claims cases, such as civil disputes involving less than $6,000 and minor offenses, such as misdemeanors, ordinance violations, and Class D felonies.

Currently there are forty-seven **City Courts** and twenty-eight **Town Courts** in Indiana. City and Town Courts handle minor offenses such as violations of city ordinances (laws), misdemeanors, and infractions. These courts commonly handle traffic matters. City and Town courts are not courts of record (their proceedings are not recorded), so appeals from city and town courts go to the circuit or superior courts and are decided as if they have never been to court before.

Note that Small Claims cases in Marion County are heard at the township and records are maintained at that level.

Record Searching Facts You Need to Know

Fees and Record Searching Tips

The Circuit Court Clerk/County Clerk in a county is the same individual and is responsible for keeping all county judicial records. However, we recommend that, when requesting a record, the request indicate which court heard the case (Circuit, Superior, or County). Many courts do not perform searches, especially criminal searches, based on a 7/8/96 statement by the State Board of Accounts. State statute sets the certification fee as $1.00 per document plus copy fee and $1.00 per page for copies. Most but not all courts follow this fee structure.

Online Access is Wide Spread but not Statewide

Implementation of an online record search system available for the public, called Odyssey, has at least thirty counties on the system with plans for more to be added. Visit http://mycase.in.gov/default.aspx.

Also, a vendor is working closely with many counties to provide electronic access. A limited free search of open case index is available at www.doxpop.com/prod/welcome.jsp. Full access to case records requires registration and subscription, the fees range from $30.00 to $1,020.00 per month depending on number of searches. Although not statewide, this is an expanding service that is also adding recording office data. At press time this system had 51 counties participating.

Note that counties must be approved by Trail Rule 77 in order to post court records on the Internet. See www.in.gov/judiciary/rules/trial_proc/index.html#r77.

Adams County

Circuit & Superior Court PO Box 189, 112 S 2nd St, Decatur, IN 46733; 260-724-5309; fax: 260-724-5313; 8AM-4:30PM (EST). *Felony, Misdemeanor, Civil, Eviction, Small Claims, Probate.*

General Information: No juvenile, adoption, mental health or sealed records released. Will fax specific case file $1.00 per page. Court makes copy: $1.00 per page. Certification fee: $1.00 per page plus copy fee. Payee: Adams County Clerk. Only cashiers checks and money orders accepted. No credit cards accepted. Prepayment required.

Civil Name Search: Access: In person, online. Visitors must perform in person searches themselves. Civil records on computer from 1992, archived from 1876. Some records on index cards. Civil PAT goes back to 1979. Public terminal has limited data available. Access civil records by subscription to Doxpop at https://www.doxpop.com/prod/court/. Free index search. Records available from 06/1990, tax warrants from 2002.

Criminal Name Search: Access: In person, online. Visitors must perform in person searches themselves. Required to search: name, years to search, DOB; SSN helpful. Criminal records computerized from 1992, archived from 1876. Some records on index cards. Criminal PAT goes back to same as civil. Public terminal has limited data available. Online is same as civil.

Allen County

Circuit & Superior Court 715 S Calhoun St, Rm 201, Courthouse, Attn; Records Mgmt Rm 202, Ft Wayne, IN 46802; 260-449-7890; fax: 260-449-7929; 8AM-4:30PM (EST). *Felony, Misdemeanor, Civil, Eviction, Small Claims, Probate.*

www.allencounty.us/courts/clerk-of-the-courts

General Information: Main number is 260-449-7245; misdemeanor & traffic 260-449-7655; small claims 260-449-7130; Court Admin.- Circuit 449-7602, Superior 449-7681. No juvenile, adoption or sealed records released. Will not fax out case files. Court makes copy: $1.00 per page. Certification fee: $1.00 per doc plus copy fee. Payee: Clerk of Allen Circuit Court. Business checks accepted. Major credit cards accepted through Government Payment Svcs, Inc. Prepayment required.

Civil Name Search: Access: In person, online. Visitors must perform in person searches themselves. Recent civil cases on computer back to 10/1995; some prior records on microfiche, archived and index from 1824. Civil PAT goes back to 10/1995. Access civil records by subscription to Doxpop at https://www.doxpop.com/prod/court/. Free index search. The probate index plus the record index from the New Haven City Court is available at http://mycase.in.gov/.

Criminal Name Search: Access: In person, online. Visitors must perform in person searches themselves. Felony cases on computer back to 2/1994; some prior records on microfiche, archived and index from 1824. Criminal PAT goes back to 2/1994. Results include next hearing date if any. The criminal and citation record index available at http://mycase.in.gov/default.aspx. Free index search.

Bartholomew County

Circuit & Superior Court PO Box 924, Columbus, IN 47202-0924; 812-379-1600; fax: 812-379-1675; 8AM-5PM (EST). *Felony, Misdemeanor, Civil, Eviction, Small Claims, Probate.*

www.bartholomewco.com

General Information: This court will only search felony and misdemeanor cases. Probate fax is same as main fax number. Online identifiers in results same as on public terminal. No juvenile, mental health, adoption or sealed released. All searches 1985 to present. Will fax out specific case files $1.00 per page. Court makes copy: no fee if less than 10 copies; if 10 or more $1.00 plus $.10 ea copy over 10. Self serve copy: same. Certification fee: $1.00 per page. Payee: Bartholomew County Clerk. Personal checks accepted. No credit cards accepted. Mail requests: SASE required.

Civil Name Search: Access: In person, online. Visitors must perform in person searches themselves. Required to search: name, DOB, SSN. Civil cases indexed by plaintiff. Civil records on computer from 1985. Civil PAT goes back to 1985. Online subscription service at https://www.doxpop.com/prod/. Fees involved. Records date from 5/85.

Criminal Name Search: Access: Fax, mail, in person, online. Visitors must perform in person searches themselves. No search fee. Required to search: name, years to search, DOB. Criminal records computerized from 1985. Criminal PAT goes back to same as civil. Online access to criminal is same as civil.

Benton County

Circuit & Superior Court 706 E 5th St, #37, Fowler, IN 47944-1556; 765-884-0930; fax: 765-884-0322; 8:30AM-4PM (EST). *Felony, Misdemeanor, Civil, Eviction, Small Claims, Probate.*

General Information: No juvenile, mental, adoption or sealed released. Will fax documents to local or toll free line, fax copy of check for searching. Court makes copy: $1.00 per page. Self serve copy: $1.00. Payee: Natalie Kidd. Only cashiers checks, business checks and money orders accepted. No credit cards accepted. Prepayment required. Mail requests: SASE required for criminal.

Civil Name Search: Access: In person, online. Visitors must perform in person searches themselves. Civil records on computer from 1992, on index books from 1860. Civil PAT goes back to 1992. The record index is available at http://mycase.in.gov/. But only several years of records are available.

Criminal Name Search: Access: Mail, in person, fax. Both court and visitors may perform in person name searches. Search fee: $8.00 per name; send search requests to attention of Natalie Kidd in clerk's office. Required to search: name, years to search, DOB. Criminal records computerized from 1992, on index books from 1860. Mail turnaround time 2-3 days. Criminal PAT goes back to same as civil. The record index is available at http://mycase.in.gov/. But only several years of records are available.

Blackford County

Circuit & Superior Court 110 W Washington St, Hartford City, IN 47348; 765-348-1130; fax: 765-348-7234; 8AM-4PM (EST). *Felony, Misdemeanor, Civil, Eviction, Small Claims, Probate.*

General Information: No juvenile, mental, adoption or sealed released. Fee to fax out file $1.00 per page. Court makes copy: $1.00 per page. Certification fee: $2.00 per cert. Payee: Clerk of Blackford County. Business and personal checks accepted. No credit cards accepted. Prepayment required. Mail requests: SASE required.

Civil Name Search: Access: Fax, mail, in person. Visitors must perform in person searches themselves. No search fee. Required to search: name. Civil records on computer from 1991, on index from 1800. Civil PAT goes back to 1991. The record index is available at http://mycase.in.gov/. But only several years of records are available.

Criminal Name Search: Access: Fax, mail, in person, Online. Visitors must perform in person searches themselves. No search fee. Required to search: name; also helpful: SSN, DOB, years to search. court records on computer from 1991, on index from 1800. Mail turnaround time 1 week. Criminal PAT goes back to same as civil. The record index is available at http://mycase.in.gov/. But only several years of records are available. Although dates of birth can be used as a search feature in criminal cases, the Indiana Supreme Court has determined that dates of birth will not be displayed in Public Access.

Boone County

Circuit & Superior Court I & II Rm 212, Courthouse Sq, Lebanon, IN 46052; 765-482-3510; fax: 765-485-0150; 8AM-4PM (EST). *Felony, Misdemeanor, Civil, Eviction, Small Claims, Probate.*

http://boonecounty.in.gov/Default.aspx?tabid=103

General Information: No juvenile, mental, adoption or sealed released. Will fax documents to local or toll free line. Court makes copy: $1.00 per page for court orders, $.10 for pleadings. Certification fee: $1.00 per cert. Payee: Boone County Clerk. Business checks accepted, no personal checks. Major credit cards accepted at www.govpay.com copy code PLC6457. Prepayment required. Mail requests: SASE required.

Civil Name Search: Access: Mail, in person, Online. Both court and visitors may perform in person name searches. No search fee. Civil docket indexed from 2002. Mail turnaround time 1 week. Civil PAT goes back to 2002. Access the civil docket index by name or case number at http://courtviewpa.boonecounty.in.gov/pa/.

Criminal Name Search: Access: Mail, in person, online. Both court and visitors may perform in person name searches. No search fee. Required to search: name, years to search; also helpful: SSN. Criminal records indexed from 1900. Mail turnaround time 1 week. Criminal PAT goes back to 2002. Access the criminal docket index by name or case number at http://courtviewpa.boonecounty.in.gov/pa/.

Brown County

Circuit Court Box 85, 20 E Main, Nashville, IN 47448; 812-988-5510; fax: 812-988-5562; 8AM-4PM (EST). *Felony, Misdemeanor, Civil, Eviction, Small Claims, Probate.*

General Information: No juvenile, mental, adoption or sealed records released. Will not fax documents. Court makes copy: $1.00 per page. Self serve copy: same. Certification fee: $1.00 plus copy fee. Payee: County Clerk. Local personal checks accepted. Major credit cards accepted through 3rd party; transaction fee applies. Prepayment required.

Civil Name Search: Access: In person, online. Visitors must perform in person searches themselves. Civil records open cases on computer from 1993, in entry books from early 1800s. Civil PAT goes back to 1993. Fee access to civil chronological back to 1993 is by subscription at https://www.doxpop.com/prod/; free access limited to only current open cases, case summary only.

Criminal Name Search: Access: In person, online. Visitors must perform in person searches themselves. Required to search: name, years to search, DOB; also helpful: SSN. Criminal records open cases on computer from 1993, in entry books from early 1800s. Criminal PAT goes back to same as civil. Fee access to criminal chronological back to 1993 is by subscription at www.doxpop.com; free access limited to only current open cases.

Carroll County

Circuit & Superior Court Courthouse, 101 W Main, Delphi, IN 46923; 765-564-4485; fax: 765-564-1835; 8AM-5PM M,T,Th,F; 8AM-N W (EST). *Felony, Misdemeanor, Civil, Eviction, Small Claims, Probate.*

General Information: No juvenile, mental, adoption or sealed released. Will not fax documents. Court makes copy: $1.00 per page. Certification fee: $1.00. Payee: Carroll County Clerk. No personal checks. Major credit cards accepted via vendor, fees charged. Prepayment required.

Civil Name Search: Access: In person, online. Visitors must perform in person searches themselves. Civil records archived from 1981, on index from 1828. Civil PAT goes back to 4/2010. The record index is available at http://mycase.in.gov/. But only several years of records are available.

Criminal Name Search: Access: In person, online. Visitors must perform in person searches themselves. Criminal records archived from 1981, on index from 1828. Criminal PAT goes back to 4/2010. The record index is available at http://mycase.in.gov/. But only several years of records are available, 4/2010.

Cass County

Circuit & Superior Court 200 Court Park, Logansport, IN 46947; 574-753-7730; fax: 574-753-3596; 8AM-4PM (EST). *Felony, Misdemeanor, Civil, Eviction, Small Claims, Probate.*

www.co.cass.in.us/dav/courts/circuit.html

General Information: No juvenile, mental, adoption or sealed released. Will not fax documents. Court makes copy: $.10 per page. Certification fee: $3.00. Payee: Cass County Clerk. No personal checks; use money order. Prepayment required. Mail requests: SASE requested.

Civil Name Search: Access: Mail, in person, online. Both court and visitors may perform in person name searches. No search fee. Civil records on computer from 1989, on index from 1830s. Mail turnaround time 2 weeks. Civil PAT goes back to 1989. The record index is available at http://mycase.in.gov/.

Criminal Name Search: Access: Mail, in person, online. Both court and visitors may perform in person name searches. No search fee. Required to search: name, years to search, DOB; also helpful: SSN, signed release. Criminal records computerized from 1989, on index from 1830s. Mail turnaround time 2 weeks. Criminal PAT goes back to same as civil. The record index is available at http://mycase.in.gov/.

Clark County

Circuit & Superior Court 501 E Court, Rm 137, Jeffersonville, IN 47130; 812-285-6244; fax: 812-285-6372; 8:30AM-4:30PM; 8:30-N Sat (EST). *Felony, Misdemeanor, Civil, Eviction, Small Claims, Probate.*

www.co.clark.in.us/governmentdirectory.html

General Information: No juvenile, mental, adoption or sealed released. Court makes copy: $.10 per page. Self serve copy: same. Certification fee: $1.00 per cert. Payee: County Clerk. Business checks not accepted. No credit cards accepted. Prepayment required.

Civil Name Search: Access: In person, online. Visitors must perform in person searches themselves. Required to search: name, years to search; also helpful: address. Civil records on computer since 8/92, on books from 1900. Civil PAT goes back to 1993. Results sometimes last 4 digits on SSN. The record index is available at http://mycase.in.gov/. But only several years of records are available.

Criminal Name Search: Access: In person, online. Visitors must perform in person searches themselves. Required to search: name, years to search; also helpful: DOB, SSN. Criminal records on computer since 8/92, on books from 1900. Criminal PAT goes back to 1992. Physical traits appear in terminal results, if in file. The record index is available at http://mycase.in.gov/. But only several years of records are available. Online results show name only.

Clay County

Circuit & Superior Court 609 E National Ave, #213, Brazil, IN 47834; 812-448-9024; fax: 812-446-9602; 8AM-4PM (EST). *Felony, Misdemeanor, Civil, Eviction, Small Claims, Probate.*

www.claycountyin.gov/metadot/index.pl

General Information: No juvenile, mental, adoption or sealed released. Court makes copy: $1.00 per page. Self serve copy: same. Certification fee: $2.00. Payee: County Clerk. Business checks accepted if in-state. No credit cards accepted. Prepayment required.

Civil Name Search: Access: Phone, In person, online. Visitors must perform in person searches themselves. No search fee. Required to search: name, years to search; also helpful: address. Civil docket indexed from 1850; on computer back to 1995. Note: Clerk will only phone search the computer for current cases only. Civil PAT goes back to 1996 but not complete. Online subscription service at https://www.doxpop.com. Fees involved. A limited free search of open cases is available. Online index goes back to 9/1994; images to 8/2000.

Criminal Name Search: Access: Phone, In person, online. Visitors must perform in person searches themselves. No search fee. Required to search:

name, years to search, address, DOB; also helpful-SSN, signed release. Criminal records indexed from 1850; on computer back to 1995. Note: Clerk will only phone search the computer for current cases only. Criminal PAT goes back to 1996 but not complete. Online subscription service at https://www.doxpop.com. Fees involved. A limited free search of open cases is available. Online index goes back to 9/1994; images to 8/2000.

Clinton County

Circuit & Superior Court 265 Courthouse Square, Frankfort, IN 46041; 765-659-6335; fax: 765-659-6347; 8AM-4PM; 8:AM-N TH (EST). *Felony, Misdemeanor, Civil, Eviction, Small Claims, Probate.*

General Information: No juvenile, mental, adoption or sealed released. Will not fax documents. Court makes copy: $1.00 per page. Certification fee: $1.00 per page plus copy fee. Payee: County Clerk. Business checks accepted. No credit cards accepted. Prepayment required.

Civil Name Search: Access: In person, online. Visitors must perform in person searches themselves. Civil records on computer from 1991, on microfiche and index from 1900s. Civil PAT goes back to 1991. Online subscription service at https://www.doxpop.com. Fees involved. Records date from 01/91. A limited free search of open cases is available. The county will be added to the states' system at http://mycase.in.gov/default.aspx in the near future.

Criminal Name Search: Access: In person, online. Visitors must perform in person searches themselves. Required to search: name, years to search, signed release; also helpful: DOB. Criminal records computerized from 1991, on microfiche and index from 1900s. Criminal PAT goes back to same as civil. Online subscription service at https://www.doxpop.com. Fees involved. Records date from 01/91. A limited free search of open cases is available. The county will be added to the states' system at http://mycase.in.gov/default.aspx in the near future. Online results show middle initial, DOB, address.

Crawford County

Circuit Court Box 375, English, IN 47118; 812-338-2565; fax: 812-338-2507; 8AM-4PM M,F; 8AM-6PM T-TH (EST). *Felony, Misdemeanor, Civil, Eviction, Small Claims, Probate.*

General Information: Probate fax is same as main fax number. No juvenile, mental, adoption or sealed released. No fee to fax documents. Court makes copy: $1.00 per page. Self serve copy: $.50 per page. Certification fee: $2.00 per document. Payee: County Clerk. Business checks accepted. No credit cards accepted. Prepayment required.

Civil Name Search: Access: In person only. Visitors must perform in person searches themselves. Civil docket indexed from 1900s.

Criminal Name Search: Access: In person only. Only the court performs in person name searches; visitors may not. Required to search: name, years to search, DOB, SSN, signed release. Criminal records indexed from 1900s. Mail turnaround time 1 week.

Daviess County

Circuit & Superior Court PO Box 739, Washington, IN 47501; 812-254-8664; criminal phone: 812-254-8669; civil phone: 812-254-8664; probate phone: 812-254-8664; fax: 812-254-8698; 8AM-4PM (EST). *Felony, Misdemeanor, Civil, Eviction, Small Claims, Probate.*

General Information: Election phone number: 812-254-8679; Small Claims phone number: 812-254-8669. No juvenile, mental, adoption or sealed records released. Will not fax documents. Court makes copy: $1.00 per page. Self serve copy: same. Certification fee: $1.00 per cert plus copy fee. Payee: Daviess County Clerk. Business checks accepted. Major credit cards accepted in person. Prepayment required. Mail requests: SASE required.

Civil Name Search: Access: Mail, in person, online. Both court and visitors may perform in person name searches. No search fee. Civil docket indexed from 1900s; recent on computer since 1993. Mail turnaround time varies. Civil PAT goes back to 1994. Online subscription service at https://www.doxpop.com. Fees involved. Records date from 02/94. A limited free search of open cases is available.

Criminal Name Search: Access: Mail, in person, online. Both court and visitors may perform in person name searches. No search fee. Criminal records indexed from 1900s; recent on computer since 1994. Mail turnaround time varies. Criminal PAT available. Online subscription service at https://www.doxpop.com. Fees involved. Records date from 02/94. A limited free search of open cases is available. Online results show name, DOB.

Dearborn County

Circuit & Superior Court 1 & 2 Courthouse, 215 W High St, Lawrenceburg, IN 47025; 812-537-8867; fax: 812-532-2021; 8:30AM-4:30PM (EST). *Felony, Misdemeanor, Civil, Eviction, Small Claims, Probate.*

www.dearborncounty.org/datafiles/judges.html

General Information: Mail searches are ONLY done for marriage licenses and FBI searches. No juvenile, mental, adoption or sealed records released. Will not fax documents. Court makes copy: $1.00 per page. Certification fee:

$1.00 per cert. Payee: Circuit Court Clerk. Only cashiers checks and money orders accepted. No credit cards accepted. Prepayment required.

Civil Name Search: Access: In person only. Visitors must perform in person searches themselves. Civil records on computer from 1992, on index from 1970s. Civil PAT goes back to 2000 countywide.

Criminal Name Search: Access: In person only. Visitors must perform in person searches themselves. Required to search: name, years to search, DOB; SSN helpful. Criminal records computerized from 1992, on index from 1970s, archived to 1930. Criminal PAT goes back to same as civil.

Decatur County

Circuit & Superior Court 150 Courthouse Square, #244, Greensburg, IN 47240; 812-663-8223/8642; fax: 812-662-6627; 8AM-4PM M-TH; 8AM-5PM F (EST). *Felony, Misdemeanor, Civil, Eviction, Small Claims, Probate.*

www.decaturcounty.in.gov

General Information: This court is in process of scanning all documents to place on the online site. No juvenile, mental, adoption or sealed released. Will fax specific case file if situation warrants. Court makes copy: $1.00 per page. Certification fee: $1.00 per page. Payee: Decatur County Clerk. No personal checks accepted. No credit cards accepted for research. Prepayment required.

Civil Name Search: Access: In person, online. Visitors must perform in person searches themselves. Civil docket indexed from 1823; on computer back to 1998. Civil PAT goes back to 1998. Online subscription service at https://www.doxpop.com. Fees involved. A limited free search of open cases is available. Online records go back to 12/1998.

Criminal Name Search: Access: In person, online. Visitors must perform in person searches themselves. Required to search: name, years to search, DOB; SSN helpful. Criminal records indexed from 1823; on computer back to 1998. Criminal PAT goes back to same as civil. Online subscription service at https://www.doxpop.com. Fees involved. A limited free search of open cases is available. Online records go back to 12/1998. Online results show name, DOB, address.

DeKalb County

Circuit & Superior Court 1 & 2 PO Box 230, Auburn, IN 46706; 260-925-0912; fax: 260-925-5126; 8:30AM-4:30PM (EST). *Felony, Misdemeanor, Civil, Eviction, Small Claims, Probate.*

General Information: There are three working courts here. Superior I has traffic and criminal. Superior II has small claims and evictions. No juvenile, mental, adoption or sealed released. Will not fax out documents. Court makes copy: $1.00 per page. Certification fee: $1.00. Payee: DeKalb County Clerk. Only cashiers checks and money orders accepted. Major credit cards accepted. Prepayment required. Mail requests: SASE required for mail return of any copies.

Civil Name Search: Access: In person, online. Visitors must perform in person searches themselves. Civil records on computer back to 1987, on index from 1913. Note: The court will not perform a name search. Civil PAT goes back to 1987. Search the civil, family and probate docket by case number, party name or attorney name at http://mycase.in.gov/default.aspx.

Criminal Name Search: Access: In person, online. Visitors must perform in person searches themselves. No search fee. Required to search: name, years to search, DOB. Criminal records computerized from 1987. Note: Court will pull a file if case number known. Criminal PAT goes back to same as civil. Access court record index free at http://mycase.in.gov/default.aspx. Although dates of birth can be used as a search feature in criminal cases, the Indiana Supreme Court has determined that dates of birth will not be displayed in Public Access.

Delaware County

Circuit Court Box 1089, 100 W Main St, Muncie, IN 47308; 765-747-7726; fax: 765-747-7768; 8:30AM-4:30PM (EST). *Felony, Misdemeanor, Civil, Small Claims, Probate.*

www.in.gov/judiciary/delaware/

General Information: No juvenile, mental, adoption or sealed released. Fee to fax out file $2.00. Court makes copy: $.10 per page. Certification fee: $1.00. Payee: Delaware County Clerk. Business checks accepted. No credit cards accepted. Prepayment required. Mail requests: SASE required.

Civil Name Search: Access: Fax, mail, in person, online. Both court and visitors may perform in person name searches. No search fee. Civil records on computer from 1989, on microfiche, archived and on index from 1800. Mail turnaround time varies. Civil PAT goes back to 1989. Online subscription service at https://www.doxpop.com. Fees involved. Records date from 1/89. A limited free search of open cases is available. Index from Muncie City court also available online.

Criminal Name Search: Access: In person, online. Visitors must perform in person searches themselves. Required to search: name, years to search, DOB, SSN. Criminal records computerized from 1989, on microfiche, archived and on index from 1800. Criminal PAT goes back to same as civil. Also, an online subscription service is at www.doxpop.com. Fees involved. Records date from 01/89. A limited free search of open cases is available. An index from the Muncie City court is also available online.

Dubois County

Circuit & Superior Court 1 Courthouse Square, Jasper, IN 47546; 812-481-7035; fax: 812-481-7044; 8AM-4PM (EST). *Felony, Misdemeanor, Civil, Eviction, Small Claims, Probate.*
www.duboiscountyin.org/
General Information: No juvenile, mental, adoption or sealed records released. Will fax documents $3.00 1st page, $1.00 ea add'l page. Court makes copy: $.50 per page. Self serve copy: same. Certification fee: $1.00. Payee: Court Clerk. Personal checks accepted. No credit cards accepted. Prepayment required. Mail requests: SASE required for mail return of any copies.
Civil Name Search: Access: In person, online. Visitors must perform in person searches themselves. Required to search: name; also helpful: years to search. Civil records on computer from 8\93, on index books from 1930. Civil PAT goes back to 1993. Terminal results may show last 4 digits of SSN. Online subscription service at https://www.doxpop.com. Fees involved. Records date back to 10/1993. A limited free search of open cases is available.
Criminal Name Search: Access: In person, online. Visitors must perform in person searches themselves. Required to search: name; also helpful: years to search. Criminal records computerized from 8\93, on index books from 1930. Criminal PAT goes back to same as civil. Online access to criminal index same as civil.

Elkhart County

Elkhart Superior Courts 1, 2, 5, 6 315 S 2nd St, Elkhart, IN 46516; 574-523-2233 (1&2 clerk) /2305 (#5 clerk); fax: 574-523-2388; 8AM-4PM T-F; 8AM-5PM M (EST). *Felony, Misdemeanor, Civil, Eviction, Small Claims, Probate.*
www.elkhartcountyindiana.com/Departments/Clerk/index.htm
General Information: Online identifiers in results same as on public terminal. No juvenile, mental, adoption or sealed records released. Will not fax documents. Court makes copy: $1.00 per page. Self serve copy: same. Certification fee: $2.00. Payee: Elkhart County Court Clerk. No personal checks. Major credit cards accepted. Prepayment required.
Civil Name Search: Access: In person, online. Both court and visitors may perform in person name searches. No search fee. Civil records archived from 1830; on computer since 1995. Civil PAT goes back to 1996. Results may also give last 4 digits of SSN. Online subscription service at https://www.doxpop.com. Fees involved. Records date from 1/92. A limited free search of open cases is available.
Criminal Name Search: Access: In person, online. Both court and visitors may perform in person name searches. No search fee. Required to search: name, years to search, DOB; also helpful: SSN. Criminal records archived from 1830; on computer since 1995. Criminal PAT goes back to same as civil. Results give last 4 digits of SSN only. Identifiers are not always available. Online subscription service at https://www.doxpop.com. Fees involved. Records date from 1/92. A limited free search of open cases is available. Online results show middle initial, DOB.
Goshen Circuit & Superior Courts 3, 4 Courthouse, 101 N Main St, Goshen, IN 46526; 574-535-6429; fax: 574-535-6471; 8AM-5PM M, 8AM-4PM T-F (EST). *Felony, Misdemeanor, Civil, Eviction, Small Claims, Probate.*
www.elkhartcountyindiana.com/Departments/Clerk/index.htm
General Information: Includes Circuit Court (Rm 204) and Superior Court 3 (Rm 205, 535-6438) and 4 (Rm 105, 535-6403). No juvenile, mental, adoption or sealed records released. Will not fax documents. Court makes copy: $1.00 per page. Certification fee: $1.00 per cert plus copy fee. Payee: Court Clerk. No personal checks or credit cards accepted. Prepayment required. Mail requests: SASE required for mail return of any copies.
Civil Name Search: Access: In person, online. Visitors must perform in person searches themselves. Civil records archived from 1830; on computer since 1996. Some records on index books. Civil PAT goes back to 1996. Online subscription service at https://www.doxpop.com. Fees involved; $39.00 per month. Records date from 01/92. A limited free search of open cases is available.
Criminal Name Search: Access: In person, online. Visitors must perform in person searches themselves. Required to search: name, years to search, DOB; also helpful: SSN. Criminal records archived from 1830; on computer since 1996. Some records on index books. Criminal PAT goes back to 1996. Online subscription service at https://www.doxpop.com. Fees involved; $39.00 per month. Records date from 01/92. A limited free search of open cases is available. Online results show middle initial, DOB.

Fayette County

Circuit & Superior Court 401 N Central Ave, Courthhouse, 2nd Fl, North, Connersville, IN 47331; 765-825-1813; fax: 765-827-4902; 8:30AM-4PM M,T,F; till 5PM W (EST). *Felony, Misdemeanor, Civil, Eviction, Small Claims, Probate.*
www.connersvillecommunity.com/pages.asp?PageName=Judicial&PageIndex=72
General Information: Note on Thursday, the office closes to the public at noon, but reopens for abstractors at 1:30 PM. The fax number is NOT to be used by the public. No juvenile, mental, adoption or sealed released. Will not fax documents. Court makes copy: $1.00 per page. Self serve copy: $1.00 per page. Certification fee: $1.00. Payee: Fayette County Clerk. Only cashiers checks and money orders accepted. No credit cards accepted. Prepayment required.
Civil Name Search: Access: In person, online. Visitors must perform in person searches themselves. Civil records on computer from 1988 (Circuit), 1992 (Superior). Civil PAT goes back to 1990. Online subscription service at https://www.doxpop.com. Fees involved; $39.00 per month. Records date from 01/96. A limited free search of open cases is available.
Criminal Name Search: Access: In person, online. Visitors must perform in person searches themselves. Criminal records computerized from 1988 (Circuit), 1992 (Superior). Criminal PAT goes back to same as civil. Online access to criminal records is the same as civil. Online also includes tax warrants.

Floyd County

Circuit & Superior Court Floyd County Clerk, 311 Hauss Sq, Rm 235, New Albany, IN 47150; 812-948-5413/5411; fax: 812-948-4711; 8AM-4PM (EST). *Felony, Misdemeanor, Civil, Eviction, Small Claims, Probate.*
www.floydcounty.in.gov/
General Information: Probate is a separate index at this same address. Probate fax is same as main fax number. No juvenile, mental, adoption or sealed released. Will not fax documents. Court makes copy: $.10 per page. Self serve copy: same. Certification fee: $1.00 per page. Payee: Court Clerk. No Personal checks and credit cards accepted. Prepayment required. Mail requests: SASE required.
Civil Name Search: Access: Mail, in person, online. Visitors must perform in person searches themselves. No search fee. Civil records on computer from 1988, archived from 1978, on index from 1819. Civil PAT goes back to 1988. Search the index at http://mycase.in.gov/default.aspx. Includes Family and Probate records.
Criminal Name Search: Access: Mail, in person, online. Visitors must perform in person searches themselves. No search fee. Required to search: name, years to search; also helpful: SSN. Criminal records computerized from 1988, archived from 1978, on index from 1819. Mail turnaround time 1-2 days. Criminal PAT goes back to same as civil. Search the index at http://mycase.in.gov/default.aspx. Although dates of birth can be used as a search feature in criminal cases, the Indiana Supreme Court has determined that dates of birth will not be displayed in Public Access.

Fountain County

Circuit Court Box 183, Covington, IN 47932; 765-793-2192; fax: 765-793-5002; 8AM-4PM (EST). *Felony, Misdemeanor, Civil, Eviction, Small Claims, Probate.*
General Information: No juvenile, mental, adoption or sealed released. Will fax documents to local or toll-free number. Court makes copy: $1.00 per page. Self serve copy: same. Certification fee: $1.00. Payee: Court Clerk. No personal checks. No credit cards accepted. Prepayment required. Mail requests: SASE required.
Civil Name Search: Access: Mail, in person, online. Both court and visitors may perform in person name searches. No search fee. Civil records on computer from 1995. Mail turnaround time 1-2 days if records after 1989, 4-5 days if prior. Civil PAT goes back to mid-1995. Online subscription service at https://www.doxpop.com. Fees involved. Records date from 9/95. A limited free search of open cases is available.
Criminal Name Search: Access: Mail, in person, online. Both court and visitors may perform in person name searches. No search fee. Criminal records computerized from 1995. Mail turnaround time 1-2 days if records after 1989, 4-5 days if prior. Criminal PAT goes back to same as civil. Online subscription service at https://www.doxpop.com. Fees involved. Records date from 9/95. A limited free search of open cases is available. Online results show name, DOB.

Franklin County

Circuit Court 459 Main, Brookville, IN 47012; 765-647-5111; fax: 765-647-3224; 8:30AM-12; 1PM-4PM (EST). *Felony, Misdemeanor, Civil, Eviction, Small Claims, Probate.*
General Information: No juvenile, mental, adoption or sealed released. Will fax documents $1.00 per page. Court makes copy: $1.00 per page.

Certification fee: $1.00. Payee: Court Clerk. Personal checks accepted. No credit cards accepted. Prepayment required.

Civil Name Search: Access: In person, online. Visitors must perform in person searches themselves. Civil records indexed. Public use terminal available, records go back to 04/00. Online subscription service at https://www.doxpop.com. Fees involved. Records date from 04/2000. A limited free search of open cases is available.

Criminal Name Search: Access: In person, online. Visitors must perform in person searches themselves. Criminal records on index. Public use terminal available, crim records go back to same. Terminal results may show last for digits of SSN. Electronic access same as civil.

Fulton County

Circuit Court/Superior Court 815 Main St, Rm 315 (Circuit);, Rochester, IN 46975; 574-223-2911; civil phone: 574-223-7712; probate phone: 574-223-7715; fax: 574-223-8304; 8AM-4PM (EST). *Felony, Misdemeanor, Civil, Eviction, Small Claims, Probate.*
www.co.fulton.in.us/Circuit%20Court/index.htm

General Information: Probate fax is same as main fax number. No juvenile, mental, adoption or sealed released. Will fax documents $4.00 per page. Court makes copy: $1.00 per page. Certification fee: $1.00 plus copy fee. Payee: County Clerk. Business checks accepted. No credit cards accepted. Prepayment required. Mail requests: SASE Required.

Civil Name Search: Access: Mail, in person, online. Both court and visitors may perform in person name searches. No search fee. Civil records on computer from 1989, on microfiche, archived and on index from 1845. Mail turnaround time 3-4 days. Civil PAT goes back to 1999. Online subscription service at https://www.doxpop.com. Fees involved. Records date back to 1/1999. A limited free search of open cases is available.

Criminal Name Search: Access: Mail, in person, online. Both court and visitors may perform in person name searches. No search fee. Criminal records computerized from 1989, on microfiche, archived and on index from 1845. Mail turnaround time 3-4 days. Criminal PAT goes back to same as civil. Online access to criminal is the same as civil.

Gibson County

Circuit & Superior Court Courthouse, PO Box 630, Princeton, IN 47670; 812-386-6474; fax: 812-385-5025; 8AM-4PM (CST). *Felony, Misdemeanor, Civil, Eviction, Small Claims, Probate.*

General Information: Probate fax is same as main fax number. No juvenile, mental, adoption or sealed records released. Will not fax out case files. Court makes copy: $.35 per page; $.25 for non-orders.Copy fee $1.00 per page with Judge's signature. Certification fee: $1.00 per doc plus copy fee. Payee: Court Clerk. Business checks accepted for copy payment. No personal checks or credit cards accepted. Prepayment required.

Civil Name Search: Access: In person, online. Visitors must perform in person searches themselves. Civil records on computer 1/1996 for Superior; 1990 for Circuit. On microfiche from 1940, on index from 1813. Civil PAT goes back to 1/1996 for superior; 1990 for Circuit. Online subscription service at https://www.doxpop.com. Fees involved. Superior records date from 1/96.; circuit from 05/05. A limited free search of open cases is available.

Criminal Name Search: Access: In person, online. Visitors must perform in person searches themselves. Criminal records on computer 1/1996 for Superior; 1990 for Circuit. On microfiche from 1940, on index from 1813. Criminal PAT goes back to same as civil. Online access to criminal is same as civil.

Grant County

Circuit & Superior Court Courthouse 101 E 4th St, Marion, IN 46952; 765-668-8121; fax: 765-668-6541; 8AM-4PM (EST). *Felony, Misdemeanor, Civil, Eviction, Small Claims, Probate.*
www.grantcounty.net

General Information: Online court records do not always show sentences, identifiers are often incomplete, and city court records are not shown. Probate is in a separate index at this address. Probate fax is same as main fax number. No juvenile, adoption, mental health or sealed records released. Will fax specific case file $1.00 per page fee. Court makes copy: $.10 per page. Self serve copy: same. Certification fee: $1.00 per certification. Payee: Court Clerk. No personal checks or credit cards accepted. Prepayment required.

Civil Name Search: Access: In person, online. Visitors must perform in person searches themselves. Required to search: name, years to search; also helpful: address. Civil records on computer from 1989, on index from 1881. Civil PAT goes back to 7/1989. Online subscription service at https://www.doxpop.com. Fees involved. Records date back to 8/1989. A limited free search of open cases is available. Index from Gas City Court also available online.

Criminal Name Search: Access: In person, online. Visitors must perform in person searches themselves. Required to search: name, years to search; also helpful: DOB, SSN. Criminal records computerized from 1989, on index from 1881. Criminal PAT goes back to same as civil. Online subscription service at https://www.doxpop.com. Fees involved. Records

date back to 8/1989. A limited free search of open cases is available. Index from Gas City Court also available online.

Greene County

Circuit & Superior Court PO Box 229, 1 Main St, Bloomfield, IN 47424; 812-384-8532; fax: 812-384-8458; 8AM-4PM (EST). *Felony, Misdemeanor, Civil, Eviction, Small Claims, Probate.*

General Information: No juvenile, mental, adoption or sealed released. Court makes copy: $1.00 per page. Certification fee: $1.00. Payee: Court Clerk. Only cash, cashiers checks and money orders accepted. No credit cards accepted. Prepayment required.

Civil Name Search: Access: In person, online. Both court and visitors may perform in person name searches. No search fee. Records in books. Civil, probate and family docket index search is free at http://mycase.in.gov/default.aspx.

Criminal Name Search: Access: In person, only. Both court and visitors may perform in person name searches. No search fee. Criminal records in books. Criminal docket index search is free at http://mycase.in.gov/default.aspx.

Hamilton County

Circuit & Superior Court One Hamilton County Square, #106, Noblesville, IN 46060-2233; 317-776-9629; fax: 317-776-9727; 8AM-4:30PM (EST). *Felony, Misdemeanor, Civil, Eviction, Small Claims, Probate.*
www.hamiltoncounty.in.gov/departments.asp?id=2100

General Information: Probate fax is same as main fax number. No juvenile, mental, adoption or sealed released. Will not fax out case files. Court makes copy: $.50 per page. Self serve copy: same. Certification fee: $1.00 plus $.50 per page. Payee: Court Clerk. Business checks accepted. No credit cards accepted. Prepayment required.

Civil Name Search: Access: In person, online. Visitors must perform in person searches themselves. Civil indices on computer from 1987, on index from 1920s. Civil PAT goes back to mid-1986. See description under Criminal.

Criminal Name Search: Access: In person, online. Visitors must perform in person searches themselves. Criminal records computerized from 1987, on index from 5/1933. Criminal PAT goes back to same as civil. Online subscription service at https://www.doxpop.com. Fees involved. Records date from 01/1987 to 9/21//2009. Note that newer cases and updates to existing cases for Hamilton County are no longer be updated on Doxpop. New cases are now shown at http://mycase.in.gov/default.aspx, there is a separate search for the Carmel City Court.

Hancock County

Circuit & Superior Court 9 E Main St, Rm 201, Greenfield, IN 46140; 317-477-1109; fax: 317-477-1163; 8AM-4PM (EST). *Felony, Misdemeanor, Civil, Eviction, Small Claims, Probate.*

General Information: No juvenile, mental, adoption or sealed released. Will not fax documents. Court makes copy: $1.00 per page if microfilm, otherwise $.25 per page. Self serve copy: $.25 per page. Certification fee: $1.00 per doc. Payee: Court Clerk. Only cashier checks or money orders accepted. No credit cards accepted; debit cards okay. Prepayment required.

Civil Name Search: Access: In person, online. Both court and visitors may perform in person name searches. No search fee. Civil records on computer from 7/88, on index and archived from 1883. Civil PAT goes back to 1988. Online subscription service at https://www.doxpop.com. Fees involved. Records date from 7/98. A limited free search of open cases is available.

Criminal Name Search: Access: In person, online. Both court and visitors may perform in person name searches. No search fee. Required to search: name, years to search, DOB; SSN helpful. Criminal records computerized from 7/88, on index and archived from 1883. Criminal PAT goes back to 1988. Online access to criminal is same as civil.

Harrison County

Circuit Court 300 N Capitol, Corydon, IN 47112; 812-738-4289; criminal phone: 812-738-8149; civil phone: 812-738-4289; probate phone: 812-738-4289; criminal fax: 812-738-2459; civil fax: 8AM-4:30PM; 8AM-4:30PM (EST). *Civil, Eviction, Probate.*
www.harrisoncounty.in.gov/circuitcourt.htm

General Information: Probate fax- 812-738-3126 No juvenile, mental, adoption or sealed released. Fee to fax out file $1.00 per page. Court makes copy: $1.00 per page. Self serve copy: same. Certification fee: $1.00 per document plus copy fee. Payee: Court Clerk. Only cashiers checks and money orders accepted. Major credit cards accepted. Prepayment required.

Civil Name Search: Access: In person, online. Visitors must perform in person searches themselves. Civil docket indexed from 1900. Note: Court personnel will only do record searching when they have time; strongly urge using a retriever. Civil PAT available. Search the civil, family and probate docket by case number, party name or attorney name at http://mycase.in.gov/default.aspx. Not very many years are online.

Criminal Name Search: Access: In person, online. Visitors must perform in person searches themselves. Required to search: name, years to search, DOB; also helpful-SSN. Criminal records indexed from 1900; on computer back to 1992. Note: Court personnel only do record searching when they have time; suggest to use a retriever. Criminal PAT available. Search docket date at http://mycase.in.gov/default.aspx, only a few years are offered. Although dates of birth can be used as a search feature in criminal cases, the Indiana Supreme Court has determined that dates of birth will not be displayed in Public Access.

Superior Court 1445 Gardner Ln, #3126, Corydon, IN 47112; 812-738-8149; fax: 812-738-2459; 8AM-4:30PM (EST). *Felony, Misdemeanor, Civil, Small Claims.*

www.harrisoncounty.in.gov/superiorcourt.htm

General Information: No juvenile, mental, adoption or sealed released. Will not fax out case files. Court makes copy: $1.00 per page. Self serve copy: same. Certification fee: $1.00 per document plus copy fee. Payee: Court Clerk. Only cashiers checks and money orders accepted. Visa/MC accepted. Prepayment required.

Civil Name Search: Access: In person, online. Visitors must perform in person searches themselves. Civil docket indexed from 1976; on computer back to 1992. Civil PAT goes back to 1992; indexes only. Public access terminal in lobby. Search the civil, family and probate docket by case number, party name or attorney name at http://mycase.in.gov/default.aspx. Not very many years are online.

Criminal Name Search: Access: In person, online. Visitors must perform in person searches themselves. Required to search: name, years to search, DOB; also helpful-SSN. Criminal records indexed from 1976; on computer back to 1992. Criminal PAT goes back to same as civil. Public access terminal in lobby. Search docket date at http://mycase.in.gov/default.aspx, only a few years are offered. Although dates of birth can be used as a search feature in criminal cases, the Indiana Supreme Court has determined that dates of birth will not be displayed in Public Access.

Hendricks County

Circuit & Superior Court 51 W Main St, #104, Danville, IN 46122; 317-745-9231; fax: 317-745-9306; 8AM-4PM (EST). *Felony, Misdemeanor, Civil, Eviction, Small Claims, Probate.*

www.co.hendricks.in.us/

General Information: Online identifiers in results same as on public terminal. No juvenile, mental, adoption or sealed released. Will not fax documents. Court makes copy: $1.00 per page. Certification fee: $1.00. Payee: Hendricks County Clerk. Business checks accepted. No credit cards accepted. Prepayment required. Mail requests: SASE not required but add'l postage may be billed for over 10 pages.

Civil Name Search: Access: In person, mail, online. Visitors must perform in person searches themselves. No search fee. Civil records on computer since late 1992, on index from 1800s. Note: Will only do mail request if out of state. Civil PAT goes back to 9/1992. Online docket found at www.co.hendricks.in.us/. There is an index to the Plainfield Town Court dockets at http://mycase.in.gov/default.aspx.

Criminal Name Search: Access: In person, mail, online. Visitors must perform in person searches themselves. No search fee. Required to search: name, years to search; also helpful: DOB, SSN. Criminal records on computer since late 1992, on index from 1800s. Note: Court will only do mail request if out of state. Mail turnaround time is 72 hours. Criminal PAT goes back to same as civil. Search docket online at www.co.hendricks.in.us/. There is an index to the Plainfield Town Court dockets at http://mycase.in.gov/default.aspx.

Henry County

Circuit & Superior Courts I & II PO Box B, 1215 Race St, New Castle, IN 47362; 765-529-6401; fax: 765-521-7046; 8AM-4PM (EST). *Felony, Misdemeanor, Civil, Eviction, Small Claims, Probate.*

www.henryco.net/

General Information: Probate fax is same as main fax number. No juvenile, mental, protective orders, adoption or any other confidential records. Will not fax out case files. Court makes copy: $1.00 per page. Certification fee: $1.00 per document plus copy fee. Payee: Henry County Clerk. Only cashiers checks and money orders accepted. Major credit cards accepted with 3% surcharge. Prepayment required.

Civil Name Search: Access: In person, online. Visitors must perform in person searches themselves. Civil cases indexed by plaintiff. Civil records on computer from 02/1991, manual records from 1822. Civil PAT goes back to 2/1991. Online subscription service at https://www.doxpop.com. Fees involved. Records date back to 1/1991. A limited free search of open cases is available. Personal identifiers usually but not always include DOB and middle initial.

Criminal Name Search: Access: In person, online. Visitors must perform in person searches themselves. Records on computer from 02/1991, manual records from 1822. Criminal PAT goes back to same as civil. Online subscription service at https://www.doxpop.com. Fees involved. Records date back to 1/1991. A limited free search of open cases is available. Personal identifiers usually but not always include DOB and middle initial.

Howard County

Circuit & Superior Court 104 N Buckeye, Rm 114, Kokomo, IN 46901; 765-456-2204; criminal phone: 765-456-2000; civil phone: 765-456-2000; fax: 765-456-2267; 8AM-4PM (EST). *Felony, Misdemeanor, Civil, Eviction, Small Claims, Probate.*

http://co.howard.in.us/clerk1/

General Information: Small claims phone-765-456-2204. Online identifiers in results same as on public terminal. No juvenile, mental, adoption or sealed records released. Will fax documents $.20 per page. Court makes copy: $.20 per page from printed records. Self serve copy: $.20 per page. Certification fee: $1.00. Payee: County Clerk. Only cashiers checks and money orders accepted. No credit cards accepted. Prepayment required. May pay through 3rd party "PayTrust".

Civil Name Search: Access: In person, online. Visitors must perform in person searches themselves. Civil records on computer since 1994, on microfiche from early 1800s. Civil PAT goes back to 1994. Online subscription service at https://www.doxpop.com. Fees involved. Records date from 07/94. A limited free search of open cases is available.

Criminal Name Search: Access: In person, online. Visitors must perform in person searches themselves. Required to search: name, years to search; also helpful: DOB. Criminal records on computer since 1992, on microfiche from early 1800s. Criminal PAT goes back to same as civil. Online subscription service at https://www.doxpop.com. Fees involved. Records date from 07/94. A limited free search of open cases is available. Online results show middle initial, DOB.

Huntington County

Circuit & Superior Court PO Box 228, Huntington, IN 46750; 260-358-4817; fax: 260-358-4880; 8AM-4:30PM (EST). *Felony, Misdemeanor, Civil, Eviction, Small Claims, Probate.*

www.huntington.in.us/county/

General Information: No juvenile, mental, adoption or sealed released. Will fax documents to local or toll free line. Court makes copy: $.25 per page. Self serve copy: same. Certification fee: $1.00 per cert. Payee: County Clerk. No personal checks. No credit cards accepted. Prepayment required.

Civil Name Search: Access: Fax, phone, mail, in person, online. Both court and visitors may perform in person name searches. No search fee. Civil records on computer from 1990, on microfiche from 1970, on index and archived from 1800s. Civil PAT goes back to 1990. Search the civil, family and probate docket by case number, party name or attorney name at http://mycase.in.gov/default.aspx. Not very many years are online. There is a separate look-up for the Roanoke Town Court.

Criminal Name Search: Access: In person, online. Visitors must perform in person searches themselves. Criminal records computerized from 1990, on microfiche from 1970, on index and archived from 1800s. Criminal PAT goes back to same as civil. Search docket date at http://mycase.in.gov/default.aspx, only a few years are offered. There is a separate look-up for the Roanoke Town Court. Although dates of birth can be used as a search feature in criminal cases, the Indiana Supreme Court has determined that dates of birth will not be displayed in Public Access.

Jackson County

Circuit Court PO Box 318, Brownstown, IN 47220; 812-358-6116; probate phone: 812-358-6133; fax: 812-358-6187; 8AM-4:30PM (EST). *Felony, Misdemeanor, Civil, Eviction, Small Claims, Probate.*

www.jacksoncounty.in.gov/index.aspx?nid=268

General Information: Court will not perform searches for private companies. Probate fax is same as main fax number. No juvenile, mental, adoption or sealed released. Will fax documents $5.00 per doc; no fee to toll-free number. Court makes copy: $1.00 per page. Self serve copy: same. Certification fee: $1.00 per document. Payee: Jackson County Clerk. No personal checks or credit cards accepted. Prepayment required.

Civil Name Search: Access: In person only. Visitors must perform in person searches themselves. Civil records on computer from 1989, on index from 1800s. Civil PAT goes back to 1989.

Criminal Name Search: Access: In person only. Visitors must perform in person searches themselves. Required to search: name, years to search; also helpful: DOB, SSN. Criminal records computerized from 1989, on index from 1800s. Note: Will recommend local document retrievers to do searches for you. Criminal PAT goes back to same as civil.

Superior Court PO Box 788, Seymour, IN 47274; 812-522-9676; fax: 812-523-6065; 8AM-4:30PM (EST). *Misdemeanor, Civil, Eviction, Small Claims, Traffic.*

General Information: No juvenile, mental, adoption or sealed released. Will fax documents $5.00 per doc; no fee to toll-free number. Court makes copy: $1.00 per page. Self serve copy: same. Certification fee: $1.00 per page. Payee: Jackson County Clerk. Only cashiers checks and money orders accepted. No credit cards accepted. Prepayment required.

Civil Name Search: Access: Mail, in person. Visitors must perform in person searches themselves. No search fee. Civil records on computer from 1989, on index from 1800s.

Criminal Name Search: Access: In person only. Visitors must perform in person searches themselves. Required to search: name, years to search; also helpful: DOB, SSN. Criminal records computerized from 1989, on index from 1800s.

Jasper County

Circuit Court 115 W Washington, Rensselaer, IN 47978; 219-866-4941; criminal phone: 219-866-4926/4921; civil phone: 219-866-4926/4921; probate phone: 218-866-4926/49219; fax: 219-866-9450; 8AM-4PM (CST). *Felony, Misdemeanor, Civil, Eviction, Small Claims, Probate.* www.jaspercountyin.gov/Default.aspx?tabid=58

General Information: This court also handles juvenile, paternity and adoption.

219-866-4909 Traffic; 219-866-4928 Child Support No juvenile, mental, adoption or sealed released. Will fax documents $5.00 per page. Court makes copy: $.50 per page. Certification fee: $1.00 per page. Payee: Jasper County Clerk. No personal or business checks accepted, must be money order or cashier check. No credit cards accepted. Prepayment required. Mail requests: SASE required.

Civil Name Search: Access: Mail, in person, online. Both court and visitors may perform in person name searches. No search fee. County records on computer from 1976, circuit from 1999. Some records on index from 1900s. Mail turnaround time 1 day. Civil PAT goes back to 1989. Search records free at http://mycase.in.gov/default.aspx.

Criminal Name Search: Access: Mail, in person, online. Both court and visitors may perform in person name searches. No search fee. Required to search: name, years to search; also helpful: DOB, SSN. County records on computer from 1976, circuit from 1989. Some records on index from 1900s. Mail turnaround time 1 day. Criminal PAT goes back to same as civil. Search records free at http://mycase.in.gov/default.aspx.

Superior Court 115 W Washington St, #103, Rensselaer, IN 47978; 219-866-4971; criminal phone: 21-866-4922/4912; civil phone: 21-866-4922/4912; probate phone: 219-866-4912; fax: 219-866-9450; 8AM-4PM (CST). *Felony, Misdemeanor, Civil, Probate.* www.jaspercountyin.gov/Default.aspx?tabid=58

General Information: No juvenile, mental, adoption or sealed released. Will fax documents $5.00 per page. Court makes copy: $.50 per page. Certification fee: $1.00 per page includes copy fee. Payee: County Clerk. Only cashiers checks and money orders accepted. No credit cards or personal checks accepted. Prepayment required. Mail requests: SASE required.

Civil Name Search: Access: Mail, in person, online. Visitors must perform in person searches themselves. No search fee. County records on computer from 1976, circuit from 1989. Some records on index from 1800s. Mail turnaround time 1 day to 1 week. Civil PAT goes back to 1989. Search records free at http://mycase.in.gov/default.aspx.

Criminal Name Search: Access: Mail, in person, online. Visitors must perform in person searches themselves. No search fee. County records on computer from 1976, circuit from 1989. Some records on index from 1800s. Mail turnaround time 1 day to 1 week. Criminal PAT goes back to same as civil. Search records free at http://mycase.in.gov/default.aspx.

Jay County

Circuit & Superior Court 120 N Court St, Courthouse, Portland, IN 47371; 260-726-4951; fax: 260-726-6922; 8:30AM-4:30PM (EST). *Felony, Misdemeanor, Civil, Eviction, Small Claims, Probate.* www.co.jay.in.us

General Information: Online identifiers in results same as on public terminal. No juvenile, mental, adoption or sealed records released. Will fax documents to local or toll-free number. Court makes copy: $1.00 per page. Certification fee: $1.00 per page. Payee: Court Clerk. Personal and business checks accepted. No credit cards accepted. Prepayment required. Mail requests: SASE required.

Civil Name Search: Access: In person, online. Visitors must perform in person searches themselves. Required to search: name, years to search; also helpful: address. Civil records on computer from 8\94, prior on microfiche from 1979, on index books from 1900. Civil PAT goes back to 1994. Online subscription service at https://www.doxpop.com. Fees involved. Records date from 03/94. A limited free search of open cases is available.

Criminal Name Search: Access: Mail, in person, online. Visitors must perform in person searches themselves. No search fee. Required to search: name, years to search, DOB; also helpful: SSN, address. Criminal records computerized from 8\94, prior on microfiche from 1979, on index books from 1900. Criminal PAT goes back to same as civil. Online subscription service at https://www.doxpop.com. Fees involved. Records date from 03/94. A limited free search of open cases is available.

Jefferson County

Circuit & Superior Court 300 E Main St, Rm 203, Courthouse, Madison, IN 47250; 812-265-8923/22; probate phone: 812-265-8928;; 8AM-4PM (EST). *Felony, Misdemeanor, Civil, Eviction, Small Claims, Probate.*

General Information: No juvenile, mental, adoption or sealed released. Will fax documents $1.00 per page. Court makes copy: $1.00 per page. Self serve copy: same. Certification fee: $1.00 per page. Payee: County Clerk. Only cashiers checks and money orders accepted. No credit cards accepted. Prepayment required.

Civil Name Search: Access: In person only. Visitors must perform in person searches themselves. Civil cases indexed by plaintiff, defendant. Civil docket indexed from 1975, computerized since 1995. Civil PAT goes back to 1995.

Criminal Name Search: Access: In person only. Visitors must perform in person searches themselves. Required to search: Name, years to search, address, DOB, SSN. Criminal records indexed from 1975, computerized since 1995. Criminal PAT goes back to same as civil.

Jennings County

Circuit Court Courthouse, PO Box 385, Vernon, IN 47282; 812-352-3070; fax: 812-352-3076; 8AM-4PM (EST). *Felony, Misdemeanor, Civil, Eviction, Small Claims, Probate.*

General Information: No juvenile, mental, adoption or sealed released. Will fax documents to local or toll-free number. Court makes copy: $.25 per page. Self serve copy: same. Certification fee: $1.00. Payee: County Clerk. Personal checks accepted. No credit cards accepted. Prepayment required.

Civil Name Search: Access: In person only. Visitors must perform in person searches themselves. Civil docket indexed from 1930; computerized since 2000. Civil PAT goes back to 10/2000. DOB will not always appear; SSNs never.

Criminal Name Search: Access: In person only. Visitors must perform in person searches themselves. Required to search: name, years to search, DOB; SSN helpful. Criminal records indexed from 1930; computerized since 2000. Criminal PAT goes back to same as civil. DOB will not always appear; sometimes last 4 of SSN will.

Johnson County

Circuit & Superior Court Courthouse, PO Box 368, Franklin, IN 46131; 317-736-3708; criminal phone: 317-736-3951; civil phone: 317-736-3708; probate phone: 317-736-3913; criminal fax: 317-736-3749; civil fax: 8AM-4:30PM; 8AM-4:30PM (EST). *Felony, Misdemeanor, Civil, Eviction, Small Claims, Probate.* www.co.johnson.in.us/

General Information: Online identifiers in results same as on public terminal. No juvenile, mental, adoption or sealed released. Will not fax out documents. Court makes copy: $1.00 per page. Self serve copy: $.50 per page. Certification fee: $1.00 per page. Payee: County Clerk. Business checks accepted, personal checks are not. Major credit cards accepted. Prepayment required. Mail requests: SASE required.

Civil Name Search: Access: Mail (as time allows), in person, online. Visitors must perform in person searches themselves. No search fee. Civil records on computer back 10 years. Mail turnaround time 2 days or more. Civil PAT goes back to 1989. Online subscription service at https://www.doxpop.com. Fees involved. Records date from 08/89. A limited free search of open cases is available. The record index from the Greenwood City Court is available at http://mycase.in.gov/. Records do not go back far.

Criminal Name Search: Access: In person, online. Visitors must perform in person searches themselves. Required to search: name, years to search; also helpful: DOB, SSN. Criminal records on computer back 15 years. Criminal PAT goes back to same as civil. Online subscription service at https://www.doxpop.com. Fees involved. Records date from 08/89. A limited free search of open cases is available. Online results show name, DOB.

Knox County

Circuit & Superior Court 101 N 7th St, #28, Vincennes, IN 47591; 812-885-2521; fax: 812-895-4929; 8AM-4PM (EST). *Felony, Misdemeanor, Civil, Eviction, Small Claims, Probate.*

General Information: A mail search request should specify to search both civil and criminal indexes. Although these courts are not online, note that the Bicknell City Court has its dockets index online at http://mycase.in.gov/default.aspx No juvenile, mental, adoption or sealed released. Will fax documents for no fee. Court makes copy: $1.00 per page. Self serve copy: same. Certification fee: $1.00 per page or per doc - court does not have a specific rule at this time. Payee: Knox County Clerk. Personal checks accepted. No credit cards accepted. Prepayment required. Mail requests: SASE required.

Civil Name Search: Access: In person, mail. Visitors must perform in person searches themselves. No search fee. Civil index on docket books from 1800s. Civil PAT goes back to 7/2010.

Criminal Name Search: Access: In person, mail. Visitors must perform in person searches themselves. No search fee. Criminal records indexed in books from 1800s. Criminal PAT goes back to 7/2010.

Kosciusko County

Circuit & Superior Court 121 N Lake, Warsaw, IN 46580; 574-372-2331; criminal phone: 574-372-2457 (1st), 372-2453 (2nd & 3rd); civil phone: 574-372-2331; probate phone: 574-372-2339; fax: 574-372-2338; 8AM-4:30PM (EST). *Felony, Misdemeanor, Civil, Eviction, Small Claims, Probate.*

www.kcgov.com/

General Information: Probate records on same computer system, same index. Probate fax is same as main fax number. No juvenile, mental, adoption or sealed released. Will fax documents to toll free number only. Court makes copy: $.05 per page, $1.00 minimum. Self serve copy: $.05 per page. Certification fee: $1.00 per certification. Payee: County Clerk. Personal checks accepted. No credit cards accepted. Prepayment required. Mail requests: SASE required for mail return of any copies.

Civil Name Search: Access: Fax, in person, online. Both court and visitors may perform in person name searches. No search fee. Civil records on computer from 10/1/93, general index from 1908. Civil PAT goes back to 1993, countywide. DOB, SSN, middle initial sometimes available. Online subscription service at https://www.doxpop.com. Fees involved. Data goes back to 10/1991.

Criminal Name Search: Access: Fax, in person, online. Both court and visitors may perform in person name searches. No search fee. Required to search: name, years to search; also helpful-DOB, SSN. DL#. Criminal records computerized from 10/1/93, general index from 1908. Criminal PAT goes back to same as civil. Online access to criminal is same as civil.

La Porte County

Circuit & Superior Court 813 Lincolnway, Ste 105, La Porte, IN 46350; 219-326-6808; fax: 219-326-6626; 8AM-4PM (CST). *Felony, Misdemeanor, Civil, Eviction, Probate.*

www.laportecounty.org/judiciary/courts/clerk.html

General Information: Microfilm department- x2435/2276. Probate fax number same as main fax. No juvenile, mental, adoption or sealed released. Will fax documents if all fees prepaid. Court makes copy: $1.00 per page. Self serve copy: $.15 per page. Certification fee: $1.00 plus $1.00 per page. Payee: Court Clerk. Business checks accepted. No credit cards accepted. Prepayment required.

Civil Name Search: Access: In person, fax, online. Visitors must perform in person searches themselves. Search fee: $1.00 per page. Civil records on microfiche and index from 1900. Civil PAT goes back to 10 years. Online subscription service at https://www.doxpop.com. Fees involved. Records date from 03/98. A limited free search of open cases is available.

Criminal Name Search: Access: In person, fax, online. Visitors must perform in person searches themselves. Search fee: $1.00 per page. Criminal records on microfiche and index from 1900. Criminal PAT goes back to same as civil. Online access is same as civil.

LaGrange County

Circuit & Superior Court 105 N Detroit St, Courthouse, LaGrange, IN 46761; 260-499-6368; civil phone: 260-499-6375; fax: 260-499-6403; 8AM-4PM M-F (EST). *Felony, Misdemeanor, Civil, Eviction, Small Claims, Probate.*

www.lagrangecounty.org/

General Information: No juvenile, mental, adoption or sealed released. Will not fax documents. Court makes copy: $1.00 per page. Self serve copy: same. Certification fee: $1.00 per cert. Payee: LaGrange County Clerk. Personal checks accepted. No credit cards accepted. Prepayment required. Mail requests: SASE requested.

Civil Name Search: Access: Phone, mail, in person, online. Visitors must perform in person searches themselves. No search fee. Civil records on computer from 1990, on books from 1900. Civil PAT goes back to 1991. Online subscription service at https://www.doxpop.com. Fees involved. Records date back to 1/1990. A limited free search of open cases is available.

Criminal Name Search: Access: Phone, mail, in person, online. Visitors must perform in person searches themselves. No search fee. Required to search: name, years to search; also helpful: DOB, SSN. Criminal records computerized from 1990, on books from 1900. Mail turnaround time 1-2 days from 1/1/90; 30 days if prior to 1/1/90. Criminal PAT goes back to

1991. Online subscription service at https://www.doxpop.com. Fees involved. Records date back to 1/1990. A limited free search of open cases is available. Online results show middle initial, DOB, address.

Lake County

Circuit & Superior Court 2293 N Main St, Courthouse, Crown Point, IN 46307; 219-755-3460; criminal phone: 219-755-3477; civil phone: 219-755-3462; probate phone: 219-755-3468; criminal fax: 219-755-3781; civil fax: 8:30AM-4PM; 8:30AM-4PM (CST). *Felony, Misdemeanor, Civil, Eviction, Small Claims, Probate.*

www.lakecountyin.org/index.jsp

General Information: Telephone of traffic, D-felonies, and misdemeanors is 219-755-3620. No juvenile, mental, adoption or sealed released. Will fax documents $1.00 per page fee. Court makes copy: $1.00 per page. Certification fee: $1.00 per page plus copy fee. Payee: Lake County Clerk. Business checks accepted. No credit cards accepted. Prepayment required.

Civil Name Search: Access: Mail, fax, in person, online. Both court and visitors may perform in person name searches. No search fee. Required to search: name, years to search; also helpful: address. Civil records go back to 1920s; on microfiche back to 1983; on computer back to 1990s. Note: Fax requests must be on letterhead. Mail turnaround time 1 week. Civil PAT goes back to 1990. Online search for docket records available at https://www.lakecountyin.org/portal/media-type/html/user/anon/page/online-docket. Search free but $.25 per page copy fee with $1.00 minimum. Results do not show the DOB.

Criminal Name Search: Access: Mail, in person, online. Both court and visitors may perform in person name searches. Search fee: $7.00. Required to search: name, years to search, DOB, SSN; also helpful: address. Criminal records go back to 1900s; on microfiche back to 1983; on computer back to 1990s. Note: Search requests for background checks are forwarded to the County Bureau of Identification, 219-755-3316. Authorization required. Mail turnaround time 1 week. Criminal PAT goes back to same as civil. Online search of docket records at https://www.lakecountyin.org/portal/media-type/html/user/anon/page/online-docket. Search free but $.25 per page copy fee with $1.00 minimum. The DOB often will show on results screen.

Lawrence County

Circuit & Superior Court 31 Courthouse, 916 15th St, Bedford, IN 47421; 812-275-7543; fax: 812-277-2024; 8AM-4PM (EST). *Felony, Misdemeanor, Civil, Eviction, Small Claims, Probate.*

General Information: Superior Court I is 812-275-3124; Superior Court II is 812-275-4161. All small claims are filed in Superior II. The County Court converted to a Superior Court on 01/01/2009. No juvenile, mental, adoption or sealed released. Court makes copy: $1.00 per page. Self serve copy: same. Certification fee: $1.00 per cert. Payee: Lawrence County Clerk. Only cashiers checks and money orders accepted. No credit cards accepted. Prepayment required.

Civil Name Search: Access: In person, online. Visitors must perform in person searches themselves. Civil cases indexed by plaintiff. Civil records on computer from 1987, on index from 1817. Civil PAT goes back to 1987. Access civil records by subscription to Doxpop at https://www.doxpop.com/prod/court/. Free index search.

Criminal Name Search: Access: In person, online. Visitors must perform in person searches themselves. Required to search: name, years to search, DOB. Criminal records computerized from 1987, on index from 1817. Criminal PAT goes back to same as civil. Access civil records by subscription to Doxpop at https://www.doxpop.com/prod/court/. Free index search.

Madison County

Circuit & Superior Court PO Box 1277, 16 E 9th St, Anderson, IN 46015-1277; 765-641-9443; probate phone: 765-641-9467; fax: 765-640-4203; 8AM-4PM (EST). *Felony, Misdemeanor, Civil, Eviction, Small Claims, Probate.*

www.madisoncountyindiana.org/Clerk.html

General Information: No juvenile, mental, adoption or sealed records released. Will not fax documents. Court makes copy: $1.00 per page. Certification fee: $2.00. Payee: County Clerk. Business checks accepted. No credit cards accepted. Prepayment required.

Civil Name Search: Access: In person, online. Visitors must perform in person searches themselves. Civil cases indexed by defendant. Civil records on microfiche and archived from 1950, on index from 1900. Civil PAT goes back to 1986. Free online service at http://mycase.in.gov/default.aspx. Includes Alexandria City Court.

Criminal Name Search: Access: In person, online. Visitors must perform in person searches themselves. Required to search: name, years to search, signed release. Criminal records on microfiche and archived from 1950, on index from 1900. Criminal PAT goes back to 1900. Free online service at http://mycase.in.gov/default.aspx. Includes Alexandria City Court.

Marion County

Circuit & Superior Court 200 E Washington St, Indianapolis, IN 46204; criminal phone: 317-327-4733; civil phone: 317-327-4740; probate phone: 317-327-4718; fax: 317-327-3893; 8AM-4:30PM (EST). *Felony, Misdemeanor, Civil, Probate.*

www.indy.gov/egov/county/clerk/Pages/home.aspx

General Information: The Municipal Court of Marion County, once separate, is now part of Superior Court. All records are merged. There are 9 different small claims courts in the county, each with its own DB for records. No juvenile, mental, adoption or sealed released. Will not fax documents. Court makes copy: $1.00 page. Certification fee: $1.00; Exemplification fee-$4.00. Payee: County Clerk. Personal checks accepted with mail requests. Major credit cards accepted both in-house and online, service fee charged. Prepayment required. Mail requests: SASE required.

Civil Name Search: Access: Mail, in person, online. Both court and visitors may perform in person name searches. No search fee. Civil records on computer back to 1991, on microfiche, archived and on index from 1912. Small claims records are held by the township in which they were filed. Mail turnaround time 1-2 days. Public use terminal available. Search names online for free at www.civicnet.net/court_records.html. See the web for fees, as there are many ways to order. One may be subscriber or use a credit card for a one-time search. Marriage records included. Also, search Townships of Center, Lawrence, Franklin, Perry, Warren, and Washington; Bunkerhill Town court; and Alexandria City civil, family, and probate dockets free at http://mycase.in.gov/default.aspx.

Criminal Name Search: Access: Mail, online, in person. Both court and visitors may perform in person name searches. No search fee. Required to search: name, years to search, DOB. Criminal records computerized from 1981, on microfiche, archived and on index from 1912. Small claims records are held by the township in which the. Mail turnaround time 1-2 days. Public use terminal available. Search names online at https://www.biz.indygov.org/civil_court_records.html. See the web for fees, as there are several ways to order. One may be a subscriber or may use a credit card for a one-time search. Also, search Townships of Center, Lawrence, Franklin, Perry, Warren, and Washington; Bunkerhill Town court; and Alexandria City criminal dockets and citations free at http://mycase.in.gov/default.aspx.

Marshall County

Circuit & Superior Court 1 & 2 211 W Madison St, Plymouth, IN 46563; 574-936-8922; fax: 574-936-8893; 8AM-4PM (EST). *Felony, Misdemeanor, Civil, Eviction, Small Claims, Probate.*

www.in.gov/judiciary/marshall/

General Information: Circuit Court address is 501 N Center St #301, Plymouth, IN 46563. No juvenile, mental, adoption or sealed released. Will fax out specific case files for $5.00 1st page; $1.00 each add'l, not to exceed $10.00. Court makes copy: $1.00 per page. Self serve copy: same. Certification fee: $2.00. Payee: Marshall County Clerk. Business checks accepted. No credit cards accepted. Prepayment required.

Civil Name Search: Access: In person, online. Visitors must perform in person searches themselves. Required to search: name, years to search; also helpful: address. Civil records on computer from 1989, on microfiche, archived and on index from 1835. Civil PAT goes back to 1991. Online subscription service at https://www.doxpop.com. Fees involved. Records date from 09/88. A limited free search of open cases is available.

Criminal Name Search: Access: In person, online. Visitors must perform in person searches themselves. Required to search: name, years to search, signed release; also helpful: address, DOB, SSN. Criminal records computerized from 1989, on microfiche, archived and on index from 1835. Criminal PAT goes back to 1988. Online subscription service at https://www.doxpop.com. Fees involved. Records date from 09/88. A limited free search of open cases is available.

Martin County

Circuit Court PO Box 120 (129 Main St), Shoals, IN 47581; 812-247-3651; fax: 812-247-2791; 8AM-4PM (EST). *Felony, Misdemeanor, Civil, Eviction, Small Claims, Probate.*

General Information: Probate fax is same as main fax number. No juvenile, mental, adoption, or sealed records released. Will fax documents to local or toll free line. Court makes copy: $1.00 per page. Certification fee: $2.00 per certification. Payee: County Clerk. Business checks accepted. No credit cards accepted. Prepayment required.

Civil Name Search: Access: In person, online. Visitors must perform in person searches themselves. Civil index on docket books and is computerized. Public use terminal available, records go back to 2003. Access civil records by subscription to Doxpop at https://www.doxpop.com/prod/court/. Free index search.

Criminal Name Search: Access: In person, online. Visitors must perform in person searches themselves. Required to search: name, years to search, DOB or SSN. Criminal records indexed in books and is computerized. Public use terminal available, crim records go back to same.

Access civil records by subscription to Doxpop at https://www.doxpop.com/prod/court/. Free index search.

Miami County

Circuit & Superior Courts PO Box 184, Peru, IN 46970; 765-472-3901; fax: 765-472-1778; 8AM-4PM (EST). *Felony, Misdemeanor, Civil, Eviction, Small Claims, Probate.*

www.miamicountyin.gov

General Information: Online identifiers in results same as on public terminal. No juvenile, mental, adoption, or sealed released. Will fax documents $1.00 per page; no fee for toll free or local call. Court makes copy: $1.00 per page. Self serve copy: same. Certification fee: $1.00. Payee: Miami County Clerk. Personal checks not accepted. Major credit cards accepted. Prepayment required.

Civil Name Search: Access: Fax, mail, in person, online. Both court and visitors may perform in person name searches. No search fee. Civil records on computer back to 4/1998, archived from 1900s. Some records on docket books by case number and alpha. Mail turnaround time 1-2 days. Civil PAT goes back to 1/1998. The court is working on adding more older records to the public system. Online subscription service at https://www.doxpop.com. Fees involved. Records date from 03/98. A limited free search of open cases is available.

Criminal Name Search: Access: Fax, mail, in person, online. Both court and visitors may perform in person name searches. No search fee. Required to search: name, years to search, DOB, SSN, signed release. Criminal records computerized from 4/1998; archived from 1900s. Some records on docket books by case number and alpha. Mail turnaround time 1-2 days. Criminal PAT goes back to same as civil. The court is working on adding more older records to the public system. Online subscription service at https://www.doxpop.com. Fees involved. Records date from 03/98. A limited free search of open cases is available. Online results show middle initial.

Monroe County

Circuit Court 301 N College Ave, Ste 201, Bloomington, IN 47402; 812-349-2600; fax: 812-349-2610; 8AM-4PM M-F (EST). *Felony, Misdemeanor, Civil, Eviction, Small Claims, Probate.*

www.co.monroe.in.us/tsd/Justice/CircuitCourt.aspx

General Information: Probate fax is same as main fax number. No juvenile, mental, adoption or sealed released. Fee to fax out file $1.00 per page. Court makes copy: $1.00 per page. Self serve copy: same. Certification fee: $1.00 per cert plus copy fee. Payee: Monroe County Clerk. No personal checks accepted. Major credit cards accepted in person. Prepayment required.

Civil Name Search: Access: Mail, fax, in person, online. Both court and visitors may perform in person name searches. No search fee. Civil records on computer from 1993. Some records on docket books by case number and alpha. In the process of putting records on microfilm. Mail turnaround time 48 hours. Civil PAT goes back to 6/1993. Search the docket by case number, party name or attorney name at http://mycase.in.gov/default.aspx.

Criminal Name Search: Access: Mail, fax, in person, online. Both court and visitors may perform in person name searches. No search fee. Required to search: name, years to search, DOB. Criminal records computerized from 1993. Some records on docket books by case number and alpha. In the process of putting records on microfilm. Mail turnaround time 72 hours. Criminal PAT goes back to same as civil. Online access by free service at http://mycase.in.gov/default.aspx. Includes criminal and citations. Although dates of birth can be used as a search feature in criminal cases, the Indiana Supreme Court has determined that dates of birth will not be displayed in Public Access.

Montgomery County

Circuit & Superior Court PO Box 768, Crawfordsville, IN 47933; 765-364-6430; fax: 765-364-6355; 8:30AM-4:30PM (EST). *Felony, Misdemeanor, Civil, Eviction, Small Claims, Probate.*

www.montgomeryco.net

General Information: Probate is a separate index at this same address. Probate fax is same as main fax number. There is a Superior Court 1 and a Superior Court 2 which was formerly known as the County Court. Online identifiers in results same as on public terminal. No juvenile, mental, adoption or sealed released. Will fax documents $1.00 per page plus $3.25 fax fee. Court makes copy: $1.00 per page. Self serve copy: same. Certification fee: $1.00 per page plus copy fee. Payee: Montgomery County Clerk. Business checks accepted. No credit cards accepted. Prepayment required. Mail requests: SASE required.

Civil Name Search: Access: Phone, fax, mail, in person, online. Both court and visitors may perform in person name searches. No search fee. Civil records on computer from 1990, some on microfiche and docket books, and archived from 1800s. Note: Indicate types of cases sought in mail search request. Mail turnaround time 1 week. Civil PAT goes back to

1990. Online subscription service at https://www.doxpop.com. Fees involved. Records date from 01/90. A limited free search of open cases is available.

Criminal Name Search: Access: Mail, fax, in person, online. Both court and visitors may perform in person name searches. No search fee. Required to search: name, years to search, DOB; also helpful: SSN. Criminal records computerized from 1990, some on microfiche and docket books, and archived from 1800s. Mail turnaround time 1 week. Criminal PAT goes back to same as civil. Online subscription service at https://www.doxpop.com. Fees involved. Records date from 01/90. A limited free search of open cases is available. Online results show middle initial, DOB, address.

Morgan County

Circuit & Superior Court PO Box 1556, 10 E Washington St, Martinsville, IN 46151; 765-342-1025; fax: 765-342-1111; 8AM-4PM M,T,TH,F; 8AM-5PM W (EST). *Felony, Misdemeanor, Civil, Eviction, Small Claims, Probate.*
www.morgancounty.in.gov/
General Information: No juvenile, mental, adoption or sealed released. Will fax documents to local or toll-free number. Court makes copy: $.10 per page. Certification fee: $1.00 per page plus copy fee. Payee: Morgan County Clerk. Personal checks accepted. Debit or debit cards accepted, excpet online. Convenience fee for credit or debit. Prepayment required. Mail requests: SASE required for mail return of any copies.
Civil Name Search: Access: In person, online. Visitors must perform in person searches themselves. Civil records archived from 1970; on computer back to 1993. Some records on index cards;. Note: In some instances, limited information is given over the phone if the docket number is known. Civil PAT goes back to 1995. Online subscription service at https://www.doxpop.com. Fees involved. Records date from 01/1997. A limited free search of open cases is available.
Criminal Name Search: Access: In person, online. Visitors must perform in person searches themselves. Required to search: name, years to search, DOB; SSN helpful, signed release. Criminal records archived from 1970; on microfilm 1992-95, on computer back to 1993. Criminal PAT goes back to same as civil. Online access is same as civil.

Newton County

Circuit & Superior Court PO Box 49, 201 N 3rd St, Kentland, IN 47951; 219-474-6081; fax: 219-474-5749; 8AM-4PM (CST). *Felony, Misdemeanor, Civil, Eviction, Small Claims, Probate.*
General Information: Search fee includes both courts, civil and criminal indexes. No juvenile, mental, adoption or sealed records released. With your letterhead request, court will fax documents to local or toll-free number. Court makes copy: $.25 per page. Certification fee: $1.25 per doc. Payee: Clerk of Newton Circuit Court. Business checks accepted. No credit cards accepted. Prepayment required. Mail requests: SASE required.
Civil Name Search: Access: Mail, in person. Both court and visitors may perform in person name searches. Search fee: $3.00 per name. Civil docket indexed from 1937, partial on microfiche; on computer back to 1996. Mail turnaround time 1-2 weeks. Civil PAT goes back to 1995.
Criminal Name Search: Access: Mail, in person. Both court and visitors may perform in person name searches. Search fee: $3.00 per name. Required to search: name, years to search, DOB, signed release; also helpful: SSN. Criminal records indexed from 1937, partial on microfiche; on computer back to 1996. Mail turnaround time 1-2 weeks. Criminal PAT goes back to same as civil. For identification purposes, find case numbers on public terminal, then clerk will pull files and match them based on personal identifiers.

Noble County

Circuit, Superior I & Superior II Court 101 N Orange St, Albion, IN 46701; 260-636-2736; fax: 260-636-4000; 8AM-4:30PM (EST). *Felony, Misdemeanor, Civil, Eviction, Small Claims, Probate.*
www.nobleco.org/
General Information: Clerk's office manages records for all three courts. Circuit Court phone is 260-636-2128. Probate fax is same as main fax number. A great number of record files are stored offsite. No juvenile, mental, adoption or sealed released. Will not fax documents. Court makes copy: $1.00 per page. Certification fee: $1.00 per certification. Payee: Noble County Clerk. No personal checks accepted. Major credit cards accepted; a usage fee applies. Prepayment required. Mail requests: SASE required for mail return of any copies.
Civil Name Search: Access: In person, online. Visitors must perform in person searches themselves. Civil index on cards and docket books to 1856; on computer back to 1992. Note: Court will accept genealogy search requests by mail. Civil PAT goes back to 1992. Public access terminal-court will assist in instructing users for genealogy purposes. Access court records free at http://noble.nasaview.com/terms.php.
Criminal Name Search: Access: In person, online. Visitors must perform in person searches themselves. Required to search: name, years to

search; also helpful: DOB. Criminal records indexed on cards and docket books to 1856; on computer back to 1992. Note: Some address and dobs appear online, but SSNs do not. Criminal PAT goes back to 1992. Public terminals located in Recorder's office. Online access to criminal same as civil, see above.

Ohio County

Circuit Court PO Box 185, Rising Sun, IN 47040; 812-438-2610; fax: 812-438-1215; 9AM-4PM M,T,TH,F 9AM-N Sat (EST). *Felony, Misdemeanor, Civil, Eviction, Small Claims, Probate.*
General Information: No juvenile, mental, adoption or sealed released. Will fax documents to local or toll-free number. Court makes copy: $1.00 per page. Self serve copy: same. Certification fee: $2.00. Payee: Ohio County Clerk. No personal checks or credit cards accepted. Prepayment required.
Civil Name Search: Access: In person only. Both court and visitors may perform in person name searches. No search fee. Civil records archived from 1844; on computer back to 8/1999. Civil PAT available.
Criminal Name Search: Access: In person only. Visitors must perform in person searches themselves. Criminal records computerized from 8/1999. Criminal PAT available.

Orange County

Circuit Court Courthouse, Court St, Paoli, IN 47454; 812-723-2649; fax: 812-723-0239; 8AM-4PM (EST). *Felony, Civil, Eviction, Small Claims, Probate.*
General Information: Probate is a separate index at this same address. See County Superior Court for misdemeanors and Class D (minor) felonies. Probate fax is same as main fax number. No juvenile, mental, adoption or sealed released. Will fax documents. Court makes copy: $1.00 per page. Self serve copy: $.10 per page. Certification fee: $5.00 per document. Payee: Orange Circuit Clerk. Only cashiers checks and money orders accepted. No credit cards accepted. Prepayment required. Mail requests: SASE required.
Civil Name Search: Access: In person only. Visitors must perform in person searches themselves. Civil records archived from 1874. Some records on docket books. Note: This court will not perform name searches for the public. Mail turnaround time 2 weeks.
Criminal Name Search: Access: In person only. Visitors must perform in person searches themselves. Criminal records archived from 1874. Some records on docket books. Note: This court will not perform name searches for the public. Mail turnaround time 2 weeks.
Superior Court 205 E Main St, Paoli, IN 47454; 812-723-3322; criminal phone: 812-723-2403; civil phone: 812-723-2403; fax: 812-723-5839; 8AM-N, 1-4PM (EST). *Felony, Misdemeanor, Civil, Eviction, Small Claims, Probate.*
General Information: The court will not perform a name search. No juvenile, mental, adoption or sealed released. Will fax documents to local or toll-free number. Court makes copy: $1.00 per page. Certification fee: $1.00 per doc plus copy fee. Payee: Orange Superior Court Clerk. Only cashiers checks and money orders accepted. No credit cards accepted. Prepayment required.
Civil Name Search: Access: In person. Visitors must perform in person searches themselves. Civil records go back to 1978.
Criminal Name Search: Access: In person. Visitors must perform in person searches themselves. Criminal records archived from 1874. Some records on docket books.

Owen County

Circuit Court PO Box 146, Courthouse, Spencer, IN 47460; 812-829-5015; fax: 812-829-5147; 8AM-4PM (EST). *Felony, Misdemeanor, Civil, Eviction, Small Claims, Probate.*
General Information: No juvenile, mental, adoption or sealed records released. Will fax documents $1.00 per page. Court makes copy: $1.00 per page. Self serve copy: same. Certification fee: $1.00 per page. Payee: Owen County Clerk. Business checks accepted. Major credit cards accepted. Prepayment required.
Civil Name Search: Access: In person, online. Visitors must perform in person searches themselves. Civil records archived from 1800s. Some records on docket books. The record index is available at http://mycase.in.gov/
Criminal Name Search: Access: In person, online. Visitors must perform in person searches themselves. Criminal records archived from 1800s. Some records on docket books. Limited as of 04/18/07. The record index is available at http://mycase.in.gov/ Although dates of birth can be used as a search feature in criminal cases, the Indiana Supreme Court has determined that dates of birth will not be displayed in Public Access.

Parke County

Circuit Court 116 W High St, Rm 204, Rockville, IN 47872; 765-569-5132; fax: 765-569-4222; 8AM-4PM (EST). *Felony, Misdemeanor, Civil, Eviction, Small Claims, Probate.*
General Information: No juvenile, mental, adoption or sealed released. Will fax documents for fee, call first. Court makes copy: n/a. Self serve

copy: $1.00 per page. Certification fee: $2.00. Payee: Parke County Clerk. No personal checks. No credit cards accepted. Prepayment required.

Civil Name Search: Access: In person, online. Visitors must perform in person searches themselves. Civil records archived from 1880s. Some records on docket books. The record index is available at http://mycase.in.gov/.

Criminal Name Search: Access: In person, online. Visitors must perform in person searches themselves. Criminal records archived from 1880s. Some records on docket books. The record index is available at http://mycase.in.gov/. Although dates of birth can be used as a search feature in criminal cases, the Indiana Supreme Court has determined that dates of birth will not be displayed in Public Access.

Perry County

Circuit Court 2219 Payne St, #219, Courthouse, Circuit Clerk, Tell City, IN 47586; 812-547-3741; fax: 812-547-9782; 8AM-4PM (CST). *Felony, Misdemeanor, Civil, Eviction, Small Claims, Probate.*
www.perrycountyin.org/

General Information: No juvenile, mental, adoption or sealed released. Court makes copy: $1.00 per page. Certification fee: $1.00 per cert. Payee: Perry County Clerk. Business checks accepted. No credit cards accepted. Prepayment required.

Civil Name Search: Access: In person, online. Both court and visitors may perform in person name searches. No search fee. Civil records archived from 1900s. Some records on dockets. Civil PAT goes back to 1997. Online subscription service at https://www.doxpop.com. Fees involved. Records date back to 7/1997.

Criminal Name Search: Access: In person, online. Both court and visitors may perform in person name searches. No search fee. Criminal records archived from 1900s. Some records on dockets. Criminal PAT goes back to same as civil. Online access same as civil.

Pike County

Circuit Court PO Box 125, Petersburg, IN 47567; 812-354-6025/6026; probate phone: 812-354-6025; fax: 812-354-6369; 8AM-4PM (EST). *Felony, Misdemeanor, Civil, Eviction, Small Claims, Probate.*

General Information: Probate fax- 812-354-6369 No juvenile, mental, adoption or sealed released. Will not fax out documents. Court makes copy: $1.00 per page. Self serve copy: same. Certification fee: $1.00 per cert. Payee: Pike County Clerk. Only cashiers checks and money orders accepted. Major credit cards accepted. Prepayment required.

Civil Name Search: Access: In person, online. Both court and visitors may perform in person name searches. No search fee. Civil records archived from 1817. Some records on docket books and index file; on computer since 7/99. Civil PAT goes back to 1999. Online subscription service at https://www.doxpop.com. Fees involved. A limited free search of open cases is available.

Criminal Name Search: Access: In person, online. Both court and visitors may perform in person name searches. No search fee. Required to search: name, years to search, DOB. Criminal records archived from 1817. Some records on docket books and index file; on computer since 7/99. Criminal PAT goes back to same. Online access to criminal same as civil. Online results show name only.

Porter County

Circuit Court County Clerk, Courthouse, 16 E Lincolnway, Valparaiso, IN 46383-5659; 219-465-3450;; 8:30AM-4:30PM (CST). *Felony, Misdemeanor, Civil, Eviction, Small Claims, Probate.*
www.porterco.org

General Information: Eviction and small claims are in Rm 211, 219-465-3413. There is also an office in Portage. No juvenile, mental, adoption or sealed released. Will not fax documents. Court makes copy: $1.00 per page. Certification fee: $1.00 per document plus copy fee. Payee: Porter County Clerk. Cashiers checks and money orders accepted, no personal checks. Prepayment required. Mail requests: SASE required.

Civil Name Search: Access: Online, in person. Visitors must perform in person searches themselves. Civil records on computer index from 1990. Circuit Court records kept from 1844, Superior Court records from 1895. Probate records from Circuit Court. Civil PAT goes back to 2000. Subscription access to court records is available via Enhanced Access for $50 per month, $25 each add'l user, see www.porterco.org/index.php?id=enhancedaccess or call 219-465-3547.

Criminal Name Search: Access: Online, in person. Visitors must perform in person searches themselves. No search fee. Criminal records on computer index since 1990. Circuit Court criminal records kept from 1877, Superior Court from 1895. Criminal PAT goes back to same as civil. Subscription access to court records is available via Enhanced Access for $50 per month, $25 each add'l user, see www.porterco.org/index.php?id=enhancedaccess or call 219-465-3547.

Superior Court 3560 Willow Creek Dr, Portage, IN 46368; 219-759-8217;; 8:30AM-4:30PM (CST). *Misdemeanor, Civil, Small Claims.*
www.porterco.org/

General Information: No juvenile, mental, adoption or sealed records released. Will not fax out documents. Court makes copy: $1.00 per page. Certification fee: $1.00 per cert. Payee: Porter County Clerk. Only cashiers checks and money orders accepted. Major credit cards accepted, service fee added. Prepayment required.

Civil Name Search: Access: Online, in person. Both court and visitors may perform in person name searches. No search fee. Civil records on computer since 1990; prior records on manual index. Mail turnaround time 1 week. Civil PAT goes back to 1990. Subscription access to court records is available via Enhanced Access for $50 per month, $25 each add'l user, see www.porterco.org/index.php?id=enhancedaccess or call 219-465-3547.

Criminal Name Search: Access: Online, in person. Both court and visitors may perform in person name searches. No search fee. Required to search: name, years to search; also helpful: DOB, SSN. Criminal records on computer since 1990; prior records on manual index. Mail turnaround time 1 week. Criminal PAT goes back to 1990. Subscription access to court records is available via Enhanced Access for $50 per month, $25 each add'l user, see www.porterco.org/index.php?id=enhancedaccess or call 219-465-3547.

Posey County

Circuit & Superior Court PO Box 606, 300 Main St, Mount Vernon, IN 47620-0606; 812-838-1306; criminal phone: 812-838-8367; civil phone: 812-838-8368; probate phone: 812-838-1306; fax: 812-838-1307; 8AM-4PM (CST). *Felony, Misdemeanor, Civil, Eviction, Small Claims, Probate.*

General Information: Probate fax is same as main fax number. No juvenile, mental, adoption or sealed released. Will fax documents $1.00 per page. Court makes copy: $1.00 per page. Self serve copy: $1.00 per page. Certification fee: $1.00 plus copy fee. Payee: Posey County Clerk. Only cashiers checks and money orders accepted. Major credit cards accepted. Prepayment required.

Civil Name Search: Access: In person, online. Only the court performs in person name searches; visitors may not. No search fee. Required to search: name, years to search; also helpful: address. Civil records on computer since 8/88, prior on docket books. Civil PAT available. Public terminal available in Superior Court. The record index is available at http://mycase.in.gov/.

Criminal Name Search: Access: In person, online. Both court and visitors may perform in person name searches. No search fee. Required to search: name, years to search; also helpful: DOB, SSN. Criminal records on computer since 8/88, prior on docket books. Criminal PAT available. The record index is available at http://mycase.in.gov/.

Pulaski County

Circuit Court 112 E Main, Rm 230, Winamac, IN 46996; 574-946-3313; fax: 574-946-4953; 8AM-4PM (EST). *Felony, Civil, Probate.*

General Information: Civil suits, eviction and small claims are managed by the Superior Court. Probate fax is same as main fax number. No juvenile, mental, adoption or sealed records released. Will fax documents $3.00 fee. Court makes copy: $.10 per page. Self serve copy: same. Certification fee: $2.00 per cert. Payee: Pulaski County Clerk. Only cashiers checks and money orders accepted. No credit cards accepted. Prepayment required.

Civil Name Search: Access: In person only. Visitors must perform in person searches themselves. Civil cases indexed by defendant. Civil records archived from 1850s. Some records indexed on docket books. On computer back to 2000. Public use terminal available, records go back to 2000.

Criminal Name Search: Access: In person only. Visitors must perform in person searches themselves. Required to search: name, years to search; SSN helpful. Criminal records archived from 1850s. Some records indexed on docket books. On computer from 2000. Public use terminal available, crim records go back to 2000.

Superior Court 112 E Main St, Winamac, IN 46996; 574-946-3371; fax: 574-946-3573; 8AM-4PM (EST). *Misdemeanor, Civil, Eviction, Small Claims, Traffic.*

General Information: Add'l current civil records can be found at the Circuit Court. The advantage this court offers is that it will do limited phone index searches and the Circuit Court will not. No juvenile, mental, adoption or sealed records released. Court makes copy: n/a. Certification fee: $1.00 plus copy fee. Payee: Pulaski County. Only cashiers checks and money orders accepted. No credit cards accepted. Prepayment required.

Civil Name Search: Access: Phone, in person. Visitors must perform in person searches themselves. No search fee. Civil cases indexed by defendant. Most records go back a maximum of two years; older records found at Circuit Court Clerk office. Civil PAT goes back to 1996.

Criminal Name Search: Access: Phone, in person. Visitors must perform in person searches themselves. No search fee. Required to search: Name only. Misdemeanor records go back a maximum of two years; older records found at Circuit Court Clerk office. Note: Clerk will do short, usually single name searches for no fee over the phone. Criminal PAT goes back to same as civil. Results include last 4 digits of SSN.

Putnam County

Circuit & Superior Court PO Box 546, Greencastle, IN 46135; 765-653-2648; probate phone: 765-653-2649; fax: 765-653-8405; 8AM-4PM (EST). *Felony, Misdemeanor, Civil, Eviction, Small Claims, Probate.*

General Information: No juvenile, mental, adoption or sealed released. Will not fax documents. Court makes copy: $1.00 per page. Self serve copy: same. Certification fee: $1.00. Payee: Putnam County Clerk. Business checks accepted. No credit cards accepted. Prepayment required. Mail requests: SASE required for mail return of any copies.

Civil Name Search: Access: In person, online. Visitors must perform in person searches themselves. Civil index on docket books from 1991, archived from 1800s. Some records on docket books. Civil PAT goes back to parts of 1998 for Circuit; 1992 for Superior. Online subscription service at https://www.doxpop.com. Fees involved. Records date from 01/92. A limited free search of open cases is available.

Criminal Name Search: Access: In person, online. Visitors must perform in person searches themselves. Required to search: name, years to search; also helpful: DOB, SSN. Criminal records indexed in books from 1991, archived from 1800s. Some records on docket books. Criminal PAT goes back to same as civil. Online access to criminal same as civil. Online results show middle initial, DOB.

Randolph County

Circuit & Superior Court PO Box 230 Courthouse, Winchester, IN 47394-0230; 765-584-7207; fax: 765-584-4320; 8AM-4PM (EST). *Felony, Misdemeanor, Civil, Eviction, Small Claims, Probate.*
www.randolphcounty.us/

General Information: No juvenile, mental, adoption or sealed released. Will fax documents $4.00 1st page, $.75 each add'l. Court makes copy: $1.00 per page. Self serve copy: same. Certification fee: $1.00. Payee: Randolph County Clerk. Checks and money orders accepted. No credit cards accepted. Prepayment required. Mail requests: SASE required.

Civil Name Search: Access: Fax, mail, in person, online. Visitors must perform in person searches themselves. No search fee. Civil records archived from early 1800s, computerized from 1994. Records on docket books and microfiche. Civil PAT goes back to 6/1994. Online subscription service at https://www.doxpop.com. Fees involved. Records date from 06/94. A limited free search of open cases is available.

Criminal Name Search: Access: Fax, mail, in person, online. Visitors must perform in person searches themselves. No search fee. Criminal records archived from early 1800s, computerized since 1994. Records on docket books and microfiche. Mail turnaround time 3 days. Criminal PAT goes back to same as civil. Online subscription service at https://www.doxpop.com. Fees involved. Records date from 06/94. A limited free search of open cases is available.

Ripley County

Circuit Court PO Box 177, Versailles, IN 47042; 812-689-6115; fax: 812-689-6000; 8AM-4PM (EST). *Felony, Misdemeanor, Civil, Eviction, Small Claims, Probate.*
www.ripleycounty.com

General Information: No juvenile, mental, adoption or sealed records released. Will fax documents $1.00 per page, prepaid. Court makes copy: $1.00 per page. Self serve copy: same. Certification fee: $3.00. Payee: Clerk of Ripley Circuit Court. Personal checks accepted. No credit cards accepted. Prepayment required. Mail requests: SASE required.

Civil Name Search: Access: Phone, mail, in person, online. Both court and visitors may perform in person name searches. No search fee. Civil records on computer since 1993, archived from 1800s. Some records on docket books. Mail turnaround time 1 week. Public use terminal available, records go back to 1993. Online subscription service at https://www.doxpop.com. Fees involved. Records date from 07/1993. A limited free search of open cases is available.

Criminal Name Search: Access: Mail, in person, online. Both court and visitors may perform in person name searches. No search fee. Required to search: name, years to search, DOB, signed release; also helpful: SSN. Criminal records on computer since 1993, archived from 1800s. Some records on docket books. Mail turnaround time 1 week. Public use terminal available, crim records go back to same. Online access to criminal is same as civil.

Rush County

Circuit & Superior Court 101 E 2nd St, Room 209, Rushville, IN 46173; 765-932-2086; fax: 765-932-4165; 8AM-4PM M-F (EST). *Felony, Misdemeanor, Civil, Eviction, Small Claims, Probate.*
www.rushcounty.in.gov/Public/Home/index.cfm

General Information: This office will not conduct general name searches, but will pull files if the specific case number is given. No juvenile, mental, adoption or sealed records released. Will not fax out documents. Court makes copy: $1.00 per page. Self serve copy: same. Certification fee: $1.00 per unit. Payee: Rush County Clerk. Business checks accepted. Major credit cards accepted. Prepayment required.

Civil Name Search: Access: In person, online. Visitors must perform in person searches themselves. Civil records archived from 1822. Some records on docket books. Search civil, family, and probate dockets free at http://mycase.in.gov/default.aspx.

Criminal Name Search: Access: In person, only. Visitors must perform in person searches themselves. Required to search: name, years to search, DOB; SSN, cause number helpful. Criminal records archived from 1822. Some records on docket books. Note: Court will only search the status of an open case, and you need to provide the case number of it. Search criminal dockets free at http://mycase.in.gov/default.aspx.

Scott County

Circuit & Superior Court 1 E McClain Ave, #120, Scottsburg, IN 47170; 812-752-8420; fax: 812-752-5459; 8:30AM-4:30PM (EST). *Felony, Misdemeanor, Civil, Eviction, Small Claims, Probate.*

General Information: No juvenile, mental, adoption or sealed released. Court makes copy: $1.00 per page. Certification fee: $2.00 per cert. Payee: Scott County Clerk. Business checks accepted. No credit cards accepted except for licenses, traffic tickets. Prepayment required.

Civil Name Search: Access: In person only. Visitors must perform in person searches themselves. Required to search: name, years to search; also helpful: address. Civil records on computer from 2/90, on docket books from 1970. Note: Court will only search if provided a case number. Civil PAT goes back to 1990.

Criminal Name Search: Access: In person only. Visitors must perform in person searches themselves. Required to search: name, years to search; also helpful: DOB, SSN. Criminal records computerized from 2/90, on docket books from 1970. Note: Court will only search if provided a case number. Criminal PAT goes back to 1990.

Shelby County

Circuit & Superior Court 407 S Harrison St, Shelbyville, IN 46176; 317-392-6320; fax: 317-392-6339; 8AM-4PM (EST). *Felony, Misdemeanor, Civil, Eviction, Small Claims, Probate.*
www.co.shelby.in.us/

General Information: No juvenile, mental, adoption or sealed released. Will not fax documents. Court makes copy: $.50 per page. Certification fee: $1.00 per page. Payee: Clerk of Court. No personal checks. No credit cards accepted. Prepayment required.

Civil Name Search: Access: In person, online. Visitors must perform in person searches themselves. Civil records on computer since 7/95. Note: Will pull case records Tues and Thurs AM only. Civil PAT goes back to 1995. Terminal results do not always show the DOB or middle initial. Online subscription service at https://www.doxpop.com. Fees involved. Records date from 07/1995. A limited free search of open cases is available. Also search civil, family, and probate dockets free at http://mycase.in.gov/default.aspx.

Criminal Name Search: Access: In person, online. Visitors must perform in person searches themselves. Criminal records on computer since 7/95. Note: Will pull case records Tues and Thurs AM only. Criminal PAT goes back to same as civil. Terminal results do not always show the DOB or middle initial. Online access to criminal is same as civil.

Spencer County

Circuit Court PO Box 12, 200 Main St, Rm 8, Rockport, IN 47635; 812-649-6027; fax: 812-649-6030; 8AM-4PM (CST). *Felony, Misdemeanor, Civil, Eviction, Small Claims, Probate.*
www.spencercounty.in.gov/

General Information: Probate is a separate index at this same address. Probate fax is same as main fax number. No juvenile, mental, adoption or sealed released. Will fax out specific case files no fee if all fees paid in advance. Court makes copy: $1.00 per page. Self serve copy: same. Certification fee: $1.00 per document plus copy fee. Payee: Spencer Circuit Court. Only cashiers checks and money orders accepted. Major credit cards accepted in person only. Prepayment required. Mail requests: SASE required for mail return of any copies.

Civil Name Search: Access: In person, online. Both court and visitors may perform in person name searches. No search fee; court will provide only limited help. Civil records archived from early 1800s. Some records on docket books. Civil cases on computer. Starting 2/02 all new cases are computerized. Civil PAT goes back to 2002. Online subscription service at https://www.doxpop.com. Fees involved. Records date from 1/02.

Criminal Name Search: Access: In person, online. Both court and visitors may perform in person name searches. No search fee; court will provide only limited help. Criminal records archived from early 1800s. Some records on docket books. Starting 2/02 all new cases are computerized. Criminal PAT goes back to same as civil. Online access to criminal is same as civil. Online results show name only.

St. Joseph County

Circuit & Superior Court 101 S Main St, South Bend, IN 46601; 574-235-9635; fax: 574-235-9838; 8AM-4:30PM (EST). *Felony, Misdemeanor, Civil, Eviction, Small Claims, Probate.*

General Information: No juvenile, mental, adoption or sealed released. Will fax documents to local or toll-free number; will not fax certified documents. Court makes copy: $1.00 per page. Certification fee: $1.00. Payee: St Joseph County Clerk. Business checks accepted. No credit cards accepted. Prepayment required. Mail requests: SASE required for civil.

Civil Name Search: Access: Mail, in person. Visitors must perform in person searches themselves. No search fee. Civil records on general index from 1962, computerized since 1992. Civil PAT goes back to 1992.

Criminal Name Search: Access: In person, online (limited). Visitors must perform in person searches themselves. Required to search: name, years to search; also helpful: address, DOB, SSN. Criminal records on general index from 1962, computerized since 1984. Criminal PAT goes back to 1986 (Misd), 1992 (Felony). The record index for infraction ordinances only is available at http://mycase.in.gov/ Although dates of birth can be used as a search feature in criminal cases, the Indiana Supreme Court has determined that dates of birth will not be displayed in Public Access.

Starke County

Circuit Court PO Box 395, 53 E Washington, Courthouse, Knox, IN 46534; 574-772-9128; probate phone: 574-772-9162; fax: 574-772-9169; 8AM-4PM (CST). *Felony, Misdemeanor, Civil, Eviction, Small Claims, Probate.*

www.co.starke.in.us/circuit-court/

General Information: No juvenile, mental, adoption or sealed released. Will fax documents $1.00 per page. Court makes copy: $1.00 per page. Self serve copy: same. Certification fee: $2.00. Payee: Clerk of Stark Circuit Court. Local business checks accepted with proper identification. No credit cards accepted. Prepayment required.

Civil Name Search: Access: In person, online. Both court and visitors may perform in person name searches. No search fee. Civil records archived from 1850s. Some records on docket books. Civil PAT goes back to 2006. Online subscription service at www.doxpop.com/prod/. Fees involved. Records date back to 9/2005 A limited free search of open cases is available. DOB on internet results shows year of birth only. Also- the Knox City Court index is viewable at http://mycase.in.gov/default.aspx.

Criminal Name Search: Access: In person, online. Both court and visitors may perform in person name searches. No search fee. Required to search: name, years to search, DOB. Criminal records archived from 1850s. Some records on docket books. Criminal PAT goes back to 2006. DOB does not always appear in results. Online subscription service at www.doxpop.com/prod/. Fees involved. Records date back to 9/2005 A limited free search of open cases is available. Also- the Knox City Court index is viewable at http://mycase.in.gov/default.aspx. Online results show middle initial.

Steuben County

Circuit & Superior Court 55 S Public Square, Courthouse, Angola, IN 46703; 260-668-1000; criminal phone: x2270; civil phone: x2240; 8AM-4:30PM (EST). *Felony, Misdemeanor, Civil, Eviction, Small Claims, Probate.*

www.steubencounty.com/departments/court/court.aspx

General Information: No juvenile, mental, adoption, some probate, or sealed released. Will not fax documents. Court makes copy: $1.00 per page. Certification fee: $2.00. Payee: Steuben County Clerk. Only cashiers checks and money orders accepted. No credit cards accepted. Prepayment required.

Civil Name Search: Access: In person only. Visitors must perform in person searches themselves. Civil records archived from 1800s. Some records on docket books. Civil PAT goes back to 1995 for civil case records - but not judgments.

Criminal Name Search: Access: In person only. Visitors must perform in person searches themselves. Criminal records archived from 1800s, computerized since 6/94. Some records on docket books. Criminal PAT goes back to same as civil. Will show DOB and address if on case file.

Sullivan County

Circuit & Superior Court PO Box 370, 100 Courthouse Sq, Rm 304, Sullivan, IN 47882-0370; 812-268-4657; probate phone: 812-268-4411; fax: 812-268-7027; 8AM-4PM (EST). *Felony, Misdemeanor, Civil, Eviction, Small Claims, Probate.*

General Information: No juvenile, mental, adoption or sealed released. Will not fax documents. Court makes copy: $1.00 per page. Self serve copy: same. Certification fee: $1.00 per page. Payee: Sullivan County. No personal checks accepted; business check okay. Major credit cards accepted at 888-604-7888; mention pay location 5208. Prepayment required.

Civil Name Search: Access: In person, online. Visitors must perform in person searches themselves. Required to search: name, years to search; also helpful: address. Civil index on docket books or general index from late 1850's; computerized from 1999. Civil PAT goes back to 1991. Online subscription service at https://www.doxpop.com. Fees involved. Records date from 04/1999. A limited free search of open cases is available.

Criminal Name Search: Access: In person, online. Visitors must perform in person searches themselves. Required to search: name, years to search, DOB, signed release; also helpful: address, SSN. Criminal docket on books or general index from late 1850's; computerized from 1999. Criminal PAT goes back to 1993. Online subscription service at https://www.doxpop.com. Fees involved. Records date from 04/1999. A limited free search of open cases is available. Online results show name only.

Switzerland County

Circuit & Superior Court Courthouse, 212 W Main St, Vevay, IN 47043; 812-427-4415; fax: 812-427-4408; 8AM-3:30PM M-W,F; 8AM-N TH (EST). *Felony, Misdemeanor, Civil, Eviction, Small Claims, Probate.*

General Information: Probate fax is same as main fax number. No juvenile, mental, adoption or sealed released. Will not fax documents. Court makes copy: first 4 pages free, $1.00 for 5th page, then $.25 each add'l. Self serve copy: same. Certification fee: $1.00 per page plus copy fee. Payee: Switzerland County Clerk. No personal checks or credit cards accepted. Prepayment required.

Civil Name Search: Access: In person only. Visitors must perform in person searches themselves. Required to search: name, years to search, DOB. Civil records archived from 1900s. All records on docket books or general index. Civil PAT goes back to 2/2001.

Criminal Name Search: Access: In person only. Visitors must perform in person searches themselves. Required to search: name, years to search, DOB. Criminal records archived from 1900s. All records on docket books or general index. Criminal PAT goes back to same as civil.

Tippecanoe County

Circuit & Superior Court PO Box 1665, Lafayette, IN 47902; 765-423-9326; probate phone: 765-423-9343; fax: 765-423-9194; 8AM-4:30PM (EST). *Felony, Misdemeanor, Civil, Eviction, Small Claims, Probate.*

www.tippecanoe.in.gov

General Information: No juvenile, mental, adoption or sealed released. Will fax documents $2.00 per page. Court makes copy: $1.00 per page. Self serve copy: $.05 per page. Certification fee: $1.00. Payee: Tippecanoe County Clerk. Business checks accepted. No credit cards accepted. Prepayment required.

Civil Name Search: Access: In person, mail, online. Visitors must perform in person searches themselves. No search fee. Civil records on computer from 1987, on microfiche from 1900. Some records on index and docket books. Civil PAT goes back to mid 1980s. identifiers on the civil docket are limited, not nearly as many as shown on the criminal docket. Online access to court records through CourtView are free at www.county.tippecanoe.in.us/court/pa.urd/pamw6500-display.

Criminal Name Search: Access: In person, mail, online. Visitors must perform in person searches themselves. No search fee. Required to search: name, years to search; also helpful: DOB, SSN, sex, signed release. Criminal records computerized from 1987, on microfiche from 1900. Some records on index and docket books. Criminal PAT goes back to same as civil. The DOB, address and middle initial only show if available, is not consistent. Online access to court records through CourtView are free at www.county.tippecanoe.in.us/court/pa.urd/pamw6500-display. Online results show middle initial, DOB, address.

Tipton County

Circuit Court 101 E Jefferson, 3rd Fl, County Courthouse, Tipton, IN 46072; 765-675-2795; fax: 765-675-6436; 8AM-4PM M-TH; 8AM-5PM F (EST). *Felony, Misdemeanor, Civil, Eviction, Small Claims, Probate.*

www.tiptoncounty.in.gov/

General Information: No juvenile, mental, adoption or sealed released. Will fax documents $1.00 per page. Court makes copy: $1.00 per page. Self serve copy: same. Certification fee: $1.00 plus copy fees. Payee: Tipton County Clerk. Personal checks accepted. No credit cards accepted. Prepayment required.

Civil Name Search: Access: In person, online. Both court and visitors may perform in person name searches. Search fee: $1.00. Civil records on card file and archived from 1930s. Civil PAT goes back to 09/22/08. Search the docket by case number, party name or attorney name at http://mycase.in.gov/default.aspx.

Criminal Name Search: Access: In person, online. Both court and visitors may perform in person name searches. Search fee: $1.00. Criminal records on card file and archived from 1930s. Criminal PAT goes back to 09/22/08. Online access by free service at http://mycase.in.gov/default.aspx. Includes criminal and citations. Although dates of birth can be used as a search feature in criminal cases, the Indiana Supreme Court has determined that dates of birth will not be displayed in Public Access.

Union County

Circuit Court 26 W Union St, Liberty, IN 47353; 765-458-6121; fax: 765-458-5263; 8AM-4PM (EST). *Felony, Misdemeanor, Civil, Eviction, Small Claims, Probate.*

General Information: No juvenile, mental, adoption or sealed records released. Will not fax documents. Court makes copy: $1.00 per page. Certification fee: $1.00 per cert. Payee: Union County Clerk. Only cashiers checks and money orders accepted. No credit cards accepted. Prepayment required.

Civil Name Search: Access: In person, online. Visitors must perform in person searches themselves. Civil records archived from 1821. Some records on docket books or entry books. Search the docket by case number, party name or attorney name at http://mycase.in.gov/default.aspx.

Criminal Name Search: Access: In person, online. Visitors must perform in person searches themselves. Required to search: name, years to search, DOB. Criminal records archived from 1821. Some records on docket books or entry books. Search the docket by case number, party name or attorney name at http://mycase.in.gov/default.aspx.

Vanderburgh County

Circuit & Superior Court PO Box 3356, Civic Ctr Courts Bldg - Rm 216, Evansville, IN 47732-3356; 812-435-5160; criminal phone: 812-435-5169; civil phone: 812-435-5722; probate phone: 812-435-5377; fax: 812-435-5849; 7:30AM-4:30PM (CST). *Felony, Misdemeanor, Civil, Eviction, Small Claims, Probate.*

www.vanderburghgov.org/index.aspx?page=66

General Information: No juvenile, mental, adoption or sealed released. Will not fax documents. Court makes copy: $1.00 per page. Self serve copy: $1.00 per page. Certification fee: $1.00. Payee: Vanderburgh County Clerk. Business checks accepted. No credit cards accepted. Prepayment required.

Civil Name Search: Access: In person , online. Visitors must perform in person searches themselves. Civil records on computer back to 1991, archived from 1900s. Some records on index books. Civil PAT goes back to 1991. Public terminal closes at 4PM. Access civil records by subscription to Doxpop at https://www.doxpop.com/prod/court/. Free index search.

Criminal Name Search: Access: In person, online. Visitors must perform in person searches themselves. Required to search: name, years to search, DOB, SSN. Criminal records computerized from 1991, archived from 1900s. Some records on index books. Criminal PAT goes back to same as civil. Public terminal closes at 4PM. Access civil records by subscription to Doxpop at https://www.doxpop.com/prod/court/. Free index search.

Vermillion County

Circuit Court PO Box 10, Newport, IN 47966-0010; 765-492-5350; fax: 765-492-5351; 8AM-4PM (EST). *Felony, Misdemeanor, Civil, Eviction, Small Claims, Probate.*

General Information: No juvenile, mental, adoption or sealed released. Will not fax documents. Court makes copy: $1.00 per page. Self serve copy: same. Certification fee: $2.00. Payee: Vermillion County Clerk. Business checks accepted. No credit cards accepted. Prepayment required.

Civil Name Search: Access: In person, online. Visitors must perform in person searches themselves. Required to search: name. Records on computer go back to 1994; archived from 1824. Some records on docket books. Civil PAT goes back to 07/94. Online subscription service at https://www.doxpop.com. Fees involved. Records date from 07/1999. A limited free search of open cases is available.

Criminal Name Search: Access: In person, online. Visitors must perform in person searches themselves. Required to search: name. Records on computer go back to 1994; archived from 1825. Some records on docket books. Criminal PAT goes back to 07/94. Electronic access same as civil.

Vigo County

Circuit Court 33 S 3rd Street, Terre Haute, IN 47807-3425; 812-462-3211; fax: 812-232-2921; 8AM-4PM (EST). *Felony, Misdemeanor, Civil, Eviction, Small Claims, Probate.*

www.vigocounty.in.gov/

General Information: No juvenile, mental, adoption or sealed released. Will not fax documents. Court makes copy: $1.00 per page. Certification fee: $1.00 per cert. Payee: Vigo County Clerk. Only cashiers checks and money orders accepted. No credit cards accepted. Prepayment required. Mail requests: SASE required.

Civil Name Search: Access: Mail, in person, online. Visitors must perform in person searches themselves. No search fee. Civil index on docket books; on computer back to 8/1996. Civil PAT goes back to 1996. Online subscription service at https://www.doxpop.com. Fees involved. Records date from 04/96. A limited free search of open cases is available.

Criminal Name Search: Access: In person, online. Visitors must perform in person searches themselves. Required to search: name, years to search; also helpful: DOB. Criminal records indexed in books; on computer back to 8/1996. Criminal PAT goes back to same as civil. Online access to criminal records is the same as civil. Depending on the age of the subject, identifiers shown online usually include DOB and last 4 digits of SSN.

Wabash County

Circuit & Superior Court 69 W Hill St, Wabash, IN 46992; 260-563-0661 X230; fax: 260-569-1352; 8AM-4PM (EST). *Felony, Misdemeanor, Civil, Eviction, Small Claims, Probate.*

General Information: Online identifiers in results same as on public terminal. No juvenile, mental, adoption or sealed records released. Will fax documents $2.00 1st page, $1.00 each add'l page. Court makes copy: $1.00 per page. Certification fee: $1.00. Payee: Wabash County Clerk. In-state business checks accepted. No credit cards accepted. Prepayment required.

Civil Name Search: Access: In person, online. Visitors must perform in person searches themselves. Civil records archived from 1800s; on computer since 1989. Some judgments on fee books. Civil PAT goes back to 1989. Online subscription service at https://www.doxpop.com . Fees involved. Records date from 08/89. A limited free search of open cases is available.

Criminal Name Search: Access: In person, online. Visitors must perform in person searches themselves. Required to search: name, years to search, DOB; also helpful: SSN. Criminal records archived from 1800s; on computer since 1989. Some judgments on fee books. Criminal PAT goes back to same as civil. Online subscription service at https://www.doxpop.com . Fees involved. Records date from 08/89. A limited free search of open cases is available. Online results show name only.

Warren County

Circuit Court 125 N Monroe, #11, Williamsport, IN 47993; 765-762-3510; fax: 765-762-7251; 8AM-4PM (EST). *Felony, Misdemeanor, Civil, Eviction, Small Claims, Probate.*

General Information: No juvenile, mental, adoption or sealed released. Fee to fax out is $1.00 per page. Court makes copy: $1.00 per page. Certification fee: $1.00 per cert. Payee: Warren County Clerk. Personal checks accepted. No credit cards accepted. Prepayment required.

Civil Name Search: Access: In person, online. Both court and visitors may perform in person name searches. No search fee. Civil records archived from 1828. Some records on docket books. Search the docket by case number, party name or attorney name at http://mycase.in.gov/default.aspx. Cases here are only since Oct 2008.

Criminal Name Search: Access: In person, online. Both court and visitors may perform in person name searches. No search fee. Required to search: name, years to search; DOB; SSN helpful. Criminal records archived from 1828. Some records on docket books. Online access by free service at http://mycase.in.gov/default.aspx. Includes criminal and citations. Reportedly, case info available are only since Oct 2008. Although dates of birth can be used as a search feature in criminal cases, the Indiana Supreme Court has determined that dates of birth will not be displayed in Public Access.

Warrick County

Circuit & Superior Court 1 County Square, #200, Boonville, IN 47601; 812-897-6160; fax: 812-897-6400; 8AM-4PM (CST). *Felony, Misdemeanor, Civil, Eviction, Small Claims, Probate.*

www.warrickcounty.gov/

General Information: No juvenile, mental, adoption or sealed released. Will not fax out case file copies. Court makes copy: $1.00 per page. Certification fee: $1.00 per cert. Payee: Warrick County Clerk. Business checks accepted; no personal checks. Major credit cards accepted online. Prepayment required. Mail requests: SASE required for mail return of any copies.

Civil Name Search: Access: In person, online. Visitors must perform in person searches themselves. No search fee. Civil records on computer from 1987, archived from 1900s. Some records on index books. Civil PAT goes back to 1987. Online subscription service at https://www.doxpop.com . Fees involved. Records date from 06/87. A limited free search of open cases is available.

Criminal Name Search: Access: In person, online. Both court and visitors may perform in person name searches. No search fee. Required to search: name, years to search; also helpful: DOB, SSN. Criminal records computerized from 1987, archived from 1900s. Some records on index books. Criminal PAT goes back to same as civil. Online subscription service at https://www.doxpop.com. Fees involved. Records date from 08/89. A limited free search of open cases is available.

Washington County

Circuit & Superior Court Courthouse, 99 Public Sq, #200, Salem, IN 47167; 812-883-5302; criminal phone: 812-883-1634; civil phone: 812-883-5748; probate phone: 812-883-5748; fax: 812-883-1933; 8AM-4PM M-F (EST). *Felony, Misdemeanor, Civil, Small Claims, Probate.*
www.washingtoncounty.in.gov/circuitcourt.html

General Information: Will only return calls to toll-free numbers. Traffic phone number same as criminal. No juvenile, mental, adoption or sealed released; no information given out via telephone. Will not fax out case files. Court makes copy: $1.00 per page. Self serve copy: same. Certification fee: $1.00. Payee: Washington County Clerk. Only cashiers checks and money orders accepted. No credit cards accepted. Prepayment required.

Civil Name Search: Access: In person, online. Visitors must perform in person searches themselves. Required to search: name, years to search; also helpful: address. Civil records on books, archived from 1820. Some records on docket books. Search the docket by case number, party name or attorney name at http://mycase.in.gov/default.aspx.

Criminal Name Search: Access: In person, online. Both court and visitors may perform in person name searches. No search fee. Required to search: name, years to search, DOB; also helpful: address, SSN. Criminal index on computer from 1980, docket books and archived from 1820. Online access by free service at http://mycase.in.gov/default.aspx. Includes criminal and citations. Although dates of birth can be used as a search feature in criminal cases, the Indiana Supreme Court has determined that dates of birth will not be displayed in Public Access.

Wayne County

Circuit & Superior Court Courthouse, 301 E Main St, Richmond, IN 47374; 765-973-9220; criminal phone: 765-973-9223/9215; fax: 765-973-9490; 8:30AM-5PM M; 8:30AM-4:30PM T-F (EST). *Felony, Misdemeanor, Civil, Eviction, Small Claims, Probate.*
www.co.wayne.in.us/courts/

General Information: Circuit clerk- 765-973-9266; Superior Ct #1 - 765-973-9259; Superior Ct #2- 765-973-9260; Small claims- 765-973-9202. No juvenile, mental, adoption or sealed released. Will not fax documents. Court makes copy: $1.00 per page. Certification fee: $1.00 per cert. Payee: Wayne County Clerk. Personal checks accepted. Prepayment required. Mail requests: SASE required.

Civil Name Search: Access: Mail, fax, in person, online. Both court and visitors may perform in person name searches. No search fee unless extensive searching required. Fee TBD. Civil records on computer from 4/90, circuit on microfiche from 1957, superior on microfiche from 1960 to 1971, all archived from 1800s. Some records. Note: Fax request must be on letterhead. Civil PAT goes back to 1990. Access records via subscription service at https://www.doxpop.com. Fees involved. Records date from 3/90; a limited free search of open cases is available.

Criminal Name Search: Access: Mail, fax, in person, online. Both court and visitors may perform in person name searches. No search fee. Required to search: name, years to search, fax request on letterhead. Criminal records computerized from 4/90, circuit on microfiche from 1957, superior on microfiche 1960-1971, all archived from 1800s. Note: Fax request must be on letterhead. Mail turnaround time 1 week. Criminal PAT goes back to same as civil. Access records via subscription service at https://www.doxpop.com. Fees involved. Records date from 3/90; a limited free search of open cases is available.

Wells County

Circuit & Superior Court 102 W Market, Rm 201, Bluffton, IN 46714; 260-824-6479; probate phone: 260-824-6480; fax: 260-824-6559; 8AM-4:30PM (EST). *Civil, Probate.*
www.wellscounty.org/superiorcourt.htm

General Information: There is also a Bluffton City Court, which is online and mentioned here. Probate fax is same as main fax number. No juvenile, mental, adoption or sealed released. Will not fax out case files. Court makes copy: $1.00 per page. Self serve copy: same. Certification fee: $1.00 plus copy fee. Payee: Wells County Clerk. Personal checks accepted. No credit cards accepted. Prepayment required.

Civil Name Search: Access: In person, online. Visitors must perform in person searches themselves. Civil records archived from 1837. Some records on docket books. Civil PAT goes back to 8/22/06, both courts. Online subscription service to courts at https://www.doxpop.com. Fees involved. A limited free search of open cases is available. Online index goes back to 1/2000.

Criminal Name Search: Access: In person, online. Visitors must perform in person searches themselves. Required to search: name, years to search, DOB; SSN helpful. Criminal records archived from 1837. Some records on docket books. Criminal PAT goes back to 8/22/06, both courts. Online access to Bluffton city criminal records is the same as civil.

White County

Circuit Court PO Box 350, 110 N Main, Monticello, IN 47960; 574-583-7032; fax: 574-583-1532; 8AM-4PM (EST). *Civil, Probate.*

General Information: No juvenile, mental, adoption or sealed released. Will not fax documents. Court makes copy: $1.00 per page. Self serve copy: same. Certification fee: $1.00. Payee: White County Clerk. Personal checks accepted. No credit cards accepted. Prepayment required.

Civil Name Search: Access: In person, online. Visitors must perform in person searches themselves. Civil records on indexes and files, some records on docket books back to 1950s. Public use terminal has civil records back to 1/2006. Online subscription service at https://www.doxpop.com. Fees involved. Index goes back to 1/2006. A limited free search of open cases is available.

Superior Court PO Box 1005, 110 N Main, Monticello, IN 47960; 574-583-9520; criminal fax: 574-583-2437; civil fax: 8AM-4PM; 8AM-4PM (EST). *Felony, Misdemeanor, Eviction, Small Claims.*

General Information: No juvenile, mental, adoption or sealed released. Will fax specific case file. Court makes copy: $1.00 per page. Certification fee: $1.00 per document plus copy fee. Payee: White County Clerk. No out-of-state checks accepted. No credit cards accepted. Prepayment required.

Civil Name Search: Access: In person, online. Both court and visitors may perform in person name searches. No search fee. Civil records on indexes and files, some records on docket books. Note: Court will perform search only if a date is provided Civil PAT goes back to 2006. Online subscription service at https://www.doxpop.com. Fees involved. Index goes back to 1/2006. A limited free search of open cases is available.

Criminal Name Search: Access: In person, online. Visitors must perform in person searches themselves. Criminal records on indexes and files, some records on docket books. Note: Court will criminal search only if a date is provided. Criminal PAT goes back to same as civil. Online access to criminal is same as civil.

Whitley County

Circuit & Superior Court 101 W Van Buren, Rm 10, Columbia City, IN 46725; 260-248-3102; fax: 260-248-3137; 8AM-4:30PM (EST). *Felony, Misdemeanor, Civil, Eviction, Small Claims, Probate.*
www.whitleygov.com/courts/

General Information: No juvenile, mental, adoption or sealed released. Will not fax documents. Court makes copy: $1.00 per page. Certification fee: $1.00. Payee: Whitley County Clerk. Only cashiers checks and money orders accepted. No credit cards accepted. Prepayment required. Mail requests: SASE required for mail return of any copies.

Civil Name Search: Access: In person, online. Visitors must perform in person searches themselves. Civil records on computer from 1999. Some records on docket books. Civil PAT goes back to 1993 (Circuit); 1988 (Superior). Online subscription service at https://www.doxpop.com. Fees involved. Records date from 01/1999. A limited free search of open cases is available.

Criminal Name Search: Access: In person, online. Visitors must perform in person searches themselves. Required to search: name, years to search; also helpful: DOB. Criminal records computerized from 1999. Some records on docket books back to 1900. Criminal PAT goes back to same as civil. Online access same as civil. Online results show middle initial, DOB.

Iowa

Time Zone:	**CST**
Capital:	**Des Moines, Polk County**
# of Counties:	**99**
State Web:	**www.iowa.gov**
Court Web:	**www.iowacourts.gov**

Administration State Court Administrator, Judicial Branch Bldg, 1111 East Court Ave, Des Moines, IA, 50319; 515-281-5241, (Supreme Ct Clerk- 515-281-5911), Fax: AOC- 515-242-0014 (Supreme Ct Clerk Fax- 515-242-6164).

The Supreme and Appellate Courts Besides being the court of last resort, the Iowa Supreme Court is responsible for licensing and disciplining attorneys, promulgating rules of procedure and practice used throughout the state courts, and overseeing the operation of the entire state court system. The Iowa Court of Appeals is an intermediate appellate court. It reviews appeals from trial court decisions that have been transferred to the Court of Appeals by the Supreme Court. From the home page above one may access Supreme Court and Appellate Court opinions.

The Iowa Courts

Court	Type	How Organized	Jurisdiction Highpoints
District*	General	100 courts in 8 Districts	Felony, Civil over $15,000, Juvenile, Domestic Relations, Estate, Probate

* = profiled in this book

Details on the Court Structure The **District Court** is the court of general jurisdiction and handles all civil, criminal, juvenile, and probate matters in the state. Vital records (except divorces) were moved from the courts to the County Recorder's office in each county. Divorce records are still held by the County Clerk of Courts.

Judicial Magistrates, part of the District Court, have jurisdiction over simple misdemeanors, including scheduled violations, county and municipal infractions, and small claims. Magistrates have authority to issue search warrants, conduct preliminary hearings, and hear certain involuntary hospitalization matters.

Record Searching Facts You Need to Know

Fees and Record Searching Tips In most courts, the copy fee is $.50 per page. By statute the certification fee is $20.00 plus copy fee. Most courts do not perform name searches and recommend the use of a record retriever. Most courts provide a public access terminal for onsite access to the index.

Online Access is Statewide District criminal, civil (including divorce cases with financials/custody data), probate, and traffic information is available from all 99 Iowa counties at www.iowacourts.state.ia.us/ESAWebApp/SelectFrame. Name searches are available on either a statewide or specific county basis. Names of juveniles aged 10 to 17 will only appear for completed cases with a guilty verdict. There is no fee for basic information. A $25.00 per month pay system is offered for more detailed requests. While this is an excellent site with much information and are updated daily, the historical records offered are from different starting dates per county.

Adair County

5th District Court 400 Public Sq, #7, Greenfield, IA 50849; 641-743-2445; fax: 641-743-2974; 8AM-4:30PM M-TH; 1PM to 4:30PM F (CST). *Felony, Misdemeanor, Civil, Eviction, Small Claims, Probate.* www.iowacourts.gov/District_Courts/District_Five/

General Information: Online identifiers in results same as on public terminal. No juvenile, sealed, dissolution of marriage, mental health domestic abuse or deferred records released. Will fax documents $.50 per page. Court makes copy: $.50 per page. Self serve copy: same. Certification fee: $20.00 per doc; exemplification is an additional $20.00. Payee: Clerk of Court. Personal checks and credit cards accepted. Prepayment required.

Civil Name Search: Access: In person, online. Both court and visitors may perform in person name searches. No search fee. Civil index in docket books from late 1800s, computerized since 11/1996. Civil PAT goes back to 1997. DOBs and middle initial appear on most records, not all. **For details about the state's online access to records, see the sections at the front or back of this chapter.**
Criminal Name Search: Access: In person, online. Visitors must perform in person searches themselves. Required to search: name, years to search, DOB, signed release; also helpful: SSN. Criminal docket on books from late 1800s, computerized since 11/1996. Criminal PAT goes back to same as civil. DOBs and middle initial appear on most records, not all. **For details about the state's online access to records, see the sections at the front or back of this chapter.**

Adams County

5th District Court PO Box 484, 500 9th St, Courthouse, Corning, IA 50841; 641-322-4711; fax: 641-322-4523; 8AM-12, 1-4:30PM M & W; closed Tu & Th at 4:30; 8AM-Noon Fri (CST). *Felony, Misdemeanor, Civil, Eviction, Small Claims, Probate.* www.iowacourts.gov/District_Courts/District_Five/

General Information: Probate fax is same as main fax number. Online identifiers in results same as on public terminal. No sealed, dissolution of marriage, mental health, sealed or expunged records released. Will fax documents $.50 per page. Court makes copy: $.50 per page. Certification fee: $20.00 per doc; exemplification is an additional $20.00. Payee: Clerk of Court. Personal checks accepted. Visa/MC accepted. Prepayment required.

Civil Name Search: Access: In person, online. Visitors must perform in person searches themselves. Civil index in docket books from late 1800s, on computer back to 11/96. Civil PAT goes back to 1996. DOBs and middle initial appear on most records, not all. **For details about the state's online access to records, see the section at the front or back of this chapter.**
Criminal Name Search: Access: In person, online. Visitors must perform in person searches themselves. Required to search: name, years to search, signed release. Criminal docket on books from late 1800s, on computer back to 11/96. Criminal PAT goes back to same as civil. DOBs and middle initial appear on most records, not all. **For details about the state's online access to records, see the section at the front or back of this chapter.**

Allamakee County

1st District Court PO Box 248, 110 Allamakee St, Waukon, IA 52172; 563-568-6351; fax: 563-568-6353; 8AM-2:30PM (CST). *Felony, Misdemeanor, Civil, Eviction, Small Claims, Probate.* www.iowacourts.gov/District_Courts/District_One/

General Information: Online identifiers in results same as on public terminal. No juvenile, adoption, sealed, pending dissolution of marriage, mental health, domestic abuse or deferred records released. Will not fax documents. Court makes copy: $.50 per page. Self serve copy: same. Certification fee: $20.00 per doc; exemplification is an additional $20.00. Payee: Clerk of Court. Personal checks accepted. Credit cards accepted for website fine payments only. Prepayment required. Mail requests: SASE required for mail return of any copies.
Civil Name Search: Access: In person, online. Visitors must perform in person searches themselves. All judgments on computer back to 4/1997; on index books back to 1880, probate back to 1852. Civil PAT goes back to 4/1997. DOBs and middle initial appear on most records, not all. **For details about the state's online access to records, see the section at the front or back of this chapter.**
Criminal Name Search: Access: In person, online. Visitors must perform in person searches themselves. Required to search: name, years to search, signed release. Criminal docket on books from 1800s; on computer back to 4/1997. Criminal PAT goes back to same as civil. DOBs and middle initial appear on most records, not all. **For details about the state's online access to records, see the section at the front or back of this chapter.**

Appanoose County

8th District Court PO Box 400, 201 N 12th St, Centerville, IA 52544; 641-856-6101; fax: 641-856-2282; 8AM-4:30PM M,W,F; 8AM-2:30PM T,TH (CST). *Felony, Misdemeanor, Civil, Eviction, Small Claims, Probate.* www.iowacourts.gov/District_Courts/District_Eight/

General Information: Online identifiers in results same as on public terminal. No juvenile, sealed, dissolution of marriage, mental health, domestic abuse or deferred records released. Will fax documents to local or toll-free number. Court makes copy: $.50 per page. Certification fee: $20.00 per doc; exemplification is an additional $20.00. Payee: Clerk of Court. Personal checks accepted. Visa/MC accepted. Prepayment required.

Civil Name Search: Access: In person, online. Visitors must perform in person searches themselves. Civil index in docket books from 1847, on computer back to 2/96. Civil PAT goes back to 1996. DOBs and middle initial appear on most records, not all. **For details about the state's online access to records, see the section at the front or back of this chapter.**
Criminal Name Search: Access: In person, online. Visitors must perform in person searches themselves. Required to search: name, years to search, signed release. Criminal docket on books from 1847, on computer back to 2/96. Criminal PAT goes back to same as civil. DOBs and middle initial appear on most records, not all. **For details about the state's online access to records, see the section at the front or back of this chapter.**

Audubon County

4th District Court 318 Leroy St, #6, Audubon, IA 50025; 712-563-4275; fax: 712-563-4276; 8AM-12, 1PM-4:30PM M,W; 8AM-Noon Fri (CST). *Felony, Misdemeanor, Civil, Eviction, Small Claims, Probate.* www.iowacourts.gov/District_Courts/District_Four/

General Information: Online identifiers in results same as on public terminal. No juvenile, sealed, dissolution of marriage, mental health, domestic abuse or deferred records released. Will fax documents $2.00 per fax. Court makes copy: $.50 per page. Certification fee: $20.00 per doc; exemplification is an additional $20.00. Payee: Clerk of Court. Personal checks accepted. No credit cards accepted. Prepayment required. Mail requests: SASE required for mail return of any copies.

Civil Name Search: Access: In person, online. Visitors must perform in person searches themselves. Required to search: name, years to search; also helpful: address. Civil index in docket books from 1930s, computerized since 1996. Civil PAT goes back to 11/1996. DOBs and middle initial appear on most records, not all. **For details about the state's online access to records, see the section at the front or back of this chapter.**
Criminal Name Search: Access: In person, online. Visitors must perform in person searches themselves. Required to search: name, years to search; also helpful: DOB, SSN, address. Criminal docket on books from late 1800s. Criminal PAT goes back to same as civil. DOBs and middle initial appear on most records, not all. **For details about the state's online access to records, see the section at the front or back of this chapter.**

Benton County

6th District Court PO Box 719, 111 E 4th St, 2nd Fl, Vinton, IA 52349; 319-472-2766; fax: 319-472-2747; 8AM-4:30PM M,W,F; 8AM-2:30PM T,TH (CST). *Felony, Misdemeanor, Civil, Eviction, Small Claims, Probate.* www.iowacourts.gov/District_Courts/District_Six/

General Information: Online identifiers in results same as on public terminal. No juvenile, sealed, dissolution of marriage, mental health, domestic abuse or deferred records released. Will fax out documents for $1.00 per page. Court makes copy: $.50 per page. Certification fee: $20.00 per doc; exemplification is an additional $20.00. Payee: Clerk of Court. Personal checks accepted. Visa/MC accepted. Prepayment required.

Civil Name Search: Access: In person, online. Visitors must perform in person searches themselves. Civil records on original record books from 1800s, index is on computer since 6/95. Civil PAT goes back to 1995. DOBs and middle initial appear on most records, not all. **For details about the state's online access to records, see the section at the front or back of this chapter.**
Criminal Name Search: Access: In person, online. Visitors must perform in person searches themselves. Criminal records on original record books from 1800s, index is on computer since 6/95. Criminal PAT goes back to 1995. DOBs and middle initial appear on most records, not all. **For details about the state's online access to records, see the section at the front or back of this chapter.**

Black Hawk County

1st District Court 316 E 5th St, PO Box 9500, Waterloo, IA 50703; 319-833-3331; probate phone: x 1856; fax: 319-833-3251; 8AM-4:30PM M,W,F; 8AM-2:30PM T,TH (CST). *Felony, Misdemeanor, Civil, Eviction, Small Claims, Probate.* www.iowacourts.gov/District_Courts/District_One/

General Information: Online identifiers in results same as on public terminal. No juvenile, sealed, dissolution of marriage, mental health, domestic abuse or deferred records released. Will not fax documents. Court makes copy: $.50 per page. Certification fee: $20.00 per doc; exemplification is an additional $20.00. Payee: District Court. Personal checks and credit cards accepted. Prepayment required.

Civil Name Search: Access: In person, online. Visitors must perform in person searches themselves. Civil records on computer from 1992, docket books from early 1900s. Civil PAT goes back to 1992. DOBs and middle initial appear on most records, not all. **For details about the state's online access to records, see the section at the front or back of this chapter.**

Criminal Name Search: Access: In person, online. Visitors must perform in person searches themselves. Required to search: name, years to search; also helpful: DOB, SSN. Criminal records computerized from 1992, docket books from early 1900s. Criminal PAT goes back to same as civil. DOBs and middle initial appear on most records, not all. **For details about the state's online access to records, see the section at the front or back of this chapter.**

Boone County

2nd District Court 201 State St, Boone, IA 50036; 515-433-0561; fax: 515-433-0563; 8AM-4:30PM M,W,F; 8AM-N T,TH (CST). *Felony, Misdemeanor, Civil, Eviction, Small Claims, Probate.* www.iowacourts.gov/District_Courts/District_Two/

General Information: Online identifiers in results same as on public terminal. No juvenile, sealed, dissolution of marriage, mental health, domestic abuse or deferred records released. Will fax documents $1.00 per page. Court makes copy: $.50 per page. Certification fee: $20.00 per doc; exemplification is an additional $20.00. Payee: Clerk of Court. Personal checks accepted. Visa/MC accepted. Prepayment required.

Civil Name Search: Access: In person, online. Visitors must perform in person searches themselves. Civil index in docket books from 1890s; computerized records go back to 1996. Civil PAT goes back to 1996. DOBs and middle initial appear on most records, not all. **For details about the state's online access to records, see the section at the front or back of this chapter.**

Criminal Name Search: Access: In person, online. Visitors must perform in person searches themselves. Required to search: name, years to search, offense, date of offense. Criminal docket on books from 1890s; computerized records go back to 1996. Criminal PAT goes back to same as civil. DOBs and middle initial appear on most records, not all. **For details about the state's online access to records, see the section at the front or back of this chapter.**

Bremer County

2nd District Court 415 E Bremer, Waverly, IA 50677; 319-352-5661; fax: 319-352-1054; 8AM-4:30PM M,W,F; 8AM-2:30PM T,TH (CST). *Felony, Misdemeanor, Civil, Eviction, Small Claims, Probate.* www.iowacourts.gov/District_Courts/District_Two/

General Information: Online identifiers in results same as on public terminal. No juvenile, sealed, dissolution of marriage, mental health, domestic abuse or deferred records released. Will fax specific file for $1.00 per page. Court makes copy: $.50 per page. Self serve copy: same. Certification fee: $20.00 per doc; exemplification is an additional $20.00. Payee: Clerk of Court. Personal checks and credit cards accepted. Prepayment required. Mail requests: SASE required for mail return of any copies.

Civil Name Search: Access: In person, online. Visitors must perform in person searches themselves. Civil records on computer since 7/97; prior records on docket books from 1900's. Civil PAT goes back to 1998. DOBs and middle initial appear on most records, not all **For details about the state's online access to records, see the section at the front or back of this chapter.**

Criminal Name Search: Access: In person, online. Visitors must perform in person searches themselves. Criminal records go back to 1900's; computerized records go back to 1996. Criminal PAT goes back to 1998. DOBs and middle initial appear on most records, not all. **For details about the state's online access to records, see the section at the front or back of this chapter.**

Buchanan County

1st District Court PO Box 259, 210 5th Ave NE, Independence, IA 50644; 319-334-2196; fax: 319-334-7455; 8AM-4:30PM M,W,F; 8AM-2:30PM T,TH (CST). *Felony, Misdemeanor, Civil, Eviction, Small Claims, Probate.* www.iowacourts.gov/District_Courts/District_One/

General Information: Probate is in a separate index at this address. Online identifiers in results same as on public terminal. No juvenile, sealed, dissolution of marriage, mental health, domestic abuse or deferred records released. Will fax documents for $1.50 1st page, $.50 ea addl. Court makes copy: $.50 per page. Self serve copy: none. Certification fee: $20.00 per doc; exemplification is an additional $20.00. Payee: Clerk of Court. Personal checks and credit cards accepted. Prepayment required. Mail requests: SASE required.

Civil Name Search: Access: In person, online. Both court and visitors may perform in person name searches. No search fee. Civil index in docket

books from 1800s; computerized since 1996. Civil PAT goes back to 1985. DOBs and middle initial appear on most records, not all. **For details about the state's online access to records, see the section at the front or back of this chapter.**

Criminal Name Search: Access: Mail, in person, online. Both court and visitors may perform in person name searches. No search fee. Criminal docket on books from 1800s; computerized since 1996. Mail turnaround time 2 days. Criminal PAT goes back to same as civil. DOBs and middle initial appear on most records, not all. **For details about the state's online access to records, see the section at the front or back of this chapter.**

Buena Vista County

3rd District Court PO Box 1186, 215 E 5th St, Storm Lake, IA 50588; 712-749-2546; fax: 712-749-2700; 8AM-4:30PM M,W,F; 8AM-2:30PM T,TH (CST). *Felony, Misdemeanor, Civil, Eviction, Small Claims, Probate.* www.iowacourts.gov/District_Courts/District_Three/

General Information: Online identifiers in results same as on public terminal. No juvenile, sealed, mental health records released. Will fax out documents no fee. Court makes copy: $.50 per page. Certification fee: $20.00 per doc; exemplification is an additional $20.00. Payee: Clerk of Court. Personal checks and credit cards accepted. Prepayment required. Mail requests: SASE required for mail return of any copies.

Civil Name Search: Access: In person, online. Visitors must perform in person searches themselves. Civil index on cards from early 1900s; on computer back to 1996. Civil PAT goes back to 1995. DOBs and middle initial appear on most records, not all. **For details about the state's online access to records, see the section at the front or back of this chapter.**

Criminal Name Search: Access: In person, online. Visitors must perform in person searches themselves. Criminal records indexed on cards from early 1900s; on computer back to 1994. Criminal PAT goes back to same as civil. DOBs and middle initial appear on most records, not all. **For details about the state's online access to records, see the section at the front or back of this chapter.**

Butler County

2nd District Court PO Box 307, 428 6th Street, Allison, IA 50602; 319-267-2487; fax: 319-267-2488; 9AM-3:30PM (Closed noon-1PM) (CST). *Felony, Misdemeanor, Civil, Eviction, Small Claims, Probate.* www.iowacourts.gov/District_Courts/District_Two/

General Information: Online identifiers in results same as on public terminal. No juvenile, sealed, dissolution of marriage, mental health, domestic abuse or deferred records released. Will fax documents $1.00 per page. Court makes copy: $.50 per page. Self serve copy: same. Certification fee: $20.00 per doc; exemplification is an additional $20.00. Payee: Clerk of Court. Personal checks accepted. Visa/MC accepted. Prepayment required. Mail requests: SASE required for mail return of any copies.

Civil Name Search: Access: In person, online. Visitors must perform in person searches themselves. Civil index in docket books from 1800s, on computer back to 4/97. Civil PAT goes back to 4/1997. DOBs and middle initial appear on most records, not all **For details about the state's online access to records, see the section at the front or back of this chapter.**

Criminal Name Search: Access: In person, online. Visitors must perform in person searches themselves. Criminal docket on books from 1800s, on computer back to 4/97. Criminal PAT goes back to same as civil. DOBs and middle initial appear on most records, not all. **For details about the state's online access to records, see the section at the front or back of this chapter.**

Calhoun County

2nd District Court 416 Fourth St #5, Rockwell City, IA 50579; 712-297-8122; fax: 712-297-5082; 9AM-3:30PM (Closed noon-1PM) (CST). *Felony, Misdemeanor, Civil, Eviction, Small Claims, Probate.* www.iowacourts.gov/District_Courts/District_Two/

General Information: Online identifiers in results same as on public terminal. No juvenile, sealed, pending dissolution of marriage, mental health, domestic abuse or deferred records released. Will fax out specific case files for $1.00 per page. Court makes copy: $.50 per page. Certification fee: $20.00 per doc; exemplification is an additional $20.00. Payee: Clerk of the Court. Personal checks and credit cards accepted. Prepayment required.

Civil Name Search: Access: In person, online. Visitors must perform in person searches themselves. Civil index in docket books from 1880s, computerized since 7/97. Civil PAT goes back to 7/1997. DOBs and middle initial appear on most records, not all. **For details about the state's online access to records, see the section at the front or back of this chapter.**

Criminal Name Search: Access: In person, online. Visitors must perform in person searches themselves. Required to search: name, years to search, DOB, signed release; also helpful: SSN. Criminal docket on books from 1880s, computerized since 7/97. Criminal PAT goes back to 7/1997. DOBs and middle initial appear on most records, not all. **For details about the state's online access to records, see the section at the front or back of this chapter.**

Carroll County

2nd District Court 114 E 6th St, Ste 5, Carroll, IA 51401; 712-792-4327; fax: 712-792-4328; 8AM-4:30PM M,W,F; 8AM-2:30PM T,TH (CST). *Felony, Misdemeanor, Civil, Eviction, Small Claims, Probate.* www.iowacourts.gov/District_Courts/District_Two/

General Information: Probate fax is same as main fax number. This court has shortened hours until further notice. Online identifiers in results same as on public terminal. No juvenile, sealed, dissolution of marriage, mental health, domestic abuse or deferred records released. Will fax out specific case files for $1.00 per page. Court makes copy: $.50 per page. Self serve copy: $.25 per page. Certification fee: $20.00 per doc; exemplification is an additional $20.00. Payee: Clerk of Court. Personal checks and credit cards accepted. Prepayment required. Mail requests: SASE required for mail return of any copies.

Civil Name Search: Access: In person, online. Visitors must perform in person searches themselves. Civil index on docket books from 1800s; computerized records go back to 1993 on a limited basis. Everything from 9/1997 to present. Civil PAT goes back to 1997. DOBs and middle initial appear on most records, not all. **For details about the state's online access to records, see the section at the front or back of this chapter.**

Criminal Name Search: Access: In person, online. Visitors must perform in person searches themselves. Criminal records computerized from 6/1993, index books from 1800s. Criminal PAT goes back to same as civil. DOBs and middle initial appear on most records, not all. **For details about the state's online access to records, see the section at the front or back of this chapter.**

Cass County

4th District Court 5 W 7th St, Courthouse, Atlantic, IA 50022; 712-243-2105; fax: 712-243-4661; 8AM-4:30PM M,W,F; 8AM-2:30PM T,TH (CST). *Felony, Misdemeanor, Civil, Eviction, Small Claims, Probate.* www.iowacourts.gov/District_Courts/District_Four/.

General Information: Online identifiers in results same as on public terminal. No juvenile, sealed, dissolution of marriage, mental health, domestic abuse or deferred records released. Will fax documents to local or toll-free number. Court makes copy: $.50 per page. Certification fee: $20.00 per doc; exemplification is an additional $20.00. Payee: Clerk of Court. Personal checks accepted. Visa/MC accepted. Prepayment required.

Civil Name Search: Access: In person, online. Visitors must perform in person searches themselves. Civil index in docket books from early 1900s; on computer back to 11/1996. Civil PAT goes back to 11/1996. DOBs and middle initial appear on most records, not all. **For details about the state's online access to records, see the section at the front or back of this chapter.**

Criminal Name Search: Access: In person, online. Visitors must perform in person searches themselves. Required to search: name, years to search, signed release; also helpful: DOB, SSN. Criminal docket on books from 1880s; on computer back to 11/1996. Criminal PAT goes back to same as civil. DOBs and middle initial appear on most records, not all. **For details about the state's online access to records, see the section at the front or back of this chapter.**

Cedar County

7th District Court 400 Cedar St, Attn: Cedar County Clerk of Court, Tipton, IA 52772; 563-886-2101; fax: 563-886-3594; 8AM-4:30PM M,W,F; 8AM-2:30PM T,TH (CST). *Felony, Misdemeanor, Civil, Eviction, Small Claims, Probate.* www.iowacourts.gov/District_Courts/District_Seven/index.asp

General Information: Magistrate Office phone number 563-886-6981. Online identifiers in results same as on public terminal. No juvenile, sealed, dissolution of marriage, mental health, domestic abuse or deferred records released. Will not fax documents. Court makes copy: $.50 per page. Self serve copy: same. Certification fee: $20.00 per doc; exemplification is an additional $20.00. Payee: Clerk of Court. Only cashiers checks and money orders accepted. No credit cards accepted. Prepayment required.

Civil Name Search: Access: In person, online. Visitors must perform in person searches themselves. Civil records on computer since 10/1996; on microfiche and docket books from 1839. Civil PAT goes back to 10/1996. DOBs and middle initial appear on most records, not all. **For details about the state's online access to records, see the section at the front or back of this chapter.**

Criminal Name Search: Access: In person, online. Visitors must perform in person searches themselves. Required to search: name, years to search; also helpful: DOB, SSN, signed release. Criminal records on computer since 7/1992; on microfiche and docket books from 1839. Criminal PAT goes back to 7/1992. DOBs and middle initial appear on most records, not all. **For details about the state's online access to records, see the section at the front or back of this chapter.**

Cerro Gordo County

2nd District Court 220 N Washington, Mason City, IA 50401; 641-424-6431; criminal phone: x3; civil phone: x4; probate phone: x7; fax: 641-424-6726; 8AM-4:30PM M,W,F; 8AM-2:30PM T,TH (CST). *Felony, Misdemeanor, Civil, Eviction, Small Claims, Probate.* www.iowacourts.gov/District_Courts/District_Two/

General Information: Online identifiers in results same as on public terminal. No Sealed, mental health, domestic abuse or deferred records that have been expunged released. Will fax documents $1.00 per page. Court makes copy: $.50 per page. Certification fee: $20.00 per doc; exemplification is an additional $20.00. Payee: Clerk of Court. Personal checks and credit cards accepted. Prepayment required.

Civil Name Search: Access: In person, online. Visitors must perform in person searches themselves. Civil records on computer since 1996: prior records on docket books from early 1900s. Civil PAT goes back to 1996. DOBs and middle initial appear on most records, not all. **For details about the state's online access to records, see the section at the front or back of this chapter.**

Criminal Name Search: Access: In person, online. Visitors must perform in person searches themselves. Required to search: name, years to search; also helpful: DOB, SSN. Criminal records on computer since 4/95; prior records on index cards from 1977; prior to 1977 on docket books. Criminal PAT goes back to 1995. DOBs and middle initial appear on most records, not all. **For details about the state's online access to records, see the section at the front or back of this chapter..**

Cherokee County

3rd District Court 520 W Main St, Cherokee, IA 51012; 712-225-6744; probate phone: 712-225-6744; fax: 712-225-6749; 8AM-4:30PM M,W,F; 8AM-2:30PM T,TH (CST). *Felony, Misdemeanor, Civil, Eviction, Small Claims, Probate.* www.iowacourts.gov/District_Courts/District_Three/

General Information: Online identifiers in results same as on public terminal. No juvenile, sealed, dissolution of marriage, mental health, domestic abuse or deferred records released. Will fax documents to local or toll-free number. Court makes copy: $.50 per page. Certification fee: $20.00 per doc; exemplification is an additional $20.00. Payee: Clerk of Court. Personal checks accepted. Visa/MC accepted. Prepayment required.

Civil Name Search: Access: In person, online. Visitors must perform in person searches themselves. Civil index in docket books from 1800s, indexed on computer since 1997. Civil PAT goes back to 1997. DOBs and middle initial appear on most records, not all. **For details about online access to records, see the section at the front or back of this chapter.**

Criminal Name Search: Access: In person, online. Visitors must perform in person searches themselves. Criminal records index is computerized since 1997. Criminal PAT goes back to 1997. DOBs and middle initial appear on most records, not all. **For details about online access to records, see the section at the front or back of this chapter.**

Chickasaw County

1st District Court County Courthouse, 8 E Prospect, New Hampton, IA 50659; 641-394-2106; fax: 641-394-5106; 8AM-2:30PM (CST). *Felony, Misdemeanor, Civil, Eviction, Small Claims, Probate.* www.iowacourts.gov/District_Courts/District_One/

General Information: Online identifiers in results same as on public terminal. No juvenile, sealed, dissolution of marriage, adoption, mental health, domestic abuse or deferred records released. Will fax documents for no fee. Court makes copy: $.50 per page. Certification fee: $20.00 per doc; exemplification is an additional $20.00. Payee: Clerk of District Court. Personal checks accepted. No credit cards accepted. Prepayment required. Mail requests: SASE required for mail return of any copies.

Civil Name Search: Access: In person, online. Visitors must perform in person searches themselves. Civil index in docket books from late 1800s; on computer back to 1996. Civil PAT goes back to 1996. DOBs and middle initial appear on most records, not all. **For details about the state's online access to records, see the section at the front or back of this chapter.**

Criminal Name Search: Access: In person, online. Visitors must perform in person searches themselves. Required to search: name, years to search, signed release. Criminal docket on books from late 1800s; on computer back to 1996. Criminal PAT goes back to same as civil. DOBs and middle initial appear on most records, not all. **For details about the state's online access to records, see the section at the front or back of this chapter.**

Clarke County

5th District Court 100 S Main St, Clarke County Courthouse, Osceola, IA 50213; 641-342-6096; fax: 641-342-2463; 8AM-4:30PM M,W,F; 8AM-2:30PM T,TH (CST). *Felony, Misdemeanor, Civil, Eviction, Small Claims, Probate.* www.iowacourts.gov/District_Courts/District_Five/

General Information: Online identifiers in results same as on public terminal. No juvenile, sealed, dissolution of marriage, mental health, domestic abuse or deferred records released. Will fax documents to local or toll-free number. Court makes copy: $.50 per page. Certification fee: $20.00 per doc; exemplification is an additional $20.00. Payee: Clerk of Court. Personal checks accepted. Visa/MC accepted. Prepayment required. Mail requests: SASE required for mail return of any copies.

Civil Name Search: Access: In person, online. Both court and visitors may perform in person name searches. No search fee. Civil index in docket books from early 1880s, on computer back to 7/96. Civil PAT goes back to 1996. DOBs and middle initial appear on most records, not all. **For details about the state's online access to records, see the section at the front or back of this chapter.**

Criminal Name Search: Access: In person, online. Both court and visitors may perform in person name searches. No search fee. Required to search: name, years to search; also helpful: SSN. Criminal docket on books from early 1880s, on computer back to 7/96. Criminal PAT goes back to 1996. DOBs and middle initial appear on most records, not all. **For details about the state's online access to records, see the section at the front or back of this chapter.**

Clay County

3rd District Court 215 W 4th St, Courthouse, Spencer, IA 51301; 712-262-4335; fax: 712-262-6042; 8AM-4:30PM M,W,F; 8AM-2:30PM T,TH (CST). *Felony, Misdemeanor, Civil, Eviction, Small Claims, Probate.* www.iowacourts.gov/District_Courts/District_Three/

General Information: Online identifiers in results same as on public terminal. No juvenile, sealed, pending dissolution of marriage, mental health, sealed domestic abuse or deferred records released. Will fax documents. Court makes copy: $.50 per page. Self serve copy: same. Certification fee: $20.00 per doc; exemplification is an additional $20.00. Payee: Clerk of Court. Personal checks accepted. Prepayment required.

Civil Name Search: Access: In person, online. Visitors must perform in person searches themselves. Civil records on microfilm from to 1972 to 1995, docket books from 1800s, on computer back to 8/18/97. Civil PAT goes back to 8/18/97. DOBs and middle initial appear on most records, not all **For details about the state's online access to records, see the section at the front or back of this chapter.**

Criminal Name Search: Access: In person, online. Visitors must perform in person searches themselves. Criminal records on microfilm from to 1972 to 1995, docket books from 1800s, on computer back to 1/7/97. Criminal PAT goes back to 1/7/1997. DOBs and middle initial appear on most records, not all. **For details about the state's online access to records, see the section at the front or back of this chapter..**

Clayton County

1st District Court PO Box 418, 111 High St NE, Courthouse, Elkader, IA 52043; 563-245-2204; fax: 563-245-1175; 8AM-4:30PM M,W,F; 8AM-2:30PM T,TH (CST). *Felony, Misdemeanor, Civil, Eviction, Small Claims, Probate.* www.iowacourts.gov/District_Courts/District_One/

General Information: Online identifiers in results same as on public terminal. No juvenile unless child is age 10 or older and offense is considered a public offense, sealed, dissolution of marriage, mental health, or deferred records released. Court makes copy: $.50 per page. Self serve copy: same. Certification fee: $20.00 per doc; exemplification is an additional $20.00. Payee: Clerk of Court. Personal checks and credit cards accepted. Prepayment required.

Civil Name Search: Access: In person, online. Visitors must perform in person searches themselves. Civil index in docket books from late 1880s, on computer back to 4/97. Civil PAT goes back to 1997. DOBs and middle initial appear on most records, not all. **For details about online access to records, see the section at the front or back of this chapter.**

Criminal Name Search: Access: In person, online. Visitors must perform in person searches themselves. Criminal docket on books from late 1880s, on computer back to 4/97. Criminal PAT goes back to same as civil. DOBs and middle initial appear on most records, not all. **For details about the state's online access to records, see the section at the front or back of this chapter..**

Clinton County

7th District Court PO Box 2957, 612 N 2nd St, Courthouse, Clinton, IA 52733; 563-243-6213 x1; criminal phone: x1; criminal fax: 563-243-3655; civil fax: 8AM-4:30PM M,W,F; 8AM-2:30PM T,TH; 8AM-4:30PM M,W,F; 8AM-2:30PM T,TH (CST). *Felony, Misdemeanor, Civil, Eviction, Small Claims, Probate.* www.iowacourts.gov/District_Courts/District_Seven/index.asp

General Information: Online identifiers in results same as on public terminal. No juvenile, adoption, sealed, dissolution of marriage before decree, mental health, domestic abuse or deferred records released. Will not fax documents. Court makes copy: $.50 per page. Certification fee: $20.00

per doc; exemplification is an additional $20.00. Payee: Clerk of Court. Personal checks accepted. Visa/MC accepted. Prepayment required.

Civil Name Search: Access: In person, online. Visitors must perform in person searches themselves. Civil cases indexed by defendant. Civil records on computer since 1993, on docket books prior. Civil PAT goes back to 1993. DOBs and middle initial appear on most records, not all. **For details about the state's online access to records, see the section at the front or back of this chapter.**

Criminal Name Search: Access: In person, online. Visitors must perform in person searches themselves. Required to search: name, years to search, DOB, signed release. Criminal records on computer since 1980, on docket books prior. Criminal PAT goes back to same as civil. DOBs and middle initial appear on most records, not all **For details about online access to records, see the section at the front or back of this chapter.**

Crawford County

3rd District Court 1202 Broadway, Ste 1P, Denison, IA 51442; 712-263-2242; fax: 712-263-5753; 8AM-4:30PM M,W,F; 8AM-2:30PM T,TH (CST). *Felony, Misdemeanor, Civil, Eviction, Small Claims, Probate.* www.iowacourts.gov/District_Courts/District_Three/

General Information: Online identifiers in results same as on public terminal. No sealed or pending dissolution of marriage decrees, domestic abuse, adoption, juvenile records released. Will fax documents if not to lengthy. Court makes copy: $.50 per page. Self serve copy: same. Certification fee: $20.00 per doc; exemplification is an additional $20.00. Exemplification fee $20.00. Payee: Clerk of Court. Personal checks accepted. Visa/MC accepted. Prepayment required.

Civil Name Search: Access: In person, online. Visitors must perform in person searches themselves. Civil records available since 1937, on docket books from 1869, on computer back to 9/2/97, Small Claims to 3/6/97, Probate to 5/8/97. Public use terminal available. DOBs and middle initial appear on most records, not all. **For details about the state's online access to records, see the section at the front or back of this chapter..**

Criminal Name Search: Access: In person, online. Visitors must perform in person searches themselves. Criminal records available since 1937, on docket books from 1869, on computer back to 10/96, Traffic to 1/16/96. Public use terminal available. DOBs and middle initial appear on most records, not all. **For details about the state's online access to records, see the section at the front or back of this chapter..**

Dallas County

5th District Court 801 Court St, Attn Court Clerk, Adel, IA 50003; criminal phone: 515-993-5816; civil phone: 515-993-6856; probate phone: 515-993-6860; criminal fax: 515-993-6991; civil fax: 8AM-4:30PM M,W,F; 8AM-2:30PM T,TH; 8AM-4:30PM M,W,F; 8AM-2:30PM T,TH (CST). *Felony, Misdemeanor, Civil, Eviction, Small Claims, Probate.* www.iowacourts.gov/District_Courts/District_Five/

General Information: Probate records are in a separate index. Probate fax-515-993-4752 Online identifiers in results same as on public terminal. No juvenile, sealed, dissolution of marriage, mental health, domestic abuse or deferred records released. Will fax documents for $.50 per page. Court makes copy: $.50 per page. Certification fee: $20.00 per doc; exemplification is an additional $20.00. Payee: Clerk of Court. Personal checks and credit cards accepted. Prepayment required.

Civil Name Search: Access: In person, online. Visitors must perform in person searches themselves. Civil index in docket books from 1800s; computerized records since 1996. Civil PAT goes back to 1996. DOBs and middle initial appear on most records, not all. **For details about online access to records, see the section at the front or back of this chapter.**

Criminal Name Search: Access: In person, online. Visitors must perform in person searches themselves. Criminal docket on books from 1800s; computerized records since 1996. Criminal PAT goes back to same as civil. DOBs and middle initial appear on most records, not all. **For details about the state's online access to records, see the section at the front or back of this chapter.**

Davis County

8th District Court 100 Courthouse Sq, Bloomfield, IA 52537; 641-664-2011; fax: 641-664-2041; 9AM-3:30PM M,W,F; 9AM-1:30PM T,TH (CST). *Felony, Misdemeanor, Civil, Eviction, Small Claims, Probate.* www.iowacourts.gov/District_Courts/District_Eight/

General Information: Office closes 12:30 to 1:30 PM daily. Online identifiers in results same as on public terminal. No juvenile, sealed, dissolution of marriage, mental health, domestic abuse or deferred records released. Will fax documents $5.00 minimum. Court makes copy: $.50 per page. Certification fee: $20.00 per doc; exemplification is an additional $20.00. Payee: Clerk of Court. Personal checks accepted. No credit cards accepted. Prepayment required.

Civil Name Search: Access: In person, online. Visitors must perform in person searches themselves. Civil index in docket books from late 1800s; computerized since 1997. Civil PAT goes back to 1997. DOBs and middle initial appear on most records, not all. **For details about the state's online access to records, see the section at the front or back of this chapter.**

Criminal Name Search: Access: In person, online. Visitors must perform in person searches themselves. Required to search: name, years to search, DOB. Criminal docket on books from late 1800s; computerized since 1997. Criminal PAT goes back to same as civil. DOBs and middle initial appear on most records, not all. **For details about the state's online access to records, see the section at the front or back of this chapter.**

Decatur County

5th District Court 207 N Main St, Leon, IA 50144; 641-446-4331; fax: 641-446-3759; 8AM-4:30PM M,W,F; 8AM-2:30PM T,TH (CST). *Felony, Misdemeanor, Civil, Eviction, Small Claims, Probate.* www.iowacourts.gov/District_Courts/District_Five/

General Information: Probate fax is same as main fax number. Online identifiers in results same as on public terminal. No juvenile, sealed, pending dissolution of marriage, mental health, domestic abuse or deferred records released. Will not fax documents. Court makes copy: $.50 per page. Certification fee: $20.00 per doc; exemplification is an additional $20.00. Payee: Clerk of Court. Personal checks and credit cards accepted. Prepayment required.

Civil Name Search: Access: In person, online. Visitors must perform in person searches themselves. Civil index on docket books since 1880; on computer back to 1996. Note: Probate is a separate index at this same address. Civil PAT goes back to 1996. DOBs and middle initial appear on most records, not all. **For details about the state's online access to records, see the section at the front or back of this chapter.**

Criminal Name Search: Access: In person, online. Visitors must perform in person searches themselves. Required to search: name, years to search, DOB or SSN. Criminal docket on books since 1880; on computer back to 1996. Criminal PAT goes back to same as civil. DOBs and middle initial appear on most records, not all. **For details about the state's online access to records, see the section at the front or back of this chapter.**

Delaware County

District Court PO Box 527, 301 E. Main St, Courthouse, Manchester, IA 52057; 563-927-4942; fax: 563-927-3074; 8AM-4:30PM M,W,F; 8AM-2:30PM T,TH (CST). *Felony, Misdemeanor, Civil, Eviction, Small Claims, Probate.* www.iowacourts.gov/District_Courts/District_One/

General Information: Online identifiers in results same as on public terminal. No juvenile, sealed, dissolution of marriage, mental health, domestic abuse or deferred records released. Will fax documents to local or toll-free number. Court makes copy: $.50 per page. Certification fee: $20.00 per doc; exemplification is an additional $20.00. Payee: Clerk of Court. Personal checks accepted. Visa/MC accepted. Prepayment required.

Civil Name Search: Access: In person, online. Visitors must perform in person searches themselves. Civil index in docket books from late 1800s; on computer back to 1996. Civil PAT goes back to 1996. DOBs and middle initial appear on most records, not all. **For details about online access to records, see the section at the front or back of this chapter.**

Criminal Name Search: Access: In person, online. Visitors must perform in person searches themselves. Criminal docket on books from late 1800s; on computer back to 1996. Criminal PAT goes back to same as civil. DOBs and middle initial appear on most records, not all. **For details about the state's online access to records, see the section at the front or back of this chapter.**

Des Moines County

8th District Court PO Box 158, 513 N Main St 3rd Floor, Burlington, IA 52601; 319-753-8262; fax: 319-753-8253; 8AM-4:30PM M,W,F; 8AM-2:30PM T,TH (CST). *Felony, Misdemeanor, Civil, Eviction, Small Claims, Probate.* www.iowacourts.gov/District_Courts/District_Eight/

General Information: City of Des Moines is not in this county; see Polk county. Online identifiers in results same as on public terminal. No juvenile, sealed, dissolution of marriage, mental health, domestic abuse or deferred records released. Will fax documents $1.00 per page, $5.00 minimum. Court makes copy: $.50 per page. Self serve copy: same. Certification fee: $20.00 per doc; exemplification is an additional $20.00. Payee: Clerk of Court. Personal checks and credit cards accepted. Prepayment required.

Civil Name Search: Access: In person, online. Visitors must perform in person searches themselves. Required to search: name, years to search; also helpful: address. Civil records on computer from 7/1992, docket books prior. Civil PAT goes back to 1992. DOBs and middle initial appear on most records, not all. **For details about the state's online access to records, see the section at the front or back of this chapter.**

Criminal Name Search: Access: In person, online. Visitors must perform in person searches themselves. Required to search: name, years to search, aliases; also helpful: DOB, SSN. Criminal records computerized from 7/1992, docket books prior. Criminal PAT goes back to same as civil. DOBs and middle initial appear on most records, not all. **For details**

about the state's online access to records, see the section at the front or back of this chapter.

Dickinson County

3rd District Court 1802 Hill Ave, Ste 2506, Spirit Lake, IA 51360; 712-336-1138; fax: 712-336-4005; 8AM-4:30PM M,W,F; 8AM-2:30PM T,TH (CST). *Felony, Misdemeanor, Civil, Eviction, Small Claims, Probate.* www.iowacourts.gov/District_Courts/District_Three/

General Information: Online identifiers in results same as on public terminal. No juvenile, sealed, dissolution of marriage, mental health, domestic abuse or deferred records released. Will fax documents $1.00 per page. Court makes copy: $.50 per page. Self serve copy: same. Certification fee: $20.00 per doc; exemplification is an additional $20.00. Payee: Clerk of Court. Personal checks accepted. No credit cards accepted. Prepayment required.

Civil Name Search: Access: In person, online. Visitors must perform in person searches themselves. Early information on microfiche, docket books from 1800s; computerized back to 1992. Civil PAT goes back to 1995. DOBs and middle initial appear on most records, not all. **For details about the state's online access to records, see the section at the front or back of this chapter.**

Criminal Name Search: Access: In person, online. Visitors must perform in person searches themselves. Criminal records early information on microfiche, docket books from 1800s; computerized back to 1992. Criminal PAT goes back to 1993. DOBs and middle initial appear on most records, not all. **For details about the state's online access to records, see the section at the front or back of this chapter.**

Dubuque County

1st District Court PO Box 1220, 720 Central Ave 2nd Floor, Dubuque, IA 52004-1220; 563-589-4418; 8AM-4:30PM M,W,F; 8AM-2:30PM T,TH (CST). *Felony, Misdemeanor, Civil, Eviction, Small Claims, Probate.* www.iowacourts.gov/District_Courts/District_One/

General Information: Online identifiers in results same as on public terminal. No juvenile, sealed, dissolution of marriage, mental health, domestic abuse or expunged records released. Will not fax documents. Court makes copy: $.50 per page. Self serve copy: same. Certification fee: $20.00 per doc; exemplification is an additional $20.00. Payee: Clerk of District Court. Local checks accepted. Visa/MC accepted. Prepayment required.

Civil Name Search: Access: In person, online. Visitors must perform in person searches themselves. Civil records on computer since 7/1994, on docket books from 1900s. Civil PAT goes back to 1994. DOBs and middle initial appear on most records, not all. **For details about the state's online access to records, see the section at the front or back of this chapter.**

Criminal Name Search: Access: In person, online. Visitors must perform in person searches themselves. Required to search: name, years to search; also helpful: DOB, SSN. Criminal records on computer since 7/1994, on docket books from 1900s. Criminal PAT goes back to same as civil. DOBs and middle initial appear on most records, not all. **For details about the state's online access to records, see the section at the front or back of this chapter..**

Emmet County

3rd District Court Emmet County, 609 1st Ave N, Estherville, IA 51334; 712-362-3325; fax: 712-362-5329; 8AM-4:30PM M,W,F; 8AM-2:30PM T,TH (CST). *Felony, Misdemeanor, Civil, Eviction, Small Claims, Probate.* www.iowacourts.gov/District_Courts/District_Three/

General Information: Online identifiers in results same as on public terminal. No juvenile, sealed, dissolution of marriage, mental health, domestic abuse or deferred records released. Will fax documents to local or toll-free number. Court makes copy: $.50 per page. Self serve copy: same. Certification fee: $20.00 per doc; exemplification is an additional $20.00. Payee: Clerk of Court. Personal checks and credit cards accepted. Prepayment required.

Civil Name Search: Access: In person, online. Visitors must perform in person searches themselves. Civil index in docket books from 1900s, on computer back to 2/96. Civil PAT goes back to 1997. DOBs and middle initial appear on most records, not all. **For details about the state's online access to records, see the section at the front or back of this chapter.**

Criminal Name Search: Access: In person, online. Visitors must perform in person searches themselves. Criminal docket on books from 1900s, on computer back to 2/96. Criminal PAT goes back to same as civil. DOBs and middle initial appear on most records, not all. **For details about the state's online access to records, see the section at the front or back of this chapter.**

Fayette County

Fayette County District Court PO Box 458, 114 N Vine St, West Union, IA 52175; 563-422-5694; fax: 563-422-3137; 8AM-4:30PM M,W,F; 8AM-2:30PM T,TH (CST). *Felony, Misdemeanor, Civil, Eviction, Small Claims, Probate, Traffic.* www.iowacourts.gov/District_Courts/District_One/

General Information: Online identifiers in results same as on public terminal. No juvenile, sealed, dissolution of marriage, mental health, domestic abuse or deferred records released. Will not fax documents. Court makes copy: $.50 per page. Certification fee: $20.00 per doc; exemplification is an additional $20.00. Payee: Clerk of Court. Personal checks accepted. No credit cards accepted. Prepayment required.

Civil Name Search: Access: In person, online. Visitors must perform in person searches themselves. Civil index in docket books from 1900s, on computer back to 8/96. Civil PAT goes back to 1996. DOBs and middle initial appear on most records, not all. **For details about the state's online access to records, see the section at the front or back of this chapter.**

Criminal Name Search: Access: In person, online. Visitors must perform in person searches themselves. Criminal docket on books from 1900s; 1940-1960 on CD-ROM, on computer back to 8/96. Criminal PAT goes back to same as civil. DOBs and middle initial appear on most records, not all. **For details about the state's online access to records, see the section at the front or back of this chapter.**

Floyd County

2nd District Court 101 S Main St #306, Charles City, IA 50616; 641-228-7777; fax: 641-228-7772; 8AM-4:30PM M,W,F; 8AM-2:30PM T,TH (CST). *Felony, Misdemeanor, Civil, Eviction, Small Claims, Probate.*
www.iowacourts.gov/District_Courts/District_Two/

General Information: Closed Thursdays. Online identifiers in results same as on public terminal. No juvenile, sealed, dissolution of marriage, mental health, domestic abuse or deferred records released. Will not fax documents. Court makes copy: $.50 per page. Self serve copy: same. Certification fee: $20.00 per doc; exemplification is an additional $20.00. Payee: Clerk of Court. Personal checks accepted. Visa/MC accepted. Prepayment required. Mail requests: SASE required for mail return of any copies.

Civil Name Search: Access: In person, online. Visitors must perform in person searches themselves. Civil records in docket books, are computerized since 1996. Civil PAT goes back to 5/1996. DOBs and middle initial appear on most records, not all. **For details about the state's online access to records, see the section at the front or back of this chapter.**

Criminal Name Search: Access: In person, online. Visitors must perform in person searches themselves. Required to search: name, years to search, DOB, signed release; also helpful: SSN. Criminal records in docket books, are computerized since 1996. Criminal PAT goes back to same as civil. DOBs and middle initial appear on most records, not all. **For details about the state's online access to records, see the section at the front or back of this chapter.**

Franklin County

2nd Judicial District Court 12 1st Ave NW Ste 203, Hampton, IA 50441; 641-456-5626; 8AM-4:00PM M,W,F; 8AM-2:30PM T,TH (CST). *Felony, Misdemeanor, Civil, Eviction, Small Claims, Probate.*
www.iowacourts.gov/District_Courts/District_Two/

General Information: Online identifiers in results same as on public terminal. No juvenile, sealed, dissolution of marriage, mental health, domestic abuse or deferred records released. Will fax out specific case files for $1.00 per page. Court makes copy: $.50 per page. Certification fee: $20.00 per doc; exemplification is an additional $20.00. Payee: Clerk of District Court. Personal checks accepted. Visa/MC accepted. Prepayment required.

Civil Name Search: Access: In person, online. Visitors must perform in person searches themselves. Civil records on microfiche and/or microfilm from 1860 to 1984, on docket books from 1984 to present. Note: The court will retrieve records if you have a case file number; get that number off the web search or PAT results. Civil PAT goes back to 4/1997. DOBs and middle initial appear on most records, not all. **For details about the state's online access to records, see the section at the front or back of this chapter.**

Criminal Name Search: Access: In person, online. Visitors must perform in person searches themselves. Criminal records on microfiche and/or microfilm from 1860 to 1984, on docket books from 1984 to present. Criminal PAT goes back to same as civil. DOBs and middle initial appear on most records, not all. **For details about the state's online access to records, see the section at the front or back of this chapter.**

Fremont County

4th District Court PO Box 549, 506 Filmore St, Sidney, IA 51652; 712-374-2232; fax: 712-374-3330; 8AM-4:30PM M,W,F; 8AM-2:30PM T,TH (CST). *Felony, Misdemeanor, Civil, Eviction, Small Claims, Probate.*
www.iowacourts.gov/District_Courts/District_Four/

General Information: Online identifiers in results same as on public terminal. No juvenile, sealed, pending, dissolution of marriage, mental health, domestic abuse or expunged records released. Will not fax documents. Court makes copy: $.50 per page. Self serve copy: same. Certification fee:

$20.00 per doc; exemplification is an additional $20.00. Payee: Clerk of Court. Personal checks accepted. No credit cards accepted. Prepayment required. Mail requests: SASE required for mail return of any copies.

Civil Name Search: Access: In person, online. Visitors must perform in person searches themselves. Required to search: name. Computerized from 11/96, civil records in docket books and microfiche from the 1930's. Civil PAT goes back to 11/1996. Middle initial appear on most records, not all. **For details about the state's online access to records, see the section at the front or back of this chapter.**.

Criminal Name Search: Access: In person, online. Visitors must perform in person searches themselves. Required to search: name. Computerized from 11/96, criminal records in docket books and microfiche from the 1930's. Criminal PAT goes back to same as civil. DOBs and middle initial appear on most records, not all. **For details about online access to records, see the section at the front or back of this chapter.**

Greene County

2nd District Court County Courthouse, 114 N Chestnut, Jefferson, IA 50129; 515-386-2516; fax: 515-386-2321; 8AM-4:30PM M,W,F; 8AM-2:30PM T,TH (CST). *Felony, Misdemeanor, Civil, Eviction, Small Claims, Probate.*
www.iowacourts.gov/District_Courts/District_Two/

General Information: Probate fax is same as main fax number. Online identifiers in results same as on public terminal. No juvenile, sealed, dissolution of marriage, mental health, domestic abuse or deferred records released. Will fax $1.00 per page. Court makes copy: $.50 per page. Self serve copy: same. Certification fee: $20.00 per doc; exemplification is an additional $20.00. Payee: Clerk of Court. Personal checks accepted. Visa/MC accepted. Prepayment required.

Civil Name Search: Access: In person, online. Visitors must perform in person searches themselves. Civil records on microfiche from 1981 back to establishment of court, docket books from 1800s, on computer back to 7/97. Civil PAT goes back to 7/1997. DOBs and middle initial appear on most records, not all. **For details about the state's online access to records, see the section at the front or back of this chapter.**

Criminal Name Search: Access: In person, online. Visitors must perform in person searches themselves. Criminal records from 1981 back to establishment of court, docket books from 1800s, on computer back to 7/97. Criminal PAT goes back to same as civil. DOBs and middle initial appear on most records, not all. **For details about the state's online access to records, see the section at the front or back of this chapter.**

Grundy County

1st District Court County Courthouse, 706 G Ave, Grundy Center, IA 50638; 319-824-5229; fax: 319-824-3447; 8AM-4:30PM M,W,F; 8AM-2:30PM T,TH (CST). *Felony, Misdemeanor, Civil, Eviction, Small Claims, Probate.*
www.grundycounty.org/

General Information: Online identifiers in results same as on public terminal. No pending, confidential, juvenile, sealed, dissolution of marriage, mental health, or expunged records released. Will not fax documents. Court makes copy: $.50 per page. Certification fee: $20.00 per doc; exemplification is an additional $20.00. Payee: Clerk of Court. Personal checks and credit cards accepted. Prepayment required. Mail requests: SASE required for mail return of any copies.

Civil Name Search: Access: In person, online. Visitors must perform in person searches themselves. Civil index in docket books from 1881, on computer back to 4/97. Civil PAT goes back to 1997. DOBs and middle initial appear on most records, not all. **For details about the state's online access to records, see the section at the front or back of this chapter.**

Criminal Name Search: Access: In person, online. Visitors must perform in person searches themselves. Criminal docket on books from 1881, on computer back to 4/97. Criminal PAT goes back to same as civil. DOBs and middle initial appear on most records, not all. **For details about the state's online access to records, see the section at the front or back of this chapter.**

Guthrie County

5th District Court Courthouse, 200 N 5th St, Guthrie Center, IA 50115; 641-747-3415; fax: 641-747-2420; 8AM-4:30PM M,W; 8AM-2:30PM T,TH, closed Fri (CST). *Felony, Misdemeanor, Civil, Eviction, Small Claims, Probate.*
www.iowacourts.gov/District_Courts/District_Five/

General Information: Online identifiers in results same as on public terminal. No juvenile, sealed, dissolution of marriage, mental health, domestic abuse or deferred records released. Will fax documents for $.50 per page. Court makes copy: $.50 per page. Certification fee: $20.00 per doc; exemplification is an additional $20.00. Payee: Clerk of Court. Personal checks accepted. Prepayment required.

Civil Name Search: Access: In person, online. Visitors must perform in person searches themselves. Required to search: name, case number, years to search. Civil records on computer since 11/96; prior records on docket books from 1880s. Civil PAT goes back to 1996. DOBs and middle initial appear on most records, not all. **For details about the state's online access to records, see the section at the front or back of this chapter.**

Criminal Name Search: Access: In person, online. Visitors must perform in person searches themselves. Required to search: name, case number, years to search. Criminal records on computer since 11/96; prior records on docket books from 1880s. Criminal PAT goes back to same as civil. DOBs and middle initial appear on most records, not all. **For details about the state's online access to records, see the section at the front or back of this chapter.**

Hamilton County

2nd District Court PO Box 845, 2300 Superior St, Ste 9, Webster City, IA 50595; 515-832-9600; fax: 515-832-9519; 8AM-4:30PM M,W,F; 8AM-2:30PM T,TH (CST). *Felony, Misdemeanor, Civil, Eviction, Small Claims, Probate.* www.iowacourts.gov/District_Courts/District_Two/

General Information: Probate fax is same as main fax number. Online identifiers in results same as on public terminal. No juvenile, sealed, dissolution of marriage, mental health, domestic abuse records released. Will fax out specific case files for $1.00 per page. Court makes copy: $.50 per page. Certification fee: $20.00 per doc; exemplification is an additional $20.00. Payee: Clerk of Court. Personal checks accepted. No credit cards accepted. Prepayment required.

Civil Name Search: Access: In person, online. Visitors must perform in person searches themselves. Civil records on microfiche from 1939, docket books from 1880s. Civil PAT goes back to 1996. DOBs and middle initial appear on most records, not all. **For details about the state's online access to records, see the section at the front or back of this chapter.**

Criminal Name Search: Access: In person, online. Visitors must perform in person searches themselves. Criminal records go back to 1996. Criminal PAT goes back to 1996. DOBs and middle initial appear on most records, not all. **For details about the state's online access to records, see the section at the front or back of this chapter.**

Hancock County

2nd District Court 855 State St, Garner, IA 50438; 641-923-2532; fax: 641-923-3521; 8AM-4:30PM M,W,F; 8AM-2:30PM T,TH (CST). *Felony, Misdemeanor, Civil, Eviction, Small Claims, Probate.* www.iowacourts.gov/District_Courts/District_Two/

General Information: Court will only retrieve cases where you provide case number info. Online identifiers in results same as on public terminal. No juvenile, sealed, dissolution of marriage, mental health, domestic abuse or deferred records released. Will fax documents $1.00 per page. Court makes copy: $.50 per page. Certification fee: $20.00 per doc; exemplification is an additional $20.00. Payee: Clerk of Court. Personal checks and credit cards accepted. Prepayment required. Mail requests: SASE required for mail return of any copies.

Civil Name Search: Access: In person, online. Visitors must perform in person searches themselves. Civil index in docket books from 1880s; on computer since 1997. Civil PAT goes back to 1997. DOBs and middle initial appear on most records, not all. **For details about the state's online access to records, see the section at the front or back of this chapter.**

Criminal Name Search: Access: In person, online. Visitors must perform in person searches themselves. Criminal docket on books from 1880s; on computer since 1997. Criminal PAT goes back to same as civil. DOBs and middle initial appear on most records, not all. **For details about the state's online access to records, see the section at the front or back of this chapter.**

Hardin County

2nd District Court PO Box 495, Courthouse, 1215 Edging Ave, Ste 7, Eldora, IA 50627; 641-858-2328; fax: 641-858-2320; 8AM-4:30PM M,W,F; 8AM-2:30PM T,TH (CST). *Felony, Misdemeanor, Civil, Eviction, Small Claims, Probate.* www.iowacourts.gov/District_Courts/District_Two/

General Information: Online identifiers in results same as on public terminal. No juvenile, sealed, dissolution of marriage, mental health, domestic abuse or deferred records released. Will fax documents to local or toll-free number. Court makes copy: $.50 per page. Certification fee: $20.00 per doc; exemplification is an additional $20.00. Payee: Clerk of Court. Personal checks accepted. No credit cards accepted. Prepayment required.

Civil Name Search: Access: In person, online. Visitors must perform in person searches themselves. Civil index in docket books from 1880s, on computer back to 2/96. Civil PAT goes back to 1996. DOBs and middle initial appear on most records, not all. **For details about the state's online access to records, see the section at the front or back of this chapter.**

Criminal Name Search: Access: In person, online. Visitors must perform in person searches themselves. Criminal docket on books from 1880s, on computer back to 2/96. Criminal PAT goes back to same as civil. DOBs and middle initial appear on most records, not all. **For**

details about the state's online access to records, see the section at the front or back of this chapter.

Harrison County

District Court Court House, 111 N 2nd Ave, Logan, IA 51546; 712-644-2665; fax: 712-644-2615; 8AM-4:30PM M,W,F; 8AM-2:30PM T,TH (CST). *Felony, Misdemeanor, Civil, Eviction, Small Claims, Probate.* www.iowacourts.gov/District_Courts/District_Four/

General Information: Online identifiers in results same as on public terminal. No juvenile, sealed, confidential, dissolution of marriage, mental health, or deferred records released. Will fax documents $2.00 fee plus copy fees. Court makes copy: $.50 per page. Certification fee: $20.00 per doc; exemplification is an additional $20.00. Payee: Clerk of Court. Personal checks and credit cards accepted. Prepayment required.

Civil Name Search: Access: In person, online. Visitors must perform in person searches themselves. Civil records on computer since 11/96; prior on docket books since 1840s in Clerk's office. Civil PAT goes back to 11/1996. DOBs and middle initial appear on most records, not all. **For details about the state's online access to records, see the section at the front or back of this chapter.**

Criminal Name Search: Access: In person, online. Visitors must perform in person searches themselves. Criminal records on computer since 11/96, prior on docket books from 1840s in Clerk's office. Criminal PAT goes back to same as civil. DOBs and middle initial appear on most records, not all. **For details about the state's online access to records, see the section at the front or back of this chapter.**

Henry County

8th District Court PO Box 176, 100 E Washington, Mount Pleasant, IA 52641; criminal phone: 319-385-3150/319-385-4203; civil/probate phone: 319-385-2632; fax: 319-385-4144; 8AM-4:30PM M,W,F; 8AM-2:30PM T,TH (CST). *Felony, Misdemeanor, Civil, Eviction, Small Claims, Probate.* www.iowacourts.gov/District_Courts/District_Eight/

General Information: Probate is a separate index at this same address. Probate fax- 319-385-4144. Online identifiers in results same as on public terminal. No juvenile, sealed, dissolution of marriage, mental health, domestic abuse or deferred records released. Will fax documents $1.00 per page, $5.00 minimum. Court makes copy: $.50 per page. Self serve copy: same. Certification fee: $20.00 per doc; exemplification is an additional $20.00. Payee: Clerk of Court. Personal checks and credit cards accepted. Prepayment required.

Civil Name Search: Access: In person, online. Visitors must perform in person searches themselves. Civil index in docket books from 1880s, on computer back to 10/1986. Civil PAT goes back to 1996. DOBs and middle initial appear on most records, not all. **For details about online access to records, see the section at the front or back of this chapter.**

Criminal Name Search: Access: In person, online. Visitors must perform in person searches themselves. Required to search: name, years to search, DOB; also helpful: address, SSN. Criminal docket on books from early 1900s, on computer back to 2/96. Criminal PAT goes back to 1996. DOBs and middle initial appear on most records, not all. **For details about the state's online access to records, see the section at the front or back of this chapter.**

Howard County

1st District Court Courthouse, 137 N Elm St, Cresco, IA 52136; 563-547-2661; fax: 563-547-3605; 8AM-4:30PM M,W,F; 8AM-2:30PM T,TH (CST). *Felony, Misdemeanor, Civil, Eviction, Small Claims, Probate.* www.iowacourts.gov/District_Courts/District_One/

General Information: Online identifiers in results same as on public terminal. No juvenile, sealed, pending, dissolution of marriage, mental health, domestic abuse or deferred records released. Will fax documents to local or toll-free number. Court makes copy: $.50 per page. Certification fee: $20.00 per doc; exemplification is an additional $20.00. Payee: Clerk of Court. Personal checks and credit cards accepted. Prepayment required.

Civil Name Search: Access: In person, online. Visitors must perform in person searches themselves. Civil index in docket books from 1900s, on computer back to 4/97. Civil PAT goes back to 1997. DOBs and middle initial appear on most records, not all. **For details about the state's online access to records, see the section at the front or back of this chapter.**

Criminal Name Search: Access: In person, online. Visitors must perform in person searches themselves. Required to search: name, years to search, DOB. Criminal docket on books from 1900s, on computer back to 4/97. Criminal PAT goes back to same as civil. DOBs and middle initial appear on most records, not all. **For details about the state's online access to records, see the section at the front or back of this chapter.**

Humboldt County

2nd District Court PO Box 100, 203 Main St, Dakota City, IA 50529; 515-332-1806; fax: 515-332-7100; 9AM-N, 1PM-3:30PM M, T, TH (CST). *Felony, Misdemeanor, Civil, Eviction, Small Claims, Probate.* www.iowacourts.gov/District_Courts/District_Two/

General Information: Online identifiers in results same as on public terminal. No juvenile, sealed, dissolution of marriage, mental health, domestic abuse or deferred records released. Will fax documents to local or toll-free number. Court makes copy: $.50 per page. Certification fee: $20.00 per doc; exemplification is an additional $20.00. Payee: Clerk of Court. Personal checks accepted. Visa/MC accepted. Prepayment required.

Civil Name Search: Access: In person, online. Visitors must perform in person searches themselves. Civil index in docket books from early 1900s; computerized records since 7/97. Civil PAT goes back to 7/1997. DOBs and middle initial appear on most records, not all. **For details about the state's online access to records, see the section at the front or back of this chapter.**

Criminal Name Search: Access: In person, online. Visitors must perform in person searches themselves. Criminal docket on books from early 1900s; computerized records since 7/97. Criminal PAT goes back to same as civil. DOBs and middle initial appear on most records, not all. **For details about the state's online access to records, see the section at the front or back of this chapter.**

Ida County

3rd District Court Courthouse, 401 Moorehead St, Ida Grove, IA 51445; 712-364-2628; fax: 712-364-2699; 8AM-4:30PM M,W,F; 8AM-2:30PM T,TH (CST). *Felony, Misdemeanor, Civil, Eviction, Small Claims, Probate.*
www.iowacourts.gov/District_Courts/District_Three/
General Information: Online identifiers in results same as on public terminal. No juvenile, sealed, dissolution of marriage, mental health, domestic abuse or deferred records released. Will fax document for $1.00 per page. Court makes copy: $.50 per page. Certification fee: $20.00 per doc; exemplification is an additional $20.00. Payee: Clerk of Court. Personal checks accepted. Visa/MC accepted. Prepayment required.
Civil Name Search: Access: In person, online. Visitors must perform in person searches themselves. Civil index in docket books from early 1800s, computerized since 7/97. Civil PAT goes back to 7/1997. DOBs and middle initial appear on most records, not all. **For details about the state's online access to records, see the section at the front or back of this chapter.**
Criminal Name Search: Access: In person, online. Visitors must perform in person searches themselves. Criminal docket on books from early 1800s, computerized since 7/97. Criminal PAT goes back to same as civil. DOBs and middle initial appear on most records, not all. **For details about the state's online access to records, see the section at the front or back of this chapter.**

Iowa County

6th District Court PO Box 266, 901 Court Ave, Marengo, IA 52301; 319-642-3914;; 8AM-4:30PM M,W,F; 8AM-2:30PM T,TH; closed 11:30AM-12:30PM (CST). *Felony, Misdemeanor, Civil, Eviction, Small Claims, Probate.*
www.iowacourts.gov/District_Courts/District_Six/
General Information: Online identifiers in results same as on public terminal. No juvenile, sealed, dissolution of marriage, mental health, domestic abuse or deferred records released. Will fax documents to local or toll-free number. Court makes copy: $.50 per page. Certification fee: $20.00 per doc; exemplification is an additional $20.00. Payee: Clerk of Court. Personal checks accepted. No credit cards accepted. Prepayment required.
Civil Name Search: Access: In person, online. Visitors must perform in person searches themselves. Civil index in docket books from early 1800s; on computer back to 2/97. Civil PAT goes back to 2/1997. DOBs and middle initial appear on most records, not all. **For details about the state's online access to records, see the section at the front or back of this chapter.**
Criminal Name Search: Access: Mail, in person, online. Visitors must perform in person searches themselves. No search fee. Criminal docket on books from early 1800s; on computer back to 2/1997. Mail Turnaround is as time permits. Criminal PAT goes back to same as civil. DOBs and middle initial appear on most records, not all. **For details about the state's online access to records, see the section at the front or back of this chapter.**.

Jackson County

7th District Court 201 W Platt, Maquoketa, IA 52060; 563-652-4946; fax: 563-652-2708; 8AM-4:30PM M,W,F; 8AM-2:30PM T,TH (CST). *Felony, Misdemeanor, Civil, Eviction, Small Claims, Probate.*
www.iowacourts.gov/District_Courts/District_Seven/index.asp
General Information: Probate is a separate index at this same address. Probate fax is same as main fax number. Online identifiers in results same as on public terminal. No juvenile, sealed, dissolution of marriage, mental health, domestic abuse or deferred records released. Court makes copy: $.50 per page. Certification fee: $20.00 per doc; exemplification is an additional $20.00. Payee: Clerk of Court. Personal checks accepted. Prepayment required.

Civil Name Search: Access: In person, online. Visitors must perform in person searches themselves. Civil records on computer since 1994, on docket books from 1900s. Civil PAT goes back to 1997. DOBs and middle initial appear on most records, not all. **For details about the state's online access to records, see the section at the front or back of this chapter.**
Criminal Name Search: Access: In person, online. Visitors must perform in person searches themselves. Required to search: name, years to search, DOB; also helpful: SSN. Criminal records on computer since 1994, on docket books from 1900s. Criminal PAT goes back to 1993. DOBs and middle initial appear on most records, not all. **For details about the state's online access to records, see the section at the front or back of this chapter.**

Jasper County

5th District Court 101 1st St N, Rm 104, Newton, IA 50208; 641-792-3255; criminal phone: 641-792-9161; civil phone: 641-792-3255; probate phone: 641-792-3255; fax: 641-792-2818; 8AM-4:30PM M,W,F; 8AM-2:30PM T,TH (CST). *Felony, Misdemeanor, Civil, Eviction, Small Claims, Probate.*
www.iowacourts.gov/District_Courts/District_Five/
General Information: Probate is a separate index at this same address. Online identifiers in results same as on public terminal. No juvenile, sealed, dissolution of marriage, mental health, or deferred records released. Will not fax documents. Court makes copy: $.50 per page. Self serve copy: same. Certification fee: $20.00 per doc; exemplification is an additional $20.00. Payee: Clerk of Court. Personal checks and credit cards accepted. Prepayment required.
Civil Name Search: Access: In person, online. Visitors must perform in person searches themselves. Civil records on computer since 1994, docket books from 1900s. Note: Court will pull file if given case number. Civil PAT goes back to 1994. DOBs and middle initial appear on most records, not all. **For details about the state's online access to records, see the section at the front or back of this chapter.**
Criminal Name Search: Access: In person, online. Visitors must perform in person searches themselves. Criminal records on computer since 1994, docket books from 1900s. Note: Court will pull file if given case number. Criminal PAT goes back to same as civil. DOBs and middle initial appear on most records, not all. **For details about the state's online access to records, see the section at the front or back of this chapter.**

Jefferson County

8th District Court PO Box 984, 51 W Briggs, #5, Fairfield, IA 52556; 641-472-3454; fax: 641-472-9472; 8AM-4:30PM (CST). *Felony, Misdemeanor, Civil, Eviction, Small Claims, Probate.*
www.iowacourts.gov/District_Courts/District_Eight/
General Information: Online identifiers in results same as on public terminal. No juvenile, sealed, dissolution of marriage, mental health, domestic abuse or deferred records released. Will fax documents $1.00 per page. Court makes copy: $.50 per page. Certification fee: $20.00 per doc; exemplification is an additional $20.00. Payee: Clerk of Court. Personal checks accepted. Visa/MC accepted. Prepayment required.
Civil Name Search: Access: In person, online. Visitors must perform in person searches themselves. Civil index in docket books from 1800s, on computer back to 2/96. Civil PAT goes back to 1/1996. DOBs and middle initial appear on most records, not all. **For details about the state's online access to records, see the section at the front or back of this chapter.**
Criminal Name Search: Access: In person, online. Visitors must perform in person searches themselves. Required to search: name, years to search, DOB. Criminal docket on books from 1800s, on computer back to 2/96. Criminal PAT goes back to same as civil. DOBs and middle initial appear on most records, not all. **For details about the state's online access to records, see the section at the front or back of this chapter.**

Johnson County

6th District Court PO Box 2510, 417 S Clinton St, Iowa City, IA 52244; 319-356-6060; fax: 319-339-6153; 8AM-4:30PM M,W,F; 8AM-2:30PM T,TH (CST). *Felony, Misdemeanor, Civil, Eviction, Small Claims, Probate.*
www.iowacourts.gov/District_Courts/District_Six/
General Information: Online identifiers in results same as on public terminal. No juvenile, sealed, dissolution of marriage, mental health, domestic abuse petition, or deferred records released. Will fax documents $5.00 plus $.50 per page fee. Court makes copy: $.50 per page. Self serve copy: same. Certification fee: $20.00 per doc; exemplification is an additional $20.00. Payee: Clerk of Court. Personal checks and credit cards accepted. Prepayment required.
Civil Name Search: Access: In person, online. Visitors must perform in person searches themselves. Search fee: $10.00, but date of filing or judgment and DOB/SSN must match. Civil index on docket books and microfilm from 1880s, on computer back to 4/93. Civil PAT goes back to 1994. DOBs and middle initial appear on most records, not all. **For**

details about the state's online access to records, see the section at the front or back of this chapter..

Criminal Name Search: Access: In person, online. Visitors must perform in person searches themselves. Search fee: $10.00, but date of filing and DOB/SSN must match. Required to search: name, years to search; also helpful: address, DOB, SSN. Criminal docket on books and microfilm from 1880s, on computer back to 4/93. Criminal PAT goes back to same as civil. DOBs and middle initial appear on most records, not all. **For details about the state's online access to records, see the section at the front or back of this chapter.**

Jones County

6th District Court PO Box 19, Attn: Clerk of District Court, 500 W Main St, Anamosa, IA 52205; 319-462-4341; fax: 319-462-5827; 8AM-4:30PM M,W,F; 8AM-2:30PM T,TH; closed Noon-1PM daily (CST). *Felony, Misdemeanor, Civil, Eviction, Small Claims, Probate.*
www.iowacourts.gov/District_Courts/District_Six/

General Information: Online identifiers in results same as on public terminal. No juvenile, sealed, dissolution of marriage (prior to decree), mental health or deferred records released. Will fax documents to local or toll-free number. Court makes copy: $.50 per page. Certification fee: $20.00 per doc; exemplification is an additional $20.00. Payee: Clerk of Court. Personal checks accepted. No credit cards accepted. Prepayment required.

Civil Name Search: Access: In person, online. Visitors must perform in person searches themselves. Civil index in docket books from mid 1800s; dockets on computer back to 6/1997. Civil PAT goes back to 1997. DOBs and middle initial appear on most records, not all. **For details about the state's online access to records, see the section at the front or back of this chapter.**

Criminal Name Search: Access: In person, online. Visitors must perform in person searches themselves. Criminal docket on books from early 1900s; dockets on computer back to 11/1996. Criminal PAT goes back to 1996. DOBs and middle initial appear on most records, not all. **For details about the state's online access to records, see the section at the front or back of this chapter.**

Keokuk County

8th District Court 101 S Main, Courthouse, Sigourney, IA 52591; 641-622-2210; fax: 641-622-2171; 8AM-3:30PM M,W,F; 8AM-2:30PM T,TH (CST). *Felony, Misdemeanor, Civil, Eviction, Small Claims, Probate.*
www.iowacourts.gov/District_Courts/District_Eight/

General Information: This court will perform no name searches. You must hire a local onsite researcher. Online identifiers in results same as on public terminal. No juvenile, sealed, dissolution of marriage, mental health, domestic abuse or deferred records released. Will fax documents $1.00 per page. Court makes copy: $.50 per page. Certification fee: $20.00 per doc; exemplification is an additional $20.00. Payee: Clerk of Court. Personal checks accepted. No credit cards accepted. Prepayment required.

Civil Name Search: Access: In person, online. Visitors must perform in person searches themselves. Civil index in docket books from 1888; on computer back to 2/1997. Civil PAT goes back to 2/1997. DOBs and middle initial appear on most records, not all. **For details about the state's online access to records, see the section at the front or back of this chapter.**

Criminal Name Search: Access: In person, online. Visitors must perform in person searches themselves. Criminal docket on books from 1888; on computer back to 2/1997. Criminal PAT goes back to same as civil. DOBs and middle initial appear on most records, not all. **For details about the state's online access to records, see the section at the front or back of this chapter.**

Kossuth County

3rd District Court County Courthouse, 114 W State St, Algona, IA 50511; 515-295-3240; fax: 515-295-2820; 8AM-4:30PM M,W,F; 8AM-2:30PM T,TH (CST). *Felony, Misdemeanor, Civil, Eviction, Small Claims, Probate.*
www.iowacourts.gov/District_Courts/District_Three/

General Information: Online identifiers in results same as on public terminal. No juvenile, sealed, dissolution of marriage, mental health, domestic abuse or deferred records released. Will not fax out documents. Court makes copy: $.50 per page. Certification fee: $20.00 per doc; exemplification is an additional $20.00. Payee: Clerk of Court. Personal checks accepted. No credit cards accepted. Prepayment required.

Civil Name Search: Access: In person, online. Visitors must perform in person searches themselves. Civil records on computer since 9/97; prior records on dockets. Civil PAT goes back to 9/1997. DOBs and middle initial appear on most records, not all. **For details about the state's online access to records, see the section at the front or back of this chapter.**

Criminal Name Search: Access: In person, online. Visitors must perform in person searches themselves. Criminal records on computer since 9/97; prior records on dockets. Criminal PAT goes back to same as

civil. DOBs and middle initial appear on most records, not all. **For details about the state's online access to records, see the section at the front or back of this chapter.**

Lee County

8th District Court District Court, 701 Ave F, Ft Madison, IA 52627; criminal phone: 319-372-4553; civil phone: 319-372-3523; fax: 319-372-2557; 8AM-4:30PM M,W,F; 8AM-2:30PM T,TH (CST). *Felony, Misdemeanor, Civil, Eviction, Small Claims, Probate.*
www.iowacourts.gov/District_Courts/District_Eight/

General Information: Online identifiers in results same as on public terminal. No sealed, pending dissolution of marriage, mental health, domestic abuse or deferred records released. Will fax documents $1.00 per page, $5.00 minimum. Court makes copy: $.50 per page. Self serve copy: same. Certification fee: $20.00 per doc; exemplification is an additional $20.00. Payee: Clerk of Court. Personal checks and credit cards accepted. Prepayment required.

Civil Name Search: Access: In person, online. Visitors must perform in person searches themselves. Civil index in docket books from early 1800s; computerized from 1996. Civil PAT goes back to 1996. DOBs and middle initial appear on most records, not all. **For details about the state's online access to records, see the section at the front or back of this chapter.**

Criminal Name Search: Access: In person, online. Visitors must perform in person searches themselves. Criminal docket on books from early 1800s; computerized from 1996. Criminal PAT goes back to same as civil. DOBs and middle initial appear on most records, not all. **For details about the state's online access to records, see the section at the front or back of this chapter.**

Linn County

District Court PO Box 1468, County Courthouse, 3rd Ave Bridge, Cedar Rapids, IA 52406-1468; 319-398-3411; criminal phone: x1132; civil phone: x1212;; 8AM-4:30PM M,W,F; 8AM-2:30PM T,TH (CST). *Felony, Misdemeanor, Civil, Eviction, Small Claims, Probate.*
www.iowacourts.gov/District_Courts/District_Six/

General Information: Online identifiers in results same as on public terminal. No juvenile, sealed, pending dissolution of marriage, mental health, or deferred records released. Will fax documents $.50 per page. Court makes copy: $.50 per page. Certification fee: $20.00 per doc; exemplification is an additional $20.00. Payee: Clerk of Court. Personal checks accepted. No credit cards accepted. Prepayment required. Mail requests: SASE required for mail return of any copies.

Civil Name Search: Access: In person, online. Visitors must perform in person searches themselves. Civil records on computer from 1995, docket books from early 1900s. Note some court files and dockets were destroyed by the 2008 flood. Civil PAT goes back to 1995. DOBs and middle initial appear on most records, not all. **For details about the state's online access to records, see the section at the front or back of this chapter.**

Criminal Name Search: Access: In person, online. Visitors must perform in person searches themselves. Required to search: name, years to search; also helpful: address, DOB. Criminal records on computer since 1993. Note some court files and dockets were destroyed by the 2008 flood. Criminal PAT goes back to 1993. DOBs and middle initial appear on most records, not all. **For details about the state's online access to records, see the section at the front or back of this chapter.**

Louisa County

8th District Court PO Box 268, 117 S Main, Wapello, IA 52653; 319-523-4541; fax: 319-523-4542; 8AM-4:30PM M,W,F; 8AM-2:30PM T,TH (CST). *Felony, Misdemeanor, Civil, Eviction, Small Claims, Probate.*
www.iowacourts.gov/District_Courts/District_Eight/

General Information: Online identifiers in results same as on public terminal. No juvenile, sealed, dissolution of marriage, mental health, domestic abuse or deferred records released. Will fax documents $1.00 per page, minimum fee- $5.00. Court makes copy: $.50 per page. Certification fee: $20.00 per doc; exemplification is an additional $20.00. Payee: Clerk of Court. Personal checks accepted. No credit cards accepted. Prepayment required.

Civil Name Search: Access: In person, online. Both court and visitors may perform in person name searches. No search fee. Civil index in docket books from 1920s, on computer since 2/97. Civil PAT goes back to 2/1997. DOBs and middle initial appear on most records, not all. **For details about the state's online access to records, see the section at the front or back of this chapter.**

Criminal Name Search: Access: In person, online. Both court and visitors may perform in person name searches. No search fee. Required to search: name, years to search, DOB, signed release; also helpful: SSN. Criminal docket on books from 1920s, on computer since 2/97. Note: Results include name, address and case number. Criminal PAT goes back to same as civil. DOBs and middle initial appear on most records, not all.

For details about the state's online access to records, see the section at the front or back of this chapter.

Lucas County

5th District Court 916 Braden, Courthouse, Chariton, IA 50049; 641-774-4421; fax: 641-774-8669; 8AM-12: 1PM-4PM M - TH (CST). *Felony, Misdemeanor, Civil, Eviction, Small Claims, Probate.* www.iowacourts.gov/District_Courts/District_Five/

General Information: Court is closed Fridays. Probate fax is same as main fax number. Online identifiers in results same as on public terminal. No juvenile, adoption, sealed, dissolution of marriage, mental health, domestic abuse or deferred records released. Will fax out specific case files for $.50 per page. Court makes copy: $.50 per page. Self serve copy: same. Certification fee: $20.00 per doc; exemplification is an additional $20.00. Payee: Clerk of District Court. Personal checks and credit cards accepted. Prepayment required.

Civil Name Search: Access: In person, online. Visitors must perform in person searches themselves. Civil index in docket books from 1880s; on computer back to 1997. Civil PAT goes back to 2/1997. DOBs and middle initial appear on most records, not all. **For details about the state's online access to records, see the section at the front or back of this chapter.**

Criminal Name Search: Access: In person, online. Visitors must perform in person searches themselves. Required to search: name, years to search, signed release; also helpful: SSN. Criminal docket on books from 1880s; on computer back to 1997. Criminal PAT goes back to same as civil. DOBs and middle initial appear on most records, not all. **For details about the state's online access to records, see the section at the front or back of this chapter.**

Lyon County

3rd District Court 206 S 2nd Ave, Courthouse, Rock Rapids, IA 51246; 712-472-8530; fax: 712-472-8537; 8AM-4:30PM M,W,F; 8AM-2:30PM T,TH (CST). *Felony, Misdemeanor, Civil, Eviction, Small Claims, Probate.* www.iowacourts.gov/District_Courts/District_Three/

General Information: Online identifiers in results same as on public terminal. No juvenile, sealed, dissolution of marriage, mental health, domestic abuse or deferred records released. Will fax documents to local or toll-free number. Court makes copy: $.50 per page. Certification fee: $20.00 per doc; exemplification is an additional $20.00. Payee: Clerk of Court. Personal checks and credit cards accepted. Prepayment required.

Civil Name Search: Access: In person, online. Visitors must perform in person searches themselves. Civil index in docket books from 1880s, on computer back to 9/97. Civil PAT goes back to 1997. DOBs and middle initial appear on most records, not all. **For details about the state's online access to records, see the section at the front or back of this chapter.**

Criminal Name Search: Access: In person, online. Visitors must perform in person searches themselves. Criminal docket on books from 1880s, on computer back to 9/97. Criminal PAT goes back to same as civil. DOBs and middle initial appear on most records, not all. **For details about the state's online access to records, see the section at the front or back of this chapter.**

Madison County

5th District Court PO Box 152, 112 N John Wayne Dr, Winterset, IA 50273; 515-462-4451; fax: 515-462-9825; 8AM-4:30PM M,W,F; 8AM-2:30PM T,TH (CST). *Felony, Misdemeanor, Civil, Eviction, Small Claims, Probate.* www.iowacourts.gov/District_Courts/District_Five/

General Information: Online identifiers in results same as on public terminal. No juvenile, sealed, dissolution of marriage, mental health, domestic abuse of deferred records released. Will fax documents back after fees paid. Court makes copy: $.50 per page. Certification fee: $20.00 per doc; exemplification is an additional $20.00. Payee: Clerk of Court. Personal checks accepted. No credit cards accepted. Prepayment required.

Civil Name Search: Access: In person, online. Visitors must perform in person searches themselves. Civil cases indexed by plaintiff. Civil index in docket books from 1880s; computerized records since 1996. Civil PAT goes back to 1996. DOBs and middle initial appear on most records, not all. **For details about the state's online access to records, see the section at the front or back of this chapter.**

Criminal Name Search: Access: In person, online. Visitors must perform in person searches themselves. Required to search: name, years to search; also helpful: DOB. Criminal docket on books from 1880s; computerized records since 1996. Misdemeanors from 1974 to present. Criminal PAT goes back to same as civil. DOBs and middle initial appear on most records, not all. **For details about the state's online access to records, see the section at the front or back of this chapter.**

Mahaska County

8th District Court Courthouse, 106 S 1st St, Oskaloosa, IA 52577; 641-673-7786; fax: 641-672-1256; 8AM-4:30PM M,W,F; 8AM-2:30PM T,TH (CST). *Felony, Misdemeanor, Civil, Eviction, Small Claims, Probate.* www.iowacourts.gov/District_Courts/District_Eight/

General Information: Online identifiers in results same as on public terminal. No juvenile, sealed, dissolution of marriage, mental health, domestic abuse or deferred records released. Will fax documents $1.00 per page, $5.00 minimum. Court makes copy: $.50 per page. Certification fee: $20.00 per doc; exemplification is an additional $20.00. Payee: Clerk of Court. Personal checks accepted. Visa/MC accepted online only. Prepayment required.

Civil Name Search: Access: In person, online. Visitors must perform in person searches themselves. Civil index in docket books from 1880s; computerized records since 1995. Civil PAT goes back to 1996. DOBs and middle initial appear on most records, not all. **For details about the state's online access to records, see the section at the front or back of this chapter.**

Criminal Name Search: Access: In person, online. Visitors must perform in person searches themselves. Criminal docket on books from 1880s; computerized records since 1995. Note: Results include case number. Criminal PAT goes back to 1995. DOBs and middle initial appear on most records, not all. **For details about the state's online access to records, see the section at the front or back of this chapter.**

Marion County

5th District Court 214 E Main St, Knoxville, IA 50138; 641-828-2207; fax: 641-828-7580; 8AM-4:30PM M,W,F; 8AM-2:30PM T,TH (CST). *Felony, Misdemeanor, Civil, Eviction, Small Claims, Probate.* www.iowacourts.gov/District_Courts/District_Five/

General Information: Online identifiers in results same as on public terminal. Delinquencies are public, not CINA, FINA, Termination or adoptions. No juvenile, sealed, dissolution of marriage, or mental health records released. Will fax documents for $.50 per page fee. Court makes copy: $.50 per page. Self serve copy: same. Certification fee: $20.00 per doc; exemplification is an additional $20.00. Payee: Clerk of Court. Personal checks accepted. Visa/MC accepted. Prepayment required. Mail requests: SASE required for mail return of any copies.

Civil Name Search: Access: In person, online. Visitors must perform in person searches themselves. Civil records on computer since 1992, docket books from 1896. Civil PAT goes back to 1994, countywide. DOBs and middle initial appear on most records, not all. **For details about the state's online access to records, see the section at the front or back of this chapter.**

Criminal Name Search: Access: In person, online. Visitors must perform in person searches themselves. Criminal records on computer since 1992, docket books from 1896. Criminal PAT goes back to 1993, countywide. DOBs and middle initial appear on most records, not all. **For details about the state's online access to records, see the section at the front or back of this chapter.**

Marshall County

2nd District Court Courthouse, 17 E Main St, Marshalltown, IA 50158; 641-754-1603; fax: 641-754-1600; 8AM-4:30PM M,W,F; 8AM-2:30PM T,TH (CST). *Felony, Misdemeanor, Civil, Eviction, Small Claims, Probate.* www.iowacourts.gov/District_Courts/District_Two/

General Information: Online identifiers in results same as on public terminal. No juvenile, sealed, pending dissolution of marriage, mental health, sealed domestic abuse and deferred records released. Will fax documents $1.00 per page. Court makes copy: $.50 per page. Self serve copy: same. Certification fee: $20.00 per doc; exemplification is an additional $20.00. Payee: Clerk of Court. Personal checks and credit cards accepted. Prepayment required.

Civil Name Search: Access: In person, online. Visitors must perform in person searches themselves. Civil records on computer since 6/1994, docket books from late 1800s. Civil PAT goes back to 1994. DOBs and middle initial appear on most records, not all. **For details about the state's online access to records, see the section at the front or back of this chapter.**

Criminal Name Search: Access: In person, online. Visitors must perform in person searches themselves. Required to search: name, years to search; also helpful: DOB, SSN. Criminal records on computer since 8/1992, docket books from late 1800s. Criminal PAT goes back to 8/1992. DOBs and middle initial appear on most records, not all. **For details about the state's online access to records, see the section at the front or back of this chapter.**

Mills County

4th District Court 418 Sharp St, Courthouse, Glenwood, IA 51534; 712-527-4880; fax: 712-527-4936; 8AM-N 1-4:30PM M,W,F; 8AM-N, 1-2:30PM T,TH (CST). *Felony, Misdemeanor, Civil, Eviction, Small Claims, Probate, Traffic.* www.iowacourts.gov/District_Courts/District_Four/

General Information: Online identifiers in results same as on public terminal. No juvenile, sealed, dissolution of marriage, mental health, domestic abuse or deferred records released. Will fax documents $2.00 per fax plus copy fees if necessary. Court makes copy: $.50 per page. Self serve copy: same. Certification fee: $20.00 per doc; exemplification is an additional $20.00. Payee: Clerk of Court. Personal checks accepted. No credit cards accepted. Prepayment required. Mail requests: SASE required for mail return of any copies.

Civil Name Search: Access: In person, online. Visitors must perform in person searches themselves. Civil index on docket books since 1880s; computerized records since 02/96. Civil PAT goes back to 2/1996. DOBs and middle initial appear on most records, not all. **For details about the state's online access to records, see the section at the front or back of this chapter.**

Criminal Name Search: Access: In person, online. Visitors must perform in person searches themselves. Criminal docket on books since 1880s; computerized records since 2/96. Criminal PAT goes back to same as civil. DOBs and middle initial appear on most records, not all. An advanced search is provided for no fee. **For details about the state's online access to records, see the section at the front or back of this chapter.**

Mitchell County

2nd District Court 508 State St, Osage, IA 50461; 641-732-3726; fax: 641-732-3728; 8AM-4:30PM M,W,F; 8AM-2:30PM T,TH (CST). *Felony, Misdemeanor, Civil, Eviction, Small Claims, Probate.* www.iowacourts.gov/District_Courts/District_Two/

General Information: Probate fax is same as main fax number. Online identifiers in results same as on public terminal. No juvenile, sealed, dissolution of marriage, mental health, domestic abuse or deferred records released. Will fax documents $1.00 per page. Court makes copy: $.50 per page. Self serve copy: same. Certification fee: $20.00 per doc; exemplification is an additional $20.00. Payee: Clerk of Court. Personal checks and credit cards accepted. Prepayment required. Mail requests: SASE required for mail return of any copies.

Civil Name Search: Access: In person, online. Visitors must perform in person searches themselves. Civil index in docket books from 1880s, computerized since 1997. Civil PAT goes back to 4/1997. DOBs and middle initial appear on most records, not all. **For details about the state's online access to records, see the section at the front or back of this chapter.**

Criminal Name Search: Access: In person, online. Visitors must perform in person searches themselves. Required to search: name, years to search, signed release. Criminal docket on books from 1880s, computerized since 1997. Criminal PAT goes back to same as civil. DOBs and middle initial appear on most records, not all. **For details about the state's online access to records, see the section at the front or back of this chapter.**

Monona County

3rd District Court 610 Iowa Ave, Attn: Clerk of Court, Onawa, IA 51040; 712-423-2491; fax: 712-423-2744; 8AM-4:30PM M,W,F; 8AM-2:30PM T,TH (CST). *Felony, Misdemeanor, Civil, Eviction, Small Claims, Probate.* www.iowacourts.gov/District_Courts/District_Three/

General Information: Online identifiers in results same as on public terminal. No juvenile, sealed, dissolution of marriage, mental health, or deferred records released. Will fax documents to local or toll-free number. Court makes copy: $.50 per page. Certification fee: $20.00 per doc; exemplification is an additional $20.00. Payee: Clerk of Court. Personal checks and credit cards accepted. Visa/MC accepted. Prepayment required.

Civil Name Search: Access: In person, online. Visitors must perform in person searches themselves. Civil records on computer since 7/97; prior records on microfiche and docket books from 1880s. Civil PAT goes back to 1997. DOBs and middle initial appear on most records, not all. **For details about the state's online access to records, see the section at the front or back of this chapter.**

Criminal Name Search: Access: In person, online. Visitors must perform in person searches themselves. Criminal records on computer since 7/97; prior records on microfiche and docket books from 1880s. Criminal PAT goes back to same as civil. DOBs and middle initial appear on most records, not all. **For details about the state's online access to records, see the section at the front or back of this chapter.**

Monroe County

8th District Court 10 Benton Ave E, Courthouse, Albia, IA 52531; 641-932-5212; fax: 641-932-3245; 8AM-3:30PM M,W,F; 8AM-2:30PM T,TH; closed N-12:30PM (CST). *Felony, Misdemeanor, Civil, Eviction, Small Claims, Probate.* www.iowacourts.gov/District_Courts/District_Eight/

General Information: Online identifiers in results same as on public terminal. No juvenile, sealed, dissolution of marriage, mental health, domestic abuse or deferred records released. Will fax documents $5.00 per page. Court makes copy: $.50 per page. Certification fee: $20.00 per doc; exemplification is an additional $20.00. Payee: Clerk of Court. Personal checks accepted. Visa/MC accepted. Prepayment required.

Civil Name Search: Access: In person, online. Visitors must perform in person searches themselves. Civil index in docket books from late 1800s, on computer back to 2/97. Civil PAT goes back to 1997. DOBs and

middle initial appear on most records, not all. **For details about the state's online access to records, see the section at the front or back of this chapter.**

Criminal Name Search: Access: In person, online. Visitors must perform in person searches themselves. Required to search: name, years to search, DOB, signed release; also helpful: SSN. Criminal docket on books from late 1800s, on computer back to 2/97. Criminal PAT goes back to same as civil. DOBs and middle initial appear on most records, not all. **For details about the state's online access to records, see the section at the front or back of this chapter.**

Montgomery County

4th District Court PO Box 469, 105 Coolbaugh St, Red Oak, IA 51566; 712-623-4986; fax: 712-623-4987; 8AM-4:30PM M,W,F; 8AM-2:30PM T,TH (CST). *Felony, Misdemeanor, Civil, Eviction, Small Claims, Probate.* www.iowacourts.gov/District_Courts/District_Four/

General Information: Online identifiers in results same as on public terminal. No juvenile, sealed, dissolution of marriage, mental health or deferred records released. Will fax documents $2.00 fax fee plus $.50 per page. Court makes copy: $.50 per page. Certification fee: $20.00 per doc; exemplification is an additional $20.00. Payee: Clerk of Court. Personal checks and credit cards accepted. Prepayment required. Mail requests: SASE required for mail return of any copies.

Civil Name Search: Access: In person, online. Visitors must perform in person searches themselves. Civil index in docket books from 1940, microfiche prior, on computer back to 6/96. Civil PAT goes back to 6/1996. DOBs and middle initial appear on most records, not all. **For details about the state's online access to records, see the section at the front or back of this chapter.**

Criminal Name Search: Access: In person, online. Visitors must perform in person searches themselves. Criminal docket on books from 1940, microfiche prior, on computer back to 6/96. Criminal PAT goes back to same as civil. DOBs and middle initial appear on most records, not all. **For details about the state's online access to records, see the section at the front or back of this chapter.**

Muscatine County

7th District Court 401 E Third St, Courthouse, Muscatine, IA 52761; 563-263-6511; criminal phone: 563-263-2447; criminal fax: 563-262-7655; civil fax: 8AM-4:30PM M,W,F; 8AM-2:30PM T,TH; 8AM-4:30PM M,W,F; 8AM-2:30PM T,TH (CST). *Felony, Misdemeanor, Civil, Eviction, Small Claims, Probate.* www.iowacourts.gov/District_Courts/District_Seven/index.asp

General Information: Season hours on T & Th are 8AM-2:30PM. Online identifiers in results same as on public terminal. No juvenile, sealed, dissolutions of marriage, mental health, domestic abuse or deferred records released. Will fax out documents for $.50 per page. Court makes copy: $.50 per page. Certification fee: $20.00 per doc; exemplification is an additional $20.00. Payee: Clerk of Court. Personal checks accepted. No credit cards accepted. Prepayment required. Mail requests: SASE required for mail return of any copies.

Civil Name Search: Access: In person, online. Visitors must perform in person searches themselves. Civil index on docket books, on computer since 10/95. Civil PAT goes back to 10/1995. DOBs and middle initial appear on most records, not all. **For details about the state's online access to records, see the section at the front or back of this chapter.**

Criminal Name Search: Access: In person, online. Visitors must perform in person searches themselves. Criminal Records are computerized since 4/94. Criminal PAT goes back to 4/1994. DOBs and middle initial appear on most records, not all. **For details about the state's online access to records, see the section at the front or back of this chapter.**

O'Brien County

3rd District Court Courthouse, Criminal Records, 155 S Hayes Ave, Primghar, IA 51245; 712-957-3255 or 5860; fax: 712-957-2965; 8AM-4:30PM M,W,F; 8AM-2:30PM T,TH (CST). *Felony, Misdemeanor, Civil, Eviction, Small Claims, Probate.* www.iowacourts.gov/District_Courts/District_Three/

General Information: Online identifiers in results same as on public terminal. No juvenile, sealed, dissolution of marriage, mental health records released. Will fax documents $1.00 1st page and $.50 per add'l page. Court makes copy: $.50 per page. Self serve copy: same. Certification fee: $20.00 per doc; exemplification is an additional $20.00. Payee: Clerk of Court. Personal checks accepted. No credit cards accepted for copies. Prepayment required.

Civil Name Search: Access: In person, online. Visitors must perform in person searches themselves. Civil index in docket books from late 1800s; computerized since 1997. Civil PAT goes back to 9/1997. DOBs and middle initial appear on most records, not all. **For details about the**

state's online access to records, see the section at the front or back of this chapter.

Criminal Name Search: Access: In person, online. Visitors must perform in person searches themselves. Required to search: name, years to search; also helpful: DOB, SSN. Criminal docket on books from late 1800s; computerized since 1997. Criminal PAT goes back to same as civil. DOBs and middle initial appear on most records, not all. **For details about the state's online access to records, see the section at the front or back of this chapter.**

Osceola County

3rd District Court Courthouse, Criminal Records, 300 7th Street, Sibley, IA 51249; 712-754-3595; fax: 712-754-2480; 8AM-4:30PM M,W,F; 8AM-2:30PM T,TH (CST). *Felony, Misdemeanor, Civil, Eviction, Small Claims, Probate.* www.iowacourts.gov/District_Courts/District_Three/

General Information: Probate fax is same as main fax number. Online identifiers in results same as on public terminal. No juvenile, sealed, dissolution of marriage, mental health, or deferred records released. Will fax documents $.50 per page. Court makes copy: $.50 per page. Self serve copy: same. Certification fee: $20.00 per doc; exemplification is an additional $20.00. Payee: Clerk of Court. Personal checks and credit cards accepted. Prepayment required.

Civil Name Search: Access: In person, online. Visitors must perform in person searches themselves. Civil index in docket books from 1883; on computer back to 1997. Civil PAT goes back to 9/1997. DOBs and middle initial appear on most records, not all. **For details about the state's online access to records, see the section at the front or back of this chapter.**

Criminal Name Search: Access: In person, online. Visitors must perform in person searches themselves. Criminal docket on books from 1883; on computer back to 1997. Criminal PAT goes back to same as civil. DOBs and middle initial appear on most records, not all. **For details about the state's online access to records, see the section at the front or back of this chapter.**

Page County

4th District Court PO Box 263, 112 E Main, Clarinda, IA 51632; 712-542-3214; fax: 712-542-5460; 8AM-N 1-4:30PM M,W,F; 8AM-N 1-2:30PM T,TH (CST). *Felony, Misdemeanor, Civil, Eviction, Small Claims, Probate.* www.iowacourts.gov/District_Courts/District_Four/

General Information: Probate records are a separate index at this address. Probate fax is same as main fax number. Online identifiers in results same as on public terminal. No juvenile, sealed dissolution of marriage, mental health or deferred records released. Will fax out specific case files for $2.00. Court makes copy: $.50 per page. Self serve copy: same. Certification fee: $20.00 per doc; exemplification is an additional $20.00. Payee: Clerk of District Court. Personal checks accepted. No credit cards accepted. Prepayment required.

Civil Name Search: Access: In person, online. Visitors must perform in person searches themselves. Civil index on docket books; on computer back to 1995. Civil PAT goes back to 1995. Results include name and DOB. **For details about the state's online access to records, see the section at the front or back of this chapter.**

Criminal Name Search: Access: In person, online. Visitors must perform in person searches themselves. Required to search: name, years to search, DOB, SSN, signed release. Criminal docket on books; on computer back to 1995. Criminal PAT goes back to same as civil. Results include name and DOB. **For details about the state's online access to records, see the section at the front or back of this chapter.**

Palo Alto County

3rd District Court 1010 Broadway, Ste 200, Emmetsburg, IA 50536; 712-852-3603; fax: 712-852-2274; 8AM-4:30PM M,W,F; 8AM-2:30PM T,TH (CST). *Felony, Misdemeanor, Civil, Eviction, Small Claims, Probate.* www.iowacourts.gov/District_Courts/District_Three/

General Information: Online identifiers in results same as on public terminal. No juvenile, sealed, dissolution of marriage, mental health, domestic abuse or deferred records released. Will not fax documents. Court makes copy: $.50 per page. Certification fee: $20.00 per doc; exemplification is an additional $20.00. Payee: Clerk of Court. Personal checks accepted. No credit cards accepted. Prepayment required. Mail requests: SASE required for mail return of any copies.

Civil Name Search: Access: In person, online. Visitors must perform in person searches themselves. Civil index in docket books from 1800s; computerized from 1997. Civil PAT goes back to 1997. DOBs and middle initial appear on most records, not all. **For details about the state's online access to records, see the section at the front or back of this chapter.**

Criminal Name Search: Access: In person, online. Visitors must perform in person searches themselves. Required to search: name, years to search, DOB, SSN. Criminal docket on books from 1800s; computerized from 1997. Criminal PAT goes back to same as civil. DOBs and middle

initial appear on most records, not all. **For details about the state's online access to records, see the section at the front or back of this chapter.**

Plymouth County

3rd Judicial District Plymouth County Clerk of District Court, 215 Fourth Ave SE, Courthouse, Le Mars, IA 51031; 712-546-4215; fax: 712-546-8430; 8AM-4:30PM M,W,F; 8AM-2:30PM T,TH (CST). *Felony, Misdemeanor, Civil, Eviction, Small Claims, Probate.* www.iowacourts.gov/District_Courts/District_Three/

General Information: Online identifiers in results same as on public terminal. No juvenile, (sealed, dissolution of marriage), mental health, domestic abuse or deferred records released. Will fax documents for no fee; large files cannot be faxed. Court makes copy: $.50 per page. Certification fee: $20.00 per doc; exemplification is an additional $20.00. Payee: Clerk of Court. Personal checks accepted. Credit cards accepted online only. Prepayment required. Mail requests: SASE required for mail return of any copies.

Civil Name Search: Access: In person, online. Visitors must perform in person searches themselves. Civil index in docket books from 1895 to 11/92, docket cards from 11/92 to 7/97, on computer back to 7/97. Civil PAT goes back to 1997. DOBs and middle initial appear on most records, not all. **For details about the state's online access to records, see the section at the front or back of this chapter.**

Criminal Name Search: Access: In person, online. Visitors must perform in person searches themselves. Criminal docket on books from 1895 to 11/92, docket cards from 11/92 to 7/97, on computer back to 7/97. Criminal PAT goes back to same as civil. DOBs and middle initial appear on most records, but not all. **For details about the state's online access to records, see the section at the front or back of this chapter.**

Pocahontas County

2nd District Court Courthouse, 99 Court Square, #6, Pocahontas, IA 50574-1629; 712-335-4208; fax: 712-335-5045; 9AM-3:30PM M,T,TH,F (closed noon-1PM) (CST). *Felony, Misdemeanor, Civil, Eviction, Small Claims, Probate.* www.iowacourts.gov/District_Courts/District_Two/

General Information: Online identifiers in results same as on public terminal. No juvenile, sealed, dissolution of marriage, mental health, domestic abuse or deferred records released. Will fax documents $1.00 per page. Court makes copy: $.50 per page. Certification fee: $20.00 per doc; exemplification is an additional $20.00. Payee: Clerk of Court. Personal checks and credit cards accepted. Prepayment required.

Civil Name Search: Access: In person, online. Visitors must perform in person searches themselves. Civil index in docket books from 1880s, on computer back to 7/97. Civil PAT goes back to 7/1997. Results include financial information. **For details about the state's online access to records, see the section at the front or back of this chapter.**

Criminal Name Search: Access: In person, online. Visitors must perform in person searches themselves. Required to search: name, years to search, DOB. Criminal docket on books from 1880s, on computer back to 7/97. Criminal PAT goes back to same as civil. Results include financial information. **For details about the state's online access to records, see the section at the front or back of this chapter.**

Polk County

District Court 500 Mulberry St, #212, Des Moines, IA 50309; 515-286-3772; criminal fax: 515-323-5250; civil fax: 8AM-4:30PM M,W,F; 8AM-2:30PM T,TH; 8AM-4:30PM M,W,F; 8AM-2:30PM T,TH (CST). *Felony, Misdemeanor, Civil, Eviction, Small Claims, Probate.* www.iowacourts.gov/District_Courts/District_Five/

General Information: Online identifiers in results same as on public terminal. No juvenile, child, sealed, pending dissolution of marriage, mental health, expunged, domestic abuse or deferred records released. Will fax documents $1.00 per page. Court makes copy: $.50 per page. Certification fee: $20.00 per doc; exemplification is an additional $20.00. Payee: Clerk of Court. Personal checks and credit cards accepted. Prepayment required.

Civil Name Search: Access: In person, online. Visitors must perform in person searches themselves. Required to search: name, years to search; also helpful: address. Civil records on computer back to 1993; docket books and index cards from 1880s and microfilm prior to 1970. Note: Mail search requests are not recommended. Civil PAT goes back to 1993. DOBs and middle initial appear on most records, not all. **For details about the state's online access to records, see the section at the front or back of this chapter.**

Criminal Name Search: Access: In person, online. Visitors must perform in person searches themselves. Required to search: name, years to search, address, DOB; also helpful: SSN. Criminal records computerized from 1993; docket books and index cards from 1880s and microfilm prior to 1970. Note: Mail search requests are not recommended. Criminal PAT goes back to same as civil. DOBs and middle initial appear on most records, not all. **For details about the state's online access to records, see the section at the front or back of this chapter.**

Pottawattamie County

4th District Court 227 S 6th St, Council Bluffs, IA 51501; 712-328-5604; fax: 712-328-4810; 8AM-4:30PM M,W,F; 8AM-2:30PM T,TH (CST). *Felony, Misdemeanor, Civil, Eviction, Small Claims, Probate.*
www.iowacourts.gov/District_Courts/District_Four/
General Information: Office is closed 12-1PM daily. Online identifiers in results same as on public terminal. No juvenile, sealed, pending dissolution of marriage, mental health, domestic abuse or deferred records released. Will fax documents $2.00. Court makes copy: $.50 per page. Certification fee: $20.00 per doc; exemplification is an additional $20.00. Payee: Clerk of Court. Personal checks and credit cards accepted. Prepayment required. Mail requests: SASE required for mail return of any copies.
Civil Name Search: Access: In person, mail, online. Visitors must perform in person searches themselves. No search fee. Civil records on computer from 1978, index books prior. Records are being microfilmed as load permits. Public use terminal available, records go back to 1995. Also DOBs and middle initial often appear, but not always. **For details about the state's online access to records, see the section at the front or back of this chapter.**
Criminal Name Search: Access: In person, online. Visitors must perform in person searches themselves. Criminal records computerized from 1978, index books prior. Records are being microfilmed as load permits. Public use terminal available, crim records go back to 1992. Also DOBs and middle initial often appear, but not always. **For details about the state's online access to records, see the section at the front or back of this chapter.**

Poweshiek County

8th District Court PO Box 218, 302 E Main St, Montezuma, IA 50171; 641-623-5644; fax: 641-623-5320; 8AM-4:30PM M,W,F; 8AM-2:30PM T,TH (CST). *Felony, Misdemeanor, Civil, Eviction, Small Claims, Probate.*
www.iowacourts.gov/District_Courts/District_Eight/
General Information: Online identifiers in results same as on public terminal. No juvenile, sealed, pending, dissolution of marriage, mental health, domestic abuse or deferred records released. Will fax documents $1.00 per page if prepaid. Court makes copy: $.50 per page. Certification fee: $20.00 per doc; exemplification is an additional $20.00. Payee: Clerk of Court. Personal checks accepted. No credit cards accepted. Prepayment required.
Civil Name Search: Access: In person, online. Visitors must perform in person searches themselves. Civil index on cards from 1980, docket books from early 1900s, computer since 7/95. Civil PAT goes back to 7/1995. DOBs and middle initial appear on most records, not all. **For details about the state's online access to records, see the section at the front or back of this chapter.**
Criminal Name Search: Access: In person, online. Visitors must perform in person searches themselves. Criminal records on computer since 1995, index cards since 1980, docket books from early 1900s. Criminal PAT goes back to same as civil. DOBs and middle initial appear on most records, not all. **For details about the state's online access to records, see the section at the front or back of this chapter.**

Ringgold County

5th District Court PO Box 523, 109 W Madison, Mount Ayr, IA 50854; 641-464-3234; fax: 641-464-2478; 9AM-3:30PM M,T,TH,F (closed noon-1PM) (CST). *Felony, Misdemeanor, Civil, Small Claims, Probate, Traffic.*
www.iowacourts.gov/District_Courts/District_Five/
General Information: Online identifiers in results same as on public terminal. No CINA, juvenile, sealed, pending dissolution of marriage, mental health or expunged records released. Will fax out documents $.50 per page. Court makes copy: $.50 per page. Certification fee: $20.00 per doc; exemplification is an additional $20.00. Payee: Clerk of Court. Personal checks accepted. Visa/MC accepted. Prepayment required.
Civil Name Search: Access: In person, online. Visitors must perform in person searches themselves. Civil index on docket books; on computer back to 11/1996. Civil PAT goes back to 11/1996. DOBs and middle initial appear on most records, not all. **For details about the state's online access to records, see the section at the front or back of this chapter.**
Criminal Name Search: Access: In person, online. Visitors must perform in person searches themselves. Criminal docket on books; on computer back to 11/1996. Criminal PAT goes back to same as civil. DOBs and middle initial appear on most records, not all. **For details about the state's online access to records, see the section at the front or back of this chapter.**

Sac County

2nd District Court 100 NW State St, Ste12, Sac City, IA 50583; 712-662-7791; fax: 712-662-7978; 8AM-4:30PM M,W,F; 8AM-2:30PM T,TH (CST). *Felony, Misdemeanor, Civil, Eviction, Small Claims, Probate.*
www.iowacourts.gov/District_Courts/District_Two/

General Information: Online identifiers in results same as on public terminal. No juvenile, sealed, pending dissolution of marriage, mental health, domestic abuse or deferred records released. Will fax documents for $1.00 per page fee. Court makes copy: $.50 per page. Certification fee: $20.00 per doc; exemplification is an additional $20.00. Payee: Clerk of Court. Personal checks accepted. Visa/MC accepted. Prepayment required.
Civil Name Search: Access: In person, online. Visitors must perform in person searches themselves. Required to search: name. Civil records go back to 1888; on computer back to 7/1997. Civil PAT goes back to 7/1997. DOBs and middle initial appear on most records, not all. **For details about the state's online access to records, see the section at the front or back of this chapter.**
Criminal Name Search: Access: In person, online. Visitors must perform in person searches themselves. Required to search: name, approximate date. Criminal records go back to 1888; on computer back to 7/1997. Note: Court may assist in search, if necessary. Criminal PAT goes back to same as civil. DOBs and middle initial appear on most records, not all. **For details about the state's online access to records, see the section at the front or back of this chapter.**

Scott County

7th District Court 416 W 4th St, Davenport, IA 52801; criminal phone: 563-326-8786; civil phone: 563-326-8647; probate phone: 563-326-8648; fax: 563-326-8298; 8AM-4:30PM M,W,F; 8AM-2:30PM T,TH (CST). *Felony, Misdemeanor, Civil, Eviction, Small Claims, Probate.*
www.iowacourts.gov/District_Courts/District_Seven/index.asp
General Information: Online identifiers in results same as on public terminal. No juvenile, sealed, dissolution of marriage, mental health, domestic abuse or deferred records released. Court makes copy: $.50 per page. Certification fee: $20.00 per doc; exemplification is an additional $20.00. Payee: Clerk of Court. Personal checks and credit cards accepted. Prepayment required. Mail requests: SASE required for mail return of any copies.
Civil Name Search: Access: In person, online. Visitors must perform in person searches themselves. Civil records on computer back to 11/1993, docket books prior. Civil PAT goes back to 1992. DOBs and middle initial appear on most records, not all. **For details about the state's online access to records, see the section at the front or back of this chapter.**
Criminal Name Search: Access: In person, online. Visitors must perform in person searches themselves. Required to search: name, years to search, DOB; also helpful: SSN. Criminal records computerized from 1992, printouts and docket books prior. Criminal PAT goes back to same as civil. DOBs and middle initial appear on most records, not all. **For details about the state's online access to records, see the section at the front or back of this chapter.**

Shelby County

4th District Court PO Box 431, 612 Court St, Harlan, IA 51537; 712-755-5543; fax: 712-755-2667; 8AM-4:30PM M,W,F; 8AM-2:30PM T,TH (CST). *Felony, Misdemeanor, Civil, Eviction, Small Claims, Probate.*
www.iowacourts.gov/District_Courts/District_Four/
General Information: The court will not perform name searches. Online identifiers in results same as on public terminal. No juvenile, sealed, dissolution of marriage, mental health, domestic abuse or deferred records released. Will fax out specific case files for $2.00 plus $.50 per page. Court makes copy: $.50 per page. Certification fee: $20.00 per doc; exemplification is an additional $20.00. Payee: Clerk of Court. Personal checks and credit cards accepted. Prepayment required.
Civil Name Search: Access: In person, online. Visitors must perform in person searches themselves. Civil records on original files back to 1999, microfilm prior, on computer back to 10/95. Public use terminal available. DOBs and middle initial appear on most records, not all. **For details about the state's online access to records, see the section at the front or back of this chapter.**
Criminal Name Search: Access: In person, online. Visitors must perform in person searches themselves. Required to search: name, years to search; also helpful: DOB. Criminal records on original files back to 1980, microfilm prior, on computer back to 10/95. Public use terminal available. DOBs and middle initial appear on most records, not all. **For details about the state's online access to records, see the section at the front or back of this chapter.**

Sioux County

3rd District Court , 210 Central Ave SW, Courthouse, Orange City, IA 51041; 712-737-2286; fax: 712-737-8908; 8AM-4:30PM M,W,F; 8AM-2:30PM T,TH (CST). *Felony, Misdemeanor, Civil, Eviction, Small Claims, Probate.* www.iowacourts.gov/District_Courts/District_Three/
General Information: Online identifiers in results same as on public terminal. No juvenile, sealed, dissolution of marriage, mental health, domestic abuse or deferred records released. Will not fax out documents. Court makes copy: $.50 per page. Certification fee: $20.00 per doc;

exemplification is an additional $20.00. Payee: Clerk of Court. Personal checks accepted. Visa/MC accepted. Prepayment required.

Civil Name Search: Access: In person, online. Visitors must perform in person searches themselves. Civil index in docket books from 1800s; computerized records since 9/97. Civil PAT goes back to 1997. DOBs and middle initial appear on most records, not all. **For details about the state's online access to records, see the section at the front or back of this chapter.**

Criminal Name Search: Access: In person, online. Visitors must perform in person searches themselves. Required to search: name, years to search, signed release. Criminal docket on books from 1800s; computerized records since 9/97. Criminal PAT goes back to same as civil. DOBs and middle initial appear on most records, not all. **For details about the state's online access to records, see the section at the front or back of this chapter.**

Story County

2nd District Court 1315 S B Ave, Nevada, IA 50201; 515-382-7410; 8AM-4:30PM M,W,F; 8AM-2:30PM T,TH (CST). *Felony, Misdemeanor, Civil, Probate.* www.iowacourts.gov/District_Courts/District_Two/
General Information: Also has a branch in Ames that handles minor misdemeanors, traffic, and small claims at 515-239-5140. Online identifiers in results same as on public terminal. No sealed, pending dissolution of marriage, mental health, or expunged records released. Will not fax documents. Court makes copy: $.50 per page. Certification fee: $20.00 per doc; exemplification is an additional $20.00. Payee: Clerk of Court. Personal checks accepted. Visa/MC accepted. Prepayment required.
Civil Name Search: Access: In person, online. Visitors must perform in person searches themselves. Civil index in docket books from 1900s; on computer back to 1995. Civil PAT goes back to 1995. DOBs and middle initial appear on most records, not all. **For details about the state's online access to records, see the section at the front or back of this chapter.**
Criminal Name Search: Access: In person, online. Visitors must perform in person searches themselves. Criminal records on computer since 1992, prior on docket books. Criminal PAT goes back to 1992. **For details about the state's online access to records, see the section at the front or back of this chapter.**

Ames Associate District Court PO Box 748, 515 Clark St, Ames, IA 50010; 515-239-5140; fax: 515-239-5141; 8AM-4:30PM M,W,F; 8AM-2:30PM T,TH (CST). *Misdemeanor (Minor), Small Claims, Eviction.* www.iowacourts.gov/District_Courts/District_Two/
General Information: A branch of the District Court in Nevada. Online identifiers in results same as on public terminal. No sealed or expunged records released. Will not fax documents. Court makes copy: $.50 per page. Self serve copy: same. Certification fee: $20.00 per doc; exemplification is an additional $20.00. Payee: Clerk of Court. Personal checks accepted. No credit cards accepted. Prepayment required.
Civil Name Search: Access: In person, online. Visitors must perform in person searches themselves. Civil records on computer back to 1995. Civil PAT goes back to 7/1995. DOBs and middle initial appear on most records, not all. **For details about the state's online access to records, see the section at the front or back of this chapter.**
Criminal Name Search: Access: In person, online. Visitors must perform in person searches themselves. Required to search: name, approx date of offense. Criminal records on computer since 1992, prior on docket books. Criminal PAT goes back to 3/1995. DOBs and middle initial appear on most records, not all. **For details about the state's online access to records, see the section at the front or back of this chapter.**

Tama County

6th Judicial District Court PO Box 306, 100 W High St, Toledo, IA 52342; 641-484-3721; fax: 641-484-6403; 8AM-4:30PM M,W,F; 8AM-2:30PM T,TH (CST). *Felony, Misdemeanor, Civil, Eviction, Small Claims, Probate.* www.iowacourts.gov/District_Courts/District_Six/
General Information: Probate fax is same as main fax number. Online identifiers in results same as on public terminal. No juvenile, sealed, dissolution of marriage, mental health, domestic abuse or deferred records released. Will fax documents for no fee. Court makes copy: $.50 per page. Self serve copy: same. Certification fee: $20.00 per doc; exemplification is an additional $20.00. Payee: Clerk of Court. Personal checks accepted. Visa/MC accepted. Prepayment required.
Civil Name Search: Access: In person, online. Visitors must perform in person searches themselves. Civil index in docket books from 1880s; computerized records since 1997. Magistrate dockets to 1972, prior to 1972, Justice of the Peace. Public use terminal has civil records back to 1997. DOBs and middle initial appear on most records, not all. **For details about the state's online access to records, see the section at the front or back of this chapter.**
Criminal Name Search: Access: In person, online. Visitors must perform in person searches themselves. Criminal docket on books from 1880s; computerized records since 1995. Magistrate dockets to 1972, prior to

1972, Justice of the Peace. Note: Results include name, DOB and case number. **For details about the state's online access to records, see the section at the front or back of this chapter.**

Taylor County

5th District Court 405 Jefferson, #4, County Courthouse, Bedford, IA 50833; 712-523-2095; fax: 712-523-2936; 8AM-4:30PM M, W, F; 8:30AM-2:30PM TH; closed during lunch (CST). *Felony, Misdemeanor, Civil, Eviction, Small Claims, Probate.*
www.iowacourts.gov/District_Courts/District_Five/
General Information: Online identifiers in results same as on public terminal. No juvenile, sealed, dissolution of marriage, mental health, domestic abuse or deferred records released. Will fax out specific case files to local or toll free line. Court makes copy: $.50 per page. Self serve copy: same. Certification fee: $20.00 per doc; exemplification is an additional $20.00. Payee: Clerk of Court. Personal checks accepted. No credit cards accepted. Prepayment required.
Civil Name Search: Access: In person, online. Visitors must perform in person searches themselves. Civil records on computer since 11/01/96; prior to 1880s. Public use terminal available, records go back to 2001. DOBs and middle initial appear on most records, not all. **For details about the state's online access to records, see the section at the front or back of this chapter.**
Criminal Name Search: Access: In person, online. Visitors must perform in person searches themselves. Criminal records on computer since 11/01/96; prior to 1880s. Public use terminal available, crim records go back to 10 years. DOBs and middle initial appear on most records, not all. **For details about the state's online access to records, see the section at the front or back of this chapter.**

Union County

5th District Court Courthouse, 300 N Pine St, Ste 6, Creston, IA 50801; 641-782-7315; fax: 641-782-8241; 8AM-4:30PM M,W,F; 8AM-2:30PM T,TH (CST). *Felony, Misdemeanor, Civil, Eviction, Small Claims, Probate.* www.iowacourts.gov/District_Courts/District_Five/
General Information: Probate fax is same as main fax number. Online identifiers in results same as on public terminal. No juvenile cases less than 10 years, sealed, pending dissolution of marriage, mental health, or deferred records released. Will fax documents for $.50 per page. Court makes copy: $.50 per page. Self serve copy: same. Certification fee: $20.00 per doc; exemplification is an additional $20.00. Payee: Clerk of Court. Personal checks and credit cards accepted. Prepayment required.
Civil Name Search: Access: In person, online. Visitors must perform in person searches themselves. Civil index in docket books from 1900s; computerized back to 10/1996. Civil PAT goes back to 10/1996. DOBs and middle initial appear on most records, not all. **For details about the state's online access to records, see the section at the front or back of this chapter.**
Criminal Name Search: Access: In person, online. Visitors must perform in person searches themselves. Criminal docket on books from 1900s; computerized back to 10/1996. Criminal PAT goes back to same as civil. DOBs and middle initial appear on most records, not all. **For details about the state's online access to records, see the section at the front or back of this chapter.**

Van Buren County

District Court PO Box 495, 902 4th St, Courthouse, Keosauqua, IA 52565; 319-293-3108; fax: 319-293-3811; 9AM-3:30PM M,W,F; 9AM-2:20PM T,TH (CST). *Felony, Misdemeanor, Civil, Eviction, Small Claims, Probate.*
www.iowacourts.gov/District_Courts/District_Eight/
General Information: Online identifiers in results same as on public terminal. No sealed, mental health, or sealed records released; will release un-sealed juvenile, marriage dissolution or DA records if after July, 2000. Will fax documents $1.00 per page. $5.00 minimum. Court makes copy: $.50 per page. Self serve copy: same. Certification fee: $20.00 per doc; exemplification is an additional $20.00. Payee: Clerk of Court. Personal checks accepted. Visa/MC accepted. Prepayment required.
Civil Name Search: Access: In person, online. Visitors must perform in person searches themselves. Civil index in docket books from 1837, computerized since 1997. Civil PAT goes back to 1997. DOBs and middle initial appear on most records, not all. **For details about the state's online access to records, see the section at the front or back of this chapter.**
Criminal Name Search: Access: In person, online. Visitors must perform in person searches themselves. Required to search: name, years to search, DOB. Criminal docket on books from 1837, computerized since 1997. Criminal PAT goes back to 1997. DOBs and middle initial appear on most records, not all. **For details about the state's online access to records, see the section at the front or back of this chapter.**

Wapello County

8th District Court 101 W 4th St, Ottumwa, IA 52501; 641-683-0060; fax: 641-683-0064; 8AM-4:30PM (Closed T, Th at 2:30PM) (CST). *Felony, Misdemeanor, Civil, Eviction, Small Claims, Probate, Domestic Abuse.*
www.iowacourts.gov/District_Courts/District_Eight/
General Information: SSNs are only maintained on a confidential sheet not available to the public. Online identifiers in results same as on public terminal. No juvenile, sealed, dissolution of marriage, mental health, domestic abuse or deferred records released. Will fax documents at $.50 per page, $5.00 minimum. Court makes copy: $.50 per page. Certification fee: $20.00 per doc; exemplification is an additional $20.00. Payee: Clerk of Court. Personal checks and credit cards accepted. Prepayment required.
Civil Name Search: Access: In person, online. Visitors must perform in person searches themselves. Civil records on computer back to 5/1994; docket books prior. Civil PAT goes back to 1995. Middle initial appears on most records, not all. **For details about the state's online access to records, see the section at the front or back of this chapter.**
Criminal Name Search: Access: In person, online. Visitors must perform in person searches themselves. Required to search: name, years to search, DOB; also helpful: SSN. Criminal records computerized from 5/1994; docket books prior. Criminal PAT goes back to same as civil. Middle initial appears on most records, not all. **For details about the state's online access to records, see the section at the front or back of this chapter.**

Warren County

5th District Court PO Box 379, 115 N Howard, Indianola, IA 50125; 515-961-1033; criminal phone: 515-961-1033; civil phone: 515-961-1027; probate phone: 515-961-1037; fax: 515-961-1071; 8AM-4:30PM M,W,F; 8AM-2:30PM T,TH (CST). *Felony, Misdemeanor, Civil, Eviction, Small Claims, Probate.*
www.iowacourts.gov/District_Courts/District_Five/
General Information: Online identifiers in results same as on public terminal. No juvenile, sealed, dissolution of marriage, mental health, domestic abuse or deferred records released. Will not fax documents. Court makes copy: $.50 per page. Certification fee: $20.00 per doc; exemplification is an additional $20.00. Payee: Clerk of Court. Personal checks and credit cards accepted. Prepayment required.
Civil Name Search: Access: In person, online. Visitors must perform in person searches themselves. Civil records on computer back to 10/1995; prior on docket books to 1925. Civil PAT goes back to 1995. DOBs and middle initial appear on most records, not all. **For details about the state's online access to records, see the section at the front or back of this chapter.**
Criminal Name Search: Access: In person, online. Visitors must perform in person searches themselves. Criminal records computerized from 10/1995; prior on docket books to 1945. Criminal PAT goes back to same as civil. DOBs and middle initial appear on most records, not all. **For details about the state's online access to records, see the section at the front or back of this chapter.**

Washington County

8th District Court 224 W Main, Washington, IA 52353; 319-653-7741; fax: 319-653-7787; 8AM-4:30PM M,W,F; 8AM-2:30PM T,TH (CST). *Felony, Misdemeanor, Civil, Eviction, Small Claims, Probate.*
www.iowacourts.gov/District_Courts/District_Eight/
General Information: Online identifiers in results same as on public terminal. No juvenile, sealed, dissolution of marriage, mental health, domestic abuse or deferred records released. Will fax documents $1.00 per page, $5.00 minimum. Court makes copy: $.50 per page. Certification fee: $20.00 per doc; exemplification is an additional $20.00. Payee: Clerk of Court. Personal checks accepted. Visa/MC accepted. Prepayment required.
Civil Name Search: Access: In person, online. Visitors must perform in person searches themselves. Civil records on computer back to 1997, microfilm from 1940, docket books since court inception. Civil PAT goes back to 1997. DOBs and middle initial appear on most records, not all. **For details about the state's online access to records, see the section at the front or back of this chapter.**
Criminal Name Search: Access: In person, online. Visitors must perform in person searches themselves. Criminal records computerized from 1997, microfilm from 1940, docket books since court inception. Criminal PAT goes back to same as civil. DOBs and middle initial appear on most records, not all. **For details about the state's online access to records, see the section at the front or back of this chapter.**

Wayne County

5th District Court PO Box 424, 101 Franklin, Corydon, IA 50060; 641-872-2264; fax: 641-872-2431; 9AM-4PM M-TH (Closed noon-1PM) (CST). *Felony, Misdemeanor, Civil, Eviction, Small Claims, Probate.*
www.iowacourts.gov/District_Courts/District_Five/

General Information: Probate fax is same as main fax number. Online identifiers in results same as on public terminal. No juvenile, sealed, dissolution of marriage, mental health, domestic abuse or deferred records released. Will not fax documents. Court makes copy: $.50 per page. Certification fee: $20.00 per doc; exemplification is an additional $40.00. Payee: Clerk of Court. Personal checks accepted. Visa/MC accepted. Prepayment required. Mail requests: SASE required for mail return of any copies.
Civil Name Search: Access: In person, online. Visitors must perform in person searches themselves. Civil records on dockets from 1890, on computer back to 2/97. Civil PAT goes back to 2/1997. DOBs and middle initial appear on most records, not all. **For details about the state's online access to records, see the section at the front or back of this chapter.**
Criminal Name Search: Access: In person, online. Visitors must perform in person searches themselves. Required to search: name, years to search, DOB. Criminal docket index from 1890, on computer back to 2/97. Criminal PAT goes back to same as civil. DOBs and middle initial appear on most records, not all. **For details about the state's online access to records, see the section at the front or back of this chapter..**

Webster County

2nd District Court 701 Central Ave, Courthouse, Ft Dodge, IA 50501; 515-576-7115; fax: 515-576-0555; 8AM-4:30PM M,W,F; 8AM-2:30PM T,TH (CST). *Felony, Misdemeanor, Civil, Eviction, Small Claims, Probate.*
www.iowacourts.gov/District_Courts/District_Two/
General Information: Probate fax is same as main fax number. Online identifiers in results same as on public terminal. No juvenile, sealed, dissolution of marriage, mental health, domestic abuse or deferred records released. Will fax documents $1.00 per page. Court makes copy: $.50 per page. Certification fee: $20.00 per doc; exemplification is an additional $20.00. Payee: Clerk of Court. Personal checks and credit cards accepted. Prepayment required.
Civil Name Search: Access: In person, online. Visitors must perform in person searches themselves. Civil index in docket books from 1800s, on computer since 1995. Civil PAT goes back to 1995. DOBs and middle initial appear on most records, not all. **For details about the state's online access to records, see the section at the front or back of this chapter.**
Criminal Name Search: Access: In person, online. Visitors must perform in person searches themselves. Required to search: name, years to search, signed release. Criminal docket on books from 1800s, on computer since 1995. Criminal PAT goes back to 1995. DOBs and middle initial appear on most records, not all. **For details about the state's online access to records, see the section at the front or back of this chapter.**

Winnebago County

2nd District Court 126 S Clark, Ste 6, Forest City, IA 50436; 641-585-4520; fax: 641-585-2615; 9AM-Noon; 1PM-3:30PM M,T,W,F (CST). *Felony, Misdemeanor, Civil, Eviction, Small Claims, Probate.*
www.iowacourts.gov/District_Courts/District_Two/
General Information: Probate fax is same as main fax number. This agency is closed to the public on Thursdays. Online identifiers in results same as on public terminal. No juvenile, pending or dismissed dissolution of marriage, mental health, criminal expunged or substance abuse records released. Domestic abuse law change states that parts of the file may be public, depending on Judge's order. Will fax documents for $1.00 per page, pre-paid. Court makes copy: $.50 per page. Certification fee: $20.00 per doc; exemplification is an additional $20.00. Payee: Clerk of Court. Personal checks and credit cards accepted. Prepayment required.
Civil Name Search: Access: In person, online. Visitors must perform in person searches themselves. Required to search: name, years to search; also helpful: address. Civil records on dockets from 1880s; on computer since 9/1997. Civil PAT goes back to 9/1997. **For details about the state's online access to records, see the section at the front or back of this chapter.**
Criminal Name Search: Access: In person, online. Visitors must perform in person searches themselves. Required to search: name, years to search; also helpful: address, DOB, aliases, offense, date of offense. Criminal docket index from 1940s; on computer since 9/1997. Criminal PAT goes back to same as civil. DOBs and middle initial appear on most records, not all. **For details about the state's online access to records, see the section at the front or back of this chapter.**

Winneshiek County

1st District Court 201 W Main St, Decorah, IA 52101; 563-382-2469; fax: 563-382-0603; 8AM-4:30PM M,W,F; 8AM-2:30PM T,TH (CST). *Felony, Misdemeanor, Civil, Eviction, Small Claims, Probate.*
www.iowacourts.gov/District_Courts/District_One/
General Information: Online identifiers in results same as on public terminal. No juvenile, sealed, dissolution of marriage, mental health, domestic abuse or deferred records released. Will fax documents to local or toll-free number. Court makes copy: $.50 per page. Self serve copy: $.25 per

page. Certification fee: $20.00 per doc; exemplification is an additional $20.00. Payee: Clerk of Court. Personal checks accepted. No credit cards accepted. Prepayment required. Mail requests: SASE required for mail return of any copies.
Civil Name Search: Access: In person, online. Visitors must perform in person searches themselves. Civil records on computer since 1992, docket books since 1860s. Civil PAT goes back to 1992. DOBs and middle initial appear on most records, not all. **For details about the state's online access to records, see the section at the front or back of this chapter..**
Criminal Name Search: Access: In person, online. Visitors must perform in person searches themselves. Required to search: name, years to search, signed release. Criminal records on computer since 1991, docket books since 1860s. Criminal PAT goes back to 1991. DOBs and middle initial appear on most records, not all. **For details about the state's online access to records, see the section at the front or back of this chapter.**

Woodbury County

3rd District Court Woodbury County Courthouse, 620 Douglas, Rm 101, Sioux City, IA 51101-1248; criminal phone: 712-279-6611; civil phone: 712-279-6612; probate phone: 712-279-6614; fax: 712-279-6021; 8AM-4:30PM M,W,F; 8AM-2:30PM T,TH (CST). *Felony, Civil, Probate.*
www.iowacourts.gov/District_Courts/District_Three/
General Information: Online identifiers in results same as on public terminal. No adoption, substance abuse, pending dissolution of marriage, or mental health records released. Will fax documents to local or toll-free number. Court makes copy: $.50 per page. Certification fee: $20.00 per doc; exemplification is an additional $20.00. Payee: Clerk of Court. Personal checks accepted. Visa/MC accepted. Prepayment required. Mail requests: SASE required for mail return of any copies.
Civil Name Search: Access: In person, online. Visitors must perform in person searches themselves. Civil index on docket books from early 1900; on computer from 7/95. Civil PAT goes back to 7/1995. DOBs and middle initial appear on most records, not all. **For details about the state's online access to records, see the section at the front or back of this chapter.**
Criminal Name Search: Access: In person, online. Visitors must perform in person searches themselves. Criminal records indexed in books from early 1900; on computer from 10/95. Note: Results include first and last name, case number. Criminal PAT goes back to 10/1995. DOBs and middle initial appear on most records, not all. **For details about the state's online access to records, see the section at the front or back of this chapter.**

Associate District Court 407 7th St RM 111, County Clerk at Law Enforcement Ctr, Sioux City, IA 51101; 712-279-6624; civil phone: 712-279-6464; fax: 712-279-9564; 8AM-4:30PM M,W,F; 8AM-2:30PM T,TH (CST). *Misdemeanor, Civil, Eviction, Small Claims.*
www.iowacourts.gov/District_Courts/District_Three/
General Information: Online identifiers in results same as on public terminal. No juvenile records released. Court makes copy: $.50 per page. Self serve copy: same. Certification fee: $20.00 per doc; exemplification is an additional $20.00. Payee: Clerk of Court. Personal checks accepted. Visa/MC accepted. Prepayment required.
Civil Name Search: Access: In person, online. Visitors must perform in person searches themselves. Civil index in docket books from early 1900; on computer from 7/95. Civil PAT goes back to 1992. DOBs and middle initial appear on most records, not all. **For details about the state's online access to records, see the section at the front or back of this chapter.**
Criminal Name Search: Access: In person, online. Visitors must perform in person searches themselves. Criminal Records indexed on computer since 1992; on computer from 7/92. Criminal PAT goes back to same as civil. DOBs and middle initial appear on most records, not all. **For details about the state's online access to records, see the section at the front or back of this chapter.**

Worth County

2nd District Court 1000 Central Ave, Northwood, IA 50459; 641-324-2840; fax: 641-324-2360; 9AM12; 1PM-3:30PM M,T,TH, F (closed W) (CST). *Felony, Misdemeanor, Civil, Eviction, Small Claims, Probate.*
www.iowacourts.gov/District_Courts/District_Two/
General Information: Case number required for documents. Online identifiers in results same as on public terminal. No juvenile, sealed, dissolution of marriage, mental health, domestic abuse, dismissed, or deferred records released. Will fax out specific case files for $1.00 per page. Court makes copy: $.50 per page. Certification fee: $20.00 per doc; exemplification is an additional $20.00. Payee: Clerk of Court. Personal checks and credit cards accepted. Prepayment required.
Civil Name Search: Access: In person, online. Visitors must perform in person searches themselves. Civil records on computer and docket books, on computer back to 4/97. Civil PAT goes back to 4/1997. DOBs and middle initial appear on most records, not all. **For details about the**

state's online access to records, see the section at the front or back of this chapter.
Criminal Name Search: Access: In person, online. Visitors must perform in person searches themselves. Criminal records on computer and docket books, on computer back to 4/97. Criminal PAT goes back to same as civil. DOBs and middle initial appear on most records, not all. **For details about the state's online access to records, see the section at the front or back of this chapter.**

Wright County

2nd District Court PO Box 306, 115 N Main St, Clarion, IA 50525; 515-532-3113; fax: 515-532-2343; 8AM-4:30PM M,W,F; 8AM-2:30PM T,TH (CST). *Felony, Misdemeanor, Civil, Eviction, Small Claims, Probate.*
www.iowacourts.gov/District_Courts/District_Two/
General Information: Probate is separate index at this same address. Probate fax is same as main fax number. Online identifiers in results same as on public terminal. No juvenile, sealed, dissolution of marriage, mental health, domestic abuse or deferred records released. Will fax out specific case files for $2.00. Court makes copy: $.50 per page. Self serve copy: same. Certification fee: $20.00 per doc; exemplification is an additional $20.00. Payee: Clerk of Court. Personal checks accepted. No credit cards accepted. Prepayment required.
Civil Name Search: Access: In person, online. Visitors must perform in person searches themselves. Civil index in docket books from 1880; on computer since 1997. Civil PAT goes back to 1997. DOBs and middle initial appear on most records, not all. **For details about the state's online access to records, see the section at the front or back of this chapter.**
Criminal Name Search: Access: In person, online. Visitors must perform in person searches themselves. Required to search: name, years to search; also helpful: DOB, SSN. Criminal docket on books from 1880s; on computer since 1997. Criminal PAT goes back to same as civil. DOBs and middle initial appear on most records, not all. **For details about the state's online access to records, see the section at the front or back of this chapter..**

About Online Access

District criminal, civil (including divorce cases with financials/custody data), probate, and traffic information is available from all 99 Iowa counties at www.iowacourts.state.ia.us/ESAWebApp/SelectFrame.

Name searches are available on either a statewide or specific county basis. Names of juveniles aged 10 to 17 will only appear for completed cases with a guilty verdict.

There is no fee for basic information. A $25.00 per month pay system is offered for more detailed requests.

While this is an excellent site with much information and are updated daily, the historical records offered are from different same starting dates per county.

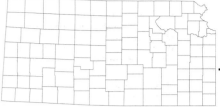

Kansas

Time Zone:	**CST & MST***

* Kansas' five western-most counties are MST:
They are: Greeley, Hamilton, Kearny, Sherman, Wallace,

Capital:	**Topeka, Shawnee County**
# of Counties:	**105**
State Web:	**www.kansas.gov**
Court Web:	**www.kscourts.org**

Administration

Office of Judicial Administration, 301 SW 10th Street, Rm 337, Topeka, KS, 66612; 785-296-2256, Fax: 785-296-7076.

The Supreme and Appellate Courts

The Supreme Court is the court of last resort. The Court of Appeals hears all appeals from orders of the State Corporation Commission and all appeals from the District Courts in both civil and criminal cases except those which may be appealed directly to the Supreme Court. It also has jurisdiction over original actions in habeas corpus.

Published opinions and case information from the Appellate Courts and Supreme Court are available at www.kscourts.org.

The Kansas Courts

Court	Type	How Organized	Jurisdiction Highpoints
District*	General	110 Courts in 31 Districts	Felony, Misdemeanor, Civil, Small Claims, Juvenile, Traffic, Eviction, Domestic Relations, Estate
Municipal	Limited	350 Courts	Municipal ordinances

* = profiled in this book

Details on the Court Structure

The **District Court** is the court of general jurisdiction. with general original jurisdiction over all civil and criminal cases, including divorce and domestic relations, damage suits, probate and administration of estates, guardianships, conservatorships, care of the mentally ill, juvenile matters, and small claims.

Municipal Courts deal with city ordinances; cases usually involve traffic and other minor offenses. If an individual in Municipal Court wants a jury trial, the request must be filed de novo in a District Court. Marriage and divorce records are with the Clerk of the District Court where they occurred as well as at the state vital records agency.

Record Searching Facts You Need to Know

Fees and Record Searching Tips

Five counties - Cowley, Crawford, Labette, Montgomery, and Neosho - have two hearing locations but only one record center, which is the location shown herein.

The Kansas Legislature's Administrative Order 156 (Fall, 2000) allows courts to charge up to $12.00 per hour for search services. Approximately 70% of the courts follow that schedule. Many Kansas courts do not provide criminal record name searches and refer requesters to the Kansas Bureau of Investigation.

Online Access is Nearly Statewide

Commercial online access for civil and criminal records is available for District Court Records (except Sedgwick County cases prior to 2003 and Wyandotte County Cases prior to July 2004) at https://www.accesskansas.org/countyCourts/. Fee is $1.00 per search and $1.00 per case retrieved for view. A credit card is required. Frequent requesters may sign-up for an annual subscription and receive monthly billing. If doing a name search, be aware the search is one county at a time and virtually no personal identifiers are shown on index results; for example the DOB is not shown. The case number is given. There is a $95 annual fee and users have access to other records such as the state criminal record repository and motor vehicle records. For additional information or a registration packet, telephone 800-4-KANSAS (800-452-6727) or visit the web page.

Allen County

District Court 1 N Washington St, Iola, KS 66749; 620-365-1425; fax: 620-365-1429; 8AM-5PM (CST). *Felony, Misdemeanor, Civil, Eviction, Small Claims, Probate.* www.31stjudicialdistrict.org

General Information: No juvenile (under the age of 15), mental health, sealed or expunged records released. Accepts requests via email, but cannot return results by email. Fee to fax out file $1.00 per page. Court makes copy: $.50 per page. Certification fee: $1.00. Payee: Clerk of Court. Personal checks accepted. No credit cards accepted. Prepayment required. Mail requests: SASE required.

Civil Name Search: Access: Fax, mail, in person, online. Both court and visitors may perform in person name searches. Search fee: $12.00 per hour. Civil records on computer from 1993, manual index from 1800s. Mail turnaround time 3-4 days Civil PAT goes back to 1993. **For details about the state's online access to records, see the section at the front or back of this chapter.** Also, court calendars, limited action hearing results, and service results appear on the court's main website.

Criminal Name Search: Access: Online. No criminal searching at this court. Search fee: $12.00 per hour. Criminal records computerized from 1993, manual index from 1800s. Note: All criminal searches are referred to the KBI, unless a case number is provided. The fees described here for criminal records only pertain if a case # is given. Criminal PAT available. **For details about the state's online access to records, see the section at the front or back of this chapter.**

Anderson County

District Court PO Box 305, Garnett, KS 66032; 785-448-6886; fax: 785-448-3230; 8AM-N, 1PM-4PM (CST). *Felony, Misdemeanor, Civil, Eviction, Small Claims, Probate.* www.franklincoks.org/4thdistrict/

General Information: Probate fax is same as main fax number. Online identifiers in results same as on public terminal. No juvenile, mental health, sealed or expunged records released. Will fax documents $2.00 1st page, $.50 each add'l. Court makes copy: $.25 per page. Self serve copy: same.If by email, no fee. Certification fee: $1.00 per document. Payee: District Court. Personal checks and credit cards accepted. Prepayment required. Mail requests: SASE required.

Civil Name Search: Access: Fax, mail, in person, online. Both court and visitors may perform in person name searches. Search fee: $12.00 per hour. Civil records on computer from 1977, index books from 1800s. Mail turnaround time 3 days. Civil PAT goes back to 1977. Public terminal includes probate, marriage, etc. **For details about the state's online access to records, see the section at the front or back of this chapter.** Also, access to old probate court records up to 8/29/2001 is free at www.kscourts.org/dstcts/4anprrec.htm as well as on the subscription service. Access marriage records by alpha search up to 8/29/2001 for free at www.kscourts.org/dstcts/4anmarec.htm.

Criminal Name Search: Access: Fax, mail, in person, online. Visitors must perform in person searches themselves. Search fee: $12.00 per hour. Criminal records computerized from 1977, index books from 1800s. Note: For criminal record searches, the court urges requesters to contact the KS Bureau of Investigations. Mail turnaround time within 3 days. Criminal PAT goes back to same as civil. **For details about the state's online access to records, see the section at the front or back of this chapter.**

Atchison County

District Court PO Box 408, Atchison, KS 66002; 913-367-7400; fax: 913-367-1171; 8AM-5PM (CST). *Felony, Misdemeanor, Civil, Eviction, Small Claims, Probate.* www.atchisoncountyks.org/

General Information: No juvenile, mental health, sealed or expunged records released. Will fax documents $1.25 per page. Court makes copy: $.25 per page. Certification fee: $1.00 plus copy fee. Payee: District Court. Personal checks accepted. No credit cards accepted. Prepayment required. Mail requests: SASE required for civil.

Civil Name Search: Access: Fax, mail, in person, online. Both court and visitors may perform in person name searches. Search fee: $12.00 per hour. Civil records on computer from 1991, index books from 1900s, archives from 1860s. Mail turnaround time 1-5 days. Civil PAT goes back to 1990. **For details about the state's online access to records, see the section at the front or back of this chapter. Criminal Name Search:** Access: In person, online. Visitors must perform in person searches themselves. Criminal records computerized from 1991, index books from 1900s, archives from 1860s. Criminal PAT goes back to same as civil. **For details about the state's online access to records, see the section at the front or back of this chapter.**

Barber County

District Court 118 E Washington, Medicine Lodge, KS 67104; 620-886-5639; fax: 620-886-5854; 8AM-N,1-5PM (CST). *Felony, Misdemeanor, Civil, Eviction, Small Claims, Probate.* www.kscourts.org/Districts/District-Info.asp?d=30

General Information: No juvenile, mental health, sealed or expunged records released. Will fax documents $1.00 per page, with a $10.00 page limit. Court makes copy: $.25 per page. Certification fee: $1.00 per cert. Payee: District Court. Personal checks accepted. No credit cards accepted. Prepayment required.

Civil Name Search: Access: In person, online. Visitors must perform in person searches themselves. Civil records from 1990, microfiche from 1900-1976, index cards from 1800s. Civil PAT goes back to 1990. **For details about the state's online access to records, see the section at the front or back of this chapter.**

Criminal Name Search: Access: In person, online. Visitors must perform in person searches themselves. Criminal records computerized from 1990, microfiche from 1900-1976, index cards from 1800s. Criminal PAT goes back to same as civil. **For details about the state's online access to records, see the section at the front or back of this chapter.**

Barton County

District Court 1400 Main, Rm 306, Great Bend, KS 67530; 620-793-1856; fax: 620-793-1860; 8AM-5PM (CST). *Felony, Misdemeanor, Civil, Eviction, Small Claims, Probate.*

General Information: Probate fax is same as main fax number. No juvenile, mental health, sealed or expunged records released. Will fax documents $.50 per page. Court makes copy: $.35 per page; $.1.00 for microfilm copies. No certification fee . Payee: Clerk of Court. Personal checks accepted. No credit cards accepted. Prepayment required. Mail requests: SASE required.

Civil Name Search: Access: Fax, mail, in person, online. Both court and visitors may perform in person name searches. Search fee: $12.00 per hour. Minimum of $12.00 in advance. Civil records on computer 1990, microfiche and archives from 1800s, index from 1987. Mail turnaround time 3 days. Civil PAT goes back to 1990. **For details about the state's online access to records, see the section at the front or back of this chapter.**

Criminal Name Search: Access: Fax, mail, in person, online. Both court and visitors may perform in person name searches. Search fee: $12.00 per hour. Minimum of $12.00 in advance. Criminal records on computer 1990, microfiche and archives from 1800s, index from 1987. Note: Screening firm and employment-related searches and bulk requests will be referred to the state criminal record agency. Mail turnaround time 3 days. Criminal PAT goes back to same as civil. **For details about the state's online access to records, see the section at the front or back of this chapter.**

Bourbon County

District Court PO Box 868, Fort Scott, KS 66701; 620-223-0780; criminal phone: 620-223-1838; civil phone: 620-223-0780; probate phone: 620-223-1380; fax: 620-223-5303; 8:30AM-4:30PM (CST). *Felony, Misdemeanor, Civil, Eviction, Small Claims, Probate.*

General Information: Probate fax is same as main fax number. No juvenile, mental health, sealed or expunged records released. Will not fax out case files. Court makes copy: $.25 per page. Self serve copy: $.10 per page. Certification fee: $1.00 per document, plus copy fee. Payee: Clerk of Court. Personal checks accepted. No credit cards accepted. Prepayment required.

Civil Name Search: Access: In person, online. Visitors must perform in person searches themselves. Civil records on computer since 1990, index on computer since 1985. Civil PAT goes back to 20 years. **For details about the state's online access to records, see the section at the front or back of this chapter.**

Criminal Name Search: Access: In person, online. Visitors must perform in person searches themselves. Required to search: name, years to search; SSN helpful. Criminal records on computer since 1990, index on computer since 1985. Criminal PAT goes back to same as civil. **For details about the state's online access to records, see the section at the front or back of this chapter.**

Brown County

District Court PO Box 417, Hiawatha, KS 66434; 785-742-7481; fax: 785-742-3506; 8AM-5PM (CST). *Felony, Misdemeanor, Civil, Eviction, Small Claims, Probate.*

General Information: Probate fax is same as main fax number. No juvenile, mental health, sealed or expunged records released. Fee to fax out file $1.00 per page. Court makes copy: $.50 first page, $.25 each add'l. Certification fee: $1.00 per document. Payee: District Court. Personal checks accepted. No credit cards accepted. Prepayment required. Mail requests: SASE required.

Civil Name Search: Access: Phone, fax, mail, in person, online. Both court and visitors may perform in person name searches. Search fee: $12.00 per hour. Civil records on computer from 1982, microfiche from 1900s, index books from 1900s. Mail turnaround time 1-2 days. Civil PAT goes back to 1982. **For details about the state's online access to records, see the section at the front or back of this chapter.**

Criminal Name Search: Access: Phone, fax, mail, in person, online. Both court and visitors may perform in person name searches. Search fee: $12.00 per hour. Required to search: name, years to search; also helpful: SSN. Criminal records computerized from 1982, microfiche and index books from 1900s. Mail turnaround time 1-2 days. Criminal PAT goes back to same as civil. **For details about the state's online access to records, see the section at the front or back of this chapter.**

Butler County

District Court 201 W Pine, #101, El Dorado, KS 67042; 316-322-4370; fax: 316-321-9486; 8AM-5PM (CST). *Felony, Misdemeanor, Civil, Eviction, Small Claims, Probate.*

General Information: No juvenile, mental health, sealed or expunged records released. Will fax documents if prepaid. Court makes copy: $.50 per page; $1.00 if from microfilm. Self serve copy: same. Certification fee: $1.00 per page. Payee: Clerk of District Court. Personal checks accepted. No credit cards accepted. Prepayment required.

Civil Name Search: Access: In person, online. Visitors must perform in person searches themselves. Civil records on computer from 1992, index cards from 1800s. Civil PAT goes back to 1992. **For details about the state's online access to records, see the section at the front or back of this chapter.**

Criminal Name Search: Access: Fax, in person, online. Visitors must perform in person searches themselves. Search fee: $12.00 per hour. Criminal records computerized from 1992, index cards from 1800s. Note: The court will not perform a name search and sends requesters to the state Bureau of Investigations. Search fees below involved records from a specific case only. Criminal PAT goes back to same as civil. **For details about the state's online access to records, see the section at the front or back of this chapter.**

Chase County

District Court PO Box 529, Cottonwood Falls, KS 66845; 620-273-6319; fax: 620-273-6890; 8AM-5PM (CST). *Felony, Misdemeanor, Civil, Eviction, Small Claims, Probate.* www.5thjd.org/

General Information: No juvenile, mental health, sealed or expunged records released. Will not fax documents. Court makes copy: $.50 per page. Certification fee: $2.00 per cert. Payee: District Court. Personal checks accepted. No credit cards accepted. Prepayment required.

Civil Name Search: Access: In person, online. Visitors must perform in person searches themselves. Civil records on computer from late 1990, microfiche from 1860, index books from 1860; visitors may search the printed index desk copy. Civil PAT goes back to 1991. **For details about the state's online access to records, see the section at the front or back of this chapter.**

Criminal Name Search: Access: In person, online. Visitors must perform in person searches themselves. Criminal records computerized from late 1990, microfiche from 1860, index books from 1860; visitors may search the printed index desk copy. Criminal PAT goes back to same as civil. **For details about the state's online access to records, see the section at the front or back of this chapter.**

Chautauqua County

District Court PO Box 306, 215 N Chautauqua St, Sedan, KS 67361; 620-725-5870; fax: 620-725-3027; 8AM-4PM (CST). *Felony, Misdemeanor, Civil, Eviction, Small Claims, Probate.* www.kscourts.org/districts/District-Info.asp?d=14

General Information: Probate fax is same as main fax number. No juvenile, mental health, sealed or expunged records released. Will fax documents. Court makes copy: $.25 per page. Self serve copy: same. Certification fee: $1.00 per certification plus copy fee. Payee: District Court. Personal checks accepted. No credit cards accepted. Prepayment required. Mail requests: SASE required.

Civil Name Search: Access: Mail, in person, online. Both court and visitors may perform in person name searches. Search fee: $12.00 per hour. Civil records on computer from 1990, archives from 1950, index cards from 1870. Mail turnaround time 1-2 weeks. Civil PAT goes back to 1990. Terminal results also show SSNs. **For details about the state's online access to records, see the section at the front or back of this chapter.**

Criminal Name Search: Access: Mail, in person, online. Both court and visitors may perform in person name searches. Search fee: $12.00 per hour. Required to search: name, years to search; also helpful: DOB. Criminal records computerized from 1990, archives from 1950, index cards from 1870. Mail turnaround time 1-2 weeks. Criminal PAT goes back to same as civil. Terminal results include SSN. **For details about the state's online access to records, see the section at the front or back of this chapter.**

Cherokee County

District Court PO Box 189, Columbus, KS 66725; 620-429-3880; fax: 620-429-1130; 8AM-5PM (CST). *Felony, Misdemeanor, Civil, Eviction, Small Claims, Probate.*

General Information: No juvenile, mental health, sealed or expunged records released. Will not fax documents. Court makes copy: $.25 per page. Certification fee: $1.25 per page includes copy. Payee: District Court. Personal checks accepted; 14-day hold. No credit cards accepted. Prepayment required. Mail requests: SASE required.

Civil Name Search: Access: Mail, fax, in person, online. Visitors must perform in person searches themselves. Search fee: $12.00 per hour. Civil records on computer back 16 years, index books from 1867. Mail turnaround time 3 days. Civil PAT goes back to 1990. **For details about the state's online access to records, see the section at the front or back of this chapter.**

Criminal Name Search: Access: Mail, fax, in person. Visitors must perform in person searches themselves. Search fee: $12.00 per hour. Required to search: name, years to search; also helpful: SSN. Criminal records on computer back 20 years, index books from 1867. Mail turnaround time 3 days. Criminal PAT goes back to same as civil. **For details about the state's online access to records, see the section at the front or back of this chapter.**

Cheyenne County

District Court PO Box 646, St Francis, KS 67756; 785-332-8850; fax: 785-332-8851; 8AM-N,1-5PM (CST). *Felony, Misdemeanor, Civil, Eviction, Small Claims, Probate.*

General Information: Probate records on a separate index. Court personnel will NOT do any record searching for the public. Probate fax is same as main fax number. No juvenile, adoptions, mental health, sealed or expunged records released. Will fax documents $1.00 per page; free if toll free line used. Court makes copy: $.25 per page. Self serve copy: same. Certification fee: $1.00 per cert. Payee: Clerk of Court. Personal checks accepted. No credit cards accepted. Prepayment required.

Civil Name Search: Access: In person, online. Visitors must perform in person searches themselves. Civil records on strip index from 1989, index cards from 1870. **For details about the state's online access to records, see the section at the front or back of this chapter.**

Criminal Name Search: Access: In person, online. Visitors must perform in person searches themselves. Criminal records on strip index from 1989, index cards from 1870. **For details about the state's online access to records, see the section at the front or back of this chapter.**

Clark County

District Court PO Box 790, Ashland, KS 67831; 620-635-2753; fax: 620-635-2155; 8AM-5PM (CST). *Felony, Misdemeanor, Civil, Eviction, Small Claims, Probate.* www.kscourts.org/Districts/District-Info.asp?d=16

General Information: Probate fax is same as main fax number. No juvenile, mental health, sealed or expunged records released. Will fax documents $2.00 first page and $.50 ea add'l. Court makes copy: $.25 per page. Self serve copy: same. Certification fee: $1.00 plus copy fee. Payee: District Court. Personal checks accepted. No credit cards accepted. Prepayment required. Mail requests: SASE required.

Civil Name Search: Access: Mail, fax, in person, online. Both court and visitors may perform in person name searches. Search fee: $12.00 per search. Civil records on computer from 2003, microfiche and archives from 1800s, index cards from 1800s. Mail turnaround time 2 days. Civil PAT goes back to 2004. **For details about the state's online access to records, see the section at the front or back of this chapter.**

Criminal Name Search: Access: Mail, fax, in person, online. Both court and visitors may perform in person name searches. Search fee: $12.00 per search. Required to search: name, years to search; also helpful: SSN. Criminal records indexed on cards. Mail turnaround time 2 days. Criminal PAT goes back to 2004. **For details about the state's online access to records, see the section at the front or back of this chapter**

Clay County

District Court PO Box 203, Clay Center, KS 67432; 785-632-3443; fax: 785-632-2651; 8AM-4PM (CST). *Felony, Misdemeanor, Civil, Eviction, Small Claims, Probate.* www.claycountykansas.org/government/district-court

General Information: No juvenile, adoption, mental health, sealed or expunged records released. Will fax out documents $2.00 1st page, $.50 each add'l. Court makes copy: $.25 per page. Self serve copy: $.25 per page. Certification fee: $1.00. Payee: Clerk of District Court. Personal checks accepted. No credit cards accepted. Prepayment required. Mail requests: SASE required.

Civil Name Search: Access: Mail, in person, online. Visitors must perform in person searches themselves. Search fee: $12.00 per name. Civil records on computer from 7/1994, index books from late 1800s. Mail turnaround time 3 days. Civil PAT goes back to 7/1994. **For details about the state's online access to records, see the section at the front or back of this chapter.**

Criminal Name Search: Access: Mail, in person, online. Visitors must perform in person searches themselves. Search fee: $12.00 per name. Required to search: name. Criminal records computerized from 7/1994, index books from late 1800s. Mail turnaround time 3 days. Criminal PAT goes back to same as civil. **For details about the state's online access to records, see the section at the front or back of this chapter.**

Cloud County

District Court 811 Washington, Ste P, Concordia, KS 66901; 785-243-8124; fax: 785-243-8188; 8AM-5PM (CST). *Felony, Misdemeanor, Civil, Eviction, Small Claims, Probate.*
www.kscourts.org/Districts/District-Info.asp?d=12

General Information: No juvenile, mental health, sealed or expunged records released. Will fax documents $2.00 per page. Court makes copy: $.25 per page.If SASE not sent will charge the cost of postage. Certification fee: $1.00 plus copy fee. Payee: Clerk of Court. Personal checks accepted. No credit cards accepted. Prepayment required. Mail requests: SASE requested.

Civil Name Search: Access: Phone, fax, mail, in person, online. Visitors must perform in person searches themselves. Search fee: $12.00 per hour. Civil records in print indexes from 1992, index books prior to 1992. Mail turnaround time 3-4 days. Civil PAT goes back to 1994. **For details about the state's online access to records, see the section at the front or back of this chapter.**

Criminal Name Search: Access: Fax, mail, in person, online. Both court and visitors may perform in person name searches. Search fee: $12.00 per hour. Required to search: name, years to search; also helpful: SSN, DOB. Criminal records in print indexes from 1992, index books prior to 1992. Mail turnaround time 3-4 days. Criminal PAT goes back to same as civil. **For details about the state's online access to records, see the section at the front or back of this chapter.**

Coffey County

District Court 110 S Sixth St, Ste 102, Burlington, KS 66839; 620-364-8628; fax: 620-364-8535; 8AM-4PM (CST). *Felony, Misdemeanor, Civil, Eviction, Small Claims, Probate.* www.franklincoks.org/4thdistrict/

General Information: Direct email record requests todistrictcourt@coffeycountyks.org. No juvenile, mental health, sealed or expunged records released. Fee to fax out file $2.00 1st page; $.50 each add'l. Court makes copy: $.25 per page. Self serve copy: same. Certification fee: $1.00. Payee: Clerk of District Court. Personal checks and credit cards accepted. Prepayment required. Mail requests: SASE required.

Civil Name Search: Access: Mail, fax, in person, email, online. Both court and visitors may perform in person name searches. Search fee: $12.00 per hour. Civil records on computer back to 1800s. Mail turnaround time 3 days. Public use terminal available, records go back to 1800's. Current court calendars are free online at www.franklincoks.org/4thdistrict/coffeybydate.html. Probate and marriage records are accessible at this website, marriages at www.kscourts.org/dstcts/4comarec.htm to 1/18/2001. **For details about the state's online access to records, see the section at the front or back of this chapter.**

Criminal Name Search: Access: Mail, fax, in person, email, online. Both court and visitors may perform in person name searches. Search fee: $12.00 per hour. Required to search: name, years to search, DOB. Criminal records computerized from 1800s. Note: The court will not do name searches for employment purposes and refers requesters to the state agency - KBI. Mail turnaround time 3 days. Public use terminal available, crim records go back to same. Online access to subscription service and the court calendar is the same as civil. Online results show name only.

Comanche County

District Court PO Box 722, 201 S New York, Coldwater, KS 67029; 620-582-2182; fax: 620-582-2603; 8AM-5PM (CST). *Felony, Misdemeanor, Civil, Eviction, Small Claims, Probate.*
www.kscourts.org/Districts/District-Info.asp?d=16

General Information: Probate fax is same as main fax number. No juvenile, mental health, sealed or expunged records released. Will fax specific case file $1.00 per page. Court makes copy: $.25 per page. Self serve copy: same. Certification fee: $1.00 per page plus copy fee. Payee: District Court. Personal checks accepted. No credit cards accepted. Prepayment required.

Civil Name Search: Access: In person, online. Both court and visitors may perform in person name searches. No search fee. Civil records on computer back to 2004 (child support only), index books from 1886. Civil PAT goes back to 2004. **For details about the state's online access to records, see the section at the front or back of this chapter.**

Criminal Name Search: Access: In person, online. Both court and visitors may perform in person name searches. No search fee. Required to search: name, years to search; SSN helpful. Criminal records indexed in books from 1886. Criminal PAT goes back to same as civil. **For details about the state's online access to records, see the section at the front or back of this chapter.**

Cowley County

Arkansas City District Court PO Box 1152, Arkansas City, KS 67005; 620-441-4520; fax: 620-442-7213; 8AM-N,1-4PM (CST). *Felony, Misdemeanor, Civil, Eviction, Small Claims, Probate.*
www.cowleycounty.org/court/

General Information: This court covers the southern part of the county. Many felony records are kept at Winfield. Probate fax is same as main fax number. No juvenile, mental health, sealed or expunged records released. Will fax documents $1.00 per page. Court makes copy: $.50 per page. Certification fee: $2.00 per doc plus copy fee. Payee: Clerk of Court. Personal checks accepted. No credit cards accepted. Prepayment required. Mail requests: SASE helpful.

Civil Name Search: Access: Fax, mail, in person, online. Both court and visitors may perform in person name searches. Search fee: $12.00 per name. Civil records from 1977. This Court facility in existence since 1977, so no records prior to that date. Computer records commencing 1994. Mail turnaround time 1 week. Civil PAT goes back to 1994. Results include docket notes. **For details about the state's online access to records, see the section at the front or back of this chapter.**

Criminal Name Search: Access: Fax, mail, in person. Both court and visitors may perform in person name searches. Search fee: $12.00 per name. Required to search: name, years to search, SSN. Criminal records from 1977. Court facility in existence since 1977, so no records prior to that date. Computer records commencing 1994. Mail turnaround time 1 week. Criminal PAT goes back to same as civil. Results include docket notes. **For details about the state's online access to records, see the section at the front or back of this chapter.**

Winfield District Court PO Box 472, Winfield, KS 67156; 620-221-5470; fax: 620-221-1097; 8AM-N,1-4PM (CST). *Felony, Misdemeanor, Civil, Eviction, Small Claims, Probate.*
www.cowleycounty.org/court/index.htm

General Information: This court covers northern part of county. No juvenile, mental health, sealed or expunged records released. Court makes copy: $.50 per page. Certification fee: $2.00 per cert. Payee: Clerk of Court. Personal checks accepted. No credit cards accepted. Prepayment required. Mail requests: SASE required.

Civil Name Search: Access: Fax, mail, in person, online. Both court and visitors may perform in person name searches. Search fee: $12.00 per name. Civil records on computer since 1994, index cards from 1874. Mail turnaround time 1 week. Civil PAT goes back to 1994. **For details about the state's online access to records, see the section at the front or back of this chapter.**

Criminal Name Search: Access: Fax, mail, in person. Both court and visitors may perform in person name searches. Search fee: $12.00 per name. Criminal records on computer since 1994, index cards from 1874. Mail turnaround time 1 week. Criminal PAT goes back to same as civil. **For details about the state's online access to records, see the section at the front or back of this chapter.**

Crawford County

Girard District Court PO Box 69, Girard, KS 66743; 620-724-6211; fax: 620-724-4987; 8AM-4PM (CST). *Felony, Misdemeanor, Civil, Probate.*

General Information: Records on computer are maintained here for the Pittsburg District Court as well since 8/92. For prior cases, search both courts separately. No confidential juvenile, mental health, sealed or expunged records released. Will fax documents $2.50 per page. Court makes copy: $.25 per page. Certification fee: $1.00. Payee: Clerk of Court. Personal checks accepted. No credit cards accepted. Prepayment required. Mail requests: SASE required.

Civil Name Search: Access: Fax, mail, in person, online. Both court and visitors may perform in person name searches. Search fee: $12.00 per hour. Civil records on computer since 8/1992, microfiche from 1977, index cards from 1977. Mail turnaround time 3 days. Civil PAT goes back to 1977. **For details about the state's online access to records, see the section at the front or back of this chapter.**

Criminal Name Search: Access: Phone, fax, in person, online. Both court and visitors may perform in person name searches. Search fee: $12.00 per hour. Criminal records on computer since 8/1992, microfiche from 1977,

index cards from 1977. Note: Employment/work-related/credit mail inquires are referred to the Kansas Bureau of Investigation. Criminal PAT goes back to same as civil. **For details about the state's online access to records, see the section at the front or back of this chapter.**
Pittsburg District Court 602 N Locust, Pittsburg, KS 66762; 620-231-0391; fax: 620-231-0316; 8AM-5PM (CST). *Misdemeanor, Civil, Eviction, Small Claims, Probate.*
www.kscourts.org/Districts/District-Info.asp?d=11
General Information: Records back to 8/92 can be searched at Girard District Court as well; Girard and Pittsburg share a computer system. For cases prior to 8/92, search both courts separately. Probate fax is same as main fax number. No juvenile, mental health, sealed or expunged records released. Will fax documents $2.50 per page. Court makes copy: $.25 per page. Self serve copy: same. Certification fee: $1.00 plus copy fee. Payee: Clerk of Court. Personal checks accepted. No credit cards accepted. Prepayment required. Mail requests: SASE required.
Civil Name Search: Access: Fax, mail, in person, online. Both court and visitors may perform in person name searches. Search fee: $12.00 per hour. Civil records on computer since 8/1992, microfiche from 1977, index cards from 1977. Mail turnaround time 3 days. Civil PAT goes back to 8/1992. **For details about the state's online access to records, see the section at the front or back of this chapter.**
Criminal Name Search: Access: Mail, in person, online. Both court and visitors may perform in person name searches. Search fee: $12.00 per hour. Criminal records on computer since 8/1992, microfiche from 1977, index cards from 1977. Note: Employment/work-related mail inquires are referred to the Kansas Bureau of Investigation. Mail requests must be on courts form, call court for form and they will fax it to you. Mail turnaround time 3 days. Criminal PAT goes back to same as civil. **For details about the state's online access to records, see the section at the front or back of this chapter.**

Decatur County

District Court PO Box 89, 120- E Hall St, Oberlin, KS 67749; 785-475-8107; fax: 785-475-8170; 8AM-5PM (CST). *Felony, Misdemeanor, Civil, Eviction, Small Claims, Probate.*
General Information: No adoption, juvenile, mental health, sealed or expunged records released. Will fax documents $1.00 1st page, $.25 each add'l page. Court makes copy: $.25 per page. Certification fee: $1.00. Payee: Clerk of District Court. Personal checks accepted. No credit cards accepted. Prepayment required.
Civil Name Search: Access: In person, online. Both court and visitors may perform in person name searches. Search fee: $4.00 per name. Civil index on docket books from 1870. Civil PAT goes back to 2004. **For details about the state's online access to records, see the section at the front or back of this chapter.**
Criminal Name Search: Access: In person, online. Both court and visitors may perform in person name searches. Search fee: $4.00 per name. Criminal records indexed in books from 1870. Criminal PAT goes back to same as civil. **For details about the state's online access to records, see the section at the front or back of this chapter.**

Dickinson County

District Court PO Box 127, Abilene, KS 67410; 785-263-3142; criminal phone: x305; civil phone: x301; probate phone: x304; fax: 785-263-4407; 8AM-5PM (CST). *Felony, Misdemeanor, Civil, Eviction, Small Claims, Probate.* www.8thjd.com
General Information: Probate fax is same as main fax number. No juvenile, mental health, sealed or expunged records released. Will fax documents $2.00 per page. Court makes copy: $1.00 for first 4 pages; $.25 each add'l. Self serve copy: same. Certification fee: $1.00 per document. Payee: Clerk of District Court. Personal checks accepted. No credit cards accepted. Prepayment required. Mail requests: SASE required.
Civil Name Search: Access: Mail, fax, in person, email, online. Both court and visitors may perform in person name searches. Search fee: $12.00 per hour. Civil records on computer since 7/92, on index books prior. Note: Direct email civil record requests to dkcdc@8thjd.com Mail turnaround time 3 days. Civil PAT goes back to 7/1992. **For details about the state's online access to records, see the section at the front or back of this chapter.**
Criminal Name Search: Access: Mail, in person, online. Visitors must perform in person searches themselves. Search fee: $12.00 per hour. Required to search: name, years to search, DOB; also helpful: SSN. Criminal records on computer since 7/92, on index books prior. Will search only if case number is provided. Court directs search requests to KBI. Criminal PAT goes back to same as civil. **For details about the state's online access to records, see the section at the front or back of this chapter.**

Doniphan County

District Court PO Box 295, Troy, KS 66087; 785-985-3582; fax: 785-985-2402; 8AM-5PM (CST). *Felony, Misdemeanor, Civil, Eviction, Small Claims, Probate.*

General Information: Probate fax is same as main fax number. No juvenile, mental health, sealed or expunged records released. Fee to fax out file $2.00 1st page, $1.00 ea add'l. Court makes copy: $.50 first page, $.25 each add'l. Self serve copy: $.25 per page. Certification fee: $1.00 per document. Payee: Clerk of Court. Personal checks accepted. No credit cards accepted. Prepayment required. Mail requests: SASE required.
Civil Name Search: Access: Phone, fax, mail, in person, online. Both court and visitors may perform in person name searches. Search fee: $12.00 per hour. Civil records on computer since 1992; index cards from 1856. Mail turnaround time 1-2 days. Civil PAT goes back to 1992. **For details about the state's online access to records, see the section at the front or back of this chapter.**
Criminal Name Search: Access: Phone, fax, mail, in person, online. Both court and visitors may perform in person name searches. Search fee: $12.00 per hour. Required to search: name, years to search; also helpful: address, DOB. Criminal records on computer since 1992; index cards from 1852. Mail turnaround time 1-2 days. Criminal PAT goes back to same as civil. **For details about the state's online access to records, see the section at the front or back of this chapter.**

Douglas County

District Court 111 E 11th St, Lawrence, KS 66044-2966; 785-832-5141; fax: 785-832-5174; 8AM-12; 1-5PM (CST). *Felony, Misdemeanor, Civil, Eviction, Small Claims, Probate.*
www.douglas-county.com/district_court/dc_home.aspx
General Information: Send questions to courtrecords@douglas-county.com. No juvenile, mental health, sealed or expunged records released. Will fax documents $1.00 per page if local, $2.00 if long distance. Court makes copy: $.25 per page. Certification fee: $1.00 per document plus copy fee. Authentications are $2.00 per document plus copy fee. Payee: Clerk of Court. Personal checks accepted. No credit cards accepted. Prepayment required. Prepayment only required for research & off site retrieval ($12.00).
Civil Name Search: Access: Phone, fax, mail, in person, online. Both court and visitors may perform in person name searches. Search fee: $12.00 per hour. Civil index on cards from 1863, archived from 1865 on film, indexed on computer since 1989. Note: All written requests must include a phone number. Add $1.00 for shipping and handling for mail requests. Mail turnaround time 3 days. Civil PAT goes back to 1992. **For details about the state's online access to records, see the section at the front or back of this chapter.**
Criminal Name Search: Access: Phone, fax, mail, in person, online. Both court and visitors may perform in person name searches. Search fee: $12.00 per hour. Required to search: name, years to search; also helpful: DOB, SSN. Criminal records computerized from 1989, index cards 1860, archived from 1865. Note: All other background check requests must be in writing. Add $1.00 for shipping and handling for mail requests. Mail turnaround time 3 days. Criminal PAT goes back to 1992. The following information is available on the public access computers: party names, case filings, document filings, court payments, criminal charges, and court dates. **For details about the state's online access to records, see the section at the front or back of this chapter.**

Edwards County

District Court PO Box 232, Kinsley, KS 67547; 620-659-2442; fax: 620-659-2998; 8AM-5PM (CST). *Felony, Misdemeanor, Civil, Eviction, Small Claims, Probate.* www.kscourts.org/Districts/District-Info.asp?d=24
General Information: No juvenile, adoption, mental health, sealed or expunged records released. Will fax documents to local or toll free line. Court makes copy: $.25 per page. Certification fee: $1.00 plus copy fee. Payee: Clerk District Court. Personal checks accepted. No credit cards accepted. Prepayment required. Mail requests: SASE required.
Civil Name Search: Access: Mail, in person, online. Both court and visitors may perform in person name searches. Search fee: $12.00 per name. Civil index on docket books from 1800s. Mail turnaround time 2 days Civil PAT goes back to 10/2002. **For details about the state's online access to records, see the section at the front or back of this chapter.**
Criminal Name Search: Access: In person, online. Visitors must perform in person searches themselves. Criminal records indexed in books from 1800s. Note: The court recommends criminal record searchers to access the state's KBI system. Mail turnaround time is 2 days. Criminal PAT goes back to same as civil. **For details about the state's online access to records, see the section at the front or back of this chapter.**

Elk County

District Court PO Box 306, 127 N Pine, Howard, KS 67349; 620-374-2370; fax: 620-374-3531; 8AM-4:30PM (CST). *Felony, Misdemeanor, Civil, Eviction, Small Claims, Probate.*
www.13thjudicial.org/
General Information: Probate fax is same as main fax number. No juvenile, mental health, sealed or expunged records released. Will fax

documents for $1.00 plus copy costs. Court makes copy: $.50 per page. Self serve copy: same. Certification fee: $1.00 per document. Payee: Clerk of District Court. Personal checks accepted. No credit cards accepted. Prepayment required. Mail requests: SASE required.

Civil Name Search: Access: Mail, in person, online. Both court and visitors may perform in person name searches. Search fee: Depending on difficulty, clerk may charge $12 per hr search fee. Civil index on docket books from 1907. Mail turnaround time 1-2 days. Civil PAT goes back to 1984. **For details about the state's online access to records, see the section at the front or back of this chapter.**

Criminal Name Search: Access: In person, online. Visitors must perform in person searches themselves. Search fee: Depending on difficulty, clerk may charge $12 per hr search fee. Criminal records indexed in books from 1956; on computer back to 1984. Note: Record searchers are encouraged to contact the state criminal record agency. Mail turnaround time 1-2 days. Criminal PAT goes back to same as civil. **For details about the state's online access to records, see the section at the front or back of this chapter.**

Ellis County

District Court PO Box 8, 1204 Fort St, 3rd Fl, Hays, KS 67601; 785-628-9415; fax: 785-628-8415; 8AM-5PM (CST). *Felony, Misdemeanor, Civil, Eviction, Small Claims, Probate.*
www.23rdjudicial.org/Ellis/Ellis.html

General Information: Probate fax is same as main fax number. No juvenile, mental health, sealed or expunged records released. Will fax documents $.50 1st page, $.25 each add'l page. Court makes copy: $.25 per page. Certification fee: $1.00 per cert plus copy fee. Payee: Clerk of Court. Personal checks accepted. Credit cards only accepted through INK. Prepayment required. Mail requests: SASE required for civil.

Civil Name Search: Access: Mail, in person, online. Both court and visitors may perform in person name searches. Search fee: $12.00 per hour. Civil records on computer from 1991, microfiche from 1900s, index cards from 1800s, archives from 1800s. Mail turnaround time 3-5 days. Civil PAT goes back to 1991. **For details about the state's online access to records, see the section at the front or back of this chapter.**

Criminal Name Search: Access: In person, online. Visitors must perform in person searches themselves. Criminal records computerized from 1991, microfiche from 1900s, index cards from 1800s, archives from 1800s. Criminal PAT goes back to same as civil. **For details about the state's online access to records, see the section at the front or back of this chapter.**

Ellsworth County

District Court 210 N Kansas St, Ellsworth, KS 67439-3118; 785-472-3832; fax: 785-472-5712; 8AM-5PM (CST). *Felony, Misdemeanor, Civil, Eviction, Small Claims, Probate.*

General Information: No juvenile, mental health, sealed or expunged records released. Will fax documents $.50 per page. Court makes copy: $.35 per page. No certification fee . Payee: District Court. Personal checks accepted. No credit cards accepted. Prepayment required. Mail requests: SASE required.

Civil Name Search: Access: Phone, fax, mail, in person, online. Both court and visitors may perform in person name searches. No search fee. Civil records on computer from 1994, microfiche from 1900s, books from late 1800s. Mail turnaround time 1-2 days. **For details about the state's online access to records, see the section at the front or back of this chapter.**

Criminal Name Search: Access: Phone, fax, mail, in person, online. Both court and visitors may perform in person name searches. No search fee. Required to search: name, years to search; also helpful: SSN. Criminal records computerized from 1994, microfiche from 1900s, books from late 1800s. Mail turnaround time 1-2 days. **For details about the state's online access to records, see the section at the front or back of this chapter.**

Finney County

District Court PO Box 798, Garden City, KS 67846; criminal phone: 620-271-6132; civil phone: 620-271-6121; fax: 620-271-6140; 8AM-4PM (CST). *Felony, Misdemeanor, Civil, Eviction, Small Claims, Probate.*

General Information: No juvenile, Mental health, sealed or expunged records released. Court makes copy: $.25 per page, $1.00 minimum. Certification fee: $1.00 per doc, plus copy fee. Payee: District Court. Personal checks accepted. Prepayment required.

Civil Name Search: Access: In person, online. Visitors must perform in person searches themselves. Civil records on computer from 1991, microfiche from 1900s, index books from 1900s. Civil PAT goes back to 1991. **For details about the state's online access to records, see the section at the front or back of this chapter.**

Criminal Name Search: Access: In person, online. Visitors must perform in person searches themselves. Criminal records computerized from 1991, microfiche from 1900s, index books from 1900s. Criminal PAT

goes back to same as civil. **For details about the state's online access to records, see the section at the front or back of this chapter.**

Ford County

District Court 101 W Spruce, Dodge City, KS 67801; 620-227-4609; criminal phone: 620-227-4608; civil phone: 620-227-4610; probate phone: 620-277-4606; fax: 620-227-6799; 8AM-5PM (CST). *Felony, Misdemeanor, Civil, Eviction, Small Claims, Probate.*
www.kscourts.org/Districts/District-Info.asp?d=16

General Information: Probate fax is same as main fax number. No juvenile, mental health, sealed or expunged records released. Fee to fax specific case file $1.00 per page. Court makes copy: $.25 per page. Self serve copy: same. Certification fee: $1.00 per document plus copy fee. Payee: Clerk of District Court. Personal checks accepted. No credit cards accepted. Prepayment required.

Civil Name Search: Access: Mail, in person, online. Both court and visitors may perform in person name searches. Search fee: $12.00 per hour. Required to search: name, case number. Civil records on computer back to 10/1991, microfiche/film from 1900s, index books from 1900s. Mail turnaround time 3 days. Civil PAT goes back to 10/1991. **For details about the state's online access to records, see the section at the front or back of this chapter.**

Criminal Name Search: Access: In person, online. Both court and visitors may perform in person name searches. Search fee: $12.00 per hour. Required to search: name, case number. Criminal records computerized from 10/1991, microfiche/film from 1900s, index books from 1900s. Note: Criminal record searches for military employment are referred to KBI or Division of Motor Vehicles. Criminal PAT goes back to same as civil. **For details about the state's online access to records, see the section at the front or back of this chapter.**

Franklin County

District Court PO Box 637 (301 S Main), Ottawa, KS 66067; 785-242-6000; fax: 785-242-5970; 8AM-N, 1PM-4PM (CST). *Felony, Misdemeanor, Civil, Eviction, Small Claims, Probate.*
www.franklincoks.org/4thdistrict/

General Information: Probate fax is same as main fax number. No juvenile, mental health, sealed or expunged records released. Will fax documents to local or toll free line. Court makes copy: $.25 per page. Certification fee: $1.00 plus copy fee. Payee: Clerk of District Court. Personal checks accepted. Credit cards accepted. Prepayment required. Mail requests: SASE required for civil.

Civil Name Search: Access: Mail, fax, in person, online. Both court and visitors may perform in person name searches. Search fee: $12.00 per hour. Civil records on computer back to 1979, index books from 1800s. Mail turnaround time 1-3 days. Civil PAT goes back to 1979. **For details about the state's online access to records, see the section at the front or back of this chapter.** Also, access to probate court records is free at www.kscourts.org/dstcts/4frprrec.htm. Access to county marriage records is by alpha search for free at www.kscourts.org/dstcts/4frmarec.htm.

Criminal Name Search: Access: In person, online. Visitors must perform in person searches themselves. Required to search: name, years to search, SSN. Criminal records computerized from 1980, index books from 1800s. Criminal PAT goes back to 1980. Online access to criminal docket and calendars is the same as civil. Online results show name only.

Geary County

District Court PO Box 1147, Junction City, KS 66441; 785-762-5221; fax: 785-762-4420; 9AM-5PM (CST). *Felony, Misdemeanor, Civil, Eviction, Small Claims, Probate.* www.8thjd.com

General Information: No juvenile, adoption, mental health, sealed or expunged records released. Fee to fax out file $2.00 per page. Court makes copy: $.25 per page, $1.00 minimum. Certification fee: $1.00. Exemplification fee- $2.00. Payee: Clerk of Court. Personal checks accepted. No credit cards accepted. Prepayment required. Mail requests: SASE required.

Civil Name Search: Access: Mail, in person, email, online. Visitors must perform in person searches themselves. Search fee: $12.00 per hour. Civil records on computer from 1992, microfiche, index books and archives from 1894. Note: Direct email record requests to gecdc@8thjd.com Mail turnaround time 3 days. Civil PAT goes back to 1992. **For details about the state's online access to records, see the section at the front or back of this chapter.**

Criminal Name Search: Access: Mail, in person, email, online. Both court and visitors may perform in person name searches. Search fee: $12.00 per hour. Required to search: name, charges, date of offense. Criminal records computerized from 1992, microfiche, index books and archives from 1894. Note: Direct email record requests to gecdc@oz-online.net. Mail turnaround time 3 days. Criminal PAT goes back to same as civil. **For details about the state's online access to records, see the section at the front or back of this chapter.**

Gove County

District Court PO Box 97, 470 Broad St, Gove, KS 67736; 785-938-2310; fax: 785-938-2312; 8AM-N, 1-5PM (CST). *Felony, Misdemeanor, Civil, Eviction, Small Claims, Probate.*
www.23rdjudicial.org

General Information: No juvenile, mental health, sealed or expunged records released. Fee to fax out file $1.00 per page. Court makes copy: $.25 per page. Self serve copy: same. Certification fee: $1.00. Payee: Clerk of District Court. Personal checks accepted. No credit cards accepted. Prepayment required. Mail requests: SASE required.

Civil Name Search: Access: Fax, mail, in person, online. Both court and visitors may perform in person name searches. Search fee: $12.00 per hour. Civil records on computer from 1992, index books from 1890 through present. Mail turnaround time 1-2 days. Civil PAT goes back to 1992. **For details about the state's online access to records, see the section at the front or back of this chapter.** Case filings from previous week available online at the county site.

Criminal Name Search: Access: Fax, mail, in person, online. Both court and visitors may perform in person name searches. Search fee: $12.00 per hour. Criminal records computerized from 1992, index books from 1890 through present. Mail turnaround time 1-2 days. Criminal PAT goes back to 1992. **For details about the state's online access to records, see the section at the front or back of this chapter.**

Graham County

District Court 410 N Pomeroy, Ste 9, Hill City, KS 67642; 785-421-3458; fax: 785-421-5463; 8AM-5PM (CST). *Felony, Misdemeanor, Civil, Eviction, Small Claims, Probate.*

General Information: Probate is a separate index at this same address. Probate fax- 785-421-5463 No juvenile, mental health, sealed or expunged records released. Will fax documents to local or toll free line. Court makes copy: $.25 per page. Certification fee: $1.00 per instrument plus copy fee. Payee: Clerk of District Court. Personal checks accepted. No credit cards accepted. Prepayment required. Mail requests: SASE required.

Civil Name Search: Access: In person, online. Visitors must perform in person searches themselves. Civil index on docket books from 1880s; computerized records go back to 2004. **For details about the state's online access to records, see the section at the front or back of this chapter.**

Criminal Name Search: Access: Mail, in person, online. Visitors must perform in person searches themselves. Search fee: $12.00 per hour. Required to search: name, years to search, DOB; also helpful: SSN, signed release. Criminal records indexed in books from 1880s; computerized records go back to 2004. Mail turnaround time 2 days. **For details about the state's online access to records, see the section at the front or back of this chapter.**

Grant County

District Court 108 S Glenn St, Ulysses, KS 67880; 620-356-1526; fax: 620-353-2131; 8AM-N, 1-5PM (CST). *Felony, Misdemeanor, Civil, Eviction, Small Claims, Probate.*

General Information: Search includes both civil and criminal indexes. Court will perform searches as time permits. No juvenile, mental health, sealed or expunged records released. Will not fax documents. Court makes copy: $.50 per page. Certification fee: $1.00 per seal. Payee: District Court. Personal checks accepted. No credit cards accepted. Prepayment required.

Civil Name Search: Access: Mail, fax, in person, online. Visitors must perform in person searches themselves. Search fee: $12.80 per hour. Civil records on computer from 1977, microfiche index from 1880s. Mail turnaround time 2-7 days. Civil PAT goes back to 1977. **For details about the state's online access to records, see the section at the front or back of this chapter.**

Criminal Name Search: Access: In person, online. Visitors must perform in person searches themselves. Search fee: $12.80 per hour. Criminal records computerized from 1977, microfiche index from 1880s. Note: This court often refers searchers to the state Bureau of investigations, including in-person searchers. Mail turnaround time 2-7 days. Criminal PAT goes back to 1977. **For details about the state's online access to records, see the section at the front or back of this chapter.**

Gray County

District Court PO Box 487, 300 S Main, Cimarron, KS 67835; 620-855-3812; fax: 620-855-7037; 8AM-5PM (CST). *Felony, Misdemeanor, Civil, Eviction, Small Claims, Probate.*
www.kscourts.org/Districts/District-Info.asp?d=16

General Information: To access public records send a fax or written request to : Gray County District Court, PO Box 487, Cimarron, KS 67835. No juvenile, mental health, sealed or expunged records released. Will fax documents $1.00 per page. Court makes copy: $.50 per page. Self serve copy: $.25 per page. Certification fee: $1.00. Payee: Clerk of District Court. Personal checks accepted. No credit cards accepted. Prepayment required. Mail requests: SASE required.

Civil Name Search: Access: Fax, mail, in person, online. Visitors must perform in person searches themselves. Search fee: $12.00 per hour. Required to search: name; also helpful: years to search. Civil records on computer from 1990, index books from 1800s. Note: To access public records send a written request to Gray County District Court, PO Box 487, Cimarron, KS 67835. Fax requests must be pre-paid. Civil PAT goes back to 1990. **For details about the state's online access to records, see the section at the front or back of this chapter.**

Criminal Name Search: Access: Fax, mail, in person, online. Visitors must perform in person searches themselves. Search fee: $12.00 per hour. Required to search: name, years to search; also helpful: address, DOB. Criminal records computerized from 1990, index books from 1800s. Note: Fax requests must be pre-paid. Criminal records search for employment, credit, and the like shall be referred to the executive branch agency most likely to have files, e.g. KS Bureau of Investigation or Division of Vehicles. Mail turnaround time 1 day. Criminal PAT goes back to same as civil. **For details about the state's online access to records, see the section at the front or back of this chapter.**

Greeley County

District Court PO Box 516, Tribune, KS 67879; 620-376-4292; fax: 620-376-2351; 8AM-N, 1-5PM (MST). *Felony, Misdemeanor, Civil, Eviction, Small Claims (limited civil), Probate.*

General Information: No juvenile, mental health, sealed or expunged records released. Will fax documents $1.00 per page. Court makes copy: $.50 per page. Certification fee: $1.00 per doc plus copy fee. Payee: Clerk of the District Court. Personal checks accepted. No credit cards accepted. Prepayment required.

Civil Name Search: Access: In person, online. Visitors must perform in person searches themselves. Required to search: name. Civil records on hardcopy index from beginning. Civil PAT goes back to 1986. **For details about the state's online access to records, see the section at the front or back of this chapter.**

Criminal Name Search: Access: In person, fax, online. Visitors must perform in person searches themselves. Required to search: name, DOB. Criminal records on hardcopy index from beginning. Criminal PAT goes back to 1986. **For details about the state's online access to records, see the section at the front or back of this chapter.**

Greenwood County

District Court 311 N Main, Eureka, KS 67045; 620-583-8153; fax: 620-583-6818; 8AM-5PM (CST). *Felony, Misdemeanor, Civil, Eviction, Small Claims, Probate.* www.13thjudicial.org/

General Information: Email questions to clerk@greenwoodcourt.com No juvenile, mental health, sealed or expunged records released. Will fax documents to local or toll free line. Court makes copy: $.50 per page. Certification fee: $1.00. Payee: Clerk of Court. Personal checks accepted. No credit cards accepted. Prepayment required. Mail requests: SASE required.

Civil Name Search: Access: Mail, in person, online. Both court and visitors may perform in person name searches. Search fee: $12.00 per hour. Required to search: name, case number. Civil records on computer from 1993, index from 1800s. Mail turnaround time 1-3 days. Civil PAT goes back to 1993. Identifiers in results varies. **For details about the state's online access to records, see the section at the front or back of this chapter.**

Criminal Name Search: Access: Mail, in person, online. Both court and visitors may perform in person name searches. Search fee: $12.00 per hour if search performed by court personnel. Required to search: name, case number. Criminal records computerized from 1993, index from 1800s. Mail turnaround time 1-3 days. Criminal PAT goes back to 1993. Identifiers in results varies. **For details about the state's online access to records, see the section at the front or back of this chapter.**

Hamilton County

District Court PO Box 745, Syracuse, KS 67878; 620-384-5159; fax: 620-384-7806; 8AM-5PM (MST). *Felony, Misdemeanor, Civil, Eviction, Small Claims, Probate.*

General Information: Probate fax is same as main fax number. No juvenile, mental health, sealed or expunged records released. Will fax specific case file $1.00 per page. Court makes copy: $.25 per page. Self serve copy: same. Certification fee: $1.00. Payee: Clerk of District Court. Personal checks accepted. No credit cards accepted. Prepayment required.

Civil Name Search: Access: In person, online. Visitors must perform in person searches themselves. Civil records on computer from 1985, microfiche, archives and index cards from 1880s. Civil PAT goes back to 1985. **For details about the state's online access to records, see the section at the front or back of this chapter.**

Criminal Name Search: Access: In person, online. Visitors must perform in person searches themselves. Criminal records computerized from 1985, microfiche, archives and index cards from 1880s. Criminal PAT goes back to same as civil. **For details about the state's online access to records, see the section at the front or back of this chapter.**

Harper County

District Court PO Box 467, 201 N Jennings, Anthony, KS 67003; 620-842-3721; fax: 620-842-6025; 8AM-N, 1-5PM (CST). *Felony, Misdemeanor, Civil, Eviction, Small Claims, Probate.*

General Information: No juvenile, mental health, sealed or expunged records released. Will fax documents $1.00 per page. Court makes copy: $.25 per page. Certification fee: $1.00 per cert. Payee: Clerk of District Court. Personal checks accepted. No credit cards accepted. Prepayment required.

Civil Name Search: Access: In person, online. Visitors must perform in person searches themselves. Civil records on computer from 1976, microfiche, index books and archives from 1887. Civil PAT goes back to 1970's. Terminal results include driver license info (height, weight, color of eyes). **For details about the state's online access to records, see the section at the front or back of this chapter.**

Criminal Name Search: Access: In person, online. Visitors must perform in person searches themselves. Required to search: name, years to search, SSN. Criminal records computerized from 1976, index books and archives from 1887. Criminal PAT goes back to same as civil. Results include driver license information (height, weight, color of eyes). **For details about the state's online access to records, see the section at the front or back of this chapter.**

Harvey County

District Court PO Box 665, Newton, KS 67114-0665; 316-284-6890; criminal phone: 316-284-6896; civil phone: 316-284-6894; probate phone: 316-284-6824; fax: 316-283-4601; 9AM-5PM (CST). *Felony, Misdemeanor, Civil, Eviction, Small Claims, Probate.*

General Information: No juvenile, mental health, sealed or expunged records released. Will fax documents $1.00 per page. Court makes copy: $.50 per page. Self serve copy: same. Certification fee: $1.00. Payee: Clerk of District Court. Personal checks accepted. No credit cards accepted. Prepayment required. Mail requests: SASE helpful.

Civil Name Search: Access: Mail, fax, in person, email, online. Both court and visitors may perform in person name searches. Search fee: $12.00 per hour. Civil index on docket books from 1800s; on computer back to mid 1970s. Note: Direct email civil record requests to deenaj@9thdistct.net Mail turnaround time 3-5 days. Public use terminal available, records go back to 1960's. **For details about the state's online access to records, see the section at the front or back of this chapter.**

Criminal Name Search: Access: Mail, fax, in person, online. Both court and visitors may perform in person name searches. Search fee: $12.00 per name. Required to search: name, years to search, DOB; also helpful-SSN, signed release. Criminal records computerized since 1960s, archived from 1800s. Note: Call KBI for thorough statewide search. Mail turnaround time 3-5 days. Public use terminal available, crim records go back to same **For details about the state's online access to records, see the section at the front or back of this chapter.**

Haskell County

District Court PO Box 146, Sublette, KS 67877; 620-675-2671; fax: 620-675-8599; 8AM-5PM (CST). *Felony, Misdemeanor, Civil, Eviction, Small Claims, Probate.*

General Information: No juvenile, mental health, sealed or expunged records released. Will fax documents $3.00 plus $.25 per page. Court makes copy: $.50 per page. Self serve copy: same. Certification fee: $1.00 per document. Payee: Clerk of District Court. Personal checks accepted. No credit cards accepted. Prepayment required. Mail requests: SASE requested for civil.

Civil Name Search: Access: Mail, fax, in person, online. Both court and visitors may perform in person name searches. Search fee: $12.00 per hour. Civil records on computer from 1990, index books from 1874. Civil PAT goes back to 1990. **For details about the state's online access to records, see the section at the front or back of this chapter.**

Criminal Name Search: Access: In person, online. Visitors must perform in person searches themselves. Criminal records computerized from 1990, index books from 1874. Criminal PAT goes back to 1990. **For details about the state's online access to records, see the section at the front or back of this chapter.**

Hodgeman County

District Court PO Box 187, Jetmore, KS 67854; 620-357-6522; fax: 620-357-6216; 8AM-5PM (CST). *Felony, Misdemeanor, Civil, Eviction, Small Claims, Probate.*
www.kscourts.org/Districts/District-Info.asp?d=24

General Information: Probate is a separate index at this same address. Probate fax is same as main fax number. No juvenile, mental health, sealed or expunged records released. Will fax documents $.50 per page. Court makes copy: $.25 per page. Certification fee: $1.00 per page plus copy fee. Payee: Clerk of Court. Personal checks accepted. No credit cards accepted.

Prepayment required. Must prepay for mail and fax. Mail requests: SASE required for civil.

Civil Name Search: Access: Phone, fax, mail, in person, online. Both court and visitors may perform in person name searches. Search fee: $12.00 per hour. Civil index on cards and books from 1800s. Mail turnaround time 1-2 days. **For details about the state's online access to records, see the section at the front or back of this chapter.**

Criminal Name Search: Access: In person, online. Visitors must perform in person searches themselves. Criminal records indexed on cards and books from 1800s. **For details about the state's online access to records, see the section at the front or back of this chapter.**

Jackson County

District Court 400 New York Ave, #311, Holton, KS 66436; 785-364-2191; fax: 785-364-3804; 8AM-4:30PM (CST). *Felony, Misdemeanor, Civil, Eviction, Small Claims, Probate.*

General Information: No juvenile, mental health, sealed or expunged records released. Will fax documents $2.00 per 10 pages. Court makes copy: $.25 per page. Self serve copy: same. Certification fee: $1.00. Payee: Clerk of District Court. Personal checks accepted. No credit cards accepted. Prepayment required.

Civil Name Search: Access: In person, online. Visitors must perform in person searches themselves. Civil index on cards from 1800s, recent records computerized. Civil PAT goes back to 1850s. Results include height, weight, race if known. **For details about the state's online access to records, see the section at the front or back of this chapter.**

Criminal Name Search: Access: In person, online. Visitors must perform in person searches themselves. Criminal records indexed on cards from 1800s, recent records computerized. Criminal PAT goes back to same as civil. Results include height, weight, race of known. **For details about the state's online access to records, see the section at the front or back of this chapter.**

Jefferson County

District Court PO Box 327, Oskaloosa, KS 66066; 785-863-2461; fax: 785-863-2369; 8AM-4PM (CST). *Felony, Misdemeanor, Civil, Eviction, Small Claims, Probate.*
www.jfcountyks.com/index.aspx?nid=174

General Information: No juvenile, mental health, sealed or expunged records released. Will fax documents to local or toll-free number. Court makes copy: $.25 per page. Self serve copy: $.10 per page. Certification fee: $1.00. Payee: District Court. Personal checks accepted. No credit cards accepted. Prepayment required.

Civil Name Search: Access: In person, online. Visitors must perform in person searches themselves. Civil records on computer since 1/77, on index books from 1855. Civil PAT goes back to 1977. **For details about the state's online access to records, see the section at the front or back of this chapter.**

Criminal Name Search: Access: In person, online. Visitors must perform in person searches themselves. Required to search: name, years to search; SSN helpful. Criminal records indexed in books from 1855, computerized since 1/77. Criminal PAT goes back to same as civil. **For details about the state's online access to records, see the section at the front or back of this chapter.**

Jewell County

District Court 307 N Commercial, Mankato, KS 66956; 785-378-4030; fax: 785-378-4035; 8AM-5PM (CST). *Felony, Misdemeanor, Civil, Eviction, Small Claims, Probate.*
www.kscourts.org/Districts/District-Info.asp?d=12

General Information: No juvenile, mental health, adoption, sealed or expunged records released. Will fax documents $3.00 per page. Court makes copy: $.25 per page. Certification fee: $1.25. Payee: District Court. Personal checks accepted. No credit cards accepted. Prepayment required. Mail requests: SASE required for mail return of any copies.

Civil Name Search: Access: In person, online. Both court and visitors may perform in person name searches. Search fee: $12.00 per hour. Civil index on docket books from 1871. Civil PAT goes back to 1995. **For details about the state's online access to records, see the section at the front or back of this chapter.**

Criminal Name Search: Access: In person, online. Both court and visitors may perform in person name searches. Search fee: $12.00 per hour. Criminal records indexed in books from 1871. Criminal PAT goes back to same as civil. **For details about the state's online access to records, see the section at the front or back of this chapter.**

Johnson County

District Court 100 N Kansas, Olathe, KS 66061; 913-715-3480; criminal phone: 913-715-3460; civil phone: 913-715-3400, or 3500; criminal fax: 913-715-3481; civil fax: 8AM-5PM; 8AM-5PM (CST). *Felony, Misdemeanor, Civil, Eviction, Small Claims, Probate.*
www.jococourts.org/

General Information: Search requests should be made to the Records Center, phone 913-715-3480. Court says that non-online requests for criminal record "searches" for employment, credit, or will be referred to Records Dept at Kansas Bureau of Investigation, 785-296-8200. Online identifiers in results same as on public terminal. No juvenile, mental health, sealed or expunged records released. No employment searches. Will fax documents $2.50 per page. Court makes copy: $.50 per page. Certification fee: $1.00 per cert, Authentication fee $2.00 per authentication. Payee: Clerk of the District Court. Cashiers checks and money orders accepted. Major credit cards accepted. Prepayment required.

Civil Name Search: Access: Phone, Mail, In person, online. Both court and visitors may perform in person name searches. Search fee: $12.00 per hour. Civil records on computer from 1980, microfiche, archives and index prior. Note: Records Management is on the 2nd Fl. Civil PAT goes back to 1968. Search Johnson County District Court records available free at www.jococourts.org with index back to 1980. **For details about the state's online access to records, see the section at the front or back of this chapter.**

Criminal Name Search: Access: In person, online. Both court and visitors may perform in person name searches. Search fee: $12.00 per hour. Criminal records computerized from 1980, microfiche, archives and index prior. Criminal PAT goes back to same as civil. Search Johnson County District Court records available free at www.jococourts.org with index back to 1980. Online results show name only.

Kearny County

District Court PO Box 64, 304 N Main, Lakin, KS 67860; 620-355-6481; fax: 620-355-7462; 8AM-N,1-5PM (CST). *Felony, Misdemeanor, Civil, Eviction, Small Claims, Probate.*

www.kscourts.org/districts/Courthouse-info.asp?d=25&cid=89

General Information: No juvenile, mental health, adoption, sealed or expunged records released. Will fax documents $1.00 per page prepaid. Court makes copy: $.25 per page. Self serve copy: same. Certification fee: $1.00. Payee: District Court. Personal checks accepted. No credit cards accepted. Prepayment required. Mail requests: SASE required.

Civil Name Search: Access: Mail, in person, online. Visitors must perform in person searches themselves. Search fee: $12.00 per hour; but court will only search if you provide a case number. Civil records on computer from 1991, index books from 1900s. Note: A case number must be provided with mail search requests. Mail turnaround time 3 days. Civil PAT goes back to 6/1991. **For details about the state's online access to records, see the section at the front or back of this chapter.**

Criminal Name Search: Access: Mail, in person, online. Visitors must perform in person searches themselves. Search fee: $12.00 per hour, but court will only search if you provide a case number. Criminal records computerized from 1991, index books from 1900s. Note: A case number must be provided with mail search requests. Mail turnaround time 3 days. Criminal PAT goes back to same as civil. **For details about the state's online access to records, see the section at the front or back of this chapter.**

Kingman County

District Court PO Box 495 (130 N Spruce St), Kingman, KS 67068; 620-532-5151; fax: 620-532-2952; 8AM-N, 1-5PM (CST). *Felony, Misdemeanor, Civil, Eviction, Small Claims, Probate.*

www.kscourts.org/Districts/District-Info.asp?d=30

General Information: Probate fax is same as main fax number. No juvenile, mental health, sealed or expunged records released. Fee to fax out file $1.00 per page. Court makes copy: $.25 per page. Self serve copy: same. Certification fee: $1.00 per pleading plus copy fee. Payee: Clerk of Court. Personal checks accepted. No credit cards accepted. Prepayment required. Mail requests: SASE required.

Civil Name Search: Access: Mail, fax, in person, online. Both court and visitors may perform in person name searches. Search fee: $12.00 per hour. Civil records on computer from 1990, microfiche, archives and index cards from 1800s. Mail turnaround time 1-2 days. Civil PAT goes back to 1980s. **For details about the state's online access to records, see the section at the front or back of this chapter.**

Criminal Name Search: Access: Mail, fax, in person. Both court and visitors may perform in person name searches. Search fee: $12.00 per hour. Required to search: name, years to search; also helpful: case type. Criminal records computerized from 1990, microfiche, archives and index cards from 1800s. Mail turnaround time 1-2 days. Criminal PAT goes back to same as civil. **For details about the state's online access to records, see the section at the front or back of this chapter.**

Kiowa County

District Court 211 E Florida, Greensburg, KS 67054; 620-723-3317; fax: 620-723-2970; 8AM-5PM (CST). *Felony, Misdemeanor, Civil, Eviction, Small Claims, Probate.*

www.kscourts.org/Districts/District-Info.asp?d=16

General Information: Probate fax is same as main fax number. No juvenile, mental health, sealed or expunged records released. Fee to fax out file $1.00 per page. Court makes copy: $.25 per page. Certification fee: $1.00. Payee: Clerk of District Court. Personal checks accepted. No credit cards accepted. Prepayment required. Mail requests: SASE required.

Civil Name Search: Access: Fax, mail, in person, online. Both court and visitors may perform in person name searches. Search fee: $12.00 per hour. Civil records archived and on index books from 1800s; computerized back to 1980. Mail turnaround time 7 days. Civil PAT goes back to 1900's. **For details about the state's online access to records, see the section at the front or back of this chapter.**

Criminal Name Search: Access: Fax, mail, in person, online. Both court and visitors may perform in person name searches. Search fee: $12.00 per hour. Required to search: name, years to search, signed release; also helpful: DOB. Criminal records archived and on index books from 1800s; computerized back to 1940. Mail turnaround time 7 days. Criminal PAT goes back to same as civil. **For details about the state's online access to records, see the section at the front or back of this chapter.**

Labette County

District Court - Oswego Courthouse, 501 Merchant, 3rd Fl, Oswego, KS 67356; 620-795-4533 x350; fax: 620-795-3056; 8AM-4PM (CST). *Felony, Misdemeanor, Civil, Eviction, Small Claims, Probate.*

General Information: Probate fax is same as main fax number. no juvenile, adoption, mental health, sealed or expunged records released. Will fax documents, fee is $2.50 per page. Court makes copy: $.25 per page. Self serve copy: same. Certification fee: $1.00 per certification. Payee: Clerk of District Court. Personal checks accepted. No credit cards accepted. Prepayment required. Mail requests: SASE required.

Civil Name Search: Access: In person, mail, fax, online. Visitors must perform in person searches themselves. Search fee: $12.00 per hr; $6.00 min. Civil records on computer since 1992. Civil PAT goes back to 1994. **For details about the state's online access to records, see the section at the front or back of this chapter.**

Criminal Name Search: Access: In person, mail, fax, online. Visitors must perform in person searches themselves. Search fee: $12.00 per hr; $6.00 min. Required to search: name, years to search; also helpful: DOB, SSN. Criminal records on computer since 1992. Criminal PAT goes back to same as civil. Results include year of birth. **For details about the state's online access to records, see the section at the front or back of this chapter.**

District Court - Parsons 201 S Central, Parsons, KS 67357; 620-421-4120; fax: 620-421-3633; 8AM-4PM (CST). *Felony, Misdemeanor, Civil, Eviction, Small Claims, Probate.*

General Information: No juvenile, adoption, mental health, sealed or expunged records released. Will fax documents $2.50 per page fee. Court makes copy: $.25 per page. Certification fee: $1.00 per cert. Payee: Clerk of District Court. Personal checks accepted. Visa/MC accepted. Prepayment required. Mail requests: SASE required.

Civil Name Search: Access: Mail, fax, in person, online. Both court and visitors may perform in person name searches. Search fee: $12.00 per hr; $6.00 min. Civil records on computer from 1992, index books from 1874. Mail turnaround time 1-2 days. Civil PAT goes back to 1992. **For details about the state's online access to records, see the section at the front or back of this chapter.**

Criminal Name Search: Access: Mail, fax, in person. Both court and visitors may perform in person name searches. Search fee: $12.00 per hr; $6.00 min. Criminal records computerized from 1992, index books from 1874. Mail turnaround time 1-2 days. Criminal PAT goes back to same as civil. **For details about the state's online access to records, see the section at the front or back of this chapter.**

Lane County

District Court PO Box 188, 144 S Lane, Dighton, KS 67839; 620-397-2805; fax: 620-397-5526; 8AM-5PM (CST). *Felony, Misdemeanor, Civil, Eviction, Small Claims, Probate.*

www.kscourts.org/Districts/District-Info.asp?d=24

General Information: No juvenile, mental health, sealed or expunged records released. Will not fax documents. Court makes copy: $.25 per page. Certification fee: $1.00 per page plus copy fee. Payee: Clerk of Court. Personal checks accepted. Money order and cash accepted. No credit cards accepted. Prepayment required. Mail requests: SASE required.

Civil Name Search: Access: Mail, in person, online. Both court and visitors may perform in person name searches. Search fee: $12.00 per name. Civil records on computer since 1993; prior records from 1800s. Mail turnaround time 1 week. Civil PAT goes back to 2000. **For details about the state's online access to records, see the section at the front or back of this chapter.**

Criminal Name Search: Access: Mail, in person, online. Visitors must perform in person searches themselves. Search fee: $12.00 per name. Required to search: name, years to search; also helpful: SSN. Criminal records on computer since 1993; prior records from 1800s. Mail turnaround time 1 week. Criminal PAT goes back to 2000. **For details about the state's online access to records, see the section at the front or back of this chapter.**

Leavenworth County

District Court Leavenworth Justice Center, 601 S 3rd St, #3051, Leavenworth, KS 66048; 913-684-0700; criminal phone: 913-684-0704; civil phone: 913-684-0701; fax: 913-684-0492; 8AM-5PM (CST). *Felony, Misdemeanor, Civil, Eviction, Small Claims, Probate.*
www.leavenworthcounty.org/home.asp

General Information: No juvenile, mental health, sealed or expunged records released. Will fax documents $1.00 per page, prepaid. Court makes copy: $.25 per page. Self serve copy: same. Certification fee: $1.00 per page plus copy fee. Payee: Clerk of District Court. Personal checks accepted. No credit cards accepted. Prepayment required. Mail requests: SASE required.

Civil Name Search: Access: Mail, in person, online. Both court and visitors may perform in person name searches. Search fee: $12.00 per hour, if extensive. Civil records on computer from 1990, microfiche to 1952 and index books from 1901. Mail turnaround time 3-4 days. Civil PAT goes back to 1990. **For details about the state's online access to records, see the section at the front or back of this chapter** s.

Criminal Name Search: Access: Mail, in person, online. Visitors must perform in person searches themselves. Search fee: $12.00 per hour, if extensive. Required to search: name, years to search; also helpful: SSN. Criminal records computerized from 1990, microfiche and index books from 1960. Mail turnaround time 3-4 days. Criminal PAT goes back to same as civil. **For details about the state's online access to records, see the section at the front or back of this chapter.**

Lincoln County

District Court 216 E Lincoln Ave, Lincoln, KS 67455; 785-524-4057; fax: 785-524-3204; 8AM-N, 1-5PM (CST). *Felony, Misdemeanor, Civil, Eviction, Small Claims, Probate.*
www.kscourts.org/Districts/District-Info.asp?d=12

General Information: Probate fax is same as main fax number. No juvenile, mental health, sealed or expunged records released. Will fax documents $3.00 per page. Court makes copy: $.25 per page. Certification fee: $1.00 per document. Payee: Clerk of Court. Personal checks accepted. No credit cards accepted. Prepayment required.

Civil Name Search: Access: Fax, mail, in person, online. Only the court performs in person name searches; visitors may not. No search fee. Required to search: name; also helpful: years to search. All records on computer. **For details about the state's online access to records, see the section at the front or back of this chapter.**

Criminal Name Search: Access: In person, phone, online. Both court and visitors may perform in person name searches. No search fee. Required to search: name; also helpful: years to search, DOB, SSN. Criminal records on computer since 1980, on index cards from 1880. Note: Will search 1 name by phone only, maybe. Public use terminal has crim records back to 2007. **For details about the state's online access to records, see the section at the front or back of this chapter.**

Linn County

District Court PO Box 350, 318 Chestnut St., Mound City, KS 66056-0350; 913-795-2660; fax: 913-795-2004; 8AM-4:30PM (CST). *Felony, Misdemeanor, Civil, Eviction, Small Claims, Probate.*
www.kscourts.org/dstcts/6linnco.htm

General Information: Probate fax is same as main fax number. No juvenile, mental health, sealed or expunged records released. Will not fax out case files. Court makes copy: $.25 per page. Certification fee: $1.50. Payee: Clerk of District Court. No personal checks or credit cards accepted. Prepayment required.

Civil Name Search: Access: In person, online. Visitors must perform in person searches themselves. Civil records on computer from 1990, archives and index books from 1854. Civil PAT goes back to 1800s. **For details about the state's online access to records, see the section at the front or back of this chapter.**

Criminal Name Search: Access: In person, online. Visitors must perform in person searches themselves. Criminal records computerized from 1990, archives and index books from 1886. Criminal PAT goes back to 1975. **For details about the state's online access to records, see the section at the front or back of this chapter.**

Logan County

District Court 710 W 2nd St, Oakley, KS 67748-1233; 785-671-3654; fax: 785-671-3517; 8:30AM-N, 1-5PM (CST). *Felony, Misdemeanor, Civil, Eviction, Small Claims, Probate.*

General Information: No juvenile, mental health, sealed or expunged records released. Will fax documents $1.00 per page. Court makes copy: $.25 per page. Certification fee: $1.00; authentication- $2.00. Payee: Clerk of

District Court. Personal checks accepted. No credit cards accepted. Prepayment required.

Civil Name Search: Access: In person, online. Visitors must perform in person searches themselves. Required to search: name; also helpful: years to search. Civil records on computer back to 1887. Civil PAT goes back to 1887. **For details about the state's online access to records, see the section at the front or back of this chapter.**

Criminal Name Search: Access: In person, online. Visitors must perform in person searches themselves. Required to search: name; SSN helpful, years to search. Criminal records computerized from 1887. Criminal PAT goes back to same as civil. **For details about the state's online access to records, see the section at the front or back of this chapter.**

Lyon County

District Court 430 Commercial St, Emporia, KS 66801; 620-341-3287; fax: 620-341-3497; 8AM-4PM (CST). *Felony, Misdemeanor, Civil, Eviction, Small Claims, Probate, Traffic.* www.5thjd.org/

General Information: Probate fax is same as main fax number. No mental health, sealed or expunged records released. Will fax documents $1.00 per page. Court makes copy: $.50 per page. Certification fee: $2.00 per document plus copy fee. Payee: Lyon County District Court. Personal checks accepted. No credit cards accepted. Prepayment required.

Civil Name Search: Access: In person, online. Visitors must perform in person searches themselves. Records maintained since 1859. Mail turnaround time 3 days maximum. Civil PAT goes back to 1998. Personal identifiers shown on terminal may or may not include DOB, address, SSN and middle initial. **For details about the state's online access to records, see the section at the front or back of this chapter.**

Criminal Name Search: Access: Fax, mail, in person, online. Both court and visitors may perform in person name searches. No search fee. Records maintained since 1859. Note: All requests for criminal searches referred to Kansas Bureau of Investigations (KBI). Criminal PAT goes back to same as civil. Personal identifiers shown on terminal may or may not include DOB, address, SSN and middle initial. **For details about the state's online access to records, see the section at the front or back of this chapter.**

Marion County

District Court 200 S Third, 201, Marion, KS 66861; 620-382-2104; fax: 620-382-2259; 8AM-5PM (CST). *Felony, Misdemeanor, Civil, Eviction, Small Claims, Probate.*
www.8thjd.com

General Information: Probate fax is same as main fax number. No juvenile, mental health, sealed or expunged records released. Will not fax out case files. Court makes copy: $1.00 per page; $.25 each after 1st 4. Certification fee: $1.00 per cert. Payee: District Court. Personal checks accepted. No credit cards accepted. Prepayment required.

Civil Name Search: Access: In person, online. Visitors must perform in person searches themselves. Civil records on computer from 7/1992, on index cards from 1800s. Civil PAT goes back to 1992. **For details about the state's online access to records, see the section at the front or back of this chapter.**

Criminal Name Search: Access: In person, online. Visitors must perform in person searches themselves. Criminal records computerized from 7/1992, on index cards from 1800s. Criminal PAT goes back to same as civil. **For details about the state's online access to records, see the section at the front or back of this chapter.**

Marshall County

District Court PO Box 149, 1201 Broadway, Office #5, Marysville, KS 66508; 785-562-5301; fax: 785-562-2458; 8AM-5PM; Search hours: 8:30AM-4:30PM (CST). *Felony, Misdemeanor, Civil, Eviction, Small Claims, Probate.* www.kansas.gov/

General Information: No juvenile, offender under 14 years of age, no child in need of care, mental health, sealed or expunged records released. Will fax documents $2.00 1st page, $1.00 each add'l. Prepayment required. Court makes copy: $.50 first page, $.25 each add'l. Certification fee: $1.00. Payee: Clerk of Court. Personal checks accepted. No credit cards accepted. Prepayment required. Mail requests: SASE required.

Civil Name Search: Access: Fax, mail, in person, online. Both court and visitors may perform in person name searches. Search fee: $12.00 per hour. Civil records on computer from 1980, microfiche from 1977 (earlier records on roll-marriage licenses on computer index 1860s, forward/naturalizations. Mail turnaround time 1-2 days. Civil PAT goes back to 1980. **For details about the state's online access to records, see the section at the front or back of this chapter.**

Criminal Name Search: Access: Fax, mail, in person, online. Both court and visitors may perform in person name searches. Search fee: $12.00 per hour. Criminal records computerized from 1986, microfiche from 1977. Mail turnaround time 1-2 days. Criminal PAT goes back to 1982. **For details about the state's online access to records, see the section at the front or back of this chapter.**

McPherson County

District Court PO Box 1106, McPherson, KS 67460; 620-241-3422; fax: 620-241-1372; 8AM-5PM (CST). *Felony, Misdemeanor, Civil, Eviction, Small Claims, Probate.*

www.mcphersoncountyks.us/index.aspx?NID=9

General Information: No juvenile, mental health, sealed or expunged records released. Will fax documents $1.00 per page. Court makes copy: $.50 per page. Certification fee: $1.00. Payee: District Court. Personal checks accepted. Prepayment required. Mail requests: SASE required.

Civil Name Search: Access: Mail, in person, online. Both court and visitors may perform in person name searches. Search fee: $12.00 per hour. Civil records on microfilm from 1953, index cards from 1900s. Mail turnaround time 1-3 days. Civil PAT goes back to 1980s. **For details about the state's online access to records, see the section at the front or back of this chapter.**

Criminal Name Search: Access: Mail, in person, online. Both court and visitors may perform in person name searches. Search fee: $12.00 per hour. Required to search: name, years to search; also helpful: SSN. Criminal records on microfilm from 1953, index cards from 1900s. Mail turnaround time 1-3 days. Criminal PAT goes back to same as civil. **For details about the state's online access to records, see the section at the front or back of this chapter.**

Meade County

District Court PO Box 623, Meade, KS 67864; 620-873-8750; fax: 620-873-8759; 8AM-5PM (CST). *Felony, Misdemeanor, Civil, Eviction, Small Claims, Probate.*

www.kscourts.org/Districts/District-Info.asp?d=16

General Information: All employment background checks requested by mail, phone, or fax are referred to the KBI (state agency for criminal records). No juvenile, mental health, sealed or expunged records released. Will fax documents $2.00 1st page, $.50 each add'l. Court makes copy: $.25 per page. Certification fee: $1.00 per page plus copy fee. Payee: Clerk of Court. Personal checks accepted. No credit cards accepted. Prepayment required. Mail requests: SASE required.

Civil Name Search: Access: Fax, mail, in person, online. Both court and visitors may perform in person name searches. Search fee: $12.00 per search. Civil records on computer from 1990, index cards from 1896. Mail turnaround time 2-3 days Civil PAT goes back to 1992. **For details about the state's online access to records, see the section at the front or back of this chapter.**

Criminal Name Search: Access: Fax, mail, in person, online. Both court and visitors may perform in person name searches. Search fee: $12.00 per search. Criminal records computerized from 1990, index cards from 1896. Mail turnaround time is 2-3 days. Criminal PAT goes back to 1992. **For details about the state's online access to records, see the section at the front or back of this chapter.**

Miami County

District Court PO Box 187, 120 S Pearl St, Paola, KS 66071; 913-294-3326; fax: 913-294-2535; 8AM-3:30PM, W closed Noon hour (CST). *Felony, Misdemeanor, Civil, Eviction, Small Claims, Probate.*

General Information: No juvenile, mental health, sealed or expunged records released. Will fax specific document for $.50 per page. Court makes copy: $.50 per page. Self serve copy: $.25 per page. Certification fee: $1.50 per page. Payee: District Court. Personal checks accepted. No credit cards accepted. Prepayment required.

Civil Name Search: Access: In person, online. Visitors must perform in person searches themselves. Civil records on computer from 1984, index cards from 1890s. Civil PAT goes back to 1987. **For details about the state's online access to records, see the section at the front or back of this chapter.**

Criminal Name Search: Access: In person, online. Both court and visitors may perform in person name searches. Required to search: name, years to search; SSN helpful. Criminal records computerized from 1984, index cards from 1890s. Criminal PAT goes back to same as civil. **For details about the state's online access to records, see the section at the front or back of this chapter.**

Mitchell County

District Court 115 S Hersey, Beloit, KS 67420; 785-738-3753; fax: 785-738-4101; 8AM-5PM (CST). *Felony, Misdemeanor, Civil, Eviction, Small Claims, Probate.* www.kscourts.org/Districts/District-Info.asp?d=12

General Information: Probate is a separate index at this same address. Probate fax is same as main fax number. No juvenile, mental health, sealed or expunged records released. Will fax documents. Court makes copy: $.25 per page. Self serve copy: same. Certification fee: $1.00 per page plus copy fee. Payee: Clerk of Court. Personal checks accepted. No credit cards accepted. Prepayment required. Mail requests: SASE required.

Civil Name Search: Access: Mail, in person, online. Both court and visitors may perform in person name searches. Search fee: $5.00 per name.

Civil index on cards from 1876. Mail turnaround time 1-2 days. Civil PAT goes back to 2003. **For details about the state's online access to records, see the section at the front or back of this chapter.**

Criminal Name Search: Access: Mail, in person, online. Both court and visitors may perform in person name searches. Search fee: $5.00 per name. Criminal records indexed on cards from 1977, archived to 1870. Mail turnaround time 1-2 days. Criminal PAT goes back to 2003. **For details about the state's online access to records, see the section at the front or back of this chapter.**

Montgomery County

Independence District Court 300 E Main St, #201, Independence, KS 67301; 620-330-1070; fax: 620-331-6120; 8AM-N 1-4PM (CST). *Felony, Misdemeanor, Civil, Eviction, Small Claims, Probate.*

General Information: No juvenile, adoptions, mental health, sealed or expunged records released. Will fax documents $5.00 1st page, $1.00 each add'l. Court makes copy: $.25 per page. Certification fee: $1.00. Payee: Clerk of Court. Personal checks accepted. No credit cards accepted. Prepayment required.

Civil Name Search: Access: Fax, mail, in person, online. Both court and visitors may perform in person name searches. Search fee: $12.00 per hour. $6.00 minimum. Civil records on computer since 1992, on microfiche from 1870-1930, archives 1930-1992, index cards from 1870. Note: This court covers civil cases for the northern part of the county. It is suggested to search both courts. Mail turnaround time 72 hours. Civil PAT goes back to 1993. **For details about the state's online access to records, see the section at the front or back of this chapter.**

Criminal Name Search: Access: Fax, mail, in person, online. Both court and visitors may perform in person name searches. Search fee: $12.00 per hour. $6.00 minimum. Required to search: name, years to search; also helpful: SSN. Criminal records on computer since 1992, on microfiche from 1870-1930, archives 1930-1992, index cards from 1870. Mail turnaround time 72 hours. Criminal PAT goes back to same as civil. **For details about the state's online access to records, see the section at the front or back of this chapter.**

Coffeyville District Court 102 W 7th St, #A, Coffeyville, KS 67337; 620-251-1060; fax: 620-251-2734; 8:AM-N, 1-4PM (CST). *Civil, Eviction, Small Claims, Probate, Traffic.*

General Information: This court covers civil cases for the southern part of the county, although cases can be filed in either court. It is recommended to search both courts No juvenile, mental health, sealed, adoption, or expunged records released. Fee to fax out file $1.00 per page. Court makes copy: $.25 per page. Certification fee: $1.00 per page plus copy fee. Payee: Clerk of Court. Personal checks accepted. No credit cards accepted. Prepayment required. Mail requests: SASE requested.

Civil Name Search: Access: Fax, mail, in person, online. Both court and visitors may perform in person name searches. Search fee: $12.80 per hour; $6.00 minimum. Civil records on computer back to 1992, on paper, fiche, etc. since 1924. Mail turnaround time 72 hours. Public use terminal has civil records. **For details about the state's online access to records, see the section at the front or back of this chapter.**

Morris County

District Court County Courthouse, 501 W Main St, Council Grove, KS 66846; 620-767-6838; fax: 620-767-6488; 8AM-5PM (CST). *Felony, Misdemeanor, Civil, Eviction, Small Claims, Probate.*

www.8thjd.com

General Information: Will fax documents $1.00 per page. Court makes copy: $.25 per page. Certification fee: $1.00. Payee: Clerk of Court. Personal checks accepted. No credit cards accepted. Prepayment required. Mail requests: SASE required.

Civil Name Search: Access: Fax, mail, in person, online. Both court and visitors may perform in person name searches. Search fee: $12.00 per hour. Civil records on computer since 1992, on microfiche, archives and index cards from 1860. Mail turnaround time 1-2 days. Civil PAT goes back to 1992. **For details about the state's online access to records, see the section at the front or back of this chapter.**

Criminal Name Search: Access: Fax, mail, in person, online. Both court and visitors may perform in person name searches. Search fee: $12.00 per hour. Criminal records on computer since 1992, on microfiche, archives and index cards from 1860. Mail turnaround time 1-2 days. Criminal PAT goes back to same as civil. **For details about the state's online access to records, see the section at the front or back of this chapter.**

Morton County

District Court PO Box 825, 1025 Morton St, Elkhart, KS 67950; 620-697-2563; fax: 620-697-4289; 8AM-N, 1-5PM (CST). *Felony, Misdemeanor, Civil, Eviction, Small Claims, Probate.*

General Information: Probate fax is same as main fax number. No juvenile, mental health, sealed or expunged records released. Fee to fax out file: $3.00 1st pg.; $.50 each add'l. Court makes copy: $.50 per page. Self serve copy: same. Certification fee: $1.00 per certification. Payee: Clerk of Court. Two party checks not accepted. No credit cards accepted. Prepayment required.

Civil Name Search: Access: Mail, fax, in person, online. Both court and visitors may perform in person name searches. Search fee: $12.80 per hour. Civil records on computer from 1800s. Mail turnaround time same day. Civil PAT goes back to 1992. **For details about the state's online access to records, see the section at the front or back of this chapter.**

Criminal Name Search: Access: In person, online. Visitors must perform in person searches themselves. Criminal records computerized from 1800s. Criminal PAT goes back to 1977. **For details about the state's online access to records, see the section at the front or back of this chapter.**

Nemaha County

District Court PO Box 213, Seneca, KS 66538; 785-336-2146; fax: 785-336-6450; 8AM-5PM (CST). *Felony, Misdemeanor, Civil, Eviction, Small Claims, Probate.*

General Information: Court also holds marriage records. No juvenile, mental health, sealed or expunged records released. Will fax documents $1.00 per page. Court makes copy: $.25 per page. Certification fee: $1.00. Payee: Clerk of District Court. Business checks accepted. No credit cards accepted for copies or searches. Prepayment required. Mail requests: SASE required.

Civil Name Search: Access: Phone, mail, in person, online. Both court and visitors may perform in person name searches. Search fee: $12.00 per hour. Civil records on computer from 1977, index cards from 1870. Mail turnaround time 1-2 days. Civil PAT goes back to 1977. The name and sex of the defendant is on search results. **For details about the state's online access to records, see the section at the front or back of this chapter.**

Criminal Name Search: Access: In person, online. Visitors must perform in person searches themselves. Required to search: name, years to search, SSN. Criminal records computerized from 1977, index cards from 1870. Criminal PAT goes back to 1977. The sex of the defendant is also on search results. **For details about the state's online access to records, see the section at the front or back of this chapter.**

Neosho County

Erie District Court PO Box 19, Neosho County Courthouse, Erie, KS 66733; 620-244-3831; fax: 620-244-3830; 8AM-N, 1-4:30PM (CST). *Felony, Misdemeanor, Civil, Eviction, Small Claims, Probate.* www.31stjudicialdistrict.org/

General Information: There are two courts for the county. The web page gives hearing results and information concerning service of process in Chapter 61 cases and includes information covering the previous month. No juvenile, mental health, sealed or expunged records released. Fee to fax out file $1.00 per page. Court makes copy: $.50 per page. Certification fee: $1.00. Payee: Clerk of Court. Personal checks accepted. No credit cards accepted. Prepayment required. Mail requests: SASE required.

Civil Name Search: Access: Fax, mail, in person, online. Both court and visitors may perform in person name searches. Search fee: $12.00 per name. Civil index on cards from 1900s; on computer back to 1993. Mail turnaround time 1-3 days. Civil PAT goes back to 1993. **For details about the state's online access to records, see the section at the front or back of this chapter.** Also, court calendars, limited action hearing results, and service results appear online on the court website.

Criminal Name Search: Access: Mail, in person, online. Visitors must perform in person searches themselves. Search fee: $12.00 per name. Required to search: name, years to search, DOB. Criminal records indexed on cards from 1900s; on computer back to 1993. Note: Limited mail searches are okay, lists should be sent to the central state agency. Searches for employment, credit or the like are referred to KBI. Mail turnaround time 1-3 days. Criminal PAT goes back to same as civil. **For details about the state's online access to records, see the section at the front or back of this chapter.**

Chanute District Court 102 S Lincoln, PO Box 889, Chanute, KS 66720; 620-431-5700; Option 2; fax: 620-431-5710; 8AM-5PM (CST). *Felony, Misdemeanor, Civil, Eviction, Small Claims.* www.31stjudicialdistrict.org

General Information: There are two courts for the county. No juvenile, mental health, sealed or expunged records released. Fee to fax out file $1.00 per page. Court makes copy: $.50 per page. Certification fee: $1.00 per cert plus copy fee. Payee: Clerk of District Court. Personal checks accepted. No credit cards accepted. Prepayment required.

Civil Name Search: Access: Mail, in person, online. Both court and visitors may perform in person name searches. Search fee: $12.00 per hour. Civil records on computer since 1993; prior back to 1955. Civil PAT goes back to 1993. **For details about the state's online access to records, see the section at the front or back of this chapter.** Also, court calendars, limited action hearing results, and service results appear on the court website.

Criminal Name Search: Access: In person, online. Both court and visitors may perform in person name searches. Search fee: $12.00 per hour per name. Criminal records on computer since 1993; prior back to 1955. Criminal PAT goes back to same as civil. Court calendars, limited action hearing results, and service results appear on the court website. **For details about the state's online access to records, see the section at the front or back of this chapter**

Ness County

District Court PO Box 445, 100 S Kansas, Courthouse, Ness City, KS 67560; 785-798-3693; fax: 785-798-3348; 8AM-5PM (CST). *Felony, Misdemeanor, Civil, Eviction, Small Claims, Probate.*

General Information: Probate is a separate index at this same address. Probate fax is same as main fax number. No juvenile, mental health, sealed or expunged records released. Fee to fax out file $1.00 per page. Court makes copy: $.25 per page. Self serve copy: same. Certification fee: $1.00 per page plus copy fee. Payee: Clerk of Court. Personal checks accepted. No credit cards accepted. Prepayment required.

Civil Name Search: Access: Fax, mail, in person, online. Both court and visitors may perform in person name searches. Search fee: $12.00 per name. Civil index on docket books from 1885. Mail turnaround time 1 week. Civil PAT goes back to 2003. **For details about the state's online access to records, see the section at the front or back of this chapter.**

Criminal Name Search: Access: Fax, mail, in person, online. Visitors must perform in person searches themselves. Search fee: $12.00 per name. Criminal records indexed in books from 1885. Note: Court prefers that you use a local retriever to do searches; the court rarely performs them for the public. Mail turnaround time 1 week. Criminal PAT goes back to same as civil. Terminal results sometimes shows DOB. **For details about the state's online access to records, see the section at the front or back of this chapter.**

Norton County

District Court PO Box 70, Norton, KS 67654; 785-877-5720; fax: 785-877-5722; 8AM-5PM (CST). *Felony, Misdemeanor, Civil, Eviction, Small Claims, Probate.*

General Information: No juvenile, mental health, sealed or expunged records released. Will fax documents to local or toll free line. Court makes copy: $.25 per page. Self serve copy: same. Certification fee: $1.00. Payee: Clerk of District Court. Personal checks accepted. No credit cards accepted. Prepayment required. Mail requests: SASE required.

Civil Name Search: Access: Mail, in person, online. Both court and visitors may perform in person name searches. Search fee: $12.00 per hour. Civil docket indexed from 1900s. Mail turnaround time 1 week. Civil PAT goes back to 2004. **For details about the state's online access to records, see the section at the front or back of this chapter.**

Criminal Name Search: Access: Mail, in person, online. Visitors must perform in person searches themselves. Search fee: $12.00 per hour. Criminal records indexed from 1900s. Mail turnaround time 1 week. Criminal PAT goes back to same as civil. **For details about the state's online access to records, see the section at the front or back of this chapter.**

Osage County

District Court PO Box 549, Lyndon, KS 66451; 785-828-4514; fax: 785-828-4704; 8AM-N,1-4PM (CST). *Felony, Misdemeanor, Civil, Eviction, Small Claims, Probate.* www.franklincoks.org/4thdistrict/

General Information: Also, see www.kscourts.org/districts/District-Info.asp?d=4. Online identifiers in results same as on public terminal. No juvenile, mental health, sealed or expunged records released. Will not fax documents. Court makes copy: $.25 per page. Certification fee: $1.00. Payee: Clerk of Court. Business checks accepted. Prepayment required.

Civil Name Search: Access: In person, online. Visitors must perform in person searches themselves. Civil records on computer from 1980. Civil PAT goes back to 1980. Current court calendars are free online at www.franklincoks.org/4thdistrict/osagebydate.html. **For details about the state's online access to records, see the section at the front or back of this chapter.**

Criminal Name Search: Access: In person, online. Visitors must perform in person searches themselves. Criminal records computerized from 1980. Note: This agency will NOT do name searches. Contact the KBI state agency. Criminal PAT goes back to 1980. Current court calendars are free online at www.franklincoks.org/4thdistrict/osagebydate.html. Also, access to old probate court and marriage records is free at www.kscourts.org/dstcts/4osco.htm. Online results show name only.

Osborne County

District Court PO Box 160, 423 W Main, Osborne, KS 67473; 785-346-5911; fax: 785-346-5992; 8AM-N, 1-5PM (CST). *Felony, Misdemeanor, Civil, Eviction, Small Claims, Probate.*

General Information: Court will search criminal and civil indexes for single fee, if requested. No juvenile, mental health, sealed or expunged records released. Will fax documents $.50 per page. Court makes copy: $.25 per page. Certification fee: $1.00 per doc. Payee: Clerk of District Court. Personal checks accepted. Money order and cash accepted. No credit cards accepted. Prepayment required.

Civil Name Search: Access: Mail, fax, in person, online. Visitors must perform in person searches themselves. Search fee: $12.00 per hour. Civil records on microfiche from 1872-1980, index books from 1981, index cards from 1872. Mail turnaround time 3 days. **For details about the state's online access to records, see the section at the front or back of this chapter.**

Criminal Name Search: Access: Mail, fax, in person, online. Both court and visitors may perform in person name searches. Search fee: $12.00 per hour. Required to search: name, years to search; also helpful: SSN. Criminal records on microfiche from 1872-1980, index books from 1981, index cards from 1872. Mail turnaround time 3 days. **For details about the state's online access to records, see the section at the front or back of this chapter.**

Ottawa County

District Court 307 N Concord, Minneapolis, KS 67467; 785-392-2917; fax: 785-392-3626; 8AM-N;1-5PM (CST). *Felony, Misdemeanor, Civil, Eviction, Small Claims, Probate.*

www.ottawacounty.org/DistrictCourt/tabid/3388/Default.aspx

General Information: Archival searches done as spare time permits. Probate fax is same as main fax number. No juvenile, mental health, sealed or expunged records released. Will fax documents to local or toll-free number. Court makes copy: $.50 per page. Self serve copy: same. Certification fee: $2.00 per doc plus copy fee. Payee: Clerk of District Court. Personal checks accepted. No credit cards accepted. Prepayment required.

Civil Name Search: Access: Mail, fax, in person, online. Both court and visitors may perform in person name searches. Search fee: $9.00 per hour. Civil docket indexed from 1800s; computerized records since 1990. Mail turnaround time 3 days. Civil PAT goes back to 2000. **For details about the state's online access to records, see the section at the front or back of this chapter.**

Criminal Name Search: Access: In person, online. Both court and visitors may perform in person name searches. No search fee. Required to search: name, years to search; SSN helpful. Criminal records indexed from 1800s; computerized records since 1990. Criminal PAT goes back to 1999. Criminal records on terminal may not be complete. **For details about the state's online access to records, see the section at the front or back of this chapter**

Pawnee County

District Court PO Box 270, Larned, KS 67550; 620-285-6937; fax: 620-285-3665; 8AM-5PM (CST). *Felony, Misdemeanor, Civil, Eviction, Small Claims, Probate.* www.kscourts.org/Districts/District-Info.asp?d=24

General Information: No juvenile, mental health, sealed or expunged records released. Will fax documents $.50 per page. Court makes copy: $.25 per page. Self serve copy: same. Certification fee: $1.00 per page plus copy fee. Payee: Clerk of District Court. Personal checks accepted. No credit cards accepted. Prepayment required. Mail requests: SASE required.

Civil Name Search: Access: Fax, mail, in person, online. Both court and visitors may perform in person name searches. Search fee: $12.00 an hour. Civil records on computer from 2002, index cards from 1900s. Mail turnaround time 1 day. Civil PAT goes back to 2002. **For details about the state's online access to records, see the section at the front or back of this chapter.**

Criminal Name Search: Access: Fax, mail, in person, online. Visitors must perform in person searches themselves. Search fee: $12.00 an hour. Required to search: name, years to search; also helpful: SSN. Criminal records computerized from 2002, index cards from 1900s. Mail turnaround time 1-2 days. Criminal PAT goes back to 2002. **For details about the state's online access to records, see the section at the front or back of this chapter.**

Phillips County

District Court PO Box 564, 301 State St, Phillipsburg, KS 67661; 785-543-6830; fax: 785-543-6832; 8AM-5PM (CST). *Felony, Misdemeanor, Civil, Eviction, Small Claims, Probate.*

General Information: No mental health, sealed or expunged records released. Will fax documents $.50 per page. Court makes copy: $.25 per page. Certification fee: $1.00 per cert. Payee: Clerk of District Court. Personal checks accepted. No credit cards accepted. Prepayment required. Mail requests: SASE required for criminal.

Civil Name Search: Access: Mail, fax, in person, online. Visitors must perform in person searches themselves. No search fee. Civil cases indexed by defendant, plaintiff; also helpful: DOB, SSN. Civil docket indexed from 1900s; on computer back to 2004. Civil PAT goes back to 2/2004. **For details about the state's online access to records, see the section at the front or back of this chapter.**

Criminal Name Search: Access: Mail, fax, in person, online. Both court and visitors may perform in person name searches. Search fee: $12.00 per hour. Required to search: name, years to search; also helpful: DOB, SSN. Criminal records indexed from 1900s; on computer back to 2004. Mail turnaround time 2 days. Criminal PAT goes back to same as civil. **For details about the state's online access to records, see the section at the front or back of this chapter.**

Pottawatomie County

District Court PO Box 129, Westmoreland, KS 66549; 785-457-3392; fax: 785-457-2107; 8AM-4PM (CST). *Felony, Misdemeanor, Civil, Eviction, Small Claims, Probate.*

General Information: No juvenile, mental health, sealed or expunged records released. Will only fax results to attorneys involved in cases for $2.00 plus $.25 per page after the 1st 2 pages. Court makes copy: $.25 per page. Self serve copy: same. Certification fee: $2.00 per doc. Payee: Clerk of District Court. Personal checks accepted. No credit cards accepted for record research. Prepayment required.

Civil Name Search: Access: In person, online. Visitors must perform in person searches themselves. Civil records computerized since 1998, on microfiche from 1800s, index from 1800s. Civil PAT goes back to 1997. **For details about the state's online access to records, see the section at the front or back of this chapter.**

Criminal Name Search: Access: In person, online. Visitors must perform in person searches themselves. Required to search: name, years to search; SSN helpful. Criminal records computerized since 1998, on microfiche from 1800s, index from 1800s. Criminal PAT goes back to same as civil. **For details about the state's online access to records, see the section at the front or back of this chapter.**

Pratt County

District Court PO Box 984, Pratt, KS 67124; 620-672-4100; fax: 620-672-2902; 8AM-N, 1-5PM (CST). *Felony, Misdemeanor, Civil, Eviction, Small Claims, Probate.*

www.kscourts.org/Districts/District-Info.asp?d=30

General Information: Probate fax is same as main fax number. No juvenile, mental health, sealed or expunged records released. Fee to fax out file $1.00 per page. Court makes copy: $.25 per page. Certification fee: $1.00 per item. Payee: Clerk of District Court. Personal checks accepted. No credit cards accepted. Prepayment required. Mail requests: SASE required.

Civil Name Search: Access: Mail, fax, in person, online. Both court and visitors may perform in person name searches. Search fee: $12.00 per hour, 15 minute minimum. Civil records on computer back to 1988, microfiche, archives, index from 1878. Mail turnaround time 48 hours. Civil PAT goes back to 1988. **For details about the state's online access to records, see the section at the front or back of this chapter.**

Criminal Name Search: Access: In person, online. Both court and visitors may perform in person name searches. Search fee: $12.00 per hour. Required to search: name, years to search, DOB; also helpful: SSN, signed release. Criminal records computerized from 1988, microfiche, archives, index from 1878. Criminal PAT goes back to same as civil. **For details about the state's online access to records, see the section at the front or back of this chapter.**

Rawlins County

District Court 607 Main, #F, Atwood, KS 67730; 785-626-3465; fax: 785-626-3350; 8AM-12; 1PM-5PM (CST). *Felony, Misdemeanor, Civil, Eviction, Small Claims, Probate.*

General Information: No juvenile, mental health, sealed or expunged records released. Court makes copy: $.25 per page. Certification fee: $1.00. Payee: Clerk of District Court. Only in-state checks accepted. No credit cards accepted. Prepayment required.

Civil Name Search: Access: In person, online. Visitors must perform in person searches themselves. Civil docket indexed from 1900s in books. Civil PAT goes back to 3/2004. **For details about the state's online access to records, see the section at the front or back of this chapter.**

Criminal Name Search: Access: In person, online. Visitors must perform in person searches themselves. Criminal records indexed from 1900s in books. Note: This agency refers requesters to the Kansas Bureau of Investigations. Criminal PAT goes back to same as civil. **For details about the state's online access to records, see the section at the front or back of this chapter.**

Reno County

District Court 206 W 1st, Hutchinson, KS 67501; 620-694-2956; fax: 620-694-2958; 8AM-N, 1-5PM (CST). *Felony, Misdemeanor, Civil, Eviction, Small Claims, Probate.*

General Information: Court will charge a $5.00 fee upfront before providing record services. No mental health, juvenile (some), sealed or expunged records released. Will not fax documents. Court makes copy: $.25 per page. Certification fee: $1.00 per certificate; $2.00 per authorization. Payee: Clerk of District Court. Personal checks accepted. No credit cards accepted. Prepayment required. Mail requests: SASE required.

Civil Name Search: Access: Mail, in person, online. Visitors must perform in person searches themselves. Search fee: $12.00 per hour, if in storage then $20.00. Civil records on computer from 1/1992, index cards from 1900s. Note: Court personnel will only search pre-1/1992 records. Mail turnaround time 3-5 days in-state; 3-10 days out-of-state. Civil PAT goes back to 1/1992. **For details about the state's online access to records, see the section at the front or back of this chapter.**

Criminal Name Search: Access: Mail, In person, online. Visitors must perform in person searches themselves. Search fee: $12.00 per hour, if in storage then $20.00. Required to search: name, years to search, DOB, signed release; also helpful: address, SSN. Criminal records computerized from 1992, index cards from 1900s. Note: Court personnel here will only search pre-1/1992 records at a rate of $1.00 per 5 minutes. Mail turnaround time 3-5 days (requestor in-state); 3-10 days (out-of-state). Criminal PAT goes back to same as civil. Online access to criminal records back to 4/2003 is the same as civil. Online results show name only. Also, court recommends the statewide criminal history check system at www.accesskansas.org/kbi/criminalhistory/.

Republic County

District Court PO Box 8, Belleville, KS 66935; 785-527-7234; fax: 785-527-5029; 8AM-5PM (CST). *Felony, Misdemeanor, Civil, Eviction, Small Claims, Probate.*

www.kscourts.org/Districts/District-Info.asp?d=12

General Information: Probate is a separate index at the same address. Probate fax is same as main fax number. No juvenile, mental health, sealed or expunged records released. Will fax documents $3.00 per page. Court makes copy: $.25 per page. Certification fee: $1.00 per document plus copy fee. Payee: Clerk of Court. Personal checks accepted. No credit cards accepted. Prepayment required. Mail requests: SASE required for civil.

Civil Name Search: Access: Mail, in person, online. Both court and visitors may perform in person name searches. Search fee: $12.00 per hour. Records computerized since 2004. Civil and probate records indexed from 1869. Mail turnaround time 3-7 days. Civil PAT goes back to 2004. **For details about the state's online access to records, see the section at the front or back of this chapter.**

Criminal Name Search: Access: In person, online. Visitors must perform in person searches themselves. Criminal records indexed from 1869. Criminal PAT goes back to 1/2004. **For details about the state's online access to records, see the section at the front or back of this chapter.**

Rice County

District Court 101 W Commercial, Lyons, KS 67554; 620-257-2383; fax: 620-257-3826; 8AM-5PM (CST). *Felony, Misdemeanor, Civil, Eviction, Small Claims, Probate.*

www.ricecounty.us

General Information: Probate fax is same as main fax number. No juvenile unless designated by judge, mental health, sealed or expunged records released. Fee to fax document $.50 per page. Court makes copy: $1.00 first page, $.25 each add'l. Self serve copy: same. No certification fee . Payee: Clerk of Court. Personal checks accepted. No credit cards accepted. Prepayment required. Mail requests: SASE required.

Civil Name Search: Access: Fax, mail, in person, online. Both court and visitors may perform in person name searches. Search fee: $12.00 per hour. Civil records on computer from 1880. Note: The court will not process lists of name searches. Mail turnaround time 3 days. Civil PAT goes back to 1880s. There are no identifiers on records up thru 2003; from 2004 some record have DOBs. **For details about the state's online access to records at the front or back of this chapter.**

Criminal Name Search: Access: In person, online. Visitors must perform in person searches themselves. Required to search: name, years to search; also helpful: SSN. Criminal records index on computer from 1880. Note: The court will not process lists of name searches. These criminal searches are referred to the KBI. Mail turnaround time 1-3 days. Criminal PAT goes back to same as civil. There are no identifiers on records up thru 2003; from 2004 some record have DOBs. **For details about the state's online access to records, see the section at the front or back of this chapter.**

Riley County

District Court PO Box 158, Manhattan, KS 66505-0158; 785-537-6364; fax: 785-537-6382; 9AM-4PM (CST). *Felony, Misdemeanor, Civil, Eviction, Small Claims, Probate.*

General Information: No mental health, sealed or expunged records released. Will not fax documents. Court makes copy: $.25 per page. Certification fee: $1.00 plus copy fee. Payee: Clerk of Court. Personal checks accepted. No credit cards accepted. Prepayment required.

Civil Name Search: Access: In person, online. Visitors must perform in person searches themselves. Civil records on computer back to 10/93; prior records in index journals. Note: The court or visitors may perform the in person search for dates after 7/2003. Civil PAT goes back to 1993. **For details about the state's online access to records, see the section at the front or back of this chapter.**

Criminal Name Search: Access: In person, online. Visitors must perform in person searches themselves. Required to search: name, years to search; also helpful: DOB, SSN. Criminal records computerized from 1986, microfiche, archives and index cards from 1900s. Note: The court or visitors may perform the in person search for dates after 7/2003. Criminal PAT goes back to 1986. **For details about the state's online access to records, see the section at the front or back of this chapter.**

Rooks County

District Court 115 N Walnut, PO Box 532, Stockton, KS 67669; 785-425-6718; fax: 785-425-6568; 8AM-5PM closed 12-1 (CST). *Felony, Misdemeanor, Civil, Eviction, Small Claims, Probate.*

www.23rdjudicial.org/Rooks/Rooks.html

General Information: No juvenile, adoption, mental health, sealed or expunged records released. Fee to fax out file $2.50 1st page and $1.50 ea add'l. Court makes copy: $.25 per page. Self serve copy: same. Certification fee: $2.00. Payee: Clerk of Court. Personal checks accepted. No credit cards accepted. Prepayment required. Mail requests: SASE required for civil.

Civil Name Search: Access: Mail, in person, online. Both court and visitors may perform in person name searches. Search fee: $12.80 per hour. Civil index on cards from 1888; on computer since 1995. Mail turnaround time 1-3 days. Civil PAT goes back to 1995. **For details about the state's online access to records, see the section at the front or back of this chapter.**

Criminal Name Search: Access: In person, online. Both court and visitors may perform in person name searches. No search fee. Required to search: name, years to search; also helpful: DOB, SSN. Criminal records indexed on cards from 1888; on computer since. Note: The court personnel will not do criminal record searches for the public. Criminal PAT goes back to 1996. Online access to criminal records is the same as civil. Case filings from previous week available on the court website. Online results show name only.

Rush County

District Court PO Box 387, 715 Elm, La Crosse, KS 67548; 785-222-2718; fax: 785-222-2748; 8AM-5PM (CST). *Felony, Misdemeanor, Civil, Eviction, Small Claims, Probate.*

www.kscourts.org/Districts/District-Info.asp?d=24

General Information: Probate is separate index at this same address. Probate fax is same as main fax number. No juvenile, mental health, sealed or expunged records released. Will fax documents $.50 per page. Court makes copy: $.25 per page. Self serve copy: same. Certification fee: $1.00 per page plus copy fee. Payee: Clerk of District Court. Personal checks accepted. No credit cards accepted. Prepayment required. Mail requests: SASE required for civil.

Civil Name Search: Access: Phone, fax, mail, in person, online. Both court and visitors may perform in person name searches. Search fee: $12.00 per hour. Civil records on computer from 4/2003, on index from 1800s. Mail turnaround time 3 days. Civil PAT goes back to 2003. **For details about the state's online access to records, see the section at the front or back of this chapter.**

Criminal Name Search: Access: In person, online. Visitors must perform in person searches themselves. Search fee: $12.00. Required to search: name, years to search; SSN helpful. Criminal records computerized from 4/2003, on index from 1800s. Criminal PAT goes back to same as civil. **For details about the state's online access to records, see the section at the front or back of this chapter.**

Russell County

District Court PO Box 876, 401 N Main St, Russell, KS 67665; 785-483-5641; fax: 785-483-2448; 8AM-5PM (CST). *Felony, Misdemeanor, Civil, Eviction, Small Claims, Probate.*

General Information: Court will search criminal and civil for the single sear fee, if asked. No juvenile, mental health, sealed or expunged records released. Fee to fax document $.50 per page. Court makes copy: $.50 per page. Self serve copy: $.50 per page. No certification fee . Payee: Clerk of Court. Personal checks accepted. No credit cards accepted. Prepayment required. Mail requests: SASE required.

Civil Name Search: Access: Fax, mail, in person, online. Both court and visitors may perform in person name searches. Search fee: $12.00 per hour. Civil records on computer from 1990, index cards from 1900s. Mail turnaround time 3 days. Civil PAT goes back to 1990. **For details about**

the state's online access to records, see the section at the front or back of this chapter.

Criminal Name Search: Access: Fax, mail, in person, online. Both court and visitors may perform in person name searches. Search fee: $12.00 per hour. Required to search: name, years to search, DOB. Criminal records computerized from 1990, index cards from 1900s. Mail turnaround time 3 days. Criminal PAT goes back to same as civil. **For details about the state's online access to records, see the section at the front or back of this chapter.**

Saline County

District Court PO Box 1760, 300 S Ash St, Salina, KS 67402-1760; 785-309-5831; civil phone: 785-309-5836; fax: 785-309-5845; 8AM-4PM (CST). *Felony, Misdemeanor, Civil, Eviction, Small Claims, Probate.*

General Information: You can fax in requests and phone the following day to follow up. Clerk recommends following up on mailed requests also via phone. No juvenile, mental health, sealed or expunged records released. Will not fax documents. Court makes copy: $.25 per page. Certification fee: $1.00 per cert. Payee: Clerk of District Court. Personal checks accepted. No credit cards accepted. Prepayment required.

Civil Name Search: Access: Mail, in person, online. Both court and visitors may perform in person name searches. Search fee: $12.00 per hour. Required to search: name, years to search, address. Civil records on computer from 1990, index from early 1900s. Mail turnaround time 1 week. Civil PAT goes back to 2003. **For details about the state's online access to records, see the section at the front or back of this chapter.**

Criminal Name Search: Access: Mail, in person, online. Both court and visitors may perform in person name searches. Search fee: $12.00 per hour. Required to search: name, years to search, address, DOB, SSN, signed release. Criminal records computerized from 1990, index from early 1900s. Mail turnaround time 1 week. Criminal PAT goes back to 2003. **For details about the state's online access to records, see the section at the front or back of this chapter.**

Scott County

District Court 303 Court St, Scott City, KS 67871; 620-872-7208; fax: 620-872-3683; 8AM-N, 1-5PM (CST). *Felony, Misdemeanor, Civil, Eviction, Small Claims, Probate.*

General Information: No juvenile, mental health, sealed or expunged records released. Fee to fax out file $1.00 per page. Court makes copy: $.25 per page. Certification fee: $1.00 per cert. Payee: Clerk of Court. Personal checks accepted. No credit cards accepted. Prepayment required. Mail requests: SASE required.

Civil Name Search: Access: Mail, fax, in person, online. Both court and visitors may perform in person name searches. Search fee: $12.00 per hour per custodian of records' estimate. Civil records on computer back to 1992, index cards from 1980s. Mail turnaround time 2-3 days. Civil PAT goes back to 1992. Results may include DOB or address, but not always. **For details about the state's online access to records, see the section at the front or back of this chapter.**

Criminal Name Search: Access: In person, online, mail. Visitors must perform in person searches themselves. Search fee: $12.00 per hour per custodian of records' estimate. Required to search: name, years to search, DOB. Criminal records computerized from 1992, index cards from 1980s. Note: Court will perform short searches only; usually directs searchers to state KBI. Mail turnaround time 2-3 days. Criminal PAT goes back to same as civil. Results may include DOB or address, but not always. **For details about the state's online access to records, see the section at the front or back of this chapter.**

Sedgwick County

District Court 525 N Main, Wichita, KS 67203; 316-660-5800; criminal phone: 316-660-5719; civil phone: 316-660-5803; probate phone: 316-660-5740; fax: 316-660-5784; 8AM-N, 1P-5P (CST). *Felony, Misdemeanor, Civil, Eviction, Small Claims, Probate.* www.dc18.org

General Information: No juvenile, adoption, mental health, sealed or expunged records released. Will fax documents $2.00 1st page, $1.00 each add'l, maximum of 10 pages. Court makes copy: $.25 per page. Self serve copy: same. Certification fee: $1.00 per cert. Payee: Clerk of Court. Personal checks accepted. No credit cards accepted. Prepayment required. Mail requests: SASE required for civil.

Civil Name Search: Access: Fax, mail, online, in person. Both court and visitors may perform in person name searches. Search fee: $12.00 per hour. Fee charged if more than 15 minutes. Required to search: name, years to search; case number helpful. Civil records on computer from 1983, microfiche from 1982, archives from 1977 and index cards from 1900s. Note: Email record requests to micro@dc18.org. Mail turnaround time 7-10 days. Civil PAT goes back to 1984. **For details about the state's online access to records, see the section at the front or back of this chapter.** Search pre-2003 cases are on a separate system. System also includes probate, traffic, domestic, and criminal cases. For more information, call 316-660-5800 or visit website.

Criminal Name Search: Access: In person, online. Both court and visitors may perform in person name searches. Search fee: $12.00 per hour. Fee charged if more than 15 minutes. Required to search: name, years to search; case number helpful. Criminal records computerized from 1983, microfiche from 1982, archives from 1977 and index cards from 1900s. Criminal PAT goes back to 1983. **For details about the state's online access to records, see the section at the front or back of this chapter.** Search pre-2003 cases are on a separate system. Online results show name only.

Seward County

District Court 415 N Washington, #103, Liberal, KS 67901; 620-626-3375; criminal phone: 620-626-3234; civil phone: 620-626-3391; probate phone: 620-626-3232; fax: 620-626-3302; 8:30AM-5PM (CST). *Felony, Misdemeanor, Civil, Eviction, Small Claims, Probate.*

General Information: Court will do searches on occasion, fee is $12.00 per hour. The Small Claims Court can be reached at 620-626-3232. No juvenile, mental health, sealed or expunged records released. Will fax specific case file $3.00 1st page; $.50 each add'l page. Court makes copy: $.50 per page. Self serve copy: same. Certification fee: $1.50 per seal plus copy fee. Payee: Clerk of District Court. Personal checks accepted. No credit cards accepted. Prepayment required.

Civil Name Search: Access: Mail, in person, online. Visitors must perform in person searches themselves. Search fee: $12.00 per name. Civil records on computer back to 1977, index from 1900s. Civil PAT goes back to 1977. **For details about the state's online access to records, see the section at the front or back of this chapter.**

Criminal Name Search: Access: Mail, in person, online. Visitors must perform in person searches themselves. Search fee: $12.00 per name. Required to search: name, years to search; SSN helpful. Criminal records computerized from 1977, index from 1900s. Criminal PAT goes back to same as civil. **For details about the state's online access to records, see the section at the front or back of this chapter.**

Shawnee County

District Court 200 E 7th Rm 209, Topeka, KS 66603; 785-233-8200 X4327; criminal phone: x5157; civil phone: x5158; probate phone: x5156; criminal fax: 785-291-4908; civil fax: 8AM-4PM; 8AM-4PM (CST). *Felony, Misdemeanor, Civil, Eviction, Small Claims, Probate, Traffic.* www.shawneecourt.org

General Information: No juvenile, mental health, sealed or expunged records released. Will fax documents to local or toll free line. Court makes copy: $.50 per page. Certification fee: $2.25 for Authentication; $1.25 for certification. Payee: Clerk of District Court. Personal checks accepted. Credit cards accepted. Prepayment required.

Civil Name Search: Access: Fax, mail, in person, online. Both court and visitors may perform in person name searches. Search fee: $12.00 per hour. Civil records on computer from 1980, microfiche from 1950, archives and index from 1800s. Note: A site only available to attorneys is at www.shawneecourt.org/img_temp.htm. Mail turnaround time 3-4 days. Civil PAT goes back to 1988. See www.shawneecourt.org/doe/index.html. Also find "viewing restricted" domestic documents here. Also, daily dockets lists free at www.shawneecourt.org/docket/. **For details about the state's online access to records, see the section at the front or back of this chapter.**

Criminal Name Search: Access: Fax, mail, in person, online. Both court and visitors may perform in person name searches. Search fee: $12.00 per hour. Required to search: name, years to search, DOB. Criminal records computerized from 1980, microfiche from 1950, archives and index from 1800s. Mail turnaround time 3-4 days. Criminal PAT goes back to 1984. Online access to criminal records and dockets is the same as civil. But the court states that online results only show name, no identifiers given. Online results show name only.

Sheridan County

District Court PO Box 753, Hoxie, KS 67740; 785-675-3451; fax: 785-675-2256; 8AM-N, 1PM-5PM (CST). *Felony, Misdemeanor, Civil, Eviction, Small Claims, Probate.*

General Information: Probate records prior to 2004 are on a separate index. Probate fax is same as main fax number. No juvenile, mental health, sealed or expunged records released. Will fax documents to local or toll free line. Court makes copy: $.25 per page. Self serve copy: same. Certification fee: $1.00 per page includes copies. Payee: Clerk of Court. Personal checks accepted. No credit cards accepted. Prepayment required. Mail requests: SASE required.

Civil Name Search: Access: Phone, fax, mail, in person. Both court and visitors may perform in person name searches. Search fee: $12.00 per hour. Civil records on strip index from 1885. Note: Mail requests require use of a special form. Mail turnaround time 1-2 days. Civil PAT goes back to 2004. **For details about the state's online access to records, see the section at the front or back of this chapter.**

Criminal Name Search: Access: Phone, fax, mail, in person, online. Both court and visitors may perform in person name searches. Search fee: $12.00 per hour. Required to search: name, years to search, signed release. Criminal records computerized from 2004; partial computer records back to 1995; on strip index from 1885. Mail turnaround time 1-2 days. Criminal PAT goes back to same as civil. **For details about the state's online access to records, see the section at the front or back of this chapter.**

Sherman County

District Court 813 Broadway, Rm 201, Goodland, KS 67735; 785-890-4850; criminal phone: 785-890-4854; civil phone: 785-890-4853; fax: 785-890-4858; 8AM-N, 1-5PM (MST). *Felony, Misdemeanor, Civil, Eviction, Small Claims, Probate.*

General Information: No juvenile before 1997, mental health, sealed or expunged records released. Will fax documents $1.00 per page. Court makes copy: $.25 per page. Certification fee: $1.00. Payee: Clerk of District Court. Personal checks accepted. No credit cards accepted. Prepayment required.

Civil Name Search: Access: In person, online. Visitors must perform in person searches themselves. Civil index in docket books from 1900s. Civil PAT goes back to 2004. **For details about the state's online access to records, see the section at the front or back of this chapter.**

Criminal Name Search: Access: In person, online. Visitors must perform in person searches themselves. Required to search: name, years to search; SSN helpful. Criminal docket on books from 1900s. Criminal PAT available. **For details about the state's online access to records, see the section at the front or back of this chapter.**

Smith County

District Court PO Box 273, 218 S Grant, Smith Center, KS 66967; 785-282-5140/41; fax: 785-282-5145; 8AM-Noon, 1PM-5PM (CST). *Felony, Misdemeanor, Civil, Eviction, Small Claims, Probate.*

General Information: No juvenile, mental health, sealed or expunged records released. Will fax documents $.75 per page. Court makes copy: $.25 per page. Self serve copy: same. Certification fee: $1.00 per page. Payee: Clerk of Court. Personal checks accepted. No credit cards accepted. Prepayment required.

Civil Name Search: Access: In person, fax, online. Visitors must perform in person searches themselves. Search fee: $5.00 with results, $3.00 without results. Civil index on cards from 1873. Civil PAT goes back to 2004. Terminal civil results can contain DOB. **For details about the state's online access to records, see the section at the front or back of this chapter.**

Criminal Name Search: Access: In person, fax, online. Visitors must perform in person searches themselves. Search fee: $5.00 with results, $3.00 without results. Required to search: name, years to search; SSN helpful. Criminal records indexed on cards from 1873. Criminal PAT goes back to 2004. **For details about the state's online access to records, see the section at the front or back of this chapter.**

Stafford County

District Court PO Box 365, St John, KS 67576; 620-549-3295; fax: 620-549-3298; 8AM-5PM (CST). *Felony, Misdemeanor, Civil, Eviction, Small Claims, Probate.* www.staffordcounty.org

General Information: Probate fax is same as main fax number. No juvenile, mental health, sealed or expunged records released. Will not fax documents. Court makes copy: $.50 per page. No certification fee . Payee: Clerk of District Court. Personal checks accepted. No credit cards accepted. Prepayment required. Mail requests: SASE required for civil.

Civil Name Search: Access: Phone, mail, fax, in person, email, online. Both court and visitors may perform in person name searches. Search fee: $12.00 per hour, 15 minutes minimum. Civil records on computer from 1988, microfiche and index from 1900s. Note: Direct email civil record requests to mgatton@embacqmail.com. Mail turnaround time 3 days. Civil PAT goes back to 1988. **For details about the state's online access to records, see the section at the front or back of this chapter.**

Criminal Name Search: Access: In person, online. Visitors must perform in person searches themselves. Criminal records computerized from 1988, microfiche and index from 1900s. Note: All other requests must go to the Kansas Bureau of Investigations. Criminal PAT goes back to same as civil. **For details about the state's online access to records, see the section at the front or back of this chapter.**

Stanton County

District Court PO Box 913, Johnson, KS 67855; 620-492-2180; fax: 620-492-6410; 8AM-12PM - 1PM-5PM (CST). *Felony, Misdemeanor, Civil, Eviction, Small Claims, Probate.*

General Information: No juvenile, mental health, sealed or expunged records released. Will fax documents $2.00 1st page, $.50 each add'l. Court makes copy: $.50 per page. Self serve copy: same. Certification fee: $1.00 per cert. Payee: Clerk of District Court. Personal checks accepted. No credit cards accepted. Prepayment required. Mail requests: SASE required.

Civil Name Search: Access: Phone, fax, mail, in person, online. Both court and visitors may·perform in person name searches. Search fee: $12.00 per hour. Civil records on computer from 1977, index from 1887. Mail turnaround time 1-3 days. Civil PAT goes back to 1977. **For details about the state's online access to records, see the section at the front or back of this chapter.**

Criminal Name Search: Access: Phone, fax, mail, in person, online. Both court and visitors may perform in person name searches. Search fee: $12.00 per hour. Required to search: name, years to search, DOB, SSN. Criminal records computerized from 1977, index from 1887. Mail turnaround time 1-3 days. Criminal PAT goes back to 1977. **For details about the state's online access to records, see the section at the front or back of this chapter.**

Stevens County

District Court 200 E 6th, Hugoton, KS 67951; 620-544-2484; fax: 620-544-2528; 8AM-5PM Closed noon-1PM (CST). *Felony, Misdemeanor, Civil, Eviction, Small Claims, Probate.*

General Information: Probate fax is same as main fax number. No juvenile, mental health, sealed or expunged records released. Fee to fax out file $3.00 plus $.50 per page. Court makes copy: $.50 per page. Self serve copy: same. Certification fee: $1.25 per page plus copy fee. Payee: Clerk of District Court. Personal checks accepted. No credit cards accepted. Prepayment required. Must prepay for fax and mail. Mail requests: SASE required.

Civil Name Search: Access: Mail, fax, in person, online. Both court and visitors may perform in person name searches. Search fee: $12.50 per hour. Civil records on computer, microfiche, archives and index from 1887. Mail turnaround time 3 days. Civil PAT goes back to 04/01/2008. **For details about the state's online access to records, see the section at the front or back of this chapter.**

Criminal Name Search: Access: Online only. Visitors must perform in person searches themselves. Required to search: name, years to search; also helpful: SSN. Criminal records computerized from 04/01/2008, microfiche, archives and index from 1887. Criminal PAT goes back to 1991 approximately. **For details about the state's online access to records, see the section at the front or back of this chapter.**

Sumner County

District Court PO Box 399, County Courthouse, Wellington, KS 67152; 620-326-5936; probate phone: 620-399-1042; fax: 620-326-5365; 8AM-N, 1-4PM (CST). *Felony, Misdemeanor, Civil, Eviction, Small Claims, Probate.* https://www.accesskansas.org/countyCourts/

General Information: Court prefers that you summit requests on their request form. Probate fax is same as main fax number. No juvenile, mental health, sealed or expunged records released. Will fax documents $1.00 per page up to 10 pages only. Court makes copy: $.25 per page. Certification fee: $2.00 plus copy fee. Payee: Clerk of Court. Personal checks accepted. No credit cards accepted. Prepayment required.

Civil Name Search: Access: Mail, fax, in person, online. Both court and visitors may perform in person name searches. Search fee: $12.00 per hour. Civil records on computer back to 1991, index cards from 1800s for probate. Note: Will not do any lien searches, no name searches over the phone, specific case number needed. Mail turnaround time 1-3 days. Civil PAT goes back to 1991. **For details about the state's online access to records, see the section at the front or back of this chapter.**

Criminal Name Search: Access: Mail, fax, in person. Both court and visitors may perform in person name searches. Search fee: $12.00 per hour. Required to search: name, years to search; also helpful: case number. Criminal records computerized from 1991, index cards from 1800s for probate. Note: Will not search any name over phone unless specific case number is given. Court will not perform searches for employment purposes. Mail turnaround time 1-3 days. Criminal PAT goes back to same as civil. **For details about the state's online access to records, see the section at the front or back of this chapter.**

Thomas County

District Court PO Box 805, 300 N Court Ave, Colby, KS 67701; 785-460-4540; fax: 785-460-2291; 8:30AM-5PM (CST). *Felony, Misdemeanor, Civil, Eviction, Small Claims, Probate.*

General Information: No juvenile, mental health, sealed or expunged records released. Will fax documents $1.00 per page. Court makes copy: $.25 per page. Certification fee: $1.00 per page plus copy fee; $2.00 for an Authentication. Payee: Clerk. Personal checks accepted. Prepayment required. Mail requests: SASE required.

Civil Name Search: Access: Fax, mail, in person, online. Both court and visitors may perform in person name searches. Search fee: $12.00 per hour. Civil docket indexed from 1887. Civil PAT goes back to 1996. **For details about the state's online access to records, see the section at the front or back of this chapter.**

Criminal Name Search: Access: Fax, mail, in person. Both court and visitors may perform in person name searches. Search fee: $12.00 per hour. Required to search: name, years to search, DOB, sex; also helpful: SSN. Criminal records indexed from 1887. Criminal PAT goes back to same as civil. **For details about the state's online access to records, see the section at the front or back of this chapter.**

Trego County

District Court 216 N Main, WaKeeney, KS 67672; 785-743-2148; fax: 785-743-2726; 8AM-N, 1-5PM (CST). *Felony, Misdemeanor, Civil, Eviction, Small Claims, Probate.* www.23rdjudicial.org

General Information: Probate fax is same as main fax number. No juvenile, mental health, sealed or expunged records released. Fee to fax out file $2.00 1st page; $.50 each add'l. Court makes copy: $.25 per page. Self serve copy: same. Certification fee: $1.00 per page plus copy fee. Payee: Clerk of Court. Personal checks accepted. No credit cards accepted. Prepayment required. Mail requests: SASE required.

Civil Name Search: Access: Phone, mail, fax, in person, online. Both court and visitors may perform in person name searches. Search fee: $12.00 per hour. Civil records on computer since 1996; prior records on card index. Mail turnaround time 1-2 days. Civil PAT goes back to 1996. 2002 to present includes DOB and SSN. **For details about the state's online access to records, see the section at the front or back of this chapter.** Also, access back to 11/1/02 is web-based at www.kansas.gov/subscribers/. A $95.00 annual subscription required plus usage fee as low as $1.00 per search.

Criminal Name Search: Access: Mail, in person, online. Both court and visitors may perform in person name searches. Search fee: $12.00 per hour. Required to search: name, years to search; also helpful: DOB, SSN, sex. Criminal records on computer since 1996; prior records on card index. Mail turnaround time 1-2 days. Criminal PAT available. 2002 to present includes DOB and SSN. **For details about the state's online access to records, see the section at the front or back of this chapter.**

Wabaunsee County

District Court Courthouse, PO Box 278, 215 Kansas Ave, Alma, KS 66401; 785-765-2406; fax: 785-765-2487; 8AM-4:00PM (CST). *Felony, Misdemeanor, Civil, Eviction, Small Claims, Probate.*

General Information: No juvenile, mental health, sealed or expunged records released. Will not fax documents. Court makes copy: $.50 per page. Certification fee: $1.25 plus copy fee. Payee: Clerk of District Court. Personal checks accepted. No credit cards accepted. Prepayment required.

Civil Name Search: Access: In person, online. Visitors must perform in person searches themselves. Civil records on book index from 1800s; on computer back to 1996. Civil PAT goes back to 1996. Terminal results also show SSNs if on documents. **For details about the state's online access to records, see the section at the front or back of this chapter**

Criminal Name Search: Access: In person, online. Visitors must perform in person searches themselves. Required to search: name, years to search; SSN helpful. Criminal docket on books index from 1800s; on computer back to 1996. Criminal PAT goes back to 1996. Terminal results also show SSN. **For details about the state's online access to records, see the section at the front or back of this chapter.**

Wallace County

District Court PO Box 8, Sharon Springs, KS 67758; 785-852-4289; fax: 785-852-4271; 8AM-N,1-5PM (MST). *Felony, Misdemeanor, Civil, Eviction, Small Claims, Probate.*

General Information: Probate fax is same as main fax number. No juvenile offender (under 14 years old), juvenile in need of care, adoption, mental health, sealed or expunged records released. Will fax documents to local or toll free line. Court makes copy: $.25 per page. Self serve copy: same. Certification fee: $1.00 per page plus copy fee. Payee: Clerk of Court. Personal checks accepted. No credit cards accepted. Prepayment required. Mail requests: SASE helpful.

Civil Name Search: Access: Mail, in person, fax, online. Visitors must perform in person searches themselves. Search fee: $12.00 per hour. Required to search: name; also helpful: years to search. Civil docket indexed from 1887. Note: A case number must be provided; court will not do name searches. Mail turnaround time 2 days. Civil PAT available. **For details about the state's online access to records, see the section at the front or back of this chapter.**

Criminal Name Search: Access: In person, online. Visitors must perform in person searches themselves. Required to search: name; also helpful: years to search. Criminal records indexed from 1887. Criminal PAT available. **For details about the state's online access to records, see the section at the front or back of this chapter.**

Washington County

District Court Courthouse, 214 C St, Washington, KS 66968; 785-325-2381; fax: 785-325-2557; 8AM-N,1-4PM (CST). *Felony, Misdemeanor, Civil, Eviction, Small Claims, Probate.* www.kscourts.org/Districts/District-Info.asp?d=12

General Information: Probate fax is same as main fax number. No juvenile, mental health, sealed or expunged records released. Fee to fax out file $3.00 per page. Court makes copy: $.25 per page. Self serve copy: same. Certification fee: $1.00 per document plus copy fee. Payee: Washington County District Court. Personal checks accepted. No credit cards accepted. Prepayment required.

Civil Name Search: Access: In person, online. Visitors must perform in person searches themselves. Civil records on card index from 1887; on computer back to 1995. Civil PAT goes back to 6/2003. **For details about the state's online access to records, see the section at the front or back of this chapter.**

Criminal Name Search: Access: In person, online. Visitors must perform in person searches themselves. Criminal records on card index from 1887; on computer back to 1995. Criminal PAT goes back to 6/2003. **For details about the state's online access to records, see the section at the front or back of this chapter.**

Wichita County

District Court PO Box 968, 206 S 4th St, Leoti, KS 67861; 620-375-4454; fax: 620-375-2999; 8AM-5PM (CST). *Felony, Misdemeanor, Civil, Eviction, Small Claims, Probate.*

General Information: This court is not in City of Wichita, KS. City of Wichita, KS is in Sedgwick County. No juvenile, mental health, sealed or expunged records released. Will fax documents $1.00 per page. Court makes copy: $.50 per page. Self serve copy: same. Certification fee: $1.00. Payee: Clerk of District Court. Personal checks accepted. No credit cards accepted. Prepayment required. Mail requests: SASE required for civil.

Civil Name Search: Access: Mail, in person, online. Both court and visitors may perform in person name searches. Search fee: $12.00 per hour. Civil records on computer back to 1986, on index from 1900. Civil PAT goes back to 1986. **For details about the state's online access to records, see the section at the front or back of this chapter.**

Criminal Name Search: Access: In person, online. Visitors must perform in person searches themselves. Required to search: name. Criminal records computerized from 1986, on index from 1900. Note: Criminal records are through the KBI. Criminal PAT goes back to same as civil. **For details about the state's online access to records, see the section at the front or back of this chapter.**

Wilson County

District Court 615 Madison, Rm 214, Fredonia, KS 66736; 620-378-4533; fax: 620-378-4531; 8AM-4PM (CST). *Felony, Misdemeanor, Civil, Eviction, Small Claims, Probate.* www.31stjudicialdistrict.org

General Information: Probate fax is same as main fax number. No juvenile, mental health, sealed or expunged records released. Will fax documents $1.00 per page. Court makes copy: $.50 per page. Certification fee: $1.00 per page. Payee: Clerk of Court. Personal checks accepted. No credit cards accepted. Prepayment required. Mail requests: SASE required.

Civil Name Search: Access: Fax, mail, in person, online. Both court and visitors may perform in person name searches. Search fee: $12.00 per hour. Required to search: name, years to search, request in writing. Civil records on computer since 1993, index cards from 1864. Mail turnaround time 1-3 weeks. Civil PAT goes back to 1993. **For details about the state's online access to records, see the section at the front or back of this chapter.** Also, access back to 11/1/02 is web-based at www.kansas.gov/subscribers/.

Criminal Name Search: Access: In person, online. Visitors must perform in person searches themselves. Required to search: name, years to search; also helpful: SSN. Criminal records on computer since 1993, manual index from 1864. Criminal PAT goes back to same as civil. Court calendars, limited action hearing results, and service results appear on the court website. **For details about the state's online access to records, see the section at the front or back of this chapter.** The staff refers criminal record name searches to KBI - the state agency. Court calendars, limited action hearing results, and service results appear on the court website. Online results show name only.

Woodson County

District Court 105 W Rutledge, Yates Center, KS 66783; 620-625-8610; fax: 620-625-8674; 8AM-N; 1-5PM (CST). *Felony, Misdemeanor, Civil, Eviction, Small Claims, Probate, Traffic.* www.31stjudicialdistrict.org

General Information: Court calendar is on website above. Probate fax is same as main fax number. No juvenile (under age 14 years), mental health, sealed or expunged records released. Fee to fax out file $1.00 per page. Court makes copy: $.50 per page. Self serve copy: same. Certification fee: $1.00 per certification. Payee: District Court. Business checks accepted. No credit cards accepted. Prepayment required. Mail requests: SASE required for civil.

Civil Name Search: Access: Mail, in person, online. Both court and visitors may perform in person name searches. Search fee: $12.00 per hour. Civil docket indexed from 1880s, on computer since 1993. Mail turnaround time 1 day. Civil PAT goes back to 1993. **For details about**

the state's online access to records, see the section at the front or back of this chapter.

Criminal Name Search: Access: In person, online. Visitors must perform in person searches themselves. Criminal records indexed from 1880s, on computer since 1993. Note: Phone inquiries referred to KBI at 785-296-8200. Criminal PAT goes back to same as civil. Court calendars, limited action hearing results, and service results appear on the website. **For details about the state's online access to records, see the section at the front or back of this chapter.**

Wyandotte County

District Court 710 N 7th St, Kansas City, KS 66101; criminal phone: 913-573-2905; civil phone: 913-573-2901; probate phone: 913-573-2834; criminal fax: 913-573-8177; civil fax: 8AM-5PM; 8AM-5PM (CST).
Felony, Misdemeanor, Civil, Eviction, Small Claims, Probate.

General Information: Fax number for the Limited Civil Division is 913-573-4135. No juvenile, mental health, sealed or expunged records released. Court makes copy: $.25 per page. Certification fee: none. Payee: Clerk of District Court. Personal checks accepted. No credit cards accepted. Prepayment required.

Civil Name Search: Access: In person, online. Both court and visitors may perform in person name searches. No search fee. Civil records on computer from 1975, microfiche, archives and index from 1900s. Note: If extensive copying or searching required, fee is $12.00 per hour. Civil PAT goes back to 1975. **For details about the state's online access to records, see the section at the front or back of this chapter.**

Criminal Name Search: Access: In person, online. Visitors must perform in person searches themselves. Required to search: name, years to search, DOB, SSN. Criminal records computerized from 1972, microfiche, archives and index from early 1900s. Note: Refer phone inquires to KBI at 785-296-8200. If extensive copying or searching required, fee is $12.00 per hour. Criminal PAT goes back to 1972. **For details about the state's online access to records, see the section at the front or back of this chapter.**

About Online Access

Commercial online access for civil and criminal records is available for District Court Records (except Sedgwick County cases prior to 2003 and Wyandotte County Cases prior to July 2004) at https://www.accesskansas.org/countyCourts/.

Fee is $1.00 per search and $1.00 per case retrieved for view. A credit card is required. Frequent requesters may sign-up for an annual subscription and receive monthly billing. If doing a name search, be aware the search is one county at a time and virtually no personal identifiers are shown on index results; for example the DOB is not shown. The case number is given.

There is a $95 annual fee and users have access to other other records such as the state criminal record repository and motor vehicle records.

For additional information or a registration packet, telephone 800-4-KANSAS (800-452-6727) or visit the web page.

Kentucky

Time Zone:	**EST & CST***

*Kentucky's forty western-most counties are CST: They are: Adair, Allen, Ballard, Barren, Breckinridge, Butler, Caldwell, Calloway, Carlisle, Christian, Clinton, Crittenden, Cumberland, Daviess, Edmonson, Fulton, Graves, Grayson, Hancock, Hart, Henderson, Hickman, Hopkins, Livingstone, Logan, Marshall, McCracken, McLean, Metcalfe, Monroe, Muhlenberg, Ohio, Russell, Simpson, Todd, Trigg, Union, Warren, Wayne, and Webster

Capital:	**Frankfort, Franklin County**
# of Counties:	**120**
State Web:	**www.kentucky.gov**
Court Web:	**http://courts.ky.gov**

Administration

Administrative Office of Courts, Pre-Trial Services Records Unit, 100 Mill Creek Park, Frankfort, KY, 40601; 502-573-1682, Fax: 502-573-1669. http://courts.ky.gov/aoc/

The Supreme and Appellate Courts

The Supreme Court is the court of last resort. The Court of Appeals hears all appeals from the lower courts. Divorces may not be appealed; however, child custody and property rights decisions may be appealed. Search opinions and case information from the Supreme Court and Court of Appeals at http://courts.ky.gov/research/.

The Kentucky Courts

Court	Type	How Organized	Jurisdiction Highpoints
Circuit*	General	120 Courts in 31 Districts	Felony, Misdemeanor, Civil, Contested Probate, Land, Family, Domestic Abuse
District*	Limited	120 Courts in 59 Districts	Misdemeanor, Civil $5,000 or less, Small Claims, Ordinances, Traffic, Eviction, Domestic Abuse

* = profiled in this book

Details on the Court Structure

The **Circuit Court** is the court of general jurisdiction and hears civil matters involving more than $5,000, capital offenses and felonies, land dispute title cases and contested probate cases. The **Family Court** is a division of the Circuit Court and has concurrent jurisdiction with certain domestic abuse matters.

District Court is the court of limited jurisdiction and handles juvenile matters, city and county ordinances, misdemeanors, violations, traffic offenses, probate of wills, arraignments, felony probable cause hearings, small claims ($2,500 or less), civil cases involving $5,000 or less, voluntary and involuntary mental commitments and cases relating to domestic violence and abuse.

Ninety percent of all Kentuckians involved in court proceedings appear in District Court

Record Searching Facts You Need to Know

Fees and Record Searching Tips

Nearly all courts will not perform a name search. Courts send criminal record search requesters to a statewide service provided by the Administrative Office of the Courts. Records may be requested via fax, standard mail, walk-in, even a drive-thru service, and online (see below). The CourtNet Criminal History database contains records from all 120 counties for at least the last five years for all misdemeanor and traffic cases and for felonies dating back to 1978. The search fee is $15.00 per request. A SASE must accompany mail requests. Call 800-928-6381 for more information.

Also, see http://courts.ky.gov/aoc/courtservices/recordsandstatistics/records.htm.

Several Online Access Programs are Available

The KY Admin. Office of Courts provides a criminal record online ordering system called AOCFastCheck. The fee is $15.00 per record, add 5% for use of a credit card. Subscribers receive an email notification when results are ready. For more information, visit http://courts.ky.gov/aoc/AOCFastCheck.htm. The following case types are not available - juvenile, mental health, and civil/domestic violence.

A Cautionary Note - The AOC is NOT the state mandated official site for criminal records. State law dictates that the Kentucky State Police Records Branch is responsible for holding records with confirmed dispositions, not the AOC.

A limited search site to find case numbers is free at http://apps.kycourts.net/CourtRecords. Search daily court calendars by county free at http://apps.kycourts.net/dockets.

Registered members of the KY Bar may use CourtNet-KBA to review pending cases at http://apps.kycourts.net/courtrecordsKBA/.

Adair County

Circuit & District Court 201 Campbellsville St, Ste 101, Columbia, KY 42728; 270-384-2626; fax: 270-384-4299; 8AM-4PM (CST). *Felony, Misdemeanor, Civil, Eviction, Small Claims, Probate.*
www.courts.ky.gov/counties/
General Information: No adoption, mental, juvenile, or sealed records released. Court makes copy: $.25 per page. Self serve copy: same. No certification fee . Payee: Circuit Clerk. No Personal checks and credit cards accepted. Prepayment required.
Civil Name Search: Access: In person, online. Visitors must perform in person searches themselves. Civil records on computer since 6/1993, prior records on docket books since 1978. Civil PAT goes back to 6/1993. **Note: For a complete description of online access see the *Online Access is Statewide* section at the front or back of this chapter.**
Criminal Name Search: Access: Mail, in person, online. Visitors must perform in person searches themselves. No search fee. Required to search: name, years to search, SSN. Criminal records on computer since 6/1993, prior records on docket books since 1978. **For details about mail, fax, phone, in-person, and online access programs offered by the KYAOC see the sections at the front or back of this chapter**.

Allen County

Circuit & District Court PO Box 477, 201 W. Main St., Room 202, Scottsville, KY 42164; 270-237-3561; fax: 270-237-9120; 8AM-4:30PM (CST). *Felony, Misdemeanor, Civil, Eviction, Small Claims, Probate.*
www.courts.ky.gov/counties/
General Information: No adoption, mental, juvenile, or sealed records released. Will fax documents for no fee. Court makes copy: $.25 per page. Certification fee: $5.00 per doc plus copy fee. Payee: Circuit Clerk. Local personal checks accepted. No credit cards accepted. Prepayment required.
Civil Name Search: Access: In person, online. Visitors must perform in person searches themselves. Civil records on computer since 1992, records on index cards from 1980 to 1992, prior records on books. Civil PAT goes back to 9/1992. **For details about mail, fax, phone, in-person, and online access programs offered by the KYAOC see the sections at the front or back of this chapter**. Criminal PAT goes back to same as civil. Results on a public terminal sometimes shows last 4 digits of SSN.

Anderson County

Circuit & District Court 151 S Main St, Courthouse, Lawrenceburg, KY 40342; 502-839-3508; fax: 502-839-4995; 8:30AM-5PM (EST). *Felony, Civil Actions over $5,000.*
www.courts.ky.gov/counties/
General Information: No adoption, mental, juvenile, or sealed records released. Court makes copy: $.25 per page. Certification fee: $5.00 per doc. Payee: Clerk of Circuit Court. Personal checks accepted. No credit cards accepted. Prepayment required.
Civil Name Search: Access: Mail, In person, online. Only the court performs in person name searches; visitors may not. No search fee. Civil records on computer since 8/1994, prior records on docket books since 1978. **Note: For a complete description of online access see the *Online Access is Statewide* section at the front or back of this chapter.**
Criminal Name Search: Access: In person, online. Only the court performs in person name searches; visitors may not. Required to search: name, years to search; also helpful: DOB, SSN. Criminal records may be on computer back to 1994. **For details about mail, fax, phone, in-person, and online access programs offered by the KYAOC see the sections at the front or back of this chapter.**

Ballard County

Circuit & District Court Box 265, Wickliffe, KY 42087; 270-335-5123; fax: 270-335-3849; 8AM-4PM; last F of month 8AM-5PM (CST). *Felony, Misdemeanor, Civil, Eviction, Small Claims, Probate.*
www.courts.ky.gov/counties/
General Information: No adoption, mental, juvenile, or sealed records released. Fee to fax out file $2.00 1st page, $1.00 each addl. Court makes copy: $.25 per page. Self serve copy: same. Certification fee: $5.00 per doc. Payee: Circuit Clerk. Only cashiers checks and money orders accepted. Major credit cards accepted. Prepayment required.
Civil Name Search: Access: In person, online. Both court and visitors may perform in person name searches. No search fee. Civil records on computer since 1992, prior records on books to 1978. Civil PAT goes back to 1992. **Note: For a complete description of online access see the *Online Access is Statewide* section at the front or back of this chapter.**
Criminal Name Search: Access: In person, online. Visitors must perform in person searches themselves. Required to search: name, years to search, DOB. Criminal records on computer since 1992, prior records on books to 1978. **For details about mail, fax, phone, in-person, and online access programs offered by the KYAOC see the sections at the front or back of this chapter**. Criminal PAT goes back to same as civil.

Barren County

Circuit & District Court PO Box 1359, 100 Courthouse Sq, Glasgow, KY 42142-1359; 270-651-3763; fax: 270-651-6203; 8AM-4:30PM (CST). *Felony, Misdemeanor, Civil, Eviction, Small Claims, Probate.*
www.courts.ky.gov
General Information: No adoption, mental, juvenile, or sealed records released. Will not fax out case files. Court makes copy: $.25 per page. Self serve copy: same. Certification fee: $5.00 per doc plus copy fee. Payee: Circuit Clerk. Personal checks accepted except for restitution payments. Major credit cards accepted. Prepayment required.
Civil Name Search: Access: In person, online. Visitors must perform in person searches themselves. Civil records on computer back to 10/1991, prior records on index books since 1800s are kept in Frankfort, KY. Civil PAT goes back to 10/1991. Results include DOB in some cases. **Note: For a complete description of online access see the *Online Access is Statewide* section at the front or back of this chapter.**
Criminal Name Search: Access: In person, online. Visitors must perform in person searches themselves. Required to search: name, years to search, DOB; SSN helpful. Criminal records computerized from 10/1991, prior records on index books since 1800s are kept in Frankfort, KY. **For details about mail, fax, phone, in-person, and online access programs offered by the KYAOC see the sections at the front or back of this chapter**. Criminal PAT goes back to same as civil. Terminal results may include DOB and SSN.

Bath County

Circuit & District Court PO Box 558, 19 E Main, Owingsville, KY 40360; 606-674-2186 X6821; fax: 606-674-3996; 8AM-4PM (EST). *Felony, Misdemeanor, Civil, Eviction, Small Claims, Probate.*
http://courts.ky.gov/counties/
General Information: No adoption, mental, juvenile, or sealed records released. Will fax documents $3.00 per page fee. Court makes copy: $.25 per page. Self serve copy: same. Certification fee: $5.00 per doc. Payee: Circuit Clerk. No personal checks accepted. Visa/MC accepted. Prepayment required.
Civil Name Search: Access: In person, mail, online. Visitors must perform in person searches themselves. Civil records computerized since 1994, on docket books since 1978, prior records archived. Mail turnaround time 3-4 days. Civil PAT goes back to 1994. **Note: For a complete**

description of online access see the *Online Access is Statewide* section at the front or back of this chapter.

Criminal Name Search: Access: In person, mail online. Visitors must perform in person searches themselves. Required to search: name, years to search, DOB, SSN. Criminal records computerized since 1994, on docket books since 1978, prior records archived. Mail turnaround time 3-4 days. Criminal PAT goes back to same as civil.**For details about mail, fax, phone, in-person, and online access programs offered by the KYAOC see the sections at the front or back of this chapter.** Mail turnaround time 3-4 days. Criminal PAT goes back to same as civil.

Bell County

Circuit & District Court Box 307, Pineville, KY 40977; 606-337-2942; probate phone: 606-337-9900; fax: 606-337-8850; 8AM-4PM (EST). *Felony, Misdemeanor, Civil, Eviction, Small Claims, Probate.*
http://courts.ky.gov/Counties/Bell/default.htm

General Information: Probate fax is same as main fax number. No adoption, mental, juvenile, or sealed records released. Will fax documents, $2.00 1st page, $1.00 each add'l. Court makes copy: $.25 per page. Self serve copy: same. Certification fee: $5.00. Payee: Circuit Clerk. Personal checks accepted. Prepayment required. Mail requests: SASE required for civil.

Civil Name Search: Access: Phone, mail, in person, online. Both court and visitors may perform in person name searches. No search fee. Civil records on computer since 8/91, prior records on docket books since 1978. Civil PAT goes back to 8/1991. **Note: For a complete description of online access see the *Online Access is Statewide* section at the front or back of this chapter.**

Criminal Name Search: Access: In person, online. Visitors must perform in person searches themselves. Search fee: Court will do a index search for the name and tell you how many records they find, for no fee. Criminal records on computer since 8/91, prior records on docket books since 1978. Criminal PAT goes back to same as civil. **For details about mail, fax, phone, in-person, and online access programs offered by the KYAOC see the sections at the front or back of this chapter.**

Boone County

Circuit & District Court 6025 Rogers Ln, #141, Burlington, KY 41005; 859-334-2286; criminal phone: 859-334-3536 District; civil phone: 859-334-2287 District; fax: 859-334-3650; 8:30AM-4:30PM (EST). *Felony, Misdemeanor, Civil, Eviction, Small Claims, Probate.*
www.courts.ky.gov/counties/

General Information: No adoption, mental, juvenile, or sealed records released. Fee to fax out file $3.00 per page. Court makes copy: $.25 per page. Self serve copy: same. Certification fee: $5.00 per doc. Payee: Circuit Clerk. Only cashiers checks and money orders accepted. Visa/MC accepted. Prepayment required.

Civil Name Search: Access: In person, online. Both court and visitors may perform in person name searches. Civil records on computer since 7/1990, on index card file since 1978, prior records on books. Civil PAT goes back to 7/1990. **Note: For a complete description of online access see the *Online Access is Statewide* section at the front or back of this chapter.**

Criminal Name Search: Access: In person, online. Visitors must perform in person searches themselves. Required to search: name, years to search, DOB; SSN helpful. Criminal records on computer since 7/1990, on index card file since 1978, prior records on books. Criminal PAT goes back to same as civil. **For details about mail, fax, phone, in-person, and online access programs offered by the KYAOC see the sections at the front or back of this chapter.**

Bourbon County

Circuit & District Court Box 740, 310 Main St, Courthouse Annex, Paris, KY 40361; 859-987-2624; fax: 859-987-6049; 8:30AM-4:30PM (EST). *Felony, Misdemeanor, Civil, Eviction, Small Claims, Probate.*
www.courts.ky.gov/counties/

General Information: No adoption, mental, juvenile, or sealed records released. Will not fax documents. Court makes copy: $.25 per page. Self serve copy: same. Certification fee: $5.00. Payee: Circuit Clerk. Local personal checks accepted. No credit cards accepted. Prepayment required.

Civil Name Search: Access: In person, online. Visitors must perform in person searches themselves. Civil records on computer since 11/1991, prior records on books. Civil PAT goes back to 1991. **Note: For a complete description of online access see the *Online Access is Statewide* section at the front or back of this chapter.**

Criminal Name Search: Access: In person, online. Visitors must perform in person searches themselves. Required to search: name, years to search; SSN helpful. Criminal records on computer since 11/1991, prior records on books. Criminal PAT goes back to same as civil. **For details about mail, fax, phone, in-person, and online access programs offered by the KYAOC see the sections at the front or back of this chapter.**

Boyd County

Circuit & District Court Box 688, Catlettsburg, KY 41129-0688; 606-739-4131, 4132, 4133; fax: 606-739-5793; 8:30AM-4PM (EST). *Felony, Misdemeanor, Civil, Eviction, Small Claims, Probate.*
www.courts.ky.gov/counties/

General Information: No adoption, mental, juvenile, or sealed records released. Court makes copy: $.25 per page. Certification fee: $5.00 per doc. Payee: Circuit Clerk. Personal checks and credit cards accepted. Prepayment required.

Civil Name Search: Access: In person, online. Visitors must perform in person searches themselves. Civil records on computer since 1991, prior records on index cards since 1978. Civil PAT goes back to 1991. **Note: For a complete description of online access see the *Online Access is Statewide* section at the front or back of this chapter.**

Criminal Name Search: Access: In person, online. Visitors must perform in person searches themselves. Required to search: name, years to search; also helpful: DOB, SSN. Criminal records on computer since 1991, on index cards since 1978; misdemeanor & traffic from 1995. Criminal PAT goes back to same as civil. **For details about mail, fax, phone, in-person, and online access programs offered by the KYAOC see the sections at the front or back of this chapter.**

Boyle County

Circuit Court 321 Main St, Danville, KY 40422; 859-239-7442; fax: 859-239-7000; 8AM-4:30PM (EST). *Felony, Civil Actions over $5,000.* www.courts.ky.gov/counties/

General Information: The District Court is also located here on the floor above. No adoption, mental, juvenile, or sealed records released. Will fax documents $1.00 per page; cannot fax certified pages. Court makes copy: $.25 per page. Self serve copy: same. Certification fee: $5.00. Payee: Circuit Clerk. No Personal checks and credit cards accepted. Prepayment required. Mail requests: SASE required for mail return of any copies.

Civil Name Search: Access: In person, online. Both court and visitors may perform in person name searches. No search fee. Civil records on computer since 8/91, prior records on index cards. Civil PAT goes back to 8/1991. Results include year of birth and last 4 numbers of SSN. **Note: For a complete description of online access see the *Online Access is Statewide* section at the front or back of this chapter.**

Criminal Name Search: Access: In person, online. Visitors must perform in person searches themselves. Required to search: name, years to search, and DOB, SSN if available. Criminal records on computer since 8/91, prior records on index cards. Note: Criminal PAT goes back to same as civil. Results include year of birth and last 4 numbers of SSN. **For details about mail, fax, phone, in-person, and online access programs offered by the KYAOC see the sections at the front or back of this chapter.**

District Court 321 W Main St, Courthouse, 3rd Fl, Danville, KY 40422; 859-239-7362; fax: 859-239-7807; 8AM-4:30PM (EST). *Misdemeanor, Civil Actions under $5,000, Eviction, Small Claims, Probate.*
www.courts.ky.gov/

General Information: Public access terminals in the Circuit Clerk's office. For most purposes, the circuit and district court are combined, with the staffs on separate floors. No adoption, mental, juvenile, or sealed records released. Will fax out documents $1.00 per page, uncertified. Court makes copy: $.25 per page. Self serve copy: $.25 per page. Certification fee: $5.00 per doc. Payee: District Clerk. Personal checks accepted. No credit cards accepted. Prepayment required.

Civil Name Search: Access: In person, online. Visitors must perform in person searches themselves. Civil records on computer since 8/91, prior records on index cards since 1977. Civil PAT goes back to 8/1991. Only year of DOB and last 4 digits of SSN appear. **Note: For a complete description of online access see the *Online Access is Statewide* section at the front or back of this chapter.**

Criminal Name Search: Access: In person, online. Visitors must perform in person searches themselves. Required to search: name, DOB, SSN. Criminal records on computer since 8/91; prior records on card index. Criminal PAT goes back to same as civil. Only year of DOB and last 4 digits of SSN appear. **For details about mail, fax, phone, in-person, and online access programs offered by the KYAOC see the sections at the front or back of this chapter.**

Bracken County

Circuit & District Court PO Box 205, 116 W. Miami St, Brooksville, KY 41004-0205; 606-735-3328; fax: 606-735-3900; 8AM-4:30PM M,T,TH,F; 8:30AM-N W,Sat (EST). *Felony, Misdemeanor, Civil, Eviction, Small Claims, Probate.* http://courts.ky.gov/Counties/Bracken/

General Information: Probate fax is same as main fax number. No adoption, mental, juvenile, or sealed records released. Will not fax documents. Court makes copy: $.25 per page. Self serve copy: same. Certification fee: $5.00 per doc. Payee: Circuit Clerk. Personal checks and credit cards accepted. Prepayment required. Mail requests: SASE required for civil.

Civil Name Search: Access: Mail, in person, online. Both court and visitors may perform in person name searches. No search fee. Civil records on computer since 1993, prior records on docket books since 1797. Mail turnaround time 3-5 days. Civil PAT goes back to 8/1992. **Note: For a complete description of online access see the** *Online Access is Statewide* **section at the front or back of this chapter**.

Criminal Name Search: Access: In person, online. Visitors must perform in person searches themselves. Criminal records on computer since 1993, prior records on docket books since 1797. Criminal PAT goes back to same as civil. Terminal usually will show year of birth. **For details about mail, fax, phone, in-person, and online access programs offered by the KYAOC see the sections at the front or back of this chapter**.

Breathitt County

Circuit & District Court 1131 Main St, Jackson, KY 41339; 606-666-5768; fax: 606-666-4893; 8AM-4PM M-F (EST). *Felony, Misdemeanor, Civil, Eviction, Small Claims, Probate.*
www.courts.ky.gov/counties/
General Information: No adoption, mental, juvenile, or sealed records released. Will not fax documents. Court makes copy: $.25 per page. Certification fee: $5.00 per cert. Payee: Circuit Clerk. Personal checks and credit cards accepted. Prepayment required. Mail requests: SASE required.
Civil Name Search: Access: Phone, fax, mail, in person, online. Both court and visitors may perform in person name searches. No search fee. Civil records in files since 1992. Mail turnaround time 2-3 days. Civil PAT goes back to 1995. **Note: For a complete description of online access see the** *Online Access is Statewide* **section at the front or back of this chapter**.
Criminal Name Search: Access: Phone, fax, mail, in person, online. Both court and visitors may perform in person name searches. No search fee. Required to search: name, years to search, DOB, SSN, signed release. Criminal records in files since 1992. Criminal PAT goes back to same as civil. **For details about mail, fax, phone, in-person, and online access programs offered by the KYAOC see the sections at the front or back of this chapter**.

Breckinridge County

Circuit & District Court PO Box 111, Hardinsburg, KY 40143; 270-756-2239; fax: 270-756-1129; 8AM-4PM M-F; 8AM-12 Sat (CST). *Felony, Misdemeanor, Civil, Eviction, Small Claims, Probate.*
www.courts.ky.gov/counties/
General Information: No adoption, mental, juvenile, or sealed records released. Will fax documents $2.00 1st page, $1.00 ea add'l, prepaid. Court makes copy: $.25 per page. Self serve copy: same. Certification fee: $5.00. Payee: Circuit Clerk. Personal checks and credit cards accepted. Prepayment required. Mail requests: SASE required for mail return of any copies.
Civil Name Search: Access: In person, online. Visitors must perform in person searches themselves. Civil records on computer back to 8/1994, on index cards since 1978, prior records in office 1992-present, Record books to 1991 bound in Archives. Public use terminal available. **Note: For a complete description of online access see the** *Online Access is Statewide* **section at the front or back of this chapter**.
Criminal Name Search: Access: In person, online. Visitors must perform in person searches themselves. Required to search: name, years to search, DOB, SSN. Criminal records computerized from 8/1994, on index cards since 1978, prior records on docket books since the 1800s. **For details about mail, fax, phone, in-person, and online access programs offered by the KYAOC see the sections at the front or back of this chapter**.

Bullitt County

Circuit & District Court Box 746, Shepherdsville, KY 40165; 502-543-7104; fax: 502-543-7158; 8AM-4PM (EST). *Felony, Misdemeanor, Civil, Eviction, Small Claims, Probate* www.courts.ky.gov/counties/bullitt/
General Information: The District Court can be reached at 502-543-2244. No adoption, mental, juvenile, or sealed records released. Fee to fax out case file is $2.00 per page. Court makes copy: $.25 per page. Self serve copy: same. Certification fee: $5.00. Payee: Circuit Clerk. Personal checks accepted. No credit cards accepted. Prepayment required.
Civil Name Search: Access: In person, online. Visitors must perform in person searches themselves. Required to search: name. Civil records on computer since 11/91, prior records on index cards since the 1800s. Civil PAT goes back to 11/1991. **Note: For a complete description of online access see the** *Online Access is Statewide* **section at the front or back of this chapter**.
Criminal Name Search: Access: In person, online. Visitors must perform in person searches themselves. Required to search: name, years to search, DOB, SSN. Criminal records on computer since 11/91, prior records on index cards since the 1800s. Criminal PAT goes back to same as civil.

For details about mail, fax, phone, in-person, and online access programs offered by the KYAOC see the sections at the front or back of this chapter.

Butler County

Circuit & District Court Box 625, 110 N Main St, Morgantown, KY 42261; 270-526-5631; fax: 270-526-6763; 8AM-4PM M-F; 9AM-N Sat (CST). *Felony, Misdemeanor, Civil, Eviction, Small Claims, Probate.*
www.courts.ky.gov/counties/
General Information: No adoption, mental, juvenile, or sealed records released. Will not fax documents. Court makes copy: $.25 per page. No certification fee . Payee: Circuit Clerk. Personal checks accepted. No credit cards accepted. Prepayment required. Mail requests: SASE required.
Civil Name Search: Access: In person, online. Both court and visitors may perform in person name searches. Civil records on computer since 1993, prior records on index cards since the 1800s. Civil PAT goes back to 1993. **Note: For a complete description of online access see the** *Online Access is Statewide* **section at the front or back of this chapter**.
Criminal Name Search: Access: In person, online. Both court and visitors may perform in person name searches. Required to search: name, years to search, DOB. Criminal records on computer since 1993, prior records on index cards since the 1800s, easily accessible from 1978. Criminal PAT goes back to same as civil. **For details about mail, fax, phone, in-person, and online access programs offered by the KYAOC see the sections at the front or back of this chapter**.

Caldwell County

Circuit & District Court 105 W Court Sq, Princeton, KY 42445; 270-365-6884; fax: 270-365-9171; 8AM-4PM (CST). *Felony, Misdemeanor, Civil, Eviction, Small Claims, Probate.* www.courts.ky.gov/counties/
General Information: Probate fax is same as main fax number. No adoption, mental, juvenile, or sealed records released. Fee to fax out file $2.00 1st page, $1.00 each add'l. Court makes copy: $.25 per page; copy request must include postage. Self serve copy: same. Certification fee: $5.00 per doc plus copy fee. Payee: Circuit Clerk. Personal checks accepted. Major credit cards accepted, except some VISAs. Prepayment required.
Civil Name Search: Access: In person, online. Visitors must perform in person searches themselves. Civil index on cards; on computer back to 9/94. Civil PAT goes back to 9/1994. **Note: For a complete description of online access see the** *Online Access is Statewide* **section at the front or back of this chapter**.
Criminal Name Search: Access: In person, online. Visitors must perform in person searches themselves. Required to search: name, years to search, DOB; also helpful: SSN. Criminal records indexed on cards; on computer back to 9/94. Criminal PAT goes back to same as civil. **For details about mail, fax, phone, in-person, and online access programs offered by the KYAOC see the sections at the front or back of this chapter**.

Calloway County

Circuit & District Court 312 N 4th St, Murray, KY 42071; 270-753-2714; fax: 270-759-9822; 8AM-5:30PM M-TH; 8AM-4:30PM F (CST). *Felony, Misdemeanor, Civil, Eviction, Small Claims, Probate.*
www.courts.ky.gov/counties/
General Information: Circuit court civil and criminal phone number is 270-753-2773. No adoption, mental, juvenile, or sealed records released. Will fax documents $3.00 1st page, $1.00 ea add'l. Court makes copy: $.25 per page. Certification fee: $5.00. Payee: Circuit Clerk. Personal checks accepted. Major credit cards accepted except VISA. Prepayment required. Mail requests: SASE required for civil.
Civil Name Search: Access: Mail, in person, online. Visitors must perform in person searches themselves. No search fee. Civil records on computer since 6/92, on index cards since 1978. Prior to 1978 records are archived in Frankfort. Civil PAT goes back to 1978. **Note: For a complete description of online access see the** *Online Access is Statewide* **section at the front or back of this chapter**.
Criminal Name Search: Access: In person, online. Visitors must perform in person searches themselves. Required to search: name, years to search, DOB; SSN helpful. Criminal records on computer since 6/92, on index cards since 1978. Prior to 1978 records are archived in Frankfort. Criminal PAT goes back to same as civil. **For details about mail, fax, phone, in-person, and online access programs offered by the KYAOC see the sections at the front or back of this chapter**.

Campbell County

Circuit Court 330 York St, Rm 8, Newport, KY 41071; 859-292-6314; probate phone: 859-292-6305; fax: 859-431-0816; 8:30AM-4PM (EST). *Felony, Civil Actions over $5,000.*
http://courts.ky.gov/Counties/Campbell/default.htm
General Information: Probate address is 600 Columbia St. No adoption, mental, juvenile, or sealed records released. Will not fax out case files. Court makes copy: $.25 per page. Self serve copy: same. Certification fee: $5.00

per doc plus copy fee. Payee: Campbell Circuit Court. Personal checks accepted. No credit cards accepted. Prepayment required.

Civil Name Search: Access: Mail, in person, online. Visitors must perform in person searches themselves. Search fee: Fee based on number of copy pages. Civil records on computer since 1992, prior records on index cards since 1978. Civil PAT goes back to 1992. Public terminal results may also show SSN. **Note: For a complete description of online access see the *Online Access is Statewide* section at the front or back of this chapter.**

Criminal Name Search: Access: Mail, in person, online. Visitors must perform in person searches themselves. Search fee: Fee based on number of copy pages. Required to search: name, years to search; SSN helpful. Criminal records on computer since 1992, prior records on index cards since 1978. Criminal PAT goes back to same as civil. Public terminal results may also show SSN. **For information about the mail, fax, phone, in-person, and online access programs offered by the KYAOC see the sections at the front or back of this chapter.**

District Court 600 Columbia St, Newport, KY 41071-1816; 859-292-6305; fax: 859-292-6593; 8AM-4PM (EST). *Misdemeanor, Civil Actions under $5,000, Eviction, Small Claims, Probate.*
http://courts.ky.gov/Counties/Campbell/default.htm
General Information: Probate fax is same as main fax number. No adoption, mental, juvenile, or sealed records released. Will not fax documents. Court makes copy: $.25 per page. Self serve copy: same. Certification fee: $5.00 per doc plus copy fees. Payee: Campbell Circuit Clerk. Business checks accepted. No credit cards accepted. Prepayment required. Mail requests: SASE required for civil.

Civil Name Search: Access: Mail, in person, online. Both court and visitors may perform in person name searches. Search fee: $10.00 (probate searches only). Civil records on computer back to 1992, prior records on index cards to 1978. Civil PAT goes back to 1992. **Note: For a complete description of online access see the *Online Access is Statewide* section at the front or back of this chapter.**

Criminal Name Search: Access: In person, online. Visitors must perform in person searches themselves. Criminal records computerized from 1992, prior records on index cards to 1978. Criminal PAT goes back to same as civil. **For information about the mail, fax, phone, in-person, and online access programs offered by the KYAOC see the sections at the front or back of this chapter.**

Carlisle County

Circuit & District Court Box 337, Bardwell, KY 42023; 270-628-5425; fax: 270-628-5456; 8AM-4PM (CST). *Felony, Misdemeanor, Civil, Eviction, Small Claims, Probate.*
www.courts.ky.gov/counties/
General Information: No adoption, mental, juvenile, or sealed records released. Will fax documents $2.00 per page. Court makes copy: $.25 per page. Self serve copy: same. Certification fee: $5.00. Payee: Circuit Clerk. Personal checks accepted. No credit cards accepted. Prepayment required. Mail requests: SASE required.

Civil Name Search: Access: Phone, fax, mail, in person, online. Both court and visitors may perform in person name searches. No search fee. Civil records on computer since 5/1993, records on docket books since 1978, prior records archived. Mail turnaround time 1-5 days. Civil PAT goes back to 1993. **Note: For a complete description of online access see the *Online Access is Statewide* section at the front or back of this chapter.**

Criminal Name Search: Access: Phone, fax, mail, in person, online. Both court and visitors may perform in person name searches. No search fee. Criminal records on computer since 5/1993, records on docket books since 1978, prior records archived. Note: Mail turnaround time 1-5 days. Criminal PAT goes back to same as civil. Terminal results include SSN. **For information about the mail, fax, phone, in-person, and online access programs offered by the KYAOC see the sections at the front or back of this chapter.**

Carroll County

Circuit & District Court 802 Clay St, Carrollton, KY 41008; 502-732-4305; fax: 502-732-8138; 8AM-4:30PM (EST). *Felony, Misdemeanor, Civil, Eviction, Small Claims, Probate.*
www.courts.ky.gov/counties/
General Information: No adoption, mental, juvenile, or sealed records released. Will not fax out case files. Court makes copy: $.25 per page. Certification fee: $5.00 per cert plus copy fee. Payee: Circuit Clerk. Personal checks and credit cards accepted. Prepayment required. Mail requests: SASE required for mail return of any copies.

Civil Name Search: Access: In person, online. Visitors must perform in person searches themselves. Civil records on computer since 1994, on docket books since 1988. Records before 1988 archived in Frankfort. Civil PAT goes back to 1994. **Note: For a complete description of online**

access see the *Online Access is Statewide* section at the front or back of this chapter.

Criminal Name Search: Access: In person, online. Visitors must perform in person searches themselves. Required to search: name, years to search, DOB; SSN helpful. Criminal records on computer since 1994, on docket books since 1988. Records before 1988 archived in Frankfort. Criminal PAT goes back to same as civil. **For information about the mail, fax, phone, in-person, and online access programs offered by the KYAOC see the sections at the front or back of this chapter.**

Carter County

Circuit Court 100 E Main St, Carter County Justice Center, Grayson, KY 41143; 606-474-5191; fax: 606-474-8826; 8:30AM-4PM; 9AM-N Sat (EST). *Felony, Civil Actions over $5,000.*
www.courts.ky.gov/counties/
General Information: No adoption, mental, juvenile, or sealed records released. Will not fax documents. Court makes copy: $.25 per page. Certification fee: $5.00 per doc plus copy fee. Payee: Carter County Circuit Clerk. Personal checks accepted. No credit cards accepted. Prepayment required.

Civil Name Search: Access: In person, online. Visitors must perform in person searches themselves. Civil records on computer since 1994, records archived since 1978, prior records are archived. Civil PAT goes back to 1994. **Note: For a complete description of online access see the *Online Access is Statewide* section at the front or back of this chapter.**

Criminal Name Search: Access: In person, online. Visitors must perform in person searches themselves. Required to search: name, years to search, DOB, SSN. Criminal records on computer since 1994, records archived since 1978, prior records are archived. Criminal PAT goes back to 1994. **For information about the mail, fax, phone, in-person, and online access programs offered by the KYAOC see the sections at the front or back of this chapter.**

District Court Carter County Justice Center, 100 E Main, Grayson, KY 41143; 606-474-6572; fax: 606-474-8584; 8:30AM-4PM (EST). *Misdemeanor, Civil Actions under $5,000, Eviction, Small Claims, Probate.*
www.courts.ky.gov/
General Information: No adoption, mental, juvenile, or sealed records released. Will fax documents $3.00 1st page, $1.00 each add'l page. Court makes copy: $.25 per page. Certification fee: $5.00. Payee: District Clerk. Personal checks accepted. No credit cards accepted. Prepayment required. Mail requests: SASE required for civil.

Civil Name Search: Access: Mail, in person, online. Both court and visitors may perform in person name searches. No search fee. Civil records on computer since 1994, prior records on index cards. Mail turnaround time 2-3 days Civil PAT goes back to 4/1994. **Note: For a complete description of online access see the *Online Access is Statewide* section at the front or back of this chapter.**

Criminal Name Search: Access: In person, online. Visitors must perform in person searches themselves. Required to search: name, years to search, DOB; SSN helpful. Criminal records on computer since 1994, prior records on index cards. Criminal PAT goes back to same as civil. Results include last 4 digits of SSN, DOB year only. **For information about the mail, fax, phone, in-person, and online access programs offered by the KYAOC see the sections at the front or back of this chapter.**

Casey County

Circuit & District Court PO Box 147, Liberty, KY 42539; 606-787-6510/606-787-6761; fax: 606-787-2497; 7AM-5PM (EST). *Felony, Misdemeanor, Civil, Eviction, Small Claims, Probate.*
www.courts.ky.gov/counties/
General Information: This court asks all pre-trial record requests go to the Administrative office of the Courts in Frankfort. No adoption, mental, juvenile, or sealed records released. Will fax documents $1.00 per page fee. Court makes copy: $.25 per page. Self serve copy: same. Certification fee: $5.00. Payee: Circuit Clerk. Personal checks accepted. No credit cards accepted. Prepayment required.

Civil Name Search: Access: In person, online. Visitors must perform in person searches themselves. Civil index on cards since 1978, prior records archived, computerized from 1995. Civil PAT goes back to 1995. **Note: For a complete description of online access see the *Online Access is Statewide* section at the front or back of this chapter.**

Criminal Name Search: Access: In person, online. Visitors must perform in person searches themselves. Required to search: name, years to search, DOB, SSN. Criminal records indexed on cards since 1978, prior records archived, computerized from 1995. Criminal PAT goes back to same as civil. **For information about the mail, fax, phone, in-person, and online access programs offered by the KYAOC see the sections at the front or back of this chapter.**

Christian County

Circuit & District Court Christian County Justice Ctr, 100 Justice Way, Hopkinsville, KY 42240; 270-889-6539; fax: 270-889-6564; 8AM-4:30PM (CST). *Felony, Misdemeanor, Civil, Eviction, Small Claims, Probate.* www.courts.ky.gov/counties/

General Information: Fax number above is for District Court. No adoption, mental, juvenile, or sealed records released. Will not fax documents. Court makes copy: $.25 per page. Certification fee: $5.00 per doc. Payee: Circuit Clerk. No personal checks accepted. Visa/MC accepted. Prepayment required.

Civil Name Search: Access: In person, online. Visitors must perform in person searches themselves. Civil records on computer since 1991, prior records on index cards since 1978. Civil PAT goes back to 1991. **Note: For a complete description of online access see the *Online Access is Statewide* section at the front or back of this chapter.**

Criminal Name Search: Access: In person, online. Visitors must perform in person searches themselves. Required to search: name, years to search; also helpful: DOB, SSN. Criminal records on computer since 1991, prior records on index cards since 1978. Criminal PAT goes back to same as civil. **For information about the mail, fax, phone, in-person, and online access programs offered by the KYAOC see the sections at the front or back of this chapter.**

Clark County

Circuit Court Box 687, Winchester, KY 40392; 859-737-7264; fax: 859-737-7005; 8AM-4PM (EST). *Felony, Civil Actions over $5,000.* www.courts.ky.gov/counties/

General Information: No adoption, mental, juvenile, or sealed records released. Will not fax documents. Court makes copy: $.25 per page. Certification fee: $5.00 per doc. Payee: Circuit Clerk. Personal checks accepted. No credit cards accepted. Prepayment required.

Civil Name Search: Access: In person, online. Visitors must perform in person searches themselves. Required to search: name, years to search; also helpful: address. Civil records on computer since 1989, on index cards since 1950, prior records archived since the 1700s. Civil PAT goes back to 1989. **Note: For a complete description of online access see the *Online Access is Statewide* section at the front or back of this chapter.**

Criminal Name Search: Access: In person, online. Visitors must perform in person searches themselves. Required to search: name, years to search; also helpful: address, DOB, SSN. Criminal records on computer since 1989, on index cards since 1950, prior records archived since the 1700s. Criminal PAT goes back to same as civil. **For information about the mail, fax, phone, in-person, and online access programs offered by the KYAOC see the sections at the front or back of this chapter**

District Court PO Box 687, 17 Cleveland Ave, Courthouse Annex, Winchester, KY 40392-0687; 859-737-7141; probate phone: 859-737-7141; fax: 859-737-7005; 8AM-4PM (EST). *Misdemeanor, Civil Actions under $5,000, Eviction, Small Claims, Probate.*

General Information: Probate fax is same as main fax number. No adoption, mental, juvenile, or sealed records released. Will not fax documents. Court makes copy: $.25 per page. Self serve copy: same. Certification fee: $5.00. Payee: District Clerk. Personal checks accepted. No credit cards accepted. Prepayment required.

Civil Name Search: Access: In person, online. Both court and visitors may perform in person name searches. No search fee. Civil records on computer since 1989, on docket books since 1978, prior records on archived. Civil PAT goes back to 1989. **Note: For a complete description of online access see the *Online Access is Statewide* section at the front or back of this chapter.**

Criminal Name Search: Access: In person, online. Both court and visitors may perform in person name searches. Required to search: name, years to search; also helpful: DOB, SSN. Criminal records on computer since 1989, on docket books since 1978, prior records on archived. Criminal PAT goes back to same as civil. **For information about the mail, fax, phone, in-person, and online access programs offered by the KYAOC see the sections at the front or back of this chapter.**

Clay County

Circuit & District Court 316 Main St #108, Manchester, KY 40962; 606-598-3663; fax: 606-598-4047; 7:30AM-4:30PM (EST). *Felony, Misdemeanor, Civil, Eviction, Small Claims, Probate.* www.courts.ky.gov/counties/

General Information: No adoption, mental, juvenile, or sealed records released. Will not fax documents. Court makes copy: $.25 per page. Self serve copy: same. Certification fee: $5.00 per doc plus copy fee. Payee: Circuit Clerk. Personal checks accepted. Visa/MC accepted. Prepayment required.

Civil Name Search: Access: In person, online. Visitors must perform in person searches themselves. Civil records on computer back to 1992, on index cards since 1978, records through 1991 in archives. Civil PAT goes back to 1992. **Note: For a complete description of online access see the *Online Access is Statewide* section at the front or back of this chapter.**

Criminal Name Search: Access: In person, online. Visitors must perform in person searches themselves. Required to search: name, years to search, DOB; SSN helpful. Criminal records computerized from 1992, on index cards since 1978, records through 1991 in archives. Criminal PAT goes back to same as civil. **For information about the mail, fax, phone, in-person, and online access programs offered by the KYAOC see the sections at the front or back of this chapter.**

Clinton County

Circuit & District Court Courthouse 2nd Fl, 100 S Cross St, Albany, KY 42602; 606-387-6424; fax: 606-387-8154; 8AM-4:30PM M-F; 8AM-N Sat (CST). *Felony, Misdemeanor, Civil, Eviction, Small Claims, Probate.* www.courts.ky.gov/Counties/Clinton/default.htm

General Information: No adoption, mental, juvenile, or sealed records released. Will not fax documents. Court makes copy: $.25 per page. Certification fee: $5.00 per doc. Payee: Circuit Clerk. Personal checks accepted. No credit cards accepted. Prepayment required. Mail requests: SASE required.

Civil Name Search: Access: Phone, mail, in person, online. Both court and visitors may perform in person name searches. No search fee. Civil records on computer since 8/92, on docket books since 1978, prior records archived to 1865. Mail turnaround time 5 days. Civil PAT goes back to 8/1992. **Note: For a complete description of online access see the *Online Access is Statewide* section at the front or back of this chapter.**

Criminal Name Search: Access: In person, online. Visitors must perform in person searches themselves. Required to search: name, years to search, SSN; also helpful: DOB. Criminal records on computer since 8/93, on docket books since 1978, prior records archive to 1865. NCriminal PAT goes back to same as civil. **For information about the mail, fax, phone, in-person, and online access programs offered by the KYAOC see the sections at the front or back of this chapter.**

Crittenden County

Circuit & District Court 107 S Main, Marion, KY 42064; 270-965-4200 (and) 270-965-4046; fax: 270-965-4572; 8AM-4:30PM (CST). *Felony, Misdemeanor, Civil, Eviction, Small Claims, Probate, Traffic.* www.courts.ky.gov/counties/

General Information: No adoption, mental, juvenile, or sealed records released. Fee to fax out file $2.00 1st page; $1.00 each add'l. Court makes copy: $.25 per page. Certification fee: $5.00. Payee: Circuit Clerk. No personal checks. No credit cards accepted. Prepayment required.

Civil Name Search: Access: In person, online. Visitors must perform in person searches themselves. Civil index on cards since 1978; on computer back to 9/94. Civil PAT goes back to 9/1994. **Note: For a complete description of online access see the *Online Access is Statewide* section at the front or back of this chapter.**

Criminal Name Search: Access: In person, online. Visitors must perform in person searches themselves. Circuit criminal records on index cards since 1978; on computer back to 9/94; District Criminal 9/94 to present. Criminal PAT goes back to same as civil. **For information about the mail, fax, phone, in-person, and online access programs offered by the KYAOC see the sections at the front or back of this chapter.**

Cumberland County

Circuit & District Court PO Box 395, Burkesville, KY 42717-0395; 270-864-2611; fax: 270-864-1227; 8AM-4PM (CST). *Felony, Misdemeanor, Civil, Eviction, Small Claims, Probate.* www.courts.ky.gov/counties/

General Information: No adoption, mental, juvenile, or sealed records released. Fee to fax out file $2.00 plus $1.00 per page. Court makes copy: $.25 per page. Self serve copy: $.25 per page. Certification fee: $5.00 per doc. Payee: Circuit Clerk. Personal checks accepted. No credit cards accepted. Prepayment required.

Civil Name Search: Access: In person, online. Visitors must perform in person searches themselves. Civil records on computer back to 6/93, on docket cards from 1978, prior records archived. Civil PAT goes back to 6/1993. **Note: For a complete description of online access see the *Online Access is Statewide* section at the front or back of this chapter.**

Criminal Name Search: Access: In person, online. Visitors must perform in person searches themselves. Required to search: name, years to search, DOB; SSN helpful. Criminal records computerized from 6/93, on docket cards from 1978, prior records archived. Criminal PAT goes back to same as civil. **For information about the mail, fax, phone, in-person, and online access programs offered by the KYAOC see the sections at the front or back of this chapter.**

Daviess County

Circuit & District Court PO Box 277, 100 E Second St, Owensboro, KY 42302; 270-687-7330-Circuit Crim; criminal phone: 270-687-7329-Circuit Crim; 270-687-7200-District Crim; civil phone: 270-687-7220-Circuit Civil; 270-687-7205-District Civil; probate phone: 270-687-7207;; 8AM-4PM (CST). *Felony, Misdemeanor, Civil, Eviction, Small Claims, Probate.* www.courts.ky.gov/counties/

General Information: These courts function as a combined court, that is, a criminal search includes Circuit and District courts, ditto for Civil. No adoption, mental, juvenile, or sealed records released. Will not fax documents. Court makes copy: $.25 per page. Certification fee: $5.00 per cert plus copy fee. Payee: Circuit Clerk. Local business checks accepted; no personal checks. No credit cards accepted. Prepayment required.

Civil Name Search: Access: In person, online. Visitors must perform in person searches themselves. Civil records on computer since 4/91, on index cards since 1978, prior records on docket books since 1809. Civil PAT goes back to 4/1991. Public terminals located on 2nd Fl and there is a person to assist you. **Note: For a complete description of online access see the** *Online Access is Statewide* **section at the front or back of this chapter.**

Criminal Name Search: Access: In person, online. Visitors must perform in person searches themselves. Required to search: name, years to search, DOB, SSN. Criminal records on computer since 4/91, on index cards since 1978, prior records on docket books since 1809. Criminal PAT goes back to 4/1991. Public terminals located on 2nd Fl and there is a person to assist you. **For information about the mail, fax, phone, in-person, and online access programs offered by the KYAOC see the sections at the front or back of this chapter.**

Edmonson County

Circuit & District Court Box 739, 110 Cross Main St., Brownsville, KY 42210; 270-597-2584; probate phone: 270-597-3918; fax: 270-597-2884; 8AM-4:30PM M-W,F; 8AM-N TH,S (CST). *Felony, Misdemeanor, Civil, Eviction, Small Claims, Probate.* www.courts.ky.gov/counties/

General Information: The court personnel will look at computer and relate limited information w/o pulling file, but the court strongly urges to hire a search firm for best information. No adoption, mental, juvenile, or sealed records released. Will not fax documents. Court makes copy: $.25 per page. Self serve copy: same. Certification fee: $5.00. Payee: Circuit Clerk. Personal checks accepted. No credit cards accepted. Prepayment required.

Civil Name Search: Access: In person, online. Visitors must perform in person searches themselves. Required to search: name, years to search, address. Civil records computerized since 1995, on index cards and docket books from 1800s. Civil PAT goes back to 1995. SSN also appears on terminal search results. **Note: For a complete description of online access see the** *Online Access is Statewide* **section at the front or back of this chapter.**

Criminal Name Search: Access: In person, online. Visitors must perform in person searches themselves. Required to search: name, years to search, DOB, SSN. Criminal records computerized since 1995, on index cards and docket books from 1800s. Criminal PAT goes back to same as civil. Terminal results include SSN. **For information about the mail, fax, phone, in-person, and online access programs offered by the KYAOC see the sections at the front or back of this chapter.**

Elliott County

Circuit & District Court PO Box 788, Corner of Main and Jane Caudill St, Sandy Hook, KY 41171; 606-738-5238; fax: 606-738-6962; 8AM-4PM M-F; 9AM-N 1st & 3rd Sat (EST). *Felony, Misdemeanor, Civil, Eviction, Small Claims, Probate.* www.courts.ky.gov/counties/

General Information: Also open first and third Sat of month from 9AM to noon. No adoption, mental, juvenile, or sealed records released. Will fax specific case file $2.00 1st page; $1.00 each add'l. Court makes copy: $.25 per page. Self serve copy: same. Certification fee: $5.00 per doc. Payee: Circuit Clerk. Personal checks accepted. No credit cards accepted. Prepayment required.

Civil Name Search: Access: In person, online. Both court and visitors may perform in person name searches. No search fee. Civil records on computer since 10/1992, prior records on index cards since 1978. Civil PAT goes back to 10/1992. Terminal results also show SSNs. **Note: For a complete description of online access see the** *Online Access is Statewide* **section at the front or back of this chapter.**

Criminal Name Search: Access: In person, online. Both court and visitors may perform in person name searches. No search fee. Required to search: name, years to search; SSN helpful. Criminal records on computer since 10/1992, prior records on index cards since 1978. Criminal PAT goes back to same as civil. **For information about the mail, fax, phone, in-person, and online access programs offered by the KYAOC see the sections at the front or back of this chapter**

Estill County

Circuit & District Court 130 Main St, Rm 207, Irvine, KY 40336; 606-723-3970; fax: 606-723-1158; 8AM-4PM M-TH; 8AM-6:30PM F (EST). *Felony, Misdemeanor, Civil, Eviction, Small Claims, Probate.* www.courts.ky.gov/counties/

General Information: Probate index is separate at this same address. No adoption, mental, juvenile, or sealed records released. Fee to fax out file $1.00 per page. Court makes copy: $.25 per page. Certification fee: $5.00 per doc includes copy fee. Payee: Circuit Clerk. Personal checks accepted. No credit cards accepted. Prepayment required. Mail requests: SASE required.

Civil Name Search: Access: Phone, fax, mail, in person, online. Both court and visitors may perform in person name searches. No search fee. Civil index on cards and computer back to 1994; older at archives. Mail turnaround time 2-4 days. Civil PAT goes back to 1994. **Note: For a complete description of online access see the** *Online Access is Statewide* **section at the front or back of this chapter.**

Criminal Name Search: Access: In person, online. Both court and visitors may perform in person name searches. No search fee. Required to search: name, years to search, DOB. Criminal records go back to 1994. Criminal PAT goes back to same as civil. **For information about the mail, fax, phone, in-person, and online access programs offered by the KYAOC see the sections at the front or back of this chapter.**

Fayette County

Circuit Court 120 N Limestone, Lexington, KY 40507; criminal phone: 859-246-2224; civil phone: 859-246-2141; fax: 859-246-2227; 8:30AM-4:30PM (EST). *Felony, Civil Actions over $5,000.* http://courts.ky.gov/Counties/Fayette/default.htm

General Information: No adoption, juvenile, mental, or sealed records released. Court makes copy: $.25 per page. Self serve copy: same. Certification fee: $5.00 per doc. Payee: Fayette County Circuit Clerk. No personal checks or credit cards accepted. Prepayment required.

Civil Name Search: Access: In person, online. Both court and visitors may perform in person name searches. Civil records on computer since 4/1993, on index cards since 1978, prior records on books and archived. Civil PAT goes back to 1988. **Note: For a complete description of online access see the** *Online Access is Statewide* **section at the front or back of this chapter.**

Criminal Name Search: Access: In person, online. Both court and visitors may perform in person name searches. Required to search: name, years to search; also helpful: DOB, SSN. Criminal records on computer since 4/1993, on index cards since 1978, prior records on books and archived. Criminal PAT goes back to 1993. Terminal results include SSN. **For information about the mail, fax, phone, in-person, and online access programs offered by the KYAOC see the sections at the front or back of this chapter.**

District Court 150 N Limestone, Lexington, KY 40507; 859-246-2141; criminal phone: 859-246-2228; civil phone: 859-246-2240; probate phone: 859-246-2242; fax: 859-246-2146; 8AM-4PM (EST). *Misdemeanor, Civil Actions under $5,000, Eviction, Small Claims, Probate.* http://courts.ky.gov/Counties/Fayette/default.htm

General Information: Probate and civil is in Rm D101; criminal and traffic in D157. No adoption, mental, juvenile, or sealed records released. Will not fax documents. Court makes copy: $.25 per page. Certification fee: $5.00 per cert, $.75 for an attested copy. Payee: District Clerk. Personal checks accepted. No credit cards accepted. Prepayment required. Mail requests: SASE required for civil.

Civil Name Search: Access: Mail, in person, online. Both court and visitors may perform in person name searches. Search fee: $5.00 per name. Civil records on computer since 1992, prior records on index cards since 1977. Mail turnaround time 1 week Civil PAT goes back to 1992. **Note: For a complete description of online access see the** *Online Access is Statewide* **section at the front or back of this chapter.**

Criminal Name Search: Access: In person, online. Visitors must perform in person searches themselves. Required to search: name, years to search, DOB; SSN helpful. Criminal records on computer since 1977. Criminal PAT goes back to same as civil. **For information about the mail, fax, phone, in-person, and online access programs offered by the KYAOC see the sections at the front or back of this chapter.**

Fleming County

Circuit & District Court Courthouse 100 Court Square, Flemingsburg, KY 41041; 606-845-7011; fax: 606-849-2400; 8AM-4:30PM (EST). *Felony, Misdemeanor, Civil, Eviction, Small Claims, Probate, Traffic.* www.courts.ky.gov/counties/

General Information: No adoption, mental, juvenile, or sealed records released. Fee to fax out file $1.00 per page. Court makes copy: $.25 per page. Self serve copy: same. Certification fee: $5.00. Payee: Circuit Clerk. Personal checks accepted. No credit cards accepted. Prepayment required. Mail requests: SASE required.

Civil Name Search: Access: Phone, mail, in person, online. Both court and visitors may perform in person name searches. No search fee. Civil records on computer since 5/1994, prior records on index cards back to 1992. Mail turnaround time 1-3 days. Civil PAT goes back to 4/1994. **Note: For a complete description of online access see the *Online Access is Statewide* section at the front or back of this chapter.**

Criminal Name Search: Access: In person, online. Both court and visitors may perform in person name searches. No search fee. Required to search: name, years to search, DOB, SSN helpful. Criminal records on computer since 5/1994, prior records on index cards since 1978. Criminal PAT goes back to same as civil. **For information about the mail, fax, phone, in-person, and online access programs offered by the KYAOC see the sections at the front or back of this chapter.**

Floyd County

Circuit Court 127 S Lake Dr, Prestonsburg, KY 41653-3368; 606-889-1658; civil phone: 606-889-1650; fax: 606-889-1666; 8AM-4PM (EST). *Felony, Civil Actions over $5,000.* www.courts.ky.gov/counties/

General Information: No adoption, mental, juvenile, or sealed records released. Will fax documents $2.00 1st page; $1.00 ea add'l page. Court makes copy: $.25 per page. Self serve copy: no charge if paper provided. Certification fee: $5.00. Payee: Clerk of Circuit Court. Personal checks accepted. No credit cards accepted. Prepayment required. Mail requests: SASE required.

Civil Name Search: Access: Mail, in person, online. Both court and visitors may perform in person name searches. No search fee. Civil records on computer since 9/1991, prior records on index cards since 1978. Mail turnaround time up to 10 days. Civil PAT goes back to 1991. **Note: For a complete description of online access see the *Online Access is Statewide* section at the front or back of this chapter.**

Criminal Name Search: Access: Mail, in person, online. Both court and visitors may perform in person name searches. No search fee. Required to search: name, years to search, DOB, SSN. Criminal records on computer since 9/1991, prior records on index cards since 1978. Mail turnaround time up to 10 days. Criminal PAT goes back to same as civil. Terminal results include SSN. **For information about the mail, fax, phone, in-person, and online access programs offered by the KYAOC see the sections at the front or back of this chapter.**

District Court 127 S Lake Dr, Prestonsburg, KY 41653; 606-889-1658; criminal phone: 606-889-1672; probate phone: 606-889-1650; fax: 606-889-1652; 8AM-4PM (EST). *Misdemeanor, Small Claims, Probate.* www.courts.ky.gov/counties/

General Information: Small claims- 606-889-1650. No adoption, mental, juvenile, or sealed records released. Will not fax documents. Court makes copy: $.25 per page. Certification fee: $5.00. Payee: Floyd District Court. Personal checks accepted. No credit cards accepted. Prepayment required. Mail requests: SASE required.

Civil Name Search: Access: Mail, in person, online. Both court and visitors may perform in person name searches. No search fee. Civil records on computer since 1991, prior records on index cards since 1978. Records are only kept for five years in this office. Mail turnaround time up to 10 days. Civil PAT available. Includes probate index as well. **Note: For a complete description of online access see the *Online Access is Statewide* section at the front or back of this chapter.**

Criminal Name Search: Access: Mail, in person, online. Both court and visitors may perform in person name searches. No search fee. Required to search: name, years to search; also helpful: SSN. Criminal records on computer since 1991, prior records in index cards since 1989. Records are only kept for five years in this office. Mail turnaround time up to 10 days. Criminal PAT goes back to 1991. **For information about the mail, fax, phone, in-person, and online access programs offered by the KYAOC see the sections at the front or back of this chapter.**

Franklin County

Circuit Court 669 Chamberlin, Frankfort, KY 40602; 502-564-8380; fax: 502-564-8188; 7:30AM-5PM (EST). *Felony, Civil Actions over $5,000.* www.courts.ky.gov/counties/

General Information: Criminal records can be done at AOC, 100 Mill Creek Park, Frankfort KY 40601- walk-in 7AM-3PM or drive thru 7AM - 10PM No adoption, mental, juvenile, or sealed records released. Will fax documents $2.00 1st page, $1.00 each add'l, limit 10 pages. Court makes copy: $.25 per page. Self serve copy: same. Certification fee: $5.00 per doc plus copy fee. Payee: Circuit Clerk. Personal checks accepted. No credit cards accepted. Prepayment required.

Civil Name Search: Access: In person, online. Both court and visitors may perform in person name searches. No search fee. Civil records on computer since 1990, prior records on index cards since 1978. Note: Court staff will assist in person requester depending on workload. Civil PAT goes back to 1990. **Note: For a complete description of online access**

see the *Online Access is Statewide* section at the front or back of this chapter.

Criminal Name Search: Access: In person, online. No search fee. Required to search: name, years to search, DOB, SSN. Criminal records on computer since 1990, prior records on index cards since 1978. Criminal PAT goes back to 1990. **For information about the mail, fax, phone, in-person, and online access programs offered by the KYAOC see the sections at the front or back of this chapter.**

District Court 669 Chamberlin Ave, Frankfort, KY 40601; 502-564-7013; fax: 502-564-8188; 8AM-4:30PM (EST). *Misdemeanor, Civil Actions under $5,000, Eviction, Small Claims, Probate.* http://courts.ky.gov/counties/franklin/

General Information: No adoption, mental, juvenile, or sealed records released. Will fax documents $2.00 1st page, $1.00 each add'l page, limit 10 pages. Court makes copy: $.25 per page. Self serve copy: same. Certification fee: $5.00 per doc plus copy fee. Payee: Franklin Circuit Clerk. Personal checks accepted. No credit cards accepted. Prepayment required.

Civil Name Search: Access: In person, online. Visitors must perform in person searches themselves. Civil records on computer since 1990, records on index cards since 1978, prior records archived. Civil PAT goes back to 1990. **Note: For a complete description of online access see the *Online Access is Statewide* section at the front or back of this chapter.**

Criminal Name Search: Access: In person, online. Visitors must perform in person searches themselves. Required to search: name, years to search, DOB. Criminal records on computer since 1990, records on index cards since 1978, prior records archived. Criminal PAT goes back to same as civil. Terminal results also include race, gender, eyes. **For details about mail, fax, phone, in-person, and online access programs offered by the KYAOC see the sections at the front or back of this chapter.**

Fulton County

Circuit & District Court Box 198, Hickman, KY 42050; 270-236-3944; fax: 270-236-3729; 8AM-4PM (CST). *Felony, Misdemeanor, Civil, Eviction, Small Claims, Probate.* www.courts.ky.gov/counties/

General Information: Six days of the court docket information can be found at www.kycourts.com. No adoption, mental, juvenile, or sealed records released. Will not fax documents. Court makes copy: $.25 per page. Self serve copy: same. Certification fee: $5.00. Payee: Circuit Clerk. Personal checks accepted. No credit cards accepted. Prepayment required. Mail requests: SASE required for civil.

Civil Name Search: Access: Mail, in person, online. Both court and visitors may perform in person name searches. No search fee. Civil docket indexed from 1980, computerized from 1995, and archived since 1843. Civil PAT goes back to 1978. **Note: For a complete description of online access see the *Online Access is Statewide* section at the front or back of this chapter.**

Criminal Name Search: Access: In person, online. Visitors must perform in person searches themselves. Criminal records indexed from 1980, computerized from 1995, and archived since 1843. Criminal PAT goes back to same as civil. **For information about the mail, fax, phone, in-person, and online access programs offered by the KYAOC see the sections at the front or back of this chapter.**

Gallatin County

Circuit Court PO Box 256, 100 Main St, Warsaw, KY 41095; 859-567-5241; fax: 859-567-7420; 8AM-4:30PM (EST). *Felony, Civil Actions over $5,000.* www.courts.ky.gov/counties/

General Information: No adoption, mental, juvenile, or sealed records released. Will fax documents $2.00 first page, $1.00 ea addl. Court makes copy: $.25 per page. Self serve copy: same. Certification fee: $5.00 per cert plus copy fee. Payee: Circuit Clerk. Personal checks and credit cards accepted. Prepayment required. Mail requests: SASE required.

Civil Name Search: Access: Mail, in person, online. Both court and visitors may perform in person name searches. No search fee. Civil records go back to 1995, computerized docket to 1993. Mail turnaround time 4 days. Civil PAT goes back to 1995. **Note: For a complete description of online access see the *Online Access is Statewide* section at the front or back of this chapter.**

Criminal Name Search: Access: Mail, in person, online. Both court and visitors may perform in person name searches. No search fee. Required to search: name, years to search; also helpful: SSN. Criminal records go back to 1995, computerized docket to 1993. Criminal PAT goes back to same as civil. **For information about the mail, fax, phone, in-person, and online access programs offered by the KYAOC see the sections at the front or back of this chapter.**

District Court PO Box 256, Town Center, Hiways 35 and 42, Warsaw, KY 41095; 859-567-2388; probate phone: 859-567-2388; fax: 859-567-1492; 8AM-4:30PM T-F; 8AM-6PM M (EST). *Misdemeanor, Civil Actions under $5,000, Eviction, Small Claims, Probate.*

www.courts.ky.gov/counties/

General Information: Probate fax- 859-567-1492. No adoption, mental, juvenile, or sealed records released. Fee to fax out file $2.00 1st page plus $1.00 each add'l. Court makes copy: $.25 per page. Certification fee: $5.00 per doc plus copy fee. Payee: District Clerk. Personal checks accepted. MC/AmEx/Discover accepted, no Visa. A 5% transaction fee added for credit card payments. Prepayment required.

Civil Name Search: Access: Fax, mail, in person, online. Both court and visitors may perform in person name searches. No search fee; limited number accepted. Civil records on computer since 10/1994, prior records on index cards since 1978. Mail turnaround time 1-2 days. Civil PAT goes back to 10/1994. **Note: For a complete description of online access see the *Online Access is Statewide* section at the front or back of this chapter.**

Criminal Name Search: Access: Fax, mail, in person, online. Both court and visitors may perform in person name searches. No search fee; onsite searches by staff are courtesy look-ups and limited to one or two. Required to search: name, years to search, DOB; also helpful: SSN. Criminal records on computer since 10/1994, prior records on index cards since 1978. Criminal PAT goes back to same as civil. **For information about the mail, fax, phone, in-person, and online access programs offered by the KYAOC see the sections at the front or back of this chapter.**

Garrard County

Circuit & District Court 7 Public Square, Courthouse Annex, Lancaster, KY 40444; 859-792-2961; fax: 859-792-6414; 8AM-4PM M,T,TH,F, 8AM-N W,Sat (EST). *Felony, Misdemeanor, Civil, Eviction, Small Claims, Probate.*

http://courts.ky.gov/counties/Garrard/

General Information: Circuit Clerk can be reached at 859-792-2961. No adoption, mental, juvenile, or sealed records released. Court makes copy: $.25 per page. Self serve copy: $.25 per page. Certification fee: $5.00 per doc. Payee: Circuit Clerk. Personal checks and money orders accepted. Major credit cards accepted. Prepayment required.

Civil Name Search: Access: In person, online. Visitors must perform in person searches themselves. Civil records in index since 1978. Civil PAT available. **Note: For a complete description of online access see the *Online Access is Statewide* section at the front or back of this chapter.**

Criminal Name Search: Access: In person, online. Visitors must perform in person searches themselves. Required to search: name, years to search; also helpful: address, DOB, SSN. Criminal records in index since 1978. Criminal PAT available. **For information about the mail, fax, phone, in-person, and online access programs offered by the KYAOC see the sections at the front or back of this chapter.**

Grant County

Circuit & District Court Courthouse, 224 S Main, Williamstown, KY 41097; 859-824-4467 (Circuit) 859-823-5251 (District); fax: 859-824-0183; 8AM-4PM M-F (EST). *Felony, Misdemeanor, Civil, Eviction, Small Claims, Probate.*

http://courts.ky.gov

General Information: District Court records destroyed before 2000. Court is also open 8:30AM to noon on the last Sat. of month. No adoption, mental, juvenile, or sealed records released. Will fax specific docket for $2.00 for 1st page; $1.00 each add'l page. Court makes copy: $.25 per page. Self serve copy: same. Certification fee: $5.00. Payee: Circuit Clerk. Personal checks accepted. No credit cards accepted for record copies. Prepayment required.

Civil Name Search: Access: In person, online. Visitors must perform in person searches themselves. Civil records on computer back to 1992, prior records on index cards since 1977. Civil PAT goes back to 7/1992. **Note: For a complete description of online access see the *Online Access is Statewide* section at the front or back of this chapter.**

Criminal Name Search: Access: In person, online. Visitors must perform in person searches themselves. Required to search: name, years to search, DOB; SSN helpful. Criminal records computerized from 1992, prior records on index cards since 1977. Criminal PAT goes back to same as civil. **For information about the mail, fax, phone, in-person, and online access programs offered by the KYAOC see the sections at the front or back of this chapter.**

Graves County

Circuit & District Court Courthouse 100 E Broadway, Mayfield, KY 42066; 270-247-1733; fax: 270-247-7358; 8AM-4:30PM (CST). *Felony, Misdemeanor, Civil, Eviction, Small Claims, Probate.*

www.courts.ky.gov/counties/

General Information: No adoption, mental, juvenile, or sealed records released. Will fax specific case file $3.00 plus $1.00 per page if specific case

docket requested. Court makes copy: $.25 per page. Certification fee: $5.00 per doc. Payee: Circuit Clerk. Personal checks and credit cards accepted. Prepayment required.

Civil Name Search: Access: In person, online. Visitors must perform in person searches themselves. Civil records on computer since 6/1994, prior records on index cards since 1978. Civil PAT goes back to 6/1994. **Note: For a complete description of online access see the *Online Access is Statewide* section at the front or back of this chapter.**

Criminal Name Search: Access: In person, online. Visitors must perform in person searches themselves. Required to search: name, years to search, DOB; SSN helpful. Criminal records on computer since 6/1994, prior records on index cards since 1978. Criminal PAT goes back to same as civil. **For information about the mail, fax, phone, in-person, and online access programs offered by the KYAOC see the sections at the front or back of this chapter.**

Grayson County

Circuit & District Court Clerk's Office, 500 Carroll Gibson Blvd, Leitchfield, KY 42754; 270-259-3040; fax: 270-259-9866; 8AM-4:30PM M,T,W,F; 8AM-5:30PM TH (CST). *Felony, Misdemeanor, Civil, Eviction, Small Claims, Probate.*

www.courts.ky.gov/counties/

General Information: No adoption, mental, juvenile, or sealed records released. Will fax documents $1.00 per page. Court makes copy: $.25 per page. Self serve copy: same. Certification fee: $5.00. Payee: Circuit Clerk. Personal checks and credit cards accepted. Prepayment required. Mail requests: SASE required.

Civil Name Search: Access: Mail, in person, online. Both court and visitors may perform in person name searches. No search fee. Civil records on computer since 5/94, prior records on index cards since 1978. Mail turnaround time 5 days. Civil PAT goes back to 5/1994. **Note: For a complete description of online access see the *Online Access is Statewide* section at the front or back of this chapter.**

Criminal Name Search: Access: Mail, in person, online. Both court and visitors may perform in person name searches. No search fee. Required to search: name, years to search; also helpful: DOB, SSN. Criminal records on computer since 5/94, prior records on index cards since 1978. Criminal PAT goes back to same as civil. **For information about the mail, fax, phone, in-person, and online access programs offered by the KYAOC see the sections at the front or back of this chapter.**

Green County

Circuit & District Court 200 W Court St, Greensburg, KY 42743; 270-932-5631; fax: 270-932-6468; 8AM-5PM (EST). *Felony, Misdemeanor, Civil, Eviction, Small Claims, Probate.*

www.courts.ky.gov/counties/

General Information: No adoption, mental, juvenile, or sealed records released. Will fax documents to local or toll-free number. Court makes copy: $.25 per page. No certification fee . Payee: Circuit Clerk. Personal checks accepted. Visa/MC accepted. Prepayment required. Mail requests: SASE required.

Civil Name Search: Access: In person, online. Both court and visitors may perform in person name searches. Civil index on cards and computer since 1978. Mail n/a. Civil PAT goes back to 1996. **Note: For a complete description of online access see the *Online Access is Statewide* section at the front or back of this chapter.**

Criminal Name Search: Access: In person, online. Both court and visitors may perform in person name searches. Required to search: name, years to search; also helpful: DOB. Criminal records indexed on cards and computer since 1978. Criminal PAT available. **For information about the mail, fax, phone, in-person, and online access programs offered by the KYAOC see the sections at the front or back of this chapter.**

Greenup County

Circuit & District Court Courthouse Annex, 101 Harrison St, Greenup, KY 41144; 606-473-9869; fax: 606-473-7388; 9AM-4:30PM (EST). *Felony, Misdemeanor, Civil, Eviction, Small Claims, Probate.*

http://courts.ky.gov/counties/Greenup/

General Information: No adoption, mental, juvenile, or sealed records released. Will fax documents $3.00 per fax. Court makes copy: $.35 per page. Self serve copy: same. Certification fee: $5.00. Payee: Circuit Clerk. Personal checks, money orders, cash and cashier checks accepted. All major credit cards accepted. Prepayment required.

Civil Name Search: Access: In person, online. Both court and visitors may perform in person name searches. No search fee. Civil records on computer since 1990, prior records on index cards since 1978. Civil PAT goes back to 1990. Results include first and last names, SSN. **Note: For a complete description of online access see the *Online Access is Statewide* section at the front or back of this chapter.**

Criminal Name Search: Access: In person, online. Visitors must perform in person searches themselves. Required to search: name, years to search, DOB; SSN helpful. Criminal records on computer since 1990, prior records on index cards since 1978. Criminal PAT goes back to same as civil. Results include first and last names. **For information about the mail, fax, phone, in-person, and online access programs offered by the KYAOC see the sections at the front or back of this chapter.**

Hancock County

Circuit & District Court 200 Court Sq, PO Box 250, Hawesville, KY 42348; 270-927-8144; fax: 270-927-8629; 7:30AM-4PM M,T,W,F; 7:30AM-5:30PM TH (CST). *Felony, Misdemeanor, Civil, Eviction, Small Claims, Probate.*

www.courts.ky.gov/counties/

General Information: No adoption, mental, juvenile, or sealed records released. Fee to fax specific case file $2.00 for 1st page; $1.00 each add'l. Court makes copy: $.25 per page. Certification fee: $5.00 per doc copy fee. Payee: Circuit Clerk. Personal checks accepted. No credit cards accepted. Prepayment required.

Civil Name Search: Access: Mail, in person, online. Both court and visitors may perform in person name searches. No search fee. Civil records on computer since 8/1994, prior records on index cards. Civil PAT goes back to 8/1994. **Note: For a complete description of online access see the *Online Access is Statewide* section at the front or back of this chapter.**

Criminal Name Search: Access: Mail, in person, online. Both court and visitors may perform in person name searches. No search fee. Required to search: name, years to search, DOB; SSN helpful. Criminal records on computer since 8/1994, prior records on index cards. Criminal PAT goes back to 8/1994. **For information about the mail, fax, phone, in-person, and online access programs offered by the KYAOC see the sections at the front or back of this chapter.**

Hardin County

Circuit & District Court Hardin County Justice Ctr, 120 E Dixie Ave, Elizabethtown, KY 42701; 270-766-5000; fax: 270-766-5243; 8AM-4:30PM (EST). *Felony, Misdemeanor, Civil, Eviction, Small Claims, Probate.* www.courts.ky.gov/counties/

General Information: No adoption, mental, juvenile, motor vehicle or sealed records released. Will fax specific document for $2.00 1st page, $1.00 each add'l page, payable in advance by money order only. Court makes copy: $.25 per page. Certification fee: $5.00 per doc. Payee: Circuit Clerk. Money orders only accepted. No credit cards accepted. Prepayment required.

Civil Name Search: Access: In person, online. Visitors must perform in person searches themselves. Civil records on computer since 3/28/94, prior records on index cards since 1978. Note: Civil cases do not always have DOB or SSN. Civil PAT goes back to 1994. **Note: For a complete description of online access see the *Online Access is Statewide* section at the front or back of this chapter.**

Criminal Name Search: Access: In person, online. Visitors must perform in person searches themselves. Required to search: name, years to search, DOB. Criminal records on computer since 3/28/94, prior records on index cards since 1978. Criminal PAT goes back to same as civil. **For information about the mail, fax, phone, in-person, and online access programs offered by the KYAOC see the sections at the front or back of this chapter.**

Radcliff District Court 220 Freedom Way, Radcliff, KY 40160; 270-351-1299/4799; fax: 270-351-1301; 8AM-N, 12:30-4PM (EST). *Eviction, Civil under $5,000, Small Claim.* http://courts.ky.gov/

Harlan County

Circuit & District Court 129 S First St., Justice Center, Harlan, KY 40831; 606-573-2680, 606-573-7114; fax: 606-573-5895; 8AM-4:30PM (EST). *Felony, Misdemeanor, Civil, Eviction, Small Claims, Probate.* www.courts.ky.gov/counties/

General Information: No adoption, mental, juvenile, sealed or domestic violence records released. Will fax specific case file $2.00 1st page, $1.00 each add'l. Court makes copy: $.25 per page. Certification fee: $5.00 per doc plus copy fee. Payee: Circuit Clerk. Local personal checks accepted only. No credit cards accepted. Prepayment required.

Civil Name Search: Access: In person, online. Visitors must perform in person searches themselves. Civil records on computer since 8/1991, on index cards since 1978, records prior to 1991 are archived in Frankfort. Civil PAT goes back to 7/1991. Only the birth year shows on terminal results. **Note: For a complete description of online access see the *Online Access is Statewide* section at the front or back of this chapter.**

Criminal Name Search: Access: In person, online. Visitors must perform in person searches themselves. Required to search: name, years to search, DOB; SSN helpful. Criminal records on computer since 8/1991, on index cards since 1978, records prior to 1991 archived in Frankfort. Criminal PAT goes back to same as civil. **For information about the mail, fax, phone, in-person, and online access programs offered by the KYAOC see the sections at the front or back of this chapter.**

Harrison County

Circuit & District Court 115 Court St #1, Cynthiana, KY 41031; 859-234-1914; fax: 859-234-6787; 8:30AM-4:30PM, 9AM-N Sat (EST). *Felony, Misdemeanor, Civil, Eviction, Small Claims, Probate.* www.courts.ky.gov/counties/

General Information: No adoption, mental, juvenile, or sealed records released. Will not fax documents. Court makes copy: $.25 per page. Self serve copy: same. Certification fee: $5.00. Payee: Circuit Clerk. Personal checks accepted. No credit cards accepted. Prepayment required. Mail requests: SASE required for civil.

Civil Name Search: Access: Mail, in person, online. Both court and visitors may perform in person name searches. No search fee. Civil index on cards since 1978 (circuit only); on computer back to 1995; others back to 1953. Mail turnaround time 1 week. Civil PAT goes back to 1995. **Note: For a complete description of online access see the *Online Access is Statewide* section at the front or back of this chapter.**

Criminal Name Search: Access: In person, online. Visitors must perform in person searches themselves. Required to searc Criminal PAT goes back to same as civil. **For information about the mail, fax, phone, in-person, and online access programs offered by the KYAOC see the sections at the front or back of this chapter.**

Hart County

Circuit & District Court PO Box 248, 117 E South St, Munfordville, KY 42765; 270-524-5181; fax: 270-524-7202; 8AM-4PM, till 5PM M (CST). *Felony, Misdemeanor, Civil, Eviction, Small Claims, Probate.* www.courts.ky.gov/counties/

General Information: No adoption, mental, juvenile, or sealed records released. Will not fax documents. Court makes copy: $.25 per page. Self serve copy: same. Certification fee: $5.00. Payee: Circuit Clerk. Business checks accepted. No credit cards accepted. Prepayment required.

Civil Name Search: Access: In person, online. Visitors must perform in person searches themselves. Required to search: name, years to search; also helpful: address. Civil index on cards since 1978, computerized since 3/95. Civil PAT goes back to 3/1995. **Note: For a complete description of online access see the *Online Access is Statewide* section at the front or back of this chapter.**

Criminal Name Search: Access: In person, online. Visitors must perform in person searches themselves. Required to search: name, years to search, DOB, SSN; also helpful: address. Criminal records indexed on cards since 1978, computerized since 3/95. Criminal PAT goes back to same as civil. **For information about the mail, fax, phone, in-person, and online access programs offered by the KYAOC see the sections at the front or back of this chapter.**

Henderson County

Circuit & District Court PO Box 675, 5 N Main, Judicial Ctr, Henderson, KY 42419; 270-826-2405/1566; fax: 270-831-2710; 8AM-4:30PM (CST). *Felony, Civil Actions over $5,000.* www.courts.ky.gov/counties/

General Information: Fax number is valid for both District and Circuit Courts. No adoption, mental, juvenile, or sealed records released. Will fax documents $2.00 1st page, $1.00 ea. add'l, including coversheet. Court makes copy: $.25 per page. Self serve copy: same. Certification fee: $5.00 per doc plus copy fee. Payee: Circuit Clerk. Personal checks accepted. No credit cards accepted. Prepayment required. Mail requests: SASE required for mail return of any copies.

Civil Name Search: Access: In person, online. Visitors must perform in person searches themselves. Civil records on computer from 3/1991, records on index cards from 1978 to 3/1991. Civil PAT goes back to 1991. **Note: For a complete description of online access see the *Online Access is Statewide* section at the front or back of this chapter.**

Criminal Name Search: Access: In person, online. Visitors must perform in person searches themselves. Required to search: name, years to search, DOB. Criminal records computerized from 3/1991, records on index cards from 1978 to 3/1991. Criminal PAT goes back to same as civil. **For information about the mail, fax, phone, in-person, and online access programs offered by the KYAOC see the sections at the front or back of this chapter.**

Henry County

Circuit & District Court PO Box 359, 30 N Main St, New Castle, KY 40050; 502-845-7551 dist; 502-845-2868 Circ; fax: 502-845-2969; 8AM-4PM (EST). *Felony, Misdemeanor, Civil, Eviction, Small Claims, Probate.* www.courts.ky.gov/counties/

General Information: No adoption, mental, juvenile, or sealed records released. Will fax documents $2.00 1st page, $1.00 each add'l. Court makes copy: $.25 per page. Self serve copy: same. Certification fee: $5.00 per doc. Payee: Circuit Clerk. Personal checks and credit cards accepted. Prepayment required.

Civil Name Search: Access: In person, online. Visitors must perform in person searches themselves. Civil records on computer since 5/1994. Civil PAT goes back to 5/1994. **Note: For a complete description of online access see the *Online Access is Statewide* section at the front or back of this chapter.**

Criminal Name Search: Access: In person, online. Visitors must perform in person searches themselves. Required to search: name, years to search; SSN helpful. Criminal records on computer since 5/1994. Criminal PAT goes back to same as civil. **For information about the mail, fax, phone, in-person, and online access programs offered by the KYAOC see the sections at the front or back of this chapter.**

Hickman County

Circuit & District Court 109 S Washington St, Clinton, KY 42031; 270-653-3901; fax: 270-653-3989; 8AM-4PM (CST). *Felony, Misdemeanor, Civil, Eviction, Small Claims, Probate.*
www.courts.ky.gov/counties/

General Information: Probate fax is same as main fax number. No adoption, mental, juvenile, or sealed records released. Will fax out documents $2.00 1st page, $1.00 each add'l. Court makes copy: $.25 per page. Certification fee: $5.00 per cert. Payee: Circuit Clerk. Personal checks accepted. No credit cards accepted. Prepayment required. Mail requests: SASE required.

Civil Name Search: Access: Mail, in person, online. Both court and visitors may perform in person name searches. No search fee. Civil records on computer from 6/94 to present, on index from 1978 to 6/94. Note: If court does search, request must be in writing. Mail turnaround time same day if possible. Civil PAT goes back to 6/1994. **Note: For a complete description of online access see the *Online Access is Statewide* section at the front or back of this chapter.**

Criminal Name Search: Access: Mail, in person, online. Both court and visitors may perform in person name searches. No search fee. Required to search: name, years to search, DOB; also helpful: SSN. Criminal records computerized from 6/94 to present, on index from 1978 to 6/94. Mail turnaround time same day. Criminal PAT goes back to same as civil. **For information about the mail, fax, phone, in-person, and online access programs offered by the KYAOC see the sections at the front or back of this chapter.**

Hopkins County

Circuit & District Court Courthouse 30 S Main St, Madisonville, KY 42431; criminal phone: 270-824-7501; civil phone: 270-824-7502; probate phone: 270-824-7509; fax: 270-824-7032; 7:30AM-4PM (CST). *Felony, Misdemeanor, Civil, Eviction, Small Claims, Probate.*
www.courts.ky.gov/counties/

General Information: Probate fax is same as main fax number. All copy requests must be submitted in writing and there could be a 5-day wait. No adoption, mental, juvenile, or sealed records released. Will fax documents to local or toll-free number, prefer to mail docs. Court makes copy: $.25 per page. Certification fee: $5.00 plus copy fee. Payee: Circuit Clerk. Personal checks accepted. Visa/MC/AmEx accepted. Prepayment required.

Civil Name Search: Access: In person, online. Visitors must perform in person searches themselves. Civil records on computer back to 6/1991; on index cards from 1978 to 1991. Note: For searches prior to 1990, fill out search requests form to search archives in Frankfort. Civil PAT goes back to 1992. **Note: For a complete description of online access see the *Online Access is Statewide* section at the front or back of this chapter.**

Criminal Name Search: Access: In person, online. Visitors must perform in person searches themselves. Required to search: name, years to search, signed release; also helpful: DOB, SSN. Criminal records computerized from 6/1991, on index cards from 1978 to 1991, archived since 1800s. Criminal PAT goes back to same as civil. **For information about the mail, fax, phone, in-person, and online access programs offered by the KYAOC see the sections at the front or back of this chapter.**

Jackson County

Circuit Court PO Box 84, McKee, KY 40447; 606-287-7783; criminal phone: 606-287-8651; civil phone: 606-287-7783; fax: 606-287-3277; 8AM-4PM M-F; 8AM-N Sat (EST). *Felony, Civil Actions over $5,000.*
www.courts.ky.gov/counties/

General Information: No adoption, mental, juvenile, or sealed records released. Fee to fax out file $1.00 per page. Court makes copy: $.25 per page. Self serve copy: same. Certification fee: $5.00 per cert. Payee: Jackson County Circuit Clerk. Personal checks accepted. No credit cards accepted. Prepayment required. Mail requests: SASE required.

Civil Name Search: Access: Fax, mail, in person, online. Both court and visitors may perform in person name searches. No search fee. Required to search: name, years to search; also helpful: address. Civil records on computer from 5/1993 to present, on index cards from 1978 to 1993. Mail turnaround time 2 days. Civil PAT goes back to 1993. **Note: For a**

complete description of online access see the *Online Access is Statewide* section at the front or back of this chapter.

Criminal Name Search: Access: Fax, mail, in person, online. Both court and visitors may perform in person name searches. No search fee. Required to search: name, years to search, DOB; also helpful: SSN. Criminal records computerized from 5/1993 to present, on index cards from 1990 to 1993. **For information about the mail, fax, phone, in-person, and online access programs offered by the KYAOC see the sections at the front or back of this chapter** Mail turnaround time 2 days. Criminal PAT goes back to same as civil. Terminal results include SSN. **For information about the mail, fax, phone, in-person, and online access programs offered by the KYAOC see the sections at the front or back of this chapter.**

District Court PO Box 84, McKee, KY 40447; 606-287-8651; fax: 606-287-3277; 8AM-4PM M-F; 8AM-N Sat (EST). *Misdemeanor, Civil Actions under $5,000, Eviction, Small Claims, Probate.*
www.courts.ky.gov/counties/

General Information: No adoption, mental, juvenile, or sealed records released. Will fax documents $2.00 1st page, $1.00 ea add'l. Court makes copy: $.25 per page. Self serve copy: same. Certification fee: $5.00. Payee: Jackson County District Clerk. Personal checks and credit cards accepted. Prepayment required. Mail requests: SASE required.

Civil Name Search: Access: Fax, mail, in person, online. Both court and visitors may perform in person name searches. No search fee. Civil records on computer back to 5/1993, on index cards from 1978. Mail turnaround time 1 week. Civil PAT goes back to 5/1993. **Note: For a complete description of online access see the *Online Access is Statewide* section at the front or back of this chapter.**

Criminal Name Search: Access: Fax, mail, in person, online. Both court and visitors may perform in person name searches. No search fee. Required to search: name, years to search, DOB; also helpful: SSN. Criminal records computerized from 5/1993; on index cards from 1990. Mail turnaround time 1 week. Criminal PAT goes back to same as civil. Terminal results include SSN. **For information about the mail, fax, phone, in-person, and online access programs offered by the KYAOC see the sections at the front or back of this chapter.**

Jefferson County

Circuit Court 600 W Jefferson St, Circuit Clerk, Louisville, KY 40202; 502-595-3055; fax: 502-595-4128; 8:30am-4:30PM . *Felony, Civil Actions over $5,000.*
www.courts.ky.gov/counties/

General Information: Contact the Records Division at 1-800-928-2350. No adoption or sealed records released. Court makes copy: $.25 per page. Certification fee: $5.00 per doc. Payee: Circuit Clerk. Personal checks accepted. Prepayment required.

Civil Name Search: Access: In person, online. Visitors must perform in person searches themselves. Civil records on computer from 1991, prior in index cards. Civil PAT goes back to 1993. **Note: For a complete description of online access see the *Online Access is Statewide* section at the front or back of this chapter.**

Criminal Name Search: Access: In person, online. Visitors must perform in person searches themselves. Criminal records computerized from 1991, prior in index cards. Criminal PAT goes back to same as civil. **For information about the mail, fax, phone, in-person, and online access programs offered by the KYAOC see the sections at the front or back of this chapter.**

District Court 600 W Jefferson St, Hall of Justice, Louisville, KY 40202; 502-595-3055; criminal phone: 502-595-3009; civil phone: 502-595-3015; fax: 502-595-4629; 8:30AM-4:30PM (EST). *Misdemeanor, Civil Actions under $5,000, Eviction, Small Claims, Probate.*
www.courts.ky.gov/counties/

General Information: No adoption, mental, juvenile, or sealed records released. Court makes copy: $.25 per page. Self serve copy: same. Certification fee: $5.00 per doc. Payee: Circuit Clerk. Personal checks accepted. Credit cards accepted for District Criminal Traffic only. Prepayment required.

Civil Name Search: Access: In person, online. Visitors must perform in person searches themselves. Civil records on computer back to 3/93; index cards 1978 to 1988. Civil PAT goes back to 1988. **Note: For a complete description of online access see the *Online Access is Statewide* section at the front or back of this chapter.**

Criminal Name Search: Access: In person, online. Visitors must perform in person searches themselves. Criminal records computerized from 3/93; on index cards 1978 to 1988. NCriminal PAT goes back to same as civil. **For information about the mail, fax, phone, in-person, and online access programs offered by the KYAOC see the sections at the front or back of this chapter.**

Jessamine County

Circuit Court 107 N Main St, Nicholasville, KY 40356; 859-885-4531, 887-1005; fax: 859-887-0425; 8AM-4:30PM M,T,W,F; 8AM-N Th (EST). *Felony, Civil Actions over $5,000, Traffic.*
www.courts.ky.gov/counties/
General Information: No adoption, mental, juvenile, or sealed records released. Court makes copy: $.25 per page. Certification fee: $5.00 per doc. Payee: Jessamine Circuit Clerk. Personal checks accepted. Visa/MC accepted. Prepayment required.
Civil Name Search: Access: In person, online. Visitors must perform in person searches themselves. Civil records on computer from 6/1992 to present, on index cards from 1978 to 1992. Civil PAT goes back to 6/1992. **Note: For a complete description of online access see the** *Online Access is Statewide* **section at the front or back of this chapter.**
Criminal Name Search: Access: In person, online. Visitors must perform in person searches themselves. Required to search: name, years to search, DOB; also helpful: SSN. Criminal records computerized from 6/1992 to present, on index cards from 1978 to 1992. Criminal PAT goes back to same as civil. **For information about the mail, fax, phone, in-person, and online access programs offered by the KYAOC see the sections at the front or back of this chapter.**

District Court 107 N Main St, Nicholasville, KY 40356; 859-887-1005; fax: 859-887-0425; 8AM-4:30PM M-W; 8AM-N TH; 8AM-4:30PM F (EST). *Misdemeanor, Civil Actions under $5,000, Eviction, Small Claims, Probate.* www.courts.ky.gov/counties/
General Information: No adoption, mental, juvenile, or sealed records released. Court makes copy: $.25 per page. Self serve copy: $.25 per page. Certification fee: $5.00 per doc. Payee: District Clerk. Personal checks accepted. Major credit cards accepted via VitalChek, 5% usage fee added. Prepayment required. Mail requests: SASE required.
Civil Name Search: Access: Mail, in person, online. Both court and visitors may perform in person name searches. No search fee. Civil records on computer since 1992, on file cards prior. Mail turnaround time 2-4 days. Civil PAT goes back to 1992. **Note: For a complete description of online access see the** *Online Access is Statewide* **section at the front or back of this chapter.**
Criminal Name Search: Access: Mail, in person, online. Both court and visitors may perform in person name searches. No search fee. Required to search: name, years to search; also helpful: DOB, SSN. Criminal records on computer since 1992, on file cards prior. Criminal PAT goes back to same as civil. **For information about the mail, fax, phone, in-person, and online access programs offered by the KYAOC see the sections at the front or back of this chapter.**

Johnson County

Circuit & District Court 908 Third St, #109, Paintsville, KY 41240; 606-297-9567; fax: 606-297-9573; 8AM-4PM (EST). *Felony, Misdemeanor, Civil, Eviction, Small Claims, Probate.*
http://courts.ky.gov/counties/Johnson/
General Information: Probate fax is same as main fax number. No adoption, mental, juvenile, or sealed records released. Will not fax documents. Court makes copy: $.25 per page. Certification fee: $5.00. Add'l fee for copies. Payee: Circuit Clerk. Personal checks accepted. No credit cards accepted. Prepayment required. Mail requests: SASE required for civil.
Civil Name Search: Access: Phone, mail, in person, online. Both court and visitors may perform in person name searches. No search fee. Civil records on computer since 9/88, on index cards from 1978 to 1995, books from 1843 to 1978. From 1992 and prior files are at the archives in Fran. Mail turnaround time 3 days. Civil PAT goes back to 10/1988. **Note: For a complete description of online access see the** *Online Access is Statewide* **section at the front or back of this chapter.**
Criminal Name Search: Access: In person, online. Visitors must perform in person searches themselves. Required to search: name, years to search, DOB, SSN. Criminal records on computer since 9/88, on index cards from 1978 to 1988, books from 1843 to 1978. From 1992 and prior files are at the archives in Frankfurt. Criminal PAT goes back to same as civil. **For information about the mail, fax, phone, in-person, and online access programs offered by the KYAOC see the sections at the front or back of this chapter.**

Kenton County

Circuit Court 230 Madison Ave, 3rd Fl, Covington, KY 41011; 859-292-6521; fax: 859-292-6611; 8AM-4:30PM (EST). *Felony, Civil Actions over $5,000.* http://courts.ky.gov/Counties/Kenton/default.htm
General Information: Civil limit raised from $4000 to $5000 6/8/2011. No adoption, mental, juvenile, or sealed records released. Will fax documents $2.00 1st page, $1.00 each add'l. Court makes copy: $.25 per page. Video of hearings are $20.00, turnaround time 14 days. Certification fee: $5.00 per cert. Payee: Kenton Circuit Clerk. Personal checks accepted. Major credit &

debit cards accepted except VISA credit. Prepayment required. Mail requests: SASE required for civil.
Civil Name Search: Access: In person, online. Both court and visitors may perform in person name searches. Civil records on computer back to 6/12/89, on index cards from 1800s. Mail turnaround time 7 days. Civil PAT goes back to 6/12/89. **Note: For a complete description of online access see the** *Online Access is Statewide* **section at the front or back of this chapter.**
Criminal Name Search: Access: In person, online. Visitors must perform in person searches themselves. Required to search: name, years to search, DOB or SSN. Criminal records computerized from 4/27/90. Criminal PAT goes back to 4/27/90. **For information about the mail, fax, phone, in-person, and online access programs offered by the KYAOC see the sections at the front or back of this chapter.**

District Court 230 Madison Ave, 3rd Fl, Covington, KY 41011; 859-292-6523; fax: 859-292-6611; 8AM-4PM (EST). *Misdemeanor, Civil Actions under $5,000, Eviction, Small Claims, Probate.*
http://courts.ky.gov/Counties/Kenton/default.htm
General Information: No adoption, mental, juvenile, or sealed records released. Fee to fax out file $3.00 each. Court makes copy: $.25 per page. Certification fee: $5.00 per doc. Payee: District Clerk. Cashiers checks, money orders, and local checks accepted. Major credit cards except VISA accepted. Prepayment required. Mail requests: SASE required for civil.
Civil Name Search: Access: Mail, in person, online. Both court and visitors may perform in person name searches. No search fee. Civil records on computer from 6/9/89 to present, on index cards from 1985. Mail turnaround time 1 week. Civil PAT goes back to 1991. Terminal show year of birth. **Note: For a complete description of online access see the** *Online Access is Statewide* **section at the front or back of this chapter.**
Criminal Name Search: Access: In person, online. Visitors must perform in person searches themselves. Required to search: name, years to search DOB; SSN helpful. Criminal records computerized from 5/20/91 to present, index cards held since 1996. Criminal PAT goes back to 1991. **For information about the mail, fax, phone, in-person, and online access programs offered by the KYAOC see the sections at the front or back of this chapter.**

Knott County

Circuit & District Court PO Box 1317, 53 W Main St, Hindman, KY 41822; 606-785-5021; fax: 606-785-3994; 8AM-4PM M-F; 8AM-N 1st & 4th Sats (EST). *Felony, Misdemeanor, Civil, Eviction, Small Claims, Probate.* www.courts.ky.gov/counties/
General Information: No adoption, mental, juvenile, or sealed records released. Will fax documents to local or toll free line. Court makes copy: $.25 per page. Certification fee: $5.00 per doc. Payee: Circuit Clerk. Personal checks accepted. No credit cards accepted. Prepayment required.
Civil Name Search: Access: In person, online. Visitors must perform in person searches themselves. Civil records in index files, computerized since 11/94. Civil PAT goes back to 11/1994. Not all public terminal results show identifiers. **Note: For a complete description of online access see the** *Online Access is Statewide* **section at the front or back of this chapter.**
Criminal Name Search: Access: In person, online. Visitors must perform in person searches themselves. Required to search: name, years to search, DOB; also helpful: SSN. Criminal records in index files; on computer back to 11/1994. Criminal PAT goes back to 11/1994. **For information about the mail, fax, phone, in-person, and online access programs offered by the KYAOC see the sections at the front or back of this chapter.**

Knox County

Circuit & District Court PO Box 760, 401 Court Sq #202, Barbourville, KY 40906; 606-546-3075 Circ. Ct; 546-3232 Dist.; fax: 606-546-7949; 8AM-4:30PM M-F; 8:30AM-N Sat (EST). *Felony, Misdemeanor, Civil, Eviction, Small Claims, Probate.* www.courts.ky.gov/counties/
General Information: No adoption, mental, juvenile, or sealed records released. Court makes copy: $.25 per page. Certification fee: $5.00 per doc. Payee: Circuit Clerk. No personal checks accepted. Visa/MC accepted. Prepayment required.
Civil Name Search: Access: In person, online. Visitors must perform in person searches themselves. Civil records go back to 1978; on computer back to 7/92. Civil PAT goes back to 7/1994. **Note: For a complete description of online access see the** *Online Access is Statewide* **section at the front or back of this chapter.**
Criminal Name Search: Access: In person, online. Visitors must perform in person searches themselves. Required to search: name, years to search, DOB; SSN helpful. Criminal records go back to 1978; on computer back to 7/92. Criminal PAT goes back to same as civil. **For information about the mail, fax, phone, in-person, and online access programs offered by the KYAOC see the sections at the front or back of this chapter.**

Larue County

Circuit & District Court PO Box 191, 209 W High St, Courthouse Annex, Hodgenville, KY 42748; 270-358-3421; fax: 270-358-3731; 8AM-4PM M-F, 9AM-Noon Sat; closed N-1PM W (EST). *Felony, Misdemeanor, Civil, Eviction, Small Claims, Probate.*

http://courts.ky.gov/counties/Larue/

General Information: Probate fax is same as main fax number. Regarding copies of specific case files - If specific case files are requested by the public, the court will only mail if less than 5 copies, otherwise an attorney must make the request on behalf of the requester. No adoption, mental, juvenile, or sealed records released. Will fax documents for $2.00 first page, $1.00 ea add'l. Court makes copy: $.25 per page. Self serve copy: same. Certification fee: $5.00. Payee: Circuit Clerk. No personal checks or credit cards accepted. Prepayment required.

Civil Name Search: Access: In person, online. Both court and visitors may perform in person name searches. No search fee. Civil records on computer since 1995. Civil PAT goes back to 1995. **Note: For a complete description of online access see the** *Online Access is Statewide* **section at the front or back of this chapter.**

Criminal Name Search: Access: In person, online. Both court and visitors may perform in person name searches. No search fee. Required to search: name, years to search, DOB; SSN helpful. Criminal records on computer since 1995. Criminal PAT goes back to same as civil. **For information about the mail, fax, phone, in-person, and online access programs offered by the KYAOC see the sections at the front or back of this chapter.**

Laurel County

Circuit & District Court PO Box 1798, 103 S Broad St, Courthouse Annex 2, London, KY 40743-1798; 606-330-2079; probate phone: 606-330-2055; fax: 606-330-2084; 8AM-4:30PM M-F (EST). *Felony, Misdemeanor, Civil, Eviction, Small Claims, Probate.*

www.courts.ky.gov/counties/

General Information: No adoption, mental, juvenile, or sealed records released. Will not fax documents. Court makes copy: $.25 per page. Self serve copy: same. Certification fee: $5.00. Payee: Circuit Clerk. Personal checks accepted. No credit cards accepted. Prepayment required.

Civil Name Search: Access: In person, online. Visitors must perform in person searches themselves. Civil records on computer from 7/94, and index books from 1992. Civil PAT goes back to 1994. **Note: For a complete description of online access see the** *Online Access is Statewide* **section at the front or back of this chapter.**

Criminal Name Search: Access: In person, online. Visitors must perform in person searches themselves. Required to search: name, years to search, DOB, SSN. Criminal records computerized from 7/94, and index books from 1987. Criminal PAT goes back to same as civil. **For information about the mail, fax, phone, in-person, and online access programs offered by the KYAOC see the sections at the front or back of this chapter.**

Lawrence County

Circuit & District Court PO Box 847, Courthouse, Louisa, KY 41230; 606-638-4215; fax: 606-638-0264; 8:30AM-4PM, 8:30AM-N 1st & last Sat of month (EST). *Felony, Misdemeanor, Civil, Eviction, Small Claims, Probate.*

www.courts.ky.gov/counties/

General Information: No adoption, mental, juvenile, or sealed records released. Fee to fax out file $2.00 per page. Court makes copy: $.25 per page. Certification fee: $5.00 per doc. Payee: Circuit Clerk. Personal checks accepted. No credit cards accepted. Prepayment required. Mail requests: SASE required for civil.

Civil Name Search: Access: Mail, fax, in person, online. Both court and visitors may perform in person name searches. No search fee. Civil records on computer from 11/94, index cards from 1978. Mail turnaround time within 1 week. Civil PAT goes back to 1995. **Note: For a complete description of online access see the** *Online Access is Statewide* **section at the front or back of this chapter.**

Criminal Name Search: Access: In person, online. Visitors must perform in person searches themselves. Required to search: name, years to search; also helpful: DOB, SSN. Criminal records computerized from 11/94, index cards from 1978. Criminal PAT goes back to 1995. **For information about the mail, fax, phone, in-person, and online access programs offered by the KYAOC see the sections at the front or back of this chapter.**

Lee County

Circuit & District Court PO Box E, 256 Main St, Beattyville, KY 41311; 606-464-8400; fax: 606-464-0144; 8AM-4PM M-F; 8:30AM-11:30AM 1st Sat of month only (EST). *Felony, Misdemeanor, Civil, Eviction, Small Claims, Probate.*

www.courts.ky.gov/counties/

General Information: No adoption, mental, juvenile, or sealed records released. Will not fax documents. Court makes copy: $.25 per page. Certification fee: $5.00 per doc. Payee: Circuit Clerk. Only cashiers checks, money orders and attorney checks accepted. No credit cards accepted. Prepayment required.

Civil Name Search: Access: In person, online. Visitors must perform in person searches themselves. Civil records on computer from 9/94 to present, on index cards from 1978. Civil PAT goes back to 9/1994. **Note: For a complete description of online access see the** *Online Access is Statewide* **section at the front or back of this chapter.**

Criminal Name Search: Access: In person, online. Visitors must perform in person searches themselves. Required to search: name, years to search, DOB; SSN helpful. Criminal records computerized from 9/94 to present, on index cards from 1978. Criminal PAT goes back to same as civil. **For information about the mail, fax, phone, in-person, and online access programs offered by the KYAOC see the sections at the front or back of this chapter.**

Leslie County

Circuit & District Court PO Box 1750, 22010 Main St, Hyden, KY 41749; 606-672-2505; probate phone: 606-672-2503; fax: 606-672-5128; 8AM-4PM M-F; 8AM-N Sat (EST). *Felony, Misdemeanor, Civil, Eviction, Small Claims, Probate.*

www.courts.ky.gov/counties/

General Information: No adoption, mental, juvenile, or sealed records released. Will not fax documents. Court makes copy: $.25 per page. Certification fee: $5.00. Payee: Circuit Clerk. Personal checks accepted. Major credit cards accepted if fee is for $500 or above. Prepayment required.

Civil Name Search: Access: In person, online. Visitors must perform in person searches themselves. Civil cases indexed by plaintiff. Civil records on computer and index books. Civil PAT goes back to 1993. **Note: For a complete description of online access see the** *Online Access is Statewide* **section at the front or back of this chapter.**

Criminal Name Search: Access: In person, online. Visitors must perform in person searches themselves. Required to search: name, years to search; also helpful: address, DOB, SSN. Criminal records on computer and index books. Criminal PAT goes back to same as civil. **For information about the mail, fax, phone, in-person, and online access programs offered by the KYAOC see the sections at the front or back of this chapter.**

Letcher County

Circuit & District Court 156 W Main St, #201, Whitesburg, KY 41858; 606-633-7559/1048; fax: 606-633-5864; 8AM-4PM; 8:30AM-12PM 1st Sat monthly (EST). *Felony, Misdemeanor, Civil, Eviction, Small Claims, Probate.*

www.courts.ky.gov/counties/

General Information: No adoption, mental, juvenile, or sealed records released. Fee to fax out file $2.00 1st page, $1.00 each add'l. Court makes copy: $.25 per page. Certification fee: $5.00 per doc. Payee: Circuit Clerk. Local personal checks accepted. Visa/MC accepted. Prepayment required. Mail requests: SASE required for civil.

Civil Name Search: Access: In person, online. Both court and visitors may perform in person name searches. Required to search: name, years to search; also helpful: address. Civil records on computer go back to 11/1991; on index books from 1986 to 1991. Files maintained in office. Records from 1985 to 1800s in archives in. Civil PAT goes back to 1991. **Note: For a complete description of online access see the** *Online Access is Statewide* **section at the front or back of this chapter.**

Criminal Name Search: Access: In person, online. Visitors must perform in person searches themselves. Required to search: name, years to search, DOB, SSN; also helpful: address. Criminal records on computer go back to 11/1991; on index cards from 1986 to 1991. Files maintained in office. Records from 1985 to 1800s in archives. Criminal PAT goes back to same as civil. **For information about the mail, fax, phone, in-person, and online access programs offered by the KYAOC see the sections at the front or back of this chapter.**

Lewis County

Circuit & District Court PO Box 70, 100 E Main St, Vanceburg, KY 41179; 606-796-3053; fax: 606-796-3030; 8AM-4:30PM M,T,TH,F 8:30-N W,Sat (EST). *Felony, Misdemeanor, Civil, Eviction, Small Claims, Probate.*

www.courts.ky.gov/counties/

General Information: No adoption, mental, juvenile, or sealed records released. Will fax documents to local or toll-free number. Court makes copy: $.25 per page. Self serve copy: same. Certification fee: $5.00. Payee: Circuit Clerk. Personal checks accepted. No credit cards accepted. Prepayment required. Mail requests: SASE required.

Civil Name Search: Access: Phone, mail, in person, online. Both court and visitors may perform in person name searches. No search fee.

Computerized from 1994, civil records on index cards back to 1955. Mail turnaround time within 1 week. Civil PAT goes back to 1994. **Note: For a complete description of online access see the *Online Access is Statewide* section at the front or back of this chapter.**
Criminal Name Search: Access: Mail, in person, online. Both court and visitors may perform in person name searches. No search fee. Required to search: name, years to search, DOB; also helpful: SSN. Computerized from 1994, criminal records on index cards back to 1960s. Criminal PAT goes back to same as civil. **For information about the mail, fax, phone, in-person, and online access programs offered by the KYAOC see the sections at the front or back of this chapter.**

Lincoln County

Circuit & District Court 101 E Main, Stanford, KY 40484; 606-365-2535; fax: 606-365-3389; 8AM-4PM; 9AM-N Sat (EST). *Felony, Misdemeanor, Civil, Eviction, Small Claims, Probate.*
www.courts.ky.gov/counties/
General Information: No adoption, mental, juvenile, or sealed records released. Will not fax documents. Court makes copy: $.25 per page. Certification fee: $5.00 per doc. Payee: Circuit Clerk. Personal checks accepted. No credit cards accepted. Prepayment required.
Civil Name Search: Access: In person, online. Visitors must perform in person searches themselves. Civil records on computer from 5/94, index cards prior, archived from 1978 to 1900. Civil PAT goes back to 1994. **Note: For a complete description of online access see the *Online Access is Statewide* section at the front or back of this chapter.**
Criminal Name Search: Access: In person, online. Visitors must perform in person searches themselves. Required to search: name, years to search; SSN helpful. Criminal records computerized from 5/94, index cards prior, archived from 1978 to 1900. Criminal PAT goes back to same as civil. **For information about the mail, fax, phone, in-person, and online access programs offered by the KYAOC see the sections at the front or back of this chapter.**

Livingston County

Circuit & District Court PO Box 160, Smithland, KY 42081; 270-928-2172; fax: 270-928-2976; 8AM-6PM M 8AM-4PM T-F (CST). *Felony, Misdemeanor, Civil, Eviction, Small Claims, Probate.*
www.courts.ky.gov/counties/
General Information: No adoption, mental, juvenile, or sealed records released. Will fax documents $2.00 1st page, $1.00 each add'l page. Court makes copy: $.25 per page. Certification fee: $5.00. Payee: Circuit Clerk. No out-of-state personal checks accepted. No credit cards accepted. Prepayment required.
Civil Name Search: Access: In person, online. Visitors must perform in person searches themselves. Civil records on computer from 1993 to present, index cards prior, archived from 1799 to 1851. Civil PAT goes back to 1993. **Note: For a complete description of online access see the *Online Access is Statewide* section at the front or back of this chapter.**
Criminal Name Search: Access: In person, online. Visitors must perform in person searches themselves. Required to search: name, years to search, DOB; SSN helpful. Criminal records computerized from 1993 to present, index cards prior, archived from 1799 to 1851. Criminal PAT goes back to same as civil. **For information about the mail, fax, phone, in-person, and online access programs offered by the KYAOC see the sections at the front or back of this chapter.**

Logan County

Circuit Court Box 420, W 4th St, Russellville, KY 42276-0420; 270-726-2424; fax: 270-726-7893; 8AM-4:30PM M-TH; 8AM-5PM F (CST). *Felony, Civil Actions over $5,000.*
www.courts.ky.gov/counties/
General Information: No adoption, mental, juvenile or sealed records released. Will not fax documents. Court makes copy: $.25 per page. Certification fee: $5.00. Payee: Circuit Clerk. Only cashiers checks and money orders accepted. No credit cards accepted. Prepayment required. Mail requests: SASE required for mail return of any copies.
Civil Name Search: Access: In person, online. Visitors must perform in person searches themselves. Civil records on computer from 4/1992 to present, on index card from 1978 to 1992. Civil PAT goes back to 1992. **Note: For a complete description of online access see the *Online Access is Statewide* section at the front or back of this chapter.**
Criminal Name Search: Access: In person, online. Visitors must perform in person searches themselves. Required to search: name, years to search, DOB, SSN. Criminal records computerized from 4/1992 to present, on index card from 1978 to 1992. Criminal PAT goes back to same as civil. **For information about the mail, fax, phone, in-person, and online access programs offered by the KYAOC see the sections at the front or back of this chapter.**

District Court Box 420, Russellville, KY 42276; 270-726-3107; probate phone: 270-726-3108; fax: 270-726-7893; 8AM-4:30PM (till 5PM on Fri) (CST). *Misdemeanor, Civil Actions under $5,000, Eviction, Small Claims, Probate.*
www.courts.ky.gov/counties/
General Information: No adoption, mental, juvenile, or sealed records released. Will not fax documents. Court makes copy: $.25 per page. Self serve copy: same. Certification fee: $5.00. Payee: Logan District Clerk. Personal checks accepted. No credit cards accepted. Prepayment required. Mail requests: SASE required for mail return of any copies.
Civil Name Search: Access: In person, online. Visitors must perform in person searches themselves. Civil records on computer since 1992, index cards from 1978 to 1992. Civil PAT goes back to 1992. **Note: For a complete description of online access see the *Online Access is Statewide* section at the front or back of this chapter.**
Criminal Name Search: Access: In person, online. Visitors must perform in person searches themselves. Required to search: name, years to search, DOB; SSN helpful. Criminal records on computer since 1992, index cards from 1978 to 1991. Criminal PAT goes back to same as civil. **For information about the mail, fax, phone, in-person, and online access programs offered by the KYAOC see the sections at the front or back of this chapter.**

Lyon County

Circuit & District Court Box 565, Eddyville, KY 42038; 270-388-7231 Circ Ct; 270-388-2727 Dist Ct; fax: 270-388-9135; 8AM-4PM (CST). *Felony, Misdemeanor, Civil, Eviction, Small Claims, Probate.*
http://courts.ky.gov/counties/Lyon/
General Information: This court also handles domestic violence, traffic, and juvenile cases. No adoption, mental, juvenile, or sealed records released. Will fax documents $3.00 per page. Court makes copy: $.25 per page. Self serve copy: same. Certification fee: $5.00 per doc. Payee: Circuit Clerk. No personal checks. No credit cards accepted. Prepayment required.
Civil Name Search: Access: In person, online. Visitors must perform in person searches themselves. Civil records on computer from 11/94 to present, on index cards from 1978 to 1994. Civil PAT goes back to 1995. **Note: For a complete description of online access see the *Online Access is Statewide* section at the front or back of this chapter.**
Criminal Name Search: Access: In person, online. Visitors must perform in person searches themselves. Required to search: name, years to search, DOB; SSN helpful. Criminal records computerized from 11/94 to present. Circuit Court records are on index cards from 1978 to 1994, but not District Court records. Criminal PAT goes back to same as civil. **For information about the mail, fax, phone, in-person, and online access programs offered by the KYAOC see the sections at the front or back of this chapter.**

Madison County

Circuit Court PO Box 813, 101 W Main St, County Courthouse, Rm 227, Richmond, KY 40476-0813; 859-624-4793; fax: 859-625-0598; 8AM-4PM (EST). *Felony, Civil Actions over $5,000.*
http://courts.ky.gov/Counties/Madison/default.htm
General Information: No adoption, mental, juvenile, or sealed records released. Will fax out documents for $3.50. Court makes copy: $.25 per page. Self serve copy: same. Certification fee: $5.00. Payee: Madison Circuit Clerk. Personal checks accepted. Visa/MC accepted. Prepayment required.
Civil Name Search: Access: In person, online. Visitors must perform in person searches themselves. Civil records on computer back to 11/1990 to present, on index cards from 1978 to 1990. Civil PAT goes back to 11/1990. **Note: For a complete description of online access see the *Online Access is Statewide* section at the front or back of this chapter.**
Criminal Name Search: Access: In person, online. Visitors must perform in person searches themselves. Required to search: name, years to search; also helpful: DOB, SSN. Criminal records computerized from 11/1990 to present, on index cards from 1978 to 1990. Criminal PAT goes back to same as civil. **For details about mail, fax, phone, in-person, and online access programs offered by the KYAOC see the sections at the front or back of this chapter.**

District Court Madison Hall of Justice, 351 W Main St, Richmond, KY 40475; 859-624-4722; fax: 859-624-4746; 8AM-4PM (EST). *Misdemeanor, Civil Actions under $5,000, Eviction, Small Claims, Probate.*
www.courts.ky.gov/counties/
General Information: No adoption, mental, juvenile, or sealed records released. Fee to fax out file $2.00 per page. Court makes copy: $.25 per page. Self serve copy: $.25 per page. Certification fee: $5.00 per doc. Payee: District Court. Personal checks accepted. Visa/MC accepted. Prepayment required.
Civil Name Search: Access: In person, online. Visitors must perform in person searches themselves. Civil records go back to 11/90; computerized. Civil PAT goes back to 1991. **Note: For a complete description of**

online access see the *Online Access is Statewide* section at the front or back of this chapter.

Criminal Name Search: Access: In person, online. Visitors must perform in person searches themselves. Required to search: name, years to search, DOB; SSN helpful. Criminal records go back to 1999; computerized Criminal PAT goes back to 1999. **For information about the mail, fax, phone, in-person, and online access programs offered by the KYAOC see the sections at the front or back of this chapter.**

Magoffin County

Circuit & District Court PO Box 147, 100 E Maple St, Salyersville, KY 41465; 606-349-2215; fax: 606-349-2209; 8AM-4PM (EST). *Felony, Misdemeanor, Civil, Eviction, Small Claims, Probate.*

General Information: No adoption, mental, juvenile, or sealed records released. Fee to fax non-certified file is $2.00 1st page, $1.00 each add'l. Court makes copy: $.25 per page. Certification fee: $5.00; per doc plus copy fees. Payee: Circuit Clerk. Personal checks accepted. No credit cards accepted. Prepayment required.

Civil Name Search: Access: In person, online. Both court and visitors may perform in person name searches. No search fee. Civil records on computer from 3/1993 to present, on index cards from 1978 to 1993. Cases before 1990 are in archives. Civil PAT goes back to 1993. **Note: For a complete description of online access see the *Online Access is Statewide* section at the front or back of this chapter.**

Criminal Name Search: Access: In person, online. Both court and visitors may perform in person name searches. No search fee. Required to search: name, years to search, DOB; also helpful: SSN. Criminal records computerized from 3/1993 to present, on index cards from 1978 to 1993. Cases before 1990 are in archives. Criminal PAT goes back to same as civil. Terminal results include SSN. **For information about the mail, fax, phone, in-person, and online access programs offered by the KYAOC see the sections at the front or back of this chapter.**

Marion County

Circuit & District Court 120 W Main St, #6, Lebanon, KY 40033; 270-692-2681; fax: 270-692-3097; 8:30AM-4:30PM; 8:30AM-N Sat (EST). *Felony, Misdemeanor, Civil, Eviction, Small Claims, Probate.* http://courts.ky.gov/

General Information: No adoption, mental, juvenile, or sealed records released. Will fax documents $2.00 1st page, $1.00 each add'l. Court makes copy: $.25 per page. Certification fee: $5.00. Payee: Circuit Clerk. Personal checks accepted. Major credit cards except VISA accepted, there is 5% fee. Prepayment required.

Civil Name Search: Access: In person, online. Visitors must perform in person searches themselves. Civil records on computer from 5/1993 to present, on index cards from 1978 to 1993. Civil PAT goes back to 1993. Terminal results may include SSN. **Note: For a complete description of online access see the *Online Access is Statewide* section at the front or back of this chapter.**

Criminal Name Search: Access: In person, online. Visitors must perform in person searches themselves. Required to search: name, years to search; SSN helpful. Criminal records computerized from 5/1993 to present, on index cards from 1978 to 1993. Criminal PAT goes back to same as civil. **For information about the mail, fax, phone, in-person, and online access programs offered by the KYAOC see the sections at the front or back of this chapter.**

Marshall County

Circuit & District Court 80 Judicial Dr, Unit #101, Benton, KY 42025; 270-527-3883/1721; fax: 270-527-5865; 8AM-4:30PM (CST). *Felony, Misdemeanor, Civil, Eviction, Small Claims, Probate, Juvenile, Domestic Violence, Traffic.* http://courts.ky.gov/Counties/Marshall/default.htm

General Information: The clerk will consider fax, mail or phone record search requests on a case-by-case basis, per your direct request. No adoption, mental, juvenile, or sealed records released. Fee to fax out file $2.00 1st page, $1.00 each add'l. Court makes copy: $.25 per page. Self serve copy: same. Certification fee: $5.00 per cert plus copy fee. Payee: Circuit Clerk. Personal checks accepted. Visa/MC accepted. Prepayment required. Mail requests: SASE required.

Civil Name Search: Access: Fax, mail, in person, online. Both court and visitors may perform in person name searches. No search fee. Civil records on computer since 8/1992 to present, on index books from 1978 to 1992. Mail turnaround time 3 days. Public use terminal has civil records back to 8/1992. Terminal results also show SSNs. **Note: For a complete description of online access see the *Online Access is Statewide* section at the front or back of this chapter.**

Criminal Name Search: Access: Phone, fax, mail, in person, online. Both court and visitors may perform in person name searches. No search fee. Required to search: name, years to search, DOB; also helpful: SSN. Criminal records on computer since 8/1992 to present, on index books from 1978 to 1992. Mail turnaround time 3 days. **For information about the mail,**

fax, phone, in-person, and online access programs offered by the KYAOC see the sections at the front or back of this chapter.

Martin County

Circuit & District Court Box 430, 14 Court St, Inez, KY 41224; 606-298-3508; fax: 606-298-4202; 8AM-4PM except 1st & 3rd Th 8AM-7PM (EST). *Felony, Misdemeanor, Civil, Eviction, Small Claims, Probate.* www.courts.ky.gov/counties/

General Information: No adoption, mental, juvenile, or sealed records released. Will fax documents to local or toll-free number. Court makes copy: $.25 per page; return postage required. Certification fee: $5.00 per doc. Payee: Circuit Clerk. Personal checks and credit cards accepted. Prepayment required. Mail requests: SASE required for civil.

Civil Name Search: Access: In person, online. Both court and visitors may perform in person name searches. Civil records on computer since 4/1994, District on index books since 1987, Circuit on index books since 1978, prior records on docket books. Civil PAT goes back to 4/1994. **Note: For a complete description of online access see the *Online Access is Statewide* section at the front or back of this chapter.**

Criminal Name Search: Access: In person, online. Visitors must perform in person searches themselves. Required to search: name, years to search; also helpful: DOB, SSN. Criminal records on computer since 4/1994, District on index books since 1987, Circuit on index books since 1978, prior records on docket books. Criminal PAT goes back to same as civil. **For information about the mail, fax, phone, in-person, and online access programs offered by the KYAOC see the sections at the front or back of this chapter.**

Mason County

Circuit Court 100 W 3rd St, Maysville, KY 41056; 606-564-4340; civil phone: 606-564-4340; fax: 606-564-0932; 8:30AM-4:30PM (EST). *Felony, Civil Actions over $5,000.* http://courts.ky.gov/Counties/Mason/default.htm

General Information: No adoption, mental, juvenile, or sealed records released. Will not fax out case files. Court makes copy: $.25 per page. Certification fee: $5.00 per cert includes copies. Payee: Kentucky State Treasurer. Business checks or money order accepted, personal checks are not. Major credit cards accepted. Prepayment required.

Civil Name Search: Access: In person, online. Visitors must perform in person searches themselves. Civil records on computer back to 4/1994, records on index books since 1929, prior records archived from 1798. Civil PAT goes back to 1994. **Note: For a complete description of online access see the *Online Access is Statewide* section at the front or back of this chapter.**

Criminal Name Search: Access: In person, online. Visitors must perform in person searches themselves. Required to search: name, years to search, DOB. Criminal records computerized from 4/1994, records on index books since 1929, prior records archived from 1798. Criminal PAT goes back to same as civil. **For information about the mail, fax, phone, in-person, and online access programs offered by the KYAOC see the sections at the front or back of this chapter.**

District Court 100 W 3rd St, Maysville, KY 41056; 606-564-4011; fax: 606-564-0932; 8AM-4:30PM (EST). *Misdemeanor, Civil Actions under $4000, Eviction, Small Claims, Probate.*

General Information: Probate fax is same as main fax number. This court WILL NOT do name searches. No adoption, mental, juvenile, or sealed records released. Will not fax out case files. Court makes copy: $.25 per page. Certification fee: $5.00 per cert plus copy fee. Payee: Kentucky State Treasurer. Personal checks accepted. Credit cards accepted. Prepayment required.

Civil Name Search: Access: In person, online. Visitors must perform in person searches themselves. Civil records on computer since 4/1994, prior records on index books from 1978. Civil PAT goes back to 1994. **Note: For a complete description of online access see the *Online Access is Statewide* section at the front or back of this chapter.**

Criminal Name Search: Access: In person, online. Visitors must perform in person searches themselves. Criminal records on computer since 4/1994, prior records on index books from 1983. Criminal PAT goes back to same as civil. **For information about the mail, fax, phone, in-person, and online access programs offered by the KYAOC see the sections at the front or back of this chapter.**

McCracken County

Circuit Court Box 1455, 301 S 6th St, Paducah, KY 42002-1455; 270-575-7280; civil phone: 270-575-7281; 8:30AM-4:30PM, 5PM Fri (CST). *Felony, Civil Actions over $5,000.* www.courts.ky.gov/counties/

General Information: No adoption, mental, juvenile, or sealed records released. Will not fax documents. Court makes copy: $.25 per page. Self serve copy: $.25 per page. Certification fee: $5.00. Payee: Circuit Clerk. Personal checks accepted. No credit cards accepted. Prepayment required.

Civil Name Search: Access: In person, online. Both court and visitors may perform in person name searches. No search fee. Civil records on computer since 9/1991, prior records on index cards since 1978. Civil PAT goes back to 1991. **Note: For a complete description of online access see the** *Online Access is Statewide* **section at the front or back of this chapter.**

Criminal Name Search: Access: In person, online. Both court and visitors may perform in person name searches. No search fee. Required to search: name, years to search; also helpful: DOB & SSN. Criminal records on computer since 9/1991, prior records on index cards since 1978. Criminal PAT goes back to same as civil. **For information about the mail, fax, phone, in-person, and online access programs offered by the KYAOC see the sections at the front or back of this chapter.**

District Court Box 1436, Paducah, KY 42002; 270-575-7270; 8:30AM-5PM; 8:30AM-4:30PM T-F (CST). *Misdemeanor, Civil Actions under $5,000, Eviction, Small Claims, Probate.*

General Information: No adoption, mental, juvenile, or sealed records released. Will not fax documents. Court makes copy: $.25 per page. Certification fee: $5.00 plus copy fee. Payee: District Clerk. Personal checks accepted. No credit cards accepted. Prepayment required.

Civil Name Search: Access: In person, online. Visitors must perform in person searches themselves. Civil records on computer since 9/91, on index books since 1978, prior records archived from the 1900s. Civil PAT goes back to 1992. **Note: For a complete description of online access see the** *Online Access is Statewide* **section at the front or back of this chapter.**

Criminal Name Search: Access: In person, online. Visitors must perform in person searches themselves. Required to search: name, years to search; SSN & DOB helpful. Criminal records on computer since 9/91, on index books since 1982, prior records archived from the 1900s. Criminal PAT goes back to same as civil. **For information about the mail, fax, phone, in-person, and online access programs offered by the KYAOC see the sections at the front or back of this chapter.**

McCreary County

Circuit & District Court Box 40, Whitley City, KY 42653; 606-376-5041; fax: 606-376-8844; 8:30AM-4:30PM (EST). *Felony, Misdemeanor, Civil, Eviction, Small Claims, Probate.*

www.courts.ky.gov/counties/

General Information: No adoption, mental, juvenile, or sealed records released. Will fax documents $2.00 per page. Court makes copy: $.25 per page. Self serve copy: same. Certification fee: $5.00 per doc plus copy fee. Payee: Circuit Clerk. Personal checks accepted. No credit cards accepted. Prepayment required. Mail requests: SASE required.

Civil Name Search: Access: Mail, in person, online. Both court and visitors may perform in person name searches. No search fee. Required to search: name, years to search; also helpful: address. Civil records go back to 1930s; on computer back to 1995. Civil PAT goes back to 1995. **Note: For a complete description of online access see the** *Online Access is Statewide* **section at the front or back of this chapter.**

Criminal Name Search: Access: In person, online. Both court and visitors may perform in person name searches. No search fee. Required to search: name, years to search, DOB, SSN; also helpful: address. Criminal records go back to 1930s; on computer back to 1995. Criminal PAT goes back to 1995. **For information about the mail, fax, phone, in-person, and online access programs offered by the KYAOC see the sections at the front or back of this chapter.**

McLean County

Circuit & District Court Box 145 (210 E Main St), Calhoun, KY 42327; 270-273-3966; fax: 270-273-5918; 8AM-4:30PM M-TH; till 6PM F (CST). *Felony, Misdemeanor, Civil, Eviction, Small Claims, Probate.*

www.courts.ky.gov/counties/

General Information: Probate fax is same as main fax number. No adoption, mental, juvenile, or sealed records released. Will fax documents to local or toll free line. Court makes copy: $.25 per page. Certification fee: $5.00 per doc plus $.25 per page. Payee: Circuit Clerk. Personal checks accepted. Major credit and debit cards accepted except VISA. There is $2.50 fee. Prepayment required.

Civil Name Search: Access: Mail, in person, online. Both court and visitors may perform in person name searches. No search fee. Civil records on computer since 1991, prior records on index cards since 1978. Civil PAT goes back to 1991. Terminal results also show SSNs. **Note: For a complete description of online access see the** *Online Access is Statewide* **section at the front or back of this chapter.**

Criminal Name Search: Access: In person, online. Both court and visitors may perform in person name searches. No search fee. Required to search: name, years to search, DOB; SSN helpful. Criminal records on computer since 1991, prior records on index cards since 1978. Criminal PAT goes back to same as civil. **For information about the mail, fax,**

phone, in-person, and online access programs offered by the KYAOC see the sections at the front or back of this chapter.

Meade County

Circuit & District Court 516 Hillcrest Dr #4, Courthouse, Brandenburg, KY 40108; 270-422-4961; fax: 270-422-2147; 8AM-4:30AM; til 6:30PM TH (EST). *Felony, Misdemeanor, Civil, Eviction, Small Claims, Probate.*

www.courts.ky.gov/counties/

General Information: No adoption, mental, juvenile, or sealed records released. Will not fax documents. Court makes copy: $.25 per page. Self serve copy: same. Certification fee: $5.00 per doc. Payee: Circuit Clerk. Personal checks accepted. No credit cards accepted. Prepayment required. Mail requests: SASE required.

Civil Name Search: Access: In person, online. Visitors must perform in person searches themselves. Civil records on computer since 2/95, prior on index cards. Civil PAT goes back to 2/1995. **Note: For a complete description of online access see the** *Online Access is Statewide* **section at the front or back of this chapter.**

Criminal Name Search: Access: In person, online. Visitors must perform in person searches themselves. Criminal records on computer since 2/95, prior on index cards. Criminal PAT goes back to same as civil. **For information about the mail, fax, phone, in-person, and online access programs offered by the KYAOC see the sections at the front or back of this chapter.**

Menifee County

Circuit & District Court PO Box 172, 12 Walnut St, Courthouse, Frenchburg, KY 40322; 606-768-2461; fax: 606-768-2462; 8AM-N, 12:30-4PM (EST). *Felony, Misdemeanor, Civil, Eviction, Small Claims, Probate.*

www.courts.ky.gov/counties/

General Information: No adoption, mental, juvenile, or sealed records released. Will not fax documents. Court makes copy: $.25 per page. Certification fee: $5.00 per doc. Payee: Circuit Clerk. Personal checks accepted, must have local contact info. No credit cards accepted. Prepayment required.

Civil Name Search: Access: In person, online. Visitors must perform in person searches themselves. Civil index on cards from 1978 to 1994. Civil PAT goes back to 1995. **Note: For a complete description of online access see the** *Online Access is Statewide* **section at the front or back of this chapter.**

Criminal Name Search: Access: In person, online. Visitors must perform in person searches themselves. Criminal records indexed on cards from 1978 to 1994. Criminal PAT goes back to same as civil. **For information about the mail, fax, phone, in-person, and online access programs offered by the KYAOC see the sections at the front or back of this chapter.**

Mercer County

Circuit & District Court 207 W Lexington St, Harrodsburg, KY 40330-1696; 859-734-6306; criminal phone: 859-734-6307; civil phone: 859-734-6305 (District); probate phone: 859-734-6305; fax: 859-734-9159; 8AM-4:30PM (EST). *Felony, Misdemeanor, Civil, Eviction, Small Claims, Probate.*

www.courts.ky.gov/counties/

General Information: Circuit Civil & Criminal 859-734-6306. No adoption, mental, juvenile, or sealed records released. Court makes copy: $.25 per page. Self serve copy: same. Certification fee: $5.00 per cert. Payee: Circuit Clerk. Personal checks accepted. No credit cards accepted. Prepayment required.

Civil Name Search: Access: In person, online. Visitors must perform in person searches themselves. Civil records on computer back to 1993; prior in index books. Civil PAT goes back to 1991. **Note: For a complete description of online access see the** *Online Access is Statewide* **section at the front or back of this chapter.**

Criminal Name Search: Access: In person, online. Visitors must perform in person searches themselves. Required to search: name, years to search; also helpful: DOB, SSN. Criminal records computerized from 1993; prior in index books. Criminal PAT goes back to same as civil. **For information about the mail, fax, phone, in-person, and online access programs offered by the KYAOC see the sections at the front or back of this chapter.**

Metcalfe County

Circuit & District Court Box 27, 201 E Stockton St, Edmonton, KY 42129; 270-432-3663; fax: 270-432-4437; 8AM-4PM (CST). *Felony, Misdemeanor, Civil, Eviction, Small Claims, Probate.*

www.courts.ky.gov/counties/

General Information: No adoption, mental, juvenile, or sealed records released. Fee to fax out file $2.00 1st page; $1.00 each add'l. Court makes copy: $.25 per page. Self serve copy: same. Certification fee: $5.00 per doc.

Payee: Circuit Clerk. Personal checks and credit cards accepted. Prepayment required. Mail requests: SASE required.

Civil Name Search: Access: Phone, fax, mail, in person, online. Both court and visitors may perform in person name searches. No search fee. Civil records on computer back to 1992, prior records on index cards since 1978. Mail turnaround time 1-2 days. Civil PAT goes back to 1992. **Note: For a complete description of online access see the** *Online Access is Statewide* **section at the front or back of this chapter.**

Criminal Name Search: Access: Phone, fax, mail, in person, online. Both court and visitors may perform in person name searches. No search fee. Required to search: name, years to search, DOB, SSN, signed release. Criminal records computerized from 1992, prior records on index cards since 1980. Mail turnaround time 1-2 days. Criminal PAT goes back to 1992. **For information about the mail, fax, phone, in-person, and online access programs offered by the KYAOC see the sections at the front or back of this chapter.**

Monroe County

Circuit & District Court 200 N Main St #B, Tompkinsville, KY 42167; 270-487-5480; fax: 270-487-0068; 8AM-4PM (CST). *Felony, Misdemeanor, Civil, Eviction, Small Claims, Probate.*

www.courts.ky.gov/counties/

General Information: No adoption, mental, juvenile, or sealed records released. Will fax back documents. Court makes copy: $.25 per page. Self serve copy: same. Certification fee: $5.00. Payee: Circuit Clerk. Personal checks accepted. No credit cards accepted. Prepayment required.

Civil Name Search: Access: In person, online. Both court and visitors may perform in person name searches. No search fee. Civil records kept in files. Civil PAT goes back to 1995. Terminal results may include last four digits of SSN. **Note: For a complete description of online access see the** *Online Access is Statewide* **section at the front or back of this chapter.**

Criminal Name Search: Access: In person, online. Both court and visitors may perform in person name searches. No search fee. Criminal records kept in files. Criminal PAT goes back to same as civil. **For information about the mail, fax, phone, in-person, and online access programs offered by the KYAOC see the sections at the front or back of this chapter.**

Montgomery County

Circuit & District Court PO Box 327, 1 Court St, Courthouse, Mt Sterling, KY 40353; 859-498-5966; fax: 859-498-9341; 8AM-4PM M,T; 8AM-5PM F (EST). *Felony, Misdemeanor, Civil, Eviction, Small Claims, Probate.*

www.courts.ky.gov/counties/

General Information: No adoption, mental, juvenile, or sealed records released. Will not fax documents. Court makes copy: $.25 per page. Certification fee: $5.00. Payee: Circuit Clerk. Personal checks accepted. No credit cards accepted. Prepayment required.

Civil Name Search: Access: In person, online. Both court and visitors may perform in person name searches. No search fee. Civil records on computer since 8/1991, on index cards from 1978-1991, prior records on docket books (at archives). Civil PAT goes back to 8/1991. **Note: For a complete description of online access see the** *Online Access is Statewide* **section at the front or back of this chapter.**

Criminal Name Search: Access: In person, online. Visitors must perform in person searches themselves. Criminal records on computer since 8/1991, on index cards from 1978-1991, prior records on docket books (at archives). Criminal PAT goes back to same as civil. **For information about the mail, fax, phone, in-person, and online access programs offered by the KYAOC see the sections at the front or back of this chapter.**

Morgan County

Circuit & District Court Box 85, West Liberty, KY 41472; 606-743-3763; fax: 606-743-2633; 8AM-4PM (EST). *Felony, Misdemeanor, Civil, Eviction, Small Claims, Probate.*

www.courts.ky.gov/counties/

General Information: Probate fax is same as main fax number. No adoption, mental, juvenile, or sealed records released. Will fax documents if they have time; fee is $2.00 1st page, $1.00 each add'l. Court makes copy: $.25 per page. Self serve copy: same. Certification fee: $5.00 per doc plus copy fee. Payee: Circuit Clerk. Personal checks accepted. No credit cards accepted. Prepayment required. Mail requests: SASE requested.

Civil Name Search: Access: Mail, in person, online. Both court and visitors may perform in person name searches. No search fee. Civil records on computer back to 9/1993. Mail turnaround time 1 day. Civil PAT goes back to 9/1992. **Note: For a complete description of online access see the** *Online Access is Statewide* **section at the front or back of this chapter.**

Criminal Name Search: Access: Mail, in person, online. Both court and visitors may perform in person name searches. Criminal

records computerized from 9/1993. Mail turnaround time 1 day. Criminal PAT goes back to same as civil. **For information about the mail, fax, phone, in-person, and online access programs offered by the KYAOC see the sections at the front or back of this chapter.**

Muhlenberg County

Circuit Court PO Box 776, Greenville, KY 42345; 270-338-4850 (Felony); fax: 270-338-0177; 8AM-4PM (CST). *Felony, Civil Actions over $5,000.*

www.courts.ky.gov/counties/

General Information: Direct mail felony record requests to state AOC. No adoption, mental, juvenile, or sealed records released. Court makes copy: $.25 per page. Certification fee: $5.00. Payee: Circuit Clerk. Personal checks accepted. Visa accepted. Prepayment required.

Civil Name Search: Access: In person, online. Visitors must perform in person searches themselves. Civil records on computer since 5/1992, records on index since 1978, records archived if before 1985. Civil PAT goes back to 1992. **Note: For a complete description of online access see the** *Online Access is Statewide* **section at the front or back of this chapter.**

Criminal Name Search: Access: In person, online. Visitors must perform in person searches themselves. Required to search: name, years to search, SSN; also helpful: DOB. Criminal records on computer since 5/1992, records on index since 1978, records archived if before 1985. Criminal PAT goes back to same as civil. **For information about the mail, fax, phone, in-person, and online access programs offered by the KYAOC see the sections at the front or back of this chapter.**

District Court Box 776, Greenville, KY 42345; 270-338-0995; fax: 270-338-0177; 8AM-4PM (CST). *Misdemeanor, Civil Actions under $5,000, Eviction, Small Claims, Probate.*

General Information: No adoption, mental, juvenile, or sealed records released. Court makes copy: $.25 per page. Self serve copy: none. Certification fee: $5.00 per doc. Payee: District Clerk. Personal checks accepted. No credit cards accepted. Prepayment required.

Civil Name Search: Access: In person, online. Visitors must perform in person searches themselves. Civil records on computer since 1992, on index books from 1978, archived if before 1985. Civil PAT goes back to 1992. **Note: For a complete description of online access see the** *Online Access is Statewide* **section at the front or back of this chapter.**

Criminal Name Search: Access: In person only. Visitors must perform in person searches themselves. Criminal records on computer since 1992, on index books from 1978, archived if before 1985. Criminal PAT goes back to same as civil. **For information about the mail, fax, phone, in-person, and online access programs offered by the KYAOC see the sections at the front or back of this chapter.**

Nelson County

Circuit & District Court 200 Nelson County Plaza, Bardstown, KY 40004; 502-348-3648;; 8:30AM-4:30PM (EST). *Felony, Misdemeanor, Civil, Eviction, Small Claims, Probate.*

www.courts.ky.gov/counties/

General Information: Personal identifiers are no longer filed with case documentation. Criminal record checks are done statewide at Pretrial Services in Frankfort. No adoption, mental, juvenile, domestic violence or sealed records released. Will not fax documents. Court makes copy: $.25 per page, but limited to 5 case files per day. A drivers' license is required before they'll make copies for you. Certification fee: $5.00 per doc plus copy fees. Payee: Circuit Clerk. Personal checks accepted. No credit cards accepted. Prepayment required.

Civil Name Search: Access: In person, online. Both court and visitors may perform in person name searches. No search fee. Civil records on computer since 1990, on index since 1978, prior records archived from 1940. Note: Only five cases may be viewed per person per day. Civil PAT goes back to 1990. **Note: For a complete description of online access see the** *Online Access is Statewide* **section at the front or back of this chapter.**

Criminal Name Search: Access: In person, online. Visitors must perform in person searches themselves. No search fee. Required to search: name, years to search, DOB; also helpful: SSN. Criminal records on computer since 1990, on index since 1978, prior records archived from 1940. Criminal PAT goes back to same as civil. **For information about the mail, fax, phone, in-person, and online access programs offered by the KYAOC see the sections at the front or back of this chapter.**

Nicholas County

Circuit & District Court 125 Main St, Carlisle, KY 40311; 859-289-2336; fax: 859-289-6141; 8:30AM-4:30PM; 1st & Last Sats- 8-11:30AM (EST). *Felony, Misdemeanor, Civil, Eviction, Small Claims, Probate.*

www.courts.ky.gov/counties/

General Information: No adoption, mental, juvenile, or sealed records released. Will fax documents $2.00 1st page, $1.00 each add'l page. Court makes copy: $.25 per page. Certification fee: $5.00 per doc. Payee: Circuit Clerk. Personal checks accepted. No credit cards accepted. Prepayment required.

Civil Name Search: Access: In person, online. Both court and visitors may perform in person name searches. No search fee. Required to search: name, years to search, written request. Civil records on computer since 3/1993, prior records on index cards. Civil PAT goes back to 1993. **Note: For a complete description of online access see the *Online Access is Statewide* section at the front or back of this chapter.**

Criminal Name Search: Access: In person, online. Both court and visitors may perform in person name searches. Required to search: name, years to search, written request. Criminal records on computer since 3/1993, prior records on index cards. Criminal PAT goes back to 1993. **For information about the mail, fax, phone, in-person, and online access programs offered by the KYAOC see the sections at the front or back of this chapter.**

Ohio County

Circuit & District Court PO Box 67, 130 E Washington, #300, Hartford, KY 42347; 270-298-3671; fax: 270-298-9565; 8:30AM-4:30PM (CST). *Felony, Misdemeanor, Civil, Eviction, Small Claims, Probate.*
www.courts.ky.gov/counties/
General Information: No adoption, mental, juvenile, or sealed records released. Will not fax out documents. Court makes copy: $.25 per page. Self serve copy: $.25 per page. Certification fee: $5.00 per doc. Payee: Circuit Clerk. No personal checks or credit cards accepted. Prepayment required.

Civil Name Search: Access: In person, online. Visitors must perform in person searches themselves. Civil records on computer since 10/91, Circuit court on index books since 1800s, District court on index books since 1987, prior records archived. Civil PAT goes back to 1992. **Note: For a complete description of online access see the *Online Access is Statewide* section at the front or back of this chapter.**

Criminal Name Search: Access: In person, online. Visitors must perform in person searches themselves. Criminal records on computer since 10/91, Circuit court on index books since 1800s, District court on index books since 1987, prior records archived. Criminal PAT goes back to same as civil. **For information about the mail, fax, phone, in-person, and online access programs offered by the KYAOC see the sections at the front or back of this chapter.**

Oldham County

Circuit & District Court 100 W Main St, La Grange, KY 40031; 502-222-9837; probate phone: 502-222-5621; fax: 502-222-3047; 8AM-4PM (EST). *Felony, Misdemeanor, Civil, Eviction, Small Claims, Probate.*
www.courts.ky.gov/counties/
General Information: Criminal record requests are referred to the AOC Pre-Trial Services in Frankfort, 800-928-6381. District Traffic phone number 222-0522. No adoption, mental, juvenile, or sealed records released. Will fax specific file data for $2.00 per doc plus $1.00 per page. Court makes copy: $.25 per page. Certification fee: $5.00. Payee: Circuit Clerk. Personal checks and credit cards accepted. Prepayment required.

Civil Name Search: Access: In person, online. Visitors must perform in person searches themselves. Civil records on computer since 1991, on index books since 1978, prior records archived since 1800s. Civil PAT goes back to 9/1991. **Note: For a complete description of online access see the *Online Access is Statewide* section at the front or back of this chapter.**

Criminal Name Search: Access: In person, online. Visitors must perform in person searches themselves. Required to search: name, years to search; DOB helpful. Circuit criminal records on computer since 9/1991, on index books since 1978. District criminal on computer since 9/1991, indexed back to 1983. Criminal PAT goes back to 9/1991. Terminal shows DOB year only. **For information about the mail, fax, phone, in-person, and online access programs offered by the KYAOC see the sections at the front or back of this chapter.**

Owen County

Circuit & District Court PO Box 473, 100 N Thomas, Owenton, KY 40359; 502-484-2232; fax: 502-484-0625; 8AM-4PM (EST). *Felony, Misdemeanor, Civil, Eviction, Small Claims, Probate.*
www.courts.ky.gov/counties/
General Information: No adoption, mental, juvenile, or sealed records released. Will not fax documents. Court makes copy: $.25 per page. Self serve copy: same. Certification fee: $5.00. Payee: Circuit Clerk. Personal checks not accepted. Money order and cash accepted. Major credit cards accepted in certain instances, fees assessed. Prepayment required. Mail requests: SASE required for mail return of any copies.

Civil Name Search: Access: In person, online. Both court and visitors may perform in person name searches. No search fee. Civil records on computer since 1992, prior records on index books since 1946. Cases before 1978 transferred to state archives. Civil PAT goes back to 1992. A **Note:**

For a complete description of online access see the *Online Access is Statewide* section at the front or back of this chapter.

Criminal Name Search: Access: In person, online. Both court and visitors may perform in person name searches. No search fee. Required to search: name, years to search, DOB, SSN. Criminal records on computer since 1992, prior records on index books since 1946. Cases before 1978 transferred to state archives. Criminal PAT goes back to same as civil. **For information about the mail, fax, phone, in-person, and online access programs offered by the KYAOC see the sections at the front or back of this chapter.**

Owsley County

Circuit & District Court PO Box 130, North Court St, Booneville, KY 41314; 606-593-6226; probate phone: 606-593-6529; fax: 606-593-6343; 8AM-4PM M-F, 8AM-N Sat (EST). *Felony, Misdemeanor, Civil, Eviction, Small Claims, Probate.*
http://courts.ky.gov/counties/owsley/default.htm
General Information: No adoption, mental, juvenile, or sealed records released. Will fax out files $2.00 1st page; $1.00 ea add'l. Court makes copy: $.25 per page. Certification fee: $5.00. Payee: Circuit Clerk. Personal checks and credit cards accepted. Prepayment required.

Civil Name Search: Access: In person, online. Visitors must perform in person searches themselves. Civil records on computer since 10/1994, prior records on index cards since 1967. Civil PAT goes back to 1994. **Note: For a complete description of online access see the *Online Access is Statewide* section at the front or back of this chapter.**

Criminal Name Search: Access: In person, online. Visitors must perform in person searches themselves. Required to search: name, years to search, DOB or SSN. Criminal records on computer since 10/1994, prior records on index cards since 1967. Criminal PAT goes back to same as civil. **For information about the mail, fax, phone, in-person, and online access programs offered by the KYAOC see the sections at the front or back of this chapter.**

Pendleton County

Circuit & District Court PO Box 69, 120 Ridgeway Ave, County Judicial Center, Falmouth, KY 41040; 859-654-3347; fax: 859-654-3405; 8AM-4PM (EST). *Felony, Misdemeanor, Civil, Eviction, Small Claims, Probate.*
www.courts.ky.gov/counties/
General Information: No adoption, mental, juvenile, or sealed records released. Will not fax documents. Court makes copy: $.25 per page. Certification fee: $5.00 per doc. Payee: Circuit Clerk. Personal checks accepted. No credit cards accepted. Prepayment required. SASE or postage included in payment.

Civil Name Search: Access: Mail, in person, online. Both court and visitors may perform in person name searches. No search fee. Civil records on computer since 1922, prior records on index books since 1978. Mail turnaround time 1 week Civil PAT goes back to 1999 for District; 1992 for Circuit. **Note: For a complete description of online access see the *Online Access is Statewide* section at the front or back of this chapter.**

Criminal Name Search: Access: In person, online. Both court and visitors may perform in person name searches. No search fee. Criminal records on computer since 1999, prior records on index books since 1978. Criminal PAT available. **For information about the mail, fax, phone, in-person, and online access programs offered by the KYAOC see the sections at the front or back of this chapter.**

Perry County

Circuit Court Box 7433, Hazard, KY 41701; 606-435-6000; fax: 606-435-6143; 8AM-4PM (EST). *Felony, Civil Actions over $5,000.*
www.courts.ky.gov/counties/
General Information: No adoption, mental, juvenile, or sealed records released. Court makes copy: $.25 per page. Certification fee: $5.00 per doc plus copy fee. Payee: Circuit Clerk. Personal checks accepted. No credit cards accepted. Prepayment required.

Civil Name Search: Access: In person, online. Visitors must perform in person searches themselves. Civil records on computer since 10/1991, prior records on index cards since 1978. Civil PAT goes back to 1992. **Note: For a complete description of online access see the *Online Access is Statewide* section at the front or back of this chapter.**

Criminal Name Search: Access: In person, online. Visitors must perform in person searches themselves. Criminal records on computer since 10/1991, prior records on index cards since 1978. Criminal PAT goes back to same as civil. **For information about the mail, fax, phone, in-person, and online access programs offered by the KYAOC see the sections at the front or back of this chapter.**

District Court PO Box 7433, 545 Main St, Hazard, KY 41702; 606-435-6002; fax: 606-435-6143; 8AM-4PM (EST). *Misdemeanor, Civil Actions under $5,000, Eviction, Small Claims, Probate.*

General Information: No adoption, mental, juvenile, or sealed records released. Will fax 1 page but not multiple pages. Court makes copy: $.25 per page. Certification fee: $5.00 per doc. Payee: District Clerk. Personal checks accepted. No credit cards accepted. Prepayment required.

Civil Name Search: Access: In person, online. No search fee. Civil records on computer since 1991, records on index books since 1978, prior records archived since 1900s. Civil PAT goes back to 1991. **Note: For a complete description of online access see the *Online Access is Statewide* section at the front or back of this chapter.**

Criminal Name Search: Access: In person, online. Visitors must perform in person searches themselves. Criminal records on computer since 1991, records on index books since 1978, prior records archived since 1900s. Criminal PAT goes back to same as civil. **For information about the mail, fax, phone, in-person, and online access programs offered by the KYAOC see the sections at the front or back of this chapter.**

Pike County

Circuit & District Court PO Box 1002, 179 Division St #336, Pikeville, KY 41502; 606-433-7557; fax: 606-433-7044; 8AM-4:30PM (EST). *Felony, Misdemeanor, Civil, Eviction, Small Claims, Probate.*
http://courts.ky.gov/

General Information: No adoption, mental, juvenile, or sealed records released. Will not fax documents. Court makes copy: $.25 per page. Certification fee: $5.00 per doc. Payee: Circuit Clerk. Personal checks and credit cards accepted. Prepayment required.

Civil Name Search: Access: In person, mail, online. Both court and visitors may perform in person name searches. No search fee. Civil records on computer since 3/1994, prior records on index cards from 1978. Mail turnaround time 2-4 days Civil PAT goes back to 3/1994. **Note: For a complete description of online access see the *Online Access is Statewide* section at the front or back of this chapter.**

Criminal Name Search: Access: In person, mail, online. Both court and visitors may perform in person name searches. No search fee. Criminal records on computer since 3/1994, prior records on index cards from 1978. Mail turnaround time 2-4 days. Criminal PAT goes back to same as civil. **For information about the mail, fax, phone, in-person, and online access programs offered by the KYAOC see the sections at the front or back of this chapter.**

Powell County

Circuit & District Court Box 578, 525 Washington St, Stanton, KY 40380; 606-663-4141; criminal phone: 606-663-4142; fax: 606-663-2710; 8AM-6PM M,F; 8AM-4:30PM T,W,TH (EST). *Felony, Misdemeanor, Civil, Eviction, Small Claims, Probate.*
http://courts.ky.gov/counties/powell/

General Information: Probate fax is same as main fax number. No adoption, mental, juvenile, or sealed records released. Will not fax documents. Court makes copy: $.25 per page. Self serve copy: same. Certification fee: $5.00 per cert. Payee: Circuit Clerk. No personal checks; money orders preferred. Major credit and debit cards accepted. Prepayment required. Mail requests: SASE required for civil.

Civil Name Search: Access: Mail, in person, online. Both court and visitors may perform in person name searches. No search fee. Civil records on computer since 1993, prior records on index cards since 1978. Civil PAT goes back to 1993. **Note: For a complete description of online access see the *Online Access is Statewide* section at the front or back of this chapter.**

Criminal Name Search: Access: In person, online. Visitors must perform in person searches themselves. Required to search: name, years to search, DOB; SSN helpful. Criminal records on computer since 1993, prior records on index cards since 1978. Criminal PAT goes back to same as civil. **For information about the mail, fax, phone, in-person, and online access programs offered by the KYAOC see the sections at the front or back of this chapter.**

Pulaski County

Circuit & District Court PO Box 664, 100 N Main, Courthouse Sq 3rd Fl, Somerset, KY 42502; 606-677-4029; fax: 606-677-4002; 8AM-4:30PM M-F, 8AM-N Sat (EST). *Felony, Misdemeanor, Civil, Eviction, Small Claims, Probate.*
www.courts.ky.gov/counties/

General Information: No adoption, mental, juvenile, or sealed records released. Court makes copy: $.25 per page. Self serve copy: same. Certification fee: $5.00 per doc. Payee: Circuit Clerk. Personal checks accepted. No credit cards accepted. Prepayment required.

Civil Name Search: Access: In person, online. Visitors must perform in person searches themselves. Civil records on computer since 1991, prior records on index books from 1978. Civil PAT goes back to 1991. **Note: For a complete description of online access see the *Online Access is Statewide* section at the front or back of this chapter.**

Criminal Name Search: Access: In person, online. Visitors must perform in person searches themselves. Criminal records on computer since 1991, prior records on index books from 1978. Criminal PAT goes back to same as civil. **For information about the mail, fax, phone, in-person, and online access programs offered by the KYAOC see the sections at the front or back of this chapter.**

Robertson County

Circuit & District Court PO Box 63, 127 E Walnut St, Mt Olivet, KY 41064; 606-724-5993; fax: 606-724-5721; 8:30AM-4:30PM M-F; Sats by app't (EST). *Felony, Misdemeanor, Civil, Eviction, Small Claims, Probate.*
www.courts.ky.gov/counties/

General Information: No adoption, mental, juvenile, or sealed records released. Will not fax documents. Court makes copy: $.25 per page. Certification fee: $5.00 per doc. Payee: Circuit Clerk. Personal checks accepted. Mc/AmEx/Discover cards accepted. Prepayment required.

Civil Name Search: Access: In person, online. Visitors must perform in person searches themselves. Civil records on computer to 1995, previous on index cards. Civil PAT goes back to 1995. **Note: For a complete description of online access see the *Online Access is Statewide* section at the front or back of this chapter.**

Criminal Name Search: Access: In person, online. Visitors must perform in person searches themselves. Required to search: name, years to search; also helpful: DOB, SSN. Criminal records on computer to 1995, previous on index cards. Criminal PAT goes back to same as civil. **For information about the mail, fax, phone, in-person, and online access programs offered by the KYAOC see the sections at the front or back of this chapter.**

Rockcastle County

Circuit & District Court Courthouse Annex, 205 E Main St., Rm 102, Mt Vernon, KY 40456; 606-256-2581; 8AM-4PM M-W & F; 8AM-5PM Th (EST). *Felony, Misdemeanor, Civil, Eviction, Small Claims, Probate.*
www.courts.ky.gov/counties/

General Information: No adoption, mental, juvenile, or sealed records released. Will not fax documents. Court makes copy: $.25 per page. Certification fee: $5.00 per doc plus copy fee. Payee: Circuit Clerk. Personal checks accepted. No credit cards accepted. Prepayment required.

Civil Name Search: Access: In person, online. Visitors must perform in person searches themselves. Civil records on computer since 1991, index cards from 1978 to 1990, prior are archived at Frankfort. Civil PAT goes back to 1991. **Note: For a complete description of online access see the *Online Access is Statewide* section at the front or back of this chapter.**

Criminal Name Search: Access: In person, online. Visitors must perform in person searches themselves. Required to search: name, years to search, DOB; SSN helpful. Criminal Records from 1991 to present are available. Criminal PAT goes back to same as civil. **For information about the mail, fax, phone, in-person, and online access programs offered by the KYAOC see the sections at the front or back of this chapter.**

Rowan County

Circuit & District Court 627 E Main, Morehead, KY 40351-1398; 606-783-8505; fax: 606-783-8504; 8:30AM-4:30PM M-TH; 8:30AM-6PM F (EST). *Felony, Misdemeanor, Civil, Eviction, Small Claims, Probate.*
http://courts.ky.gov/Counties/Rowan/default.htm

General Information: No adoption, mental, juvenile, or sealed records released. Will not fax out documents. Court makes copy: $.25 per page. Certification fee: $1.00 per page. Payee: Circuit Clerk. Only cashiers checks and money orders accepted. No credit cards accepted. Prepayment required.

Civil Name Search: Access: In person, online. Visitors must perform in person searches themselves. Civil records on computer from 1991, index cards from 1989, archived from 1900. Civil PAT goes back to 1991. **Note: For a complete description of online access see the *Online Access is Statewide* section at the front or back of this chapter.**

Criminal Name Search: Access: In person, online. Visitors must perform in person searches themselves. Criminal records computerized from 1991, index cards from 1989, archived from 1900. Criminal PAT goes back to 1991. **For information about the mail, fax, phone, in-person, and online access programs offered by the KYAOC see the sections at the front or back of this chapter.**

Russell County

Circuit & District Court 410 Monument Square, #203, Jamestown, KY 42629; 270-343-2185; probate phone: 270-343-2185; fax: 270-343-5808; 8AM-4:30PM (CST). *Felony, Misdemeanor, Civil, Eviction, Small Claims, Probate.*
http://courts.ky.gov/

General Information: Probate fax is same as main fax number. The agency is open the 1st and 3rd Sat each month from 8AM-11AM. No adoption, mental, juvenile, or sealed records released. Will not fax

documents. Court makes copy: $.25 per page. Self serve copy: same. Certification fee: $5.00. Payee: Circuit Clerk. Personal checks accepted. Discover, AMEX and MC accepted. Prepayment required.
Civil Name Search: Access: In person, online. Visitors must perform in person searches themselves. Civil records on computer from 8/1994, index cards from 1978-1994, prior archived at Frankfort. Civil PAT goes back to 1994. **Note: For a complete description of online access see the** *Online Access is Statewide* **section at the front or back of this chapter.**
Criminal Name Search: Access: In person, online. Visitors must perform in person searches themselves. Criminal records computerized from 8/1994, index cards from 1978-1994, prior archived at Frankfort. Criminal PAT goes back to same as civil. **For information about the mail, fax, phone, in-person, and online access programs offered by the KYAOC see the sections at the front or back of this chapter.**

Scott County

Circuit & District Court 119 N Hamilton, Georgetown, KY 40324; 502-863-0474; fax: 502-863-9089; 8:30AM-4:30PM (EST). *Felony, Misdemeanor, Civil, Eviction, Small Claims, Probate.*
http://courts.ky.gov/Counties/Scott/default.htm
General Information: No adoption, mental, juvenile, paternity and domestic violence records released. Will fax documents for $2.00 first page and $1.00 ea add'l. Court makes copy: $.25 per page. Self serve copy: same. Certification fee: $5.00. Payee: Circuit Clerk. Local Personal checks and credit cards accepted. Prepayment required. Mail requests: SASE required.
Civil Name Search: Access: Mail, in person, online. Both court and visitors may perform in person name searches. No search fee. Civil records on computer since 1992, index cards from 1978 to 1992, in books prior. Mail turnaround time varies. Civil PAT goes back to 1992. Terminal results also show SSNs. **Note: For a complete description of online access see the** *Online Access is Statewide* **section at the front or back of this chapter.**
Criminal Name Search: Access: Mail, in person, online. Both court and visitors may perform in person name searches. No search fee. Required to search: name, years to search; also helpful: SSN. Criminal records on computer since 1992, index cards from 1978 to 1992, in books prior. Mail turnaround time varies. Criminal PAT goes back to same as civil. Terminal results include SSN. **For information about the mail, fax, phone, in-person, and online access programs offered by the KYAOC see the sections at the front or back of this chapter.**

Shelby County

Circuit & District Court 501 Main St, Shelbyville, KY 40065; 502-633-1287; civil phone: 502-633-4736 (Dist Ct); fax: 502-633-0146; 8:30AM-4:30PM (EST). *Felony, Misdemeanor, Civil, Eviction, Small Claims, Probate.*
www.courts.ky.gov/counties/
General Information: Dist Ct- 502-633-4736. Fax for misdemeanor clerk is 502-633-6421. No adoption, mental, juvenile, or sealed records released. Will fax documents $2.00 per page. Court makes copy: $.25 per page. Certification fee: $5.00 per doc plus copy fee. Payee: Circuit Clerk. Personal checks accepted. No credit cards accepted. Prepayment required. Mail requests: SASE required for civil.
Civil Name Search: Access: Mail, in person, online. Both court and visitors may perform in person name searches. No search fee. Civil records on computer back to 9/91; index cards from 1978 to 1991. Civil PAT goes back to 1991. **Note: For a complete description of online access see the** *Online Access is Statewide* **section at the front or back of this chapter.**
Criminal Name Search: Access: In person, online. Visitors must perform in person searches themselves. Required to search: name, years to search, DOB. Criminal records computerized from 9/91; index cards from 1978 to 1991. Criminal PAT goes back to same as civil. **For information about the mail, fax, phone, in-person, and online access programs offered by the KYAOC see the sections at the front or back of this chapter.**

Simpson County

Circuit & District Court 101 N Court St, Franklin, KY 42135-0261; 270-586-8910/4241; fax: 270-586-0265; 8AM-4PM (CST). *Felony, Misdemeanor, Civil, Eviction, Small Claims, Probate.*
http://courts.ky.gov/Counties/Simpson/default.htm
General Information: No adoption, mental, juvenile, or sealed records released. Court makes copy: $.25 per page. Certification fee: $5.00. Payee: Circuit Clerk. Only cashiers checks and money orders accepted. Major credit cards accepted. Prepayment required.
Civil Name Search: Access: In person, online. Both court and visitors may perform in person name searches. No search fee. Civil records on computer since 11/92, manual prior to 1978. Civil PAT goes back to 11/1992. **Note: For a complete description of online access see the** *Online Access is Statewide* **section at the front or back of this chapter.**

Criminal Name Search: Access: In person, online. Visitors must perform in person searches themselves. Required to search: name, years to search, DOB, SSN. Criminal records on computer since 11/92, card index back to 1978. Criminal PAT goes back to same as civil. **For information about the mail, fax, phone, in-person, and online access programs offered by the KYAOC see the sections at the front or back of this chapter.**

Spencer County

Circuit & District Court Box 282, Taylorsville, KY 40071; 502-477-3220; fax: 502-477-9368; 7AM-4PM M-F (EST). *Felony, Misdemeanor, Civil, Eviction, Small Claims, Probate.*
www.courts.ky.gov/counties/
General Information: Court personnel will not provide name searches of records. No adoption, mental, juvenile, or sealed records released. Will not fax documents. Court makes copy: $.25 per page. Certification fee: $5.00. Payee: Circuit Clerk. Personal checks accepted. No credit cards accepted. Prepayment required. Mail requests: SASE required.
Civil Name Search: Access: In person, online. Visitors must perform in person searches themselves. Civil records on computer from 8/94 to present, index cards from 1978 to 1994. Civil PAT goes back to 1995. **Note: For a complete description of online access see the** *Online Access is Statewide* **section at the front or back of this chapter.**
Criminal Name Search: Access: In person, online. Visitors must perform in person searches themselves. Required to search: name, years to search, DOB; also helpful: SSN. Criminal records computerized from 1995 to present, index cards from 1978 to 1994. Criminal PAT goes back to same as civil. **For information about the mail, fax, phone, in-person, and online access programs offered by the KYAOC see the sections at the front or back of this chapter.**

Taylor County

Circuit & District Court 300 E Main St, Campbellsville, KY 42718; 270-465-6686; fax: 270-789-4356; 8AM-4:30PM (EST). *Felony, Misdemeanor, Civil, Eviction, Small Claims, Probate.*
www.courts.ky.gov/counties/
General Information: No adoption, mental, juvenile, or sealed records released. Will fax documents $2.00 1st page, $1.00 ea add'l. Court makes copy: $.25 per page. Self serve copy: $.15 per page. Certification fee: $5.00 per doc. Payee: Circuit Clerk. Personal checks accepted. No credit cards accepted. Prepayment required.
Civil Name Search: Access: In person, online. Both court and visitors may perform in person name searches. No search fee. Civil records on computer from 1993 to present, index cards from 1978 to 1993. Civil PAT goes back to mid-1993. **Note: For a complete description of online access see the** *Online Access is Statewide* **section at the front or back of this chapter.**
Criminal Name Search: Access: In person, online. Visitors must perform in person searches themselves. Required to search: name, years to search, DOB, SSN. Criminal records computerized from 1993 to present, index cards from 1978 to 1993. Criminal PAT goes back to same as civil. **For information about the mail, fax, phone, in-person, and online access programs offered by the KYAOC see the sections at the front or back of this chapter.**

Todd County

Circuit & District Court Box 337, 202 E Washington St, Elkton, KY 42220; 270-265-2343 Circ Ct; 270-265-5631 Dist Ct; fax: 270-265-2122; 8AM-4:30PM (CST). *Felony, Misdemeanor, Civil, Eviction, Small Claims, Probate.*
www.courts.ky.gov/counties/
General Information: No adoption, mental, juvenile, or sealed records released. Will fax back documents. Court makes copy: $.25 per page. Certification fee: no fee. Payee: Circuit Clerk. Personal checks accepted. No credit cards accepted. Prepayment required.
Civil Name Search: Access: In person, online. Visitors must perform in person searches themselves. Civil records on computer since 1/1993, index cards from 1978-1993, index books prior to 1978. Civil PAT goes back to 1993. **Note: For a complete description of online access see the** *Online Access is Statewide* **section at the front or back of this chapter.**
Criminal Name Search: Access: In person, online. Visitors must perform in person searches themselves. Criminal records on computer since 1/1993, index cards from 1978-1993, index books prior to 1978. Criminal PAT goes back to same as civil.

Trigg County

Circuit & District Court Box 673, 41 Main St, Cadiz, KY 42211; 270-522-6270; probate phone: 270-522-7070; fax: 270-522-5828; 8AM-4PM (CST). *Felony, Misdemeanor, Civil, Eviction, Small Claims, Probate.*
http://courts.ky.gov/counties/Trigg/
General Information: District Court can be reached at 270-522-7070. Probate is a separate index at this same address. No adoption, mental,

juvenile, or sealed records released. Will not fax out case files. Court makes copy: $.25 per page. Self serve copy: same. Certification fee: $5.00 per doc plus copy fee. Payee: Circuit Clerk. Only cashiers checks and money orders accepted. No credit cards accepted. Prepayment required.

Civil Name Search: Access: In person, online. Visitors must perform in person searches themselves. Civil records on computer from 4/1993 to present, index cards from 1978 to 1993. Civil PAT goes back to 4/1993. **Note: For a complete description of online access see the *Online Access is Statewide* section at the front or back of this chapter.**

Criminal Name Search: Access: In person, online. Visitors must perform in person searches themselves. Required to search: name, years to search, DOB; SSN helpful. Criminal records computerized from 4/1993 to present, index cards from 1978 to 1993. Criminal PAT goes back to same as civil. **For information about the mail, fax, phone, in-person, and online access programs offered by the KYAOC see the sections at the front or back of this chapter.**

Trimble County

Circuit & District Court Box 248, Bedford, KY 40006; 502-255-3213, 502-255-3525 (District); criminal phone: 502-255-3213; civil phone: 502-255-3525; probate phone: 502-255-3525; criminal fax: 502-255-4953; civil fax: 8AM-4:30PM M-F; 8AM-N 1st Sat of month; 8AM-4:30PM M-F; 8AM-N 1st Sat of month (EST). *Felony, Misdemeanor, Civil, Eviction, Small Claims, Probate.*

www.courts.ky.gov/counties/

General Information: Probate records in separate index at this same address. Probate fax- 502-255-4953 No adoption, mental, juvenile, or sealed records released. Will not fax documents. Court makes copy: $.25 per page. Certification fee: $5.00 per doc includes copies. Payee: Circuit Clerk. Only cashiers checks and money orders accepted. No credit cards accepted. Prepayment required. Mail requests: SASE required for civil.

Civil Name Search: Access: Mail, in person, online. Both court and visitors may perform in person name searches. No search fee. Civil records on computer and in folders from 1993 to present, folders 1978 to 1992, everything is archives prior to 1992. Mail turnaround time 2-4 days. Civil PAT goes back to 1993. **Note: For a complete description of online access see the *Online Access is Statewide* section at the front or back of this chapter.**

Criminal Name Search: Access: In person, online. Visitors must perform in person searches themselves. Required to search: name, years to search, DOB; SSN helpful. Criminal records on computer and in folders from 1993 to present, folders 1978 to 1992, archives prior to 1978. Criminal PAT goes back to same as civil. **For information about the mail, fax, phone, in-person, and online access programs offered by the KYAOC see the sections at the front or back of this chapter.**

Union County

Circuit & District Court PO Box 59, Morganfield, KY 42437; 270-389-0800/0804; fax: 270-389-9887; 8AM-4PM (CST). *Felony, Misdemeanor, Civil, Eviction, Small Claims, Probate.*

www.courts.ky.gov/counties/

General Information: No searches performed on Thursday. Circuit Court phone- 270-389-1811. Probate fax is same as main fax number. No adoption, mental, juvenile, or sealed records released. Will not fax documents. Court makes copy: $.25 per page. Certification fee: $5.00 per doc plus copy fee. Payee: Circuit Clerk. Business checks accepted. No credit cards accepted. Prepayment required. Mail requests: SASE required for civil.

Civil Name Search: Access: Mail, in person, online. Both court and visitors may perform in person name searches. No search fee. Civil records on computer since 6/1994 (new records only); prior on index cards and archived. Mail turnaround time 1 week. Civil PAT goes back to 6/1994. **Note: For a complete description of online access see the *Online Access is Statewide* section at the front or back of this chapter.**

Criminal Name Search: Access: In person, online. Visitors must perform in person searches themselves. Required to search: name, years to search, DOB, SSN. Criminal records on computer since 6/1994 (new records only); prior on index cards and archived. Criminal PAT goes back to same as civil. **For information about the mail, fax, phone, in-person, and online access programs offered by the KYAOC see the sections at the front or back of this chapter.**

Warren County

Circuit & District Court 1001 Center St #102, Bowling Green, KY 42101-2184; 270-746-7400; fax: 270-746-7501; 8AM-4:30PM (CST). *Felony, Misdemeanor, Civil, Eviction, Small Claims, Probate.*

www.courts.ky.gov/counties/

General Information: No adoption, mental, juvenile, or sealed records released. Will fax documents $2.00 1st page, $1.00 ea add'l. Court makes copy: $.25 per page. Self serve copy: same. Certification fee: $5.00. Payee: Circuit Clerk. Personal checks accepted. All major credit cards accepted. Prepayment required.

Civil Name Search: Access: In person, online. Visitors must perform in person searches themselves. Civil records on computer since 1989. Civil PAT goes back to 1999. Small Claims court records only go back to 2001. Some results may include SSN. **Note: For a complete description of online access see the *Online Access is Statewide* section at the front or back of this chapter.**

Criminal Name Search: Access: In person, online. Visitors must perform in person searches themselves. Required to search: name, years to search; also helpful: DOB, SSN. Criminal records on computer since 1990. Criminal PAT goes back to 1990. Misdemeanor court records only go back to 2001. **For information about the mail, fax, phone, in-person, and online access programs offered by the KYAOC see the sections at the front or back of this chapter.**

Washington County

Circuit & District Court 100 E Main St, #100, Springfield, KY 40069; 859-336-3761; fax: 859-336-9824; 8:30 AM-4:30PM; 9AM-N on 2nd Sat of month (EST). *Felony, Misdemeanor, Civil, Eviction, Small Claims, Probate.*

www.courts.ky.gov/counties/

General Information: No adoption, mental, juvenile, or sealed records released. Will not fax documents. Court makes copy: $.25 per page. Self serve copy: same. Certification fee: $5.00. Payee: Circuit Clerk. Personal checks and credit cards accepted. Prepayment required.

Civil Name Search: Access: In person, online. Both court and visitors may perform in person name searches. No search fee. Civil records on computer, index cards and archived. Civil PAT goes back to 1994. **Note: For a complete description of online access see the *Online Access is Statewide* section at the front or back of this chapter.**

Criminal Name Search: Access: In person, online. Both court and visitors may perform in person name searches. No search fee. Required to search: name, years to search, DOB. Criminal records on computer, index cards and archived. Criminal PAT goes back to same as civil. **For information about the mail, fax, phone, in-person, and online access programs offered by the KYAOC see the sections at the front or back of this chapter.**

Wayne County

Circuit & District Court 125 W Columbia Ave, Monticello, KY 42633-1448; 606-348-5841/or/5983; fax: 606-348-4225; 8AM-4PM M-F; 9-11:45AM 1st & 3rd Sats (EST). *Felony, Misdemeanor, Civil, Eviction, Small Claims, Probate.*

http://courts.ky.gov/counties/Wayne/

General Information: No adoption, mental, juvenile, or sealed records released. Will not fax documents. Court makes copy: $.25 per page. Certification fee: $5.00 per doc. Payee: Circuit Clerk. Personal checks accepted. No credit cards accepted. Prepayment required. Mail requests: SASE required.

Civil Name Search: Access: Fax, in person, online. Visitors must perform in person searches themselves. No search fee. Civil records on computer from 10/92 to present, index cards from 1978 to 1992. Mail turnaround time 5 days. Civil PAT goes back to 1993. **Note: For a complete description of online access see the *Online Access is Statewide* section at the front or back of this chapter.**

Criminal Name Search: Access: Fax, in person, online. Visitors must perform in person searches themselves. No search fee. Required to search: name, years to search; also helpful: DOB, SSN. Criminal records computerized from 10/92 to present, index cards from 1978 to 1992. Criminal PAT goes back to same as civil. **For information about the mail, fax, phone, in-person, and online access programs offered by the KYAOC see the sections at the front or back of this chapter.**

Webster County

Circuit & District Court PO Box 290, 35 US Hwy 41A South, Dixon, KY 42409; 270-639-9160; probate phone: 270-639-9300- district ct; fax: 270-639-6757; 8AM-4PM (CST). *Felony, Misdemeanor, Civil, Eviction, Small Claims, Probate.*

http://courts.ky.gov/counties/webster/

General Information: No adoption, mental, juvenile, or sealed records released. Fee to fax out file $2.00 1st page, $1.00 each add'l. Court makes copy: $.25 per page. Self serve copy: same. Certification fee: $5.00. Payee: Circuit Clerk. Personal checks and credit cards accepted. Prepayment required. Mail requests: SASE required.

Civil Name Search: Access: Fax, mail, in person, online. Both court and visitors may perform in person name searches. No search fee. Civil records in office from 1987 to present, prior records are at Frankfort archives. Mail turnaround time 1 day. Civil PAT goes back to 6/1994. **Note: For a complete description of online access see the *Online Access is Statewide* section at the front or back of this chapter.**

Criminal Name Search: Access: Fax, mail, in person, online. Both court and visitors may perform in person name searches. No search fee. Circuit criminal records in office from 1987 to present, prior records are at Frankfort archives; District Court to 1999. Mail turnaround time 1 day. Criminal PAT goes back to same as civil. Results include last 4 digits of SSN. **For information about the mail, fax, phone, in-person, and online access programs offered by the KYAOC see the sections at the front or back of this chapter.**

Whitley County

Williamsburg Circuit & District Court Box 329, 200 Main St, Courthouse Sq, Williamsburg, KY 40769; 606-549-2973; fax: 606-549-3393; 8AM-4PM (EST). *Felony, Misdemeanor, Civil, Eviction, Small Claims, Probate.*
www.courts.ky.gov/counties/
General Information: Circuit court can be reached at 606-549-2973. District court can be reached at 606-549-5162. No adoption, mental, juvenile, or sealed records released. Will not fax documents. Court makes copy: $.25 per page. Certification fee: $5.00 per doc. Payee: Whitley Circuit Clerk. Personal checks accepted. Visa/MC and debit cards accepted. Prepayment required.
Civil Name Search: Access: In person, online. Visitors must perform in person searches themselves. Civil records on computer from 1993 to present, index cards from 1978 to 1993. Civil PAT goes back to 1993. **Note: For a complete description of online access see the** *Online Access is Statewide* **section at the front or back of this chapter.**
Criminal Name Search: Access: In person, online. Visitors must perform in person searches themselves. Required to search: name, years to search; also helpful: DOB, SSN. Criminal records computerized from 1993 to present, index cards from 1978 to 1993. Note: Criminal PAT goes back to same as civil. **For information about the mail, fax, phone, in-person, and online access programs offered by the KYAOC see the sections at the front or back of this chapter.**

District Court - Corbin 805 S Main St #10, City Hall, Corbin, KY 40701; 606-523-1085/or/1771; fax: 606-523-2049; 8AM-4PM M-F; 8:30-11:30AM 1st Sats (EST). *Felony, Misdemeanor, Civil, Eviction, Small Claims, Probate.*
www.courts.ky.gov/counties/
General Information: No adoption, mental, juvenile or sealed records released. Will not fax documents. Court makes copy: $.25 per page. Certification fee: $5.00 per doc. Payee: Whitley District Court. Personal checks accepted. Visa/MC accepted. Prepayment required.
Civil Name Search: Access: In person, online. Visitors must perform in person searches themselves. Civil records on computer from 1993 to present, index books prior. Civil PAT goes back to 1993. **Note: For a complete description of online access see the** *Online Access is Statewide* **section at the front or back of this chapter.**
Criminal Name Search: Access: In person, online. Visitors must perform in person searches themselves. Criminal records computerized from 1993 to present, index books prior. Criminal PAT goes back to same as civil. **For information about the mail, fax, phone, in-person, and online access programs offered by the KYAOC see the sections at the front or back of this chapter.**

Wolfe County

Circuit & District Court Box 296, Campton, KY 41301; 606-668-3736; fax: 606-668-3198; 8AM-4PM (till 5PM first Friday of month) (EST). *Felony, Misdemeanor, Civil, Eviction, Small Claims, Probate.*
http://courts.ky.gov/Counties/Wolfe/default.htm
General Information: No adoption, mental, juvenile, or sealed records released. Court makes copy: $.25 per page. Self serve copy: same. Certification fee: $5.00. Payee: Circuit Clerk. Personal checks and credit cards accepted. Prepayment required. Mail requests: SASE required.
Civil Name Search: Access: Mail, in person, online. Visitors must perform in person searches themselves. No search fee. Civil records on computer from 1992 to present, index books prior. Civil PAT goes back to 1992. **Note: For a complete description of online access see the** *Online Access is Statewide* **section at the front or back of this chapter.**
Criminal Name Search: Access: Mail, in person, online. Visitors must perform in person searches themselves. No search fee. Required to search: name, years to search; also helpful: DOB, SSN. Criminal records computerized from 1992 to present, index books prior. Mail turnaround time same day. Criminal PAT goes back to same as civil. Sex and race also indicated on the public terminal. **For information about the mail, fax, phone, in-person, and online access programs offered by the KYAOC see the sections at the front or back of this chapter.**

Woodford County

Circuit & District Court 130 Court St, Versailles, KY 40383; 859-873-3711; fax: 859-879-8531; 8AM-4PM M-TH; 8AM-5:30PM F (EST). *Felony, Misdemeanor, Civil, Eviction, Small Claims, Probate.*
www.courts.ky.gov/counties/
General Information: No adoption, mental, juvenile, or sealed records released. Will not fax documents. Court makes copy: $.25 per page. Self

serve copy: same. Certification fee: $5.00. Payee: Circuit Clerk. Personal checks accepted. No credit cards accepted. Prepayment required.
Civil Name Search: Access: In person, online. Visitors must perform in person searches themselves. Civil records on computer from 2/91 to present, index cards from 1978 to 1991. Civil PAT goes back to 1991. **Note: For a complete description of online access see the** *Online Access is Statewide* **section at the front or back of this chapter.**
Criminal Name Search: Access: In person, online. Visitors must perform in person searches themselves. Required to search: name, years to search; SSN helpful. Criminal records computerized from 2/91 to present, index cards from 1978 to 1991. Criminal PAT goes back to same as civil. **For information about the mail, fax, phone, in-person, and online access programs offered by the KYAOC see the sections at the front or back of this chapter.**

About Searching Criminal Records in KY

Courts send criminal record search requesters to a statewide service provided by the Administrative Office of the Courts. Records may be requested via fax, standard mail, walk-in, even a drive-thru service, and online (see below). The CourtNet Criminal History database contains records from all 120 counties for at least the last five years for all misdemeanor and traffic cases and for felonies dating back to 1978. The search fee is $15.00 per request. A SASE must accompany mail requests.

See http://courts.ky.gov/ and click on *Obtain a Criminal Record Report*

About Online Access in KY

- The KY Admin. Office of Courts provides a criminal record online ordering system called AOCFastCheck. The fee is $15.00 per record; add 5% for use of a credit card. Subscribers receive an email notification when results are ready. For more information, visit http://courts.ky.gov/aoc/AOCFastCheck.htm. The following case types are not available - juvenile, mental health, and civil/domestic violence.

  A Cautionary Note - The AOC is NOT the state mandated official site for criminal records. State law dictates that the Kentucky State Police Records Branch is responsible for holding records with confirmed dispositions, not the AOC.

- A limited search site to find case numbers is free at http://apps.kycourts.net/CourtRecords. Search daily court calendars by county free at http://apps.kycourts.net/dockets.

- Registered members of the KY Bar may use CourtNet-KBA to review pending cases at http://apps.kycourts.net/courtrecordsKBA/.

Louisiana

Time Zone:	**CST**
Capital:	**Baton Rouge, East Baton Rouge Parish**
# of Parishes:	**64**
State Web:	**www.louisiana.gov**
Court Web:	**www.lasc.org**

Administration	Office of Judicial Administrator, Judicial Council of the Supreme Court, 400 Royal St, Suite 1190, New Orleans, LA, 70130; 504-310-2550, Fax: 504-310-2587.
The Supreme and Appellate Courts	The Supreme Court is the highest court. There are five Court of Appeals that are the intermediate courts of appeal between the District Courts and the Supreme Court. Search opinions at www.lasc.org/opinion_search.asp.

The Louisiana Courts

Court	Type	How Organized	Jurisdiction Highpoints
District*	General	65 Courts in 43 Districts	Felony, Misdemeanor, Civil, Probate, Eviction, Domestic Relations
City*	Limited	49 Courts	Misdemeanor, Limited Civil, Traffic, Eviction
Parish*	Limited	3	Misdemeanor, Limited Civil, Traffic, Eviction
Juvenile/Family	Special	5	Juvenile , Divorce, Child Custody
Justice of the Peace	Limited	382	Ordinance, Traffic
Mayor	Limited	250	Ordinance, Traffic

* = profiled in this book

Details on the Trial Court Structure	The trial court of general jurisdiction in Louisiana is the **District Court**. A District Court Clerk in each Parish holds all the records for that Parish. Each Parish has its own clerk and courthouse.

City Courts are courts of record and handle misdemeanors, limited civil, juvenile, traffic and evection. The amount of civil is concurrent with the District Court based where the amount in controversy does not exceed $15,000 to $35,000 depending on the court. (See CCP 4843 - http://www.legis.state.la.us/lss/lss.asp?doc=112087).

In criminal matters, City Courts generally have jurisdiction over ordinance violations and misdemeanor violations of state law. City judges also handle a large number of traffic cases.

Parish Courts exercise jurisdiction in civil cases worth up to $10,000 to 25,000 and criminal cases punishable by fines of $1,000 or less, or imprisonment of six months or less. Cases are appealable from the Parish Courts directly to the courts of appeal. A municipality or local may have a **Mayor's Court** or **Justice of the Peace Court** which handle certain traffic cases and minor infractions.

Record Searching Facts You Need to Know

Fees and Record Searching Tips	The fees for criminal record searches, copies and certifications for the Parish District Courts are set by statute; however, the courts do not always follow these standards. The fee

for a criminal record search is $20.00, copy fee is $1.00, and $5.00 to certify. 80% of the courts offer a public access terminal. Many City Courts are not computerized; records must be researched using non-electronic indices.

Online Access is Limited

There is no statewide system open to the public for trial court dockets, but a number of parishes offer online access.

Acadia Parish

15th District Court PO Box 922, Crowley, LA 70527; 337-788-8881; fax: 337-788-1048; 8:30AM-4:30PM (CST). *Felony, Misdemeanor, Civil, Probate.*

www.acadiaparishclerk.com

General Information: No adoption or juvenile records released. Fee to fax out file $6.00 1st page, $2.00 add'l page; includes copies. Court makes copy: $1.00 per page, $2.00 per page is mailed. Self serve copy: $.75 per page. If copies are to be returned by mail and you do not provide an SASE, add $1.00 per page mailing fee. Certification fee: $6.00 per document. Payee: Acadia Parish Clerk of Court. Personal checks accepted. No credit cards accepted. Prepayment required. Mail requests: SASE required.

Civil Name Search: Access: Phone, fax, mail, in person, online. Both court and visitors may perform in person name searches. Search fee: $20.00 per name. Civil records on computer from 1985, archived from 1800s. Mail turnaround time civil 1-2 days. Civil PAT goes back to 1999. Online access to record information is by subscription. There is a set-up fee and a monthly fee. Call the court for details.

Criminal Name Search: Access: Fax, mail, in person, online. Both court and visitors may perform in person name searches. Search fee: $20.00 per name per year. Required to search: name, years to search, DOB; also helpful: SSN. Criminal records computerized from 1979, archived from 1800s. Note: Copy of check must be faxed with fax request. Mail turnaround time 1-2 days. Criminal PAT goes back to 1979. Terminal results include SSN. Online access to record information is by subscription. There is a set-up fee and a monthly fee. Call the court for details.

Crowley City Court PO Box 225, 426 North Ave F, Crowley, LA 70526; 337-788-4118; *Misdemeanor, Civil to $30,000, Eviction, Traffic.*

Rayne City Court PO Box 31, Rayne, LA 70578; 337-334-9677; *Misdemeanor, Civil to $30,000, Eviction, Traffic.*

Allen Parish

33rd District Court PO Box 248, 400 W 6th Ave, Oberlin, LA 70655; 337-639-4351; fax: 337-639-2030; 8AM-4:30PM (CST). *Felony, Misdemeanor, Civil, Probate.*

General Information: Probate is in a separate index. Probate fax is same as main fax number. No adoption or juvenile records released. Fee to fax out file $5.00 and $2.00 each add'l page. Court makes copy: $1.00 per page. Certification fee: $5.00 per certification. Payee: Allen Parish Clerk of Court. Personal checks accepted. No credit cards accepted. Prepayment required. Mail requests: SASE requested.

Civil Name Search: Access: Mail, in person. Both court and visitors may perform in person name searches. Search fee: $10.00 per name. Fee is for a 10 year search. Civil records archived back to 1913; on computer back to 1985. Mail turnaround time 2 days. Civil PAT goes back to 1985.

Criminal Name Search: Access: Mail, in person. Both court and visitors may perform in person name searches. Search fee: $20.00 per name. Fee is for a 10 year search. Required to search: name, years to search, DOB, SSN. Criminal records archived back to 1913; on computer back to 7/94. Mail turnaround time 2 days. Criminal PAT goes back to 1994. Personal identifiers on terminal results vary; SSNs may appear.

Oakdale City Court PO Box 565, 333 E 6th Ave, Oakdale, LA 71463; 318-335-1121; *Misdemeanor, Civil to $30,000, Eviction, Traffic.*

Ascension Parish

23rd District Court PO Box 192, 300 Houmas St, Donaldsonville, LA 70346; 225-473-9866; criminal fax: 225-473-8641; civil fax: 8:30AM-4:30PM; 8:30AM-4:30PM (CST). *Felony, Misdemeanor, Civil, Probate.*

www.ascensionclerk.com/default.aspx

General Information: Online identifiers in results same as on public terminal. No adoption or juvenile records released. Will fax documents $5.00 1st page, $1.00 each add'l. Court makes copy: $1.00 per page; $.50 per page after 1st 15. Self serve copy: $.50 per page. Certification fee: $5.00. Payee: Ascension Parish Clerk of Court. In state personal checks accepted. No credit cards accepted. Prepayment required. Mail requests: SASE requested.

Civil Name Search: Access: Fax, mail, in person, online. Both court and visitors may perform in person name searches. Search fee: $20.00 per name. Civil records on computer from 1987, index books back to 1800s. Mail turnaround time 2 days. Civil PAT goes back to 1987. Access to civil judgments, etc, available by subscription; $100 set-up charge single user; $250 multiple user up to 5, plus $50.00 monthly and $.50 per image printed; includes recorded document index; see www.ascensionclerk.com/onlineservices.aspx.

Criminal Name Search: Access: Fax, mail, in person, online. Both court and visitors may perform in person name searches. Search fee: $20.00 per name. Required to search: name, years to search, DOB; also helpful: SSN. Criminal Records go back to 1800s; computerized records since 11/86. Mail turnaround time 2 days. Criminal PAT goes back to 11/1986. the criminal docket is available online, see civil section for details.

Ascension Parish Court 828 S Irma Blvd Bldg 2, Gonzales, LA 70737; 225-473-9866; *Misdemeanor, Civil to $15,000, Eviction, Traffic.*

Assumption Parish

23rd District Court PO Box 249, Napoleonville, LA 70390; 985-369-6653; fax: 985-369-2032; 8:30AM-4:30PM (CST). *Felony, Misdemeanor, Civil, Probate.* www.assumptionclerk.com/

General Information: No adoption or juvenile records released. Will fax documents $2.00 1st page, $1.00 each add'l. Court makes copy: $1.00 per page. Self serve copy: $.75 per page. Certification fee: $5.00 per document. Payee: Assumption Parish Clerk of Court. Personal checks accepted. No credit cards accepted. Prepayment required. Mail requests: SASE requested.

Civil Name Search: Access: Fax, mail, in person, online. Both court and visitors may perform in person name searches. Search fee: $20.00 per name per 10 years. Civil records archived back to 1800s; on computer back to 1990. Mail turnaround time 1 day. Civil PAT goes back to 1990. After registration you may search civil court records and probate records back to 4/16/2005 at http://97.89.251.18/resolution/ or call 985-369-6653 for info or signup. Registration is $50 with monthly charges as well.

Criminal Name Search: Access: Fax, mail, in person, online. Both court and visitors may perform in person name searches. Search fee: $20.00 per name; is for 10 years. Required to search: name, years to search, DOB. Criminal records archived back to 1900s; on computer back to 1994. Mail turnaround time 1 day. Criminal PAT goes back to 1994. After registration you may login to search criminal records at http://97.89.251.18:80/qGov/Verdict/Criminal/Index.aspx or call 985-369-6653 for info or signup. Registration is $50 with monthly charges as well. Online results show middle initial, DOB.

Avoyelles Parish

12th District Court PO Box 219, 300 N Main, Courthouse Bldg, Marksville, LA 71351; 318-253-7523; probate phone: 318-253-7523; 8:30AM-5PM (CST). *Felony, Misdemeanor, Civil, Probate.*

General Information: No adoption or juvenile records released. Will not fax documents. Court makes copy: $1.00 per page. Certification fee: $5.00 per page. Payee: Clerk of Court. Personal checks accepted. No credit cards accepted. Prepayment required.

Civil Name Search: Access: Mail, in person, online. Both court and visitors may perform in person name searches. Search fee: $20.00 per name, per search. Civil records on computer from 1985, microfiche back to 1800s. Mail turnaround time 1 day. Civil PAT goes back to 1985. An online subscription service to record images is available at http://cotthosting.com/laavoyelles. Monthly rate is $75.00, other fees are $.50 for each printed page plus a service fee to use PayPal.

Criminal Name Search: Access: Mail, in person, online. Both court and visitors may perform in person name searches. Search fee: $20.00 per name, per search. Required to search: name, years to search, DOB; also helpful: SSN. Criminal records computerized from 1985, microfiche back to 1800s. Mail turnaround time 1 day. Criminal PAT goes back to 1995. An online subscription service to record images is available at http://cotthosting.com/laavoyelles. Monthly rate is $75.00, other fees are $.50 for each printed page plus a service fee to use PayPal.

Bunkie City Court PO Box 74, Bunkie, LA 71322; 318-346-7250; *Misdemeanor, Civil to $25,000, Eviction, Traffic.*

Marksville City Court PO Box 429, 116 W Bon Bempt St, Marksville, LA 71351; 318-253-7860; *Misdemeanor, Civil to $25,000, Eviction, Traffic.*

Beauregard Parish

36th District Court PO Box 100, 201 W 1st St, DeRidder, LA 70634; 337-463-8595; fax: 337-462-3916; 8AM-4:30PM (CST). *Felony, Misdemeanor, Civil, Probate.*

General Information: No adoption or juvenile records released. Will not fax documents. Court makes copy: $1.25 per page. Certification fee: $5.00 per doc plus copy fee. Payee: Clerk of Court. Personal checks accepted. No credit cards accepted. Prepayment required. Mail requests: SASE required.

Civil Name Search: Access: Mail, in person. Both court and visitors may perform in person name searches. Search fee: $15.00 per name. Fee is per 10 years searched. Civil records on computer since 1985, archived from 1913. Mail turnaround time 1 week. Civil PAT available.

Criminal Name Search: Access: Mail, in person. Both court and visitors may perform in person name searches. Search fee: $15.00 per name. Fee is per 10 years searched. Required to search: name, years to search, DOB; also helpful: SSN. Criminal record index in books. Mail turnaround time 1 week. Criminal PAT available.

Bienville Parish

2nd District Court 100 Courthouse Dr, Rm 100, Arcadia, LA 71001; 318-263-2123; fax: 318-263-7426; 8:30AM-4:30PM (CST). *Felony, Misdemeanor, Civil, Probate.*

http://clerk.bienvilleparish.org/

General Information: Online identifiers in results same as on public terminal. No adoption or juvenile records released. Will fax documents $2.00 plus $1.50 per page. Court makes copy: $1.50 per page. Self serve copy: $1.00 per page. Certification fee: $5.00 per cert. Payee: Clerk of Court. Personal checks accepted. No credit cards accepted. Prepayment required. Mail requests: SASE required.

Civil Name Search: Access: Fax, mail, in person, online. Both court and visitors may perform in person name searches. Search fee: $10.00 per name. Civil records on computer from 1989, index books prior. Mail turnaround time 2-3 days. Public use terminal has civil records back to 1/1989. An online subscription service to view images is available. Contact the Clerk of Court for details and pricing.

Criminal Name Search: Access: Fax, mail, in person, online. Both court and visitors may perform in person name searches. Search fee: $10.00 per name. Required to search: name, years to search, DOB; also helpful: SSN. Criminal records computerized from 1991, index books prior. Mail turnaround time 2-3 days. An online subscription service to view images is available. Contact the Clerk of Court for details and pricing.

Bossier Parish

26th District Court PO Box 430, 204 Burt Blvd, 3rd Fl, Benton, LA 71006; 318-965-2336; fax: 318-965-2713; 8:30AM-4:30PM (CST). *Felony, Misdemeanor, Civil, Probate, Traffic.*

www.bossierclerk.com

General Information: No adoption or juvenile records released. Will fax documents for $5.00 local or $8.00 long distance plus copy fee. Court makes copy: $.50 per page; $1.00 if for criminal record. Self serve copy: same. Certification fee: $2.00; but $5.00 if for criminal record. Payee: Clerk of Court. Business checks accepted. No credit cards accepted. Prepayment required. Mail requests: SASE requested.

Civil Name Search: Access: Mail, in person, online. Both court and visitors may perform in person name searches. Search fee: $15.00 per name. Civil records on computer from 1987, index books back to 1843. Note: There is a print image fee of $.25 per page. Mail turnaround time same or next day. Civil PAT goes back to 1987. Sometimes the DOB appears. Access to the Parish Clerk of Court online records requires $85 setup fee and a $35 monthly flat fee, see the home page. Civil, criminal, probate (1982 forward), traffic and domestic index information is by name or case number. Call 318-965-2336 for more information. The system occasionally has records missing or lack identifiers that would otherwise be found in person.

Criminal Name Search: Access: Mail, online, in person. Both court and visitors may perform in person name searches. Search fee: $20.00 per name. Required to search: name, years to search: also helpful: DOB. Criminal records on computer since 1982. Note: There is a print image fee of $.25 per page. Mail turnaround time same or next day. Criminal PAT goes back to 1982. Sometimes the DOB appears. Access to the Parish Clerk of Court online records requires $85 setup fee and a $35 monthly flat fee, see the home page. Online results show middle initial.

Bossier City Court 620 Benton Rd, Bossier City, LA 71111; 318-332-4117; *Misdemeanor, Civil to $15,000, Eviction, Traffic.*

Caddo Parish

1st District Court 501 Texas St, Rm 103, Texas St Courthouse, Shreveport, LA 71101-5408; 318-226-6791; criminal phone: 318-226-6786; civil phone: 318-226-6776; probate phone: 318-226-6778; fax: 318-227-9080; 8:30AM-5PM (CST). *Felony, Misdemeanor, Civil, Probate.*

www.caddoclerk.com

General Information: No adoption or juvenile records released. Will fax documents to local or toll-free number. Court makes copy: $.50 per page. Self serve copy: $.50 per page. Certification fee: $2.00 per cert plus copy fee. Payee: Clerk of Court. Personal checks accepted. Prepayment required. Mail requests: SASE required.

Civil Name Search: Access: Mail, in person, online. Both court and visitors may perform in person name searches. Search fee: $10.00 per name. Civil records on computer from 1984; images go back to 2000. Mail

turnaround time 1-2 days. Civil PAT goes back to 1984. Online access to civil records back to 1994 and name index back to 1984 is through county internet service. Registration and $100 set-up fee and $30 monthly usage fee is required. Marriage and recording information is also available. Online images $.25 each to print. For information and sign-up, call 318-226-6523. The online system for the District Court may occasionally have court records missing or lack identifiers that would otherwise be found in person.

Criminal Name Search: Access: Mail, in person, online. Both court and visitors may perform in person name searches. Search fee: $10.00 per name. For criminal computer printouts, fee is $2.00 for first page and $1.00 each add'l. Required to search: name, years to search, DOB; also helpful: SSN. Criminal records computerized from 1984; images go back to 2000. Mail turnaround time 1-2 days. Criminal PAT goes back to same as civil. Online access to civil records back to 1994 and name index back to 1984 is through county internet service. Registration and $100 set-up fee and $30 monthly usage fee is required. Marriage and recording information is also available. Online images $.25 each to print. For information and sign-up, call 318-226-6523. The online system for the District Court may occasionally have court records missing or lack identifiers that would otherwise be found in person.

Shreveport City Court Civil Division, 1244 Texas Ave, Shreveport, LA 71101; 318-673-5800; criminal phone: 313-673-5830; fax: 318-673-5813; 8AM-5PM (CST). *Civil Actions under $25,000, Small Claims.*

www.shreveportla.gov/citycourt/

General Information: No sealed records released. Will not fax documents. Court makes copy: $.50 per page. Certification fee: $2.50. Payee: Shreveport City Court. Personal checks accepted. Major credit cards accepted, surcharges apply. Prepayment required. Mail requests: SASE required.

Civil Name Search: Access: Mail, in person. Visitors must perform in person searches themselves. No search fee. Civil records on computer back to 1987. Note: Must provide case number for mail searches. Public use terminal has civil records back to 1987.

Calcasieu Parish

14th District Court PO Box 1030, 1000 Ryn St, Courthouse, Lake Charles, LA 70602; 337-437-3550; civil phone: x126; fax: 337-437-3833; 8:30AM-4:30PM (CST). *Felony, Misdemeanor, Civil, Probate.*

www.calclerkofcourt.com

General Information: Search fee for each index searched. Probate fax is same as main fax number. Online identifiers in results same as on public terminal. No adoption or juvenile records released. Will fax documents $5.00 1st page, $.50 each add'l. Court makes copy: $1.00 per page. Self serve copy: same. Certification fee: $5.00 per cert plus copy fee. Payee: Clerk of Court. Personal checks accepted with ID. No credit cards accepted. Prepayment required. Mail requests: SASE required.

Civil Name Search: Access: Fax, mail, in person, online. Both court and visitors may perform in person name searches. Search fee: $15.00 per name. Additional fee of $1.00 per year after 1st 10 years. Civil records on computer back to 2000; older records are archived. Mail turnaround time 24 hours. Civil PAT goes back to 1987. Online access to civil records is the same as criminal, see below.

Criminal Name Search: Access: Fax, mail, in person, online. Both court and visitors may perform in person name searches. Search fee: $15.00 per name. Additional fee of $1.00 per year after 1st 10 years. Required to search: name, years to search, DOB; also helpful: SSN. Criminal records on computer since 1987. Mail turnaround time 24 hours. Criminal PAT goes back to same as civil. Online access to court record indices is free at http://207.191.42.34/resolution/. Registration and password required. Full documents requires $100.00 per month subscription. Online results show middle initial, DOB.

Lake Charles City Court PO Box 1664, Lake Charles, LA 70602; criminal phone: 337-491-1565; civil phone: 337-491-1564; criminal fax: 337-491-8745; civil fax: 8AM-4:30PM; 8AM-4:30PM (CST). *Misdemeanor, Civil Actions under $25,000, Small Claims.*

www.lccitycourt.org/

General Information: No sealed records released. Will not fax documents. Court makes copy: $1.00 per page. Self serve copy: same. Certification fee: $5.00. Certification included in copy fee. Payee: Lake Charles City Court. Personal checks and credit cards accepted. Prepayment required.

Civil Name Search: Access: Mail, in person. Both court and visitors may perform in person name searches. No search fee. Civil records kept on paper for 10 years, older records archived on computer. Mail turnaround time 2-5 days. Public use terminal has civil records back to 1989.

Criminal Name Search: Access: Mail, in person. Both court and visitors may perform in person name searches. No search fee. Criminal records kept on paper for 10 years, older records archived on computer. Mail turnaround time 2-3 days.

Sulphur City Court 802 S Huntington St, Sulphur, LA 70663; 337-527-7006; *Misdemeanor, Civil to $25,000, Eviction, Traffic.*

Caldwell Parish

37th District Court Clerk of Court, PO Box 1327, Columbia, LA 71418; 318-649-2272; fax: 318-649-2037; 8AM-4:30PM (CST). *Felony, Misdemeanor, Civil, Probate.*

General Information: All record requests must be in writing. Probate fax is same as main fax number. No adoption or juvenile records released. Will fax documents $3.00 1st page, $1.00 each add'l plus costs for the copies. Court makes copy: $1.00 per page. Self serve copy: same. Certification fee: $5.00 per document plus copy fee. Payee: Clerk of Court. Personal checks accepted. No credit cards accepted. Prepayment required. Mail requests: SASE helpful.

Civil Name Search: Access: Fax, mail, in person. Both court and visitors may perform in person name searches. Search fee: $20.00 per name. Civil records on books from 1910, computerized since 11/84. Note: Requests for court performed searches must be in writing. Mail turnaround time 1 day. Civil PAT available.

Criminal Name Search: Access: Mail, in person. Both court and visitors may perform in person name searches. Search fee: $20.00 per name. Required to search: name, years to search, DOB; also helpful: SSN. Note that some criminal records don't contain DOB or SSN. Criminal records kept on books since 1970, computerized since 1998. Note: Requests for court performed searches must be in writing. Mail turnaround time 1 day. Criminal PAT available.

Cameron Parish

38th District Court PO Box 549, Cameron, LA 70631; 337-775-5316; fax: 337-775-2838; 8:30AM-4:30PM (CST). *Felony, Misdemeanor, Civil, Probate.*

General Information: No adoption, interdiction or juvenile records released. Fee to fax out file $5.00 1st page, $1.00 each add'l. Court makes copy: $1.00 per page. Self serve copy: same. Certification fee: $5.00. Payee: Cameron Parish Clerk of Court. Personal checks accepted. No credit cards accepted. Prepayment required. Mail requests: SASE required.

Civil Name Search: Access: Phone, mail, fax, in person, online. Both court and visitors may perform in person name searches. Search fee: $10.00. Civil records from 1874; on computer back to 7/1994. Mail turnaround time 2 days. Civil PAT goes back to 1994. Online access is offered, but by contract only and fees involved. The court asks to Susan Racca at 337-775-5316 for details.

Criminal Name Search: Access: Fax, mail, in person, online. Both court and visitors may perform in person name searches. Search fee: $10.00 per name. Required to search: name, years to search, DOB. Criminal records from 1874; on computer back to 1980. Mail turnaround time 2 days. Criminal PAT goes back to 1981. See civil for online access.

Catahoula Parish

7th District Court PO Box 654, Harrisonburg, LA 71340; 318-744-5497; fax: 318-744-5488; 8AM-4:30PM (CST). *Felony, Misdemeanor, Civil, Probate.*

General Information: No adoption or juvenile records released. Will fax documents $5.00 plus $1.00 per page. Court makes copy: $1.00 per page. Self serve copy: same. Certification fee: $5.00. Payee: Clerk of Court. Personal checks accepted. No credit cards accepted. Prepayment required. Mail requests: SASE required.

Civil Name Search: Access: Mail, in person. Both court and visitors may perform in person name searches. Search fee: $20.00 per name per year. Civil records minute entries back to 1800s. Public use terminal has civil records back to 5/13/1998.

Criminal Name Search: Access: Mail, in person. Both court and visitors may perform in person name searches. Search fee: $20.00 per name per year. Required to search: name, years to search, DOB. Criminal records minute entries back to 1800s.

Claiborne Parish

2nd District Court PO Box 330, Homer, LA 71040; 318-927-9601; fax: 318-927-2345; 8:30AM-4:30PM (CST). *Felony, Misdemeanor, Civil, Probate.*

General Information: Probate is a separate index at this same address. Probate fax is same as main fax number. No adoption or juvenile records released. Fee to fax out doc $10.00 each. Court makes copy: $1.00 per page. Certification fee: $5.00 per document plus copy fee. Payee: Clerk of Court. Personal checks accepted. No credit cards accepted. Prepayment required. Mail requests: SASE required.

Civil Name Search: Access: Mail, in person. Both court and visitors may perform in person name searches. Search fee: $10.00 per name. Civil index on docket books back to early 1900s. Mail turnaround time 1-2 days.

Criminal Name Search: Access: Mail, in person. Both court and visitors may perform in person name searches. Search fee: $20.00 per name.

Required to search: name, years to search, DOB; also helpful: SSN. Criminal records on computer 1993 forward. Mail turnaround time 1-2 days.

Concordia Parish

7th District Court PO Box 790, Vidalia, LA 71373; 318-336-4204; fax: 318-336-8777; 8:30AM-4:30PM (CST). *Felony, Misdemeanor, Civil, Probate.* www.concordiaclerk.org

General Information: No adoption or juvenile records released. Will fax documents $5.00 per doc plus $1.00 per page. Court makes copy: $1.00 per page. Self serve copy: same. Certification fee: $5.00. Payee: Clerk of Court. Personal checks accepted. No credit cards accepted. Prepayment required.

Civil Name Search: Access: Mail, in person. Both court and visitors may perform in person name searches. Search fee: $25.00 per name. Civil records on computer from 1980, index books back to 1800s. Mail turnaround time 3-4 days. Civil PAT goes back to 1983.

Criminal Name Search: Access: Mail, in person. Visitors must perform in person searches themselves. Search fee: $20.00 per name. Required to search: name, years to search, DOB; also helpful: SSN. Criminal records computerized from 1980, index books back to 1800s. Mail turnaround time 3-4 days. Criminal PAT goes back to same as civil.

Vidalia City Court 409 Texas St, Vidalia, LA 71373; 318-336-6255; *Misdemeanor, Civil to $15,000, Eviction, Traffic.*

De Soto Parish

42nd District Court PO Box 1206, Mansfield, LA 71052; 318-872-3110; criminal phone: 318-872-3181; civil phone: 318-872-3788; fax: 318-872-4202; 8:30AM-4:30PM (CST). *Felony, Misdemeanor, Civil, Probate.* www.desotoparishclerk.org/

General Information: Probate fax- 318-872-4202 No adoption or juvenile records released. Fee to fax out doc $10.00 plus $1.00 per page. Court makes copy: $1.00 per page. Self serve copy: $.50 per page. Certification fee: $5.00 per doc. Payee: Clerk of Court. Personal checks accepted. No credit cards accepted. Prepayment required. Mail requests: SASE Required.

Civil Name Search: Access: Mail, in person, online. Both court and visitors may perform in person name searches. Search fee: $10.00 per name. Civil records on computer from 1991, index books back to 1843. Mail turnaround time 2-4 days. Civil PAT goes back to 1991. Access index via a web-based subscription service. Search index, view, & print image fee is $100.00 per month, plus a one-time setup fee of $150.00. Contact Jayme, Katie or Valerie at 318-872-3110 to set-up an account of visit www.desotoparishclerk.org/online.html.

Criminal Name Search: Access: Mail, in person, online. Both court and visitors may perform in person name searches. Search fee: $10.00 per name. Required to search: name, years to search, DOB. Criminal records on computer since 1991, archived or in books to 1950's. Mail turnaround time 2-4 days. Criminal PAT goes back to same as civil. Online access same as civil.

East Baton Rouge Parish

19th District Court PO Box 1991, Baton Rouge, LA 70821; 225-389-3950; criminal phone: 225-389-3964; probate phone: 225-389-5118; fax: 225-389-3392; 7:30AM-5:30PM (CST). *Felony, Misdemeanor, Civil, Probate.* www.ebrclerkofcourt.org

General Information: Probate fax- 225-389-2372 No adoption or juvenile records released. Fee to fax out file $5.00 each plus $.50 per page. Court makes copy: $.50 per page civil; $1.00 per page criminal. Self serve copy: $1.00 per page. Certification fee: $5.00. Payee: East Baton Rouge Parish. Only cashiers checks, business checks, and money orders accepted. Major credit cards accepted. Prepayment required. Mail requests: SASE helpful.

Civil Name Search: Access: Fax, mail, online, in person. Both court and visitors may perform in person name searches. Search fee: $22 per name per index, if certificate issued. Civil records in index books from 1810. Mail turnaround time 3-5 days. Public use terminal has civil records back to 1988. Online access to the clerk's database is by subscription. Civil record indexes go back to '88; case tracking of civil and probate back to 1988. Setup fee is $100.00 plus $50.00 per month for 1st password, $25.00 for each add'l passwords. Call MIS Dept at 225-389-5295 for info or visit the website.

Criminal Name Search: Access: Mail, online, in person. Only the court performs in person name searches; visitors may not. Search fee: $20.00 per name, if certificate issued. Required to search: name, years to search, DOB; also helpful: SSN. Criminal docket on books from 1942; on computer back to 1990. Mail turnaround time 3-5 days. Online access to criminal records is the same as civil. Criminal case tracking goes back to 8/1990.

Baton Rouge City Court PO Box 3438, 233 St Louis St, Baton Rouge, LA 70802; 225-389-5279; criminal phone: 225-389-5294; civil phone: 225-389-3017; criminal fax: 225-389-7619; civil fax: 8AM-5PM; 8AM-5PM (CST). *Misdemeanors, Civil Actions up tor $15,000, Small Claims, Criminal Traffic.* www.brgov.com/dept/citycourt/

General Information: Criminal Dept is #145; Civil is on 2nd Fl. Records Dept phone- 225-389-8388. No sealed records released. Will fax documents

for no fee. Court makes copy: $.50 per page. Certification fee: $1.00 per page plus copy fee. Payee: City of Baton Rouge. Personal checks accepted. Accepts Visa/MC. Amex plus 5% surcharge. Prepayment required.
Civil Name Search: Access: Mail, in person, fax, online. Visitors must perform in person searches themselves. Search fee: $20.00 per name. Civil records on computer back to 1990. Mail turnaround time 2-5 days. Civil PAT goes back to 1990. Access city court's database including attorneys and warrants free at from the web page.
Criminal Name Search: Access: In person, online. Both court and visitors may perform in person name searches. Search fee: $20 per name. Required to search: name, DOB, years to search. Note: Background checks for the City are performed in the Criminal Records Division at the Baton Rouge Police Dept located at 504 Mayflower or at Parish Prison. Criminal PAT goes back to 2000. Access city court's criminal dockets database and warrants free at http://brgov.com/dept.citycourt.

Baker City Court PO Box 1, Baker, LA 70704-0001; 225-778-1866; *Misdemeanor, Civil to $35,000, Eviction, Traffic.*

Baton Rouge City Court 233 St Louis St, PO Box 3438 (70821), Baton Rouge, LA 70802; 225-389-5279; fax: 225-389-7656; *Misdemeanor, Civil to $35,000, Eviction, Traffic.*

Zachary City Court PO Box 310, 4510 Main St, Zachary, LA 70791; 225-654-0044; *Misdemeanor, Civil to $35,000, Eviction, Traffic.*

East Carroll Parish

6th District Court 400 1st St, Lake Providence, LA 71254; 318-559-2399; fax: 318-559-1502; 8:30AM-4:30PM (CST). *Felony, Misdemeanor, Civil, Probate.*
General Information: No adoption or juvenile records released. Will fax documents $5.00 plus $2.00 per page. Court makes copy: $2.00 per page. Certification fee: $5.00 per cert. plus copy fee. Payee: Clerk of Court. No personal checks. No credit cards accepted. Prepayment required. Mail requests: SASE required.
Civil Name Search: Access: Mail, in person. Both court and visitors may perform in person name searches. Search fee: $20.00 per name per 10 years. Civil index on docket books back to 1832. Mail turnaround time same day.
Criminal Name Search: Access: Mail, in person. Both court and visitors may perform in person name searches. Search fee: $20.00 for 10 yr check. Required to search: name, years to search, DOB; also helpful: SSN. Criminal records indexed in books back to 1832. Mail turnaround time same day.

East Feliciana Parish

20th District Court PO Box 599, Clinton, LA 70722; 225-683-5145; fax: 225-683-3556; 8:30AM-4:30PM (CST). *Felony, Misdemeanor, Civil, Probate.*
www.eastfelicianaclerk.org/court.html
General Information: Probate fax is same as main fax number. No adoption or juvenile records released. Will fax documents $5.00 1st page, $1.00 each add'l. Court makes copy: $1.00 per page. Certification fee: $5.00 per doc. Payee: Clerk of Court. Personal checks accepted. No credit cards accepted. Prepayment required. Mail requests: SASE required.
Civil Name Search: Access: Mail, in person, online. Both court and visitors may perform in person name searches. Search fee: $10.00 per name per ten years. Required to search: name, years to search; also helpful: address. Civil records on computer from 1980, index books back to 1825. Mail turnaround time 1-2 days. Civil PAT goes back to 1988. Online subscription service is available. $400.00 per quarter permits access to viewable documents; $250 per quarter permits access in indices. This database also includes recordings, conveyances, mortgages, and marriage records.
Criminal Name Search: Access: Fax, mail, in person, online. Both court and visitors may perform in person name searches. Search fee: $10.00 per name. Required to search: name, years to search, DOB, SSN. Criminal records computerized from 1990, index books back to 1825. Mail turnaround time 1-2 days. Criminal PAT goes back to 1990. Criminal online also requires a subscription for full access, must be approved. Call for details.

Evangeline Parish

13th District Court PO Drawer 347, Ville Platte, LA 70586; 337-363-5671; fax: 337-363-5780; 8AM-4:30PM (CST). *Felony, Misdemeanor, Civil, Probate.*
General Information: Probate fax is same as main fax number. No adoption or juvenile records released. Will fax copies for $10.00 1st 5 pages, then $1.00 each add'l. Court makes copy: $1.00 per page. Self serve copy: same.To mail copies-$10.00 for 1st 5 pages, $1.00 each add'l page. Certification fee: $2.00 per page includes copy. Payee: Clerk of Court. Personal checks accepted. No credit cards accepted. Prepayment required.
Civil Name Search: Access: Fax, mail, in person. Both court and visitors may perform in person name searches. Search fee: $15.00 per name. Fee is for first 7 years searched. Add $2.00 per add'l year. Civil records on

computer back to 1989; prior records archived from 1911. Mail turnaround time 1-2 days. Public use terminal has civil records back to 1989. Results include complete name (1st, middle, last name).
Criminal Name Search: Access: Fax, mail, in person. Only the court performs in person name searches; visitors may not. Search fee: $15.00 per name. Fee is for first 7 years searched. Add $2.00 per add'l year. Required to search: name, years to search; also helpful: DOB, SSN. Criminal records computerized from 1989, prior records archived from 1911. Mail turnaround time 1-2 days.

Ville Platte City Court PO Box 147, Ville Platte, LA 70586; 337-363-1500; *Misdemeanor, Civil to $15,000, Eviction, Traffic.*

Franklin Parish

5th District Court PO Box 1564, Winnsboro, LA 71295; 318-435-5133; fax: 318-435-6792; 8:30AM-4:30PM (CST). *Felony, Misdemeanor, Civil, Probate.*
General Information: Probate fax is same as main fax number. No adoption or juvenile records released. Will fax documents $5.00 1st page, $1.00 each add'l. Court makes copy: $1.00 per page. Certification fee: $5.00 per document plus copy fee. Payee: Clerk of Court. Business checks accepted. No credit cards accepted. Prepayment required. Mail requests: SASE required.
Civil Name Search: Access: Mail, in person. Both court and visitors may perform in person name searches. Search fee: $20.00 per name. Civil records on computer from 1989, index books back to 1843. Mail turnaround time 1-2 days.
Criminal Name Search: Access: Mail, in person. Both court and visitors may perform in person name searches. Search fee: $20.00 per name. Fee includes 10 year search. Required to search: name, years to search, DOB; also helpful: SSN. Criminal records on computer since 1995. Mail turnaround time 1-2 days.

Winnsboro City Court 1308 Cornell St, Winnsboro, LA 71295; 318-435-4508; *Misdemeanor, Civil to $25,000, Eviction, Traffic.*

Grant Parish

35th District Court PO Box 263, Colfax, LA 71417; 318-627-3246; fax: 318-627-3201; 8:30AM-4:30PM (CST). *Felony, Misdemeanor, Civil, Probate.*
General Information: No adoption or juvenile records released without approval of a judge. Will fax documents $5.00 1st page, $2.00 each add'l, prepaid. Court makes copy: $1.00 per page. Self serve copy: $.50 per page. Certification fee: $5.00. Payee: Grant Parish Clerk of Court. Personal checks accepted. No credit cards accepted. Prepayment required. Mail requests: SASE required.
Civil Name Search: Access: Phone, fax, mail, in person. Both court and visitors may perform in person name searches. Search fee: $10.00 per name. Civil records on computer back to 1989; index books back to 1878. Mail turnaround time 1-2 days. Public use terminal has civil records. Terminal shows largely land-related documents.
Criminal Name Search: Access: Phone, fax, mail, in person. Both court and visitors may perform in person name searches. Search fee: $20.00 per name. Required to search: name, years to search, DOB; also helpful: SSN. Criminal index goes back to 1904; on computer back to 1996. Mail turnaround time 1-2 days.

Iberia Parish

16th District Court PO Drawer 12010, 300 Iberia St, New Iberia, LA 70562-2010; 337-365-7282; fax: 337-365-0737; 8:30AM-4:30PM (CST). *Felony, Misdemeanor, Civil, Probate.*
www.iberiaclerk.com
General Information: Probate fax is same as main fax number. No adoption or juvenile records released. Will fax specific case file data to local or toll-free number. Civil fax- $5.75 for 1st page, $1.50 each add'l. Court makes copy: $.75 per page. Self serve copy: $.50 per page. Certification fee: $5.00 per document. Payee: Clerk of Court. Personal checks accepted. Prepayment required.
Civil Name Search: Access: Mail, in person, online. Both court and visitors may perform in person name searches. Search fee: $20.00 per name. Required to search: name, years to search, SSN or DOB; also helpful: address. Civil records on computer back to 1974, index books back to 1868. Civil PAT goes back to 30 years. Search the civil index to 01/01/09 and probate to 01/01/2000 at www.iberiaclerk.com/resolution/default.asp. A user ID and password are required, it may be necessary to call for help on obtaining.
Criminal Name Search: Access: Mail, in person, online. Both court and visitors may perform in person name searches. Search fee: $20.00 per name. Required to search: name, years to search, DOB, SSN; also helpful: address. Criminal records computerized from 1994, index books back to 1868. Criminal PAT goes back to 10 years. search criminal record index from 01/01/2000 to the last day of the previous month. A user ID and password are required, it may be necessary to call for help on obtaining.

Jeanerette City Court PO Box 268, Jeanerette, LA 70544; 337-276-5603; *Misdemeanor, Civil to $30,000, Eviction, Traffic.*

New Iberia City Court 457 E Main St, Rm 206, New Iberia, LA 70560; 337-369-2334; *Misdemeanor, Civil to $30,000, Eviction, Traffic.*

Iberville Parish

18th District Court PO Box 423, 58050 Meriam, Plaquemine, LA 70764; 225-687-5160; fax: 225-687-5260; 8:30AM-4:30PM (CST). *Felony, Misdemeanor, Civil, Probate.*
www.ibervilleclerk.com/
General Information: Criminal department on 3rd Fl. No adoption or juvenile records released. Fee to fax out file $5.00 1st page, $1.00 each add'l. Court makes copy: $1.00 per page. Self serve copy: same. Certification fee: $5.00 per doc for certified, $3.00 if confirmed. Payee: Clerk of Court. Personal checks accepted. No credit cards accepted. Prepayment required. Mail requests: SASE required.
Civil Name Search: Access: Fax, mail, in person, online. Both court and visitors may perform in person name searches. Search fee: $10.00 per name. Civil records on computer back to 1990, books back to 1700. Mail turnaround time 1-2 days. Civil PAT goes back to 1990. Access to civil records online by subscription, contact clerk for details. See page at http://cotthosting.com/laiberia/User/Login.aspx?ReturnUrl=%2flaiberia%2findex.aspx.
Criminal Name Search: Access: Mail, in person. Both court and visitors may perform in person name searches. Search fee: $20.00 per name. Required to search: name, years to search, DOB; also helpful: SSN, address. Criminal docket on books back to 1900 or so. Mail turnaround time 1-2 days. Criminal PAT goes back to same as civil. Online results show name only.

Plaquemine City Court PO Box 1017, Plaquemine, LA 70765; 225-687-7236; *Misdemeanor, Civil to $25,000, Eviction, Traffic.*

Jackson Parish

2nd District Court PO Drawer 730, Jonesboro, LA 71251; 318-259-2424; fax: 318-395-0386; 8:30AM-4:30PM (CST). *Felony, Misdemeanor, Civil, Probate.*
www.jacksonparishclerk.org/
General Information: Probate fax is same as main fax number. No adoption or juvenile records released. Will fax documents $5.00 minimum; $2.00 1st pg; $1.00 each add'l. Court makes copy: $1.00 per page. Self serve copy: same. Certification fee: $5.00 per certification plus copy fee. Payee: Clerk of Court. Personal checks accepted. No credit cards accepted. Prepayment required. Mail requests: SASE required.
Civil Name Search: Access: Phone, mail, in person. Both court and visitors may perform in person name searches. Search fee: $20.00 per name; search includes 1988 to present. Civil index on docket books from 1880 and on computer since 1988. Mail turnaround time immediate. Civil PAT goes back to 1988.
Criminal Name Search: Access: Phone, mail, in person. Both court and visitors may perform in person name searches. Search fee: $20.00 per name; search includes 1988 to present. Required to search: name, years to search, DOB; also helpful: SSN. Criminal records on computer since 1988. Mail turnaround time 1-2 days. Criminal PAT goes back to same as civil.

Jefferson Davis Parish

31st District Court PO Box 799, Jennings, LA 70546; 337-824-8340; fax: 337-824-1354; 8:30AM-4:30PM (CST). *Felony, Misdemeanor, Civil, Probate.*
www.jeffdavisclerk.com/
General Information: No adoption or juvenile records released. Will fax documents $1.00 per page plus $10.00 fax fee. Court makes copy: $1.00 per page. Self serve copy: $.50 per page. Certification fee: $5.00. Payee: Clerk of Court. Personal checks accepted. No credit cards accepted. Prepayment required.
Civil Name Search: Access: Mail, in person. Both court and visitors may perform in person name searches. Search fee: $10.00 per name for 10 years. Required to search: name, years to search; also helpful: address. Civil records archived from 1913, on computer back to 1991. Mail turnaround time 2 days.
Criminal Name Search: Access: Mail, in person. Both court and visitors may perform in person name searches. Search fee: $20.00 per name for 10 years. Required to search: name, years to search; also helpful: DOB, SSN. Include city of residence of subject in your search request. Criminal records archived from 1913, on computer back to 1991. Mail turnaround time 2 days.

Jennings City Court PO Box 609, Jennings, LA 70546; 337-821-5514; *Misdemeanor, Civil to $30,000, Eviction, Traffic.*

Jefferson Parish

24th District Court PO Box 10, 200 Derbigny St, Gretna, LA 70054; 504-364-2900; criminal phone: 504-364-2992; civil phone: 504-364-3740/2611; probate phone: same as civil; criminal fax: 504-364-3797; civil fax: 8:30AM-4:30PM; 8:30AM-4:30PM (CST). *Felony, Misdemeanor, Civil, Probate.*
www.jpclerkofcourt.us
General Information: No adoption, juvenile or grand jury records released. Will fax documents $5.00 1st page, $1.00 each add'l. Court makes copy: $1.00 per page. Certification fee: $5.00 per page. Payee: Clerk of Court. Only cashiers checks and money orders accepted. No credit cards accepted. Prepayment required. Mail requests: SASE required.
Civil Name Search: Access: Phone, fax, mail, online, in person. Both court and visitors may perform in person name searches. Search fee: $5.00 per name. Civil records on computer from 1986, in index books back to 1972, prior records archived. Note: Phone search requests on computer are free, but only a couple names per request. Mail turnaround time 1-2 days. Civil PAT goes back to 1986 but older cases added as accessed. Access to court records on JeffNet is $100, plus $50.00 monthly, $.25 per printed page. Includes recordings, marriage index, and assessor rolls. For further information and sign-up, visit the website and click on "Jeffnet" or call 504-364-2976.
Criminal Name Search: Access: Mail, fax, online, in person. Both court and visitors may perform in person name searches. Search fee: $20.00 per case number. Required to search: name, years to search, DOB; also helpful: SSN. Criminal records computerized from 05/1994 to present, active cases are in books from 1972. Mail turnaround time 1-2 days. Criminal PAT goes back to 5/1994. Online access via internet, see civil. Online results show middle initial, DOB.

1st Parish Court 924 David Dr, Metairie, LA 70003; 504-736-8900; *Misdemeanor, Civil to $15,000, Eviction, Traffic.*

2nd Parish Court 100 Huey P Long Ave, Gretna, LA 22051; 504-364-2800; *Misdemeanor, Civil to $15,000, Eviction, Traffic.*

La Salle Parish

28th District Court PO Box 1316, Jena, LA 71342; 318-992-2158; fax: 318-992-2157; 8:30AM-4:30PM (CST). *Felony, Misdemeanor, Civil, Probate.*
General Information: No adoption or juvenile records released. Fee to fax out doc $10.00 each. Court makes copy: $1.00 per page. Self serve copy: same. Certification fee: $5.00 per cert plus copy fee. Payee: Clerk of Court. Personal checks accepted. No credit cards accepted. Prepayment required. Mail requests: SASE required.
Civil Name Search: Access: Phone, fax, mail, in person. Both court and visitors may perform in person name searches. Search fee: $20.00 1st name, $10.00 additional name. Fee is for 10 year search per name with certificate. Civil records archived from 1916; on computer since 6/95. Mail turnaround time 1-2 weeks; will release results sooner by phone. Public use terminal has civil records back to 1995.
Criminal Name Search: Access: Phone, fax, mail, in person. Both court and visitors may perform in person name searches. Search fee: $20.00 1st name, $10.00 additional name. Fee is for 10 year search per name with certificate. Required to search: name, years to search, DOB; also helpful: SSN. Criminal records archived from 1936; on computer since 1999. Mail turnaround time 1-2 weeks; will release results sooner by phone.

Lafayette Parish

15th District Court PO Box 2009, c/o Clerk of Court, Lafayette, LA 70502; 337-291-6400; criminal phone: 337-291-6329; civil phone: 337-291-6303; probate phone: 337-291-6303; criminal fax: 337-291-6475; civil fax: 8:30AM-4:30PM; 8:30AM-4:30PM (CST). *Felony, Misdemeanor, Civil, Probate.*
www.lafayetteparishclerk.com
General Information: Probate fax- 337-291-6480 No adoption or juvenile records released. Will fax documents to local or toll free line for $1.00 per page, 2 page minimum. Court makes copy: $1.00 per page. Self serve copy: $.50 per page. Certification fee: $5.00 per certification. Payee: Clerk of Court. Personal checks accepted. Prepayment required.
Civil Name Search: Access: Phone, fax, mail, online, in person. Both court and visitors may perform in person name searches. Search fee: $20.00 per name. Civil records archived from 1923; on computer back to 1986. Mail turnaround time 1-2 days. Civil PAT goes back to 1986. Access to the remote online system requires $100 setup fee plus $65 subscription fee per month. Civil index goes back to 1986. For more information, call 337-291-6435 or visit www.lafayetteparishclerk.com/onlineIndex.cfm. The system includes scanned images and pleadings back to May 2006.
Criminal Name Search: Access: Phone, fax, mail, in person. Both court and visitors may perform in person name searches. Search fee: $20.00 per name. Required to search: name, years to search, DOB. Criminal records

archived from 1966; on computer back to 1986. Mail turnaround time 1-2 days. Criminal PAT goes back to 1986. Online access to criminal index is not available at this time.

Lafayette City Court PO Drawer 3344, 105 E Convent St, Lafayette, LA 70502-3344; 337-291-8735; *Misdemeanor, Civil to $15,000, Eviction, Traffic.*

Lafourche Parish

17th District Court PO Box 818, Thibodaux, LA 70302; 985-447-4841; criminal phone: 985-448-0591; civil phone: 985-447-5550; probate phone: 985-447-5550; fax: 985-447-5800; 8:30AM-4:30PM (CST). *Felony, Misdemeanor, Civil, Probate.*
www.lafourcheclerk.com/
General Information: Probate is separate index at this same address. Probate fax is same as main fax number. No adoption or juvenile records released. Fee to fax out file $2.00 per page, includes copy fee. Court makes copy: $1.00 per page. Certification fee: $5.00 per certification plus $1.00 per page. Payee: Lafourche Parish Clerk of Court. Personal checks accepted. No credit cards accepted. Prepayment required.
Civil Name Search: Access: Fax, mail, in person, online. Both court and visitors may perform in person name searches. Search fee: $20.00 per name for a 10 year search. Civil records on computer back to 7/1982, microfiche from 1970, index books to early 1800s. Wills from 1817 and court orders from 07/01/1994 are available on a subscription system at https://www.lafourcheclerk.com/eSearch/User/Login.aspx?ReturnUrl=/esearch/default.aspx.
Criminal Name Search: Access: Fax, mail, in person. Both court and visitors may perform in person name searches. Search fee: $20.00 per name. Fee is for 10 year search. Required to search: name, years to search, DOB; also helpful: SSN, race, sex. Criminal records computerized from 7/1982, index books back to 1800s. Public use terminal has crim records back to 7/82. Results include race/sex. Criminal record docket is not available online.

Thibodaux City Court PO Box 568, 1309 Canal Blvd, Thibodaux, LA 70302; 985-446-7250; *Misdemeanor, Civil to $15,000, Eviction, Traffic.*

Lincoln Parish

3rd District Court PO Box 924, Ruston, LA 71273-0924; 318-251-5130; fax: 318-255-6004; 8:30AM-4:30PM (CST). *Felony, Misdemeanor, Civil, Probate.*
General Information: No adoption or juvenile records released. Fee to fax out file $5.00 for 1st page, $1.00 each add'l. Court makes copy: $2.00 per page. Self serve copy: $1.00 per page. Certification fee: $5.00 per doc. Payee: Clerk of Court. No personal checks or credit cards accepted. Prepayment required.
Civil Name Search: Access: Mail, in person. Both court and visitors may perform in person name searches. Search fee: $10.00 per name. Fee is per 10 years searched. Civil records on computer since 1985, index books back to 1800s. Mail turnaround time 1-2 days. Civil PAT goes back to 1984.
Criminal Name Search: Access: Mail, in person. Both court and visitors may perform in person name searches. Search fee: $10.00 per name. Fee is per 10 years searched. Required to search: name, years to search, DOB; also helpful: SSN. Criminal records on computer since 1992. Mail turnaround time 1-2 days. Criminal PAT goes back to 1992.

Ruston City Court PO Box 1821, Ruston, LA 22061; 318-251-8614; *Misdemeanor, Civil to $25,000, Eviction, Traffic.*

Livingston Parish

21st District Court PO Box 1150, Livingston, LA 70754; 225-686-2216; fax: 225-686-1867; 8AM-4PM (CST). *Felony, Misdemeanor, Civil, Probate.*
www.livclerk.org
General Information: There is also a web page for the 21st Judicial District at www.21stjdc.org. No adoption or juvenile records released. Will not fax documents. Court makes copy: $1.00 per page. Self serve copy: $.50 per page. Certification fee: $5.00 per doc plus copy fee. Payee: 21st District Court. Personal checks accepted. Visa/MC accepted for online copies only. Prepayment required.
Civil Name Search: Access: Mail, in person. Visitors must perform in person searches themselves. Search fee: $15.00. Civil index on docket books since 1800s; computerized records from 1982 to current. Mail turnaround time 1-2 days. Civil PAT goes back to 1989. Civil indexing is available to online subscribers. Civil images are available to online subscribers with a Louisiana Bar Number. Call 225-686-2216 for more information.
Criminal Name Search: Access: Mail, in person. Visitors must perform in person searches themselves. Search fee: $20.00. Required to search: name, years to search, DOB; also helpful: SSN, race, sex. Criminal records indexed in books since 1958; computerized records past 20 years. Note: Copies of pleadings pertaining to the search may be purchased at an

additional charge of $1.00 per page. Mail turnaround time 1-2 days. Criminal PAT goes back to same as civil. Online access is available to local attorneys only, with registration, call 225-686-2216 x1107. $50.00 per year fee for online access. Online results show middle initial.

Denham Springs City Court 400 Mayor Herbert Hoover Ave, Denham Springs, LA 70726; 225-665-1253; *Misdemeanor, Civil to $15,000, Eviction, Traffic.*

Madison Parish

6th District Court PO Box 1710, Tallulah, LA 71282; 318-574-0655; fax: 318-574-3961; 8:30AM-4:30PM (CST). *Felony, Misdemeanor, Civil, Probate.*
General Information: No adoption or juvenile records released. Will fax documents $2.00 per page. Court makes copy: $2.00 per page. Self serve copy: same. Certification fee: $5.00. Payee: Clerk of Court. Personal checks accepted. No credit cards accepted. Prepayment required. Mail requests: SASE required.
Civil Name Search: Access: Phone, mail, in person. Both court and visitors may perform in person name searches. Search fee: $10.00 per name. Civil records kept on computer since 7/93. Mail turnaround time 1-2 days. Civil PAT goes back to 1993.
Criminal Name Search: Access: Phone, mail, in person, fax. Both court and visitors may perform in person name searches. Search fee: $10.00 per name. Required to search: name, years to search, DOB; also helpful: SSN. Criminal records on index, computerized since 1999. Mail turnaround time 1-2 days. Criminal PAT goes back to 1998.

Morehouse Parish

4th District Court PO Box 1543, Bastrop, LA 71221; 318-281-3343; fax: 318-281-3775; 8:30AM-4:30PM (CST). *Felony, Misdemeanor, Civil, Probate.*
General Information: Probate fax is same as main fax number. No adoption, juvenile or judicial commitment records released. Will fax documents $5.00 1st page, $1.00 each add'l. Court makes copy: $1.00 per page. Self serve copy: same. Certification fee: $5.00 per document plus copy fee. Payee: Clerk of Court. Personal checks accepted. No credit cards accepted. Prepayment required. Mail requests: SASE required.
Civil Name Search: Access: Phone, fax, mail, in person. Both court and visitors may perform in person name searches. Search fee: $20.00 per name. Fee is per 10 years searched. Required to search: name, years to search; also helpful: address. Civil records on computer since 1987, in books since 1898, some on microfilm. Mail turnaround time 2-3 days. Civil PAT goes back to 1987.
Criminal Name Search: Access: Phone, fax, mail, in person. Both court and visitors may perform in person name searches. Search fee: $20.00 per name. Fee is per 10 years searched. Required to search: name, years to search, DOB; also helpful: address, SSN. Criminal records in books since 1926 and on microfilm since 1974; computerized records go back to 1994. Mail turnaround time 2-3 days. Criminal PAT goes back to 1994.

Bastrop City Court PO Box 391, Bastrop, LA 71221-0391; 318-283-0257; *Misdemeanor, Civil to $15,000, Eviction, Traffic.*

Natchitoches Parish

10th District Court PO Box 476, Natchitoches, LA 71458; 318-352-8152; civil phone: 318-357-2293; fax: 318-352-9321; 8:30AM-4:30PM (CST). *Felony, Misdemeanor, Civil, Small Claims, Probate.*
www.npclerkofcourt.org/
General Information: No adoption or juvenile records released. Will fax civil documents only for $5.00 1st page, $2.00 each add'l. Court makes copy: $1.00 per page. Self serve copy: same. Certification fee: $5.00 per document plus copy fee. Payee: Clerk of Court. Personal checks accepted. No credit cards accepted. Prepayment required. Mail requests: SASE required.
Civil Name Search: Access: Phone, fax, mail, in person, online. Both court and visitors may perform in person name searches. Search fee: $10.00 per name. Civil records on computer back to 6/1991, archived from 1950, index books back to 1700s. Mail turnaround time 1 week. Civil PAT goes back to 1986. With username and password to WebView you can search and access civil records, judgments. $50 setup fee, then $50.00 monthly, plus $.50 per image. Includes conveyance and marriage records. Direct subscription inquires to Linda Cockrell at 318-352-8152.
Criminal Name Search: Access: Phone, mail, in person. Both court and visitors may perform in person name searches. Search fee: $10.00 per name. Required to search: name, years to search, DOB; also helpful: SSN. Criminal records computerized from 6/1991, archived from 1950, index books back to 1800s. Mail turnaround time 1 week. Criminal PAT goes back to 1991.

Natchitoches City Court PO Box 70, Natchitoches, LA 71458-0070; 318-352-6666; *Misdemeanor, Civil to $25,000, Eviction, Traffic.*

Orleans Parish

Civil District Court 421 Loyola Ave, Rm 402, Attn: Clerk of Civil Dist. Ct., New Orleans, LA 70112; 504-592-9100; fax: 504-592-9128; 8:30AM-5PM (CST). *Civil, Probate, Domestic Relations.*
www.orleanscdc.com/

General Information: The Civil Court also oversees Conveyances, Mortgages, and Notaries Archives. Online identifiers in results same as on public terminal. No adoption or juvenile released. Will not fax out documents, but will accept fax documents for $5.00 per fax plus $2.50 per page. Court makes copy: $1.00 per page. Certification fee: $3.00 per page includes copy fee. Exemplification is $12.00 plus $3.00 per page. Payee: Clerk of Court. Only attorneys' checks, cashiers checks and money orders accepted. Major credit cards accepted. Prepayment required. Mail requests: SASE required.

Civil Name Search: Access: Phone, mail, online, in person. Both court and visitors may perform in person name searches. No search fee. Civil records on computer since 1985, in books back to early 1800s. Mail turnaround time 1-2 days. Public use terminal has civil records back to 1985. CDC Remote provides access to civil case index from 1985 and First City Court cases as well as parish mortgage and conveyance indexes. Case files are not provided. The annual fee is $500 or monthly is $100. Credit cards are accepted. Call 504-592-9264 for more information.

Criminal District Court 2700 Tulane Ave, Rm 115, New Orleans, LA 70119; 504-658-9000; records- 658-9028; fax: 504-658-9183; 8:15AM-3PM clerk; 8AM-4PM records (CST). *Felony, Misdemeanor.*

General Information: Records Dept phone- 504-658-9028, open till 4PM. No adoption or juvenile records released. Records Rm will fax out documents. Court makes copy: $1.50 per page. Certification fee: $2.00 per document. Payee: Clerk of Court. Business checks accepted. No credit cards accepted. Prepayment required. Mail requests: SASE required.

Criminal Name Search: Access: Mail, in person. Both court and visitors may perform in person name searches. Search fee: $10.00 per name. Required to search: name, DOB, SSN. SSN must be included. If you do not specify the years to search, then the search will include their complete records. Criminal records on computer past 8 years, books and files go back to early 1900s. Note: Only government agencies may fax in requests. Mail turnaround time 2 days.

New Orleans City Court 421 Loyola Ave, Rm 201, New Orleans, LA 70112; 504-592-9155; fax: 504-592-9281; 9AM-4PM (CST). *Civil Actions under $25,000, Small Claims, Eviction.*
www.orleanscdc.com/

General Information: Will receive fax docs for $5.00 1st 2 pages then $2.50 each add'l. Small claims phone-504-592-9154. Online identifiers in results same as on public terminal. No sealed records released. Will not fax documents. Court makes copy: $2.00 per page. Certification fee: $4.00 per page. Payee: New Orleans First City Court. No personal checks. Credit cards accepted. Prepayment required. Mail requests: SASE requested.

Civil Name Search: Access: Mail, in person, online. Both court and visitors may perform in person name searches. No search fee. Civil records on computer back to 1988. Mail turnaround time 5-10 days. Public use terminal has civil records back to 1988. Public terminal includes eviction and small claims records filed in FCC. CDC Remote provides access to First City Court cases from 1988 as well as civil cases, parish mortgage and conveyance indexes. The fee is $250 or $300 per year. Call 504-592-9264 for more information.

New Orleans Municipal Court 727 S Broad St, New Orleans, LA 70119; 504-658-9700; *Misdemeanor, Civil to $25,000, Eviction, Traffic.*

New Orleans Traffic Court 727 S Broad St, Violations Bureau, New Orleans, LA 70119; 504-827-5091; *Traffic.*

Second City Court of New Orleans 225 Morgan St, New Orleans, LA 70114; 504-368-4245; *Misdemeanor, Civil to $15,000, Eviction, Traffic.*

Ouachita Parish

4th District Court PO Box 1862, Monroe, LA 71210-1862; 318-327-1444; fax: 318-327-1462; 8:30AM-5PM (CST). *Felony, Misdemeanor, Civil, Probate.*
www.opclerkofcourt.com/

General Information: No adoption or juvenile records released. Will fax documents $2.00 1st page, $1.00 each add'l. Court makes copy: $1.00 per page. Self serve copy: $.50 per page. Certification fee: $5.00 per page plus copy fee. Payee: Clerk of Court. Business checks accepted. Checks accepted up to $50.00. No credit cards accepted unless online sub. secured. Prepayment required. Mail requests: SASE requested.

Civil Name Search: Access: Fax, mail, in person. Both court and visitors may perform in person name searches. Search fee: $10.00 per name. Civil records on computer from 1991, index books back to 1800s. Mail

turnaround time 1-2 days. Civil PAT goes back to 1989. Online access to the civil index is no longer available.

Criminal Name Search: Access: Fax, mail, in person, online. Both court and visitors may perform in person name searches. Search fee: $20.00 per name. Required to search: name, years to search, DOB; also helpful: SSN. Criminal records computerized from 1991, index books back to 1800s. Mail turnaround time 1-2 days. Criminal PAT goes back to 1991. A subscription service to the record index is at www.opclerkofcourt.com/online_records.htm. There is a one day ($12.50) or one month ($100) or one year ($1080) unlimited access fee to the index and images. There is an additional $.50 per page fee to print. Establish an account with a credit card. The there a $10.00 minimum for copies, before they will print.

Monroe City Court PO Box 777, Monroe, LA 71210; 318-329-2580; *Misdemeanor, Civil to $30,000, Eviction, Traffic.*

West Monroe City Court 2303 N 7th St, West Monroe, LA 71291; 318-396-2767; *Misdemeanor, Civil to $15,000, Eviction, Traffic.*

Plaquemines Parish

25th District Court PO Box 40, 301 Maine St, Belle Chasse, LA 70037; 504-297-5180; fax: 504-297-5195; 8:30AM-4:30PM (CST). *Felony, Misdemeanor, Civil, Probate.*
www.plaqueminesparishclerkofcourt.com/

General Information: Probate fax- 504-297-5195. Court will search probate records by written request only. The fee is $10.00 per name. No adoption or juvenile records released. Will not fax documents. Court makes copy: $1.00 per page. Self serve copy: No self serve criminal copier; Civil self serve- $1.00 each. Certification fee: $5.00 per document. Payee: Clerk of Court. Personal checks accepted. No credit cards accepted. Prepayment required.

Civil Name Search: Access: In person, online. Visitors must perform in person searches themselves. Civil index on docket books back to 1800s; computerized since 1/1977. Note: Court will search probate records by written request only. The fee is $10 per name. Civil PAT goes back to 1977. Search the docket index online from the home page.

Criminal Name Search: Access: In person, online. Visitors must perform in person searches themselves. Criminal records indexed in books back to 1966; computerized records go back to 1/1966. Note: This agency suggests to also reach the Plaquemines Sheriff's Office for a criminal search, 504-297-5114. Criminal PAT goes back to 1966 (index only). Search the docket index online from the home page.

Pointe Coupee Parish

18th District Court PO Box 86, New Roads, LA 70760; 225-638-9596; criminal phone: x3; civil phone: x1; fax: 225-638-9590; 8:30AM-4:30PM (CST). *Felony, Misdemeanor, Civil, Probate.*

General Information: No adoption or juvenile records released. Will fax documents to local or toll free line. Court makes copy: $1.25 per page. Certification fee: $5.00 per doc plus copy fee. Payee: Clerk of Court. Personal checks accepted. No credit cards accepted. Prepayment required.

Civil Name Search: Access: Mail, in person. Both court and visitors may perform in person name searches. Search fee: $10.00 per name. Civil index on docket books back to 1800s. Mail turnaround time 1-5 days. Civil PAT available.

Criminal Name Search: Access: In person only. Visitors must perform in person searches themselves. Required to search: name, years to search, DOB; SSN helpful. Criminal records indexed in books back to 1800s. Criminal PAT available.

Rapides Parish

9th District Court PO Box 952, Alexandria, LA 71309; 318-473-8153; criminal phone: 318-619-5860; civil phone: 318-619-5852; probate phone: 318-619-5852; fax: 318-473-4667; 8:30AM-4:30PM (CST). *Felony, Misdemeanor, Civil, Probate.*
www.rapidesclerk.org

General Information: Probate fax is same as main fax number. Another contact number is 318-619-5845 (Public Service). If questions, email info@rapidesclerk.org. No adoption, juvenile, or judicial commitment records released. Will fax documents to local or toll free line, fee is $2.25 per page. Court makes copy: $1.00 per page. Self serve copy: same. A copy of the Criminal Minutes is $10.00. Certification fee: $5.00 per civil cert, $10.00 per criminal cert; plus copy fee. Payee: Rapides Parish Clerk of Court. Personal checks accepted. No credit cards accepted. Prepayment required.

Civil Name Search: Access: Mail, in person. Both court and visitors may perform in person name searches. Search fee: $20.00 per name. Fee is per separate index. Civil index on docket books since 1864, civil in computer since 10/84. Mail turnaround time within 72 hours. Civil PAT goes back to 1984.

Criminal Name Search: Access: Mail, in person. Both court and visitors may perform in person name searches. Search fee: $20.00 per name. Fee is per separate index. Required to search: name, years to search, DOB; also helpful: SSN. Criminal records on computer since 1984; prior records in index books back to 1864. Mail turnaround time 72 hours. Criminal PAT goes back to same as civil.

Alexandria City Court PO Box 30, Alexandria, LA 71309; 318-449-5146; *Misdemeanor, Civil to $15,000, Eviction, Traffic.*

Pineville City Court PO Box 3671, Pineville, LA 71361; 318-449-5656; *Misdemeanor, Civil to $15,000, Eviction, Traffic.*

Red River Parish

39th District Court PO Box 485, Coushatta, LA 71019; 318-932-6741; fax: 318-932-3126; 8:30AM-4:30PM (CST). *Felony, Misdemeanor, Civil, Probate.*

General Information: No adoption or juvenile records released. Will fax documents to local or toll-free number. Court makes copy: $2.00 per page. Self serve copy: $1.00 per page. Certification fee: $5.00 per document. Payee: Clerk of Court. Personal checks only accepted. No credit cards accepted. Prepayment required. Mail requests: SASE required.

Civil Name Search: Access: Mail, in person. Both court and visitors may perform in person name searches. Search fee: $10.00 per name. Civil index on docket books. Mail turnaround time 1-2 days. Public use terminal has civil records back to 2000.

Criminal Name Search: Access: Mail, in person. Only the court performs in person name searches; visitors may not. Search fee: $10.00 per name. Required to search: name, years to search, DOB; also helpful: SSN. The index is kept in the DA's office. Mail turnaround time 1-2 days.

Richland Parish

5th District Court PO Box 119, Rayville, LA 71269; 318-728-4171, 318-728-7000; fax: 318-728-7020; 8:30AM-4:30PM (CST). *Felony, Misdemeanor, Civil, Probate.*

General Information: No adoption or juvenile records released. Will fax documents for a $5.00 fee. Court makes copy: $2.00 per page. Self serve copy: $.50 per page. Certification fee: $5.00. Payee: Clerk of Court. Personal checks accepted. No credit cards accepted. Prepayment required. Mail requests: SASE required.

Civil Name Search: Access: Mail, in person. Both court and visitors may perform in person name searches. Search fee: $20.00 per name. Civil records on since 1/94, prior on books to 1800s. Mail turnaround time 1-2 days.

Criminal Name Search: Access: Mail, in person. Both court and visitors may perform in person name searches. Search fee: $20.00 per name. Required to search: name, years to search, DOB, SSN. Criminal records on since 1/94, prior on books to 1800s. Note: Extract of court minutes is $10.00. Mail turnaround time 1-2 days.

Sabine Parish

11th District Court Sabine Clerk of Court, PO Box 419, Many, LA 71449; 318-256-6223; fax: 318-256-9037; 8AM-4:30PM (CST). *Felony, Misdemeanor, Civil, Probate.*
www.sabineparishclerk.com/

General Information: Probate fax is same as main fax number. No adoption or juvenile records released. Will fax documents $5.00 1st page, $2.00 each add'l. Court makes copy: $1.00 per page. Self serve copy: same. Certification fee: $5.00 per cert; $15.00 for exemplification. Payee: Sabine Parish Clerk. Personal checks accepted. No credit cards accepted. Prepayment required. Mail requests: SASE required.

Civil Name Search: Access: Fax, mail, in person, online. Both court and visitors may perform in person name searches. Search fee: $20.00 per name. Civil records index on computer back to 1985. Mail turnaround time 5-10 days. Public use terminal has civil records back to 01/1985. Access civil and succession-probate court records by subscription at www.sabineparishclerk.com/online.htm. $50.00 one-time setup fee plus $100 per month, includes conveyance, mortgage, marriage records. Civil suits go back to 1/1985; Probate to 1920.

Criminal Name Search: Access: Fax, mail, in person. Both court and visitors may perform in person name searches. Search fee: $20.00 per name. Criminal records on computer by name go back to 1990. Mail turnaround time 5-10 days. Access to criminal records online not available.

St. Bernard Parish

34th District Court PO Box 1746, 9061 W Judge Perez Dr (70043), Chalmette, LA 70044; 504-271-3434; fax: 504-278-4380; 8:30AM-4:30PM (CST). *Felony, Misdemeanor, Civil, Probate.*
www.stbclerk.com/modules.php?name=system

General Information: No adoption or juvenile records. Will not fax documents. Court makes copy: $1.00 per page. Certification fee: $5.00. Payee: Clerk of Court. No personal checks or credit cards accepted. Prepayment required. Mail requests: SASE required.

Civil Name Search: Access: Mail, in person, online. Both court and visitors may perform in person name searches. Search fee: $10.00 per

name. Fee is per 10 years searched. Civil index on docket books back to 1800s, on computer since 1989. Mail turnaround time 2-3 days. Civil PAT goes back to 1989. Search Civil suits back to 1/1989 free at http://records.stbclerk.com/LandRecords/protected/SrchQuickName.aspx.

Criminal Name Search: Access: Mail, in person, online. Both court and visitors may perform in person name searches. Search fee: $10.00 per name. Fee is per 10 years searched. Required to search: name, years to search, DOB; also helpful: SSN, address. Criminal records indexed in books back to 1800s, on computer since 1989. Mail turnaround time 2-3 days. Criminal PAT goes back to same as civil. Search index to 1/1989 free at http://records.stbclerk.com/LandRecords/protected/SrchQuickName.aspx.

St. Charles Parish

29th District Court PO Box 424, 15045 River Rd, Hahnville, LA 70057; 985-783-6632; fax: 985-783-2005; 8:30AM-4:30PM (CST). *Felony, Misdemeanor, Civil, Probate.*
www.stcharlesgov.net/

General Information: Probate is a separate index at this same address. Probate fax is same as main fax number. No adoption or juvenile records released. Fee to fax out file $4.00 per page. Court makes copy: $1.00 per page. Certification fee: $5.00 plus copy fees. Payee: Clerk of Court. Personal checks accepted. No credit cards accepted except online civil records. Prepayment required.

Civil Name Search: Access: Mail, fax, in person, online. Both court and visitors may perform in person name searches. Search fee: $10.00 per name. Civil records on computer back to 1982, on index books back to 1890. Mail turnaround time 1 day. Civil PAT goes back to 1982. Results may or may not include identifiers.

Criminal Name Search: Access: Mail, fax, in person. Both court and visitors may perform in person name searches. Search fee: $10.00 per name. Required to search: name, years to search, DOB; also helpful: SSN, race, sex. Criminal records computerized from 1990, on index books back to 1900s. Mail turnaround time 1 day. Criminal PAT goes back to 5/1990. Results may or may not include identifiers. The log-in page is at https://records.stcharlesparish-la.gov/User/Login.aspx?ReturnUrl=%2findex.aspx. Images to 1999, index to 1988. Fee is $50 per month plus $1.00 per page for copies. All fees paid by credit card via Pay pal.

St. Helena Parish

21st District Court PO Box 308, 369 Mitnan St, Greensburg, LA 70441; 225-222-4514; criminal fax: 225-222-3443; civil fax: 8:30AM-4:30PM; 8:30AM-4:30PM (CST). *Felony, Misdemeanor, Civil, Probate.*

General Information: Search fee applies for each division. Probate fax is same as main fax number. No adoption or juvenile records released. Will not fax out documents. Court makes copy: $1.00 per page. Self serve copy: $1.00 per page. Certification fee: $5.00 per seal. Payee: Clerk of Court. Personal checks accepted. No credit cards accepted. Prepayment required. Mail requests: SASE required.

Civil Name Search: Access: Phone, mail, fax, in person. Both court and visitors may perform in person name searches. Search fee: $20.00 per name. Civil index on docket books back to 1800s. Mail turnaround time 1-2 days.

Criminal Name Search: Access: Mail, in person. Both court and visitors may perform in person name searches. Search fee: $20.00 per name. Required to search: name, years to search, DOB; also helpful: SSN. Criminal records indexed in books back to 1800s. Mail turnaround time 1-2 days.

St. James Parish

23rd District Court PO Box 63, 5800 Louisiana Hwy 44, River Rd, Convent, LA 70723; 225-562-7496; criminal phone: 225-562-2271; civil phone: 225-562-2360; probate phone: 225-562-2360; fax: 225-562-2383; 8AM-4:30PM (CST). *Felony, Misdemeanor, Civil, Probate.*

General Information: Probate is a separate index at this same address. Probate fax is same as main fax number. No adoption or juvenile records released. Will fax documents for $5.00 per doc fee. Court makes copy: $1.00 per page. Self serve copy: same. Certification fee: $5.00 per document plus copy fee. Payee: Clerk of Court. Only cashiers checks and money orders accepted. No credit cards accepted. Prepayment required. Mail requests: SASE required.

Civil Name Search: Access: Mail, in person. Both court and visitors may perform in person name searches. Search fee: $15.00 per name. Civil index on docket books back to early 1900s; on computer back to 1988. Mail turnaround time 1-2 days. Civil PAT goes back to 1990.

Criminal Name Search: Access: Mail, in person. Both court and visitors may perform in person name searches. Search fee: $15.00 per name. Required to search: name, years to search, DOB. Criminal records indexed in books back to early 1900s; on computer back to 1988. Mail turnaround time 1-2 days. Criminal PAT goes back to 1990.

St. John the Baptist Parish

40th District Court PO Box 280, Edgard, LA 70049; 985-497-3331; fax: 985-497-3972; 8:30AM-4:30PM (CST). *Felony, Misdemeanor, Civil, Probate.*
www.stjohnclerk.org

General Information: Court is planning to offer online searches eventually. No adoption or juvenile records released. Fee to fax out file $5.00 first page. $1.00 ea add'l. Court makes copy: $1.00 per page. Certification fee: $5.00 per doc. Payee: Clerk of Court. No Personal checks and credit cards accepted. Prepayment required. Mail requests: SASE required.

Civil Name Search: Access: Mail, fax, in person. Both court and visitors may perform in person name searches. Search fee: $15.00 per name. Fee is for first 15 years. Add $1.00 per add'l year. Civil records on computer since 11/2/1982. Mail turnaround time 3-4 days. Civil PAT goes back to 1982.

Criminal Name Search: Access: Mail, fax, in person. Both court and visitors may perform in person name searches. Search fee: $20.00 per name. Fee is for first 15 years. Add $1.00 per add'l year. Required to search: name, years to search, DOB; also helpful: SSN. Felony records on computer since 1983, misdemeanors since 3/91. Mail turnaround time 3-4 days. Criminal PAT goes back to same as civil.

St. Landry Parish

27th District Court PO Box 750, Courthouse, Opelousas, LA 70570; 337-942-5606; fax: 337-948-1653; 8AM-4:30PM (CST). *Felony, Misdemeanor, Civil, Probate.*
www.stlandry.org

General Information: Online identifiers in results same as on public terminal. No adoption or juvenile records released. Fee to fax out file $5.00 1st page, $1.00 each add'l. Court makes copy: $1.00 per page. Self serve copy: $.50 per page. Certification fee: $5.50. Payee: Clerk of Court. Personal checks accepted. No credit cards accepted. Prepayment required. Mail requests: SASE required.

Civil Name Search: Access: Mail, fax, in person, online. Both court and visitors may perform in person name searches. Search fee: $20.00 per name. Additional $1.00 fee per year after 1st 10 years. Civil index on docket books back to 1800s, on computer back to 1992. Mail turnaround time 1-2 days. Civil PAT goes back to 07/1992. Results include plaintiff names. Online subscription access program to civil cases is available. The fee ranges from $50.00 to $300 per month. Includes civil court records back to 1997, also includes land indexes and images. Contact the court or visit the web page for details.

Criminal Name Search: Access: Mail, fax, in person. Both court and visitors may perform in person name searches. Search fee: $20.00 per name. Additional $1.00 fee per year after 1st 10 years. Required to search: name, years to search, DOB; also helpful: SSN. Criminal records indexed in books back to 1800s, on computer back to 1995. Mail turnaround time 1-3 days. Criminal PAT goes back to 1995. Online results show name only.

Eunice City Court PO Box 591, Eunice, LA 70535; 337-457-6535; *Misdemeanor, Civil to $25,000, Eviction, Traffic.*

Opelousas City Court PO Box 1999, Opelousas, LA 70571-1999; 337-948-2570; *Misdemeanor, Civil to $25,000, Eviction, Traffic.*

St. Martin Parish

16th District Court PO Box 308, St. Martinville, LA 70582; 337-394-2210; fax: 337-394-7772; 8:30AM-4:30PM (CST). *Felony, Misdemeanor, Civil, Probate.*
www.stmartinparishclerkofcourt.com

General Information: No adoption, sealed records, expunged or juvenile records released. Will fax documents $.75 per page. Court makes copy: $1.00 per page. Self serve copy: same. Certification fee: $6.00 per doc. Payee: Clerk of Court. Personal checks accepted. No credit cards accepted. Prepayment required.

Civil Name Search: Access: In person, online. Both court and visitors may perform in person name searches. Search fee: $10.00 per name. Required to search: name, years to search; also helpful: DOB. Civil records archived from 1760, on computer since 1990. Civil PAT goes back to 1990. The online system is by subscription only, Fee is $100 per month. Data available images back to 1989/1990. Judgments are found with Recorder's Office data indices available at www.stmartinparishclerkofcourt.com.

Criminal Name Search: Access: In person, online. Both court and visitors may perform in person name searches. Search fee: $10.00 per name. Required to search: name, years to search, DOB; also helpful: address, SSN. Criminal records archived from 1760, on computer since 1990. Criminal PAT goes back to same as civil. The online system is by subscription only, Fee is $100 per month. Data available images back to 1989/1990. Note if both civil and criminal data wanted, then fee is $200 per month. Online results show middle initial, DOB, address.

Breaux Bridge City Court 101 Berard St, Breaux Bridge, LA 70517; 337-332-4117; *Misdemeanor, Civil to $15,000, Eviction, Traffic.*

St. Mary Parish

16th Judicial District Court PO Drawer 1231, Franklin, LA 70538; 337-828-4100 X200; fax: 337-828-2509; 8:30AM-4:30PM (CST). *Felony, Misdemeanor, Civil, Probate.*

General Information: No adoption or juvenile records released. Will not fax documents. Court makes copy: $1.00 per page. Self serve copy: $.50 per page. Certification fee: $5.00. Payee: St. Mary Parish Clerk of Court. Personal checks, money order, cash accepted. No credit cards accepted. Prepayment required.

Civil Name Search: Access: In person only. Visitors must perform in person searches themselves. Civil index on docket books back to 1800s. Civil PAT goes back to 1980. Public terminal is located in record room.

Criminal Name Search: Access: In person only. Visitors must perform in person searches themselves. Required to search: name, years to search, DOB; SSN helpful. Criminal records indexed in books back to 1800s. Criminal PAT goes back to 1983. Public terminal is located in record room.

Franklin City Court 317 Willow St, PO Box 343, Franklin, LA 70538; 337-828-3858; *Misdemeanor, Civil to $15,000, Eviction, Traffic.*

Morgan City Court 7261 Hwy 182 E, PO Box 1577, Morgan City, LA 70381; 985-384-2718; *Misdemeanor, Civil to $15,000, Eviction, Traffic.*

St. Tammany Parish

22nd District Court PO Box 1090, Covington, LA 70434; 985-809-8700; fax: 985-809-8777; 8:30AM-4:30PM (CST). *Felony, Misdemeanor, Civil, Probate.*
www.sttammanyclerk.org/main/index.asp

General Information: No adoption or juvenile records released. Will fax documents if name search pre-paid. Court makes copy: $.50 per page. Self serve copy: same. Certification fee: $3.00 per doc. Payee: Clerk of Court. Personal checks accepted. Credit cards only accepted for online access payments. Prepayment required. Mail requests: SASE required.

Civil Name Search: Access: Mail, in person, online. Both court and visitors may perform in person name searches. No search fee, unless extensive. Civil records archived on index books back to 1810, on computer since 1992, document images scanned since 1995. Mail turnaround time 1-2 days. Civil PAT goes back to 1992. Internet access to civil records is from the Clerk of Court. $50 initial setup fee, $50.00 per month and $.35 to print a page. For information, call Kristie Howell at 985-809-8787. Civil index goes back to 1992; images to 1995. Search index free at https://www.sttammanyclerk.org/liveapp/default.asp.

Criminal Name Search: Access: Mail, in person, online. Both court and visitors may perform in person name searches. No search fee, unless extensive or if for background check then $20.00. Required to search: name, years to search, DOB; also helpful: SSN. Criminal records on computer since 10/87, archived to 1915 but must be searched by court. Mail turnaround time 2-3 days. Criminal PAT goes back to 10/1987. Internet access to criminal records is the same as civil, indices go back to 1988. Online results show name, DOB.

lidell City Court 501 Bouscaren St, Slidell, LA 70459; 985-643-1274; *Misdemeanor, Civil to $35,000, Eviction, Traffic.*

Tangipahoa Parish

21st District Court PO Box 667, Amite, LA 70422; 985-748-4146; criminal fax: 985-747-3387; civil fax: 8:30AM-4:30PM; 8:30AM-4:30PM (CST). *Felony, Misdemeanor, Civil, Probate.*
www.tangiclerk.org

General Information: No adoption or juvenile records released. Fee to fax out file $5.00 1st page, $1.00 each add'l. Court makes copy: $1.00 per page. Self serve copy: same. Certification fee: $5.00 per document plus copy fee. Payee: Clerk of Court. Personal checks and credit cards accepted. Prepayment required. Mail requests: SASE required.

Civil Name Search: Access: Mail, in person, online. Both court and visitors may perform in person name searches. Search fee: $10.00 per name per 10 years. Civil records archived back to early 1900s; on computer back to 1974. Mail turnaround time 3-4 days. Civil PAT goes back to 1974. Online access to index of civil records is at www.tangiclerk.org/eSearch. You can "Sign in as a Guest" to view indexes at no cost; images are only available with a paid subscription). Index back to 1974. There are no civil suit histories or images available. For subscription information and list of fees, click on "Online" at home page, or call Andi Matheu: 985-748-4146.

Criminal Name Search: Access: Mail, in person. Both court and visitors may perform in person name searches. Search fee: $20.00 per name. Required to search: name, years to search, DOB, SSN. Criminal records archived back to early 1900s; on computer back to 1994. Mail turnaround time 3-4 days. Criminal PAT goes back to same as civil. Online results show name only.

Hammond City Court-7th Ward 303 E Thomas St, Hammond, LA 70401; 985-542-3455; *Misdemeanor, Civil to $30,000, Eviction, Traffic.*

Tensas Parish

6th District Court PO Box 78, 201 Hancock St, St. Joseph, LA 71366; 318-766-3921; fax: 318-766-3926; 8:30AM-3:30PM (CST). *Felony, Misdemeanor, Civil, Probate.*

General Information: No adoption or juvenile records released. Will not fax documents. Court makes copy: $3.00 1st page, $2.00 ea add'l. Certification fee: $5.50. Payee: Clerk of Court. Personal checks accepted. No credit cards accepted. Prepayment required.

Civil Name Search: Access: In person only. Visitors must perform in person searches themselves. Civil records archived back to 1800s, on computer since mid-1998.

Criminal Name Search: Access: In person only. Visitors must perform in person searches themselves. Required to search: name, years to search; also helpful: DOB, SSN. Criminal records on computer since 1998; archived back to 1800s.

Terrebonne Parish

32nd District Court PO Box 1569, 7856 Main St, Houma, LA 70361; 985-868-5660; criminal fax: 985-868-5143; civil fax: 8:30AM-4:30PM; 8:30AM-4:30PM (CST). *Felony, Misdemeanor, Civil, Probate, Traffic.*
www.terrebonneclerk.org/

General Information: Search fee is per index. Probate is separate index at this same address. No adoption or juvenile records released. Will fax documents $2.00 per page up to 5 pages, then $1.00 ea addl. Court makes copy: $1.00 per page. Certification fee: $5.00 per cert plus copy fee. Payee: Terrebonne Parish Clerk of Court. Personal checks accepted. No credit cards accepted. Prepayment required. Mail requests: SASE required.

Civil Name Search: Access: Mail, fax, in person. Both court and visitors may perform in person name searches. Search fee: $25.00 per name. Civil records on computer since 1986, in books to 1823. Note: Will accept fax search request if prepaid. Mail turnaround time 1 week. Civil PAT available. Public terminal on 1st Fl.

Criminal Name Search: Access: Mail, in person. Both court and visitors may perform in person name searches. Search fee: $25.00 per name. Required to search: name, years to search, DOB; also helpful: SSN, race, sex. Criminal records archived to 1800s. Mail turnaround time 1 week. Criminal PAT available.

Houma City Court 7887 Main St, Houma, LA 70360; 985-868-4232; *Misdemeanor, Civil to $20,000, Eviction, Traffic.*

Union Parish

3rd District Court Courthouse Bldg, 100 E Bayou #105, Farmerville, LA 71241; 318-368-3055; fax: 318-368-3861; 8:30AM-4:30PM (CST). *Felony, Misdemeanor, Civil, Probate.*
www.upclerk.com/

General Information: Probate fax uses same fax number. No adoption or juvenile records released. Will fax documents $5.00 per doc. Court makes copy: $2.00 per page. Self serve copy: $1.00 per page. Certification fee: $5.00 per instrument. Payee: Clerk of Court. Personal checks and credit cards accepted. Prepayment required. Mail requests: SASE required.

Civil Name Search: Access: Mail, in person, online. Both court and visitors may perform in person name searches. No search fee. Civil index on docket books back to 1839. Mail turnaround time same day. Public use terminal has civil records back to 1978. From the home page click on "Online Index Search. This is a subscription service or on a $5.00 per record basis.

Criminal Name Search: Access: Mail, fax, in person. Both court and visitors may perform in person name searches. Search fee: $20.00 per name. Required to search: name, years to search, SSN. Criminal records indexed in books back to 1839; computerized records go back to 1978. Note: The criminal record index will become available online in the fall of 2011. Mail turnaround time same day.

Vermilion Parish

15th District Court 100 N State St, #101, Abbeville, LA 70510; 337-898-1992; civil phone: 337-898-4550; criminal fax: 337-740-8803; civil fax: 8:30AM-4:30PM; 8:30AM-4:30PM (CST). *Felony, Misdemeanor, Civil, Probate.*
www.vermilionparishclerkofcourt.com/

General Information: No adoption or juvenile records released. Will fax back documents $5.00 plus $1.00 per page. Court makes copy: $1.00 per page. Certification fee: $5.00 per certification. Payee: Vermilion Parish Clerk of Court. Personal checks, money order or cash accepted. No credit cards accepted. Prepayment required. Mail requests: SASE required.

Civil Name Search: Access: Phone, fax, mail, in person. Both court and visitors may perform in person name searches. Search fee: $20.00 per name. Required to search: name, years to search, DOB, SSN. Civil records on computer since 1983, in books since 1885, on microfilm since 1885. Mail turnaround time 1-2 days after payment.

Criminal Name Search: Access: Phone, fax, mail, in person. Both court and visitors may perform in person name searches. Search fee: $20.00 per name. Required to search: name, years to search; also helpful: SSN, DOB, race, sex. Criminal records on computer since 1983, in books since 1885, on microfilm since 1885. Mail turnaround time 1-2 days after payment. Public use terminal has crim records back to 1993.

Abbeville City Court 208 S State St, PO Box 251 (70511), Abbeville, LA 70510; 337-893-1513; *Misdemeanor, Civil to $25,000, Eviction, Traffic.*

Kaplan City Court 511 N Cushing Ave, PO Box 121, Kaplan, LA 70548; 337-643-6611; *Misdemeanor, Civil to $25,000, Eviction, Traffic.*

Vernon Parish

30th District Court PO Box 40, Leesville, LA 71496; 337-238-1384; probate phone: 337-238-4345; fax: 337-238-9902; 8AM-4:30PM (CST). *Felony, Misdemeanor, Civil, Probate.*
www.vernonclerk.com/

General Information: Probate fax is same as main fax number. No adoption or juvenile records released. Will fax documents to local or toll free line. Court makes copy: $1.25 per page. Self serve copy: $.75 per page. Certification fee: $5.00. Payee: Clerk of Court. Personal checks accepted. No credit cards accepted. Prepayment required. Mail requests: SASE required.

Civil Name Search: Access: Mail, fax, in person. Both court and visitors may perform in person name searches. Search fee: $10.00 per name. Civil records on computer from 11/1985, archived back to 1900. Mail turnaround time same day. Civil PAT goes back to 1986.

Criminal Name Search: Access: Mail, in person. Both court and visitors may perform in person name searches. Search fee: $20.00 per name. Required to search: name, years to search, DOB, SSN. Criminal records computerized from 11/1985, archived back to 1900. Mail turnaround time same day. Criminal PAT goes back to 11/1985.

Leesville City Court PO Box 1486, Leesville, LA 71496-1486; 337-238-1531; *Misdemeanor, Civil to $35,000, Eviction, Traffic.*

Washington Parish

22nd District Court PO Box 607, Franklinton, LA 70438; 985-839-4663/7821; criminal fax: 985-839-7271; civil fax: 8AM-4:30PM; 8AM-4:30PM (CST). *Felony, Misdemeanor, Civil, Probate.*
www.wpclerk.org/CustomPage.aspx?Title=Home

General Information: No adoption or juvenile records released. Will not fax documents. Court makes copy: $1.00 per page. Self serve copy: $.50 per page. Certification fee: $5.00. Payee: Washington Parish Clerk of Court. Personal checks accepted. No credit cards accepted. Prepayment required. Mail requests: SASE requested.

Civil Name Search: Access: Mail, in person, online. Both court and visitors may perform in person name searches. Search fee: $10.00 per name per index. Civil records on computer from 1993, archived 4/1967, index books back to 1800s. Mail turnaround time 1-2 days. Civil PAT goes back to 1988. The index and images are searchable online. The fee is $100 per month to view plus $1.00 for each printed page. Sign-up is at https://search.wpclerk.org/external/User/Login.aspx?ReturnUrl=%2fexternal%2findex.aspx.

Criminal Name Search: Access: Mail, fax, in person, online. Both court and visitors may perform in person name searches. Search fee: $20.00 per name per index. Required to search: name, years to search, DOB; also helpful- SSN. Criminal records computerized from 1993, archived 4/1967, index books back to 1800s. Mail turnaround time 1-2 days. Criminal PAT goes back to 8/1989; newer cases have show more info. The records index only are searchable online. The fee is $100 per month to view plus $1.00 for each printed page. The sign-up is at https://search.wpclerk.org/external/User/Login.aspx?ReturnUrl=%2fexternal%2findex.aspx.

Bogalusa City Court PO Box 518, Bogalusa, LA 70429-0518; 985-732-6204; *Misdemeanor, Civil to $25,000, Eviction, Traffic.*

Webster Parish

26th District Court PO Box 370, Minden, LA 71058-0370; 318-371-0366; fax: 318-371-0226; 8:30AM-4:30PM (CST). *Felony, Misdemeanor, Civil, Probate.*
www.websterclerk.org/

General Information: Probate is a separate index at this same address. No adoption or juvenile records released. Will fax documents $5.00 per page. Court makes copy: $1.00 per page. Self serve copy: $.50 per page. Certification fee: $5.00 per document. Payee: Clerk of Court. Personal checks accepted. No credit cards accepted. Prepayment required.

Civil Name Search: Access: Fax, mail, in person, online. Both court and visitors may perform in person name searches. Search fee: $10.00 per name. Civil records archived back to 1800s, on computer since 1986. Mail turnaround time 2-3 days. Civil PAT goes back to 01/1986. Access court records by subscription; fee is $50.00 per month for index searches and images. Civil index goes back to 01/1986; images back to 2005. Sub includes criminal, probate, civil, traffic, also marriages and conveyances. Login, signup or find more information at www.websterclerk.org/records.html.

Criminal Name Search: Access: Mail, fax, in person, online. Both court and visitors may perform in person name searches. Search fee: $20.00 per name. Required to search: name; also helpful: years to search. Criminal records not on computer, in books to 1871. Mail turnaround time 2-3 days. Criminal PAT goes back to 11/1992. Access to criminal index and images is included in the general subscription service described in the civil section, above. The criminal subscription index goes back to 11/28/1992; images go back to early 2007.

Minden City Court PO Box 968, Minden, LA 71058-0968; 318-377-4308; *Misdemeanor, Civil to $35,000, Eviction, Traffic.*

Springhill City Court PO Box 86, Springhill, LA 71075; 318-539-4213; *Misdemeanor, Civil to $35,000, Eviction, Traffic.*

West Baton Rouge Parish

18th District Court PO Box 107, Port Allen, LA 70767; 225-383-0378; fax: 225-383-3694; 8:30AM-4:30PM (CST). *Felony, Misdemeanor, Civil, Probate.*

www.wbrclerk.org/

General Information: Probate fax is same as main fax number. No adoption or juvenile records released. Will fax documents $5.00 each. Court makes copy: $2.00 per page. Self serve copy: $1.00 per page. Certification fee: $5.00 per doc. Payee: Clerk of Court. Personal checks accepted. No credit cards accepted. Prepayment required. Mail requests: SASE required.

Civil Name Search: Access: Phone, mail, in person. Both court and visitors may perform in person name searches. Search fee: $20.00 per name. Civil records on computer from 1983. Mail turnaround time 1-2 days. Civil PAT goes back to 1983.

Criminal Name Search: Access: Phone, mail, in person. Both court and visitors may perform in person name searches. Search fee: $20.00 per name. Required to search: name, years to search, DOB; also helpful: SSN. Criminal records computerized from 1983. Mail turnaround time 1-2 days. Criminal PAT goes back to same as civil.

Port Allen City Court PO Box 93, 330 S Alexander Ave, Port Allen, LA 70767; 225-346-4702; *Misdemeanor, Civil to $25,000, Eviction, Traffic.*

West Carroll Parish

5th District Court PO Box 1078, Oak Grove, LA 71263; 318-428-3281/2369; fax: 318-428-9896; 8:30AM-4:30PM (CST). *Felony, Misdemeanor, Civil, Probate.*

General Information: No adoption or juvenile records released. Will fax documents for $5.00 fee plus $2.00 per page. Court makes copy: $2.00 per page. Certification fee: $5.00 per certification plus copy fee. Payee: Clerk of Court. Only cashiers checks and money orders accepted. No credit cards accepted. Prepayment required. Mail requests: SASE required.

Civil Name Search: Access: Mail, in person. Both court and visitors may perform in person name searches. Search fee: $1.00 per name per year. Civil index on docket books back to 1800s. Mail turnaround time 1-2 days.

Criminal Name Search: Access: Mail, in person. Both court and visitors may perform in person name searches. Search fee: $1.00 per name per year. Required to search: name, years to search, DOB. Criminal records indexed in books back to 1800s. Mail turnaround time 1-2 days. Public use terminal has crim records back to same as civil.

West Feliciana Parish

20th District Court PO Box 1843, St Francisville, LA 70775; 225-635-3794; fax: 225-635-3770; 8:30AM-4:30PM (CST). *Felony, Misdemeanor, Civil, Probate.*

General Information: No adoption, juvenile or juvenile records released. Will fax documents $5.00 1st page, $1.00 ea add'l. Court makes copy: $1.00 per page. Self serve copy: same. Certification fee: $5.00. Payee: Clerk of Court. Business checks accepted. No credit cards accepted. Prepayment required. Mail requests: SASE required.

Civil Name Search: Access: Mail, in person. Both court and visitors may perform in person name searches. Search fee: $10.00 per name. Fee is per 10 years searched. Required to search: name, years to search; also helpful: address. Civil records on computer from 1984, index books back to 1800s. Mail turnaround time 3-5 days. Civil PAT goes back to 1990.

Criminal Name Search: Access: Mail, in person. Both court and visitors may perform in person name searches. Search fee: $10.00 per name. Fee is per 10 years searched. Required to search: name, years to search, DOB; also helpful: address. Criminal records on computer since 1992; prior on cards and dockets back to 1800s. Mail turnaround time 3-5 days. Criminal PAT goes back to 1991.

Winn Parish

8th District Court 100 Main St, #103, Winnfield, LA 71483; 318-628-3515; fax: 318-628-3527; 8AM-4:30PM (CST). *Felony, Misdemeanor, Civil, Probate.*

General Information: No adoption or juvenile records released. Fee to fax out file $5.00 each plus $1.00 per page. Court makes copy: $1.00 per page. Self serve copy: same. Certification fee: $5.00. Payee: Winn Parish Clerk of Court. Personal checks accepted. No credit cards accepted. Prepayment required. Mail requests: SASE required.

Civil Name Search: Access: Mail, in person. Both court and visitors may perform in person name searches. Search fee: $20.00 per name for 10 year search. Required to search: name, years to search, address. Civil records on books from 1886 to present, on computer from 1988, mortgages since 1981, conveyances since 1993. Mail turnaround time 2-3 days.

Criminal Name Search: Access: Mail, in person. Both court and visitors may perform in person name searches. Search fee: $20.00 per name for 10 year search. Required to search: name, years to search, address, DOB; also helpful: SSN. Criminal records in books since 1886, computerized since 1997. Mail turnaround time 2-3 days.

Winnfield City Court PO Box 908, 700 Church St, Winnfield, LA 71483; 318-628-4844; *Misdemeanor, Civil to $30,000, Eviction, Traffic.*

Common Abbreviations in Text

- DL   Driver's license
- PAT   Public use access terminal
- SASE Self-addressed, stamped envelope
- SSN   Social Security Number

Maine

Time Zone:	**EST**
Capital:	**Augusta, Kennebec County**
# of Counties:	**16**
State Web:	**www.maine.gov**
Court Web:	**www.courts.state.me.us**

Administration

State Court Administrator, PO Box 4820, Portland, ME, 04112-4820; 207-822-0792, Fax: 207-822-0781.

The Supreme Court & Appellate Division

The Supreme Court is the court of last resort. An Appellate Division of the Court hears appeals from criminal sentences when the penalty is one year or more of incarceration. The website offers access to Maine Supreme Court opinions and administrative orders, but not all documents are available online.

The Maine Courts

Court	Type	How Organized	Jurisdiction Highpoints
Superior*	General	17 Courts in 16 Counties	Felony, Misdemeanor, Civil,
District*	Limited	31 Courts in 13 Districts	Felony, Misdemeanor, Civil, Small Claims, Family, Juvenile
Probate	Special	One per County	Probate

* = profiled in this book

Details on the Trial Court Structure

A **Superior Court** – the court of general jurisdiction – is located in each of Maine's sixteen counties, except for Aroostook County which has two Superior Courts. A Superior Court may hear almost any kind of civil or criminal case that may be brought to trial.

Both Superior and District Courts handle misdemeanor and felony cases, with jury trials being held in Superior Court only.

The **District Court** hears both civil and criminal and always sits without a jury. Within the District Court is the Family Division, which hears all divorce and family matters, including child support and paternity cases. The District Court also hears child protection cases, and serves as Maine's juvenile court. Actions for protection from abuse or harassment, mental health, small claims cases, and money judgments are filed in the District Court. Traffic violations are processed primarily through a centralized Violations Bureau, part of the District Court system. Prior to year 2001, District Courts accepted civil cases involving claims less than $30,000. Now, District Courts have jurisdiction concurrent with that of the Superior Court for all civil actions, except cases vested in the Superior Court by statute.

Probate Courts are part of the county's court system, not the state system. Although the Probate Court may be housed with other state courts, the court is generally on a different phone system and calls may not be transferred.

Record Searching Facts You Need to Know

Fees and Record Searching Tips

Per administrative order, Maine Superior and District Court search fees are as follows: 1) $15.00 for a search; 2) copy fee: 1st page is $2.00, $1.00 each additional; 3) if your mail request does not include a self-addressed stamped envelope, then add an additional $5.00. Some courts offer a free search if only one name is submitted. Some courts indicate they will search both the civil and criminal indices for $15.00, when asked.

Most mail requests of a name search for full criminal history record information are returned to the sender, referring them to the State Bureau of Investigation. Mail requests that make a specific inquiry related to an identified case are responded to in writing. You must also include all appropriate copy and/or attestation fees.

Online Access is Not Widespread

The state court system does not offer online access to trial court records. Some county level courts are online through a private vendor.

Search probate records free at https://www.maineprobate.net/index.html. Images are $2.00 each if not registered; $1.00 each if you subscribe.

Androscoggin County

Androscoggin Superior Court PO Box 3660, Auburn, ME 04212-3660; 207-783-5450; 8AM-4PM (EST). *Felony, Misdemeanor, Civil*

General Information: Search fees and copy fees listed are mandatory per administrative rule. If a SASE is not supplied for mail searches, court may charge add'l $5.00. No adoption, juvenile, impounded by judge, certain domestic matters. Will not fax documents. Court makes copy: $2.00 1st page, $1.00 each add'l. Certification fee: $5.00 per doc plus copy fee. Payee: Androscoggin Superior Court. Personal checks and credit cards accepted. Prepayment required. Mail requests: SASE required.

Civil Name Search: Access: Mail, in person. Only the court performs in person name searches; visitors may not. Search fee: $15.00, includes both civil and criminal. Required to search: name, years to search; also helpful: address. Civil index on cards since 1977. Mail turnaround time 1 week.

Criminal Name Search: Access: Mail, in person. Only the court performs in person name searches; visitors may not. Search fee: $15.00, includes both civil and criminal. Required to search: name, years to search; also helpful: DOB. Criminal records go back to 1920s; on computer back to 1998. Mail turnaround time 1 week.

Lewiston District Court - South 8 PO Box 1345, 71 Lisbon St, Lewiston, ME 04243-1345; criminal phone: 207-795-4800; civil phone: 207-795-4801; 8AM-4PM (EST). *Misdemeanor, Civil Actions, Eviction, Small Claims.*

General Information: Search fees and copy fees listed are mandatory per administrative rule. If a SASE is not supplied for mail searches, court may charge add'l $5.00. No juvenile, protective custody records released. Will not fax documents. Court makes copy: $2.00 1st page, $1.00 each add'l. Certification fee: $5.00 per doc plus copy fee. Payee: Maine District Court. Personal checks and credit cards accepted. Prepayment required. Mail requests: SASE required.

Civil Name Search: Access: Mail, in person. Both court and visitors may perform in person name searches. Search fee: $15.00, includes both civil and criminal. Required to search: name, years to search; also helpful: address. Civil cases indexed by defendant. Civil index in docket books from 1980-1987; on computer back to 1987. Mail turnaround time up to 2 weeks.

Criminal Name Search: Access: Mail, in person. Both court and visitors may perform in person name searches. Search fee: $15.00, includes both civil and criminal. Required to search: name, years to search, DOB; also helpful: address, SSN. Criminal records computerized from 1987, docket books from 1984. Mail turnaround time up to 2 weeks.

Probate Court 2 Turner St, Unit 5, Auburn, ME 04210; 207-782-0281; fax: 207-782-1135; 8:30AM-5PM (EST). *Probate.*

General Information: Search probate records free at https://www.maineprobate.net/index.html. An account is $10.00 per month; $2.00 fee for images, $1.00 if account holder. Also have guardianship, conservatorship, name changes and adoption records at this court.

Aroostook County

Caribou Superior Court 144 Sweden St, #101, Caribou, ME 04736; 207-498-8125; 8AM-4PM (EST). *Felony, Misdemeanor, Civil Actions.*

General Information: Search fees and copy fees listed are mandatory per administrative rule. If a SASE is not supplied for mail searches, court may charge add'l $5.00. No juvenile, protective custody records released. Will not fax documents. Court makes copy: $2.00 1st page, $1.00 each add'l. Certification fee: $5.00. Payee: Treasurer, State of Maine or Superior Court. Personal checks accepted. Credit cards accepted. Prepayment required. Mail requests: SASE required.

Civil Name Search: Access: Mail, in person. Only the court performs in person name searches; visitors may not. Search fee: One name no fee, two or more $15.00 each, includes both civil and criminal. Required to search: name, DOB, years to search. Civil index on docket books since 1960. Mail turnaround time 1 week.

Criminal Name Search: Access: Mail, in person. Only the court performs in person name searches; visitors may not. Search fee: One name no fee, two or more $15.00 each, includes both civil and criminal. Required to search: name, years to search; also helpful: DOB. Criminal docket on books since 1960. Mail turnaround time 1 week.

Caribou District Court - East 1 144 Sweden St, Caribou, ME 04736; 207-493-3144; 8AM-4PM (EST). *Misdemeanor, Civil Actions, Eviction, Small Claims.*

General Information: Search fees and copy fees listed are mandatory per administrative rule. If a SASE is not supplied for mail searches, court will charge add'l $5.00. No juvenile or child protective records released. Will not fax documents. Court makes copy: $2.00 1st page, $1.00 each add'l. Certification fee: $5.00 per page. Payee: Maine District Court. Personal checks accepted. Credit cards accepted. Prepayment required. Mail requests: SASE required.

Civil Name Search: Access: Mail, in person. Only the court performs in person name searches; visitors may not. Search fee: First name free, then $15.00, includes both civil and criminal. Civil cases indexed by defendant. Civil index on docket books since 1963, on computer from 10/01. Mail turnaround time 1 week.

Criminal Name Search: Access: Mail, in person. Only the court performs in person name searches; visitors may not. Search fee: First name free, then $15.00, includes both civil and criminal. Required to search: name, years to search; also helpful: DOB. Criminal records on computer since 1987 (includes traffic), docket books since 1963. Note: DOB appears on criminal search result. Mail turnaround time 1 week.

District Court 2 PO Box 794, 27 Riverside Dr, Presque Isle, ME 04769; 207-764-2055; fax: 207-764-2057; 8AM-4PM (EST). *Misdemeanor, Civil Actions, Eviction, Small Claims.*

www.courts.state.me.us

General Information: Search fees and copy fees listed are mandatory per administrative rule. If a SASE is not supplied for mail searches, court may charge add'l $5.00. No juvenile or child protective records released. Will not fax documents. Court makes copy: $2.00 1st page, $1.00 each add'l. Certification fee: $5.00. Payee: Maine District Court. Personal checks accepted. Visa/MC accepted. Prepayment required. Mail requests: SASE required or $5.00 postage fee.

Civil Name Search: Access: Mail, in person. Both court and visitors may perform in person name searches. Search fee: $15.00 per name (first name if free). Civil cases indexed by defendant. Civil records on computer since 1999, docket books since 1963. Mail turnaround time 1 week.

Criminal Name Search: Access: Mail, in person. Both court and visitors may perform in person name searches. Search fee: $15.00 per name (first name is free). Required to search: name, years to search; also helpful: DOB. Criminal records on computer since 1987, docket books since 1963. Mail turnaround time 1 week.

Fort Kent District Court - District 1 Division of Western Aroostook, 139 Market St #101, Fort Kent, ME 04743; 207-834-5003; 8AM-4PM (EST). *Misdemeanor, Civil Actions, Eviction, Small Claims.*

General Information: Search fees and copy fees listed are mandatory per administrative rule. If a SASE is not supplied for mail searches, court may charge add'l $5.00. No juvenile, protective custody, impounded, mental health records released. Will not fax documents. Court makes copy: $2.00 1st page, $1.00 each add'l. Certification fee: $5.00 for attestation. Payee: Maine District Court. Personal checks accepted. Credit cards accepted. Prepayment required. Mail requests: SASE required.

Civil Name Search: Access: Phone, mail, in person. Only the court performs in person name searches; visitors may not. Search fee: $15.00, includes both civil and criminal. Civil records are computerized since 8/2001. Mail turnaround time within 5 days.

Criminal Name Search: Access: Phone, mail, in person. Only the court performs in person name searches; visitors may not. Search fee: $15.00, includes both civil and criminal. Criminal records computerized from 1988, on docket books from 1960-1988. Mail turnaround time 2-3 days.

Houlton District Court - South 2 26 Court St, Ste 201, Houlton, ME 04730; 207-532-2147; 8AM-4PM (EST). *Misdemeanor, Civil Actions, Eviction, Small Claims.*

General Information: Search fees and copy fees listed are mandatory per administrative rule. If a SASE is not supplied for mail searches, court may charge add'l $5.00. No Juvenile or protective custody records released. Will not fax documents. Court makes copy: $2.00 first page, $1.00 ea add'l.

Certification fee: $5.00. Payee: Maine District Court. Personal checks accepted. Credit cards accepted. Prepayment required. Mail requests: SASE required.

Civil Name Search: Access: Mail, in person. Both court and visitors may perform in person name searches. Search fee: $15.00, includes both civil and criminal. Required to search: name, years to search; also helpful: address. Civil index on docket books since 1960. Mail turnaround time 5-7 days.

Criminal Name Search: Access: Mail, in person. Only the court performs in person name searches; visitors may not. Search fee: $15.00, includes both civil and criminal. Required to search: name, years to search; also helpful: address, DOB. Criminal records on computer since 6/1987, docket books since 1960. Mail turnaround time 5-7 days.

Caribou-Houlton Superior Court 144 Sweden St, #101, Caribou, ME 04736; 207-532-6563; 8AM-4PM (EST). *Felony, Misdemeanor, Civil Actions.*

General Information: The Court only holds record prior to 1990. All cases are located at the Superior Court in Caribou, address Given here.

Madawaska District Court - West This court, physically located at 645 E Main in Madawaska, is only open 2 days a month. All case files are in Fort Kent; see that District Court to obtain records.

Probate Court 26 Court St, #103, Houlton, ME 04730; 207-532-1502; 8AM-4:30PM (EST). *Probate.* www.aroostook.me.us/probate.html

General Information: Search probate records free at https://www.maineprobate.net/index.html. An account is $10.00 per month: $2.00 fee for images, $1.00 if account holder.

Cumberland County

Superior Court - Civil 142 Federal St, Portland, ME 04101; 207-822-4105; criminal phone: 207-822-4113; civil phone: 207-822-4105; 8AM-4PM (EST). *Civil Actions.*

General Information: Search fees and copy fees listed are mandatory per administrative rule. The Portland District Court consolidated with this court effective 04/01/2010. Records are held here. No juvenile, medical malpractice, impounded records released. Will not fax documents. Court makes copy: $2.00 1st page, $1.00 each add'l. Certification fee: $5.00. Payee: Superior Court. Personal checks accepted. Credit cards accepted. Prepayment required.

Civil Name Search: Access: In person. Both court and visitors may perform in person name searches. Search fee: $15.00 per name, but if only one name then free. If a SASE not supplied for mail searches, court will charge an add'l $5.00. Civil index on cards since 1975, prior records archived. Note: Court will only answer general questions on filing and hearing dates by phone or mail.

Unified Superior Court - Criminal Criminal Docket, 142 Federal St, Portland, ME 04101; 207-822-4204; 8AM-12; 1PM-4:30PM (EST). *Felony, Misdemeanor.* www.cumberlandcounty.org/

General Information: Holds records for the old Portland District Court - South 9 Criminal (Misdemeanors). Search fees and copy fees listed are mandatory per administrative rule. If a SASE is not supplied for mail searches, court may charge add'l $5.00. Will not fax documents. Court makes copy: $2.00 1st page, $1.00 each add'l. Certification fee: $5.00. Payee: Clerk of Courts. Personal checks accepted. No credit cards accepted. Prepayment required.

Criminal Name Search: Access: Mail, in person. Only the court performs in person name searches; visitors may not. Search fee: $15.00, includes both felonies and misdemeanors. Submit DOB with search. Criminal records indexed on cards since 1900s, some records from 8/98 to present are computerized. Note: Note that juvenile records are held by the Portland District Court. Mail turnaround time 1-5 days, but can vary by number of names submitted. The search includes search of records from the old Portland District Court.

Portland District Court - South 9 Civil PO Box 412, 205 Newbury St, Portland, ME 04112; 207-822-4200; 8AM-4PM (EST). *Eviction, Small Claims, Family.*

General Information: The civil cases were consolidated into the Superior Court effective 04/01/2010.

Bath District Court 101 New Meadows Rd, West Bath, ME 04530; 207-442-0200; 8AM-4PM . *Misdemeanor, Eviction, Civil & Small Claims.*

General Information: Combined with West Bath District Court 6 in Sagadahoc County.

Bridgton District Court - North 9 3 Chase St, #2, Bridgton, ME 04009; 207-647-3535; fax: 207-647-5457; 8AM-4PM (EST). *Misdemeanor, Civil Actions, Eviction, Small Claims.*

General Information: Search fees and copy fees listed are mandatory per administrative rule. If a SASE is not supplied for mail searches, court may charge add'l $5.00. No juvenile, protective custody, financial affidavits, impounded or domestic records released. Will not fax documents. Court makes copy: $2.00 1st page, $1.00 each add'l. Certification fee: $5.00 per doc

plus copy fee. Payee: Maine District Court. Personal checks and credit cards accepted. Prepayment required. Mail requests: SASE required.

Civil Name Search: Access: Phone, mail, in person. Both court and visitors may perform in person name searches. Search fee: $15.00, includes both civil and criminal. Civil cases indexed by defendant. Civil records go back to 1990; on computer back to 2001. Mail turnaround time 5 days.

Criminal Name Search: Access: Phone, mail, in person. Only the court performs in person name searches; visitors may not. Search fee: $15.00, includes both civil and criminal. Required to search: name, years to search; also helpful: DOB. Criminal records computerized from 1986, records go back to 1980. Mail turnaround time 5 days.

Probate Court 142 Federal St, #125, Portland, ME 04101-4196; 207-871-8382 x3301; fax: 207-791-2658; 8:30AM-4:15PM (EST). *Probate.* http://cumberlandcounty.org/Probate/index.htm

General Information: Search probate index free at https://www.maineprobate.net/index.html. Account is $10.00 per month., Copies w/account $1.00 per page; Copies w/no account $2.00 per page.

Franklin County

Superior Court 140 Main St, Farmington, ME 04938; 207-778-3346; 8AM-4PM (EST). *Felony, Misdemeanor, Civil Actions.*

General Information: Search fees and copy fees listed are mandatory per administrative rule. If a SASE is not supplied for mail searches, court may charge add'l $5.00. No juvenile, impounded or medical malpractice records released. Will not fax documents. Court makes copy: $2.00 1st page, $1.00 each add'l. Certification fee: $5.00 per doc plus copy fee. Payee: Superior Court. Personal checks accepted. Credit cards accepted. Prepayment required. Mail requests: SASE required.

Civil Name Search: Access: Mail, in person. Both court and visitors may perform in person name searches. Search fee: $15.00 per name. Civil index on docket books and index cards since 1900s. Mail turnaround time 1 week.

Criminal Name Search: Access: Mail, in person. Only the court performs in person name searches; visitors may not. Search fee: $15.00 per name if the request is for more than one name. Required to search: name, DOB, years to search. Criminal docket on books and index cards since 1900s. Mail turnaround time 1 week.

Franklin District Court 12 129 Main St, Farmington, ME 04938; 207-778-2119; 8AM-4PM (EST). *Misdemeanor, Civil- Small Claims, Eviction.*

General Information: Search fees and copy fees listed are mandatory per administrative rule. No impounded records released. Will not fax documents. Court makes copy: $2.00 1st page, $1.00 each add'l. Certification fee: $5.00 per doc plus copy fee. Payee: Maine District Court. Personal checks accepted. Credit cards accepted. Prepayment required.

Civil Name Search: Access: Mail, in person. Visitors must perform in person searches themselves. Search fee: $15.00 per name if request for more than one name. Civil cases indexed by defendant. Civil index on docket books since 1965 (index cards in front). Mail turnaround time 1 week.

Criminal Name Search: Access: Mail, in person. Only the court performs in person name searches; visitors may not. Search fee: $15.00 per name if request for more than one name. Submit DOB with search. Criminal records on computer since 1987, on docket books since 1965 (index cards in front). Mail turnaround time 1 week.

Probate Court 140 Main St, #6, County Courthouse, Farmington, ME 04938; 207-778-5888; fax: 207-778-5899; 8:30AM-4PM (EST). *Probate.*

General Information: Search probate records free at https://www.maineprobate.net/index.html. An account is $10.00 per month: $2.00 fee for images, $1.00 if account holder.

Hancock County

Superior Court 50 State St, Ellsworth, ME 04605-1926; 207-667-7176; 8AM-4PM (EST). *Felony, Misdemeanor, Civil Actions.*

General Information: Search fees and copy fees listed are mandatory per administrative rule. No protective custody records released. Will not fax documents. Court makes copy: $2.00 1st page, $1.00 each add'l.They will bill you for copies, but search fee must be paid up front. Certification fee: $5.00 per cert plus copy fee. Payee: State of Maine. Personal checks and credit cards accepted. Prepayment required. Mail requests: SASE required.

Civil Name Search: Access: Mail, in person. Only the court performs in person name searches; visitors may not. Search fee: $15.00 per name, if multiples. Civil records on card files since 1960. Mail turnaround time 1 day time permitting.

Criminal Name Search: Access: Mail, person only. Only the court performs in person name searches; visitors may not. Search fee: $15.00 per name, if multiples. Submit DOB with search. Criminal records on card files since 1960. Mail turnaround time 1 day time permitting.

Ellsworth District Court - Central 5 50 State St #2, Ellsworth, ME 04605; 207-667-7141; 8AM-4PM (EST). *Misdemeanor, Civil Actions, Eviction, Small Claims.*

General Information: Search fees and copy fees listed are mandatory per administrative rule. The Bar Harbor District Court - South 5 merged with this court in July 2005. Records are co-mingled. No juvenile, child protection, adoption or mental health records released. Will not fax documents. Court makes copy: $2.00 1st page, $1.00 each add'l. Certification fee: $5.00 per doc plus copy fee. Payee: Maine District Court. Personal checks accepted. Visa/MC accepted. Prepayment required. Mail requests: SASE required.

Civil Name Search: Access: Mail, in person. Both court and visitors may perform in person name searches. Search fee: $15.00, includes both civil and criminal. Need to know names of both parties to search. Civil index on docket books since 1965; on computer back to 10/01. Mail turnaround time 1 week.

Criminal Name Search: Access: Mail, in person. Only the court performs in person name searches; visitors may not. Search fee: $15.00, includes both civil and criminal. Submit DOB with search. Criminal records computerized from 1987, docket books since 1965. Mail turnaround time 1 week.

Probate Court 50 State St, #6, Ellsworth, ME 04605; 207-667-9098; fax: 207-667-5316; 8:30AM-4PM (EST). *Probate.*

General Information: Search probate records free at https://www.maineprobate.net/index.html. An account is $10.00 per month: $2.00 fee for images, $1.00 if account holder. This court also handles guardianships, estates, and adoptions.

Kennebec County

Superior Court 95 State St, Clerk of Court, Augusta, ME 04330; 207-624-5800; fax: 207-287-9057; 8AM-4PM (EST). *Felony, Misdemeanor, Civil Actions.*

www.maine.gov/tools/whatsnew/index.php?topic=Court_Courthouse_Direct ory&id=44271&v=article

General Information: Search fees and copy fees listed are mandatory per administrative rule. No protective custody or juvenile records released. Will not fax documents. Court makes copy: $2.00 1st page, $1.00 each add'l. Certification fee: $5.00 per doc. Payee: Treasurer State of Maine. Personal checks and credit cards accepted. Prepayment required.

Civil Name Search: Access: In person only. Only the court performs in person name searches; visitors may not. Search fee: 1st search free, then $15.00 per case. Civil index on cards since 1977, docket books since 1970, on computer 2 years.

Criminal Name Search: Access: In person only. Only the court performs in person name searches; visitors may not. Search fee: 1st search free, then $15.00 per case. Required to search: name, years to search; also helpful: DOB, docket number. Criminal records indexed on cards since 1977, docket books since 1978, on computer 5 years.

Maine District Court 7 Division of Southern Kennebec, 145 State St, Augusta, ME 04330-7495; 207-287-8075; fax: 207-287-8082; 8AM-4PM (EST). *Misdemeanor, Civil Actions, Eviction, Small Claims.*

General Information: Search fees and copy fees listed are mandatory per administrative rule. If a SASE is not supplied for mail searches, court may charge add'l $5.00. No juvenile, mental health, protective custody and closed proceeding case records released. Will not fax documents. Court makes copy: $2.00 1st page, $1.00 each add'l. Certification fee: $5.00 per doc plus copy fee. Payee: Maine District Court. Personal checks accepted. Visa/MC/Discover accepted. Prepayment required. Mail requests: SASE required.

Civil Name Search: Access: Mail, in person. Only the court performs in person name searches; visitors may not. Search fee: $15.00, includes both civil and criminal per name. Civil cases indexed by defendant. Civil records kept 10 years. Mail turnaround time 1 week.

Criminal Name Search: Access: Mail, in person. Only the court performs in person name searches; visitors may not. Search fee: $15.00, includes both civil and criminal per name. Required to search: name, years to search, DOB; also helpful: SSN. Criminal records computerized from 1987, docket books since 1963. Mail turnaround time 1 week.

Waterville District Court - District 7 18 Colby St, Waterville, ME 04901; 207-873-2103; 8AM-4PM (EST). *Misdemeanor, Civil Actions, Eviction, Small Claims.*

www.maine.gov/tools/whatsnew/index.php?topic=Court_Courthouse_Direct ory&id=44267&v=article

General Information: Search fees and copy fees listed are mandatory per administrative rule. No juvenile, protective custody records released. Court reserves the right to restrict the number of record requests. Will not fax documents. Court makes copy: $2.00 1st page, $1.00 each add'l PLUS $5.00 to mail. Certification fee: $5.00 per doc plus copy fee. Payee: Maine District Court. Personal checks accepted. Visa/MC accepted. Prepayment required. Mail requests: SASE required.

Civil Name Search: Access: Mail, in person. Both court and visitors may perform in person name searches. Search fee: $15.00 per name, includes both civil and criminal. Required to search: name, years to search; also helpful: address. Civil cases indexed by defendant. Civil records on computer

since 2001. Docket books from 1979-1987 are archived. Mail turnaround time 1 week.

Criminal Name Search: Access: Mail, in person. Both court and visitors may perform in person name searches. Search fee: $15.00 per name, includes both civil and criminal. Required to search: name, years to search, DOB; also helpful: address, SSN. Criminal records on computer since 1999. Docket books from 1979-1987 are archived. Mail turnaround time 2 weeks.

Probate Court 95 State St, Augusta, ME 04330; 207-622-7558 or 207-622-7559; fax: 207-621-1639; 8AM-4PM (EST). *Probate.* www.maineprobate.net/Kennebec.html

General Information: Search probate records free at https://www.maineprobate.net/index.html. An account is $10.00 per month: $2.00 fee for images, $1.00 if account holder.

Knox County

Superior Court 62 Union St, Rockland, ME 04841-2836; 207-594-2576; fax: 207-596-2251; 8AM-4PM (EST). *Felony, Misdemeanor, Civil Actions.*

General Information: Search fees and copy fees listed are mandatory per administrative rule. If a SASE is not supplied for mail searches, court may charge add'l $5.00. District Ct is a separate search and fee. though records are both at this location. No Impounded or pre-sentence records released. Will not fax documents. Court makes copy: $2.00 1st page, $1.00 each add'l. Certification fee: $5.00 plus copy fees. Payee: State Treasurer. Personal checks accepted. Visa/MC accepted. Prepayment required. Mail requests: SASE required.

Civil Name Search: Access: Mail, in person. Only the court performs in person name searches; visitors may not. Search fee: $15.00, includes both civil and criminal. Civil index on docket books since 1930s, index cards (in office) since mid-1970s; on computer back to 1999. Mail turnaround time 1 week.

Criminal Name Search: Access: Mail, in person. Only the court performs in person name searches; visitors may not. Search fee: $15.00, includes both civil and criminal. Required to search: name, years to search; also helpful: DOB, middle initial. Criminal docket on books since 1930s, index cards (in office) since mid-1970s; on computer back to 1999. Mail turnaround time 1 week.

District Court 6 62 Union St, Rockland, ME 04841; 207-596-2240; probate phone: 207-594-0427; 8AM-4PM (EST). *Misdemeanor, Civil Actions, Eviction, Small Claims.*

General Information: Search fee includes both District Ct civil and criminal indexes, but not Superior Ct which is separate search. Search fees and copy fees are mandatory per administrative rule. If a SASE is not supplied for mail searches, court may charge add'l $5.00. No impounded records released. Will not fax documents. Court makes copy: $2.00 1st page, $1.00 each add'l. Certification fee: $5.00 per cert. Payee: Maine District Court. Personal checks accepted. Visa/MC accepted. Prepayment required. Mail requests: SASE required.

Civil Name Search: Access: Mail, in person. Only the court performs in person name searches; visitors may not. Search fee: First search is free, each add'l search $15.00 per name. Civil index on docket books back to the 1970's. Mail turnaround time 3-4 days.

Criminal Name Search: Access: Mail, in person. Only the court performs in person name searches; visitors may not. Search fee: First search is free, each add'l search $15.00 per name. Submit DOB with search. Criminal docket on books back to 1989. Mail turnaround time 3-4 days.

Probate Court 62 Union St, Rockland, ME 04841; 207-594-0427; fax: 207-594-0863; 8AM-4PM (EST). *Probate.*

General Information: Search probate records free at https://www.maineprobate.net/index.html. An account is $10.00 per month: $2.00 fee for images, $1.00 if account holder.

Lincoln County

County Combined Court PO Box 249, 25 High St, Wiscasset, ME 04578; 207-882-7517, 207-882-6363; criminal phone: x3; fax: 207-882-7741; 8AM-4PM (EST). *Felony, Misdemeanor, Civil Actions, Eviction, Small Claims.*

General Information: This is now a combined court, with combined indexes. Search fees and copy fees listed are mandatory per administrative rule. If a SASE is not supplied for mail searches, court may charge add'l $5.00. No protective custody records released. Will not fax documents. Court makes copy: $2.00 1st page, $1.00 each add'l. Certification fee: $5.00 per doc. Payee: Lincoln County Superior Court. Personal checks accepted. Visa/MC/Discover cards accepted. Prepayment required. Mail requests: SASE required.

Civil Name Search: Access: Mail, in person. Only the court performs in person name searches; visitors may not. Search fee: No fee to search 1 case per day; each add'l search is $15.00, includes both civil and criminal. Civil index on docket books and index cards since 1960s. Mail turnaround time 1-2 days.

Criminal Name Search: Access: +Mail, in person. Only the court performs in person name searches; visitors may not. Search fee: No fee to search 1 case per day; each add'l search is $15.00, includes both civil and criminal. Submit DOB with search. Criminal docket on books and index cards since 1960s. Mail turnaround time 1-2 days.

Probate Court 32 High St, PO Box 249, Wiscasset, ME 04578; 207-882-7392; fax: 207-882-4324; 8AM-4PM (EST). *Probate.*
www.co.lincoln.me.us/dep.html
General Information: Search probate records free at https://www.maineprobate.net/index.html. An account is $10.00 per month: $2.00 fee for images, $1.00 if account holder..

Oxford County

Superior Court PO Box 179, 26 Western Ave, Courthouse, South Paris, ME 04281-0179; 207-743-8936; fax: 207-743-0544; 8AM-4PM (EST). *Felony, Misdemeanor, Civil Actions over $30,000.*
General Information: Search fees and copy fees listed are mandatory per administrative rule. If a SASE is not supplied for mail searches, court may charge add'l $5.00. The search fee includes both the civil and criminal indexes. No protective custody or protection from abuse records released. Will fax back documents $2.00 first page, $1.00 ea add'l. Court makes copy: $2.00 first page, $1.00 ea add'l. Certification fee: $5.00 per doc plus copy fee. Payee: Clerk of Superior Court. Personal checks and credit cards accepted. Prepayment required. Mail requests: SASE requested.
Civil Name Search: Access: Mail, in person. Both court and visitors may perform in person name searches. Search fee: $15.00, includes both civil and criminal. Submit DOB with search. Mail turnaround time 5-10 days.
Criminal Name Search: Access: Mail, in person. Both court and visitors may perform in person name searches. Search fee: $15.00, includes both civil and criminal. Submit DOB with search. Criminal docket on books since 1960. Mail turnaround time 5-10 days.

Rumford District Court - Div. of North Oxford 145 Congress St, Municipal Bldg, Rumford, ME 04276; 207-364-7171; 8AM-4PM (EST). *Misdemeanor, Civil Actions, Eviction, Small Claims.*
General Information: Search fees and copy fees listed are mandatory per administrative rule. Search includes both civil and criminal index. If a SASE is not supplied for mail searches, court may charge add'l $5.00. No impounded records released. Will not fax documents. Court makes copy: $2.00 1st page, $1.00 each add'l. Certification fee: $5.00 per cert plus copy fee. Payee: Maine District Court. Personal checks and credit cards accepted. Prepayment required. Mail requests: SASE required.
Civil Name Search: Access: Mail, in person. Only the court performs in person name searches; visitors may not. Search fee: $15.00 per name. Civil index on docket books since 1966. Mail turnaround time 1 week.
Criminal Name Search: Access: Mail, in person. Only the court performs in person name searches; visitors may not. Search fee: $15.00 per name. Submit DOB with search. Criminal records on computer since 3/1988, docket books since 1966. Mail turnaround time 1 week.

South Paris District Court - South 11 26 Western Ave, South Paris, ME 04281; 207-743-8942; fax: 207-744-0362; 8AM-4PM (EST). *Misdemeanor, Civil Actions, Eviction, Small Claims.*
General Information: Search fees and copy fees listed are mandatory per administrative rule. If a SASE is not supplied for mail searches, court may charge add'l $5.00. No juvenile or child protective records released. Will not fax documents. Court makes copy: $2.00 first page, the $1.00 ea add'l. Certification fee: $5.00 per doc plus copy fee. Payee: Maine District Court. Personal checks and credit cards accepted. Prepayment required. Mail requests: SASE required.
Civil Name Search: Access: Mail, in person. Both court and visitors may perform in person name searches. Search fee: $15.00, includes both civil and criminal. Civil cases indexed by defendant. Civil index on docket books back 5 years. Mail turnaround time 5-10 days.
Criminal Name Search: Access: Mail, in person. Both court and visitors may perform in person name searches. Search fee: $15.00, includes both civil and criminal. Required to search: name, years to search; also helpful: DOB. Criminal records on computer since 4/99, docket books back to 1966. Note: Records after 4/99 cannot be accessed on the public access computer; request a search in writing. Mail turnaround time 5-10 days.

Probate Court PO Box 179, 26 Western Ave, South Paris, ME 04281; 207-743-6671; fax: 207-743-4255; 8AM-4PM (EST). *Probate.*
www.oxfordcounty.org/probate.php
General Information: Search probate records free at https://www.maineprobate.net/index.html. An account is $10.00 per month: $2.00 fee for images, $1.00 if account holder.

Penobscot County

Superior Court 78 Exchange St, Bangor, ME 04401-6504; 207-561-2300; 8AM-4PM (EST). *Felony, Misdemeanor, Civil Actions.*
www.maine.gov/tools/whatsnew/index.php?topic=Court_Courthouse_Direct ory&id=44272&v=article

General Information: Index now unified with District Court. Search fees and copy fees listed are mandatory per administrative rule. If a SASE is not supplied for mail searches, court may charge add'l $5.00. No impounded records released. Will not fax documents. Court makes copy: $2.00 1st page, $1.00 each add'l. Certification fee: $5.00 per doc. Payee: Treasurer, State of Maine. Personal checks accepted. Credit cards accepted. Prepayment required. Mail requests: SASE required or pay $5.00 add'l for mail return.
Civil Name Search: Access: Mail, in person. Only the court performs in person name searches; visitors may not. Search fee: $15.00 per name, includes Superior and District unified index; includes both civil and criminal if asked. Civil index on docket books since 1976 (76-82 at Maine Archives); on computer back to 2002; archived back to 1927.
Criminal Name Search: Access: Mail, in person. Only the court performs in person name searches; visitors may not. Search fee: $15.00 per name, includes Superior and District unified index; includes both civil and criminal if asked. Submit DOB with search. Criminal docket on books since 1976; on computer back to 1998; archived back to 1927.

Central District Court - Central 13 52 Main St, Lincoln, ME 04457; 207-794-8512; 8AM-4PM (EST). *Misdemeanor, Civil Actions, Eviction, Small Claims.*
General Information: Search fees and copy fees listed are mandatory per administrative rule. If a SASE is not supplied for mail searches, court may charge add'l $5.00. No juvenile or protective custody records released. Court makes copy: $2.00 1st page, $1.00 each add'l. Certification fee: $5.00 per piece plus copy fee. Payee: Maine District Court. Personal checks accepted. Credit cards accepted. Prepayment required.
Civil Name Search: Access: In person only. Only the court performs in person name searches; visitors may not. Search fee: $15.00 per name. Civil cases indexed by defendant. Civil index on docket books since 1964.
Criminal Name Search: Access: In person only. Only the court performs in person name searches; visitors may not. Search fee: $15.00 per name. Submit DOB with search. Criminal records on computer since 1987, docket books since 1984.

Newport District Court - West 3 12 Water St, Newport, ME 04953; 207-368-5778; fax: 207-368-7724; 8AM-4PM (EST). *Misdemeanor, Civil Actions, Eviction, Small Claims.*
General Information: Search fees and copy fees listed are mandatory per administrative rule. If a SASE is not supplied for mail searches, court may charge add'l $5.00. No impounded records released. Will not fax documents. Court makes copy: $2.00 1st page, $1.00 each add'l. Certification fee: $5.00 per cert plus copy fee. Payee: Maine District Court. Personal checks accepted. Credit cards accepted. Prepayment required. Mail requests: SASE required.
Civil Name Search: Access: Mail, in person. Both court and visitors may perform in person name searches. Search fee: $15.00, includes both civil and criminal. Civil index on docket books back to 1965; computerized back to 2001. Mail turnaround time 1 week. Civil PAT goes back to 2001.
Criminal Name Search: Access: Mail, in person. Both court and visitors may perform in person name searches. Search fee: $15.00, includes both civil and criminal. Submit DOB with search. Criminal records on computer for 5 years, on docket books since 1987. Mail turnaround time 1 week. Criminal PAT goes back to 1987.

Millinocket District Court - North 13 207 Penobscot Ave, Millinocket, ME 04462; 207-723-4786; 8AM-4PM (EST). *Misdemeanor, Civil Actions, Eviction, Small Claims.*
General Information: On July 1, 2010, the Millinocket District Court Clerk's office was consolidated with the Lincoln District Court Clerk's office. Although this address remains open for limited time periods, all case inquires should be sent to the Court in Lincoln.

Bangor Unified District Court 78 Exchange St #100, Bangor, ME 04401-6504; 207-561-2300; 8AM-4PM (EST). *Misdemeanor, Civil Actions, Eviction, Small Claims.*
General Information: Search fee includes both Superior and District unified index, also both civil and criminal indexes, if asked. If a SASE is not supplied for mail searches, court may charge add'l $5.00. See Superior Court.

Probate Court 97 Hammond St, Bangor, ME 04401-4996; 207-942-8769; fax: 207-941-8499; 8AM-4:30PM (EST). *Probate.*
https://www.maineprobate.net/Penobscot.html
General Information: Search probate records free at https://www.maineprobate.net/index.html. An account is $10.00 per month: $2.00 fee for images, $1.00 if account holder.

Piscataquis County

County Combined Court 159 E Main St, Dover-Foxcroft, ME 04426; 207-564-8419; 8AM-4PM (EST). *Felony, Misdemeanor, Civil Actions, Eviction, Small Claims.*
General Information: This is now a combined court, with combined indexes. Search fees and copy fees listed are mandatory per administrative rule. If a SASE is not supplied for mail searches, court may charge add'l $5.00. No pre-sentence report records released. Will not fax documents. Court makes copy: $2.00 1st page, $1.00 each add'l. Certification fee: $5.00

per doc. Payee: State of Maine Superior Court. Personal checks accepted. Visa/MC accepted. Prepayment required. Mail requests: SASE required.

Civil Name Search: Access: Mail, in person. Only the court performs in person name searches; visitors may not. Search fee: $15.00 per name includes both civil and criminal. Civil index on docket books since 1960; computerized records since 1998. Mail turnaround time 1 week.

Criminal Name Search: Access: Mail, in person. Only the court performs in person name searches; visitors may not. Search fee: $15.00 per name includes both civil and criminal. Required to search: name, years to search; also helpful: DOB. Criminal docket on books since 1960; computerized records since 1998. Mail turnaround time 1 week.

Probate Court 159 E Main St, Dover-Foxcroft, ME 04426; 207-564-2431; fax: 207-564-3022; 8:30AM-4PM (EST). *Probate.* http://piscataquis.us/Pages/probate.html
General Information: Search probate records free at https://www.maineprobate.net/index.html. An account is $10.00 per month: $2.00 fee for images, $1.00 if account holder.

Sagadahoc County

Superior Court 101 New Meadows Rd, West Bath, ME 04530; 207-443-9733; 8AM-4:00PM (EST). *Felony, Misdemeanor, Civil Actions.* www.maine.gov/tools/whatsnew/index.php?topic=Court_Courthouse_Direct ory&id=44273&v=article
General Information: Search fees and copy fees listed are mandatory per administrative rule. If a SASE is not supplied for mail searches, court may charge add'l $5.00. No impounded records released. Will not fax documents. Court makes copy: $2.00 1st page, $1.00 each add'l. Certification fee: $5.00 per doc plus copy fee. Payee: Clerk of Superior Court. Cash, checks, or money orders accepted. Major credit cards accepted. Prepayment required. Mail requests: SASE required.

Civil Name Search: Access: Mail, in person. Both court and visitors may perform in person name searches. Search fee: $15.00, includes both civil and criminal. Civil index on docket books since 1976; on computer back to 1999. Mail turnaround time 7 days.

Criminal Name Search: Access: Mail, in person. Both court and visitors may perform in person name searches. Search fee: $15.00, includes both civil and criminal. Submit DOB with search. Criminal docket on books since 1900s; on computer back to 1999. Mail turnaround time 7 days.

West Bath District Court 6 101 New Meadows Rd, West Bath, ME 04530-6297; 207-442-0200; criminal phone: 207-442-0205; civil phone: 207-442-0202; 8AM-4PM (EST). *Misdemeanor, Civil Actions, Eviction, Small Claims.* www.maine.gov/tools/whatsnew/index.php?topic=Court_Courthouse_Direct ory&id=44268&v=article
General Information: This court handles the eastern part of Cumberland County and all of Sagadahoc County. No protective custody or juvenile records released. Will not fax documents. Court makes copy: $2.00 1st page, $1.00 each add'l. Certification fee: $5.00. Payee: Maine District Court. Personal checks accepted. Credit cards accepted. Prepayment required.

Civil Name Search: Access: In person only. Both court and visitors may perform in person name searches. Search fee: $15.00, includes both civil and criminal. Civil index on docket books since 1980's; prior archived. Note: Search fees and copy fees listed are mandatory per administrative rule. If a SASE not supplied for mail searches, court may charge add'l $5.00.

Criminal Name Search: Access: In person only. Both court and visitors may perform in person name searches. Search fee: $15.00, includes both civil and criminal. Required to search: name, years to search; also helpful: DOB. Criminal records on computer since 1987, docket books back to 1975; prior archived. Note: The search fees and copy fees listed are mandatory per administrative rule.

Probate Court 752 High St, Bath, ME 04530; 207-443-8218; fax: 207-443-8217; 8:30AM-4:30PM (EST). *Probate.* www.maineprobate.net
General Information: Search probate records free at https://www.maineprobate.net/index.html. An account is $10.00 per month: $2.00 fee for images, $1.00 if account holder.

Somerset County

Superior Court PO Box 725, 41 Court St, Skowhegan, ME 04976; 207-474-5161; probate phone: 207-474-3322; 8AM-4PM (EST). *Felony, Misdemeanor, Civil Actions.*
General Information: Search fees and copy fees listed are mandatory per administrative rule. No impounded, present investigations, psychological evaluations or child support records released. Will not fax documents. Court makes copy: $2.00 1st page, $1.00 each add'l. Certification fee: $5.00 per doc plus copy fee. Payee: Clerk of Superior Court. Personal checks accepted. Visa/MC accepted. Prepayment required.

Civil Name Search: Access: Mail, in person. Only the court performs in person name searches; visitors may not. Search fee: $15.00 per name; no fee for searching one name only. Civil records archived in Augusta back to

1800s, docket books and index cards back to 1900s. Mail turnaround time 2-3 days; archived records longer.

Criminal Name Search: Access: Mail, in person. Only the court performs in person name searches; visitors may not. Search fee: $15.00 per name; no fee for searching one name only. Required to search: name, years to search; also helpful: DOB. Criminal records archived in Augusta back to 1800s, docket books and index cards back to 1900s; on computer back to 1998. Mail turnaround time 2-3 days, longer if record in archives.

District Court 12 PO Box 525, 47 Court St, Skowhegan, ME 04976; 207-474-9518; 8AM-4PM (EST). *Misdemeanor, Civil Actions, Eviction, Small Claims.*
General Information: Search fees and copy fees listed are mandatory per administrative rule. If a SASE is not supplied for mail searches, court may charge add'l $5.00. No juvenile records released. Will not fax documents. Court makes copy: $2.00 1st page, $1.00 each add'l. Certification fee: $5.00 per doc plus copy fee. Payee: Maine District Court. Personal checks accepted. Visa/MC accepted. Prepayment required. Mail requests: SASE required.

Civil Name Search: Access: Mail, in person. Both court and visitors may perform in person name searches. Search fee: $15.00, includes both civil and criminal. Civil cases indexed by defendant. Civil index on docket books since 1960s, divorces since 1970s. Mail turnaround time 2-4 weeks.

Criminal Name Search: Access: Mail, in person. Both court and visitors may perform in person name searches. Search fee: $15.00, includes both civil and criminal. Required to search: name, years to search; also helpful: DOB. Criminal records on computer since 1987, docket books since 1960s. Mail turnaround time 2-4 weeks.

Probate Court 41 Court St, Skowhegan, ME 04976; 207-474-3322; fax: 207-858-4235; 8:30AM-4:30PM (EST). *Probate.* www.somersetcounty-me.org/index.cfm?PageContent=Department.cfm&DeptID=21
General Information: Search probate records free at https://www.maineprobate.net/index.html. An account is $10.00 per month: $2.00 fee for images, $1.00 if account holder.

Waldo County

Superior Court/Belfast 103 Church St, Belfast, ME 04915; 207-338-1940; fax: 207-338-1086; 8AM-4PM (EST). *Felony, Misdemeanor, Civil Actions.* www.waldocountyme.gov/html/contact_us.html
General Information: Physical add: 137 Church St. Search fees and copy fees listed are mandatory per administrative rule. If a SASE is not supplied for mail searches, court may charge add'l $5.00. No protective custody records released. Will not fax documents. Court makes copy: $2.00 1st page, $1.00 each add'l. Certification fee: $5.00 per doc plus copy fee. Payee: State Treasurer. Personal checks accepted. Visa/MC accepted. Prepayment required. Mail requests: SASE required.

Civil Name Search: Access: Mail, in person. Only the court performs in person name searches; visitors may not. Search fee: $15.00, includes both civil and criminal. Allows 1 name free search. Civil records archived back to 1980 (not in office), on docket books since 1980; on computer back to 12/99. Mail turnaround time 5 days.

Criminal Name Search: Access: Mail, in person. Only the court performs in person name searches; visitors may not. Search fee: $15.00, includes both civil and criminal. Allows 1 name free search. Required to search: name, years to search; also helpful: DOB. Criminal records archived back to 1975 (not in office), on docket books since 1975; on computer back to 12/99. Mail turnaround time 5 days. Request criminal and juvenile crime information www10.informe.org/PCR/. This is a request site, (for the information) not the direct information.

District Court 5/Belfast 103 Church St, Belfast, ME 04915; 207-338-3107; 8AM-4PM (EST). *Misdemeanor, Civil Actions, Eviction, Small Claims.*
General Information: Search fees and copy fees listed are mandatory per administrative rule. If a SASE is not supplied for mail searches, court may charge add'l $5.00. No juvenile or impounded records released. Will not fax documents. Court makes copy: $2.00 1st page, $1.00 each add'l. Certification fee: $5.00 per doc plus copy fee. Payee: Maine District Court. Personal checks accepted. Visa/MC accepted. Prepayment required. Mail requests: SASE required.

Civil Name Search: Access: Mail only. Only the court performs in person name searches; visitors may not. Search fee: $15.00, includes both civil and criminal. Civil index on docket books since 1966, computerized since 2001. Mail turnaround time 1 week.

Criminal Name Search: Access: Mail only. Only the court performs in person name searches; visitors may not. Search fee: $15.00, includes both civil and criminal. Submit DOB on search. Records on computer since 1987, docket books since 1966. Mail turnaround time 1 week.

Probate Court 39A Spring St, PO Box 323, Belfast, ME 04915-0323; 207-338-2780; fax: 207-338-2360; 8AM-4PM (EST). *Probate.* www.waldocountyme.gov/rop/index.html

General Information: Search probate records free at https://www.maineprobate.net/index.html. An account is $10.00 per month: $2.00 fee for images, $1.00 if account holder.

Washington County

Superior Court PO Box 526, Clerk of Court, 85 Court St, Machias, ME 04654; 207-255-3044; 8AM-4PM (EST). *Felony, Misdemeanor, Civil.*

General Information: Search fees and copy fees listed are mandatory per administrative rule. If a SASE is not supplied for mail searches, court may charge add'l $5.00. No impounded records released. Will not fax documents. Court makes copy: $2.00 1st page, $1.00 each add'l. Certification fee: $5.00 per doc plus copy fee. Payee: Treasurer, State of Maine. Personal checks accepted. Visa/MC and Discover accepted but there is a minimum. Prepayment required. Mail requests: SASE required.

Civil Name Search: Access: Mail, in person. Only the court performs in person name searches; visitors may not. Search fee: $15.00, includes both civil and criminal. Civil index on docket books and index cards since 1930s. Mail turnaround time 1 week.

Criminal Name Search: Access: Mail, in person. Only the court performs in person name searches; visitors may not. Search fee: $15.00, includes both civil and criminal. Submit DOB with search. Criminal docket on books and index cards since 1930s. Mail turnaround time 1 week.

Calais District Court - North 4 382 South Street, #B, Calais, ME 04619-1123; 207-454-2055; TTY# 207-454-0085; 8AM-4PM (EST). *Misdemeanor, Civil Actions, Eviction, Small Claims.*

General Information: No juvenile or protective custody records released. Will not fax documents. Court makes copy: $2.00 1st page, $1.00 each add'l. Certification fee: $5.00 per doc. Payee: Maine District Court. Personal checks accepted. Credit cards accepted. Prepayment required.

Civil Name Search: Access: In person only. Both court and visitors may perform in person name searches. Search fee: $15.00 per name, if more than 1 name. Civil index on docket books since 1983, on computer back to 2001.

Criminal Name Search: Access: In person only. Both court and visitors may perform in person name searches. Search fee: $15.00 per name, if more than 1 name. Submit DOB with search. Criminal records on computer since 1987, docket books since 07/79.

Maine District Court 4 85 Court St, PO Box 526, Machias, ME 04654; 207-255-3044; 8AM-4PM (EST). *Misdemeanor, Civil Actions, Eviction, Small Claims.*

General Information: Search fees and copy fees listed are mandatory per administrative rule. If a SASE is not supplied for mail searches, court may charge add'l $5.00. No protective custody or juvenile records released. Will not fax documents. Court makes copy: $2.00 1st page, $1.00 each add'l. Certification fee: $5.00 per doc plus copy fee. Payee: Maine District Court. Personal checks and credit cards accepted. Prepayment required. Mail requests: SASE required.

Civil Name Search: Access: Mail, in person. Only the court performs in person name searches; visitors may not. Search fee: 1st name free; add'l $15.00 per name. Civil index on docket books since 1985; on computer back to 2001. Mail turnaround time 4 days.

Criminal Name Search: Access: Mail, in person. Only the court performs in person name searches; visitors may not. Search fee: 1st name free add'l $15.00. Submit DOB with search. Criminal records on computer 1987-1999, docket books since 1985. Mail turnaround time 4 days.

Probate Court PO Box 297, 85 Court St, Machias, ME 04654; 207-255-6591; fax: 207-255-3999; 8AM-4PM (EST). *Probate.*
www.washingtoncountymaine.com/probate/

General Information: Search probate records free at https://www.maineprobate.net/index.html. An account is $10.00 per month: $2.00 fee for images, $1.00 if account holder.

York County

Superior Court Clerk of Court, PO Box 160, Alfred, ME 04002; 207-324-5122; 8AM-4PM (EST). *Felony, Misdemeanor, Civil Actions.*

General Information: Search fees and copy fees listed are mandatory per administrative rule. If a SASE is not supplied for mail searches, court may charge add'l $5.00. No juvenile, or protective custody records released. Will not fax documents. Court makes copy: $2.00 1st page, $1.00 each add'l. Certification fee: $5.00 per attestation. Payee: Clerk of Courts. Cashiers checks and money orders accepted. Major credit cards accepted. Prepayment required. Mail requests: SASE required.

Civil Name Search: Access: Mail, in person. Only the court performs in person name searches; visitors may not. Search fee: $15.00, includes both civil and criminal. Civil index on docket books since 1960; computerized records go back to 2002. Note: No faxes are accepted or sent. Mail turnaround time- 1-5 names is 5 days; 6-10 names 30 working days.

Criminal Name Search: Access: Mail, in person. Only the court performs in person name searches; visitors may not. Search fee: $15.00, includes both civil and criminal. Submit DOB with search. Criminal docket on books since 1966; computerized records go back to 1998. Note: No faxes are accepted or sent. Mail turnaround time: 1-5 names is 5 days; 6-10 names 30 working days.

Biddeford District Court - East 10 25 Adams St, Biddeford, ME 04005; 207-283-1147; 8AM-4PM (EST). *Misdemeanor, Civil Actions, Eviction, Small Claims.*

General Information: Search fees and copy fees listed are mandatory per administrative rule. If a SASE is not supplied for mail searches, court may charge add'l $5.00. No child protection or juvenile records released. Will not fax documents. Court makes copy: $2.00 1st page, $1.00 each add'l. Certification fee: $5.00 per doc plus copy fee. Payee: Maine District Court. Personal checks accepted. Visa/MC accepted. Prepayment required. Mail requests: SASE required.

Civil Name Search: Access: Mail, in person. Visitors must perform in person name searches. Search fee: First name search is free, then $15.00 each add'l, includes both civil and criminal. Civil cases indexed by defendant. Civil index on docket books since 1989, prior on docket books. Note: Court will do up to 3 searches only. Mail turnaround time 4-5 days.

Criminal Name Search: Access: Mail, in person. Only the court performs in person name searches; visitors may not. Search fee: First name search is free, then $15.00 each add'l, includes both civil and criminal. Required to search: name, years to search; also helpful: DOB. Criminal records on computer since 1986, prior on docket books. Mail turnaround time is 5 days.

Springvale District Court - West 10 447 Main St, Springvale, ME 04083; 207-459-1400; 8AM-4PM (EST). *Misdemeanor, Civil Actions, Eviction, Small Claims.*

General Information: Search fees and copy fees listed are mandatory per administrative rule. If a SASE is not supplied for mail searches, court may charge add'l $5.00. No impounded, juvenile, mental health or protective custody records released. Will not fax documents. Court makes copy: $2.00 1st page, $1.00 each add'l. Certification fee: $5.00 per doc plus copy fee. Payee: Maine District Court. Personal checks and credit cards accepted. Prepayment required. Mail requests: SASE required.

Civil Name Search: Access: Mail, in person. Both court and visitors may perform in person name searches. Search fee: $15.00 per name after 1st name free; includes both civil and criminal index, if asked. Civil cases indexed by defendant. Civil records on computer since 1985, docket books since 1985. Mail turnaround time 3-4 days.

Criminal Name Search: Access: Mail, in person. Both court and visitors may perform in person name searches. Search fee: $15.00 per name after 1st name free; includes both civil and criminal index, if asked. Submit DOB with search. Criminal records on computer since 1997, dockets books since 1980. Mail turnaround time 3-4 days.

York District Court - South 10 11 Chases Pond Rd, York, ME 03909; 207-363-1230; 8AM-4PM (EST). *Misdemeanor, Civil Actions, Eviction, Small Claims.*

General Information: Search fees and copy fees listed are mandatory per administrative rule. No impounded, juvenile and protective custody records released. Will not fax documents. Court makes copy: $2.00 1st page, $1.00 each add'l. Certification fee: $5.00 per doc plus copy fee. Payee: Maine District Court. Personal checks accepted. Visa/MC/Discover accepted. Prepayment required. Mail requests: SASE required.

Civil Name Search: Access: Mail, in person. Visitors must perform in person searches themselves. Search fee: $15.00, includes both civil and criminal. Allows 1 name free search. Add $5.00 if mailed. Civil index on docket books since 1965; on computer back to 1987. Mail turnaround time 2-4 days.

Criminal Name Search: Access: Mail, in person. Visitors must perform in person searches themselves. Search fee: $15.00, includes both civil and criminal. Allows 1 name free search. Add $5.00 if mailed. Submit DOB with search. Criminal records computerized from 1987. Mail turnaround time 2-4 days.

Probate Court 45 Kennebunk Rd, Alfred, ME 04002; 207-324-1577; fax: 207-324-0163; 8AM-4:30PM (EST). *Probate.*
www.maineprobate.net

General Information: Search probate records free at https://www.maineprobate.net/index.html. An account is $10.00 per month: $2.00 fee for images, $1.00 if account holder.

Maryland

Time Zone:	**EST**
Capital:	**Annapolis, Anne Arundel County**
# of Counties:	**23**
State Web:	**www.maryland.gov**
Court Web:	**www.mdcourts.gov**

Administration

Court Administrator, Administrative Office of the Courts, 580 Taylor Ave, Annapolis, MD, 21401; 410-260-1400, 410-260-1488, Fax: 410-974-5291.

The Appellate Courts

The Maryland Court of Appeals is the highest court in the state (commonly called the Supreme Court in other states). The Court of Special Appeals is Maryland's intermediate appellate court, and it generally considers any reviewable judgment, decree, order, or other action of the circuit and orphans' courts. The web page above gives access to opinions.

The Maryland Courts

Court	Type	How Organized	Jurisdiction Highpoints
Circuit*	General	24 Courts in 8 Circuits	Felony, Misdemeanor, Civil, Domestic, Juvenile
District*	Limited	34 Courts in 12 Districts	Misdemeanor, Limited Civil, Small Claims, Eviction, Juvenile
Orphans'	Special	24 Courts	Estates, Probate

* = profiled in this book

Details on the Court Structure

Circuit Courts generally handle the State's major civil cases and more serious criminal matters, along with juvenile cases, family matters such as divorce, and most appeals from the District Court, orphans' courts and administrative agencies. The Circuit Courts also can hear cases from the District Court (civil or criminal) in which one of the parties has requested a jury trial, under certain circumstances.

The **District Court** hears both civil and criminal cases involving claims up to $30,000, and has exclusive jurisdiction over peace order cases and landlord/tenant, replevin (recovery of goods claimed to be wrongfully taken or detained), and other civil cases involving amounts at or less than $5,000. The District Court also handles motor vehicle/boating violations and other misdemeanors and limited felonies, although the circuit courts share jurisdiction if the penalties authorized are three years or more in prison, a fine of $2,500 or more, or both. Both trial courts can hear domestic violence cases.

Orphans' Courts handle wills, estates, and other probate matters. In addition, they have jurisdiction—along with the circuit courts—to appoint guardians of the person, and to protect the estates of un-emancipated minors (minors who remain under parental authority).

The Circuit Court handles **probate** in only Montgomery and Harford counties. In other counties, probate is handled by the **Orphan's Court**. The clerk is called the **Register of Wills** and is a county, not a court, function.

Note there is a Baltimore County and the City of Baltimore; each has its own courts.

Record Searching Facts You Need to Know

Fees and Record Searching Tips

A fee schedule dictates that courts must charge $5.00 for document certification in all courts. Most courts charge $.50 per page for a copy. Most courts will not do a name search for the public, those that do rarely charge a search fee.

Online Access is Statewide

See http://casesearch.courts.state.md.us/inquiry/inquiry-index.jsp for a free search of dockets of the trial courts. The search includes all District and Circuit courts in the state. Note the DOB is shown on some but not all dockets. Records are updated daily, but case information from Montgomery and Prince George's counties usually lag one additional day. All case information may be searched by party name or case number.

Bulk subscription data of civil record information from the District Courts can be requested for an annual and monthly fee - see www.courts.state.md.us/district/forms/acct/dca107.pdf. Reportedly, plans are underway for subscribing parties to access statewide Case Search bulk data and data extracts through a standards-based interface in XML format. Also, there is an Attorney Calendar Service that displays information related to an attorney's trial and hearing schedule such as case number, attorney name, trial or hearing date, defendant name, time, room, etc.

A free statewide or single county docket search of the Register of Wills records is offered at http://jportal.mdcourts.gov/willsandtrusts/index.jsf. One may search by Decedent, Guardian, Interested Party, Minor, or Personal Representative. Records from the Register of Wills of all counties go back to at least 1998.

Allegany County

4th Judicial Circuit Court 30 Washington St, Cumberland, MD 21502; 301-777-5922; fax: 301-777-2100; 8AM-4:30PM (EST). *Felony, Misdemeanor, Civil Actions over $25,000.* www.mdcourts.gov/

General Information: No adoption, juvenile, sealed, expunged or mental records released. Will not fax documents. Court makes copy: $.50 per page. Self serve copy: $.25 per page. Certification fee: $5.00 per instrument. Payee: Circuit Court. Personal checks accepted. No credit cards accepted. Prepayment required.

Civil Name Search: Access: In person, online. Visitors must perform in person searches themselves. Civil records on computer since 06/1997, archived and indexed from 1790. Civil PAT goes back to 6/1997. Free case look-up at http://casesearch.courts.state.md.us/inquiry/inquiry-index.jsp/inquiry/inquiry-index.jsp

Criminal Name Search: Access: In person, online. Visitors must perform in person searches themselves. Required to search: name, years to search; also helpful: DOB. Criminal records on computer since 9/99, archived and indexed from 1790. Criminal PAT goes back to 6/1996. Online access to criminal is same as civil, results show middle initial, DOB.

District Court 123 S Liberty St, 2nd Fl, Cumberland, MD 21502; 301-723-3100; 8:30AM-4:30PM (EST). *Misdemeanor, Civil Actions under $30000, Eviction, Small Claims.* www.mdcourts.gov/

General Information: No adoption, juvenile, sealed, expunged or mental records released. Will not fax documents. Court makes copy: $.50 per page. Certification fee: $5.00 per page. Payee: District Court of MD. Personal checks accepted. Credit cards accepted. Prepayment required.

Civil Name Search: Access: Online, in person. Visitors must perform in person searches themselves. Civil cases indexed by defendant. Civil records on computer from 1990, on index books from 1970. Civil PAT available. Free case look-up at http://casesearch.courts.state.md.us/inquiry/inquiry-index.jsp.

Criminal Name Search: Access: Online, in person. Visitors must perform in person searches themselves. Required to search: name, years to search; SSN helpful. Criminal records computerized from 1980, index books. Note: Court requires a case number for a search. Criminal PAT available. Online access to criminal is same as civil, results show middle initial, DOB.

Register of Wills 59 Prospect Sq, 1st Fl, Cumberland, MD 21502; 301-724-3760, 888-724-0148 in MD; fax: 301-724-1249; 8:30AM-4:30PM (EST). *Probate.* http://registers.maryland.gov/main/allegany.html

General Information: Search by name or estate, this county or all counties at http://jportal.mdcourts.gov/willsandtrusts/index.jsf.

Anne Arundel County

5th Judicial Circuit Court PO Box 71, 7 Church Circle, Annapolis, MD 21401; 410-222-1397; criminal phone: 410-222-1420; civil phone: 410-222-1431; 8:30AM-4:30PM; phones- 9AM-3:30PM (EST). *Felony, Misdemeanor, Civil Actions over $25,000.* www.mdcourts.gov/

General Information: Online identifiers in results same as on public terminal. No adoption, juvenile, sealed, expunged or mental records released. Will not fax documents. Court makes copy: $.50 per page. Certification fee: $5.00 per cert. Payee: Clerk of Circuit Court. Personal checks accepted. No credit cards accepted. Prepayment required. Mail requests: SASE required for civil.

Civil Name Search: Access: In person, online. Both court and visitors may perform in person name searches. No search fee. Civil records on computer from 1991, on index from 1900. Note: Search civil for liens and judgments, etc. at Document Control Dept, 410-222-1394. Mail turnaround time 2 days. Civil PAT goes back to 1991. Results include name and case number. Free case look-up at http://casesearch.courts.state.md.us/inquiry/inquiry-index.jsp.

Criminal Name Search: Access: In person, online. Both court and visitors may perform in person name searches. No search fee. Required to search: name, years to search; also helpful: SSN. Criminal records computerized from 1988, indexed from 1960, archived from 1900. Note: Results include name, address and case number. Criminal PAT goes back to 1988. Online access to criminal is same as civil, results show middle initial, DOB.

District Court 251 Rowe Blvd, #141, Annapolis, MD 21401; criminal phone: 410-260-1370; civil phone: 410-260-1800; 8:30AM-4:30PM (EST). *Misdemeanor, Civil Actions under $25,000, Eviction, Small Claims.* www.mdcourts.gov/

General Information: Court makes copy: $.50 per page. Certification fee: $5.00 per doc plus copy fee. Payee: District Court. Personal checks and credit cards accepted. Prepayment required. Mail requests: SASE required.

Civil Name Search: Access: In person, online. Both court and visitors may perform in person name searches. No search fee. Civil cases indexed by defendant. Civil records on computer from 1982, archived and indexed from 1900s. Note: This court suggests that civil searches be made at Glen Burnie. Civil PAT goes back to 1987. Free case look-up at http://casesearch.courts.state.md.us/inquiry/inquiry-index.jsp.

Criminal Name Search: Access: Phone, online, in person. Both court and visitors may perform in person name searches. No search fee. Criminal records computerized from 1982, archived and indexed from 1900s. Note: Phone search is only to see if a case exists or if case number known. Mail turnaround time 7 days. Criminal PAT goes back to 1982. Online access to criminal is same as civil, results show middle initial, DOB.

Register of Wills PO Box 2368, 7 Church Cir, Circuit Courthouse, Annapolis, MD 21404-2368; 410-222-1430, 800-679-6665 in MD; fax: 410-222-1467; 8AM-4:30PM (EST). *Probate.* http://registers.maryland.gov/main/

General Information: Search by name or estate, this county or all counties at http://jportal.mdcourts.gov/willsandtrusts/index.jsf.

Baltimore County

3rd Judicial Circuit Court 401 Bosley Ave, 2nd Fl, Towson, MD 21204; 410-887-2601; criminal phone: 410-887-2627; civil phone: 410-887-2614; fax: 410-887-3062; 8:30AM-4:30PM (EST). *Felony, Civil Actions over $30,000.* www.mdcourts.gov/

General Information: No adoption, juvenile, sealed, expunged or mental records released. Will not fax documents. Court makes copy: $.50 per page. Certification fee: $5.00 per page. Payee: Julie Ensor, Clerk. Personal checks accepted. Out of state checks not accepted. No credit cards accepted. Prepayment required.

Civil Name Search: Access: Online, in person. Visitors must perform in person searches themselves. Required to search: name, years to search; also helpful: address. Civil records in books, file jackets. Civil PAT goes back to 1995. Free case look-up at http://casesearch.courts.state.md.us/inquiry/inquiry-index.jsp.

Criminal Name Search: Access: In person, online. Visitors must perform in person searches themselves. Required to search: name, years to search; also helpful: address, DOB, SSN. Criminal records computerized from 1984, prior on books. Note: Results include name, address and case number. Criminal PAT goes back to 1985. Online access to criminal is same as civil, results show middle initial, DOB.

District Court 120 E Chesapeake Ave, Towson, MD 21286-5307; 410-512-2000; criminal phone: x3; civil phone: x2; 8:30AM-4:30PM (EST). *Misdemeanor, Civil Actions under $30,000, Eviction, Small Claims.* www.mdcourts.gov/

General Information: Court will not perform name search but will provide case file information. No adoption, juvenile, sealed, expunged or medical records released. Will not fax out documents. Court makes copy: $.50 per page. Certification fee: $5.00 per case plus copy fee. Payee: District Court of MD. Personal checks accepted. No credit cards accepted. Prepayment required.

Civil Name Search: Access: Online, in person. Visitors must perform in person searches themselves. Required to search: name, years to search; also helpful: address. Civil records on computer from 1985, on microfiche from 1971, archived from 1970, on card index from 1971. Civil PAT goes back to 1985. Addresses are not always available on terminal search results. Free case look-up at http://casesearch.courts.state.md.us/inquiry/inquiry-index.jsp.

Criminal Name Search: Access: Online, in person. Visitors must perform in person searches themselves. Criminal records on computer since 1981. Criminal PAT goes back to 1981. Online access to criminal is same as civil, results show middle initial, DOB.

Register of Wills 401 Bosley Ave, Rm 500, County Courts Bldg, Towson, MD 21204-4403; 410-887-6680/6681, 888-642-5387 in MD; fax: 410-583-2517; 8AM-4:30PM (EST). *Probate.* http://registers.maryland.gov/main/baltimore.html

General Information: Search by name or estate, this county or all counties at http://jportal.mdcourts.gov/willsandtrusts/index.jsf.

Baltimore City County

8th Judicial Circuit Court - Civil Division 111 N Calvert, Rm 409, Baltimore, MD 21202; 410-333-3722; civil phone: 410-369-3045; fax: 410-333-6986; 8:30AM-4:30PM (EST). *Civil Actions over $25,000.* www.baltcts.state.md.us

General Information: Civil clerk in Rm 462. No adoption, juvenile, sealed, expunged or mental records released. Will not fax documents. Court makes copy: $.50 per page. Certification fee: $5.00 per cert. Payee: Clerk of the Circuit Court. Business checks accepted. No credit cards accepted. Prepayment required.

Civil Name Search: Access: Phone, mail, online, in person. Both court and visitors may perform in person name searches. No search fee. Required to search: name, years to search; also helpful: address. Civil cases indexed by defendant. Civil records on computer from 1983. Note: Court conducts searches on a limited basis. Mail turnaround time 5 days. Public use terminal has civil records back to 10 years. Free case look-up at http://casesearch.courts.state.md.us/inquiry/inquiry-index.jsp.

8th Judicial Circuit Court - Criminal Division 110 N Calvert Rm 200, Baltimore, MD 21202; 410-333-3750; 8:30AM-4:30PM (EST). *Felony, Misdemeanor-(Limited).* www.mdcourts.gov/baltcity.html

General Information: No adoption, juvenile, sealed, expunged or mental records released. Will not fax documents. Court makes copy: $.50 per page. Self serve copy: same. Certification fee: $5.00 per case. Payee: Clerk of Circuit Court. Business checks accepted. No credit cards accepted. Prepayment required.

Criminal Name Search: Access: Online, in person. Visitors must perform in person searches themselves. Required to search: name, years to search; also helpful: address, DOB. Criminal records computerized from 1994, on microfilm from 1972. Public use terminal has crim records. The court warns there is limited information available on the one public terminal. Search court records free at http://casesearch.courts.state.md.us/inquiry/inquiry-index.jsp. Updated nightly. Online results show middle initial, DOB.

District Court - Civil Division 501 E Fayette St, Baltimore, MD 21202; 410-878-8900; 8:30AM-4:30PM (EST). *Civil Actions under $25,000, Eviction, Small Claims.* www.mdcourts.gov/

General Information: No medical or sealed records released. Will not fax documents. Court makes copy: $.50 per page. Certification fee: $5.00 per doc. Payee: District Court of MD. Personal checks accepted. No credit cards accepted. Prepayment required. Mail requests: SASE required.

Civil Name Search: Access: Mail, in person, online. Both court and visitors may perform in person name searches. No search fee. Civil cases indexed by defendant. Civil records on computer from 1986, on card index from 1971. Mail turnaround time 5-10 days. Public use terminal has civil records back to 1991. Free case look-up at http://casesearch.courts.state.md.us/inquiry/inquiry-index.jsp. Updated nightly.

District Court - Criminal Division 1400 E North Ave, Eastside District Court Building, Baltimore, MD 21213; 410-878-8500; 8:30AM-4:30PM (EST). *Misdemeanor.* www.mdcourts.gov/baltcity.html

General Information: Most questions can be answered by the court's 'information center.' No adoption, juvenile, sealed, expunged, medical or mental records released. Will not fax documents. Court makes copy: $.50 per page. Certification fee: $5.00 per doc. Payee: District Court. Personal checks accepted. Visa/Vida Debit accepted. Prepayment required. Mail requests: SASE required.

Criminal Name Search: Access: Mail, online, in person. No search fee. Criminal records computerized from 1982, prior on index cards from 1970. Mail turnaround time 1 week. Public use terminal has crim records back to 1982. Public terminal located at 700 E Patapsco Ave. Search court records free at http://casesearch.courts.state.md.us/inquiry/inquiry-index.jsp. Online results show middle initial, DOB.

Register of Wills 111 N Calvert St, 3rd Fl, Courthouse East, Rm 352, Baltimore, MD 21202; 410-752-5131, 888-876-0035 in MD; fax: 410-752-3494; 8:30AM-4:30PM (EST). *Probate.* http://registers.maryland.gov/main/

General Information: Search by name or estate, this county or all counties at http://jportal.mdcourts.gov/willsandtrusts/index.jsf.

Calvert County

7th Judicial Circuit Court 175 Main St Courthouse, Prince Frederick, MD 20678; 410-535-1660; criminal phone: x2266; civil phone: x2404; fax: 410-535-6245; 8:30AM-4:30PM (EST). *Felony, Misdemeanor, Civil Actions over $25,000.* www.mdcourts.gov/clerks/calvert/

General Information: Court personnel will not perform name searches. Online identifiers in results same as on public terminal. No adoption, juvenile, sealed, expunged or mental records released. Will not fax documents. Court makes copy: $.25 per page. Self serve copy: same. Certification fee: $5.00. Payee: Clerk of Circuit Court. Personal checks accepted. No credit cards accepted. Prepayment required.

Civil Name Search: Access: Online, in person. Visitors must perform in person searches themselves. Civil records on computer back to 10/1997, prior on index books back to 1959. Civil PAT goes back to 10/1997. Free case look-up at http://casesearch.courts.state.md.us/inquiry/inquiry-index.jsp.

Criminal Name Search: Access: In person, online. Visitors must perform in person searches themselves. Required to search: name, years to search; SSN helpful. Criminal records computerized from 4/2000; prior in books back to 1967, on CD to 1948. Note: Public is referred to CJIS Central Repository in Pikesville, 888-795-0011, 410-764-4501. Criminal PAT goes back to 4/2000. Online access to criminal is same as civil, results show middle initial, DOB.

District Court 200 Duke St Rm 2200, Prince Frederick, MD 20678; 443-550-6700; 8:30AM-4:30PM (EST). *Misdemeanor, Civil Actions under $30,000, Eviction, Small Claims.* www.mdcourts.gov

General Information: No adoption, juvenile, sealed, expunged or medical records released. Will not fax documents. Court makes copy: $.50 per page. Certification fee: $5.00 per cert plus copy fee. Payee: District Court of Maryland. Personal checks accepted. Credit cards accepted, fees apply. Prepayment required.

Civil Name Search: Access: In person, online. Visitors must perform in person searches themselves. Required to search: name; also helpful: address. Civil cases indexed by defendant. Civil records on computer from mid-80s, archived from 1971 to 1981, prior on Cot index. Civil PAT goes back to 1991. Free case look-up at http://casesearch.courts.state.md.us/inquiry/inquiry-index.jsp.

Criminal Name Search: Access: In person, online. Visitors must perform in person searches themselves. Required to search: name; also helpful: address, DOB. Criminal records computerized from 1981, archived from 1971-1981, prior on archived index. Criminal PAT goes back to same as civil. Terminal results will include DOB if it was provided; address is usually included. Online access to criminal is same as civil, results show middle initial, DOB.

Register of Wills 175 Main St, Courthouse, Prince Frederick, MD 20678; 410-535-1600 x2256, 888-374-0015 in MD; fax: 410-414-3952; 8:30AM-4:30PM (EST). *Probate.* http://registers.maryland.gov/main/calvert.html

General Information: Search by name or estate, this county or all counties at http://jportal.mdcourts.gov/willsandtrusts/index.jsf.

Caroline County

2nd Judicial Circuit Court Box 458, Denton, MD 21629; 410-479-1811; fax: 410-479-1142; 8:30AM-4:30PM (EST). *Felony, Misdemeanor, Civil Actions over $25,000.* www.mdcourts.gov/

General Information: Misdemeanor case records held at District Court until appealed, then stored at Circuit Court. No adoption, juvenile, sealed, expunged or mental records released. Will not fax documents. Court makes copy: $.50 per page. Self serve copy: $.25 per page. Certification fee: $5.00 per cert plus copy fee. Payee: F Dale Minner, Clerk. Personal checks accepted. No credit cards accepted. Prepayment required.

Civil Name Search: Access: Online, in person. Visitors must perform in person searches themselves. Required to search: name, years to search; also helpful: address. Civil records on computer from 10/98, card index archived from 1774. Civil PAT goes back to 10/2000. Results are not printable. Free case look-up at http://casesearch.courts.state.md.us/inquiry/inquiry-index.jsp.

Criminal Name Search: Access: In person, online. Visitors must perform in person searches themselves. Required to search: name, years to search; also helpful: address, DOB, SSN. Criminal records computerized from 2000, card index archived from 1774. Criminal PAT goes back to same as civil. Results are not printable. Online access to criminal is same as civil, results show middle initial, DOB.

District Court 207 S 3rd St, Denton, MD 21629; 410-819-4600; 8:30AM-4:30PM (EST). *Misdemeanor, Civil Actions under $25,000, Eviction, Small Claims.* www.mdcourts.gov/

General Information: No adoption, juvenile, sealed, expunged or mental records released. Will not fax documents. Court makes copy: $.50 per page. Certification fee: $5.00 per doc plus copy fee. Payee: District Court. Personal checks accepted. AmEx, Discover, MC cards accepted; There is an add'l usage fee if credit card used. Visa cards accepted only if a debit card. Prepayment required.

Civil Name Search: Access: Online, in person. Visitors must perform in person searches themselves. Required to search: name, years to search; also helpful: address. Civil cases indexed by defendant. Civil records on cards from 1971, computerized since 1981. Civil PAT goes back to at least 3 years. Public terminal includes traffic records. Identifiers on public terminal results do not always appear. Free case look-up at http://casesearch.courts.state.md.us/inquiry/inquiry-index.jsp.

Criminal Name Search: Access: Online, in person. Visitors must perform in person searches themselves. Required to search: name, years to search; also helpful: address, DOB. Criminal records on cards from 1971, computerized since 1981. Criminal PAT goes back to at least 3 years. Identifiers on public terminal results do not always appear. Online access to criminal is same as civil, results show middle initial, DOB.

Register of Wills 109 Market St, Rm 119, County Courthouse, Denton, MD 21629; 410-479-0717, 888-786-0019 in MD; fax: 410-479-4983; 8AM-4:30PM (EST). *Probate.*
http://registers.maryland.gov/main/caroline.html

General Information: Search by name or estate, this county or all counties at http://jportal.mdcourts.gov/willsandtrusts/index.jsf.

Carroll County

Judicial Circuit Court 55 N Court St, Westminster, MD 21157; criminal phone: 410-386-2025; civil phone: 410-386-2326; 8:30AM-4:30PM (EST). *Felony, Misdemeanor, Civil Actions over $25,000.*
www.mdcourts.gov/clerks/carroll/index.html

General Information: No adoption, juvenile, sealed, expunged or mental records released. Will not fax documents. Court makes copy: $.50 per page. Self serve copy: $.25 per page. Certification fee: $5.00 per doc; Exemplification fee- $10.00 per doc. Payee: Clerk of Court. Personal checks accepted. Visa/MC accepted. Prepayment required.

Civil Name Search: Access: Online, in person. Visitors must perform in person searches themselves. Required to search: name; also helpful: years to search. Civil records on computer from 1990, on card books from 1837 to 1990. Note: Will return documents by email if related to lien satisfaction. Civil PAT goes back to 1990. Free case look-up at http://casesearch.courts.state.md.us/inquiry/inquiry-index.jsp.

Criminal Name Search: Access: In person, online. Visitors must perform in person searches themselves. Required to search: name; also helpful: years to search. Criminal records computerized from 1990, on card books from 1837 to 1990. Criminal PAT goes back to same as civil. Online access to criminal is same as civil, results show middle initial, DOB.

District Court 101 N Court St, Westminster, MD 21157; 410-871-3500; 8:30AM-4:30PM (EST). *Misdemeanor, Civil Actions under $25,000, Eviction, Small Claims.* www.mdcourts.gov/

General Information: No adoption, juvenile, sealed, shielded, expunged or mental records released. Will not fax documents. Court makes copy: $.50 per page. Certification fee: $5.00 per document plus copy fee. Payee: District Court. Personal checks accepted. Credit cards accepted. Prepayment required.

Civil Name Search: Access: Online, in person. Visitors must perform in person searches themselves. Civil records on computer back to 1991; on

card index from 1971. Civil PAT goes back to 1991. Free case look-up at http://casesearch.courts.state.md.us/inquiry/inquiry-index.jsp.

Criminal Name Search: Access: Online, in person. Visitors must perform in person searches themselves. Required to search: name, years to search; also helpful: DOB. Criminal records computerized from 1982; on card index from 1971. Criminal PAT goes back to 1982. Online access to criminal is same as civil, results show middle initial, DOB.

Register of Wills 55 N Court St, Rm 124, Courthouse Annex, Westminster, MD 21157; 410-848-2586, 888-876-0034 in MD; fax: 410-876-0657; 8:30AM-4:30PM (EST). *Probate.*
http://registers.maryland.gov/main/carroll.html

General Information: Search by name or estate, this county or all counties at http://jportal.mdcourts.gov/willsandtrusts/index.jsf.

Cecil County

2nd Judicial Circuit Court 129 E Main St, Rm 112, Elkton, MD 21921; 410-996-1021; criminal phone: 410-996-5373; civil phone: 410-996-5377; fax: 410-392-6032; 8:30AM-4:30PM (EST). *Felony, Misdemeanor, Civil Actions over $25,000.* www.mdcourts.gov/clerks/cecil/index.html

General Information: Online identifiers in results same as on public terminal. No adoption, juvenile, sealed, expunged or mental records released. Will not fax documents. Court makes copy: $.50 per page. Self serve copy: $.50 per page. Certification fee: $5.00 per page plus copy fee. Payee: Clerk of Court. Personal checks accepted. No credit cards accepted. Prepayment required.

Civil Name Search: Access: Online, in person. Visitors must perform in person searches themselves. Civil cases indexed by defendant. Civil records on card index and books from 1948. Civil PAT goes back to 1988. Free case look-up at http://casesearch.courts.state.md.us/inquiry/inquiry-index.jsp.

Criminal Name Search: Access: In person, online. Visitors must perform in person searches themselves. Required to search: name, years to search; also helpful: DOB, SSN. Criminal records on card index from 1948; computerized records since 1998. Criminal PAT goes back to same as civil. Online access to criminal is same as civil, results show middle initial, DOB.

District Court 170 E Main St, Elkton, MD 21921; 410-996-2700; 8:30AM-4:30PM (EST). *Misdemeanor, Civil Actions under $30,000, Eviction, Small Claims.* www.mdcourts.gov/

General Information: No adoption, juvenile, sealed, expunged or mental records released. Will not fax documents. Court makes copy: $.50 per page. Certification fee: $5.00. Payee: District Court. Personal checks accepted. Credit cards accepted. Prepayment required.

Civil Name Search: Access: Online, in person. Visitors must perform in person searches themselves. Civil cases indexed by defendant. Civil records on computer from 1987, on card index from 1971. Civil PAT goes back to 1987. Free case look-up http://casesearch.courts.state.md.us/inquiry/inquiry-index.jsp. at

Criminal Name Search: Access: In person, online. Visitors must perform in person searches themselves. Criminal records computerized from 1981, on card index from 1971. Criminal PAT goes back to 1981. Online access to criminal is same as civil.

Register of Wills 129 E Main St, Ste 102, Circuit Courthouse, Elkton, MD 219221; 410-996-5330, 888-398-0301 in MD; fax: 410-996-1039; 8AM-4:30PM (EST). *Probate.*
http://registers.maryland.gov/main/cecil.html

General Information: Search by name or estate, this county or all counties at http://jportal.mdcourts.gov/willsandtrusts/index.jsf.

Charles County

Circuit Court for Charles County PO Box 970, 200 Charles Street, La Plata, MD 20646; 301-932-3202; 8:30AM-4:30PM (EST). *Felony, Misdemeanor, Civil Actions over $2,500.*
www.mdcourts.gov/clerks/charles/

General Information: Court personnel will not do record searches. No adoption, juvenile, sealed, expunged or medical records released. Court makes copy: $.50 per page. Self serve copy: $.25 per page. Certification fee: $5.00 per certification, $10 for exemplification. Payee: Clerk of the Circuit Court. Personal checks accepted. Prepayment required.

Civil Name Search: Access: Online, in person. Visitors must perform in person searches themselves. Civil index on docket books from 1950, on computer back to 1996. Civil PAT goes back to 1996. Free case look-up at http://casesearch.courts.state.md.us/inquiry/inquiry-index.jsp.

Criminal Name Search: Access: In person, online. Visitors must perform in person searches themselves. Criminal records indexed in books from 1950, on computer back to 1996. Criminal PAT goes back to same as civil. Online access to criminal is same as civil, results show middle initial, DOB.

District Court PO Box 3070, 200 Charles St, La Plata, MD 20646; 301-932-3300 x3 criminal, x2 civil; criminal phone: 301-932-3295; civil phone: 301-932-3290; 8:30AM-4:30PM (EST). *Misdemeanor, Civil Actions under $25,000, Eviction, Small Claims.* www.mdcourts.gov/
General Information: No unserved warrants, medical records released. Will not fax documents. Court makes copy: $.50 per page. Certification fee: $5.00 per doc plus copy fee; triple seal is $10.00. Payee: District Court. Personal checks and credit cards accepted. Prepayment required.
Civil Name Search: Access: Online, in person. Visitors must perform in person searches themselves. Civil records on computer from 1987, on index from 1971. Civil PAT goes back to 1981. Free case look-up at http://casesearch.courts.state.md.us/inquiry/inquiry-index.jsp.
Criminal Name Search: Access: Online, in person. Visitors must perform in person searches themselves. Criminal records computerized from 1984, on index from 1971. Criminal PAT goes back to 09/1998. Online access to criminal is same as civil, results show middle initial, DOB.

Register of Wills/Orphans' Court PO Box 3080, La Plata, MD 20646-3080; 301-932-3345; fax: 301-932-3349; 8:30AM-4:30PM (EST). *Probate.* http://registers.maryland.gov/main/charles.html

Dorchester County

1st Judicial Circuit Court Box 150, 206 High St, Cambridge, MD 21613; 410-228-0481; fax: 410-228-1860; 8:30AM-4:30PM (EST). *Felony, Misdemeanor, Civil Actions over $25,000.* www.mdcourts.gov/
General Information: Online identifiers in results same as on public terminal. No adoption, juvenile, sealed, expunged or mental records released. Court makes copy: $.25 per page. Self serve copy: same. Certification fee: $5.00 plus copy fee. Payee: Clerk of Circuit Court. Personal checks accepted. No credit cards accepted. Prepayment required.
Civil Name Search: Access: Online, in person. Visitors must perform in person searches themselves. Civil records on computer from 1993. Civil PAT goes back to 1993. Results include name and case number. Free case look-up at http://casesearch.courts.state.md.us/inquiry/inquiry-index.jsp.
Criminal Name Search: Access: In person, online. Visitors must perform in person searches themselves. Criminal records computerized from 1993. Note: Results include address and case number. Criminal PAT goes back to 1993. Online access to criminal is same as civil, results show middle initial, DOB.

District Court 310 Gay St, Cambridge, MD 21613; 410-901-1420; 8:30AM-4:30PM (EST). *Misdemeanor, Civil Actions under $30,000, Eviction, Small Claims.* www.mdcourts.gov/
General Information: No adoption, sealed, juvenile, expunged or mental records released. Will not fax documents. Court makes copy: $.50 per page. Certification fee: $5.00 per page. Payee: District Court. Personal checks accepted. No credit cards accepted for copy fee payment. Prepayment required.
Civil Name Search: Access: Phone, online, in person. Visitors must perform in person searches themselves. Required to search: name, years to search; also helpful: address. Civil cases indexed by defendant. Civil records archived and indexed from 1971; computerized records since 1985. Note: Phone search requests accepted to see if a case exists. Civil PAT goes back to 1985. Free case look-up at http://casesearch.courts.state.md.us/inquiry/inquiry-index.jsp.
Criminal Name Search: Access: Phone, online, in person. Visitors must perform in person searches themselves. Required to search: name, years to search; also helpful: address, DOB, SSN. Criminal records on card index from 1971; computerized records since 1985. Note: Phone search requests accepted to see if a case exists. Criminal PAT goes back to same as civil. Online access to criminal is same as civil, results show middle initial, DOB.

Register of Wills 206 High St, Courthouse, Cambridge, MD 21613; 410-228-4181, 888-242-6257 in MD; fax: 410-228-4988; 8AM-4:30PM; Public- 8:30AM-4:30PM (EST). *Probate.*
http://registers.maryland.gov/main/dorchester.html
General Information: Search by name or estate, this county or all counties at http://jportal.mdcourts.gov/willsandtrusts/index.jsf.

Frederick County

6th Judicial Circuit Court 100 W Patrick St, Frederick, MD 21701; 301-600-1970; criminal phone: 301-600-1973; civil phone: 301-600-1977; fax: 301-600-2245; 8:30AM-4:30PM (EST). *Felony, Misdemeanor, Civil Actions over $25,000.* www.mdcourts.gov/
General Information: No adoption, juvenile, sealed, expunged or mental records released. Will not fax documents. Court makes copy: $.25 per page.

Certification fee: $5.00 per doc plus copy fee. Payee: Clerk of Circuit Court. Personal checks accepted. No credit cards accepted. Prepayment required.
Civil Name Search: Access: Online, in person. Visitors must perform in person searches themselves. Civil records on computer from 2/98, prior on card books. Civil PAT goes back to 1998. Free case look-up at http://casesearch.courts.state.md.us/inquiry/inquiry-index.jsp.
Criminal Name Search: Access: In person, online. Visitors must perform in person searches themselves. Criminal records computerized from 12/81, prior on index books. Criminal PAT goes back to 3/2000. Online access to criminal is same as civil, results show middle initial, DOB.

District Court 100 W Patrick St, Frederick, MD 21701; 301-600-2000; 8:30AM-4:30PM (EST). *Misdemeanor, Civil Actions under $30,000, Eviction, Small Claims.* www.mdcourts.gov/
General Information: If the case number is known, the court will supply a copy of the disposition for $.50 per page; turnaround time is 30 days. No adoption, juvenile, sealed, expunged or mental records released. Will not fax documents. Court makes copy: $.50 per page. Certification fee: $5.00 per doc plus copy fee. Payee: District Court. Personal checks accepted. Credit cards accepted. Prepayment required.
Civil Name Search: Access: Online, in person. Visitors must perform in person searches themselves. Required to search: name; also helpful: years to search. Civil records on computer and microfiche from 1986, archived and on card index from 1971. Civil PAT goes back to 1986. Results include name and case number. Free case look-up at http://casesearch.courts.state.md.us/inquiry/inquiry-index.jsp.
Criminal Name Search: Access: Online, in person, phone. Visitors must perform in person searches themselves. Required to search: name, DOB; also helpful: years to search. Criminal records on computer and microfiche from 1982, archived and on card index from 1971. Note: Results include address and case number. Criminal PAT goes back to 1982. Online access to criminal is same as civil, results show middle initial, DOB.

Register of Wills 100 W Patrick St, Courthouse, Frederick, MD 21701; 301-600-6565, 888-258-0526; fax: 301-600-6580; 8AM-4:30PM (EST). *Probate.* http://registers.maryland.gov/main/frederick.html
General Information: Search by name or estate, this county or all counties at http://jportal.mdcourts.gov/willsandtrusts/index.jsf.

Garrett County

4th Judicial Circuit Court PO Box 447, 203 S 4th St, Oakland, MD 21550; 301-334-1937; criminal phone: 301-334-5016; civil phone: 301-334-1944; fax: 301-334-5017; 8:30AM-4:30PM (EST). *Felony, Civil Actions over $25,000, Criminal, Equity Types.* www.mdcourts.gov/
General Information: Online identifiers in results same as on public terminal. No adoption, juvenile, sealed, expunged or mental records released. Will not fax documents. Court makes copy: $.50 per page. Self serve copy: $.25 per page. Certification fee: $5.00 per page. Payee: Sondra R Buckel, Clerk. Personal checks accepted. No credit cards accepted. Prepayment required.
Civil Name Search: Access: Mail, in person, online. Both court and visitors may perform in person name searches. No search fee. Civil records on computer since 11/97. Mail turnaround time 1 day. Civil PAT goes back to 11/1997. Free case look-up at http://casesearch.courts.state.md.us/inquiry/inquiry-index.jsp.
Criminal Name Search: Access: Mail, in person, online. Both court and visitors may perform in person name searches. No search fee. Required to search: name, years to search, DOB. Criminal records on computer since 11/99. Mail turnaround time 1 day. Criminal PAT goes back to 10/25/1999. Search court records free at http://casesearch.courts.state.md.us/inquiry/inquiry-index.jsp. Online results show middle initial, DOB.

District Court 205 S 3rd St, Oakland, MD 21550; 301-334-8020; 8:30AM-4:30PM (EST). *Misdemeanor, Civil Actions under $30,000, Eviction, Small Claims.* www.mdcourts.gov/
General Information: No adoption, juvenile, sealed, expunged or mental records released. Will not fax documents. Court makes copy: $.50 per page. Certification fee: $5.00 per page. Payee: District Court. Personal checks accepted. Credit cards accepted. Prepayment required.
Civil Name Search: Access: In person, online. Visitors must perform in person searches themselves. Civil cases indexed by defendant. Civil records on computer from 1990, on index books from 1971. Free case look-up at http://casesearch.courts.state.md.us/inquiry/inquiry-index.jsp.
Criminal Name Search: Access: In person, online. Visitors must perform in person searches themselves. Required to search: name, years to search, DOB. Criminal records computerized from 1981. Online access to criminal is same as civil, results show middle initial, DOB.

Register of Wills 313 E Alder St, Rm 103, Courthouse, Oakland, MD 21550; 301-334-1999, 888-334-2203 in MD; fax: 301-334-1984; 8:30AM-4:30PM (EST). *Probate.* http://registers.maryland.gov/main/garrett.html
General Information: Search by name or estate, this county or all counties at http://jportal.mdcourts.gov/willsandtrusts/index.jsf.

Harford County

3rd Judicial Circuit 20 W Courtland St, Bel Air, MD 21014; 410-638-3426; criminal phone: 410-638-3472; civil phone: 410-638-3430; probate phone: 410-638-3275; fax: 410-420-8389; 8:30AM-4:30PM (EST). *Felony, Misdemeanor, Civil Actions over $30,000.*
www.mdcourts.gov/clerks/harford/
General Information: Online identifiers in results same as on public terminal. No adoption, presentence investigations, juvenile, sealed, expunged or mental records released. Will not fax documents. Court makes copy: $.50 per page. Self serve copy: $.25 per page. Certification fee: $5.00 per cert; $10.00 for exemplification; plus copy fees. Payee: Clerk of the Circuit Court. Only cashiers checks and money orders accepted. No credit cards accepted. Prepayment required.
Civil Name Search: Access: Online, in person. Visitors must perform in person searches themselves. Required to search: name, years to search; also helpful: address. Civil records on computer since 05/04/1998 and on books prior. Civil PAT goes back to 5/4/1998. Results include name and case number. Free case look-up at http://casesearch.courts.state.md.us/inquiry/inquiry-index.jsp.
Criminal Name Search: Access: In person, online. Visitors must perform in person searches themselves. Required to search: name, years to search; also helpful: DOB. Criminal records on computer since 06/1999 and on books prior. Criminal PAT goes back to 6/1999. Online access to criminal is same as civil, results show middle initial, DOB.
District Court 2 S Bond St, Bel Air, MD 21014; 410-836-4545; 8:30AM-4:30PM (EST). *Misdemeanor, Civil Actions under $30,000, Eviction, Small Claims.* www.mdcourts.gov/
General Information: No motor vehicle, sealed, expunged or mental records released. Will not fax documents. Court makes copy: $.50 per page. Certification fee: $5.00. Payee: District Court of MD. Personal checks accepted. Credit cards accepted. Prepayment required. Mail requests: SASE required.
Civil Name Search: Access: Mail, in person, online. Visitors must perform in person searches themselves. No search fee. Civil cases indexed by defendant. Civil records on computer from 1989, on microfiche from 1972, archived from 1900. Civil PAT goes back to 1981. printouts are not available. Free case look-up at http://casesearch.courts.state.md.us/inquiry/inquiry-index.jsp.
Criminal Name Search: Access: Mail, online, in person. Visitors must perform in person searches themselves. No search fee. Required to search: name, years to search; also helpful: address, DOB. Criminal records computerized from 1981, on microfiche from 1972, archived from 1900. Note: Results include name and case number. Mail turnaround time 3-7 days. Criminal PAT goes back to same as civil. Online access to criminal is same as civil, results show middle initial, DOB.

Register of Wills 20 W Courtland St, Rm 304, Courthouse, Bel Air, MD 21014; 410-638-3275, 888-258-0525 in MD; fax: 410-893-3177; 8:30AM-4:00PM (EST). *Probate.* http://registers.maryland.gov/main/harford.html
General Information: Search by name or estate, this county or all counties at http://jportal.mdcourts.gov/willsandtrusts/index.jsf.

Howard County

5th Judicial Circuit Court 8360 Court Ave, Ellicott City, MD 21043; 410-313-2111; 888-313-0197; criminal phone: 410-313-3824; civil phone: 410-313-3844; 8:30AM-4:30PM (EST). *Felony, Misdemeanor, Civil Actions over $30,000.*
www.mdcourts.gov/clerks/howard/
General Information: No adoption, juvenile, sealed, expunged or mental records released. Will not fax documents. Court makes copy: $.50 per page. Self serve copy: $.25 per page. Certification fee: $5.00 per page. Payee: Office of Clerk. Personal checks accepted. No credit cards accepted. Prepayment required.
Civil Name Search: Access: Online, in person. Visitors must perform in person searches themselves. Civil records on computer from 1977. Civil PAT goes back to 1997. Free case look-up at http://casesearch.courts.state.md.us/inquiry/inquiry-index.jsp/inquiry/inquiry-index.jsp.
Criminal Name Search: Access: In person, online. Visitors must perform in person searches themselves. Required to search: name, years to search; also helpful: address, DOB. Criminal records on card index to 1971, prior may or may not be archived; on computer since 1999. Criminal PAT

goes back to 1998. Online access to criminal is same as civil, results show middle initial, DOB.
District Court 3451 Courthouse Dr, Ellicott City, MD 21043; 410-480-7700; 8:30AM-4:30PM (EST). *Misdemeanor, Civil Actions under $30,000, Eviction, Small Claims.* www.mdcourts.gov/
General Information: No adoption, juvenile, sealed, expunged or mental records released. Will not fax documents. Court makes copy: $.50 per page. Self serve copy: same. Certification fee: $5.00 plus copy fee. Payee: District Court of MD. Personal checks accepted. Credit cards accepted. Prepayment required. Mail requests: SASE required if return receipt requested.
Civil Name Search: Access: Mail, in person. Both court and visitors may perform in person name searches. No search fee. Civil cases indexed by defendant. Civil records on computer from 1992, on card index prior from 1971. Mail turnaround time before 1989 3-4 weeks, 1989-present 7 days. Civil PAT goes back to 1990. Free case look-up at http://casesearch.courts.state.md.us/inquiry/inquiry-index.jsp.
Criminal Name Search: Access: Mail, online, in person. Both court and visitors may perform in person name searches. No search fee. Criminal records computerized from 1989, on card index prior from 1971. Mail turnaround time before 1989- 3-4 weeks; 1989-present- 7 days. Criminal PAT goes back to 1985. Online access to criminal is same as civil, results show middle initial, DOB.

Register of Wills 8360 Court Ave, Ellicott City, MD 21043; 410-313-2133, 888-848-0136 in MD; fax: 410-313-3409; 8:30AM-4:30PM (EST). *Probate.* http://registers.maryland.gov/main/howard.html
General Information: Search by name or estate, this county or all counties at http://jportal.mdcourts.gov/willsandtrusts/index.jsf.

Kent County

2nd Judicial Circuit Court 103 N Cross St Courthouse, Chestertown, MD 21620; 410-778-7460; criminal phone: 410-778-7477; civil phone: 410-778-7461; fax: 410-778-7412; 8:30AM-4:30PM (EST). *Felony, Misdemeanor, Civil Actions over $25,000.*
www.mdcourts.gov/clerks/kent/records.html
General Information: No adoption, juvenile, sealed, expunged or mental records released. Will not fax documents. Court makes copy: $.50 per page. Self serve copy: $.25 per page. Certification fee: $5.00 per cert. Payee: Mark L Mumford, Clerk. Personal checks accepted. No credit cards accepted. Prepayment required.
Civil Name Search: Access: Online, in person. Visitors must perform in person searches themselves. Civil records on computer from 1998, on card index from 1656. Civil PAT goes back to 5/1998. Free case look-up at http://casesearch.courts.state.md.us/inquiry/inquiry-index.jsp.
Criminal Name Search: Access: In person, online. Visitors must perform in person searches themselves. Required to search: name, years to search; also helpful: DOB, SSN. Criminal records computerized from 05/2000, on card index from 1949, archived to 1656. Criminal PAT goes back to 5/2000. Online access to criminal is same as civil, results show middle initial, DOB.

District Court 103 N Cross St, Chestertown, MD 21620; 410-810-3362; fax: 410-810-3361; 8:30AM-4:30PM (EST). *Misdemeanor, Civil Actions under $30,000, Eviction, Small Claims, Traffic.* www.mdcourts.gov/
General Information: No sealed, expunged, mental records or judge's notes released. Will not fax documents. Court makes copy: $.50 per page. Certification fee: $5.00. Payee: District Court of MD. Personal checks accepted. Credit & debit cards accepted in person only. Prepayment required.
Civil Name Search: Access: Online, in person. Visitors must perform in person searches themselves. Civil cases indexed by defendant. Civil records on computer from 1989; on card index from 1971. Note: A printout from the computer is $.50 per page. Free case look-up at http://casesearch.courts.state.md.us/inquiry/inquiry-index.jsp.
Criminal Name Search: Access: Online, in person. Visitors must perform in person searches themselves. Required to search: name, years to search, DOB. Criminal records computerized from 1988, on card index from 1971. Note: A printout from the computer is $.50 per page. Public use terminal has crim records. Online access to criminal is same as civil, results show middle initial, DOB.

Register of Wills 103 N Cross St, Courthouse, Chestertown, MD 21620; 410-778-7466, 888-778-0179 in MD; probate phone: 410-778-7465 & 410-778-7463; fax: 410-778-2466; 8AM-4:30PM (EST). *Probate.* http://registers.maryland.gov/main/kent.html
General Information: Search by name or estate, this county or all counties at http://jportal.mdcourts.gov/willsandtrusts/index.jsf.

Montgomery County

Circuit Court 50 Maryland Ave, Rockville, MD 20850; 240-777-9466; criminal phone: 240-777-9440; civil phone: 240-777-9401; criminal fax: 240-777-9444; civil fax: 8:30AM-4:30PM; 8:30AM-4:30PM (EST). *Felony, Civil Actions over $30,000.*
www.montgomerycountymd.gov/ciatmpl.asp?url=/content/circuitcourt/index.asp
General Information: No adoption, juvenile, sealed, expunged or mental records released. Will not fax documents. Court makes copy: $.50 per page. Certification fee: $5.00 per doc plus copy fee. Payee: Clerk of Circuit Court. Personal checks accepted. No credit cards accepted. Prepayment required.
Civil Name Search: Access: In person, online. Visitors must perform in person searches themselves. Required to search: name, years to search; also helpful: case number. Civil records on computer from 1977, archived from 1900, on card index from 1977. Note: Court personnel will not provide name searches, but will assist the public with case numbers and on the use of on-site terminals. Civil PAT goes back to 1977. Terminals in Rm 218. Free case look-up at http://casesearch.courts.state.md.us/inquiry/inquiry-index.jsp. Also, the daily calendar is free at www.montgomerycountymd.gov/mc/judicial/circuit/docket.html.
Criminal Name Search: Access: In person, online. Visitors must perform in person searches themselves. Required to search: name, years to search; also helpful: case number. Criminal records computerized from 1973, archived from 1900, on card index from 1977. Note: Court personnel will not provide name searches, but will assist the public with case numbers and on the use of on-site terminals. Criminal PAT goes back to 1973. Terminals in Rm 218. Search court records free at http://casesearch.courts.state.md.us/inquiry/inquiry-index.jsp. Address usually appears in online criminal results. Online results show middle initial, DOB.

District Court 8552 Second Ave., Silver Spring, MD 20910; 301-563-8500, 866-873-9785; 8:30AM-4:30PM (EST). *Misdemeanor, Civil Actions under $30,000, Eviction, Small Claims.* www.mdcourts.gov/
General Information: No juvenile, sealed, expunged or mental records or judge's notes released. Will not fax documents. Court makes copy: $.50 per page. Certification fee: $5.00 per cert plus copy fee. Payee: District Court. Personal checks accepted. Major credit cards accepted, surcharge added. Prepayment required. Mail requests: SASE required.
Civil Name Search: Access: In person, online. Both court and visitors may perform in person name searches. No search fee. Civil records on computer from 1986, in book index and case folder to at least 1986. Mail turnaround time 2-4 weeks. Civil PAT goes back to 1986. Free case look-up at http://casesearch.courts.state.md.us/inquiry/inquiry-index.jsp.
Criminal Name Search: Access: Online, in person. Both court and visitors may perform in person name searches. No search fee. Criminal records on computer, index book and case folder. Mail turnaround time 2-4 weeks. Criminal PAT goes back to 1987. Online access to criminal is same as civil, results show middle initial, DOB.

Rockville District Court 27 Courthouse Square, Rockville, MD 20850; criminal phone: 301-279-1565; civil phone: 301-279-1500; 8AM-4:30PM (EST). *Misdemeanor, Civil Actions under $30,000, Eviction, Small Claims, Traffic.* www.mdcourts.gov/
General Information: For Landlord/Tenant matters call 301-279-1555. No juvenile, sealed, expunged, mental records or judge's notes released. Will not fax documents. Court makes copy: $.50 per page. Self serve copy: same. Certification fee: $5.00 per case. Payee: District Court. Personal checks accepted. Major credit cards accepted, surcharge added. Prepayment required. Mail requests: SASE required.
Civil Name Search: Access: Mail, in person, online. Both court and visitors may perform in person name searches. No search fee. Civil cases indexed by defendant. Civil records go back to 1971; on computer back to 1990, prior in case folder. Mail turnaround time 2-4 weeks. Civil PAT goes back to 2000. Free case look-up at http://casesearch.courts.state.md.us/inquiry/inquiry-index.jsp/inquiry/inquiry-index.jsp.
Criminal Name Search: Access: Mail, online, in person. Both court and visitors may perform in person name searches. No search fee. Required to search: name, years to search; also helpful: DOB. Criminal records on computer back to 1991, prior on docket books. Mail turnaround time 2-4 weeks. Criminal PAT goes back to 1991. Online access to criminal is same as civil, results show middle initial, DOB.

Register of Wills 50 Maryland Ave, #322, Judicial Ctr, Rockville, MD 20850; 240-777-9600; 888-892-2180 in MD; fax: 240-777-9602; 8:30AM-4:30PM (EST). *Probate.*
http://registers.maryland.gov/main/montgomery.html
General Information: Search by name or estate, this county or all counties at http://jportal.mdcourts.gov/willsandtrusts/index.jsf.

Prince George's County

7th Judicial Circuit Court 14735 Main St, Upper Marlboro, MD 20772; 301-952-3655; criminal phone: 301-952-3344; civil phone: 301-952-3240; 8:30AM-4:30PM (EST). *Felony, Misdemeanor, Civil Actions over $25,000.* www.co.pg.md.us/Government/JudicialBranch/circuit.asp?nivel=foldmenu(1)
General Information: No adoption, juvenile, sealed, expunged or mental records released. Court makes copy: $.50 per page. Certification fee: $5.00 per page. Payee: Clerk of Circuit Court. Personal checks accepted. Visa/MC accepted. Prepayment required.
Civil Name Search: Access: In person, online. Visitors must perform in person searches themselves. Civil records on computer from 1984, on microfiche from 1979, on card index prior. Civil PAT goes back to 1984. For case searches for the state go to http://casesearch.courts.state.md.us/inquiry/inquiry-index.jsp/inquiry/inquiry-index.jsp. Includes defendant name, city and state, case number, date of birth, plaintiff name (civil cases only), trial date, charge, cas
Criminal Name Search: Access: Phone. in person, online. Visitors must perform in person searches themselves. Required to search: name, years to search, DOB; SSN helpful. Criminal records computerized from 1984, on microfiche from 1979, on card index prior. Note: Phone search request is to see if a case exists and its case number only. Criminal PAT goes back to 1984. For case searches for the state go to http://casesearch.courts.state.md.us/inquiry/inquiry-index.jsp/inquiry/inquiry-index.jsp. Includes defendant name, city and state, case number, date of birth, trial date, charge, case disposition. Online results show middle initial, DOB.

District Court 14735 Main St, Rm 173B, Upper Marlboro, MD 20772; 301-952-4080 x5; 8:30AM-4:30PM (EST). *Misdemeanor, Civil Actions under $25,000, Eviction, Small Claims.* www.mdcourts.gov/
General Information: Local toll-free number- 800-943-8853. This court will perform NO name searches. A court case number must be provided. No adoption, juvenile, sealed, expunged or mental records released. Will not fax documents. Court makes copy: $.50 per page. Certification fee: $5.00 per case plus copy fees. Payee: District Court of Maryland. Personal checks accepted. Major credit cards and VISA debit cards accepted, with surcharge. Prepayment required. Mail requests: SASE required.
Civil Name Search: Access: In person, online. Visitors must perform in person searches themselves. Civil cases indexed by defendant. Civil records on computer from 1988, on card index from 1970. Mail turnaround time 1-2 weeks. Civil PAT goes back to 1988. Free case look-up at http://casesearch.courts.state.md.us/inquiry/inquiry-index.jsp.
Criminal Name Search: Access: In person, online. Visitors must perform in person searches themselves. No search fee. Criminal records computerized from 1981, on cards from 1970. Mail turnaround time 1-2 weeks. Criminal PAT goes back to 1981. Online access to criminal is same as civil, results show middle initial, DOB.

Register of Wills PO Box 1729, 14735 Main Street, Rm D4001, Upper Marlboro, MD 20772; 301-952-3250, 888-464-4219 in MD; fax: 301-952-4489; 8:30AM-4:30PM M-F; 8:30AM-5PM W; 8AM-N 1st Sat every month (EST). *Probate.*
http://registers.maryland.gov/main/princegeorges.html
General Information: Search by name or estate, this county or all counties at http://jportal.mdcourts.gov/willsandtrusts/index.jsf.

Queen Anne's County

2nd Judicial Circuit Court Courthouse, 100 Courthouse Sq, Centreville, MD 21617; 410-758-1773, 800-987-7591; 8:30AM-4:30PM (EST). *Felony, Misdemeanor, Civil Actions over $25,000.* www.mdcourts.gov/clerks/queenannes/index.html
General Information: Misdemeanor case records held at District Court until appealed, then stored at Circuit Court. Online identifiers in results same as on public terminal. No adoption, juvenile, sealed, expunged or mental records released. Court makes copy: $.50 per page. Certification fee: $5.00 per cert plus copy fee. Payee: Clerk of Circuit Court. Personal checks accepted. No credit cards accepted. Prepayment required.
Civil Name Search: Access: Online, in person. Visitors must perform in person searches themselves. Civil records on computer from 11/92; on index books from 1978. Civil PAT goes back to 11/1992. Results include name and case number. Free case look-up at http://casesearch.courts.state.md.us/inquiry/inquiry-index.jsp.
Criminal Name Search: Access: In person, online. Visitors must perform in person searches themselves. Required to search: name, years to search, SSN. Criminal records computerized from 11/92; on index books from 1978. Criminal PAT goes back to same as civil. Online access to criminal is same as civil, results show middle initial, DOB.

District Court 120 Broadway, Ste1, Centreville, MD 21617; 410-819-4000; fax: 410-819-4001; 8:30AM-4:30PM (EST). *Misdemeanor, Civil Actions under $30,000, Eviction, Small Claims.*
www.mdcourts.gov/
General Information: No adoption, juvenile, sealed, expunged or mental records released. Will not fax documents. Will not accept or receive faxes for pleadings. Court makes copy: $.50 per page. Certification fee: $5.00. Payee: District Court of Maryland. Personal checks accepted. All major credit and debit cards accepted. Prepayment required.
Civil Name Search: Access: Online, in person. Visitors must perform in person searches themselves. Required to search: name, years to search; also helpful: address. Civil cases indexed by defendant. Civil records on computer from 1988, archived from 1974, prior on index books. Civil PAT goes back to 1988. Free case look-up at http://casesearch.courts.state.md.us/inquiry/inquiry-index.jsp.
Criminal Name Search: Access: Online, in person. Visitors must perform in person searches themselves. Required to search: name, years to search; also helpful: address, DOB, SSN. Criminal records computerized from 1981, prior on index books. Criminal PAT goes back to 1981. Online access to criminal is same as civil, results show middle initial, DOB.

Register of Wills Liberty Bldg, 107 N Liberty St, #220, PO Box 59, Centreville, MD 21617; 410-758-0585, 888-758-0010 in MD; fax: 410-758-4408; 8AM-4:30PM (EST). *Probate.*
http://registers.maryland.gov/main/queenannes.html
General Information: Search by name or estate, this county or all counties at http://jportal.mdcourts.gov/willsandtrusts/index.jsf.

Somerset County

1st Judicial Circuit Court PO Box 99, Princess Anne, MD 21853; 410-845-4840; criminal phone: 410-845-4850; civil phone: 410-845-4855; probate phone: 410-651-1696; fax: 410-845-4841; 8AM-4:30PM (EST). *Felony, Misdemeanor, Civil Actions over $25,000.*
www.mdcourts.gov/
General Information: No adoption, juvenile, sealed, expunged or mental records released. Will not fax documents. Court makes copy: $.50 per page. Self serve copy: $.25 per page. Certification fee: $5.00 plus copy fee. Payee: Clerk of Circuit Court. Personal checks accepted. No credit cards accepted. Prepayment required.
Civil Name Search: Access: Online, in person. Visitors must perform in person searches themselves. Required to search: name, years to search; also helpful: address. Civil records on computer from 9/93; prior archived and on index books. Civil PAT goes back to 1999. Free case look-up at http://casesearch.courts.state.md.us/inquiry/inquiry-index.jsp.
Criminal Name Search: Access: In person, online. Visitors must perform in person searches themselves. Required to search: name, years to search; also helpful: address, DOB, SSN. Criminal records computerized from 1992; prior archived and on index books. Criminal PAT goes back to 1992. Online access to criminal is same as civil, results show middle initial, DOB.

District Court 12155 Elm St #C, Princess Anne, MD 21853; 800-939-7306, 410-845-4700; 8:30AM-4:30PM (EST). *Misdemeanor, Civil Actions under $25,000, Eviction, Small Claims.* www.mdcourts.gov/
General Information: Felony cases go to Circuit Court if preliminary hearing waived or cause found. Records held at court where trial heard. Online identifiers in results same as on public terminal. No adoption, juvenile, sealed, expunged or mental records released. Will not fax documents. Court makes copy: $.50 per page. Certification fee: $5.00 per doc plus copy fee. Payee: District Court. Personal checks and credit cards accepted. Prepayment required.
Civil Name Search: Access: Online, in person. Visitors must perform in person searches themselves. Civil records on computer from 1987, archived and on index books from 1971. Civil PAT goes back to 1987. Free case look-up at http://casesearch.courts.state.md.us/inquiry/inquiry-index.jsp.
Criminal Name Search: Access: Online, in person. Visitors must perform in person searches themselves. Required to search: name, years to search; also helpful: SSN. Criminal records computerized from 1987, archived and on index books from 1971. Criminal PAT goes back to same as civil. Online access to criminal is same as civil, results show middle initial, DOB.

Register of Wills 30512 Prince William St, Courthouse, Princess Anne, MD 21853; 410-651-1696, 888-758-0039 in MD; fax: 410-651-3873; 8AM-4:30PM (EST). *Probate.*
http://registers.maryland.gov/main/somerset.html
General Information: Search by name or estate, this county or all counties at http://jportal.mdcourts.gov/willsandtrusts/index.jsf.

St. Mary's County

7th Judicial Circuit Court PO Box 676, 41605 Courthouse Dr., Leonardtown, MD 20650; 301-475-7844 x1; 8:30AM-4:30PM (EST). *Felony, Misdemeanor, Civil Actions over $30,000.*

www.mdcourts.gov/
General Information: No adoption, juvenile, sealed, expunged or mental/medical records released. Will not fax documents. Court makes copy: $.50 per page. Self serve copy: $.25 per page. A self serve copier is also available if you purchase a copier drawn down account. Certification fee: $5.00 per cert plus copy fee. Payee: Clerk of the Circuit Court. Personal checks accepted. No credit cards accepted. Prepayment required.
Civil Name Search: Access: Online, in person. Visitors must perform in person searches themselves. Civil records on computer from 1997, on card index from 1970. Civil PAT goes back to 1997. Free case look-up at http://casesearch.courts.state.md.us/inquiry/inquiry-index.jsp.
Criminal Name Search: Access: In person, online. Visitors must perform in person searches themselves. Required to search: name, years to search; SSN helpful. Criminal records computerized from 1997, on card index from 1970. Criminal PAT goes back to 2000. Online access to criminal is same as civil, results show middle initial, DOB.

District Court Carter State Office Bldg, 23110 Leonard Hall Dr, Leonardtown, MD 20650; 301-880-2700; fax: 301-880-2701; 8:30AM-4:30PM (EST). *Misdemeanor, Civil Actions under $30,000, Eviction, Small Claims.* www.msa.md.gov/msa/mdmanual/36loc/sm/html/smj.html
General Information: No adoption, juvenile, sealed, expunged or mental records released. Will not fax out documents. Court makes copy: $.50 per page. Certification fee: $5.00 per doc or triple seal for $10.00, plus copy fee. Personal checks accepted. Credit cards accepted in person; add $6.50 processing fee, $5.50 if debit card. Prepayment required.
Civil Name Search: Access: Online, in person. Visitors must perform in person searches themselves. Civil cases indexed by defendant. Civil records on computer from 1987, archived from 1971. Civil PAT goes back to 1983. Free case look-up at http://casesearch.courts.state.md.us/inquiry/inquiry-index.jsp.
Criminal Name Search: Access: Online, in person. Visitors must perform in person searches themselves. Required to search: name, years to search; also helpful: DOB. Criminal records computerized from 1985, archived from 1971. Criminal PAT goes back to 1983. Search results may also include physical identifiers. Online access to criminal is same as civil, results show middle initial, DOB.

Register of Wills 41605 Courthouse Dr, PO Box 602, Leonardtown, MD 20650; 301-475-5566; 888-475-4821 in MD; fax: 301-475-4968; 8:30AM-4:30PM (EST). *Probate.*
http://registers.maryland.gov/main/stmarys.html
General Information: Search by name or estate, this county or all counties at http://jportal.mdcourts.gov/willsandtrusts/index.jsf.

Talbot County

Circuit Court 11 N Washington St, #16, Easton, MD 21601-3195; 410-822-2611; fax: 410-820-9518; 8:30AM-4:30PM (EST). *Felony, Misdemeanor, Civil Actions over $25,000.*
www.mdcourts.gov/clerks/talbot/index.html
General Information: Online identifiers in results same as on public terminal. No adoption, juvenile, sealed, expunged or mental records released. Will not fax documents. Court makes copy: $.50 per page. Certification fee: $.50. Payee: Mary Ann Shortall, Clerk of Court. Personal checks accepted. No credit cards accepted. Prepayment required. Mail requests: SASE required for mail return of any copies.
Civil Name Search: Access: Online, in person. Visitors must perform in person searches themselves. Required to search: name, years to search; also helpful: address. Civil records on card index from 1993. Civil PAT goes back to 1997. Free case look-up at http://casesearch.courts.state.md.us/inquiry/inquiry-index.jsp.
Criminal Name Search: Access: In person, online. Visitors must perform in person searches themselves. Required to search: name, years to search; also helpful: address, DOB, SSN. Criminal records on card index from 1993. Criminal PAT goes back to same as civil. Online access to criminal is same as civil, results show middle initial, DOB.

District Court 108 W Dover St, Easton, MD 21601; 410-819-5850; 8:30AM-4:30PM (EST). *Misdemeanor, Civil Actions under $30,000, Eviction, Small Claims.* www.mdcourts.gov/
General Information: No adoption, juvenile, sealed, expunged or mental records released. Will not fax documents. Court makes copy: $.50 per page. Certification fee: $5.00 per doc. Payee: District Court of MD. Personal checks accepted. MasterCard accepted and VISA debit cards only. Prepayment required.
Civil Name Search: Access: Online, in person. Visitors must perform in person searches themselves. Civil cases indexed by defendant. Civil records go back to 1971; on computer back to 1988. Civil PAT goes back to 1988. Free case look-up at http://casesearch.courts.state.md.us/inquiry/inquiry-index.jsp.
Criminal Name Search: Access: Online, in person. Visitors must perform in person searches themselves. Criminal records go back to 1971;

on computer back to 1984. Criminal PAT goes back to 1988. Online access to criminal is same as civil, results show middle initial, DOB.

Register of Wills PO Box 816, Courthouse, 11 N Washington St, Easton, MD 21601; 410-770-6700, fax: 410-822-5452; 8:30AM-4:30PM (EST). *Probate.* http://registers.maryland.gov/main/talbot.html

General Information: Search by name or estate, this county or all counties at http://jportal.mdcourts.gov/willsandtrusts/index.jsf.

Washington County

Washington County Circuit Court Box 229, 24 Summit Ave, Hagerstown, MD 21741; 301-733-8660; criminal: 301-790-7941; civil: 301-790-4972; fax: 301-791-1151; 8AM-4:30PM (EST). *Felony, Misdemeanor, Civil Actions over $25,000.* www.mdcourts.gov/

General Information: Records prior to 1900 available at Maryland State Archives. Online identifiers in results same as on public terminal. No adoption, juvenile, sealed, expunged or mental records released. Will fax documents $3.00 up to 20 pages, then $.10 add'l page. Court makes copy: $.50 per page. Self serve copy: $.25 per page. Certification fee: $5.00 plus copy fee. Payee: Clerk of Circuit Court. No personal checks or credit cards accepted. Prepayment required.

Civil Name Search: Access: Online, in person. Visitors must perform in person searches themselves. Civil cases indexed by defendant. Civil records on case files, docket books to 1900; on computer back to 1985. Civil PAT goes back to 1996. The public access index for "Law and Criminal" go back to 1954. Search court records back to 1997 free at http://casesearch.courts.state.md.us/inquiry/inquiry-index.jsp. Some information "shielded" online but available on public access terminal.

Criminal Name Search: Access: In person, online. Visitors must perform in person searches themselves. Required to search: name, years to search; also helpful: DOB. Criminal records on case files, docket books to 1900; on computer back to 1985. Note: The complete case history is not always shown. Criminal PAT goes back to same as civil. The public access index for "Law and Criminal" go back to 1954. Search court records back to 1999 free at http://casesearch.courts.state.md.us/inquiry/inquiry-index.jsp. Online results show middle initial, DOB.

District Court 36 W Antietam St, Hagerstown, MD 21740; 800-945-1406, 240-420-4600; 8:30AM-4:30PM (EST). *Misdemeanor, Civil Actions under $25,000, Eviction, Small Claims.* www.mdcourts.gov/

General Information: No adoption, juvenile, sealed, expunged or mental records released. Will not fax documents. Court makes copy: $.50 per page. Certification fee: $5.00 per doc. Payee: District Court. Personal checks accepted. Major credit cards and debit cards accepted. Prepayment required. Mail requests: SASE required for civil.

Civil Name Search: Access: Phone, mail, online, in person. Both court and visitors may perform in person name searches. No search fee. Required to search: name, years to search; also helpful: address. Civil cases indexed by defendant. Civil records on computer from 1986, archived and on index books from 1971. Mail turnaround time 30 days. Civil PAT goes back to 1986. Free case look-up at http://casesearch.courts.state.md.us/inquiry/inquiry-index.jsp.

Criminal Name Search: Access: In person, online. Visitors must perform in person searches themselves. Required to search: name, years to search; also helpful: address, DOB, SSN, case number. Criminal records computerized from 1982, on index books from 1971. Criminal PAT goes back to 1982. Online access to criminal is same as civil, results show middle initial, DOB.

Register of Wills 24 Summit Ave, Rm 213, Courthouse, Hagerstown, MD 21740; 301-739-3612/3619, 888-739-0013 in MD; fax: 301-733-8636; 8:30AM-4:30PM (EST). *Probate.*
http://registers.maryland.gov/main/washington.html

General Information: Search by name or estate, this county or all counties at http://jportal.mdcourts.gov/willsandtrusts/index.jsf.

Wicomico County

1st Judicial Circuit Court PO Box 198, Salisbury, MD 21803-0198; 410-543-6551; fax: 410-546-8590; 8:30AM-4:30PM (EST). *Felony, Misdemeanor, Civil Actions over $25,000.*
www.mdcourts.gov/clerks/wicomico/index.html

General Information: The court will not do name searches. All requests must include a case number. All phone record requests must include case number. No adoption, juvenile, sealed, expunged or mental records released. Court makes copy: $.50 per page. Self serve copy: $.25 per page. Certification fee: $5.00, for exemplification $10.00. Payee: Clerk of Circuit Court. Personal checks accepted. Out of state checks not accepted. No credit cards accepted. Prepayment required.

Civil Name Search: Access: Online, in person. Visitors must perform in person searches themselves. Civil records on books since 1867, cases filed after 5/93 on computer. Note: Will permit phone request if case number

provided. Civil PAT goes back to 1993. Free case look-up at http://casesearch.courts.state.md.us/inquiry/inquiry-index.jsp.

Criminal Name Search: Access: Online, in person. Both court and visitors may perform in person name searches. Required to search: name, years to search; also helpful: DOB, SSN. Criminal docket on books since 1867, cases filed after 5/93 on computer. Note: Will permit phone request if case number provided. Criminal PAT goes back to same as civil. Free case look-up at http://casesearch.courts.state.md.us/inquiry/inquiry-index.jsp. Online results show middle initial, DOB.

District Court 201 Baptist St, Salisbury, MD 21801; 410-713-3500; 8:30AM-4:30PM (EST). *Misdemeanor, Civil Actions under $25,000, Eviction, Small Claims.* www.mdcourts.gov/

General Information: No adoption, juvenile, sealed, expunged or mental records released. Will not fax documents. Court makes copy: $.50 per page. Certification fee: $5.00. Payee: District Court. Personal checks accepted. Major credit and debit cards accepted. Prepayment required.

Civil Name Search: Access: Online, in person. Visitors must perform in person searches themselves. Required to search: name, years to search; also helpful: address. Civil records on computer go back to 1985, archived from 1984, on card index from 1971. Civil PAT goes back to 1982. Free case look-up at http://casesearch.courts.state.md.us/inquiry/inquiry-index.jsp.

Criminal Name Search: Access: Online, in person. Visitors must perform in person searches themselves. Required to search: name, years to search; also helpful: address, DOB. Criminal records go back to 1971; on computer back 1983. Note: Sometimes the DOB is provided on the public access terminal. Criminal PAT goes back to 1985. Online access to criminal is same as civil, results show middle initial, DOB.

Register of Wills 101 N Division St, Rm 102, Salisbury, MD 21801; 410-543-6635; fax: 410-334-3440; 8:30AM-4:30PM (EST). *Probate.* http://registers.maryland.gov/main/wicomico.html

General Information: Search by name or estate, this county or all counties at http://jportal.mdcourts.gov/willsandtrusts/index.jsf.

Worcester County

1st Judicial Circuit Court PO Box 40. Clerk of Circuit Court, 1 W Market St, Snow Hill, MD 21863; criminal phone: 410-632-5502; civil phone: 410-632-5501; 8:30AM-4:30PM (EST). *Felony, Misdemeanor, Civil Actions over $25,000.* www.mdcourts.gov/

General Information: No adoption, juvenile, sealed or expunged records released. Will not fax out case files. Court makes copy: $.50 per page. Self serve copy: $.25 per page. Certification fee: $5.00 per cert, exemplification fee is $10.00. Payee: Clerk of Circuit Court. Personal checks accepted. No credit cards accepted. Prepayment required.

Civil Name Search: Access: In person, online. Visitors must perform in person searches themselves. Civil cases indexed by defendant and plaintiff. Civil records indexed on computer since 7/93, on docket books prior. Civil PAT goes back to 1993. Free case look-up at http://casesearch.courts.state.md.us/inquiry/inquiry-index.jsp.

Criminal Name Search: Access: In person, online. Visitors must perform in person searches themselves. Criminal records indexed on computer since 7/93, on docket books prior. Criminal PAT goes back to same as civil. Online access to criminal is same as civil, results show middle initial, DOB.

District Court 301 Commerce St, Snow Hill, MD 21863-1007; 800-941-0282, 410-219-7830; fax: 410-219-7840; 8:30AM-4:30PM (EST). *Misdemeanor, Civil Actions under $30,000, Eviction, Small Claims.* www.mdcourts.gov/

General Information: No sealed or juvenile records released. Court makes copy: $.50 per page. Certification fee: $5.00 per page. Payee: District Court. Personal checks accepted. Major credit cards accepted with fee. Prepayment required. Mail requests: SASE required for mail return of any copies.

Civil Name Search: Access: Online, in person. Visitors must perform in person searches themselves. Required to search: name, years to search; also helpful: address. Civil cases indexed by defendant. Civil records on computer since 1988. Note: Records can be researched via books in the lobby. Civil PAT goes back to 1993. Free case look-up at http://casesearch.courts.state.md.us/inquiry/inquiry-index.jsp.

Criminal Name Search: Access: Online, in person. Visitors must perform in person searches themselves. Required to search: name, years to search; also helpful: address, DOB. Criminal records on computer since 1982. Note: Records can be researched via books or terminal in the lobby. Criminal PAT goes back to same as civil. Online access to criminal is same as civil, results show middle initial, DOB.

Register of Wills 1 W Market St, Rm 102, Courthouse, Snow Hill, MD 21863-1074; 410-632-1529, 888-256-0047 in MD; fax: 410-632-5600; 8:30AM-4:30PM (EST). *Probate.*
http://registers.maryland.gov/main/worcester.html

General Information: Search by name or estate, this county or all counties at http://jportal.mdcourts.gov/willsandtrusts/index.jsf.

Massachusetts

Time Zone:	**EST**
Capital:	**Boston, Suffolk County**
# of Counties:	**14**
State Web:	**www.mass.gov**
Court Web:	**www.mass.gov/courts**

Administration

Chief Justice for Administration and Management, 2 Center Plaza, Room 540, Boston, MA, 02108; 617-742-8575, Fax: 617-742-0968.

The Supreme and Appellate Court

The Supreme Judicial Court is the court of last resort. Search the Appeals Court docket and calendar at www.ma-appellatecourts.org/index.php. Appellate Courts and Supreme Court opinions are available at http://massreports.com/.

The Massachusetts Courts

Department	Type	How Organized	Jurisdiction Highpoints
Superior*	General	20 Courts in 14 Counties	Felony, Civil Actions over $25,000
District*	Special	62 Courts in 59 Geographic Divisions	Felony, Misdemeanor, Civil, Small Claims, Eviction, Domestic Relations, Juvenile
Boston Municipal *	General	8 Courts in 8 Divisions	Felony, Misdemeanor, Civil, Small Claims, Eviction, Domestic Relations, Juvenile
Housing*	General	9 Courts in 6 Divisions	Felony, Misdemeanor, Civil, Small Claims, Eviction
Probate and Family*	General and Limited	17 Courts in 14 Divisions	Estate, Domestic Relations
Juvenile	Special	41 Courts in 11 Divisions	Juvenile
Land	Special	1 Court	Real Estate

* = profiled in this book

Details on the Court Structure

The Massachusetts Trial Court is organized by "Departments" and within each department there are "Divisions." The **Superior Court** has concurrent civil jurisdiction with the **District** and **Boston Municipal Court** departments; however, most plaintiffs seeking damages of $25,000 or less file in the District, the **Boston Municipal Court**, or the **Housing Court**. District, Boston Municipal, and Housing Court departments resolve small claims matters which are $7,500 or less.

Criminal jurisdiction in the District and Boston Municipal Court departments extend to all city and town ordinances, all misdemeanors, all felonies punishable by a sentence up to five years, as well as other specifically enumerated felonies carrying greater potential penalties.

Eviction cases may be filed at a county District Court or at the regional "**Housing Court.**" A case may be moved from a District Court to a Housing Court, but never the reverse. Housing Courts also hear misdemeanor *Code Violation* cases and prelims for these. There are six Housing Court Regions - Boston (Suffolk County), Worcester (Worcester County and 5 towns from Middlesex and Norfolk), Southeast (Plymouth and Bristol Counties), Northeast (Essex County and parts of Middlesex County), and Western (Berkshire, Franklin, Hampden and Hampshire Counties). The Southeast Housing Court has three branches - Brockton, Fall River, and New Bedford.

There is one **Probate and Family Court** per county, but several counties have additional full sessions and satellite office locations – including Essex, Bristol Middlesex, and Plymouth.

Circuit Courts have original jurisdiction in all civil and criminal matters within the state, including probate, juvenile, and some traffic matters, as well as civil and criminal jury trials. The Clerk of Court is the record custodian.

The majority of **Municipal Court** cases involve traffic and ordinance matters.

Probate filing is a function of the Circuit Court; however, each county has a **Register in Probate** who maintains and manages the probate records, guardianship, and mental health records.

Record Searching Facts You Need to Know

Fees and Record Searching Tips

Massachusetts courts attest or confirm document; a certificate is a separate authentication page with a gold seal. Since July 2003, the state mandated the this fee at $2.50 per page (includes copy fee) and the copy fee at $1.00 per page for all Superior and District Courts. Most but not all courts follow this schedule.

Online Access is Limited

Online access to records is on the statewide Trial Courts Information Center website with both criminal and civil superior court cases, BUT the site is ONLY available to attorneys and law firms. Visit www.ma-trialcourts.org/tcic/welcome.jsp. Access is free but the BBO number is a requisite. Middlesex, Suffolk, Worcester indices go back to 1990s; other counties go back to active cases as of 2000-2001. For more information contact Victoria Palmarcci at victoria.palmacci@jud.state.ma.us. Site is updated daily.

Barnstable County

Superior Court 3195 Main St, PO Box 425, Barnstable, MA 02630; 508-375-6684; criminal fax: 508-362-1658; civil fax: 8:30AM-4:30PM; 8:30AM-4:30PM (EST). *Felony, Civil Actions over $25,000.*

General Information: Their public access terminal is connected to the statewide Superior Court system. Call court to recommend document retriever who can perform search for you. Court personnel often refuse to respond to questions. No victims names released. Will not fax out case files. Court makes copy: $1.00 per page. Self serve copy: $.50 per page. Certification fee: $2.50. Payee: Barnstable Superior Court. Business checks not accepted. No credit cards accepted. Prepayment required. Mail requests: SASE required for mail return of any copies.

Civil Name Search: Access: In person, online. Visitors must perform in person searches themselves. Required to search: name, years to search; also helpful: address. Civil records on computer back to 1/2001; on index cards from 1985 and books from 1830s. Civil PAT goes back to 1995. Online only for attorneys and law firms at www.ma-trialcourts.org/tcic/.

Criminal Name Search: Access: In person, online. Visitors must perform in person searches themselves. Required to search: name, years to search, DOB; also helpful: address, SSN. Criminal records computerized from 1975; books from 1830s. Criminal PAT goes back to 1975. Online for attorneys and law firms only with registration at www.ma-trialcourts.org/tcic/.

Barnstable District Court PO Box 427, Route 6A, Barnstable, MA 02630; 508-375-6600; criminal phone: 508-375-6776; civil phone: 508-375-6785; fax: 508-362-0213; 8:30AM-4:30PM (EST). *Felony, Misdemeanor, Civil, Eviction, Small Claims.*

General Information: Includes Barnstable, Yarmouth, and Sandwich. No impounded records released. Will not fax documents. Court makes copy: $1.00 per page. Certification fee: $2.50 includes copy fee. Payee: District Court. Only cashiers checks and money orders accepted. No credit cards accepted. Prepayment required. Mail requests: SASE required.

Civil Name Search: Access: Phone, mail, in person. Both court and visitors may perform in person name searches. No search fee. Civil records indexed on computer; older on cards and docket books. Mail turnaround time 1-2 weeks. Public use terminal has civil records back to 2003.

Criminal Name Search: Access: Mail, in person. Both court and visitors may perform in person name searches. No search fee. Required to search: name, years to search, DOB. Criminal records on computer since 1996; prior records on index cards and docket books. Mail turnaround time 1-2 weeks.

Falmouth District Court 161 Jones Rd, Falmouth, MA 02540; 508-495-1500; criminal phone: x225; civil phone: x230; fax: 508-495-0992; 8:30AM-4:30PM (EST). *Felony, Misdemeanor, Civil, Eviction, Small Claims.*

General Information: Includes Falmouth, Mashpee, and Bourne. No impounded records released. Will not fax documents. Court makes copy: $1.00 per page. Certification fee: $2.50. Cert fee includes copies. Payee: Falmouth District Court. Personal checks accepted. No credit cards accepted. Prepayment required.

Civil Name Search: Access: Phone, in person. Only the court performs in person name searches; visitors may not. No search fee. Civil records computerized since 1996.

Criminal Name Search: Access: Phone, in person. Only the court performs in person name searches; visitors may not. No search fee. Criminal records computerized since 1996.

Orleans District Court 237 Rock Harbor Rd, Orleans, MA 02653; 508-255-4700/1; fax: 508-240-5024; 8:30AM-4:30PM (EST). *Felony, Misdemeanor, Civil, Eviction, Small Claims.*

General Information: Includes Brewster, Chatham, Dennis, Eastham, Orleans, Truro, Wellfleet, Harwich, and Provincetown. No impounded records released. Will not fax documents. Court makes copy: $1.00 per page. Certification fee: $2.50. Payee: Orleans District Court. Personal checks accepted. No credit cards accepted. Prepayment required.

Civil Name Search: Access: In person only. Visitors must perform in person searches themselves. Civil records kept in storage from 1978. Some prior records destroyed. Public use terminal has civil records.

Criminal Name Search: Access: In person only. Visitors must perform in person searches themselves. Criminal records kept in storage from 1978. Some prior records destroyed.

Probate & Family Court PO Box 346, 3195 Main St, Route 6A, Barnstable, MA 02630; 508-375-6710; fax: 508-362-3662; 8:30AM-4PM (EST). *Probate.* http://barnstablecountypfc.com/

Berkshire County

Superior Court 76 East St, Pittsfield, MA 01201; 413-499-7487; fax: 413-442-9190; 8:30AM-4:30PM (EST). *Felony, Civil Actions over $25,000.*

General Information: No impounded records released. Will not fax documents. Court makes copy: $1.00 per page. Certification fee: $2.50 per document. Payee: Berkshire Superior Court. Personal checks accepted. No credit cards accepted. Prepayment required. Mail requests: SASE required.

Civil Name Search: Access: Mail, online. Both court and visitors may perform in person name searches. No search fee. Civil index on cards from 1900s, on computer back to 2000. Mail turnaround time 3-4 weeks. Civil PAT goes back to 2000. Sometimes DOB is shown, but not often. Only attorneys and law firms may access records online after registration at www.ma-trialcourts.org/tcic/.

Criminal Name Search: Access: Mail, in person, online. Both court and visitors may perform in person name searches. No search fee. Criminal records indexed on cards from 1900s, on computer back to 2000. Note: Because their index does not contain DOBs or SSNs, they cannot verify the subject, thus they recommend you contact the Criminal History Board in Boston, MA. Mail turnaround time 3-4 weeks. Criminal PAT available. Sometimes DOB is shown, otherwise searcher must review probation records. Only attorneys and law firms may access records online after registration at www.ma-trialcourts.org/tcic/.

Northern Berkshire District Court #28 111 Holden St, North Adams, MA 01247; 413-663-5339; fax: 413-664-7209; 8AM-4:30PM (EST). *Felony, Misdemeanor, Civil, Eviction, Small Claims.*

General Information: Handles cases for Adams, Cheshire, Clarksburg, Florida, Hancock, New Ashford, North Adams, Savoy, Williamstown, and Windsor. Exercises concurrent jurisdiction over Hancock and Windsor with the Pittsfield Division. Includes cases from closed Court #30. No impounded records released. Will fax documents to local or toll free line. Court makes copy: $1.00 per page. Certification fee: $2.50. Payee: District Court. Business checks accepted. Credit cards accepted in person. Prepayment required. Mail requests: SASE required.

Civil Name Search: Access: Fax, mail, in person. Only the court performs in person name searches; visitors may not. No search fee. Civil index on cards from 1983, docket books to 1900. Mail turnaround time 1-2 weeks. Public use terminal has civil records back to 2004.

Criminal Name Search: Access: Fax, mail, in person. Only the court performs in person name searches; visitors may not. No search fee. Required to search: name, years to search, DOB, and SSN if available. Criminal records indexed on cards from 1983, docket books to 1900. Mail turnaround time 1-2 weeks.

Pittsfield District Court #27 24 Wendell Ave, Pittsfield, MA 01201; criminal phone: 413-442-5468; civil phone: 413-499-0558; criminal fax: 413-499-7327; civil fax: 8:30AM-4:30PM; 8:30AM-4:30PM (EST). *Felony, Misdemeanor, Civil, Eviction, Small Claims.*

General Information: Includes Dalton, Hinsdale, Lanesborough, Peru, Pittsfield, Richmond, and Washington. This court exercises concurrent jurisdiction over Hancock and Windsor with the North Berkshire Div. and over Becket and Lenox with Southern Berkshire Div. No juvenile or sealed records released. Will fax documents $1.00 per page. Court makes copy: $1.00 per page. Self serve copy: same. Certification fee: $2.50 per page. Payee: Pittsfield District Court. Personal checks accepted. No credit cards accepted. Prepayment required. Mail requests: SASE required.

Civil Name Search: Access: Phone, mail, in person. Both court and visitors may perform in person name searches. No search fee. Civil index on docket books and in recent years in the computer. Mail turnaround time 1-2 weeks. Public use terminal has civil records back to 2001.

Criminal Name Search: Access: Phone, mail, in person. Both court and visitors may perform in person name searches. No search fee. Required to search: name, years to search; DOB. Criminal docket on books and in recent years in the computer. Mail turnaround time 1-2 weeks.

Southern Berkshire District Court 9 Gilmore Ave, Great Barrington, MA 01230; 413-528-3520; fax: 413-528-0757; 8:30AM-4:30PM (EST). *Felony, Misdemeanor, Civil, Eviction, Small Claims.*

General Information: Includes Alford, Becket, Egremont, Great Barrington, Lee, Lenox, Monterey, Mt. Washington, New Marlborough, Otis, Sandisfield, Sheffield, Stockbridge, Tyringham, and West Stockbridge. Shares jurisdiction of Becket and Lenox with Pittsfield Dist. Court. No juvenile, impounded records released. Will not fax documents. Court makes copy: $1.00 per page. Self serve copy: same. Certification fee: $2.50 per cert. Payee: District Court. Personal checks accepted. No credit cards accepted. Prepayment required. Mail requests: SASE required.

Civil Name Search: Access: Fax, mail, in person. Both court and visitors may perform in person name searches. No search fee. Court will only perform search if given the docket number. Civil index on cards from 1984, docket books to 1900. Mail turnaround time 1-2 weeks. Public use terminal available.

Criminal Name Search: Access: Fax, mail, in person. Both court and visitors may perform in person name searches. No search fee. Required to search: name, years to search, DOB. Criminal records indexed on cards from 1984, docket books to 1900. Note: Court will only do search if given docket number. Mail turnaround time 1-2 weeks. Public use terminal available.

Probate & Family Court 44 Bank Row, Pittsfield, MA 01201; 413-442-6941; fax: 413-443-3430; 8:30AM-4PM (EST). *Probate, Domestic, Adoptions.*

Western Housing Court , MA; . *Eviction, Misdemeanor (Code Violations), Small Claims.*

General Information: See Hampden County Western Housing Court. This court handles many housing code cases, real estate-related small claims and eviction cases for this county; also see district courts in this county.

Bristol County

Superior Court - Taunton 9 Court St, Taunton, MA 02780; 508-823-6588 x1; 8AM-4:30PM (EST). *Felony, Civil Actions over $25,000.*

General Information: No impounded records released. Will not fax documents. Court makes copy: $1.00 per page. Certification fee: $2.50 per cert. Payee: Clerk of Superior Court of Bristol County. Personal checks accepted. No credit cards accepted. Prepayment required.

Civil Name Search: Access: Mail, in person, online. Both court and visitors may perform in person name searches. No search fee. Civil records on computer link to Boston from 1985, index books from 1935. Mail turnaround time 2 weeks. Civil PAT goes back to 1980. Online only for attorneys and law firms at www.ma-trialcourts.org/tcic/.

Criminal Name Search: Access: Mail, in person, online. Both court and visitors may perform in person name searches. No search fee. Required to search: name, years to search; also helpful: DOB. Criminal records on computer link to Boston from 1985, index books from 1935. Mail turnaround time 2 weeks. Criminal PAT goes back to 2000. Online for attorneys and law firms only with registration at www.ma-trialcourts.org/tcic/.

Attleboro District Court 34 Courthouse, 88 N Main St, Attleboro, MA 02703; 508-222-5900; criminal phone: x390; civil phone: x392; fax: 508-226-3916; 8AM-4:30PM (EST). *Felony, Misdemeanor, Civil, Eviction, Small Claims.*
www.mass.gov/courts/courtsandjudges/courts/attleborodistrictmain.html

General Information: Includes Attleboro, Mansfield, North Attleboro, and Norton. No impounded records released. Will not fax documents. Court makes copy: $1.00 per page. Certification fee: $2.50. Payee: District Court, Attleboro District Court. Business checks accepted. Visa/MC accepted. Prepayment required.

Civil Name Search: Access: Phone, mail, in person. Only the court performs in person name searches; visitors may not. No search fee. Civil records on computer since 1995; prior records on index cards from 1983, docket books from 1900. Mail turnaround time 1-2 weeks.

Criminal Name Search: Access: Phone, mail, in person. Only the court performs in person name searches; visitors may not. No search fee. Required to search: name, years to search, DOB, SSN. Criminal records on computer since 1995; prior records on index cards from 1983, docket books from 1900. Mail turnaround time 1-2 weeks.

Fall River District Court 186 South Main Street, Fall River, MA 02721; 508-491-3200; criminal phone: 508-491-3225; civil phone: 508-491-3235; criminal fax: 508-646-3596; civil fax: 8:30AM-4:30PM; 8:30AM-4:30PM (EST). *Felony, Misdemeanor, Civil, Eviction, Small Claims.*
www.mass.gov/courts/courtsandjudges/courts/fallriverdistrict.html

General Information: Includes Fall River, Freetown, Somerset, Swansea, and Westport. No sealed, minor, confidential address records released. Fee to fax document $.50 per page. Court makes copy: $1.00 per page. Certification fee: $2.50 per page. Payee: District Court. Only cashiers checks and money orders accepted. No credit cards accepted. Prepayment required.

Civil Name Search: Access: In person only. Both court and visitors may perform in person name searches. No search fee. Civil records on index on computer from 2004, on card files prior and are archived or destroyed. Note: Office may do search; they are short-staffed and may not be able.

Criminal Name Search: Access: In person only. Both court and visitors may perform in person name searches. No search fee. Required to search: name, years to search, DOB or SSN. Criminal records on index on computer from 2000. Go to Probate to locate crims before 2000. Note: Office may do search; they are short-staffed and may not be able.

New Bedford District Court 33 75 N 6th St, New Bedford, MA 02740; 508-999-9700; criminal phone: 508-990-9353; civil phone: 508-990-9351; fax: 508-990-8094; 8AM-4:30PM (EST). *Felony, Misdemeanor, Civil, Eviction, Small Claims.*

General Information: Includes Acushnet, Dartmouth, Fairhaven, and New Bedford. Small claims phone: 508-990-9333. No impounded records released. Will not fax documents. Court makes copy: $1.00 per page. Certification fee: $2.50 per cert. Payee: New Bedford District Court. Business checks accepted. No credit cards accepted. Prepayment required. Mail requests: SASE required.

Civil Name Search: Access: Mail, in person. Visitors must perform in person searches themselves. No search fee. Civil records filed from 1989, prior on docket books; on computer back to 1995. Public use terminal has civil records back to 2004 (Bascot System).

Criminal Name Search: Access: Mail, in person, fax. Visitors must perform in person searches themselves. No search fee. Required to search: name, years to search, DOB; also helpful: SSN. Criminal records filed from 1989, prior on docket books; on computer back to 1999. Note: Searches are limited to pending charges; this agency recommends searching elsewhere for closed case files. Mail turnaround time 1-2 weeks.

Taunton District Court 120 Cohannet St, Taunton, MA 02780; 508-977-6000; fax: 508-824-2282; 8AM-4:30PM (EST). *Felony, Misdemeanor, Civil, Eviction, Small Claims.*

General Information: Includes Berkley, Dighton, Easton, Raynham, Rehoboth, Seekonk, and Taunton. Mental health records restricted. Will fax documents. Court makes copy: $1.00 per page. Certification fee: $2.50. Payee: District Court. Personal checks not accepted. Major credit cards accepted in person only. Prepayment required.

Civil Name Search: Access: Phone, mail, fax, in person. Only the court performs in person name searches; visitors may not. No search fee. Civil index on cards for 6 years. In person searchers must drop-off search request.

Criminal Name Search: Access: Phone, mail, in person. Visitors must perform in person searches themselves. No search fee. Required to search:

name, years to search, DOB. Criminal records indexed on cards for 6 year. Mail turnaround time 1-2 days.

New Bedford Probate & Family Court 505 Pleasant St, New Bedford, MA 02740; 508-999-5249; fax: 508-999-1211; 8AM-1PM; 2PM-4:30PM (EST). *Probate.*
www.mass.gov/courts/courtsandjudges/courts/bristolprobmain.html

Probate & Family Court 21 Father DeValles Blvd, Fall River, MA 02780; 508-672-4669; fax: 508-672-0043; 9AM-4PM,M-TH, 8:30AM-4PM F (EST). *Probate, Domestic Relations.*
www.mass.gov/courts/courtsandjudges/courts/bristolprobmain.html
General Information: There are satellite offices in New Bedford (508-999-5249), and one on Rock Street in Fall River (508-672-17510).

Southeast Housing Court - Fall River 289 Rock St., 2nd FL, Fall River, MA 02720; 508-677-1505; fax: 508-672-9621; 8:30AM-4:30PM (EST). *Eviction, Misdemeanor (Code Violations), Small Claims.*
www.mass.gov/courts/courtsandjudges/courts/southeasthousingmain.html
General Information: Also known as Fall River Trial Court. Includes housing code cases, real estate-related small claims, and many eviction cases for Bristol County except the New Bedford area; also see district courts.

Southeast Housing Court - New Bedford 139 Hathaway Rd, New Bedford, MA 02740; 508-994-0156; 8:30AM-4:30PM M,F (EST). *Eviction, Misdemeanor (Code Violations), Small Claims.*
www.mass.gov/courts/courtsandjudges/courts/southeasthousingmain.html
General Information: Open Mondays and Fridays only. Includes many code, real estate-related small claims, and eviction cases for the New Bedford area only; also see area district court.

Dukes County

Superior Court PO Box 1267, Edgartown, MA 02539; 508-627-4668; 8AM-4PM (EST). *Felony, Civil Actions over $25,000.*
General Information: No sealed records released. Will not fax documents. Court makes copy: $1.00 per page. Certification fee: $2.50 per page of document. Payee: Clerk of Superior Court. Personal checks accepted. No credit cards accepted. Prepayment required. Mail requests: SASE required.
Civil Name Search: Access: Mail, in person, online. Both court and visitors may perform in person name searches. No search fee. Civil index on cards from 1976 and books from 1695. Mail turnaround time 1-2 days. Online only for attorneys and law firms at www.ma-trialcourts.org/tcic/.
Criminal Name Search: Access: Mail, in person, online. Both court and visitors may perform in person name searches. No search fee. Criminal records indexed on cards from 1976 and books from 1695. Mail turnaround time 1-2 days. Online for attorneys and law firms only with registration at www.ma-trialcourts.org/tcic/.

Edgartown District Court PO Box 1284, 81 Main St, Courthouse, Edgartown, MA 02539-1284; 508-627-3751; fax: 508-627-7070; 8:30AM-4:30PM (EST). *Felony, Misdemeanor, Civil, Eviction, Small Claims.*
www.mass.gov/courts/courtsandjudges/courts/edgartowndistrictmain.html
General Information: Includes Edgartown, Oak Bluffs, Tisbury, West Tisbury, Aquinnah (formerly Gay Head), Gosnold, and Elizabeth Islands. No sealed records released. Will not fax out documents. Court makes copy: $1.00 per page. Certification fee: $2.50 includes copy fee. Payee: District Court. No personal checks accepted. Visa/MC accepted in person only. Prepayment required.
Civil Name Search: Access: In person only. Visitors must perform in person searches themselves. Civil index on cards from 1990, docket books to 2006. Note: The public may view paper index of files to 1990.
Criminal Name Search: Access: In person only. Both court and visitors may perform in person name searches. No search fee. Required to search: name, years to search, DOB; SSN helpful. Criminal records indexed on cards from 1990, docket books to 2006. Note: The public may view paper index of files to 1990.

Probate & Family Court PO Box 237, 81 Main St, #104, 1st Fl, Edgartown, MA 02539; 508-627-4703; fax: 508-627-7664; 8:30AM-4:30PM (EST). *Probate, Domestic Relations.*
www.mass.gov/courts/courtsandjudges/courts/dukesprobmain.html
General Information: Also holds change of names, partitions, sales of real estate, and equity records in this court.

Essex County

Superior Court - Salem 34 Federal St, Salem, MA 01970; 978-744-5500; criminal phone: x8; civil phone: x6; fax: 978-741-0691; 8AM-4:30PM (EST). *Felony, Civil Actions over $25,000.*
www.mass.gov/courts/courtsandjudges/courts/essexsupmain.html
General Information: Impounded cases are not released. Will not fax out documents. Court makes copy: $1.00 per page side. Certification fee: $2.00 per cert plus $1.00 copy fee. Payee: Clerk of Superior Court. Personal checks accepted. No credit cards accepted. Prepayment required. Mail requests: SASE requested.

Civil Name Search: Access: Mail, in person, online. Visitors must perform in person searches themselves. No search fee. Civil records are entered on computer for civil actions from all three Superior courts in this county. Computer records go back to 1985, older records on docket books. Civil PAT goes back to 1985. Online access for attorneys and law firms only with registration at www.ma-trialcourts.org/tcic/.
Criminal Name Search: Access: In person, online. Visitors must perform in person searches themselves. Criminal computer records go back to 1985, older records on docket books. Criminal PAT goes back to 2000. Online access for attorneys and law firms only with registration at www.ma-trialcourts.org/tcic/.

Superior Court - Lawrence 43 Appleton Way, Lawrence, MA 01840; 978-687-7463 x4; fax: 978-687-7869; 8AM-4:30PM (EST). *Civil Actions over $25,000.*
General Information: Index cards records prior to 1985 are found in the Salem office; criminal records also in Salem Court. No impounded records released. Will fax documents back. Court makes copy: $1.00 per page. Certification fee: $2.50 per cert. Payee: Clerk of Superior Court. Personal checks accepted. No credit cards accepted. Prepayment required.
Civil Name Search: Access: In person, online. Both court and visitors may perform in person name searches. No search fee. Civil records on computer since 1985; prior records on index cards in Salem office. Public use terminal has civil records back to 10 years. Online only for attorneys and law firms at www.ma-trialcourts.org/tcic/.

Superior Court - Newburyport 145 High St, Newburyport, MA 01950; 978-462-4474; fax: 978-462-0432; 8AM-4:30PM (EST). *Felony, Civil Actions over $25,000.*
www.mass.gov/courts/courtsandjudges/courts/essexsupmain.html
General Information: All finished criminal record files are in Salem and civil case records Session A in Salem, Session B in Newburyport and Session C & D in Lawrence. This court suggest to search at the main office in Salem. No impounded records released. Court makes copy: $1.00 per page. Certification fee: $2.50 per cert. Payee: Clerk of Superior Court. Personal checks accepted. No credit cards accepted. Prepayment required.
Civil Name Search: Access: Mail, in person, online. Both court and visitors may perform in person name searches. No search fee. Civil records on computer back to 1988. Online only for attorneys and law firms at www.ma-trialcourts.org/tcic/.
Criminal Name Search: Access: In person, online. Visitors must perform in person searches themselves. Note: The court will not perform criminal name searches for the public. Online for attorneys and law firms only with registration at www.ma-trialcourts.org/tcic/.

Gloucester District Court 197 Main St, Gloucester, MA 01930; 978-283-2620 x4; fax: 978-283-8784; 8:30AM-4:30PM (EST). *Felony, Misdemeanor, Civil, Eviction, Small Claims.*
www.mass.gov/courts/courtsandjudges/courts/gloucesterdistrictmain.html
General Information: Includes Essex, Gloucester, and Rockport. No juvenile records released. Will not fax documents. Court makes copy: $1.00 per page. Certification fee: $2.50 per cert/page. Payee: Gloucester District Court. Personal checks accepted. No credit cards accepted. Prepayment required.
Civil Name Search: Access: Mail, fax, in person. Visitors must perform in person searches themselves. No search fee. Required to search: name, years to search; also helpful: DOB. Civil records go back to 1975. Public use terminal has civil records back to 2003.
Criminal Name Search: Access: In person only. Visitors must perform in person searches themselves. Required to search: name, years to search; also helpful: DOB. Criminal records go back to 1975.

Haverhill District Court PO Box 1389, Haverhill, MA 01831; 978-373-4151; fax: 978-521-6886; 8:30AM-4:30PM (EST). *Felony, Misdemeanor, Civil, Eviction, Small Claims.*
General Information: Includes Boxford, Bradford, Georgetown, Groveland, and Haverhill. No juvenile, sealed cases, confidential records released. Will fax documents to local or toll-free number. Court makes copy: $1.00 per page. Certification fee: $2.50. Payee: Commonwealth of mass. No personal checks or credit cards accepted. Prepayment required. Mail requests: SASE required.
Civil Name Search: Access: Phone, fax, mail, in person. Both court and visitors may perform in person name searches. No search fee. Civil index on cards from 1983. Non-active in storage. Mail turnaround time 1-2 weeks. Public use terminal has civil records.
Criminal Name Search: Access: Phone, fax, mail, in person. Only the court performs in person name searches; visitors may not. No search fee. Required to search: name, years to search; also helpful: DOB. Criminal records indexed on cards from 1992, computerized since 2000. Non-active in storage. Mail turnaround time 1-2 weeks.

Ipswich District Court 188 State St, Newburyport, MA 01950; 978-462-2652; fax: 978-462-5641; 8:30AM-4:30PM (EST). *Felony, Misdemeanor, Civil, Eviction, Small Claims.*

General Information: Includes Hamilton, Ipswich, Topsfield, and Wenham. No juvenile records released. Will not fax documents. Court makes copy: $1.00 per page. Certification fee: $2.50 per page. Payee: District Court. Personal checks accepted. No credit cards accepted. Prepayment required.
Civil Name Search: Access: In person, mail. Visitors must perform in person searches themselves. No search fee. Civil index on cards and computer, small claims from 1984, civil from 1964. Civil on docket books from 1970. Public use terminal has civil records.
Criminal Name Search: Access: In person, mail. Visitors must perform in person searches themselves. No search fee. Required to search: name, years to search; also helpful: DOB. Criminal records indexed on cards from 1979.

Lawrence District Court 2 Appleton St., Lawrence, MA 01840; 978-687-7184; criminal phone: x1; civil phone: x2; criminal fax: 978-687-0794; civil fax: 8AM-4:30PM; 8AM-4:30PM (EST). *Felony, Misdemeanor, Civil, Eviction, Small Claims.*
www.mass.gov/courts/courtsandjudges/courts/lawrencedistrictmain.html
General Information: Includes Andover, Lawrence, Methuen, and North Andover. No medical, police reports, impounded, juvenile records released. Will not fax documents. Court makes copy: $1.00 per page. Certification fee: $2.50 per page includes copy fee. Payee: District Court. Personal checks and credit cards accepted. Prepayment required. Mail requests: SASE requested for criminal.
Civil Name Search: Access: In person only. Visitors must perform in person searches themselves. Civil index on cards from 1983, docket books from 1900, on computer since 1990. Public use terminal has civil records.
Criminal Name Search: Access: Mail, in person. Both court and visitors may perform in person name searches. No search fee. Required to search: name, years to search, DOB; also helpful: address, SSN. Criminal records indexed on cards from 1983, docket books from 1900, on computer since 1999. Mail turnaround time 1-2 weeks.

Lynn District Court 580 Essex St, Lynn, MA 01901; 781-598-5200; fax: 781-598-4350; 8AM-4:30PM (EST). *Felony, Misdemeanor, Civil, Eviction, Small Claims.*
www.mass.gov/courts/courtsandjudges/courts/lynndistrictmain.html
General Information: Includes Lynn, Marblehead, Nahant, Saugus, Swampscott. No juvenile, impounded or sealed records released. Will not fax documents. Court makes copy: $1.00 per page. Certification fee: $2.50 per cert. Payee: Lynn District Court. Personal checks accepted. Major credit cards accepted in person only. Prepayment required. Mail requests: SASE required.
Civil Name Search: Access: Mail, in person. Visitors must perform in person searches themselves. No search fee. Civil index on cards from 1983, docket books from approx 1900. Records older than 15 years are difficult to find and may take longer. Public use terminal has civil records back to 2001.
Criminal Name Search: Access: Mail, in person. Visitors must perform in person searches themselves. No search fee. Required to search: name, years to search; also helpful: DOB, SSN. Criminal records computerized from 1997, on index cards from 1983, docket books from approx 1900. Records older than 15 years are difficult to find an. Mail turnaround time 5 days.

Newburyport District Court 22 188 State St, Newburyport, MA 01950; 978-462-2652; fax: 978-463-0438; 8:30AM-4:30PM (EST). *Felony, Misdemeanor, Civil, Eviction, Small Claims.*
General Information: Includes Amesbury, Merrimac, Newbury, Newburyport, Rowley, Salisbury, and West Newbury. No juvenile or impounded records released. Will fax documents to local or toll-free number. Court makes copy: $1.00 per page. Certification fee: $2.50 per cert; exemplification is $50.00. Payee: District Court. Personal checks and credit cards accepted. Prepayment required.
Civil Name Search: Access: Mail, in person. Both court and visitors may perform in person name searches. No search fee. Civil index on cards from 1983. Mail turnaround time 1-2 weeks. Civil PAT goes back to 1996.
Criminal Name Search: Access: Mail, in person. Both court and visitors may perform in person name searches. No search fee. Required to search: name, years to search, DOB. Criminal records indexed on cards from 1983. Mail turnaround time 1-2 weeks. Criminal PAT goes back to same as civil.

Peabody District Court 86 1 Lowell St, Courthouse, Peabody, MA 01960; 978-532-3100; fax: 978-531-8524; 8:30AM-4:30PM (EST). *Felony, Misdemeanor, Civil, Eviction, Small Claims.*
www.mass.gov/courts/courtsandjudges/courts/peabodydistrictmain.html
General Information: Includes Lynnfield and Peabody. No juvenile or impounded records released. Will not fax out documents. Court makes copy: $1.00 per page. Certification fee: $2.50 per cert/page. Payee: District Court. No personal checks accepted. Visa/MC accepted in person only, not over phone. Prepayment required.

Civil Name Search: Access: In person only. Visitors must perform in person searches themselves. Civil records stored in office for 10 years, prior stored in basement and are difficult to find. Public use terminal has civil records back to 2003.
Criminal Name Search: Access: Mail, in person. Visitors must perform in person searches themselves. No search fee. Required to search: name, years to search, DOB. Criminal records stored in office for 10 years, prior stored in basement and are difficult to find. Note: Will do mail search for 1 name only.

Salem District Court 36 65 Washington St, Salem, MA 01970; 978-744-1167; fax: 978-744-3211; 8:30AM-4:30PM (EST). *Felony, Misdemeanor, Civil, Eviction, Small Claims.*
www.mass.gov/courts/courtsandjudges/courts/salemdistrictmain.html
General Information: Includes Beverly, Danvers, Manchester by the Sea, Middleton, and Salem. No juvenile or impounded records released. Will not fax out documents. Court makes copy: $1.00 per page. Certification fee: $2.50. Payee: District Court. No Personal checks and credit cards accepted. Prepayment required.
Civil Name Search: Access: In person only. Visitors must perform in person searches themselves. Civil index on cards and docket books. Note: Visitors must perform in person searches Thursday or Friday 2-4:30PM Civil PAT goes back to 2003.
Criminal Name Search: Access: In person. Visitors must perform in person searches themselves. Required to search: name, years to search, DOB, SSN. Criminal records indexed on cards and docket books 1998 to present. Note: In person criminal searches on Thursday or Friday 2-4:30PM. Criminal PAT goes back to same as civil.

Northeast Housing Court 2 Appleton St, Fenton Judicial Ctr, Lawrence, MA 01840; 978-689-7833; 8:30AM-4:30PM (EST). *Eviction, Misdemeanor, Code Violations, Housing, Small Claims.*
www.mass.gov/courts/courtsandjudges/courts/northeasthousingmain.html
General Information: Includes Middlesex County towns Acton, Ayer, Billerica, Boxborough, Carlisle, Chelmsford, Concord, Dracut, Dunstable, Groton, Littleton, Lowell, Maynard, Pepperell, Shirley, Stow, Tewksbury, Tyngsboro, and Westford. District courts have same case types.

Probate & Family Court 36 Federal St, Salem, MA 01970; 978-744-1020; probate phone: x5; fax: 978-741-2957; 8:30AM-4:30PM (EST). *Probate, Domestic Relations.*
General Information: There is a satellite office in Lawrence (978-975-2429).

Franklin County

Superior Court PO Box 1573, 425 Main St, Greenfield, MA 01302; 413-774-5535; fax: 413-774-4770; 8:30AM-4:30PM (EST). *Felony, Civil Actions over $25,000.*
General Information: No impounded or juvenile records released. Will fax documents for $1.00 per page (name) if pre-paid to toll-free line. Court makes copy: $1.00 per page. Certification fee: $2.50 per page attested includes copy fee. What is known as a certified copy in most states is known as a attested copy in Mass. What Mass. calls a single page "Certificate" with gold seal is $20.00. Payee: Franklin County Superior Court. Personal checks accepted. No credit cards accepted. Prepayment required. Mail requests: SASE required.
Civil Name Search: Access: Fax, in person, online. Both court and visitors may perform in person name searches. Search fee: $1.00. Civil records in files; on computer back 15 years. Civil PAT goes back to 15 years. Online only for attorneys and law firms at www.ma-trialcourts.org/tcic.
Criminal Name Search: Access: Fax, in person, online. Both court and visitors may perform in person name searches. Search fee: $1.00. Required to search: name, years to search, DOB. Criminal records in files; on computer back 12 years. Criminal PAT goes back to 12 years. Online for attorneys and law firms only with registration at www.ma-trialcourts.org/tcic/.

Greenfield District Court 425 Main St, Greenfield, MA 01301; 413-774-5533; probate phone: 413-774-7011; fax: 413-774-5328; 8:30AM-4:30PM (EST). *Felony, Misdemeanor, Civil, Eviction, Small Claims.*
General Information: Includes Ashfield, Bernardston, Buckland, Charlemont, Colrain, Conway, Deerfield, Gill, Greenfield, Hawley, Heath, Leyden, Monroe, Montague, Northfield, Rowe, Shelburne, Sunderland, and Whately. No juvenile records released. Will not fax documents. Court makes copy: $1.00 per page. Certification fee: $2.50. Payee: Greenfield District Court. Personal checks accepted. No credit cards accepted. Prepayment required.
Civil Name Search: Access: In person only. Visitors must perform in person searches themselves. Civil index on docket books or index cards; on computer back to 1998. Public use terminal has civil records back to 2004.
Criminal Name Search: Access: In person only. Visitors must perform in person searches themselves. Required to search: name, years to search, DOB. Criminal docket on books or index cards; on computer back to 1994.

Orange District Court #42 One Court Square, Orange, MA 01364; 978-544-8277; fax: 978-544-5204; 8:30AM-4:30PM (EST). *Felony, Misdemeanor, Civil, Eviction, Small Claims.*
www.mass.gov/courts/courtsandjudges/courts/orangedistrictmain.html
General Information: Includes Athol, Erving, New Salem, Orange, Warwick, and Wendell, Shutesbury, Leverett. No juvenile records released. Will fax documents to local or toll-free number. Court makes copy: $1.00 per page. Certification fee: $2.50 per page. Payee: District Court. No personal checks accepted. Visa/MC accepted. Prepayment required.
Civil Name Search: Access: Phone, mail, in person. Both court and visitors may perform in person name searches. No search fee. Civil index in docket books from 1975. Mail turnaround time 1-2 weeks. Public use terminal has civil records back to 19902.
Criminal Name Search: Access: Phone, mail, in person. Only the court performs in person name searches; visitors may not. No search fee. Criminal docket on books from 1975. Mail turnaround time 1-2 weeks.

Probate & Family Court PO Box 590, 425 Main St, Greenfield, MA 01302-0590; 413-774-7011; fax: 413-774-3829; 8AM-4:30PM (EST). *Probate, Domestic Relations.*
www.mass.gov/courts/courtsandjudges/courts/frankprobmain.html
General Information: This court also holds estate, domestic relations, equity, name change and domestic violence records.

Western Housing Court , MA; . *Eviction, Misdemeanor (Code Violations), Small Claims.*
General Information: See the Hampden County Western Housing Court. This court see many housing code cases, real estate-related small claims and eviction cases for this county; also see district courts in this county.

Hampden County

Superior Court 50 State St, PO Box 559, Springfield, MA 01102-0559; criminal phone: 413-735-6017; civil phone: 413-735-6016; fax: 413-737-1611; 8:30AM-4:30PM (EST). *Felony, Civil Actions over $25,000.*
General Information: No impounded case records released. Will fax documents. Court makes copy: $1.00 per page. Certification fee: $2.50. Payee: Clerk of Superior Court. Personal checks accepted. No credit cards accepted. Prepayment required. Mail requests: SASE requested for civil.
Civil Name Search: Access: Phone, mail, in person, online. Both court and visitors may perform in person name searches. No search fee. Civil records on computer from 1989 to present; prior on index cards from 1930s, books from 1812. Civil PAT goes back to 1981. Online only for attorneys and law firms at www.ma-trialcourts.org/tcic/.
Criminal Name Search: Access: In person, online. Visitors must perform in person searches themselves. Criminal records computerized from 1992 to present; prior on index cards from 1930s. Criminal PAT goes back to 1990. Online for attorneys and law firms only with registration at www.ma-trialcourts.org/tcic/.

Chicopee District Court #20 30 Church St, Chicopee, MA 01020; 413-598-0099; fax: 413-594-6187; 8:30AM-4:30PM (EST). *Felony, Misdemeanor, Civil, Eviction, Small Claims.*
General Information: No juvenile records released. Will not fax documents. Court makes copy: $1.00 per page. Certification fee: $2.50 per cert. Payee: District Court. Personal checks accepted. No credit cards accepted. Prepayment required. Mail requests: SASE required for civil.
Civil Name Search: Access: Mail, in person. Both court and visitors may perform in person name searches. No search fee. Civil index on cards from 1983, docket books to 1960; computerized since 2004. Public use terminal has civil records back to 2004.
Criminal Name Search: Access: In person. Visitors must perform in person searches themselves. Required to search: name, years to search, DOB. Criminal records indexed on cards from 1983, docket books to 1900.

Holyoke District Court 20 Court Sq, Holyoke, MA 01041-5075; 413-538-9710; fax: 413-533-7165; 9AM-4:30PM (EST). *Felony, Misdemeanor, Civil, Eviction, Small Claims.*
General Information: No juvenile, sealed records released. Will fax documents to local or toll-free number. Court makes copy: $1.00 per page. Certification fee: $2.50. Payee: District Court. Only cashiers checks and money orders accepted. Major credit cards accepted. Prepayment required. Mail requests: SASE requested.
Civil Name Search: Access: Phone, mail, fax, in person. Both court and visitors may perform in person name searches. No search fee. Civil index on cards and docket books back to 1989. Mail turnaround time 1-2 weeks. Public use terminal has civil records back to 1989.
Criminal Name Search: Access: Fax, mail, in person. Only the court performs in person name searches; visitors may not. No search fee. Required to search: name, years to search, DOB or SSN, signed release. Criminal records indexed on cards and docket books since 1976; on computer back to 1986. Mail turnaround time 1-2 weeks.

Palmer District Court 235 Sykes St, Ste 3, Palmer, MA 01069; 413-283-8916 x1; fax: 413-283-6775; 8:30AM-4:30PM (EST). *Felony, Misdemeanor, Civil, Eviction, Small Claims.*
www.mass.gov/courts/courtsandjudges/courts/palmerdistrictmain.html
General Information: Includes Ludlow, Monson, Wilbraham, Palmer, Wales, Brimfield, Holland, and Hampden. No sealed or juvenile records released. Will not fax out documents. Court makes copy: $1.00 per page. Certification fee: $2.50 per cert/page. Payee: Palmer District Court. Personal checks accepted. No credit cards accepted. Prepayment required.
Civil Name Search: Access: In person only. Visitors must perform in person searches themselves. Civil index on cards back to 1982. Public use terminal has civil records back to 2002.
Criminal Name Search: Access: In person only. Visitors must perform in person searches themselves. Criminal records indexed on cards for 10 years; on computer back to 1995.

Springfield District Court PO Box 2421, 50 State St, Springfield, MA 01101-2421; 413-745-6000; criminal phone: x1; civil phone: x2; criminal fax: 413-747-4842; civil fax: 8:30AM-4:30PM; 8:30AM-4:30PM (EST). *Felony, Misdemeanor, Civil, Eviction, Small Claims.*
www.mass.gov/courts/courtsandjudges/courts/springfielddistrictmain.html
General Information: Includes Agawam, East Longmeadow, Longmeadow, Springfield, West Springfield. No sealed, expunged, or adoption records released. Will not fax out documents. Court makes copy: $1.00 per page. Certification fee: $2.50 per cert/page. Payee: District Court. Business checks accepted. Visa/MC accepted in cash office for criminal only. Prepayment required.
Civil Name Search: Access: In person only. Visitors must perform in person searches themselves. Civil index on cards; computerized records since 7/03, small claims since 2001. Public use terminal has civil records back to 2003.
Criminal Name Search: Access: In person only. Visitors must perform in person searches themselves. Criminal records indexed on cards; computerized records since 1992.

Westfield District Court 224 Elm St, Westfield, MA 01085; 413-568-8946; fax: 413-568-4863; 8AM-4PM (EST). *Felony, Misdemeanor, Civil, Eviction, Small Claims.*
www.mass.gov/courts/courtsandjudges/courts/westfielddistrictmain.html
General Information: Includes Blandford, Chester, Granville, Montgomery, Russell, Southwick, Tolland, and Westfield. No sealed or juvenile records released. Will not fax documents. Court makes copy: $1.00 per page. Certification fee: $2.50 per cert/page. Payee: District Court. Cashiers checks and money orders accepted. Visa/MC accepted. Prepayment required.
Civil Name Search: Access: Mail, in person. Both court and visitors may perform in person name searches. No search fee. Civil index on cards and in files. Public use terminal has civil records back to 2004.
Criminal Name Search: Access: In person only. Both court and visitors may perform in person name searches. No search fee. Criminal records indexed on cards and in files.

Probate & Family Court 50 State St #4, Springfield, MA 01103-0559; 413-748-7758; fax: 413-781-5605; 8AM-4:25PM (EST). *Probate, Domestic Relations.*

Western Housing Court 37 Elm St, 01103, Springfield, MA 01103; 413-748-7838; fax: 413-732-4607; 8:30AM-4:30PM (EST). *Civil, Eviction, Misdemeanor (Code Violations), Small Claims.*
General Information: Includes many housing code cases, real estate-related small claims and eviction cases for counties of Berkshire, Franklin, Hampden, and Hampshire Counties. Also see district courts for these type of cases.

Hampshire County

Superior Court PO Box 1119, Northampton, MA 01061; 413-584-5810 x331; probate phone: 413-586-8500; fax: 413-586-8217; 9AM-4PM (EST). *Felony, Civil Actions over $25,000.*
www.mass.gov/courts/courtsandjudges/courts/hampsupmain.html
General Information: Online identifiers in results same as on public terminal. No impounded case records released. Will fax documents to local or toll free line. Court makes copy: $1.00 per page. Certification fee: $20.00. Payee: Clerk of Superior Court. Personal checks accepted. No credit cards accepted. Prepayment required.
Civil Name Search: Access: Mail, fax, in person, online. Both court and visitors may perform in person name searches. No search fee. Civil records in files, index cards from 1800s; on computer back to 2000. Mail turnaround time 1 week. Civil PAT goes back to 2000. Results include name and docket number. Online only for attorneys and law firms at www.ma-trialcourts.org/tcic/.
Criminal Name Search: Access: Mail, fax, in person, online. Both court and visitors may perform in person name searches. No search fee. Criminal records in files, index cards from 1800s; on computer back to 1983.

Mail turnaround time 1 week. Criminal PAT goes back to 1983. Results include name and docket number. Online for attorneys and law firms only with registration at www.ma-trialcourts.org/tcic/.

Belchertown/Hadley District Court 205 State St, Route 202, Belchertown, MA 01007; 413-323-4056; criminal phone: x2239; civil phone: x2245; fax: 413-323-6803; 8:30AM-4:30PM (EST). *Felony, Misdemeanor, Civil, Eviction, Small Claims.*

General Information: Formerly Hadley Dist. Ct. Includes Amherst, Belchertown, Granby, Hadley, South Hadley, Pelham, Ware, all the MDC Quabbin Reservoir and Watershed Area. Includes cases formerly heard at the closed court in Ware and Hadley. No sealed, impounded, confidential or juvenile records released. Will fax documents $1.00 per page, prepaid. Court makes copy: $1.00 per page. Self serve copy: same. Certification fee: $2.50. Payee: Eastern Hampshire District Court. Personal checks accepted. Credit cards accepted in person. Prepayment required. Mail requests: SASE helpful.

Civil Name Search: Access: Fax, mail, in person. Both court and visitors may perform in person name searches. No search fee. Civil index on cards or docket books back to 1960. Some records sent to archives in Worcester. Note: In person searchers may use computer only. Mail turnaround time 1-2 weeks. Public use terminal has civil records back to 1993.

Criminal Name Search: Access: Fax, mail, in person. Only the court performs in person name searches; visitors may not. No search fee. Required to search: name, years to search, DOB, SSN. Criminal records indexed on cards or docket books back to 1920; on computer back to 1996. Some records sent to archives in Worcester. Mail turnaround time 1-2 weeks.

Northampton District Court Courthouse, 15 Gothic St, Northampton, MA 01060; 413-584-7776; criminal phone: 413-584-7400; civil phone: 413-584-7400; criminal fax: 413-586-1980; civil fax: 8:30AM-4:30PM; 8:30AM-4:30PM (EST). *Felony, Misdemeanor, Civil, Eviction, Small Claims.*

General Information: Includes Chesterfield, Cummington, Easthampton, Goshen, Hatfield, Huntington, Middlefield, Northampton, Plainfield, Southampton, Westhampton, Williamsburg, and Worthington. No CHINS-care & protection, show cause-mental health records released. No fee to fax documents. Court makes copy: $1.00 per page. Self serve copy: same. Certification fee: $2.50 per page. Payee: District Court. No personal checks. Visa/MC pr debit cards accepted in person only. Prepayment required. Mail requests: SASE requested.

Civil Name Search: Access: Fax, mail, in person. Both court and visitors may perform in person name searches. No search fee. Required to search: name, years to search, address. Civil index on cards and docket books back to 1970, computerized since 5/02. Mail turnaround time 1-2 weeks. Public use terminal has civil records back to 2001.

Criminal Name Search: Access: Fax, mail, in person. Both court and visitors may perform in person name searches. No search fee. Required to search: name, years to search, DOB, SSN. Criminal docket on books go back to 1970, on computer since 1997. Mail turnaround time 1-2 weeks.

Probate & Family Court 33 King St #3, Northampton, MA 01060-3297; 413-586-8500; fax: 413-584-1132; 8AM-4:30PM (EST). *Probate, Domestic Relations.*
www.hampshireprobate.com/

Western Housing Court , MA; . *Eviction, Misdemeanor (Code Violations), Small Claims.*

General Information: See Hampden County Western Housing Court. Sees many housing code cases, real estate-related small claims and eviction cases for this county. Also see district courts in this county for these type of cases.

Middlesex County

Superior Court - Lowell 360 Gorham St, Lowell, MA 01852; 978-453-0201; criminal phone: x259; civil phone: x280; 8:30AM-4:30PM (EST). *Felony, Civil Actions over $25,000.*
www.mass.gov/courts/courtsandjudges/courts/middsupmain.html

General Information: Will not fax documents. Court makes copy: $1.00 per page. Certification fee: $2.50 per page. Payee: Clerk of Superior Court. Personal checks accepted. No credit cards accepted. Prepayment required.

Civil Name Search: Access: Mail, in person, online. Both court and visitors may perform in person name searches. No search fee. Civil records on computer since 1988; prior records kept at East Cambridge Middlesex Superior Ct, 40 Thorndike, Cambridge, MA 02141. Mail turnaround time 1-2 days. Civil PAT available. Public access terminal only available at Woburn Branch. Online only for attorneys and law firms at www.ma-trialcourts.org/tcic/welcome.jsp.

Criminal Name Search: Access: Mail, in person, online. Both court and visitors may perform in person name searches. No search fee. Criminal records on computer since 1988; prior records kept at East Cambridge Middlesex Superior Court, Cambridge, MA. Mail turnaround time 1-2 days. Criminal PAT available. Public access terminal only available at Woburn Branch. Online for attorneys and law firms only with registration at www.ma-trialcourts.org/tcic/welcome.jsp

Superior Court - Woburn 200 TradeCenter, Woburn, MA 01801; 781-939-2700/2800; criminal phone: x4; civil phone: x5; fax: 781-939-0872; 8:30AM-4:30PM (EST). *Felony, Civil Actions over $25,000.*
www.mass.gov/courts/courtsandjudges/courts/middsupmain.html

General Information: Up until 3/17/2008 this court was located in East Cambridge. No impounded or those restricted by statute records released. Will not fax documents. Court makes copy: $1.00 per page. Self serve copy: $.25 per page. Certification fee: $2.50 per page. Payee: Clerk of Superior Court. Personal checks accepted. No credit cards accepted. Prepayment required.

Civil Name Search: Access: Mail, in person, online. Both court and visitors may perform in person name searches. No search fee. Required to search: name, years to search; also helpful: address. Civil records on computer from 1986, rest on card indexes to 1986. Mail turnaround time 3-5 days. Civil PAT goes back to 1991. Court is planning to have public internet access. Online for attorneys and law firms only with registration at www.ma-trialcourts.org/tcic/welcome.jsp.

Criminal Name Search: Access: Mail, in person, online. Both court and visitors may perform in person name searches. No search fee. Required to search: name, years to search; also helpful: address. Criminal records computerized from 1991, rest on card indexes to 1986. Mail turnaround time 3-5 days. Criminal PAT goes back to 1991. Court plans to have public internet access; is online for attorneys and law firms only with registration at www.ma-trialcourts.org/tcic/welcome.jsp.

Ayer District Court 25 E Main St, Ayer, MA 01432; 978-772-2100; fax: 978-772-5345; 8:30AM-4:30PM (EST). *Felony, Misdemeanor, Civil, Eviction, Small Claims.*
www.mass.gov/courts/courtsandjudges/courts/ayerdistrictmain.html

General Information: Includes Ayer, Ashby, Boxborough, Dunstable, Groton, Littleton, Pepperell, Shirley, Townsend, Westford and Devens Regional Enterprise Zone. Juvenile records not released. Will not fax documents. Court makes copy: $1.00 per page. Certification fee: $2.50 per page plus copy fee. Payee: Ayer District Court. Personal checks accepted. Major credit cards accepted in person only. Prepayment required. Mail requests: SASE required.

Civil Name Search: Access: Mail, in person. Both court and visitors may perform in person name searches. No search fee. Required to search: name, years to search, DOB. Civil index on cards from 1977 to present; only required to keep case files 20 years, dockets kept permanently. Mail turnaround time 1-2 weeks. Public use terminal has civil records back to limited number of years. Civil and small claims cases only appear on results.

Criminal Name Search: Access: Mail, in person. Both court and visitors may perform in person name searches. No search fee. Required to search: name, years to search, DOB. Criminal records indexed on cards from 1977 to 1995, computerized 1996 forward; Only required to keep case files 10 years. Mail turnaround time 1-2 weeks.

Cambridge District Court 52 4040 Mystic Valley Parkway, Medford, MA 02155; 781-306-2715; criminal phone: x1; civil phone: x2; fax: 781-395-2035; 8:30AM-4:30PM (EST). *Felony, Misdemeanor, Civil, Eviction, Small Claims.*
www.mass.gov/courts/courtsandjudges/courts/cambridgedistrictmain.html

General Information: Includes Cambridge, Arlington, Belmont. Formerly located in Cambridge, pre-2009. The main phone number is 781-306-2710. No sealed or juvenile records released. Will fax documents to local or toll free line. Court makes copy: $1.00 per page. Certification fee: $2.50 per cert. Payee: District Court. Personal checks accepted. Visa/MC accepted. Prepayment required.

Civil Name Search: Access: In person. However, as a public service this office may honor a mail, fax, or phone request for one or two names.Visitors must perform in person searches themselves. Civil index on cards or docket books. State law requires records be retained 10 years.

Criminal Name Search: Access: In person. However, as a public service this office may honor a mail, fax, or phone request for one or two names.Visitors must perform in person searches themselves. Required to search: name, years to search, DOB. Criminal records indexed on cards or docket books; computerized records since 1997. State law requires records be retained 10 years.

Concord District Court 47 305 Walden St, Concord, MA 01742; 978-369-0500; fax: 978-371-2945; 8:30AM-4:30PM (EST). *Felony, Misdemeanor, Civil, Eviction, Small Claims.*
www.mass.gov/courts/courtsandjudges/courts/concorddistrictmain.html

General Information: Includes Concord, Carlisle, Lincoln, Lexington, Bedford, Acton, Maynard, Stow and State PD. No impounded files released. Will not fax documents. Court makes copy: $1.00 per page. Certification fee: $2.50 per cert. Payee: Commonwealth of Massachusetts. Personal checks accepted. No credit cards accepted. Prepayment required. Mail requests: SASE requested.

Civil Name Search: Access: Mail, in person. Visitors must perform in person searches themselves. No search fee. Required to search: name, years to search; also helpful: address. Civil records computerized, searchable by public only on index cards and books from 1950, archived from 1643. Note: In person searches performed from 10AM-4PM only.

Criminal Name Search: Access: Mail, in person. Visitors must perform in person searches themselves. No search fee. Required to search: name, years to search; also helpful: address, DOB, SSN. Criminal records index printed from computer from 1998, index cards and books from 1950, archived from 1643. Note: In person searches performed from 10AM-4PM only. Public can only search the docket books. Mail turnaround time 1-2 weeks.

Framingham District Court PO Box 1969, 600 Concord St, Framingham, MA 01701; 508-875-7461; fax: 508-626-2503; 8:30AM-4:30PM (EST). *Felony, Misdemeanor, Civil, Eviction, Small Claims.*
www.mass.gov/courts/courtsandjudges/courts/framinghamdistrictmain.html
General Information: Includes Ashland, Framingham, Holliston, Hopkinton, Sudbury, and Wayland. No sealed, expunged or juvenile records released. Will not fax documents. Court makes copy: $1.00 per page. Certification fee: $2.50 per page. Payee: District Court. Only cashiers checks and money orders accepted. Visa/MC accepted. Prepayment required. Mail requests: SASE requested.
Civil Name Search: Access: Mail, fax, in person. Both court and visitors may perform in person name searches. No search fee. Civil index on docket books back to 1957; on computer back to 2002. Note: Special form required for mail request. Mail turnaround time 14 days. Civil PAT goes back to 2002.
Criminal Name Search: Access: Mail, in person, fax. Both court and visitors may perform in person name searches. No search fee. Criminal records indexed on docket books back to 1957; on computer back to 2002. Note: Special form required for mail request. Mail turnaround time 7 days. Criminal PAT goes back to 2002. Terminal results include SSN.

Lowell District Court 41 Hurd St, Lowell, MA 01852; 978-459-4101; criminal phone: X204; civil phone: x235; fax: 978-937-2486; 8:30AM-4:30PM (EST). *Felony, Misdemeanor, Civil, Eviction, Small Claims.*
www.mass.gov/courts/courtsandjudges/courts/lowelldistrictmain.html
General Information: Includes Billerica, Chelmsford, Dracut, Lowell, Tewksbury, and Tyngsboro. No impounded records released. Will fax documents. Court makes copy: $1.00 per page. Certification fee: $2.50. Payee: District Court, Lowell Division. Business checks accepted. Major credit cards accepted. Prepayment required.
Civil Name Search: Access: In person only. Visitors must perform in person searches themselves. Civil index on cards or docket books. Records retained for 10 years. Public use terminal has civil records.
Criminal Name Search: Access: In person. Visitors must perform in person searches themselves. Required to search: name, years to search, DOB. Criminal records indexed on cards or docket books. Records retained for 10 years.

Malden District Court 89 Summer St., Malden, MA 02148; 781-322-7500; criminal phone: x3; civil phone: x4; fax: 781-322-0169; 8:30AM-4:30PM (EST). *Felony, Misdemeanor, Civil, Eviction, Small Claims.*
www.mass.gov/courts/courtsandjudges/courts/maldendistrictmain.html
General Information: Includes Malden, Melrose, Everett, and Wakefield. No juvenile records released. Will not fax documents. Court makes copy: $1.00 per page. Certification fee: $2.50 per cert/page. Payee: District Court. Personal checks accepted. No credit cards accepted. Prepayment required.
Civil Name Search: Access: Mail, fax, In person. Only the court performs in person name searches; visitors may not. No search fee. Civil index on cards or docket books back to 1970; on computer back to 1992. Mail turnaround time 3-5 days.
Criminal Name Search: Access: In person only. Both court and visitors may perform in person name searches. Required to search: name, years to search, DOB. Criminal records indexed on cards or docket books back to 1970; on computer back to 1999.

Marlborough District Court 21 45 Williams St, Marlborough, MA 01752; 508-485-3700; fax: 508-485-1575; 8:30AM-4:30PM (EST). *Felony, Misdemeanor, Civil, Eviction, Small Claims.*
www.mass.gov/courts/courtsandjudges/courts/marlboroughdistrictmain.html
General Information: Includes Marlborough and Hudson. No juvenile records released. Court makes copy: $1.00 per page. Certification fee: $2.50 per cert. Payee: District Court. Personal checks accepted. No credit cards accepted. Prepayment required.
Civil Name Search: Access: Phone, mail, in person. Both court and visitors may perform in person name searches. No search fee. Civil index on cards or docket books. State law requires records be retained for 10 years. Mail turnaround time 1-2 weeks. Civil PAT goes back to 2000.
Criminal Name Search: Access: Phone, mail, in person. Both court and visitors may perform in person name searches. Required to search: name, years to county search, DOB. Criminal records indexed on cards or

docket books. State law requires records be retained for 10 years. Mail turnaround time 1-2 weeks. Criminal PAT goes back to 2000.

Natick District Court 600 Concord St, Framingham, MA 01701; 508-620-9110; fax: 508-620-9118; 8:30AM-4:30PM (EST). *Felony, Misdemeanor, Civil, Eviction, Small Claims.*
www.mass.gov/courts/courtsandjudges/courts/natickdistrictmain.html
General Information: Includes Natick and Sherborn. Since 10/2009 this Natick District Court is in same courthouse as Framingham Court, but indexes and offices are separate. No juvenile records released. Will not fax documents. Court makes copy: $1.00 per page. Certification fee: $2.50 per cert/page. Payee: District Court. Personal checks accepted. Visa/MC accepted. Prepayment required.
Civil Name Search: Access: In person only. Visitors must perform in person searches themselves. Civil index on cards and docket books, back for 10 years.
Criminal Name Search: Access: In person only. Visitors must perform in person searches themselves. Required to search: name, years to search, DOB. Criminal records indexed on cards and docket books, back for 10 years.

Newton District Court 1309 Washington St, West Newton, MA 02465; 617-244-3600 x4; fax: 617-243-7291; 8:30AM-4:30PM (EST). *Felony, Misdemeanor, Civil, Eviction, Small Claims.*
www.mass.gov/courts/courtsandjudges/courts/newtondistrictmain.html
General Information: No juvenile, (some) 209-A cases or mental health records released. Will not fax documents. Court makes copy: $1.00 per page. Certification fee: $2.50 per cert/page. Payee: District Court of Newton. Personal checks accepted. Visa/MC accepted in person only. Prepayment required.
Civil Name Search: Access: Mail, fax, in person. Both court and visitors may perform in person name searches. No search fee. Civil index on cards back to 1900. Mail turnaround time 1 week. Public use terminal has civil records back to 2002.
Criminal Name Search: Access: Mail, fax, in person. Both court and visitors may perform in person name searches. No search fee. Criminal records indexed in books back to 1900. Mail turnaround time 1 week.

Somerville District Court 175 Fellsway, Somerville, MA 02145; 617-666-8000; fax: 617-776-2111; 8:30AM-4:30PM (EST). *Felony, Misdemeanor, Civil, Eviction, Small Claims.*
www.mass.gov/courts/courtsandjudges/courts/somervilledistrictmain.html
General Information: Includes Medford and Somerville. Will search only one or two names. No juvenile or impounded records released. Will not fax documents. Court makes copy: $1.00 per page. Certification fee: $2.50 per cert/page. Payee: District Court. Personal checks accepted. No credit cards accepted. Prepayment required.
Civil Name Search: Access: Phone, Mail, In person. Visitors must perform in person searches themselves. No search fee. Civil index on cards or docket books. State law requires records be retained for 20 years.
Criminal Name Search: Access: Phone, Mail, In Person. Visitors must perform in person searches themselves. No search fee. Required to search: name, years to search, DOB. Criminal records on computer since 1997; prior records on index cards or docket books. State law requires records be retained for 20 years.

Waltham District Court 51 38 Linden St, Waltham, MA 02452; 781-894-4500 x4; fax: 781-894-4360; 8:30AM-4:30PM (EST). *Felony, Misdemeanor, Civil, Eviction, Small Claims.*
www.mass.gov/courts/courtsandjudges/courts/walthamdistrictmain.html
General Information: Includes Waltham, Watertown, and Weston. No juvenile records released. Court makes copy: $1.00 per page. Certification fee: $2.50 per cert. Payee: District Court. Personal checks accepted. No credit cards accepted. Prepayment required. Mail requests: SASE required.
Civil Name Search: Access: Mail, in person. Both court and visitors may perform in person name searches. No search fee. Civil index on cards and docket books, back for 10 years. Mail turnaround time 1 week. Public use terminal available.
Criminal Name Search: Access: Mail, in person. Both court and visitors may perform in person name searches. No search fee. Required to search: name, years to search; also helpful: DOB. Criminal records indexed on cards and docket books, back for 10 years. Mail turnaround time 1 week. Public use terminal available.

Woburn District Court 53 30 Pleasant St, Woburn, MA 01801; 781-935-4000; fax: 781-933-4404; 8:30AM-4:30PM (EST). *Felony, Misdemeanor, Civil, Eviction, Small Claims.*
www.mass.gov/courts/courtsandjudges/courts/woburndistrictmain.html
General Information: Includes Burlington, North Reading, Reading, Stoneham, Wilmington, Winchester, and Woburn. No statutorily non-public records released. Will not fax documents. Court makes copy: $1.00 per page. Certification fee: $2.50 per cert. Payee: District Court. Personal checks

accepted. Visa/MC accepted. Prepayment required. Mail requests: SASE requested.

Civil Name Search: Access: Mail, fax, in person. Both court and visitors may perform in person name searches. No search fee. Civil index on cards, computer listing or docket books back 30 years. Mail turnaround time 1-2 weeks. Public use terminal has civil records back to 2000 for some records.

Criminal Name Search: Access: Mail, fax, in person. Both court and visitors may perform in person name searches. No search fee. Required to search: name, years to search; also helpful: DOB. Criminal records indexed on cards, computer listing or docket books back 30 years. Mail turnaround time 1-2 weeks.

Probate & Family Court 208 Cambridge St, PO Box 410480, East Cambridge, MA 02141-0006; 617-768-5800; fax: 617-225-0781; 8AM-4:30PM (EST). *Probate, Domestic Relations.*
www.mass.gov/courts/courtsandjudges/courts/middprobmain.html
General Information: There are a number of satellite offices as well, in Cambridge, Concord, Marlbough, and Lowell.

Nantucket County

Superior Court PO Box 967, Nantucket, MA 02554; 508-228-2559; fax: 508-228-3725; 8:30AM-4PM (EST). *Felony, Civil Actions over $25,000.*

General Information: This office is now staffed by only one person, turnaround time or requests may be delayed. No impounded records released. No fee to fax documents; in-state faxing only. Court makes copy: $1.00 per page. Self serve copy: same. Certification fee: $2.50 per attested copy; $20.00 certification fee. Payee: Nantucket Superior Court. Personal checks accepted. No credit cards accepted. Prepayment required. Mail requests: SASE required.

Civil Name Search: Access: Phone, fax, mail, in person, online. Both court and visitors may perform in person name searches. No search fee. Civil index on docket books from 1762. Mail turnaround time 1 week. Online only for attorneys and law firms at www.ma-trialcourts.org/tcic/.

Criminal Name Search: Access: Phone, fax, mail, in person, online. Both court and visitors may perform in person name searches. No search fee. Criminal records indexed in books from 1762. Mail turnaround time 1 week. Online for attorneys and law firms only with registration at www.ma-trialcourts.org/tcic/.

Nantucket District Court 16 Broad St, PO Box 1800, Nantucket, MA 02554; 508-228-0460; fax: 508-325-5759; 8AM-4PM (EST). *Felony, Misdemeanor, Civil, Eviction, Small Claims.*

General Information: Will not fax documents. Court makes copy: $1.00 per page. Certification fee: $2.50 per cert. Payee: Nantucket District Court. Personal checks accepted. No credit cards accepted. Prepayment required.

Civil Name Search: Access: In person only. Visitors must perform in person searches themselves. Civil index on cards or docket books. State law requires records be retained for 10 years. Public use terminal has civil records back to 2004.

Criminal Name Search: Access: In person only. Visitors must perform in person searches themselves. Criminal records indexed on cards or docket books back to 1917. State law requires records be retained for 10 years.

Probate & Family Court PO Box 1116, 16 Broad St, Nantucket, MA 02554; 508-228-2669; fax: 508-228-3662; 8AM-4PM (EST). *Probate, Domestic Relations.*
General Information: Send all mail to the PO Box.

Norfolk County

Superior Court 650 High St, Dedham, MA 02026; 781-326-1600; criminal phone: x2; civil phone: x1; criminal fax: 781-320-9726; civil fax: 8:30AM-4:30PM; 8:30AM-4:30PM (EST). *Felony, Civil Actions over $25,000.*
www.mass.gov/courts/courtsandjudges/courts/norfsupmain.html
General   Information: Includes Avon,Bellingham,Braintree,Brookline,Canton,Cohasset,Dedham,Dover,Foxborough,Franklin,Hilbrook,Medfield,Medway, Millis,Milton,Needham,Norfolk, Norwood,Plainville,Quincy,Randolph,Sharon,Stoughton,Walpole,Wellesley, Westwood, Weymouth, Wrentham. No impounded records released. No one may view a file of a sex-related crime without authorization from a judge. Will not fax documents. Court makes copy: $1.00 per page. Self serve copy: $.50 per page. Certification fee: $2.50 per cert. Payee: Clerk of Superior Court. Personal checks accepted for copies only. No credit cards accepted. Prepayment required.

Civil Name Search: Access: Phone, mail, in person, online. Both court and visitors may perform in person name searches. No search fee. Civil index on docket books from 1900, on computer back to 9/2000. Mail turnaround time 1 week; 1-2 days for criminal phone in requests. Civil PAT goes back to 9/2000. Online only for attorneys and law firms at www.ma-trialcourts.org/tcic/.

Criminal Name Search: Access: In person, online. Visitors must perform in person searches themselves. Required to search: name, years to search; also helpful: address, DOB, SSN. Criminal records indexed in books from 1900; on computer back to 9/2000. Criminal PAT goes back to same as civil. Online for attorneys and law firms only with registration at www.ma-trialcourts.org/tcic/.

Brookline District Court 360 Washington St, Brookline, MA 02445; 617-232-4660; fax: 617-739-0734; 8:30AM-4:30PM (EST). *Felony, Misdemeanor, Civil, Eviction, Small Claims.*
www.mass.gov/courts/courtsandjudges/courts/brooklinedistrictco.html
General Information: No sealed case records released. Will not fax documents. Court makes copy: $1.00 per page. Certification fee: $2.50 per cert/page. Payee: Brookline District Court. Personal checks accepted. Visa/MC accepted in person only. Prepayment required.

Civil Name Search: Access: In person only. Visitors must perform in person searches themselves. Civil index on cards and docket books back for 10 years.

Criminal Name Search: Access: In person only. Visitors must perform in person searches themselves. Required to search: name, years to search; also helpful: DOB. Criminal records indexed on cards and docket books back for 10 years.

Dedham District Court 631 High St, Dedham, MA 02026; 781-329-4777; criminal phone: x338; fax: 781-320-8249; 8:15AM-4:30PM (EST). *Felony, Misdemeanor, Civil, Eviction, Small Claims.*
www.mass.gov/courts/courtsandjudges/courts/dedhamdistrictmain.html
General Information: Includes Dedham, Dover, Medfield, Needham, Norwood, Wellesley, and Westwood. No juvenile records released. Court makes copy: $1.00 per page. Certification fee: $2.50 per cert/page. Payee: District Court. Personal checks accepted. Visa/MC accepted for payment over $20.00 only; picture ID required. Prepayment required.

Civil Name Search: Access: In person only. Visitors must perform in person searches themselves. Civil records on computer since 1997, and on index cards or docket books prior to that. State law requires records be retained for 10 years. Public use terminal has civil records back to 2003.

Criminal Name Search: Access: In person only. Visitors must perform in person searches themselves. Criminal records on computer since 1997, and on index cards or docket books prior to that. State law requires records be retained for 10 years.

Quincy District Court One Dennis Ryan Parkway, Quincy, MA 02169; 617-471-1650; fax: 617-472-1924; 8:30AM-4:30PM (EST). *Felony, Misdemeanor, Civil, Eviction, Small Claims.*
General Information: Includes Braintree, Cohasset, Holbrook, Quincy, Randolph, and Weymouth, Quincy. No fax search requests accepted at this court. Juvenile records current now with Norfolk Juv. Court; no juvenile records released. Will not fax documents. Court makes copy: $1.00 per page. Certification fee: $2.50 per cert. Payee: District Court. Only cashiers checks and money orders accepted. No credit cards accepted. Prepayment required.

Civil Name Search: Access: In person only. Visitors must perform in person searches themselves. Civil index on cards or docket books. State law requires records be retained for 10 years.

Criminal Name Search: Access: In person only. Visitors must perform in person searches themselves. Required to search: name, years to search; also helpful: DOB. Criminal records on computer since 1996; prior records on index cards or docket books. State law requires records be retained for 10 years.

Stoughton District Court 1288 Central St, #16, Stoughton, MA 02072; 781-344-2131; fax: 781-341-8744; 8:30AM-4:30PM (EST). *Felony, Misdemeanor, Crim Supplemental, Civil, Eviction, Small Claims.*
General Information: Includes Avon, Canton, Sharon, and Stoughton. All fax search requests must include docket numbers. No juvenile records released. Will fax documents $1.00 per page if prepaid. Court makes copy: $1.00 per page. Certification fee: $2.50 per page; $20 for exemplified copy. Payee: District Court. Personal checks accepted. No credit cards accepted. Prepayment required. Mail requests: SASE requested.

Civil Name Search: Access: Mail, fax, in person. Both court and visitors may perform in person name searches. No search fee. Civil index on cards or docket books for 10 years or more. Mail turnaround time 1 week; if archived- 6 weeks. Public use terminal has civil records back to 2005.

Criminal Name Search: Access: Mail, fax, in person. Only the court performs in person name searches; visitors may not. No search fee. Required to search: name, years to search; also helpful: DOB. Criminal records on computer since 1995; prior records on index cards or docket books for 10 years or more. Note: Only the court may perform in person criminal searches for pre-1995 cases. Visitors may search books 1995 to present. Mail turnaround time 1 week; 6 weeks if archived.

Wrentham District Court 60 East St, Wrentham, MA 02093; 508-384-3106; criminal fax: 508-384-5052; civil fax: 8:30AM-4:30PM; 8:30AM-4:30PM (EST). *Felony, Misdemeanor, Civil, Eviction, Small Claims.*

General Information: Includes Foxborough, Franklin, Medway, Millis, Norfolk, Plainville, Walpole, and Wrentham. No show cause hearing or juvenile records released. Will not fax documents. Court makes copy: $1.00 per page. Certification fee: $2.50 per page. Payee: District Court. Personal checks accepted. No credit cards accepted. Prepayment required.

Civil Name Search: Access: In person only. Visitors must perform in person searches themselves. Civil records retained 20 years. Physical records go back to 1985; pre-1985 on docket books.

Criminal Name Search: Access: In person only. Visitors must perform in person searches themselves. Required to search: name, years to search; also helpful: DOB. Criminal records retained 20 years. Physical records go back to 1985; on computer back to 1999; pre-1985 on docket books.

Probate & Family Court 35 Shawmut Rd, Canton, MA 02021; 781-830-1200; fax: 781-830-4310; 8:30AM-4:30PM (EST). *Probate, Domestic Relations.*

www.mass.gov/courts/courtsandjudges/courts/norfolkprobmain.html

Plymouth County

Superior Court - Brockton 72 Belmont St, Brockton, MA 02401; 508-583-8250; fax: 508-584-5639; 8:30AM-4:30PM (EST). *Felony, Civil Actions over $25,000.*

General Information: No impounded records released. Court makes copy: $1.00 per page. Certification fee: $2.50 per cert. Payee: Clerk of Superior Court. Personal checks accepted. No credit cards accepted. Prepayment required.

Civil Name Search: Access: In person, mail, online. Both court and visitors may perform in person name searches. No search fee. Civil records for current civil cases are here and Plymouth, closed case are in Plymouth and Brockton; computerized records since 2000. Note: Civil record index is comingled with the Brockton court, but case files are at the court where case took place. Civil PAT goes back to 2000. Online only for attorneys and law firms at www.ma-trialcourts.org/tcic/.

Criminal Name Search: Access: In person, online. Visitors must perform in person searches themselves. Criminal records here, but some in Plymouth, some pending; computerized records since 2000. Criminal PAT goes back to same as civil. Online for attorneys and law firms only with registration at www.ma-trialcourts.org/tcic/.

Superior Court - Plymouth Plymouth Superior Court, 52 Obery Street - Suite 2041, Plymouth, MA 02360; 508-747-8400; fax: 508-830-0676; 8:30AM-4:30PM (EST). *Civil Actions over $25,000.*

www.mass.gov/courts/courtsandjudges/courts/plymouthsupmain.html

General Information: Record index is comingled with the Brockton court, but case files are at the court where case took place. No impounded records released. Court makes copy: $1.00 per page. Certification fee: $2.50. Payee: Clerk of Superior Court. Personal checks accepted. No credit cards accepted. Prepayment required. Mail requests: SASE requested.

Civil Name Search: Access: Phone, mail, in person, online. Both court and visitors may perform in person name searches. No search fee. Civil records for all closed cases are kept here; computerized records since 1983 (approx). Note: Will look-up by phone, but only one name at a time. Is willing to call other court for you. Public use terminal available, records go back to 2003. There is no DOB on this terminal. Online is only for attorneys and law firms at www.ma-trialcourts.org/tcic/, goes back to 1999.

Brockton District Court PO Box 7610, 215 Main St, Brockton, MA 02303-7610; 508-587-8000; probate phone: 508-897-5400; criminal fax: 508-587-6791; civil fax: 8:30AM-4:30PM; 8:30AM-4:30PM (EST). *Felony, Misdemeanor, Civil, Eviction, Small Claims, Probate.*

www.mass.gov/courts/courtsandjudges/courts/brocktondistrictmain.html

General Information: Includes Abington, Bridgewater, Brockton, East Bridgewater, West Bridgewater, and Whitman. Probate is on 2nd floor. No juvenile or impounded records released. Will not fax documents. Court makes copy: $1.00 per page. Certification fee: $2.50 per page includes copy fee. Payee: District Court. Personal checks accepted. Prepayment required.

Civil Name Search: Access: Mail, in person. Both court and visitors may perform in person name searches. No search fee. Civil index on cards or docket books, retained for 10 years; on computer back to 1994. Mail turnaround time 1-2 weeks. Civil PAT goes back to 1995.

Criminal Name Search: Access: Mail, in person. Both court and visitors may perform in person name searches. No search fee. Required to search: name, years to search; also helpful: DOB. Criminal records indexed on cards or docket books, retained for 10 years; on computer back to 1994. Note: There are some dispositions of felony records at this court, but most disposition are at the Superior Court. Mail turnaround time 1-2 weeks. Criminal PAT goes back to 1994. Terminal results include SSN, will also state if case moved to Superior Court.

Hingham District Court 28 George Washington Blvd, Hingham, MA 02043; 781-749-7000; fax: 781-740-8390; 8:30AM-4:30PM (EST). *Felony, Misdemeanor, Civil, Eviction, Small Claims.*

General Information: Includes Hanover, Hingham, Hull, Norwell, Rockland, and Scituate. No juvenile records released. Will not fax documents. Court makes copy: $1.00 per page. Certification fee: $2.50 per cert. Payee: District Court. Personal checks accepted. No credit cards accepted. Prepayment required.

Civil Name Search: Access: Mail, in person. Both court and visitors may perform in person name searches. No search fee. Civil index on cards or docket books, retained for 10 years or more. Mail turnaround time 1-2 weeks.

Criminal Name Search: Access: Mail, in person. Only the court performs in person name searches; visitors may not. No search fee. Required to search: name, years to search; also helpful: DOB. Criminal records indexed on cards or docket books, retained for 10 years or more. Mail turnaround time 1-2 weeks.

Plymouth 3rd District Court Courthouse, S Russell St, 11 S Russell St, Plymouth, MA 02360; 508-747-8400; fax: 508-830-9303; 8:30AM-4:30PM (EST). *Felony, Misdemeanor, Civil, Eviction, Small Claims.*

General Information: Includes Duxbury, Halifax, Hanson, Kingston, Marshfield, Pembroke, Plymouth, and Plympton. No juvenile or impounded records released. Court makes copy: $1.00 per page. Certification fee: $2.50. Payee: Plymouth District Court. Personal checks accepted. No credit cards accepted. Prepayment required. Mail requests: SASE required for mail return of any copies.

Civil Name Search: Access: Mail, in person. Only the court performs in person name searches; visitors may not. No search fee. Civil index on cards or docket books. State law requires records be retained for 10 years. Visitors can only access the index cards. Mail turnaround time 3-4 days.

Criminal Name Search: Access: Mail, in person. Only the court performs in person name searches; visitors may not. No search fee. Required to search: name, years to search; also helpful: DOB. Criminal records indexed on cards or docket books. State law requires records be retained for 10 years. Visitors can only access the index cards. Mail turnaround time 3-4 days.

Wareham District Court 2200 Cranberry Hwy, Junction Routes 28 & 58, West Wareham, MA 02576; 508-295-8300 x315; fax: 508-291-6376; 8AM-4:30PM (EST). *Felony, Misdemeanor, Civil, Eviction, Small Claims.*

www.mass.gov/courts/courtsandjudges/courts/warehamdistrictmain.html

General Information: Includes Carver, Lakeville, Marion, Mattpoinsett, Middleboro, Rochester, and Wareham. No juvenile records released. Will not fax documents. Court makes copy: $1.00 per page. Self serve copy: same. Certification fee: $2.50 per page includes copy fee. Payee: District Court. Personal checks accepted. Visa/MC accepted. Prepayment required. Mail requests: SASE requested.

Civil Name Search: Access: Phone, mail, in person. Both court and visitors may perform in person name searches. No search fee. Mail turnaround time 1-2 weeks. Civil PAT goes back to 2004.

Criminal Name Search: Access: Phone, mail, in person. Both court and visitors may perform in person name searches. No search fee. Required to search: name, years to search; also helpful: DOB. Criminal records back to 1960. Computerized records back to 1995. Mail turnaround time 1-2 weeks. Criminal PAT goes back to 2004.

Probate & Family Court 52 Obery St, #1130, Plymouth, MA 02360; 508-747-6204; fax: 508-746-6846; 8:30AM-4:30PM (EST). *Probate, Domestic Relations.*

www.pcpfc.com

General Information: There is also a location in Brockton, but records appear on the PATs and are indexed at Plymouth.

Southeast Housing Court 215 Main St, 1st Fl, Ste 160, Brockton, MA 02301; 508-894-4170; fax: 508-894-4168; 8:30AM-4:30PM (EST). *Eviction, Misdemeanor (Code Violations), Small Claims.*

www.mass.gov/courts/courtsandjudges/courts/southeasthousingmain.html

General Information: Includes housing code cases, real estate-related small claims, and many eviction cases for Plymouth County; also see district courts for these type of cases.

Suffolk County

Superior Court - Civil 3 Pemberton Sq, Superior Court Clerk, Copy Dept, Boston, MA 02108; 617-788-8175; fax: 617-788-7667; 8:30AM-4:30PM (EST). *Civil.*

www.mass.gov/courts/courtsandjudges/courts/suffsupcivmain.html

General Information: No impounded records released. Will not fax documents. Court makes copy: $1.00 per page. Self serve copy: $.25 per page. Certification fee: $2.50. Payee: Clerk of Superior Court. Business checks accepted. No credit cards accepted. Prepayment required.

Civil Name Search: Access: Mail, in person, online. Both court and visitors may perform in person name searches. No search fee. Civil records on computer from 1991, index cards and books from 1860. Mail turnaround time 1 week. Public use terminal has civil records back to 7/1990.

Terminal results may include address. Online only for attorneys and law firms at www.ma-trialcourts.org/tcic/.

Superior Court - Criminal Superior Court Clerk, Three Pemberton Sq, 14th Fl, Boston, MA 02108; 617-788-8160; 8:30AM-4:30PM (EST). *Felony.*
www.mass.gov/courts/courtsandjudges/courts/suffsupcrimmain.html
General Information: Includes Boston, Chelsea, Revere, Winthrop. Will not fax documents. Court makes copy: $1.00 per page (attested). Certification fee: $20.00. Payee: Superior Court. Personal checks accepted. No credit cards accepted. Prepayment required.
Criminal Name Search: Access: Phone, in person, online. Both court and visitors may perform in person name searches. No search fee. Criminal records computerized from 1991, index cards and books from 1950, archived from 1864. Note: Court will look up one or two names as a courtesy over the phone. Mail turnaround time 1-2 weeks. Public use terminal has crim records back to 1991. Online for attorneys and law firms only with registration at www.ma-trialcourts.org/tcic/.

Chelsea District Court 120 Broadway, Chelsea, MA 02150; 617-660-9200; criminal phone: x1; civil phone: x8; probate phone: x300; fax: 617-660-9215; 8:30AM-4:30PM (EST). *Felony, Misdemeanor, Civil, Eviction, Small Claims.*
www.mass.gov/courts/courtsandjudges/courts/chelseadistrictmain.html
General Information: Includes Chelsea and Revere. No closed cases, impounded, sealed, mental health commitment, alcoholic or victim of sexual offense records released. Will not fax documents. Court makes copy: $1.00 per page. Certification fee: $2.50 per cert/page. Payee: District Court. Personal checks accepted. No credit cards accepted. Prepayment required. Mail requests: SASE required for mail return of any copies.
Civil Name Search: Access: Phone, mail, in person. Only the court performs in person name searches; visitors may not. No search fee. Civil index on cards or docket books back to 1900; on computer back to 1990. Mail turnaround time 1-2 weeks.
Criminal Name Search: Access: Phone, mail, in person. Only the court performs in person name searches; visitors may not. No search fee. Required to search: name, years to search; also helpful: address, DOB. Criminal records indexed on cards or docket books back to 1900; on computer back to 1990. Mail turnaround time 1-2 weeks.

Brighton Division Boston Municipal Court 52 Academy Hill Rd, Brighton, MA 02135; 617-782-6521; fax: 617-254-2127; 8:30AM-4:30PM (EST). *Felony, Misdemeanor, Civil, Eviction, Small Claims.*
www.mass.gov/courts/courtsandjudges/courts/brightondistrictmain.html
General Information: Includes Allston and Brighton. Also known as Brighton District Court. No sealed or impounded records released. Will not fax documents. Court makes copy: $1.00 per page. Certification fee: $2.50 per cert/page. Payee: BMC- Brighton. Personal checks accepted. No credit cards accepted. Prepayment required. Mail requests: SASE required for mail return of any copies.
Civil Name Search: Access: In person only. Visitors must perform in person searches themselves. Civil index on cards or docket books back to 1980. State law requires records be retained for 10 years. Public use terminal has civil records.
Criminal Name Search: Access: Phone, mail, in person. Visitors must perform in person searches themselves. No search fee. Required to search: name, years to search, DOB. Computerized records from 1990, criminal records on index cards or docket books back to 1978. State law requires records be retained for 10 years. Mail turnaround time 1-2 weeks.

Central Division Boston Municipal Court Office of Clerk-Magistrate, 24 New Chardon St, 6th Fl, Boston, MA 02114; criminal phone: 617-788-8600; civil phone: 617-788-8400; criminal fax: 617-788-8465; civil fax: 8:30AM-4:30PM; 8:30AM-4:30PM (EST). *Misdemeanor, Civil, Small Claims.*
www.mass.gov/courts/courtsandjudges/courts/bostonmunicipalcourt/index.html#jurisdiction
General Information: Small Claims phone number 617-788-8411. Misdemeanor records are located on the 6th Fl in a separate index. No impounded records released. Will fax documents $.00 per page fax fee. Court makes copy: $1.00 per page. Certification fee: $2.50 per cert/page. Payee: District Court. Personal checks accepted. Prepayment required.
Civil Name Search: Access: Mail, in person. Both court and visitors may perform in person name searches. No search fee. Civil records on computer back to 1995; only court searches those records. Public can search prior records on index cards. Mail turnaround time 1-2 weeks.
Criminal Name Search: Access: Mail, in person. Both court and visitors may perform in person name searches. No search fee. Required to search: name, years to search; also helpful: DOB. Criminal records computerized from 1995; only court searches those records. Public can search prior records on index cards. Mail turnaround time 1-2 weeks.

Charlestown Division Boston Municipal Court 3 City Square, Charlestown, MA 02129; 617-242-5400; fax: 617-242-1677; 8:30AM-4:30PM (EST). *Felony, Misdemeanor, Civil, Eviction, Small Claims.*
www.mass.gov/courts/courtsandjudges/courts/charlestowndistrictmain.html
General Information: No juvenile records released. Will not fax documents. Court makes copy: $1.00 per page. Certification fee: $2.50 per cert/page. Payee: District Court. Personal checks accepted. No credit cards accepted. Prepayment required.
Civil Name Search: Access: Fax, mail, in person. Only the court performs in person name searches; visitors may not. No search fee. Civil index on cards or docket books. State law requires records be retained for 10 years. Mail turnaround time 1-2 weeks.
Criminal Name Search: Access: Fax, mail, in person. Only the court performs in person name searches; visitors may not. No search fee. Required to search: name, years to search; also helpful: DOB. Criminal records indexed on cards or docket books. State law requires records be retained for 10 years. Mail turnaround time 1-2 weeks.

Dorchester Division Boston Municipal Court 510 Washington St, Dorchester, MA 02124; 617-288-9500 x6; criminal phone: x1; civil phone: x1; fax: 617-436-8250; 8:30AM-4:30PM (EST). *Felony, Misdemeanor, Civil, Eviction, Small Claims.*
www.mass.gov/courts/courtsandjudges/courts/dorchesterdistrictmain.html
General Information: Send fax request to 'Attention Records Department.' No juvenile records released. Will fax documents to local or toll free line. Court makes copy: $1.00 per page. Certification fee: $2.50 per cert/page. Payee: District Court. Personal checks accepted. No credit cards accepted. Prepayment required. Mail requests: SASE required for mail return of any copies.
Civil Name Search: Access: Mail, fax, in person. Both court and visitors may perform in person name searches. No search fee. Civil index on cards or docket books from 1970. State law requires records be retained for 20 years. Mail turnaround time 1-2 weeks. Civil PAT goes back to 2000.
Criminal Name Search: Access: Mail, fax, in person. Both court and visitors may perform in person name searches. No search fee. Required to search: name, years to search, DOB. Criminal records indexed on cards or docket books to 1950's; on computer since 1998. State law requires records be retained for 20 years. Mail turnaround time 1-2 weeks. Criminal PAT goes back to 2000.

East Boston Division Boston Municipal Court 37 Meridian St, East Boston, MA 02128; 617-569-7550 x5; criminal phone: x4; civil phone: x117; fax: 617-561-4988; 8:30AM-4:30PM (EST). *Felony Pre-lims, Misdemeanor, Civil Actions under $25,000, Eviction, Small Claims.*
www.mass.gov/courts/courtsandjudges/courts/eastbostondistrictmain.html
General Information: Includes East Boston and Winthrop. No juvenile records released. Will fax documents. Court makes copy: $1.00 per page. Certification fee: $2.50 per cert/page. Payee: Boston Municipal Court/ East Boston Division. Personal checks accepted. Visa/MC accepted. Prepayment required. Mail requests: SASE required for mail return of any copies.
Civil Name Search: Access: In person. Visitors must perform in person searches themselves. Civil index on cards or docket books since 1965, not computerized. State law requires records be retained for 20 years.
Criminal Name Search: Access: In person. Visitors must perform in person searches themselves. Criminal records indexed on cards or docket books, computerized since 1997. State law requires records be retained 20 years. Clerk may do a phone lookup of only one name for you, at their discretion.

Roxbury Division Boston Municipal Court 85 Warren St, Roxbury, MA 02119; 617-427-7000; fax: 617-541-0286; 8:30AM-4:30PM (EST). *Felony, Misdemeanor, Civil, Eviction, Small Claims.*
www.mass.gov/courts/courtsandjudges/courts/roxburydistrictmain.html
General Information: No juvenile records released. Fee to fax out file $1.00 per page. Court makes copy: $1.00 per page. Certification fee: $2.50 per cert/page. Payee: Roxbury Court. No personal checks accepted. Prepayment required. Mail requests: SASE required for mail return of any copies.
Civil Name Search: Access: Phone, fax, mail, in person. Only the court performs in person name searches; visitors may not. No search fee. Civil index on cards or docket books since 1981; on computer back to 1999. Records retained 10 years. Mail turnaround time 1-2 weeks.
Criminal Name Search: Access: Fax, mail, in person. Only the court performs in person name searches; visitors may not. No search fee. Required to search: name, years to search, DOB; also helpful: address. Criminal records indexed on cards or docket books since 1981; on computer back to 1999. Records retained 10 years. Note: Criminal searches restricted at this time; call court for exact search procedure, extension 532. Mail turnaround time 1-2 weeks.

South Boston Division Boston Municipal Court 535 E Broadway #F2, South Boston, MA 02127; 617-268-9292/9293; fax: 617-268-7321; 8:30AM-4:30PM (EST). *Felony, Misdemeanor, Civil, Eviction, Small Claims.*

www.mass.gov/courts/courtsandjudges/courts/southbostondistrictmain.html

General Information: No juvenile or medical records released. Will not fax documents. Court makes copy: $1.00 per page. Certification fee: $2.50 per cert/page. Payee: District Court. Personal checks accepted. No credit cards accepted. Prepayment required.

Civil Name Search: Access: In person only. Visitors must perform in person searches themselves. Required to search: name, years to search, address. Civil index on cards or docket books. Records go back 20 years.

Criminal Name Search: Access: In person only. Visitors must perform in person searches themselves. Required to search: name, years to search, address, DOB. Criminal records indexed on cards or docket books. Records go back 20 years; from 2000 on computer.

West Roxbury Division Boston Municipal Court 445 Arborway, Courthouse, Jamaica Plain, MA 02130; 617-971-1200; fax: 617-983-0243; 8:30AM-4:30PM (EST). *Felony, Misdemeanor, Civil, Eviction, Small Claims.*

www.mass.gov/courts/courtsandjudges/courts/westroxburydistrictmain.html

General Information: Includes West Roxbury, Jamaica Plain, Hyde Park, Roslindale, Parts of Mission Hill, and Mattapan sections of Boston. No juvenile records released. Will not fax documents. Court makes copy: $1.00 per page. Certification fee: $2.50 per cert/page. Payee: District Court. Personal checks accepted. No credit cards accepted. Prepayment required.

Civil Name Search: Access: In person only. Visitors must perform in person searches themselves. Required to search: name, years to search, type of civil action; also helpful: address. Civil index on cards or docket books. State law requires records be retained for 10 years.

Criminal Name Search: Access: In person. Visitors must perform in person searches themselves. Required to search: name, years to search; also helpful: DOB. Criminal records indexed on cards or docket books. State law requires records be retained for 10 years.

Boston Housing Court 24 New Chardon St, 3rd Fl, Edward W Brooke Courthouse, Boston, MA 02114; 617-788-8485; criminal phone: 617-788-8515; civil phone: 617-788-8487; fax: 617-788-8981; 8:30AM-4:30PM (EST). *Eviction, Misdemeanor (Code Violations) for residential, Housing Civil Unlimited.*

www.mass.gov/courts/courtsandjudges/courts/bostonhousingmain.html

General Information: Small claims phone is 617-788-8515. Includes many housing code cases, real estate-related small claims and eviction cases for Suffolk County, except Revere, Winthrop and Chelsea.

Probate & Family Court P.O. Box 9667, Edward W Brooke Courthouse, 24 New Chardon St, 3rd Fl, Boston, MA 02114-4703; 617-788-8300; fax: 617-788-8962; 8AM-5PM (EST). *Probate, Domestic Relations.*

www.mass.gov/courts/courtsandjudges/courts/suffprobmain.html

General Information: Jurisdiction includes Boston, Brighton, Charlestown, Chelsea, Dorchester, East Boston, Hyde Park, Jamaica Plain, Revere, Roslindale, South Boston, Winthrop.

Worcester County

Superior Court 225 Main St, Rm 1008, Worcester, MA 01608; 508-831-2000; 8AM-4:30PM (EST). *Felony, Civil Actions over $25,000.*

www.mass.gov/courts/courtsandjudges/courts/worcsupmain.html

General Information: No impounded or juvenile records released. Will not fax documents. Court makes copy: $1.00 per page. Certification fee: $2.50 per cert. Payee: Clerk of Superior Court. No personal checks or credit cards accepted. Prepayment required.

Civil Name Search: Access: Mail, in person, online. Both court and visitors may perform in person name searches. No search fee. Civil records on computer from 1990, index books from 1900. Mail turnaround time 1 week. Civil PAT goes back to 1990. Online only for attorneys and law firms at www.ma-trialcourts.org/tcic/.

Criminal Name Search: Access: Mail, in person, online. Both court and visitors may perform in person name searches. No search fee. Criminal records computerized from 1990, index books from 1900. Mail turnaround time 1 week. Criminal PAT goes back to same as civil. Online for attorneys and law firms only with registration at www.ma-trialcourts.org/tcic/.

Clinton District Court 300 Boylston St, Clinton, MA 01510; 978-368-7811; fax: 978-368-7827; 8:30AM-4:30PM (EST). *Felony, Misdemeanor, Civil, Eviction, Small Claims.*

General Information: Includes Berlin, Bolton, Boylston, Clinton, Harvard, Lancaster, Sterling, and West Boylston. No juvenile records released. Will not fax documents. Court makes copy: $1.00 per page. Self serve copy: same. Certification fee: $2.50 per page. Payee: Clerk Magistrate. Personal checks accepted. No credit cards accepted. Prepayment required. Mail requests: SASE required.

Civil Name Search: Access: Mail, in person. Only the court performs in person name searches; visitors may not. No search fee. Required to search: name, years to search; also helpful: DOB, SSN. Civil index on cards or docket books back to 1987. Mail turnaround time 1-2 weeks.

Criminal Name Search: Access: Mail, in person. Only the court performs in person name searches; visitors may not. No search fee. Required to search: name, years to search, address, DOB, SSN, signed release. Criminal records indexed on cards or docket books back to 1987. Mail turnaround time 1-2 weeks.

Dudley District Court 64 279 W Main, Dudley, MA 01571; 508-943-7123; fax: 508-949-0015; 8AM-4:30PM (EST). *Felony, Misdemeanor, Civil, Eviction, Small Claims.*

General Information: Includes Charlton, Dudley, Oxford, Southbridge, Sturbridge, and Webster. No juvenile records released. Court makes copy: $1.00 per page. Self serve copy: same. Certification fee: $2.50. Payee: District Court. Business checks accepted. All major credit cards accepted in person only. Prepayment required.

Civil Name Search: Access: Phone, fax, mail, in person. Both court and visitors may perform in person name searches. No search fee. Civil records on computer back to 2002; prior on index cards or docket books; records retained 10 years. Mail turnaround time 1-2 weeks. Public use terminal has civil records back to 2002 to 2010. cases since 2010 are not on terminal.

Criminal Name Search: Access: Phone, fax, mail, in person. Both court and visitors may perform in person name searches. No search fee. Required to search: name, years to search, DOB. Criminal records computerized from 6/96; on index cards or docket books back 10 years. Note: Public may research record data by viewing docket books. Mail turnaround time 1-2 weeks.

East Brookfield District Court 544 E Main St, East Brookfield, MA 01515-1701; criminal phone: 508-885-6305 x109; civil phone: 508-885-6395 x 107; fax: 508-885-7623; 8:30AM-4:30PM (EST). *Felony, Misdemeanor, Civil, Eviction, Small Claims.*

General Information: Includes Barre, Brookfield, East Brookfield, Hardwick, Leicester, New Braintree, North Brookfield, Oakham, Paxton, Rutland, Spencer, Warren, and West Brookfield. No juvenile, mental health records released. Will not fax documents. Court makes copy: $1.00 per page. Certification fee: $2.50 per cert. Payee: District Court. No personal checks accepted, business check only. Visa/MC accepted. Prepayment required. Mail requests: SASE requested.

Civil Name Search: Access: Mail, in person. Both court and visitors may perform in person name searches. No search fee. Civil index on cards or docket books and computer. Mail turnaround time 1-2 weeks; use a retriever when possible suggested.

Criminal Name Search: Access: Mail, in person. Both court and visitors may perform in person name searches. No search fee. Required to search: name, years to search; also helpful: DOB. Criminal records indexed on cards or docket books to 1945, computerized since 1999. Mail turnaround time 1-2 weeks; strongly suggest to use a retriever when possible.

Fitchburg District Court 16 100 Elm St, Fitchburg, MA 01420; 978-345-2111; fax: 978-342-2461; 8:30AM-4:30PM (EST). *Felony, Misdemeanor, Civil, Eviction, Small Claims.*

General Information: Includes Fitchburg and Lunenburg. No juvenile or mental health records released. Will not fax out case files. Court makes copy: $1.00 per page. Certification fee: $2.50 per page. Payee: District Court. Business checks accepted, personal checks are not. Visa/MC/Carte Blanche cards accepted. Prepayment required.

Civil Name Search: Access: In person only. Visitors must perform in person searches themselves. Civil index on cards or docket books back 10 years, also on computer. Civil PAT goes back to 2002.

Criminal Name Search: Access: In person only. Visitors must perform in person searches themselves. Criminal records indexed on cards or docket books back 10 years; on computer back to 1994. Note: If a requester has the docket number, the court will pull the file on Fridays, will take longer if at archives. Criminal PAT goes back to 10 years.

Gardner District Court 108 Matthews St, Gardner, MA 01440-0040; 978-632-2373; fax: 978-630-3902; 8:30AM-4:30PM (EST). *Felony, Misdemeanor, Civil, Small Claims.*

www.mass.gov/courts/courtsandjudges/courts/gardnerdistrictmain.html

General Information: Includes Gardner, Hubbardston, Petersham, and Westminster. No juvenile records released. No fee to fax documents. Court makes copy: $1.00 per page. Certification fee: $2.50 per cert. Payee: District Court. Personal checks accepted. No credit cards accepted. Prepayment required.

Civil Name Search: Access: Mail, in person. Visitors must perform in person searches themselves. No search fee. Required to search: name, years to search, address. Civil index on cards or docket books back 10 years, also on computer. Public use terminal has civil records.

Criminal Name Search: Access: Fax, mail, in person. Visitors must perform in person searches themselves. No search fee. Required to search: name, years to search, DOB. Criminal records indexed on cards or docket books back 10 years.

Leominster District Court 25 School St, Leominster, MA 01453; 978-537-3722; fax: 978-537-3970; 8:30AM-4:30PM (EST). *Felony, Misdemeanor, Civil, Eviction, Small Claims.*

General Information: Includes Princeton, Holden and Leominster. No juvenile or impounded records released. Will not fax documents. Court makes copy: $1.00 per page. Certification fee: $2.50 per cert. Payee: District Court. Personal checks accepted. No credit cards accepted. Prepayment required. Mail requests: SASE required.

Civil Name Search: Access: Mail, in person. Both court and visitors may perform in person name searches. No search fee. Civil index on cards or docket books back 10 years, also on computer. Mail turnaround time 1-2 weeks. Public use terminal has civil records back to 2005.

Criminal Name Search: Access: Mail, in person. Both court and visitors may perform in person name searches. No search fee. Required to search: name, years to search; also helpful: DOB. Criminal records on computer since 1987; index cards or docket books back 10 years. Note: Public may view the docket books. Mail turnaround time 1-2 weeks.

Milford District Court 161 West St, Milford, MA 01757; 508-473-1260; fax: 508-634-8477; 8:30AM-4:30PM (EST). *Felony, Misdemeanor, Civil, Eviction, Small Claims.*

www.mass.gov/courts/courtsandjudges/courts/milforddistrictmain.html

General Information: Includes Mendon, Upton, Hopedale, and Milford in Worcester County; also includes Bellingham in Norfolk County. No mental health, impounded, alcohol, commitment, sexual abuse victim, waivers of fees or costs for indigents, delinquency, C & P, CHINS, 209A minor or 209A address records released. Will fax documents to local or toll-free number if all fees paid first. Court makes copy: $1.00 per page. Certification fee: $2.50. Payee: District Court. Business checks accepted. Visa/MC accepted in person only with photo ID. Prepayment required.

Civil Name Search: Access: In person only. Both court and visitors may perform in person name searches. No search fee. Civil index on cards or docket books back 10 years; on computer back to 2004. Public use terminal has civil records back to 2004. Terminal has small claims & civil records countywide.

Criminal Name Search: Access: In person only. Both court and visitors may perform in person name searches. No search fee. Required to search: name, years to search, DOB; also helpful: aliases. Criminal records computerized from 1998; prior records on index cards & docket books; computer indexes only searchable by court.

Uxbridge District Court 261 S Main St, Uxbridge, MA 01569; 508-278-2454; fax: 508-278-2929; 8:30AM-4:30PM (EST). *Felony, Misdemeanor, Civil, Eviction, Small Claims.*

General Information: Includes Blackstone, Douglas, Millville, Northbridge, Sutton, and Uxbridge. Impounded records. Will not fax out documents. Court makes copy: $1.00 per cert. Certification fee: $2.50 per cert. Payee: District Court. Personal checks accepted. No credit cards accepted. Prepayment required.

Civil Name Search: Access: Mail, in person. Only the court performs in person name searches; visitors may not. No search fee. Civil records indexed on computer. Note: All requests must be in writing. Mail turnaround time 1-2 weeks. Public use terminal has civil records back to 7/1/2004. Terminal has small claims & civil records.

Criminal Name Search: Access: Mail, in person. Only the court performs in person name searches; visitors may not. No search fee. Required to search: name, years to search; also helpful: DOB. Criminal records indexed on cards or docket books back 20 years or so. Note: All requests must be in writing. Mail turnaround time 1-2 weeks.

Westborough District Court 186 Oak St, Westborough, MA 01581; 508-366-8266 x2; criminal phone: x2; civil phone: x1; fax: 508-366-8268; 8:30AM-4:30PM (EST). *Felony, Misdemeanor, Civil, Eviction, Small Claims.*

General Information: Includes Grafton, Northborough, Shrewsbury, Southborough, and Westborough. Searches of Civil and Criminal indexes are two searches. No impounded, juvenile records released. Will not fax documents. Court makes copy: $1.00 per page. Certification fee: $2.50 per cert/page. Payee: District Court Westborough Division. Personal checks accepted. No credit cards accepted. Prepayment required.

Civil Name Search: Access: Mail, Fax, in person. Both court and visitors may perform in person name searches. No search fee. Civil index on cards or docket books back 10 years; also on computer. Public use terminal has civil records back to 2004.

Criminal Name Search: Access: Mail, Fax, in person. Both court and visitors may perform in person name searches. No search fee. Required to search: name, years to search; also helpful: DOB. Criminal records indexed on cards or docket books back 10 years; also on computer.

Winchendon District Court 108 Matthews, Gardner, MA 01440; 978-632-6326; fax: 978-632-3580; 8:30AM-4:30PM (EST). *Felony, Misdemeanor, Civil, Eviction, Small Claims.*

General Information: Includes Ashburnham, Phillipston, Royalston, Templeton, and Winchendon. This court moved its operation to Gardner on June 22, 2009. Previously the court's location was in Winchendon. Winchendon's records are kept separate from Gardner. Will not fax documents. Court makes copy: $1.00 per page. Certification fee: $2.50 per page. Payee: District Court. Personal checks accepted. No credit cards accepted. Prepayment required. Mail requests: SASE required.

Civil Name Search: Access: Phone, mail, in person. Visitors must perform in person searches themselves. No search fee. Civil index on cards or docket books back 10 years; also on computer. Note: Court will assist public if search is prior to docket books. Mail turnaround time 1-2 weeks. Civil PAT goes back to 2004. The further back, the less complete the case record database on the public terminal is. Results on terminal includes plaintiff names.

Criminal Name Search: Access: Mail, in person. Both court and visitors may perform in person name searches. No search fee. Required to search: name, years to search; also helpful: DOB, docket number. Criminal records indexed on docket books back 10 years. Mail turnaround time 1-2 weeks. Criminal PAT goes back to 1995. The further back, the less complete the case record database on the public terminal is. Results on terminal include PCF#.

Worcester District Court 225 Main St, Rm 1019, Worcester, MA 01608; 508-831-2010; criminal phone: x3; civil phone: x4; fax: 508-797-0716; 8AM-4:30PM (EST). *Felony, Misdemeanor, Civil, Eviction, Small Claims.*

www.mass.gov/courts/courtsandjudges/courts/worcesterdistrictmain.html

General Information: Includes Auburn, Millbury, and Worcester. No sealed, expunged, adoption or sex offense records released. Will not fax documents. Court makes copy: $1.00 per page. Certification fee: $2.50 per cert/page. Payee: District Court. In-state personal checks accepted; no out-of-state. Visa/MC accepted in person only. Prepayment required.

Civil Name Search: Access: In person only. Both court and visitors may perform in person name searches. No search fee. Civil index on cards 1987-1998; docket books 1999-2008, also on computer. Mail turnaround time 1-2 weeks. Civil PAT goes back to 2001.

Criminal Name Search: Access: In person only. Both court and visitors may perform in person name searches. No search fee. Criminal records on computer since 1999; prior records on docket books since 1982. Criminal PAT goes back to 1999.

Probate & Family Court 225 Main St, Worcester, MA 01608; 508-831-2200; fax: 508-752-6138; 8AM-4:30PM (EST). *Probate, Domestic Relations.*

Worcester Housing Court 225 Main St, Worcester, MA 01608; 508-831-2050; fax: 508-792-1170; 8:30AM-4:30PM (EST). *Eviction, Misdemeanor (Code Violations), Small Claims.*

General Information: Includes housing code cases, real estate-related small claims and many eviction cases for Worcester County. Also includes Asby, Hudson, Marlborough, and Townsend in Middles and Bellingham in Norfolk. Also see district courts for similar types of cases.

Michigan

Time Zone:	**EST & CST***
	*Four Northwestern Michigan counties are CST: They are: Dickinson, Gogebic, Iron, Menominee.
Capital:	**Lansing, Ingham County**
# of Counties:	**83**
State Web:	**www.michigan.gov**
Court Web:	**http://courts.michigan.gov**

Administration

State Court Administrator, PO Box 30048, Lansing, MI, 48909; 517-373-0130, Fax: 517-373-7517.

The Supreme Court and the Court of Appeals

The Supreme Court is Michigan's court of last resort. The Court of Appeals is the intermediate appellate court between the Supreme Court and the Michigan trial courts. Final decisions resulting from a circuit or probate court hearing may be appealed to the Court of Appeals. Court of Appeals opinions are free online to view at http://coa.courts.mi.gov/resources/opinions.htm. Subscribe to free email updates of appellate opinions at http://coa.courts.mi.gov/resources/subscribe.htm.

The Michigan Courts

Court	Type	How Organized	Jurisdiction Highpoints
Circuit*	General	83 Courts in 57 Circuits	Felony, Civil, Domestic, Juvenile
District*	Limited	105 Courts in 98 Districts	Misdemeanor, Civil to $25,000, Small Claims, Eviction, Traffic
Municipal*	Limited	4 Courts	Ordinance
Probate*	Special	79	Probate

* = profiled in this book

Details on the Court Structure

The **Circuit Court** is the court of general jurisdiction. In general, the Circuit Court handles all civil cases with claims of more than $25,000 and all felony criminal cases (cases where the accused, if found guilty, could be sent to prison). The **Family Division** of Circuit Court handles all cases regarding divorce, paternity, adoptions, personal protection actions, emancipation of minors, treatment and testing of infectious disease, safe delivery of newborns, name changes, juvenile offenses, and child abuse and neglect. In addition, the Circuit Court hears cases appealed from the other trial courts or from administrative agencies.

The **District Court** handles most traffic violations, civil cases with claims up to $25,000, landlord-tenant matters, most traffic tickets, and all misdemeanor criminal cases (generally, cases where the guilty, cannot be sentenced to more than one year in jail). Small claims cases are heard by a division of the District Court.

Four municipalities have chosen to retain a **Municipal Court** rather than create a District Court. The Municipal Courts have limited powers and are located in Grosse Pointe, Grosse Pointe Farms, Grosse Pointe Park, and Grosse Point Shores/Grosse Pointe Woods.

The **Probate Court** handles wills, administers estates and trusts, appoints guardians and conservators, and orders treatment for mentally ill and developmentally disabled persons.

There is a **Court of Claims** in Lansing that is a function of the 30th Circuit Court with jurisdiction over claims against the state of Michigan.

Record Searching Facts You Need to Know

Fees and Record Searching Tips

Court records are considered public except for specific categories: controlled substances, spousal abuse, Holmes youthful trainee, parental kidnapping, set aside convictions and probation, and sealed records. Courts will, however, affirm that cases exist and provide case numbers. Some courts will not perform criminal searches, rather they refer requests to the State Police. Although most courts charge $10.00 for certification, search requirements, and procedures vary widely because each jurisdiction may create its own administrative orders.

Several counties (Barry, Berrien, Iron, Isabella, Lake, and Washtenaw) and the 46th Circuit Court are participating in a *Demonstration Pilot* project designed to streamline court services and consolidate case management. These courts may refer to themselves as County Trial Courts.

Online Access is Limited

There is a wide range of online computerization of the judicial system from "none" to "fairly complete," but there is no statewide court records network. Some Michigan courts provide public access terminals in clerk's offices, and some courts are developing off-site electronic filing and searching capability.

Alcona County

23rd Circuit Court PO Box 308, Harrisville, MI 48740; 989-724-9410; fax: 989-724-9419; 8:30AM-N, 1-4:30PM (EST). *Felony, Civil Actions over $25,000, Vital Statistics.*

General Information: No suppressed, juvenile, sex offenders, mental health, or adoption records released. Will fax documents for fee, not disclosed, call. Court makes copy: $1.00 per page. Certification fee: $10.00 plus $1.00 per page copy fee after first page. Payee: Alcona County Clerk. Personal checks accepted. Credit card payments accepted via GPS. Prepayment required. Mail requests: SASE required.
Civil Name Search: Access: Fax, mail, in person. Only the court performs in person name searches; visitors may not. Search fee: $10.00 per name. Civil records on computer since 1990, pleading headings in books since 1869. Mail turnaround time 1-2 days.
Criminal Name Search: Access: Fax, mail, in person. Only the court performs in person name searches; visitors may not. Search fee: $10.00 per name. Required to search: name, years to search, DOB. Criminal records on computer since 1990, pleading headings in books since 1869. Mail turnaround time 1-2 days.

81st District Court PO Box 385, Harrisville, MI 48740; 989-724-9500; fax: 989-724-9509; 8:30AM-4:30PM (EST). *Misdemeanor, Civil Actions under $25,000, Eviction, Small Claims.*
General Information: No suppressed, juvenile, sex offenders, mental health, or adoption records released. Fee to fax out doc $10.00 each. Court makes copy: $1.00 per page. Certification fee: $10.00. Payee: 81st District Court. No personal checks or credit cards accepted. Prepayment required. Mail requests: SASE required.
Civil Name Search: Access: Phone, fax, mail, in person. Only the court performs in person name searches; visitors may not. Search fee: $10.00. Civil records on books since 1980; on computer back to 1997. Mail turnaround time 1 week.
Criminal Name Search: Access: Fax, mail, in person. Only the court performs in person name searches; visitors may not. Search fee: $10.00. Required to search: name, years to search, DOB. Criminal docket on books since 1980; on computer back to 1997. Mail turnaround time 1 week.

Probate Court PO Box 328, 106 Fifth St, Harrisville, MI 48740; 989-724-9490; fax: 989-724-9499; 8:30AM-4:30PM (EST). *Probate.*

Alger County

11th Circuit Court 101 Court St, PO Box 538, Munising, MI 49862; 906-387-2076; fax: 906-387-2156; 8AM-4PM (EST). *Felony, Civil Actions over $25,000, Vital Statistics.*
General Information: No juvenile, sex offenders, mental health, or adoption records released. Will fax documents to toll-free number. Court makes copy: $1.00 per page. Certification fee: $10.00 per document. Payee: Alger County Clerk. Personal checks accepted. Prepayment required. Mail requests: SASE required.
Civil Name Search: Access: Mail, in person. Only the court performs in person name searches; visitors may not. Search fee: $5.00 per name. Civil index on docket books back to 1884; on computer back to 2000. Mail turnaround time 1 week.
Criminal Name Search: Access: Mail, in person. Only the court performs in person name searches; visitors may not. Search fee: $5.00 per name. Criminal records indexed in books back to 1884; on computer back to 2000. Mail turnaround time 1 week.

93rd District Court PO Box 186, Munising, MI 49862; 906-387-3879; fax: 906-387-2688; 8AM-4PM (EST). *Misdemeanor, Civil Actions under $25,000, Eviction, Small Claims.* www.algercourthouse.com/
General Information: No suppressed records released. Will fax documents to local or toll free line. Court makes copy: $.25 per page. Certification fee: $10.00 per document plus copy fee for any add'l pages. Payee: District Court. Business checks accepted. Major credit cards accepted. Prepayment required. Mail requests: SASE required.
Civil Name Search: Access: Mail, in person. Only the court performs in person name searches; visitors may not. Search fee: $10.00 per name. Civil index on docket books back 10 years; on computer back to 2000. Mail turnaround time 5-7 days.
Criminal Name Search: Access: Fax, mail, in person. Only the court performs in person name searches; visitors may not. Search fee: $10.00 per name. Required to search: name, years to search, DOB. Criminal records indexed in books back 6 years; on computer back to 2000. Mail turnaround time 5-7 days.

Probate Court 101 Court St, Munising, MI 49862; 906-387-2080; fax: 906-387-4134; 8AM-N, 1-4PM (EST). *Probate.*

Allegan County

48th Circuit Court 113 Chestnut St, Allegan, MI 49010; 269-673-0300 x2; fax: 269-673-0298; 8AM-5PM (EST). *Felony, Civil Actions over $25,000, Vital Statistics.*
General Information: No suppressed, juvenile, sex offenders, mental health, or adoption records released. Will fax documents to local or toll free line. Court makes copy: $1.00 per page. Certification fee: $10.00 per doc. Payee: Allegan County Clerk. Personal checks accepted. No credit cards accepted. Prepayment required. Mail requests: SASE required.
Civil Name Search: Access: Mail, fax, in person. Only the court performs in person name searches; visitors may not. Search fee: $5.00 per name. Civil records on computer since 1985. Mail turnaround time 1-7 days.
Criminal Name Search: Access: Mail, fax, in person. Only the court performs in person name searches; visitors may not. Search fee: $5.00 per name. Required to search: name, years to search, DOB. Criminal records on computer since 1985. Mail turnaround time 1-7 days.

57th District Court 113 Chestnut St, Allegan, MI 49010; 269-673-0400; criminal phone: 269-673-0400; civil phone: 269-673-0355; fax: 269-673-0490; 8:30AM-4:30PM (EST). *Misdemeanor, Civil Actions under $25,000, Eviction, Small Claims.*
www.allegancounty.org/Government/DC/
General Information: No non-public records released. Will fax documents to local or toll free line. Court makes copy: $1.00 per page. Certification fee: $10.00. Payee: 57th District Court. Personal checks accepted. Major credit cards accepted via GPS. Prepayment required. Mail requests: SASE required for mail return of any copies.
Civil Name Search: Access: In person only. Both court and visitors may perform in person name searches. No search fee. Civil PAT goes back to 1980s, countywide available. Find case number on public terminal, then clerk can retrieve full record. Records on terminal are less complete the further back you look.
Criminal Name Search: Access: In person only. Both court and visitors may perform in person name searches. No search fee. Required to search: name, years to search, DOB. . Criminal PAT goes back to same as civil. Find case number on public terminal, then clerk can retrieve full record. Records on terminal are less complete the further back you look.

Probate Court 113 Chestnut Street, Allegan, MI 49010; 269-673-0250; fax: 269-686-5157; 8AM-5PM (EST). *Probate.*

Alpena County

26th Circuit Court 720 W Chisholm #2, Alpena, MI 49707; 989-354-9520; fax: 989-354-9644; 8:30AM-4:30PM (EST). *Felony, Civil Actions over $25,000, Vital Statistics.*
www.alpenacounty.org/circuit%20court.html
General Information: No suppressed, juvenile, sex offenders, mental health, or adoption records released. Will fax documents $5.00 plus $1.00 per page. Court makes copy: $2.00 per page. Certification fee: $10.00. Payee: County Clerk. Personal checks accepted. No credit cards accepted. Prepayment required.
Civil Name Search: Access: Fax, mail, in person. Both court and visitors may perform in person name searches. Search fee: $10.00 per name. Civil records on computer since 1988, prior on docket books. Mail turnaround time 3 days or less. Civil PAT goes back to 1988, images since 2005.
Criminal Name Search: Access: Fax, mail, in person. Both court and visitors may perform in person name searches. Search fee: $10.00 per name. Criminal records on computer since 1988; prior on docket books. Mail turnaround time 2-3 days. Criminal PAT goes back to 1988, images since 2005.

88th District Court 719 W Chisholm #3, Alpena, MI 49707; 989-354-9678; criminal: 989-354-9686; civil: 989-354-9685; fax: 989-354-9785; 8:30AM-4:30PM (EST). *Misdemeanor, Civil Actions under $25,000, Eviction, Small Claims.* www.alpenacounty.org/district%20court.html
General Information: No suppressed records released. Will fax documents to local or toll free line. Court makes copy: $1.00 per page. Certification fee: $5.00. Payee: 88th District Court. Only cashiers checks and money orders accepted. Prepayment required. Mail requests: SASE required.
Civil Name Search: Access: Fax, mail, in person. Only the court performs in person name searches; visitors may not. Search fee: $5.00 per name. Civil records on computer back to 1989, prior on cards back to 1970s. Mail turnaround time 1-2 days.
Criminal Name Search: Access: Fax, mail, in person. Only the court performs in person name searches; visitors may not. Search fee: $5.00 per name. Required to search: name, years to search, DOB; also helpful: SSN. Criminal records computerized from 1989, prior on cards back to 1970s. Mail turnaround time 1-2 days.

Probate Court 719 W Chisholm, Suite 4, County Office Bldg, Alpena, MI 49707; 989-354-9650; fax: 989-354-9782; 8:30AM-4:30PM (EST). *Probate.* www.alpenacounty.org/probate%20court.html

Antrim County

13th Circuit Court PO Box 520, Bellaire, MI 49615; 231-533-6353; probate phone: 231-533-6681; fax: 231-533-6935; 8:30AM-5PM (EST). *Felony, Civil Actions over $25,000, Vital Statistics.*
www.antrimcounty.org/circuitcourt.asp
General Information: No suppressed, juvenile, sex offenders, mental health, or adoption records released. Will fax documents $5.00 per doc. Court makes copy: $.25 per page. Certification fee: $10.00 plus $1.00 per page. Payee: Antrim County Clerk. Personal checks accepted. No credit cards accepted. Prepayment required. Mail requests: SASE required.
Civil Name Search: Access: Fax, mail, in person, online. Both court and visitors may perform in person name searches. Search fee: $5.00 per name. Civil records on computer since 1997, prior on books. Note: Only court can search on computer, in person searchers may look at old records on docket books. Mail turnaround time 1 week. Access to a record index is at http://online.co.grand-traverse.mi.us/iprod/clerk/cccivil.html .
Criminal Name Search: Access: Fax, mail, in person, online. Both court and visitors may perform in person name searches. Search fee: $5.00 per name. Required to search: name, years to search; also helpful: DOB. Criminal docket on books from 1800s, on computer since 1997. Note: Only court can search on computer, in person searchers may review old docket books. Mail turnaround time 1 week. Access to criminal record index is found at http://online.co.grand-traverse.mi.us/iprod/clerk/cccriminal.html.

86th District Court PO Box 597, Bellaire, MI 49615; 231-533-6441; civil phone: 231-533-6842; fax: 231-533-6322; 8AM-4:30PM (EST). *Misdemeanor, Civil Actions under $25,000, Eviction, Small Claims.*
www.co.grand-traverse.mi.us/courts/86th_District_Court.htm
General Information: No suppressed, sex offenders records released. Will fax documents. Court makes copy: $1.00 per page. Certification fee: $10.00 per doc plus copy fee. Payee: District Court. Business checks accepted. Major credit cards accepted via GPS. Prepayment required. Mail requests: SASE required.
Civil Name Search: Access: Fax, mail, in person, online. Only the court performs in person name searches; visitors may not. Search fee: $10.00. Civil records on computer since 1986, prior on cards. Mail turnaround time usually same day. Access to a list of cases is found at http://districtcourt.co.grand-traverse.mi.us/c86_cases/. A second site is at http://online.co.grand-traverse.mi.us/iprod/clerk/cccivil.html

Criminal Name Search: Access: Fax, mail, in person, online. Only the court performs in person name searches; visitors may not. Search fee: $10.00 per name. Required to search: name, years to search, DOB; also helpful: SSN. Criminal records on computer since 1986, prior on cards. Mail turnaround time usually same day. Access online is same as civil. Online results show middle initial, DOB.

Probate Court PO Box 130, 205 E Cayuga St, Bellaire, MI 49615; 231-533-6681; fax: 231-533-6600; 8:30AM-N,12:30-4:30PM (EST). *Probate.* www.antrimcounty.org/probate.asp

Arenac County

23rd Circuit Court 120 N Grove St, PO Box 747, Standish, MI 48658; 989-846-9186; fax: 989-846-9199; 9AM-4:30PM (EST). *Felony, Civil Actions over $25,000, Vital Statistics.*
General Information: No suppressed, juvenile, mental health, or adoption records released. Will not fax documents. Court makes copy: $1.00 per page. Certification fee: $10.00 first page, $1.00 ea add'l. Payee: Arenac County Clerk. Personal checks accepted. Major credit cards accepted via GPS. Prepayment required. Mail requests: SASE required.
Civil Name Search: Access: Mail, in person. Both court and visitors may perform in person name searches. Search fee: $10.00 per name. Civil records go back to 1883, civil records on computer back to 1991, prior on index books. Mail turnaround time 1-5 days. Civil PAT goes to 1991.
Criminal Name Search: Access: Mail, in person. Both court and visitors may perform in person name searches. Search fee: $10.00 per name. Required to search: name, years to search, DOB; also helpful: SSN. Criminal records go back to 1883, Criminal records computerized from 1991, prior on index books. Mail turnaround time 1-5 days. Criminal PAT goes back to same as civil.

81st District Court PO Box 129, Standish, MI 48658; 989-846-9538; fax: 989-846-2008; 8:30AM-4:30PM (EST). *Misdemeanor, Civil Actions under $25,000, Eviction, Small Claims.*
General Information: No suppressed, juvenile, sex offenders, mental health, or adoption records released. Will fax documents $2.00 1st page, $.50 each add'l. No charge for fax cover sheet. Court makes copy: $1.00 1st page, $.25 each add'l. Certification fee: $10.00 per doc. Payee: 81st District Court. Personal checks accepted. Major credit cards accepted via GPS. Prepayment required. Mail requests: SASE required.
Civil Name Search: Access: Phone, fax, mail, in person. Only the court performs in person name searches; visitors may not. Search fee: $10.00. Civil records on computer since 1990, prior on docket books. Mail turnaround time 5 days.
Criminal Name Search: Access: Phone, fax, mail, in person. Only the court performs in person name searches; visitors may not. Search fee: $10.00. Required to search: name, years to search, DOB; also helpful: SSN. Criminal records on computer since 1990, prior on cards by name. Mail turnaround time 5 days.

Probate Court 120 N Grove, PO Box 666, Standish, MI 48658; 989-846-6941; fax: 989-846-9199; 9AM-4:30PM (EST). *Probate.*

Baraga County

12th Circuit Court 16 N 3rd St, L'Anse, MI 49946; 906-524-6183; fax: 906-524-6432; 8:30AM-4:30PM (EST). *Felony, Civil Actions over $25,000, Vital Statistics.*
General Information: No suppressed records released. Will fax documents. Court makes copy: $1.00 per page. Self serve copy: same. Certification fee: $10.00 per doc; add copy fee for add'l pages. Payee: County Clerk. Personal checks accepted. No credit cards accepted. Prepayment required. Mail requests: SASE required.
Civil Name Search: Access: Phone, mail, in person. Only the court performs in person name searches; visitors may not. Search fee: $5.00. Civil index on docket books, are computerized since 1998. Mail turnaround time same day.
Criminal Name Search: Access: Phone, mail, in person. Only the court performs in person name searches; visitors may not. Search fee: $5.00 per name. Required to search: name, years to search, DOB; also helpful: SSN. Criminal docket on books, are computerized since 1998. Mail turnaround time same day.

97th District Court 16 N 3rd St, L'Anse, MI 49946; 906-524-6109; fax: 906-524-7017; 8:30AM-N, 1-4:30PM (EST). *Misdemeanor, Civil Actions under $25,000, Eviction, Small Claims.*
General Information: No suppressed, sex offenders records released. Will fax documents to local or toll-free number. Court makes copy: $1.00 per page. Certification fee: $10.00 plus $1.00 per page after first. Payee: 97th District Court. Personal checks accepted. No credit cards accepted. Prepayment required. Mail requests: SASE requested.
Civil Name Search: Access: Mail, in person. Only the court performs in person name searches; visitors may not. Search fee: $10.00 per name. Civil records listed on docket books back 10 years. Mail turnaround time 2-3 days.
Criminal Name Search: Access: Mail, in person. Only the court performs in person name searches; visitors may not. Search fee: $10.00

per name. Required to search: name, years to search, DOB; also helpful: SSN. Criminal records listed on docket books back 10 years. Mail turnaround time 2-3 days.

Probate Court County Courthouse, 16 N 3rd St, L'Anse, MI 49946; 906-524-6390; fax: 906-524-2052; 8:30AM-N, 1-4:30PM (EST). *Probate.*

Barry County

5th Circuit Court 220 W State St, Hastings, MI 49058; 269-945-1285; fax: 269-945-0209; 8AM-5PM (EST). *Felony, Civil Actions over $25,000, Vital Statistics.* www.barrycounty.org

General Information: No suppressed, juvenile, sex offenders, mental health, or adoption records released. Will fax back documents $1.00 per page. Court makes copy: $1.00 per page. Certification fee: $10.00 per doc plus $1.00 per page. Payee: County Clerk. Personal checks accepted. Credit card payments accepted via GPS. Prepayment required. Mail requests: SASE or toll-free fax number required.

Civil Name Search: Access: Fax, mail, in person. Both court and visitors may perform in person name searches. Search fee: $5.00 per name; entitled to 5 pages of Register of Actions or copies from file. Civil records on computer since 1992, card index back to 1977, prior on books. Mail turnaround time 2 days.

Criminal Name Search: Access: Fax, mail, in person. Both court and visitors may perform in person name searches. Search fee: $5.00 per name; entitled to 5 pages of Register of Actions or copies from file. Required to search: name, years to search, DOB; also helpful: SSN. Criminal records on computer since 1992, card index back to 1977, prior on books. Mail turnaround time 2 days.

56B District Court 206 W Court St #202, Hastings, MI 49058; 269-945-1404; fax: 269-948-3314; 8AM-5PM (EST). *Misdemeanor, Civil Actions under $25,000, Eviction, Small Claims.*
www.barrycounty.org/courts-and-law-enforcement/56b-district-court/

General Information: No suppressed, sex offenders, or mental health records released. Will fax documents $1.00 per page. Court makes copy: $1.00 per page. Certification fee: $10.00 plus $1.00 per page after first. Payee: 56B District Court. Personal checks accepted. Credit card payments accepted via GPS. Prepayment required. Mail requests: SASE required.

Civil Name Search: Access: Phone, fax, mail, in person. Only the court performs in person name searches; visitors may not. Search fee: $5.00 per name. Civil records on computer since 1990, prior on index books. Mail turnaround time 2 days.

Criminal Name Search: Access: Phone, fax, mail, in person. Only the court performs in person name searches; visitors may not. Search fee: $5.00 per name. Required to search: name, years to search, DOB. Criminal records on computer since 1990, prior on index books. Mail turnaround time 2 days.

Probate Court 206 W Court St, #302, Hastings, MI 49058; 269-945-1390; fax: 269-948-3322; 8AM-5PM (EST). *Probate.*
www.barrycounty.org/courts-and-law-enforcement/family-division/probate-court/

General Information: Also handles name changes, adoptions, emancipations.

Bay County

18th Circuit Court 1230 Washington Ave #725, Bay City, MI 48708-5737; 989-895-4265; fax: 989-895-4099; 8AM-5PM (EST). *Felony, Civil Actions over $25,000, Vital Statistics.* www.baycountycourts.com/

General Information: No suppressed records released. Will not fax documents. Court makes copy: $1.00 per page. Certification fee: $10.00, $1.00 each add'l. Payee: 18th Circuit Court. Personal checks accepted. No credit cards accepted. Prepayment required. Mail requests: SASE requested.

Civil Name Search: Access: Phone, fax, mail, in person. Both court and visitors may perform in person name searches. No search fee. Required to search: Name. Civil records on computer for the last since 1986. Mail turnaround time same day. Civil PAT goes back to 1986. Access the county court records for free at from home page or http://12.221.137.17/c74/c74_cases.php. Calendar of scheduled cases at home page.

Criminal Name Search: Access: Phone, fax, mail, in person, online. Both court and visitors may perform in person name searches. Search fee: $10.00. Required to search: Name, DOB. Criminal records on computer for the last since 1986. Mail turnaround time same day. Criminal PAT goes back to same as civil. Access the county courts' records for free from home page or at http://12.221.137.17/c74/c74_cases.php. Calendar of scheduled cases at home page.

74th District Court 1230 Washington Ave, Bay City, MI 48708; 989-895-4232; criminal phone: 989-895-4229; civil phone: 989-895-4203; fax: 989-895-4233; 8AM-5PM (EST). *Misdemeanor, Civil Actions under $25,000, Eviction, Small Claims.*
www.baycountycourts.com/

General Information: No suppressed, juvenile, sex offenders, mental health, or adoption records released. Will not fax documents. Court makes copy: $1.00 per page. Self serve copy: $.25 per page. Certification fee: $10.00. Payee: 74th District Court. Personal checks accepted. Visa/MC accepted. Prepayment required.

Civil Name Search: Access: In person, online. Visitors must perform in person searches themselves. No search fee. Civil records on computer since 1992, listed on index cards prior. Civil PAT goes back to 1994. Access the county court records for free at http://12.221.137.17/c74/c74_cases.php. Calendar of scheduled cases at http://12.221.137.17/c74/c74_calendar.php.

Criminal Name Search: Access: In person, online. Visitors must perform in person searches themselves. Required to search: name, years to search, DOB; SSN helpful. Criminal records on computer since 1992, listed on index cards prior. Criminal PAT goes to 1992. Online same as civil.

Probate Court 1230 Washington, #715, Bay City, MI 48708; 989-895-4205; fax: 989-895-4194; 8AM-5PM (EST). *Probate.*

General Information: Access the county courts' calendar of scheduled cases for free at www.baycountycourts.com.

Benzie County

19th Circuit Court 448 Court Place, Beulah, MI 49617; 231-882-9671 & 800-315-3593; fax: 231-882-5941; 8AM-5PM (EST). *Felony, Civil Actions over $25,000, Vital Statistics.*

General Information: No suppressed or home-youthful training case records released. Will fax documents $3.00 1st page, $1.00 each add'l. Court makes copy: $.50 per page. Certification fee: $10.00 1st page; $1.00 each add'l. Payee: Benzie County Clerk. Personal checks accepted. Credit card payments may be accepted via GPS. Prepayment required. Mail requests: SASE required.

Civil Name Search: Access: Phone, fax, mail, in person. Both court and visitors may perform in person name searches. No search fee. Civil records on computer since 1980, records go back to 1869. Mail turnaround time 1-2 days.

Criminal Name Search: Access: Phone, fax, mail, in person. Both court and visitors may perform in person name searches. No search fee. Criminal records on computer since 1980, records go back to 1869. Mail turnaround time 1-2 days.

85th District Court 448 Court Place, Beulah, MI 49617; 231-882-0019; fax: 231-882-0022; 9AM-N, 1-5PM (EST). *Misdemeanor, Civil Actions under $25,000, Eviction, Small Claims.*
www.benzieco.net/

General Information: No suppressed, juvenile, sex offenders, mental health, or adoption records released. Will fax documents $3.00 per page. Court makes copy: $1.00 per page. Certification fee: $10.00 per page includes copies. Payee: 85th District Court. Personal checks accepted. Out of state checks accepted. Credit card payments may be accepted via GPS but not by court. Prepayment required. Mail requests: SASE required.

Civil Name Search: Access: Mail, in person. Both court and visitors may perform in person name searches. No search fee. Civil records on computer back to 1990, prior on cards to 1965. Mail turnaround time 4 days. Civil PAT goes back to 1990. Use public access terminal to look up by case number.

Criminal Name Search: Access: Mail, in person. Both court and visitors may perform in person name searches. Required to search: name, years to search, DOB. Criminal records computerized from 1990, prior on cards to 1965. Mail turnaround time 4 days. Criminal PAT goes back to same as civil. Use public access terminal to look up by case number.

Probate Court 448 Court Pl, County Gov't Ctr., Beulah, MI 49617; 231-882-9675; fax: 231-882-5987; 8:30AM-N, 1-5PM (EST). *Probate.*
www.benzieco.net/dept_probate_court.htm

Berrien County

2nd Circuit Court 811 Port St, St Joseph, MI 49085; 269-983-7111 x8368; criminal phone: x8227; civil phone: x8382; criminal fax: 269-982-8642; civil fax: 8:30AM-5PM; 8:30AM-5PM (EST). *Felony, Civil Actions over $25,000, Vital Statistics.*
www.berriencounty.org

General Information: No suppressed, juvenile, mental health, or adoption records released. Will fax documents to local or toll free line. Court makes copy: $1.00 per page. Certification fee: $10.00 plus copy fee. Payee: Berrien County Clerk. Personal checks accepted. Credit card payments accepted via GPS #4078. Prepayment required.

Civil Name Search: Access: Mail, in person. Only the court performs in person name searches; visitors may not. Search fee: $10.00 per name. Civil records on computer since 1981, prior on books (domestic) back to 1835, (civil & criminal) back to 1837. Mail turnaround time same or next day.

Criminal Name Search: Access: Mail, in person. Only the court performs in person name searches; visitors may not. Search fee: $10.00 per name. Required to search: name, years to search, DOB; also helpful: SSN. Criminal records on computer since 1981, prior on books to 1837. Mail turnaround time 1-2 days.

Berrien County Trial Court Attn: Records, 811 Port St, St Joseph, MI 49085; 269-983-7111; fax: 269-982-8643; 8:30AM-5PM (EST). *Misdemeanor, Civil Actions under $25,000, Eviction, Small Claims.* http://berriencounty.org/Courts

General Information: No suppressed or mental health records released. Will fax documents if prepaid. Court makes copy: $1.00 per page; microfilm copies are $2.00 per page. Certification fee: Included in search fee. $10.00 plus $1.00 per page. Payee: Berrien County Trial Court. Personal checks accepted. Credit card payments accepted via GPS. Prepayment required.

Civil Name Search: Access: Mail, in person. Only the court performs in person name searches; visitors may not. Search fee: $11.00 per name. Required to search: name, years to search; also helpful: address. Civil records on computer back to 1988, on logs from 1976-87, index cards from 1969-75. Will do civil record check searches for only seven years. Note: In person requesters must call ahead five days in advance; records held for 3 add'l days. File review is supervised. Mail turnaround time 3 days.

Criminal Name Search: Access: Mail, in person. Only the court performs in person name searches; visitors may not. Search fee: $11.00 per name. Required to search: name, years to search, DOB or last 4 digits of SSN; also helpful: signed release, address. Criminal records on computer or microfilm back to 1979. Note: In person requesters must call ahead 3 days in advance; records held for 3 add'l days. Mail turnaround time 3 days.

Probate Court Family Division, 811 Port St, St Joseph, MI 49085; 269-982-8613; fax: 269-982-8644; 8:30AM-5PM (EST). *Probate.* www.berriencounty.org/?dept=8&pid=239

Branch County

15th Circuit Court 31 Division St, Coldwater, MI 49036; 517-279-4306; fax: 517-278-5627; 8AM-5PM (EST). *Felony, Civil Actions over $25,000, Vital Statistics.* www.countyofbranch.com/

General Information: No suppressed records released. Will fax documents if all fees prepaid. Court makes copy: $1.00 per page. Certification fee: $10.00 per document plus copy fee. Payee: Branch County Clerk. Business checks accepted. Prepayment required. Mail requests: SASE required.

Civil Name Search: Access: Mail, in person. Both court and visitors may perform in person name searches. Search fee: $10.00 for 10 year search; $1.00 per name per each add'l year. Civil records on computer since 1988, prior in books back to 1830s. Mail turnaround time 1-5 days. Civil PAT goes back to 1988.

Criminal Name Search: Access: Mail, in person. Both court and visitors may perform in person name searches. Search fee: $10.00 for 10 year search; $1.00 per name per each add'l year. Required to search: name, years to search, DOB. Criminal records on computer since 1988, prior in books back to 1830s. Mail turnaround time 1-5 days. Criminal PAT goes back to same as civil.

3A District Court 31 Division St, Coldwater, MI 49036; 517-279-4308; criminal phone: 517-279-4329; civil phone: 517-279-4331; fax: 517-279-4333; 8AM-5PM (EST). *Misdemeanor, Civil Actions under $25,000, Eviction, Small Claims.* www.branchcountycourts.com/

General Information: Small Claims is 279-4330 and Traffic is 279-4328. No suppressed or non-public records released. Will fax documents if search fee prepaid. Court makes copy: $1.00 per page. Certification fee: $10.00 + copy fee. Payee: 3A District Court. Personal checks accepted. Visa/MC accepted. Credit card payments accepted via GPS. Prepayment required.

Civil Name Search: Access: Mail, in person. Only the court performs in person name searches; visitors may not. Search fee: $10.00 per name. Civil records on computer since 6/1991, prior on index books. Mail turnaround time immediate if possible, otherwise 2-3 days.

Criminal Name Search: Access: Mail, in person. Only the court performs in person name searches; visitors may not. Search fee: $10.00 per name. Required to search: name, years to search, DOB; also helpful: SSN. Criminal records on computer since 10/1988. Mail turnaround time immediate if possible, otherwise 2-3 days.

Probate Court 31 Division St, Coldwater, MI 49036; 517-279-4318; fax: 517-279-6444; 8AM-5PM (EST). *Probate.* www.countyofbranch.com/dept.taf?dept_id=116

Calhoun County

37th Circuit Court 161 E Michigan Ave, Battle Creek, MI 49014-4066; 269-969-6518; fax: 269-969-6922; 8AM-5PM (EST). *Felony, Civil Actions over $25,000, Vital Statistics.* www.calhouncountymi.gov/government/circuit_court/

General Information: Expect some delays on phone calls to this jurisdiction. No suppressed, juvenile, sex offenders, mental health, or adoption records released. Will fax documents $3.00 plus $1.00 per copy. Court makes copy: $1.00 per page. $10.00 charge if file is retrieved from storage. Certification fee: $10.00 per doc plus copy fee. Payee: 37th Circuit Court Clerk. Personal checks accepted. Major credit cards accepted via in-person or fax. Prepayment required. Mail requests: SASE required for civil.

Civil Name Search: Access: Mail, in person, online. Both court and visitors may perform in person name searches. Search fee: $5.00 per name,

$10 per name if from microfilm. Civil records on computer since 1984, prior on microfilm. Note: Court will provide case number, filed date, case title, case status, and date of final judgment for the search fee. Mail turnaround time 2- 3 days. Civil PAT available. the DOB will appear on some records. Search civil case index and many related county records at https://mcc.co.calhoun.mi.us/.

Criminal Name Search: Access: In person, online. Both court and visitors may perform in person name searches. Search fee: $5.00 per name. Required to search: name, years to search, DOB. Criminal records on computer since 1984, prior on microfilm. Note: Court prefers requests go to State Police (517-322-5531). Searcher may view public court file if case number known. Criminal PAT available. Search criminal case index and traffic at https://mcc.co.calhoun.mi.us/.

10th District Court 161 E Michigan Ave, Battle Creek, MI 49014; 269-969-6666; criminal phone: 269-969-6678; civil phone: 269-969-6683; probate phone: 269-969-6794; fax: 269-969-6717; 8AM-4:30PM (EST). *Misdemeanor, Civil Actions under $25,000, Eviction, Small Claims.* www.calhouncountymi.gov/government/district_court/

General Information: Clerk will search both criminal and civil indexes if asked. The 10th District Court Marshall Branch's records and administration is now housed here. No suppressed or non-public records released. Will fax documents $1.00 per page. Court makes copy: $1.00 per page. Certification fee: $10.00 plus copy fee after first page. Payee: 10th District Court. Personal checks accepted. Major credit cards accepted via GPS. Prepayment required. Mail requests: SASE required.

Civil Name Search: Access: Mail, fax, in person. Visitors must perform in person searches themselves. No search fee, unless case is in archives, then $15.00. Civil records on computer back to 1986, prior on docket books. Public access terminal searches back to 10/1997. Note: Fax requests must be signed. Mail turnaround time 5 days. Civil PAT goes back to 1997.

Criminal Name Search: Access: Fax, mail, in person. Visitors must perform in person searches themselves. No search fee, unless case is in archives, then $15.00. Required to search: name, DOB; also helpful-case number. Criminal records computerized from 1986, prior on docket books. Public access terminal searches back to 10/1997. Note: One to five requests per day are accepted. Fax requests must be signed. Mail turnaround time 5 days. Criminal PAT goes back to same as civil.

Probate Court 161 E Michigan Ave, Justice Ctr, Battle Creek, MI 49014; 269-969-6794; fax: 269-969-6797; 8AM-5PM MTh; 9AM-5PM F (EST). *Probate.* www.calhouncountymi.gov/government/probate_court/

Cass County

43rd Circuit Court 120 N Broadway, File Room; 60296 M-62, #10, Cassopolis, MI 49031; 269-445-4412; criminal phone: 269-445-4416; civil phone: 269-445-4416; fax: 269-445-4453; 8AM-5PM (EST). *Felony, Civil Actions over $25,000, Vital Statistics.* www.casscountymi.org/DepartmentsandCourts.aspx

General Information: No suppressed, juvenile, sex offenders, mental health, or adoption records released. No fee to fax to a toll-free number. Court makes copy: $1.00 per page. Certification fee: $10.00 plus copy fee. Payee: Cass County Clerk. Business checks accepted. No credit cards accepted. Prepayment required. Mail requests: SASE required.

Civil Name Search: Access: Phone, fax, mail, in person. Both court and visitors may perform in person name searches. Search fee: $10.00 per name. Civil records on computer back to 1988; books since 1963. Mail turnaround time 2 weeks by mail.

Criminal Name Search: Access: Mail, in person. Only the court performs in person name searches; visitors may not. Search fee: $10.00 per name. Required to search: name, years to search, DOB. Criminal records computerized from 1988; books since 1963. Mail turnaround time 2 weeks by mail.

4th District Court 60296 M 62 #10, Cassopolis, MI 49031-8716; 269-445-4424/30; fax: 269-445-4486; 8AM-5PM (EST). *Misdemeanor, Civil Actions under $25,000, Eviction, Small Claims, Traffic.* www.casscountymi.org/DepartmentsandCourts/DistrictCourt.aspx

General Information: No suppressed, juvenile, sex offenders, mental health, or adoption records released. Will not fax out documents. Court makes copy: $1.00 first page, $.50 each add'l. Certification fee: $10.00 per document plus $1.00 per page after first. Payee: 4th District Court. Personal checks and credit cards accepted. Prepayment required.

Civil Name Search: Access: Phone, mail, fax, in person. Only the court performs in person name searches; visitors may not. Search fee: $10.00 per name. Required to search: name, years to search; also helpful: address. Civil records on computer since 1988, indexed on cards prior back to 1969. Note: You can fax requests, but results will not be returned by fax. Mail turnaround time 2 weeks.

Criminal Name Search: Access: Phone, mail, fax, in person. Only the court performs in person name searches; visitors may not. Search fee: $10.00 per name. Required to search: name, years to search, DOB; also helpful: address. Criminal records on computer since 1988, indexed on cards prior back to 1969. Note: Must use court-supplied form for record checks. Mail turnaround time 2 weeks.

Probate Court 60296 - M62, #10, Cassopolis, MI 49031; 269-445-4454; fax: 269-445-4453; 8AM-5PM (EST). *Probate.*
www.casscountymi.org

Charlevoix County

33rd Circuit Court 203 Antrim St, Charlevoix, MI 49720; 231-547-7200; criminal phone: x14; civil phone: x16; fax: 231-547-7217; 9AM-5PM (EST). *Felony, Civil Actions over $25,000, Vital Statistics.*
www.charlevoixcounty.org/clerk.asp
General Information: No suppressed, juvenile, adoption records released. Will fax documents, usually same day. Court makes copy: $1.00 per page. Certification fee: $10.00 first page plus $1.00 each add'l. Payee: Charlevoix County Clerk. Personal checks accepted. Major credit cards accepted via GPS. Prepayment required. Mail requests: SASE requested.
Civil Name Search: Access: Mail, by fax, in person. Only the court performs in person name searches; visitors may not. No search fee. Civil records on computer from 1990, microfiche and archives from 1868. Mail turnaround time 1 week.
Criminal Name Search: Access: Mail, by fax, in person. Only the court performs in person name searches; visitors may not. No search fee. Required to search: name, years to search, DOB. Criminal records computerized from 1991, microfiche and archives from 1868. Mail turnaround time 1 week.

90th District Court 301 State St, Court Bldg, Charlevoix, MI 49720; 231-547-7227; civil phone: 231-547-7254; fax: 231-547-7253; 9AM-5PM (EST). *Misdemeanor, Civil Actions under $25,000, Eviction, Small Claims.*
General Information: No suppressed records released. Will fax documents $5.00 per name. Court makes copy: $1.00 per page. Certification fee: $10.00. Payee: 90th District Court. Personal checks accepted. Credit card payments may be accepted via GPS.
Civil Name Search: Access: Phone, mail, fax, in person. Only the court performs in person name searches; visitors may not. Search fee: $5.00 per name. Required to search: name only. Civil records on computer back to 1987, listed on index cards/books to 1969. Mail turnaround time 1-2 days.
Criminal Name Search: Access: Mail, fax, in person. Only the court performs in person name searches; visitors may not. Search fee: $5.00 per name. Required to search: name, DOB. Criminal records computerized from 1987, listed on index cards/books to 1969. Mail turnaround time 1-2 days.

Probate Court 301 State St, County Bldg, Charlevoix, MI 49720; 231-547-7214; 547-7215; fax: 231-547-7256; 9AM-5PM (EST). *Probate.*
General Information: Shares the same judge with Emmet County.

Cheboygan County

53rd Circuit Court PO Box 70, Cheboygan, MI 49721; 231-627-8818; fax: 231-627-8453; 8AM-5PM (EST). *Felony, Civil Actions over $25,000, Vital Statistics.* www.cheboygancounty.net/53rd_circuit_court/
General Information: No suppressed records released. Will fax document for $1.00 prepaid plus copy fee. Court makes copy: $1.00 per page. Certification fee: $10.00 1st page plus $1.00 each add'l page. Cert fee includes copies. Payee: County Clerk. Personal checks accepted. No credit cards accepted. Prepayment required. Mail requests: SASE required.
Civil Name Search: Access: Phone, mail, in person. Both court and visitors may perform in person name searches. No search fee. Civil records on computer from 1987, index books from 1886. Mail turnaround time 3-4 days. Civil PAT goes back to 1987.
Criminal Name Search: Access: Phone, mail, in person. Both court and visitors may perform in person name searches. No search fee. Required to search: name, years to search, DOB. Criminal records computerized from 1987, index books from 1886. Mail turnaround time 3-4 days. Criminal PAT goes back to same as civil.

89th District Court PO Box 70, 870 S Main St, Cheboygan, MI 49721; 231-627-8809; criminal phone: 231-627-8840; civil phone: 231-627-8839; fax: 231-627-8444; 8:30AM-4PM (EST). *Misdemeanor, Civil Actions under $25,000, Eviction, Small Claims.*
www.cheboygancounty.net/89th_district_court/
General Information: No suppressed, juvenile, sex offenders, mental health, or adoption records released. Will fax out documents $1.00 1st page, $.25 each add'l. Court makes copy: $1.00 1st page, $.25 each add'l. Certification fee: $10.00 per doc. Payee: 89th District Court. Personal checks accepted. Credit cards accepted. Prepayment required. Mail requests: SASE required.
Civil Name Search: Access: Phone, fax, mail, in person, online. Both court and visitors may perform in person name searches. Search fee: $5.00 per name. Civil records on computer back to 1988, microfilmed prior. Mail turnaround time 3-4 days. Civil PAT available. Court dispositions are searchable at http://216.109.207.50/c89_cases/. Calendars are at the home page.
Criminal Name Search: Access: Phone, fax, mail, in person, online. Both court and visitors may perform in person name searches. Search fee: $5.00

per name. Required to search: name, years to search, DOB, address. Criminal records computerized from 1985. Mail turnaround time 3-4 days. Criminal PAT goes back to 1985. Court dispositions are searchable at http://216.109.207.50/c89_cases/. Calendars are at the home page.

Probate Court 870 S Main St, PO Box 70, Cheboygan, MI 49721; 231-627-8823; fax: 231-627-8868; 8:30AM-4:30PM (EST). *Probate.*

Chippewa County

50th Circuit Court 319 Court St, Sault Ste Marie, MI 49783; 906-635-6338; fax: 906-635-6385; 8AM-4:30PM (EST). *Felony, Civil Actions over $25,000, Vital Statistics.*
www.chippewacountymi.gov/circuit_court.html
General Information: The docket cannot be searched by the public, the court does all searching. No suppressed, juvenile, sex offenders, mental health, or adoption records released. Will fax documents to local or toll free line. Court makes copy: $1.00 per page. Certification fee: $10.00 plus $1.00 per page after first. Payee: County Clerk. Personal checks accepted. No credit cards accepted. Prepayment required.
Civil Name Search: Access: Mail, in person. Only the court performs in person name searches; visitors may not. No search fee. Civil records on computer since 1990, prior on index books to late 1800s. Mail turnaround time 1-2 days.
Criminal Name Search: Access: Mail, in person. Only the court performs in person name searches; visitors may not. No search fee. Required to search: name, years to search, DOB; also helpful: SSN. Criminal records on computer since 1990, prior on index books to late 1800s. Mail turnaround time 1-2 days.

91st District Court 325 Court St, Sault Ste Marie, MI 49783; 906-635-6320; criminal phone: 906-635-6322; civil phone: 906-635-7614; fax: 906-635-7605; 9AM-4:30PM (EST). *Misdemeanor, Civil Actions under $25,000, Eviction, Small Claims.*
www.chippewacountymi.gov/district_court.html
General Information: Call before faxing for instructions. No suppressed records released. Will fax documents to toll-free number. Court makes copy: $1.00 per page. Certification fee: $10.00 plus copy fee after 1st page. Payee: 91st District Court. Only cashiers checks and money orders accepted. No credit cards accepted. Prepayment required. Mail requests: SASE required.
Civil Name Search: Access: Mail, fax, in person. Both court and visitors may perform in person name searches. Search fee: $5.00 per name. Civil records on computer since 1989, prior on index books to 1969. Mail turnaround time 10 days. Civil PAT goes back to 1989. some terminal records include phone numbers.
Criminal Name Search: Access: Mail, fax, in person. Both court and visitors may perform in person name searches. Search fee: $5.00 per name. Required to search: name, years to search, DOB; also helpful: SSN. Criminal records on computer since 1989, prior on index books to 1969. Mail turnaround time 10 days. Criminal PAT goes back to 1989.

Probate Court 319 Court St, Basement - Garden Level, Sault Ste Marie, MI 49783; 906-635-6314; fax: 906-635-6852; 8AM-5PM (EST). *Probate.*
www.chippewacountymi.gov/probate_court.html
General Information: The Probate Court has jurisdiction over deceased estates, guardianships, conservatorships, and other miscellaneous matters.

Clare County

55th Circuit Court 225 W Main St, PO Box 438, Harrison, MI 48625; 989-539-7131; fax: 989-539-6616; 8AM-4:30PM (EST). *Felony, Civil Actions over $25,000, Vital Statistics.* www.clareco.net/
General Information: No suppressed, juvenile, sex offenders, mental health, or adoption records released. Will fax out documents for a $5.00 fee. Court makes copy: $1.00 per page. Certification fee: $10.00 per document plus $1.00 per page. Payee: Clare County Clerk. Personal checks accepted. No credit cards accepted at this office. Prepayment required. Mail requests: SASE required.
Civil Name Search: Access: Mail, in person. Court or public may perform in person name searches visitors can access the books themselves, not computer. Search fee: $6.00 per name. Add $1.00 per year if more than five. Required to search: name, years to search DOB. Civil records on computer since 1992, on books from 1925; visitors can access the books themselves, not computer. Mail turnaround time 1-5 days.
Criminal Name Search: Access: Mail, in person. Only the court performs in person name searches; visitors may not. Search fee: $6.00 per name. Add $1.00 per year if more than five. Required to search: name, years to search, DOB. Criminal records on computer since 1992, on books from 1925, visitors can access the books themselves, not computer. Mail turnaround time 1-5 days.

80th District Court 225 W. Main St, Harrison, MI 48625; 989-539-7173; fax: 989-539-4036; 8AM-4:30PM (EST). *Misdemeanor, Civil Actions under $25,000, Eviction, Small Claims.*
www.clareco.net/courts/80th_district.htm
General Information: No suppressed, juvenile, sex offenders, mental health, or adoption records released. Will fax documents. Court makes copy:

$1.00 per page. Certification fee: $10.00 per doc includes copy fee. Payee: 80th District Court. Personal checks accepted. No credit cards accepted. Prepayment required. Mail requests: SASE required.

Civil Name Search: Access: Mail, fax, in person. Only the court performs in person name searches; visitors may not. Search fee: $6.00 per name; $1.00 per yr over 5 years. Civil records go back to 1969; on computer back to 1988. Mail turnaround time 5 days.

Criminal Name Search: Access: Mail, fax, in person. Only the court performs in person name searches; visitors may not. Search fee: $6.00 per name; $1.00 per yr over 5 years. Required to search: name, years to search, DOB, SSN. Criminal records go back to 1969; on computer back to 1988. Mail turnaround time 5 days.

Probate and Family Court 225 W Main St., PO Box 96, Harrison, MI 48625; 989-539-7109; 8AM-4:30PM (EST). *Probate, Family.*

General Information: This is combined with Gladwin County Probate Court.

Clinton County

29th Circuit Court 100 E State St, #2600, St Johns, MI 48879-1580; 989-224-5140; fax: 989-227-6421; 8AM-5PM (EST). *Felony, Civil Actions over $25,000, Vital Statistics.* www.clinton-county.org

General Information: No suppressed or non public records released. Will fax documents $3.00 up to 20 pages, plus copy fee. Court makes copy: $1.00 per page 1st 10, $.50 each add'l. Certification fee: $10.00 per document plus $1.00 per page. Payee: Clinton County Clerk. Personal checks accepted. Debit card payments accepted via GPS. Prepayment required. Mail requests: SASE requested.

Civil Name Search: Access: Mail, in person. Both court and visitors may perform in person name searches. Search fee: $10.00 per name. Fee is for 10 year search. Civil records in calendar books since 1800s, some on microfiche; on computer since 1996. Mail turnaround time 24 hours. Civil PAT goes back to 1996.

Criminal Name Search: Access: Mail, in person. Both court and visitors may perform in person name searches. Search fee: $10.00 per name. Fee is for 10 year search. Required to search: name, years to search; also helpful: DOB. Criminal records in calendar books since 1800s, some on microfiche; on computer since 1996. Mail turnaround time 24 hours. Criminal PAT goes back to 1996.

65th District Court 100 E State St, #3400, St Johns, MI 48879-1571; 989-224-5150; criminal phone: 989-224-5153; civil phone: 989-224-5152; fax: 989-224-5154; 8AM-5PM (EST). *Misdemeanor, Civil Actions under $25,000, Eviction, Small Claims.* www.clinton-county.org

General Information: No suppressed, juvenile, sex offenders, mental health, or adoption records released. Will not fax out case files. Court makes copy: $1.00 per page. Certification fee: $10.00 per document. Payee: 65th District Court. No personal checks accepted. Major credit cards accepted via GPS. Prepayment required.

Civil Name Search: Access: In person only. Visitors must perform in person searches themselves. Civil records on computer since 1989-90. Civil PAT goes back to 1996+. Terminal results show middle initial if available.

Criminal Name Search: Access: In person only. Visitors must perform in person searches themselves. Required to search: name, years to search, DOB, SSN. Criminal records on computer since 1986. Criminal PAT goes back to 1996+. Terminal results show middle initial if available.

Probate Court 100 E State St #4300, St Johns, MI 48879; 989-224-5190; fax: 989-227-6565; 8AM-5PM (EST). *Probate.* www.clinton-county.org

General Information: Also in this court are: guardianship, conservatorship, mentally ill, safety deposit boxes, assignment of properties and infectious disease records.

Crawford County

46th Circuit Court 200 W Michigan Ave, Grayling, MI 49738; 989-348-2841; fax: 989-344-3223; 8:30AM-N, 1PM-4:30PM (EST). *Felony, Civil Actions over $25,000, Vital Statistics.* www.Circuit46.org

General Information: No suppressed records released. Will fax documents $3.00 per page or to toll-free number at no charge. Court makes copy: $1.00 per page. Certification fee: $10.00 plus copy fee. Payee: Crawford County. Personal checks and credit cards accepted. Prepayment required. Mail requests: SASE required.

Civil Name Search: Access: Mail, in person, online. Only the court performs in person name searches; visitors may not. Search fee: $5.00 per name. Civil records on computer since 1990, prior on books to 1930s. Mail turnaround time 2-3 days. Online access to court case records (closed cases for 90 days only) is free at www.circuit46.org/Crawford/c46c_cases.php.

Criminal Name Search: Access: Mail, in person, online, phone, fax. Only the court performs in person name searches; visitors may not. Search fee: $5.00 per name. Required to search: name, years to search, DOB. Criminal

records on computer since 1990, prior on books to 1960. Mail turnaround time 2-3 days. Online access to court case records (closed cases for 90 days only) is free at www.circuit46.org/Crawford/c46c_cases.php.

87-C District Court 200 W Michigan Ave., Grayling, MI 49738; 989-344-3242; fax: 989-344-3290; 8AM-4:30PM (EST). *Misdemeanor, Civil Actions under $25,000, Eviction, Small Claims.* www.Circuit46.org

General Information: No suppressed, juvenile, sex offenders, mental health, or adoption records released. Will not fax documents. Court makes copy: $1.00 per page. Self serve copy: same. Certification fee: $10.00 plus $1.00 each add'l page. Payee: 87-C District Court. Personal checks accepted. No credit cards accepted. Prepayment required. Mail requests: SASE required.

Civil Name Search: Access: Phone, mail, fax, in person, online. Only the court performs in person name searches; visitors may not. No search fee. Civil records on computer since 1990, books from 1969. Mail turnaround time 1-4 days. Online access to limited index of court records is free at www.circuit46.org/Crawford/c46c_cases.php.

Criminal Name Search: Access: Phone, mail, fax, in person, online. Only the court performs in person name searches; visitors may not. No search fee. Required to search: name, years to search, DOB. Criminal records on computer since 1989. Mail turnaround time 1-4 days. Online access to criminal records is the same as civil. There are limitations, this system is not meant to be used for background checks; it is supplemental only.

Probate Court 200 W Michigan Ave., Grayling, MI 49738; 989-344-3237; fax: 989-344-3277; 8AM-4:30PM (EST). *Probate.* www.Circuit46.org

General Information: Limited online access to index at www.circuit46.org/Crawford/c46c_cases.php.

Delta County

47th Circuit Court 310 Ludington St, Escanaba, MI 49829; 906-789-5105; fax: 906-789-5196; 8AM-4PM (EST). *Felony, Civil Actions over $25,000, Vital Statistics.* www.deltacountymi.org/

General Information: No suppressed, juvenile, sex offenders, mental health, or adoption records released. Will fax documents no add'l fee. Court makes copy: $1.00 per page. Certification fee: $10.00 plus $1.00 per page after first. Payee: Delta County. Personal checks accepted. No credit cards accepted. Prepayment required. Mail requests: SASE required.

Civil Name Search: Access: Mail, in person. Both court and visitors may perform in person name searches. Search fee: $20.00 per name. Required to search: name; also helpful: years to search, address. Civil records on computer from 1986, archived into 1800s. Mail turnaround time same day.

Criminal Name Search: Access: Mail, in person. Both court and visitors may perform in person name searches. Search fee: $20.00 per name. Required to search: name; also helpful: years to search, DOB, SSN. Criminal records computerized from 1989, archived into 1800s. Mail turnaround time same day.

94th District Court 310 Ludington St., Escanaba, MI 49829; criminal phone: 906-789-5108; civil phone: 906-789-5106; fax: 906-789-5198; 8AM-4PM (EST). *Misdemeanor, Civil Actions under $25,000, Eviction, Small Claims.*

General Information: No suppressed, juvenile, sex offenders, mental health, or adoption records released. Will fax documents to toll-free number. Court makes copy: $.25 per page. Certification fee: $10.00 per document. Payee: 94th District Court. Personal checks accepted. Major credit cards accepted via GPS. Prepayment required. Mail requests: SASE required.

Civil Name Search: Access: Mail, in person. Only the court performs in person name searches; visitors may not. Search fee: $10.00. Required to search: name, years to search; also helpful: address. Civil records on computer back to 1988, prior on books to 1968. Mail turnaround time 3 days.

Criminal Name Search: Access: Mail, in person. Only the court performs in person name searches; visitors may not. Search fee: $10.00 per name. Required to search: name, years to search, DOB; also helpful: address, SSN. Criminal records computerized from 1988, prior on books to 1968. Mail turnaround time 5 days.

Probate Court 310 Ludington St., Escanaba, MI 49829; 906-789-5114; fax: 906-789-5140; 8AM-N, 1-4PM (EST). *Probate.* http://courts.michigan.gov/scao/services/dirs/ctdirn.asp?cono=21

Dickinson County

41st Circuit Court PO Box 609, 705 S Stephenson Ave, Iron Mountain, MI 49801; 906-774-0988; fax: 906-774-4660; 8AM-4:30PM (CST). *Felony, Civil Actions over $25,000, Vital Statistics.* www.dickinsoncountymi.gov/?41stcircuit

General Information: No suppressed, juvenile, sex offenders, mental health, or adoption records released. Fee to fax back $1.50 per page. Court makes copy: $1.00 per page. Certification fee: $10.00 per doc plus copy fee. Payee: County Clerk. Business checks accepted. Credit card payments accepted via GPS. Prepayment required. Mail requests: SASE required if results to be mailed.

Civil Name Search: Access: Mail, in person. Both court and visitors may perform in person name searches. Search fee: $20.00 per name. Fee is for 10 year search. Civil index on docket books since 1891; on computer since 5/95. Mail turnaround time 1-2 days.

Criminal Name Search: Access: Mail, in person. Both court and visitors may perform in person name searches. Search fee: $10.00 per name. Fee is for 10 year search. Required to search: name, years to search, DOB; also helpful: SSN. Criminal docket on books since 1891; on computer since 5/95. Mail turnaround time 1-2 days.

95 B District Court County Courthouse, PO Box 609, Iron Mountain, MI 49801; 906-774-0506; fax: 906-774-8560; 8AM-4:30PM (CST). *Misdemeanor, Civil Actions under $25,000, Eviction, Small Claims.*
www.dickinsoncountymi.gov/?95bdistrictcourt

General Information: May require a signed release for certain records. No suppressed, juvenile, sex offenders, mental health, or adoption records released. Will fax documents for no fee. Court makes copy: $1.00 1st page; $.50 each add'l. Certification fee: $10.00 per document. Payee: 95-B District Court. Only cashiers checks and money orders accepted. No credit cards accepted. Prepayment required. Mail requests: SASE required.

Civil Name Search: Access: Phone, mail, fax. Only the court performs in person name searches; visitors may not. Search fee: $10.00 per name. Required to search: name, years to search; also helpful: address. Civil index on cards from 1981; on computer back to 2/1995. Mail turnaround time 1 week.

Criminal Name Search: Access: Mail, fax, in person. Only the court performs in person name searches; visitors may not. Search fee: $10.00 per name. Required to search: name, years to search, DOB; also helpful: address, SSN. Criminal records indexed on cards from 1981; on computer back to 2/1995. Mail turnaround time 1 week.

Probate Court PO Box 609, 705 S Stephenson, Iron Mountain, MI 49801; 906-774-1555; fax: 906-774-1561; 8AM-4:30PM (CST). *Probate.*
www.dickinsoncountymi.gov/?probatecourt

Eaton County

56th Circuit Court 1045 Independence Blvd, Charlotte, MI 48813; 517-543-4335; fax: 517-543-4475; 8AM-5PM (EST). *Felony, Civil Actions over $25,000, Vital Statistics.*
www.eatoncounty.org/index.php/courts.html

General Information: Email questions to CircuitCourtClerk@eatoncounty.org. No suppressed, juvenile, sex offenders, mental health, or adoption records released. Will not fax out documents. Court makes copy: $1.00 first page, $.50 each add'l. Certification fee: $10.00 for 1st page, $1.00 each add'l page. Payee: Eaton County Circuit Court Clerk. Personal checks accepted. Credit card payments accepted via GPS. Prepayment required. Mail requests: SASE required.

Civil Name Search: Access: Phone, fax, mail, in person. Both court and visitors may perform in person name searches. Search fee: $8.00 per name if by fax or mail. Civil records on computer back to 1988, microfilm since 1930s, books from 1848. Note: If faxing in a search request, also fax copy of your payment check. Mail turnaround time 1-3 days.

Criminal Name Search: Access: Fax, mail, in person. Both court and visitors may perform in person name searches. Search fee: $8.00 per name if by fax or mail. Required to search: name, years to search, DOB. Criminal records computerized from 1969, microfilm since 1930s, books from 1860s. Note: There is no charge to do a name search if in person. If faxing request, also fax copy of your payment check. Mail turnaround time 1-3 days. Public use terminal has crim records.

56A District Court 1045 Independence Blvd, Charlotte, MI 48813; 517-543-7520; civil phone: 517-543-4097; fax: 517-543-1469; 8AM-5PM (EST). *Misdemeanor, Civil Actions under $25,000, Eviction, Small Claims.*
www.eatoncounty.org/index.php/courts.html

General Information: No suppressed, sex offenders, mental health, or adoption records released. Will not fax documents. Court makes copy: $1.00 per page. Certification fee: $10.00 per doc plus copy fee. Payee: 56A District Court. Personal checks accepted. Visa/MC accepted in person only. Prepayment required.

Civil Name Search: Access: In person only. Visitors must perform in person searches themselves. Civil records on computer back to 1990; prior in books. Civil PAT goes back to 1990.

Criminal Name Search: Access: Mail, fax, in person. Visitors must perform in person searches themselves. Search fee: $15.00. Required to search: name, years to search, DOB. Criminal records computerized from 1987. Criminal PAT goes back to same as civil.

Probate Court 1045 Independence Blvd, Probate Court, Charlotte, MI 48813; 517-543-4185; 8AM-5PM (EST). *Probate.*
www.eatoncounty.org/index.php/courts/probate-court.html

General Information: All juvenile matters and adoptions have been transferred to the Family Division. The Probate Court continues to have jurisdiction over wills and estates, guardianships and mental health commitment petitions.

Emmet County

57th Circuit Court 200 Division St, Petoskey, MI 49770; 231-348-1744; fax: 231-348-0602; 8AM-5PM (EST). *Felony, Civil Actions over $25,000, Vital Statistics.*
www.emmetcounty.org/circuitcourt/

General Information: The search fee includes the civil and criminal indexes. No suppressed records released. Will not fax documents. Court makes copy: $.50 per page. Certification fee: $10.00 per cert plus $1.00 per page, includes copy fee. Payee: Emmet County Clerk. Local personal checks or money orders accepted. No credit cards accepted. Prepayment required. Mail requests: SASE required.

Civil Name Search: Access: Mail, in person. Only the court performs in person name searches; visitors may not. Search fee: $5.00 per name. Civil records on computer from 1867 to present. Mail turnaround time 5 days.

Criminal Name Search: Access: Mail, in person. Only the court performs in person name searches; visitors may not. Search fee: $5.00 per name. Required to search: name, years to search, DOB. Criminal records computerized from 1867 to present. Mail turnaround time 5 days.

90th District Court 200 Division St., #G12, Petoskey, MI 49770; 231-348-1750; criminal phone: 231-348-1752; civil phone: 231-348-1753; fax: 231-348-0616; 8AM-5PM (EST). *Misdemeanor, Civil Actions under $25,000, Eviction, Small Claims.*

General Information: No suppressed, juvenile, sex offenders, mental health, or adoption records released. Will fax documents $6.00 1st page, $1.00 each add'l. Court makes copy: $1.00 per page. Certification fee: $10.00 plus copy fee. Payee: 90th District Court. Business checks accepted. Major credit cards accepted. Prepayment required.

Civil Name Search: Access: Fax, mail, in person. Only the court performs in person name searches; visitors may not. Search fee: $5.00 per name. Civil records on computer since 1981, prior listed in books. Mail turnaround time 48 hours.

Criminal Name Search: Access: Fax, mail, in person. Only the court performs in person name searches; visitors may not. Search fee: $5.00 per name. Required to search: name, years to search, DOB. Criminal records on computer since 1981, prior listed on microfiche. Mail turnaround time on all Division searches is 48 hours.

Probate Court 200 Division St, #280, Petoskey, MI 49770; 231-348-1764; fax: 231-348-0672; 8AM-5PM (EST). *Probate.*
www.emmetcounty.org/7th-probate-court-184/
General Information: Shares the same judge with Charlevoix County Probate Court.

Genesee County

7th Circuit Court 900 S Saginaw, Flint, MI 48502; 810-257-3220; 8AM-4PM (EST). *Felony, Civil Actions over $25,000, Domestic.*
www.co.genesee.mi.us
General Information: Probate court is located in a separate office at the same address. No suppressed, juvenile, adoption, or mental health records released. Will not fax documents. Court makes copy: $1.00 per page. Certification fee: $10.00 per doc plus copy fee. Payee: Genesee County Clerk. Business checks and money orders accepted. No credit cards accepted. Prepayment required. Mail requests: SASE required.

Civil Name Search: Access: Mail, in person, online. Visitors must perform in person searches themselves. Search fee: $5.00 per name. Civil records on computer since 1979, prior on index cards. Mail turnaround time 1-2 weeks. Civil PAT goes back to 1979. Online access to court records is free at www.co.genesee.mi.us/clerk; click on "Circuit Court Records."

Criminal Name Search: Access: Mail, in person, online. Visitors must perform in person searches themselves. Search fee: $5.00 per name. Required to search: name, years to search, DOB. Criminal records on computer since 1979, prior on index cards. Mail turnaround time 1-2 weeks. Criminal PAT goes back to same as civil. Online access to court records is free at www.co.genesee.mi.us/clerk; click on "Circuit Court Records."

67th District Court 630 S Saginaw, Ste 124, Central Court, Flint, MI 48502; 810-257-3170; 8AM-4PM (EST). *Misdemeanor, Civil Actions under $25,000, Eviction, Small Claims.*
www.co.genesee.mi.us/districtcourt/
General Information: Cases files can be located at any one of seven 67th-district courts in county; all indexes combined on computer. Clerk's index will indicate exact location. Search includes civil and criminal indexes. Do not confuse this court with 68th District in Flint. No drug related case records released. Will not fax documents. Court makes copy: $1.00 per page. Certification fee: $11.00 per cert. Payee: 67th District Court. Cashiers checks, business checks, and money orders accepted. Major credit cards accepted in person only. Prepayment required. Mail requests: SASE required.

Civil Name Search: Access: Mail, in person, online. Only the court performs in person name searches; visitors may not. Search fee: $15.00

per name; includes civil and criminal, $2.00 for a computer printout. Required to search: name, years to search; also helpful: address. Civil records on computer since 1983, on microfilm since 1969, prior archived. Mail turnaround time 1 week. Search by name or case number at www.co.genesee.mi.us/districtcourt/recordschk.htm.
Criminal Name Search: Access: Mail, in person, online. Only the court performs in person name searches; visitors may not. Search fee: $15.00 per name, includes civil and criminal, $2.00 for a computer printout. Required to search: name, years to search, DOB, offense; also helpful: address. Criminal records on computer since 1983, on microfilm since 1969, prior archived. Mail turnaround time 1 week. Search by name or case number at www.co.genesee.mi.us/districtcourt/recordschk.htm. Also includes traffic.

68th District Court 630 S Saginaw, Flint, MI 48502; 810-766-8968; criminal phone: 810-766-8968 x1; civil phone: 810-766-8968 x2; fax: 810-766-8967; 8AM-4PM (EST). *Misdemeanor, Civil Actions under $25,000, Eviction, Small Claims.* www.ci.flint.mi.us/68th/68th.asp
General Information: The 68th District Court consists of the City of Flint and is a district of the third class with five judges. Do not confuse with 67th district which is also located in Flint City. No drug related case records released. Will fax documents. Court makes copy: $1.00 per page. Certification fee: $10.00. Payee: 68th District Court. Only cashiers checks, business checks, and money orders accepted. Credit card payments accepted via GPS or Western Union over phone. Prepayment required.
Civil Name Search: Access: Mail, in person. Both court and visitors may perform in person name searches. Search fee: $15.00 per name. Required to search: name, years to search; also helpful: address. Civil records on computer since 1989, on microfilm since 1969, prior archived. Mail turnaround time 1 week.
Criminal Name Search: Access: Mail, in person. Both court and visitors may perform in person name searches. Search fee: $15.00 per name. Required to search: name, years to search, DOB, offense; also helpful: address, SSN. Criminal records on computer since 1989, on microfilm since 1969, prior archived. Note: Court has jurisdiction over felony arraignments and criminal cases punishable by one year or less in jail. Mail turnaround time 1 week.

Probate Court 900 S Saginaw St #502, Flint, MI 48502; 810-257-3528; fax: 810-257-2713; 8:30AM-3:30PM (EST). *Probate.* www.co.genesee.mi.us/probate/index.htm
General Information: Access records free at www.co.genesee.mi.us/probate/index.htm -click on Probate Court Records,

Gladwin County

55th Circuit Court 401 W Cedar, Gladwin, MI 48624; 989-426-7351; fax: 989-426-6917; 8:30AM-4:30PM (EST). *Felony, Civil Actions over $25,000, Vital Statistics.*
General Information: No suppressed, juvenile, sex offenders, mental health, or adoption records released. Will fax documents. Court makes copy: $1.00 per page. Certification fee: $10.00 1st page, $1.00 each add'l page. Payee: Gladwin County Clerk. No personal checks accepted. Credit card payments accepted via GPS. Prepayment required. Mail requests: SASE required.
Civil Name Search: Access: Fax, mail. Only the court performs in person name searches; visitors may not. No search fee, but if search requirements are not met, fee is $5.00. Civil records on computer since 1994, prior on books. Mail turnaround time 2-3 days.
Criminal Name Search: Access: Fax, mail. Only the court performs in person name searches; visitors may not. No search fee, but if search requirements are not met, fee is $5.00. Required to search: name, years to search, DOB; also helpful: SSN. Criminal records on computer since 1994, prior on books. Mail turnaround time 2-3 days.

80th District Court 401 W Cedar, Gladwin, MI 48624; 989-426-9207; fax: 989-246-0894; 8:30AM-4:30PM (EST). *Misdemeanor, Civil Actions under $25,000, Eviction, Small Claims.* www.gladwinco.com/d80.htm
General Information: No suppressed, juvenile, sex offenders, mental health, or adoption records released. Will fax documents to local or toll-free number. Court makes copy: $1.00 per page. Certification fee: $10.00 per doc plus copy fee for add'l pages. Payee: 80th District Court. Personal checks accepted. No credit cards accepted. Prepayment required. Mail requests: SASE required.
Civil Name Search: Access: Mail, fax, in person. Only the court performs in person name searches; visitors may not. Search fee: $1.00 per year, $5.00 minimum per case. Civil records on computer since 1988, prior on index cards and docket books, archived to late 1968. Mail turnaround time same day when possible.
Criminal Name Search: Access: Mail, fax, in person. Only the court performs in person name searches; visitors may not. Search fee: $1.00 per year, $5.00 minimum per case. Required to search: name, years to search, DOB; also helpful: SSN. Criminal records on computer since 1988, prior on index cards and docket books, archived to late 1968. Mail turnaround time same day if possible.

Probate Court 401 W Cedar, Gladwin, MI 48624; 989-426-7451; fax: 989-426-6936; 8:30AM-4:30PM (EST). *Probate.*
General Information: This is combined with Clare County Probate Court.

Gogebic County

32nd Circuit Court 200 N Moore St, Bessemer, MI 49911; 906-663-4518; probate phone: 906-667-0421; fax: 906-663-4660; 8:30AM-4:30PM (CST). *Felony, Civil Actions over $25,000, Vital Statistics.* www.gogebic.org/circuit.htm
General Information: Probate fax is same as main fax number. District Court phone#: 906-663-4611. No suppressed, juvenile, sex offenders, mental health, or adoption records released. Will fax documents $1.50 per page. Court makes copy: $1.00 per page. Certification fee: $10.00 per doc plus copy fee. Payee: Gogebic County Clerk's Office. Personal checks accepted. No credit cards accepted. Prepayment required. Mail requests: SASE required.
Civil Name Search: Access: Fax, mail, in person. Only the court performs in person name searches; visitors may not. Search fee: $25.00 per name per 7 year search. Civil records in books since 1887, computerized since 1997. Mail turnaround time 1-2 days.
Criminal Name Search: Access: Fax, mail, in person. Only the court performs in person name searches; visitors may not. Search fee: $25.00 per name per 7 year search. Required to search: name, years to search, DOB. Criminal records in books since 1887, computerized since 1997. Mail turnaround time 1-2 days.

98th District Court 200 N Moore St, Bessemer, MI 49911; 906-663-4611; fax: 906-667-1124; 8:30AM-N, 1-4:30PM (CST). *Misdemeanor, Civil Actions under $25,000, Eviction, Small Claims.* www.gogebic.org/district.htm
General Information: No suppressed, juvenile, sex offenders, mental health, or adoption records released. Court makes copy: $1.00 per page. Certification fee: $10.00 per doc plus copy fee. Payee: District Court. Business checks accepted. No credit cards accepted. Prepayment required.
Civil Name Search: Access: Mail, in person. Only the court performs in person name searches; visitors may not. Search fee: $25.00 per name. Civil records on computer since 6/88. Mail turnaround time 10 days.
Criminal Name Search: Access: Mail, in person. Only the court performs in person name searches; visitors may not. Search fee: $25.00 per name. Required to search: name, years to search, DOB, SSN. Criminal records on computer since 6/88. Mail turnaround time 10 days.

Probate Court 200 N Moore St., Bessemer, MI 49911; 906-667-0421; fax: 906-663-4660; 8:30AM-N, 1-4:30PM (CST). *Probate.* www.gogebic.org/probate.htm

Grand Traverse County

13th Circuit Court 328 Washington St, Ste 300, Traverse City, MI 49684; 231-922-4710; fax: 231/922-4519; 8AM-5PM (EST). *Felony, Civil Actions over $25,000, Vital Statistics.* www.13thcircuitcourt.org/
General Information: Family Division records are located at 280 Washington St, #202. The phone# is 231-922-4640. No suppressed records released. Will fax documents. Court makes copy: $.50 per page. Certification fee: $10.00 plus $1.00 per page after first. Payee: 13th Circuit Court. Personal checks accepted. Prepayment required. Mail requests: SASE required.
Civil Name Search: Access: Phone, mail, in person, online. Only the court performs in person name searches; visitors may not. Search fee: $10.00 per name. Civil records on computer since 1964, prior on books since 1859. Mail turnaround time 1 week. Search civil records free at http://online.co.grand-traverse.mi.us/iprod/clerk/cccivil.html . 1964 through 1985 contain only index information. 1986 to present include case information and register of actions. Database updated nightly.
Criminal Name Search: Access: Phone, mail, in person, online. Only the court performs in person name searches; visitors may not. Search fee: $10.00 per name. Required to search: name, years to search; also helpful: DOB, SSN. Criminal records on computer since 1977. Mail turnaround time 1 week. Access to a record index is found at http://online.co.grand-traverse.mi.us/iprod/clerk/cccriminal.html.

86th District Court 280 Washington St., Traverse City, MI 49684; 231-922-4580; civil phone: 231-922-4413; fax: 231-922-4454; 8AM-5PM (EST). *Misdemeanor, Civil Actions under $25,000, Eviction, Small Claims.* www.co.grand-traverse.mi.us/courts/86th_District_Court.htm
General Information: Criminal Division at #114B; Civil at #114C; Traffic at #114A No suppressed, juvenile, sex offenders, mental health, or adoption records released. Will fax documents to local or toll-free number. Court makes copy: $1.00 per page. Copies can be printed from the PAT, bring your own paper and it is free. Certification fee: $10.00 per doc plus copy fee. Payee: 86th District Court. Business checks accepted. No credit cards accepted. Prepayment required. Mail requests: SASE required.
Civil Name Search: Access: Phone, mail, in person, online. Both court and visitors may perform in person name searches. No search fee. Civil records on computer since 1988, prior on books. Mail turnaround time up to

5 days. Civil PAT goes back to 1988. Access to a list of cases is found at http://districtcourt.co.grand-traverse.mi.us/c86_cases/. A second site is at http://online.co.grand-traverse.mi.us/iprod/clerk/cccivil.html

Criminal Name Search: Access: Phone, mail, in person, online. Both court and visitors may perform in person name searches. Search fee: $10.00. Required to search: name, years to search, DOB; also helpful: SSN. Most criminal records on computer form 1984. Mail turnaround time up to 5 days. Criminal PAT goes back to 1984. Access online is same as civil.

Probate Court 280 Washington St #223, Traverse City, MI 49684; 231-922-6862; fax: 231-922-4458; 8AM-5PM (EST). *Probate.*
www.co.grand-traverse.mi.us/courts/Probate_Court.htm

General Information: Direct questions to probate@grandtraverse.org.

Gratiot County

29th Circuit Court 214 E Center St, Ithaca, MI 48847; 989-875-5215; fax: 989-875-5254; 8AM-N, 1-4:30PM (EST). *Felony, Civil Actions over $25,000, Vital Statistics.*
www.co.gratiot.mi.us/Law-Justice/29th-Circuit-Court

General Information: No suppressed, juvenile, sex offenders, mental health, or adoption records released. Will fax documents to local or toll free line. Court makes copy: $1.00 per page. Certification fee: $10.00 per doc plus copy fee. Payee: Gratiot County Clerk. Personal checks accepted. Some major credit cards & debits accepted. Prepayment required. Mail requests: SASE required.

Civil Name Search: Access: Mail, in person. Only the court performs in person name searches; visitors may not. Search fee: $12.00 per name. Fee is for 10 years, $1.00 each additional year. Records computerized back 10 years. Mail turnaround time 1-3 days.

Criminal Name Search: Access: Mail, in person. Only the court performs in person name searches; visitors may not. Search fee: $12.00 per name. Fee is for 15 years, $1.00 each additional year. Records computerized back 10 years. Mail turnaround time 1-3 days.

65-B District Court 245 E Newark St, Ithaca, MI 48847; 989-875-5240; fax: 989-875-5290; 8AM-4:30PM (EST). *Misdemeanor, Civil Actions under $25,000, Eviction, Small Claims.*
http://gratiotmi.com/Law-Justice/65th-District-Court

General Information: No non-public records released. Will not fax out case files. Court makes copy: $1.00 per page. Certification fee: $10.00 plus $1.00 per page after first. Payee: 65B District Court. Personal checks accepted. No credit cards accepted. Prepayment required.

Civil Name Search: Access: In person only. Visitors must perform in person searches themselves. Civil index on docket books from 1969 to present, computerized since 1996. Civil PAT goes back to 1996.

Criminal Name Search: Access: In person only. Visitors must perform in person searches themselves. Required to search: name, years to search, DOB. Criminal records on computer since 2/20/96, in books since 1969. Criminal PAT goes back to same as civil.

Probate Court PO Box 217, 214 E Center St, Ithaca, MI 48847; 989-875-5231; fax: 989-875-5331; 8AM-4:30PM (EST). *Probate.*
http://gratiotmi.com/Law-Justice/Probate-Court

Hillsdale County

1st Circuit Court 29 N Howell, Hillsdale, MI 49242; 517-437-3391; fax: 517-437-3392; 8:30AM-5PM (EST). *Felony, Civil Actions over $25,000, Vital Statistics.*

General Information: No suppressed, juvenile, sex offenders, mental health, or adoption records released. Will fax documents to local or toll free line. Court makes copy: $.50 per page. Certification fee: $10.00 per doc plus $1 each add'l page. Payee: Hillsdale County Clerk. Personal checks accepted; out-of-state personal checks not accepted. No credit cards accepted. Prepayment required. Mail requests: SASE required.

Civil Name Search: Access: Mail, in person. Only the court performs in person name searches; visitors may not. Search fee: $10.00 per name. Civil records on computer back to 1844. Mail turnaround time 1-2 days.

Criminal Name Search: Access: Mail, in person. Only the court performs in person name searches; visitors may not. Search fee: $10.00 per name. Required to search: name, years to search, DOB; also helpful: SSN. Criminal records computerized from 1844. Mail turnaround time 1-2 days.

2nd District Court 49 N Howell, Hillsdale, MI 49242; 517-437-7329; fax: 517-437-2908; 8AM-4:30PM; 8AM-5PM Traffic (EST). *Misdemeanor, Civil Actions under $25,000, Eviction, Small Claims.*
www.co.hillsdale.mi.us/

General Information: No suppressed records released. Will fax documents to local or toll free line. Court makes copy: $.25 per page. Certification fee: $10.00 plus $1.00 each add'l page. Payee: Hillsdale District Court. Personal checks accepted. No credit cards accepted. Prepayment required.

Civil Name Search: Access: Phone, mail, in person. Only the court performs in person name searches; visitors may not. Search fee: $10.00. Civil records kept in docket books back to 1969; on computer back to 2001. A request in writing may be required. Mail turnaround time 1 week.

Criminal Name Search: Access: Phone, mail, in person. Only the court performs in person name searches; visitors may not. Search fee: $10.00. Required to search: name, years to search, DOB. Criminal records kept in docket books back to 1969; on computer back to 2001. Mail turnaround time 1 week.

Probate Court 29 N Howell, Hillsdale, MI 49242; 517-437-4643; fax: 517-437-4148; 8:30AM-N, 1-5PM (EST). *Probate.*

Houghton County

12th Circuit Court 401 E Houghton Ave, Houghton, MI 49931; 906-482-5420; fax: 906-483-0364; 8AM-4:30PM (EST). *Felony, Civil Actions over $25,000, Vital Statistics.*
www.houghtoncounty.net/directory-12jcc.shtml

General Information: No suppressed, juvenile, sex offenders, mental health, or adoption records released. Will fax documents to local or toll free line. Court makes copy: $1.00 per page. Certification fee: $10.00 plus copy fee. Payee: Clerk of Circuit Court. Personal checks accepted. No credit cards accepted. Prepayment required.

Civil Name Search: Access: Mail, in person. Only the court performs in person name searches; visitors may not. Search fee: $20.00 per name. Civil records kept on docket books, cards since 6/76; are computerized as of 1997. Mail turnaround time 1-2 days.

Criminal Name Search: Access: Mail, in person. Only the court performs in person name searches; visitors may not. Search fee: $20.00 per name. Required to search: name, years to search, DOB; also helpful: SSN. Criminal records kept on docket books, cards since 11/63; are computerized as of 1997. Mail turnaround time 1-2 days.

97th District Court 401 E Houghton Ave., Houghton, MI 49931; 906-482-4980; fax: 906-482-5270; 8AM-4:30PM (EST). *Misdemeanor, Civil Actions under $25,000, Eviction, Small Claims.*

General Information: Will fax uncertified documents after all fees paid. Court makes copy: $1.00 first page, $.50 each add'l. Certification fee: $10.00. Payee: 97th District Court. Business checks accepted. No credit cards accepted. Prepayment required. Mail requests: SASE required.

Civil Name Search: Access: Mail, fax, in person. Only the court performs in person name searches; visitors may not. Search fee: $20.00 per name. Required to search: name, years to search; also helpful: address. Civil records listed in "Registers of Actions." Records on computer back to 1998; others back to 1969. Mail turnaround time up to 1 week.

Criminal Name Search: Access: Mail, fax, in person. Only the court performs in person name searches; visitors may not. Search fee: $20.00 per name. Required to search: name, years to search, DOB, SSN; also helpful: address, signed release. Criminal records listed in "Registers of Actions." Records on computer back to 1998; others back to 1969. Mail turnaround time up to 1 week.

Probate Court 401 E. Houghton Ave., Houghton, MI 49931; 906-482-3120; fax: 906-487-5964; 8AM-4:30PM (EST). *Probate.*

Huron County

52nd Circuit Court 250 E Huron Ave, #201, Bad Axe, MI 48413; 989-269-9942; fax: 989-269-6160; 8:30AM-5PM (EST). *Felony, Civil Actions over $25,000, Vital Statistics.*
www.co.huron.mi.us/Clerks.asp

General Information: No suppressed, juvenile, sex offenders, mental health, or adoption records released. Will fax documents to local or toll free line. Court makes copy: $1.00 per page. Certification fee: $15.00 per doc. Payee: Huron County Clerk. Personal checks accepted; DL# required. Major credit cards except Visa accepted in person only. Prepayment required.

Civil Name Search: Access: Fax, In person. Only the court performs in person name searches; visitors may not. Search fee: $5.00 per name. Civil records on computer since 1992, prior on books to 1867. Note: Fax requests accepted but results not released until payment received. Mail turnaround time 2-3 days.

Criminal Name Search: Access: Mail, fax, in person. Only the court performs in person name searches; visitors may not. Search fee: $5.00 per name. Required to search: name, years to search, DOB; also helpful: SSN. Criminal records on computer since 1992, prior on books to 1867. Note: Fax requests accepted but results not released until payment received. Mail turnaround time 2-3 days.

73B District Court 250 E Huron Ave., Bad Axe, MI 48413; 989-269-9987; fax: 989-269-6167; 8:30AM-4:30PM (EST). *Misdemeanor, Civil Actions under $25,000, Eviction, Small Claims.*
www.co.huron.mi.us/district_court.asp

General Information: No suppressed, juvenile, sex offenders, mental health, or adoption records released. No fee to fax documents. Court makes copy: $1.00 per page. Certification fee: $10.00. Payee: 73B District Court. Business checks accepted. No credit cards accepted. Prepayment required. Mail requests: SASE required.

Civil Name Search: Access: Phone, fax, mail, in person. Only the court performs in person name searches; visitors may not. Search fee: $5.00 per name. Civil records on computer since 6/1992, prior on books since 1969. Mail turnaround time 1-5 days.

Criminal Name Search: Access: Phone, fax, mail, in person. Only the court performs in person name searches; visitors may not. Search fee: $5.00 per name. Required to search: name, years to search, DOB. Criminal records on computer since 6/1992, prior on books since 1969. Mail turnaround time 1-5 days.

Probate Court 250 E. Huron Ave, Rm 206, Bad Axe, MI 48413; 989-269-9944; fax: 989-269-0004; 8:30AM-N, 1-5PM (EST). *Probate.*

Ingham County

30th Circuit Court PO Box 40771, 313 W. Kalamazoo, Lansing, MI 48933; 517-483-6500; fax: 517-483-6501; 9:00AM-5:00PM (EST). *Felony, Civil Actions over $25,000, Vital Statistics.*
www.ingham.org/cc/circuit.htm
General Information: All circuit court files are public record unless specifically suppressed by Law. Will not fax documents. Court makes copy: $1.00 per page. Certification fee: $10.00 plus copy fee. Payee: Ingham County Circuit Court. Personal checks accepted. Credit card payments accepted via GPS. Prepayment required. Mail requests: SASE required.
Civil Name Search: Access: Phone, mail, in person, online. Both court and visitors may perform in person name searches. Search fee: $9.00 per name search fee for records after 1986. Civil records on computer since 1986. Mail turnaround time 1-2 days; if file is in storage, then 1 week. Civil PAT goes back to 1986. Results include name. Access court records and schedules at https://courts.ingham.org/. Schedules search free; record search is not; register or search by credit card, $11 fee per name and $2.50 for each Register of Action viewed. Cases go back to 1986. Search by case number free at https://courts.ingham.org/CourtRecordSearch/searchByCase.do. Note this search is NOT countywide.
Criminal Name Search: Access: Mail, in person, online. Both court and visitors may perform in person name searches. Search fee: $9.00 per name search fee for records after 1986. Required to search: name, years to search; also helpful: DOB. Criminal records on computer since 1986. Mail turnaround time 1-2 days; if file is in storage, then 1 week. Criminal PAT goes back to same as civil. Access to criminal records online is same as civil, see above.

54 A District Court 124 W Michigan Ave, 6th Floor City Hall, Lansing, MI 48933; 517-483-4433; criminal phone: 517-483-4445; civil phone: 517-483-4426; fax: 517-483-4108; 8AM-4:30PM (EST). *Misdemeanor, Civil Actions under $25,000, Eviction, Small Claims.*
www.lansingmi.gov/court/
General Information: This court covers the City of Lansing. No suppressed, juvenile, sex offenders, mental health, or adoption, non-public records released. Will not fax out case files. Court makes copy: $1.00 per page. Certification fee: $10.00 plus $1.00 per page after first. Payee: 54A District Court. No personal checks accepted. Visa/MC accepted. Credit card payments accepted via Western Union Speedpay. Prepayment required.
Civil Name Search: Access: In person. Visitors must perform in person searches themselves. Civil records on computer since July 1990, microfiche from 1985, prior archived in hand written index. Note: Access court record index online for part of the county, but not records from this court. See https://courts.ingham.org/. Civil PAT goes back to July 1990.
Criminal Name Search: Access: In person. Visitors must perform in person searches themselves. Required to search: name, years to search, DOB, offense, date of offense. Criminal records on computer since 1990, microfiche from 1985, prior not archived may be available on microfiche before 1969. Note: Access court record index online for part of the county, but not records from this court. See https://courts.ingham.org/. Criminal PAT goes back to same as civil.

54 B District Court 101 Linden St, East Lansing, MI 48823; 517-351-7000; criminal phone: 517-336-8630; civil phone: 517-351-1730; fax: 517-351-3371; 8AM-4:30PM (EST). *Misdemeanor, Civil Actions under $25,000, Eviction, Small Claims.*
www.cityofeastlansing.com/Home/Departments/54BDistrictCourt/
General Information: This court covers the City of East Lansing. No suppressed, juvenile, sex offenders, mental health, or adoption records released. Will not fax documents. Court makes copy: $.25 per page. Certification fee: $10.00 plus $1.00 per page after first. Payee: 54-B District Court. Credit card payments accepted in person. Prepayment required. Mail requests: SASE required.
Civil Name Search: Access: Mail, in person. Both court and visitors may perform in person name searches. No search fee. Required to search: name, years to search, also helpful- case number. Civil cases indexed by defendant, plaintiff, case number. Civil records on computer since 1991. ROA's also on computer but not accessible by the public. Note: Older records must be searched by court personnel and can take 1-3 days. Mail turnaround time 1 hour to 1 week; depends on availability. Civil PAT goes back to 1991. Access court records is online for part of the county, but not records from this court. See https://courts.ingham.org/.
Criminal Name Search: Access: Mail, in person, online. Both court and visitors may perform in person name searches. No search fee. Required to

search: name, DOB; if prior to 1989 give years needed. Criminal records on computer since 1989. ROA's also on computer but not accessible by the public. Mail turnaround time 1 hour to 1 week; depends on file availability. Criminal PAT goes back to 1989 or older. PAT results may show vehicle info. Access to criminal records online is for other courts in this county, but not this court, is at https://courts.ingham.org/.

55th District Court 700 Buhl St., Mason, MI 48854; 517-676-8400; civil phone: 517-676-8401; fax: 517-676-8241; 8:30AM-5PM (EST). *Misdemeanor, Civil Actions under $25,000, Eviction, Small Claims.*
www.ingham.org/dc/
General Information: This court covers all of Ingham County except for Lansing and East Lansing. No suppressed, juvenile, sex offenders, mental health, or adoption records released. Will fax documents $1.00 per page. Court makes copy: $1.00 per page. Certification fee: $10.00 plus $1.00 each add'l page. Payee: 55th District Court. Personal checks accepted. No credit cards accepted. Prepayment required. Mail requests: SASE helpful.
Civil Name Search: Access: Mail, in person, online. Both court and visitors may perform in person name searches. No search fee. Civil records on computer since 11/91, prior listed in index books. Mail turnaround time varies. Civil PAT goes back to 11/1991. Access court records and schedules at https://courts.ingham.org/. Schedules search free; record search is not; register or search by credit card, $10.00 fee per name plus $2.50 for each Register of Action. Cases go back to 1991. Search free at https://courts.ingham.org/CourtRecordSearch/searchByCase.do.
Criminal Name Search: Access: Mail, in person, online. Both court and visitors may perform in person name searches. No search fee. Required to search: name, years to search, DOB; case number; also helpful: SSN. Criminal records on computer since 1994, prior on books. Mail turnaround time varies. Criminal PAT goes back to 1994. Access to criminal records online is same as civil, see above.

Lansing Probate Court 313 W Kalamazoo St, Veterans Memorial Courthouse, Lansing, MI 48933; 517-483-6300 x8; fax: 517-483-6150; 8AM-N, 1PM-5PM (EST). *Probate.*
www.ingham.org/PR/Default.htm
General Information: The probate court located in Mason was closed; all of their records reside here. Schedules search free online at https://courts.ingham.org/. Register or search by credit card, $10.00 fee per name plus $2.50 for each Register of Action.

Ionia County

8th Circuit Court 100 Main, Ionia, MI 48846; 616-527-5322; probate phone: 616-527-5326; fax: 616-527-8201; 8:30AM-5PM (EST). *Felony, Civil Actions over $25,000, Vital Statistics.*
www.ioniacounty.org/circuit-court/default.aspx
General Information: Probate fax is same as main fax number. No suppressed records released. Will fax uncertified documents with payment. Court makes copy: $1.00 per page. Certification fee: $10.00 plus $1.00 per page copy fee after first. Payee: Ionia County Clerk. Personal checks accepted. Credit card payments accepted via GPS only. Prepayment required.
Civil Name Search: Access: Fax, mail, in person. Only the court performs in person name searches; visitors may not. Search fee: $5.00 per name. Civil records on computer since 1990; prior records kept in books and files, archived to 1800s. Mail turnaround time 1 week.
Criminal Name Search: Access: Fax, mail, in person. Only the court performs in person name searches; visitors may not. Search fee: $5.00 per name. Required to search: name, years to search in 5 year span; also helpful: DOB. Criminal records on computer since 1990; in books and files prior. Mail turnaround time 1 week.

64 A District Court 101 W Main, Ionia, MI 48846; 616-527-5346; civil phone: 616-527-5349; fax: 616-527-5343; 8AM-5PM (EST). *Misdemeanor, Civil Actions under $25,000, Eviction, Small Claims.*
www.ioniacounty.org/district-court/default.aspx
General Information: No suppressed, juvenile, sex offenders, mental health, or adoption records released. Will fax documents to local or toll-free number. Court makes copy: $.50 per page. Certification fee: $10.00 plus $1.00 per page after first. Payee: 64-A District Court. Personal checks accepted. Credit card payments accepted via GPS. Prepayment required. Mail requests: SASE requested.
Civil Name Search: Access: Fax, mail, in person. Only the court performs in person name searches; visitors may not. Search fee: $3.00 per name. Civil records in files and books available since 1969. Note: Fax request must be followed up by originals. Mail turnaround time 10 days.
Criminal Name Search: Access: Fax, mail, in person. Only the court performs in person name searches; visitors may not. Search fee: $3.00 per name. Required to search: name, years to search, DOB; also helpful: address. Criminal records in files and books available since 1969. Note: Fax must be followed up by originals. Mail turnaround time 10 days.

Probate Court 100 Main St, Courthouse, Ionia, MI 48846; 616-527-5326; fax: 616-527-5321; 8:30AM-5PM (EST). *Probate.*
www.ioniacounty.org/probate-court/default.aspx
General Information: Email questions to probate@ioniacounty.org.

Iosco County

23rd Circuit Court PO Box 838, Tawas City, MI 48764; 989-362-3497; fax: 989-984-1012; 9AM-5PM (EST). *Felony, Civil Actions over $25,000, Vital Statistics.* www.iosco.net

General Information: No suppressed, parental waivers, mental health, or adoption records released. Will not fax documents. Court makes copy: $1.00 per page. Certification fee: $10.00 plus $1.00 per page. Payee: Iosco County Clerk. Cashiers checks and money orders accepted. Credit cards accepted through GPS, 888-604-7888. Prepayment required.

Civil Name Search: Access: Phone, mail, in person. Only the court performs in person name searches; visitors may not. Search fee: $10.00 per name. Civil records on computer since 1987, prior on books. Mail turnaround time 1 week.

Criminal Name Search: Access: Phone, mail, in person. Only the court performs in person name searches; visitors may not. Search fee: $10.00 per name. Required to search: name, years to search, DOB; also helpful: SSN. Criminal records on computer since 1983. Mail turnaround time 1 week.

81st District Court PO Box 388, 422 Lake St, Tawas City, MI 48764; 989-362-4441; fax: 989-984-1021; 8:30AM-4:30PM (EST). *Misdemeanor, Civil Actions under $25,000, Eviction, Small Claims.*

General Information: Court will search both criminal and civil if asked. No suppressed, juvenile, sex offenders, mental health, or adoption records released. Will fax documents to local or toll free line. Court makes copy: $1.00 first page, $.50 each add'l. Certification fee: $10.00 plus $1.00 per page copy fee after first. Payee: 81st District Court. No personal checks. Major credit cards accepted via GPS. Prepayment required. Mail requests: SASE required.

Civil Name Search: Access: Mail, in person. Only the court performs in person name searches; visitors may not. Search fee: $10.00 per name. Civil records on computer since 1987, prior on books. Mail turnaround time 2-3 days.

Criminal Name Search: Access: Mail, in person. Only the court performs in person name searches; visitors may not. Search fee: $10.00 per name. Required to search: name, years to search, DOB; also helpful: SSN. Criminal records on computer since 1987, prior on books. Mail turnaround time 2-3 days.

Probate Court PO Box 421, 422 W Lake St, Tawas City, MI 48764; 989-362-3991; fax: 989-984-1035; 8AM-5PM (EST). *Probate.* http://iosco.m33access.com/circuitcourt.htm

Iron County

41st Circuit Court 2 South 6th St #9, Crystal Falls, MI 49920; 906-875-3221; fax: 906-875-0125; 8AM-N; 12:30-4PM (CST). *Felony, Civil Actions over $25,000, Vital Statistics.* www.iron.org/gov-clerk.php

General Information: Search fee includes both civil and criminal indexes. No suppressed, juvenile, sex offenders, mental health, or adoption records released. Will fax documents $1.50 per page. Court makes copy: $.25 per page. Certification fee: $10.00 plus $1.00 per page after first. Payee: Iron County Clerk. Personal checks accepted. Credit card payments accepted via GPS. Prepayment required. Mail requests: SASE requested.

Civil Name Search: Access: Fax, mail, in person. Only the court performs in person name searches; visitors may not. Search fee: $15.00 per name. Most records on books, on microfiche 1958-67. Mail turnaround time 2-3 days.

Criminal Name Search: Access: Fax, mail, in person. Only the court performs in person name searches; visitors may not. Search fee: $15.00 per name. Required to search: name, years to search, DOB. Most records on books, on microfiche 1958-67. Mail turnaround time 2-3 days.

95 B District Court 2 S 6th St., Crystal Falls, MI 49920; 906-875-0619; fax: 906-875-0656; 8AM-4PM (CST). *Misdemeanor, Civil Actions under $25,000, Eviction, Small Claims.* www.iron.org

General Information: No suppressed, juvenile, sex offenders, mental health, or adoption records released. Will fax documents $1.00 per page. Court makes copy: $.25 per page. Certification fee: $10.00 plus $1.00 per page after first. Payee: 95-B District Court. Personal checks accepted. Credit card payments accepted via GPS. Prepayment required.

Civil Name Search: Access: Mail, in person. Only the court performs in person name searches; visitors may not. Search fee: $10.00. Civil records computerized since 1999, earlier records index kept on cards, accessible from 1970. Note: There is no search fee if a name and DOB are submitted for a Yes or No answer. The fee kicks in for accessing details of the case. Mail turnaround time 1 week.

Criminal Name Search: Access: Mail, in person. Only the court performs in person name searches; visitors may not. Search fee: $10.00. Required to search: name, years to search, DOB; also helpful: SSN. Criminal records computerized since 1999, earlier records index kept on cards, accessible from 1970. Note: There is no search fee if a name and DOB are submitted for a Yes or No answer. The fee kicks in for accessing details of the case. Mail turnaround time 1 week.

Probate Court 2 S 6th St, #10, Crystal Falls, MI 49920; 906-875-0659; fax: 906-875-0656; 8AM-N, 12:30-4PM (CST). *Probate.* www.iron.org

Isabella County

21st Circuit Court 200 N Main St, Mount Pleasant, MI 48858; 989-772-0911 X346; fax: 989-779-8022; 8AM-4:30PM (EST). *Felony, Civil Actions over $25,000, Vital Statistics.* www.isabellacounty.org/trial.html

General Information: No suppressed, juvenile, sex offenders, mental health, or adoption records released. Will fax to local or toll-free line. Court makes copy: $1.00 per page. Certification fee: $10.00 plus $1.00 per page after first. Payee: Isabella County Court. Personal checks accepted. Prepayment required. Mail requests: SASE helpful.

Civil Name Search: Access: Mail, in person. Both court and visitors may perform in person name searches. Search fee: $5.00 from 1980 to present. Prior years $1.00 per year. Civil records on computer since 1980, archived from 1900. Mail turnaround time 1-2 weeks. Civil PAT available.

Criminal Name Search: Access: Mail, in person. Both court and visitors may perform in person name searches. Search fee: $5.00 from 1980 to present. Prior years $1.00 per year. Required to search: name, years to search, DOB; also helpful: SSN. Criminal records on computer since 1980, archived from 1900. Mail turnaround time 1-2 weeks. Criminal PAT goes to 1986.

76th District Court 300 N Main St., Mount Pleasant, MI 48858; 989-772-0911 X490; probate phone: x316; fax: 989-779-8022; 8AM-4:30PM (EST). *Misdemeanor, Civil Actions under $25,000, Eviction, Small Claims.* www.isabellacounty.org/trial.html

General Information: No suppressed, juvenile, sex offenders, or adoption records released. Will fax documents. Court makes copy: $1.00 per page. Certification fee: $10.00 per doc. Payee: Isabella County Trial Court. Business checks accepted. Credit card payments accepted via GPS. Prepayment required. Mail requests: SASE required.

Civil Name Search: Access: Mail, in person. Both court and visitors may perform in person name searches. Search fee: $5.00 per name. Civil records on computer since 1988, on books since 1969. Mail turnaround time 5-7 days. Civil PAT available.

Criminal Name Search: Access: Mail, in person. Both court and visitors may perform in person name searches. Search fee: $5.00 per name. Required to search: name, years to search, DOB; also helpful: SSN. Criminal records on computer back 10 years, on books since 1969. Mail turnaround time 5-7 days. Criminal PAT available.

Probate Court 300 N Main St, Mount Pleasant, MI 48858; 989-772-0911 x276; fax: 989-779-8022; 8AM-4:30PM (EST). *Probate.* www.isabellacounty.org/dept/courts/probate.html

General Information: Copies are $1.00 per page, if certified then $10 first plus $1.00 per page.

Jackson County

4th Circuit Court 312 S Jackson St, Jackson, MI 49201; 517-788-4268; criminal phone: 517-788-4260; fax: 517-788-4601; 8AM-5PM (EST). *Felony, Civil Actions over $25,000, Vital Statistics.* www.co.jackson.mi.us/CCinfo.asp

General Information: No adoption or juvenile records released. Will fax documents $3.00 1st page, $1.00 each add'l. Court makes copy: $.50 per page. Certification fee: $10.00 plus $2.00 per page after first. Payee: Jackson County Clerk. Cashiers checks and money orders accepted. No credit cards accepted. Prepayment required. Prepayment of fax and mail service required.

Civil Name Search: Access: Phone, mail, in person, online. Only the court performs in person name searches; visitors may not. No search fee. Civil records on computer since 1982, prior on index cards and docket books since 1800s. Mail turnaround time 1 week. Access court records free at http://96.61.192.32/c12/c12_cases.php.

Criminal Name Search: Access: Phone, mail, in person, online. Only the court performs in person name searches; visitors may not. No search fee. Required to search: name, years to search; also helpful: DOB, SSN. Criminal records on computer since 1982, prior on index cards and docket books since 1800s. Mail turnaround time 1 week. Access court records free at http://96.61.192.32/c12/c12_cases.php.

12th District Court 312 S Jackson St., Jackson, MI 49201; 517-788-4260; criminal phone: 517-788-4260; civil phone: 517-788-4037; criminal fax: 517-788-4262; civil fax: 8AM-5PM; 8AM-5PM (EST). *Misdemeanor, Civil Actions under $25,000, Eviction, Small Claims.* www.d12.com/county_courts/d12/index.asp

General Information: No suppressed, juvenile, sex offenders, mental health, or probation records released. Will fax documents $5.00 1st page, $1.00 each add'l. Court makes copy: $.25 per page, first 10 free to county resident. Certification fee: $10.00 plus $1.00 per page after first. Payee: 12th District Court. Personal checks accepted. Visa/MC accepted. Prepayment required. Mail requests: SASE helpful.

Civil Name Search: Access: Fax, mail, in person, online. Only the court performs in person name searches; visitors may not. No search fee. Civil

records on computer since 1986; microfilm to 1969. Mail turnaround time 2 days. Access court records free at http://96.61.192.51/c12/c12_cases.php.
Criminal Name Search: Access: Fax, mail, in person, online. Only the court performs in person name searches; visitors may not. No search fee. Required to search: name, years to search, DOB; also helpful: SSN. Criminal records on computer since 1986; microfilm from 1969. Mail turnaround time 2 days. Access court records free at http://96.61.192.51/c12/c12_cases.php.

Probate Court 312 S Jackson St, 1st Fl, Jackson, MI 49201; 517-788-4290; fax: 517-788-4291; 8AM-5PM (EST). *Probate.*
www.co.jackson.mi.us/CCinfo.asp
General Information: Access probate court records free at http://96.61.192.32/c12/c12_cases.php.

Kalamazoo County

9th Circuit Court 227 W Michigan Ave, Kalamazoo, MI 49007; 269-383-8837; fax: 269-383-8647; 8AM-5PM (EST). *Felony, Civil Actions over $25,000, Vital Statistics.* www.kalcounty.com/courts/
General Information: No suppressed or non-public records released. Will not fax documents. Court makes copy: $1.00 per page. Certification fee: $13.00 per doc for seal includes copy fee. Payee: 9th Circuit Court Clerk. Personal checks accepted except for criminal payments. Major credit cards accepted. Prepayment required. Mail requests: SASE required.
Civil Name Search: Access: Mail, in person. Visitors must perform in person searches themselves. Search fee: $1.00 per name if over one. Civil records stored as hard copies, some records kept off-site; computerized records go back to 1984. Note: Clerks may do name search for public if not busy and if only for 1 name. Mail turnaround time 3to 21 days. Civil PAT goes back to 1984 for all branches in this Circuit. Public terminal has index of case numbers only.
Criminal Name Search: Access: Mail, in person. Visitors must perform in person searches themselves. Search fee: $1.00 per name. Required to search: name, years to search, DOB. Criminal records stored as hard copies, some records kept off-site; computerized records go back to 1984. Note: May search 1-2 names for free, depending how busy, but will not do lists. Mail turnaround time 3-21 days. Criminal PAT goes back to same as civil. Results also show race and gender. Public terminal has index of case numbers only.

8th District Court - Crosstown 150 E Crosstown Parkway, Kalamazoo, MI 49001; 269-384-8171; fax: 269-383-8899; 8AM-5PM (EST). *Civil Actions under $25,000, Eviction, Small Claims, Traffic Citations.* www.kalcounty.com/courts/district/index.htm
General Information: This court covers Kalamazoo County. No suppressed or non-public records released. No fee to fax documents if local or toll-free call. Court makes copy: $1.00 per page. Certification fee: $10.00 1st page plus copy fee for add'l pages. Payee: 8th District Court. Personal checks accepted. Visa/MC accepted. Prepayment required.
Civil Name Search: Access: In person only. Visitors must perform in person searches themselves. Civil records on computer back to 1998, prior on index books to 1969. Note: All requests to review files or obtain document copies must be made on the File/Copy Request Form. Each requester may only request 5 case files per day. Public use terminal has civil records back to 1/1999.

8th District Court - North 227 W Michigan Ave, Kalamazoo, MI 49007; 269-384-8171; fax: 269-384-8047; 8AM-5PM (EST). *Misdemeanor.* www.kalcounty.com
General Information: This court covers Kalamazoo County. No suppressed or non-public records released. No fee to fax documents. Court makes copy: $1.00 per page. Certification fee: $10.00 1st page plus copy fee for add'l pages. Payee: 8th District Court. Personal checks accepted. No credit cards accepted. Prepayment required.
Criminal Name Search: Access: In person only. Visitors must perform in person searches themselves. Required to search: name, years to search, DOB. Some Criminal records computerized from 1991, prior on books to 1969. Note: All requests to review files or obtain document copies must be made on the File/Copy Request Form. Each requester may only request 5 case files per day. Public use terminal has crim records back to 1991.

8th District Court - South 7810 Shaver Rd., Portage, MI 49024; 269-383-6460; criminal phone: x2; fax: 269-321-3645; 8AM-5PM (EST). *Misdemeanor, Civil Actions under $25,000, Eviction, Small Claims.* www.kalcounty.com/
General Information: This court covers Kalamazoo County South of N Ave/Kilgore Rd. No suppressed or non-public records released. Will fax documents to local or toll-free number. Court makes copy: $1.00 per page. Certification fee: $10.00 1st page plus copy fee for add'l pages. Payee: 8th District Court. Personal checks accepted. No credit cards accepted. Prepayment required.
Civil Name Search: Access: In person only. Visitors must perform in person searches themselves. Civil records on computer back to 1998, prior on index books to 1969. Civil PAT goes back to 1/1999.

Criminal Name Search: Access: In person. Visitors must perform in person searches themselves. Required to search: name, years to search, DOB. Some Criminal records computerized from 1991, prior on books to 1969. Note: All requests to review files or obtain document copies must be made on the File/Copy Request Form. Mail turnaround time 5 days. Criminal PAT goes back to 1991.

Probate Court 150 E Crosstown Parkway, Kalamazoo, MI 49001; 269-383-8666; fax: 269-383-8685; 9AM-N, 1-5PM (EST). *Probate.*
www.kalcounty.com/courts/probate/default.asp

Kalkaska County

46th Circuit Court 605 N Birch St, Kalkaska, MI 49646; 231-258-3300; probate phone: 231-258-3314; fax: 231-258-3337; 8:30AM-4;30PM (EST). *Felony, Civil Actions over $25,000, Vital Statistics.*
www.circuit46.org/Kalkaska/c46k_home.html
General Information: Probate records located at 605 N Birch St. No suppressed records released. Will fax documents $5.00 plus $1.00 per page. Not all docs can be returned by fax. Court makes copy: $1.00 per page. Certification fee: $10.00 per document plus copy fee. Payee: Kalkaska County Clerk. Personal checks accepted. No credit cards accepted. Prepayment required. Mail requests: SASE required.
Civil Name Search: Access: Mail, in person, online. Only the court performs in person name searches; visitors may not. No search fee. Civil records on computer since 1989, prior on books, indexed to late 1800s. Mail turnaround time 1-3 days. Online access to court case records (open or closed cases for 90 days only) is free at www.circuit46.org/Kalkaska/c46k_cases.php.
Criminal Name Search: Access: Mail, in person, online. Only the court performs in person name searches; visitors may not. No search fee. Required to search: name, years to search, DOB; also helpful: SSN. Criminal records on computer since 1989, prior on books, indexed to 1800s. Mail turnaround time 1-3 days. Online access to court case records (open or closed cases for 90 days only) is free at www.circuit46.org/Kalkaska/c46k_cases.php.

87-B District Court 605 N Birch St., Kalkaska, MI 49646; 231-258-9031; fax: 231-258-2424; 8AM-4:30PM (EST). *Misdemeanor, Civil Actions under $25,000, Eviction, Small Claims, Traffic.*
www.Circuit46.org
General Information: Online identifiers in results same as on public terminal. No suppressed records released. Will fax documents to local or toll free line. Court makes copy: $1.00 per page. Certification fee: $10.00 plus $1.00 per page after first. Payee: 87-B District Court. Cashiers checks and money orders accepted. No credit cards accepted. Prepayment required. Mail requests: SASE required.
Civil Name Search: Access: Phone, mail, in person, online. Both court and visitors may perform in person name searches. No search fee. Civil records on computer since 1989, prior on books. Mail turnaround time 4 days plus mailing time. Civil PAT goes back to 1989. Public terminal is in a secured area, available by approved appointment only. Online access to limited index of court records is free at www.circuit46.org/Kalkaska/c46k_cases.php.
Criminal Name Search: Access: Phone, mail, in person, online. Both court and visitors may perform in person name searches. No search fee. Required to search: name, years to search, DOB. Criminal records on computer since 1989, prior on books. Mail turnaround time 4 days plus mailing time. Criminal PAT goes back to same as civil. Public terminal is in a secured area, available by approved appointment only. Online access to criminal records is the same as civil. There are limitations, this system is not meant to be used for background checks, it is supplemental only. Online results show middle initial, DOB.

46th Circuit Ct - Probate Division 605 N Birch St, Kalkaska, MI 49646; 231-258-3330 x2; fax: 231-258-3329; 8AM-4:30PM (EST). *Probate.*
www.circuit46.org/Kalkaska/c46k_probate.html
General Information: Limited search by name free at www.circuit46.org/Kalkaska/c46k_cases.php.

Kent County

17th Circuit Court 180 Ottawa Ave NW, #2400, Grand Rapids, MI 49503; 616-632-5480; fax: 616-632-5458; 8AM-5PM (EST). *Felony, Civil Actions over $25,000.*
www.accesskent.com/CourtsAndLawEnforcement/17thCircuitCourt/17cc_index.htm
General Information: Search fee includes both civil and criminal indexes. No suppressed records released. Will not fax documents. Court makes copy: $1.00 per page. Certification fee: $10.00 plus copy fee after 1st page. Payee: Kent County Clerk. Personal checks accepted. No credit cards accepted. Prepayment required. Mail requests: SASE required.
Civil Name Search: Access: Mail, in person, online. Only the court performs in person name searches; visitors may not. Search fee: $5.00 per name. Required to search: name, DOB, years to search. Civil records on computer since 1986, prior on books. Mail turnaround time 2-3 days.

Search for $6.00 per name at https://www.accesskent.com/CourtNameSearch/. DOB not required but credit card is for record found. Also, search hearings schedule free at https://www.accesskent.com/CCHearing/

Criminal Name Search: Access: Mail, in person, online. Only the court performs in person name searches; visitors may not. Search fee: $5.00 per name. Required to search: name, years to search, DOB. Criminal records on computer since 1986, prior on books. Mail turnaround time 2-3 days. Search for $6.00 per name at https://www.accesskent.com/CourtNameSearch/. DOB and credit card required for results. Also, search for accident reports at $3.00 per name at https://www.accesskent.com/AccidentReports/

59th District Court - Walker 4343 Remembrance Rd NW, Walker, MI 49534; 616-453-5765; fax: 616-791-6851; 8AM--5PM M-Th; 8AM-3PM F (EST). *Misdemeanor, Civil Actions under $25,000, Eviction, Small Claims.*

General Information: City of Walker page is www.ci.walker.mi.us/. No suppressed, juvenile, sex offenders, mental health, or adoption records released. Will fax documents $1.00 per name. Court makes copy: $1.00 per page. Certification fee: $10.00 plus $1.00 per page after first. Payee: 59th District Court. Personal checks accepted. Major credit cards accepted via GPS. Prepayment required. Mail requests: SASE required.

Civil Name Search: Access: Mail, in person. Only the court performs in person name searches; visitors may not. Search fee: $1.00 per name. Add $1.00 per add'l year requested. Required to search: name, years to search; also helpful: address. Civil records on computer from 1989, docket books and cards prior. Mail turnaround time varies.

Criminal Name Search: Access: Mail, in person. Only the court performs in person name searches; visitors may not. Search fee: $1.00 per name. Add $1.00 per add'l year requested. Required to search: name, years to search, DOB; also helpful: address, SSN. Criminal records computerized from 1989, docket books and cards prior. Mail turnaround time varies.

59th District Court - Grandville 3161 Wilson Ave SW, Grandville, MI 49418; 616-538-9660; fax: 616-538-5144; 8:30AM-5PM (EST). *Misdemeanor, Civil Actions under $25,000, Eviction, Small Claims.* www.cityofgrandville.com/Services/Courts/OverviewCourts.htm

General Information: No suppressed, juvenile, sex offenders, mental health, or adoption records released. Court makes copy: $1.00 per page. Certification fee: $10.00 plus $1.00 per page after first. Payee: 59th District Court. Personal checks accepted. Credit card payments accepted via GPS. Prepayment required. Mail requests: SASE helpful.

Civil Name Search: Access: Mail, in person. Only the court performs in person name searches; visitors may not. Search fee: $8.00. Required to search: name, years to search; also helpful: address. Civil records on computer from 1986, docket books and cards prior. Mail turnaround time 1-2 days.

Criminal Name Search: Access: Mail, in person. Only the court performs in person name searches; visitors may not. Search fee: $8.00. Required to search: name, years to search, DOB; also helpful: address. Criminal records computerized from 1986, docket books and cards prior. Mail turnaround time 1-2 days.

61st District Court - Grand Rapids 180 Ottawa Ave NW #1400, County Courthouse, Grand Rapids, MI 49503; 616-632-5700; criminal phone: 616-632-5525; civil phone: 616-632-5555; criminal fax: 616-632-5584; civil fax: 7:45AM-4:45PM; 7:45AM-4:45PM (EST). *Misdemeanor, Civil Actions under $25,000, Eviction, Small Claims.* www.grcourt.org/

General Information: No suppressed, juvenile, sex offenders, mental health, or adoption records released. Will fax documents to local or toll-free number. Court makes copy: $1.00 first page. Certification fee: $10.00 plus $1.00 per page after first. Payee: 61st District Court. Personal checks accepted. Visa/MC accepted. Prepayment required. Prepayment of mail service required.

Civil Name Search: Access: Mail, fax, in person, online. Both court and visitors may perform in person name searches. No search fee. Civil records kept in files and books, computerized since 1999. Mail turnaround time 7-10 days. Civil PAT goes back to 10/1999. Search online at https://www.grcourt.org/CourtPayments/

Criminal Name Search: Access: Mail, fax, in person, online. Both court and visitors may perform in person name searches. No search fee. Required to search: name, years to search, DOB; also helpful: SSN. Criminal records are automated from 1999, images on microfiche from 1980. Mail turnaround time 7-10 days. Criminal PAT goes back to same as civil. Search at https://www.grcourt.org/CourtPayments/ Online results show middle initial, DOB.

62 A District Court - Wyoming 2650 De Hoop Ave SW, Wyoming, MI 49509; criminal phone: 616-257-9814; civil phone: 616-530-7386; fax: 616-249-3419; 8AM-5PM M-Th, 8AM-3PM Fri (EST). *Misdemeanor, Civil Actions under $25,000, Eviction, Small Claims.* www.ci.wyoming.mi.us/DistrictCourt/d-court.asp

General Information: No suppressed, juvenile, sex offenders, mental health, or adoption records released. Will not fax documents. Court makes copy: $1.00 per page. Certification fee: $10.00 plus $1.00 per page after first. Payee: 62 A District Court. Personal checks accepted. Accepts Visa credit cards in person only. Prepayment required. Mail requests: SASE required.

Civil Name Search: Access: Mail, fax, in person. Both court and visitors may perform in person name searches. Search fee: $1.00 per name plus $.50 per year. Civil records kept on docket books since 1980; on computer back to 1997. Note: The judge must approve all requests from collection agencies. Mail turnaround time 2-3 days. Civil PAT goes back to 1997.

Criminal Name Search: Access: Mail, fax, in person. Both court and visitors may perform in person name searches. Search fee: $1.00 per name plus $.50 per year. Required to search: name, years to search, DOB; also helpful: Case #. Criminal docket books kept since 1980; on computer back to 1997. Note: The court suggests mail requests be sent to the state police. Mail turnaround time 2-3 days. Criminal PAT goes back to same as civil.

62 B District Court - Kentwood 4740 Walma Ave, Kentwood, MI 49512; 616-698-9310; fax: 616-698-8199; 8AM-5PM (EST). *Misdemeanor, Civil Actions under $25,000, Eviction, Small Claims.* www.ci.kentwood.mi.us/cityhall/Departments/court.asp

General Information: No suppressed, juvenile, sex offenders, mental health, or adoption records released. Will not fax documents. Court makes copy: $2.00 1st page, $.25 each add'l. Self serve copy: same. Certification fee: $10.00. Payee: 62 B District Court. Personal checks accepted. Visa/MC accepted. Credit card payments also accepted via GPS. Prepayment required. Mail requests: SASE helpful.

Civil Name Search: Access: Mail, in person. Both court and visitors may perform in person name searches. Search fee: $5.00 per name. Civil records on computer since 11/88, prior on books. Mail turnaround time 1-2 days. Civil PAT goes back to 11/1988.

Criminal Name Search: Access: Mail, in person. Both court and visitors may perform in person name searches. Search fee: $5.00 per name. Required to search: name, years to search, DOB. Criminal records on computer since 11/88, prior on books. Mail turnaround time 1-2 days. Criminal PAT goes back to same as civil.

63rd District Court 1950 East Beltline Ave NE, Grand Rapids, MI 49525; 616-632-7770; 8AM-5PM (EST). *Misdemeanor, Civil Actions under $25,000, Eviction, Small Claims.*

General Information: No suppressed, juvenile, sex offenders, mental health, or adoption records released. Will not fax documents. Court makes copy: $1.00 per page. Certification fee: $10.00. Payee: 63rd District Court. Personal checks and credit cards accepted. Prepayment required.

Civil Name Search: Access: In person only. Visitors must perform in person searches themselves. Required to search: n/a. Civil records on computer since 8/94, prior on books. Civil PAT goes back to 1996.

Criminal Name Search: Access: In person only. Visitors must perform in person searches themselves. Required to search: n/a. Criminal records on computer since 8/94, prior on books. Criminal PAT goes back to 1996.

Probate Court 180 Ottawa Ave NW #2500, Grand Rapids, MI 49503; 616-632-5440; fax: 616-632-5430; 8AM-5PM (EST). *Probate.* www.accesskent.com/CourtsAndLawEnforcement/ProbateCourt/

General Information: Free online records at www.accesskent.com/CourtsAndLawEnforcement/ProbateCourt/probate_index.htm. This court also hold estates, trust, guardianships, conservatorships, mental commitments & name change records.

Keweenaw County

12th Circuit Court 5095 4th St., Eagle River, MI 49950-9624; 906-337-2229; fax: 906-337-2795; 9AM-4PM (EST). *Felony, Civil Actions over $25,000, Vital Statistics.*

General Information: No suppressed, juvenile, sex offenders, mental health, or adoption records released. Will fax documents. Court makes copy: $1.00 per page. Self serve copy: same. Certification fee: $10.00 per document plus copy fee. Payee: Keweenaw County. Personal checks accepted. No credit cards accepted. Prepayment required. Mail requests: SASE requested.

Civil Name Search: Access: Mail, fax, in person. Only the court performs in person name searches; visitors may not. Search fee: $10.00. Civil records kept on index books since 1963. Mail turnaround time 1-2 days.

Criminal Name Search: Access: Mail, fax, in person. Only the court performs in person name searches; visitors may not. Search fee: $10.00. Required to search: name, years to search, DOB. Criminal index on books since 1964. Mail turnaround time 1-2 days.

97th District Court 5095 4th St., Eagle River, MI 49950; 906-337-2229; fax: 906-337-2795; 9AM-4PM (EST). *Misdemeanor, Civil Actions under $25,000, Eviction, Small Claims.*

General Information: No suppressed, juvenile, sex offenders, mental health, or adoption records released. Will fax documents if not lengthy, but search results cannot be faxed. Court makes copy: $1.00 per page. Self serve copy: same. Certification fee: $10.00 per document plus copy fee. Payee:

Keweenaw County. Personal checks accepted. No credit cards accepted. Prepayment required. Mail requests: SASE required.

Civil Name Search: Access: Fax, mail, in person. Only the court performs in person name searches; visitors may not. Search fee: $10.00 per name. Civil records kept on books to 1970's. Note: Results cannot be faxed. Mail turnaround time 1-2 days.

Criminal Name Search: Access: Fax, mail, in person. Only the court performs in person name searches; visitors may not. Search fee: $10.00 per name. Required to search: name, years to search, DOB; also helpful: SSN. Criminal records kept on books to 1970's. Mail turnaround time 1-2 days.

Probate Court 5095 4th St, Eagle River, MI 49950; 906-337-1927; fax: 906-337-2795; 9AM-4PM (EST). *Probate, Juvenile.*
www.keweenawcountyonline.org/department-probate.php

Lake County

Lake County Trial Court 800 10th St, #300, Baldwin, MI 49304; 231-745-4614; fax: 231-745-6232; 8AM-5PM (EST). *Felony, Misdemeanor, Civil Actions, Eviction, Small Claims, Probate, Vital Statistics.*

General Information: No suppressed, sex offenders, mental health, or adoption records released. Fee to fax document $1.00 each. Court makes copy: $1.00 per page. Certification fee: $10.00. Payee: Lake County Trial Court. Personal checks accepted. Major credit cards accepted via GPS. Prepayment required.

Civil Name Search: Access: Mail, in person. Only the court performs in person name searches; visitors may not. Search fee: $5.00 per name per year. Civil records on computer since 7/89, prior on books to 1876. Mail turnaround time 1-2 days.

Criminal Name Search: Access: Mail, in person. Only the court performs in person name searches; visitors may not. Search fee: $5.00 per name per year. Required to search: name, years to search, DOB; also helpful: SSN. Criminal records on computer since 7/89, prior on books to 1876. Mail turnaround time 1-2 days.

Lapeer County

40th Circuit Court Clerk's Office, 255 Clay St, Lapeer, MI 48446; 810-667-0358; fax: 810-667-0264; 8AM-5PM, counter til 4:30 PM (EST). *Felony, Civil Actions over $25,000, Vital Statistics.*
www.lapeercountyweb.org/court.htm

General Information: No suppressed records released. Will not fax documents. Court makes copy: $1.00 per page. Certification fee: $10.00 1st page; $1.00 per page after first. Payee: 40th Circuit Court. Personal checks accepted. No credit cards accepted. Prepayment required. Mail requests: SASE required.

Civil Name Search: Access: Mail, in person. Visitors must perform in person searches themselves. Search fee: $5.00 search fee covers 10 year span. Civil records on computer since 1994, prior on index cards and books. Mail turnaround time 48 hours. Civil PAT goes back to 1994. The terminal is located at the Clerk's office, same address.

Criminal Name Search: Access: Mail, in person. Visitors must perform in person searches themselves. Search fee: $5.00 search fee covers 10 year span. Required to search: name, years to search; DOB. Criminal records on computer since 1996, prior on index cards and books. Mail turnaround time 48 hours. Criminal PAT goes back to 1996. The terminal is located at the Clerk's office, same address.

71 A District Court 255 Clay St., Lapeer, MI 48446; 810-667-0314; criminal phone: x2; civil phone: x3; 8AM-5PM (EST). *Misdemeanor, Civil Actions under $25,000, Eviction, Small Claims.*
http://lapeercountyweb.org/district_court.htm

General Information: No suppressed, juvenile, sex offenders, mental health, or adoption records released. Will not fax documents. Court makes copy: $1.00 per page. Certification fee: $10.00 plus $1.00 per page after first. Payee: 71 A District Court. Third party checks not accepted. Visa/MC cards accepted. Credit card payments accepted via GPS. Prepayment required. Mail requests: SASE required.

Civil Name Search: Access: Mail, in person. Only the court performs in person name searches; visitors may not. Search fee: $5.00 per name. Civil records on computer since 1992, cards and dockets from 1969. Mail turnaround time 10 days.

Criminal Name Search: Access: Mail, in person. Only the court performs in person name searches; visitors may not. Search fee: $5.00 per name. Required to search: name, years to search, DOB; also helpful: SSN. Criminal records on computer since 1992, cards and dockets from 1969. Mail turnaround time 10 days.

Probate Court 255 Clay St., Lapeer, MI 48446; 810-667-0261; fax: 810-667-0271; 8AM-5PM (EST). *Probate.*

Leelanau County

13th Circuit Court 8527 E Gov't Ctr Dr, #103, Suttons Bay, MI 49682; 231-256-9824; fax: 231-256-8295; 9AM-5PM (EST). *Felony, Civil Actions over $25,000, Vital Statistics.*
www.leelanau.cc/coclerk.asp

General Information: Formerly located in Leland. No suppressed, juvenile, sex offenders, mental health, or adoption records released. Will not fax out documents. Court makes copy: $.50 per page. Certification fee: $10.00 plus $1.00 per page. Payee: County Clerk. Personal checks accepted. No credit cards accepted. Prepayment required. Mail requests: SASE required.

Civil Name Search: Access: Mail, fax, in person, online. Both court and visitors may perform in person name searches. Search fee: $3.00 per name. Civil records on computer since 1/93, prior on docket books. Mail turnaround time 2-3 days. Access to a record index is at http://online.co.grand-traverse.mi.us/iprod/clerk/cccivil.html . Family court records also included. Search by name or case number.

Criminal Name Search: Access: Mail, fax, in person, online. Both court and visitors may perform in person name searches. Search fee: $3.00 per name. Criminal records on computer since 1/97; prior records on books. Mail turnaround time 2-3 days. Access to a record index is found at http://online.co.grand-traverse.mi.us/iprod/clerk/cccriminal.html. Search by name or case number to 1981.

86th District Court 8527 E Gov't Center Dr, #201, Leland, MI 49682; 231-256-8250; fax: 231-256-8275; 8AM-4PM (EST). *Misdemeanor, Civil Actions under $25,000, Eviction, Small Claims, Traffic.*
www.co.grand-traverse.mi.us/courts/86th_District_Court.htm

General Information: No suppressed, sex offenders records released. Fee to fax document $.25 per page. Court makes copy: $1.00 per page. Certification fee: $10.00 per document plus copy fee. Payee: 86th District Court. Business checks accepted. Credit cards accepted; usage fee applies. Prepayment required. Mail requests: SASE requested.

Civil Name Search: Access: Fax, mail, in person, online. Both court and visitors may perform in person name searches. No search fee. Civil records on computer since 1991, prior on books to 1969. Mail turnaround time 3 days. Civil PAT goes back to 1990. Access to a list of cases is found at http://districtcourt.co.grand-traverse.mi.us/c86_cases/. A second site is at http://online.co.grand-traverse.mi.us/iprod/clerk/cccivil.html

Criminal Name Search: Access: Phone, fax, mail, in person, online. Both court and visitors may perform in person name searches. No search fee. Required to search: name, years to search, DOB; also helpful: SSN. Criminal records on computer since 1991, prior on books to 1969. Mail turnaround time 3 days. Criminal PAT goes to 1990. Access online is same as civil.

Probate Court 8527 E Gov't Center Dr, #203, Suttons Bay, MI 49682; 231-256-9803; fax: 231-256-9845; 9AM-5PM (EST). *Probate, Family.*
General Information: Formerly located in Leland.

Lenawee County

39th Circuit Court 425 N Main St, Judicial Bldg, 3rd Fl, Adrian, MI 49221; 517-264-4597; fax: 517-264-4790; 8AM-4:30PM (EST). *Felony, Civil Actions over $25,000, Vital Statistics.*
www.lenawee.mi.us/government/county-courts?id=244

General Information: The court refers to the index as the 'Name Index" and not the docket index. No suppressed, juvenile, sex offenders, mental health, or adoption records released. Will fax documents. Court makes copy: $1.00 per page. Certification fee: $16.00 per doc includes copy fee. Payee: Lenawee County Clerk or 39th Circuit Court. Personal checks accepted. No credit cards accepted. Prepayment required. Mail requests: SASE helpful.

Civil Name Search: Access: Mail, in person. Both court and visitors may perform in person name searches. Search fee: $10.00 per name. Fee is for ten years. Civil records on computer back to 1/89, prior on books. Mail turnaround time 1-2 days. Civil PAT goes back to 1989.

Criminal Name Search: Access: Mail, in person. Both court and visitors may perform in person name searches. Search fee: $10.00 per name. Fee is for 10 years. Criminal records computerized from 1/89, prior on books. Mail turnaround time 1-2 days. Criminal PAT goes back to same as civil.

2A District Court 425 N Main St., Rex B Martin Courthouse, Adrian, MI 49221; 517-264-4668; criminal phone: 517-264-4673; civil phone: 517-264-4662; fax: 517-264-4665; 8AM-4:30PM (EST). *Misdemeanor, Civil Actions under $25,000, Eviction, Small Claims.*

General Information: Civil and criminal indexes are separate search fees. No suppressed, juvenile, sex offenders, mental health, or adoption records released. Will fax documents to local or toll free line. Court makes copy: $.25 per page. Certification fee: $10.00 per doc. Payee: 2A District Court. Personal checks accepted. Visa/MC accepted. Prepayment required. Mail requests: SASE required.

Civil Name Search: Access: Fax, mail, in person. Both court and visitors may perform in person name searches. Search fee: $10.00 per name. Civil records on computer since 1988, prior on index books, cards and microfilm back to 1968. Mail turnaround time 2 days. Civil PAT goes back to 1987.

Criminal Name Search: Access: Fax, mail, in person. Both court and visitors may perform in person name searches. Search fee: $10.00 per name. Required to search: name, years to search, DOB. Criminal records on computer since 1988, prior on index books, cards and microfilm back to 1969. Mail turnaround time 2 days. Criminal PAT goes back to 1987.

Probate Court 425 N Main St, Adrian, MI 49221; 517-264-4614; fax: 517-264-4616; 8AM-4:30PM (EST). *Probate.*

Livingston County

44th Circuit Court 204 S Highlander Way #4, Howell, MI 48843; 517-546-9816; probate phone: 517-546-3750; fax: 517-548-4219; 8AM-5PM (EST). *Felony, Civil Actions over $25,000, Domestic.*
www.co.livingston.mi.us
General Information: Juvenile Unit records are at 517-546-1500. Probate in a separate index at this same address. Probate fax- 517-552-2510 All records released unless suppressed. Will not fax out documents. Court makes copy: $1.00 per page. Certification fee: $10.00 per document plus copy fee. Payee: Livingston County Clerk. Personal checks accepted if in state. Major credit cards accepted. Prepayment required. Mail requests: SASE required.
Civil Name Search: Access: Mail, in person, online. Both court and visitors may perform in person name searches. Search fee: $6.00 record verification cost per name. Civil records computerized from 1987, on microfiche and archived from 1900s. Mail turnaround time 5 days. Civil PAT goes back to 1987. Access civil name index and abbreviated case summary online free or by more detailed data subscription at https://www.livingstonlive.org/CourtRecordValidation/. The subscription fee is $6.00 for the verification and $2.50 for an abbreviated summary. Search cases for the 53rd District, 44th Circuit Court, Juvenile & Family Courts.
Criminal Name Search: Access: Mail, in person, online. Both court and visitors may perform in person name searches. Search fee: $6.00 record verification cost per name. Criminal records computerized from 1987, microfiche and archived from 1900s. Mail turnaround time 5 days. Criminal PAT goes back to same as civil. Access criminal name index and abbreviated case summary back to 1997 free or more detailed by subscription at https://www.livingstonlive.org/CourtRecordValidation/; a DOB is required to search. The subscription fee is $6.00 for the verification and $2.50 for an abbreviated summary. Online results show name only.

53 A District Court 204 S Highlander Way #1, Howell, MI 48843; 517-548-1000; criminal phone: x7; civil phone: x8; criminal fax: 517-548-9445; civil fax: 8AM-5PM; 8AM-5PM (EST). *Misdemeanor, Civil Actions under $25,000, Eviction, Small Claims.*
http://co.livingston.mi.us/DistrictCourt/
General Information: No suppressed, juvenile, sex offenders, mental health, or adoption records released. Will fax documents to local or toll-free number. Court makes copy: $1.00 per page. Certification fee: $10.00. Payee: 53 District Court. Personal checks and credit cards accepted. Prepayment required.
Civil Name Search: Access: In person, online. Visitors must perform in person searches themselves. Required to search: name, years to search; also helpful: address. Civil records on computer since 1982. Civil PAT goes back to 10 years. Access civil records after registration or by subscription at https://www.livingstonlive.org/CourtRecordValidation/. $6 fee for each name and court searched; $2.50 for each summary or case history. Search cases for the 53rd District, 44th Circuit Court, Juvenile & Family Courts.
Criminal Name Search: Access: In person, online. Visitors must perform in person searches themselves. Required to search: name, years to search, DOB; also helpful: address, SSN. Criminal records on computer since 1982. Criminal PAT goes back to Open and pending cases but not all closed cases. The PAT here also has Brighton records. Access criminal records back to 1997 after registration or by subscription at https://www.livingstonlive.org/CourtRecordValidation/ but a DOB is required to search on the free access. $6 fee for each name and court searched; $2.50 for each summary or case history.

53 B District Court 224 N1st St, Brighton, MI 48116; 810-229-6615; criminal phone: x6; civil phone: x7; fax: 810-229-1770; 8AM-12; 1-5PM (EST). *Misdemeanor, Civil Actions under $25,000, Eviction, Small Claims.*
http://co.livingston.mi.us/DistrictCourt/brighton.htm
General Information: This Brighton Court's records also appear on the Howell Division public access terminals. No suppressed, juvenile, sex offenders, mental health, or adoption records released. Will not fax documents. Court makes copy: $1.00 per page. Certification fee: $10.00. Payee: 53rd District Court. Personal checks accepted. Credit card payments accepted for online requests only. Prepayment required. Mail requests: SASE required for civil.
Civil Name Search: Access: Mail, in person, online. Visitors must perform in person searches themselves. No search fee. Civil records on computer since 1985, prior on index books. Mail turnaround time 1 week. Civil PAT goes back to 10 years. Access civil records after registration or by subscription at https://www.livingstonlive.org/CourtRecordValidation/. Search cases for the 53rd District, 44th Circuit Court, Juvenile & Family Courts.
Criminal Name Search: Access: In person, online. Visitors must perform in person searches themselves. Required to search: name, years to search, DOB; also helpful: SSN. Criminal records on computer since 1985,

prior on index books and microfilm. Criminal PAT goes back to same as civil. Access criminal records back to 1997 after registration or by subscription at https://www.livingstonlive.org/CourtRecordValidation/ but a DOB is required to search on the free access.

Probate Court 204 S. Highlander Way #2, Judicial Center Bldg, Howell, MI 48843; 517-546-3750; fax: 517-552-2510; 8AM-5PM (EST). *Probate.*
http://co.livingston.mi.us/probatecourt/default.asp

Luce County

11th Circuit Court 407 W Harrie, Newberry, MI 49868; 906-293-5521; probate phone: 906-293-5601; fax: 906-293-5553; 8AM-4PM (EST). *Felony, Civil Actions over $25,000, Vital Statistics.*
www.lucecountymi.org/
General Information: No suppressed, juvenile, sex offenders, mental health, or adoption records released. Will fax documents $1.00 per page plus $1.00 fax fee. Court makes copy: $1.00 per page. Certification fee: $10.00. Payee: 11th Circuit Court. Personal checks accepted. No credit cards accepted. Prepayment required. Mail requests: SASE required.
Civil Name Search: Access: Mail, in person. Only the court performs in person name searches; visitors may not. No search fee. Civil records listed on cards since 1876. Mail turnaround time 4-5 days.
Criminal Name Search: Access: Mail, in person. Only the court performs in person name searches; visitors may not. No search fee. Required to search: name, years to search, DOB. Criminal records listed on cards since 1876. Mail turnaround time 4-5 days.

92nd District Court 407 W Harrie, Newberry, MI 49868; 906-293-5531; fax: 906-293-5773; 8AM-4PM (EST). *Misdemeanor, Civil Actions under $25,000, Eviction, Small Claims.* http://92nd.lucecountymi.org/
General Information: Will fax documents $1.00 per page. Court makes copy: $1.00 per page. Certification fee: $10.00. Payee: 92nd District Court. In state personal checks accepted. Credit card payments accepted via GPS. Prepayment required. Government Payment Services plan participant. Mail requests: SASE preferred.
Civil Name Search: Access: Phone, fax, mail, in person. Only the court performs in person name searches; visitors may not. No search fee. Civil records to 1969, some on computer. Mail turnaround time 1 week.
Criminal Name Search: Access: Phone, fax, mail, in person. Only the court performs in person name searches; visitors may not. No search fee. Required to search: name, years to search, DOB; also helpful: SSN. Criminal records to 1969, some on computer. Mail turnaround time 1 week.

Probate Court 407 W. Harrie, Newberry, MI 49868; 906-293-5601; fax: 906-293-5665; 8AM-N, 1-4PM (EST). *Probate.*
www.lucecountymi.org/
General Information: This is a combined court with Mackinac County Probate Court.

Mackinac County

11th Circuit Court 100 S Marley St, Rm 10, St Ignace, MI 49781; 906-643-7300; fax: 906-643-7302; 8:30AM-4:30PM (EST). *Felony, Civil Actions over $25,000, Vital Statistics.*
www.mackinaccounty.net/courts.html
General Information: No suppressed, juvenile, sex offenders, mental health, or adoption records released. Will not fax documents. Court makes copy: $1.00 per page. Certification fee: $10.00 per cert plus copy fee. Payee: County Clerk. Personal checks accepted. Credit card payments accepted via GPS. Prepayment required. Mail requests: SASE required.
Civil Name Search: Access: Mail, in person. Only the court performs in person name searches; visitors may not. Search fee: $10.00. Civil records on docket book; on computer back to 1998. Mail turnaround time 10 days.
Criminal Name Search: Access: Mail, in person. Only the court performs in person name searches; visitors may not. Search fee: $10.00. Required to search: name, years to search, DOB. Criminal records on docket book; on computer back to 1998. Mail turnaround time 10 days.

92nd District Court 100 S Marley, Rm 55, St Ignace, MI 49781; 906-643-7321; fax: 906-643-7326; 8:30AM-4:30PM (EST). *Misdemeanor, Civil Actions under $25,000, Eviction, Small Claims.*
www.mackinaccounty.net/courts.html
General Information: No suppressed, juvenile, sex offenders, mental health, or adoption records released. Will not fax out documents. Court makes copy: $1.00 per page. Certification fee: $10.00. Payee: 92nd District Court. Personal checks accepted. Credit card payments accepted via GPS, pay location code 1432. Prepayment required. Mail requests: SASE required.
Civil Name Search: Access: Mail, in person, fax, phone. Visitors must perform in person searches themselves. No search fee. Civil cases indexed by defendant. Civil records on computer since 11/92, prior in files to 1969.
Criminal Name Search: Access: Fax, mail, in person. Visitors must perform in person searches themselves. No search fee. Required to search: name, years to search, DOB. Criminal records on computer since 11/92, prior in files to 1969. Mail turnaround time 1 week.

Probate Court 100 S Marley St Rm 15, St Ignace, MI 49781; 906-643-7303; fax: 906-643-8861; 8:30AM-N, 1-4:30PM (EST). *Probate.* www.mackinaccounty.net/courts.html

General Information: This is a combined court with Luce County Probate Court.

Macomb County

16th Circuit Court 40 N Main St, Mount Clemens, MI 48043; 586-469-5199; fax: 586-783-8184; 8AM-4:15PM M-W-F; 8AM-1:30PM Tu-Th (EST). *Felony, Civil Actions over $25,000.* www.macombcountymi.gov/clerksoffice/

General Information: A record request form is at www.macombcountymi.gov/clerksoffice/pdf/FaxOrMailFileRequestForm.pdf. Online identifiers in results same as on public terminal. No suppressed, juvenile, sex offenders, mental health, or adoption records released. Will fax documents $10.00 plus $1.00 per page. Court makes copy: $1.00 per page. Certification fee: $10.00 per doc plus $1.00 per page. Payee: Macomb County Clerk. Personal checks and credit cards accepted. Prepayment required. Mail requests: SASE required.

Civil Name Search: Access: Mail, fax, in person, online. Both court and visitors may perform in person name searches. Search fee: $1.00 per name. Required to search: name or case number. Civil records on computer since 1977, on microfiche to 1969, prior to 1800s archived. Mail turnaround time 1 week. Civil PAT goes back to 1980. Civil online access is the same as criminal, see below. Online records include divorces.

Criminal Name Search: Access: Mail, fax, in person, online. Both court and visitors may perform in person name searches. Search fee: $1.00 per name. Required to search: name or case number. Criminal records on computer since 1970, on microfiche to 1969, prior to 1800s archived. Mail turnaround time 1 week. Criminal PAT goes back to same as civil. Access Circuit Court index for free at http://macombcountymi.gov/pa/. From this site one may order document copies. Online results show middle initial.

37th District Court - Center Line 7070 E Ten Mile Rd, Center Line, MI 48015; 586-757-8333; fax: 586-759-9611; 8:30AM-4:30PM (EST). *Misdemeanor.* http://37thdistrictcourt.net/

General Information: Shares 37th District with Warren. Each court has to be searched separately. No suppressed, juvenile, sex offenders, mental health, or adoption records released. Will not fax documents. Court makes copy: $1.00 per page. Certification fee: $10.00. Payee: 37th District Court. Personal checks and credit cards accepted. Prepayment required.

Criminal Name Search: Access: Mail, in person, fax. Only the court performs in person name searches; visitors may not. Search fee: $10.00 per name. Required to search: name, years to search, DOB; also helpful: SSN. Criminal records on computer since 1992, prior on index cards. Mail turnaround time 2 weeks.

39th B District Court - Fraser PO Box 10, 33000 Garfield Rd, Fraser, MI 48026; 586-293-3137; fax: 586-296-8499; 8AM-4:30PM (EST). *Misdemeanor, Infractions.* www.macombcountymi.gov/district_court/court39b.htm

General Information: All civil actions, eviction, and small claims cases now handled by 39-A District Court in Roseville. No suppressed, juvenile, sex offenders, mental health, or adoption records released. Will fax documents to local or toll-free number. Court makes copy: $1.00 per page, $2.00 if on microfilm. Certification fee: $10.00 per doc. Payee: 39th District Court. Personal checks accepted. Credit card payments accepted via GPS. Prepayment required.

Criminal Name Search: Access: Mail, in person. Only the court performs in person name searches; visitors may not. No search fee. Required to search: name, years to search, DOB; also helpful: SSN. Criminal records on computer since 1988, prior on microfilm. Mail turnaround time 1-2 days.

37th District Court - Warren 8300 Common Rd., Warren, MI 48093; 586-574-4900; criminal phone: x3; civil phone: x2; fax: 586-574-4932; 8:30AM-4:30PM (EST). *Misdemeanor, Civil Actions under $25,000, Eviction, Small Claims.* http://37thdistrictcourt.net/

General Information: Shares 37th District with Center Line. Each court has to be searched separately, but you can request your search to include a court's criminal and civil indexes. No suppressed, juvenile, sex offenders, mental health, or adoption records released. Will not fax documents. Court makes copy: $1.00 per page. Certification fee: $10.00 per cert. Payee: 37th District Court. Personal checks accepted. No credit cards accepted. Prepayment required.

Civil Name Search: Access: Mail, in person. Only the court performs in person name searches; visitors may not. Search fee: $10.00 per name. Civil records on computer since 1992, prior on index cards. Mail turnaround time 2 weeks.

Criminal Name Search: Access: Mail, fax, in person. Only the court performs in person name searches; visitors may not. Search fee: $10.00 per name. Required to search: name, years to search, DOB; also helpful:

SSN. Criminal records on computer since 1992, prior on index cards. Mail turnaround time 2 weeks.

38th District Court - Eastpointe 16101 Nine Mile Rd, Eastpointe, MI 48021; 586-445-5020; criminal phone: x4; civil phone: x7; fax: 586-445-5060; 8AM-4:15PM (EST). *Misdemeanor, Civil Actions under $25,000, Eviction, Small Claims* www.macombcountymi.gov/district_court/court38.htm

General Information: No suppressed, sex offenders, mental health records released. Will fax documents to local or toll-free number. Court makes copy: $1.00 per page. Certification fee: $10.00 per doc plus copy fee. Payee: 38th District Court. Personal checks accepted. Major credit cards accepted via GPS. Prepayment required. Mail requests: SASE required.

Civil Name Search: Access: Mail, in person, online. Both court and visitors may perform in person name searches. No search fee. Civil records on computer since 1996, prior on index cards. Mail turnaround time 10 days. Civil PAT goes back to 1997. Access case name look-ups free at https://secure.courts.michigan.gov/jis/

Criminal Name Search: Access: Mail, in person, online. Both court and visitors may perform in person name searches. No search fee. Required to search: name, years to search, DOB. Criminal records on computer since 1996, prior on index cards. Mail turnaround time 10 days. Criminal PAT goes back to 1997. Access case name look-ups at https://secure.courts.michigan.gov/jis/ Online results show name only.

39th District Court - Roseville 29733 Gratiot Ave, Roseville, MI 48066; 586-773-2010; criminal phone: 586-447-4430; civil phone: 586-447-4420; fax: 586-445-5070; 8AM-4:30PM (EST). *Misdemeanor, Civil Actions under $25,000, Eviction, Small Claims.* www.macombcountymi.gov/district_court/index.htm

General Information: All civil actions, eviction, and small claims cases from the Fraser location are now located here. No suppressed, juvenile, sex offenders, mental health, or adoption records released. Will fax documents to local or toll-free number. Court makes copy: $1.00 per page, $2.00 if on microfilm. Certification fee: $10.00. Payee: 39th District Court. Personal checks accepted. No credit cards accepted. Prepayment required.

Civil Name Search: Access: Mail, in person. Only the court performs in person name searches; visitors may not. No search fee. Civil records on computer since 1985, prior on microfilm. Mail turnaround time 1-2 days.

Criminal Name Search: Access: Mail, in person. Only the court performs in person name searches; visitors may not. No search fee. Required to search: name, years to search, DOB; also helpful: SSN. Records on computer since 1985, prior on microfilm. Mail turnaround time 1-2 days.

40th District Court - St. Clair Shores 27701 Jefferson, St. Clair Shores, MI 48081; 586-445-5280; criminal phone: 586-445-5281; civil phone: 586-445-5282; fax: 586-445-4003; 8:30AM-4:30PM (EST). *Misdemeanor, Civil Actions under $25,000, Eviction, Small Claims.* http://macombcountymi.gov/district_court/court40.htm

General Information: No suppressed, juvenile, sex offenders, mental health, or adoption records released. Will not fax documents. Court makes copy: $1.00 per page. Certification fee: $10.00 per certification plus copy fee. Payee: 40th District Court. Personal checks accepted. Credit card payments accepted via GPS. Prepayment required.

Civil Name Search: Access: Mail, in person. Visitors must perform in person searches themselves. Search fee: $10.00 per name. Civil records on computer since 1991; prior records on index books. Note: The court has a request form that must be used with all searches. Mail turnaround time 2 weeks.

Criminal Name Search: Access: Mail, in person, fax. Only the court performs in person name searches; visitors may not. Search fee: $10.00 per name. Required to search: name, years to search, DOB; also helpful: SSN. Criminal records on computer since 1991; prior records on index books. Note: Mail requests must have case number. The court has a request form that must be used with all searches. Mail turnaround time 2 weeks.

41 A District Court - Shelby 51660 Van Dyke, Shelby Township, MI 48316; 586-739-7325; criminal phone: x5; civil phone: x6; fax: 586-726-4555; 8AM-Noon; 1-4PM (EST). *Misdemeanor, Civil Actions under $25,000, Eviction, Small Claims.* www.macombcountymi.gov/district_court/court41a.htm

General Information: Serving Macomb Township, Shelby Township, Utica. Court will search both criminal and civil if requested. No suppressed, sex offenders, mental health records released. Will fax documents to local or toll-free number. Court makes copy: $1.00 per page. Certification fee: $10.00 1st page, $1.00 copy fee for each add'l page. Payee: 41A District Court. No personal checks accepted. Visa/MC accepted. Prepayment required.

Civil Name Search: Access: Mail, in person. Both court and visitors may perform in person name searches. No search fee. Civil records on computer since 1992, prior on index cards. Civil PAT goes back to 1997. Public terminal available M,T,TH from 9AM-1PM/1 hour limit.

Criminal Name Search: Access: Mail, in person. Both court and visitors may perform in person name searches. No search fee. Required to search:

name, years to search, DOB. Criminal records on computer since 1992, prior on index cards. Criminal PAT goes back to same as civil. Public terminal available M,T,TH from 9AM-1PM/1 hour limit. Public Terminal located in the civil division.

41 A District Court - Sterling Heights 40111 Dodge Park, Sterling Heights, MI 48313; 586-446-2500; criminal phone: 586-446-2550; civil phone: 586-446-2535; fax: 586-276-4074; 8:30AM-4:30PM (EST). *Misdemeanor, Civil Actions under $25,000, Eviction, Small Claims.*
www.macombcountymi.gov/district_court/index.htm
General Information: No suppressed, juvenile, sex offenders, mental health, or adoption records released. Will fax documents to local or toll-free number. Court makes copy: $1.00 per page. Certification fee: $10.00. Payee: 41A District Court. Personal checks and credit cards accepted. Prepayment required. Mail requests: SASE required.
Civil Name Search: Access: Mail, in person. Only the court performs in person name searches; visitors may not. No search fee. Civil records on computer since 1992; prior records on books. Mail turnaround time 1 week.
Criminal Name Search: Access: Mail, in person. Only the court performs in person name searches; visitors may not. No search fee. Required to search: name, years to search, DOB; also helpful: SSN. Criminal records on computer since 1986; prior records on books. Mail turnaround time 1 week.

41 B District Court 22380 Starks Dr, Clinton Township, MI 48036; 586-469-9300; fax: 586-469-1651; 8:30AM-4:30PM (EST). *Misdemeanor, Civil Actions under $25,000, Eviction, Small Claims, Traffic.*
www.41bdistrictcourt.com/
General Information: Serving Clinton Township, Harrison Township, Mount Clemens. The court staff will not provide a name search. No suppressed, juvenile, sex offenders, mental health, or adoption records released. Will not fax documents. Court makes copy: $.50 per page. Certification fee: $10.00. Payee: 41 B District Court. Personal or cashiers checks and money orders accepted. Visa/MC accepted. Credit card payments accepted via GPS. Prepayment required.
Civil Name Search: Access: In person. Visitors must perform in person searches themselves. No search fee. Civil PAT goes back to 1996.
Criminal Name Search: Access: In person only. Visitors must perform in person searches themselves. Required to search: name, years to search, DOB. Criminal records computerized from 1996, prior on microfilm to 1970s. Criminal PAT goes back to 1996.

42nd District Court Division 1 PO Box 6, 14713 Thirty-three Mile Rd, Romeo, MI 48065; 586-752-9679; fax: 586-752-1906; 8:30AM-4:45PM (EST). *Misdemeanor, Civil Actions under $25,000, Eviction, Small Claims.*
www.macombcountymi.gov/district_court/index.htm
General Information: Serving Armada and Armada Township, Bruce Township, Memphis, Ray Township, Richmond and Richmond Township, Romeo, Washington Township. Will not fax documents. Court makes copy: $1.00 per page. Certification fee: $10.00. Payee: 42-1 District Court. Personal checks accepted. Visa/MC accepted; Call ahead for instructions. Credit card payments accepted via GPS. Prepayment required. Mail requests: SASE requested.
Civil Name Search: Access: Mail, in person. Only the court performs in person name searches; visitors may not. Search fee: $10.00 per name. Civil records on computer since 1990, prior on index books. Mail turnaround time 2-3 days.
Criminal Name Search: Access: Mail, in person. Only the court performs in person name searches; visitors may not. Search fee: $10.00 per name. Required to search: name, years to search, DOB; also helpful: SSN, sex, signed release. Criminal records on computer since 1990, prior on index books. Mail turnaround time 2-3 days.

42nd District Court Division 2 35071 Twenty-three Mile Rd, New Baltimore, MI 48047; 586-725-9500; criminal phone: x3; civil phone: x4; fax: 586-725-1404; 8:30AM-5PM (EST). *Misdemeanor, Civil Actions under $25,000, Eviction, Small Claims.*
www.macombcountymi.gov/district_court/index.htm
General Information: Includes city of New Baltimore, Village of New Haven, and townships of Lenox and Chesterfield. Will fax case file $.50 per page. Court makes copy: $1.00 per page. Certification fee: $10.00 per doc plus copy fees. Payee: 42nd District Court. No Personal checks and credit cards accepted. Prepayment required. Prepayment of mail search required. Mail requests: SASE required.
Civil Name Search: Access: Mail, in person. Only the court performs in person name searches; visitors may not. No search fee. Civil records on computer back to 1990. Mail turnaround time 1 week.
Criminal Name Search: Access: Mail, in person. Only the court performs in person name searches; visitors may not. No search fee. Required to search: name, years to search, DOB; also helpful: SSN. Criminal records computerized from 1990. Mail turnaround time 1 week.

41 B District Court - Mt Clemens , MI; . *Civil Actions under $25,000, Eviction, Small Claims.*

General Information: Court combined with 41 B District Court - Clinton TWP.

Probate Court 21850 Dunham Rd, Mount Clemens, MI 48043-1075; 586-469-5290; fax: 586-783-0971; 8:30AM-4:30PM (EST). *Probate.*
www.macombcountymi.gov/probatecourt/index.htm

Manistee County

19th Circuit Court 415 3rd St, Manistee, MI 49660; 231-723-3331; fax: 231-723-1492; 8:30AM-5PM (EST). *Felony, Civil Actions over $25,000, Vital Statistics.*
www.manisteecountymi.gov/
General Information: No suppressed, juvenile, sex offenders, mental health, or adoption records released. Will fax documents $2.00 per page. Court makes copy: $.50 per page. Certification fee: $13.00 1st page, includes copy fee. Add $2.00 each add'l page. Payee: Manistee County Clerk. Personal checks accepted. No credit cards accepted. Prepayment required.
Civil Name Search: Access: Mail, in person. Only the court performs in person name searches; visitors may not. No search fee. Civil records on computer since 7/90, index books from 1867. Mail turnaround time 1 days.
Criminal Name Search: Access: Mail, in person. Only the court performs in person name searches; visitors may not. No search fee. Required to search: name, years to search, DOB. Criminal records on computer since 7/90, index books from 1867. Mail turnaround time 1 days.

85th District Court 415 3rd St, Manistee, MI 49660; 231-723-5010; fax: 231-723-1491; 8:30AM-N, 1-5PM (EST). *Misdemeanor, Civil Actions under $25,000, Eviction, Small Claims.*
www.manisteecountymi.gov/
General Information: No suppressed, juvenile, sex offenders, mental health, or adoption records released. Will fax documents no fee. Court makes copy: $1.00 per page. Certification fee: $10.00 per document. Payee: 85th District Court. Personal checks accepted. No credit cards accepted. Prepayment required. Mail requests: SASE required.
Civil Name Search: Access: Fax, mail, in person. Both court and visitors may perform in person name searches. No search fee. Civil records on computer since 4/89, prior on index books. Mail turnaround time 21 days maximum. Civil PAT goes back to 4/1989.
Criminal Name Search: Access: Fax, mail, in person. Both court and visitors may perform in person name searches. No search fee. Required to search: name, years to search, DOB. Criminal records on computer since 4/89, prior on index books. Mail turnaround time 5-7 days; 21 days max. Criminal PAT goes back to same as civil.
Probate Court 415 3rd St, Manistee, MI 49660; 231-723-3261; fax: 231-398-3558; 8:30AM-N, 1-5PM (EST). *Probate.*
www.manisteecountymi.gov/

Marquette County

25th Circuit Court 234 W Baraga Ave, Marquette, MI 49855; 906-225-8330; fax: 906-228-1572; 8AM-5PM (EST). *Felony, Civil Actions over $25,000, Vital Statistics.*
General Information: No suppressed, juvenile, sex offenders, mental health, or adoption records released. Will fax documents to local or toll free line. Court makes copy: $1.00 per page. Certification fee: $10.00 plus $1.00 per page. Payee: County Clerk. Personal checks accepted. No credit cards accepted. Prepayment required.
Civil Name Search: Access: Mail, in person. Only the court performs in person name searches; visitors may not. Search fee: $10.00 per name. Civil records on books since 1852, on computer from 4/95. Mail turnaround time 1-2 days.
Criminal Name Search: Access: Mail, in person. Only the court performs in person name searches; visitors may not. Search fee: $10.00 per name. Required to search: name, years to search, DOB. Docket on books since 1852, on computer from 4/95. Mail turnaround time 1-2 days.

96th District Court County Courthouse, Marquette, MI 49855; 906-225-8235; fax: 906-225-8255; 8AM-5PM (EST). *Misdemeanor, Civil Actions under $25,000, Eviction, Small Claims.*
General Information: No suppressed records released. Will fax documents for add'l $5.00 fee. Court makes copy: $1.00 per page. Certification fee: $10.00 plus $1.00 per page after first. Payee: 96th District Court. Business checks accepted. Credit cards accepted, extra fees involved. Credit card payments accepted via GPS. Prepayment required. Mail requests: SASE required.
Civil Name Search: Access: Fax, mail, in person. Only the court performs in person name searches; visitors may not. Search fee: $5.00 per name by mail, $10.00 by fax. Required to search: name, years to search; also helpful: address. Civil records on computer since 1995, prior on docket books and microfiche. Mail turnaround time 1-2 weeks.
Criminal Name Search: Access: Fax, mail, in person. Only the court performs in person name searches; visitors may not. Search fee: $5.00 per name by mail, $10.00 by fax. Required to search: name, years to search, DOB. Criminal records on computer since 1995, prior on docket books and microfiche. Mail turnaround time 1-2 weeks.

Probate Court 234 W Baraga, Marquette, MI 49855; 906-225-8300; fax: 906-228-1533; 8AM-5PM (EST). *Probate.*
General Information: Copy fee is $1.00 per page.

Mason County

51st Circuit Court 304 E Ludington Ave, Ludington, MI 49431; 231-845-1445; fax: 231-843-1972; 8AM-5PM (EST). *Felony, Civil Actions over $25,000, Vital Statistics.*
General Information: No suppressed, juvenile, sex offenders, mental health, or adoption records released. Court makes copy: $1.00 per page, but can vary w/type of doc. Self serve copy: same. Certification fee: $10.00 per doc plus copy fee. Payee: Mason County Clerk. Personal checks accepted. No credit cards accepted. Prepayment required. Prepayment of mail service required. Mail requests: SASE required.
Civil Name Search: Access: Phone, fax, mail, in person. Only the court performs in person name searches; visitors may not. No search fee. Civil records on file since 1867. Mail turnaround time 1 week.
Criminal Name Search: Access: Phone, fax, mail, in person. Only the court performs in person name searches; visitors may not. No search fee. Required to search: name, years to search, DOB. Criminal records on file since 1867. Mail turnaround time 1 week.

79th District Court County Court, 304 E Ludington Ave, Ludington, MI 49431; 231-843-4130; fax: 231-845-9076; 9AM-5PM (EST). *Misdemeanor, Civil Actions under $25,000, Eviction, Small Claims.*
General Information: No suppressed, juvenile, sex offenders, mental health, or adoption records released. No fee to fax documents locally only. Court makes copy: $1.00 per page. Certification fee: $10.00 plus $1.00 per page after first. Payee: 79th District Court. Only cashiers checks and money orders accepted. Credit card payments accepted via GPS. Prepayment required.
Civil Name Search: Access: In person only. Both court and visitors may perform in person name searches. No search fee. Civil records on Register of Action Docket Cards since 1969, computerized since 10/96. Civil PAT goes back to 1996.
Criminal Name Search: Access: In person only. Both court and visitors may perform in person name searches. No search fee. Required to search: name, years to search, DOB. Criminal records on Register of Action Docket Cards since 1969, computerized since 10/96. Criminal PAT goes to 1996.

Probate Court 304 E Ludington Ave, Ludington, MI 49431; 231-843-8666; fax: 231-843-1972; 9AM-N, 1-5PM (EST). *Probate.*

Mecosta County

49th Circuit Court 400 Elm, Rm 131, Big Rapids, MI 49307; 231-592-0783; fax: 231-592-0193; 8:30AM-5PM (EST). *Felony, Civil Actions over $25,000, Vital Statistics.*
www.co.mecosta.mi.us/clerk.asp
General Information: No suppressed, juvenile, mental health, or adoption records released. Will fax documents to local or toll free line. Court makes copy: $1.00 per page. Certification fee: $10.00 per page includes copy fee. Payee: Mecosta County Clerk. No personal checks; money orders and cashiers checks preferred. Prepayment required. Mail requests: SASE required.
Civil Name Search: Access: Fax, mail, in person. Only the court performs in person name searches; visitors may not. Search fee: $5.00 per name. Civil records on computer since 10/70, archived and microfiche since 1900s. Mail turnaround time 1 week.
Criminal Name Search: Access: Fax, mail, in person. Only the court performs in person name searches; visitors may not. Search fee: $5.00 per name. Criminal records on computer since 10/70, archived and microfiche since 1900s. Mail turnaround time 1 week.

77th District Court 400 Elm, Big Rapids, MI 49307; 231-592-0799; civil phone: 231-592-0796; fax: 231-796-2180; 8:30AM-4:30PM (EST). *Misdemeanor, Civil Actions under $25,000, Eviction, Small Claims.*
www.co.mecosta.mi.us/
General Information: No suppressed, juvenile, sex offenders, mental health, or adoption records released. Will fax documents to local or toll free line. Court makes copy: $1.00 per page. Certification fee: $10.00. Payee: 77th District Court. Business checks accepted. Major credit cards accepted via GPS. Prepayment required. Mail requests: SASE required.
Civil Name Search: Access: Mail, fax, in person. Only the court performs in person name searches; visitors may not. Search fee: $5.00 per name. Civil records on computer to 1995. Mail turnaround time 7 days.
Criminal Name Search: Access: Mail, in person. Only the court performs in person name searches; visitors may not. Search fee: $5.00 per name. Required to search: name, years to search, DOB. Criminal records on computer for 10 years, archived and microfiche prior. Note: Signed release required if request is for employment screening purposes. Mail turnaround time 7 days.

Probate Court 400 Elm St, Big Rapids, MI 49307; 231-592-0135; fax: 231-592-0191; 8:30AM-5PM T,TH,F (EST). *Probate.*
www.co.mecosta.mi.us/probate.asp

General Information: Shares the same judge with Osceola County Probate Court.

Menominee County

41st Circuit Court 839 10th Ave, Menominee, MI 49858; 906-863-9968; fax: 906-863-5819; 8AM-4:30PM (CST). *Felony, Civil Actions over $25,000, Vital Statistics.*
www.menomineecounty.com/
General Information: No suppressed, juvenile, sex offenders, mental health, or adoption records released. Will fax documents for no fee. Court makes copy: $1.00 per page. Certification fee: $10.00 per document plus copy fee. Payee: 41st Circuit Court. Personal checks accepted. Credit card payments accepted via GovPay. Prepayment required.
Civil Name Search: Access: Mail, in person. Only the court performs in person name searches; visitors may not. Search fee: $1.00 per year per person (as plaintiff or defendant). Civil records kept by docket entry in file folders, state archived to 1940, computerized since 1998. Mail turnaround time 2-3 days.
Criminal Name Search: Access: Mail, in person. Only the court performs in person name searches; visitors may not. Search fee: $5.00 per person for the first 5 years (minimum search), $1.00 each add'l year. Required to search: name, years to search, DOB; also helpful: SSN. Criminal records kept by docket entry in file folders from 1900; computerized back to 1998. Mail turnaround time 2-3 days.

95 A District Court 839 10th Ave, Menominee, MI 49858; 906-863-8532; fax: 906-863-2023; 8AM-4:30PM (CST). *Misdemeanor, Civil Actions under $25,000, Eviction, Small Claims.*
www.menomineecounty.com/departments/
General Information: No suppressed, juvenile, sex offenders, mental health, or adoption records released. Will fax documents for $1.00 per page. Court makes copy: $1.00 per page. Certification fee: $10.00 plus copy fee. Payee: District Court 95A. Personal checks accepted. No credit cards accepted. Prepayment required. Mail requests: SASE required for mail return of any copies.
Civil Name Search: Access: Fax, mail, in person. Only the court performs in person name searches; visitors may not. Search fee: $5.00 per name back to 2000. Civil index on docket books since 1969, computerized to 2000. Mail turnaround time 1 week.
Criminal Name Search: Access: Fax, mail, in person. Only the court performs in person name searches; visitors may not. Search fee: $5.00 per name back to 2000. Required to search: name, years to search, DOB. Criminal records indexed in books since 1969, computerized to 2000. Mail turnaround time 1 week.

Probate Court 839 10th Ave, Menominee, MI 49858; 906-863-2634; fax: 906-863-9904; 8AM-4:30PM (CST). *Probate, Juvenile.*
General Information: They also hold guardianships, conservatorships, adoptions, name changes, emancipations, mentally ill individuals records at this court.

Midland County

42nd Circuit Court Courthouse, 301 W Main St, Midland, MI 48640; 989-832-6735; fax: 989-832-6610; 8AM-5PM (EST). *Felony, Civil Actions over $25,000.*
http://co.midland.mi.us/departments/home.php?id=4
General Information: No suppressed records released. Will fax documents $1.00 per page. Court makes copy: $1.00 per page. Certification fee: $15.00 plus $1.00 per page. Payee: Clerk of Circuit Court. Personal checks accepted. Visa/MC accepted. Credit card payments accepted via GPS. Prepayment required. Mail requests: SASE required.
Civil Name Search: Access: Phone, mail, in person. Only the court performs in person name searches; visitors may not. Search fee: $5.00 per name. Civil records on computer from 1988, prior on books since 1800s. Mail turnaround time same day. Search court calendars free at http://co.midland.mi.us/court_calendar.php.
Criminal Name Search: Access: Phone, mail, in person. Only the court performs in person name searches; visitors may not. Search fee: $5.00 per name. Required to search: name, years to search, DOB. Criminal records computerized from 1988, prior on books since 1800s. Mail turnaround time same day. Search court calendars free at http://co.midland.mi.us/court_calendar.php.

75th District Court - Criminal Division 301 W Main St, Midland, MI 48640-5183; 989-832-6702 (6714-traffic); fax: 989-832-6601; 8:00AM-5PM (EST). *Misdemeanor.*
General Information: No suppressed, sex offenders or mental health records released. Will fax documents. Court makes copy: $1.00 per page after 5 pages. Certification fee: $5.00 per name. Payee: 75th District Court. Personal checks accepted. Visa/MC accepted. Prepayment required.
Criminal Name Search: Access: Mail, in person. Only the court performs in person name searches; visitors may not. Search fee: $5.00 per name (includes cert if asked for). Required to search: name, years to search, DOB. Criminal records on computer since 1991, prior on docket books and

paper index. Mail turnaround time 1 week. Search court calendars free at http://co.midland.mi.us/court_calendar.php.

75th District Court - Civil Division 301 W Main St, Midland, MI 48640; 989-832-6701; fax: 989-967-3712; 8:00AM-5PM (EST). *Civil Actions under $25,000, Eviction, Small Claims.*

General Information: Small Claims can be reached at 989-832-6717. No suppressed, juvenile, sex offenders, mental health, or adoption records released. Will not fax documents. Court makes copy: $1.00 per page. Certification fee: $5.00. Payee: 75th District Court. Personal checks accepted. Credit card payments accepted for criminal & traffic only. Prepayment required. Mail requests: SASE required.

Civil Name Search: Access: Mail, in person. Both court and visitors may perform in person name searches. Search fee: $1.00 per name. Required to search: name, years to search; also helpful: address. Civil records on computer since 6/89; on index books until 6/89. Mail turnaround time 5-7 days.

Probate Court 301 W Main St, Midland, MI 48640; 989-832-6880; fax: 989-832-6607; 8AM-5PM (EST). *Probate.*

http://co.midland.mi.us/departments/home.php?id=23

General Information: Search court calendars free at http://co.midland.mi.us/court_calendar.php.

Missaukee County

28th Circuit Court PO Box 800, 111 South Canal, Lake City, MI 49651; 231-839-4967; fax: 231-839-3684; 9AM-5PM (EST). *Felony, Civil Actions over $25,000, Vital Statistics.*

www.missaukee.org/court.htm?

General Information: No suppressed, juvenile, sex offenders, mental health, or adoption records released. Will fax documents $5.00 plus $1.00 per page. Court makes copy: $1.00 per page. Self serve copy: available. Certification fee: $10.00 per document plus copy fee. Payee: Missaukee County Clerk. Personal checks accepted. Debit cards accepted in person. Prepayment required. Mail requests: SASE required.

Civil Name Search: Access: Phone, fax, mail, in person. Both court and visitors may perform in person name searches. Search fee: $5.00 per name. Civil records on computer since 1965, prior on books. Mail turnaround time 2 days. Civil PAT goes back to 1965.

Criminal Name Search: Access: Phone, fax, mail, in person. Both court and visitors may perform in person name searches. Search fee: $5.00 per name. Required to search: name, years to search; also helpful: DOB, SSN. Criminal records on computer since 1988, prior on books. Mail turnaround time 2 days. Criminal PAT goes back to 1988.

84th District Court PO Box 800, Lake City, MI 49651; criminal phone: 231-839-5851; civil phone: 231-839-4590; fax: 231-839-8821; 9AM-5PM (EST). *Misdemeanor, Civil Actions under $25,000, Eviction, Small Claims.*

General Information: No suppressed, juvenile, sex offenders, mental health, or adoption records released. Will fax documents to local or toll free line. Court makes copy: $1.00 per page. Certification fee: $10.00 plus $1.00 per page after first. Payee: District Court. Personal checks accepted. Credit card payments accepted via GPS. Prepayment required. Mail requests: SASE required.

Civil Name Search: Access: Fax, mail, in person. Only the court performs in person name searches; visitors may not. No search fee. Civil records on computer since 1989. Mail turnaround time 1 week.

Criminal Name Search: Access: Fax, mail, in person. Only the court performs in person name searches; visitors may not. No search fee. Required to search: name, years to search, DOB, SSN. Criminal records on computer since 1988. Mail turnaround time 1-2 days.

Probate Court PO Box 800, 111 S Canal St, Lake City, MI 49651; 231-839-2266 x208; fax: 231-839-5856; 9AM-N, 1-5PM (EST). *Probate.*

General Information: Will accept email search requests to probate@missaukee.org

Monroe County

38th Circuit Court 106 E 1st St, Monroe, MI 48161; 734-240-7020; fax: 734-240-7045; 8:30AM-N, 1PM-5PM; closed W (EST). *Felony, Civil Actions over $25,000, Vital Statistics.*

www.co.monroe.mi.us/government/courts/circuit_court/index.html

General Information: No suppressed records released. Will not fax documents. Court makes copy: $1.00 per page. Certification fee: $10.00. Payee: 38th Circuit Court. No personal checks or credit cards accepted. Prepayment required.

Civil Name Search: Access: Mail, in person. Both court and visitors may perform in person name searches. Search fee: $8.00 per name. Fee is per name per 5 years. Civil records on computer back to 1991; prior on docket books. Mail turnaround time same or next day Civil PAT goes back to 1991.

Criminal Name Search: Access: Mail, in person. Both court and visitors may perform in person name searches. Search fee: $8.00 per name. Fee is per name per 5 years. Required to search: name, years to search, DOB.

Criminal records computerized from 1991; prior on docket books. Mail turnaround time same or next day . Criminal PAT goes back to 1991.

1st District Court 106 E 1st St, Monroe, MI 48161; 734-240-7075; criminal phone: 734-240-7080; civil phone: 734-240-7090; fax: 734-240-7098; 8:30AM-4:45PM (EST). *Misdemeanor, Civil Actions under $25,000, Eviction, Small Claims.*

www.co.monroe.mi.us/government/courts/district_court/index.html

General Information: No suppressed, juvenile, sex offenders, mental health, or adoption records released. Will not fax documents. Court makes copy: $1.00 per page; 3 page minimum for criminal, 2 for civil. Certification fee: $10.00 per page. Payee: 1st District Court. Business checks accepted. Credit card payments accepted via GovPay. Prepayment required. Mail requests: SASE required.

Civil Name Search: Access: Mail, in person. Both court and visitors may perform in person name searches. No search fee. Required to search: name, years to search, address. Civil records on computer since 1993; prior records to 1969 on microfilm. Mail turnaround time 1 week. Civil PAT goes back to 10+ years.

Criminal Name Search: Access: Mail, in person. Both court and visitors may perform in person name searches. No search fee. Required to search: name, years to search, DOB; also helpful: address. Criminal records on computer since 1993; prior records to 1969 on microfilm. Mail turnaround time 1 week. Criminal PAT goes back to 10+ years.

Probate Court 106 E 1st St, Monroe, MI 48161; 734-240-7346; fax: 734-240-7354/7355; 9AM-N 1PM-5PM (EST). *Probate.*

www.co.monroe.mi.us/government/courts/probate_court/index.html

General Information: Access probate court index free at www.co.monroe.mi.us/egov/probate/accept.aspx.

Montcalm County

8th Circuit Court 639 N State St, Stanton, MI 48888; 989-831-3520; fax: 989-831-3525; 8AM-5PM (EST). *Felony, Civil Actions over $25,000, Vital Statistics.* www.montcalm.org

General Information: The office closes for lunch hour at noon. No suppressed, juvenile, sex offenders, mental health, adoption, birth or DD214 records released. Will fax documents to local or toll-free number. Court makes copy: $1.00 per page. Certification fee: $10.00 plus $1.00 per page after first. Payee: Montcalm County Clerk. Personal checks accepted. Credit card payments accepted via GPS. Prepayment required. Mail requests: SASE required.

Civil Name Search: Access: Mail, in person. Only the court performs in person name searches; visitors may not. Search fee: $10.00 for 1st. yr. $1.00 each yr after. Civil index on docket books to 1867, computerized since 1990. Mail turnaround time 1-3 days.

Criminal Name Search: Access: Mail, in person, fax. Only the court performs in person name searches; visitors may not. Search fee: $10.00 for 1st. yr. $1.00 each yr after. Required to search: name, years to search, DOB. Criminal docket on books to 1867, computerized since 1990. Mail turnaround time 1-3 days.

64 B District Court 617 N State Rd, Stanton, MI 48888; criminal phone: 989-831-7450; civil phone: 989-831-7452; fax: 989-831-7453; 8AM-5PM (EST). *Misdemeanor, Civil Actions under $25,000, Eviction, Small Claims, Traffic.*

General Information: Probation phone- 989-831-7434. No suppressed records released. Will not fax out documents. Court makes copy: $1.00 per page. Self serve copy: same. Certification fee: $10.00 plus $1.00 each add'l page. Payee: 64 B District Court. Personal checks accepted. No credit cards accepted. Prepayment required. Mail requests: SASE required.

Civil Name Search: Access: Mail, in person. Only the court performs in person name searches; visitors may not. Search fee: $1.00 per name. Civil records on computer back 15 years, prior on books and microfiche. Mail turnaround time 7 days.

Criminal Name Search: Access: Mail, in person, fax. Only the court performs in person name searches; visitors may not. Search fee: $1.00 per name. Required to search: name, DOB. Criminal records on computer since 1989, prior on books and microfiche. Mail turnaround time 7 days.

Probate Court 625 N State St., Stanton, MI 48888; 989-831-7316; fax: 989-831-7314; 8AM-5PM (EST). *Probate.*

www.montcalm.org/probate.asp

Montmorency County

26th Circuit Court PO Box 789, Atlanta, MI 49709; 989-785-8022; probate phone: 989-785-8064; fax: 989-785-8023; 8:30AM-N, 1-4:30PM (EST). *Felony, Civil Actions over $25,000, Vital Statistics.*

General Information: No suppressed, birth certificate (except to heir or parent) adoption records released. Fee to fax out file $1.00 per page. Court makes copy: $1.00 per page. Certification fee: $10.00 plus $1.00 each add'l page. Payee: County Clerk. Personal checks accepted. Credit and debit cards accepted, except VISA. Prepayment required. Mail requests: SASE required.

Civil Name Search: Access: Mail, in person. Both court and visitors may perform in person name searches. Search fee: $5.00 per name. Civil records on computer since 1990, prior on books since 1940s, microfiche to 1970. Note: For in person searches, call ahead two days in advance. Mail turnaround time 3-5 days.

Criminal Name Search: Access: Mail, in person. Both court and visitors may perform in person name searches. Search fee: $5.00 per name. Required to search: name, years to search; also helpful: DOB. Criminal records on computer since 1990, prior on books since 1940s. Note: For in person searches, call ahead two days in advance. Mail turnaround time 3-5 days.

88-2 District Court County Courthouse, PO Box 789 (12265 M32), Atlanta, MI 49709; 989-785-8035; fax: 989-785-8036; 8:30AM-N, 1-4:30PM (EST). *Misdemeanor, Civil Actions under $25,000, Eviction, Small Claims, Traffic.*
www.montmorencycountymichigan.us/DistrictCourt.html
General Information: No suppressed, juvenile, sex offenders, mental health, or adoption records released. Fee to fax back doc $1.00 each. Court makes copy: $1.00 per page. Self serve copy: same. Certification fee: $10.00 per page. Payee: 88th District Court-Montmorency County. Personal checks accepted. Major credit cards accepted via GPS. Prepayment required. Mail requests: SASE required.
Civil Name Search: Access: Mail, in person. Both court and visitors may perform in person name searches. Search fee: $5.00 per name. Required to search: name, years to search; also helpful: address. Civil records on computer back to 1990, prior on books and card file since 1969. Mail turnaround time 2-5 days. Civil PAT available.
Criminal Name Search: Access: Mail, in person. Both court and visitors may perform in person name searches. Search fee: $5.00 per name. Required to search: name, years to search, DOB; also helpful: address, SSN, signed release. Criminal records computerized from 1990, prior on books and card file since 1969. Mail turnaround time 2-5 days. Criminal PAT available.

Probate Court PO Box 789, 12265 M-32, Judicial Annex, Atlanta, MI 49709-0789; 989-785-8064; fax: 989-785-8065; 8:30AM-N, 1-4:30PM (EST). *Probate.*
www.montmorencycountymichigan.us/PROBATE.html
General Information: Court jurisdiction in probating wills and administration of estate and trust; cases for guardianships and conservatorships of adults, minors, and developmentally disabled adults; and commitment for hospitalization or treatment of mentally ill persons.

Muskegon County

14th Circuit Court County Bldg, 6th Fl, 990 Terrace St, Muskegon, MI 49442; 231-724-6251; criminal phone: 231-724-1124; civil phone: 231-724-6173; fax: 231-724-6695; 8:30AM-5PM (EST). *Felony, Civil Actions over $25,000, Vital Statistics.*
General Information: No suppressed, juvenile, sex offenders, mental health, or adoption records released. Fee to fax out file $1.00 per page. Court makes copy: $1.00 per page. Certification fee: $10.00 per doc plus copy fee. Payee: Circuit Court Records. No personal checks. Major credit cards accepted via GPS. Prepayment required. Mail requests: SASE required.
Civil Name Search: Access: Phone, mail, fax, in person, online. Both court and visitors may perform in person name searches. Search fee: $10.00 per name. Civil records on computer back to 1984, prior on books since 1853. Mail turnaround time 2-3 days. Civil PAT goes back to 1984. There is a subscription based online record search at https://www.muskegongov.org/MCCircuitSearch/. The fee for each name searched is $6.00 and $2.50 for each Register of Action viewed.
Criminal Name Search: Access: Phone, mail, fax, in person, online. Both court and visitors may perform in person name searches. Search fee: $10.00 per name. Required to search: name, years to search, DOB; also helpful: SSN. Criminal records computerized from 1984, prior on books since 1853. Mail turnaround time 2-3 days. Criminal PAT goes back to same as civil. There is a subscription based online record search at https://www.muskegongov.org/MCCircuitSearch/. The fee for each name searched is $6.00 and $2.50 for each Register of Action viewed.

60th District Court 990 Terrace, 1st Fl, Muskegon, MI 49442; 231-724-6294; criminal phone: 231-724-6258; fax: 231-724-3489; 8:30AM-4:30PM (EST). *Misdemeanor, Civil Actions under $25,000, Eviction, Small Claims.*
www.co.muskegon.mi.us/60thdistrict/
General Information: No suppressed, juvenile, sex offenders, mental health, or adoption records released. Will not fax documents. Court makes copy: $1.00 per page. Certification fee: $10.00. Payee: 60th District Court. Personal checks accepted. No credit cards accepted for record searching. Prepayment required. Mail requests: SASE required.
Civil Name Search: Access: Mail, in person. Both court and visitors may perform in person name searches. No search fee. Civil records on computer since 5/93, prior on hard copy. Mail turnaround time 3 days. Civil PAT goes back to 5/1993. The terminal is on the 19th floor. Online access to the court weekly docket is free at www.co.muskegon.mi.us/60thdistrict/docket.htm.

Criminal Name Search: Access: Mail, in person, online. Both court and visitors may perform in person name searches. No search fee. Required to search: name, years to search, DOB. Criminal records on computer since 5/93, prior on hard copy. Mail turnaround time 3 days. Criminal PAT goes back to same as civil. Online access to court weekly docket is free at www.co.muskegon.mi.us/60thdistrict/docket.htm. Online results show name only.

Probate Court 990 Terrace St, 5th Fl, Muskegon, MI 49442; 231-724-6241; fax: 231-724-6232; 8AM-N, 1-5PM (EST). *Probate.*
www.co.muskegon.mi.us/probatecourt/
General Information: Subscription based record search at https://www.muskegongov.org/MCProbSearch/.

Newaygo County

27th Circuit Court PO Box 885, White Cloud, MI 49349-0885; 231-689-7269; criminal phone: 231-689-7269; fax: 231-689-7007; 8AM-N; 1-5PM (EST). *Felony, Civil Actions over $25,000, Vital Statistics.*
www.countyofnewaygo.com/Clerk/ClerkHome.htm
General Information: No suppressed records released. Will fax documents to toll-free number. Court makes copy: $1.00 per page. Certification fee: $10.00 plus $1.00 per page for copy after first. Payee: County Circuit Court Clerk. Personal checks accepted. No credit cards accepted. Prepayment required. Mail requests: SASE requested.
Civil Name Search: Access: Mail, fax, in person. Only the court performs in person name searches; visitors may not. No search fee. Civil records archived since 1880s; on computer since 7/1994. Mail turnaround time 2-5 days.
Criminal Name Search: Access: Mail, fax, in person. Only the court performs in person name searches; visitors may not. No search fee. Required to search: name, years to search; also helpful: DOB. Criminal records archived since 1880s; on computer since 7/1994. Mail turnaround time 2-5 days.

78th District Court 1092 Newell St, White Cloud, MI 49349; 231-689-7257; fax: 231-689-7258; 8AM-N, 1-5PM (EST). *Misdemeanor, Civil Actions under $25,000, Eviction, Small Claims.*
www.countyofnewaygo.com/Courts/District/DCHome.htm
General Information: No suppressed records released. No fee to fax documents. Court makes copy: $1.00 per page. Self serve copy: same. Certification fee: $10.00 plus $1.00 per page after first. Payee: 78th District Court. Personal checks accepted. Credit card payments accepted via GPS. Visa/MC/Discover/AmEx cards accepted. Prepayment required. Mail requests: SASE required.
Civil Name Search: Access: Fax, mail, in person. Both court and visitors may perform in person name searches. No search fee. Required to search: name, years to search; also helpful: address. Civil records on computer since 7/27/89, prior in folders. Mail turnaround time 7-10 days. Civil PAT goes back to 1989.
Criminal Name Search: Access: Fax, mail, in person. Both court and visitors may perform in person name searches. No search fee. Required to search: name, years to search, DOB; also helpful: address. Criminal records on computer since 7/27/89, prior in folders. Mail turnaround time 7-10 days. Criminal PAT goes back to same as civil.

Probate Court PO Box 885, 1092 Newell St., White Cloud, MI 49349; 231-689-7270; fax: 231-689-7276; 8AM-N, 1-5PM (EST). *Probate.*
www.countyofnewaygo.com/Courts/Probate/ProbateHome.htm
General Information: This court also holds guardianship, conservatorship, mentally ill and estate records.

Oakland County

6th Circuit Court County Clerk of the Court, 1200 N Telegraph Rd, Pontiac, MI 48341; 248-858-0581; fax: 248-452-9221; 8AM-4:30PM (EST). *Felony, Civil Actions over $25,000, Domestic Actions.*
www.oakgov.com/courts/
General Information: Email questions to clerklegal@oakgov.com. Will fax documents to local or toll free line. Court makes copy: $1.00 per page. Copies can be mailed or ordered online. Certification fee: $10.00 plus $1.00 per page. Payee: Oakland County Clerk's Office. Personal checks not accepted. Visa/MC accepted. Prepayment required. Mail requests: SASE required.
Civil Name Search: Access: Mail, in person, online. Both court and visitors may perform in person name searches. Search fee: $1.00 per name. Civil records on computer since 1963, prior on microfilm. Mail turnaround time 7 days. Civil PAT goes back to 1963. Register of Actions free at www.oakgov.com/clerkrod/courtexplorer. Order document copies online, plus enhanced access fee starting at $2.50.
Criminal Name Search: Access: Mail, in person, online. Both court and visitors may perform in person name searches. Search fee: $1.00 per name. Required to search: name; also helpful: years to search, DOB, SSN. Criminal records on computer since 1963, prior on microfilm & books. Mail turnaround time 7 days. Criminal PAT goes back to same as civil. Personal identifiers include name and birth year only. Online criminal access is the same as civil see above.

50th District Court - Pontiac Criminal Division 70 N Saginaw, Pontiac, MI 48342; 248-758-3800 x3; criminal phone: 248-758-3820; 8AM-4:30PM (EST). *Misdemeanor.* www.pontiac.mi.us/Court/index.html

General Information: No suppressed, juvenile, sex offenders, mental health, or adoption records released. Court makes copy: $1.00 per page. Self serve copy: same. Certification fee: $10.00 per doc. Payee: 50th District Court. Personal checks accepted. Credit card payments accepted via GPS. Prepayment required.

Criminal Name Search: Access: In person only. Both court and visitors may perform in person name searches. Required to search: name, years to search, DOB; also helpful: SSN. Criminal records on computer since 1984, prior on index cards since 1975. Public use terminal has crim records back to 4/2004.

43rd District Court 43 E Nine Mile Rd, Hazel Park, MI 48030; 248-547-3034; fax: 248-546-4088; 8AM-4:15PM (EST). *Misdemeanor, Civil Actions under $25,000, Eviction, Small Claims.* www.oakgov.com/courts/

General Information: No suppressed, juvenile, sex offenders, mental health, or adoption records released. Court makes copy: $1.00 per page. Certification fee: $10.00 per doc includes copy fee. Payee: 43rd District Court. Only cashiers checks, cash or money orders accepted. Credit card payments accepted via GPS. Prepayment required.

Civil Name Search: Access: In person only. Both court and visitors may perform in person name searches. No search fee. Civil records on computer since 1989, prior on books since 1970.

Criminal Name Search: Access: In person only. Both court and visitors may perform in person name searches. No search fee. Required to search: name, years to search, DOB. Criminal records on computer since 1989, prior on books since 1970.

44th District Court - Royal Oak 400 E Eleven Mile Rd, Royal Oak, MI 48067; 248-246-3600; fax: 248-246-3601; 8AM-4:30PM (EST). *Misdemeanor, Civil Actions under $25,000, Eviction, Small Claims.* www.oakgov.com/courts/

General Information: No suppressed, juvenile, sex offenders, mental health, or adoption records released. Will not fax documents. Court makes copy: $1.00 per page. Certification fee: $10.00 per page, includes copy fee. Payee: 44th District Court. Personal checks accepted. Major credit cards accepted via GPS. Prepayment required. Mail requests: SASE required.

Civil Name Search: Access: Mail, in person. Only the court performs in person name searches; visitors may not. Search fee: $10.00 per name. Civil records on computer since 1983s, prior on docket books and index cards. Mail turnaround time 5 days.

Criminal Name Search: Access: Mail, in person. Only the court performs in person name searches; visitors may not. Search fee: $10.00 per name. Required to search: name, years to search, DOB, signed release, offense; also helpful: address. Criminal records on computer since 1983s, prior on docket books and index cards. Mail turnaround time 5 days.

45 A District Court - Berkley 3338 Coolidge, Berkley, MI 48072; 248-658-3400; criminal phone: 248-658-3404; civil phone: 248-658-3405; fax: 248-658-3401; 8:15AM-4:45PM (EST). *Misdemeanor, Civil Actions under $25,000, Civil Infractions, Eviction, Small Claims.* www.oakgov.com/courts/

General Information: No suppressed records released. Will fax documents. Court makes copy: $2.00 per page. Certification fee: $10.00 per request plus copy fee. Payee: 45 A District Court. Personal checks accepted. Credit cards and debit cards accepted w/service fees. Prepayment required. Mail requests: SASE required.

Civil Name Search: Access: Mail, in person. Only the court performs in person name searches; visitors may not. Search fee: $10.00 per name, per search. Civil records on computer since 1994 prior on books. Mail turnaround time 1 week.

Criminal Name Search: Access: Mail, in person. Only the court performs in person name searches; visitors may not. Search fee: $10.00 per name, per search. Required to search: name, years to search, DOB; also helpful: SSN. Criminal records on computer since 1994, prior on books. Mail turnaround time 1 week.

45 B District Court 13600 Oak Park Blvd, City Hall Bldg, Oak Park, MI 48237; 248-691-7440; criminal phone: x3; civil phone: x2; fax: 248-691-7158; 8AM-5PM (EST). *Misdemeanor, Civil Actions under $25,000, Eviction, Small Claims.* www.oakgov.com/courts/

General Information: Court covers Huntington Woods, Oak Park, Pleasant Ridge, and Royal Oak Township. No suppressed records released. Will not fax documents. Court makes copy: $1.00 per page. Certification fee: $10.00. Payee: 45 B District Court. Business checks accepted. Major credit cards accepted via GPS. Prepayment required. Mail requests: SASE required.

Civil Name Search: Access: Mail, in person. Both court and visitors may perform in person name searches. No search fee. Civil records on computer back to 1988. Docket books and index cards back to 1987. Mail turnaround time varies. Civil PAT goes back to 1988.

Criminal Name Search: Access: Mail, in person. Both court and visitors may perform in person name searches. No search fee. Required to search: name, years to search, DOB. Criminal records computerized from 1993. Docket books and index cards go back to 1988. Mail turnaround time varies. Criminal PAT goes back to 1988.

46th District Court - Southfield 26000 Evergreen Rd, Southfield, MI 48076; 248-796-5800; criminal phone: 248-796-5880; civil phone: 248-796-5870; fax: 248-796-5875; 8AM-4:30PM (counter) (EST). *Misdemeanor, Civil Actions under $25,000, Eviction, Small Claims.* www.oakgov.com/courts/

General Information: No suppressed or "non-public" records released, such as juvenile, sex offenders, mental health, or adoption records. Will not fax documents. Court makes copy: $.50 per page.If copies are made from microfilm, the copy fee is $1.00 per page. Certification fee: $10.00 per document. Payee: 46th District Court. Personal checks accepted. Major credit cards accepted via GPS. Mail requests: SASE requested.

Civil Name Search: Access: Mail, in person. Both court and visitors may perform in person name searches. No search fee. Required to search: name or case number. Civil records prior to 1992 are on microfilm; most recent records are computerized. Mail turnaround time varies. Public use terminal has civil records back to 1992.

Criminal Name Search: Access: Mail, in person. Both court and visitors may perform in person name searches. Search fee: $1.00 per name. Required to search: name, years to search, DOB. Criminal records on computer since 1992, prior on microfiche. Mail turnaround time varies.

47th District Court - Farmington, Farmington Hills 31605 W 11 Mile Rd, Farmington Hills, MI 48336; 248-871-2900; criminal phone: 248-871-2920; civil phone: 248-871-2910; fax: 248-871-2901; 8:30AM-4:30PM (EST). *Misdemeanor, Civil Actions under $25,000, Eviction, Small Claims.* www.fhgov.com/Services/47thDistrictCourt/OverviewCourt.asp

General Information: No suppressed, sex offenders or mental health records released. Court makes copy: $1.00 per page. Certification fee: $10.00 plus $1.00 per page after first. Payee: 47th District Court. Personal checks accepted. Major credit cards accepted via GPS. Prepayment required.

Civil Name Search: Access: In person only. Visitors must perform in person searches themselves. Required to search: name, years to search, case number. Civil records on computer since 7/19/93; prior on microfiche since 1975. Civil PAT goes back to 7/19/93.

Criminal Name Search: Access: In person only. Visitors must perform in person searches themselves. Required to search: name, years to search, case number DOB; also helpful: offense. Criminal records on computer since 7/19/93; prior on microfiche since 1975. Criminal PAT goes to 7/19/93.

48th District Court - Bloomfield Hills 4280 Telegraph Rd, Bloomfield Hills, MI 48302; 248-647-1141; civil phone: 248-433-9343; fax: 248-647-8955; 8:30AM-4:30PM (EST). *Misdemeanor, Civil Actions under $25,000, Eviction, Small Claims.* www.oakgov.com/dc48/index.html

General Information: No suppressed, juvenile, sex offenders, mental health, victim or adoption records released. Will not fax documents. Court makes copy: $1.00 per page. Certification fee: $10.00 plus $1.00 per page after first - this applies to civil, eviction and small claims cases only. No fee to certify a criminal record. Payee: 48th District Court. Personal checks accepted. Credit cards accepted via GPS, call 888-604-7888. Prepayment required.

Civil Name Search: Access: Phone, mail, in person. Both court and visitors may perform in person name searches. No search fee. Required to search: name, years to search, address. Civil records on computer since 1980. Note: Limited data is given over the phone. Mail turnaround time varies. Civil PAT goes back to 1980. Terminal results may or may not show full name.

Criminal Name Search: Access: Phone, mail, in person. Both court and visitors may perform in person name searches. No search fee. Required to search: name, years to search, address, DOB. Criminal records on computer since 1980. Mail turnaround time varies. Criminal PAT goes back to same as civil. Terminal results may or may not show full name.

50th District Court - Pontiac Civil Division 70 N Saginaw, Pontiac, MI 48342; 248-758-3820 x4; civil phone: 248-758-3880; fax: 248-758-3888; 8AM-4:30PM (EST). *Civil Actions under $25,000, Eviction, Small Claims.* www.pontiac.mi.us/Court/index.html

General Information: No suppressed, juvenile, sex offenders, mental health, or adoption records released. Court makes copy: $1.00 per page. Certification fee: $10.00 per doc includes copies. Payee: 50th District Court. Personal checks accepted. Credit card payments accepted via GPS. Prepayment required.

Civil Name Search: Access: Fax, mail, in person. Both court and visitors may perform in person name searches. Search fee: $1.00 per name plus cost of copies. Civil records on computer since 1985. Mail turnaround time 3-4 days. Public use terminal has civil records back to 2004.

51st District Court - Waterford 5100 Civic Center Dr, Waterford, MI 48329; 248-674-4655; criminal phone: x3; civil phone: x4; fax: 248-674-4476; 8:30AM-4:45PM (EST). *Misdemeanor, Civil Actions under $25,000, Eviction, Small Claims.* www.twp.waterford.mi.us/Departments/51st-District-Court.aspx

General Information: Search the current docket online free at http://jisweb.twp.waterford.mi.us/jisdocket/jisdocket.aspx. No suppressed, juvenile, sex offenders, mental health, or adoption records released. Will fax documents to local number. Court makes copy: $1.00 per page. Certification fee: $10.00 per doc plus copy fee. Payee: 51st District Court. Personal checks accepted. Major credit cards accepted via GPS. Prepayment required.
Civil Name Search: Access: Mail, in person. Only the court performs in person name searches; visitors may not. No search fee, minimum $1.00 copy fee. Civil records on computer since 1980s, prior on docket books and index cards back 10 years. Mail turnaround time 10 days.
Criminal Name Search: Access: Mail, in person. Only the court performs in person name searches; visitors may not. No search fee, minimum $1.00 copy fee. Required to search: name, years to search, DOB; also helpful: SSN. Criminal records on computer since 1980s, prior on docket books and index cards to 1985. Mail turnaround time 10 days.

52nd District Court - Division 1, Novi 48150 Grand River Ave, Novi, MI 48374; criminal phone: 248-305-6460; civil phone: 248-305-6080; 8AM-4:15PM (EST). *Misdemeanor, Civil Actions under $25,000, Eviction, Small Claims.* www.52-1districtcourt.com

General Information: No suppressed, juvenile, sex offenders or mental health records released. Will not fax documents. Court makes copy: $1.00 per page. Certification fee: $10.00 per cert of disposition. Payee: 52-1 District Court. Personal checks accepted. Visa/MC/Discover Major credit cards accepted via GPS. Prepayment required. Mail requests: SASE required.
Civil Name Search: Access: Phone, mail, in person. Only the court performs in person name searches; visitors may not. Search fee: For written requests there is $1.00 per name fee; no charge for phone search. Prefers to do large name lists on Fridays - must reserve time. Civil records on computer since 1987, prior on books. Mail turnaround time 1 month.
Criminal Name Search: Access: Phone, mail, in person. Only the court performs in person name searches; visitors may not. Search fee: For written requests there is $1.00 per name fee; no charge for phone search. Best to do large name lists on Thursday & Friday. Required to search: name, years to search; also helpful: DOB. Criminal records on computer since 1987, prior on books. Mail turnaround time 1 month.

52nd District Court - Division 2 5850 Lorac, Clarkston, MI 48346; 248-625-4880; fax: 248-625-5602; 8:30AM-4:30PM (EST). *Misdemeanor, Civil Actions under $25,000, Eviction, Small Claims.* www.oakgov.com/courts/

General Information: Court covers Springfield, Holly, Groveland, Brandon, Independence, Clarkston & Ortonville and Townships of White Lake and Rose. No suppressed, juvenile or sex offender records released. Will not fax out documents. Court makes copy: $1.00 per page. Certification fee: $10.00. No personal checks accepted. Visa/MC accepted in person only. Prepayment required. Mail requests: SASE required.
Civil Name Search: Access: Phone, fax, mail, in person. Only the court performs in person name searches; visitors may not. No search fee. Civil records on computer since 1982, prior on microfiche since 1976. Mail turnaround time 3-5 days.
Criminal Name Search: Access: Phone, fax, mail, in person. Only the court performs in person name searches; visitors may not. No search fee. Required to search: name, years to search, DOB. Criminal records on computer since 1982, prior on microfiche since 1976. Mail turnaround time 3-5 days.

52nd District Court - Division 3 700 Barclay Circle, Rochester Hills, MI 48307; 248-853-5553; fax: 248-853-3277; 8:30AM-4:30PM (EST). *Misdemeanor, Civil Actions under $25,000, Eviction, Small Claims.* www.oakgov.com/courts/dcourt/

General Information: No suppressed records released. Will not fax documents. Court makes copy: $1.00 per page. Certification fee: $10.00 plus copy fee. Payee: 52-3 District Court. Personal checks accepted. Credit cards accepted in person only. Prepayment required.
Civil Name Search: Access: Phone, fax, mail, in person. Only the court performs in person name searches; visitors may not. No search fee. Required to search: name; also helpful: years to search. Civil records on computer for 10 years, prior on docket books and index cards. Mail turnaround time varies.
Criminal Name Search: Access: Phone, fax, mail, in person. Only the court performs in person name searches; visitors may not. No search fee. Required to search: name, DOB; also helpful: years to search. Criminal records on computer for 10 years, prior on docket books and index cards. Mail turnaround time varies.

52nd District Court - Division 4 520 W Big Beaver Rd, Troy, MI 48084; 248-528-0400; civil phone: 248-528-0404; fax: 248-528-3588; 8:15AM-4:15PM (EST). *Misdemeanor, Civil Actions under $25,000, Eviction, Small Claims.* www.oakgov.com/dc52div4/

General Information: Division 4 is Troy, Clawson. No suppressed, juvenile, sex offenders, mental health, or adoption records released. No fee to fax documents for criminal records and local calls only. Court makes copy: $1.00 per page. Certification fee: $10.00 per doc plus copy fee. Payee: 52-4 District Court. Personal checks accepted. Visa/MC/AmEx accepted. Prepayment required. Mail requests: SASE required.
Civil Name Search: Access: Mail, fax, in person. Only the court performs in person name searches; visitors may not. Search fee: $1.00 per name. Civil records go back to 1995. Mail turnaround time 1 week.
Criminal Name Search: Access: Fax, mail, in person. Only the court performs in person name searches; visitors may not. Search fee: $1.00 per name. Required to search: name; also helpful: years to search, DOB, SSN. Mail turnaround time 1 week.

Probate Court 1200 N Telegraph Rd, 1st Fl, Oakland County Complex, East Wing, Pontiac, MI 48341; 248-858-0260; fax: 248-452-2016; 8AM-4:30PM (EST). *Probate.* www.oakgov.com/probate/

Oceana County

27th Circuit Court 100 State St, #M-10, Hart, MI 49420; 231-873-3977; 9AM-5PM (EST). *Felony, Civil Actions over $25,000, Vital Statistics.* www.co.oceana.mi.us/circuitcourt

General Information: No suppressed, juvenile, sex offenders, mental health, or adoption records released. Will not fax documents. Court makes copy: $1.00 per page. Certification fee: $10.00 plus $1.00 per page. Payee: Oceana County Circuit Court. Personal checks accepted if local. Major credit cards accepted. Prepayment required. Mail requests: SASE requested.
Civil Name Search: Access: Mail, in person. Only the court performs in person name searches; visitors may not. Search fee: $5.00 per name. Civil records on computer since 1994, paper records to 1800s. Mail turnaround time same day.
Criminal Name Search: Access: Mail, in person. Only the court performs in person name searches; visitors may not. Search fee: $5.00 per name. Required to search: name, years to search; also helpful: DOB. Criminal records on computer since 1994, paper records to 1800s. Mail turnaround time same day.

78th District Court PO Box 471, Hart, MI 49420; 231-873-4530; fax: 231-873-1861; 8AM-5PM (EST). *Misdemeanor, Civil Actions under $25,000, Eviction, Small Claims.* www.oceana.mi.us/district_court/
General Information: No suppressed records released. Will fax documents to local or toll-free number on Fridays only. Court makes copy: $5.00 for 1st page; $1.00 each add'l; Civil- $1.00 per page. Certification fee: $10.00 1st page $1.00 each add'l page. Payee: 78th District Court. No personal checks or credit cards accepted. Prepayment required.
Civil Name Search: Access: Fax, mail, in person. Only the court performs in person name searches; visitors may not. Search fee: $1.00 per charge found. Civil cases indexed by plaintiff. Civil records on file cards and in file folders since 1967; on computer back to 1999. Mail turnaround time same day.
Criminal Name Search: Access: Fax, mail, in person. Only the court performs in person name searches; visitors may not. Search fee: $1.00 per charge found. Required to search: name, years to search, DOB. Criminal records on file cards and in file folders since 1967; on computer back to 1999. Mail turnaround time same day.

Probate Court County Bldg, 100 S State St, #M-10, Hart, MI 49420; 231-873-3666; fax: 231-873-1943; 9AM-5PM (EST). *Probate.*

Ogemaw County

34th Circuit Court 806 W Houghton, #101, West Branch, MI 48661; 989-345-0215; fax: 989-345-7223; 8:30AM-4:30PM (EST). *Felony, Civil Actions over $25,000, Vital Statistics.* www.ogemawcountymi.gov/

General Information: No suppressed, juvenile, sex offenders, mental health, or adoption records released. Will fax documents $2.00 1st page, $1.00 each add'l. Court makes copy: $.50 per page. Certification fee: $10.00 plus $1.00 per page. Payee: Ogemaw County Clerk. Personal checks accepted. No credit cards accepted for record searches. Prepayment required. Mail requests: SASE required.
Civil Name Search: Access: Phone, fax, mail, in person. Only the court performs in person name searches; visitors may not. Search fee: $10.00 per name for search of records prior to 1990, otherwise no charge. Civil index on cards since 1970, library books in vault since 1960; on computer back to 1993. Mail turnaround time 1-3 weeks.
Criminal Name Search: Access: Phone, fax, mail, in person. Only the court performs in person name searches; visitors may not. Search fee: $10.00 per name for search of records prior to 1990, otherwise no charge. Required to search: name, years to search, DOB; also helpful: SSN. Criminal

records indexed on cards since 1970, library books in vault since 1960; on computer back to 1990. Mail turnaround time 1-3 weeks.

82nd District Court PO Box 365, West Branch, MI 48661; 989-345-5040; fax: 989-345-5910; 8:30AM-4:30PM (EST). *Misdemeanor, Civil Actions under $25,000, Eviction, Small Claims.*

General Information: No suppressed records released. No fee to fax documents. Court makes copy: $.50 per page. Certification fee: $10.00 per case includes copy fee. Payee: 82nd District Court. Personal checks accepted. No credit cards accepted for record searches. Prepayment required. Prepayment of mail search required. Mail requests: SASE requested.

Civil Name Search: Access: Fax, mail, in person. Only the court performs in person name searches; visitors may not. Search fee: $5.00 per name. Civil records on computer since 1990, prior on books since 1969. Mail turnaround time 2-3 days.

Criminal Name Search: Access: Fax, mail, in person. Only the court performs in person name searches; visitors may not. Search fee: $5.00 per name. Required to search: name, years to search, DOB. Criminal records on computer since 1990, prior on books since 1969. Mail turnaround time 2-3 days.

Probate Court County Courthouse, Rm 203, 806 W Houghton Ave, West Branch, MI 48661; 989-345-0145; fax: 989-345-5901; 8:30AM-4:30PM (EST). *Probate.* www.ogemawcountymi.gov/probate/index.php

Ontonagon County

32nd Circuit Court 725 Greenland Rd, Ontonagon, MI 49953; 906-884-4255; fax: 906-884-6796; 8:30AM-4:30PM (EST). *Felony, Civil Actions over $25,000, Vital Statistics.*

General Information: No suppressed records released. Will fax documents $2.00 each. Court makes copy: $1.00 per page. Self serve copy: same. Certification fee: $10.00. Payee: County Clerk. Personal checks accepted. No credit cards accepted. Prepayment required.

Civil Name Search: Access: Mail, fax, in person. Both court and visitors may perform in person name searches. Search fee: $5.00 per name. Civil index on docket books and in folders. Mail turnaround time 2-3 days.

Criminal Name Search: Access: Mail, fax, in person. Both court and visitors may perform in person name searches. Search fee: $5.00 per name. Criminal records in folders. Mail turnaround time 2-3 days.

98th District Court 725 Greenland Rd, Ontonagon, MI 49953; 906-884-2865; fax: 906-884-2865; 8:30AM-4:30PM (EST). *Misdemeanor, Civil Actions under $25,000, Eviction, Small Claims.*

General Information: No suppressed records released. Will fax documents. Court makes copy: $1.00 per page. Certification fee: $10.00 plus $1.00 each additional copy. Payee: 98th District Court. Business checks accepted. No credit cards accepted. Prepayment required. Mail requests: SASE required.

Civil Name Search: Access: Mail, in person. Only the court performs in person name searches; visitors may not. Search fee: $5.00 each name. Civil records kept for 10 years then destroyed. Small claims kept 6 years only. Mail turnaround time 1 week.

Criminal Name Search: Access: Mail, in person. Only the court performs in person name searches; visitors may not. Search fee: $5.00 each name. Required to search: name, years to search, DOB. Criminal records kept for 10 years then destroyed. Mail turnaround time 1 week.

Probate Court 725 Greenland Rd, Ontonagon, MI 49953; 906-884-4117; fax: 906-884-2916; 8:30AM-N, 1-4:30PM (EST). *Probate.*

Osceola County

49th Circuit Court 301 W Upton, Reed City, MI 49677; 231-832-6103; fax: 231-832-6149; 9AM-5PM (EST). *Felony, Civil Actions over $25,000, Vital Statistics.*

General Information: No suppressed or adoption records released. Will fax uncertified pages $1.00 per page. Court makes copy: $1.00 per page. Certification fee: $10.00 plus $1.00 per page after first. Payee: 49th Circuit Court. Personal checks accepted. Prepayment required. Mail requests: SASE required.

Civil Name Search: Access: Phone, fax, mail, in person. Both court and visitors may perform in person name searches. Search fee: $5.00 per name. Civil records on computer since 1992, prior on docket books. Mail turnaround time 1-2 days.

Criminal Name Search: Access: Phone, fax, mail, in person. Both court and visitors may perform in person name searches. Search fee: $5.00 per name. Required to search: name, years to search, DOB. Criminal records on computer since 1992, prior on docket books back to 1967. Mail turnaround time 1-2 days.

77th District Court 410 W Upton, Reed City, MI 49677; 231-832-6155; fax: 231-832-9190; 8:30AM-4:30PM (EST). *Misdemeanor, Civil Actions under $25,000, Eviction, Small Claims.*

General Information: Court will search both criminal and civil for one search fee, if requested. No suppressed records released. May fax documents for no fee. Court makes copy: $1.00 per page. Certification fee: $10.00 per doc includes copy fee. Payee: 77th District Court. Only cashiers checks and

money orders accepted. Major credit cards accepted. Prepayment required. Mail requests: SASE required.

Civil Name Search: Access: Phone, mail, fax, in person. Only the court performs in person name searches; visitors may not. Search fee: $5.00 per name. Civil records on computer since 6/91. Mail turnaround time 2 days.

Criminal Name Search: Access: Phone, mail, fax, in person. Only the court performs in person name searches; visitors may not. Search fee: $5.00 per name. Required to search: name, DOB. Criminal records on computer since 6/91. Mail turnaround time 2 days.

Probate Court 410 W Upton, Reed City, MI 49677; 231-832-6124; fax: 231-832-6181; 8:30AM-N, 1-4:30PM (EST). *Probate.*

General Information: Shares the same judge with Mecosta County Probate Court.

Oscoda County

23rd Circuit Court PO Box 399, 311 S. Morenci Ave, Mio, MI 48647; 989-826-1110; probate phone: 989-826-1107; fax: 989-826-1136; 8:30AM-4:30PM (EST). *Felony, Civil Actions over $25,000, Vital Statistics.* www.oscodacountymi.com/Circuit%20Court.html

General Information: Probate fax- 989-826-1158 No suppressed records released. Will fax documents $5.00 1st page, $2.00 each add'l. Court makes copy: $1.00 per page. Certification fee: $10.00 plus $1.00 per page copy fee after first. Payee: Oscoda County Clerk. Personal checks accepted. Credit card payments accepted via GPS. Prepayment required. Mail requests: SASE required.

Civil Name Search: Access: Mail, in person. Only the court performs in person name searches; visitors may not. Search fee: $10.00 per name per year. Civil records on computer since 1989, prior on docket books to 1880s. Mail turnaround time 2-3 weeks.

Criminal Name Search: Access: Mail, in person. Only the court performs in person name searches; visitors may not. Search fee: $10.00 per name per year. Required to search: name, years to search, DOB. Criminal records on computer since 1989, prior on docket books to 1880s. Mail turnaround time 2-3 weeks.

81st District Court PO Box 625, Mio, MI 48647; criminal phone: 989-826-1105; civil phone: 989-826-1106; fax: 989-826-1188; 8:30AM-4:30PM (EST). *Misdemeanor, Civil Actions under $25,000, Eviction, Small Claims.*

General Information: No suppressed records released. Will fax documents to local or toll free line. Court makes copy: $.50 per page. Certification fee: $10.00 plus $1.00 per page after first. Payee: 81st District Court. No personal checks. Credit card payments accepted via GPS. Prepayment required. Mail requests: SASE required.

Civil Name Search: Access: Mail, in person. Only the court performs in person name searches; visitors may not. Search fee: $10.00 per name. Civil records on computer back to 1990, prior on index cards. Mail turnaround time 1-2 days.

Criminal Name Search: Access: Mail, in person. Only the court performs in person name searches; visitors may not. Search fee: $10.00 per name. Required to search: name, years to search, DOB. Criminal records computerized from 1990, prior on index cards. Mail turnaround time 1-2 days.

Probate Court PO Box 399, 105 S Court St, Mio, MI 48647; 989-826-1107; fax: 989-826-1158; 8:30AM-N, 1-4:30PM (EST). *Probate.* www.oscodacountymi.com/

Otsego County

46th Circuit Court 225 Main St, Gaylord, MI 49735; 989-731-7500(Clerk); fax: 989-731-7519; 8AM-4:30PM (EST). *Felony, Civil Actions over $25,000, Vital Statistics.* www.Circuit46.org

General Information: Record index is not online, but open cases and case calendars are found at www.circuit46.org/Otsego/c46g_home.html. No suppressed, juvenile, mental health, or adoption records released. Will fax documents to local or toll-free number; all others $5.00 fee per page. Court makes copy: $1.00 per page. Certification fee: $10.00 per document. Payee: Otsego County Clerk. No personal checks accepted. Credit card payments accepted via GPS. Prepayment required. Mail requests: SASE required.

Civil Name Search: Access: Mail, in person. Both court and visitors may perform in person name searches. Search fee: $5.00 per name. Civil records on computer since 1984, prior on indexes since 1800s. Mail turnaround time varies.

Criminal Name Search: Access: Mail, in person. Both court and visitors may perform in person name searches. Search fee: $5.00 per name. Required to search: name, years to search, DOB. Criminal records on computer since 1984, prior on indexes since 1800s. Mail turnaround time varies.

46th Circuit Trial Court - District Court 87-A District Court, 800 Livingston Blvd, #1C, Gaylord, MI 49735; 989-731-0201; fax: 989-732-5130; 8AM-4:30PM (EST). *Misdemeanor, Civil Actions under $25,000, Eviction, Small Claims.* www.circuit46.org

General Information: No suppressed records released. Will not fax out documents. Court makes copy: $1.00 per page. Certification fee: $10.00 plus $1.00 per page after first. Payee: 87-A District Court. Personal checks accepted. Visa/MC accepted. Prepayment required. Mail requests: SASE required.

Civil Name Search: Access: Mail, in person, online. Both court and visitors may perform in person name searches. Search fee: $5.00. Civil records on computer since 1985, prior index cards. Mail turnaround time 4 days. Civil PAT goes back to 1985. Online access to limited index (generally only open cases) is free at www.circuit46.org/Otsego/c46g_home.html.

Criminal Name Search: Access: Mail, fax, in person, online. Both court and visitors may perform in person name searches. Search fee: $5.00. Required to search: name, years to search, DOB. Criminal records on computer since 1985, prior index cards to 1969. Mail turnaround time 4 days. Criminal PAT goes back to same as civil. Access to online criminal records is the same as civil. There are limitations, this system is not meant to be used for background checks, it is supplemental only.

Probate Court 800 Livingston Blvd, #1C, Gaylord, MI 49735; 989-731-0204, 989-731-0201; fax: 989-732-5130; 8AM-4:30PM (EST). *Probate.* www.Circuit46.org

Ottawa County

20th Circuit Court 414 Washington Ave, Records - Rm 320, Grand Haven, MI 49417; 616-846-8315; fax: 616-846-8138; 8AM-5PM M-Th; 9AM-5PM F (EST). *Felony, Civil Actions over $25,000, Vital Statistics.* www.miottawa.org/CourtsLE/20thcircuit/

General Information: No suppressed, juvenile, sex offenders, mental health, or adoption records released. Will not fax documents. Court makes copy: $.50 per page. Self serve copy: same. Certification fee: $10.00 per doc plus copy fee. Payee: Ottawa County Clerk. No personal checks accepted. Major credit cards accepted via GPS. Prepayment required. Mail requests: SASE requested.

Civil Name Search: Access: Mail, fax, in person, online. Visitors must perform in person searches themselves. Search fee: $10.00 per name per decade. No fee if you provide case number. Civil cases indexed by defendant, plaintiff, number. Civil records on computer since 1998. Mail turnaround time 2-3 days; phone search - 24 hours. Civil PAT goes back to 1998. A fee-service is offered at https://www.miottawa.org/CourtRecordLookup/. One may set-up an account. Search by name or case numbers. There is a $12 cost for each name searched and a $2.50 cost for each case history or summary viewed.

Criminal Name Search: Access: Mail, fax, in person, online. Visitors must perform in person searches themselves. Search fee: $10.00 per name per decade. No fee if you provide case number. Required to search: name, years to search, DOB; also helpful: SSN. Criminal records on computer since 1990. Mail turnaround time 2-3 days; phone search - 24 hours. Criminal PAT goes back to same as civil. Same online access as civil. Includes traffic. Includes traffic. Online results show name only.

58th District Court - Grand Haven 414 Washington Ave, Grand Haven, MI 49417; 616-846-8280; criminal phone: 616-846-8127; civil phone: 616-846-8289; criminal fax: 616-846-8291; civil fax: 8AM-5PM M-TH; 9AM-5PM F; 8AM-5PM M-TH; 9AM-5PM F (EST). *Misdemeanor, Civil Actions under $25,000, Eviction, Small Claims.* www.co.ottawa.mi.us/CourtsLE/58thDistrict/

General Information: Search fee includes both civil and criminal indexes No suppressed records released. Will fax documents $3.00 per page. Court makes copy: $1.00 per page. Certification fee: $10.00 plus $1.00 per page after first. Payee: 58th District Court. Personal checks accepted, but not out-of-state. Major credit cards accepted via GPS. Prepayment required. Mail requests: SASE required.

Civil Name Search: Access: Mail, fax, in person. Both court and visitors may perform in person name searches. Search fee: $3.00. Civil records on computer back to 1993, prior on index cards since 1969. Mail turnaround time 4 days. Civil PAT goes back to 1993. A fee-service is offered at https://www.miottawa.org/CourtRecordLookup/. One may set-up an account. Search by name or case numbers. There is a $12 cost for each name searched and a $2.50 cost for each case history or summary viewed.

Criminal Name Search: Access: Mail, fax, in person, online. Both court and visitors may perform in person name searches. Search fee: $3.00 per name. Required to search: name, years to search, DOB. Criminal records computerized from 1990, prior on index cards since 1969. Mail turnaround time 4 days. Criminal PAT goes back to 1990. Same online access as civil. Includes traffic.

58th District Court - Holland 85 W 8th St, Holland, MI 49423; 616-392-6991; fax: 616-392-5013; 8AM-5PM (EST). *Misdemeanor, Civil Actions under $25,000, Eviction, Small Claims.* www.miottawa.org/CourtsLE/58thDistrict/

General Information: No suppressed records released. Will not fax out documents. Court makes copy: $1.00 per page. Certification fee: $10.00 per doc includes copies. Payee: 58th District Court. Personal checks accepted. Out of state checks not accepted. Visa/MC accepted. Prepayment required. Mail requests: SASE required.

Civil Name Search: Access: Fax, mail, in person. Both court and visitors may perform in person name searches. Search fee: $3.00 per name. Civil records on computer since 1988, prior on books since 1969. Mail turnaround time varies. Civil PAT goes back to 1989. A fee-service is offered at https://www.miottawa.org/CourtRecordLookup/. One may set-up an account. Search by name or case numbers. There is a $12 cost for each name searched and a $2.50 cost for each case history or summary viewed.

Criminal Name Search: Access: Fax, mail, in person. Both court and visitors may perform in person name searches. Search fee: $3.00 per name. Required to search: name, years to search, DOB; also helpful: SSN. Criminal records on computer since 1988, prior on books since 1969. Mail turnaround time varies. Criminal PAT goes back to 1989. Same online access as civil. Includes traffic.

58th District Court - Hudsonville 3100 Port Sheldon, Hudsonville, MI 49426; 616-662-3100 x2; fax: 616-669-2950; 8AM-Noon; 1-5PM (EST). *Misdemeanor, Civil Actions under $25,000, Eviction, Small Claims.* www.miottawa.org/CourtsLE/58thDistrict/

General Information: No suppressed records released. Will fax documents $3.00 per name. Court makes copy: $1.00 per page. Certification fee: $10.00. Payee: 58th District Court. Personal checks accepted. Credit card payments accepted via GPS. Prepayment required.

Civil Name Search: Access: Mail, in person. Both court and visitors may perform in person name searches. Search fee: $3.00 per name. Required to search: name, years to search; also helpful: address. Civil records on computer since 7/1993, prior on index file. Mail turnaround time 2 days. Civil PAT goes back to 1990. A fee-service is offered at https://www.miottawa.org/CourtRecordLookup/. One may set-up an account. Search by name or case numbers. There is a $12 cost for each name searched and a $2.50 cost for each case history or summary viewed.

Criminal Name Search: Access: Mail, in person, online. Both court and visitors may perform in person name searches. Search fee: $3.00 per name. Required to search: name, years to search, DOB; also helpful: address. Criminal records on computer since 1990. Mail turnaround time 2 days. Criminal PAT goes back to 1990. Same online access as civil. Includes traffic.

Probate Court 12120 Fillmore St, West Olive, MI 49460; 616-786-4110; fax: 616-738-4624; 8AM-5PM M-F (EST). *Probate.* www.miottawa.org/CourtsLE/Probate/

General Information: This court also holds deceased estates, guardianships, conservatorships and mentally ill records.

Presque Isle County

53rd Circuit Court PO Box 110, 151 E Huron, Rogers City, MI 49779; 989-734-3288; probate phone: 989-734-3268; fax: 989-734-7635; 8:30AM-4:30PM (EST). *Felony, Civil Actions over $25,000, Vital Statistics.* www.presqueislecounty.org/

General Information: No suppressed, juvenile, mental health, or adoption records released. Will fax documents $1.00 per page if prepaid. Court makes copy: $1.00 per page. Certification fee: $10.00 plus $1.00 per page. Payee: Presque Isle County Clerk. Personal checks accepted up to $249.99. Credit card payments may be accepted via GPS but not by court. Prepayment required. Mail requests: SASE required.

Civil Name Search: Access: Phone, fax, mail, in person. Only the court performs in person name searches; visitors may not. No search fee. Civil index on docket books since 1871. Mail turnaround time 1 week.

Criminal Name Search: Access: Phone, fax, mail, in person. Only the court performs in person name searches; visitors may not. No search fee. Required to search: name, years to search, DOB. Criminal docket on books since 1871. Mail turnaround time 1 week.

89th District Court PO Box 110, Rogers City, MI 49779; 989-734-2411; fax: 989-734-3400; 8AM-4PM (EST). *Misdemeanor, Civil Actions under $25,000, Eviction, Small Claims.* www.cheboygancounty.net/pages/89th_district_court/index.php

General Information: No suppressed records released. Will not fax documents. Court makes copy: $1.00 first page, $.50 each add'l. Self serve copy: same. Certification fee: $10.00 plus $1.00 per page after first. Payee: 89th District Court. Personal checks accepted. No credit cards accepted. Prepayment required. Mail requests: SASE required.

Civil Name Search: Access: Mail, in person. Only the court performs in person name searches; visitors may not. Search fee: $5.00. Civil records on computer since 7/94, prior on index books. Mail turnaround time 2 weeks. Dockets for 2 weeks ahead are available at www.89thdistrictcourt.org/scheduling.htm.

Criminal Name Search: Access: Mail, in person. Only the court performs in person name searches; visitors may not. Search fee: $5.00. Required to search: name, years to search, DOB. Criminal records on computer since 7/94, prior on index books. Mail turnaround time 2 weeks or less. Dockets for 2 weeks ahead are available at www.89thdistrictcourt.org/scheduling.htm.

Probate Court 151 Huron Ave, PO Box 110, Rogers City, MI 49779; 989-734-3268; fax: 989-734-4420; 8:30AM-4:30PM (EST). *Probate.*

Roscommon County

34th Circuit Court 500 Lake St #1, Attn: County Clerk Reg of Deeds, Roscommon, MI 48653; 989-275-1902; fax: 989-275-0602; 8:30AM-4:30PM (EST). *Felony, Civil Actions over $25,000, Vital Statistics.*
General Information: No suppressed, sex offenders or mental health records released. Fee to fax out file $3.00 1st page, $1.00 each add'l. Court makes copy: $.50 per page. Certification fee: $11.00 plus $1.00 per page after first. Payee: 34th Circuit Court. Personal checks accepted. No credit cards accepted. Prepayment required. Mail requests: SASE required.
Civil Name Search: Access: Fax, mail, in person. Both court and visitors may perform in person name searches. Search fee: $5.00 per name. Civil records on computer since 3/94, prior on docket books and cards. Mail turnaround time 24 hours. Civil PAT available.
Criminal Name Search: Access: Fax, mail, in person. Both court and visitors may perform in person name searches. Search fee: $5.00 per name. Required to search: name, years to search, DOB. Criminal records on computer since 3/94, prior on docket books and cards. Mail turnaround time 24 hours. Criminal PAT available.

83rd District Court 500 Lake St, Roscommon, MI 48653; 989-275-5312; fax: 989-275-6033; 8:30AM-4:30PM (EST). *Misdemeanor, Civil Actions under $25,000, Eviction, Small Claims.*
www.roscommoncounty.net/
General Information: No suppressed, juvenile, sex offenders, mental health, or adoption records released. No fee to fax documents. Court makes copy: $.50 per page. Certification fee: $10.00 first page, $1.00 ea add'l. Payee: 83rd District Court. Personal checks accepted. Credit card payments accepted via GPS. Prepayment required.
Civil Name Search: Access: Phone, fax, mail, in person. Only the court performs in person name searches; visitors may not. No search fee. Civil records on computer since 1988, prior on index cards since 1969. Mail turnaround time same day.
Criminal Name Search: Access: Phone, fax, mail, in person. Only the court performs in person name searches; visitors may not. No search fee. Required to search: name, years to search, DOB; also helpful: SSN. Criminal records on computer since 1988, prior on index cards since 1969. Mail turnaround time same day.

Probate Court 500 Lake St, Roscommon, MI 48653; 989-275-5221; fax: 989-275-8537; 8:30AM-4:30PM (EST). *Probate.*
www.roscommoncounty.net/

Saginaw County

10th Circuit Court 111 S Michigan Ave, Saginaw, MI 48602; 989-790-5470; probate phone: 989-790-5320; fax: 989-790-5248; 8AM-5:00PM (EST). *Felony, Civil Actions over $25,000, Vital Statistics.*
www.saginawcounty.com/CircuitCourt.aspx?AspxAutoDetectCookieSupport=1
General Information: No suppressed, sex offenders, mental health or guardianship records released. Will fax documents, up to 5 pages. Court makes copy: $1.00 per page. Certification fee: $10.00 plus $1.00 per page. Payee: Saginaw County Clerk. Personal checks accepted. Credit card payments accepted via GPS and online. In person searches limited to debit cards only. Prepayment required. Mail requests: SASE required.
Civil Name Search: Access: Mail, in person, online. Both court and visitors may perform in person name searches. No search fee at this time. Civil records on computer since 1985, prior on index books, microfilm. Mail turnaround time 2 days. Civil PAT goes back to 1986. Search civil records from 2000 forward online free at www.saginawcounty.com/Clerk/Court/CivilRecords.aspx
Criminal Name Search: Access: Mail, in person, online. Both court and visitors may perform in person name searches. No search fee at this time. Required to search: name, years to search, DOB. Criminal records on computer since 1986, prior on index books. Mail turnaround time 2 days. Criminal PAT goes back to same as civil. Search criminal records online free at www.saginawcounty.com/Clerk/Court/CriminalRecords.aspx. Records shown are from 2000 to present. Online results show name, DOB.

70th District Court - Criminal Division 111 S Michigan Ave, 3rd Fl, County Governmental Ctr, Saginaw, MI 48602; 989-790-5385; fax: 989-790-5589; 8AM-4:45PM (EST). *Misdemeanor.*
www.saginawcounty.com/DistrictCourt/CriminalDivision.aspx
General Information: No suppressed, juvenile, sex offenders, mental health, or adoption records released. Will fax documents to local or toll free line for a fee depending on how many pages. Prepayment required of $10.00 plus fax fee. Court makes copy: $1.00 per page. Certification fee: $10.00 for 1st page, $1.00 per page after. Payee: 70th District Court. Business checks

accepted. Major credit cards accepted in person only. Prepayment required. Mail requests: SASE required.
Criminal Name Search: Access: Fax, mail, in person. Both court and visitors may perform in person name searches. Search fee: $10.00 per name. Required to search: name, years to search, DOB, signed release; also helpful: address. Criminal records computerized from 1986, prior on microfiche since 1970. Note: Fax information received only if pre-paid. Mail turnaround time 1 week. Public use terminal has crim records back to 1986.

70th District Court - Civil Division 111 S Michigan Ave, Saginaw, MI 48602; 989-790-5380; fax: 989-790-5562; 8AM-4:45PM (EST). *Civil Actions under $25,000, Eviction, Small Claims.*
www.saginawcounty.com/DistrictCourt/Default.aspx
General Information: No suppressed records released. Will fax documents to local or toll free line for a fax fee. Court makes copy: $1.00 per page. Certification fee: $10.00. Payee: 70th District court. Personal checks accepted. No credit cards accepted. Prepayment required. Mail requests: SASE required.
Civil Name Search: Access: Mail, in person. Only the court performs in person name searches; visitors may not. Search fee: $10.00 per name. Civil records on computer since 1982, prior on docket books. Mail turnaround time 1 week. Public use terminal has civil records back to 1988. Terminal results show middle initial if one was provided.

Probate/Family Court 111 S Michigan St, 2nd Fl, Rm 204, Saginaw, MI 48602; 989-790-5328; fax: 989-790-5328; 8AM-5PM (EST). *Probate.*
www.saginawcounty.com/Probate/Default.aspx

Sanilac County

24th Circuit Court 60 W Sanilac, Rm 203, Sandusky, MI 48471; 810-648-3212 x8227; fax: 810-648-5466; 8AM-4:30PM (EST). *Felony, Civil Actions over $25,000, Vital Statistics.*
www.sanilaccounty.net/PublicPages/Entity.aspx?ID=131
General Information: No suppressed, juvenile, sex offenders, mental health, or adoption records released. Will fax documents to local or toll free line. Court makes copy: $1.00 per page. Certification fee: $10.00 plus $1.00 per page. Payee: Sanilac County Clerk. Personal checks accepted. Credit card payments go through GPS. Prepayment required. Mail requests: SASE required.
Civil Name Search: Access: Mail, in person. Both court and visitors may perform in person name searches. Search fee: $10.00 per name. Civil records on computer since 1993. Mail turnaround time 2-3 days.
Criminal Name Search: Access: Mail, in person. Both court and visitors may perform in person name searches. Search fee: $10.00 per name. Criminal records on computer since 1993. Mail turnaround time 2-3 days.

73A District Court 60 W Sanilac, Sandusky, MI 48471; 810-648-3250; civil phone: 810-648-3250; fax: 810-648-3271; 8AM-4:30PM (EST). *Misdemeanor, Civil Actions under $25,000, Eviction, Small Claims.*
General Information: Traffic phone is 810-648-3424. No suppressed records released. Will fax documents to local or toll free line. Fax fee included in search. Court makes copy: $1.00 per page. Certification fee: $10.00 plus $1.00 per page after first. Payee: 73A District Court. Personal checks accepted. No credit cards accepted. Prepayment required. Mail requests: SASE required.
Civil Name Search: Access: Mail, in person. Only the court performs in person name searches; visitors may not. Search fee: $1.00 per name per year. Required to search: name, years to search; also helpful: address, DOB. Civil records on computer back to 1989, prior on docket books to 1969. Mail turnaround time 1 week.
Criminal Name Search: Access: Mail, in person. Only the court performs in person name searches; visitors may not. Search fee: $1.00 per name per year. Required to search: name, years to search, DOB; also helpful: address. Criminal records computerized from 1989, prior on docket books to 1969. Mail turnaround time 1 week.

Probate Court 60 W Sanilac Ave, Rm 203, Sandusky, MI 48471-1096; 810-648-3221; fax: 810-648-5466; 8AM-N, 1-4:30PM (EST). *Probate.*
www.sanilaccounty.net/

Schoolcraft County

11th Circuit Court 300 Walnut St, Rm 164, Manistique, MI 49854; 906-341-3618; probate phone: 906-341-3644; fax: 906-341-5680; 8AM-4PM (EST). *Felony, Civil Actions over $25,000, Vital Statistics.*
General Information: Probate is a separate index in Rm 129. Probate fax-906-341-3627 No suppressed, juvenile, sex offenders, mental health, or adoption records released. Will fax documents to local or toll free line. Court makes copy: $1.00 per page. Certification fee: $10.00 per document plus copy fee. Exemplification fee is $29.00. Payee: Schoolcraft County Clerk. Personal checks accepted. Credit card payments accepted via GPS. Prepayment required.
Civil Name Search: Access: Phone, fax, mail, in person. Both court and visitors may perform in person name searches. Search fee: $10.00 per

name. Civil index on docket books and index since 1881. Mail turnaround time 2-3 days.

Criminal Name Search: Access: Phone, fax, mail, in person. Only the court performs in person name searches; visitors may not. Search fee: $10.00 per name. Criminal docket on books and index since 1881. Mail turnaround time 2-3 days.

93rd District Court 300 Walnut St, Rm 135, Manistique, MI 49854; 906-341-3630; fax: 906-341-8006; 8AM-4PM (EST). *Misdemeanor, Civil Actions under $25,000, Eviction, Small Claims.*
www.schoolcraftcounty.net/departments_1.asp?go=District Court

General Information: No suppressed, sex offenders or mental health records released. Will fax documents. Court makes copy: $1.00 per page. Self serve copy: same. Certification fee: $10.00 plus copy fee if more than 1 page. Payee: 93rd District Court. Business checks accepted. Major credit cards accepted. Prepayment required. Mail requests: SASE required.

Civil Name Search: Access: Mail, in person. Both court and visitors may perform in person name searches. Search fee: $10.00. Civil records computerized since 1999, also kept on index cards. Mail turnaround time 2-3 days.

Criminal Name Search: Access: Mail, in person. Only the court performs in person name searches; visitors may not. Search fee: $10.00. Required to search: name, years to search, DOB. Criminal records computerized since 1999, also kept on index cards. Mail turnaround time 2-3 days.

Probate Court 300 Walnut St, Rm 129, Manistique, MI 49854; 906-341-3641; fax: 906-341-3627; 8AM-N 1PM-4PM (EST). *Probate.*
www.schoolcraftcounty.net/departments_1.asp?go=Probate%20Court

Shiawassee County

35th Circuit Court 208 N Shiawassee St, Corunna, MI 48817; 989-743-2262; fax: 989-743-2241; 8AM-5PM, may close for lunch hour (EST). *Felony, Civil Actions over $25,000, Vital Statistics.*

General Information: No suppressed records released. Will fax documents for $10.00 fee. Court makes copy: $1.00 per page 1st 5 pages; $.15 each add'l. Certification fee: $10.00 per document. A Register of Action fee is $10.00. Payee: 35th Circuit Court. Personal checks and credit cards accepted. Prepayment required. Mail requests: SASE required.

Civil Name Search: Access: Phone, fax, mail, in person. Both court and visitors may perform in person name searches. Search fee: $10.00 for up to 10 years. Civil records on computer since 9/87, prior on docket books and cards. Mail turnaround time 1 week.

Criminal Name Search: Access: Phone, fax, mail, in person. Both court and visitors may perform in person name searches. Search fee: $10.00 for up to 10 years. Required to search: name, years to search, DOB. Criminal records on computer since 10/93; prior on docket books. Mail turnaround time 1 week.

66th District Court 110 E Mack St, Corunna, MI 48817; 989-743-2395; fax: 989-743-2469; 8AM-5PM (EST). *Misdemeanor, Civil Actions under $25,000, Eviction, Small Claims.*

General Information: No suppressed records released. Faxes out documents Fridays only. Court makes copy: $1.00 per page. Certification fee: $10.00 plus any copy fees. Payee: 66th District Court. Personal checks accepted. Major credit cards accepted in person only. Prepayment required. Mail requests: SASE required.

Civil Name Search: Access: Phone, fax, mail, in person. Both court and visitors may perform in person name searches. No search fee. Required to search: name, years to search; also helpful: DOB, SSN. Civil records on computer back to 1995, prior on microfiche. Mail turnaround time 1 week.

Criminal Name Search: Access: Phone, fax, mail, in person. Both court and visitors may perform in person name searches. No search fee. Required to search: name, years to search, DOB. Case number required for pre-1995 research. Criminal records computerized from 1995, prior on microfiche to 1969. Mail turnaround time 1 week.

Probate Court 110 E Mack St, Courts & Health Bldg, Corunna, MI 48817; 989-743-2211; fax: 989-743-2349; 8AM-5PM (EST). *Probate.*
www.shiawassee.net/Law-Justice/Probate-Court

St. Clair County

31st Circuit Court 201 McMorran Blvd, Port Huron, MI 48060; 810-985-2200; fax: 810-985-4796; 8AM-4:30PM (EST). *Felony, Civil Actions over $25,000, Vital Statistics.*
www.stclaircounty.org/Offices/courts/

General Information: Online identifiers in results same as on public terminal. No suppressed, juvenile, mental health, or adoption records released. Will fax documents $10.00 per searched name. Court makes copy: $1.00 per page. Certification fee: $10.00. Payee: St. Clair Clerk of Court. Will accept In state checks. Credit cards accepted. Prepayment required. Mail requests: SASE required.

Civil Name Search: Access: Mail, fax, in person, online. Both court and visitors may perform in person name searches. No search fee. Required to search: name, years to search; also helpful: address. Civil records on

computer back to 1987, non computerized records back to 1936. Mail turnaround time 24 hours. Civil PAT available. A index of records can be viewed at www.stclaircounty.org/Offices/courts/circuit/records.asp.

Criminal Name Search: Access: Mail, fax, in person, online. Both court and visitors may perform in person name searches. No search fee. Required to search: name, years to search, DOB; also helpful: address. Criminal records computerized from 1987, non computerized records back to 1936. Mail turnaround time 24 hours. Criminal PAT available. Records index can be viewed at www.stclaircounty.org/Offices/courts/circuit/records.asp. Online results show middle initial, DOB, address.

72nd District Court 201 McMorran Blvd, Rm 2900, Port Huron, MI 48060; 810-985-2076; criminal phone: 810-985-2072; civil phone: 810-985-2077; fax: 810-982-1260; 8AM-4:30PM M-TH; 9AM-4:30PM (EST). *Misdemeanor, Civil Actions under $25,000, Eviction, Small Claims.*
www.stclaircounty.org/Offices/courts/

General Information: No suppressed records released. Will fax documents $1.00 per page. Court makes copy: $1.00 per page. Certification fee: $10.00 per doc includes copy fee. Payee: 72nd District Court. Personal checks and credit cards accepted. Prepayment required. Mail requests: SASE required for mail return of any copies.

Civil Name Search: Access: In person, online. Visitors must perform in person searches themselves. Civil records on computer since 1987, prior on docket books back to 1969. Civil PAT goes back to 1989, countywide. Access court case index free at www.stclaircounty.org/DCS/search.aspx.

Criminal Name Search: Access: In person, online. Visitors must perform in person searches themselves. Required to search: name, years to search, DOB; SSN helpful. Criminal records on computer since 1987, prior on docket books back to 1969. Criminal PAT goes back to same as civil. Access court case index free at www.stclaircounty.org/DCS/search.aspx.

Probate Court 201 McMorran Blvd, Rm 2600, Port Huron, MI 48060; 810-985-2066; fax: 810-985-2179; 8AM-4:30PM (EST). *Probate.*
www.stclaircounty.org/Offices/courts/probate/
General Information: Probate cases may be included in the online search at www.stclaircounty.org/DCS/search.aspx.

St. Joseph County

45th Circuit Court PO Box 189, 125 W Main St, 2nd Fl, Centreville, MI 49032; 269-467-5542; fax: 269-467-5558; 8AM-5PM (EST). *Felony, Civil Actions over $25,000, Vital Statistics.*
www.stjosephcountymi.org/circuit/

General Information: No suppressed records released. Will fax documents $2.00 1st page, $1.00 each add'l. Court makes copy: $1.00 per page. Certification fee: $10.00 per certification plus $1.00 per page. Payee: St. Joseph County Clerk. Business checks accepted. Credit card payments accepted via GPS and telephone. Prepayment required.

Civil Name Search: Access: Mail, in person. Both court and visitors may perform in person name searches. Search fee: $1.00 per name. For records prior to 1988, fee is $1.00 per year searched. Civil records on computer since 1988, prior on books from 1900, earlier in archives. Note: Visitors can do in person searches after 1988. Mail turnaround time 1 day. Civil PAT goes back to 1988.

Criminal Name Search: Access: Mail, in person. Both court and visitors may perform in person name searches. Search fee: $1.00 per name. For records prior to 1988, fee is $1.00 per year searched. Criminal records on computer since 1988, prior on books from 1900, earlier in archives. Note: Court can do in person searches of indexes after 1988. Mail turnaround time same day. Criminal PAT goes back to same as civil.

3-B District Court PO Box 67, Centreville, MI 49032; 269-467-5627; criminal phone: 269-467-5585; civil phone: 269-467-5623; fax: 269-467-5611; 8AM-5PM (EST). *Misdemeanor, Civil Actions under $25,000, Eviction, Small Claims.*
www.stjosephcountymi.org/district/

General Information: No suppressed records released. Will not fax documents. Court makes copy: $.25 per page. Certification fee: $10.00 per doc copy fee. Payee: 3-B District Court. Business checks accepted. Credit card payments accepted via GPS. Prepayment required.

Civil Name Search: Access: Phone, mail, in person. Both court and visitors may perform in person name searches. No search fee. Required to search: name, years to search; also helpful: address. Civil records on computer since 1988, prior in archives. Note: Phone search access limited. Mail turnaround time minimum 72 hours. Civil PAT goes back to 1988.

Criminal Name Search: Access: Fax, mail, in person. Both court and visitors may perform in person name searches. No search fee. Required to search: name, years to search, DOB, date of offense. Criminal records on computer since 1988, prior in archives. Note: Signed release required for some searches. Mail turnaround time minimum 72 hours. Criminal PAT goes back to same as civil.

Probate Court PO Box 190, 125 W Main St, 2nd Fl, Courts Bldg, Centreville, MI 49032; 269-467-5538; fax: 269-467-5560; 8AM-5PM (EST). *Probate.* www.stjosephcountymi.org/probate/

Tuscola County

54th Circuit Court 440 N State St, Caro, MI 48723; 989-673-3330; 989-672-3780 county clerk; criminal phone: 989-672-3775; civil phone: 989-672-3775; probate phone: 989-672-3850; fax: 989-672-4266; 8AM-N, 1-4:30PM (EST). *Felony, Civil Actions over $25,000, Vital Statistics.*
www.tuscolacounty.org

General Information: No suppressed, juvenile, sex offenders, mental health, or adoption records released. Will not fax documents. Court makes copy: $1.00 per page. Certification fee: $10.00 plus $1.00 per page after first. Payee: County Clerk. No personal checks. Credit card payments accepted via Govexp. Prepayment required. Mail requests: SASE required.

Civil Name Search: Access: Mail, in person. Only the court performs in person name searches; visitors may not. Search fee: $5.00 per name. Fee is $1.00 for each year prior to 1989. Civil records on computer since 1989, prior on books since beginning. Mail turnaround time 3-4 days.

Criminal Name Search: Access: Mail, in person. Only the court performs in person name searches; visitors may not. Search fee: $5.00 per name. Fee is $1.00 for each year prior to 1989. Required to search: name, years to search, DOB. Criminal records on computer since 1989, prior on books since beginning. Mail turnaround time 3-4 days.

71 B District Court 440 N State St., Caro, MI 48723; 989-672-3800; criminal phone: 989-672-3790; civil phone: 989-672-3800; criminal fax: 989-672-4526; civil fax: 8AM-4:30PM; 8AM-4:30PM (EST). *Misdemeanor, Civil Actions under $25,000, Eviction, Small Claims.*

General Information: Staff will check records as time permits, but no more than 5 per day. No suppressed records released. Will fax documents for $1.00 per page plus purchase of search or copies. Court makes copy: $.50 per page.Copy fee is only of on site. Certification fee: $10.00 plus $1.00 per page after first. Payee: 71 B District Court. Personal checks accepted. Credit cards accepted; a surcharge applies. Credit card payments accepted via GPS. Prepayment required. Mail requests: SASE required.

Civil Name Search: Access: Mail, in person. Only the court performs in person name searches; visitors may not. No search fee. Civil records on computer since 1998, prior on cards. Mail turnaround time 5-10 days.

Criminal Name Search: Access: Fax, Mail, in person. Only the court performs in person name searches; visitors may not. Search fee: $5.00 for Defendant History Inquiry plus $1.00 per page of other records needed if faxed - $.50 if on site. Required to search: name, years to search, DOB; also helpful: SSN. Criminal records on computer since 1998; others back to 1969. Note: The fax must include a copy of the check that will be mailed. Mail turnaround time 1-3 days.

Probate Court 440 N State St, Caro, MI 48723; 989-672-3850; fax: 989-672-2057; 8AM-N, 1-4:30PM (EST). *Probate.*

Van Buren County

36th Circuit Court 212 Paw Paw St #101, Paw Paw, MI 49079; 269-657-8218 #6; criminal fax: 269-657-8298; civil fax: 8:30AM-5PM; 8:30AM-5PM (EST). *Felony, Civil Actions over $25,000, Vital Statistics.*
www.vbco.org/government0093.asp

General Information: No suppressed, sex offender records released. Will phone when documents ready if toll-free number provided. Court makes copy: $1.00 per page. Certification fee: $10.00 plus $1.00 per page after first. Payee: Van Buren County Clerk. Personal checks accepted. Credit card payments accepted via GPS. Prepayment required. Mail requests: SASE required.

Civil Name Search: Access: Mail, in person. Only the court performs in person name searches; visitors may not. Search fee: $1.00 per name per year. Fee includes combined civil and criminal search. Civil records on computer back to 1990, prior on docket books since 1800s. Mail turnaround time 1 day.

Criminal Name Search: Access: Mail, in person. Only the court performs in person name searches; visitors may not. Search fee: $1.00 per name per year. Required to search: name, years to search, DOB, signed release. Criminal records computerized from 1990, prior on docket books since 1800s. Mail turnaround time 1 day.

7th District Court - East 212 Paw Paw St, #130, Paw Paw, MI 49079; 269-657-8222; fax: 269-657-0719; 9AM-4:30PM (EST). *Misdemeanor, Civil Actions under $25,000, Eviction, Small Claims.*
www.vbco.org/government0093.asp

General Information: No suppressed records released. Court makes copy: $1.00 per page. Certification fee: $10.00 per doc plus copy fee. Payee: 7th District Court. No personal checks accepted. Credit card payments accepted via GPS. Prepayment required. Mail requests: SASE required.

Civil Name Search: Access: Mail, fax, in person. Both court and visitors may perform in person name searches. No search fee. Civil records kept in file folder; computerized records since 1999. Mail turnaround time 1-2 days.

Criminal Name Search: Access: Mail, fax, in person. Both court and visitors may perform in person name searches. No search fee. Required to search: name, years to search, DOB, SSN. Criminal records kept in file folder; computerized since 1999. Mail turnaround time 1-2 days.

7th District Court - West Division 1007 E Wells, PO Box 311, South Haven, MI 49090; 269-637-5258; fax: 269-639-4517; 8:30AM-4:30PM (EST). *Misdemeanor, Civil Actions under $25,000, Eviction, Small Claims.*
www.vbco.org/government0093.asp

General Information: No suppressed, juvenile, sex offenders, mental health, or adoption records released. Court makes copy: $1.00 per page. Certification fee: $10.00 plus $1.00 per page after first. Payee: 7th District Court. Personal checks accepted. Credit card payments accepted via GPS. Prepayment required. Mail requests: SASE required.

Civil Name Search: Access: Mail, in person. Only the court performs in person name searches; visitors may not. Search fee: $1.00 per name plus copy fee. Civil records on computer since 1991, prior on index cards since 1982. Mail turnaround time 3 days.

Criminal Name Search: Access: Mail, in person. Only the court performs in person name searches; visitors may not. Search fee: $1.00 per name plus copy fee. Required to search: name, years to search, DOB. Criminal records on computer since 1991, prior on index cards since 1982. Mail turnaround time 3 days.

Probate Court 212 Paw Paw St, Ste 220, Paw Paw, MI 49079; 269-657-8225; fax: 269-657-7573; 8:30AM-5PM (EST). *Probate.*
www.vbco.org/government0093.asp

Washtenaw County

22nd Circuit Court PO Box 8645, 101 E Huron St, Ann Arbor, MI 48107-8645; 734-222-3001/3270; fax: 734-222-3089; 8:30AM-4:45PM (EST). *Felony, Civil Actions over $25,000.*
www.washtenawtrialcourt.org

General Information: Weekly court dockets listed by judge are free at http://washtenawtrialcourt.org/calendar. Records from the year 1883 to older then 25 years have been purged. No suppressed records released. Will not fax documents. Court makes copy: $1.00 per page.The court is entitled to collect $2.00 per copy. Certification fee: $10.00 per doc plus copy fee. Payee: Clerk of Court. Personal checks and credit cards accepted. Prepayment required. Mail requests: SASE required.

Civil Name Search: Access: Mail, in person, online. Both court and visitors may perform in person name searches. Search fee: $5.00 per name from 1979 to present; add $1.00 per name per year prior to 1979. Civil records kept as originals in file folders, records go back to 1900; computerized since 1979. Mail turnaround time 2-3 weeks. Civil PAT goes back to 1979. Results from PAT do not always include DOB or address. Only signed orders back 30 days are free online at http://washtenawtrialcourt.org/signed_orders; search by judge.

Criminal Name Search: Access: Mail, in person, online. Both court and visitors may perform in person name searches. Search fee: $5.00 per name from 1979 to present; add $1.00 per name per year prior to 1979. Required to search: name, years to search, DOB. Criminal records kept as originals in file folders, records go back to 1900; computerized since 1979. Mail turnaround time 2-3 weeks. Criminal PAT goes back to 1979. Results from PAT do not always include DOB or address. Only signed orders back 30 days are free online at http://washtenawtrialcourt.org/signed_orders; search by judge. Listed only, cannot view the orders.

14B District Court - Criminal Division 7200 S Huron River Dr, Ypsilanti, MI 48197; 734-483-1333; fax: 734-483-3630; 8AM-5PM (EST). *Misdemeanor.*
http://14adistrictcourt.org/locations/14a-2

General Information: 14B District Court covers the township of Ypsilanti which surrounds the city of Ypsilanti including Eastern Michigan University. No suppressed, probation, juvenile, sex offenders, probation, mental health, or adoption records released. Will not fax documents. Court makes copy: $1.00 per page.The court is entitled to collect $2.00 per copy. Certification fee: $10.00 per doc. Payee: 14-B District Court. Personal checks accepted. Major credit cards accepted via GPS. Prepayment required.

Criminal Name Search: Access: Fax, mail, in person. Only the court performs in person name searches; visitors may not. No search fee. Required to search: name, years to search, DOB; also helpful: SSN. Criminal records on computer since 1990, prior records kept by name. Mail turnaround time 1 week; phone turnaround 1 day.

15th District Court - Criminal Division 301 E Huron, Ann Arbor, MI 48107-8650; 734-794-6750; 8AM-4:30PM M-TH; 8AM-3PM F (EST). *Misdemeanor, Traffic.*
www.a2gov.org/services/OtherServices/15D/Pages/default.aspx

General Information: The Traffic/Criminal Division maintains the records for all traffic and criminal misdemeanors, civil infractions, ordinance violations, and University of Michigan Regents violations. No suppressed, juvenile, sex offenders, mental health, or adoption records released. Will not fax documents. Court makes copy: $.25 per page.The court is entitled to collect $2.00 per copy. Certification fee: $10.00 per doc plus $1.00 per page. Payee: 15th District Court. Checks accepted. Major credit cards accepted via telecheck. Prepayment required. Mail requests: SASE required.

Criminal Name Search: Access: Mail, fax, in person, online. Only the court performs in person name searches; visitors may not. No search fee.

Required to search: name, years to search, DOB; also helpful: offense. Criminal records computerized back to 1992; prior on docket cards since 1969. Note: The court will not do a name search; either a case number or charge and incident date is required. Mail turnaround time 2-3 days. Access court records free at www.a2gov.org/services/OtherServices/15D/Pages/OnlineCaseSearch.aspx. Includes cases files on or after 08/05/2006. Online results show name only.

14A-1 District Court 4133 Washtenaw, Ann Arbor, MI 48107-8645; 734-973-4545; fax: 734-973-4693; 8AM-4:30PM (EST). *Misdemeanor, Civil Actions under $25,000, Eviction, Small Claims.*
http://14adistrictcourt.org/locations/14a-1
General Information: 14A-1 District Court presides over the Townships of Ann Arbor, Augusta, Pittsfield, Salem, and Superior, and the Village of Barton Hills. All Preliminary Examinations for Washtenaw County are heard at this location. No suppressed records released. Will fax documents to local number. Court makes copy: $1.00 per page.The court is entitled to collect $2.00 per copy. Certification fee: $10.00 per doc plus copy fee. Payee: 14 A District Court. Personal checks accepted. Visa/MC/Discover accepted. Prepayment required. Mail requests: SASE required.
Civil Name Search: Access: Mail, in person, online. Both court and visitors may perform in person name searches. No search fee. Civil records on computer since 1985, prior on index cards. Mail turnaround time 1-2 weeks. Civil PAT goes back to 1985. Dockets and calendars are searchable at www.14adistrictcourt.org/cases.
Criminal Name Search: Access: Mail, in person, online. Both court and visitors may perform in person name searches. No search fee. Required to search: name, years to search, DOB. Criminal records on computer since 1985, prior on index cards. Mail turnaround time 1-2 weeks. Criminal PAT goes back to same as civil. Dockets and calendars are searchable at www.14adistrictcourt.org/cases. Online results show middle initial.

14A-4 District Court 1000 N Maple Rd, Saline, MI 48176; 734-429-2504; fax: 734-429-2879; 8AM-4:30PM (EST). *Misdemeanor, Civil Actions under $25,000, Eviction, Small Claims.*
http://14adistrictcourt.org
General Information: This District Court presides over the cities of Saline and Milan, the Townships of Bridgewater, Freedom, Lodi, Manchester, Saline, Sharon and York, and the Village of Manchester. Prior to 2009, cases for these jurisdictions are in 14-A3. No suppressed records released. Will not fax documents. Court makes copy: $1.00 for 1st copy, $.25 each add'l.The court is entitled to collect $2.00 per copy. Certification fee: $10.00 per doc plus $1.00 per page. Payee: 14A District Court. Personal checks and credit cards accepted. Prepayment required. Mail requests: SASE required for civil.
Civil Name Search: Access: Mail, fax, in person, online. Only the court performs in person name searches; visitors may not. No search fee. Civil records on computer since 08/2009. Note: Court will perform search time permitting. Dockets and calendars are searchable at www.14adistrictcourt.org/cases.
Criminal Name Search: Access: In person, mail, fax, online. Both court and visitors may perform in person name searches. No search fee. Required to search: name, years to search, DOB. Criminal records on computer since 08/2009. Dockets and calendars are searchable at www.14adistrictcourt.org/cases.

14A2 District Court 415 W Michigan Ave, Ypsilanti, MI 48197; 734-484-6690; fax: 734-484-6697; 8AM-4:30PM (EST). *Misdemeanor, Civil Actions under $25,000, Eviction, Small Claims.*
http://14adistrictcourt.org/locations/14a-2
General Information: 14B District Court covers the city of Ypsilanti and includes Eastern Mich Univ. No suppressed, juvenile, sex offenders, mental health, or adoption records released. Will not fax documents. Court makes copy: $1.00 first page, $.25 ea add'l.The court is entitled to collect $2.00 per copy. Certification fee: $10.00 per case plus $1.00 per page. Payee: 14 A-2 District Court. Personal checks accepted. Major credit cards accepted; $10.00 minimum. Credit card payments accepted via GPS. Prepayment required. Mail requests: SASE requested.
Civil Name Search: Access: Mail, in person. Only the court performs in person name searches; visitors may not. No search fee. Civil records on computer since 1985, prior on file cards since 1969. Note: Specific docket information must be given; court will not do name searches. Historical data on viewable online - only current dockets and calendars are searchable online at www.14adistrictcourt.org/cases. Mail turnaround time 1 week; phone turnaround can be immediate up to 2 days. Only current dockets and calendars are searchable online at www.14adistrictcourt.org/cases.
Criminal Name Search: Access: Mail, in person. Only the court performs in person name searches; visitors may not. No search fee. Required to search: name, years to search, DOB. Criminal records on computer since 1985, prior on file cards since 1969. Note: This court will not do name searches. Historical data on viewable online - only current dockets and calendars are searchable online at

www.14adistrictcourt.org/cases. Mail turnaround time 1 week; phone turnaround immediate up to 2 days.

14A3 District Court 122 S Main St, Chelsea, MI 48118; 734-475-8606; fax: 734-475-0460; 8AM-4:30PM (EST). *Misdemeanor, Civil Actions under $25,000, Eviction, Small Claims.*
http://14adistrictcourt.org/locations/14a-3
General Information: 14A-3 District Court presides over the City of Chelsea, the Townships of Dexter, Lima, Lyndon, Northfield, Scio, Sylvan and Webster, as well as the Village of Dexter. No suppressed records released. Will not fax documents. Court makes copy: $1.00 for 1st copy, $.25 each add'l.The court is entitled to collect $2.00 per copy. Certification fee: $10.00 per doc. Payee: 14A District Court. Personal checks and credit cards accepted. Prepayment required. $10.00 minimum on credit card orders. Mail requests: SASE required for civil.
Civil Name Search: Access: Mail, fax, in person, online. Both court and visitors may perform in person name searches. No search fee. Civil records on computer since 1986; prior on index cards. Note: Court will perform search time permitting. Civil PAT goes back to 1986. Terminals here may be temporarily down. Dockets and calendars are searchable at www.14adistrictcourt.org/cases.
Criminal Name Search: Access: In person, online. Both court and visitors may perform in person name searches. Required to search: name, years to search, DOB; SSN helpful. Criminal records on computer since 1986; prior on index cards. Criminal PAT goes back to same. Dockets and calendars are searchable at www.14adistrictcourt.org/cases.

14B District Court - Civil Division 7200 S Huron River Dr, Ypsilanti, MI 48197; 734-483-5300 x3; fax: 734-483-3630; 8AM-5PM (EST). *Civil Actions under $25,000, Eviction, Small Claims.*
http://14adistrictcourt.org/locations/14a-2
General Information: 14B District Court covers the township of Ypsilanti which surrounds the city of Ypsilanti including Eastern Michigan University. No suppressed, juvenile, sex offenders, probation, mental health, or adoption records released. Will not fax out documents as a general rule. Court makes copy: $1.00 per page.The court is entitled to collect $2.00 per copy. Certification fee: $10.00 per doc. Payee: 14-B District Court. Personal checks accepted. Visa/MC accepted. Prepayment required. Mail requests: SASE required for civil.
Civil Name Search: Access: Phone, mail, in person. Only the court performs in person name searches; visitors may not. No search fee. Civil records on computer since 1990, prior on card files from 1985-1989. Mail turnaround time 1 week, phone turnaround 1 day.

15th District Court - Civil Division PO Box 8650, 301 E Huron St, Ann Arbor, MI 48107; 734-794-6752; fax: 734-794-6753; 8AM-4:30PM (EST). *Civil Actions under $25,000, Eviction, Small Claims.*
www.a2gov.org/services/OtherServices/15D/Pages/default.aspx
General Information: No suppressed records released. Will not fax documents. Court makes copy: $.25 per page.The court is entitled to collect $2.00 per copy. Certification fee: $10.00 per doc plus $1.00 per page. Payee: 15th District Court. Personal checks and credit cards accepted. Prepayment required. Mail requests: SASE required for civil.
Civil Name Search: Access: Phone, fax, mail, in person, online. Only the court performs in person name searches; visitors may not. No search fee. Civil records on computer since 1990, prior on docket books. Mail turnaround time 3-4 days. Access court records free at www.a2gov.org/services/OtherServices/15D/Pages/OnlineCaseSearch.aspx. Includes cases filed on or after 08/05/2006.

Probate Court PO Box 8645, 101 E Huron St, Rm 314, Ann Arbor, MI 48107; 734-222-3072; fax: 734-222-3019; 8AM-4:30PM (EST). *Probate.*
http://washtenawtrialcourt.org/probate/index_html

Wayne County

3rd Circuit Court - Criminal Div Frank Murphy Hall of Justice, 1441 St Antoine, Rm 901, Detroit, MI 48226; 313-224-2500; criminal phone: 313-224-2502/2503; fax: 313-224-2786; 8:30AM-4:30PM (EST). *Felony.*
https://www.3rdcc.org/
General Information: No suppressed, juvenile, sex offenders, mental health, or adoption records released. Will not fax documents. Court makes copy: $1.00 per page. Certification fee: $10.00 per doc plus copy fee. Payee: Wayne County Clerk. No personal checks accepted. Credit card payments accepted via GPS; office preparing to accept CCs in near future. Prepayment required. Mail requests: SASE required.
Criminal Name Search: Access: Mail, in person. Both court and visitors may perform in person name searches. Search fee: $5.00 per name. Required to search: full name (no initials), years to search, DOB, race sex - all are required. Also helpful: city where crime occurred. Criminal records on computer since mid 1974, prior on microfiche through 1976, archives off-site 1800s to 2000. Note: Mail requests should be on a letterhead Mail turnaround time 3-4 days. Public use terminal has crim records back to mid-1974.

3rd Circuit Court - Civil Div 2 Woodward Ave, Rm 201, Attn: Rosa, Coleman A Young Municipal Ctr, Detroit, MI 48226; 313-224-5530; fax: 313-967-3712; 8AM-4:30PM (EST). *Civil Actions over $25,000, Vital Statistics.*
www.3rdcc.org
General Information: No suppressed records released. Will not fax documents. Court makes copy: $2.25 per page. Certification fee: $10.00 plus $1.00 per page. Payee: 3rd Circuit Court. No personal checks accepted. Major credit cards accepted in person only. Prepayment required.
Civil Name Search: Access: Mail, in person. Both court and visitors may perform in person name searches. Search fee: $1.00 per name. Civil records on computer since 1984, prior on index cards. Mail turnaround time 1 week. Public use terminal has civil records back to 1985.

16th District Court 32765 Five Mile Rd, Livonia, MI 48154-5498; 734-466-2500; 466-2550 Probation; criminal phone: X3542; civil phone: X3541; 8:30AM-4:30PM (EST). *Misdemeanor, Civil Actions under $25,000, Eviction, Small Claims.*
www.ci.livonia.mi.us/
General Information: No suppressed records released. Will fax documents to local or toll free line. Court makes copy: $1.00 per page. Certification fee: $10.00 per cert plus copy fee. Payee: 16th District Court. Personal checks accepted. Visa/MC accepted. Credit card payments accepted via GPS. Prepayment required. Mail requests: SASE required for civil.
Civil Name Search: Access: Mail, in person. Both court and visitors may perform in person name searches. No search fee. Civil records on computer since 1990, prior on microfiche. Mail turnaround time 1 week. Civil PAT goes back to 1990.
Criminal Name Search: Access: In person only. Visitors must perform in person searches themselves. Required to search: name, years to search, DOB; also helpful: offense, date of offense, case number. Criminal records on computer since 1991, prior on microfiche. Note: Court will process request if case number is provided. Criminal PAT goes back to 1991.

17th District Court 15111 Beech-Daly Rd, Redford, MI 48239; 313-387-2790; fax: 313-387-2712; 8:30AM-4:15PM (EST). *Misdemeanor, Civil Actions under $25,000, Eviction, Small Claims.*
www.redfordtwp.com/
General Information: No suppressed, child and spousal abuse records released. Court makes copy: $1.00 per page. Certification fee: $10.00 per doc plus copy fee. Payee: 17th District Court. Personal checks accepted. Visa/MC and debit cards accepted. Prepayment required. Mail requests: SASE required.
Civil Name Search: Access: Phone, mail, in person. Only the court performs in person name searches; visitors may not. No search fee. Civil records on computer since 1990, prior on index cards. Note: Will do single name lookups over the phone. Mail turnaround time 2 days.
Criminal Name Search: Access: Fax, mail, in person. Both court and visitors may perform in person name searches. Search fee: $10.00 per name. Required to search: name, years to search, DOB, SSN. Criminal records on computer since 1990, prior on index cards. Mail turnaround time 2 days.

18th District Court 36675 Ford Rd, Westland, MI 48185; 734-595-8720; fax: 734-595-0160; 8AM-4PM, till 5:30 on TH (Apr-Sept is 8AM-4PM) (EST). *Misdemeanor, Civil Actions under $25,000, Eviction, Small Claims.*
www.18thdistrictcourt.com
General Information: No suppressed records released. Will fax documents to local or toll free line. Court makes copy: $1.00 per page. Certification fee: $10.00 per doc plus copy fee. Payee: 18th District Court. Local personal checks accepted. No credit cards accepted. Prepayment required. Mail requests: SASE required.
Civil Name Search: Access: Phone, mail, fax, in person. Only the court performs in person name searches; visitors may not. No search fee. Required to search: name, years to search; also helpful: case number or title. Civil records on computer since 1997. Note: Will name search free, but cert fee applied to copy. Mail turnaround time 1-2 weeks.
Criminal Name Search: Access: Phone, mail, in person. Only the court performs in person name searches; visitors may not. No search fee. Required to search: name, years to search, DOB; also helpful: case number. Criminal records on computer since 1992, prior on microfilm back to 1969. Note: Will name search free, but cert fee applied to copy. Mail turnaround time 1-2 weeks.

19th District Court 16077 Michigan Ave, Dearborn, MI 48126; 313-943-2060; fax: 313-943-3071; 8AM-4:30PM (EST). *Misdemeanor, Civil Actions under $25,000, Eviction, Small Claims.*
www.cityofdearborn.org
General Information: No suppressed records released. Court makes copy: $1.00 per page. Certification fee: $10.00. Payee: 19th District Court. Cashiers checks and money orders accepted. Visa/MC accepted. Credit card payments accepted via GPS. Prepayment required. Also, pay online at www.officialpayments.com. Mail requests: SASE helpful.
Civil Name Search: Access: Fax, mail, in person. Visitors must perform in person searches themselves. No search fee. Civil records on computer since 1986. Mail turnaround time 3 days. Civil PAT available.
Criminal Name Search: Access: Fax, mail, in person. Visitors must perform in person searches themselves. No search fee. Required to search: name, years to search, DOB, offense, date of offense. Criminal records on computer since 1987, prior on docket books. Mail turnaround time 3 days. Criminal PAT available.

20th District Court 25637 Michigan Ave, Dearborn Heights, MI 48125; 313-277-7480; fax: 313-277-7141; 9AM-5PM (EST). *Misdemeanor, Civil Actions under $25,000, Eviction, Small Claims.*
www.ci.dearborn-heights.mi.us/20th.cfm
General Information: No suppressed, juvenile, sex offenders, mental health, or adoption records released. Will fax documents. Court makes copy: $1.00 per page. Self serve copy: same. Certification fee: $10.00. Payee: 20th District Court. Business checks accepted. Visa/MC accepted. Credit card payments accepted via GPS. Prepayment required.
Civil Name Search: Access: In person only. Only the court performs in person name searches; visitors may not. No search fee. Required to search: name, years to search; also helpful: address. Civil records on computer since 4/1991, prior records on microfiche or books.
Criminal Name Search: Access: In person only. Only the court performs in person name searches; visitors may not. No search fee. Required to search: name, years to search, DOB; also helpful: SSN. Criminal records on computer since 4/1991, prior records on microfiche or books.

21st District Court 6000 Middlebelt Rd, Garden City, MI 48135; 734-793-1680; criminal phone: x2; civil phone: x3; fax: 734-793-1681; 8:30AM-5PM (EST). *Misdemeanor, Civil Actions under $25,000, Eviction, Small Claims.*
General Information: No suppressed records released. Will not fax documents. Court makes copy: $1.00 per page. Certification fee: $10.00 per cert includes copies. Payee: 21st District Court. Personal checks accepted. Credit card payments accepted via GPS or in person. Prepayment required. Mail requests: SASE required.
Civil Name Search: Access: Mail, in person. Only the court performs in person name searches; visitors may not. No search fee. Civil records on computer back to 1989, prior on books, microfilm, and cards. Note: In person searchers must fill out a "File/copy Request Form." Visitors can search the printed case index to locate a case number. Mail turnaround time 1-4 days.
Criminal Name Search: Access: Mail, in person. Only the court performs in person name searches; visitors may not. No search fee. Required to search: name, years to search, DOB. Criminal records computerized from 1989, prior on books, microfilm, and cards. Note: In person searchers must fill out a "File/copy Request Form." Visitors can first search the printed case index to locate a criminal case number. Mail turnaround time 1-4 days.

22nd District Court 27331 S River Park Dr, Inkster, MI 48141; 313-277-8200; fax: 313-277-8221; 8:30AM-4:30PM (EST). *Misdemeanor, Civil Actions under $25,000, Eviction, Small Claims.*
General Information: No suppressed records released. Will not fax out documents. Court makes copy: $1.00 per page. Certification fee: $10.00 per doc plus copy fee. Payee: 22nd District Court. Personal checks accepted. Credit card payments accepted via GPS. Prepayment required. Credit card usage fee is $7.00 plus 2.75%. Mail requests: SASE required.
Civil Name Search: Access: Mail, in person. Only the court performs in person name searches; visitors may not. Search fee: Search fee determined on case by case basis. Civil records on computer since 1996, prior on docket books. Mail turnaround time 2 weeks.
Criminal Name Search: Access: Mail, in person. Only the court performs in person name searches; visitors may not. Search fee: Search fee determined on case by case basis. Required to search: name, years to search, DOB; also helpful: SSN. Criminal records on computer since 1996, prior on books. Mail turnaround time 2 weeks.

23rd District Court 23365 Goddard Rd, Taylor, MI 48180; 734-374-1334; criminal phone: 734-374-1334; civil phone: 734-374-1328; fax: 734-374-1303; 8:15AM-4:45PM (EST). *Misdemeanor, Civil Actions under $25,000, Eviction, Small Claims.*
General Information: No suppressed, sexual abuse or drug abuse records released. Will fax documents. Court makes copy: $1.00 per page. Certification fee: $10.00. Payee: 23rd District Court. Personal checks accepted. Visa/MC/Discover credit cards accepted in criminal division only. Prepayment required.
Civil Name Search: Access: Mail, in person. Only the court performs in person name searches; visitors may not. No search fee. Civil records on computer since 1993, prior on books. Mail turnaround time 1-2 days.
Criminal Name Search: Access: Mail, in person. Only the court performs in person name searches; visitors may not. No search fee.

Required to search: name, years to search, DOB. Criminal records on computer since 1993, prior on index cards. Mail turnaround time 1-2 days.

24th District Court - Allen Park & Melvindale 6515 Roosevelt, Allen Park, MI 48101-2524; 313-928-0535; criminal phone: x225 or x226; civil phone: 313-928-1899; fax: 313-928-1860; 8:30AM-4:30PM (EST). *Misdemeanor, Civil Actions under $25,000, Eviction, Small Claims.* www.24thdiscourt.org

General Information: No non-public records, including driving and probation records, released. Will fax documents to local or toll free line. Court makes copy: $.50 per page. Self serve copy: same. Certification fee: $10.00. Payee: 24th District Court. Personal checks accepted. Credit cards accepted in person. Credit card payments accepted via GPS. Prepayment required. Mail requests: SASE required if return mail requested.

Civil Name Search: Access: Phone, mail, fax, in person. Only the court performs in person name searches; visitors may not. No search fee. Required to search: name, years to search, case number. Civil records on computer since 1992, prior records stored as hard-copies. Mail turnaround time 1 week.

Criminal Name Search: Access: Fax, mail, in person. Only the court performs in person name searches; visitors may not. No search fee. Required to search: name, years to search, DOB. Criminal records on computer since 1993, prior records stored as hard-copies. Mail turnaround time 1 week.

25th District Court 1475 Cleophus, Lincoln Park, MI 48146; 313-382-8603; civil phone: 313-382-9365; fax: 313-382-9361; 9AM-4:30PM (EST). *Misdemeanor, Civil Actions under $25,000, Eviction, Small Claims.*

General Information: No suppressed or expunged records released. Will fax documents for no fee. Court makes copy: $.50 per page. Certification fee: $11.00 per doc. Payee: 25th District Court. Personal checks accepted. Visa/MC cards accepted. Credit card payments accepted via GPS. Prepayment required. Mail requests: SASE required.

Civil Name Search: Access: Mail, phone, fax, in person. Only the court performs in person name searches; visitors may not. No search fee. Civil records on computer since 1988, prior records stored as hard-copies. Mail turnaround time 1 week.

Criminal Name Search: Access: Mail, phone, fax, in person. Only the court performs in person name searches; visitors may not. No search fee. Required to search: name, years to search, DOB. Criminal records on computer since 1987, prior on docket books and cards. Mail turnaround time 1 week.

26-1 District Court 10600 W Jefferson, River Rouge, MI 48218; 313-842-7819; criminal phone: 313-297-0024; civil phone: 313-297-0023; fax: 313-842-5923; 8:30AM-4:30PM (EST). *Misdemeanor, Civil Actions under $25,000, Eviction, Small Claims.*

General Information: No suppressed records released. Will fax documents $2.00. Court makes copy: $1.00 per page. Self serve copy: same. Certification fee: $10.00 per doc plus copy fee. Payee: 26-1 District Court. No Personal checks and credit cards accepted. Prepayment required. Mail requests: SASE helpful.

Civil Name Search: Access: Fax, mail, in person. Only the court performs in person name searches; visitors may not. No search fee. Civil records on computer since 11/93; prior records on cards. Mail turnaround time 1 week.

Criminal Name Search: Access: Fax, mail, in person. Only the court performs in person name searches; visitors may not. No search fee. Required to search: name, years to search, DOB. Criminal records on computer since 1993, prior on index cards. Mail turnaround time 1 week.

26-2 District Court 3869 W Jefferson, Ecorse, MI 48229; 313-386-7900; fax: 313-928-5956; 9AM-4PM (EST). *Misdemeanor, Civil Actions under $25,000, Eviction, Small Claims.*

General Information: No suppressed records released. Will not fax out documents. Court makes copy: $1.00 per page. Certification fee: $10.00 per doc plus copy fee. Payee: 26-2 District Court. Business checks accepted. No credit cards accepted. Prepayment required. Mail requests: SASE required.

Civil Name Search: Access: Mail, in person, fax. Only the court performs in person name searches; visitors may not. No search fee. Civil records on computer back to 1992, prior on index cards. Mail turnaround time 1 week.

Criminal Name Search: Access: Mail, in person, fax. Only the court performs in person name searches; visitors may not. No search fee. Required to search: name, years to search, DOB; also helpful: SSN. Criminal records computerized from 1992, prior on index cards. Mail turnaround time 1 week.

27th District Court 2015 Biddle Ave, Wyandotte, MI 48192; 734-324-4475; criminal phone: 734-324-4477; civil phone: 734-324-4491; fax: 734-324-4472; 8:30AM-4PM (EST). *Misdemeanor, Civil Actions under $25,000, Eviction, Small Claims.* www.wyandotte.net/Departments/PublicSafety/27thDistrictCourt.asp

General Information: Phone for record checks is 734-327-4495. The 27-2 District Court in Riverview was closed as of 12/31/02. All of their records are at this court. No suppressed records released. Will fax documents to local or toll free line. Court makes copy: $1.00 per page. Certification fee: $10.00 plus copy fee for add'l pages. Payee: 27th District Court. Money order or in person cash accepted. Credit card payments accepted via GPS. Prepayment required. Mail requests: SASE required.

Civil Name Search: Access: Mail, in person. Only the court performs in person name searches; visitors may not. Search fee: $1.00. Civil records on computer since 1988, prior on index cards. Mail turnaround time varies.

Criminal Name Search: Access: Mail, in person. Only the court performs in person name searches; visitors may not. Search fee: $1.00. Required to search: name, years to search, DOB. Criminal records on computer since 1988, prior on index cards. Mail turnaround time varies.

28th District Court 14720 Reaume Parkway, Southgate, MI 48195; 734-258-3068; criminal phone: x3631; civil phone: x3632; fax: 734-246-1405; 8:30AM-4:30PM (EST). *Misdemeanor, Civil Actions under $25,000, Eviction, Small Claims.* http://28thdistrictcourt.com/index.html

General Information: No suppressed, probation, sex offenders, or mental health records released. Will not fax out case files. Court makes copy: $1.00 per page. Certification fee: $10.00 per document includes copies. Payee: 28th District Court. Cash, cashiers check or money order accepted. Major credit cards accepted in person and by phone. Credit card payments accepted via GPS. Prepayment required.

Civil Name Search: Access: In person only. Both court and visitors may perform in person name searches. No search fee. Required to search: name, years to search; also helpful: address. Civil records on computer back to 1987, prior on card files by party back to 1979.

Criminal Name Search: Access: In person only. Only the court performs in person name searches; visitors may not. No search fee. Required to search: name, years to search, DOB; also helpful: address, case number. Criminal records go back to 1979; on computer back to 1986.

29th District Court 34808 Sims Ave, Wayne, MI 48184; 734-722-5220; fax: 734-722-7003; 8AM-4PM (EST). *Misdemeanor, Civil Actions under $25,000, Eviction, Small Claims.* www.ci.wayne.mi.us/court.shtml

General Information: No suppressed, juvenile, sex offenders, mental health, or adoption records released. Will fax documents to local or toll free line. Court makes copy: $1.00 per page. Certification fee: $10.00. Payee: 29th District Court. Personal checks accepted. No credit cards accepted for record searches or copies. Prepayment required. Mail requests: SASE required.

Civil Name Search: Access: Phone, mail, in person. Only the court performs in person name searches; visitors may not. No search fee. Civil records on computer since 1990. Note: Will name search free, but a copy fee applies. Mail turnaround time 1 week.

Criminal Name Search: Access: Phone, mail, in person. Only the court performs in person name searches; visitors may not. No search fee. Required to search: name, years to search, DOB; also helpful: address. Criminal records on computer since 1990. Mail turnaround time 1 week, phone turnaround 1 day.

30th District Court 12050 Wood Ward Ave, Highland Park, MI 48203; 313-252-0300; fax: 313-865-1115; 8AM-4:30PM M-F (EST). *Misdemeanor, Civil Actions under $25,000, Eviction, Small Claims.* www.highlandparkcity.us/Government/30thDistrictCourt.asp

General Information: No suppressed records released. Will fax documents. Court makes copy: $1.00 per page. Certification fee: $5.00. Payee: 30th District Court. Personal checks and credit cards accepted. Prepayment required. Mail requests: SASE required.

Civil Name Search: Access: Mail, in person. Only the court performs in person name searches; visitors may not. Search fee: $5.00 per name. Required to search: name, years to search, DOB. Civil records on computer since 1989, prior on index cards or docket books. Mail turnaround time 1-2 weeks.

Criminal Name Search: Access: Mail, in person. Only the court performs in person name searches; visitors may not. Search fee: $5.00 per name. Required to search: name, years to search, DOB. Criminal records on computer since 1989, prior on index cards or docket books. Mail turnaround time 1-2 weeks.

31st District Court 3401 Evaline Ave, Hamtramck, MI 48212; 313-876-7710; fax: 313-876-7724; 8AM-4PM (EST). *Misdemeanor, Civil Actions under $25,000, Eviction, Small Claims.*

General Information: No suppressed records released. Will fax documents $1.00 per page. Court makes copy: $1.00 per page. Self serve copy: none. Certification fee: $10.00 plus copy fee after first page. Payee: 31st District Court. Personal checks and credit cards accepted. Prepayment required. Mail requests: SASE required.

Civil Name Search: Access: Mail, in person. Only the court performs in person name searches; visitors may not. No search fee. Civil records on computer since 1989, prior on index cards. Mail turnaround time 1-2 days.

Criminal Name Search: Access: Mail, in person. Only the court performs in person name searches; visitors may not. No search fee.

Required to search: name, years to search, DOB. Criminal records on computer since 1989, prior on index cards. Mail turnaround time 1-2 days.

32 A District Court 19617 Harper Ave, Harper Woods, MI 48225; 313-343-2590; civil phone: 313-343-2592; fax: 313-343-2594; 8:30AM-4:30PM (EST). *Misdemeanor, Civil Actions under $25,000, Small Claims.*
General Information: No suppressed records released. Will fax documents, no fee. Court makes copy: $1.00 per page. Certification fee: $11.00 per doc. Payee: 32A District Court. Personal checks accepted. Visa/MC accepted. Prepayment required. Mail requests: SASE requested.
Civil Name Search: Access: Phone, fax, mail, in person. Only the court performs in person name searches; visitors may not. No search fee. Civil records indexed by name and case number on computer, microfiche, and paper. Mail turnaround time same day.
Criminal Name Search: Access: Phone, fax, mail, in person. Only the court performs in person name searches; visitors may not. No search fee. Criminal records indexed by name and case number on computer, microfiche, and paper. Mail turnaround time same day.

33rd District Court 19000 Van Horn Rd, Woodhaven, MI 48183; 734-671-0201; criminal phone: 734-671-0201; civil phone: 734-671-0225; fax: 734-671-0307; 8:30AM-4:30PM (EST). *Misdemeanor, Civil Actions under $25,000, Eviction, Small Claims.*
www.d33.courts.mi.gov/
General Information: The 33rd District Court serves the Townships of Brownstown and Grosse Ile, and the Cities of Flat Rock, Gibraltar, Rockwood, Trenton, and Woodhaven. A search of the current docket calendar is offered, but not historical data. No suppressed records released. Will not fax documents. Court makes copy: $.25 per page. Certification fee: $10.00 plus $1.00 per page after first. Payee: 33rd District Court. Business checks accepted. Major credit cards accepted. Prepayment required.
Civil Name Search: Access: In person, online. Visitors must perform in person name searches themselves. Civil records on computer since 1999, prior on microfilm and microfiche but only court can search on these. Civil PAT goes back to 1999 countywide. Docket information is offered at www.d33.courts.mi.gov/jisdocket/jisdocket.aspx, searchable by name, attorney, judge or case number.
Criminal Name Search: Access: In person, online. Visitors must perform in person searches themselves. Required to search: name, years to search, DOB. Criminal records on computer since 1995, prior on microfilm and microfiche. Criminal PAT goes back to same as civil. Docket information is offered at www.d33.courts.mi.gov/jisdocket/jisdocket.aspx, searchable by name, attorney, judge or case number.

34th District Court 11131 Wayne Rd, Romulus, MI 48174-1491; 734-941-4462; fax: 734-941-7530; 8:30AM-4PM (EST). *Misdemeanor, Civil Actions under $25,000, Eviction, Small Claims.*
General Information: No suppressed records released. Will fax civil documents to local or toll-free number, limited to 5 pages. Will not fax out criminal. Court makes copy: $1.00 per page. Certification fee: $10.00 plus $1.00 per page. Payee: 34th District Court. Personal checks and credit cards accepted. Prepayment required. Mail requests: SASE required.
Civil Name Search: Access: Mail, in person. Only the court performs in person name searches; visitors may not. No search fee. Civil records on computer since 1984, prior on index cards and docket books. Mail turnaround time 2 weeks.
Criminal Name Search: Access: Mail, in person. Only the court performs in person name searches; visitors may not. Search fee: $24.00 per name. Required to search: name, years to search, DOB; also helpful: SSN. Criminal records on computer back to 2006, limited back further; index cards onsite, docket books offsite. Mail turnaround time 1 week.

35th District Court 660 Plymouth Rd, Plymouth, MI 48170; 734-459-4740; fax: 734-454-9303; 8:30AM-4:30PM (EST). *Misdemeanor, Civil Infractions, Civil Actions under $25,000, Eviction, Small Claims.*
www.35thdistrictcourt.org
General Information: No suppressed, juvenile, sex offenders, mental health, or adoption records released. Fee to fax document $1.00 each. Court makes copy: $1.00 per page. Certification fee: $10.00 for a certification plus copy fee. Payee: 35th District Court. Third party checks not accepted. Visa/MC and debit cards accepted. Prepayment required.
Civil Name Search: Access: Fax, mail, in person. Both court and visitors may perform in person name searches. No search fee. Civil records on computer since 1990. Mail turnaround time 1 week. Civil PAT goes back to 1998.
Criminal Name Search: Access: Fax, mail, in person. Both court and visitors may perform in person name searches. No search fee. Required to search: name, years to search, DOB; also helpful: SSN, sex, signed release. Criminal records on computer since 1990. Mail turnaround time 1 week. Criminal PAT goes back to same as civil.

36th District Court 421 Madison, Detroit, MI 48226; 313-965-2200; criminal phone: 313-965-5029; civil phone: 313-965-6098; fax: 313-965-4074; 8AM-4:30PM (EST). *Felony, Misdemeanor, Civil Actions under $25,000, Eviction, Small Claims Under $3000.*

General Information: Small Claims phone number is 313-965-5972. No suppressed records released. Will not fax documents. Court makes copy: $1.00 per page. Certification fee: $10.00 per doc plus copy fee. Payee: 36th District Court. No personal checks or credit cards accepted. Prepayment required.
Civil Name Search: Access: In person only. Visitors must perform in person searches themselves. Required to search: name, years to search, address. Civil cases indexed by name, case number. Civil records on computer since 1985, prior kept in file folders. Note: If a case number is provided, then court will retrieve records. Public use terminal has civil records back to 1981. Civil records public terminal is on 2nd Fl.
Criminal Name Search: Access: In person only. Both court and visitors may perform in person name searches. Required to search: name, DOB; SSN helpful. Criminal records go back to 1987. Note: Will do a single name search over the phone to let you know index numbers, if any. Criminal public terminal on 1st Fl.

Probate Court Coleman A Young Muni. Ctr, 13th Fl, 2 Woodward Ave, Detroit, MI 48226; 313-224-5706; 8AM-4:30PM (EST). *Probate.*
www.wcpc.us/
General Information: Search probate records at http://public.wcpc.us/pa/pa.urd/pamw6500.display. Summary, party, event, docket, disposition, costs available. Records go back into 1980s.

Wexford County

28th Circuit Court PO Box 490, Cadillac, MI 49601; 231-779-9450; fax: 231-779-0447; 8:30AM-5PM (EST). *Felony, Civil Actions over $25,000, Vital Statistics.*
www.wexfordcounty.org
General Information: No suppressed, YTA files, juvenile, sex offenders, mental health, or adoption records released. Will not fax documents. Court makes copy: $1.00 per page. Certification fee: $10.00, plus $1.00 each add'l page. Payee: Wexford County Clerk. Checks and money orders accepted. Credit card payments accepted via VitalChek. Prepayment required. Mail requests: SASE required.
Civil Name Search: Access: Mail, in person. Only the court performs in person name searches; visitors may not. Search fee: $5.00 per name for 10 year search. Civil records go back to 1868, civil records on computer since 1977. Mail turnaround time same day if possible.
Criminal Name Search: Access: Mail, in person. Only the court performs in person name searches; visitors may not. Search fee: $5.00 per name for 10 year search. Criminal records go back to 1868, criminal records on computer since 1977. Mail turnaround time same day.

84th District Court 437 E Division St, Cadillac, MI 49601; 231-779-9515; fax: 231-779-5396; 8:30AM-5PM (EST). *Misdemeanor, Civil Actions under $25,000, Eviction, Small Claims.*
General Information: No suppressed, juvenile, sex offenders, mental health, or adoption records released. Will fax documents to local or toll-free number. Court makes copy: $1.00 per page. Certification fee: $10.00 per doc plus copy fee. Payee: 84th District Court. Personal checks accepted. No credit cards accepted. Prepayment required. Mail requests: SASE required.
Civil Name Search: Access: Phone, fax, mail, in person. Both court and visitors may perform in person name searches. Search fee: $1.00 per page found. Civil records on computer since 1984; on index from 1969 to 1984. Mail turnaround time 1 week.
Criminal Name Search: Access: Mail, fax, in person. Both court and visitors may perform in person name searches. Search fee: $1.00 per name found. Required to search: name, years to search, DOB; also helpful: SSN. Criminal records on computer since 1984; prior records on blue cards. Mail turnaround time 1 week.

Probate Court 437 E Division, Cadillac, MI 49601; 231-779-9510; probate phone: 231-779-9511; fax: 231-779-9485; 8:30AM-5PM (EST). *Probate.*
www.wexfordcounty.org/

Minnesota

Time Zone:	CST
Capital:	St Paul, Ramsey County
# of Counties:	87
State Web:	www.state.mn.us
Court Web:	www.mncourts.gov

Administration

State Court Administrator, 25 Rev. Dr. Martin Luther King Jr. Blvd., St Paul, MN, 55155; Telephone: 651-296-2474, Fax: 651-297-5636.

The Supreme Court and the Court of Appeals

The Supreme Court is the highest court in the state. The Court of Appeals reviews all final decisions of the trial courts, state agencies and local governments, except from the Minnesota Tax Court, the Minnesota Workers' Compensation Court of Appeals, first-degree murder cases and statewide election contests. Opinions are found at the home page mentioned above.

The Minnesota Courts

Court	Type	How Organized	Jurisdiction Highpoints
District*	General	97 Courts in 10 Circuits	Felony, Misdemeanor, Civil, Small Claims, Domestic, Juvenile, Probate
Tribal*	General	11 Courts	Felony, Misdemeanor, Civil, Small Claims, Domestic, Juvenile, Probate

* = profiled in this book

Details on the Trial Court Structure

District Courts hear everything from traffic tickets, to civil and family conflicts, to first degree murder trials. Some District Courts may have separate divisions, such as criminal, civil, probate, family, and juvenile courts.

There are 97 District Courts (some counties have divisional courts) comprising 10 judicial districts. The limit for small claims is $7500 unless the case involves a consumer credit transaction, then the limit is $4000.

There are eleven **Tribal Courts** that have jurisdiction on tribal land.

Record Searching Facts You Need to Know

Fees and Record Searching Tips

Most Judicial Districts no longer perform criminal record name searches for the public, but may do civil name searches. In general, the search fee is $5.00. Some courts charge an additional $10.00 plus the copy fee. Copy fees are charged by the "document" not by the page and the fee is generally $8.00. A document will often contain multilple pages and there can be multiple documentin a case file. Certification of a document is generally $14.00 per document.

An exact name is required to search, e.g., a request for "Robert Smith" will not result in finding "Bob Smith." The requester must request both names and pay two search and copy fees. When a search is permitted by "plaintiff or defendant," most jurisdictions state that a case is indexed by only the first plaintiff or defendant. Second or third party names would not be sufficient information for a search.

All courts provide public access terminals. The terminal provides statewide access – not just data from the county. Most courts accept personal checks.

Online Access is Statewide, but Caution Needed

Minnesota offers the Trial Court Public Access (MPA) of searchinh statewide or by county. Records available include criminal, civil, family, and probate. Searches can be performed using a case number or by name. See http://pa.courts.state.mn.us/default.aspx.

However searchers should first know there are a number of caveats; certain publicly-accessible case records or data fields found at the courthouse cannot be viewed online. For example, comment fields for all case types are not available online but are available at the courthouse. Party street address and name searches on criminal, traffic, and petty misdemeanor pre-conviction case records are not accessible online, but are at the courthouse. A criminal/traffic/petty search excludes all Hennepin County and Ramsey County payable citations except: 1) those that result in a court appearance; and 2) Ramsey DNR payable citations. Also, Party street address and name searches on criminal pre-conviction case records are publicly accessible and available at the courthouse, but not online. The federal Violence Against Women Act (VAWA) prevents the state (all states) from displaying harassment and domestic abuse case records online, but these convictions are available at the courthouse. The bottom line is the public access terminals found at the courthouses provide more information than found on the online system.

The public access terminals found at courthouses are considered the most accurate searching locations. The online system is a supplemental search.

Aitkin County

9th Judicial District Court 209 Second St NW, Aitkin, MN 56431; 218-927-7350; fax: 218-927-4535; 8AM-4:30PM (CST). *Felony, Misdemeanor, Civil, Eviction, Small Claims, Probate.* www.mncourts.gov/district/9/

General Information: Week ahead court calendars available online. No adoption, juvenile, sex offender or sealed records released. Fee to fax back- $25.00 per doc up to 25 pgs. Court makes copy: $8.00 per doc. Certification fee: $14.00 per doc. Payee: Aitkin District Court. Personal checks accepted. Visa/MC/Discover accepted. Prepayment required. Mail requests: SASE required.

Civil Name Search: Access: Mail, in person, online. Both court and visitors may perform in person name searches. Search fee: $5.00 per name. Civil records on computer from 2/90, cards to 1982, index books prior. Mail turnaround time 1 week. Civil PAT goes back to 2/1990. Public terminal allows for a statewide search and is more extensive than online search. **For details about the state's online access to records, see the sections at the front or back of this chapter.**

Criminal Name Search: Access: Mail, in person, online. Both court and visitors may perform in person name searches. Search fee: $5.00 per name. Required to search: name, years to search, DOB. Criminal records computerized from 2/90, cards to 1982, index books prior. Mail turnaround time 1 week. Criminal PAT goes back to 2/1990. Public terminal allows for a statewide search and is more extensive than online search. **For details about the state's online access to records, see the sections at the front or back of this chapter.**

Anoka County

10th Judicial District Court Attn: File Room, 325 E Main St, Anoka, MN 55303; 763-422-7350; criminal phone: 763-422-7385; civil phone: 763-323-5939; probate phone: 763-422-7471; criminal fax: 763-422-6919; civil fax: 8AM-4:30PM; 8AM-4:30PM (CST). *Felony, Misdemeanor, Civil, Eviction, Small Claims, Probate.* www.co.anoka.mn.us/departments/courts/index.htm

General Information: Probate fax- 763-422-7085. No adoption, juvenile, sex offender or sealed records released. Will not fax documents. Court makes copy: $8.00 per doc. Certification fee: $14.00 per doc; exemplification $26.00. Cert fee includes copies. Payee: Court Administrator. Personal checks and credit cards accepted. Prepayment required.

Civil Name Search: Access: Mail, in person, online. Both court and visitors may perform in person name searches. No search fee. Civil records on computer from 1985, prior on microfiche. Note: Weekly calendars free at www.mncourts.gov/district/10/?page=1326. Mail turnaround time 2 weeks. Civil PAT goes back to 1985. Public terminal allows for a statewide search and is more extensive than online search. **For details about the state's online access to records, see the sections at the front or back of this chapter.**

Criminal Name Search: Access: In person, online. Visitors must perform in person searches themselves. Required to search: name, years to search, DOB. Criminal records computerized from 1985, prior on microfiche. Criminal PAT goes back to 1985. Public terminal allows for a statewide search and is more extensive than online search. **For details about the state's online access to records, see the sections at the front or back of this chapter.**

Becker County

7th Judicial District Court 913 Lake Ave, Detroit Lakes, MN 56501; 218-846-7305; fax: 218-847-7620; 8AM-4:30PM (CST). *Felony, Misdemeanor, Civil, Eviction, Small Claims, Probate.* www.mncourts.gov/district/7/

General Information: No adoption, juvenile, sex offender or sealed records released. Fee to fax back- $25.00 per doc. Court makes copy: $8.00 per doc w/ judge's signature; $.25 per page all other docs. Certification fee: $14.00 per doc. Payee: Becker County. Personal checks and credit cards accepted. Prepayment required.

Civil Name Search: Access: In person, online. Both court and visitors may perform in person name searches. No search fee. Required to search: name; also helpful: years to search. Civil records on computer from 8/86, prior on books from 1891. Civil PAT goes back to 1986. Public terminal allows for a statewide search and is more extensive than online search. **For details about the state's online access to records, see the sections at the front or back of this chapter.**

Criminal Name Search: Access: In person, online. Visitors must perform in person searches themselves. Criminal records computerized from 8/86, prior on books from 1891. Criminal PAT goes back to 1986. Public terminal allows for a statewide search and is more extensive than online search. **For details about the state's online access to records, see the sections at the front or back of this chapter.**

White Earth Band of Chippewa Tribal Court PO Box 418, Reservation Tribal Council Bldg, White Earth, MN 56591; 218-983-3285 x1246; fax: 218-983-3294; 8AM-4:30PM (CST). *Criminal, Civil, Juvenile, Traffic, Estate, Eviction.* www.whiteearthtribalcourt.com/

Beltrami County

District Court c/o Court Admin, Judicial Ctr, 600 Minnesota Ave NW, #108, Bemidji, MN 56601; 218-333-4120; criminal phone: 281-333-4125; civil phone: 218-333-4128; probate phone: 218-333-4123; fax: 218-333-4209; 8AM-4:30PM (CST). *Felony, Misdemeanor, Civil, Eviction, Small Claims, Probate.* www.mncourts.gov/district/9/

General Information: Probate fax is same as main fax number. Week ahead court calendars available online. No adoption, juvenile, sex offender or sealed records released. Will fax documents to local or toll free line. Court makes copy: $8.00 per doc. Certification fee: $14.00 per doc. Payee: Court Administrator. Personal checks and credit cards accepted. Prepayment required. Mail requests: SASE required for civil.

Civil Name Search: Access: Mail, in person, online. Both court and visitors may perform in person name searches. Search fee: $5.00 per name. Civil records on computer back to 1983. Mail turnaround time 1-5 days. Civil PAT goes back to 1983. Public terminal allows for a statewide search and is more extensive than online search. **For details about the state's online access to records, see the sections at the front or back of this chapter.**

Criminal Name Search: Access: In person, online. Visitors must perform in person searches themselves. Required to search: name, years to search, DOB. Criminal records computerized from 1983. Criminal PAT goes back to 1983. Public terminal allows for a statewide search and is more extensive than online search. **For details about the state's online access to records, see the sections at the front or back of this chapter.**

Red Lake Nation Tribal Court PO Box 572, Red Lake, MN 56671; 218-679-3303; fax: 218-679-2683; www.redlakenation.org (CST). *Criminal, Civil, Juvenile, Traffic, Estate, Eviction.*

Benton County

7th Judicial District Court 615 Highway 23, PO Box 189, Foley, MN 56329-0189; 320-968-5205; fax: 320-968-5353; 8AM-4:30PM (CST). *Felony, Misdemeanor, Civil, Eviction, Small Claims, Probate, Family.* www.mncourts.gov/district/7/

General Information: No adoption, juvenile records released. Will not fax out case files. Court makes copy: $8.00 per doc. Self serve copy: no charge if off computer. Certification fee: $14.00 per doc. Payee: Court Administrator. Personal checks, Visa/MC accepted. Prepayment required.

Civil Name Search: Access: In person, online. Visitors must perform in person searches themselves. Civil records on computer from 1986. Civil PAT goes back to 1986. Public terminal allows for a statewide search and is more extensive than online search. **For details about the state's online access to records, see the sections at the front or back of this chapter.**

Criminal Name Search: Access: In person, online. Visitors must perform in person searches themselves. Required to search: name, years to search, DOB. Criminal records computerized from 1986. Note: Court recommends searching via the BCA at 651-642-0610. Criminal PAT goes back to 1986. Public terminal allows for a statewide search and is more extensive than online search. **For details about the state's online access to records, see the sections at the front or back of this chapter.**

Big Stone County

Big Stone District Court 20 2nd St SE, #107, Ortonville, MN 56278; 320-839-2536; fax: 320-839-2537; 8AM-4:30PM M-TH; 8AM-2PM F (CST). *Felony, Misdemeanor, Civil, Eviction, Small Claims, Probate.* www.mncourts.gov/district/8/

General Information: Probate fax is same as main fax number. No adoption, juvenile, sex offender or sealed records released. Will not fax documents. Court makes copy: $8.00 per doc. Certification fee: $14.00 per doc. Payee: Court Administrator. Personal checks, Visa/MC accepted. Prepayment required. Mail requests: SASE required for civil.

Civil Name Search: Access: Mail, in person, online. Both court and visitors may perform in person name searches. Search fee: $5.00. Civil records on computer from 1989, prior on cards and in books. Civil PAT goes back to 1990. Public terminal allows for a statewide search and is more extensive than online search. **For details about the state's online access to records, see the sections at the front or back of this chapter.**

Criminal Name Search: Access: In person, online. Visitors must perform in person searches themselves. Required to search: name, years to search, DOB; SSN helpful. Criminal records computerized from 1989, prior on cards and in books. Criminal PAT goes back to 1990. his court is on the MNCIS system; records can be accessed by public terminal from other counties. **For details about the state's online access to records, see the sections at the front or back of this chapter.**

Blue Earth County

5th Judicial District Court 401 Carver, Mankato, MN 56001; 507-304-4650; 8AM-4:30PM (CST). *Felony, Misdemeanor, Civil, Eviction, Small Claims, Probate.* www.co.blue-earth.mn.us/dept/courts.php

General Information: No juvenile, adoption, sealed records released. Fee to fax back- $25.00 per doc up to 25 pgs. Court makes copy: $8.00 per doc. Certification fee: $14.00 per doc plus copy fee. Payee: Court Administrator. Personal checks, Visa/MC accepted. Prepayment required.

Civil Name Search: Access: Mail, in person, online. Both court and visitors may perform in person name searches. Search fee: $5.00 per name. Required to search: name, exact dates to search. Civil records on computer from 8/85, prior in books and cards. Mail turnaround time 7-10 days. Civil PAT goes back to 1985. Public terminal allows for a statewide search more extensive than online search. **For details about the state's online access to records, see the sections at the front or back of this chapter.**

Criminal Name Search: Access: In person, online. Visitors must perform in person searches themselves. Required to search: name, exact dates to search; also helpful: DOB. Criminal records computerized from 8/85, prior in books and cards. Note: The county forwards mail requests to State Bureau of Criminal Apprehension. Criminal PAT goes back to 1985. Public terminal allows for a statewide search. **For details about the state's online access to records, see the sections at the front or back of this chapter.**

Brown County

5th Judicial District Court PO Box 248, 14 S State St, New Ulm, MN 56073-0248; 507-233-6670; fax: 507-359-9562; 8AM-5PM (CST). *Felony, Misdemeanor, Civil, Eviction, Small Claims, Probate.* www.mncourts.gov/district/5/

General Information: No adoption, juvenile, sex offender or sealed records released. Fee to fax back- $25.00 per doc up to 50 pgs. Court makes copy: $8.00 per doc. Certification fee: $14.00 per doc includes copies. Payee: Court Administrator. Personal checks and credit cards accepted. Prepayment required. Mail requests: SASE required for civil.

Civil Name Search: Access: Mail, in person, online. Both court and visitors may perform in person name searches. Search fee: $10.00 per name. Civil records on computer from 1988, microfiche 1981-1988, prior on books. Mail turnaround time 3 days. Civil PAT goes back to 1988. Records available at any 5th District courthouse public access terminals. Results may show DOB or address but not always. **For details about the state's online access to records, see the sections at the front or back of this chapter.**

Criminal Name Search: Access: In person, online. Visitors must perform in person searches themselves. Criminal records computerized from 1988, microfiche 1981-1988, prior on books. Note: Make written requests to the State Bureau of Criminal Apprehension. Criminal PAT goes back to 1988. Records available at any 5th District courthouse public access terminals. Public terminal allows for a statewide search. Results may show DOB or address but not always. **For details about the state's online access to records, see the sections at the front or back of this chapter.**

Carlton County

6th Judicial District Court PO Box 190, 301 Walnut Ave, Carlton, MN 55718; 218-384-4281; criminal phone: 218-384-9109; civil phone: 218-384-9139; probate phone: 218-384-9113; criminal fax: 218-384-9182; civil fax: 8AM-4PM; 8AM-4PM (CST). *Felony, Misdemeanor, Civil, Eviction, Small Claims, Probate.* www.mncourts.gov/district/6/

General Information: No adoption, juvenile, sex offender or sealed records released. Fee to fax back- $25.00 per doc up to 25 pgs. Court makes copy: $8.00 per doc. Certification fee: $14.00 per doc. Payee: Court Administrator. Personal checks accepted. Most credit cards accepted. Prepayment required. Mail requests: SASE required for civil.

Civil Name Search: Access: Mail, fax, in person, online. Both court and visitors may perform in person name searches. Search fee: $5.00 per name. Required to search: name, years to search; also helpful: address. Civil records on computer from 1985, in books from 1982. Mail turnaround time 3 days. Civil PAT goes back to 1986. Public terminal allows for a statewide search and is more extensive than online search. **For details about the state's online access to records, see the sections at the front or back of this chapter.**

Criminal Name Search: Access: In person, online. Visitors must perform in person searches themselves. Required to search: name, years to search; also helpful: address, DOB. Criminal records computerized from 1985, in books from 1972. Criminal PAT goes back to 1986. Public terminal allows for a statewide search and is more extensive than online search. **For details about the state's online access to records, see the sections at the front or back of this chapter.**

Fond Du Lac Band of Chippewa Tribal Court 1720 Big Lake Rd, Cloquet, MN 55720; 218-878-2767; fax: 218-878-2684;*Criminal, Civil, Juvenile, Traffic, Estate, Eviction.* www.fdlrez.com/

Carver County

1st Judicial District Court 604 E 4th St, Chaska, MN 55318-2183; 952-361-1420; fax: 952-361-1491; 8AM-4:30PM (CST). *Felony, Misdemeanor, Civil, Eviction, Small Claims, Probate.* www.mncourts.gov/district/1/

General Information: No adoption, juvenile, sex offender or sealed records released. Will not fax documents. Court makes copy: $8.00 per doc. Certification fee: $14.00 per doc. Payee: Court Administrator. Personal checks, Visa/MC accepted. Prepayment required.

Civil Name Search: Access: In person, online. Visitors must perform in person searches themselves. Civil records on computer from 2/92, prior on books. Note: Note that court will do a "judgment search" for $5.00, but not a name search of civil records. Public use terminal available, records go back to 1992. Results include name, city, state, zip. **For details about the state's online access to records, see the sections at the front or back of this chapter.**

Criminal Name Search: Access: In person, online. Visitors must perform in person searches themselves. Criminal records computerized from 2/92, prior on books. Note: Results include name, city, state, zip. Public use terminal available, crim records go back to 1992. Results include name, city, state, zip. Public terminal allows for a statewide search. **For details about the state's online access to records, see the sections at the front or back of this chapter.**

Cass County

9th Judicial District Court PO Box 3000, 300 Minnesota Ave, Walker, MN 56484; 218-547-7200; fax: 218-547-1904; 8AM-4:30PM (CST). *Felony, Misdemeanor, Civil, Eviction, Small Claims, Probate.* www.mncourts.gov/district/9/

General Information: Week ahead court calendars available online. No adoption, juvenile or sealed records released. Will fax documents for $5.00 per document. Court makes copy: $8.00 per doc. Certification fee: $14.00 per doc. Payee: District Court. Personal checks and credit cards accepted. Prepayment required. Mail requests: SASE required for civil.

Civil Name Search: Access: Mail, in person, online. Visitors must perform in person searches themselves. Search fee: $5.00 per name. Required to search: full name, years to search; also helpful: address. Civil records on computer from March 1990, on index cards from 1983-1990, on books to 1983-1900. Mail turnaround time 5 days Civil PAT goes back to 03/1990. Public terminal allows for a statewide search and is more extensive than online search. **For details about the state's online access to records, see the sections at the front or back of this chapter.**

Criminal Name Search: Access: In person, online. Visitors must perform in person searches themselves. Criminal records computerized from March 1990, on index cards from 1983-1990, on books to 1983-1900. Criminal PAT goes back to 03/1990. Public terminal allows for a statewide search and is more extensive than online search. **For details about the state's online access to records, see the sections at the front or back of this chapter.**

Leech Lake Bank of Ojibwe Tribal Court 6520 US Hwy 2 NW, Cass Lake, MN 56633; 218-335-3682; fax: 218-335-3685; 8AM-4:30PM (CST). *Criminal, Civil, Juvenile, Traffic, Estate, Eviction.* www.llojibwe.com/law/court.html

General Information: Physical address: 16126 John Moose Dr, Cass Lake. Coverage includes-Leech Lake Reservation, Beltrami County, Cass County, Hubbard County, Itasca County.

Chippewa County

8th Judicial District Court Chippewa County Court Administer, 629 N 11th St Ste 9, Montevideo, MN 56265; 320-269-7774; fax: 320-269-7733; 8AM-4:30PM M-TH; 8AM-2PM F (CST). *Felony, Misdemeanor, Civil, Eviction, Small Claims, Probate.* www.mncourts.gov/district/8/

General Information: No adoption, juvenile, sex offender or sealed records released. Will not fax documents. Court makes copy: $8.00 per doc. Certification fee: $14.00 per doc. Payee: Court Administrator. Personal checks accepted. Prepayment required. Mail requests: SASE required for civil.

Civil Name Search: Access: Mail, in person, online. Both court and visitors may perform in person name searches. Search fee: $5.00 per name. Civil records on computer from 1988, but regularly purged, in books from 1870 (probate only). Mail turnaround time 1 week. Civil PAT goes back to 1988. Public terminal allows for a statewide search and is more extensive than online search. **For details about the state's online access to records, see the sections at the front or back of this chapter.**

Criminal Name Search: Access: Mail, in person, online. Both court and visitors may perform in person name searches. Search fee: $5.00 per name. Required to search: name, years to search, DOB. Criminal records computerized from 1988. Mail turnaround time 1 week. Criminal PAT goes back to 1988. Public terminal allows for a statewide search and is more extensive than online search. **For details about the state's online access to records, see the sections at the front or back of this chapter.**

Chisago County

10th Judicial District Court 313 N Main St, Rm 358, Center City, MN 55012; 651-213-8650; fax: 651-213-8651; 8AM-4:30PM M, T, W, F; 11AM-4:30PM TH (CST). *Felony, Misdemeanor, Civil, Eviction, Small Claims, Probate.* www.mncourts.gov/district/10/

General Information: No adoption, juvenile, sex offender or sealed records released. Fee to fax back- $25.00 per doc up to 25 pgs. Court makes copy: $8.00 per doc. Only the court can make a copy of a file, but visitors can make copies of copies free in the Law Library. Certification fee: $14.00 per doc includes copy fee. Payee: Court Administrator. Personal checks and credit cards accepted. Prepayment required. Mail requests: SASE required for civil.

Civil Name Search: Access: Mail, fax, in person, online. Both court and visitors may perform in person name searches. Search fee: $5.00 per name. Civil records on computer from 09/1984, prior on index cards. Note: Weekly calendars free at www.mncourts.gov/district/10/?page=1326. Civil PAT goes back to late 1980s. Public terminal allows for a statewide search and is more extensive than online search. **For details about the state's online access to records, see the sections at the front or back of this chapter.**

Criminal Name Search: Access: In person, online. Visitors must perform in person searches themselves. Required to search: name, years to search; also helpful: DOB. Criminal records computerized from 09/1984, prior on index cards. Criminal PAT goes back to late 1980s. Public terminal allows for a statewide search and is more extensive than online search. **For details about the state's online access to records, see the sections at the front or back of this chapter.**

Clay County

7th Judicial District Court PO Box 280, 807 11th St N, Clay County Ct Admin, Moorhead, MN 56561; 218-299-5065; fax: 218-299-7307; 8AM-4:30PM (CST). *Felony, Misdemeanor, Civil, Eviction, Small Claims, Probate.* www.co.clay.mn.us/Depts/CourtAdm/CourtAdm.htm

General Information: Court personnel do not perform searches for the public. No adoption or sealed records released. Fee to fax back- $25.00 per doc up to 25 pgs. Court makes copy: $8.00 per doc. Certification fee: $14.00 per doc plus copy fee. Payee: Court Administrator. Personal checks and credit cards accepted. Prepayment required.

Civil Name Search: Access: In person, online. Visitors must perform in person searches themselves. Required to search: name; also helpful: years to search. Civil records on computer back to 1982; prior on microfiche, microfilm and docket books. Civil PAT goes back to 1982. Public terminal allows for a statewide search and is more extensive than online search. **For details about the state's online access to records, see the sections at the front or back of this chapter.**

Criminal Name Search: Access: In person, online. Visitors must perform in person searches themselves. Required to search: name, years to search, DOB. Criminal records computerized from 1982; prior on microfiche and microfilm. Criminal PAT goes back to 1982. Public terminal allows for a statewide search and is more extensive than online search. **For details about the state's online access to records, see the sections at the front or back of this chapter.**

Clearwater County

9th Judicial District Court 213 Main Ave North, Dept 303, Bagley, MN 56621; 218-694-6177; fax: 218-694-6213; 8AM-4:30PM (CST). *Felony, Misdemeanor, Civil, Eviction, Small Claims, Probate.* www.mncourts.gov/district/9/

General Information: Week ahead court calendars available online. No adoption, juvenile or sealed records released. Fee to fax back- $25.00 per doc up to 25 pgs. Court makes copy: $8.00 per doc. Certification fee: $14.00 per doc. Payee: Court Administrator. Personal checks and credit cards accepted. Prepayment required.

Civil Name Search: Access: Mail, in person, online. Both court and visitors may perform in person name searches. Search fee: $5.00 per name, by court. Civil records on computer from 1990, on cards and books prior back to 1903. Mail turnaround time 1 week. Civil PAT goes back to 1990. Public terminal allows for a statewide search and is more extensive than online search. **For details about the state's online access to records, see the sections at the front or back of this chapter.**

Criminal Name Search: Access: In person, online. Visitors must perform in person searches themselves. Required to search: name, years to search; also helpful: DOB. Criminal records computerized from 1990, on cards and books prior back to 1903. Note: Court personnel will not perform name searches. Requests are referred to the state criminal agency. Criminal PAT goes back to 1990. Public terminal allows for a statewide search and is more extensive than online search. **For details about the state's online access to records, see the sections at the front or back of this chapter.**

Cook County

6th Judicial District Court 411 W 2nd St, Grand Marais, MN 55604-2307; 218-387-3610; fax: 218-387-3007; 8AM-4PM (CST). *Felony, Misdemeanor, Civil, Eviction, Small Claims, Probate, Traffic.* www.mncourts.gov/district/6/

General Information: No adoption, juvenile, sex offender or sealed records released. Fee to fax back- $25.00 per doc up to 50 pgs. Court makes copy: $8.00 per doc. Certification fee: $14.00 per doc. Payee: Court Administrator. Business checks accepted. Visa/MC accepted. Prepayment required.

Civil Name Search: Access: In person, online. Visitors must perform in person searches themselves. Search fee: $5.00 for a judgment search. Civil records on computer back to 2/91, prior on card files. Civil PAT goes back to 1991. Public terminal allows for a statewide search and is more extensive than online search. **For details about the state's online access to records, see the sections at the front or back of this chapter.**

Criminal Name Search: Access: In person, online. Visitors must perform in person searches themselves. Required to search: name, years to search, DOB. Criminal records computerized from 2/91, prior on card files. Criminal PAT goes back to 1991. Public terminal allows for a statewide search and is more extensive than online search. **For details about the state's online access to records, see the sections at the front or back of this chapter.**

Grand Portage Tribal Court Hwy 61, PO Box 428, Grand Portage, MN 55605; 218-475-2239; fax: 2180475-2284;*Criminal, Civil, Juvenile, Traffic, Estate, Eviction.* www.grandportage.com/tribalgovernment.php

Cottonwood County

5th Judicial District Court PO Box 97, Windom, MN 56101; 507-831-4551; fax: 507-831-1425; 8AM-4:30PM (CST). *Felony, Misdemeanor, Civil, Eviction, Small Claims, Probate.* www.mncourts.gov/district/5/

General Information: No adoption, juvenile, sex offender or sealed records released. Will fax documents to local or toll free line. Court makes copy: $8.00 per doc. Certification fee: $14.00 per doc includes copy fee. Payee: Court Administrator. Personal checks, Visa/MC accepted. Prepayment required. Mail requests: SASE required.

Civil Name Search: Access: Mail, fax, in person, online. Both court and visitors may perform in person name searches. Search fee: $10.00 per name. Required to search: name; also helpful: years to search. Civil records on computer back to 1989; probate on microfilm. There is a $5.00 fee to certify a judgment search done on computer. Mail turnaround time 2-3 days. Civil PAT goes back to 1989. Public terminal allows for a statewide search and is more extensive than online search. **For details about the state's online access to records, see the sections at the front or back of this chapter.**

Criminal Name Search: Access: Mail, fax, in person, online. Both court and visitors may perform in person name searches. Search fee: $10.00 per name. Required to search: name, years to search, DOB. Criminal records computerized from 1989; prior records on card file. Note: Court will only do searches if caseload permits. Mail turnaround time 2-3 days. Criminal PAT goes back to 1989. Public terminal allows for a statewide search and is more extensive than online search. **For details about the state's online access to records, see the sections at the front or back of this chapter.**

Crow Wing County

District Court Crow Wing County Judicial Center, 213 Laurel St, #11, Brainerd, MN 56401; 218-824-1310; fax: 218-824-1311; 8AM-5PM (CST). *Felony, Misdemeanor, Civil, Eviction, Small Claims, Probate.* www.mncourts.gov/district/9/

General Information: Week ahead court calendars available online. No adoption, juvenile, sex offender or sealed records released. Will not fax documents. Court makes copy: $8.00 per doc. Certification fee: $14.00 per doc plus copy fee. Payee: Court Administrator. Personal checks accepted. No credit cards accepted. Prepayment required. Mail requests: SASE required for civil.

Civil Name Search: Access: Mail, in person, online. Both court and visitors may perform in person name searches. Search fee: $5.00 per name. Civil records on computer from 1989, prior in books from 1873. Mail turnaround time 5 days Civil PAT goes back to 1989. Public terminal allows for a statewide search and is more extensive than online search. **For details about the state's online access to records, see the sections at the front or back of this chapter.**

Criminal Name Search: Access: In person, online. Both court and visitors may perform in person name searches. Search fee: $5.00 per name. Required to search: name, years to search; also helpful: DOB. Criminal records computerized from 1989, prior in books from 1873. Criminal PAT goes back to 1989. Public terminal allows for a statewide search and is more extensive than online search. **For details about the state's online access to records, see the sections at the front or back of this chapter.**

Dakota County

1st Judicial District Court - Apple Valley 14955 Galaxie Ave, Apple Valley, MN 55124; 952-891-7256; criminal phone: 952-891-7239; civil phone: 952-891-7244; criminal fax: 952-891-7312; civil fax: 8AM-4:30PM; 8AM-4:30PM (CST). *Misdemeanor, Civil, Eviction, Small Claims, Traffic.* www.mncourts.gov/default.aspx?siteID=1

General Information: No adoption, juvenile, sex offender or sealed records released. Will not fax out documents. Court makes copy: $8.00 per doc. Self serve copy: $.50 per page. Certification fee: $14.00 per doc. Payee: District Court. Personal checks and credit cards accepted. Prepayment required.

Civil Name Search: Access: In person, online. Visitors must perform in person searches themselves. Civil records on computer back to 1988, prior in files in index books back to 1969. Civil PAT goes back to 1988. Public terminal allows for a statewide search and is more extensive than online search. **For details about the state's online access to records, see the sections at the front or back of this chapter.**

Criminal Name Search: Access: In person, online. Visitors must perform in person searches themselves. Required to search: name, years to search, DOB. Criminal records computerized from 1988, prior in files to 1987 if not destroyed. Criminal PAT goes back to 1988. Public terminal allows for a statewide search and is more extensive than online search. **For details about the state's online access to records, see the sections at the front or back of this chapter.**

1st Judicial District Court - Division 3 1 Mendota Rd West, #140, West St Paul, MN 55118-4767; 651-554-6200; fax: 651-554-6226; 8AM-4:30PM (CST). *Misdemeanor, Civil, Eviction, Small Claims.* www.mncourts.gov/default.aspx?siteID=1

General Information: Formerly located at 125 3rd Ave North, S. St. Paul. No adoption, juvenile, sex offender or sealed records released. Will not fax out case files. Court makes copy: $8.00 per doc. Certification fee: $14.00 per doc plus copy fee. Payee: Court Administrator. Personal checks and credit cards accepted. Prepayment required.

Civil Name Search: Access: In person, online. Visitors must perform in person searches themselves. Civil records on computer from 12/87, prior on ledgers. Civil PAT goes back to 1/1988. Public terminal allows for a statewide search and is more extensive than online search. **For details about the state's online access to records, see the sections at the front or back of this chapter.**

Criminal Name Search: Access: In person, online. Visitors must perform in person searches themselves. Criminal records computerized from 12/87, prior on ledgers. Criminal PAT goes back to 1/1988. Public terminal allows for a statewide search and is more extensive than online search. **For details about the state's online access to records, see the sections at the front or back of this chapter.**

District Court Judicial Center, 1560 Hwy 55, Hastings, MN 55033; 651-438-8100; criminal fax: 651-438-8160; civil fax: 8AM-4:30PM; 8AM-4:30PM (CST). *Felony, Misdemeanor, Civil, Eviction, Small Claims, Probate.* www.mncourts.gov/default.aspx?siteID=1

General Information: Probate fax- 651-438-8161 No adoption, juvenile, sealed records released. Will not fax out case files. Court makes copy: $8.00 per doc. Certification fee: $14.00 per doc plus copy fee. Payee: District Court. Personal checks, Visa/MC accepted. Prepayment required.

Civil Name Search: Access: In person, online. Visitors must perform in person searches themselves. Civil records on computer from 1/88, on ledgers prior. Civil PAT goes back to 1/1988. Public terminal allows for a statewide search and is more extensive than online search. **For details about the state's online access to records, see the sections at the front or back of this chapter.**

Criminal Name Search: Access: In person, online. Visitors must perform in person searches themselves. Criminal records computerized from 1/88, on ledgers prior. Criminal PAT goes back to 1/1988. Public terminals at 3 locations- Judicial Ctr, 1560 W Hwy 55 in Hastings; Western Svc Ctr, 14955 Galaxie Ave in Apple Valley; Northern Svc Ctr, 1 Mendot Rd W, #140 in West St Paul. Public terminal allows for a statewide search. **For details about the state's online access to records, see the sections at the front or back of this chapter.**

Dodge County

3rd Judicial District Court 22 Sixth St E, Dept. 12, Mantorville, MN 55955; 507-635-6260; fax: 507-635-6271; 8AM-4:30PM (CST). *Felony, Misdemeanor, Civil, Eviction, Small Claims, Probate.* www.mncourts.gov/district/3/

General Information: No adoption, juvenile, sex offender or sealed records released. Fee to fax back- $25.00 per doc up to 25 pgs. Court makes copy: $8.00 per doc. Certification fee: $14.00 per doc. Payee: Court Administrator. Personal checks, Visa/MC accepted. Prepayment required. Mail requests: SASE required for civil.

Civil Name Search: Access: In person, online. Visitors must perform in person searches themselves. Civil records on computer back to 1989, on cards from 1984, on books from 1972. Mail turnaround time 3 days. Civil PAT goes back to 1989. Public terminal allows for a statewide search and is more extensive than online search. . Search by case number or by name. Daily Court calendar is posted at www.mncourts.gov/default.aspx?page=512.

Criminal Name Search: Access: In person, online. Visitors must perform in person searches themselves. Required to search: name, years to search, DOB. Criminal records computerized from 1984, on cards from 1984, on books from 1972. Criminal PAT goes back to 1989. Public terminal allows for a statewide search and is more extensive than online search. **For details about the state's online access to records, see the sections at the front or back of this chapter.**

Douglas County

7th Judicial District Court 305 8th Ave West, Alexandria, MN 56308; 320-762-3882; fax: 320-762-8863; 8AM-4:30PM (CST). *Felony, Misdemeanor, Civil, Eviction, Small Claims, Probate.* www.mncourts.gov/district/7/

General Information: Probate fax is same as main fax number. No adoption, juvenile or sealed records released. Will not fax documents. Court makes copy: $8.00 per doc. Certification fee: $14.00 plus copy fee. Payee: Court Administrator. Personal checks, Visa/MC accepted. Prepayment required.

Civil Name Search: Access: In person, online. Both court and visitors may perform in person name searches. No search fee. Civil records on computer from 1987, on microfiche from 1951, books prior. The books are grouped by letter, but not alphabetized. Civil PAT goes back to 1987. Public terminal allows for a statewide search and is more extensive than online search. **For details about the state's online access to records, see the sections at the front or back of this chapter.**

Criminal Name Search: Access: In person, online. Visitors must perform in person searches themselves. Required to search: name. Criminal records computerized from 1987, on microfiche from 1951, books prior. The books are grouped by letter, but not alphabetized. Note: Court recommends search through BCA. Criminal PAT goes back to 1987. Public terminal allows for a statewide search and is more extensive than online search. **For details about the state's online access to records, see the sections at the front or back of this chapter.**

Faribault County

5th Judicial District Court PO Box 130, Blue Earth, MN 56013; 507-526-6273; fax: 507-526-3054; 8AM-4:30PM (CST). *Felony, Misdemeanor, Civil, Eviction, Small Claims, Probate.* www.mncourts.gov/district/5/

General Information: No adoption, juvenile, sex offender or sealed records released. Fee to fax back- $25.00 per doc up to 25 pgs. Court makes copy: $8.00 per doc. Certification fee: $14.00 per doc. Payee: Court Administrator. Personal checks and credit cards accepted. Prepayment required. Mail requests: SASE required for civil.

Civil Name Search: Access: Mail, fax, in person, online. Both court and visitors may perform in person name searches. Search fee: $5.00 per name for a judgment search. Civil records on computer from 1989, in books from 1870. Mail turnaround time 1 week. Civil PAT goes back to 1989. Public terminal allows for a statewide search and is more extensive than online search. **For details about the state's online access to records, see the sections at the front or back of this chapter.**

Criminal Name Search: Access: In person, online. Visitors must perform in person searches themselves. Required to search: name, years to search; also helpful: DOB. Criminal records computerized from 1989, in books from 1870. Note: The county suggests sending requests to the state Bureau of Criminal Apprehension. Criminal PAT goes back to 1989. Public terminal allows for a statewide search and is more extensive than online search. **For details about the state's online access to records, see the sections at the front or back of this chapter.**

Fillmore County

3rd Judicial District Court 101 Fillmore St, PO Box 436, Preston, MN 55965; 507-765-4483; fax: 507-765-4571; 8AM-4:30PM; 12:30PM-4:30PM TH (CST). *Felony, Misdemeanor, Civil, Eviction, Small Claims, Probate.* www.mncourts.gov/district/3/

General Information: Probate fax is same as main fax number. No adoption, juvenile or sealed records released. Fee to fax back- $2.00 first pg, $1.00 ea. add'l. Court makes copy: $8.00 per doc. Certification fee: $14.00 per doc plus copy fee. Payee: Court Administrator. Personal checks and credit cards accepted. Prepayment required.

Civil Name Search: Access: Mail, in person, online. Both court and visitors may perform in person name searches. Search fee: $5.00 per name. Civil records on computer from 1990, books from 1860s. Mail turnaround time 1-2 days. Civil PAT goes back to 1990. Public terminal allows for a statewide search and is more extensive than online search. **For details about the state's online access to records, see the sections at the front or back of this chapter.**

Criminal Name Search: Access: In person, online. Visitors must perform in person searches themselves. Required to search: name, years to search, DOB. Criminal records computerized from 1990, books from 1860s. Criminal PAT goes back to 1990. Public terminal allows for a statewide search and is more extensive than online search. **For details about the state's online access to records, see the sections at the front or back of this chapter.**

Freeborn County

3rd Judicial District Court 411 S Broadway, Albert Lea, MN 56007; 507-377-5153; fax: 507-377-5260; 8AM-5PM (CST). *Felony, Misdemeanor, Civil, Eviction, Small Claims, Probate.* www.mncourts.gov/district/3/

General Information: No adoption, juvenile, sex offender or sealed records released. Will not fax documents. Court makes copy: $8.00 per doc. Certification fee: $14.00 per doc. Payee: Court Administrator. Personal checks, Visa/MC accepted. Prepayment required. Mail requests: SASE required for civil.

Civil Name Search: Access: Mail, in person, online. Both court and visitors may perform in person name searches. Search fee: $5.00 per name. Civil records on computer from 11/89. Civil PAT goes back to 11/1989. Public terminal allows for a statewide search and is more extensive than

online search. **For details about the state's online access to records, see the sections at the front or back of this chapter.**

Criminal Name Search: Access: In person, online. Visitors must perform in person searches themselves. Required to search: name, years to search, DOB. Criminal records computerized from 11/89. Criminal PAT goes back to 11/1989. Public terminal allows for a statewide search and is more extensive than online search. **For details about the state's online access to records, see the sections at the front or back of this chapter.**

Goodhue County

District Court 454 W 6th St, Red Wing, MN 55066; 651-267-4800; probate phone: 651-267-4810; fax: 651-267-4989; 8AM-4:30PM (CST). *Felony, Misdemeanor, Civil, Eviction, Small Claims, Probate.* www.mncourts.gov/district/1/

General Information: Probate fax is same as main fax number. No adoption, juvenile, sex offender or sealed records released. Will fax documents to local or toll-free number. Court makes copy: $8.00 per doc. Certification fee: $14.00 per doc. Payee: Court Administrator. Personal checks accepted. Visa/MC/Discover accepted. Prepayment required.

Civil Name Search: Access: Mail, in person, online. Both court and visitors may perform in person name searches. No search fee. Civil records on computer from 3/92, prior records on docket books. Mail turnaround time 1 week. Civil PAT goes back to 1992. Public terminal allows for a statewide search and is more extensive than online search. **For details about the state's online access to records, see the sections at the front or back of this chapter.**

Criminal Name Search: Access: In person, online. Visitors must perform in person searches themselves. Required to search: name. Criminal records computerized from 3/92, prior records on docket books. Criminal PAT goes back to 1992. Public terminal allows for a statewide search and is more extensive than online search. **For details about the state's online access to records, see the sections at the front or back of this chapter.**

Prairie Island Indian Community Tribal Court 5636 Sturgeon Lake Rd, Welch, MN 55089; 651-385-4161; 800-554-5473; fax: 651-385-4160;*Criminal, Civil, Juvenile, Traffic, Estate, Eviction.* www.prairieisland.org/tribal_court%20Ver%20A.htm

Grant County

8th Judicial District Court PO Box 1007, 10 2nd St NE, Elbow Lake, MN 56531; 218-685-4825; fax: 218-685-5349; 8AM-4PM (CST). *Felony, Misdemeanor, Civil, Eviction, Small Claims, Probate.* www.mncourts.gov/district/8/

General Information: No adoption, juvenile, sex offender or sealed records released. Fee to fax back- $25.00 per doc up to 50 pgs. Court makes copy: $8.00 per doc. Certification fee: $14.00 per doc includes copy fees. Payee: Court Administrator. Personal checks, Visa/MC accepted. Prepayment required. Mail requests: SASE required for civil.

Civil Name Search: Access: Mail, fax, in person, online. Both court and visitors may perform in person name searches. Search fee: $5.00 per name. Civil records on computer from 6/89, on cards from 1930, prior at Historical Society. Mail turnaround time 3-4 days. Civil PAT goes back to 1989. Public terminal allows for a statewide search and is more extensive than online search. **For details about the state's online access to records, see the sections at the front or back of this chapter.**

Criminal Name Search: Access: In person, online. Visitors must perform in person searches themselves. Required to search: name, years to search; also helpful: DOB. Criminal records computerized from 6/89, on cards from 1930, prior at Historical Society. Criminal PAT goes back to 1989. Public terminal allows for a statewide search and is more extensive than online search. **For details about the state's online access to records, see the sections at the front or back of this chapter.**

Hennepin County

4th Judicial District Court - Criminal Division 300 S 6th St, PSL-2nd Floor HCGC, Minneapolis, MN 55487; 612-348-4849/2612; fax: 612-348-6099; 8AM-4:30PM (CST). *Felony, Misdemeanor.* www.mncourts.gov/district/4/

General Information: This is the central location for all criminal record searching in this county. If a misdemeanor case file is needed at one of the other District Courts, this court will retrieve it. For more info see www.mncourts.gov/district/4/?page=1865. No sex offender or sealed records released. Will fax documents. Court makes copy: $8.00 per doc. Self serve copy: same. Certification fee: $14.00 per case. Cert fee includes search fee. Payee: Court Administrator. Personal checks accepted. Credit cards accepted in person. Prepayment required. Mail requests: SASE required.

Criminal Name Search: Access: Fax, mail, in person, online. Both court and visitors may perform in person name searches. Search fee: $14.00 per name. Required to search: name, years to search, DOB. Felony record index back to 1886. Computerized records back to 1978. Files copies held up to 30 years per state law. Mail turnaround time 14-21 days. Public use terminal has crim records back to 1989. Public terminal allows for a statewide search and is more extensive than online search. **For details about the state's online access to records, see the sections at the front or back of this chapter.**

4th Judicial District Court - Division 1 Civil 3 C Government Ctr, 300 S 6th St, Minneapolis, MN 55487; 612-348-3164; fax: 612-348-2131; 8AM-4:30PM (closed Wed at 1:30) (CST). *Civil, Small Claims, Eviction.* www.mncourts.gov/district/4/

General Information: The Housing Court handles evictions countywide and is located at Courts Tower, Floor 3 (C3) of the Hennepin County Government Center, 612-348-5186. Conciliation Court (Small Claims is 350 South 5th Street, Rm. #306, 612-348-2713. No sex offender or sealed records released, domestic abuse and paternity cases are limited. Will not fax out documents. Court makes copy: $8.00 per doc. Certification fee: $14.00 per doc. Payee: Court Administrator. Personal checks accepted. No credit cards accepted. Prepayment required. Mail requests: SASE required.

Civil Name Search: Access: Fax, mail, in person, online. Both court and visitors may perform in person name searches. Search fee: $5.00 per name by mail. Civil records on computer from 1978, prior on microfilm. Civil judgments kept 10 years then paper files destroyed if not renewed. Mail turnaround time 7-10 days. Public use terminal has civil records back to 1978. No address, DOB generally not available. PAT results statewide. Civil, small claims, family and probate index free at . Search by case number or by name. Electronic filings and abuse cases not shown. Search judgments free at . See records center webpage for record specifics at www.mncourts.gov/district/4/?page=1865.

4th Judicial District Court - Division 3 Ridgedale 12601 Ridgedale Dr, Minnetonka, MN 55305-1912; 612-543-1400; fax: 952-541-6297; 8AM-4:30PM (Wed: 8AM-1:30PM) (CST). *Misdemeanor, Traffic.* www.mncourts.gov/district/4/

General Information: Juris- Deephaven, Eden Prairie, Excelsior, Golden Vly, Greenwood, Hopkins, Independence, Long Lk, Loretto, Maple Grove, Maple Plain, Medina, Minnetonka, Minnetrista, Mound, Orono, Plymouth, Shorewood, Spring Pk, St Bonifacius, Tonka Bay, Wayzata, Woodland No police reports, juvenile or sealed records released. Will not fax out documents. Court makes copy: $8.00 per doc. Certification fee: $14.00 per doc. Payee: Hennepin County District Court. Personal checks accepted. Credit cards accepted in person only. Prepayment required. Mail requests: SASE required.

Criminal Name Search: Access: Phone, fax, mail, in person, online. Both court and visitors may perform in person name searches. Search fee: $5.00 per name. Required to search: name, years to search; also helpful: DOB. Criminal records on computer since 1989; prior records on microfiche. Note: The court refers requesters to the criminal record center in Minneapolis or online system. Mail turnaround time 3-4 weeks. Public use terminal has crim records back to 1986. Public terminal, which does not always work, has limited data available. See records center webpage for record specifics at www.mncourts.gov/district/4/?page=1865. Online results show middle initial, DOB.

4th Judicial District Court - Division 2 Brookdale 6125 Shingle Creek Parkway #200, Brooklyn Center, MN 55430; 612-543-2140; fax: 763-569-3697; 8AM-4:30PM M,T,TH,F; W 1:30PM (CST). *Misdemeanor, Traffic.* www.mncourts.gov/district/4/

General Information: The court refers requesters to the criminal record center in Minneapolis or online system. Jurisdiction area- Brooklyn Center, Brooklyn Park, Champlin, Corcoran, Crystal, Dayton, Greenfield, Hanover, Hassan, New Hope, Osseo, Robbinsdale, Rockford, Rogers.

4th Judicial District Court - Division 4 Southdale 7009 York Ave S, Edina, MN 55435; 612-348-2040; fax: 952-830-4993; 8AM-4:30PM, W- 8AM-1:30PM (CST). *Misdemeanor, Traffic.* www.mncourts.gov/district/4/

General Information: The court refers requesters to the criminal record center in Minneapolis or online system. Jurisdictional area- Airport (MAC), Bloomington, Edina, Richfield, St Louis Pk.

4th Judicial District Court C400 Government Ctr, 300 S 6th St, Minneapolis, MN 55487-0340; 612-348-3244; fax: 612-348-2130; 8:30AM-4:30PM (Probate closed W 1:30-4:30) (CST). *Probate, Mental Health.* www.mncourts.gov/district/4/

General Information: Search Probate and Family cases free at www.mncourts.gov/default.aspx?page=1927. Mental health can be reached at 612-348-6868

Houston County

3rd Judicial District Court 304 S Marshall, Rm 204, Caledonia, MN 55921; 507-725-5806; fax: 507-725-5550; 8AM-4:30PM, Tues- 12:30-4:30PM (CST). *Felony, Misdemeanor, Civil, Eviction, Small Claims, Probate.* www.mncourts.gov/district/3/

General Information: No adoption, juvenile, sex offender or sealed records released. Fee to fax back- $1.00 per page in-state, $2.00 out-of-state.

Court makes copy: $8.00 per doc. Certification fee: $14.00 per doc plus copy fee. Payee: Court Administrator. Personal checks, Visa/MC accepted. Prepayment required. Mail requests: SASE required for civil.

Civil Name Search: Access: Mail, in person, online. Both court and visitors may perform in person name searches. No search fee. Required to search: name, years to search, DOB. Civil records on computer back to 8/89, prior on cards and books. Probate on microfilm to 1990. Mail turnaround time 2 days. Civil PAT goes back to 1989. Public terminal allows for a statewide search and is more extensive than online search. **For details about the state's online access to records, see the sections at the front or back of this chapter.**

Criminal Name Search: Access: In person, online. Visitors must perform in person searches themselves. Required to search: name, years to search; also helpful: DOB. Criminal records computerized from 8/89, prior on cards and books. Criminal PAT goes back to 1989. Public terminal allows for a statewide search and is more extensive than online search. **For details about the state's online access to records, see the sections at the front or back of this chapter.**

Hubbard County

9th Judicial District Court 301 Court Ave, Park Rapids, MN 56470; 218-732-5286; fax: 218-732-0137; 8AM-4:30PM (CST). *Felony, Misdemeanor, Civil, Eviction, Small Claims, Probate.* www.mncourts.gov/district/9/?page=3916

General Information: Week ahead court calendars available online. No adoption, juvenile, sex offender or sealed records released. Fee to fax back- $25.00 per doc up to 25 pgs. Court makes copy: $8.00 per doc. Certification fee: $14.00 per doc. Payee: Court Administrator. Personal checks accepted. Visa/MC/Discover accepted. Prepayment required.

Civil Name Search: Access: Mail, in person, online. Visitors must perform in person searches themselves. Search fee: $5.00 per name. Civil records on computer since 1990, prior on index cards. Civil PAT goes back to 1990. Public terminal allows for a statewide search and is more extensive than online search. **For details about the state's online access to records, see the sections at the front or back of this chapter.**

Criminal Name Search: Access: In person, online. Visitors must perform in person searches themselves. Required to search: name, DOB. Criminal records on computer since 1990, prior on index cards. Criminal PAT goes back to 1990. Public terminal allows for a statewide search and is more extensive than online search. **For details about the state's online access to records, see the sections at the front or back of this chapter.**

Isanti County

10th Judicial District Court 555 18th Ave SW, Cambridge, MN 55008; 763-689-2292; fax: 763-689-8340; 8AM-4:30PM (CST). *Felony, Misdemeanor, Civil, Eviction, Small Claims, Probate.* www.mncourts.gov/district/10/

General Information: Probate fax is same as main fax number. No adoption, juvenile, sex offender or sealed records released. Will fax free to local or toll-free numbers. Court makes copy: $8.00 uncertified. Certification fee: $14.00 per doc. Payee: Court Administrator. Personal checks, Visa/MC accepted. Prepayment required. Mail requests: SASE required for civil.

Civil Name Search: Access: Mail, in person, online. Both court and visitors may perform in person name searches. No search fee. Civil records on computer from 12/84, prior on microfiche. Note: Weekly calendars free at www.mncourts.gov/district/10/?page=1326. Civil PAT goes back to 1985. Public terminal allows for a statewide search and is more extensive than online search. **For details about the state's online access to records, see the sections at the front or back of this chapter.**

Criminal Name Search: Access: In person, online. Visitors must perform in person searches themselves. Criminal records computerized from 12/84, prior on microfiche. Criminal PAT goes back to 1985. Public terminal allows for a statewide search and is more extensive than online search. **For details about the state's online access to records, see the sections at the front or back of this chapter.**

Itasca County

9th Judicial District Court 123 4th St NE, Grand Rapids, MN 55744-2600; 218-327-2870; fax: 218-327-2897; 8AM-4:30PM (CST). *Felony, Misdemeanor, Civil, Eviction, Small Claims, Probate, Family.* www.co.itasca.mn.us/Home/Departments/Court%20Administration/Pages/default.aspx

General Information: Week ahead court calendars available online. No adoption, juvenile or sealed records released. Fee to fax back- $5.00. Court makes copy: $8.00 per doc. Certification fee: $14.00. Payee: Court Administrator. Personal checks accepted. Visa/MC/Discover accepted. Prepayment required.

Civil Name Search: Access: Mail, in person, online. Both court and visitors may perform in person name searches. Search fee: $5.00 per name. Required to search: name, years to search, DOB. Civil records on computer from 4-87, on microfiche to 1982, on books prior. Mail turnaround time 20

days, 24 hours more to pull from off-site storage. Civil PAT goes back to 4/1987. Public terminal allows for a statewide search and is more extensive than online search. **For details about the state's online access to records, see the sections at the front or back of this chapter.**
Criminal Name Search: Access: In person, online. Visitors must perform in person searches themselves. Required to search: name, years to search, DOB. Criminal records computerized from 4-87, on microfiche to 1982, on books prior. Note: This agency will not perform a record search. Record checks should made through the Bureau of Criminal Apprehension; see state section on criminal records. Criminal PAT goes back to 4/1987. Public terminal allows for a statewide search and is more extensive than online search. **For details about the state's online access to records, see the sections at the front or back of this chapter.**

Jackson County

5th Judicial District Court PO Box 177, Jackson, MN 56143; criminal phone: 507-847-2566; civil phone: 507-847-4400; fax: 507-847-5433; 8AM-4:30PM (CST). *Felony, Misdemeanor, Civil, Eviction, Small Claims, Probate.*
www.mncourts.gov/district/5/
General Information: Probate is a separate index at this same address. No adoption, juvenile, sex offender or sealed records released. Fee to fax back- $25.00 per doc up to 25 pgs. Court makes copy: $8.00 per doc. Certification fee: $14.00 per doc. Payee: Court Administrator. Personal checks and credit cards accepted. Prepayment required.
Civil Name Search: Access: Fax, mail, in person, online. Both court and visitors may perform in person name searches. Search fee: $10.00 per name. Required to search: name, years to search, address. Civil records on computer from 5/89. Probate on microfiche from 1870. Mail turnaround time 2-3 days. Civil PAT goes back to 5/1989. Public terminal allows for a statewide search and is more extensive than online search. **For details about the state's online access to records, see the sections at the front or back of this chapter.**
Criminal Name Search: Access: Fax, mail, in person, online. Visitors must perform in person searches themselves. Search fee: $10.00 per name. Required to search: name, years to search, DOB. Criminal records computerized from 5/89. Probate on microfiche from 1870. Mail turnaround time 2-3 days. Criminal PAT goes back to 5/1989. Public terminal allows for a statewide search and is more extensive than online search. **For details about the state's online access to records, see the sections at the front or back of this chapter.**

Kanabec County

District Court 18 N Vine, #318, Mora, MN 55051-1385; 320-679-6400; fax: 320-679-6411; 8AM-4:30PM (CST). *Felony, Misdemeanor, Civil, Eviction, Small Claims, Probate.* www.mncourts.gov/district/10/
General Information: No adoption, juvenile or sealed records released. Will not fax documents. Court makes copy: $8.00 per doc; exemplification $10.00. Certification fee: $14.00 per doc plus copy fee. Payee: Court Administrator. Personal checks, Visa/MC accepted. Prepayment required.
Civil Name Search: Access: In person, online. Visitors must perform in person searches themselves. Civil records on computer from 1986, prior on books and microfiche. Note: Weekly calendars free at www.mncourts.gov/district/10/?page=1326. Civil PAT goes back to 1986. Public terminal allows for a statewide search and is more extensive than online search. **For details about the state's online access to records, see the sections at the front or back of this chapter.**
Criminal Name Search: Access: In person, online. Visitors must perform in person searches themselves. Required to search: name, years to search; also helpful: DOB. Criminal records computerized from 1986, prior on books and microfiche. Criminal PAT goes back to 1986. Public terminal allows for a statewide search and is more extensive than online search. **For details about the state's online access to records, see the sections at the front or back of this chapter.**

Kandiyohi County

Kandiyohi District Court 505 Becker Ave SW, Willmar, MN 56201; 320-231-6206; fax: 320-231-6276; 8AM-4:30PM (CST). *Felony, Misdemeanor, Civil, Eviction, Small Claims, Probate.*
www.mncourts.gov/district/8/
General Information: No adoption, juvenile, sex offender or sealed records released. Fee to fax back- $25.00 per doc up to 50 pgs. Court makes copy: $8.00 per doc. Certification fee: $14.00 per doc. Payee: Court Administrator. Personal checks accepted. No credit cards accepted. Prepayment required.
Civil Name Search: Access: Mail, in person, online. Both court and visitors may perform in person name searches. Search fee: $5.00 per name. Civil records on computer from 1986, prior on microfilm. Mail turnaround time 48 hours. Civil PAT goes back to 1986. Public terminal allows for a statewide search and is more extensive than online search. **For details about the state's online access to records, see the sections at the front or back of this chapter.**

Criminal Name Search: Access: In person, online. Visitors must perform in person searches themselves. Required to search: name, years to search; DOB helpful. Criminal records computerized from 1986, prior on microfilm. Criminal PAT goes back to 1986. Public terminal allows for a statewide search and is more extensive than online search. **For details about the state's online access to records, see the sections at the front or back of this chapter.**

Kittson County

9th Judicial District Court 410 Fifth St S, #204, Hallock, MN 56728; 218-843-3632; fax: 218-843-3634; 8AM-4:30PM (CST). *Felony, Misdemeanor, Civil, Eviction, Small Claims, Probate.*
www.mncourts.gov/district/9/
General Information: Week ahead court calendars available online. No adoption, juvenile, sex offender or sealed records released. Fee to fax back- $25.00 per doc up to 25 pgs. Court makes copy: $8.00 per doc. Certification fee: $14.00 per doc. Payee: Court Administrator. Personal checks and credit cards accepted. Prepayment required.
Civil Name Search: Access: In person, online. Both court and visitors may perform in person name searches. Search fee: $5.00 per name. Will charge $20.00 per hour for extensive searches. Civil records on computer from 9/90, prior on books and index cards. Note: Visitors may look at judgment docket. Civil PAT goes back to 1990. Public terminal allows for a statewide search and is more extensive than online search. **For details about the state's online access to records, see the sections at the front or back of this chapter.**
Criminal Name Search: Access: In person, online. Visitors must perform in person searches themselves. Required to search: name, years to search, DOB, offense. Criminal records computerized from 9/90, prior on books and index cards. Criminal PAT goes back to 1990. Public terminal allows for a statewide search and is more extensive than online search. **For details about the state's online access to records, see the sections at the front or back of this chapter.**

Koochiching County

9th Judicial District Court Court House, 715 4th St, International Falls, MN 56649; criminal phone: 218-283-1163; civil phone: 218-283-1160; probate phone: 218-283-1160; fax: 218-283-1162; 8AM-4PM (CST). *Felony, Misdemeanor, Civil, Eviction, Small Claims, Probate.*
www.mncourts.gov/district/9/
General Information: Week ahead court calendars available online. Misdemeanor records- 218-283-1164. Probate fax is same as main fax number. No adoption, juvenile, sex offender or sealed records released. Fee to fax back- $25.00 per doc up to 50 pgs. Court makes copy: $8.00 per doc. Certification fee: $14.00 per doc plus copy fee. Payee: Court Administrator. Personal checks and credit cards accepted. Prepayment required. Mail requests: SASE required for civil.
Civil Name Search: Access: Mail, fax, in person, online. Both court and visitors may perform in person name searches. No search fee. Required to search: name, years to search, DOB. Civil records on computer from 8/90, on TCIS cards from 1984, on books from 1906. Note: Search daily court calendar at the website. Civil PAT goes back to 8/1990. Public terminal allows for a statewide search and is more extensive than online search. **For details about the state's online access to records, see the sections at the front or back of this chapter.**
Criminal Name Search: Access: In person, online. Visitors must perform in person searches themselves. Required to search: name, years to search, DOB. Criminal records computerized from 8/90, on TCIS cards from 1984, on books from 1906. Note: Criminal record checks can be done via BCA. Criminal PAT goes back to 8/1990. Public terminal allows for a statewide search and is more extensive than online search. **For details about the state's online access to records, see the sections at the front or back of this chapter.**

Lac qui Parle County

8th Judicial District Court PO Box 36, 600 6th St, Madison, MN 56256; 320-598-3536; fax: 320-598-3915; 8AM-4:30PM (CST). *Felony, Misdemeanor, Civil, Eviction, Small Claims, Probate.*
www.mncourts.gov/district/8/
General Information: No adoption, juvenile, sex offender or sealed records released. Fee to fax back- $25.00 per doc up to 25 pgs. Court makes copy: $8.00 per doc. Certification fee: $14.00 per doc. Payee: Court Administrator. Personal checks accepted. Visa/MC accepted for fine payments only. Prepayment required. Mail requests: SASE required for civil.
Civil Name Search: Access: Fax, phone, mail, in person. Visitors must perform in person searches themselves. No search fee. Civil records on computer from 1988, prior on index cards. Mail turnaround time 2-3 days. Civil PAT goes back to 1988. Public terminal allows for a statewide search and is more extensive than online search. **For details about the state's online access to records, see the sections at the front or back of this chapter.**

Criminal Name Search: Access: In person, online. Visitors must perform in person searches themselves. No search fee. Required to search: name, years to search, DOB; SSN helpful. Criminal records computerized from 1988, prior on index cards. Note: Court may refer criminal searches requests to the sheriff's office, 320-598-3720. Sheriff address is 600 6th St. Criminal PAT goes back to 1988. Public terminal allows for a statewide search and is more extensive than online search. **For details about the state's online access to records, see the sections at the front or back of this chapter.**

Lake County

6th Judicial District Court 601 3rd Ave, Two Harbors, MN 55616; 218-834-8330; probate phone: 218-834-8329; fax: 218-834-8397; 8AM-4:30PM (CST). *Felony, Misdemeanor, Civil, Eviction, Small Claims, Probate.* www.mncourts.gov/district/6/

General Information: Probate fax is same as main fax number. No adoption, juvenile, sex offender or sealed records released. Fee to fax back-$25.00 per doc up to 25 pgs. Court makes copy: $8.00 per doc. Certification fee: $14.00 per doc. Payee: Court Administrator. Personal checks and credit cards accepted. Prepayment required. Mail requests: SASE required for civil.

Civil Name Search: Access: Fax, mail, in person, online. Both court and visitors may perform in person name searches. Search fee: $5.00 per name. Civil records on computer back to 1991, prior on imaging or microfilm. Mail turnaround time 7-10 days. Civil PAT goes back to 1991. Public terminal allows for a statewide search and is more extensive than online search. **For details about the state's online access to records, see the sections at the front or back of this chapter.**

Criminal Name Search: Access: In person, online. Visitors must perform in person searches themselves. Required to search: name, years to search, DOB. Criminal records computerized from 1991, imaging or microfilm. Criminal PAT goes back to 1991. Public terminal allows for a statewide search and is more extensive than online search. **For details about the state's online access to records, see the sections at the front or back of this chapter.**

Lake of the Woods County

9th Judicial District Court 206 8th Ave SE, #250, Baudette, MN 56623; 218-634-1451; fax: 218-634-9444; 7:30AM-4PM (CST). *Felony, Misdemeanor, Civil, Eviction, Small Claims, Probate.* www.mncourts.gov/district/9/

General Information: Week ahead court calendars available online. No adoption, juvenile, sex offender or sealed records released. Will fax documents for $25.00 per doc. Court makes copy: $8.00 per doc. Certification fee: $14.00 per doc. Payee: Court Administrator. Personal checks, Visa/MC accepted. Prepayment required.

Civil Name Search: Access: Fax, mail, in person, online. Both court and visitors may perform in person name searches. Search fee: $5.00 per name. Civil records on computer back to 1990; on microfilm to 1923. Mail turnaround time 2 days. Civil PAT goes back to 1990. Public terminal allows for a statewide search and is more extensive than online search. **For details about the state's online access to records, see the sections at the front or back of this chapter.**

Criminal Name Search: Access: In person, online. Visitors must perform in person searches themselves. Required to search: name, years to search, DOB. Criminal records computerized from 1990; on microfilm back to 1923. Note: Criminal searches referred to BCA. Criminal PAT goes back to 1990. Public terminal allows for a statewide search and is more extensive than online search. **For details about the state's online access to records, see the sections at the front or back of this chapter.**

Le Sueur County

1st Judicial District Court 88 S Park Ave, Le Center, MN 56057; 507-357-8252; fax: 507-357-6433; 8AM-4:30PM (CST). *Felony, Misdemeanor, Civil, Eviction, Small Claims, Probate.* www.mncourts.gov/district/1/

General Information: No adoption, juvenile, sex offender or sealed records released. Will fax documents. Court makes copy: $8.00 per doc. Certification fee: $14.00 per doc includes copies. Payee: Court Administrator. Personal checks, Visa/MC accepted. Prepayment required.

Civil Name Search: Access: In person, online. Both court and visitors may perform in person name searches. Required to search: name. Civil records on computer from 1994, prior on books. Civil PAT goes back to 1992. Public terminal allows for a statewide search and is more extensive than online search. **For details about the state's online access to records, see the sections at the front or back of this chapter.**

Criminal Name Search: Access: In person, online. Visitors must perform in person searches themselves. Required to search: name, DOB. Criminal records computerized from 1992, prior on books. Criminal PAT goes back to 1992. Public terminal allows for a statewide search and is more extensive than online search. **For details about the state's online access to records, see the sections at the front or back of this chapter.**

Lincoln County

5th Judicial District Court PO Box 15, 319 N Rebecca St, Ivanhoe, MN 56142-0015; 507-694-1355 or 507-694-1505; probate phone: 507-694-1355; fax: 507-694-1717; 8AM-4:30PM (CST). *Felony, Misdemeanor, Civil, Eviction, Small Claims, Probate, Family.* www.mncourts.gov/district/5/

General Information: Probate fax is same as main fax number. No adoption, juvenile, sex offender or sealed records released. Fee to fax back-$25.00 per doc up to 50 pgs. Court makes copy: $8.00 per doc. Certification fee: $14.00 per doc plus copy fee. Payee: Court Administrator. Personal checks, Visa/MC accepted. Prepayment required. Mail requests: SASE required for civil.

Civil Name Search: Access: Mail, in person, online. Both court and visitors may perform in person name searches. Search fee: $5.00 per name. Public terminal is available to access cases from 1/1989, on TCIS manual index cards from 12/82, on books from late 1800. Civil PAT goes back to 1989. Public terminal allows for a statewide search and is more extensive than online search. **For details about the state's online access to records, see the sections at the front or back of this chapter.**

Criminal Name Search: Access: In person, online. Both court and visitors may perform in person name searches. No search fee. Required to search: name, years to search, DOB. Criminal records computerized from 1989, on TCIS from 12/82, on books from late 1800. Note: All written requests for criminal records are referred to statewide BCA; call for form, 650-793-2420, but if you have a case number this court will pull the public file for you for inspection. Criminal PAT goes back to 1989. Public terminal allows for a statewide search and is more extensive than online search. **For details about the state's online access to records, see the sections at the front or back of this chapter.**

Lyon County

5th Judicial District Court 607 W Main St, Marshall, MN 56258; 507-537-6734; fax: 507-537-6150; 8:30AM-4:30PM (CST). *Felony, Misdemeanor, Civil, Eviction, Small Claims, Probate.* www.mncourts.gov/district/5/

General Information: No adoption, juvenile, sex offender or sealed records released. Will fax documents for $25.00 per doc up to 25 pgs. Court makes copy: $8.00 per doc. Certification fee: $14.00 per doc. Payee: Court Administrator. Personal checks and credit cards accepted. Prepayment required. Mail requests: SASE required for civil.

Civil Name Search: Access: Mail, fax, in person, online. Both court and visitors may perform in person name searches. Search fee: $10.00. Civil records on computer from 1987, prior on index cards. Mail turnaround time 1 week Civil PAT goes back to 1997. Public terminal allows for a statewide search and is more extensive than online search. **For details about the state's online access to records, see the sections at the front or back of this chapter.**

Criminal Name Search: Access: In person, online. Visitors must perform in person searches themselves. Criminal records go back to 1987. Note: The court asks requests be sent to the state Bureau of Criminal Apprehension. Criminal PAT goes back to 1997. Public terminal allows for a statewide search and is more extensive than online search. **For details about the state's online access to records, see the sections at the front or back of this chapter.**

Mahnomen County

9th Judicial District Court PO Box 459, 311 N Main, Mahnomen, MN 56557; 218-935-2251; fax: 218-935-2851; 8AM-4:30PM (CST). *Felony, Misdemeanor, Civil, Eviction, Small Claims, Probate.* www.mncourts.gov/district/9/

General Information: Week ahead court calendars available online. No adoption, juvenile, sex offender or sealed records released. Will not fax documents. Court makes copy: $8.00 per doc. Certification fee: $14.00 per doc plus copy fee. Payee: Court Administrator. Personal checks, Visa/MC accepted. Prepayment required.

Civil Name Search: Access: In person, online. Both court and visitors may perform in person name searches. Civil records on computer from 8/90, prior on books from 1907. Civil PAT goes back to 1990. Public terminal allows for a statewide search and is more extensive than online search. **For details about the state's online access to records, see the sections at the front or back of this chapter.**

Criminal Name Search: Access: In person, online. Both court and visitors may perform in person name searches. Criminal records computerized from 8/90, prior on books from 1907. Criminal PAT goes back to 1990. Public terminal allows for a statewide search and is more extensive than online search. **For details about the state's online access to records, see the sections at the front or back of this chapter.**

Marshall County

9th Judicial District Court Court Administrator - Records, 208 E Colvin, Ste 18, Warren, MN 56762; 218-745-4921; fax: 218-745-4343; 8AM-4:30PM (CST). *Felony, Misdemeanor, Civil, Eviction, Small Claims, Probate.* www.mncourts.gov/district/9/

General Information: Week ahead court calendars available online. No adoption, juvenile, sex offender or sealed records released. Will fax documents for fee. Court makes copy: $8.00 per doc. Certification fee: $14.00 per doc. Payee: Court Administrator. Personal checks and credit cards accepted. Prepayment required. Mail requests: SASE required.

Civil Name Search: Access: Mail, in person, online. Both court and visitors may perform in person name searches. Search fee: $5.00 per name. Required to search: name, years to search; also helpful: address. Civil records on computer from 5/90, on cards from 1982, on books from 1885. Mail turnaround time same day. Civil PAT goes back to 1990. Public terminal allows for a statewide search and is more extensive than online search. **For details about the state's online access to records, see the sections at the front or back of this chapter.**

Criminal Name Search: Access: Mail, in person, online. Visitors must perform in person searches themselves. Search fee: $5.00 per name. Required to search: name, years to search; also helpful: address, DOB. Criminal records computerized from 5/90, on cards from 1982, on books from 1885. Note: Most name searchers with written requests are asked to contact the BCA State repository. Mail turnaround time same day. Criminal PAT goes back to 1990. Public terminal allows for a statewide search and is more extensive than online search. **For details about the state's online access to records, see the sections at the front or back of this chapter.**

Martin County

5th Judicial District Court 201 Lake Ave, Rm 304, Martin County Court Admin., Fairmont, MN 56031; 507-238-3205; fax: 507-238-1913; 8AM-5PM (CST). *Felony, Misdemeanor, Civil, Eviction, Small Claims, Probate.* www.mncourts.gov/district/5/

General Information: Probate fax is same as main fax number. No adoption, most juvenile, or sealed records released. Will fax civil search results or specific case files for $25.00 per fax if prepaid. Court makes copy: $8.00 per doc. Certification fee: $14.00 per doc. Payee: Court Administrator. Personal checks and credit cards accepted. Prepayment required. Mail requests: SASE required for civil.

Civil Name Search: Access: Mail, in person, online. Both court and visitors may perform in person name searches. Search fee: $10.00 per name. Required to search: name, years to search; also helpful: address. Civil records on computer from 7/89, on cards from 1986, on books from 1800s. Mail turnaround time 2 weeks. Civil PAT goes back to 7/1989. Public terminal allows for a statewide search and is more extensive than online search. **For details about the state's online access to records, see the sections at the front or back of this chapter.**

Criminal Name Search: Access: In person, online. Visitors must perform in person searches themselves. Required to search: name, years to search, DOB; also helpful: address, SSN. Criminal records computerized from 7/89, on cards from 1986, on books from 1800s. Note: Court suggests sending requests to State Bureau of Criminal Apprehension. Criminal PAT goes back to 7/1989. Public terminal allows for a statewide search and is more extensive than online search. **For details about the state's online access to records, see the sections at the front or back of this chapter.**

McLeod County

1st Judicial District Court 830 E 11th, Glencoe, MN 55336; 320-864-1281; fax: 320-864-5905; 8AM-4:30PM (CST). *Felony, Misdemeanor, Civil, Eviction, Small Claims, Probate.* www.co.mcleod.mn.us/mcleodco.cfm?pageID=14&sub=yes

General Information: No adoption, juvenile, sex offender or sealed records released. Will not fax documents. Court makes copy: $8.00 per doc.The public is able to print copies from the public terminal at no cost. A separate copy machine is not available to the public. Certification fee: $14.00 per doc plus copy fee. Payee: Court Administrator. Personal checks, Visa/MC accepted. Prepayment required. Mail requests: SASE required for civil.

Civil Name Search: Access: Mail, in person, online. Both court and visitors may perform in person name searches. No search fee. Civil records on computer from 4/92, prior on books. Mail turnaround time 3-5 days. Civil PAT goes back to 1991. Public terminal allows for a statewide search and is more extensive than online search. **For details about the state's online access to records, see the sections at the front or back of this chapter.**

Criminal Name Search: Access: In person, online. Visitors must perform in person searches themselves. Criminal records computerized from 4/92, prior on books. Criminal PAT goes back to 1991. Public terminal allows for a statewide search and is more extensive than online

search. **For details about the state's online access to records, see the sections at the front or back of this chapter.**

Meeker County

8th Judicial District Court 325 N Sibley, Litchfield, MN 55355; 320-693-5230; fax: 320-693-5254; 8AM-4:30PM M-Th; 8AM-2PM F (CST). *Felony, Misdemeanor, Civil, Eviction, Small Claims, Probate.* www.mncourts.gov/district/8/

General Information: No adoption, juvenile, sex offender or sealed records released. Fee to fax back- $25.00 per doc up to 25 pgs. Court makes copy: $8.00 per doc. Certification fee: $14.00 per doc plus copy fee. Payee: Court Administrator. Personal checks, Visa/MC accepted. Prepayment required. Mail requests: SASE required for civil.

Civil Name Search: Access: Mail, in person, online. Both court and visitors may perform in person name searches. Search fee: $5.00 per name. Required to search: name; also helpful: years to search, address. Civil records on computer from 11/88, prior on index cards. Mail turnaround time 2-3 days. Civil PAT goes back to 11/1988. Public terminal allows for a statewide search and is more extensive than online search. **For details about the state's online access to records, see the sections at the front or back of this chapter.**

Criminal Name Search: Access: In person, online. Visitors must perform in person searches themselves. Required to search: name; also helpful: years to search, DOB. Criminal records computerized from 11/88, prior on index cards back to 1880s. Criminal PAT goes back to 11/1988. Public terminal allows for a statewide search and is more extensive than online search. **For details about the state's online access to records, see the sections at the front or back of this chapter.**

Mille Lacs County

7th Judicial District Court Mille Lacs County Justice Center, 225 6th Ave SE, Milaca, MN 56353; 320-983-8313; fax: 320-983-8384; 8AM-4:30PM (CST). *Felony, Misdemeanor, Civil, Eviction, Small Claims, Probate.* www.mncourts.gov/district/7/

General Information: No adoption, juvenile, sex offender or sealed records released. There is a $8.00 copy fee per doc faxed. Court makes copy: $8.00 per doc. Self serve copy: available. Certification fee: $14.00 per doc plus copy fee; exemplification if $16.00. Payee: District Court. Personal checks, Visa/MC accepted. Prepayment required. Mail requests: SASE required for civil.

Civil Name Search: Access: Mail, in person, online. Both court and visitors may perform in person name searches. Search fee: $5.00. Civil records on computer from 4/86, cards from 1981, books prior. Mail turnaround time 2 weeks. Civil PAT goes back to 1986. Public terminal allows for a statewide search and is more extensive than online search. **For details about the state's online access to records, see the sections at the front or back of this chapter.**

Criminal Name Search: Access: In person, online. Visitors must perform in person searches themselves. Criminal records computerized from 4/86, cards from 1981, books prior. Criminal PAT goes back to 1986. Public terminal allows for a statewide search and is more extensive than online search. **For details about the state's online access to records, see the sections at the front or back of this chapter.**

Mille Lacs Band of Ojibwe Tribal Court 43408 Oodena Dr, Onamia, MN 56359; 320-532-7404; fax: 320-532-3153;*Criminal, Civil, Juvenile, Traffic, Estate, Eviction.* www.millelacsband.com/Page_TribalCourt.aspx

Morrison County

7th Judicial District Court 213 SE 1st Ave, Little Falls, MN 56345; 320-632-0327; probate phone: 320-632-0327; fax: 320-632-0340; 8AM-4:30PM (CST). *Felony, Misdemeanor, Civil, Eviction, Small Claims, Probate.* www.mncourts.gov/district/7/

General Information: No adoption, juvenile, sex offender or sealed records released. Fee to fax back- $25.00 per doc up to 25 pgs. Court makes copy: $8.00 per doc. Certification fee: $14.00 per doc plus copy fee. Payee: Court Administrator. Personal checks and credit cards accepted. Prepayment required. Mail requests: SASE required for civil.

Civil Name Search: Access: Fax, mail, in person, online. Both court and visitors may perform in person name searches. No search fee. Civil records on computer from 5/86, prior on cards and books. Civil PAT goes back to 5/1986. Public terminal allows for a statewide search and is more extensive than online search. **For details about the state's online access to records, see the sections at the front or back of this chapter.**

Criminal Name Search: Access: In person, online. Visitors must perform in person searches themselves. Required to search: name, years to search, DOB. Criminal records computerized from 5/86, prior on cards and books. Criminal PAT goes back to 5/1986. Public terminal allows for a statewide search and is more extensive than online search. **For details**

about the state's online access to records, see the sections at the front or back of this chapter.

Mower County

Mower County District Court 201 2nd Ave NE, Austin, MN 55912; 507-437-9465; fax: 507-434-2702; 8AM-4:30PM M, T, TH, F; 12:30PM-4:30PM W (CST). *Felony, Misdemeanor, Civil, Eviction, Small Claims, Probate, Family.* www.mncourts.gov/district/3/

General Information: No adoption, juvenile, paternity or sealed records released. Fee to fax back- $25.00 per doc up to 50 pgs. Court makes copy: $8.00 per doc. Certification fee: $14.00 per doc. Payee: Court Administrator. Personal checks and credit cards accepted. Prepayment required. Mail requests: SASE required for civil.

Civil Name Search: Access: Mail, in person, online. Both court and visitors may perform in person name searches. Search fee: $5.00. Civil records on computer from 1989. Civil PAT goes back to 1989. Public terminal allows for a statewide search and is more extensive than online search. **For details about the state's online access to records, see the sections at the front or back of this chapter.**

Criminal Name Search: Access: In person, online. Visitors must perform in person searches themselves. Required to search: name, years to search, DOB. Criminal records computerized from 1989. Criminal PAT goes back to 1989. Public terminal allows for a statewide search and is more extensive than online search. **For details about the state's online access to records, see the sections at the front or back of this chapter.**

Murray County

5th Judicial District Court PO Box 57, Slayton, MN 56172-0057; 507-836-1120; fax: 507-836-6019; 8:30AM-4:30PM (CST). *Felony, Misdemeanor, Civil, Eviction, Small Claims, Probate.* www.mncourts.gov/district/5/

General Information: No adoption, juvenile, or sealed records released. Fee to fax back- $25.00 per doc up to 25 pgs. Court makes copy: $8.00 per doc. Certification fee: $14.00 per doc plus copy fee. Payee: Court Administrator. Personal checks, Visa/MC accepted. Prepayment required.

Civil Name Search: Access: Fax, mail, in person, online. Both court and visitors may perform in person name searches. Search fee: $10.00 per name. Civil records on computer from 7/88. Mail turnaround time 7 days Civil PAT available. Public terminal allows for a statewide search and is more extensive than online search. **For details about the state's online access to records, see the sections at the front or back of this chapter.**

Criminal Name Search: Access: In person, online. Visitors must perform in person searches themselves. Required to search: name, years to search; SSN helpful. Criminal records computerized from 7/88. Note: The court suggests sending requests to Bureau of Criminal Apprehension. Criminal PAT available. Public terminal allows for a statewide search and is more extensive than online search. **For details about the state's online access to records, see the sections at the front or back of this chapter.**

Nicollet County

5th Judicial District Court PO Box 496, St Peter, MN 56082; 507-931-6800; criminal phone: 507-934-0388; civil phone: 507-934-0386; probate phone: 507-934-0380; fax: 507-931-4278; 8AM-5PM (CST). *Felony, Misdemeanor, Civil, Eviction, Small Claims, Probate.* www.mncourts.gov/district/5/

General Information: Fine Inquiry telephone is 507-934-7503. The court in North Mankato is closed. All records from that District Court branch are located here. No adoption, juvenile, sex offender or sealed records released. Will not fax documents. Court makes copy: $8.00 per doc. Certification fee: $14.00 per doc includes copies. Payee: Court Administrator. Personal checks, Visa/MC accepted. Prepayment required. Mail requests: SASE required for civil.

Civil Name Search: Access: Mail, in person, online. Both court and visitors may perform in person name searches. Search fee: $5.00 per name. Civil records on computer from 9/25/88, on books from 1890. The civil records prior to 9/25/88 for the entire county are located here. Mail turnaround time 2 weeks. Civil PAT goes back to 1988. Public terminal allows for a statewide search and is more extensive than online search. **For details about the state's online access to records, see the sections at the front or back of this chapter.**

Criminal Name Search: Access: In person, online. Visitors must perform in person searches themselves. Required to search: name, years to search, DOB. Criminal records on computer since 9/25/88. Prior records for this court only are located here on books and cards. Note: The court will not do criminal searches. Criminal PAT goes back to 1988. Public terminal allows for a statewide search and is more extensive than online search. **For details about the state's online access to records, see the sections at the front or back of this chapter.**

Nobles County

5th Judicial District Court PO Box 547, 1530 Airport Rd, Worthington, MN 56187; 507-372-8263; fax: 507-372-4994; 8AM-4:30PM (CST). *Felony, Misdemeanor, Civil, Eviction, Small Claims, Probate.* www.mncourts.gov/district/5/

General Information: No adoption, juvenile, sex offender or sealed records released. Will not fax documents. Court makes copy: $8.00 per doc. Self serve copy: No self serve criminal copier; Civil self serve- $1.00 each. Certification fee: $14.00 per doc plus copy fee. Payee: Court Administrator. Personal checks accepted. Credit cards accepted in person only. Prepayment required. Mail requests: SASE required for civil.

Civil Name Search: Access: Mail, in person, online. Both court and visitors may perform in person name searches. Search fee: $5.00 per name. Civil records on computer from 7/88, on books and index cards prior. Mail turnaround time 5 days Civil PAT goes back to 7/1988. Public terminal allows for a statewide search and is more extensive than online search. **For details about the state's online access to records, see the sections at the front or back of this chapter.**

Criminal Name Search: Access: In person, online. Visitors must perform in person searches themselves. Required to search: name, years to search; SSN helpful. Criminal records computerized from 7/88, on books and index cards prior. Note: The court suggests sending requests to the state Bureau of Criminal Apprehension. Criminal PAT goes back to 7/1988. Public terminal allows for a statewide search and is more extensive than online search. **For details about the state's online access to records, see the sections at the front or back of this chapter.**

Norman County

9th Judicial District Court 16 3rd Ave E, Courthouse, Ada, MN 56510-0146; 218-784-5458; fax: 218-784-3110; 8AM-4:30PM (CST). *Felony, Misdemeanor, Civil, Eviction, Small Claims, Probate.* www.mncourts.gov/district/9/

General Information: Week ahead court calendars available online. Probate fax is same as main fax number. No adoption, juvenile, sex offender or sealed records released. Fee to fax back- $25.00 per doc up to 25 pgs. Court makes copy: $8.00 per doc. Certification fee: $14.00 per doc includes copies. Payee: Court Administrator. Business checks accepted. Visa/MC accepted. Prepayment required.

Civil Name Search: Access: Mail, in person, online. Both court and visitors may perform in person name searches. Search fee: $5.00 per name. Civil records on computer since 5/1990, prior on index cards. Civil PAT goes back to 1990. Public terminal allows for a statewide search and is more extensive than online search. **For details about the state's online access to records, see the sections at the front or back of this chapter.**

Criminal Name Search: Access: In person, online. Visitors must perform in person searches themselves. Required to search: name, years to search, DOB. Criminal records on computer since 5/90, prior on index cards. Note: Criminal searches directed to BCA- 1-800-832-6446, fax 218-935-9999. Criminal PAT goes back to 1990. Public terminal allows for a statewide search and is more extensive than online search. **For details about the state's online access to records, see the sections at the front or back of this chapter.**

Olmsted County

Olmsted County District Court 151 4th St SE, Rochester, MN 55904; criminal phone: 507-206-2496; civil phone: 507-206-2499; probate phone: 507-206-2489; fax: 507-285-8996; 9AM-4:30PM (CST). *Felony, Misdemeanor, Civil, Eviction, Small Claims, Probate.* www.mncourts.gov/district/3/?page=222

General Information: No adoption, juvenile, sex offender or sealed records released. Fee to fax back- $25.00 per doc up to 25 pgs. Court makes copy: $8.00 per doc. Certification fee: $14.00 per doc plus copy fee. Payee: Court Administrator. Personal checks accepted. Visa/MC/Discover accepted. Prepayment required.

Civil Name Search: Access: In person, online. Both court and visitors may perform in person name searches. No search fee. Civil records on computer from mid-1989, prior to 1856 on index cards. Note: Probate files vary greatly, but most contain date and place of death, list of heirs, copy of will (if one was written), inventory of personal property, and final disposition of the estate. Civil PAT goes back to 1983. Public terminal allows for a statewide search and is more extensive than online search. www.mncourts.gov/default.aspx?page=1927**For details about the state's online access to records, see the sections at the front or back of this chapter.**

Criminal Name Search: Access: In person, online. Visitors must perform in person searches themselves. Required to search: name, DOB. Criminal records computerized from mid-1989, prior to 1856 on index cards. Note: Access the daily court calendar at the website. Criminal PAT goes back to 1983. Public terminal allows for a statewide search and is more extensive than online search. **For details about the state's online access to records, see the sections at the front or back of this chapter.**

Otter Tail County

Otter Tail County District Court 121 W Junius Ave #310, Fergus Falls, MN 56538-0417; 218-998-8420; fax: 218-998-8438; 8AM-4:30PM (CST). *Felony, Misdemeanor, Civil, Eviction, Small Claims, Probate, Traffic.* www.mncourts.gov/district/7/

General Information: No adoption, certain juvenile or sealed records released. Fee to fax back- $25.00 per doc up to 50 pgs. Court makes copy: $8.00 per doc. Certification fee: $14.00 per doc. Payee: Court Administrator. Personal checks and credit cards accepted. Prepayment required. Mail requests: SASE required for civil.

Civil Name Search: Access: Mail, in person, online. Both court and visitors may perform in person name searches. Search fee: $5.00 per name. Required to search: name; also helpful: years to search. Civil records on computer from 1987, prior on index books. Civil PAT goes back to 10/1987. Public terminal allows for a statewide search and is more extensive than online search. **For details about the state's online access to records, see the sections at the front or back of this chapter.**

Criminal Name Search: Access: In person, online. Visitors must perform in person searches themselves. Required to search: name, years to search, DOB; also helpful: address. Criminal records computerized from 1987, prior on index books. Criminal PAT goes back to 10/1987. Public terminal allows for a statewide search and is more extensive than online search. **For details about the state's online access to records, see the sections at the front or back of this chapter.**

Pennington County

9th Judicial District Court Court Admin Office, 101 N Main, Thief River Falls, MN 56701; 218-683-7023; fax: 218-681-0907; 8AM-4:30PM (CST). *Felony, Misdemeanor, Civil, Family, Eviction, Small Claims, Probate.* www.mncourts.gov/district/9/

General Information: Week ahead court calendars available online. No adoption, juvenile, or sealed records released. Fee to fax back- $25.00 per doc up to 25 pgs. Court makes copy: $8.00 per doc. Self serve copy: same. Certification fee: $14.00 per doc copy fee. Payee: Court Administrator. Personal checks and credit cards accepted. Prepayment required.

Civil Name Search: Access: In person, online. Both court and visitors may perform in person name searches. Search fee: $5.00 per name. Civil records on computer back to 1990, prior on TCIS cards and books to 1911. Civil PAT goes back to 1990. Public terminal allows for a statewide search and is more extensive than online search. **For details about the state's online access to records, see the sections at the front or back of this chapter.**

Criminal Name Search: Access: In person, online. Visitors must perform in person searches themselves. Required to search: name, years to search, DOB. Criminal records computerized from 1990, prior on TCIS cards and books to 1911. Criminal PAT goes back to 1990. Public terminal allows for a statewide search and is more extensive than online search. **For details about the state's online access to records, see the sections at the front or back of this chapter.**

Pine County

10th Judicial District Court 635 Northridge Dr NW, #320, Pine City, MN 55063; 320-591-1500; fax: 320-591-1524; 8AM-4:30PM (CST). *Felony, Misdemeanor, Civil, Eviction, Small Claims, Probate.* www.mncourts.gov/district/10/

General Information: No adoption, juvenile, or sealed records released. Will fax documents. Court makes copy: $8.00 per doc; exemplification $12.00. Certification fee: $14.00 per doc. Payee: Court Administrator. Personal checks, Visa/MC accepted. Prepayment required.

Civil Name Search: Access: Mail, In person, online. Visitors must perform in person searches themselves. Search fee: No civil searches, but judgment search is $5.00 per name. Civil records on computer from 2/85. Note: Weekly calendars free at www.mncourts.gov/district/10/?page=1326. Civil PAT goes back to 2/1985. Public terminal allows for a statewide search and is more extensive than online search. **For details about the state's online access to records, see the sections at the front or back of this chapter.**

Criminal Name Search: Access: In person, online. Visitors must perform in person searches themselves. Criminal records computerized from 2/85. Criminal PAT goes back to 2/1985. Public terminal allows for a statewide search and is more extensive than online search. **For details about the state's online access to records, see the sections at the front or back of this chapter.**

Pipestone County

5th Judicial District Court PO Box 337, 416 S Hiawatha Ave, Pipestone, MN 56164; 507-825-6730; fax: 507-825-6733; 8:30AM-4:30PM (CST). *Felony, Misdemeanor, Civil, Eviction, Small Claims, Probate.* www.mncourts.gov/district/5/

General Information: No adoption, juvenile, sex offender victims or sealed records released. Fee to fax back- $25.00 per doc up to 25 pgs. Court

makes copy: $8.00 per doc. Certification fee: $14.00 per doc plus copy fee. Payee: Court Administrator. Personal checks, Visa/MC accepted. Prepayment required. Mail requests: SASE required for civil.

Civil Name Search: Access: Mail, in person, online. Both court and visitors may perform in person name searches. Search fee: $5.00 per name. Civil records on computer from 1989, prior on books. Mail turnaround time 7 days Civil PAT goes back to 1989. Public terminal allows for a statewide search and is more extensive than online search. Search civil, family and probate records and calendars at . This search is not an official record search, per MN. **For details about the state's online access to records, see the sections at the front or back of this chapter.**

Criminal Name Search: Access: In person, online. Visitors must perform in person searches themselves. Criminal records computerized from 1989, prior on books. Note: Court suggests sending requests to State Bureau of Criminal Apprehension. Criminal PAT goes back to 1989. Public terminal allows for a statewide search and is more extensive than online search. **For details about the state's online access to records, see the sections at the front or back of this chapter.**

Polk County

9th Judicial District Court Court Administrator, 816 Marin Ave, #210, Crookston, MN 56716; 218-281-2332; fax: 218-281-2204; 8AM-4:30PM (CST). *Felony, Misdemeanor, Civil, Eviction, Small Claims, Probate.* www.mncourts.gov/district/9/

General Information: Week ahead court calendars available online. No adoption, non-felony under age 16 juvenile or sealed records released. Fee to fax back- $25.00 per doc up to 25 pgs. Court makes copy: $8.00 per doc. Certification fee: $14.00 per doc plus copy fee. Payee: Court Administrator. Personal checks accepted. Visa/MC/Discover accepted. Prepayment required. Mail requests: SASE required.

Civil Name Search: Access: Mail, in person, online. Visitors must perform in person searches themselves. Search fee: $5.00 per name. Civil records on computer from 1990, prior on index cards or books. Note: Child protection and child service cases are available since 7/1/2002. Mail turnaround time 3-5 days. Civil PAT goes back to 1990. Public terminal allows for a statewide search and is more extensive than online search. **For details about the state's online access to records, see the sections at the front or back of this chapter.**

Criminal Name Search: Access: Mail, in person, online. Visitors must perform in person searches themselves. Search fee: $5.00 per name. Required to search: name, years to search, DOB. Criminal records computerized from 1990, prior on index cards or books. Mail turnaround time 3-5 days. Criminal PAT goes back to 1990. Public terminal allows for a statewide search and is more extensive than online search. **For details about the state's online access to records, see the sections at the front or back of this chapter.**

Pope County

8th Judicial District Court 130 E Minnesota Ave, Glenwood, MN 56334; 320-634-5222; fax: 320-634-5527; 8AM-4:30PM (till 2PM on Fri) (CST). *Felony, Misdemeanor, Civil, Eviction, Small Claims, Probate.* www.mncourts.gov/district/8/

General Information: No adoption, juvenile, sex offender or sealed records released. Will fax documents for $25.00. Court makes copy: $8.00 per doc. Certification fee: $14.00 per doc. Payee: Court Administrator. Personal checks and credit cards accepted. Prepayment required. Mail requests: SASE required for civil.

Civil Name Search: Access: Mail, in person, online. Both court and visitors may perform in person name searches. Search fee: $5.00 per name. Civil records on computer from 1988, prior on TCIS cards ad books. Mail turnaround time 1 week Civil PAT goes back to 1990. Public terminal allows for a statewide search and is more extensive than online search. **For details about the state's online access to records, see the sections at the front or back of this chapter.**

Criminal Name Search: Access: In person, online. Visitors must perform in person searches themselves. Criminal records computerized from 1988, prior on TCIS cards ad books. Criminal PAT goes back to 1990. Public terminal allows for a statewide search and is more extensive than online search. **For details about the state's online access to records, see the sections at the front or back of this chapter.**

Ramsey County

2nd Judicial District Court 1700 Ramsey County Courthouse, 15 Kellogg Blvd West, St Paul, MN 55102; criminal phone: 651-266-8180; civil phone: 651-266-8253; criminal fax: 651-266-8172; civil fax: 8AM-4:30PM; 8AM-4:30PM (CST). *Felony, Misdemeanor, Civil, Probate.* www.mncourts.gov/district/2/

General Information: No adoption, juvenile, sex offender or sealed records released. Fee to fax back- $25.00 per doc up to 25 pgs. Court makes copy: $8.00 per doc. Certification fee: $14.00 per doc. Payee: Court

Administrator. Personal checks, Visa/MC accepted. Prepayment required. Mail requests: SASE required for civil.

Civil Name Search: Access: Mail, in person, online. Both court and visitors may perform in person name searches. Search fee: $10.00 per name. Civil records on computer from 5/88, prior on books. Mail turnaround time 1-2 days. Civil PAT goes back to 1993. Public terminal allows for a statewide search and is more extensive than online search. **For details about the state's online access to records, see the sections at the front or back of this chapter.**

Criminal Name Search: Access: In person, online. Visitors must perform in person searches themselves. Required to search: name, years to search, DOB. Felony records on computer go back to 1987; misdemeanors go back to 1985, prior on books to 1953 felonies only. Criminal PAT goes back to 1986. Public terminal allows for a statewide search and is more extensive than online search. **For details about the state's online access to records, see the sections at the front or back of this chapter.**

2nd Judicial District Court - Maplewood Area 2050 White Bear Ave, Maplewood, MN 55109; 651-266-1999; fax: 651-266-1978; 8AM-4:30PM (CST). *Misdemeanor.* www.mncourts.gov/district/2/
General Information: This court holds the records for the closed New Brighton Court. No adoption, juvenile, sex offender victim, sealed or medical records released. Will not fax documents. Court makes copy: $8.00 per doc. Certification fee: $14.00 per doc. Payee: Ramsey County District Court. Personal checks accepted. Credit cards accepted but not over phone. Prepayment required.
Criminal Name Search: Access: In person, online. Visitors must perform in person searches themselves. Required to search: name; also helpful: address, DOB, offense, date of offense. Criminal records computerized from 11/90. Public use terminal has crim records back to 11/1990. Terminal results include date of offense. Public terminal allows for a statewide search. **For details about the state's online access to records, see the sections at the front or back of this chapter.**

Shakopee Mdewakanton Sioux Community Tribal Court 335 Atrium Office Bldg, 1295 Bandana Blvd, St Paul, MN 55108; 651-357-1496; fax: 651-644-5904;*Criminal, Civil, Juvenile, Traffic, Estate, Eviction.*

Red Lake County

9th Judicial District Court PO Box 339, 124 Langevin Ave, Red Lake Falls, MN 56750; 218-253-4281; fax: 218-253-4287; 8AM-4:30PM (CST). *Felony, Misdemeanor, Civil, Eviction, Small Claims, Probate.* www.mncourts.gov/district/9/
General Information: Week ahead court calendars available online. Probate fax is same as main fax number. No adoption, juvenile, sex offender or sealed records released. Will fax documents for $5.00 per doc fee. Court makes copy: $8.00 per doc. Certification fee: $14.00 per doc includes search fee. Payee: Court Administrator. Personal checks and credit cards accepted. Prepayment required. Mail requests: SASE required for civil.
Civil Name Search: Access: Mail, in person, online. Both court and visitors may perform in person name searches. Search fee: $5.00 per name. Civil records on computer and microfiche from 1990, on books from 1897. Mail turnaround time 2-5 days. Civil PAT goes back to 1990. Public terminal allows for a statewide search and is more extensive than online search. **For details about the state's online access to records, see the sections at the front or back of this chapter.**
Criminal Name Search: Access: In person, online. Visitors must perform in person searches themselves. Required to search: name, years to search, DOB. Criminal records on computer and microfiche from 1990, on books from 1897. Note: Court suggest you perform in criminal search through BCA. Criminal PAT goes back to 1990. Public terminal allows for a statewide search and is more extensive than online search. **For details about the state's online access to records, see the sections at the front or back of this chapter.**

Redwood County

5th Judicial District Court PO Box 130, 3rd & Jefferson Strs, Redwood Falls, MN 56283; 507-637-4020; probate phone: 507-637-4018; fax: 507-637-4021; 8AM-4:30PM (CST). *Felony, Misdemeanor, Civil, Eviction, Small Claims, Probate.* www.mncourts.gov/district/5/
General Information: Probate fax is same as main fax number. No adoption, juvenile, sex offender or sealed records released. Fee to fax back- $25.00 per doc up to 25 pgs. Court makes copy: $8.00 per doc. Certification fee: $14.00 per doc plus copy fee. Payee: Court Administrator. Personal checks and credit cards accepted. Prepayment required.
Civil Name Search: Access: In person, online. Both court and visitors may perform in person name searches. No search fee. Civil records on computer from 11/88, prior on card and books. Civil PAT goes back to 1988. Public terminal allows for a statewide search and is more extensive than online search. **For details about the state's online access to records, see the sections at the front or back of this chapter.**

Criminal Name Search: Access: In person, online. Visitors must perform in person searches themselves. Criminal records computerized from 11/88, prior on card and books. Note: No felony or gross misdemeanor searches will be performed. Criminal PAT goes back to 1988. Public terminal allows for a statewide search and is more extensive than online search. **For details about the state's online access to records, see the sections at the front or back of this chapter.**

Renville County

8th Judicial District Court 500 E DePue Ave, 3rd level, Olivia, MN 56277; 320-523-3680; fax: 320-523-3689; 8AM-4:30PM (CST). *Felony, Misdemeanor, Civil, Eviction, Small Claims, Probate.* www.mncourts.gov/district/8/
General Information: No adoption, juvenile or sealed records released. Fee to fax back- $25.00 up to 20 pgs, if over 25 pages then $50.00. Court makes copy: $8.00 per doc. Certification fee: $14.00 per doc plus copy fee. Payee: Court Administrator. Personal checks accepted. No credit cards accepted. Prepayment required. Mail requests: SASE required for civil.
Civil Name Search: Access: Mail, in person, online. Both court and visitors may perform in person name searches. Search fee: $5.00 per name. Civil records on computer from 1988, prior on index cards. Civil PAT goes back to 1/1988. Public terminal allows for a statewide search and is more extensive than online search. **For details about the state's online access to records, see the sections at the front or back of this chapter.**
Criminal Name Search: Access: In person, online. Visitors must perform in person searches themselves. Required to search: name. Criminal records computerized from 1988, prior on index cards. Note: Court recommends that written requests be submitted to the MN Bureau of Criminal Apprehension. Criminal PAT goes back to 1/1988. Public terminal allows for a statewide search and is more extensive than online search. **For details about the state's online access to records, see the sections at the front or back of this chapter.**

Lower Sioux Community Tribal Court PO Box 308, 39527 Res Hwy 1, Morton, MN 56270; 507-697-6185; fax: 507-697-8621;*Criminal, Civil, Juvenile, Traffic, Estate, Eviction.* www.lowersioux.com/d-tribalcourt.html

Rice County

3rd Judicial District Court 218 NW 3rd St, Faribault, MN 55021; 507-332-6107; fax: 507-332-6199; 8AM-4:30PM M-Th, 12:30-4:30PM Fri (CST). *Felony, Misdemeanor, Civil, Eviction, Small Claims, Probate.* www.mncourts.gov/district/3/
General Information: Many county offices are now relocated to the new government services building, but not the court, as yet. No adoption, juvenile, sex offender or sealed records released. Will fax documents for $5.00 fee. Court makes copy: $8.00 per doc. Certification fee: $14.00 per doc. Payee: Court Administrator. Personal checks accepted. Visa/MC/Discover accepted. Prepayment required. Mail requests: SASE required for civil.
Civil Name Search: Access: Mail, in person, online. Both court and visitors may perform in person name searches. Search fee: $5.00 per name. Civil records on computer from 1990, prior on index cards. Mail turnaround time 3 days. Civil PAT available. Public terminal connects to statewide online system. **For details about the state's online access to records, see the sections at the front or back of this chapter.**
Criminal Name Search: Access: In person, online. Visitors must perform in person searches themselves. Required to search: name, years to search; SSN helpful. Criminal records computerized from 1990, prior on index cards. Criminal PAT available. Public terminal connects to statewide online system. **For details about the state's online access to records, see the sections at the front or back of this chapter.**

Rock County

5th Judicial District Court PO Box 745, Luverne, MN 56156; 507-283-5020; fax: 507-283-5017; 8AM-5PM (CST). *Felony, Misdemeanor, Civil, Eviction, Small Claims, Probate.* www.mncourts.gov/district/5/
General Information: Probate fax is same as main fax number. No adoption, juvenile, sex offender or sealed records released. Fee to fax back- $25.00 per doc up to 25 pgs. Court makes copy: $8.00 per doc. Certification fee: $14.00 (includes the copy fee, if ordered at same time). Payee: Court Administrator. Personal checks, Visa/MC accepted. Prepayment required. Mail requests: SASE required.
Civil Name Search: Access: Mail, in person, online. Both court and visitors may perform in person name searches. Search fee: $10.00 per name. Civil records on computer from 1989, prior on books. Note: Visitors may search in books for records prior to 1985. Mail turnaround time same day if possible. Civil PAT goes back to 1989. **For details about the state's online access to records, see the sections at the front or back of this chapter.**
Criminal Name Search: Access: Mail, in person, online. Both court and visitors may perform in person name searches. Search fee: $10.00 per name. Required to search: name, years to search; also helpful: SSN. Criminal

records computerized from 1989, prior on books. Note: Visitors may search in books for records prior to 1985. Mail turnaround time same day if possible. Criminal PAT goes back to 1989. Public terminal allows for a statewide search and is more extensive than online search. **For details about the state's online access to records, see the sections at the front or back of this chapter.**

Roseau County

9th Judicial District Court 606 5th Ave SW Rm 20, Roseau, MN 56751; 218-463-2541; fax: 218-463-1889; 8AM-4:30PM (CST). *Felony, Misdemeanor, Civil, Eviction, Small Claims, Probate.*
www.mncourts.gov/district/9/
General Information: Week ahead court calendars available online. No adoption, juvenile, paternity or sealed records released. Will fax documents for $1.00 per page plus copy fee. Court makes copy: $8.00 per doc. Certification fee: $14.00 per doc includes copy fee. Payee: Court Administrator. Personal checks accepted. Visa/MC/Discover accepted. Prepayment required. Mail requests: SASE required for civil.
Civil Name Search: Access: Mail, in person, online. Both court and visitors may perform in person name searches. Search fee: $5.00 per name. Civil records on computer back to 1990, prior on index cards or imaging to 1895. Mail turnaround time same day if possible. Civil PAT goes back to 1991. Public access terminal is made available to ongoing, experienced requesters. **For details about the state's online access to records, see the sections at the front or back of this chapter.**
Criminal Name Search: Access: In person, online. Visitors must perform in person searches themselves. Required to search: name, years to search; also helpful: DOB. Criminal records computerized from 1990, prior on imaging or thru state historical society. Note: Court will perform only statutorily required criminal searches. Criminal PAT goes back to 1991. Public access terminal is made available to ongoing, experienced requesters. Public terminal allows for a statewide search. **For details about the state's online access to records, see the sections at the front or back of this chapter.**

Scott County

1st Judicial District Court Scott County Justice Ctr, 200 Fourth Ave W, Shakopee, MN 55379; 952-496-8200; fax: 952-496-8211; 8AM-4:30PM (CST). *Felony, Misdemeanor, Civil, Eviction, Small Claims, Probate.* www.mncourts.gov/district/1/
General Information: No adoption, juvenile or sealed records released. Fee to fax back- $25.00 for each 50 pages or portions thereof. Court makes copy: $8.00 per doc. Certification fee: $14.00 per doc. Payee: Scott County District Court. Personal checks and credit cards accepted. Prepayment required. Mail requests: SASE required.
Civil Name Search: Access: Mail, in person, online. Both court and visitors may perform in person name searches. Search fee: $5.00 per name. Civil records on computer from 1981, prior on books. Mail turnaround time 5 days Civil PAT goes back to 1996. Public terminal located in Library. **For details about the state's online access to records, see the sections at the front or back of this chapter.**
Criminal Name Search: Access: Mail, in person, online. Both court and visitors may perform in person name searches. Search fee: $5.00 per name. Required to search: name, years to search, DOB. Criminal records computerized from 1981, prior on books. Criminal PAT goes back to 1996. Public terminal located in Library. Public terminal allows for a statewide search. **For details about the state's online access to records, see the sections at the front or back of this chapter.**

Sherburne County

10th Judicial District Court Sherburne County Government Ctr, 13880 Business Ctr Dr, Elk River, MN 55330-4608; 763-241-2800; fax: 763-241-2816; 8AM-4:30PM (CST). *Felony, Misdemeanor, Civil, Eviction, Small Claims, Probate.* www.mncourts.gov/district/10/
General Information: No adoption, juvenile, confidential or sealed records released. Will not fax documents. Court makes copy: $8.00 per doc. Certification fee: $14.00 per doc includes copy fee; exemplification $12.00. Payee: Court Administrator. Personal checks, Visa/MC accepted. Prepayment required. Mail requests: SASE required for civil.
Civil Name Search: Access: Mail, in person, online. Both court and visitors may perform in person name searches. Search fee: $5.00 per name. Civil records on computer from 1985, prior on books. Note: Weekly calendars free at www.mncourts.gov/district/10/?page=1326. Mail turnaround time 1 week Civil PAT goes back to 1985. Public terminal allows for a statewide search and is more extensive than online search. **For details about the state's online access to records, see the sections at the front or back of this chapter.**
Criminal Name Search: Access: In person, online. Both court and visitors may perform in person name searches. Search fee: $5.00 per name. Required to search: name, years to search, DOB. Criminal records computerized from 1985, prior on books back to 1930s. Criminal PAT goes back to 1985. Public terminal allows for a statewide search and is more

extensive than online search. **For details about the state's online access to records, see the sections at the front or back of this chapter.**

Sibley County

1st Judicial District Court PO Box 867, 400 Court St, Gaylord, MN 55334; 507-237-4051; fax: 507-237-4062; 8AM-4:30PM (CST). *Felony, Misdemeanor, Civil, Eviction, Small Claims, Probate.*
www.mncourts.gov/district/1/
General Information: Probate fax is same as main fax number. No adoption, juvenile, or sealed records released. Fee to fax back- $25.00 per doc up to 25 pgs. Court makes copy: $8.00 per doc. Certification fee: $14.00 per doc. Payee: Court Administrator. Personal checks, Visa/MC accepted. Prepayment required. Mail requests: SASE required.
Civil Name Search: Access: Mail, in person, online. Both court and visitors may perform in person name searches. Search fee: $5.00 per name. Civil records on computer from 5/92, prior on books to 1800s. Mail turnaround time 2-3 weeks. Civil PAT goes back to 1992. Public terminal allows for a statewide search and is more extensive than online search. This search is not an official record search, per MN**For details about the state's online access to records, see the sections at the front or back of this chapter.**
Criminal Name Search: Access: Mail, in person, online. Both court and visitors may perform in person name searches. Search fee: $5.00 per name. Required to search: name, years to search, DOB. Criminal records computerized from 5/92, prior on books to 1800s. Mail turnaround time 2-3 weeks, . Criminal PAT goes back to 1992. Public terminal allows for a statewide search and is more extensive than online search. **For details about the state's online access to records, see the sections at the front or back of this chapter.**

St. Louis County

6th Judicial District Court 100 N 5th Ave W, Rm 320, Duluth, MN 55802-1294; 218-726-2430; probate phone: 218-726-2521; criminal fax: 218-726-2473; civil fax: 8AM-4:30PM; 8AM-4:30PM (CST). *Felony, Misdemeanor, Civil, Eviction, Small Claims, Probate.*
www.mncourts.gov/district/6/
General Information: All 3 St Louis County courts can access computer records for the county and direct you to the appropriate court to get the physical file. Probate fax is same as main fax number. No adoption, juvenile, juvenile victim of sex offense, sealed records released. Will not fax documents. Court makes copy: $8.00 per doc. Certification fee: $14.00 (includes search fee). Payee: Court Administrator. Personal checks accepted. No credit cards accepted. Prepayment required.
Civil Name Search: Access: Mail, in person, online. Both court and visitors may perform in person name searches. Search fee: $5.00 per name or name variation. Civil records on computer from 1976. Mail turnaround time 1 week. Civil PAT goes back to 1976. Public terminal allows for a statewide search and is more extensive than online search. **For details about the state's online access to records, see the sections at the front or back of this chapter.**
Criminal Name Search: Access: Mail, in person, online. Both court and visitors may perform in person name searches. Search fee: $5.00 per name or name variation. Required to search: name. Criminal records computerized from 1976. Criminal PAT goes back to 1976. Public terminal allows for a statewide search and is more extensive than online search. **For details about the state's online access to records, see the sections at the front or back of this chapter.**

6th Judicial District Court - Hibbing Branch 1810 12th Ave East, Hibbing, MN 55746; 218-262-0105; probate phone: 218-726-2400; fax: 218-262-0219; 8AM-4:30PM (CST). *Felony, Misdemeanor, Civil, Eviction, Small Claims, Probate.* www.mncourts.gov/district/6/
General Information: All 3 St Louis County courts can access county computer records and direct you to the appropriate court for the physical file. Probate fax is same as main fax number. No adoption, juvenile, sex offender or sealed records released. Fee to fax back- $25.00 per doc up to 25 pgs. Court makes copy: $8.00 per doc. Certification fee: $14.00 per doc plus copy fee. Payee: Court Administrator. Personal checks accepted. Credit cards not accepted for copies or searches. Prepayment required. Mail requests: SASE required for civil.
Civil Name Search: Access: Mail, in person, online. Both court and visitors may perform in person name searches. Search fee: $5.00 per name/per judgment. Civil records on computer from 1985, prior on card or books. Civil PAT goes back to 1991. Public terminal allows for a statewide search and is more extensive than online search. **For details about the state's online access to records, see the sections at the front or back of this chapter.**
Criminal Name Search: Access: In person, online. Visitors must perform in person searches themselves. Criminal records computerized from 1985, all on image system. Criminal PAT goes back to 1991. Results include charges. Public terminal allows for a statewide search. **For**

details about the state's online access to records, see the sections at the front or back of this chapter.

6th Judicial District Court - Virginia Branch 300 S 5th Ave, Court Administrator, Virginia, MN 55792; 218-749-7106; criminal phone: x4; probate phone: x7; fax: 218-749-7109; 8AM-4:30PM (CST). *Felony, Misdemeanor, Civil, Eviction, Small Claims, Probate.* www.mncourts.gov/district/6/

General Information: All three St Louis County courts can access computer records for the county and direct you to the appropriate court for the physical files. No adoption, juvenile, sex offender or sealed records released. Fee to fax back- $25.00 per doc up to 25 pgs. Court makes copy: $8.00 per doc. Certification fee: $14.00 per doc plus copy fee. Payee: Court Administrator. Personal checks accepted. No credit cards accepted. Prepayment required.

Civil Name Search: Access: Mail, in person, online. Both court and visitors may perform in person name searches. Search fee: $5.00 per name. Civil records on computer back 15 years, prior on books. Mail turnaround time 1-2 days. Civil PAT goes back to 1990. Public terminal allows for a statewide search and is more extensive than online search. **For details about the state's online access to records, see the sections at the front or back of this chapter.**

Criminal Name Search: Access: In person, online. Visitors must perform in person searches themselves. Required to search: name, years to search, DOB. Criminal records on computer back 15 years, prior on books. Criminal PAT goes back to 1990. Public terminal allows for a statewide search and is more extensive than online search. **For details about the state's online access to records, see the sections at the front or back of this chapter.**

Bois Forte Tribal Court Res Hwy 1, PO Box 25, Nett Lake, MN 55772; 218-757-3462; fax: 218-757-3166;*Criminal, Civil, Juvenile, Traffic, Estate, Eviction.* www.boisforte.com/

Stearns County

Stearns County District Court 725 Courthouse Square, St Cloud, MN 56303; 320-656-3620; fax: 320-656-6335; 8AM-4:30PM (CST). *Felony, Misdemeanor, Civil, Small Claims, Eviction, Probate, Traffic.* www.mncourts.gov/district/7/

General Information: Court calendars free at website. No adoption or other sealed records released without court petition. Fee to fax back- $25.00 per doc up to 25 pgs. Court makes copy: $8.00 per doc. Certification fee: $14.00. Payee: District Court. Personal checks, Visa/MC accepted. Prepayment required.

Civil Name Search: Access: Mail, in person, online. Both court and visitors may perform in person name searches. Search fee: $5.00 per name. Civil records on computer back to 1984, on books from the 1920s. Civil PAT goes back to 1984. Public terminal allows for a statewide search and is more extensive than online search. **For details about the state's online access to records, see the sections at the front or back of this chapter.**

Criminal Name Search: Access: In person, online. Visitors must perform in person searches themselves. No search fee. Required to search: name. Criminal records computerized from 1984, on books from the 1920s. Criminal PAT goes back to 1984. Public terminal allows for a statewide search and is more extensive than online search. **For details about the state's online access to records, see the sections at the front or back of this chapter.**

Steele County

3rd Judicial District Court PO Box 487 (111 E Main St), Owatonna, MN 55060; 507-444-7700; probate phone: 507-444-7707; fax: 507-444-7491; 8AM-4:30PM (CST). *Felony, Misdemeanor, Civil, Eviction, Small Claims, Probate.* www.mncourts.gov/district/3/

General Information: No adoption, juvenile, sex offender or sealed records released. Will not fax documents. Court makes copy: $8.00 per doc. Certification fee: $14.00 per doc. Payee: Court Administrator. Personal checks, Visa/MC accepted. Prepayment required. Mail requests: SASE required for civil.

Civil Name Search: Access: Mail, in person, online. Both court and visitors may perform in person name searches. Search fee: $5.00. Civil records on computer from 1990, on books from 1870. Civil PAT goes back to 1990. Public terminal allows for a statewide search and is more extensive than online search. **For details about the state's online access to records, see the sections at the front or back of this chapter.**

Criminal Name Search: Access: In person, online. Visitors must perform in person searches themselves. Required to search: name, years to search; SSN helpful. Criminal records computerized from 1990, on books from 1870. Criminal PAT goes back to 1990. Public terminal allows for a statewide search and is more extensive than online search. **For details about the state's online access to records, see the sections at the front or back of this chapter.**

Stevens County

8th Judicial District Court PO Box 530, 400 Colorado Ave, Ste 307, Morris, MN 56267; 320-208-6640; fax: 320-589-7288; 8AM-4:30PM (7:30AM-4PM Summer) (CST). *Felony, Misdemeanor, Civil, Eviction, Small Claims, Probate.* www.mncourts.gov/district/8/

General Information: No adoption, juvenile, sex offender or sealed records released. Will fax documents $25.00 each. Court makes copy: $8.00 per doc. Certification fee: $14.00 per doc. Payee: Court Administrator. Personal checks, Visa/MC accepted. Prepayment required. Mail requests: SASE required for civil.

Civil Name Search: Access: Mail, in person, online. Both court and visitors may perform in person name searches. Search fee: $5.00 per name. Civil records on computer from 2/89, on cards from 5/86, on books from 1900. Mail turnaround time 2 days. Civil PAT goes back to 2/1989. Public terminal allows for a statewide search and is more extensive than online search. **For details about the state's online access to records, see the sections at the front or back of this chapter.**

Criminal Name Search: Access: In person, online. Visitors must perform in person searches themselves. Criminal records computerized from 2/89, on cards from 5/86, on books from 1900. Note: For access to criminal history information, the court recommends the BCA at 651-642-0610. Criminal PAT goes back to 2/1989. Public terminal allows for a statewide search and is more extensive than online search. **For details about the state's online access to records, see the sections at the front or back of this chapter.**

Swift County

8th Judicial District Court 301 14th St N Ste 6, Benson, MN 56215; 320-843-2744; fax: 320-843-4124; 8AM-N, 1PM-4:30PM M-TH; 8AM-N, 1PM-2PM F (CST). *Felony, Misdemeanor, Civil, Eviction, Small Claims, Probate.* www.mncourts.gov/district/8/

General Information: Probate records prior to 1983 are in a separate index. Probate fax is same as main fax number. No adoption, juvenile, minor victim of sex offense, sealed records released. Fee to fax back- $25.00 per doc up to 25 pgs. Court makes copy: $8.00 per doc. Certification fee: $14.00 per doc plus copy fee. Payee: Court Administrator. Personal checks and credit cards accepted. Prepayment required. Mail requests: SASE required for civil.

Civil Name Search: Access: Phone, fax, mail, in person, online. Both court and visitors may perform in person name searches. No search fee. Civil records on computer back to 8/1988, prior in files and books from 1800s. Mail turnaround time 1-2 weeks Civil PAT goes back to 8/1988. Public terminal allows for a statewide search and is more extensive than online search. Limited search of civil and family are found at **For details about the state's online access to records, see the sections at the front or back of this chapter.**

Criminal Name Search: Access: Mail, in person, online. Visitors must perform in person searches themselves. Search fee: $5.00 per name. Required to search: name, years to search; also helpful: DOB. Criminal records computerized from 1988, prior in files and books from 1800s except those destroyed per retention schedule. Criminal PAT goes back to 8/1988. Public terminal allows for a statewide search and is more extensive than online search. **For details about the state's online access to records, see the sections at the front or back of this chapter.**

Todd County

7th Judicial District Court 221 1st Ave South, #100, Long Prairie, MN 56347; 320-732-7800; fax: 320-732-2506; 8AM-4:30PM (CST). *Felony, Misdemeanor, Civil, Eviction, Small Claims, Probate.* www.mncourts.gov/district/7/

General Information: Probate fax is same as main fax number. No adoption, juvenile or sealed records released. Fee to fax back- $25.00 per doc up to 25 pgs. Court makes copy: $8.00 per doc. Certification fee: $14.00 per document, includes copy fee. Payee: Court Administrator. Personal checks, Visa/MC accepted. Prepayment required. Mail requests: SASE required.

Civil Name Search: Access: Mail, in person, online. Both court and visitors may perform in person name searches. Search fee: $5.00 per name. Required to search: name, years to search, address. Civil records on computer 7/86, prior on index cards and books. Mail turnaround time 5-7 days. Civil PAT goes back to 1986. Public terminal allows for a statewide search and is more extensive than online search. **For details about the state's online access to records, see the sections at the front or back of this chapter.**

Criminal Name Search: Access: Mail, in person, online. Both court and visitors may perform in person name searches. Search fee: $5.00 per name. Required to search: name, years to search, address, DOB. Criminal records on computer 7/86, prior on index cards and books. Mail turnaround time 5-7 days. Criminal PAT goes back to 1986. Public terminal allows for a statewide search and is more extensive than online search. **For details about the state's online access to records, see the sections at the front or back of this chapter.**

Traverse County

8th Judicial District Court 702 2nd Ave N, PO Box 867, Wheaton, MN 56296; 320-563-4343; fax: 320-563-4311; 8AM-N, 12:30-4:30PM (CST). *Felony, Misdemeanor, Civil, Eviction, Small Claims, Probate.* www.mncourts.gov/district/8/

General Information: Probate fax is same as main fax number. No adoption, juvenile, sex offender or sealed records released. Fee to fax back-$5.00 for 1-9 pages, $10 for 10 pages or more. Court makes copy: $8.00 per doc. Certification fee: $14.00 per document. Payee: Court Administrator. Personal checks, Visa/MC accepted. Prepayment required. Mail requests: SASE required for civil.

Civil Name Search: Access: Mail, in person, online. Both court and visitors may perform in person name searches. Search fee: $5.00 per name. Civil records on computer from 6/89, prior on index cards and books, and on images. Note: Only judgment searches accepted by mail. Mail turnaround time 1-2 days. Civil PAT goes back to 6/1989. Public terminal allows for a statewide search and is more extensive than online search. The terminal shows city and gender. **For details about the state's online access to records, see the sections at the front or back of this chapter.**

Criminal Name Search: Access: In person, online. Visitors must perform in person searches themselves. Criminal records computerized from 6/89, prior on index cards and books. Criminal PAT goes back to 6/1989. Public terminal allows for a statewide search and is more extensive than online search. The terminal shows city and gender. **For details about the state's online access to records, see the sections at the front or back of this chapter.**

Wabasha County

3rd Judicial District Court 848 17th Street East, Ste 4, Wabasha, MN 55981; 651-565-3524; criminal phone: 651-565-3011; probate phone: 651-565-3087; fax: 651-565-8214; 8AM-4:30PM (CST). *Felony, Misdemeanor, Civil, Eviction, Small Claims, Probate.* www.mncourts.gov/district/3/

General Information: Probate fax is same as main fax number. No adoption, juvenile, sex offender or sealed records released. Fee to fax back-$25.00 per doc up to 25 pgs. Court makes copy: $8.00 per doc. Certification fee: $14.00 per doc plus copy fee. Payee: Wabasha District Court. Personal checks and credit cards accepted. Prepayment required. Mail requests: SASE requested.

Civil Name Search: Access: Phone, fax, mail, in person, online. Both court and visitors may perform in person name searches. Search fee: $5.00 for judgment searches. Civil records on computer from 6/89, prior on index cards and books. Note: Search daily court calendar at the website. Civil PAT goes back to 6/1989. Public terminal allows for a statewide search and is more extensive than online search. **For details about the state's online access to records, see the sections at the front or back of this chapter.**

Criminal Name Search: Access: In person, online. Visitors must perform in person searches themselves. Required to search: name, years to search; also helpful: DOB. Criminal records computerized from 6/89, prior on index cards and books. Note: View weekly court calendar at the website. Criminal PAT goes back to 6/1989. Public terminal allows for a statewide search and is more extensive than online search. **For details about the state's online access to records, see the sections at the front or back of this chapter.**

Wadena County

7th Judicial District Court County Courthouse, 415 S Jefferson St, Wadena, MN 56482; 218-631-7633; fax: 218-631-7635; 8AM-4:30PM (CST). *Felony, Misdemeanor, Civil, Eviction, Small Claims, Probate.* www.mncourts.gov/district/7/

General Information: Note that the search fee is $5.00 and the copy fee is an additional $5.00. No adoption, juvenile, or sealed records released. Fee to fax back- $25.00 per doc up to 25 pgs. Court makes copy: $8.00 per doc. Certification fee: $14.00, includes copy fee. Payee: Court Administrator. Personal checks, Visa/MC accepted. Prepayment required.

Civil Name Search: Access: Mail, in person, online. Both court and visitors may perform in person name searches. Search fee: $5.00 per name. Civil records on computer from 7/86; prior on books, cards and microfiche. Mail turnaround time 7 to 10 days. Civil PAT goes back to 7/1986. Public terminal allows for a statewide search and is more extensive than online search. **For details about the state's online access to records, see the sections at the front or back of this chapter.**

Criminal Name Search: Access: Mail, in person, online. Both court and visitors may perform in person name searches. Search fee: $5.00 per name. Required to search: name, years to search, DOB; also helpful: address. Criminal records computerized from 7/86; prior on books, cards and microfiche. Mail turnaround time 7-10 days. Criminal PAT goes back to 7/1986. Public terminal allows for a statewide search and is more extensive than online search. **For details about the state's online access to records, see the sections at the front or back of this chapter.**

Waseca County

3rd Judicial District Court 307 N State St, Waseca, MN 56093; 507-835-0540; criminal phone: x7; civil phone: x4; fax: 507-837-5317; 8AM-4:30PM; 12:30-4:30PM TH (CST). *Felony, Misdemeanor, Civil, Eviction, Small Claims, Probate, Family.* www.mncourts.gov/district/3/

General Information: No adoption, juvenile, sex offender victim or sealed records released. Fee to fax back- $25.00 per doc up to 25 pgs. Court makes copy: $8.00 per doc. Certification fee: $14.00 per doc plus copy fee. Payee: Court Administrator. Personal checks, Visa/MC accepted. Prepayment required. Mail requests: SASE required for civil.

Civil Name Search: Access: Mail, in person, online. Both court and visitors may perform in person name searches. Search fee: $5.00 per name. Civil records on computer from 1990, prior on TCIS cards and books. Mail turnaround time 5 days. Civil PAT goes back to 1990. Public terminal allows for a statewide search and is more extensive than online search. **For details about the state's online access to records, see the sections at the front or back of this chapter.**

Criminal Name Search: Access: In person, online. Visitors must perform in person searches themselves. Required to search: name, years to search, DOB. Criminal records computerized from 1990, prior on TCIS cards and books. Criminal PAT goes back to 1990. Public terminal allows for a statewide search and is more extensive than online search. **For details about the state's online access to records, see the sections at the front or back of this chapter.**

Washington County

10th Judicial District Court 14949 62nd St North, PO Box 3802, Stillwater, MN 55082-3802; 651-430-6263; fax: 651-430-6300; 8:30AM-4:30PM, closed Tues AM (CST). *Felony, Misdemeanor, Civil, Eviction, Small Claims, Probate.* www.mncourts.gov/district/10/

General Information: No adoption, juvenile, sex offender or sealed records released. Will not fax documents. Court makes copy: $8.00 per doc; exemplification $20.00. Certification fee: $14.00 per doc. Payee: Court Administrator. Personal checks, Visa/MC accepted. Prepayment required.

Civil Name Search: Access: Mail, in person, online. Both court and visitors may perform in person name searches. Search fee: $5.00 per name. Civil records on computer back to 12/83, prior on books. Note: Weekly calendars free at www.mncourts.gov/district/10/?page=1326. Civil PAT goes back to 1991. Public terminal allows for a statewide search and is more extensive than online search. **For details about the state's online access to records, see the sections at the front or back of this chapter.**

Criminal Name Search: Access: In person, online. Visitors must perform in person searches themselves. Required to search: name, years to search, DOB. Criminal records computerized from 12/83, prior on books. Note: Fax and mail access limited to statute requirements. Criminal PAT goes back to 1991. Public terminal allows for a statewide search and is more extensive than online search. **For details about the state's online access to records, see the sections at the front or back of this chapter.**

Watonwan County

5th Judicial District Court PO Box 518, 710 2nd Ave South, St James, MN 56081; 507-375-1236; criminal phone: x3; civil phone: x2; probate phone: x1; fax: 507-375-5010; 8AM-5PM (CST). *Felony, Misdemeanor, Civil, Eviction, Small Claims, Probate.* www.mncourts.gov/district/5/

General Information: The Jury Office can be reached at 507-375-1236. No adoption, juvenile, sex offender or sealed records released. Fee to fax back- $5.00 per doc. Court makes copy: $8.00 per doc. Certification fee: $14.00 per doc includes copy fee. Payee: Court Administrator. Personal checks and credit cards accepted. Prepayment required. Mail requests: SASE required for civil.

Civil Name Search: Access: Fax, mail, in person, online. Both court and visitors may perform in person name searches. Search fee: $5.00 per name. Civil records on computer from 5/89, prior on index cards. Mail turnaround time 5 business days. Civil PAT goes back to 4/1988. Public terminal allows for a statewide search and is more extensive than online search. **For details about the state's online access to records, see the sections at the front or back of this chapter.**

Criminal Name Search: Access: Mail, in person, online. Visitors must perform in person searches themselves. Search fee: $15.00 per name. Required to search: name, years to search; also helpful: DOB. Criminal records computerized from 5/89, prior on index cards. Mail turnaround time 5 business days. Criminal PAT goes back to 4/1988. Public terminal allows for a statewide search and is more extensive than online search. **For details about the state's online access to records, see the sections at the front or back of this chapter.**

Wilkin County

8th Judicial District Court PO Box 219, Breckenridge, MN 56520; 218-643-7172; fax: 218-643-7167; 8AM-4:30PM m-TH; 8AM-2PM F (CST). *Felony, Misdemeanor, Civil, Eviction, Small Claims, Probate.* www.mncourts.gov/district/8/

General Information: No adoption, juvenile, sex offender or sealed records released. Fee to fax back- $25.00 per doc up to 50 pgs. Court makes copy: $8.00 per doc. Certification fee: $14.00 per doc plus copy fee. Payee: Court Administrator. Personal checks, Visa/MC accepted. Prepayment required. Mail requests: SASE required.

Civil Name Search: Access: Phone, mail, in person, online. Both court and visitors may perform in person name searches. No search fee. Required to search: name; also helpful: years to search. Civil records on computer from 1989, prior on books. Mail turnaround time 7-14 days. Civil PAT goes back to 1989. Public terminal allows for a statewide search and is more extensive than online search. **For details about the state's online access to records, see the sections at the front or back of this chapter.**

Criminal Name Search: Access: In person, online. Both court and visitors may perform in person name searches. Required to search: name; also helpful: years to search. Criminal records computerized from 1989, prior on books. Criminal PAT goes back to 1989. Public terminal allows for a statewide search and is more extensive than online search. **For details about the state's online access to records, see the sections at the front or back of this chapter.**

Winona County

3rd Judicial District Court 171 W 3rd St, Winona, MN 55987; 507-457-6385; criminal fax: 507-457-6392; civil fax: 8AM-4:30PM Except 12:30PM-4:30 PM on W; 8AM-4:30PM Except 12:30PM-4:30 PM on W (CST). *Felony, Misdemeanor, Civil, Eviction, Small Claims, Probate.* www.mncourts.gov/district/3/

General Information: No adoption, juvenile or sealed records released. Will not fax documents. Court makes copy: $8.00 per doc. Certification fee: $14.00 per case. Cert fee includes original $5.00 search fee. Payee: Court Administrator. Personal checks, Visa/MC accepted. Prepayment required.

Civil Name Search: Access: Mail, in person, online. Both court and visitors may perform in person name searches. Search fee: $10.00 per hour if extensive. Civil records on computer from 1986, on books from 1962. Note: Only in person civil searches by public computer, not older book indices. Mail turnaround time 5-10 working days. Civil PAT goes back to 1986. identifiers on terminal results vary by case type. **For details about the state's online access to records, see the sections at the front or back of this chapter.**

Criminal Name Search: Access: In person, online. Visitors must perform in person searches themselves. Required to search: name, years to search, DOB. Criminal records computerized from 1986, on books from 1962. Note: Criminal searchers are usually referred to the MN State BCA. Court accepts phone requests to lookup specific offenses, 502-457-6570; case number very helpful. Criminal PAT goes back to 1986. Terminal results can include addresses. Public terminal allows for a statewide search. **For details about the state's online access to records, see the sections at the front or back of this chapter.**

Wright County

10th Judicial District Court 10 NW 2nd St, Rm 201, Buffalo, MN 55313-1192; 763-682-7539; fax: 763-682-7300; 8AM-4:30PM (CST). *Felony, Misdemeanor, Civil, Eviction, Small Claims, Probate.* www.mncourts.gov/district/10/

General Information: No adoption, juvenile, confidential or sealed records released. Fee to fax back- $25.00 per doc up to 25 pgs; prepay by credit card. Court makes copy: $8.00 per doc; exemplification $12.00. Certification fee: $14.00 per doc plus copy fee. Payee: Court Administrator. Personal checks accepted. VISA, MC, and Discover accepted. Prepayment required.

Civil Name Search: Access: In person, online. Visitors must perform in person searches themselves. Required to search: name, years to search, approx. date. Civil records on computer from 8/84, prior on books, cards & microfiche. Note: Certificates for outstanding docketed money judgments may be requested by mail. Each name variation requires $5.00 fee. Weekly calendars free at www.mncourts.gov/district/10/?page=1326. Civil PAT goes back to 1984. DOB and full name may be on party record. **For details about the state's online access to records, see the sections at the front or back of this chapter.**

Criminal Name Search: Access: In person, online. Visitors must perform in person searches themselves. Required to search: name, years to search; also helpful: DOB, approx. date. Criminal records computerized from 8/84, prior on books, cards & microfiche. Criminal PAT goes back to 1984. Public terminal allows for a statewide search and is more extensive than online search. **For details about the state's online access to records, see the sections at the front or back of this chapter.**

Yellow Medicine County

8th Judicial District Court 415 9th Ave, #103, Granite Falls, MN 56241; 320-564-3325; fax: 320-564-4435; 8AM-4PM (CST). *Felony, Misdemeanor, Civil, Eviction, Small Claims, Probate.* www.mncourts.gov/district/8/

General Information: No adoption, juvenile or sealed records released. Fee to fax back- $25.00 per doc up to 25 pgs. Court makes copy: $8.00 per doc. Certification fee: $14.00 per doc plus copy fee. Payee: Court Administrator. Personal checks and credit cards accepted. Prepayment required. Mail requests: SASE required for civil.

Civil Name Search: Access: Mail, in person, online. Both court and visitors may perform in person name searches. Search fee: $10.00 for certified search. Required to search: name, years to search; also helpful: address. Civil records on computer from 1988. Civil PAT goes back to 1988. Public terminal allows for a statewide search and is more extensive than online search. **For details about the state's online access to records, see the sections at the front or back of this chapter.**

Criminal Name Search: Access: In person, online. Visitors must perform in person searches themselves. Criminal records computerized from 1988. Criminal PAT goes back to 1988. Public terminal allows for a statewide search and is more extensive than online search. **For details about the state's online access to records, see the sections at the front or back of this chapter.**

Upper Sioux Community Tribal Court PO Box 155, 2499 564th St, Granite Falls, MN 56241; 320-564-6317; fax: 320-564-4915; *Criminal, Civil, Juvenile, Traffic, Estate, Eviction.* www.uppersiouxcommunity-nsn.gov/pages/tribalcourt.htm

---

About the Statewide Online Access

Minnesota offers the Trial Court Public Access (MPA) of searching statewide or by county. Records available include criminal, civil, family, and probate. Searches can be performed using a case number or by name. See http://pa.courts.state.mn.us/default.aspx.

However searchers should first know there are several caveats.

- Certain publicly-accessible case records or data fields found at the courthouse cannot be viewed online. For example, comment fields for all case types are not available online but are available at the courthouse.

- Party street address and name searches on criminal, traffic, and petty misdemeanor pre-conviction case records are not accessible online, but are at the courthouse.

- A criminal/traffic/petty search excludes all Hennepin County and Ramsey County payable citations except: 1) those that result in a court appearance; and 2) Ramsey DNR payable citations.

- Also, Party street address and name searches on criminal pre-conviction case records are publicly accessible and available at the courthouse, but not online.

- The federal Violence Against Women Act (VAWA) prevents the state (all states) from displaying harassment and domestic abuse case records online, but these convictions are available at the courthouse.

The bottom line is the public access terminals found at the courthouses provide more information than found on the online system.

The public access terminals found at courthouses are considered the most accurate searching locations. The online system is a supplemental search.

Mississippi

Time Zone:	CST
Capital:	Jackson, Hinds County
# of Counties:	82
State Web:	www.mississippi.gov
Court Web:	www.mssc.state.ms.us

Administration

Court Administrator, Supreme Court, Box 117, Jackson, MS, 39205; 601-354-7406, Fax: 601-354-7459.

The Supreme Court and the Court of Appeals

The Supreme Court is the highest court in the state. The Court of Appeals hears cases assigned by the Supreme Court. The Court of Appeals is an error correction court. Decisions of the Chancery, Circuit and County Courts and of the Court of Appeals may be appealed to the Supreme Court. The website offers searching of the MS Supreme Court and Court of Appeals decisions and dockets.

The Mississippi Courts

Court	Type	How Organized	Jurisdiction Highpoints
Circuit*	General	70 Courts in 22 Districts	Felony, Civil
Chancery*	Special	91 Courts in 20 Districts	Probate, Divorce, Equity, Domestic, Wills, Juvenile
County*	Limited	21 Courts	Misdemeanor, Civil Actions under $3,500, Eviction, Small Claims, Juvenile, Eminent Domain
Justice*	Limited	82 Courts	Misdemeanor, Civil Actions under $3,500, Eviction, Small Claims, Traffic
Municipal	Limited	226	Local ordinance, Traffic

* = profiled in this book

Details on the Court Structure

Circuit Courts hear felony criminal prosecutions and civil lawsuits.

Chancery Courts have jurisdiction over matters involving equity; domestic matters including adoptions, custody disputes and divorces; guardianships; sanity hearings; probate, wills; and challenges to constitutionality of state laws. Land records are filed in Chancery Court. Chancery Courts have jurisdiction over juvenile matters in counties which have no County Court.

County Courts have exclusive jurisdiction over eminent domain proceedings and juvenile matters, among other things. In counties which have a County Court, a County Court judge also serves as the Youth Court judge. County Courts share jurisdiction with Circuit and Chancery Courts in some civil matters. The jurisdictional limit of County Courts is up to $200,000, The traditional limit is $75,000 max for a County Court, but this is not adhered to at all counties. County Courts may handle non-capital felony cases transferred from Circuit Court. County Courts have concurrent jurisdiction with Justice Courts in all matters, civil and criminal.

Justice Courts have jurisdiction over small claims civil cases involving amounts of $3,500 or less, misdemeanor criminal cases and any traffic offense that occurs outside a municipality

Civil cases under $3,500 are usually found in Justice Courts as filing fees are less there than at Circuit Courts. Jasper County added a 2nd Justice Court in 5/2008; it is located in City of Paulding. Since July 2008, there is a $3,500 case limit (formerly $2,500) for both civil and small claims cases at the Justice Courts. Circuit and County Courts are usually combined, except in Harrison County.

Municipal Courts have jurisdiction over misdemeanor crimes, municipal ordinances and city traffic violations.

Drug Courts are special courts which address crimes committed by persons addicted to drugs or alcohol. **Youth Courts** generally deal with matters in involving abuse and neglect of juveniles, as well as offenses committed by juveniles.

Record Searching Facts You Need to Know

Fees and Record Searching Tips

A number of Mississippi counties have two Circuit Court Districts. A search of either court in such a county will include the index from the other court. Full name is a search requirement for all courts. DOB and SSN are very helpful for differentiating between like-named individuals.

The Administrative Office of Courts offers a statewide search of civil, probate, or felony records by a fax request with a 24 hour turnaround time. Only criminal felony cases with dispositions are reported, misdemeanor cases are not. Request should include the name, DOB and full or partial SSN. The results report the county and docket number of the case. There is a $25.00 start-up fee and a $5.00 fee per name search. Call 601-576-4630 or fax 601-576-4639 for details.

Online Access is Limited

Certain courts in Adams, DeSoto, Jackson and Oktibbeha counties offer online access to the public. Also, Mississippi is in the midst of implementing a Pilot Testing of the Mississippi Electronic Courts System (MEC). The system allows web-based document filing and case management. Courts can make case information available on the web for practicing attorneys in MS. A number of courts have been authorized to participate. At press time, active courts include Madison County Chancery and Circuit (civil only), Scott County Chancery, Warren County Chancery, and Warren County Circuit (county and civil only). Other entities authorized to participate include courts in DeSoto, Harrison, and Holmes counties. At present there are no fees associated with using this system. For details visit www.mssc.state.ms.us/mec/mec.html.

Adams County

Circuit & County Court PO Box 1224, 115 S Wall, Natchez, MS 39121; 601-446-6326; fax: 601-445-7955; 8AM-5PM (CST). *Felony, Misdemeanor, Civil (usually over $3,500).*
www.adamscountyms.net/index.php
General Information: No sealed, adoptions, mental health, juvenile, sex, or expunged records released. Will not fax documents. Court makes copy: $1.00 per page. Certification fee: $2.00 per cert plus copy fee. Payee: Circuit Clerk. Personal checks accepted. No credit cards accepted. Prepayment required. Mail requests: SASE required.
Civil Name Search: Access: Mail, in person, online. Both court and visitors may perform in person name searches. Search fee: $10.00 per name. Civil records on computer; docket books to 1950s; records stored in basement to 1799. Mail turnaround time 1-2 days if on computer. Civil PAT goes back to 1997. The Circuit Court Case and Judgment Roll Information is $25/monthly or $275/yearly. A user account must be created and subscription purchased to use this service at www.deltacomputersystems.com/MS/MS01/
Criminal Name Search: Access: Mail, in person, online. Both court and visitors may perform in person name searches. Search fee: $10.00 per name. Required to search: name, years to search; also helpful: SSN. Criminal records on computer; docket books to 1950s; records stored in basement to 1799. Mail turnaround time 1-2 days if on computer. Criminal PAT goes back to same as civil. The Circuit Court Case and Judgment Roll Information is $25/monthly or $275/yearly. A user account must be created and subscription purchased to use this service at www.deltacomputersystems.com/MS/MS01/
Justice Court 114 S Wall St, Natchez, MS 39121; 601-442-0199; fax: 601-445-7902; 8AM-5PM (CST). *Misdemeanor, Civil Actions under $3,500, Eviction, Small Claims.*
Chancery Court PO Box 1006, 1 Courthouse Sq, Natchez, MS 39121; 601-446-6684; fax: 601-445-7913; 8AM-5PM (CST). *Probate, Civil Land, Divorce, Family.*

Alcorn County

Circuit Court PO Box 430 Attn: Circuit Clerk, Corinth, MS 38835; 662-286-7740; fax: 662-286-7767; 8AM-5PM (CST). *Felony, Civil (usually over $3,500).*
General Information: No sealed, adoptions, mental health, juvenile, sex, or expunged records released. Fee to fax document $1.00 each. Court makes copy: $1.00 per page. Self serve copy: $.50 per page. No certification fee . Payee: Circuit Clerk. Personal checks accepted. No credit cards accepted. Prepayment required. Mail requests: SASE required.
Civil Name Search: Access: Mail, fax, in person. Both court and visitors may perform in person name searches. Search fee: $10.00 per name. Civil index in docket books from the 1930s. Mail turnaround time varies. Civil PAT goes back to 2/2003. Results include address if given by attorneys.
Criminal Name Search: Access: Mail, fax, in person. Both court and visitors may perform in person name searches. Search fee: $10.00 per name. Required to search: name, years to search, DOB; also helpful: SSN, sex. Criminal docket on books from the 1930s. Mail turnaround time varies. Criminal PAT goes back to same as civil.

Justice Court PO Box 226, 600 E Waldron St, Corinth, MS 38835; 662-286-7776; fax: 662-286-2157; 8AM-5PM (CST). *Misdemeanor, Civil Actions under $3,500, Eviction, Small Claims, Traffic.*
www.alcorncounty.org/justice.aspx

Chancery Court PO Box 69, 501 Waldron St, Corinth, MS 38835-0069; 662-286-7700; fax: 662-286-7706; 8AM-5PM (CST). *Probate, Civil Land, Divorce, Family.*

Amite County

Circuit Court PO Box 312, 243 W Main St, Liberty, MS 39645; 601-657-8932; fax: 601-657-1082; 8AM-5PM (CST). *Felony, Civil (usually over $3,500).*
General Information: Marriage records from 1809 - present. Will fax documents $3.00. Court makes copy: $.50 per page. Self serve copy: $.25 per page. Certification fee: $10.00 per document. Payee: Circuit Clerk. Personal checks accepted. No credit cards accepted.

Civil Name Search: Access: Phone, fax, mail, in person. Both court and visitors may perform in person name searches. Search fee: $10.00 per name. Civil index on docket books since 1976; judgments on computer back to 1990. Mail turnaround time same day.

Criminal Name Search: Access: Fax, mail, in person. Both court and visitors may perform in person name searches. Search fee: $10.00 per name. Required to search: name, years to search, DOB; also helpful: SSN. Criminal docket on books since 1976. Mail turnaround time same day.

Justice Court PO Box 362, 243 Broad St, Liberty, MS 39645; 601-657-4527; fax: 601-657-8604; 8AM-4:30PM (CST). *Misdemeanor, Civil Actions under $3,500, Eviction, Small Claims.*

Chancery Court Courthouse Square, 243 W Main St, Liberty, MS 39645; 601-657-8022; fax: 601-657-8288; 8AM-5PM (CST). *Probate, Civil Land, Divorce, Family.* www.amitecounty.ms/court-systems/chancery/

General Information: Cases include domestic/family, divorce, child custody, property division, adoptions, alimony, estates, land issues, emancipation, property title confirmation, property disputes over $50,000, and insurance settlements to minors.

Attala County

Circuit Court 100 Courthouse, #1, Kosciusko, MS 39090; 662-289-1471; fax: 662-289-7666; 8AM-5PM (CST). *Felony, Civil (usually over $3,500).*

General Information: Will fax documents. Court makes copy: $.50 per page. Self serve copy: same. Certification fee: $1.00 per document. Payee: Circuit Clerk. Business checks accepted. No credit cards accepted. Prepayment required. Mail requests: SASE required.

Civil Name Search: Access: Fax, mail, in person. Both court and visitors may perform in person name searches. Search fee: $10.00 per name. Civil records kept on docket books since 1915. Mail turnaround time same day.

Criminal Name Search: Access: Fax, mail, in person. Both court and visitors may perform in person name searches. Search fee: $10.00 per name. Required to search: name, years to search, DOB; also helpful: SSN. Criminal docket books kept since 1915. Mail turnaround time same day.

Justice Court 100 Courthouse, #4, Kosciusko, MS 39090; 662-289-7272; fax: 662-289-0105; 8AM-5PM (CST). *Misdemeanor, Civil Actions under $3,500, Eviction, Small Claims.*

Chancery Court 230 W. Washington, Kosciusko, MS 39090; 662-289-2921; fax: 662-289-7662; 8AM-5PM (CST). *Probate, Civil Land, Divorce, Family.*

Benton County

Circuit Court PO Box 262, 190 Ripley Ave, Ashland, MS 38603; 662-224-6310; fax: 662-224-6312; 8AM-5PM (CST). *Felony, Civil (usually over $3,500).*

General Information: No sealed, adoptions, mental health, juvenile, sex, or expunged records released. Will fax documents for fee. Court makes copy: $2.00 per page. Self serve copy: $.25 per page. Certification fee: $1.00. Payee: Circuit Court. Only cashiers checks and money orders accepted. No credit cards accepted. Prepayment required. Mail requests: SASE required.

Civil Name Search: Access: Mail, in person. Both court and visitors may perform in person name searches. Search fee: $10.00 per name. Required to search: name, years to search, address. Civil records kept on index books since 1871. Mail turnaround time same day. Civil PAT goes to 1999.

Criminal Name Search: Access: Mail, in person. Both court and visitors may perform in person name searches. Search fee: $10.00 per name. Required to search: name, years to search, DOB; also helpful: SSN. Criminal records kept on index books since 1871. Mail turnaround time same day. Criminal PAT goes back to same as civil.

Justice Court PO Box 152, 190 Ripley Ave, Ashland, MS 38603; 662-224-6320; fax: 662-224-6313; 8AM-5PM (CST). *Misdemeanor, Civil Actions under $3,500, Eviction, Small Claims.*

Chancery Court PO Box 218, 190 Ripley Ave, Ashland, MS 38603; 662-224-6300; fax: 662-224-6303; 8AM-5PM (CST). *Probate, Civil Land, Divorce, Family.*

Bolivar County

Circuit & County Court - 1st District PO Box 205, 801 Main St, Rosedale, MS 38769; 662-759-6521; fax: 662-759-3717; 8AM-N, 1PM-5PM (CST). *Felony, Misdemeanor, Civil (usually over $3,500).* www.co.bolivar.ms.us/circuitclerk.htm

General Information: No sealed, juvenile, sex, or expunged records released. Will fax documents to local or toll-free number. Court makes copy: $.50 per page. Self serve copy: $.25 per page. Certification fee: $1.50. Payee: Circuit Clerk. Only agency checks and money orders accepted. No credit cards accepted. Prepayment required. Mail requests: SASE required for criminal.

Civil Name Search: Access: mail, in person. Visitors must perform in person searches themselves. Search fee: $10.00 per name for 7 year search. Civil index on docket books since 1900s. Mail turnaround time 2-3 days. Civil PAT goes back to 2002. Name listed is name given by filing party.

Criminal Name Search: Access: Mail, in person. Both court and visitors may perform in person name searches. Search fee: $10.00 per name for 7 year search. Criminal docket on books since 1900s. Mail turnaround time 2-3 days. Criminal PAT goes back to same as civil. Name listed is name given by filing party.

Circuit & County Court - 2nd District PO Box 670, 200 S Court St, Cleveland, MS 38732; 662-843-2061; fax: 662-846-2943; 8AM-5PM (CST). *Felony, Misdemeanor, Civil (usually over $3,500).* www.co.bolivar.ms.us/circuitclerk.htm

General Information: No sealed, juvenile or expunged records released. Will fax documents to local or toll-free number. Court makes copy: $.50 per page. Self serve copy: $.25 per page. Certification fee: $1.50 per cert. Payee: Circuit Clerk. No personal checks or credit cards accepted. Prepayment required. Mail requests: SASE required for criminal record return.

Civil Name Search: Access: In person only. Both court and visitors may perform in person name searches. Search fee: $10.00. Civil index on docket books since 1940. Civil PAT goes back to 2002.

Criminal Name Search: Access: Mail, in person. Both court and visitors may perform in person name searches. Search fee: $10.00 per name; fee is for 7 year search. Criminal docket on books since 1940. Mail turnaround time 2-3 days. Criminal PAT goes back to 2000.

Justice Court PO Box 1507, 404 MLK Dr, Cleveland, MS 38732; 662-843-4008; fax: 662-846-6783; 8AM-5PM (CST). *Misdemeanor, Civil Actions under $3,500, Eviction, Small Claims.*

Cleveland Chancery Court PO Box 789, 200 Court St, Cleveland, MS 38732; 662-843-2071; fax: 662-846-2940; 8AM-5PM (CST). *Probate, Divorce, Family.*

Rosedale Chancery Court PO Box 238, 801 Main St, Rosedale, MS 38769; 662-759-3762; fax: 662-759-3467; 8AM-N, 1-5PM (CST). *Probate, Divorce, Family.*

Calhoun County

Circuit Court PO Box 25, Pittsboro, MS 38951; 662-412-3101; fax: 662-412-3103; 8AM-5PM (CST). *Felony, Civil (usually over $3,500).*

General Information: No sealed, mental health, juvenile, sex, or expunged records released. Fee to fax out file $2.00 per page. Court makes copy: $1.00 per page. Self serve copy: $.25 per page. There is also an Archive Fee of $1.00 on civil copies and filings. Certification fee: $1.50. Payee: Circuit Clerk. Personal checks accepted. No credit cards accepted. Prepayment required.

Civil Name Search: Access: Mail, in person. Both court and visitors may perform in person name searches. Search fee: $10.00 per name. Required to search: name, years to search, DOB or SSN. Civil index on docket books since 1922; computerized records go back to 1922. Mail turnaround time 1 day. Civil PAT goes back to 12 years.

Criminal Name Search: Access: Mail, in person. Both court and visitors may perform in person name searches. Search fee: $10.00 per name. Required to search: name, years to search, DOB; also helpful: SSN. Criminal docket on books since 1922; computerized records go back to 1922. Mail turnaround time 1 day; phone search info released after payment received. Criminal PAT goes back to same as civil.

Justice Court PO Box 7, Hwy 9 Courthouse Sq, Pittsboro, MS 38951; 662-412-3134; fax: 662-412-3136; 8AM-5PM (CST). *Misdemeanor, Civil Actions under $3,500, Eviction, Small Claims.*

Chancery Court PO Box 8, 103 W Main, Pittsboro, MS 38951; 662-412-3117; fax: 662-412-3111; 8AM-5PM (CST). *Probate, Civil Land, Divorce, Family.*

Carroll County

Circuit Court PO Box 6, Vaiden, MS 39176; 662-464-5476; fax: 662-464-5407; 8AM-5PM (CST). *Felony, Civil (usually over $3,500).*

General Information: No adoption, mental health or juvenile records released. Will fax documents to local or toll free line. Court makes copy: $.50 per page. Self serve copy: $.25 per page. Certification fee: $2.00. Payee: Circuit Court. Personal checks accepted. No credit cards accepted. Prepayment required. Mail requests: SASE required.

Civil Name Search: Access: Mail, in person. Both court and visitors may perform in person name searches. Search fee: $10.00 per name. Civil records on books since 1900s. Mail turnaround time 2 days.

Criminal Name Search: Access: Mail, in person. Both court and visitors may perform in person name searches. Search fee: $10.00 per name. Required to search: name, years to search; also helpful: SSN. Criminal docket on books since 1900s. Mail turnaround time 2 days.

Justice Court PO Box 10, Courthouse, 600 Lexington St, Carrollton, MS 38917; 662-237-9285; fax: 662-237-6833; 8AM-5PM (CST). *Misdemeanor, Civil Actions under $3,500, Eviction, Small Claims.*

Chancery Court PO Box 60, 600 Lexington St, Carrollton, MS 38917; 662-237-9274; fax: 662-237-9642; 8AM-N; 1-5PM (CST). *Probate, Civil Land, Divorce, Family.*

Chickasaw County

Circuit Court - 1st District 1 Pinson Sq, Rm 2, Houston, MS 38851; 662-456-2331; fax: 662-456-4831; 8AM-5PM (CST). *Felony, Civil (usually over $3,500).*

General Information: No sealed, adoptions, mental health, juvenile, sex, or expunged records released. Will not fax out documents. Court makes copy: $1.00 per page. Self serve copy: $.50 per page. Certification fee: $1.00 plus $.50 per page after first. Payee: Circuit Clerk. Business checks accepted. No credit cards accepted. Prepayment required. Mail requests: SASE required.

Civil Name Search: Access: Mail, in person. Both court and visitors may perform in person name searches. Search fee: $10.00 per name. Required to search: name, years to search; also helpful: address, DOB, DL. Civil index on docket books since mid-1800s. Mail turnaround time 2-3 days. Civil PAT goes back to 2004, countywide on this terminal.

Criminal Name Search: Access: Mail, in person. Both court and visitors may perform in person name searches. Search fee: $10.00 per name. Required to search: name, years to search, DOB; also helpful: address, SSN. Criminal docket on books since 1900. Mail turnaround time 2-3 days. Criminal PAT goes back to same as civil.

Circuit Court - 2nd District Courthouse, 234 W Main St Rm #203, Okolona, MS 38860; 662-447-2838; fax: 662-447-2504; 8AM-5PM (CST). *Felony, Civil (usually over $3,500).*

General Information: No sealed, adoptions, mental health, juvenile, sex, or expunged records released. Will not fax out documents. Court makes copy: $1.00 per page. Self serve copy: $.50 per page. Certification fee: $1.00 plus $.50 per page after first. Payee: Circuit Clerk. Business checks accepted. No credit cards accepted. Prepayment required. Mail requests: SASE required.

Civil Name Search: Access: Fax, mail, in person. Both court and visitors may perform in person name searches. Search fee: $10.00 per name. Required to search: name, years to search; also helpful: address. Civil records on computer. Mail turnaround time 2-3 days. Civil PAT goes back to 2003, countywide.

Criminal Name Search: Access: Fax, mail, in person. Both court and visitors may perform in person name searches. Search fee: $10.00 per name. Required to search: name, years to search, DOB; also helpful: SSN. Criminal records on computer. Mail turnaround time 2-3 days. Criminal PAT goes back to 2002, countywide.

Justice Court District 1 Courthouse, 1 Pinson Sq, Houston, MS 38851; 662-456-3941; fax: 662-448-8122; 8AM-5PM (CST). *Misdemeanor, Civil Actions under $3,500, Eviction, Small Claims.*

Justice Court District 2 236 W Main, Okolona, MS 38860; 662-447-3402; fax: 662-447-5020; 8AM-N; 1-5PM (CST). *Misdemeanor, Civil Actions under $3,500, Eviction, Small Claims.*

General Information: The court charges a copy fee of $2.00 per page. The search fee is $25.00.

Chancery Court- District 1 Courthouse Bldg, 1 Pinson Square, Houston, MS 38851; 662-456-2513; fax: 662-456-5295; 8AM-5PM (CST). *Probate, Divorce, Family.*

Chancery Court- District 2 234 W Main, Rm 201, Okolona, MS 38860-1438; 662-447-2092; fax: 662-447-5024; 8AM-N;1-5PM (CST). *Probate, Divorce, Family.*

Choctaw County

Circuit Court PO Box 34, Ackerman, MS 39735; 662-285-6245; fax: 662-285-2196; 8AM-5PM (CST). *Felony, Civil (usually over $3,500).*

General Information: No sealed, adoptions, mental health, juvenile, sex, or expunged records released. Will fax documents to local or toll free line. Court makes copy: $1.00 per page. Self serve copy: $.50 per page. Certification fee: $1.00 per page. Payee: Choctaw County Circuit Clerk. Personal checks accepted. No credit cards accepted. Prepayment required. Mail requests: SASE required.

Civil Name Search: Access: Mail, in person. Both court and visitors may perform in person name searches. Search fee: $10.00 per name. Civil records in books back to 1926. Mail turnaround time 14 days legal maximum. Civil PAT goes back to 2003.

Criminal Name Search: Access: Mail, in person. Both court and visitors may perform in person name searches. Search fee: $10.00 per name. Same fee for in person search. Required to search: name, years to search; also helpful: DOB, SSN. Criminal records in books back to 1926. Mail turnaround time 14 days legal maximum. Criminal PAT goes to 2003.

Justice Court 140 Jailhouse Rd, Ackerman, MS 39735; 662-285-3599; fax: 662-285-9039; 8AM-5PM (CST). *Misdemeanor, Civil Actions under $3,500, Eviction, Small Claims.*

Chancery Court PO Box 250, 22 Quinn St, Ackerman, MS 39735; 662-285-6329; fax: 662-285-3444; 8AM-5PM (CST). *Probate, Civil Land, Divorce, Family.*

Claiborne County

Circuit Court PO Box 549, Port Gibson, MS 39150; 601-437-5841; fax: 601-437-4543; 8AM-5PM (CST). *Felony, Civil (usually over $3,500).*

General Information: No sealed, adoptions, mental health, juvenile, sex, or expunged records released. Will fax documents $2.00 per page, if not extensive. Court makes copy: $1.00 per page; docket sheets $2.00 per page. Certification fee: $1.50 per case. Payee: Sammie L Good, Circuit Clerk. Personal checks accepted. No credit cards accepted. Prepayment required.

Civil Name Search: Access: Mail, in person. Both court and visitors may perform in person name searches. Search fee: $10.00 per name. Required to search: name, years to search, address. Civil index on docket books since 1820. Mail turnaround time varies.

Criminal Name Search: Access: Mail, in person. Both court and visitors may perform in person name searches. Search fee: $10.00 per name. Required to search: name, years to search, address, DOB, signed release. Criminal docket on books since 1820. Mail turnaround time varies.

Justice Court P O Box 497, 510 Market St, Port Gibson, MS 39150; 601-437-4478; fax: 601-437-3833; 8AM-4:30PM (CST). *Misdemeanor, Civil Actions under $3,500, Eviction, Small Claims.*

Chancery Court PO Box 449, 410 Market St, Port Gibson, MS 39150; 601-437-4992; fax: 601-437-3137; 8AM-5PM (CST). *Probate, Civil Land, Divorce, Family.*

Clarke County

Circuit Court PO Box 216, 101 S Archusa Ave, Quitman, MS 39355; 601-776-3111; fax: 601-776-1001; 8AM-5PM (CST). *Felony, Civil (usually over $3,500).*

General Information: No sealed, adoptions, mental health, juvenile, sex, or expunged records released. No fee to fax documents. Court makes copy: $.50 per page. Self serve copy: $.25 per page. Certification fee: $1.00 per page plus copy fee. Payee: Circuit Clerk. Personal checks accepted. No credit cards accepted. Prepayment required.

Civil Name Search: Access: Fax, mail, in person. Both court and visitors may perform in person name searches. Search fee: $10.00 per name. Required to search: name, years to search; also helpful: address. Civil records kept on docket books since 1950s. Mail turnaround time 1 day. Public use terminal has civil records back to Judgements only back to 1995. Results sometimes include the SSN.

Criminal Name Search: Access: Fax, mail, in person. Both court and visitors may perform in person name searches. Search fee: $10.00 per name. Required to search: name, years to search; also helpful: address, DOB, SSN, sex. Criminal docket books kept since 1950s. Mail turnaround time 1 day.

Justice Court PO Box 4, 100 E Church St, Quitman, MS 39355; 601-776-5371; fax: 601-776-1014; 8AM-5PM (CST). *Misdemeanor, Civil Actions under $3,500, Eviction, Small Claims.*

Chancery Court PO Box 689, 101 S Archusa, Quitman, MS 39355; 601-776-2126; fax: 601 -776-2756; 8AM-5PM (CST). *Probate, Civil Land, Divorce, Family.*

Clay County

Circuit Court PO Box 364, West Point, MS 39773; 662-494-3384; fax: 662-495-2057; 8AM-5PM (CST). *Felony, Civil (usually over $3,500).* www.claycountyms.com/courts/

General Information: Public must search using docket books. No sealed, adoptions, mental health, juvenile, sex, or expunged records released. Will fax documents. Court makes copy: $1.00 per page. Self serve copy: $.25 per page. Certification fee: $1.00 per page. Payee: Clay County Circuit Clerk. Personal checks accepted. No credit cards accepted. Prepayment required.

Civil Name Search: Access: Phone, mail, in person. Both court and visitors may perform in person name searches. Search fee: $10.00 per name. Civil index on docket books back to 1962; archived since mid-1800s. Note: Public must search using docket books. Mail turnaround time same day.

Criminal Name Search: Access: Mail, in person. Both court and visitors may perform in person name searches. Search fee: $10.00 per name. Required to search: name, years to search, address, DOB; also helpful: SSN. Criminal docket on books back to 1962; archived since late-1800s. Mail turnaround time same day.

Justice Court PO Box 674, 218 W Broad St, West Point, MS 39773; 662-494-6141; fax: 662-494-6141; 8AM-5PM (CST). *Misdemeanor, Civil Actions under $3,500, Eviction, Small Claims.*

Chancery Court PO Box 815, 205 Court St, West Point, MS 39773; 662-494-3124; fax: 662-492-4059; 8AM-5PM (CST). *Probate, Civil Land, Divorce, Family.* www.claycountyms.com/index.php

General Information: Send faxes to Attention Chancery Court. A private company permits online access to civil records; go to www.recordsusa.com or call Rob at 888-633-4748 x17 for info and demo.

Coahoma County

Circuit & County Court PO Box 849, Clarksdale, MS 38614-0849; 662-624-3014; fax: 662-624-3075; 8AM-5PM (CST). *Felony, Civil (usually over $3,500).*

General Information: No sealed, adoptions, mental health, juvenile, sex, or expunged records released. No fee to fax documents. Court makes copy: $1.00 per page. Self serve copy: $.50 per page. Certification fee: $1.00. Payee: Circuit Clerk. Personal checks accepted. Prepayment required.

Civil Name Search: Access: Fax, mail, in person. Both court and visitors may perform in person name searches. Search fee: $10.00 per name. Required to search: name, years to search, address. Civil records on dockets since 1950, archived since 1836. Note: Will also search judgment rolls. Mail turnaround time 2 days.

Criminal Name Search: Access: Fax, mail, in person. Both court and visitors may perform in person name searches. Search fee: $10.00 per name. Required to search: name, years to search, DOB, signed release; also helpful: SSN. Criminal records on dockets since 1910, archived since 1836. Mail turnaround time 2 days.

Justice Court 144 Ritch St, Clarksdale, MS 38614; 662-624-3060; fax: 662-624-5528; 8AM-5PM (CST). *Misdemeanor, Civil Actions under $3,500, Eviction, Small Claims.*
www.coahomacounty.net/justicecourt.html

Chancery Court PO Box 98, 115 1st St, Clarksdale, MS 38614; 662-624-3000; fax: 662-624-3040; 8AM-5PM (CST). *Probate, Civil, Divorce, Family.*
General Information: Also hold child support and adoption records.

Copiah County

Circuit Court PO Box 467, Hazlehurst, MS 39083; 601-894-1241; fax: 601-894-3026; 8AM-5PM (CST). *Felony, Civil (usually over $3,500).*

General Information: Also, use 601-894-3301 for the 22nd Circuit Court District. No sealed, adoptions, mental health, juvenile, sex, or expunged records released. No fee to fax documents. Court makes copy: $.50 per page. Self serve copy: $.25 per page. Certification fee: $1.50. Payee: Circuit Clerk. Business checks accepted. No credit cards accepted. Prepayment required.

Civil Name Search: Access: Fax, mail, in person. Both court and visitors may perform in person name searches. Search fee: $10.00 per name. Civil cases indexed by defendant. Civil index on docket books since late 1800s. Mail turnaround time 1-2 days.

Criminal Name Search: Access: Fax, mail, in person. Both court and visitors may perform in person name searches. Search fee: $10.00 per name. Required to search: name, years to search; also helpful: DOB, SSN. Criminal docket on books since late 1800s. Mail turnaround time 1-2 days.

Justice Court PO Box 798, 121 W Frost St, Hazlehurst, MS 39083; 601-894-3218; fax: 601-894-6038; 8AM-5PM (CST). *Misdemeanor, Civil Actions under $3,500, Eviction, Small Claims.*

Chancery Court PO Box 507, 122 S Lowe St, Hazlehurst, MS 39083; 601-894-3021; fax: 601-894-4081; 8AM-5PM (CST). *Probate, Civil Land, Divorce, Family.*
General Information: The calendar is online at www.deltacomputersystems.com/ms/ms15/index.html.

Covington County

Circuit Court PO Box 667, Collins, MS 39428; 601-765-6506; fax: 601-765-5012; 8AM-5PM (CST). *Felony, Civil (usually over $3,500).*

General Information: No sealed, adoptions, mental health, juvenile, sex, or expunged records released. No fee to fax documents. Court makes copy: $.50 per page. Self serve copy: $.25 per page. Certification fee: $3.00. Payee: Circuit Clerk. Personal checks accepted. No credit cards accepted. Prepayment required. Mail requests: SASE required.

Civil Name Search: Access: Fax, mail, in person. Both court and visitors may perform in person name searches. Search fee: $10.00 per name. Civil index on docket books since 1915. Mail turnaround time 2-3 days.

Criminal Name Search: Access: Fax, mail, in person. Both court and visitors may perform in person name searches. Search fee: $10.00 per name. Required to search: name, years to search, DOB; also helpful: SSN. Criminal docket on books since 1915. Mail turnaround time 2-3 days.

Justice Court PO Box 665, 101 Dogwood Ave, Collins, MS 39428; 601-765-6581; fax: 601-765-5014; 8AM-5PM (CST). *Misdemeanor, Civil Actions under $3,500, Eviction, Small Claims.*

Chancery Court PO Box 1679, 101 S Elm St, Collins, MS 39428; 601-765-4242; fax: 601-765-5016; 8AM-5PM (CST). *Probate, Civil Land, Divorce, Family.*

De Soto County

Circuit & County Court 2535 Hwy 51 South, Hernando, MS 38632; 662-429-1325; criminal phone: 662-429-1325; civil phone: 662-429-1326; criminal fax: 662-449-1416; civil fax: 8AM-5PM; 8AM-5PM (CST). *Felony, Misdemeanor, Civil (usually over $3,500).*
www.desotoms.com/departments/courts/circuit-court

General Information: No sealed, juvenile, sex, or expunged records released. Will not fax documents. Court makes copy: $1.00 per page. Self serve copy: same. Certification fee: $2.50 per doc. No personal checks accepted. Cash or money order only. No credit cards accepted. Prepayment required.

Civil Name Search: Access: Mail, in person, online. Both court and visitors may perform in person name searches. Search fee: $10.00 per name. Required to search: name, years to search; also helpful: address. Civil index on docket books since 1895, online index since 1987. Mail turnaround time 3 days. Civil PAT goes back to 1990-2002; partial from 2003 forward. Search docket information, records and judgments at www.deltacomputersystems.com/MS/MS17/INDEX.HTML/ Fee is $30 monthly or $360 annually.

Criminal Name Search: Access: Mail, in person, online. Both court and visitors may perform in person name searches. Search fee: $10.00 per name. Required to search: name, years to search, DOB; also helpful: SSN. Criminal docket on books since 1915, online index since 1980. Mail turnaround time 3 days. Criminal PAT goes back to same as civil. Search docket info and records online same as civil.

Justice Court 8525 Highway 51 North, Southaven, MS 38671; 662-393-5810; fax: 662-393-5859; 8AM-5PM (CST). *Misdemeanor, Civil Actions under $3,500, Eviction, Small Claims.*
www.desotoms.com/departments/courts/justice-court
General Information: Records maintained since 1984, search fee is $5.00. Search docket free online at www.desotoms.info/.

Chancery Court PO Box 949, Rm 100, 2535 Hwy 51 South, Hernando, MS 38632; 662-429-1320; fax: 662-449-1420; 8AM-5PM (CST). *Probate, Civil Land, Divorce, Family.*
www.desotoms.com/departments/courts/chancery-court

Forrest County

Circuit & County Court PO Box 992, 630 Main St, Hattiesburg, MS 39403; 601-582-3213; fax: 601-545-6065; 8AM-5PM (CST). *Felony, Civil (usually over $3,500).*

General Information: No juvenile or expunged records released. Will fax back documents no fee. Court makes copy: $1.00 per page. Self serve copy: $.50 per page. Certification fee: $1.50 per cert plus copy fee; is included in copy fee. Payee: Circuit Clerk. Business checks or attorney checks accepted. No credit cards accepted. Prepayment required.

Civil Name Search: Access: Phone, mail, in person. Both court and visitors may perform in person name searches. Search fee: $10.00 per name includes copies and cert. Required to search: name, years to search; also helpful: address. Civil index on docket books since 1900s. Note: Limited phone access. Mail turnaround time 10 days. Civil PAT goes back to 2000.

Criminal Name Search: Access: Mail, in person. Both court and visitors may perform in person name searches. Search fee: $10.00 per name includes copies and cert. Required to search: name, years to search, DOB, SSN; also helpful: address. Criminal docket on books since 1900s; on computer since 1995. Mail turnaround time 10 days. Criminal PAT goes back to same as civil.

Justice Court 700 Main St, Hattiesburg, MS 39401; 601-544-3136 x500; fax: 601-545-6114; 8AM-5PM (CST). *Misdemeanor, Civil Actions under $3,500, Eviction, Small Claims.*
General Information: Searches performed by the court only on Thursdays, or after 2PM rest of week (if time allows).

Chancery Court PO Box 951, 641 Main St, Hattiesburg, MS 39403; 601-545-6040; fax: 601-545-6043; 8AM-5PM (CST). *Probate, Civil Land, Divorce, Family.*

Franklin County

Circuit Court PO Box 267, Meadville, MS 39653; 601-384-2320; fax: 601-384-8244; 8AM-5PM (CST). *Felony, Civil (usually over $3,500).*

General Information: No sealed, adoptions, mental health, juvenile, sex, or expunged records released. Will fax documents to local or toll free line. Court makes copy: $1.00 per page. Self serve copy: $.50 per page. Certification fee: $.50 per page. Payee: Circuit Clerk. Personal checks accepted. No credit cards accepted. Prepayment required.

Civil Name Search: Access: Phone, fax, mail, in person. Both court and visitors may perform in person name searches. Search fee: $10.00 per name. Civil records on books since 1944. Mail turnaround time 2-3 days. Public use terminal has civil records back to 1994. Judgments only on public access terminal. Terminal results may also show address.

Criminal Name Search: Access: Fax, mail, in person. Both court and visitors may perform in person name searches. Search fee: $10.00 per name. Required to search: name, years to search, DOB or SSN; also helpful: address. Criminal docket on books since 1944. Mail turnaround time 2-3 days.

Justice Court PO Box 365, Courthouse Sq/Main, Meadville, MS 39653; 601-384-2002; fax: 601-384-2253; 8AM-5PM (CST). *Misdemeanor, Civil Actions under $3,500, Eviction, Small Claims.*

Chancery Court PO Box 297, 36 Main St E, Meadville, MS 39653; 601-384-2330; fax: 601-384-5864; 8AM-5PM (CST). *Probate, Civil Land, Divorce, Family.*

George County

Circuit Court 355 Cox St, #C, Lucedale, MS 39452; 601-947-4881; fax: 601-947-8804; 8AM-5PM M-F, 9AM-N Sat (CST). *Felony, Civil (usually over $3,500).*

General Information: No sealed, adoptions, mental health, juvenile, sex, or expunged records released. Will fax documents for no add'l fee. Court makes copy: $1.00 per page. Certification fee: $2.00 per cert plus copy fee. Payee: Circuit Clerk. Personal checks accepted. No credit cards accepted. Prepayment required. Mail requests: SASE requested.

Civil Name Search: Access: Fax, mail, in person. Both court and visitors may perform in person name searches. Search fee: $10.00 per name. Civil index on docket books since 1910. Mail turnaround time 1-2 days.

Criminal Name Search: Access: Fax, mail, in person. Both court and visitors may perform in person name searches. Search fee: $10.00 per name. Required to search: name, years to search; also helpful: SSN. Criminal docket on books since 1910. Mail turnaround time 1-2 days.

Justice Court 368 Cox St, Lucedale, MS 39452; 601-947-4834; fax: 601-947-1911; 8AM-5PM (CST). *Misdemeanor, Civil Actions under $3,500, Eviction, Small Claims.*

General Information: Records on computer (5/92 forward) are $4.00 per name. Prior to 5/92, searches are $20 for first 1/2 hour then $5.00 each 1/4 hour.

Chancery Court 355 Cox St, #A, Lucedale, MS 39452; 601-947-4801; fax: 601-947-1300; 8AM-5PM (CST). *Probate, Civil Land, Divorce, Family.*

Greene County

Circuit Court PO Box 310, 400 Main St, Leakesville, MS 39451; 601-394-2379; fax: 601-394-2334; 8AM-5PM (CST). *Felony, Civil (usually over $3,500).*

General Information: No sealed, adoptions, mental health, juvenile, sex, or expunged records released. No fee to fax documents. Court makes copy: $1.00 per page. Self serve copy: $.25 per page. Certification fee: $1.00 per doc. Payee: Circuit Clerk. Personal checks accepted. No credit cards accepted. Prepayment required. Mail requests: SASE requested.

Civil Name Search: Access: Phone, fax, mail, in person. Both court and visitors may perform in person name searches. Search fee: $10.00 per name. Required to search: name, years to search; also helpful: address. Civil index on docket books since early 1900s. Mail turnaround time 1-2 days.

Criminal Name Search: Access: Phone, fax, mail, in person. Both court and visitors may perform in person name searches. Search fee: $10.00 per name. Required to search: name, years to search; also helpful: SSN. Criminal docket on books since early 1900s. Misdemeanor records kept in Greene County Justice Court, 601-394-2347. Mail turnaround time 1-2 days.

Justice Court PO Box 547, 416 Main St, Leakesville, MS 39451; 601-394-2347; fax: 601-394-2114; 8AM-5PM (CST). *Misdemeanor, Civil Actions under $3,500, Eviction, Small Claims.*

General Information: For payments only use www.greenecotix.com.

Chancery Court PO Box 610, 400 Main St, Leakesville, MS 39451; 601-394-2377; fax: 601-394-4445; 8AM-5PM (CST). *Probate, Civil Land, Divorce, Family.*

Grenada County

Circuit Court PO Box 1517, 59 Green St Courthouse, Grenada, MS 38902-1517; 662-226-1941; fax: 662-227-2865; 8AM-5PM (CST). *Felony, Civil (usually over $3,500).*
www.grenadacircuitclerk.webs.com/

General Information: Public access terminal has only civil judgments. No sealed, juvenile, or expunged records released. Will fax documents $3.00 per page. Court makes copy: $1.00 per page. Self serve copy: $.25 per page. Certification fee: $2.00. Payee: Circuit Clerk. No personal checks or credit cards accepted. Prepayment required.

Civil Name Search: Access: In person only. Visitors must perform in person searches themselves. Civil index on docket books since mid-1970s. Civil PAT goes back to 1999. Use terminal to search for judgments.

Criminal Name Search: Access: In person only. Visitors must perform in person searches themselves. Criminal docket on books since mid-1970s. Criminal PAT goes back to 1999.

Justice Court 16 First St, Grenada, MS 38901; 662-226-3331; fax: 662-227-5513; 8AM-5PM (CST). *Misdemeanor, Civil Actions under $3,500, Eviction, Small Claims.*

General Information: Will hear preliminary felonies.

Chancery Court PO Box 1208, 59 Green St, Rm 1, Grenada, 662-226-1821; fax: 662-227-2860; 8AM-5PM (CST). *Probate, C Divorce, Family.*

Hancock County

Circuit Court 152 Main St, #B, Bay St. Louis, MS 39520; 228-467-5265; probate phone: 228-467-5404; fax: 228-467-2779; 8AM-5PM (CST). *Felony, Civil.*

General Information: No sealed, adoptions, mental health, juvenile, sex, or expunged records released. Will not fax documents. Court makes copy: $1.00 per page. Self serve copy: same. Certification fee: $1.50 per page. Payee: Circuit Clerk. Personal checks accepted. No credit cards accepted. Prepayment required.

Civil Name Search: Access: Mail, in person. Both court and visitors may perform in person name searches. Search fee: $10.00 per name. Civil index on docket books since 1975. Mail turnaround time 2 days to 1 week. Civil PAT goes back to 2000.

Criminal Name Search: Access: Mail, in person. Both court and visitors may perform in person name searches. Search fee: $10.00 per name. Required to search: name, years to search, DOB; also helpful: SSN. Criminal docket on books since 1970. Mail turnaround time 2 days to 1 week. Criminal PAT goes back to same as civil.

Justice Court PO Box 698, 17343 Hiway 603, Kiln, MS 39556; 228-255-5808; fax: 228-255-5851; 8AM-5PM (CST). *Misdemeanor, Civil Actions under $3,500, Eviction, Small Claims.*

Chancery Court 152 Main St, #A, Bay St. Louis, MS 39520; 228-467-5406; fax: 228-467-3159; 8AM-5PM (CST). *Probate, Civil Land, Divorce, Family.* www.hancockcountyms.gov/chancery.htm

Harrison County

Circuit & County Court - 1st District PO Box 998, 1801 23rd Av, Gulfport, MS 39502; 228-865-4147, 228-865-4010; fax: 228-865-4009; 8AM-5PM (CST). *Felony, Misdemeanor, Civil Actions.*

General Information: No sealed, adoptions, mental health, juvenile, sex, or expunged records released. Will fax documents for fee. Court makes copy: $.50 per page. Self serve copy: $.25 per page. Certification fee: $2.50 per cert. Payee: Circuit Clerk. Attorney's business checks, money orders, cash or certified checks accepted. No credit cards accepted. Prepayment required. Mail requests: SASE requested.

Civil Name Search: Access: Fax, mail, in person, online. Both court and visitors may perform in person name searches. Search fee: $10.00 per name. Civil records on computer back to 7/1991, prior on docket books, older records are archived. Mail turnaround time 2-3 days. Civil PAT goes back to 10 years. Access to Judicial District judgments are free at http://co.harrison.ms.us/elected/circuitclerk/jroll/. Search current court dockets free by date at http://co.harrison.ms.us/dockets/.

Criminal Name Search: Access: Fax, mail, in person. Both court and visitors may perform in person name searches. Search fee: $10.00 per name. Required to search: name, years to search, DOB; also helpful: SSN. Criminal records computerized from 7/1991, prior on docket books, older records are archived. Mail turnaround time 2-3 days. Criminal PAT goes back to same as civil. Search current court dockets free by date at http://co.harrison.ms.us/dockets/.

Circuit & County Court - 2nd District PO Box 235, 730 Martin Luther King Jr Blvd, Biloxi, MS 39533; 228-435-8293/8258; fax: 228-435-8277; 8AM-5PM (CST). *Felony, Misdemeanor, Civil Actions.*

General Information: This is a Circuit and County Court under one clerk. No sealed or expunged records released. Will fax documents $.50 per page. Court makes copy: $.50 per page. Self serve copy: $.25 per page on your paper. Certification fee: $1.00 per cert. Payee: Circuit Clerk. No personal checks or credit cards accepted. Prepayment required. Mail requests: SASE required.

Civil Name Search: Access: Fax, mail, in person, online. Both court and visitors may perform in person name searches. Search fee: $10.00 per name. Civil records on computer since 3/91, prior on docket books. Mail turnaround time 3 days. Civil PAT goes back to 2005. Access to Judicial District judgments are free at http://co.harrison.ms.us/elected/circuitclerk/jroll/. Search current court dockets free by date at http://co.harrison.ms.us/dockets/.

Criminal Name Search: Access: Fax, mail, in person. Both court and visitors may perform in person name searches. Search fee: $10.00 per name. Required to search: name, years to search, DOB; also helpful: SSN, aliases. Criminal records on computer since 3/91, prior on books. Mail turnaround time 3 days. Criminal PAT goes back to same as civil. Terminal results include SSN. Search current court dockets by date free at http://co.harrison.ms.us/dockets/.

Justice Court District 1 PO Box 1754, Gulfport, MS 39502; 228-865-4213; criminal phone: 228-865-4214; civil phone: 228-865-4193; fax: 228-865-4216; 8AM-5PM (CST). *Misdemeanor, Civil Actions under $3,500, Eviction, Small Claims.*
http://co.harrison.ms.us/departments/justice%20court/

Search Justice court tickets free at
...departments/justice%20court/.

...strict 2 PO Box 1141, Biloxi, MS 39533; criminal
...251; civil phone: 228-435-8250; fax: 228-435-8279;
...). *Misdemeanor, Civil Actions under $3,500, Eviction,*

...rison.ms.us/departments/justice%20court/
Information: Traffic is reached at 228-435-8252. Search Justice
tickets free at
http://co.harrison.ms.us/departments/justice%20court/tickets/.

Biloxi Chancery Court PO Box 544, 730 Martin Luther King Jr Blvd
(39530), Biloxi, MS 39533; 228-435-8228; fax: 228-435-8281; 8AM-5PM
(CST). *Probate, Divorce, Family.*
http://co.harrison.ms.us/elected/chanceryclerk/chancourt.asp
General Information: Search Chancery Court dockets for free at
http://co.harrison.ms.us/dockets/.

Gulfport Chancery Court Harrison County Judicial 1, 1801 23rd Ave,
Gulfport, MS 39501; 228-865-4095; fax: 228-865-4054; 8AM-5PM
(CST). *Probate, Divorce, Family.*
http://co.harrison.ms.us/elected/chanceryclerk/
General Information: Search Chancery Court dockets for free at
http://co.harrison.ms.us/dockets/.

Hinds County

Circuit & County Court - 1st District PO Box 327, Jackson, MS
39205; 601-968-6628; fax: 601-973-5547; 8AM-5PM (CST). *Felony,
Misdemeanor, Civil (usually over $3,500).*
www.co.hinds.ms.us/pgs/index.asp
General Information: No sealed, adoptions, mental health, juvenile, sex,
or expunged records released. Will not fax documents. Court makes copy:
$1.00 per page. Self serve copy: $.50 per page. Certification fee: $1.00 plus
copy fee. Payee: Circuit Clerk. Personal checks accepted. No credit cards
accepted. Prepayment required. Mail requests: SASE required.
Civil Name Search: Access: Mail, in person, online. Both court and
visitors may perform in person name searches. Search fee: $9.00 per name.
Civil index on docket books back to 1900s. Mail turnaround time 14 days.
Civil PAT goes back to 1993. Search civil and county case info at
www.co.hinds.ms.us/pgs/apps/gindex.asp. Judgment information is also
available.
Criminal Name Search: Access: Mail, in person. Both court and visitors
may perform in person name searches. Search fee: $9.00 per name.
Required to search: name, years to search, DOB; also helpful: SSN. Criminal
docket on books back to 1900s. Note: The court does not offer online but
the Sheriff's Office offers an inmate and sex offender search at
www.co.hinds.ms.us/pgs/apps/gindex.asp. Mail turnaround time 14 days.
Criminal PAT goes back to 1981.

Circuit & County Court - 2nd District PO Box 999, Raymond, MS
39154; 601-857-8038; fax: 601-857-0535; 8AM-N, 1-5PM (CST). *Felony,
Misdemeanor, Civil (usually over $3,500).*
www.co.hinds.ms.us/pgs/index.asp
General Information: No sealed, adoptions, mental health, juvenile, sex,
expunged or some preliminary criminal records released. Will fax documents
$1.00 per page prepaid. Court makes copy: $1.00 per page. Certification fee:
$1.50 per cert. Payee: Circuit Clerk. Personal checks accepted. No credit
cards accepted. Prepayment required. Mail requests: SASE requested.
Civil Name Search: Access: In person, online. Visitors must perform in
person searches themselves. Civil records on computer since 1994, prior on
docket books since late 1800s. Access the clerk's judgment rolls free at
www.co.hinds.ms.us/pgs/apps/jridx_query.asp.
Criminal Name Search: Access: Mail, in person. Both court and visitors
may perform in person name searches. Search fee: $9.00 per name.
Required to search: name, years to search; also helpful: DOB, SSN. Criminal
records on computer since 1994, prior on docket books since late 1800s. Mail
turnaround time 1 week.

Justice Court 407 E Pascagoula, 3rd Fl, PO Box 3490, Jackson, MS
39207; 601-965-8800; civil phone: x3; fax: 601-973-5532; 8AM-5PM
(CST). *Misdemeanor, Civil Actions under $3,500, Eviction, Small Claims.*
www.co.hinds.ms.us/pgs/ctydivision/justicecourt.asp

Chancery Court- Jackson PO Box 686, 316 S President St, Jackson,
MS 39205; 601-968-6540; fax: 601-973-5554; 8AM-5PM (CST). *Probate,
Divorce, Family.*

Chancery Court- Raymond PO Box 88, 127 W Main St, Annex Bldg,
Raymond, MS 39154; 601-857-8055; fax: 601-857-4953 or 3123; 8AM-
5PM (CST). *Probate, Divorce, Family.*
www.co.hinds.ms.us/pgs/elected/chanceryclerk.asp
General Information: This court also holds records of land disputes.

Holmes County

Circuit Court PO Box 718, Lexington, MS 39095; 662-834-2476;
fax: 662-834-3870; 8AM-5PM (CST). *Felony, Civil (usually over $3,500).*
General Information: No sealed or expunged records released. No fee to
fax documents. Court makes copy: $1.00 per page. Self serve copy: $.50 per
page. Certification fee: $1.50 plus copy fee; Exemplification fee $30.00.
Payee: Holmes County Circuit Clerk. Business checks accepted. No credit
cards accepted. Prepayment required.
Civil Name Search: Access: Fax, mail, in person. Both court and visitors
may perform in person name searches. Search fee: $10.00 per name. Civil
index on docket books since 1940s. Mail turnaround time 1-2 days.
Criminal Name Search: Access: Fax, mail, in person. Both court and
visitors may perform in person name searches. Search fee: $10.00 per
name. Required to search: name, years to search; also helpful: DOB, SSN.
Criminal docket on books since 1940s. Mail turnaround time 1-2 days.

Justice Court PO Box 99, 200 Court St, Lexington, MS 39095; 662-834-
4565; fax: 662-834-1402; 8AM-5PM (CST). *Misdemeanor, Civil Actions
under $3,500, Eviction, Small Claims.*

Chancery Court PO Box 239, 2 Court Sq, Lexington, MS 39095; 662-
834-2508; fax: 662-834-1872; 8AM-5PM (CST). *Probate, Civil Land,
Divorce, Family.*

Humphreys County

Circuit Court PO Box 696, Belzoni, MS 39038; 662-247-3065; fax: 662-
247-3906; 8AM-5PM (CST). *Felony, Civil (usually over $3,500).*
General Information: No sealed, adoptions, mental health, juvenile, sex,
or expunged records released. Will fax documents $1.00. Court makes copy:
$1.00 per page. Self serve copy: $.50 per page. Certification fee: $1.00 per
page if you perform search. No cert fee if court performs search. Payee:
Circuit Clerk. Personal checks accepted. No credit cards accepted.
Prepayment required. Mail requests: SASE required.
Civil Name Search: Access: Fax, mail, in person. Both court and visitors
may perform in person name searches. Search fee: $10.00 per name. Civil
records on books since 1918. Mail turnaround time 1 day.
Criminal Name Search: Access: Fax, mail, in person. Both court and
visitors may perform in person name searches. Search fee: $10.00 per
name. Required to search: name, years to search; also helpful: DOB, SSN.
Criminal docket on books since 1918. Mail turnaround time 1 day; phone
turnaround 30 minutes.

Justice Court 102 Castleman St, Belzoni, MS 39038; 662-247-4337;
fax: 662-247-1095; 8AM-5PM (CST). *Misdemeanor, Civil Actions under
$3,500, Eviction, Small Claims.*

Chancery Court PO Box 547, 102 Castleman St, Belzoni, MS 39038;
662-247-1740; fax: 662-247-0101; 8AM-N, 1-5PM (CST). *Probate, Civil
Land, Divorce, Family.*

Issaquena County

Circuit Court PO Box 27, 129 Court St, Mayersville, MS 39113; 662-
873-2761; fax: 662-873-2061; 8AM-Noon; 1-5PM (CST). *Felony, Civil
(usually over $3,500).*
General Information: No sealed, adoptions, mental health, juvenile, sex,
or expunged records released. Will fax documents to local or toll free line.
Court makes copy: $.50 per page. Self serve copy: $.25 per page.
Certification fee: $1.00 per cert. Payee: Circuit Clerk. Personal checks
accepted. No credit cards accepted. Mail requests: SASE requested.
Civil Name Search: Access: Fax, mail, in person. Both court and visitors
may perform in person name searches. Search fee: $20.00 per name. Civil
index on docket books since 1846. Mail turnaround time 1 week.
Criminal Name Search: Access: Fax, mail, in person. Both court and
visitors may perform in person name searches. Search fee: $20.00 per
name. Required to search: name, years to search; also helpful: DOB, SSN.
Criminal docket on books since 1846. Mail turnaround time 1 week.

Justice Court PO Box 58, 129 Court St, Mayersville, MS 39113; 662-
873-6287; fax: 662-873-2094; 8AM-N, 1-5PM (CST). *Misdemeanor, Civil
Actions under $3,500, Eviction, Small Claims.*

Chancery Court PO Box 27, 129 Court St, Mayersville, MS 39113; 662-
873-2761; fax: 662-873-2061; 8AM-N, 1-5PM (CST). *Probate, Civil
Land, Divorce, Family.*

Itawamba County

Circuit Court 201 W Main, Fulton, MS 38843; 662-862-3511; fax: 662-
862-4006; 8AM-5PM (CST). *Felony, Civil (usually over $3,500).*
General Information: Will fax documents to local or toll free line. Court
makes copy: $.25 per page. No certification fee . Payee: Itawamba County
Circuit Court. No personal checks or credit cards accepted. Prepayment
required. Mail requests: SASE required.
Civil Name Search: Access: Phone, fax, mail, in person. Both court and
visitors may perform in person name searches. Search fee: $10.00 with a
written request. Civil records on books since 1940s, index may be viewed on

judgment roll. Mail turnaround time 1 week. Civil PAT goes back to 2007.

Criminal Name Search: Access: Phone, fax, mail, in person. Both court and visitors may perform in person name searches. Search fee: $10.00 with a written request. Required to search: name, years to search, DOB; also helpful: SSN. Criminal docket on books since 1940s. Mail turnaround time 1 week. Criminal PAT goes back to 2007.

Justice Court 304 D W Wiygul St., Fulton, MS 38843; 662-862-4315; fax: 662-862-5805; 8AM-5PM (CST). *Misdemeanor, Civil Actions under $3,500, Eviction, Small Claims.*

Chancery Court PO Box 776, 201 W Main, Fulton, MS 38843; 662-862-3421; fax: 662-862-3421; 8AM-5PM M-F; 8AM-N Sat (CST). *Probate, Civil Land, Divorce, Family.*

Jackson County

Circuit Court PO Box 998, Pascagoula, MS 39568-0998; 228-769-3025; fax: 228-769-3180; 8AM-5PM (CST). *Felony, Civil (usually over $3,500).*
www.co.jackson.ms.us/DS/CircuitCourt.html
General Information: No sealed or expunged records released. Will not fax documents. Court makes copy: $1.00 per page. Self serve copy: $.25 per page. Certification fee: $2.00 per page, includes copy fee. Payee: Circuit Clerk. Business checks accepted. No credit cards accepted. Prepayment required. Mail requests: SASE required.
Civil Name Search: Access: Mail, in person, online. Both court and visitors may perform in person name searches. Search fee: $10.00 per name per 10 years searched. Civil records on computer back to 1993, prior on docket books since 1920s. Mail turnaround time varies. Civil PAT goes back to 1992. Access to only Circuit Court monthly dockets is free at www.co.jackson.ms.us/courts/circuit-court/Docket.aspx
Criminal Name Search: Access: Mail, in person, online. Both court and visitors may perform in person name searches. Search fee: $10.00 per name, per 10 years searched. Required to search: name, years to search, DOB; also helpful: SSN. Criminal records computerized from 1992, prior on docket books since 1920s. Mail turnaround time varies. Criminal PAT goes back to same as civil. Online access to criminal dockets only is the same as civil.

County Court PO Box 998, 3104 Magnolia St, Pascagoula, MS 39568; 228-769-3181; fax: 228-769-3180; 8AM-5PM (CST). *Misdemeanor, Civil Actions (usually over $3,500).*
www.co.jackson.ms.us/courts/county-court.php
General Information: No sealed, adoptions, mental health, juvenile, sex, or expunged records released. Will not fax documents. Court makes copy: $1.00 per page. Self serve copy: $.25 per page. Certification fee: $2.00. Payee: Clerk of County Court. Only cashiers checks and money orders accepted. No credit cards accepted. Prepayment required.
Civil Name Search: Access: Mail, in person. Both court and visitors may perform in person name searches. Search fee: $10.00 per name per 10 years. Civil records files go back 20 years; on computer back to 2001. Mail turnaround time 1 week. Civil PAT goes back to 2001.
Criminal Name Search: Access: Mail, in person. Both court and visitors may perform in person name searches. Search fee: $10.00 per name per 10 years. Required to search: name, years to search, DOB. Criminal records go back 12 years; on computer back to 2000 (county), 1992 (circuit). Mail turnaround time 1 week. Criminal PAT goes back to 2000.

Justice Court 5343 Jefferson St, Moss Point, MS 39563; criminal phone: 228.769.3080, 3387; civil phone: 228.769.3086, 3087, 3399; fax: 228-769-3364; 8AM-5PM (CST). *Misdemeanor, Civil Actions under $3,500, Eviction, Small Claims.*
www.co.jackson.ms.us/courts/justice-court.php

Chancery Court PO Box 998, 3104 Magnolia St, Pascagoula, MS 39568; 228-769-3124, 769-3125; fax: 228-769-3397; 8AM-5PM (CST). *Probate, Civil Land, Divorce, Family.*
www.co.jackson.ms.us/DS/ChanceryCourts.html
General Information: Access Chancery Court cases and docket schedule free at www.deltacomputersystems.com/MS/MS30/INDEX.HTML.

Jasper County

Circuit Court - 1st District PO Box 58, 1782 Hwy 503, Paulding, MS 39348; 601-727-4941; fax: 601-727-4475; 8AM-5PM (CST). *Felony, Civil (usually over $3,500).*
General Information: No sealed or expunged records released. Will fax documents $5.00 per doc. Court makes copy: $.50 per page. Self serve copy: $.25 per page. Certification fee: $1.50 per doc. Payee: Circuit Clerk. Personal checks accepted. No credit cards accepted. Prepayment required. Mail requests: SASE required.
Civil Name Search: Access: Fax, mail, in person. Both court and visitors may perform in person name searches. Search fee: $10.00 per name. Fee includes a search of both districts in the county. Civil index on docket books since 1932. Mail turnaround time 1 week.

Criminal Name Search: Access: Fax, mail, in person. Both court and visitors may perform in person name searches. Search fee: $10.00 per name. Fee includes a search of both districts in the county. Required to search: name, years to search; also helpful: DOB, SSN. Criminal docket on books since 1932. Mail turnaround time 1 week.

Circuit Court - 2nd District PO Box 447, Bay Springs, MS 39422; 601-764-2245; fax: 601-764-3078; 8AM-5PM (CST). *Felony, Civil (usually over $3,500).*
www.co.jasper.ms.us/circuit_clerk.html
General Information: No sealed, adoptions, mental health, juvenile, sex, or expunged records released. Will fax documents to local or toll free line. Court makes copy: $1.00 per page. Self serve copy: $.25 per page. Certification fee: $2.00 per page. Payee: Circuit Clerk. Personal checks accepted. No credit cards accepted. Prepayment required. Mail requests: SASE requested.
Civil Name Search: Access: Mail, in person. Both court and visitors may perform in person name searches. Search fee: $10.00 per name. Fee includes a search of both districts in the county. Civil index on docket books since 1932. Mail turnaround time 1-2 days. Public use terminal has civil records back to 7 years. Search for judgments only.
Criminal Name Search: Access: Mail, in person, fax. Both court and visitors may perform in person name searches. Search fee: $10.00 per name. Fee includes a search of both districts in the county. Required to search: name, years to search; also helpful: SSN. Criminal docket on books since 1932. Mail turnaround time 1-2 days.

Justice CourtDistrict 1 PO Box 39, Paulding, MS 39348; 601-727-2247; fax: 601-727-2246; 8AM-5PM (CST). *Misdemeanor, Civil Actions under $3,500, Eviction, Small Claims.*
www.co.jasper.ms.us/courthouses.html
General Information: This court is new as of 5/1/08. Prior to that date, all records are found at Justice Court District 2 in Bay Springs. Paulding has only new cases of 5/1/08.

Justice Court District 2 PO Box 1054, 27 W 8th Ave, Bay Springs, MS 39422; 601-764-2065; fax: 601-764-3402; 8AM-5PM (CST). *Misdemeanor, Civil Actions under $3,500, Eviction, Small Claims.*
www.co.jasper.ms.us/courthouses.html
General Information: This is the original Justice Court for Jasper County. As of 5/1/2008, a second Justice Court was added in Paulding. All Justice Court records prior to that date are at Justice Court District 2.

Bay Springs Chancery Court PO Box 1047, 27 W 8th Ave, Bay Springs, MS 39422; 601-764-3368; fax: 601-764-3999; 8AM-5PM (CST). *Probate, Divorce, Family, Civil Land.*

Chancery Court- First District PO Box 38, 1782 Highway 503, Paulding, MS 39348; 601-727-4940; fax: 601-727-4475; 8AM-5PM M_F (CST). *Probate, Divorce, Family.*

Jefferson County

Circuit Court PO Box 305, Fayette, MS 39069; 601-786-3422; fax: 601-786-9676; 8AM-5PM (CST). *Felony, Civil (usually over $3,500).*
General Information: No sealed, adoptions, mental health, juvenile, sex, or expunged records released. Will fax documents to local or toll free line. Court makes copy: $.50 per page. Self serve copy: same. Certification fee: $1.50. Payee: Jefferson County Circuit Court. Business checks accepted. No credit cards accepted. Prepayment required. Mail requests: SASE required.
Civil Name Search: Access: Phone, mail, in person. Both court and visitors may perform in person name searches. Search fee: $10.00 per name. Required to search: name, years to search, DOB; also helpful: SSN, sex, signed release. Civil index on docket books since 1966, prior archived. Mail turnaround time same day. Civil PAT goes back to 1971.
Criminal Name Search: Access: Phone, mail, in person. Both court and visitors may perform in person name searches. Search fee: $10.00 per name. Required to search: name, years to search, DOB; also helpful: SSN. Criminal docket on books since 1971, prior archived. Mail turnaround time same day. Criminal PAT goes back to 1971.

Justice Court PO Box 1047, 1483 S Main St, Fayette, MS 39069; 601-786-8594; criminal phone: 601-786-8601; fax: 601-786-6017; 8AM-5PM (CST). *Misdemeanor, Civil Actions under $3,500, Eviction, Small Claims.*

Chancery Court PO Box 145, 1483 Main St, Fayette, MS 39069; 601-786-3021; fax: 601-786-6009; 8AM-5PM (CST). *Probate, Civil Land, Divorce, Family.*

Jefferson Davis County

Circuit Court PO Box 1090, Prentiss, MS 39474; 601-792-4231; fax: 601-792-4957; 8AM-5PM (CST). *Felony, Civil (usually over $3,500).*
http://da15thdistrict.org/
General Information: No sealed, adoptions, mental health, juvenile, sex, or expunged records released. Fee to fax out file $1.00 per page. Court makes copy: $.50 per page. Self serve copy: $.25 per page. Certification fee: $2.00. Payee: Circuit Clerk. Personal checks accepted. No credit cards accepted. Prepayment required.

Civil Name Search: Access: Phone, fax, mail, in person. Both court and visitors may perform in person name searches. Search fee: $10.00 per name. Civil index on docket books since 1906. Mail turnaround time 1-2 days.

Criminal Name Search: Access: Phone, fax, mail, in person. Both court and visitors may perform in person name searches. Search fee: $10.00 per name. Required to search: name, years to search; also helpful: SSN. Criminal docket on books since 1906. Mail turnaround time 1-2 days.

Justice Court PO Box 1407, 2335 Columbia Ave, Prentiss, MS 39474; 601-792-5129; fax: 601-792-5128; 8AM-N, 1-5PM (CST). *Misdemeanor, Civil Actions under $3,500, Eviction, Small Claims.*

Chancery Court PO Box 1137, 2426 Pearl Ave, Prentiss, MS 39474; 601-792-4204; fax: 601-792-2894; 8AM-5PM (CST). *Probate, Civil Land, Divorce, Family.*

Jones County

Circuit & County Court - 1st District 101 N. Court St., #B, Ellisville, MS 39437; 601-477-8538; fax: 601-477-8539; 8AM-5PM (CST). *Felony, Misdemeanor, Civil (usually over $3,500).*

General Information: No sealed, adoptions, mental health, juvenile, sex, or expunged records released. Will fax documents to local or toll free line. Court makes copy: $1.00 per page. Self serve copy: $.25 per page. Certification fee: $2.00. Payee: Circuit Clerk. Personal checks accepted. No credit cards accepted. Prepayment required. Mail requests: SASE required.

Civil Name Search: Access: Mail, fax, in person, online. Visitors must perform in person searches themselves. Search fee: $10.00. Civil index on docket books since 1960s. Mail turnaround time 1-2 days. Access the circuit court judgment roll free at www.deltacomputersystems.com/MS/MS34/INDEX.HTML.

Criminal Name Search: Access: Mail, fax, in person. Both court and visitors may perform in person name searches. Search fee: $10.00 per name. Criminal docket on books since 1960s. Mail turnaround time 1-2 days.

Circuit & County Court - 2nd District PO Box 1336, Laurel, MS 39441; 601-425-2556; fax: 601-399-4774; 8AM-5PM (CST). *Felony, Misdemeanor, Civil (usually over $3,500).*

www.co.jones.ms.us

General Information: No sealed or Juvenile Youth Court records released. Will fax documents to local or toll free line. Court makes copy: $1.00 per page. Self serve copy: $.25 per page. Certification fee: $1.50. Payee: Jones County Circuit Clerk. Personal checks accepted. No credit cards accepted. Prepayment required. Mail requests: SASE required for criminal.

Civil Name Search: Access: In person, online. Visitors must perform in person searches themselves. Civil index on docket books since 1960s. Note: The court will not search civil records for the public. Civil PAT goes back to 2003. Access the circuit court judgment roll free at www.deltacomputersystems.com/MS/MS34/JRLINKQUERYM.HTML.

Criminal Name Search: Access: Mail, in person. Both court and visitors may perform in person name searches. Search fee: $10.00 per name. Fee is per district. Required to search: name, years to search; also helpful: SSN. Criminal docket on books since 1960s. Note: Only misdemeanors here are cases appealed from lower court. Mail turnaround time 2 days. Criminal PAT goes back to 2003.

Justice Court PO Box 1997, Laurel, MS 39441; 601-428-3137; fax: 601-428-0526; 8AM-5PM (CST). *Misdemeanor, Civil Actions under $3,500, Eviction, Small Claims.*

General Information: This Justice Court houses all the Justices for Jones County. The street address of 402 Central Ave has ZIP of 39440.

Ellisville Chancery Court 101 N Court St. #D, PO Box 248, Ellisville, MS 39437; 601-477-3307; fax: 601-477-1240; 8AM-5PM (CST). *Probate, Divorce, Family.*

Laurel Chancery Court 2nd District PO Box 1468, 415 N 5th Ave, Laurel, MS 39441; 601-428-0527; probate phone: 602-428-3182; fax: 601-428-3610; 8AM-5PM (CST). *Probate, Divorce, Family.*

Kemper County

Circuit Court PO Box 130, De Kalb, MS 39328; 601-743-2224; fax: 601-743-4173; 8AM-5PM (CST). *Felony, Civil (usually over $3,500).*

General Information: No sealed, adoptions, mental health, juvenile, sex, or expunged records released. Will fax documents $.25 per page. Court makes copy: $.50 per page. Self serve copy: $.25 per page. Certification fee: $1.00 per page. Payee: Circuit Clerk. Business checks accepted. No credit cards accepted. Prepayment required. Mail requests: SASE requested.

Civil Name Search: Access: Phone, fax, mail, in person. Both court and visitors may perform in person name searches. Search fee: $10.00 per name. Required to search: name, years to search, address. Civil index on docket books since 1960s, archived since 1912. Mail turnaround time 1 week.

Criminal Name Search: Access: Fax, mail, in person. Both court and visitors may perform in person name searches. Search fee: $10.00 per name. Required to search: name, years to search, address, DOB; also helpful: SSN. Criminal docket on books since 1960s, archived since 1912. Mail turnaround time 1 week.

Justice Court PO Box 661, Courthouse, Hwy 39, Main St, De Kalb, MS 39328; 601-743-2793; fax: 601-743-4893; 8AM-5PM (CST). *Misdemeanor, Civil Actions under $3,500, Eviction, Small Claims.*

Chancery Court PO Box 188, Main St Courthouse, De Kalb, MS 39328; 601-743-2460; fax: 601-743-2789; 8AM-5PM (CST). *Probate, Civil Land, Divorce, Family.*

Lafayette County

Circuit Court LaFayette County Courthouse, One Courthouse Sq, #201, Oxford, MS 38655; 662-234-4951; fax: 662-236-0238; 8AM-5PM (CST). *Felony, Civil (usually over $3,500).*

General Information: No sealed, adoptions, mental health, juvenile, or expunged records released. Will fax documents to local or toll free line. Court makes copy: $1.00 per page. Self serve copy: $.25 per page. Certification fee: $1.50. Payee: Circuit Clerk. Business checks accepted. No credit cards accepted. Prepayment required.

Civil Name Search: Access: Mail, in person. Both court and visitors may perform in person name searches. Search fee: $10.00 per name. Fee is per 10 years searched. Required to search: name, years to search; also helpful: address. Civil index in docket books from 1900; on computer back to 1997. Mail turnaround time next day. Civil PAT goes back to 1997.

Criminal Name Search: Access: Mail, in person. Both court and visitors may perform in person name searches. Search fee: $10.00 per name. Fee is per 10 years searched. Required to search: name, years to search, DOB; also helpful: address, SSN. Criminal docket on books from 1900, on computer back to 1995. Mail turnaround time 1-2 days. Criminal PAT goes back to 1995.

Justice Court 713 Jackson Ave, Oxford, MS 38655; 662-234-1545; fax: 662-238-7990; 8AM-5PM (CST). *Misdemeanor, Civil Actions under $3,500, Eviction, Small Claims.*

Chancery Court 300 N Lamar Blvd, Oxford, MS 38655; 662-234-2131; fax: 662-234-5038; 8AM-5PM (CST). *Probate, Civil Land, Divorce, Family.*

www.lafayettecoms.com/HTML/Main.html?Chancery%20Court%20Page

Lamar County

Circuit Court PO Box 369, Purvis, MS 39475; 601-794-8504; fax: 601-794-3905; 8AM-5PM (CST). *Felony, Civil (usually over $3,500).*

General Information: No sealed, adoptions, mental health, juvenile, sex, or expunged records released. Will not fax documents. Court makes copy: $1.00 per page. Self serve copy: $.25 per page. No certification fee . Payee: Circuit Clerk. Business checks accepted. No credit cards accepted. Prepayment required. Mail requests: SASE requested.

Civil Name Search: Access: Mail, in person. Both court and visitors may perform in person name searches. Search fee: $10.00 per name. Civil index on docket books since 1904. Mail turnaround time 1-2 days. Public use terminal has civil records. Terminal shows judgments only, must search civil record index by hand.

Criminal Name Search: Access: Mail, in person. Both court and visitors may perform in person name searches. Search fee: $10.00 per name. Required to search: name, years to search; also helpful: SSN. Criminal docket on books since 1904. Mail turnaround time 1-2 days.

Justice Court PO Box 1010, 205 Main St, #A, Purvis, MS 39475; 601-794-2950; fax: 601-794-1076; 8AM-5PM (CST). *Misdemeanor, Civil Actions under $3,500, Eviction, Small Claims.*

Chancery Court PO Box 247, 403 Main St, Purvis, MS 39475; 601-794-8504; fax: 601-794-3903; 8AM-5PM (CST). *Probate, Civil Land, Divorce, Family.*

Lauderdale County

Circuit & County Court PO Box 1005, Meridian, MS 39302-1005; 601-482-9738; fax: 601-484-3970; 8AM-5PM (CST). *Felony, Civil (usually over $3,500).* www.lauderdalecounty.org/

General Information: County Court can be reached at 601-482-9715. No sealed, adoptions, mental health, juvenile, sex, or expunged records released. Will fax documents to local or toll-free number. Court makes copy: $.50 per page. Self serve copy: $.25 per page. No certification fee . Payee: Circuit Clerk. Business checks accepted. No credit cards accepted. Prepayment required. Will bill complete files to attorneys. Mail requests: SASE requested.

Civil Name Search: Access: Phone, mail, fax, in person. Both court and visitors may perform in person name searches. Search fee: $10.00 per name. Required to search: name, years to search, SSN. Civil index on docket books back to 1950s, on computer back to 1992. Court will only search computer records. Mail turnaround time 1 week. Civil PAT goes back to 1992.

Criminal Name Search: Access: Mail, fax, in person. Both court and visitors may perform in person name searches. Search fee: $10.00 per name. Required to search: name, years to search, DOB; also helpful: SSN.

Criminal records on computer (Felony) back to 1965. Mail turnaround time 1 week, phone turnaround 1 week. Criminal PAT goes back to 1965.

Justice Court PO Box 5126, Meridian, MS 39302; 601-482-9879; fax: 601-482-9813; 8AM-5PM (CST). *Misdemeanor, Civil Actions under $3,500, Eviction, Small Claims, Traffic.*
www.lauderdalecounty.org/officeservices/justice_court.htm
General Information: Physical Address: 410 Constitution Ave, 6th Fl, Meridian, MS 39301.

Chancery Court PO Box 1587, 500 Constitution Ave, 1st Fl, Meridian, MS 39302; 601-482-97-1; fax: 601-486-4921; 8AM-5PM (CST). *Probate, Civil Land, Divorce, Family.*
www.lauderdalecounty.org/officeservices/chancery_clerk.htm

Lawrence County

Circuit Court PO Box 1249, 517 E Broad St, Monticello, MS 39654; 601-587-4791 or 0112; fax: 601-587-4405; 8AM-5PM (CST). *Felony, Civil (usually over $3,500).*
General Information: No sealed, adoptions, mental health, juvenile, sex, or expunged records released. Will fax out documents if all fees paid. Court makes copy: $1.00 per page. Self serve copy: $.50 per page. Certification fee: $1.00. Payee: Circuit Clerk. Local personal checks accepted with ID. No credit cards accepted. Prepayment required. Mail requests: SASE helpful.
Civil Name Search: Access: Phone, mail, in person. Both court and visitors may perform in person name searches. Search fee: $10.00 per name. Required to search: name, years to search; also helpful: address. Civil index on docket books since late 1970's, available to public to view. Note: For fax request, fax copy of check for fee. Mail turnaround time 1 week.
Criminal Name Search: Access: Phone, mail, in person. Both court and visitors may perform in person name searches. Search fee: $10.00 per name. Required to search: name, years to search, DOB; also helpful: address, SSN. Criminal docket on books since late 1970's, available to public to view. Note: In fax request send copy of payment check Mail turnaround time 1 week, phone turnaround 1-2 days.

Justice Court PO Box 903, 435 Brinson St, Monticello, MS 39654; 601-587-7183, 587-4854; civil phone: 601-587-4854/7183; fax: 601-587-0755; 8AM-5PM (CST). *Misdemeanor, Civil Actions under $3,500, Eviction, Small Claims.*

Chancery Court PO Box 821, 517 E Broad St, Courthouse Sq, Monticello, MS 39654; 601-587-7162; fax: 601-587-0767; 8AM-5PM (CST). *Probate, Civil Land, Divorce, Family.*

Leake County

Circuit Court PO Box 67, Court Sq on Main St, Carthage, MS 39051; 601-267-8357; fax: 601-267-8889; 8AM-5PM (CST). *Felony, Civil (usually over $3,500).*
General Information: No sealed, adoptions, mental health, juvenile, sex, or expunged records released. Court makes copy: $1.00 per page. Self serve copy: $.25 per page. Certification fee: $1.50 per cert. Payee: Circuit Clerk. Personal checks accepted, but good to ask for approval first. No credit cards accepted. Prepayment required. Mail requests: SASE required for criminal.
Civil Name Search: Access: In person only. Visitors must perform in person searches themselves. Civil index on docket books since 1970s. Public use terminal has civil records. Public terminal has voting and Judgments only.
Criminal Name Search: Access: Mail, in person. Both court and visitors may perform in person name searches. Search fee: $10.00 per name. Required to search: name, years to search, DOB; also helpful: SSN. Criminal docket on books since 1977. Mail turnaround time 1-2 days.

Justice Court PO Box 69, 215 W Main St, Carthage, MS 39051; 601-267-5677; fax: 601-267-6134; 8AM-5PM (CST). *Misdemeanor, Civil Actions $3,500 (as of 7/1/08), Eviction, Small Claims.*

Chancery Court PO Box 72, County Courthouse, Court Sq, Carthage, MS 39051; 601-267-7371/72; fax: 601-267-6137; 8AM-5PM (CST). *Probate, Civil Land, Divorce, Family.*
www.co.leake.ms.us
General Information: Records also include divorce, custody, land disputes, mental and drug commitments.

Lee County

Circuit & County Court PO Box 762, 200 W Jefferson, Circuit Court, Tupelo, MS 38802; 662-841-9022/9023(Circuit) 9730 (County); fax: 662-680-6089; 8AM-5PM (CST). *Felony, Civil (usually over $3,500).*
General Information: Mailing address for County Court - PO Box 736. Phone-662-841-9049. The courts are separate. Clerks will search both criminal and civil indexes one fee, if requested. No sealed or expunged records released. Will not fax documents. Court makes copy: $.25 per page. Certification fee: $3.00. Payee: Lee County & Circuit Court. Business checks accepted. No credit cards accepted. Prepayment required. Mail requests: SASE required.

Civil Name Search: Access: Mail, in person. Both court and visitors may perform in person name searches. Search fee: $10.00 per name. Circuit records on computer since 1990, others on docket books since 1987. County records not on computer. Mail turnaround time 1-2 days. Civil PAT goes back to 2003.
Criminal Name Search: Access: Mail, in person. Both court and visitors may perform in person name searches. Search fee: $10.00 per name. Required to search: name, years to search; also helpful: DOB, SSN. Circuit records on computer since 1990, others on docket books since 1987. County records not on computer. Mail turnaround time 1-2 days. Criminal PAT goes back to same as civil.

Justice Court PO Box 108, 331 N Broadway St, Tupelo, MS 38802; 662-841-9014; fax: 662-680-6021; 8AM-5PM (CST). *Misdemeanor, Civil Actions under $3,500, Eviction, Small Claims.*

Chancery Court PO Box 7127, 200 W Jefferson, Tupelo, MS 38802; 662-841-9100; fax: 662-680-6091; 8AM-5PM (CST). *Probate, Civil Land, Divorce, Family.*

Leflore County

Circuit & County Court PO Box 1953, 310 W Market St, Greenwood, MS 38935-1953; 662-453-1435; fax: 662-455-1278; 8AM-5PM (CST). *Felony, Civil (usually over $3,500).*
General Information: Court will search criminal and civil indexes as one search, if requested. No sealed or expunged records released. Will fax documents for free. Court makes copy: $1.00 per page. Self serve copy: $.50 per page. Certification fee: $2.00 to notarize. Payee: Circuit Clerk. Personal checks accepted. No credit cards accepted. Prepayment required.
Civil Name Search: Access: Phone, fax, mail, in person, online. Both court and visitors may perform in person name searches. Search fee: $10.00 per name. Civil records on computer index goes back 10 years; prior records on docket books since mid-1800s. Mail turnaround time 1-2 days. Civil PAT goes back to 1990s. A private company permits online access to civil records; go to www.recordsusa.com or call Rob at 888-633-4748 x17 for info and demo.
Criminal Name Search: Access: Fax, mail, in person. Both court and visitors may perform in person name searches. Search fee: $10.00 per name. Required to search: name, years to search; also helpful: DOB, SSN. Criminal records on computer index goes back 10 years; prior records on docket books since mid-1800s. Mail turnaround time 1-2 days. Criminal PAT goes back to same as civil.

Justice Court PO Box 8056, 3600 CR 540 - Baldwin Rd, Greenwood, MS 38935; 662-453-1605; fax: 662-455-8759; 8AM-5PM (CST). *Misdemeanor, Civil Actions under $3,500, Eviction, Small Claims.*

Chancery Court PO Box 1579, 310 W Market St, County Courthouse, Greenwood, MS 38935-1579; 662-453-1432; fax: 662-455-7959; 8AM-5PM (CST). *Probate, Civil Land, Divorce, Family.*
http://7chancerycourt.com/

Lincoln County

Circuit Court PO Box 357, 301 S 1st St Rm 205, Brookhaven, MS 39602; 601-835-3435; fax: 601-835-3482; 8AM-5PM (CST). *Felony, Civil (usually over $3,500).*
General Information: No sealed or expunged records released. Will fax documents $10.00 per doc. Court makes copy: $1.00 per page. Self serve copy: $.50 per page. Certification fee: none. Payee: Circuit Clerk. Personal checks accepted. Out of state checks not accepted. Visa/MC accepted. Prepayment required.
Civil Name Search: Access: Mail, in person. Both court and visitors may perform in person name searches. Search fee: $10.00 per name. Civil records on computer since 1986, prior on docket books. Mail turnaround time 1-2 days. Civil PAT goes back to 1982.
Criminal Name Search: Access: Mail, in person. Both court and visitors may perform in person name searches. Search fee: $10.00 per name. Required to search: name, years to search; also helpful: DOB, SSN. Criminal records on computer since 1982, prior on docket books. Mail turnaround time 1-2 days. Criminal PAT goes back to same as civil.

Justice Court PO Box 767, Brookhaven, MS 39602; 601-835-3474; fax: 601-835-3494; 8AM-5PM (CST). *Misdemeanor, Civil Actions under $3,500, Eviction, Small Claims.*
General Information: Physical Address: 308 S. 2nd St, Brookhaven, MS 39601

Chancery Court PO Box 555, 300 S 1st St, Brookhaven, MS 39602; 601-835-3412; fax: 601-835-3423; 8AM-5PM (CST). *Probate, Civil Land, Divorce, Family.*

Lowndes County

Circuit & County Court PO Box 31, Columbus, MS 39703; 662-329-5900;; 8AM-5PM (CST). *Felony, Civil (usually over $3,500).*
General Information: No sealed, adoption, mental health, juvenile, sex or expunged cases released. Will fax documents to local or toll free line. Court makes copy: $1.00 per page. Self serve copy: No self serve criminal copier;

Civil self serve- $.25 each. Certification fee: $1.00. Payee: Clerk of Court. Personal checks accepted. No credit cards accepted. Prepayment required. Mail requests: SASE required.

Civil Name Search: Access: Mail, in person. Both court and visitors may perform in person name searches. Search fee: $10.00 per name. Civil records on computer from 2/94, on docket books from 1900s. Mail turnaround time 7 to 14 days. Civil PAT goes back to 1996.

Criminal Name Search: Access: Mail, in person. Both court and visitors may perform in person name searches. Search fee: $10.00 per name. Required to search: name, years to search, DOB; also helpful: SSN. Criminal records on computer since 11/93; prior on docket books. Mail turnaround time 14 days. Criminal PAT goes back to 1993.

Justice Court 11 Airline Rd, Columbus, MS 39702; 662-329-5929; fax: 662-245-4619; 8AM-5PM (CST). *Misdemeanor, Civil Actions under $3,500, Eviction, Small Claims.*

Chancery Court PO Box 684, 515 S 2nd Ave North, Columbus, MS 39703; 662-329-5800; 8AM-5PM (CST). *Probate, Civil Land, Divorce, Family.*

Madison County

Circuit & County Court PO Box 1626, Canton, MS 39046; 601-859-4365; fax: 601-859-8555; 8AM-5PM (CST). *Felony, Civil (usually over $3,500).*

General Information: No sealed, adoptions, mental health, juvenile, sex, or expunged records released. Will fax documents to local or toll free line. Court makes copy: $.50 per page. Self serve copy: $.25 per page. Certification fee: $1.50. Payee: Circuit Clerk. Personal checks accepted. No credit cards accepted. Prepayment required. Mail requests: SASE requested.

Civil Name Search: Access: Phone, fax, mail, in person, online. Both court and visitors may perform in person name searches. No search fee. Civil records on computer since 1987, prior on docket books since 1950. Mail turnaround time 1 week. Civil PAT goes back to 1989. The Circuit Court participates in the Pilot MEC program for online filing and case record view but only for attorneys. See www.mssc.state.ms.us/mec/mec.html.

Criminal Name Search: Access: Mail, in person. Both court and visitors may perform in person name searches. Search fee: $10.00 per name. Criminal records on computer since 1992, prior on docket books since 1945. Mail turnaround time 1 week. Criminal PAT goes back to 1984.

Justice Court 2961 N Liberty Street, Canton, MS 39046; 601-859-6337; fax: 601-859-2570; 8AM-5PM (CST). *Misdemeanor, Civil Actions under $3,500, Eviction, Small Claims.*

General Information: Request for history must be in writing with a $6.00 fee made out to Madison County Justice Court.

Chancery Court PO Box 404, 146 W Center St, Canton, MS 39046; 601-859-1177; fax: 601-859-0795; 8AM-5PM (CST). *Probate, Civil Land, Divorce, Family.*
www.madison-co.com/court_systems/chancery_court/index.php

General Information: Search chancery cases free from the home page www.madison-co.com/court_systems/chancery_court/index.php. This court also participates in the Pilot MEC program for attorneys - see www.mssc.state.ms.us/mec/mec.html.

Marion County

Circuit Court 250 Broad St, #1, Columbia, MS 39429; 601-736-8246; fax: 601-731-6344; 8AM-5PM (CST). *Felony, Civil (usually over $3,500).*

General Information: No sealed, adoptions, mental health, juvenile, sex, or expunged records released. Will fax documents to local or toll free line. Court makes copy: $.50 per page. Self serve copy: $.25 per page. No certification fee . Payee: Circuit Clerk. Personal checks accepted. No credit cards accepted. Prepayment required. Mail requests: SASE required.

Civil Name Search: Access: Mail, in person. Both court and visitors may perform in person name searches. Search fee: $10.00 per name. Civil index on docket books since 1800s. Mail turnaround time 3 days.

Criminal Name Search: Access: Mail, in person, fax. Both court and visitors may perform in person name searches. Search fee: $10.00 per name. Required to search: name, years to search; also helpful: SSN. Criminal docket on books since 1800s. Mail turnaround time 1-2 days.

Justice Court 500 Courthouse Square #2, Columbia, MS 39429; 601-736-2572; fax: 601-731-3781; 8AM-5PM (CST). *Misdemeanor, Civil Actions under $3,500, Eviction, Small Claims, Ordinance, Traffic.*

Chancery Court 250 Broad St, #2, Columbia, MS 39429; 601-444-0205; fax: 601-444-0206; 8AM-5PM (CST). *Probate, Civil Land, Divorce, Family.*

General Information: Court records and calendars online at www.deltacomputersystems.com/MS/MS46/INDEX.html.

Marshall County

Circuit Court PO Box 459, 128 E Vandorn Ave, Holly Springs, MS 38635; 662-252-3434; fax: 662-252-5951; 8AM-5PM (CST). *Felony, Civil (usually over $3,500).*

General Information: No sealed or expunged records released. No fee to fax back document; prepay or fax copy of your search fee check. Court makes copy: $1.00 per page. Self serve copy: $.50 per page. Certification fee: $3.50 per doc. Payee: Circuit Court Clerk. Personal checks accepted. No credit cards accepted. Prepayment required. Mail requests: SASE requested.

Civil Name Search: Access: Fax, mail, in person. Both court and visitors may perform in person name searches. Search fee: $10.00 per name. Civil index on docket books since 1960s; computerized records go back to 1999. Note: Fax requests- include copy of payment check. Mail turnaround time 1-2 days. Civil PAT goes back to 1999.

Criminal Name Search: Access: Fax, mail, in person. Both court and visitors may perform in person name searches. Search fee: $10.00 per name. Required to search: name, years to search; also helpful: DOB, SSN. Criminal docket on books since 1960s; computerized records go back to 1999. Note: Fax requests-must include copy of payment check. Mail turnaround time 1-2 days. Criminal PAT goes back to same as civil.

Justice Court- North & South Districts PO Box 729, 819 West St, #B, Holly Springs, MS 38635; 662-252-3585; fax: 662-252-0028; 8AM-5PM (CST). *Misdemeanor, Civil Actions under $3,500, Eviction, Small Claims.*

Chancery Court PO Box 219, 128 E Van Dorn, Court Sq, Holly Springs, MS 38635; 662-252-4431; fax: 662-551-3302; 8AM-5PM (CST). *Probate, Civil Land, Divorce, Family.*

Monroe County

Circuit Court PO Box 843, Aberdeen, MS 39730; 662-369-2732; fax: 662-319-5993; 8AM-5PM (CST). *Felony, Civil (usually over $3,500).*

General Information: No sealed, adoptions, mental health, juvenile, sex, or expunged records released. Will not fax out case files. Court makes copy: $1.00 per page. Self serve copy: $.25 per page. Certification fee: $3.00. Payee: Monroe County Circuit Clerk. Only cashiers checks and money orders accepted. No credit cards accepted. Prepayment required.

Civil Name Search: Access: In person only. Visitors must perform in person searches themselves. Required to search: name, years to search; also helpful: address. Civil index on docket books since 1821. Civil PAT goes back to 2002.

Criminal Name Search: Access: In person only. Visitors must perform in person searches themselves. Required to search: name, years to search, DOB; also helpful: address, SSN. Criminal docket on books since 1821. Criminal PAT goes back to 2002.

Justice Court PO Box 518, 1619 Hwy 25 N, Amory, MS 38821; 662-256-8493; fax: 662-256-7876; 8AM-5PM (CST). *Misdemeanor, Civil Actions under $3,500, Eviction, Small Claims.*

General Information: Aberdeen Justice Court Dist. 2 is closed; records here.

Chancery Court PO Box 578, 201 W Commerce St, Aberdeen, MS 39730; 662-369-8143; fax: 662-369-7928; 8AM-5PM (CST). *Probate, Civil Land, Divorce, Family.*

Montgomery County

Circuit Court PO Box 765, Winona, MS 38967; 662-283-4161; fax: 662-283-3363; 8AM-5PM (CST). *Felony, Civil (usually over $3,500).*

General Information: No sealed or expunged records released. Will fax documents to local or toll free line. Court makes copy: $1.00 per page. Self serve copy: $.25 per page. Certification fee: $2.00. Payee: Circuit Clerk. Personal checks accepted. No credit cards accepted. Prepayment requested. Mail requests: SASE required.

Civil Name Search: Access: Mail, in person. Both court and visitors may perform in person name searches. Search fee: $10.00 per name. Civil index on docket books since early 1900s. Mail turnaround time 1-2 days.

Criminal Name Search: Access: Mail, in person. Both court and visitors may perform in person name searches. Search fee: $10.00 per name. Criminal docket on books since early 1900s. Mail turnaround time 1-2 days.

Justice Court PO Box 229, 706 Alberta Dr, Winona, MS 38967; 662-283-2290; fax: 662-283-2052; 8AM-5PM (CST). *Misdemeanor, Civil Actions under $3,500, Eviction, Small Claims.*

Chancery Court PO Box 71, 614 Summit St, Winona, MS 38967; 662-283-2333; fax: 662-283-2233; 8AM-5PM (CST). *Probate, Civil Land, Divorce, Family.*

General Information: Will not do searches.

Neshoba County

Circuit Court 401 E Beacon St #110, Philadelphia, MS 39350; 601-656-4781; fax: 601-650-3997; 8AM-5PM (CST). *Felony, Civil (usually over $3,500).*

General Information: No sealed, adoptions, mental health, juvenile, sex, or expunged records released. Will not fax out documents. Court makes copy: $1.00 per page. Certification fee: $1.00 per certification. Payee: Circuit Clerk.

Business checks accepted. No credit cards accepted. Prepayment required. Mail requests: SASE requested.

Civil Name Search: Access: Mail, in person. Both court and visitors may perform in person name searches. Search fee: $10.00 per name. Civil cases indexed by defendant. Civil records in-house back 10 years; indexed back 50 years. Mail turnaround time 1-2 days. Public use terminal has civil records back to 1993 on civil judgments only.

Criminal Name Search: Access: Mail, in person. Both court and visitors may perform in person name searches. Search fee: $10.00 per name. Required to search: name, years to search, DOB; also helpful: SSN. Criminal records in-house back 20 years; on docket books back 50 years. Mail turnaround time approx. 5 days.

Justice Court 200 Byrd Ave, Philadelphia, MS 39350; 601-656-5361/1101; fax: 601-656-6482; 8AM-5PM (CST). *Misdemeanor, Civil Actions under $3,500, Eviction, Small Claims.*

Chancery Court 401 Beacon St #107, Philadelphia, MS 39350; 601-656-3581; fax: 601-656-5915; 8AM-5PM (CST). *Probate, Civil Land, Divorce, Family.* www.neshobacounty.net/court-systems/chancery-court.php

Newton County

Circuit Court PO Box 447, Decatur, MS 39327; 601-635-2368; fax: 601-635-3210; 8AM-5PM (CST). *Felony, Civil (usually over $3,500).*

General Information: No sealed, adoptions, mental health, juvenile, sex, or expunged records released. Will fax documents to local or toll free line. Court makes copy: $.50 per page. Certification fee: $1.50 per cert. Payee: Circuit Court. Personal checks accepted. No credit cards accepted. Prepayment required. Mail requests: SASE required.

Civil Name Search: Access: Mail, in person. Both court and visitors may perform in person name searches. Search fee: $10.00 per name. Civil index on docket books since 1968. Mail turnaround time same day. Civil PAT goes back to 2003.

Criminal Name Search: Access: Mail, in person. Both court and visitors may perform in person name searches. Search fee: $10.00 per name. Required to search: name, years to search, DOB; also helpful: SSN. Criminal docket on books since 1968. Mail turnaround time same day. Criminal PAT goes back to same as civil. Some results do no include full name.

Justice Court PO Box 69, 11 4th Ave, Decatur, MS 39327; 601-635-2740; fax: 601-635-4047; 8AM-5PM (CST). *Misdemeanor, Civil Actions under $3,500, Eviction, Small Claims.*

Chancery Clerk Office PO Box 68, 92 W Broad St, Decatur, MS 39327; 601-635-2367; fax: 601-635-3479; 8AM-5PM (CST). *Probate, Divorce, Family.*

Noxubee County

Circuit Court PO Box 431, 505 S Jefferson, Macon, MS 39341; 662-726-5737; fax: 662-726-2938; 8AM-5PM (CST). *Felony, Civil (usually over $3,500).*

General Information: No sealed, adoptions, mental health, juvenile, sex, or expunged records released. Will not fax documents. Court makes copy: $.25 per page. Self serve copy: same. Certification fee: $15.00 per doc. Payee: Circuit Clerk. Business checks accepted. No credit cards accepted. Prepayment required. Mail requests: SASE required.

Civil Name Search: Access: Mail, fax, in person. Both court and visitors may perform in person name searches. Search fee: $10.00 per name. Civil cases indexed by defendant. Civil index on docket books since 1800s. Mail turnaround time 1 week. Civil PAT goes back to 1970.

Criminal Name Search: Access: Mail, fax, in person. Both court and visitors may perform in person name searches. Search fee: $10.00 per name. Required to search: name, years to search; also helpful: SSN. Criminal docket on books since 1800s. Mail turnaround time 1 week. Criminal PAT goes back to 1965.

Justice Court- North & South Districts 507 S Jefferson, PO Box 550, Macon, MS 39341; 662-726-5834; fax: 662-726-2944; 8AM-5PM (CST). *Misdemeanor, Civil Actions under $3,500, Eviction, Small Claims.*

Chancery Court PO Box 147, County Courthouse, 505 S Jefferson St, Macon, MS 39341; 662-726-4243; fax: 662-726-2272; 8AM-5PM (CST). *Probate, Civil Land, Divorce, Family.*

Oktibbeha County

Circuit Court 108 W Main, #118, Starkville, MS 39759; 662-323-1400, 662-323-1356; fax: 662-323-1121; 8AM-5PM (CST). *Felony, Civil (usually over $3,500).* www.oktibbehacountyms.org/circuit_clerk/index.htm

General Information: No sealed, adoptions, mental health, juvenile, sex, or expunged records released. Will fax out documents no fee. Court makes copy: $1.00 per page. Self serve copy: $.25 per page. Certification fee: $1.50. Payee: Circuit Clerk. No personal checks or credit cards accepted. Prepayment required. Mail requests: SASE required.

Civil Name Search: Access: Mail, fax, in person, online. Both court and visitors may perform in person name searches. Search fee: $10.00 per name. Required to search: name, years to search; also helpful: address. Civil index on docket books since 1938. Mail turnaround time 1 week. Civil PAT goes to 1990. Access the civil circuit records per subscription at www.deltacomputersystems.com/MS/MS53/mclinkquerycc.html. Fee is $25 monthly or $275 annual. Access the county judgment roll www.deltacomputersystems.com/MS/MS53/jrlinkquerym.html, same fees.

Criminal Name Search: Access: Mail, fax, in person, online. Both court and visitors may perform in person name searches. Search fee: $10.00 per name. Required to search: name, years to search; also helpful: DOB, SSN. Criminal records on docket since 1950. Mail turnaround time 1 week. Criminal PAT goes to 1997. Access the county criminal circuit records at www.deltacomputersystems.com/MS/MS53/mclinkquerycr.html. Fee is $25 monthly or $275 annual.

Justice Court- Districts 1-3 104 Felix Long Dr, Starkville, MS 39759; 662-324-3032; criminal phone: 662-324-3040; fax: 662-338-1078; 8AM-5PM (CST). *Misdemeanor, Civil Actions under $3,500, Eviction, Small Claims.*

Chancery Court Courthouse, 101 E Main, Starkville, MS 39759; 662-323-5834; fax: 662-338-1064; 8AM-5PM (CST). *Probate, Civil Land, Divorce, Family.* www.oktibbehachanceryclerk.com/index.php

Panola County

Circuit Court - 1st District 215 S Pocahontas St, Sardis, MS 38666; 662-487-2073; fax: 662-487-3595; 8AM-5PM (CST). *Felony, Civil (usually over $3,500).*

General Information: No sealed, adoptions, mental health, juvenile, sex, or expunged records released. No fee to fax documents. Prepay or fax copy of your search fee check. Court makes copy: $1.00 per page criminal; Civil $.50 per page. Self serve copy: $.50 per page criminal; Civil self serve- $.25 each. Certification fee: $5.00 per doc. Payee: Circuit Clerk. Business checks accepted. No credit cards accepted. Prepayment required. Mail requests: SASE required.

Civil Name Search: Access: Fax, mail, in person. Both court and visitors may perform in person name searches. Search fee: $10.00 per name. Fee is for each district searched. Civil index on docket books since 1970s, archived since 1925. Mail turnaround time 1-2 days.

Criminal Name Search: Access: Fax, mail, in person. Both court and visitors may perform in person name searches. Search fee: $10.00 per name. Fee is for each district searched. Required to search: name, years to search, DOB; also helpful: SSN. Criminal docket on books since 1970, archived since 1925, records are not computerized. Mail turnaround time 1-2 days.

Circuit Court - 2nd District PO Box 346, 151 Public Sq, Batesville, MS 38606; 662-563-6210; fax: 662-563-8233; 8AM-5PM (CST). *Felony, Civil (usually over $3,500).*

General Information: No sealed, adoptions, mental health, juvenile, sex, or expunged records released. Will fax documents $1.00 per page. Court makes copy: $1.00 per page criminal; Civil $.50 per page. Self serve copy: $.25 per page. Certification fee: $1.50 per cert. Payee: Circuit Clerk's Office. Personal checks accepted. No credit cards accepted. Prepayment required. Mail requests: SASE required.

Civil Name Search: Access: Phone, fax, mail, in person. Both court and visitors may perform in person name searches. Search fee: $10.00 per name. Fee is per district. Civil records on computer go back to 2004, Civil records on docket books since 1900. Mail turnaround time same day.

Criminal Name Search: Access: Fax, mail, in person. Both court and visitors may perform in person name searches. Search fee: $10.00 per name. Fee is per district. Required to search: name, years to search, address, DOB; also helpful: SSN. Criminal records on computer go back to 2004, Criminal records on docket books since 1900. Mail turnaround time same day.

Justice Court PO Box 249, 619 E Lee St, Sardis, MS 38666; 662-487-2080; criminal phone: 662-487-2080; civil phone: 662-487-2082; fax: 662-487-2008; 8AM-5PM (CST). *Misdemeanor, Civil Actions under $3,500, Eviction, Small Claims.*

General Information: This Justice Court houses all the Justices for Panola County.

Panola County Chancery Clerk 151 Public Square, Suite B, Batesville, MS 38606; 662-563-6205; fax: 662-563-6277; 8AM-5PM (CST). *Probate, Divorce, Family.*

Sardis Chancery Court 215 S Pocahontas St, Sardis, MS 38666; 662-487-2070; fax: 662-487-3559; 8AM-N, 1-5PM (CST). *Probate, Divorce, Family.*

Pearl River County

Circuit Court Courthouse, Poplarville, MS 39470; 601-403-2300; criminal phone: x323; civil phone: Ext 324; fax: 601-403-2327; 8AM-5PM (CST). *Felony, Civil (usually over $3,500).* www.pearlrivercounty.net/circuit/index.htm

General Information: No sealed, adoptions, mental health, juvenile, sex, or expunged records released. Will fax documents to local or toll free line. Court makes copy: $1.00 per page. Self serve copy: $.50 per page. Certification fee: $2.50. Payee: Circuit Clerk. Personal checks accepted. No credit cards accepted. Prepayment required.

Civil Name Search: Access: Mail, fax, in person. Both court and visitors may perform in person name searches. Search fee: $10.00 per name. Required to search: name, years to search, DOB, SSN. Civil index on docket books since 1890. Mail turnaround time 1-2 days. Civil PAT goes back to 2003.

Criminal Name Search: Access: Mail, fax, in person. Both court and visitors may perform in person name searches. Search fee: $10.00 per name. Criminal records on computer since late 1960s, prior on docket books since 1890. Mail turnaround time 1-2 days. Criminal PAT goes back to same as civil. DOB and SSN shown only if provided by the arresting agency.

Justice Court- Northern, Southeastern & Southwestern Districts 169 Savannah Millard Rd, Ste A, Poplarville, MS 39470; 601-403-2500; fax: 601-403-2553; 8AM-5PM (CST). *Misdemeanor, Civil Actions under $3,500, Eviction, Small Claims.* www.pearlrivercounty.net/

Chancery Court PO Box 431, 200 S Main St, Poplarville, MS 39470; 601-403-2300; fax: 601-403-2317; 8AM-5PM (CST). *Probate, Civil Land, Divorce, Family.*

General Information: Search court cases free at www.deltacomputersystems.com/search.html and click on Pearl River.

Perry County

Circuit Court PO Box 198, New Augusta, MS 39462; 601-964-8663; fax: 601-964-8740; 8AM-5PM (CST). *Felony, Civil (usually over $3,500).*

General Information: No sealed, adoptions, mental health, juvenile, sex, or expunged records released. Will fax documents to local or toll free line. Court makes copy: $.50 per page. Self serve copy: $.25 per page. Certification fee: $2.50 per document. Payee: Circuit Clerk. Personal checks accepted. No credit cards accepted. Prepayment required. Mail requests: SASE required.

Civil Name Search: Access: Mail, fax, in person. Both court and visitors may perform in person name searches. Search fee: $10.00 per name. Fee is per 10 years searched. Civil index on docket books since 1980. Mail turnaround time 1-2 days.

Criminal Name Search: Access: Mail, fax, in person. Both court and visitors may perform in person name searches. Search fee: $10.00 per name. Fee is per 10 years searched. Required to search: name, years to search, DOB; also helpful: SSN, sex, signed release. Criminal docket on books since 1971; on computer since. Mail turnaround time 1-2 days.

Justice Court PO Box 455, 103 1st St W, New Augusta, MS 39462; 601-964-8366; fax: 601-964-8368; 8AM-5PM (CST). *Misdemeanor, Civil Actions under $3,500, Eviction, Small Claims.*

General Information: Civil Actions Limit raised from $2500 to $3500 7/1/2008.

Chancery Court PO Box 198, 103 Main St, New Augusta, MS 39462; 601-964-8398; fax: 601-964-8746; 8AM-5PM (CST). *Probate, Civil Land, Divorce, Family.*

Pike County

Circuit & County Court PO Drawer 31, 218 E Bay St, Magnolia, MS 39652; 601-783-2581; fax: 601-783-6322; 8AM-5PM (CST). *Felony, Civil (usually over $3,500)* www.co.pike.ms.us/

General Information: No sealed, adoptions, mental health, juvenile, sex, or expunged records released. Will fax documents to local or toll-free number. Court makes copy: $1.00 per page. Self serve copy: same. Certification fee: none. Payee: Circuit Clerk. Personal checks accepted. No credit cards accepted. Prepayment required. Mail requests: SASE required.

Civil Name Search: Access: Fax, mail, in person, online. Both court and visitors may perform in person name searches. Search fee: $6.00 per name. Civil index on docket books since 1950s; on computer from 2000 to present. Mail turnaround time 1-2 days. Civil PAT goes back to 1971. Search the judgment roll free at www.co.pike.ms.us/jrlinkquerym.html, The civil index is available by subscription at www.co.pike.ms.us/mclinkqueryc.html. Fee is either $25 monthly or $275 annually.

Criminal Name Search: Access: Fax, mail, in person. Both court and visitors may perform in person name searches. Search fee: $6.00 per name. Required to search: name, years to search, DOB; also helpful: SSN. Criminal docket on books and computerized since 1960s. Mail turnaround time 1-2 days. Criminal PAT goes back to same as civil. The civil index is available by subscription at www.co.pike.ms.us/mclinkqueryc.html. Fee is either $25 monthly or $275 annually.

Justice Court- Divisions 1-3 PO Box 509, 2109 Jesse Hall Memorial Dr, Magnolia, MS 39652; 601-783-5333; fax: 601-783-4181; 8AM-5PM (CST). *Misdemeanor, Civil Actions under $3,500, Eviction, Small Claims.* www.co.pike.ms.us/

Chancery Court PO Box 309, 175 S Cherry St, Magnolia, MS 39652; 601-783-3362; fax: 601-783-5982; 8AM-5PM (CST). *Probate, Civil Land, Divorce, Family.* www.co.pike.ms.us/

General Information: Records are available online for a subscription at www.co.pike.ms.us/mclinkquerych.html.

Pontotoc County

Circuit Court PO Box 428, Pontotoc, MS 38863; 662-489-3908; fax: 662-489-2318; 8AM-5PM (CST). *Felony, Civil (usually over $3,500).*

General Information: No sealed, adoptions, mental health, juvenile, sex, or expunged records released. Will fax documents to local or toll free line. Court makes copy: $.50 per page. Self serve copy: $.50 first page, $.25 ea add'l. No certification fee . Payee: Circuit Clerk. No personal checks or credit cards accepted. Prepayment required. Mail requests: SASE required.

Civil Name Search: Access: Mail, in person. Both court and visitors may perform in person name searches. Search fee: $5.00 per name. Civil records on books from 1849. Mail turnaround time 1 week. Civil PAT goes back to 2003.

Criminal Name Search: Access: Mail, in person. Both court and visitors may perform in person name searches. Search fee: $5.00 per name. Required to search: name, years to search, DOB; also helpful: SSN. Computerized back to 2003; criminal docket on books from 1849. Mail turnaround time 1 week. Criminal PAT goes back to same as civil.

Justice Court- East & West Districts 29 E Washington St, Pontotoc, MS 38863; 662-489-3920; fax: 662-488-2986; 8AM-5PM (CST). *Misdemeanor, Civil Actions under $3,500, Eviction, Small Claims.*

Chancery Court PO Box 209, 34 S Liberty, Pontotoc, MS 38863; 662-489-3900; fax: 662-489-3940; 8AM-5PM (CST). *Probate, Civil Land, Divorce, Family.*

Prentiss County

Circuit Court PO Box 727, 101A N Main St, Booneville, MS 38829; 662-728-4611; fax: 662-728-2006; 8AM-5PM (CST). *Felony, Civil (usually over $3,500).* http://co.prentiss.ms.us/circuit.html

General Information: No sealed, adoptions, mental health, juvenile, sex, or expunged records released. Will fax documents. Court makes copy: $.50 per page. Self serve copy: $.25 per page. Certification fee: $2.00. Payee: Circuit Clerk. Personal checks accepted. No credit cards accepted. Prepayment required. Mail requests: SASE required.

Civil Name Search: Access: Mail, in person. Both court and visitors may perform in person name searches. Search fee: $10.00 per name. Civil index on docket books; judgments only on computer since 1985. Mail turnaround time varies. Public use terminal available, records go back to 2007.

Criminal Name Search: Access: Fax, mail, in person. Both court and visitors may perform in person name searches. Search fee: $10.00 per name. Required to search: name, years to search; also helpful: DOB, SSN. Criminal docket on books. Mail turnaround time varies. Public use terminal available, crim records go back to 2007.

Justice Court 1901C E Chambers Dr, Booneville, MS 38829; 662-728-8696; civil phone: 662-728-2011; fax: 662-728-2009; 8AM-5PM (CST). *Misdemeanor, Civil Actions under $3,500, Eviction, Small Claims.*

Chancery Court PO Box 477, 100 N Main St, Booneville, MS 38829; 662-728-8151; fax: 662-728-2007; 8AM-5PM (CST). *Probate, Civil Land, Divorce, Family.*

Quitman County

Circuit Court Courthouse, 220 Chestnut St, #4, Marks, MS 38646; 662-326-8003; fax: 662-326-8004; 8AM-5PM (CST). *Felony, Civil (usually over $3,500).*

General Information: No sealed, adoptions, mental health, juvenile, sex, or expunged records released. No fax fee when $10.00 has been paid. Court makes copy: $.50 per page. Self serve copy: $.25 per page. Certification fee: $1.50 per document. Payee: Circuit Clerk. Business checks accepted. No credit cards accepted. Prepayment required.

Civil Name Search: Access: Fax, mail, in person. Both court and visitors may perform in person name searches. Search fee: $10.00 per name. Civil records on books and files since 1890. Mail turnaround time 2 days; phone results 10 minutes.

Criminal Name Search: Access: Fax, mail, in person. Both court and visitors may perform in person name searches. Search fee: $10.00 per name. Required to search: name, years to search, DOB; also helpful: SSN. Criminal docket on books and files since 1890. Mail turnaround time 2 days; phone results- 10 minutes.

Justice Court- Districts 1 & 2 275 E Main St, Marks, MS 38646; 662-326-2104/7906; fax: 662-326-2330; 8AM-N, 1-5PM (CST). *Misdemeanor, Civil Actions under $3,500, Eviction, Small Claims.*

Chancery Court 220 Chestnut St, Ste 2, Marks, MS 38646; 662-326-2661; fax: 662-326-8004; 8AM-N, 1-5PM (CST). *Probate, Civil Land, Divorce, Family.*

Rankin County

Circuit & County Court PO Drawer 1599, 215 E Government St, Brandon, MS 39043; 601-825-1466; criminal fax: 601-824-2445; civil fax: 8AM-5PM; 8AM-5PM (CST). *Felony, Misdemeanor, Civil (usually over $3,500).* www.rankincounty.org

General Information: Circuit and county are two different searches, You can request a combined criminal and civil search. No sealed or expunged records released. Will fax documents to local or toll free line. Court makes copy: $1.00 per page. Self serve copy: No self serve criminal copier; Civil self serve- $.25 each. Certification fee: $1.00 per doc. Payee: Circuit Clerk. Personal checks accepted. No credit cards accepted. Prepayment required. Mail requests: SASE required.

Civil Name Search: Access: Mail, in person. Both court and visitors may perform in person name searches. Search fee: $10.00 per name. Civil records on computer since 1990, prior on docket books. Mail turnaround time 1-2 days. Civil PAT goes back to 1990.

Criminal Name Search: Access: Mail, in person. Both court and visitors may perform in person name searches. Search fee: $10.00 per name. Required to search: name, years to search; also helpful: DOB, SSN. Criminal records on computer since 1990, prior on docket books. Mail turnaround time 1-2 days. Criminal PAT goes back to same as civil.

Justice Court- Districts 1-4 117 N. Timber, Brandon, MS 39042; 601-824-2665; fax: 601-824-2668; 8AM-5PM (CST). *Misdemeanor, Civil Actions under $3,500, Eviction, Small Claims.* www.rankincounty.org

Chancery Court 203 Town Sq, Brandon, MS 39042; 601-825-1649; 8AM-5PM (CST). *Probate, Civil Land, Divorce, Family.* www.rankincounty.org/chcourt/

General Information: Mailing address is PO Box 700, Zip is 39043.

Scott County

Circuit Court PO Box 371, 100 E 1st St, Courthouse, Forest, MS 39074; 601-469-3601;; 8AM-5PM (CST). *Felony, Civil (usually over $3,500).*

General Information: No sealed, adoptions, mental health, juvenile, sex, or expunged records released. Will fax documents to local or toll free line. Court makes copy: $.50 per page. Self serve copy: $.25 per page. Certification fee: $1.50 per page. Payee: Circuit Clerk. Personal checks accepted. No credit cards accepted. Prepayment required. Mail requests: SASE required.

Civil Name Search: Access: Mail, in person. Both court and visitors may perform in person name searches. Search fee: $10.00 per name. Fee is for 7 year search. Civil index on docket books since 1865, on computer back to 2002. Mail turnaround time 1 week. Public use terminal available, records go back to 2002.

Criminal Name Search: Access: Mail, in person. Both court and visitors may perform in person name searches. Search fee: $10.00 per name. Fee is for 7 year search. Required to search: name, years to search, DOB; also helpful: SSN. Criminal docket on books since 1965, on computer back to 2002. Mail turnaround time 1 week. Public use terminal available, crim records go back to 2002.

Justice Court PO Box 371, 100 Main St, Forest, MS 39074; 601-469-4555; fax: 601-469-5193; 8AM-5PM (CST). *Misdemeanor, Civil Actions under $3,500, Eviction, Small Claims.*

Chancery Court 100 Main St, PO Box 630, Forest, MS 39074; 601-469-1922, 601-469-1927; fax: 601-469-5180; 8AM-5PM (CST). *Probate, Civil Land, Divorce, Family.*

General Information: The Court participates in the Pilot MEC program for online filing and case record view but only for attorneys. See www.mssc.state.ms.us/mec/mec.html.

Sharkey County

Circuit Court PO Box 218 (120 Locust St), Rolling Fork, MS 39159; 662-873-2766; criminal phone: 662-873-2755; civil phone: 662-873-2755; fax: 662-873-6045; 8AM-N, 1-5PM (CST). *Felony, Civil (usually over $3,500).*

General Information: No sealed, adoptions, mental health, juvenile, sex, or expunged records released. Fee to fax out file $2.00 per page. Court makes copy: $.50 per page. Self serve copy: $.25 per page. Certification fee: $3.00 per document. Payee: Circuit Clerk. Business checks accepted. No credit cards accepted. Prepayment required. Mail requests: SASE required.

Civil Name Search: Access: Fax, mail, in person. Both court and visitors may perform in person name searches. Search fee: $10.00 per name. Civil index on docket books since 1893. Mail turnaround time 1 week.

Criminal Name Search: Access: Fax, mail, in person. Both court and visitors may perform in person name searches. Search fee: $10.00 per name. Required to search: name, years to search, DOB; also helpful: SSN. Criminal docket on books since 1893. Mail turnaround time 1 week.

Justice Court PO Box 235, 120 Locust St, Rolling Fork, MS 39159; 662-873-6140; fax: 662-873-0154; 8AM-N 1PM-5PM (CST). *Misdemeanor, Civil Actions under $3,500, Eviction, Small Claims.*

Chancery Court 120 Locust St, PO Box 218, Rolling Fork, MS 39159; 662-873-2755; fax: 662-873-6045; 8AM-N,1-5PM (CST). *Probate, Civil Land, Divorce, Family.*

Simpson County

Circuit Court PO Box 307, Mendenhall, MS 39114; 601-847-2474; fax: 601-847-4011; 8AM-5PM (CST). *Felony, Civil (usually over $3,500).*

General Information: No sealed or expunged records released. No fee to fax documents. Court makes copy: $.50 per page. Self serve copy: $.25 per page. Certification fee: $1.50 per page. Payee: Circuit Clerk. Business checks accepted. No credit cards accepted. Prepayment required.

Civil Name Search: Access: Fax, mail, in person. Both court and visitors may perform in person name searches. Search fee: $10.00 per name. Civil index on docket books since 1978. Mail turnaround time 1-2 days.

Criminal Name Search: Access: Fax, mail, in person. Both court and visitors may perform in person name searches. Search fee: $10.00 per name. Required to search: name, years to search; also helpful: DOB, SSN. Criminal docket on books since 1978. Mail turnaround time 1-2 days.

Justice Court 1498 Simpson Highway 149, Mendenhall, MS 39114; 601-847-5848; fax: 601-847-5856; 8AM-4:45PM (CST). *Misdemeanor, Civil Actions under $3,500, Eviction, Small Claims.*

Chancery Court PO Box 367, 111 W Pine, Mendenhall, MS 39114; 601-847-2626; fax: 601-847-7004; 8AM-5PM (CST). *Probate, Civil Land, Divorce, Family.*

Smith County

Circuit Court PO Box 517, 123 Main St, Raleigh, MS 39153; 601-782-4751; fax: 601-782-4007; 8AM-5PM (CST). *Felony, Civil (usually over $3,500).*

General Information: No sealed or expunged records released. Fee to fax out file $5.00 1st page, $1.00 each add'l. Court makes copy: $1.00 per page. Self serve copy: $.25 per page. Certification fee: $5.00 per document. Payee: Circuit Clerk. Personal checks accepted. No credit cards accepted. Prepayment required. Mail requests: SASE required.

Civil Name Search: Access: Mail, in person. Both court and visitors may perform in person name searches. Search fee: $10.00 per name. Civil index on docket books since 1912. Mail turnaround time 2 days. Civil PAT goes back to 1997.

Criminal Name Search: Access: Mail, in person. Both court and visitors may perform in person name searches. Search fee: $10.00 per name. Required to search: name, years to search, DOB; also helpful: SSN. Criminal docket on books since 1912. Mail turnaround time 2 days. Criminal PAT goes back to 1997.

Justice Court PO Box 171, 123 Main St, Raleigh, MS 39153; 601-782-4005/4334; fax: 601-782-5899; 8AM-5PM (CST). *Misdemeanor, Civil Actions under $3,500, Eviction, Small Claims.*

Chancery Court 201 Courthouse Sq., PO Box 39, Raleigh, MS 39153; 601-782-9811; fax: 601-782-4690; 8AM-5PM (CST). *Probate, Civil Land, Divorce, Family.*

Stone County

Circuit Court Courthouse, 323 Cavers Ave, Wiggins, MS 39577; 601-928-5246; fax: 601-928-5248; 8AM-5PM (CST). *Felony, Civil (usually over $3,500).*

General Information: No sealed, adoptions, mental health, juvenile, sex, or expunged records released. Will fax documents $3.00 1st page, $.50 each add'l. Court makes copy: $.50 per page. Certification fee: $1.50. Payee: Circuit Clerk. Business checks accepted. No credit cards accepted. Prepayment required. Mail requests: SASE required.

Civil Name Search: Access: Fax, mail, in person. Both court and visitors may perform in person name searches. Search fee: $10.00 per name. Civil index on docket books since 1945. Mail turnaround time same day.

Criminal Name Search: Access: Fax, mail, in person. Both court and visitors may perform in person name searches. Search fee: $10.00 per name. Required to search: name, years to search, DOB, notarized release; also helpful: SSN. Criminal docket on books since 1945. Mail turnaround time same day.

Justice Court 231 3rd St South, Wiggins, MS 39577-2808; 601-928-4415; fax: 601-928-2114; 8AM-5PM (CST). *Misdemeanor, Civil Actions under $3,500, Eviction, Small Claims.*

Chancery Court 323 E Cavers, PO Drawer 7, Wiggins, MS 39577; 601-928-5266; fax: 601-928-6464; 8AM-5PM (CST). *Probate, Civil Land, Divorce, Family.*

Sunflower County

Circuit Court PO Box 880, Indianola, MS 38751; 662-887-1252; fax: 662-887-7077; 8AM-5PM (CST). *Felony, Civil (usually over $3,500).*
General Information: No sealed, adoptions, mental health, juvenile, sex, or expunged records released. Fee to fax out file $1.00 per page. Court makes copy: $.50 per page. Self serve copy: $.25 per page. Certification fee: $1.50 per document. Payee: Circuit Clerk. Personal checks accepted. No credit cards accepted. Prepayment required. Mail requests: SASE required.
Civil Name Search: Access: Mail, in person. Both court and visitors may perform in person name searches. Search fee: $10.00 per name. Fee is for 7 year search. Civil index on docket books since 1881; on computer since 2000. Mail turnaround time 2 days. Civil PAT goes back to 2000. Public fax terminal also has partial civil records back to 1996.
Criminal Name Search: Access: Mail, in person. Both court and visitors may perform in person name searches. Search fee: $10.00 per name. Fee is for 7 year search. Required to search: name, years to search, DOB; also helpful: SSN. Criminal docket on books since 1913; on computer since 2000. Mail turnaround time 1-3 days. Criminal PAT goes back to 10/1999. Public terminal also has partial criminal records back to 1996.

Justice Court- Northern District PO Box 52, 119 N Chester, Ruleville, MS 38771; 662-756-2835; fax: 662-756-4175; 8AM-N, 1-5PM (CST). *Misdemeanor, Eviction, Small Claims.*
Justice Court- Southern District PO Box 487, 202 Main St, Indianola, MS 38751; 662-887-6921; fax: 662-887-2798; 8AM-N, 1-5PM (CST). *Misdemeanor, Civil Actions under $3,500, Eviction, Small Claims.*
Chancery Court 200 Main St, PO Box 988, Indianola, MS 38751; 662-887-4703; 8AM-5PM (CST). *Probate, Civil Land, Divorce, Family.*

Tallahatchie County

Charleston Circuit Court PO Box 86, Charleston, MS 38921; 662-647-8758; probate phone: 662-647-5551; fax: 662-647-8490; 8AM-5PM (CST). *Felony, Civil (usually over $3,500).*
General Information: No sealed, adoptions, mental health, juvenile, sex, or expunged records released. Will fax documents for fee. Court makes copy: $.50 per page. Certification fee: $1.00 per cert plus copy fee. Payee: Circuit Clerk. Personal checks accepted. No credit cards accepted. Prepayment required. Mail requests: SASE requested.
Civil Name Search: Access: Fax, mail, in person. Both court and visitors may perform in person name searches. Search fee: $10.00 per name. Civil records on books since 1920s. Mail turnaround time 3 days.
Criminal Name Search: Access: Fax, mail, in person. Both court and visitors may perform in person name searches. Search fee: $10.00 per name. Required to search: name, years to search, DOB; also helpful: SSN. Criminal docket on books since 1920s. Mail turnaround time 3 days.

Tallahatchie Justice Court District 1 PO Box 440, 1 Main St, 2nd Fl, Charleston, MS 38921; 662-647-3477/3478; fax: 662-647-2208; 8AM-5PM (CST). *Misdemeanor, Civil Actions under $3,500, Eviction, Small Claims.*
General Information: Court is located upstairs of the Charleston court house; records are not co-mingled. Call before faxing.
Tallahatchie Justice Court District 2 PO Box 155, 401 Court Sq, Sumner, MS 38957; 662-375-9452; fax: 662-375-8200; 8AM-N; 1-5PM (CST). *Misdemeanor, Civil Actions under $3,500, Eviction, Small Claims.*
General Information: Also known as Sumner Justice Court.
Charleston Chancery Court #1 Court Sq, PO Box 350, Charleston, MS 38921; 662-647-5551; fax: 662-647-3702; 8AM-5PM (CST). *Probate, Divorce, Family.*
Sumner Chancery Court PO Box 180, 100 N Main Court Square, Sumner, MS 38957; 662-375-8731; fax: 662-375-7252; 8AM-N, 1-5PM (CST). *Probate, Divorce, Family.*

Tate County

Circuit Court 201 Ward St, Senatobia, MS 38668; 662-562-5211; fax: 662-562-7486; 8AM-5PM (CST). *Felony, Civil (usually over $3,500).*
General Information: No sealed, adoptions, mental health, juvenile, sex, or expunged records released. Will not fax documents. Court makes copy: $.50 first page, $.25 each add'l. Self serve copy: $.25 per page. Certification fee: $1.00 per page. Payee: Circuit Clerk. Personal checks accepted. No credit cards accepted. Prepayment required. Mail requests: SASE requested.
Civil Name Search: Access: Mail, in person. Both court and visitors may perform in person name searches. Search fee: $10.00 per name. Civil records on books since 1872. Mail turnaround time same day. Civil PAT goes back to 1990.
Criminal Name Search: Access: Mail, in person. Both court and visitors may perform in person name searches. Search fee: $10.00 per name. Required to search: name, years to search; also helpful: SSN. Criminal docket on books since 1872. Mail turnaround time same day. Criminal PAT goes back to same as civil.

Justice Court 103 Preston McKay Dr, Senatobia, MS 38668; 662-562-7626; fax: 662-562-7663; 8AM-N,1-5PM (CST). *Misdemeanor, Civil Actions under $3,500, Eviction, Small Claims.*
Chancery Court 201 Ward St, PO Box 309, Senatobia, MS 38668; 662-562-5661; fax: 662-560-6205; 8AM-5PM (CST). *Probate, Civil Land, Divorce, Family.*

Tippah County

Circuit Court Courthouse, 102A N Main St, Ripley, MS 38663; 662-837-7370; fax: 662-837-1030; 8AM-5PM (CST). *Felony, Civil (usually over $3,500).*
General Information: Probate fax is same as main fax number. No sealed, adoptions, mental health, juvenile, sex or expunged records released. Will fax documents $1.00 per page. Court makes copy: civil court- no charge; criminal court $.50 per page. Self serve copy: Criminal self serve copy $.25 per page; No civil self serve. No certification fee . Payee: Circuit Clerk. Personal checks accepted. No credit cards accepted. Prepayment required. Mail requests: SASE required.
Civil Name Search: Access: Phone, fax, mail, in person. Both court and visitors may perform in person name searches. Search fee: $5.00 per name. Civil cases indexed by defendant. Civil index on docket books since 1800s. Mail turnaround time 1 week; phone turnaround 30 minutes.
Criminal Name Search: Access: Phone, fax, mail, in person. Both court and visitors may perform in person name searches. Search fee: $5.00 per name. Required to search: name, years to search, DOB; also helpful: SSN. Criminal docket on books since 1800s. Mail turnaround time 1 week; phone turnaround 30 minutes.

Justice Court Justice Court, 205-B Spring Ave, Ripley, MS 38663; 662-837-8842; fax: 662-837-1398; 8AM-5PM (CST). *Misdemeanor, Civil Actions under $3,500, Eviction, Small Claims.*
Chancery Court 101 East Spring St, Ripley, MS 38663; 662-837-7374; fax: 662-837-7148; 8AM-5PM (CST). *Probate, Civil Land, Divorce, Family.*

Tishomingo County

Circuit Court 1008 Battleground Dr, Iuka, MS 38852; 662-423-7026; fax: 662-423-1667; 8AM-5PM (CST). *Felony, Civil (usually over $3,500).*
General Information: No sealed, adoptions, mental health, juvenile, sex, or expunged records released. Will fax documents $10.00 per name. Court makes copy: $1.00 per page. Self serve copy: $.25 per page. Certification fee: $1.00 per page. Payee: Circuit Clerk. Business checks accepted. No credit cards accepted. Prepayment required. Mail requests: SASE requested.
Civil Name Search: Access: Mail, in person. Both court and visitors may perform in person name searches. Search fee: $10.00 per name. Civil records on computer back to 2000, in docket books since 1950s, others in storage. Mail turnaround time 1-2 days. Civil PAT goes back to 2000.
Criminal Name Search: Access: Mail, in person. Both court and visitors may perform in person name searches. Search fee: $10.00 per name. Required to search: name, years to search, DOB; also helpful: SSN, signed release. Criminal records computerized from 2000, in docket books since 1950s, others in storage. Mail turnaround time 1-2 days. Criminal PAT goes back to same as civil.

Justice Court- Northern & Southern Districts 1008 Battleground Drive, Rm 212, Iuka, MS 38852; 662-423-7033; fax: 662-423-7094; 8AM-5PM (CST). *Misdemeanor, Civil Actions under $3,500, Eviction, Small Claims.*
Chancery Court 1008 Battleground Dr, Iuka, MS 38852; 662-423-7010; fax: 662-423-7005; 8AM-5PM (CST). *Probate, Civil Land, Divorce, Family.*

Tunica County

Circuit Court PO Box 184, Tunica, MS 38676; 662-363-2842; fax: 662-363-2413; 8AM-5PM (CST). *Felony, Civil (usually over $3,500).* www.tunicacountycircuitclerk.com/
General Information: No sealed, adoptions, mental health, juvenile, sex, or expunged records released. Will fax documents to local or toll free line. Court makes copy: $1.00 per page, add'l fee for postage. Self serve copy: $.50 per page. Certification fee: $3.50. Payee: Circuit Clerk. Personal checks accepted. No credit cards accepted. Prepayment required. Mail requests: SASE requested.
Civil Name Search: Access: Mail, in person. Both court and visitors may perform in person name searches. Search fee: $10.00 per name. Civil index on docket books for 10 years; archived prior. Mail turnaround time 1 week.
Criminal Name Search: Access: Mail, in person. Both court and visitors may perform in person name searches. Search fee: $10.00 per name. Required to search: name, years to search, DOB; also helpful: SSN. Criminal docket on books for 10 years. Mail turnaround time 1 week.

Justice Court 5130 Old Moon Landing Rd., Tunica, MS 38676; 662-363-2178; fax: 662-363-4234; 8AM-5PM (CST). *Misdemeanor, Civil Actions Under $3,500, Eviction, Small Claims.*

General Information: Traffic tickets also included in jurisdiction.

Chancery Court PO Box 217, 1300 School St, Rm 104, Tunica, MS 38676; 662-363-2451; fax: 662-357-5934; 8AM-N, 1PM-5PM (CST). *Probate, Civil Land, Divorce, Family.*

Union County

Circuit Court PO Box 298, 114 Bankhead St, New Albany, MS 38652; 662-534-1910; fax: 662-534-2059; 8AM-5PM (CST). *Felony, Civil (usually over $3,500).*

General Information: No adoption, mental health or juvenile records released. No fee to fax documents. Court makes copy: $.50 per page. Self serve copy: $.25 per page. Certification fee: $10.00 per doc. Payee: Union County Circuit Clerk. Personal checks accepted. No credit cards accepted. Prepayment required. Mail requests: SASE requested.

Civil Name Search: Access: Fax, mail, in person. Both court and visitors may perform in person name searches. Search fee: $10.00 per name. Includes certification fee. Required to search: name, years to search, address. Civil index on docket books since early 1900s. Mail turnaround time 1 week. Civil PAT goes back to 2000.

Criminal Name Search: Access: Fax, mail, in person. Both court and visitors may perform in person name searches. Search fee: $10.00 per name. Fee includes certification. Required to search: name, years to search, DOB; also helpful: SSN. Criminal docket on books since early 1900s. Mail turnaround time 1 week. Criminal PAT goes back to 2000.

Justice Court- East & West Posts PO Box 27, 300 Carter Ave, New Albany, MS 38652; 662-534-1951; fax: 662-534-1935; 8AM-5PM (CST). *Misdemeanor, Civil Actions under $3,500, Eviction, Small Claims.*

Chancery Court PO Box 847, 109 E Main St, New Albany, MS 38652; 662-534-1900; fax: 662-534-1907; 8AM-5PM (CST). *Probate, Civil Land, Divorce, Family.*

General Information: Misdemeanor records phone is 662-534-1951.

Walthall County

Circuit Court 200 Ball Ave, Tylertown, MS 39667; 601-876-5677; fax: 601-876-4077; 8AM-N; 1-5PM (CST). *Felony, Civil (usually over $3,500).*

General Information: No sealed, adoptions, mental health, juvenile, sex, or expunged records released. Will fax documents. Court makes copy: $.50 per page. Self serve copy: $.25 per page. Certification fee: $1.50 per document. Payee: Circuit Clerk. Personal checks accepted. No credit cards accepted. Prepayment required.

Civil Name Search: Access: Mail, in person. Both court and visitors may perform in person name searches. Search fee: $10.00 per name includes copies. Civil index on docket books since 1914, records are not computerized. Mail turnaround time 1-2 days.

Criminal Name Search: Access: Mail, in person. Both court and visitors may perform in person name searches. Search fee: $10.00 per name includes copies. Required to search: name, years to search; also helpful: SSN. Criminal docket on books since 1914, records are not computerized. Mail turnaround time 1-2 days.

Justice Court- Districts 1 & 2 PO Box 507, 807 Magnolia Ave, Tylertown, MS 39667; 601-876-2311; fax: 601-876-6866; 8AM-N, 1-5PM (CST). *Misdemeanor, Civil Actions under $3,500, Eviction, Small Claims.*

General Information: Traffic tickets are also held at this court.

Chancery Court PO Box 351, 200 Ball Ave, Tylertown, MS 39667; 601-876-3553; fax: 601-876-6026; 8AM-5PM (CST). *Probate, Civil Land, Divorce, Family.*

Warren County

Circuit & County Court PO Box 351, 1009 Cherry St, Vicksburg, MS 39181; 601-636-3961; fax: 601-630-4100; 8AM-5PM (CST). *Felony, Misdemeanor, Civil (usually over $3,500).*

General Information: No sealed or expunged records released. Will fax documents $5.00 per page. Court makes copy: $1.00 per page. Self serve copy: $.25 per page. Certification fee: $1.00 per page. Payee: Circuit Clerk. No personal checks or credit cards accepted. Prepayment required. Mail requests: SASE required.

Civil Name Search: Access: Mail, in person, online. Both court and visitors may perform in person name searches. Search fee: $10.00 per name. Civil records on books since 1970s. Mail turnaround time 1 day. Civil PAT goes back to 2002. The Circuit and County Court participates in the Pilot MEC program for online filing and case record view but only for attorneys. See www.mssc.state.ms.us/mec/mec.html.

Criminal Name Search: Access: Mail, in person. Both court and visitors may perform in person name searches. Search fee: $10.00 per name. Required to search: name, years to search; also helpful: DOB, SSN. Criminal docket on books since 1970s. Mail turnaround time 1 day. Criminal PAT goes back to same as civil.

Justice Court- Northern, Central & Southern Districts PO Box 1598, 919 Farmer St, Vicksburg, MS 39181; 601-634-6402; fax: 601-630-

8015; 8AM-5PM (CST). *Misdemeanor, Civil Actions under $3,500, Eviction, Small Claims.*

Chancery Court PO Box 351, 1009 Cherry St, Vicksburg, MS 39181; 601-636-4415; fax: 601-630-8185; 8AM-5PM (CST). *Probate, Civil Land, Divorce, Family.*

www.co.warren.ms.us/ChanceryClerk/ChanceryClerk.htm

General Information: Also handles adoption, divorce, lunacy, Uresa, and minor settlements

Washington County

Circuit & County Court PO Box 1276, Greenville, MS 38702; 662-378-2747; fax: 662-334-2698; 8AM-5PM (CST). *Felony, Misdemeanor, Civil.*

General Information: No sealed or expunged records released. No fee to fax documents. Court makes copy: $1.00 per page. Self serve copy: $.25 per page. Certification fee: $1.50. Payee: Circuit Clerk. Business checks accepted. No credit cards accepted. Prepayment required. Mail requests: SASE required.

Civil Name Search: Access: Fax, mail, in person. Both court and visitors may perform in person name searches. Search fee: $15.00 per name per court. Civil records on books since 1964. Mail turnaround time 5-10 days. Public use terminal available, records go back to 9/2006.

Criminal Name Search: Access: Fax, mail, in person. Both court and visitors may perform in person name searches. Search fee: $15.00 per name for 7 years, $1.00 each add'l year. Required to search: name, years to search; also helpful: DOB, SSN. Criminal docket on books since 1978. Mail turnaround time 5-10 days. Public use terminal available, crim records go back to same as civil.

Justice Court- Districts 1-3 905 W Alexander, Greenville, MS 38701; 662-332-0633; fax: 662-390-4760; 8AM-5PM (CST). *Misdemeanor, Civil Actions under $3,500, Eviction, Small Claims.*

Chancery Court PO Box 309, 900 Washington Ave, Greenville, MS 38720-0309; 662-332-1595; fax: 662-334-2725; 8AM-5PM (CST). *Probate, Civil Land, Divorce, Family.*

Wayne County

Circuit Court PO Box 428, Waynesboro, MS 39367; 601-735-1171; fax: 601-735-6261; 8AM-5PM (CST). *Felony, Civil (usually over $3,500).*

General Information: This court is in process of computerizing their records. No sealed or expunged records released. Fee to fax out file $1.00 per page. Court makes copy: $.50 per page. Self serve copy: $.25 per page. Certification fee: $1.50. Payee: Circuit Clerk. Business checks accepted. No credit cards accepted. Prepayment required. Mail requests: SASE required.

Civil Name Search: Access: Phone, fax, mail, in person. Both court and visitors may perform in person name searches. Search fee: $10.00 per name. Civil index on docket books since 1980, others in storage. Mail turnaround time 1-2 days. Civil PAT goes back to 1999.

Criminal Name Search: Access: Fax, mail, in person. Both court and visitors may perform in person name searches. Search fee: $10.00 per name. Required to search: name, years to search; also helpful: DOB, SSN, signed release. Criminal docket on books since 1980, others in storage. Mail turnaround time 1-2 days. Criminal PAT goes back to 1996.

Justice Court- Posts 1 & 2 810 Chickasawhay St, #C, Waynesboro, MS 39367; 601-735-3118; fax: 601-735-6266; 8AM-5PM (CST). *Misdemeanor, Civil Actions under $3,500, Eviction, Small Claims.*

Chancery Court Courthouse, 609 Azalea Dr, Waynesboro, MS 39367; 601-735-2873; fax: 601-735-6224; 8AM-5PM (CST). *Probate, Civil Land, Divorce, Family.*

Webster County

Circuit Court PO Box 308, 515 Carroll St, Walthall, MS 39771; 662-258-6287; fax: 662-258-7686; 8AM-5PM (CST). *Felony, Civil (usually over $3,500).*

General Information: No sealed, adoptions, mental health, juvenile, sex, or expunged records released. No fee to fax documents. Court makes copy: $1.00 per page. Self serve copy: $.50 per page. Certification fee: $1.00 per page. Payee: Circuit Clerk. Business checks accepted. No credit cards accepted. Prepayment required.

Civil Name Search: Access: Phone, fax, mail, in person. Both court and visitors may perform in person name searches. Search fee: $10.00 per name. Civil index on docket books since 1874. Mail turnaround time 1-2 days.

Criminal Name Search: Access: Fax, mail, in person. Both court and visitors may perform in person name searches. Search fee: $10.00 per name. Required to search: name, years to search, DOB; also helpful: SSN. Criminal docket on books since 1874. Mail turnaround time 1-2 days.

Justice Court- Districts 1 & 2 24 E Fox Ave, Eupora, MS 39744; 662-258-2590; fax: 662-258-3093; 8AM-5PM (CST). *Misdemeanor, Civil Actions under $3,500, Eviction, Small Claims.*

Chancery Court PO Box 398, 515 Carroll Street, Walthall, MS 39771; 662-258-4131; fax: 662-258-9635; 8AM-5PM (CST). *Probate, Civil Land, Divorce, Family.*

Wilkinson County

Circuit Court PO Box 327, 525 Main St, Woodville, MS 39669; 601-888-6697; fax: 601-888-6984; 8AM-5PM (CST). *Felony, Civil (usually over $3,500).*

General Information: No sealed or expunged records released. Will fax documents $5.00 per page. Court makes copy: $.50 per page. Self serve copy: $.25 per page. Certification fee: $10.00 per doc. Payee: Circuit Clerk. Personal checks accepted. No credit cards accepted. Prepayment required.

Civil Name Search: Access: Mail, in person. Both court and visitors may perform in person name searches. Search fee: $10.00 per name. Civil index on docket books since 1940s. Mail turnaround time 1-2 days. Civil PAT goes back to 2008.

Criminal Name Search: Access: Mail, in person. Both court and visitors may perform in person name searches. Search fee: $10.00 per name. Required to search: name, years to search; also helpful: DOB, SSN. Criminal docket on books since 1940s. Mail turnaround time 1-2 days. Criminal PAT goes back to 2008.

Justice Court PO Box 40, 1389 Highway 61 South, Woodville, MS 39669; 601-888-3538, 601-888-3972; fax: 601-888-7591; 8AM-5PM (CST). *Misdemeanor, Civil Actions under $3,500, Eviction, Small Claims.*

Chancery Court PO Box 516, 525 Main St, Woodville, MS 39669; 601-888-4381; fax: 601-888-6776; 8AM-5PM (CST). *Probate, Civil Land, Divorce, Family.*

Winston County

Circuit Court PO Box 785, Louisville, MS 39339; 662-773-3581; fax: 662-773-7192; 8AM-5PM (CST). *Felony, Civil (usually over $3,500).*

General Information: You may email requests to kim@winstoncounty.org. No sealed, adoptions, or expunged records released. Will fax documents $5.00 1st page, $1.00 each add'l. Court makes copy: $1.00 per page. Self serve copy: $.25 per page. Certification fee: $3.00 per doc. Payee: Circuit Clerk. Personal checks accepted. No credit cards accepted. Prepayment required. Mail requests: SASE requested.

Civil Name Search: Access: Phone, fax, mail, in person. Both court and visitors may perform in person name searches. Search fee: $10.00 per name. Civil index on docket books since early 1950s; some on computer back to 1994; all since 2000. Note: If faxing, please include a copy of the check to be mailed. Mail turnaround time 14 day maximum. Civil PAT goes back to 2000.

Criminal Name Search: Access: Fax, mail, in person. Both court and visitors may perform in person name searches. Search fee: $10.00 per name. Required to search: name, years to search, DOB; also helpful: SSN. Criminal docket on books since early 1800s; on computer back to 2000. Note: If faxing, please include a copy of the check to be mailed. Mail turnaround time 14 day maximum . Criminal PAT goes back to 2000.

Justice Court PO Box 327, 115 S Court St, Louisville, MS 39339; 662-773-6016; fax: 662-773-8817; 8AM-5PM (CST). *Misdemeanor, Civil Actions under $3,500, Eviction, Small Claims.*

Chancery Court PO Drawer 69, 115 S Court St, Louisville, MS 39339; 662-773-3631; fax: 662-773-8814; 8AM-5PM (CST). *Probate, Civil Land, Divorce, Family.*

Yalobusha County

Coffeeville Circuit Court PO Box 260, Coffeeville, MS 38922; 662-675-8187; fax: 662-675-8004; 8AM-5PM (CST). *Felony, Civil (usually over $3,500).*

General Information: No sealed, adoptions, mental health, juvenile, sex, or expunged records released. Will fax documents to local or toll free line. Court makes copy: $.50 per page. Self serve copy: $.25 per page. Certification fee: $10.00. Payee: Circuit Clerk. Personal checks accepted. No credit cards accepted. Prepayment required. Mail requests: SASE requested.

Civil Name Search: Access: Phone, fax, mail, in person. Both court and visitors may perform in person name searches. Search fee: $10.00 per name. May mail request with check or fax request with copy of check to be mailed. Civil index on docket books since 1930s. Mail turnaround time 1-2 days.

Criminal Name Search: Access: Phone, fax, mail, in person. Both court and visitors may perform in person name searches. Search fee: $10.00 per name. May mail request with check or fax request with copy of check to be mailed. Required to search: name, years to search; also helpful: DOB. Criminal docket on books since 1930s. Mail turnaround time 1-2 days.

Water Valley Circuit Court PO Box 1431, 201 Blackmer Dr, Water Valley, MS 38965; 662-473-1341; fax: 662-473-5020; 8AM-5PM (CST). *Felony, Civil over $3,500.*

General Information: No sealed, adoptions, mental health, juvenile, sex, or expunged records released. No fee to fax documents to toll-fee number. Court makes copy: $.50 per page. Self serve copy: same. Certification fee: No cert fee if a search fee paid. Payee: Circuit Clerk. Personal checks accepted. No credit cards accepted. Prepayment required.

Civil Name Search: Access: Fax, mail, in person. Both court and visitors may perform in person name searches. Search fee: $10.00 per name. Includes certification fee. Civil index on docket books since 1930s. Mail turnaround time 1 week.

Criminal Name Search: Access: Fax, mail, in person. Both court and visitors may perform in person name searches. Search fee: $10.00 per name. Fee includes certification. Required to search: name, years to search, DOB; also helpful: SSN. Criminal docket on books since 1930s. Mail turnaround time 1 week.

Justice Court- District 1 PO Box 218, 7092 County Rd 436,(Water Valley, 38965), Coffeeville, MS 38922; 662-473-2790; fax: 662-473-5016; 8AM-5PM (CST). *Misdemeanor, Civil Actions under $3,500, Eviction, Small Claims.*

General Information: 14400 Main St, Coffeeville, MS 38922 is the courthouse address. Records kept at above address.

Justice Court- Division 2 PO Box 918, 205 Blackmur Dr, Water Valley, MS 38965; 662-473-4502; fax: 662-473-5016; 8AM-5PM (CST). *Misdemeanor, Civil Actions under $3,500, Eviction, Small Claims.*

Chancery Court PO Box 664, 201 Blackmur Dr, Water Valley, MS 38965; 662-473-2091; fax: 662-473-3622; 8AM-N 1PM-5PM (CST). *Probate, Civil Land, Divorce, Family.*

Chancery Court PO Box 260, 14400 Main St, Coffeeville, MS 38922; 662-675-2716; fax: 662-675-8004; 8AM-N, 1-5PM (CST). *Probate, Civil Land, Divorce, Family.*

Yazoo County

Circuit & County Court PO Box 108, 211 E Broadway, Yazoo City, MS 39194; 662-746-1872; fax: 662-716-0113; 8AM-5PM (CST). *Felony, Misdemeanor, Civil (usually over $3,500).*

General Information: No sealed, adoptions, mental health, juvenile, sex, or expunged records released. Will fax documents. Court makes copy: $.50 per page. Self serve copy: $.25 per page. Certification fee: $1.00 per page. Payee: Circuit Clerk. Business checks accepted. No credit cards accepted. Prepayment required. Mail requests: SASE required.

Civil Name Search: Access: Mail, in person. Both court and visitors may perform in person name searches. Search fee: $10.00 per name. Civil records for Civil Circuit on docket books since 1973; for Civil County on docket books since 1977. Mail turnaround time 1 day. Civil PAT available.

Criminal Name Search: Access: Mail, in person. Both court and visitors may perform in person name searches. Search fee: $10.00 per name. Required to search: name, years to search, DOB; also helpful: SSN. Criminal records for Criminal Circuit from 1975; Criminal County on docket books since 1975. Mail turnaround time 1 day. Criminal PAT available.

Justice Court- Northern & Southern Districts PO Box 798, 211 E Broadway, Yazoo City, MS 39194; 662-746-8181; fax: 662-746-2186; 8AM-5PM (CST). *Misdemeanor, Civil Actions under $3,500, Eviction, Small Claims.*

Chancery Court PO Box 68, 211 E Broadway, Yazoo City, MS 39194; 662-746-2661; fax: 662-746-3893; 8AM-5PM (CST). *Probate, Civil Land, Divorce, Family.*

General Information: Physical address for court is 211 E Broadway.

Missouri

Time Zone:	CST
Capital:	Jefferson City, Cole County
# of Counties:	114
State Web:	www.mo.gov
Court Web:	www.courts.mo.gov

Administration

State Court Administrator, 2112 Industrial Dr., PO Box 104480, Jefferson City, MO, 65109; 573-751-4377, Fax: 573-751-5540.

The Supreme and Appellate Courts

The Supreme Court is the court of last resort. The Missouri Court of Appeals is the intermediate appellate court and handles appeals from the Circuit Courts and all other appeals except those in the Supreme Court's exclusive jurisdiction. Appellate and Supreme Court opinions are available at the web page.

The Missouri Courts

Court	Type	How Organized	Jurisdiction Highpoints
Circuit *	General	106 Courts (with Divisions) in 45 Districts	Felony, Misdemeanor, Civil, Small Claims, Eviction, Family, Probate, Juvenile
Municipal	Limited	470	Ordinance

* = profiled in this book

Details on the Court Structure

The **Circuit Courts** are the primary trial courts in Missouri, and they have general jurisdiction over almost all civil and criminal matters. Each circuit court consists of divisions including associate circuit, small claims, municipal, criminal, family, probate and juvenile. The type of case determines the division to which a particular case is assigned.

At one time, every county had an **Associate Circuit Court**. Over the past few years the Associate Courts has been consolidated into the Circuit Court, with the Associate Court beginning a division of the Circuit Court. Since 01/01/2010, all Associate Courts are supposedly absorbed into the Circuit Court as Divisions. Herein we have segregated the Associate Courts when record keeping, fees and phone numbers indicated are completely comingled with the Circuit Court.

The **Municipal Court** has original jurisdiction on municipal ordinance violations.

Record Searching Facts You Need to Know

Fees and Record Searching Tips

Many Circuit Courts do not accept mail or fax requests to perform criminal record searches and refer requesters to the MO State Highway Patrol Criminal Records Division. Those courts which will do a name search charge between $1.00 and $10.00, or no fee at all.

All courts participate in the Missouri CaseNet online system (see below). The public access terminals found in the court houses generally reflect the same content as found on the CaseNet access. However, since few identifiers are given, often an onsite search is needed to view file to confirm identity is needed.

Online Access is Statewide for Trial Courts

Available at https://www.courts.mo.gov/casenet/base/welcome.do is Missouri CaseNet, an online system for access to docket data. The system includes all Circuit Courts, City of St. Louis, the Eastern, Western, and Southern Appellate Courts, the Supreme Court, and Fine Collection Center. Cases can be searched case number, filing date, or litigant name. A number of Municipal Courts also participate. CaseNet search results show full name, address, and usually year of birth only (click on Parties and Attorneys at case result page). Note some individual courts offer access to probate records outside of CaseNet.

Adair County

Consolidated Circuit Court PO Box 690, 106 W Washington, Kirksville, MO 63501; 660-665-2552; fax: 660-665-3420; 8AM-5PM (CST). *Felony, Civil Actions, Small Claims, Probate.*
www.courts.mo.gov/page.jsp?id=1534
General Information: The court consolidated on 06/01/2008. No juvenile, mental, expunged, sealed, dismissed or suspended records released. Will not fax documents. Court makes copy: $.25 per page. Certification fee: $2.50 per cert. Payee: Circuit Clerk. No personal checks or credit cards accepted. Prepayment required.
Civil Name Search: Access: In person, online. Visitors must perform in person searches themselves. No search fee. Prior on index cards. Civil PAT goes back to 09/2005, but judgments go back further. Case lookup is at https://www.courts.mo.gov/casenet/base/welcome.do. Online records go back to 9/6/2005. Online search results show full name, address, and year of birth only.
Criminal Name Search: Access: In person, online. Visitors must perform in person searches themselves. Criminal records on computer since 1991, prior on index cards. Note: Criminal search requests are forwarded to MO State Highway Patrol. Criminal PAT goes back to 09/2005. Both the terminal and CaseNet only show year of birth. For common names, one must ask the Clerk for more identifiers to correctly do a search. Online access to criminal records same as civil, above.

Andrew County

Consolidated Circuit Court PO Box 318, Savannah, MO 64485; 816-324-4221; fax: 816-324-5667; 8AM-5PM (CST). *Felony, Civil Actions, Small Claims, Probate.* www.courts.mo.gov/page.jsp?id=1561
General Information: The Circuit and Associate Courts consolidated effective Jan 1, 2011. Online identifiers in results same as on public terminal. No juvenile, mental, expunged, sealed, dismissed or suspended imposition of sentence records released. Will not fax documents. Court makes copy: $.25 per page first 10 pages, then $.10 ea add'l. Certification fee: $2.50 per cert plus copy fees. Payee: Andrew County. Personal checks accepted. No credit cards accepted. Prepayment required.
Civil Name Search: Access: In person, online. Both court and visitors may perform in person name searches. No search fee. Civil index on cards since 1976, archived since 1850, computerized since 6/00. Civil PAT goes back to 10 years. Sometimes older judgment will be displayed. Case lookup is at https://www.courts.mo.gov/casenet/base/welcome.do. Online records go back to 1993. Online search results show full name, address, and year of birth only.
Criminal Name Search: Access: In person, online. Visitors must perform in person searches themselves. Required to search: name, years to search; also helpful: DOB. Criminal records on computer ten years, archived from 1841. Criminal PAT goes back to same as civil. Both the terminal and CaseNet only show year of birth. For common names, one must ask the Clerk for more identifiers to correctly do a search. Case lookup is at https://www.courts.mo.gov/casenet/base/welcome.do. Online records go back to 1993. Online search results show full name, address, and year of birth only.

Atchison County

Combined Circuit Court PO Box 280, Rock Port, MO 64482; 660-744-2707, 660-744-2700; fax: 660-744-6100; 8:30AM-4:30PM (CST). *Felony, Misdemeanor, Civil Actions, Small Claims, Eviction, Probate, Traffic.*
www.courts.mo.gov/page.jsp?id=1543
General Information: Combined with the Associate Circuit Ct 2/2009. Online identifiers in results same as on public terminal. No juvenile, mental, expunged, sealed, dismissed or suspended imposition of sentence records released. Will fax documents for $1.00 per page. Court makes copy: $1.00 per page. Certification fee: $1.00 per cert. Payee: Circuit Clerk. Personal checks accepted. No credit cards accepted. Prepayment required. Mail requests: SASE helpful for mail return of any copies.
Civil Name Search: Access: In person, online. Visitors must perform in person searches themselves. Civil index on docket books, and archived from 1845. Civil PAT available. Case lookup is at https://www.courts.mo.gov/casenet/base/welcome.do. Online records go back to 3/20/2006. The online system does not always include the DOB.
Criminal Name Search: Access: In person, online. Visitors must perform in person searches themselves. Criminal records indexed in books, and archived from 1845. Note: Court recommends to search at MO State Highway Patrol, 573-526-6153. Criminal PAT available. Both the terminal and CaseNet only show year of birth. For common names, one must ask the Clerk for more identifiers to correctly do a search. Online access to criminal records same as civil, above. Online results show middle initial.

Audrain County

Consolidated Circuit Court Courthouse, 101 N Jefferson, Mexico, MO 65265; 573-473-5850; criminal phone: 573-473-5840; civil phone: 573-473-5842; fax: 573-581-3237; 8AM-5PM (CST). *Felony, Misdemeanor, Civil Actions, Small Claims, Probate.*
www.courts.mo.gov/page.jsp?id=1592
General Information: Online identifiers in results same as on public terminal. No juvenile, mental, expunged, sealed, dismissed or suspended imposition of sentence records released. Will fax documents for $1.00 per page. Court makes copy: $.25 per page. Certification fee: $1.50 for first 2 pages; $.25 each add'l. Payee: Circuit Clerk. Personal checks accepted. No credit cards accepted. Prepayment required. Mail requests: SASE required for mail return of any copies.
Civil Name Search: Access: In person, online. Visitors must perform in person searches themselves. Civil records on computer since 8/92, prior on index cards, older records archived at Genealogy Club in Mexico, MO. Civil PAT goes back to 2003. Often older judgment will be displayed. Participates in the state online court record system at https://www.courts.mo.gov/casenet/base/welcome.do. Online records go back to 5/19/2003. Online search results show full name, address, and year of birth only.
Criminal Name Search: Access: In person, online. Visitors must perform in person searches themselves. Required to search: name, years to search; also SSN, case number. Criminal records on computer since 8/92, stored for 25 years on site then archived (back to 1800s). Criminal PAT goes back to same as civil. Both the terminal and CaseNet only show year of birth. For common names, one must ask the Clerk for more identifiers to correctly do a search. Participates in the state online court record system at https://www.courts.mo.gov/casenet/base/welcome.do. Online records go back to 5/19/2003. Online search results show full name, address, and year of birth only.

Barry County

Combined Circuit Court 102 West St #1 (Criminal Div) #2 (Civil Div), Barry County Judicial Center, Cassville, MO 65625; 417-847-3133, 417-847-6557; criminal phone: x2627; civil phone: x2626; criminal fax: 417-847-6298; civil fax: 8AM-4PM; 8AM-4PM (CST). *Felony, Misdemeanor, Civil Actions, Eviction, Small Claims, Probate.*
www.courts.mo.gov/page.jsp?id=1660
General Information: The Circuit Court and Assoc Circuit Court combined 1/2007. Online identifiers in results same as on public terminal. No juvenile, mental expunged, sealed, dismissed or suspended imposition of sentence records released. Will fax documents. Court makes copy: $.25 per page. Certification fee: $1.00 per doc. Payee: Circuit Clerk. No personal checks. No credit cards accepted. Prepayment required. Mail requests: SASE required for civil.
Civil Name Search: Access: Mail, fax, in person, online. Both court and visitors may perform in person name searches. No search fee. Civil index on cards, archived since mid-1800s. Civil PAT goes back to 2005. Often older judgment will be displayed. Case lookup is at https://www.courts.mo.gov/casenet/base/welcome.do. Online records go back to 7/11/2005. Online search results show full name, address, and year of birth only.
Criminal Name Search: Access: In person, online (Mail, fax if case number known). Both court and visitors may perform in person name searches. No search fee. Required to search: case number. Criminal records indexed on cards, archived since mid-1800s; on computer back to 1995. Note: Call ahead for approval of a mail or fax request, and fee. Often, this court directs requests to Highway Patrol for criminal background checks. Criminal PAT goes back to 2005. Both the terminal and CaseNet only show year of birth. For common names, one must ask the Clerk for more identifiers to correctly do a search. Online access to criminal records same as civil, above.

Barton County

Consolidated Circuit Court 1007 Broadway, Rm 204, County Courthouse, Lamar, MO 64759; 417-682-2444; fax: 417-682-2960; 8AM-N, 1-4:30PM (CST). *Felony, Misdemeanor, Civil, Eviction, Small Claims, Probate.*
www.courts.mo.gov/page.jsp?id=1633
General Information: Online identifiers in results same as on public terminal. No juvenile, mental, expunged, dismissed, or suspended imposition of sentence records released. Will fax out documents $1.00 1st page, $.50 each add'l. Court makes copy: $.25 per page. Self serve copy: same. Certification fee: $2.50. Payee: Circuit Court. Personal checks accepted. No credit cards accepted. Prepayment required. Mail requests: SASE required.
Civil Name Search: Access: Mail, in person, online. Both court and visitors may perform in person name searches. No search fee. Required to search: name, years to search; also helpful: address. Civil records on computer since 1999; prior from 1880 on books or archived. Mail

turnaround time 2 weeks. Civil PAT goes back to 1880. Often older judgment will be displayed. Case lookup is at https://www.courts.mo.gov/casenet/base/welcome.do. Results show DOB day and month only. Online records go back to 4/1/1999. Online search results show full name, address, and year of birth only.

Criminal Name Search: Access: Mail, online, in person. Both court and visitors may perform in person name searches. No search fee. Required to search: name, years to search; also helpful: address, DOB, SSN. Criminal records on computer since 1993; prior from 1880on books or archived. Mail turnaround time 2 weeks. Criminal PAT goes back to 1999 countywide. Both the terminal and CaseNet only show year of birth. For common names, one must ask the Clerk for more identifiers to correctly do a search. Case lookup is at https://www.courts.mo.gov/casenet/base/welcome.do. Results show DOB day and month only. Online records go back to 4/1/1999. Online search results show full name, address, and year of birth only.

Bates County

Consolidated Circuit Court 1 N Delaware St, Bates County Courthouse, Butler, MO 64730; 660-679-5171 or 3311; fax: 660-679-4446; 8AM-4:30PM (CST). *Felony, Misdemeanor, Civil, Eviction, Small Claims, Probate.* http://tacnet.missouri.org/~court27/

General Information: Online identifiers in results same as on public terminal. No juvenile, mental, expunged, dismissed, or suspended imposition of sentence records released. No fee to fax documents. Court makes copy: $.25 per page. Self serve copy: same. Certification fee: $1.50 per certification. Payee: Circuit Court. Only cashiers checks and money orders accepted. No credit cards accepted. Prepayment required. Mail requests: SASE required.

Civil Name Search: Access: Fax, mail, in person, online. Both court and visitors may perform in person name searches. No search fee. Civil records on computer since 9/1/92, prior on books since 1858. Mail turnaround time within 48 hours. Civil PAT goes back to 8/13/2003. Often older judgment will be displayed. Case lookup is at https://www.courts.mo.gov/casenet/base/welcome.do. Online records go back to 8/18/2003. Online search results show full name, address, and year of birth only.

Criminal Name Search: Access: Fax, mail, in person, online. Both court and visitors may perform in person name searches. No search fee. Criminal records on computer since 9/1/92, prior on books since 1858. Mail turnaround time within 48 hours. Criminal PAT goes back to same as civil. Both the terminal and CaseNet only show year of birth. For common names, one must ask the Clerk for more identifiers to correctly do a search. Case lookup is at https://www.courts.mo.gov/casenet/base/welcome.do. Online records go back to 8/18/2003. Online search results show full name, address, and year of birth only.

Benton County

Consolidated Circuit Court PO Box 37, 316 Van Buren, Warsaw, MO 65355; 660-438-7712; fax: 660-438-5755; 8AM-5PM (CST). *Felony, Misdemeanor, Civil, Eviction, Small Claims, Probate.* http://home.positech.net/~dcourt/

General Information: Online identifiers in results same as on public terminal. No juvenile, mental, expunged, dismissed, or suspended imposition of sentence records released. Will fax back documents. Court makes copy: $.15 per page. Self serve copy: same. Certification fee: $2.50 per cert plus copy fee. Payee: Clerk of Circuit Court. Personal checks accepted. No credit cards accepted. Prepayment required.

Civil Name Search: Access: Mail, in person, online. Visitors must perform in person searches themselves. No search fee. Civil records on computer since 1993, prior on index cards since 1800. Civil PAT goes back to 11/2001. Often older judgment will be displayed. The statewide CaseNet system at https://www.courts.mo.gov/casenet/base/welcome.do provides back to 11/13/2001. Online search results show full name, address, and year of birth only.

Criminal Name Search: Access: In person, online. Visitors must perform in person searches themselves. Required to search: name, years to search, DOB; also helpful: SSN. Criminal records on computer since 1993, prior on index cards since 1800. Note: Court may perform search if time permits. Court will only indicate if subject is on probation or has open case. Court recommends criminal searches at MO State Hwy Patrol, 573-526-6288. Criminal PAT goes back to same as civil. Both the terminal and CaseNet only show year of birth. For common names, one must ask the Clerk for more identifiers to correctly do a search. Online access to criminal same as civil, above.

Bollinger County

Consolidated Circuit Court 204 High St, Ste 6, Marble Hill, MO 63764; 573-238-1900 x6; criminal fax: 573-238-2773; civil fax: 8AM-4PM; 8AM-4PM (CST). *Felony, Misdemeanor, Civil, Eviction, Small Claims, Probate.* www.courts.mo.gov/page.jsp?id=1640

General Information: Associate Court combined 2011. Online identifiers in results same as on public terminal. No juvenile, mental, expunged, dismissed, or suspended imposition of sentence records released. Will not fax documents. Court makes copy: $1.00 per page. Self serve copy: same. Certification fee: $1.00 per cert. Payee: Circuit Clerk. Personal checks accepted. No credit cards accepted. Prepayment required.

Civil Name Search: Access: In person, online. Visitors must perform in person searches themselves. Civil records on computer since 1990, prior on index cards 1976-1990. Public use terminal has civil records back to 1990 to July 1, 2001 only - for notes and judgments. Access to civil records is free at https://www.courts.mo.gov/casenet/base/welcome.do. Online records go back to 7/1/2001. Online search results show full name, address, and year of birth only.

Criminal Name Search: Access: In person, online. Visitors must perform in person searches themselves. Criminal records on computer since 1990, prior on index cards 1976-1990. Both the terminal and CaseNet only show year of birth. For common names, one must ask the Clerk for more identifiers to correctly do a search. Access to civil records is free at https://www.courts.mo.gov/casenet/base/welcome.do. Online records go back to 7/1/2001. Online search results show full name, address, and year of birth only.

Boone County

Consolidated Circuit Court 705 E Walnut, Columbia, MO 65201; 573-886-4000; probate phone: 573-886-4090; fax: 573-886-4044; 8AM-5PM (CST). *Felony, Misdemeanor, Civil, Eviction, Small Claims, Probate.* www.courts.mo.gov/hosted/circuit13/

General Information: Online identifiers in results same as on public terminal. No juvenile, mental, paternity, expunged, dismissed, or suspended imposition of sentence records released. Will not fax documents. Court makes copy: $1.00 1st page; $.10 each add'l. Certification fee: $1.00 per cert. Payee: Boone County Circuit Clerk. Business checks accepted. Visa/MC accepted. Prepayment required.

Civil Name Search: Access: In person, online. Visitors must perform in person searches themselves. Civil records on computer for recent cases, others on books. Civil PAT goes back to 1985. Often older judgments will be displayed. Case lookup is at https://www.courts.mo.gov/casenet/base/welcome.do. Online civil records go back to 1986; probate back to 1986. Online search results show full name, address, and year of birth only.

Criminal Name Search: Access: In person, online. Visitors must perform in person searches themselves. Required to search: name, years to search, DOB. Criminal records on computer for recent cases, others on books. Criminal PAT goes back to same as civil. Both the terminal and CaseNet only show year of birth. For common names, one must ask the Clerk for more identifiers to correctly do a search. Case lookup is at https://www.courts.mo.gov/casenet/base/welcome.do. Online civil records go back to 1986; probate back to 1986. Online search results show full name, address, and year of birth only.

Buchanan County

Consolidated Circuit Court 411 Jules St, Rm 331, St Joseph, MO 64501; 816-271-1462; fax: 816-271-1538; 8AM-5PM (CST). *Felony, Misdemeanor, Civil, Eviction, Small Claims.* www.courts.mo.gov/page.jsp?id=1563

General Information: Online identifiers in results same as on public terminal. No juvenile, mental, expunged, dismissed, or suspended imposition of sentence records released. Will fax documents $1.00 per page. Court makes copy: $.25 per page for 1st 10 copies, $.10 per page add'l. Self serve copy: same. Certification fee: $2.50 per doc. Payee: Buchanan Circuit Clerk. Personal checks accepted. No credit cards accepted. Prepayment required.

Civil Name Search: Access: In person, online. Visitors must perform in person searches themselves. Civil records on computer since 2/92, on index cards since 1976, prior archived. Civil PAT goes back to 1992. Often older judgment will be displayed. Case lookup is at https://www.courts.mo.gov/casenet/base/welcome.do. Online records go back to 2000. Online search results show full name, address, and year of birth only.

Criminal Name Search: Access: In person, online. Visitors must perform in person searches themselves. Criminal records on computer since 2/92, on index cards since 1976, prior archived. Criminal PAT goes back to same as civil. Both the terminal and CaseNet only show year of birth. For common names, one must ask the Clerk for more identifiers to correctly do a search. Case lookup is at https://www.courts.mo.gov/casenet/base/welcome.do. Online records go back to 2000. Online search results show full name, address, and year of birth only.

Probate Court Buchanan County Courthouse, 411 Jules St, Rm 333, St Joseph, MO 64501; 816-271-1477; fax: 816-271-1538; 8AM-5PM (CST). *Probate.* www.courts.mo.gov/page.jsp?id=1563

Butler County

Consolidated Circuit Court Courthouse, 100 N Main, Poplar Bluff, MO 63901; criminal phone: 573-686-8087; civil phone: 573-686-8082; probate phone: 573-686-8073; criminal fax: 573-686-8093; civil fax: 8AM-4PM; 8AM-4PM (CST). *Felony, Misdemeanor, Civil, Eviction, Small Claims, Probate.* www.courts.mo.gov/page.jsp?id=1650

General Information: Circuit and Associate courts combined 12/1/2004. Probate fax- 573-686-0056 Online identifiers in results same as on public terminal. No juvenile, mental, expunged, dismissed, or suspended imposition of sentence records released. Will fax documents $1.00 per page. Court makes copy: $.25 per page. Self serve copy: same. Certification fee: $2.50 plus copy fee. Payee: Clerk of Circuit Court. Business checks accepted. No credit cards accepted. Prepayment required.

Civil Name Search: Access: Fax, mail, in person, online. Visitors must perform in person searches themselves. Search fee: $1.00 per name per year. Civil records on computer since 9/91, prior on cards and books since 1865. Civil PAT goes back to 1992. Often older judgment will be displayed. Case lookup is at https://www.courts.mo.gov/casenet/base/welcome.do, records from 9/2005. Online search results show full name, address, and year of birth only.

Criminal Name Search: Access: In person, fax, mail, online. Visitors must perform in person searches themselves. Search fee: $1.00 per name per year. Criminal records on computer since 9/91, prior on cards and books since 1865. Mail turnaround time is 1-3 days. Criminal PAT goes back to same as civil. Both the terminal and CaseNet only show year of birth. For common names, one must ask the Clerk for more identifiers to correctly do a search. Case lookup is at https://www.courts.mo.gov/casenet/base/welcome.do, records from 9/2005. Online search results show full name, address, and year of birth only. Online access to probate records is free at www.16thcircuit.org/publicaccess.asp. This includes private process servers, jury verdicts, criminal traffic, and criminal sureties.

Caldwell County

Consolidated Circuit Court PO Box 68, 49 E Main, Kingston, MO 64650; 816-586-2581/2771; fax: 816-586-2333; 8AM-4:30PM (CST). *Felony, Misdemeanor, Civil, Eviction, Small Claims, Probate.* www.courts.mo.gov/page.jsp?id=1673

General Information: Online identifiers in results same as on public terminal. No juvenile, mental, expunged, dismissed, or suspended imposition of sentence records released. Will fax documents $1.00 per fax. Court makes copy: $1.00 per page. Certification fee: $1.50 per doc. Payee: Circuit Clerk. Personal checks accepted. No credit cards accepted. Prepayment required. Mail requests: SASE required.

Civil Name Search: Access: Phone, mail, in person, online. Both court and visitors may perform in person name searches. No search fee. Civil records on computer back to 1995. Mail turnaround time 3 days. Civil PAT goes back to 1995. Often older judgment will be displayed. Case lookup is at https://www.courts.mo.gov/casenet/base/welcome.do. Online records go back to 1/23/2006. Online search results show full name, address, and year of birth only.

Criminal Name Search: Access: Phone, mail, in person, online. Both court and visitors may perform in person name searches. No search fee. Criminal records computerized from 1995. Mail turnaround time 3 days. Criminal PAT goes back to 2006. Both the terminal and CaseNet only show year of birth. For common names, one must ask the Clerk for more identifiers to correctly do a search. Case lookup is at https://www.courts.mo.gov/casenet/base/welcome.do. Online records go back to 1/23/2006. Online search results show full name, address, and year of birth only.

Callaway County

Consolidated Circuit Court 10 E 5th St, Fulton, MO 65251; 573-642-0780; probate phone: 573-642-7080; fax: 573-642-0700; 8AM-5PM (CST). *Felony, Misdemeanor, Civil, Eviction, Small Claims, Probate.* www.courts.mo.gov/hosted/circuit13/

General Information: Online identifiers in results same as on public terminal. No juvenile, mental, expunged, dismissed, or suspended imposition of sentence records released. Will fax documents $.10 per page to local phone. Court makes copy: $1.00 for 1st page, $.10 per add'l pages. Self serve copy: $.10 per page. Certification fee: $1.50. Payee: Circuit Clerk. Business checks accepted. Attorney/law firm checks accepted. Major credit cards accepted. Prepayment required.

Civil Name Search: Access: Fax, mail, in person, online. Both court and visitors may perform in person name searches. No search fee. Civil index on docket books and cards since 1821. Note: Court will only perform searches as time permits Mail turnaround time 5 days. Civil PAT goes back to 2000. Often older judgment will be displayed. Case lookup is at https://www.courts.mo.gov/casenet/base/welcome.do. Online cases go

back to 2000; online probate to 1977. Online search results show full name, address, and year of birth only.

Criminal Name Search: Access: In person, online. Visitors must perform in person searches themselves. Required to search: name, years to search; also helpful: DOB, SSN. Criminal records on computer since 1993, prior on index books and cards since 1821. Criminal PAT goes back to same as civil. Both the terminal and CaseNet only show year of birth. For common names, one must ask the Clerk for more identifiers to correctly do a search. Case lookup is at https://www.courts.mo.gov/casenet/base/welcome.do. Online cases go back to 2000; online probate to 1977. Online search results show full name, address, and year of birth only.

Camden County

Consolidated Circuit Court 1 Court Circle, #8, Camdenton, MO 65020; 573-346-4440; fax: 573-346-5422; 8:30AM-4:30PM (CST). *Felony, Misdemeanor, Civil, Eviction, Small Claims, Probate.* www.courts.mo.gov/page.jsp?id=1628

General Information: A 2nd court website is www.camdenmo.org/circuitcourt/index.htm. Online identifiers in results same as on public terminal. No juvenile, mental, expunged, dismissed, or suspended imposition of sentence records released. Will fax documents $1.00 per page. Court makes copy: $.25 per page. Certification fee: $1.50 per cert. Payee: Circuit Clerk. Only cashiers checks and money orders accepted. Credit cards accepted for copies and certifications.

Civil Name Search: Access: Mail, in person, online. Both court and visitors may perform in person name searches. No search fee. Civil records on computer since 1989, on index cards from 1965 to 1989, prior on index books since 1903. Mail turnaround time 1 day, if possible. Civil PAT goes back to 1988. Often older judgment will be displayed. Case lookup is at https://www.courts.mo.gov/casenet/base/welcome.do. Online records go back to 11/28/2005. Online search results show full name, address, and year of birth only.

Criminal Name Search: Access: In person, online. Both court and visitors may perform in person name searches. No search fee. Required to search: name, years to search; also helpful: DOB, SSN. Criminal records on computer since 1989, on index cards from 1965 to 1989, prior on index books since 1903. Criminal PAT goes back to same as civil. Both the terminal and CaseNet only show year of birth. For common names, one must ask the Clerk for more identifiers to correctly do a search. Case lookup is at https://www.courts.mo.gov/casenet/base/welcome.do. Online records go back to 11/28/2005. Online search results show full name, address, and year of birth only.

Cape Girardeau County

Circuit Court - Civil Division 44 N Lorimier, Ste 1, Cape Girardeau, MO 63701; 573-335-8253; fax: 573-331-2565; 8AM-4:30PM (CST). *Civil, Eviction, Small Claims, Probate.* www.courts.mo.gov/page.jsp?id=1641

General Information: Probate located here at a separate court, 573-334-6249, and online. Online identifiers in results same as on public terminal. No juvenile, mental, expunged, dismissed, or suspended imposition of sentence, paternity, cases where one party on AFDC records released. Will fax documents to local or toll free line, fee is $1.00 per page. Court makes copy: $1.00 per page. Certification fee: $1.00 per cert; if probate then $1.50 per page. Payee: Circuit Clerk. Personal checks accepted. No credit cards accepted. Prepayment required. Mail requests: SASE required.

Civil Name Search: Access: Mail, in person, online. Both court and visitors may perform in person name searches. No search fee. Civil records on computer since 1994, prior on index cards since 10/75. Mail turnaround time 1 week. Public use terminal has civil records back to 1994. Often older judgment will be displayed. Access to civil records is free at https://www.courts.mo.gov/casenet/base/welcome.do. Online records go back to 7/1/2001. Online search results show full name, address, and year of birth only.

Circuit Court - Criminal Division I, II., III 100 Court St, Ste 301, Jackson, MO 63755; 573-243-8446 (misdemeanors); criminal phone: 573-243-1755 (felony); fax: 573-204-2405; 8AM-4:30PM (CST). *Felony, Misdemeanor.* www.courts.mo.gov/page.jsp?id=1641

General Information: Fax for misdemeanors is 578-204-2367. Online identifiers in results same as on public terminal. No juvenile, mental, expunged, dismissed, or suspended imposition of sentence records released. Will fax documents to local or toll free line. Court makes copy: $1.00 per page. Self serve copy: same. Certification fee: $1.00 per cert seal. Payee: Circuit Clerk. Personal checks accepted. No credit cards accepted. Prepayment required. Mail requests: SASE required.

Criminal Name Search: Access: Mail, in person, online. Both court and visitors may perform in person name searches. Search fee: $10.00 per name. Required to search: name, years to search, last four digits of SSN. Criminal records on computer since 1991, prior on books. Mail turnaround time 2 weeks. Public use terminal has crim records back to 8/23/93 in this court, countywide to 07/01/2001. Both the terminal and CaseNet only show year of birth. For common names, one must ask the Clerk for more identifiers to correctly do a search. Access to criminal records is free at www.courts.mo.gov/casenet/base/welcome.do. Online public case records go back to 7/1/01; Circuit court criminal judgments to 8/23/1993. Online search results show full name, address, and year of birth only.

Carroll County

Circuit Court 8 S Main St, Ste 3, Carrollton, MO 64633; 660-542-1466; fax: 660-542-1444; 8:30AM-4:30PM (CST). *Felony, Civil Actions over $25,000.* www.courts.mo.gov/page.jsp?id=1568

General Information: Online identifiers in results same as on public terminal. No juvenile, mental, expunged, dismissed, or suspended imposition of sentence records released. Will not fax out documents. Court makes copy: $.35 per page. Self serve copy: same. Certification fee: $.35 per document includes copy fee. Payee: Circuit Clerk. Personal checks accepted. Prepayment required.

Civil Name Search: Access: Fax, mail, in person, online. Both court and visitors may perform in person name searches. No search fee. Civil records on books since 1833. Mail turnaround time varies. Civil PAT goes back to 2001. Often older judgment will be displayed. Case lookup is at https://www.courts.mo.gov/casenet/base/welcome.do. Online records go back to 9/19/01. Online search results show full name, address, and year of birth only.

Criminal Name Search: Access: Fax, mail, in person, online. Both court and visitors may perform in person name searches. No search fee. Criminal docket on books since 1833. Mail turnaround time varies. Criminal PAT available. Both the terminal and CaseNet only show year of birth. For common names, one must ask the Clerk for more identifiers to correctly do a search. Case lookup is at https://www.courts.mo.gov/casenet/base/welcome.do. Online records go back to 9/19/01. Online search results show full name, address, and year of birth only.

Associate Circuit Division Courthouse, 8 S Main, #1, Carrollton, MO 64633; 660-542-1818; criminal phone: 660-542-2494; civil phone: 660-542-1818; probate phone: 660-542-1818; fax: 660-542-1877; 8:30AM-4:30PM (CST). *Misdemeanor, Civil Actions under $25,000, Eviction, Small Claims, Probate.* www.courts.mo.gov/page.jsp?id=1568

General Information: Probate fax is same as main fax number. Online identifiers in results same as on public terminal. No juvenile, mental, expunged, dismissed, or suspended imposition of sentence records released. Will fax documents for no fee. Court makes copy: $.35 per page. Certification fee: $2.50 per document plus copy fee. Payee: Associate Circuit Court. Only cashiers checks and money orders accepted. No credit cards accepted. Prepayment required. Mail requests: SASE required for mail return of any copies.

Civil Name Search: Access: Mail, in person, online. Visitors must perform in person searches themselves. No search fee. Required to search: name, years to search, address. Civil records go back to 1990; on computer back to 12/2001. Civil PAT goes back to 12/2001. Often older judgment will be displayed. Case lookup is at https://www.courts.mo.gov/casenet/base/welcome.do. Online records go back to 09/19/01. Online search results show full name, address, and year of birth only.

Criminal Name Search: Access: In person, online. Visitors must perform in person searches themselves. Required to search: name, years to search, address, DOB. Criminal records go back to 1990; on computer back to 12/2001. Criminal PAT goes back to same as civil. Both the terminal and CaseNet only show year of birth. For common names, one must ask the Clerk for more identifiers to correctly do a search. Case lookup is at https://www.courts.mo.gov/casenet/base/welcome.do. Online records go back to 09/19/01. Online search results show full name, address, and year of birth only.

Carter County

Combined Circuit Court PO Box 578, 105 Main St, Van Buren, MO 63965; 573-323-4513; fax: 573-323-8914; 8AM-4PM (CST). *Felony, Civil , Eviction, Small Claims, Probate.* www.courts.mo.gov/page.jsp?id=1652

General Information: The Associated Court combined with the Circuit Court. No juvenile, mental, paternity, expunged, dismissed, or suspended imposition of sentence records released. Will fax document for $2.00 per doc plus $1.00 each add'l page. Court makes copy: $.25 per page. Certification fee: $1.00 per cert plus copy fee. Payee: Circuit Clerk. Personal checks accepted. No credit cards accepted. Prepayment required. Mail requests: SASE required.

Civil Name Search: Access: Mail, in person, online. Both court and visitors may perform in person name searches. No search fee. Civil records on computer since 1979, on index cards since 1988, archived since late-1800s. Associate Court civil records on index since 1994. Case lookup is at

https://www.courts.mo.gov/casenet/base/welcome.do. Online records go back to 4/17/2000. Online search results show full name, address, and year of birth only.

Criminal Name Search: Access: Mail, in person, online. Visitors must perform in person searches themselves. No search fee. Criminal records on computer since 1979, on index cards since 1988, archived since late-1800s. Associate Court criminal records on index since 1999. Both the terminal and CaseNet only show year of birth. For common names, one must ask the Clerk for more identifiers to correctly do a search. Case lookup is at https://www.courts.mo.gov/casenet/base/welcome.do. Online records go back to 4/17/2000. Online search results show full name, address, and year of birth only. Online access to probate records is free at www.16thcircuit.org/publicaccess.asp. This includes private process servers, jury verdicts, criminal traffic, and criminal sureties.

Cass County

Consolidated Circuit Court 2501 W Mechanic, Harrisonville, MO 64701; 816-380-8227/8200; probate phone: 816-380-8218; fax: 816-380-8225; 8AM-4:30PM (CST). *Felony, Civil Actions over $25,000.* www.courts.mo.gov/page.jsp?id=1902

General Information: Online identifiers in results same as on public terminal. No juvenile, mental, expunged, dismissed, or suspended imposition of sentence records released. Will fax documents $3.00 1st page, $1.00 ea add'l. Court makes copy: $.25 per page. Certification fee: $1.50 per page plus copy fee. Payee: Cass County Circuit Clerk. No personal checks. No credit cards accepted. Prepayment required. Mail requests: SASE required.

Civil Name Search: Access: Phone, mail, in person, online. Both court and visitors may perform in person name searches. No search fee. Civil records on computer since 6/2005, on index cards since 1976, prior on judgment books since 1800s. Mail turnaround time 1 week. Civil PAT goes back to 6/2005. Often older judgment will be displayed. Case lookup is at https://www.courts.mo.gov/casenet/base/welcome.do. Online records go back to 6/6/2005. Online search results show full name, address, and year of birth only.

Criminal Name Search: Access: Phone, mail, in person, online. Both court and visitors may perform in person name searches. No search fee. Criminal records on computer since 6/2005, on index cards since 1976, prior on judgment books since 1800s. Mail turnaround time 1 week. Criminal PAT goes back to same as civil. Both the terminal and CaseNet only show year of birth. For common names, one must ask the Clerk for more identifiers to correctly do a search. Case lookup is at https://www.courts.mo.gov/casenet/base/welcome.do. Online records go back to 6/6/2005. Online search results show full name, address, and year of birth only.

Probate Court Cass County Justice Center, 501 W. Mechanic St, Harrisonville, MO 64701; 816-380-8217; fax: 816-380-8215; 8AM-N, 1-4:30PM (CST). *Probate.*

General Information: Participates in the free state online court record system at https://www.courts.mo.gov/casenet. Online records go back to 6/6/2005.

Cedar County

Consolidated Circuit Court PO Box 665, 113 South St, Stockton, MO 65785; 417-276-6700; fax: 417-276-5001; 8AM-4:30PM (CST). *Felony, Misdemeanor, Civil, Eviction, Small Claims, Probate.* www.courts.mo.gov/page.jsp?id=1635

General Information: Online identifiers in results same as on public terminal. No juvenile, mental, expunged, dismissed, or suspended imposition of sentence records released. Fee to fax out file $1.00 per page. Court makes copy: $.25 per page; Probate $1.00 per page. Self serve copy: $.25 per page. Certification fee: $1.50 per cert plus copy fee. Payee: Cedar County Circuit Court. Personal checks accepted. No credit cards accepted. Prepayment required.

Civil Name Search: Access: Fax, mail, in person, online. Visitors must perform in person searches themselves. No search fee. Civil index on cards since 1979, prior on docket books to 1830. Civil PAT goes back to 9/11/2000. Often older judgment will be displayed. Case lookup is at https://www.courts.mo.gov/casenet/base/welcome.do. Online records go back to 9/11/2000. Online include Probate. Online search results show full name, address, and year of birth only.

Criminal Name Search: Access: Mail, fax, In person, online. Visitors must perform in person searches themselves. No search fee. Criminal records indexed on cards since 1979, prior on docket books. Criminal PAT goes back to same as civil. Both the terminal and CaseNet only show year of birth. For common names, one must ask the Clerk for more identifiers to correctly do a search. Case lookup is at https://www.courts.mo.gov/casenet/base/welcome.do. Online records go back to 9/11/2000. Online include Probate. Online search results show full name, address, and year of birth only.

Chariton County

Consolidated Circuit Court 306 S Cherry, Keytesville, MO 65261; 660-288-3602; criminal phone: 660-288-3271; civil phone: 660-288-3602; fax: 660-288-3763; 8:30AM-4:30PM (CST). *Felony, Misdemeanor, Civil, Eviction, Small Claims, Probate.* www.courts.mo.gov/page.jsp?id=1570

General Information: The Circuit Court and Associate Division consolidated on 1/1/2006. Online identifiers in results same as on public terminal. No juvenile, mental, expunged, dismissed, or suspended imposition of sentence records released. Fee to fax out file $1.00 per page. Court makes copy: $1.00 per page. Self serve copy: same. Certification fee: $1.50 per page plus copy fee. Payee: Chariton County Circuit Clerk. Personal checks accepted. No credit cards accepted. Prepayment required. Mail requests: SASE required.

Civil Name Search: Access: Fax, mail, in person, online. Both court and visitors may perform in person name searches. Search fee: $4.00 per name. Civil records computerized since 5/13/2002; on index books since 1975, prior on docket books to 1827. Mail turnaround time same day. Civil PAT goes back to 2002. Often older judgment will be displayed. Participates in the free online court records system at https://www.courts.mo.gov/casenet/base/welcome.do. Online records go back to 5/13/2002. Online search results show full name, address, and year of birth only.

Criminal Name Search: Access: Fax, mail, in person, online. Both court and visitors may perform in person name searches. Search fee: $4.00 per name. Required to search: name, years to search; also helpful: DOB, SSN. Criminal records computerized since 5/13/2002; on index books since 1975, prior on docket books to 1827. Mail turnaround time same day. Criminal PAT goes back to same as civil. Both the terminal and CaseNet only show year of birth. For common names, one must ask the Clerk for more identifiers to correctly do a search. Participates in the free online court records system at https://www.courts.mo.gov/casenet/base/welcome.do. Online records go back to 5/13/2002. Online search results show full name, address, and year of birth only.

Christian County

Consolidated Circuit Court PO Box 278, 110 W Elm, Rm 205, Ozark, MO 65721; 417-581-6372; probate phone: 417-581-4523; fax: 417-581-0391; 8AM-4:30PM (CST). *Felony, Misdemeanor, Civil Actions over $25,000, Probate, Eviction.* http://courts.christiancountymo.gov/

General Information: Online identifiers in results same as on public terminal. No juvenile, mental, expunged, dismissed, or suspended imposition or execution of sentence records released. Will not fax out documents. Court makes copy: $.30 per page. Certification fee: $1.00 per cert plus copy fee; if Associate Court record then $1.50 per cert plus $1.00 per page. Payee: Christian County Circuit Clerk. No personal checks or credit cards accepted. Prepayment required. Mail requests: SASE required.

Civil Name Search: Access: Mail, in person, online. Both court and visitors may perform in person name searches. Search fee: $6.00 per name. Civil records on computer since 9/97, judgments since 1991; pending cases indexed on computer. Old case card files back to 1979. Note: Results include full name and/or case number. Mail turnaround time 1 week. Civil PAT goes back to 1991. Often older judgment will be displayed. Case lookup is at https://www.courts.mo.gov/casenet/base/welcome.do. Online records go back to 6/13/03. Online search results show full name, address, and year of birth only.

Criminal Name Search: Access: Mail, in person, online. Both court and visitors may perform in person name searches. Search fee: $6.00 per name. Criminal records on computer since 9/97, pending cases indexed in card files. Old case card files back to 1979. Note: Results include full name and/or case number. Mail turnaround time 1 week. Criminal PAT goes back to same as civil. Both the terminal and CaseNet only show year of birth. For common names, one must ask the Clerk for more identifiers to correctly do a search. Online access to criminal same as civil, above.

Clark County

Consolidated Circuit Court 510 N Johnson, Kahoka, MO 63445; 660-727-3292; fax: 660-727-1051; 8AM-4PM (CST). *Felony, Civil Actions over $45,000.* www.courts.mo.gov/page.jsp?id=321

General Information: While the Associate Court has consolidated with the Circuit Court, record searches must be performed on both databases - the records have not been comingled as of yet. Online identifiers in results same as on public terminal. No juvenile, mental, expunged, dismissed, or suspended imposition of sentence records released. Fee to fax out file $1.00 per page. Court makes copy: $.50 per page. Self serve copy: same. Certification fee: $3.00 per document. Payee: Clerk of Circuit Court. Personal checks accepted. No credit cards accepted. Prepayment required. Mail requests: SASE required.

Civil Name Search: Access: Phone, fax, mail, in person, online. Both court and visitors may perform in person name searches. No search fee. Civil records on books since 1991 (1988 Assoc Court), prior archived since

1836. Mail turnaround time 4 days. Civil PAT goes back to 9/19/2001. Often older judgment will be displayed. Case lookup is at https://www.courts.mo.gov/casenet/base/welcome.do. Online records go back to 09/19/01. Online search results show full name, address, and year of birth only.

Criminal Name Search: Access: Phone, fax, mail, in person, online. Both court and visitors may perform in person name searches. No search fee. Criminal docket on books since 1991 (1988 Assoc Court), prior archived since 1836. Mail turnaround time 4 days. Criminal PAT goes back to same as civil. Both the terminal and CaseNet only show year of birth. For common names, one must ask the Clerk for more identifiers to correctly do a search. Case lookup is at https://www.courts.mo.gov/casenet/base/welcome.do. Online records go back to 09/19/01. Online search results show full name, address, and year of birth only.

Clay County

Consolidated Circuit Court 11 S Water St, Liberty, MO 64068; 816-407-3900; fax: 816-407-3888; 8AM-5PM (CST). *Felony, Misdemeanor, Civil, Eviction, Small Claims, Probate.* www.circuit7.net

General Information: Online identifiers in results same as on public terminal. No juvenile, mental, expunged, dismissed, or suspended imposition of sentence records released. Will fax documents; cannot fax certified copies. Court makes copy: $1.00 per page. Certification fee: $5.00 per cert plus copy fee. Payee: Clay County Circuit Clerk. No personal checks or credit cards accepted. Prepayment required. Mail requests: SASE required for civil.

Civil Name Search: Access: Mail, in person, online. Both court and visitors may perform in person name searches. No search fee. Civil records on computer since 1987; prior records on index. Civil PAT goes back to 1987. Often older judgment will be displayed. Case lookup is at https://www.courts.mo.gov/casenet/base/welcome.do. Online index dates back to 1978 for civil and 1977 for probate. Online search results show full name, address, and year of birth only.

Criminal Name Search: Access: In person, online. Visitors must perform in person searches themselves. Required to search: name, years to search, DOB. Criminal records on computer since 1994, prior on index cards. Criminal PAT goes back to 1992. Both the terminal and CaseNet only show year of birth. For common names, one must ask the Clerk for more identifiers to correctly do a search. Case lookup is at https://www.courts.mo.gov/casenet/base/welcome.do. Online index dates back to 1978 for civil and 1977 for probate. Online search results show full name, address, and year of birth only. Online access to probate records is free at www.16thcircuit.org/publicaccess.asp. This includes private process servers, jury verdicts, criminal traffic, and criminal sureties.

Clinton County

Consolidated Circuit Court PO Box 275, Plattsburg, MO 64477; criminal phone: 816-539-3755; civil phone: 816-539-3731; fax: 816-539-3893; 8AM-5PM (CST). *Felony, Misdemeanor, Civil, Eviction, Small Claims, Probate.* www.courts.mo.gov/page.jsp?id=1674

General Information: The Associate Division and Circuit Court consolidated in 10/2005. Online identifiers in results same as on public terminal. No juvenile, mental, expunged, dismissed, or suspended imposition of sentence records released. Will fax documents $2.00 per page. Court makes copy: $1.00 per page. Certification fee: $1.50. Payee: Circuit Clerk. No personal checks. No credit cards accepted. Prepayment required.

Civil Name Search: Access: Mail, fax, in person, online. Visitors must perform in person searches themselves. No search fee. Civil records (Judgments) on computer from 1976, archived since 1833. Civil PAT goes back to 1976. Often older judgment will be displayed. Case lookup is at https://www.courts.mo.gov/casenet/base/welcome.do. Online records go back to 1/23/2006. Online search results show full name, address, and year of birth only.

Criminal Name Search: Access: Mail, fax, in person, online. Visitors must perform in person searches themselves. No search fee. Criminal records (Judgments) on computer from 1976, archived since 1833. Mail turnaround time 1 week. Criminal PAT goes back to same as civil. Both the terminal and CaseNet only show year of birth. For common names, one must ask the Clerk for more identifiers to correctly do a search. Case lookup is at https://www.courts.mo.gov/casenet/base/welcome.do. Online records go back to 1/23/2006. Online search results show full name, address, and year of birth only.

Cole County

Consolidated Circuit Court PO Box 1870, 301 E High St, Jefferson City, MO 65102-1870; 573-634-9100; criminal phone: 573-634-9171; civil phone: 573-634-9151; criminal fax: 573-635-5376; civil fax: 7:30AM-4:30PM; 7:30AM-4:30PM (CST). *Felony, Misdemeanor, Civil, Eviction, Small Claims, Probate.* www.courts.mo.gov/page.jsp?id=1905

General Information: The Circuit Court and Associate Division consolidated on 01/01. Criminal clerk- #208; Civil- #305 Online identifiers in results same as on public terminal. No juvenile, mental, expunged, dismissed, or suspended imposition of sentence records released. Other access to criminal records: the court prefers that requesters go to the state highway patrol. Will fax documents to local or toll-free number. Court makes copy: $.20 per page for crim, $.40 per page civ. Certification fee: $1.00 per page plus copy fee. Payee: Cole County Circuit Clerk. No personal checks or credit cards accepted. Prepayment required. Mail requests: SASE requested for civil.

Civil Name Search: Access: Fax, mail, in person, online. Both court and visitors may perform in person name searches. No search fee. Civil records (pending) on computer, on books since 1820. Mail turnaround time 2-5 days. Public use terminal has civil records back to 2000. Often older judgment will be displayed. Case lookup is at https://www.courts.mo.gov/casenet/base/welcome.do. Online records go back to 1/1980; probate to 6/2/72. Online search results show full name, address, and year of birth only. Online access to probate records is free at www.16thcircuit.org/publicaccess.asp. This includes private process servers, jury verdicts, criminal traffic, and criminal sureties.

Criminal Name Search: Access: Mail, fax, In person, online. Both court and visitors may perform in person name searches. No search fee. Required to search: name, years to search; also helpful: DOB, SSN. Criminal records on computer since 1989, prior on book since 1820. Note: Online results include name and case number. Both the terminal and CaseNet only show year of birth. For common names, one must ask the Clerk for more identifiers to correctly do a search. Online access same as civil.

Cooper County

Consolidated Circuit Court 200 Main St, Rm 31, Boonville, MO 65233; 660-882-2232; fax: 660-882-2043; 8:30AM-5PM (CST). *Felony, Misdemeanor, Civil, Eviction, Small Claims, Probate.*
www.courts.mo.gov/page.jsp?id=1614

General Information: Online identifiers in results same as on public terminal. No juvenile, mental, expunged, dismissed, or suspended imposition of sentence records released. Will fax out documents $1.00 per page. Court makes copy: $1.00 per page. Certification fee: $1.50 per cert. Payee: Circuit Clerk. No personal checks or credit cards accepted. Prepayment required. Mail requests: SASE required for civil.

Civil Name Search: Access: Phone, fax, mail, in person, online. Both court and visitors may perform in person name searches. No search fee. Civil records on cards since 1975, case files from 1819 forward; on computer back to 2001. Mail turnaround time 1-2 days. Can tell if record is available and cost over phone. Civil PAT goes back to 4/2001. Often older judgment will be displayed. Access to civil records is free at https://www.courts.mo.gov/casenet/base/welcome.do. Online records go back to 4/2001. Online search results show full name, address, and year of birth only. Online access to probate records is free at www.16thcircuit.org/publicaccess.asp. This includes private process servers, jury verdicts, criminal traffic, and criminal sureties.

Criminal Name Search: Access: In person, online. Both court and visitors may perform in person name searches. No search fee. Required to search: name, years to search, DOB; also helpful: SSN. Criminal records on cards since 1975, case files from 1819 forward; on computer back to 2001 for Circuit, mid-1990s for Associate Ct. Note: Court can say if record is available and cost over phone. Criminal PAT goes back to same as civil. Both the terminal and CaseNet only show year of birth. For common names, one must ask the Clerk for more identifiers to correctly do a search. Online access to criminal same as civil, above.

Crawford County

Circuit Court PO Box 1550, 111 Third Street, Steelville, MO 65565; 573-775-2866; fax: 573-775-2452; 8AM-4:30PM (CST). *Felony, Civil, Eviction, Small Claims, Probate.* www.courts.mo.gov/page.jsp?id=1668
General Information: The Associate Court has consolidated with the Circuit Court. Online identifiers in results same as on public terminal. No juvenile, mental, expunged, dismissed, or suspended imposition of sentence records released. Will fax documents $1.00 per page. Court makes copy: $.30 per page. Certification fee: $1.50 per seal plus copy fee. Payee: Crawford County Circuit Clerk. No personal checks. No credit cards accepted. Prepayment required. Mail requests: SASE required.

Civil Name Search: Access: Mail, fax, in person, online. Both court and visitors may perform in person name searches. No search fee. Civil records on computer from 3/02/92 for judgments only, archived from 1800s, some records on index cards and books. Mail turnaround time as time permits. Civil PAT goes back to 3/1992. Often older judgment will be displayed. Participates in the state court record system at https://www.courts.mo.gov/casenet/base/welcome.do. Online records go back to 4/9/2001. Online search results show full name, address, and year of birth only.

Criminal Name Search: Access: Mail, fax, in person, online. Both court and visitors may perform in person name searches. No search fee. Required to search: name, years to search, offense, date of offense. Criminal

records on computer since 3/02/92, prior on cards. Mail turnaround time as time permits. Criminal PAT goes back to same as civil. Both the terminal and CaseNet only show year of birth. For common names, one must ask the Clerk for more identifiers to correctly do a search. Participates in the state court record system at https://www.courts.mo.gov/casenet/base/welcome.do. Online records go back to 4/9/2001. Online search results show full name, address, and year of birth only.

Dade County

Consolidated Circuit Court Courthouse, 300 W Water, Greenfield, MO 65661; 417-637-2271; fax: 417-637-5055; 8AM-4PM (CST). *Felony, Misdemeanor, Civil, Eviction, Small Claims, Probate.*
www.courts.mo.gov/page.jsp?id=1636
General Information: Online identifiers in results same as on public terminal. No juvenile, mental, expunged, dismissed, or suspended imposition of sentence records released. Will fax documents. Court makes copy: $.10 per page. Self serve copy: same. Certification fee: $2.50. Payee: Dade County Circuit Clerk. Personal checks accepted. No credit cards accepted. Prepayment required. Mail requests: SASE required.

Civil Name Search: Access: Mail, in person, online. Both court and visitors may perform in person name searches. Search fee: $5.00. Civil records in index cards since 1982, prior on books to 1800s; on computer back to 2000. Mail turnaround time 2-3 days. Civil PAT goes back to 2000. Terminal results also show SSNs. Case lookup is at https://www.courts.mo.gov/casenet/base/welcome.do. Online records go back to 9/20/1999. Online records include Probate Court. Online search results show full name, address, and year of birth only.

Criminal Name Search: Access: Mail, in person, online. Both court and visitors may perform in person name searches. Search fee: $5.00. Required to search: name, years to search; also helpful-DOB, SSN, signed release. Criminal records in index cards since 1982, prior on book to 1800s; on computer back to 2000. Mail turnaround time 2-3 days. Criminal PAT goes back to same as civil. Both the terminal and CaseNet only show year of birth. For common names, one must ask the Clerk for more identifiers to correctly do a search. Case lookup is at https://www.courts.mo.gov/casenet/base/welcome.do. Online records go back to 9/20/1999. Online records include Probate Court. Online search results show full name, address, and year of birth only.

Dallas County

Circuit Court PO Box 1910, 108 S Maple St, Buffalo, MO 65622; 417-345-2243; fax: 417-345-5539; 7:30AM-4PM (CST). *Felony, Misdemeanor, Civil Actions, Eviction, Small Claims, Probate.*
www.courts.mo.gov/page.jsp?id=4835
General Information: Online identifiers in results same as on public terminal. No juvenile, mental, expunged, dismissed, or suspended imposition of sentence records released. Fee to fax out file $1.00 per page, 10 page limit. Court makes copy: $.25 per page. Self serve copy: same. Certification fee: $1.00 per document. Payee: Circuit Clerk. Personal checks accepted. No credit cards accepted. Prepayment required.

Civil Name Search: Access: In person, online. Visitors must perform in person searches themselves. Civil records on computer since 11/2011, prior on book since 1951. Civil PAT goes back to 11/13/01. Often older judgment will be displayed. Case lookup is at https://www.courts.mo.gov/casenet/base/welcome.do. Online records go back to 11/13/2001. Online search results show full name, address, and year of birth only.

Criminal Name Search: Access: In person, online. Visitors must perform in person searches themselves. Required to search: name, years to search; also helpful: DOB. Criminal records on computer since 2001, prior on book since 1951. Criminal PAT goes back to same as civil. Both the terminal and CaseNet only show year of birth. For common names, one must ask the Clerk for more identifiers to correctly do a search. Case lookup is at https://www.courts.mo.gov/casenet/base/welcome.do. Online records go back to 11/13/2001. Online search results show full name, address, and year of birth only.

Daviess County

Circuit Court PO Box 337, Gallatin, MO 64640; 660-663-2932; fax: 660-663-3876; 8AM-4:30PM (CST). *Felony, Civil Actions over $25,000.* www.courts.mo.gov/page.jsp?id=1675
General Information: The Associate Circuit Court consolidated with the Circuit Court in November 2009. Online identifiers in results same as on public terminal. No juvenile, mental, expunged, dismissed, or suspended imposition of sentence records released. Will fax documents $2.00 per page. Court makes copy: $1.00 per page. Certification fee: none. Payee: Daviess County Circuit Clerk. Business checks accepted. No credit cards accepted. Prepayment required. Mail requests: SASE required.

Civil Name Search: Access: Phone, fax, mail, in person, online. Both court and visitors may perform in person name searches. Search fee: $10.00 per name. Civil records on records books since 1839. Mail turnaround time 1 day; phone turnaround 1 day with request filed. Civil PAT goes back to 1/2006. Often older judgment will be displayed. Case lookup is at https://www.courts.mo.gov/casenet/base/welcome.do. Online records go back to 1/23/2006. Online search results show full name, address, and year of birth only.

Criminal Name Search: Access: Phone, fax, mail, in person, online. Both court and visitors may perform in person name searches. Search fee: $10.00 per name. Required to search: name, years to search, DOB. Criminal records on records books since 1839. Note: Results include name, year filed, type of case. Mail turnaround time 1 day; phone turnaround 1 day after request filed. Criminal PAT goes back to 1/2006. Both the terminal and CaseNet only show year of birth. For common names, one must ask the Clerk for more identifiers to correctly do a search. Online access to criminal same as civil, above.

De Kalb County

Circuit Consolidated Court PO Box 248, 109 W Main, Maysville, MO 64469; 816-449-2602; probate phone: 816-449-2602; fax: 816-449-5400; 8AM-4:30PM (CST). *Felony, Misdemeanor, Civil Actions, Small Claims, Probate.* www.courts.mo.gov/page.jsp?id=1676

General Information: No juvenile or suspended imposition of sentence records released. Will fax specific case file for $1.00. Court makes copy: $1.00 per page. Self serve copy: same. Certification fee: $1.50 per doc. Payee: Circuit Clerk. Personal checks accepted. No credit cards accepted. Prepayment required.

Civil Name Search: Access: In person, online. Visitors must perform in person searches themselves. Civil index on cards since 1970, computerized since 2003. Note: If specific case file documents are requested, mail back requests must include postage costs and copy fees. Case lookup is at https://www.courts.mo.gov/casenet/base/welcome.do. Online records go back to 1/23/2006. Online search results show full name, address, and year of birth only.

Criminal Name Search: Access: In person, online. Visitors must perform in person searches themselves. Criminal records indexed on cards since 1970, computerized since 2003. Note: If specific case file documents are requested, mail back requests must include postage costs and copy fees. Both the terminal and CaseNet only show year of birth. For common names, one must ask the Clerk for more identifiers to correctly do a search. Online access to criminal same as civil, above.

Dent County

Consolidated Circuit Court 112 E 5th St, Salem, MO 65560; 573-729-3931; probate phone: 573-729-3134; fax: 573-729-9414; 8AM-4:30PM (CST). *Felony, Misdemeanor, Civil Actions, Small Claims, Probate.* www.courts.mo.gov/page.jsp?id=1669

General Information: Online identifiers in results same as on public terminal. No juvenile, mental, expunged, dismissed, or suspended imposition of sentence records released. Will not fax documents. Court makes copy: $.25 per page. Certification fee: $2.00 per cert plus copy fee. Payee: Dent County Circuit Clerk. Only cashiers checks and money orders accepted. No credit cards accepted. Prepayment required. Mail requests: SASE required for civil.

Civil Name Search: Access: Mail, fax, in person, online. Both court and visitors may perform in person name searches. No search fee. Civil records on computer since 1993, on index cards since 1978. Mail turnaround time 2 days. Civil PAT goes back to 1996 but often older judgments may be displayed. Case lookup is at https://www.courts.mo.gov/casenet/base/welcome.do. Online records go back to 4/9/2001. Online search results show full name, address, and year of birth only.

Criminal Name Search: Access: In person, online. Visitors must perform in person searches themselves. Criminal records on computer since 1993, on index cards since 1978. Criminal PAT goes back to same as civil. Both the terminal and CaseNet only show year of birth. For common names, one must ask the Clerk for more identifiers to correctly do a search. Case lookup is at https://www.courts.mo.gov/casenet/base/welcome.do. Online records go back to 4/9/2001. Online search results show full name, address, and year of birth only.

Douglas County

Consolidated Circuit Court PO Box 249, Ava, MO 65608; 417-683-4713; fax: 417-683-2794; 8AM-4:30PM (CST). *Felony, Misdemeanor, Civil Actions, Small Claims, Probate.* www.courts.mo.gov/page.jsp?id=1678

General Information: Online identifiers in results same as on public terminal. No juvenile, mental, expunged, dismissed, or suspended imposition of sentence records released. Will fax documents to local or toll free line. Court makes copy: $.25 per page. Certification fee: $2.50. Payee: Circuit Clerk. Personal checks accepted. No credit cards accepted. Prepayment required. Mail requests: SASE required.

Civil Name Search: Access: Phone, mail, in person, online. Visitors must perform in person searches themselves. Search fee: $10.00 per hour. Civil

records on alpha cards since 1977. Mail turnaround time 1 week. Civil PAT goes back to 2006. Often older judgment will be displayed. Case lookup is at https://www.courts.mo.gov/casenet/base/welcome.do. Civil results give address. Online records go back to 2/20/2006. Online search results show full name, address, and year of birth only.

Criminal Name Search: Access: Phone, mail, in person, online. Visitors must perform in person searches themselves. Search fee: $10.00 per hour. Required to search: name, years to search; also helpful: DOB, SSN. Criminal records on alpha cards since 1977. Mail turnaround time 1 week. Criminal PAT goes back to 5 years. Both the terminal and CaseNet only show year of birth. For common names, one must ask the Clerk for more identifiers to correctly do a search. Case lookup is at https://www.courts.mo.gov/casenet/base/welcome.do. Civil results give address. Online records go back to 2/20/2006. Online search results show full name, address, and year of birth only.

Dunklin County

Consolidated Circuit Court PO Box 567, Kennett, MO 63857; 573-888-2456; civil phone: 573-888-3378; probate phone: 573-888-3272; fax: 573-888-0319; 8:30AM-4:30PM (CST). *Felony, Misdemeanor, Civil, Eviction, Small Claims, Probate.* www.courts.mo.gov/page.jsp?id=1647

General Information: All searches require a written request, and requests can be faxed to the court. The Circuit Court and Associate Division consolidated 01/01/2006. Probate and Juvenile #202, Criminal #301/302, Civil #103. Online identifiers in results same as on public terminal. No juvenile, mental, expunged or dismissed records released. Will fax documents $1.00 per page. Court makes copy: $.50 per page. Self serve copy: $.25 per page. Certification fee: $2.00 per document. Payee: Circuit Clerk. Personal checks accepted. Prepayment required. Will bill attorneys, courts and abstract companies.

Civil Name Search: Access: In person, online. Visitors must perform in person searches themselves. Civil index on cards back to 1900; on computer back to 1990. Civil PAT goes back to 1990. Often older judgment will be displayed. Access to civil records is free at https://www.courts.mo.gov/casenet/base/welcome.do. Online records go back to 7/1/2001. Online search results show full name, address, and year of birth only. Online access to probate records is free at www.16thcircuit.org/publicaccess.asp. This includes private process servers, jury verdicts, criminal traffic, and criminal sureties.

Criminal Name Search: Access: In person, online. Visitors must perform in person searches themselves. Required to search: name, years to search, DOB, SSN. Criminal records computerized from 8/2001. Note: Court only performs records searches for Law Enforcement Agencies. Criminal PAT goes back to 8/1994. Both the terminal and CaseNet only show year of birth. For common names, one must ask the Clerk for more identifiers to correctly do a search. Online access to criminal same as civil, above.

Franklin County

Consolidated Circuit Court 401 E Main St, #100A, Union, MO 63084; criminal phone: 636-583-7365; civil phone: 636-583-7366; probate phone: 636-583-6312; 8AM-4:30PM (CST). *Felony, Misdemeanor, Civil Actions, Eviction, Small Claims, Probate.* www.courts.mo.gov/page.jsp?id=1616

General Information: Consolidated May, 2008. Assoc. Circuit and Probate courts now also located here. Probate fax- 636-583-7368. For criminal searches, this court refers you to CaseNet or the state criminal record repository- 573-526-6153; 751-9382-fax. Online identifiers in results same as on public terminal. No juvenile, mental, expunged, dismissed, or suspended imposition of sentence records released. Will not fax documents. Court makes copy: $1.00 per page. Self serve copy: same. Certification fee: $1.00. Payee: Circuit Clerk. Personal checks accepted. No credit cards accepted. Prepayment required.

Civil Name Search: Access: Online, in person. Visitors must perform in person searches themselves. Civil records on computer back to 1995; others filed as originals to 1821. Civil PAT goes back to 1995. Often older judgment will be displayed. Case lookup is at https://www.courts.mo.gov/casenet/base/welcome.do. Online records go back to 1/1995. Online search results show full name, address, and year of birth only.

Criminal Name Search: Access: Online, in person. Visitors must perform in person searches themselves. Required to search: name, years to search, DOB. Criminal records computerized from 1995; others filed as originals to 1940. Criminal PAT goes back to same as civil. Both the terminal and CaseNet only show year of birth. For common names, one must ask the Clerk for more identifiers to correctly do a search. Case lookup is at https://www.courts.mo.gov/casenet/base/welcome.do. Online records go back to 1/1995. Online search results show full name, address, and year of birth only.

Gasconade County

Consolidated Circuit Court 119 E 1st St, Rm 6, Hermann, MO 65041-1182; 573-486-2632; fax: 573-486-5812; 8AM-4:30PM (CST). *Felony, Misdemeanor, Civil Actions, Small Claims, Probate.*
www.courts.mo.gov/page.jsp?id=1617
General Information: Online identifiers in results same as on public terminal. No juvenile, mental, expunged, dismissed, or suspended imposition of sentence records released. Will fax documents $2.00 1st page, $1.00 each add'l. Court makes copy: $.10 per page. Certification fee: $1.50 per cert seal. Payee: Gasconade Circuit Court. Personal checks accepted. No credit cards accepted. Prepayment required. Mail requests: SASE required.
Civil Name Search: Access: Mail, in person, online. Both court and visitors may perform in person name searches. No search fee. Civil index on cards since 1976, prior on books stored at archives, computerized storage since 09/2000. Mail turnaround time 2-3 days. Civil PAT goes back to 1990 countywide. Often older judgment will be displayed. Case lookup is at https://www.courts.mo.gov/casenet/base/welcome.do. Online records go back to 9/1/2000, Online search results show full name, address, and year of birth only.
Criminal Name Search: Access: In person, online. Visitors must perform in person searches themselves. Criminal records indexed on cards since 1976, prior on books stored in archives, computerized storage since 09/2000. Note: If there is a common name, For common names, the Clerk cannot provide more identifiers to correctly do a search. Criminal PAT goes back to same as civil. Both the terminal and CaseNet only show year of birth. For common names, one must ask the Clerk for more identifiers to correctly do a search. Case lookup is at https://www.courts.mo.gov/casenet/base/welcome.do. Online records go back to 9/1/2000. Online search results show full name, address, and year of birth only.

Gentry County

Circuit Court PO Box 32, Gentry County Courthouse, Albany, MO 64402; 660-726-3618; fax: 660-726-4102; 8AM-4:30PM (CST). *Felony, Civil Actions, Probate, Small Claims.*
www.courts.mo.gov/page.jsp?id=1544
General Information: Online identifiers in results same as on public terminal. No juvenile, mental, expunged, dismissed, or suspended imposition of sentence records released. Fee to fax out file $1.00 per page. Court makes copy: $.30 per page. Self serve copy: same. Certification fee: $1.00 per page plus copy fee. Payee: Circuit Clerk. Personal checks accepted. No credit cards accepted. Prepayment required. Mail requests: SASE required.
Civil Name Search: Access: Mail, fax, in person, online. Both court and visitors may perform in person name searches. Search fee: $5.00 per name. Civil records archived since 1885. Mail turnaround time 5 working days. Civil PAT goes back to 3/2006. Often older judgment will be displayed. Case lookup is at https://www.courts.mo.gov/casenet/base/welcome.do. Online records go back to 3/20/2006. Online search results show full name, address, and year of birth only.
Criminal Name Search: Access: Mail, in person, online. Both court and visitors may perform in person name searches. Search fee: $5.00 per name. Required to search: name, years to search; also helpful: DOB, SSN. Criminal records archived since 1885. Mail turnaround time 5 working days. Criminal PAT goes back to 3/2006. Both the terminal and CaseNet only show year of birth. For common names, one must ask the Clerk for more identifiers to correctly do a search. Case lookup is at https://www.courts.mo.gov/casenet/base/welcome.do. Online records go back to 3/20/2006. Online search results show full name, address, and year of birth only.

Greene County

Circuit Court 1010 Booneville, Springfield, MO 65802; 417-868-4074; criminal phone: x4; civil phone: x2;; 8AM-5AM (CST). *Felony, Misdemeanor, Civil, Eviction, Small Claims, Probate.*
www.greenecountymo.org/circuit_clerk/index.php
General Information: This court consolidated with the Assoc. Circuit Court in 2007. A criminal search includes felony and misdemeanor; civil includes all civil records. Add'l phones- Domestic- x4, Traffic- x5. Online identifiers in results same as on public terminal. No juvenile, mental, expunged, sealed, dismissed or suspended imposition of sentence records released. Will fax documents if fax account has been established. Court makes copy: $.10 per page. Self serve copy: same. Certification fee: $1.10 per seal. Payee: Circuit Clerk. Business checks accepted. Discover and MC accepted with valid ID. Prepayment required. Mail requests: SASE required.
Civil Name Search: Access: Mail, in person, online. Visitors must perform in person searches themselves. No search fee. Civil records on computer back to 7/89, prior on index cards. Mail turnaround time 1 week. Civil PAT goes back to 1989. Public terminal does not always include address. Access records back to 1990 at https://www.courts.mo.gov/casenet/base/welcome.do. Online search results show full name, address, and year of birth only.

Criminal Name Search: Access: In person, online. Visitors must perform in person searches themselves. Required to search: name, years to search; also helpful: address, DOB, SSN. Criminal records computerized from 7/89, prior on index cards. Mail turnaround time 1 week. Criminal PAT goes back to same as civil. Both the terminal and CaseNet only show year of birth. For common names, one must ask the Clerk for more identifiers to correctly do a search. Access records back to 1990 at https://www.courts.mo.gov/casenet/base/welcome.do.

Grundy County

Consolidated Circuit Court Courthouse, 700 Main St, PO Box 196, Trenton, MO 64683; 660-359-6605/4040; fax: 660-359-6604; 8:30AM-4:30PM (CST). *Felony, Misdemeanor, Civil Actions, Small Claims, Probate, Domestic.* www.courts.mo.gov/page.jsp?id=1538
General Information: Online identifiers in results same as on public terminal. No juvenile, Title 4D, child support, mental, expunged, dismissed, or suspended imposition of sentence cases. Will fax specific file data for $2.00 per document. Court makes copy: $.25 per page. Certification fee: $2.00 per cert. Payee: Circuit Clerk. Personal checks accepted. No credit cards accepted. Prepayment required. Mail requests: SASE required for mail return of any copies.
Civil Name Search: Access: In person, online. Visitors must perform in person searches themselves. Civil records archived since 1841; on computer back to 2000. Civil PAT goes back to 3/2000. Often older judgment will be displayed. Case lookup is at https://www.courts.mo.gov/casenet/base/welcome.do. Online records go back to 3/2000. Online search results show full name, address, and year of birth only.
Criminal Name Search: Access: In person, online. Visitors must perform in person searches themselves. Criminal records archived since 1841; on computer back to 2000. Criminal PAT goes back to same as civil. Both the terminal and CaseNet only show year of birth. For common names, one must ask the Clerk for more identifiers to correctly do a search. Case lookup is at https://www.courts.mo.gov/casenet/base/welcome.do. Online records go back to 3/2000. Online search results show full name, address, and year of birth only.

Harrison County

Consolidated Circuit Court PO Box 189, 1500 Central, Bethany, MO 64424; 660-425-6425/6432; fax: 660-425-6390; 8AM-4:30PM (CST). *Felony, Misdemeanor, Civil, Eviction, Small Claims, Probate.*
www.courts.mo.gov/page.jsp?id=1539
General Information: Online identifiers in results same as on public terminal. No juvenile, mental, expunged, dismissed, or suspended imposition of sentence records released. Will not fax documents. Court makes copy: $.25 per page. Certification fee: $1.00 plus copy fee. Payee: Harrison County Circuit Court. Personal checks accepted. No credit cards accepted. Prepayment required. Mail requests: SASE required for civil.
Civil Name Search: Access: Mail, in person, online. Both court and visitors may perform in person name searches. No search fee. Civil index on cards since 1979, prior on index books. Mail turnaround time 2 days. Civil PAT goes back to 2000. Often older judgment will be displayed. Case lookup is at https://www.courts.mo.gov/casenet/base/welcome.do. Online records go back to 3/29/2000. Online search results show full name, address, and year of birth only.
Criminal Name Search: Access: In person, online. Visitors must perform in person searches themselves. Criminal records indexed on cards since 1979, prior on index books. Criminal PAT goes back to same as civil. Both the terminal and CaseNet only show year of birth. For common names, one must ask the Clerk for more identifiers to correctly do a search. Case lookup is at https://www.courts.mo.gov/casenet/base/welcome.do. Online records go back to 3/29/2000. Online search results show full name, address, and year of birth only.

Henry County

Consolidated Circuit Court PO Box 487, Clinton, MO 64735; 660-885-7232; fax: 660-885-8247; 8AM-4:30PM (CST). *Felony, Misdemeanor, Civil, Eviction, Small Claims, Probate.*
http://tacnet.missouri.org/~court27/
General Information: The Circuit Court and Associate Division consolidated as of 01/03. Online identifiers in results same as on public terminal. No juvenile, mental, expunged, dismissed, or suspended imposition of sentence records released. Will not fax documents. Court makes copy: $.25 per page. $2.50 fee for records copied from big books. Certification fee: $1.50. Payee: Henry County Circuit Court. Personal checks accepted. Prepayment required. Copy fees may be billed. Mail requests: SASE required for civil.
Civil Name Search: Access: Mail, in person, online. Only the court performs in person name searches; visitors may not. No search fee as long

as search takes 15 minutes or less. Civil records on computer since 8/92, on index cards since 1979, archived since 1877. Mail turnaround time 5-10 days Often older judgment will be displayed. Case lookup is at https://www.courts.mo.gov/casenet/base/welcome.do. Online records go back to 8/18/2003.

Criminal Name Search: Access: In person, online. Only the court performs in person name searches; visitors may not. No search fee. Criminal records on computer since 8/92, on index cards since 1979, archived since 1877. Note: This court suggests criminal search requests should go to the MO Highway Patrol. Both the terminal and CaseNet only show year of birth. For common names, one must ask the Clerk for more identifiers to correctly do a search. Online access to criminal same as civil, above.

Hickory County

Circuit Court PO Box 345, Court House Sq, Hermitage, MO 65668; 417-745-6421; fax: 417-745-6670; 8AM-N, 12:30-4PM (CST). *Felony, Civil Actions, Eviction, Small Claims, Probate.* www.positech.net/~dcourt/

General Information: Online identifiers in results same as on public terminal. No juvenile, mental, expunged, dismissed, or suspended imposition of sentence records released. Fee to fax back is $1.00 per page. Court makes copy: $1.00 per page microfilm; $.25 per page paper. Certification fee: $1.00 per cert. plus copy fee. Payee: Hickory County Circuit Clerk. Personal checks accepted. No credit cards accepted. Prepayment required.

Civil Name Search: Access: In person, online. Both court and visitors may perform in person name searches. No search fee. Civil records on computer since 11/2001, prior on index books since 1976. Civil PAT goes back to 2001. Often older judgment will be displayed. Case lookup is at https://www.courts.mo.gov/casenet/base/welcome.do. Online records go back to 11/13/2001. Online search results show full name, address, and year of birth only. Probate Court also participates in the CaseNet system; also, access probate records at www.16thcircuit.org/publicaccess.asp.

Criminal Name Search: Access: In person, online. Both court and visitors may perform in person name searches. No search fee. Required to search: name, years to search, signed release. Criminal records on computer since 11/2001, prior on index books since 1976. Criminal PAT goes back to same as civil. Both the terminal and CaseNet only show year of birth. For common names, one must ask the Clerk for more identifiers to correctly do a search. Case lookup is at https://www.courts.mo.gov/casenet/base/welcome.do. Online records go back to 11/13/2001. Online search results show full name, address, and year of birth only.

Holt County

Circuit Court PO Box 318, 102 W Nodaway, Oregon, MO 64473; 660-446-3301; fax: 660-446-3328; 8AM-4:30PM (CST). *Felony, Civil Actions over $25,000.* www.courts.mo.gov/page.jsp?id=1547

General Information: Online identifiers in results same as on public terminal. No juvenile, mental, expunged, dismissed, or suspended imposition of sentence records released. Will fax documents $2.00 each. Court makes copy: $1.00 per page. Certification fee: $1.00 per page plus copy fee. Payee: Recorder. Personal checks accepted. No credit cards accepted. Prepayment required. Mail requests: SASE required.

Civil Name Search: Access: Mail, in person, online. Both court and visitors may perform in person name searches. Search fee: $4.00. Civil records on books. Mail turnaround time varies. Civil PAT goes back to 3/20/06. The terminal connects to CaseNet. Participates in the statewide MO CaseNet record system at https://www.courts.mo.gov/casenet/base/welcome.do. Online records go back to 3/20/2006. Online search results show full name, address, and year of birth only.

Criminal Name Search: Access: Mail, in person, online. Both court and visitors may perform in person name searches. Search fee: $4.00. Criminal docket on books. Mail turnaround time varies. Criminal PAT goes back to 3/20/2006. Both the terminal and CaseNet only show year of birth. For common names, one must ask the Clerk for more identifiers to correctly do a search. Participates in the statewide MO Casenet record system at https://www.courts.mo.gov/casenet/base/welcome.do. Online records go back to 3/20/2006. Online search results show full name, address, and year of birth only.

Associate Circuit Division PO Box 173, 102 W. Nodaway, Oregon, MO 64473; 660-446-3380; fax: 660-446-3588; 8:30AM-4:30PM (CST). *Misdemeanor, Civil Actions under $25,000, Eviction, Small Claims, Probate.* www.courts.mo.gov/page.jsp?id=1547

General Information: Online identifiers in results same as on public terminal. No juvenile, mental, expunged, dismissed, or suspended imposition of sentence records released. Will not fax documents. Court makes copy: $.25 per page. Certification fee: $1.50 per cert plus $1.00 per page. Payee: Associate Circuit Court. Personal checks accepted. No credit cards accepted. Prepayment required. Mail requests: SASE required for civil.

Civil Name Search: Access: Mail, fax, in person, online. Both court and visitors may perform in person name searches. No search fee. Civil index on cards since 1979. Mail turnaround time 2 days. Civil PAT goes back to 3/2006. Often older judgment will be displayed. Case lookup is at https://www.courts.mo.gov/casenet/base/welcome.do. Online records go back to 3/20/2006. Online search results show full name, address, and year of birth only.

Criminal Name Search: Access: In person, online. Visitors must perform in person name searches. Criminal records on computer since 1991, prior on index cards since 1979. Criminal PAT goes back to 3/2006. Both the terminal and CaseNet only show year of birth. Case lookup is at https://www.courts.mo.gov/casenet/base/welcome.do. Online records go back to 3/20/2006. Online search results show full name, address, and year of birth only.

Howard County

Circuit Court 1 Courthouse Square, Fayette, MO 65248; 660-248-2194; fax: 660-248-5009; 8:30AM-4:30PM (CST). *Felony, Civil Actions over $30,000.* www.courts.mo.gov/page.jsp?id=1599

General Information: Office will not do certified searches, only simple searches to see if a name exists. Online identifiers in results same as on public terminal. No juvenile, mental, expunged, dismissed, or suspended imposition of sentence records released. Will fax out specific case files for $2.00 per document. Court makes copy: $.25 per page. Self serve copy: same. Certification fee: $2.00 per doc. Payee: Circuit Clerk. Personal checks accepted. No credit cards accepted. Prepayment required. Mail requests: SASE required.

Civil Name Search: Access: Mail, fax, in person, online. Visitors must perform in person searches themselves. No search fee. Civil index on cards; computer records go back to the 1970's. Civil PAT goes back to 1970s. Often older judgment will be displayed. Case lookup is at https://www.courts.mo.gov/casenet/base/welcome.do. Online records go back to 10/01. Online search results show full name, address, and year of birth only.

Criminal Name Search: Access: In person, online, mail, fax. Visitors must perform in person searches themselves. No search fee. Criminal records indexed on cards; computer records go back to the 1970's. Note: Results include address. Criminal PAT goes back to same as civil. Both the terminal and CaseNet only show year of birth. For common names, one must ask the Clerk for more identifiers to correctly do a search. Online access to criminal same as civil, above, records start 11/01/2001.

Howell County

Circuit Court PO Box 967, West Plains, MO 65775; 417-256-3741; fax: 417-256-4650; 8AM-4:30PM (CST). *Felony, Civil Actions, Eviction, Small Claims, Probate.* www.courts.mo.gov/page.jsp?id=1653

General Information: The Associate Court was consolidated into the Circuit Court. Online identifiers in results same as on public terminal. No juvenile, mental, expunged, dismissed, or suspended imposition of sentence records released. Will fax documents $1.00 per page. Court makes copy: $.10 per page. Certification fee: $1.50 per doc plus copy fee. Payee: Howell County Circuit Clerk. Personal checks accepted. No credit cards accepted. Prepayment required. Will bill to attorneys. Mail requests: SASE required for civil.

Civil Name Search: Access: Phone, fax, mail, in person, online. Both court and visitors may perform in person name searches. No search fee. Civil index on cards since 1977. Mail turnaround time 2 days. Civil PAT goes back to 2000. Often older judgment will be displayed. Case lookup is at https://www.courts.mo.gov/casenet/base/welcome.do. Online records go back to 4/17/2000. Online search results show full name, address, and year of birth only.

Criminal Name Search: Access: In person, online. Both court and visitors may perform in person name searches. No search fee. Criminal records indexed on cards since 1977. Criminal PAT goes back to 2000+. Both the terminal and CaseNet only show year of birth. For common names, one must ask the Clerk for more identifiers to correctly do a search. Case lookup is at https://www.courts.mo.gov/casenet/base/welcome.do. Online records go back to 4/17/2000. Online search results show full name, address, and year of birth only.

Iron County

Circuit Court 250 S Main, Ste 220, Ironton, MO 63650; 573-546-2511; fax: 573-546-6006; 7:30AM-4:30PM (CST). *Felony, Misdemeanor, Civil Actions, Eviction, Small Claims, Probate.* www.courts.mo.gov/page.jsp?id=1670

General Information: The Circuit and Associate Circuit Court have consolidated. Court personnel will not perform name searches for the public. Online identifiers in results same as on public terminal. No juvenile, mental, expunged, dismissed, or suspended imposition of sentence records released. Will fax documents for $5.00 fee. Court makes copy: $.30 per page.

Certification fee: $1.50 plus $1.00 per page. Payee: Iron County Circuit Clerk. Personal checks accepted. No credit cards accepted. Prepayment required. Mail requests: SASE required.

Civil Name Search: Access: In person, online. Visitors must perform in person searches themselves. Civil index on cards since 1976, prior on books. Note: Files requested by case number take 10 days turnaround. Civil PAT goes back to 4/2001. Often older judgment will be displayed. Case lookup is at https://www.courts.mo.gov/casenet/base/welcome.do. Online records go back to 4/9/2001. Online search results show full name, address, and year of birth only.

Criminal Name Search: Access: In person, online. Visitors must perform in person searches themselves. Criminal records indexed on cards since 1976, prior on books to 1856. Note: 10 day turnaround on files requested by case number. Criminal PAT goes back to 4/2001. Both the terminal and CaseNet only show year of birth. For common names, one must ask the Clerk for more identifiers to correctly do a search. Participates in the free statewide Casenet court record system at www.courts.mo.gov/casenet/base/welcome.do. Online records go back to 4/9/2001.

Jackson County

Circuit Court - Civil Division 415 E 12th, 3rd Fl, Kansas City, MO 64106; 816-881-3522; probate phone: 816-881-3755; fax: 816-881-3635; 8AM-5PM (CST). *Civil, Eviction, Small Claims, Probate, Domestic.* www.16thcircuit.org

General Information: There is a combined computer system with the Independence civil court. Online identifiers in results same as on public terminal. No juvenile, mental, expunged, dismissed, or suspended imposition of sentence records released. Will not fax documents. Court makes copy: $1.00 per page. Certification fee: $4.00 per cert plus copy fee. Payee: Dept of Civil Records. Business checks accepted. No credit cards accepted. Prepayment required.

Civil Name Search: Access: Online, in person. Visitors must perform in person searches themselves. Civil records on computer since 1973, some records on microfiche and books, older records archived off-site. Public use terminal has civil records back to 1989. Often older judgment will be displayed. Case lookup is at https://www.courts.mo.gov/casenet/base/welcome.do. Jackson CaseNet records go back to 1/1989, but judgments only go back to 2/15/1989. Online search results show full name, address, and year of birth only. Probate Court also participates in the CaseNet system; also, access probate records at www.16thcircuit.org/Depts/PRB/prb_inquiry.asp?dept=prb.

Independence Circuit Court - Civil Annex 308 W Kansas #310, Independence, MO 64050; 816-881-4573; probate phone: 816-881-4552; fax: 816-881-4410; 8AM-5PM (CST). *Civil, Eviction, Small Claims, Probate.* www.16thcircuit.org

General Information: Direct civil search requests to Rm 204. This court on the same computer system as Kansas City for civil cases, but files maintained separately. Online identifiers in results same as on public terminal. No sealed records released. Will not fax documents. Court makes copy: $1.00 per page. Certification fee: $3.00 per cert plus copy fee. Payee: Civil Records. Only cashiers checks and money orders accepted. No credit cards accepted. Prepayment required. Mail requests: SASE required for mail return of any copies.

Civil Name Search: Access: In person, online. Visitors must perform in person searches themselves. Civil records on computer since 1989. Note: The court will not do background checks, except for attorneys. You must have case number if the court is to pull a record. Public use terminal has civil records back to 1989. Often older judgment will be displayed. Case lookup is at https://www.courts.mo.gov/casenet/base/welcome.do. Online records go back to 1/1989. Online search results show full name, address, and year of birth only. Online access to probate records is free at www.16thcircuit.org/Depts/PRB/prb_inquiry.asp?dept=prb

Circuit Court - Criminal Division 1315 Locust, 1st Fl, Kansas City, MO 64106-2937; 816-881-4350; fax: 816-881-3420; 8AM-5PM (CST). *Felony, Misdemeanor.* www.16thcircuit.org

General Information: All background checks (name searches) are sent to the Missouri Highway Patrol in Jefferson City. Court will only pull file or give copies if a specific case number is given. Will not fax documents. Court makes copy: $1.00 per page. Certification fee: $4.00 per doc, authentication-$6.00. Only cashiers checks and money orders accepted. No credit cards accepted. Prepayment required. Mail requests: SASE required.

Criminal Name Search: Access: Online, mail, fax, in person. Visitors must perform in person searches themselves. No search fee. Criminal records on computer since 1968 for felonies, 1980 for misdemeanors. Note: Fax or mail requests must include a case or file number; form found at court website criminal records, forms page. Mail turnaround time 10-14 days. Both the terminal and CaseNet only show year of birth. For

common names, one must ask the Clerk for more identifiers to correctly do a search. Participates in the free state online court record system at www.courts.mo.gov/casenet/base/welcome.do. Online records go back to 1/1989. Also, current criminal docket calendar is available from the home page. Online search results show full name, address, and year of birth only. Online access to probate records is free at www.16thcircuit.org/publicaccess.asp. This includes private process servers, jury verdicts, criminal traffic, and criminal sureties.

Jasper County

Carthage Circuit Court Courthouse, Rm 303, 302 S Main St, Carthage, MO 64836; 417-358-0441; fax: 417-358-0461; 8AM-5PM (CST). *Felony, Civil Actions over $25,000.* www.courts.mo.gov/page.jsp?id=1638

General Information: Although the Carthage Circuit and Associate Division merged, the records are only co-mingled from 7/2000 forward. Each of the 3 courts in the county must be searched for an accurate overall search. Probate is separate index, separate address. Online identifiers in results same as on public terminal. No juvenile, mental, expunged, dismissed, or suspended imposition of sentence records released. Will fax documents to local number only. Court makes copy: $.25 per page. Self serve copy: same. Certification fee: $1.50 per page plus copy fee; Exemplification fee- $3.00. Payee: Jasper County Circuit Clerk. Business checks accepted. No credit cards accepted. Prepayment required. Mail requests: SASE required.

Civil Name Search: Access: Mail, in person, online. Both court and visitors may perform in person name searches. No search fee. Civil records on computer since 7/1/91, prior on cards since 1975. Mail turnaround time 1 week. Civil PAT goes back to 1991. Often older judgment will be displayed. Case lookup is at https://www.courts.mo.gov/casenet/base/welcome.do. Online records go back to 6/26/2000. Online search results show full name, address, and year of birth only.

Criminal Name Search: Access: Mail, in person, online. Both court and visitors may perform in person name searches. No search fee. Criminal records on computer since 7/1/91, prior on cards since 1975. Mail turnaround time 1 week. Criminal PAT goes back to same as civil. Both the terminal and CaseNet only show year of birth. For common names, one must ask the Clerk for more identifiers to correctly do a search. Case lookup is at https://www.courts.mo.gov/casenet/base/welcome.do. Online records go back to 6/26/2000. Online search results show full name, address, and year of birth only.

Joplin Consolidated Circuit Court Courthouse, 3rd Fl, 601 S Pearl, Rm 300, Joplin, MO 64801; 417-625-4310/4316; fax: 417-782-7172; 8:30AM-N, 1PM-4:30PM (CST). *Felony, Misdemeanor, Civil Actions, Small Claims, Probate.* www.courts.mo.gov/page.jsp?id=1638

General Information: Although the Joplin Circuit and Associate Division merged, the records are only co-mingled from 07/00 forward. Each of the 3 courts in the county must be searched for an accurate overall search. Online identifiers in results same as on public terminal. No juvenile, mental, expunged, dismissed, or suspended imposition of sentence records released. Will fax out specific case files. Court makes copy: $.25 per page. Certification fee: $1.50 per document plus copy fee. Payee: Jasper County Circuit Clerk. No personal checks or credit cards accepted. Prepayment required.

Civil Name Search: Access: In person, online. Visitors must perform in person searches themselves. Civil records on computer since 1991, prior on cards since 1975. Civil PAT goes back to ten years or more. Often older judgment will be displayed. Case lookup is at https://www.courts.mo.gov/casenet/base/welcome.do. Online records go back to 6/26/2000. Online search results show full name, address, and year of birth only.

Criminal Name Search: Access: In person, online. Visitors must perform in person searches themselves. Criminal records computerized from 1991, prior on cards back to 1975. Criminal PAT goes back to same as civil. CaseNet only shows year of birth. For common names, one must ask the Clerk for more identifiers to correctly do a search. Case lookup is at https://www.courts.mo.gov/casenet/base/welcome.do. Online records go back to 6/26/2000. Online search results show full name, address, and year of birth only.

Carthage Associate Division Court Courthouse, Rm 304, 302 S. Main St, Carthage, MO 64836; 417-358-0450; fax: 417-358-0461; 8:30AM-N, 1-4:30PM (CST). *Misdemeanor, Civil Actions under $25,000, Eviction, Small Claims, Probate.* www.courts.mo.gov/page.jsp?id=1638

General Information: Although Carthage Circuit and Associate Division merged, the records are co-mingled from 7/2000 forward only. Each of the 3 courts in the county must be searched for an accurate overall search. Online identifiers in results same as on public terminal. No juvenile, mental, expunged, dismissed, or suspended imposition of sentence records released. Will not fax documents. Court makes copy: $.25 per page. Certification fee:

$1.50 per cert includes copy fee. Payee: Associate Court. No personal checks accepted. Visa/MC accepted. Prepayment required.

Civil Name Search: Access: In person, online. Visitors must perform in person searches themselves. Civil records on computer back to 2000, prior on cards back to 1979. Civil PAT goes back to 1999. Often older judgment will be displayed. Participates in the free statewide CaseNet record system at https://www.courts.mo.gov/casenet/base/welcome.do. Online records go back to 6/26/2000. Online search results show full name, address, and year of birth only.

Criminal Name Search: Access: In person, online. Visitors must perform in person searches themselves. Criminal records computerized from 2000, prior on cards back to 1979. Note: Will possibly help public with a search, depending on how busy the staff is. Criminal PAT goes back to same as civil. Both the terminal and CaseNet only show year of birth. For common names, one must ask the Clerk for more identifiers to correctly do a search. Participates in the free statewide Casenet record system at https://www.courts.mo.gov/casenet/base/welcome.do. Online records go back to 6/26/2000. Online search results show full name, address, and year of birth only.

Jefferson County

Circuit Court - Civil Division PO Box 100, 300 Main St, Hillsboro, MO 63050; 636-797-5443, 636-797-5060; fax: 636-797-5073; 8AM-5PM (CST). *Civil Actions, Eviction, Small Claims, Probate.* www.courts.mo.gov/page.jsp?id=1620

General Information: Online identifiers in results same as on public terminal. No juvenile, mental, expunged, dismissed, or suspended imposition of sentence records released. Court makes copy: $1.00 per page. Certification fee: $.50 per page plus copy fee. Payee: Circuit Clerk. Business checks accepted. No credit cards accepted. Prepayment required. Mail requests: SASE required.

Civil Name Search: Access: Phone, fax, mail, in person, online. Both court and visitors may perform in person name searches. Search fee: $1.00 per name. Civil records on computer since 10/90, prior on books since 1966. Mail turnaround time 1-2 days. Public use terminal has civil records back to 1985. Often older judgment will be displayed. Case lookup is at https://www.courts.mo.gov/casenet/base/welcome.do. Records go back to 5/9/2006. Online search results show full name, address, and year of birth only.

Circuit Court - Criminal Division PO Box 100, 300 2nd St, Hillsboro, MO 63050; 636-797-5370; fax: 636-797-5073; 8AM-5PM (CST). *Felony, Misdemeanor.* www.courts.mo.gov/page.jsp?id=1620

General Information: Court personnel will not perform name searches. Online identifiers in results same as on public terminal. No juvenile, mental, expunged, dismissed, or suspended imposition of sentence records released. Will not fax documents. Court makes copy: $1.00 per page. Certification fee: $.50 per file; $2.00 per page if microfilm. Payee: Circuit Clerk. Business checks accepted. No credit cards accepted. Prepayment required. Mail requests: SASE required for civil.

Criminal Name Search: Access: In person, online. Visitors must perform in person searches themselves. Required to search: name, years to search, signed release, DOB or SSN. Criminal records on computer since 1989, on index cards 1976 to 1988, prior on books or microfilm. Public use terminal has crim records back to 1989. Both the terminal and CaseNet only show year of birth. For common names, one must ask the Clerk for more identifiers to correctly do a search. Participates in the free state online court record system at www.courts.mo.gov/casenet/base/welcome.do. Online records go back to 5/9/2006. Online search results show full name, address, and year of birth only. Online access to probate records is free at www.16thcircuit.org/publicaccess.asp. This includes private process servers, jury verdicts, criminal traffic, and criminal sureties.

Johnson County

Consolidated Circuit Court Johnson County Justice Ctr, 101 W Market, Warrensburg, MO 64093; 660-422-7413/or/7410; fax: 660-422-7417; 8AM-4:30PM (CST). *Felony, Misdemeanor, Civil, Eviction, Small Claims, Probate.* www.courts.mo.gov/page.jsp?id=1610

General Information: Fax to 660-422-7412 as well. Online identifiers in results same as on public terminal. No juvenile, adoptions, mental, expunged, dismissed, or suspended imposition of sentence records released. Will fax documents for $.50 per page. Court makes copy: $.25 per page. Self serve copy: same. Certification fee: none. Payee: Circuit Clerk. No personal checks or credit cards accepted. Prepayment required.

Civil Name Search: Access: Mail, fax, in person, online. Visitors must perform in person searches themselves. Search fee: $10.00 per name. Civil records on file since 1800s, microfilmed from 1950s to 1988. Note: Only the court can pull records prior to 1976. Mail turnaround time 1 week. Civil PAT goes back to 1994. Often older judgment will be displayed. Case lookup is at https://www.courts.mo.gov/casenet/base/welcome.do.

Online records go back to 6/6/2005. Online search results show full name, address, and year of birth only.

Criminal Name Search: Access: Mail, fax, in person, online. Visitors must perform in person searches themselves. Search fee: $10.00 per name. Required to search: name, years to search, DOB, SSN. Criminal records on file since 1800s, microfilmed through 1988. Note: Court will perform search if prior to 1976. Mail turnaround time 1 week. Criminal PAT goes back to same as civil. Both the terminal and CaseNet only show year of birth. For common names, one must ask the Clerk for more identifiers to correctly do a search. Online access to criminal records same as civil, above.

Knox County

Consolidated Circuit Court PO Box 116, 107 N 4th St, Edina, MO 63537; 660-397-2305; fax: 660-397-3331; 8:30AM-N, 1-4PM (CST). *Felony, Misdemeanor, Civil, Eviction, Small Claims, Probate.* www.courts.mo.gov/page.jsp?id=1535

General Information: The Circuit Court and Associate Division consolidated 3/01/2006. Records keeping is still separated at this location however. Online identifiers in results same as on public terminal. No juvenile, mental, expunged, dismissed, or suspended imposition of sentence records released. Will fax documents; fee varies but usually $3.50 per doc. Court makes copy: $1.00 per page. Self serve copy: same. Certification fee: $2.00. Payee: Circuit Court. Personal checks accepted. No credit cards accepted. Prepayment required.

Civil Name Search: Access: Mail, in person, online. Both court and visitors may perform in person name searches. No search fee. Civil records on microfiche since 3/83, archived since 1845, no computerization. Mail turnaround time same day. Civil PAT goes back to 9/6/2005. Often older judgment will be displayed. Case lookup is at https://www.courts.mo.gov/casenet/base/welcome.do. Online records go back to 9/6/2005. Online search results show full name, address, and year of birth only.

Criminal Name Search: Access: Mail, in person, online. Both court and visitors may perform in person name searches. No search fee. Criminal records archived since 1845, no computerization. Mail turnaround time same day. Criminal PAT goes back to same as civil. Both the terminal and CaseNet only show year of birth. For common names, one must ask the Clerk for more identifiers to correctly do a search. Case lookup is at https://www.courts.mo.gov/casenet/base/welcome.do. Online records go back to 9/6/2005. Online search results show full name, address, and year of birth only.

Laclede County

Consolidated Circuit Court 200 N Adams St, Lebanon, MO 65536; 417-532-2471, 532-9196; criminal phone: 417-532-2471; fax: 417-532-3683; 8AM-4PM (CST). *Felony, Misdemeanor, Civil. Eviction, Small Claims, Probate.* www.courts.mo.gov/page.jsp?id=1629

General Information: Probate fax is same as main fax number. Online identifiers in results same as on public terminal. No juvenile, mental, expunged, dismissed, or suspended imposition of sentence records released. Will fax documents $3.00 1st page, $1.00 each add'l. Court makes copy: $.25 per page. Self serve copy: same. Certification fee: $1.50 per document plus copy fee. Payee: Laclede County Circuit Clerk. Personal checks accepted. No credit cards accepted. Prepayment required. Copy fees may be billed to Attorneys only. Mail requests: SASE required.

Civil Name Search: Access: Phone, fax, mail, in person, online. Both court and visitors may perform in person name searches. No search fee. Civil records on cards since 1979, prior on books. Mail turnaround time varies. Civil PAT goes back to 1995; judgment index only. Often older judgment will be displayed. Case lookup is at https://www.courts.mo.gov/casenet/base/welcome.do. Online records go back to 11/28/2005. Online search results show full name, address, and year of birth only.

Criminal Name Search: Access: Phone, fax, mail, in person, online. Both court and visitors may perform in person name searches. No search fee. Required to search: name, years to search; also helpful: SSN. Criminal records on cards since 1979, prior on books. Mail turnaround time varies. Criminal PAT available. Both the terminal and CaseNet only show year of birth. For common names, one must ask the Clerk for more identifiers to correctly do a search. Case lookup is at https://www.courts.mo.gov/casenet/base/welcome.do. Online records go back to 11/28/2005. Online search results show full name, address, and year of birth only.

Lafayette County

Consolidated Circuit Court PO Box 10, County Clerk's Office, Lexington, MO 64067; 660-259-6101; probate phone: 660-259-2324; fax: 660-259-6148; 8AM-4:30PM (CST). *Felony, Misdemeanor, Civil, Eviction, Small Claims, Probate.* www.lafayettecountymo.com/

General Information: The Circuit Court and Associate Division consolidated as of 9/2004. Probate fax- 660-259-4997 Online identifiers in results same as on public terminal. No juvenile, mental, expunged, dismissed, or suspended imposition of sentence records released. Will fax back documents $1.00 per page. Court makes copy: $.25 per page; Probate-$1.00 per page. Certification fee: $2.50 per document plus copy fee. Payee: Circuit Clerk. Personal checks only accepted from county residents; money orders or cashiers checks preferred. Major credit cards accepted for searches and copies. Attorney of record and copy fees will be billed. Mail requests: SASE required.

Civil Name Search: Access: Mail, fax, in person, online. Both court and visitors may perform in person name searches. No search fee. Civil cases indexed by defendant, plaintiff, case number. Civil records on books, archived since 1821; on computer back to 1987. Note: All search requests to clerk must be in writing. Forms available online. Mail turnaround time 3-5 days. Civil PAT goes back to 2002. Often older judgment will be displayed. Case lookup is at https://www.courts.mo.gov/casenet/base/welcome.do. Online records go back to 04/01/02. Online search results show full name, address, and year of birth only.

Criminal Name Search: Access: In person, online. Both court and visitors may perform in person name searches. No search fee. Required to search: name, years to search; also helpful-case number. Criminal docket on books, archived since 1823; on computer back to 1987. Criminal PAT goes back to same as civil. Both the terminal and CaseNet only show year of birth. For common names, one must ask the Clerk for more identifiers to correctly do a search. Case lookup is at https://www.courts.mo.gov/casenet/base/welcome.do. Online records go back to 04/01/02. Online search results show full name, address, and year of birth only.

Lawrence County

Circuit Court 240 N Main, #110, Mt Vernon, MO 65712; 417-466-2471; fax: 417-466-7899; 7:30AM-4PM (CST). *Felony, Misdemeanor, Civil, Eviction, Small Claims, Probate, Traffic.* www.courts.mo.gov/page.jsp?id=1661

General Information: Court consolidated with Associate Circuit Court Online identifiers in results same as on public terminal. No juvenile, mental, expunged, dismissed, or suspended imposition of sentence records released. Will fax out documents if all fees prepaid and not a lot of copies to fax. Court makes copy: $.25 per page. Self serve copy: same. Certification fee: $2.00 per cert plus copy fee. Payee: Circuit Court. Business checks or money orders accepted, no personal checks please. Major credit cards accepted. Prepayment required. Mail requests: SASE helpful.

Civil Name Search: Access: Mail, in person, online. Both court and visitors may perform in person name searches. Search fee: $5.00 per name. Civil records on computer back to 7/1991. Mail turnaround time 1 week. Civil PAT goes back to 7/1991. Often older judgment will be displayed. Case lookup is at https://www.courts.mo.gov/casenet/base/welcome.do. Online records go back to 7/11/2005 and includes probate. Online search results show full name, address, and year of birth only.

Criminal Name Search: Access: Mail, in person, online. Both court and visitors may perform in person name searches. Search fee: $5.00 per name. Required to search: name, years to search, DOB; also helpful: SSN. Criminal records computerized from July 1, 1991. Mail turnaround time 1 week. Criminal PAT goes back to same as civil. Both the terminal and CaseNet only show year of birth. For common names, one must ask the Clerk for more identifiers to correctly do a search. Case lookup is at https://www.courts.mo.gov/casenet/base/welcome.do. Online records go back to 7/11/2005 and includes probate. Online search results show full name, address, and year of birth only.

Lewis County

Consolidated Circuit Court PO Box 8, Monticello, MO 63457; 573-767-5232; fax: 573-767-5342; 8AM-N,1-4PM (CST). *Felony, Misdemeanor, Civil, Eviction, Small Claims, Probate.* www.courts.mo.gov/page.jsp?id=1537

General Information: Consolidated court on 4-1-03. Online identifiers in results same as on public terminal. No juvenile, mental, expunged, dismissed, or suspended imposition of sentence records released. Will fax documents. Court makes copy: $.25 per page plus $.20 per minute. Self serve copy: $.25 per page. Certification fee: $2.50. Payee: Lewis County Circuit Court. Personal checks not accepted. No credit cards accepted. Prepayment required.

Civil Name Search: Access: Mail, in person, online. Visitors must perform in person searches themselves. No search fee. Civil records on computer back to 1976 (judgments) and index books, archived since 1830s. Civil PAT goes back to 9/6/05. Often older judgment will be displayed. Case lookup is at https://www.courts.mo.gov/casenet/base/welcome.do. Online records go back to 9/6/2005. Online search results show full name, address, and year of birth only.

Criminal Name Search: Access: In person, online. Visitors must perform in person searches themselves. Criminal records on computer and index books, archived since 1830s. Criminal PAT goes back to same as civil. Both the terminal and CaseNet only show year of birth. For common names, one must ask the Clerk for more identifiers to correctly do a search. Case lookup is at https://www.courts.mo.gov/casenet/base/welcome.do. Online records go back to 9/6/2005. Online search results show full name, address, and year of birth only.

Lincoln County

Consolidated Circuit Court Lincoln County Justice Ctr, 45 Business park Dr, Troy, MO 63379; 636-528-6300; fax: 636-528-9168; 8AM-4:30PM (CST). *Felony, Misdemeanor, Civil, Eviction, Small Claims, Probate.* www.courts.mo.gov/page.jsp?id=1682

General Information: Online identifiers in results same as on public terminal. No juvenile, mental, expunged, dismissed, or suspended imposition of sentence records released. Will fax specific case file only; not search documents. Court makes copy: $.25 per page. Self serve copy: same. Certification fee: $.50 per page includes copies. Payee: Lincoln County Circuit Clerk. Personal checks accepted. No credit cards accepted. Prepayment required.

Civil Name Search: Access: In person, online. Visitors must perform in person searches themselves. Civil records on computer since 2002, prior on index cards since 1978. Civil PAT goes back to 4/2002. Often older judgment will be displayed. Record access free at https://www.courts.mo.gov/casenet/base/welcome.do. Online records go back to 04/03/02. Online search results show full name, address, and year of birth only.

Criminal Name Search: Access: In person, online. Visitors must perform in person searches themselves. Criminal records on computer since 8/98, prior on index cards since 1978. Criminal PAT goes back to same as civil. Both the terminal and CaseNet only show year of birth. For common names, one must ask the Clerk for more identifiers to correctly do a search. Record access free at https://www.courts.mo.gov/casenet/base/welcome.do. Online records go back to 04/03/02. Online search results show full name, address, and year of birth only.

Linn County

Consolidated Circuit Court PO Box 84, 108 N High St, Linneus, MO 64653-0084; 660-895-5212; fax: 660-895-5277; 8AM-N, 1-4:30PM (CST). *Felony, Misdemeanor, Civil, Eviction, Small Claims, Probate.* www.courts.mo.gov/page.jsp?id=1573

General Information: Online identifiers in results same as on public terminal. No juvenile, mental, expunged, dismissed, or suspended imposition of sentence records released. No fee to fax documents. Court makes copy: $1.00 per page. Certification fee: $1.50 per page includes copies. Payee: Linn County Circuit Court. Only cashiers checks and money orders accepted. No credit cards accepted. Prepayment required. Mail requests: SASE required.

Civil Name Search: Access: Fax, mail, in person, online. Both court and visitors may perform in person name searches. No search fee. Civil records on books. Mail turnaround time 1 week. Civil PAT goes back to 5/2001. Case lookup is at https://www.courts.mo.gov/casenet/base/welcome.do. Online records go back to 5/13/2002. Online search results show full name, address, and year of birth only.

Criminal Name Search: Access: Fax, mail, in person, online. Both court and visitors may perform in person name searches. No search fee. Criminal docket on books. Mail turnaround time 1 week. Criminal PAT goes back to same as civil. Both the terminal and CaseNet only show year of birth. For common names, one must ask the Clerk for more identifiers to correctly do a search. Case lookup is at https://www.courts.mo.gov/casenet/base/welcome.do. Online records go back to 5/13/2002. Online search results show full name, address, and year of birth only.

Livingston County

Combined Circuit Court 700 Webster St, Chillicothe, MO 64601; 660-646-8000 x1; fax: 660-646-2734; 8AM-5PM (CST). *Felony, Misdemeanor, Civil Actions, Eviction, Small Claims, Probate.* www.courts.mo.gov/page.jsp?id=1677

General Information: Combined with Assoc Circuit Ct 4/1/2009. Online identifiers in results same as on public terminal. No juvenile, mental, expunged, dismissed, or suspended imposition of sentence records released. Will fax documents to local or toll free line. Court makes copy: $1.00 per page. Self serve copy: same. Certification fee: $1.50. Payee: Livingston County Circuit Clerk. Personal checks accepted. No credit cards accepted. Prepayment required. Attorneys may be billed for copy fees. Mail requests: SASE required.

Civil Name Search: Access: Mail, fax, in person, online. Visitors must perform in person searches themselves. No search fee. Required to search:

name, years to search, any personal identifiers. Civil index on cards since 1974, prior on record books. Civil PAT goes back to 1/23/2006. Often older judgment will be displayed. Case lookup is at https://www.courts.mo.gov/casenet/base/welcome.do. Online records go back to 1/23/2006. Online search results show full name, address, and year of birth only.
Criminal Name Search: Access: Mail, fax, in person, online. Visitors must perform in person searches themselves. No search fee. Required to search: name, years to search, any personal identifiers. Criminal records indexed on cards since 1974, prior on record books. Criminal PAT goes back to 1/23/2006. Both the terminal and CaseNet only show year of birth. For common names, one must ask the Clerk for more identifiers to correctly do a search. Case lookup is at https://www.courts.mo.gov/casenet/base/welcome.do. Online records go back to 1/23/2006. Online search results show full name, address, and year of birth only.

Macon County

Combined Circuit Court PO Box 382, 101 E Washington St, Bldg 2, Macon, MO 63552; 660-385-4631; criminal phone: 660-385-4631; civil phone: 660-385-4631; fax: 660-385-4235; 8AM-4:30PM (CST). *Felony, Misdemeanor, Civil Actions, Small Claims, Eviction, Probate.* www.maconcountymo.com/Government/CircuitClerk/tabid/82/language/en-US/Default.aspx
General Information: The Associate Court is a Division of the Circuit Court, but the courts have combined at this location Online identifiers in results same as on public terminal. No juvenile, mental, expunged, dismissed, or suspended imposition of sentence records released. Will fax documents $1.00 1st page, $.25 each add'l. Court makes copy: $.25 per page. Self serve copy: same. Certification fee: $3.00 per doc. Payee: Clerk of Circuit Court. Personal checks accepted. No credit cards accepted. Prepayment required. Mail requests: SASE required.
Civil Name Search: Access: Fax, mail, in person, online. Visitors must perform in person searches themselves. Search fee: $3.00. Civil records on computer since 1/1/91, on index cards from 1976-1990, prior on books. Mail turnaround time 7 days. Civil PAT goes back to 11/2003. Case lookup is at https://www.courts.mo.gov/casenet/base/welcome.do. Online records go back to 4/17/2000. Online search results show full name, address, and year of birth only.
Criminal Name Search: Access: Mail, in person, online. Visitors must perform in person searches themselves. Search fee: $3.00. Criminal records on computer since 1/1/91, on index cards from 1976-1990, prior on books. Note: Court directs criminal name search requests to CaseNet or the MO State Hiway Patrol. Mail turnaround time 7 days. Criminal PAT goes back to same as civil. Both the terminal and CaseNet only show year of birth. For common names, one must ask the Clerk for more identifiers to correctly do a search. Online access to criminal records same as civil, above.

Madison County

Consolidated Circuit Court PO Box 470, Fredericktown, MO 63645-0470; 573-783-2102; fax: 573-783-5920; 8AM-5PM (CST). *Felony, Misdemeanor, Civil, Small Claims, Probate.* www.courts.mo.gov/page.jsp?id=1624
General Information: The Associates court was merged into the Circuit Court effective 01/01/2006. All records are co-mingled. Online identifiers in results same as on public terminal. No juvenile, mental, expunged, dismissed, or suspended imposition of sentence records released. Will not fax documents. Court makes copy: $.10 per page. Certification fee: $2.00 per page includes copy. Payee: Madison County Circuit Clerk. Personal checks accepted. No credit cards accepted. Prepayment required. Mail requests: SASE required for mail return of any copies.
Civil Name Search: Access: In person, online. Visitors must perform in person searches themselves. Civil records on computer back to 1993, prior on index cards from 1979-1992. Civil PAT goes back to 1993. Often older judgment will be displayed. Case lookup is at https://www.courts.mo.gov/casenet/base/welcome.do. Records go back to 11/01/00. Online search results show full name, address, and year of birth only.
Criminal Name Search: Access: In person, online. Visitors must perform in person searches themselves. Criminal records computerized from 1993, prior on index cards from 1979-1993. Criminal PAT goes back to same as civil. Both the terminal and CaseNet only show year of birth. For common names, one must ask the Clerk for more identifiers to correctly do a search. Case lookup is at https://www.courts.mo.gov/casenet/base/welcome.do. Records go back to 11/01/00. Online search results show full name, address, and year of birth only.

Maries County

Consolidated Circuit Court PO Box 213, 211 Fourth St, Vienna, MO 65582; 573-422-3338; fax: 573-422-3976; 8AM-4PM (CST). *Felony, Civil Actions over $25,000.* www.courts.mo.gov/page.jsp?id=4754
General Information: Online identifiers in results same as on public terminal. No juvenile, mental, expunged, dismissed, or suspended imposition of sentence records released. Will fax documents $1.00 per page. Court makes copy: $.50 per page. Self serve copy: same. Certification fee: $1.50 per cert plus copy fee. Payee: Maries County Circuit Clerk. Personal checks accepted. No credit cards accepted. Prepayment required. Mail requests: SASE required.
Civil Name Search: Access: Fax, mail, in person, online. Both court and visitors may perform in person name searches. No search fee. Civil records go back to 1940. Mail turnaround time 1-3 days. Civil PAT goes back to 1/07. Often older judgment will be displayed. Case lookup is at https://www.courts.mo.gov/casenet/base/welcome.do. Records go back to 1/22/2007. Online search results show full name, address, and year of birth only.
Criminal Name Search: Access: Fax, mail, in person, online. Both court and visitors may perform in person name searches. No search fee. Criminal records go back 10 1940. Mail turnaround time 1-3 days. Criminal PAT goes back to same. Both the terminal and CaseNet only show year of birth. For common names, one must ask the Clerk for more identifiers to correctly do a search. Case lookup is at https://www.courts.mo.gov/casenet/base/welcome.do. Records go back to 1/22/2007. Online search results show full name, address, and year of birth only.

Marion County

Consolidated Circuit Court District 1 PO Box 431, 100 S Main St, Palmyra, MO 63461; 573-769-2550; fax: 573-769-4558; 8AM-N, 1PM-5PM (CST). *Felony, Misdemeanor, Civil, Eviction, Small Claims, Probate.* www.courts.mo.gov/page.jsp?id=1580
General Information: Online identifiers in results same as on public terminal. No juvenile, mental, expunged, dismissed, or suspended imposition of sentence records released. Will not fax documents. Court makes copy: $.25 per page. Self serve copy: same. Certification fee: none. Payee: Marion County Circuit Clerk of Division I. Business checks accepted. No credit cards accepted. Prepayment required. Mail requests: SASE required for mail return of any copies.
Civil Name Search: Access: In person, online. Visitors must perform in person searches themselves. Civil index on cards since 1977, prior on judgment books. Civil PAT goes back to 1987. Often older judgment will be displayed. Case lookup is at https://www.courts.mo.gov/casenet/base/welcome.do. Online records go back to 9/12/2005. Online search results show full name, address, and year of birth only.
Criminal Name Search: Access: In person, online. Visitors must perform in person searches themselves. Required to search: name, years to search, DOB. Criminal records indexed on cards since 1977, prior on judgment books. Criminal PAT goes back to 2000. Both the terminal and CaseNet only show year of birth. For common names, one must ask the Clerk for more identifiers to correctly do a search. Case lookup is at https://www.courts.mo.gov/casenet/base/welcome.do. Online records go back to 9/12/2005. Online search results show full name, address, and year of birth only. Online results show middle initial.
Consolidated Circuit Court District 2 906 Broadway, Rm 105, Hannibal, MO 63401; 573-221-0198; fax: 573-221-9328; 8AM-Noon, 1-5PM (CST). *Felony, Misdemeanor, Civil, Eviction, Small Claims, Probate.* www.courts.mo.gov/page.jsp?id=1580
General Information: Jurisdiction is Twps of Miller and Mason only. The Associate Circuit Court consolidate with this court in July 2005. Online identifiers in results same as on public terminal. No juvenile, mental, expunged, dismissed, or suspended imposition of sentence records released. Will not fax out documents. Court makes copy: $.50 per page. Certification fee: $5.00 per document plus copy fee. Payee: Circuit Clerk District II. No personal checks accepted. Cash, money orders or cashier checks only accepted. No credit cards accepted.
Civil Name Search: Access: Fax, mail, in person, online. Both court and visitors may perform in person name searches. No search fee. Civil records on computer since 1991, prior on index cards. Mail turnaround time 5 days. Civil PAT goes back to 1976. Often older judgment will be displayed. Case lookup is at https://www.courts.mo.gov/casenet/base/welcome.do. Online records go back to 9/12/2005. Online search results show full name, address, and year of birth only.
Criminal Name Search: Access: In person, online. Visitors must perform in person searches themselves. Criminal records on computer. Criminal PAT goes back to same as civil. Both the terminal and CaseNet only show year of birth. For common names, one must ask the Clerk for more identifiers to correctly do a search. Case lookup is at

https://www.courts.mo.gov/casenet/base/welcome.do. Online records go back to 9/12/2005. Online search results show full name, address, and year of birth only.

McDonald County

Consolidated Circuit Court PO Box 157, Pineville, MO 64856; 417-223-7515; fax: 417-223-4125; 8AM-4:30PM (CST). *Felony, Misdemeanor, Civil, Small Claims, Probate.*
www.courts.mo.gov/page.jsp?id=1663
General Information: Online identifiers in results same as on public terminal. No juvenile, mental, expunged, dismissed, paternity or suspended imposition of sentence records released. Court makes copy: $.25 per page. Certification fee: $2.00; Probate is $1.00 per page. Payee: McDonald County Circuit Clerk. Business checks accepted. No credit cards accepted. Prepayment required. Mail requests: SASE required.
Civil Name Search: Access: Fax, mail, in person, online. Visitors must perform in person searches themselves. No search fee. Civil records on computer since 1979, prior on index cards. Civil PAT goes back to 8/1991. Often older judgment will be displayed. Case lookup is at https://www.courts.mo.gov/casenet/base/welcome.do. Online records go back to 1/21/2004 Online search results show full name, address, and year of birth only.
Criminal Name Search: Access: In person, online. Visitors must perform in person searches themselves. Criminal records on computer since 1991, on index cards since 1979, prior on index cards. Note: Criminal search requests are directed to the MO Highway Patrol. Criminal PAT goes back to 10/1991. Both the terminal and CaseNet only show year of birth. For common names, one must ask the Clerk for more identifiers to correctly do a search. Online access to criminal records same as civil, above.

Mercer County

Circuit Court Courthouse, 802 E Main, Princeton, MO 64673; 660-748-4335/4232; fax: 660-748-4339; 8:30AM-N, 1-4:30PM (CST). *Felony, Misdemeanor, Civil, Eviction, Small Claims, Probate.*
www.courts.mo.gov/page.jsp?id=1540
General Information: Online identifiers in results same as on public terminal. No juvenile, mental, expunged, dismissed, or suspended imposition of sentence records released. Will fax documents $2.00 per page. Court makes copy: $1.00 per page. Self serve copy: same. Certification fee: $1.50 plus copy fee. Payee: Mercer County Circuit Clerk. Personal checks not accepted if out of state; money orders preferred. No credit cards accepted. Prepayment required. Mail requests: SASE required for mail return of any copies.
Civil Name Search: Access: In person, online. Visitors must perform in person searches themselves. Civil records on computer since 1991, on index cards since 1977, prior on books. Civil PAT goes back to 2000. Often older judgment will be displayed. Case lookup is at https://www.courts.mo.gov/casenet/base/welcome.do. Online records go back to 3/29/2000. Online search results show full name, address, and year of birth only.
Criminal Name Search: Access: In person, online. Visitors must perform in person searches themselves. Required to search: name, years to search, DOB. Criminal records on computer since 1991, on index cards since 1977, prior on books. Criminal PAT goes back to same as civil. Both the terminal and CaseNet only show year of birth. For common names, one must ask the Clerk for more identifiers to correctly do a search. Case lookup is at https://www.courts.mo.gov/casenet/base/welcome.do. Online records go back to 3/29/2000. Online search results show full name, address, and year of birth only.

Miller County

Consolidated Circuit Court PO Box 11, Tuscumbia, MO 65082; 573-369-1980; fax: 573-369-1894; 8AM-4:30PM (CST). *Felony, Misdemeanor, Civil, Small Claims, Eviction, Probate.*
www.courts.mo.gov/page.jsp?id=1630
General Information: The Circuit Court and Associate Division consolidated 11/28/2005. Online identifiers in results same as on public terminal. No juvenile, mental, expunged, dismissed, or suspended imposition of sentence records released. No fee to fax documents if other fees prepaid. Will fax to local and toll-free numbers only. Court makes copy: $.50 per page. Self serve copy: same. Certification fee: $2.00. Payee: Miller County Circuit Court. Personal checks accepted. No credit cards accepted. Prepayment required. Mail requests: SASE required for civil.
Civil Name Search: Access: Phone, fax, mail, in person, online. Both court and visitors may perform in person name searches. Search fee: $4.00 per name. Civil index on cards since 1976, prior on books. Civil PAT goes back to 1991. Often older judgment will be displayed. Case lookup is at https://www.courts.mo.gov/casenet/base/welcome.do. Online records go back to 11/28/2005. Online search results show full name, address, and year of birth only.

Criminal Name Search: Access: In person, online. Visitors must perform in person searches themselves. Criminal records indexed on cards since 1976, prior on books. Note: Court refers background checkers to the State Highway Patrol. Criminal PAT goes back to same as civil. Both the terminal and CaseNet only show year of birth. For common names, one must ask the Clerk for more identifiers to correctly do a search. Online access to criminal records same as civil, above.

Mississippi County

Consolidated Circuit Court PO Box 369, Charleston, MO 63834; 573-683-2146 x1; fax: 573-683-7696; 8AM-4:30PM (CST). *Felony, Misdemeanor, Civil, Small Claims, Eviction, Probate.*
www.courts.mo.gov/page.jsp?id=1643
General Information: Online identifiers in results same as on public terminal. No juvenile, mental, expunged, dismissed, or suspended imposition of sentence records released. Will fax out specific case files. Court makes copy: $1.00 1st page; $.25 each add'l page. Certification fee: $.50 per cert plus copy fee. Payee: Circuit Clerk. Personal checks accepted. No credit cards accepted. Prepayment required.
Civil Name Search: Access: In person, online. Visitors must perform in person searches themselves. Civil records in case files since 1976. Civil PAT goes back to 1979. Often older judgment will be displayed. Access to civil records is free at https://www.courts.mo.gov/casenet/base/welcome.do. Online records go back to 6/15/2001. Online search results show full name, address, and year of birth only.
Criminal Name Search: Access: In person, online. Visitors must perform in person searches themselves. Required to search: name, years to search, DOB. Criminal records in case files since 1951. Criminal PAT goes back to same as civil. Both the terminal and CaseNet only show year of birth. For common names, one must ask the Clerk for more identifiers to correctly do a search. Access to civil records is free at https://www.courts.mo.gov/casenet/base/welcome.do. Online records go back to 6/15/2001. Online search results show full name, address, and year of birth only.

Moniteau County

Circuit Court 200 E Main, California, MO 65018; 573-796-2071; fax: 573-796-2591; 8AM-N, 1-4:30PM (CST). *Felony, Civil Actions over $25,000.* www.courts.mo.gov/page.jsp?id=1631
General Information: Online identifiers in results same as on public terminal. No juvenile, mental, expunged, dismissed, or suspended imposition of sentence records released. Will not fax out up to a 5-page document. Court makes copy: $.50 per page. Self serve copy: same. Certification fee: $1.00 per doc. Payee: Moniteau County Circuit Court. Personal checks accepted. No credit cards accepted. Prepayment required.
Civil Name Search: Access: In person, online. Both court and visitors may perform in person name searches. No search fee. Required to search: name, years to search; also helpful: case number. Civil cases indexed by plaintiff only. Civil records on computer since 11/2005, prior on index cards and books. Civil PAT goes back to 11/2005. Often older judgment will be displayed. Case lookup is at https://www.courts.mo.gov/casenet/base/welcome.do. Online records go back to 11/28/2005. Online search results show full name, address, and year of birth only.
Criminal Name Search: Access: In person, online. Both court and visitors may perform in person name searches. No search fee. Required to search: name, years to search; also helpful: case number. Criminal records on computer since 11/2005, prior on index cards and books to 1845. Criminal PAT goes back to 11/2005. Both the terminal and CaseNet only show year of birth. For common names, one must ask the Clerk for more identifiers to correctly do a search. Case lookup is at https://www.courts.mo.gov/casenet/base/welcome.do. Online records go back to 11/28/2005. Online search results show full name, address, and year of birth only.
Associate Circuit Division 200 E Main, California, MO 65018; 573-796-4671; probate phone: 573-796-2814; 8AM-N, 1PM-4:30PM (CST). *Misdemeanor, Civil Actions under $25,000, Eviction, Small Claims, Probate.*
www.courts.mo.gov/page.jsp?id=1631
General Information: The court will not do probate record searches. Online identifiers in results same as on public terminal. No juvenile, mental, expunged, dismissed, or suspended imposition of sentence records released. Will not fax documents. Court makes copy: $.25 per page. Self serve copy: same. Certification fee: $1.50 for 1st page, $1.00 each add'l. Payee: Moniteau Court. Personal checks accepted. No credit cards accepted. Prepayment required.
Civil Name Search: Access: In person, online. Visitors must perform in person searches themselves. Civil index on cards since 1979, prior on index books from 1948 to 1979, archived before. Civil PAT goes back to 11/2005. Often older judgment will be displayed. Case lookup is at

https://www.courts.mo.gov/casenet/base/welcome.do. Online records go back to 11/28/2005 and includes probate. Online search results show full name, address, and year of birth only.

Criminal Name Search: Access: In person, online. Visitors must perform in person searches themselves. Criminal records indexed on cards since 1979, prior on index books from 1948 to 1979, archived before. Criminal PAT goes back to 11/2005. Both the terminal and CaseNet only show year of birth. For common names, one must ask the Clerk for more identifiers to correctly do a search. Case lookup is at https://www.courts.mo.gov/casenet/base/welcome.do. Online records go back to 11/28/2005 and includes probate. Online search results show full name, address, and year of birth only.

Monroe County

Consolidated Circuit Court 300 N Main, Ste 201, Paris, MO 65275; 660-327-5204/5220; criminal fax: 660-327-5781; civil fax: 8AM-4:30PM; 8AM-4:30PM (CST). *Felony, Misdemeanor, Civil, Small Claims, Eviction, Probate, Traffic.* www.courts.mo.gov/page.jsp?id=1582

General Information: Online identifiers in results same as on public terminal. No juvenile, mental, expunged, dismissed, or suspended imposition of sentence records released. Fee to fax out file $1.00 per page. Court makes copy: $1.00 per page. Self serve copy: $.50 per page. Certification fee: $2.00. Payee: Monroe County Circuit Court. Personal checks accepted. No credit cards accepted. Prepayment required. Mail requests: SASE required.

Civil Name Search: Access: Mail, in person, online. Both court and visitors may perform in person name searches. Search fee: $14.00 per name. Civil records on computer since 1996; index cards since 1979, prior on index books. Mail turnaround time 1 week. Public use terminal available, records go back to 7/1/05. Often older judgment will be displayed. Case lookup is at https://www.courts.mo.gov/casenet/base/welcome.do. Online records go back to 9/12/2005. Online search results show full name, address, and year of birth only.

Criminal Name Search: Access: Mail, in person, online. Both court and visitors may perform in person name searches. Search fee: $14.00 per name. Required to search: name, years to search, SSN, signed release. Criminal records on computer since 1996, on index cards from 1979 to 1990. Mail turnaround time 1 week. Public use terminal available, crim records go back to same. Both the terminal and CaseNet only show year of birth. For common names, one must ask the Clerk for more identifiers to correctly do a search. Case lookup is at https://www.courts.mo.gov/casenet/base/welcome.do. Online records go back to 9/12/2005. Online search results show full name, address, and year of birth only.

Montgomery County

Circuit Court 211 E 3rd, #301, Montgomery City, MO 63361; 573-564-3341; fax: 573-564-3914; 8AM-4:30PM (CST). *Felony, Civil Actions, Eviction, Small Claims, Probate.* www.courts.mo.gov/page.jsp?id=1593

General Information: The Circuit and Associate Circuit Court are now consolidated at this office. Online identifiers in results same as on public terminal. No juvenile, mental, expunged, dismissed, or suspended imposition of sentence records released. Will fax documents $5.00 1st page, $2.00 each add'l page. Court makes copy: $.25 per page. Self serve copy: same. Certification fee: $1.50 per doc. Payee: Montgomery County Circuit Court. No personal checks or credit cards accepted. Prepayment required.

Civil Name Search: Access: Online, in person. Visitors must perform in person searches themselves. Civil records on computer since 1987 for judgments, on index cards since 1979, prior on books to 1864. Civil PAT goes back to 1996. Results include name, action, docket entries, case number, parties. Case lookup is at https://www.courts.mo.gov/casenet/base/welcome.do. Online records go back to 7/1/1997. Online search results show full name, address, and year of birth only.

Criminal Name Search: Access: Online, in person. Visitors must perform in person searches themselves. Criminal records on computer since 1987 for judgments, on index cards since 1979, prior on books. Criminal PAT goes back to same as civil. Both the terminal and CaseNet only show year of birth. For common names, one must ask the Clerk for more identifiers to correctly do a search. Case lookup is at https://www.courts.mo.gov/casenet/base/welcome.do. Online records go back to 7/1/1997. Online search results show full name, address, and year of birth only.

Morgan County

Consolidated Circuit Court 211 E Newton, Versailles, MO 65084; 573-378-4413; criminal phone: 573-378-4060; civil phone: 573-378-4235; fax: 573-378-5356; 8AM-5PM (CST). *Felony, Civil Actions, Eviction, Small Claims, Probate.* www.courts.mo.gov/page.jsp?id=1632

General Information: Online identifiers in results same as on public terminal. No juvenile, mental, expunged, dismissed, or suspended imposition of sentence records released. Will not fax documents. Court makes copy: $.50

per page. Self serve copy: $.25 per page. Certification fee: $1.50. Payee: Circuit Court. Personal checks accepted. No credit cards accepted. Prepayment required. Copy fees may be billed. Mail requests: SASE required.

Civil Name Search: Access: Phone, mail, in person, online. Visitors must perform in person searches themselves. No search fee. Civil records on computer since 11/2005, on index cards since 1979, prior archived since mid-1800s. Civil PAT goes back to 11/2005. Often older judgment will be displayed. Case lookup is at https://www.courts.mo.gov/casenet/base/welcome.do. Online records go back to 11/28/2005. Online search results show full name, address, and year of birth only.

Criminal Name Search: Access: Phone, mail, in person, online. Visitors must perform in person searches themselves. No search fee. Criminal records on computer since 11/2005, on index cards since 1979, prior archived since mid-1800s. Mail turnaround time 1 week; phone turnaround immediate. Criminal PAT goes back to same as civil. Both the terminal and CaseNet only show year of birth. For common names, one must ask the Clerk for more identifiers to correctly do a search. Case lookup is at https://www.courts.mo.gov/casenet/base/welcome.do. Online records go back to 11/28/2005. Online search results show full name, address, and year of birth only.

New Madrid County

Consolidated Circuit Court County Courthouse, 450 Main St, New Madrid, MO 63869; 573-748-2228; fax: 573-748-5409; 8AM-4:30PM (CST). *Felony, Misdemeanor, Civil, Eviction, Small Claims, Probate.* www.courts.mo.gov/page.jsp?id=1645

General Information: Online identifiers in results same as on public terminal. No juvenile, mental, expunged, dismissed, or suspended imposition of sentence records released. Will fax out specific case files. Court makes copy: $1.00 per page. Certification fee: $5.00 per doc. Payee: Circuit Clerk. No personal checks. Major credit cards accepted. Prepayment required.

Civil Name Search: Access: In person, online. Visitors must perform in person searches themselves. Associate civil records on Cot index since 1979, Circuit and all prior on books. Civil PAT goes back to 2/2001. only year of birth shows; often older judgment will be displayed. Access to civil records is free at https://www.courts.mo.gov/casenet/base/welcome.do. Online records go back to 2/7/2001. Online search results show full name, address, and year of birth only.

Criminal Name Search: Access: In person, online. Visitors must perform in person searches themselves. Associate criminal records on Cot index since 1979, Circuit and all prior on books. Criminal PAT goes back to same as civil. Both the terminal and CaseNet only show year of birth. For common names, one must ask the Clerk for more identifiers to correctly do a search. Access to civil records is free at https://www.courts.mo.gov/casenet/base/welcome.do. Online records go back to 2/7/2001. Online search results show full name, address, and year of birth only.

Newton County

Consolidated Circuit Court PO Box 170, Criminal Div. (PO Box 130 for civil), 101 S Wood St, Courthouse, Neosho, MO 64850; 417-451-8210; criminal fax: 417-451-8272; civil fax: 8AM-5PM; 8AM-5PM (CST). *Felony, Misdemeanor, Civil, Eviction, Small Claims, Probate.* www.courts.mo.gov/page.jsp?id=1664

General Information: Probate is a separate division; probate address is 101 S Wood, #204. Probate fax- 417-451-8265 Online identifiers in results same as on public terminal. No juvenile, mental, expunged, dismissed, or suspended imposition of sentence records released. Will not fax documents. Court makes copy: $.25 per page. Certification fee: $1.00 per document plus copy fee. Payee: Newton County Circuit Clerk. Business checks accepted. No credit cards accepted. Prepayment required.

Civil Name Search: Access: In person, online. Visitors must perform in person searches themselves. Civil records on computer since 1991, microfilm since 1860, prior on index cards and books. Civil PAT goes back to 1991. Often older judgment will be displayed. Case lookup is at https://www.courts.mo.gov/casenet/base/welcome.do. Online records go back to 1/21/2004. Online search results show full name, address, and year of birth only.

Criminal Name Search: Access: In person, online. Visitors must perform in person searches themselves. Criminal records on computer since 1991, microfilm since 1860, prior on index cards and books. Criminal PAT goes back to same as civil. Both the terminal and CaseNet only show year of birth. For common names, one must ask the Clerk for more identifiers to correctly do a search. Case lookup is at https://www.courts.mo.gov/casenet/base/welcome.do. Online records go back to 1/21/2004. Online search results show full name, address, and year of birth only.

Nodaway County

Consolidated Circuit Court 305 N Main, Maryville, MO 64468; 660-582-5431; probate phone: 660-582-4221; fax: 660-582-2047; 8AM-12; 1PM-4:30PM (CST). *Felony, Misdemeanor, Civil, Eviction, Small Claims, Probate.* www.courts.mo.gov/page.jsp?id=1549

General Information: The Circuit Court and Associate Division consolidated 10/2005. Online identifiers in results same as on public terminal. No juvenile, mental, expunged, dismissed, or suspended imposition of sentence records released. Fee to fax out file $1.00 per page. Court makes copy: $.10 per page. Certification fee: $.50. Payee: Circuit Clerk. Personal checks accepted. No credit cards accepted. Prepayment required. Mail requests: SASE required.

Civil Name Search: Access: Phone, mail, in person, online. Visitors must perform in person searches themselves. No search fee. Civil records on computer back to 5/91, archived since 1845. Civil PAT goes back to 5/1991. Often older judgment will be displayed. Case lookup is at https://www.courts.mo.gov/casenet/base/welcome.do. Online records go back to 3/20/2006. Online search results show full name, address, and year of birth only.

Criminal Name Search: Access: In person, online. Visitors must perform in person searches themselves. Required to search: name, years to search, DOB. Criminal records computerized from 5/91, archived since 1845. Criminal PAT goes back to same as civil. Both the terminal and CaseNet only show year of birth. For common names, one must ask the Clerk for more identifiers to correctly do a search. Case lookup is at https://www.courts.mo.gov/casenet/base/welcome.do. Online records go back to 3/20/2006. Online search results show full name, address, and year of birth only.

Oregon County

Consolidated Circuit Court PO Box 406, Courthouse Sq, Alton, MO 65606; 417-778-7460/61; fax: 417-778-7206; 8AM-4PM (CST). *Felony, Misdemeanor, Civil, Eviction, Small Claims, Probate.* www.courts.mo.gov/page.jsp?id=1654

General Information: Online identifiers in results same as on public terminal. No juvenile, mental, expunged, dismissed, or suspended imposition of sentence records released. Will fax documents $1.00 1st page, $.50 each add'l. Court makes copy: $.25 per page. Certification fee: $2.00 per cert plus copy fee. Payee: Circuit Court. Personal checks and cash accepted. No credit cards accepted. Prepayment required.

Civil Name Search: Access: In person, online. Both court and visitors may perform in person name searches. No search fee. Civil records on books. Civil PAT goes back to 2000. Often older judgment will be displayed. Case lookup is at https://www.courts.mo.gov/casenet/base/welcome.do. Online records go back to 1991. Online search results show full name, address, and year of birth only.

Criminal Name Search: Access: In person, online. Both court and visitors may perform in person name searches. No search fee. Criminal docket on books. Note: Court will only search if not busy, and may refer you to State Highway Patrol. Criminal PAT goes back to same as civil. Both the terminal and CaseNet only show year of birth. For common names, one must ask the Clerk for more identifiers to correctly do a search. Online access to criminal same as civil, above.

Osage County

Consolidated Circuit Court PO Box 825, Linn, MO 65051; 573-897-3114; fax: 573-897-4075; 8AM-4:30PM (CST). *Felony, Misdemeanor, Civil, Eviction, Small Claims, Probate.* www.courts.mo.gov/page.jsp?id=1618

General Information: The Associate Division consolidated into the Circuit Court on 01/01/2006. Online identifiers in results same as on public terminal. No juvenile, mental, expunged, dismissed, or suspended imposition of sentence records released. Fee to fax out file $1.00 per page. Court makes copy: $.25 per page. Self serve copy: same. Certification fee: $2.00 per cert plus copy fee. Payee: Circuit Clerk. Personal checks accepted. Visa/MC/Discover accepted. Prepayment required. Mail requests: SASE required.

Civil Name Search: Access: Phone, mail, in person, online. Both court and visitors may perform in person name searches. No search fee. Civil index on cards and books. Mail turnaround time ASAP. Civil PAT goes back to 1992, some to 2000. Often older judgment will be displayed. Probate is on terminal back to 2000. Case lookup is at https://www.courts.mo.gov/casenet/base/welcome.do. Online civil records go back to 9/01/2000.

Criminal Name Search: Access: Phone, mail, fax, in person, online. Both court and visitors may perform in person name searches. No search fee. Required to search: name, years to search, DOB; also helpful: SSN. Criminal records indexed on cards and books, computerized since 1992. Mail turnaround time ASAP. Criminal PAT goes back to same as civil. Both the terminal and CaseNet only show year of birth. For common names,

one must ask the Clerk for more identifiers to correctly do a search. Online access to criminal same as civil, above. Online criminal records go back to 8/28/1992. Online results show middle initial, DOB.

Ozark County

Consolidated Circuit Court PO Box 869, Gainesville, MO 65655; 417-679-4232; fax: 417-679-4554; 8AM-N, 12:30-4:30PM (CST). *Felony, Misdemeanor, Civil, Eviction, Small Claims, Probate.* www.courts.mo.gov/page.jsp?id=1679

General Information: Online identifiers in results same as on public terminal. No juvenile, mental, expunged, dismissed, or suspended imposition of sentence records released. Will fax documents $.50 per page. Court makes copy: $1.00 per page. Certification fee: $1.50. Payee: Ozark County Circuit Court. Personal checks accepted. No credit cards accepted. Prepayment required.

Civil Name Search: Access: Mail, in person, online. Both court and visitors may perform in person name searches. No search fee. Civil index on cards since 1979, archived since 1933. Civil PAT goes back to 2/2006. The terminal is in the recorder's office and connects to CaseNet. Case lookup is at https://www.courts.mo.gov/casenet/base/welcome.do. Online records go back to 2/20/2006. Online search results show full name, address, and sometimes year of birth.

Criminal Name Search: Access: In person, online. Both court and visitors may perform in person name searches. No search fee. Required to search: name, years to search, DOB. Criminal records indexed on cards since 1979, archived since 1933. Criminal PAT goes back to 2/2006. The terminal is in the recorder's office and connects to CaseNet, will show year of birth. Case lookup is at https://www.courts.mo.gov/casenet/base/welcome.do. Online records go back to 2/20/2006. Online search results show full name, address, and year of birth only.

Pemiscot County

Circuit Court 610 Ward St - County Courthouse, PO Box 34, Caruthersville, MO 63830; 573-333-0187; fax: 573-333-1272; 8AM-4:30PM (CST). *Felony, Civil Actions over $25,000.* www.courts.mo.gov/page.jsp?id=1646

General Information: Online identifiers in results same as on public terminal. No juvenile, mental, expunged, dismissed, or suspended imposition of sentence records released. Will not fax documents. Court makes copy: $.50 per page. No certification fee . Payee: Pemiscot County Circuit Clerk. No personal checks or credit cards accepted. Prepayment required.

Civil Name Search: Access: In person, online. Visitors must perform in person searches themselves. Civil index on cards since 1979, prior on books. Civil PAT goes back to 1/7/2001. Often older judgment will be displayed. Case lookup is at https://www.courts.mo.gov/casenet/base/welcome.do. Online records go back to 2/7/2001. Online search results show full name, address, and year of birth only.

Criminal Name Search: Access: In person, online. Visitors must perform in person searches themselves. Criminal records indexed on cards since 1979, prior on books. Criminal PAT goes back to same as civil. Both the terminal and CaseNet only show year of birth. For common names, one must ask the Clerk for more identifiers to correctly do a search. Case lookup is at https://www.courts.mo.gov/casenet/base/welcome.do. Online records go back to 2/7/2001. Online search results show full name, address, and year of birth only.

Associate Circuit Division PO Drawer 228, 800 Ward Ave, County Courthouse, Caruthersville, MO 63830; 573-333-2784; fax: 573-333-4722; 8AM-4:30PM (CST). *Misdemeanor, Civil Actions under $45,000, Eviction, Small Claims, Probate.* www.courts.mo.gov/page.jsp?id=1646

General Information: No juvenile, mental, expunged, dismissed, or suspended imposition of sentence records released. Will fax documents to local or toll-free number. Court makes copy: $1.00 per page. No certification fee . Payee: Pemiscot County Clerk. Only cashiers checks and money orders accepted. No credit cards accepted. Prepayment required.

Civil Name Search: Access: In person, fax, online. Only the court performs in person name searches; visitors may not. Civil records on computer back to 2001, index cards since 1979, prior on books. Case lookup is at https://www.courts.mo.gov/casenet/base/welcome.do. Online records go back to 2/14/2001. Online search results show full name, address, and year of birth only.

Criminal Name Search: Access: In person, online. Only the court performs in person name searches; visitors may not. Criminal records on computer since 5/90, on index cards from 1979-1990, prior on books. Both the terminal and CaseNet only show year of birth. For common names, one must ask the Clerk for more identifiers to correctly do a search. Case lookup is at https://www.courts.mo.gov/casenet/base/welcome.do. Online records go back to 2/14/2001. Online search results show full name, address, and year of birth only.

Perry County

Consolidated Circuit Court 15 W Saint Maries St #2, Perryville, MO 63775-1399; 573-547-6581; criminal phone: x5; civil phone: x3; probate phone: x7; fax: 573-547-9323; 8AM-5PM (CST). *Felony, Misdemeanor, Civil, Eviction, Small Claims, Probate.*
www.courts.mo.gov/page.jsp?id=1642
General Information: The Associate Division consolidated into the Circuit Court on 07/01/2003. Online identifiers in results same as on public terminal. No juvenile, mental, paternity (except final judgment), expunged, dismissed, or suspended imposition of sentence records released. Will fax documents $1.00 per page. Court makes copy: $1.00 per page. Certification fee: $1.00 per cert plus copy fee. Payee: Perry County Circuit Clerk. Personal checks accepted. No credit cards accepted. Prepayment required.
Civil Name Search: Access: In person, online. Visitors must perform in person searches themselves. Civil records on computer since 1994, prior on index cards. Civil PAT goes back to 1994. Often older judgment will be displayed. Access to civil records is free at https://www.courts.mo.gov/casenet/base/welcome.do. Online civil records go back to 7/1/2001.
Criminal Name Search: Access: In person, online. Both court and visitors may perform in person name searches. No search fee. Criminal records on computer since 1993, prior on index cards. Criminal PAT goes back to same as civil. Both the terminal and CaseNet only show year of birth. For common names, one must ask the Clerk for more identifiers to correctly do a search. Online access to criminal same as civil, above, criminal case records go back to 1993.

Pettis County

Circuit Court - Civil 415 S Ohio, Sedalia, MO 65301; 660-826-5000 x926; probate phone: x924; fax: 660-826-4520; 8AM-5PM (CST). *Civil Actions, Eviction, Small Claims, Probate.*
www.courts.mo.gov/page.jsp?id=1615
General Information: Online identifiers in results same as on public terminal. No juvenile, mental, expunged, dismissed, or suspended imposition of sentence records released. Will fax documents $2.50 1st page, $1.50 each add'l. Court makes copy: $1.00 1st page, $.50 each add'l. Certification fee: $1.50 plus copy fee. Payee: Pettis County Circuit Clerk. Personal checks accepted. No credit cards accepted. Prepayment required. Mail requests: SASE required.
Civil Name Search: Access: Phone, fax, mail, in person, online. Both court and visitors may perform in person name searches. No search fee. Civil index on docket books since 9/75, prior on judgment books. Mail turnaround time 1-2 days. Public use terminal has civil records back to 4/2001; judgments back to 1991. Often older judgment will be displayed. Access to civil records is free at https://www.courts.mo.gov/casenet/base/welcome.do back to 4/1/2001. Online search results show full name, address, and year of birth only.

Circuit Court - Criminal 415 S Ohio, Sedalia, MO 65301; 660-826-5000 x924; fax: 660-827-8613; 7:30AM-5PM (CST). *Felony, Misdemeanor, Traffic.*
www.courts.mo.gov/page.jsp?id=1615
General Information: Online identifiers in results same as on public terminal. No juvenile, mental, expunged, dismissed, or suspended imposition of sentence records released. Will fax documents for free. Court makes copy: $1.00 1st page; $.50 each add'l. Certification fee: $1.50 per page plus copy fee. Payee: Circuit Clerk. Only cashiers checks and money orders accepted. No credit cards accepted. Prepayment required. Mail requests: SASE required.
Criminal Name Search: Access: Phone, fax, mail, in person, online. Both court and visitors may perform in person name searches. No search fee. Required to search: name, years to search, DOB, SSN; on some cases: signed release. Criminal records computerized from 1993, on index cards from 1975-1993, prior on judgment books. Mail turnaround time 1-2 weeks. Public use terminal has crim records back to 1995. Both the terminal and CaseNet only show year of birth. For common names, one must ask the Clerk for more identifiers to correctly do a search. Access to criminal records is free at https://www.courts.mo.gov/casenet/base/welcome.do back to 1/1992. Online search results show full name, address, and year of birth only. Online access to probate records is free at www.16thcircuit.org/publicaccess.asp. This includes private process servers, jury verdicts, criminal traffic, and criminal sureties.
Probate Court 415 S. Ohio St, Sedalia, MO 65301; 660-826-5000 x470; fax: 660-827-8613; 8AM-5PM (CST). *Probate.* www.courts.mo.gov
General Information: Access to probate records is available free at https://www.courts.mo.gov/casenet.

Phelps County

Consolidated Circuit Court 200 N Main St, Ste 201, Rolla, MO 65401; 573-458-6210; criminal phone: 573-458-6202; civil phone: 573-458-6204; probate phone: 573-458-6245; fax: 573-458-6224; 8AM-5PM (CST). *Felony, Misdemeanor, Civil, Small Claims, Eviction, Probate.*
www.courts.mo.gov/page.jsp?id=4755
General Information: Probate fax- 573-458-6235 Online identifiers in results same as on public terminal. No juvenile, mental, expunged or dismissed records released. Will fax documents $1.00 per page. Court makes copy: $.25 per page. Self serve copy: same. Certification fee: $1.00 per page does include copies. Payee: Circuit Clerk. Personal checks accepted. No credit cards accepted. Prepayment required. Mail requests: SASE required for mail return of any copies.
Civil Name Search: Access: In person, online. Visitors must perform in person searches themselves. Civil records on computer since 1992; prior on books to 1957. Civil PAT goes back to 1992. Often older judgment will be displayed. Case lookup is at https://www.courts.mo.gov/casenet/base/welcome.do. Online records go back to 1/22/2007. Online search results show full name, address, and year of birth only.
Criminal Name Search: Access: In person, online. Visitors must perform in person searches themselves. Required to search: names, years to search. Criminal records computerized since 1991, prior indexed on books to 1957. Criminal PAT goes back to same as civil. Both the terminal and CaseNet only show year of birth. For common names, one must ask the Clerk for more identifiers to correctly do a search. Case lookup is at https://www.courts.mo.gov/casenet/base/welcome.do. Online records go back to 1/22/2007. Online search results show full name, address, and year of birth only.

Pike County

Consolidated Circuit Court 115 W Main, Bowling Green, MO 63334; 573-324-3112; fax: 573-324-3150; 8AM-4:30PM (CST). *Felony, Misdemeanor, Civil, Small Claims, Eviction, Probate, Traffic.*
www.courts.mo.gov/page.jsp?id=1683
General Information: This court consolidated with the Associate Court in June 2006. Online identifiers in results same as on public terminal. No juvenile, mental, expunged, dismissed, or suspended imposition of sentence records released. Will not fax out documents. Court makes copy: $.50 per page. Self serve copy: same. Certification fee: $1.00 per doc. Payee: Pike County Circuit Clerk. Personal checks accepted. No credit cards accepted. Prepayment required. Mail requests: SASE required for civil.
Civil Name Search: Access: Mail, in person, online. Visitors must perform in person searches themselves. No search fee. Required to search: name, years to search; also helpful: address. Civil index on cards since 1977, prior on books; Associate court records indexed on cards since 1979, archived since 1819. Note: Court will help with simple searches only, will not do judgments of lien searches. Civil PAT goes back to 1992. Often older judgment will be displayed. Case lookup is at https://www.courts.mo.gov/casenet/base/welcome.do. Online records go back 4/2002. Online search results show full name, address, and year of birth only.
Criminal Name Search: Access: In person, online. Visitors must perform in person searches themselves. Required to search: name, years to search; also helpful: DOB. Criminal records indexed on cards since 1977, prior on books; Associate court records indexed on cards since 1979, archived since 1819. Note: Criminal searches should be directed to the MO Highway Patrol. Criminal PAT goes back to same as civil. Both the terminal and CaseNet only show year of birth. For common names, one must ask the Clerk for more identifiers to correctly do a search. Online access to criminal same as civil, above.

Platte County

Consolidated Circuit Court 415 Third St #5, Platte City, MO 64079; 816-858-2232; fax: 816-858-3392; 8AM-5PM (CST). *Felony, Misdemeanor, Civil, Eviction, Small Claims.*
www.courts.mo.gov/page.jsp?id=1567
General Information: Associate court consolidated with Circuit court in 2006. Online identifiers in results same as on public terminal. No juvenile, mental, expunged, dismissed, or suspended imposition of sentence records released. Will not fax documents. Court makes copy: $.25 per page. Certification fee: $1.00. Payee: Platte County Circuit Clerk. Only cashiers checks and money orders accepted. No credit cards accepted. Prepayment required.
Civil Name Search: Access: Online, in person. Visitors must perform in person searches themselves. Civil records on computer since 10/91. Civil PAT goes back to 10/1991. Often older judgment will be displayed. Case lookup is at https://www.courts.mo.gov/casenet/base/welcome.do. Cases go back to 10/1/1991. Online search results show full name, address, and year of birth only.

Criminal Name Search: Access: Online, in person. Visitors must perform in person searches themselves. Required to search: name, years to search, DOB; also helpful: SSN. Criminal records on computer since 10/91. Criminal PAT goes back to 10/1991. Both the terminal and CaseNet only show year of birth. For common names, one must ask the Clerk for more identifiers to correctly do a search. Case lookup is at https://www.courts.mo.gov/casenet/base/welcome.do. Cases go back to 10/1/1991. Online search results show full name, address, and year of birth only.

Probate Court 415 Third St, #95, Platte City, MO 64079; 816-858-3438; probate phone: 816-858-3440; fax: 816-858-3392; 8AM-5PM (CST). *Probate.*

General Information: Can search by name or case number at https://www.courts.mo.gov/casenet. Cases go back to 1/1/1991.

Polk County

Consolidated Circuit Court 102 E Broadway, Rm 14, Bolivar, MO 65613; 417-326-4912; fax: 417-326-4194; 8AM-5PM (CST). *Felony, Misdemeanor, Civil, Eviction, Small Claims, Probate.* www.positech.net/~dcourt/

General Information: The Circuit Court and Associate Division consolidated as of 01/03. Online identifiers in results same as on public terminal. No juvenile, mental, expunged, dismissed, or suspended imposition of sentence records released. Will fax documents to local or toll-free number. Court makes copy: $.25 per page. Self serve copy: $.10 per page. Certification fee: $2.00 per cert. Payee: Circuit Clerk. Personal checks accepted. No credit cards accepted. Prepayment required. Mail requests: SASE required for mail return of any copies.

Civil Name Search: Access: In person, online. Visitors must perform in person searches themselves. Civil records on computer since 1991, prior on card index since 1979. Civil PAT goes back to 2001. Often older judgment will be displayed. Case lookup is at https://www.courts.mo.gov/casenet/base/welcome.do. Online records go back to 11/13/2001. Online search results show full name, address, and year of birth only.

Criminal Name Search: Access: In person, online. Visitors must perform in person searches themselves. Criminal records on computer since 1991, prior on card index since 1979. Criminal PAT goes back to same as civil. Both the terminal and CaseNet only show year of birth. For common names, one must ask the Clerk for more identifiers to correctly do a search. Case lookup is at https://www.courts.mo.gov/casenet/base/welcome.do. Online records go back to 11/13/2001. Online search results show full name, address, and year of birth only.

Pulaski County

Consolidated Circuit Court 301 Historic Rt 66 E, #202, Waynesville, MO 65583; 573-774-4755; probate phone: 573-774-4784; fax: 573-774-6967; 8AM-4:30PM (CST). *Felony, Misdemeanor, Civil, Eviction, Small Claims.* www.courts.mo.gov/page.jsp?id=4756

General Information: Online identifiers in results same as on public terminal. No juvenile, mental, paternity, expunged, dismissed, or suspended imposition of sentence records released. Will fax specific case files for $2.00 per 5 pages. Court makes copy: $.25 per page. Certification fee: $2.00 per cert plus copy fee. Payee: Circuit Clerk. No personal or business checks accepted. Prepayment required.

Civil Name Search: Access: In person, online. Visitors must perform in person searches themselves. Required to search: name, years to search; also helpful: address. Civil records on computer since 1990, prior on books since 1903. Civil PAT goes back to 1991. Often older judgment will be displayed. Case lookup is at https://www.courts.mo.gov/casenet/base/welcome.do. Online records go back to 1/22/2007 Online search results show full name, address, and year of birth only.

Criminal Name Search: Access: In person, online. Visitors must perform in person searches themselves. Required to search: name, years to search; also helpful: DOB, SSN. Criminal records on computer since 1991, prior on books since 1903. Criminal PAT goes back to same as civil. Both the terminal and CaseNet only show year of birth. For common names, one must ask the Clerk for more identifiers to correctly do a search. Participates in the free state online court record system at www.courts.mo.gov/casenet/base/welcome.do. Online records go back to 1/22/2007

Probate Court 301 Historic 66 East, #316, Waynesville, MO 65583; 573-774-4784; fax: 573-774-6673; 8AM-4:30PM (CST). *Probate.*

General Information: Participates in the free state online court record system at https://www.courts.mo.gov/casenet.

Putnam County

Circuit Court Courthouse Rm 204, Unionville, MO 63565; 660-947-2071; fax: 660-947-2320; 8AM-N; 1-5PM (CST). *Felony, Civil , Eviction, Small Claims, Probate.* www.courts.mo.gov/page.jsp?id=1541

General Information: This is now a consolidated court. The Associate Court merged with the Circuit Court in December 2009. Records are combined. The direct phone to Division 2 (formerly Associate Court) is 660-947-2117. Online identifiers in results same as on public terminal. No juvenile, mental, expunged, dismissed, or suspended imposition of sentence records released. Will fax documents $1.00 1st page; $50 each add'l; plus copy fee. Court makes copy: $.25 per page. Self serve copy: same. Certification fee: $1.00. Payee: Circuit Clerk. Business checks accepted. No credit cards accepted. Prepayment required. Mail requests: SASE required for civil.

Civil Name Search: Access: Mail, in person, online. Both court and visitors may perform in person name searches. No search fee. Civil index on cards since 1848; on computer since 3/00. Mail turnaround time same day. Civil PAT goes back to 1990. Often older judgment will be displayed. Case lookup is at https://www.courts.mo.gov/casenet/base/welcome.do. Online records go back to 3/29/2000. Online search results show full name, address, and year of birth only.

Criminal Name Search: Access: In person, online. Visitors must perform in person searches themselves. Criminal records indexed on cards since 1848; on computer since 3/00. Note: No criminal histories are researched by court staff. Requesters referred to the State Hwy Patrol. Criminal PAT goes back to same as civil. Both the terminal and CaseNet only show year of birth. For common names, one must ask the Clerk for more identifiers to correctly do a search. Online access to criminal records same as civil, above.

Ralls County

Consolidated Circuit Court PO Box 466, New London, MO 63459; criminal phone: 573-985-5641; civil phone: 573-985-5633; fax: 573-985-3446; 8AM-N, 1-4:30PM (CST). *Felony, Misdemeanor, Civil, Eviction, Small Claims, Probate.* www.courts.mo.gov/page.jsp?id=1585

General Information: The Associate Division consolidated into this court on 08/01/2005. Online identifiers in results same as on public terminal. No juvenile, mental, expunged, dismissed, or suspended imposition of sentence records released. Court makes copy: $.25 per page. Self serve copy: same. Certification fee: $1.00. Payee: Ralls County Circuit Court. In-state personal checks accepted. No credit cards accepted. Prepayment required. Mail requests: SASE required for civil.

Civil Name Search: Access: Mail, in person, online. Both court and visitors may perform in person name searches. No search fee. Required to search: name, years to search, DOB, SSN and signed release. Civil index on cards since 1976, prior on books. Mail turnaround time varies. Civil PAT goes back to 1990. Often older judgment will be displayed. Case lookup is at https://www.courts.mo.gov/casenet/base/welcome.do. Online records go back to 9/12/2005. Online search results show full name, address, and year of birth only.

Criminal Name Search: Access: In person, online. Visitors must perform in person searches themselves. Required to search: name, years to search, signed release and SSN. Criminal records indexed on cards 1976 to 9/12/05, now online, prior on books. Criminal PAT goes back to 9/12/2005. Both the terminal and CaseNet only show year of birth. For common names, one must ask the Clerk for more identifiers to correctly do a search. Case lookup is at https://www.courts.mo.gov/casenet/base/welcome.do. Online records go back to 9/12/2005. Online search results show full name, address, and year of birth only.

Randolph County

Consolidated Circuit Court 372 Highway JJ Ste A, Huntsville, MO 65259; 660-277-4601; fax: 660-277-4636; 8AM-4:30PM (CST). *Felony, Misdemeanor, Civil, Eviction, Small Claims, Probate.* www.courts.mo.gov/page.jsp?id=1600

General Information: Court formerly located in Moberly. Online identifiers in results same as on public terminal. No juvenile, mental, expunged, dismissed, or suspended imposition of sentence records released. Will fax out document $4.00 per page. Court makes copy: $.25 per page. Certification fee: $1.50 per page. Payee: Randolph County Circuit Clerk. No personal checks or credit cards accepted. Prepayment required. Mail requests: SASE required.

Civil Name Search: Access: Fax, mail, in person, online. Both court and visitors may perform in person name searches. No search fee. Required to search: name, years to search, address. On index since 1975, prior on record books. Mail turnaround time 1 week. Public use terminal available. Often older judgment will be displayed. Participates in the free court record system at https://www.courts.mo.gov/casenet/base/welcome.do.

Online civil records go back to 10/31/2001. Online search results show full name, address, and year of birth only.

Criminal Name Search: Access: Fax, mail, in person, online. Both court and visitors may perform in person name searches. No search fee. Required to search: name, years to search, address, DOB; also helpful- SSN. Criminal records computerized from 1994, prior on index books. Mail turnaround time 1 week. Public use terminal available. Both the terminal and CaseNet only show year of birth. For common names, one must ask the Clerk for more identifiers to correctly do a search. Participates in the free court record system at www.courts.mo.gov/casenet/base/welcome.do. Online criminal records go back to 5/1/1994.

Ray County

Consolidated Circuit Court PO Box 594, 100 E Main, Richmond, MO 64085; 816-776-3377; fax: 816-776-6016; 8AM-4PM (CST). *Felony, Misdemeanor, Civil, Eviction, Small Claims, Probate.*
www.courts.mo.gov/page.jsp?id=1569
General Information: The Associate Division consolidated into this court on 01/01/2006. Online identifiers in results same as on public terminal. No juvenile, mental, expunged, dismissed, or suspended imposition of sentence records released. Fee to fax out file $1.00 per page. Court makes copy: $.25 per page. Certification fee: $1.50 per cert plus copy fee. Payee: Ray County Circuit Clerk. Business checks accepted. No credit cards accepted. Prepayment required. Mail requests: SASE required for civil.
Civil Name Search: Access: Phone, fax, mail, in person, online. Both court and visitors may perform in person name searches. No search fee. Civil index on cards since 1977, prior on judgment books. Probate records are in a separate index. Mail turnaround time 2-4 weeks. Civil PAT goes back to 12/2001. Often older judgment will be displayed. Case lookup is at https://www.courts.mo.gov/casenet/base/welcome.do. Online records go back to 2001. Online search results show full name, address, and year of birth only.
Criminal Name Search: Access: In person, online. Both court and visitors may perform in person name searches. No search fee. Required to search: name, years to search; also helpful: DOB, SSN. Criminal records indexed on cards since 1977, prior on judgment books. Note: The court refers criminal record search requesters to contact the MO Highway Patrol, 573-751-3313. Criminal PAT goes back to same as civil. Both the terminal and CaseNet only show year of birth. For common names, one must ask the Clerk for more identifiers to correctly do a search. Online access to criminal records same as civil, above.

Reynolds County

Circuit Court PO Box 39, Centerville, MO 63633; 573-648-2494 x34; fax: 573-648-1002; 8AM-4PM (CST). *Felony, Civil, Eviction, Small Claims, Probate.*
www.courts.mo.gov/page.jsp?id=1671
General Information: The Associate Circuit Court consolidated with Circuit Court. Online identifiers in results same as on public terminal. No juvenile, mental, expunged, dismissed, or suspended imposition of sentence records released. Fee to fax out file $2.00 each plus $1.00 per page. Court makes copy: $2.00 per doc. Self serve copy: $.50 per page. Certification fee: $2.00 per document. Payee: Randy L Cowin. Personal checks not accepted, money orders preferred. Prepayment required. Mail requests: SASE required.
Civil Name Search: Access: Phone, mail, in person, online. Both court and visitors may perform in person name searches. Search fee: $10.00. Civil records on cards and books, archived since 1872. Mail turnaround time 2 days. Civil PAT goes back to 2001. Often older judgment will be displayed. Case lookup is at https://www.courts.mo.gov/casenet/base/welcome.do. Online records go back to 4/9/2001. Online search results show full name, address, and year of birth only.
Criminal Name Search: Access: Phone, mail, in person, online. Both court and visitors may perform in person name searches. Search fee: $10.00. Required to search: name, years to search, DOB; also helpful: SSN, sex, signed release. Criminal records on cards and books, archived since 1872. Mail turnaround time 2 days. Criminal PAT goes back to same as civil. Both the terminal and CaseNet only show year of birth. Case lookup is at https://www.courts.mo.gov/casenet/base/welcome.do. Online records go back to 4/9/2001. Online search results show full name, address, and year of birth only.

Ripley County

Consolidated Circuit Court 100 Courthouse Sq, Doniphan, MO 63935; 573-996-2818, 573-996-2013; probate phone: 573-996-2013; fax: 573-996-5014; 7AM-4PM (CST). *Felony, Misdemeanor, Civil, Eviction, Small Claims, Probate.*
www.courts.mo.gov/page.jsp?id=1651
General Information: This court consolidated on 12/1/2004. 2nd fax number is 573-996-5014. Probate is a separate index at this same address. Online identifiers in results same as on public terminal. No juvenile,

mental, expunged, dismissed, or suspended imposition of sentence records released. Will not fax documents. Court makes copy: $.25 per page; probate is $1.00 per doc. Self serve copy: same. Certification fee: $1.50 if done by in-person searcher. Payee: Circuit Clerk. Personal checks accepted. No credit cards accepted. Prepayment required.
Civil Name Search: Access: In person, online. Both court and visitors may perform in person name searches. Civil records on cards and books since 1976, archived since 1850s. Civil PAT goes back to 1979. Often older judgment will be displayed. Case lookup is at https://www.courts.mo.gov/casenet/base/welcome.do. Online records go back to 9/26/05. Online search results show full name, address, and year of birth only.
Criminal Name Search: Access: In person, online. Visitors must perform in person searches themselves. Required to search: name, years to search, DOB. Criminal records on cards and books since 1976, archived since 1850s. Criminal PAT goes back to 2005. Both the terminal and CaseNet only show year of birth. For common names, one must ask the Clerk for more identifiers to correctly do a search. Case lookup is at https://www.courts.mo.gov/casenet/base/welcome.do. Online records go back to 9/26/05. Online search results show full name, address, and year of birth only.

Saline County

Circuit Court PO Box 670, 19 E Arrow, Rm 205, Marshall, MO 65340; 660-886-2300; fax: 660-831-5360; 8AM-4:30PM (CST). *Felony, Civil Actions over $25,000.* www.courts.mo.gov/page.jsp?id=1607
General Information: Online identifiers in results same as on public terminal. No juvenile, mental, expunged, dismissed, or suspended imposition of sentence records released. Will fax documents $1.00 per page. Court makes copy: $.25 per page. Self serve copy: same. Certification fee: $2.50 per cert plus copy fee. Payee: Saline County Circuit Court. Personal checks accepted. No credit cards accepted. Prepayment required.
Civil Name Search: Access: Mail, in person, online. Visitors must perform in person searches themselves. No search fee. Civil index on cards since 1974, prior on books since 1820. Civil PAT goes back to 1985. Often older judgment will be displayed. Search free on state online court record system at https://www.courts.mo.gov/casenet/base/welcome.do. Online records go back to 4/2002. Online search results show full name, address, and year of birth only.
Criminal Name Search: Access: In person, online. Visitors must perform in person searches themselves. Criminal records indexed on cards since 1974, prior on books since 1820. Criminal PAT goes back to same as civil. Both the terminal and CaseNet only show year of birth. For common names, one must ask the Clerk for more identifiers to correctly do a search. Search free on state online court record system at https://www.courts.mo.gov/casenet/base/welcome.do. Online records go back to 4/2002. Online search results show full name, address, and year of birth only.
Associate Circuit Division PO Box 670, Marshall, MO 65340; 660-886-6988; probate phone: 660-886-8808; fax: 660-886-2919; 8AM-4:30PM (CST). *Misdemeanor, Civil Actions under $25,000, Eviction, Small Claims.*
www.courts.mo.gov/page.jsp?id=1607
General Information: Also known as Circuit Division 6. Is part of the 15th Judicial Circuit. No juvenile, mental, expunged, dismissed, or suspended imposition of sentence records released. Will fax documents, no fax copy. Court makes copy: none. No certification fee . Mail requests: SASE required.
Civil Name Search: Access: Phone, mail, in person, online. Only the court performs in person name searches; visitors may not. No search fee. Civil index on cards since 1979, prior on books. Mail turnaround time 1-2 days. Case lookup is at https://www.courts.mo.gov/casenet/base/welcome.do. Online records go back to 4/1/2002. Online search results show full name, address, and year of birth only.
Criminal Name Search: Access: Phone, mail, in person, online. Only the court performs in person name searches; visitors may not. No search fee. Criminal records on computer since 1993, prior on cards and books. Mail turnaround time 1-2 days. Both the terminal and CaseNet only show year of birth. For common names, one must ask the Clerk for more identifiers to correctly do a search. Case lookup is at https://www.courts.mo.gov/casenet/base/welcome.do. Online records go back to 4/1/2002. Online search results show full name, address, and year of birth only.

Schuyler County

Circuit Court PO Box 417, Lancaster, MO 63548; 660-457-3784; fax: 660-457-3016; 8AM-4PM (CST). *Felony, Civil Actions, Eviction, Small Claims, Probate.* www.courts.mo.gov/page.jsp?id=1521
General Information: Misdemeanor and probate phone is 660-457-3755. This court consolidated the Associate Court with the Circuit Court. Online identifiers in results same as on public terminal. No juvenile, mental,

expunged, dismissed, or suspended imposition of sentence records released. Will fax documents $2.00 plus $1.00 per page. Court makes copy: $1.00 per page. Self serve copy: same. Certification fee: $1.00. Payee: Schuyler County Circuit Clerk. Personal checks accepted. No credit cards accepted. Prepayment required. Mail requests: SASE required.

Civil Name Search: Access: Mail, in person, online. Both court and visitors may perform in person name searches. Search fee: $5.00 per name. Civil index computerized back to 2001, on cards & books. Mail turnaround time 1-2 days. Civil PAT goes back to 9/19/01. Often older judgment will be displayed. Case lookup is at https://www.courts.mo.gov/casenet/base/welcome.do. Online records go back to 9/19/01. Online search results show full name, address, and year of birth only.

Criminal Name Search: Access: Mail, in person, online. Both court and visitors may perform in person name searches. Search fee: $5.00 per name. Criminal computerized back to 2001, records indexed on cards & books. Note: Phone request callers are referred to the MO Highway Patrol. Mail turnaround time 4 days. Criminal PAT goes back to same as civil. Both the terminal and CaseNet only show year of birth. For common names, one must ask the Clerk for more identifiers to correctly do a search. Online access to criminal same as civil, above.

Scotland County

Consolidated Circuit Court Courthouse, Rm 200, 117 S Market, Memphis, MO 63555; 660-465-2404, 660-465-8605; probate phone: 660-465-2404; fax: 660-465-8673; 8AM-4PM (CST). *Felony, Misdemeanor, Civil, Eviction, Small Claims, Probate.* www.courts.mo.gov/page.jsp?id=1527

General Information: Circuit Court consolidated with Associate Court 1/2007. Online identifiers in results same as on public terminal. No juvenile, mental, expunged, dismissed, or suspended imposition of sentence records released. Fee to fax out file $1.00 per page, prepaid. Court makes copy: $.25 per page. Self serve copy: same. Certification fee: $1.50 plus $.25 per page; $1.00 per page for Probate certified copies. Payee: Scotland County Circuit Clerk. Personal checks accepted. No credit cards accepted. Prepayment required. Mail requests: SASE required.

Civil Name Search: Access: Mail, fax, in person, online. Both court and visitors may perform in person name searches. No search fee. Civil records on computer since 2001, prior civil back to 1947 on cards and books to 1841, probate back to 1841. Mail turnaround time 2-7 days. Civil PAT goes back to 2001. Public terminal located in main Circuit Court Clerk office. Case lookup is at https://www.courts.mo.gov/casenet/base/welcome.do. Online records go back to 09/19/01. Online search results show full name, address, and year of birth only.

Criminal Name Search: Access: Mail, fax, in person, online. Both court and visitors may perform in person name searches. No search fee. Criminal records on computer since 2001, prior on cards and books to 1847. Mail turnaround time ASAP . Criminal PAT goes back to same as civil. Both the terminal and CaseNet only show year of birth. For common names, one must ask the Clerk for more identifiers to correctly do a search. Case lookup is at https://www.courts.mo.gov/casenet/base/welcome.do. Online records go back to 09/19/01. Online search results show full name, address, and year of birth only.

Scott County

Consolidated Circuit Court PO Box 587, 131 S Winchester, Benton, MO 63736; 573-545-3596; criminal phone: 573-545-3576; civil phone: 573-545-3596- Assoc Ct; probate phone: 573-545-3511; criminal fax: 573-545-3597; civil fax: 8AM--4:30PM; 8AM--4:30PM (CST). *Felony, Misdemeanor, Civil, Eviction, Small Claims, Probate.* www.scottcountymo.com/circuitclerk.html

General Information: The Associate, Probate, and the Circuit Court were consolidated 1/2007. Online identifiers in results same as on public terminal. No juvenile, mental, expunged, dismissed, or suspended imposition of sentence records released. Will fax out documents but only if small number of pages. Court makes copy: $1.00 first page, $.25 each add'l (Probate- $.50 each add'l). Certification fee: Certification including in copy fee. Payee: Clerk of Court. Personal checks accepted. Major credit cards accepted, 5% surcharge. Prepayment required.

Civil Name Search: Access: In person, online. Visitors must perform in person searches themselves. Civil records on computer back to 1980, prior on index cards and books. Note: Copies of domestic judgments are $3.00, if with parenting plan or separation agreement then $5.00. Civil PAT goes back to 1980. Often older judgment will be displayed. Access to civil records is free at https://www.courts.mo.gov/casenet/base/welcome.do. Online records go back to 6/15/2001. Online search results show full name, address, and year of birth only.

Criminal Name Search: Access: In person, online. Visitors must perform in person searches themselves. Required to search: name, years to

search, DOB. Criminal records on computer since 1980, prior on index cards and books. Note: The court refers criminal record searches to the MO State Highway Patrol. Criminal PAT goes back to 1980. Both the terminal and CaseNet only show year of birth. Access to criminal records is free at https://www.courts.mo.gov/casenet/base/welcome.do. Online records go back to 6/15/2001.

Shannon County

Consolidated Circuit Court PO Box 148, Courthouse, South Side Entrance, Eminence, MO 65466; 573-226-3315; fax: 573-226-5321; 8AM-4:30PM (CST). *Felony, Misdemeanor, Civil, Eviction, Small Claims, Probate.* www.courts.mo.gov/page.jsp?id=1655

General Information: The Associate Division consolidated with this court on 08/01/2005. Online identifiers in results same as on public terminal. No juvenile, mental, expunged, dismissed, or suspended imposition of sentence records released. Fee to fax out file $2.00 per page. Court makes copy: $.25 per page. Certification fee: $2.00 per cert plus copy fee. Payee: Shannon County Circuit Clerk. Personal checks accepted. No credit cards accepted. Prepayment required. Mail requests: SASE required.

Civil Name Search: Access: Mail, in person, online. Both court and visitors may perform in person name searches. No search fee. Civil index on cards and books. Record index on computer back to 1980. Note: Also, visitors may perform in person probate records searches themselves. Mail turnaround time 1 week. Civil PAT goes back to 4/2000. Often older judgment will be displayed. Case lookup is at https://www.courts.mo.gov/casenet/base/welcome.do. Online records go back to 1992. Online search results show full name, address, and year of birth only.

Criminal Name Search: Access: Mail, in person, online. Both court and visitors may perform in person name searches. No search fee. Required to search: name, years to search, offense. Criminal records indexed on cards and books. Record index on computer back to 1980. Mail turnaround time 1 week. Criminal PAT goes back to same as civil. Both the terminal and CaseNet only show year of birth. For common names, one must ask the Clerk for more identifiers to correctly do a search. Case lookup is at https://www.courts.mo.gov/casenet/base/welcome.do. Online records go back to 1992. Online search results show full name, address, and year of birth only. Online access to probate records is free at www.16thcircuit.org/publicaccess.asp. This includes private process servers, jury verdicts, criminal traffic, and criminal sureties.

Shelby County

Consolidated Circuit Court PO Box 176, Shelbyville, MO 63469; 573-633-2151; fax: 573-633-2142; 8AM-4:30PM (CST). *Felony, Misdemeanor, Civil, Eviction, Small Claims, Probate.* www.courts.mo.gov/page.jsp?id=1667

General Information: The Associate Division consolidated with this court on 01/01/2006. Online identifiers in results same as on public terminal. No juvenile, mental, expunged, dismissed, or suspended imposition of sentence records released. Fee to fax out file $3.00 each. Court makes copy: $.25 per page. Self serve copy: $.10 per page. Certification fee: $1.50 per cert. Payee: Shelby County Circuit Clerk. Personal checks accepted. No credit cards accepted. Prepayment required. Mail requests: SASE required.

Civil Name Search: Access: Mail, fax, in person, online. Both court and visitors may perform in person name searches. No search fee. Civil index on cards since 1975, prior on books since 1835. Mail turnaround time 1 day. Public use terminal available. Often older judgment will be displayed. Case lookup is at https://www.courts.mo.gov/casenet/base/welcome.do. Online records go back to 4/17/2000. Online search results show full name, address, and year of birth only.

Criminal Name Search: Access: Mail, fax, in person, online. Both court and visitors may perform in person name searches. No search fee. Criminal records indexed on cards since 1975, prior on books since 1835. Mail turnaround time 1 day. Public use terminal available. Both the terminal and CaseNet only show year of birth. For common names, one must ask the Clerk for more identifiers to correctly do a search. Case lookup is at https://www.courts.mo.gov/casenet/base/welcome.do. Online records go back to 11-12-2003. Online search results show full name, address, and year of birth only. Online access to probate records is free at www.16thcircuit.org/publicaccess.asp. This includes private process servers, jury verdicts, criminal traffic, and criminal sureties.

St. Charles County

Consolidated Circuit Court 300 N 2nd St, St. Charles, MO 63301; 636-949-3098; criminal phone: 636-949-7380; probate phone: 636-949-3086; fax: 636-949-7390; 8:30AM-5PM (CST). *Felony, Misdemeanor, Civil, Eviction, Small Claims, Probate.* www.courts.mo.gov/page.jsp?id=1588

General Information: The Circuit Court and Associate Division consolidated as of 01/03. Traffic Court is reached at 636-949-7385. Probate fax- 636-949-3070 Online identifiers in results same as on public terminal. No juvenile, mental, expunged, dismissed, or suspended imposition of sentence records released. Will fax documents. Court makes copy: $.25 per page. Certification fee: $1.50. Payee: St. Charles Circuit Clerk. No personal checks. No credit cards accepted for record searches. Prepayment required. Mail requests: SASE required for civil.

Civil Name Search: Access: Mail, in person, online. Both court and visitors may perform in person name searches. No search fee. Civil index on cards since 1971, prior on books; judgment records (A-M) on computer since 1987. Mail turnaround time 1 day. Civil PAT goes back to 1994. Often older judgment will be displayed. Case lookup is at https://www.courts.mo.gov/casenet/base/welcome.do. Online civil records form 01/1994 forward. Probate data from 10/10/2000 forward. Municipal court cases now on CaseNet.

Criminal Name Search: Access: In person, online. Visitors must perform in person searches themselves. Required to search: name, years to search; also helpful: DOB. Criminal records indexed on cards since 1971, prior on books; judgment records (A-M) on computer since 1987. Criminal PAT goes back to 1992. Both the terminal and CaseNet only show year of birth. For common names, one must ask the Clerk for more identifiers to correctly do a search. Online access to criminal records is the same as civil. Online criminal records back to 10/1992. Misdemeanor and traffic back to 01/1996. Municipal court cases now on CaseNet. Municipal court cases now on CaseNet.

St. Clair County
Consolidated Circuit Court PO Box 493, Osceola, MO 64776; 417-646-2226; fax: 417-646-2401; 8AM-4:30PM (CST). *Felony, Misdemeanor, Civil, Eviction, Small Claims, Probate.*
http://stclaircountymissouri.com/default.aspx
General Information: Online identifiers in results same as on public terminal. No juvenile, mental, expunged, dismissed, or suspended imposition of sentence records released. Will fax documents. Court makes copy: $1.00 per page. Certification fee: $.50 per document. Payee: St Clair County Circuit Clerk. Personal checks accepted. No credit cards accepted. Prepayment required. Mail requests: SASE required.
Civil Name Search: Access: Mail, in person, online. Both court and visitors may perform in person name searches. Search fee: $2.00 per name. Civil judgment records on computer since 1991, on index cards since 1980, prior records on index books. Mail turnaround time 1-2 days. Civil PAT goes back to 8/2003; Casenet from 2003. Often older judgment will be displayed. Case lookup is at https://www.courts.mo.gov/casenet/base/welcome.do. Index goes back to 8/18/2003. Online search results show full name, address, and year of birth only.
Criminal Name Search: Access: Mail, in person, online. Both court and visitors may perform in person name searches. Search fee: $2.00 per name. Required to search: name, years to search, DOB. Criminal records on computer since 1991, on index cards since 1980, prior records on index books. Mail turnaround time 1-2 days. Criminal PAT goes back to same as civil. Both the terminal and CaseNet only show year of birth. For common names, one must ask the Clerk for more identifiers to correctly do a search. Case lookup is at https://www.courts.mo.gov/casenet/base/welcome.do. Index goes back to 8/18/2003. Online search results show full name, address, and year of birth only.

St. Francois County
Circuit Court - Division I & II 1 N Washington, Rm 303, Farmington, MO 63640; 573-756-4551; probate phone: 573-756-6601; fax: 573-756-3733; 8AM-5PM (CST). *Felony, Civil, Small Claims, Probate.*
www.courts.mo.gov/page.jsp?id=1626
General Information: This court consolidated the Circuit and Associate Circuit Court. Online identifiers in results same as on public terminal. No juvenile, mental, expunged, dismissed, or suspended imposition of sentence records released. Will not fax documents. Court makes copy: $.25 per page. Self serve copy: same. Attorney copy fee is $1.00 per page. Certification fee: $1.50 per document plus copy fee. Payee: Clerk of Circuit Court. Business checks accepted. No credit cards accepted. Prepayment required. Mail requests: SASE required for civil.
Civil Name Search: Access: Fax, mail, in person, online. Both court and visitors may perform in person name searches. No search fee. Civil records on computer since 6/90, on microfiche since 1970, archived since 1821. Mail turnaround time 1-2 weeks. Civil PAT goes back to 6/1990. Often older judgment will be displayed. Case lookup is at https://www.courts.mo.gov/casenet/base/welcome.do. Online records go back to 11/01/00. Online search results show full name, address, and year of birth only.
Criminal Name Search: Access: In person, online. Both court and visitors may perform in person name searches. No search fee. Required to search: name, years to search; also helpful: DOB, SSN. Criminal records on computer since 3/1/93. Criminal PAT goes back to 3/1993. Both the terminal and CaseNet only show year of birth. For common names, one

must ask the Clerk for more identifiers to correctly do a search. Online access to criminal records same as civil, above. Online search results show full name, address, and year of birth only. Online access to probate records is free at www.16thcircuit.org/publicaccess.asp. This includes private process servers, jury verdicts, criminal traffic, and criminal sureties.

St. Louis County
Circuit Court of St. Louis County - Civil 7900 Carondelet Ave, Clayton Government Center, Clayton, MO 63105-1766; 314-615-8029; fax: 314-615-8739; 8AM-5PM (CST). *Civil Actions over $25,000.*
www.stlouisco.com/lawandpublicsafety/circuitcourt
General Information: Records Rm phone- 314-615-8034. When faxing a search request, fax to "Attn Certified Copies." Online identifiers in results same as on public terminal. No juvenile, paternity, mental, expunged, dismissed, or suspended imposition of sentence records released. Will not fax documents. Court makes copy: $.30 per page. Certification fee: $1.80; authenticated copy is $3.50. Payee: Circuit Clerk. Personal checks accepted. Credit cards accepted in person only. Prepayment required.
Civil Name Search: Access: Phone, fax, mail, in person, online. Both court and visitors may perform in person name searches. No search fee. Required to search: name, years to search; also helpful: address. Civil records on computer back to 1978, prior on index cards. Case files archived for 25 years. Mail turnaround time up to 3 days. Public use terminal has civil records back to 1978. Often older judgment will be displayed. Access court records free at https://www.courts.mo.gov/casenet/base/welcome.do - records go back to 10/1/2007. Search limited closed cases probate index free at www.stlouisco.com/CourtCaseSearch/frmProbateSearch.aspx?TabId=pr.

Associate Circuit - Civil Division 7900 Carondelet, Clayton, MO 63105; 314-615-8090; probate phone: 314-615-2629; fax: 314-615-2689; 8AM-5PM (CST). *Civil Actions under $25,000, Eviction, Small Claims, Probate.*
www.stlouisco.com/circuitcourt
General Information: Small claims court phone- 314-615-2658. Probate office is on 5th Fl. Online identifiers in results same as on public terminal. No juvenile, mental, expunged, dismissed, paternity, suspended imposition of sentence records released. Will not fax documents. Court makes copy: $.30 per page. Self serve copy: $.10 per page. Certification fee: $1.80, authenticated copy is $3.50. Payee: Circuit Clerk-Civil Division. Personal checks accepted. Major credit cards accepted in person only, not over the phone. Prepayment required. Mail requests: SASE required.
Civil Name Search: Access: Phone, mail, in person, online. Both court and visitors may perform in person name searches. No search fee. Civil records on computer since 1986, prior on cards. Mail turnaround time 1 week. Public use terminal has civil records back to 1986. Often older judgment will be displayed. Access Court records back to 7/6/2004 free on the state online court record system at https://www.courts.mo.gov/casenet/base/welcome.do. Search probate index up to 12/10/2004 free at www.stlouisco.com/CourtCaseSearch/frmProbateSearch.aspx?TabId=pr.

Circuit Court of St. Louis County - Criminal 7900 Carondelet Ave, Clayton, MO 63105; 314-615-2675; fax: 314-615-2689; 8AM-5PM (CST). *Felony, Misdemeanor, Traffic.*
www.stlouisco.com/YourGovernment/CountyDepartments/StLouisCountyCircuitCourt
General Information: Online identifiers in results same as on public terminal. No juvenile, mental, expunged, dismissed, or suspended imposition of sentence records released. Will fax non-certified documents to local or toll-free number. Court makes copy: $.30 per page. Certification fee: $1.50; authenticated copy is $3.50. Payee: St Louis County Circuit Clerk. Personal checks and credit cards accepted. Prepayment required. Mail requests: SASE required.
Criminal Name Search: Access: Phone, mail, fax, in person, online. Both court and visitors may perform in person name searches. No search fee. Required to search: name, years to search, DOB, offense, date of offense. Criminal records computerized from 1986, prior on index cards. Permanent records on microfiche since 1978, earlier in books. Case files archived for. Mail turnaround time varies. Public use terminal has crim records back to 1986. Both the terminal and CaseNet only show year of birth. For common names, one must ask the Clerk for more identifiers to correctly do a search. Participates in the free state online court record system at www.courts.mo.gov/casenet/base/welcome.do. Online records go back to 6/4/2007. Online search results show full name, address, and year of birth only. Online access to probate records is free at www.16thcircuit.org/publicaccess.asp. This includes private process servers, jury verdicts, criminal traffic, and criminal sureties.

St. Louis City County

Circuit Courts - Civil 10 N Tucker Blvd, 3rd Fl, Civil Courts Bldg, St Louis, MO 63101; 314-622-4405; probate phone: 314-622-4301; fax: 314-622-4537; 8AM-5PM (CST). *Civil, Eviction, Small Claims, Probate.* www.courts.mo.gov/hosted/circuit22/

General Information: Small Claims telephone is 314-622-3788. Probate is located on the 10th Fl. Circuit Clerk's website is www.stlcitycircuitcourt.com/. Online identifiers in results same as on public terminal. No sealed or confidential records released. Will not fax documents. Court makes copy: $.30 per page. Certification fee: $3.50 for 1st page; $.50 each add'l. Payee: City of St. Louis Circuit Clerk. Only cashiers checks and money orders accepted. No credit cards accepted. Prepayment required. Mail requests: SASE required.

Civil Name Search: Access: Mail, in person, online. Both court and visitors may perform in person name searches. No search fee. Civil records on computer since 1/80, on index cards since early 1800s. Note: Mail search is for older, pre-1980s records only. Mail turnaround time usually 1 week. Public use terminal has civil records back to 1982. Often older judgment will be displayed. Online access to civil records back to 10/1/2007 is free at https://www.courts.mo.gov/casenet/base/welcome.do. Remote access is also through MoBar Net and is open only to attorneys. Call 314-535-1950 for information. Also, probate records are free online at www.courts.mo.gov/casenet/base/welcome.do. Online probate records go back to 1/1990.

City of St Louis Circuit Court - Criminal 1114 Market St, 2nd Fl, Carnahan Courthouse, Attn: Case Records/File Section, St Louis, MO 63101; 314-622-4195 gen info); criminal phone: 314-622-3341; fax: 314-613-7486; 8AM-5PM (CST). *Felony, Misdemeanor.* www.courts.mo.gov/hosted/circuit17/

General Information: The Certified/Record Copy Dept and Court Clerk's Admin. Office and Civil Div. is located 10 N Tucker St, St Louis, 63101. Online identifiers in results same as on public terminal. No juvenile, mental, expunged, dismissed, or suspended imposition of sentence records released. Will not fax out documents. Court makes copy: $.30 per page. Certification fee: $3.50 per cert plus $.50 per page. Payee: City of St. Louis Circuit Clerk. Business/attorneys checks accepted. No credit cards accepted. Prepayment required. Mail requests: SASE required.

Criminal Name Search: Access: In person, mail, fax, online. Both court and visitors may perform in person name searches. No search fee. Required to search: name, years to search, DOB, signed release; also helpful: address, SSN. Criminal records on computer since 1990 for misdemeanor; since 1992 for felony. Note: Courts criminal case records/copy section telephone is 714-613-4156 or 4408. Fax is given above. Public use terminal has crim records back to 1980. Both the terminal and CaseNet only show year of birth. For common names, one must ask the Clerk for more identifiers to correctly do a search. Participates in the free state online court record system at www.courts.mo.gov/casenet/base/welcome.do. Online search results show full name, address, and year of birth only. Online access to probate records is free at www.16thcircuit.org/publicaccess.asp. This includes private process servers, jury verdicts, criminal traffic, and criminal sureties.

Ste. Genevieve County

Circuit Court 55 S 3rd, Rm 23, Ste Genevieve, MO 63670; 573-883-2705/2265; fax: 573-883-9351; 8AM-5PM (CST). *Felony, Misdemeanor, Civil, Eviction, Small Claims, Probate.* www.courts.mo.gov/page.jsp?id=1625

General Information: Online identifiers in results same as on public terminal. No juvenile, mental, expunged, paternity, dismissed, or suspended imposition of sentence records released. Will fax documents to local or toll-free number. Court makes copy: $1.00 per page. Self serve copy: $.25 per page. Certification fee: $1.50 per cert. Payee: St Genevieve County Circuit Clerk. Business checks accepted. No credit cards accepted. Prepayment required. Mail requests: SASE required for mail return of any copies.

Civil Name Search: Access: In person, online. Visitors must perform in person searches themselves. Civil records on books since early 1800s, recent civil records (1995) computerized. Civil PAT goes back to 1997. Often older judgment will be displayed. Case lookup is at https://www.courts.mo.gov/casenet/base/welcome.do. Online records go back to 11/06/00. Online search results show full name, address, and year of birth only.

Criminal Name Search: Access: In person, online. Visitors must perform in person searches themselves. Criminal Record indexes on books, not computerized. Criminal PAT goes back to 1994. Both the terminal and CaseNet only show year of birth. For common names, one must ask the Clerk for more identifiers to correctly do a search. Case lookup is at https://www.courts.mo.gov/casenet/base/welcome.do. Online records go back to 11/06/00. Online search results show full name, address, and

year of birth only. Online access to probate records is free at www.16thcircuit.org/publicaccess.asp. This includes private process servers, jury verdicts, criminal traffic, and criminal sureties.

Stoddard County

Consolidated Circuit Court PO Box 30, Bloomfield, MO 63825; 573-568-4640; probate phone: x3; fax: 573-568-2271; 8AM-4:30PM (CST). *Felony, Misdemeanor, Civil Actions, Eviction, Small Claims, Probate.* www.courts.mo.gov/page.jsp?id=1648

General Information: Civil, criminal, and probate divisions are combined into one consolidated unit. Online identifiers in results same as on public terminal. No juvenile, mental, expunged, dismissed, or suspended imposition of sentence records released. Will fax documents to local or toll-free number. Court makes copy: $.25 per page. Certification fee: $2.00 per cert. Payee: Stoddard County Circuit Clerk. Personal checks accepted. No credit cards accepted. Prepayment required. Mail requests: SASE required.

Civil Name Search: Access: Fax, mail, in person, online. Both court and visitors may perform in person name searches. No search fee. Civil records on computer since 1991, prior on cards and books. Mail turnaround time 1-3 days. Civil PAT goes back to 1991. Often older judgment will be displayed. Access to civil records is free at https://www.courts.mo.gov/casenet/base/welcome.do. Online records go back to 7/1/2001. Online search results show full name, address, and year of birth only.

Criminal Name Search: Access: Mail, in person, online. Both court and visitors may perform in person name searches. No search fee. Required to search: name, years to search; also helpful: DOB, SSN. Criminal records on computer since 1991, prior on cards and books. Mail turnaround time 1-3 days. Criminal PAT goes back to 1991. Both the terminal and CaseNet only show year of birth. For common names, one must ask the Clerk for more identifiers to correctly do a search. Access to civil records is free at https://www.courts.mo.gov/casenet/base/welcome.do. Online records go back to 7/1/2001. Online search results show full name, address, and year of birth only.

Stone County

Consolidated Circuit Court PO Box 18, 110 S Maple, Judicial Ctr, 2nd Fl, Galena, MO 65656; 417-357-6114; fax: 417-357-6163; 7:30AM-4:00PM (CST). *Felony, Misdemeanor, Civil, Eviction, Small Claims, Probate.* www.courts.mo.gov/page.jsp?id=1662

General Information: Consolidated with Divisions II and III in 2007. Online identifiers in results same as on public terminal. No juvenile, mental, expunged, dismissed, or suspended imposition of sentence records released. Will not fax out documents. Court makes copy: $.25 per page. Certification fee: $1.50 per cert plus copy fee. Payee: Circuit Court. No personal checks or credit cards accepted. Prepayment required. Mail requests: SASE required.

Civil Name Search: Access: Phone, fax, mail, in person, online. Both court and visitors may perform in person name searches. No search fee. Civil records on cards and books, archived since 1852; computerized records since 1992. Mail turnaround time 1 week. Civil PAT goes back to 1992. Often older judgment will be displayed. Case lookup is at https://www.courts.mo.gov/casenet/base/welcome.do. Online records go back to 7/11/2005 and includes probate. Online search results show full name, address, and year of birth only.

Criminal Name Search: Access: Phone, fax, mail, in person, online. Both court and visitors may perform in person name searches. No search fee. Required to search: name, years to search; also helpful: DOB, SSN. Criminal records on cards and books, archived since 1852; computerized records since 1992. Mail turnaround time 1 week. Criminal PAT goes back to same as civil. Both the terminal and CaseNet only show year of birth. For common names, one must ask the Clerk for more identifiers to correctly do a search. Case lookup is at https://www.courts.mo.gov/casenet/base/welcome.do. Online records go back to 7/11/2005 and includes probate. Online search results show full name, address, and year of birth only.

Sullivan County

Consolidated Circuit Court 109 N Main, Courthouse, Milan, MO 63556-1358; 660-265-4717; criminal phone: 660-265-3303; civil phone: 660-265-4717; probate phone: 660-265-3303; fax: 660-265-5071; 9:00AM-4:30PM (CST). *Felony, Misdemeanor, Civil, Eviction, Small Claims, Probate.* www.courts.mo.gov/page.jsp?id=1576

General Information: Online identifiers in results same as on public terminal. No juvenile, mental, expunged, dismissed, or suspended imposition of sentence records released. Will not fax documents. Court makes copy: $1.00 per page. Self serve copy: $.25 per page. Certification fee: $1.50. Payee: Consolidated Circuit Court of Sullivan County. Personal checks accepted. No credit cards accepted. Prepayment required.

Civil Name Search: Access: In person, online. Visitors must perform in person searches themselves. Civil index on cards since 1979, prior on books. Civil PAT goes back to 2002. Often older judgment will be displayed. Participates in the statewide CaseNet court record system at https://www.courts.mo.gov/casenet/base/welcome.do. Online records go back to 5/13/2002. Online search results show full name, address, and year of birth only.

Criminal Name Search: Access: In person, online. Visitors must perform in person searches themselves. Required to search: name, years to search; also helpful: DOB, SSN. Criminal records indexed on cards since 1979, prior on books. Criminal PAT goes back to same as civil. Both the terminal and CaseNet only show year of birth. For common names, one must ask the Clerk for more identifiers to correctly do a search. Participates in the statewide Casenet court record system at https://www.courts.mo.gov/casenet/base/welcome.do. Online records go back to 5/13/2002. Online search results show full name, address, and year of birth only. Online access to probate records is free at www.16thcircuit.org/publicaccess.asp. This includes private process servers, jury verdicts, criminal traffic, and criminal sureties.

Taney County

Consolidated Circuit Court PO Box 335, 110 W Elm, Forsyth, MO 65653; 417-546-7230; fax: 417-546-6133; 8AM-5PM (CST). *Felony, Misdemeanor, Civil, Eviction, Small Claims, Probate.* www.courts.mo.gov/page.jsp?id=1658

General Information: The Associate Division was consolidated with this court. Online identifiers in results same as on public terminal. No juvenile, mental, expunged, dismissed, or suspended imposition of sentence records released. Will fax documents. Court makes copy: $.25 per page. Certification fee: $1.50 per cert plus copy fee. Payee: Circuit Clerk. Personal checks accepted. No credit cards accepted. Prepayment required. Mail requests: SASE required for mail return of any copies.

Civil Name Search: Access: Mail, in person, online. Visitors must perform in person searches themselves. Search fee: $4.00 per name. Civil records on computer since 1/95, prior on index cards and books since 1885. Civil PAT goes back to 1995. Often older judgment will be displayed. Participates in the state online court record system at https://www.courts.mo.gov/casenet/base/welcome.do. Online records include probate court. Online search results show full name, address, and year of birth only.

Criminal Name Search: Access: In person, online. Visitors must perform in person searches themselves. Required to search: name, years to search, DOB. Criminal records on computer since 1/95, prior on index cards and books since 1885. Note: For information on criminal records call MO State Highway Patrol at 573-526-6153. Criminal PAT goes back to same as civil. Both the terminal and CaseNet only show year of birth. For common names, one must ask the Clerk for more identifiers to correctly do a search. Online access to criminal records same as civil, above.

Texas County

Circuit Court 519 N Grand, Ste 202, Houston, MO 65483; 417-967-3742/3663; fax: 417-967-4220; 8:30-N; 12:30PM-4:30PM (CST). *Felony, Misdemeanor, Civil, Eviction, Small Claims, Probate.* www.courts.mo.gov/page.jsp?id=4757

General Information: No juvenile, mental, expunged, dismissed, or suspended imposition of sentence records released. Will not fax documents. Court makes copy: $1.00 per page. Certification fee: $2.50. Payee: Texas County Circuit Clerk. Personal checks accepted. No credit cards accepted. Prepayment required.

Civil Name Search: Access: In person, online. Visitors must perform in person searches themselves. Civil index on docket books since 1900s. Participates in the state online court record system at https://www.courts.mo.gov/casenet/base/welcome.do. Online records go back to 1/22/2007. Online search results show full name, address, and year of birth only.

Criminal Name Search: Access: In person, online. Visitors must perform in person searches themselves. Criminal records indexed in books since 1900s. Both the terminal and CaseNet only show year of birth. For common names, one must ask the Clerk for more identifiers to correctly do a search. Participates in the free state online court record system at www.courts.mo.gov/casenet/base/welcome.do. Records go back to 1/22/2007.

Vernon County

Consolidated Circuit Court Courthouse, Suite 15, 100 W Cherry St, Nevada, MO 64772; 417-448-2525/2550; fax: 417-448-2512; 8AM-4:30PM (CST). *Felony, Misdemeanor, Civil, Eviction, Small Claims, Probate.* www.courts.mo.gov/

General Information: Probate fax is same as main fax number. Online identifiers in results same as on public terminal. No juvenile, mental, expunged, dismissed, or suspended imposition of sentence records released. Will fax documents. Court makes copy: $.20 per page; microfilmed records $1.00 per page. Self serve copy: $.20 per page. Certification fee: $1.50.

Payee: Vernon County Circuit Clerk. Personal checks accepted. No credit cards accepted. Prepayment required. Mail requests: SASE required.

Civil Name Search: Access: In person, online, email. Visitors must perform in person searches themselves. No search fee. Civil records go back to 1863; on computer back to 2000. Judgments on index cards up until 1992. Civil PAT goes back to 1990. Often older judgment will be displayed. Participates in the state online court record system at https://www.courts.mo.gov/casenet/base/welcome.do. Online records go back to 9/11/2000. Online records include probate court. Direct email civil search requests to vickie.erwin@courts.mo.gov.

Criminal Name Search: Access: Mail, in person, online. Visitors must perform in person searches themselves. Search fee: $5.00 per name. Required to search: name, years to search, DOB. Criminal records go back to 1863; on computer back to 1990 for Assoc. Court records, back to 2000 for Circuit Court records. Criminal PAT goes back to 1990. Both the terminal and CaseNet only show year of birth. For common names, one must ask the Clerk for more identifiers to correctly do a search. Online access to criminal records same as civil, above. Online results show middle initial, DOB, address.

Warren County

Consolidated Circuit Court 104 W Main, Warrenton, MO 63383; 636-456-3363, 636-456-3375; fax: 636-456-2422; 8AM-4:30PM (CST). *Felony, Misdemeanor, Civil, Eviction, Small Claims, Probate.* www.courts.mo.gov/page.jsp?id=1595

General Information: The Associated Circuit Court has consolidated with the main Circuit Court. Probate fax is same as main fax number. Online identifiers in results same as on public terminal. No juvenile, mental, expunged, dismissed, or suspended imposition of sentence records released. Will fax documents to local or toll-free number. Court makes copy: $.50 per page. Certification fee: $1.00 per certification. Payee: Warren County Circuit Clerk. Attorney checks accepted. Major credit cards accepted; $4.00 courtesy fee applies for credit or debit cards. Prepayment required.

Civil Name Search: Access: Online, in person. Visitors must perform in person searches themselves. Civil index on cards since 1976, prior on books. Public use terminal available, records go back to 1975 Circuit; 5/2003 Assoc. Often older judgment will be displayed. Participates in the state online court record system at https://www.courts.mo.gov/casenet/base/welcome.do. Online records go back to 9/20/1999. Online search results show full name, address, and year of birth only.

Criminal Name Search: Access: Online, in person. Visitors must perform in person searches themselves. Criminal records indexed on cards since 1976, prior on books. Public use terminal available, crim records go back to 1975 Circuit; 5/2003 Assoc. Both the terminal and CaseNet only show year of birth. For common names, one must ask the Clerk for more identifiers to correctly do a search. Participates in the state online court record system at https://www.courts.mo.gov/casenet/base/welcome.do. Online records go back to 9/20/1999. Online search results show full name, address, and year of birth only.

Washington County

Circuit Court PO Box 216, Potosi, MO 63664; 573-438-6111; fax: 573-438-7900; 8AM-5PM (CST). *Felony, Civil Actions over $45,000.* www.courts.mo.gov/page.jsp?id=1627

General Information: Online identifiers in results same as on public terminal. No juvenile, mental, expunged, dismissed, or suspended imposition of sentence records released. Will not fax documents. Court makes copy: $1.00 per page. Certification fee: $2.00 per doc. Payee: Washington County Circuit Clerk. Personal checks accepted. No credit cards accepted. Prepayment required. Mail requests: SASE required.

Civil Name Search: Access: Mail, in person, online. Both court and visitors may perform in person name searches. No search fee. Civil index on cards since 1976, prior on books. Mail turnaround time 5-10 days. Civil PAT goes back to 11/2000. Often older judgment will be displayed. Participates in the state online court record system at https://www.courts.mo.gov/casenet/base/welcome.do. Online records go back to 11/09/00. Online search results show full name, address.

Criminal Name Search: Access: Mail, in person, online. Both court and visitors may perform in person name searches. No search fee. Criminal records indexed on cards since 1976, prior on books. Mail turnaround time 5-10 days. Criminal PAT goes back to 11/2000. Both the terminal and CaseNet only show year of birth. For common names, one must ask the Clerk for more identifiers to correctly do a search. Participates in the state online court record system at https://www.courts.mo.gov/casenet/base/welcome.do. Online records go back to 11/09/00. Online search results show full name, address.

Wayne County

Consolidated Circuit Court PO Box 78, 109 Walnut St, Greenville, MO 63944; 573-224-35600 opt1; fax: 573-224-3225; 8AM-5PM (CST). *Felony, Misdemeanor, Civil, Eviction, Small Claims, Probate, Traffic.* www.courts.mo.gov/page.jsp?id=1672

General Information: Divisions were consolidated 10/2005. Online identifiers in results same as on public terminal. No juvenile, mental, expunged, dismissed, or suspended imposition of sentence records released. Will fax documents to local or toll-free number. Court makes copy: $.50 per page. Certification fee: $2.00 per cert plus copy fee. Payee: Wayne County Circuit Clerk. Personal checks accepted. No credit cards accepted. Prepayment required. Mail requests: SASE required for civil.

Civil Name Search: Access: Mail, in person, online. Both court and visitors may perform in person name searches. No search fee. Civil index on cards since 1978, prior on books and manual card file. Mail turnaround time 1 week. Civil PAT goes back to 2001. Often older judgment will be displayed. Participates in the statewide CaseNet court record system at https://www.courts.mo.gov/casenet/base/welcome.do. Online records go back to 4/9/2001. Online search results show full name, address, and year of birth only.

Criminal Name Search: Access: In person, online. Both court and visitors may perform in person name searches. No search fee. Required to search: name, years to search; also helpful: DOB. Criminal records indexed on cards since 1978, prior on books. Criminal PAT goes back to 2000. Both the terminal and CaseNet only show year of birth. For common names, one must ask the Clerk for more identifiers to correctly do a search. Participates in the statewide Casenet court record system at https://www.courts.mo.gov/casenet/base/welcome.do. Online records go back to 4/9/2001. Online search results show full name, address, and year of birth only.

Webster County

Circuit Court - Civil PO Box B, Courthouse, Marshfield, MO 65706; 417-859-2006; fax: 417-859-6265; 8AM-5PM (CST). *Civil Actions, Eviction, Small Claims, Probate.* http://home.positech.net/~dcourt/

General Information: Online identifiers in results same as on public terminal. No juvenile, mental, expunged, dismissed, or suspended imposition of sentence records released. Will fax documents $2.00 per page. Court makes copy: $.25 per page. Self serve copy: same. Certification fee: $2.50 plus copy fee, no limit on pages. Payee: Webster County Circuit Clerk. Personal checks accepted. No credit cards accepted. Prepayment required. Mail requests: SASE required.

Civil Name Search: Access: Fax, mail, in person, online. Both court and visitors may perform in person name searches. No search fee. Civil records on computer since 1976 (judgment index). Mail turnaround time 5 days Public use terminal has civil records back to 1976, judgments only. Often older judgment will be displayed. Access to civil records back to 11/13/2001 is free at https://www.courts.mo.gov/casenet/base/welcome.do. Online search results show full name, address, and year of birth only.

Circuit Court - Criminal PO Box B, Courthouse, Marshfield, MO 65706; 417-859-2041; fax: 417-859-6265; 8AM-5PM (CST). *Felony, Misdemeanor.* http://home.positech.net/~dcourt/

General Information: No juvenile, mental, expunged, dismissed, or suspended imposition of sentence records released. Will not fax documents. Court makes copy: $.25 per page. Certification fee: No certification fee. Payee: Associate Circuit Court. Only cashiers checks and money orders accepted. No credit cards accepted. Prepayment required. Mail requests: SASE required.

Criminal Name Search: Access: Mail, in person, online. Only the court performs in person name searches; visitors may not. No search fee. Required to search: name, years to search; also helpful: DOB, SSN. Criminal records on computer since 1992. Mail turnaround time varies. Both the terminal and CaseNet only show year of birth. For common names, one must ask the Clerk for more identifiers to correctly do a search. Access to criminal records back to 11/13/2001 is free at https://www.courts.mo.gov/casenet/base/welcome.do. Online search results include year of birth only. Online results show name, DOB.

Worth County

Circuit Court PO Box 350, 11 W 4th St, Grant City, MO 64456; 660-564-2210/2152; fax: 660-564-3394; 8AM-4:30PM (CST). *Felony, Misdemeanor, Civil, Eviction, Small Claims, Probate.* www.courts.mo.gov/page.jsp?id=1558

General Information: Online identifiers in results same as on public terminal. No juvenile, mental, expunged, dismissed, or suspended imposition of sentence records released. Will fax documents to local or toll-free number. Court makes copy: $1.00 per page. Certification fee: $2.50 per cert plus copy fee. Payee: Worth County Circuit Clerk. Personal checks accepted. No credit cards accepted. Prepayment required. Mail requests: SASE required.

Civil Name Search: Access: Fax, mail, in person, online. Both court and visitors may perform in person name searches. Search fee: $5.00 per name. Civil records on computer since 1990, prior on index cards. Mail turnaround time same day. Civil PAT goes back to 1996. Often older judgment will be displayed. Participates in the statewide MO CaseNet record system at https://www.courts.mo.gov/casenet/base/welcome.do. Online records go back to 3/20/2006. Online search results show full name, address, and year of birth only.

Criminal Name Search: Access: Fax, mail, in person, online. Both court and visitors may perform in person name searches. Search fee: $5.00 per name. Criminal records on computer since 1990, prior on index cards. Mail turnaround time same day. Criminal PAT goes back to same as civil. Both the terminal and CaseNet only show year of birth. For common names, one must ask the Clerk for more identifiers to correctly do a search. Participates in the statewide MO Casenet record system at www.courts.mo.gov/casenet/base/welcome.do. Online records go back to 3/20/2006.

Wright County

Circuit Court PO Box 39, Hartville, MO 65667; 417-741-7121; fax: 417-741-7504; 8AM-4:30PM (CST). *Felony, Misdemeanor, Civil, Eviction, Small Claims, Probate.* www.courts.mo.gov/page.jsp?id=1680

General Information: Online identifiers in results same as on public terminal. No juvenile, mental, expunged, dismissed, or suspended imposition of sentence records released. Will fax documents $5.00. Court makes copy: $.25 per page. Self serve copy: same. Certification fee: $1.00 per cert. Payee: Wright County Circuit Clerk. Personal checks accepted. No credit cards accepted. Prepayment required.

Civil Name Search: Access: Mail, in person, online. Both court and visitors may perform in person name searches. No search fee. Civil index on cards since 1979, prior on books to 1900s. Mail turnaround time 1 day. Public use terminal has civil records back to 2/20/06. Judgment index, court records available on public access terminal since 2/20/06. Participates in the state online court record system at https://www.courts.mo.gov/casenet/base/welcome.do. Online records go back to 2/20/2006. Online search results show full name, address, and year of birth only.

Criminal Name Search: Access: Mail, in person, online. Both court and visitors may perform in person name searches. No search fee. Criminal records indexed on cards since 1979, prior on books to 1900s. Mail turnaround time 1 day. Both the terminal and CaseNet only show year of birth. For common names, one must ask the Clerk for more identifiers to correctly do a search. Online access to criminal records same as civil, above. For criminal searches contact Highway Patrol at 573-526-6153.

Common Abbreviations Found in Text

- **DL**   Driver's license
- **PAT**   Public use access terminal
- **SASE**   Self-addressed, stamped envelope
- **SSN**   Social Security Number

Montana

Time Zone:	MST
Capital:	Helena, Lewis and Clark County
# of Counties:	56
State Web:	http://mt.gov
Court Web:	www.courts.mt.gov

Administration

Court Administrator, Park Avenue Building, Room 328 (PO Box 203005), Helena, MT, 59620; 406-841-2950, Fax: 406-841-2955.

The Supreme and Appellate Courts

The Supreme Court is the court of last resort. Montana does not have an intermediate appellate court. Consequently, the Supreme Court hears direct appeals from all of the District Courts across Montana, as well as from the Workers' Compensation Court and the Water Court. Supreme Court opinions, orders, and recently filed briefs may be found http://searchcourts.mt.gov.

The Montana Courts

Court	Type	How Organized	Jurisdiction Highpoints
District *	General	106 Courts (with Divisions) in 45 Districts	Felony, Civil $12,000 or above, Family, Probate, Juvenile
Justice*	Limited	66	Misdemeanor, Limited Civil, Small Claims Eviction
Municipal	Limited	5	Ordinance, (Some Misdemeanor, Limited Civil, Small Claims Eviction)
City	Limited	81	Ordinance, (Some Misdemeanor, Limited Civil, Small Claims Eviction)

* = profiled in this book

Details on the Court Structure

The **District Courts,** the courts of general jurisdiction, handle all felony cases and probate cases, most civil cases at law and in equity, and other special actions and proceedings.

The courts of limited jurisdiction are **Justice Courts**, **City Courts** and **Municipal Courts**. Although the jurisdiction of these courts differs slightly, collectively they address cases involving misdemeanor offenses, civil cases for amounts up to $12,000, small claims valued up to $7,000, landlord/tenant disputes, local ordinances, forcible entry and detainer, protection orders, certain issues involving juveniles, and other matters. Some Justice Courts and City Courts have consolidated.

Note - Effective July 1, 2011, the District Court's minimum civil limit amount was raised from $7,000 to $12,000; the lower courts maximum from $7,000 to $12,000; small claims from 3,000 to $7,000, and City Court jurisdiction on certain matters from increased from $5,000 to $9,500.

There is also a **Water Court** and a **Workers' Compensation Court** in Montana.

Record Searching Facts You Need to Know

Fees and Record Searching Tips

Most District Courts charge $2.00 per name per year, first 7 years, then $1.00 per year for searching. Copies are usally $1.00 per page first 10 pages, then $.50 per page after. Certification is usually $2.00. A document titled *Access to Court Records* is found at http://courts.mt.gov/crt_records/faq.asp. The document advises that all documents filed with the court should not contain the full DOB, unless required by law.

Many Montana Justices of the Peace maintain case record indexes on their personal computers, which does speed the retrieval process.

Online Access is Non-Existent

There is no statewide access to docket information from the trial courts. Several courts respond to email requests, but none offer online access to records.

Beaverhead County

District Court Beaverhead County Courthouse, 2 S Pacific St, Dillon, MT 59725; 406-683-3725; fax: 406-683-3728; 8AM-5PM (MST). *Felony, Civil Actions over $12,000, Probate.* www.beaverheadcounty.org/
General Information: Probate fax is same as main fax number. No adoption, juvenile, sanity, paternity or dismissed criminal records released. Will fax documents $1.00 per page. Court makes copy: $1.00 per page 1st 10 pages, then $.50 each add'l. Self serve copy: same. Certification fee: $2.00; exemplification is $6.00. Payee: Clerk of Court. No personal checks. No credit cards accepted. Prepayment required. Mail requests: SASE required.
Civil Name Search: Access: Fax, mail, in person. Both court and visitors may perform in person name searches. Search fee: $2.00 per name per year, first 7 years, then $1.00 per year. Civil records in books back to 1870s; on computer since 1997. Note: For fax access, include fax copy of check for fee. Mail turnaround time 1-2 days. Civil PAT goes back to 7/1997.
Criminal Name Search: Access: Fax, mail, in person. Both court and visitors may perform in person name searches. Search fee: $2.00 per name per year, first 7 years, then $1.00 per year. Criminal records in books back to 1870s; on computer since 1997. Note: For fax request, include copy of check for fee. Mail turnaround time 1-2 days. Criminal PAT goes back to same as civil.
County Justice Court 2 S Pacific, Cluster #16, Dillon, MT 59725; 406-683-3755; fax: 406-683-3736; 8AM-5PM (MST). *Misdemeanor, Civil Actions under $12,000, Eviction, Small Claims.*
www.beaverheadcounty.org

Big Horn County

District Court 121 W 3rd St, Rm 221, PO Box 908, Hardin, MT 59034; 406-665-9750; fax: 406-665-9755; 8AM-5PM (MST). *Felony, Civil Actions over $12,000, Probate.*
General Information: No adoption, sanity, pre-sentence, psychiatric evaluation, dependent & neglected, or confidential criminal justice records released. Fee to fax out file $1.00 per page. Court makes copy: $1.00 per page 1st 10 pages, then $.50 each add'l. Self serve copy: same. Certification fee: $2.00. Payee: Clerk of Court. No personal checks or credit cards accepted. Prepayment required. Will bill government agencies. Mail requests: SASE required.
Civil Name Search: Access: Fax, mail, in person. Both court and visitors may perform in person name searches. Search fee: $2.00 per name per year, first 7 years, then $1.00 per year. Civil records in books, microfilm, and computer back to 1913. Mail turnaround time same day. Civil PAT goes back to 1913.
Criminal Name Search: Access: Fax, mail, in person. Both court and visitors may perform in person name searches. Search fee: $2.00 per name per year, first 7 years, then $1.00 per year. Required to search: name, years to search, DOB; also helpful, SSN. Criminal records in books and on microfilm back to 1913; on computer back to 1913. Note: Court order required for confidential information. Mail turnaround time same day. Criminal PAT goes back to same as civil.
Justice Court PO Box 908, 121 W 3rd, Rm 210, Courthouse, Hardin, MT 59034; 406-665-9760; fax: 406-665-9764; 8AM-5PM (MST). *Misdemeanor, Civil Actions under $12,000, Eviction, Small Claims.*
http://bighorn.mt.gov/justice_court.htm

Blaine County

District Court PO Box 969, 420 Ohio Street, Chinook, MT 59523; 406-357-3230; fax: 406-357-3109; 8AM-5PM (MST). *Felony, Civil Actions over $12,000, Eviction, Probate.*
www.co.blaine.mt.gov/district.html
General Information: Probate fax is same as main fax number. No adoption, juvenile, neglect, dependent, or sanity records released. Fee to fax out file $1.00 per page. Court makes copy: $1.00 per page 1st 10 pages, then $.50 each add'l. Certification fee: $2.00 per certification. Payee: Clerk of Court. No personal checks. No credit cards accepted. Prepayment required. Mail requests: SASE required.
Civil Name Search: Access: Fax, mail, in person. Both court and visitors may perform in person name searches. Search fee: $2.00 per name per year, first 7 years, then $1.00 per year. Civil records in books from 1912; on computer back to 1995. Mail turnaround time same day. Civil PAT goes back to 1995.
Criminal Name Search: Access: Fax, mail, in person. Both court and visitors may perform in person name searches. Search fee: $2.00 per name per year, first 7 years, then $1.00 per year. Required to search: name, years to search, signed release. Criminal records in books from 1912; on computer

back to 1995. Mail turnaround time same day. Criminal PAT goes back to same as civil.
Justice Court PO Box 1266, 420 Ohio St, Chinook, MT 59523; 406-357-2335; fax: 406-357-2361; 8AM-5PM (MST). *Misdemeanor, Civil Actions under $12,000, Small Claims. Eviction.*
www.co.blaine.mt.gov/justice.html
General Information: Ordinance Violations are not handled here. There is also a Harlem Justice Court, at Harlem City Hall, 406-353-2361, only open 10AM-N on the 2nd & 4th Wednesdays of each month.

Broadwater County

District Court 515 Broadway, Townsend, MT 59644; 406-266-9236; fax: 406-266-4720; 8AM-N, 1-5PM (MST). *Felony, Civil Actions, Probate.*
General Information: No adoption, juvenile or sanity records released. Will fax documents. Court makes copy: $1.00 per page 1st 10 pages, then $.50 each add'l. Certification fee: $2.00. Payee: Clerk of Court. Personal checks accepted. No credit cards accepted. Prepayment required. Mail requests: SASE required.
Civil Name Search: Access: Fax, mail, in person. Both court and visitors may perform in person name searches. Search fee: $2.00 per name per year, first 7 years, then $1.00 per year. Required to search: name, years to search, DOB. Civil records on microfiche and archives back to 1897; on computer back to 1997. Mail turnaround time same day. Civil PAT goes back to 1997.
Criminal Name Search: Access: Fax, mail, in person. Both court and visitors may perform in person name searches. Search fee: $2.00 per name per year, first 7 years, then $1.00 per year. Required to search: name, years to search, DOB. Criminal records on microfiche and archives back to 1897; on computer back to 1997. Mail turnaround time same day. Criminal PAT goes back to same as civil.
Justice Court 515 Broadway, Townsend, MT 59644; 406-266-9231; fax: 406-266-4720; 8AM-5PM (MST). *Misdemeanor, Civil Actions under $12,000, Eviction, Small Claims.*

Carbon County

District Court PO Box 948, Red Lodge, MT 59068; 406-446-1225; fax: 406-446-0103; 8AM-5PM (MST). *Felony, Civil Actions, Probate.*
General Information: No adoption, juvenile or sanity records released. Will fax documents $1.00 per page; no charge to toll free number. Court makes copy: $1.00 per page 1st 10 pages, then $.50 each add'l. Certification fee: $2.00, for exemplified record fee is $6.00. Payee: Clerk of Court. Personal checks accepted. No credit cards accepted. Prepayment required. Mail requests: SASE required.
Civil Name Search: Access: Phone, fax, mail, in person. Both court and visitors may perform in person name searches. Search fee: $2.00 per name per year, first 7 years, then $1.00 per year. Civil index in docket books from 1895; on computer back to 1995. Mail turnaround time 1-2 days. Civil PAT goes back to 1995.
Criminal Name Search: Access: Fax, mail, in person. Both court and visitors may perform in person name searches. Search fee: $2.00 per name per year, first 7 years, then $1.00 per year. Criminal docket on books from 1895; on computer back to 1995. Mail turnaround time 1-2 days. Criminal PAT goes back to 1995.
Carbon County Justice Court PO Box 2, 102 N Broadway, Red Lodge, MT 59068; 406-446-1440; fax: 406-446-9175; 8AM-5PM (MST). *Misdemeanor, Civil Actions under $12,000, Eviction, Small Claims.*
www.co.carbon.mt.us
Joliet City Court PO Box 210, 116 S main St, Joliet, MT 59041; 406-962-3567; fax: 406-962-9803; 8AM-N Wed only (MST). *Misdemeanor, Civil Actions under $12,000.*

Carter County

District Court PO Box 322, Ekalaka, MT 59324; 406-775-8714; fax: 406-775-8703; 8AM-5PM (MST). *Felony, Civil Actions over $12,000, Eviction, Probate.*
General Information: Probate is separate index at this same address. No adoption, juvenile or sanity records released. Will fax documents $1.00 per page. Court makes copy: $1.00 per page 1st 10 pages, then $.50 each add'l. Self serve copy: same. Certification fee: $2.00 per instrument plus copy fee. Payee: Clerk of Court. Personal checks accepted. No credit cards accepted. Prepayment required. Mail requests: SASE required.
Civil Name Search: Access: Phone, fax, mail, in person. Both court and visitors may perform in person name searches. Search fee: $2.00 per name per year, first 7 years, then $1.00 per year. Civil records in books from 1917; computerized back to 1996. Mail turnaround time same or next day.

Criminal Name Search: Access: Phone, fax, mail, in person. Only the court performs in person name searches; visitors may not. Search fee: $2.00 per name per year, first 7 years, then $1.00 per year. Required to search: name, years to search, signed release; also helpful: SSN. Criminal records in books from 1917; computerized back to 1996. Mail turnaround time 1-2 days; same or next day for phone requests.

Justice Court PO Box 72, Ekalaka, MT 59324-0072; 406-775-8754, 406-775-8838; fax: 406-775-8703; 8AM-5PM 1st,2nd,3rd W of month; 10AM-3:PM 4th W (MST). *Misdemeanor, Small Claims, Eviction, Ordinance.*

Cascade County

District Court County Courthouse, 415 2nd Ave North, Great Falls, MT 59401; 406-454-6780; fax: 406-454-6907; 8AM-5PM (MST). *Felony, Civil Actions over $12,000, Probate.* www.co.cascade.mt.us/

General Information: No adoption or sanity records released. Will not fax documents. Court makes copy: $1.00 per page; $.50 per page after 1st 10. Certification fee: $2.00 per document plus copy fee, exemplification fee is $6.00. Payee: Clerk of Court. No personal checks accepted; business checks, cashier's checks and money orders accepted. No credit cards accepted. Prepayment required. Mail requests: SASE required.

Civil Name Search: Access: Fax, mail, in person. Both court and visitors may perform in person name searches. Search fee: $2.00 per name per year, first 7 years, then $1.00 per year. Civil records on computer from 1987; on docket books to 1889. Mail turnaround time 3-4 days. Civil PAT goes back to 1987.

Criminal Name Search: Access: Fax, mail, in person. Both court and visitors may perform in person name searches. Search fee: $2.00 per name per year, first 7 years, then $1.00 per year. Criminal records computerized from 1987; on docket books to 1889. Mail turnaround time 1-2 days. Criminal PAT goes back to 1987.

Cascade Justice Court Cascade County Courthouse, 415 2nd Ave N, Great Falls, MT 59401; 406-454-6873; fax: 406-454-6877; 8AM-5PM (MST). *Misdemeanor, Civil Actions under $12,000, Eviction, Small Claims.*

General Information: Public terminal located in law library.

Chouteau County

District Court PO Box 459, Ft Benton, MT 59442; 406-622-5024; fax: 406-622-3028; 8AM-5PM (MST). *Felony, Civil Actions over $12,000, Eviction, Probate.*

General Information: No adoption, paternity, juvenile or sanity records released. Will fax documents , fees same as copy fee schedule. Court makes copy: $1.00 per page 1st 10 pages, then $.50 each add'l. Certification fee: $2.00 per cert plus copy fee. Payee: Clerk of Court. Business and personal checks accepted. No credit cards accepted. Prepayment required. Mail requests: SASE required.

Civil Name Search: Access: Fax, mail, in person. Both court and visitors may perform in person name searches. Search fee: $2.00 per name per year, first 7 years, then $1.00 per year. Civil records on books from 1886; on computer from 1997 forward. Mail turnaround time 1 day. Civil PAT goes back to 1997.

Criminal Name Search: Access: Fax, mail, in person. Both court and visitors may perform in person name searches. Search fee: $2.00 per name per year, first 7 years, then $1.00 per year. Criminal docket on books from 1886; on computer from 1997 forward. Mail turnaround time 1 day. Criminal PAT goes back to same as civil. Online results show name only.

Chouteau County Justice Court PO Box 459, 1215 Washington, Ft Benton, MT 59442; 406-622-5502; fax: 406-622-3815; 9AM-4PM (MST). *Misdemeanor, Civil Actions under $12,000, Eviction, Small Claims, Ordinance.*

General Information: As of 12/2002, the records from the former Justice Court in Big Sandy are housed at this location.

Custer County

District Court 1010 Main, Miles City, MT 59301-3419; 406-874-3326; fax: 406-874-3451; 8AM-5PM (MST). *Felony, Civil Actions over $12,000, Probate.*

General Information: Probate fax is same as main fax number. No dependent & neglected, juvenile or sanity records released. Will fax documents $1.00 per page. Court makes copy: $1.00 per page 1st 10 pages, then $.50 each add'l. Self serve copy: same. Certification fee: $2.00 per document. Payee: Clerk of District Court. Personal checks accepted. No credit cards accepted. Prepayment required. Mail requests: SASE required.

Civil Name Search: Access: Phone, fax, mail, in person. Both court and visitors may perform in person name searches. Search fee: $2.00 per name per year, first 7 years, then $1.00 per year. Civil records on computer back to 1990; also in books. Mail turnaround time 1-2 days. Civil PAT goes back to 1990.

Criminal Name Search: Access: Mail, in person. Both court and visitors may perform in person name searches. Search fee: $2.00 per name per year, first 7 years, then $1.00 per name per year. Criminal records computerized from 1990; also in books. Mail turnaround time 1-2 days. Criminal PAT goes back to same as civil.

Justice Court 1010 Main St, Miles City, MT 59301; 406-874-3408; fax: 406-874-3452; 8AM-5PM (MST). *Misdemeanor, Civil Actions under $12,000, Eviction, Small Claims, Traffic.* www.co.custer.mt.us

General Information: Record search request must be in writing; fee is $25.00 per search.

Daniels County

District Court PO Box 67, Scobey, MT 59263; 406-487-2651; fax: 406-487-5432; 8AM-N, 1-5PM (MST). *Felony, Civil Actions over $12,000, Probate.*

General Information: Probate fax is same as main fax number. No adoption, juvenile or sanity records released. Fee to fax document $.50 per page. Court makes copy: $1.00 per page 1st 10 pages, then $.50 each add'l. Certification fee: $2.00 per document. Payee: Clerk of Court. Personal checks accepted. No credit cards accepted. Prepayment required. Mail requests: SASE required.

Civil Name Search: Access: Phone, mail, in person. Both court and visitors may perform in person name searches. Search fee: $2.00 per name per year, first 7 years, then $1.00 per year. Civil records on books since 1920; on computer back to 1997. Mail turnaround time same day.

Criminal Name Search: Access: Mail, in person, fax. Only the court performs in person name searches; visitors may not. Search fee: $2.00 per name per year, first 7 years, then $1.00 per year. Criminal docket on books since 1920; on computer back to 1986. Mail turnaround time 1-2 days.

Justice Court PO Box 838, County Courthouse, Upstairs, Scobey, MT 59263; 406-487-5432; fax: 406-487-5432; 8AM-10AM (MST). *Misdemeanor, Civil Actions under $12,000, Eviction, Small Claims.*

Dawson County

District Court 207 W Bell, Glendive, MT 59330; 406-377-3967; fax: 406-377-7280; 8AM-5PM (MST). *Felony, Civil Actions over $12,000, Probate.* www.dawsoncountymontana.com/clerk_of_court.htm

General Information: No adoption, juvenile, sanity or expunged records released. Will fax documents to local or toll free line. Court makes copy: $1.00 per page 1st 10 pages, then $.50 each add'l. Self serve copy: same.Marriage license copy-$5.00 plus cert fee; divorce decree copy-$10.00 plus cert fee. Certification fee: $2.00 per document. If they prepare authenticated copies fee is $6.00 for seal plus copy fee. Payee: Clerk of District Court. Only cashiers checks and money orders accepted. No credit cards accepted. Prepayment required. Mail requests: SASE required.

Civil Name Search: Access: Mail, in person. Both court and visitors may perform in person name searches. Search fee: $2.00 per name per year, first 7 years, then $1.00 per year. Civil records on computer from 1997, on card index prior. Mail turnaround time usually same or next day. Civil PAT goes back to 1997.

Criminal Name Search: Access: Mail, in person. Both court and visitors may perform in person name searches. Search fee: $2.00 per name per year, first 7 years, then $1.00 per year. Required to search: name, years to search, DOB, SSN. Criminal records computerized from 1997, on card index prior. Mail turnaround time usually same or next day. Criminal PAT goes back to same as civil.

Justice Court 207 W Bell St, Glendive, MT 59330; 406-377-5425; fax: 406-377-1869; 8AM-5PM (MST). *Misdemeanor, Civil Actions under $12,000, Eviction, Small Claims.*

Deer Lodge County

District Court 800 S Main, Anaconda, MT 59711; 406-563-4041; fax: 406-563-4077; 8AM-5PM (MST). *Felony, Civil Actions over $12,000, Probate.*

General Information: No adoption, juvenile or sanity records released. Fee to fax out $1.00 1st pg, $.50 each add'l. Court makes copy: $1.00 per page 1st 10 pages, then $.50 each add'l. Certification fee: $2.00. Payee: Clerk of Court. Personal checks accepted. No credit cards accepted. Prepayment required. Mail requests: SASE required.

Civil Name Search: Access: Phone, mail, in person. Both court and visitors may perform in person name searches. Search fee: $2.00 per name per year, first 7 years, then $1.00 per year. Civil records in archives and index books; on computer back to 1993. Mail turnaround time 2-3 days. Civil PAT goes back to 1993.

Criminal Name Search: Access: Mail, in person. Both court and visitors may perform in person name searches. Search fee: $2.00 per name per year, first 7 years, then $1.00 per year. Criminal records in archives and index books; on computer back to 1993. Mail turnaround time 2-3 days. Criminal PAT goes back to same as civil.

Justice Court 800 Main Street, Anaconda, MT 59711; 406-563-4025; fax: 406-563-4028; 8AM-N, 1-5PM (MST). *Misdemeanor, Civil Actions under $12,000, Eviction, Small Claims.*

Fallon County

District Court PO Box 1521, Baker, MT 59313; 406-778-8114; fax: 406-778-2815; 8AM-5PM (MST). *Felony, Civil Actions over $12,000, Eviction, Probate.*

General Information: Probate fax is same as main fax number. No confidential records released. Fee to fax out file $1.00 per page. Court makes copy: $1.00 per page 1st 10 pages, then $.50 each add'l. Certification fee: $2.00. Payee: Clerk of Court. Personal checks accepted. No credit cards accepted. Prepayment required. Mail requests: SASE required.

Civil Name Search: Access: Mail, in person. Both court and visitors may perform in person name searches. Search fee: $2.00 per name per year, first 7 years, then $1.00 per year. Required to search: name, years to search, address. Civil records in books. Mail turnaround time same day. Civil PAT goes back to 1913.

Criminal Name Search: Access: Mail, in person. Both court and visitors may perform in person name searches. Search fee: $2.00 per name per year, first 7 years, then $1.00 per year. Criminal records in books. Mail turnaround time same day. Criminal PAT goes back to 1914.

Justice Court Box 846, 10 W Fallon, Baker, MT 59313; 406-778-7128; fax: 406-778-4414; 2PM-5PM Wed; 11AM-5PM Th, Fri (MST). *Misdemeanor, Civil Actions under $12,000, Eviction, Small Claims.*

Fergus County

District Court PO Box 1074, 712 W Main, Lewistown, MT 59457; 406-535-5026; fax: 406-535-6076; 8AM-5PM (MST). *Felony, Civil Actions over $12,000, Eviction, Probate.*

www.co.fergus.mt.us

General Information: Probate fax is same as main fax number. No adoption, juvenile, sanity or expunged records released. Fee to fax out file $1.00 per page. Court makes copy: $1.00 per page 1st 10 pages, then $.50 each add'l. Self serve copy: same. Certification fee: $2.00 per document. Payee: Clerk of Court. Personal checks and credit cards accepted. Prepayment required. Mail requests: SASE required.

Civil Name Search: Access: Phone, fax, mail, in person. Both court and visitors may perform in person name searches. Search fee: $2.00 per name per year, first 7 years, then $1.00 per year. Civil records on computer back to 1997; prior on docket books, microfiche. Mail turnaround time 1 day. Civil PAT goes back to 1996.

Criminal Name Search: Access: Phone, fax, mail, in person. Both court and visitors may perform in person name searches. Search fee: $2.00 per name per year, first 7 years, then $1.00 per year. Criminal records computerized from 1997; prior on docket books, microfiche. Mail turnaround time 1 day. Criminal PAT goes back to same as civil.

Justice Court 121 8th Ave South, Lewistown, MT 59457; 406-535-5418; fax: 406-535-3860; 9AM-4PM (MST). *Misdemeanor, Civil under 7,000, Eviction, Small Claims, Ordinance.*

www.midrivers.com/~fergusco/jpcourt/jpcourt.html

General Information: You may email requests to jpcourt@co.fergus.mt.us

Flathead County

District Court 800 S Main, Kalispell, MT 59901; 406-758-5660; fax: 406-758-5652; 8AM-5PM (MST). *Felony, Civil Actions over $10,000, Probate.*

http://flathead.mt.gov/clerk_of_court/

General Information: The address above should be used for mail requests. Court clerk location is 920 S. Main, 3rd Fl. No adoption, dependent/neglected children or sanity records released. Fee to fax out file $1.00 per page. Court makes copy: $1.00 per page; $.50 per page after first 10. Certification fee: $2.00 per doc plus copy fee. Payee: Clerk of Court. Personal checks accepted. No credit cards accepted. Prepayment required. Mail requests: SASE required.

Civil Name Search: Access: Mail, in person. Both court and visitors may perform in person name searches. Search fee: $2.00 per name per year, first 7 years, then $1.00 per year. Civil records on computer since 1990; records go back to 1893. Mail turnaround time 10 days. Civil PAT goes back to 1990. Public terminal results do not always include identifiers.

Criminal Name Search: Access: Mail, in person. Both court and visitors may perform in person name searches. Search fee: $2.00 per name per year, first 7 years, then $1.00 per year. Criminal records on computer since 1990; records go back to 1893. Note: In person searchers will not be able to view confidential criminal records. Mail turnaround time 24-48 hours. Criminal PAT goes back to 1990.

County Justice Court 800 S Main, Kalispell, MT 59901; 406-758-5649; fax: 406-758-5842; 8AM-5PM (MST). *Misdemeanor, Civil Actions under $12,000, Eviction, Small Claims.*

http://flathead.mt.gov/justice_court/

Gallatin County

Clerk of District Court 615 S 16th St, Rm 302, Bozeman, MT 59715; 406-582-2165; fax: 406-582-2176; 8AM-5PM (MST). *Felony, Civil Actions over $12,000, Probate.*

www.gallatin.mt.gov

General Information: No adoption or sanity records released. Fee to fax out file $2.00 1st page, $1.00 ea add'l page. Court makes copy: $1.00 per page; $.50 per page after 1st 10 pages. Certification fee: $2.00. Payee: Clerk of Court. Personal checks accepted. No credit cards accepted. Prepayment required. If not sure of correct check amount, leave amount blank and put in 'not to exceed $30.00.'. Mail requests: SASE required.

Civil Name Search: Access: Phone, mail, fax, in person. Both court and visitors may perform in person name searches. Search fee: $2.00 per name per year, first 7 years, then $1.00 per year. Civil records on computer back to 1985; docket books back to 1860. Mail turnaround time 1-3 days. Civil PAT goes back to 1985. 2 access terminal available.

Criminal Name Search: Access: Mail, in person. Both court and visitors may perform in person name searches. Search fee: $2.00 per name per year, first 7 years, then $1.00 per year. Criminal records computerized from 1985; docket books back to 1860. Mail turnaround time 1-3 days. Criminal PAT goes back to same as civil.

Belgrade City Court 91 E Central, Belgrade, MT 59714; 406-388-3774; fax: 406-388-3779; 8AM-N; 1PM-5PM (MST). *Misdemeanor, Civil Actions under $12,000, Eviction, Ordinance.*

www.ci.belgrade.mt.us

Gallatin County Justice Court 615 S 16th St, Rm 168, Bozeman, MT 59715; 406-582-2191; fax: 406-582-2163; 8AM-4PM (MST). *Misdemeanor, Civil Actions under $12,000, Eviction, Small Claims.*

www.gallatin.mt.gov/Public_Documents/gallatincomt_justice/justcourt

Garfield County

District Court PO Box 8, 352 Leavitt Ave, Jordan, MT 59337; 406-557-6254; fax: 406-557-2323; 8AM-5PM (MST). *Felony, Civil Actions over $12,000, Eviction, Probate.*

General Information: No adoption, juvenile or sanity records released. Will fax documents to local or toll free line. Court makes copy: $1.00 per page 1st 10 pages, then $.50 each add'l. Certification fee: $2.00 per cert plus copy fee. Payee: Clerk of Court. Personal checks accepted. No credit cards accepted. Prepayment required.

Civil Name Search: Access: Phone, mail, in person. Both court and visitors may perform in person name searches. Search fee: $2.00 per name per year, first 7 years, then $1.00 per year. Civil cases indexed by plaintiff. Civil records in books from early 1900s; computerized records go back to 1998. Note: Some records lost due to fire in December, 1997. Mail turnaround time 1 week.

Criminal Name Search: Access: Phone, mail, in person. Both court and visitors may perform in person name searches. Search fee: $2.00 per name per year, first 7 years, then $1.00 per year. Required to search: name, years to search; also helpful: DOB. Criminal records in books from early 1900s, computerized records go back to 1998. Note: Some records lost due to fire in December, 1997. Mail turnaround time 1 week.

Justice Court PO Box 482, 352 Leavitt St, Jordan, MT 59337; 406-557-2733; fax: 406-557-2735; 8AM-5PM W (MST). *Misdemeanor, Civil Actions under $12,000, Eviction, Small Claims.*

Glacier County

District Court 512 E Main St, Cut Bank, MT 59427; 406-873-3619; fax: 406-873-5627; 8AM-5PM (MST). *Felony, Civil Actions, Probate.*

General Information: Probate fax is same as main fax number. No adoption, juvenile, sanity or paternity records released without court order. Fee to fax out file $1.00 per page. Court makes copy: $1.00 per page 1st 10 pages, then $.50 each add'l. Self serve copy: $1.00 per page. Certification fee: $2.00 per cert plus copy fee. Payee: Clerk of District Court. Personal checks accepted. No credit cards accepted. Prepayment required. Mail requests: SASE requested.

Civil Name Search: Access: Phone, fax, mail, in person, email. Both court and visitors may perform in person name searches. Search fee: $2.00 per name per year, first 7 years, then $1.00 per year. Civil records in books from 1919; on computer since 1992. Note: Direct email search requests to dianderson@mt.gov Mail turnaround time usually same day, 2-3 hours for phone requests depending on workload. Civil PAT goes back to 1919.

Criminal Name Search: Access: Fax, mail, in person. Both court and visitors may perform in person name searches. Search fee: $2.00 per name per year, first 7 years, then $1.00 per year. Required to search: name, years to search, DOB, SSN. Criminal records in books from 1919; on computer since 1992. Note: Written request required. Mail turnaround time usually same day, 2-3 hours for phone requests depending on workload. Criminal PAT goes back to 1919.

Justice Court 512 E Main St, Cut Bank, MT 59427; 406-873-3631; fax: 406-873-3659; 8AM-N, 1-5PM (MST). *Misdemeanor, Civil Actions under $12,000, Eviction, Small Claims.*

Golden Valley County

District Court PO Box 10, Ryegate, MT 59074; 406-568-2231; fax: 406-568-2428; 8AM-5PM (MST). *Felony, Civil Actions over $12,000, Eviction, Probate.*

General Information: No adoption, juvenile or sanity records released. Will fax documents $1.00 per page. Same fee applies to send them a fax. Court makes copy: $1.00 per page 1st 10 pages, then $.50 each add'l. Self serve copy: same. Certification fee: $2.00. Payee: Clerk of Court. Personal checks accepted. No credit cards accepted. Prepayment required. Mail requests: SASE required.

Civil Name Search: Access: Fax, mail, in person. Only the court performs in person name searches; visitors may not. Search fee: $2.00 per name per year, first 7 years, then $1.00 per year. Required to search: name, years to search, signed release. Civil records on books back to 1923. Computerized records back to 1997. Mail turnaround time 2-3 days.

Criminal Name Search: Access: Fax, mail, in person. Only the court performs in person name searches; visitors may not. Search fee: $2.00 per name per year, first 7 years, then $1.00 per year. Required to search: name, years to search, signed release. Criminal docket on books to 1923. Computerized records go back to 1997. Mail turnaround time 2-3 days.

Justice Court PO Box 10, 104 Kemp, Ryegate, MT 59074; 406-568-2102; fax: 406-568-2428; 9AM-5PM Tues (MST). *Misdemeanor, Civil Actions under $12,000, Eviction, Small Claims.*

Granite County

District Court PO Box 399, 220 N Sansome, Philipsburg, MT 59858-0399; 406-859-3712; fax: 406-859-3817; 8AM-N, 1-5PM (MST). *Felony, Civil Actions over $12,000, Eviction, Probate.*

General Information: No adoption, juvenile or sanity records released. Will fax documents $1.00 per page. Court makes copy: $1.00 per page 1st 10 pages, then $.50 each add'l. Self serve copy: same. Certification fee: $2.00. Payee: Clerk of Court. Personal checks accepted. No credit cards accepted. Prepayment required. Mail requests: SASE required.

Civil Name Search: Access: Phone, fax, mail, in person. Both court and visitors may perform in person name searches. Search fee: $2.00 per name per year, first 7 years, then $1.00 per year. Civil index on docket books since 1893. Mail turnaround time 1-4 days. Civil PAT goes back to 1990.

Criminal Name Search: Access: Phone, fax, mail, in person. Both court and visitors may perform in person name searches. Search fee: $2.00 per name per year, first 7 years, then $1.00 per year. Criminal docket on books since 1893. Mail turnaround time 1-4 days. Criminal PAT goes back to same as civil.

Drummond Justice Court #2 - See Philipsburg , MT; .
General Information: Court is closed, case files are at the Justice Court in Philipsburg.

Philipsburg Justice Court PO Box 356, 330 N Sansom, Philipsburg, MT 59858; 406-859-3006; fax: 406-859-7025; 10AM-12, 1-5PM M,W,F (MST). *Misdemeanor, Civil Actions under $12,000, Eviction, Small Claims.*

Hill County

District Court 315 Fourth St, Havre, MT 59501; 406-265-5481 X224; fax: 406-265-3693; 8AM-5PM (MST). *Felony, Civil Actions over $12,000, Eviction, Probate.*
http://co.hill.mt.us

General Information: No adoption, juvenile, paternity, sanity records released. Will fax documents $1.00 per page. Court makes copy: $1.00 per page 1st 10 pages, then $.50 each add'l. Certification fee: $2.00. Payee: Clerk of Court. Business checks accepted. No credit cards accepted. Prepayment required. Mail requests: SASE required.

Civil Name Search: Access: Phone, fax, mail, in person. Both court and visitors may perform in person name searches. Search fee: $2.00 per name per year, first 7 years, then $1.00 per year. Required to search: name, years to search; also very helpful- maiden name. Civil records on computer since 1985; prior records on docket books to 1912. Mail turnaround time same day. Civil PAT goes back to 1985.

Criminal Name Search: Access: Fax, mail, in person. Both court and visitors may perform in person name searches. Search fee: $2.00 per name per year, first 7 years, then $1.00 per year. Required to search: name, years to search; also helpful: maiden name. Criminal records on computer since 1988; prior records on docket books to 1912. Note: Absolutely no criminal record checks by phone. Mail turnaround time same day. Criminal PAT goes back to 1988.

Justice Court Hill County Courthouse, 315 4th St, Havre, MT 59501; 406-265-5481 X240; fax: 406-262-9441; 8AM-5PM (MST). *Misdemeanor, Civil Actions under $12,000, Eviction, Small Claims.*
http://co.hill.mt.us

Jefferson County

District Court PO Box H, 201 W Centennial, Boulder, MT 59632; 406-225-4041/4042; fax: 406-225-4044; 8AM-N, 1-5PM (MST). *Felony, Civil Actions over $12,000, Eviction, Probate.*
www.jeffco.mt.gov/county/courts.html

General Information: Juvenile, sanity or adoption records not released. Will fax documents to local or toll-free number, otherwise $1.00 per page. Court makes copy: $1.00 per page 1st 10 pages, then $.50 each add'l. Certification fee: $2.00 per doc. Payee: Clerk of Court. Personal checks accepted. No credit cards accepted. Prepayment required. Mail requests: SASE required.

Civil Name Search: Access: Mail, fax, in person. Both court and visitors may perform in person name searches. Search fee: $2.00 per name per year, first 7 years, then $1.00 per year. Civil records on computer since 1993, on microfilm since 1925. Mail turnaround time same day. Civil PAT goes back to 1993.

Criminal Name Search: Access: Mail, fax, in person. Both court and visitors may perform in person name searches. Search fee: $2.00 per name per year, first 7 years, then $1.00 per year. Criminal records on computer since 1992, on microfilm since 1925. Mail turnaround time same day. Criminal PAT goes back to 1992.

Justice Court PO Box H, 108 S Washington, Boulder, MT 59632; 406-225-4055; 8AM-N, 1-5PM (MST). *Misdemeanor, Civil Actions under $12,000, Eviction, Small Claims.*

Judith Basin County

District Court PO Box 307, Stanford, MT 59479; 406-566-2277 X113; fax: 406-566-2211; 8AM-5PM (MST). *Felony, Civil Actions over $12,000, Probate.*

General Information: Probate is a separate index at this same address. Probate fax is same as main fax number. No adoption, sanity records released. Will fax documents. Court makes copy: $1.00 per page 1st 10 pages, then $.50 each add'l. Self serve copy: Criminal self serve copy $1.00 per page; No civil self serve. Certification fee: $2.00 per document plus copy fee. Payee: Clerk of Court. Business checks accepted. No credit cards accepted. Prepayment required. Mail requests: SASE required.

Civil Name Search: Access: Phone, fax, mail, in person. Both court and visitors may perform in person name searches. Search fee: $2.00 per name per year, first 7 years, then $1.00 per year. Civil records on books back to 1920; on computer back to 1996. Mail turnaround time 10 days.

Criminal Name Search: Access: Phone, mail, in person. Both court and visitors may perform in person name searches. Search fee: $2.00 per name per year, first 7 years, then $1.00 per year. Required to search: name, years to search, signed release. Criminal docket on books back to 1920; on computer back to 1996. Mail turnaround time 10 days.

Justice Court PO Box 339, 91Third St North, Stanford, MT 59479; 406-566-2277 X117; fax: 406-566-2211; 8AM-5PM (MST). *Misdemeanor, Civil Actions under $12,000, Eviction, Small Claims.*

Lake County

District Court Clerk of District Court Office, 106 4th Ave E, Polson, MT 59860; 406-883-7254; fax: 406-883-8582; 8AM-5PM (MST). *Felony, Civil Actions over $12,000, Probate.*

General Information: No adoption, juvenile, sanity or expunged records released. Will fax documents $1.00 per page. Court makes copy: $1.00 per page 1st 10 pages, then $.50 each add'l. Certification fee: $2.00. Payee: Clerk of Court. Business checks accepted. No credit cards accepted. Prepayment required. Mail requests: SASE required.

Civil Name Search: Access: Phone, fax, mail, in person. Both court and visitors may perform in person name searches. Search fee: $2.00 per name per year, first 7 years, then $1.00 per year. Civil records on books since 1923; on computer since 1990. Mail turnaround time 3 days; 2 hours for phone requests. Civil PAT goes back to 1989.

Criminal Name Search: Access: Phone, fax, mail, in person. Both court and visitors may perform in person name searches. Search fee: $2.00 per name per year, first 7 years, then $1.00 per year. Criminal docket on books since 1923; on computer since 1990. Mail turnaround time 3 days; 2 hours for phone requests. Criminal PAT goes back to same as civil.

Justice Court 106 4th Ave E, Polson, MT 59860; 406-883-7258; fax: 406-883-7343; 8AM-5PM (MST). *Misdemeanor, Civil Actions under $12,000, Eviction, Small Claims.*

Lewis and Clark County

District Court 228 Broadway, PO Box 158, Helena, MT 59624; 406-447-8216; fax: 406-447-8275; 8AM-5PM (MST). *Felony, Civil Actions over $12,000, Eviction, Probate, Small Claims.* www.co.lewis-clark.mt.us

General Information: No adoption or sanity records released. Fee to fax out file $1.00 per page. Court makes copy: $1.00 per page 1st 10 pages, then $.50 each add'l. Self serve copy: same. Certification fee: $2.00. Payee: Clerk of Court. Personal and business checks accepted. Visa/MC accepted. Prepayment required. Mail requests: SASE required.

Civil Name Search: Access: Fax, mail, in person, email. Both court and visitors may perform in person name searches. Search fee: $2.00 per name per year, first 7 years, then $1.00 per year. Civil records on computer since 1991, microfilm prior to 1/99. Mail turnaround time 2 days. Civil PAT goes back to 1991. Will accept email record requests to cpotuzak@co.lewis-clark.mt.us.

Criminal Name Search: Access: Fax, mail, in person, email. Both court and visitors may perform in person name searches. Search fee: $2.00 per name per year, first 7 years, then $1.00 per year. Criminal records on computer since 1993, microfilm prior to 1/97. Mail turnaround time 2 days. Criminal PAT goes back to 1993. Will accept email record requests to cpotuzak@co.lewis-clark.mt.us Online results show name only.

Justice Court 228 Broadway, Helena, MT 59601; 406-447-8202; fax: 406-447-8269; 8AM-4PM M-F (MST). *Misdemeanor, Civil Actions under $12,000, Eviction, Small Claims, Ordinance.* www.co.lewis-clark.mt.us/

Liberty County

District Court PO Box 549, Chester, MT 59522; 406-759-5615; fax: 406-759-5996; 8AM-5PM (MST). *Felony, Civil Actions over $12,000, Eviction, Probate.*

General Information: With fax requests include copy of your check. No adoption, juvenile or sanity records released. Will fax documents to local or toll free line. Court makes copy: $1.00 per page 1st 10 pages, then $.50 each add'l. Certification fee: $2.00 per cert plus copy fee. Payee: Clerk of Court. Personal checks accepted. No credit cards accepted. Prepayment required. Mail requests: SASE required.

Civil Name Search: Access: Fax, mail, in person. Both court and visitors may perform in person name searches. Search fee: $2.00 per name per year, first 7 years, then $1.00 per year. Required to search: name, years to search, address. Civil records on books since 1920. Mail turnaround time 2-3 days.

Criminal Name Search: Access: Fax, mail, in person, fax. Both court and visitors may perform in person name searches. Search fee: $2.00 per name per year, first 7 years, then $1.00 per year. Required to search: name, years to search, signed release. Criminal docket on books since 1920. Mail turnaround time 2-3 days.

Justice Court PO Box 161, 311 1/2 Adams Ave, Chester, MT 59522; 406-759-5213; fax: 406-759-5455; 9AM-N, 1-5PM Tues (MST). *Misdemeanor, Civil Actions under $12,000, Eviction, Small Claims.*

Lincoln County

District Court 512 California Ave, Libby, MT 59923; 406-293-7781; probate phone: x224; fax: 406-293-9816; 8AM-5PM (MST). *Felony, Civil Actions over $12,000, Probate.* www.lincolncountymt.us/clerkofcourt/index.html

General Information: No adoption, juvenile or sanity records released. Will fax out results for price of copies. Court makes copy: $1.00 per page, divorce decree- $10.00. Certification fee: $2.00. Payee: Clerk of Court. Personal checks accepted. No credit cards accepted. Prepayment required. Mail requests: SASE required.

Civil Name Search: Access: Mail, in person. Both court and visitors may perform in person name searches. Search fee: $2.00 per name per year, first 7 years, then $1.00 per year. Civil records on computer from 1996, prior on docket books. Mail turnaround time 1 week. Civil PAT goes back to 1996.

Criminal Name Search: Access: Mail, in person. Both court and visitors may perform in person name searches. Search fee: $2.00 per name per year, first 7 years, then $1.00 per year. Criminal records computerized from 1996, prior on docket books. Mail turnaround time 1 week. Criminal PAT goes back to same as civil.

Eureka Justice Court #2 PO Box 403, Eureka, MT 59917; 406-297-2622; fax: 406-297-3829; 8AM-N, 1-5PM (MST). *Misdemeanor, Civil Actions under $12,000, Eviction, Small Claims.*
General Information: This court covers the Eastern portion of the county.

Libby Justice Court #1 418 Mineral Ave, Libby, MT 59923; 406-283-2411/2412/2413; fax: 406-293-5948; 8AM-5PM (MST). *Misdemeanor, Civil Actions under $12,000, Eviction, Small Claims.*
General Information: This court covers the Western portion of the county.

Madison County

District Court PO Box 185, Virginia City, MT 59755; 406-843-4230; fax: 406-843-5207; 8AM-5PM (MST). *Felony, Civil Actions over $12,000, Eviction, Probate.* www.madison.mt.gov/departments/district_court/district_court.asp

General Information: No adoption, juvenile or sanity records released. Fee to fax out file $4.00 1st page, $1.00 each add'l. Court makes copy: $1.00 per page 1st 10 pages, then $.50 each add'l. Self serve copy: same. Certification

fee: $2.00. Payee: Clerk of Court. Personal checks accepted. No credit cards accepted. Prepayment required. Mail requests: SASE required for mail return of any copies.

Civil Name Search: Access: Phone, fax, mail, in person. Both court and visitors may perform in person name searches. Search fee: $2.00 per name per year, first 7 years, then $1.00 per year. Civil records on books since 1864; on computer back to 1990. Mail turnaround time 1 week. Civil PAT goes back to 1990.

Criminal Name Search: Access: Fax, mail, in person. Both court and visitors may perform in person name searches. Search fee: $2.00 per name per year, first 7 years, then $1.00 per year. Criminal docket on books since 1864; on computer back to 1990. Mail turnaround time 1 week. Criminal PAT goes back to same as civil.

Madison County Justice Court PO Box 277, 100 W Wallace St, Virginia City, MT 59755; 406-843-4237; fax: 406-843-4219; 8AM-5PM (MST). *Misdemeanor, Civil Actions under $12,000, Eviction, Small Claims.* www.madison.mt.gov/departments/justice_court/justice_ct.asp

McCone County

District Court PO Box 199, 1004 C Ave, Circle, MT 59215; 406-485-3410; fax: 406-485-3436; 8AM-5PM (MST). *Felony, Civil Actions over $12,000, Eviction, Probate.* www.mccone.mt.gov/

General Information: No adoption, juvenile, sanity or mental health records released. Will fax documents to local or toll free line. Court makes copy: $1.00 per page 1st 10 pages, then $.50 each add'l. Certification fee: $2.00 per cert plus copy fee. Payee: Clerk of Court. Personal checks accepted. No credit cards accepted. Prepayment required. Mail requests: SASE helpful.

Civil Name Search: Access: Mail, in person. Only the court performs in person name searches; visitors may not. Search fee: $2.00 per name per year, first 7 years, then $1.00 per year. Civil records in books from 1919, computerized since 1996. Mail turnaround time 1-2 days.

Criminal Name Search: Access: Mail, in person. Only the court performs in person name searches; visitors may not. Search fee: $2.00 per name per year, first 7 years, then $1.00 per year. Criminal records in books and microfilm since 1919, computerized since 1996. Mail turnaround time 1-2 days.

Justice Court PO Box 192, 1004 C Ave, Circle, MT 59215; 406-485-3548; fax: 406-485-2689; 9AM-N Tues& W (MST). *Misdemeanor, Civil Actions under $12,000, Eviction, Small Claims.*

Meagher County

District Court PO Box 443, White Sulphur Springs, MT 59645; 406-547-3612 x110; fax: 406-547-3836; 7:30AM-4PM (MST). *Felony, Civil Actions over $12,000, Eviction, Probate.*

General Information: No adoption, juvenile or sanity records released. Will fax documents to local or toll-free number. Court makes copy: $1.00 per page 1st 10 pages, then $.50 each add'l. Certification fee: $2.00. Payee: Clerk of Court. Personal checks accepted. No credit cards accepted. Prepayment required. Mail requests: SASE required.

Civil Name Search: Access: Phone, mail, fax, in person. Both court and visitors may perform in person name searches. Search fee: $2.00 per name per year, first 7 years, then $1.00 per year. Civil index on docket books or microfiche to 1900; on computer back to 1996. Mail turnaround time 1 day or same day.

Criminal Name Search: Access: Phone, mail, fax, in person. Both court and visitors may perform in person name searches. Search fee: $2.00 per name per year, first 7 years, then $1.00 per year. Required to search: name, years to search, DOB. Criminal docket on books or microfiche to 1900; on computer back to 1996. Mail turnaround time 3 days.

Justice Court PO Box 698, Justice Court, 15 W Main St, White Sulphur Springs, MT 59645; 406-547-3612 x5; fax: 406-547-3961; 8AM-N (MST). *Misdemeanor, Civil Actions under $12,000, Eviction, Small Claims.*

Mineral County

District Court PO Box 129, Superior, MT 59872; 406-822-3538; fax: 406-822-3822; 8AM-N,1-5PM (MST). *Felony, Civil Actions over $12,000, Probate.* www.co.mineral.mt.us/

General Information: Probate is a separate index at this same address. 2nd fax is 406-822-3822. No adoption, sanity records released. Fee to fax out file $5.00 each. You must fax request with copy of payment check. Court makes copy: $1.00 per page 1st 10 pages, then $.50 each add'l. Certification fee: $2.00 per document plus copy fee. Payee: Clerk of Court. Personal checks accepted. No credit cards accepted. Prepayment required. Mail requests: SASE required.

Civil Name Search: Access: Fax, mail, in person. Only the court performs in person name searches; visitors may not. Search fee: $2.00 per name per year, first 7 years, then $1.00 per year. Civil index in docket books from 1914, on computer back to 1990. Mail turnaround time same day after payment received.

Criminal Name Search: Access: Fax, mail, in person. Only the court performs in person name searches; visitors may not. Search fee: $2.00 per name per year, first 7 years, then $1.00 per year. Criminal docket on books from 1914, on computer back to 1990. Mail turnaround time same day after payment received.

Justice Court PO Box 658, 300 River St, Superior, MT 59872; 406-822-3550; fax: 406-822-3821; 8AM-N, 1-5PM (MST). *Misdemeanor, Civil Actions under $12,000, Eviction, Small Claims.*

Missoula County

District Court 200 W Broadway, 2nd Fl, Courthouse, Missoula, MT 59802; 406-258-4780; fax: 406-258-4899; 8AM-5PM (MST). *Felony, Civil Actions over $12,000, Probate.*

www.co.missoula.mt.us/coc/

General Information: No adoption, juvenile, sealed, expunged or pre-sentence psychiatric records released. Will fax documents $2.00 each; no fee if returning on toll free line. Court makes copy: $1.00 per page 1st 10 pages, then $.50 each add'l. Certification fee: $2.00. Exemplification fee- $4.00 plus copy fee. Payee: Clerk of Court. Personal checks accepted. Visa/MC accepted. Prepayment required. Mail requests: SASE requested.

Civil Name Search: Access: Fax, mail, in person. Both court and visitors may perform in person name searches. Search fee: $2.00 per name per year, first 7 years, then $1.00 per year. Civil records on computer from 10/89, microfilm from 1970s, archived to late 1800s. Mail turnaround time up to 2 weeks. Civil PAT goes back to 1989. Images on the public access terminals can be printed out, also emailed.

Criminal Name Search: Access: Fax, mail, in person. Both court and visitors may perform in person name searches. Search fee: $2.00 per name per year, first 7 years, then $1.00 per year. Criminal records computerized from 10/89, microfilm from 1970s, archived to late 1800s. Mail turnaround time up to 2 weeks. Criminal PAT goes back to same as civil. Images on the public access terminals can be printed out, also emailed.

Limited Jurisdiction Court - Dept 1 200 W Broadway, Missoula County Courthouse, 3rd Fl, Missoula, MT 59802; 406-258-4871; fax: 406-258-3935; 8AM-5PM (MST). *Misdemeanor, Civil Actions under $12,000, Eviction, Small Claims.*

www.co.missoula.mt.us/jp1/

Musselshell County

District Court 506 Main St, Roundup, MT 59072; 406-323-1413; fax: 406-323-1710; 8AM-N, 1-5PM (MST). *Felony, Civil Actions over $12,000, Eviction, Probate.*

General Information: Include copy of the fees check with any fax requests. Probate fax is same as main fax number. No adoption, (some) juvenile or sanity records released. Will fax documents to local or toll free line. Court makes copy: $1.00 per page 1st 10 pages, then $.50 each add'l. Self serve copy: same. Certification fee: $2.00 per document plus copy fee. Payee: Clerk of Court. Personal checks accepted. No credit cards accepted. Prepayment required. Mail requests: SASE required.

Civil Name Search: Access: Mail, fax, in person. Both court and visitors may perform in person name searches. Search fee: $2.00 per name per year, first 7 years, then $1.00 per year. Computerized records from 7/96, civil records on docket books from 1911 searchable by visitors. Mail turnaround time 2-3 days.

Criminal Name Search: Access: Mail, fax, in person. Both court and visitors may perform in person name searches. Search fee: $2.00 per name per year, first 7 years, then $1.00 per year. Criminal docket on books from 1911. Mail turnaround time 2-3 days.

Justice Court PO Box 660, 34 2nd Ave W, Roundup, MT 59072; 406-323-1078; fax: 406-323-1734; 9AM-4PM (MST). *Misdemeanor, Civil Actions under $12,000, Eviction, Small Claims.*

Park County

District Court PO Box 437, Livingston, MT 59047; 406-222-4125; fax: 406-222-4128; 8AM-5PM (MST). *Felony, Civil Actions over $12,000, Eviction, Probate.*

General Information: No adoption, juvenile or sanity records released. Court makes copy: $1.00 per page first 10 pages, then $.50 each add'l. Certification fee: $2.00. Payee: Clerk of Court. Personal checks accepted. No credit cards accepted. Prepayment required.

Civil Name Search: Access: Fax, mail, in person. Both court and visitors may perform in person name searches. Search fee: $2.00 per name per year, first 7 years, then $1.00 per year. Civil records on computer, microfiche, and docket books from 1889 to present. Mail turnaround time 1-2 days for all requests. Civil PAT goes back to 1980.

Criminal Name Search: Access: Fax, mail, in person. Both court and visitors may perform in person name searches. Search fee: $2.00 per name per year, first 7 years, then $1.00 per year. Criminal records on computer, microfiche, and docket books from 1889 to present. Mail turnaround time 1-2 days for all requests. Criminal PAT goes back to 1996.

Justice Court 414 E Callender, Livingston, MT 59047; 406-222-4169/4170; civil phone: 406-222-4149; fax: 406-222-4103; 8AM-N, 1PM-4:30PM (MST). *Misdemeanor, Civil Actions under $12,000, Eviction, Small Claims.*

www.parkcounty.org/Departments/JUSTICEOFTHEPEACE/JUSTICEOFTHEPEACE.html

Petroleum County

District Court PO Box 226, Winnett, MT 59087; 406-429-5311; fax: 406-429-6328; 8AM-4PM (MST). *Felony, Civil Actions over $12,000, Eviction, Probate.*

General Information: No adoption, juvenile or sanity records released. Will fax documents to local or toll free line. Court makes copy: $1.00 per page 1st 10 pages, then $.50 each add'l. Self serve copy: same. Certification fee: $2.00. Payee: Clerk of Court. Personal checks accepted. No credit cards accepted. Prepayment required. Mail requests: SASE required.

Civil Name Search: Access: Phone, mail, in person. Both court and visitors may perform in person name searches. Search fee: $2.00 per name per year, first 7 years, then $1.00 per year. Civil index in docket books from 1924. Mail turnaround time 1 day.

Criminal Name Search: Access: Phone, mail, in person. Only the court performs in person name searches; visitors may not. Search fee: $2.00 per name per year, first 7 years, then $1.00 per year. Criminal docket on books from 1924. Mail turnaround time 1 day.

Justice Court PO Box 226, 201 E Main, Winnett, MT 59087; 406-429-5311; fax: 406-429-6328; 9AM-4PM TH (MST). *Misdemeanor, Civil Actions under $12,000, Eviction, Small Claims.*

Phillips County

District Court PO Box 530, 314 S 2nd Ave W, Malta, MT 59538; 406-654-1023; fax: 406-654-1023; 8AM-5PM (MST). *Felony, Civil Actions over $12,000, Eviction, Probate.*

General Information: Probate fax is same as main fax number. No adoption, juvenile or sanity records released. Will fax documents $5.00; no charge to toll free number. Court makes copy: $1.00 per page 1st 10 pages, then $.50 each add'l. Certification fee: $2.00 per document. Payee: Clerk of Court. Personal checks accepted. No credit cards accepted. Prepayment required. Mail requests: SASE required.

Civil Name Search: Access: Mail, in person. Only the court performs in person name searches; visitors may not. Search fee: $2.00 per name per year, first 7 years, then $1.00 per year. Civil records on computer back to 1997; prior on books. Mail turnaround time 1-2 days.

Criminal Name Search: Access: Mail, in person. Only the court performs in person name searches; visitors may not. Search fee: $2.00 per name per year, first 7 years, then $1.00 per year. Required to search: name, years to search, signed release. Criminal records computerized from 1997; books, microfilm back to 1915. Mail turnaround time 1-2 days.

Justice Court PO Box 1396, 314 S 2nd Ave West, Malta, MT 59538; 406-654-1118; fax: 406-654-1213; 9AM-3PM M-TH (MST). *Misdemeanor, Civil Actions under $12,000, Eviction, Small Claims.*

Pondera County

District Court 20 Fourth Ave SW, Conrad, MT 59425; 406-271-4026; fax: 406-271-4081; 8AM-5PM (MST). *Felony, Civil Actions over $12,000, Eviction, Probate.*

General Information: Probate fax is same as main fax number. No adoption, neglect, or juvenile, sanity records released. Will fax documents $3.00 1st page, $1.00 ea add'l. Court makes copy: $1.00 per page 1st 10 pages, then $.50 each add'l. Certification fee: $2.00 per document plus copy fee. Payee: Clerk of Court. Personal checks accepted, some restrictions apply. No credit cards accepted. Prepayment required. Mail requests: SASE required.

Civil Name Search: Access: Fax, mail, in person. Both court and visitors may perform in person name searches. Search fee: $2.00 per name per year, first 7 years, then $1.00 per year. Civil index in docket books from 1919; on computer back to 1995. Mail turnaround time 2-3 days. Civil PAT available.

Criminal Name Search: Access: Fax, mail, in person. Both court and visitors may perform in person name searches. Search fee: $2.00 per name per year, first 7 years, then $1.00 per year. Criminal docket on books from 1919; on computer back to 1995. Mail turnaround time 2-3 days. Criminal PAT available.

Justice Court 20 Fourth Ave SW, Conrad, MT 59425; 406-271-4030; fax: 406-271-4031; 9AM-N, 1-4PM (MST). *Misdemeanor, Civil Actions under $12,000, Eviction, Small Claims.*

Powder River County

District Court PO Box 200, Broadus, MT 59317; 406-436-2320; fax: 406-436-2325; 8AM-N, 1-5PM (MST). *Felony, Civil Actions over $12,000, Probate.*

http://prco.mt.gov/departments/ClerkofDistrictCourt.asp

General Information: Probate is a separate index at this same address. Probate fax is same as main fax number. No adoption, juvenile, sanity, dismissed criminal records released. Fee to fax out file $1.00 per page. Court makes copy: $1.00 per page 1st 10 pages, then $.50 each add'l. Certification fee: $2.00 per cert plus copy fee. Payee: Clerk of Court. Only cashiers checks and money orders accepted. No credit cards accepted. Prepayment required. Mail requests: SASE required.

Civil Name Search: Access: Fax, mail, in person. Both court and visitors may perform in person name searches. Search fee: $2.00 per name per year, first 7 years, then $1.00 per year. Civil records on computer since 1993, microfiche since 1974, and books since 1919. Mail turnaround time same day. Civil PAT goes back to 1993.

Criminal Name Search: Access: Fax, mail, in person. Both court and visitors may perform in person name searches. Search fee: $2.00 per name per year, first 7 years, then $1.00 per year. Criminal records on computer since 1993, microfiche since 1974, and books since 1919. Mail turnaround time same day if prepaid. Criminal PAT goes back to same as civil.

Justice Court PO Box 692, Courthouse Sq, Broadus, MT 59317; 406-436-2503; fax: 406-436-2866; 8AM-5PM M-W, 8AM-N Th (MST). *Misdemeanor, Civil Actions under $12,000, Eviction, Small Claims.* http://prco.mt.gov

General Information: Record requests must in writing on letterhead. $25.00 per person includes 10 year search & 10 copies; after 10 copies $.45 per page (certified) or $.25 per page (non-certified).

Powell County

District Court 409 Missouri Ave, Deer Lodge, MT 59722; 406-846-3680 X234/235; fax: 406-846-1031; 8AM-5PM (MST). *Felony, Civil Actions over $12,000, Eviction, Probate.*

General Information: No adoption, juvenile or sanity records released. Will fax documents $1.00 per page. Court makes copy: $1.00 per page 1st 10 pages, then $.50 each add'l. Certification fee: $2.00. Payee: Clerk of Court. Personal checks accepted. No credit cards accepted. Prepayment required. Mail requests: SASE required.

Civil Name Search: Access: Mail, in person. Both court and visitors may perform in person name searches. Search fee: $2.00 per name per year, first 7 years, then $1.00 per year. Civil index on docket books since turn of century, on computer since 1996. Mail turnaround time 2-3 days. Civil PAT goes back to 1996.

Criminal Name Search: Access: Mail, in person. Both court and visitors may perform in person name searches. Search fee: $2.00 per name per year, first 7 years, then $1.00 per year. Required to search: name, years to search, DOB, SSN. Criminal docket on books since turn of century, on computer since 1996. Mail turnaround time 2-3 days. Criminal PAT goes back to same as civil.

Justice Court, City Court 409 Missouri, Powell County Courthouse, Deer Lodge, MT 59722; 406-846-3680; fax: 406-846-1031; 8AM-5PM (MST). *Misdemeanor, Civil Actions under $12,000, Eviction, Small Claims, Ordinance.*

General Information: $25.00 per name fee per 7 years for court to record search, even if request is in person; includes both courts.

Prairie County

District Court PO Box 125, Terry, MT 59349; 406-635-5575; fax: 406-635-5576; 8AM-N; 1PM-5PM (MST). *Felony, Civil Actions over $12,000, Eviction, Probate.*

General Information: No adoption, juvenile or sanity records released. Will fax documents to local or toll free line. Court makes copy: $1.00 1st 10 pages, $.50 each add'l page. Self serve copy: same. Certification fee: $2.00 per cert plus copy fee. Payee: Clerk of Court. Personal checks and credit cards accepted. Prepayment required. Mail requests: SASE requested.

Civil Name Search: Access: Fax, mail, in person. Both court and visitors may perform in person name searches. Search fee: $2.00 per name per year, first 7 years, then $1.00 per year. Civil records on books since 1915; computerized records go back to 1997. Mail turnaround time 5 days.

Criminal Name Search: Access: Fax, mail, in person. Both court and visitors may perform in person name searches. Search fee: $2.00 per name per year, first 7 years, then $1.00 per year. Required to search: name, years to search, DOB, SSN. Criminal docket on books since 1915; computerized records go back to 1997. Mail turnaround time 5 days.

Justice Court PO Box 124, 217 Park, Terry, MT 59349; 406-635-4466; fax: 406-635-4126; 12:30-3:30PM (MST). *Misdemeanor, Civil Actions under $12,000, Eviction, Small Claims, Ordinance.* www.prairie.mt.gov

Ravalli County

District Court Ravalli County Courthouse, 205 Bedford St. #D, Hamilton, MT 59840; 406-375-6710; fax: 406-375-6721; 9AM-5PM (MST). *Felony, Civil Actions over $12,000, Probate.* http://courts.mt.gov/locator/dist21.mcpx

General Information: Probate fax is same as main fax number. No adoption, juvenile, psychological, medical or expunged records released. Will fax documents $1.00 per page. Court makes copy: $1.00 per page 1st 10 pages, then $.50 each add'l. Self serve copy: same. Certification fee: $2.00 per cert plus copy fee; authentication or exemplification fee $6.00 plus copy fee. Payee: Clerk of Court. Personal checks accepted. No credit cards accepted. Prepayment required. Mail requests: SASE required.

Civil Name Search: Access: Mail, in person. Both court and visitors may perform in person name searches. Search fee: $2.00 per name per year, first 7 years, then $1.00 per year. Civil records on microfiche (1989), docket books (1914). Mail turnaround time 4-5 days. Civil PAT goes back to 1996.

Criminal Name Search: Access: Mail, in person. Both court and visitors may perform in person name searches. Search fee: $2.00 per name per year, first 7 years, then $1.00 per year. Criminal records on microfiche (1989), docket books (1914). Mail turnaround time 4-5 days. Criminal PAT goes back to same as civil.

Justice Court Dept. #1 and #2 205 Bedford St., Hamilton, MT 59840; 406-375-6755; fax: 406-375-6759; 9AM-5PM (MST). *Misdemeanor, Civil Actions under $12,000, Eviction, Small Claims.* http://rc.mt.gov/justicecourt/default.mcpx

Richland County

District Court 201 W Main, Sidney, MT 59270; 406-433-1709; fax: 406-433-6945; 8AM-5PM (MST). *Felony, Civil Actions over $12,000, Probate.*

General Information: Probate fax is same as main fax number. Evictions are handled by Justice and Small Claims Court, 406-433-2815. No adoption, juvenile, paternity, sanity, dismissed or expunged records released. Will fax documents $1.00 per page. Court makes copy: $1.00 per page 1st 10 pages, then $.50 each add'l. Self serve copy: same. Certification fee: $2.00 per seal. Payee: Clerk of Court. Personal checks accepted. No credit cards accepted. Prepayment required. Mail requests: SASE required.

Civil Name Search: Access: Phone, fax, mail, in person. Both court and visitors may perform in person name searches. Search fee: $2.00 per name per year, first 7 years, then $1.00 per year. Civil records in books since 1914; on computer back to 1997. Mail turnaround time 1-3 days.

Criminal Name Search: Access: Phone, fax, mail, in person. Both court and visitors may perform in person name searches. Search fee: $2.00 per name per year, first 7 years, then $1.00 per year. Criminal records in books since 1914; on computer back to 1997. Mail turnaround time 1-3 days.

Justice Court Sideny City Court, 300 12th Ave NW, Ste 6, Sidney, MT 59270; 406-433-2815; fax: 406-433-4021; 8AM-5PM (MST). *Misdemeanor, Civil Actions under $12,000, Eviction, Small Claims.*

Roosevelt County

District Court County Courthouse, 400 2nd Ave S, Wolf Point, MT 59201; 406-653-6266; fax: 406-653-6203; 8AM-5PM (MST). *Felony, Civil Actions over $12,000, Probate.*

General Information: No adoption, juvenile or sanity records released. Will fax documents $3.00 plus $1.00 per page. Court makes copy: $1.00 per page 1st 10 pages, then $.50 each add'l. Certification fee: $2.00. Payee: Clerk of Court. Personal checks accepted. No credit cards accepted. Prepayment required. Mail requests: SASE required.

Civil Name Search: Access: Phone, fax, mail, in person. Both court and visitors may perform in person name searches. Search fee: $2.00 per name per year, first 7 years, then $1.00 per year. Civil records on books and microfiche back to 1919, computerized back to 1996. Mail turnaround time 2-3 days after payment receipt.

Criminal Name Search: Access: Fax, mail, in person. Only the court performs in person name searches; visitors may not. Search fee: $2.00 per name per year, first 7 years, then $1.00 per year. Required to search: name, years to search; also helpful: DOB. Criminal docket on books and microfiche back to 1919, computerized back to 1996. Mail turnaround time 2-3 days after payment received.

Culbertson Justice Court Post #2 PO Box 421, 307 Broadway, Culbertson, MT 59218; 406-787-6607; fax: 406-787-6608; 9AM-3PM M-TH (MST). *Misdemeanor, Civil Actions under $12,000, Eviction, Small Claims.*

Wolf Point Justice Court Post #1 County Courthouse, 400 Second Ave. S., Wolf Point, MT 59201; 406-653-6261, 406-653-6258; fax: 406-653-6236; 8AM-N (MST). *Misdemeanor, Civil Actions under $12,000, Eviction, Small Claims, County Ordinance.*

General Information: This location is also home to Wolf Point City Court where city ordinances.

Rosebud County

District Court PO Box 48, 1200 Main St, Forsyth, MT 59327; 406-346-7322; fax: 406-346-2719; 8AM-5PM (MST). *Felony, Civil Actions over $12,000, Eviction, Probate.*

General Information: Search fee includes both civil and criminal indexes. No adoption, juvenile, sanity or sealed records released. Will fax out documents. Court makes copy: $1.00 per page 1st 10 doc pages, then $.50 each add'l. Self serve copy: same. Certification fee: $2.00 per doc. Payee: Clerk of Court. No personal checks or credit cards accepted. Prepayment required. Mail requests: SASE required.

Civil Name Search: Access: Fax, mail, in person. Both court and visitors may perform in person name searches. Search fee: $2.00 per name per year, first 7 years, then $1.00 per year. Written requests only. Civil records in books, on microfiche back to 1901; on computer back to 1996. Mail turnaround time 2 days. Civil PAT goes back to 1996.

Criminal Name Search: Access: Fax, mail, in person. Both court and visitors may perform in person name searches. Search fee: $2.00 per name per year, first 7 years, then $1.00 per year. Written requests only. Required to search: name, years to search, signed release. Criminal records in books, on microfiche back to 1901; on computer back to 1996. Mail turnaround time 2 days. Criminal PAT goes back to 1996.

Limited Jurisdiction Court #1 PO Box 504, 1200 Main St, County Courthouse, Forsyth, MT 59327; 406-346-2638; fax: 406-346-7551; 8AM-5PM (MST). *Misdemeanor, Civil Actions under $12,000, Eviction, Small Claims.*

General Information: Also has records for the Limited Jurisdiction Court in Colstrip, which was closed in 2006. The clerk expects to have all Colstrip records eventually; now only has Colstrip records back to 2003.

Limited Jurisdiction Court #2 Colstrip, MT; 406-346-2638; . *Misdemeanor, Civil Actions under $12,000, Eviction, Small Claims.*

General Information: Court closed 2006; records back to 2003 at Limited Jurisdiction Court #1 in Forsyth, phone numbers given here. All records available at Forsyth.

Sanders County

District Court PO Box 519, 1111 Main St, Rm 320, Thompson Falls, MT 59873; 406-827-6962; fax: 406-827-6973; 8AM-5PM (MST). *Felony, Civil Actions over $12,000, Eviction, Probate.*

General Information: No adoption, juvenile, neglect/abuse, sanity or pre-sentence investigation records released. Will fax documents to local or toll free line. Court makes copy: $1.00 per page 1st 10 pages, then $.50 each add'l. Self serve copy: same. Certification fee: $2.00. Payee: Clerk of Court. Personal checks accepted. No credit cards accepted. Prepayment required. Mail requests: SASE required.

Civil Name Search: Access: Mail, in person. Both court and visitors may perform in person name searches. Search fee: $2.00 per name per year, first 7 years, then $1.00 per year. Civil index on docket books since 1906, on computer since 1999. Mail turnaround time 1-4 days. Civil PAT goes back to 1999.

Criminal Name Search: Access: Mail, in person. Both court and visitors may perform in person name searches. Search fee: $2.00 per name per year, first 7 years, then $1.00 per year. Criminal docket on books since 1906, on computer since 1999. Mail turnaround time 1-4 days. Criminal PAT goes back to 1999.

Justice Court PO Box 519, 1111 Main St, Thompson Falls, MT 59873; 406-827-6941; fax: 406-827-6987; 8AM-N, 1-5PM (MST). *Misdemeanor, Civil Actions under $12,000, Eviction, Traffic.* www.mt.gov/

Sheridan County

District Court 100 W Laurel, Plentywood, MT 59254; 406-765-3404; fax: 406-765-2602; 8AM-N, 1-5PM (MST). *Felony, Civil Actions over $12,000, Eviction, Probate.* www.co.sheridan.mt.us

General Information: No adoption, juvenile or sanity records released. Will fax documents to toll free line if prepaid. Court makes copy: $1.00 per page 1st 10 pages, then $.50 each add'l. Certification fee: $2.00. Payee: Clerk of District Court. Personal checks accepted. No credit cards accepted. Prepayment required. Mail requests: SASE required.

Civil Name Search: Access: Phone, mail, in person. Both court and visitors may perform in person name searches. Search fee: $2.00 per name per year, first 7 years, then $1.00 per year. Civil index on docket books since 1913. Mail turnaround time 1-2 days.

Criminal Name Search: Access: Phone, mail, in person. Both court and visitors may perform in person name searches. Search fee: $2.00 per name per year, first 7 years, then $1.00 per year. Criminal docket on books since 1913. Mail turnaround time 1-2 days.

Justice Court 100 W Laurel Ave, Plentywood, MT 59254; 406-765-3409; fax: 406-765-3489; 8AM-5PM (MST). *Misdemeanor, Civil Actions under $12,000, Eviction, Small Claims up to $3,000.*

General Information: Records also in this court are traffic tickets, restraining orders and criminal misc.

Silver Bow County

District Court 155 W Granite St, Rm 313, Butte, MT 59701; 406-497-6350; fax: 406-497-6358; 8AM-5PM (MST). *Felony, Civil Actions over $12,000, Probate.*

General Information: No adoption, juvenile or sanity records released. Fee to fax in or out file $1.00 per page. Court makes copy: $1.00 per page 1st 10 pages, then $.50 each add'l. Certification fee: $2.00. Payee: Clerk of Court. Personal checks accepted. No credit cards accepted. Prepayment required. Mail requests: SASE required.

Civil Name Search: Access: Fax, mail, in person. Both court and visitors may perform in person name searches. Search fee: $2.00 per name per year, first 7 years, then $1.00 per year. Civil records in original files since 1970, on microfilm back to 1887; on computer back to 1996. Mail turnaround time 3 days. Civil PAT goes back to 1996.

Criminal Name Search: Access: Fax, mail, in person. Both court and visitors may perform in person name searches. Search fee: $2.00 per name per year, first 7 years, then $1.00 per year. Criminal records in original files since 1970, on microfilm back to 1887; on computer back to 1995. Mail turnaround time 1-3 days; will not do phone searches. Criminal PAT goes back to 1996.

Limited Jurisdiction Court #1 & #2 155 W Granite St, Rm 305, Silver Bow County Courthouse, Butte, MT 59701; 406-497-6390; fax: 406-497-6468; 8AM-5PM (MST). *Misdemeanor, Civil Actions under $12,000, Eviction, Small Claims.*

General Information: Two Justice Courts at this location; both courts must be searched for records. #1 phone- 406-497-6391; #2 is 6392.

Stillwater County

District Court PO Box 367, Columbus, MT 59019; 406-322-8030; fax: 406-322-8048; 8AM-N, 1-5PM (MST). *Felony, Civil Actions over $12,000, Probate.*

General Information: Search Evictions at local courts. No adoption, juvenile or sanity records released. Will fax documents $1.00 per page. Court makes copy: $1.00 per page 1st 10 pages, then $.50 each add'l. Certification fee: $2.00. Payee: Clerk of Court. Personal checks accepted. No credit cards accepted. Prepayment required. Mail requests: SASE required.

Civil Name Search: Access: Phone, mail, in person. Both court and visitors may perform in person name searches. Search fee: $2.00 per name per year, first 7 years, then $1.00 per year. Civil index on docket books since 1913; on computer back to 1997. Mail turnaround time 1-2 days. Public use terminal available, records go back to 1997.

Criminal Name Search: Access: Phone, mail, in person. Both court and visitors may perform in person name searches. Search fee: $2.00 per name per year, first 7 years, then $1.00 per year. Criminal docket on books since 1913; on computer back to 1997. Mail turnaround time 1-2 days. Public use terminal available, crim records go back to 1997.

Justice Court PO Box 77, 400 E 3rd Ave N, Columbus, MT 59019; 406-322-8040; fax: 406-322-8048; 8AM-N, 1-5PM (MST). *Misdemeanor, Civil Actions under $12,000, Eviction, Small Claims.*

Sweet Grass County

District Court PO Box 698, Big Timber, MT 59011; 406-932-5154; fax: 406-932-5433; 8AM-N, 1-5PM (MST). *Felony, Civil Actions over $12,000, Eviction, Probate.*

General Information: Probate records in a separate index at same address. Probate fax is same as main fax number. No adoption, juvenile or sanity records released. Will fax documents free locally, add $1.50 if not a toll free number. Court makes copy: $1.00 per page 1st 10 pages, then $.50 each add'l. Certification fee: $2.00 per document. Payee: Clerk of Court. Personal checks accepted. No credit cards accepted. Prepayment required. Mail requests: SASE required.

Civil Name Search: Access: Phone, mail, in person. Only the court performs in person name searches; visitors may not. Search fee: $2.00 per name per year, first 7 years, then $1.00 per year. Civil records in books since 1895, on microfiche since 1972, computerized since 1996. Mail turnaround time 1 day.

Criminal Name Search: Access: Phone, mail, in person. Only the court performs in person name searches; visitors may not. Search fee: $2.00 per name per year, first 7 years, then $1.00 per year. Criminal records in books since 1895, on microfiche since 1972, computerized since 1996. Mail turnaround time 1 day.

Justice Court PO Box 1432, 200 West 1st, Big Timber, MT 59011; 406-932-5150; fax: 406-932-5433; 8AM-5PM (MST). *Misdemeanor, Traffic Complaints, Civil Actions under $12,000, Eviction, Small Claims.*

General Information: This is also the Big Timber City Court.

Teton County

District Court PO Box 487, Choteau, MT 59422; 406-466-2909; fax: 406-466-2910; 8AM-N, 1-5PM (MST). *Felony, Civil Actions over $12,000, Eviction, Probate.*

General Information: No adoption, juvenile or sanity records released. Fee to fax out file $1.00 per page. Court makes copy: $1.00 per page 1st 10, $.50 each add'l. Certification fee: $2.00 per document. Payee: Clerk of Court. Personal checks accepted. No credit cards accepted. Prepayment required. Mail requests: SASE required.

Civil Name Search: Access: Phone, fax, mail, in person. Only the court performs in person name searches; visitors may not. Search fee: $2.00 per name per year, first 7 years, then $1.00 per year. Civil records on books from 1893; on computer back to 1995. Mail turnaround time 1 day.

Criminal Name Search: Access: Phone, mail, in person. Only the court performs in person name searches; visitors may not. Search fee: $2.00 per name per year, first 7 years, then $1.00 per year. Criminal docket on books from 1893; on computer back to 1995. Mail turnaround time 1 day.

Justice Court PO Box 337, 1 Main Ave S, Choteau, MT 59422; 406-466-5611; fax: 406-466-2138; 8AM-N, 1-5PM (MST). *Misdemeanor, Civil Actions under $12,000, Eviction, Small Claims.*

Toole County

District Court PO Box 850, Shelby, MT 59474; 406-424-8330; fax: 406-424-8331; 8AM-5PM (MST). *Felony, Civil Actions over $12,000, Probate.*

General Information: Probate fax is same as main fax number. Eviction at local level. No adoption, juvenile or sanity records released. Will fax documents $1.00 per page. Court makes copy: $1.00 per page 1st 10 pages, then $.50 each add'l. Self serve copy: $1.00 per page. Certification fee: $2.00 per document plus copy fee. Payee: Clerk of Court. Personal checks accepted. No credit cards accepted. Prepayment required. Mail requests: SASE required.

Civil Name Search: Access: Phone, fax, mail, in person. Both court and visitors may perform in person name searches. Search fee: $2.00 per name per year, first 7 years, then $1.00 per year. Civil records in books from 1914; on computer since 1997. Note: Will email for cost of copies. Mail turnaround time same day as request received.

Criminal Name Search: Access: Phone, fax, mail, in person. Both court and visitors may perform in person name searches. Search fee: $2.00 per name per year, first 7 years, then $1.00 per year. Required to search: name, years to search, DOB. Criminal records in books from 1914; on computer since 1997. Note: Will email for cost of copies. Mail turnaround time same day as received.

Justice Court PO Box 738, 226 1st St S, Rm 104, Shelby, MT 59474; 406-424-8315; fax: 406-424-8316; 8AM-5PM (MST). *Misdemeanor, Civil Actions under $12,000, Eviction, Small Claims.*

Treasure County

District Court PO Box 392, Hysham, MT 59038; 406-342-5547; fax: 406-342-5445; 8AM-5PM (MST). *Felony, Civil Actions over $12,000, Eviction, Probate.*

General Information: No adoption or sanity records released. Fee to fax out file- $1.50 per page. Court makes copy: $1.00 per page 1st 10 pages, then $.50 each add'l. Certification fee: $2.00. Payee: Clerk of Court. Personal checks accepted. No credit cards accepted. Prepayment required. Mail requests: SASE required.

Civil Name Search: Access: Fax, mail, in person. Both court and visitors may perform in person name searches. Search fee: $2.00 per name per year, first 7 years, then $1.00 per year. Civil records on books since 1919, on microfilm from 1985 to present; on computer back to 1996. Mail turnaround time usually 1 day.

Criminal Name Search: Access: Fax, mail, in person. Both court and visitors may perform in person name searches. Search fee: $2.00 per name per year, first 7 years, then $1.00 per year. Required to search: name, years to search, DOB. Criminal docket on books since 1919, on microfilm from 1985 to present; on computer back to 1996. Mail turnaround time 1 day.

Justice Court PO Box 297, 307 Rapelje Ave, Hysham, MT 59038-0297; 406-342-5532; fax: 406-342-5212; 9AM-Noon (MST). *Misdemeanor, Civil Actions under $12,000, Eviction, Small Claims.*

Valley County

Clerk of District Court 501 Court Sq #6, Glasgow, MT 59230; 406-228-6268; fax: 406-228-6212; 8AM-5PM (MST). *Felony, Civil Actions over $12,000, Eviction, Probate.*

General Information: Probate fax is same as main fax number. No adoption, juvenile or sanity records released. Fee to fax out file $1.00 per page. Court makes copy: $1.00 per page 1st 10 pages, then $.50 each add'l. Certification fee: $2.00 per document plus copy fee. Payee: Clerk of Court. Business checks accepted. No credit cards accepted. Prepayment required. Mail requests: SASE required.

Civil Name Search: Access: Phone, fax, mail, in person. Only the court performs in person name searches; visitors may not. Search fee: $2.00 per name per year, first 7 years, then $1.00 per year. Civil records in books since 1893; on computer back to 1996. Mail turnaround time same day.

Criminal Name Search: Access: Fax, mail, in person. Only the court performs in person name searches; visitors may not. Search fee: $2.00 per

name per year, first 7 years, then $1.00 per year. Required to search: name, years to search, signed release. Criminal records in books since 1893; on computer back to 1996. Mail turnaround time same day.

Justice Court 501 Court Sq #10, Glasgow, MT 59230; 406-228-6271; fax: 406-228-4601; 8AM-N (MST). *Misdemeanor, Civil Actions under $12,000, Eviction, Small Claims.*

Wheatland County

District Court Box 227, Harlowton, MT 59036; 406-632-4893; fax: 406-632-4873; 8AM-N, 1-5PM (MST). *Felony, Civil Actions over $12,000, Eviction, Probate.*

General Information: Probate fax is same as main fax number. No adoption, juvenile or sanity records released. Will fax documents to local or toll free line. Court makes copy: $1.00 per page 1st 10 pages, then $.50 each add'l. Certification fee: $2.00. Payee: Clerk of Court. Personal checks accepted. No credit cards accepted. Prepayment required. Mail requests: SASE required.

Civil Name Search: Access: Fax, mail, in person. Both court and visitors may perform in person name searches. Search fee: $2.00 per name per year, first 7 years, then $1.00 per year. Computerized records back to 1996, civil records on docket books since 1917, probate on microfiche from 1984. Mail turnaround time next day.

Criminal Name Search: Access: Mail, in person. Both court and visitors may perform in person name searches. Search fee: $2.00 per name per year, first 7 years, then $1.00 per year. Computerized records back to 1996, criminal records on docket books since 1917, probate on microfiche from 1984. Mail turnaround time next day.

Justice Court PO Box 524, 201 A Ave NW, Harlowton, MT 59036; 406-632-4821; fax: 406-632-4873; 10AM-1PM T,TH (MST). *Misdemeanor, Civil Actions under $12,000, Eviction, Small Claims.*

Wibaux County

District Court PO Box 292, 200 S Wibaux St, Courthouse, Wibaux, MT 59353; 406-796-2484; fax: 406-796-2484; 8AM-N, 1-5PM (MST). *Felony, Civil Actions over $12,000, Eviction, Probate.*

General Information: No adoption, juvenile or sanity records released. Will fax documents $2.00 1st page, $.50 each add'l, turnaround time is 2-3 days. Court makes copy: $1.00 per page 1st 10 pages, then $.50 each add'l. Self serve copy: No self serve criminal copier; Civil self serve- $.15 each. Certification fee: $2.00 per doc. Payee: Clerk of Court. Personal checks accepted. No credit cards accepted. Prepayment required. Arrangements must first be made for payment for fax and phone requests. Mail requests: SASE required.

Civil Name Search: Access: Phone, fax, mail, in person. Both court and visitors may perform in person name searches. Search fee: $2.00 per name per year, first 7 years, then $1.00 per year. Civil index on docket books since 1914, on computer since 1/97. Mail turnaround time 1 week.

Criminal Name Search: Access: Phone, fax, mail, in person. Only the court performs in person name searches; visitors may not. Search fee: $2.00 per name per year, first 7 years, then $1.00 per year. Criminal docket on books since 1914, on computer since 1/97. Mail turnaround time 1 week.

Justice Court PO Box 445, 203 S Wibaux St, Wibaux, MT 59353; 406-796-7671; fax: 406-796-2484; 1-5PM M&W, 8AM-N F (MST). *Misdemeanor, Civil Actions under $12,000, Eviction, Small Claims.*

Yellowstone County

District Court PO Box 35030, 217 N 27 St, 7th Fl, Billings, MT 59107; criminal phone: 406-256-2860; civil phone: 406-256-2851; probate phone: 406-256-2865; fax: 406-256-2995; 8AM-5PM (MST). *Felony, Civil Actions over $12,000, Probate.*
www.co.yellowstone.mt.gov/clerk_court/

General Information: No adoption, juvenile or sanity records released. Will not fax documents. Court makes copy: $1.00 per page 1st 10 pages, then $.50 each add'l. Certification fee: $2.00 per cert plus copy fee. Payee: Clerk of Court. No personal checks. No credit cards accepted. Prepayment required. Mail requests: SASE required.

Civil Name Search: Access: Mail, in person. Both court and visitors may perform in person name searches. Search fee: $2.00 per name per year, first 7 years, then $1.00 per year. Civil records in books, on microfilm back to 1800s; on computer back to 1992. Mail turnaround time 1 day if record less than 10 years old. Civil PAT goes back to 1990.

Criminal Name Search: Access: Mail, in person. Both court and visitors may perform in person name searches. Search fee: $2.00 per name per year, first 7 years, then $1.00 per year. Criminal records in books, on microfilm back to 1800s; on computer back to 1990. Mail turnaround time 1 day if record less than 10 years old. Criminal PAT goes back to same as civil.

Justice Court PO Box 35032, 217 N 27th, Rm 603, Billings, MT 59107; 406-256-2998; fax: 406-256-2898; 9AM-5PM (MST). *Misdemeanor, Civil Actions under $12,000, Eviction, Small Claims.*
www.co.yellowstone.mt.gov/justicecourt/

Nebraska

Time Zone: **CST & MST***

* Nebraska's nineteen western-most counties are MST: They are: Arthur, Banner, Box Butte, Chase, Cherry, Cheyenne, Dawes, Deuel, Dundy, Garden, Grant, Hooker, Keith, Kimball, Morrill, Perkins, Scotts. Bluff, Sheridan, and Sioux.

Capital:	**Lincoln, Lancaster County**
# of Counties:	**93**
State Web:	**www.nebraska.gov**
Court Web:	**http://court.nol.org**

Administration

Court Administrator, PO Box 98910, Lincoln, NE, 68509-8910; 402-471-3730, Fax: 402-471-2197

The Supreme and Appellate Courts

The Supreme Court is the court of last resort. The Court of Appeals is generally the first court to hear appeals of judgments and orders in criminal, juvenile, civil, domestic relations and probate matters. In addition, the Court of Appeals has appellate jurisdiction over decisions originating in a number of state administrative boards and agencies. Opinions are available from http://court.nol.org/opinions under *Quick Links*.

The Nebraska Courts

Court	Type	How Organized	Jurisdiction Highpoints
District *	General	93 Courts in 12 Districts	Felony, Civil $52,000 or above, Family, Probate
County*	Limited	93 Courts in 12 Districts	Misdemeanor, Limited Civil, Small Claims Eviction, Juvenile, Probate, Ordinances Estate
Juvenile	Special	3 Courts in 3 Counties	Juvenile

* = profiled in this book

Details on the Court Structure

District Courts have original jurisdiction in all felony cases, equity cases, domestic relations cases, and civil cases where the amount in controversy involves more than $52,000. District Courts also have appellate jurisdiction in certain matters arising out of County Courts.

County Courts have original jurisdiction in probate matters, violations of city or village ordinances, juvenile court matters without a separate juvenile court, adoptions, preliminary hearings in felony cases, and eminent domain proceedings. The County Courts have concurrent jurisdiction in civil matters when the amount in controversy is $52,000 or less, criminal matters classified as misdemeanors or infractions, some domestic relations matters, and paternity actions. Nearly all misdemeanor cases are tried in the County Courts. As a rule of thumb, only District Courts can enter a sentence which incarcerates a defendant for more than one year.

County Courts have juvenile jurisdiction in all but 3 counties. Douglas, Lancaster, and Sarpy counties have separate **Juvenile Courts**. Also, there is a separate Workers' Compensation Court – see www.wcc.ne.gov.

Record Searching Facts You Need to Know

Fees and Record Searching Tips

The State Attorney General has recommended that courts not perform record searches for the public. Therefore nearly all Nebraska courts will not respond to written search requests and also require the public to do their own in person searches. In general, the copy fee is $.25 per page and the certification fee is $1.00.

Online Access is Nearly Statewide

An online access subscription service is available for all Nebraska County Courts and all District Courts. Douglas County District Court was the last county added in April 2011. Case details, all party listings, payments, and actions taken for criminal, civil, probate, juvenile, and traffic are available. District Courts and County Courts must be searched separately. The system starts with a name search and resulting list gives full DOB. Both convictions and pending cases are available in the criminal search. The fee for a onetime search using a credit card is $15.00. Ongoing users may register with Nebraska.gov and have an account that also gives access to other records. There is a start-up/annual fee for $50.00. For court record access the fee is $1.00 per record or a flat rate of $300.00 per month. Go to www.nebraska.gov/faqs/justice or call 402-471-7810 for more information.

Adams County

District Court PO Box 9, Hastings, NE 68902; 402-461-7264; fax: 402-461-7269; 8:30AM-5PM (CST). *Felony, Civil Actions over $52,000.* www.adamscounty.org/DistrictCOURT.html

General Information: No juvenile, search warrants or mental health records released. Will not fax documents. Court makes copy: $.25 per page. Certification fee: $1.00 per page plus copy fee. Payee: Clerk of District Court. Personal checks accepted, credit cards are not. Prepayment required.

Civil Name Search: Access: In person, online. Visitors must perform in person searches themselves. Civil records on microfiche from 1800s, 5 yrs on index cards, on docket books from 1800s. Civil PAT goes back to 07/1997. **See front or rear of chapter for detailed description of state's online access.** Online records date from 07/97.

Criminal Name Search: Access: In person, online. Visitors must perform in person searches themselves. Criminal records on microfiche from 1800s, 5 yrs on index cards, on docket books from 1800s. Criminal PAT goes back to 07/1997. **See front or rear of chapter for detailed description of state's online access.** Online records date from 07/97. Online results show middle initial, DOB.

County Court PO Box 95, Hastings, NE 68902-0095; 402-461-7143; fax: 402-461-7144; 8AM-5PM (CST). *Misdemeanor, Civil Actions under $52,000, Eviction, Small Claims, Probate.* www.district10.us/

General Information: No adoption or juvenile records released. Will not fax documents. Court makes copy: $.25 per page. Self serve copy: same. Certification fee: $1.00 per page plus copy fee. Payee: Adams County Court. Business checks accepted. No credit cards accepted. Prepayment required.

Civil Name Search: Access: In person, online. Visitors must perform in person searches themselves. Required to search: name, years to search; also helpful: address. Civil cases indexed by defendant. Civil index on cards and files from 1970s. Civil PAT goes back to 1999. **See front or rear of chapter for detailed description of state's online access.** Online civil records date from 10/99 forward, probate from 05/98.

Criminal Name Search: Access: In person, online. Visitors must perform in person searches themselves. Required to search: name, years to search; also helpful: DOB, SSN. Criminal records indexed on cards and files from 1970s. Criminal PAT goes back to same as civil. **See front or rear of chapter for detailed description of state's online access.** Online criminal and traffic records date from 07/97. Online results show middle initial, DOB.

Antelope County

District Court PO Box 45, Neligh, NE 68756; 402-887-4508; fax: 402-887-4870; 8AM-4:30PM (CST). *Felony, Civil Actions over $52,000.*

General Information: No juvenile, sealed, search warrants, or mental health record released. Will fax specific case file for $1.00 per page. Court makes copy: $.25 per page. Self serve copy: same. Certification fee: $1.00 per certificate plus copy fee. Payee: Clerk of District Court. Personal checks accepted, credit cards are not. Prepayment required. Mail requests: SASE required.

Civil Name Search: Access: In person, online. Visitors must perform in person searches themselves. Civil index on docket books from 1872, computerized since 1999. Civil PAT goes back to 1999. **See front or rear of chapter for detailed description of state's online access.** Online records date from 03/99.

Criminal Name Search: Access: In person, online. Visitors must perform in person searches themselves. Criminal records indexed in books from 1872, computerized since 1999. Criminal PAT goes back to same as civil. **See front or rear of chapter for detailed description of state's online access.** Online records date from 03/99. Online results show middle initial, DOB, address.

Antelope County Court 501 Main, Neligh, NE 68756; 402-887-4650; fax: 402-887-4160; 8:30AM-5PM (CST). *Misdemeanor, Civil Actions under $52,000, Eviction, Small Claims, Probate.* http://supremecourt.ne.gov/county-court/

General Information: Probate fax is same as main fax number. No adoption, or sealed records released. Will fax out specific case files for $1.00 per page. Court makes copy: $.25 per page. Self serve copy: same. Certification fee: $1.00 per doc plus copy fee. Payee: Antelope County Court. Personal checks accepted, credit cards are not. Prepayment required.

Civil Name Search: Access: In person, online. Visitors must perform in person searches themselves. Civil records on computer from 1999, probate on microfiche from 1876, civil and small claims indexed from 1983. Civil PAT available. **See front or rear of chapter for detailed description of state's online access.** Online civil and probate records date from 12/99.

Criminal Name Search: Access: In person, online. Visitors must perform in person searches themselves. Required to search: name, years to search, DOB, signed release. Criminal index on computer from 1999, indexed from 1800s. Criminal PAT available. **See front or rear of chapter for detailed description of state's online access.** Online criminal and traffic records date from 12/99. Online results show middle initial, DOB.

Arthur County

District & County Court PO Box 126, 205 Fir St., Arthur, NE 69121; 308-764-2203; fax: 308-764-2216; 8AM-4PM (MST). *Felony, Misdemeanor, Civil, Eviction, Small Claims, Probate.* http://supremecourt.ne.gov/county-court/

General Information: The PO to use if sending to the County Court is PO 146. No search warrants, juvenile, adoption, mental health, or sealed records released. Will fax documents $1.00 per page. Court makes copy: $.20 per page if mailed. Self serve copy: $.10 per page. Certification fee: $1.50 first page; $.50 each add'l. Payee: Arthur County Clerk. Personal checks accepted, credit cards are not. Prepayment required.

Civil Name Search: Access: In person, online. Both court and visitors may perform in person name searches. No search fee. Civil index on docket books from 1987, on docket books from 1913. Civil PAT goes back to 1999. **See front or rear of chapter for detailed description of state's online access.** County court online records date from 09/99 forward; District Court records from 06/00.

Criminal Name Search: Access: In person, online. Both court and visitors may perform in person name searches. No search fee. Criminal records indexed in books from 1987, on docket books from 1913. Criminal PAT goes back to same as civil. **See front or rear of chapter for detailed description of state's online access.** Online criminal and traffic records date from 09/99 forward; District Court records from 6/2000. Online results show middle initial, DOB.

Banner County

District Court PO Box 67, 206 State St, Harrisburg, NE 69345; 308-436-5265; fax: 308-436-4180; 8AM-4:30PM (MST). *Felony, Civil Actions over $52,000.*

General Information: No search warrants, mental health, or sealed records released. Will fax documents $.50 per page. Court makes copy: $.50 per page. Certification fee: $1.50 per instrument. Payee: Banner County Clerk. Personal checks accepted, credit cards are not. Prepayment required. Mail requests: SASE required.

Civil Name Search: Access: Fax, mail, in person, online. Both court and visitors may perform in person name searches. No search fee. Required to search: name, years to search; also helpful: address. Civil index in docket books from 1800s. Mail Turnaround time 5-7 days. Civil PAT goes back to 2004. **See front or rear of chapter for detailed description of state's online access.** Online civil records date from 06/00 forward.

Criminal Name Search: Access: Fax, mail, in person, online. Both court and visitors may perform in person name searches. No search fee. Required to search: name, years to search, DOB; also helpful: address. Criminal docket on books from 1800s. Mail Turnaround time 5-7 days. Criminal PAT goes back to same as civil. **See front or rear of chapter for detailed description of state's online access.** Online records date from 06/00 forward. Online results show middle initial, DOB.

Banner County Court PO Box 2, 206 State St, Harrisburg, NE 69345; 308-436-5268; probate phone: 308-436-5268.; fax: 308-436-4180; 8:30AM-4:30PM Thursdays only (MST). *Misdemeanor, Civil Actions under $52,000, Eviction, Small Claims, Probate.* http://supremecourt.ne.gov/county-court/

General Information: For assistance on days other than Thursday, contact the Circuit Court, 308-436-5265. No adoption, sealed records released. Court makes copy: $.50 per page. Certification fee: $1.50 per doc. Payee: Banner County Court. Personal checks accepted, credit cards are not. Prepayment required.

Civil Name Search: Access: In person, online. Both court and visitors may perform in person name searches. No search fee. Civil records on register of action cards from 1992, prior on docket books, on computer from 12/2000. **See front or rear of chapter for detailed description of state's online access.** Online civil and probate records date from 01/01 forward.

Criminal Name Search: Access: In person, online. Both court and visitors may perform in person name searches. No search fee. Required to search: name, years to search, signed release; also helpful: address, DOB. Criminal records on register of action cards from 1992, prior on docket books, on computer from 6/2000. **See front or rear of chapter for detailed description of state's online access.** Online criminal and traffic records date from 04/00. Online results show middle initial, DOB.

Blaine County

District Court 145 Lincoln Ave, Brewster, NE 68821; 308-547-2222 x201; fax: 308-547-2228; 8AM-4PM (CST). *Felony, Civil Actions over $52,000.* http://dc8.nol.org

General Information: No search warrants, mental health, or sealed records released. Will fax documents $3.00 1st page. $1.00 ea add'l. Court makes copy: $.25 per page. Certification fee: $1.50. Payee: Blaine County Clerk. Personal checks accepted, credit cards are not. Prepayment required. Mail requests: SASE required.

Civil Name Search: Access: Fax, mail, in person, online. Both court and visitors may perform in person name searches. Search fee: $1.00 per name. Civil index on docket books from late 1800s. Mail Turnaround time 1-2 days. Civil PAT goes back to 6/2000. **See front or rear of chapter for detailed description of state's online access.** Online records date from 06/00 forward.

Criminal Name Search: Access: Fax, mail, in person, online. Both court and visitors may perform in person name searches. Search fee: $1.00 per name. Required to search: name, years to search, DOB. Criminal records indexed in books from late 1800s. Mail Turnaround time 1-2 days. Criminal PAT goes back to same as civil. **See front or rear of chapter for detailed description of state's online access.** Online records date from 06/00 forward. Online results show name only.

Blaine County Court 145 Lincoln Ave, Brewster, NE 68821; 308-547-2222 x211; probate phone: x202; fax: 308-547-2226; 8AM-4PM (CST). *Misdemeanor, Civil Actions under $52,000, Eviction, Small Claims, Probate.* http://supremecourt.ne.gov/county-court/

General Information: Probate fax is same as main fax number. No juvenile, adoption, or sealed records released. Will fax documents $1.00 per page. Court makes copy: $.25 per page. Self serve copy: same. Certification fee: $1.00 per page plus copy fee. Payee: Blaine County Court. Personal checks accepted, credit cards are not. Mail requests: SASE required.

Civil Name Search: Access: Phone, fax, mail, in person, online. Only the court performs in person name searches; visitors may not. No search fee. Required to search: name, years to search; also helpful: address. Civil index on docket books from 1960. on microfiche prior to 1960. Mail Turnaround time 2 days. **See front or rear of chapter for detailed description of state's online access.** Online civil and probate records date from 01/01 forward.

Criminal Name Search: Access: Phone, fax, mail, in person, online. Only the court performs in person name searches; visitors may not. No search fee. Required to search: name, years to search; also helpful: address, DOB, SSN. Criminal records indexed in books from 1960. on microfiche prior to 1960. Mail Turnaround time 2 days. **See front or rear of chapter for detailed description of state's online access.** Online criminal and traffic records date from 08/00. Online results show middle initial, DOB.

Boone County

District Court 222 S 4th St, Albion, NE 68620; 402-395-2057; fax: 402-395-6592; 8:30AM-5PM (CST). *Felony, Civil Actions over $52,000.*

General Information: No search warrants, mental health, or sealed records released. Will fax documents $3.00 1st page, $1.00 each add'l. Court makes copy: $.25 per page. Certification fee: $1.00 per page plus copy fee. Payee: Clerk of District Court. Personal checks accepted, credit cards are not. Prepayment required.

Civil Name Search: Access: In person, online. Visitors must perform in person searches themselves. Civil records in general index and dockets from 1800s, computerized records since 2001. Civil PAT goes back to 2000. Civil records online; see criminal access. Online records date from 12/99 forward.

Criminal Name Search: Access: In person, online. Visitors must perform in person searches themselves. Required to search: name, years to

search; also helpful: DOB. Criminal records in general index and dockets from 1800s, computerized records since 2001. Criminal PAT goes back to same as civil. **See front or rear of chapter for detailed description of state's online access.** Online records date from 12/99 forward. Online results show middle initial, DOB.

Boone County Court 222 S 4th St, Albion, NE 68620; 402-395-6184; fax: 402-395-6592; 8AM-5PM (CST). *Misdemeanor, Civil Actions under $52,000, Eviction, Small Claims, Probate.* http://supremecourt.ne.gov/county-court/

General Information: Online identifiers in results same as on public terminal. No adoption, or sealed records released. No fee to fax documents. Court makes copy: $.25 per page. Self serve copy: same. Certification fee: $1.00. Payee: Clerk of County Court. Personal checks accepted, credit cards are not. Prepayment required.

Civil Name Search: Access: In person, online. Visitors must perform in person searches themselves. Civil records on general index and docket books from late 1800s; computerized back to 2000; probate on microfiche from late 1800s. Civil PAT goes back to 6/2000. **See front or rear of chapter for detailed description of state's online access.** Online civil records date from 10/00 forward, probate from 01/01.

Criminal Name Search: Access: In person, online. Visitors must perform in person searches themselves. Required to search: name, years to search; also helpful: DOB. Criminal records on general index and docket books from late 1800s; computerized back to 2000. Criminal PAT goes back to same as civil. **See front or rear of chapter for detailed description of state's online access.** Online criminal and traffic records date from 06/00. Online results show middle initial, DOB.

Box Butte County

District Court 515 Box Butte #300, Alliance, NE 69301; 308-762-6293; fax: 308-762-5700; 8AM-5PM (MST). *Felony, Civil Actions over $52,000.*

General Information: No mental health, or sealed records released. Will fax out specific case files for $1.00 per page. Court makes copy: $.25 per page. Self serve copy: same. Certification fee: $1.00 per page plus copy fee. Personal checks accepted, credit cards are not. Prepayment required.

Civil Name Search: Access: In person, online. Visitors must perform in person searches themselves. Civil general index and docket books from late 1800s. Civil PAT goes back to 1890. **See front or rear of chapter for detailed description of state's online access.** Online records date from 10/97.

Criminal Name Search: Access: In person, online. Visitors must perform in person searches themselves. Criminal records on general index and docket books from late 1800s. Criminal PAT goes back to 1890. **See front or rear of chapter for detailed description of state's online access.** Online records date from 10/97. Online results show middle initial, DOB.

Box Butte County Court PO Box 613, Alliance, NE 69301; 308-762-6800; fax: 308-762-2650; 8:30AM-5PM (MST). *Misdemeanor, Civil Actions under $52,000, Eviction, Small Claims ($3,500), Probate.* http://supremecourt.ne.gov/county-court/

General Information: No adoption or sealed records released. Will fax documents $2.75 per page. Court makes copy: $.25 per page. Certification fee: $1.00. Payee: Box Butte County Court. Personal checks accepted, credit cards are not. Prepayment required.

Civil Name Search: Access: in person, online. Visitors must perform in person searches themselves. Civil records on microfiche for 10 years, on index cards to docket books from late 1800s; computerized records since 2000. Civil PAT goes back to 4/2000. **See front or rear of chapter for detailed description of state's online access.** Online records date from 11/00 forward.

Criminal Name Search: Access: In person, online. Visitors must perform in person searches themselves. Required to search: name, years to search, DOB. Criminal records on microfiche for 10 years, on index cards to docket books from late 1800s; computerized records since 2000. Criminal PAT goes back to same as civil. **See front or rear of chapter for detailed description of state's online access.** Online criminal and traffic records date from 04/00. Online results show middle initial, DOB.

Boyd County

District Court PO Box 26, 401 N Thayer St, Butte, NE 68722; 402-775-2391; fax: 402-775-2146; 8:15AM-4PM (CST). *Felony, Civil Actions over $52,000.*

General Information: No search warrants, mental health, or sealed records released. Will fax documents $3.00 1st page, $1.00 ea add'l. Court makes copy: $.25 per page. Self serve copy: same. Certification fee: $1.50. Payee: Boyd County Clerk. Personal checks accepted, credit cards are not. Prepayment required. Mail requests: SASE required.

Civil Name Search: Access: Mail, fax, in person, online. Both court and visitors may perform in person name searches. Search fee: $3.00 per name. Required to search: name, years to search, address. Civil general index and docket books from late 1800s. Mail Turnaround time 3-4 days. Civil PAT goes back to 2000. **See front or rear of chapter for detailed description of state's online access.** Online records date from 07/00.

Criminal Name Search: Access: Mail, fax, in person, online. Both court and visitors may perform in person name searches. Search fee: $3.00 per name. Required to search: name, years to search, address. Criminal records on general index and docket books from late 1800s. Mail Turnaround time 3-4 days. Criminal PAT goes back to same as civil. **See front or rear of chapter for detailed description of state's online access.** Online records date from 07/00 forward. Online results show middle initial, DOB.

Boyd County Court PO Box 396, 401 Thayer, Butte, NE 68722; 402-775-2211; fax: same as voice number; 8:14AM-4PM M,W; F (CST). *Misdemeanor, Civil Actions under $52,000, Eviction, Small Claims, Probate.* http://supremecourt.ne.gov/county-court/
General Information: Send questions to cathy.reiman@nebraska.gov. No adoption, juvenile, or sealed records released. Will fax documents for no fee. Court makes copy: $.25 per page. Certification fee: $1.00. Payee: Boyd County Court. Personal checks accepted, credit cards are not. Prepayment required.
Civil Name Search: Access: In person, online. Visitors must perform in person searches themselves. Required to search: name, years to search; also helpful: address. Civil general index and docket books from late 1800s, on computer back 12 years. Civil PAT goes back to 1998. **See front or rear of chapter for detailed description of state's online access.** Online civil records date from 11/00 forward, probate from 10/00.
Criminal Name Search: Access: In person, online. Visitors must perform in person searches themselves. Required to search: name, years to search; also helpful: address, DOB, SSN. Criminal records on general index and docket books from late 1800s, on computer back 12 years. Criminal PAT goes back to 1998. **See front or rear of chapter for detailed description of state's online access.** Online criminal and traffic records date from 08/00. Online results show middle initial, DOB.

Brown County

District Court 148 W Fourth St, Ainsworth, NE 69210; 402-387-2705; fax: 402-387-0918; 8AM-5PM (CST). *Felony, Civil Actions over $52,000.*
General Information: No search warrants, mental health, or sealed records released. Fee to fax out file $3.00 1st page, $1.50 each add'l. Court makes copy: $.25 per page. Self serve copy: $.25 per page. Certification fee: $5.00 1st page, $1 each add'l, includes copies. Payee: Clerk of District Court, Brown County. Personal checks accepted, credit cards are not. Prepayment required. Mail requests: SASE required.
Civil Name Search: Access: Phone, fax, mail, in person, online. Both court and visitors may perform in person name searches. No search fee. Required to search: name, years to search; also helpful: address. Civil records on general index and docket books from late 1886s; on computer back to 2000. Mail Turnaround time 3-4 days. Civil PAT goes back to 2001. **See front or rear of chapter for detailed description of state's online access.** Online records date from 02/00.
Criminal Name Search: Access: Fax, mail, in person, online. Both court and visitors may perform in person name searches. No search fee. Required to search: name, years to search, signed release; also helpful: address, DOB, SSN. Criminal records on general index and docket books from late 1886; on computer back to 2000. Mail Turnaround time 3-4 days. Criminal PAT goes back to 2001. **See front or rear of chapter for detailed description of state's online access.** Online records date from 02/00. Online results show middle initial, DOB.
Brown County Court 148 W Fourth St, Ainsworth, NE 69210; 402-387-2864; fax: 402-387-0918; 8AM-4:30PM (CST). *Misdemeanor, Civil Actions under $52,000, Eviction, Small Claims, Probate.*
General Information: No adoption, juvenile, or sealed records released. Will not fax documents. Court makes copy: $.25 per page. Certification fee: $1.00 per page plus copy fee. Payee: Brown County Court. Personal checks accepted, credit cards are not. Prepayment required.
Civil Name Search: Access: In person, online. Both court and visitors may perform in person name searches. No search fee. Civil records in boxes in office since 1980; on computer since 2001. Civil PAT goes back to 2000. **See front or rear of chapter for detailed description of state's online access.** Online civil records date from 04/01 forward, probate from 03/01.
Criminal Name Search: Access: In person, online. Both court and visitors may perform in person name searches. No search fee. Required to search: name, years to search, DOB. Criminal records in boxes in office since 1979; on computer since 2000. Criminal PAT goes back to same as civil. **See front or rear of chapter for detailed description of state's online access.** Online criminal and traffic records date from 08/00. Online results show middle initial, DOB.

Buffalo County

District Court PO Box 520, Kearney, NE 68848; 308-236-1246; fax: 308-233-3693; 8AM-5PM (CST). *Felony, Civil Actions over $52,000.*

www.buffalocounty.ne.gov/offices/ClerkDistrictCourt/
General Information: No juvenile, mental health, search warrants or sealed records released. Will fax out specific case files for $3.00 for 1st page, $1.00 each add'l. Court makes copy: $.25 per page. Self serve copy: same. Certification fee: $1.00 per doc plus copy fee. Payee: Clerk of District Court. Business checks accepted. No credit cards accepted. Prepayment required.
Civil Name Search: Access: In person, online. Visitors must perform in person searches themselves. Required to search: name only. Civil records on computer from 1993, on microfiche through 1991, on books from 1800s. Civil PAT goes back to 1997. Public terminal in courthouse lobby. **See front or rear of chapter for detailed description of state's online access.** Online records date from 05/97.
Criminal Name Search: Access: In person, online. Visitors must perform in person searches themselves. Required to search: name, DOB. Criminal records computerized from 1997; on microfiche 1991-current; on books from 1800s. Criminal PAT goes back to same as civil. Public terminal in courthouse lobby. **See front or rear of chapter for detailed description of state's online access.** Online records date from 05/97. Online results show middle initial, DOB.

Buffalo County Court PO Box 520, Kearney, NE 68848; 308-236-1220; criminal phone: 308-236-1232; probate phone: 308-236-1229; fax: 308-236-1243; 8AM-5PM (CST). *Misdemeanor, Civil Actions under $52,000, Eviction, Small Claims, Probate.*
www.supremecourt.ne.gov/county-court/county-court-website/buffalopub.htm
General Information: No adoption, or sealed records released. Will not fax documents. Court makes copy: $.25 per page. Certification fee: $1.00 per seal plus copy fee. Payee: County Court. Personal checks accepted, credit cards are not. Prepayment required.
Civil Name Search: Access: In person, online. Visitors must perform in person searches themselves. Civil docket on computer from 4/94, on microfiche, general index, and docket books from late 1800s. Record files kept 15 years. Civil PAT goes back to 1994. **See front or rear of chapter for detailed description of state's online access.** Online civil and probate records date from 04/94.
Criminal Name Search: Access: In person, online. Visitors must perform in person searches themselves. Criminal docket computerized from 4/94, on microfiche, general index, and docket books from late 1800s. Record files kept 15 years. Criminal PAT goes back to 1994. **See front or rear of chapter for detailed description of state's online access.** Online criminal and traffic records date from 04/94. Online results show middle initial, DOB.

Burt County

District Court 111 N 13th St #11, Tekamah, NE 68061; 402-374-2905; fax: 402-374-2906; 8AM-4:30PM (CST). *Felony, Civil Actions over $52,000, Domestic.* www.burtcounty.ne.gov/court.html
General Information: No mental health records released. Will fax documents to local or toll free line. Court makes copy: $.25 per page. Certification fee: $1.00 per document. Payee: Clerk of District Court. Personal checks accepted. No credit cards accepted for record searches. Prepayment required. Mail requests: SASE required for mail return of any copies.
Civil Name Search: Access: In person, online. Visitors must perform in person searches themselves. Civil records on books from 1800s. Civil PAT goes back to 1999. **See front or rear of chapter for detailed description of state's online access.** Online records date from 3/1999.
Criminal Name Search: Access: In person, online. Visitors must perform in person searches themselves. Required to search: name, years to search; also helpful: DOB, SSN. Criminal docket on books from 1800s. Criminal PAT goes back to same as civil. **See front or rear of chapter for detailed description of state's online access.** Online records date from 3/1999. Online results show middle initial, DOB.

Burt County Court 111 N 13th St, #9, Tekamah, NE 68061; 402-374-2950; fax: 402-374-2951; 8AM-4:30PM (CST). *Misdemeanor, Civil Actions under $52,000, Eviction, Small Claims, Probate.*
http://supremecourt.ne.gov/county-court/
General Information: Closed 1/2 hour at lunch. Online identifiers in results same as on public terminal. No adoption records released. Will not fax documents. Court makes copy: $.25 per page. Self serve copy: same. Certification fee: $1.00 per page. Payee: Burt County Court. No personal checks or credit cards accepted. Prepayment required.
Civil Name Search: Access: In person, online. Visitors must perform in person searches themselves. Required to search: name, years to search, address. Civil index on cards back to 1867, computerized back to 1998. Civil PAT goes back to 1998 using District Court terminal. **See front or rear of chapter for detailed description of state's online access.** Online civil records date from 03/00 forward, probate from 05/98.
Criminal Name Search: Access: In person, online. Visitors must perform in person searches themselves. Required to search: name, years to

search, address, DOB. Criminal records indexed on cards back to 1867, computerized back to 1998. Criminal PAT goes back to same as civil. **See front or rear of chapter for detailed description of state's online access.** Online criminal and traffic records date from 02/98. Online results show middle initial, DOB.

Butler County

District Court 451 5th St, David City, NE 68632-1666; 402-367-7460; fax: 402-367-3249; 8:30AM-5PM (CST). *Felony, Civil Actions over $52,000.*

General Information: No juvenile or mental health records released. No fee to fax documents. Court makes copy: $.25 per page. Self serve copy: $.10 per page. Certification fee: $1.50 per document. Payee: District Court. Personal checks accepted, credit cards are not. Prepayment required. Mail requests: SASE required.

Civil Name Search: Access: Mail, in person, online. Both court and visitors may perform in person name searches. Search fee: $2.00 per name. Civil records on books. Mail Turnaround time 1-2 days. Civil PAT goes back to 2001. **See front or rear of chapter for detailed description of state's online access.** Online records date from 03/99.

Criminal Name Search: Access: Mail, in person, online. Both court and visitors may perform in person name searches. Search fee: $2.00 per name. Required to search: name, years to search; also helpful: DOB, SSN. Criminal docket on books. Mail Turnaround time 1-2 days. Criminal PAT goes back to same. **See front or rear of chapter for detailed description of state's online access.** Online records date from 03/99. Online results show middle initial, DOB.

Butler County Court 451 5th St, David City, NE 68632-1666; 402-367-7480; fax: 402-367-3249; 8AM-N, 1-5PM (CST). *Misdemeanor, Civil Actions under $52,000, Eviction, Small Claims, Probate, Juvenile.*

http://supremecourt.ne.gov/county-court/

General Information: Online identifiers in results same as on public terminal. No adoption records released. Some juvenile requires signed release. Will fax case file $3.00 first page and $1.00 ea add'l, if pre-paid. Court makes copy: $.25 per page. Certification fee: $1.00. Payee: Butler County Court. Personal checks accepted, credit cards are not. Prepayment required. Mail requests: SASE required for mail return of any copies.

Civil Name Search: Access: In person, online. Visitors must perform in person searches themselves. Civil records on computer since 1998, docket books from late 1800s, probate on microfiche. Note: They can refer requestors to parties who perform searches at the court. Civil PAT goes back to 1998. **See front or rear of chapter for detailed description of state's online access.** Online civil records date from 10/99 forward, probate from 03/98.

Criminal Name Search: Access: In person, online. Visitors must perform in person searches themselves. Required to search: name, years to search; also helpful: DOB. Criminal records on computer since 1998, docket books from late 1800s, probate on microfiche. Note: Court can refer requestors to parties who perform searches at the court. Criminal PAT goes back to same as civil. Results include driver's license number. **See front or rear of chapter for detailed description of state's online access.** Online criminal and traffic records date from 03/98. Online results show middle initial, DOB.

Cass County

District Court Cass County Courthouse, 346 Main St, Plattsmouth, NE 68048; 402-296-9339; fax: 402-296-9345; 8AM-5PM (CST). *Felony, Civil Actions over $52,000.* www.cassne.org/distcourt.html

General Information: Online identifiers in results same as on public terminal. Will fax out specific case files for $1.50 1st page; $.50 each add'l. Court makes copy: $.25 per page. Certification fee: $1.00 per seal plus copy fee. Payee: Clerk of District Court. Personal checks accepted, credit cards are not. Prepayment required.

Civil Name Search: Access: In person, online. Visitors must perform in person searches themselves. Civil index on docket books from 1860s, index on computer since 9/97. Civil PAT goes back to 8/1997. **See front or rear of chapter for detailed description of state's online access.** Online records date from 08/97.

Criminal Name Search: Access: In person, online. Visitors must perform in person searches themselves. Criminal records indexed in books from 1860s, index on computer since 9/97. Criminal PAT goes back to 8/1997. **See front or rear of chapter for detailed description of state's online access.** Online records date from 08/97. Online results show middle initial, DOB.

Cass County Court Cass County Courthouse, 346 Main St Rm 301, Plattsmouth, NE 68048; 402-296-9334; probate phone: 402-296-9334; fax: 402-296-9545; 8AM-5PM (CST). *Misdemeanor, Civil Actions under $52,000, Eviction, Small Claims, Probate.*

http://supremecourt.ne.gov/county-court/

General Information: Will not fax documents. Court makes copy: $.25 per page. Certification fee: $1.00. Payee: Cass County Court. No personal checks or credit cards accepted. Prepayment required.

Civil Name Search: Access: In person, online. Visitors must perform in person searches themselves. Civil index on cards for 5 years then sent to Capital for storage; computerized records since 2000. Civil PAT goes back to 2000. **See front or rear of chapter for detailed description of state's online access.** Online civil records date from 01/00 forward, probate from 05/98.

Criminal Name Search: Access: In person, online. Visitors must perform in person searches themselves. Criminal records on computer since 1/97. Criminal PAT goes back to 2000. **See front or rear of chapter for detailed description of state's online access.** Online criminal and traffic records date from 01/97. Online results show middle initial, DOB.

Cedar County

District Court PO Box 796, Hartington, NE 68739-0796; 402-254-6957; fax: 402-254-6954; 8AM-5PM (CST). *Felony, Civil Actions over $52,000, Domestic, Appeals.*

General Information: Online identifiers in results same as on public terminal. No mental health records released. Will fax documents for $3.00 for first page and $1.00 ea add'l. Court makes copy: $.25 per page. Certification fee: $1.00. Payee: District Court. Personal checks accepted. Prepayment required.

Civil Name Search: Access: In person, online. Visitors must perform in person searches themselves. Civil records prior to 11/1999 are available in book form. Civil PAT goes back to 11/1999. **See front or rear of chapter for detailed description of state's online access.** Online records date from 11/99.

Criminal Name Search: Access: In person, online. Visitors must perform in person searches themselves. Required to search: name, years to search; also helpful: SSN. Criminal records prior to 11/1999 are available in book form. Criminal PAT goes back to same as civil. **See front or rear of chapter for detailed description of state's online access.** Online records date from 11/99. Online results show middle initial, DOB.

Cedar County Court PO Box 695, Hartington, NE 68739; 402-254-7441; fax: 402-254-7447; 8AM-5PM (CST). *Misdemeanor, Civil Actions under $55,000, Eviction, Small Claims, Probate, Traffic.*

http://supremecourt.ne.gov/county-court/

General Information: Online identifiers in results same as on public terminal. No juvenile or judge sealed records released. Will fax out specific case files for $3.00 for 1st page, $1.00 each add'l. Court makes copy: $.25 per page. Self serve copy: same. Certification fee: $1.00. Payee: Cedar County Court. Personal checks accepted, credit cards are not. Prepayment required. Mail requests: SASE required for mail return of any copies.

Civil Name Search: Access: In person, online. Visitors must perform in person searches themselves. Civil cases indexed by defendant. Civil records on general index, docket books 15 years; some on microfiche to 1983. Civil PAT goes back to 2000. **See front or rear of chapter for detailed description of state's online access.** Online civil and probate records from 11/00 forward.

Criminal Name Search: Access: In person, online. Visitors must perform in person searches themselves. Required to search: name, years to search, offense; also helpful: DOB. Criminal records indexed in books since 1983. Computerized records go back to 2000. Criminal PAT goes back to same as civil. **See front or rear of chapter for detailed description of state's online access.** Online criminal and traffic records date from 6/200. Online results show middle initial, DOB.

Chase County

District Court PO Box 1299, Imperial, NE 69033; 308-882-7500; fax: 308-882-7552; 8AM-4PM (MST). *Felony, Civil Actions over $52,000.*

General Information: County and District records must be searched separately. Online identifiers in results same as on public terminal. Will fax documents $1.00 per page. Court makes copy: $.50 per page. Self serve copy: same. Certification fee: $1.00 plus copy fee for each document. Payee: Chase County Clerk. Personal checks accepted, credit cards are not. Prepayment required. Mail requests: SASE required.

Civil Name Search: Access: Phone, fax, mail, in person, online. Both court and visitors may perform in person name searches. No search fee. Civil records general index, docket books from early 1900s. Mail Turnaround time up to 5 days. Civil PAT goes back to 2000. **See front or rear of chapter for detailed description of state's online access.** Online records date from 05/00.

Criminal Name Search: Access: Phone, fax, mail, in person, online. Both court and visitors may perform in person name searches. No search fee. Required to search: name, years to search; also helpful: DOB, SSN. Criminal records general index, docket books from early 1900s, computerized since 2000. Mail Turnaround time 5 days. Criminal PAT goes back to same as civil. Results include some drivers license numbers. **See front or rear of**

chapter for detailed description of state's online access. Online records date from 05/00. Online results show middle initial, DOB.

Chase County Court PO Box 1299, 921 Broadway, Imperial, NE 69033; 308-882-7519; fax: 308-882-7554; 8AM-4PM (MST). *Misdemeanor, Civil Actions under $52,000, Eviction, Small Claims, Probate.* http://supremecourt.ne.gov/county-court/

General Information: No adoption, juvenile. Will fax documents to local or toll free line. Court makes copy: $.25 per page. Certification fee: $1.00 per doc plus copy fee. Payee: Chase County Court. Personal checks accepted, credit cards are not. Prepayment required.

Civil Name Search: Access: In person, online. Both court and visitors may perform in person name searches. No search fee. Civil records on general index, docket books from 1910; prior incomplete. Some probate on microfiche. Civil PAT goes back to 1/2001. **See front or rear of chapter for detailed description of state's online access.** Online civil and probate records date from 1/2001 forward.

Criminal Name Search: Access: In person, online. Both court and visitors may perform in person name searches. No search fee. Required to search: name, years to search, DOB. Criminal records indexed in books from 1910; prior incomplete. Some probate on microfiche. Criminal PAT goes back to 9/2000. Public access terminal located at courthouse. **See front or rear of chapter for detailed description of state's online access.** Online criminal and traffic records date from 09/00. Online results show middle initial, DOB.

Cherry County

District Court 365 N Main St, Valentine, NE 69201; 402-376-1840; fax: 402-376-3830; 8AM-4:30PM (MST). *Felony, Civil Actions over $52,000.*

General Information: No juvenile records. Will not fax documents. Court makes copy: $.25 per page. Certification fee: $1.00 per page plus copy fee. Payee: Clerk of District Court. Personal checks accepted, credit cards are not. Prepayment required.

Civil Name Search: Access: In person, online. Visitors must perform in person searches themselves. Required to search: name, years to search; also helpful: address. Civil cases indexed by petitioner, respondent. Civil index on docket books from late 1800s. Civil PAT goes back to 3/1999. **See front or rear of chapter for detailed description of state's online access.** Justice records date from 03/99.

Criminal Name Search: Access: In person, online. Visitors must perform in person searches themselves. Criminal records indexed in books from late 1800s; computerized records since 1999. Criminal PAT goes back to same as civil. **See front or rear of chapter for detailed description of state's online access.** Online records date from 03/99. Online results show middle initial, DOB.

Cherry County Court 365 N Main St, Valentine, NE 69201; 402-376-2590; fax: 402-376-5942; 8AM-5PM (CST). *Misdemeanor, Civil Actions under $52,000, Eviction, Small Claims, Probate.* http://supremecourt.ne.gov/county-court/

General Information: Online identifiers in results same as on public terminal. No adoption records released. Juvenile released only to parties involved. Will fax out docs no add'l fee. Court makes copy: $.25 per page. Self serve copy: same. Certification fee: $1.25. Payee: Cherry County Court. Personal checks accepted, credit cards are not. Prepayment required.

Civil Name Search: Access: In person, online. Visitors must perform in person searches themselves. Civil records on docket card file from 1986, general index prior from late 1800s. Civil PAT goes back to 11/2000. **See front or rear of chapter for detailed description of state's online access.** Online civil and probate records from 11/00 forward.

Criminal Name Search: Access: In person, online. Visitors must perform in person searches themselves. Required to search: name, years to search, DOB. Criminal records on docket card file from 1986, general index prior from late 1800s; on computer since 8/2000. Criminal PAT goes back to 8/2000. **See front or rear of chapter for detailed description of state's online access.** Online criminal and traffic records date from 08/20 Online results show middle initial, DOB.

Cheyenne County

District Court PO Box 217, 1000 10th Ave, Sidney, NE 69162; 308-254-2814; fax: 308-254-7832; 8AM-5PM (MST). *Felony, Civil Actions over $52,000.* www.co.cheyenne.ne.us/court.html

General Information: No mental health or search warrants released. Will fax documents to local or toll-free number for $2.00 first page and $.50 ea add'l. Court makes copy: $.50 per page. Certification fee: $1.00 per doc plus copy fee. Payee: Clerk of District Court. No personal checks. No credit cards accepted. Prepayment required. Attorneys may be billed.

Civil Name Search: Access: In person, online. Visitors must perform in person searches themselves. Civil records on general index, docket books going back to late 1800s, on computer since 9/98. Civil PAT goes back to 1997. **See front or rear of chapter for detailed description of state's online access.** Online records date from 08/98.

Criminal Name Search: Access: In person, online. Visitors must perform in person searches themselves. Required to search: name, years to search; also helpful: DOB, SSN. Criminal records indexed in books going back to late 1800s, on computer since 9/98. Criminal PAT goes back to same as civil. **See front or rear of chapter for detailed description of state's online access.** Online records date from 08/98. Online results show middle initial, DOB.

Cheyenne County Court 1000 10th Ave, Sidney, NE 69162; 308-254-2929; fax: 308-254-2312; 8AM-5PM (MST). *Misdemeanor, Civil Actions under $52,000, Eviction, Small Claims, Probate.* http://supremecourt.ne.gov/county-court/

General Information: Must first receive permission to fax to the court. No adoption, juvenile, confidential records released. Court makes copy: $.25 per page. Certification fee: $1.00 per page plus copy fee. Payee: Cheyenne County Court. Personal checks accepted, credit cards are not. Prepayment required. Mail requests: SASE required.

Civil Name Search: Access: Fax, mail, in person, online. Both court and visitors may perform in person name searches. No search fee. Civil index on docket books from late 1800s. Mail Turnaround time within 1 week. Civil PAT goes back to 6/2000. Civil records online: see criminal access. Online records date from 12/00, including probate.

Criminal Name Search: Access: Fax, mail, in person, online. Both court and visitors may perform in person name searches. No search fee. Required to search: name, years to search; also helpful: DOB. Criminal records indexed in books from late 1800s; computerized records since 2000. Mail Turnaround time within 1 week. Criminal PAT goes back to same as civil. **See front or rear of chapter for detailed description of state's online access.** Online criminal and traffic records date from 06/00. Online results show middle initial, DOB.

Clay County

District Court Clerk of The District Court, 111 W Fairfield St, Clay Center, NE 68933; 402-762-3595; fax: 402-762-3604; 8:30AM-5PM (CST). *Felony, Civil Actions over $52,000.* www.claycounty.ne.gov/webpages/district_court/district_court.html

General Information: Online identifiers in results same as on public terminal. No mental health records released. Will fax documents $3.00 1st page, $1.00 ea add'l. Court makes copy: $.25 per page. Certification fee: $1.00. Payee: Clerk of District Court. Personal checks accepted, credit cards are not. Prepayment required.

Civil Name Search: Access: In person, online. Visitors must perform in person searches themselves. Required to search: name; also helpful: years to search. Civil index on docket books from late 1800s, on microfiche from 1986, computerized since 1998. Civil PAT goes back to 1998. **See front or rear of chapter for detailed description of state's online access.** Online records date from 09/98.

Criminal Name Search: Access: In person, online. Visitors must perform in person searches themselves. Required to search: name, DOB; also helpful: years to search, SSN. Criminal records indexed in books from late 1800s, on microfiche from 1986, computerized since 1998. Criminal PAT goes back to 9/1998. **See front or rear of chapter for detailed description of state's online access.** Online records date from 09/98. Online results show middle initial, DOB.

Clay County Court 111 W Fairfield St, Clay Center, NE 68933; 402-762-3651; fax: 402-762-3250; 8:30AM-5PM (CST). *Misdemeanor, Civil Actions under $52,000, Eviction, Small Claims, Probate, Traffic.* www.claycounty.ne.gov/webpages/county_court/county_court.html

General Information: Online identifiers in results same as on public terminal. No adoption or juvenile records released. Will not fax documents. Court makes copy: $.25 per page. Self serve copy: same. Certification fee: $1.00. Payee: Clay County. Personal checks accepted, credit cards are not. Prepayment required.

Civil Name Search: Access: In person, online. Visitors must perform in person searches themselves. Civil cases indexed by defendant. Civil records in index books from late 1800s, on computer from 4/2000. Civil PAT goes back to 4/2000. **See front or rear of chapter for detailed description of state's online access.** Online records date from 4/2000, including probate.

Criminal Name Search: Access: In person, online. Visitors must perform in person searches themselves. Required to search: name, years to search; also helpful: DOB, SSN. Criminal docket on books back 15 years from judgment. Criminal PAT goes back to same as civil. **See front or rear of chapter for detailed description of state's online access.** Online criminal and traffic records date from 4/2000. Online results show middle initial, DOB.

Colfax County

District Court 411 E 11th St, Schuyler, NE 68661; 402-352-8506; fax: 402-352-8550; 8:30AM-4:30PM (CST). *Felony, Civil Actions over $52,000.* www.colfaxcounty.ne.gov

General Information: The court and clerk only have the record files, not the indexes. The indexes are located in the NE State Historical Society Archives, 1500 R St, Lincoln, NE 68501. No juvenile or mental health records released. Will fax out specific case files for $1.00 per page. Court makes copy: $.30 per page. Certification fee: $1.50. Payee: Clerk of District Court. Business checks and local personal checks accepted. Prepayment required.

Civil Name Search: Access: In person, online. Visitors must perform in person searches themselves. Required to search: name, years to search; also helpful: address. Civil index on docket books back to 1880. Civil PAT goes back to 4/1997. **See front or rear of chapter for detailed description of state's online access.** Online records date back to 4/97.

Criminal Name Search: Access: In person, online. Visitors must perform in person searches themselves. Required to search: name, years to search; also helpful: address, DOB, SSN. Criminal records indexed in books back to 1880. Criminal PAT goes back to same as civil. **See front or rear of chapter for detailed description of state's online access.** Online records date back to 4/97. Online results show middle initial, DOB.

Colfax County Court PO Box 191, 411 E 11th St, Schuyler, NE 68661; 402-352-8511; fax: 402-352-8535; 8AM-4:30PM (CST). *Misdemeanor, Civil Actions under $52,000, Eviction, Small Claims, Probate.*

http://supremecourt.ne.gov/county-court/

General Information: No juvenile records released. Will not fax documents. Court makes copy: $.25 per page. Certification fee: $1.00 per doc plus copy fee. Payee: Colfax County Court. Personal checks accepted, credit cards are not. Prepayment required.

Civil Name Search: Access: In person, online. Visitors must perform in person searches themselves. Civil index on docket books from 1880s; computerized records since 1996. Civil PAT goes back to 1997. **See front or rear of chapter for detailed description of state's online access.** Online civil records date from 10/99 forward, probate from 05/98.

Criminal Name Search: Access: In person, online. Visitors must perform in person searches themselves. Required to search: name, years to search; also helpful: DOB, SSN. Criminal records indexed in books from 1880s; computerized records since 1996. Criminal PAT goes back to same as civil. **See front or rear of chapter for detailed description of state's online access.** Online criminal and traffic records date from 10/96. Online results show middle initial, DOB.

Cuming County

District Court 200 S Lincoln, Rm 200, West Point, NE 68788; 402-372-6004; fax: 402-372-6017; 8:30AM-4:30PM (CST). *Felony, Civil Actions over $51,000.*

General Information: No mental health records released. Will fax documents if you provide copy of your check for services. Court makes copy: $.25 per page. Self serve copy: same. Certification fee: $1.00. Payee: Clerk of District Court. Personal checks accepted, credit cards are not. Prepayment required.

Civil Name Search: Access: Mail, fax, in person. Visitors must perform in person searches themselves. Civil records in books from 1939; on computer back to 2000. Mail Turnaround time 1-5 days. Civil PAT goes back to 11/1999. **See front or rear of chapter for detailed description of state's online access.** Online records date from 11/99.

Criminal Name Search: Access: Fax, in person, online. Visitors must perform in person searches themselves. No search fee. Criminal records in books from 1939; on computer back to 2000. Mail Turnaround time 1-5 days. Criminal PAT goes back to same as civil. **See front or rear of chapter for detailed description of state's online access.** Online records date from 11/99. Online results show middle initial, DOB.

Cuming County Court 200 S Lincoln, Rm 103, West Point, NE 68788; 402-372-6003; probate phone: 402-372-6003; fax: 402-372-6030; 8:30AM-4:30PM (CST). *Misdemeanor, Civil Actions under $51,000, Eviction, Small Claims Under $35, Probate, Traffic.*

www.co.cuming.ne.us/county_court.html

General Information: Online identifiers in results same as on public terminal. No mental health records released. Will not fax documents. Court makes copy: $.25 per page. Certification fee: $1.00. Payee: Cuming County Court. Personal checks accepted; ID required. No credit cards accepted. Prepayment required.

Civil Name Search: Access: In person, online. Visitors must perform in person searches themselves. Civil index on cards, also on computer since 4/2000. Civil PAT goes back to 04/2000. Public terminal located in the District Court office. **See front or rear of chapter for detailed description of state's online access.** Online records date from 4/2000, including probate.

Criminal Name Search: Access: In person, online. Visitors must perform in person searches themselves. Required to search: name, years to search; also helpful: DOB, SSN. Criminal records indexed on cards, also on computer since 4/2000. Criminal PAT goes back to 04/2000. Public

terminal located in the District Court office. **See front or rear of chapter for detailed description of state's online access.** Online criminal and traffic records date from 3/2000. Online results show middle initial, DOB.

Custer County

District Court 431 S 10th Ave, Broken Bow, NE 68822; 308-872-2121; fax: 308-872-5826; 9AM-5PM (CST). *Felony, Civil Actions over $52,000.*

General Information: No search warrants, mental health, or sealed records released. Fee to fax out file $3.00 per page. Court makes copy: $.25 per page. Self serve copy: same. Certification fee: $1.25 per page plus copy fee. Payee: Clerk of District Court. Business checks accepted. No credit cards accepted. Prepayment required. Mail requests: SASE required.

Civil Name Search: Access: Phone, fax, mail, in person, online. Both court and visitors may perform in person name searches. No search fee. Required to search: name, years to search; also helpful: address. Civil index on docket books and docket books from late 1800s; on computer back to 4/1998. Mail Turnaround time 3-4 days. Civil PAT goes back to 4/1998. **See front or rear of chapter for detailed description of state's online access.** Online records date from 03/98.

Criminal Name Search: Access: Phone, fax, mail, in person, online. Both court and visitors may perform in person name searches. No search fee. Required to search: name, years to search; also helpful: address, DOB, SSN. Criminal records indexed in books and docket books from late 1800s; on computer back to 4/1998. Mail Turnaround time 3-4 days. Criminal PAT goes back to same as civil. Results include charges. **See front or rear of chapter for detailed description of state's online access.** Online records date from 03/98. Online results show middle initial, DOB.

Custer County Court 431 S 10th Ave, Broken Bow, NE 68822; 308-872-5761; fax: 308-872-6052; 8AM-N, 1-5PM (CST). *Misdemeanor, Civil Actions under $52,000, Eviction, Small Claims, Probate.*

http://supremecourt.ne.gov/county-court/

General Information: Probate fax is same as main fax number. No adoption records released. Will not fax documents. Court makes copy: $.25 per page. Certification fee: $1.00 per doc plus copy fee. Payee: Custer County Court. Personal checks accepted, credit cards are not. Prepayment required.

Civil Name Search: Access: In person, online. Visitors must perform in person searches themselves. Civil records on computer back to 2000, on index books from 1988, probate from 1986, balance are archived. Civil PAT goes back to 2000. **See front or rear of chapter for detailed description of state's online access.** Online records date from 1/01, including probate.

Criminal Name Search: Access: In person, online. Visitors must perform in person searches themselves. Criminal records computerized from 2000, index books from 1988, probate from 1986, balance are archived. Criminal PAT goes back to 2000. PA terminal is in Circuit Court. **See front or rear of chapter for detailed description of state's online access.** Online criminal and traffic records date from 7/17/00. Online results show middle initial, DOB.

Dakota County

District Court PO Box 66, Dakota City, NE 68731; 402-987-2115; fax: 402-987-2117; 8AM-4:30PM (CST). *Felony, Civil Actions over $52,000.*

General Information: No juvenile or mental health records released. Court makes copy: $.25 per page. Self serve copy: same. Certification fee: $1.00. Payee: Clerk of District Court. Personal checks accepted, credit cards are not. Prepayment required. Mail requests: SASE required.

Civil Name Search: Access: In person, online. Visitors must perform in person searches themselves. Civil index on docket books from 1985, prior records archived at NE State Historical Society, Lincoln, NE; computerized records since 1998. Note: This office will not do name searches. Civil PAT goes back to 1988. **See front or rear of chapter for detailed description of state's online access.** Online records date from 03/98.

Criminal Name Search: Access: Online, in person. Visitors must perform in person searches themselves. Criminal records indexed in books from 1985, prior records archived at NE State Historical Society, Lincoln, NE; computerized records since 1998. Note: This office will not do name searches. Criminal PAT goes back to same as civil. **See front or rear of chapter for detailed description of state's online access.** Online records date from 03/98. Online results show middle initial, DOB.

Dakota County Court PO Box 385, 1601 Broadway, Dakota City, NE 68731; 402-987-2115; fax: 402-987-2185; 8AM-4:30PM (CST). *Misdemeanor, Civil Actions under $52,000, Eviction, Small Claims, Probate.* http://supremecourt.ne.gov/county-court/

General Information: No adoption or juvenile records released. Will fax documents $3.00 1st page, $1.00 each add'l. Court makes copy: $.25 per page. Certification fee: $1.00 per doc plus copy fee. Payee: Dakota County Court. Personal checks accepted, credit cards are not. Prepayment required. Mail requests: SASE not required.

Civil Name Search: Access: In person, online. Visitors must perform in person searches themselves. Civil index on docket books from late 1800s. Civil PAT goes back to 1998. **See front or rear of chapter for detailed description of state's online access.** Online civil records date from 10/99 forward, probate from 05/98.

Criminal Name Search: Access: In person, online. Visitors must perform in person searches themselves. Criminal records indexed in books from late 1800s. Criminal PAT goes back to same as civil. **See front or rear of chapter for detailed description of state's online access.** Online criminal and traffic records date from 10/97. Online results show middle initial, DOB.

Dawes County

District Court 451 Main St, Ste B, Chadron, NE 69337; 308-432-0109; fax: 308-432-0110; 8:30AM-4:30PM (MST). *Felony, Civil Actions over $52,000.*

General Information: No mental health records released. Will fax documents to local or toll-free number. Court makes copy: $.25 per page. Certification fee: $1.00 plus copy fee. Payee: Clerk of District Court. Personal checks accepted, credit cards are not. Prepayment required. Mail requests: SASE required for mail return of any copies.

Civil Name Search: Access: In person, online. Visitors must perform in person searches themselves. Civil records on general index, docket books from 1886. Civil PAT goes back to 2001. **See front or rear of chapter for detailed description of state's online access.** Online records date from 08/98.

Criminal Name Search: Access: Fax, mail, in person, online. Visitors must perform in person searches themselves. Search fee: $10.00 per name. Criminal records indexed in books from 1886. Criminal PAT goes back to same as civil. **See front or rear of chapter for detailed description of state's online access.** Online records date from 08/98. Online results show name only.

Dawes County Court 451 Main St, Ste D, Chadron, NE 69337; 308-432-0116; fax: 308-432-0118; 7:30AM-4:30PM (MST). *Misdemeanor, Civil Actions under $52,000, Eviction, Small Claims, Probate.* http://supremecourt.ne.gov/county-court/

General Information: Online identifiers in results same as on public terminal. No confidential records released. Will fax out documents. Court makes copy: $.25 per page. Self serve copy: same. Certification fee: $1.00. Payee: Dawes County Court. Personal checks accepted, credit cards are not. Prepayment required. Mail requests: SASE required for mail return of any copies.

Civil Name Search: Access: In person, online. Visitors must perform in person searches themselves. Civil records on case cards, case files kept since 1993; on computer back to 2001. Civil PAT goes back to 11/2000. **See front or rear of chapter for detailed description of state's online access.** Online civil and probate records from 11/00 forward.

Criminal Name Search: Access: In person, online. Visitors must perform in person searches themselves. Required to search: name, years to search, DOB; also helpful: address. Criminal records on case cards, case files kept since 11991; on computer back to 2000. Criminal PAT goes back to 4/2000. **See front or rear of chapter for detailed description of state's online access.** Online criminal and traffic records date from 04/00. Online results show middle initial, DOB.

Dawson County

District Court 700 N Washington 3rd Fl, Rm E, Lexington, NE 68850; 308-324-4261; fax: 308-324-9876; 8AM-N, 1-5PM (CST). *Felony, Civil Actions over $52,000.* www.dawsoncountyne.org/

General Information: No juvenile or mental health records released. Will fax out documents. Court makes copy: $.25 per page. Certification fee: $1.00 plus copy fee. Payee: Clerk of District Court. Personal checks accepted, credit cards are not. Prepayment required. Mail requests: SASE required.

Civil Name Search: Access: Fax, mail, in person, online. Visitors must perform in person searches themselves. No search fee. Recent civil records on microfiche, some older records on microfilm, index books date to late 1800s. Mail Turnaround time 2 days. Civil PAT goes back to 5/1997. **See front or rear of chapter for detailed description of state's online access.** Online records date from 06/97.

Criminal Name Search: Access: Fax, mail, in person, online. Visitors must perform in person searches themselves. No search fee. Recent records on microfiche, some older records on microfilm, index books date to late 1800s. Mail Turnaround time 2 days. Criminal PAT goes back to same as civil. **See front or rear of chapter for detailed description of state's online access.** Online records date from 6/1997. Online results show middle initial, DOB.

Dawson County Court 700 N Washington St, Rm J, Lexington, NE 68850; 308-324-5606; fax: 308-324-9837; 8AM-5PM (CST). *Misdemeanor, Civil Actions under $52,000, Eviction, Small Claims, Probate.* www.supremecourt.ne.gov/county-court/county-court-website/dawson.shtml

General Information: Court personnel will only search records if specific case # given; turnaround time is 3-5 days. No adoption or juvenile records released. Will fax specific case for $3.00 1st page, $1.00 ea add'l. Court makes copy: $.25 per page. Self serve copy: same. Certification fee: $1.00. Payee: Dawson County Court. Personal checks accepted, credit cards are not. Prepayment required. Mail requests: SASE required for mail return of any copies.

Civil Name Search: Access: In person, online. Visitors must perform in person searches themselves. Required to search: name, years to search; also helpful: address. Civil records on books from late 1800s, docket books 15 years back; on computer since 1998. Civil PAT goes back to late 1997. **See front or rear of chapter for detailed description of state's online access.** Online civil records date from 10/99 forward, probate from 05/98.

Criminal Name Search: Access: In person, online. Visitors must perform in person searches themselves. Required to search: name, years to search, offense, DOB; also helpful: address. Criminal docket on books from late 1800s, docket books 15 years back; on computer since 1998. Criminal PAT goes back to same as civil. **See front or rear of chapter for detailed description of state's online access.** Online criminal and traffic records date from 05/00. Online results show middle initial, DOB.

Deuel County

District Court PO Box 327, 718 Third St, Chappell, NE 69129; 308-874-3308/2818; fax: 308-874-3472; 8AM-4PM (MST). *Felony, Civil Actions over $52,000.* www.co.deuel.ne.us/court.html

General Information: No mental health or service discharge records released. Will fax documents for $1.50 per page. Court makes copy: $.50 per page. Self serve copy: $.25 per page. Certification fee: $1.50 per page. Payee: Clerk of District Court. Personal checks accepted, credit cards are not. Prepayment required. Mail requests: SASE required.

Civil Name Search: Access: Phone, fax, mail, in person, online. Both court and visitors may perform in person name searches. No search fee. Required to search: name; also helpful: years to search. Civil records on general index and docket books from late 1800s. Mail Turnaround time 1 week. Civil PAT goes back to 2000. **See front or rear of chapter for detailed description of state's online access.** Online records date from 05/00.

Criminal Name Search: Access: Phone, fax, mail, in person, online. Both court and visitors may perform in person name searches. No search fee. Required to search: name; also helpful: years to search, DOB, SSN. Criminal records on general index and docket books from late 1800s. Mail Turnaround time 1 week. Criminal PAT goes back to same as civil. **See front or rear of chapter for detailed description of state's online access.** Online records date from 05/00. Online results show middle initial, DOB.

Deuel County Court PO Box 514, Chappell, NE 69129; 308-874-2909; fax: 308-874-3472; 8AM-4PM (MST). *Misdemeanor, Civil Actions under $52,000, Eviction, Small Claims, Probate.* http://supremecourt.ne.gov/county-court/

General Information: Online identifiers in results same as on public terminal. No juvenile records released. Will fax documents. Court makes copy: $.50 per page. Self serve copy: same. Certification fee: $1.00 per seal plus $.25 per page. Payee: Deuel County Court. Personal & business checks accepted. No credit cards accepted. Prepayment required.

Civil Name Search: Access: In person, online. Visitors must perform in person searches themselves. Required to search: name only. Civil index on cards from 1989, computerized since 2001. Civil PAT goes back to 12/2000. **See front or rear of chapter for detailed description of state's online access.** Online civil and probate records from 12/00 forward.

Criminal Name Search: Access: In person, online. Visitors must perform in person searches themselves. Required to search: name, DOB. Criminal records indexed on cards from 1989, computerized since 2001. Criminal PAT goes back to same as civil. **See front or rear of chapter for detailed description of state's online access.** Online criminal and traffic records date from 12/00. Online results show middle initial, DOB.

Dixon County

District Court PO Box 395, Ponca, NE 68770; 402-755-5604; fax: 402-755-5651; 8AM-N, 1-5PM (CST). *Felony, Civil Actions over $52,000.*

General Information: No mental health records released. Will fax out documents. Court makes copy: $.25 per page. Self serve copy: same. Certification fee: $1.00 per page plus copy fee. Payee: Clerk of District Court. Personal checks accepted, credit cards are not. Will bill copy fees.

Civil Name Search: Access: In person, online. Visitors must perform in person searches themselves. Civil records on books from 1876; computerized records go back to 1999. Civil PAT goes back to 1999, includes Dixon County Court. **See front or rear of chapter for detailed description of state's online access.** Online records date from 11/99.

Criminal Name Search: Access: In person, online. Visitors must perform in person searches themselves. Required to search: name, years to search, DOB. Criminal docket on books from 1876; computerized records go back to 1999. Criminal PAT goes back to same as civil. Single use or subscribe at https://www.nebraska.gov/justicecc/ccname.cgi for court access. Single search is $15.00 a record or open an account for $1 per record plus $50 annual fee. Online records date from 11/99. Online results show middle initial, DOB.

Dixon County Court PO Box 497, Ponca, NE 68770; 402-755-5607; fax: 402-755-5651; 8AM-N. 1PM-4:30PM (CST). *Misdemeanor, Civil Actions under $52,000, Eviction, Small Claims, Probate.*
http://supremecourt.ne.gov/county-court/
General Information: No adoption or juvenile records released. Will not fax documents. Court makes copy: $.25 per page. Certification fee: $1.00 per doc. Payee: Dixon County Court. Personal checks accepted, credit cards are not. Prepayment required.
Civil Name Search: Access: In person, online. Visitors must perform in person searches themselves. Civil and probate docket on cards from 1987; prior in dockets from 1836 civil and 1876 probate; computerized since 2001. Public use terminal available, records go back to 2000. **See front or rear of chapter for detailed description of state's online access.** Online civil records date from 01/01 forward, probate from 1/2001.
Criminal Name Search: Access: In person, online. Visitors must perform in person searches themselves. Required to search: name, years to search, DOB. Criminal records in files, cards from 1987; prior in dockets from 1933; computerized since 2000. Public use terminal available, crim records go back to same. **See front or rear of chapter for detailed description of state's online access.** Online criminal and traffic records date from 7/2000. Online results show middle initial, DOB.

Dodge County

District Court 428 N Broad, Fremont, NE 68026; 402-727-2780; fax: 402-727-2773; 8:30AM-4:30PM (CST). *Felony, Civil Actions over $52,000, Divorce.*
General Information: No mental health records released. Will fax documents $2.00 each in state; $5.00 out of state. Court makes copy: $.25 per page. Certification fee: $1.50 plus copy fee. Payee: District Court. Personal checks accepted, credit cards are not. Prepayment required.
Civil Name Search: Access: In person, online. Visitors must perform in person searches themselves. Civil records on general index, docket books from late 1800s; computerized records since 1997. Civil PAT goes back to 7/1997. **See front or rear of chapter for detailed description of state's online access.** Online records date from 7/1997.
Criminal Name Search: Access: In person, online. Visitors must perform in person searches themselves. Criminal records indexed in books from late 1800s; computerized records since 1997. Criminal PAT goes back to same as civil. **See front or rear of chapter for detailed description of state's online access.** Online records date from 7/1997. Online results show middle initial, DOB.

Dodge County Court 428 N Broad St, Fremont, NE 68025; 402-727-2755; criminal phone: 402-727-2758; civil phone: 402-727-2756; probate phone: 402-727-2755; fax: 402-727-2762; 8AM-5PM (CST). *Misdemeanor, Civil Actions under $52,000, Eviction, Small Claims, Probate.* http://supremecourt.ne.gov/county-court/
General Information: Probate is separate index at this same address. Probate fax is same as main fax number. Online identifiers in results same as on public terminal. No adoption or juvenile records released. Will fax documents $3.00 1st page, $1.00 ea add'l page. Court makes copy: $.25 per page. Self serve copy: same. Certification fee: $1.00 per document plus copy fee. Payee: Dodge County Court. Personal checks accepted, credit cards are not. Prepayment required.
Civil Name Search: Access: In person, online. Visitors must perform in person searches themselves. Civil cases indexed by defendant. Civil records on general index; on computer back to 1998. Probate on microfilm from early 1900s. Civil PAT goes back to 1998. **See front or rear of chapter for detailed description of state's online access.** Online civil records date from 01/00 forward, probate from 05/98.
Criminal Name Search: Access: In person, online. Visitors must perform in person searches themselves. Required to search: name, years to search; also helpful: DOB. Criminal records on general index; on computer back to 1998. Criminal PAT goes back to same as civil. **See front or rear of chapter for detailed description of state's online access.** Online criminal and traffic records date from 1/20/97. Online results show middle initial, DOB.

Douglas County

District Court 1701 Farnam, Hall of Justice, Rm 300, Omaha, NE 68183; 402-444-7018; fax: 402-444-1757; 8AM-4:30PM (CST). *Felony, Civil Actions over $52,000.* http://omaha-douglasconnection.com/courts
General Information: One may request a file from the clerk from the web page. You must have the docket number. No juvenile records released. Will

not fax documents. Court makes copy: $.25 per page. Add $1.00 postage fee. Self serve copy: same. Certification fee: $5.50 for 1-5 pages, $.25 each add'l, plus postage or SASE if mailing. Payee: Clerk of District Court. Personal checks accepted, credit cards are not. Prepayment required. Mail requests: SASE required or must send funds for postage.
Civil Name Search: Access: Mail, in person, online. Both court and visitors may perform in person name searches. Search fee: $5.00 per name. Required to search: name, years to search; also helpful: address. Civil records on computer from 1980, on books back to late 1800s. Mail Turnaround time 1-2 days. Civil PAT goes back to 1974. **See front or rear of chapter for detailed description of state's online access.** Online criminal and traffic records date from 01/1992. Online results show middle initial, DOB.
Criminal Name Search: Access: Mail, in person, online. Visitors must perform in person searches themselves. Search fee: $5.00 per name. Required to search: name, years to search; also helpful: address, DOB, SSN. Criminal records computerized from 1980, on books back to late 1800s. Mail Turnaround time 1-2 days. Criminal PAT goes back to 1981. **See front or rear of chapter for detailed description of state's online access.** Online criminal and traffic records date from 01/1992. Online results show middle initial, DOB.

County Court Criminal 1701 Farnham St, 2 East, Omaha, NE 68183; 402-444-5387; fax: 402-444-3608; 8AM-4:30PM (CST). *Misdemeanor, Traffic.* http://omaha-douglasconnection.com/courts
General Information: Court handles criminal traffic. Online identifiers in results same as on public terminal. Will not fax documents. Court makes copy: $.25 per page. Certification fee: $1.25; Authentication is $3.25. Payee: Douglas County Court. Personal checks accepted, credit cards are not. Prepayment required. Mail requests: SASE required.
Criminal Name Search: Access: Mail, in person, online. Visitors must perform in person searches themselves. No search fee. Required to search: name, years to search; also helpful: DOB. Criminal records computerized from 1980s. Mail Turnaround time 1-5 days. Public use terminal has crim records back to 4/1996. **See front or rear of chapter for detailed description of state's online access.** Online results show middle initial, DOB.

County Court Civil 1819 Farnam, #F03, Hall of Justice, Omaha, NE 68183; 402-444-5424; fax: 402-996-8326; 8AM-4:30PM (CST). *Civil Actions under $52,000, Eviction, Small Claims.*
http://omaha-douglasconnection.com/courts
General Information: Will not fax documents. Court makes copy: $.25 per page. Certification fee: $1.25; Authentication is $3.25. Payee: Douglas County Court. Personal checks accepted, credit cards are not. Mail requests: SASE required.
Civil Name Search: Access: Mail, in person, online. Visitors must perform in person searches themselves. No search fee. Civil records on computer from 1987 (small claims), from 1983 (civil). Civil records are purged after about 20 years. Public use terminal has civil records back to late 1990s. **See front or rear of chapter for detailed description of state's online access.**

County Court Probate 1701 Farnam, 3 West, Omaha, NE 68183; 402-444-7152; fax: 402-444-4019; 8AM-4:30PM (CST). *Probate.*
http://omaha-douglasconnection.com/courts
General Information: Copies are $25 each.

Dundy County

District Court PO Box 506, 112 Seventh Ave W, Benkelman, NE 69021; 308-423-2058; fax: 308-423-2325; 8AM-4PM (MST). *Felony, Civil Actions over $52,000.*
General Information: No juvenile records released. Will not fax documents. Court makes copy: $1.00 per page. Self serve copy: available. Certification fee: $1.50 plus $.50 each add'l page. Payee: Clerk of District Court. Personal checks accepted, credit cards are not. Prepayment required.
Civil Name Search: Access: In person, online. Visitors must perform in person searches themselves. Required to search: name, years to search; also helpful: address. Civil index on docket books from late 1800s. Civil PAT goes back to 8/2000. **See front or rear of chapter for detailed description of state's online access.** Online records date from 8/2000.
Criminal Name Search: Access: Mail, in person, online. Visitors must perform in person searches themselves. No search fee. Required to search: name, years to search; also helpful: address, DOB, SSN. Criminal records indexed in books from late 1800s. Mail Turnaround time 1 day. Criminal PAT goes back to same as civil. **See front or rear of chapter for detailed description of state's online access.** Online records date from 8/2000. Online results show middle initial, DOB.

Dundy County Court PO Box 378, Benkelman, NE 69021; 308-423-2374; fax: 308-423-2325; 8AM-4PM (MST). *Misdemeanor, Civil Actions under $52,000, Eviction, Small Claims, Probate.*
http://supremecourt.ne.gov/county-court/
General Information: No adoption or juvenile records released. Will fax out specific case files for $3.00 charge for 1st page, $1.00 each add'l. Court

makes copy: $.25 per page. Certification fee: $1.00 per document plus copy fee. Payee: Dundy County Court. Business checks accepted. No credit cards accepted for record searches. Prepayment required.

Civil Name Search: Access: In person, online. Visitors must perform in person searches themselves. Civil records on general index, docket books from late 1800s; some probate, civil on microfiche. Civil PAT goes back to 2000. **See front or rear of chapter for detailed description of state's online access.** Online civil records date from 11/00 forward, probate from 12/00.

Criminal Name Search: Access: In person, online. Visitors must perform in person searches themselves. Required to search: name, years to search, DOB, signed release; also helpful: address. Criminal records indexed in books from late 1800s, computerized since 2001. Criminal PAT goes back to 2001. **See front or rear of chapter for detailed description of state's online access.** Online criminal and traffic records date from 08/00. Online results show middle initial, DOB.

Fillmore County

District Court PO Box 147, 900 G St, Geneva, NE 68361-0147; 402-759-3811; fax: 402-759-4440; 8AM-N, 1-4:30PM (CST). *Felony, Civil Actions over $52,000.*

www.fillmorecounty.org/webpages/district_court/district_court.html

General Information: No juvenile or mental health records released. Will fax documents $3.00 1st page, $1.00 ea add'l, prepaid. Court makes copy: $.25 per page. Certification fee: $1.00 plus copy fees. Payee: Clerk of District Court. Personal checks accepted, credit cards are not. Prepayment required. Mail requests: SASE required.

Civil Name Search: Access: Fax, mail, in person, online, email. Visitors must perform in person searches themselves. No search fee. Civil index on docket books to late 1800s, on computer since 1998. Mail Turnaround time 1-5 days. Civil PAT goes back to 1998. **See front or rear of chapter for detailed description of state's online access.** Online records date from 06/98.

Criminal Name Search: Access: Fax, mail, in person, online, email. Visitors must perform in person searches themselves. No search fee. Required to search: name, years to search, DOB. Criminal records indexed in books to late 1800s, on computer since 1998. Mail Turnaround time 1-5 days. Criminal PAT goes back to same as civil. **See front or rear of chapter for detailed description of state's online access.** Online records date from 06/98. Online results show middle initial, DOB.

Fillmore County Court PO Box 66, 900 G St, Geneva, NE 68361; 402-759-3514; fax: 402-759-4440; 8AM-n, 1PM-4:30PM (CST). *Misdemeanor, Civil Actions under $52,000, Eviction, Small Claims, Probate.* www.district10.us/

General Information: No adoption or juvenile records released. Will fax documents $2.00 1st page, $1.00 each add'l. Court makes copy: $.25 per page. Certification fee: $1.00 per doc plus copy fee. Payee: County Court. Personal checks accepted, credit cards are not. Prepayment required.

Civil Name Search: Access: In person, online. Both court and visitors may perform in person name searches. No search fee. Civil records on general index, docket books from late 1800s; probate on microfiche. Civil PAT goes back to 2000. **See front or rear of chapter for detailed description of state's online access.** Online civil and probate records from 02/00 forward.

Criminal Name Search: Access: In person, online. Both court and visitors may perform in person name searches. No search fee. Criminal records indexed in books from late 1800s; probate on microfiche. Criminal PAT goes back to same as civil. **See front or rear of chapter for detailed description of state's online access.** Online criminal and traffic records date from 02/00. Online results show middle initial, DOB.

Franklin County

District Court PO Box 146, 405 15th Ave, Franklin, NE 68939; 308-425-6202; fax: 308-425-6093; 8:30AM-4:30PM (CST). *Felony, Civil Actions over $52,000.*

General Information: No adoption or juvenile records released. Will fax documents $1.50 per page. Court makes copy: $1.00 per page. Self serve copy: $.25 per page. Certification fee: $1.50 per page. Payee: Clerk of District Court or County Clerk. Personal checks accepted, credit cards are not. Prepayment required.

Civil Name Search: Access: In person, online. Visitors must perform in person searches themselves. Civil index on docket books back to turn of century; on computer back to 2/2000. Civil PAT goes back to 2000. **See front or rear of chapter for detailed description of state's online access.** Online records date from 02/00.

Criminal Name Search: Access: In person, online. Visitors must perform in person searches themselves. Criminal records indexed in books back to turn of century; on computer back to 2/2000. Criminal PAT goes back to same as civil. **See front or rear of chapter for detailed description of state's online access.** Online records date from 02/00. Online results show middle initial, DOB.

Franklin County Court PO Box 174, 405 15th Ave, Franklin, NE 68939; 308-425-6288; fax: 308-425-6289; 8AM-4:30PM (CST). *Misdemeanor, Civil Actions under $52,000, Eviction, Small Claims, Probate.* www.district10.us/franklin_county.htm

General Information: Court personnel not permitted to do name searches. No juvenile, adoption records released. Will not fax documents. Court makes copy: $.25 per page. Certification fee: $1.25. Payee: Franklin County Court. Personal checks accepted, credit cards are not. Prepayment required.

Civil Name Search: Access: In person, online. Visitors must perform in person searches themselves. Civil records on computer since 5/2000, on docket cards since 1988, prior on docket books. Civil PAT goes back to 5/2000. **See front or rear of chapter for detailed description of state's online access.** Online civil from 04/09 and probate records from 05/00 forward.

Criminal Name Search: Access: In person, online. Visitors must perform in person searches themselves. Criminal records on computer since 5/2000, docket cards since 1988, prior on docket books. Criminal PAT goes back to same as civil. **See front or rear of chapter for detailed description of state's online access.** Online criminal and traffic records date from 04/09. Online results show middle initial, DOB.

Frontier County

District Court PO Box 40, Courthouse, Stockville, NE 69042; 308-367-8641; fax: 308-367-8730; 9AM-4:30PM (CST). *Felony, Civil Actions over $52,000.* www.co.frontier.ne.us/court.html

General Information: Will fax documents $3.00 per page. Court makes copy: $.25 per page. Self serve copy: same. Certification fee: $1.00 per page plus copy fee. Payee: Clerk of District Court. Only cashiers checks and money orders accepted. No credit cards accepted. Prepayment required. Mail requests: SASE required.

Civil Name Search: Access: Mail, in person, online. Both court and visitors may perform in person name searches. No search fee. Civil records on general index, docket books from late 1800s; computerized records since 6/00. Mail Turnaround time 5 days. Civil PAT goes back to 6/2000. **See front or rear of chapter for detailed description of state's online access.** Online records date from 06/00.

Criminal Name Search: Access: Mail, in person, online. Both court and visitors may perform in person name searches. No search fee. Required to search: name, years to search, DOB, signed release. Criminal records indexed in books from late 1800s; computerized records since 6/00. Mail Turnaround time 5 days. Criminal PAT goes back to same as civil. **See front or rear of chapter for detailed description of state's online access.** Online records date from 06/00. Online results show middle initial, DOB.

Frontier County Court PO Box 38, Stockville, NE 69042; 308-367-8629; fax: 308-367-8730; 9AM-4:30PM (CST). *Misdemeanor, Civil Actions under $52,000, Eviction, Small Claims, Probate.* http://supremecourt.ne.gov/county-court/

General Information: No adoption or juvenile records released. Fee to fax out file $3.00 per page then $1.00 ea add'l. Court makes copy: $.25 per page. Self serve copy: same. Certification fee: $1.00 per copy. Payee: County Court. Only cashiers checks and money orders accepted. No credit cards accepted. Prepayment required. Mail requests: SASE required.

Civil Name Search: Access: Fax, mail, in person, online. Both court and visitors may perform in person name searches. No search fee. Civil cases indexed by plaintiff. Civil records on general index, docket books from late 1800s; on computer back to 10/2000. Mail Turnaround time 5 days. Civil PAT goes back to 10/2000. **See front or rear of chapter for detailed description of state's online access.** Online civil and probate records from 09/00 forward.

Criminal Name Search: Access: Fax, mail, in person, online. Both court and visitors may perform in person name searches. No search fee. Required to search: name, years to search, DOB; also helpful-signed release. Criminal records indexed in books from late 1800s; on computer back to 10/2000. Mail Turnaround time 5 days. Criminal PAT goes back to same as civil. Results sometimes include address. **See front or rear of chapter for detailed description of state's online access.** Online criminal and traffic records date from 09/00. Online results show middle initial, DOB.

Furnas County

District Court PO Box 413, Beaver City, NE 68926; 308-268-4015; fax: 308-268-4015; 10AM-N, 1-3PM (CST). *Felony, Civil Actions over $52,000.*

General Information: No mental health records released. Will fax documents. Court makes copy: $.25 per page. Self serve copy: same. Certification fee: $1.00. Payee: Clerk of District Court. Personal checks accepted, credit cards are not. Prepayment required.

Civil Name Search: Access: In person, online. Both court and visitors may perform in person name searches. No search fee. Civil records in general index books and files from late 1800s. Civil PAT goes back to

2000. **See front or rear of chapter for detailed description of state's online access.** Online records date from 04/00.

Criminal Name Search: Access: In person, online. Both court and visitors may perform in person name searches. No search fee. Criminal records in general index books and files from late 1800s. Criminal PAT goes back to same as civil. **See front or rear of chapter for detailed description of state's online access.** Online records date from 04/00. Online results show middle initial, DOB.

Furnas County Court PO Box 373, 912 R St, Beaver City, NE 68926; 308-268-4025; fax: 308-268-4025; 8AM-4PM (CST). *Misdemeanor, Civil Actions under $52,000, Eviction, Small Claims, Probate.*
www.furnascounty.ne.gov/index_html?page=content/magistrate.html

General Information: No adoption, juvenile or sealed records released. Court makes copy: $.25 per page. Self serve copy: same. Certification fee: $1.00 per page plus copy fee. Payee: County Court. Personal checks accepted, credit cards are not. Prepayment required.

Civil Name Search: Access: In person, online. Visitors must perform in person searches themselves. Civil records on card system from 1984, docket books back to late 1800s. Note: Court will search only if you provide a case number. Civil PAT goes back to 9/2000. Civil records online- see criminal access. Online civil and probate records from 01/01 forward.

Criminal Name Search: Access: In person, online. Visitors must perform in person searches themselves. Required to search: name, years to search; also helpful: DOB. Criminal records on card system from 1984, docket books back to late 1800s. Note: Court will search only if you provide a case number. Criminal PAT goes back to same as civil. **See front or rear of chapter for detailed description of state's online access.** Online criminal and traffic records date from 09/00. Online results show middle initial, DOB.

Gage County

District Court 612 Grant St, #11, Beatrice, NE 68310-2946; 402-223-1332; fax: 402-223-1313; 8AM-5PM (CST). *Felony, Civil Actions over $52,000.*

General Information: No juvenile or mental health records released. Will fax documents for no fee. Court makes copy: $.50 per page. Certification fee: $1.00 per cert plus copy fee. Payee: Clerk of District Court. Personal checks accepted, credit cards are not. Prepayment required.

Civil Name Search: Access: In person, online. Both court and visitors may perform in person name searches. No search fee. Civil index on docket books from late 1800s; on computer back to 1997. Civil PAT goes back to 1997. Public terminal search results may include DOB or address. **See front or rear of chapter for detailed description of state's online access.** Online records date from 11/96.

Criminal Name Search: Access: In person, online. Both court and visitors may perform in person name searches. No search fee. Required to search: name, years to search, DOB. Criminal records indexed in books from late 1800s; on computer back to 1997. Criminal PAT goes back to same as civil. Public terminal search results may include DOB or address. **See front or rear of chapter for detailed description of state's online access.** Online records date from 11/96. Online results show middle initial, DOB.

Gage County Court 612 Grant St, #17, Beatrice, NE 68310-2946; 402-223-1323; criminal phone: x1; civil phone: x4; probate phone: 402-223-1327; fax: 402-223-1374; 8AM-5PM (CST). *Misdemeanor, Civil Actions under $52,000, Eviction, Small Claims, Probate.*

General Information: Online identifiers in results same as on public terminal. No adoption or juvenile records released. Will not fax documents. Court makes copy: $.25 per page. Certification fee: $1.00 per doc plus copy fee. Payee: Gage County Court. Personal checks accepted, credit cards are not. Prepayment required. Mail requests: SASE required.

Civil Name Search: Access: In person, online. Visitors must perform in person searches themselves. Civil records go back to 1987; on computer back to 1999. Probate records from 1860, probate on microfiche. Note: Court personnel will not perform name searches. Civil PAT goes back to 9/1996. **See front or rear of chapter for detailed description of state's online access.** Online civil records date from 11/16/98 forward, probate from 05/98.

Criminal Name Search: Access: In person, online. Visitors must perform in person searches themselves. Required to search: name, years to search, DOB. Criminal records go back to 1976; on computer back to 1996. Note: Court personnel will not perform name searches. Criminal PAT goes back to same as civil. **See front or rear of chapter for detailed description of state's online access.** Online criminal and traffic records date from 09/09/96. Online results show middle initial, DOB.

Garden County

District Court PO Box 486, 611 Main, Oshkosh, NE 69154; 308-772-3924; fax: 308-772-0124; 8AM-4PM (MST). *Felony, Civil Actions over $52,000.*

General Information: No confidential records released. Will fax documents $2.00 1st page, $1.00 each add'l. Court makes copy: $.50 per page. Self serve copy: $.25 per page. Certification fee: $5.00. Payee: Clerk of District Court. Personal checks accepted, credit cards are not. Prepayment required. Mail requests: SASE required.

Civil Name Search: Access: Fax, mail, in person, online. Both court and visitors may perform in person name searches. Search fee: $5.00. Civil records in files, docket books back to 1910; on computer back to 1998. Mail Turnaround time same day. Civil PAT goes back to 1998. **See front or rear of chapter for detailed description of state's online access.** Online records date from 08/98.

Criminal Name Search: Access: Fax, mail, in person, online. Both court and visitors may perform in person name searches. Search fee: $5.00. Criminal records in files, docket books back to 1910; on computer back to 1998. Mail Turnaround time same day. Criminal PAT goes back to same as civil. **See front or rear of chapter for detailed description of state's online access.** Online records date from 08/98. Online results show middle initial, DOB.

County Court PO Box 465, Oshkosh, NE 69154; 308-772-3696; fax: 308-772-4143; 8AM-4:30PM Tu/W/Th (MST). *Misdemeanor, Civil Actions under $52,000, Eviction, Small Claims, Probate.*
http://supremecourt.ne.gov/county-court/

General Information: Clerk only available 3 days per week: Tu/W/Th. Clerk may also be contacted at 308-772-2909. No adoption or juvenile records released. Will fax documents $.25 per page fee. Court makes copy: $.25 per page. Self serve copy: same. Certification fee: $3.25 per doc. Payee: Garden County Court. Personal checks accepted, credit cards are not. Prepayment required.

Civil Name Search: Access: In person, online. Visitors must perform in person searches themselves. Civil records on general index, docket books from 1993, computerized since 1998. Note: Phone access limited to short searches. **See front or rear of chapter for detailed description of state's online access.** Online civil and probate records from 01/01 forward.

Criminal Name Search: Access: In person, online. Visitors must perform in person searches themselves. Criminal records indexed in books from 1992, computerized since 1998. **See front or rear of chapter for detailed description of state's online access.** Online criminal and traffic records date from 06/00. Online results show middle initial, DOB.

Garfield County

District Court PO Box 218, 250 S 8 Ave, Burwell, NE 68823; 308-346-4161; fax: 308-346-4651; 9AM-12; 1PM-5PM (CST). *Felony, Civil Actions over $52,000.*

General Information: Will fax documents $3.00 per page. Court makes copy: $.25 per page. Self serve copy: same. Certification fee: $1.50 per page plus copy fee. Payee: Clerk of District Court. Personal checks accepted, credit cards are not. Prepayment required. Mail requests: SASE required with civil search request.

Civil Name Search: Access: Mail, in person, online. Both court and visitors may perform in person name searches. Search fee: $5.00 per name may be charged to search. Required to search: name, years to search; also helpful: address. Civil index on docket books from 1885. Mail Turnaround time 3-4 days. Civil PAT available. Public terminal search results may include DOB or address. **See front or rear of chapter for detailed description of state's online access.** Online records date from 07/00.

Criminal Name Search: Access: In person, online. Visitors must perform in person searches themselves. Required to search: name, years to search; also helpful: address, DOB, SSN. Criminal records indexed in books from 1885. Criminal PAT available. Public terminal search results may include DOB or address. **See front or rear of chapter for detailed description of state's online access.** Online records date from 07/00. Online results show middle initial, DOB.

Garfield County Court PO Box 431, Burwell, NE 68823; 308-346-4123; fax: 308-346-4069; 9AM-4PM (CST). *Misdemeanor, Civil Actions under $52,000, Eviction, Small Claims, Probate.*
http://supremecourt.ne.gov/county-court/

General Information: No juvenile records released. Will fax documents $3.00 1st page, $1.00 each add'l. Court makes copy: $.25 per page. Certification fee: $1.00. Payee: County Court. Personal checks accepted. Prepayment required.

Civil Name Search: Access: In person, online. Visitors must perform in person searches themselves. Civil cases indexed by defendant. Civil index on docket books, from 1885 (probate), 25 years for civil; on computer back to 2000. Civil PAT goes back to 2000. **See front or rear of chapter for detailed description of state's online access.** Online civil and probate records from 10/00 forward.

Criminal Name Search: Access: In person, online. Visitors must perform in person searches themselves. Criminal record keeping back for 25 years; on computer back to 2000. Criminal PAT goes back to same as civil. **See front or rear of chapter for detailed description of state's online access.** Online criminal and traffic records date from 07/00. Online results show middle initial, DOB.

Gosper County

District Court PO Box 136, 507 Smith St, Elwood, NE 68937; 308-785-2611; fax: 308-785-2300; 8:30AM-4:30PM (CST). *Felony, Civil Actions over $52,000.*

www.co.gosper.ne.us/webpages/district_court/district_court.html

General Information: Online identifiers in results same as on public terminal. No juvenile records or search warrants released. Will fax documents for $3.00 1st page and $1.00 ea add'l. Court makes copy: $.25 per page. Self serve copy: same. Certification fee: $1.00 per page plus copy fee. Payee: Clerk of District Court. Personal checks accepted, credit cards are not. Prepayment required. Mail requests: SASE requested.

Civil Name Search: Access: Fax, mail, in person, online. Visitors must perform in person searches themselves. No search fee. Civil records in general index books since late 1800s. Civil PAT goes back to 2000. **See front or rear of chapter for detailed description of state's online access.** Online records date from 07/00.

Criminal Name Search: Access: Fax, mail, in person, online. Visitors must perform in person searches themselves. No search fee. Required to search: name, years to search; also helpful: DOB. Criminal records in general index books since late 1800s. Criminal PAT goes back to same as civil. **See front or rear of chapter for detailed description of state's online access.** Online records date from 07/00. Online results show middle initial, DOB.

Gosper County Court PO Box 55, 507 Smith St, Elwood, NE 68937; 308-785-2531; fax: 308-785-2300; 8:30AM-4:30PM (CST). *Misdemeanor, Civil Actions under $52,000, Eviction, Small Claims, Probate.* http://supremecourt.ne.gov/county-court/

General Information: Always call first before faxing. No adoption or juvenile records released. Will fax documents $3.00 1st page, $1.00 ea add'l. Court makes copy: $.25 per page. Self serve copy: same. Certification fee: $1.00. Payee: Gosper County Court. Personal checks accepted. Out of state checks not accepted. No credit cards accepted. Prepayment required.

Civil Name Search: Access: In person, online. Visitors must perform in person searches themselves. Civil index on cards, docket books kept for 10 years (civil), to late 1800s (probate). Note: Mail access limited to short searches. Civil PAT goes back to 2000. **See front or rear of chapter for detailed description of state's online access.** Online civil and probate records from 11/00 forward.

Criminal Name Search: Access: In person, online. Visitors must perform in person searches themselves. Required to search: name, years to search, DOB. Criminal record keeping back for 15 years, computerized back to 2001. Criminal PAT goes back to same as civil. **See front or rear of chapter for detailed description of state's online access.** Online criminal and traffic records date from 02/00.

Grant County

District Court PO Box 139, Hyannis, NE 69350; 308-458-2488; fax: 308-458-2780; 8AM-4PM (MST). *Felony, Civil.*

General Information: No mental health records released. Will fax documents $.50 per page. Court makes copy: $.20 per page; $.50 if to be mailed. Self serve copy: same. Certification fee: $1.50 includes copy fee. Payee: Grant County Clerk. Personal checks accepted, credit cards are not. Prepayment required. Mail requests: SASE required.

Civil Name Search: Access: Fax, mail, in person, online. Both court and visitors may perform in person name searches. No search fee. Civil index on docket books from 1888. Mail Turnaround time 3-4 days. Public use terminal available, records go back to 2000. **See front or rear of chapter for detailed description of state's online access.** Online records date from 06/00.

Criminal Name Search: Access: Fax, mail, in person, online. Both court and visitors may perform in person name searches. No search fee. Criminal records indexed in books from 1888. Mail Turnaround time 3-4 days. Public use terminal available, crim records go back to 2000. **See front or rear of chapter for detailed description of state's online access.** Online records date from 06/00. Online results show middle initial, DOB.

Grant County Court PO Box 437, Hyannis, NE 69350; 308-458-2433; fax: 308-327-5623; 10AM-4PM only on 2nd Tues of month (MST). *Misdemeanor, Civil Actions under $52,000, Eviction, Small Claims, Probate.* http://supremecourt.ne.gov/county-court/

General Information: This court administered by Sheridan County by Julie Krotz at 308-327-5656. Court will not do record searches by name, etc. but will send and certify copies of specific records. No adoption records released without court order. Will not fax documents. Court makes copy: none. Certification fee: $1.00. Payee: Grant County Court. Personal checks accepted, credit cards are not. Prepayment required.

Civil Name Search: Access: in person, online. Visitors must perform in person searches themselves. Required to search: name, years to search; also helpful: address. Civil records in files, docket books from 1888, computerized since 7/00. Note: Limited phone searching for specific records. **See front or rear of chapter for detailed description of state's online access.** Online civil records date from 11/00 forward, probate from 01/01.

Criminal Name Search: Access: In person, online. Visitors must perform in person searches themselves. Required to search: name, years to search, DOB; also helpful: address. Criminal records in files, docket books from 1888, computerized since 7/00. Note: Limited phone searching for specific records. **See front or rear of chapter for detailed description of state's online access.** Online criminal and traffic records date from 07/00. Online results show middle initial, DOB.

Greeley County

District Court PO Box 287, 101 S Kildare, Greeley, NE 68842; 308-428-3625; fax: 308-428-3022; 8AM-N; 1PM-4PM (CST). *Felony, Civil Actions over $52,000.*

www.supremecourt.ne.gov/district-court/district-court-website/greeley.shtml

General Information: No mental health records released. Will fax back docs $1.00 per page. Court makes copy: $.25 per page, max of $10.00. Self serve copy: same. Certification fee: $2.50 per doc. Payee: Clerk of District Court. Only cashiers checks and money orders accepted. No credit cards accepted. Prepayment required. Mail requests: SASE required.

Civil Name Search: Access: Mail, in person, online. Visitors must perform in person searches themselves. No search fee. Required to search: name, years to search, address. Civil records on general index books from late 1800s. Mail Turnaround time 1 day. Civil PAT goes back to 7/2000. **See front or rear of chapter for detailed description of state's online access.** Online records date from 07/00.

Criminal Name Search: Access: Fax, mail, in person, online. Visitors must perform in person searches themselves. No search fee. Required to search: name, years to search, DOB, signed release. Criminal records on general index books from late 1800s. Mail Turnaround time 1 day. Criminal PAT goes back to same as civil. **See front or rear of chapter for detailed description of state's online access.** Online records date from 07/00. Online results show middle initial, DOB.

Greeley County Court PO Box 302, 2 Kildare, Greeley, NE 68842; 308-428-2705; fax: 308-428-6500; 8AM-5PM M,T; 1PM-5PM Th (CST). *Misdemeanor, Civil Actions under $52,000, Eviction, Small Claims, Probate.* http://supremecourt.ne.gov/county-court/

General Information: Probate fax is same as main fax number. No adoption records released. Will fax out specific case files; fee varies by job. Court makes copy: $.25 per page. Certification fee: $1.00 per page. Payee: County Court. Only cashiers checks and money orders accepted. No credit cards accepted. Prepayment required. Mail requests: SASE required for mail return of any copies.

Civil Name Search: Access: In person, online. Visitors must perform in person searches themselves. Civil index on cards, kept from late 1800s, computerized since 5/2000. Civil PAT goes back to 5/2000. **See front or rear of chapter for detailed description of state's online access.** Online civil and probate records from 5/2000 forward.

Criminal Name Search: Access: In person, online. Visitors must perform in person searches themselves. Criminal records indexed on cards, kept from late 1800s, computerized since 5/2000. Criminal PAT goes back to 5/2000. **See front or rear of chapter for detailed description of state's online access.** Online criminal and traffic records date from 05/00. Online results show middle initial, DOB.

Hall County

District Court 111 W First St, Grand Island, NE 68802; 308-385-5144; fax: 308-385-5110; 8AM-5PM (CST). *Felony, Civil Actions over $52,000.*

General Information: Also, 800-508-0064. No mental health records released. Fee to fax out file $3.00 1st page, $1.00 each add'l. Court makes copy: $.25 per page. Certification fee: $1.00 per cert. Payee: Clerk of District Court. Personal checks accepted, credit cards are not. Prepayment required. Mail requests: SASE required.

Civil Name Search: Access: Fax, mail, in person, online. Visitors must perform in person searches themselves. No search fee. Many records on computer since 1985, some on microfilm, original index books back to late 1800s. Note: Court performs searches for government/law enforcement only. Mail Turnaround time 3-4 days. Civil PAT goes back to 1989. **See front or rear of chapter for detailed description of state's online access.** Online records date from 10/97.

Criminal Name Search: Access: Fax, mail, in person, online. Visitors must perform in person searches themselves. No search fee. Many records on computer since 1985, some on microfilm, original index books back to late 1800s. Note: Court performs searches for government/law enforcement only. Mail Turnaround time 3-4 days. Criminal PAT goes back to same as civil. **See front or rear of chapter for detailed description of state's online access.** Online records date from 10/97. Online results show middle initial, DOB.

Hall County Court 111 W 1st St, Grand Island, NE 68801; 308-385-5135; fax: 308-385-5138; 8AM-5PM (CST). *Misdemeanor, Civil Actions under $52,000, Eviction, Small Claims, Probate.*

http://supremecourt.ne.gov/county-court/

General Information: No confidential records released. Will not fax documents. Court makes copy: $.25 per page. Certification fee: $1.00 plus copy fee. Payee: County Court. Personal checks accepted, credit cards are not. Prepayment required.

Civil Name Search: Access: In person, online. Visitors must perform in person searches themselves. Civil cases indexed by defendant. Civil index on docket books, on computer after 1/24/00. Civil PAT goes back to 1/2000. **See front or rear of chapter for detailed description of state's online access.** Online civil records date from 01/00 forward, probate from 08/98.

Criminal Name Search: Access: Fax, mail, in person, online. Visitors must perform in person searches themselves. No search fee. Required to search: name, years to search, DOB. Criminal records indexed in books; on computer after 5/19/97. Mail Turnaround time 1 day. Criminal PAT goes back to 5/1997. **See front or rear of chapter for detailed description of state's online access.** Online criminal and traffic records date from 05/97. Online results show middle initial, DOB.

Hamilton County

District Court 1111 13th Street, Aurora, NE 68818; 402-694-3533; fax: 402-694-2250; 8AM-5PM (CST). *Felony, Civil Actions over $51,000.*

www.co.hamilton.ne.us/clerkdistrictcourt.html

General Information: Email questions to dcourt@hamilton.net. No mental health board hearing records released. Will fax documents $1.00 per page. Court makes copy: $.25 per page. Self serve copy: same. Certification fee: $1.00. Payee: Clerk of District Court. Personal checks accepted, credit cards are not. Prepayment required.

Civil Name Search: Access: In person, online. Visitors must perform in person searches themselves. Civil index on docket books and files from late 1800s. Civil PAT goes back to 1998. **See front or rear of chapter for detailed description of state's online access.** Online records date from 03/98.

Criminal Name Search: Access: In person, online. Visitors must perform in person searches themselves. Criminal records indexed in books and files from late 1800s. Criminal PAT goes back to same as civil. **See front or rear of chapter for detailed description of state's online access.** Online records date from 03/98. Online results show middle initial, DOB.

Hamilton County Court PO Box 323, 1111 13th St, Aurora, NE 68818; 402-694-6188; fax: 402-694-2250; 8AM-5PM (CST). *Misdemeanor, Civil Actions under $52,000, Eviction, Small Claims, Probate.*

General Information: No adoption records released. Will fax documents for $3.00 fee. Court makes copy: $.25 per page. Certification fee: $1.00 per page plus copy fee. Payee: Hamilton County Court. Personal checks accepted, credit cards are not. Prepayment required.

Civil Name Search: Access: In person, online. Visitors must perform in person searches themselves. Civil records computerized since 1998, older on docket books, probate on microfiche from late 1800s. Civil PAT goes back to 4/1998. **See front or rear of chapter for detailed description of state's online access.** Online civil records date from 10/99 forward, probate from 05/98.

Criminal Name Search: Access: In person, online. Visitors must perform in person searches themselves. Computerized since 1997. Criminal PAT goes back to same as civil. **See front or rear of chapter for detailed description of state's online access.** Online criminal and traffic records date from 07/97. Online results show name only.

Harlan County

District Court PO Box 698, 706 W 2nd St, Alma, NE 68920; 308-928-2173; fax: 308-928-2079; 8:30AM-4:30PM (CST). *Felony, Civil Actions over $52,000.*

General Information: No juvenile records released. Will fax documents $1.00 per page. Court makes copy: $.25 per page. Self serve copy: same. Certification fee: $1.00. Payee: Clerk of District Court. Personal checks accepted, credit cards are not. Prepayment required. Mail requests: SASE not required.

Civil Name Search: Access: Phone, mail, in person, online. Both court and visitors may perform in person name searches. Search fee: $5.00 per name. Civil records on books and in files from late 1800s, on computer back to 3/2000. Mail Turnaround time 1 day. Civil PAT goes back to 3/2000. **See front or rear of chapter for detailed description of state's online access.** Online records date from 04/00.

Criminal Name Search: Access: Phone, mail, in person, online. Both court and visitors may perform in person name searches. Search fee: $5.00 per name. Criminal docket on books and in files from late 1800s; on computer back to 3/2000. Mail Turnaround time 1 day. Criminal PAT goes back to same as civil. **See front or rear of chapter for detailed**

description of state's online access. Online records date from 4/2000. Online results show middle initial, DOB.

Harlan County Court PO Box 379, 706 2nd St, Alma, NE 68920; 308-928-2179; fax: 308-928-2170; 8:30AM-4:30PM (CST). *Misdemeanor, Civil Actions under $52,000, Eviction, Small Claims, Probate.*

www.district10.us/harlan_county.htm

General Information: No adoption records released. Limited access to juvenile records. Will not fax documents. Court makes copy: $.25 per page. Self serve copy: same. Certification fee: $1.00. Payee: Harlan County Court. Business checks accepted. No credit cards accepted. Prepayment required.

Civil Name Search: Access: In person, online. Visitors must perform in person searches themselves. Required to search: name, years to search; also helpful: address. Civil cases indexed by defendant. Civil index on cards from 1900; computerized since 2000. Civil PAT goes back to 2000. Public data available on CD-ROM for legal research only. **See front or rear of chapter for detailed description of state's online access.** Online civil and probate records from 11/00 forward.

Criminal Name Search: Access: In person, online. Visitors must perform in person searches themselves. Required to search: name, years to search; also helpful: address, DOB. Criminal records indexed on cards from 1900, computerized since 2000. Criminal PAT goes back to same as civil. Public data available on CD-ROM for legal research only. **See front or rear of chapter for detailed description of state's online access.** Online criminal and traffic records date from 03/00. Online results show middle initial, DOB.

Hayes County

District Court PO Box 370, 505 Trouth St, Hayes Center, NE 69032; 308-286-3413; fax: 308-286-3208; 8AM-4PM (CST). *Felony, Civil Actions over $52,000.*

General Information: Online identifiers in results same as on public terminal. No sealed records released. Will not fax out documents. Court makes copy: none, donation based. Self serve copy: same. Certification fee: none. Payee: Clerk of District Court. Personal checks accepted, credit cards are not. Prepayment required. Mail requests: SASE required.

Civil Name Search: Access: Fax, mail, in person, online. Visitors must perform in person searches themselves. No search fee. Required to search: name; also helpful: years to search, address. Civil index on docket books back to late 1800s. Mail Turnaround time 2 days. Civil PAT goes back to 6/2000. **See front or rear of chapter for detailed description of state's online access.** Online records date from 06/00.

Criminal Name Search: Access: Fax, mail, in person, online. Visitors must perform in person searches themselves. No search fee. Criminal records indexed in books back to late 1800s. Mail Turnaround time 2 days. Criminal PAT goes back to same as civil. **See front or rear of chapter for detailed description of state's online access.** Online records date from 6/2000. Online results show middle initial, DOB.

Hayes County Court PO Box 370, Hayes Center, NE 69032; 308-286-3315; fax: 308-286-3208; Call for hours. (CST). *Misdemeanor, Civil Actions under $52,000, Eviction, Small Claims, Probate.*

http://supremecourt.ne.gov/county-court/

General Information: Email kathy.j.jones@nebraska.gov if questions. No juvenile or adoption records released. Will not fax documents. Court makes copy: $.25 per page. Self serve copy: same. Certification fee: $1.00. Payee: County Court. Personal checks accepted, credit cards are not. Prepayment required. Mail requests: SASE required for mail return of any copies.

Civil Name Search: Access: In person, online. Visitors must perform in person searches themselves. Civil records on general index books and files back to late 1800s; on computer back to mid-2000. **See front or rear of chapter for detailed description of state's online access.** Online civil records date from 11/00 forward, probate from 12/00.

Criminal Name Search: Access: In person, online. Visitors must perform in person searches themselves. Required to search: name, years to search, DOB. Criminal records on general index books and files back to late 1800s; on computer back to mid-2000. **See front or rear of chapter for detailed description of state's online access.** Online criminal and traffic records date from 08/00. Online results show middle initial, DOB.

Hitchcock County

District Court PO Box 248, 229 E "D" St, Trenton, NE 69044; 308-334-5646; fax: 308-334-5398; 8:30AM-4PM (CST). *Felony, Civil Actions over $52,000.*

www.co.hitchcock.ne.us/court.html

General Information: No sealed records released. Will fax documents $3.00 1st page, $1.50 each add'l. Court makes copy: $.50 per page. Certification fee: $1.00 per cert plus copy fee. Payee: Clerk of District Court. Personal checks accepted, credit cards are not. Prepayment required. Mail requests: SASE required.

Civil Name Search: Access: Phone, fax, mail, in person, online. Both court and visitors may perform in person name searches. No search fee. Civil records on books from late 1800s; on computer back to 1999. Mail

Turnaround time 2 days. Civil PAT goes back to 2000. **See front or rear of chapter for detailed description of state's online access.** Online records date from 06/00.

Criminal Name Search: Access: Phone, fax, mail, in person, online. Both court and visitors may perform in person name searches. No search fee. Criminal docket on books from late 1800s; on computer back to 1999. Mail Turnaround time 2 days. Criminal PAT goes back to same as civil. **See front or rear of chapter for detailed description of state's online access.** Online records date from 6/2000. Online results show middle initial, DOB.

Hitchcock County Court PO Box 248, Trenton, NE 69044; 308-334-5383; fax: 308-334-5398; 8:30AM-4:30PM (CST). *Misdemeanor, Civil Actions under $52,000, Eviction, Small Claims, Probate.*

General Information: Probate is a separate index at this same address. No adoption or juvenile records released. Will not fax documents. Court makes copy: $.25 per page. Self serve copy: same. Certification fee: $1.00. Payee: County Court. Personal checks accepted. Prepayment required.

Civil Name Search: Access: In person, online. Both court and visitors may perform in person name searches. No search fee. Civil index on docket books, cards go back to 1960s; on computer back to 2000. Probate records go back to late 1800s. Civil PAT goes back to 2000. Public terminal is across the hall. **See front or rear of chapter for detailed description of state's online access.** Online civil and probate records from 1/2001 forward.

Criminal Name Search: Access: In person, online. Both court and visitors may perform in person name searches. No search fee. Required to search: name, years to search, DOB. Criminal records go back to 1989 approx. on docket books, cards; on computer back to 2000. Criminal PAT goes back to 2000. Public terminal is across the hall. **See front or rear of chapter for detailed description of state's online access.** Online criminal and traffic records date from 09/00. Online results show middle initial, DOB.

Holt County

District Court PO Box 755, 204 N 4th St, O'Neill, NE 68763; 402-336-2840; fax: 402-336-3601; 8AM-4:30PM (CST). *Felony, Civil Actions over $52,000.*

General Information: No juvenile or mental health records released. Will fax documents $3.00 1st page, $1.00 each add'l. Court makes copy: $.20 per page. Self serve copy: same. Certification fee: $1.00 per page. Payee: Clerk of District Court. Personal checks accepted, credit cards are not. Prepayment required. Mail requests: SASE required.

Civil Name Search: Access: Phone, fax, mail, in person, online. Both court and visitors may perform in person name searches. No search fee. Required to search: name, years to search; also helpful: address. Civil index on docket books and general index books since late 1800, search last 15 years only. Mail Turnaround time 1 week or less. Civil PAT goes back to 1980s. **See front or rear of chapter for detailed description of state's online access.** Online records date from 6/98.

Criminal Name Search: Access: Phone, fax, mail, in person, online. Both court and visitors may perform in person name searches. No search fee. Required to search: name, years to search, DOB. Criminal docket on books and general index books archived since late 1800s, search last 15 years only. Mail Turnaround time 1 week or less. Criminal PAT goes back to 1997. **See front or rear of chapter for detailed description of state's online access.** Online records date from 6/98. Online results show middle initial, DOB.

Holt County Court 204 N 4th St, O'Neill, NE 68763; 402-336-1662; fax: 402-336-1663; 8AM-4:30PM (CST). *Misdemeanor, Civil Actions under $52,000, Eviction, Small Claims, Probate.*
http://supremecourt.ne.gov/county-court/

General Information: No adoption records released. Will not fax documents unless have an account with ne.gov. Court makes copy: $.25 per page. Certification fee: $1.00 per doc plus copy fee. Payee: Holt County Court. Personal checks accepted, credit cards are not. Prepayment required. Mail requests: SASE required for mail return of any copies.

Civil Name Search: Access: In person, online. Visitors must perform in person searches themselves. Civil cases indexed by defendant. Civil records go back to 1970; on computer back to 2000; probate from 1880. Civil PAT goes back to 7/2000. **See front or rear of chapter for detailed description of state's online access.** Online civil records date from 10/00 forward, probate from 11/00.

Criminal Name Search: Access: In person, online. Visitors must perform in person searches themselves. Required to search: name, years to search, DOB. Criminal records go back to 1885, on computer back to 2000. Criminal PAT goes back to same as civil. **See front or rear of chapter for detailed description of state's online access.** Online criminal and traffic records date from 07/00. Online results show middle initial, DOB.

Hooker County

District Court PO Box 184, Mullen, NE 69152; 308-546-2244; fax: 308-546-2490; 8:30AM-N, 1-4:30PM (MST). *Felony, Civil Actions over $52,000.*

General Information: No mental health records released. Will fax documents $2.00 fee per page. Court makes copy: $1.00 per page. Self serve copy: $.25 per page. Certification fee: $1.50 per cert. Payee: Clerk of District Court. Personal checks accepted, credit cards are not. Prepayment required.

Civil Name Search: Access: In person, online. Visitors must perform in person searches themselves. Civil index on docket books since late 1800s. Civil PAT goes back to 6/2000. **See front or rear of chapter for detailed description of state's online access.** Online records date from 06/00.

Criminal Name Search: Access: In person, online. Visitors must perform in person searches themselves. Criminal records indexed in books since late 1800s. Criminal PAT goes back to same as civil. **See front or rear of chapter for detailed description of state's online access.** Online records date from 6/2000. Online results show middle initial, DOB.

Hooker County Court PO Box 184, 303 NW 1st St, Mullen, NE 69152; 308-546-2249; fax: 308-546-2490; 8:30AM-4:30PM (MST). *Misdemeanor, Civil Actions under $52,000, Eviction, Small Claims, Probate.*
http://supremecourt.ne.gov/county-court/

General Information: Fax number is located at sheriff's office. No adoption or juvenile records released. No fee to fax out. Court makes copy: $.25 per page. Certification fee: $1.00 per cert plus copy fee. Payee: County Court. Business checks accepted. No credit cards accepted. Prepayment required.

Civil Name Search: Access: In person, online. Visitors must perform in person searches themselves. Civil index on cards and books from late 1800s. Civil PAT available. Some identifiers may be viewable, most are not. **See front or rear of chapter for detailed description of state's online access.** Online civil records date from 11/99 forward, probate from 08/98.

Criminal Name Search: Access: In person, online. Both court and visitors may perform in person name searches. No search fee. Required to search: name, years to search; also helpful: DOB, SSN. Criminal records indexed on cards and books from late 1800s, computerized 1998. Criminal PAT available. Some identifiers may be viewable, most are not. **See front or rear of chapter for detailed description of state's online access.** Online criminal and traffic records date from 08/98. Online results show middle initial, DOB.

Howard County

District Court PO Box 25, 612 Indian St, St Paul, NE 68873; 308-754-4343; fax: 308-754-4266; 8AM-5PM (CST). *Felony, Civil Actions over $52,000.*

General Information: No pending case records released. Will not fax documents. Court makes copy: $.25 per page. Certification fee: $5.00 per cert. Payee: Clerk of District Court. Personal checks accepted, credit cards are not. Prepayment required.

Civil Name Search: Access: In person, online. Both court and visitors may perform in person name searches. No search fee. Civil records on microfiche from 1986, books prior. The microfiche machine is not working as of Summer 2011. Civil PAT goes back to 2002. **See front or rear of chapter for detailed description of state's online access.** Online records date from 06/98.

Criminal Name Search: Access: Fax, mail, in person, online. Both court and visitors may perform in person name searches. No search fee. Required to search: name, years to search, DOB. Criminal records on microfiche from 1986, books prior; on computer back to 9/1998. The microfiche machine is not working as of Summer 2011. Criminal PAT goes back to 9/1998. **See front or rear of chapter for detailed description of state's online access.** Online records date from 06/98. Online results show middle initial, DOB.

Howard County Court 612 Indian St #6, St Paul, NE 68873; 308-754-4192; fax: 308-754-4727; 8AM-N; 1PM-4PM (CST). *Misdemeanor, Civil Actions under $52,000, Eviction, Small Claims, Probate.*
http://supremecourt.ne.gov/county-court/

General Information: Will not fax documents. Court makes copy: $.25 per page. Certification fee: $1.00 per page plus copy fee. Payee: Howard County Court. Business checks accepted. Major credit cards accepted online for traffic only. Prepayment required.

Civil Name Search: Access: In person, online. Visitors must perform in person searches themselves. Civil cases indexed by defendant. Civil records on docket cards since 1982; computerized records since 2000. Civil PAT goes back to 2000. **See front or rear of chapter for detailed description of state's online access.** Online civil records date from 05/01 forward, probate from 08/00.

Criminal Name Search: Access: In person, online. Visitors must perform in person searches themselves. Required to search: name, years to search; also helpful: DOB. Criminal records on docket cards since 1982; computerized records since 2000. Criminal PAT goes back to same as civil. **See front or rear of chapter for detailed description of state's online access.** Online criminal and traffic records date from 08/00. Online results show middle initial, DOB.

Jefferson County

District Court Jefferson County Courthouse, 411 Fourth St, Fairbury, NE 68352; 402-729-6807; fax: 402-729-6808; 8AM-5PM (CST). *Felony, Civil Actions over $52,000.* www.co.jefferson.ne.us/

General Information: No mental health records released. Fee to fax out file $2.00 per page. Court makes copy: $.25 per page. Certification fee: $1.00. Payee: Clerk of District Court. Personal checks accepted. Major credit cards accepted. Prepayment required. Mail requests: SASE required for civil.

Civil Name Search: Access: Fax, mail, in person, online. Both court and visitors may perform in person name searches. No search fee. Civil index on docket books from 1870s; on computer back to 1996. Mail Turnaround time 1-3 days. Civil PAT goes back to 1996, countywide. **See front or rear of chapter for detailed description of state's online access.** Online records date from 11/96.

Criminal Name Search: Access: In person, online. Visitors must perform in person searches themselves. Required to search: name, years to search, DOB. Criminal records indexed in books from 1870s; on computer back to 1996. Criminal PAT goes back to 1996, countywide. **See front or rear of chapter for detailed description of state's online access.** Online records date from 11/96. Online results show name only.

Jefferson County Court 411 Fourth St, Fairbury, NE 68352; 402-729-6801; fax: 402-729-6802; 8AM-N, 1-5PM (CST). *Misdemeanor, Civil Actions under $52,000, Eviction, Small Claims, Probate.* www.co.jefferson.ne.us/

General Information: County Court employees will not search for court records or provide information or documentation of court records for any person or agency unless a specific case number is presented. No adoption or sealed records released. Will fax back documents for $2.00 per page. Court makes copy: $.25 per page. Certification fee: $1.00 per seal plus copy fee. Payee: County Court. Personal checks accepted. Major credit cards accepted online only. Prepayment required.

Civil Name Search: Access: In person, online. Visitors must perform in person searches themselves. Civil records on cards from 1988, prior on docket books; computerized records from 10/1999. Civil PAT goes back to 1996, countywide, on the JUSTICE access terminal. **See front or rear of chapter for detailed description of state's online access.** Online civil records date from 10/99 forward, probate from 05/98.

Criminal Name Search: Access: In person, online. Visitors must perform in person searches themselves. Required to search: name, years to search, DOB, signed release. Criminal records on cards from 1988, prior on docket books; computerized records from 9/1996. Criminal PAT goes back to 1996, countywide on the JUSTICE access terminal. **See front or rear of chapter for detailed description of state's online access.** Phone number in Lincoln for subscription is 402-471-7185 or 800-747-8177. Online criminal and traffic records date from 09/96. Online results show middle initial, DOB.

Johnson County

District Court PO Box 416, Tecumseh, NE 68450; 402-335-6301; fax: 402-335-6311; 8AM-N, 1-4:30PM (CST). *Felony, Civil Actions over $52,000.*

General Information: No juvenile records released. Fee to fax out file $2.00 each. Court makes copy: $.50 per page. Self serve copy: same. Certification fee: $1.50. Payee: Clerk of District Court. Personal checks accepted, credit cards are not. Prepayment required.

Civil Name Search: Access: Mail, in person, online. Both court and visitors may perform in person name searches. No search fee. Civil index and docket books from late 1800s, microfiche back 7 years. Civil PAT goes back to 1998. **See front or rear of chapter for detailed description of state's online access.** Online civil and probate records from 04/01 forward.

Criminal Name Search: Access: In person, online. Both court and visitors may perform in person name searches. No search fee. Criminal records on index and docket books from late 1800s, microfiche back 7 years. Criminal PAT goes back to same as civil. **See front or rear of chapter for detailed description of state's online access.** Online records date from 4/2000. Online results show middle initial, DOB.

Johnson County Court PO Box 285, 3rd and Broadway, Tecumseh, NE 68450; 402-335-6313; fax: 402-335-6314; 8AM-4:30PM (CST). *Misdemeanor, Civil Actions under $52,000, Eviction, Small Claims, Probate.* http://supremecourt.ne.gov/county-court/

General Information: The court is in the process of computerizing their records. No adoption or juvenile records released. Will not fax documents.

Court makes copy: $.25 per page. Certification fee: $1.00 per page plus copy fee. Payee: County Court. Personal checks accepted, credit cards are not. Prepayment required.

Civil Name Search: Access: Mail, in person, online. Both court and visitors may perform in person name searches. No search fee. Required to search: name, years to search; also helpful: address. Civil index on cards back 15 years, microfiche back to late 1800s for probate. Mail Turnaround time 1 day. Civil PAT goes back to 4/2000. **See front or rear of chapter for detailed description of state's online access.** Online records date from 02/98.

Criminal Name Search: Access: Mail, in person, online. Both court and visitors may perform in person name searches. No search fee. Required to search: name, years to search, DOB, signed release; also helpful: address, SSN. Criminal records indexed on cards back 15 years. Mail Turnaround time 1 day. Criminal PAT goes back to same as civil. **See front or rear of chapter for detailed description of state's online access.** Online criminal and traffic records date from 02/98. Online results show middle initial, DOB.

Kearney County

District Court PO Box 208, 424 N Colorado, Minden, NE 68959; 308-832-1742; fax: 308-832-0636; 8:30AM-5PM (CST). *Felony, Civil Actions over $52,000.* www.kearneycounty.ne.gov/webpages/district_court/district_court.html

General Information: Online identifiers in results same as on public terminal. No mental health records released. Court makes copy: $.25 per page. Certification fee: $1.00 per doc. Payee: Clerk of District Court. Personal checks accepted, credit cards are not. Prepayment required.

Civil Name Search: Access: In person, online. Visitors must perform in person searches themselves. All records on microfilm since 1800s; on computer back to 9/1998. Note: Mail access to attorneys only. Civil PAT goes back to 9/1998. **See front or rear of chapter for detailed description of state's online access.** Online records date from 08/98.

Criminal Name Search: Access: In person, online. Visitors must perform in person searches themselves. Criminal records on microfilm since 1800s; on computer back to 9/1998. Criminal PAT available. **See front or rear of chapter for detailed description of state's online access.** Online records date from 08/98. Online results show middle initial, DOB.

Kearney County Court PO Box 377, 426 N Colorado, Minden, NE 68959; 308-832-2719; fax: 308-832-0636; 8AM-N, 1-5PM (CST). *Misdemeanor, Civil Actions under $52,000, Eviction, Small Claims, Probate.* www.district10.us/kearney_county.htm

General Information: Court makes copy: $.25 per page. Certification fee: $1.00 per page. Payee: Kearney County Court. Personal checks accepted. Prepayment required. Mail requests: SASE requested.

Civil Name Search: Access: In person, online. Visitors must perform in person searches themselves. Civil cases indexed by defendant. Civil records computerized since 10/99, rest on index cards, some probate on microfiche. Public use terminal available. **See front or rear of chapter for detailed description of state's online access.** Online civil records date from 10/99 forward, probate from 05/98.

Criminal Name Search: Access: Mail, in person, online. Visitors must perform in person searches themselves. No search fee. Criminal records computerized since 3/97, indexes available since 1988. Mail Turnaround time 1 week. Public use terminal available. **See front or rear of chapter for detailed description of state's online access.** Online criminal and traffic records date from 03/97. Online results show middle initial, DOB.

Keith County

District Court 511 N Spruce St, #202, Ogallala, NE 69153; 308-284-3849; fax: 308-284-3978; 8AM-4PM (MST). *Felony, Civil Actions over $52,000.* www.co.keith.ne.us/

General Information: No juvenile or mental health records released. No fee to fax documents. Fee is charged if long distance. Court makes copy: $.25 per page. Self serve copy: same. Certification fee: $1.00 per cert. Payee: Clerk of District Court. Personal checks accepted. Major credit cards accepted. Prepayment required. Mail requests: SASE not required.

Civil Name Search: Access: Fax, mail, in person, online. Both court and visitors may perform in person name searches. No search fee. Required to search: name, years to search, DOB. Civil index on docket books from late 1800s; on computer back to 1975. Mail Turnaround time 2-3 days. Civil PAT goes back to 1975. **See front or rear of chapter for detailed description of state's online access.** Online records date from 06/97.

Criminal Name Search: Access: Fax, mail, in person, online. Both court and visitors may perform in person name searches. No search fee. Required to search: name, years to search, DOB. Criminal records indexed in books from late 1800s; on computer back to 1975. Mail Turnaround time 2-3 days. Criminal PAT goes back to same as civil. **See front or rear of**

chapter for detailed description of state's online access. Online records date from 06/97. Online results show middle initial, DOB.

Keith County Court PO Box 358, 511 N Spruce, Ogallala, NE 69153; 308-284-3693; fax: 308-284-6825; 7:30AM-4:30PM (MST). *Misdemeanor, Civil Actions under $52,000, Eviction, Small Claims, Probate.* http://supremecourt.ne.gov/county-court/

General Information: No adoption records released. Will fax documents $3.00 first page and $1.00 ea add'l. Court makes copy: $.25 per page. Certification fee: $1.00 per certification plus $.25 per page. Payee: County Court. Local checks accepted only. No credit cards accepted. Prepayment required.

Civil Name Search: Access: In person, online. Visitors must perform in person searches themselves. Civil index on cards, files; computerized records since 1997. Civil PAT goes back to 2000. **See front or rear of chapter for detailed description of state's online access.** Online civil records date from 10/99 forward, probate from 05/98.

Criminal Name Search: Access: In person, online. Visitors must perform in person searches themselves. Criminal records indexed on cards, files; computerized records since 1997. Criminal PAT goes back to 2000. **See front or rear of chapter for detailed description of state's online access.** Online criminal and traffic records date from 06/97. Online results show middle initial, DOB.

Keya Paha County

District Court PO Box 349, Springview, NE 68778; 402-497-3791; fax: 402-497-3799; 8AM-5PM (CST). *Felony, Civil Actions over $52,000.* www.co.keya-paha.ne.us

General Information: No confidential records released. Will fax documents $2.00 1st page, $1.00 each add'l. Court makes copy: $.25 per page. Legal size- $.30 per page. Self serve copy: same. Certification fee: $4.00 per document includes copies. Payee: Clerk of District Court. Personal checks accepted, credit cards are not. Prepayment required. Mail requests: SASE required.

Civil Name Search: Access: Fax, mail, in person, online. Both court and visitors may perform in person name searches. No search fee. Civil records on microfiche 7-9 years, on docket books since late 1800s. Mail Turnaround time 3-4 days. Civil PAT goes back to 1999. **See front or rear of chapter for detailed description of state's online access.** Online records date from 07/00.

Criminal Name Search: Access: Fax, mail, in person, online. Both court and visitors may perform in person name searches. No search fee. Computerized back to 2000, criminal records on microfiche 7-9 years, on docket books since late 1800s. Mail Turnaround time 3-4 days. Criminal PAT goes back to same as civil. **See front or rear of chapter for detailed description of state's online access.** Online records date from 7/2000. Online results show middle initial, DOB.

Keya Paha County Court PO Box 275, Courthouse Ln, Springview, NE 68778; 402-497-3021; probate phone: 402-684-3021; fax: 402-497-3799; every 2nd Friday, 8AM-4:30PM (CST). *Misdemeanor, Civil Actions under $52,000, Eviction, Small Claims, Probate.* http://supremecourt.ne.gov/county-court/

General Information: Court Ofc is rarely manned. Clerk is usually at Brown County Courthouse. To search at Keya Paha, contact Roxanne Philben, 402-387-2864; she will call the treasurer and instruct them to let you in Keya Paha court to perform your in person search. No juvenile records released. Will not fax documents. Court makes copy: $.25 per page. Certification fee: $1.00 per page plus copy fee. Payee: County Clerk. Personal checks accepted, credit cards are not. Prepayment required.

Civil Name Search: Access: In person, online. Visitors must perform in person searches themselves. Required to search: name, years to search; also helpful: address. Civil records in index books and files, many records on microfiche, back to late 1800s. Civil PAT goes back to 2000. **See front or rear of chapter for detailed description of state's online access.** Online civil and probate records from 01/01 forward.

Criminal Name Search: Access: In person, online. Visitors must perform in person searches themselves. Required to search: name, years to search; also helpful: address, DOB, SSN. Criminal docket on books and files, many records on microfiche, back to late 1800s. Criminal PAT goes back to same as civil. **See front or rear of chapter for detailed description of state's online access.** Online criminal and traffic records date from 08/00. Online results show middle initial, DOB.

Kimball County

District Court 114 E 3rd St, #7, Kimball, NE 69145; 308-235-3591; fax: 308-235-3190; 8AM-5PM M-TH, 8AM-4PM F (MST). *Felony, Civil Actions over $52,000.* www.co.kimball.ne.us/

General Information: No mental health records released. Will fax documents $3.00 1st page, $1.00 ea add'l page. Court makes copy: $.50 per page in person, $1.00 if mailed. Certification fee: $1.50. Payee: Clerk of

District Court. Personal checks accepted, credit cards are not. Prepayment required.

Civil Name Search: Access: In person, online. Visitors must perform in person searches themselves. Civil records on microfiche from 1960 forward, prior in books from early 1900s, computerized since 10/97. Civil PAT goes back to 10/1997. Civil records online - see criminal access.

Criminal Name Search: Access: In person, online. Visitors must perform in person searches themselves. Criminal records on microfiche from 1960 forward, prior in books from early 1900s, computerized since 10/97. Criminal PAT goes back to 10/1997. **See front or rear of chapter for detailed description of state's online access.** Also, for $15.00 fee per search, you may access the JUSTICE Court Case system statewide at https://www.nebraska.gov/justicecc/ccname.cgi. Online results show middle initial, DOB.

Kimball County Court 114 E 3rd St, Kimball, NE 69145; 308-235-2831; fax: 308-235-3927; 8AM-N, 1-5PM, closes 4PM F (MST). *Misdemeanor, Civil Actions under $52,000, Small Claims, Probate, Traffic.* http://supremecourt.ne.gov/county-court/

General Information: Will not fax documents as a rule. Court makes copy: $.25 per page. Certification fee: $1.00 per doc plus copy fee. Payee: County Court. Personal checks accepted, credit cards are not. Prepayment required.

Civil Name Search: Access: In person, online. Visitors must perform in person searches themselves. Civil index on cards and original files, also state computer. Civil PAT goes back to 2000. **See front or rear of chapter for detailed description of state's online access.** Online civil and probate records from 11/00 forward.

Criminal Name Search: Access: In person, online. Visitors must perform in person searches themselves. Criminal records indexed on cards and original files. Criminal PAT goes back to 2000. **See front or rear of chapter for detailed description of state's online access.** Online criminal and traffic records date from 04/00. Online results show middle initial, DOB.

Knox County

District Court PO Box 126, 206 Main St, Center, NE 68724; 402-288-5606; fax: 402-288-5609; 8:30AM-4:30PM (CST). *Felony, Civil Actions over $52,000.*

General Information: No mental health records released. Will fax documents $.25 per page. Court makes copy: $.25 per page. Self serve copy: $.10 per page. Certification fee: $1.00 per doc. Payee: Clerk of District Court. Personal checks accepted, credit cards are not. Prepayment required.

Civil Name Search: Access: Online, in person. Visitors must perform in person searches themselves. Civil index on docket books from 1874; on computer back to 9/98. Civil PAT goes back to 9/1998. Both District and County Court case index are available, but each has to be searched separately. **See front or rear of chapter for detailed description of state's online access.** Online records date from 09/98.

Criminal Name Search: Access: In person, online. Visitors must perform in person searches themselves. Required to search: name, years to search; also helpful: DOB. Criminal records indexed in books from 1874; on computer back to 9/1998. Criminal PAT goes back to same as civil. Both District and County Court case index are available, but each has to be searched separately. **See front or rear of chapter for detailed description of state's online access.** Online records date from 09/98. Online results show middle initial, DOB.

Knox County Court PO Box 125, Center, NE 68724; 402-288-5607; fax: 402-288-5609; 8:30AM-4:30PM (CST). *Misdemeanor, Civil Actions under $52,000, Eviction, Small Claims, Probate.* www.supremecourt.ne.gov

General Information: Online identifiers in results same as on public terminal. No adoption records released. Will not fax documents. Court makes copy: $.25 per page. Self serve copy: same. Certification fee: $1.00. Payee: County Court. Personal checks accepted, credit cards are not. Prepayment required.

Civil Name Search: Access: In person, online. Visitors must perform in person searches themselves. Civil index on cards and general docket books from late 1800s; on computer from 8/2000. Civil PAT goes back to 8/2000. Both District and County Court case index are available, but each has to be searched separately. **See front or rear of chapter for detailed description of state's online access.** Online civil records date from 11/00 forward, probate from 09/00.

Criminal Name Search: Access: In person, online. Visitors must perform in person searches themselves. Required to search: name, years to search; also helpful: DOB. Criminal records indexed on cards and general docket books from late 1800s; on computer from 8/2000. Criminal PAT goes back to same as civil. **See front or rear of chapter for detailed description of state's online access.** Online criminal and traffic records date from 08/00. Online results show middle initial, DOB.

Lancaster County

District Court 575 S 10th St, Lincoln, NE 68508-2810; 402-441-7328; fax: 402-441-6190; 8AM-4:30PM (CST). *Felony, Civil Actions over $52,000.* http://lancaster.ne.gov/districtcourt/index.htm

General Information: Online identifiers in results same as on public terminal. No mental health or grand jury records released. Will fax documents $5.00 fee. Court makes copy: $.50 per page. Certification fee: $1.00 per cert. Payee: Clerk of District Court. Personal checks accepted. No credit cards accepted for record searches, except online. Prepayment required. Mail requests: SASE requested.

Civil Name Search: Access: Mail, in person, online. Both court and visitors may perform in person name searches. Search fee: No search fee 1st half hour; add $4.25 per each 15 minutes add'l; with $20 deposit required for jobs estimated over half hour. Civil records on computer from 1984, microfiche 1972 to 12/1975, docket books 1865 to 1984. Mail Turnaround time 5 days. Civil PAT goes back to 1984. Civil court records online - see front or rear of chapter for detailed description of state's online access. Online records date from 06/99.

Criminal Name Search: Access: Mail, in person, online. Both court and visitors may perform in person name searches. Search fee: No search fee 1st half hour; add $4.25 per each 15 minutes add'l; with $20 deposit required for jobs estimated over half hour. Required to search: name, years to search, DOB. Criminal records computerized from 1984, microfiche 1972 to 12/1975, docket books 1865 to 1984. Mail Turnaround time 5 days. Criminal PAT goes back to same as civil. **See front or rear of chapter for detailed description of state's online access.** Online records date from 06/99. Online results show name only.

Lancaster County Court 575 S 10th St, 2nd Fl, Lincoln, NE 68508; 402-441-7291; criminal phone: 402-441-8959; civil phone: 402-441-7271; probate phone: 402-441-7443; criminal fax: 402-441-6056; civil fax: 8AM-4:30PM; 8AM-4:30PM (CST). *Misdemeanor, Civil Actions under $52,000, Eviction, Small Claims, Probate.* http://supremecourt.ne.gov/county-court/

General Information: No adoption records released. Will not fax documents. Court makes copy: $.25 per page. Certification fee: $1.00 per cert. Payee: Lancaster County Court. Personal checks, Visa/MC accepted. Prepayment required.

Civil Name Search: Access: Mail, in person, online. Visitors must perform in person searches themselves. No search fee. Civil index on docket books back to 1988, computerized since 11/98. Civil PAT goes back to 1995. Single use or subscribe at https://www.nebraska.gov/justicecc/ccname.cgi for court access. Single use is $15.00 a record or pay a monthly flat rate. Online civil records go back to 11/16/98, probate back to 05/98.

Criminal Name Search: Access: Mail, in person, online. Visitors must perform in person searches themselves. No search fee. Required to search: name, years to search, DOB. Criminal records on computer since 2/95; prior records are available if the case number is known. Note: Only mailed criminal records requested will be accepted. Mail Turnaround time 7-10 working days. Criminal PAT goes back to same as civil. Online access to criminal records is the same as civil. Online criminal and traffic records date from 2/28/95. Online results show middle initial, DOB.

Lincoln County

District Court PO Box 1616, 301 N Jeffers St, North Platte, NE 69103-1616; 308-534-4350 x301 & X303; fax: 308-535-3527; 8AM-5PM (CST). *Felony, Civil Actions over $52,000.* www.co.lincoln.ne.us/index.php?option=com_content&view=article&id=63%3Adistrict-court&catid=28&Itemid=16

General Information: No sealed, court ordered or mental health records released. Will fax documents to local or toll-free number. Court makes copy: $.25 per page. Certification fee: $1.00. Payee: Clerk of District Court. Personal checks accepted, credit cards are not. Prepayment required.

Civil Name Search: Access: In person, online. Visitors must perform in person searches themselves. Civil records on computer back to 5/1997; books from 1866. Civil PAT goes back to 1997. **See front or rear of chapter for detailed description of state's online access.** Online records date from 04/97.

Criminal Name Search: Access: In person, online. Visitors must perform in person searches themselves. Criminal records computerized from 5/1997; books from 1866. Criminal PAT goes back to 1997. **See front or rear of chapter for detailed description of state's online access.** Online records date from 04/97. Online results show middle initial, DOB.

Lincoln County Court PO Box 519, 301 N Jeffers St, North Platte, NE 69103; 308-534-4350; fax: 308-535-3525; 8AM-5PM (CST). *Misdemeanor, Civil Actions under $51,000, Eviction, Small Claims, Probate.* www.co.lincoln.ne.us/index.php?option=com_content&view=article&id=55%3Acounty-court&catid=6%3Acounty-court&Itemid=27

General Information: No adoption records released. Will fax documents for fee. Court makes copy: $.25 per page, free if printed from public access terminal. Certification fee: $1.00 per doc plus copy fee. Payee: County Court. Personal checks accepted. Visa, MC, Discover accepted. Prepayment required.

Civil Name Search: Access: In person, online. Visitors must perform in person searches themselves. Civil records kept on index books back 20-25 years. Civil PAT goes back to 1997. **See front or rear of chapter for detailed description of state's online access.** Online civil records date from 10/99 forward, probate from 05/98.

Criminal Name Search: Access: Mail, fax, in person, online. Visitors must perform in person searches themselves. No search fee. Required to search: name, years to search, DOB. Criminal records on computer since 4/97. Note: No fee if record printed from public access terminal. Criminal PAT goes back to same as civil. **See front or rear of chapter for detailed description of state's online access.** Online criminal and traffic records date from 04/97. Online results show middle initial, DOB.

Logan County

District Court PO Box 8, 317 Main St, Stapleton, NE 69163; 308-636-2311; 8:30AM-N; 1-4:30PM M-TH; 8:30AM-N; 1PM-4PM F (CST). *Felony, Civil Actions over $52,000.*

General Information: Will fax documents $2.50 1st page, $1.00 each add'l. Court makes copy: $.25 per page. Certification fee: $1.00 per cert plus $.50 per page includes copy. Payee: Clerk of the District Court. Personal checks accepted, credit cards are not. Prepayment required. Mail requests: SASE helpful.

Civil Name Search: Access: Fax, mail, in person, online. Both court and visitors may perform in person name searches. No search fee. Civil index on docket books; computerized records since 2000. Mail Turnaround time same day. Civil PAT goes back to 1997. **See front or rear of chapter for detailed description of state's online access.** Online records date from 04/97.

Criminal Name Search: Access: Fax, mail, in person, online. Both court and visitors may perform in person name searches. No search fee. Criminal docket on books; computerized records since 2000. Mail Turnaround time same day. Criminal PAT goes back to same as civil. **See front or rear of chapter for detailed description of state's online access.** Online records date from 04/97. Online results show middle initial, DOB.

Logan County Court PO Box 8, 317 Main St, Stapleton, NE 69163; 308-636-2677; 8:30AM-4:30PM call to verify if open (CST). *Misdemeanor, Civil Actions under $52,000, Eviction, Small Claims, Probate.* www.supremecourt.ne.gov/county-court/county-court-website/logan.shtml

General Information: This office is staffed by two persons and only open for business on certain days of the week (which sometimes vary). Please phone ahead to make an appointment or leave a message. Adoption and juvenile records are not released. Fee to fax out file $3.00 1st page, $1.00 each add'l. Court makes copy: $.25 per page. Certification fee: $1.00. Payee: County Court. Personal checks accepted. Visa/MC accepted for traffic only. Prepayment required.

Civil Name Search: Access: In person, online. Both court and visitors may perform in person name searches. No search fee. Required to search: name, years to search; also helpful: address. Civil index on docket books since 1837. **See front or rear of chapter for detailed description of state's online access.** Online civil records date from 01/00 forward, probate from 09/98.

Criminal Name Search: Access: In person, online. Both court and visitors may perform in person name searches. No search fee. Required to search: name, years to search, signed release; also helpful: DOB. Criminal docket on books since 1837. Public use terminal has crim records back to 1998. **See front or rear of chapter for detailed description of state's online access.** Online criminal and traffic records date from 09/98. Online results show middle initial, DOB.

Loup County

District Court PO Box 187, Taylor, NE 68879; 308-942-3135; fax: 308-942-3103; 8:30AM-5PM M-TH, 8:30AM-N F (CST). *Felony, Civil Actions over $52,000.*

General Information: No juvenile or adoption records released. Will not fax documents. Court makes copy: $.25 per page. Self serve copy: same. Certification fee: $1.00. Payee: Clerk of District Court. Personal checks accepted, credit cards are not. Prepayment required.

Civil Name Search: Access: In person, online. Visitors must perform in person searches themselves. Civil records in index books from late 1800s. Civil PAT goes back to 2000. **See front or rear of chapter for detailed description of state's online access.** Online records date from 06/00.

Criminal Name Search: Access: In person, online. Visitors must perform in person searches themselves. Required to search: name, years to search; also helpful: address, DOB, SSN. Criminal docket on books from late 1800s. Criminal PAT goes back to same as civil. **See front or rear of**

chapter for detailed description of state's online access. Online records date from 6/2000. Online results show middle initial, DOB.

Loup County Court PO Box 146, 408 4th St, Taylor, NE 68879; 308-942-6035; fax: 308-942-3103; 8:30AM-N. 1PM-4:30PM M-TH; 8:30AM-N F (CST). *Misdemeanor, Civil Actions under $52,000, Eviction, Small Claims, Probate.*

http://supremecourt.ne.gov/county-court/

General Information: the court is in process of scanning all images into a searchable database. Will not fax documents. Court makes copy: $.25 per page. Self serve copy: same. Certification fee: $1.00. Payee: County Court. Personal checks accepted, credit cards are not. Prepayment required.

Civil Name Search: Access: In person, online. Visitors must perform in person searches themselves. Civil index on docket books since late 1800s. Some records have been filmed and forwarded to state archives. Civil PAT goes back to 2000. **See front or rear of chapter for detailed description of state's online access.** Online civil records date from 10/00 forward, probate from 11/00.

Criminal Name Search: Access: In person, online. Visitors must perform in person searches themselves. Criminal records indexed in books since late 1800s. Some records have been filmed and forwarded to state archives. Criminal PAT goes back to 2000. **See front or rear of chapter for detailed description of state's online access.** Online criminal and traffic records date from 08/00. Online results show middle initial, DOB.

Madison County

District Court PO Box 249, 1313 N Main St, Madison, NE 68748; 402-454-3311 X140; fax: 402-454-6528; 8AM-5PM (CST). *Felony, Civil Actions over $52,000.*

http://co.madison.ne.us/clerkdiscrt.htm

General Information: Online identifiers in results same as on public terminal. No mental health records released. Will fax out specific case documents for $1.00 per page if prepaid. Court makes copy: $.25 per page. Certification fee: $1.50. Payee: Clerk of District Court. Personal checks accepted. Major credit cards accepted. Prepayment required.

Civil Name Search: Access: In person, online. Visitors must perform in person searches themselves. Civil records on microfiche from late 1970s, prior on docket books from late 1800s; computerized records go back to 1987. Civil PAT goes back to 9/1997. **See front or rear of chapter for detailed description of state's online access.** Online records date from 09/97.

Criminal Name Search: Access: In person, online. Visitors must perform in person searches themselves. Criminal records on microfiche from late 1970s, prior on docket books from late 1800s; computerized records go back to 1987. Criminal PAT goes back to 9/1997. **See front or rear of chapter for detailed description of state's online access.** Online records date from 09/97. Online results show middle initial, DOB.

Madison County Court PO Box 230, Madison, NE 68748; 402-454-3311; criminal phone: x181; civil phone: x142; probate phone: x165; fax: 402-454-3438; 8:30AM-5PM (CST). *Misdemeanor, Civil Actions under $52,000, Eviction, Small Claims, Probate.*

http://supremecourt.ne.gov/county-court/

General Information: Probate fax is same as main fax number. No adoption records released. Will fax documents to local or toll free line. Court makes copy: $.25 per page. Self serve copy: same. Certification fee: $1.00 per certification. Payee: Madison County Court. Personal checks accepted, credit cards are not. Prepayment required.

Civil Name Search: Access: In person, online. Visitors must perform in person searches themselves. Civil records on computer since 1996, prior on docket book, cards. Civil PAT goes back to 2000. The terminal is located at the District Court. **See front or rear of chapter for detailed description of state's online access.** Online civil records date from 01/99 forward, probate from 05/98.

Criminal Name Search: Access: In person, online. Visitors must perform in person searches themselves. Required to search: name, years to search, DOB. Criminal records computerized from 1996. Criminal PAT goes back to 2000. The terminal is located at the District Court. **See front or rear of chapter for detailed description of state's online access.** Online criminal and traffic records date from 10/96. Online results show middle initial, DOB.

McPherson County

District Court PO Box 122, Tryon, NE 69167; 308-587-2363; fax: 308-587-2363; 8:30AM-N, 1-4:30PM (CST). *Felony, Civil Actions over $52,000.*

General Information: Call before faxing. No adoption records released. Will fax documents $2.00 1st page, $1.00 each add'l. Court makes copy: $.50 per page. Self serve copy: same. Certification fee: $1.50 per page plus copy fee. Payee: Clerk of District Court. Business checks accepted. No credit cards accepted. Prepayment required. Mail requests: SASE required for mail return of any copies.

Civil Name Search: Access: In person, online. Visitors must perform in person searches themselves. Required to search: name, years to search; also helpful: address. Civil index on docket books since late 1800s. Civil PAT goes back to 6/2000. **See front or rear of chapter for detailed description of state's online access.** Online records date from 06/00.

Criminal Name Search: Access: In person, online. Visitors must perform in person searches themselves. Required to search: name, years to search; also helpful: address, DOB, SSN. Criminal records indexed in books since late 1800s. Criminal PAT goes back to 6/2000. **See front or rear of chapter for detailed description of state's online access.** 800-747-8177 or 402-471-7185. Online records date from 6/2000. Online results show middle initial, DOB.

McPherson County Court PO Box 122, 500 Anderson, Tryon, NE 69167; 308-587-2363; 8:30AM-N, 1-4:30PM (CST). *Misdemeanor, Civil Actions under $52,000, Eviction, Small Claims, Probate.*

http://supremecourt.ne.gov/county-court/

General Information: Call for fax number before faxing. Adoption and juvenile records are not released. Fee to fax out file $2.00 1st page, $1.00 each add'l. Court makes copy: $.50 per page. Self serve copy: same. Certification fee: $1.25 per doc. Payee: County Court. Personal checks accepted, credit cards are not. Prepayment required.

Civil Name Search: Access: In person, online. Both court and visitors may perform in person name searches. No search fee. Required to search: name, years to search; also helpful: address. Civil records computerized since 6/99, rest on index cards, are not computerized. **See front or rear of chapter for detailed description of state's online access.** Online civil records date from 01/009 forward, probate from 08/98.

Criminal Name Search: Access: In person, online. Both court and visitors may perform in person name searches. No search fee. Required to search: name, years to search, signed release; also helpful: address, DOB. Criminal records computerized since 8/98. Public use terminal has crim records. **See front or rear of chapter for detailed description of state's online access.** Online criminal and traffic records date from 08/98. Online results show middle initial, DOB.

Merrick County

District Court PO Box 27, Central City, NE 68826; 308-946-2461; fax: 308-946-3692; 8AM-5PM (CST). *Felony, Civil Actions over $52,000.*

General Information: No probation or mental health records released. Will fax out specific case files $3.00 first page and $1.00 ea add'l. Court makes copy: $.25 per page. Self serve copy: same. Certification fee: $1.00. Payee: Clerk of District Court. Personal checks accepted, credit cards are not. Prepayment required.

Civil Name Search: Access: In person, online. Visitors must perform in person searches themselves. Civil index on docket books from 1860; on computer back to 1994. Civil PAT goes back to 7/1994. Terminal results also show SSNs. **See front or rear of chapter for detailed description of state's online access.** Online records date from 07/94.

Criminal Name Search: Access: In person, online. Visitors must perform in person searches themselves. Required to search: name, years to search, signed release. Criminal records indexed in books from 1860; on computer back to 1994. Criminal PAT goes back to same as civil. **See front or rear of chapter for detailed description of state's online access.** Online records date from 07/94. Online results show middle initial, DOB.

Merrick County Court County Courthouse, PO Box 27, Central City, NE 68826; 308-946-2812; fax: 308-946-3838; 8AM-5PM (CST). *Misdemeanor, Civil Actions under $52,000, Eviction, Small Claims, Probate.* http://supremecourt.ne.gov/county-court/

General Information: No financial affidavits or sealed records released. Will not fax documents. Court makes copy: $.25 per page. Certification fee: $1.00. Payee: County Court. Personal checks accepted, credit cards are not. Prepayment required.

Civil Name Search: Access: In person, online. Visitors must perform in person searches themselves. Civil index on docket books also on computer back to 1994. Civil PAT goes back to 1/1994. **See front or rear of chapter for detailed description of state's online access.** Online civil and probate records from 03/94 forward.

Criminal Name Search: Access: In person, online. Visitors must perform in person searches themselves. Required to search: name, years to search, DOB. Criminal records indexed in books from 1860; on computer back to 1994. Criminal PAT goes back to same as civil. **See front or rear of chapter for detailed description of state's online access.** Online criminal and traffic records date from 01/94. Online results show middle initial, DOB.

Morrill County

District Court PO Box 824, Bridgeport, NE 69336; 308-262-1261; fax: 308-262-1799; 8AM-N, 1-4:30PM (MST). *Felony, Civil Actions over $52,000.*

General Information: No mental health records released. Will not fax documents. Court makes copy: $.25 per page. Certification fee: $1.00. Payee: Clerk of District Court. Personal checks accepted, credit cards are not. Prepayment required.

Civil Name Search: Access: In person, online. Visitors must perform in person searches themselves. Computerized records back to 11/97; civil records on microfilm, books dating back to early 1900. Civil PAT goes back to 1997. Sometimes the DOB may show. **See front or rear of chapter for detailed description of state's online access.** Online records date from 10/97.

Criminal Name Search: Access: In person, online. Visitors must perform in person searches themselves. Criminal records on microfilm, books dating back to early 1900. Criminal PAT goes back to same as civil. Sometimes the DOB will show. **See front or rear of chapter for detailed description of state's online access.** Online records date from 10/97. Online results show middle initial, DOB.

Morrill County Court PO Box 418, Bridgeport, NE 69336; 308-262-0812; 8AM-4:30PM (MST). *Misdemeanor, Civil Actions under $52,000, Eviction, Small Claims, Probate.*

http://supremecourt.ne.gov/county-court/

General Information: No adoption records released. Court makes copy: $.25 per page. Certification fee: $1.00. Payee: County Court. Personal checks accepted, credit cards are not. Prepayment required.

Civil Name Search: Access: In person, online. Visitors must perform in person searches themselves. Civil index on docket books to 1908; probate on microfiche. Public use terminal available. **See front or rear of chapter for detailed description of state's online access.** Online civil and probate records from 01/01 forward.

Criminal Name Search: Access: In person, online. Visitors must perform in person searches themselves. Criminal records indexed in books to 1908; probate on microfiche. Public use terminal available. **See front or rear of chapter for detailed description of state's online access.** Online criminal and traffic records date from 04/00. Online results show middle initial, DOB.

Nance County

District Court PO Box 338, Fullerton, NE 68638; 308-536-2365; fax: 308-536-2742; 8AM-4:30PM (CST). *Felony, Civil Actions over $52,000.*

www.supremecourt.ne.gov/district-court/district-court-website/nance.shtml

General Information: No mental health records released. Will fax out documents $2.50 1st page, $1.50 each add'l. Court makes copy: $.25 per page. Certification fee: $1.00. Payee: Clerk of District Court. Personal checks accepted, credit cards are not. Prepayment required. Mail requests: SASE required for civil.

Civil Name Search: Access: Phone, fax, mail, in person, online. Both court and visitors may perform in person name searches. No search fee. Required to search: name, years to search; also helpful: address. Civil index on docket books from late 1800s. Mail Turnaround time 1 day. Civil PAT goes back to 1999. Public terminal in District Court Office- County staff will perform searches. **See front or rear of chapter for detailed description of state's online access.** Online records date from 12/99.

Criminal Name Search: Access: In person, online. Both court and visitors may perform in person name searches. No search fee. Required to search: name, years to search; also helpful: address, DOB, SSN. Criminal records indexed in books from late 1800s. Criminal PAT goes back to same as civil. Public terminal in District Court Office- County staff will perform searches. **See front or rear of chapter for detailed description of state's online access.** Online records date from 12/99. Online results show middle initial, DOB.

Nance County Court PO Box 837, Fullerton, NE 68638; 308-536-2675; fax: 308-536-2742; 8AM-5PM (CST). *Misdemeanor, Civil Actions under $52,000, Eviction, Small Claims, Probate.*

http://supremecourt.ne.gov/county-court/

General Information: Must have case number, or court personnel will not research for the public. Online identifiers in results same as on public terminal. No juvenile, psychological reports or adoption records released. Will not fax documents. Court makes copy: $.25 per page. Certification fee: $1.00 per cert plus copy fee. Payee: County Court. Personal checks accepted. Major credit cards accepted for online system. Prepayment required. Mail requests: SASE required for civil.

Civil Name Search: Access: In person, online. Both court and visitors may perform in person name searches. Required to search: name, years to search; also helpful: address. Civil index on cards since late 1800s, computerized since 1/01, probate on microfilm. Civil PAT goes back to 2001. **See front or rear of chapter for detailed description of state's online access.** Online civil and probate records from 08/00 forward.

Criminal Name Search: Access: In person, online. Both court and visitors may perform in person name searches. Required to search: name, years to search; also helpful: address, DOB. Criminal records available since

1985, computerized since 2002, probate on microfilm. Note: Court will not pull records unless provided a case number. Criminal PAT goes back to same as civil. **See front or rear of chapter for detailed description of state's online access.** Online criminal and traffic records date from 08/00.Also, for $15.00 fee per search, you may access the JUSTICE Court Case system statewide at https://www.nebraska.gov/justicecc/ccname.cgi. Online results show middle initial, DOB.

Nemaha County

District Court 1824 N St, Auburn, NE 68305; 402-274-3616; fax: 402-274-5583; 8AM-N, 1-5PM (CST). *Felony, Civil Actions over $52,000.*

General Information: Online identifiers in results same as on public terminal. No mental, juvenile records released. Will fax documents to local or toll free line. Court makes copy: $.25 per page. Certification fee: $1.00 plus copy fee. Payee: Clerk of District Court. Personal checks accepted, credit cards are not. Prepayment required.

Civil Name Search: Access: In person, mail, online. Both court and visitors may perform in person name searches. No search fee. Required to search: name, years to search; also helpful: address. Civil records on general index and docket books since the late 1800s; computerized records go back to 06/1998. Note: Court will search on a time available basis. Mail Turnaround time 1 to 3 days, more if busy. Civil PAT goes back to 06/1998. **See front or rear of chapter for detailed description of state's online access.** Online records date from 6/98.

Criminal Name Search: Access: In person, mail, online. Both court and visitors may perform in person name searches. No search fee. Required to search: name, years to search; also helpful: address, DOB, SSN. Criminal records on general index and docket books since1950; computerized records go back to 06/1998. Note: Court will only criminal search time permitting. Mail Turnaround time 1 to 3 days, more if busy. Criminal PAT goes back to same as civil. **See front or rear of chapter for detailed description of state's online access.** Online records date from 6/98. Online results show middle initial, DOB.

Nemaha County Court 1824 N St, Auburn, NE 68305; 402-274-3008; fax: 402-274-4605; 8AM-N, 1-5PM (CST). *Misdemeanor, Civil Actions under $52,000, Eviction, Small Claims, Probate.*

http://supremecourt.ne.gov/county-court/

General Information: This court also handles adoption, juvenile, and preliminary felony hearings. Probate fax is same as main fax number. No adoption records released. Will not fax documents. Court makes copy: $.25 per page. Certification fee: $1.00 per page plus copy fee. Payee: Clerk of County Court. Personal checks accepted, credit cards are not. Prepayment required. Mail requests: SASE required for mail return of any copies.

Civil Name Search: Access: In person, online. Visitors must perform in person searches themselves. Civil index on docket books since late 1800s, computerized records go back to 4/2000. **See front or rear of chapter for detailed description of state's online access.** Online civil and probate records from 04/00 forward.

Criminal Name Search: Access: In person, online. Visitors must perform in person searches themselves. Required to search: name, years to search; also helpful: DOB, SSN. Criminal records indexed in books since late 1800s, computerized records go back to 4/2000. Public use terminal has crim records back to 4/2000. **See front or rear of chapter for detailed description of state's online access.** Online criminal and traffic records date from 04/00. Online results show middle initial, DOB.

Nuckolls County

District Court PO Box 362, 150 S Main, Nelson, NE 68961; 402-225-4341; fax: 402-225-2373; 8:30AM-4:30PM (CST). *Felony, Civil Actions over $52,000.*

www.nuckollscounty.ne.gov

General Information: Court's search services not available to employers using employment agencies. Will fax documents $3.00 1st page, $1.00 ea add'l. Court makes copy: $.25 per page. Self serve copy: same. Certification fee: $1.00 per cert plus copy fee. Payee: Clerk of District Court. Personal checks accepted, credit cards are not. Prepayment required.

Civil Name Search: Access: In person, online. Visitors must perform in person searches themselves. Civil index on docket books since late 1800s, computerized since 2000. Civil PAT goes back to 2000. **See front or rear of chapter for detailed description of state's online access.** Online records date from 03/00.

Criminal Name Search: Access: In person, online. Visitors must perform in person searches themselves. Criminal records indexed in books since late 1800s, computerized since 2000. Criminal PAT goes back to same as civil. **See front or rear of chapter for detailed description of state's online access.** Online records date from 03/00. Online results show middle initial, DOB.

Nuckolls County Court PO Box 372, 105 S Main, Nelson, NE 68961; 402-225-2371; fax: 402-225-2373; 8AM-4:30PM (CST). *Misdemeanor, Civil Actions under $52,000, Eviction, Small Claims, Probate.* www.district10.us/

General Information: Mail access limited to short searches. No adoption or juvenile records released. Will fax out documents $3.00 per page. Court makes copy: $.25 per page. Self serve copy: same. Certification fee: $1.00 per cert plus copy fee. Payee: County Court. Personal checks accepted. Major credit cards accepted. Prepayment required.

Civil Name Search: Access: In person, online. Visitors must perform in person searches themselves. Civil index on cards, probate on microfilm. Civil PAT goes back to 2000. **See front or rear of chapter for detailed description of state's online access.** Online civil records date from 12/00 forward, probate from 01/01.

Criminal Name Search: Access: In person, online. Visitors must perform in person searches themselves. Criminal records indexed on cards, probate on microfilm. Criminal PAT goes back to same as civil. **See front or rear of chapter for detailed description of state's online access.** Online criminal and traffic records date from 08/00. Online results show middle initial, DOB.

Otoe County

District Court 1021 Central Ave, Rm 209, PO Box 726, Nebraska City, NE 68410; 402-873-9550; fax: 402-873-9583; 8AM-5PM Courthouse doors close at 4:30PM (CST). *Felony, Dissolutions, Civil Actions over $52,000.* www.co.otoe.ne.us/court.html

General Information: Online identifiers in results same as on public terminal. Will fax documents if fees prepaid. Court makes copy: $.25 per page. Self serve copy: same. Certification fee: $1.00 plus copy fee. Payee: Clerk of District Court. Personal checks accepted, credit cards are not. Prepayment required. Mail requests: SASE required for mail return of any copies.

Civil Name Search: Access: In person, online. Visitors must perform in person searches themselves. Required to search: name, years to search, address. Civil index on docket books from late 1800s, computerized from 8/97. Civil PAT goes back to 8/1997. **See front or rear of chapter for detailed description of state's online access.** Online records date from 08/97.

Criminal Name Search: Access: In person, online. Visitors must perform in person searches themselves. Criminal records indexed in books from late 1800s, computerized from 8/97. Criminal PAT goes back to same as civil. **See front or rear of chapter for detailed description of state's online access.** Online records date from 08/97. Online results show middle initial, DOB.

Otoe County Court 1021 Central Ave, Rm 109, PO Box 487, Nebraska City, NE 68410-0487; 402-873-9575; fax: 402-873-9030; 8AM-5PM (CST). *Misdemeanor, Civil Actions under $52,000, Eviction, Small Claims, Probate.* http://supremecourt.ne.gov/county-court/

General Information: No adoption records released without court order; juvenile records only released with signed release statement. Will fax documents $1.00 per page. Court makes copy: $.25 per page. Certification fee: $1.00 per cert plus copy fee. Payee: County Court. Personal checks accepted. No credit cards accepted for copies or certifications. Prepayment required. Mail requests: SASE required.

Civil Name Search: Access: Phone, fax, mail, in person, online. Both court and visitors may perform in person name searches. No search fee. Civil records go back to 1974; computerized records go to 1999. Mail Turnaround time 2-3 days. Civil PAT goes back to 2000. Showing of identifiers varies widely on terminal. **See front or rear of chapter for detailed description of state's online access.** Online civil records date from 10/99 forward, probate from 05/98.

Criminal Name Search: Access: Fax, mail, in person, online. Both court and visitors may perform in person name searches. No search fee. Required to search: name, offense; also helpful: years to search, address, DOB. Criminal records go back to 1981; computerized since 1997. Mail Turnaround time 2-3 days. Criminal PAT goes back to 1997. Showing of identifiers varies widely on terminal. **See front or rear of chapter for detailed description of state's online access.** Online criminal and traffic records date from 02/97. Online results show middle initial, DOB.

Pawnee County

District Court PO Box 431, Pawnee City, NE 68420; 402-852-2963; criminal phone: 402-852-2969; fax: 402-852-2963; 8AM-4PM (CST). *Felony, Civil Actions over $52,000.*

General Information: No mental health records released. Will not fax documents. Court makes copy: $.25 per page. Self serve copy: $.25 per page. Certification fee: $1.00. Payee: Clerk of District Court. Personal checks accepted, credit cards are not. Prepayment required.

Civil Name Search: Access: In person, online. Both court and visitors may perform in person name searches. No search fee. Civil index on docket books since late 1800s. Public use terminal available. **See front or rear of chapter for detailed description of state's online access.** Online records date from 03/98.

Criminal Name Search: Access: In person, online. Visitors must perform in person searches themselves. Criminal records indexed in books since late 1800s. Public use terminal available. **See front or rear of chapter for detailed description of state's online access.** Online records date from 03/98. Online results show middle initial, DOB.

Pawnee County Court PO Box 471, 625 6th St, Pawnee City, NE 68420; 402-852-2388; 8AM-Noon (CST). *Misdemeanor, Civil Actions under $52,000, Eviction, Small Claims, Probate.* http://supremecourt.ne.gov/county-court/

General Information: Probate requests are accepted by mail with prepayment. No adoption records released. Will not fax documents. Court makes copy: $.25 per page. Self serve copy: same. Certification fee: $1.00. Payee: Pawnee County Court. Personal checks accepted, credit cards are not. Prepayment required.

Civil Name Search: Access: In person, online. Visitors must perform in person searches themselves. Required to search: name, years to search; also helpful: address. Civil records indexed on computer since late 1980s and books back to late 1800s. Civil PAT goes back to 7/2000. **See front or rear of chapter for detailed description of state's online access.** Online civil and probate records from 06/00 forward.

Criminal Name Search: Access: In person, online. Visitors must perform in person searches themselves. Required to search: name, years to search; also helpful: SSN. Criminal records indexed on computer since late 1980s and books back to late 1800s. Criminal PAT goes back to same as civil. **See front or rear of chapter for detailed description of state's online access.** Online criminal and traffic records date from 06/00. Online results show middle initial, DOB.

Perkins County

District Court PO Box 156, 200 Lincoln Ave, Grant, NE 69140; 308-352-4643; fax: 308-352-2455; 8AM-4PM (MST). *Felony, Civil Actions over $52,000.*

General Information: Court requests no phone calls please. All records public. Will fax documents $3.00 prepaid. Court makes copy: $.50 per page. Self serve copy: same. Certification fee: $3.00 per cert plus copy fee. Payee: Clerk of District Court. Personal checks accepted, credit cards are not. Prepayment required. Mail requests: SASE required.

Civil Name Search: Access: Fax, mail, in person, online. Both court and visitors may perform in person name searches. No search fee. Civil index on docket books since late 1800s. Mail Turnaround time 2-4 days. Civil PAT goes back to 2000. **See front or rear of chapter for detailed description of state's online access.** Online records date from 06/00.

Criminal Name Search: Access: Fax, mail, in person, online. Both court and visitors may perform in person name searches. No search fee. Criminal records indexed in books since late 1800s. Mail Turnaround time 2-4 days. Criminal PAT goes back to same as civil. **See front or rear of chapter for detailed description of state's online access.** Online records date from 6/2000. Online results show middle initial, DOB.

Perkins County Court PO Box 222, 200 Lincoln Ave, Grant, NE 69140; 308-352-4415; fax: 308-352-4415; 8AM-45PM M-TH (MST). *Misdemeanor, Civil Actions under $52,000, Eviction, Small Claims, Probate.* http://supremecourt.ne.gov/county-court/

General Information: No sealed records released. Court makes copy: $.25 per page. Certification fee: $1.00. Payee: Perkins County Court. Personal checks accepted, credit cards are not. Prepayment required.

Civil Name Search: Access: In person, online. Visitors must perform in person searches themselves. Civil index on cards from 1987, prior on books; probate on microfilm & hard copy. Civil PAT goes back to 6/2000. **See front or rear of chapter for detailed description of state's online access.** Online civil and probate records from 11/00 forward.

Criminal Name Search: Access: In person, online. Visitors must perform in person searches themselves. Required to search: name, years to search; also helpful: DOB. Criminal records indexed on cards from 1987, prior on books; probate on microfilm & hard copy. Criminal PAT goes back to same as civil. **See front or rear of chapter for detailed description of state's online access.** Online criminal and traffic records date from 06/00. Online results show middle initial, DOB.

Phelps County

District Court PO Box 462, Holdrege, NE 68949; 308-995-2281; fax: 308-995-2282; 9AM-5PM (CST). *Felony, Civil Actions over $52,000.* www.phelpsgov.org/

General Information: No mental health, sealed records released. Will fax specific case files to local or toll-free number. Court makes copy: $.25 per page. Certification fee: $1.00. Payee: Clerk of District Court. Personal checks accepted, credit cards are not. Prepayment required.

Civil Name Search: Access: In person, online. Visitors must perform in person searches themselves. Civil records on computer from 3/1998, on books back to 1885. Public use terminal available, records go back to 3/1998. **See front or rear of chapter for detailed description of state's online access.** Online records date from 03/98.

Criminal Name Search: Access: In person, online. Visitors must perform in person searches themselves. Required to search: name, years to search; also helpful: DOB. Criminal records computerized from 3/1998, on books prior back to 1885. Public use terminal available, crim records go back to 3/1998. **See front or rear of chapter for detailed description of state's online access.** Online records date from 03/98. Online results show middle initial, DOB.

Phelps County Court PO Box 255, 715 Fifth Ave, Holdrege, NE 68949; 308-995-6561; fax: 308-995-6562; 8AM-N, 1-5PM (CST). *Misdemeanor, Civil Actions under $52,000, Eviction, Small Claims, Probate.* www.district10.us/

General Information: Requests for specific record files must be placed in writing. These documents will be mailed within one week. Online identifiers in results same as on public terminal. No adoption records released. Will not fax documents. Court makes copy: $.25 per page. Self serve copy: same. Certification fee: $1.00 per cert plus copy fee. Payee: Phelps County Court. Personal checks accepted, credit cards are not. Prepayment required. Mail requests: SASE required for mail return of any copies.

Civil Name Search: Access: In person, online. Visitors must perform in person searches themselves. Civil records computerized since 1999, on index cards going back to late 1970s; probate on microfiche to late 1800s. Civil PAT goes back to 3/1998. **See front or rear of chapter for detailed description of state's online access.** Online civil records date from 10/99 forward, probate from 06/98. Results include name and address only.

Criminal Name Search: Access: In person, online. Visitors must perform in person searches themselves. Required to search: name, years to search, DOB. Criminal records computerized since 1998, in files to 1987. Criminal PAT goes back to same as civil. **See front or rear of chapter for detailed description of state's online access.** Online criminal and traffic records date from 06/98. Online results show middle initial, DOB.

Pierce County

District Court 111 W Court St, Rm 12, Pierce, NE 68767; 402-329-4335; fax: 402-329-6412; 8:30AM-4:30PM (CST). *Felony, Civil Actions over $52,000.*

General Information: No mental health records released. Will fax out documents $3.00 1st page, $1.00 each add'l. Court makes copy: $.25 per page. Certification fee: $1.00 plus copy fee. Payee: Clerk of District Court. Personal checks accepted, credit cards are not. Prepayment required. Mail requests: SASE required for mail return of any copies.

Civil Name Search: Access: In person, online. Visitors must perform in person searches themselves. Civil index on docket books from 1870s; on computer back to 3/1999. Civil PAT goes back to 3/1999. **See front or rear of chapter for detailed description of state's online access.** Online records date from 03/99.

Criminal Name Search: Access: In person, online. Visitors must perform in person searches themselves. Required to search: name, years to search; also helpful: address, DOB, SSN. Criminal records indexed in books from 1870s; on computer back to 3/1999. Criminal PAT goes back to same as civil. Subscribe to JUSTICE at https://www.nebraska.gov/justicecc/ccname.cgi for court access. Single use is $15.00 a record or open an account for $1 per record plus $50 annual fee. Online records date from 03/99. Also, you may access the JUSTICE Court Case system statewide at https://www.nebraska.gov/justicecc/ccname.cgi. Online results show middle initial, DOB.

Pierce County Court 111 W Court St, Rm 11, Pierce, NE 68767; 402-329-6245; fax: 402-329-6412; 8:30AM-4:30PM (CST). *Misdemeanor, Civil Actions under $52,000, Eviction, Small Claims, Probate.* http://supremecourt.ne.gov/county-court/

General Information: Online identifiers in results same as on public terminal. No adoption records released. Will not fax documents. Court makes copy: $.25 per page. Self serve copy: same. Certification fee: $1.00. Payee: County Court. Personal checks accepted. No credit cards accepted for record searches. Prepayment required.

Civil Name Search: Access: In person, online. Visitors must perform in person searches themselves. Civil index on docket books back about 15 years, computerized since 5/2000. Civil PAT goes back to 5/2000. **See front or rear of chapter for detailed description of state's online access.** Online civil and probate records from 05/00 forward.

Criminal Name Search: Access: In person, online. Visitors must perform in person searches themselves. Criminal records indexed in books back about 15 years, computerized since 5/00. Criminal PAT goes back to same as civil. **See front or rear of chapter for detailed description of state's online access.** Online criminal and traffic records date from 05/00. Online results show middle initial, DOB.

Platte County

District Court PO Box 1188, Columbus, NE 68602-1188; 402-563-4906; fax: 402-562-6718; 8:30AM-5PM (CST). *Felony, Civil Actions over $52,000.* www.plattecounty.net/district.htm

General Information: Online identifiers in results same as on public terminal. No juvenile or sealed records released. Will not fax documents. Court makes copy: $.25 per page. Certification fee: $1.00 per certification plus copy fee. Payee: District Court. Only cashiers checks and money orders accepted. No credit cards accepted. Prepayment required.

Civil Name Search: Access: In person, online. Visitors must perform in person searches themselves. Civil records go back to 1800, civil records filed as hard copies; also on computer after 8/1/97. Civil PAT goes back to 1997. **See front or rear of chapter for detailed description of state's online access.** Online records date from 09/97. Court Calendar for month available at www.plattecounty.net/district/calendar.htm.

Criminal Name Search: Access: In person, online. Visitors must perform in person searches themselves. Required to search: name, years to search, DOB. Criminal records go back to 1880's , criminal records filed as hard copies; also on computer after 8/1/97. Criminal PAT goes back to same as civil. **See front or rear of chapter for detailed description of state's online access.** Online records date from 09/97. Court Calendar for month available at www.plattecounty.net/district/calendar.htm. Online results show middle initial, DOB.

Platte County Court PO Box 538, 2610 14th St, Columbus, NE 68602-0538; 402-563-4905; fax: 402-562-8158; 8AM-5PM (CST). *Misdemeanor, Civil Actions under $52,000, Eviction, Small Claims, Probate.* http://supremecourt.ne.gov/county-court/

General Information: Probate fax is same as main fax number. No adoption records released. Will not fax documents. Court makes copy: $.25 per page. Certification fee: $1.00 per seal. Payee: Platte County Court. Personal checks accepted, credit cards are not. Prepayment required.

Civil Name Search: Access: In person, online. Visitors must perform in person searches themselves. Civil index on docket books from 1980; on computer back to 1996. Civil PAT goes back to 10/1999. Terminal results may also include address. **See front or rear of chapter for detailed description of state's online access.** Online civil records date from 10/99 forward, probate from 05/98.

Criminal Name Search: Access: In person, online. Visitors must perform in person searches themselves. Required to search: name, years to search, DOB. Criminal records indexed in books from 1980; on computer back to 1996. Criminal PAT goes back to 10/1996. Terminal results may also include address. **See front or rear of chapter for detailed description of state's online access.** Online criminal and traffic records date from 10/96. Online results show middle initial, DOB.

Polk County

District Court PO Box 447, Osceola, NE 68651; 402-747-3487; fax: 402-747-8299; 8AM-N,1-5PM (CST). *Felony, Civil Actions over $52,000.*

General Information: Will fax documents $1.00 1st page, $.50 ea add'l. Court makes copy: $.25 per page. Certification fee: $1.00. Payee: Clerk of District Court. Personal checks accepted, credit cards are not. Prepayment required.

Civil Name Search: Access: In person, online. Visitors must perform in person searches themselves. Civil index on docket books from 1871. Civil PAT goes back to 4/9/1998. **See front or rear of chapter for detailed description of state's online access.** Online records date from 04/98.

Criminal Name Search: Access: In person, online. Visitors must perform in person searches themselves. Required to search: name. Criminal records indexed in books from 1871. Criminal PAT goes back to 4/1998. **See front or rear of chapter for detailed description of state's online access.** Online records date from 04/98. Online results show middle initial, DOB.

Polk County Court PO Box 506, Osceola, NE 68651; 402-747-5371; fax: 402-747-2656; 8AM-5PM (CST). *Misdemeanor, Civil Actions under $52,000, Eviction, Small Claims, Probate.* http://supremecourt.ne.gov/county-court/

General Information: Probate is a separate index at this same address. Probate fax is same as main fax number. Online identifiers in results same as on public terminal. No adoption, juvenile records released. Will fax out specific case files. Court makes copy: $.25 per page. Self serve copy: same. Certification fee: $1.00 per seal plus copy fee. Payee: County Court. Personal checks accepted, credit cards are not. Prepayment required. Mail requests: SASE required for mail return of any copies.

Civil Name Search: Access: In person, online. Visitors must perform in person searches themselves. Civil index on cards back to late 1970s; probate records back to late 1800s. Civil PAT goes back to 2000. **See front or rear of chapter for detailed description of state's online access.** Online civil and probate records from 01/01 forward.
Criminal Name Search: Access: In person, online. Visitors must perform in person searches themselves. Required to search: name, years to search, DOB. Criminal records indexed on cards back to late 1970s; on computer back to 8/2000. Criminal PAT goes back to same as civil. **See front or rear of chapter for detailed description of state's online access.** Online criminal and traffic records date from 08/00. Online results show middle initial, DOB.

Red Willow County

District Court 520 Norris Ave, McCook, NE 69001; 308-345-4583; fax: 308-345-7907; 8AM-4PM (CST). *Felony, Civil Actions over $52,000.* www.co.red-willow.ne.us/court.html
General Information: Online identifiers in results same as on public terminal. Will fax documents $3.00 1st page, $1.00 each add'l. Court makes copy: $.50 per page. Certification fee: $1.00. Payee: Clerk of District Court. Personal checks accepted, credit cards are not. Prepayment required. Mail requests: SASE required.
Civil Name Search: Access: Mail, in person, online. Both court and visitors may perform in person name searches. No search fee. Civil index on docket books since 1871, on microfiche since mid 1980s, computerized since 1998. Mail Turnaround time 2-4 days. Civil PAT goes back to 1998. **See front or rear of chapter for detailed description of state's online access.** Online records date from 06/98.
Criminal Name Search: Access: Mail, in person, online. Both court and visitors may perform in person name searches. No search fee. Criminal records indexed in books since 1871, on microfiche since mid 1980s, computerized since 1998. Mail Turnaround time 2-4 days. Criminal PAT goes back to same as civil. **See front or rear of chapter for detailed description of state's online access.** Online records date from 06/98. Online results show middle initial, DOB.

Red Willow County Court PO Box 199, 502 Norris Ave, McCook, NE 69001; 308-345-1904; fax: 308-345-1904; 8AM-5PM (CST). *Misdemeanor, Civil Actions under $52,000, Eviction, Small Claims, Probate.* http://supremecourt.ne.gov/county-court/
General Information: Online identifiers in results same as on public terminal. No adoption, juvenile, convictions set aside on misdemeanor offense, sealed records released. Will fax documents to local or toll-free number. Court makes copy: $.25 per page. Certification fee: $1.00 per cert plus copy fee. Payee: County Court. Personal checks accepted, credit cards are not. Prepayment required.
Civil Name Search: Access: In person, online. Visitors must perform in person searches themselves. Required to search: name, years to search, case number. Civil records on case files and docket cards since 1984, probate on microfilm since 1977; on computer back to 1998. Civil PAT goes back to 1998. **See front or rear of chapter for detailed description of state's online access.** Online civil records date from 01/00 forward, probate from 08/98.
Criminal Name Search: Access: In person, online. Visitors must perform in person searches themselves. Required to search: name, years to search, DOB, case number. Criminal docket on books since 1984; on computer back to 1998. Criminal PAT goes back to same as civil. **See front or rear of chapter for detailed description of state's online access.** Online criminal and traffic records date from 06/98. Online results show middle initial, DOB.

Richardson County

District Court 1700 Stone St, Falls City, NE 68355; 402-245-2023; fax: 402-245-3725; 8:30AM-n, 1PM-5PM (CST). *Felony, Civil Actions over $52,000.* www.co.richardson.ne.us/
General Information: No sealed records released. Will not fax documents. Court makes copy: $.25 per page. Certification fee: $1.00. Payee: Clerk of District Court. Personal checks accepted, credit cards are not. Prepayment required.
Civil Name Search: Access: In person, online. Visitors must perform in person searches themselves. Civil records on microfiche and at state archives to 1930; on computer back to 1998. Civil PAT goes back to 1998. **See front or rear of chapter for detailed description of state's online access.** Online records date from 02/98.
Criminal Name Search: Access: In person, online. Visitors must perform in person searches themselves. Required to search: name, years to search, DOB, signed release. Criminal records on microfiche and at state archives to 1930; on computer back to 1998. Criminal PAT goes back to 1998. **See front or rear of chapter for detailed description of state's online access.** Online records date from 02/98. Online results show middle initial, DOB.

Richardson County Court 1700 Stone St Rm 205, Falls City, NE 68355; 402-245-2812; fax: 402-245-3352; 8AM-N, 1-5PM (CST). *Misdemeanor, Civil Actions under $52,000, Eviction, Small Claims, Probate.* http://supremecourt.ne.gov/county-court/
General Information: No adoption records released. Will not fax documents. Court makes copy: $.25 per page. Certification fee: $1.00 per cert plus copy fee. Payee: County Court. Only cashiers checks and money orders accepted. No credit cards accepted except for traffic fines. Prepayment required.
Civil Name Search: Access: In person, online. Visitors must perform in person searches themselves. Civil index on cards back to 1970s. Civil PAT goes back to 2000. **See front or rear of chapter for detailed description of state's online access.** Online civil and probate records from 11/00 forward.
Criminal Name Search: Access: In person, online. Visitors must perform in person searches themselves. Required to search: name, years to search; also helpful: DOB. Criminal records indexed on cards back to 1970s. Criminal PAT goes back to same as civil. **See front or rear of chapter for detailed description of state's online access.** Online criminal and traffic records date from 06/00. Online results show middle initial, DOB.

Rock County

District Court PO Box 367, 400 State St, Bassett, NE 68714; 402-684-3933; fax: 402-684-2741; 9AM-N, 1PM-5PM (CST). *Felony, Civil Actions over $52,000.*
General Information: No juvenile or sealed records released. Will fax documents $2.00 1st page, $1.00 each add'l. Court makes copy: $.25 per page. Certification fee: $1.50 per cert. Payee: Clerk of District Court. Personal checks accepted, credit cards are not. Prepayment required. Mail requests: SASE required.
Civil Name Search: Access: Fax, mail, in person, online. Both court and visitors may perform in person name searches. No search fee. Civil index on docket books since 1800s. Mail Turnaround time 1-2 days. Civil PAT goes back to 1996. **See front or rear of chapter for detailed description of state's online access.** Online records date from 08/00.
Criminal Name Search: Access: Fax, mail, in person, online. Both court and visitors may perform in person name searches. No search fee. Required to search: name, years to search, DOB. Criminal records indexed in books since 1800s. Mail Turnaround time 1-2 days. Criminal PAT goes back to 1996. **See front or rear of chapter for detailed description of state's online access.** Online records date from 8/2000. Online results show name only.

Rock County Court PO Box 249, 400 State St, Bassett, NE 68714; 402-684-3601; fax: 402-684-2741; 8AM-5PM M,W,F (CST). *Misdemeanor, Civil Actions under $52,000, Eviction, Small Claims, Probate.* http://supremecourt.ne.gov/county-court/
General Information: Will not fax documents. Court makes copy: $.25 per page. Certification fee: $1.50 per cert plus copy fee. Payee: County Court. Personal checks accepted, credit cards are not. Prepayment required.
Civil Name Search: Access: In person, online. Visitors must perform in person searches themselves. Civil index on docket books from 1800s, index cards from 1985; on computer back to 8/2000. Civil PAT goes back to 2000. **See front or rear of chapter for detailed description of state's online access.** Online civil and probate records from 10/00 forward.
Criminal Name Search: Access: In person, online. Visitors must perform in person searches themselves. Required to search: name, years to search, DOB. Criminal records indexed in books from 1800s, index cards from 1985; on computer back to 8/2000. Criminal PAT goes back to same as civil. **See front or rear of chapter for detailed description of state's online access.** Online criminal and traffic records date from 08/00. Online results show middle initial, DOB.

Saline County

District Court Clerk of District Court, PO Box 865, Wilber, NE 68465; 402-821-2823; fax: 402-821-3179; 8AM-N, 1-5PM (CST). *Felony, Civil Actions over $52,000.* www.co.saline.ne.us/webpages/district_court/district_court.html
General Information: This court will not perform name searches. No sealed or mental health records released. Will fax specific case for $1.00 1st page $.25 ea add'l, but not name-search results. Court makes copy: $.25 per page. Self serve copy: same. Certification fee: $1.00. Payee: Clerk of District Court. Personal checks accepted, credit cards are not. Prepayment required. Mail requests: SASE required for mail return of any copies.
Civil Name Search: Access: In person, online. Visitors must perform in person searches themselves. Civil records being entered on computer beginning 8/94, index in dockets books from 1800s. Civil PAT goes back to 8/1994. **See front or rear of chapter for detailed description of state's online access.** Online records date from 7/94.
Criminal Name Search: Access: In person, online. Visitors must perform in person searches themselves. Required to search: name, years to search; also helpful: DOB. Criminal records being entered on computer

beginning 8/94, index in dockets books from 1800s. Criminal PAT goes back to 8/1994. **See front or rear of chapter for detailed description of state's online access.** Online records date from 7/94.

Saline County Court PO Box 865, 215 S Court St, Wilber, NE 68465; 402-821-2131; fax: 402-821-2132; 8AM-N; 1PM-5PM (CST). *Misdemeanor, Civil Actions under $52,000, Eviction, Small Claims, Probate.* http://supremecourt.ne.gov/county-court/
General Information: Court will not provide name searches and ask all requesters to use the on-site terminals or online system. No juvenile or sealed records released. No fee to fax documents. Court makes copy: $.25 per page. Certification fee: $1.00 per cert plus copy fee. Payee: County Court. Personal checks accepted, credit cards are not. Prepayment required. Mail requests: SASE required.
Civil Name Search: Access: In person, online. Visitors must perform in person searches themselves. Civil index on docket books from 1860s; computerized records since 1994. Civil PAT goes back to 1994. Public terminal available in District Court. **See front or rear of chapter for detailed description of state's online access.** Online civil and probate records from 06/94 forward.
Criminal Name Search: Access: In person, online. Both court and visitors may perform in person name searches. Criminal records indexed in books from 1860s; computerized records since 1994. Criminal PAT goes back to same as civil. Public terminal available in District Court. **See front or rear of chapter for detailed description of state's online access.** Online criminal and traffic records date from 07/94. Online results show middle initial, DOB.

Sarpy County

District Court 1210 Golden Gate Dr, #3141, Papillion, NE 68046; 402-593-2267; fax: 402-593-4403; 8AM-4:45PM (CST). *Felony, Civil Actions over $52,000.* www.sarpy.com
General Information: No mental health or search warrant records released. Will not fax documents. Court makes copy: $.75 first page, $.25 each add'l (per pleading). Certification fee: $1.00. Payee: Clerk of District Court. Only cashiers checks and money orders accepted. No credit cards accepted. Prepayment required. Mail requests: SASE required.
Civil Name Search: Access: Phone, mail, in person, online. Both court and visitors may perform in person name searches. No search fee. Civil records on computer from 1979 forward, on books prior. Mail Turnaround time 1-2 days. Civil PAT goes back to 1979. **See front or rear of chapter for detailed description of state's online access.** Online records date from 12/98.
Criminal Name Search: Access: Phone, mail, in person, online. Both court and visitors may perform in person name searches. No search fee. Criminal records computerized from 1979 forward, on books prior. Note: For phone requests, will only verify from computer index. Mail Turnaround time 1-2 days. Criminal PAT goes back to same as civil. **See front or rear of chapter for detailed description of state's online access.** Online records date from 12/98. Online results show middle initial, DOB.

Sarpy County Court 1210 Golden Gate Dr, #3142, Papillion, NE 68046; 402-593-5775; fax: 402-593-2193; 8AM-4:45PM (CST). *Misdemeanor, Civil Actions under $50,000, Eviction, Small Claims, Probate.* www.sarpy.com
General Information: No adoption records released. Will not fax documents. Court makes copy: $.25 per page. Certification fee: $1.00 per cert plus copy fee. Payee: County Court. Personal checks, Visa/MC accepted. Prepayment required.
Civil Name Search: Access: Fax, mail, in person, online. Visitors must perform in person searches themselves. No search fee. Civil records on docket books and cards 15 years, archived from 1800s. Mail Turnaround time 1 day. Civil PAT goes back to 1997. Single use or subscribe at https://www.nebraska.gov/justicecc/ccname.cgi for court access. Single use is $15.00 a record or pay a monthly flat rate.
Criminal Name Search: Access: Fax, mail, in person, online. Visitors must perform in person searches themselves. No search fee. Required to search: name, years to search, DOB. Criminal records on docket books and cards from 1800s. Mail Turnaround time 1 day. Criminal PAT goes back to same as civil. Online access to criminal records is the same as civil. Online criminal and traffic records date from 8/97. Online results show middle initial, DOB.

Saunders County

District Court County Courthouse, 387 N Chestnut St #6, Wahoo, NE 68066; 402-443-8113; fax: 402-443-8170; 8AM-5PM (CST). *Felony, Civil Actions over $52,000.*
General Information: No mental health records released. Will fax documents $3.00 1st page; $1.00 each add'l pg, prepaid. Court makes copy: $.25 per page. Self serve copy: $.25 per page. Certification fee: $1.00 per doc plus copy fee. Payee: Clerk of District Court. Personal checks accepted, credit cards are not. Prepayment required.

Civil Name Search: Access: In person, online. Visitors must perform in person searches themselves. Civil index on docket books to late 1800s; on computer back to 1998. Civil PAT goes back to 1998. No SSNs should appear, but results can show whatever identifiers the attorney puts in. **See front or rear of chapter for detailed description of state's online access.** Online records date from 6/98.
Criminal Name Search: Access: In person, online. Visitors must perform in person searches themselves. Required to search: name, years to search; also helpful: DOB, SSN. Criminal records indexed in books to late 1800s; on computer back to 1998. Criminal PAT goes back to 1998. **See front or rear of chapter for detailed description of state's online access.** Online records date from 6/98. Online results show name only.

Saunders County Court 387 N Chestnut, Ste 5, Wahoo, NE 68066; 402-443-8119; fax: 402-443-8121; 8AM-5PM (CST). *Misdemeanor, Civil Actions under $52,000, Eviction, Small Claims, Probate.* http://supremecourt.ne.gov/county-court/
General Information: No adoption or sealed records released. Will fax documents $3.00 per page. Court makes copy: $.25 per page. Self serve copy: same. Certification fee: $1.00. Payee: County Court. Personal checks accepted. No credit cards accepted except online. Prepayment required.
Civil Name Search: Access: In person, online. Visitors must perform in person searches themselves. Civil record file copies maintained 15 years. Civil PAT goes back to 2001. **See front or rear of chapter for detailed description of state's online access.** Online civil and probate records from 11/00 forward.
Criminal Name Search: Access: In person, online. Visitors must perform in person searches themselves. Criminal records indexed in books. Criminal PAT goes back to 2000. **See front or rear of chapter for detailed description of state's online access.** Online criminal and traffic records date from 06/26/00. Online results show middle initial, DOB.

Scotts Bluff County

District Court 1725 10th St, Gering, NE 69341; 308-436-6641; fax: 308-436-6759; 8AM-4:30PM (MST). *Felony, Civil Actions over $52,000.* www.scottsbluffcounty.org/court-district/court-district.html
General Information: No juvenile or mental health records released. Will fax out specific case files for $3.50 plus copy fee. Court makes copy: $.25 per page. Certification fee: $1.00 per page. Exemplification fee is $3.00. Payee: Clerk of District Court. Business checks accepted. No credit cards accepted. Prepayment required.
Civil Name Search: Access: In person, online. Visitors must perform in person searches themselves. Civil index on docket books to 1800s; on computer back to 1997. Note: Mail search done only if case number provided. Civil PAT goes back to 1997. Results include judgment information. Civil records online - see criminal access.
Criminal Name Search: Access: In person, online. Visitors must perform in person searches themselves. Required to search: name. Criminal records indexed in books to 1800s; on computer back to 1997. Note: Results include judgment information. Mail search done only if case number provided. Criminal PAT goes back to same as civil. Results include judgment information. **See front or rear of chapter for detailed description of state's online access.** Also, for $15.00 fee per search, you may access the JUSTICE Court Case system statewide at https://www.nebraska.gov/justicecc/ccname.cgi. Online results show name only.

Scotts Bluff County Court Scotts Bluff County Court House - 1st Level, 1725 10th St, Gering, NE 69341; 308-436-6648; criminal phone: 308-436-6649; civil phone: 308-436-6770; fax: 308-436-6872; 7:30AM-4:30PM (MST). *Misdemeanor, Civil Actions under $52,000, Eviction, Small Claims, Probate.* www.scottsbluffcounty.org/court-county/court-county.html
General Information: No adoption records released. Will not fax out documents. Court makes copy: $.25 per page. Certification fee: $1.00 per cert plus copy fee. Payee: County Court. Personal checks accepted, credit cards are not. Prepayment required.
Civil Name Search: Access: In person, online. Visitors must perform in person searches themselves. Civil records computerized since 2000. Civil PAT goes back to 5/2000. Probate and juvenile record index is also shown. **See front or rear of chapter for detailed description of state's online access.** Online civil and probate records from 03/01 forward.
Criminal Name Search: Access: In person, online. Visitors must perform in person searches themselves. Required to search: name, years to search, DOB. Criminal records computerized since 2000. Criminal PAT goes back to same as civil. **See front or rear of chapter for detailed description of state's online access.** Online criminal and traffic records date from 05/00. Online results show middle initial, DOB.

Seward County

District Court PO Box 36, Seward, NE 68434; 402-643-4895; fax: 402-643-2950; 8AM-5PM (CST). *Felony, Civil Actions over $52,000.*

General Information: Will fax out specific case files for $3.00 1st page, $1.00 each add'l. Court makes copy: $.30 per page. Certification fee: $1.00. Payee: Clerk of District Court. No personal checks. No credit cards accepted. Prepayment required.

Civil Name Search: Access: In person, online. Visitors must perform in person searches themselves. Civil index on docket books since late 1800s; computerized since 6/98. Public use terminal available, records go back to 6/98. **See front or rear of chapter for detailed description of state's online access.** Online records date from 06/98.

Criminal Name Search: Access: In person, online. Visitors must perform in person searches themselves. Criminal records indexed in books since late 1800s; computerized since 6/98. Public use terminal available, crim records go back to same. **See front or rear of chapter for detailed description of state's online access.** Online records date from 06/98. Online results show middle initial, DOB.

Seward County Court PO Box 37, 529 Seward St, Seward, NE 68434; 402-643-3341; fax: 402-643-2950; 8AM-5PM (CST). *Misdemeanor, Civil Actions under $52,000, Eviction, Small Claims, Probate.* www.connectseward.org/cgov/countycourt.htm

General Information: No adoption, juvenile or sealed records released. Will not fax documents. Court makes copy: $.25 per page. Certification fee: $1.00 per page plus copy fee. Payee: County Court. Personal checks accepted, credit cards are not. Prepayment required.

Civil Name Search: Access: Mail, in person, online. Visitors must perform in person searches themselves. No search fee. Civil index on docket books, cards back to 1975, computerized back to 1997. Mail Turnaround time 1 week. Civil PAT goes back to 1997. **See front or rear of chapter for detailed description of state's online access.** Online civil records date from 10/99 forward, probate from 05/98.

Criminal Name Search: Access: Mail, in person, online. Visitors must perform in person searches themselves. No search fee. Criminal records indexed in books, cards back to 1950. Mail Turnaround time 1 week. Criminal PAT goes back to same as civil. **See front or rear of chapter for detailed description of state's online access.** Online criminal and traffic records date from 03/97. Online results show middle initial, DOB.

Sheridan County

District Court PO Box 581, Rushville, NE 69360; 308-327-5654; fax: 308-327-5618; 8:30AM-4:30PM (MST). *Felony, Civil Actions over $52,000.*

General Information: No mental health, grand jury records released. Will fax documents to local and toll free lines. Court makes copy: $.10 per page. Self serve copy: same. Certification fee: $1.00 per case plus copy fee. Payee: Clerk of District Court. Personal checks accepted, credit cards are not. Mail requests: SASE required.

Civil Name Search: Access: Mail, fax, in person, online. Both court and visitors may perform in person name searches. Search fee: $5.00 per name. Civil index and docket books since 1800s, computerized since 1998. Mail Turnaround time 1-2 days. Civil PAT goes back to 8/1998. **See front or rear of chapter for detailed description of state's online access.** Online records date from 08/98.

Criminal Name Search: Access: Mail, fax, in person, online. Both court and visitors may perform in person name searches. Search fee: $5.00 per name. Required to search: name, years to search, signed release; also helpful: DOB. Criminal records on index and docket books since 1800s, computerized since 1998. Mail Turnaround time 1-2 days. Criminal PAT goes back to same as civil. **See front or rear of chapter for detailed description of state's online access.** Online records date from 08/98. Online results show middle initial, DOB.

Sheridan County Court PO Box 430, 303 E 2nd St, Rushville, NE 69360; 308-327-5656; fax: 308-327-5623; 8AM-4:30PM (MST). *Misdemeanor, Civil Actions under $52,000, Eviction, Small Claims, Probate.* http://supremecourt.ne.gov/county-court/

General Information: Online identifiers in results same as on public terminal. No adoption or confidential records released. No fee to fax back documents. Court makes copy: none. Certification fee: $1.00 per cert. Payee: Sheridan County Court. Personal checks accepted, credit cards are not. Prepayment required.

Civil Name Search: Access: In person, online. Visitors must perform in person searches themselves. Civil index on docket books, on microfiche from 1920 forward; on computer back to 6/2000. Civil PAT goes back to 1/2001. **See front or rear of chapter for detailed description of state's online access.** Online civil and probate records from 11/00 forward.

Criminal Name Search: Access: In person, online. Visitors must perform in person searches themselves. Criminal records indexed in books, on microfiche from 1920 forward; on computer back to 6/2000. Criminal PAT goes back to 6/12/2000. **See front or rear of chapter for detailed description of state's online access.** Online criminal and traffic records date from 06/00. Online results show name only.

Sherman County

District Court 630 O St, PO Box 456, Loup City, NE 68853; 308-745-1513 x103; fax: 308-745-0157; 8:30AM-4:30PM (CST). *Felony, Civil Actions over $52,000.*

General Information: Online identifiers in results same as on public terminal. No mental health records released. Will not fax documents. Court makes copy: $.50 per page. Self serve copy: $.25 per page. Certification fee: $1.00. Payee: Clerk of District Court. Personal checks accepted, credit cards are not. Prepayment required.

Civil Name Search: Access: In person, online. Visitors must perform in person searches themselves. Civil index and docket books since late 1800s; on computer back to 4/2000. Civil PAT goes back to 4/17/2000. **See front or rear of chapter for detailed description of state's online access.** Online records date from 04/00.

Criminal Name Search: Access: In person, online. Visitors must perform in person searches themselves. Criminal records on index and docket books since late 1800s; on computer back to 4/2000. Criminal PAT goes back to same as civil. DL, sex, hair, eyes, etc., also used as identifiers. **See front or rear of chapter for detailed description of state's online access.** Online records date from 04/00. Online results show middle initial, DOB.

Sherman County Court 630 O St, PO Box 55, Loup City, NE 68853; 308-745-1513 x102; fax: 308-745-1510; 8:30AM-4:30PM (CST). *Misdemeanor, Civil Actions under $52,000, Eviction, Small Claims, Probate.* http://supremecourt.ne.gov/county-court/

General Information: Juvenile and Traffic cases are also held at this court. No adoption records released. Fee to fax out file $3.00 1st page; $1.00 each add'l. Court makes copy: $.25 per page. Self serve copy: $.25 per page. Certification fee: $1.00 for seal, $.25 per page. Payee: Sherman County Court. Business checks accepted. No credit cards accepted. Prepayment required.

Civil Name Search: Access: In person, online. Visitors must perform in person searches themselves. Civil cases indexed by defendant and plaintiff from 2000 forward. Civil index on docket books from late 1800s; on computer back to 5/2000 in DC office. Civil PAT goes back to 4/2000. Public terminal located in District Court Office. **See front or rear of chapter for detailed description of state's online access.** Online civil and probate records from 05/00 forward.

Criminal Name Search: Access: In person, online. Visitors must perform in person searches themselves. Required to search: name, years to search, DOB. Criminal records indexed in books from late 1800s; on computer back to 5/2000. Criminal PAT goes back to same as civil. Public terminal located in District Court Office. **See front or rear of chapter for detailed description of state's online access.** Online criminal and traffic records date from 05/00. Online results show name only.

Sioux County

District Court PO Box 158, 325 Main St, Harrison, NE 69346; 308-668-2443; 8AM-4:30PM (MST). *Felony, Civil Actions over $52,000.*

General Information: No adoption or sealed records released. Will fax documents $1.00 per page. Court makes copy: $.50 per page. Self serve copy: $.25 per page. Certification fee: $6.00 per page. Payee: Clerk of District Court. Personal checks accepted, credit cards are not. Prepayment required.

Civil Name Search: Access: In person, online. Both court and visitors may perform in person name searches. No search fee. Civil records in index and docket books since 1800s; computerized records since 1992. Civil PAT goes back to 1992. **See front or rear of chapter for detailed description of state's online access.** Online records date from 06/00.

Criminal Name Search: Access: In person, online. Both court and visitors may perform in person name searches. No search fee. Required to search: name, years to search; also helpful: DOB, SSN. Criminal records in index and docket books since 1800s; computerized records since 1992. Criminal PAT goes back to same as civil. **See front or rear of chapter for detailed description of state's online access.** Online records date from 06/00. Online results show middle initial, DOB.

Sioux County Court PO Box 158, 325 Main St, Harrison, NE 69346; 308-668-2443; fax: 308-668-2443; 8AM-4:30PM (MST). *Misdemeanor, Civil Actions under $52,000, Eviction, Small Claims, Probate.* http://supremecourt.ne.gov/county-court/

General Information: No sealed, expunged, or adoption records released. Will fax documents $1.00 per page. Court makes copy: $1.00 per page. Self serve copy: same. Certification fee: $1.00 per document. Payee: County Court. Personal checks accepted, credit cards are not. Prepayment required.

Civil Name Search: Access: In person, online. Both court and visitors may perform in person name searches. No search fee. Civil index on docket books from late 1800s. Note: This court prefers to take phone requests. Very few civil cases handled each year. Civil PAT goes back to 1992. **See front or rear of chapter for detailed description of state's online access.** Online civil and probate records are from 01/01 forward.

Criminal Name Search: Access: In person, online. Both court and visitors may perform in person name searches. No search fee. Criminal records indexed in books from late 1800s. Criminal PAT goes back to same as civil. **See front or rear of chapter for detailed description of state's online access.** Online criminal and traffic records date from 08/00. Online results show middle initial, DOB.

Stanton County

District Court PO Box 347, 804 Ivy St, Stanton, NE 68779; 402-439-2222; fax: 402-439-2200; 8:30AM-4:30PM (CST). *Felony, Civil Actions over $52,000.*

www.co.stanton.ne.us/court.html

General Information: Online identifiers in results same as on public terminal. No juvenile records released. Will fax documents $2.50 1st page, $1.00 each add'l. Court makes copy: $.25 per page. Self serve copy: same. Certification fee: $1.00 per page plus copy fee. Payee: Clerk of District Court. Personal checks accepted, credit cards are not. Prepayment required. Mail requests: SASE required.

Civil Name Search: Access: Fax, mail, in person, online. Visitors must perform in person searches themselves. No search fee. Civil records on books from 1867, on computer from 12/1999. Mail Turnaround time 3-4 days. Civil PAT goes to 12/1999. **See front or rear of chapter for detailed description of state's online access.** Online records from 12/99.

Criminal Name Search: Access: Fax, mail, in person, online. Visitors must perform in person searches themselves. No search fee. Required to search: name, years to search; also helpful: address, DOB, SSN. Criminal docket on books from 1867, on computer from 12/1999. Mail Turnaround time 3-4 days. Criminal PAT goes back to same as civil. **See front or rear of chapter for detailed description of state's online access.** Online records date from 12/99, results show middle initial, DOB.

Stanton County Court 804 Ivy St, PO Box 536, Stanton, NE 68779; 402-439-2221; probate phone: 402-439-2221; fax: 402-439-2227; 8:30AM-4:30PM (CST). *Misdemeanor, Civil Actions under $52,000, Eviction, Small Claims, Probate.* www.co.stanton.ne.us/cntycourt.html

General Information: No adoption records released. Will fax documents to local or toll-free number. Court makes copy: $.25 per page. Certification fee: $1.00. Payee: Stanton County. Personal checks accepted, credit cards are not. Prepayment required. Mail requests: SASE required for mail return of any copies.

Civil Name Search: Access: In person, online. Visitors must perform in person searches themselves. Civil records on docket cards and books back to 1950s; probate on microfilm. Civil PAT goes back to 7/2000. **See front or rear of chapter for detailed description of state's online access.** Online civil and probate records from 10/00 forward.

Criminal Name Search: Access: In person, online. Visitors must perform in person searches themselves. Required to search: name, years to search, DOB. Criminal records on docket cards and books back to 1900s; criminal records computerized back to 1999. Criminal PAT goes back to same as civil. **See front or rear of chapter for detailed description of state's online access.** Online criminal and traffic records date from 06/00. Online results show name only.

Thayer County

District Court 225 N 4th St, Rm 302, Hebron, NE 68370; 402-768-6116; fax: 402-768-6128; 7:30AM-4:30PM (CST). *Felony, Civil Actions over $52,000.*

General Information: No mental health or sealed records released. Will not fax documents. Court makes copy: $.25 per page. Certification fee: $1.00. Payee: Thayer County District Court. Personal checks accepted, credit cards are not. Mail requests: SASE required for Naturalization Records only.

Civil Name Search: Access: In person, online. Visitors must perform in person searches themselves. Civil records on books from 1900s; computerized records go back 3/2000. Civil PAT goes back to 3/2000. **See front or rear of chapter for detailed description of state's online access.** Online records from 03/00.

Criminal Name Search: Access: In person, online. Visitors must perform in person searches themselves. Criminal docket on books from 1900; computerized records go back 3/2000. Criminal PAT goes back to same as civil. Results include name and case number. **See front or rear of chapter for detailed description of state's online access.** Online records date from 03/00. Online results show middle initial, DOB.

Thayer County Court 225 N 5th St, Rm 203, Hebron, NE 68370; 402-768-6325; fax: 402-768-7232; 7:30AM-4:30PM (CST). *Misdemeanor, Civil Actions under $52,000, Eviction, Small Claims, Probate.* http://supremecourt.ne.gov/county-court/

General Information: Send questions to thayercountycourt@hotmail.com. No adoption or juvenile records released. Will not fax documents. Court makes copy: $.25 per page. Certification fee: $1.00. Payee: County Court. No personal checks or credit cards accepted. Prepayment required.

Civil Name Search: Access: In person, online. Visitors must perform in person searches themselves. Required to search: name, years to search, address. Civil records on docket cards from 1871; probate on microfiche. Civil PAT goes back to 2000. **See front or rear of chapter for detailed description of state's online access.** Online civil and probate records from 02/00 forward.

Criminal Name Search: Access: In person, online. Visitors must perform in person searches themselves. Required to search: name, years to search, DOB. Criminal records on docket cards from 1871; probate on microfiche. Criminal PAT goes to 2000. **See front or rear of chapter for detailed description of state's online access.** Online criminal & traffic records date from 02/00, results show middle initial, DOB.

Thomas County

District Court PO Box 226, 503 Main St, Thedford, NE 69166; 308-645-2261; fax: 308-645-2623; 8AM-N, 1-4PM M-TH; till 3PM F (CST). *Felony, Civil Actions over $52,000.*

General Information: The District Court no longer performs name searches. No sealed or juvenile records released. Will fax documents $5.00 per fax. Court makes copy: $.50 per page. Self serve copy: same. Certification fee: $5.00 per cert. Payee: Clerk of District Court. Personal checks accepted, credit cards are not. Prepayment required.

Civil Name Search: Access: In person, online. Visitors must perform in person searches themselves. Civil records indexed in books and in case files since 1800s; on computer back to 6/2000. Civil PAT goes back to 6/2000. **See front or rear of chapter for detailed description of state's online access.** Online records date from 06/00.

Criminal Name Search: Access: In person, online. Visitors must perform in person searches themselves. Required to search: name, years to search, DOB; also helpful- SSN, signed release. Criminal records indexed in books and in case files since 1800s; on computer back to 6/2000. Criminal PAT goes back to same as civil. **See front or rear of chapter for detailed description of state's online access.** Online records date from 06/00. Online results show middle initial, DOB.

Thomas County Court PO Box 233, 503 Main St, Thedford, NE 69166; 308-645-2266 or 2273; fax: 308-645-2623; 8AM-4PM M-TH; 8AM-3PM F (CST). *Misdemeanor, Civil Actions under $52,000, Eviction, Small Claims, Probate.* http://supremecourt.ne.gov/county-court/

General Information: No adoption or juvenile records released. Will not fax documents. Court makes copy: $.25 per page. Self serve copy: same. Certification fee: $1.00 per cert. Payee: County Court. Personal checks, Visa/MC accepted. Prepayment required. Mail requests: SASE required.

Civil Name Search: Access: Phone, fax, mail, in person, online. Both court and visitors may perform in person name searches. No search fee. Civil index on cards and books from late 1800s. Mail Turnaround time 2 days. Civil PAT goes back to 6/2000. **See front or rear of chapter for detailed description of state's online access.** Online civil records date from 10/99 forward, probate from 07/98.

Criminal Name Search: Access: Fax, mail, in person, online. Both court and visitors may perform in person name searches. No search fee. Required to search: name, years to search, DOB, signed release. Criminal records indexed on cards and books from late 1800s. Mail Turnaround time 2 days. Criminal PAT goes back to same as civil. **See front or rear of chapter for detailed description of state's online access.** Online criminal and traffic records date from 07/98. Online results show middle initial, DOB.

Thurston County

District Court PO Box 216, Pender, NE 68047; 402-385-3318; fax: 402-385-2762; 8:30AM-N, 1-5PM (CST). *Felony, Civil Actions over $52,000.*

General Information: No mental health records released. Will not fax documents. Court makes copy: $.25 per page. Self serve copy: same. Certification fee: $1.00 per certification plus copy fee. Payee: Clerk of District Court. No personal checks or credit cards accepted. Prepayment required.

Civil Name Search: Access: In person, online. Visitors must perform in person searches themselves. Civil index on docket books from late 1800s; on computer back to 1998. Civil PAT goes back to 1998. **See front or rear of chapter for detailed description of state's online access.** Online records date from 03/98.

Criminal Name Search: Access: In person, online. Visitors must perform in person searches themselves. Criminal records indexed in books from late 1800s; on computer back to 1998. Criminal PAT goes back to same as civil. **See front or rear of chapter for detailed description of state's online access.** Online records date from 03/98. Online results show middle initial, DOB.

Thurston County Court County Courthouse, PO Box 129, Pender, NE 68047; 402-385-3136; fax: 402-385-3143; 8AM-N,1-5PM (CST). *Misdemeanor, Civil Actions under $52,000, Eviction, Small Claims, Probate.* http://supremecourt.ne.gov/county-court/

General Information: Probate fax is same as main fax number. Online identifiers in results same as on public terminal. No adoption or juvenile records released. Will not fax documents. Court makes copy: $.25 per page. Self serve copy: $.10 per page. Certification fee: $1.00 per seal. Payee: County Court. Personal checks accepted if in state. No credit cards accepted. Prepayment required.

Civil Name Search: Access: In person, online. Visitors must perform in person searches themselves. Civil records on books; probate on microfiche since 1800s; on computer back to 1/2000. Civil PAT goes back to 1/2000. **See front or rear of chapter for detailed description of state's online access.** Online civil and probate records from 01/00 forward.

Criminal Name Search: Access: In person, online. Visitors must perform in person searches themselves. Criminal docket on books per state requirement; on computer back to 1/2000. Criminal PAT goes back to same as civil. **See front or rear of chapter for detailed description of state's online access.** Online criminal and traffic records date from 01/00. Online results show middle initial, DOB.

Valley County

District Court 125 S 15th St, Ord, NE 68862; 308-728-3700; fax: 308-728-7725; 8AM-5PM (CST). *Felony, Civil Actions over $52,000.*

General Information: Will fax to toll-free number. Court makes copy: $.10 per page; $.15 per page legal size. Self serve copy: same. Certification fee: $1.00 per page plus copy fee. Payee: Valley County Clerk. Personal checks accepted, credit cards are not. Prepayment required.

Civil Name Search: Access: In person, online. Visitors must perform in person searches themselves. Civil records in general index books since late 1800s. Civil PAT to 3/2000. **See front or rear of chapter for detailed description of state's online access.** Online records date from 3/2000.

Criminal Name Search: Access: In person, online. Visitors must perform in person searches themselves. Required to search: name, years to search; also helpful: DOB, SSN. Criminal records in general index books since late 1800s; on computer back to 3/2000. Criminal PAT goes back to same as civil. **See front or rear of chapter for detailed description of state's online access.** Online records date from 3/2000. Online results show middle initial, DOB.

Valley County Court 125 S 15th St, Ord, NE 68862; 308-728-3831; fax: 308-728-7725; 8AM-5PM (CST). *Misdemeanor, Civil Actions under $52,000, Eviction, Small Claims, Probate.*

http://supremecourt.ne.gov/county-court/

General Information: No adoption records released. Will fax documents $3.00 1st page, $1.00 each add'l. Court makes copy: $.25 per page. Self serve copy: same. Certification fee: $1.00 per doc. Payee: Valley County Court. Personal checks accepted. Prepayment required. Mail requests: SASE required.

Civil Name Search: Access: Phone, fax, mail, in person, online. Both court and visitors may perform in person name searches. No search fee. Civil records on books and in files since 1890s; probate on microfiche. Mail Turnaround time 1 week. Civil PAT goes back to 9 years. **See front or rear of chapter for detailed description of state's online access.** Online civil and probate records from 05/00 forward.

Criminal Name Search: Access: Phone, fax, mail, in person, online. Both court and visitors may perform in person name searches. No search fee. Criminal docket on books and in files since 1890s; probate on microfiche. Mail Turnaround time 1 week. Criminal PAT goes back to same as civil. **See front or rear of chapter for detailed description of state's online access.** Online criminal and traffic records date from 05/00. Online results show middle initial, DOB.

Washington County

District Court PO Box 431, Blair, NE 68008; 402-426-6899; fax: 402-426-6898; 8AM-N; 1PM-4:30PM (CST). *Felony, Civil Actions over $52,000.* www.co.washington.ne.us/court.html

General Information: No juvenile, mental health records released. Will fax documents $3.00 1st page, $1.00 ea add'l. Court makes copy: $.25 per page. Certification fee: $1.00. Payee: Clerk of District Court. Personal checks accepted, credit cards are not. Prepayment required.

Civil Name Search: Access: In person, online. Visitors must perform in person searches themselves. Civil index on docket books and in files since 1930s; computerized records since 1997, prior sent to capitol. Civil PAT goes back to 7/1997. **See front or rear of chapter for detailed description of state's online access.** Online records date from 07/97.

Criminal Name Search: Access: In person, online. Visitors must perform in person searches themselves. Required to search: name, years to search, DOB. Criminal records indexed in books and in files since 1930s; computerized records since 1997, prior sent to capitol. Criminal PAT goes back to same as civil. **See front or rear of chapter for detailed description of state's online access.** Online records date from 06/97. Online results show middle initial, DOB.

Washington County Court 1555 Colfax St, Blair, NE 68008; 402-426-6833; fax: 402-426-6840; 8AM-4:30PM (CST). *Misdemeanor, Civil Actions under $52,000, Eviction, Small Claims, Probate.*

http://supremecourt.ne.gov/county-court/

General Information: Probate records are on a separate index at this address. Probate fax is same as main fax number. Online identifiers in results same as on public terminal. No adoption records released. Will not fax documents. Court makes copy: $.25 per page. Self serve copy: same. Certification fee: $1.00 per certification. Payee: Washington County Court. No personal checks; must be money order or cashier check. No credit cards accepted. Prepayment required.

Civil Name Search: Access: In person, online. Visitors must perform in person searches themselves. Civil index on docket books, cards; probate on microfilm since 1867; on computer back to 1997. Civil PAT goes back to 12/1999, countywide. **See front or rear of chapter for detailed description of state's online access.** Online civil records date from 12/99 forward, probate from 5/98.

Criminal Name Search: Access: In person, online. Visitors must perform in person searches themselves. Required to search: name, years to search, DOB, SSN. Criminal records indexed in books, cards; probate on microfilm since 1867; on computer back to 1997. Criminal PAT goes back to 2/1997, countywide. **See front or rear of chapter for detailed description of state's online access.** Online criminal and traffic records date from 2/97. Online results show middle initial, DOB.

Wayne County

District Court 510 Pearl St, #6, Wayne, NE 68787; 402-375-2260; fax: 402-375-0103; 8:30AM-5PM (CST). *Felony, Civil Actions over $51,000.* www.waynecountyne.org/index.aspx?nid=90

General Information: Court personnel will not do searches for the public. No mental health records released. Will fax out documents $2.00 1st page, $1.00 each add'l, prepaid. Court makes copy: $.25 per page. Self serve copy: same. Certification fee: $1.00. Payee: Clerk of District Court. Only cashiers checks and money orders accepted. No credit cards accepted. Prepayment required.

Civil Name Search: Access: In person, online. Visitors must perform in person searches themselves. Civil index on docket books from late 1800s, computerized since 3/99. Civil PAT goes back to 3/1999. Not all records show personal identifiers. **See front or rear of chapter for detailed description of state's online access.** Online records date from 03/99.

Criminal Name Search: Access: In person, online. Visitors must perform in person searches themselves. Criminal records indexed in books from late 1800s, computerized since 3/99. Criminal PAT goes back to same as civil. Not all records show personal identifiers. **See front or rear of chapter for detailed description of state's online access.**

Wayne County Court 510 Pearl St, #B, Wayne, NE 68787; 402-375-1622; fax: 402-375-2342; 8:30AM-5PM (CST). *Misdemeanor, Civil Actions under $52,000, Eviction, Small Claims, Probate.*
www.waynecountyne.org/index.aspx?nid=85

General Information: No adoption records released. Will not fax documents. Court makes copy: $.25 per page. Self serve copy: $.25 per page. Certification fee: $1.00. Payee: County Court. Personal checks accepted, credit cards are not. Prepayment required.

Civil Name Search: Access: In person, online. Visitors must perform in person searches themselves. Required to search: name, years to search, DOB. Civil index on docket books, cards from late 1800s. Civil PAT goes back to 1999. **See front or rear of chapter for detailed description of state's online access.** Online civil and probate records from 2/2000 forward.

Criminal Name Search: Access: In person, online. Visitors must perform in person searches themselves. Required to search: name, years to search, DOB. Criminal records indexed in books, cards from late 1800s. Criminal PAT goes back to same as civil. **See front or rear of chapter for detailed description of state's online access.** Online criminal and traffic records date from 2/2000. Online results show middle initial, DOB.

Webster County

District Court 621 N Cedar, Red Cloud, NE 68970; 402-746-2716; fax: 402-746-2710; 8:30AM-4:30PM (CST). *Felony, Civil Actions over $52,000.*

General Information: No mental health records released. Will not fax documents. Court makes copy: $1.00 per page. Certification fee: $1.50 per cert plus copy fee. Payee: Clerk of District Court. Personal checks, Visa/MC accepted. Prepayment required.

Civil Name Search: Access: Fax, mail, in person, online. Visitors must perform in person searches themselves. No search fee. Civil records indexed on microfiche; in files back to 1800s. Civil PAT goes back to 10/2000. **See front or rear of chapter for detailed description of state's online access.** Online records date from 10/00.

Criminal Name Search: Access: Fax, mail, in person, online. Visitors must perform in person searches themselves. No search fee. Required to search: name, years to search; also helpful: address, DOB, SSN. Criminal records indexed on microfiche; in files back to 1800s. Criminal PAT goes back to same as civil. **See front or rear of chapter for detailed description of state's online access.** Online records date from 10/2000. Online results show middle initial, DOB.

Webster County Court 621 N Cedar, Red Cloud, NE 68970; 402-746-2777; fax: 402-746-2771; 8AM-4:30PM (CST). *Misdemeanor, Civil Actions under $52,000, Eviction, Small Claims, Probate.* www.district10.us/

General Information: Probate fax is same as main fax number. Online identifiers in results same as on public terminal. No adoption or juvenile records released. Will fax out specific case files for $3.00 for 1st page; $1.00 each add'l. Court makes copy: $.25 per page. Self serve copy: same. Certification fee: $1.00 plus copy fee. Payee: County Court. Business checks accepted. No credit cards accepted. Prepayment required.

Civil Name Search: Access: In person, online. Visitors must perform in person searches themselves. Required to search: name, years to search; also helpful: address. Civil cases indexed by defendant. Civil index on cards and books; probate on microfiche since late 1930, indexed on computer since 7/00. Civil PAT goes back to 1/2001. **See front or rear of chapter for detailed description of state's online access.** Online civil records date from 01/00 forward, probate from 02/00.

Criminal Name Search: Access: In person, online. Visitors must perform in person searches themselves. Required to search: name, years to search, DOB. Criminal records indexed on cards and books; probate on microfiche since late 1930, indexed on computer since 7/00. Criminal PAT goes back to 7/2000. **See front or rear of chapter for detailed description of state's online access.** Online criminal and traffic records date from 07/00. Online results show middle initial, DOB.

Wheeler County

District Court PO Box 127, Bartlett, NE 68622; 308-654-3235; 9AM-N, 1-5PM (CST). *Felony, Civil Actions over $52,000.*

General Information: No juvenile or adoption records released. Will fax out specific case files for $3.00. Court makes copy: $.50 per page. Self serve copy: $.20 per page. Certification fee: $8.00 per doc. Payee: Clerk of District Court. Personal checks accepted, credit cards are not. Prepayment required.

Civil Name Search: Access: Mail, in person, online. Visitors must perform in person searches themselves. No search fee. Civil index on docket books from late 1800s. Note: Mail access limited to short searches. Civil PAT goes back to 2000. Civil records online - see criminal access.

Criminal Name Search: Access: In person, online. Visitors must perform in person searches themselves. Criminal records indexed in books from late 1800s. Criminal PAT goes back to 2000. **See front or rear of chapter for detailed description of state's online access.** Online records date from 7/2000. Online results show middle initial, DOB.

Wheeler County Court PO Box 127, 1st and Main St, Bartlett, NE 68622; 308-654-3376; fax: 308-654-3176; 9AM-4PM TH; and 1st & 2nd M (CST). *Misdemeanor, Civil Actions under $52,000, Eviction, Small Claims, Probate.* http://supremecourt.ne.gov/county-court/

General Information: Court clerk also serves Garfield County Court and may be contacted there, 308-346-4123 No adoption records released. Will fax documents $3.00 1st page; $1.00 each add'l. Court makes copy: $.25 per page. Self serve copy: same. Certification fee: $1.00. Payee: County Court. Personal checks accepted, credit cards are not. Prepayment required.

Civil Name Search: Access: In person, online. Visitors must perform in person searches themselves. No search fee. Civil index on docket books from late 1800s. Public use terminal has civil records back to 2000. **See front or rear of chapter for detailed description of state's online access.** Online civil records date from 1/2001 forward, probate from 1/02.

Criminal Name Search: Access: In person, online. Visitors must perform in person searches themselves. Criminal records indexed in books from late 1800s. **See front or rear of chapter for detailed description of state's online access.** Online criminal and traffic records date from 7/2000.

York County

District Court 510 Lincoln Ave, York, NE 68467; 402-362-4038; fax: 402-362-2577; 8:30AM-5PM (CST). *Felony, Civil Actions over $52,000.*

General Information: The SSN does not show up in the computer index, but will show in the case files. Online identifiers in results same as on public terminal. mental health records are restricted from public view. Will fax documents. Court makes copy: $.25 per page. Self serve copy: same. Certification fee: $1.00. Payee: Clerk of District Court. Personal checks accepted, credit cards are not. Prepayment required.

Civil Name Search: Access: In person, online. Visitors must perform in person searches themselves. Civil index on docket books and in files from 1875, computerized go back to 1998. Civil PAT goes back to 1998. **See front or rear of chapter for detailed description of state's online access.** Online records date from 06/98.

Criminal Name Search: Access: In person, online. Visitors must perform in person searches themselves. Criminal records indexed in books and in files from 1875, computerized records go back to 1998. Criminal PAT goes back to 1998. **See front or rear of chapter for detailed description of state's online access.** Online records date from 06/98. Online results show middle initial, DOB.

York County Court 510 Lincoln Ave, York, NE 68467; 402-362-4925; fax: 402-362-2577; 8AM-5PM (CST). *Misdemeanor, Civil Actions under $52,000, Eviction, Small Claims, Probate.* http://supremecourt.ne.gov/county-court/

General Information: Court staff will only assist public with records if case number given. No adoption or sealed records released. Will not fax documents. Court makes copy: $.25 per page. Certification fee: $1.00. Payee: York County Court. Personal checks accepted, credit cards are not. Prepayment required.

Civil Name Search: Access: In person, online. Visitors must perform in person searches themselves. Civil records accessible for 15 years, prior on docket cards, files from 1875. Civil PAT goes back to 1997. **See front or rear of chapter for detailed description of state's online access.** Online civil records date from 10/99 forward, probate from 05/98.

Criminal Name Search: Access: In person, online. Visitors must perform in person searches themselves. Criminal records easily accessible for 15 years, prior on docket cards, files from 1875. Criminal PAT goes back to 3/1997. **See front or rear of chapter for detailed description of state's online access.** Online criminal and traffic records date from 03/97. Online results show middle initial, DOB.

About Online Access

An online access subscription service is available for all Nebraska County Courts and all District Courts. Douglas County District Court was the last county added in April 2011. Case details, all party listings, payments, and actions taken for criminal, civil, probate, juvenile, and traffic are available. District Courts and County Courts must be searched separately. Both convictions and pending cases are available in the criminal search.

The system starts with a name search and resulting list gives full DOB. The fee for a onetime search using a credit card is $15.00. Ongoing users may register with Nebraska.gov and have an account that also gives access to other records. There is a start-up/annual fee for $50.00. For court record access the fee is $1.00 per record or a flat rate of $300.00 per month.

Go to www.nebraska.gov/faqs/justice or call 402-471-7810 for more info.

Nevada

Time Zone:	**PST**
Capital:	**Carson City, Carson City County**
# of Counties:	**17**
State Web:	**www.nv.gov**
Court Web:	**www.nevadajudiciary.us**

Administration

Supreme Court of Nevada, Administrative Office of the Courts, 201 S Carson St #250, Carson City, NV, 89701; 775-684-1700, Fax: 775-684-1723.

The Supreme Court

The primary constitutional function of the Supreme Court is to review appeals from decisions of the District Courts. Currently there is not an intermediate Court of Appeals in Nevada, but there is ongoing discussion of the formation of one. Opinions are accessible from the web page.

The Nevada Courts

Court	Type	How Organized	Jurisdiction Highpoints
District*	General	17 Courts in 9 Districts	Felony, Gross Misdemeanor, Civil Actions over $10,000, Probate
Justice*	Limited	43 Courts by Township	Misdemeanor, Civil Actions under $10,000, Eviction, Small Claims
Municipal*	Limited	20 Courts	Misdemeanor, Traffic, Ordinance

* = profiled in this book

Details on the Court Structure

Note that Nevada does NOT have a unified court system.

The **District Courts** are the courts of general jurisdiction. Probate is handled by the District Courts, as are divorce records. The judges also hear appeals from Justice and Municipal Court cases.

The **Justice Courts** are generally named for the township of jurisdiction. Due to their small populations, some townships no longer have Justice Courts. The Justice Courts handle misdemeanor crime and traffic matters, small claims disputes, evictions, and other civil matters less than $10,000, the maximum amount for Small Claims increased from $5,000 to $7,500 in July 2011. The Justices of the Peace also preside over felony and gross misdemeanor arraignments and conduct preliminary hearings to determine if sufficient evidence exists to hold criminals for trial at District Court.

The **Municipal Courts** manage cases involving violations of traffic and misdemeanor ordinances that occur within the city limits of incorporated municipalities. Generally they do not oversee civil matters.

Record Searching Facts You Need to Know

Fees and Record Searching Tips

Many Nevada Justice Courts are small and have very few records. Their hours of operation vary widely and contact is difficult. It is recommended that requesters call ahead for information prior to submitting a written request or attempting an in person retrieval. Fees will vary; many Justice Courts charge $1.00 per name per year to do a name search.

Online Access is Limited

Some Nevada courts have internal online computer systems, but only Clark and Washoe counties offer online access to the public. A state-sponsored court automation system is being implemented.

Carson City

1st Judicial District Court 885 E Musser St, #3031, Carson City, NV 89701-4775; 775-887-2082; fax: 775-887-2177; 9AM-5PM (PST). *Felony, Gross Misdemeanor, Civil Actions over $10,000, Probate.* www.carson.org/Index.aspx?page=240

General Information: The Justice Courts retain records for minor misdemeanors. No sealed or juvenile records released. Will fax documents to local or toll free line. Court makes copy: $1.00 per page. Certification fee: $5.00 if copy is presented to this office, $3.00 if they make the copies plus copy fees. Payee: Carson City. Personal check accepted with check guarantee card only. Credit and debit cards accepted. Prepayment required. Mail requests: SASE required.

Civil Name Search: Access: Mail, in person. Only the court performs in person name searches; visitors may not. Search fee: $1.00 per name per year. Civil records on computer from 1987, on microfiche and archives from 1861. Mail Turnaround time 4-5 days.

Criminal Name Search: Access: Mail, in person. Only the court performs in person name searches; visitors may not. Search fee: $1.00 per name per year. Criminal records computerized from 1987, on microfiche and archives from 1861. Mail Turnaround time 4-5 days.

Justice Court 885 E Musser St, #2007, Carson City, NV 89701-4775; 775-887-2121; fax: 775-887-2351; 8AM-5PM; closed 11AM-N F (PST). *Misdemeanor, Civil Actions under $10,000, Eviction, Small Claims.* www.carson.org/Index.aspx?page=822

General Information: Also, try www.carson.org/ for information about this jurisdiction. No sealed, sexual victims, juvenile records released. Will fax documents to local or toll free line. Court makes copy: $.30 per page. Certification fee: $3.00 per doc. Payee: Carson City. Personal checks accepted. Visa/MC accepted in person only. Prepayment required. Mail requests: SASE required.

Civil Name Search: Access: Mail, in person. Only the court performs in person name searches; visitors may not. Search fee: $1.00 per name per year. Required to search: name, years to search, DOB. Mail Turnaround time 48 hours.

Criminal Name Search: Access: Mail, in person. Only the court performs in person name searches; visitors may not. Search fee: $1.00 per name per year. Required to search: name, years to search, DOB. Criminal records on computer alpha index from 1991. Note: In person is not while you wait. Mail Turnaround time 48 hours.

Carson City Municipal Court 885 E Musser St, Ste 2007, Carson City, NV 89701; 775-887-2121; fax: 775-887-2351; *Misdemeanor, Traffic.* www.nevadajudiciary.us/index.php/municipal

Churchill County

3rd Judicial District Court 73 N Maine St, #B, Fallon, NV 89406; 775-423-6080; fax: 775-423-8578; 8AM-N, 1-5PM (PST). *Felony, Gross Misdemeanor, Civil Actions over $10,000, Probate.* www.churchillcounty.org/dcourt/

General Information: Probate fax is same as main fax number. No juvenile, adoption or sealed records released. No fee to fax documents to local or toll free numbers only. Court makes copy: $1.00 per page. Certification fee: $5.00 per document plus copy fee. Payee: Office of Court Clerk. Business checks accepted; no personal checks. No credit cards accepted. Prepayment required. Mail requests: SASE required.

Civil Name Search: Access: Fax, mail, in person. Only the court performs in person name searches; visitors may not. Search fee: $1.00 per name per year. Civil records on computer from 1989, prior on books, microfiche. Mail Turnaround time 1-2 days.

Criminal Name Search: Access: Fax, mail, in person. Only the court performs in person name searches; visitors may not. Search fee: $1.00 per name per year. Required to search: name, years to search, DOB; also helpful: SSN. Criminal records computerized from 1989, prior on books, microfiche to 1910. Mail Turnaround time 1-2 days.

New River Justice Court 71 N Maine St, Fallon, NV 89406; 775-423-2845; fax: 775-423-0472; 8AM-12, 1-5PM (PST). *Misdemeanor, Civil Actions under $10,000, Eviction, Small Claims.* www.churchillcounty.org/jcourt/

General Information: No sealed records released. Will fax search results to toll-free line. Court makes copy: $.30 per page. Certification fee: $3.00 per doc; Exemplification- $6.00 per doc. Payee: Justice Court. Personal checks, Visa/MC accepted. Prepayment required. Mail requests: SASE not required.

Civil Name Search: Access: Mail, fax, in person. Only the court performs in person name searches; visitors may not. Search fee: $1.00 per name per year. Civil records on computer from 1987, prior on microfiche back to 1980. Note: Fax search requests must be prepaid; use credit card. Use fax number for search request and include credit card for payment. Mail Turnaround time 1 day.

Criminal Name Search: Access: Mail, fax, in person. Only the court performs in person name searches; visitors may not. Search fee: $1.00 per name per year. Required to search: name, years to search, DOB. Criminal records computerized from 1987, prior on microfiche back to 1980. Note: Fax search requests must be prepaid; use credit card. Use fax number for search request and include credit card for payment. Mail Turnaround time 1 day.

Fallon Municipal Court 55 W Williams Ave, Fallon, NV 89406; 775-423-6244; fax: 775-867-2378; *Misdemeanor, Traffic.* http://nevadajudiciary.us/index.php/municipal/

Clark County

8th Judicial District Court 200 Lewis Ave, 3rd Fl, Records Dept, Las Vegas, NV 89155; 702-671-4554; criminal phone: 702-671-0501; civil phone: 702-671-0530; probate phone: 702-455-2373 family ct; fax: 702-474-2434; 8AM-4PM (PST). *Felony, Gross Misdemeanor, Civil Actions over $10,000, Probate.* www.clarkcountycourts.us/

General Information: Records Dept is on the 3rd Fl. All probate records, including microfilm, and with the Family Court - call 703-455-2373. No sealed records released. Will not fax out documents. Court makes copy: $1.00 per page. Self serve copy: $.10 per page but cannot be used to copy from files. Certification fee: $3.00 to Certify or $6.00 to Exemplify when copies supplied by court. If own copies, $5.00 to Cert, $9.00 to Exempt. Payee: 8th Judicial District Court. Personal checks accepted if pre-printed. No credit cards accepted. Prepayment required. Mail requests: SASE required.

Civil Name Search: Access: Mail, in person, online. Both court and visitors may perform in person name searches. Search fee: $1.00 per name per year. Fee is per case type. Civil records on computer back to 11/90, prior records on microfilm to 1909. Note: Clerks will search several names in person but if 5 or more names presented, wait is 1-2 days. Mail Turnaround time 10 working days. Civil PAT goes back to 1/1990. Case records are searchable free at https://www.clarkcountycourts.us/Anonymous/default.aspx. Search by case number or party name or attorney. A wealth of data is available including calendars, but few personal identifiers. Online access to probate cases filed prior to 01/01/2009 are found at http://courtgate.coca.co.clark.nv.us/DistrictCourt/asp/CaseNo.asp. Otherwise use site above.

Criminal Name Search: Access: Mail, in person, online. Both court and visitors may perform in person name searches. Search fee: $1.00 per name per year. Fee is per case type, i.e.: crim, civil. Required to search: name, years to search, DOB, alias, charges. Criminal records computerized from 11/90, prior records on microfilm to 1909. Note: Clerks will search 1 to 2 names in person but if a list is presented, expect to wait 24-48 hours for results. Personal identifiers most likely found in case pleadings and in police reports. Mail Turnaround time 10 working days. Criminal PAT goes back to 1/1991. Online access to criminal cases filed prior to 01/01/2009 at http://courtgate.coca.co.clark.nv.us/DistrictCourt/asp/CaseNo.asp. Online results show name only.

Boulder Township Justice Court 505 Ave G, Boulder City, NV 89005; 702-455-8000; fax: 702-455-8003; 7:30AM-5PM M-TH (PST). *Misdemeanor, Civil Actions under $10,000, Eviction, Small Claims.* www.clarkcountycourts.us

General Information: No financial records released. Will not fax documents. Court makes copy: $.30 per page. Certification fee: $3.00. Payee: Justice Court. Personal checks, Visa/MC accepted. Prepayment required. Mail requests: SASE required.

Civil Name Search: Access: Fax, mail, in person, online. Both court and visitors may perform in person name searches. Search fee: $1.00 per name per year. Required to search: name, years to search; also helpful: address. Civil cases indexed by defendant. Civil records on microfiche varies depending on subject. Mail Turnaround time 1 week. Access civil cases at http://cvpublicaccess.co.clark.nv.us/pa/. Search calendars free at http://redrock.co.clark.nv.us/jcCalendar/CalendarSearch.aspx.

Criminal Name Search: Access: Fax, mail, in person, online. Only the court performs in person name searches; visitors may not. Search fee: $1.00 per name per year. Required to search: name, years to search, DOB, date of offense; also helpful: SSN. Criminal records on microfiche varies depending on subject. Mail Turnaround time 1 week. Access to Misdemeanor cases online is same as civil, see above. Online results show middle initial, DOB.

Bunkerville Justice Court 190 W Virgin St, PO Box 7185, Bunkerville, NV 89007; 702-346-5711; fax: 702-346-7212; 7AM-4PM M-TH (PST). *Misdemeanor, Civil Actions under $10,000, Eviction, Small Claims.* www.clarkcountycourts.us/

General Information: No sealed or confidential records released. Will fax documents. Court makes copy: $.30 per page. Certification fee: $3.00 per cert plus copy fee. Payee: Bunkerville Justice Court. No Personal checks, Visa/MC accepted. Prepayment required. Mail requests: SASE not required.

Civil Name Search: Access: Mail, in person, online. Only the court performs in person name searches; visitors may not. Search fee: $1.00 per name per year. Civil cases indexed by case number. Civil records (citations)

on computer from 1991, on docket books. Mail Turnaround time 2 weeks. Access civil cases at http://cvpublicaccess.co.clark.nv.us/pa/. Search calendars free at http://redrock.co.clark.nv.us/jcCalendar/CalendarSearch.aspx.

Criminal Name Search: Access: Mail, in person, online. Only the court performs in person name searches; visitors may not. Search fee: $1.00 per name per year. Required to search: name, years to search, DOB; also helpful: SSN. Criminal records (citations) on computer from 1997, on docket books. Mail Turnaround time 2 weeks. Access to Misdemeanor cases online is same as civil, see above. Online results show middle initial, DOB.

Goodsprings Township Justice Court PO Box 19155, 23120 Las Vegas Blvd South, Jean, NV 89019; 702-874-1405; fax: 702-874-1612; 6:30AM-4:30PM M-TH (PST). *Misdemeanor, Civil Actions under $10,000, Eviction, Small Claims.* www.clarkcountynv.gov/depts/justicecourt/goodsprings/Pages/default.aspx

General Information: Also known as Jean Justice Court. No sealed records released. Will not fax documents. Court makes copy: $.50 per page. Certification fee: $3.00 per doc plus copy fee. Payee: Goodsprings Justice Court. Business checks accepted. Visa/MC accepted. Prepayment required. Mail requests: SASE required.

Civil Name Search: Access: Fax, mail, in person, online. Only the court performs in person name searches; visitors may not. Search fee: $1.00 per name per year. Required to search: name, years to search, case number. Civil records on computer for 10 years, file reports for 10 years after closed. Mail Turnaround time within 2 weeks. Court cases and calendars free at http://cvpublicaccess.co.clark.nv.us/pa/.

Criminal Name Search: Access: Fax, mail, in person, online. Only the court performs in person name searches; visitors may not. Search fee: $1.00 per name per year. Required to search: name, years to search, DOB, case number; also helpful: SSN. Criminal records on computer for 10 years, file reports for 10 years after closed. Mail Turnaround time within 2 weeks. Court cases and calendars free at http://cvpublicaccess.co.clark.nv.us/pa/. Online results show middle initial.

Henderson Township Justice Court 243 S Water St, Henderson, NV 89015; 702-455-7980; fax: 702-455-7977; 7AM-5:20PM M-TH (PST). *Misdemeanor, Civil Actions under $10,000, Eviction, Small Claims, Felony Prelim.* www.clarkcountycourts.us/

General Information: Traffic can be reached at 702-455-7980. Also www.clarkcountynv.gov/depts/justicecourt/henderson/Pages/default.aspx Will not fax documents. Court makes copy: $.30 per page. Certification fee: $3.00. Payee: Henderson Justice Court. Personal checks, Visa/MC accepted. Prepayment required. Mail requests: SASE required.

Civil Name Search: Access: Mail, in person, online. Only the court performs in person name searches; visitors may not. Search fee: $1.00 per name per year. Required to search: name, years to search, DOB, SSN. Civil cases indexed by defendant. Civil index on cards and docket books. Evictions kept for 2-6 years; civil and small claims for 6 years. Mail Turnaround time 2 weeks. Access civil cases at http://cvpublicaccess.co.clark.nv.us/pa/. Search calendars free at http://redrock.co.clark.nv.us/jcCalendar/CalendarSearch.aspx.

Criminal Name Search: Access: Mail, in person, online. Only the court performs in person name searches; visitors may not. Search fee: $1.00 per name per year. Required to search: name, years to search, DOB; also helpful: SSN. Criminal records go back 10 years. Mail Turnaround time 2 weeks. Access to Misdemeanor cases online is same as civil, see above. Online results show middle initial, DOB.

Las Vegas Township Justice Court PO Box 552511, 200 Lewis Ave, Regional Justice Center, Las Vegas, NV 89155; 702-671-3116; criminal phone: 702-671-3201; civil phone: 702-671-6478; fax: 702-671-3342; 8AM-3PM (PST). *Misdemeanor, Civil Actions under $10,000, Eviction, Small Claims, Traffic.* www.clarkcountycourts.us/lvjc/index.html

General Information: The Las Vegas Justice Court is housed at the same location, call 702-671-3192 x2. No sealed, confidential or judge's notes records released. Will fax documents to local or toll free line. Court makes copy: $.30 per page. Certification fee: $3.00 per doc plus copy fee. Payee: Justice Court, Las Vegas Township. Personal checks accepted. Prepayment required. Mail requests: SASE requested.

Civil Name Search: Access: Phone, fax, mail, in person, online. Both court and visitors may perform in person name searches. Search fee: $1.00 per name per year. Civil records go back 8 years. Note: Court will search up to 5 names in person but if more, expect a multi-day turnaround time. Mail Turnaround time 3 weeks. Name or case number search at https://www.clarkcountycourts.us/Anonymous/default.aspx for traffic citations, family court. Also, calendars ONLY free at http://redrock.co.clark.nv.us/jcCalendar/CalendarSearch.aspx.

Criminal Name Search: Access: Phone, fax, mail, in person. Only the court performs in person name searches; visitors may not. Search fee: $1.00 per name per year. Required to search: name, years to search, DOB;

also helpful: SSN. Criminal records go back 10 years, per state law. Note: Court will search up to 5 names in person but if more, expect a multi-day turnaround time. Also, Court says for background checks- call the Metro Police, 702-229-3271. Mail Turnaround time 3 weeks. Access to misdemeanor traffic records and schedules is same as civil, see above. Online results show middle initial, DOB.

Laughlin Township Justice Court 101 Civic Way, #2, Laughlin, NV 89029; 702-298-4622; civil phone: 702-298-6130; fax: 702-298-7508; 8AM-4PM M-TH, closed F (PST). *Misdemeanor, Civil Actions under $10,000, Eviction, Small Claims.* www.clarkcountycourts.us/

General Information: No sealed records released. Will not fax out documents. Court makes copy: $.30 per page. Certification fee: $3.00 per cert plus copy fee. Payee: Laughlin Justice Court. No checks accepted. Visa/MC cards accepted. Prepayment required. Mail requests: SASE required.

Civil Name Search: Access: Mail, in person, online. Only the court performs in person name searches; visitors may not. Search fee: $1.00 per name per year. Civil records on docket book by name and case number. Note: All closed files are shredded 10 years from closed date. Mail Turnaround time 2 weeks. Access civil cases at http://cvpublicaccess.co.clark.nv.us/pa/. Search calendars free at http://redrock.co.clark.nv.us/jcCalendar/CalendarSearch.aspx.

Criminal Name Search: Access: Mail, in person, online. Only the court performs in person name searches; visitors may not. Search fee: $1.00 per name per year. Required to search: name, years to search, DOB. Criminal records computerized from 1990, prior in files and must be cross referenced. Note: All closed files are shredded 10 years from closed date. Mail Turnaround time 2 weeks. Access to Misdemeanor cases online is same as civil, see above. Online results show middle initial, DOB.

Mesquite Township Justice Court 500 Hillside Dr, Mesquite, NV 89027-3116; 702-346-5298; fax: 702-346-7319; 7AM-5PM M-TH (PST). *Felony, Civil Actions under $10,000, Eviction, Small Claims.* www.clarkcountycourts.us/

General Information: All requests must be in writing. Please supply SASE or toll-free fax number. Misdemeanor cases are handled at the Mesquite Municipal Court. No sealed records released. Will fax documents $1.00 each. Court makes copy: $.30 per page. Certification fee: $3.00. Payee: Mesquite Justice Court. Only cashiers checks and money orders accepted. No credit cards accepted. Prepayment required. Mail requests: SASE required.

Civil Name Search: Access: Fax, mail, in person, online. Only the court performs in person name searches; visitors may not. Search fee: $1.00 per name per year. Civil cases indexed by defendant. Mail Turnaround time approx. 1-2 weeks. Access civil cases at http://cvpublicaccess.co.clark.nv.us/pa/. Search calendars free at http://redrock.co.clark.nv.us/jcCalendar/CalendarSearch.aspx.

Criminal Name Search: Access: Phone, fax, mail, in person, online. Only the court performs in person name searches; visitors may not. Search fee: $1.00 per name per year. Required to search: name, years to search, DOB; also helpful: SSN. Criminal records computerized from 2001. Mail Turnaround time approx. 1-2 weeks. Access to Misdemeanor cases online is same as civil, see above. Online results show middle initial, DOB.

Moapa Township Justice Court PO Box 280, 1340 E Hwy 168, Moapa, NV 89025; 702-864-2333; fax: 702-864-2585; 7:30AM-5:30PM (PST). *Misdemeanor, Civil Actions under $10,000, Eviction, Small Claims.* www.clarkcountycourts.us/

General Information: You may email the court at moapajusticecourt@co.clark.nv.us. The Clerk County web page is at www.accessclarkcounty.com/. No sealed records released. No fee to fax documents. Court makes copy: $.30 per page. Certification fee: $3.00 per cert plus copy fee. Payee: Moapa Township Justice Court. Personal checks accepted. Credit cards accepted. Prepayment required. Mail requests: SASE required.

Civil Name Search: Access: Fax, mail, in person, online. Only the court performs in person name searches; visitors may not. Search fee: $1.00 per name per year. Civil records on computer from 10/90, prior records on index cards and docket books. Archives flooded in 1980s. Mail Turnaround time 1-5 days. Access civil cases at http://cvpublicaccess.co.clark.nv.us/pa/. Search calendars free at http://redrock.co.clark.nv.us/jcCalendar/CalendarSearch.aspx.

Criminal Name Search: Access: Fax, mail, in person, online. Only the court performs in person name searches; visitors may not. Search fee: $1.00 per name per year. Required to search: name, years to search; also helpful: DOB, SSN. Criminal records computerized from 10/90, prior records on index cards and docket books. Archives flooded in 1980s. Mail Turnaround time 1-5 days. Access to Misdemeanor cases online is same as civil, see above. Online results show middle initial, DOB.

Moapa Valley Township Justice Court 320 N Moapa Valley Blvd, PO Box 337, Overton, NV 89040; 702-397-2840; fax: 702-397-2842; 7AM-4PM M-TH (PST). *Misdemeanor, Civil Actions under $10,000, Eviction, Small Claims, Traffic.* www.clarkcountycourts.us/
General Information: No sealed records released. Will fax documents $1.00 per page. Court makes copy: $.30 per page. Certification fee: $3.00. Payee: Moapa Valley Justice Court. Personal checks, Visa/MC accepted. Prepayment required. Mail requests: SASE required.
Civil Name Search: Access: Mail, in person, online. Only the court performs in person name searches; visitors may not. Search fee: $1.00 per name per year. Civil records on computer from 1991, prior on docket books. Mail Turnaround time approx. 1-2 weeks. Access civil cases at http://cvpublicaccess.co.clark.nv.us/pa/. Search calendars free at http://redrock.co.clark.nv.us/jcCalendar/CalendarSearch.aspx.
Criminal Name Search: Access: Mail, in person, online. Only the court performs in person name searches; visitors may not. Search fee: $1.00 per name per year. Required to search: name, years to search, DOB; also helpful: SSN. Criminal records computerized from 1991, prior on docket books. Mail Turnaround time 1-2 weeks. Access to Misdemeanor cases online is same as civil, see above. Online results show middle initial, DOB.

North Las Vegas Township Justice Court 2428 N Martin L King Blvd, N Las Vegas, NV 89032-3700; 702-455-7802; civil phone: 702-455-7801; fax: 702-455-7832; 7:15AM-5:45PM (PST). *Misdemeanor, Civil Actions under $10,000, Eviction, Small Claims.* www.clarkcountycourts.us/
General Information: No sealed records or protective orders released. Will not fax documents. Court makes copy: $.30 per page. Certification fee: $3.00 per document. Payee: North Las Vegas Justice Court. Personal check accepted with bankcard. Visa/MC credit cards accepted. Prepayment required. Mail requests: SASE required.
Civil Name Search: Access: Mail, in person, online. Both court and visitors may perform in person name searches. Search fee: $1.00 per name per year. Civil index on docket books. Mail Turnaround time 2 weeks. Public use terminal has civil records. Access civil cases at http://cvpublicaccess.co.clark.nv.us/pa/. Search calendars free at http://redrock.co.clark.nv.us/jcCalendar/CalendarSearch.aspx. DOB may sometimes appear in index search results.
Criminal Name Search: Access: Mail, in person, online. Only the court performs in person name searches; visitors may not. Search fee: $1.00 per name per year. Required to search: name, years to search, DOB, SSN. Criminal docket on books, microfilm. Note: Only court personnel can search for cases prior to Oct 2008. Mail Turnaround time 1-10 days. Access to criminal cases online is same as civil, see above. Online results show middle initial.

Searchlight Justice Court PO Box 815, 1090 Cottonwood Cove Rd, Searchlight, NV 89046; 702-297-1252; fax: 702-297-1022; 7AM-5PM M-TH (PST). *Misdemeanor, Civil Actions under $10,000, Eviction, Small Claims.* www.clarkcountycourts.us/
General Information: No sealed records released. Will not fax documents. Court makes copy: $1.00 per page. Certification fee: $3.00 per cert plus copy fee. Payee: Searchlight Justice Court. No Personal checks, Visa/MC accepted. Prepayment required. Mail requests: SASE required.
Civil Name Search: Access: Fax, mail, in person, online. Only the court performs in person name searches; visitors may not. Search fee: $1.00 per name per year. Civil records on computer from 1988, prior to 1988 filed by case number. Mail Turnaround time 1-2 weeks. Access civil cases at http://cvpublicaccess.co.clark.nv.us/pa/. Search calendars free at http://redrock.co.clark.nv.us/jcCalendar/CalendarSearch.aspx.
Criminal Name Search: Access: Fax, mail, in person, online. Only the court performs in person name searches; visitors may not. Search fee: $1.00 per name per year. Required to search: name, years to search, DOB; also helpful: SSN. Criminal records computerized from 1988, prior to 1988 filed by case number. Mail Turnaround time 1-2 weeks. Access to Misdemeanor cases online is same as civil, see above. Online results show middle initial, DOB.

Boulder City Municipal Court 501 Avenue G, Boulder City, NV 89005; 702-293-9278; fax: 702-293-9345; 7AM-6PM M-TH (PST). *Misdemeanor, Traffic, Infractions.* www.bcnv.org/MunicipalCourt/
General Information: Citation inquiry online at www.bouldercity-nv.gov/municipalcourt/CitationInquiry.asp coming soon.

Boulder Township Municipal Court 501 Avenue G, Boulder City, NV 89005; 702-455-8000; fax: 702-455-8003; *Misdemeanor, Traffic, Infractions.* http://nevadajudiciary.us/index.php/municipal/

Henderson Municipal Court PO Box 95959 MS621, 243 Water St, 2nd Fl, Henderson, NV 89015; 702-267-3300; fax: 702-267-3303; 7:45-5PM M-Th, closed Fri (PST). *Misdemeanor, Traffic, Infractions.* www.cityofhenderson.com/municipal_court/index.php

General Information: Online access to court records and calendars is free at http://hmc.cityofhenderson.com/pa/.

Las Vegas Municipal Court 200 Lewis Ave, Regional Justice Center, 1st Fl, Las Vegas, NV 89155; 702-229-6421; fax: 702-464-2538; 8AM-5PM (PST). *Misdemeanor, Traffic, Infractions.* www.lasvegasnevada.gov/Government/municipalcourt.htm
General Information: Helpful records research form is free at www.lasvegasnevada.gov/files/Public_Records_Request_Form.pdf.

Mesquite Municipal Court 500 Hillside Dr, Mesquite, NV 89027; 702-346-5291; fax: 702-346-6587; 8AM-5PM (PST). *Misdemeanor, Traffic, Infractions.* www.mesquitenv.com/GeneralInfo/MunicipalCourt

North Las Vegas Municipal Court 2332 Las Vegas Blvd. North, Ste 100, North Las Vegas, NV 89030; 702-633-1130; fax: 702-399-6296; 7AM-5PM (PST). *Misdemeanor, Traffic, Infractions.* www.cityofnorthlasvegas.com/Departments/MunicipalCourt/MunicipalCourt.shtm
General Information: Search names online free at www.cityofnorthlasvegas.com/pa/.

Douglas County

9th Judicial District Court PO Box 218, Minden, NV 89423; 775-782-9820; fax: 775-782-9954; 8AM-5PM (PST). *Felony, Gross Misdemeanor, Civil Actions over $10,000, Probate.*
http://cltr.co.douglas.nv.us/courtclerk/default.asp
General Information: Misdemeanors are handled by the East Fork Justice Court and Tahoe Township Justice Court. Probate uses same fax number. No sealed records released. Will fax documents after all payments received. Court makes copy: $1.00 per page. Certification fee: $3.00 per document plus copy fee. If document is presented to clerk for certification (no reproduction needed) fee is $5.00. Exemplification is $6.00. Payee: Douglas County Court Clerk. Business checks accepted. No credit cards accepted. Prepayment required. Mail requests: SASE required.
Civil Name Search: Access: Mail, in person. Only the court performs in person name searches; visitors may not. Search fee: $1.00 per name per year. Civil index on cards from 1962, docket books prior to 1962, archived from mid-1850s. On computer back to 1996. Mail Turnaround time 2 days.
Criminal Name Search: Access: Mail, in person. Only the court performs in person name searches; visitors may not. Search fee: $1.00 per name per year. Required to search: name, years to search, DOB. Criminal records indexed on cards from 1962, docket books prior to 1962, archived from mid-1850s. On computer back to 1996. Mail Turnaround time 2 days.

East Fork Justice Court PO Box 218, 1625 8th St, Minden, NV 89423; 775-782-9955; fax: 775-782-9947; 8AM-5PM (PST). *Misdemeanor, Civil Actions under $10,000, Eviction, Small Claims.*
www.douglascountynv.gov/sites/EFJC/Contact_Us_EFJC.cfm
General Information: No sealed records released. Will fax out docs if prepaid. Court makes copy: $.30 per page. Certification fee: $3.00 per doc plus copy fee; Exemplification fee, $6.00. Payee: East Fork Justice Court. Local personal or business checks accepted. Visa/MC accepted. Prepayment required. Mail requests: SASE required.
Civil Name Search: Access: Mail, in person. Only the court performs in person name searches; visitors may not. Search fee: $1.00 per name per year per index. Required to search: name, years to search, DOB or SSN. Computerized records from 1996. Mail Turnaround time 5-7 days.
Criminal Name Search: Access: Mail, in person. Only the court performs in person name searches; visitors may not. Search fee: $1.00 per name per year per index. Required to search: name, years to search, DOB or SSN. Computerized records from 1996. Mail Turnaround time 5-7 days.

Tahoe Justice Court PO Box 7169, 175 US Hwy 50, Stateline, NV 89449; 775-586-7200; fax: 775-586-7203; 8AM-5PM (PST). *Misdemeanor, Civil Actions under $10,000, Eviction, Small Claims.*
www.douglascountynv.gov/sites/main/
General Information: Window for walk-in service opens at 8:45. No sealed records released. Will not fax documents. Court makes copy: $.30 per page. Certification fee: $3.00 per doc. Payee: Tahoe Justice Court. Local Personal checks, Visa/MC accepted. Prepayment required. Mail requests: SASE required.
Civil Name Search: Access: Phone, mail, in person. Only the court performs in person name searches; visitors may not. Search fee: $1.00 per name per year per case. Required to search: name or case number, years to search. Civil index on cards from 1985-1995; 1995-present on computer. Prior to 1985 some records in docket books, some on microfilm. Mail Turnaround time 2 weeks or less.
Criminal Name Search: Access: Phone, mail, in person. Only the court performs in person name searches; visitors may not. Search fee: $1.00 per name per year. Required to search: name or case number, years to search, DOB. Criminal records on docket cards 1985-1995; 1995 to present on

computer. Pre-1985 records on books and microfilm. Mail Turnaround time 2 weeks.

Elko County

4th Judicial District Court 571 Idaho St, 3rd Fl, Elko, NV 89801; 775-753-4600; fax: 775-753-4610; 9AM-5PM (PST). *Felony, Gross Misdemeanor, Civil Actions over $10,000, Probate.*
www.elkocountynv.net/
General Information: Probate fax is same as main fax number. The clerk's office is separate from the court No sealed records released. Fee to fax out file $1.00 per page. Court makes copy: $1.00 per page. Self serve copy: $.50 per page.Exemplified copies are $6.00 Certification fee: $3.00 for cert plus copy fee if court prepares copies; $5.00 cert if you prepare copies. Payee: Elko County Clerk. Personal checks, Visa/MC accepted. Prepayment required. Prepay accounts are available. Mail requests: SASE required.
Civil Name Search: Access: Phone, mail, in person, email. Both court and visitors may perform in person name searches. Search fee: $1.00 per name per year. Fee is for years prior to 10/01/91. Civil records on computer back to 1970; prior on index cards. Note: Direct email requests to clerk@elkocountynv.net. Mail Turnaround time 1-2 days.
Criminal Name Search: Access: Phone, mail, in person. Both court and visitors may perform in person name searches. Search fee: $1.00 per name per year. Fee is for years prior to 1980. Criminal records computerized from 1970; prior on index cards. Mail Turnaround time 1 day.

Carlin Justice Court PO Box 789, Carlin, NV 89822; 775-754-6321; fax: 775-754-6893; 9AM-5PM (PST). *Misdemeanor, Civil Actions under $10,000, Eviction, Small Claims.*
General Information: Court may be combined with Carlin Municipal Court. Court requires all record requests to be in writing. Will fax documents to local or toll-free number. Court makes copy: $.30 per page. Self serve copy: same. Certification fee: $3.00 per document plus copy fee. Payee: Carlin Court. Personal checks accepted upon approval. Major credit cards accepted. Prepayment required. Mail requests: SASE required.
Civil Name Search: Access: Mail, in person. Both court and visitors may perform in person name searches. Search fee: $1.00 per name per year. Civil records on computer starting in 1994, prior are in books. Mail Turnaround time 1 week.
Criminal Name Search: Access: Mail, in person. Only the court performs in person name searches; visitors may not. Search fee: $1.00 per name per year. Required to search: name, years to search, DOB, SSN. Criminal records on computer starting in 1994, prior are in books. Mail Turnaround time 1 week.

Eastline Justice Court PO Box 2300, West Wendover, NV 89883; 775-664-2305; fax: 775-664-2979; 8AM-5PM (PST). *Misdemeanor, Civil Actions under $10,000, Eviction, Small Claims.*
General Information: Has a sister court named West Wendover Municipal. The court does not charge separately for the Justice or Municipal Court. No open case records released. Will fax documents to local or toll-free number. Court makes copy: $.30 per page.If a copy is required for all documents in a file, the fee is $5.00. Certification fee: $3.00 per document. Payee: Eastline Justice Court. Personal checks accepted. Major credit and debit cards accepted, there is a $5.00 processing fee. Prepayment required. Mail requests: SASE required.
Civil Name Search: Access: Mail, in person. Only the court performs in person name searches; visitors may not. Search fee: $7.00 per name. Civil cases indexed by defendant. Civil records on computer from 1992, prior on index, docket book. Mail Turnaround time 1 week.
Criminal Name Search: Access: Mail, in person. Only the court performs in person name searches; visitors may not. Search fee: $7.00 per name. Required to search: name, years to search; also helpful: DOB. Criminal records computerized from 1992, prior on index, docket book. Mail Turnaround time 1 week.

Elko Justice Court PO Box 176, 571 Idaho St, Elko, NV 89803; 775-738-8403; fax: 775-738-8416; 8AM-5PM (PST). *Misdemeanor, Civil Actions under $10,000, Eviction, Small Claims.*
www.elkojusticeandmunicipalcourt.net/
General Information: Court is co-located with Elko Municipal Court. No confidential evaluations or sealed records released. Will fax documents to local or toll-free number. Court makes copy: $1.00 per page. Certification fee: $3.00; exemplification fee- $5.00. Payee: Elko Justice Court. Personal checks accepted. Major credit cards accepted. Prepayment required. Mail requests: SASE required.
Civil Name Search: Access: Fax, mail, in person. Both court and visitors may perform in person name searches. Search fee: $1.00 per name per year. Fee is per court. Civil records on computer after 1994, on docket books after 1980s, prior in county archives. Mail Turnaround time 7-10 days.
Criminal Name Search: Access: Mail, in person. Both court and visitors may perform in person name searches. Search fee: $1.00 per name per year. Fee is per court. Required to search: name, years to search; DOB or

SSN also required. Criminal records on computer after 1994, on docket books after 1980s, prior in county archives. Mail Turnaround time 7-10 days.

Jackpot Justice Court PO Box 229, Jackpot, NV 89825; 775-755-2456; fax: 775-755-2455; 9AM-N, 1-5PM (PST). *Misdemeanor, Civil Actions under $10,000, Eviction, Small Claims.*
General Information: Restrictions on active cases. No fee to fax documents. Court makes copy: $.25 per page. Certification fee: $3.00. Payee: Jackpot Justice Court. Business checks accepted. No credit cards accepted. Prepayment required. Mail requests: SASE required.
Civil Name Search: Access: Mail, in person. Only the court performs in person name searches; visitors may not. Search fee: $7.00 per name per year. Civil cases indexed by defendant. Civil index on docket books per year since 1988; on computer back to 1995. Mail Turnaround time 1 week.
Criminal Name Search: Access: Fax, mail, in person. Only the court performs in person name searches; visitors may not. Search fee: $7.00 per name per year. Required to search: name, years to search, DOB. Criminal docket on books per year since 1988; on computer back to 1995. Mail Turnaround time 1 week.

Wells Township Justice and Municipal Court PO Box 297, Wells, NV 89835; 775-752-3726; fax: 775-752-3363; 9AM-N,1-5PM (PST). *Misdemeanor, Civil Actions under $10,000, Eviction, Small Claims, Traffic, Ordinance.*
General Information: Court is a combined Justice and Municipal Court. No pending, confidential records released. Will not fax documents. Court makes copy: $.30 per page. Certification fee: $3.00. Payee: Wells Justice Court. Personal checks not accepted. No credit cards accepted. Prepayment required. Mail requests: SASE required.
Civil Name Search: Access: Mail, in person. Only the court performs in person name searches; visitors may not. Search fee: $1.00 per name per year. Civil records on computer from 1989, prior on docket books. Note: In person access may require fee for clerical assistance. Mail Turnaround time 2 weeks.
Criminal Name Search: Access: Mail, in person. Only the court performs in person name searches; visitors may not. Search fee: $1.00 per name per year. Required to search: name, years to search; also DOB or SSN. Criminal records computerized from 1989, prior on docket books. Note: In person access may require fee for clerical assistance. Mail Turnaround time 2 weeks.

Jarbidge Justice Court.
General Information: This is an "unincorporated ghost town." No criminal or civil cases in more than 20 years. Mostly marriages, fish and game violations. Only 40 year round residents. All records at the Elko Justice Court.

Mountain City Justice Court.
General Information: Closed. Records held in Elko Justice Court, 775-738-8403.

Carlin Municipal Court PO Box 789, Carlin, NV 89822; 775-754-6321; fax: 775-754-6893; *Misdemeanor, Traffic, Infraction.*
http://nevadajudiciary.us/index.php/municipal/
General Information: Records here may now be combined with those of the Carlin Justice Court Clerk.

Eastline Township Municipal Court PO Box 2300, West Wendover, NV 89883; 775-664-2305; fax: 775-664-2979; *Misdemeanor, Traffic, Infraction.* http://nevadajudiciary.us/index.php/municipal/
General Information: This court is co-located with Wet Wendover Municipal Court.

Elko Municipal Court PO Box 176, 571 Idaho St, Elko, NV 89801; 775-738-8403; fax: 775-738-8416; *Misdemeanor, Traffic, Infraction.*
www.elkojusticeandmunicipalcourt.net/
General Information: Court is co-located with Elko Township Justice Court.

West Wendover Municipal Court PO Box 2300, West Wendover, NV 89773; 775-664-2305; fax: 775-664-2979; *Misdemeanor, Traffic, Infraction.* http://nevadajudiciary.us/index.php/municipal/
General Information: Records for Eastline Municipal Court also here.

Esmeralda County

5th Judicial District Court PO Box 547, Goldfield, NV 89013; 775-485-6309; fax: 775-485-6376; 8AM-5PM; Closed 12-1PM (PST). *Felony, Gross Misdemeanor, Civil Actions over $10,000, Probate.*
www.accessesmeralda.com/Court.htm
General Information: No juvenile or pre-sentence records released. Fee to fax out file $1.00 per page. Court makes copy: $1.00 per page. Certification fee: $3.00. Payee: Esmeralda County Clerk. Personal checks accepted. Credit cards accepted. Prepayment required. Mail requests: SASE required.
Civil Name Search: Access: Fax, mail, in person. Both court and visitors may perform in person name searches. Search fee: $1.00 per name per

year. Civil index in docket books from 1800s. Mail Turnaround time 2 weeks.

Criminal Name Search: Access: Fax, mail, in person. Both court and visitors may perform in person name searches. Search fee: $1.00. Criminal docket on books from 1800s. Mail Turnaround time 2 weeks.

Esmeralda Justice Court PO Box 370, Goldfield, NV 89013; 775-485-6359; fax: 775-485-3462; 8AM-5PM (PST). *Misdemeanor, Civil Actions under $10,000, Eviction, Small Claims.*

General Information: No sealed records released. Will fax documents $1.00 per page. Court makes copy: $.30 per page. Certification fee: $3.00. Payee: Justice Court. Only cashiers checks and money orders accepted. No credit cards accepted. Prepayment required. Mail requests: SASE required.

Civil Name Search: Access: Phone, fax, mail, in person. Only the court performs in person name searches; visitors may not. Search fee: $1.00 per name per year. Civil cases indexed by plaintiff. Civil index on docket books since 1987. Mail Turnaround time 1 day.

Criminal Name Search: Access: Phone, fax, mail, in person. Only the court performs in person name searches; visitors may not. Search fee: $1.00 per name per year. Criminal docket on books since 1987. Mail Turnaround time 1 day.

Eureka County

7th Judicial District Court PO Box 677, Eureka, NV 89316; 775-237-5262; fax: 775-237-6015; 8AM-N, 1-5PM (PST). *Felony, Gross Misdemeanor, Civil Actions over $10,000, Probate.*

General Information: No juvenile, sealed records released. Will fax to toll-free number. Court makes copy: $1.00 per page. Certification fee: $5.00 per document includes copy fee. Payee: Eureka County Clerk. Personal checks, Visa/MC accepted. Prepayment required. Mail requests: SASE required.

Civil Name Search: Access: Phone, fax, mail, in person. Both court and visitors may perform in person name searches. Search fee: $1.00 per name per year. Civil records archived from 1873. Note: Public can search docket books. Mail Turnaround time 1 day.

Criminal Name Search: Access: Phone, fax, mail, in person. Both court and visitors may perform in person name searches. Search fee: $1.00 per name per year. Criminal records archived from 1873. Note: Public can search docket books. Mail Turnaround time 1 day.

Beowawe Justice Court PO Box 211338, Crescent Valley, NV 89821; 775-468-0244; fax: 775-468-0323; 6AM-N, 12:30PM-4:30PM (PST). *Misdemeanor, Civil Actions under $10,000, Eviction, Small Claims.*
www.co.eureka.nv.us/court/beowawe.htm

General Information: All records are open to the public, no records are restricted. Will fax documents to local or toll-free number. Court makes copy: $.30 per page. Certification fee: $3.00. Payee: Beowawe Justice Court. Only cashiers checks and money orders accepted. Visa/MC accepted. Prepayment required. Mail requests: SASE required.

Civil Name Search: Access: Mail, in person. Only the court performs in person name searches; visitors may not. Search fee: $1.00 per name per year. Civil cases indexed by plaintiff. Civil records go back to 2/1994; computerized records go back to 1997. Mail Turnaround time 5 days.

Criminal Name Search: Access: Mail, in person. Only the court performs in person name searches; visitors may not. Search fee: $1.00 per name per year. Criminal records go back to 11/1993; computerized records go back to 1997. Mail Turnaround time 5 days.

Eureka Justice Court PO Box 496, Eureka, NV 89316; 775-237-5540; fax: 775-237-6016; 8AM-N,1-5PM (PST). *Misdemeanor, Civil Actions under $10,000, Eviction, Small Claims.*

General Information: Will fax documents $1.00 per page. Court makes copy: $.25 per page for 1-10 pages, $.20 per page for 11-25, $.15 per page for 26-50, and $.10 per page over 50. Certification fee: $3.00. Payee: Eureka Justice Court. Cashiers checks and money orders accepted. Major credit cards accepted. Prepayment required. Mail requests: SASE required.

Civil Name Search: Access: Phone, mail, in person. Only the court performs in person name searches; visitors may not. Search fee: $1.00 per year searched. Civil records on computer since 1995; on docket books, archived from 1940. Mail Turnaround time 2 days.

Criminal Name Search: Access: Phone, mail, in person. Only the court performs in person name searches; visitors may not. Search fee: $1.00 per year searched. Criminal records on computer since 1995; on docket books, archived from 1940. Mail Turnaround time 2 days.

Humboldt County

6th Judicial District Court 50 W 5th St, Winnemucca, NV 89445; 775-623-6343; fax: 775-623-6309; 8AM-5PM (PST). *Felony, Gross Misdemeanor, Civil Actions over $10,000, Probate.*

General Information: No adoption, sealed records released. Will fax documents $1.00 per page, prepaid only. Court makes copy: $1.00 per page. Certification fee: $3.00 per cert plus copy fee. Payee: Humboldt County

Clerk. Personal checks accepted, credit cards are not. Prepayment required. Mail requests: SASE not required.

Civil Name Search: Access: Phone, fax, mail, in person. Only the court performs in person name searches; visitors may not. No search fee unless old record then $1.00 per name per year if over 22 years ago. Required to search: name, years to search; also helpful- any personal identifiers- DOB, etc. Civil records on computer from 1984, on microfiche from 1900. Mail Turnaround time 1 day. Older records - over 10 years old - may not contain DOB.

Criminal Name Search: Access: Phone, fax, mail, in person. Both court and visitors may perform in person name searches. No search fee unless old record then $1.00 per name per year if over 22 years ago. Required to search: name, years to search; also helpful- any personal identifiers- DOB, etc. Criminal records computerized from 1984, on microfiche from 1900. Mail Turnaround time 1 day, immediate if phone request and record on computer. Older records - over 10 years old - may not contain DOB.

Union Justice Court PO Box 1218, Winnemucca, NV 89446; 775-623-6059; civil phone: 775-623-6379; fax: 775-623-6458; 8AM-5PM (PST). *Misdemeanor, Civil Actions under $10,000, Eviction, Small Claims.*
www.hcnv.us/justice/justice_home.htm

General Information: May also fax to 775-623-6439. No fee to fax documents. Court makes copy: $.30 per page. Certification fee: $3.00 per cert plus copy fee; exemplified- $9.00. Payee: Justice Court. Personal checks accepted. Add a $3.00 processing fee if you pay via credit card. Prepayment required. Mail requests: SASE required.

Civil Name Search: Access: Fax, mail, in person. Only the court performs in person name searches; visitors may not. Search fee: $1.00 per name per year; minimum of $7.00. Required to search: name, years to search; also helpful: address. Civil records on computer from 1988, prior on docket books. Mail Turnaround time 1-2 days.

Criminal Name Search: Access: Fax, mail, in person. Only the court performs in person name searches; visitors may not. Search fee: $1.00 per name per year; minimum of $7.00. Required to search: name, years to search, DOB; also helpful: address, SSN. Criminal records computerized from 1988. Mail Turnaround time 1-2 days.

McDermitt Justice Court *Misdemeanor, Civil Actions under $10,000, Eviction, Small Claims.*
General Information: Closed case records are at the Union Justice Court.

Paradise Valley Justice Court *Misdemeanor, Civil Actions under $10,000, Eviction, Small Claims.*
General Information: Closed case records are at the Union Justice Court.

Lander County

6th Judicial District Court 315 S Humboldt, Battle Mountain, NV 89820; 775-635-5738; fax: 775-635-5761; 8AM-5PM (PST). *Felony, Gross Misdemeanor, Civil Actions over $10,000, Probate.*
http://landercountynv.org/lander-county-elected-officials/county-clerk

General Information: Probate fax is same as main fax number. For questions, email clerk@landercountynv.org. No juvenile, sealed records released. Fee to fax out file $1.00 per page. Court makes copy: $1.00 per page. Certification fee: $3.00 per document plus copy fee. Payee: Lander County Clerk. Personal checks accepted, credit cards are not. Prepayment required. Mail requests: SASE required.

Civil Name Search: Access: Phone, fax, mail, in person. Only the court performs in person name searches; visitors may not. No search fee. Civil records on computer from 1990, on index from 1986-1990, on microfiche until 1985, prior records on docket books. Mail Turnaround time 7 days.

Criminal Name Search: Access: Phone, fax, mail, in person. Only the court performs in person name searches; visitors may not. No search fee. Criminal records computerized from 1990, on index from 1986-1990, on microfiche until 1985, prior records on docket books. Mail Turnaround time 7 days.

Argenta Justice Court 315 S Humboldt, Battle Mountain, NV 89820; 775-635-5151; fax: 775-635-0604; 8AM-5PM (PST). *Misdemeanor, Civil Actions under $10,000, Eviction, Small Claims.*

General Information: No unserved search warrant records released. Fee to fax out file $1.00 per page. Court makes copy: $.50 per page. Certification fee: $1.00 per page plus copy fee. Payee: Argenta Justice Court. Only cashiers checks and money orders accepted. No credit cards accepted. Prepayment required. Mail requests: SASE required.

Civil Name Search: Access: Phone, mail, in person. Only the court performs in person name searches; visitors may not. Search fee: $1.00 per name per year. Civil records on computer from 1988, prior on docket books. Mail Turnaround time 1 day.

Criminal Name Search: Access: Phone, mail, in person. Only the court performs in person name searches; visitors may not. Search fee: $1.00 per name per year. Required to search: name, years to search; also helpful: DOB, SSN. Criminal records computerized from 1988, prior on docket books. Mail Turnaround time 1 day.

Austin Justice Court PO Box 100, Austin, NV 89310; 775-964-2380; fax: 775-964-2327; 8AM-4PM M, 8AM-N T-TH (PST). *Misdemeanor, Civil Actions under $10,000, Eviction, Small Claims.*

General Information: No fees for requests from government agencies. Access to view records with SSNs is restricted. Will fax documents to local or toll free line. Court makes copy: $.25 per page. Self serve copy: same. No certification fee . Payee: Austin Justice Court. Personal checks accepted, credit cards are not. Mail requests: SASE required.

Civil Name Search: Access: Phone, mail, fax, in person. Only the court performs in person name searches; visitors may not. No search fee. Civil cases indexed by plaintiff and defendant. Civil index on docket books, computerized since 1988. Mail Turnaround time 1 week.

Criminal Name Search: Access: Phone, mail, fax, in person. Only the court performs in person name searches; visitors may not. No search fee. Criminal records computerized from 1988, easily available since 1976. Mail Turnaround time 1 week.

Lincoln County

7th Judicial District Court PO Box 90, 181 N Main St, Ste 101, Pioche, NV 89043; 775-962-5390; fax: 775-962-5180; 8AM-5PM (PST). *Felony, Gross Misdemeanor, Civil Actions over $10,000, Probate.*
www.lincolncountynv.org/clerk/index.html

General Information: No juvenile, sealed records released. Fee to fax out file $1.00 per page. Court makes copy: $1.00 per page. Self serve copy: same. Certification fee: $5.00. Payee: Lincoln County Clerk. Personal checks accepted, credit cards are not. Prepayment required. Mail requests: SASE required.

Civil Name Search: Access: Mail, in person. Both court and visitors may perform in person name searches. Search fee: $1.00 per name per year. Civil index in docket books from 1876. Records are computerized since 2001. Mail Turnaround time 1-2 days.

Criminal Name Search: Access: Mail, in person. Both court and visitors may perform in person name searches. Search fee: $1.00 per name per year. Criminal docket on books from 1876. Records are computerized since 2001. Mail Turnaround time 1-2 days.

Meadow Valley Justice Court PO Box 36, Pioche, NV 89043; 775-962-5140; fax: 775-962-5559; 8AM-5PM (PST). *Misdemeanor, Civil Actions under $10,000, Eviction, Small Claims.*

General Information: Juvenile records are not released. Will fax documents to local or toll-free number. Court makes copy: $.30 per page. Self serve copy: same. Certification fee: $3.00. Payee: Meadow Valley Justice Court. Personal checks accepted. Major credit cards accepted. Prepayment required. Mail requests: SASE required.

Civil Name Search: Access: Fax, mail, in person. Only the court performs in person name searches; visitors may not. Search fee: $1.00 per name per year. Civil records archived from 1982 on docket books. Mail Turnaround time 1-5 days.

Criminal Name Search: Access: Fax, mail, in person. Only the court performs in person name searches; visitors may not. Search fee: $1.00 per name per year. Criminal records are all originals; they go back to 1982; on computer back to 2000. Mail Turnaround time 1-5 days.

Pahranagat Valley Justice Court PO Box 449, Alamo, NV 89001; 775-725-3357; fax: 775-725-3566; 8AM-5PM (PST). *Misdemeanor, Civil Actions under $10,000, Eviction, Small Claims.*

General Information: No personal notes released. Will fax out documents $1.00 per page. Court makes copy: $.30 per page. Certification fee: $3.00 per page. Payee: Pahranagat Valley Justice Court. Personal checks accepted, but cashiers ck and money orders preferred. Visa/MC accepted. Prepayment required. Mail requests: SASE required.

Civil Name Search: Access: Fax, mail, in person. Only the court performs in person name searches; visitors may not. Search fee: $1.00 per name per year. Civil cases indexed by defendant. Civil index on docket books to 1980; on computer back to 1997. Mail Turnaround time 1-3 days.

Criminal Name Search: Access: Fax, mail, in person. Only the court performs in person name searches; visitors may not. Search fee: $1.00 per name per year. Required to search: name, years to search, DOB; also helpful: SSN, signed release. Criminal docket on books to 1980; on computer back to 1997. Mail Turnaround time 1-3 days.

Caliente Municipal Court PO Box 1006, Caliente, NV 89008; 775-726-3193; ; 8AM-5PM (PST). *Misdemeanor, Traffic, Infractions.*
http://nevadajudiciary.us/index.php/municipal/

Lyon County

3rd Judicial District Court 27 S Main St, Yerington, NV 89447; 775-463-6503; fax: 775-463-3643; 8AM-5PM (PST). *Felony, Gross Misdemeanor, Civil Actions over $10,000, Probate.*
www.lyon-county.org/index.asp?nid=675

General Information: No adoption, juvenile or sealed records released. Will fax documents $3.00 per page. Court makes copy: $1.00 per page. Certification fee: $3.00 per document plus copy fee. Payee: Lyon County

Clerk. Personal checks accepted. Major credit cards accepted. Prepayment required. Mail requests: SASE required.

Civil Name Search: Access: Phone, mail, in person. Only the court performs in person name searches; visitors may not. Search fee: $1.00 per name per year. Civil records on computer back to 1989. Mail Turnaround time 1 week for mail requests, immediate by phone if on computer.

Criminal Name Search: Access: Phone, mail, in person. Only the court performs in person name searches; visitors may not. Search fee: $1.00 per name per year. Criminal records computerized from 1985. Mail Turnaround time 1 week for mail requests, immediate for phone request if on computer.

Canal Township Justice Court 565 E Main St, Fernley, NV 89408; 775-575-3355; fax: 775-575-3359; 8AM-5PM (PST). *Misdemeanor, Civil Actions under $10,000, Eviction, Small Claims.*
www.lyon-county.org/index.asp?nid=235

General Information: No police reports or sealed records released. Will fax documents $3.00 per page. Court makes copy: $.30 per page. Certification fee: $3.00 per cert. Payee: Fernley Justice Court. Personal checks accepted. Out of state checks not accepted. Visa/MC accepted. Prepayment required. Mail requests: SASE required.

Civil Name Search: Access: Phone, mail, in person. Only the court performs in person name searches; visitors may not. Search fee: $1.00 per name per year. Civil records on computer from 1992, prior on docket books. Mail Turnaround time 1 week.

Criminal Name Search: Access: Phone, mail, in person. Only the court performs in person name searches; visitors may not. Search fee: $1.00 per name per year. Required to search: name, years to search; also helpful: SSN. Criminal records computerized from 1992, prior on docket books. Mail Turnaround time 1 week.

Dayton Township Justice Court 235 Main St, Dayton, NV 89403; 775-246-6233; fax: 775-246-6203; 8AM-5PM (PST). *Misdemeanor, Civil Actions under $10,000, Eviction, Small Claims.*
www.lyon-county.org/index.asp?nid=230

General Information: No sealed records released. Will fax back documents for no fee. Court makes copy: $.30 per page. Certification fee: $3.00 per certification. Payee: Dayton Township Justice Court. Personal checks accepted. Visa/MC accepted with $3.00 surcharge. Prepayment required. Mail requests: SASE required.

Civil Name Search: Access: Phone, fax, mail, in person. Only the court performs in person name searches; visitors may not. Search fee: $1.00 per name per year,. Civil records on computer from 1991, prior on docket books by year. Mail Turnaround time within 1 week.

Criminal Name Search: Access: Phone, fax, mail, in person. Only the court performs in person name searches; visitors may not. Search fee: $1.00 per name per year, back 7 years. Criminal records computerized from 1991, prior on docket books by year. Mail Turnaround time within 1 week.

Walker River Justice Court 30 Nevin Way, Yerington, NV 89447; 775-463-6639; fax: 775-463-6638; 8AM-5PM (PST). *Misdemeanor, Civil Actions under $10,000, Eviction, Small Claims.*
www.lyon-county.org/index.asp?nid=240

General Information: Effective July 1, 2006 the Smith Valley Justice Court and the Mason Valley Justice Court merged to form the Walker River Justice Court in Yerington. Records to be consolidated, but a separate index search is suggested. No police, sheriff reports released. Will fax documents $1.00 per page. Court makes copy: $.30 per page. Certification fee: $3.00. Payee: Walker River Justice Court. No personal checks. Major credit cards accepted. Prepayment required. Mail requests: SASE required.

Civil Name Search: Access: Phone, mail, in person. Only the court performs in person name searches; visitors may not. Search fee: $1.00 per name per year. Civil records on computer from 1992, archives from 1900s. Mail Turnaround time 3 days, immediate for phone requests.

Criminal Name Search: Access: Fax, mail, in person, Fax. Only the court performs in person name searches; visitors may not. Search fee: $1.00 per name per year. Required to search: name, years to search; also helpful: DOB, SSN. Criminal records computerized from 1992, archives from 1900s. Mail Turnaround time 3 days, immediate for phone requests.

Fernley Municipal Court 595 Silver Lace Blvd, Fernley, NV 89408; 775-784-9879; fax: 775-784-9879 *Misdemeanor, Traffic, Infractions.*
http://nevadajudiciary.us/index.php/municipal/

Yerington Municipal Court 102 S Main, Yerington, NV 89447; 775-463-351; *Misdemeanor, Traffic, Infractions.*
http://nevadajudiciary.us/index.php/municipal/

Mineral County

5th Judicial District Court PO Box 1450, Hawthorne, NV 89415; 775-945-2446; fax: 775-945-0706; 8AM-5PM (PST). *Felony, Gross Misdemeanor, Civil Actions over $10,000, Probate.*

General Information: Probate fax is same as main fax number. No juvenile records released. Will fax documents $1.50 per page. Court makes copy: $1.00 per page. Self serve copy: same. Certification fee: $3.00 per certification plus copy fee. Payee: Mineral County Clerk. Personal checks accepted, credit cards are not. Prepayment required. Mail requests: SASE not required.

Civil Name Search: Access: Phone, fax, mail, in person. Both court and visitors may perform in person name searches. Search fee: $1.00 per name per year. Civil records go back to 1911; computerized records since 1993. Mail Turnaround time 1 day.

Criminal Name Search: Access: Phone, fax, mail, in person. Both court and visitors may perform in person name searches. Search fee: $1.00 per name per year. Criminal records go back to 1911; computerized records since 1993. Mail Turnaround time 1 day.

Hawthorne Justice Court PO Box 1660, Hawthorne, NV 89415; 775-945-3859; fax: 775-945-0700; 8AM-5PM (PST). *Misdemeanor, Civil Actions under $10,000, Eviction, Small Claims.*

General Information: This court holds records from Schurz Justice Court. No pending case or sealed records released. Will fax documents to local or toll-free number. Court makes copy: $.25 per page. Legal size- $1.00 per page. No certification fee . Payee: Hawthorne Justice Court. Personal checks accepted, credit cards are not. Prepayment required. Mail requests: SASE required.

Civil Name Search: Access: Phone, mail, in person. Both court and visitors may perform in person name searches. No search fee. Civil cases indexed by defendant. Civil records on computer from 1994, prior on docket books. Mail Turnaround time 1-5 days.

Criminal Name Search: Access: Phone, mail, in person, fax. Both court and visitors may perform in person name searches. No search fee. Criminal records computerized from 1992. Mail Turnaround time 1-5 days.

Mina Justice Court.
General Information: Closed. All records at the Hawthorne Justice Court.

Schurz Justice Court.
General Information: Closed - records now housed at Hawthorne Justice Court

Nye County

5th Judicial District Court PO Box 1031, Tonopah, NV 89049; 775-482-8131; probate phone: 775-482-8127; fax: 775-482-8133; 8AM-5PM (PST). *Felony, Gross Misdemeanor, Civil Actions over $10,000, Probate.* www.nyecounty.net/index.asp?NID=92

General Information: Probate fax- 775-482-8133 No adoption or juvenile records released. Will fax documents $2.00 1st page, $1.00 each add'l. Court makes copy: $1.00 per page. Self serve copy: same. Certification fee: $3.00. Payee: Nye County Clerk. Business checks or in state Personal checks accepted, credit cards are not. Prepayment required. Mail requests: SASE required.

Civil Name Search: Access: Phone, fax, mail, in person. Only the court performs in person name searches; visitors may not. Search fee: $1.00 per name per year. Civil records on computer from 1991, on docket books from 1864, some are microfilmed. Mail Turnaround time 1 day.

Criminal Name Search: Access: Phone, fax, mail, in person. Only the court performs in person name searches; visitors may not. Search fee: $1.00 per name per year. Records computerized from 1991, on docket books from 1800s, many are microfilmed. Mail Turnaround time 1 day.

Beatty Justice Court PO Box 805, Beatty, NV 89003; 775-553-2951; fax: 775-553-2136; 8AM-5PM (PST). *Misdemeanor, Civil Actions up to $10,000, Eviction, Small Claims.*

General Information: No sealed, confidential records released. Will fax documents if all fees paid; fax copies are $0.25 per page (no charge to fax original). If project more than 15 minutes, add'l fees may apply. Court makes copy: $.30 per page. Self serve copy: same. Certification fee: $3.00 per document. Payee: Beatty Justice Court. No Personal checks, Visa/MC accepted. Prepayment required. Mail requests: SASE required.

Civil Name Search: Access: Phone, mail, in person. Only the court performs in person name searches; visitors may not. Search fee: $1.00 per name per year. Computer printouts on all civil actions (no way to segregate small claims or evictions) is $0.16 per page. Civil records on computer from 1989, archived from 1950s, some on docket books. Mail Turnaround time 1 week for mail requests, same day for phone requests when possible.

Criminal Name Search: Access: Phone, mail, in person. Only the court performs in person name searches; visitors may not. Search fee: $1.00 per name per year. Required to search: name, years to search, DOB. Criminal records computerized from 1989. Mail Turnaround time 1 week for mail requests, same day for phone request, when possible.

Pahrump Township Justice Court 1520 E Basin Ave, Pahrump, NV 89060; 775-751-7050; fax: 775-751-7059; 8AM-5PM (PST). *Misdemeanor, Civil Actions up to $10,000, Eviction, Small Claims.* www.pahrumpjusticecourt.com/

General Information: Calendar posted Friday for following week. No sealed, confidential records released. Court makes copy: $.30 per page. Self serve copy: same. Certification fee: $3.00 per document. Payee: Pahrump Justice Court. Visa/MC accepted. Prepayment required. Mail requests: SASE required.

Civil Name Search: Access: Phone, mail, in person. Only the court performs in person name searches; visitors may not. Search fee: $1.00 per name per year. Computer printouts on all civil actions (no way to segregate small claims or evictions) is $0.30 per page. Civil records on computer from 1989, archived from 1950s on docket books. Mail Turnaround time 2 weeks for mail requests.

Criminal Name Search: Access: Phone, mail, in person. Only the court performs in person name searches; visitors may not. Search fee: $1.00 per name per year. Required to search: name, years to search, DOB. Criminal records computerized from 1989. Mail Turnaround time 2 weeks for mail requests.

Tonopah Justice Court PO Box 1151, Tonopah, NV 89049; 775-482-8155; fax: 775-482-7349; 8AM-N, 1-5PM (PST). *Misdemeanor, Civil Actions under $10,000, Eviction, Small Claims.* www.nyecounty.net/

General Information: No sealed or confidential records released. Will fax documents to local or toll free line. Will accept fax requests if proof of payment attached. Court makes copy: $.30 per page. Certification fee: $3.00 per cert. Payee: Tonopah Justice Court. Business checks accepted. Major credit cards accepted, 3% fee may be added. Prepayment required. Mail requests: SASE required.

Civil Name Search: Access: Fax, mail, in person. Only the court performs in person name searches; visitors may not. Search fee: $1.00 per name per year. Civil cases indexed by plaintiff. Civil records on computer from 1992, on archives from 1950s, some on docket books. Mail Turnaround time 1-2 weeks if older than 1992.

Criminal Name Search: Access: Fax, mail, in person. Only the court performs in person name searches; visitors may not. Search fee: $1.00 per name per year. Required to search: name, years to search, offense, date of offense; also helpful: DOB, SSN. Criminal records computerized from 1992, on docket books from 1943. Mail Turnaround time 1-2 weeks if older than 1992.

Gabbs Justice Court.
General Information: This court is closed; any records are now at Tonopah 775-482-8155.

Pershing County

6th Judicial District Court PO Box 820, Lovelock, NV 89419; 775-273-2410; fax: 775-273-2434; 9AM-5PM (PST). *Felony, Civil Actions over $10,000, Probate.* http://pershingcounty.net/index.php/District-Court/sixth-judicial-district-court.html

General Information: Misdemeanors are handled by the Lake Township Justice Court. No adoption, juvenile or sealed records released. Will fax documents for $1.00 per page. Court makes copy: $1.00 per page. Self serve copy: same. Certification fee: $3.00 per doc; exemplification- $6.00. Payee: Pershing County District Court. Personal checks accepted, credit cards are not. Prepayment required. Mail requests: SASE required.

Civil Name Search: Access: Phone, fax (3 names or less), mail, in person. Only the court performs in person name searches; visitors may not. Search fee: $1.00 per year per name. Civil records on computer from 1992, microfilmed from 1919-1938, books from 1919. Court will do up to 3 or more searches by phone. Mail Turnaround time 1-3 days.

Criminal Name Search: Access: Phone, fax (3 names or less), mail, in person. Only the court performs in person name searches; visitors may not. Search fee: $1.00 per year per name. Criminal records computerized from 1992, microfilmed from 1919-1938, books from 1919. Note: Court will do up to 3 or more searches by phone. Mail Turnaround time 1-3 days.

Lake Township Justice Court PO Box 8, Lovelock, NV 89419; 775-273-2753; fax: 775-273-0416; 7AM-5:30PM M-TH (PST). *Misdemeanor, Civil Actions under $10,000, Eviction, Small Claims.* http://pershingcounty.net/index.php/Justice-Court/

General Information: No sealed, driver's history or highway patrol records released. Will fax documents to local or toll-free number. Court makes copy: $.30 per page. Certification fee: $3.00. Payee: Lake Township Justice Court. Personal checks accepted; ID required. No credit cards accepted. Prepayment required. Mail requests: SASE required.

Civil Name Search: Access: Phone, mail, in person. Visitors must perform in person searches themselves. Search fee: $1.00 per name per year. Required to search: name, years to search; also helpful: address. Civil records on computer from 1988, on docket books prior. Mail Turnaround time 2 days.

Criminal Name Search: Access: Phone, mail, in person. Visitors must perform in person searches themselves. Search fee: $1.00 per name per year. Required to search: name, years to search; also helpful: DOB. Criminal records computerized from 1988, on docket books prior. Mail Turnaround time 2 days, 30 minutes for phone requests for records prior to 1988.

Storey County

1st Judicial District Court PO Drawer D, Virginia City, NV 89440; 775-847-0969; fax: 775-847-0921; 9AM-5PM (PST). *Felony, Gross Misdemeanor, Civil Actions over $10,000, Probate.*
General Information: Will accept email request - wbacus@storeycounty.org. No juvenile or sealed records released. Will fax documents to local or toll free line, will fax long distance with copy of check. Court makes copy: $1.00 per page. Self serve copy: same. Certification fee: $6.00 per document or $5.00 if copy provided. Payee: Storey County Clerk. Personal checks, Visa/MC accepted. Prepayment required. Mail requests: SASE required.
Civil Name Search: Access: Phone, mail, fax, in person. Both court and visitors may perform in person name searches. Search fee: $1.00 per name per year. Civil records on computer since 1997; prior years on books. Note: Accepts phone search requests only if paid in advance. Will accept email request - wbacus@storeycounty.org. Mail Turnaround time 1 week; 1 day by fax; 5 minutes for phone requests when possible.
Criminal Name Search: Access: Phone, mail, fax, in person. Both court and visitors may perform in person name searches. Search fee: $1.00 per name per year. Required to search: name, years to search, signed release; also helpful: DOB, SSN. Criminal records on computer since 1997; prior years on books. Note: Search by phone only if pre-paid. Mail Turnaround time 1 week; 1 day by fax; 5 minutes for phone requests when possible.

Virginia Township Justice Court PO Box 674, Virginia City, NV 89440; 775-847-0962; fax: 775-847-0915; 9AM-5PM (PST). *Misdemeanor, Civil Actions under $10,000, Eviction, Small Claims.* www.storeycounty.org/
General Information: Will fax documents to local or toll free line. Court makes copy: $.30 per page. Certification fee: $3.00. Payee: Justice Court. Personal checks accepted. Major credit cards accepted for record searches, not for civil fees. Prepayment required. Mail requests: SASE required.
Civil Name Search: Access: Phone, mail, in person. Only the court performs in person name searches; visitors may not. Search fee: $1.00 per name per year. Civil records retained for 7 years, some on docket books. Mail Turnaround time 1 week.
Criminal Name Search: Access: Phone, mail, in person. Only the court performs in person name searches; visitors may not. Search fee: $1.00 per name per year. Required to search: name, years to search, DOB; also helpful: SSN. Criminal records on computer since 1988. Mail Turnaround time 1 week.

Washoe County

2nd Judicial District Court PO Box 30083, 75 Court St, Rm 131, Reno, NV 89520; 775-328-3110; fax: 775-325-6658; 8AM-5PM (PST). *Felony, Gross Misdemeanor, Civil Actions over $10,000, Probate.* www.washoecourts.com
General Information: From 1985 to 1999 need to do self search because computer crashed and cannot be recovered for those years. Family Court located at 1 S Sierra St. No sealed or juvenile records released. Will not fax documents. Court makes copy: $1.00 per page. Certification fee: $3.00 per page plus copy fee. Payee: Washoe County District Court, or WCDC. Business checks, cashiers checks and money orders accepted. Major credit cards accepted in person only. Prepayment required. Mail requests: SASE required.
Civil Name Search: Access: Mail, online, in person. Both court and visitors may perform in person name searches. Search fee: $1.00 per name per year. Civil records on computer back to 1984, microfiche from 1983, archives from 1920. Mail Turnaround time 2-4 weeks. Civil PAT goes back to 2000. CourtConnect online access is at the website. Case data in CourtConnect includes cases filed after 1/2000. From the home page, one can search for detailed case information, but the case number is needed. Calendars also free at website. The states that any commercial use of data obtained through the use of this site is strictly prohibited.
Criminal Name Search: Access: Mail, online, in person. Both court and visitors may perform in person name searches. Search fee: $1.00 per name per year. Criminal records computerized from 1984, microfiche from 1983, archives from 1920. Mail Turnaround time 2-4 weeks. Criminal PAT goes back to same as civil. CourtConnect online access is at the website. Case data in CourtConnect includes cases filed after 1/2000. The states that any commercial use of data obtained through the use of this site is strictly prohibited. Calendars also free at website. Online results show name only.

Incline Village Justice Court 865 Tahoe Blvd, #301, Incline Village, NV 89451; 775-832-4100; fax: 775-832-4162; 9AM-5PM (PST). *Misdemeanor, Civil Actions under $10,000, Eviction, Small Claims.* www.co.washoe.nv.us/ijc

General Information: The court records are not computerized for searching. Paper records must be searched in binders. Will fax documents if prepaid. Court makes copy: $.30 per page. Certification fee: $3.00. Payee: Justice Court. Personal checks accepted; check guarantee card required. No credit cards accepted. Prepayment required. Mail requests: SASE required.
Civil Name Search: Access: Mail, in person. Both court and visitors may perform in person name searches. Search fee: $2.00 per name per year. Civil records on dockets to 1980's. Mail Turnaround time 1-3 days.
Criminal Name Search: Access: Mail, in person. Both court and visitors may perform in person name searches. Search fee: $2.00 per name per year. Required to search: name, years to search; also helpful: DOB. Full dockets of criminal records searchable for 6-7 years, docket sheets available from 1980 to present. Mail Turnaround time 1-3 days.

Reno Justice Court PO Box 30083, Reno, NV 89520; 775-325-6501; criminal phone: 775-325-6500; civil phone: 775-325-6501; criminal fax: 775-325-6510; civil fax: 8AM-4PM M,T, TH, F; 8AM-5PM W; 8AM-4PM M,T, TH, F; 8AM-5PM W (PST). *Misdemeanor, Civil Actions under $10,000, Eviction, Small Claims.* www.washoecounty.us/rjc
General Information: Also hold records for Verdi Justice Court which closed 05/2005. No sealed records released. Will fax documents to local or toll-free number. Court makes copy: $.30 per page. Certification fee: $3.00 per document. Payee: Reno Justice Court. Only cashiers checks and money orders accepted by mail. Major credit cards accepted at the counter. Prepayment required. Mail requests: SASE required.
Civil Name Search: Access: Mail, in person. Both court and visitors may perform in person name searches. Search fee: $2.00 per calendar year. If retrieved from storage add $40.00 per trip. Then $6.00 first file and $3.00 ea add'l if in sequential order, $6.00 if not. Civil cases indexed by plaintiff and defendant. Civil records archived from 1997, on docket book; computerized records since 1997. Note: For mail access call first. Court will send form (also found on website) to be filled out & returned with payment. Mail Turnaround time 2-5 days depending on workload.
Criminal Name Search: Access: Mail, in person. Only the court performs in person name searches; visitors may not. Search fee: $2.00 per calendar year. If retrieved from storage add $40.00 per trip. Then $6.00 first file and $3.00 ea add'l if in sequential order, $6.00 if not. Required to search: name, years to search; also helpful: DOB, SSN, aliases. Criminal records archived from 1982, on docket books; computerized records since 1986. Note: For mail access call first. Court will send form to be filled out and returned with payment. Mail Turnaround time 2-5 days depending on workload.

Sparks Justice Court 630 Greenbrae Dr, Sparks, NV 89431; 775-353-7600; civil phone: 775-353-7603; fax: 775-352-3004; 8AM-5PM (PST). *Misdemeanor, Civil Actions under $10,000, Eviction, Small Claims.* www.co.washoe.nv.us/sjc
General Information: The court charges additional fees to retrieve archived files. They will only disclose these fees when told which files are needed. Will fax documents if prepaid. Court makes copy: $.30 per page. Certification fee: $3.00 per cert. Payee: Justice Court. Personal checks accepted; check guarantee card required. No credit cards accepted. Prepayment required.
Civil Name Search: Access: Mail, in person. Both court and visitors may perform in person name searches. Search fee: $1.00 per name per year. Civil records on computer 1990 to present, prior in books and on cards. Note: Case number required to search pre-1990 records. Mail Turnaround time 1-3 days. Civil PAT goes back to 1990.
Criminal Name Search: Access: Phone, mail, in person. Both court and visitors may perform in person name searches. Search fee: $1.00 per name per year. Required to search: name, years to search; also helpful: DOB, SSN. Full dockets of criminal records on computer last 10 years, 1990-1996 partially on computer, prior in books and on cards. Note: Case number required to search pre-1990 records. Traffic record search fees are same. Mail Turnaround time 1-3 days. Criminal PAT goes back to 1993.

Wadsworth Justice Court PO Box 68, Wadsworth, NV 89442; 775-575-4585; fax: 775-575-0253; 8AM-5PM M-TH (PST). *Misdemeanor, Civil Actions under $10,000, Eviction, Small Claims.*
General Information: Closed Fridays. No sealed records. PC sheets released. Will fax documents if prepaid. Court makes copy: $.30 per page. Certification fee: $3.00 per page plus copy fee. Payee: Justice Court. Personal checks accepted; check guarantee card required. No credit cards accepted. Prepayment required.
Civil Name Search: Access: Mail, in person. Both court and visitors may perform in person name searches. Search fee: $1.00 per name. Civil records go back to 2001. Mail Turnaround time 5-10 days.
Criminal Name Search: Access: Mail, in person. Both court and visitors may perform in person name searches. Search fee: $1.00 per name. Required to search: name, years to search; also helpful: DOB. Criminal records go back to 2001. Mail Turnaround time 5-10 days.

Reno Municipal Court PO Box 1900, 1 S Sierra St, Reno, NV 89505; 775-334-2296; fax: 775-334-3859; 7:30AM-5PM M-Th, 7:30AM-N Fri (PST). *Misdemeanor, Traffic, Infractions.*
www.reno.gov/Index.aspx?page=183

Sparks Municipal Court 1450 C St, Sparks, NV 89431; 775-353-2286; ; 7:30AM-6PM (PST). *Misdemeanor, Traffic, Infractions.*
www.cityofsparks.us/departments/municipal-court

White Pine County

7th Judicial District Court 801 Clark St, Ste. #4, Ely, NV 89301; 775-289-2341; fax: 775-289-2544; 8AM-5PM (PST). *Felony, Gross Misdemeanor, Civil Actions over $10,000, Probate.*

General Information: No sealed or juvenile records released. Will fax documents to local or toll-free number, otherwise fee is $1.00 per page. Court makes copy: $1.00 per page. Certification fee: $6.00 per doc. Payee: White Pine County Clerk. Will not accept personal checks, except local; business check OK. Major credit cards accepted. Prepayment required. They prefer prepayment, but will sent without it if they know and trust you. Mail requests: SASE required.

Civil Name Search: Access: Mail, fax, in person. Only the court performs in person name searches; visitors may not. Search fee: $1.00 per name per year per add'l name. Civil records on computer back to 1991; older records go back to the beginning. Mail Turnaround time 1-3 days.

Criminal Name Search: Access: Mail, fax, in person. Only the court performs in person name searches; visitors may not. Search fee: $1.00 per name per year per add'l name. Criminal records computerized from 1991; older records go back to the beginning. Mail Turnaround time 1-3 days.

Ely Justice Court 801 Clark St, #6, Ely, NV 89301; 775-289-2678; fax: 775-289-3392; 9AM-5PM (PST). *Misdemeanor, Civil Actions under $10,000, Eviction, Small Claims.*

General Information: This court holds the records for Baker Justice Court (Baker Justice Court closed June, 2006). No sealed records released. Will fax documents to toll-free number. Court makes copy: $.30 per page. Certification fee: $3.00. Payee: Ely Justice Court. Only cashiers checks and money orders accepted. Accepts any credit card accepted by Western Union Quick Collect Svc. Prepayment required. Mail requests: SASE required.

Civil Name Search: Access: Phone, fax, mail, in person. Only the court performs in person name searches; visitors may not. Search fee: $1.00 per name per year. Required to search: name, case number, years to search. Civil records on computer from 1988, archived from 1899. Mail Turnaround time 1-5 days.

Criminal Name Search: Access: Phone, fax, mail, in person. Only the court performs in person name searches; visitors may not. Search fee: $1.00 per name per year. Required to search: name, case number, years to search; also helpful: DOB, SSN. Criminal records computerized from 1988, archived from 1899. Mail Turnaround time 1-5 days.

Lund Justice Court PO Box 87, Lund, NV 89317; 775-238-5400;; 10AM-2:30PM Mon & Fri (PST). *Misdemeanor, Civil Actions under $10,000, Eviction, Small Claims.*

General Information: Will not fax documents. Court makes copy: $1.00 per page. Certification fee: $2.00. Payee: Lund Justice Court. No personal checks accepted. Money orders required. No credit cards accepted. Prepayment required. Mail requests: SASE required.

Civil Name Search: Access: Mail only. Only the court performs in person name searches; visitors may not. Search fee: $1.00 per name per year. Civil records only kept in files, archives from 1899. Mail Turnaround time 5 days.

Criminal Name Search: Access: Mail only. Only the court performs in person name searches; visitors may not. Search fee: $1.00 per name per year. Required to search: name, years to search, DOB; also helpful: SSN. Criminal records only kept in files, archives from 1899. Mail Turnaround time 5 days.

Baker Justice Court *Misdemeanor, Civil Actions under $10,000, Eviction, Small Claims.*

General Information: Baker court is now closed; cases heard at Ely Justice Court in Ely, records located there.

Ely Municipal Court PO Box 151055, 1785 Great Basin Blvd, Ely, NV 89315; 775-289-4838; fax: 775-289-8225; *Misdemeanor, Traffic, Infractions.*
http://nevadajudiciary.us/index.php/municipal/

New Hampshire

Time Zone:	EST
Capital:	**Concord, Merrimack County**
# of Counties:	**10**
State Web:	**www.nh.gov**
Court Web:	**www.courts.state.nh.us**

Administration

Administrative Office of the Courts, Supreme Court Bldg, 2 Charles Doe, Concord, NH, 03301; Phone: 603-271-2521, Fax: 603-271-3977.

The Supreme Court

The Supreme Court is the appellate court and has jurisdiction to review appeals from the State trial courts and from many State administrative agencies. It also has original jurisdiction to issue writs of certiorari, prohibition, habeas corpus and other writs. There is not an intermediate Court of Appeals. Opinions are accessible from the web page.

The New Hampshire Courts

Court	Type	How Organized	Jurisdiction Highpoints
Superior*	General	11Courts in 10 Districts	Felony, Civil
Circuit*	Limited	10 Courts with Multiple Divisions in 10 Districts	Misdemeanor, Civil, Eviction, Small Claims, Family, Probate

* = profiled in this book

Details on the Court Structure

The **Superior Court** is the court of General Jurisdiction and has jurisdiction over a wide variety of cases, including criminal, domestic relations, and civil cases, and provides the only forum in this state for trial by jury. Felony cases include Class A misdemeanors. The Superior Court has exclusive jurisdiction over cases in which the damage claims exceed $25,000.

Effective July 1, 2011, a new **Circuit Court** system was established that consolidated the then existing 32 **District Courts**, 10 **Probate Courts**, and 25 **Family Courts**. Under the new rules, each county now has a Circuit Court with three Divisions: District, Family and Probate. All the current District Court locations remained open. In Cheshire County, the marital division continues to operate as part of the Cheshire County Superior Court. In all other counties, the Circuit Court Family Division operates at the same locations as before.

Probate cases are filed in the Circuit Court located at the county seat.

Record Searching Facts You Need to Know

Fees and Record Searching Tips

Since Circuit Courts (formerly District Courts) are organized by town and not by county, each Circuit Court Division has maintained its own database of records. Thus a search of misdemeanor records in a county would require a search at each of the Circuit Courts in that county. However, with the reorganization it is expected that records will eventually be consolidated by county.

Searching, copies, and certification fees are set by the New Hampshire Supreme Court. The search fee structure is: computer search - $20.00 per name for up to 5 names, then $5.00 each add'l name in that request; manual search - $25.00, usually when archived or paper records are included. Most courts follow this fee schedule, but not all do. Some courts will still charge the older fee of $20.00 for the one to four names, then $5.00 ea add'l. Copies are usually $.50 per page; a few offer self serve copying. Certification fee is $5.00 and may or may not include the copy fee. No public access terminals are found at NH courts. Most Circuit Court case files are non-electronic.

Also of note is the current jurisdiction of the Franklin Circuit Court includes towns from two counties – Merrimack and Belknap.

Online Access is Extremely Limited

While there is no statewide access available for historical trial court records. The home page has information on current dockets of the Superior Courts.

Hillsborough County

Superior Court - Northern District PO Box 2143, Manchester, NH 03051-2143; 603-669-7410; criminal phone: x3; civil phone: x2; ; 8AM-4PM M,W,F; 8AM-1PM Tu,Th (EST). *Felony, Civil Actions over $1,500.*
www.courts.state.nh.us/superior/index.htm
General Information: Search fee includes all indexes, if asked. The Family/Marital Division now at 35 Amherst St, Manchester, 603-624-0015. No sealed, juvenile, mental health records released. Will not fax documents. Court makes copy: $.50 per page. Self serve copy: $.25 per page. Certification fee: $5.00 per seal. Payee: Hillsborough Superior Court-Northern District. Personal checks accepted. Major credit cards accepted. Prepayment required. Mail requests: SASE required.
Civil Name Search: Access: Mail, in person. Only the court performs in person name searches; visitors may not. Search fee: Computer search is $20.00 per name for first 5 names then $5.00 each add'l name in that request. Court may charge less. Civil records on computer from 5/85, index cards from 1980s, index books from 1900s; organized 1769. Mail Turnaround time 3 days.
Criminal Name Search: Access: Mail, in person. Only the court performs in person name searches; visitors may not. Search fee: Computer search is $20.00 per name for first 5 names then $5.00 each add'l name in that request. Court may charge less. Required to search: name, years to search, DOB. Criminal records computerized from 5/85, index cards from 1980s, index books from 1900s; organized 1769. Mail Turnaround time 3 days.

Superior Court - Southern District 30 Spring St, Nashua, NH 03061; 603-883-6461;; 8AM-4PM M,W,F; 8AM-1PM Tu,Th (EST). *Felony, Civil Actions over $1,500.*
www.courts.state.nh.us/superior/index.htm
General Information: Search fee includes all indexes, if asked. No sealed, juvenile or annulled records released. Will not fax documents. Court makes copy: $.50 per page. Self serve copy: $.05 per page. Certification fee: $5.00 per seal. Payee: Superior Court. Personal checks accepted. Credit cards accepted. Prepayment required.
Civil Name Search: Access: Mail, in person. Only the court performs in person name searches; visitors may not. Search fee: Computer search is $20.00 per name for first 5 names then $5.00 each add'l name in that request. Court may charge less. Civil records on computer back to 3/92; overall records go back to 1992. Mail Turnaround time 2-3 days.
Criminal Name Search: Access: Mail, in person. Only the court performs in person name searches; visitors may not. Search fee: Computer search is $20.00 per name for first 5 names then $5.00 each add'l name in that request. Court may charge less. Required to search: name, years to search; also helpful: DOB. Criminal records computerized from 3/92; overall records go back to 1992. Mail Turnaround time 2-3 days.

Goffstown Circuit Court - District and Family Divisions 329 Mast Rd, Goffstown, NH 03045; 603-621-2211;; 8AM-4PM (EST). *Misdemeanor, Civil Actions under $25,000, Eviction, Small Claims, Domestic, Juvenile.*
www.courts.state.nh.us/circuitcourt/index.htm
General Information: Includes towns of Goffstown, Weare, New Boston, and Francestown. Search fee includes all 4 indexes, if asked. No sealed, juvenile, mental health, expunged or dismissed records released. Court makes copy: $.50 per page. Certification fee: $5.00 per cert. Payee: Goffstown District Court. Personal checks accepted. Major credit cards accepted. Prepayment required. Mail requests: SASE helpful.
Civil Name Search: Access: Mail, in person. Only the court performs in person name searches; visitors may not. Search fee: Computer search is $20.00 per name for first 5 names then $5.00 each add'l name in that request. Court may charge less. Civil records on computer from 3/92, kept in files prior. Mail Turnaround time 2 weeks.
Criminal Name Search: Access: Mail, in person. Only the court performs in person name searches; visitors may not. Search fee: Computer search is $20.00 per name for first 5 names then $5.00 each add'l name in that request. Court may charge less. Required to search: name, years to search, DOB. Criminal records computerized from 3/92, kept in files prior. Mail Turnaround time 2 weeks.

Manchester Circuit Court - District and Family Divisions 35 Amherst St, Manchester, NH 03101-1801; 603-624-6510;; 8AM-4PM (EST). *Misdemeanor, Civil Actions under $25,000, Eviction, Small Claims, Domestic, Juvenile.*
www.courts.state.nh.us/circuitcourt/index.htm
General Information: Includes city of Manchester. They have a Records Research & Report Form to use for search requests. The Family Court can be reached at 603-624-0015. No adoption, sealed, juvenile, mental health, expunged or dismissed records released. Will fax documents to local or toll-free number. Court makes copy: $.50 per page. Certification fee: $5.00 per document plus copy fee; exemplification- $25.00. Payee: Manchester District Court. Personal checks accepted. Major credit cards accepted. Prepayment required. Mail requests: SASE required.
Civil Name Search: Access: Mail, in person. Only the court performs in person name searches; visitors may not. Search fee: Computer search is $20.00 per name for first 5 names then $5.00 each add'l name in that request. Court may charge less. Required to search: name, years to search, DOB. Civil records on computer from 6//15/1992, on index cards from 1960. Note: All requests must be in writing. Mail Turnaround time 2-3 weeks.
Criminal Name Search: Access: Mail, in person. Only the court performs in person name searches; visitors may not. Search fee: Computer search is $20.00 per name for first 5 names then $5.00 each add'l name in that request. Court may charge less. Required to search: name, years to search, DOB. Criminal records computerized from 6/15/1992, on index cards from 1960. Note: All requests must be in writing. Manual record searches would be searches back to 1980, unless otherwise specified. Mail Turnaround time 2-3 weeks.

Merrimack Circuit Court - District and Family Divisions PO Box 324, Merrimack, NH 03054-0324; 603-424-9916;; 8AM-4PM (EST). *Misdemeanor, Civil Actions under $25,000, Eviction, Small Claims, Domestic, Juvenile.*
www.courts.state.nh.us/circuitcourt/index.htm
General Information: Includes towns of Merrimack, Litchfield, and Bedford. The Family Division can be reached at 603-423-8592. No adoption, sealed, juvenile, mental health, expunged or dismissed records released. Will not fax documents. Court makes copy: $.50 per page. Certification fee: $5.00 per doc. Payee: Merrimack District Court. Personal checks accepted. Major credit cards accepted. Prepayment required. Mail requests: SASE required.
Civil Name Search: Access: Mail, in person. Only the court performs in person name searches; visitors may not. Search fee: Computer search is $20.00 per name for first 5 names then $5.00 each add'l name in that request. Court may charge less. Civil records on computer from 7/92, on index cards from 1972, index books in archives at Concord. Note: All requests must be in writing. Mail Turnaround time 1-2 days.
Criminal Name Search: Access: Mail, in person. Both court and visitors may perform in person name searches. Search fee: Computer search is $20.00 per name for first 5 names then $5.00 each add'l name in that request. Court may charge less. Required to search: name, years to search; also helpful: DOB. Criminal records computerized from 7/92, on index cards from 1972, index books in archives at Concord. Note: Requests must be in writing. Mail Turnaround time 1-2 days.

Milford Circuit Court - District and Family Divisions PO Box 943, 180 Elm St, Milford, NH 03055-0943; 603-673-2900; ; 8AM-4PM (EST). *Misdemeanor, Civil Actions under $25,000, Eviction, Small Claims, Domestic, Juvenile.*
www.courts.state.nh.us/circuitcourt/index.htm
General Information: Includes towns of Milford, Brookline, Amherst, Mason, Wilton, Lyndeborough, and Mont Vernon. Search fee includes all 4 indexes, if asked. No adoption, sealed, juvenile, mental health, expunged or dismissed records released. Will not fax documents. Court makes copy: $.50 per page. Certification fee: $5.00 per cert/page. Payee: Milford District Court. Personal checks accepted. Visa/MC/Discover accepted. Prepayment required. Mail requests: SASE required.
Civil Name Search: Access: Mail, in person. Only the court performs in person name searches; visitors may not. Search fee: Computer search is $20.00 per name for first 5 names then $5.00 each add'l name in that request. Court may charge less. Civil records on computer from 8/92, on index cards from 1950s, prior records may or may not be at old courthouse. Mail Turnaround time 7 days.

Criminal Name Search: Access: Mail, in person. Only the court performs in person name searches; visitors may not. Search fee: Computer search is $20.00 per name for first 5 names then $5.00 each add'l name in that request. Court may charge less. Required to search: name, years to search; also helpful: DOB, SSN. Criminal records computerized from 8/92, on index cards from 1950s, prior records may or may not be at old courthouse. Mail Turnaround time 14 days.

Nashua Circuit Court - District and Family Divisions PO Box 310, 25 Walnut St, Nashua, NH 03061-0310; 603-880-3333;; 8AM-4PM; irregular due to budget restraints (EST). *Misdemeanor, Civil Actions under $25,000, Eviction, Small Claims, Domestic, Juvenile.*
www.courts.state.nh.us/courtlocations/hillsdistdir.htm#Nashua

General Information: Includes city of Nashua and the towns of Hudson and Hollis. Search fee includes all 4 indexes, if asked. No adoption, sealed, juvenile, mental health, expunged records released. Will not fax documents. Court makes copy: $.50 per page. Certification fee: $5.00 per cert. Payee: Nashua District Court. Personal checks accepted. Major credit cards accepted. Prepayment required. Mail requests: SASE required.

Civil Name Search: Access: Mail, in person. Only the court performs in person name searches; visitors may not. Search fee: Computer search is $20.00 per name for first 5 names then $5.00 each add'l name in that request. Court may charge less. Required to search: name, years to search, DOB. Civil records on computer from 1993, index cards from 1982. Note: All requests must be in writing. Mail Turnaround time 5 days.

Criminal Name Search: Access: Mail, in person. Only the court performs in person name searches; visitors may not. Search fee: Computer search is $20.00 per name for first 5 names then $5.00 each add'l name in that request. Court may charge less. Required to search: name, years to search; also helpful: DOB, SSN. Criminal records computerized from 8/1992, index cards from 1982. Note: All requests must be in writing. Mail Turnaround time 5 days.

Hillsborough Circuit Court - District Division , , NH; ; .
Misdemeanor, Civil Actions under $25,000, Eviction, Small Claims.
General Information: Effective December 23, 2008, the Hillsborough District Court merged with the Henniker District Court in Merrimack county. Records there.

Probate Division PO Box 387, Nashua, NH 03061-0387; 603-882-1231; fax: 603-882-1620; 8AM-4PM (EST). *Probate.*
www.courts.state.nh.us/probate/
General Information: The physical address is 30 Spring St. Zip is 03061.

Merrimack County

Superior Court PO Box 2880, Concord, NH 03302-2880; 603-225-5501;; 8AM-4PM (EST). *Felony, Civil Actions over $1,500.*
www.courts.state.nh.us/superior/index.htm
General Information: Actual records kept off site - files prior to 1983 are at State Archives. Files more than 5 years old but not prior to 1983 are retrieved by courier with 3-5 day wait. Search fee includes all indexes, if asked. No adoption, sealed, juvenile, mental health, expunged or dismissed records released. Will not fax documents. Court makes copy: $.50 per page. Self serve copy: $.15 per page. Certification fee: $5.00 per cert plus copy fee. Payee: Merrimack Superior Court. Personal checks accepted. Major credit cards accepted. Prepayment required. Mail requests: SASE required.

Civil Name Search: Access: Mail, in person. Only the court performs in person name searches; visitors may not. Search fee: Computer search is $20.00 per name for first 5 names then $5.00 each add'l name in that request. Court may charge less. Civil records on computer from 1983, index cards from 1950, index books from 1800s; organized 1823. Mail Turnaround time 2-3 weeks.

Criminal Name Search: Access: Phone, mail, in person. Only the court performs in person name searches; visitors may not. Search fee: Computer search is $20.00 per name for first 5 names then $5.00 each add'l name in that request. Court may charge less. Required to search: name, years to search, DOB; also helpful: SSN. Criminal records on computer since 1984. Mail Turnaround time 2-3 weeks.

Concord Circuit Court - District and Family Divisions PO Box 3420, 32 Clinton St, Concord, NH 03302-3420; 603-271-6400; criminal phone: x3; civil phone: x4;; 8AM-4PM (EST). *Misdemeanor, Civil Actions under $25,000, Eviction, Small Claims, Traffic.*
www.courts.state.nh.us/circuitcourt/index.htm
General Information: The Family Division is reached at 603-271-0630. The former Pittsfield District Court has been combined with this court. Includes city of Concord, and the towns of Loudon, Canterbury, Dunbarton, Bow, Hopkinton, Pittsfield, Chichester, and Epsom. No sealed, juvenile, mental health, expunged or dismissed records released. Will not fax documents. Court makes copy: $.50 per page. Self serve copy: $.15 per page in Family Div. Certification fee: $5.00 per page includes copy fee. Payee:

Concord District Court. Personal checks accepted. Major credit cards accepted. Prepayment required. Mail requests: SASE requested.

Civil Name Search: Access: Mail, in person. Only the court performs in person name searches; visitors may not. Search fee: Computer search is $20.00 per name for first 5 names then $5.00 each add'l name in that request. Court may charge less. Civil records on computer from 1989, index cards from 1978, docket books from 1800. Mail Turnaround time 10 days.

Criminal Name Search: Access: Mail, in person. Only the court performs in person name searches; visitors may not. Search fee: Computer search is $20.00 per name for first 5 names then $5.00 each add'l name in that request. Court may charge less. Required to search: name, years to search, DOB. Criminal records computerized from 1989, index cards from 1978, docket books from 1800. Note: In person search requests are not same day; they're treated same as a mail request. Mail Turnaround time 10 days.

Franklin Circuit Court - District and Family Divisions 7 Hancock Terrace, Franklin, NH 03235; 603-934-3290; fax: 603-934-7255; 8AM-4PM (EST). *Misdemeanor, Civil Actions under $25,000, Eviction, Small Claims, Domestic, Juvenile.*
www.courts.state.nh.us/circuitcourt/index.htm
General Information: Search fee includes all 4 indexes, if asked. Includes city of Franklin and the towns of Northfield, Danbury, Andover, Boscawen, Salisbury, Hill, Webster and both Sanbornton and Tilton which are in Belknap County. No adoption, sealed, juvenile, mental health, expunged or dismissed records released. Will not fax documents. Court makes copy: $.50 per page. Certification fee: $5.00 per doc. Payee: Franklin District Court. Personal checks, Visa/MC accepted. Prepayment required. Mail requests: SASE required.

Civil Name Search: Access: Mail, in person. Only the court performs in person name searches; visitors may not. Search fee: Computer search is $20.00 per name for first 5 names then $5.00 each add'l name in that request. Court may charge less. Civil cases indexed by plaintiff. Civil records on computer from 1/91, index cards from 1/80, index books from 1960s. Mail Turnaround time 2-3 days.

Criminal Name Search: Access: Mail, in person. Only the court performs in person name searches; visitors may not. Search fee: Computer search is $20.00 per name for first 5 names then $5.00 each add'l name in that request. Court may charge less. Required to search: name, years to search; also helpful: DOB, SSN. Criminal records computerized from 1/91, index cards from 1/80, index books from 1960s. Mail Turnaround time 2-3 days.

Henniker Circuit Court - District and Family Divisions 41 Liberty Hill Rd, Bldg #2, Henniker, NH 03242; 603-428-3214 x1;; 8AM-4PM (EST). *Misdemeanor, Civil Actions under $25,000, Eviction, Small Claims, Domestic, Juvenile.*
www.courts.state.nh.us/circuitcourt/index.htm
General Information: Search fee includes all 4 indexes, if asked. Includes towns of Henniker, Hillsborough, Deering, Antrim, Bennington, Windsor, Warner, Sutton, and Bradford. Includes closed District Court cases from Hillsborough. No adoption, sealed, juvenile, mental health, expunged or dismissed records released. Will not fax documents. Court makes copy: $.50 per page. Certification fee: $5.00 per cert; attestation includes copy fee. Payee: Henniker District Court. Personal checks accepted, credit cards are not. Prepayment required. Mail requests: SASE required.

Civil Name Search: Access: Mail, in person. Only the court performs in person name searches; visitors may not. Search fee: Computer search is $20.00 per name for first 5 names then $5.00 each add'l name in that request. Court may charge less. Civil index on cards from 1988, index books from 1960s; on computer back to 1992. Mail Turnaround time can take as long as 6 weeks.

Criminal Name Search: Access: Mail, in person. Only the court performs in person name searches; visitors may not. Search fee: Computer search is $20.00 per name for first 5 names then $5.00 each add'l name in that request. Court may charge less. Required to search: name, years to search, DOB; also helpful: SSN. Criminal records indexed on cards from 1988, index books from 1960s; on computer back to 1992. Mail Turnaround time can take as long as 6 weeks.

Hooksett Circuit Court - District and Family Divisions 101 Merrimack, Hooksett, NH 03106; 603-485-9901;; 8AM-4PM (EST). *Misdemeanor, Civil Actions under $25,000, Eviction, Small Claims, Domestic, Juvenile.*
www.courts.state.nh.us/circuitcourt/index.htm
General Information: Includes towns of Allenstown, Pembroke, and Hooksett. Search fee includes all 4 indexes, if asked. No sealed, juvenile, mental health, expunged or dismissed records released. Will not fax documents. Court makes copy: $.50 per page. Certification fee: $5.00 per page. Cert fee includes copies. Payee: Hooksett District Court. Personal checks accepted. Major credit cards accepted. Prepayment required. Mail requests: SASE required.

Civil Name Search: Access: Mail, in person. Only the court performs in person name searches; visitors may not. Search fee: Computer search is $20.00 per name for first 5 names then $5.00 each add'l name in that request. Court may charge less. Civil records on computer from 1993, on index cards from 1980, index books from 1975. Note: All requests must be in writing. Mail Turnaround time 1-2 months.

Criminal Name Search: Access: Mail, in person. Only the court performs in person name searches; visitors may not. Search fee: Computer search is $20.00 per name for first 5 names then $5.00 each add'l name in that request. Court may charge less. Required to search: name, years to search; also helpful: DOB, SSN. Criminal records computerized from 1993, on index cards from 1980, index books from 1975. Mail Turnaround time 1-2 months.

New London Circuit (District) Court 55 Main Street, New London, NH 03773-1519; ; 8:30AM-4PM (EST). *Misdemeanor, Civil Actions under $25,000, Eviction, Small Claims.*

General Information: Closed 10/22/2009. Case files for New London, Wilmot, Newbury sent to the Newport Court in Sullivan county. Sutton cases now in the District Court in Henniker.

Probate Division 163 N Main St, Concord, NH 03301; 603-224-9589; fax: 603-225-0179; 8AM-4PM (EST). *Probate.*
www.courts.state.nh.us/probate/

Rockingham County

Superior Court PO Box 1258, 10 Route 125, Kingston, NH 03848-1258; 603-642-5256;; 8AM-4PM M, TH, F; 8AM-N T, W (EST). *Felony, Civil Actions over $1,500.*
www.courts.state.nh.us/superior/index.htm

General Information: Search fee includes all indexes, if asked. No sealed, juvenile, mental health, expunged, annulled records released. Will not fax documents. Court makes copy: $.50 per page. Self serve copy: $.25 per page. Certification fee: $5.00 per cert. Payee: Clerk Superior Court. Personal checks accepted. Credit cards accepted. Prepayment required.

Civil Name Search: Access: Mail, in person. Only the court performs in person name searches; visitors may not. Search fee: Computer search is $20.00 per name for first 5 names then $5.00 each add'l name in that request. Court may charge less. Civil records on computer from 1988, index cards from 1958-1987, organized 1769.

Criminal Name Search: Access: Mail, in person. Only the court performs in person name searches; visitors may not. Search fee: Computer search is $20.00 per name for first 5 names then $5.00 each add'l name in that request. Court may charge less. Required to search: name, years to search; also helpful: DOB. Criminal records computerized from 1988, index cards from 1920, organized 1769.

Brentwood Circuit Court 10 Route 125, Brentwood, NH 03833; 603-642-9173, 642-9145;; 8AM-4PM (EST). *Misdemeanor, Civil Actions under $25,000, Eviction, Small Claims, Domestic, Juvenile, Probate.*
www.courts.state.nh.us/circuitcourt/index.htm

General Information: All three Divisions located here. Mailing address for District Division is PO Box 1149, Kingston 03848. Jurisdiction includes towns of Exeter, Newmarket, Stratham, Newfields, Fremont, East Kingston, Kensington, Epping, and Brentwood. No adoption, sealed, juvenile, mental health, expunged or dismissed records released. Will fax documents to local or toll-free number, all fees prepaid. Court makes copy: $.50 per page. Certification fee: $5.00 per cert. Payee: Exeter District Court. Personal checks accepted. Major credit cards accepted. Prepayment required. Mail requests: SASE not required.

Civil Name Search: Access: Mail, in person. Only the court performs in person name searches; visitors may not. Search fee: Computer search is $20.00 per name for first 5 names then $5.00 each add'l name in that request. Court may charge less. Required to search: name, years to search; also helpful: address. Civil records on computer back to 1991. Mail Turnaround time 3 days.

Criminal Name Search: Access: Mail, in person. Both court and visitors may perform in person name searches. Search fee: Computer search is $20.00 per name for first 5 names then $5.00 each add'l name in that request. Court may charge less. Required to search: name, years to search, DOB. Criminal records computerized from 1991. Mail Turnaround time 3 days.

Candia Circuit Court - District and Family Divisions 110 Raymond Rd, Candia, NH 03034; 603-483-2789; criminal phone: x1; civil phone: x2; ; 8AM-4PM (EST). *Misdemeanor, Civil Actions under $25,000, Eviction, Small Claims, Domestic, Juvenile.*
www.courts.state.nh.us/circuitcourt/index.htm

General Information: Includes towns of Auburn, Candia, Deerfield, Northwood, Nottingham, and Raymond. This court was formerly located in Auburn, NH. No adoption, sealed, juvenile, mental health, expunged or dismissed records released. Will not fax documents. Court makes copy: $.50 per page. Certification fee: $5.00 per page includes copy fee. Payee: Auburn

District Court. Personal checks accepted, credit cards are not. Prepayment required. Mail requests: SASE required.

Civil Name Search: Access: Mail, in person. Only the court performs in person name searches; visitors may not. Search fee: Computer search is $20.00 per name for first 5 names then $5.00 each add'l name in that request. Court may charge less. Required to search: name, years to search; also helpful: address. Civil records on computer from 5/92, index cards from 1980, index books from 1968. Mail Turnaround time 10 days.

Criminal Name Search: Access: Mail, in person. Only the court performs in person name searches; visitors may not. Search fee: Computer search is $20.00 per name for first 5 names then $5.00 each add'l name in that request. Court may charge less. Required to search: name, years to search, DOB, signed release. Criminal records computerized from 5/92, index cards from 1980, index books from 1968. Mail Turnaround time 10 days.

Derry Circuit Court - District and Family Divisions 10 Manning St, Derry, NH 03038; 603-434-4676;; 8AM-4PM (EST). *Misdemeanor, Civil Actions under $25,000, Eviction, Small Claims, Domestic, Juvenile.*
www.courts.state.nh.us/circuitcourt/index.htm

General Information: Includes towns of Derry, Londonderry, Chester, and Sandown. Family Division is reached at 603-421-0077. No adoption, sealed, juvenile, mental health, expunged, dismissed or annulment records released. Will not fax documents. Court makes copy: $.50 per page. Certification fee: $5.00 per cert. Payee: Derry District Court. Personal checks accepted. Major credit cards accepted. Prepayment required. Mail requests: SASE required.

Civil Name Search: Access: Phone, mail, in person. Only the court performs in person name searches; visitors may not. Search fee: Computer search is $20.00 per name for first 5 names then $5.00 each add'l name in that request. Court may charge less. Civil records on computer from 10/92, on index cards prior. Mail Turnaround time 1 week or more.

Criminal Name Search: Access: Phone, mail, in person. Only the court performs in person name searches; visitors may not. Search fee: Computer search is $20.00 per name for first 5 names then $5.00 each add'l name in that request. Court may charge less. Required to search: name, years to search; also helpful: DOB, SSN. Criminal records computerized from 10/92, on index cards prior. Mail Turnaround time 1 week.

Plaistow Circuit Court - District Division PO Box 129, 14 Elm St, Plaistow, NH 03865; 603-382-4651; fax: 603-382-4952; 8AM-4PM (EST). *Misdemeanor, Civil Actions under $25,000, Eviction, Small Claims.*
www.courts.state.nh.us/circuitcourt/index.htm

General Information: Includes towns of Plaistow, Hampstead, Kingston, Newton, Atkinson, and Danville. No adoption, sealed, juvenile, mental health, expunged or dismissed records released. Will not fax documents. Court makes copy: $.50 per page. Certification fee: $5.00 per cert. Payee: Plaistow District Court. Personal checks accepted. Major credit cards accepted. Prepayment required. Mail requests: SASE required.

Civil Name Search: Access: Mail, in person. Only the court performs in person name searches; visitors may not. Search fee: Computer search is $20.00 per name for first 5 names then $5.00 each add'l name in that request. Court may charge less. Civil records on computer from 7/91, index cards from 1980, index books from 1960s. Mail Turnaround time 2-3 days.

Criminal Name Search: Access: Mail, in person. Only the court performs in person name searches; visitors may not. Search fee: Computer search is $20.00 per name for first 5 names then $5.00 each add'l name in that request. Court may charge less. Required to search: name, years to search, DOB. Criminal records computerized from 7/91, index cards from 1980, index books from 1960s. Mail Turnaround time 2-3 days.

Portsmouth Circuit Court - District and Family Divisions 111 Parrott Ave, Portsmouth, NH 03801-4490; 603-431-2192; criminal phone: x230; civil phone: x230; ; 8AM-4PM (EST). *Misdemeanor, Civil Actions under $25,000, Eviction, Small Claims, Domestic, Juvenile.*
www.courts.state.nh.us/circuitcourt/index.htm

General Information: Includes city of Portsmouth and the towns of Newington, Greenland, Rye, and New Castle. Family Division is reached at 603-433-8518. No adoption, sealed, juvenile, mental health, expunged or dismissed records released. Will not fax documents. Court makes copy: $.50 per page. Certification fee: $1.00 per page included in search fee plus $.30 per page after first. Payee: Portsmouth District Court. Personal checks accepted, credit cards are not. Prepayment required. Mail requests: SASE required.

Civil Name Search: Access: Mail, in person. Only the court performs in person name searches; visitors may not. Search fee: Computer search is $20.00 per name for first 5 names then $5.00 each add'l name in that request. Court may charge less. Civil records on computer from 4/92, docket cards from 1980, index books from 1960s. Mail Turnaround time 2-3 days.

Criminal Name Search: Access: Mail, in person. Only the court performs in person name searches; visitors may not. Search fee: Computer search is $20.00 per name for first 5 names then $5.00 each add'l name in that request. Court may charge less. Required to search: name, years to search; also helpful: DOB, SSN. Criminal records computerized from 4/92, docket cards from 1980, index books from 1960s. Mail Turnaround time 2-3 days.

Salem Circuit Court - District and Family Divisions 35 Geremonty Dr, Salem, NH 03079; 603-893-4483;; 8AM-4PM (EST). *Misdemeanor, Civil Actions under $25,000, Eviction, Small Claims, Domestic, Juvenile.*
www.courts.state.nh.us/circuitcourt/index.htm
General Information: Includes towns of Salem, Windham, and Pelham. The Family Court is reached at 603-893-2084. No adoption, sealed, juvenile, mental health, expunged or dismissed records released. May fax documents $3.00. Court makes copy: $.50 per page. Certification fee: $5.00 per cert. Payee: Salem District Court. Personal checks accepted, credit cards are not. Prepayment required. Mail requests: SASE required.
Civil Name Search: Access: Mail, in person. Only the court performs in person name searches; visitors may not. Search fee: Computer search is $20.00 per name for first 5 names then $5.00 each add'l name in that request. Court may charge less. Required to search: name, years to search, DOB. Civil records on computer from 4/92, docket cards from 1980, docket books from 1950. Note: Record requests may be dropped off, an appointment is not necessary. Mail Turnaround time 2-3 weeks.
Criminal Name Search: Access: Mail, in person. Only the court performs in person name searches; visitors may not. Search fee: Computer search is $20.00 per name for first 5 names then $5.00 each add'l name in that request. Court may charge less. Required to search: name, years to search, DOB. Criminal records computerized from 4/92, docket cards from 1980, docket books from 1950. Mail Turnaround time 2-3 weeks.

Seabrook Circuit Court - District Division 130 Ledge Rd, Seabrook, NH 03874-4322; 603-474-2637/2653;; 8AM-4PM (EST). *Misdemeanor, Civil Actions under $25,000, Eviction, Small Claims.*
www.courts.state.nh.us/circuitcourt/index.htm
General Information: Jurisdiction includes towns of Hampton, Hampton Falls, North Hampton, South Hampton, and Seabrook. No adoption, sealed, juvenile, mental health, expunged or dismissed records released. Will fax documents to local or toll-free number. Court makes copy: $.50 per page but may be less. Certification fee: $5.00 per cert. Payee: Hampton District Court. Personal checks, Visa/MC accepted. Prepayment required. Mail requests: SASE required.
Civil Name Search: Access: Mail, in person. Only the court performs in person name searches; visitors may not. Search fee: Computer search is $20.00 per name for first 5 names then $5.00 each add'l name in that request. Court may charge less. Civil cases indexed by defendant. Civil records on computer from 4/91, index cards from 1979, index books from 1900s. Mail Turnaround time 1 week.
Criminal Name Search: Access: Mail, in person. Only the court performs in person name searches; visitors may not. Search fee: Computer search is $20.00 per name for first 5 names then $5.00 each add'l name in that request. Court may charge less. Required to search: name, years to search; also helpful: DOB, SSN. Criminal records computerized from 4/91, index cards from 1979, index books from 1900s. Mail Turnaround time 1 week.

Strafford County

Superior Court PO Box 799, 259 County Farm Rd, Dover, NH 03821-0799; 603-742-3065; criminal phone: x305; civil phone: x350; probate phone: 603-742-2550; ; 8AM-4PM (EST). *Felony, Civil Actions over $1,500, DR.*
www.courts.state.nh.us/superior/index.htm
General Information: Search fee includes all indexes, if asked. No sealed, juvenile, mental health, expunged or dismissed records released. Will not fax documents. Court makes copy: $.50 per page. Self serve copy: $.25 per page. Certification fee: $5.00 per cert plus their copy fee. Payee: Strafford Superior Court. Personal checks, Visa/MC accepted. Prepayment required. Mail requests: SASE not required.
Civil Name Search: Access: Mail, in person. Only the court performs in person name searches; visitors may not. Search fee: Computer search is $20.00 per name for first 5 names then $5.00 each add'l name in that request. Court may charge less. Civil records on computer from 3/89, index cards from 1970, index books from 1900s, organized 1769. Note: For court assisted name searches, the spelling of name must match exactly. Mail Turnaround time 1 week.
Criminal Name Search: Access: Mail, in person. Only the court performs in person name searches; visitors may not. Search fee: Computer search is $20.00 per name for first 5 names then $5.00 each add'l name in that request. Court may charge less. Required to search: name, years to search; also helpful: DOB, SSN. Criminal records computerized from 3/89, index cards from 1970, index books from 1900s, organized 1769. Mail Turnaround time 1 week.

Dover Circuit Court - District and Family Divisions 25 St Thomas St, Dover, NH 03820; 603-742-7202; fax: 603-742-5956; 8AM-4PM (EST). *Misdemeanor, Civil Actions under $20,000, Eviction, Small Claims, Domestic, Juvenile.*
www.courts.state.nh.us/circuitcourt/index.htm
General Information: Includes cases from the closed Durham District Court. Includes Cities of Dover, Somersworth, towns of Rollinsford, Durham, Lee and Madbury. There is also a Family Court at 279 County Farm Rd in Diver at the County Bldg - 603-742-5341. No adoption, sealed, juvenile, mental health, expunged or dismissed records released. May fax documents if not busy. Court makes copy: $.50 per doc. Certification fee: $5.00 per doc. Payee: Dover District Court. Personal checks accepted. Major credit cards accepted. Prepayment required. Mail requests: SASE required.
Civil Name Search: Access: Mail, in person. Only the court performs in person name searches; visitors may not. Search fee: Computer search is $20.00 per name for first 5 names then $5.00 each add'l name in that request. Court may charge less. Civil records on computer from 1993, on index cards from 1980, index books from 1970. Mail Turnaround time 1-2 days.
Criminal Name Search: Access: Mail, in person. Only the court performs in person name searches; visitors may not. Search fee: Computer search is $20.00 per name for first 5 names then $5.00 each add'l name in that request. Court may charge less. Required to search: name, years to search, DOB. Criminal records computerized from 1993, on index cards from 1980, index books from 1970. Mail Turnaround time 1-2 days.

Rochester Circuit Court - District Division 76 N Main St, Rochester, NH 03867; 603-332-3516;; 8AM-4PM (EST). *Misdemeanor, Civil Actions under $25,000, Eviction, Small Claims.*
www.courts.state.nh.us/courtlocations/straffdistdir.htm#Rochester
General Information: Includes city of Rochester and the towns of Barrington, Milton, New Durham, Farmington, Strafford, and Middleton. No sealed, juvenile, mental health, expunged records released. Will not fax out documents. Court makes copy: $.50 per page. Certification fee: $5.00 per page. Payee: Rochester District Court. Personal checks accepted. Visa/MC and Discover accepted. Prepayment required. Mail requests: SASE not required.
Civil Name Search: Access: Mail, in person. Only the court performs in person name searches; visitors may not. Search fee: Computer search is $20.00 per name for first 5 names then $5.00 each add'l name in that request. Court may charge less. Required to search: name, years to search; also helpful DOB. Civil records on computer from 1989, index cards from 7/80, index books from 1960s. Note: Requests must be in writing. Mail Turnaround time 1 week.
Criminal Name Search: Access: Mail, in person. Only the court performs in person name searches; visitors may not. Search fee: Computer search is $20.00 per name for first 5 names then $5.00 each add'l name in that request. Court may charge less. Required to search: name, years to search; also helpful: DOB. Criminal records computerized from 1989, index cards from 7/80, index books from 1960s. Note: Requests must be in writing. Mail Turnaround time 1 week.

Durham District Court *Misdemeanor, Civil Actions under $25,000, Eviction, Small Claims.*
General Information: Closed 02/03/2009. Case files for Durham, Lee and Madbury now at the Dover District Court.

Durham District Court - Closed, see Dover Closed 02/03/2009. **Case files for Durham, Lee and Madbury now at the Dover District Court.**

Probate Division 259 County Farm Rd, Dover, NH 03820; 603-742-2550; ; 8AM-4PM (EST). *Probate.*
www.courts.state.nh.us/probate/

Sullivan County

Superior Court 22 Main St, Newport, NH 03773; 603-863-3450;; 8AM-12:30PM; 1PM-4:00PM (EST). *Felony, Civil Actions over $1,500.*
www.courts.state.nh.us/superior/index.htm
General Information: Search fee includes all indexes, if asked. No adoption, sealed, juvenile, mental health, expunged or dismissed records released. Will not fax documents. Court makes copy: $.50 per page. Self serve copy: $.25 per page. Certification fee: $5.00 for attestation; copy fee not included. Payee: Sullivan County Superior Court. Personal checks, Visa/MC accepted. Prepayment required. Mail requests: SASE required.
Civil Name Search: Access: Mail, in person. Only the court performs in person name searches; visitors may not. Search fee: Computer search is $20.00 per name for first 5 names then $5.00 each add'l name in that request. Court may charge less. Required to search: name, DOB. Civil records on computer from 1989, on index cards from 1980s, index books from 1800s. Mail Turnaround time 1 week.
Criminal Name Search: Access: Mail, in person. Only the court performs in person name searches; visitors may not. Search fee: Computer search is $20.00 per name for first 5 names then $5.00 each add'l name in

that request. Court may charge less. Required to search: name, DOB. Criminal records computerized from 1989, on index cards from 1980s, index books from 1800s. Mail Turnaround time 1 week.

Claremont Circuit Court - District and Family Divisions 1 Police Court, Claremont, NH 03743; 603-542-6064;; 8AM-4PM (EST). *Misdemeanor, Civil Actions under $25,000, Eviction, Small Claims, Domestic, Juvenile.*
www.courts.state.nh.us/circuitcourt/index.htm
General Information: Search fee includes all 4 indexes, if asked. Jurisdiction area includes city of Claremont and the towns of Cornish, Unity, Charlestown, Acworth, Langdon, and Plainfield. No adoption, sealed, juvenile, mental health, expunged or dismissed records released. Will fax documents to local or toll-free number. Court makes copy: $.50 per page. Certification fee: $5.00 per cert. Payee: Claremont District Court. Personal checks, Visa/MC accepted. Prepayment required. Mail requests: SASE required.
Civil Name Search: Access: Phone, mail, in person. Only the court performs in person name searches; visitors may not. Search fee: Computer search is $20.00 per name for first 5 names then $5.00 each add'l name in that request. Court may charge less. Required to search: name, years to search, DOB. Civil records on computer from 10/92, on index cards from 1980, index books from 1960. Mail Turnaround time 1 week.
Criminal Name Search: Access: Phone, mail, in person. Only the court performs in person name searches; visitors may not. Search fee: Computer search is $20.00 per name for first 5 names then $5.00 each add'l name in that request. Court may charge less. Required to search: name, years to search, DOB. Criminal records computerized from 10/92, on index cards from 1980, index books from 1960. Mail Turnaround time 1 week.

Newport Circuit Court - District and Family Divisions 55 Main St, Newport, NH 03773; 603-863-1832;; 8AM-4PM (EST). *Misdemeanor, Civil Actions under $25,000, Eviction, Small Claims, Domestic, Juvenile.*
www.courts.state.nh.us/circuitcourt/index.htm
General Information: Jurisdiction includes towns of Grantham, Croydon, Springfield, Sunapee, Goshen, Lempster, Newport, New London, Newbury, Springfield, Sunapee, Washington and Wilmot. Includes cases from closed court in New London (New London, Newbury, Wilmot). No adoption, sealed, juvenile, mental health, expunged or dismissed records released. Will fax documents by special request. Court makes copy: $.50 per page. Certification fee: $5.00 per cert. Payee: Newport District Court. Personal checks, Visa/MC accepted. Prepayment required. Mail requests: SASE required.
Civil Name Search: Access: Mail, in person. Only the court performs in person name searches; visitors may not. Search fee: Computer search is $20.00 per name for first 5 names then $5.00 each add'l name in that request. Court may charge less. Civil records on computer from 1993, on index cards from 1980. Note: All requests must be in writing. Search fee includes all 4 indexes, if asked. Mail Turnaround time 2-3 days.
Criminal Name Search: Access: Mail, in person. Only the court performs in person name searches; visitors may not. Search fee: Computer search is $20.00 per name for first 5 names then $5.00 each add'l name in that request. Court may charge less. Required to search: name, years to search, DOB. Criminal records computerized from 1993, on index cards from 1980. Note: Requests must be in writing. Search fee includes all 4 indexes, if asked. Mail Turnaround time 2-3 days.

Probate Division 14 Main St, 3rd Fl, Newport, NH 03773; 603-863-3150; ; 8AM-4PM (EST). *Probate.*
www.courts.state.nh.us/probate/

New Jersey

Time Zone:	**EST**
Capital:	**Trenton, Mercer County**
# of Counties:	**83**
State Web:	**www.state.nj.us**
Court Web:	**www.judiciary.state.nj.us**

Administration

Administrative Office of the Courts, RJH Justice Complex, Courts Bldg 7th Fl, PO Box 037, Trenton, NJ, 08625; 609-984-0275, Fax: 609-984-6968.

The Supreme Court and the Court of Appeals

The New Jersey Supreme Court is the highest appellate court. The Appellate Division of the Superior Court is New Jersey's intermediate Appellate Court. Appellate Division judges hear appeals from decisions of the trial courts, the Tax Court and State administrative agencies. Opinions from the Supreme or Appellate Court are viewable from the home page above – click on *Opinions*.

The New Jersey Courts

Court	Type	How Organized	Jurisdiction Highpoints
Superior*	General	21 Courts in 21 Counties	Felony, Misdemeanor, Civil, Domestic, Family, Juvenile
Special Civil Part*	Limited	21 Courts in 21 Counties	Civil to $15,000, Small Claims, Eviction,
Municipal*	Limited	535 Courts	Misdemeanor, Ordinance, Traffic
Tax*	Special	1	Probate

* = profiled in this book

Details on the Court Structure

Each **Superior Court** has 3 divisions; Civil, Criminal, and Family. Search requests should be addressed separately to each division. Criminal cases are those in which a defendant stands accused of a serious crime, such as assault, theft, robbery, fraud, or murder. Civil cases in which the amount in controversy exceeds $15,000 are heard in the Civil Division of Superior Court.

Cases in which the amounts in controversy are between $3,000 and $15,000 are heard in the **Special Civil Part** of the Civil Division. Those in which the amounts in controversy are less than $3,000 also are heard in the Special Civil Part and are known as Small Claims cases.

Civil cases in which monetary damages are not being sought are heard in the General Equity Division of Superior Court. General Equity judges handle non-jury cases such as those involving trade secrets, labor matters, foreclosures and other disputes in which court relief, often in the form of restraining orders, is sought on an emergency basis.

Family related cases, such as those involving divorce, domestic violence, juvenile delinquency, child support, foster-care placements and termination of parental rights, are heard by the Family Division. Probate is handled by the Surrogates Court.

The **Municipal Courts** are courts of limited jurisdiction with responsibility for motor vehicle and parking tickets, minor criminal offenses (see Promis/Gavel below), municipal ordinance offenses, and other offenses, such as fish and game violations.

Record Searching Facts You Need to Know

Fees and Record Searching Tips

Note that Cape May County offices are located in City of Cape May Court House, and not in City of Cape May.

There are state guidelines for certain court record fees. Copies of paper records provided to the public are $.05 per page for letter size and $.07 per page for legal size. A certified copy is $5.00 for the first 5 pages plus $.75 for each additional page. But be aware that not all courts necessarily follow the pricing mandates. See www.judiciary.state.nj.us/superior/copies_court_rec.htm#caf .

The Superior Court Records Center in Trenton will provide copies of civil, divorce, and general equity records statewide. The case number must be supplied first. Call 609-292-4804 for further details.

Criminal name searches may be done in person at the court house using the public access terminals. But the data provided is not necessarily complete (see *About Promis/Gavel* below). Many Superior Courts direct non-in person searches to the New Jersey State Police (NJSP) Records and ID Section at 609-882-2000, x2991 or x2918. This organization reportedly has the most complete database publicly available.

About Promis/Gavel and Criminal Record Searches

Originally developed for county prosecutors, the Promis/Gavel is an automated criminal case tracking system providing the case management functions including docketing, indexing, noticing, calendaring, statistical reporting, etc. Promis/Gavel is interactive with the courts as well as with the NJSP. However, the public cannot access the complete Promis/Gavel system—only a filtered Promis/Gavel Public Access (PGPA) system is available to the public. The filtered system is the data shown on the public access terminals at court locations.

The reason this system is referred to as "filtered" is because the PGPA does not include soundex name searching. Also it does not show offenses or petty offenses recorded in the 530+ Municipal Courts, unless they are filed with indictables. The more serious of these petty offenses include drug offenses, violence, theft, sexual assault, and pedophilia. An AOC press release about the PGPA states, "The court records obtained from Promis/Gavel do not constitute a criminal history records check, which must be obtained through law enforcement." However be advised that professionals in New Jersey recommend to proceed with caution if you are only using PGPA for a criminal record search.

Online Access is Limited to Primarily Civil Records

A free statewide access service to civil cases and civil judgments is available at http://njcourts.judiciary.state.nj.us/web1/ACMSPA/. One may search by name or docket number. If a name search is performed, it is name only - no personal identifiers are shown except an address on docket.

Also, the State offers an Electronic Access Program to civil case docket and summary information from four separate state information systems. Included are the Automated Case Management Systems (ACMS), the Civil Judgment and Order Docket, the Family Automated Case Tracking System (FACTS), and the Automated Traffic System (ATS). The fee is $1.00 per minute. Subscribers receive only a screen view; downloads and data extraction (screen-scraping) are not available. For more information and enrollment forms see www.judiciary.state.nj.us/superior/eap_main.htm.

The Judiciary's civil motion calendar and schedule is searchable at www.judiciary.state.nj.us/calendars.htm. The database includes all Superior Court Motion calendars for the Civil Division (Law-Civil Part, Special Civil Part and Chancery-General Equity), and proceeding information for a six-week period (two weeks prior to the current date and four weeks following the current date).

Atlantic County

Superior Court - Criminal Criminal Courthouse, 4997 Unami Blvd, Mays Landing, NJ 08330; criminal phone: 609-909-8154; fax: 609-909-8190; 8:30AM-4:30PM (EST). *Felony, Misdemeanor.* www.judiciary.state.nj.us/atlantic/index.htm

General Information: No sealed, expunged, judges notes, PSI's, or mental illness records released. Will not fax documents. Court makes copy: $.05 per page letter size: $.07 per page legal size. Certification fee: Per statewide mandate fee $5.00 for the first 5 pages plus $.75 for each additional page. Payee: Treasurer, State of NJ. Personal checks accepted, credit cards are not. Prepayment required.

Criminal Name Search: Access: In person only. Visitors must perform in person searches themselves. Required to search: name, years to search, DOB; SSN helpful. Criminal records computerized from 1985, prior on docket books and index cards back to 1940. Public use terminal has crim records back to 1985. Aliases also shown in results.

Superior Court - Civil 1201 Bacharach Blvd., Atlantic City, NJ 08401; 609-345-6700; fax: 609-343-2326; 8:30AM-4:30PM (EST). *Civil Actions over $15,000, Probate.* www.judiciary.state.nj.us/atlantic/index.htm

General Information: As a practical matter, searching any civil court can be preformed at any civil court location. No sealed, expunged, judges notes, PSI's, or mental illness records released. Will not fax documents unless special circumstance. Court makes copy: $.05 per page letter size: $.07 per page legal size. Self serve copy: $.15 per page. Certification fee: Per statewide mandate fee $5.00 for the first 5 pages plus $.75 for each additional page. Payee: Clerk of Special Civil Ct. Personal checks accepted, credit cards are not. Prepayment required. Mail requests: SASE required.

Civil Name Search: Access: In person, online. Both court and visitors may perform in person name searches. Civil records on computer from 9/84, on dockets from 1960, prior to 1960 archived. Prior to 1960 records are for public review only in large books. In order to review index books, call in advance for an appointment. Mail Turnaround time 1 day. Public use terminal has civil records back to 1985. **See the front or back of the chapter for details about online access to civil dockets, calendar, and a subscription service.**

Superior Court Special Civil Part 1201 Bacharach Blvd., Atlantic City, NJ 08401; 609-345-6700 X3347; fax: 609-343-2326; 8:30AM-4:30PM (EST). *Civil Actions under $15,000, Eviction, Small Claims.* www.judiciary.state.nj.us/atlantic/index.htm

General Information: As a practical matter, searching any civil court can be preformed at any county civil court location. No adoption, sealed, juvenile, expunged, dismissed, or mental health records released. Will not fax documents unless special circumstance. Court makes copy: $.05 per page letter size: $.07 per page legal size. Self serve copy: $.15 per page. Certification fee: Per statewide mandate fee $5.00 for the first 5 pages plus $.75 for each additional page. Payee: Clerk, Special Civil Part. Personal checks accepted, credit cards are not. Prepayment required. Mail requests: SASE required.

Civil Name Search: Access: In person, online. Both court and visitors may perform in person name searches. Civil records on computer from 1985 (some from 1987), prior on index books. In order to review index books, call in advance for an appointment. Mail Turnaround time 1 week. Public use terminal has civil records back to 1987. **See the front or back of the chapter for details about online access to civil dockets, calendar, and a subscription service.**

Bergen County

Superior Court - Criminal 10 Main St, Rm 124, Justice Ctr, Hackensack, NJ 07601; 201-527-2445; criminal phone: x3; fax: 201-371-1118; 8:30AM-4:30PM (EST). *Felony, Misdemeanor.* www.judiciary.state.nj.us/bergen/index.htm

General Information: No sealed, expunged, dismissed, judges notes, PSI's, or discovery packets records released. Will not fax documents. Court makes copy: $.05 per page letter size: $.07 per page legal size. Certification fee: $5.00 per case. Payee: Bergen County Clerk. Personal checks accepted, credit cards are not. Prepayment required.

Criminal Name Search: Access: Mail, in person. Both court and visitors may perform in person name searches. No search fee. Criminal records computerized from 1995. Public use terminal has crim records. Public record terminal located in the Library.

Superior Court - Civil 10 Main St. Rm 111, Justice Ctr, Hackensack, NJ 07601; 201-527-2700; civil phone: x2601; probate phone: 201-646-2252;; 8:30AM-4:30PM (EST). *Civil Actions over $15,000, Probate.* www.judiciary.state.nj.us/bergen/index.htm

General Information: Probate records managed by Surrogate's Court. No sealed, expunged, dismissed, judges notes, PSI's, or discovery packets records released. Will not fax documents. Court makes copy: $.05 per page letter size: $.07 per page legal size. Self serve copy: $.25 per page. Certification fee: Per statewide mandate fee $5.00 for the first 5 pages plus $.75 for each additional page. Payee: Bergen County Clerk. Personal checks accepted, credit cards are not. Prepayment required. Mail requests: SASE required for civil.

Civil Name Search: Access: Mail, in person, online. Only the court performs in person name searches; visitors may not. Civil records on computer for 2-5 years, on dockets from 1900s. Mail Turnaround time 1 week. Public use terminal has civil records back to 2-5 years. Public terminals in law library. S **See the front or back of the chapter for details about online access to civil dockets, calendar, and a subscription service.**

Superior Court Special Civil Part 10 Main St, Rm 427, Justice Ctr, Hackensack, NJ 07601; 201-527-2700; civil phone: x2;; 8:30AM-4:30PM (EST). *Civil Actions under $15,000, Eviction, Small Claims.* www.judiciary.state.nj.us/bergen/index.htm

General Information: No adoption, sealed, juvenile, expunged, dismissed, or mental illness records released. Will not fax documents. Court makes copy: $.05 per page letter size: $.07 per page legal size. Certification fee: Per statewide mandate fee $5.00 for the first 5 pages plus $.75 for each additional page. Payee: Bergen County Special Civil Part. Personal checks accepted, credit cards are not. Prepayment required. Mail requests: SASE required.

Civil Name Search: Access: In person, phone, online. Both court and visitors may perform in person name searches. No search fee. Required to search: name, years to search, case identifiers. Civil records on computer from 1990, prior on index cards. Note: Due to identity matching problems, this Special Civil Parts prefer not to perform name searches; please provide a case or docket number. Public use terminal has civil records. Public terminal is located in the law library. **See the front or back of the chapter for details about online access to civil dockets, calendar, and a subscription service.**

Burlington County

Superior Court - Criminal 49 Rancocas Rd, Mount Holly, NJ 08060; 609-518-2560; fax: 609-518-2569; 8AM-5PM (EST). *Felony, Misdemeanor.* www.judiciary.state.nj.us/burlington/index.htm

General Information: No sealed, expunged, judges notes, PSI's, or discovery packets released. Will not fax documents. Court makes copy: $.05 per page letter size: $.07 per page legal size. Certification fee: Per statewide mandate fee $5.00 for the first 5 pages plus $.75 for each additional page. Payee: State of New Jersey Treasurer. Personal checks accepted, credit cards are not. Prepayment required.

Criminal Name Search: Access: In person only. Visitors must perform in person searches themselves. Required to search: name, years to search; also helpful: DOB, SSN. Criminal records computerized from 1986, on docket books from 1954, archived from early 1900s. Public use terminal has crim records.

Superior Court - Civil 49 Rancocas Rd, Mount Holly, NJ 08060; 609-518-2815; fax: 609-518-2826; 8:30AM-4:30PM (EST). *Civil Actions over $15,000, Probate.* www.judiciary.state.nj.us/burlington/index.htm

General Information: No sealed, expunged, judges notes, PSI's, or discovery packets released. Court makes copy: $.05 per page letter size: $.07 per page legal size. Certification fee: Per statewide mandate fee $5.00 for the first 5 pages plus $.75 for each additional page. Payee: State of New Jersey Treasurer. Personal checks accepted, credit cards are not. Prepayment required. Mail requests: SASE required for civil.

Civil Name Search: Access: Mail, in person, online. Both court and visitors may perform in person name searches. No search fee.Local judgment records on computer since 1989, all others from 1954 to present. Mail Turnaround time 10 days. Public use terminal has civil records back to 1989. **See the front or back of the chapter for details about online access to civil dockets, calendar, and a subscription service.**

Superior Court Special Civil Part 49 Rancocas Rd., Mount Holly, NJ 08060; 609-518-2865; fax: 609-518-2872; 8:30AM-4:30PM (EST). *Civil Actions under $15,000, Eviction, Small Claims.* www.njcourtsonline.com

General Information: This court does not handle criminal matters in the Special Civil Part. No fee to fax documents. Court makes copy: $.05 per page letter size: $.07 per page legal size. Certification fee: Per statewide mandate fee $5.00 for the first 5 pages plus $.75 for each additional page. Payee: Treasurer, State of NJ. Personal checks accepted, credit cards are not. Prepayment required. Mail requests: SASE required.

Civil Name Search: Access: Phone, fax, mail, in person. Both court and visitors may perform in person name searches. No search fee. Civil records on computer from 1995, microfilm from 1984, prior on index books by docket number. Mail Turnaround time 1-2 weeks. Public use terminal has civil records back to 1995. **See the front or back of the chapter for details about online access to civil dockets, calendar, and a subscription service.**

Camden County

Superior Court - Criminal Hall of Justice, 101 S 5th St, Camden, NJ 08103; 856-379-2200; criminal phone: x3343; fax: 856-379-2255; 8:30AM-4:30PM (EST). *Felony, Misdemeanor.* www.judiciary.state.nj.us/camden/index.htm

General Information: No sealed, expunged, dismissed, judges notes, PSI's or discovery packets records released. Will not fax documents. Court makes copy: $.05 per page letter size: $.07 per page legal size. Certification fee: Per statewide mandate fee $5.00 for the first 5 pages plus $.75 for each additional page. Payee: NJ State Treasurer. Cash, money orders or business checks accepted - no personal checks. No credit cards accepted. Prepayment required. Mail requests: SASE required.

Criminal Name Search: Access: Mail, fax, in person. Both court and visitors may perform in person name searches. Search fee: None, but a fee is to be implemented soon. Required to search: name, years to search, DOB, SSN. Criminal records computerized from 1986, on docket books from 1940. Mail Turnaround time 3-5 days. Public use terminal has crim records back to 1986.

Superior Court - Civil Hall of Justice, Ste 670, 101 S 5th St, Camden, NJ 08103; 856-379-2200; civil phone: 856-379-2202; fax: 856-379-2255; 8:30AM-4:30PM (EST). *Civil Actions over $15,000, Probate.* www.judiciary.state.nj.us/camden/index.htm

General Information: No sealed, dismissed, judges notes, or discovery packets records released. Will not fax documents. Court makes copy: $.05 per page letter size: $.07 per page legal size. Certification fee: Per statewide mandate fee $5.00 for the first 5 pages plus $.75 for each additional page. Payee: Clerk of Superior Court. Personal checks accepted, credit cards are not. Prepayment required. Mail requests: SASE required.

Civil Name Search: Access: Mail, in person, online. Both court and visitors may perform in person name searches. No search fee. Civil records on computer from 1987. Note: Also, mail or in person judgment searches are directed to Trenton. Mail Turnaround time 5 days. Public use terminal has civil records back to 1987. **See the front or back of the chapter for details about online access to civil dockets, calendar, and a subscription service.**

Superior Court Special Civil Part Hall of Justice Complex, 101 S. 5th St., Camden, NJ 08103; 856-379-2202; fax: 856-379-2252; 8:30AM-4:30PM (EST). *Civil Actions under $15,000, Eviction, Small Claims.*
www.judiciary.state.nj.us/camden/index.htm
General Information: Alternate fax number- 856-379-2253. Docket numbers with "DC" indicates cases under $15,000; if "SC" then under $3,000. No adoption, sealed, juvenile, expunged, restricted, or mental health records released. Will not fax documents. Court makes copy: $.05 per page letter size: $.07 per page legal size. Certification fee: $5.00 for the first 5 pages plus $.75 for each additional page. Payee: Treasurer, State of NJ. Personal checks accepted, credit cards are not. Prepayment required. Mail requests: SASE required for mail return of any copies.

Civil Name Search: Access: Mail, in person. Both court and visitors may perform in person name searches. No search fee. Civil records on computer from 1988. Prior records on docket books. Note: In person access is limited to one name. Mail Turnaround time varies; larger orders take longer. Public use terminal has civil records back to 1988. **See the front or back of the chapter for details about online access to civil dockets, calendar, and a subscription service..**

Cape May County

Superior Court - Criminal 9 N Main St, Superior Court, Cape May Court House, NJ 08210; 609-463-6550; criminal phone: 609-463-6500; fax: 609-463-6458; 8:30AM-4:30PM (EST). *Felony, Misdemeanor.*
www.judiciary.state.nj.us/atlantic/index.htm
General Information: No sealed, expunged, dismissed, judges notes, PSI's, or discovery packets records released. Court makes copy: $.05 per page letter size: $.07 per page legal size. Certification fee: Per statewide mandate fee $5.00 for the first 5 pages plus $.75 for each additional page. Payee: State of New Jersey Treasurer. Personal checks accepted, credit cards are not. Prepayment required.

Criminal Name Search: Access: In person only. Visitors must perform in person searches themselves. Required to search: name, years to search, DOB; SSN helpful. Criminal records computerized from 1985; on index books back to 1950. Public use terminal has crim records back to 1985.

Superior Court - Civil Civil/Equity Division-Law, DN-203, 9 N Main St, Cape May Court House, NJ 08210; 609-463-6514; fax: 609-463-6465; 8:30AM-4:30PM (EST). *Civil Actions over $15,000, Probate.*
www.judiciary.state.nj.us/atlantic/index.htm
General Information: No sealed records released. Will not fax documents. Court makes copy: $.05 per page letter size: $.07 per page legal size. Certification fee: Per statewide mandate fee $5.00 for the first 5 pages plus $.75 for each additional page. Payee: Treasurer, State of NJ. Personal checks accepted, credit cards are not. Prepayment required.

Civil Name Search: Access: In person only. Visitors must perform in person searches themselves. Civil records on computer from 4/91, on index books and archived from 1900s. Public use terminal has civil records back to 1991. **See the front or back of the chapter for details about online access to civil dockets, calendar, and a subscription service.**

Superior Court Special Civil Part DN-203, 9 N. Main St, Cape May Court House, NJ 08210; 609-463-6522; fax: 609-463-6465; 8:30AM-4:30PM (EST). *Civil Actions under $15,000, Eviction, Small Claims.*
www.judiciary.state.nj.us/atlantic/index.htm
General Information: No sealed records released. Will not fax documents. Court makes copy: $.05 per page letter size: $.07 per page legal size. Certification fee: Per statewide mandate fee $5.00 for the first 5 pages plus $.75 for each additional page. Payee: Treasurer, State of NJ. Personal checks accepted, credit cards are not. Prepayment required.

Civil Name Search: Access: In person only. Visitors must perform in person searches themselves. Required to search: name, years to search; also helpful: address. Civil records on computer from 4/1991, on index from 1973. Public use terminal has civil records. **See the front or back of the chapter for details about online access to civil dockets, calendar, and a subscription service.**

Cumberland County

Superior Court - Criminal 60 W. Beral, Courthouse, Broad/Fayette Strs, Bridgeton, NJ 08302; 856-453-4300; fax: 856-451-7152; 8:30AM-4:30PM (EST). *Felony, Misdemeanor.*
www.judiciary.state.nj.us/gloucester/cum/index.htm
General Information: NJ State Police Search, PO Box 7068, West Trenton, NJ 08625. Phone number is 609-882-2000. No sealed, expunged, dismissed, judges notes, PSI's, or discovery packets records released. Will not fax documents. Court makes copy: $.05 per page letter size: $.07 per page legal size. Certification fee: Per statewide mandate fee $5.00 for the first 5 pages plus $.75 for each additional page. Payee: State of New Jersey, Misc Fund. Personal checks accepted, credit cards are not. Prepayment required. Mail requests: SASE required.

Criminal Name Search: Access: Mail, in person. Both court and visitors may perform in person name searches. Search fee: $4.00 per name. Required to search: name, years to search, DOB, SSN, signed release; also helpful: address. Criminal records computerized from 1986, on index from 1900. Mail Turnaround time 1 week. Public use terminal has crim records back to 1986. Public access terminal in Law Library.

Superior Court - Civil 60 W Broad St, Bridgeton, NJ 08302; 856-453-4330; civil phone: 856-453-4350; fax: 856-453-4349; 8:30AM-4:30PM (EST). *Civil Actions over $15,000, Probate.*
www.judiciary.state.nj.us/gloucester/index.htm
General Information: No sealed, expunged, dismissed, judges notes, PSI's, or discovery packets records released. Court makes copy: $.05 per page letter size: $.07 per page legal size. Certification fee: $5.00. Payee: Treasurer - State of New Jersey. Personal checks accepted, credit cards are not. Prepayment required. Mail requests: SASE required.

Civil Name Search: Access: Mail, in person, online. Both court and visitors may perform in person name searches. Search fee: $4.00 per name. Civil records on computer from 1986, on index from 1900. Mail Turnaround time 1 week. **See the front or back of the chapter for details about online access to civil dockets, calendar, and a subscription service.**

Superior Court Special Civil Part 60 W Broad, Bridgeton, NJ 08302; 856-453-4350; fax: 856-453-4349; 8:30AM-4:30PM (EST). *Civil Actions under $15,000, Eviction, Small Claims.*
www.judiciary.state.nj.us/gloucester/index.htm
General Information: Judgment Unit Information phone number is 609-421-6100 No adoption, sealed, juvenile, expunged, dismissed, or mental illness records released. Court makes copy: $.05 per page letter size: $.07 per page legal size. Certification fee: $5.00. Payee: Treasurer, State of NJ. Personal checks accepted, credit cards are not. Prepayment required. Mail requests: SASE requested.

Civil Name Search: Access: Phone, mail, in person. Both court and visitors may perform in person name searches. No search fee. Civil records on computer from 12/89, on docket books from 1949 to 11/89. Note: Phone access is limited to 1 or 2 searches. Mail Turnaround time 1 week. Public use terminal has civil records. **See the front or back of the chapter for details about online access to civil dockets, calendar, and a subscription service.**

Essex County

Superior Court - Criminal 50 W Market St, Rm 1012, County Court Bldg, Veterans Ct, Newark, NJ 07102-1681; 973-693-5965, 973-693-5700-switchboard; fax: 973-693-5963; 8:30AM-4:30PM (EST). *Felony, Misdemeanor.* www.judiciary.state.nj.us/essex/index.htm
General Information: No sealed, expunged, dismissed, judges notes, PSI's, or discovery packets records released. Will fax documents to local or toll free line. Court makes copy: $.05 per page letter size: $.07 per page legal size. Certification fee: Per statewide mandate fee $5.00 for the first 5 pages plus $.75 for each additional page. Payee: State of New Jersey Treasurer. Only cashiers checks and money orders accepted. No credit cards accepted. Prepayment required. Mail requests: SASE required.

Criminal Name Search: Access: Mail, in person. Both court and visitors may perform in person name searches. Search fee: $5.00 per indictment. Required to search: name, years to search, DOB, SSN. Criminal records computerized from 1985. Note: All records requests must be mailed with pre-payment. Mail Turnaround time 1 week. Public use terminal has crim records back to 1985.

Superior Court - Civil 465 Dr. Martin Luther King Blvd, Rm 201, Newark, NJ 07102-1681; 973-693-5529; ; 8:30AM-4:30PM (EST). *Civil Actions, Law, Probate.*
www.judiciary.state.nj.us/essex/civil/home.htm
General Information: No sealed, expunged, dismissed, judges notes, PSI's, or discovery packets records released. Will fax documents $3.00 per page. Court makes copy: $.05 per page letter size: $.07 per page legal size. Self serve copy: $.10 per copy; machine accepts up to $5.00 bills. Certification fee: $5.00 for the first 5 pages plus $.75 for each additional page. Payee: State

of New Jersey Treasurer. Business checks accepted. No credit cards accepted. Prepayment required. Mail requests: SASE required.

Civil Name Search: Access: In person, online. Only the court performs in person name searches; visitors may not. No search fee. Civil records on computer from 1984, on index from 1930. Note: Visitors may perform their own searches at the Ombudsman Office, Rm 132, 50 W Market St, Newark. **See the front or back of the chapter for details about online access to civil dockets, calendar, and a subscription service.**

Superior Court Special Civil Part 465 Martin Luther King Blvd, Rm 240, Hall of Records, Newark, NJ 07102; 973-693-6494; 693-6460- recs; ; 8:30AM-4:30PM (EST). *Civil Actions under $15,000, Eviction, Small Claims.* www.judiciary.state.nj.us/essex/civil/home.htm
General Information: No adoption, sealed, juvenile, expunged, dismissed, or mental illness records released. Will not fax out documents. Court makes copy: $.05 per page letter size: $.07 per page legal size. Certification fee: Per statewide mandate fee $5.00 for the first 5 pages plus $.75 for each additional page. Payee: Essex County Special Civil Part. Personal checks accepted, credit cards are not. Prepayment required. Mail requests: SASE helpful.
Civil Name Search: Access: Mail, fax, in person, online. Both court and visitors may perform in person name searches. No search fee. Civil records on computer from 1986 and archived 1982-2004. Note: Pre- 2005 records are in storage and will take longer to process. Mail Turnaround time 7-10 days. Public use terminal has civil records back to 1990's. Search PAT index free in Rm 132 only. **See the front or back of the chapter for details about online access to civil dockets, calendar, and a subscription service.**

Gloucester County

Superior Court - Criminal PO Box 187, 70 Hunter St, Woodbury, NJ 08096; 856-856-686-7500; fax: 856-853-3735; 8:30AM-4:30PM (EST). *Felony, Misdemeanor.* www.judiciary.state.nj.us/gloucester/glo/index.htm
General Information: No sealed, expunged, dismissed, judges notes, PSI's, or discovery packets records released. Will not fax documents. Court makes copy: $.05 per page letter size: $.07 per page legal size. Certification fee: Per statewide mandate fee $5.00 for the first 5 pages plus $.75 for each additional page. Payee: State of New Jersey, Miscellaneous. Personal checks accepted, credit cards are not. Prepayment required. Mail requests: SASE required.
Criminal Name Search: Access: In person. Visitors must perform in person searches themselves. Required to search: name, years to search, DOB, SSN, signed release. Criminal records computerized from 1982, on index from 1955. Mail Turnaround time 1-3 days. Public use terminal has crim records back to 1982. Terminal in Family Court location or at Law Library in building complex.

Superior Court - Civil 1 N Broad St, Woodbury, NJ 08096; 856-853-3232; civil phone: 856-853-3392; fax: 856-853-3429; 8:30AM-4:30PM (EST). *Civil Actions, Probate.*
www.judiciary.state.nj.us/gloucester/glo/index.htm
General Information: Probate files with Surrogate Court. No sealed, expunged, dismissed, judges notes, PSI's, or discovery packets records released. Will not fax documents. Court makes copy: $.05 per page letter size: $.07 per page legal size. Certification fee: Per statewide mandate fee $5.00 for the first 5 pages plus $.75 for each additional page. Payee: Treasurer State of New Jersey. Personal checks accepted, credit cards are not. Prepayment required. Mail requests: SASE required.
Civil Name Search: Access: Mail, in person, online. Only the court performs in person name searches; visitors may not. No search fee. Civil records on computer from 1988, prior records on county books. Note: Searches are done looking at the electronic filing system. Mail Turnaround time ASAP. **See the front or back of the chapter for details about online access to civil dockets, calendar, and a subscription service.**

Superior Court Special Civil Part 1 N Broad St., Woodbury, NJ 08096; 856-853-3392; fax: 856-853-3416; 8:30AM-4:30PM (EST). *Civil Actions under $15,000, Eviction, Small Claims.*
www.judiciary.state.nj.us/gloucester/glo/index.htm
General Information: Court makes copy: $.05 per page letter size: $.07 per page legal size. Certification fee: $5.00 for the first 5 pages plus $.75 for each additional page. Payee: Clerk, Superior Court of NJ. Personal checks accepted. Prepayment required. Mail requests: SASE required.
Civil Name Search: Access: Mail, in person, online. Only the court performs in person name searches; visitors may not. No search fee. Civil records on computer from 8/89, on index books from 1900. **See the front or back of the chapter for details about online access to civil dockets, calendar, and a subscription service.**

Hudson County

Superior Court - Criminal Record Office 595 Newark Ave, Rm 101, Jersey City, NJ 07306; 201-795-6659; fax: 201-795-6121; 8:30AM-4:30PM (EST). *Felony, Misdemeanor.*

www.judiciary.state.nj.us/hudson/index.htm
General Information: No sealed, expunged, dismissed, judges notes, PSI's, or discovery packets records released. Will not fax documents. Court makes copy: $.05 per page letter size: $.07 per page legal size. Certification fee: Per statewide mandate fee $5.00 for the first 5 pages plus $.75 for each additional page. Payee: Treasurer, State of NJ. Personal checks accepted, credit cards are not. Prepayment required. Mail requests: SASE not required.
Criminal Name Search: Access: Mail, in person. Visitors must perform in person searches themselves. No search fee. Required to search: name, years to search, DOB, SSN. Criminal records computerized from 1985, on index books from 1956. Note: Court suggests access for a fee via www.state.nj.us/lps/njsp/about/serv_chrc.html - the NJ State Police. Mail Turnaround time 1 week. Public use terminal has crim records back to 1985. Public may search index books or terminal by name and dob.

Superior Court - Civil 595 Newark Ave, Jersey City, NJ 07306; 201-217-5162; 201-217-5163 (Records Rm); fax: 201-217-5241; 8:30AM-4:30PM (EST). *Civil Actions over $15,000, Probate.*
www.judiciary.state.nj.us/hudson/index.htm
General Information: No sealed, expunged, dismissed, judges notes, PSI's, or discovery packets records released. Will not fax documents. Court makes copy: $.05 per page letter size: $.07 per page legal size. Certification fee: Per statewide mandate fee $5.00. Payee: Treasurer, State of NJ. Personal checks accepted, credit cards are not. Prepayment required.
Civil Name Search: Access: In person, online. Both court and visitors may perform in person name searches. No search fee. Civil record images on computer for 18 months after disposition. Public use terminal has civil records to 1992. **See the front or back of the chapter for details about online access to civil dockets, calendar, and a subscription service.**

Superior Court Special Civil Part 595 Newark Ave, Rm G-9, Jersey City, NJ 07306; 201-795-6000; criminal phone: 201-217-5162; fax: 201-795-6053; 8:30AM-4:30PM (EST). *Civil Actions under $15,000, Eviction, Small Claims.* www.judiciary.state.nj.us/hudson/index.htm
General Information: The web page for the county is www.hudsoncountynj.org/. Any inquires concerning court records should be addressed to the Court Administrator's Office. No adoption, sealed, juvenile, expunged, dismissed, or mental illness released. Court makes copy: $.05 per page letter size: $.07 per page legal size. Self serve copy: Self serve copier in 5th Fl Library. Certification fee: Per statewide mandate fee $5.00 for the first 5 pages plus $.75 for each additional page. Payee: Treasurer, State of NJ. Personal checks accepted, credit cards are not. Prepayment required.
Civil Name Search: Access: In person, online. Visitors must perform in person searches themselves. Required to search: name, years to search, address. Civil index on cards from 1993, prior on docket books. Public use terminal has civil records back to 1995. **See the front or back of the chapter for details about online access to civil dockets, calendar, and a subscription service.**

Hunterdon County

Superior Court - Criminal 65 Park Ave, Flemington, NJ 08822; 908-237-5840; fax: 908-237-5841; 8:30AM-4:30PM (EST). *Felony, Misdemeanor.* www.judiciary.state.nj.us/somerset/index.htm
General Information: No sealed, expunged, dismissed, judges notes, PSI's, or discovery packets records released. Will fax documents, no charge. Court makes copy: $.05 per page letter size: $.07 per page legal size. Certification fee: Per statewide mandate fee $5.00 for the first 5 pages. Payee: Treasurer, State of New Jersey. Personal checks accepted, credit cards are not. Prepayment required. Mail requests: SASE required.
Criminal Name Search: Access: Fax, mail, in person. Visitors must perform in person searches themselves. Search fee: $6.00 per name. Required to search: name, years to search, DOB; also helpful: SSN. Criminal records computerized from 1987, prior on index books. Mail Turnaround time 1-3 weeks. Public use terminal has crim records back to 1987.

Superior Court - Civil Hunterdon County Justice Ctr, 65 Park Ave, Flemington, NJ 08822; 908-237-5820; probate phone: 908-788-1156; fax: 908-237-5821; 8:30AM-4:30PM (EST). *Civil Actions over $15,000, Probate.* www.judiciary.state.nj.us/somerset/index.htm
General Information: Probate records are indexed separately and are located on the 2nd Fl Surrogate/Probate office. No sealed, expunged, dismissed, judges notes, PSI's, or discovery packets records released. Will not fax documents. Court makes copy: $.05 per page letter size: $.07 per page legal size. Certification fee: Per statewide mandate fee $5.00 for the first 5 pages plus $.75 for each additional page. Payee: Treasurer State of New Jersey. Personal checks accepted, credit cards are not. Prepayment required. Mail requests: SASE required.
Civil Name Search: Access: Mail, in person, phone, online. Both court and visitors may perform in person name searches. No search fee. Civil records on computer since 1990, on index from 1950. Mail Turnaround time 1-2 weeks. Public use terminal has civil records back to 1990. **See the**

front or back of the chapter for details about online access to civil dockets, calendar, and a subscription service.

Superior Court Special Civil Part Hunterdon County Justice Ctr, 65 Park Ave, 2nd Fl, Flemington, NJ 08822; 908-237-5820; fax: 908-237-5821; 8:30AM-4:30PM (EST). *Civil Actions under $15,000, Eviction, Small Claims.* www.judiciary.state.nj.us/somerset/index.htm

General Information: No protective order files records released. Will not fax documents. Court makes copy: $.05 per page letter size: $.07 per page legal size. Self serve copy: $.15 per page. Certification fee: $5.00 for the first 5 pages plus $.75 for each additional page. Payee: Treasurer, State of NJ. Money orders, cash or personal checks accepted, credit cards are not. Prepayment required. Mail requests: SASE required.

Civil Name Search: Access: Phone, mail, in person, online. Both court and visitors may perform in person name searches. No search fee. Civil cases indexed by plaintiff, defendant. Civil records on computer from 1991, on index books from 1900. Mail Turnaround time 1 week. Public use terminal has civil records back to 1991. **See the front or back of the chapter for details about online access to civil dockets, calendar, and a subscription service.**

Mercer County

Superior Court - Criminal 209 S. Broad St, 2nd Fl, PO Box 8068, Trenton, NJ 08650-0068; 609-571-4000 x5; Crim Recs 609-571-4107; fax: 609-571-4161; 8:30AM-4:30PM; Search hrs- 9AM-3:30PM (EST). *Felony, Misdemeanor.*
www.judiciary.state.nj.us/mercer/index.htm

General Information: No sealed, expunged, judges notes, PSI's, or discovery packets records released. Will fax documents to local or toll-free number. Court makes copy: $.05 per page letter size: $.07 per page legal size. Certification fee: Per statewide mandate fee $5.00 for the first 5 pages plus $.75 for each additional page. Payee: Treasurer, State of NJ. Personal checks accepted, credit cards are not. Prepayment required. Mail requests: SASE not required.

Criminal Name Search: Access: In person only. Visitors must perform in person searches themselves. Required to search: name, years to search, DOB, SSN. Criminal records computerized from 1985, on docket books from 1900s. Note: Court will pull files and make copies, but will not search. Public use terminal has crim records back to 1985.

Superior Court - Civil 175 S Broad, #152, PO Box 8068, Trenton, NJ 08650-0068; 609-571-4490 3; fax: 609-571-4473; 8:30AM-4:30PM (EST). *Civil Actions over $15,000, Probate.*
www.judiciary.state.nj.us/mercer/index.htm

General Information: No sealed, expunged, dismissed, judges notes, PSI's, or discovery packets records released. Will fax documents to local or toll-free number but page number limit. Court makes copy: $.05 per page letter size: $.07 per page legal size. Certification fee: Per statewide mandate fee $5.00 for the first 5 pages plus $.75 for each additional page. Payee: Treasurer, State of NJ. Personal checks accepted, credit cards are not. Prepayment required. Mail requests: SASE required for Civil.

Civil Name Search: Access: Fax, mail, in person, online. Only the court performs in person name searches; visitors may not. No search fee. Civil records on computer since 1995, archived from 1972, on microfiche from 1965, prior indexed from 1894. Mail Turnaround time up to 2 weeks. Public use terminal has civil records back to 1995. Public terminal show address, usually. **See the front or back of the chapter for details about online access to civil dockets, calendar, and a subscription service.**

Superior Court Special Civil Part Box 8068, 175 S Broad St, 1st Fl, Trenton, NJ 08650; 609-571-4490 x1; civil phone: 609-571-4484; fax: 609-571-4489; 8:30AM-4:30PM (EST). *Civil Actions under $15,000, Eviction, Small Claims.* www.judiciary.state.nj.us/mercer/index.htm

General Information: Record index on a public access terminal at Hughes Justice Ctr, 25 Market St. No adoption, sealed, juvenile, expunged, dismissed, or mental illness records released. Will not fax documents. Court makes copy: $.05 per page letter size: $.07 per page legal size. Certification fee: Per statewide mandate fee $5.00 for the first 5 pages plus $.75 for each additional page. Payee: State of New Jersey. Only cash and money orders accepted - no personal checks. No credit cards accepted. Prepayment required.

Civil Name Search: Access: In person, online. Visitors must perform in person searches themselves. Civil records on computer from 1989, on index from 1984, some data on microfiche. Public use terminal has civil records back to 1989. **See the front or back of the chapter for details about online access to civil dockets, calendar, and a subscription service.**

Middlesex County

Superior Court - Criminal PO Box 964, New Brunswick, NJ 08901; 732-519-3853; ; 8:30AM-4:30PM (EST). *Felony, Misdemeanor.*
www.judiciary.state.nj.us/middlesex/index.htm

General Information: Physical address is 56 Paterson St. No sealed, expunged, PSI records released. Will not fax out documents. Court makes

copy: $.05 per page letter size. Self serve copy: same. Certification fee: $5.00 per cert. Payee: State of New Jersey Treasurer. Cash, personal checks, or money order accepted. No credit cards accepted. Prepayment required. Mail requests: SASE required.

Criminal Name Search: Access: Mail, in person. Visitors must perform in person searches themselves. No search fee. Required to search: name and DOB. Criminal records computerized from 1981, prior on index books back to 1956. Note: Court will only search if provided with arrest date, summons, indictment or prosecutor case number; no name searches performed. Mail Turnaround time up to 2 weeks. Public use terminal has crim records back to 1981.

Superior Court - Civil PO Box 2633, 56 Patterson St, 2nd Fl Tower, New Brunswick, NJ 08903; 732-981-2464, 519-3737, 519-3678; probate phone: 732-745-3055;; 8:15AM-4:30PM (EST). *Civil Actions over $15,000.* www.judiciary.state.nj.us/middlesex/index.htm

General Information: Probate is located at 75 Bayard St. No sealed, expunged, dismissed, judges notes, PSI's, on discovery packets records released. Will not fax documents. Court makes copy: $.05 per page letter size: $.07 per page legal size. Certification fee: Per statewide mandate fee $5.00 for the first 5 pages. Payee: Treasurer of The State of New Jersey. Personal checks accepted (no starter checks). No credit cards accepted. Prepayment required. Mail requests: SASE required.

Civil Name Search: Access: Mail, in person, online. Both court and visitors may perform in person name searches. No search fee. Required to search: name, years to search, if copies needed place request in writing. Civil records on computer from 1992, on docket books from 1940. Note: Place all requests in writing. Mail Turnaround time up to 3 weeks. Public use terminal has civil records back to 1992. **See the front or back of the chapter for details about online access to civil dockets, calendar, and a subscription service.**

Superior Court Special Civil Part PO Box 1146, 56 Paterson St, New Brunswick, NJ 08901; 732-519-3200; civil phone: x3301;; 8:30AM-4:30PM (EST). *Civil Actions under $15,000, Eviction, Small Claims.* www.judiciary.state.nj.us/middlesex/index.htm

General Information: No adoption, sealed, juvenile, expunged, dismissed, or mental health records released. Will not fax documents. Court makes copy: $.05 per page letter size: $.07 per page legal size. Certification fee: Per statewide mandate fee $5.00 for the first 5 pages plus $.75 for each additional page. Payee: Treasurer, State of NJ. Personal checks accepted, credit cards are not. Prepayment required.

Civil Name Search: Access: Mail, in person, online. Both court and visitors may perform in person name searches. No search fee. Civil records on computer from 1985, on docket books from 1960 (offsite). Mail Turnaround time 30 days. Public use terminal has civil records back to 1985. **See the front or back of the chapter for details about online access to civil dockets, calendar, and a subscription service.**

Monmouth County

Superior Court - Criminal 71 Monument Park, Rm 149, 1st Fl, E Wing, PO Box 1271, Freehold, NJ 07728-1271; 732-677-4300; fax: 732-677-4358; 8:30AM-4:30PM (EST). *Felony (indictable).*
www.judiciary.state.nj.us/monmouth/index.htm

General Information: This court holds only indictable case records. Will accept fax requests but only for specific case files. No sealed or expunged, judges notes, PSI's, or discovery packets records released. Will not fax back documents. Court makes copy: $.05 per page letter size: $.07 per page legal size. Certification fee: Per statewide mandate fee $5.00 per indictment. Cert fee includes copies. Payee: State of New Jersey Treasurer. Personal checks accepted; ID required. No credit cards accepted. Prepayment required.

Criminal Name Search: Access: In person only. Visitors must perform in person searches themselves. Criminal records computerized from 1986, on index books from 1956. Note: The agency asks requester to use the Records Request Form . Public use terminal has crim records back to 1986. Also terminal shows sex, race, weight, height, hair, eyes, SBI #.

Superior Court - Civil PO Box 1269, 71 Monument Pk, Freehold, NJ 07728-1255; 732-677-4298; civil phone: 732-677-4240; Special civil- 732-677-4270; Sm Claims- 732-677-4292; fax: 732-677-4369; 8:30AM-4:30PM (EST). *Civil Actions over $15,000; Special Civil.*
www.judiciary.state.nj.us/monmouth/index.htm

General Information: Direct civil search questions to Jennifer Oliver at 732-677-4257. No sealed, expunged, dismissed, judges notes, PSI's, or discovery packets records released. Court makes copy: $.05 per page letter size: $.07 per page legal size. Certification fee: Per statewide mandate fee $5.00 for the first 5 pages plus $.75 for each additional page. Payee: Treasurer State of New Jersey. Personal checks accepted, credit cards are not. Prepayment required. Mail requests: SASE required.

Civil Name Search: Access: Mail, fax, in person, online. Visitors must perform in person searches themselves. Search fee: Fee depends on nature of job. Clerk will call back with cost. Accounts available. Civil records on computer from 1991, on index books from 1956. Mail Turnaround time 48 hours. Public use terminal has civil records back to 1991. **See the front or back of the chapter for details about online access to civil dockets, calendar, and a subscription service.**

Superior Court Special Civil Part Courthouse, 71 Monument Pk., PO Box 1270, Freehold, NJ 07728; 732-677-4223; civil phone: 732-677-4290 Small Claims; fax: 732-677-4362; 8:30AM-4:30PM (EST). *Civil Actions under $15,000, Eviction, Small Claims.*
www.judiciary.state.nj.us/monmouth/index.htm

General Information: Will not fax documents. Court makes copy: $.05 per page letter size: $.07 per page legal size. Self serve copy: Self serve copier located in Rm 143 East Central. There is a charge. Certification fee: Per statewide mandate fee $5.00. Payee: Treasurer State of New Jersey. Personal checks accepted, credit cards are not. Prepayment required. Mail requests: SASE required.

Civil Name Search: Access: Mail, in person, online. Both court and visitors may perform in person name searches. No search fee. Civil records on computer from 1996, on index books from 1985, prior in archives. Mail Turnaround time 1 day to weeks; longer if archived. Public use terminal has civil records back to 1985. **See the front or back of the chapter for details about online access to civil dockets, calendar, and a subscription service.**

Morris County

Superior Court - Criminal PO Box 910, Washington & Court St, Morristown, NJ 07963-0910; 973-326-6950; fax: 973-326-6973; 8:30AM-4:30PM (EST). *Felony, Misdemeanor.*
www.judiciary.state.nj.us/morris/index.htm

General Information: No sealed, expunged, dismissed, judges notes, PSI's, or discovery packets records released. Will not fax documents. Court makes copy: $.05 per page letter size: $.07 per page legal size. Certification fee: Per statewide mandate fee $5.00 for the first 5 pages plus $.75 for each additional page. Payee: State of New Jersey Treasurer. Personal checks accepted, credit cards are not. Prepayment required. Mail requests: SASE required.

Criminal Name Search: Access: Fax, mail, in person. Both court and visitors may perform in person name searches. No search fee. Required to search: name, years to search, DOB, SSN, signed release. Criminal records computerized from 1984, on index books from 1966. Mail Turnaround time 1-3 weeks.

Superior Court - Civil PO Box 910, Washington St Courthouse, 2nd Fl, Morristown, NJ 07963-0910; 973-656-4115; fax: 973-656-4123; 8:30AM-4:30PM (EST). *Civil Actions over $15,000, Probate.*
www.judiciary.state.nj.us/morris/index.htm

General Information: No sealed, expunged, dismissed, judges notes, PSI's, or discovery packets records released. Will fax documents for $.75 per page fee (1-2 pages max). Court makes copy: $.05 per page letter size: $.07 per page legal size. Self serve copy: $.05 per page. Certification fee: $5.00 per doc. Payee: State of New Jersey Treasurer. No personal checks or credit cards accepted. Prepayment required.

Civil Name Search: Access: In person, online. Visitors must perform in person searches themselves. Required to search: name, years to search; also helpful: address. Civil records on computer from 1984, on index books from 1966 in archives, but is in process of destroying older records. Public use terminal has civil records back to 1990. **See the front or back of the chapter for details about online access to civil dockets, calendar, and a subscription service.**

Superior Court Special Civil Part PO Box 910, Court and Washington Sts, Morristown, NJ 07963-0910; 973-656-4125; fax: 973-656-4123; 8:30AM-4:30PM (EST). *Civil Actions under $15,000, Eviction, Small Claims.*

General Information: No adoption, sealed, juvenile, expunged, dismissed, or mental illness records released. Will not fax documents. Court makes copy: $.05 per page letter size: $.07 per page legal size. Self serve copy: $.05 per page. Certification fee: First doc if free, then $5.00 per doc. Payee: State of New Jersey Treasurer. Personal checks accepted, credit cards are not. Prepayment required. Mail requests: SASE required.

Civil Name Search: Access: Mail, in person, online. Visitors must perform in person searches themselves. No search fee. Civil records on computer from 8/1988, on index books from 1979. Mail Turnaround time 1 week. Public use terminal has civil records back to 8/1988. **See the front or back of the chapter for details about online access to civil dockets, calendar, and a subscription service.**

Ocean County

Superior Court - Criminal PO Box 2191, 120 Hooper Ave, Justice Complex, Rm 220, Toms River, NJ 08754-2191; 732-929-4780; fax: 732-506-5067; 8:30AM-4:30PM (EST). *Felony, Misdemeanor.*
www.judiciary.state.nj.us/ocean/index.htm

General Information: No sealed, expunged, judges notes, PSI's, or discovery packets records released. Will fax reply if no record found. Court makes copy: $.05 per page letter size: $.07 per page legal size. Certification fee: Per statewide mandate fee $5.00 for the first 5 pages plus $.05 for each additional page. Payee: NJ State Treasurer. Personal checks accepted, credit cards are not. Prepayment required.

Criminal Name Search: Access: In person only. Visitors must perform in person searches themselves. Required to search: name, years to search; also helpful: address, DOB, SSN. Criminal records computerized from 1990, on index books from 1920. Public use terminal has crim records back to 1990. Public access terminal allows you to search statewide.

Superior Court - Civil 118 Washington #121, Toms River, NJ 08753; 732-929-2016; fax: 732-506-5398; 8:30AM-4:30PM (EST). *Civil Actions over $15,000, Probate.* www.judiciary.state.nj.us/ocean/index.htm

General Information: Will not fax documents. Court makes copy: $.05 per page letter size: $.07 per page legal size. Certification fee: Per statewide mandate fee $5.00 for the first 5 pages plus $.75 for each additional page. Payee: Treasurer, State of NJ. Personal checks accepted, credit cards are not. Prepayment required.

Civil Name Search: Access: In person, online. Visitors must perform in person searches themselves. Search fee: Court charges no fee if and when they assist you with search. Civil records on computer from 1989, on index books from 1920. Public use terminal has civil records back to 1989. **See the front or back of the chapter for details about online access to civil dockets, calendar, and a subscription service.**

Superior Court Special Civil Part 118 Washington St, Rm 121, Toms River, NJ 08753; 732-929-2016; fax: 732-506-5398; 8:30AM-4:30PM (EST). *Civil Actions under $15,000, Eviction, Small Claims.*
www.judiciary.state.nj.us/ocean/index.htm

General Information: Also, use PO Box 2191 with ZIP of 08754. No adoption, sealed, juvenile, expunged, dismissed, or mental illness records released. Will not fax documents. Court makes copy: $.05 per page letter size: $.07 per page legal size. Certification fee: Per statewide mandate fee $5.00 for the first 5 pages plus $.75 for each additional page. Payee: Treasurer, State of NJ. Personal checks accepted, credit cards are not. Prepayment required. Mail requests: SASE requested.

Civil Name Search: Access: In person, online. Both court and visitors may perform in person name searches. No search fee. Required to search: name, years to search, address. Civil records on computer from 1985, on index books from 1972, on microfilm prior. Public use terminal has civil records back to 1985. **See the front or back of the chapter for details about online access to civil dockets, calendar, and a subscription service.**

Passaic County

Superior Court - Criminal 77 Hamilton St. 2nd Fl, Paterson, NJ 07505-2108; 973-247-8404; fax: 973-247-8401; 8:30AM-4:30PM (EST). *Felony, Misdemeanor.* www.judiciary.state.nj.us/passaic/index.htm

General Information: No sealed, expunged, judges notes, PSI's, or discovery packets records released. Will fax documents. Court makes copy: $.05 per page letter size: $.07 per page legal size. Self serve copy: $.25 per page. Certification fee: Per statewide mandate fee $5.00 for the first 5 pages plus $.75 for each additional page. The Seal of the Court is $5.00. Payee: Treasurer, State of New Jersey. Personal and business checks accepted. No credit cards accepted. Prepayment required. Mail requests: SASE not required.

Criminal Name Search: Access: In person only. Visitors must perform in person searches themselves. Required to search: name; also helpful: DOB. Criminal records computerized from 1986, on microfiche prior. Note: Court will only retrieve a record if you provide an indictment or accusation or complaint number, which can be garnered from state police or the public access terminal. Public use terminal has crim records back to 1986.

Superior Court - Civil 77 Hamilton St, 1st Fl, Paterson, NJ 07505-2108; 973-247-8000; civil phone: 973-247-8227; probate phone: 973-881-4760; fax: 973-247-8186; 8:30AM-4:30PM (EST). *Civil Actions over $15,000, Probate.* www.judiciary.state.nj.us/passaic/index.htm

General Information: Civil records and Civil Special Part records are now co-located in the same area. Probate is located on the 2nd Fl. No sealed, expunged, dismissed, judges notes, PSI's, or discovery packets records released. Will fax documents for fee same as copy fee. Court makes copy: $.05 per page letter size: $.07 per page legal size. Certification fee: Per statewide mandate fee $5.00 for the first 5 pages plus $.75 for each additional page. Payee: Treasurer State of New Jersey. Personal checks accepted, credit cards are not. Prepayment required.

Civil Name Search: Access: Mail, in person, online. Visitors must perform in person searches themselves. No search fee. Civil records on computer from 1986, on index books from 1979. Mail Turnaround time up to 1 week. Public use terminal has civil records back to 1993. Public terminal results may show address, sometime DOB and other identifiers. **See the front or back of the chapter for details about online access to civil dockets, calendar, and a subscription service.**

Superior Court Special Civil Part 77 Hamilton St., New Courthouse, 1st Fl, Paterson, NJ 07505; 973-247-8000, 973-247-3259; fax: 973-247-3250; 8:30AM-4:30PM (EST). *Civil Actions under $15,000, Eviction, Small Claims.* www.judiciary.state.nj.us/passaic/index.htm

General Information: Civil records and Civil Special Part records are now co-located in the same area. No adoption, sealed, juvenile, expunged, dismissed, or mental illness records released. Will fax documents for fee same as copy fee. Court makes copy: $.05 per page letter size: $.07 per page legal size. Certification fee: $5.00 for the first 5 pages plus $.75 for each additional page. Payee: Treasurer, State of New Jersey. Personal checks accepted, credit cards are not. Prepayment required.

Civil Name Search: Access: Mail, in person, online. Both court and visitors may perform in person name searches. No search fee. Civil records on computer from 1993, on index from 1980, prior archived. Note: Include your phone number with written requests. It may take up to 2 days for court to retrieve case files. Mail Turnaround time 2-3 days. Public use terminal has civil records to 1993, results may show address, sometime DOB and other identifiers. **See the front or back of the chapter for details about online access to civil dockets, calendar, and a subscription service.**

Salem County

Superior Court - Criminal 92 Market St, Salem, NJ 08079-1913; 856-935-7510 x8212; fax: 856-935-8291; 8:30AM-4:30PM (EST). *Felony, Misdemeanor.* www.judiciary.state.nj.us/gloucester/sal/index.htm

General Information: No sealed, expunged, dismissed, judges notes, PSI's, or discovery packets records released. Will not fax documents. Court makes copy: $.05 per page letter size: $.07 per page legal size. Certification fee: Per statewide mandate fee $5.00 for the first 5 pages plus $.75 for each additional page. Payee: State of New Jersey Treasurer. Personal checks accepted, credit cards are not. Prepayment required. Mail requests: SASE required for civil.

Criminal Name Search: Access: In person only. Visitors must perform in person searches themselves. Required to search: name, years to search, DOB, SSN; indictment number helpful. Criminal records computerized from 1989; indexed from 1957. Public use terminal has crim records back to 1989.

Superior Court - Civil 92 Market St, Salem, NJ 08079-1913; 856-935-7510 x8210, x8214; criminal phone: x 832; probate phone: 856-935-7510 x8322; fax: 856-935-6551; 8:30AM-4:30PM (EST). *Civil Actions over $15,000, Probate.* www.judiciary.state.nj.us/gloucester/sal/index.htm

General Information: Probate located at the County Surrogate's office at this 92 Market St address. No sealed, expunged, dismissed, judges notes, PSI's, or discovery packets records released. Will fax documents if fees prepaid. Court makes copy: $.05 per page letter size: $.07 per page legal size. Certification fee: Per statewide mandate fee $5.00 for the first 5 pages plus $.75 for each additional page. Payee: Superior Court of NJ. Personal checks accepted. Prepayment required.

Civil Name Search: Access: In person, online. Both court and visitors may perform in person name searches. No search fee. Civil records on computer from 1987, older records on microfilm in Trenton. Public use terminal has civil records back to 1987. **See the front or back of the chapter for details about online access to civil dockets, calendar, and a subscription service.**

Superior Court Special Civil Part 92 Market St, Salem, NJ 08079; 856-935-7510 x8385; fax: 856-935-6551; 8:30AM-4:30PM (EST). *Civil Actions under $15,000, Eviction, Small Claims.* www.judiciary.state.nj.us/gloucester/sal/index.htm

General Information: No adoption, sealed, juvenile, expunged, dismissed, or mental illness records released. Court makes copy: $.05 per page letter size: $.07 per page legal size. Certification fee: Per statewide mandate fee $5.00 for the first 5 pages plus $.75 for each additional page. Payee: Special Civil Part. Personal checks accepted. Prepayment required.

Civil Name Search: Access: Phone, fax, mail, in person, online. Both court and visitors may perform in person name searches. No search fee. Civil records on computer from 1990, on index from 1953. Mail Turnaround time 1-2 days. Public use terminal has civil records back to 1990. **See the front or back of the chapter for details about online access to civil dockets, calendar, and a subscription service.**

Somerset County

Superior Court - Criminal PO Box 3000 (20 N Bridge St, 2nd Fl), Somerville, NJ 08876-1262; 908-231-7666; fax: 908-231-9276; 8:30AM-4:30PM (EST). *Felony, Misdemeanor.* www.judiciary.state.nj.us/somerset/index.htm

General Information: No sealed, expunged, judges notes, PSI's, or discovery packets records released. Will not fax documents. Court makes copy: $.05 per page letter size: $.07 per page legal size.There is a self-service copy machine in the law library. Certification fee: Per statewide mandate fee $5.00 for the first 5 pages plus $.75 for each additional page. Payee: State of New Jersey Treasurer. Personal checks accepted, credit cards are not. Prepayment required. Mail requests: SASE required.

Criminal Name Search: Access: Phone, fax, mail, in person. Both court and visitors may perform in person name searches. Search fee: $6.00 per name. Required to search: name, years to search, DOB; also helpful: SSN. Criminal records computerized from 1981, prior on index books. Mail Turnaround time 2-3 days. Public use terminal has crim records to 1981.

Superior Court - Civil PO Box 3000, Civil Division, 40 N Bridge St,, Somerville, NJ 08876-1262; 908-231-7054; fax: 908-231-7167; 8:30AM-4:30PM (EST). *Civil Actions, Probate, Equity.* www.judiciary.state.nj.us/somerset/index.htm

General Information: No sealed, expunged, dismissed, judges notes, PSI's, or discovery packets records released. Will not fax documents. Court makes copy: $.05 per page letter size: $.07 per page legal size. Certification fee: Per statewide mandate fee $5.00 for the first 5 pages plus $.75 for each additional page. Payee: Treasurer, State of NJ. Personal checks accepted, credit cards are not. Prepayment required. Mail requests: SASE required.

Civil Name Search: Access: Phone, mail, in person. Both court and visitors may perform in person name searches. No search fee. Required to search: name; also helpful: years to search. Civil records on computer from 1990. Note: Civil cases are archived 18 months after their last activity. Mail Turnaround time 1-2 days. Public use terminal has civil records back to 1990. Terminal located at 40 N Brady St. **See the front or back of the chapter for details about online access to civil dockets, calendar, and a subscription service.**

Superior Court Special Civil Part PO Box 3000, 20 North Bridge St, Somerville, NJ 08876-1262; 908-231-7014;; 8:30AM-4:30PM (EST). *Civil Actions under $15,000, Llandlord/Tenant, Small Claims.* www.judiciary.state.nj.us/somerset/index.htm

General Information: No adoption, sealed, juvenile, expunged, dismissed, or mental illness records released. Will not fax documents. Court makes copy: $.05 per page letter size: $.07 per page legal size. Certification fee: Per statewide mandate fee $5.00 for the first 5 pages plus $.75 for each additional page. Payee: Treasurer, State of NJ. Personal checks accepted, credit cards are not. Prepayment required. Mail requests: SASE required.

Civil Name Search: Access: Mail, in person, online. Visitors must perform in person searches themselves. No search fee. Civil records on computer from 1990, prior on index books. Note: In person access requires an appointment. Mail Turnaround time 1-2 days. Public use terminal has civil records back to 1995. Public terminal at counter provides visitor with book lookup help only. **See the front or back of the chapter for details about online access to civil dockets, calendar, and a subscription service.**

Sussex County

Superior Court - Criminal 43-47 High St, Sussex Judicial Ctr, Newton, NJ 07860; 973-579-0696; fax: 973-579-0767; 8:30AM-4:30PM (EST). *Felony, Misdemeanor.* www.judiciary.state.nj.us/morris/index.htm

General Information: No sealed, expunged, dismissed, judges notes, PSI's, or discovery packets records released. Will not fax out documents. Court makes copy: $.05 per page letter size: $.07 per page legal size.If file copy is extensive, minimum fee is $5.00 for copies. Certification fee: Per statewide mandate fee $5.00 for the first 5 pages plus $.75 for each additional page. Payee: Treasurer, State of NJ. Only cashiers checks and money orders accepted. No credit cards accepted. Prepayment required.

Criminal Name Search: Access: In person only. Both court and visitors may perform in person name searches. Search fee: None; copy fee only. Required to search: name, years to search, DOB; the court prefers that you provide the case number, complaint number, arrest date, etc; get that info off public access terminal. Criminal records computerized from 1986, on docket books to 1950s. Public use terminal has crim records back to 1956 approx.

Superior Court - Civil 43-47 High St, Sussex Judicial Ctr, Newton, NJ 07860; 973-579-0914/0915; fax: 973-579-0736; 8:30AM-4:30PM (EST). *Special Civil Actions, Eviction, Probate.* www.judiciary.state.nj.us/morris/index.htm

General Information: No sealed, expunged, dismissed, judges notes, PSI's, or discovery packets records released. Will fax documents if prepaid depending on amount of pages. Court makes copy: $.05 per page letter size: $.07 per page legal size. Certification fee: $5.00 for the first 5 pages plus $.75 for each additional page. Payee: Treasurer State of New Jersey. Personal checks accepted, credit cards are not. Prepayment required.

Civil Name Search: Access: Phone, mail, in person, online. Only the court performs in person name searches; visitors may not. No search fee. Civil records on computer from 1989, on microfiche by plaintiff prior to

1989, closed cases archived yearly and sent to Trenton. Mail Turnaround time up to 1 week. Public use terminal has civil records. Public access terminal located in Law Library. **See the front or back of the chapter for details about online access to civil dockets, calendar, and a subscription service.**

Superior Court Special Civil Part 43-47 High St., Newton, NJ 07860; 973-579-0918; fax: 973-579-0736; 8:30AM-4:30PM (EST). *Civil Actions under $15,000, Eviction, Small Claims.*
www.judiciary.state.nj.us/morris/index.htm
General Information: No adoption, sealed, juvenile, expunged, dismissed, or mental illness records released. Will not fax documents. Court makes copy: $.05 per page letter size: $.07 per page legal size. Certification fee: Per statewide mandate fee $5.00 for the first 5 pages plus $.75 for each additional page. Payee: State of New Jersey Treasurer. Personal checks accepted, credit cards are not. Prepayment required.
Civil Name Search: Access: Phone, fax, mail, in person, online. Both court and visitors may perform in person name searches. No search fee. Civil records on computer from mid 1989, on index books from 1940. Note: Court will accept name phone and fax search requests for up to 3 names. Mail Turnaround time up to 2 weeks. Public use terminal has civil records. Public access terminal located in law library. **See the front or back of the chapter for details about online access to civil dockets, calendar, and a subscription service.**

Union County

Superior Court - Criminal County Courthouse, 2 Broad St - Tower Bldg 7th Fl, Elizabeth, NJ 07207; 908-659-4660; ; 8:30AM-4:30PM (EST). *Felony, Misdemeanor.* www.judiciary.state.nj.us/union/index.htm
General Information: No sealed, expunged, dismissed, judges notes, PSI's, warrants, or discovery packets records released. Will not fax documents. Court makes copy: $.05 per page letter size: $.07 per page legal size. Self serve copy: $.75 per page. Certification fee: Per statewide mandate fee $5.00 for the first 5 pages plus $.75 for each additional page. Payee: Treasurer, State of NJ. Business checks and money orders accepted. No credit cards accepted. Prepayment required.
Criminal Name Search: Access: In person only. Visitors must perform in person searches themselves. Required to search: name, years to search; also helpful: DOB, SSN. Criminal records computerized from 1985-prior with name and indictment # from 1967. Note: In person access: 9AM-3:30PM. For any requests regarding records prior to 1985, contact the NJ State Police for a criminal history sheet, and from the IND/ACC# this court can quickly find the reference in their records. Public use terminal has crim records back to 1985.

Superior Court - Civil 2 Broad St, Elizabeth, NJ 07207; 908-659-4810; probate phone: 908-527-4270;; 8:30AM-4:30PM (EST). *Civil Actions over $15,000, Probate.* www.judiciary.state.nj.us/union/civil.htm
General Information: The probate phone is for the Surrogate Div who holds probate court records; located at same address. No sealed, expunged, dismissed, judges notes, PSI's, or discovery packets records released. Will not fax documents. Court makes copy: $.05 per page letter size: $.07 per page legal size. Certification fee: Per statewide mandate fee $5.00 for the first 5 pages plus $.75 for each additional page. Payee: Treasurer, State of NJ. Personal checks accepted, credit cards are not. Prepayment required.
Civil Name Search: Access: Phone, mail, in person, online. Visitors must perform in person searches themselves. No search fee. Required to search: name, years to search, or docket number. Civil records on computer from 1984, prior records archived in Trenton. Mail Turnaround time 1-2 days. Public use terminal has civil records back to 1984. **See the front or back of the chapter for details about online access to civil dockets, calendar, and a subscription service.**

Superior Court Special Civil Part 2 Broad St, Elizabeth, NJ 07207; 908-659-4900; ; 8:30AM-4:30PM (EST). *Civil Actions under $15,000, Eviction, Small Claims.* www.judiciary.state.nj.us/union/index.htm
General Information: No adoption, sealed, juvenile, expunged, dismissed, or mental illness records released. Will not fax documents. Court makes copy: $.05 per page letter size: $.07 per page legal size. Certification fee: Per statewide mandate fee $5.00 for the first 5 pages plus $.75 for each additional page. Payee: Treasurer, State of NJ. Personal checks accepted, credit cards are not. Prepayment required. Mail requests: SASE required.
Civil Name Search: Access: In person, online. Both court and visitors may perform in person name searches. Civil records on computer from 1993, on index books 1965, prior archived. Note: Phone access limited to info after 11/93. Mail Turnaround time varies. Public use terminal has civil records. **See the front or back of the chapter for details about online access to civil dockets, calendar, and a subscription service.**

Warren County

Warren County Superior Court Criminal Case Management Division, PO Box 900, Belvidere, NJ 07823; 908-475-6990; criminal phone: 908-475-6990; fax: 908-475-6982; 8:30AM-4:30PM (EST). *Felony, Misdemeanor.* www.judiciary.state.nj.us/somerset/index.htm
General Information: No sealed, expunged, dismissed, judges notes, PSI's, or discovery packets records released. Will fax documents to local or toll free line. Court makes copy: $.05 per page letter size: $.07 per page legal size. Certification fee: Per statewide mandate fee $5.00 for the first 5 pages plus $.75 for each additional page. Payee: State of New Jersey Judiciary. Personal checks accepted, credit cards are not. Prepayment required.
Criminal Name Search: Access: Phone, mail, fax, in person. Both court and visitors may perform in person name searches. Search fee: $6.00 per name. Required to search: name, years to search, DOB; also helpful: signed release. Criminal records computerized from 1985; prior on microfilm to 1927. Mail Turnaround time 2-5 days. Public use terminal has crim records back to 1985.

Superior Court - Civil PO Box 900, 413 2nd St, Belvidere, NJ 07823; 908-475-6140; probate phone: 908-475-6223; ; 8:30AM-4:30PM (EST). *Civil Actions over $15,000, Probate.* www.judiciary.state.nj.us/somerset/index.htm
General Information: Surrogates/Probate court is located at 413 2nd St in the courthouse. Probate fax- 908-475-6319 No sealed, expunged, or dismissed records released. Will not fax documents. Court makes copy: $.05 per page letter size: $.07 per page legal size. Certification fee: $5.00 for the first 5 pages plus $.75 for each additional page. Payee: Treasurer, State of NJ. Personal checks accepted, credit cards are not. Prepayment required.
Civil Name Search: Access: Mail, in person, online. Only the court performs in person name searches; visitors may not. Search fee: $6.00, but court will perform one search no fee. Civil records on computer from 1991, prior on index books from 1951. Note: In person access requires an appointment. Mail Turnaround time 2 days. Public use terminal has civil records back to - closed cases in last 18 months. **See the front or back of the chapter for details about online access to civil dockets, calendar, and a subscription service.**

Superior Court Special Civil Part PO Box 900, 413 2nd St, Belvidere, NJ 07823; 908-475-6140;; 8:30AM-4:30PM (EST). *Civil Actions under $15,000, Eviction, Small Claims.* www.judiciary.state.nj.us/somerset/index.htm
General Information: No adoption, sealed, juvenile, expunged, dismissed, or mental illness records released. Will not fax documents. Court makes copy: $.05 per page letter size: $.07 per page legal size. Certification fee: Per statewide mandate fee $5.00 for the first 5 pages plus $.75 for each additional page. Payee: Treasurer, State of NJ. Personal checks accepted, credit cards are not. Prepayment required. Mail requests: SASE required.
Civil Name Search: Access: Mail, in person, online. Only the court performs in person name searches; visitors may not. Search fee: $6.00, but will perform one search no fee. Civil records on computer from 10/91, prior on index books from 1951. Note: In person access requires an appointment. Mail Turnaround time 2-3 days. Public use terminal has civil records. **See the front or back of the chapter for details about online access to civil dockets, calendar, and a subscription service.**

___

About Online Access

A free statewide access service to civil cases and civil judgments is available at http://njcourts.judiciary.state.nj.us/web1/ACMSPA/. One may search by name or docket number. If a name search is performed, it is name only - no personal identifiers are shown except an address on docket.

Also, the State offers an Electronic Access Program to civil case docket and summary information from four separate state information systems. Included are the Automated Case Management Systems (ACMS), the Civil Judgment and Order Docket, the Family Automated Case Tracking System (FACTS), and the Automated Traffic System (ATS). The fee is $1.00 per minute. Subscribers receive only a screen view; downloads and data extraction (screen-scraping) are not available. For more information and enrollment forms see www.judiciary.state.nj.us/superior/eap_main.htm.

The Judiciary's civil motion calendar and schedule is searchable at www.judiciary.state.nj.us/calendars.htm. The database includes all Superior Court Motion calendars for the Civil Division (Law-Civil Part, Special Civil Part and Chancery-General Equity), and proceeding information for a six-week period (two weeks prior to the current date and four weeks following the current date).

New Mexico

Time Zone:	MST
Capital:	Santa Fe, Santa Fe County
# of Counties:	33
State Web:	www.newmexico.gov
Court Web:	www.nmcourts.gov

Administration

Administrative Office of the Courts, Judicial Information Division, 2905 Rodeo Park Dr East, Bldg #5, Santa Fe, NM, 87505; 505-476-6900, Fax: 505-476-6952.

The Supreme and Appellate Courts

The Supreme Court is the court of last resort and has superintending control over all lower courts and attorneys licensed in the state. The Court of Appeals has mandatory jurisdiction for civil, non-capital criminal, juvenile cases; discretionary jurisdiction in interlocutory decision cases and administrative agency appeals. Find their opinions at http://coa.nmcourts.gov/

The New Mexico Courts

Court	Type	How Organized	Jurisdiction Highpoints
District*	General	30 Courts in 13 Districts	Felony, Civil, Juvenile, Domestic Relations, Estate
Magistrate*	Limited	54 Courts in 32 Districts	Misdemeanor, Civil up to $10,000, Small Claims, Traffic, Eviction, Contract
Municipal	Limited	80 Courts	Ordinances, Traffic. Petty Misdemeanors
Metropolitan Court of Bernalillo County	Limited	1	Misdemeanor, Civil to $10,000, Eviction, Tort, Contract
Probate	Special	30 Courts by County	Probate, Uncontested Estate

* = profiled in this book

Details on the Court Structure

The **District Courts** hear felony, civil, tort, contract, real property rights, estate, exclusive domestic relations, mental health. They handle appeals for administrative agencies and lower courts, miscellaneous civil jurisdiction; and misdemeanors.

The **Magistrate Court** handles tort, contract, landlord/tenant rights, civil, ($0-10,000); small claims, felony preliminary hearings; misdemeanor, DWI/DUI and other traffic violations.

Municipal Courts handle petty misdemeanors, DWI/DUI, traffic violations, and other municipal ordinance violations. The **Bernalillo Metropolitan Court** has jurisdiction in cases up to $10,000.

County Clerks hold the case files for "informal" or "uncontested" probate cases seen by the Probate Judge. The District Courts hold case files for "formal" or "contested" probate cases.

Record Searching Facts You Need to Know

Fees and Record Searching Tips

In low-populated counties in New Mexico there are some "shared courts" – meaning one county handling cases arising in another. Records are held at the locations indicated in the text. Of the courts who will do a search, only a handful charge a search fee. Most District Courts charge $.35 per copy and Magistrate Courts $.50 per copy. Most District Courts charge $1.50 for certification; the certification fee at Magistrate Courts varies widely.

Online Access is Statewide, But Not From One Site

The home page at www.nmcourts.gov offers free access to District Courts and Magistrate Courts case information statewide except Bernalillo Metropolitan Court (see below). There is also a separate look-up for DWI Reports and DWI Offenders. Municipal Court data is limited to criminal Domestic Violence and DWI historic convictions from September 1, 1991 forward. In general, the other records are available from June 1997 forward. The search is inclusive of all counties participating. Search by name & DL and/or DOB, and by county and type of case or by case number. Case lookup does not display the full date of birth, it displays only the year of birth. In addition, driver's license numbers are not displayed on records. The site also offers a DWI Offender History tool for researching DWI history; search by name.

A commercial online service is available for the Metropolitan Court of Bernalillo County, via a vendor. There is a $35.00 set up fee, a connect time fee based on usage. The system is available 24 hours daily. Call 505-345-6555 for more information.

Bernalillo County

2nd Judicial District Court PO Box 488, 400 Lomas NW, Albuquerque, NM 87103; 505-841-7425 (Administration); fax: 505-841-6705; 8AM-5PM; clerk office: 10AM-4PM (MST). *Felony, Civil, Family, Juvenile, Contested Probate.*
www.nmcourts.gov/seconddistrictcourt/
General Information: The clerk's office hours are 10AM-4PM. Online identifiers in results same as on public terminal. No sequestered or juvenile records released. Will not fax documents. Court makes copy: $.35 per page. Certification fee: $1.50, Exemplification fee: $4.50. Payee: Clerk of the Court. Only cashiers checks and money orders accepted. No credit cards accepted. Prepayment required. Mail requests: SASE requested.
Civil Name Search: Access: Mail, in person, online. Both court and visitors may perform in person name searches. Search fee: $1.50 per name. Civil records on computer from 1984, prior on docket books/microfiche. Mail Turnaround time up to 10 days. Civil PAT goes back to 1984. Online access is free at www.nmcourts.gov Most data goes back to 6/1985. Case look-up displays the year of birth.
Criminal Name Search: Access: Mail, online, in person. Both court and visitors may perform in person name searches. Search fee: $1.50 per name. Required to search: name, years to search; also helpful: DOB, SSN. Criminal records computerized from 1979, prior on docket books/microfiche. Mail Turnaround time up to 10 days. Criminal PAT goes back to 1979. Terminal results may or may not have complete name or a DOB. Online access to criminal records is free at www.nmcourts.gov. Most data goes back to 6/1979. Case look-up displays the year of birth.

Metropolitan Court 401 Lomas NW, Albuquerque, NM 87102; 505-841-8151; fax: 505-222-4831; 7:30AM-5PM (MST). *Misdemeanor, Civil Actions under $10,000, Eviction, Small Claims.*
www.metrocourt.state.nm.us
General Information: Records phone is 505-841-8230. Online identifiers in results same as on public terminal. No pre-sentence reports, psychological evaluations, confidential records released. Will fax out documents. Court makes copy: $1.00 per page. Computer printout $.50 per page. Certification fee: $1.50 per cert. Payee: Metro Court. Personal checks, Visa/MC accepted. Prepayment required. Mail requests: SASE not required.
Civil Name Search: Access: Phone, fax, mail, online, in person. Both court and visitors may perform in person name searches. Search fee: $1.00 per page found. Required to search: name, years to search; you give identifiers to help court match the results to the person. Civil records on computer from 1987. Max. 5 years back except uncollected judgments which stay open 14 years from date of judgment. Note: Visit the viewing room to examine current cases and cases back to 1989. Mail Turnaround time 3-5 days. Civil PAT goes back to 1987. Access Metropolitan court civil records online at www.metrocourt.state.nm.us.
Criminal Name Search: Access: Phone, fax, mail, online, in person. Both court and visitors may perform in person name searches. Search fee: $1.00 per page found. Required to search: name, SSN, DOB; you give identifiers to help court match the results to the person. Criminal records computerized from 1983. Note: Visit the viewing room to examine current cases and cases back to 1989. Mail Turnaround time 3-5 days. Criminal PAT goes back to same as civil. Terminal results may or may not have complete name or a DOB. Search Metro Court criminal case records free at www.metrocourt.state.nm.us. The DWI data is available at www2.nmcourts.gov/caselookup/app

Catron County

Quemado Magistrate Court PO Box 283, Quemado, NM 87829; 575-773-4604; fax: 575-773-4688; 8AM- Noon M-T-TH; 8AM-5PM W (MST). *Misdemeanor, Civil Actions under $10,000, Eviction, Small Claims.*

General Information: Online identifiers in results same as on public terminal. Fee to fax out file $1.00 per page. Court makes copy: $.10 per page. Certification fee: $.50 per page includes copy fee. Payee: Magistrate Court. Personal checks accepted, credit cards are not. Prepayment required.
Civil Name Search: Access: Mail, fax, in person, online. Both court and visitors may perform in person name searches. No search fee. Required to search: name, years to search; also helpful-DOB, SSN, address. Civil cases indexed by defendant, plaintiff and docket number. Records computerized since 1997. Mail Turnaround time 1-2 weeks. Civil PAT goes back to 1996. Terminal results may or may not have complete name or a DOB. Case lookup from 1997 forward is free at www.nmcourts.gov. Case look-up displays the year of birth.
Criminal Name Search: Access: Mail, fax, in person, online. Both court and visitors may perform in person name searches. No search fee. Required to search: name, years to search, DOB; also helpful: SSN. Records computerized since 1997. Mail Turnaround time 1-2 weeks. Criminal PAT goes back to 1996. Terminal results may or may not have complete name or a DOB. Online access to criminal records is free at www.nmcourts.gov. Case look-up displays the year of birth.

Reserve Magistrate Court PO Box 447, Reserve, NM 87830; 575-533-6474; fax: 575-533-6623; 8AM-5PM (MST). *Misdemeanor, Civil Actions under $10,000, Eviction, Small Claims.*
General Information: Online identifiers in results same as on public terminal. Will fax $.50 per page. Court makes copy: $.50 per page. Self serve copy: same. Certification fee: $1.00 per page includes copy fee. Payee: Magistrate Court. Personal checks accepted, credit cards are not. Prepayment required.
Civil Name Search: Access: Mail, fax, in person, online. Both court and visitors may perform in person name searches. No search fee. Required to search: name, years to search, address, other names used. Records computerized since 1996. Mail Turnaround time 1 week. Civil PAT goes back to 1996 countywide. Case lookup from 1997 forward is free at www.nmcourts.gov. Case look-up displays the year of birth.
Criminal Name Search: Access: Mail, fax, in person, online. Both court and visitors may perform in person name searches. No search fee. Required to search: name, years to search; also helpful: DOB, SSN. Records computerized since 1996. Mail Turnaround time 1 week. Criminal PAT goes back to same as civil. Terminal results may or may not have complete name or a DOB. Online access to criminal records is free at www.nmcourts.gov. Case look-up displays the year of birth.

7th Judicial District Court PO Drawer 1129, Socorro, NM 87801; 575-835-0050 x10; fax: 575-838-5217; 8AM-4PM (MST). *Felony, Civil Actions over $7,500, Probate.*
General Information: Case hearings and trials for Catron County may be in Socorro; all civil and criminal case files are housed at the Socorro County District Court. The physical address for this court is 200 Church St, Socorro. Index at www.nmcourts.gov/caselookup/.

County Clerk PO Box 197, 100 N main St, Reserve, NM 87830; 575-533-6400; fax: 575-533-6400; 8AM-4:30PM (MST). *Probate.*
General Information: The County Clerk holds the case files for "informal" or "uncontested" probate cases seen by the Probate Judge. The District Court holds case files for "formal" or "contested" probate cases.

Chaves County

5th Judicial District Court Box 1776, 400 N Virginia Ave, Roswell, NM 88202; 575-622-2212; fax: 575-624-9510; 8AM-N,1-5PM (MST). *Felony, Civil, Contested Probate.*
www.fifthdistrictcourt.com
General Information: No sequestered records released. Will not fax out documents. Court makes copy: $.35 per page.Photo ID required to receive copies from any file. Certification fee: $1.50 per document. Payee: District

Court Clerk. Only cashiers checks and money orders accepted. No credit cards accepted. Prepayment required. Mail requests: SASE required for mail return of any copies.

Civil Name Search: Access: Online, in person. Visitors must perform in person searches themselves. Civil records on computer from 1996, on microfiche and archived from 1891. Case lookup from 1997 forward is free at www.nmcourts.gov. Case look-up displays the year of birth.

Criminal Name Search: Access: Online, in person. Visitors must perform in person searches themselves. Required to search: name, years to search, DOB, aliases. Criminal records computerized from 1996, on microfiche and archived from 1891. Online access to criminal records is free at www.nmcourts.gov. Case look-up displays the year of birth.

Magistrate Court 400 N Virginia St, # G-1, Roswell, NM 88201; 575-624-6088; fax: 575-624-6092; 8AM-4PM M-TH; 8AM-N F (MST). *Misdemeanor, Civil Actions under $10,000, Eviction, Small Claims.*

General Information: Will fax documents to local or toll-free number. Court makes copy: $.50 per page. Certification fee: $1.00 per doc. Payee: Magistrate Court. Personal checks accepted, credit cards are not. Prepayment required.

Civil Name Search: Access: Online, in person. Only the court performs in person name searches; visitors may not. No search fee. Civil cases indexed by defendant. Case lookup from 1997 forward is free at www.nmcourts.gov. Case look-up displays the year of birth.

Criminal Name Search: Access: Online, in person. Only the court performs in person name searches; visitors may not. No search fee. Required to search: name, years to search, DOB; also helpful: SSN. Criminal records are keep 2 years (except DUIs and domestic) before being destroyed. Online access to criminal records is free at www.nmcourts.gov. Case look-up displays the year of birth.

County Clerk Box 580, #1 St Mary's Pl #110, 88203, Roswell, NM 88202; 575-624-6614; fax: 575-624-6523; 8AM-5PM (MST). *Probate.* www.co.chaves.nm.us/county/Departments/Clerk/

General Information: The County Clerk holds the case files for "informal" or "uncontested" probate cases seen by the Probate Judge. The District Court holds case files for "formal" or "contested" probate cases.

Cibola County

13th Judicial District Court Box 758, Grants, NM 87020; 505-287-8831; fax: 505-285-5755; 9AM-N, 1-5PM (MST). *Felony, Civil, Contested Probate.* www.13districtcourt.com

General Information: Probate fax is same as main fax number. No sequestered records released. Will fax documents; unless toll-free number provided, fee is $2.50 in-state; $5.00 out-of-state. Court makes copy: $.35 per page; if from micro then $.50. Self serve copy: same. Certification fee: $1.50 per page plus copy fee. Payee: District Court Clerk. Only cashier checks or money orders accepted. No credit cards accepted. Prepayment required.

Civil Name Search: Access: Fax, mail, online, in person. Both court and visitors may perform in person name searches. Search fee: $5.00 per name. Civil records on microfiche from 1981; prior to 1981 belong to Valencia County. Mail Turnaround time 2-3 days. Case lookup from 1997 forward is free at www.nmcourts.gov. Also, view all civil jury verdicts in the 13th Judicial District Court free back to 1995 at www.13districtcourt.com/verdict/jury_verdict_intro.php. Case look-up displays the year of birth.

Criminal Name Search: Access: Fax, mail, online, in person. Only the court performs in person name searches; visitors may not. Search fee: $5.00 per name. Criminal records on microfiche from 1981; prior to 1981 belong to Valencia County. Mail Turnaround time 2-3 days. Online access to criminal records is free at www.nmcourts.gov. Case look-up displays the year of birth.

Magistrate Court 114 McBride Rd, Ste B, Grants, NM 87020; 505-285-4605; fax: 505-285-6485; 8AM-4PM (MST). *Misdemeanor, Civil Actions under $10,000, Eviction, Small Claims.* www.13districtcourt.com/court-info-magistrate-cibola.htm

General Information: Will fax documents $1.00 per page. Court makes copy: $.50 per page. No certification fee . Payee: Magistrate Court. Personal checks accepted, credit cards are not. Prepayment required. Mail requests: SASE required.

Civil Name Search: Access: Fax, mail, in person, online. Only the court performs in person name searches; visitors may not. Search fee: $5.00. Records indexed from 1997. Mail Turnaround time up to 2 weeks. Case lookup from 1997 forward is free at www.nmcourts.gov. Case look-up displays the year of birth.

Criminal Name Search: Access: Fax, mail, in person, online. Only the court performs in person name searches; visitors may not. No search fee. Records indexed from 1997. Mail Turnaround time up to 2 weeks. Online access to criminal records is free at www.nmcourts.gov. Case look-up displays the year of birth.

County Clerk PO Box 190, 515 W. High St, Grants, NM 87020; 505-285-2535; fax: 505-285-2562; 8AM-5PM (MST). *Probate.*

General Information: The County Clerk holds the case files for "informal" or "uncontested" probate cases seen by the Probate Judge. The District Court holds case files for "formal" or "contested" probate cases.

Colfax County

8th Judicial District Court Box 160, Raton, NM 87740; 575-445-5585; fax: 575-445-2626; 8AM-4PM (MST). *Felony, Civil, Contested Probate.* www.nmcourts.gov/index.php

General Information: Online identifiers in results same as on public terminal. No adoption, mental, guardianship, children's cases (neglect & child in need of supervision) records released. Fee to fax out file $2.00 per page. Court makes copy: $.35 per page. Self serve copy: same. Certification fee: $1.50. Payee: District Court. Business checks accepted. No credit cards accepted. Prepayment required. Mail requests: SASE required.

Civil Name Search: Access: Fax, mail, online, in person. Both court and visitors may perform in person name searches. No search fee. Civil records archived from 1912. Mail Turnaround time 1 week. Civil PAT goes back to 1997. Case lookup from 1997 forward is free at www.nmcourts.gov Pleadings are unavailable. Case look-up displays the year of birth.

Criminal Name Search: Access: Fax, mail, online, in person. Both court and visitors may perform in person name searches. No search fee. Required to search: name, years to search; also helpful: DOB, SSN. Criminal records archived from 1912; computerized records go back to 1996/97. Mail Turnaround time 1 week. Criminal PAT goes back to same as civil. Terminal results may or may not have complete name or a DOB. Online access to criminal records is free at www.nmcourts.gov. Pleadings are unavailable. Case look-up displays the year of birth.

Raton Magistrate Court PO Box 68, Raton, NM 87740; 575-445-2220; fax: 575-445-8966; 8AM-4PM (MST). *Misdemeanor, Civil Actions under $10,000, Eviction, Small Claims.*

General Information: Will fax documents $1.00 per page. Court makes copy: $.50 per page. No certification fee . Payee: Magistrate Court. No personal checks or credit cards accepted. Prepayment required.

Civil Name Search: Access: Phone, mail, fax, in person, online. Only the court performs in person name searches; visitors may not. No search fee. Required to search: name, years to search; also helpful: DOB, SSN. Records held for 14 years. Mail Turnaround time within 1 week. Case lookup from 1997 forward is free at www.nmcourts.gov. Case look-up displays the year of birth.

Criminal Name Search: Access: Phone, mail, fax, in person, online. Only the court performs in person name searches; visitors may not. No search fee. Required to search: name, years to search; also helpful: DOB, SSN. Hard copies are kept on file for one year. Mail Turnaround time within 1 week. Online access to criminal records is free at www.nmcourts.gov. Case look-up displays the year of birth.

Springer Magistrate Court 300 Colbert Ave. PO Box 760, Springer, NM 87747; 575-483-2417; fax: 575-483-0127; 8AM-4PM (MST). *Misdemeanor, Civil Actions under $10,000, Eviction, Small Claims.*

General Information: Includes case files from the closed Cimarron Magistrate Court. Will fax documents. Court makes copy: none. Certification fee: No charge. Payee: Magistrate Court. Personal checks accepted, credit cards are not.

Civil Name Search: Access: Online, in person. Both court and visitors may perform in person name searches. No search fee. Required to search: name, years to search; also helpful: DOB. Records indexed by plaintiff and defendant. On computer back to 3/1997. Case lookup from 1997 forward is free at www.nmcourts.gov. Case look-up displays the year of birth.

Criminal Name Search: Access: Online, in person. Both court and visitors may perform in person name searches. No search fee. Required to search: name, years to search; also helpful: DOB, SSN. On computer back to 3/1997, DUI kept longer. Online access to criminal records is free at www.nmcourts.gov. Case look-up displays the year of birth.

Cimarron Magistrate Court *Misdemeanor, Civil Actions under $10,000, Eviction, Small Claims.*

General Information: Closed. Case files at the Springer Magistrate Court - 575-483-2417.

County Clerk PO Box 159, 230 N 3rd St, Raton, NM 87740; 575-445-5551; fax: 575-445-4031; 8AM-N, 1-5PM (MST). *Probate.*

General Information: The County Clerk holds the case files for "informal" or "uncontested" probate cases seen by the Probate Judge. The District Court holds case files for "formal" or "contested" probate cases.

Curry County

9th Judicial District Court Curry County Courthouse, 700 N Main, #11, Clovis, NM 88101; 575-762-9148; fax: 575-763-5160; 8AM-4PM (MST). *Felony, Civil, Contested Probate.* www.nmcourts9thjdc.com

General Information: Online identifiers in results same as on public terminal. No adoption, insanity, sequestered, neglect or abuse released. Court makes copy: $.35 per page. Certification fee: $1.50. Payee: 9th Judicial District Court. Only cashiers checks and money orders accepted. No credit cards accepted. Prepayment required. Mail requests: SASE required for mail return of any copies.

Civil Name Search: Access: Online, in person. Visitors must perform in person searches themselves. Required to search: name, years to search, address. Civil records on computer from 1997, on microfiche and archived from 1910. Civil PAT goes back to 1997. Case lookup from 1997 forward is free at www.nmcourts.gov. Case look-up displays the year of birth.

Criminal Name Search: Access: Online, in person. Visitors must perform in person searches themselves. Required to search: name, years to search; also helpful: SSN. Criminal records computerized from 1997, on microfiche and archived from 1910. Criminal PAT goes back to same as civil. Terminal results may or may not have complete name or a DOB. Online access to criminal records is free at www.nmcourts.gov. Case look-up displays the year of birth.

Magistrate Court 221 Pile, Clovis, NM 88101; 575-762-3766; fax: 575-769-1437; 8AM-4PM M-Th; 9AM-4PM F (MST). *Misdemeanor, Civil Actions under $10,000, Eviction, Small Claims.*

General Information: Online identifiers in results same as on public terminal. Will fax documents for fee of $1.00 per page. Court makes copy: $.50 per page. Certification fee: $.50 per page. Payee: Magistrate Court. Prefer cashiers checks and money orders. Regular checks incur $5.00 fee. Major credit cards accepted with a $10.00 fee. Prepayment required. Mail requests: SASE required.

Civil Name Search: Access: Phone, mail, fax, online, in person. Both court and visitors may perform in person name searches. No search fee. Civil cases indexed by plaintiff and defendant. Records stored back to 1993. Mail Turnaround time 1 week. Case lookup from 1997 forward is free at www.nmcourts.gov. Case look-up displays the year of birth.

Criminal Name Search: Access: Phone, mail, fax, online, in person. Both court and visitors may perform in person name searches. No search fee. Required to search: name, years to search; also helpful: DOB, SSN. Mail Turnaround time 1-3 days. Public use terminal has crim records back to 1995. Terminal results may or may not have complete name or a DOB. Online access to criminal records is free at www.nmcourts.gov. Case look-up displays the year of birth.

De Baca County

10th Judicial District Court Box 910, Ft. Sumner, NM 88119; 575-355-2896; fax: 575-355-2899; 9AM-1PM (MST). *Felony, Civil, Contested Probate.* http://nmcourts.gov

General Information: No mental, adoptions, or juvenile released. Fee to fax out file $2.00 first page, $1.00 ea addl. Court makes copy: $.35 per page. Certification fee: $1.50 per cert plus copy fee. Payee: District Court. Only cash, cashiers checks and money orders accepted. No credit cards accepted. Prepayment required. Mail requests: SASE required.

Civil Name Search: Access: Phone, mail, online, in person. Only the court performs in person name searches; visitors may not. No search fee. Civil index on cards and docket books archived from 1917; on computer since 1997. Mail Turnaround time 2 days. Case lookup from 1997 forward is free at www.nmcourts.gov. Case look-up displays the year of birth.

Criminal Name Search: Access: Phone, mail, online, in person. Only the court performs in person name searches; visitors may not. No search fee. Criminal records indexed on cards and docket books archived from 1917; on computer since 1997. Mail Turnaround time 2 days. Online access to criminal records is free at www.nmcourts.gov. Case look-up displays the year of birth.

Magistrate Court Box 24, Ft Sumner, NM 88119; 575-355-7371; fax: 575-355-7149; 8AM-5PM (MST). *Misdemeanor, Civil Actions under $10,000, Eviction, Small Claims.*

General Information: Online identifiers in results same as on public terminal. Will fax documents. Court makes copy: $.50 per page. Certification fee: $.50 per page. Payee: Magistrate Court. No personal checks or credit cards accepted. Prepayment required. Mail requests: SASE not required.

Civil Name Search: Access: In person, mail, online. Both court and visitors may perform in person name searches. No search fee. Required to search: name, COB; SSN is helpful. Online records go back to 1997. Mail Turnaround time 1 week. Civil PAT goes back to 1997. Case lookup from 1997 forward is free at www.nmcourts.gov. Case look-up displays the year of birth.

Criminal Name Search: Access: In person, mail, online. Both court and visitors may perform in person name searches. No search fee. Required to search: name, years to search, DOB, SSN. Online records go back to 1997. Mail Turnaround time 1 week. Criminal PAT goes back to same as civil. Terminal results may or may not have complete name or a DOB. Online

access to criminal records is free at www.nmcourts.gov. Case look-up displays the year of birth.

County Clerk PO Box 347, 248 E Ave C, Ft. Sumner, NM 88119; 575-355-2601; fax: 575-355-2441; 8AM-N, 1-4:30PM (MST). *Probate.*

General Information: The County Clerk holds the case files for "informal" or "uncontested" probate cases seen by the Probate Judge. The District Court holds case files for "formal" or "contested" probate cases.

Dona Ana County

3rd Judicial District Court 201 W Picacho, Las Cruces, NM 88005; 575-523-8200; criminal phone: 575-523-8358; civil phone: 575-523-8255; fax: 575-523-8290; 8AM-N, 1-5PM (MST). *Felony, Civil, Contested Probate.* www.thirddistrictcourt.com

General Information: Online identifiers in results same as on public terminal. No adoption, mental health, or juvenile released. Court makes copy: $.35 per page. Self serve copy: same. Certification fee: $1.50 plus copy fee. Payee: 3rd Judicial District. Only cashiers checks, cash and money orders accepted. No credit cards accepted. Prepayment required. Mail requests: SASE required.

Civil Name Search: Access: Mail, fax, online, in person. Both court and visitors may perform in person name searches. Search fee: $1.50 per name. Civil records on computer from 1986 (clerk's index 1986 to 9/96), on microfiche and archived from 1912. Note: There is a $4.00 fee or give record on a tape or CD. Mail Turnaround time 2-3 days. Civil PAT goes back to 9/1996. Access to court records back to 9/1996 is free at www.nmcourts.gov. Case look-up displays the year of birth.

Criminal Name Search: Access: Mail, fax, online, in person. Both court and visitors may perform in person name searches. Search fee: $1.50 per name. Required to search: name, years to search; also helpful: DOB, SSN. Criminal records computerized from 1986 (clerk's index 1977 to 9/96), on microfiche and archived from 1912. Note: There is a $4.00 fee or give record on a tape or CD. Mail Turnaround time 2-3 days. Criminal PAT goes back to 9/1996. Terminal results may or may not have complete name or a DOB. Online access to criminal records back to 9/1996 is free at www.nmcourts.gov. Case look-up displays the year of birth.

Anthony Magistrate Court PO Box 1259, 935 Anthony Dr, Anthony, NM 88021; 575-233-3147; fax: 575-882-0113; 8AM-4PM M,T,TH; 8AM-Noon Wed, Fri (MST). *Misdemeanor, Civil Actions under $10,000, Eviction, Small Claims.*

General Information: Will not fax documents. Court makes copy: $.50 per page. No certification fee . Payee: Anthony Magistrate Court. Personal checks accepted, credit cards are not. Prepayment required.

Civil Name Search: Access: Online, mail, in person. Only the court performs in person name searches; visitors may not. No search fee. Civil cases indexed by plaintiff & defendant. Civil records go back to 1999. Mail Turnaround time 3 days Case lookup from 1997 forward is free at www.nmcourts.gov. Case look-up displays the year of birth.

Criminal Name Search: Access: Mail, in person, online. Only the court performs in person name searches; visitors may not. No search fee. Required to search: name, years to search, DOB, SSN. Criminal records go back to 1999. Mail Turnaround time is 3 days. Online access to criminal records is free at www.nmcourts.gov. Case look-up displays the year of birth.

Hatch Magistrate Court PO Box 896, Hatch, NM 87937; 575-267-5202; 9AM-Noon 2nd & 4th Mondays (MST). *Misdemeanor, Civil Actions under $10,000, Eviction, Small Claims.* www.nmcourts.gov/

General Information: Note that this court is only open on Mondays. Will fax documents to local or toll-free number. Court makes copy: $.50 per page. No certification fee . Payee: Magistrate Court. Only cashiers checks and money orders accepted. No credit cards accepted. Prepayment required. Mail requests: SASE required.

Civil Name Search: Access: Mail, in person, online. Only the court performs in person name searches; visitors may not. No search fee. Records go back 1-14 years. Mail Turnaround time 1 week. Case lookup from 1997 forward is free at www.nmcourts.gov. Case look-up displays the year of birth.

Criminal Name Search: Access: Mail, in person, online. Only the court performs in person name searches; visitors may not. No search fee. Required to search: name, years to search, DOB, SSN. Mail Turnaround time 1 week. Online access to criminal records is free at www.nmcourts.gov. Case look-up displays the year of birth.

Las Cruces Magistrate Court 110 Calle de Alegra, Las Cruces, NM 88005; 575-524-2814; civil phone: 575-647-3816; fax: 575-525-2951; 8AM-4PM (MST). *Misdemeanor, Civil Actions under $10,000, Eviction, Small Claims.*

General Information: Online identifiers in results same as on public terminal. Will fax out docs no add'l fee. Court makes copy: $.50 by copy machine; free from computer. No certification fee . Payee: Magistrate Court. Personal checks accepted, credit cards are not.

Civil Name Search: Access: Fax, mail, in person, online. Both court and visitors may perform in person name searches. No search fee. Required to search: Civil records go back 14 years. Mail Turnaround time 72 hours. Civil PAT goes back to 1997. Case lookup from 1997 forward is free at www.nmcourts.gov. Case look-up displays the year of birth.

Criminal Name Search: Access: Fax, mail, in person, online. Both court and visitors may perform in person name searches. No search fee. Required to search: name, years to search; also helpful: DOB, SSN. Petty misdemeanor and traffic records go back 1 year. DUIs and domestic go back to 2004. Mail Turnaround time 72 hours. Criminal PAT goes back to same as civil. Terminal results may or may not have complete name or a DOB. Online access to criminal records is free at www.nmcourts.gov. Case look-up displays the year of birth.

Eddy County

5th Judicial District Court 102 N Canal St #240, Carlsbad, NM 88220; 575-885-4740; criminal phone: x135; civil phone: x123; fax: 575-887-7095; 8AM-N, 1-5PM (MST). *Felony, Civil, Contested Probate.* www.fifthdistrictcourt.com

General Information: Online identifiers in results same as on public terminal. No adoption, SS case w/children, or guardianship released. Will fax out specific case files if urgent for $1.00 per page. Court makes copy: $.35 per page. Certification fee: $1.50 per pleading plus copy fee, exemplification fee is $4.50 plus copy fee. Payee: District Court Clerk. Only cash, cashiers checks, money orders and law firm checks accepted. No credit cards accepted. Prepayment required.

Civil Name Search: Access: In person, online. Both court and visitors may perform in person name searches. Civil cases indexed by defendant. Civil records are computerized, on microfiche from 1891. Public use terminal has civil records back to 1986. Terminal results may or may not have complete name or a DOB. Case lookup from 1994 forward is free at www.nmcourts.gov, or via the court website above. All searching referred to record retrievers. Case look-up displays the year of birth.

Criminal Name Search: Access: In person, online. Both court and visitors may perform in person name searches. Required to search: name, years to search, SSN or DOB. Criminal records computerized from 1986, microfiche from 1900s. Online access to criminal records from 1994 forward is free at www.nmcourts.gov. Case look-up displays the year of birth.

Artesia Magistrate Court 109 N 15th St, Artesia, NM 88210; 575-746-2481; fax: 575-746-6763; 8AM-4PM (MST). *Misdemeanor, Civil Actions under $10,000, Eviction, Small Claims.* www.nmcourts.gov

General Information: This court also handles preliminary felonies, traffic, and DUI cases. Will fax out documents $1.00 per page. Court makes copy: $.50 per page. Certification fee: $.50 per page. Payee: Magistrate Court. Personal checks accepted, credit cards are not. Prepayment required. Mail requests: SASE required for mail return of any copies.

Civil Name Search: Access: Phone, mail, online. Only the court performs in person name searches; visitors may not. No search fee. Required to search: name, and DOB or SSN. Records available from 1992, computerized since 1996. Mail Turnaround time 1-2 days. Case lookup from 1997 forward is free at www.nmcourts.gov. Case look-up displays the year of birth.

Criminal Name Search: Access: Phone, mail, online. Only the court performs in person name searches; visitors may not. No search fee. Required to search: name, years to search; also helpful: DOB, SSN. Records computerized since 1996. Mail Turnaround time 1-2 days. Online access to criminal records is free at www.nmcourts.gov. Case look-up displays the year of birth.

Carlsbad Magistrate Court 1949 S Canal St, Carlsbad, NM 88220; 575-885-3218; fax: 575-887-3460; 8AM-4PM (till noon on Wed) (MST). *Misdemeanor, Civil Actions under $10,000, Eviction, Small Claims.*

General Information: Will fax documents $.50 per page. Court makes copy: $.50 per page. Certification fee: $.50 per page. Payee: Magistrate Court. No personal checks or credit cards accepted. Prepayment required.

Civil Name Search: Access: Phone, mail, fax, in person, online. Only the court performs in person name searches; visitors may not. No search fee. Required to search: name, DOB, SSN, address, other names used. Records held 14 years, computerized since 1996. Mail Turnaround time 1-4 days. Case lookup from 1997 forward is free at www.nmcourts.gov. Case look-up displays the year of birth.

Criminal Name Search: Access: Online, mail, in person. Only the court performs in person name searches; visitors may not. No search fee. Required to search: name, years to search, DOB, SSN, other names used. Records held 1 year, computerized since 1996. Domestic violence and DWI retained indefinitely. Mail Turnaround time 1-5 days. Online access to criminal records is free at www.nmcourts.gov. Case look-up displays the year of birth.

County Clerk Eddy County Probate, 325 S Main St, Carlsbad, NM 88220; 575-885-3383; fax: 575-234-1793; 8AM-5PM (MST). *Probate.* www.co.eddy.nm.us/departments.html

General Information: The County Clerk holds the case files for "informal" or "uncontested" probate cases seen by the Probate Judge. The District Court holds case files for "formal" or "contested" probate cases.

Grant County

6th Judicial District Court Box 2339, 201 N Cooper St, Silver City, NM 88062; 575-538-3250; fax: 575-388-5439; 8AM-N, 1-5PM (MST). *Felony, Civil, Contested Probate.*

General Information: Online identifiers in results same as on public terminal. No adoption, guardianship or abuse records released. Will fax documents $2.50 per page. Court makes copy: $.35 per page. Certification fee: $1.50. Payee: District Court Clerk. Only cashiers checks and money orders accepted. No credit cards accepted. Prepayment required. Mail requests: SASE required.

Civil Name Search: Access: Fax, mail, online, in person. Both court and visitors may perform in person name searches. No search fee. Civil records on microfiche from 1942-1987, on books from 1987; on computer back to 1997. Note: The clerk will assist in finding identifiers when necessary. Mail Turnaround time 2 weeks. Civil PAT goes back to 1997. Terminal is same as statewide online, results may or may not have complete name or a DOB. Case lookup from 1997 forward is free at www.nmcourts.gov. Case look-up displays the year of birth.

Criminal Name Search: Access: Fax, mail, online, in person. Both court and visitors may perform in person name searches. No search fee. Criminal records on microfiche from 1942-1987, on books from 1987; on computer back to 1996. Note: The clerk will assist in finding identifiers when necessary. Mail Turnaround time 2 weeks. Criminal PAT goes back to 1996. Terminal results may or may not have complete name or a DOB. Online access to criminal records is free at www.nmcourts.gov. Case look-up displays the year of birth.

Bayard Magistrate Court 701 Central Ave, Bayard, NM 88023; 575-537-3042; fax: 575-537-7365; 8AM-4PM (MST). *Misdemeanor, Civil Actions under $10,000, Eviction, Small Claims.*

General Information: Will not fax documents. Court makes copy: $.50 per page. No certification fee . Payee: Bayard Magistrate Court. Local Personal checks accepted, credit cards are not. Prepayment required. Mail requests: SASE required.

Civil Name Search: Access: Mail, fax, in person, online. Only the court performs in person name searches; visitors may not. No search fee. Civil cases indexed by plaintiff & defendant. Civil records go back to 1992. Mail Turnaround time 3 days. Case lookup from 1997 forward is free at www.nmcourts.gov. Case look-up displays the year of birth.

Criminal Name Search: Access: Mail, fax, in person, online. Only the court performs in person name searches; visitors may not. No search fee. Criminal records go back to 1999. Mail Turnaround time is 3 days. Online access to criminal records is free at www.nmcourts.gov. Case look-up displays the year of birth.

Silver City Magistrate Court 1620 E Pine St, Silver City, NM 88061; 575-538-3811; fax: 575-538-8079; 8AM-4PM (MST). *Misdemeanor, Civil Actions under $10,000, Eviction, Small Claims.*

General Information: Will fax back $1.00 per page. Court makes copy: $.50 per page. No certification fee . Payee: Magistrate Court. Personal checks accepted, credit cards are not. Prepayment required.

Civil Name Search: Access: Mail, fax, in person, online. Only the court performs in person name searches; visitors may not. No search fee. Required to search: name, years to search, DOB, SSN. Records computerized since 1995. Mail Turnaround time 2 days. Case lookup from 1997 forward is free at www.nmcourts.gov. Case look-up displays the year of birth.

Criminal Name Search: Access: Mail, fax, in person, online. Only the court performs in person name searches; visitors may not. No search fee. Required to search: name, years to search, DOB; also helpful: SSN. Records held here from 1988, computerized since 6/16/95. Mail Turnaround time 2 days. Online access to criminal records is free at www.nmcourts.gov. Case look-up displays the year of birth.

County Clerk PO Box 898, 1400 Hwy 180 E (88061), Silver City, NM 88062; 575-574-0042; fax: 575-574-0076; 8AM-5PM (MST). *Probate.* www.grantcountynm.com/grant_county_nm_info.php?CID=372

General Information: The County Clerk holds the case files for "informal" or "uncontested" probate cases seen by the Probate Judge. The District Court holds case files for "formal" or "contested" probate cases.

Guadalupe County

4th Judicial District Court 420 Parker Ave #5, County Courthouse, Santa Rosa, NM 88435; 575-472-3888; fax: 575-472-4451; 8AM-N, 1PM-4PM (MST). *Felony, Civil, Contested Probate, Domestic.*

General Information: To avoid confusion, all records requests must include a search/copy request form. Submit search request, then clerk will compute cost and call you. Microfiche search of older records is add'l $5.00 per roll. No adoption, insanity, guardianship records released. Will fax documents to local number for $2.00 1st page and $1.00 ea add'l page fee. Will fax out-of-state for $2.00 per page. Court makes copy: $.35 per page. Self serve copy: same. Certification fee: $1.50 per seal plus copy fee. Payee: District Court Clerk Office. No personal or business checks accepted. No credit cards accepted. Prepayment required. Mail requests: SASE required.

Civil Name Search: Access: Fax, mail, in person, online. Only the court performs in person name searches; visitors may not. Search fee: Fee based on scope of search. Required to search: name, years to search, DOB. Civil index in docket books from 1912, computer back to 1997. Mail Turnaround time 3 days. Access to court records from 1997 to present is free at www.nmcourts.gov Case look-up displays the year of birth.

Criminal Name Search: Access: Fax, mail, in person, online. Only the court performs in person name searches; visitors may not. Search fee: Fee based on scope of search. Required to search: name, years to search, DOB; also helpful: SSN. Criminal docket on books from 1912, computer back to 1997. Mail Turnaround time 3 days. Online access to criminal records is free at www.nmcourts.gov. Case look-up displays the year of birth.

Santa Rosa Magistrate Court 603 Parker Ave, Santa Rosa, NM 88435; 575-472-3237; fax: 575-472-3592; 8AM-4PM M-Th, 8AM-N F (MST). *Misdemeanor, Civil Actions under $10,000, Eviction, Small Claims.*

General Information: Holds records for the Vaughn Magistrate Court, which closed 2008. Will fax documents $10.00 each. Court makes copy: $.50 per page. No certification fee . Payee: Santa Rosa Magistrate Court. No personal checks or credit cards accepted. Mail requests: SASE required.

Civil Name Search: Access: Online, mail, in person. Only the court performs in person name searches; visitors may not. No search fee. Civil cases indexed by both plaintiff and defendant. Mail Turnaround time 3 days. Case lookup from 1997 forward is free at www.nmcourts.gov. Case look-up displays the year of birth.

Criminal Name Search: Access: Online, mail, in person. Only the court performs in person name searches; visitors may not. No search fee. Required to search: name, years to search, DOB, offense, date of offense; also helpful: SSN. Mail Turnaround time 3 days. Online access to criminal records is free at www.nmcourts.gov. Case look-up displays the year of birth.

Vaughn Magistrate Court - (Closed - See Santa Rosa) , , NM; . *Misdemeanor, Civil Actions under $10,000, Eviction, Small Claims.*
General Information: The Vaughn court has been closed. Records are at Santa Rosa Magistrate Court in this county.

County Clerk 1448 Historic Route 66, #1, Santa Rosa, NM 88435; 575-472-3791; fax: 575-472-4791; 8AM-N, 1-5PM (MST). *Probate.*
General Information: The County Clerk holds the case files for "informal" or "uncontested" probate cases seen by the Probate Judge. The District Court holds case files for "formal" or "contested" probate cases.

Harding County

10th Judicial District Court Box 1002, Mosquero, NM 87733; 575-673-2252; fax: 575-673-0333; 9AM-1PM (MST). *Felony, Civil, Contested Probate.*
General Information: No adoption or sealed records released. Will fax documents for $2.00 first page, $1.00 ea addl. Court makes copy: $.35 per page. Self serve copy: same. Certification fee: $1.50. Payee: District Court Clerk. Business checks accepted from attorneys only. No personal checks, no cash accepted. Court asks for money orders,. No credit cards accepted. Prepayment required. Mail requests: SASE required.
Civil Name Search: Access: Phone, fax, mail, online, in person. Only the court performs in person name searches; visitors may not. No search fee. Required to search: name; also helpful: years to search. Civil records on books from 1927. Computerized records go back to 1997. Mail Turnaround time 1 week. Case lookup from 1997 forward is free at www.nmcourts.gov. Most but not all online results show middle initial.
Criminal Name Search: Access: Phone, fax, mail, online, in person. Only the court performs in person name searches; visitors may not. No search fee. Required to search: name, DOB, SSN; also helpful: years to search. Criminal docket on books from 1927. Computerized records go back to 1997. Mail Turnaround time 1 week. Online access to criminal records is free at www.nmcourts.gov. Case look-up displays the year of birth.

Magistrate Court Box 9, 355 Chicosa St, Roy, NM 87743; 575-485-2549; fax: 575-485-2407; 8AM-4PM (MST). *Misdemeanor, Civil Actions under $10,000, Eviction, Small Claims.*
www.hardingcounty.org/Government/magistrate_court.htm
General Information: Online identifiers in results same as on public terminal. Sequestered records not released. Will fax documents. Court makes copy: $.50 per page. No certification fee . Payee: Magistrate Court. Personal

checks accepted, credit cards are not. Prepayment required. Mail requests: SASE not required.

Civil Name Search: Access: Mail, phone, in person, fax, online. Both court and visitors may perform in person name searches. No search fee. Required to search: name, DOB, years to search, other names used; also helpful-SSN, address. Records indexed by plaintiff and defendant. Records computerized since 1996. Mail Turnaround time 2 days. Civil PAT goes back to 1997. Case lookup from 1997 forward is free at www.nmcourts.gov. Case look-up displays the year of birth.

Criminal Name Search: Access: Mail, phone, in person, fax, online. Both court and visitors may perform in person name searches. No search fee. Required to search: name, years to search, DOB; also helpful: address, SSN. Records computerized since 1996. Mail Turnaround time 2 days. Criminal PAT goes back to same as civil. Terminal results may or may not have complete name or a DOB. Online access to criminal records is free at www.nmcourts.gov. Case look-up displays the year of birth.

County Clerk PO Box 1002, County Clerk, 35 Pine St, Mosquero, NM 87733; 575-673-2301; fax: 575-673-2922; 8AM-4PM (MST). *Probate.*
General Information: The County Clerk holds the case files for "informal" or "uncontested" probate cases seen by the Probate Judge. The District Court holds case files for "formal" or "contested" probate cases.

Hidalgo County

6th Judicial District Court PO Box 608, Lordsburg, NM 88045; 575-542-3411; fax: 575-542-3481; 8AM-4PM (MST). *Felony, Civil, Contested Probate.*
General Information: No juvenile or adoption records released. Fee to fax $5.00 1st page, $.35 each add'l page. Court makes copy: $.35 per page. Certification fee: $1.50. Payee: District Court Clerk. Business checks accepted. No personal checks or credit cards accepted. Prepayment required. Mail requests: SASE required.
Civil Name Search: Access: Phone, fax, mail, online, in person. Only the court performs in person name searches; visitors may not. No search fee. Civil records on microfiche and archived from 1920. Mail Turnaround time 3-5 days. Case lookup from 1997 forward is free at www.nmcourts.gov. Case look-up displays the year of birth.
Criminal Name Search: Access: Phone, fax, mail, online, in person. Only the court performs in person name searches; visitors may not. No search fee. Required to search: name, years to search; also helpful: alias. Criminal records on microfiche and archived from 1920. Mail Turnaround time 3-5 days. Online access to criminal records is free at www.nmcourts.gov. Case look-up displays the year of birth.

Magistrate Court 420 Wabash Ave, Lordsburg, NM 88045; 575-542-3582; fax: 575-542-3596; 8AM-4PM (MST). *Misdemeanor, Civil Actions under $10,000, Eviction, Small Claims.*
General Information: Fee to fax out file $1.00 per page. Court makes copy: $.50 per page. No certification fee . Payee: Magistrate Court. Only cashiers checks and money orders accepted. No credit cards accepted. Prepayment required. Mail requests: SASE required.
Civil Name Search: Access: Online, mail, in person. Only the court performs in person name searches; visitors may not. No search fee. Mail Turnaround time 1 week. Case lookup from 1997 forward is free at www.nmcourts.gov. Case look-up displays the year of birth.
Criminal Name Search: Access: Mail, in person, fax, online. Only the court performs in person name searches; visitors may not. No search fee. Required to search: name, years to search; also helpful: DOB, SSN. Mail Turnaround time 1 week. Online access to criminal records is free at www.nmcourts.gov. Case look-up displays the year of birth.

County Clerk 300 S Shakespeare, Lordsburg, NM 88045; 575-542-9213; fax: 575-542-3193; 9AM-5PM (MST). *Probate.*
General Information: The County Clerk holds the case files for "informal" or "uncontested" probate cases seen by the Probate Judge. The District Court holds case files for "formal" or "contested" probate cases.

Lea County

5th Judicial District Court Box #6-C, 100 N Main, Lovington, NM 88260; 575-396-8571; fax: 575-396-2428; 8AM-N. 1PM-5PM (MST). *Felony, Civil, Contested Probate.*
www.fifthdistrictcourt.com
General Information: Online identifiers in results same as on public terminal. No adoption, mental, abuse records released. Will not fax documents. Court makes copy: $.35 per page. Self serve copy: same. Certification fee: $1.50 per cert. Payee: District Court Clerk. Only cashiers checks and money orders accepted. No credit cards accepted. Prepayment required.
Civil Name Search: Access: Online, in person. Both court and visitors may perform in person name searches. No search fee. Civil records on computer from 1990, on microfiche from 1912. Civil PAT goes back to 1990. Case lookup from 1997 forward is free at www.nmcourts.gov. Case look-up displays the year of birth.

Criminal Name Search: Access: Online, in person. Both court and visitors may perform in person name searches. No search fee. Criminal records computerized from 1997, on microfiche from 1912. Criminal PAT goes back to same as civil. Terminal results may or may not have complete name or a DOB. Online access to criminal records is free at www.nmcourts.gov. Case look-up displays the year of birth.

Eunice Magistrate Court PO Box 240, 2200 W Ave "O", Eunice, NM 88231; 575-394-3368; fax: 575-394-3335; 8AM-4PM M,W, 8AM-N F (MST). *Misdemeanor, Civil Actions under $10,000, Eviction, Small Claims.*

General Information: Closed Tuesdays and Thursdays Will fax documents for $1.00 per page. Court makes copy: $.50 per page. Certification fee: $1.00 per copy. Payee: Eunice Magistrate Court. No personal or business checks accepted. No credit cards accepted. Mail requests: SASE required.

Civil Name Search: Access: Online, mail, fax, in person. Only the court performs in person name searches; visitors may not. No search fee. Required to search: name only. Civil cases indexed by both plaintiff & defendant. Mail Turnaround time 3 days. Case lookup from 1997 forward is free at www.nmcourts.gov. Case look-up displays the year of birth.

Criminal Name Search: Access: Online, mail, fax, in person. Only the court performs in person name searches; visitors may not. No search fee. Required to search: name, years to search, DOB; also helpful: SSN. Criminal records go back 10 years, case files held one year after disposition. Mail Turnaround time 3 days. Online access to criminal records is free at www.nmcourts.gov. Case look-up displays the year of birth.

Hobbs Magistrate Court 2110 N Alto Dr, Hobbs, NM 88240-3455; 575-397-3621; fax: 575-393-9121; 8AM-4PM (MST). *Misdemeanor, Civil Actions under $10,000, Eviction, Small Claims.*

General Information: Sealed records not available. Will fax documents to local or toll free line for $1.00 per fax. Court makes copy: $.50 per page. Self serve copy: same. No certification fee Certification included in copy fee. Payee: Magistrate Court. No personal checks or credit cards accepted. Prepayment required. Mail requests: SASE required.

Civil Name Search: Access: Online, mail, in person. Only the court performs in person name searches; visitors may not. No search fee. Required to search: name, years to search, signed release, address, other names used; DOB, SSN helpful. Civil records held 14 years, computerized since July, 1996. Mail Turnaround time seven days for mail; 3 days for fax. Case lookup from 1997 forward is free at www.nmcourts.gov. Case look-up displays the year of birth.

Criminal Name Search: Access: Online, mail, in person. Only the court performs in person name searches; visitors may not. No search fee. Required to search: name, years to search, DOB; SSN and signed release helpful. Criminal records held 1 year after disposition; computerized since July, 1996. Mail Turnaround time 3-5 days. Online access to criminal records is free at www.nmcourts.gov. Case look-up displays the year of birth.

Jal Magistrate Court PO Box 507, Jal, NM 88252; 575-395-2740; fax: 575-395-2595; 8AM-4PM Tues, 8AM-1PM Th (MST). *Misdemeanor, Civil Actions under $10,000, Eviction, Small Claims.*

General Information: All record requests must be in writing. Will not fax documents. Court makes copy: $.50 per page. Certification fee: $.50 per page. Payee: Jal Magistrate Court. . Mail requests: SASE required.

Civil Name Search: Access: Mail, in person, online. Only the court performs in person name searches; visitors may not. No search fee. Civil cases indexed by both plaintiff & defendant. Mail Turnaround time 3 days. Case lookup from 1997 forward is free at www.nmcourts.gov. Case look-up displays the year of birth.

Criminal Name Search: Access: Mail, in person, online. Only the court performs in person name searches; visitors may not. No search fee. Required to search: name, years to search, DOB; also helpful: SSN. Mail Turnaround time 3 days. Online access to criminal records is free at www.nmcourts.gov. Case look-up displays the year of birth.

Lovington Magistrate Court 100 W Central St, #D, Lovington, NM 88260; 575-396-6677; fax: 575-396-6163; 8AM-4PM M-Th; 8AM-12 F (MST). *Misdemeanor, Civil Actions under $10,000, Eviction, Small Claims.*

General Information: The Magistrate Court in Tatum has closed, the record are located here. Online identifiers in results same as on public terminal. Will fax documents per arrangement. Court makes copy: $.50 per page. Certification fee: $1.00 per copy. Payee: Magistrate Court. Business checks accepted. Prepayment required. Mail requests: SASE required.

Civil Name Search: Access: Phone, fax, mail, in person, online. Both court and visitors may perform in person name searches. No search fee. Mail Turnaround time 3 days. Public use terminal available. Case lookup from 1997 forward is free at www.nmcourts.gov. Case look-up displays the year of birth.

Criminal Name Search: Access: Phone, fax, mail, in person, online. Both court and visitors may perform in person name searches. No search fee.

Required to search: name, years to search, DOB. Mail Turnaround time 3 days. Public use terminal available. Terminal results may or may not have complete name or a DOB. Online access to criminal records is free at www.nmcourts.gov. Court warns to be cautious to match the name to the right record. Case look-up displays the year of birth.

County Clerk Box 1507, 100 N Main St, #1C, Lovington, NM 88260; 575-396-8614; fax: 575-396-3293; 8AM-5PM (MST). *Probate, Ordinance.* www.leacounty.net/clerk.htm

General Information: The County Clerk holds the case files for "informal" or "uncontested" probate cases seen by the Probate Judge. The District Court holds case files for "formal" or "contested" probate cases.

Lincoln County

12th Judicial District Court Box 725, Carrizozo, NM 88301; 575-648-2432; fax: 575-648-2581; 8AM-5PM (MST). *Felony, Civil, Contested Probate.* www.12thdistrict.net

General Information: Online identifiers in results same as on public terminal. No juvenile, adoption, or mental records released. Will fax documents to toll free number. Court makes copy: $.35 per page. Certification fee: $1.50 per stamp plus copy fee. Payee: District Court Clerk. No personal checks accepted. Money orders or cashier's checks accepted. No credit cards accepted. Prepayment required. Mail requests: SASE required.

Civil Name Search: Access: Online, mail, in person. Both court and visitors may perform in person name searches. No search fee. Civil records on computer from 1991, docket books from 1960, microfiche to 1960. Civil PAT goes back to 1991. Case lookup from 1997 forward is free at www.nmcourts.gov. Case look-up displays the year of birth.

Criminal Name Search: Access: Online, in person. Both court and visitors may perform in person name searches. No search fee. Criminal records computerized from 1991, docket books from 1960, microfiche to 1960. Criminal PAT goes back to same as civil. Terminal results may or may not have complete name or a DOB. Online access to criminal records is free at www.nmcourts.gov. Case look-up displays the year of birth.

Carrizozo Magistrate Court 310 11th St, PO Box 488, Carrizozo, NM 88301; 575-648-2389; fax: 575-648-2695; 8AM-Noon; 1-5PM M-Th, 8AM-4PM Fri (MST). *Misdemeanor, Civil Actions under $10,000, Eviction, Small Claims, Traffic.*

General Information: Will not fax documents. Court makes copy: $.50 per page. No certification fee . Payee: Carrizozo Magistrate Court. No personal checks or credit cards accepted. Mail requests: SASE required.

Civil Name Search: Access: Mail, in person, online. Both court and visitors may perform in person name searches. No search fee. Civil cases indexed by both plaintiff & defendant. Mail Turnaround time 3 days. Case lookup from 1997 forward is free at www.nmcourts.gov. Case look-up displays the year of birth.

Criminal Name Search: Access: Fax, in person, mail, online. Visitors must perform in person searches themselves. Search fee: $7.00 per name, if more than 1 name. Required to search: name, years to search; also helpful: DOB, SSN. Mail Turnaround time 3 days. Online access to criminal records for past 10 years is free at www.nmcourts.gov. Case look-up displays the year of birth.

Ruidoso Magistrate Court 301 W Highway 70 #2, Ruidoso, NM 88345; 575-378-7022; fax: 575-378-8508; 8AM-4PM M, T, TH; 9AM-4PM W; 8AM-N F (MST). *Misdemeanor, Civil Actions under $10,000, Eviction, Small Claims.*

General Information: Will not fax documents. Court makes copy: $.50 per page. Certification fee: $1.00 per cert. Payee: Ruidoso Magistrate Court. No personal checks or credit cards accepted. Prepayment required.

Civil Name Search: Access: Online, mail, in person. Both court and visitors may perform in person name searches. No search fee. Civil cases indexed by both plaintiff & defendant. Mail Turnaround time 3 days. Case lookup from 1997 forward is free at www.nmcourts.gov. Case look-up displays the year of birth.

Criminal Name Search: Access: Online, mail, in person. Visitors must perform in person searches themselves. No search fee. Required to search: name, years to search; also helpful: DOB, SSN. Mail Turnaround time 3 days. Online access to criminal records is free at www.nmcourts.gov. Case look-up displays the year of birth.

County Clerk PO Box 338, 300 Central Ave, Carrizozo, NM 88301; 575-648-2394 X6; fax: 575-648-2576; 8AM-5PM (MST). *Probate.*

General Information: The County Clerk holds the case files for "informal" or "uncontested" probate cases seen by the Probate Judge. The District Court holds case files for "formal" or "contested" probate cases.

Los Alamos County

Magistrate Court 2500 Trinty Dr, # D, Los Alamos, NM 87544; 505-662-2727; fax: 505-661-6258; 8AM-4PM (MST). *Misdemeanor, Civil Actions under $10,000, Eviction, Small Claims.*

General Information: Will fax documents $1.00 per page. Court makes copy: $.50 per page. No certification fee . Payee: Los Alamos Magistrate Court. Personal checks accepted, credit cards are not. Prepayment required. Mail requests: SASE required for mail return of any copies.

Civil Name Search: Access: Online, in person. Only the court performs in person name searches; visitors may not. No search fee. Required to search: name, years to search, address, other names used, signed release. 1997 records forward are on database. Case lookup from 1997 forward is free at www.nmcourts.gov. Case look-up displays the year of birth.

Criminal Name Search: Access: Online, in person. Only the court performs in person name searches; visitors may not. No search fee. Required to search: name, years to search, address, DOB, signed release; also helpful: SSN. Normally destroyed after 1 years from closure; except DWIs and domestic violence cases. Online access to criminal records is free at www.nmcourts.gov. Case look-up displays the year of birth.

1st Judicial District Court - See Santa Fe c/o Santa Fe 1st District Court, PO Box 2268, Santa Fe, NM 87504 http://firstdistrictcourt.com
General Information: All civil and criminal cases now handled by Santa Fe District Court.

County Clerk-Probate 2451 Central Ave, #D, Los Alamos, NM 87544; 505-662-8013, 8010; fax: 505-662-8008; 8AM-5PM (MST). *Probate.* www.losalamosnm.us/clerk/Pages/ProbateCourt.aspx

Luna County

6th Judicial District Court 855 S Platinum, Deming, NM 88030; 575-546-9611; fax: 575-543-1605; 8AM-4PM (MST). *Felony, Civil, Contested Probate.* www.nmcourts.gov/
General Information: Online identifiers in results same as on public terminal. No adoption, mental, sequestered or juvenile records released. Will fax documents $.35 per page. Court makes copy: $.35 per page. Self serve copy: same. Certification fee: $1.50 per document plus copy fee. Payee: District Court Clerk. Only cashiers checks and money orders accepted. No credit cards accepted. Prepayment required. Mail requests: SASE required.

Civil Name Search: Access: Mail, in person, online. Both court and visitors may perform in person name searches. No search fee. Civil records on microfiche from 1911; on computer back to 1997. Mail Turnaround time 5 days. Civil PAT goes back to 1997. Case lookup from 1997 forward is free at www.nmcourts.gov. Case look-up displays the year of birth.

Criminal Name Search: Access: Mail, online, in person. Both court and visitors may perform in person name searches. No search fee. Criminal records on microfiche from 1911; on computer back to 1997. Mail Turnaround time 5 days. Criminal PAT goes back to same as civil. Terminal results may or may not have complete name or a DOB. Online access to criminal records is free at www.nmcourts.gov. Case look-up displays the year of birth.

Magistrate Court 912 S Silver St, Deming, NM 88030; 575-546-9321; fax: 575-546-4896; 8AM-N, 1-5PM M-TH; 8AM-N Fri (MST). *Misdemeanor, Civil Actions under $10,000, Eviction, Small Claims.*
General Information: Will fax documents $1.00 per page. Court makes copy: $.50 per page includes certification. No certification fee . Payee: Luna Magistrate Court. Personal checks are accepted. No credit cards accepted. Prepayment required. Mail requests: SASE required.

Civil Name Search: Access: Mail, in person, online. Only the court performs in person name searches; visitors may not. No search fee. Required to search: name, years to search, if judgment was rendered. Civil records can go back 14 years, since 1996 are computerized. Mail Turnaround time 2-3 days. Case lookup from 1997 forward is free at www.nmcourts.gov. Case look-up displays the year of birth.

Criminal Name Search: Access: Mail, in person, online. Only the court performs in person name searches; visitors may not. No search fee. Criminal records computerized from 1/1996. Physical files are maintained for 1 fiscal year. Mail Turnaround time 2-3 days. Online access to criminal records is free at www.nmcourts.gov. Case look-up displays the year of birth.

County Clerk PO Box 1838, 700 S Silver, Deming, NM 88031; 575-546-0491; fax: 575-543-6617; 8AM-5PM (MST). *Probate.* www.lunacountynm.us/index.html
General Information: The County Clerk holds the case files for "informal" or "uncontested" probate cases seen by the Probate Judge. The District Court holds case files for "formal" or "contested" probate cases.

McKinley County

11th Judicial District Court 207 W. Hill, Rm 200, Gallup, NM 87301; 505-863-6816; fax: 505-722-3401; 8AM-N, 1-5PM (MST). *Felony, Civil, Contested Probate.*
General Information: No adoption or juvenile records released. Fee to fax out file $5.00 per call. Court makes copy: $.35 per page. Self serve copy: same. Certification fee: $1.50. Payee: McKinley County District Court. No

personal checks or credit cards accepted. Prepayment required. Mail requests: SASE required.

Civil Name Search: Access: Phone, mail, online, in person. Both court and visitors may perform in person name searches. No search fee. Civil records on computer from 1989, on microfiche from 1923. Note: One name only by phone. Mail Turnaround time 3-5 days. Public use terminal has civil records back to 1988. Case lookup from 1997 forward is free at www.nmcourts.gov. Case look-up displays the year of birth.

Criminal Name Search: Access: Phone, mail, online, in person. Both court and visitors may perform in person name searches. No search fee. Required to search: name, years to search, DOB; also helpful: SSN. Criminal records computerized from 1989, on microfiche from 1923. Note: Will search one name only by phone. Mail Turnaround time 3-5 days. Online access to criminal records is free at www.nmcourts.gov. Case look-up displays the year of birth.

Magistrate Court 285 Boardman Dr, Gallup, NM 87301; 505-722-6636; fax: 505-863-3510; 8AM-4PM M-Th 8AM-12 F (MST). *Misdemeanor, Civil Actions under $10,000, Eviction, Small Claims.* www.nmcourts.gov/
General Information: Felony preliminary hearings held here. Will not fax documents. Court makes copy: $.50 per page. No certification fee . Payee: Magistrate Court. Personal checks accepted. Major credit cards accepted in person only. Prepayment required.

Civil Name Search: Access: Online, in person. Only the court performs in person name searches; visitors may not. Record images go back 14 years. Case lookup from 1997 forward is free at www.nmcourts.gov. Online results show only the last 4 digits of the SSN, if available. Not all results and records show full name and/or DOB.

Criminal Name Search: Access: Online, in person. Only the court performs in person name searches; visitors may not. No search fee. Required to search: name, years to search, DOB; also helpful: SSN. Online access to criminal records is free at www.nmcourts.gov. Online results show only the last 4 digits of the SSN, if available. Not all results and records show full name and/or DOB.

Thoreau Magistrate Court Thoreau, NM 87323. *Misdemeanor, Civil Actions under $10,000, Eviction, Small Claims.*
General Information: See Gallup Magistrate clerk; ask for Deloria. Index at www.nmcourts.gov/caselookup/.

County Clerk PO Box 1268, 207 W Hill St, #100, Gallup, NM 87305; 505-863-6866; fax: 505-863-1419; 8AM-5PM (MST). *Probate, Ordinance.* www.co.mckinley.nm.us/clerk.htm
General Information: The County Clerk holds the case files for "informal" or "uncontested" probate cases seen by the Probate Judge. The District Court holds case files for "formal" or "contested" probate cases.

Mora County

4th Judicial District Court (Records in San Miguel County) , , NM; . *Felony, Civil.*
General Information: Mora District Court records are maintained at the Court in Las Vegas, County of San Miguel. See that profile for details.

Magistrate Court PO Box 131, Mora, NM 87732; 575-387-2937; fax: 575-387-9081; 8AM-4PM (MST). *Misdemeanor, Civil Actions under $10,000, Eviction, Small Claims.*
General Information: Will fax documents to local or toll-free number. Court makes copy: $.50 per page. No certification fee . Payee: Magistrate Court. Only cashiers checks and money orders accepted. Major credit cards accepted. Prepayment required.

Civil Name Search: Access: In person, online. Both court and visitors may perform in person name searches. No search fee. Records maintained for 16 years. Case lookup from 1997 forward is free at www.nmcourts.gov. Case look-up displays the year of birth.

Criminal Name Search: Access: In person, online. Both court and visitors may perform in person name searches. No search fee. File copies kept here for 3 years only. Online access to criminal records is free at www.nmcourts.gov. Case look-up displays the year of birth.

Otero County

12th Judicial District Court 1000 New York Ave, Rm 209, Alamogordo, NM 88310-6940; 575-437-7310; fax: 575-434-8886; 8AM-5PM (MST). *Felony, Civil, Contested Probate.* www.12thdistrict.net
General Information: No sealed, adoption records released. Will not fax documents. Court makes copy: $.35 per page. Self serve copy: same. Certification fee: $1.50; exemplification- $4.50. Payee: District Court. Only cashiers checks, cash or money orders accepted. No credit cards accepted. Prepayment required.

Civil Name Search: Access: Online, mail, in person, email. Only the court performs in person name searches; visitors may not. No search fee. Civil records on computer from 1991, on microfiche from 1926. Note: Phone & mail access limited to 5 names each. Email requests to aladresearch@nmcourts.gov. Case lookup from 1991 forward is free at www.nmcourts.gov Also, current court dockets are at the court website. Case look-up displays the year of birth.

Criminal Name Search: Access: Online, mail, in person, email. Only the court performs in person name searches; visitors may not. No search fee. Criminal records computerized from 1991, on microfiche from 1926. Note: Only court performs searches prior to March 1986. Email requests to aladresearch@nmcourts.gov. Mail Turnaround time 48 hours. Driver License number may also appear on terminal result. Terminal results may or may not have complete name or a DOB. Online access to criminal records is free at www.nmcourts.gov. Case look-up displays the year of birth.

Magistrate Court 263 Robert H Bradley Dr, Alamogordo, NM 88310-8288; 575-437-9000; fax: 575-439-1365; 8AM-4PM (opens 9AM on Tues) (MST). *Misdemeanor, Civil Actions under $10,000, Eviction, Small Claims.*

General Information: Will fax documents, a fee may be required. Court makes copy: $.50 per page. Certification fee: $.50 per page plus copy fee. Payee: Magistrate Court. Personal checks accepted, credit cards are not. Mail requests: SASE required.

Civil Name Search: Access: Online, mail, fax, in person. Only the court performs in person name searches; visitors may not. No search fee. Civil cases indexed by both plaintiff & defendant. Records placed in storage after one year. Mail Turnaround time 3 days. Case lookup from 1997 forward is free at www.nmcourts.gov. Case look-up displays the year of birth.

Criminal Name Search: Access: Online, mail, fax, in person. Only the court performs in person name searches; visitors may not. No search fee. Required to search: name, years to search, DOB; also helpful: SSN. Records placed in storage after one year. Mail Turnaround time 3 days. Online access to criminal records is free at www.nmcourts.gov. Case look-up displays the year of birth.

County Clerk 1104 N White Sands Blvd, Ste C, Alamogordo, NM 88310-6932; 575-437-4942; fax: 575-443-2922; 7:30AM-6PM (MST). *Probate.*

General Information: The County Clerk holds the case files for "informal" or "uncontested" probate cases seen by the Probate Judge. The District Court holds case files for "formal" or "contested" probate cases.

Quay County

10th Judicial District Court Box 1067, Tucumcari, NM 88401; 575-461-2764; fax: 575-461-4498; 8AM-Noon, 1PM-4PM (MST). *Felony, Civil, Contested Probate.*

General Information: Online identifiers in results same as on public terminal. No adoption, juvenile, guardianship, insanity records released. Will fax documents $2.00 1st page, $1.00 each add'l. Court makes copy: $.35 per page. Certification fee: $1.50. Payee: District Court Clerk. No personal checks or credit cards accepted. Prepayment required. Mail requests: SASE required.

Civil Name Search: Access: Phone, fax, mail, online, in person. Both court and visitors may perform in person name searches. No search fee. Civil records on file from 1912 to present. Mail Turnaround time same day. Civil PAT goes back to 1912. 4 digits of the DOB are provided if on the file. Case lookup from 1997 forward is free at www.nmcourts.gov. Case look-up displays the year of birth.

Criminal Name Search: Access: Phone, fax, mail, online, in person. Both court and visitors may perform in person name searches. No search fee. Required to search: name; also helpful: years to search, DOB, SSN. Criminal records on file from 1912 to present. Mail Turnaround time same day. Criminal PAT available. Terminal results may or may not have complete name or a DOB. Online access to criminal records is free at www.nmcourts.gov. Case look-up displays the year of birth.

Tucumcari Magistrate Court PO Box 1301, Tucumcari, NM 88401; 575-461-1700; fax: 575-461-4522; 8AM-4PM M-TH; till 3PM F (MST). *Misdemeanor, Civil Actions under $10,000, Eviction, Small Claims.*

General Information: San Jon Magistrate Court (closed) records are found here, if not purged. Year of birth may still be available. Will fax documents $1.00 per page. Court makes copy: $.50 per page. Certification fee: $1.00 per page. Payee: Quay County Magistrate Court. Personal checks accepted, credit cards are not. Prepayment required.

Civil Name Search: Access: Online, in person. Only the court performs in person name searches; visitors may not. No search fee. Case lookup from 1997 forward is free at www.nmcourts.gov. Case look-up displays the year of birth.

Criminal Name Search: Access: Online, in person. Only the court performs in person name searches; visitors may not. No search fee. Required to search: name, years to search, DOB, SSN. Online access to criminal records is free at www.nmcourts.gov. Case look-up displays the year of birth.

County Clerk 300 S 3rd St, PO Box 1225, Tucumcari, NM 88401; 575-461-0510; fax: 575-461-0513; 8AM-N, 1-5PM (MST). *Probate.* http://quaycounty-nm.gov/clerk.html

General Information: The County Clerk holds the case files for "informal" or "uncontested" probate cases seen by the Probate Judge. The District Court holds case files for "formal" or "contested" probate cases.

Rio Arriba County

1st Judicial District Court PO Drawer 40, Tierra Amarilla, NM 87575; 575-588-0058; fax: 575-588-9898; 8AM-N, 1-4PM (MST). *Felony, Misdemeanor, Civil, Contested Probate.* http://firstdistrictcourt.com

General Information: Will not fax documents. Court makes copy: $.35 per page. Certification fee: $1.50 per page. Payee: 1st Judicial District Court. No personal checks or credit cards accepted. Prepayment required. Mail requests: SASE required.

Civil Name Search: Access: Phone, mail, fax, in person, online. Only the court performs in person name searches; visitors may not. No search fee. Required to search: Name, years to search, SSN, DOB. Records on computer back to 1997. Case lookup from 1997 forward is free at www.nmcourts.gov. Case look-up displays the year of birth.

Criminal Name Search: Access: Phone, mail, fax, in person, online. Only the court performs in person name searches; visitors may not. No search fee. Records on computer back to 1997. Access to court records from 1997 forward is free at www.nmcourts.gov. Case look-up displays the year of birth.

Rio Arriba Magistrate Court - Division 1 PO Box 538, 2332 Hwy 17, Chama, NM 87520; 575-756-2278; fax: 575-756-2477; 8AM-N, 1-4PM (MST). *Misdemeanor, Civil Actions under $10,000, Eviction, Small Claims.*

General Information: Will not fax documents. Court makes copy: $.50 per page. No certification fee . Payee: Rio Arriba Magistrate Ct. Personal checks accepted, credit cards are not. Prepayment required. Mail requests: SASE required.

Civil Name Search: Access: Mail, fax, in person, online. Both court and visitors may perform in person name searches. No search fee. On computer back to 1997. Mail Turnaround time 1 week. Case lookup from 1997 forward is free at www.nmcourts.gov. Case look-up displays the year of birth.

Criminal Name Search: Access: Mail, fax, in person, online. Only the court performs in person name searches; visitors may not. No search fee.On computer back to 1997. Mail Turnaround time 1 week. Online access to criminal records is free at www.nmcourts.gov. Case look-up displays the year of birth.

Rio Arriba Magistrate Court - Division 2 410 Paseo de Onate, Espanola, NM 87532; 505-753-2532; fax: 505-753-4802; 8AM-4PM (MST). *Misdemeanor, Civil Actions under $10,000, Eviction, Small Claims.*

General Information: Will fax documents. Court makes copy: $.50 per page. Self serve copy: same. Certification fee: $.50 per copy. Payee: RA Magistrate Court. Personal checks accepted, credit cards are not. Prepayment required.

Civil Name Search: Access: Mail, in person, online. Only the court performs in person name searches; visitors may not. No search fee. Case records available from 1990. Mail Turnaround time 3 days. Case lookup from 1997 forward is free at www.nmcourts.gov. Case look-up displays the year of birth.

Criminal Name Search: Access: Mail, in person, online. Only the court performs in person name searches; visitors may not. No search fee. Case records available from 1997. Mail Turnaround time within 1 week. Online access to criminal records is free at www.nmcourts.gov. Case look-up displays the year of birth.

County Clerk PO Box 158, 7 Main St, Tierra Amarilla, NM 87575; 575-588-7724; fax: 575-588-7418; 8AM-5PM (MST). *Probate.*

General Information: The County Clerk holds the case files for "informal" or "uncontested" probate cases seen by the Probate Judge. The District Court holds case files for "formal" or "contested" probate cases.

Roosevelt County

9th Judicial District Court 109 W 1st St, #207, Portales, NM 88130; 575-359-6920; fax: 575-359-2140; 8AM-4PM (MST). *Felony, Civil, Contested Probate.* www.nmcourts9thjdc.com

General Information: Online identifiers in results same as on public terminal. No adoption, guardianship, insanity records released. Will fax documents $2.00 1st page, $1.00 each add'l page. Court makes copy: $.35 per page. Self serve copy: same. Certification fee: $1.50; Exemplification fee-$4.50. Payee: 9th Judicial District Court. Only cashiers checks and money orders accepted. No credit cards accepted. Prepayment required. Mail requests: SASE required for mail return of any copies.

Civil Name Search: Access: Online, in person. Visitors must perform in person searches themselves. Civil records on microfiche from 1912, archived before 1912. Civil PAT goes back to 1997. Case lookup from

1997 forward is free at www.nmcourts.gov. Case look-up displays the year of birth.

Criminal Name Search: Access: Online, in person. Visitors must perform in person searches themselves. Criminal records on microfiche from 1912, archived before 1912. Criminal PAT goes back to 1997. Terminal results may or may not have complete name or a DOB. Online access to criminal records is free at www.nmcourts.gov. Case look-up displays the year of birth.

Magistrate Court 42427 US Hwy 70, Portales, NM 88130; 575-356-8569; fax: 575-359-6883; 8AM-4PM (MST). *Misdemeanor, Civil Actions under $10,000, Eviction, Small Claims, Felony Prelim.*

General Information: Will fax documents $1.00 per page. Court makes copy: $.50 per page. No certification fee . Payee: Magistrate Court. Personal checks accepted, credit cards are not. Prepayment required. Mail requests: SASE required.

Civil Name Search: Access: Phone, mail, fax, in person, online. Only the court performs in person name searches; visitors may not. Records computerized since 1995. Mail Turnaround time 5 days. Case lookup from 1997 forward is free at www.nmcourts.gov. Case look-up displays the year of birth.

Criminal Name Search: Access: Phone, mail, fax, in person, online. Only the court performs in person name searches; visitors may not. No search fee. Required to search: name, DOB; also helpful: SSN. Records computerized since 1995. Mail Turnaround time 5 days. Online access to criminal records is free at www.nmcourts.gov. Case look-up displays the year of birth.

County Clerk Lobby Box 4, County Courthouse, 109 W 1st St, Portales, NM 88130; 575-356-8562; fax: 575-356-3560; 8AM-5PM (MST). *Probate.*

General Information: The County Clerk holds the case files for "informal" or "uncontested" probate cases seen by the Probate Judge. The District Court holds case files for "formal" or "contested" probate cases.

San Juan County

11th Judicial District Court 103 S Oliver, Aztec, NM 87410; 505-334-6151; fax: 505-334-1940; 8AM-N, 1-5PM (MST). *Felony, Civil, Contested Probate.*

www.11thjdc.com/

General Information: Online identifiers in results same as on public terminal. No adoption, insanity, sealed, expunged records released. Will fax documents $5.00 plus $.70 per page. Court makes copy: $.35 per page. Self serve copy: same. Certification fee: $1.50 per document; if each pages needs to be certified, then $1.50 per page. Payee: Eleventh District Court. No personal or out-of-state checks accepted. No credit cards accepted. Prepayment required. Mail requests: SASE required for criminal.

Civil Name Search: Access: Online, in person. Visitors must perform in person searches themselves. Required to search: name, years to search; also helpful: address. Civil records on computer from 1986, on microfiche from 1925; card file from 1912. Civil PAT goes back to 1986. Case lookup from 1997 forward is free at www.nmcourts.gov. Case look-up displays the year of birth.

Criminal Name Search: Access: Online, in person, mail, fax. Visitors must perform in person searches themselves. Required to search: name, years to search, DOB; also helpful: address, SSN. Criminal records computerized from 1986, on microfiche from 1925; card file from 1912. Mail Turnaround time 3 days. Criminal PAT goes back to same as civil. Terminal results may or may not have complete name or a DOB. Online access to criminal records is free at www.nmcourts.gov. Case look-up displays the year of birth.

Aztec Magistrate Court 200 Gossett, Aztec, NM 87410; 505-334-9479; fax: 505-334-2178; 8AM-4PM (MST). *Misdemeanor, Civil Actions under $10,000, Eviction, Small Claims.*

General Information: All records open except sealed records. Will not fax documents. Court makes copy: $.50 per page. No certification fee . Payee: Aztec Magistrate Court. Personal checks accepted, credit cards are not. Prepayment required.

Civil Name Search: Access: Online, in person. Both court and visitors may perform in person name searches. No search fee. Civil cases indexed by both plaintiff & defendant. Case lookup from 1997 forward is free at www.nmcourts.gov. Case look-up displays the year of birth.

Criminal Name Search: Access: Online, in person. Both court and visitors may perform in person name searches. No search fee. Required to search: name, years to search; also helpful: DOB, SSN. . Online access to criminal records is free at www.nmcourts.gov. Case look-up displays the year of birth.

Farmington Magistrate Court 950 W Apache St, Farmington, NM 87401; 505-326-4338; criminal phone: 2017; civil phone: 2010; criminal fax: 505-325-2618; civil fax: 8AM-4PM; 8AM-4PM (MST). *Misdemeanor, Civil Actions under $10,000, Eviction, Small Claims.*

General Information: medical information and sealed records are restricted. Will fax documents $1.00 per page. Court makes copy: $.50 per page; $1.00 per page if computer generated. No certification fee . Payee: Magistrate Court. Personal checks accepted, credit cards are not. Prepayment required.

Civil Name Search: Access: Online, in person. Both court and visitors may perform in person name searches. No search fee. Required to search: name; also helpful-years to search, other names used, address. Civil records go back 14 years for open cases. Closed case records go back to 6-30-07. Access to court records are free at www.nmcourts.gov. Records are removed from display according to retention schedule. Civil cases that have a satisfaction of judgments or dismissal filed can only be viewed online for one year after closing document is Case look-up displays the year of birth.

Criminal Name Search: Access: Online, in person. Both court and visitors may perform in person name searches. No search fee. Required to search: name, years to search, DOB; also helpful: SSN. Criminal records go back to 6-30-07; DWI's 1986; domestic violence to 2004. Online access to criminal records is free at www.nmcourts.gov. Case look-up displays the year of birth.

County Clerk PO Box 550, 100 S Oliver, #200, Aztec, NM 87410; 505-334-9471; fax: 505-334-3635; 7AM-5:30PM (MST). *Probate.* www.sjcclerk.net./

General Information: The County Clerk holds the case files for "informal" or "uncontested" probate cases seen by the Probate Judge. The District Court holds case files for "formal" or "contested" probate cases.

San Miguel County

4th Judicial District Court PO Box 1540, Las Vegas, NM 87701; 505-425-7281 x40; fax: 505-454-8611; 8AM-4PM (MST). *Felony, Civil, Contested Probate.*

General Information: Also handles cases for Mora County. All records are co-mingled. All records requests must be submitted in writing. No adoption, insanity, sealed, or guardianship records released without court approval. Will fax documents for $2.50 per page. Court makes copy: $.35 per page. Certification fee: $1.50 per doc plus copy fee. Payee: Fourth Judicial District Court Clerk. Cashiers check, money order, or exact cash accepted. No personal checks or credit cards accepted. Prepayment required. Mail requests: SASE not required.

Civil Name Search: Access: Mail, in person, online, fax. Both court and visitors may perform in person name searches. No search fee. Required to search: name, years to search, DOB, County. Civil records available back to 1912. Note: Files and records that are not sealed can be viewed in the Clerk's office upon receipt of written request. Access civil court case information from 1997 to present is free at www.nmcourts.gov under the case-lookup option. Case look-up displays the year of birth.

Criminal Name Search: Access: Fax, mail, in person, online. Only the court performs in person name searches; visitors may not. No search fee. Required to search: name, years to search, DOB, County; also helpful: SSN. Criminal records available back to 1918. Note: Files and records that are not sealed can be viewed in the Clerk's office upon receipt of written request. Online access to criminal case information is free at www.nmcourts.gov, see civil above. Case look-up displays the year of birth.

Magistrate Court 1927 7th St, Las Vegas, NM 87701-4957; 505-425-5204; civil phone: x112; fax: 505-425-0422; 8AM-4PM M-Th, 8AM-Noon Fri (MST). *Misdemeanor, Civil Actions under $10,000, Eviction, Small Claims.*

General Information: Will fax documents free. Court makes copy: $.50 per page. No certification fee . Payee: Magistrate Court. No personal checks or credit cards accepted. Prepayment required. Mail requests: SASE required.

Civil Name Search: Access: Phone, mail, fax, online, in person. Only the court performs in person name searches; visitors may not. No search fee. Civil cases indexed by both plaintiff & defendant. Physical records kept for 2 years then purged. Case lookup from 1997 forward is free at www.nmcourts.gov. Case look-up displays the year of birth.

Criminal Name Search: Access: Phone, mail, fax, online, in person. Only the court performs in person name searches; visitors may not. No search fee. Required to search: name, years to search, DOB; also helpful: address, SSN. Physical records kept for 2 years then purged. Online access to criminal records is free at www.nmcourts.gov. Case look-up displays the year of birth.

County Clerk San Miguel County Clerk, 500 W National Ave, #113, Las Vegas, NM 87701; 505-425-9331; fax: 505-454-1799; 8AM-N, 1-5PM, M-TH, 8AM-4PM, F (MST). *Probate.*

General Information: The County Clerk holds the case files for "informal" or "uncontested" probate cases seen by the Probate Judge. The District Court holds case files for "formal" or "contested" probate cases.

Sandoval County

13th Judicial District Court PO Box 600, 1500 Idalia, Bldg A, Bernalillo, NM 87004; 505-867-2376; fax: 505-867-5161; 8AM-N, 1-5PM (MST). *Felony, Civil, Contested Probate, Domestic.*
www.13districtcourt.com

General Information: Uncontested probate is with clerk, with hours 7AM-6PM. No adoption, neglect and abuse records released. Fee to fax out file $2.50 per page; out of state $5.00 per page. Court makes copy: $.35 per page. Microfilm copies $.50 per page; computer generated copies are $1.00 per page. Certification fee: $1.50 per page plus copy fee. Payee: 13th Judicial District Court. Business checks accepted. No personal checks or credit cards accepted. Prepayment required.

Civil Name Search: Access: Fax, mail, online, in person. Both court and visitors may perform in person name searches. Search fee: $5.00 search fee. Civil records indexed on computer back to 11/96; prior on microfiche. Mail Turnaround time 3-8days. Case lookup from 1997 forward is free at www.nmcourts.gov. Also, view all civil jury verdicts in the 13th Judicial District Court free back to 1995 at www.13districtcourt.com/verdict/jury_verdict_intro.php. Case look-up displays the year of birth.

Criminal Name Search: Access: Fax, mail, online, in person. Both court and visitors may perform in person name searches. Search fee: $5.00 per name. Criminal records computerized from 11/96. Mail Turnaround time 3-5 days. Online access to criminal records is free at www.nmcourts.gov. Case look-up displays the year of birth.

Bernalillo Magistrate Court 1000 Montoya Rd, Bernalillo, NM 87004; 505-867-5202 x2-6; fax: 505-867-0970; 8AM-4PM (MST). *Misdemeanor, Civil Actions under $10,000, Eviction, Small Claims.*
www.13districtcourt.com/court-info-magistrate-sandoval.htm

General Information: Will not fax documents. Court makes copy: $.35 per page. Self serve copy: same. Certification fee: $1.50 per doc. Payee: Magistrate Court. Personal checks, Visa/MC accepted. Prepayment required.

Civil Name Search: Access: Mail, fax, in person, online. Only the court performs in person name searches; visitors may not. No search fee. Civil records go back to 12/1996. Paper case file destroyed after one year. Mail Turnaround time 1-2 weeks. Case lookup from 1997 forward is free at www.nmcourts.gov. Case look-up displays the year of birth.

Criminal Name Search: Access: Online, mail, in person. Only the court performs in person name searches; visitors may not. No search fee. Criminal records go back to 12/1996. Paper case file destroyed after one year. Mail Turnaround time 1-2 weeks. Online access to criminal records is free at www.nmcourts.gov. Case look-up displays the year of birth.

Cuba Magistrate Court PO Box 1497, Cuba, NM 87013; 575-289-3519; fax: 575-289-3013; 8AM-4PM (MST). *Misdemeanor, Civil Actions under $10,000, Eviction, Small Claims.*

General Information: Online identifiers in results same as on public terminal. Will fax documents to local or toll-free number. Court makes copy: $.50 per page. Self serve copy: same. Payee: Cuba Magistrate Court. No personal checks or credit cards accepted. Prepayment required.

Civil Name Search: Access: Online, in person. Visitors must perform in person searches themselves. Civil records available from 1997. Civil PAT goes back to 14 years. Case lookup from 1997 forward is free at www.nmcourts.gov. Case look-up displays the year of birth.

Criminal Name Search: Access: Online, in person. Visitors must perform in person searches themselves. Criminal PAT goes back to 3 years. Terminal results may or may not have complete name or a DOB. Online access to criminal records is free at www.nmcourts.gov. Case look-up displays the year of birth.

Santa Fe County

First Judicial District Court Box 2268, Santa Fe, NM 87504-2268; 505-455-8250; fax: 505-455-8280; 8AM-4PM (MST). *Felony, Civil, Family, Contested Probate.* http://firstdistrictcourt.com

General Information: Because this court also handles the counties of Los Alamos and Rio Arriba, you must indicate which county you are searching. Public Records Request Email:gfedrequests.gov Online identifiers in results same as on public terminal. No adoption, juvenile, mental or abuse records released. Will not fax documents. Court makes copy: $.35 per page. Certification fee: $1.50 per seal. Payee: First Judicial District Court. Business checks accepted from law firms. No credit cards accepted. Prepayment required. Mail requests: SASE required.

Civil Name Search: Access: Phone, mail, online, in person. Both court and visitors may perform in person name searches. No search fee. Civil records on computer from 1984, older records on docket books. Note: Requests to court must be in writing. Mail Turnaround time 2 days. Civil PAT goes back to 1995. Access to index of court records from 1984 forward is free at www.nmcourts.gov Case look-up displays the year of birth.

Criminal Name Search: Access: Phone, mail, fax, email, online, in person. Both court and visitors may perform in person name searches. No search fee. Required to search: name, years to search, county; also helpful: DOB, SSN. Criminal records computerized from 1984, older records on docket books. Mail Turnaround time 2 days. Criminal PAT goes back to same as civil. Terminal results may or may not have complete name or a DOB. Online access to index of criminal records is free at www.nmcourts.gov. Case look-up displays the year of birth.

Santa Fe Magistrate Court 2056 Galisteo St, Santa Fe, NM 87505; 505-984-9914; fax: 505-986-5866; 7:30AM-4PM M, T, TH, F; 7:30AM-N W (MST). *Misdemeanor, Civil Actions under $10,000, Eviction, Small Claims.*
www.nmcourts.gov

General Information: Also, the clerk for the Pojaoque Magistrate Court may be contacted here. Year of birth may still be available. Will fax documents for no fee. Court makes copy: $.50 per page. No certification fee . Payee: Santa Fe Magistrate Court. Personal checks accepted. Major credit cards accepted.

Civil Name Search: Access: Fax, mail, in person, online. Both court and visitors may perform in person name searches. No search fee. Civil records on computer back to 1997. Mail Turnaround time 2 weeks. Case lookup from 1997 forward is free at www.nmcourts.gov Case look-up displays the year of birth.

Criminal Name Search: Access: Fax, mail, in person, online. Both court and visitors may perform in person name searches. No search fee. Required to search: name, years to search, DOB; also helpful: SSN. Criminal records computerized from 1997. Mail Turnaround time 2 weeks. Online access to criminal records is free at www.nmcourts.gov. Case look-up displays the year of birth.

Pojoaque Magistrate Court *Misdemeanor, Civil Actions under $10,000, Eviction, Small Claims.*
General Information: The Court In Pojoaque is often closed; the clerk can be contacted at the Santa Fe Magistrate Court.

County Clerk PO Box 195, 102 Grant Ave, Santa Fe, NM 87504-0276; 505-992-1636; fax: 505-995-2767; 8AM-5PM (MST). *Probate.*
www.santafecounty.org/

General Information: The County Clerk holds the case files for "informal" or "uncontested" probate cases seen by the Probate Judge. The District Court holds case files for "formal" or "contested" probate cases.

Sierra County

7th Judicial District Court PO Box 3009, 311 N Date, Truth or Consequences, NM 87901; 575-894-7167; fax: 575-894-7168; 8AM-4PM (MST). *Felony, Civil, Contested Probate.*

General Information: Online identifiers in results same as on public terminal. No adoption, insanity, juvenile, guardianship records released. Court makes copy: $.35 per page. Certification fee: $1.50 plus copy fee. Payee: Sierra County District Court. Only cashiers checks and money orders accepted. No credit cards accepted. Prepayment required. Mail requests: SASE required.

Civil Name Search: Access: Mail, online, in person. Both court and visitors may perform in person name searches. No search fee. Required to search: name, years to search, address. Civil records on microfiche from 1920, archived before 1920. Mail Turnaround time 2 days. Civil PAT goes back to 1997. Case lookup from 1997 forward is free at www.nmcourts.gov. Case look-up displays the year of birth.

Criminal Name Search: Access: Mail, online, in person. Both court and visitors may perform in person name searches. No search fee. Required to search: name, years to search, address, SSN. Criminal records on microfiche from 1920, archived before 1920. Mail Turnaround time 2 days. Criminal PAT goes back to same as civil. Terminal results may or may not have complete name or a DOB. Online access to criminal records is free at www.nmcourts.gov. Case look-up displays the year of birth.

Magistrate Court 155 W Barton, Truth or Consequences, NM 87901; 575-894-3051; fax: 575-894-0476; 8AM-4PM M,T,TH,F - 8AM-12 W (MST). *Misdemeanor, Civil Actions under $10,000, Eviction, Small Claims.*

General Information: Will fax documents $.50 per page. Court makes copy: $.50 per page. No certification fee . Payee: Magistrate Court. Personal checks accepted, credit cards are not. Prepayment required. Mail requests: SASE required for mail return of any copies.

Civil Name Search: Access: Online, in person. Both court and visitors may perform in person name searches. No search fee.. Physical paper records kept for 1 year then purged, on June 30th when over 1 year. Case lookup from 1997 forward is free at www.nmcourts.gov. Case look-up displays the year of birth.

Criminal Name Search: Access: Mail, online, in person. Both court and visitors may perform in person name searches. No search fee. Physical records kept for 2 years then purged. Note: Mail requests accepted if copy fee included. Mail Turnaround time 1-3 days . Online access to criminal records is free at www.nmcourts.gov. Case look-up displays the year of birth.

County Clerk 100 N Date St, Ste 6, Probate Records, Truth or Consequences, NM 87901; 575-894-2840; fax: 575-894-2516; 8AM-5PM (MST). *Probate.*

General Information: The County Clerk holds the case files for "informal" or "uncontested" probate cases seen by the Probate Judge. The District Court holds case files for "formal" or "contested" probate cases.

Socorro County

7th Judicial District Court PO Drawer 1129, Socorro, NM 87801; 575-835-0050 x10; fax: 575-838-5217; 8AM-4PM (MST). *Felony, Civil, Contested Probate.*

General Information: This court is responsible for Socorro County and Catron County. Online identifiers in results same as on public terminal. No sequestered records released. Will fax documents to local or toll free line. Court makes copy: $.35 per page. Certification fee: $1.50; exemplification is $4.50. Payee: Seventh Judicial District Court. Only business checks accepted. No credit cards accepted. Prepayment required. Mail requests: SASE required.

Civil Name Search: Access: Phone, fax, mail, online, in person. Both court and visitors may perform in person name searches. No search fee. Civil records on microfiche and hard copies from 1917; on computer back to 1997. Mail Turnaround time 1 day. Civil PAT goes back to 1997. Results include case type. Case lookup from 1997 forward is free at www.nmcourts.gov. Case look-up displays the year of birth.

Criminal Name Search: Access: Phone, fax, mail, online, in person. Both court and visitors may perform in person name searches. No search fee. Required to search: name, years to search, DOB; also helpful-SSN, signed release. Criminal records on microfiche and hard copies from 1917; on computer back to 1997. Mail Turnaround time 1 day. Criminal PAT goes back to 1997. Terminal results may or may not have complete name or a DOB, may show last 4 digits of SSN. Online access to criminal records is free at www.nmcourts.gov. Case look-up displays the year of birth.

Magistrate Court 102 Winkler St, Socorro, NM 87801; 575-835-2500; fax: 575-838-0428; 8AM-4PM (MST). *Misdemeanor, Civil Actions under $10,000, Eviction, Small Claims.*

General Information: Will fax back to gov't agencies only. Court makes copy: $.50 per page. Certification fee: $1.00 plus copy fee. Payee: Magistrate Court. Personal checks accepted, credit cards are not. Prepayment required. Mail requests: SASE required.

Civil Name Search: Access: Mail, in person, online. Only the court performs in person name searches; visitors may not. No search fee. Required to search: name, years to search, address, other names used. Civil records on computer back to 1997; judgments back 14 years or until satisfied. Mail Turnaround time 1-5 days. Case lookup from 1997 forward is free at www.nmcourts.gov. Case look-up displays the year of birth.

Criminal Name Search: Access: Mail, in person, online. Only the court performs in person name searches; visitors may not. No search fee. Required to search: name, years to search, other names used; also helpful-DOB, SSN. Criminal records computerized from 1997; files destroyed 2 years after closure. Mail Turnaround time 1-5 days. Online access to criminal records is free at www.nmcourts.gov. Case look-up displays the year of birth.

County Clerk PO Box I, 200 Church St, Socorro, NM 87801; 575-835-3263; fax: 575-835-1043; 8AM-5PM (MST). *Probate.*
http://sites.google.com/site/socorrocountyintranet/elected-offices/office-of-the-clerk
General Information: The County Clerk holds the case files for "informal" or "uncontested" probate cases seen by the Probate Judge. The District Court holds case files for "formal" or "contested" probate cases.

Taos County

8th Judicial District Court 105 Albright St, #N, Taos, NM 87571; 575-758-3173 x1; fax: 575-751-1281; 8AM-4PM (MST). *Felony, Civil, Contested Probate.*

General Information: No adoption, juvenile, abuse or sequestered case records released. Will fax documents $2.00 per page. Court makes copy: $.35 per page. Self serve copy: same. Certification fee: $1.50 per doc. Payee: District Court. Only cashiers checks, cash and money orders accepted. Prepayment required.

Civil Name Search: Access: In person, online. Visitors must perform in person searches themselves. Civil records on computer since 1993, books since 1912, microfiche from 1912-1980. Access to court records from 1993 forward is free at www.nmcourts.gov. Case look-up displays the year of birth.

Criminal Name Search: Access: In person, online. Visitors must perform in person searches themselves. Required to search: name, years to search, DOB; also helpful: signed release, SSN. Criminal records on

computer since 1993, books since 1912, microfiche from 1912-1950. Online access to criminal records is free at www.nmcourts.gov. Case look-up displays the year of birth.

Questa Magistrate Court PO Box 586, State Rd 522 and Hwy 230, Questa, NM 87556; 575-586-0761; fax: 575-586-0428; 8AM-4PM M,W; 8AM-N, 1PM-4PM T,TH; F closed (MST). *Misdemeanor, Civil Actions under $10,000, Eviction, Small Claims.*

General Information: Online identifiers in results same as on public terminal. Fee to fax out file $1.00 per page. Court makes copy: $.50 per page. Certification fee: $3.00 per copy. Payee: Taos Circuit Court. Personal checks accepted, credit cards are not. Prepayment required. Mail requests: SASE required.

Civil Name Search: Access: Mail, in person, online. Both court and visitors may perform in person name searches. No search fee. Required to search: name, signed release, address. Civil records go back to mid 1990's. Mail Turnaround time 23 days. Civil PAT goes back to 1999. Case lookup from 1997 forward is free at www.nmcourts.gov. Case look-up displays the year of birth.

Criminal Name Search: Access: Mail, in person, online. Both court and visitors may perform in person name searches. No search fee. Required to search: name, years to search; also helpful: DOB, SSN. Criminal records go back to 1998. Note: Results include case number. Mail Turnaround time 23 days. Criminal PAT goes back to 1999. Terminal results may or may not have complete name or a DOB. Can show race, color eyes, hair, height, weight, tattoos, etc. Online access to criminal records is free at www.nmcourts.gov. Case look-up displays the year of birth.

Taos Magistrate Court 105 Albright St, Ste M, Taos, NM 87571; 575-758-4030; fax: 575-751-0983; 8AM-4PM M-TH (MST). *Misdemeanor, Civil Actions under $10,000, Eviction, Small Claims.*

General Information: Will not fax documents. Court makes copy: $.50 per page. Certification fee: $1.00 for a certification plus all copy fees. Payee: Taos Magistrate Court. No personal checks or credit cards accepted. Prepayment required.

Civil Name Search: Access: Online, in person. Both court and visitors may perform in person name searches. No search fee. Civil cases indexed by both plaintiff & defendant. Civil records go back to 1997. Case lookup from 1997 forward is free at www.nmcourts.gov. Case look-up displays the year of birth.

Criminal Name Search: Access: Online, in person. Both court and visitors may perform in person name searches. No search fee. Required to search: name, years to search, DOB; also helpful: SSN. Criminal records go back to 1997. Online access to criminal records is free at www.nmcourts.gov. Case look-up displays the year of birth.

County Clerk 105 Albright, #D, Taos, NM 87571; 575-737-6391; fax: 575-737-6390; 8AM (Noon-1PM closed) 2PM-4PM (MST). *Probate.*
www.taoscounty.org/index.aspx?nid=111
General Information: The County Clerk holds the case files for "informal" or "uncontested" probate cases seen by the Probate Judge. The District Court holds case files for "formal" or "contested" probate cases.

Torrance County

7th Judicial District Court Neil Mertz Judicial Complex, PO Box 78, Estancia, NM 87016; 505-384-2974; fax: 505-384-2229; 8AM-4PM (MST). *Felony, Civil, Contested Probate.*

General Information: Online identifiers in results same as on public terminal. No juvenile, neglect, adoption, mental health records released. Will fax documents for $.35 per page. Court makes copy: $.35 per page. Self serve copy: same. Certification fee: $1.50 per cert. Payee: Seventh Judicial District Court. Only cashiers checks, money orders, and exact change accepted. No credit cards accepted. Prepayment required. Mail requests: SASE required.

Civil Name Search: Access: Mail, in person, online. Both court and visitors may perform in person name searches. No search fee. Civil records on hard copy until filmed, microfiche from 1912; on computer back to 1997. Mail Turnaround time 1 week. Civil PAT goes back to 1997. Case lookup from 1997 forward is free at www.nmcourts.gov. Case look-up displays the year of birth.

Criminal Name Search: Access: Mail, online, in person. Both court and visitors may perform in person name searches. No search fee. Required to search: name, years to search; also helpful: SSN, DOB. Criminal records on hard copy until filmed, microfiche from 1912; on computer back to 1997. Mail Turnaround time 1 week. Criminal PAT goes back to same as civil. Terminal results may or may not have complete name or a DOB. Online access to criminal records is free at www.nmcourts.gov. Case look-up displays the year of birth.

Estancia Magistrate Court Neil Mertz Judicial Complex, 903 N 5th St, PO Box 274, Estancia, NM 87016; 505-384-2926; fax: 505-384-3157; 8AM-4PM W-F (MST). *Misdemeanor, Civil Actions under $10,000, Eviction, Small Claims.* www.nmcourts.gov/

General Information: All record requests must be in writing. Will fax documents $1.00 per page. Court makes copy: $.50 per page. Certification fee: $.50. Payee: Magistrate court. No personal checks or credit cards accepted. Prepayment required. Mail requests: SASE required.

Civil Name Search: Access: Mail, fax, in person, online. Both court and visitors may perform in person name searches. No search fee. Closed case files maintained 1 year then archived, record index on computer since 1997. Mail Turnaround time 3-5 days. Case lookup from 1997 forward is free at www.nmcourts.gov. Case look-up displays the year of birth.

Criminal Name Search: Access: Mail, fax, in person, online. Both court and visitors may perform in person name searches. No search fee. Required to search: name, years to search; also helpful: DOB, SSN. Closed case files maintained 1 years then destroyed 1 year from date of closure; record index on computer since 1997 (DWI and VR {domestic cases retained}). Mail Turnaround time up to 3 days. Online access to criminal records is free at www.nmcourts.gov. Case look-up displays the year of birth.

Moriarty Magistrate Court PO Box 2027, 1100 W Rte 66, Moriarty, NM 87035; 505-832-4476; fax: 505-832-1563; 8AM-4PM (MST). *Misdemeanor, Civil Actions under $10,000, Eviction, Small Claims.*

General Information: Will fax documents $1.00 per page. Court makes copy: $.50 per page. No certification fee . Payee: Magistrate Court. No personal checks or credit cards accepted. Prepayment required. Mail requests: SASE required.

Civil Name Search: Access: Mail, fax, mail, in person, online. Visitors must perform in person searches themselves. No search fee. Required to search: name, DOB, SSN, years to search. Closed case files maintained 1 year, record index on computer since 1997. Judgments held for 14 years. Mail Turnaround time up to 3 days. Case lookup from 1997 forward is free at www.nmcourts.gov. Case look-up displays the year of birth.

Criminal Name Search: Access: Online, mail, in person. Both court and visitors may perform in person name searches. No search fee. Required to search: name, years to search; also helpful: DOB, SSN. Closed case files maintained 1 year, record index on computer since 1997. Mail Turnaround time up to 3 days. Online access to criminal records is free at www.nmcourts.gov. Case look-up displays the year of birth.

County Clerk PO Box 767, 205 9th St and Allen, Estancia, NM 87016; 505-246-4735; fax: 505-384-4080; 7:30AM-5:30 PM M-TH (MST). *Probate.*

General Information: The County Clerk holds the case files for "informal" or "uncontested" probate cases seen by the Probate Judge. The District Court holds case files for "formal" or "contested" probate cases.

Union County

8th Judicial District Court Box 310, Clayton, NM 88415; 575-374-9577; fax: 575-374-2089; 8AM-N, 1-5PM (MST). *Felony, Civil, Contested Probate.*

General Information: Online identifiers in results same as on public terminal. No adoption, juvenile records released. Will fax documents for $2.00 first page and $1.00 ea addl. Court makes copy: $.35 per page. Self serve copy: same. Certification fee: $1.50 per cert plus copy fee. Payee: Clerk of District Court. Only cashiers checks and money orders accepted. No credit cards accepted. Prepayment required. Mail requests: SASE required.

Civil Name Search: Access: Mail, in person, online. Both court and visitors may perform in person name searches. No search fee. Civil records on cards from 1981. Computerized records start from 1997. Mail Turnaround time 1-2 days. Civil PAT goes back to 1997. Case lookup from 1997 forward is free at www.nmcourts.gov. Case look-up displays the year of birth.

Criminal Name Search: Access: Mail, online, in person. Both court and visitors may perform in person name searches. No search fee. Criminal records on docket sheets from 1981. Computerized records start from 1997. Mail Turnaround time 1-2 days. Criminal PAT goes back to same as civil. Terminal results may or may not have complete name or a DOB. Online access to criminal records is free at www.nmcourts.gov. Case look-up displays the year of birth.

Magistrate Court 836 Main St, Clayton, NM 88415; 575-374-9472; fax: 575-374-9368; 8AM-N, 12:30-4:30PM (MST). *Misdemeanor, Civil Actions under $10,000, Eviction, Small Claims.*

General Information: The court also handles preliminary felony hearings and felony probable cause. Will fax documents $1.00 per page. Court makes copy: $.50 per page. Payee: Magistrate Court. No personal checks or credit cards accepted. Prepayment required. Mail requests: SASE required.

Civil Name Search: Access: Mail, in person, online. Only the court performs in person name searches; visitors may not. No search fee. Records available since 6/30/92, computerized since 3/13/97. Mail Turnaround time 3 days. Access to court records from 3/13/1997 forward is free at www.nmcourts.gov Case look-up displays the year of birth.

Criminal Name Search: Access: Mail, in person, online. Only the court performs in person name searches; visitors may not. No search fee.

Required to search: name, years to search; also helpful: address, DOB, SSN. Records computerized since 1/1/03. Mail Turnaround time 3 days. Online access to criminal records is free at www.nmcourts.gov. Case look-up displays the year of birth.

County Clerk PO Box 430, 200 Court St, Clayton, NM 88415; 575-374-9491; fax: 575-374-9591; 9AM-N, 1-5PM (MST). *Probate.*

General Information: The County Clerk holds the case files for "informal" or "uncontested" probate cases seen by the Probate Judge. The District Court holds case files for "formal" or "contested" probate cases.

Valencia County

13th Judicial District Court Box 1089, Los Lunas, NM 87031; 505-865-4291; fax: 505-865-8801; 9AM-12; 1PM-5PM (MST). *Felony, Civil, Contested Probate.*

www.13districtcourt.com

General Information: Online identifiers in results same as on public terminal. No adoption, sequestered or juvenile records released. Will fax documents $2.50 in-state; $5.00 out-of-state. Court makes copy: $.35 per page; $.50 from microfilm. Self serve copy: same. Certification fee: $1.50 per cert. Payee: 13th Judicial District Court. Only cashiers checks, cash and money orders accepted. No credit cards accepted. Prepayment required. Mail requests: SASE required.

Civil Name Search: Access: Fax, mail, online, in person. Both court and visitors may perform in person name searches. Search fee: $2.50 per name; 5.00 for 2, $10.00 for 3-10 names. Civil records on microfiche from 1915. Mail Turnaround time 10 days. Civil PAT goes back to 1996. Access to court records from 1996 forward is free at www.nmcourts.gov. Also, view all civil jury verdicts in the 13th Judicial District Court free back to 1995 at www.13districtcourt.com/verdict/jury_verdict_intro.php.

Criminal Name Search: Access: Mail, online, in person. Both court and visitors may perform in person name searches. Search fee: $2.50 per name; 5.00 for 2, $10.00 for 3-10 names. Criminal records on microfiche from 1915. Mail Turnaround time 2-10 days. Criminal PAT goes back to 1996. Terminal results may or may not have complete name or a DOB. Online access to criminal records is free at www.nmcourts.gov. Case look-up displays the year of birth.

Belen Magistrate Court 901 W Castillo, Belen, NM 87002; 505-864-7509; fax: 505-864-9532; 8AM-4PM (MST). *Misdemeanor, Civil Actions under $10,000, Eviction, Small Claims.*

General Information: Will fax documents to local or toll-free number. Court makes copy: $.50 per page. No certification fee . No personal checks or credit cards accepted. Prepayment required. Mail requests: SASE required.

Civil Name Search: Access: Online, mail, in person. Only the court performs in person name searches; visitors may not. No search fee. Physical records held 1 year, domestic violence 2 years. Mail Turnaround time 1 day. Case lookup from 1997 forward is free at www.nmcourts.gov. Case look-up displays the year of birth.

Criminal Name Search: Access: Online, mail, in person. Only the court performs in person name searches; visitors may not. No search fee. Required to search: name, years to search, DOB, date of offense; also helpful: address, SSN. Physical records held 2 years, DUI held since 1997. Mail Turnaround time 2 days. Online access to criminal records is free at www.nmcourts.gov. Case look-up displays the year of birth.

Los Lunas Magistrate Court 1206 Main St, Los Lunas, NM 87031; 505-865-4637; fax: 505-865-0639; 8AM-4PM M-TH; 8AM-12 F (MST). *Misdemeanor, Civil Actions under $10,000, Eviction, Small Claims.*

General Information: Will not fax documents. Court makes copy: $.50 per page. Certification fee: $1.00 per copy. Payee: Los Lunas Magistrate Court. Personal checks accepted, credit cards are not. Prepayment required.

Civil Name Search: Access: Online, mail, in person. Only the court performs in person name searches; visitors may not. No search fee. Civil cases indexed by both plaintiff & defendant. Case files kept back to 1995. Mail Turnaround time 3 days. Case lookup from 1997 forward is free at www.nmcourts.gov. Case look-up displays the year of birth.

Criminal Name Search: Access: Online, mail, in person. Only the court performs in person name searches; visitors may not. No search fee. Required to search: name, years to search, DOB; also helpful: SSN. Mail Turnaround time 3 days. Online access to criminal records is free at www.nmcourts.gov. Case look-up displays the year of birth.

County Clerk PO Box 969, 444 Luna Ave, Los Lunas, NM 87031; 505-866-2073; fax: 505-866-2023; 8AM-4:30PM (MST). *Probate.*

www.co.valencia.nm.us/departments/clerk/County_Clerk.html

General Information: The County Clerk holds the case files for "informal" or "uncontested" probate cases seen by the Probate Judge. The District Court holds case files for "formal" or "contested" probate cases.

New York

Time Zone:	**EST**
Capital:	**Albany, Albany County**
# of Counties:	**62**
State Web:	**www.iloveny.gov**
Court Web:	**www.nycourts.gov**

Administration

New York State Unified Court System, Office of Court Administration (OCA), 25 Beaver St, 8th Floor, New York, NY 10004.

The Court of Appeals and the Appellate Divisions of the Supreme Court

The Court of Appeals is the state's highest court. The next step down is the four Appellate Divisions of the Supreme Court, one in each of the State's four Judicial Departments. These Courts resolve appeals from judgments or orders of the courts of original jurisdiction in civil and criminal cases, and review civil appeals taken from the Appellate Terms and the County Courts acting as appellate courts.

Appellate Terms of the Supreme Court in the First and Second Departments hear appeals from civil and criminal cases originating in the Civil and Criminal Courts of the City of New York. In the Second Department, the Appellate Terms also have jurisdiction over appeals from civil and criminal cases originating in District, City, Town and Village Courts.

The County Courts in the Third and Fourth Departments (although primarily trial courts), hear appeals from cases originating in the City, Town and Village Courts.

Find decisions at www.nycourts.gov/decisions/index.shtml.

The New York Courts

Court	Type	How Organized	Jurisdiction Highpoints
Supreme*	General	62 Courts	Felony, Civil, Juvenile, Domestic Relations, Estate
Courts of New York City*	Limited	Civil, Criminal, Family, Surrogate by Borough	Misdemeanor, Civil up to $25,000, Family, Probate, Estate
County*	Limited	57, can be Combined with Supreme	Felony, Misdemeanor, Civil up to $25,000, Small Claims, Traffic, Eviction, Contract
City*	Limited	61 Courts	Misdemeanor, Civil Actions under $15,000, Eviction, Small Claims, Traffic.
District*	Limited	In Nassau, Suffolk	Misdemeanor, Civil to $15,000, Small Claims, Eviction, Tort, Contract
Surrogate*	Special	62	Probate, Uncontested Estate
Court of Claims	Special	1	Suits brought Against NYS Public Authorities
Family	Special	62	Family
Town and Village*	Municipal	1400 Approx.	Ordinance, Traffic, Small Claims

* = profiled in this book

Details on the Trial Court Structure

Supreme and County Courts are the highest trial courts in the state, equivalent to what may be called circuit or district in other states. New York's Supreme and County Courts may be administered together or separately. When separate, there is a clerk for each. Supreme and/or County Courts are not appeals courts. Supreme Courts handle civil cases – usually civil cases over $25,000 – but there are many exceptions. The County Courts handle felony cases and, in many counties, these County Courts also handle misdemeanors. The New York City Courts are structured differently.

For non-NYC courts (called Upstate Courts), **City Courts** handle misdemeanors and civil case claims up to $15,000, small claims, and eviction cases. Not all counties have City Courts, thus cases there fall to the Supreme and County Courts for civil and criminal respectively, or, in many counties, to the small **Town and Village Courts**, which can number in the dozens within a county.

Probate is handled by **Surrogate Courts**. Surrogate Courts may also hear Domestic Relations cases in some counties.

In **New York City**, the Supreme Court is the trial court with unlimited jurisdiction. The Civil Court of the City of New York has jurisdiction on civil matters up to $25,000. The Criminal Court of the City of New York has jurisdiction over misdemeanors and minor violations. The Family Court hears matters involving children and families. Probate is handled by the Surrogate's Court.

In the five boroughs of New York City the courts records are administered directly by the state OCA – Office of Court Administration.

Record Searching Facts You Need to Know

More About Upstate Courts and Record Keeping

Record keeping at Upstate Courts is different than in New York City. The staff at the Upstate Superior Courts are NY state employees. **But records for Supreme and County Courts are maintained by the County Clerks**, who are county employees. This is important because the OCA directs it employees to forward all search requests to the OCA, while county employees are often instructed to service record request in order to maintain revenue for budgets. To make this more confusing is the fact that in some counties (usually less-populated counties), the clerk for Supreme and County Courts may also be the County Clerk - these duo-role clerks are employed partly by the county, and partly by the state. This may create a question of whose directives and rules do they follow in regard to court record search procedures.

As a result, you will find separate entries for "County Clerks" for most NY counties in the court profiles since. While not a "court," this is where the records are kept.

The methods for searching at the County Clerk office are far different from searching at the Courts themselves. In counties where the County Clerk and the Chief Court Clerk are one in the same, you will find only the standard Supreme & County Court listing. Note that in some NY counties the address for the County Clerk is the same as for the Supreme and County Courts. Exceptions are noted in the court profiles, and a separate profile is provided that lists the County Clerk and the county rules for a countywide record search. Note also that, due to limitations in the receiving of records from the Chief Court Clerks, the County Clerk may only be able to do a civil record search, or, rarely, only a criminal record search.

While all **City Courts** are administered by state employees, there are a few City Courts that will still do a city-only record check despite the edict to state employees that they must direct all record searches to the OCA for the statewide record check. Records from City Courts do not go to the County Clerk -- records from City Courts go directly to the OCA.

In at least 20 New York counties, misdemeanor records are only available at city, town, or village courts. This is also true of small claims and eviction records. **Town and Village Courts** are listed at the end of each county section.

Fees and Record Searching Tips

As mentioned, in all but a few NY counties, the records of cases held in the Supreme and County Court are maintained at the County Clerk's office. Civil cases are often indexed by the *clerk* by defendant, whereas the *courts* themselves maintain only a plaintiff index. And, while most criminal courts in the state are indexed by defendant and plaintiff, many New York City courts are indexed by plaintiff only.

Most courts will not perform name searches and instruct requesters to contact the OCA.

When a County Clerk will search records, most often the criminal fee is $5.00 per name for every 2 years searched and $16.00 for civil. Almost all County Courts (felony records) will provide a Certificate of Disposition. This certified document indicates the disposition of a case. The fee for a Certificate of Disposition is either $5.00 or $6.00, depending upon the county. To obtain a Certificate of Disposition, you must prepay, include the name and an exact as possible date (either the disposition date or the arrest date - this requirement varies from county to county), or provide the case number. Some counties also ask for a signed release (this and other details will be noted in the individual court profiles).

Certification fees can vary depending on how the clerk office interprets the rules. Fortunately, most court clerk offices will simply apply a flat $5.00 per document certification fee, however, at some offices, if a document is more than 4 pages, then an add'l $1.25 per page is added for certification. If the certified document is to be mailed, the certification fee may be $6.00 or $5.00, depending if the court recognized the requester has provided a SASE.

Criminal Record Access From the OCA

In addition to the OCA's online access program (see below), the OCA will accept mail and in-person requests for a statewide electronic search for criminal history information. The search uses a database of criminal case records from all boroughs and all counties, including Supreme Courts, County Courts, and City Courts. (**Editor's Note**: Based on comments by record searchers, although the web page states that the record search includes all Town and Village cases, it is not clear that all Town, City, and Village Courts actually submit ALL misdemeanors to this database.)

The OCA search fee, payable by check, is $65.00 per name. The Criminal History Record Search Unit can be reached at 212-428-2943 or www.nycourts.gov/apps/chrs. Direct mail and in person requests to: Office of Court Administration (OCA), Criminal History Search, 25 Beaver St, 8th Floor, New York, NY 10004.

Online Access is Also Statewide,

The OCA offers online access to criminal records. Requesters must apply for an account. There is a weekly minimum of searches required. This is not an interactive system - the search results are sent via email. Call the OCA at 212-428-2916 or visit www.nycourts.gov/apps/chrs/ for details on how to set up an account.

Visit http://iapps.courts.state.ny.us/webcivil/ecourtsMain for five excellent resources. WebCrims provides pending criminal case data in 13 local and Supreme Courts. WebFamily provides information on active Family Court cases in all 62 counties of New York State and Integrated Domestic Violence (IDV) Court cases in those counties with IDV Courts. WebCivil Supreme contains information on both Active and Disposed Civil Supreme Court cases in all 62 counties of New York State. The WebCivil Local link gives access civil case data from 50 plus City Courts and several County Courts. WebHousing offers information on pending Landlord Tenant cases in the Housing Part of New York City Civil Court (Bronx, Kings, New York, Queens and Richmond Counties) as well as the Buffalo City Court in Erie County. There is also a case tracking service called eTrack.

Search http://decisions.courts.state.ny.us/search/query3.asp for Supreme Court Civil and Criminal decisions, dating back to 2001. **Civil Cases** are from the following counties: Allegany, Bronx, Broome, Cattaraugus, Chautauqua, Cortland, Delaware, Erie, Kings, Livingston, Madison, Monroe, Nassau, New York, Niagara, Oneida, Onondaga, Ontario, Orange, Putnam, Queens, Richmond, Schuyler, Seneca, Steuben, Suffolk, Westchester and Wyoming Counties. **Criminal Cases** are from the following counties: Albany, Bronx, Broome, Cattaraugus, Cayuga, Chautauqua, Chemung, Delaware, Erie, Kings, Monroe, Nassau, New York, Oneida, Onondaga, Ontario, Orange, Oswego, Queens, Richmond, Seneca, Suffolk, and Wayne Counties.

Albany County

County Clerk 32 N Russell Rd, Albany, NY 12206; 518-487-5101; criminal phone: 518-487-5118; civil phone: 518-487-5118; fax: 518-487-5099; 9AM-4:45PM (recordings until 3PM) (EST). *Felony, Civil.* www.albanycounty.com/clerk/
General Information: Countywide search requests made to the County Clerk are processed in the manner described below. No sealed, expunged, adoption, sex offense, juvenile, mental health or divorce records released. Will not fax documents. Court makes copy: $.65 per page; minimum $1.30. Certification fee: $1.25 per page minimum of $5.00 for cert copy. Payee: County Clerk. Personal checks accepted, credit cards are not. Prepayment required. Mail requests: SASE appreciated.
Civil Name Search: Access: Mail, in person, online. Both court and visitors may perform in person name searches. Search fee: $5.00 per name. Fee is for each two years requested. Civil records on computer from 1981, prior in books. Mail turnaround Time 5-7 days, large files longer. Civil PAT goes back to 1980. Historical records are not online, but access to current/pending Supreme Court civil cases is at http://iapps.courts.state.ny.us/webcivil/FCASMain.
Criminal Name Search: Access: Mail, in person. Both court and visitors may perform in person name searches. Search fee: $5.00 per name. Fee is per two years requested. Required to search: name, years to search, DOB. Criminal records computerized from 1981, prior in books. Mail turnaround

Time 5-7 days; large files longer. Criminal PAT goes back to same as civil. This court does not participate in eCourt criminal records system at this time.
Albany City Court - Civil Part City Hall, Rm 209, Albany, NY 12207; 518-4453-4640; fax: 518-434-5034; 8:30AM-5PM (EST). *Civil Actions under $15,000, Eviction, Small Claims, Commercial Claims Under $5000.*
General Information: No code enforcement records released. Will not fax out documents. Court makes copy: $1.30 first page, $.65 each add'l. Certification fee: $6.00 per doc. Payee: Albany City Court. Business checks accepted. Visa/MC accepted. Prepayment required. Mail requests: SASE required.
Civil Name Search: Access: Mail, in person, online. Only the court performs in person name searches; visitors may not. No search fee. Required to search: name, years to search, case type. Civil cases indexed by plaintiff, defendant. Civil records on computer from 1993, records go back 25 years. Mail turnaround Time varies. WebCivil Local at http://iapps.courts.state.ny.us/webcivil/ecourtsMain contains information on both active and disposed Civil Court cases. Search by index number, party name, attorney/firm name or judge. No fee.
Albany City Court - Misdemeanors 1 Morton Ave, Albany, NY 12202; 518-453-5520; fax: 518-447-8778; 8:30AM-4:30PM (EST). *Misdemeanor.*

General Information: No sealed, expunged, adoption, sex offense, juvenile, or mental health records released without a signed release. Will not fax documents. Court makes copy: $.65 per page with cap of $30.00. Certification fee: Certificate of Disposition fee is $10.00. Payee: Albany City Court Criminal Part. Business checks accepted. Major credit cards accepted. Prepayment required. Mail requests: SASE required.

Criminal Name Search: Access: Mail, in person, online. Only the court performs in person name searches; visitors may not. Search fee: $5.00 per name per certificate of disposition. Required to search: name, date of arrest, DOB. Criminal records on computer since mid-'93, on index cards prior. Note: Court will search but you must provide the date of arrest; no name only searches. Mail turnaround Time 1-5 days. Name search requests are often directed to the OCA for statewide record search, $65.00 search fee. See www.nycourts.gov/apps/chrs.

Supreme & County Court County Court, Courthouse, Rm 102, 16 Eagle St, Albany, NY 12207; 518-285-8777 county court; 518-285-8989 Supreme; civil phone: 518-285-8989 Supreme; fax: 518-487-5020; 9AM-5PM (EST). *Felony, Civil.*
General Information: This court does not hold closed case records. It directs criminal search requests to the OCA for a $65.00 statewide record check. However, for an Albany countywide search, see the County Clerk in a separate listing.

Cohoes City Court PO Box 678, 97 Mohawk St, Cohoes, NY 12047-0678; 518-453-5501; fax: 518-233-8202; 8:15AM-3:30PM (EST). *Misdemeanor, Civil Actions under $15,000, Eviction, Small Claims.*
General Information: Criminal searches are done by: NYS Office of Court Administration, Office of Administrative Services, Criminal History Record Search, 25 Beaver St, Rm 840, New York, NY 10004. $65.00 for statewide search fee. No sealed or expunged records released. Will not fax documents. Court makes copy: $.65 per page with $1.30 minimum. Certification fee: $5.00, Court provides certificate of disposition or letter of disposition for $6.00 or free to defendant. Payee: Cohoes County Court. Only cashiers checks and money orders accepted. Visa/MC accepted. Prepayment required.
Civil Name Search: Access: In person, mail, online. Only the court performs in person name searches; visitors may not. No search fee. Civil records on computer from 1/95, prior in books, on cards. Note: When case number given, they will provide documents by mail within 5 days, longer if retrieved from storage. This court recommends searching for judgments through the County Clerk's office. WebCivil Local at http://iapps.courts.state.ny.us/webcivil/ecourtsMain contains information on both active and disposed Civil Court cases. Search by index number, party name, attorney/firm name or judge. No fee.
Criminal Name Search: Access: Online. Criminal records computerized from 1/96, earlier in storage. Note: Will not permit access to records. All criminal record name search requests are directed to the OCA for statewide record search, $65.00 search fee. See www.nycourts.gov/apps/chrs.

Watervliet City Court 2 15th St, Watervliet, NY 12189; 518-270-3803; fax: 518-270-3812; 8AM-3PM (EST). *Misdemeanor, Civil Actions under $15,000, Eviction, Small Claims.*
www.nycourts.gov/courts/3jd
General Information: No fee to fax out. Court makes copy: $.65 per page. Certification fee: $6.00 per document plus copy fee. Payee: City Court. Business checks accepted. Visa/MC accepted in person only. Prepayment required. Mail requests: SASE required.
Civil Name Search: Access: Phone, fax, mail, in person, online. Only the court performs in person name searches; visitors may not. Search fee: $5.00 per name per 2 year period. Civil cases indexed by plaintiff. Civil records on computer from 1991, prior on index cards back to 1975. Mail turnaround Time 1-2 weeks. WebCivil Local at http://iapps.courts.state.ny.us/webcivil/ecourtsMain contains information on both active and disposed Civil Court cases. Search by index number, party name, attorney/firm name or judge. No fee.
Criminal Name Search: Access: Mail, in person, online. Only the court performs in person name searches; visitors may not. Search fee: $5.00. Required to search: name, years to search, DOB. Criminal records computerized from 1991, prior on index cards back to 1975. Mail turnaround Time 1-2 weeks. Name search requests are often directed to the OCA for statewide record search, $65.00 search fee. See www.nycourts.gov/apps/chrs.

Surrogate's Court 30 Clinton Ave, Albany, NY 12207; 518-285-8585; 8:30AM-4PM (EST). *Probate.*
www.nycourts.gov/courts/3jd/surrogates/albany/index.shtml
General Information: A county search of the probate court index by mail for 25-year search is $30.00 fee. A full county probate search of all years is $90.00.

Albany Town/Village Courts- Altamont Village Court PO Box 643, 115 Main St, Altamont, NY 12009; 518-861-8554 9AM-1PM W,F.

Berne Town Court PO Box 57, Town Hall, Berne, NY 12023; 518-872-1448 6Pm Tues. **Bethlehem Town Court** 447 Delaware Ave, Delmar, NY 12054; 518-439-9717 8:30 - 4:00 Monday - Friday. **Coeymans Town Court** 18 Russell Ave, Town Bldg, Ravena, NY 12143; 518-756-8480 8:30AM-12:30PM 1:30PM-4:30PM M-TH; 8:30AM-N F. **Colonie Town Court** 312 Wolf Rd, Public Safety Bldg, Latham, NY 12110-4814; 518-783-2714 8:30AM-4PM. **Green Island Town Court** 69 Hudson Ave, Green Island, NY 12183; 518-273-0661 9AM-N; 1-4PM. **Guilderland Town Court** PO Box 339, Town Hall, Route 20, Guilderland, NY 12084; 518-356-1980 9AM-4:30PM. **Menands Village Court** 250 Broadway, Menands, NY 12204; 518-434-3992 8:00 - 4:00 M-F. **New Scotland Town Court** 2029 New Scotland Rd, Town Hall, Slingerlands, NY 12159; 518-475-0493 8AM-3PM M-TH; 8AM-1PM F. **Ravena Village Court** 15 Mountain Rd., Ravena, NY 12143; 518-756-2313 8:30AM-N 1PM-4PM. **Rensselaerville Town Court** 87 Barger Rd, Town Bldg, Medusa, NY 12120; 518-239-4225 9AM-4:30PM - Court held 4th Mon of month at 7PM. **Town of Knox Justice Court** PO Box 124, 2292 Berne-Altamont Rd (12009), Knox, NY 12107; 518-872-9183 6PM-? W. **Voorheesville Village Court** PO Box 367, 29 Voorheesville Ave, Voorheesville, NY 12186; 518-765-5524 6PM 1st & 3rd M. **Westerlo Town Court** 671 County Rte 401, Westerlo, NY 12193; 518-797-3239 7-8:30PM M & W.

Allegany County

County Court Clerk 7 Court St, Belmont, NY 14813; 585-268-9270; fax: 585-268-9659; 9AM-N, 1-5PM (EST). *Civil.*
www.alleganyco.com/default.asp?show=btn_county_clerk
General Information: Felony records in Allegany County are managed by the County Court Clerk who directs criminal search requests to OCA for $65.00 statewide search. No sealed records released. Will fax documents $3.00 per page, prepaid. Court makes copy: $.65 per page; $1.30 minimum. Certification fee: $5.00 per doc. Over 5 pgs, add $1.25 each add'l page. Payee: County Clerk. Personal checks accepted, credit cards are not. Prepayment required.
Civil Name Search: Access: In person, online. Visitors must perform in person searches themselves. Civil cases prior to 1990 indexed by defendant only. Civil records on computer back to 1990; prior on docket books. Public use terminal has civil records back to 1990. Lookup pending Supreme Court civil cases at http://iapps.courts.state.ny.us/webcivil/FCASMain. These are only cases where a judge has been assigned.

Supreme & County Court 7 Court St, Belmont, NY 14813; 585-268-9270; fax: 585-268-7090; 9AM-5PM; 8:30AM-4PM Summer hours (EST). *Felony, Civil.*
General Information: This court does not hold closed records. Direct civil record requests to County Court Clerk, see separate listing. The County Court directs criminal search requests to the OCA for a $65.00 statewide record check.

Surrogate's Court Courthouse, 7 Court St, Belmont, NY 14813; 585-268-5815; fax: 585-268-7090; 9AM-5PM Sept-May; 8:30AM-4PM June-Aug (EST). *Probate.*
General Information: A county search of the probate court index by mail for 25-year search is $30.00 fee. A full county probate search of all years is $90.00.

Allegany Town/Village Courts- Alfred Village & Town Courts 7 W University St, Alfred, NY 14802; 607-587-9142 9AM-12:30PM M-F; 7-9PM M. **Allen Town Court** 4967 Klein Rd, Fillmore, NY 14735; 585-567-8436 6PM-? 2nd & 4th W. **Alma Town Court** PO Box 67, 5858 Allen St, Allentown, NY 14707; 585-593-4021 to 8PM Thursdays. **Almond Town & Village Courts** Route 21, Box 25B, Town Hall, Almond, NY 14804; 607-276-6665 8AM-2PM T-TH. **Amity Town Court** 1 Schuyler St, Belmont, NY 14813; 585-268-5305/5423 5:30 PM last W. **Andover Town & Village Courts** 22 E Greenwood St, Andover, NY 14806; 607-478-8446 8AM-N. **Angelica Town & Village Courts** 49 Park Circle, Angelica, NY 14709; 585-466-7928 8AM-N M,TH,F; 8:30-11:30AM T; 8AM-N W. **Belfast Town Court** PO Box 472, 9 Merton Ave, Belfast, NY 14711; 585-365-9903 8AM-N;1-4PM M&TH, 9AM-N T; 4-7PM W. **Belmont Village Court** 1 Schuyler St, Belmont, NY 14813; 585-268-5305 7PM-10PM W. **Birdsall Town Court** PO Box 222, Canaseraga, NY 14822; 607-545-8998 5:30PM 3rd M; 2nd & 4th Sat 10AM-9PM. **Bolivar Town Court** 252 Main St, Bolivar, NY 14715; 585-928-1860 8AM-N; 1-4PM. **Bolivar Village Court** 252 Main St., Bolivar, NY 14715; 585-928-2234 5AM-7PM; court opens 7PM. **Burns Town Court** 1682 Rte. 70, Canaseraga, NY 14822; 607-545-8998 **Caneadea Town Court** PO Box 596, Caneadea, NY 14717; 585-365-8240 Wed 7:30PM. **Centerville Town Court** PO Box 94, Centerville, NY 14029; 585-567-8424 by appointment. **Clarksville Town Court** PO Box 69, School St 2980, West Clarksville, NY 14786; 585-968-2031 7PM W court hours. **Cuba Town Court** 5 Bull St, Cuba, NY 14727; 585-968-1690 8:30AM-2:00PM. **Friendship Town Court** 50 W Main St, Friendship,

NY 14739; 585-973-7566 11AM-2PM M,TH,F; 11AM-9PM T. **Genesee Town Court** PO Box 40, 8296 Main St, Little Genesee, NY 14754; 585-928-2914 5-9PM TH. **Granger Town Court** PO Box 132, RD #1, Fillmore, NY 14735; 585-567-8155 **Grove Town Court** Town Hall, 1682 State Rt 70, Canseraga, NY 14822; 607-545-8998 court- 2nd & 4th Sat of Month. **Hume Town Court** PO Box 302, 20 N Genessee St, Fillmore, NY 14735; 585-567-2666 9AM-N; 1-5PM M-F; 9AM-N Sat. **Independence Town Court** 38 Marrietta Ave, Whitesville, NY 14897; 607-356-3608 8:30AM-1PM M,W; 8:30AM-N T,TH. **New Hudson Town Court** PO Box 109, Black Creek, NY 14714; 585-968-2179 7-9PM M,TH court. **Richburg Village Court** PO Box 248, 210 Main St, Town Hall, Richburg, NY 14774; 585-928-2130 Wed Eve. **Rushford Town Court** PO Box 38, 8999 Main St, Rushford, NY 14777; 585-437-5137 1-5PM 1st&3rd M. **Scio Town Court** PO Box 105, 4355 Vandermark Rd, Scio, NY 14880; 585-593-9072 7PM Tues. **Ward Town Court** 4414 County Road 10, Scio, NY 14880; 585-610-7503 6AM-2PM -these hours vary. **Wellsville Town Court** 46 S Main St, Wellsville, NY 14895; 585-593-1750 8AM-1PM W. **Wellsville Village Court** 46 S Main St, Wellsville, NY 14895; 585-593-5609 1-3PM T. **West Almond Town Court** 2701 Karr Valley Rd, West Almond, NY 14804; 607-276-2629 7-9PM W court. **Willing Town Court** 1431 State Rt. 19 South, Wellsville, NY 14895; 585-593-3210 7-9PM W court. **Wirt Town Court** PO Box 245, 210 Main St, Town Hall, Richburg, NY 14774; 585-928-2130 6-8PM W.

Bronx County

Supreme Court - Civil Division 851 Grand Concourse, Mezzanine, Rm 118, Bronx, NY 10451; 866-797-7214; fax: 718-590-8122; 9AM-5PM (EST). *Civil Actions over $25,000.*
www.courts.state.ny.us/courts/12jd
General Information: No marriage or divorce records released. Will not fax documents. Court makes copy: $.25 per page. Self serve copy: $.25 per page. Certification fee: $8.00 per doc includes copy fee at Cert Window 2. Payee: Bronx County Clerk. Only attorney checks, cashiers checks and money orders accepted. No personal checks. Visa/MC accepted. Prepayment required. Mail requests: SASE required for mail return of any copies.
Civil Name Search: Access: In person, online. Both court and visitors may perform in person name searches. Civil records on computer back to 1996; prior records on offsite archives. Public use terminal has civil records back to 1996. Terminal located at County Clerk Office. Lookup current or pending Supreme Court civil cases at http://iapps.courts.state.ny.us/webcivil/FCASMain. Also, access docket data free on the law case search at www.bronxcountyclerkinfo.com/law/UI/Admin/login.aspx and sign in as guest.

Supreme Court - Criminal Division 265 E 161st St, Bronx, NY 10451; 718-618-3010; fax: 718-618-3585; 9AM-5PM (EST). *Felony.*
www.courts.state.ny.us/courts/12jd/
General Information: Central felony records search phone is 212-428-2810 and is a statewide system. No sealed, expunged, juvenile or sex offense records released. Will not fax documents. Court makes copy: $.75 per page. Self serve copy: $.15 per page. Certification fee: $10.00 per doc. Payee: Bronx County Clerk. Only cashiers checks and money orders accepted. Prepayment required. Mail requests: SASE required.
Criminal Name Search: Access: Online. No in person or mail access says this court. Required to search: name, years to search, DOB. Criminal records computerized from 1977, prior on microfiche. Public use terminal has crim records back to 1995. No in person or mail access says this court. Online access is via the state OCA statewide system. Fee is $65.00 per search. See www.nycourts.gov/apps/chrs/. Register and access docket data free on the law case search at www.bronxcountyclerkinfo.com/law/UI/Admin/login.aspx and sign in as guest.

Civil Court of the City of New York - Bronx Branch 851 Grand Concourse, Window 6, Basement, Bronx, NY 10451; 718-618-2500, Records-718-618-2563; 9AM-5PM; 4PM for rec requests (EST). *Civil Actions under $25,000, Eviction, Small Claims.*
www.courts.state.ny.us/courts/12jd/index.shtml
General Information: General civil dial-up info line- 212-791-6000. Small claims- 718-618-2518. Court holds records 3 years then sends to archives. Resi. Evictions/Housing phone- 718-466-3025 located at 1118 Grand Concourse at 166th St. Will not fax documents. Court makes copy: Court gives you file to copy. Self serve copy: $.25 per page.Copy machine located in B-125. Certification fee: $6.00 per doc. Payee: Clerk of the Court. Only money orders and cash accepted. No credit cards accepted. Prepayment required.
Civil Name Search: Access: Phone, in person, online. Visitors must perform in person searches themselves. No search fee. Small claims in docket books. Pre-1998 records archived in Queens; 1998 to present in Brooklyn. Civil records in books, file cards back to the 1970's; computerized

records since 1998. Records archived after five years, requiring 4-8 weeks to retrieve. Note: To view files, call ahead so that clerk can schedule a time and have files available. Record requests via phone may be accepted in the Records Rm only. Public use terminal has civil records back to 1998. Public terminal has landlord/tenant, civil, and small claims. WebCivil Local at http://iapps.courts.state.ny.us/webcivil/ecourtsMain contains information on both active and disposed Civil Court cases. Search by index number, party name, attorney/firm name or judge. No fee.

Supreme Court - Criminal Div. - Misdemeanors Central Clerk's Office, 215 E 161st St, Bronx, NY 10451; 718-618-3100; fax: 718-537-5164; 9AM-1PM, 2-4:30PM (EST). *Misdemeanor.*
www.courts.state.ny.us/courts/12jd/criminal.shtml
General Information: No sealed, expunged, juvenile or sex offense records released. Court makes copy: $10.00 per copy. Certification fee: $10.00 per doc. Payee: Bronx Supreme Court. Only cashiers checks and money orders accepted. No credit cards accepted. Prepayment required. Mail requests: SASE required for civil.
Criminal Name Search: Access: In person, online. Only the court performs in person name searches; visitors may not. No search fee. Required to search: name, years to search, DOB. Some Criminal records computerized from 1976, prior on microfiche. Note: Unless a specific docket number given, this court directs all criminal record name search requests to the OCA for statewide record search. Subscribe or login as guest to search eCourts WebCrims future appearances system at http://iapps.courts.state.ny.us/webcrim_attorney/Login. Also, access docket data free on the law case search at www.bronxcountyclerkinfo.com/law/UI/Admin/login.aspx. Sign in as guest. Also, access records on the statewide CHRS system; fee is $65.00 per statewide search per name; call 212-428-2943 for info and sign-up or visit www.courts.state.ny.us/apps/chrs/.

Surrogate's Court 851 Grand Concourse, Bronx, NY 10451; 718-618-2300; 9AM-5PM (EST). *Probate.*
www.nycourts.gov/courts/nyc/surrogates/
General Information: A county search of the probate court index by mail for 25-year search is $30.00 fee. A full county probate search of all years is $90.00.

Broome County

County Clerk PO Box 2062, Broome County Clerk, County Office Bldg, Binghamton, NY 13902; 607-778-2255; fax: 607-778-2243; 9AM-4:45PM; (9AM-3:45PM June-August) (EST). *Felony, Civil.*
www.gobcclerk.com
General Information: Countywide search requests made to the County Clerk are processed in the manner described below. No sealed or youthful offender records released. Will fax documents $1.00 per page plus copy fee. Court makes copy: $.65 per page, $1.30 minimum. Self serve copy: $.25 per page from book. Certification fee: $5.20 per 8-page document includes copy fee, then $.65 per page. Payee: Broome County Clerk. No personal checks over $1000.00. Visa/MC accepted. Prepayment required. Mail requests: SASE required.
Civil Name Search: Access: Fax, mail, in person, online. Both court and visitors may perform in person name searches. Search fee: $5.00 per name. Fee is per 2 years searched, 10 years maximum. Civil records on computer from 1987, prior in books. Mail turnaround Time 5 days. Civil PAT goes back to 1986. Lookup Supreme Court civil cases at http://iapps.courts.state.ny.us/webcivil/FCASMain. Cases go back to 2002. Also, search clerk's court and judgment indexes free at www.gobcclerk.com/cgi/Official_Search_Types.html/input; records go back to 1987. Also, access to civil (judgment) records are available.
Criminal Name Search: Access: Fax, mail, in person, online. Both court and visitors may perform in person name searches. Search fee: $5.00 per name. Fee is per 2 years searched, 10 year maximum. Required to search: name, years to search, DOB. Criminal records computerized from 1987, prior in books. Mail turnaround Time 3-5 days. Criminal PAT goes back to same as civil. Name search requests are often directed to the OCA for statewide record search, $65.00 search fee. See www.nycourts.gov/apps/chrs. Online results show middle initial.

Supreme & County Court PO Box 1766, 92 Court St, County Courthouse, Binghamton, NY 13902; 607-778-2448; fax: 607-778-6426; 9AM-5PM; 8AM-4PM June-August (EST). *Felony, Civil.*
General Information: This court does not hold closed case records. The Supreme Court directs criminal record search requests to the OCA for processing. However, countywide search requests can be made to the County Clerk, see separate listing.

Binghamton City Court Governmental Plaza, 38 Holley St, Binghamton, NY 13901; 607-772-7006; fax: 607-772-7041; 8:45AM-4:45PM (EST). *Misdemeanor, Civil Actions under $15,000, Eviction, Small Claims.* www.nycourts.gov/courts/6jd/

General Information: No sealed records released. May fax documents; this is done irregularly. Court makes copy: $.65 per page; $1.30 minimum. Certification fee: $6.00 per cert civil; $5.00 if criminal. Payee: Binghamton City Court. Only cashiers checks and money orders accepted. Major credit cards accepted. Prepayment required. Mail requests: SASE required.

Civil Name Search: Access: Phone, mail, in person, online. Both court and visitors may perform in person name searches. No search fee. Civil cases indexed by defendant. Civil records on computer from 1990, prior in books, index cards. Note: In person searching only for 04/21/99 forward. Mail turnaround Time 1-2 weeks. Public use terminal has civil records back to 1996. WebCivil Local at http://iapps.courts.state.ny.us/webcivil/ecourtsMain contains information on both active and disposed Civil Court cases. Search by index number, party name, attorney/firm name or judge. No fee.

Criminal Name Search: Access: Mail, in person, online. Only the court performs in person name searches; visitors may not. No search fee. Required to search: notarized signature of requester (mail searches only), name, years to search, DOB. Criminal records computerized from 1990. Mail turnaround Time 1-2 weeks. Unless a specific docket number given, all criminal record name search requests are directed to the OCA for statewide record search, $65.00 search fee. See www.nycourts.gov/apps/chrs.

Surrogate's Court 92 Court St, Binghamton, NY 13901; 607-778-2111; 9AM-5PM; 8AM-4PM June-Sept (EST). *Probate.*
www.nycourts.gov/courts/6jd/broome/Surrogate.shtml
General Information: A county search of the probate court index by mail for 25-year search is $30.00 fee. A full county probate search of all years is $90.00. Also hold estate records here.

Broome Town/Village Courts- Barker Town Court PO Box 66, 151 Hyde St, Castle Creek, NY 13744; 607-648-6961 6PM T. **Binghamton Town Court** 279 Park Ave, Binghamton, NY 13903; 607-772-0357 9AM M. **Chenango Town Court** 1529 Route 12, Binghamton, NY 13901; 607-648-4809 ext1 9AM-4PM. **Colesville Town Court** PO Box 166, 780 Welton St, Harpursville, NY 13787; 607-693-1172 9AM-N, 1-4PM M-TH. **Conklin Town Court** PO Box 182, 1271 Conklin Rd, Conklin, NY 13748; 607-775-5244 9AM-12:30PM; 1:30-3:30PM T, Wed, Th. **Deposit Village Court** 146 Front St, Deposit, NY 13754; 607-467-4240 8AM-4PM. **Dickinson Town Court** 531 Old Front St, Binghamton, NY 13905; 607-723-9403 9AM-4PM M-F. **Endicott Village Court** 225 Jefferson Ave, Endicott, NY 13760; 607-757-2483 8:00-3:30 M -Thurs. 8:00-12:00 Friday. **Fenton Town Court** 44 Park St, Port Crane, NY 13833; 607-648-4801 x1 8AM-Noon. **Johnson City Village Court** 31 Avenue C, #2, Johnson City, NY 13790; 607-798-0002 8:30AM-4PM. **Kirkwood Town Court** 70 Crescent Dr, Town Hall, Kirkwood, NY 13795; 607-775-2653 8AM-4PM (Clerk's hrs) 8AM03:30PM (Office hrs). **Lisle Town Court** PO Box 247, Lisle, NY 13797; 607-849-4685 9:30AM-1:30PM M; 11;30AM-1:30PM W; 9AM-11AM F. **Maine Town Court** PO Box 141, 12 Lewis St, Maine, NY 13802-0141; 607-862-3427 9AM-N M-F. **Nanticoke Town Court** PO Box 71, 755 Cherry Valley Hill Rd, Glen Aubrey, NY 13777-0071; 607-692-4041 x21 10AM-N; 1-3PM TH; 4th Mon 2-4PM. **Sanford Town Court** 18 Church St, Deposit, NY 13754; 607-467-2516 7-8PM M; 1-2PM W. **Triangle Town Court** PO Box 289, 2612 Liberty St, Whitney Point, NY 13862; 607-692-4332 10AM-4PM M,W. **Union Town Court** 3121 E Main St, Endwell, NY 13760; 607-786-2965 ext1 8:30AM-4:00PM. **Vestal Town Court** 605 Vestal Pkwy West, Vestal, NY 13850; 607-748-1514 8AM-4PM M,W,F; 8AM-5PM T,TH. **Windsor Town Court** 124 Main St, Rm #2, Windsor, NY 13865; 607-655-1973 9AM-4PM M,W; 9AM-N T,TH; Closed F.

Cattaraugus County

County Clerk 303 Court St, Little Valley, NY 14755; 716-938-9111 x2297; probate phone: x2327; fax: 716-938-2773; 9AM-5PM (EST). *Felony, Civil.*
General Information: Countywide search requests made to the County Clerk are processed in the manner described below. No sealed or youthful offender records released. Will fax documents to local or toll free line for $3.00 add'l per page. Court makes copy: $1.00 per page. Certification fee: $5.00. Payee: County Clerk. Business checks accepted. No credit cards accepted. Prepayment required. Mail requests: SASE required.
Civil Name Search: Access: Mail, in person, online. Both court and visitors may perform in person name searches. Search fee: $5.00 per name. Fee is per 2 years searched. Civil records on computer from 1987, prior in books, index cards from 1900. Mail turnaround Time 2-3 days. Public use terminal has civil records back to 1995, judgments to 1987. Lookup current or pending Supreme Court civil cases at http://iapps.courts.state.ny.us/webcivil/FCASMain.
Criminal Name Search: Access: Mail, in person. Both court and visitors may perform in person name searches. Search fee: $5.00 per name. Fee is per 2 years searched. Required to search: name, years to search, DOB. Criminal records in books, index cards from 1900. Mail turnaround Time 2-3 days.

Supreme & County Court 303 Court St, Little Valley, NY 14755; 716-938-9111 x2378; fax: 716-938-6413; 9AM-5PM (EST). *Felony, Civil.*
www.nycourts.gov/litigants/courtguides/8thJD_cattaraugus.pdf
General Information: This court does not hold closed case records. It directs search criminal requests to the OCA for a $65.00 statewide record check. However, for a countywide search, see the County Clerk in separate listing.

Olean City Court PO Box 631, 101 E State St, Olean, NY 14760; 716-376-5620; fax: 716-376-5623; 8:30AM-4:30PM (EST). *Misdemeanor, Civil Actions under $15,000, Eviction, Small Claims, Traffic.*
General Information: The court is in the process of computerizing the docket. No sealed or youthful offender records released. Will fax documents to local or toll free line, if prepaid. Court makes copy: $1.30 per page. Certification fee: $6.00. Payee: Olean City Court. Business & personal checks not accepted unless if attorney. Visa/MC accepted. Prepayment required. Mail requests: SASE required.
Civil Name Search: Access: Mail, in person. Only the court performs in person name searches; visitors may not. Search fee: $5.00 per name. Required to search: name, years to search, signed release; also helpful-case number. Civil cases indexed by defendant or docket number. Civil index on docket books. Mail turnaround Time 1 week.
Criminal Name Search: Access: Mail, in person, online. Search fee: $5.00 for Certificate of Disposition; same fee if court agrees to perform a name search. Required to search: Name, years to search; also helpful- case number. Criminal records computerized from 1990, prior in books. Note: Need signed release if case files released. Name search requests are often directed to the OCA for statewide record search, $65.00 search fee. See www.nycourts.gov/apps/chrs.

Salamanca City Court Municipal Center, 225 Wildwood Ave, Salamanca, NY 14779; 716-945-4153; fax: 716-945-2362; 8AM-4PM Summer; 9AM-5PM Winter (EST). *Misdemeanor, Civil Actions under $15,000, Eviction, Small Claims.*
General Information: No sealed records released. Will fax documents. Court makes copy: $.65 per page, minimum $1.30. Self serve copy: same. Certification fee: $6.00 per doc plus copy fee. Payee: Salamanca City Court. No personal checks accepted. Visa/MC/Discover accepted. Prepayment required. Mail requests: SASE required.
Civil Name Search: Access: Mail, in person, online. Only the court performs in person name searches; visitors may not. No search fee. Civil cases indexed by defendant. Civil records on dockets from 1930s; on computer back to 1995. Mail turnaround Time 1-2 weeks. WebCivil Local at http://iapps.courts.state.ny.us/webcivil/ecourtsMain contains information on both active and disposed Civil Court cases. Search by index number, party name, attorney/firm name or judge. No fee.
Criminal Name Search: Access: Mail, in person, online. Only the court performs in person name searches; visitors may not. Search fee: A Certificate of Disposition is $5.00; signed release required. Required to search: name, years to search, DOB, case number. Criminal docket index from 1930s; on computer back to 1995. Mail turnaround Time 1-2 weeks. Name search requests are often directed to the OCA for statewide record search, $65.00 search fee. See www.nycourts.gov/apps/chrs.

Surrogate's Court 303 Court St, Little Valley, NY 14755; 716-938-2327; fax: 716-938-6983; 9AM-5PM (EST). *Probate.*
General Information: Public can search, but if court has to search there is a fee. A county search of the probate court index by mail for 25-year search is $30.00 fee. A full county probate search of all years is $90.00.

Cattaraugus Town/Village Courts- Allegany Town Court PO Box 254, 3790 Birch Run Rd, Allegany, NY 14706; 716-373-3670 8AM-N M; 8AM-4:30PM T-F. **Allegany Village Court** 106 E Main St, Allegany, NY 14706; 716-373-1460 8AM-4PM. **Ashford Town Court** 9224 Rte 240, West Valley, NY 14171; 716-942-6016 6:30-9PM TH. **Carrollton Town Court** PO Box 146, 640 Main St, Limestone, NY 14753; 716-925-7772 7PM-? M. **Coldspring Town Court** PO Box J, 2604 Lebanon Rd, Steamburg, NY 14783; 716-354-5752; criminal phone: 716-354-2012; 7-9PM T. **Conewango Town Court** 4762 Route 241, Town Hiway Bldg, Conewango Valley, NY 14726; 716-358-9321, 716-358-9152 5-7PM T (when court held). **Dayton Town Court** 9100 Route 62, South Dayton, NY 14138; 716-532-3758 8:30AM-12:30PM M-TH; 1PM-4PM F. **East Otto Town Court** PO Box 24, 9014 E Otto-Springville Rd, East Otto, NY 14729; 716-257-9071 **Ellicottville Town Court** PO Box 600, 1 W Washington St, Ellicottville, NY 14731; 716-498-0418 9AM-4PM M-TH. **Ellicottville Village Court** 1 W Washington St, Ellicottville, NY 14731; 716-699-4513 9AM-4PM M,T. **Farmersville Town Court** 8963 Lake St, Route 98, Farmersville, NY 14737; 716-676-3030 9AM-1PM M,TH; 9AM-N T,F; 9-11AM Sat. **Franklinville Town Court** PO Box 146, 11 Park Sq, Franklinville, NY 14737; 716-676-3077 9AM-12:30PMN;1:30-4:30 PM (closed W). **Freedom Town Court** 1188 Eagle St, Sandusky, NY 14133; 716-492-5828 6-8PM T. **Great Valley Town Court** PO Box 172, Town Hall, Great Valley, NY 14741; 716-699-4135 8:30AM-1PM M,T,TH. **Hinsdale Town Court** PO Box 95, 4129 Route 16, Hinsdale, NY 14743;

716-372-3918 **Humphrey Town Court** 4525 Pumpkin Hollow Rd, Great Valley, NY 14741; 716-945-1010 **Ischua Town Court** 1850 Mill St, Hinsdale, NY 14743; 716-557-8787 6:30AM-4:30PM M-TH. **Leon Town Court** 12195 Leon-New Albion Rd, Town Hall, Leon, NY 14751; 716-296-8132 Monday 7:00PM. **Little Valley Town Court** 201 Third St, Little Valley, NY 14755; 716-938-6882 2nd & 4th W eved 7-?PM. **Lyndon Town Court** 852 Lyndon Center Rd, Cuba, NY 14727; 716-676-9928 7PM W. **Machias Town Court** 3438 Roszyk Hill Rd, Machias, NY 14101; 716-353-8207 Wed 7-9PM. **Mansfield Town Court** 7660 Hollister Hill, Little Valley, NY 14755; 716-257-9288 **Napoli Town Court** 4672 Allegany Rd, Little Valley, NY 14755; 716-938-6836 1st&3rd Tues. 6;00pm -9:00pm. **New Albion Town Court** 14 Main St, Cattaraugus, NY 14719; 716-257-5387 10AM-2PM T,W. **Olean Town Court** 2634 Rte 16 N, Town Hall, Olean, NY 14760; 716-373-2727 8AM-1PM. **Otto Town Court** PO Box 66, 8842 Otto Maple Rd, Otto, NY 14766; 716-257-8251 Monday evenings. **Perrysburg Town Court** PO Box 244, 10460 Peck Hill Rd, Perrysburg, NY 14129; 716-532-4090 9:30AM=5PM Court Thursday 6:00PM. **Persia Town Court** 8 W Main St, Gowanda, NY 14070; 716-532-4042 7PM 1st, 2nd, 3rd, 4th T. **Portville Town Court** PO Box 630, 1102 Portville-Olean Rd, Portville, NY 14770; 716-933-6432 Noon-5PM M; 8AM-N T,TH; Court- 5:30PM M. **Portville Village Court** 1 Main St, Portville, NY 14770; 716-933-6288 8-10AM M,W,F; 6:30PM M. **Randolph Town Court** 72 Main St, Randolph, NY 14772; 716-358-4515 9AM-3PM T,TH,F; 9AM-N W; Court 6PM TH. **Red House Town Court** 8619 Longto Hollow Rd, Salamanca, NY 14779; 716-354-5052 1st & 3rd Mondays. **Salamanca Town Court** 4295 Center St Extension, Town Hall, Salamanca, NY 14779; 716-945-4775 7-? PM M. **South Dayton Village Court** PO Box 269, 17 Park St, South Dayton, NY 14138; 716-988-3132 7:30-9:30PM MH. **South Valley Town Court** 11888 Sawmill Run Rd, Frewsburg, NY 14738; 716-354-2335 No set hours. **Yorkshire Town Court** 82 Main St, PO Box 6, Delevan, NY 14042; 716-492-4831 9AM-12:30PM M-TH; TH @ 7PM.

Cayuga County

County Clerk 160 Genesee St, Attn: County Clerk, Auburn, NY 13021; 315-253-1271; fax: 315-253-1653; 9AM-5PM Sept-June; 8AM-4PM July-Aug (EST). *Felony, Misdemeanor, Civil.*
General Information: This County Clerk will not do a felony record name search. Access to criminal records, including name searching, must be done at the OCA in New York City. The fees is $65.00 for a statewide search. No sealed records released. Will not fax documents. Court makes copy: $.65 per page; $1.30 minimum. Certification fee: $5.00 up to 4 pages, then $1.25 ea add'l page. Payee: County Clerk. Personal checks accepted, credit cards are not. Prepayment required. Mail requests: SASE required.
Civil Name Search: Access: Mail, in person, online. Both court and visitors may perform in person name searches. Search fee: $5.00 per name per 5 years searched. Civil records on computer from 1986, prior in books. Public use terminal has civil records back to 1987. Lookup Supreme Court civil cases at http://iapps.courts.state.ny.us/webcivil/FCASMain. Cases go back to 2002.
Criminal Name Search: Access: In person. Visitors must perform in person searches themselves. Access to records must be done at the OCA in New York City.

Supreme & County Court 152 Genesee St, Auburn, NY 13021-3424; 315-255-4320; fax: 315-255-4322; 9AM-5PM Sept-June; 8AM-4PM July-Aug (EST). *Felony, Misdemeanor, Civil.*
General Information: This court does not hold closed case records. It directs criminal search requests to the OCA for a $65.00 statewide record check. However, for a countywide search, see the County Clerk in a separate listing.

Auburn City Court 157 Genesee St, Auburn, NY 13021-3434; 315-253-1570; fax: 315-253-1085; 8AM-4PM; window- 8:15AM-3:45PM (EST). *Misdemeanor, Civil Actions under $15,000, Eviction, Small Claims.*
www.nycourts.gov/courts/7jd/Auburn/index.shtml
General Information: No sealed, expunged, adoption, sex offense, juvenile or mental health records released. Will fax documents, no fee. Court makes copy: $.65 per page; $1.30 minimum. Certification fee: $6.00 per civil doc; $5.00 for criminal cert. Payee: City Court Clerk. No personal checks. Visa/MC accepted in person only. Prepayment required.
Civil Name Search: Access: Mail, fax, in person, online. Only the court performs in person name searches; visitors may not. No search fee. Civil cases indexed by defendant. Civil records on computer from 1986. WebCivil Local at http://iapps.courts.state.ny.us/webcivil/ecourtsMain contains information on both active and disposed Civil Court cases. Search by index number, party name, attorney/firm name or judge. No fee.
Criminal Name Search: Access: In person (limited), online. Search fee: Certificate of Disposition is $5.00. Note: The court does not to permit access to records unless specific case file number or an arrest date is given. All criminal record name search requests are directed to the OCA for statewide record search, $65.00 search fee. See www.nycourts.gov/apps/chrs.

Surrogate's Court Courthouse, 152 Genesee St, Auburn, NY 13021-3471; 315-255-4316; fax: 315-255-4324; 8:30AM-4:30PM (8AM-4PM summer hrs) (EST). *Probate.*
General Information: A county search of the probate court index by mail for up to 25-year search is $30.00 fee. A full county probate search of over 25 years is $90.00.

Cayuga Town/Village Courts- Aurelius Town Court 1241 W Genesee St Rd, Auburn, NY 13021; 315-255-0065 8AM & 7PM W. **Brutus Town Court** 9021 N Seneca St, Weedsport, NY 13166; 315-834-6618 9AM-3PM, T, W, TH, F. **Cato Town Court** 11320 Shortcut Rd, Cato, NY 13033; 315-626-6904 9AMN M,TH. **Conquest Town Court** 1289 Fuller Rd, Port Byron, NY 13140; 315-776-5703 **Fleming Town Court** 2433 Dublin Rd, Auburn, NY 13021; 315-252-1204 6-8PM T. **Genoa Town Court** 1000 Bartnick Rd, Genoa, NY 13071; 315-364-6722 9AM-12 TH. **Ira Town Court** 2487 W Main St, Cato, NY 13033; 315-626-3500 Tues: 9am-12; court hours- 7-9PM 2nd & 4th M. **Ledyard Town Court** 1099 Poplar Ridge Rd, Aurora, NY 13026; 315-364-5708 9:00am - 12:00 Tues. Thurs. Fri. **Locke Town Court** PO Box 29, 703 State Rte 38, Locke, NY 13092; 315-497-9338 (AM-2PM M, F; 3PM-7PM W. **Mentz Town Court** PO Box 798, 14 Sponable Dr, Port Byron, NY 13140; 315-776-9920 9AM-1PM M; court- 6-8PM Mon. **Meridian Village Court** 11320 Short Cut Rd, Cato, NY 13033; 315-626-6904 9AM-N M,TH. **Montezuma Town Court** PO Box 392, 8102 Dock St, Montezuma, NY 13117; 315-776-9163 6:30PM W. **Moravia Town Court** PO Box 1146, 139 Main St, Moravia, NY 13118; 315-497-0968 Town-2nd&4th Th 7PM; Village-Tues 7PM. **Moravia Village Court** PO Box 858, 48 W Cayuga St, Moravia, NY 13118; 315-497-0968 Evening hours vary. **Niles Town Court** 5923 New Hope Rd, Moravia, NY 13118; 315-497-0066 10AM-Noon 2nd & 4th Sat. **Owasco Town Court** 2 Bristol Ave, Auburn, NY 13021; 315-255-0446 5PM-? T. **Port Byron Village Court** PO Box 398, 52 Utica St, Port Byron, NY 13140; 315-776-9692 68:30T. **Scipio Town Court** PO Box 61, 3705 State Route 34, Scipio Center, NY 13147; 315-364-5325 7-9PM M. **Semperonius Town Court** 2274 State Rte 41A, Moravia, NY 13118; 315-496-2376 ext11 7PM-? 2nd & 4th W. **Sennett Town Court** 6931 Cherry St Rd, Auburn, NY 13021; 315-253-3712 10AM-4PM M-F; W 7PM. **Springport Town Court** 859 St Rte 326, Cayuga, NY 13034; 315-889-5020 4-7PM W. **Sterling Town Court** 1290 State Rte 104-A, Sterling, NY 13156; 315-947-6602 7PM Wed. **Summerhill Town Court** 13606 State Rte 90, Locke, NY 13092; 315-497-3496 5:30PM T. **Throop Town Court** 7471 Robinson Rd, Auburn, NY 13021; 315-252-7373 ext 106 9AM-2PM Wed. **Venice Town Court** 2479 State Rte 34, Venice Center, NY 13147; 315-364-6875 1st&3rd M 5PM-7PM. **Victory Town Court** 1323 Town Barn Rd, Red Creek, NY 13143; 315-754-8238 1st & 3rd Wed. 7:00PM. **Weedsport Village Court** PO Box 190, 8892 South St, Weedsport, NY 13166; 315-834-8634 8AM-1PM T,TH; 7PM M Court.

Chautauqua County

County Clerk PO Box 170, 1 N Erie St, Courthouse, Mayville, NY 14757; 716-753-4331; probate phone: 716-753-4339; fax: 716-753-4293; 9AM-5PM/Summer 8:30AM-4:30PM (EST). *Felony, Civil.*
www.co.chautauqua.ny.us/departments/clerk/Pages/default.aspx
General Information: Non in-person felony record requests are managed by the Supreme Court clerk who directs searches to OCA for $65.00 statewide search. This court will not perform name searches. No sealed records released. Will not fax documents. Court makes copy: $1.00 per page. No certification fee . Payee: County Clerk. Personal checks accepted, credit cards are not. Prepayment required.
Civil Name Search: Access: In person, online. Visitors must perform in person searches themselves. Civil cases indexed by plaintiff and defendant. Civil PAT goes back to 8/1997. Lookup Supreme Court civil cases at http://iapps.courts.state.ny.us/webcivil/FCASMain. Cases go back to 2002.
Criminal Name Search: Access: In person only. Visitors must perform in person searches themselves. Required to search: name, years to search, DOB. Criminal records on court's computer system from 8/1987; prior on docket books and cards. Note: Court will not search felony records. A Certificate of Conviction can be ordered for $5.00. Criminal PAT goes back to same as civil.

Supreme Court PO Box 292, 1 N Erie St, Mayville, NY 14757; 716-753-4266; fax: 716-753-4993; 9AM-5PM; Summer 8:30AM-4:30PM (EST). *Felony, Civil.*
www.nycourts.gov/courts/8jd/Chautauqua/index.shtml
General Information: This court does not hold closed case records. It directs criminal search requests to the OCA for a $65.00 statewide record check.

Dunkirk City Court City Hall, 342 Central Ave, Dunkirk, NY 14048; 716-366-2055; fax: 716-366-3622; 9AM-5PM (EST). *Misdemeanor, Civil Actions under $15,000, Eviction, Small Claims.*
General Information: No sealed, expunged, adoption, sex offense, juvenile or mental health records released. Will not fax documents. Court

makes copy: $.65 per page; $1.30 minimum. Certification fee: $6.00 per doc plus copy fee. Payee: Dunkirk City Court. Only cashiers checks and money orders accepted. Visa/MC accepted. Prepayment required. Mail requests: SASE required.

Civil Name Search: Access: Mail, in person. Only the court performs in person name searches; visitors may not. No search fee. Civil cases indexed by defendant. Civil records on computer back to 1990, prior in books. Note: Make appointment to search.

Criminal Name Search: Access: Online. No criminal searching at this court. Required to search: name, DOB, arrest date (for Cert of Disposition). Criminal records go back to 1930s. Note: A Certificate of Disposition is $6.00. Court will not do a name search, must have unless specific case file given. Also, record checks from local Police Dept.- 716-366-2266. All criminal record name search requests are directed to the OCA for statewide record search, $65.00 search fee. See www.nycourts.gov/apps/chrs.

Jamestown City Court City Hall, Jamestown, NY 14701; 716-483-7561/7562; fax: 716-483-7519; 8:30AM-5PM (EST). *Misdemeanor, Civil Actions under $15,000, Eviction, Small Claims.*

General Information: No sealed records released. Will fax documents to local or toll free line. Court makes copy: $.65 per page; $1.30 minimum. Certification fee: $6.00 per document plus copy fee. Payee: City Court. Business checks accepted. Visa/MC accepted. Prepayment required. Mail requests: SASE required.

Civil Name Search: Access: Fax, mail, in person, online. Only the court performs in person name searches; visitors may not. No search fee. Civil cases indexed by defendant. Civil records on computer back to 1989, prior in books. WebCivil Local at http://iapps.courts.state.ny.us/webcivil/ecourtsMain contains information on both active and disposed Civil Court cases. Search by index number, party name, attorney/firm name or judge. No fee.

Criminal Name Search: Access: Online. Only the court performs in person name searches; visitors may not. Search fee: $5.00 fee for certification of conviction or disposition. Required to search: Name, DOB. Criminal records computerized from 1989, prior in books to 1965. Note: The court refuses to permit access to records unless specific case file given. All criminal record name search requests are directed to the OCA for statewide record search, $65.00 search fee. See www.nycourts.gov/apps/chrs.

Surrogate's Court PO Box C, 3 N Erie St, Gerace Office Bldg, Mayville, NY 14757; 716-753-4339; fax: 716-753-4600; 9AM-5PM Summer; 8:30AM-4:30PM, July-Sept 3 (EST). *Probate.*

General Information: A county search of the probate court index by mail for 25-year search is $30.00 fee. A full county probate search of all years is $90.00.

Chautauqua Town/Village Courts- Arkwright Town Court 9543 Center Rd, Fredonia, NY 14063; 716-672-8672 **Brocton Village Court** 87 W Main St, Brocton, NY 14716; 716-792-4189 **Busti Town Court** 121 Chautauqua Ave, Lakewood, NY 14750; 716-763-4695 8:30AM-5PM M; 8:30AM-3PM T-F. **Carroll Town Court** PO Box 630, 5 Main St, Frewsburg, NY 14738; 716-569-5365 3-6 PM T. **Charlotte Town Court** PO Box 895, 8 Lester St, Sinclairville, NY 14782; 716-962-2004 9AM-N T,TH. **Chautauqua Town Court** 2 Academy St, #A, Mayville, NY 14757; 716-753-5245 / 753-7342 ext 17 1:30-4:30PM. **Cherry Creek Town Court** PO Box 98, 6845 Main St, Rte 83, Cherry Creek, NY 14723; 716-296-8050 6PM-? 1st TH, 2nd T, 3rd T. **Clymer Town Court** Clymer Community Bldg, PO Box 44, Clymer, NY 14724; 716-355-6331 7PM M. **Dunkirk Town Court** 4737 Willow Rd, Dunkirk, NY 14048; 716-366-3945 9AM-3PM M-F. **Ellery Town Court** PO Box 429, 25 Sunnyside Ave, Bemus Point, NY 14712; 716-386-2521 9:30PM-3:30PM, 6PM M. **Ellicott Town Court** 215 S Work St, Falconer, NY 14733; 716-665-5319 8AM-5PM M-TH;8AM-3PM F. **Ellington Town Court** 813 W Main St, Ellington, NY 14732; 716-287-2026 9AM-5PM M,T; 9AM-3PM W,F; 1PM-7PM TH. **Fredonia Village Court** 9-11 Church St, PO Box 31, Fredonia, NY 14063-0031; 716-679-2312 9AM-4PM. **French Creek Town Court** 10073 King Rd, Clymer, NY 14724; 716-355-8801 **Gerry Town Court** PO Box 163, 4519 Rte 60, Gerry, NY 14740; 716-985-4323 Monday 3:30-5:00pm. **Hanover Town Court** 68 Hanover St, Silver Creek, NY 14136; 716-934-4770 M-T-F 9AM-4PM,W-9AM-2PM,TH-9AM-3PM 6:30-10PM. **Harmony Town Court** 2 East Main Street, Panama, NY 14767; 716-488-1178 6:30PM-? M. **Kiantone Town Court** 1521 Peck Settlement Rd, Jamestown, NY 14701; 716-488-0383 Tues.1-5pm Wed. 9am-12 Thurs. 8am-11am. **Mina Town Court** PO Box 417, Mann Rd, Community Bldg, Findley Lake, NY 14736; 716-769-7250 8AM TH. **North Harmony Town Court** PO Box 167, 3445 Old Bridge Rd, Stow, NY 14785; 716-789-2174 9:30AM-3:30PM M,T,TH,F; closed W. **Poland Town Court** PO Box 4, 3593 Church St, Kennedy, NY 14747; 716-267-3809 5PM TH. **Pomfret Town Court** 9-11 Church St, Village Hall, 3rd Fl, Fredonia, NY 14063; 716-672-6878 M-Fri. 8am-4pm. **Portland Town Court** 87 W Main St, Brocton, NY 14716; 716-792-4111 8AM-4PM M-TH; 8AM-12PM F; Court-T,W. **Ripley Town Court** PO Box 573, 1 Park Ave, Ripley, NY 14775; 716-736-7575 6-8PM W; clerk hours vary, call for app't. **Sheridan Town Court** PO Box 73, 2702 Rte 20, Sheridan, NY 14135; 716-672-2600 8:30AM-N. **Sherman Town Court** PO Box 542, 111A Mill St, Sherman, NY 14781; 716-761-6770 9AM-4PM M,T,TH; 9AM-2PM F. **Silver Creek Village Court** 172 Central Ave, Silver Creek, NY 14136; 716-934-3558 8AM-4PM. **Stockton Town Court** PO Box 43, 22 N Main St, Stockton, NY 14784; 716-595-3192 7PM-? M. **Villenova Town Court** 1094 Butcher Rd, South Dayton, NY 14138; 716-988-3678 9am-12:30pm M-Thurs. **Westfield Town Court** 23 Elm St, Westfield, NY 14787; 716-326-6255 N-4:30PM. **Westfield Village Court** 23 Elm St, Westfield, NY 14787; 716-326-6135 9:30AM-1:30PM M,W,F.

Chemung County

County Clerk PO Box 588, 210 Lake St, Elmira, NY 14902; 607-737-2920; fax: 607-737-2897; 8:30AM-4:30PM (EST). *Misdemeanor, Civil.* www.chemungcounty.com/

General Information: Search requests made to the County Clerk are processed in the manner described below. No sealed, divorce or adoption records released. Will fax documents $1.00 per page. Court makes copy: $.65 per page, $1.30 minimum. Self serve copy: $.65 per page. Certification fee: $5.00 up to 4 pages, $1.25 each add'l page, includes copies. Payee: County Clerk. Personal checks accepted, credit cards are not. Prepayment required. Mail requests: SASE required.

Civil Name Search: Access: In person, online (limited). Both court and visitors may perform in person name searches. Search fee: $5.00 per name. Fee is per 2 years searched. Civil records on computer from 1994, prior in books to 1800s. Public use terminal has civil records. Public access terminal is in the Supreme & County Court clerk office. Access to current/pending WebCivil Supreme Court civil cases on the statewide system is at http://iapps.courts.state.ny.us/webcivil/FCASMain.

Criminal Name Search: Search fee: $5.00 for every 2 years searched or $20.00 for a seven year search. Searches with both maiden and married names are considered two searches. Required to search: name, years to search, DOB, SSN. Criminal records in docket books back to 1979. Mail turnaround Time 4-6 weeks.

Supreme & County Court PO Box 588, Hazlett Bldg, 6th Fl, Elmira, NY 14902-0588; 607-737-2084; probate phone: 607-737-2873; fax: 607-646-963-6605; 9AM-5PM (EST). *Felony, Civil.*

General Information: This court does not hold closed case records. It directs criminal search requests to the OCA for a $65.00 statewide record check. However County Clerk may perform record search, see separate listing.

Elmira City Court 317 E Church St, Elmira, NY 14901; 607-737-5681; 8:30AM-4:30PM (EST). *Misdemeanor, Civil Actions under $15,000, Eviction, Small Claims.* www.nycourts.gov/courts/6jd/

General Information: No sealed records released. Will fax documents to local or toll free line. Court makes copy: $.65 per page; $1.30 minimum. Certification fee: $6.00 per doc. Payee: Elmira City Court. No Personal checks, Visa/MC accepted. Prepayment required. Mail requests: SASE required for mail return of any copies.

Civil Name Search: Access: In person, online. Visitors must perform in person searches themselves. Civil cases indexed by defendant. Civil records on computer back to 1997; prior records on index cards. Note: If searching for records prior to 1997, call office to make appointment to search. Public use terminal has civil records back to 1997. Terminal results gives address. WebCivil Local at http://iapps.courts.state.ny.us/webcivil/ecourtsMain contains information on both active and disposed Civil Court cases. Search by index number, party name, attorney/firm name or judge. No fee.

Criminal Name Search: Access: Online. Only the court performs in person name searches; visitors may not. Search fee: A Certificate of Disposition is $5.00. Required to search: name, years to search, date of arrest (for Cert of Disposition). Criminal records computerized from 1987; prior on books. Note: Court does not permit access to records unless specific case file given. All criminal record name search requests are directed to the OCA for statewide record search, $65.00 search fee. See www.nycourts.gov/apps/chrs.

Surrogate's Court PO Box 588, 224 Lake St, Elmira, NY 14902; 607-737-2946/2819; fax: 607-737-2874; 9:15AM-12; 1PM-4PM (EST). *Probate.*

General Information: Public access terminal located in basement has complete index. A county search of the probate court index by mail for 25-year search is $30.00 fee. A full county probate search of all years is $90.00

Chemung Town/Village Courts- Ashland Town Court 3663 6th St, Wellsburg, NY 14894; 607-398-7119 9AM-2PM M-T; N-5PM W-TH. **Baldwin Town Court** 622 Breesport N Chemung Rd, Lowman, NY 14861; 607-398-7208 ext 1 1st & 3rd Tuesday 6:00PM. **Big Flats Town Court** 476 Maple St, PO Box 449, Big Flats, NY 14814; 607-562-8443 x233 8AM-N; 12:45PM-4PM. **Catlin Town Court** 1448 Chambers Rd, Beaver Dams, NY 14812; 607-739-5598 6:30PM-? W. **Chemung Town Court** 48 Rotary Rd Ext, Chemung, NY 14825; 607-529-3532 x2 Clerk hours 10am - 4pm M-Thursday Court 7:00pm Thursday. **Elmira Heights Village Court** 215 Elmwood Ave, Elmira Heights, NY 14903; 607-737-6750 9!M-4PM T,W; 9-11AM TH. **Elmira Town Court** 1255 W Water St, Elmira, NY 14905; 607-734-5971 8:30AM-3:30PM; W eve- 7:30PM. **Erin Town Court** 1138 Breesport Rd, Erin, NY 14838; 607-739-3313 x2 3:30-9PM M. **Horseheads Town Court** 150 Wygant Rd, Horseheads, NY 14845; 607-739-2113 8am-11:30 & 1:00-3:45 M-F. **Horseheads Village Court** 202 S Main St, Horseheads, NY 14845; 607-739-0158 9AM-12:30PM; 1:30-3PM. **Southport Town Court** 1139 Pennsylvania Ave, Elmira, NY 14904; 607-734-4446 8:30AM-4:30PM. **Van Etten Town Court** PO Box 177, 83 Main St., Van Etten, NY 14889; 607-589-4925 6PM-7PM W. **Veteran Town Court** 4049 Watkins Rd, PO Box 92, Millport, NY 14864; 607-739-3337 6:30-8PM W. **Wellsburg Village Court** 3663 6th St, Wellsburg, NY 14894; 607-732-0723 ext 6 M-T9-2pm W-Thru 12-5pm closed Fri..

Chenango County

County Clerk County Office Bldg, 1st Fl, 5 Court St, Norwich, NY 13815-1676; 607-337-1450; fax: 607-337-1455; 8:30AM-5PM (EST). *Felony, Civil.*

www.co.chenango.ny.us

General Information: Countywide search requests made to the County Clerk are processed in the manner described below. No sealed, expunged, adoption, sex offense, juvenile or mental health records released. Will fax documents $4.00 per page plus copy fee. Court makes copy: $.65 per page, $1.30 minimum. Certification fee: $1.25 per page, $5.00 minimum. Payee: County Clerk. Personal checks accepted, credit cards are not. Prepayment required. Mail requests: SASE required.

Civil Name Search: Access: Mail, in person, online. Both court and visitors may perform in person name searches. Search fee: $5.00 per name. Fee is per 2 years searched. Civil records on computer from 1990, prior in books since 1880. Mail turnaround Time 1 week. Civil PAT goes back to 1994. Lookup current or pending Supreme Court civil cases at http://iapps.courts.state.ny.us/webcivil/FCASMain.

Criminal Name Search: Access: Mail, in person. Both court and visitors may perform in person name searches. Search fee: $5.00 per name. Fee is per 2 years searched. Required to search: name, years to search, DOB. Criminal records in docket books. Mail turnaround Time 1 week. Criminal PAT goes back to 2004.

Supreme & County Court County Office Bldg, 5 Court St, Norwich, NY 13815-1676; 607-337-1457; fax: 607-337-1835; 8:30AM-5PM (EST). *Felony, Civil.*

General Information: This court does not hold closed case records. It directs criminal search requests to the OCA for a $65.00 statewide record check. However, for a countywide search, see the County Clerk in a separate listing.

Norwich City Court One Court Plaza, Norwich, NY 13815; 607-334-1224; fax: 607-334-8494; 8:45AM-4PM (EST). *Misdemeanor, Civil Actions under $15,000, Eviction, Small Claims, Traffic.*

www.nycourts.gov/courts/6jd/chenango/norwich/index.shtml

General Information: No sealed, expunged, adoption, sex offense, juvenile or mental health records released. Will fax documents to local or toll free line. Court makes copy: $.65 per page; minimum $1.30. Certification fee: $5.00 per doc plus copy fee. Payee: Norwich City Court. Business checks accepted. No personal check accepted. Visa/MC accepted. Prepayment required. Mail requests: SASE required.

Civil Name Search: Access: Fax, mail, in person, online. Only the court performs in person name searches; visitors may not. No search fee. Civil cases indexed by defendant. Civil records on computer from 1990, prior in books. Mail turnaround Time 5-7 days. WebCivil Local at http://iapps.courts.state.ny.us/webcivil/ecourtsMain contains information on both active and disposed Civil Court cases. Search by index number, party name, attorney/firm name or judge. No fee.

Criminal Name Search: Access: Mail, in person, online. Only the court performs in person name searches; visitors may not. Search fee: Clerk here will provide $5.00 Certificate of Disposition only. Criminal records go back to 1930's. Name search requests are often directed to the OCA for statewide record search, $65.00 search fee. See www.nycourts.gov/apps/chrs.

Surrogate's Court County Office Bldg, 5 Court St, Norwich, NY 13815; 607-337-1822/1827; fax: 646-963-6603; 8:30AM-4:30PM (EST). *Probate.*

www.nycourts.gov/courts/6jd/chenango/surrogate.shtml

General Information: A county search of the probate court index by mail for 25-year search is $30.00 fee. A full county probate search of all years is $90.00.

Chenango Town/Village Courts Afton Town Court PO Box 108, 19 Court St, Afton, NY 13730; 607-639-2505; 4-9PM W (EST). **Bainbridge Town & Village Court** 15 N Main St, Bainbridge, NY 13733; 607-967-7465; 9AM-4PM M; 9AM-N T,F; 1-4PM TH (EST). **Columbus Town Court** P.O. Box 916,, New Berlin, NY 13411; 607-847-9970; 1st and 3rd Monday (EST). **Coventry Town Court** 1839 State Highway 235, Greene, NY 13778; 607-656-8602; 7-9PM W (EST). **Earlville Village Court** PO Box 88, 8 North Main St, Earlville, NY 13332; 315-691-6020. **German Town Court** 227 Maroney Rd, McDonough, NY 13801; 607-863-3299. **Greene Town Court** PO Box 129, 51 Genesee St, Greene, NY 13778; 607-656-4333; 7 PM TH (EST). **Greene Village Court** 49 Genesee St, Greene, NY 13778; 607-656-4544; 9AM-N (EST). **Guilford Town Court** 233Marble Rd, Town Hall, Guilford, NY 13780; 607-895-6831; 7-8PM T-TH (EST). **Lincklaen Town Court** 1675 County Rte 12, Lincklaen Town Hall, DeRuyter, NY 13052; 315-852-6043; 7-9PM T (EST). **McDonough Town Court** PO Box 75, McDonough, NY 13801; 607-843-9772. **New Berlin Town Court** PO Box 308, 30 N Main St, New Berlin, NY 13411; 607-847-8962; 9AM-N M,W,TH,F; 1PM-4PM T (EST). **North Norwich Town Court** PO Box 176, North Norwich, NY 13814; 607-334-5994; 6:30PM-? TH (EST). **Norwich Town Court** 157 County Rd 32A, Town Hall, Norwich, NY 13815; 607-337-2305; W, TH 5:30PM-? (EST). **Otselic Town Court** 133 County Rd 13, South Otselic, NY 13155; 315-653-7201; 7PM T (EST). **Oxford Town Court** PO Box 1224, 20 Lafayette Park, Oxford, NY 13830; 607-843-9757; 4-6PM M&TH (EST). **Oxford Village Court** PO Box 1203, 20 Lafayette Park, Rear, Oxford, NY 13830; 607-843-9772; 6PM-? T (EST). **Pharsalia Town Court** PO Box 39, 1050 County Rd 8, East Pharsalia, NY 13758; 607-647-5081; 7PM TH (EST). **Pitcher Town Court** PO Box 97, 145 Town Hall Rd, Pitcher, NY 13136; 607-863-4350; 9AM-5PM (EST). **Plymouth Town Court** 3461 State Hwy 23, PO Box 27, Plymouth, NY 13832-0027; 607-334-3938. **Preston Town Court** 387 County Rte 10A, Norwich, NY 13815-3613; 607-334-9334; 7PM T (EST). **Sherburne Town & Village Court** PO Box 860, Canal St Town Hall, Sherburne, NY 13460; 607-674-4827. **Smithville Town Court** PO Box 217, 5285 State Hwy 41, Smithville, NY 13841; 607-656-7969; 7PM Th (EST). **Smyrna Town Court** 103 Quaker Hill Rd, Smyrna, NY 13464; 607-627-6808.

Clinton County

County Clerk County Government Ctr, 137 Margaret St, 1st Fl, Plattsburgh, NY 12901; 518-565-4700; fax: 518-565-4718; 8AM-5PM (EST). *Civil.*

www.clintoncountygov.com

General Information: This County Clerk does not have a separate index of felony records; see the Supreme and County Court. No sealed or sex case records released. Will fax out specific case files for a fee, call first. Court makes copy: $.65 per page; $1.30 minimum. Certification fee: $1.25 per page, minimum $5.00. Payee: County Clerk. Personal checks accepted, credit cards are not. Prepayment required.

Civil Name Search: Access: Mail, in person, online. Visitors must perform in person searches themselves. Search fee: $5.00. Civil cases indexed by defendant, plaintiff; by defendant only pre-May 2004. Civil records in docket books up to 2003; on computer 2003 to present. Public use terminal has civil records back to 2003. Online access to current/pending civil cases is free at http://iapps.courts.state.ny.us/webcivil/ecourtsMain.

Criminal Name Search: Access: Mail, in person. Both court and visitors may perform in person name searches. Criminal records computerized from 1986, prior in docket books from 1961. Note: Will not perform name searches.

Supreme Court County Government Ctr, 137 Margaret St, #311, Plattsburgh, NY 12901; 518-565-4715; fax: 518-565-4708; 9AM-4:45PM (EST). *Felony, Civil.*

www.nycourts.gov/courts/4jd/clinton/index.shtml

General Information: This court directs criminal search requests to the OCA for a $65.00 statewide record check. However, for a countywide search of civil records, see the County Clerk in a separate listing. No sealed or sex case records released. Will fax out specific case files to local or toll free line. Court makes copy: $.50 per page. Certification fee: $5.00 up to 4 pages, $1.25 each add'l page. Payee: County Clerk. Personal checks accepted. Prepayment required. Mail requests: SASE required.

Civil Name Search: Access: In person, online. Visitors must perform in person searches themselves. Civil cases indexed by defendant. Civil records in docket books. Historical records are not online, but access to current/pending Supreme Court civil cases is at http://iapps.courts.state.ny.us/webcivil/FCASMain

Criminal Name Search: Access: In person, online. Visitors must perform in person searches themselves. Required to search: name, years to search, DOB. Criminal records computerized from 1986, prior in docket books from 1961. Mail turnaround Time 3-4 days. Online access is via the state OCA statewide system. Fee is $65.00 per search. See www.nycourts.gov/apps/chrs/.

Plattsburg City Court 24 US Oval, Plattsburgh, NY 12903; 518-563-7870; fax: 518-563-3124; 8AM-3:45PM (EST). *Misdemeanor, Civil Actions under $15,000, Eviction, Small Claims, Traffic.* www.nycourts.gov/courts/4jd/plattsburgh_city/index.shtml

General Information: No sealed records released. Court makes copy: $.65 per page.Minimum $1.30 Certification fee: $15.00 per certificate. Payee: City Court. Only cashiers checks and money orders accepted. Visa/MC accepted. Prepayment required. Mail requests: SASE required.

Civil Name Search: Access: Mail, in person, online. Only the court performs in person name searches; visitors may not. Search fee: $5.00. A Certificate of Disposition is $6.00 per name. Civil cases indexed by defendant. Civil records on computer back to 1985, prior in books. WebCivil Local at http://iapps.courts.state.ny.us/webcivil/ecourtsMain contains information on both active and disposed Civil Court cases. Search by index number, party name, attorney/firm name or judge. No fee.

Criminal Name Search: Access: Online. Only the court performs in person name searches; visitors may not. Records available on computer since 1986, prior in books. Note: The court will not support name searches unless specific case file given. All criminal record name search requests are directed to the OCA for statewide record search, $65.00 search fee. See www.nycourts.gov/apps/chrs. Be aware that the state system does not include certain "violation" records, this court does allow an in person hand search.

Surrogate's Court 137 Margaret St, #315, Plattsburgh, NY 12901-2933; 518-565-4630; fax: 518-565-4769; 9AM-5PM (EST). *Probate.*

General Information: A county search of the probate court index by mail for 25-year search is $30.00 fee. A full county probate search of all years is $90.00. Records also in the court are guardianship and adoption.

Clinton Town/Village Courts- Altona Town Court PO Box 79, Altona, NY 12910; 518-236-7035 7PM T. **Au Sable Town Court** 111 Au Sable St, Keeseville, NY 12944; 518-834-6095 7:30AM-4:30PM. **Beekmantown Town Court** 571 Spellman Rd, West Chazy, NY 12992; 518-563-9930 7AM-3PM M,T,TH; 10AM-6PM W; Closed F. **Black Brook Town Court** PO Box 715, Au Sable Forks, NY 12912; 518-647-5411 x25 Wed 4PM. **Champlain Town Court** PO Box 3144, 729 Route 9, Champlain, NY 12919; 518-298-8160 x207 8AM-2PM. **Chazy Town Court** PO Box 219, 9631 Rte 9, Chazy, NY 12921; 518-846-8600 6:30PM T. **Clinton Town Court** 470 Campbell ', PO Box 141, Churubusco, NY 12923; 518-497-3015 Open 1st & 3rd Sat of month. **Dannemora Town Court** PO Box 658, 1168 Cook St, Dannemora, NY 12929; 518-492-7541 ext: 105 **Dannemora Village Court** PO Box 566, 121 Emman St, Dannemora, NY 12929; 518-492-7000 7-9PM T. **Ellenburg Town Court** PO Box 142, 16 St Edmunds Way #9, Ellenburg, NY 12933; 518-594-7177 6PM TH. **Keeseville Village Court** 1790 Main St, Keeseville, NY 12944; 518-834-9059 10:30AM-1:30PM. **Mooers Town Court** PO Box 403, 2508 Rte 11, Mooers, NY 12958; 518-236-7927 8AM-4:30PM M,W,TH; 6PM-? TH. **Peru Town Court** 3036 Main St, Peru, NY 12972; 518-643-2745 x1 Noon-3PM Mon; 8AM-1PM T,W,TH; Fri by appointment. **Plattsburgh Town Court** 151 Banker Rd, Plattsburgh, NY 12901; 518-562-6870 9AM-4PM. **Rouses Point Village Court** PO Box 185, 39 Lake St, Rouses Point, NY 12979; 518-297-6648 x334 8AM-3PM M-W; T eve 5PM-?. **Saranac Town Court** PO Box 147, Town Hall, Saranac, NY 12981; 518-293-8082 **Schuyler Falls Town Court** PO Box 99, 997 Mason St, Morrisonville, NY 12962; 518-563-9066 5 PM-TH.

Columbia County

County Clerk 560 Warren St, Hudson, NY 12534; 518-828-3339; fax: 518-828-5299; 9AM-4:45PM (EST). *Felony, Civil.*

General Information: Supreme and County courts are actually located at 401 Union in Hudson, but records for both courts are located at the County Clerk's Office as listed above. No sealed records released. Will not fax documents. Court makes copy: $.65 per page. Self serve copy: $.25 per page. Certification fee: $5.00. Payee: Columbia County Clerk. Personal checks accepted if name imprinted. No credit cards accepted. Prepayment required. Mail requests: SASE required.

Civil Name Search: Access: Mail, in person, online. Both court and visitors may perform in person name searches. Search fee: $5.00 per name. Fee is per 2 years searched. Civil cases indexed by defendant. Civil records on computer from 1993, prior on cards to 1985. Mail turnaround Time 1 week. Civil PAT goes back to 1993. Lookup current or pending Supreme Court civil cases at http://iapps.courts.state.ny.us/webcivil/FCASMain.

Criminal Name Search: Access: Mail, in person. Both court and visitors may perform in person name searches. Search fee: $5.00 per name. Fee is for 10 years searched. Criminal records computerized from 1993, prior on cards to 1985. Note: Supreme and County courts are actually located at 401 Union in Hudson, but records for both courts are located at the County Clerk's Office as listed above. Mail turnaround Time 3 weeks. Criminal PAT goes back to same as civil.

Supreme & County Court 401 Union St, Hudson, NY 12534; 518-828-7858; fax: 518-828-1603; 9AM-5PM (EST). *Felony, Civil.*

General Information: This court does not hold closed case records. It directs criminal search requests to the OCA for a $65.00 statewide record check. However, for a countywide search, see the County Clerk in a separate listing.

Hudson City Court 429 Warren St, Hudson, NY 12534; 518-828-3100; fax: 518-828-3628; 8AM-3:30PM (EST). *Misdemeanor, Civil Actions under $15,000, Eviction, Small Claims.* www.nycourts.gov/courts/3jd/

General Information: No sealed, expunged, adoption, sex offense, juvenile or mental health records released. Will fax documents to local or toll free line. Court makes copy: $.65 per page. Certification fee: $5.00. Payee: Hudson City Court. Business checks accepted. Major credit cards accepted. Prepayment required. Mail requests: SASE required for civil.

Civil Name Search: Access: Fax, mail, in person, online. Only the court performs in person name searches; visitors may not. Search fee: $16.00 per name. Required to search: name, years to search; also helpful: address. Civil records on computer from 1991, prior in books. Mail turnaround Time 5-7 days. WebCivil Local at http://iapps.courts.state.ny.us/webcivil/ecourtsMain contains information on both active and disposed Civil Court cases. Search by index number, party name, attorney/firm name or judge. No fee.

Criminal Name Search: Access: Online. Criminal records computerized from 1991, prior in books. All criminal record name search requests are directed to the OCA for statewide record search, $65.00 search fee. See www.nycourts.gov/apps/chrs.

Surrogate's Court 401 Union St, Courthouse, Hudson, NY 12534; 518-828-0414; fax: 518-828-1603; 9AM-5PM (EST). *Probate.*

General Information: A county search of the probate court index by mail for 25-year search is $30.00 fee. A full county probate search of all years is $90.00.

Columbia Town/Village Courts-Ancram Town Court 1416 County Rte 7, Ancram, NY 12502; 518-329-6512 2 6-8PM W. **Austerlitz Town Court** PO Box 119, 812 Route 203, Spencertown, NY 12165; 518-392-3260 x 302 3:30PM-8PM W; 2PM-6PM F. **Canaan Town Court** PO Box 59, County Rte 5, Canaan, NY 12029; 518-781-3749 10AM-2PM M,W,TH,F. **Chatham Town Court** PO Box 326, 77 Main St, 2nd Fl, Chatham, NY 12037; 518-392-5440 8AM-4PM. **Chatham Village Court** 77 Main St, Chatham, NY 12037; 518-392-5821 8:30AM-4:00PM. **Claverack Town Court** PO Box 823, 836 Route 217, Philmont, NY 12565; 518-672-4468 8:30AM-2:30PM M-TH; 8AM-N F. **Clermont Town Court** 1795 RR 9, Town Hall, Germantown, NY 12526; 518-537-6868 x503/x505 1st 2nd & 3rd Thurs 6pm-8pm 4th Thurs 5pm-6:30pm Sat.10am-12. **Copake Town Court** 230 Mountain View Rd, Town Hall, Copake, NY 12516; 518-329-1234 x3 9AM-12:30PM 1PM-3PM M-TH; 9AM-1 F;. **Gallatin Town Court** PO Box 240, Town Hall, County Rte 2 and Jackson Cors Rd, Ancram, NY 12502; 518-398-7690 4PM- W. **Germantown Town Court** 50 Palatine Park Rd, Germantown, NY 12526; 518-537-6687 ext303 or 304 Wed 6-8PM. **Ghent Town Court** 2306 Rte 66, Ghent, NY 12075; 518-392-2706 6:30PM M. **Greenport Town Court** 600 Town Hall Dr, Hudson, NY 12534; 518-828--0138 8:30AM-4PM M-W; 1:30PM-4PM F. **Hillsdale Town Court** PO Box 305, 2684 Route 23, Town Hall, Hillsdale, NY 12529; 518-325-5073 8:30AM-N; 1-4:00PM M,T,Thur,Fri. **Kinderhook Town & Village Court** PO Box 325, 6 Chatham St, Kinderhook, NY 12106; 518-758-8778 ext 303 T-Thurs 9:30 - 12:30. **Livingston Town Court** PO Box 44, 119 County Rte 19, Town Hall, Livingston, NY 12541; 518-851-7210 x312 7PM-? TH Court; Clerk-10AM-2PM F. **New Lebanon Town Court** PO Box 247, 7 Mill Rd, New Lebanon, NY 12125; 518-794-9456 11AM-5PM T; Court on TH 4PM. **Philmont Village Court** PO Box 822, 122 Main St, Philmont, NY 12565; 518-672-4886 9:30AM-3PM TH-F; Thurs eves 6PM-?. **Stockport Town Court** 2787 Atlantic Ave, Hudson, NY 12534; 518-822-8009 6:30PM-9PM M (Court hrs). **Stuyvesant Town Court** PO Box 33, 5 Sunset Dr, Stuyvesant, NY 12173; 518-758-6248 x12 **Taghkanic Town Court** 909 Rt 82, Town Hall, Ancram, NY 12502; 518-851-7638 ext 305 6PM TH. **Valatie Village Court** PO Box 122, Spring & Main St, Valatie, NY 12184; 518-758-9806 10AM-4PM M-TH; 6PM-8PM W.

Cortland County

County Clerk 46 Greenbush St, #105, Cortland, NY 13045; 607-753-5021; fax: 607-753-5378; 9PM-5PM (EST). *Felony, Civil.* www.cortland-co.org/cc/index.htm

General Information: Countywide search requests made to the County Clerk are processed in the manner described below. The fax number is not for public use. No sealed or youthful offender records released. Will not fax documents. Court makes copy: $.65 per page. $1.30 minimum. Self serve copy: same. Certification fee: $1.25 per page, $5.00 minimum. Payee: County Clerk. Personal checks accepted. Major credit cards accepted but there is a surcharge. Prepayment required. Mail requests: SASE required.

Civil Name Search: Access: Mail, in person, online. Both court and visitors may perform in person name searches. Search fee: $5.00 per name per 2 years. Civil records on computer from 5/94, prior in books. Mail turnaround Time 2 days. Public use terminal has civil records back to May 1994. Online access to index on a number of records is at www.searchiqs.com/cortland/login.aspx Also, access to current/pending WebCivil Supreme Court civil cases is at http://iapps.courts.state.ny.us/webcivil/FCASMain.

Criminal Name Search: Access: Mail, in person, online. Only the court performs in person name searches; visitors may not. Search fee: $5.00 per name per 2 years. Required to search: name, years to search, DOB. Criminal records in books. Mail turnaround Time 2 days. Access to county criminal courts index at www.searchiqs.com/cortland/login.aspx

Supreme & County Court 46 Greenbush St, #301, Cortland, NY 13045; 607-753-5013; fax: 646-963-6452; 9AM-5PM (in July/Aug 8:30AM-4:30PM) (EST). *Felony, Civil.*
www.courts.state.ny.us/courts/6jd/cortland/supreme.shtml
General Information: Direct record search requests to the County Clerk, see separate listing. Online access to current/pending Supreme Court civil cases is at http://iapps.courts.state.ny.us/webcivil/FCASMain. Criminal online access is via the state OCA statewide system.

Cortland City Court 25 Court St, Cortland, NY 13045; 607-428-5420; fax: 607-428-5435; 8:15AM-4PM (EST). *Misdemeanor, Civil Actions under $15,000, Eviction, Small Claims.*
www.cortland.org/city/court.htm
General Information: No sealed records released. Will fax documents to local or toll free line. Court makes copy: $.65 per page; $1.65 minimum. Certification fee: $6.00 per doc; may be $5.00 if in person. Payee: Cortland City Court. No Personal checks, Visa/MC accepted. Prepayment required. Mail requests: SASE required.
Civil Name Search: Access: Mail, in person, online. Only the court performs in person name searches; visitors may not. Search fee: $5.00 per name per 2 years. Civil cases indexed by defendant. Civil records on computer from 1991, prior in books. Mail turnaround Time 10 days. WebCivil Local at http://iapps.courts.state.ny.us/webcivil/ecourtsMain contains information on both active and disposed Civil Court cases form 2007. Search by index number, party name, attorney/firm name or judge. No fee.
Criminal Name Search: Access: Mail, in person, online. Only the court performs in person name searches; visitors may not. Search fee: For violations only- $5.00 per name per 2 years. Certificate of Disposition- $5.00. Required to search: name, years to search, DOB. Criminal records computerized from 1991, prior in books. Note: The court does not permit access to "fingerprint able records" unless specific case file given. Mail turnaround Time 10 days. All criminal record name search requests are directed to the OCA for statewide record search, $65.00 search fee. See www.nycourts.gov/apps/chrs.

Surrogate's Court 46 Greenbush St, #301, Cortland, NY 13045; 607-759-5556; fax: 607-753-1899; 9AM-5PM; 8:30-4:30 July-Sept 3 (EST). *Probate.*
www.nycourts.gov/courts/6jd/cortland/surrogate.shtml
General Information: A county search of the probate court index by mail for 25-year search is $30.00 fee. A full county probate search of all years is $90.00.
Cortland Town/Village Courts-Cincinnatus Town Court 3228 Route 26, Box 202, Cincinnatus, NY 13040; 607-863-4466 7PM-9PM W. **Cortlandville Town Court** 3577 Terrace Rd, Cortland, NY 13045; 607-756-2352 8:30AM-4:30PM. **Cuyler Town Court** PO Box 363, 4710 Route 13, Cuyler, DeRuyter, NY 13052; 607-423-1985 cell No set hours. **Freetown Town Court** 3900 Freetown Crossing Rd, Town Hall, Marathon, NY 13803; 607-849-6350 . 1st Wed 9AM-?. **Harford Town Court** PO Box 10, Harford, NY 13784; 518-844-4091 8AM-3PM T-F. **Homer Town Court** 4 Water St, Homer, NY 13077; 607-749-2326 9AM-2PM T&TH. **Lapeer Town Court** 1269 Parker St, Clarks Corners Rd Town Garage, Marathon, NY 13803; 607-743-3313 **Marathon Town Court** PO Box 366, 18 Brink St, Marathon, NY 13803; 607-849-6966/6960 9AM-N M-F; Wed-6:30PM. **Preble Town Court** PO Box 117, Preble, NY 13141; 607-749-2377 9AM-N ; 1PM-4PM M,W. **Scott Town Court** Town Hall, 6689 Route 41, Homer, NY 13077; 607-749-2902 6-8PM M,TH court hours. **Solon Town Court** 4012 N Tower Rd, Cincinnatus, NY 13040; 607-836-6798 **Taylor Town Court** 3854 Cheningo Solon Pond Rd, Town Barn, Cincinnatus, NY 13040; 607-863-3556 2nd Tues 7:00PM. **Truxton Town Court** PO Box 84, 3767 Prospect St, Truxton, NY 13158; 607-842-6262 or 6984 3rd Wed 7:00PM. **Virgil Town Court** 1176 Church St, Cortland, NY 13045; 607-835-6587 5PM-7PM T, 9AM-N Wed. **Willet Town Court** PO Box 37, 1425-1427 Route 41, Town Hall, Willet, NY 13863; 607-863-3261 2nd & 4th W 6-8PM.

Delaware County

County Clerk PO Box 426, 3 Court St, Delhi, NY 13753; 607-746-2123; fax: 607-746-6924; 8:30AM-5PM; Bldg hours- 9:15AM-4:30PM (EST). *Felony, Civil.*
www.co.delaware.ny.us/departments/clerk/clerk.htm
General Information: Countywide search requests made to the County Clerk are processed in the manner described below. No sealed records released. Will not fax documents. Court makes copy: $1.00 per page. Certification fee: $4.00 for judge's signature, then $1.00 per page. Payee: Delaware County Clerk. Personal checks accepted, credit cards are not. Prepayment required. Mail requests: SASE required.
Civil Name Search: Access: In person, online. Visitors must perform in person searches themselves. Civil cases indexed by defendant. Civil records in books. Civil PAT goes back to 2/2008. Lookup current or pending Supreme Court civil cases at http://iapps.courts.state.ny.us/webcivil/FCASMain.
Criminal Name Search: Access: Mail, in person. Visitors must perform in person searches themselves. Search fee: $10.00 per name. Required to search: name, years to search, DOB. Criminal records in books. Note: Misdemeanor records are maintained by city, town, and village courts. Mail turnaround Time 2 days. Criminal PAT goes back to 2/2008.

Supreme & County Court 3 Court St, Delhi, NY 13753; 607-746-2131; 9AM-5PM (EST). *Felony, Civil.*
www.co.delaware.ny.us/
General Information: Direct record search requests to the County Clerk, see separate listing. Online access to current/pending Supreme Court civil cases is at http://iapps.courts.state.ny.us/webcivil/FCASMain. Criminal online access is via the state OCA statewide system.

Surrogate's Court 3 Court St, Delhi, NY 13753; 607-746-2126; fax: 607-963-6403; 9AM-12; 1PM-5PM (EST). *Probate.*
General Information: A county search of the probate court index by mail for 25-year search is $30.00 fee. A full county probate search of all years is $90.00.
Delaware Town/Village Courts- Andes Town Court PO Box 335, 580 State Hwy 28, Andes, NY 13731; 845-676-3550 7PM TH; ofc open 2PM TH. **Bovina Town Court** PO Box 1, Bovina Center, NY 13740; 607-832-4500 **Colchester Town Court** PO Box 321, 72 Tannery Rd, Downsville, NY 13755; 607-363-7169 **Davenport Town Court** PO Box 131, 11790 St Hwy 23, Davenport Center, NY 13751; 607-278-5101 2-4PM. **Delhi Town Court** 9 Court St, Delhi, NY 13753; 607-746-7278 8AM-4PM. **Deposit Town Court** 333 State Highway 10, Deposit, NY 13754; 607-467-3233 4:30-7PM T. **Franklin Town Court** PO Box 941, Franklin, NY 13775; 607-829-3440 8:30AM-11AM M,T. **Hamden Town Court** PO Box 37, Hamden, NY 13782; 607-746-6660 M 5:30PM. **Hancock Town Court** 661 W Main St, Hancock, NY 13783; 607-637-3650 7PM-9PM 10AM-2PM Tues. 3 - 5PM TH. **Hancock Village Court** 85 E Front St, Hancock, NY 13783; 607-637-5789 5-7PM W. **Harpersfield Town Court** 25399 State Hwy 23, Harpersfield, NY 13786; 607-652-5060 **Kortright Town Court** PO Box 6, 51702 State Highway 10, Bloomville, NY 13739; 607-538-9319 4-9PM 1st, 2nd, 3rd T. **Masonville Town Court** PO Box 63, Town Bldg-Route 206 West, Masonville, NY 13804; 607-265-9249 **Meredith Town Court** PO Box 116, 4247 Turnpike Rd, Meridale, NY 13806; 607-746-2431 9AM-3PM T,W, TH; 10AM-2PM Mon. **Middletown Town Court** PO Box 839, 42339 State Hwy 28, Margaretville, NY 12455; 845-586-2575 9AM-Noon. **Roxbury Town Court** PO Box C, Grand Gorge Civic Ctr, Grand Gorge, NY 12434; 607-588-7507 M 7PM W 9AM. **Sidney Town Court** Civic Center, 21 Liberty St #4, Sidney, NY 13838; 607-561-2309 2nd &4th Th 9AM-N. **Sidney Village Court** 21 Liberty St, #4, Sidney, NY 13838; 607-561-2309 9AM-N Tue. **Stamford Town Court** PO Box M, 101 Maple Ave, Hobart, NY 13788; 607-538-1825 2nd T monthly. **Stamford Village Court** 84 Main St, Village Hall, Stamford, NY 12167; 607-652-2804 8:30AM-4:30PM. **Tompkins Town Court** PO Box 78, 8688 St Hwy 206, Sidney Center, NY 13839; 607-865-4949 1PM-? T,TH. **Walton Town Court** 129 North St, Walton, NY 13856; 607-865-5182 7PM-? W. **Walton Village Court** PO Box 27, 21 North St, Walton, NY 13856; 607-865-6150 9-11AM, 6-8PM TH.

Dutchess County

County Clerk 22 Market St, 2nd Fl, Poughkeepsie, NY 12601-3203; 845-486-2139- records; main- 845-486-2120; 9AM-5PM (EST). *Felony, Civil.*
www.co.dutchess.ny.us/CountyGov/Departments/CountyClerk/CCIndex.htm
General Information: Countywide search requests made to the County Clerk are processed in the manner described below. Civil search requests are considered separate for criminal searches. No sealed or youthful offender records released. Will not fax documents. Court makes copy: $.65 per page; $1.30 minimum. Self serve copy: $.25 per page. Certification fee: $5.00 per doc for 4 pages ($11.00 if mailed); add $1.25 each add'l page. Payee:

Dutchess County Clerk. Personal checks accepted, credit cards are not. Prepayment required. Mail requests: SASE required.

Civil Name Search: Access: Mail, in person, online. Visitors must perform in person searches themselves. Search fee: $5.00 per name per every two years or part of two years searched. Civil records in books back to 1847; on computer back to 1986. Mail turnaround Time 1 week Public use terminal available, records go back to 1987. Access to current/pending WebCivil Supreme Court civil cases is free at http://iapps.courts.state.ny.us/webcivil/FCASMain. Also, access to civil, criminal and recording office records is to be available by subscription from the county. Fee will be $35.00 monthly; civil records back to 1986 and criminal back to 1987. Contact Andee Fountain (845-486-2397) for additional information.

Criminal Name Search: Access: Mail, in person. Both court and visitors may perform in person name searches. Search fee: $5.00 per name per every two years or part of two years searched. Required to search: name, years to search, aliases. Criminal records go back to 1847; on computer back to 1987. Note: They will only create a certificate if their staff performs the search. Mail turnaround Time 2 weeks. Public use terminal available, crim records go back to 1987. Online access is the same as civil; subscriber or login as guest to search eCourts WebCrims future appearances system at http://iapps.courts.state.ny.us/webcrim_attorney/Login.

Supreme & County Court 10 Market St, Poughkeepsie, NY 12601-3203; 845-4431-1710; fax: 845-473-5403; 9AM-5PM (EST). *Felony, Civil.*

www.nycourts.gov/courts/9jd/dutchess/index.shtml

General Information: For countywide record search, see the County Clerk, otherwise this court recommends the $65.00 statewide search via the OCA. Current/pending Supreme Court civil cases are online at http://iapps.courts.state.ny.us/webcivil/FCASMain.

Beacon City Court 1 Municipal Plaza, #2, Beacon, NY 12508; 845-838-5030; fax: 845-838-5041; 8AM-4PM (EST). *Misdemeanor, Civil Actions under $15,000, Eviction, Small Claims.*

https://www.nycourts.gov/courts/9jd/dutchess/Beacon.shtml

General Information: No sealed or youthful offender records released. Will fax documents to local or toll-free number. Court makes copy: $.65 per page; $1.30 minimum. Certification fee: $5.00 for criminal; $6.00 if civil. Payee: City Court of Beacon. Only cashiers checks and money orders accepted. Visa/MC accepted. Prepayment required.

Civil Name Search: Access: Mail, fax, in person, online. Both court and visitors may perform in person name searches. No search fee. Required to search: name, DOB, years to search; also helpful- address. Civil records on computer from 1996, prior in books and cards. Mail turnaround Time 2 weeks Civil PAT goes back to 1996. Public terminal is in the County Clerk's office. WebCivil Local at http://iapps.courts.state.ny.us/webcivil/ecourtsMain contains information on both active and disposed Civil Court cases. Search by index number, party name, attorney/firm name or judge. No fee.

Criminal Name Search: Access: Mail, in person, online. Search fee: $5.00 per 2 years. A Certificate of Disposition is $5.00; signed release required. Mail turnaround Time is 2 weeks. Criminal PAT goes back to same as civil. Limited name searches, most name search requests are directed to the OCA for statewide record search, $65.00 search fee. See www.nycourts.gov/apps/chrs.

Poughkeepsie City Court 62 Civic Center Plaza, Poughkeepsie, NY 12601; 845-483-8200; fax: 845-485-6795; 8AM-4PM; counter until 3:30PM (EST). *Misdemeanor, Civil Actions under $15,000, Eviction, Small Claims.*

General Information: No sealed, expunged, adoption, sex offense, juvenile or mental health records released. Will not fax documents. Court makes copy: $.65 per page, $1.30 minimum. Certification fee: $5.00. Payee: Poughkeepsie City Court. Cashiers checks and money orders accepted. Visa/MC accepted. Prepayment required. Mail requests: SASE required.

Civil Name Search: Access: Mail, in person, online. Both court and visitors may perform in person name searches. Search fee: $5.00 per name per 2 years searched. $5.00 for certificate of disposition. Civil cases indexed by defendant. Civil records on computer from 1993. WebCivil Local at http://iapps.courts.state.ny.us/webcivil/ecourtsMain contains information on both active and disposed Civil Court cases. Search by index number, party name, attorney/firm name or judge. No fee.

Criminal Name Search: Access: Mail, in person, online. Both court and visitors may perform in person name searches. Search fee: $5.00 per name for Certificate of Disposition only. Criminal records computerized from 1990. Mail turnaround Time 2 weeks. Name search requests are often directed to the OCA for statewide record search, $65.00 search fee. See www.nycourts.gov/apps/chrs.

Surrogate's Court 10 Market St, Poughkeepsie, NY 12601; 845-431-1770; fax: 845-486-2234; 9AM-5PM (EST). *Probate.*

www.nycourts.gov/courts/9jd/dutchess/index.shtml

General Information: A county search of the probate court index by mail for 25-year search is $30.00 fee. A full county probate search of all years is $90.00.

Dutchess Town/Village Courts- **Amenia Town Court** Town Hall, Mechanic St, PO Box 36, Amenia, NY 12501; 845-373-7017 7PM T. **Beekman Town Court** 4 Main St, Poughquag, NY 12570; 845-724-5300 x3 9AM-6PM M; 8AM-4PM TU.W; 8AM-6PM TH. **Clinton Town Court** PO Box 208, Clinton Corners, NY 12514; 845-266-5988 12-4PM M; 10AM-2PM T-W. **Dover Town Court** 126 E Duncan Hill Rd, Dover Plains, NY 12522; 845-832-3461 By app't. **East Fishkill Town Court** Town Hall, 330 Route 376, Hopewell Junction, NY 12533; 845-226-4229 8AM-3PM; court W 4PM. **Fishkill Town Court** 807 Route 52, Fishkill, NY 12524; 845-831-7860 8AM-5:15PM M-TH. **Fishkill Village Court** 1095 Main St, Fishkill, NY 12524; 845-897-2103 9AM-3PM. **Hyde Park Town Court** Town Hall, 4383 Albany Post Rd, Hyde Park, NY 12538; 845-229-5111 x106/107/108 5PM T,TH; 2nd & 4th T 8:30AM. **La Grange Town Court** 120 Stringham Rd, LaGrangeville, NY 12540; 845-452-1837 8:30AM-4PM; in session 1st & 3rd T 4PM. **Milan Town Court** 20 Wilcox Circle, Milan, NY 12571; 845-758-6960 9AM-1PM. **Millbrook Village Court** PO Box 349, 35 Merritt Ave, Millbrook, NY 12545; 845-677-8277 9AM-2PM M, 9AM-11AM & 5:30PM-6:30PM T; Court- 6PM T. **North East Town Justice Court** PO Box 516, 19 N Maple Ave, Millerton, NY 12546; 518-789-3080 9AM-2PM M-TH; T 7PM; court- 7PM T. **Pawling Town Court** 160 Charles Coleman Blvd, Pawling, NY 12564; 845-855-3516 8:30AM-4PM. **Pawling Village Court** 9 Memorial Ave, Pawling, NY 12564; 845-855-5602 8AM-N. **Pine Plains Town Court** PO Box 320, 3284 Rt. 199, Pine Plains, NY 12567; 518-398-7194 **Pleasant Valley Town Court** Town Hall, Rte 44, Main St, Pleasant Valley, NY 12569; 845-635-2856 9AM-4PM. **Poughkeepsie Town Court** 17 Tucker Dr, Poughkeepsie, NY 12603; 845-485-3690/3696 8AM-3PM M-TH; 8AM-N F. **Red Hook Town Court** 7340 S Broadway, Red Hook, NY 12571; 845-758-4611/758-4609 9AM-N Tues,TH. **Red Hook Village Court** 7467 S Broadway, Red Hook, NY 12571; 845-758-4113 1-4PM T,W; court- 1st W 6PM & 3rd W 4PM. **Rhinebeck Town Court** 80 E Market St, Rhinebeck, NY 12572; 845-876-3858 9:30AM-2:30PM M.T,W,TH. **Rhinebeck Village Court** 76 E Market St, Rhinebeck, NY 12572; 845-876-4119 9AM-12:30PM 1PM-4PM, 2nd & 4th W 7PM;. **Stanford Town Court** 26 Town Hall Rd, Stanfordville, NY 12581; 845-868-2269 9AM-1PM, 5PM-8PM. **Tivoli Village Court** PO Box 397, 86 Broadway, Tivoli, NY 12583; 845-757-3219 10AM -1:00PM Mondays. **Union Vale Town Court** Town Hall-Tymor Park, 249 Duncan Rd, LaGrangeville, NY 12540; 845-724-3288 6:30PM-9:30PM. **Wappinger Town Court** 20 Middlebush Rd, Town Hall, Wappingers Falls, NY 12590; 845-297-6070 8:30AM-4PM. **Wappingers Falls Village Court** 7 Mill St, Wappingers Falls, NY 12590; 845-297-6777 9AM-3PM M-F; Court-T,Th 6PM. **Washington Town Court** PO Box 667, 10 Reservoir Dr, Millbrook, NY 12545; 845-677-6366 1:30-3PM M-F , Court T 5PM.

Erie County

County Clerk 92 Franklin St, 1st Fl, Buffalo, NY 14202; 716-858-8865; criminal phone: 716-858-7877; civil phone: 716-858-7766; fax: 716-858-6550; 9AM-4:30PM (EST). *Felony, Civil.*

www.erie.gov/depts/government/clerk/civil_criminal.phtml

General Information: Countywide search requests made to the County Clerk are processed in the manner described below. Office now located near the 92 Franklin St entrance in old section of courthouse. No misdemeanor records located here. Online identifiers in results same as on public terminal. No sealed records released. Will not fax documents. Court makes copy: $1.00 per page. Certification fee: $4.00 per doc plus copy fee. Payee: County Clerk. Personal checks accepted, credit cards are not. Prepayment required. Mail requests: SASE required for civil.

Civil Name Search: Access: Mail, in person, online. Both court and visitors may perform in person name searches. Search fee: $5.00 per name per 2 years. Civil cases indexed by defendant. Civil records on computer from 1993, prior in books back to 1900's. Mail turnaround Time 1 week. Public use terminal has civil records back to 1993. Online access to the county clerk's database of civil judgments is free at http://ecclerk.erie.gov. Records go back to 01/93. Also, access to current/pending Supreme Court civil cases is at http://iapps.courts.state.ny.us/webcivil/ecourtsMain.

Criminal Name Search: Access: In person. Both court and visitors may perform in person name searches. No search fee. Required to search: name, years to search, DOB. Criminal records in books back to 1900's. Note: Mailed search requests directed to the OCA for $65.00 statewide record search, but Erie County clerk's office can provide a search of closed criminal records. District Attorney Offices will not supply County Clerk with conviction records. Subscribe or login as guest to search eCourts WebCrims future appearances system at http://iapps.courts.state.ny.us/webcrim_attorney/Login.

Supreme & County Court 92 Franklin St, Buffalo, NY 14202; 716-858-8865; fax: 716-858-6550; 9AM-4:45PM (EST). *Felony, Civil.*
www2.erie.gov/clerk/
General Information: Court directs civil search requests to county clerk, for crim to OCA for $65.00 state record check. Access current/pending Supreme Ct cases at http://iapps.courts.state.ny.us/ and also search pending criminal appearances.

Buffalo City Court 50 Delaware Ave, Buffalo, NY 14202; 716-845-2689; criminal phone: 716-845-2661; civil phone: 716-845-2662; criminal fax: 716-847-8257; civil fax: 9AM-5PM; 9AM-5PM (EST). *Misdemeanor, Civil Actions under $15,000, Eviction, Small Claims.*
www.city-buffalo.com/
General Information: No sealed or youthful offender records released. Will not fax documents. Court makes copy: $.65 per page; $1.30 minimum. Certification fee: $6.00 per cert. Payee: City Court. Business checks accepted. Visa/MC and debit cards accepted.
Civil Name Search: Access: In person, online. Visitors must perform in person searches themselves. Public use terminal has civil records back to 1996. WebCivil Local at http://iapps.courts.state.ny.us/webcivil/ecourtsMain contains information on both active and disposed Civil Court cases. Search by index number, party name, attorney/firm name or judge. No fee.
Criminal Name Search: Access: In person, online. Only the court performs in person name searches; visitors may not. Search fee: Clerk will do Certificate of Disposition for $5.00 per arrest. Required to search: name, DOB, date of offense. Criminal records computerized from 1983, prior in books back to 1974. Note: No general searches are performed. Search future court appearances at http://iapps.courts.state.ny.us/webcrim_attorney/Login. All criminal record name search requests are directed to the OCA for statewide record search, $65.00 search fee. See www.nycourts.gov/apps/chrs.

Lackawanna City Court 714 Ridge Rd, Lackawanna, NY 14218; 716-827-6486; criminal phone: 716-827-6487; civil phone: 716-827-6661; fax: 716-825-1874; 8:30AM-4:30PM (EST). *Misdemeanor, Civil Actions under $15,000, Eviction, Small Claims.*
www.ci.lackawanna.ny.us/
General Information: No sealed or youthful offender records released. Will not fax documents. Court makes copy: $.65 per page, $1.30 minimum. Certification fee: $6.00 per document. Payee: City Court. Cash, cashiers checks and money orders accepted for court fees. Visa/MC accepted for court fees. Prepayment required. Mail requests: SASE required.
Civil Name Search: Access: Mail, in person. Only the court performs in person name searches; visitors may not. No search fee. Required to search: name; also helpful: years to search. Civil cases indexed by defendant. Civil records on computer from 1994, prior on docket books. Note: Mail access available to government agencies only.
Criminal Name Search: Access: Online. Criminal records computerized from 1994, prior on docket books. Note: The court refuses to permit access to court records unless specific case file given; a Certificate of Disposition is $6.00. All criminal record name search requests are directed to the OCA for statewide record search, $65.00 search fee. See www.nycourts.gov/apps/chrs.

Tonawanda City Court 200 Niagara St, Tonawanda, NY 14150; 716-845-2160; fax: 716-693-1612; 8:30AM-4:30PM (EST). *Misdemeanor, Civil Actions under $15,000, Eviction, Small Claims.*
www.ci.tonawanda.ny.us/
General Information: Preliminary felonies heard here. No sealed records released. Will fax documents to local or toll-free number. Court makes copy: $.65 per page. $1.30 minimum. Certification fee: $5.00. Payee: City Court of Tonawanda. Business checks accepted. Visa/MC accepted. Prepayment required. Mail requests: SASE required.
Civil Name Search: Access: Mail, in person, online. Only the court performs in person name searches; visitors may not. No search fee. Civil records on computer since 1996, prior on index cards, in books. Mail turnaround Time 3-5 days. WebCivil Local at http://iapps.courts.state.ny.us/webcivil/ecourtsMain contains information on both active and disposed Civil Court cases. Search by index number, party name, attorney/firm name or judge. No fee.
Criminal Name Search: Access: Mail, in person, online. Only the court performs in person name searches; visitors may not. Search fee: $5.00 per name each 2 years searched. A Certificate of Disposition is $5.00. Required to search: name, years to search (case number, arrest date if Cert of Disposition). Criminal records on computer since 1986, prior on index cards, in books. Note: As a rule, the court will not permit access to its records unless specific case file given. Mail turnaround Time 3-5 days. Name

search requests are often directed to the OCA for statewide record search, $65.00 search fee. See www.nycourts.gov/apps/chrs.

Surrogate's Court 92 Franklin St, Buffalo, NY 14202; 716-845-2560; fax: 716-845-7565; 9AM-5PM (EST). *Probate.*
www.courts.state.ny.us
General Information: Public access terminals located in records room & at main desk; index goes back to 1800s. A county search of the probate court index by mail for 25-year search is $30.00 fee. A full county probate search of all years is $90.00.

Erie Town/Village Courts Akron Village Court 21 Main St, Akron, NY 14001; 716-542 9636 x3; 9AM-2PM T,W,TH (EST). **Alden Town Court** 3311 Wende Rd, Alden, NY 14004; 716-937-6969 x6; 9AM-4:30PM (EST). **Alden Village Court** 13336 Broadway, Alden, NY 14004; 716-937-9216 x14; 8AM-1PM; Court- M 7PM (EST). **Amherst Town Court** 400 John James Audubon Pkwy, Amherst, NY 14228; 716-689-4200; 8:30AM-4PM (EST). **Angola Village Court** 41 Commercial St, Angola, NY 14006; 716-549-4035; 10AM-12 M,TH (EST). **Aurora Town Court** 571 Main St, East Aurora, NY 14052; 716-652-5275; 9AM-3PM M-TH (EST). **Blasdell Village Court** 121 Miriam Ave, Blasdell, NY 14219; 716-821-7908; 8:30AM-4:30PMPM M,W,F; 1PM-9PM T; 12-8PM Th (EST). **Boston Town Court** 8500 Boston State Rd, Boston, NY 14025; 716-941-6115; 9AM-2PM (EST). **Brant Town Court** PO Box 232, 1294 Brant-North Collins Rd, Brant, NY 14027; 716-549-0300; 9AM-3PM M-F; 2nd & 4th Weds- 6:30PM-? (EST). **Cheektowaga Town Court** 3223 Union Rd, Cheektowaga, NY 14227; 716-686-3436; 9AM-4PM (EST). **Clarence Town Court** 1 Town Pl, Clarence, NY 14031; 716-741-8948; 8:30AM-4:30PM (EST). **Colden Town Court** 8812 State Rd, PO Box 335, Colden, NY 14033; 716-941-6242; 9AM-5PM (EST). **Collins Town Court** PO Box 420, 14093 Mill St, Collins, NY 14034; 716-532-3340; 6PM Wed (EST). **Concord Town Court** PO Box 368, 86 Franklin St, Springville, NY 14141; 716-592-9898; 10AM-end of evening court M; 9AM-4PM T; 8AM-4PM F (EST). **Depew Village Court** 85 Manitou St, Depew, NY 14043; 716-683-0978; 8:30AM-4:30PM (EST). **Eden Town Court** 2795 E Church St, Eden, NY 14057; 716-992-3559; 9AM-4PM M,T,TH, F; 9AM-N W (EST). **Elma Town Court** 1600 Bowen Rd, Elma, NY 14059; 716-652-1855; 8AM-4PM (EST). **Evans Town Court** 8787 Erie Rd, Angola, NY 14006; 716-549-3707; 8AM-4PM; Court- M 6:30PM (EST). **Grand Island Town Court** 2255 Baseline Rd, Grand Island, NY 14072; 716-773-9600 ext 650; 9AM-5PM (EST). **Hamburg Town Court** 6100 S Park Ave, Hamburg, NY 14075; 716-649-6111x2399; 8:30AM-5:45PM M; 8:30-4:30PM T-F (EST). **Hamburg Village Court** 100 Main St, Hamburg, NY 14075; 716-649-7204; 9AM-4PM (EST). **Holland Town Court** PO Box 70, 47 Pearl St, Holland, NY 14080; 716-537-2770; 9AM-3PM (EST). **Kenmore Village Court** Municipal Court Bldg, 2919 Delaware Ave, Kenmore, NY 14217; 716-873-4554; 9AM-5PM M,W,TH; 3PM-9PM Tu (EST). **Lancaster Town Court** 525 Pavement Rd, Lancaster, NY 14086; 716-683-1814; 8:30-4:15 (EST). **Lancaster Village Court** 5423 Broadway, Lancaster, NY 14086; 716-683-6780; 8:30-4:30 (EST). **Marilla Town Court** PO Box 120, 1740 Two Rod Rd, Marilla, NY 14102; 716-652-1213 x415; 9AM-4PM M-T, Th-F; 9AM-12 W (EST). **Newstead Town Court** PO Box 227, 5 Clarence Cntr Rd, Akron, NY 14001; 716-542-4575; 9AM-3PM M-T, 12PM F, W -7PM (EST). **North Collins Town Court** PO Box 51, 10543 Main St, North Collins, NY 14111; 716-337-3712; 7PM-? M,TH (EST). **Orchard Park Town & Village Court** 4295 S Buffalo St, Orchard Park, NY 14127; 716-662-6415; 8:30AM-4:30PM M,W,F (EST). **Sardinia Town Court** PO Box 205, 12320 Savage Rd, Sardinia, NY 14134; 716-496-8900 x13; 5:30PM-9PM T, Messages can be left on voice mail (EST). **Springville Village Court** 65 Franklin St, PO Box 362, Springville, NY 14141; 716-592-5360; 9AM-N T-F (EST). **Tonawanda Town Court** 1835 Sheridan Dr, Buffalo, NY 14223; 716-876-5536; 8:30AM-4:30PM (EST). **Wales Town Court** Wales Memorial Bldg, 11006 Emery Rd, South Wales, NY 14139; 716-652-3320; 7PM TH (EST). **West Seneca Town Court** 1250 Union Rd, West Seneca, NY 14224; 716-558-3248; 9AM-4PM; Traffic Fri- 4PM; Criminal T & F till 6:30PM (EST). **Williamsville Village Court** 5565 Main St, Williamsville, NY 14221; 716-632-0450; 8AM-3PM (EST).

Essex County

County Clerk PO Box 247, 7559 Court St, Essex County Government Ctr, Elizabethtown, NY 12932; 518-873-3606; criminal phone: 518-873-3370; civil phone: 518-873-3600, 518-873-3601; criminal fax: 518-873-3376; civil fax: 8AM-5PM; 8AM-5PM (EST). *Civil, Felony.*
www.co.essex.ny.us/
General Information: County Clerk will not do felony record searches for County Court felony records; clerk will only do civil. You may search felony books in person. No sealed or youthful offender records released. Will not fax documents. Court makes copy: $.65 per page; $1.30 minimum. Self serve copy: $.65 per page. Certification fee: $1.25 per page; minimum $5.00. Payee: Essex County Clerk. Personal checks accepted. No credit or debit cards accepted. Prepayment required. Mail requests: SASE required for civil.

Civil Name Search: Access: Mail, in person, online. Both court and visitors may perform in person name searches. Search fee: $5.00. Civil records on computer from 11/93, prior in books. Mail turnaround Time 1 day. Public use terminal has civil records back to 1993. Lookup Supreme Court civil cases at http://iapps.courts.state.ny.us/webcivil/FCASMain. Cases go back to 2002.

Criminal Name Search: Access: In person. Visitors must perform in person searches themselves. Required to search: name, years to search, DOB. Criminal records computerized from 1950s, prior in books; you may search the books. Note: County Clerk will not do felony record searches for County Court felony records; clerk will only do civil. You may search felony books in person.

Supreme & County Court PO Box 217, 7559 Court St, Essex County Government Ctr, Elizabethtown, NY 12932; criminal phone: 518-873-3370; civil phone: 518-873-3370; criminal fax: 518-873-3376; civil fax: 8AM-5PM; 8AM-5PM (EST). *Felony, Civil.*

General Information: Direct record search requests to the County Clerk, see separate listing. Online access to current/pending Supreme Court civil cases is at http://iapps.courts.state.ny.us/webcivil/FCASMain. Criminal online access is via the state OCA statewide system.

Surrogate's Court PO Box 217, 7559 Court St, Elizabethtown, NY 12932; 518-873-3384; fax: 518-873-3731; 9AM-5PM (EST). *Probate.* www.courts.state.ny.us/courts/4jd/essex/index.shtml

General Information: A county search of the probate court index by mail for 25-year search is $30.00 fee. A full county probate search of all years is $90.00.

Essex Town/Village Courts- Chesterfield Town Court PO Box 456, 1 Vine St, Keeseville, NY 12944; 518-834-9211 9:30AM-4:30PM. **Crown Point Town Court** PO Box 408, 17 Monitor Bay, Crown Point, NY 12928; 518-597-4144 5PM W. **Elizabethtown Town Court** PO Box 265, 7563 Court St, Elizabethtown, NY 12932; 518-873-2047 3-5PM TH. **Essex Town Court** PO Box 355, Main St, Essex, NY 12936; 518-963-8016 1st & 3rd M 6PM-?. **Jay Town Court** PO Box 730, 11 School Ln, Community Ctr, Au Sable Forks, NY 12912; 518-647-5574 4PM-8PM M. **Keene Town Court** 10829 Route 9 N, Town Hall, PO Box 89, Keene, NY 12942; 518-576-4556 7PM M. **Lake Placid Village Court** 2693 Main St, #103, Lake Placid, NY 12946; 518-523-2004 8AM-4PM M,Th, on W 8AM-N, 7-9PM. **Lewis Town Court** Route 9, PO Box 28, Lewis, NY 12950; 518-873-3204 7-9PM TH. **Minerva Town Court** PO Box 937, 5 Morse Memorial Highway, Minerva, NY 12851; 518-251-2869 Wed Eve 7PM-9PM. **Moriah Town Court** 42 Park Place, Port Henry, NY 12974; 518-546-9955 10AM-5PM M; 11AM-8PM T;N-4PM W; 11AM-7PM TH; 10AM-5PM F. **Newcomb Town Court** PO Box 405, Newcomb, NY 12852; 518-582-4255 3PM-? 3rd M. **North Elba Town Court** 2693 Main St, Lake Placid, NY 12946; 518-523-2141 8:30AM-3:30PM. **North Hudson Town Court** 2946 Rt 9, PO Box 28, North Hudson, NY 12855; 518-532-0587 8AM-5PM M,T,F 8AM-1PM Sat. **Schroon Town Court** PO Box 578, 15 Leland Ave, Town Hall, Schroon Lake, NY 12870; 518-532-7337 x17 7:30AM-2PM M,W,F. **St Armand Town Court** PO Box 66, Bloomingdale, NY 12913; 518-891-3189 x4 10AM-6PM W. **Ticonderoga Town Court** PO Box 471, 132 Montcalm St, Ticonderoga, NY 12883; 518-585-7141 8AM-4PM; W till 6:30PM. **Westport Town Court** PO Box 465, 22 Champlain Ave, Westport, NY 12993; 518-962-4882 2PM-5PM M; 2PM-4PM TH. **Willsboro Town Court** 5 Farrell Rd, PO Box 370, Willsboro, NY 12996; 518-963-4014 5PM TH. **Wilmington Town Court** PO Box 180, Town Hall, 7 Community Circle, Wilmington, NY 12997; 518-946-7129 5:30PM TH.

Franklin County

County Clerk 355 W Main St, Attn: County Clerk, Malone, NY 12953-1817; 518-481-1681; fax: 518-483-9143; 8AM-4PM (EST). *Felony, Civil.* http://franklincony.org/content/Departments/View/4?

General Information: Felony records are managed by the Supreme Court clerk who directs search requests to OCA for a $65.00 statewide search. However, county's felony record index is accessible in person at County Clerk Office's on the public access terminal. No sealed or youthful offender records released. Will fax documents $2.60 per page. Court makes copy: $.65 per page. Self serve copy: same. Certification fee: $1.00 per page, $5.00 minimum fee. Payee: Franklin County Clerk. Personal checks accepted, credit cards are not. Prepayment required. Mail requests: SASE required for civil.

Civil Name Search: Access: Mail, in person, online. Both court and visitors may perform in person name searches. Search fee: $5.00 per name per 2 years. Civil cases indexed by defendant. Civil index of dockets on computer from 1996, prior in file folders in Clerk's office. Mail turnaround Time same day. Civil PAT goes back to 1966. Separate public terminals for criminal records and civil records. Lookup Supreme Court civil cases at http://iapps.courts.state.ny.us/webcivil/FCASMain. Cases go back to 2002.

Criminal Name Search: Access: Mail, fax, in person. Visitors must perform in person searches themselves. Search fee: $5.00 per name per 2 years. Required to search: name, years to search, DOB. Criminal records computerized from 1962. Criminal PAT goes back to same as civil. Separate public terminals for criminal records and civil records.

Supreme Court 355 W Main St, #3223, Court Clerk, Malone, NY 12953-1817; 518-481-1748; criminal phone: 518-481-1749; fax: 518-481-5456; 9AM-5PM; 8AM-4PM Summer hours (EST). *Felony, Civil.* www.nycourts.gov/courts/4jd/franklin/index.shtml

General Information: Public terminals available to search felonies here. Or, search records at County Clerk, see separate listing. No sealed or youthful offender records released. Will fax out specific case files for $1.30 per page in this area code, $2.60 per page long distance, with 10 page limit. Fees must be paid first. Court makes copy: $.65 per page, minimum 2 pages. Certification fee: $5.00 for 5 pages, then add $1.00 ea add'l page with a maximum of $40.00. Payee: County Clerk. Personal checks accepted. Prepayment required.

Civil Name Search: Access: In person, online. Visitors must perform in person searches themselves. Civil cases indexed by defendant. Civil index of dockets on computer back to 1996, prior in file folders in Clerk's office. Current or pending only Supreme Court civil case look-up is at http://iapps.courts.state.ny.us/webcivil/FCASMain.

Criminal Name Search: Access: In person, online. Visitors must perform in person searches themselves. Required to search: name, years to search, DOB. Criminal records computerized from 1962. Note: Unless you search here in person, all criminal record name search requests are directed to the OCA for $65.00 statewide record search. Public use terminal has crim records back to 1962. Online access is via the state OCA statewide system. Fee is $65.00 per search. See www.nycourts.gov/apps/chrs/.

Surrogate's Court 355 W Main St, #3223, Malone, NY 12953-1817; 518-481-1736/1737; fax: 518-481-1443; 9AM-5PM Summer; 8-4PM June-Aug (EST). *Probate.* www.nycourts.gov/courts/4jd/franklin/surrogates.shtml

General Information: A county search of the Surrogate's court index by mail for 25-year search is $30.00 fee. A full county probate search of all years is $90.00.

Franklin Town/Village Courts- Bangor Town Court PO Box 337, North Bangor, NY 12966; 518-483-2749 6PM M. **Bellmont Town Court** PO Box 54, 6755 State Rte 374, Brainardsville, NY 12915; 518-425-3461 #2 2nd&4th M 7-8PM. **Bombay Town Court** PO Box 208, Bombay, NY 12914; 518-358-9968 5PM-7:30PM T. **Brandon Town Court** 203 County Rte 13, North Bangor, NY 12966; 518-483-7503 **Brighton Town Court** PO Box 260, 12 County Rd 31 aka Jonas Pond Rd, Paul Smiths, NY 12970; 518-327-3202 Town Clerk- N-5PM T,TH; Court- 7PM W. **Burke Town Court** PO Box 157, Burke, NY 12917; 518-483-5497 7-9 PM 2nd & 4th W. **Chateaugay Town Court** PO Box 9, 191 E Main St, Town Hall, Chateaugay, NY 12920; 518-497-3429 6PM M. **Constable Town Court** Town Hall, Route 122 & 30, Constable, NY 12926; 518-481-6113; 483-5186 **Dickinson Town Court** PO Box 83, 339 Aikens Rd, Dickinson Center, NY 12930; 518-856-0201 every other Wed, 7PM-?. **Duane Town Court** 172 County Rte 26, Duane Fire Station, Malone, NY 12953; 518-483-0386 1st&3rd TH 7PM; last TH at 6PM.. **Fort Covington Town Court** 2510 Chateaugay St, Fort Covington, NY 12937; 518-358-4629 6PM-? T. **Franklin Town Court** PO Box 62, Vermontville, NY 12989; 518-891-2189 7PM-? TH. **Harrietstown Town Court** 39 Main St, Saranac Lake, NY 12983; 518-891-4500 10AM W. **Malone Town Court** 27 Airport Rd, Malone, NY 12953; 518-481-6634 9AM-4PM. **Moira Town Court** PO Box 150, 522 County Rte 6, Moira, NY 12957; 518-529-6080 3:30-7PM. **Santa Clara Town Court** 439 Gilpin Bay Rd, Saranac Lake, NY 12983; 518-891-4656 7PM-? 2nd & 4th W. **Saranac Lake Village Court** 39 Main St, Saranac Lake, NY 12983; 518-891-4423 9AM-3PM M-TH. **Tupper Lake Town Court** 120 Demars Blvd, Tupper Lake, NY 12986; 518-359-9278 4PM-6PM W. **Tupper Lake Village Court** PO Box 1290, 53 Park St, Tupper Lake, NY 12986; 518-359-9161 5PM-7PM M. **Waverly Town Court** PO Box 47, Main St, St Regis Falls, NY 12980; 518-856-9249 call for hours; court- 7PM Tues. **Westville Town Court** 936 County Rte 19, Westville-Constable, NY 12926; 518-358-2499, 518-358-3432 1st & 2nd Tues at 7PM.

Fulton County

Supreme & County Court 223 W Main St, County Bldg, Johnstown, NY 12095; 518-736-5539 (court) 518-736-5555 (county clerk); fax: 518-762-5078 (Supreme); 9AM-5PM (EST). *Felony, Civil.*

General Information: Hamilton County Supreme Court cases are heard here. The County Clerk fax is 578-762-9214. No sealed, expunged, adoption, sex offense, juvenile or mental health records released. Will fax documents after payment received. Court makes copy: $.50 per page. Self serve copy: same. Certification fee: $5.00 per page. Payee: County Clerk. Business checks only accepted. No credit cards accepted. Prepayment required. Mail requests: SASE required for civil.

Civil Name Search: Access: Phone, mail, fax, in person, online. Both court and visitors may perform in person name searches. Search fee: $3.00 per name per five years. Civil records computerized since 1994. Mail turnaround Time same day. No historical records online but current or pending only Supreme Court civil case look-up is at http://iapps.courts.state.ny.us/webcivil/FCASMain.

Criminal Name Search: Access: In person, online. Only the court performs in person name searches; visitors may not. Search fee: $16.00 per name. Required to search: name, years to search, DOB. Criminal records in file folders since 1915, computerized since 1977. Note: While the court recommends the $65 statewide search, in person searchers may view court clerk's alpha list free. See www.nycourts.gov/apps/chrs/.

Gloversville City Court 3 Frontage Rd, City Hall, Gloversville, NY 12078; 518-773-4527; fax: 518-773-4599; 8AM-4PM; window closes at 3:30 (EST). *Misdemeanor, Civil Actions under $15,000, Eviction, Small Claims.*

General Information: No sealed, youthful offender records released. Will fax documents to local or toll-free number. Court makes copy: $.65 per page; $1.30 minimum. Certification fee: $5.00 per doc criminal; $6.00 if civil, plus copy fee. Payee: Gloversville City Court. No Personal checks, Visa/MC accepted. Prepayment required. Mail requests: SASE required.

Civil Name Search: Access: Mail, in person, online. Only the court performs in person name searches; visitors may not. No search fee. Civil cases indexed by plaintiff. Civil records in books; on computer since 1990s. Mail turnaround Time less than 1 week. WebCivil Local at http://iapps.courts.state.ny.us/webcivil/ecourtsMain contains information on both active and disposed Civil Court cases. Search by index number, party name, attorney/firm name or judge. No fee.

Criminal Name Search: Access: Online. Search fee: n/a, but a Certificate of Disposition is $5.00. Required to search: name, years to search, charge, date of arrest or sentence. Note: The court refuses to permit access to records unless specific case file given. All criminal record name search requests are directed to the OCA for statewide record search, $65.00 search fee. See www.nycourts.gov/apps/chrs.

Johnstown City Court 33-41 E Main St, Johnstown, NY 12095; 518-762-0007; fax: 518-762-2720; 8AM-4PM (EST). *Misdemeanor, Civil Actions under $15,000, Eviction, Small Claims.*

General Information: No sealed or youthful offender records released. Will not fax documents. Court makes copy: $.65 per page, $1.30 minimum. Certification fee: $5.00 per document plus copy fee. Payee: Johnstown City Court. Only cashiers checks and money orders accepted. Visa/MC accepted. Prepayment required. Mail requests: SASE required.

Civil Name Search: Access: Mail, in person, online. Only the court performs in person name searches; visitors may not. No search fee. Civil cases indexed by plaintiff. Civil records in file folders, computerized since 1995. WebCivil Local at http://iapps.courts.state.ny.us/webcivil/ecourtsMain contains information on both active and disposed Civil Court cases. Search by index number, party name, attorney/firm name or judge. No fee.

Criminal Name Search: Access: Online. Only the court performs in person name searches; visitors may not. Criminal records computerized from 1990. Note: The court does not permit access to court records unless specific case file number given. All criminal record name search requests are directed to the OCA for statewide record search, $65.00 search fee. See www.nycourts.gov/apps/chrs.

Surrogate's Court 223 W Main St, Johnstown, NY 12095; 518-736-5685; fax: 518-762-6372; 9AM-5PM (8AM-4PM July-August) (EST). *Probate.*

General Information: A county search of the probate court index by mail for 25-year search is $30.00 fee. A full county probate search of over 25 years is $90.00.

Fulton Town/Village Courts - Bleecker Town Court PO Box 1049, Gloversville, NY 12078; 518-773-8786 Varies. **Broadalbin Town & Village Court** PO Box 852, 229 Union Mills Rd, Broadalbin, NY 12025; 518-883-5131 9AM-1PM M-TH. **Caroga Town Court** PO Box 328, 1840 State Hwy 10, Caroga Lake, NY 12032; 518-835-4211 x28 7PM-? M. **Ephratah Town Court** 3782 State Highway 10, Town Barn, St Johnsville, NY 13452; 518-568-7333 6-8PM TH. **Johnstown Town Court** PO Box 88, 2753 State Highway 29, Johnstown, NY 12095; 518-762-6904 10AM-4PM. **Mayfield Town Court** PO Box 308, 75 N Main St, Mayfield, NY 12117; 518-661-5254 3PM-? M. **Oppenheim Town Court** 110 State Hwy 331, St Johnsville, NY 13452; 518-568-2837 6-8PM W. **Perth Town Court** 1849 County Hwy 107, Municipal Bldg, Amsterdam, NY 12010; 518-843-6977 x14 5:30PM-? M. **Stratford Town Court** 120 Piseco Rd, Town Hall, Stratford, NY 13470; 315-429-8612 7PM-? T.

Genesee County

County Clerk PO Box 379,, 15 Main St,, Batavia, NY 14021-0379; 585-344-2550; criminal phone: x2245; civil phone: x2242; fax: 585-344-8521; 8:30AM-5PM (EST). *Felony, Civil.*
www.co.genesee.ny.us/

General Information: Countywide criminal search requests made to the County Clerk are processed in the manner described below. No sealed, expunged, adoption, sex offense, juvenile or mental health records released. Will fax out $5.00 per doc. Court makes copy: $.65 per page, $1.30 minimum. Certification fee: $5.00 per doc plus $1.25 per page after first 4. Exemplification fee- $10.00 plus copies. Payee: County Clerk. Personal checks accepted, credit cards are not. Prepayment required. Mail requests: SASE required.

Civil Name Search: Access: Mail, in person, online. Both court and visitors may perform in person name searches. Search fee: $10.00 per name per 5 year period. Required to search: name, years to search; also helpful: address. Civil cases indexed by defendant, plaintiff; indexed by defendant only prior to 1995. Civil records in books from 1802; on computer back to 1995. Mail turnaround Time 1-3 days. Civil PAT goes back to 1/1995. Lookup Supreme Court civil cases at http://iapps.courts.state.ny.us/webcivil/FCASMain. Cases go back to 2002.

Criminal Name Search: Access: Fax, mail, in person. Both court and visitors may perform in person name searches. Search fee: $10.00 per name per 5 year period, $15.00 for 6-10 years, $20.00 for 11-20 years. Required to search: name, years to search, DOB. Criminal records in books from 1802; on computer back to 1995. Note: With fax requests, include a photocopy of your fee payment check and they will entertain your search request and speed up the process. Mail turnaround Time 1-3 days. Criminal PAT goes back to same as civil.

Supreme & County Court One W Main St, Batavia, NY 14020; 585-344-2550 x2239; fax: 585-344-8517; 9AM-5PM (EST). *Felony, Civil.*

General Information: Direct record search requests to the County Clerk, see separate listing. Online access to current/pending Supreme Court civil cases is at http://iapps.courts.state.ny.us/webcivil/FCASMain. Criminal online access is via the state OCA statewide system.

Batavia City Court Genesee County Courts Facility, 1 W Main St, Batavia, NY 14020; 585-344-2550 x2416, 2417, 2418, 2415; fax: 585-344-8556; 9AM-5PM (EST). *Misdemeanor, Civil Actions under $15,000, Eviction, Small Claims.*
www.nycourts.gov/courts/8jd/genesee/batavia.shtml

General Information: No sealed, expunged, sex offense or mental health records released. Will fax documents to local or toll free line only. Court makes copy: $.65 per page. Certification fee: $6.00 per seal. Payee: Batavia City Court. Only cashiers checks and money orders accepted. Visa/MC accepted. Prepayment required. Mail requests: SASE required.

Civil Name Search: Access: Fax, mail, in person. Only the court performs in person name searches; visitors may not. Search fee: A Certificate of Disposition available for $5.00. Civil cases indexed by plaintiff. Civil records on computer from 1990, in books from 1957. Mail turnaround Time 1-3 days.

Criminal Name Search: Access: Mail, in person, online. Only the court performs in person name searches; visitors may not. Search fee: A Certificate of Disposition available for $5.00. Required to search: name, years to search, DOB. Criminal records computerized from 1993, in books from 1947. Mail turnaround Time 1-3 days. All criminal record name search requests are directed to the OCA for statewide record search, $65.00 search fee. See www.nycourts.gov/apps/chrs/.

Surrogate's Court 1 W Main St, Batavia, NY 14020; 585-344-2550 x2237; fax: 585-344-8517; 9AM-5PM (EST). *Probate.*

General Information: A county search of the probate court index by mail for 25-year search is $30.00 fee. A full county probate search of all years is $90.00.

Genesee Town/Village Courts- Alabama Town Court PO Box 476, Town Court, Alabama, NY 14013; 585-948-8132 TH. **Alexander Town Court** PO Box 248, 3350 Church St, Alexander, NY 14005; 585-591-8165 6PM-? T. **Batavia Town Court** 3833 W Main St Rd, Batavia, NY 14020; 585-343-1729 10AM-3PM. **Bergen Town Court** PO Box 249, 10 Hunter St, Bergen, NY 14416; 585-494-1221 1PM-7PM W; 1PM-5PM Th. **Bethany Town Court** 10510 Bethany Center Rd, East Bethany, NY 14054; 585-343-3325 7-9PM T. **Byron Town Court** 7028 Byron Holley Rd, Byron, NY 14422; 585-548-7123 9AM-N; 1PM-4PM M,T,W,F. **Corfu Village Court** 116 E Main St, Corfu, NY 14036; 585-599-3380 8AM-4PM. **Darien Town Court** 10569 Allegany Rd, Darien Center, NY 14040; 585-547-2274 x21 9AM-3PM M-TH. **Elba Town Court** PO Box 295, 7 Maple Ave, Elba, NY 14058-0295; 585-757-2762 9AM-N 1PM-4PM M-F; 7PM W (court). **Leroy Town & Village Court** 48 Main St, Leroy, NY 14482; 585-768-6910 8AM-4:30PM. **Oakfield Town Court**

3219 Drake St Rd, Oakfield, NY 14125; 585-948-5835 x1 9AM-N, 1-4PM. **Pavilion Town Court** PO Box 126, 1 Woodrow Dr, Pavilion, NY 14525; 585-584-2025 4PM T. **Pembroke Town Court** 116 E Main St, Corfu, NY 14036; 585-599-4817 8:30AM-4:30PM T-F. **Stafford Town Court** 8903 Rte 237, Stafford, NY 14143; 585-344-4020 8:30AM-3:30PM M,TH; 8:30AM-4:30PM T,W; 9AM-3PM F.

Greene County

Supreme & County Court County Clerk, Courthouse, 411 Main St, Catskill, NY 12414; 518-719-3255, (county clerk) 518-943-2230 (court clerk); fax: 518-719-3284; 9AM-5PM; 8:30AM-4:30PM June-Aug hours (EST). *Felony, Civil.*

General Information: Search requests are processed by the County Clerk office in the manner described below. Courts are located at 320 Main St. Fax to the County clerk office is 518-719-3284. No sealed or youthful offender records released. Will not fax documents. Court makes copy: $1.00 per page. Self serve copy: $.25 per page. Certification fee: $5.00 per doc plus copy fee. Payee: County Clerk. Personal checks accepted, credit cards are not. Prepayment required.

Civil Name Search: Access: In person, online. Both court and visitors may perform in person name searches. No search fee. Civil records in file folder, computerized since 6/13/97. Public use terminal has civil records back to 1999 for index. Historical records are not online, but access to current/pending Supreme Court civil cases is at http://iapps.courts.state.ny.us/webcivil/FCASMain.

Criminal Name Search: Access: In person, online. Only the court performs in person name searches; visitors may not. Search fee: $17.50 per name for 7-20 years. May also do search for $5.00 per name for 2 years;. Required to search: name, years to search, DOB. Criminal records indexed on cards. Online access is via the state OCA statewide system. Fee is $65.00 per search. See www.nycourts.gov/apps/chrs/.

Surrogate's Court 320 Main Street, Catskill, NY 12414; 518-444-8750; fax: 518-943-5811; 9AM-4:30PM (EST). *Probate.*

General Information: A county search of the probate court index by mail for 25-year search is $30.00 fee. A full county probate search of all years is $90.00.

Greene Town/Village Courts Ashland Town Court PO Box 129, 11980 Rte 23, Ashland, NY 12407; 518-734-4760 9AM-2PM M,W $ by app't. **Athens Town Court** PO Box 132, 2 First St, 2nd Fl, Athens, NY 12015; 518-945-3360 8AM-4PM; 3PM-? Court hrs. **Athens Village Court** 2 First St, Village Court, Athens, NY 12015; 518-945-3002 #4/11 **Cairo Town Court** PO Box 755, 512 Main St, Cairo, NY 12413; 518-622-3388 M-TH 9AM-N; T 7PM. **Catskill Town Court** 441 Main St, Catskill, NY 12414; 518-943-2142 8AM-4PM; TH to 6PM. **Catskill Village Court** 422 Main St, Catskill, NY 12414; 518-943-9544 #3/13 8AM-3:30PM. **Coxsackie Town Court** 119 Mansion St, Coxsackie, NY 12051; 518-731-6934 9PM-4PM. **Durham Town Court** 7309 St Route 81, East Durham, NY 12423; 518-239-8260 Ext 3 9-11AM M,T. **Greenville Town Court** PO Box 38, 11159 Routes 32 , Pioneer Bldg, Greenville, NY 12083; 518-966-5055 #6 1-3:30PM M,W,TH; 7PM W Court. **Halcott Town Court** 813 Route 3, Halcott Center, NY 12430; 845-254-9920 **Hunter Town Court** PO Box 70, 5748 Rte 23-A, Tannersville, NY 12485; 518-589-5882 x305/306 8AM-4PM; Court- 1PM-? Wed. **Jewett Town Court** PO Box 132, Jewett, NY 12444; 518-263-4626 #5 7-8PM T. **Lexington Town Court** PO Box 92, 3542 State Hwy 42, Lexington, NY 12452; 518-989-6303 7PM-8PM M. **New Baltimore Town Court** PO Box 67, 3809 County Rt 51, Hannacroix, NY 12087; 518-756-2079 9-4PM. **Prattsville Town Court** PO Box 418, 14517 Main St., Prattsville, NY 12468; 518-299-3125 ext 3 **Windham Town Court** PO Box 96, 371 State Rte 296, Hensonville, NY 12439; 518-734-3431 9AM-N M,W,F.

Hamilton County

County Clerk & County Court Hamilton County Clerk, PO Box 204, Rte 8, Lake Pleasant, NY 12108; 518-548-7111; fax: 518-548-9740; 8:30AM-4:30PM (EST). *Felony, Civil.*

General Information: Countywide record search requests are processed in the manner described below. Civil cases are heard in Fulton County (518-736-5539, Patricia, for info). Once closed, civil case records are returned to Hamilton County clerk. No sealed or youthful offender records released. Fee to fax document $1.00 each. Court makes copy: $.65 per page, $1.30 minimum. Certification fee: $1.25 per page; $5.00 minimum. Payee: Hamilton County Clerk. Personal checks accepted, credit cards are not. Prepayment required. Mail requests: SASE required.

Civil Name Search: Access: Mail, phone, in person, online. Both court and visitors may perform in person name searches. No search fee. Civil cases indexed by defendant. Civil records in books, records go back to 1850's. Mail turnaround Time 2-3 days. Lookup current or pending Supreme Court civil cases at http://iapps.courts.state.ny.us/webcivil/FCASMain.

Criminal Name Search: Access: Mail, in person. Only the court performs in person name searches; visitors may not. Search fee: $5.00 per name. Fee is per two years searched. Required to search: name, years to search, DOB. Criminal records go back to 1878; no computerized records. Note: Record search request must be in writing. Mail turnaround Time 2-3 days.

Supreme Court PO Box 204, County Clerk, Rte 8, Lake Pleasant, NY 12108; 518-548-7111 (Hamilton county clerk) 518-736-5539 (Fulton court clerk); fax: 518-548-9740; 8:30AM-4:30PM (EST). *Civil.* www.nycourts.gov/courts/4jd/hamilton/index.shtml

General Information: Supreme court (civil cases) in Hamilton County are heard in Fulton County. Civil records eventually returned to Hamilton County Clerk once the case is completed in Fulton. Original filings made in Hamilton, but subsequent filings usually made at Fulton. No sealed or youthful offender records released. Fee to fax out is $1.00 per doc, prepayment required. Court makes copy: $.65 per page, $1.30 minimum. Certification fee: $1.00 per page; $5.00 minimum. Payee: Hamilton County Clerk. Personal checks accepted, credit cards are not. Prepayment required. Mail requests: SASE not required.

Civil Name Search: Access: In person, online. Visitors must perform in person searches themselves. Civil cases indexed by defendant. Civil records in books, records go back to 1850's. Note: The court's records are not computerized here. Mail turnaround Time 2-3 days. Hamilton County civil cases heard in Fulton County may be available on Fulton County civil records computer system. No public terminal in Hamilton County. Historical records are not online, but access to current/pending Supreme Court civil cases is at http://iapps.courts.state.ny.us/webcivil/FCASMain.

Surrogate's Court PO Box 780, 179 White Birch Ln, Indian Lake, NY 12842; 518-648-5411; fax: 518-648-6286; 8:30AM-4:30PM (EST). *Probate.* www.courts.state.ny.us/courts/4jd/hamilton/index.shtml

General Information: Court is located in Hamilton County Ofc. A county search of the probate court index by mail for 25-year search is $30.00 fee. A full county probate search of all years is $90.00.

Hamilton Town/Village Courts - Arietta Town Court PO Box 4, Old Piseco Rd, Piseco, NY 12139; 518-548-5703 **Benson Town Court** PO Box 1017, 2189 County Highway 6, Northville, NY 12134; 518-863-4969 **Hope Town Court** Town Hall, 548 St. Route 30, Northville, NY 12134; 518-863-6493 3-6PM M-F; Court- 7PM-9PM T. **Indian Lake Town Court** PO Box 730, Pelon Rd, Town Hall, Indian Lake, NY 12842; 518-648-6226 6-8PM T,TH. **Inlet Town Court** Municipal Bldg, 160 Route 28, Inlet, NY 13360; 315-357-6121 7AM-3PM Sun-TH. **Lake Pleasant Town Court** PO Box 358, Speculator, NY 12164; 518-548-3625 9AM-1PM, 1-3PM. **Long Lake Town Court** PO Box 697, Town Hall, Long Lake, NY 12847; 518-624-3761 by appointm't; court- TH 7PM. **Morehouse Town Court** PO Box 5, Town Court, RR 8, Hoffmeister, NY 13353; 315-826-7093 **Wells Town Court** PO Box 222, 1382 St Rte 30, Wells, NY 12190; 518-924-7407 7PM-? T.

Herkimer County

County Clerk 109 Mary St, #1111, County Office Bldg, Herkimer, NY 13350-2923; 315-867-1133; criminal phone: 315-867-1137; civil phone: 315-867-1338; fax: 315-867-1189; 9AM-5PM Sept-May; 8:30AM-4PM June-Aug (EST). *Felony, Civil.*

General Information: Countywide search requests made to the County Clerk are processed in the manner described below. No sealed, expunged, adoption, sex offense, juvenile or mental health records released. Will fax out documents, fax fee same as copy fee total. Court makes copy: $.65 per page, $1.30 minimum. Certification fee: 1-4 pages is $5.00; $1.25 each add'l page. Payee: County Clerk. Personal checks accepted, credit cards are not. Prepayment required. Mail requests: SASE required.

Civil Name Search: Access: Mail, in person. Both court and visitors may perform in person name searches. Search fee: $5.00 per name per 2 year period. Civil index on docket books since 1800s. Mail turnaround Time varies- ASAP to days. Civil PAT goes back to mid-1990s. Lookup Supreme Court civil cases at http://iapps.courts.state.ny.us/webcivil/FCASMain. Cases go back to 2002.

Criminal Name Search: Access: mail, in person. Both court and visitors may perform in person name searches. Search fee: $5.00 per name per 2 year period. Required to search: name, years to search, DOB. Criminal records indexed in books since 1800s. Mail turnaround Time varies- ASAP to days. Criminal PAT goes back to 1800s.

Supreme & County Court 301 N Washington St, %th Floor, Herkimer, NY 13350-1993; criminal phone: 315-867-1282; civil phone: 315-867-1209; fax: 315-866-1802; 8:30AM-4:30PM; 8:30AM-4PM Summer hours (EST). *Felony, Civil.*

General Information: The County Court clerk directs felony requests to the OCA for a $65.00 statewide record check. See also separate listing for

County Clerk. Access to current/pending Supreme Court civil cases is at http://iapps.courts.state.ny.us/webcivil/FCASMain.

Little Falls City Court 659 E Main St, Little Falls, NY 13365; 315-823-1690; fax: 315-823-1623; 8:30AM-4:30PM (EST). *Misdemeanor, Civil Actions under $15,000, Eviction, Small Claims.*

General Information: No sealed, expunged, adoption, sex offense, juvenile or mental health records released. Will fax documents to local or toll free line. Court makes copy: $.65 per page; minimum $1.30. Certification fee: $6.00 per document. Payee: Little Falls City Court. Only cashiers checks and money orders accepted. Visa/MC accepted in person only. Prepayment required. Mail requests: SASE required.

Civil Name Search: Access: Mail, fax, in person, online. Only the court performs in person name searches; visitors may not. Search fee: $2.50 per name per year. Civil cases indexed by defendant. Civil records go back to 1973; on computer back to 4/02. Mail turnaround Time 1 week. WebCivil Local at http://iapps.courts.state.ny.us/webcivil/ecourtsMain contains information on both active and disposed Civil Court cases. Search by index number, party name, attorney/firm name or judge. No fee.

Criminal Name Search: Access: Mail, in person, online. Only the court performs in person name searches; visitors may not. Search fee: $2.50 per name per year. Required to search: name, years to search, DOB, signed release. Criminal records go back to 1948; on computer back to 4/02. Mail turnaround Time 1 week. Name search requests are often directed to the OCA for statewide record search, $65.00 search fee. See www.nycourts.gov/apps/chrs.

Surrogate's Court 301 N Washington St, #5550, Herkimer, NY 13350; 315-867-1170; fax: 315-866-1802; 8:30AM-4:30PM Sept-May; 8:00AM-4PM June-Aug (EST). *Probate.*

General Information: Access to limited (some, not all) 5th District Surrogate's Court records is free after registration at http://surrogate5th.courts.state.ny.us/Public/Login.aspx.

Herkimer Town/Village Courts - Columbia Town Court 147 Columbia Center Rd, Mohawk, NY 13407; 315-866-1309 *2 5:30-7:30PM T. **Danube Town Court** , 438 Creek Rd, Little Falls, NY 13365; 315-823-4210 9:15AM-12:15PM M&W; call for app't. **Fairfield Town Court** 439 Kelly Rd, Little Falls, NY 13365; 315-823-1383 7PM W. **Frankfort Town Court** Town Hall, 142 S Litchfield St, Frankfort, NY 13340; 315-895-7267 9AM-1PM W-F; court- 7PM-? M,T. **Frankfort Village Court** 110 Railroad St #6, Frankfort, NY 13340; 315-894-8513 8AM-3PM M-T; court-7PM T; 8AM-N W. **German Flatts Town Court** PO Box 57, 66 E Main St, Mohawk, NY 13407; 315-866-3571 4-7PM M/Criminal & Traffic; 6-9PM T/Civil/Small Claims. **Herkimer Town Court** 114 N Prospect St, Herkimer, NY 13350; 315-866-1280 M-TH 9AM-5PM, 9AM-4PM F. **Herkimer Village Court** 120 Green St., Herkimer, NY 13350; 315-866-0604 4PM W. **Ilion Village Court** PO Box 270, 49 Morgan St, Ilion, NY 13357; 315-894-4175 10AM-N. **Litchfield Town Court** 1403 Cedarville Rd, Frankfort, NY 13340; 315-894-4111 5PM Tuesdays. **Little Falls Town Court** 478 Flint Ave, Town Hall, Little Falls, NY 13365; 315-823-1202 5:30PM court hours M,TH. **Manheim Town Court** PO Box 32, 6356 St Rte 167, Dolgeville, NY 13329; 315-429-9631 9AM-12:30PM M-TH. **Middleville Village Court** Village Court, S Main St, PO Box 76, Middleville, NY 13406; 315-823-2747 9AM-4PM. **Newport Town Court** , PO Box 534, Newport, NY 13416; 315-845-8938 **Newport Village Court** PO Box 335, 8219 St Rt 28, Newport, NY 13416; 315-845-1680 / 8605 7-9PM T. **Norway Town Court** 3013 Military Rd, Newport, NY 13416; 315-845-6107 **Ohio Town Court** 234 Nellis Rd., Ohio, NY 13324; 315-826-3466 7PM-? T. **Russia Town Court** PO Box 126, 8916 N Main St, Municipal Bldg, Poland, NY 13431; 315-826-3074 10AM-3PM W. **Salisbury Town Court** PO Box 241, 126 State Rt 29A, Salisbury Center, NY 13454; 315-429-8581 11AM-1PM, 2PM-5PM T-F. **Schuyler Town Court** 2090 State Route 5, Utica, NY 13502; 315-733-1093 M-TH 9AM-3PM; 8AM-3PM F; court- 6PM Mon. **Stark Town Court** PO Box 115, Van Hornesville, NY 13475; 315-858-2091 10AM W court. **Warren Town Court** Town Court, 175 Little Lakes Rd, Richfield Spgs., NY 13439; 315-858-1283 7PM TH. **Webb Town Court** PO Box 157, Route 28, Main St, Old Forge, NY 13420; 315-369-3321 7:30PM T&TH. **Winfield Town Court** PO Box 161, West Winfield, NY 13491; 315-822-5759 6PM-9PM W.

Jefferson County

County Court Jefferson County Clerk's Office-Court Records, 175 Arsenal St, County Bldg, Watertown, NY 13601-3783; 315-785-3200; probate phone: 315-785-3019; fax: 315-785-5145; 9AM-5PM; 8:30AM-4PM July-Aug hours (EST). *Felony, Civil.*
www.co.jefferson.ny.us/index.aspx?page=51

General Information: Countywide record search requests are processed in the manner described below by the County Clerk, phone above, or 785-3200. No sealed, expunged, adoption, sex offense, juvenile or mental health records released. Will fax out specific case files. Court makes copy: $.65 per page; $1.30 minimum. Self serve copy: same. Certification fee: $1.25 per page, $5.00 minimum. with copies. Payee: County Clerk of Jefferson County.

Personal checks accepted, credit cards are not. Prepayment required. Mail requests: SASE required.

Civil Name Search: Access: In person, online. Visitors must perform in person searches themselves. Civil records on computer back to 1/1992; prior in books from 1805 by first defendant name only. Note: Civil phone for the Supreme Court clerk 315-785-7912. Civil PAT goes back to 1992. Current or pending Supreme Court civil case look-up is at http://iapps.courts.state.ny.us/webcivil/FCASMain.

Criminal Name Search: Access: Mail, in person. Both court and visitors may perform in person name searches. Search fee: $5.00 per name. Fee is per 2 years searched. Required to search: name, years to search; also helpful: DOB, signed release. Criminal records computerized from 1/1992; prior in books from 1805 by first defendant name only. Note: County court clerk is 315-785-3044. Mail turnaround Time 1 week. Criminal PAT goes back to same as civil.

Supreme Court Jefferson County Clerk's Office-Court Records, 175 Arsenal St, County Bldg, Watertown, NY 13601-3783; 315-785-3200 County Clerk; fax: 315-785-5145; 9AM-5PM; 8:30AM-4PM July-Aug hours (EST). *Felony, Civil.*
www.nycourts.gov/courts/5jd/index.shtml

General Information: Countywide record search requests are processed in the manner described below by the County Clerk, phone above, or 785-3081. No sealed, expunged, adoption, sex offense, juvenile or mental health records released. Will fax out specific case files. Court makes copy: $.65 per page; $1.30 minimum. Self serve copy: same. Certification fee: $1.25 per page, $5.00 minimum. with copies. Payee: Jefferson County Clerk. Personal checks accepted, credit cards are not. Prepayment required. Mail requests: SASE required.

Civil Name Search: Access: In person, online. Visitors must perform in person searches themselves. Civil records on computer back to 1/1992; prior in books from 1805 by first defendant name only. Note: Civil phone for the Supreme Court clerk 315-785-7912. Civil PAT goes back to 1992. Current or pending only Supreme Court civil case look-up is at http://iapps.courts.state.ny.us/webcivil/FCASMain.

Criminal Name Search: Access: Mail, in person, online. Both court and visitors may perform in person name searches. Search fee: $5.00 per name. Fee is per 2 years searched. Required to search: name, years to search; also helpful: DOB, signed release. Criminal records computerized from 1/1992; prior in books from 1805 by first defendant name only. Note: County court clerk is 315-785-3044. Mail turnaround Time 1 week. Criminal PAT goes back to same as civil. Online access is via the state OCA statewide system. Fee is $65.00 per search. See www.nycourts.gov/apps/chrs/.

Watertown City Court 245 Washington St, Municipal Bldg, Watertown, NY 13601; 315-785-7785; fax: 315-785-7856; 8:30AM4:30PM (EST). *Misdemeanor, Civil Actions under $15,000, Eviction, Small Claims.*
www.watertown-ny.gov/index.asp?NID=76

General Information: No sealed records released. Will fax documents to local or toll free line. Court makes copy: $.65 per page, but $1.30 minimum. Certification fee: $6.00. Payee: City Court. Only cashiers checks and money orders accepted. Visa/MC accepted. Prepayment required. Mail requests: SASE required.

Civil Name Search: Access: Mail, in person, online. Only the court performs in person name searches; visitors may not. Search fee: $6.00 per name. Fee is per name & docket. Civil cases indexed by defendant. Civil records in docket books and computerized. Mail turnaround Time 2 days. WebCivil Local at http://iapps.courts.state.ny.us/webcivil/ecourtsMain contains information on both active and disposed Civil Court cases. Search by index number, party name, attorney/firm name or judge. No fee.

Criminal Name Search: Access: Online. Only the court performs in person name searches; visitors may not. Search fee: $16.00 per name. Criminal records in docket books and computerized. Note: The court refuses to permit access to court records unless specific case file given. All criminal record name search requests are directed to the OCA for statewide record search, $65.00 search fee. See www.nycourts.gov/apps/chrs.

Surrogate's Court County Court Complex, 163 Arsenal St, 3rd Fl, Watertown, NY 13601-2562; 315-785-3019; fax: 315-785-5194; 8:30AM-4:30PM Sept-May; 8:30AM-4PM June-Aug (EST). *Probate.*
www.nycourts.gov/courts/5jd/index.shtml

General Information: A county search of the probate court index by mail for 25-year search is $30.00 fee. A full county probate search of all years is $90.00.

Jefferson Town/Village Courts - Adams Town Court 3 S Main St, Adams, NY 13605-0024; 315-232-2467 9AM-1PM M-F; 7PM every Wed. **Alexandria Bay Village Court** PO Box 809, 10 Walton St, Alexandria Bay, NY 13607; 315-482-4786 7PM W. **Alexandria Town Court** P.O. Box 130, 46372 Co. Rt 1, Alexandria Bay, NY 13607; 315-482-9637 8AM-4PM. **Antwerp Town Court** 45 Main St, PO Box 9, Town

Hall, Antwerp, NY 13608; 315-659-8989 6:30-9PM T, also 4th TH. **Brownville Town Court** 16431 Star School House Rd., Dexter, NY 13634; 315-767-6940 6:30PM TH. **Brownville Village Court** 16431 Star School Rd, Dexter, NY 13634; 315-767-6940 6:30PM TH. **Cape Vincent Town Court** PO Box 680, 1964 NYS Rte 12E, Cape Vincent, NY 13618; 315-654-3883 **Carthage Village Court** 120 S Mechanic St, Carthage, NY 13619; 315-493-2890 M 6PM. **Champion Town Court** 10 N Broad St, Carthage, NY 13619; 315-493-2687 **Clayton Town and Village Court** 401 Mary St, Clayton, NY 13624; 315-686-2427 9AM-N. **Ellisburg Town Court** PO Box 113, Main St, Town Hall, Ellisburg, NY 13636; 315-846-9216 9AM-2PM M-F. **Glen Park Village Court** 16431 Star School House Rd., Town Office, Dexter, NY 13634; 315-767-6940 6:30PM TH. **Henderson Town Court** PO Box 259, 12105 Town Barn Rd, Henderson, NY 13650; 315-938-5542 ext 26 **Hounsfield Town Court** PO Box 306, 411 W Washington St, Sackets Harbor, NY 13685; 315-646-2767 9AM-N, 1-4PM T,TH; Court-6-8PM Th. **LeRay Town Court** 8650 Leray St., Evans Mills, NY 13637; 315-629-0228 9AM-3PM. **Lorraine Town Court** PO Box 52, 17676 County Rte 189, Lorraine, NY 13659; 315-232-2548 7PM-9PM T. **Lyme Town Court** PO Box 66, Chaumont, NY 13622; 315-649-2788 9AM-3PM M-W. **Orleans Town Court** PO Box 206, 20558 Sunrise Ave, Lafargeville, NY 13656; 315-658-2272 9AM-12; 1PM-5PM M-T, Th-F. **Pamelia Town Court** 25859 NY Route 37, Watertown, NY 13601; 315-785-9794 M-TH 7:30AM-2:30PM; 7:30-1PM F. **Philadelphia Town Court** 33019 US Route 11, Philadelphia, NY 13673; 315-642-3421 Court W 6PM. **Rodman Town Court** PO Box 431, 12509 School St, Rodman, NY 13682; 315-232-2522 Court- 1st & 3rd TH 7PM. **Rutland Town Court** 28411 State Route 126, Black River, NY 13612; 315-788-1265 7-9PM T. **Theresa Town Court** 215 Riverside Ave, PO Box 675, Theresa, NY 13691; 315-628-4148 10AM-2PM T. **Theresa Village Court** PO Box 299, 124 Commercial St, Theresa, NY 13691; 315-628-4425 7PM-? 1st, 3rd T; Clerk- TH. **Watertown Town Court** 22869 County Route 67, Watertown, NY 13601; 315-782-0412 8AM-3PM. **West Carthage Village Court** 23 Franklin St, West Carthage, NY 13619; 315-493-6345 6PM T. **Wilna Town Court** 120 S. Mechanic St, Carthage, NY 13169; 315-493-2890 9AM-4PM.

Kings County

Supreme Court - Civil Division 360 Adams St, #189, c/o County Clerk office, Brooklyn, NY 11201; 718-404-9820 clerk; 718-675-7699 ct; 9AM-5PM, 9AM-3PM for records (EST). *Civil Actions over $25,000.*
www.courts.state.ny.us/courts/2jd/kings.shtml

General Information: Supreme Ct civil records are managed by the County Clerk's office. Address and phone and searching methods at County Clerk are given here. See www.courts.state.ny.us/courts/2jd/kingsclerk/index.shtml for add'l info. No sealed, expunged, adoption, juvenile or mental health records released. Will not fax documents. Court makes copy: $.35 per page. Self serve copy: same. Certification fee: $8.00 per doc plus $25 per page copies. $25.00 for exemplification. Payee: County Clerk. Only attorney checks and money orders accepted. Visa/MC accepted. Prepayment required. Mail requests: SASE required for civil.

Civil Name Search: Access: In person, online. Visitors must perform in person searches themselves. Required to search: name, years to search; also requested by clerk- index number. Civil cases indexed by defendant. Civil records on computer back to 1993; in books, on microfiche back to 1900's. Note: Picture ID required for in person searchers for matrimonial cases. Public use terminal has civil records back to 1993. Results may include address and attorney. 9AM-6PM, 347-296-1144. Access to current/pending Supreme Court civil cases is at http://iapps.courts.state.ny.us/webcivil/FCASMain.

Brooklyn Criminal Court 120 Schermerhorn St, Brooklyn, NY 11201; 347-404-9400/02; fax: 718-643-7733; 9AM-5PM (EST). *Misdemeanor.*
www.courts.state.ny.us/courts/2jd/kings.shtml#sup

General Information: Alt fax-643-5234. Court will not perform crim searches; direct search requests to OCA, 25 Beaver St, NYC, 212-428-2810. Also subscribe or guest login to search eCourts WebCrims appearances system at http://iapps.courts.state.ny.us/webcrim_attorney/Login.

Civil Court of the City of New York - Kings Branch, Brooklyn 141 Livingston St, #303, Brooklyn, NY 11201; 347-404-9123; civil phone: 347-404-9015 records rm; 9AM-5PM (EST). *Civil Actions under $25,000, Eviction, Small Claims.*
www.courts.state.ny.us/courts/2jd/kings.shtml

General Information: Searching performed in the basement record Rm-007 or on Civil Dept. public access terminal in #302. General civil info line-212-791-6000. Sm Claims phone- 347-404-9021; housing ct- 347-404-9201; Admin- 347-404-9133. All records public. Will not fax documents. Court makes copy: Record Room gives you file to copy, once you present a case number. Self serve copy: $.25 per page. Certification fee: $6.00 per doc. Payee: NYC Civil Court. Only cashiers checks and money orders accepted. No credit cards accepted. Prepayment required.

Civil Name Search: Access: Phone, in person, online. Visitors must perform in person searches themselves. No search fee. Civil cases indexed by plaintiff. Pre-1998 records archived in Queens; 1998 to present in Brooklyn. Civil records on computer from 1987 for small claims, 1990 for tenant/landlord, and from 1/1998 for civil. Note: When not busy the civil department is known to be able to do a computer lookup while you wait on the phone. Public use terminal has civil records back to 1997. Public terminal has Landlord/tenant, civil, and small claims. 1 PAT in basement, 3 on 3rd Fl. Access civil records free at http://iapps.courts.state.ny.us/webcivil/ecourtsMain. Landlord/Tenant index can also be found on the internet.

Supreme Court - Criminal 320 Jay St, Brooklyn, NY 11201; 347-296-1076; direct- 347-296-1122; criminal phone: x3 felony; x3 then x4 records rm; 9AM-4:30PM (EST). *Felony.*
www.courts.state.ny.us/courts/2jd/kings.shtml#sup

General Information: This court does not perform criminal searches; direct search requests to the OCA, 25 Beaver St, NYC, 212-428-2810. Also, search online for future court appearances and summons case info at http://iapps.courts.state.ny.us/webcrim_attorney/Login.

Surrogate's Court 2 Johnson St, Brooklyn, NY 11201; 347-404-9700; fax: 718-643-6237; 9AM-5PM (EST). *Probate.*
www.nycourts.gov/courts/nyc/surrogates/

General Information: A county search of the probate court index by mail for 25-year search is $30.00 fee. A full county probate search of all years is $90.00.

Lewis County

Supreme & County Court Courthouse, County Clerk, PO Box 232, Lowville, NY 13367; 315-376-5333 (County); 315-376-5380 (Supreme); fax: 315-376-3768; 8:30AM-4:30PM (EST). *Felony, Civil.*

General Information: Countywide search requests are processed in the manner described below by the County Clerk. No sealed, youthful offender or sex abuse case records released. Will fax documents $1.00 per page. Court makes copy: $.65 per page. Self serve copy: same. Certification fee: $5.00 per document. Payee: County Clerk. Personal checks accepted, credit cards are not. Prepayment required. Mail requests: SASE required.

Civil Name Search: Access: Mail, in person, online. Both court and visitors may perform in person name searches. Search fee: $10.00 per name. Civil cases indexed by defendant only. Civil index on cards from 1935. Mail turnaround Time 2 days. Civil PAT goes back to 2002. Historical records are not online, but access to current/pending Supreme Court civil cases is at http://iapps.courts.state.ny.us/webcivil/FCASMain.

Criminal Name Search: Access: Mail, in person, online. Both court and visitors may perform in person name searches. Search fee: $10.00 per name. Criminal records indexed on cards from 1935. Mail turnaround Time 2 days. Criminal PAT goes back to same as civil. Online access is via the state OCA statewide system. Fee is $65.00 per search. See www.nycourts.gov/apps/chrs/.

Surrogate's Court Courthouse, 7660 State St, Lowville, NY 13367; 315-376-5344; fax: 315-376-1647; 8:30AM-4:30PM; Jun-July-Aug 8:30-4PM (EST). *Probate, Guardianships, Small Estates.*
www.nycourts.gov/courts/5jd/lewis/

General Information: Search Fee: $30 for under 25 yrs to $90 for over 70 yrs. Records available on Public Terminal in Cty Law Lib, also online free with registration at http://surrogate5th.courts.state.ny.us/Public/Login.aspx but records are not all inclusive.

Lewis Town/Village Courts - Croghan Town Court PO Box 532, 9882 State Rte 126, Croghan, NY 13327; 315-346-1272 9:30-11:30AM Tues. **Denmark Town Court** PO Box 44, 3707 Roberts Rd (13619), Copenhagen, NY 13626; 315-493-1302 9AM-N, and 7PM-9PM W, or by appm't. **Diana Town Court** PO Box 271, 5952 Old State Ext Rd, Harrisville, NY 13648; 315-543-2312 9AM-4PM. **Greig Town Court** PO Box 56, Glenfield, NY 13343; 315-348-8272 **Harrisburg Town Court** PO Box 208, 7886 Cobb Rd, Lowville, NY 13367; 315-688-4193 **Lewis Town Court** 5213 Osceola Rd,, West Leyden, NY 13489; 315-942-2371 **Leyden Town Court** R1 Box 116, 3387 Douglas St, Port Leyden, NY 13433; 315-348-6215 Every other Wed 4PM. **Lowville Town Court** 5533 Bostwick St, Lowville, NY 13367; 315-376-8070 6PM 1st & 3rd W,TH. **Lowville Village Court** 5535 Bostwick St, Lowville, NY 13367; 315-376-2834 8AM-3:30PM M; 4-6PM Tu; 8AM-3:30PM W-TH; 8AM-1PM F. **Lyonsdale Town Court** PO Box 313, 3364 Pearl St, Port Leyden, NY 13433; 315-348-8666 DA Night - 1st W. **Martinsburg Town Court** PO Box 16, 6682 State Rt 26, Martinsburg, NY 13404; 315-376-2299 Court 1st & 3rd M 6PM. **New Bremen Town Court** 8420 State Rd 812, Lowville, NY 13367; 315-376-3752 10AM-3PM, 7PM-? W only. **Osceola Town Court** 1711 Florence Rd, Camden, NY 13316; 315-599-8891 **Pinckney Town Court** 307 State Rte 177, PO Box 208, Lowville, NY 13367; 315-688-2076 **Port Leyden Village Court** PO Box 116, 3387 Douglas St, Port Leyden, NY 13433; 315-348-6215 Every other W 4PM. **Turin Town Court** PO Box 236, 6312 E Main St, Turin, NY 13473; 315-348-6073 **Watson Town Court** 6971 #4

Rd, Lowville, NY 13367; 315-376-8132 9-11:30AM M,T,W. **West Turin Town Court** PO Box 703, 4059 Cherry St, Lyons Falls, NY 13368; 315-348-5553 9AM-4PM.

Livingston County

County Clerk 6 Court St, Rm 201, Geneseo, NY 14454; 585-243-7010; fax: 585-243-7928; 8:30AM-4:30PM Oct-May; 8AM-4PM June-Sept (EST). *Felony, Civil.*
www.co.livingston.state.ny.us/clerk.htm
General Information: Countywide search requests made to the County Court Clerk are processed in the manner described below. No sealed or youthful offender records released. Will not fax out documents. Court makes copy: $.65 per page. Self serve copy: self serve available if you have a copy code or button, prefunded, prepaid. Certification fee: $5.00 up to 4 pages, $.65 each add'l page. Payee: County Clerk. Personal checks, money orders accepted. No credit cards accepted. Prepayment required. Mail requests: SASE required.
Civil Name Search: Access: Mail, fax, in person, online. Both court and visitors may perform in person name searches. Search fee: $2.50 per name per year if a written request. Civil cases indexed by defendant only. Civil records on computer since 1996. Plaintiff index available only on computer searches. Mail turnaround Time same day. Civil PAT goes back to 1996. Lookup Supreme Court civil cases at http://iapps.courts.state.ny.us/webcivil/FCASMain. Cases go back to 2002.
Criminal Name Search: Access: Mail, fax, in person. Both court and visitors may perform in person name searches. Criminal records on computer since 1996. Plaintiff index available only on computer searches. Note: One may view the index, the court performs no searches for the public. Mail turnaround Time same day. Criminal PAT goes back to same as civil.

Supreme & County Court 2 Court St, Geneseo, NY 14454; 585-243-7060; fax: 585-243-7067; 9AM-5PM (EST). *Felony, Civil.*
www.nycourts.gov/litigants/courtguides/7thJD_livingston.pdf
General Information: County Court directs felony search requests to the OCA for a $65.00 statewide search fee. See also County Clerk in separate listing. Access current/pending Supreme Court civil cases is at http://iapps.courts.state.ny.us/webcivil/FCASMain.

Surrogate's Court 2 Court St, Geneseo, NY 14454; 585-243-7095; fax: 585-243-7583; 9AM-5PM (EST). *Probate.*
General Information: A county search of the probate court index by mail for 25-year search is $30.00 fee. A full county probate search of all years is $90.00.

Livingston Town/Village Courts - Avon Town Court 23 Genesee St, Avon, NY 14414; 585-226-2425 M,T,TH, 9-4PM; W 9AM-Noon. **Avon Village Court** 23 Genesee St, Opera Block Bldg, Avon, NY 14414; 585-226-2425 x13 9AM-N M,T,W; Closed TH,F. **Caledonia Town Court** 3095 Main St, Caledonia, NY 14423; 585-538-4800 8AM-2PM M-TH; till noon F. **Caledonia Village Court** 3095 Main St, Caledonia, NY 14423; 585-538-4800 8AM-4PN M-TH, 8AM-2PM F. **Conesus Town Court** 6210 S Livonia Rd, Conesus, NY 14435; 585-346-9240 3-7PM 4th W. **Dansville Village Court** 14 Clara Barton St, Dansville, NY 14437; 585-335-2460 1-6PM W. **Geneseo Town & Village Court** 119 Main St, Geneseo, NY 14454; 585-243-4530 8AM-3PM M-F. **Groveland Town Court** 4955 Aten Rd., Groveland, NY 14462; 585-243-3782 8:30AM-3PM (till 2:30 F). **Leicester Town Court** 132 Main St, PO Box 226, Leicester, NY 14481; 585-382-9419 8AM-4PM M-TH; Closed F. **Lima Town Court** 7321 E Main St, PO Box 513, Lima, NY 14485; 585-582-1011 9AM-N. **Livonia Town Court** PO Box 33, 4705 Main St, Hemlock, NY 14487; 585-346-0221 9AM-3PM M-TH. **Mount Morris Village & Town Courts** 117 Main St, Mount Morris, NY 14510; 585-658-3249 8AM-1:30PM M-Th. **North Dansville Town Court** 14 Clara Barton St, Dansville, NY 14437; 585-335-2460 1-5PM W. **Nunda Village & Town Courts** 4 Massachusetts St, Nunda, NY 14517; 585-468-5177 **Ossian Town Court** 4706 Ossian Hill Rd, Dansville, NY 14437; 585-335-8040 1st Th 5PM. **Portage Town Court** 9907 N Church St, Hunt, NY 14846; 585-476-5910 **Sparta Town Court** 7351 Route 256, Scottsburg, NY 14545; 585-335-2860 3PM-? 2nd & 4th M; or call for app'm't. **Springwater Town Court** 8022 S. Main St., Springwater, NY 14560; 585-669-2635 M 10-2PM; W 4:30-8:30PM; TH 10-2PM; Sat 9-12PM. **West Sparta Town Court** 8302 Kysorville/Beyersville Rd, Dansville, NY 14437; 585-335-2443 call clerk for app't. **York Town Court** PO Box 187, 2668 Main St, Rte 36, York, NY 14592; 585-243-3128 M,T,TH,F 9-Noon, 1-4PM; W 9AM-Noon.

Madison County

County Clerk County Office Bldg #4, PO Box 668, Wampsville, NY 13163-0668; 315-366-2261; probate phone: 315-366-2392; fax: 315-366-2615; 9AM-5PM (EST). *Felony, Civil.*
www.madisoncounty.org/
General Information: Countywide search requests made to the County Clerk are processed in the manner described below. No sealed, expunged,

adoption, sex offense, juvenile or mental health records released. Court makes copy: $1.00 per page. Certification fee: Minimum $5.00; $1.00 per page if over 4 pages. Payee: County Clerk. Personal checks accepted, credit cards are not. Prepayment required. Mail requests: SASE required.
Civil Name Search: Access: Mail, in person, online (limited). Both court and visitors may perform in person name searches. Search fee: $5.00 per name. Fee is per 5 years searched. Civil cases indexed by defendant. Judgment records on computer from 1992, prior in books. Mail turnaround Time 1 day. Public use terminal has civil records back to 1/1997. Lookup Supreme Court civil cases at http://iapps.courts.state.ny.us/webcivil/FCASMain. Cases go back to 2002.
Criminal Name Search: Access: Mail, in person. Only the court performs in person name searches; visitors may not. Search fee: $5.00 per name per 5 years. Required to search: name, years to search, DOB. Criminal records on computer to 1984, previous years in books. Mail turnaround Time 2 days.

Supreme & County Court PO Box 545, Wampsville, NY 13163; 315-366-2267; fax: 315-366-2539; 9AM-5PM (EST). *Felony, Civil.*
www.nycourts.gov/courts/6jd/madison/index.shtml
General Information: Direct record search requests to the County Clerk (315-366-2261), see separate listing. Criminal online access is via the state OCA statewide system.

Oneida City Court 108 Main St, Oneida, NY 13421; 315-266-4740; fax: 646-963-6435; 8:30AM-4:30PM M-TH; 8AM-4PM F (EST). *Misdemeanor, Civil Actions under $15,000, Eviction, Small Claims.*
www.nycourts.gov/courts/6jd/madison/oneida/
General Information: No sealed, expunged, sex offense, mental health or youthful offender records released. Will fax documents to local or toll free line. Court makes copy: $.65 per page. Certification fee: $5.00 per document; Exemplification fee $15.00. Payee: City Court. Personal checks, Visa/MC accepted. Prepayment required. Mail requests: SASE required.
Civil Name Search: Access: Mail, in person, online. Both court and visitors may perform in person name searches. Search fee: $5.00 per name per 2 years searched. Civil cases indexed by plaintiff. Civil records on computer from 1990, prior in books back to 1950s. Mail turnaround Time 1-2 days. Public use terminal has civil records back to 07/2007. WebCivil Local at http://iapps.courts.state.ny.us/webcivil/ecourtsMain contains information on both active and disposed Civil Court cases. Search by index number, party name, attorney/firm name or judge. No fee.
Criminal Name Search: Access: Online. Only the court performs in person name searches; visitors may not. Criminal records computerized from 1989; prior in books back to 1950s. Mail turnaround Time 1-2 days. All criminal record search requests made to the Court Clerk are forwarded to the OCA for processing. There is a $65.00 fee. See www.nycourts.gov/apps/chrs.

Surrogate's Court PO Box 607, 138 N Court St, Wampsville, NY 13163; 315-366-2392; fax: 315-963-6594; 8:30AM-4:30PM (EST). *Probate.*
General Information: A county search of the probate court index by mail for 25-year search is $30.00 fee. A full county probate search of all years is $90.00.

Madison Town/Village Courts Brookfield Town Court PO Box 103, Main St, Brookfield, NY 13314; 315-899-5856; varies (EST). **Canastota Village Court** 205 S Peterboro St, Canastota, NY 13032; 315-697-9410; 8AM-4PM (EST). **Cazenovia Town Court** 7 Albany St, Cazenovia, NY 13035; 315-655-9213; call for availability (EST). **Cazenovia Village Court** 90 Albany St, Cazenovia, NY 13035; 315-655-4011; 9830AM-1PM M-TH; 8:30-10:30AM F (EST). **Chittenango Village Court** 222 Genesee St, Municipal Bldg, Chittenango, NY 13037; 315-687-3937; 9AM-4PM (EST). **De Ruyter Town Court** 735 Utica St, Town Hall, De Ruyter, NY 13052; 315-852-9650; . **Eaton Town Court** PO Box 66, 35 Cedar St, Morrisville, NY 13408; 315-684-3154; 9AM-4PM (EST). **Fenner Town Court** 3151 East Rd, Cazenovia, NY 13035; 315-655-2705; 9AM-N (EST). **Georgetown Town Court** PO Box 127, 460 Route 26, Main St, Georgetown, NY 13072; 315-837-4795; 10AM 2nd & 4th WH (EST). **Hamilton Town Court** 60 Montgomery St, Hamilton, NY 13346; 315-824-3508; M 9AM-8PM; T W 9AM-3PM (EST). **Hamilton Village Court** PO Box 119, 60 Montgomery St, Hamilton, NY 13346; 315-824-3508; M 9-8PM; T W 9-3PM (EST). **Lebanon Town Court** 1210 Bradley Brook Rd, Earlville, NY 13332; 315-837-4844; 6:30PM 2nd & 4th TH (EST). **Lenox Town Court** 205 S Peterboro St, Canastota, NY 13032; 315-697-9410; 8AM-4PM (EST). **Lincoln Town Court** PO Box 101, Wampsville, NY 13163; 315-363-6837; 10AM-4PM (EST). **Madison Town Court** Box 42, 7358 Route 20, Madison, NY 13402; 315-893-7544; 7PM M (EST). **Morrisville Village Court** PO Box 66, 23 Cedar St, Morrisville, NY 13408; 315-684-3154; 6:00PM Wed. (EST). **Nelson Town Court** 4085 Nelson Rd., Cazenovia, NY 13035; 315-655-8582; 2-4PM T; Court-4PM 1st & 3rd T (EST). **Stockbridge Town Court** PO Box 143, 5324 N Main St, Munnsville, NY 13409; 315-495-2686; .

Sullivan Town Court 7507 Lakeport Rd., Chittenango, NY 13037; 315-687-3347; 9AM-4PM (EST).

Monroe County

County Clerk 101 County Office Bldg, 39 W Main St #101, Rochester, NY 14614; 585-753-1600; fax: 585-753-1624; 9AM-5PM; 10AM-2PM last Saturday of month (EST). *Felony, Civil.*
www.monroecounty.gov/clerk-index.php
General Information: Countywide search requests made to the County Clerk are processed in the manner described below. Online identifiers in results same as on public terminal. No sealed, divorce records, confidential files released. Will not fax documents. Court makes copy: $.65 per page, $1.30 minimum. Certification fee: $5.00 up to 4 pages, $1.25 each add'l page; includes copy fee. Payee: County Clerk. Personal checks, Visa/MC accepted. Prepayment required. Mail requests: SASE required.
Civil Name Search: Access: Fax, mail, in person. Both court and visitors may perform in person name searches. Search fee: $5.00 per name per 2 years. Civil cases indexed by defendant only prior to 1993. Civil records on computer since 6/93, prior in books. Mail turnaround Time 2 weeks. Civil PAT goes back to 1993.
Criminal Name Search: Access: Fax, mail, online, in person. Both court and visitors may perform in person name searches. Search fee: $5.00 per name; fee is per 2 years searched. A $5.00 blanket index search is also available. Required to search: name, years to search, DOB. Criminal records on computer since 6/93, prior in books. Mail turnaround Time 2 weeks. Criminal PAT goes back to same as civil. Online criminal record name search requests are directed to the OCA for statewide record search, $65.00 search fee. See www.nycourts.gov/apps/chrs. Online results show middle initial.

Supreme Court 545 Hall of Justice, 99 Exchange Blvd, Rochester, NY 14614; 585-753-1645; fax: 585-753-1650; 9AM-5PM (EST). *Felony, Civil.*
www.courts.state.ny.us/courts/7jd/monroe/
General Information: This court does not hold closed case records. It directs criminal search requests to the OCA for a $65.00 statewide record check. However, for a countywide search, see the County Clerk in a separate listing.

Rochester City Court - Civil 99 Exchange Blvd, Rm 6, Hall of Justice, Rochester, NY 14614; 585-428-2444; fax: 585-428-2588; 9AM-5PM (EST). *Civil Actions under $15,000, Eviction, Small Claims.*
www.courts.state.ny.us/courts/7jd/rochester/index.shtml
General Information: Will not fax documents. Court makes copy: $.65 per page with $1.30 minimum. Certification fee: $6.00 per document. Payee: Rochester City Court. Cashiers checks and money orders accepted. Visa/MC accepted. Prepayment required.
Civil Name Search: Access: In person, online. Both court and visitors may perform in person name searches. Search fee: None, but there is a $2.00 per case retrieval fee. Civil records on computer from 1983, prior in books from 1973. Public use terminal has civil records back to 1983. WebCivil Local at http://iapps.courts.state.ny.us/webcivil/ecourtsMain contains information on both active and disposed Civil Court cases. Search by index number, party name, attorney/firm name or judge. No fee.

Rochester City Court - Criminal 150 S Plymouth, Rm 123, Public Safety Bldg, Rochester, NY 14614; 585-428-2447; fax: 585-428-2732; 8:30AM-5PM (EST). *Misdemeanor.*
General Information: No sealed, expunged, probation reports, adoption, sex offense, juvenile or mental health records released. Will fax back to attorneys only. Court makes copy: none for Certificate of Disposition. No certification fee . Payee: Rochester City Court. Only certified checks and money orders accepted. No credit cards accepted. Prepayment required.
Criminal Name Search: Access: In person, online. Search fee: $5.00 per name for Certificate of Disposition. Required to search: Name, years to search, date, any exact details (for Certificate of Disposition). Criminal records on computer since 1986, prior on books from 1980. Note: In person searches limited to pending and current cases on the public access terminal. Public use terminal has crim records back to 1986. All criminal record name search requests are directed to the OCA for statewide record search, $65.00 search fee. See www.nycourts.gov/apps/chrs.

Surrogate's Court 541 Hall of Justice, 99 Exchange Blvd, Rochester, NY 14614; 585-428-5200; fax: 585-428-2650; 9AM-5PM (EST). *Probate.*
www.courts.state.ny.us/courts/7jd/courts/surrogates/
General Information: A county search of the probate court index by mail for 25-year search is $30.00 fee. A full county probate search of all years is $90.00.

Monroe Town/Village Courts Brighton Town Court 2300 Elmwood Ave, Rochester, NY 14618; 585-784-5152; 9AM-5PM (EST). **Chili Town Court** 3235 Chili Ave, Rochester, NY 14624; 585-889-1999; 9AM-5PM (EST). **Clarkson Town Court** PO Box 803, 3655 Lake Rd, Clarkson, NY 14430; 585-637-1134; 8AM-4PM M-TH; 8AM-1PM F (EST). **East Rochester Town Court** 120 W Commercial St, East Rochester, NY 14445; 585-385-2576; 9AM-4PM (EST). **Fairport Village Court** 31 S Main St, Fairport, NY 14450; 585-223-0316; 9AM-3PM M-F (EST). **Gates Town Court** 1605 Buffalo Rd, Rochester, NY 14624; 585-247-6106; 426-0410; 9AM-5PM (EST). **Greece Town Court** 4 Vince Tofany Blvd, Rochester, NY 14612; 585-227-3110; 9AM-5PM (EST). **Hamlin Town Court** 1 650 Lake Rd, Hamlin, NY 14464; 585-964-8641; 8AM-1PM M-TH; 8AM-N F (EST). **Henrietta Town Court** 135 Calkins Rd, #G, Rochester, NY 14623; 585-359-2640; M-TH 9AM-5PM, 9AM-4PM F (EST). **Honeoye Falls Village Court** 5 East St, Honeoye Falls, NY 14472; 585-624-1711; 1st & 3rd W (EST). **Irondequoit Town Court** 1300 Titus Ave, Rochester, NY 14617; 585-336-6040; 8AM-5PM; till 4PM F (EST). **Mendon Town Court** 16 W Main St, Honeoye Falls, NY 14472; 585-624-6064; 9-12PM M,W,TH,F; 1PM-4PM T (EST). **Ogden Town Court** 269 Ogden Center Rd, Spencerport, NY 14559; 585-617-6118; 9AM-3PM (EST). **Parma Town Court** 1300 Hilton-Parma Corners Rd, Hilton, NY 14468; 585-392-9470; 7:30AM-12PM (EST). **Penfield Town Court** 1985 Baird Rd, Penfield, NY 14526; 585-340-8623 or 340-8624; 8AM-4PM (EST). **Perinton Town Court** 1350 Turk Hill Rd, Fairport, NY 14450; 585-223-0770; 9AM - 5PM (EST). **Pittsford Town Court** 3750 Monroe Ave, Ste 950, Pittsford, NY 14534; 585-248-6238; 9AM-5PM; Court TH 6PM (EST). **Riga Town Court** 6460 Buffalo Road, Churchville, NY 14428; 585-293-3884; 9AM-4PM (EST). **Rush Town Court** 5977 E Henrietta Rd, Rush, NY 14543; 585-533-1130; 9AM-1:30PM (EST). **Sweden Town Court** 18 State St, Brockport, NY 14420; 585-637-1070; 9AM-5PM (EST). **Webster Town Court** 1002 Ridge Rd, Webster, NY 14580; 585-872-7020/; 8:30AM-4:30PM (EST). **Wheatland Town Court** PO Box 28 (22 Main St), Scottsville, NY 14546; 585-889-3074; 9AM-1PM (EST).

Montgomery County

County Clerk PO Box 1500, 64 Broadway, County Office Bldg, Fonda, NY 12068; 518-853-8113; 8:30AM-4PM; summer- 9AM-4PM (EST). *Felony, Misdemeanor, Civil.*
www.co.montgomery.ny.us/clerk/
General Information: Countywide civil search requests made to the County Clerk are processed in the manner described below. No sealed or youthful offender records released. Will not fax documents. Court makes copy: $1.00 per page. Self serve copy: $.25 per page. Certification fee: $4.00 per doc plus copy fee. Payee: County Clerk. Personal checks accepted, credit cards are not. Prepayment required. Mail requests: SASE required for civil.
Civil Name Search: Access: Mail, in person, online. Both court and visitors may perform in person name searches. Search fee: $5.00 per name per 5 years. Required to search: name, years to search, address. Civil records in books and on index cards back to 1965; on computer back to 1992. Mail turnaround Time 3 days Public use terminal has civil records back to 1992. Lookup Supreme Court civil cases at http://iapps.courts.state.ny.us/webcivil/FCASMain. Cases go back to 2002.
Criminal Name Search: Access: In person only. Visitors must perform in person searches themselves. Required to search: name, years to search, DOB. Criminal records computerized from 1992; file index back to 1965. Note: County clerk directs criminal searches to OCA for $65.00 statewide search. See the County Clerk for an in person criminal search, call 518-853-4516.

Supreme & County Court PO Box 1500, 58 Broadway - County Courthouse, Fonda, NY 12068; 518-853-4516; fax: 518-853-3596; 9AM-5PM (EST). *Felony, Misdemeanor (limited), Civil.*
General Information: See County Clerk listing for civil search. See state OCA for $65.00 felony search. Court keeps its own Misdemeanor cases only, usually only drug cases; also search city, town, village courts for add'l misdemeanors.

Amsterdam City Court Public Safety Bldg, Rm 208, One Guy Park Ave Ext, Amsterdam, NY 12010; 518-842-9510; fax: 518-843-8474; 8AM-3:45PM (public window closes 3:30PM) (EST). *Misdemeanor, Civil Actions under $15,000, Eviction, Small Claims.*
General Information: No sealed, expunged, adoption, sex offense, juvenile or mental health records released. Will fax documents to local or toll free line. Court makes copy: $.65 per page. Certification fee: $10.00 per document plus copy fee. Payee: City Court. Cashiers checks and money orders accepted. Major credit cards accepted. Prepayment required. Mail requests: SASE required.
Civil Name Search: Access: Mail, in person, online. Only the court performs in person name searches; visitors may not. Search fee: $5.00 per name per very two years searched. Civil cases indexed by defendant. Civil records on computer since 1995, prior on index cards. Mail turnaround Time 3 weeks. WebCivil Local at http://iapps.courts.state.ny.us/webcivil/ecourtsMain contains information on both active and disposed Civil Court cases. Search by index number, party name, attorney/firm name or judge. No fee.

Criminal Name Search: Access: Online. Only the court performs in person name searches; visitors may not. Search fee: A Certificate of Disposition from this court is $6.00. Required to search: name, DOB, years to search. Criminal records computerized from 11/93, prior on index cards. Note: This court does not have access to county records. Mail turnaround Time 3 weeks. All criminal record name search requests are directed to the OCA for statewide record search, $65.00 search fee. See www.nycourts.gov/apps/chrs. These are request forms only.

Surrogate's Court New Court House, 58 Broadway, Rm 50, PO Box 1500, Fonda, NY 12068; 518-853-8108; fax: 518-853-8230; 9AM-5PM; 8AM-4PM summer hours (EST). *Probate.*

General Information: A county search of the probate court index by mail for 25-year search is $30.00 fee. A full county probate search of all years is $90.00.

Montgomery Town/Village Courts - Amsterdam Town Court 283 Mannys Corners Rd, Amsterdam, NY 12010; 518-842-7411 8AM-12:30PM M-F; Court Tu 6PM, TH 7PM. **Canajoharie Town Court** 12 Mitchell St, Canajoharie, NY 13317; 518-673-3013 9AM - 3PM M-TH. **Canajoharie Village Court** 75 Erie Blvd, Canajoharie, NY 13317; 518-673-5116 9AM-4PM. **Charleston Town Court** 480 Corbin Hill Rd, Municipal Bldg, Sprakers, NY 12166; 518-922-6279 1-5PM T; 1PM-9PM TH. **Florida Town Court** 214 Fort Hunter Rd, Amsterdam, NY 12010; 518-843-6468 8AM-2PM. **Fultonville Village Court** PO Box 223, 10 Erie St, Fultonville, NY 12072; 518-853-3166 7AM-4PM (closed F). **Glen Town Court** 7 Erie St, Fultonville, NY 12072; 518-853-4825 7AM-3PM. **Minden Town Court** 136 State Hwy 80, Fort Plain, NY 13339; 518-993-3616 9:30AM-2PM M,T. **Mohawk Town Court** PO Box 415, 2 Park St, Fonda, NY 12068; 518-853-8865 x20 9AM-3PM, 7-9 PM T & TH. **Palatine Town Court** PO Box 40, 141 W Grand St, Palatine Bridge, NY 13428; 518-673-1003 7-9PM M,TH court. **Root Town Court** 1048 Carlisle Rd, Sprakers, NY 12166; 518-673-3549 4PM-9PM M. **St Johnsville Town Court** 7431 State Hiy 5, St Johnsville, NY 13452; 518-568-2662 9AM-1PM M,W,F; 7PM TH. **St Johnsville Village Court** 16 Washington St, St Johnsville, NY 13452; 518-568-5298 9AM-1PM T-TH Office hrs; 6PM-9PM W Court hrs.

Nassau County

County Clerk 240 Old Country Rd, Mineola, NY 11501; 516-571-2272; criminal phone: 516-571-2800; fax: 516-742-4099; 9AM-4:30PM (EST). *Felony, Civil Actions over $15,000.*

www.nassaucountyny.gov/

General Information: Holds records for Supreme Court and County Court. As a rule, this office directs felony record search requests to the OCA for the $65.00 statewide search, however, the records department can perform in person felony searches as described below. No sealed, expunged, adoption, sex offense, juvenile or mental health records released. Will not fax documents. Court makes copy: $.65 per page; $1.30 minimum. Self serve copy: $.25 per page. Certification fee: $5.00 per doc includes 4 copy pgs; $1.25 each add'l page, includes copy fee. Payee: Nassau County Clerk's Office. Personal checks accepted, credit cards are not. Prepayment required. Mail requests: SASE required for civil.

Civil Name Search: Access: Mail, in person, online. Both court and visitors may perform in person name searches. Search fee: $25.00 for judgment search. Civil records on computer from 1992, prior in books. Note: For answers to record search questions call Bob Grabel at County Clerk's office Rm 106 at 516-571-1448. Onsite docket searching available 9AM-3:30PM. Mail turnaround Time 1-2 weeks. Public use terminal has civil records back to 1992. Search supreme court decisions for free from the web page.

Criminal Name Search: Access: In person, online. Only the court performs in person name searches; visitors may not. Required to search: name, DOB. Records stored back to 1800s, computerized since 1980s. The county clerk has felony case "minutes" from the County Court, but "minutes" data is only accessible by attorney's with a written letter of request. For full records, contact the County Court.

County Court 262 Old Country Rd, Mineola, NY 11501; 516-571-2800; fax: 516-571-2802; 9AM-4:40PM (EST). *Felony.*

www.nassaucountyny.gov/

General Information: The County Court Clerk directs felony search requests to the OCA for a statewide record search. However, the court will search pre-1982 records (provide arrest date), which are on books only. No sealed, expunged, sex offense, juvenile, or mental health records released. Will not fax documents. Court makes copy: $.65 per page, $1.30 minimum. Certification fee: $5.20 per cert. Payee: Clerk of Court. No personal checks accepted. Visa/MC accepted, but only with ID presented. Prepayment required.

Criminal Name Search: Access: In person only. Only the court performs in person name searches; visitors may not. Search fee: A Certificate of Disposition may be available from the court. Required to search: name, years to search, DOB. Criminal records computerized from 1982, prior in archives or on microfilm. Note: Also, for "minutes," you may contact records

section of the County Clerk office at 240 Old Country Rd, Mineola, NY, 11501, 516-571-2272. Minutes records are restricted to attorneys only. Public use terminal has crim records. Only registered attorneys may use public access terminal. Search future court appearances at http://iapps.courts.state.ny.us/webcrim_attorney/Login. Some records up to 1984 can be count on the state system as http://courts.state.ny.us.

District Court 99 Main St, Hempstead, NY 11550; 516-572-2355; civil phone: 516-572-2266; fax: 516-572-2291; 9AM-5PM, transactions until 4:30PM (EST). *Civil Actions under $15,000, Eviction, Small Claims, Ordinance.*

General Information: There are 4 Districts. Records for 2nd District are separate prior to 1980. 1st District handles misdemeanor cases. Sm Claims phone- 516-572-2261. Will fax back documents if prepaid. Court makes copy: $1.30 each page; $.65 per page after first 2. Self serve copy: $.25 per page. Certification fee: $6.00; exemplification- $15.00. Payee: Clerk of District Court. No personal or business checks accepted. Major credit cards accepted in person only. Prepayment required. Mail requests: SASE required.

Civil Name Search: Access: Mail, fax, in person. Only the court performs in person name searches; visitors may not. No search fee. Civil records on computer back to 1990; prior in books. Mail turnaround Time 1 week.

District Court 99 Main St, Hempstead, NY 11550; 516-572-2293; criminal phone: 516-572-2293; 9AM-5PM, transactions until 4:30PM (EST). *Misdemeanor.*

www.courts.state.ny.us/courts/10jd/nassau/district.shtml

General Information: Will fax back documents if prepaid. Court makes copy: $1.30 each page; $.65 per page after first 2. Self serve copy: $.25 per page. Certification fee: $6.00; exemplification- $15.00. Payee: Clerk of District Court. No personal or business checks accepted. No credit cards accepted in person only. Prepayment required. Mail requests: SASE required for civil.

Criminal Name Search: Access: In person, online. Only the court performs in person name searches; visitors may not. Search fee: $65.00 per name, statewide search. Required to search: name, DOB; also helpful: address. Criminal records computerized from 1980, prior on books back to 1960. Note: Only minor misdemeanors found here. As a rule, the court directs requests to OCA for $65.00 statewide search. Online access is via the state OCA statewide system. See www.nycourts.gov/apps/chrs/.

Supreme & County Court Supreme Court Bldg, 100 Supreme Court Dr, Mineola, NY 11501; civil phone: 516-571-2904; fax: 516-571-1575; 9AM-5PM (EST). *Civil Actions over $15,000.*

www.nassaucountyny.gov/

General Information: All physical records are maintained at the County Clerk's Office (see entry for County Clerk) 240 Old Country Rd, Mineola, 516-571-2272.

Glen Cove City Court 13 Glen St, Glen Cove, NY 11542; 516-676-0109/1955; fax: 516-676-1570; 9AM-5PM (EST). *Misdemeanor, Civil Actions under $15,000, Eviction, Small Claims, Traffic.*

www.glencove-li.com/

General Information: No sealed, expunged, adoption, sex offense, juvenile or mental health records released. Will not fax documents. Court makes copy: $1.00 per page. Certification fee: $6.00. Payee: Glen Cove City Court. No Personal checks, Visa/MC accepted. Prepayment required. Mail requests: SASE required for civil.

Civil Name Search: Access: Mail, fax, in person, online. Only the court performs in person name searches; visitors may not. Search fee: $16.00 per name. Civil records go back to 1970; on computer back to 1996. WebCivil Local at http://iapps.courts.state.ny.us/webcivil/ecourtsMain contains information on both active and disposed Civil Court cases. Search by index number, party name, attorney/firm name or judge. No fee.

Criminal Name Search: Access: Online. Only the court performs in person name searches; visitors may not. Required to search: DOB, years to search. Criminal records go back to 1966; on computer back to 1996. Note: The court refuses to permit access to court records unless specific case file given. All criminal record name search requests are directed to the OCA for statewide record search, $65.00 search fee. See www.nycourts.gov/apps/chrs.

Long Beach City Court 1 W Chester St, Long Beach, NY 11561; 516-431-1000; criminal phone: x7500; civil phone: x7510; fax: 516-889-3511; 9AM-5PM (EST). *Misdemeanor, Civil Actions under $15,000, Eviction, Small Claims, Traffic.*

General Information: No sealed, expunged, adoption, sex offense, juvenile or mental health records released. Will not fax documents. Court makes copy: $.65 per page, $1.30 minimum. Self serve copy: $.65 per page. Certification fee: $5.00 per doc plus copy fee if criminal; $6.00 if civil. Payee: City Court of Long Beach. Only cashiers checks and money orders accepted. Visa/MC accepted if in person. Prepayment required.

Civil Name Search: Access: In person, online. Only the court performs in person name searches; visitors may not. Search fee: Best to get Certificate of Disposition for $6.00, then get case numbers to make in person request. Civil records are indexed by Plaintiff, Defendant. Civil records go back 25 years. Note: Court recommends the $65.00 statewide search at the OCA. WebCivil Local at http://iapps.courts.state.ny.us/webcivil/ecourtsMain contains information on both active and disposed Civil Court cases. Search by index number, party name, attorney/firm name or judge. No fee.

Criminal Name Search: Access: In person, online. Search fee: $6.00 for Certificate of Disposition. Criminal records computerized for 25 years. Note: The court will not permit access to court records unless specific case file given. First, get Cert. of Disposition. All criminal record name search requests are directed to the OCA for statewide record search, $65.00 search fee. See www.nycourts.gov/apps/chrs.

Surrogate's Court 262 Old Country Rd, Mineola, NY 11501; 516-571-2082; fax: 516-571-2997; 9AM-4:45PM (EST). *Probate.*

General Information: Public access terminal available - index goes way back. A county search of the probate court index by mail for 25-year search is $30.00 fee.

Nassau Town/Village Courts - Atlantic Beach Village Court 65 The Plaza, PO Box 189, Atlantic Beach, NY 11509; 516-371-4552 ext 4 9-5PM; Court Wed 7PM Biweekly. **Brookville Village Court** 18 Horse Hill Rd, Brooksville, NY 11545; 516-922-8198 Call for Court date. **Cove Neck Village Court** PO Box 299, 2 Cove Neck Rd, Oyster Bay, NY 11771; 516-922-1885 9:30AM - 12:30PM. **East Hills Village Court** 209 Harbor Hill Rd., East Hills, NY 11576; 516-621-6117 9-4:30PM. **East Rockaway Village Court** PO Box 189, 376 Atlantic Ave, East Rockaway, NY 11518; 516-887-6312 9AM-4:45PM. **East Williston Village Court** , 2 Prospect St, East Wiliston, NY 11596; 516-922-9154 **Farmingdale Village Court** 361 Main St, Village Hall, Farmingdale, NY 11735; 516-293-2292 9AM-3PM. **Flower Hill Village Court** 1 Bonnie Heights Rd, Manhasset, NY 11030; 516-627-5000 9AM-4:30PM. **Garden City Village Court** 351 Stewart Ave, Garden City, NY 11530; 516-742-9886 8:30-4:00PM M-F. **Hempstead Village Court** 99 Nichols Ct, Hempstead, NY 11550; 516-478-6254 /6257 8:30-4PM. **Kings Point Village Court** 32 Steppingstone Ln, Kings Point, NY 11024; 516-482-7872 #302 9:30AM-4:30PM. **Lake Success Village Court** 15 Vanderbilt Dr, Lake Success, NY 11020; 516-482-7430 varies. **Lattingtown Village Court** PO Box 201, Locust Valley, NY 11560; 516-681-9271 9AM-N M,W,F. **Lawrence Village Court** 196 Central Ave, Lawrence, NY 11559; 516-239-9166 8AM-4PM M-F. **Malverne Village Court** 99 Church St, Malverne, NY 11565; 516-599-1200 9AM - 5PM. **Manorhaven Village Court** 33 Manorhaven Blvd, Port Washington, NY 11050; 516-883-7000 9AM-4PM. **Massapequa Park Village Court** 151 Front St, Village Hall, Massapequa Park, NY 11762; 516- 798-0244 x118 9AM-5PM. **Munsey Park Village Court** 1777 Northern Blvd, Manhasset, NY 11030; 516-365-7790 9AM-4PM. **Muttontown Village Court** 1 Raz Tafuro Way, Muttontown, NY 11791; 516-364-2240 9:30AM-12:30PM. **Old Brookville Village Court** 201 McCouns Ln, Old Brookville, NY 11545; 516-681-9271 9:30AM-12:30PM M-F. **Oyster Bay Cove Village Court** 25B Rte 25A, Oyster Bay, NY 11771; 516-922-1016 8AM-04PM M,W,F. **Plandome Heights Village Court** PO Box 1384, 37 Orchard St, Manhasset, NY 11030; 516-627-1136 9:00-4:00. **Plandome Manor Village Court** PO Box 952, 1526 N Plandome Rd, Plandome Manor, NY 11030; 516-627-3701 9:00 - 4:00. **Plandome Village Court** PO Box 930, 65 South Dr, Plandome, NY 11030; 516-627-1748 **Rockville Centre Village Court** PO Box 950 (One College Pl), Rockville Centre, NY 11571; 516-678-9233 8AM-3:30PM. **Sea Cliff Village Court** PO Box 340, Sea Cliff, NY 11579; 516-671-0328 M 1-6PM; T-F 9-4:30PM. **South Floral Park Village Court** 383 Roquette Ave, South Floral Park, NY 11001; 516-352-8047 9AM-N, 1-4PM. **Stewart Manor Village Court** 120 Covert Ave, Stewart Manor, NY 11530; 516-354-1800 9AM-4PM. **Upper Brookville Village Court** PO Box 436, 1395 Planting Fields Rd, Annex Bldg (Oyster Bay), Glen Head, NY 11545; 516-624-7715 9:30AM - 12:30PM. **Valley Stream Village Court** 123 S Central Ave, Valley Stream, NY 11580; 516-825-4200 8AM-4PM. **Westbury Village Court** 235 Lincoln Pl, Westbury, NY 11590; 516-334-1700 x116 9AM-4:30PM

New York County

Supreme Court - Civil Division County Clerk, 60 Centre St, Rm 103, New York City, NY 10007; 646-386-5955 x8; civil phone: 646-386-5942 records; 386-5940 (docket Section); 9AM-3PM county clerk; 9AM-5PM Supreme Ct Office (EST). *Civil Actions over $25,000.*
www.nycourts.gov/supctmanh/

General Information: Record search requests are managed by the County Clerk's office; information here is for that County Clerk office. The Supreme Ct clerk office phone is 636-386-3160 but they will refer you to the County Clerk. Will not fax documents. Court makes copy: $.35 per page. Self serve copy: $.25 per page. Certification fee: $8.00 per doc plus copy fee. Payee: County Clerk. Cashiers checks, attorney checks and money orders accepted;

no personal checks. No credit cards accepted, except Visa/MC in person only. Prepayment required.

Civil Name Search: Access: Mail, In person, online. Both court and visitors may perform in person name searches. Search fee: $5.00 per 2 years per name. Civil records on computer from 1993, prior in books; records go back to 1971. Note: Direct mail requests to the Mail Clerk, Rm 141B, certification phone 646-386-5935/36 (Law & Equity) Mail turnaround Time 7-10 days Public use terminal has civil records back to 1993. Public terminal located in Rm 103B. Search the Sup. Ct Online records CCIS (back to 1986) or CCOP (back to 1972) free at http://iapps.courts.state.ny.us/iscroll/index.jsp. Click Advanced Search. $39.90 monthly sub; $19.95 base rate to purchase case file copy. Also, access to current/pending Supreme Court civil cases is at http://iapps.courts.state.ny.us/webcivil/FCASMain. Opinions/decisions free at www.nycourts.gov/supctmanh/Decisions_Online.htm.

Supreme Court - Criminal Division 100 Centre St, Rm 1000, New York, NY 10013; 646-386-4000; criminal phone: 646-386-3860 correspondence sec.; fax: 212-374-3177; 9AM-5PM (EST). *Felony, Misdemeanor.*

General Information: The Court will only process mail or in person requests for specific documents or papers related to felony cases. Copies may possibly be purchased from the County Clerk. No sealed, expunged, adoption, sex offense, juvenile or mental health records released. Will not fax documents. Court makes copy: n/a. Self serve copy: $.15 per page. Certification fee: $8.00 per document. Note that court will only make copies if certified. Payee: County Clerk. No personal checks. No credit cards accepted. Prepayment required. Mail requests: SASE requested.

Criminal Name Search: Access: Mail, fax, in person. Visitors must perform in person searches themselves. Search fee: No search fee if in person. A Certificate of Disposition is $10.00. Required to search: name, years to search, DOB. Case number or other case identifiers are required for Certificate of Disposition; get case number from OCA or online search. Physical records back to 1999. Criminal records computerized from 1980s (less complete the further back), prior records archived. Note: Written requests for name searches should be directed to OCA for $65.00 statewide search. With case number, the correspondence section will accept requests for specific document via fax, mail or phone. Mail turnaround Time is 1 day; older records from archives- 1 week. Public use terminal has crim records back to only current cases. Docket or case number required for a terminal search; no name searching. Only name, birth year and NYSID# will appear for identifiers. Online access is via the state OCA statewide system. Fee is $65.00 per search. See www.nycourts.gov/apps/chrs/. Subscribe or login as guest to search eCourts WebCrims future appearances system at http://iapps.courts.state.ny.us/webcrim_attorney/Login.

Civil Court of the City of New York 111 Centre St, Rm 118, New York, NY 10013; 646-386-5700- info; 646-386-5730 Admin; civil phone: 646-386-5600; fax: 212-374-8053; 9AM-5PM, open til 7PM TH (EST). *Civil Actions under $25,000, Eviction, Small Claims.*
www.courts.state.ny.us/courts/1jd/index.shtml

General Information: Use 646-386-5750 for landlord/tenant records. Small Claims- 646-386-5480. Archives phone- 646-386-5515. General NYC civil dial-up info line- 212-791-6000. Fax number is for Admin Ofc who distributes the faxes. no sealed records released. Will not fax documents. Court makes copy: n/a. Self serve copy: $.10 per page. Self-serve copier located outside Rm 118. Certification fee: $6.00 per doc. Payee: Clerk of Civil Court. Only cashiers checks and money orders accepted. Attorney's checks accepted. No credit cards accepted. Prepayment required. Mail requests: SASE required for civil.

Civil Name Search: Access: Phone, in person, online. Visitors must perform in person searches themselves. No search fee. Required to search: name, years to search; also helpful: address. Civil cases indexed by plaintiff; computerized records since 1994. Pre-1998 records archived in Queens; 1998 to present in Brooklyn. Landlord/Tenant records on computer from 1984, civil from 1994, prior in books. Records are archived after 3 years. Note: Clerk's office will do a name lookup to see if a case exists and its number. Public use terminal has civil records back to 1994. Results may include calendar number, partial address. Public terminal has Landlord/tenant, civil, and small claims. Located on 1st Fl. Court decisions at http://decisions.courts.state.ny.us/search/query3.asp. WebCivil Local at http://iapps.courts.state.ny.us/webcivil/ecourtsMain contains information on both active and disposed Civil Court cases. Search by index number, party name, attorney/firm name or judge. No fee.

Surrogate's Court 31 Chambers St, #402, New York City, NY 10007; 646-386-5000; 9AM-5PM (EST). *Probate.*
www.courts.state.ny.us/courts/nyc/surrogates/index.shtml

General Information: Public terminal has index back to 1968. Mail search requests for past 25 years are $30.00; you may include your email address in your written request for fast reply. Make check to NY Surrogates Ct, but no personal checks accepted.

Niagara County

County Court County Clerk, 175 Hawley St - Courthouse, Lockport, NY 14094; 716-439-7022; criminal phone: 726-439-7065; civil phone: 716-439-7029; probate phone: 716-439-7135; fax: 716-439-7066; 9AM-5PM (EST). *Felony, Civil Actions over $25,000.*
www.niagaracounty.com

General Information: This court also directs criminal search requests to the OCA for a $65.00 statewide record check. Online identifiers in results same as on public terminal. No sealed or youthful offender records released. Will fax documents for add'l $3.00 per name. Court makes copy: $1.30 1st page, $.65 ea add'l. Certification fee: $5.00 minimum; up to 5 pages. Payee: County Clerk. Personal checks, money orders accepted. Visa/MC accepted, small fee charged. Prepayment required. Mail requests: SASE not required.

Civil Name Search: Access: Mail, fax, in person, online. Both court and visitors may perform in person name searches. Search fee: $5.00 per name per 2 years. Civil cases indexed by defendant. Civil index in docket books from 1950, computerized since 1997. Note: Will accept fax requests if payment arrangement is made in advance. Mail turnaround Time 3-5 days. Civil PAT goes back to 1997. Lookup Supreme Court civil cases at http://iapps.courts.state.ny.us/webcivil/FCASMain. Cases go back to 2002.

Criminal Name Search: Access: In person, online. Visitors must perform in person searches themselves. Required to search: name, years to search, DOB. Criminal records on computer since 1/97; prior records in books. Note: Unless given very specific info such as case number, this court limits itself to issuing only Certificates of Disposition for $5.00. Criminal PAT goes back to 10/1997. Name search requests are often directed to the OCA for statewide record search, $65.00 search fee. See www.nycourts.gov/apps/chrs.

Supreme & County Court 775 3rd St, Niagara Falls, NY 14302; 716-278-1800; fax: 716-278-1809; 9AM-5PM (EST). *Felony, Civil Actions over $25,000.*

General Information: This court will not provide records to the public. All records are maintained at County Clerk office, 175 Hawley St, Lockport, NY 14094, 716-439-7030.

Lockport City Court One Locks Plaza, Municipal Bldg, Lockport, NY 14094; 716-439-6660; criminal phone: x501; fax: 716-439-6684; 8:30AM-4:30PM (EST). *Misdemeanor, Civil Actions under $15,000, Eviction, Small Claims.*

General Information: No sealed, expunged, adoption, sex offense, juvenile or mental health records released. Will fax documents to local or toll free line. Court makes copy: $1.00 per page. Certification fee: $6.00. Payee: City Court of Lockport. Cashiers checks and money orders accepted. Major credit cards accepted. Prepayment required. Mail requests: SASE required for civil.

Civil Name Search: Access: Phone, fax, mail, in person, online. Both court and visitors may perform in person name searches. Search fee: $16.00 per name. Civil cases indexed by defendant. Civil records on computer from 1988, prior in books from 1900s. Mail turnaround Time 14 days. WebCivil Local at http://iapps.courts.state.ny.us/webcivil/ecourtsMain contains information on both active and disposed Civil Court cases. Search by index number, party name, attorney/firm name or judge. No fee.

Criminal Name Search: Access: Online. Only the court performs in person name searches; visitors may not. Criminal records in books from 1977 forward; computerized since 1988. Note: The court is unable to search criminal records unless specific case file given. All criminal record name search requests are directed to the OCA for statewide record search, $65.00 search fee. See www.nycourts.gov/apps/chrs.

Niagara Falls City Court Niagara Falls Municipal Center, 1925 Main St, Niagara Falls, NY 14305; 716-278-9800; criminal phone: 716-278-9800; civil phone: 716-278-9860; fax: 716-278-9809; 9AM-5PM (EST). *Misdemeanor, Civil Actions under $15,000, Eviction, Small Claims.*
www.nycourts.gov/courts/8jd/Niagara/niagarafalls.shtml

General Information: No sealed, expunged, adoption, sex offense, juvenile or mental health records released. Will not fax documents. Court makes copy: $.65 per page, $130 minimum. Certification fee: $6.00per page. Payee: City Court of Niagara Falls. No checks accepted. Visa/MC accepted. Prepayment required. Mail requests: SASE not required.

Civil Name Search: Access: Mail, in person. Both court and visitors may perform in person name searches. Search fee: $5.00 per name for 2 years; computer search is $16.00. Civil cases indexed by defendant. Civil records on microfilm from 1985, in books since 1970. Mail turnaround Time 7-10 working days.

Criminal Name Search: Access: Mail, in person, online. Only the court performs in person name searches; visitors may not. Search fee: A

certificate of Disposition is $5.00. Criminal records in books from 1970. Note: The court refuses to permit access to criminal court records unless specific case file given. Mail turnaround Time 7-10 working days. Name search requests are often directed to the OCA for statewide record search, $65.00 search fee. See www.nycourts.gov/apps/chrs.

North Tonawanda City Court 216 Payne Ave, City Hall, North Tonawanda, NY 14120; 716-693-1010; criminal phone: x504; civil phone: x501; fax: 716-743-1754; 8AM-4PM; 8AM-4PM Summer hrs (EST). *Misdemeanor, Civil Actions under $15,000, Eviction, Small Claims.*

General Information: No sealed, expunged, adoption, sex offense, juvenile or mental health records released. Will fax documents $5.00 fee. Court makes copy: $.65 per page, $1.30 minimum. Certification fee: $5.00 per document. Payee: City Court. Only cashiers checks and money orders accepted. Visa/MC accepted in person only or for traffic in person, fax, or mail only. Prepayment required. Mail requests: SASE requested.

Civil Name Search: Access: Mail, fax, in person. Only the court performs in person name searches; visitors may not. Search fee: $6.00 for transcript. Civil cases indexed by defendant. Civil records on computer from 1993, prior in books. Mail turnaround Time 2-5 days.

Criminal Name Search: Access: Mail, fax, in person, online. Only the court performs in person name searches; visitors may not. Search fee: $5.00 per name for Cert of Disposition only and date of arrest must be included. Required to search: Name, exact date of arrest, DOB. Criminal records computerized from 1986, prior in books back to late 1970s. Mail turnaround Time 2-5 days. Name search requests are often directed to the OCA for statewide record search, $65.00 search fee. See www.nycourts.gov/apps/chrs.

Surrogate's Court Niagara's County Courthouse, 175 Hawley St, Lockport, NY 14094; 716-439-7130; fax: 716-439-7319; 9AM-5PM (EST). *Probate.*
http://courts.state.ny.us/

General Information: A search of the probate court index by mail for 25-year search is $30.00 fee. A full county probate search for more that 25 years is $90.00. Copy cost $.25 per page. Searches are done as Court Staff time permits.

Niagara Town/Village Courts - Cambria Town Court 4160 Upper Mt Road, Sanborn, NY 14132; 716-433-7664 1st T- 2-7:30PM; 2nd T-6:30PM; 5th T- 7:30PM. **Hartland Town Court** 8942 Ridge Rd, Gasport, NY 14067; 716-735-7239 9AM-12PM T,W,TH,; Court 7PM-? Tu. **Lewiston Town Court** 1375 Ridge Rd, PO Box 330, Lewiston, NY 14092; 716-754-8213 x1 8AM-4PM. **Lockport Town Court** 6564 Dysinger Rd, Lockport, NY 14094; 716-439-9528 8AM-4PM. **Newfane Town Court** 2896 Transit Rd, Newfane, NY 14108; 716-778-9292 9-12PM. **Niagara Town Court** 7105 Lockport Rd, Niagara Falls, NY 14305; 716-215-1480 8AM-4:30PM, public hours 8AM-4PM. **Pendleton Town Court** 6570 Campbell Blvd, Lockport, NY 14094; 716-625-8833 9-3PM. **Porter Town Court** 3265 Creek Rd, Youngstown, NY 14174; 716-745-7036 x6 8AM-N 1PM-4PM. **Royalton Town Court** 5316 Royalton Center Rd, Middleport, NY 14105; 716-772-2588 11AM-4PM T,W,TH. **Somerset Town Court** PO Box 368, 8700 Haight Rd, Barker, NY 14012; 716-795-9193 10AM-2PM M-T. **Wheatfield Town Court** 2800 Church Rd, North Tonawanda, NY 14120; 716-694-6793 10AM-2PM. **Wilson Town Court** PO Box 537, 375 Lake St, Wilson, NY 14172; 716-751-0549 9AM-11AM M-TH.

Oneida County

County Clerk 800 Park Ave, Utica, NY 13501; criminal phone: 315-798-5797; civil phone: 315-798-5797; fax: 315-798-6440; 8:30AM-5PM:8:30AM-4:30PM Summer hours (EST). *Felony, Civil.*

General Information: Countywide search requests made to the County Clerk are processed in the manner described below. Online identifiers in results same as on public terminal. No sealed, expunged, adoption, sex offense, juvenile or mental health records released. Will fax documents $1.00 per page plus copy fee. Court makes copy: $.65 per page, $5.00 minimum. Self serve copy: $.65 per page, $5.20 minimum. Certification fee: $5.00 includes copy fee. Payee: County Clerk. Personal checks accepted, credit cards are not. Prepayment required. Mail requests: SASE required.

Civil Name Search: Access: Mail, fax, in person, online. Both court and visitors may perform in person name searches. Search fee: $5.00 per name. Fee is for 2 year search. Civil records on computer from 1992, prior in books by plaintiff only. Mail turnaround Time 1 week. Civil PAT goes back to 1992. Lookup current or pending Supreme Court civil cases at http://iapps.courts.state.ny.us/webcivil/FCASMain.

Criminal Name Search: Access: Mail, fax, in person. Both court and visitors may perform in person name searches. Search fee: $5.00 per name. Fee is for 2 years searched. Required to search: name, years to search, DOB, signed release. Criminal records computerized from 1992, prior in books by defendant only. Mail turnaround Time 1 week. Criminal PAT goes back to 1992.

Supreme & County Court 200 Elizabeth St, Utica, NY 13501; 315-7266-4200; fax: 315-798-6436; 8:30AM-4:30PM (EST). *Felony, Civil.*
General Information: Direct record search requests to the County Clerk, see separate listing. Access to current/pending Supreme Court civil cases is at https://iapps.courts.state.ny.us/caseTrac/jsp/ecourt.htm.

Rome City Court 100 W Court St, Rome, NY 13440; 315-337-6440; fax: 315-338-0343; 8:30AM-4:30PM; 8:30AM-4PM Summer Hours (EST). *Misdemeanor, Civil Actions under $15,000, Eviction, Small Claims, Traffic.*
General Information: No sealed or youthful offender records released. Will fax documents to local or toll free line. Court makes copy: $.65 per page, $1.30 minimum. Certification fee: $6.00 per doc. Exemplification fee $1.00. Payee: Rome City Court. Only cashiers checks and money orders accepted. Visa/MC accepted. Prepayment required.
Civil Name Search: Access: In person, online. Only the court performs in person name searches; visitors may not. No search fee. Civil records in books and some on computer. WebCivil Local at http://iapps.courts.state.ny.us/webcivil/ecourtsMain contains information on both active and disposed Civil Court cases. Search by index number, party name, attorney/firm name or judge. No fee.
Criminal Name Search: Access: In person, online. Only the court performs in person name searches; visitors may not. Search fee: A Certificate of Disposition is $6.00. Required to search: name, years to search, (case number, arrest date for Cert. of Disposition). Note: As a rule, this court does not permit access to court records unless specific case file given. All criminal record name search requests are directed to the OCA for statewide record search, $65.00 search fee. See www.nycourts.gov/apps/chrs. Be aware that the state system does not include certain "violation" records, this court does allow an in person search.

Sherrill City Court 373 Sherrill Rd, Sherrill, NY 13461; 315-363-0996; fax: 315-363-1176; 8:30AM-4:30PM (EST). *Misdemeanor, Civil Actions under $15,000, Eviction, Small Claims.*
General Information: No sealed, expunged, adoption, sex offense, juvenile or mental health records released. Will not fax documents. Court makes copy: $.65 per page. Certification fee: $6.00 per document plus copy fee. Payee: Sherrill City Court. Personal checks accepted, credit cards are not. Prepayment required. Mail requests: SASE required.
Civil Name Search: Access: Mail, in person, online. Only the court performs in person name searches; visitors may not. Search fee: $5.00 per name per 2 year period. Civil cases indexed by defendant only. Civil records in books since 1988, rest archived. Mail turnaround Time 1-2 days. WebCivil Local at http://iapps.courts.state.ny.us/webcivil/ecourtsMain contains information on both active and disposed Civil Court cases. Search by index number, party name, attorney/firm name or judge. No fee.
Criminal Name Search: Access: Mail, in person, online. Only the court performs in person name searches; visitors may not. Search fee: $5.00 per name per 2 year period. Also, a Certificate of Disposition is $6.00. Required to search: name, DOB, years to search. Criminal records in books since 1800s. The court will do a name search of their records. Mail turnaround Time 1-2 days. But many name search requests are often directed to the OCA for statewide record search, $65.00 search fee. See www.nycourts.gov/apps/chrs.

Utica City Court 411 Oriskany St W, Utica, NY 13502; criminal phone: 315-266-4602; civil phone: 315-266-4603; criminal fax: 315-724-0762; civil fax: 8:30AM-4:30PM; 8:30AM-4:30PM (EST). *Misdemeanor, Civil Actions under $15,000, Eviction, Small Claims,.*
General Information: No sealed, expunged, adoption, sex offense, juvenile or mental health records released. Will not fax documents. Court makes copy: $.65 per page. $1.30 minimum. Certification fee: $5.00 per cert plus copy fee. Payee: City Court of Utica. Only cashiers checks and money orders accepted. Visa/MC accepted. Prepayment required.
Civil Name Search: Access: In person, online. Both court and visitors may perform in person name searches. No search fee. Required to search: name, years to search, address. Civil cases indexed by defendant. Civil records in books from 1900s, computerized records back to 1980's. Civil PAT goes back to 1998. WebCivil Local at http://iapps.courts.state.ny.us/webcivil/ecourtsMain contains information on both active and disposed Civil Court cases. Search by index number, party name, attorney/firm name or judge. No fee.
Criminal Name Search: Access: In person, online. Both court and visitors may perform in person name searches. Search fee: $6.00 for certificate of disposition. Required to search: name, years to search, address. Criminal records in books from 1900s, computerized records back to 1980's. Note: The court refuses to permit access to court records unless specific case file given. Criminal PAT goes back to 1998. All criminal record name search requests are directed to the OCA for statewide record search, $65.00 search fee. See www.nycourts.gov/apps/chrs.

Surrogate's Court Oneida County Office Bldg 8th Fl, 800 Park Ave, Utica, NY 13501; 315-266-4550; fax: 315-797-9237; 8:30AM-4:30PM (EST). *Probate.*
General Information: Access to some, not all 5th District Surrogate's records is free after registration at http://surrogate5th.courts.state.ny.us/Public/Login.aspx. A mail search of the index for up to 25-year search is $30.00 fee; all over 25 years $90.00 per name.

Oneida Town/Village Courts - Annsville Town Court PO Box 61, 9196 Main St, Taberg, NY 13471; 315-336-1295 6-7:30PM M. **Augusta Town Court** PO Box 671, 185 N Main St, Oriskany Falls, NY 13362; 315-821-3814 4PM-? 1st & 3rd TH. **Ava Town Court** PO Box 94, 14468 St Rte 26, Ava, NY 13303; 315-942-5669 6PM 2nd TH monthly or by appoin't, call 315-942-6195. **Boonville Town Court** 13149 St Rte 12, Boonville, NY 13309; 315-943-2071 6PM-? T. **Boonville Village Court** 13149 State Rte 12, Boonville, NY 13309; 315-943-2070 3:30-5:30PM M-TH; court- 6PM W. **Bridgewater Town Court** Municipal Bldg. Route 8, Bridgewater, NY 13313; 315-822-5909 M 7PM. **Camden Town Court** Church St, Town Hall, Camden, NY 13316; 315-245-4033 7PM-? M-W. **Deerfield Town Court** 6329 Walker Rd, Deerfield, NY 13502; 315-5073058 1PM-6PM. **Florence Town Court** 11352 Thomson Corners, Florence Rd, Camden, NY 13316; 315-245-4256 **Floyd Town Court** 8299 Old Floyd Rd, Rome, NY 13440; 315-865-4256 x25 6-8PM M,W. **Forestport Town Court** PO Box 137, 12012 Woodhull Rd, Forestport, NY 13338; 315-392-2801 ext 5 7PM-8:30PM T, and as needed. **Kirkland Town Court** PO Box 87, Franklin Springs, NY 13341; 315-853-4538 6:30PM T. **Lee Town Court** 5808 Stokes-Lee Center Rd, PO Box 122, Lee Center, NY 13363; 315-336-1585 10AM-6PM W. **Marcy Town Court** Town Court, 8801 Paul Becker Rd, Marcy, NY 13403; 315-768-4800 x223/224 9AM-4PM M-TH; 9AM-N F. **Marshall Town Court** 2641 St Rte 12B, Deansboro, NY 13328; 315-841-4473 x12 5:30PM-? W (court). **New Hartford Town Court** 30 Kellogg Rd, New Hartford, NY 13413; 315-732-5924 9AM-4PM. **New Hartford Village Court** 30 Kellogg Rd, New Hartford, NY 13413; 315-732-5924 9AM-4PM. **New York Mills Village Court** 1 Maple St, New York Mills, NY 13417; 315-736-7811 3:30-6PM M. **Oriskany Village Court** Municipal Bldg, 708 Utica St, PO Box 904, Oriskany, NY 13424; 315-736-2725 4PM-? W. **Paris Town Court** 2580 Sulpher Springs Rd, Sauquoit, NY 13456; 315-839-6208 or 5678 x4 M 6PM. **Remsen Town Court** 10540 Academy Ln, Remsen, NY 13438; 315-831-8710 6PM-? T. **Sangerfield Town Court** PO Box 34, 1084 State Rte 12, Sangerfield, NY 13455; 315-841-4108 2nd TH 7PM; 4th TH 3PM. **Steuben Town Court** 9458 Soule Rd, Remsen, NY 13438; 315-865-5508 7PM T. **Sylvan Beach Village Court** 808 Marina Dr, PO Box 580, Sylvan Beach, NY 13157; 315-762-4246 10AM-3PM W-TH; court- 4PM-? TH except 3rd TH. **Trenton Town Court** Town Hall, 8520 Old Poland Rd, PO Box 521, Barneveld, NY 13304; 315-896-4510 7PM-? M,T. **Vernon Town Court** PO Box 643, 4305 Peterboro Rd, Vernon, NY 13476; 315-829-4481 1PM-? W. **Verona Town Court** PO Box 165, Verona, NY 13478; 315-363-4394 9AM-3:30PM M-TH. **Vienna Town Court** PO Box 376, 2083 State Rt 49, Town Hall, North Bay, NY 13123; 315-245-2191 Court Tues Night. **Waterville Village Court** 122 Barton Ave, Waterville, NY 13480; 315-841-8737 2nd T, 4th TH each month - 5PM till done. **Western Town Court** 9219 Main St, Town Court, Westernville, NY 13486; 315-827-4548 7PM-9PM T. **Westmoreland Town Court** PO Box 238, 100 Station Rd, Westmoreland, NY 13490; 315-853-4333 M-TH 9AM-3PM. **Whitesboro Village Court** PO Box 73, 8 Park Ave, Whitesboro, NY 13492; 315-736-4353 9:30AM-Noon T. **Whitestown Town Court** 1 Championship Way, Whitesboro, NY 13492; 315-736-0564/1251 5PM-7PM M.

Onondaga County

County Clerk 401 Montgomery St, Rm 200, Syracuse, NY 13202; 315-435-2229; criminal phone: 315-435-2236; civil phone: 315-435-2234; fax: 315-435-3455; 8AM-4PM (EST). *Felony, Civil.*
General Information: Countywide search requests made to the County Clerk are processed in the manner described below. All requests must be in writing. No sealed, divorce, judgment or sexual abuse records released. Will not fax documents. Court makes copy: $.65 per page, $1.30 minimum. Certification fee: $5.00 minimum; $1.25 per page over 4. Payee: County Clerk. Personal checks accepted; $60.00 limit. Visa and Discover accepted. Prepayment required. Mail requests: SASE required.
Civil Name Search: Access: Mail, in person, online. Both court and visitors may perform in person name searches. Search fee: $2.50 per name per year. Civil records on computer from 1989, prior in books but can only search by plaintiff name. Mail turnaround Time 2-3 days. Civil PAT goes back to 1989. At a site maintained by the state, lookup current or pending Supreme Court civil cases at http://iapps.courts.state.ny.us/webcivil/FCASMain.
Criminal Name Search: Access: Mail, in person. Both court and visitors may perform in person name searches. Search fee: $2.50 per name per year. Required to search: name, years to search; also helpful: DOB. Criminal

records computerized from 1990, prior in books. Mail turnaround Time 2-3 days. Criminal PAT goes back to 1990. Online results show name only.

Supreme & County Court 401 Montgomery St, 3rd Fl, Syracuse, NY 13202; 315-671-1030; fax: 315-671-1176; 8:30AM-4:30PM (EST). *Civil.*
www.nycourts.gov/courts/
General Information: Search requests to Supreme Court forwarded to the OCA for processing. Countywide only searches can be performed at the County Clerk, see separate listing. Access current/pending Supreme Court cases at http://iapps.courts.state.ny.us/webcivil/FCASMain.

County Court 505 S State St, Rm 110, Syracuse, NY 13202; 315-671-1020; fax: 315-671-1191; 8:30AM-4:30PM (EST). *Felony.*
www.nycourts.gov/courts/
General Information: Search requests made to County Court are forwarded to the OCA for processing of $65.00 statewide record search. Countywide only searches can be performed at the County Clerk office, see separate listing.

Syracuse City Court 505 S State St, Rm 130, Syracuse, NY 13202-2104; 315-671-2700; criminal phone: 315-671-2760; civil phone: 315-671-2782; criminal fax: 315-671-2743; civil fax: 8:30AM-4:30PM; closes to public- 3:30PM; 8:30AM-4:30PM; closes to public- 3:30PM (EST). *Misdemeanor, Civil Actions under $15,000, Eviction, Small Claims.*
www.nycourts.gov/courts/5jd/onondaga/syracuse/
General Information: Small claims phone is 315-671-3982; civil fax is 315-671-2741. Traffic phone- 315-671-2770. No sealed, expunged, adoption, sex offense, juvenile or mental health records released. Will not fax documents. Court makes copy: $.65 per page. $1.30 minimum. Certification fee: $6.00 fee per case. Payee: Syracuse City Court. Only cashiers checks, money orders and attorney checks accepted. Visa/MC accepted. Prepayment required. Mail requests: SASE required.
Civil Name Search: Access: Mail, in person, online. Only the court performs in person name searches; visitors may not. Search fee: $16.00 per name. Required to search: name, years to search; also helpful: address. Civil cases indexed by defendant, plaintiff or index number. Civil records on computer from 1993, from 1980-2000 on fiche or microfilm. Mail turnaround Time 1-2 weeks. WebCivil Local at http://iapps.courts.state.ny.us/webcivil/ecourtsMain contains information on both active and disposed Civil Court cases. Search by index number, party name, attorney/firm name or judge. No fee.
Criminal Name Search: Access: Online. No criminal searching at this court. Required to search: name, years to search, DOB; also helpful: offense. Criminal records from 1960 to present are on either computer, dockets or manual books. Mail turnaround Time 1-2 weeks. Name search requests are directed to the OCA for statewide record search, $65.00 search fee, unless the case is very current. See www.nycourts.gov/apps/chrs. Also the court will sometimes direct requesters to the local sheriff's office.

Surrogate's Court Onondaga Courthouse, Rm 209, 401 Montgomery St, Syracuse, NY 13202; 315-671-2100; fax: 315-671-1162; 8:30AM-4:30PM (EST). *Probate.*
http://surrogate5th.courts.state.ny.us/public/
General Information: Access to some, not all 5th District Surrogate's records is free after registration at http://surrogate5th.courts.state.ny.us/Public/Login.aspx. A county search of the probate court index by mail for 25-year search- $30.00 fee; all years is $90.00.

Onondaga Town/Village Courts - Baldwinsville Village Court 16 W Genesee St, Baldwinsville, NY 13027; 315-635-6355 8:30AM-4PM M-F. **Camillus Town Court** 4600 W Genesee St, Syracuse, NY 13219; See comments 8:30-4:30PM. **Cicero Town Court** PO Box 151, 8236 S Main St, Cicero, NY 13039; 315-699-8478 8:30-4:30PM. **Clay Town Court** 4401 Rte 31, Clay, NY 13041; 315-652-3800 8:30AM-4:30PM M-F. **De Witt Town Court** 5400 Butternut Dr, East Syracuse, NY 13057; 315-446-3910 x2 8:30AM-4:30PM. **East Syracuse Village Court** 204 N Center St, East Syracuse, NY 13057; 315-437-3541 x3300 8AM-4PM M-TH; 8AM-2PM F (court-4PM-? T). **Elbridge Town Court** PO Box 568, 5 Route 31 West, Jordan, NY 13080; 315-689-7380 9AM-N, 1-4:30PM. **Fabius Town Court** 7786 Main St, Fabius Community Ctr (off Rte 80), PO Box 164, Fabius, NY 13063; 315-683-9847 Thurs 7PM. **Fayetteville Village Court** 425 E Genesee St, Fayetteville, NY 13066; 315-637-8070 M-TH 8AM-4PM; 2nd & 4th Tu 5:30PM. **Geddes Town Court** 1000 Woods Rd, Solvay, NY 13209; 315-468-3613 x5 8:30AM-4:30PM M-TH; 8:30AM-4:30PM F. **Jordan Village Court** PO Box 561, 7 Mechanic St, Jordan, NY 13080; 315-689-3483 Court Office- 10AM-N T,TH; Court- 6PM 1st and 3rd T /month. **La Fayette Town Court** 2577 Rte 11 North, PO Box 135, La Fayette, NY 13084; 315-677-9350 9AM-5PM M-TH; Court- 6PM Wed. **Liverpool Village Court** 310 Sycamore Street, Liverpool, NY 13088; 315-457-5379 x3 8AM-4PM M-TH; 8AM-N FH. **Lysander Town Court** 8220 Loop Rd, Baldwinsville, NY 13027; 315-638-1308 9AM-2PM; T 7PM; W 7:30PM. **Manlius Town Court** 301 Brooklea Dr, Fayetteville, NY 13066; 315-637-3251 9AM-4PM. **Manlius Village Court** 1 Arkie Albanese Ave,

Manlius, NY 13104; 315-682-7245 9AM-4PM M-TH, 9AM-N F. **Marcellus Town Court** 24 E Main St, Marcellus, NY 13108; 315-673-3269 x3 9AM-2:30PM. **Minoa Village Court** 240 N Main St, Minoa, NY 13116; 315-656-2203 8:30AM-N T,W,TH. **North Syracuse Justice Court** Municipal Bldg, 600 S Bay Rd, North Syracuse, NY 13212; 315-458-4695 8AM-4PM; 6PM M. **Onondaga Town Court** 5020 Ball Rd, Syracuse, NY 13215-1605; 315-469-1674 9AM-4PM. **Otisco Town Court** 1924 Barker St, Tully, NY 13159; 315-696-6771 9AM-1PM T,TH; 2PM-5PM W. **Pompey Town Court** 8354 Route 20, Manlius, NY 13104; 315-682-9877 6PM T. **Salina Town Court** 201 School Rd, Liverpool, NY 13090; 315-457 4252 9-4:30PM; TH 3:30PM+. **Skaneateles Town Court** 24 Jordan St, Skaneateles, NY 13152; 315-685-5880 8AM-4:30PM. **Solvay Village Court** 1100 Woods Rd, Solvay, NY 13209; 315-468-1608 8:30AM-4:30PM. **Spafford Town Court** 1984 Route 174, Skaneateles, NY 13152; 315-673-0710 1PM-4PM Tu; 6PM 1st,3rd M. **Tully Town Court** Box 126, 5833 Meetinghouse Rd, Tully, NY 13159; 315-696-5884 9AM-1PM M-F; T to 7PM. **Van Buren Town Court** 7575 Van Buren Rd, Baldwinsville, NY 13027; 315-635-3523 8:30AM-4PM.

Ontario County

County Clerk 20 Ontario St, Municipal Bldg, Canandaigua, NY 14424; 585-396-4251; criminal phone: 585-393-2953; civil phone: 585-396-4205; fax: 585-393-2951; 8:30AM-5PM (EST). *Felony, Civil.*
General Information: Felony search requests made to the County Court Clerk are processed by the County Clerk's office. No sealed, youthful offender, sex abuse, sex crime, divorce or sealed records released. Will fax search results for $2.00 per page. Court makes copy: $.65 per page. $1.30 minimum. Self serve copy: same. Certification fee: $.65 per page with a $5.20 minimum if you prepare; $1.25 per page with $5.00 minimum if they prepare. Payee: County Clerk. Personal checks accepted, credit cards are not. Prepayment required. Mail requests: SASE required.
Civil Name Search: Access: Fax, mail, in person. Both court and visitors may perform in person name searches. No search fee. Civil records on computer from 1992, records go back to 1887. Mail turnaround Time 1 week. Civil PAT goes back to 1992.
Criminal Name Search: Access: Fax, mail, in person. Both court and visitors may perform in person name searches. Search fee: $5.00 per name. Required to search: name, years to search; also helpful-DOB. Criminal records computerized from 1990, records go back to 1919. Mail turnaround Time 1 week. Criminal PAT goes back to 1990.

Supreme & County Court 27 N Main St, Rm 130, Canandaigua, NY 14424-1447; 585-396-4239; criminal phone: 585-396-4239; fax: 585-396-4576; 9AM-5PM (EST). *Felony, Civil.*
www.nycourts.gov/courts/7jd/
General Information: Direct search requests to the County Clerk, see separate listing. Access to current/pending Supreme Court civil cases is at https://iapps.courts.state.ny.us/caseTrac/jsp/ecourt.htm.

Canandaigua City Court 2 N Main St, City Hall, Canandaigua, NY 14424-1448; 585-396-5011; fax: 585-396-5012; 8AM-4PM (EST). *Misdemeanor, Civil Actions under $15,000, Eviction, Small Claims.*
www.canandaiguanewyork.gov/index.asp
General Information: The above web page is a city site, there is no site for the court. No sealed, expunged, adoption, sex offense, juvenile or mental health records released. Will fax back documents. Court makes copy: $.65 per page; minimum $1.30. Certification fee: $5.00 per document includes copy fee. Payee: Canandaigua City Court. Only cashiers checks, cash and money orders accepted. Visa/MC accepted. Prepayment required. Mail requests: SASE required.
Civil Name Search: Access: Mail, in person, online. Only the court performs in person name searches; visitors may not. No search fee. Civil records on computer from 1986, prior in books from 1960. Records are not kept on-site; as fee may apply to retrieve records from them. WebCivil Local at http://iapps.courts.state.ny.us/webcivil/ecourtsMain contains information on both active and disposed Civil Court cases. Search by index number, party name, attorney/firm name or judge. No fee.
Criminal Name Search: Access: In person, online. Only the court performs in person name searches; visitors may not. Required to search: name, arrest/and/or conviction dates. Criminal records computerized from 1986, prior in books from 1960. Books not kept on-site. Note: The court refuses to permit access to court records unless specific case file given. All criminal record name search requests are directed to the OCA for statewide record search, $65.00 search fee. See www.nycourts.gov/apps/chrs.

Geneva City Court 255 Exchange St, Public Safety Bldg, Geneva, NY 14456; 315-789-6560; fax: 315-781-2802; 8AM-4PM (EST). *Misdemeanor, Civil Actions under $15,000, Eviction, Small Claims.*
www.co.ontario.ny.us/index.html
General Information: No youthful offender records released. Will fax documents to local or toll free line. Court makes copy: $.65 per page, $1.30

minimum. Certification fee: $5.00 per doc plus copy fee. Payee: City Court. Only cashiers checks and money orders accepted. Visa/MC accepted. Prepayment required. Mail requests: SASE required.

Civil Name Search: Access: Mail, in person, online. Only the court performs in person name searches; visitors may not. Search fee: $16.00 per name. Civil cases indexed by plaintiff. Civil records on computer from 1994. Mail turnaround Time 1 week. WebCivil Local at http://iapps.courts.state.ny.us/webcivil/ecourtsMain contains information on both active and disposed Civil Court cases. Search by index number, party name, attorney/firm name or judge. No fee.

Criminal Name Search: Access: Online. Both court and visitors may perform in person name searches. Criminal records computerized from 1992. Note: The court refuses to permit access to court records unless specific case file given. All criminal record name search requests are directed to the OCA for statewide record search, $65.00 search fee. See www.nycourts.gov/apps/chrs.

Surrogate's Court 27 N Main St, Canandaigua, NY 14424-1447; 585-396-4054/4055; fax: 585-396-4812; 9AM-5PM (EST). *Probate, Guardianship.*

General Information: A county search of the probate court index by mail for 25-year search is $30.00 fee. A full county probate search of all years is $90.00.

Ontario Town/Village Courts - **Bristol Town Court** 6740 County Road 32, Town Hall, Canandaigua, NY 14424; 585-229-4523 x15 9AM-N M-W (court, 7:30PM-? TH). **Canadice Town Court** 5949 County Rd 37, Springwater, NY 14560; 585-367-3590 2PM-5PM TH,F (clerk); 7PM-? 1st & 2nd TH (court). **Canandaigua Town Court** 5440 Rts 5 & 20 West, Canandaigua, NY 14424; 585-394-9040 9AM-N T,W,F; 1PM-5PM TH. **Clifton Springs Village Court** 1 W Main St., Village Hall, Clifton Springs, NY 14432; 315-462-3048 6PM-? T (court). **East Bloomfield Town Court** PO Box 85, 99 Main St, Bloomfield, NY 14443; 585-657-7248 5-8PM TH. **Farmington Town Court** 1000 County Rd 8, Farmington, NY 14425; 315-986-3113 or 8195 9AM-3:30PM M-TH, 7PN-? M,W. **Geneva Town Court** 3750 County Rd 6, Geneva, NY 14456; 315-789-1100 x310 or 311 5:30PM M; 6PM TH. **Gorham Town Court** PO Box 224, 4736 South St, Gorham, NY 14461; 585-526-6298 7PM-? T. **Hopewell Town Court** 2716 County Rd 47, Canandaigua, NY 14424; 585-394-1963 x6 8AM-N, 1-7:30PM T; 9AM-4PM W. **Manchester Town Court** 1272 County Road 7, Clifton Springs, NY 14432; 585-289-3010 x103/111 & 315-462-6224 x103/111 10AM-4:30PM M-TH. **Naples Town Court** PO Box 535, 106 S Main St, Naples, NY 14512; 585-374-2111 7PM TH. **Phelps Town Court** PO Box 219, 1331 Rte 88, Phelps, NY 14532; 315-548-2090 9AM-11:45AM M-F. **Richmond Town Court** PO Box 145, 8690 Main St, Honeoye, NY 14471; 585-229-4006 7-?PM W (traffic); 5PM-? 2nd & 3rd W (criminal). **Seneca Town Court** 4224 South St, Stanley, NY 14561; 585-526-4780 6PM-7:30PM T; 7PM-? W. **South Bristol Town Court** 6500 Gannett Hill Rd West, Naples, NY 14512; 585-374-6355 7PM TH. **Victor Town Court** 11 Franark Dr, Victor, NY 14564; 585-924-5262; civil phone: 585-924-5262; 9AM-N, 1-4PM. **West Bloomfield Town Court** PO Box 82, 2560 County Rd 37, West Bloomfield, NY 14585-0087; 585-624-9860 Random.

Orange County

County Clerk 255 Main St, Goshen, NY 10924; 845-291-3080; fax: 845-291-2691; 9AM-5PM (EST). *Felony, Civil.*

General Information: Search requests made to the County Clerk are processed in the manner described below. No sealed records released. Will not fax documents. Court makes copy: $.65 per page. Self serve copy: $.25 per page. Certification fee: $5.00 plus $1.25 per page after 1st 8 pgs; exemplification fee is $15.00. Payee: Orange County Clerk. Business checks accepted. No credit cards accepted. Prepayment required. Mail requests: SASE required.

Civil Name Search: Access: Mail, in person. Both court and visitors may perform in person name searches. Search fee: $2.50 per name. Civil records on computer from 1994; prior indexed only by plaintiff. Mail turnaround Time 2 weeks. Civil PAT goes back to 8/1993.

Criminal Name Search: Access: Mail, in person. Both court and visitors may perform in person name searches. Search fee: $2.50 per name per year. Required to search: name, years to search, DOB. Criminal records on computer since 1994; prior on index Rolodex cards. Mail turnaround Time 2 weeks. Criminal PAT goes back to same as civil. Subscribe or login as guest to search eCourts WebCrims future appearances system at http://iapps.courts.state.ny.us/webcrim_attorney/Login.

Supreme & County Court 255-285 Main St, Goshen, NY 10924; criminal phone: 845-291-3100; civil phone: 845-291-3111; fax: 845-291-2525; 9AM-5PM (EST). *Felony, Civil.*

General Information: Civil fax- 845-291-2595. Direct search requests to County Clerk; see separate listing. The County Court (criminal court) is at 285 Main St., but records at County Clerk office.

Middletown City Court 2 James St, Middletown, NY 10940; 845-346-4050; fax: 845-343-5737; 8:30AM-4PM (EST). *Misdemeanor, Civil Actions under $15,000, Eviction, Small Claims, Traffic.*

General Information: No sealed or youthful offender records released. Will not fax documents. Court makes copy: $.65 per page, $1.30 minimum. Certification fee: $5.00 per doc plus copy fee. Payee: City Court of Middletown. Only cashiers checks and money orders accepted. Visa/MC accepted. Prepayment required. Mail requests: SASE required.

Civil Name Search: Access: Mail, in person, online. Only the court performs in person name searches; visitors may not. No search fee. Civil records on computer from 1994, prior on cards. Mail turnaround Time 1 week. WebCivil Local at http://iapps.courts.state.ny.us/webcivil/ecourtsMain contains information on both active and disposed Civil Court cases. Search by index number, party name, attorney/firm name or judge. No fee.

Criminal Name Search: Access: In person, online. Only the court performs in person name searches; visitors may not. Criminal records computerized from 1986, prior on cards. Note: The court refuses to permit access to court records unless specific case file given. All criminal record name search requests are directed to the OCA for statewide record search, $65.00 search fee. See www.nycourts.gov/apps/chrs.

Newburgh City Court 300 Broadway, Newburgh, NY 12550; 845-483-8100; criminal phone: 845-565-0421; civil phone: 845-565-0230; 8AM-4PM (EST). *Misdemeanor, Civil Actions up to $15,000, Eviction, Small Claims, Traffic.*

www.courts.state.ny.us/courts/9jd/Orange/Newburgh.shtml

General Information: Specialty Court can be reached at 845-565-0292. No sealed, youthful offender or sex abuse victim records released. Will fax documents to local or toll free line. Court makes copy: $.65 per page. Certification fee: $6.00 per doc includes copy fee. Payee: Newburgh City Court. Only cashiers checks and money orders accepted. Visa/MC for fees and fines only. Prepayment required.

Civil Name Search: Access: In person, online. Only the court performs in person name searches; visitors may not. Required to search: name, years to search; also helpful- case caption. Civil cases indexed by defendant. Civil records on computer from 1997, prior in docket books or on index cards. Note: The court does not permit access to court records unless specific case file given. WebCivil Local at http://iapps.courts.state.ny.us/webcivil/ecourtsMain contains information on both active and disposed Civil Court cases. Search by index number, party name, attorney/firm name or judge. No fee.

Criminal Name Search: Access: Online. Only the court performs in person name searches; visitors may not. Criminal records computerized from 1986. Note: The court does not permit access to court records unless specific case file given. All criminal record name search requests are directed to the OCA for statewide record search, $65.00 search fee. See www.nycourts.gov/apps/chrs.

Port Jervis City Court 20 Hammond St, Port Jervis, NY 12771-2495; 845-858-4034; fax: 845-858-9883; 9AM-5PM (EST). *Misdemeanor, Civil Actions under $15,000, Eviction, Small Claims.*

General Information: No sealed, expunged, adoption, sex offense, juvenile or mental health records released. Will not fax documents. Court makes copy: $.65 per page, $1.30 minimum. Certification fee: $6.00. Payee: City Court of Port Jervis. Only cashiers checks and money orders accepted. Visa/MC accepted. Prepayment required. Mail requests: SASE required.

Civil Name Search: Access: Mail, in person, online. Both court and visitors may perform in person name searches. No search fee. Civil cases indexed by defendant. Civil records on dockets from 1978, computerized since 1996. Mail turnaround Time 3 weeks. WebCivil Local at http://iapps.courts.state.ny.us/webcivil/ecourtsMain contains information on both active and disposed Civil Court cases. Search by index number, party name, attorney/firm name or judge. No fee.

Criminal Name Search: Access: Mail, in person, online. Search fee: $5.00 per name per 2 years for "violations" only, no misdemeanors. Criminal docket index from 1978, computerized since 1996. Note: The court refuses to permit access to misdemeanor records unless specific case file given. Mail turnaround Time 3 weeks. Name search requests are often directed to the OCA for statewide record search, $65.00 search fee. See www.nycourts.gov/apps/chrs.

Surrogate's Court 30 Park Pl, Surrogate's Courthouse, Goshen, NY 10924; 845-291-2193; fax: 845-291-2196; 9AM-5PM; Vault closes at 4PM (EST). *Probate.*

www.nycourts.gov/courts/

General Information: A county search of the probate court index by mail for 25-year search is $30.00 fee. A full county probate search of all years is $90.00.

Orange Town/Village Courts - **Blooming Grove Town Court** PO Box 358, 6 Horton Rd, Blooming Grove, NY 10914; 845-496-7631 8:30AM-4:30PM. **Chester Town Court** 1786 Kings Hwy, Chester, NY 10918; 845-

469-9541 8:30AM-4PM (court 6PM-?). **Chester Village Court** 47 Main St, Chester, NY 10918; 845-469-8584 9AM-5PM M-TH; 9AM-12PM F. **Cornwall Town Court** 183 Main St, Cornwall, NY 12518; 845-534-8717 8:30AM-4:30PM. **Crawford Town Court** 121 Route 302, Pine Bush, NY 12566; 845-744-2435 8:30AM-4PM. **Deerpark Town Court** PO Box 621, 420 Route 209, Huguenot, NY 12746; 845-856-2928 x7 or x8 9AM T; 7PM W. **Florida Village Court** PO Box 451, 33 S Main St, Florida, NY 10921; 845-651-4940 6PN-8PM TH. **Goshen Town Court** PO Box 667, 41 Webster Ave, Goshen, NY 10924; 845-294-6477 9AM-4:30PM M-F. **Goshen Village Court** Village Hall, 276 Main St, Goshen, NY 10924; 845-294-5826 8:30-3:30 M-F (court on W). **Greenville Town Court** 1537 US Hwy 6, Port Jervis, NY 12771; 845-856-4813 10AM-3PM M-F. **Greenwood Lake Village Court** PO Box 1705, 47 Waterstone Rd, Greenwood Lake, NY 10925; 845-477-9215 8-11:30AM, 1-4PM. **Hamptonburgh Town Court** 18 Bull Rd, Campbell Hall, NY 10916; 845-427-2424 x3 10AM-4PM M-TH. **Harriman Village Court** PO Box 706, 1 Church St, Harriman, NY 10926; 845-782-6853 8:30AM-N 1PM-4PM M,T,W; 6PM-8PM TH; 9AM-N F. **Highlands Town Court** PO Box277, Highland Falls, NY 10928; 845-446-4280 8-4:30PM. **Maybrook Village Court** 111Schipps lane, Maybrook, NY 12543; 845-427-2224 M 9AM-5PM; T 1AM-N 5-9PM; TH 9AM-1PM; F9AM-1PM. **Minisink Town Court** PO Box 349, 20 Roy Smith Dr, Westtown, NY 10998; 845-726-3700 7PM TH. **Monroe Town Court** 17 Lake St, Monroe, NY 10950; 845-783-9733 8:30-12PM 1PM-4PM; Court-Must call to verify Court time.. **Montgomery Town Court** 110 Bracken Rd, Montgomery, NY 12549; 845-457-2620 8:15-4PM M-TH ; 8:15-12PM F; T&W 7PM-?. **Montgomery Village Court** 133 Clinton St., Montgomery, NY 12549; 845-457-9037 9AM-4PM. **Mount Hope Town Court** PO Box 872, Baker St, Otisville, NY 10963; 845-386-5303 7PM-? 2nd & 3rd T; 1st & 3rd TH. **New Windsor Town Court** Town Hall, 555 Union Ave, New Windsor, NY 12553; 845-563-4682/845-563-4684 8:30-4PM. **Newburgh Town Court** 311 Route 32, Newburgh, NY 12550; 845-564-7161 8:30AM-4:30PM. **Otisville Village Court** 66 Highland Ave, Otisville, NY 10963; 845-386-1004 1st & 4th T 7PM. **Tuxedo Park Village Court** PO Box 31, Tuxedo Park, NY 10987; 845-928-2311 4th TH clerk; 3rd TH for court. **Tuxedo Town Court** 1 Temple Dr., Tuxedo, NY 10987; 845-351-5655 9-3PM, Court T9:30AM; TH 5PM. **Walden Village Court** 1 Municipal Square, Walden, NY 12586; 845-778-1632 7AM-3:30PM. **Wallkill Town Court** 99 Tower Dr, Bldg B, Middletown, NY 10941-2005; 845-692-7822 9AM-4PM M-TH; 9AM-3:30 F. **Warwick Town Court** 132 Kings Hwy, Warwick, NY 10990; 845-986-1128 x8 8:30AM-4PM; court- T 7PM. **Warwick Village Court** 77 Main St, PO Box 369, Warwick, NY 10990; 845-986-2031 8:30AM-4PM. **Washingtonville Village Court** 29 W Main St, Washingtonville, NY 10992; 845-496-9797 8:30AM-3:30PM. **Wawayanda Town Court** 80 Ridgebury Hill Rd, Slate Hill, NY 10973; 845-355-5706 9AM-4PM. **Woodbury Justice Court** PO Box 509, 511 Rt 32, Highland Mills, NY 10930; 845-928-2311 8AM-4PM.

Orleans County

County Clerk Courthouse, Attn: County Clerk, 3 S Main St, #1, Albion, NY 14411-9998; 585-589-5334; fax: 585-589-0181; 9AM-5PM; July/Aug is 8:30AM-4PM) (EST). *Civil.*
www.orleansny.com/Departments/PublicRecords/CountyClerk/tabid/93/Default.aspx
General Information: For felony records see the County Court clerk at the Supreme and County Court in separate listing. No sealed or divorce records released. Will fax documents if all fees prepaid. Court makes copy: $1.00 per page. Self serve copy: same. Certification fee: $4.00 plus $1.00 per page after first 4. Payee: Orleans County Clerk. Personal checks accepted, credit cards are not. Prepayment required. Mail requests: SASE required.
Civil Name Search: Access: Mail, in person. Both court and visitors may perform in person name searches. Search fee: $5.00 per name. Fee is for 2 year search. Civil cases indexed by defendant. Civil records in books to 1940s; on computer back to 1998. Mail turnaround Time 1 week. Public use terminal has civil records back to 1998.

Supreme & County Court Courthouse, 1 S Main, #3, Albion, NY 14411-9998; 585-589-5458; fax: 585-589-0632; 9AM-5PM (EST). *Felony, Civil.*
General Information: This court does not hold closed case records. It directs criminal search requests to the OCA for a $65.00 statewide record check. However, for a countywide search, see the County Clerk in a separate listing.

Surrogate's Court 1 S Main St, #3, Albion, NY 14411; 585-589-4457; fax: 585-589-0632; 9AM-5PM (EST). *Probate.*
General Information: A county search of the probate court index by mail for 25-year search is $30.00 fee. A full county probate search of all years is $90.00.

Orleans Town/Village Courts - Albion Town Court 3665 Clarendon Rd, Albion, NY 14411; 585-589-7048 x18 8AM-2:30PM except Wed; Court- 6PM-? T, 9AM-? W. **Barre Town Court** 14317 W Barre Rd, Albion, NY 14411; 585-589-5100 6PM TH. **Carlton Town Court** Carlton

Town Hall, 14341 Waterport/Carlton Rd, Albion, NY 14411; 585-682-4517 6PM-? M, TH. **Clarendon Justice Court** PO Box 145, 16385 Church St, Clarendon, NY 14429; 585-638-6371 x102 M 9AM-2:30PM; T 12-6PM. **Gaines Town Court** 14087 Ridge Rd, Albion, NY 14411; 585-589-4592 8AM-3PM M-TH; 8AM-N F. **Kendall Town Court** 1873 Kendall Rd, Kendall, NY 14476; 585-659-8546 Call for appointment; 7PM-? (court). **Medina Village Court** 600 Main St, Medina, NY 14103; 585-798-4875 9AM-N, 1-4:30PM. **Murray Town Court** 3840 Fancher Rd, Holley, NY 14470; 585-638-6570 x105 7PM M. **Ridgeway Town Court** 4062 Salt Works Rd, Medina, NY 14103; 585-798-3282 9AM-4PM M-F. **Shelby Town Court** 4062 Salt Works, PO Box 348, Medina, NY 14103; 585-798-3120 x309 9AM-N M; 9AM-4PM TH,F. **Yates Town Court** 8 S Main St, Lyndonville, NY 14098; 585-765-9603 9AM-10:30AM.

Oswego County

County Clerk 46 E Bridge St, Oswego, NY 13126; 315-349-8738; fax: 315-349-8692; 9AM-5PM (EST). *Felony, Civil.*
www.oswegocounty.com/clerk.shtml
General Information: Online identifiers in results same as on public terminal. No sealed, youthful offender or divorce records released. Will not fax documents. Court makes copy: $.65 per page, $1.30 minimum. Certification fee: $5.00 minimum, includes 4 pages copies; $1.25 per page after 4. Payee: County Clerk. Personal checks accepted up to $350.00. No credit cards accepted. Prepayment required. Mail requests: SASE required.
Civil Name Search: Access: In person, online. Visitors must perform in person searches themselves. Civil records on computer from 1/90, prior in books from 1896. Public use terminal has civil records back to 1990. Lookup Supreme Court civil cases at http://iapps.courts.state.ny.us/webcivil/FCASMain. Cases go back to 2002.
Criminal Name Search: Access: Mail, in person. Only the court performs in person name searches; visitors may not. Search fee: $5.00 per name for every 2 years searched. Required to search: name, years to search, DOB. Criminal records computerized from 1973; prior in docket books from 1939. Mail turnaround Time 2-3 days.

Supreme & County Court 25 E Oneida St, Oswego, NY 13126; 315-349-3280; civil phone: 315-349-3277; fax: 315-349-8513; 8:30AM-4:30PM (EST). *Felony, Civil.*
General Information: Direct search requests to the County Clerk, see separate listing. Access to current/pending Supreme Court civil cases is at https://iapps.courts.state.ny.us/caseTrac/jsp/ecourt.htm.

Fulton City Court 141 S 1st St, Fulton, NY 13069; 315-593-8400; fax: 315-592-3415; 8:30AM-4:30PM; Summer 8:30AM-4PM (EST). *Misdemeanor, Civil Actions under $15,000, Eviction, Small Claims.*
www.nycourts.gov/courts/5jd/oswego/fulton/
General Information: No sealed, expunged, adoption, sex offense, juvenile or mental health records released. Will fax documents to local or toll free line. Court makes copy: $.65 per page; $1.30 minimum. Certification fee: $6.00 per doc plus copy fee; exemplification fee is $15.00. Payee: Fulton City Court. Only cashiers checks and money orders accepted. Visa/MC accepted. Prepayment required. Mail requests: SASE requested for civil.
Civil Name Search: Access: Mail, in person, online. Only the court performs in person name searches; visitors may not. No search fee. Civil cases indexed by defendant. Civil records on dockets from 1991; computerized records since 1998. Mail turnaround Time 2 weeks or less. WebCivil Local at http://iapps.courts.state.ny.us/webcivil/ecourtsMain contains information on both active and disposed Civil Court cases. Search by index number, party name, attorney/firm name or judge. No fee.
Criminal Name Search: Access: Online. Only the court performs in person name searches; visitors may not. Search fee: $6.00 for 2 year search. Required to search: name, DOB, charge. Criminal records go back to 1918, computerized records since 1997, criminal records on dockets from 1987. Note: The court refuses to permit access to court records unless specific charge is given. All criminal record name search requests are directed to the OCA for statewide record search, $65.00 search fee. See www.nycourts.gov/apps/chrs.

Oswego City Court Conway Municipal Bldg, 20 W Oneida St, Oswego, NY 13126; 315-343-0415; fax: 315-343-0531; 8:30AM-4:30PM (EST). *Misdemeanor, Civil Actions under $15,000, Eviction, Small Claims.*
www.nycourts.gov/courts/5jd/Oswego/oswego/index.shtml
General Information: No sealed or youthful offender records released. Will fax documents to local or toll-free number. Court makes copy: $.65 per page; $1.30 minimum. Certification fee: $6.00 plus copy fees. Payee: Oswego City Court. Only cashiers checks and money orders accepted. Visa/MC/Discover accepted. Prepayment required. Mail requests: SASE required.
Civil Name Search: Access: Mail, in person, online. Only the court performs in person name searches; visitors may not. No search fee. Civil

cases indexed by defendant. Civil records on computer from 1987, prior in books. WebCivil Local at http://iapps.courts.state.ny.us/webcivil/ecourtsMain contains information on both active and disposed Civil Court cases. Search by index number, party name, attorney/firm name or judge. No fee.

Criminal Name Search: Access: Mail, in person, online. Search fee: $5.00 for each 2 years searched. Criminal records computerized from 1987, prior in books. Name search requests are often directed to the OCA for statewide record search, $65.00 search fee. See www.nycourts.gov/apps/chrs.

Surrogate's Court Courthouse, 25 E Oneida St, 25 E Oneida St, Oswego, NY 13126; 315-349-3295; fax: 315-349-8514; 8:30AM-4:30PM Sept-May; 8:30AM-4PM June-Aug (EST). *Probate.*

General Information: A county search of the probate court index by mail for 25-year search is $30.00 fee. A full county probate search of all years is $90.00.

Oswego Town/Village Courts - Albion Town Court PO Box 127, Altmar, NY 13302-0127; 315-298-6325 **Amboy Town Court** 822 State Route 69, Amboy Town Hall, Williamstown, NY 13493; 315-964-7799 7PM-? 3rd T. **Boylston Town Court** Town Court, 912 County Rt 13, Lacona, NY 13083; 315-387-2320 **Constantia Town Court** 14 Frederick St, Constantia, NY 13044; 315-243-2600 or 440-2842 5PM-? M. **Granby Town Court** 820 County Rte 8, Fulton, NY 13069; 315-598-2958 10AM-2PM M-F; 4:30PM-6:30PM TU. **Hannibal Town Court** Drawer B, 824 County Route 34, Hannibal, NY 13074; 315-564-6798 1-3:30PM M,T,W; 7PM T. **Hastings Town Court** Town Hall, 1134 U S Rte 11, Central Square, NY 13036; 315-676-4317 8:30AM-N 1PM-4PM. **Mexico Town Court** 3245 Main St, PO Box 98, Mexico, NY 13114; 315-963-3785 7-9PM T. **Minetto Town Court** PO Box 220, Minetto, NY 13115; 315-326-0030 7PM 1st & 3rd TH. **New Haven Town Court** Route 104E, PO Box 141, New Haven, NY 13121; 315-963-8886 7PM TH. **Orwell Town Court** Town Hall, Orwell, NY 13426; 315-298-3040 7PM-9PM W. **Oswego Town Court** 640 County Rte 20, #2, Oswego, NY 13126; 315-343-7249/343-0588 9AM-4PM 6:30PM M (court). **Palermo Town Court** 53 County Rte 35, Fulton, NY 13069; 315-593-2333 x222 3-8:30PM M. **Parish Town Court** PO Box 406, 2938 E Main St, Parish, NY 13131; 315-625-7282 7PM T. **Pulaski Village Court** PO Box 227, 4917 Jefferson St, Snow Memorial Bldg, Pulaski, NY 13142; 315-298-7431 6PM-? 1st & 3rd W. **Redfield Town Court** Town Municipal Bldg, 4830 County Rt 17, Redfield, NY 13437; 315-599-7125 varies. **Richland Town Court** PO Box 29, 1 Bridge St, H Douglas Barclay Courthouse, Pulaski, NY 13142; 315-298-5174 x25 or 27 1st&3rd M 7PM. **Sandy Creek Town Court** 1992 Harwood Dr, PO Box 341, Sandy Creek, NY 13145; 315-387-5456 x1 8:45AM-3:45PM. **Schroeppel Town Court** Rd #3-Route 57A-Box 9B, Town Ofc. Bldg, 69 County Rt 57A, Phoenix, NY 13135; 315-695-6177 x4 8AM-N 1PM-3:30PM. **Scriba Town Court** 42 Creamery Rd., Oswego, NY 13126; 315-343-3250/1503 M-TH 8AM-12PM, Court Th 7PM. **Volney Town Court** 1445 County Rte 6, Fulton, NY 13069; 315-598-7082 11:30AM-3:30PM M-T-TH. **West Monroe Town Court** County Route 11, West Monroe, NY 13167; 315-676-3522 Court Mon- 5PM. **Williamstown Town Court** 2910 County Route 17N, Williamstown, NY 13493; 315-964-2279 4:30-8PM.

Otsego County

County Clerk 197 Main St, Public Office Bldg, Cooperstown, NY 13326; 607-547-4276; fax: 607-547-7544; 9AM-5PM; (9AM-4PM in July-Aug) (EST). *Felony, Civil.*

General Information: Countywide search requests made to the county clerk are processed in the manner described below. No sealed, expunged, adoption, sex offense, juvenile or mental health records released. Will fax documents on criminal cases. Court makes copy: $1.00 per page. Certification fee: $5.00. Payee: Otsego County Clerk. Business checks accepted. Prepayment required. Mail requests: SASE required.

Civil Name Search: Access: Mail, in person, online. Both court and visitors may perform in person name searches. Search fee: $5.00 per name. Civil cases indexed by defendant. Civil records on computer back to 1997; prior in books. Mail turnaround Time 1-2 days. Public use terminal has civil records back to 5/1/1997. Lookup Supreme Court civil cases at http://iapps.courts.state.ny.us/webcivil/FCASMain. Cases go back to 2002.

Criminal Name Search: Access: Mail, in person. Both court and visitors may perform in person name searches. Search fee: $5.00 per name. Required to search: name, years to search, address, DOB. Criminal records computerized from 1997; prior in books. Note: Misdemeanor records are maintained by city, town and village courts. In person criminal record searches should be performed over at the Supreme and County Court office at the courthouse. Mail turnaround Time 1-2 days.

Supreme & County Court PO Box 710, 193 Main St, Cooperstown, NY 13326; 607-547-4364; criminal phone: 607-547-4388; civil phone: 607-547-4364; probate phone: 607-547-4213; fax: 607-547-7567; 9AM-5PM; 8AM-4PM Summer hours (EST). *Felony, Civil.*
www.nycourts.gov/courts/6jd/otsego/index.shtml

General Information: This court does not hold closed case records. It directs criminal search requests to the OCA for a $65.00 statewide record check. However, for a countywide search, see the County Clerk in a separate listing.

Oneonta City Court 81 Main St, Oneonta, NY 13820; 607-432-4480; 8AM-4PM (EST). *Misdemeanor, Civil Actions under $15,000, Eviction, Small Claims.*

General Information: No sealed or youthful offender records released. Will fax documents to local or toll-free number. Court makes copy: $.65 per page, $1.30 minimum. Certification fee: $6.00 per page plus copy fee. Payee: Oneonta City Court. Required payment in certified funds only. No Personal checks, Visa/MC accepted. Prepayment required. Mail requests: SASE required for civil.

Civil Name Search: Access: Mail, in person, online. Only the court performs in person name searches; visitors may not. Search fee: $5.00 per name per 2 years. Civil cases indexed by defendant. Civil records on computer from 1987, prior in books. Mail turnaround Time 1 week from receipt. WebCivil Local at http://iapps.courts.state.ny.us/webcivil/ecourtsMain contains information on both active and disposed Civil Court cases. Search by index number, party name, attorney/firm name or judge. No fee.

Criminal Name Search: Access: Online. Only the court performs in person name searches; visitors may not. Search fee: A Certificate of Disposition is available for $5.00. Required to search: Name, case number, signed release. A release form is available from the clerk or online. Date of Birth required for accurate search. Most records go back 6 years; DWI 25 years, DWAI 10 years. Note: Court performs Certificate of Disposition searches only. Court does not have access to county records. All criminal record name search requests are directed to the OCA for statewide record search, $65.00 search fee. See www.nycourts.gov/apps/chrs.

Surrogate's Court Surrogate's Office, 197 Main St, Cooperstown, NY 13326; 607-547-4338/4213; fax: 607-547-7566; 9AM-N, 1-5PM, Reg Hrs, 8AM-4PM July -Aug (EST). *Probate.*

General Information: A county search of the probate court index by mail for 25-year search is $30.00 fee. A full county probate search of all years is $90.00.

Otsego Town/Village Courts - Burlington Town Court Municipal Bldg, Route 51, Burlington Flats, NY 13315; 607-965-2344 8:30AM-N T,TH; 6-8PM M. **Butternuts Town Court** PO Box 26, 1234 State Hwy 51, Gilbertsville, NY 13776; 607-783-2758 7-9PM 2 & 4 T. **Cherry Valley Town Court** PO Box243, Main St, Cherry Valley, NY 13320; 607-264-8324 7PM-9PM W. **Cooperstown Village Court** PO Box 346, 22 Main St, Cooperstown, NY 13326; 607-547-9597 8AM-4PM. **Decatur Town Court** 104 County Rte 37, PO Box 463, Worcester, NY 12197; 607-397-8298, 397-7365 7PM-? 2nd TH. **Edmeston Town Court** 2 West St, Edmeston, NY 13335; 607-965-9823 7PM-? 1st M; 6PM-? M (court). **Exeter Town Court** PO Box 223, 7411 Rte 28, Schuyler Lake, NY 13457; 315-858-3905 Court Wed 7-9PM. **Hartwick Town Court** PO Box 106, Hartwick, NY 13348; 607-293-8133 7PM-? W court. **Laurens Town Court & Village Court** 37 Brook St, Laurens, NY 13796; 607-433-1053 6PM-? TH Court. **Maryland Town Court** PO Box 42, Schenevus, NY 12155; 607-638-9495 6-8PM T. **Middlefield Town Court** 2671 County Highway 33, Cooperstown, NY 13326; 607-547-2239 5:30PM-? M. **Milford Town Court** PO Box 328, 2859 Rte 28, Portlandville, NY 13834; 607-286-7773 3-6PM T. **Morris Town Court & Village Court** PO Box 524, 93 Main St, Morris, NY 13808; 607-263-2224 M 7PM. **New Lisbon Town Court** PO Box 242, 908 County Hwy 16, Garrattsville, NY 13342; 607-965-8627 7PM-? W. **Oneonta Town Court** 3966 State Hwy #23, West Oneonta, NY 13861; 607-432-0124 8:30AM-5PM. **Otego Town Court** PO Box 468, 3526 State Hwy 7, Otego, NY 13825; 607-988-2698 9AM-1PM M-F; Court TH 7:00PM. **Otsego Town Court** PO Box 57, 811 Co Hwy 26, Fly Creek, NY 13337; 607-547-5689 M 12-4PM; W 11AM-2PM; TH 12-4PM. **Pittsfield Town Court** PO Box 368, New Berlin, NY 13411; 607-847-6524 **Plainfield Town Court** 129 Co Hwy 18A, West Winfield, NY 13491; 315-855-4150 **Richfield Springs Village Court** PO Box 271, 102 Main St, Richfield Springs, NY 13439; 315-858-2048 6:30-8PM 1st, 3rd TH. **Richfield Town Court** PO Box 786, Richfield Springs, NY 13439; 315-858-2830 Court W 6-8PM. **Springfield Town Court** PO Box 325, Town Court, Elementary School CR 29A, Springfield, NY 13468; 315-858-1508 7-8PM M. **Unadilla Town Court** PO Box 334, 1648 State Hwy 7, Unadilla, NY 13849; 607-369-7458 After 1:30PM M; 9:30AM-12:30PM T-F. **Westford Town Court** PO Box 165, 1812 County Hwy 34, Westford, NY 13488; 607-638-9972 (Home Phone) 7PM-? 1st & 3rd T. **Worcester Town Court** PO Box 294, 29 Katie Lane, Worcester, NY 12197; 607-397-8476 4PM-6:30PM T; 9AM-N F.

Putnam County

County Clerk 40 Gleneida Ave, County Clerk Office, Carmel, NY 10512; 84845-808-1142; fax: 845-228-0231; 9AM-5PM; 8AM-4PM Summer hours (EST). *Felony, Civil.*
www.putnamcountyny.com/countyclerk/index.htm

General Information: Countywide search requests made to the County Court Clerk are processed in the manner described below. No sealed or youthful offender records released. Will fax documents $1.00 per page. Court makes copy: $1.00 per page. Self serve copy: $.25 per page. Certification fee: $4.00 per doc; Exemplification fee- $10.00. Payee: County Clerk. Personal checks accepted, credit cards are not. Prepayment required. Mail requests: SASE required.

Civil Name Search: Access: Mail, in person, online. Both court and visitors may perform in person name searches. Search fee: $5.00 per name. Fee is per 2 years searched. Civil records on computer from 4/93, prior in books. Mail turnaround Time 2 days. Civil PAT goes back to 1983. Lookup Supreme Court civil cases at http://iapps.courts.state.ny.us/webcivil/FCASMain. Cases go back to 2002. Access to the clerk's records index (but not images except judgments) is via subscription service at www2.landaccess.com/cgibin/homepage?County=8002. Pay per use ($5.00 to view doc) or $100 per month plan available.

Criminal Name Search: Access: Mail, in person, online. Both court and visitors may perform in person name searches. Search fee: $5.00 per name per certificate of search. Required to search: name, years to search, DOB. Criminal records computerized since 1983. Mail turnaround Time 2 days. Criminal PAT goes back to 1983. Access to the clerk's records index but not images is via subscription service at www2.landaccess.com/cgibin/homepage?County=8002. Pay per use ($5.00 to view doc) or $100 per month plan available. Also, subscribe or login as guest to search eCourts WebCrims future appearances system at http://iapps.courts.state.ny.us/webcrim_attorney/Login.

Supreme & County Court 20 County Center, Supreme and County Court, Carmel, NY 10512; 845-208-7805; fax: 845-228-9611; 9AM-5PM (EST). *Felony, Civil.*

General Information: This court does not hold closed case records. It directs criminal search requests to the OCA for a $65.00 statewide record check. However, for a countywide search, see the County Clerk in a separate listing.

Surrogate's Court Historic Courthouse, 44 Gleneida Ave, Carmel, NY 10512; 845-208-7860; fax: 845-228-5761; 9AM-5PM (EST). *Probate.*

General Information: A county search of the probate court index by mail for 25-year search is $30.00 fee. A full county probate search of all years is $90.00.

Putnam Town/Village Courts - Brewster Village Court 50 Main St, Brewster, NY 10509; 845-278-2401 8:30AM-4PM. **Carmel Town Court** Town Hall, 60 McAlpin Ave, Mahopac, NY 10541; 845-628-1500 9:30AM-4PM. **Cold Spring Village Court** 85 Main St, Cold Spring, NY 10516; 845-265-9070 x3 9AM-4PM. **Kent Town Court** 25 Sybil's Crossing, Kent Lakes, NY 10512; 845-225-1606 9AM-5PM. **Patterson Town Court** PO Box 416, 1144 Rte 311, Justice Court, Patterson, NY 12563; 845-878-1080 9AM-5PM. **Philipstown Town Court** Town Hall, 238 Main St, Cold Spring, NY 10516; 845-265-2951 9AM-4PM. **Putnam Valley Town Court** 265 Oscawana Lake Rd, Putnam Valley, NY 10579; 845-526-3050 8AM-4PM. **Southeast Town Court** 1360 Rte 22, Brewster, NY 10509; 845-279-8939 9AM-4:30PM M-TH; 9AM-2PM F.

Queens County

Supreme Court - Civil Division 88-11 Sutphin Blvd, #106, County Clerk Records Rm, Jamaica, NY 11435; 718-298-0601, 718-298-0615 Records Rm; civil phone: 718-298-1009 Supreme Ct Clerk; fax: 718-520-4731; 9AM-5PM, no cashier transactions after 4:45PM (EST). *Civil Actions over $25,000.*
www.courts.state.ny.us/courts/11jd/index.shtml

General Information: Records managed by County Clerk Office. Information here is for the County Clerk Records Rm. To identify a record, first search at the Search Dept, 718-298-0609; with a case number, go to records room (9AM-3PM only) who will pull record for you to copy. No marriage or incompetence records released. Identification required to review confidential matrimonial case records. Will not fax documents. Court makes copy: $.25 per page. Self serve copy: $.15 per page.mail request copies are $.65 per page Certification fee: $8.00 per doc. Payee: County Clerk. Only postal money orders accepted. No credit cards accepted. Prepayment required. Mail requests: SASE required.

Civil Name Search: Access: Mail, in person, online. Both court and visitors may perform in person name searches. Search fee: $10.00 per name. Fee is for first two years; add $5.00 per add'l 2 years. Required to search: name, years to search, address. Civil cases indexed by plaintiff. Civil records on computer from 1992, prior in books back through 1980s. The records dept in basement has records on computer, PAT, and microfiche. Mail turnaround Time 1 week. Public use terminal has civil records back to 1992. Public terminal in Search Dept, Rm #106. Access to current/pending Supreme Court civil cases is at http://iapps.courts.state.ny.us/webcivil/FCASMain.

Supreme Court - Criminal Term 125-01 Queens Blvd, Kew Gardens, NY 11415; 718-298-1400 records; fax: 718-520-2494; 9:30AM-4:30PM operating; 9AM-5PM public (EST). *Felony.*
www.courts.state.ny.us/courts/11jd/index.shtml

General Information: For Cert of Disposition, contact Correspondence Section at 718-298-1319; in person or written requests cost $10.00 postal money order or cash. For general into, Finance Unit at 718-298-1317. Will fax documents to local or toll-free number. Court makes copy: $.25 per page. Certification fee: $10.00 for 1st page, $1.00 each add'l. Certification only available through the County Clerk Office - 718-298-2943. Payee: Queens County Clerk. Personal checks accepted, credit cards are not. Prepayment required. Mail requests: SASE required for civil.

Criminal Name Search: Access: In person, online. Visitors must perform in person searches themselves. Required to search: name, DOB, years to search. Records Rm records go back to 2005. Note: With indictment number or arrest info you may obtain certified copies at the Queens County Clerk office, 718-298-0601. At the Correspondence section you may make an in person written search request, or a $10.00 Cert of Disposition request. Public use terminal has crim records back to 1984, but you need to be an attorney. Public terminal located in Rm 17. Online access is via the state OCA statewide system. Fee is $65.00 per search. See www.nycourts.gov/apps/chrs/. Subscribe or login as guest to search eCourts WebCrims future appearances system at http://iapps.courts.state.ny.us/webcrim_attorney/Login.

Supreme Court - Long Is. City 25-10 Court Sq, Long Island City, NY 11101; 718-298-1616; fax: 718-520-2539; 9AM-5PM (EST). *Civil Actions over $25,000.*

General Information: Trials only here, civil records available at Queens County Clerk, or at Jamaica Supreme Court.

Civil Court of the City of New York - Queens Branch 89-17 Sutphin Blvd, Jamaica, NY 11435; 718-262-7100; fax: 718-262-7107; 9AM-5PM; small claims & housing open later on TH (EST). *Civil Actions under $25,000, Small Claims.*
www.courts.state.ny.us/courts/11jd/index.shtml

General Information: General housing court and eviction info phone- 646-386-5750. General civil dial-up info line- 212-791-6000. Will not fax documents. Court makes copy: Court gives you file to copy. Self serve copy: $.25 per page. Certification fee: $6.00 per doc. Payee: Clerk of Civil Court. Only cashiers checks and money orders accepted. No credit cards accepted. Prepayment required.

Civil Name Search: Access: In person, online. Visitors must perform in person searches themselves. Required to search: name, years to search; also helpful- case number. Civil cases indexed by plaintiff. Civil records indexed on computer. computer files keep 20 years then archived. Pre-1998 records archived in Queens; 1998 to present in Brooklyn. Note: No searching unless specific case number given. If the case file is archived, it will take 3 weeks to retrieve. Only 2006 and 2007 and current case at court; remainder in archives. Public use terminal has civil records back to 1997; no judgments on terminal. Public terminal includes housing and civil records only. Sum Claims on separate system in Rm #116, 9AM-4:30PM. Access civil records free at http://iapps.courts.state.ny.us/webcivil/ecourtsMain.

Surrogate's Court 88-11 Sutphin Blvd, 7th Fl, Jamaica, NY 11435; 718-298-0500; 9AM-1PM, 2-4:30PM (til 4:10PM Fri) (EST). *Probate.*
www.courts.state.ny.us/courts/nyc/surrogates/index.shtml

General Information: Public access terminal is available. Mail requests accepted, fee $30,00 for index search back 25 years.

Rensselaer County

County Clerk 105 3rd St, Troy, NY 12180; 518-270-4080; fax: 518-271-7998; 8:30AM-5PM (EST). *Felony, Civil.*
www.rensco.com

General Information: Countywide record search requests made to the county clerk are processed in the manner described below. Civil and criminal divisions are separate and managed by separate clerks. No sealed, open/pending cases, youthful offender records released. Will fax documents. Court makes copy: $1.00 per page. Self serve copy: $.50 per page. Certification fee: $4.00 per cert. Payee: County Clerk. Personal checks accepted, credit cards are not. Prepayment required. Mail requests: SASE required.

Civil Name Search: Access: Mail, in person, online. Visitors must perform in person searches themselves. Search fee: $10.00 per name. Civil cases indexed by plaintiff pre-1996; by defendant & plaintiff after 1996. Civil records on computer back to 1997; prior in books to 1930s. Mail turnaround Time 1 week. Lookup Supreme Court civil cases at http://iapps.courts.state.ny.us/webcivil/FCASMain. Cases go back to 2002.

Criminal Name Search: Access: Mail, in person. Only the court performs in person name searches; visitors may not. Search fee: $5.00 per name per 2 years. Required to search: name, years to search; also helpful-DOB. Criminal records computerized from 1986; prior in books to 1976. Note: An email search account can be set-up with this office. Mail turnaround Time 1 week.

Supreme & County Court 80 2nd St, Troy, NY 12180; 518-285-5025; fax: 518-270-3714; 8:30AM-5PM (EST). *Felony, Civil.*
General Information: This court does not hold closed case records. It directs criminal search requests to the OCA for a $65.00 statewide record check. However, for a countywide search, see the County Clerk in a separate listing.

Rensselaer City Court 62 Washington St, Rensselaer, NY 12144; 518-453-4680; fax: 518-462-3307; 8AM-3PM (EST). *Misdemeanor, Civil Actions under $15,000, Eviction, Small Claims, Traffic.*
General Information: No sealed, expunged, adoption, sex offense, juvenile or mental health records released. Will not fax documents. Court makes copy: $.65 per page. Certification fee: $6.00. Payee: Rensselaer City Court. No personal checks accepted. Major credit cards accepted. Prepayment required.
Civil Name Search: Access: Mail, in person, online. Only the court performs in person name searches; visitors may not. Search fee: $6.00 per name. Civil cases indexed by defendant. Civil records back 20 years. Mail turnaround Time 2-5 days WebCivil Local at http://iapps.courts.state.ny.us/webcivil/ecourtsMain contains information on both active and disposed Civil Court cases. Search by index number, party name, attorney/firm name or judge. No fee.
Criminal Name Search: Access: Mail, in person, online. Only the court performs in person name searches; visitors may not. Search fee: $6.00 for a Certificate of Disposition only. Criminal records back 20 years. Note: Court will only confirm convictions. Mail turnaround Time 2-5 days . Name search requests are often directed to the OCA for statewide record search, $65.00 search fee. See www.nycourts.gov/apps/chrs.

Troy City Court 51 State St, 2nd Fl, Troy, NY 12180; 518-453-5900; fax: 518-274-2816; 8:30AM-4PM (EST). *Misdemeanor, Civil Actions under $15,000, Eviction, Small Claims.*
General Information: No sealed records released. Will fax documents. Court makes copy: $.65 per page. Certification fee: $5.00 per doc plus copy fee. Exemplification fee $15.00. Payee: Troy City Court. No personal checks accepted. Credit cards accepted. Prepayment required.
Civil Name Search: Access: In person, online. No search fee.WebCivil Local at http://iapps.courts.state.ny.us/webcivil/ecourtsMain contains information on both active and disposed Civil Court cases. Search by index number, party name, attorney/firm name or judge. No fee.
Criminal Name Search: Access: In person, online. Only the court performs in person name searches; visitors may not. Search fee: $5.00 per docket for certificate of disposition. Required to search: name, approx or exact date of arrest, DOB, aliases, offense. Criminal records computerized from 1989, prior in books. Note: Court will only confirm convictions. All criminal record name search requests are directed to the OCA for statewide record search, $65.00 search fee. See www.nycourts.gov/apps/chrs.

Surrogate's Court County Courthouse, 80 2nd St, Troy, NY 12180; 518-285-6100; fax: 518-272-5452; 9AM-5PM (EST). *Probate.*
www.courts.state.ny.us/courts/3jd/surrogates/rensselaer/index.shtml
General Information: A county search of the probate court index by mail for 25-year search is $30.00 fee. A full county probate search of all years is $90.00.

Rensselaer Town/Village Courts -Berlin Town Court PO Box 488, 65 S Main St, Berlin, NY 12022; 518-658-2020 x3 7PM W?; 3rd W 5:30PM (criminal cases). **Brunswick Town Court** 336 Town Office Rd, Troy, NY 12180; 518-279-3461 x113 8AM-4PM. **Castleton-on-Hudson Village Court** PO Box 126, 85 S Main St, Castleton, NY 12033; 518-732-2211 6PM-? T. **East Greenbush Town Court** 225 Columbia Turnpike, Rensselaer, NY 12144; 518-477-5412 8:30-4:30PM. **Grafton Town Court** PO Box 1, Grafton, NY 12082; 518-279-3565 x2 7-9PM T. **Hoosick Falls Village Court** 24 Main St, Hoosick Falls, NY 12090; 518-686-4399 10AM-1PM M-TH; Closed F. **Hoosick Town Court** 80 Church St, PO Box 17, Hoosick Falls, NY 12090; 518-686-3335 9AM-4PM TH. **Nassau Town Court** 29 Church St, PO Box 587, Nassau, NY 12123; 518-766-2343 x4 Court- 7 PM Wed. **Nassau Village Court** 40 Malden St, PO Box 452, Nassau, NY 12123; 518-766-3044 x1 8AM-N. **North Greenbush Town Court** 2 Douglas St, Wynantskill, NY 12198; 518-283-2789 x28 or x29 8:30AM-N M,T,TH; 3:30AM-4:15 W; Closed F. **Petersburgh Town Court** Town Hall, 65 Main St, PO Box 233, Petersburgh, NY 12138; 518-658-3777 7PM T; 2nd T 6PM. **Pittstown Town Court** 123 Tomhannock Rd, Valley Falls, NY 12185; 518-753-4222 x 305 10AM-1PM M,W. **Poestenkill Town Court** PO Box 164, 38 Davis Dr, Poestenkill, NY 12140; 518-283-5100 8AM-5PM M-F (court- 6:30PM M). **Sand Lake Town Court** PO Box 273, 8428 NY Rte 66, Sand Lake, NY 12153; 518-674-3033 8AM-5PM M; 8AM-2PM T-F. **Schaghticoke Town Court** 290 Northline Dr, Melrose, NY 12121; 518-753-6915 x106 or 107 9AM-N

M,W,F; Court- 7PM M; 6-8PM Wed. **Schodack Justice Court** 265 Schuurman Rd, Castleton, NY 12033; 518-477-9390 9AM-4PM M-F (court 6PM-? W). **Stephentown Town Court** Grange Hall Rd, PO Box 268, Stephentown, NY 12168; 518-733-5636 7PM-? 1st, 2nd, 3rd W.

Richmond County

County Civil Court 927 Castleton Ave, Staten Island, NY 10301; 646-386-5700; fax: 718-390-8108; 9AM-5PM (EST). *Civil Actions, Small Claims, Housing.*
www.nycourts.gov/courts/13jd
General Information: The court for Housing/Landlord/Tenant actions can be reached at 718-675-5750. No matrimonial records released. Will not fax documents. Self serve copy: $.15 per page. Court gives you file to copy. Certification fee: $6.00 per doc includes copy fee. Payee: Clerk of Civil Clerk. Only cashier's checks and money orders accepted. No credit cards accepted. Prepayment required.
Civil Name Search: Access: In person, online. Visitors must perform in person searches themselves. Civil cases indexed by plaintiff. Civil records on computer back to 1993. Public use terminal has civil records back to 1993. Also, access to statewide Supreme Court civil cases to 2002 is at http://iapps.courts.state.ny.us/webcivil/FCASMain.

Supreme Court - Civil Division 18 Richmond Terrace, Staten Island, NY 10301; 718-675-8700; 9AM-5PM (EST). *Civil Actions.*
www.nycourts.gov/courts/13jd
General Information: The court for Housing/Landlord/Tenant actions can be reached at 718-675-5750. No matrimonial records released. Will not fax documents. Court makes copy: $.25 per page. Self serve copy: $.25 per page. Certification fee: $8.00 per doc includes copy fee. Payee: Richmond County Clerk. Only attorney's checks and money orders accepted. No credit cards accepted. Prepayment required.
Civil Name Search: Access: Phone, in person, online. Visitors must perform in person searches themselves. Search fee: $5.00 per name per 2 years. Civil cases indexed by plaintiff. Civil records on computer back to 1993. Public use terminal has civil records back to 1993. Also, access to current/pending Supreme Court civil cases is at http://iapps.courts.state.ny.us/webcivil/FCASMain.

Supreme Court - Criminal Division 18 Richmond Terrace, Staten Island, NY 10304; 718-675-8700; fax: 718-390-8405; 9AM-5PM (EST). *Felony, Misdemeanor.*
www.nycourts.gov/courts/13jd/
General Information: Court will not perform name searches. Must request all criminal record name searches from the OCA for statewide record search, $65.00 search fee. No sealed or youthful offender records released unless to subject. Will not fax documents. Court makes copy: $.65 per page. Certification fee: $10.00 per doc plus copy fee. Payee: County Clerk, Richmond County. Only cashiers checks and money orders accepted. No credit cards accepted. Prepayment required. Mail requests: SASE required.
Criminal Name Search: Access: In person, online. Visitors must perform in person searches themselves. Required to search: name, DOB, years to search. Criminal records computerized from 1975, prior archived back to 1960. Note: Will provide a Certificate of Disposition for $10.00. Will not allow in person or mail access to case files without a specific case number. All criminal record name search requests directed to the OCA for statewide record search, $65.00 search fee. Online access is via the state OCA statewide system. Fee is $65.00 per search. See www.nycourts.gov/apps/chrs/. Subscribe or login as guest to search eCourts WebCrims future appearances system at http://iapps.courts.state.ny.us/webcrim_attorney/Login.

Surrogate's Court 18 Richmond Terrace, Rm 201, Staten Island, NY 10301; 718-675-8500; fax: 718-390-8741; 9AM-5PM (EST). *Probate, Adoption, Guardianship.*
www.nycourts.gov/courts/13jd/
General Information: A county search of the probate court index by mail for 25-year search is $30.00 fee. A full county probate search of all years is $90.00.

Rockland County

County Clerk 1 S. Main, Ste.100, New City, NY 10956; 845-638-5070; criminal phone: 845-638-5094; civil phone: 845-638-5094; fax: 845-638-5647; 7AM-6PM (EST). *Felony, Misdemeanor, Civil.*
www.rocklandcountyclerk.com
General Information: Countywide search requests made to the county clerk are processed here. Misdemeanor records maintained by city, town, village courts, but this clerk may have a misdemeanor record if your provide an index number. Online identifiers in results same as on public terminal. No detention records release. Will not fax documents. Court makes copy: $1.00 per page. Self serve copy: $.25 per page. Certification fee: $1.25 per page, $5.00 minimum; exemplification- $15.00. Payee: Rockland County

Clerk. Personal checks accepted, credit cards are not. Prepayment required. Mail requests: SASE required.

Civil Name Search: Access: Mail, in person, online. Both court and visitors may perform in person name searches. Search fee: $5.00 per each 2 years. Civil indexed by defendant, plaintiff. Civil records on computer from 1982. Mail turnaround Time approx. 10 days. Civil PAT goes back to 1982. Online access to county clerk index is free at www.rocklandcountyclerk.com/court_records.html. Online includes civil judgments, real estate records, tax warrants. Call 845-638-5221 for info. Also, access to current Supreme court cases is at https://iapps.courts.state.ny.us/caseTrac/jsp/ecourt.htm.

Criminal Name Search: Access: Mail, online, in person. Both court and visitors may perform in person name searches. Search fee: $5.00 each 2 years. Criminal records computerized from 1982. Mail turnaround Time approx. 10 days. Criminal PAT goes back to same as civil. Free acces to index at www.rocklandcountyclerk.com/court_records.html. Index includes criminal records back to 1982. Free registration required. Also, subscribe or login as guest to search eCourts WebCrims system at http://iapps.courts.state.ny.us/webcrim_attorney/Login. Also, access calendar of current Supreme court cases at https://iapps.courts.state.ny.us/caseTrac/jsp/ecourt.htm. Online results show name only.

Supreme & County Court 1 S Main St, #200, New City, NY 10956; 845-638-5393; fax: 845-638-5312; 9AM-5PM (EST). *Felony, Civil.* www.nycourts.gov/courts/9jd/rockland/index.shtml
General Information: Direct all search requests to the County Clerk office, see separate listing. County Court is located in #400.

Surrogate's Court 1 S Main St, #270, New City, NY 10956; 845-638-5330; fax: 845-638-5632; 9AM-5PM (EST). *Probate.*
General Information: A county search of the probate court index by mail for 25-year search is $30.00 fee. A full county probate search of all years is $90.00. Also this court holds administration and guardianship records.

Rockland Town/Village Courts - Chestnut Ridge Village Court 277 Old Nyack Turnpike, Chestnut Ridge, NY 10977; 845-425-3108 9AM-4PM. **Clarkstown Town Court** 20 Maple Ave, New City, NY 10956; 845-639-5960/5970 9AM-4PM. **Grand View-on-Hudson Court** 282 S Broadway, South Nyack, NY 10960; 845-358-5078 9AM-5PM. **Haverstraw Town Court** 1 Rosman Rd, Garnerville, NY 10923; 845-947-0020 8AM-4PM. **Haverstraw Village Justice Court** 40 New Main St, Haverstraw, NY 10927; 845-947-4063 9AM-5PM. **Hillburn Village Court** 31 Mountain Ave, Hillburn, NY 10931; 845-357-2036 9AM-4:30PM. **Nyack Village Court** 9 N Broadway, Nyack, NY 10960; 845-358-4464 9AM-5PM. **Orangetown Town Court** Town Hall, 26 Orangeburg Rd, Orangeburg, NY 10962; 845-359-5100 9-4PM. **Piermont Village Court** 478 Piermont Ave, Piermont, NY 10968; 845-359-0345 9AM-3PM. **Ramapo Town Court** 237 Route 59, Suffern, NY 10901; 845-357-5100 9-5PM. **Sloatsburg Village Court** 96 Orange Turnpike, Sloatsburg, NY 10974; 845-753-5506 8AM-4PM. **South Nyack Village Court** 282 Broadway, South Nyack, NY 10960; 845-358-5078 9-12PM M,T,TH. **Spring Valley Village Court** 200 N Main St, Spring Valley, NY 10977; 845-573-5820 8:30AM-4:30PM ofc; 9AM-3PM Window. **Stony Point Town Court** 6 Patriot Hill Dr., Stony Point, NY 10980; 845-786-2506 8AM-4PM M-F (except trial days, usually T&TH). **Suffern Village Court** 61 Washington Ave, Suffern, NY 10901; 845-357-6424 8AM-3:30PM. **Upper Nyack Village Court** 328 N Broadway, Upper Nyack, NY 10960; 845-358-0202 9AM-N M-F. **Wesley Hills Justice Court** 432 Route 306, Wesley Hills, NY 10952; 845-354-0404 2nd Wed, 4th Tu of month. **West Haverstraw Village Court** Village Court, 130 Samsondale Ave., West Haverstraw, NY 10993; 845-947-1013 8:30AM-4:30PM.

Saratoga County

County Clerk 40 McMaster St, Ballston Spa, NY 12020; 518-885-2213 X4410; civil phone: x4410; fax: 518-884-4726; 8AM-5PM (EST). *Felony, Civil.*
General Information: This County Clerk does not have a separate index of felony records; in person searching only, or contact the state OCA. No youthful offender or divorce records released. Will fax back documents. Court makes copy: $1.25 per page. Self serve copy: $.50 per page. Certification fee: $5.00 per cert includes 4 copy pages; $1.25 each add'l page; max $40.00. Payee: County Clerk. Only in-state personal checks with name/address and phone accepted. No credit cards accepted. Prepayment required. Mail requests: SASE required.
Civil Name Search: Access: Mail, in person, online. Both court and visitors may perform in person name searches. Search fee: $5.00 per name per 2 years. Required to search: name, years to search; also helpful: address. Civil records on computer from 3/88, prior in books. Mail turnaround Time 3-4 days. Public use terminal has civil records back to 1987. Lookup Supreme Court civil cases at http://iapps.courts.state.ny.us/webcivil/FCASMain. Cases go back to 2002.

Criminal Name Search: Access: In person only. Both court and visitors may perform in person name searches. No search fee. Required to search: name, years to search; DOB; also helpful: address. Criminal records not computerized here, on books. Note: The clerk's office has the records but they will not search them.

Supreme & County Court 30 McMaster St, Ballston Spa, NY 12020; 518-451-8840; fax: 528-884-4758; 9AM-5PM (EST). *Felony, Civil.* www.nycourts.gov/courts/4jd/saratoga/index.shtml
General Information: This court does not hold closed case records. See separate County Clerk entry for Supreme civil records. Access to current/pending Supreme Court civil at http://iapps.courts.state.ny.us/webcivil/FCASMain. Criminal online via state OCA statewide system.

Mechanicville City Court 36 N Main St, Mechanicville, NY 12118; 518-664-9876; fax: 518-664-8606; 8AM-4PM (EST). *Misdemeanor, Civil Actions under $15,000, Eviction, Small Claims.*
General Information: No sealed, expunged, adoption, sex offense, juvenile or mental health records released. Will fax documents to local or toll free line. Court makes copy: $.65 per page; $1.30 minimum. Certification fee: $6.00 per doc plus copy fee. Payee: City Court. No Personal checks, Visa/MC accepted. Prepayment required.
Civil Name Search: Access: In person, online. Both court and visitors may perform in person name searches. No search fee. Civil cases indexed by defendant. Civil records on computer since 1/94; records go back to 1900. WebCivil Local at http://iapps.courts.state.ny.us/webcivil/ecourtsMain contains information on both active and disposed Civil Court cases. Search by index number, party name, attorney/firm name or judge. No fee.
Criminal Name Search: Access: Online. Only the court performs in person name searches; visitors may not. No search fee. Criminal records computerized from 9/93; records go back to 1900. Note: The court refuses to permit access to court records unless specific case file given. All criminal record name search requests are directed to the OCA for statewide record search, $65.00 search fee. See www.nycourts.gov/apps/chrs.

Saratoga Springs City Court City Hall, 474 Broadway, Ste #3, Saratoga Springs, NY 12866; 518-451-8780; fax: 518-584-3097; 8AM-4PM; ofc- 9AM-3:45PM (EST). *Misdemeanor, Civil Actions under $15,000, Eviction, Small Claims, Traffic.*
General Information: Sealed files not released. Will not fax documents. Court makes copy: $1.30 1st page; $.65 each add'l. Certification fee: $5.00. Payee: City Court. Only cashiers checks and money orders accepted. Credit cards not accepted via phone. Prepayment required. Mail requests: SASE required for civil.
Civil Name Search: Access: Mail, in person, online. Only the court performs in person name searches; visitors may not. No search fee. Civil cases indexed by defendant. Civil records on computer back to 10/94; prior records on index cards. Note: Make search requests in writing. Mail turnaround Time 1 week WebCivil Local at http://iapps.courts.state.ny.us/webcivil/ecourtsMain contains information on both active and disposed Civil Court cases. Search by index number, party name, attorney/firm name or judge. No fee.
Criminal Name Search: Access: In person, online. Only the court performs in person name searches; visitors may not. Search fee: Certificate of Disposition is $5.00 per name. Criminal records computerized from 8/93. All criminal record name search requests are directed to the OCA for statewide record search, $65.00 search fee. See www.nycourts.gov/apps/chrs.

Surrogate's Court 30 McMaster St, Bldg 3, Ballston Spa, NY 12020; 518-451-8830; fax: 518-884-4774; 9AM-5PM (EST). *Probate.*
General Information: Public access terminal back to 1990. Older records being added. County search of the probate court index by mail for 25-yr search is $30 fee. Full county probate search of all yrs is $90. Also found in this court are voluntary admins & guardianships.

Saratoga Town/Village Courts - Ballston Spa Village Court 30 Bath St, Ballston Spa, NY 12020; 518-885-6393 **Ballston Town Court** PO Box 67, 323 Charlton Rd, Ballston Spa, Burnt Hills, NY 12027; 518-885-8559 9AM-N M,T; Court-5:30PM-? Wed, 7PM-? TH. **Charlton Town Court** 758 Charlton Rd, Charlton, NY 12019; 518-384-0152 x201 9AM-1PM M-F; 6PM -8PM T; 9AM-N Sat (except July & Aug). **Clifton Park Town Court** Public Safety Bldg, 5 Municipal Plaza, Clifton Park, NY 12065; 518-371-6668 9AM-5PM; Court 7PM W&TH. **Corinth Town Court** 600 Palmer Ave, Corinth, NY 12822; 518-654-9232 x4 8AM-N, 12:30PM-4PM. **Day Town Court** 1652 N Shore Rd, Hadley, NY 12835; 518-696-3789 #306/316 5PM-? W (court). **Galway Town Court** PO Box 219, 5910 Sacandaga Rd, Galway, NY 12074; 518-882-6070 x15 6PM-? TH. **Galway Village Court** PO Box 219, 5910 Sacandaga Rd, Galway, NY 12074; 518-882-6070 5PM TH. **Greenfield Town Court** PO Box 10, 7 Wilton Rd, Greenfield Center, NY 12833; 518-893-7432 x310 9AM-2PM M-Th. **Hadley Town Court** PO Box 323, 4 Stony Creek Rd, Hadley, NY

12835-0323; 518-696-4379 x8 3PM-? W; 9AM-N TH. **Halfmoon Town Court** 1 Halfmoon town Plza, Halfmoon, NY 12065; 518-371-2592 9AM-4PM M-F. **Malta Town Court** 2538 Route 9, Ballston Spa, NY 12020; 518-899-6121 9AM-5PM. **Milton Town Court** 345 Rowland St., Ballston Spa, NY 12020; 518-885-9267 1PM-4PM M,T,W. **Moreau Town Court** 1390 Rt 9, Gansevoort, NY 12831; 518-793-3188 8:AM-4PM. **Northumberland Town Court** 17 Catherine St, PO Box 128, Gansevoort, NY 12831; 518-745-0178 8AM-3PM M,T,W. **Providence Town Court** 7187 Barkersville Rd, Middle Grove, NY 12850-1411; 518-882-6753 9AM-2:30PM W,F; 3PM-7PM TH; 8AM-N F. **Saratoga Town Court** 12 Spring St, Schuylerville, NY 12871; 518-695-6887 x315 10AM-3PM M-F. **Stillwater Town Court** PO Box 700, 66 East St, Town Court (Mechanicville 12118), Stillwater, NY 12170; 518-664-6946 9AM-2PM M T TH. **Waterford Town Court** 65 Broad St, Waterford, NY 12188; 518-237-6788 8AM-4PM (court 6PM-?). **Wilton Town Court** 20 Traver Rd, Gansevoort, NY 12831; 518-587-1980 8:30AM-4PM.

Schenectady County

County Clerk 620 State St, 3rd Fl, Attn: County Clerk, Schenectady, NY 12305; 518-388-4220; fax: 518-388-4224; 9AM-5PM; July-Aug-9AM-4PM; file papers 1/2 hour before close (EST). *Civil from Supreme Ct.* http://schenectadycounty.com/FullStory.aspx?m=47&amid=2070

General Information: For felony records see the County Court clerk at the Supreme and County Court in separate listing. No sealed, youthful offenders, infant compromise or divorce records released. Will not fax out documents. Court makes copy: $1.00 per page off computer. Self serve copy: $.50 per page. Certification fee: $1.00 per page; exemplification- add $10.00. Payee: County Clerk. Personal checks accepted, credit cards are not. Prepayment required. Mail requests: SASE required.

Civil Name Search: Access: Mail, in person, online. Both court and visitors may perform in person name searches. Search fee: $5.00 per name per 2 years. They can verify a no record found via the phone. Civil cases indexed by plaintiff. Civil records on computer from 1989, prior on index cards. Note: In person access is only here at the County Clerk, not the Supreme Court Clerk. Mail turnaround Time 4 days. Will expedite requests if requested. Public use terminal has civil records back to 1995 but may include some records back to 1988. Results may include other personal identifiers, depending on what data is originally entered. Online access to current/pending Supreme Court civil cases is at http://iapps.courts.state.ny.us/webcivil/ecourtsMain.

Supreme & County Court 612 State St, 4th Fl, Schenectady, NY 12305; 518-285-8401; civil phone: 518-388-4222; fax: 518-388-4520; 9AM-5PM (EST). *Felony.*

General Information: This court does not hold closed civil case records - see separate County Clerk entry. Access to current/pending Supreme Court civil at http://iapps.courts.state.ny.us/webcivil/FCASMain. Criminal online via state OCA statewide system. No sealed, youthful offenders, infant compromise or divorce records released. Notarized, signed release required to access sealed records. Will not fax out documents. Court makes copy: $.65 per page. Certification fee: $5.00 per doc at court. Payee: County Clerk. Personal checks accepted, credit cards are not. Prepayment required. Mail requests: SASE required.

Criminal Name Search: Access: Mail, in person, online. Only the court performs in person name searches; visitors may not. Search fee: $5.00 per name for Cert of Disposition. Required to search: name, years to search, DOB; include indictment number for Cert of Disposition. Criminal records computerized from 1989, prior in index books. Mail turnaround Time 4 days. Online access is via the state OCA statewide system. Fee is $65.00 per search. See www.nycourts.gov/apps/chrs/.

Schenectady City Court - Civil Jay St, City Hall, #215, Schenectady, NY 12305; 518-382-5077; fax: 518-382-5080; 8AM-4PM (EST). *Civil Actions under $15,000, Eviction, Small Claims.*

General Information: No sealed or youthful offender records released. Will fax documents to local or toll-free number. Court makes copy: $.65 per page. Certification fee: $6.00. Payee: City Court. Only cashiers checks and money orders accepted - except will take checks form attorneys. Visa/MC accepted. Prepayment required. Mail requests: SASE required.

Civil Name Search: Access: Mail, in person, online. Only the court performs in person name searches; visitors may not. Search fee: $16.00 per name. Civil cases indexed by docket #. Civil records on computer from 1998, prior in books. Mail turnaround Time 2 weeks. WebCivil Local at http://iapps.courts.state.ny.us/webcivil/ecourtsMain contains information on both active and disposed Civil Court cases. Search by index number, party name, attorney/firm name or judge. No fee.

Schenectady City Court - Criminal 531 Liberty St, Schenectady, NY 12305; 518-382-5239; fax: 518-382-5241; 8AM-4PM (EST). *Misdemeanor.*

General Information: No sealed or youthful offender records released. Will not fax documents. Court makes copy: $.65 per page. Certification fee:

$6.00. Payee: City Court. Only cashiers checks and money orders accepted. Visa/MC accepted. Prepayment required. Mail requests: SASE required.

Criminal Name Search: Access: Online. Only the court performs in person name searches; visitors may not. Search fee: A certificate of Disposition is $6.00. Required to search: Name, DOB, case number. Criminal records computerized from 1995, prior in books. All criminal record name search requests are directed to the OCA for statewide record search, $65.00 search fee. See www.nycourts.gov/apps/chrs.

Surrogate's Court 612 State St, Judicial Bldg, Schenectady, NY 12305; 518-285-8455; fax: 518-377-6378; 9AM-5PM (EST). *Probate, Administration, Guardianship, Adoption.*

General Information: A county search of the probate court index by mail for 25-year search is $30.00 fee. A full county probate search of all years is $90.00.

Schenectady Town/Village Courts - Duanesburg Town Court Town Hall, Route 20, Duanesburg, NY 12056; 518-895-8922 x105 or 106 10AM-3PM M-TH (court 7PM M & W). **Glenville Town Court** Municipal Ctr, 18 Glenridge Rd, Glenville, NY 12302; 518-688-1200 x409 9AM-5PM; 9AM-4PM July/Aug (court 5:30PM-? T&TH). **Niskayuna Town Court** One Niskayuna Circle, Niskayuna, NY 12309; 518-386-4560 9AM-4PM, W till 6PM. **Princetown Town Court** 165 Princetown Plaza, Schenectady, NY 12306; 518-357-4047 10AM-4PM M or TH; court- W 7PM. **Rotterdam Town Court** 101 Princetown Rd, Schenectady, NY 12306; 518-355-7911 8AM-5PM M-F (8AM-4PM Summer). **Scotia Village Court** 4 Ten Broek St, Scotia, NY 12302; 518-374-2099 9AM-1PM 2PM-5PM M,T,W,F; 1PM-6PM TH.

Schoharie County

Supreme & County Court PO Box 549, 284 Main St, Attn: County Clerk, Schoharie, NY 12157; 518-295-8316 (County Clerk); 518-295-8342 (Supreme); fax: 518-295-8338; 8:30AM-5PM; 8:30AM-7:00PM W (EST). *Felony, Civil, Misdemeanor, Eviction, Small Claims.* www.schohariecounty-ny.gov

General Information: Direct search requests to the County Clerk who processes requests in the manner described below. No sealed criminal or divorce records released. Fee to fax out file $1.00 per page. Court makes copy: $.50 per page. Self serve copy: same. Certification fee: $4.00. Payee: County Clerk. Personal checks accepted. Prepayment required. Mail requests: SASE required.

Civil Name Search: Access: Fax, mail, in person, online. Both court and visitors may perform in person name searches. Search fee: $5.00 per name. Civil records on computer from 1994, prior in books. Mail turnaround Time 24-48 hours. Civil PAT goes back to 1994. Current or pending only Supreme Court civil case look-up is at http://iapps.courts.state.ny.us/webcivil/FCASMain.

Criminal Name Search: Access: Fax, mail, in person, Online. Both court and visitors may perform in person name searches. Search fee: $5.00 per name. Required to search: name, years to search, DOB or SSN. Criminal records in books back to 1930; on computer back to 2000. Mail turnaround Time 24-48 hours. Criminal PAT goes back to 2000. Terminal results include SSN. Online access is via the state OCA statewide system. Fee is $65.00 per search. See www.nycourts.gov/apps/chrs/.

Surrogate's Court Courthouse, 290 Main St, PO Box 669, Schoharie, NY 12157; 518-295-8387; fax: 518-295-8451; 9AM-5PM (EST). *Probate.* www.courts.state.ny.us/courts/3jd/surrogates/schoharie/index.shtml

General Information: A county search of the probate court index by mail for 25-year search is $30.00 fee. A full county probate search of all years is $90.00.

Schoharie Town/Village Courts - Blenheim Town Court 2153 State Rte 30, Fultonham, NY 12071; 518-827-6115 **Broome Town Court** 914 State Rte 145, Middleburg, NY 12122; 518-827-8777 Hours vary. **Carlisle Town Court** PO Box 104, Carlisle, NY 12031; 518-234-7080 4PM W court. **Cobleskill Town Court and Village Court** 378 Mineral Springs Rd #3, Cobleskill, NY 12043; 518-234-7886 9-12PM,1-3PM M,T,TH. **Conesville Town Court** 1306 State Route 990V, Gilboa, NY 12076; 607-588-7211 Evenings on 2nd and 4th Tuesday of each month. **Esperance Town Court** 104 Charleston St, PO Box 226, Esperance, NY 12066; 518-875-6109 6PM-8:30PM W. **Fulton Town Court** 1168 Bear Ladder Rd, West Fulton, NY 12194; 518-827-6391 2nd & 4th T 9AM-?. **Gilboa Town Court** PO Box 105, 373 State Rte 990V, #1, Gilboa, NY 12076; 607-588-7604 10AM-2PM M,T,W,F; 6:30-9PM TH. **Jefferson Town Court** 142 Campo Rd, Jefferson, NY 12093; 607-652-2109 Wed Eve. **Middleburgh Town Court** 143 Railroad Ave, PO Box 946, Middleburgh, NY 12122; 518-827-7433 7PM-9PM W and by appointment. **Middleburgh Village Court** 309 Main St, PO Box 789, Middleburgh, NY 12122; 518-827-7433 **Richmondville Town Court** PO Box 7, 340 Main St, Richmondville, NY 12149; 518-294-8851 9AM-11:30AM M,T,W. **Schoharie Town Court and Village Court** PO Box 865, Schoharie, NY 12157; 518-296-6575 4PM-6PM Monday only. **Seward Town Court** 795 Lowe Rd, #1, Cobleskill, NY 12043; 518-234-3144, 234-2292 Court- 7PM-? Wed. **Sharon Town Court** PO Box 96, 106 Park St, Sharon Springs, NY

13459; 518-284-3419 1PM TH except holidays. **Summit Town Court** PO Box 132, 1580 Charlotte Valley Rd, Summit, NY 12175; 518-287-1194 10AM 1st & 3rd TH. **Wright Town Court** PO Box 43, 913 SR 443, Gallupville, NY 12073; 518-872-1705 7PM T + by appointment.

Schuyler County

County Clerk Courthouse, 105 9th St, Unit 8, Watkins Glen, NY 14891; 607-535-8133; 9AM-5PM (EST). *Felony, Civil.*
General Information: Countywide search requests made to the county clerk are processed in the manner described below. No sealed or youthful offender records released. Will not fax out documents. Court makes copy: $.65 per page. Certification fee: $5.00 per doc. Cert fee is for 1st 4 pages, add'l pages are $1.25 each, copies included. Payee: County Clerk. Personal checks accepted, credit cards are not. Prepayment required. Mail requests: SASE required.
Civil Name Search: Access: Mail, in person, online. Both court and visitors may perform in person name searches. Search fee: $5.00 per name. Civil cases indexed by defendant. Civil records are indexed in books; on computer back to 1987. Mail turnaround Time 2-3 days. Lookup current or pending Supreme Court civil cases at http://iapps.courts.state.ny.us/webcivil/FCASMain.
Criminal Name Search: Access: Mail, in person. Only the court performs in person name searches; visitors may not. Search fee: $5.00 per name. Required to search: name, years to search, DOB. Criminal records are indexed in books; on computer back to 1987. Misdemeanors go back to 1971. Mail turnaround Time 2-3 days.

Supreme & County Court Courthouse, 105 9th St, Unit 35, Watkins Glen, NY 14891; criminal phone: 607-535-7015; civil phone: 607-535-7760; fax: 607-535-4918; 9AM-5PM (EST). *Felony, Civil.*
General Information: This court does not hold closed case records. See separate County Clerk entry for Supreme Court civil records. Access to current/pending Supreme Court civil at http://iapps.courts.state.ny.us/webcivil/FCASMain. Criminal online via state OCA statewide system.

Surrogate's Court County Courthouse, 105 9th St, Unit 35, Watkins Glen, NY 14891; 607-535-7144; fax: 607-535-4918; 9AM-5PM (8:30AM-4:30 PM in Summer) (EST). *Probate.*
General Information: A county search of the probate court index by mail for 25-year search is $30.00 fee. Estate searches for estates older than 25 years is $90.00. Also, records at this court are administration, guardianships and adoptions.

Schuyler Town/Village Courts - Catharine Town Court 106 Grant Rd, Odessa, NY 14869; 607-594-2273 9-2PM M,T,TH, 4-7PM W. **Cayuta Town Court** PO Box 22, Town Court, Cayuta, NY 14824; 607-594-2507 10AM-N M&TH. **Dix Town Court** Town Hall c/o A. Gregory, 304 7th St, Watkins Glen, NY 14891; 607-535-7973 x204 Wed 7PM. **Hector Town Court** 5097 Route 227, Burdett, NY 14818; 607-546-5286 9AM-4PM. **Montour Falls Village Court** 408 W Main St, PO Box 744, Montour Falls, NY 14865; 607-535-7362 2PM - ?. **Montour Town Court** PO Box 579, Montour Falls, NY 14865; 607-535-9476 8AM-1PM M,T,TH,F; 3PM-6PM W. **Odessa Village Court** Village Court, 106 Grant Rd, Odessa, NY 14869; 607-594-2273 9AM-2PM M,T,TH; 4-7PM W. **Reading Town Court** PO Box 5, Reading Center, NY 14876; 607-535-7459 x101 **Tyrone Town Court** 457 County Rte 23, PO Box 169 (Tyrone, NY 14887), Dundee, NY 14837; 607-292-6695 6PM-? M. **Watkins Glen Village Court** 303 N Franklin St, Watkins Glen, NY 14891; 607-535-9717 Sat 9AM.

Seneca County

County Clerk 1 DiPronio Dr, County Office Bldg, Attn: Seneca County Clerk, Waterloo, NY 13165-1396; 315-539-1771; fax: 315-539-3789; 8:30AM-5PM (EST). *Felony, Civil.*
General Information: Countywide search requests made to the county clerk are processed in the manner described below. No divorce records released. Will fax documents to local or toll free line. Court makes copy: $.65 per page;. Self serve copy: $.40 per page. Certification fee: $5.00; if exemplification then $10.00. Payee: Seneca County Clerk. Personal checks accepted, credit cards are not. Prepayment required. Mail requests: SASE required.
Civil Name Search: Access: Mail, in person, online. Both court and visitors may perform in person name searches. Search fee: $10.00 per name. Civil cases indexed by defendant. Civil records on computer since 3/1997; prior records in books. Mail turnaround Time 1 week. Civil PAT goes back to 3/1997. Lookup Supreme Court civil cases at http://iapps.courts.state.ny.us/webcivil/FCASMain. Cases go back to 2002.
Criminal Name Search: Access: Mail, in person. Both court and visitors may perform in person name searches. Search fee: $10.00 per name. Required to search: name, years to search, signed release. Criminal records on computer since 3/1997; prior records in books. Mail turnaround Time 1 week. Criminal PAT goes back to same as civil.

Supreme & County Court 48 W Williams St, Courthouse, Waterloo, NY 13165; 315-539-7021; fax: 315-539-3267; 9AM-5PM (EST). *Felony, Civil.*
www.nycourts.gov/courts/7jd/seneca/index.shtml
General Information: This court does not hold closed case records. See separate County Clerk entry for Supreme civil records. Access to current/pending Supreme Court civil at http://iapps.courts.state.ny.us/webcivil/FCASMain. Criminal online via state OCA statewide system.

Surrogate's Court 48 W Williams St, Waterloo, NY 13165; 315-539-7531; fax: 315-539-3267; 9AM-5PM (EST). *Probate.*
www.nycourts.gov/courts/7jd/
General Information: A county search of the probate court index requires a fee of $30.00 for under 25 years and $90.00 for over 25 years.
Seneca Town/Village Courts - Covert Town Court PO Box 220, 8469 S Main St, Municipal Bldg, Interlaken, NY 14847; 607-532 4091 10AM-4PM M. **Fayette Town Court** 1439 Yellow Tavern Rd, Waterloo, NY 13165; 315-585-6282 7:30AM-4PM T,TH. **Junius Town Court** 655 Dublin Rd, Clyde, NY 14433; 315-539-4667 9AM-12 Th. **Lodi Town Court** 8440 Main St, PO Box 33, Lodi, NY 14860; 607-582-7730 10AM-? W. **Ovid Town Court** PO Box 35, 7160 Main St, Municipal Bldg, Ovid, NY 14521; 607-869-9845 7-9PM Mon; 7-8PM TH. **Romulus Town Court** PO Box 274, 1435 Prospect St, Willard, NY 14588; 607-869-9650 11AM-2PM M,W; 10AM-2PM F. **Seneca Falls Town Court** 81 W Bayard, Seneca Falls, NY 13148; 315-568-9234 9AM-4PM. **Tyre Town Court** 1315 Middle Black Brook Rd, Seneca Falls, NY 13148; 315-568-1221, 568-9417 varies. **Varick Town Court** 4782 Rte 96, Romulus, NY 14541; 315-585-6018 7PM-? W (court-No court 3rd W). **Waterloo Town Court** 66 Virginia St, Waterloo, NY 13165; 315-539-3213 10AM-N 1PM-4PM M,T,TH; 1PM-4PM W (court-2PM W). **Waterloo Village Court** 41 W Main St, Waterloo, NY 13165; 315-539-2512 9AM-N 1PM-4PM M-TH (court 9AM-N W).

St. Lawrence County

Supreme & County Court 48 Court St, Canton, NY 13617-1169; 315-379-2237 (County Clerk); 315-379-2219 (Court Clerk); probate phone: 315-379-2217; fax: 315-379-2302; 8AM-5PM (Thurs til 7PM) (EST). *Felony, Civil.*
General Information: Direct all search requests to the via the County Clerk's office; information given here is for that County Clerk office. This court does not hold closed case records. No sealed or divorce records released. Will fax documents $4.00 each; no fee to toll-free numbers. Court makes copy: $.65 per page. Self serve copy: $.50 per page. Certification fee: $5.00. Payee: County Clerk. Personal checks accepted, credit cards are not. Prepayment required. Mail requests: SASE required.
Civil Name Search: Access: Fax, mail, in person, online. Both court and visitors may perform in person name searches. Search fee: $5.00 per name. Civil records go back to 1986; on computer since 1990, prior in books. Mail turnaround Time 2-3 days. Civil PAT goes back to 1986. Historical records are not online, but access to current/pending Supreme Court civil cases is at http://iapps.courts.state.ny.us/webcivil/FCASMain.
Criminal Name Search: Access: Fax, mail, in person, online. Both court and visitors may perform in person name searches. Search fee: $15.00 per name. Required to search: name, years to search, DOB. Criminal records on computer since 1985, prior in books. Mail turnaround Time 2-3 days. Criminal PAT goes back to 1985. Online access is via the state OCA statewide system. Fee is $65.00 per search. See www.nycourts.gov/apps/chrs/.

Ogdensburg City Court 330 Ford St, Ogdensburg, NY 13669; 315-393-3941; fax: 315-393-6839; 8AM-4PM (EST). *Misdemeanor, Civil Actions under $15,000, Eviction, Small Claims.*
www.nycourts.gov/courts/4jd/stlawrence/ogdensburg.shtml
General Information: No youthful offender records released. Will fax documents. Court makes copy: $.65 per page, minimun-$1.30 fee. Certification fee: $5.00. Payee: City Court. Business checks accepted. Visa/MC/Discover accepted. Prepayment required. Mail requests: SASE required.
Civil Name Search: Access: Mail, in person, online. Both court and visitors may perform in person name searches. No search fee. Civil cases indexed by defendant. Civil records on computer since 1995; prior records in books. Mail turnaround Time 1 week. WebCivil Local at http://iapps.courts.state.ny.us/webcivil/ecourtsMain contains information on both active and disposed Civil Court cases. Search by index number, party name, attorney/firm name or judge. No fee.
Criminal Name Search: Access: Mail, in person, online. Both court and visitors may perform in person name searches. Computerized records go back to 1992; archives back to 19th Century. All criminal record name search requests are directed to the OCA for statewide record search, $65.00 search fee. See www.nycourts.gov/apps/chrs.

Surrogate's Court 48 Court St, Courthouse, Canton, NY 13617; 315-379-2217; fax: 315-379-2372; 9AM-5PM Sept-June; 8AM-4PM July-Aug (EST). *Probate.*

General Information: A county search of the probate court index by mail for 25-year search is $30.00 fee. A full county probate search of all years is $90.00. Also has administration, small estates and guardianship records. **St. Lawrence Town/Village Courts - Brasher Town Court** 11 Factory St, PO Box 358, Brasher Falls, NY 13613; 315-389-4223 x5 10AM-2PM 6PM-8PM T. **Canton Town Court** Municipal Bldg, 60 Main St, Canton, NY 13617; 315-379-9844 9AM-4PM. **Canton Village Court** Municipal Bldg, 60 Main St, Canton, NY 13617; 315-379-9844 9AM-4PM. **Clare Town Court** 3441 County Rd 27, Russell, NY 13684; 315-386-3084 8AM-N. **Clifton Town Court** Community Center, PO Box 679, Cranberry Lake, NY 12927-0679; 315-848-5522 7PM-? 1st & 3rd T. **Colton Town Court** PO Box 475, 9 Sugar Bush Ln, South Colton, NY 13687; 315-262-2380 2nd & 4th T 7PM. **De Peyster Town Court** PO Box 41, Town Hall, County Route 10, De Peyster, NY 13633; 315-344-7259 **DeKalb Town Court** DeKalb Town Complex, DeKalb, NY 13630; 315-347-2119 -clerk (after 5:30PM); 347-2071 -court 7:30PM-? T. **Depeyster Town Court** 303 Plimpton Rd, Heuvelton, NY 13654; 315-344-7259 varies. **Edwards Town Court** 161 Main St, PO Box 118, Edwards, NY 13635; 315-562-8113 6PM T. **Fine Town Court** 4078 S Hwy 3, Star Lake, NY 13690; 315-848-3121 6:30PM-? T 2nd & 4th T. **Fowler Town Court** 87 Little York Rd., Gouverneur, NY 13642; 315-287-9996 6PM-? W. **Gouverneur Town Court** 33 Clinton St, Gouverneur, NY 13642; 315-287-4623 9AM-N, 1-4PM. **Hammond Town Court** PO Box 219, 17 N Main St, Hammond, NY 13646; 315-324-5321 9AM-N M,T,W, 9AM-N 1PM-4PM F. **Hopkinton Town Court** 7 Church St, Hopkinton, NY 12965; 315-328-4211 9AM-3:30PM M,W,F; 7:30-9PM Wed Court. **Lawrence Town Court** 11403 US Hwy 11, North Lawrence, NY 12967; 315-389-4487 8AM-12:30PM 1PM-4PM M,T,W. **Lisbon Town Court** PO Box 8, 6963 CR 10, Lisbon, NY 13658; 315-393-0489 9AM-2:30PM M-TH (court 7PM-? T). **Louisville Town Court** 14810 State Hwy 37, Massena, NY 13662; 315-764-1424 1PM-6PM W; Court- 5:30PM-? W. **Macomb Town Court** 6663 State Hwy 58, Hammond, NY 13646; 315-578-2212 x3 7:30AM-2PM M,W,F. **Madrid Town Court** 3529 County Rt. 14, Madrid, NY 13660; 315-528-3399 6-8PM 2nd & 4th T for Court; records by app't only.. **Massena Town Court and Village Court** Town Hall, 60 Main St, Massena, NY 13662; 315-769-5431 8:30-12:00PM,1-4PM. **Morristown Town Court** Town Hall- 604 Main St, PO Box 240, Morristown, NY 13664; 315-375-4148 11-4PM. **Norfolk Town Court** 5 W Main St, Box 481, Norfolk, NY 13667; 315-384-4721 M-TH 9AM-N. **Oswegatchie Town Court** 51 State St, Heuvelton, NY 13654; 315-344-7284 8AM-4PM. **Parishville Town Court** Catherine St-Box 155, Parishville, NY 13672; 315-268-1722 x5 6-9PM 1st and 3rd T. **Piercefield Town Court** PO Box 220, 48 Waller St, Piercefield, NY 12973; 518-359-2237 1st & last TH 5PM. **Pierrepont Town Court** 864 State Hwy 68, Canton, NY 13617; 315-379-0415 9AM-4PM M-TH, 9AM-1PM F. **Pitcairn Town Court** 10 Edwards Rd., Harrisville, NY 13648; 315-543-2111 x12 9AM-3PM M; 9AM-4PM W. **Potsdam Town Court** 35 Market St, Potsdam, NY 13676; 315-265-4318 9-4PM. **Potsdam Village Court** PO Box 5168, Park St Civic Center, Potsdam, NY 13676; 315-265-5890 8AM-4PM; (court- 8PM-9:30PM W). **Rossie Town Court** Town Court, 908 County Rte 3, Redwood, NY 13679; 315-324-5166 9AM 1st & 3rd Wed. **Russell Town Court** Box 628, 4 Pestle St, Russell, NY 13684; 315-347-4824 6:00-7:30PM 1st & 3rd M for court. **Stockholm Justice Court** 607 State Hwy 11C, Municipal Bldg, PO Box 206, Winthrop, NY 13697; 315-389-5171 X3 9AM-N 1PM-4PM M-TH. **Waddington Town Court** Box 338, Maple St, Waddington, NY 13694; 315-388-5629 8AM-1PM W,TH; court 5:30 on 1st & 3rd W.

Steuben County

Supreme & County Court 3 E Pulteney Sq - County Clerk, Bath, NY 14810; 607-776-9631 x2563; fax: 607-664-2157; 8:30AM-5PM (EST). *Felony, Civil.*

General Information: This court does not hold closed case records. See separate County Clerk entry for Supreme civil records. Access to current/pending Supreme Court civil at http://iapps.courts.state.ny.us/webcivil/FCASMain. No sealed, expunged, adoption, sex offense, juvenile or mental health records released. Will fax documents $3.00 each plus $1.00 per page. Court makes copy: $.65 per page. $1.30 minimum. Self serve copy: same. Certification fee: $5.00. Payee: Steuben County Clerk. Personal checks accepted, credit cards are not. Prepayment required. Mail requests: SASE required.

Civil Name Search: Access: Fax, mail, in person, online. Both court and visitors may perform in person name searches. Search fee: $10.00 per name. Civil cases indexed by defendant. Civil records on computer from 1965, in book from 1931, prior archived. Note: Visitors are not allowed to search divorce files themselves. Mail turnaround Time 1 day. If searched in Archives will take longer. Public use terminal has civil records back to 1960. Current or pending only Supreme Court civil case look-up is at http://iapps.courts.state.ny.us/webcivil/FCASMain.

Criminal Name Search: Access: Fax, mail, in person, online. Only the court performs in person name searches; visitors may not. Search fee: $10.00 per name. Required to search: name, years to search, DOB. Criminal records computerized from 1965, in books from 1931, prior archived. Mail turnaround Time 1 day. If searched in Archives will take longer. Online access is via the state OCA statewide system. Fee is $65.00 per search. See www.nycourts.gov/apps/chrs/.

Corning City Court 12 Civic Center Plaza, Corning, NY 14830-2884; 607-936-4111; fax: 607-936-0519; 8AM-4PM (EST). *Misdemeanor, Civil Actions under $15,000, Eviction, Small Claims.* www.nycourts.gov/courts/7jd/corning/

General Information: No sealed or youthful offender records released. Will fax documents to local or toll free line. Court makes copy: $.65 per page; $1.30 minimum. Certification fee: $5.00. Payee: Corning City Court. No personal checks accepted. Visa/MC/Discover accepted. Prepayment required. Mail requests: SASE required for civil.

Civil Name Search: Access: Mail, in person, online. Only the court performs in person name searches; visitors may not. Search fee: Fees subject to change; call for details. Civil cases indexed by defendant. Civil records on computer from 1986, prior in books. Note: Request must be in writing. WebCivil Local at http://iapps.courts.state.ny.us/webcivil/ecourtsMain contains information on both active and disposed Civil Court cases. Search by index number, party name, attorney/firm name or judge. No fee.

Criminal Name Search: Access: Online. Criminal records computerized from 1986, prior in books. Note: The court refuses to permit access to court records unless specific case file given. All criminal record name search requests are directed to the OCA for statewide record search, $65.00 search fee. See www.nycourts.gov/apps/chrs.

Hornell City Court 82 Main St, Hornell, NY 14843-0627; 607-324-7531; fax: 607-324-6325; 8AM-4PM (EST). *Misdemeanor, Civil Actions under $15,000, Eviction, Small Claims.* www.nycourts.gov/courts/7jd/hornell/index.shtml

General Information: No sealed or sexual offense records released. Will fax documents to local or toll free line. Court makes copy: $.65 per page, minimum $1.30, maximum $40.00. Certification fee: $6.00. Payee: Hornell City Court. Cashiers checks and money orders accepted. Visa/MC accepted. Prepayment required.

Civil Name Search: Access: Fax, mail, in person, online. Only the court performs in person name searches; visitors may not. No search fee. Civil records on computer from 1985, prior in books, folders and index cards go back 25 years. Mail turnaround Time 5 days WebCivil Local at http://iapps.courts.state.ny.us/webcivil/ecourtsMain contains information on both active and disposed Civil Court cases. Search by index number, party name, attorney/firm name or judge. No fee.

Criminal Name Search: Access: Online. Criminal records computerized from 1985, records go back 25 years. Note: The court will not permit access to court records. All criminal record name search requests are directed to the OCA for statewide record search, $65.00 search fee. See www.nycourts.gov/apps/chrs.

Surrogate's Court 3 E Pulteney Sq, Bath, NY 14810-1598; 607-664-2287; fax: 607-776-4987; 9AM-5PM (EST). *Estate, guardianship.*

General Information: A county search of the probate court index by mail for 25-year search is $30.00 fee. A full county probate search of all years is $90.00. Records also at this court are administration, small estate and guardianship 17 and 17A.

Steuben Town/Village Courts - Addison Town Court 21 Main St, Addison, NY 14801; 607-359-3615 M-TH 9AM-2PM. **Avoca Town Court** PO Box 463, 3 Chase St, Avoca, NY 14809; 607-566-2093 7AM-3PM M-TH. **Bath Town Court and Village Court** 110 Liberty St, PO Box 327, Bath, NY 14810; 607-776-3192 9AM-4PM. **Bradford Town Court** 7620 County Rte 20, Bradford, NY 14815; 607-583-4270, 607-776-6776 5-8PM M. **Cameron Town Court** PO Box 1932, 4091 Bath St, Cameron, NY 14819; 607-695-9022 Court- 6PM Mon. **Campbell Town Court** Town Hall, 8529 Main St, Campbell, NY 14821; 607-527-8244 #1 x503 8AM-4PM. **Canisteo Town Court** Town Court, 6 S Main St, Canisteo, NY 14823; 607-698-2129 7PM-? M court. **Caton Town Court** 11161 Hendy Hollow Rd, Corning, NY 14830; 607-524-6303 x3 M 6PM. **Cohocton Town Court** PO Box 221 (Atlanta, NY 14808), 19 S Main St, Atlanta, NY 14808; 585-534-5100 9:30AM-12:30PM M,W. **Corning Town Court** 20 S Maple St, Corning, NY 14830; 607-936-9062 10AM-4:30PM M; 9:30AM-4:30PM T-F. **Dansville Town Court** 1487 Day Rd., Arkport, NY 14807; 607-295-9917 7PM-? T (Clerk-W morning). **Erwin Justice Court** Town Hall, 117 W Water St, Painted Post, NY 14870; 607-936-3122 10AM M/ 11AM W till ?. **Fremont Town Court** 8217 Cream Hill Rd-RD #2, Arkport, NY 14807; 607-324-0009 5PM-? M. **Greenwood Town Court** PO Box 764, 2698 State Rte 248, Greenwood, NY 14839; 607-225-4654 x3 7PM-? W. **Hartsville Town Court** 5150 Purdy Creek Rd, Hornell, NY 14843; 607-698-4940 **Hornby Town Court** 4830 Hornby Rd, Beaver Dams, NY 14812; 607-962-0683 8AM-N Wed.

Hornellsville Town Court PO Box 1, 4 Park Ave, Arkport, NY 14807; 607-295-8207 9AM-1PM. **Howard Town Court** 3725 Mill Rd, Avoca, NY 14809; 607-566-2058 9:30AM-3:30PM T; 9:30AM-12:30PM F. **Jasper Town Court** Drawer 10, 3807 Preacher St, Jasper, NY 14855; 607-792-3576 1st & 3rd T. **Lindley Town Court** PO Box 62, 637 US 15, Lindley, NY 14858; 607-523-8816 6-9PM T. **Prattsburgh Town Court** PO Box 372, 19 N Main St, Prattsburgh, NY 14873; 607-522-3731 9AM 2nd W; 7PM 4th W. **Pulteney Town Court** PO Box 214, 9226 County Rte 74, Pulteney, NY 14874; 607-868-3931 8:30AM-11PM W. **Rathbone Town Court** 8088 County Rte 21, Addison, NY 14801; 607-359-2258 6PM-? 2nd & 4th M. **Savona Village Court** PO Box 763, 15 McCoy St, Savona, NY 14879; 607-583-7618 10-6PM (office hrs). **Thurston Town Court** PO Box 467, 7475 Rte 333 (Thurston, NY), Campbell, NY 14821; 607-527-6157 6PM 1st & 3rd T court. **Troupsburg Town Court** PO Box 83, 873 Main St, Troupsburg, NY 14885; 607-525-6403 court 9AM-? Weds. **Tuscarora Town Court** 1094 Gill Rd, Addison, NY 14801; 607-359-2066 6-8PM T. **Urbana Town Court** 8014 Pleasant Valley Rd, PO Box 186, Hammondsport, NY 14840; 607-569 2709 5PM & 6:15PM M. **Wayland Town Court and Village Court** PO Box 515, 17 N Main St, Wayland, NY 14572; 585-728-3504 9AM-5:30PM W; 1st&3rd W at 5:30PM. **Wayne Town Court** PO Box 182, Sisbee Road, Wayne, NY 14893; 607-292-6003 7PM TH. **West Union Town Court** 1328 State Rte 248, Rexville, NY 14877-9780; 607-225-4321, 225-4429 1st & 3rd W-7PM; 2nd W- 4:30PM. **Wheeler Town Court** 6439 Gardner Rd, Bath, NY 14810; 607-776-7208 1PM-4:30PM T,TH. **Woodhull Town Court** PO Box 56, 1585 Academy St, Woodhull, NY 14898; 607-458-5252 7PM M court hrs.

Suffolk County

Supreme & County Court - Main 310 Centre Dr, Riverhead County Ctr, Attn: Court Actions, Riverhead, NY 11901; 631-852-2000; criminal phone: 631-852-2000 x854; civil phone: 631-852-2000 x857; fax: 631-852-2004; 9AM-5PM; file rm- to 4:30PM only (EST). *Felony, Civil over $15,000.*

www.suffolkcountyny.gov/departments/countyclerk.aspx   (AND)
www.courts.state.ny.us/courts/10jd/suffolk/supreme.shtml

General Information: Records are managed by the County Clerk; information for County Clerk office is given here. Faxes accepted from gov't agencies only. Supreme Ct clerk info-631-852-2334; County Ct Clerk info-631-852-1462. No sealed or divorce records released. Clerk may fax back documents time permitting and if you're really sweet, no fee. Court makes copy: $1.25 per page. Self serve copy: $.25 per page. Certification fee: $5.00 per cert plus copy fee. Payee: County Clerk. Personal checks accepted with proper ID on check. No credit cards accepted. Prepayment required. Mail requests: SASE required.

Civil Name Search: Access: Mail, in person, online. Both court and visitors may perform in person name searches. Search fee: $5.00 per name per 2 years searched. $9.00 fee for Certificate of Search. Civil records on computer back to 4/84; prior in books. Mail turnaround Time 7-14 days. Civil PAT goes back to 1984. Access to current/pending Supreme Court civil cases is at http://iapps.courts.state.ny.us/webcivil/FCASMain.

Criminal Name Search: Access: Mail, in person, online. Both court and visitors may perform in person name searches. Search fee: Felony- $9.00 per name (computer back to 1980s, paper back to '60s). $5.00 fee for Certificate of Disposition. $9.00 fee for Certificate of Search. Required to search: name, years to search, DOB. Criminal records computerized from 1984. Note: Clerk may restrict searcher's number of records pulled to 10 per day. Clerk recommends $65.00 statewide record search through OCA for 1985 to present. Mail turnaround Time 7-14 days. Criminal PAT goes back to 1984; records may not be on the terminal at this time. Online access is via the state OCA statewide system. Fee is $65.00 per search. See www.nycourts.gov/apps/chrs/. Also, subscribe or login as guest to search eCourts WebCrims future appearances system at http://iapps.courts.state.ny.us/webcrim_attorney/Login. Online results show name only.

County Court & 1st District Court 400 Carleton Ave, Central Islip, NY 11722; 631-853-7500; 8:30AM-4:30PM (EST). *Misdemeanor.*

http://courts.state.ny.us/courts/10jd/suffolk/dist/

General Information: No sealed or youthful offender records released. Will not fax documents. Court makes copy: $.65 per page. Certification fee: $5.00 per doc. Payee: Clerk of the District Court. Personal checks accepted with proper ID. Credit cards accepted. Prepayment required.

Criminal Name Search: Access: Mail (not always available), in person. Only the court performs in person name searches; visitors may not. Search fee: $6.00 for Certificate of Disposition only. Required to search: Name, DOB, approx date of arrest and charge. Criminal records go back to 1971; on computer back to 3/2000. Note: Court will pull record if docket number and proper identifiers are provided. Name search requesters are directed to send requests to OCA for $65.00 statewide search. Also, a Suffolk County only search is through the local Police Dept- 631-852-6015. Online access to active criminal court dates only listed by defendant or docket are free at http://iapps.courts.state.ny.us/webcrim_attorney/Login.

2nd District Court 30 E Hoffman Ave, Lindenhurst, NY 11757; 631-854-1121; fax: 631-854-1127; 9AM-1PM, 2-5PM; window closes at 12:30 and 4:30PM (EST). *Civil Actions under $15,000, Eviction, Small Claims, Ordinances, Traffic.*

http://courts.state.ny.us/courts/10jd/suffolk/

General Information: Also handles Babylon Town ordinance cases. Use your paid receipt for a civil search from any Suffolk District Court to search at any other Suffolk District courts for free. No sealed records released. Will not fax documents. Court makes copy: $.65 per page, $1.30 minimum. Certification fee: $6.00 per doc plus copy fee. Payee: Clerk of Court. Only cashiers checks and money orders accepted. Major credit cards accepted in person only. Prepayment required. Mail requests: SASE required.

Civil Name Search: Access: Mail, in person. Only the court performs in person name searches; visitors may not. Search fee: $16.00 per name. Civil cases indexed by plaintiff. Civil records on computer from 1996, prior in books, on cards. Mail turnaround Time 2 weeks.

3rd District Court 1850 New York Ave, Huntington Station, NY 11746; 631-854-4545; fax: 631-854-4549; 9AM-12:30PM, 2-4:30PM (EST). *Civil Actions under $15,000, Eviction, Small Claims, Traffic.*

http://courts.state.ny.us/courts/10jd/suffolk/

General Information: Use your paid receipt for a civil search from any Suffolk District Court to search at any other Suffolk District courts for free. No sealed records released. Will not fax documents. Court makes copy: $.65 per page. $1.30 minimum. Certification fee: $6.00 per doc plus $.65 copy fee. Payee: Clerk of the Court. Business and Personal checks, Visa/MC accepted. Prepayment required.

Civil Name Search: Access: Mail, in person. Only the court performs in person name searches; visitors may not. No search fee. Civil cases indexed by defendant. Civil records on computer from 1988, prior in books, on microfilm. Note: This court suggests a wider civil record search be performed at the County Clerk office. This court's civil records are indexed by key letters "HU" Currently adding public access terminals.

4th District Court N County Complex Bldg 158, Veteran's Memorial Highway, Hauppauge, NY 11788-0099; 631-853-5400; fax: 631-853-5951; 9AM-1PM; 2PM-5PM (EST). *Civil Actions under $15,000, Eviction, Small Claims.*

http://courts.state.ny.us/courts/10jd/suffolk/

General Information: No sealed records released. Will not fax documents. Court makes copy: $.65 per page. Certification fee: $6.00 per cert; exemplification- $16.00. Payee: Clerk of Court. Personal checks, Visa/MC accepted. Prepayment required. Mail requests: SASE required.

Civil Name Search: Access: Mail, in person. Only the court performs in person name searches; visitors may not. No search fee. Civil records on computer from 1987, prior in books.

6th District Court 150 W Main St, Patchogue, NY 11772; 631-854-1440; auto- 631-853-7500; fax: 631-854-1444; 9AM-1PM, 2PM-5PM (EST). *Civil Actions under $15,001, Eviction, Small Claims.*

http://courts.state.ny.us/courts/10jd/suffolk/

General Information: Use your paid receipt for a civil search from any Suffolk District Court to search at any other Suffolk District courts for free. Note some misdemeanor records here, but are only Brookhaven Town Ordinance violations. No sealed or youthful offender records released. Will not fax out documents. Court makes copy: $.65 per page. Certification fee: $6.00 per doc; exemplification- $15.00. Payee: Clerk of Court. Personal checks accepted. Visa/MC accepted in person. Prepayment required. Mail requests: SASE required.

Civil Name Search: Access: Mail, in person. Only the court performs in person name searches; visitors may not. No search fee. Civil records on computer from 1989, prior on microfilm. Note: Public terminals to be added some time in the future. Web access is in development.

Suffolk District Courts 1 & 5 - Civil 3105-1 Veterans Memorial Hwy, Ronkonkoma, NY 11779-7614; 631-854-9676 (1st); 631-854-9673 (5th); fax: 631-854-9681; 9AM-1PM, 2-5PM (EST). *Civil Actions under $15,000, Eviction, Small Claims.*

http://courts.state.ny.us/courts/10jd/suffolk/

General Information: Use your paid receipt for a civil search from any Suffolk District Court to search at any other Suffolk District courts for free. No sealed or youthful offender records released. Will fax documents for no fee. Court makes copy: $1.30 first page, $.65 each add'l. Certification fee: $6.00 per page includes copy fee. Exemplification fee- $15.00. Payee: Clerk of the Court. Cash, checks, or money orders accepted. Visa/MC accepted. Prepayment required. Mail requests: SASE required.

Civil Name Search: Access: Mail, in person. Only the court performs in person name searches; visitors may not. No search fee. Civil cases indexed by defendant. Civil records on computer back to 1989, prior in books back to 1969. Mail turnaround Time 2 weeks.

Surrogate's Court 320 Centre Dr, Riverhead, NY 11901; 631-852-1746; fax: 631-852-1414; 9AM-5PM (EST). *Probate.*
www.courts.state.ny.us/courts/10jd/suffolk/surrogates.shtml
General Information: A county search of the probate court index by mail for 25-year search is $30.00 fee. A full county probate search of all years is $90.00. Records Dept phone # 631-852-1724.

Suffolk Town/Village Courts - Asharoken Village Court 1 Asharoken Ave, Asharoken, NY 11768; 631-261-8677 7PM W court; clerk hours varies. **Belle Terre Village Court** 55 Cliff Rd, Town Hall, Belle Terre, NY 11777; 631-473-5105 Morning-varies. **Bellport Village Court** 29 Bellport Ln, Bellport, NY 11713; 631-286-0327 x22 irregular. **East Hampton Town Court** 159 Pantigo Rd, Justice Court Bldg, East Hampton, NY 11937; 631-324-4134 9AM-4PM. **Greenport Village Court** 236 Third St, Greenport, NY 11944; 631-477-0248 **Head of the Harbor Village Court** 500 N Country Rd, St James, NY 11780; 631-584-2034 9:30AM-2:30PM M,T,TH. **Islandia Village Court** 1100 Old Nichols Rd, Islandia, NY 11749; 631-348-0470 8:30AM-4:30PM. **Lake Grove Justice Court** PO Box 1231, 980 Hawkins Ave, Lake Grove, NY 11755-0531; 631-585-2008 10AM-2PM T,TH. **Nissequogue Village Court** PO Box 184, 631 Moritches Rd, Nissiquagua, St James, NY 11780; 631-862-8576 11AM-3PM T-W; court- 2nd W 7PM; and by app't. **Ocean Beach Village Court** PO Box 433, Ocean Beach, NY 11770; 631-583-0104 10 AM-?. **Old Field Village Court** PO Box 2724, Setauket, NY 11733; 631-941-9416 9AM-3PM M,T,TH. **Patchogue Village Court** 14 Baker St, PO Box 719, Patchogue, NY 11772; 631-475-2753 9-4:30PM. **Poquott Village Court** PO Box 813, 45 Birchwood Ave, East Setauket, NY 11733; 631-476-4043 9AM-5PM. **Port Jefferson Village Court** 121 W Broadway, Port Jefferson, NY 11777; 631-473-8382 9-5PM. **Quogue Village Justice Court** PO Box 926, 123 Jessup Ave, Quogue, NY 11959; 631-653-9400 9AM-12 (M,F); 9AM-4PM W. **Riverhead Justice Court** 210 Howell Ave, Riverhead, NY 11901; 631-727-3200 x229 8:30-4:30PM. **Shelter Island Town Court** PO Box 1632, 46 N Ferry Rd, Justice Hall-Rte 114, Shelter Island, NY 11964; 631-749-8989 8AM-4:30PM M-F. **Shoreham Village Court** PO Box 389, Shoreham, NY 11786; 631-821-0680 9:30AM-12:30PM T,W,F. **Southampton Town Court** 32 Jackson Ave, Hampton Bays, Southampton, NY 11968; 631-702-2990 8:30AM-4PM M-F. **Southampton Village Court** 151 Windmill Lane, Southampton, NY 11968; 631-204-2140 9AM-4PM. **Southold Town Justice Court** 53095 Main Rd, Route 25, PO Box 1179, Southold, NY 11971; 631-765-1852 8AM-4PM. **West Hampton Dunes Village Court** PO Box 306, West Hampton Beach, NY 11978; 631-288-6571 9AM-5PM. **Westhampton Beach Village Court** 165 Mill Rd, Westhampton Beach, NY 11978; 631-288-3980 9AM-3PM M-F.

Sullivan County

County Clerk 100 North St, Sullivan Gov't Ctr, Monticello, NY 12701; 845-807-0411; 9AM-4:45PM (EST). *Felony, Civil.*
General Information: Countywide search requests made to the county clerk are processed in the manner described below. Supreme Court phone- 845-794-4066. County Ct phone- 845-794-1248. No sealed, expunged, adoption, sex offense, juvenile or mental health records released. Will not fax documents. Court makes copy: $1.00 per page. Self serve copy: $.25 per page. Certification fee: $5.20, if over 6 pages add $.85 per page. Payee: Sullivan County Clerk. Personal checks accepted, credit cards are not. Prepayment required. Mail requests: SASE not required.
Civil Name Search: Access: Mail, in person, online. Both court and visitors may perform in person name searches. Search fee: $5.00 per name on computer only. Civil cases indexed by plaintiff. Civil records on computer from 1990, prior in books from 1800s. Note: This office may search off the computer. Mail turnaround Time 1-2 weeks. Public use terminal has civil records back to 1990. The court does not offer its online access but participates with a state site. Lookup current or pending Supreme Court civil cases at http://iapps.courts.state.ny.us/webcivil/FCASMain.
Criminal Name Search: Access: In person only. Only the court performs in person name searches; visitors may not. Search fee: A Certificate of Disposition, by mail or in person, is $6.00. Required to search: name, years to search, DOB. The county clerk only holds criminal records that are older than 10 years. Note: The county clerk holds records that are older than 10 years. Criminal name search requests are directed to the OCA for a $65.00 statewide record check.

Supreme Court County Courthouse, 414 Broadway, Monticello, NY 12701; 845-794-4066; probate phone: 845-794-3000 x3450; fax: 845-791-6170; 9AM-12:30PM, 1:30PM-4:30PM (EST). *Felony, Civil, Misdemeanor.*
General Information: No sealed, expunged, adoption, sex offense, juvenile or mental health records released. Court makes copy: $.65 per page, $1.30 minimum; maximum is $40.00 per file. Certification fee: $5.00, Criminal Certificate of Disposition- $6.00. Payee: County Clerk for civil; to

Court Clerk for criminal. Personal checks accepted. Credit cards accepted. Prepayment required. Mail requests: SASE not required.
Civil Name Search: Access: Mail, in person. Only the court performs in person name searches; visitors may not. Civil cases indexed by plaintiff. Civil records on computer from 1990, prior in books from 1800s. Note: Perform civil searches at the County Clerk's office. Mail turnaround Time 2-3 weeks. Public use terminal has civil records back to 4/1/1990. Current or pending only Supreme Court civil case look-up is at http://iapps.courts.state.ny.us/webcivil/FCASMain.
Criminal Name Search: Access: Mail (limited), in person, online. Only the court performs in person name searches; visitors may not. Search fee: $16.00. Required to search: name, years to search, DOB, approx date of arrest. Criminal records go back to 1967; on computer back to 4/1990. Note: For mail request, County Court directs search requests to OCA for $65.00 statewide check. In person search: 1st find case number by search at County Clerk office (see separate entry), then ask County Court clerk office (address above) for case file. Mail turnaround Time is 2-3 weeks. Online access is via the state OCA statewide system. Fee is $65.00 per search. See www.nycourts.gov/apps/chrs/.

Surrogate's Court County Government Ctr, 100 North St, Monticello, NY 12701; 845-807-0690; fax: 845-794-0310; 9AM-5PM may be closed for lunch N-1PM (EST). *Probate.*
www.nycourts.gov/courts/3jd/surrogates/sullivan/index.shtml
General Information: A county search of the probate court index by mail for 25-year search is $30.00 fee. A full county probate search of all years is $90.00.

Sullivan Town/Village Courts - Bethel Town Court PO Box 691, 3586 State Route 55, Kauneonga Lake, NY 12749; 845-583-7420 9:30AM-4:30PM M,T,TH,F; 3PM-9PM W. **Bloomingburg Justice Court** PO Box 341, Village Hall, 13 North Road, Bloomingburg, NY 12721; 845-733-1400 By Appointment Only. **Callicoon Town Court** PO Box 687, 19 Legion St, Jeffersonville, NY 12748; 845-482-5390 x301 M,W,F 11:30-4PM. **Delaware Justice Court** PO Box 129, 104 Main St, Hortonville, NY 12745; 845-887-5849 x8 1PM-4PM M, T, TH. **Fallsburg Town Court** PO Box 2019, 19 Railroad Plaza, South Fallsburg, NY 12779; 845-434-4574 8:30AM-4PM T-F. **Forestburgh Town Court** King Rd, PO Box 114, Forestburgh, NY 12777-0114; 845-794-0611 x 12 5:30 PM Monday. **Fremont Town Court** Town Court, County Rd 95, Fremont Center, NY 12736; 845-887-6605 (Town Hall) **Highland Town Court** 4 Schoolhouse Rd, Barryville, NY 12719; 845-557-8132 9AM-11AM T,TH; 5PM-? M,W. **Liberty Town Court** 120 N Main St, Liberty, NY 12754; 845-292-6980 M 8:30-4:30. **Lumberland Town Court** PO Box 226, 1052 Proctor Rd, Glen Spey, NY 12737; 845-858-8548 x3 7PM-? T; 9AM-2PM W. **Mamakating Town Court** 2948 Rte 209, Wurtsboro, NY 12790; 845-888-3038 9AM-4PM M-F. **Monticello Village Court** 18 Pleasant St, Monticello, NY 12701; 845-794-1222 8AM-4PM. **Neversink Town Court** 273 Main St, PO Box 307, Grahamsville, NY 12740; 845-985-7685 x311 7:30PM M&T, 10AM-1PM F. **Rockland Town Court** 1939 Old Rte 17, PO Box 28, Roscoe, NY 12776; 607-498-4320 9AM-2:45PM MTWF ; 2-8PM TH. **Thompson Town Court** 4052 Route 42, Monticello, NY 12701; 845-794-7130 8:30AM-4:30PM. **Tusten Town Court** Box 195, Town Court, 210 Bridge St, Narrowsburg, NY 12764; 845-252-3310 12:30PM-2:30PM T; 1PM-5PM TH; N-2PM F.

Tioga County

County Clerk PO Box 307, 16 Court St, Owego, NY 13827; 607-687-8660; fax: 607-687-8686; 9AM-5PM (EST). *Civil.*
General Information: Countywide civil record search requests made to the county clerk are processed in the manner described below. County clerk has only a paper index list of felony proceedings. Felony records are managed by the Court Clerk, see separate listing. No sealed, expunged, adoption, sex offense, juvenile or mental health records released. Will not fax documents. Court makes copy: $.65 per page. Self serve copy: $.25 per page. Certification fee: $5.00 per doc includes copy fee. Payee: Tioga County Clerk. Personal checks accepted, credit cards are not. Prepayment required. Mail requests: SASE required for mail return of any copies.
Civil Name Search: Access: In person. Visitors must perform in person searches themselves. Civil cases indexed by defendant. Civil records in books. Visitor can search in County Clerk's Office. Public use terminal has civil records back to 9/2003.

Supreme & County Court PO Box 307, 16 Court St, Owego, NY 13827; 607-687-0544; fax: 607-687-5680; 9AM-5PM (EST). *Felony, Civil.*
General Information: This court does not hold closed case records. See separate County Clerk entry for Supreme civil records. Access to current/pending Supreme Court civil at http://iapps.courts.state.ny.us/webcivil/FCASMain. Criminal online via state OCA statewide system.

Surrogate's Court PO Box 10, 20 Court St, Owego, NY 13827; 607-687-1303; fax: 646-963-6398; 9AM-5PM (EST). *Probate.*

www.nycourts.gov/courts/6jd/

General Information: Court is located in the County Court Annex Bldg. A county search of the probate court index by mail for 25-year search is $30.00 fee. A full county probate search of all years is $90.00.

Tioga Town/Village Courts - Barton Town Court 304 Route 17C, Waverly, NY 14892; 607-565-8609 x1 5:30-7:30PM T. **Berkshire Town Court** 18 Railroad Ave, Berkshire, NY 13736; 607-657-8286/8601 7PM-? 1st M; 5:30PM-? 3rd M. **Candor Town Court and Village Court** 33 Humiston St, PO Box 6, Candor, NY 13743-0006; 607-659-3175 9AM-4:30PM M. **Newark Valley Town Court** 109 Whig St, Newark Valley, NY 13811; 607-642-5278 Tues. **Nichols Town Court** Town Hall, PO Box 219, Nichols, NY 13812; 607-642-5278 6PM T, 7PM TH. **Owego Town Court** 2354 State Route 434, Apalachin, NY 13732; 607-687-0123 x4 8AM-4:30PM. **Owego Village Court** 90 Temple St, Owego, NY 13827; 607-687-2236 9AM-4:30PM M-F. **Richford Town Court** PO Box 170, 7 Bowery Ln, Town Hall, Richford, NY 13835-0170; 607-657-8090 5:30PM-8PM 1st,3rd & 4th M. **Spencer Town Court** 81 E Tioga St, Spencer, NY 14883; 607-589-7342 **Spencer Village Court** PO Box 346, 84 N Main St, Spencer, NY 14883; 607-589-4310 7PM 2nd & 4th W. **Tioga Town Court** PO Box 32, 54 5th Ave, Tioga Center, NY 13845; 607-687-9577 1:30-5PM T,W,TH. **Waverly Village Court** 32 Ithaca St, Waverly, NY 14892; 607-565-4771 8:30AM-5PM M-F (court-4PM-? T,TH).

Tompkins County

Supreme & County Court Tomkins County Clerk, 320 N Tioga St, Ithaca, NY 14850; 607-274-5431 (County Clerk); 607-272-0466 (Court Clerks); criminal phone: 607-274-5453; civil phone: 607-274-5453; fax: 607-274-5445; 9AM-5PM (Court Clerks have Summer hours-8:30AM-4:30PM) (EST). *Felony, Civil.*

www.tompkins-co.org/cclerk/

General Information: Direct all search requests to the County Clerk office; information given here is for that County Clerk office. No sealed, expunged, adoption, sex offense, juvenile or mental health records released. Will fax documents to local or toll free line. Court makes copy: $.65 per page, $1.30 minimum. Self serve copy: same. Certification fee: $5.00 per document plus copy fee. Payee: County Clerk. Personal checks accepted, credit cards are not. Prepayment required. Mail requests: SASE required.

Civil Name Search: Access: Fax, mail, in person, online. Both court and visitors may perform in person name searches. Search fee: $5.00 per name if court does search. Fee is per 2 years searched. Civil records in books. Note: Before faxing, you must first be approved with a credit account. Mail turnaround Time 1-2 days. Public use terminal has civil records back to 7/7/1999. Historical records are not online, but access to current/pending Supreme Court civil cases is at http://iapps.courts.state.ny.us/webcivil/FCASMain.

Criminal Name Search: Access: Fax, mail, in person, online. Only the court performs in person name searches; visitors may not. Search fee: $5.00 per name if court does search. Fee is per 2 years searched. Required to search: name, years to search, signed release; also helpful: DOB. Felony records in books. Note: Before faxing, you must first be approved with a credit account. Mail turnaround Time 1-2 days. Online access is via the state OCA statewide system. Fee is $65.00 per search. See www.nycourts.gov/apps/chrs/.

Ithaca City Court 118 E Clinton St, Ithaca, NY 14850; 607-273-2263; fax: 607-277-3702; 8AM-4PM (EST). *Misdemeanor, Civil Actions under $15,000, Eviction, Small Claims.*

www.nycourts.gov/ithaca/city/

General Information: Local search is for violation level convictions only. No sealed, youthful offender records released. Will fax documents to local or toll free line. Court makes copy: $.65 per page; $1.30 minimum. Certification fee: $6.00 per cert plus copy fee. Payee: Ithica City Court. Only cashiers checks and money orders accepted by mail; cash in person. Visa/MC accepted. Prepayment required. Mail requests: SASE required.

Civil Name Search: Access: Mail, in person, online. Only the court performs in person name searches; visitors may not. Search fee: $5.00 per each 2 year period. Civil cases indexed by defendant. Civil records on computer since 1996; prior records in books. Mail turnaround Time 7-10 days. WebCivil Local at http://iapps.courts.state.ny.us/webcivil/ecourtsMain contains information on both active and disposed Civil Court cases. Search by index number, party name, attorney/firm name or judge. No fee.

Criminal Name Search: Access: Mail, in person, online. Search fee: $5.00 per each 2 year period. Criminal records computerized from 1990, prior in books. Mail turnaround Time 7-10 days. Name search requests are often directed to the OCA for statewide record search, $65.00 search fee. See www.nycourts.gov/apps/chrs.

Surrogate's Court 320 N Tioga St, Ithaca, NY 14850; 607-277-0622; fax: 212-457-2952; 9AM-5PM (EST). *Probate.*

General Information: A county search of the probate court index by mail for 25-year search is $30.00 fee. A full county probate search of all years is $90.00.

Tompkins Town/Village Courts - Caroline Town Court PO Box 121, 2670 Slaterville Rd, Slaterville Springs, NY 14881; 607-539-7796 Court M 5PM; W 8AM. **Cayuga Heights Village Court** 836 Hanshaw Rd, Ithaca, NY 14850; 607-257-3944 6PM T. **Danby Town Court** 1830 Danby Rd, Ithaca, NY 14850; 607-277-0095 12:00-2:30PM; Court night: 7PM T. **Dryden Town Court** 65 E Main St, Dryden, NY 13053; 607-844-8888 x1 8:30AM-4PM; court-6AM M; 9AM T. **Enfield Town Court** 182 Enfield Main Rd, Ithaca, NY 14850; 607-272-0529 5PM-? M,TH. **Freeville Village Court** PO Box 288, Freeville, NY 13068; 607-844-8470 9AM-10AM M; 4PM-&PM 1st W. **Groton Town Court** 101 Conger Blvd, PO Box 5, Groton, NY 13073; 607-898-5273/3711 8AM-4PM t-TH, 1PM-4PM M; 8AM-12 F. **Ithaca Town Court** 215 N Tioga St, Ithaca, NY 14850; 607-273-0493 8AM-3:30PM M-TH; 8AM-N F. **Lansing Town Court** PO Box 186, 29 Auburn Rd, Lansing, NY 14882; 607-533-4776 M-TH 7:30AM-4PM, 7:30AM-N F. **Newfield Town Court** 166 Main St, Newfield, NY 14867; 607-564-9982 M 9AM-5PM; W 9AM-2PM; Th 9AM-2PM. **Ulysses Town Court** 10 Elm St, Trumansburg, NY 14886; 607-387-5411 10AM-7PM M; 8AM-N, 1-4PM T-TH; 8AM-N F.

Ulster County

County Clerk PO Box 1800, 244 Fair St, Kingston, NY 12401; 845-340-3288 (Clerk); 845-340-3000 (Switchboard); fax: 845-340-3299; 9AM-4:45PM (EST). *Felony, Civil.*

www.co.ulster.ny.us

General Information: Countywide search requests made to the County Clerk are processed in the manner described below. No sealed, expunged, adoption, sex offense, juvenile or mental health records released. Will fax out documents for $2.00 per page. Court makes copy: $1.25 per page, minimum $5.00. Self serve copy: $.65 per page, 2 page minimum. Certification fee: $5.00. Payee: Ulster County Clerk. Personal checks accepted, credit cards are not. Prepayment required. Mail requests: SASE required.

Civil Name Search: Access: Phone, mail, in person, online. Both court and visitors may perform in person name searches. Search fee: $5.00 per name per 2 years searched; county clerk may perform 1 search from 1987 forward for free over phone. Civil records on computer from 1987, in books from 1920s, prior archived. Mail turnaround Time 5 days. Civil PAT goes back to 1987. Access to current Supreme court cases is at http://iapps.courts.state.ny.us/webcivil/ecourtsMain.

Criminal Name Search: Access: Phone, mail, in person. Both court and visitors may perform in person name searches. Search fee: $5.00 per name. Fee is per 2 years searched. Criminal records computerized from 1987, in books from 1920s, prior archived. Mail turnaround Time 5 days. Criminal PAT goes back to same as civil.

Supreme & County Court 285 Wall St, Kingston, NY 12401; 845-340-3377; fax: 845-340-3387; 9AM-5PM (EST). *Felony, Civil.*

www.nycourts.gov/courts/3jd/supreme/ulster/index.shtml

General Information: This court does not hold closed case records. See separate County Clerk entry for Supreme civil records. Access to current/pending Supreme Court civil at http://iapps.courts.state.ny.us/webcivil/FCASMain. Criminal online via state OCA statewide system.

Kingston City Court One Garraghan Dr, Kingston, NY 12401; 845-338-2974; fax: 845-338-1443; 8:30AM-4:30PM; Doors close 3:45 (EST). *Misdemeanor, Civil Actions under $15,000, Eviction, Small Claims.*

General Information: Generally, they will not search beyond 25 years back. No sealed or youthful offender records released. Will not fax documents. Court makes copy: $1.00 per page. Certification fee: $5.00. Payee: City Court. No Personal checks, Visa/MC accepted. Prepayment required. Mail requests: SASE required.

Civil Name Search: Access: Mail, in person, online. Only the court performs in person name searches; visitors may not. Search fee: $5.00 per name per 2 years. Civil cases indexed by plaintiff. Civil records on computer from 1995. Overall records go back to 1983. Note: Request must be in writing. Generally, they will not search beyond 25 years back. Mail turnaround Time 1-2 weeks. WebCivil Local at http://iapps.courts.state.ny.us/webcivil/ecourtsMain contains information on both active and disposed Civil Court cases. Search by index number, party name, attorney/firm name or judge. No fee.

Criminal Name Search: Access: Mail, in person, online. Only the court performs in person name searches; visitors may not. Search fee: $5.00 per name per 2 years. Required to search: Name, years to search, DOB. Criminal records computerized from 1995. Overall records go back to 1983. Note: The court sometimes directs requesters to send requests to OCA for the statewide search. Generally, they will not search beyond 25 years back. Mail turnaround Time 1-2 weeks. Name search requests are often directed to the OCA for statewide record search, $65.00 search fee. See www.nycourts.gov/apps/chrs.

Surrogate's Court PO Box 1800, 240 Fair St, Kingston, NY 12402; 845-340-3348; fax: 845-340-3352; 9AM-5PM (EST). *Probate.*

General Information: A county search of the probate court index by mail for 25-year search is $30.00 fee. A full county probate search of all years is $90.00.

Ulster Town/Village Courts - Crawford Town Court PO Box 109, 121 State Route 302, Pine Bush, NY 12566; 845-744-2435 8:30AM-4PM; (court 6:30PM-? M,T). **Denning Town Court** PO Box 66, 1567 Denning Rd, Claryville, NY 12725; 845-985-2100 9AM-N 1st & 3rd T. **Ellenville Village Court** 2 Elting Ct, Ellenville, NY 12428; 845-647-7080 8AM-3:30PM. **Esopus Town Court** PO Box 700, 284 Broadway, Port Ewen, NY 12466; 845-331-5776 6PM-? M-T. **Gardiner Town Court** PO Box 289, 2340 Route 44-55, Gardiner, NY 12525; 845-256-0017 x106 9:30AM-3:30PM. **Hardenburgh Town Court** , 51 Rider Hallow Rd, Arkville, NY 12406; 845-586-1010 10AM-? 1st M; 6PM-? 3rd Mo. **Hurley Town Court** PO Box 325, 10 Wamsley Pl, Hurley, NY 12443; 845-331-9229 ext 1 9AM-1PM M-F; tll 4:30 TH. **Kingston Town Court** 906 Sawkill Rd, Kingston, NY 12401; 845-336-8853 x12 2PM-? T. **Lloyd Town Court** 12 Church St, #2, Rear of Bldg Entrance, 2nd Fl, Highland, NY 12528; 845-691-7544 8:30AM-4:30PM. **Marbletown Town Court** PO Box 128, 3775 Main St, Town Hall, Stone Ridge, NY 12484; 845-687-4328 x8 8:30AM-4:30PM. **Marlborough Town Court** PO Box 305, Route 9 W, Milton, NY 12547; 845-795-2256 8AM-2:30PM. **New Paltz Town Court** 23 Plattekill Ave., New Paltz, NY 12561; 845-255-0041/0043 8:30AM-3:30PM M-F. **Olive Town Court** PO Box 201, 50 Bostock Rd, Shokan, NY 12481; 845-657-2912 9AM-1PM. **Plattekill Town Court** PO Box 45, 1915 Rte 44-55, Modena, NY 12548; 845-883-5805 10AM-9PM M; 10AM-4PM T. **Rochester Town Court** PO Box 167, 140 Samsonville Rd, Kerhonkson, NY 12446; 845-626-2522 8AM-N M-TH. **Rosendale Town Court** PO Box 423, 520 LeFever Fall Rd, Rosendale, NY 12472; 845-658-3686 9AM-5PM M-TH. **Saugerties Town Court** 4 High St, Saugerties, NY 12477; 845-246-2800 x325 8AM-4PM. **Saugerties Village Court** 43 Partition St, Municipal Bldg, Saugerties, NY 12477; 845-246-3958 6PM-? M court. **Shandaken Town Court** PO Box 6, Town Hall, 7209 Rte 28, Shandaken, NY 12480; 845-688-5005 10AM-5PM T,TH; 1PM-3:30PM 3rd TH. **Shawangunk Town Court** PO Box 247, 14 Central Ave, Wallkill, NY 12589; 845-895-2111 9AM-12:30PM, 1:15-4PM. **Ulster Town Court** 1 Town Hall Dr, Lake Katrine, NY 12449; 845-382-1737 8AM-4PM. **Wawarsing Town Court** PO Box 671, 108 Canal St, Ellenville, NY 12428; 845-647-4770 8AM-4PM M-TH; 7AM-3PM F. **Woodstock Town Court** 76 Tinker St, Woodstock, NY 12498; 845-679-6345 8:30AM-12:30PM.

Warren County

County Clerk 1340 State Route 9, Attn: County Clerk, Lake George, NY 12845; 518-761-6426; fax: 518-761-6551; 9AM-5PM (EST). *Civil, Felony.*

General Information: Countywide civil record search requests made to the county clerk are processed in the manner described below. No adoption, juvenile or mental health records released. Will not fax documents. Court makes copy: $.65 per page, mailed copies $1.30 per page. Self serve copy: same. Certification fee: $5.00 for 1st four pages, $1.25 each add'l page. Payee: Warren County Clerk. Personal checks accepted, credit cards are not. Prepayment required. Mail requests: SASE required for civil.

Civil Name Search: Access: Mail, in person, online. Both court and visitors may perform in person name searches. Search fee: $5.00 per name for each 2 years. Civil cases indexed by plaintiff & defendant. Civil records index on computer from 1917 to present. Mail turnaround Time 1-2 days. Public use terminal has civil records back to 1900s. Get index numbers from PAT, then clerk will pull files. Lookup Supreme Court civil cases at http://iapps.courts.state.ny.us/webcivil/FCASMain. Cases go back to 2002.

Criminal Name Search: Access: In person only. Both court and visitors may perform in person name searches. No search fee. Required to search: name, years to search, DOB. Criminal records not on computer, on index from 1929. Note: The clerk directs criminal search requests to the OCA for the $65.00 statewide search. Court clerk office will not do Certificate of Conviction reports. They may direct you to sheriff's office for record searches; first call sheriff's office-518-743-2500.

Supreme & County Court 1340 State Rte 9, Lake George, NY 12845; 518-761-6430/6431 county clerk; fax: 518-761-6253; 9AM-5PM (EST). *Felony.*

General Information: This court does not hold closed case records. See separate County Clerk entry for Supreme civil records. Access to current/pending Supreme Court civil at http://iapps.courts.state.ny.us/webcivil/FCASMain. Criminal online via state OCA statewide system.

Glens Falls City Court 42 Ridge St, Glens Falls, NY 12801; 518-798-4714; fax: 518-798-0137; 8:30AM-4:30PM (EST). *Misdemeanor, Civil Actions under $15,000, Eviction, Small Claims.*

General Information: No sealed records released. Will fax documents to local or toll free line. Court makes copy: $.65 per page; $1.30 minimum. Certification fee: $6.00 per document plus copy fee for civil, $5.00 per document plus copy fee for all others. Payee: City Court. Only cashiers checks and money orders accepted. Prepayment required.

Civil Name Search: Access: Online. Only the court performs in person name searches; visitors may not. Civil records go back to 1975; on computer from 1987, prior on microfilm. Note: This court will only provide record is a case number is provided. Because judgment releases are not always filed with this court, the court will not name search. This court will refer you to the County Clerk for civil searches. WebCivil Local at http://iapps.courts.state.ny.us/webcivil/ecourtsMain contains information on both active and disposed Civil Court cases. Search by index number, party name, attorney/firm name or judge. No fee.

Criminal Name Search: Access: Online. Only the court performs in person name searches; visitors may not. Criminal records go back to the late 1960's; on computer from 1990, prior on microfilm. Note: The court does not permit access to court records unless specific case file given. Results include case number. All criminal record name search requests are directed to the OCA for statewide record search, $65.00 search fee. See www.nycourts.gov/apps/chrs.

Surrogate's Court 1340 State Rte 9, County Municipal Ctr, Lake George, NY 12845-9803; 518-761-6514; fax: 518-761-6511; 9AM-5PM (EST). *Probate.*

General Information: Public terminal available back to 1995 with older records being added. Cards go back to 1800s. A county search of the probate court index by mail for 25-year search is $30.00 fee. A full county probate search of all years is $90.00.

Warren Town/Village Courts -Bolton Town Court PO Box 478, Bolton Landing, NY 12814; 518-644-2202 9AM-4PM M-F (3PM-? 2nd & 4th W). **Chester Justice Court** PO Box 486, 6307 State Rt 9, Chestertown, NY 12817; 518-494-3133 8AM-3:30PM. **Hague Town Court** PO Box 509, 9793 Graphite Mtn Rd, Hague, NY 12836; 518-543-6161 5:30PM TH. **Horicon Town Court** PO Box 31, 6604 State Rte 8, Brant Lake, NY 12815; 518-585-2749 10AM-1PM T,W,TH. **Johnsburg Town Court** PO Box 178, 2370 State Rte 28, Wevertown, NY 12886; 518-251-3029 7PM W. **Lake George Town Court** PO Box 392, 20 Old Post Rd, Lake George, NY 12845; 518-668-5420 8:30-4:30PM. **Lake Luzerne Town Court** PO Box 31, 14 School St, Lake Luzerne, NY 12846-0370; 518-696-4294 9AM-2PM M,T; 10AM-4PM W. **Queensbury Town Court** 81 Glenwood Ave, Queensbury, NY 12804; 518-745-5571 8AM-4PM T-F. **Stony Creek Town Court** 52 Hadley Rd, Town Hall, PO Box 96, Stony Creek, NY 12878; 518-696-2508 M 7PM-?. **Thurman Town Court** 303 Athol Rd, PO Box 134, Athol, NY 12810; 518-623-9660 7PM-? M. **Warrensburg Town Court** 3797 Main St, Warrensburg, NY 12885; 518-623-9776 8:30AM-4:30PM.

Washington County

County Clerk 383 Broadway, Bldg A, Fort Edward, NY 12828; 518-746-2170; fax: 518-746-2177; 8:30AM-4:30PM (EST). *Civil.*

General Information: For felony records see the County Court clerk at the Supreme and County Court in separate listing. No sealed or youthful offender records released. Will not fax documents. Court makes copy: $1.00 per page. Self serve copy: $.50 per page. Certification fee: $5.00 per doc; add $10 for exemplification. Payee: County Clerk. Business checks accepted. No credit cards accepted. Prepayment required. Mail requests: SASE required.

Civil Name Search: Access: Mail, in person, online (limited). Visitors must perform in person searches themselves. No search fee. Generally, court will answer mailed civil records requests but you must at least provide year to search. Civil cases indexed by defendant. Civil records on books from 1800s. Mail turnaround Time 1-2 days. Public use terminal has civil records. Access to current/pending WebCivil Supreme Court civil cases may be online at http://iapps.courts.state.ny.us/webcivil/FCASMain.

Supreme & County Court 383 Broadway, Fort Edward, NY 12828; criminal phone: 518-746-2521; civil phone: 518-746-2520; fax: 518-746-2519; 8:30AM-4:30PM (EST). *Felony, Civil.*

General Information: No sealed or youthful offender records released. Will not fax documents. Court makes copy: $1.00 per page. Certification fee: none at this court office. Payee: County Clerk. Business checks accepted at county clerk office. No credit cards accepted. Prepayment required.

Civil Name Search: Access: In person, online. Visitors must perform in person searches themselves. Records available from early 1800's. Note: For access to physical court records, direct civil record search requests to the County Clerk, see separate listing. Historical records are not online, but access to current/pending Supreme Court civil cases is at http://iapps.courts.state.ny.us/webcivil/FCASMain.

Criminal Name Search: Access: In person, mail, online. Visitors must perform in person searches themselves. Search fee: No fee if you search; $5.00 for Certificate of Disposition. Criminal docket on books from 1800s, on computer back to late 1989. Note: Visitors may search the Book of Convictions. All mail criminal record name search requests are directed to the OCA for the $65.00 statewide record search. Online access is via the state OCA statewide system. Fee is $65.00 per search. See www.nycourts.gov/apps/chrs/.

Surrogate's Court 383 Broadway, Fort Edward, NY 12828; 518-746-2546; fax: 518-746-2547; 8:30AM-4:30PM (EST). *Probate, Estate.*

General Information: A county search of the probate court index by mail for 25-year search is $30.00 fee. A full county probate search of all years is $90.00.

Washington Town/Village Courts - Argyle Town Court 41 Main St, PO Box 38, Argyle, NY 12809; 518-638-8681 x13 Every Tues 5PM; Civil 1st & 3rd TH 5PM. **Cambridge Town Court** 2 Academy St, Cambridge, NY 12816; 518-677-5896 6PM 1st & 3rd T. **Cambridge Village Court** 56 N Park St, Cambridge, NY 12816; 518-677-2622 M 7PM. **Dresden Town Court** 46 Pike Brook Rd, Town Hall, Clemons, NY 12819; 518-499-1382 7PM-? TH (court). **Easton Town Court** 1071 State Route 40, Greenwich, NY 12834; 518-692-0027 9AM-1PM T & W. **Fort Ann Town Court** PO Box 314, 80 George St, Town Hall, Fort Ann, NY 12827; 518-639-4088 3:15-5PM T, TH. **Fort Edward Town Court and Village Court** 118 Broadway, Fort Edward, NY 12828; 518-747-2252 8AM-4PM. **Granville Town Court** PO Box 177, Granville, NY 12832; 518-642-9243 x3 8AM-3:30PM (court- 5PM-? M). **Granville Village Court** PO Box 208, 51 Quaker St, Granville, NY 12832; 518-642-9386 5PM T. **Greenwich Town Court** 2 Academy St, Greenwich, NY 12834; 518-692-7611 9AM-N 1PM-4PM T. **Greenwich Village Court** 6 Academy St, Greenwich, NY 12834; 518-692-2755 10AM-2PM T. **Hampton Town Court** Rte 22-A, Hampton, NY 12837; 518-282-9830 6:30PM TH. **Hartford Town Court** PO Box 14, 165 County Route 23, Main St, Hartford, NY 12838; 518-632-9274 4:30PM TH. **Hebron Town Court** PO Box 415, Salem, NY 12832; 518-854-9300 N-2PM W (clerk); 7PM-? W (court). **Hudson Falls Village Court** 218 Main St, Village Hall, Hudson Falls, NY 12839; 518-747-3292 8:30-4PM. **Jackson Town Court** Town Court, 2355 State Rte 22, Cambridge, NY 12816; 518-677-8896 7PM TH. **Kingsbury Town Court** 210 Main St, Hudson Falls, NY 12839; 518-747-2188 x3010 8:30AM-3:30PM M-TH. **Putnam Court** Box 96, Putnam Station, NY 12861; 518-547-8317 No set hrs (clerk); 6PM-8PM 1st & 3rd T (court). **Salem Town & Village Court** 181 Main St, Salem, NY 12865; 518-854-9215 6PM M. **White Creek Town Court** PO Box 213, 28 Mountain View Dr, Town Hall, Cambridge, NY 12816; 518-677-8545 7PM TH. **Whitehall Town Court** PO Box 272, 1 Saunders St, Whitehall Village Building, Whitehall, NY 12887; 518-499-0772 9AM-N Tues. **Whitehall Village Court** PO Box 272, 1 Saunders St, Whitehall, NY 12887; 518-499-0772 9AM-N Wed.

Wayne County

Supreme & County Court 9 Pearl St, PO Box 608, Lyons, NY 14489-0608; 315-946-7470; probate phone: 315-946-5430; fax: 315-946-5978; 9AM-5PM (EST). *Felony, Civil.*

General Information: Direct all search requests to the County Clerk office; information given here is for that County Clerk office. Eviction and small claims records are found at the Justice Courts in this county. No matrimonial records released. Fax out fee long distance within Wayne County $2.00 1st page, $1.00 each add'l page; long distance outside County $3.00 1st page, $1.00 each add'l page; no fax charge for 800 number. Court makes copy: $.65 per page; $1.30 minimum. Self serve copy: $.25 per page. Certification fee: $5.00 up to 4 pages, $1.25 each add'l page includes copy fee. Exemplification- $10.00. Payee: County Clerk. Personal checks accepted, credit cards are not. Prepayment required. Mail requests: SASE requested.

Civil Name Search: Access: Phone, fax, mail, in person. Both court and visitors may perform in person name searches. Search fee: $5.00 per name per every 2 years. Civil records on computer back to 1985, prior in books. Mail turnaround Time 5-7 days. Civil PAT goes back to 1985. Current or pending only Supreme Court civil case look-up is at http://iapps.courts.state.ny.us/webcivil/FCASMain.

Criminal Name Search: Access: Fax, mail, in person, only. Both court and visitors may perform in person name searches. Search fee: $5.00 per name uncertified back to 1979. $5.00 per name for every 2 years certified search. Required to search: name, years to search, DOB; also helpful: gender. Criminal records computerized from 1979. Mail turnaround Time 5-7 days. Criminal PAT goes back to 1979. Online access is via the state OCA statewide system. Fee is $65.00 per search. See www.nycourts.gov/apps/chrs/.

Surrogate's Court 54 Broad St, Rm 106, Hall of Justice, Lyons, NY 14489; 315-946-5430; fax: 315-946-5433; 9AM-5PM (EST). *Probate.* www.nycourts.gov/courts/7jd/courts/surrogates/

General Information: A county search of the probate court index by mail for 25-year search is $30.00 fee. A full county probate search of all years is $90.00.

Wayne Town/Village Courts - Arcadia Town Court 100 E Miller St, Newark, NY 14513; 315-331-7666 9AM-4PM. **Butler Town Court** 4576 Butler Center Rd, Wolcott, NY 14590; 315-594-2719 5:30PM W. **Galen Town Court** #6 S Park St, Clyde, NY 14433; 315-923-9375 8AM-4PM M T,TH,F; 8AM-12PM W. **Huron Town Court** 10880 Lummisville Rd, Wolcott, NY 14590; 315-594-6511 10AM:30PM M-TH. **Lyons Town Court** 43 Phelps St, Lyons, NY 14489; 315-946-4076 8AM-Noon. **Lyons Village Court** 76 William St, Lyons, NY 14489; 315-946-4565 8AM-4PM. **Macedon Town Court** 32 Main St, Macedon, NY 14502; 315-986-5932 x208 9AM-4PM M-TH. **Macedon Village Court** Village Court, 81 Main St, Macedon, NY 14502; 315-986-1597 5:30PM-8:30PM T,TH; 5PM-6PM 2nd & 4th W. **Marion Town** 3827 N Main St, Marion, NY 14505; 315-926-4461 8AM-1PM M-TH; Closed F. **Newark Village Court** 100 E Miller St, Newark, NY 14513; 315-331-7666 8AM-4PM. **Ontario Justice Court** 1846 Ridge Rd, PO Box 580, Ontario, NY 14519; 315-524-6511 x757 9AM-N 1PM-4PM. **Palmyra Town Court** 144 E Main St, Palmyra, NY 14522; 315-597-5431 9AM-3PM M-TH. **Rose Town Court** PO Box 310, 5074 N Main St, North Rose, NY 14516; 315-587-4418 9AM-4:30PM M,T,W,F, 7PM M. **Savannah Town Court** PO Box 296, Savannah, NY 13146; 315-365-2811 7PM TH. **Sodus Point Village Court** 8356 Bay St, PO Box 159, Sodus Point, NY 14555; 315-483-6217 irregular. **Sodus Town Court** 1416 Mill St, Sodus, NY 14551; 315-483-6807 9AM-3PM M-TH; 9AM-1:30PM F. **Walworth Town Court** 3600 Lorraine Dr, Town Hall, Walworth, NY 14568; 315-986-1400 x316 9AM-5PM M-TW; 9AM-2:30PM TH; Closed F. **Williamson Town Court** 6380 State Route 21, #2, Williamson, NY 14589; 315-589-8250 9AM-3PM. **Wolcott Town Court** 6070 Lake Ave, PO Box 237, Wolcott, NY 14590; 315-594-8257 9AM-3PM M-TH; 7PM 1st & 3rd TH court. **Wolcott Village Court** PO Box 85, 6015 New Hartford St, Wolcott, NY 14590; 315-594-6437 1st & 3rd TH 5PM.

Westchester County

County Clerk 110 Dr Martin L King Blvd, Rm 330, White Plains, NY 10601; 914-995-3070; fax: 914-995-3172; 8AM-5:00PM (EST). *Felony, Civil.* www.westchesterclerk.com

General Information: Countywide search requests made to the County Clerk are processed in the manner described below. Fax number above is not for the public - do not use. No sealed, expunged, adoption, sex offense, juvenile or mental health records released. Will not fax documents. Court makes copy: $.65 per page, minimum $1.00. Self serve copy: $.25 per page. Certification fee: $5.00 per doc, if over 8 pages add $.65 per page. Payee: County Clerk. Personal checks, Visa/MC accepted. Prepayment required. Mail requests: SASE required.

Civil Name Search: Access: Mail, in person, online. Both court and visitors may perform in person name searches. Search fee: $5.00 per name per 2 years. Civil records on computer from 1980, prior in books from 1847. Mail turnaround Time 1 week. Civil PAT goes back to 1978. Access civil cases on the county clerk database search site back to 2002 at http://wro.westchesterclerk.com/landsearch.aspx. Data includes liens, judgments, tax warrants, foreclosures, Divorces (no images). Also, access current/pending WebCivil Supreme Court civil cases at http://iapps.courts.state.ny.us/webcivil/FCASMain.

Criminal Name Search: Access: Mail, in person, online. Both court and visitors may perform in person name searches. Search fee: $5.00 per name per 2 years. Criminal records computerized from 1978, prior in books from 1847. Mail turnaround Time 1 week. Criminal PAT goes back to same as civil. Access criminal records on the county clerk database search site back to 2002 at http://ccpv.westchesterclerk.com. Search is free, but registration and fees for images. Also, subscribe or login as guest to search eCourts WebCrims future appearances system at http://iapps.courts.state.ny.us/webcrim_attorney/Login. Online results show middle initial.

Supreme Court 111 Dr Martin L King Blvd, Rm 900, White Plains, NY 10601; criminal phone: 914-824-5400; civil phone: 914-9824-5300; criminal fax: 914-995-4323; civil fax: 9AM-5PM; 9AM-5PM (EST). *Felony, Civil.* www.courts.state.ny.us/courts/9jd/Westchester/supremecounty.shtml

General Information: This court doesn't hold closed records, see County Clerk listing. See http://wro.westchesterclerk.com/legalsearch.aspx. Current/pending Supreme civil at http://iapps.courts.state.ny.us/webcivil/FCASMain. Criminal online via state OCA statewide system.

Mt Vernon City Court Ronald Blackwood Bldg, 2 Roosevelt Square, 2nd Fl, Mt Vernon, NY 10550-2019; 914-831-6440; criminal phone: 914-831-6420; fax: 914-699-1230; 9AM-5PM (payments to 4PM only) (EST). *Misdemeanor, Civil Actions under $15,000, Eviction, Small Claims.*

General Information: Small claims: 831-6411; Landlord/Tenant: 831-6413; Traffic: 831-6430. No sealed records released. Will not fax documents.

Court makes copy: $1.30 1st page, $.65 each add'l. Certification fee: $6.00. Payee: City Court. Cashiers checks and money orders accepted. Visa/MC accepted. Prepayment required. Mail requests: SASE required for civil.

Civil Name Search: Access: Mail, in person. Only the court performs in person name searches; visitors may not. No search fee. Required to search: name, years to search; also helpful: address. Civil records on computer since 1986, prior in books. Note: Court holds records for 3 years and then send to archives Mail turnaround Time 1 week.

Criminal Name Search: Access: In person, online. Only the court performs in person name searches; visitors may not. Criminal records on computer since 1986, prior in books. All criminal record name search requests are directed to the OCA for statewide record search, $65.00 search fee. See www.nycourts.gov/apps/chrs.

New Rochelle City Court 475 North Ave, New Rochelle, NY 10801; 914-654-2291; criminal phone: 914-654-2311; civil phone: 914-654-2299; fax: 914-654-0344; 9AM-5PM; entry gate closes at 4:30PM (EST). *Misdemeanor, Civil Actions under $15,000, Small Claims.*
www.courts.state.ny.us/courts/9jd/Westchester/NewRochelle.shtml
General Information: Traffic phone- 914-654-2292. No sealed records released. Will not fax documents. Court makes copy: $.65 per page. Certification fee: $10.00 per doc for criminal, $6.00 civil. Payee: City Court of New Rochelle. No personal checks accepted. Visa/MC accepted if criminal division; not accepted for civil. Prepayment required.

Civil Name Search: Access: Mail, in person. Only the court performs in person name searches; visitors may not. Search fee: $16.00 per name. Civil records retained for 20 years.

Criminal Name Search: Access: Phone, mail, in person, online. Search fee: $16.00 per name. Certificate of Disposition- $10.00 with release. Note: It has been found that this court may do short phone request lookups. Name search requests are often directed to the OCA for statewide record search, $65.00 search fee. See www.nycourts.gov/apps/chrs.

Peekskill City Court 2 Nelson Ave, Peekskill, NY 10566; 914-831-6480; fax: 914-736-1889; 9AM-4:30PM (EST). *Misdemeanor, Civil Actions under $15,000, Eviction, Small Claims.*
General Information: No sealed records released. Will not fax documents. Court makes copy: $.65 per page; $1.30 minimum. Certification fee: $6.00 per doc plus copy fee. Payee: Peekskill City Court. No personal or business checks accepted. Visa/MC/Discover accepted. Prepayment required. Mail requests: SASE required for criminal.

Civil Name Search: Access: In person only. Only the court performs in person name searches; visitors may not. No search fee. Civil cases indexed by plaintiff. Civil records on computer back to 1994, prior in books.

Criminal Name Search: Access: Mail, in person, online. Both court and visitors may perform in person name searches. Search fee: Certificate of Disposition- $6.00 and you must supply specific case info. Required to search: name, years to search, DOB. Criminal records computerized from 1990, prior on cards. Mail turnaround Time 1-5 days. Name search requests are often directed to the OCA for statewide record search, $65.00 search fee. See www.nycourts.gov/apps/chrs.

Rye City Court 21 3rd St, 21 McCullough Place, Rye, NY 10580; 914-831-6400; 9AM-5PM (EST). *Misdemeanor, Civil Actions under $15,000, Eviction, Small Claims.*
www.ryeny.gov
General Information: No sealed records released. Court makes copy: $.65 per page; $1.30 minimum. Certification fee: $5.00 per cert plus copy fee. Payee: City Court. No personal checks accepted. Major credit cards accepted. Prepayment required.

Civil Name Search: Access: In person, online. Only the court performs in person name searches; visitors may not. No search fee. Civil cases indexed by plaintiff. Civil records on computer from 1994, prior on index cards. Note: Make an appointment to search in person. WebCivil Local at http://iapps.courts.state.ny.us/webcivil/ecourtsMain contains information on both active and disposed Civil Court cases. Search by index number, party name, attorney/firm name or judge. No fee.

Criminal Name Search: Access: In person, online. Only the court performs in person name searches; visitors may not. Search fee: Certificate of Disposition- $5.00 per name. Required to search: DOB, years to search. Criminal records computerized from 1986. Note: The court will perform limited name searches. All criminal record name search requests are directed to the OCA for statewide record search, $65.00 search fee. See www.nycourts.gov/apps/chrs.

White Plains City Court 77 S Lexington Ave, Main Fl, White Plains, NY 10601; 914-824-5675; criminal phone: 914-824-5688; fax: 914-422-6058; 8:45AM-5PM; registers close- 4:45PM (EST). *Misdemeanor, Civil Actions under $15,000, Eviction, Small Claims, Traffic.*
General Information: No sealed, youthful offender or sex case records released. Will fax documents no fee, all fees paid. Court makes copy: $1.00 1st page; $.50 each add'l. Certification fee: $6.00 per doc. Payee: City Court. Cashiers checks and money orders accepted. Visa/MC accepted in person

only. Prepayment required. Credit cards not accepted for Certificates of Disposition. Mail requests: SASE required.

Civil Name Search: Access: Mail, fax, in person, online. Only the court performs in person name searches; visitors may not. Search fee: $16.00 per name. Civil cases indexed by defendant. Civil records on docket cards and computer. Mail turnaround Time 1-2 days. WebCivil Local at http://iapps.courts.state.ny.us/webcivil/ecourtsMain contains information on both active and disposed Civil Court cases. Search by index number, party name, attorney/firm name or judge. No fee.

Criminal Name Search: Access: Mail, in person, online. Search fee: Certificate of Disposition- $5.00 per name. Required to search: name, years to search, DOB. Criminal records computerized from 1988, prior on cards. Note: Except for certificate of disposition, the court does not permit access to court records unless specific case file given. Mail turnaround Time 1-2 days. Name search requests are often directed to the OCA for statewide record search, $65.00 search fee. See www.nycourts.gov/apps/chrs.

Yonkers City Court 100 S Broadway, Yonkers, NY 10701; 914-831-6450; criminal phone: 914-831-6930; civil phone: 914-831-6920; fax: 914-377-6395; 9AM-5PM (EST). *Misdemeanor, Civil Actions under $15,000, Eviction, Small Claims.*
General Information: No sealed records released. Will not fax documents. Court makes copy: $.65 per page; $1.30 minimum. Certification fee: $6.00 per document. Payee: City Court. Cashiers checks and money orders accepted. Visa/MC accepted. Prepayment required. Mail requests: SASE not required.

Civil Name Search: Access: Mail, in person, online. Only the court performs in person name searches; visitors may not. Search fee: $16.00 per name. Civil cases indexed by plaintiff. Civil records on computer since 1/95. Mail turnaround Time 2-3 weeks. WebCivil Local at http://iapps.courts.state.ny.us/webcivil/ecourtsMain contains information on both active and disposed Civil Court cases. Search by index number, party name, attorney/firm name or judge. No fee.

Criminal Name Search: Access: Mail, in person, online. Only the court performs in person name searches; visitors may not. Search fee: $16.00, if specific case # given. Criminal records on computer since 1993. Note: The court does not permit access to court records unless specific case file given. Mail turnaround Time 2-3 weeks. Requesters are directed to the OCA for $65.00 statewide search.

Surrogate's Court 111 Dr Martin Luther King Jr Blvd, 10th Fl, White Plains, NY 10601; 914-824-5656; fax: 914-995-3728; 9AM-5PM (EST). *Probate.*
General Information: A county search of the probate court index by mail for 25-year search is $30.00 fee. A full county probate search of all years is $90.00.

Westchester Town/Village Courts - Ardsley Village Court 507 Ashford Ave, Ardsley, NY 10502-2222; 914-693-1703 9AM-4PM. **Bedford Town Court** 321 Bedford Rd, Bedford Hills, NY 10507; 914-666-6965 8:30AM-4:30PM. **Briarcliff Manor Village Court** 1111 Pleasantville Rd, Briarcliff Manor, NY 10510; 914-944-2788 8:30AM-4:30PM M,T,TH,F; Court in session W. **Bronxville Village Court** 200 Pondfield Rd, Bronxville, NY 10708; 914-337-2454 9-4PM. **Buchanan Village Court** Municipal Bldg, 236 Tate Ave, Buchanan, NY 10511; 914-737-1033 7PM-? T court. **Cortlandt Town Court** One Heady St, Cortlandt Manor, NY 10567; 914-734-1090 8:30AM-4PM. **Croton-on-Hudson Village Court** Municipal Bldg, 1 Van Wyck St, Croton-on-Hudson, NY 10520; 914-271-6266 8:30-4PM. **Dobbs Ferry Village Court** PO Box 122, 112 Main St, Dobbs Ferry, NY 10522; 914-693-6161 8:30AM-4PM. **Eastchester Town Court** 40 Mill Rd, Town Hall, Eastchester, NY 10709; 914-771-3354 8:30AM-4:30PM. **Elmsford Village Court** 15 S Stone Ave, Elmsford, NY 10523; 914-592-8949 8:30-4PM. **Greenburgh Town Court** 188 Tarrytown Rd, White Plains, NY 10607; 914-682-5365 9AM-4:30PM. **Harrison Town Court** Municipal Bldg, 1 Heineman Pl, Harrison, NY 10528; 914-670-3010 9AM-4PM (3PM in summer months). **Hastings-on-Hudson Village Court** 7 Maple Ave, Municipal Bldg, Hastings-on-Hudson, NY 10706; 914-478-3403 8:30AM-5PM M-TH; 8:30AM-N F. **Irvington Village Court** 85 Main St, Irvington, NY 10533; 914-591-7095 9AM-4PM M-TH. **Larchmont Village Court** Municipal Bldg, 120 Larchmont Ave, Larchmont, NY 10538; 914-834-6230 8:30-4:30PM. **Lewisboro Justice Court** 11 Main St, PO Box 500, South Salem, NY 10590-0405; 914-763-5417 9AM-5PM. **Mamaroneck Town Court** 740 W Boston Post Rd, Town Center, 2nd Fl, Rm 215, Mamaroneck, NY 10543; 914-381-7875 8:30-4PM. **Mamaroneck Village Court** 169 Mt Pleasant Ave, Village Hall, 2nd Fl, Mamroneck, NY 10543; 914-777-7710 9AM-4:30PM. **Mount Kisco Town Court** 40 Green St., Mount Kisco, NY 10549; 914-241-7033 8:30AM-4:30PM. **Mount Pleasant Town Court** 1 Town Hall Plaza, Valhalla, NY 10595; 914-742-2324 8:30AM-4:30PM. **New Castle Justice Court** 200 S Greeley Ave, Chappaqua, NY 10514; 914-238-4726 8:45-4PM. **North Castle Justice Court** 15 Bedford Rd, Armonk, NY 10504; 914-273-8627 8:30-4PM. **North Salem Town Court** PO Box 365, 274 Titicus Rd, Town Hall

Annex, North Salem, NY 10560; 914-669-9691 9-12PM,1-4PM. **Ossining Town Court** 86-88 Spring St, Ossining, NY 10562; 914-762-8562 8:30AM-4:30PM. **Ossining Village Court** 86 Spring St., Ossining, NY 10562; 914-941-3067 9AM-4PM. **Pelham Town Court** 34 5th Ave, Pelham, NY 10803; 914-738-7030 9AM-4PM. **Pleasantville Village Court** 80 Wheeler Ave, Pleasantville, NY 10570; 914-769-2027 8:30AM-4PM. **Port Chester Justice Court** 350 N Main St, Port Chester, NY 10573; 914-939-8220 8:30AM-4PM. **Pound Ridge Justice Court** Town House, 179 Westchester Ave, Pound Ridge, NY 10576; 914-764-3983 9AM-4:30PM. **Rye Town Court** 10 Pearl St, Port Chester, NY 10573; 914-939-3305 8:30AM-4PM. **Scarsdale Village Court** 1001 Post Rd, Scarsdale, NY 10583; 914-722-1120/1123 9AM-5PM. **Sleepy Hollow Village Court** 28 Beekman Ave, Sleepy Hollow, NY 10591; 914-631-2783 8:30-4:30PM. **Somers Town Court** 335 Route 202, Somers, NY 10589; 914-277-8225 9AM-4:30PM. **Tarrytown Village Court** One Depot Plaza, Tarrytown, NY 10591; 914-631-5215 8:30AM-4:30PM. **Tuckahoe Village Court** 65 Main St, Tuckahoe, NY 10707; 914-961-4787 8:30-4:30. **Yorktown Justice Court** 2295 Crompond Rd, Yorktown Heights, NY 10598; 914-962-6216 9AM-4PM.

Wyoming County

Supreme & County Court 143 N Main St, Ste 104, Warsaw, NY 14569; 585-786-8810-county clerk, 585-786-3148-court clerks); fax: 585-786-3703; 9AM-5PM (EST). *Felony, Civil.*
www.wyomingco.net/cclerk/main.html
General Information: This court does not hold closed case records. See separate County Clerk entry for Supreme civil records. Access to current/pending Supreme Court civil at http://iapps.courts.state.ny.us/webcivil/FCASMain. No sealed, divorce or sexual abuse records released. Fee to fax out file $1.00 per page. Court makes copy: $.50 per page for walk-ins. Certification fee: $5.00. Payee: County Clerk. Personal checks accepted, credit cards are not. Prepayment required. Mail requests: SASE required for mail return of any copies.
Civil Name Search: Access: In person, online. Visitors must perform in person searches themselves. Civil cases indexed by defendant. Civil records on computer back to 2/14/2001; prior on books. Public use terminal has civil records back to 2001. Results often include address. Civil records available by subscription through ACS; contact Donna Hart 800-800-7009 for info and registration. Historical records are not online, but access to current/pending Supreme Court civil cases is at http://iapps.courts.state.ny.us/webcivil/FCASMain.
Criminal Name Search: Access: Phone, fax, mail, in person, online. Only the court performs in person name searches; visitors may not. Search fee: $10.00 for 1-5 years searched per name; 6-10 years is $15.00; 11-20 years is $20.00. Required to search: name, years to search, DOB. Criminal records in books. Note: Address requests to County Clerk. Phone or fax searching allowed once you have an account setup. Mail turnaround Time 2-3 days. Online access is via the state OCA statewide system. Fee is $65.00 per search. See www.nycourts.gov/apps/chrs/.

Surrogate's Court 147 N Main St, Courthouse, Warsaw, NY 14569; 585-786-3148/2253; fax: 585-786-2818; 9AM-5PM (EST). *Probate, Guardianship.*
www.nycourts.gov/courts/8jd/Wyoming/index.shtml
General Information: A county search of the probate court index by mail for 25-year search is $30.00 fee. A full county probate search of all years is $90.00.
Wyoming Town/Village Courts - Arcade Justice Court 17 Church St, Arcade, NY 14009; 585-492-4479 7AM-5PM T-Wed; 12-5PM th; 12-4PM F. **Arcade Town Court** 17 Church St, Arcade, NY 14009; 585-492-4479 7AM-5PM T-Wed; 12-5PM th; 12-4PM F. **Attica Town Court** 9 Water St, Attica, NY 14011; 585-591-4613 7PM-? M court. **Attica Village Court** PO Box 163, 9 Water St, Attica, NY 14011; 585-591-2957 4:30-7PM M; 9:30AM-1PM F. **Bennington Town Court** 4076 E Blood Rd., Cowlesville, NY 14037; 716-652-5585 9AM-5PM. **Castile Town Court** 51-53 N Main St, Castile, NY 14427; 585-493-5875 **Covington Town Court** PO Box 128, 7083 Court Rd, Pavilion, NY 14525; 585-584-8498 7-9PM M. **Eagle Town Court** 3560 E Main St, Bliss, NY 14024; 585-322-7667 **Gainesville Town Court** PO Box 351, 43 N Main St, Silver Springs, NY 14550; 585-493-3395 5:30-9PM M. **Genesee Falls Town Court** 6635 Church St, Portageville, NY 14536; 585-468-5015 7PM-? W court. **Java Town Court** PO Box 46, 1428 Main St, Java Center, NY 14082; 585-457-3233 7:30PM-? 1st & 3rd W. **Middlebury Town Court** 51 Sherman Ave, PO Box 274, Wyoming, NY 14591-0274; 585-495-6040 **Orangeville Town Court** 3529 Route 20A, Warsaw, NY 14569; 585-786-2883 **Perry Town Court and Village Courts** 46 N Main St, Perry, NY 14530; 585-237-2149 (4090 is Town Court) M&T 9-1PM; W 9-7PM. **Pike Town Court** PO Box 157, Main St, Pike, NY 14130; 585-493-5140 6PM-8PM T; 9-11AM Sat. **Sheldon Town Court** 1380 Centerline Rd, Strykersville, NY 14145; 585-535-0468 6:30PM-? M. **Silver Springs Village Court** 43 N Main St, PO Box 317, Silver Springs, NY 14550; 585-493-3395 5:30-9PM M. **Warsaw Town**

Court and Village Court 27 N Main St, Warsaw, NY 14569; 585-786-3361 N-4PM M; N-4:30PM T,W,TH; Closed F. **Wethersfield Town Court** Hermitage Town Bldg, 4362 Route 78, Gainesville, NY 14066; 585-322-7233 irregular.

Yates County

County Clerk 415 Liberty St, #1107, Penn Yan, NY 14527; 315-536-5120; fax: 315-536-5545; 9AM-5PM; (8:30AM-4:30PM in July & Aug) (EST). *Felony, Civil.*
www.yatescounty.org/display_page.asp?pID=78
General Information: Countywide search requests made to the County Clerk are processed in the manner described here, also see Supreme & County Court. No divorce records outside parties involved, sealed records released. Will fax out specific case files for $.65 a page to non-toll-free number; add'l $2.00 for toll number. Court makes copy: $.65 per page, $1.30 minimum. Certification fee: $1.25 per page, $5.00 minimum includes cost of copies. Exemplification fee $10.00. Payee: Yates County Clerk. Personal checks accepted, credit cards are not. Prepayment required. Mail requests: SASE not required.
Civil Name Search: Access: In person, online. Both court and visitors may perform in person name searches. Search fee: $10.00 per name. Civil record indices on computer back to 1/88, prior in books. Public use terminal has civil records back to 1/1988. Lookup Supreme Court civil cases at http://iapps.courts.state.ny.us/webcivil/FCASMain. Cases go back to 2002.
Criminal Name Search: Access: Mail, fax, in person. Both court and visitors may perform in person name searches. Search fee: $10.00 per name for 7 year search. Criminal docket on books; not computerized. Mail turnaround Time 2-3 days.

Supreme & County Court 415 Liberty St, Penn Yan, NY 14527; 315-536-5126/5129; fax: 315-536-5190; 9AM-5PM; 8:30AM-4:30PM Summer Hours (EST). *Felony, Civil.*
General Information: This court does not hold closed case records. See separate County Clerk entry for Supreme civil records. Access to current/pending Supreme Court civil at http://iapps.courts.state.ny.us/webcivil/FCASMain. Criminal online via state OCA statewide system.

Surrogate's Court 415 Liberty St, Penn Yan, NY 14527; 315-536-5130; fax: 315-536-5190; 9AM-5PM (EST). *Probate.*
General Information: Hours are 8:30AM-4:30PM in July and August. A county search of the probate court index by mail for 25-year search is $30.00 fee. A full county probate search of all years is $90.00.
Yates Town/Village Courts - Barrington Town Court 4424 Old Bath Rd., Pen Yan, NY 14837; 607-243-5323 6PM T. **Benton Town Court** Town Hall, 1526 Route 14A, Penn Yan, NY 14527; 315-536-2320 5:30 PM W. **Dundee Village Court** 12 Union St, Dundee, NY 14837; 607-243-5551 9AM-4PM. **Italy Town Court** 6060 Italy Valley Road, Naples, NY 14512; 585-374-6194 7PM 1st & 3rd W; Sm Claims 3rd M. **Jerusalem Town Court** 3816 Italy Hill Rd, Branchport, NY 14418; 315-595-6102 6PM-? M. **Middlesex Town Court** Box 147, Middlesex, NY 14507; 585-554-3607 7PM T&TH. **Milo Town Court** 137 Main St., Penn Yan, NY 14527; 315-531-8816 9AM T. **Penn Yan Village Court** 127 Main St, Penn Yan, NY 14527; 315-536-7243 4PM-7PM M; 5-9PM W. **Potter Town Court** 1226 Phelps Rd, Middlesex, NY 14507; 585-554-6758 9-12PM,2-6PM M,T,THh 9-12PM Sat. **Starkey Town Court** 40 Seneca St, Dundee, NY 14837; 607-243-5344 6pm-? W court. **Torrey Town Court** PO Box 74, 56 Geneva St, Dresden, NY 14441; 315-536-5655 9AM-4:30PM.

North Carolina

Time Zone:	EST
Capital:	Raleigh, Wake County
# of Counties:	100
State Web:	www.ncgov.gov
Court Web:	www.nccourts.org

Administration

Administrative Office of the Courts (AOC), 901 Corporate Center Drive, Raleigh, NC 27607-5045; 919- 890-1000

The Supreme and Appellate Courts

The Supreme Court is the court of last resort. The Court of Appeals is the state's only intermediate appellate court. Opinions are available from the home page.

The North Carolina Courts

Court	Type	How Organized	Jurisdiction Highpoints
Superior *	General	100 Courts in 46 Districts	Felony, Civil $10,000 or above
District*	Limited	100 Courts in 39 Districts	Misdemeanor, Limited Civil, Small Claims Juvenile, Traffic, Ordinances, Evictions

* = profiled in this book

Details on the Court Structure

All felony criminal cases, civil cases involving more than $10,000 and misdemeanor and infraction appeals from District Court are tried in the **Superior Court**.

District Courts handle civil, misdemeanors and infractions, juvenile and magistrate. Civil cases include divorce, custody, child support and cases involving less than $10,000 or small claims ($5,000 or less). A **Magistrate** is a judicial officer of the District Court and the Magistrate presides over Small Claims Court and evictions. The principal relief sought in Small Claims Court is money, the recovery of specific personal property, or summary ejectment (eviction).

Uncontested Probate is handled by County Clerks.

Record Searching Facts You Need to Know

Fees and Record Searching Tips

The counties combine the courts in one courthouse and one record database, thus searching is done through one court, not two, within the county. Many courts recommend that civil searches be done in person or by a retriever and that criminal searches only be requested in writing. Very few courts will do a civil record name search.

A fee structure is in place that mandates copy fees to be $2.00 for the first page and $.25 each additional page, and $25.00 for a criminal record search, which in most jurisdictions includes certification. Most courts have adopted these rules. Many courts have archived their records prior to 1968 in the Raleigh State Archives, 919-807-7280.

Online Access is Statewide

The state AOC provides ongoing, high volume requesters and vendors with portions of electronic criminal and civil records on an ongoing basis pursuant to a licensing agreement. A Daily Criminal access is supplied. However starting in 2011 case dispositions were removed from the extract. Users must now access a secondary source - known as the Green Screen - to find the case details. The Green Screen is a cumbersome system using technology from the 1970's. The requirement to using the Green Screen has increased the turnaround time and fees charged by vendors. To obtain cost and connectivity information contact the NCAOC Remote Public Access team at 919-890-2220 or via email at rpa@nccourts.org. For a list of the participating vendors visit the web at www.nccourts.org/Citizens/GoToCourt/Default.asp?topic=1.

There are several other North Carolina online services that are free. Search civil and criminal court calendars at www1.aoc.state.nc.us/www/calendars.html. Search the District and Superior Court Query system for current criminal defendants at http://www1.aoc.state.nc.us/www/calendars/CriminalQuery.html. At this site there are also queries for Impaired Driving, Citations, and Current Civil and Criminal Calendars.

Alamance County

Superior-District Court - Criminal 212 W Elm St, #105, Graham, NC 27253; 336-438-1001; fax: 336-570-6991; 8AM-5PM (EST). *Felony, Misdemeanor.* www.nccourts.org/County/Alamance/Default.asp
General Information: Search criminal court calendars at www1.aoc.state.nc.us/www/calendars.html. Probate is in a separate index at this courthouse. No sealed case records released. Will not fax documents. Court makes copy: $2.00 1st page, $.25 ea add'l. Self serve copy: $.25 per page. Certification fee: $3.00 per cert; exemplification- $10.00. Payee: Clerk of Superior Court. Only cashiers checks and money orders accepted. No credit cards accepted. Prepayment required.
Criminal Name Search: Access: Mail, in person, online. Both court and visitors may perform in person name searches. Search fee: $25.00 per name, includes certification. Required to search: name, years to search, DOB; also helpful: address, SSN. Criminal records on computer since 1985, on index cards back to 1975. Mail turnaround time 1 week. Public use terminal has crim records back to 3/1985, includes countywide. **See details about online access to criminal records at front or back of this chapter.**

Superior-District Court - Civil 1 Court Square, Graham, NC 27253; 336-570-5203; probate phone: 336-570-5204; fax: 336-570-5201; 8AM-5PM (EST). *Civil, Eviction, Small Claims, Probate.*
www.nccourts.org/County/Alamance/Default.asp
General Information: No adoption, sealed cases, juvenile, or mental records released. Will not fax documents. Court makes copy: $2.00 1st page, $.25 ea add'l page. Self serve copy: $.25 per page. Certification fee: $3.00. Payee: Clerk of Superior Court. No personal checks or credit cards accepted. Prepayment required.
Civil Name Search: Access: Mail, in person, online. Visitors must perform in person searches themselves. No search fee. Civil records computerized since 1988, prior indexed on books. Public use terminal has civil records back to 1988. **See details about online access to civil records at front or back of this chapter. .**

Alexander County

Superior-District Court PO Box 100, Taylorsville, NC 28681; 828-632-2215; fax: 828-632-3550; 8AM-5PM (EST). *Felony, Misdemeanor, Civil, Eviction, Small Claims, Probate.*
www.nccourts.org/County/Alexander/Default.asp
General Information: Search civil and criminal court calendars at www1.aoc.state.nc.us/www/calendars.html. No adoption, sealed cases, juvenile, sex offenders, mental, expunged records released. Will fax documents for $1.00 per page. Court makes copy: $2.00 1st page, $.25 ea add'l. Self serve copy: $.25 per page. Certification fee: $3.00. Payee: Clerk of Superior Court. Business checks accepted. No credit cards accepted. Prepayment required. Mail requests: SASE required.
Civil Name Search: Access: Mail, in person, online. Both court and visitors may perform in person name searches. No search fee. Required to search: name, years to search, address. Civil records on computer since 10/1989, prior on books to 1865. Mail turnaround time 1-3 days. Civil PAT goes back to 1989. **See details about online access to civil records at front or back of this chapter.**
Criminal Name Search: Access: Mail, in person, online. Both court and visitors may perform in person name searches. Search fee: $25.00 per name, includes certification. Required to search: name, years to search, address, DOB. Criminal records on computer since 10/1989, prior on books to 1865. Mail turnaround time 1-3 days. Criminal PAT goes back to same as civil. **See details about online access to criminal records at front or back of this chapter.**

Alleghany County

Superior-District Court PO Box 61, 12 N Main St, Sparta, NC 28675; 336-372-8949; fax: 336-372-4899; 8AM-5PM (EST). *Felony, Misdemeanor, Civil, Eviction, Small Claims, Probate.*
www.nccourts.org/County/Alleghany/Default.asp
General Information: Search civil and criminal court calendars at www1.aoc.state.nc.us/www/calendars.html. No adoption, sealed cases, juvenile, mental or expunged records released. Will not fax documents. Court makes copy: $2.00 1st page, $.25 ea add'l. Certification fee: $3.00 per doc. Payee: Clerk of Superior Court. Business checks and in-state Personal checks

accepted, credit cards are not. Prepayment required. Mail requests: SASE required for criminal.
Civil Name Search: Access: In person, online. Visitors must perform in person searches themselves. Required to search: name, years to search; also helpful: address. Civil records on computer from 11/1988, index books prior. Civil PAT goes back to 1988. **See details about online access to civil records at front or back of this chapter.**
Criminal Name Search: Access: Mail, fax, in person, online. Both court and visitors may perform in person name searches. Search fee: $25.00 per name, includes certification. Required to search: name, years to search, DOB; also helpful: address, SSN. Criminal records computerized from 11/ 1988, index books prior. Mail turnaround time 2 days. Criminal PAT goes back to same as civil. **See details about online access to criminal records at front or back of this chapter.**

Anson County

Superior-District Court PO Box 1064 (114 N Greene St), Wadesboro, NC 28170; 704-994-3800; fax: 704-994-3801; 8:30AM-5PM (EST). *Felony, Misdemeanor, Civil, Eviction, Small Claims, Probate.*
www.nccourts.org/County/Anson/Default.asp
General Information: Search civil and criminal court calendars at www1.aoc.state.nc.us/www/calendars.html. No adoption, sealed cases, juvenile, mental, or expunged records released. Will not fax documents. Court makes copy: $2.00 1st page, $.25 ea add'l. Self serve copy: same. Certification fee: $3.00. Payee: Clerk of Superior Court. Business checks accepted. No personal checks. No credit cards accepted. Prepayment required. Mail requests: SASE required.
Civil Name Search: Access: In person, online. Visitors must perform in person searches themselves. Civil records on computer since 11/1989, in books prior. Civil PAT goes back to 1989. Public terminal has Estates/Special Proceedings. SSNs and middle initials do not appear on all records. **See details about online access to civil records at front or back of this chapter.**
Criminal Name Search: Access: Mail, in person, online. Both court and visitors may perform in person name searches. Search fee: $25.00 per name, includes certification. Required to search: name, years to search, DOB; also helpful: SSN. Criminal records on computer since 10/89, on microfilm 1982-89, in books prior. Mail turnaround time 2-5 days. Criminal PAT goes back to 1989. **See details about online access to criminal records at front or back of this chapter.**

Ashe County

Superior-District Court 150 Government Circle #3100, Jefferson, NC 28640-9378; 336-246-5641; fax: 336-246-4276; 8AM-5PM (EST). *Felony, Misdemeanor, Civil, Eviction, Small Claims, Probate.*
www.nccourts.org/County/Ashe/Default.asp
General Information: Search civil and criminal court calendars at www1.aoc.state.nc.us/www/calendars.html. No adoption, sealed cases, juvenile, sex offenders, mental or expunged records released. Will fax out documents; fax fee varies from case to case. Court makes copy: $2.00 1st page, $.25 ea add'l. Self serve copy: $.25 per page. Certification fee: $3.00. Payee: Clerk of Superior Court. Only cashiers checks and money orders accepted. No credit cards accepted. Prepayment required.
Civil Name Search: Access: Mail, in person, online. Both court and visitors may perform in person name searches. No search fee. Civil records on computer from 12/89, on index books back to 1900s. Mail turnaround time 1-3 days. Civil PAT goes back to 1989. **See details about online access to civil records at front or back of this chapter.**
Criminal Name Search: Access: Mail, in person, online. Both court and visitors may perform in person name searches. Search fee: $25.00 per name, includes certification. Criminal records computerized from 12/89, on index books back to 1900s. Note: Court will search records after 1988; visitors or researchers must search themselves for records prior to 1988. Mail turnaround time 1-3 days. Criminal PAT goes back to 1988. **See details about online access to criminal records at front or back of this chapter.**

Avery County

Superior-District Court PO Box 115, Newland, NC 28657; 828-733-2900; fax: 828-733-8410; 8AM-4:30PM (EST). *Felony, Misdemeanor, Civil, Eviction, Small Claims, Probate.*
www.nccourts.org/County/Avery/Default.asp

General Information: Search civil and criminal court calendars at www1.aoc.state.nc.us/www/calendars.html. No adoption, sealed cases, juvenile, sex offenders, mental or expunged records released. Will not fax documents. Court makes copy: $2.00 1st page, $.25 ea add'l. Self serve copy: $.25 per page. Certification fee: $3.00 if you perform search in person. Payee: Clerk of Superior Court. Only cashiers checks and money orders accepted. No credit cards accepted. Prepayment required. Will bill copy fees.
Civil Name Search: Access: In person, online. Visitors must perform in person searches themselves. Required to search: name, years to search; also helpful: address. Civil records on computer since 1988, on index books to 1968. Civil PAT goes back to 10/1988. **See details about online access to civil records at front or back of this chapter.**
Criminal Name Search: Access: Mail, in person, online. Both court and visitors may perform in person name searches. Search fee: $25.00 per name, includes certification. Required to search: name, years to search; also helpful: address. Criminal records computerized from 11/88; on cards and books back to 1968. Mail turnaround time 2-3 days. Criminal PAT goes back to 11/1988. **See details about online access to criminal records at front or back of this chapter.**

Beaufort County

Superior-District Court PO Box 1403, 112 W 2nd St, Washington, NC 27889-1403; 252-940-4000; fax: 252-940-4001; 8AM-5PM (EST). *Felony, Misdemeanor, Civil, Eviction, Small Claims, Probate.*
www.nccourts.org/County/Beaufort/Default.asp
General Information: Search civil and criminal court calendars at www1.aoc.state.nc.us/www/calendars.html. No adoption, sealed cases, juvenile, sex offenders, mental or expunged records released. Will not fax documents. Court makes copy: $2.00 1st page, $.25 ea add'l. Certification fee: $3.00 per doc. Payee: Clerk of Superior Court. Business checks accepted; no personal checks. No credit cards accepted. Prepayment required.
Civil Name Search: Access: In person, online. Visitors must perform in person searches themselves. Required to search: name, years to search, address. Civil records on computer since 6/87, docket books to 1800s. Civil PAT goes back to 6/1987. **See details about online access to civil records at front or back of this chapter.**
Criminal Name Search: Access: Mail, in person, online. Both court and visitors may perform in person name searches. Search fee: $25.00 per name, includes certification. Required to search: name; also helpful: years to search, address, DOB, SSN. Criminal records on computer since 5/87, docket books to 1800s. Mail turnaround time 5 days. Criminal PAT goes back to 1987. **See details about online access to criminal records at front or back of this chapter.**

Bertie County

Superior-District Court PO Box 370, 108 Dundee St, Windsor, NC 27983; 252-794-6800; criminal phone: 252-794-3039; civil phone: 252-794-3030; fax: 252-794-6801; 8AM-5PM (EST). *Felony, Misdemeanor, Civil, Eviction, Small Claims, Probate.*
www.nccourts.org/County/Bertie/Default.asp
General Information: Search civil and criminal court calendars at www1.aoc.state.nc.us/www/calendars.html. No adoption, sealed cases, juvenile, mental, expunged records released. Fee to fax document $1.00 1st page; $.25 each add'l. Court makes copy: $2.00 1st page, $.25 ea add'l. Certification fee: $3.00 per doc. Court will not certify any in person searches. Payee: Clerk of Superior Court. Only cashiers checks and money orders accepted. No credit cards accepted. Prepayment required. Mail requests: SASE requested for criminal.
Civil Name Search: Access: In person, online. Both court and visitors may perform in person name searches. No search fee. Civil records on computer from 11/96, prior on books to 1968. Note: Court will do a civil search if it is conjunction with a criminal search. Civil PAT goes back to 6/1989. **See details about online access to civil records at front or back of this chapter.**
Criminal Name Search: Access: Mail, in person, online. Both court and visitors may perform in person name searches. Search fee: $25.00 per name, includes certification. Required to search: name, years to search, DOB; also helpful: address, SSN. Criminal records computerized from 3/89, prior on books to 1968. Mail turnaround time 1-2 days. Criminal PAT goes back to 3/1989. **See details about online access to criminal records at front or back of this chapter.**

Bladen County

Superior-District Court PO Box 2619, Elizabethtown, NC 28337; 910-872-7200; probate phone: 910-872-7202; fax: 910-872-7218; 8:30AM-5PM (EST). *Felony, Misdemeanor, Civil, Eviction, Small Claims, Probate.*
www.nccourts.org/County/Bladen/Default.asp
General Information: Search civil and criminal court calendars at www1.aoc.state.nc.us/www/calendars.html. No adoption, sealed cases, juvenile, sex offenders, mental or expunged records released. Will not fax

documents. Court makes copy: $2.00 1st page, $.25 ea add'l. Certification fee: None; $3.00 if you perform search in person. Only cashiers checks and money orders accepted. No credit cards accepted for record searches. Prepayment required.
Civil Name Search: Access: In person, online. Visitors must perform in person searches themselves. Civil records on computer since 1989, prior on judgment books back to 1896 (fire). Civil PAT goes back to 1989. **See details about online access to civil records at front or back of this chapter.**
Criminal Name Search: Access: Mail, in person, online. Both court and visitors may perform in person name searches. Search fee: $25.00 per name, includes certification. Required to search: name, years to search, DOB. Criminal records computerized from 5/89, on books to 1968. Mail turnaround time 5 days. Criminal PAT goes to 1988. **See details about online access to criminal records at front or back of this chapter.**

Brunswick County

Superior-District Court 310 Goverment Ctr Dr, Unit 1, Attn: Clerk, Bolivia, NC 28422; 910-253-3900; criminal phone: 910-253-3902; civil phone: 910-253-3903; probate phone: 910-253-3904; criminal fax: 910-253-3901; civil fax: 8:30AM-5PM; 8:30AM-5PM (EST). *Felony, Misdemeanor, Civil, Eviction, Small Claims, Probate.*
www.nccourts.org/County/Brunswick/Default.asp
General Information: Search civil and criminal court calendars at www1.aoc.state.nc.us/www/calendars.html. No adoption, sealed cases, juvenile, mental or expunged records. Will fax documents $1.00 1st page, $.25 each add'l page to gov't agencies only. Court makes copy: $2.00 1st page, $.25 ea add'l. Self serve copy: available with "copy key". Certification fee: $3.00 per doc. Payee: Clerk of Court. Business checks accepted. No personal checks or credit cards accepted. Prepayment required. Mail requests: SASE helpful.
Civil Name Search: Access: In person, online. Visitors must perform in person searches themselves. Civil records on computer since 1989, prior on books to 1968. Civil PAT goes back to 1989. **See details about online access to civil records at front or back of this chapter.**
Criminal Name Search: Access: Mail, in person, online. Both court and visitors may perform in person name searches. Search fee: $25.00 per name, includes certification. Criminal records on computer since 1989, prior on microfiche and books to 1968. Mail turnaround time 5 days. Criminal PAT goes back to same as civil. Results include driver's license number. **See details about online access to criminal records at front or back of this chapter.**

Buncombe County

Superior-District Court 60 Court Plaza, Asheville, NC 28801; 828-259-3400; criminal fax: 828-259-3374; civil fax: 8:30AM-5PM; 8:30AM-5PM (EST). *Felony, Misdemeanor, Civil, Eviction, Small Claims, Probate.*
www.nccourts.org/County/Buncombe/Default.asp
General Information: Search civil and criminal court calendars at www1.aoc.state.nc.us/www/calendars.html. No adoption, sealed cases, juvenile, sex offenders, mental or expunged records required. Will not fax out documents. Court makes copy: $2.00 1st page, $.25 ea add'l. Certification fee: $3.00 per page. Payee: Clerk of Court. No personal checks accepted except for law firm filings. No credit cards accepted. Prepayment required. Prepayment required only for background checks. Mail requests: SASE required.
Civil Name Search: Access: Mail, fax, in person, online. Both court and visitors may perform in person name searches. No search fee. Civil records on computer since 1/88; on books or dockets to 1915; judgment books in archives. Mail turnaround time 1 week. Civil PAT goes back to 1988. **See details about online access to civil records at front or back of this chapter.**
Criminal Name Search: Access: Mail, fax, in person, online. Both court and visitors may perform in person name searches. Search fee: $25.00 per name, includes certification. Required to search: name, years to search, DOB. Criminal records on computer since 11/82; on books or dockets to 12/70. Note: Court personnel will assist public with a name search. Mail turnaround time 1 week. Criminal PAT goes back to 12/82. **See details about online access to criminal records at front or back of this chapter.**

Burke County

Superior-District Court PO Box 796, Morganton, NC 28680; 828-433-3200; fax: 828-433-3201; 8AM-5PM (EST). *Felony, Misdemeanor, Civil, Eviction, Small Claims, Probate.*
www.nccourts.org/County/Burke/Default.asp
General Information: Direct connection to court reports: 828-297-6358 or 828-855-0876. Search civil and criminal court calendars at www1.aoc.state.nc.us/www/calendars.html. No adoption, sealed cases, juvenile, sex offenders, mental or expunged records released. Fee to fax out file $3.00 each. Court makes copy: $2.00 1st page, $.25 ea add'l. Certification

fee: $10.00 per doc. Payee: Clerk of Court. Business checks accepted. Prepayment required. Mail requests: SASE required.
Civil Name Search: Access: In person, mail, online. Visitors must perform in person searches themselves. No search fee. Required to search: name, years to search; also helpful: address. Civil records on computer since 10/1988, on index books to 1890s. Civil PAT goes back to 10/1988. **See details about online access to civil records at front or back of this chapter.**
Criminal Name Search: Access: Mail, in person, online. Both court and visitors may perform in person name searches. Search fee: $25.00 per name, includes certification. Required to search: name, years to search, DOB; also helpful: address, SSN. Criminal records on computer since 6/1986, on cards or books back to 1900s. Mail turnaround time 1-2 days. Criminal PAT goes back to 6/1986. **See details about online access to criminal records at front or back of this chapter.**

Cabarrus County

Superior-District Court PO Box 70, 77 Union St South, Concord, NC 28026-0070; 704-262-5500; fax: 704-262-5501; 8:30AM-5PM (EST). *Felony, Misdemeanor, Civil, Eviction, Small Claims, Probate.* www.nccourts.org/County/Cabarrus/Default.asp
General Information: Search includes both indexes, also civil and criminal if requested. Search civil and criminal court calendars at www1.aoc.state.nc.us/www/calendars.html. Estates & Special Proceed phone- 704-786-4137. No adoption, sealed cases, juvenile, sex offenders, mental or expunged records released. Will not fax documents. Court makes copy: $2.00 1st page, $.25 ea add'l. Certification fee: $3.00 per page includes copy fee. Payee: Clerk of Superior Court. Only cashiers checks, cash and money orders accepted. No credit cards accepted. Prepayment required.
Civil Name Search: Access: In person, online. Visitors must perform in person searches themselves. Required to search: name, years to search; also helpful: address. Civil records go back to 1900s; on computer since 2/13/89. Civil PAT goes back to 1989. **See details about online access to civil records at front or back of this chapter.**
Criminal Name Search: Access: Mail, in person, online. Both court and visitors may perform in person name searches. Search fee: $25.00 per name, includes certification. Required to search: name, DOB; also helpful: address, SSN, maiden name. Criminal records go back to 12/70; on computer back to 1/85. Mail turnaround time 2-3 days. Criminal PAT goes back to 1985. **See details about online access to criminal records at front or back of this chapter.**

Caldwell County

Superior-District Court PO Box 1376, Lenoir, NC 28645; criminal phone: 828-759-3502; civil phone: 828-759-3503; fax: 828-759-3501; 8AM-5PM (EST). *Felony, Misdemeanor, Civil, Eviction, Small Claims, Probate.* www.nccourts.org/County/Caldwell/Default.asp
General Information: Search civil and criminal court calendars at www1.aoc.state.nc.us/www/calendars.html. No adoption, sealed cases, juvenile, sex offenders, mental or expunged records released. Fee to fax out file $2.00 1st page; $.25 each add'l. Court makes copy: $2.00 1st page, $.25 ea add'l. Self serve copy: $.25 per page. Certification fee: $3.00. Payee: Clerk of Superior Court. Only cashiers checks and money orders accepted. No credit cards accepted. Prepayment required. Mail requests: SASE required.
Civil Name Search: Access: In person, online. Visitors must perform in person searches themselves. Civil records on computer since 11/1988, prior on books to 1849. Civil PAT goes back to 11/1988. **See details about online access to civil records at front or back of this chapter.**
Criminal Name Search: Access: Mail, in person, online. Both court and visitors may perform in person name searches. Search fee: $25.00 per name, includes certification. Required to search: name. Criminal records computerized from 8/86, prior in books to 1966. Mail turnaround time 1-2 days. Criminal PAT goes back to 8/1986. **See details about online access to criminal records at front or back of this chapter.**

Camden County

Superior-District Court PO Box 219, 117 Hwy 343 North, Camden, NC 27921; 252-331-4871; fax: 252-331-4827; 8AM-5PM (EST). *Felony, Misdemeanor, Civil, Eviction, Small Claims, Probate.* www.nccourts.org/County/Camden/Default.asp
General Information: Search criminal court calendars at www1.aoc.state.nc.us/www/calendars.html. No adoption, sealed cases, juvenile, sex offenders, mental or expunged records released. Will fax documents to local or toll-free number. Court makes copy: $2.00 1st page, $.25 ea add'l. Self serve copy: $.25 per page with Hecon Key.You must acquire a HECON key to use self-serve copier. Certification fee: $3.00. Payee: Clerk of Superior Court. Business checks accepted. No credit cards accepted. Prepayment required. Mail requests: SASE not required.

Civil Name Search: Access: In person, online. Visitors must perform in person searches themselves. Civil records on computer since 11/27/1989, prior on index books to 12/05/1966. Civil PAT goes back to 1989. **See details about online access to civil records at front or back of this chapter.**
Criminal Name Search: Access: Mail, fax, in person, online. Both court and visitors may perform in person name searches. Search fee: $25.00 per name, includes certification. Required to search: name, years to search, DOB. Criminal record index on computer, on index books to 1966. Note: Fax search requests must be prepaid. Mail turnaround time 1-2 days. Criminal PAT goes back to 1990. **See details about online access to criminal records at front or back of this chapter.**

Carteret County

Superior-District Court - Carteret County 300 Courthouse Square, Beaufort, NC 28516; 252-504-4400; criminal phone: 252-504-4444; civil phone: 252-504-4422; fax: 252-504-4401; 8AM-5PM (EST). *Felony, Misdemeanor, Civil, Eviction, Small Claims, Probate.* www.nccourts.org/County/Carteret/
General Information: No adoption, sealed cases, juvenile, sex offenders, mental or expunged records released. Will fax out docs no add'l fee. Court makes copy: $2.00 1st page, $.25 ea add'l. Certification fee: None; $3.00 if you perform search in person. Payee: Clerk of Superior Court. Attorney business checks accepted. No credit cards accepted. Prepayment required.
Civil Name Search: Access: In person, online. Visitors must perform in person searches themselves. Civil records on computer back to 1988, prior on books to 1800s. Note: This court will not perform a name search of the civil index. Civil PAT goes back to 1988. **See details about online access to civil records at front or back of this chapter.**
Criminal Name Search: Access: Mail, fax, in person, online. Visitors must perform in person searches themselves. Search fee: $25.00 per name, includes certification. Required to search: name, years to search; also helpful: address, DOB, SSN. Criminal records computerized from 1/87. Mail turnaround time 1 week. Criminal PAT goes back to 1987. **See details about online access to criminal records at front or back of this chapter.**

Caswell County

Superior-District Court PO Drawer 790, 139 E Church St, Yanceyville, NC 27379; 336-694-4171; fax: 336-694-7338; 8AM-5PM (EST). *Felony, Misdemeanor, Civil, Eviction, Small Claims, Probate.* www.nccourts.org/County/Caswell/Default.asp
General Information: No adoption, sealed cases, juvenile, mental or expunged records released. Will fax documents $2.00 per page. Court makes copy: $2.00 1st page, $.25 ea add'l. Self serve copy: $.25 per page. Certification fee: $3.00 per doc. Payee: Clerk of Superior Court. Business checks accepted. No credit cards accepted. Prepayment required. Mail requests: SASE required for criminal.
Civil Name Search: Access: In person, online. Visitors must perform in person searches themselves. Civil records on computer from 3/89 to present, on index books back to 1970, prior records in civil summons book. Civil PAT goes back to 3/1989. **See details about online access to civil records at front or back of this chapter.**
Criminal Name Search: Access: Mail, in person, online. Both court and visitors may perform in person name searches. Search fee: $25.00 per name, includes certification. Required to search: name, years to search, DOB; also helpful: address. Criminal records on computer since 5/88, prior on books and cards. Mail turnaround time 1-2 days. Criminal PAT goes back to 5/18/1988. **See details about online access to criminal records at front or back of this chapter.**

Catawba County

Superior-District Court PO Box 790, Newton, NC 28658; 828-466-6100; ; 8AM-5PM (EST). *Felony, Misdemeanor, Civil, Eviction, Small Claims, Probate.* www.catawbacountync.gov/state/clerk/default.asp
General Information: No adoption, sealed cases, juvenile, sex offenders, mental or expunged records released. Will not fax documents. Court makes copy: $2.00 1st page, $.25 ea add'l. Self serve copy: with Copy Key. Certification fee: $3.00 includes copies, but if over $3.00 worth of copies, add on add'l copy fee. Payee: Clerk of Court. Only cashiers checks and money orders accepted. No credit cards accepted. Prepayment required. Mail requests: SASE required for criminal.
Civil Name Search: Access: In person, online. Visitors must perform in person searches themselves. Civil records on computer since 3/1988, prior on books. Civil PAT goes back to 1988. Terminal results also show SSNs. **See details about online access to civil records at front or back of this chapter.**
Criminal Name Search: Access: Mail, in person, online. Both court and visitors may perform in person name searches. Search fee: $25.00 per name, includes certification. Required to search: name, years to search, DOB. Criminal records on computer since 4/85, on books to 1966, archived prior.

Mail turnaround time 5 days. Criminal PAT goes back to 4/1985. Terminal results include SSN. **See details about online access to criminal records at front or back of this chapter.**

Chatham County

Superior-District Court PO Box 369, 12 East St, Pittsboro, NC 27312; 919-542-3240; fax: 919-542-1402; 8:30AM-5PM (EST). *Felony, Misdemeanor, Civil, Eviction, Small Claims, Probate.*
www.nccourts.org/County/Chatham/Default.asp
General Information: No adoption, sealed cases, juvenile, sex offenders, mental or expunged records released. Will fax documents $1.00 1st page, $.25 each add'l page. Court makes copy: $2.00 1st page, $.25 ea add'l. Certification fee: $3.00. Will not certify civil. Payee: Clerk of Superior Court. No personal checks or credit cards accepted. Prepayment required. Mail requests: SASE required.
Civil Name Search: Access: In person, online. Both court and visitors may perform in person name searches. No search fee. Civil records on computer since 4/1989, prior on books, archived 1968 back in Raleigh. Civil PAT goes back to 4/1989. **See details about online access to civil records at front or back of this chapter.**
Criminal Name Search: Access: Mail, in person, online. Both court and visitors may perform in person name searches. Search fee: $25.00 per name, includes certification. Required to search: name, years to search; also helpful: address, DOB, SSN. Criminal records on computer since 7/1987, prior on books or cards to 1968. Mail turnaround time 1 day. Criminal PAT goes back to 7/1987. **See details about online access to criminal records at front or back of this chapter.**

Cherokee County

Superior-District Court 75 Peachtree St, Rm 201, Murphy, NC 28906; 828-837-2522; fax: 828-837-8178; 8AM-5PM (EST). *Felony, Misdemeanor, Civil, Eviction, Small Claims, Probate.*
www.nccourts.org/County/Cherokee/Default.asp
General Information: No adoption, sealed cases, juvenile or mental records released. Will not fax out documents. Court makes copy: $2.00 1st page, $.25 ea add'l. No certification fee . Payee: Clerk of Superior Court. No personal checks or credit cards accepted. Prepayment required. Mail requests: SASE required.
Civil Name Search: Access: Phone, fax, mail, in person, online. Visitors must perform in person searches themselves. No search fee. Required to search: name, years to search, address. Civil records on computer since 5/89, on index books to 1867. Note: Will not do title searches. Mail turnaround time 1-2 days. Public use terminal has civil records back to 5/1989. **See details about online access to civil records at front or back of this chapter.**
Criminal Name Search: Access: Mail, in person, online. Only the court performs in person name searches; visitors may not. Search fee: $25.00 per name, includes certification. Required to search: name, years to search, DOB. Criminal records on computer since 5/89, index cards to 1985, index books to 1966. Note: Criminal calendars online at www1.aoc.state.nc.us/www/calendars/Contacts.html. Mail turnaround time 1-2 days. **See details about online access to criminal records at front or back of this chapter.**

Chowan County

Superior-District Court Clerk of Superior Ct; N.C. Courier Box 106319, PO Box 588, Edenton, NC 27932; 252-368-5000; fax: 252-368-5001; 9AM-5PM (EST). *Felony, Misdemeanor, Civil, Eviction, Small Claims, Probate.* www.nccourts.org/County/Chowan/Default.asp
General Information: Search criminal court calendars at www1.aoc.state.nc.us/www/calendars.html. Probate fax is same as main fax number. No adoption, sealed cases, juvenile, sex offenders, mental or expunged records released. Will not fax documents. Court makes copy: $2.00 1st page, $.25 ea add'l. Certification fee: $3.00; exemplification fee- $10.00. Payee: Clerk of Superior Court. Only cashiers checks and money orders accepted. No credit cards accepted. Prepayment required. Mail requests: SASE required for criminal.
Civil Name Search: Access: In person, online. Visitors must perform in person searches themselves. Required to search: name, years to search; also helpful: address. Civil records on computer since 1990, prior on books to 1800s. Civil PAT goes back to 1990. **See details about online access to civil records at front or back of this chapter.**
Criminal Name Search: Access: Mail, in person, online. Both court and visitors may perform in person name searches. Search fee: $25.00 per name, includes certification. Required to search: name, years to search, DOB; also helpful: address, SSN. Criminal records computerized from 1/90, prior as civil. Mail turnaround time 3-5 days. Criminal PAT goes back to same as civil. Terminal results include SSN. **See details about online access to criminal records at front or back of this chapter.**

Clay County

Superior-District Court 261 Courthouse Dr, Ste#1, Hayesville, NC 28904; 828-389-8334; fax: 828-389-3329; 8:30AM-5PM (EST). *Felony, Misdemeanor, Civil, Eviction, Small Claims, Probate.*
www.nccourts.org/County/Clay/Default.asp
General Information: Search civil and criminal court calendars, etc. at www1.aoc.state.nc.us/www/calendars.html. No adoption, sealed cases, juvenile, sex offenders, mental or expunged records released. Fee to fax document $.25 per page. Court makes copy: $2.00 1st page, $.25 ea add'l. Self serve copy: $.25 per page. Certification fee: $3.00 per doc. Payee: Clerk of Court. Business checks accepted. No credit cards accepted. Prepayment required. Mail requests: SASE required for criminal.
Civil Name Search: Access: In person, online. Visitors must perform in person searches themselves. Required to search: name, years to search; also helpful: address. Civil records on computer since 1989, on books since 1888. Public use terminal has civil records back to 1989. **See details about online access to civil records at front or back of this chapter.**
Criminal Name Search: Access: Mail, in person, online. Only the court performs in person name searches; visitors may not. Search fee: $25.00 per name, includes certification. Required to search: name, years to search, DOB; also helpful: address, SSN. Criminal records computerized from 1989, on books since 1888. Mail turnaround time 1 days. **See details about online access to criminal records at front or back of this chapter.**

Cleveland County

Superior-District Court 100 Justice Pl, Shelby, NC 28150; 704-484-4862; fax: 704-480-5487; 8:30AM-5PM (EST). *Felony, Misdemeanor, Civil, Eviction, Small Claims, Probate.*
www.nccourts.org/County/Cleveland/Default.asp
General Information: No adoption, sealed cases, juvenile, sex offenders, mental or expunged records released. Will not fax out documents. Court makes copy: $2.00 1st page, $.25 ea add'l. Certification fee: $3.00; Exemplification fee- $10.00. Payee: Clerk of Superior Court. No out-of-state or personal checks accepted. Certified funds, money orders and bank checks accepted. No credit cards accepted. Prepayment required. Mail requests: SASE requested for criminal.
Civil Name Search: Access: In person, online. Visitors must perform in person searches themselves. Civil records on computer since 1988, books to 1968, archived prior. Civil PAT goes back to 1988. **See details about online access to civil records at front or back of this chapter.**
Criminal Name Search: Access: Mail, in person, online. Both court and visitors may perform in person name searches. Search fee: $25.00 per name, includes certification. Required to search: name, years to search, DOB; also helpful: address, SSN. Criminal records on computer since 6/86, on books to 1972, archived prior. Mail turnaround time 1-2 days. Criminal PAT goes back to 6/1988. **See details about online access to criminal records at front or back of this chapter.**

Columbus County

Superior-District Court PO Box 1587, Whiteville, NC 28472; 910-641-4400; fax: 910-641-4401; 8AM-5PM (EST). *Felony, Misdemeanor, Civil, Eviction, Small Claims, Probate.*
www.nccourts.org/County/Columbus/Default.asp
General Information: No adoption, sealed, juvenile, sex offender, mental, expunged or dismissed. Will not fax documents. Court makes copy: $2.00 per doc, $.25 ea add'l pg. Self serve copy: $.25 per page. Certification fee: $3.00. Payee: Clerk of Superior Court. Only cashiers checks and money orders accepted. No credit cards accepted. Prepayment required. Mail requests: SASE required.
Civil Name Search: Access: Mail, fax, in person, online. Visitors must perform in person searches themselves. No search fee. Required to search: name, years to search; also helpful: address. Civil records on computer from 1989, prior on books to 1968. Civil PAT goes back to 5/1989. **See details about online access to civil records at front or back of this chapter.**
Criminal Name Search: Access: Mail, fax, in person, online. Both court and visitors may perform in person name searches. Search fee: $25.00 per name, includes certification. Required to search: name, years to search, DOB; also helpful: address, SSN. Criminal records computerized from 1987, prior on books or cards to 1968. Mail turnaround time 2-5 days. Criminal PAT goes back to 6/1987. **See details about online access to criminal records at front or back of this chapter.**

Craven County

Superior-District Court PO Box 1187, New Bern, NC 28563; 252-639-3000; fax: 252-639-3131; 8AM-5PM (EST). *Felony, Misdemeanor, Civil, Eviction, Small Claims, Probate.*
www.nccourts.org/County/Craven/Default.asp
General Information: No adoption, sealed cases, juvenile, sex offenders, mental, expunged, or dismissed. $1.60 per page. Court makes copy: $2.00 1st page, $.25 ea add'l. Self serve copy: $.25 per page. Certification fee: None;

$3.00 if you perform search in person. Payee: Clerk of Superior Court. Only cashiers checks and money orders accepted. No credit cards accepted. Prepayment required. Mail requests: SASE required.

Civil Name Search: Access: In person, online. Visitors must perform in person searches themselves. Required to search: name, years to search; also helpful: address. Civil records on computer from 10/88, prior to 1968 are archived. Mail n/a. Civil PAT goes back to 1997. **See details about online access to civil records at front or back of this chapter.**

Criminal Name Search: Access: Mail, in person, online. Both court and visitors may perform in person name searches. Search fee: $25.00 per name, includes certification. Required to search: name, years to search, DOB; also helpful: address, SSN. Criminal records on computer since 1/87, prior on books and cards to 1968. Mail turnaround time 1-2 days. Criminal PAT goes back to 1988. **See details about online access to criminal records at front or back of this chapter.**

Cumberland County

Superior-District Court PO Box 363, 117 Dick St, Fayetteville, NC 28302; 910-678-2902; criminal phone: 910-678-2906; civil phone: 910-678-2909; probate phone: 910-678-2904; fax: 910-678-2989; 8AM-5PM (EST). *Felony, Misdemeanor, Civil, Eviction, Small Claims, Probate.*
www.aoc.state.nc.us/district12/

General Information: Search court calendars at www1.aoc.state.nc.us/www/calendars.html. No adoption, sealed cases, juvenile, sex offenders, mental or expunged records released. Court makes copy: $2.00 1st page, $.25 ea add'l. Certification fee: $3.00 for 1st 5 pages. Cert fee includes copies. Payee: Clerk of Superior Court. No personal checks accepted, must be money order or certified. No credit cards accepted. Prepayment required.

Civil Name Search: Access: Mail, in person, online. Both court and visitors may perform in person name searches. No search fee. Required to search: name, years to search; also helpful: address. Civil records on computer since 1988, books back to 1956. Mail turnaround time 5-10 days. Civil PAT goes back to 7/1988. **See details about online access to civil records at front or back of this chapter.**

Criminal Name Search: Access: Mail, in person, online. Both court and visitors may perform in person name searches. Search fee: $25.00 per name, includes certification. Required to search: name, years to search; also helpful: address, DOB, SSN. Criminal records on computer since 5/82, books and microfilm to 1920s. Mail turnaround time 2 weeks. Criminal PAT goes back to 1982. **See details about online access to criminal records at front or back of this chapter.**

Currituck County

Superior-District Court PO Box 175, Currituck, NC 27929; 252-232-6200; fax: 252-232-6201; 8:30AM-5PM (EST). *Felony, Misdemeanor, Civil, Eviction, Small Claims, Probate.*
www.nccourts.org/County/Currituck/Default.asp

General Information: Search criminal court calendars at www1.aoc.state.nc.us/www/calendars.html. No adoption, sealed cases, juvenile, sex offenders, mental or expunged records released. Court makes copy: $2.00 1st page, $.25 ea add'l. Self serve copy: $.25 per page. Certification fee: $3.00. Payee: Clerk of Superior Court. Only cashiers checks and money orders accepted. No credit cards accepted. Prepayment required. Mail requests: SASE required.

Civil Name Search: Access: In person, online. Visitors must perform in person searches themselves. Civil records on computer back to 1990, books to 1968, prior archived. Civil PAT goes back to 1990. **See details about online access to civil records at front or back of this chapter.**

Criminal Name Search: Access: Mail, in person, online. Both court and visitors may perform in person name searches. Search fee: $25.00 per name, includes certification. Required to search: name, years to search, DOB, signed release. Criminal records computerized from 11/27/89, books to 1968, prior archived. Note: Mail search requests must be on letterhead and include signed release. Mail turnaround time 1 day. Criminal PAT goes back to same as civil. **See details about online access to criminal records at front or back of this chapter.**

Dare County

Superior-District Court PO Box 1849, 962 Marshall Collins Dr, Manteo, NC 27954; 252-475-9100; fax: 252-473-1620; 8AM-5PM (EST). *Felony, Misdemeanor, Civil, Eviction, Small Claims, Probate.*
www.nccourts.org/County/Dare/Default.asp

General Information: No adoption, sealed cases, juvenile, sex offenders, mental or expunged records released. Fee to fax document $.25 per page. Court makes copy: $2.00 1st page, $.25 ea add'l. Self serve copy: $.25 per page. Certification fee: $3.00 per doc. Payee: Superior District Court. Business checks accepted. No personal checks accepted. Prepayment required.

Civil Name Search: Access: In person, online. Visitors must perform in

person searches themselves. Required to search: name, years to search; also helpful: address, DOB. Civil records on computer since 1985, on books to 1966. Civil PAT goes back to 1987. **See details about online access to civil records at front or back of this chapter.**

Criminal Name Search: Access: Mail, in person, online. Both court and visitors may perform in person name searches. Search fee: $25.00 per name, includes certification. Required to search: name, years to search, DOB. Criminal records on computer since 1987, on books and cards to 1966. Mail turnaround time 2 days. Criminal PAT goes back to 1989. **See details about online access to criminal records at front or back of this chapter.**

Davidson County

Superior-District Court PO Box 1064, 110 W Center St, Lexington, NC 27293-1064; 336-242-6701; criminal phone: x1; civil phone: x2; probate phone: x3; fax: 336-242-6759; 8AM-5PM (EST). *Felony, Misdemeanor, Civil, Eviction, Small Claims, Probate.*
www.nccourts.org/County/Davidson/Default.asp

General Information: There is also a 2nd court location at 22 Randolph St in Thomasville, 336-474-3185 but records and mailing address here in Lexington. No adoption, sealed cases, juvenile, sex offenders, mental or expunged records released. Will not fax documents. Court makes copy: $2.00 1st page, $.25 ea add'l. Certification fee: $3.00 per page. Payee: Clerk of Superior Court. Business checks accepted, if pre-approved. No credit cards accepted. Prepayment required. Mail requests: SASE requested for criminal.

Civil Name Search: Access: Mail, in person, online. Visitors must perform in person searches themselves. Required to search: name, years to search; also helpful: address. Civil records on computer since 5/16/1988, prior on books. Civil PAT goes back to 1985. **See details about online access to civil records at front or back of this chapter.** Civil and criminal indexes are two separate searches.

Criminal Name Search: Access: Mail, in person, online. Both court and visitors may perform in person name searches. Search fee: $25.00 per name, includes certification. Required to search: name, DOB, years to search; also helpful: address, SSN. Criminal records on computer since 10/1985, on books and cards to 1952. Mail turnaround time 2-3 days. Criminal PAT goes back to same as civil. **See details about online access to criminal records at front or back of this chapter.**

Davie County

Superior-District Court 140 S Main St, Mocksville, NC 27028; 336-751-3507; criminal phone: 336-751-3508; probate phone: 336-751-3508; fax: 336-751-4720; 8:30AM-5PM (EST). *Felony, Misdemeanor, Civil, Eviction, Small Claims, Probate.*
www.nccourts.org/County/Davie/Default.asp

General Information: No adoption, sealed cases, juvenile, sex offenders, mental or expunged records released. Court makes copy: $2.00 1st page, $.25 ea add'l. Self serve copy: same. Certification fee: $3.00. Payee: Clerk of Superior Court. No personal checks or credit cards accepted. Prepayment required. Mail requests: SASE required for criminal.

Civil Name Search: Access: In person, online. Visitors must perform in person searches themselves. Civil records on computer back to 10/89; on books to 1970. Civil PAT goes back to 11/1989. **See details about online access to civil records at front or back of this chapter.**

Criminal Name Search: Access: Mail, in person, online. Both court and visitors may perform in person name searches. Search fee: $25.00 per name, includes certification. Required to search: name, years to search, DOB, signed release. Criminal records computerized from 11/89. Mail turnaround time 5 days. Criminal PAT goes back to same as civil. **See details about online access to criminal records at front or back of this chapter.**

Duplin County

Superior-District Court PO Box 189, 112 Duplin St, Kenansville, NC 28349; 910-275-7000; fax: 910-275-7001; 8AM-5PM (EST). *Felony, Misdemeanor, Civil, Eviction, Small Claims, Probate.*
www.nccourts.org/County/Duplin/Default.asp

General Information: No adoption, sealed cases, juvenile, sex offenders, mental or expunged records released. Will not fax documents. Court makes copy: $2.00 1st page, $.25 ea add'l. Certification fee: $3.00. Payee: Clerk of Superior Court. No personal checks. No credit cards accepted. Prepayment required. Mail requests: SASE required for criminal.

Civil Name Search: Access: In person, online. Visitors must perform in person searches themselves. Civil records on computer since 1989, prior on books to early 1900s. Note: Court personnel will not perform name searches for the public. Civil PAT goes back to 1989. **See details about online access to civil records at front or back of this chapter.**

Criminal Name Search: Access: In person, online. Visitors must perform in person searches themselves. Required to search: name, years to search, DOB. Criminal records on computer since 5/1988, on cards and books to 1927. Note: Court personnel will not perform name searches for the public. Criminal PAT goes back to 5/1988. **See details about online access to criminal records at front or back of this chapter.**

Durham County

Superior-District Court 201 E Main St, Durham, NC 27701; criminal phone: 919-564-7270; civil phone: 919-564-7050; fax: 919-560-3341; 8:30AM-5PM (EST). *Felony, Misdemeanor, Civil, Eviction, Small Claims, Probate.* www.nccourts.org/County/Durham/Default.asp

General Information: No adoption, sealed cases, juvenile, sex offenders, mental or expunged records released. Will not fax documents. Court makes copy: $2.00 1st page, $.25 ea add'l. Certification fee: $3.00. Payee: Clerk of Superior Court. Only cashiers checks and money orders accepted. No credit cards accepted. Prepayment required. Mail requests: SASE required.

Civil Name Search: Access: Mail, in person, online. Visitors must perform in person searches themselves. No search fee. Required to search: name, years to search; also helpful: address. Civil records computerized since 1988, on books to late 1800s. Civil PAT goes back to 1988. **See details about online access to civil records at front or back of this chapter.**

Criminal Name Search: Access: Mail, in person, online. Both court and visitors may perform in person name searches. Search fee: $25.00 per name, includes certification. Required to search: name, years to search, DOB; also helpful: address. Criminal records on microfiche since 1982, prior on books to 1979. There is no fee for a simple computer printout. Mail turnaround time 3-4 days. Criminal PAT goes back to 1980s. **See details about online access to criminal records at front or back of this chapter.**

Edgecombe County

Superior-District Court PO Drawer 9, 301 St Andrews St, Tarboro, NC 27886; 252-824-3200; criminal phone: 252-823-2056; civil phone: 252-823-6161; criminal fax: 252-824-3201; civil fax: 8AM-5PM; 8AM-5PM (EST). *Felony, Misdemeanor, Civil, Eviction, Small Claims, Probate.* www.nccourts.org/County/Edgecombe/Default.asp

General Information: No adoption, sealed cases, juvenile, sex offenders, mental or expunged records required. Court makes copy: $2.00 1st page, $.25 ea add'l. Certification fee: $3.00. Payee: Clerk of Superior Court. Only certified check or money order accepted. No credit cards accepted. Prepayment required. Mail requests: SASE helpful.

Civil Name Search: Access: In person, online. Visitors must perform in person searches themselves. Required to search: name, years to search, address. Civil records on computer since 1988. Civil PAT goes back to 1988. **See details about online access to civil records at front or back of this chapter.**

Criminal Name Search: Access: Mail, in person, online. Both court and visitors may perform in person name searches. Search fee: $25.00 per name, includes certification. Required to search: name, DOB; also helpful: address, former names. Criminal records on computer since 4/87, on books and cards to 1900s. Mail turnaround time 1-2 days. Criminal PAT goes back to 1987. **See details about online access to criminal records at front or back of this chapter.**

Forsyth County

Superior-District Court PO Box 20099, 200 N Main, Hall of Justice, Winston Salem, NC 27120-0099; 336-761-2250; criminal phone: 336-761-2366; civil phone: 336-761-2340; probate phone: 336-761-2470; fax: 336-761-2018; 8AM-5PM (EST). *Felony, Misdemeanor, Civil, Eviction, Small Claims, Probate.* www.nccourts.org/County/Forsyth/Default.asp

General Information: Civil index is searched separately from the criminal index. No adoption, sealed cases, juvenile, sex offenders, mental or expunged records released. Will not fax documents. Court makes copy: $2.00 1st page, $.25 ea add'l. Certification fee: $3.00. Payee: Clerk of Superior Court. Business checks accepted. No credit cards accepted. Prepayment required. Mail requests: SASE required.

Civil Name Search: Access: In person, online. Both court and visitors may perform in person name searches. Search fee: $25.00 per name, includes certification. Civil records on computer since 4/1989, prior on books to 1968, on microfiche prior. Mail turnaround time 1-2 days. Civil PAT goes back to 4/1989. **See details about online access to civil records at front or back of this chapter.**

Criminal Name Search: Access: Mail, in person, online. Both court and visitors may perform in person name searches. Search fee: $25.00 per name, includes certification. Required to search: DOB. Criminal records on computer since 10/1983, prior on books to 1968, on microfiche prior. Mail turnaround time 1-2 days. Criminal PAT goes back to 10/1983. **See details about online access to criminal records at front or back of this chapter.**

Franklin County

Superior-District Court 102 S Main St, Louisburg, NC 27549; 919-497-4200; fax: 919-497-4201; 8:30AM-5PM (EST). *Felony, Misdemeanor, Civil, Eviction, Small Claims, Probate.* www.nccourts.org/County/Franklin/Default.asp

General Information: No adoption, sealed cases, juvenile, mental or expunged records released. Will not fax documents. Court makes copy: $2.00 1st page, $.25 ea add'l. Self serve copy: $.25 per page. Certification fee: $3.00; for exemplification fee $10.00. Payee: Clerk of Superior Court. No personal checks or credit cards accepted. Prepayment required. Mail requests: SASE requested.

Civil Name Search: Access: Mail, in person, online. Visitors must perform in person searches themselves. No search fee. Required to search: name, years to search; also helpful: address. Civil records on computer since 6/1989, prior on books. Mail turnaround time 1-2 days. Civil PAT goes back to 1997. **See details about online access to civil records at front or back of this chapter.**

Criminal Name Search: Access: Mail, in person, online. Both court and visitors may perform in person name searches. Search fee: $25.00 per name, includes certification. Required to search: name, years to search, DOB; also helpful: address. Criminal records on computer since 1980, on index books back to 1968. Mail turnaround time 1-2 days. Criminal PAT goes back to 1980. **See details about online access to criminal records at front or back of this chapter.**

Gaston County

Superior-District Court Gaston County Court House, 325 N Marietta St. #1004, Gastonia, NC 28052-2331; 704-852-3100; fax: 704-852-3267; 8:30AM-5PM (EST). *Felony, Misdemeanor, Civil, Eviction, Small Claims, Probate.* www.nccourts.org/County/Gaston/Default.asp

General Information: No adoption, sealed cases, juvenile, mental or expunged records released. Will not fax documents. Court makes copy: $2.00 1st page, $.25 ea add'l. Certification fee: $3.00. Exemplification of records is $10.00. No out-of-state checks accepted. No credit cards accepted. Prepayment required. Mail requests: SASE required.

Civil Name Search: Access: In person, online. Visitors must perform in person searches themselves. Required to search: name, years to search; also helpful: address. Civil records on computer since 1988, prior on books to 1891. Civil PAT goes back to 1988. **See details about online access to civil records at front or back of this chapter.**

Criminal Name Search: Access: Mail, in person, online. Both court and visitors may perform in person name searches. Search fee: $25.00 per name, includes certification. Required to search: name, address, DOB; also helpful: years to search, SSN. Criminal records on criminal terminal from 1/83, on books and microfilm to 1973. Mail turnaround time 1-2 days. Criminal PAT goes back to 1983. **See details about online access to criminal records at front or back of this chapter.**

Gates County

Superior-District Court PO Box 31, Gatesville, NC 27938; 252-357-1365; fax: 252-357-1047; 8:30AM-5PM (EST). *Felony, Misdemeanor, Civil, Eviction, Small Claims, Probate.* www.nccourts.org/County/Gates/Default.asp

General Information: No adoption, sealed cases, juvenile, sex offenders, mental or expunged records released. Court makes copy: $2.00 1st page, $.25 ea add'l. Self serve copy: $.25 per page. Certification fee: $3.00 per doc. Payee: Clerk of Superior Court. Business checks accepted. No credit cards accepted. Prepayment required. SASE required for mail return of any copies.

Civil Name Search: Access: In person, online. Visitors must perform in person searches themselves. Required to search: name, years to search; also helpful: address. Civil records on computer since 1990, prior on books to 1966. Civil PAT goes back to 1989. **See details about online access to civil records at front or back of this chapter.**

Criminal Name Search: Access: Mail, in person, online. Both court and visitors may perform in person name searches. Search fee: $25.00 per name, includes certification. Required to search: name, years to search, DOB; also helpful: address, SSN. Criminal records on computer since 1990, prior on books to 1966. Mail turnaround time 1-2 days. Criminal PAT goes back to 1990. **See details about online access to criminal records at front or back of this chapter.**

Graham County

Superior-District Court PO Box 1179, Robbinsville, NC 28771; 828-479-7986; criminal phone: X7975; civil phone: X7973; fax: 828-479-6417; 8AM-5PM (EST). *Felony, Misdemeanor, Civil, Eviction, Small Claims, Probate.* www.nccourts.org/County/Graham/Default.asp

General Information: No adoption, sealed cases, juvenile, sex offenders, mental or expunged records released. Will fax documents to local or toll-free number. Court makes copy: $2.00 1st page, $.25 ea add'l. Self serve copy: same. Certification fee: $3.00. Payee: Clerk of Superior Court. Only cashiers checks and money orders accepted. No credit cards accepted. Prepayment required. Mail requests: SASE required for criminal.

Civil Name Search: Access: In person, online. Visitors must perform in person searches themselves. Civil records on computer since 1989, on books since 1920s. Civil PAT goes back to 1989. **See details about online access to civil records at front or back of this chapter.**

Criminal Name Search: Access: Mail, in person, online. Both court and visitors may perform in person name searches. Search fee: $25.00 per name, includes certification. Required to search: name, years to search; also helpful: address, DOB, SSN. Criminal records on computer since 1984, on books to 1920s. Mail turnaround time 3-5 days. Criminal PAT goes back to 1984. **See details about online access to criminal records at front or back of this chapter.**

Granville County

Superior-District Court 101 Main St, Courthouse, Oxford, NC 27565; 919-690-4800; fax: 919-690-4801; 8:30AM-5PM (EST). *Felony, Misdemeanor, Civil, Eviction, Small Claims, Probate.*
www.nccourts.org/County/Granville/Default.asp

General Information: No adoption, sealed cases, juvenile, mental or expunged records released. Will not fax documents. Court makes copy: $2.00 1st page, $.25 ea add'l. Certification fee: $3.00. Payee: Clerk of Superior Court. No personal checks. Money order or cash only. No credit cards accepted. Prepayment required. Mail requests: SASE helpful.

Civil Name Search: Access: In person, online. Both court and visitors may perform in person name searches. No search fee. Required to search: name, years to search; also helpful: address. Civil records on computer since 6/12/1989, on books & nicer film to 1968, prior files destroyed. Civil PAT goes back to 6/1989. **See details about online access to civil records at front or back of this chapter.**

Criminal Name Search: Access: Mail, in person, online. Both court and visitors may perform in person name searches. Search fee: $25.00 per name, includes certification. Required to search: name, years to search, DOB; also helpful: address. Criminal records on computer since 2/29/1988, prior on books on cards to 1968. Mail turnaround time 1 day. Criminal PAT goes back to 3/1988. **See details about online access to criminal records at front or back of this chapter.**

Greene County

Superior-District Court PO Box 675, Snow Hill, NC 28580; 252-747-3505; fax: 252-747-2700; 8AM-5PM (EST). *Felony, Misdemeanor, Civil, Eviction, Small Claims, Probate.*
www.nccourts.org/County/Greene/Default.asp

General Information: Probate fax is same as main fax number. No adoption, sealed cases, juvenile, sex offenders, mental or expunged records released. Will not fax out documents. Court makes copy: $2.00 1st page, $.25 ea add'l. Self serve copy: $.25 per page. Certification fee: $3.00 if you perform search in person. Payee: Clerk of Superior Court. Business checks accepted. No credit cards accepted. Prepayment required.

Civil Name Search: Access: In person, online. Both court and visitors may perform in person name searches. No search fee. Required to search: name, years to search; also helpful: address. Civil records on computer since 10/1989. Civil PAT goes back to 1986, can vary - all non-confidential records are viewable. **See details about online access to civil records at front or back of this chapter.**

Criminal Name Search: Access: Mail, in person, online. Both court and visitors may perform in person name searches. Search fee: $25.00 per name, includes certification. Required to search: name, years to search; also helpful: address, DOB, SSN. Criminal records on computer since 10/1989, prior on books to 1968. Mail turnaround time 1-2 days. Criminal PAT goes back to 1989. **See details about online access to criminal records at front or back of this chapter.**

Guilford County

Superior-District Court PO Box 3008, 201 S Eugene St, Greensboro, NC 27402; 336-412-7997; criminal phone: 336-412-7444; civil phone: 336-412-7400; fax: 336-412-7302; 8:30AM-5PM (EST). *Felony, Misdemeanor, Civil, Eviction, Small Claims, Probate.*
www.nccourts.org/County/Guilford/Default.asp

General Information: No adoption, sealed cases, juvenile, sex offenders, mental or expunged records released. Will not fax documents. Court makes copy: $2.00 1st page, $.25 ea add'l. Certification fee: $3.00; Exemplified copy $10.00. Payee: Clerk of Superior Court. Only cashiers checks and money orders accepted. No credit cards accepted. Prepayment required. Mail requests: SASE required for criminal.

Civil Name Search: Access: In person, online. Visitors must perform in person searches themselves. Required to search: name, years to search; also helpful: address. Civil records on computer since 9/88, on books to late 1800s. Civil PAT goes back to 9/1988. **See details about online access to civil records at front or back of this chapter.**

Criminal Name Search: Access: Mail, in person, online. Both court and visitors may perform in person name searches. Search fee: $25.00 per name, includes certification. Required to search: name, years to search, DOB; also helpful: address, full name. Criminal records on computer since 5/83, on cards and books to late 1800s. Mail turnaround time 1 week. Criminal PAT

goes back to 5/1983. **See details about online access to criminal records at front or back of this chapter.**

Halifax County

Superior-District Court PO Box 66, 257 Ferrell Lane, Halifax, NC 27839; 252-593-3000; fax: 252-593-3001; 8:15AM-5:15PM crim; to 5PM civil (EST). *Felony, Misdemeanor, Civil, Eviction, Small Claims, Probate.*
www.nccourts.org/County/Halifax/Courthouse/Default.asp

General Information: No adoption, sealed cases, juvenile, sex offenders, mental or expunged records released. Will fax documents $2.00 1st page, $.25 each add'l page. Court makes copy: $2.00 1st page, $.25 ea add'l. Self serve copy: $.25 per page from the public terminal, uncertified; public key required. Certification fee: $3.00 per doc; exemplification- $10.00. Payee: Clerk of Superior Court. No attorney checks accepted. No credit cards accepted. Prepayment required.

Civil Name Search: Access: In person, online. Both court and visitors may perform in person name searches. No search fee. Required to search: name, years to search; also helpful: address. Civil records on computer since 1988, on books to 1968, prior archived. Note: Visitors use only the public access terminal for civil searching. Civil PAT goes back to 1988. **See details about online access to civil records at front or back of this chapter.**

Criminal Name Search: Access: Mail, in person, online. Both court and visitors may perform in person name searches. Search fee: $25.00 per name, includes certification. Required to search: name, years to search; also helpful: address, DOB, SSN. Criminal records on computer since 9/1987, on books to 1968, prior archived. Note: There is no fee for a simple printout. Mail turnaround time 1-2 days. Criminal PAT goes back to 1987. **See details about online access to criminal records at front or back of this chapter.**

Harnett County

Superior-District Court 301 W Cornelius Harnett Blvd, Ste 100, Lillington, NC 27546; 910-814-4600; criminal phone: 910-814-4601; civil phone: 910-814-4602; probate phone: 910-814-4603; fax: 910-814-4560; 8:30AM-5PM (EST). *Felony, Misdemeanor, Civil, Eviction, Small Claims, Probate.*
www.nccourts.org/County/Harnett/Default.asp

General Information: No adoption, sealed cases, juvenile, mental or expunged records released. Will fax documents $2.00 1st page, $.25 each add'l. Court makes copy: $2.00 1st page, $.25 ea add'l. Certification fee: $3.00 plus copy fee; exemplification fee $10.00 plus copy fee. Payee: Clerk of Superior Court. Cash, cashiers checks and money orders accepted. No credit cards accepted. Prepayment required. Mail requests: SASE required for mail returns of criminal results.

Civil Name Search: Access: In person, online. Visitors must perform in person searches themselves. Required to search: name, years to search; also helpful: address. Civil records on computer since 4/17/1989, prior on books from 1938. Civil PAT goes back to 4/1989. Results include case name. **See details about online access to civil records at front or back of this chapter.**

Criminal Name Search: Access: Mail, in person, online. Both court and visitors may perform in person name searches. Search fee: $25.00 per name, includes certification. Required to search: name, years to search, address, DOB. Criminal records on computer since 5/87, on books from 1968. Mail turnaround time 1 week-10 days. Criminal PAT goes back to 5/1987. Results include case name. **See details about online access to criminal records at front or back of this chapter.**

Haywood County

Superior-District Court 285 N. Main, Ste. 1500, Waynesville, NC 28786; 828-454-6501; criminal phone: x1; civil phone: x2;; 8AM-5PM (EST). *Felony, Misdemeanor, Civil, Eviction, Small Claims, Probate.*
www.nccourts.org/County/Haywood/Default.asp

General Information: No adoption, sealed cases, juvenile, sex offenders, mental or expunged records released. Will not fax documents. Court makes copy: $2.00 1st page, $.25 ea add'l. Self serve copy: $.25 per page.Can buy a "key" to make own copies at reduced rate. Certification fee: $3.00. Payee: Clerk of Superior Court. Only cashiers checks and money orders accepted. No credit cards accepted. Prepayment required. Mail requests: SASE required.

Civil Name Search: Access: Mail, in person, online. Both court and visitors may perform in person name searches. Search fee: $25.00 per name. Required to search: name, years to search; also helpful: address. Civil records on computer since 10/1987, prior on books to 1955. Mail turnaround time 1-2 days. Civil PAT goes back to 10/1987. **See details about online access to civil records at front or back of this chapter.**

Criminal Name Search: Access: Mail, in person, online. Both court and visitors may perform in person name searches. Search fee: $25.00 per name, includes certification. Required to search: name, years to search, DOB; also helpful: address, SSN. Criminal records computerized from 5/87, on books or cards from 1800s. Mail turnaround time 1-2 days. Criminal PAT goes back to 10/1981. **See details about online access to criminal records at front or back of this chapter.**

Henderson County

Superior-District Court PO Box 965, 200 N Grove St, #163, Hendersonville, NC 28793; 828-694-4100; fax: 828-694-4107; 8AM-5PM (EST). *Felony, Misdemeanor, Civil, Eviction, Small Claims, Probate.*
www.nccourts.org/County/Henderson/Default.asp
General Information: No adoption, sealed cases, juvenile, sex offenders, mental or expunged records released. Will not fax documents. Court makes copy: $2.00 1st page, $.25 ea add'l. Certification fee: $3.00; Exemplified copy $10.00. Payee: Clerk of Superior Court. No personal checks or credit cards accepted. Prepayment required. Mail requests: SASE required.
Civil Name Search: Access: In person, online. Both court and visitors may perform in person name searches. No search fee. Required to search: name, years to search; also helpful: address. Civil records on computer back to 1988, prior on books to 1968. Civil PAT goes back to 10/1988. **See details about online access to civil records at front or back of this chapter.**
Criminal Name Search: Access: Mail, in person, online. Both court and visitors may perform in person name searches. Search fee: $25.00 per name, includes certification. Required to search: full name; also helpful: address, DOB, SSN, years to search. Criminal records computerized from 9/86, prior on books to 1968. Mail turnaround time 1 week. Criminal PAT goes back to 9/1986. **See details about online access to criminal records at front or back of this chapter.**

Hertford County

Superior-District Court PO Box 86, 701 King St, Winton, NC 27986; 252-358-7100; fax: 252-358-7101; 8AM-5PM (EST). *Felony, Misdemeanor, Civil, Eviction, Small Claims, Probate.*
www.nccourts.org/County/Hertford/Default.asp
General Information: No adoption, sealed cases, juvenile, sex offenders, mental or expunged records released. Court makes copy: $2.00 1st page, $.25 ea add'l. Certification fee: $3.00 per doc. Payee: Clerk of Superior Court. Only cashiers checks and money orders accepted. No credit cards accepted. Prepayment required. Mail requests: SASE helpful.
Civil Name Search: Access: In person, online. Visitors must perform in person searches themselves. Required to search: name, years to search; also helpful: address. Civil records on computer back to 4/1989, prior on index cards and judgment books to 1968. Civil PAT goes back to 1989. **See details about online access to civil records at front or back of this chapter.**
Criminal Name Search: Access: Mail, in person, online. Both court and visitors may perform in person name searches. Search fee: $25.00 per name, includes certification. Required to search: name, years to search, DOB; also helpful: address, SSN. Criminal records computerized from 4/1989, prior on index cards or judgment books to 1968. Mail turnaround time 1-2 days. Criminal PAT goes back to same as civil. **See details about online access to criminal records at front or back of this chapter.**

Hoke County

Superior-District Court PO Drawer 1569, 304 Main St, Raeford, NC 28376; 910-878-4100; fax: 910-878-4102; 8:30AM-5PM (EST). *Felony, Misdemeanor, Civil, Eviction, Small Claims, Probate.*
www.nccourts.org/County/Hoke/Default.asp
General Information: No adoption, sealed cases, juvenile, mental or expunged records released. Will not fax documents. Court makes copy: $2.00 1st page, $.25 ea add'l. Certification fee: None; $3.00 if you perform search in person. Payee: Clerk of Superior Court. Business checks accepted, credit cards are not. Prepayment required. Mail requests: SASE required for criminal.
Civil Name Search: Access: Mail, in person, online. Both court and visitors may perform in person name searches. Search fee: $15.00. Required to search: name, years to search; also helpful: address. Civil records on computer since 10/89, on books to 1967. Civil PAT goes back to 10/1989. **See details about online access to civil records at front or back of this chapter.**
Criminal Name Search: Access: Mail, in person, online. Both court and visitors may perform in person name searches. Search fee: $25.00 per name, includes certification. Required to search: name, years to search, DOB; also helpful: address, SSN. Criminal records on computer since 10/89, on books to 1967. Mail turnaround time 1-2 days. Criminal PAT goes back to same as civil. **See details about online access to criminal records at front or back of this chapter.**

Hyde County

Superior-District Court PO Box 337, 30 Oyster Creek St, Swanquarter, NC 27885; 252-926-4101; fax: 252-926-1002; 8AM-5PM (EST). *Felony, Misdemeanor, Civil, Eviction, Small Claims, Probate.*
www.nccourts.org/County/Hyde/Default.asp
General Information: No adoption, sealed cases, juvenile, sex offenders, mental, involuntary commitments, or expunged records released. Will fax documents if copy fee prepaid. Court makes copy: $2.00 1st page, $.25 ea add'l. Self serve copy: $.25 per page. Certification fee: $3.00 per page. Payee: Clerk of Superior Court. Only cash, cashiers checks and money orders accepted. No credit cards accepted. Prepayment required. Mail requests: SASE required.
Civil Name Search: Access: In person, online. Visitors must perform in person searches themselves. Civil records on computer since 7/89, on books to 1968; estate and special proceedings back to 1996. Civil PAT goes back to 1996. **See details about online access to civil records at front or back of this chapter.**
Criminal Name Search: Access: Mail, in person, online. Visitors must perform in person searches themselves. Search fee: $25.00 per name, includes certification. Required to search: name, years to search, DOB; also helpful- signed release. Criminal records on computer since 7/89, on books to 1968. Note: Court refers to criminal searches as criminal background checks, not name searches. Criminal PAT goes back to 1989. **See details about online access to criminal records at front or back of this chapter.** Online results show name only.

Iredell County

Superior-District Court 221 E Water St, Statesville, NC 28677; 704-832-6600; fax: 704-832-6601; 8AM-5PM (EST). *Felony, Misdemeanor, Civil, Eviction, Small Claims, Probate.*
www.nccourts.org/County/Iredell/Default.asp
General Information: Direct requests to Attention of Iredell County Clerk of Courts. No adoption, sealed cases, juvenile, sex offenders, mental or expunged records released. Will fax documents to local or toll free line, will not fax certified pages. Court makes copy: $2.00 1st page, $.25 ea add'l. Self serve copy: $.25 per page with copy button. Certification fee: $3.00 per page; exemplifications $10.00. Cert fee includes copy fee. Payee: Clerk of Superior Court. Only cashiers checks and money orders accepted. No credit cards accepted. Prepayment required. Mail requests: SASE required.
Civil Name Search: Access: In person, online. Both court and visitors may perform in person name searches. Search fee: $25.00 per name for certified search results, otherwise just fee for the copies. Civil records on computer since 07/88, in books since, 1786, on microfiche since 1971. Civil PAT goes back to 1985. **See details about online access to civil records at front or back of this chapter.**
Criminal Name Search: Access: Mail, in person, online. Both court and visitors may perform in person name searches. Search fee: $25.00 per name for certified search results, otherwise just fee for the copies. Required to search: name, years to search, DOB. Criminal records on computer since 1985, prior on books and cards to 1970. Mail turnaround time 2 days. Criminal PAT goes back to same as civil. **See details about online access to criminal records at front or back of this chapter.**

Jackson County

Superior-District Court 401 Grindstaff Cove Rd, Sylva, NC 28779; criminal phone: 828-586-7512; civil phone: 828-586-7512; fax: 828-586-9009; 8:30AM-5PM (EST). *Felony, Misdemeanor, Civil, Eviction, Small Claims, Probate.*
www.nccourts.org/County/Jackson/Default.asp
General Information: Probate fax is same as main fax number. No adoption, sealed cases, juvenile, mental or expunged records released. Will not fax documents. Court makes copy: $2.00 1st page, $.25 ea add'l. Self serve copy: $.25 per page. Certification fee: $10.00 per document includes copies. Payee: Clerk of Superior Court. Only cashiers checks and money orders accepted. No credit cards accepted. Prepayment required. Mail requests: SASE required for criminal.
Civil Name Search: Access: In person, online. Visitors must perform in person searches themselves. Required to search: name, years to search; also helpful: address. Civil records on computer since 6/30/97, prior on books from 1966. Civil PAT goes back to 6/30/97. **See details about online access to civil records at front or back of this chapter.**
Criminal Name Search: Access: Mail, in person, online. Both court and visitors may perform in person name searches. Search fee: $25.00 per name, includes certification. Required to search: name, years to search, DOB; also helpful: address, SSN. Criminal records on computer since 5/01/1989, prior on books from 1966. Mail turnaround time 1-2 days. Criminal PAT goes back to 6/30/97. **See details about online access to criminal records at front or back of this chapter.**

Johnston County

Superior-District Court PO Box 297, Johnson and 2nd Strs, Smithfield, NC 27577; 919-209-5400 x5442; criminal phone: x5422; civil phone: x5412; fax: 919-209-5401; 8AM-5PM (EST). *Felony, Misdemeanor, Civil, Eviction, Small Claims, Probate.*

www.nccourts.org/County/Johnston/Default.asp

General Information: Probate is in a separate index at this courthouse. Probate fax is same as main fax number. No adoption, sealed cases, juvenile, sex offenders, mental or expunged records released. Will fax documents. Court makes copy: $2.00 1st page, $.25 ea add'l. Certification fee: $3.00 per document unless copy fee exceeds $3.00, then no cert fee. Payee: Clerk of Superior Court. Business checks accepted; no out-of-state checks accepted. No credit cards accepted. Prepayment required. Mail requests: SASE requested.

Civil Name Search: Access: Fax, mail, in person, online. Visitors must perform in person searches themselves. No search fee. Required to search: name, years to search; also helpful: address. Civil records on computer since 1989, prior on books to 1930s. Civil PAT goes back to 1982. **See details about online access to civil records at front or back of this chapter.**

Criminal Name Search: Access: Mail, fax, in person, online. Both court and visitors may perform in person name searches. Search fee: $25.00 per name, includes certification. Required to search: name, DOB; also helpful: years to search, address, SSN. Criminal records computerized from 5/86, prior on books and cards to 1968. Mail turnaround time 1-2 days. Criminal PAT goes back to same as civil. **See details about online access to criminal records at front or back of this chapter.**

Jones County

Superior-District Court PO Box 280, Trenton, NC 28585; 252-448-7351; criminal phone: x1; civil phone: x3; fax: 252-448-1607; 8AM-5PM (EST). *Felony, Misdemeanor, Civil, Eviction, Small Claims, Probate.*

www.nccourts.org/County/Jones/Default.asp

General Information: No adoption, sealed cases, juvenile, sex offenders, mental or expunged records released. Will not fax documents. Court makes copy: $2.00 1st page, $.25 ea add'l. Certification fee: $3.00. Payee: Clerk of Court. Only cashiers checks and money orders accepted. No credit cards accepted. Prepayment required. Mail requests: SASE required for criminal.

Civil Name Search: Access: In person, online. Visitors must perform in person searches themselves. Civil records on computer since 1994, prior on microfilm. Civil PAT goes back to 1989. **See details about online access to civil records at front or back of this chapter.**

Criminal Name Search: Access: Mail, in person, online. Both court and visitors may perform in person name searches. Search fee: $25.00 per name, includes certification. Required to search: name, years to search; also helpful: DOB. Criminal records on computer since 1989, prior on microfilm. Mail turnaround time 5 days. Criminal PAT goes back to same as civil. **See details about online access to criminal records at front or back of this chapter.**

Lee County

Superior-District Court PO Box 4209, 1400 S Horner Blvd, Sanford, NC 27331; 919-718-6333; fax: 919-718-6301; 8AM-5PM (EST). *Felony, Misdemeanor, Civil, Eviction, Small Claims, Probate.*

www.nccourts.org/County/Lee/Default.asp

General Information: No adoption, sealed cases, juvenile, mental or expunged records released. Will fax documents $2.00 1st page, $.25 ea add'l; prepaid. Court makes copy: $2.00 1st page, $.25 ea add'l. Self serve copy: same; or $.25 per page is you have purchased a copy key. Certification fee: $3.00. Payee: Clerk of Superior Court. Only cashiers checks and money orders accepted. No credit cards accepted. Prepayment required.

Civil Name Search: Access: In person, online. Visitors must perform in person searches themselves. Civil records on computer since 1989, prior on books to 1967, index to 1907. Civil PAT goes back to 1989. **See details about online access to civil records at front or back of this chapter.**

Criminal Name Search: Access: Mail, in person, online. Both court and visitors may perform in person name searches. Search fee: $25.00 per name, includes certification. Required to search: name, years to search, DOB. Criminal records on computer since 6/87, prior on books to 12/68, index to criminal actions books from 8/84 to 6/87. Mail turnaround time 1-3 days. Criminal PAT goes back to 6/1987. **See details about online access to criminal records at front or back of this chapter.**

Lenoir County

Superior-District Court 130 S Queen St, Kinston, NC 28502-0068; 252-520-5300; fax: 252-520-5385; 8AM-5PM (EST). *Felony, Misdemeanor, Civil, Eviction, Small Claims, Probate.*

www.nccourts.org/County/Lenoir/Default.asp

General Information: No adoption, sealed cases, juvenile, sex offenders, mental or expunged records released. Will not fax out documents. Court makes copy: $2.00 1st page, $.25 ea add'l. Self serve copy: purchase $10.00 copy key. Certification fee: $3.00. Payee: Clerk of Superior Court. Only cashiers checks and money orders accepted. No credit cards accepted. Prepayment required. Mail requests: SASE required.

Civil Name Search: Access: In person, online. Both court and visitors may perform in person name searches. No search fee. Required to search: name, years to search; also helpful: address. Civil records on computer since 10/24/1988, prior on books to 1900s, prior destroyed due to fire. Public use terminal has civil records back to 1988. **See details about online access to civil records at front or back of this chapter.**

Criminal Name Search: Access: Mail, in person, online. Only the court performs in person name searches; visitors may not. Search fee: $25.00 per name, includes certification. Required to search: name, years to search, DOB; also helpful: address. Criminal records on computer since 8/86, prior records on books and cards to 1925. Mail turnaround time 1-2 days. **See details about online access to criminal records at front or back of this chapter.**

Lincoln County

Superior-District Court PO Box 8, 1 Courthouse Sq, Lincolnton, NC 28093; 704-742-7800; fax: 704-742-7801; 8AM-5PM (EST). *Felony, Misdemeanor, Civil, Eviction, Small Claims, Probate.*

www.nccourts.org/County/Lincoln/Default.asp

General Information: No adoption, sealed cases, juvenile, sex offenders, mental or expunged records released. Will fax documents $2.00 per page. Court makes copy: $2.00 1st page, $.25 ea add'l. Certification fee: None; $3.00 if you perform search in person. Payee: Clerk of Court. Business checks accepted. No personal checks or credit cards accepted. Prepayment required. Mail requests: SASE required for criminal.

Civil Name Search: Access: In person, online. Visitors must perform in person searches themselves. Civil records on computer since 11-1-87, in books since mid-1800s, on microfiche from 1-1-68 to present. Civil PAT goes back to 11/1987. **See details about online access to civil records at front or back of this chapter.**

Criminal Name Search: Access: Mail, in person, online. Both court and visitors may perform in person name searches. Search fee: $25.00 per name, includes certification. Required to search: name, DOB; Also helpful: years to search. Criminal records on computer since 1987, prior on books and cards to 1968. Mail turnaround time 2 days to 1 week. Criminal PAT goes back to same as civil. **See details about online access to criminal records at front or back of this chapter.**

Macon County

Superior-District Court 5 W Main St, Franklin, NC 28744; 828-349-2000; fax: 828-369-2515; 8AM-5PM (EST). *Felony, Misdemeanor, Civil, Eviction, Small Claims, Probate.*

www.nccourts.org/County/Macon/Default.asp

General Information: No adoption, sealed cases, juvenile, sex offenders, mental or expunged records released. Will fax documents $1.00 1st page, $.25 each add'l page. Court makes copy: $2.00 1st page, $.25 ea add'l. Certification fee: $3.00 per cert. Payee: Clerk of Superior Court. No personal checks or credit cards accepted. Prepayment required. Mail requests: SASE required.

Civil Name Search: Access: In person, online. Visitors must perform in person searches themselves. Required to search: name, years to search; also helpful: address. Civil records on computer since 5/1989, prior on books to 1968. Public use terminal has civil records back to 5/1989. **See details about online access to civil records at front or back of this chapter.**

Criminal Name Search: Access: Mail, in person, online. Only the court performs in person name searches; visitors may not. Search fee: $25.00 per name, includes certification. Required to search: name, DOB, years to search; also helpful- file number. Criminal records on computer since 5/1989, prior on books to 1968. Mail turnaround time 1-2 days. **See details about online access to criminal records at front or back of this chapter.**

Madison County

Superior-District Court PO Box 217, 2 N Main St, Marshall, NC 28753; 828-649-2531; fax: 828-649-2829; 8AM-5PM (EST). *Felony, Misdemeanor, Civil, Eviction, Small Claims, Probate.*

www.nccourts.org/County/Madison/Default.asp

General Information: No adoption, sealed cases, juvenile, sex offenders, mental, expunged, or dismissed records released. Will fax documents $1.00 1st page, $.25 each add'l page. Court makes copy: $2.00 1st page, $.25 ea add'l. Certification fee: $3.00; Exemplified copy $10.00. Payee: Clerk of Superior Court. Only cashiers checks and money orders accepted. No credit cards accepted. Prepayment required.

Civil Name Search: Access: In person, online. Visitors must perform in person searches themselves. Required to search: name, years to search; also helpful: address. Civil records on computer back to 10/88, prior on books to 1968. Civil PAT goes back to 10/1988. **See details about online access to civil records at front or back of this chapter.**

Criminal Name Search: Access: Mail, in person, online. Visitors must perform in person searches themselves. Search fee: $25.00 per name, includes certification. Required to search: name, DOB; also helpful: years to search. Criminal records on computer since 10/88, prior on books to 1968. Mail turnaround time 1-2 days. Criminal PAT goes back to same as civil. **See details about online access to criminal records at front or back of this chapter.**

Martin County

Superior-District Court PO Box 807, Williamston, NC 27892; 252-809-5100; fax: 252-809-5101; 8AM-5PM (EST). *Felony, Misdemeanor, Civil, Eviction, Small Claims, Probate.*

www.nccourts.org/County/Martin/Default.asp

General Information: Search criminal court calendars at www1.aoc.state.nc.us/www/calendars.html. No adoption, sealed cases, juvenile, mental or expunged records released. Will not fax documents. Court makes copy: $2.00 1st page, $.25 ea add'l. Certification fee: $3.00; Exemplified copy $10.00. Payee: Clerk of Court. Only cashiers checks and money orders accepted. No credit cards accepted. Prepayment required. Mail requests: SASE required for criminal.

Civil Name Search: Access: In person, online. Both court and visitors may perform in person name searches. No search fee. Required to search: name, years to search, address. Civil records go back to 1800s, civil records on computer since 1989, in books since 1968. Public use terminal available. **See details about online access to civil records at front or back of this chapter.**

Criminal Name Search: Access: Mail, in person, online. Both court and visitors may perform in person name searches. Search fee: $25.00 per name, includes certification. Required to search: name, years to search, address, DOB; also helpful: SSN. Criminal records go back to 1800s criminal records on computer since 1996 in books since 1968. Mail turnaround time 1 week. Public use terminal available. **See details about online access to criminal records at front or back of this chapter.**

McDowell County

Superior-District Court 21 S Main St, Marion, NC 28752; 828-652-7717 x201; criminal phone: x228; civil phone: x208; fax: 828-659-2641; 8:30AM-5PM (EST). *Felony, Misdemeanor, Civil, Eviction, Small Claims, Probate.*

www.nccourts.org/County/McDowell/Default.asp

General Information: No adoption, sealed cases, juvenile, sex offenders, mental or expunged records released. Court makes copy: $2.00 1st page, $.25 ea add'l. Certification fee: $3.00; Exemplified copy $10.00. Payee: Clerk of Superior Court. Business checks accepted. Prepayment required. Mail requests: SASE required.

Civil Name Search: Access: Mail, in person, online. Both court and visitors may perform in person name searches. No search fee. Required to search: name, years to search; also helpful: address. Civil records on computer since 11/88, prior on books to 1930. Mail turnaround time 1-2 days. Public use terminal available. **See details about online access to civil records at front or back of this chapter.**

Criminal Name Search: Access: Mail, in person, online. Both court and visitors may perform in person name searches. Search fee: $25.00 per name, includes certification. Required to search: name, DOB; also helpful: years to search, address, SSN. Criminal records on computer since 10/1987, prior on books to 1968. Mail turnaround time 1-2 days. Public use terminal available. **See details about online access to criminal records at front or back of this chapter.**

Mecklenburg County

Superior-District Court PO Box 37971, 832 E 4th St, Rm 2132, Charlotte, NC 28237; 704-686-0400 (info); criminal phone: 704-686-0600; civil phone: 704-686-0520; criminal fax: 704-686-0601; civil fax: 9AM-5PM; 9AM-5PM (EST). *Felony, Misdemeanor, Civil, Eviction, Small Claims, Probate.* www.nccourts.org/County/Mecklenburg/Staff/Clerk.asp

General Information: No adoption, sealed cases, juvenile, sex offenders, mental or expunged records released. Will not fax documents. Court makes copy: $2.00 1st page, $.25 ea add'l. Certification fee: $3.00 per page. Payee: Clerk of Superior Court. Only cashiers checks and money orders accepted. No credit cards accepted. Prepayment required. Mail requests: SASE requested for criminal.

Civil Name Search: Access: In person, online. Visitors must perform in person searches themselves. Required to search: name. Civil records on computer since 4/1988, prior on books to 1940s. Civil PAT goes back to 1988. **See details about online access to civil records at front or back of this chapter.**

Criminal Name Search: Access: Mail, in person, online. Both court and visitors may perform in person name searches. Search fee: $25.00 per name, includes certification. Required to search: name, years to search, address, DOB; also helpful: SSN. Criminal records computerized from 1/83, prior on cards and books to 1930s. Mail turnaround time 1-2 days.

Criminal PAT goes back to 1983. **See details about online access to criminal records at front or back of this chapter.**

Mitchell County

Superior-District Court 328 Longview Dr, Bakersville, NC 28705; 828-688-2161; fax: 828-688-2168; 8:30AM-5PM M-TH; 8:30AM-4:30PM F (EST). *Felony, Misdemeanor, Civil, Eviction, Small Claims, Probate.*

www.nccourts.org/County/Mitchell/Default.asp

General Information: No adoption, sealed cases, juvenile, sex offenders, mental or expunged records released. Will not fax documents. Court makes copy: $2.00 1st page, $.25 ea add'l. Certification fee: None; $3.00 if you perform search in person. Payee: Superior-District Court. No personal checks accepted, certified funds and money orders preferred. No credit cards accepted. Prepayment required. Mail requests: SASE required for criminal.

Civil Name Search: Access: In person, online. Visitors must perform in person searches themselves. Required to search: name, years to search; also helpful: address. Civil records on computer since 1988, prior on books since 1968. Civil PAT goes back to 1988. **See details about online access to civil records at front or back of this chapter.**

Criminal Name Search: Access: Mail, in person, online. Both court and visitors may perform in person name searches. Search fee: $25.00 per name, includes certification. Required to search: name, years to search, DOB; also helpful- address. Criminal records on computer since 1988, prior on books since 1968; 1984-1988 on microfilm. Mail turnaround time 1-2 days. Criminal PAT goes back to same as civil. **See details about online access to criminal records at front or back of this chapter.**

Montgomery County

Superior-District Court PO Box 527, Troy, NC 27371; 910-576-4211; fax: 910-576-5020; 8:30AM-5PM (EST). *Felony, Misdemeanor, Civil, Eviction, Small Claims, Probate.*

www.nccourts.org/County/Montgomery/Default.asp

General Information: Address mail to Clerk of Superior Court. No adoption, sealed cases, juvenile, sex offenders, mental or expunged records released. Will fax documents $2.00 per page. Court makes copy: $2.00 1st page, $.25 ea add'l. Self serve copy: $.25 per page. Certification fee: $3.00; Exemplification fee- $10.00 each. Payee: Clerk of Superior Court. Only cashiers checks and money orders accepted. No credit cards accepted. Prepayment required. Mail requests: SASE required for mail return of any copies.

Civil Name Search: Access: In person, online. Visitors must perform in person searches themselves. Civil records on computer since 4/1989, archived in Raleigh to 1843, prior records destroyed in fire. Civil PAT available. **See details about online access to civil records at front or back of this chapter.**

Criminal Name Search: Access: Phone, fax, mail, in person, online. Both court and visitors may perform in person name searches. Search fee: $25.00 per name, includes certification. Required to search: name, years to search, address, DOB, signed release. Criminal records on computer since 4/1989, archived in Raleigh to 1843, prior records destroyed in fire. Mail turnaround time 1-2 days. Criminal PAT goes back to 1988. **See details about online access to criminal records at front or back of this chapter.**

Moore County

Superior-District Court PO Box 936, Carthage, NC 28327; 910-722-5000; fax: 910-722-5001; 8AM-5PM (EST). *Felony, Misdemeanor, Civil, Eviction, Small Claims, Probate.*

www.nccourts.org/County/Moore/Default.asp

General Information: No adoption, sealed cases, juvenile, mental or expunged records released. Will not fax documents. Court makes copy: $2.00 1st page, $.25 ea add'l. Certification fee: $3.00 per cert. Payee: Clerk of Superior Court. Cashiers checks and money orders accepted. No credit cards accepted. Prepayment required. Mail requests: SASE required.

Civil Name Search: Access: In person, online. Both court and visitors may perform in person name searches. No search fee. Required to search: name, DOB, years to search. Civil records on computer since 3/1989, prior on books, older records in basement. Civil PAT goes 1987. **See details about online access to civil records at front or back of this chapter.**

Criminal Name Search: Access: Mail, in person, online. Both court and visitors may perform in person name searches. Search fee: $25.00 per name, includes certification. Required to search: name, years to search, DOB, signed release; also helpful: maiden name, address. Criminal records on computer since 5/1987, prior on books to 1968, older records in basement. Mail turnaround time 2-4 days. Criminal PAT goes back to 1989. **See details about online access to criminal records at front or back of this chapter.**

Nash County

Superior-District Court PO Box 759, 234 W Washington St, Nashville, NC 27856; 252-459-4081; criminal phone: 252-459-4085; fax: 252-459-6050; 8AM-5PM (EST). *Felony, Misdemeanor, Civil, Eviction, Small Claims, Probate.* www.nccourts.org/County/Nash/Default.asp

General Information: No adoption, sealed cases, juvenile, mental or expunged records released. Will not fax documents. Court makes copy: $2.00 1st page, $.25 ea add'l. Certification fee: $3.00; Exemplified copy $10.00. If certified copy exceeds 6 pages, then add $.25 for each add'l page. Payee: Clerk of Superior Court. Only cashiers checks and money orders accepted. No credit cards accepted. Prepayment required. Mail requests: SASE required for criminal.

Civil Name Search: Access: In person, online. Both court and visitors may perform in person name searches. No search fee. Required to search: name, years to search; also helpful: address. Civil records on computer since 6/1988, prior in books. Civil PAT goes back to 6/1988. **See details about online access to civil records at front or back of this chapter.**

Criminal Name Search: Access: Mail, in person, online. Both court and visitors may perform in person name searches. Search fee: $25.00 per name, includes certification. Required to search: name, years to search, DOB; also helpful: address. Criminal records on computer since 5/1980, prior on books and cards dating back to late 1800s. Mail turnaround time 1 week. Criminal PAT goes back to 1980. **See details about online access to criminal records at front or back of this chapter.**

New Hanover County

Superior-District Court PO Box 2023, 316 Princess St, Wilmington, NC 28402; 910-341-1111; criminal phone: 910-341-1301; civil phone: 910-341-1302; probate phone: 910-341-1304; criminal fax: 910-251-2676; civil fax: 8AM-5PM; 8AM-5PM (EST). *Felony, Misdemeanor, Civil, Eviction, Small Claims, Probate.*
www.nccourts.org/County/NewHanover/Default.asp

General Information: No adoption, sealed cases, juvenile, sex offenders, mental or expunged records released. Court makes copy: $2.00 1st page, $.25 ea add'l. Certification fee: $3.00 per doc. Payee: Clerk of Superior Court. Only cashiers checks and money orders accepted. Prepayment required. Mail requests: SASE required for criminal.

Civil Name Search: Access: In person, online. Visitors must perform in person searches themselves. Required to search: name, years to search; also helpful: address. Civil records on computer since 1988, on books to late 1800s. Public use terminal available. **See details about online access to civil records at front or back of this chapter.**

Criminal Name Search: Access: Mail, in person, online. Both court and visitors may perform in person name searches. Search fee: $25.00 per name, includes certification. Required to search: name, years to search, DOB; also helpful: address, SSN. Criminal records on computer since 11/83, prior on books and files to late 1800s. Mail turnaround time 1-2 days. Public use terminal available. **See details about online access to criminal records at front or back of this chapter.**

Northampton County

Superior-District Court PO Box 217, 102 W Jefferson St, Jackson, NC 27845; 252-574-3100; fax: 252-574-3101; 8:30AM-5PM (EST). *Felony, Misdemeanor, Civil, Eviction, Small Claims, Probate.*
www.nccourts.org/County/Northampton/Default.asp

General Information: No adoption, sealed cases, juvenile, sex offenders, mental or expunged records released. Will not fax documents. Court makes copy: $2.00 1st page, $.25 ea add'l. Self serve copy: $.25 each copy with a purchase of a key at $10.00. Certification fee: $3.00 per doc. Payee: Clerk of Superior Court. Only cash or certified checks accepted. No personal checks or credit cards accepted. Prepayment required. Mail requests: SASE required.

Civil Name Search: Access: Mail, in person, online. Visitors must perform in person searches themselves. Search fee: $15.00 per name. Required to search: name, years to search; also helpful: address. Civil records on computer back to 1993, prior on books to 1968. Mail turnaround time 3-10 days Civil PAT goes back to 1989. **See details about online access to civil records at front or back of this chapter.**

Criminal Name Search: Access: Mail, in person, online. Visitors must perform in person searches themselves. Search fee: $25.00 per name, includes certification. Required to search: name, years to search, DOB; also helpful: address, SSN. Criminal records computerized from 1989, prior on books to 1968. Mail turnaround time 3-10 days. Criminal PAT goes back to same as civil. **See details about online access to criminal records at front or back of this chapter.**

Onslow County

Superior-District Court 625 Court St, Jacksonville, NC 28540; 910-478-3600; fax: 910-455-6285; 8AM-5PM (EST). *Felony, Misdemeanor, Civil, Eviction, Small Claims, Probate.*
www.nccourts.org/County/Onslow/Default.asp

General Information: No adoption, sealed cases, juvenile, sex offenders, mental or expunged records released. Will fax documents $1.00 1st page, $.25 each add'l page. Court makes copy: $2.00 1st page, $.25 ea add'l.A copy key may be purchased from CSC & used in person only to make copies or print from public terminals, fee for photocopier key is $110.00 per key purchase, for printer key $60.00 per key purchase. Certification fee: $3.00; Exemplified copy $10.00. Payee: Clerk of Superior Court. Business checks accepted if in state. No credit cards accepted. Prepayment required.

Civil Name Search: Access: In person, online. Visitors must perform in person searches themselves. Required to search: name, years to search; also helpful: address. Civil records on computer since 1988, prior on books to 1920s. Civil PAT goes back to 1988. **See details about online access to civil records at front or back of this chapter.**

Criminal Name Search: Access: Mail, in person, online. Both court and visitors may perform in person name searches. Search fee: $25.00 per name, includes certification of first copy. Required to search: name, years to search, DOB; also helpful: address, SSN. Criminal records on computer since 2/83, prior on books to 1920s. Mail turnaround time 1-2 days. Criminal PAT goes back to same as civil. **See details about online access to criminal records at front or back of this chapter.**

Orange County

Superior-District Court 106 E Margaret Lane, Hillsborough, NC 27278; 919-644-4700; fax: 919-644-4501; 8:30AM-5PM (EST). *Felony, Misdemeanor, Civil, Eviction, Small Claims, Probate.*
www.nccourts.org

General Information: No adoption, sealed cases, juvenile, sex offenders, mental or expunged records released. Will not fax documents. Court makes copy: $2.00 1st page, $.25 ea add'l page. Certification fee: $3.00. Payee: Clerk of Superior Court. Only cashiers checks and money orders accepted. No credit cards accepted. Prepayment required. Mail requests: SASE required.

Civil Name Search: Access: In person, online. Visitors must perform in person searches themselves. Required to search: name, years to search; also helpful: address. Civil records on computer since 5/1989. Civil PAT goes back to 1989. **See details about online access to civil records at front or back of this chapter.**

Criminal Name Search: Access: Mail, in person, online. Both court and visitors may perform in person name searches. Search fee: $25.00 per name, includes certification. Required to search: name, DOB; also helpful: address, SSN, race, sex. computer records go to 3/87. Mail turnaround time 4-5 days. Criminal PAT goes back to 1987. Results include driver's license number. **See details about online access to criminal records at front or back of this chapter.**

Pamlico County

Superior-District Court PO Box 38, 202 Main St, Bayboro, NC 28515; 252-745-6600; criminal phone: 252-745-6632; probate phone: 252-745-6600; fax: 252-745-6601; 8AM-5PM (EST). *Felony, Misdemeanor, Civil, Eviction, Small Claims, Probate.*
www.nccourts.org/County/Pamlico/Default.asp

General Information: Probate fax is same as main fax number. No adoption, sealed cases, juvenile, sex offenders, mental or expunged records released. Will fax documents $1.00 1st page, $.25 each add'l page. Court makes copy: $2.00 1st page, $.25 ea add'l. Certification fee: $3.00. Payee: Pamlico Clerk of Court. Only cashiers checks and money orders accepted. No credit cards accepted. Prepayment required. Mail requests: SASE required for criminal.

Civil Name Search: Access: In person, online. Visitors must perform in person searches themselves. Required to search: name, years to search, address. Civil records go back to 1988. Civil PAT goes back to 1989. **See details about online access to civil records at front or back of this chapter.**

Criminal Name Search: Access: Mail, in person, online. Both court and visitors may perform in person name searches. Search fee: $25.00 per name, includes certification. Required to search: name, years to search, DOB. Criminal records on computer since 9/84, prior on books to 1968. Mail turnaround time 1-2 days. Criminal PAT goes back to same as civil. **See details about online access to criminal records at front or back of this chapter.**

Pasquotank County

Superior-District Court PO Box 449, Elizabeth City, NC 27907-0449; 252-331-4600; fax: 252-331-4680; 8AM-5PM (EST). *Felony, Misdemeanor, Civil, Eviction, Small Claims, Probate.*
www.nccourts.org

General Information: The District Court direct phone number is 252-331-4500. No adoption, sealed cases, juvenile, sex offenders, mental or expunged records released. Will not fax documents. Court makes copy: $3.00 1st page, $.25 ea add'l. Self serve copy: same. No certification fee . Payee: Clerk of

Superior Court. Business checks accepted. No credit cards accepted. Prepayment required.

Civil Name Search: Access: In person, online. Visitors must perform in person searches themselves. Required to search: name, years to search; also helpful: address. Civil records on computer since 3/6/1989, books prior to 1800s (some in Raleigh). Civil PAT goes back to 1993. **See details about online access to civil records at front or back of this chapter.**

Criminal Name Search: Access: Mail, in person, online. Both court and visitors may perform in person name searches. Search fee: $25.00 per name, includes certification. Required to search: name, years to search, DOB; also helpful: address, SSN, race, sex. Criminal records on computer since 4/88, prior on books and microfiche. Mail turnaround time 2 days. Criminal PAT goes back to 1989. **See details about online access to criminal records at front or back of this chapter.**

Pender County

Superior-District Court PO Box 310, Burgaw, NC 28425; 910-663-3900; fax: 910-663-3901; 8AM-5PM (EST). *Felony, Misdemeanor, Civil, Eviction, Small Claims, Probate.*

www.nccourts.org/County/Pender/Default.asp

General Information: No adoption, sealed cases, juvenile, sex offenders, mental or expunged records released. Will fax documents $2.00 1st page, $.25 each add'l. Court makes copy: $2.00 1st page, $.25 ea add'l. Self serve copy: same. Certification fee: $3.00. Exemplification fee- $10.00. Payee: Clerk of Superior Court. Business checks accepted. No credit cards accepted. Prepayment required. Mail requests: SASE required for mail return of any copies.

Civil Name Search: Access: In person, online. Visitors must perform in person searches themselves. Required to search: name, years to search; also helpful: address. Civil records on computer since 1989, prior in books from 1875. Note: Civil search can be done statewide from any Clerk of Courts office. Civil PAT goes back to 1989. **See details about online access to civil records at front or back of this chapter.**

Criminal Name Search: Access: Mail, fax, in person, online. Both court and visitors may perform in person name searches. Search fee: $25.00 per name, includes certification. Required to search: name, years to search, DOB; also helpful: address, SSN. Criminal records on computer since 9/89, prior in books from 1968. Mail turnaround time 1 week. Criminal PAT goes back to 7/89. **See details about online access to criminal records at front or back of this chapter.**

Perquimans County

Superior-District Court PO Box 33, 128 N Church St, Hertford, NC 27944; 252-426-1505; fax: 252-426-1901; 8AM-5PM (EST). *Felony, Misdemeanor, Civil, Eviction, Small Claims, Probate.*

www.nccourts.org/County/Perquimans/Default.asp

General Information: No adoption, sealed cases, juvenile, sex offenders, mental or expunged records released. Court makes copy: Per docket - $2.00 1st page, $.25 ea add'l. Certification fee: None; $3.00 if you perform search in person. Payee: Clerk of Superior Court. Only cashiers checks and money orders accepted. No credit cards accepted. Prepayment required. Mail requests: SASE required.

Civil Name Search: Access: Mail, in person, online. Both court and visitors may perform in person name searches. Search fee: $25.00 per name, includes certification. Civil records on computer since 1989, prior in books to 1966, rest archived and must be searched in person only. Civil PAT goes back to 10/23/89. Terminal results also show SSNs. **See details about online access to civil records at front or back of this chapter.**

Criminal Name Search: Access: Mail, in person, online. Both court and visitors may perform in person name searches. Search fee: $25.00 per name, includes certification. Required to search: name, years to search, DOB. Criminal records on computer since 1989, prior in books to 12/1966, rest archived and must be searched in person only. Mail turnaround time 1-2 days. Criminal PAT goes back to same as civil. Terminal results include SSN. **See details about online access to criminal records at front or back of this chapter.**

Person County

Superior-District Court 105 S Main St, Roxboro, NC 27573; 336-503-5200; fax: 336-503-5229; 8AM-5PM (EST). *Felony, Misdemeanor, Civil, Eviction, Small Claims, Probate.*

www.nccourts.org/County/Person/Default.asp

General Information: No adoption, sealed cases, juvenile, sex offenders, mental or expunged records released. Will not fax out documents. Court makes copy: $2.00 1st page, $.25 ea add'l. Certification fee: $3.00; Exemplified copy $10.00. Payee: Clerk of Superior Court. Business checks accepted. No credit cards accepted. Prepayment required. Mail requests: SASE required.

Civil Name Search: Access: In person, online. Visitors must perform in person searches themselves. Civil records on microfiche since 4/89, prior in

index books to 1968. Civil PAT goes back to 4/1997. **See details about online access to civil records at front or back of this chapter.**

Criminal Name Search: Access: Mail, in person, online. Both court and visitors may perform in person name searches. Search fee: $25.00 per name, includes certification. Required to search: name, DOB; also helpful: years to search. Criminal records on computer since 3/88, index cards and books prior to 1968. Mail turnaround time 5-7 days. Criminal PAT goes back to 3/1988. **See details about online access to criminal records at front or back of this chapter.**

Pitt County

Superior-District Court PO Box 6067, 100 W Third St, Greenville, NC 27835; 252-695-7100; criminal phone: 252-695-7117; civil phone: 252-695-7150; fax: 252-695-7376; 8AM-5PM (EST). *Felony, Misdemeanor, Civil, Eviction, Small Claims, Probate.*

www.nccourts.org/County/Pitt/Default.asp

General Information: No adoption, sealed cases, juvenile, sex offenders, mental or expunged records released. Will not fax documents. Court makes copy: $2.00 1st page, $.25 ea add'l. Certification fee: $3.00. Payee: Clerk of Court. No personal checks or credit cards accepted. Prepayment required. Mail requests: SASE required.

Civil Name Search: Access: In person, online. Visitors must perform in person searches themselves. Required to search: name, years to search; also helpful: address. Civil records on computer back to 1988, on books to 1968. Civil PAT goes back to 1988. **See details about online access to civil records at front or back of this chapter.**

Criminal Name Search: Access: Mail, in person, online. Both court and visitors may perform in person name searches. Search fee: $25.00 per name, includes certification. Required to search: name, years to search, DOB; also helpful: address, SSN. Criminal records computerized from 2/85, on books and cards to early 1900s. Mail turnaround time 1-2 days. Criminal PAT goes back to 2/1985. **See details about online access to criminal records at front or back of this chapter.**

Polk County

Superior-District Court PO Box 38, Columbus, NC 28722; 828-894-8231; fax: 828-894-5752; 8AM-5PM (EST). *Felony, Misdemeanor, Civil, Eviction, Small Claims, Probate.*

www.nccourts.org/County/Polk/Default.asp

General Information: No adoption, sealed cases, juvenile, sex offenders, mental, expunged or dismissed records released. Will fax documents $1.00 1st page, $.25 each add'l page. Court makes copy: $2.00 1st page, $.25 ea add'l. Certification fee: $3.00. Payee: Clerk of Superior Court. Business checks accepted. No credit cards accepted. Prepayment required. Mail requests: SASE required.

Civil Name Search: Access: Mail, in person, online. Visitors must perform in person searches themselves. No search fee. Civil records on computer since 5/89, prior on books to 1968. Civil PAT goes back to 1989. **See details about online access to civil records at front or back of this chapter.**

Criminal Name Search: Access: Mail, in person, online. Both court and visitors may perform in person name searches. Search fee: $25.00 per name, includes certification. Required to search: name, years to search, DOB. Criminal records on computer since 5/89, prior on books to 1968. Mail turnaround time 1-2 days. Criminal PAT goes back to same as civil. **See details about online access to criminal records at front or back of this chapter.**

Randolph County

Superior-District Court 176 E Salisbury St #201, Asheboro, NC 27203; 336-328-3000; criminal phone: 336-328-3005; civil phone: 336-328-3004; fax: 336-328-3131; 8AM-5PM (EST). *Felony, Misdemeanor, Civil, Eviction, Small Claims, Probate.*

www.nccourts.org/County/Randolph/Default.asp

General Information: No adoption, sealed cases, juvenile, sex offenders, mental or expunged records released. Will not fax documents. Court makes copy: $2.00 1st page, $.25 ea add'l. Certification fee: $3.00 per doc. Payee: Clerk of Superior Court. Only cashiers checks and money orders accepted. No credit cards accepted. Prepayment required. Mail requests: SASE required for criminal.

Civil Name Search: Access: In person, online. Visitors must perform in person searches themselves. Civil records on computer since 2/89, prior on books to 1800s archived in Raleigh. **See details about online access to civil records at front or back of this chapter.**

Criminal Name Search: Access: Mail, in person, online. Only the court performs in person name searches; visitors may not. Search fee: $25.00 per name, includes certification. Required to search: name, years to search, address, DOB. Criminal records on computer since 6/85, prior on books and cards from 1970 to 1981. Microfilm from 1981 to 6/85. Mail turnaround time 1-2 days. **See details about online access to criminal records at front or back of this chapter.**

Richmond County

Superior-District Court 105 W Franklin St, Rockingham, NC 28379; 910-419-7400; fax: 910-419-7402; 8AM-5PM (EST). *Felony, Misdemeanor, Civil, Eviction, Small Claims, Probate.*
www.nccourts.org/County/Richmond/Default.asp

General Information: No adoption, sealed cases, juvenile, sex offenders, mental or expunged records released. Will not fax documents. Court makes copy: $3.00 per doc; divorces- $2.50 1st page, $.25 each add'l. Self serve copy: same. Certification fee: $3.00. Payee: Clerk of Superior Court. Business checks accepted. No credit cards accepted. Prepayment required. Mail requests: SASE required for criminal.

Civil Name Search: Access: In person, online. Visitors must perform in person searches themselves. Required to search: name, years to search; also helpful- address. Civil records on computer since 4/89, prior on books since 1968. Civil PAT goes back to 1988. **See details about online access to civil records at front or back of this chapter.**

Criminal Name Search: Access: Mail, in person, online. Both court and visitors may perform in person name searches. Search fee: $25.00 per name, includes certification. Required to search: name, years to search, DOB; also helpful: address, SSN. Criminal records on computer since 1988, cards to 1977, books 1969 to 1977, prior archived. Mail turnaround time 1-2 days. Criminal PAT goes back to same as civil. **See details about online access to criminal records at front or back of this chapter.**

Robeson County

Superior-District Court PO Box 1084, Lumberton, NC 28359; 910-272-5900; fax: 910-272-5901; 8:15AM-5:15PM (EST). *Felony, Misdemeanor, Civil, Eviction, Small Claims, Probate.*
www.nccourts.org/County/Robeson/Default.asp

General Information: Will not fax documents. Court makes copy: $2.00 1st page, $.25 ea add'l. Certification fee: Certification is $3.00; Exemplification is $10.00. Payee: Clerk of Superior Court. Business checks accepted if in state. No credit cards accepted for records searches or copies. Prepayment required. Mail requests: SASE required for criminal.

Civil Name Search: Access: In person, online. Visitors must perform in person searches themselves. Required to search: name, years to search; also helpful: address. Civil records on computer since 1988, prior on books since 1966. Civil PAT goes back to 1988. **See details about online access to civil records at front or back of this chapter.**

Criminal Name Search: Access: Mail, in person, online. Both court and visitors may perform in person name searches. Search fee: $25.00 per name, includes certification. Required to search: name, years to search; also helpful: address, DOB. Criminal records on computer since 1983, index books prior. Mail turnaround time 1-2 days. Criminal PAT goes back to 1983. **See details about online access to criminal records at front or back of this chapter.**

Rockingham County

Superior-District Court PO Box 127, Wentworth, NC 27375; 336-634-6000; fax: 336-634-6001; 8:30AM-5PM (EST). *Felony, Misdemeanor, Civil, Eviction, Small Claims, Probate.*
www.nccourts.org/County/Rockingham/Default.asp

General Information: Physical address is 170 Highway 65, Wentworth 27320. No adoption, sealed cases, juvenile, sex offenders, mental or expunged records released. Will not fax documents. Court makes copy: $2.00 1st page, $.25 ea add'l. Self serve copy: same. Certification fee: $3.00 per doc. Cert fee includes copies. Payee: Clerk of Superior Court. Only cashiers checks and money orders accepted. No credit cards accepted. Prepayment required. Mail requests: SASE required.

Civil Name Search: Access: In person, online. Both court and visitors may perform in person name searches. No search fee. Civil records on computer since 2/89, prior on books. Civil PAT goes back to 1989. Terminal results also show SSNs. **See details about online access to civil records at front or back of this chapter.**

Criminal Name Search: Access: Mail, in person, online. Both court and visitors may perform in person name searches. Search fee: $25.00 per name, includes certification. Required to search: name, years to search, DOB. Criminal records on computer since 5/85, prior on cards and books. Mail turnaround time 1-2 days. Criminal PAT goes back to 1985. **See details about online access to criminal records at front or back of this chapter.**

Rowan County

Superior-District Court 210 N Main St, Salisbury, NC 28144; 704-797-3001; criminal phone: 704-797-3016 (Supr), 3015 (Dist); civil phone: 704-797-3003; probate phone: 704-797-3005; fax: 704-797-3050; 8AM-5PM (EST). *Felony, Misdemeanor, Civil, Eviction, Small Claims, Probate.*
www.nccourts.org/County/Rowan/Default.asp

General Information: No adoption, sealed cases, juvenile, sex offenders, mental or expunged records released. Will fax documents $2.00 1st page,

$.25 each add'l. Court makes copy: $2.00 1st page, $.25 ea add'l. Certification fee: $3.00; Exemplified copy $10.00. Payee: Clerk of Superior Court. Local and some business checks accepted. No credit cards accepted. Prepayment required.

Civil Name Search: Access: Mail, in person, online. Both court and visitors may perform in person name searches. No search fee. Required to search: name, years to search; also helpful: address. Civil records on computer since 1989, prior on books to 1800s. Mail turnaround time 1-3 days. Civil PAT goes back to 1987. **See details about online access to civil records at front or back of this chapter.**

Criminal Name Search: Access: Mail, in person, online. Both court and visitors may perform in person name searches. Search fee: $25.00 per name, includes certification. Required to search: name; also helpful: DOB, years to search, address, SSN. Criminal records computerized from 5/85, prior on books and cards to 1970. Mail turnaround time 1-3 days. Criminal PAT goes back to 1985. **See details about online access to criminal records at front or back of this chapter.**

Rutherford County

Superior-District Court PO Box 630, 229 N Main St, Rutherfordton, NC 28139; 828-286-9136; criminal phone: 828-286-3243; civil phone: 828-286-9136; fax: 828-286-4322; 8AM-5PM (EST). *Felony, Misdemeanor, Civil, Eviction, Small Claims, Probate.*
www.nccourts.org/County/Rutherford/Default.asp

General Information: No adoption, sealed cases, juvenile, mental or expunged records released. Will not fax documents. Court makes copy: $2.00 1st page, $.25 ea add'l. Certification fee: $3.00; Exemplified copy $6.00. Payee: Clerk of Superior Court. Business checks accepted. No credit cards accepted. Prepayment required. Mail requests: SASE required for criminal.

Civil Name Search: Access: In person, online. Visitors must perform in person searches themselves. Required to search: name, years to search; also helpful: address. Civil records on computer 10/1988, prior on books, some records to 1700s. Civil PAT goes back to 10/1988. **See details about online access to civil records at front or back of this chapter.**

Criminal Name Search: Access: Mail, in person, online. Both court and visitors may perform in person name searches. Search fee: $25.00 per name, includes certification. Required to search: name, years to search, DOB; also helpful: address, SSN. Criminal records on computer since 6/87, prior on microfiche and books dating to 1800s. Mail turnaround time 1-2 days. Criminal PAT goes back to 6/1987. Terminal results also include DL#, Race, Sex. **See details about online access to criminal records at front or back of this chapter.**

Sampson County

Superior-District Court County Courthouse, 101 E Main St, Clinton, NC 28328; 910-592-5191; criminal phone: 910-592-6981; fax: 910-592-5502; 8AM-5PM (EST). *Felony, Misdemeanor, Civil, Eviction, Small Claims, Probate.*
www.sampsoncountyclerkofcourt.org

General Information: No adoption, sealed cases, juvenile, mental or expunged records released. Will fax documents. Court makes copy: $2.00 1st page, $.25 ea add'l. Certification fee: $3.00 per doc. Payee: Clerk of Superior Court. No personal checks or credit cards accepted. Prepayment required. Mail requests: SASE requested for criminal.

Civil Name Search: Access: In person, online. Visitors must perform in person searches themselves. Required to search: name, years to search; also helpful: address. Civil records on computer since 1989, prior on books. Civil PAT goes back to 1989. **See details about online access to civil records at front or back of this chapter.**

Criminal Name Search: Access: Mail, in person, online. Both court and visitors may perform in person name searches. Search fee: $25.00 per name, includes certification. Required to search: name, years to search, DOB; also helpful: address, SSN. Criminal records on computer since 7/87, prior on books. Mail turnaround time 1-2 days. Criminal PAT goes back to 1987. **See details about online access to criminal records at front or back of this chapter.**

Scotland County

Superior-District Court PO Box 769, 212 Biggs St, Laurinburg, NC 28353; 910-266-4400; criminal phone: 910-266-4401; civil phone: 910-266-4402; fax: 910-266-4466; 8:30AM-5PM (EST). *Felony, Misdemeanor, Civil, Eviction, Small Claims, Probate.*
www.nccourts.org/County/Scotland/Default.asp

General Information: Probate fax is same as main fax number. No adoption, sealed cases, juvenile, sex offenders, mental or expunged records released. Will not fax documents. Court makes copy: $2.00 1st page, $.25 ea add'l. Certification fee: $3.00; Exemplified copy $10.00. Payee: Clerk of Court. Only cashiers checks and money orders accepted. No credit cards accepted. Prepayment required. Mail requests: SASE required.

Civil Name Search: Access: In person, online. Visitors must perform in person searches themselves. Civil records on computer since 1988, in books

since 1966. Civil PAT goes back to 1989. **See details about online access to civil records at front or back of this chapter.**
Criminal Name Search: Access: Mail, in person, online. Both court and visitors may perform in person name searches. Search fee: $25.00 per name, includes certification. Required to search: name, years to search, DOB; SSN helpful. Criminal records on computer since 1988, in books 1966-1988, on microfiche 1984-1988. Mail turnaround time 1-2 days. Criminal PAT goes back to 1988. **See details about online access to criminal records at front or back of this chapter.**

Stanly County

Superior-District Court PO Box 668, 201 S 2nd St, Albemarle, NC 28002-0668; 704-986-7000; fax: 704-986-7001; 8:30AM-5PM (EST). *Felony, Misdemeanor, Civil, Eviction, Small Claims, Probate.*
www.nccourts.org/County/Stanly/Default.asp
General Information: No adoption, sealed cases, juvenile, sex offenders, mental or expunged records released. Court makes copy: $2.00 1st page, $.25 ea add'l. Certification fee: None; $3.00 if you perform search in person. Payee: Clerk of Superior Court. Only in-state checks, cashiers checks and money orders accepted. No credit cards accepted. Prepayment required. Mail requests: SASE required.
Civil Name Search: Access: In person, online. Visitors must perform in person searches themselves. Required to search: name, years to search; also helpful: address. Civil records on computer since 1989, books to 1968. Civil PAT goes back to 1989. **See details about online access to civil records at front or back of this chapter.**
Criminal Name Search: Access: Mail, in person, online. Both court and visitors may perform in person name searches. Search fee: $25.00 per name, includes certification. Required to search: name, years to search, DOB. Criminal records on computer since 1989; books from 1968 to May, 1983; microfilm from 1983 to Sept, 1989. Mail turnaround time 1-2 days. Criminal PAT goes back to same as civil. **See details about online access to criminal records at front or back of this chapter.**

Stokes County

Superior-District Court PO Box 250, 1012 Main St, Danbury, NC 27016; 336-593-4400; fax: 336-593-4401; 8:30AM-5PM (EST). *Felony, Misdemeanor, Civil, Eviction, Small Claims, Probate.*
www.stokesclerk.com/
General Information: No adoption, sealed cases, juvenile, sex offenders, mental or expunged records released. Will not fax documents. Court makes copy: $2.00 1st page, $.25 ea add'l. Certification fee: $3.00; exemplification-$20.00 per doc. Payee: Clerk of Superior Court. Only cashiers checks and money orders accepted. No credit cards accepted. Prepayment required. Mail requests: SASE required for criminal.
Civil Name Search: Access: In person, online. Visitors must perform in person searches themselves. Required to search: name, years to search; also helpful: address. Civil records on computer since 9/1988, prior on books to early 1900s. Note: Civil background checks not performed. Civil PAT goes back to 9/1988. **See details about online access to civil records at front or back of this chapter.**
Criminal Name Search: Access: Mail, in person, online. Both court and visitors may perform in person name searches. Search fee: $25.00 per name, includes certification. Required to search: name; also helpful: address, DOB. Criminal records on computer since 9/1988, prior on books to early 1900s. Mail turnaround time 1 week. Criminal PAT goes back to same as civil. **See details about online access to criminal records at front or back of this chapter.**

Surry County

Superior-District Court PO Box 345, 201 E. Kapp St, Dobson, NC 27017; 336-386-3700; fax: 336-386-3701; 8AM-5PM (EST). *Felony, Misdemeanor, Civil, Eviction, Small Claims, Probate.*
www.nccourts.org/County/Surry/Default.asp
General Information: No adoption, sealed cases, juvenile, sex offenders, mental or expunged records released. Will fax documents $1.00 1st page, $.25 each add'l. Court makes copy: $2.00 1st page, $.25 ea add'l. Certification fee: $3.00; Exemplified copy $10.00. Payee: Clerk of Superior Court. Business checks accepted. No personal checks. No credit cards accepted. Prepayment required. Mail requests: SASE required for criminal.
Civil Name Search: Access: In person. Visitors must perform in person searches themselves. Required to search: name, years to search, DOB; also helpful: address. Civil records on computer since 10/88, on books to 1970, must know township for earlier records. Civil PAT goes back to 1987. **See details about online access to civil records at front or back of this chapter.**
Criminal Name Search: Access: Mail, in person, online. Both court and visitors may perform in person name searches. Search fee: $25.00 per name, includes certification. Required to search: name, years to search, DOB. Criminal records on computer since 10/88, on books to 1970, must know township for earlier records. Mail turnaround time 1-2 days. Criminal PAT

goes back to same as civil. **See details about online access to criminal records at front or back of this chapter.**

Swain County

Superior-District Court PO Box 1397, Clerk of Superior Ct, 101 Mitchell St, Admin Bldg, Bryson City, NC 28713; 828-488-2288; fax: 828-488-9360; 8:30AM-5PM (EST). *Felony, Misdemeanor, Civil, Eviction, Small Claims, Probate.*
www.nccourts.org/County/Swain/Default.asp
General Information: No adoption, sealed cases, juvenile, mental or expunged records released. Will fax specific case file $10.00 per page, prepaid. Court makes copy: $2.00 1st page, $.25 ea add'l. Self serve copy: $.25 per page. Certification fee: $3.00; Exemplified copy $10.00. Payee: Clerk of Superior Court. No personal checks accepted. No credit or debit cards accepted. Prepayment required.
Civil Name Search: Access: In person, online. Both court and visitors may perform in person name searches. Search fee: $25.00. Civil records on computer since 5/1989, prior on books to 1920. Public use terminal has civil records back to 5/8/89. **See details about online access to civil records at front or back of this chapter.**
Criminal Name Search: Access: Mail, in person, online. Both court and visitors may perform in person name searches. Search fee: $25.00 per name, includes certification. Required to search: name, years to search, DOB; also helpful-signed release. Criminal records computerized from 8/1984, prior on books to 1969. **See details about online access to criminal records at front or back of this chapter.**

Transylvania County

Superior-District Court 7 E Main St, Brevard, NC 28712; 828-884-3120; criminal phone: 828-884-3128; civil phone: 828-884-3125; fax: 828-883-2161; 8:30AM-5PM (EST). *Felony, Misdemeanor, Civil, Eviction, Small Claims, Probate.* www.nccourts.org/County/Transylvania/Default.asp
General Information: No adoption, sealed cases, juvenile, mental or expunged records released. Will not fax documents. Court makes copy: $2.00 1st page, $.25 ea add'l. Certification fee: $3.00 plus $.25 each add'l page. Exemplification fee- $10.00. Payee: Clerk of Superior Court. In state Personal checks accepted, credit cards are not. Prepayment required. Mail requests: SASE required for criminal.
Civil Name Search: Access: In person, online. Visitors must perform in person searches themselves. Required to search: name, years to search; also helpful: address. Civil records on computer from 11/89, on books from 1968. Civil PAT goes back to 11/1989. **See details about online access to civil records at front or back of this chapter.**
Criminal Name Search: Access: Mail, in person, online. Both court and visitors may perform in person name searches. Search fee: $25.00 per name, includes certification. Required to search: name, years to search, DOB; also helpful: address,. Criminal records computerized from 6/89, on books 1968-1989. Mail turnaround time 1-3 days. Criminal PAT goes back to 6/1989. **See details about online access to criminal records at front or back of this chapter.**

Tyrrell County

Superior-District Court PO Box 406, 403 Main St, Columbia, NC 27925; 252-796-6281; fax: 252-796-0008; 8:30AM-5PM (EST). *Felony, Misdemeanor, Civil, Eviction, Small Claims, Probate.*
www.nccourts.org/County/Tyrrell/Default.asp
General Information: No adoption, sealed cases, juvenile, sex offenders, mental records expunged. Will fax documents for $2.00 first page, $1.00 ea add'l. Court makes copy: $2.00 1st page, $.25 ea add'l. Certification fee: $6.00 per doc. Payee: County Clerk of Court. Business checks accepted. No personal checks. No credit cards accepted. Prepayment required. Mail requests: SASE required.
Civil Name Search: Access: In person, online. Visitors must perform in person searches themselves. Required to search: name, years to search; also helpful: address. Civil records on computer since 10/89, prior on microfilm, books to 1968. Civil PAT goes back to 1996. **See details about online access to civil records at front or back of this chapter.**
Criminal Name Search: Access: Mail, in person, online. Both court and visitors may perform in person name searches. Search fee: $25.00 per name, includes certification. Required to search: name, years to search, DOB; also helpful: address, SSN. Criminal records on computer since 10/89, prior on books to 1968. Mail turnaround time 1-2 days. Criminal PAT goes back to 1990. **See details about online access to criminal records at front or back of this chapter.**

Union County

Superior-District Court PO Box 5038, 400 N Main St (28112), Monroe, NC 28111; 704-698-3100; criminal phone: 704-296-4602; civil phone: 704-296-4601; fax: 704-698-3101; 8:30AM-5PM (EST). *Felony, Misdemeanor, Civil, Eviction, Small Claims, Probate.*
www.nccourts.org/County/Union/Default.asp

General Information: No adoption, sealed cases, juvenile, sex offenders, mental or expunged records released. Will not fax documents. Court makes copy: $2.00 1st page, $.25 ea add'l. Certification fee: $3.00 or copy fee if greater. Payee: Clerk of Superior Court. Will accept local business checks only for civil cases. No credit cards accepted for record searches. Prepayment required.

Civil Name Search: Access: In person, online. Visitors must perform in person searches themselves. Required to search: name, years to search; also helpful: address. Civil records on computer since 3/1989, prior on books to 1968. Civil PAT goes back to 1987. **See details about online access to civil records at front or back of this chapter.**

Criminal Name Search: Access: Mail, in person, online. Both court and visitors may perform in person name searches. Search fee: $25.00 per name, includes certification. Required to search: name, years to search; also helpful: address, DOB. Criminal record on computer since 1989; prior on books to 1968. Mail turnaround time 1-2 weeks. Criminal PAT goes back to 1987. **See details about online access to criminal records at front or back of this chapter.**

Vance County

Superior-District Court 156 Church St. #101, Henderson, NC 27536; 252-738-9000; criminal phone: x1; civil phone: x4; fax: 252-492-6666; 8:30AM-5PM (EST). *Felony, Misdemeanor, Civil, Eviction, Small Claims, Probate.*

www.nccourts.org/County/Vance/Default.asp

General Information: No adoption, sealed cases, juvenile, sex offenders, mental or expunged records released. Will fax documents $1.00 1st page, $.25 each add'l page. Court makes copy: $2.00 1st page, $.25 ea add'l. Certification fee: $3.00; exemplification fee is $10.00. Payee: Clerk of Superior Court. Local checks accepted. No credit cards accepted. Prepayment required.

Civil Name Search: Access: In person, online. Visitors must perform in person searches themselves. Required to search: name, years to search; also helpful: address. Civil records on computer since 1989, prior on books to 1881. Civil PAT goes back to 3/27/1898. Also allows tracking of civil cases from filing to disposition after 01/29/1997. **See details about online access to civil records at front or back of this chapter.**

Criminal Name Search: Access: Mail, in person, online. Both court and visitors may perform in person name searches. Search fee: $25.00 per name, includes certification. Required to search: name, years to search, address, DOB; also helpful: SSN. Criminal records on computer to 12/80, prior on books and cards to 1881. Mail turnaround time 1-2 days. Criminal PAT goes back to same as civil 1979. **See details about online access to criminal records at front or back of this chapter.**

Wake County

Superior-District Court PO Box 351, 316 Fayetteville St Mall, Raleigh, NC 27602; 919-792-4000; criminal phone: 919-792-4300; civil phone: 919-792-4125; probate phone: 919-792-4450;; 8:30AM-5PM (EST). *Felony, Misdemeanor, Civil, Eviction, Small Claims, Probate.*

http://web.co.wake.nc.us/courts/

General Information: Civil Div on 11th Fl; criminal on 1st. Juvenile, judicial waivers, involuntary commitments are confidential. No sealed cases, juvenile, mental or expunged records released. Will not fax documents. Court makes copy: $2.00 1st page, $.25 ea add'l. Certification fee: $3.00 per doc. Payee: Clerk of Superior Court. Business checks accepted with prior registration. No personal checks accepted. No credit cards accepted for record searching or copies. Prepayment required.

Civil Name Search: Access: In person, online. Visitors must perform in person searches themselves. Civil records on computer since 1987, prior on books to 1920s. Civil PAT goes back to 2/1988. **See details about online access to civil records at front or back of this chapter.**

Criminal Name Search: Access: Mail, in person, online. Both court and visitors may perform in person name searches. Search fee: $25.00 per name, includes certification. Criminal records computerized from 5/82, prior on books and cards from 1968. Mail turnaround time 3 days. Criminal PAT goes back to 1982. **See details about online access to criminal records at front or back of this chapter.**

Warren County

Superior-District Court PO Box 709, Warrenton, NC 27589; 252-257-3261; fax: 252-257-5529; 8:30AM-5PM (EST). *Felony, Misdemeanor, Civil, Eviction, Small Claims, Probate.*

www.nccourts.org/County/Warren/Default.asp

General Information: Probate fax is same as main fax number. No adoption, sealed cases, juvenile, sex offenders, mental or expunged records released. Will fax documents $2.00 per page. Court makes copy: $2.00 1st page, $.25 ea add'l. Self serve copy: $.25 per page. Certification fee: $3.00 per copy; Exemplification fee- $10.00. Payee: Clerk of Superior Court.

Business checks accepted; no personal checks. No credit cards accepted. Prepayment required. Mail requests: SASE required.

Civil Name Search: Access: In person, online. Visitors must perform in person searches themselves. Civil records on computer since 1989, prior on books to 1968. Civil PAT goes back to 1989. **See details about online access to civil records at front or back of this chapter.**

Criminal Name Search: Access: Mail, in person, online. Both court and visitors may perform in person name searches. Search fee: $25.00 per name, includes certification. Required to search: name, years to search, DOB. Criminal records computerized from 5/81, prior on books to 1968. Mail turnaround time 1-2 days. Criminal PAT goes back to 1981. **See details about online access to criminal records at front or back of this chapter.**

Washington County

Superior-District Court PO Box 901, Plymouth, NC 27962; 252-793-3013; fax: 252-793-1081; 8AM-5PM (EST). *Felony, Misdemeanor, Civil, Eviction, Small Claims, Probate.*

www.nccourts.org/County/Washington/Default.asp

General Information: No adoption, sealed, juvenile, mental health, expunged records released. Will not fax documents. Court makes copy: $2.00 1st page, $.25 ea add'l. Self serve copy: $.25 per page. Certification fee: $3.00. Payee: Clerk of Court. Business checks accepted. No personal checks or credit cards accepted. Prepayment required. Mail requests: SASE required for criminal.

Civil Name Search: Access: In person, online. Visitors must perform in person searches themselves. Civil records on computer back to 12/89, prior on books. Civil PAT goes back to 12/1989. **See details about online access to civil records at front or back of this chapter.**

Criminal Name Search: Access: Mail, in person, online. Both court and visitors may perform in person name searches. Search fee: $25.00 per name, includes certification. Required to search: name, years to search; also helpful: address, DOB, SSN. Criminal records computerized from 12/89, prior on books. Mail turnaround time 2-3 days. Criminal PAT goes back to same as civil. **See details about online access to criminal records at front or back of this chapter.**

Watauga County

Superior-District Court Courthouse #13, 842 W King St, Boone, NC 28607-3525; 828-268-6600; fax: 828-268-6601; 8AM-5PM (EST). *Felony, Misdemeanor, Civil, Eviction, Small Claims, Probate.*

www.nccourts.org/County/Watauga/Default.asp

General Information: No adoption, sealed, juvenile, sex offenders, mental, expunged or dismissed records released. Will not fax documents. Court makes copy: $2.00 1st page, $.25 ea add'l. Self serve copy: $.25 per page. Certification fee: None; $3.00 if you perform search in person. Payee: Clerk of Court. Only cashiers checks and money orders accepted. No credit cards accepted. Prepayment required. Mail requests: SASE requested for criminal.

Civil Name Search: Access: In person, online. Visitors must perform in person searches themselves. Civil records on computer since 12/5/88, on books to 1872, prior destroyed by fire. Civil PAT goes back to 1988. **See details about online access to civil records at front or back of this chapter.**

Criminal Name Search: Access: Mail, in person, online. Both court and visitors may perform in person name searches. Search fee: $25.00 per name, includes certification. Required to search: name, years to search, DOB, SSN. Criminal records computerized from 11/88, prior on cards and books to 1968. Mail turnaround time 1-2 days. Criminal PAT goes back to same as civil. **See details about online access to criminal records at front or back of this chapter.**

Wayne County

Superior-District Court Clerk of Court, 224 E Walnut St, Rm 230, Goldsboro, NC 27530; 919-722-6100; criminal phone: ext 1; civil phone: ext 3; probate phone: ext4; fax: 919-722-6180; 8AM-5PM (EST). *Felony, Misdemeanor, Civil, Eviction, Small Claims, Probate, Special Proceedings.*

www.nccourts.org/County/Wayne/Default.asp

General Information: Reach Family Division at 919-722-6100 ext2. No adoption, sealed, juvenile, sex offenders, mental, expunged or dismissed. Will fax documents $2.00 1st page, $.25 each add'l. Court makes copy: $2.00 1st page, $.25 ea add'l. Add $1.00 to first page if out of state. Self serve copy: same. Certification fee: $3.00. Payee: Clerk of Superior Court. Business checks accepted. No credit cards accepted. Prepayment required. Mail requests: SASE requested for criminal.

Civil Name Search: Access: In person, online. Visitors must perform in person searches themselves. Required to search: name, years to search; also helpful: address. Civil records on computer since 7-18-88, on books since 1968, open to public prior. Note: Court will not do a search unless book and page number or a year of judgment given. Civil PAT goes back to

1985. **See details about online access to civil records at front or back of this chapter.**

Criminal Name Search: Access: Mail, in person, online. Both court and visitors may perform in person name searches. Search fee: $25.00 per name, includes certification. Required to search: name, years to search, DOB; also helpful: address, aliases. Criminal records on computer since 1985, on books prior1985, open to public prior. Mail turnaround time 1-2 days. Criminal PAT goes back to same as civil. **See details about online access to criminal records at front or back of this chapter.**

Wilkes County

Superior-District Court 500 Courthouse Drive, #1115, Wilkesboro, NC 28697; 336-651-4400; fax: 336-651-4401; 8AM-5PM (EST). *Felony, Misdemeanor, Civil, Eviction, Small Claims, Probate.*
www.nccourts.org/County/Wilkes/
General Information: No adoption, sealed cases, juvenile, sex offenders, mental or expunged records released. Will fax documents $1.00 1st page, $.25 each add'l page. Court makes copy: $2.00 1st page, $.25 ea add'l. Certification fee: $3.00. Payee: Clerk of Superior Court. Only cashiers checks and money orders accepted. No credit cards accepted. Prepayment required. Mail requests: SASE requested for criminal.
Civil Name Search: Access: In person, online. Visitors must perform in person searches themselves. Civil records on computer since 07/87, prior on books to early 1900s. Civil PAT goes back to 1987. **See details about online access to civil records at front or back of this chapter.**
Criminal Name Search: Access: Mail, in person, online. Both court and visitors may perform in person name searches. Search fee: $25.00 per name, includes certification. Required to search: name, years to search, DOB; also helpful: address. Criminal records on computer since 07/87, prior on books to early 1900s. Mail turnaround time 1-2 days. Criminal PAT goes back to same as civil. **See details about online access to criminal records at front or back of this chapter.**

Wilson County

Superior-District Court PO Box 1608, 115 E Nash St, Wilson, NC 27894; 252-291-7500; civil phone: 252-291-7502; probate phone: 252-291-7502; criminal fax: 252-291-8049; civil fax: 8;30AM-5PM; 8;30AM-5PM (EST). *Felony, Misdemeanor, Civil, Eviction, Small Claims, Probate.*
www.nccourts.org/County/Wilson/Default.asp
General Information: No adoption, sealed cases, juvenile, sex offenders, mental, or expunged records released. Will not fax documents. Court makes copy: $2.00 1st page, $.25 ea add'l. Certification fee: $3.00; Exemplified copy $10.00. Payee: Clerk of Court. Only cashiers checks and money orders accepted. No credit cards accepted. Prepayment required. Mail requests: SASE requested for criminal.
Civil Name Search: Access: In person, online. Visitors must perform in person searches themselves. Required to search: name, years to search; also helpful: address. Civil records on computer since 8/88, prior on books to 1968, public viewing from 1915 to 1968. Civil PAT goes back to 10/1989. **See details about online access to civil records at front or back of this chapter.**
Criminal Name Search: Access: Mail, fax, in person, online. Both court and visitors may perform in person name searches. Search fee: $25.00 per name, includes certification. Required to search: name, years to search, DOB; also helpful: address, SSN. Criminal records on computer since 5/86, Index cards to 9/76, books to 1918. Mail turnaround time 2-4 days. Criminal PAT goes back to 5/1986. **See details about online access to criminal records at front or back of this chapter.**

Yadkin County

Superior-District Court PO Box 95, Yadkinville, NC 27055; 336-679-3600; fax: 336-679-3601; 8AM-5PM (EST). *Felony, Misdemeanor, Civil, Eviction, Small Claims, Probate.*
www.nccourts.org/County/Yadkin/Default.asp
General Information: No adoption, sealed cases, juvenile, sex offenders, mental or expunged records released. Will not fax documents. Court makes copy: $2.00 1st page, $.25 ea add'l. Certification fee: $3.00. Payee: Clerk of Superior Court. Business checks or certified funds and money orders accepted. No credit cards accepted. Prepayment required. Mail requests: SASE required for criminal.
Civil Name Search: Access: In person, online. Visitors must perform in person searches themselves. Required to search: name, years to search; also helpful: address. Civil records on computer since 8/89, prior on books to 1970. Public use terminal available. **See details about online access to civil records at front or back of this chapter.**
Criminal Name Search: Access: Mail, in person, online. Both court and visitors may perform in person name searches. Search fee: $25.00 per name, includes certification. Required to search: name, years to search, DOB; also helpful: address. Criminal records on computer since 8/89, prior on books to 1970. Mail turnaround time 1-2 days. Public use terminal

available. **See details about online access to criminal records at front or back of this chapter.**

Yancey County

Superior-District Court 110 Town Square, Rm 5, Burnsville, NC 28714; 828-678-5700; fax: 828-678-5701; 8AM-5PM (EST). *Felony, Misdemeanor, Civil, Eviction, Small Claims, Probate.*
www.nccourts.org/County/Yancey/Default.asp
General Information: No adoption, sealed cases, juvenile, sex offenders, mental, expunged or dismissed records released. Will not fax documents. Court makes copy: $2.00 1st page, $.25 ea add'l. Certification fee: $3.00; Exemplified copy $10.00. Payee: Clerk of Superior Court. Business checks accepted. No personal checks. No credit cards accepted. Prepayment required.
Civil Name Search: Access: In person, online. Visitors must perform in person searches themselves. Required to search: name, years to search; also helpful: address. Civil records on computer since 1988, prior on books. **See details about online access to civil records at front or back of this chapter.**
Criminal Name Search: Access: Mail, in person, online. Only the court performs in person name searches; visitors may not. Search fee: $25.00 per name, includes certification. Required to search: name, years to search, DOB; also helpful: address, SSN. Criminal records on computer since 1998, prior on books. Mail turnaround time depends on ease of access, can take up to 2 weeks. **See details about online access to criminal records at front or back of this chapter.**

About Online Access

The state AOC provides ongoing, high volume requesters and vendors with portions of electronic criminal and civil records on an ongoing basis pursuant to a licensing agreement. A Daily Criminal access is supplied.

However starting in 2011 case dispositions were removed from the extract. Users must now access a secondary source - known as the Green Screen - to find the case details. The Green Screen is a cumbersome system using technology from the 1970's. The requirement of using the Green Screen has increased the turnaround time and fees charged by vendors. To obtain cost and connectivity information contact the NCAOC Remote Public Access team at 919-890-2220 or via email at rpa@nccourts.org.

For a list of the participating vendors visit the web at www.nccourts.org/Citizens/GoToCourt/Default.asp?topic=1.

There are several other North Carolina online services that are free. Search civil and criminal court calendars at www1.aoc.state.nc.us/www/calendars.html. Search the District-Superior system for current criminal defendants at www1.aoc.state.nc.us/www/calendars/CriminalQuery.html.

At thsi site there are also querys for Impaired Driving, Citations, and Current Civil and Criminal Calendars.

North Dakota

Time Zone:	**CST**
Capital:	**Bismarck, Burleigh County**
# of Counties:	**53**
State Web:	**www.nd.gov**
Court Web:	**www.ndcourts.gov**

Administration

State Court Administrator, North Dakota Judiciary, 600 E Blvd, 1st Floor Judicial Wing, Dept. 180, Bismarck, ND, 58505-0530; 701-328-4216, Fax: 701-328-2092.

The Supreme and Appellate Courts

The Supreme Court is the court of last resort. The Court of Appeals only hears cases assigned to it by the Supreme Court. Some years no cases are assigned. One may search North Dakota Supreme Court dockets and opinions at www.ndcourts.gov. Search by docket number, party name, or anything else that may appear in the text. Records are from 1982 forward. Email notification of new opinions is also available.

The North Dakota Courts

Court	Type	How Organized	Jurisdiction Highpoints
District*	General	53Courts in 7 Districts	Felony, Misdemeanor, Civil, Small Claims Juvenile, Evictions
Municipal*	Limited	88 Courts in 88 Towns	Traffic, Ordinance

* = profiled in this book

Details on the Court Structure

The **District Courts** have general jurisdiction over criminal, civil, and juvenile matters. At one time there were County Courts, but these courts merged with the District Courts statewide in 1995. These older County Court records are held by the 53 District Court Clerks in the 7 judicial districts.

Municipal Courts in North Dakota have jurisdiction for all violations of traffic and municipal ordinances, with some exceptions.

Record Searching Facts You Need to Know

Fees and Record Searching Tips

Since 1997, the standardized search fee in District Courts is $10.00 per name and the certification fee is $10.00 per document. The standard copy fee is $.50 per page but most courts charge less. For search requests for records previous to 1995, it is recommended to include the phrase "include all County Court cases" in the request.

Online Access is Statewide

In the Spring of 2011, the state completed the migration to the new online access system for court record index data, including civil, criminal, probate, traffic, family case files as well as judgments. All District Courts as well as thirteen Muncipal Courts participate. The web page is found at http://publicsearch.ndcourts.gov/. There are a variety of searches, including by name, case number, attorney, and date filed. Results will provide year of birth. If full DOB is input at time of search, results will show full DOB if matching. Data throughput varies by each county; most counties go back at least 7 years.

Adams County

Southwest Judicial District Court PO Box 469, Attn- Clerk of Court, 602 Adams Ave, Hettinger, ND 58639; 701-567-2537; fax: 701-567-2910; 8:00AM-N; 12:30PM-5PM (MST). *Felony, Misdemeanor, Civil, Eviction, Small Claims, Probate.*

General Information: Search requests must be in writing. Probate fax is same as main fax number. No adoption, sealed, juvenile, mental health, expunged, DV or dismissed records released. Fee to fax out file $3.00 1st 2 pages, $.50 each add'l. Court makes copy: $1.00 per page, if over 5 pgs $.25 per add'l page. Certification fee: $10.00 per document, copy fee included. Payee: Clerk of District Court. Personal checks accepted, credit cards are not. Prepayment required. Mail requests: SASE required.

Civil Name Search: Access: Fax, mail, in person, online. Both court and visitors may perform in person name searches. Search fee: $10.00 per name. Required to search: name, years to search; also helpful: address. Civil index on cards from 1990, on docket books in vault from 1900s. Mail turnaround time 1-2 days. Civil PAT goes back to 1/1995. Year of birth is only identifier shown. Access civil index on the state system at http://publicsearch.ndcourts.gov/default.aspx. Index goes back to 12/2001. Search by name and case number, an advanced search allows search with year of birth.

Criminal Name Search: Access: Fax, mail, in person, online. Both court and visitors may perform in person name searches. Search fee: $10.00 per name. Required to search: name, years to search, DOB; also helpful: address. Criminal records indexed on cards from 1990, on docket books in vault from 1900s. Mail turnaround time 1-2 days. Criminal PAT goes back to 1/1995. Year of birth is only identifier shown. Access criminal index on the state system at http://publicsearch.ndcourts.gov/default.aspx. Index goes back to 12/2001. Search by name and case number, an advanced search allows search with year of birth. Online results show name only.

Barnes County

Southeast Judicial District Court PO Box 774, Valley City, ND 58072; 701-845-8512; fax: 701-845-1341; 8AM-5PM (CST). *Felony, Misdemeanor, Civil, Eviction, Small Claims, Probate.*

General Information: No adoption, paternity, sealed, juvenile, mental health, expunged or dismissed records released. Will fax documents to local or toll-free number. Court makes copy: $.25 per page. Self serve copy: same. Certification fee: $10.00 per document. $5.00 for second copy same doc. Payee: Clerk of District Court. Personal checks and major credit cards accepted. Prepayment required. Mail requests: SASE required.

Civil Name Search: Access: Fax, mail, in person, online. Both court and visitors may perform in person name searches. Search fee: $10.00 per name. Required to search: name, years to search; also helpful: address. Civil index on docket books from early 1900s; on computer back to March, 1997. Mail turnaround time 1-2 days. Civil PAT goes back to 1997. If civil money judgment, on computer back to the 1980's. Access civil index on the state system at http://publicsearch.ndcourts.gov/default.aspx. Index goes back to 3/1997. The site includes separate search for Valley City Municipal Court. Search by name and DOB and case type, results may show city of residence.

Criminal Name Search: Access: Fax, mail, in person, online. Both court and visitors may perform in person name searches. Search fee: $10.00 per name. Required to search: name, years to search; also helpful: address, DOB, SSN. Criminal records maintained here for 10 years, archived on index books from early 1900s; on computer back to March, 1997. Mail turnaround time 1-2 days. Criminal PAT goes back to same as civil. Access criminal index on the state system at http://publicsearch.ndcourts.gov/default.aspx. Index goes back to 3/1997. The site includes separate search for Valley City Municipal Court. Search by name and DOB and case type, results may show city of residence. Online results show name only.

Benson County

Northeast Judicial District Court PO Box 213, Minnewaukan, ND 58351; 701-473-5345; fax: 701-473-5345; 8:30AM-4:30PM (CST). *Felony, Misdemeanor, Civil, Eviction, Small Claims, Probate.*

General Information: No adoption, sealed, juvenile, mental health, expunged or dismissed records released. Will fax documents $1.00 per page. Court makes copy: $.25 per page. Certification fee: $10.00 per doc includes copy fee. Payee: Benson County Court. Personal checks accepted. Major credit cards accepted, minimum fee $10.00. Prepayment required. Mail requests: SASE required.

Civil Name Search: Access: Fax, mail, in person, online. Only the court performs in person name searches; visitors may not. Search fee: $10.00 per name. Required to search: name, years to search; also helpful: address. Civil index on docket books and index books from early 1900s, on index cards from 6/10/91. Note: Visitors must do their own judgment searching. Mail turnaround time 5 days. Online access to civil is same as criminal. Search by name and DOB and case type, results may show city of residence.

Criminal Name Search: Access: Fax, mail, in person, online. Only the court performs in person name searches; visitors may not. Search fee: $10.00 per name. Required to search: name, years to search, DOB, signed release; also helpful: address. Criminal docket on books and index books from early 1900s, on index cards from 6/10/91. Note: Signed release required for juvenile cases. Mail turnaround time 5 days. Access criminal index on the state system at http://publicsearch.ndcourts.gov/default.aspx. Index goes back to 4/2000. Search by name and DOB and case type, results may show city of residence. Online results show name only.

Billings County

Southwest Judicial District Court PO Box 138, Medora, ND 58645; 701-623-4492; fax: 701-623-4382; 8AM-N, 4PM Labor to Mem Day; Summer- 8AM-5PM M,TH; 8AM-N F (MST). *Felony, Misdemeanor, Civil, Eviction, Small Claims, Probate.*

General Information: No adoption, sealed, juvenile, mental health, expunged or dismissed records released. Will fax documents $2.00 1st 4 pages, $.50 each add'l. Court makes copy: $1.00 per page. Self serve copy:

$.25 per page. Certification fee: $10.00 plus $5.00 each add'l page. Payee: Clerk of District Court. No out-of-state checks accepted unless pre-approved; fax copy of check to clerk. Major credit cards accepted. Prepayment required. Copy of check maybe faxed to 701-623-4382. Mail requests: SASE required.

Civil Name Search: Access: Fax, mail, in person, online. Both court and visitors may perform in person name searches. Search fee: $10.00 per name. Required to search: name, years to search; also helpful: address. Civil index on docket books from 1800s; on computer back to 1996. Mail turnaround time 1 day. Civil PAT goes back to 1996. Can only view, cannot print from the terminal. Access criminal index on the state system at http://publicsearch.ndcourts.gov/default.aspx. Index goes back to 1/2003. Search by name and case number, an advanced search allows search with DOB, often year only.

Criminal Name Search: Access: Fax, mail, in person, online. Both court and visitors may perform in person name searches. Search fee: $10.00 per name. Required to search: name, years to search; also helpful: address, DOB, SSN. Criminal records in books. Mail turnaround time 1 day. Criminal PAT goes back to same as criminal. Can only view, cannot print from the terminal. Access criminal index on the state system at http://publicsearch.ndcourts.gov/default.aspx. Index goes back to 1/2003. Search by name and case number, an advanced search allows search with DOB, often year only. Online results show name only.

Bottineau County

Northeast Judicial District Court 314 W 5th St, #12, Bottineau, ND 58318; 701-228-3983; fax: 701-228-2336; 8AM-5PM (CST). *Felony, Misdemeanor, Civil, Eviction, Small Claims, Probate.*

General Information: No adoption, paternity, sealed, juvenile, mental health, expunged or dismissed records released. Will fax documents $4.00 1st page, $2.00 each add'l. Court makes copy: $.25 per page. Certification fee: $10.00 per doc. Payee: Clerk of the Court. Personal checks accepted, credit cards are not. Prepayment required. Mail requests: SASE required.

Civil Name Search: Access: Fax, mail, in person, online. Only the court performs in person name searches; visitors may not. Search fee: $10.00 per name. Required to search: name, years to search; also helpful: address. Civil index on cards from 1987, on docket books from 1972. Mail turnaround time 1 day. Online access to civil is same as criminal. Search by name and DOB and case type, results may show city of residence.

Criminal Name Search: Access: Fax, mail, in person, online. Only the court performs in person name searches; visitors may not. Search fee: $10.00 per name. Required to search: name, years to search; also helpful: address, DOB, SSN. Criminal docket on books from 1885. Mail turnaround time 1 day. Access criminal index on the state system at http://publicsearch.ndcourts.gov/default.aspx. Index goes back to 11/1997. Search by name and DOB and case type, results may show city of residence. Online results show name only.

Bowman County

Southwest Judicial District Court 104 1st Street NW, #3, Bowman, ND 58623; 701-523-3450; fax: 701-523-5443; 8AM-N, 1-4:30PM (MST). *Felony, Misdemeanor, Civil, Eviction, Small Claims, Probate.*

General Information: Probate fax is same as main fax number. No adoption, sealed, juvenile, mental health, expunged or dismissed records released. Will fax documents to local or toll free line. Court makes copy: $.25 per page. Certification fee: $10.00 per document; add'l document copies $5.00 each. Payee: Clerk of Court. Personal checks accepted, credit cards are not. Prepayment required. Mail requests: SASE required.

Civil Name Search: Access: Mail, in person, phone, fax, online. Both court and visitors may perform in person name searches. Search fee: $10.00 per name. Required to search: name, years to search; also helpful: address. Civil records on dockets from 1907; computerized records back to 1995. Mail turnaround time 1-2 days. Online access is same as criminal. Search by name and case number, result may show city of residence. An advanced search allows search with DOB.

Criminal Name Search: Access: Mail, in person, online. Only the court performs in person name searches; visitors may not. Search fee: $10.00 per name. Required to search: name, years to search, DOB; also helpful: address. Criminal records on microfiche from 1978, on dockets from 1907; computerized records back to 1995. Mail turnaround time 1-2 days. Access criminal index on the state system at http://publicsearch.ndcourts.gov/default.aspx. Index goes back to 12/1996. Search by name and case number, result may show city of residence. Online results show name only. An advanced search allows search with DOB.

Burke County

Northwest Judicial District Court PO Box 219, 103 Main St, Bowbells, ND 58721; 701-377-2718; fax: 701-377-2020; 8:30AM-N, 1-5 PM (CST). *Felony, Misdemeanor, Civil, Eviction, Small Claims, Probate.*

General Information: No adoption, sealed, juvenile, mental health, expunged or dismissed records released. Will fax back docs for $2.00 per page. Court makes copy: $.50 per page. Certification fee: $10.00 per doc includes copies. Payee: Clerk of Court. Personal checks accepted, credit cards are not. Prepayment required.

Civil Name Search: Access: Fax, mail, in person, online. Both court and visitors may perform in person name searches. Search fee: $10.00 if a written reply is required. Required to search: name, years to search; also helpful: address. Civil records for county civil, probate, and district from 1910, county small claims from 1980. Mail turnaround time 1-3 days. Civil PAT goes back to 2005. Access Civil index on the state system at http://publicsearch.ndcourts.gov/default.aspx. Index goes back to 4/2002. Search by name and case number, result may show city of residence. An advanced search allows search with DOB.

Criminal Name Search: Access: Fax, mail, in person, online. Both court and visitors may perform in person name searches. Search fee: $10.00 if a written reply is required. Required to search: name, years to search; also helpful: address, DOB, SSN. Criminal records for from 1910, county criminal from 1980. Mail turnaround time 1-3 days. Criminal PAT goes back to 2005. Access criminal index on the state system at http://publicsearch.ndcourts.gov/default.aspx. Index from 4/2002. Search by name and case number, result may show city of residence. Online results show name only. An advanced search allows search with DOB.

Burleigh County

South Central Judicial District Court PO Box 1055, 514 East Thayer Ave, Bismarck, ND 58502; 701-222-6690; criminal phone: #2; civil phone: #1; probate phone: 701-222-6690; fax: 701-222-6689; 8AM-5PM (CST). *Felony, Misdemeanor, Civil, Eviction, Small Claims, Probate.*

General Information: No adoption, sealed, juvenile, mental health, expunged or dismissed records released. Will fax documents to local or toll free line. Court makes copy: $.10 per page; $1.00 minimum. Certification fee: $10.00 plus $5.00 each add'l Cert copy. Payee: Clerk of Court. Personal checks, Visa/MC accepted. Prepayment required.

Civil Name Search: Access: Mail, in person, online. Both court and visitors may perform in person name searches. Search fee: $10.00 per name. Required to search: name; also helpful: years to search. Civil records on computer back to 1/91; in books from 1890s. Mail turnaround time 2 days. Civil PAT goes back to 1991. DOB and Initials do not always appear on results. Access criminal index on the state system at http://publicsearch.ndcourts.gov/default.aspx. Index goes back to 12/1990. Online includes Bismarck Muni Court and Lincoln Muni Court. Search by name and case number, result may show city of residence. An advanced search allows search with DOB.

Criminal Name Search: Access: Mail, in person, online. Both court and visitors may perform in person name searches. Search fee: $10.00 per name. Required to search: name; also helpful: years to search, address, DOB, SSN. Criminal records computerized from 1/91; in books from early 1900s. Mail turnaround time 1-2 days. Criminal PAT goes back to same as civil. DOB and Initials do not always appear on results. Access criminal index on the state system at http://publicsearch.ndcourts.gov/default.aspx. Index goes back to 12/1990. Online includes municipal courts in Bismarck and Lincoln. Search by name and case number, result may show city of residence. An advanced search allows search with DOB.

Cass County

East Central Judicial District Court PO Box 2806, 211 9th St, Fargo, ND 58108; criminal phone: 701-241-5660; civil phone: 701-241-5645; probate phone: 701-241-5655; 8AM-5PM (CST). *Felony, Misdemeanor, Civil, Eviction, Small Claims, Probate.*

General Information: Older case data can be accessed form the ND Archives or North Dakota University web pages. No adoption, sealed, juvenile, mental health, expunged or dismissed records released. Court makes copy: $.10 per page, $1.00 minimum. Self serve copy: same. Certification fee: $10.00 per doc includes copy fee. Payee: Clerk of District Court. Personal checks accepted. Credit cards accepted. Prepayment required. Mail requests: SASE required.

Civil Name Search: Access: Mail, fax, in person, online. Both court and visitors may perform in person name searches. Search fee: $10.00 per name. Required to search: name, years to search; also helpful: address. Civil records index on computer from 1988, on index books from late 1800s. Mail turnaround time 3-5 days. Civil PAT goes back to 1988. Access civil index on the state system at http://publicsearch.ndcourts.gov/default.aspx. Index goes back to 11/2002. Online includes West Fargo Muni Court. Search probate records from the 1870s to 1951 online at http://library.ndsu.edu/db/probate/. There is no fee.

Criminal Name Search: Access: Mail, fax, in person, online. Both court and visitors may perform in person name searches. Search fee: $10.00 per name. Required to search: name, DOB, years to search. Criminal records computerized from 1988, on index cards from 1980. Mail turnaround time 3-5 days. Criminal PAT goes back to same as civil. Access criminal index on the state system at http://publicsearch.ndcourts.gov/default.aspx. Index goes back to 11/2002. Online includes West Fargo Muni Court. Search by name and

DOB and case type, results may show city of residence. Online results show name only.

Cavalier County

Northeast Judicial District Court 901 Third St, Ste 1, Langdon, ND 58249; 701-256-2124; fax: 701-256-3468; 8:30AM-4:30PM (CST). *Felony, Misdemeanor, Civil, Eviction, Small Claims, Probate.* www.ndcourts.gov/court/counties/cavalier.htm

General Information: No adoption, sealed, juvenile, mental health, expunged or dismissed records released. Will fax documents for fee for $.25 per page. Court makes copy: $.10 per page but $1.00 minimum charge. Certification fee: $10.00. Payee: Clerk of Court. Personal checks and major credit cards accepted. Prepayment required. Mail requests: SASE required.

Civil Name Search: Access: Fax, mail, in person, online. Both court and visitors may perform in person name searches. Search fee: $10.00 per name. Required to search: name, years to search; also helpful: address. Civil records going on computer, prior stored. Mail turnaround time 1 week. Civil PAT goes back to 1997. Online access to civil is same as criminal. Search by name and DOB and case type, results may show city of residence.

Criminal Name Search: Access: Fax, mail, in person, online. Both court and visitors may perform in person name searches. Search fee: $10.00 per name. Required to search: name, years to search; also helpful: address, DOB. Criminal records for District Court on index books from 1937, for County Court on index books from 1983, prior stored. Mail turnaround time 1 week. Criminal PAT goes back to 1997. Access criminal index on the state system at http://publicsearch.ndcourts.gov/default.aspx. Index goes back to 11/1997. Search by name and DOB and case type, results may show city of residence. Online results show name only.

Dickey County

Southeast Judicial District Court Clerk of Court, PO Box 336, Ellendale, ND 58436; 701-349-3249 X4; fax: 701-349-3560; 9AM-N, 1-4:30PM (CST). *Felony, Misdemeanor, Civil, Eviction, Small Claims, Probate.*

General Information: Probate uses the same fax number. No adoption, sealed, juvenile, mental health, expunged or dismissed-deferred records released. Will fax documents to local or toll free line. Court makes copy: $.25 per page. Certification fee: $10.00 per document. Payee: Clerk of Court. Personal checks and major credit cards accepted. Prepayment required.

Civil Name Search: Access: Mail, in person, online. Only the court performs in person name searches; visitors may not. Search fee: $10.00 per name. Required to search: name, years to search; also helpful: address. Civil index on docket books to 1983; 1997-present. Old district court records have no index and are very hard to search prior to 1925. Probate from 1800s. Mail turnaround time 3-5 days. Online access to civil is same as criminal. Search by name and DOB and case type, results may show city of residence.

Criminal Name Search: Access: Mail, in person, online. Only the court performs in person name searches; visitors may not. Search fee: $10.00 per name. Required to search: name, years to search, DOB; also helpful: address, SSN. Criminal records indexed in books to 1983, 1997- present. Old district court records have no index and are very hard to search. Mail turnaround time 1-2 days. Access criminal index on the state system at http://publicsearch.ndcourts.gov/default.aspx. Index goes back to 5/1997. Search by name and DOB and case type, results may show city of residence. Online results show name only.

Divide County

Northwest Judicial District Court PO Box 68, Crosby, ND 58730; 701-965-6831; fax: 701-965-6943; 8:30AM-N, 1-5PM (CST). *Felony, Misdemeanor, Civil, Eviction, Small Claims, Probate.*

General Information: No adoption, sealed, juvenile, mental health, expunged or dismissed records released. Will fax documents $3.00 1st page, $1.00 each add'l. Also a $1.00 charge per incoming fax page. Court makes copy: $.25 per page, $2.00 minimum if by mail. Certification fee: $10.00 per doc. Payee: Clerk of District Court. Personal checks accepted, credit cards are not. Prepayment required. Mail requests: SASE required.

Civil Name Search: Access: Fax, mail, in person, online. Both court and visitors may perform in person name searches. Search fee: $10.00 per name. Required to search: name, years to search; also helpful: address. Civil index on docket books from 1910. Note: Visitor can check for judgments. Records for eviction, small claims and probate are an additional $10.00 if full certification needed. Mail turnaround time 1-2 days. Civil PAT available. Online access to civil is same as criminal via the statewide court website. Search by name and case number, result may show city of residence. An advanced search allows search with DOB.

Criminal Name Search: Access: Fax, mail, in person, online. Both court and visitors may perform in person name searches. Search fee: $10.00 per name. Required to search: name, years to search; also helpful: address, DOB, SSN. Criminal records indexed in books from 1910. Mail turnaround time 1-2 days. Criminal PAT available. Access criminal index on the state system at http://publicsearch.ndcourts.gov/default.aspx. Index goes back to 4/2003. Search by name and case number, result may show city of residence. An advanced search allows search of traffic citation with DOB. Online results show name only.

Dunn County

District Court PO Box 136, 205 Owens St, Manning, ND 58642-0136; 701-573-4447; fax: 701-573-4444; 8AM-N,12:30-4:30PM (MST). *Felony, Misdemeanor, Civil, Small Claims, Probate.*

General Information: Probate fax is same as main fax number. Adoptions, paternity, juvenile, mental health, deferred impositions, and termination of parental rights are restricted access files. Will fax documents $2.00 plus $1.00 per page. Court makes copy: $1.00 per page. Self serve copy: same. Certification fee: $10.00 per document includes copy fee. Payee: Dunn County Clerk of Court. In state Personal checks accepted, credit cards are not. Prepayment required.

Civil Name Search: Access: Fax, mail, in person, online. Both court and visitors may perform in person name searches. Search fee: $10.00 per name. Required to search: name, years to search; also helpful: address. Civil records on plaintiff/defendant index cards from 1988, on docket books from 1900s, on computer since 1/97. Note: Fax requests must include copy of the check to be mailed. Mail turnaround time 2 days. Civil PAT goes back to 1/1997. Online access to civil is same as criminal via the statewide court website. Search by name and case number, result may show city of residence. An advanced search allows search with DOB.

Criminal Name Search: Access: Fax, mail, in person, online. Both court and visitors may perform in person name searches. Search fee: $10.00 per name. Required to search: name, years to search, DOB; also helpful: address, SSN. Criminal records on plaintiff/defendant index cards from 1988, on docket books from 1900s, on computer since 1/97. Note: Fax requesters must fax copy of the check, which can be mailed. Mail turnaround time 2 days. Criminal PAT goes back to same as civil. Access criminal index on the state system at http://publicsearch.ndcourts.gov/default.aspx. Index goes back to 1/1997. Search by name and case number, result may show city of residence. Online results show name only. An advanced search allows search with DOB.

Eddy County

Southeast Judicial District Court 524 Central Ave, c/o Clerk of District Court, New Rockford, ND 58356; 701-947-2813 x2013; fax: 701-947-2067; 8AM-4PM (CST). *Felony, Misdemeanor, Civil, Eviction, Small Claims, Probate.*

General Information: No adoption, sealed, juvenile, mental health, expunged or dismissed records released. Fee to fax out file $4.00 1st 3 pages, $1.00 each add'l page. Court makes copy: $1.00 per document. Certification fee: $10.00. Payee: Eddy County District Court. Personal checks accepted, credit cards are not. Prepayment required. Mail requests: SASE required.

Civil Name Search: Access: Fax, mail, in person, online. Both court and visitors may perform in person name searches. Search fee: $10.00 per name. Required to search: name, years to search; also helpful: address. Civil index on cards from 4/92, on index books from early 1900s. Note: All requests must be in writing. Mail turnaround time 1-2 days. Online access to civil is same as criminal. Search by name and DOB and case type, results may show city of residence.

Criminal Name Search: Access: Fax, mail, in person, online. Both court and visitors may perform in person name searches. Search fee: $10.00 per name. Required to search: name, years to search; also helpful: address, DOB, SSN. Criminal records indexed on cards from 4/92, on index books from early 1900s. Note: All requests must be in writing. Mail turnaround time 1-2 days. Access criminal index on the state system at http://publicsearch.ndcourts.gov/default.aspx. Index goes back to 8/1997. Search by name and DOB and case type, results may show city of residence. Online results show name only.

Emmons County

South Central Judicial District Court PO Box 905, Linton, ND 58552; 701-254-4812; fax: 701-254-4012; 8:30AM-N, 1-5PM (CST). *Felony, Misdemeanor, Civil, Eviction, Small Claims, Probate.*
http://emmonscounty.tripod.com/

General Information: Probate fax is same as main fax number. No adoption, sealed, juvenile, mental health, expunged or dismissed records released. Fee to fax out file $3.00 1st page, $1.00 each add'l. Court makes copy: $.20 per page. Certification fee: $10.00 per document. Payee: Clerk of Courts. Personal checks accepted. Visa/MC/Discover accepted. Prepayment required. Mail requests: SASE required.

Civil Name Search: Access: Fax, mail, in person, online. Only the court performs in person name searches; visitors may not. Search fee: $10.00 per name. Required to search: name, years to search; also helpful: address. Civil index on cards from 1988, on index books from 1914, on computer back to 1995. Mail turnaround time 1-2 days. Public use terminal has civil records. Online access to civil is same as criminal via the statewide court website. Search by name and case number, result may show city of residence. An advanced search allows search with DOB.

Criminal Name Search: Access: Fax, mail, in person, online. Only the court performs in person name searches; visitors may not. Search fee: $10.00 per name. Required to search: name, years to search, DOB; also helpful: address, SSN. Criminal records indexed in books back to 1983; on computer back to 1995. Mail turnaround time 1-2 days. Access criminal index back to 1/1996 on the state system at http://publicsearch.ndcourts.gov/default.aspx. Search by name and case number. Online results show name only. An advanced search allows search with DOB.

Foster County

Southeast Judicial District Court PO Box 257, Attn: Foster County Clerk of Court, Carrington, ND 58421; 701-652-1001; fax: 701-652-2173; 8:30AM-4:30PM (CST). *Felony, Misdemeanor, Civil, Eviction, Small Claims, Probate.*
https://mylocalgov.com/FosterCountyND/index.asp

General Information: No adoption, sealed, juvenile, mental health, expunged or dismissed records released. Will fax documents $3.00 each. Court makes copy: $1.00 per page. Self serve copy: same. Certification fee: $10.00. Payee: Clerk of Courts. Personal checks accepted. Credit cards accepted. Prepayment required. Mail requests: SASE required.

Civil Name Search: Access: Mail, in person, online. Both court and visitors may perform in person name searches. Search fee: $10.00 per name. Required to search: name, years to search; also helpful: address. Civil index on docket books from early 1900s. Mail turnaround time 1-2 days. Civil PAT available. The public terminal connects to the statewide system. Access civil index back to 5/2000 on the state system at http://publicsearch.ndcourts.gov/default.aspx. Search by name and DOB and case type, results may show city of residence.

Criminal Name Search: Access: Mail, in person, online. Both court and visitors may perform in person name searches. Search fee: $10.00 per name. Required to search: name, years to search, DOB; also helpful: address. Felony records available for past 10 years, misdemeanors for 7, infractions for 3. Mail turnaround time 1-2 days. Criminal PAT available. The public terminal connects to the statewide system. Access criminal index on the state system at http://publicsearch.ndcourts.gov/default.aspx. Index goes back to 5/2000. Search by name and DOB and case type, results may show city of residence. Online results show name only.

Golden Valley County

Southwest Judicial District Court PO Box 9, Beach, ND 58621-0009; 701-872-3713; fax: 701-872-4383; 8AM-N, 1-4PM (MST). *Felony, Misdemeanor, Civil, Eviction, Small Claims, Probate.*

General Information: No adoption, sealed, juvenile, mental health, expunged or dismissed records released. Will fax documents $1.00 per page. Court makes copy: $.50 per page. Self serve copy: same. Certification fee: $10.00. Payee: Clerk of Court. Personal checks accepted, credit cards are not. Prepayment required. Mail requests: SASE required.

Civil Name Search: Access: Fax, mail, in person, online. Both court and visitors may perform in person name searches. Search fee: $10.00 per name. Required to search: name, years to search; also helpful: address. Civil index on cards from 1987, on index books from 1913 to 1960. From 1960 to 1987, records are hard to find; there is no indexing. Note: Fax request must include copy of check. Mail turnaround time 3-4 days. Civil PAT goes back to 2003. Online access to civil is same as criminal via the statewide court website. Search by name and case number, result may show city of residence. An advanced search allows search with DOB.

Criminal Name Search: Access: Fax, mail, in person, online. Both court and visitors may perform in person name searches. Search fee: $10.00 per name. Required to search: name, years to search, DOB; also helpful: address, SSN. Criminal records indexed on cards from 1987, on index books 1913 to 1960. From 1960 to 1987, records are hard to find; there is no indexing. Note: Fax request must include copy of check. Statewide records on computer since 04/04/03. Mail turnaround time 3-4 days. Criminal PAT goes back to 2003. Access criminal index on the state system at http://publicsearch.ndcourts.gov/default.aspx. Index goes back to 4/2003. Search by name and case number, result may show city of residence. Online results show name only. An advanced search allows search with DOB.

Grand Forks County

Northeast Central Judicial District Court PO Box 5939, Grand Forks, ND 58206-5939; criminal phone: 701-787-2700; civil phone: 701-787-2715; probate phone: 701-787-2715; criminal fax: 701-787-2701; civil fax: 8AM-5PM; 8AM-5PM (CST). *Felony, Misdemeanor, Civil, Eviction, Small Claims, Probate.*

General Information: Probate fax- 701-787-2716 No adoption, sealed, juvenile, mental health, expunged or dismissed records released. Will fax documents for no fee. Court makes copy: $.10 per page; $1.00 minimum. Certification fee: $10.00. Payee: Clerk of District Court. Personal checks and major credit cards accepted. Prepayment required.

Civil Name Search: Access: Mail, in person, online. Both court and visitors may perform in person name searches. Search fee: $10.00 per name. Required to search: name, years to search; also helpful: address. Civil records on computer from 11/91, on index books from early 1900s. Mail turnaround time 1-2 days. Civil PAT goes back to 10/1991. Access criminal index on the state system at http://publicsearch.ndcourts.gov/default.aspx. Index goes back to 10/1991. Search by name and DOB and case type, results may show city of residence.

Criminal Name Search: Access: Mail, in person, online. Both court and visitors may perform in person name searches. Search fee: $10.00 per name. Required to search: name, years to search, DOB, signed release; also helpful: address, SSN. Criminal records computerized from 10/91, on index books from early 1900s. Mail turnaround time 1-2 days. Criminal PAT goes back to same as civil. Access criminal index on the state system at http://publicsearch.ndcourts.gov/default.aspx. Index goes back to 10/1991. Search by name and DOB and case type, results may show city of residence. Online results show name only.

Grant County

South Central Judicial District Court PO Box 258, 106 2nd Ave NE, Carson, ND 58529; 701-622-3615; fax: 701-622-3717; 8AM-N, 12:30-4PM (MST). *Felony, Misdemeanor, Civil, Eviction, Small Claims, Probate.*

General Information: No adoption, sealed, juvenile, mental health, expunged or dismissed records released. Will fax documents $3.00 each. Court makes copy: $.25 per page. Certification fee: $10.00 per doc includes copy fee. Payee: Clerk of Grant County Court. Personal checks, Visa/MC accepted. Prepayment required.

Civil Name Search: Access: Fax, mail, in person, online. Both court and visitors may perform in person name searches. Search fee: $10.00 per name. Required to search: name, years to search; also helpful: address. Civil index on cards from 1990, on docket books in vault from 1900s. Mail turnaround time 1 day. Online access to civil is same as criminal via the statewide court website. Search by name and case number, result may show city of residence. An advanced search allows search with DOB.

Criminal Name Search: Access: Fax, mail, in person, online. Both court and visitors may perform in person name searches. Search fee: $10.00 per name. Required to search: name, years to search; also helpful: address, DOB, SSN. Criminal records indexed on cards from 1990, on docket books in vault from 1900s. Mail turnaround time 1 day. Access criminal index back to 2003 on the state system at http://publicsearch.ndcourts.gov/default.aspx. Search by name and case number. An advanced search allows search with DOB.

Griggs County

Southeast Judicial District Court PO Box 326, 808 Rollin, Cooperstown, ND 58425; 701-797-2772; fax: 701-797-3587; 8AM-N, 1-4:30PM (CST). *Felony, Misdemeanor, Civil, Eviction, Small Claims, Probate.*

General Information: No adoption, sealed, juvenile, mental health, expunged or dismissed records released. Will fax documents $1.00 per page. Incoming fax- $1.00 per page; free for state attorneys. Court makes copy: $.25 per page, $1.00 minimum. Certification fee: $10.00 per doc. Payee: Clerk of Courts. Personal checks accepted, credit cards are not. Prepayment required. Mail requests: SASE required.

Civil Name Search: Access: Fax, mail, in person, online. Both court and visitors may perform in person name searches. Search fee: $10.00 per name. Required to search: name, years to search; also helpful: address. Civil records in docket books from 1890 to 2001 and UCIS 2001 to present. Note: Phone access discouraged. Mail turnaround time 1-2 days. Online access to civil is same as criminal. Search by name and DOB and case type, results may show city of residence.

Criminal Name Search: Access: Fax, mail, in person, online. Both court and visitors may perform in person name searches. Search fee: $10.00 per name. Required to search: name, years to search; also helpful: address, DOB, SSN. Criminal docket on books from 1890 to 2001 and UCIS 2001 to present. Note: Phone access discouraged. Mail turnaround time 1-2 days. Access criminal index on the state system at http://publicsearch.ndcourts.gov/default.aspx. Index goes back to 1/2002. Search by name and DOB and case type, results may show city of residence. Online results show name only.

Hettinger County

Southwest Judicial District Court PO Box 668, 336 Pacific Ave, Mott, ND 58646; 701-824-2645; fax: 701-824-2717; 8AM-N, 1-4:30PM (MST). *Felony, Misdemeanor, Civil, Eviction, Small Claims, Probate.*

General Information: No adoption, sealed, juvenile, mental health, expunged or dismissed records released. Will fax documents $3.00 per doc; fee is for up to 20 pages. Court makes copy: $1.00 per page. Certification fee: $10.00 per doc includes copies. Payee: Hettinger Court Clerk. Personal checks accepted, credit cards are not. Prepayment required. Mail requests: SASE required.

Civil Name Search: Access: Fax, mail, in person, online. Both court and visitors may perform in person name searches. Search fee: $10.00 per name. Required to search: name, years to search; also helpful: address. Civil

index on cards from 1987, on index books from 1908. Mail turnaround time 1 day. Online access to civil is same as criminal via the statewide court website. Search by name and case number, result may show city of residence. An advanced search allows search with DOB.

Criminal Name Search: Access: Fax, mail, in person, online. Both court and visitors may perform in person name searches. Search fee: $10.00 per name. Required to search: name, years to search, DOB; also helpful: address. Criminal records indexed on cards from 1987, on index books from 1908. Mail turnaround time 1 day. Access criminal index on the state system at http://publicsearch.ndcourts.gov/default.aspx. Index goes back to 3/2003. Search by name and case number, result may show city of residence. Online results show name only. An advanced search allows search with DOB.

Kidder County

District Court PO Box 66, 120 E Broadway, Steele, ND 58482; 701-475-2632 x9224; fax: 701-475-2202; 9AM-5PM (CST). *Felony, Misdemeanor, Civil, Eviction, Small Claims, Probate.*

General Information: No adoption, sealed, juvenile, mental health, expunged or dismissed records released. Will fax documents $3.00 plus the copy fee. Court makes copy: $1.00 per document. Certification fee: $10.00. Payee: Clerk of Court. Personal checks and major credit cards accepted. Prepayment required. Mail requests: SASE required.

Civil Name Search: Access: Fax, mail, in person, online. Both court and visitors may perform in person name searches. Search fee: $10.00 per name. Required to search: name, years to search; also helpful: address. Civil records on index book from 1800s, on computer since 1990. Mail turnaround time 1-2 days. Civil PAT goes back to 1990. Identifier shown includes only year of birth. Online access to civil is same as criminal via the statewide court website. Search by name and case number, result may show city of residence. An advanced search allows search with DOB.

Criminal Name Search: Access: Mail, in person, online. Both court and visitors may perform in person name searches. Search fee: $10.00 per name. Required to search: name, years to search, DOB; also helpful: address. Records on index book from 1900s, on computer since 1990. Mail turnaround time 1-2 days. Criminal PAT goes back to same as civil. Year of birth only shown on terminal. Access criminal index on the state system at http://publicsearch.ndcourts.gov/default.aspx. Index goes back to 1/2000. Search by name and case number, result may show city of residence. Online results show name only. An advanced search allows search with DOB.

La Moure County

Southeast Judicial District Court PO Box 128, LaMoure, ND 58458; 701-883-5301; fax: 701-883-4240; 8:30AM-N, 1-4:30PM (CST). *Felony, Misdemeanor, Civil, Eviction, Small Claims, Probate.*

General Information: Probate fax is same as main fax number. Email questions to 23clerk@ndcourts.gov No adoption, sealed, juvenile, mental health, expunged or dismissed records released. Will not fax out docs without pre-payment or copy of payment check. Court makes copy: $.10 per page. Self serve copy: same. Certification fee: $10.00. Payee: Clerk of Court. Personal checks accepted, credit cards are not. Prepayment required. Mail requests: SASE required.

Civil Name Search: Access: Fax, mail, in person, online. Only the court performs in person name searches; visitors may not. Search fee: $10.00 per name. Required to search: name, years to search; also helpful: address, SSN, DOB. Civil index in docket books from 1800s; on computer back to 2002. Mail turnaround time usually same day. Online access to civil is same as criminal. Search by name and DOB and case type, results may show city of residence.

Criminal Name Search: Access: Fax, mail, in person, online. Only the court performs in person name searches; visitors may not. Search fee: $10.00 per name. Required to search: name, years to search; also helpful: address, DOB. Felony records go back 21 years; misdemeanors back 15 years. Mail turnaround time 1 day. Access criminal index on the state system at http://publicsearch.ndcourts.gov/default.aspx. Index goes back to 2/2002. Search by name and DOB and case type, results may show city of residence. Online results show name only.

Logan County

South Central Judicial District Court 301 Broadway, Napoleon, ND 58561; 701-754-2751; fax: 701-754-2270; 8:30AM-4:30PM (closed at noon) (CST). *Felony, Misdemeanor, Civil, Eviction, Small Claims, Probate.*

General Information: Probate fax is same as main fax number. No adoption, sealed, juvenile, mental health, expunged or dismissed records released. Fee to fax out file $3.00 1st page, $1.00 each add'l. Court makes copy: $1.00 per document. Self serve copy: same. Certification fee: $10.00 per document. Payee: Clerk of Court. Business checks accepted. No credit cards accepted. Prepayment required. Mail requests: SASE requested.

Civil Name Search: Access: Fax, mail, in person, online. Only the court performs in person name searches; visitors may not. Search fee: $10.00 per name. Required to search: name, years to search; also helpful: address, signed release. Civil index on docket books from 1884. Mail turnaround time 1 day. Online access to civil is same as criminal via the statewide court website. Search by name and case number, result may show city of residence. An advanced search allows search with DOB.

Criminal Name Search: Access: Fax, mail, in person, online. Only the court performs in person name searches; visitors may not. Search fee: $10.00 per name. Required to search: name, years to search, DOB; also helpful: address, signed release. Criminal records indexed in books from 1890. Mail turnaround time 1 day. Access criminal index to 5/2003 at http://publicsearch.ndcourts.gov/default.aspx. Search by name and case number, result may show city of residence. Online results show name only. An advanced search allows search with DOB.

McHenry County

Northeast Judicial District Court 407 Main St S, Rm 203, Towner, ND 58788; 701-537-5729; fax: 701-537-0555; 8AM-4:30PM (CST). *Felony, Misdemeanor, Civil, Eviction, Small Claims, Probate.*

General Information: Probate in a separate index at this same address. Probate fax is same as main fax number. No adoption, sealed, juvenile, mental health, expunged or dismissed records released. Will fax documents $1.00 1st page, $.50 each add'l. Court makes copy: $.25 per page. Certification fee: $10.00 includes copies. Payee: Clerk of Courts. Personal checks and major credit cards accepted. Prepayment required. Mail requests: SASE required.

Civil Name Search: Access: Fax, mail, in person, online. Only the court performs in person name searches; visitors may not. Search fee: $10.00 per name. Required to search: name, years to search; also helpful: address. Civil index on cards from 1991, on index books from 1905. Mail turnaround time 1-2 days. Online access to civil is same as criminal. Search by name and DOB and case type, results may show city of residence.

Criminal Name Search: Access: Fax, mail, in person, online. Both court and visitors may perform in person name searches. Search fee: $10.00 per name. Required to search: name, years to search; also helpful: address, DOB, SSN. Criminal records indexed on cards from 1991, on index books from 1905. Mail turnaround time 1-2 days. Access criminal index on the state system at http://publicsearch.ndcourts.gov/default.aspx. Index goes back to 1/2000. Search by name and DOB and case type, results may show city of residence. Online results show name only.

McIntosh County

McIntosh County District Court PO Box 179, Ashley, ND 58413; 701-288-3450; fax: 701-288-3671; 8AM-4:30PM (CST). *Felony, Misdemeanor, Civil, Eviction, Small Claims, Probate.*

General Information: No adoption, sealed, juvenile, mental health, expunged or dismissed records released. Will fax documents to local or toll free line. Court makes copy: $.25 per page. Certification fee: $10.00 per doc. Payee: Clerk of Court. Only cashiers checks and money orders accepted. No credit cards accepted. Prepayment required.

Civil Name Search: Access: Phone, fax, mail, in person, online. Visitors must perform in person searches themselves. Search fee: $10.00 per name. Required to search: name, years to search; also helpful: address. Civil index on cards from 1987, on index books from 1930s. Mail turnaround time 1-2 days. Civil PAT goes back to 1995. Online access to civil is same as criminal via the statewide court website. Search by name and case number, result may show city of residence. An advanced search allows search with DOB.

Criminal Name Search: Access: Fax, mail, in person, online. Both court and visitors may perform in person name searches. Search fee: $10.00 per name. Required to search: name, years to search, DOB; also helpful: address. Criminal records indexed on cards from 1987, on index books from 1930s. Mail turnaround time 1-2 days. Criminal PAT goes back to 1995. Access criminal index back to 1995 on the state system at http://publicsearch.ndcourts.gov/default.aspx. Search by name and case number, result may show city of residence. Online results show name only. An advanced search allows search with DOB.

McKenzie County

McKenzie County District Court PO Box 524, Watford City, ND 58854; 701-444-3616 Dept 287; criminal phone: 701-444-3616 Dept 287; fax: 701-444-3916; 8AM-4PM (CST). *Felony, Misdemeanor, Civil, Eviction, Small Claims, Probate, Traffic.*

General Information: No adoption, juvenile, mental health, expunged or dismissed records released. Fee to fax out file $2.00 1st page, $1.00 ea add'l. Court makes copy: $.25 per page. Self serve copy: same.Charge of $25.00 per hour will be assessed after the first hour of copying time. Certification fee: $10.00 per document. Payee: Clerk of Court, McKenzie County. Personal checks accepted. Credit cards accepted. Prepayment required. Mail requests: SASE required.

Civil Name Search: Access: Mail, in person, online. Both court and visitors may perform in person name searches. Search fee: $10.00 per name. Required to search: name, years to search; also helpful: address, SSN if available. Civil records on computer back to 1/96. Note: Documents may be returned by email for $1.00 per page. Mail turnaround time 1-2 days. Online access to civil is same as criminal via the statewide court website.

Calendars also available online. Search by name and case number. An advanced search allows search with DOB.

Criminal Name Search: Access: Mail, in person, online. Only the court performs in person name searches; visitors may not. Search fee: $10.00 per name. Required to search: name, years to search, DOB. Criminal records computerized from 12/87; on books back to 1908. Note: Documents may be returned by email for $1.00 per page. Mail turnaround time 1-2 days. Access criminal index on the state system back to 1/2000 at http://publicsearch.ndcourts.gov/default.aspx. Search by name and case number, result may show city of residence. Online results show name only. An advanced search allows search with DOB.

McLean County

South Central Judicial District Court PO Box 1108, Washburn, ND 58577; 701-462-8541; fax: 701-462-8212; 8AM-N, 12:30-4:30PM (CST). *Felony, Misdemeanor, Civil, Eviction, Small Claims, Probate.*

General Information: Probate fax is same as main fax number. No adoption, sealed, juvenile, mental health, expunged or deferred imposition dismissed records released. Will fax documents to toll free line. Court makes copy: $.10 per page, $1.00 minimum. Self serve copy: $.25 per page. Certification fee: $10.00 per document. Payee: Clerk of Courts. Personal checks accepted, credit cards are not. Prepayment required.

Civil Name Search: Access: Mail, in person, online. Both court and visitors may perform in person name searches. Search fee: $10.00 per name. Required to search: name, years to search; also helpful: address. Civil index on docket books from early 1900s; on computer back to 1996. Mail turnaround time 1-2 days. Civil PAT goes back to 1996. Online access to civil is same as criminal via the statewide court website. Search by name and case number, result may show city of residence. An advanced search allows search with DOB.

Criminal Name Search: Access: Mail, in person, online. Both court and visitors may perform in person name searches. Search fee: $10.00 per name. Required to search: name, years to search, DOB; also helpful: address, SSN. Criminal records indexed on cards from 1983, on index books from early 1900s; on computer back to 1996. Mail turnaround time 1-2 days. Criminal PAT goes back to same as civil. Access criminal index on the state system at http://publicsearch.ndcourts.gov/default.aspx. Index goes back to 8/1995. Search by name and case number, result may show city of residence. Online results show name only. An advanced search allows search with DOB.

Mercer County

District Court PO Box 39, 1021 Arthur St, Stanton, ND 58571; 701-745-3262; fax: 701-745-3710; 8AM-4PM (MST). *Felony, Misdemeanor, Civil, Eviction, Small Claims, Probate.* www.mercercountynd.com/?id=25

General Information: No adoption, sealed, juvenile, mental health, expunged or dismissed records released. Will fax documents $5.00 per doc. Court makes copy: $.25 per page. Self serve copy: $.25 per page. Certification fee: $10.00 per doc. Payee: Mercer County Clerk of Court. Personal checks accepted, credit cards are not. Prepayment required. Mail requests: SASE required.

Civil Name Search: Access: Fax, mail, in person, online. Both court and visitors may perform in person name searches. Search fee: $10.00 per name. Required to search: name, years to search; also helpful: address. Civil index on cards from 1979, on index books from 1889, computerized since 1990. Mail turnaround time 1-2 days. Civil PAT goes back to 1992. Online access to civil is same as criminal via the statewide court website. Search by name and case number, result may show city of residence. An advanced search allows search with DOB.

Criminal Name Search: Access: Fax, mail, in person, online. Both court and visitors may perform in person name searches. Search fee: $10.00 per name. Required to search: name, years to search, signed release; also helpful: address, DOB, SSN. Criminal records indexed on cards from 1979, on index books from 1889, computerized since 1990. Mail turnaround time 1-2 days. Criminal PAT goes back to same as civil. Access criminal index on the state system at http://publicsearch.ndcourts.gov/default.aspx. Index goes back to 3/1991. Search by name and case number, result may show city of residence. Online results show name only. An advanced search allows search with DOB.

Morton County

District Court 210 2nd Ave NW, Mandan, ND 58554; 701-667-3358; criminal phone: 701-667-3355; fax: 701-667-3474; 8AM-5PM (MST). *Felony, Misdemeanor, Civil, Eviction, Small Claims, Probate.* www.ndcourts.gov/court/Counties/Morton.htm

General Information: No adoption, sealed, juvenile, mental health, expunged or dismissed records released. Will fax case files to local or toll free number. Court makes copy: $.10 per page, $1.00 min. Certification fee: $10.00. Cert fee includes copies. Payee: Clerk of District Court. Personal checks accepted, credit cards are not. Prepayment required. Mail requests: SASE helpful.

Civil Name Search: Access: Mail, in person, online. Both court and visitors may perform in person name searches. Search fee: $10.00 per name. Required to search: name, years to search; also helpful: address. Civil records on computer from 1990; on index books from 1985. Mail turnaround time 1-2 days. Civil PAT goes back to 1990. Online access to civil is same as criminal via the statewide court website. Includes Mandan Municipal Court. Search by name and case number, result may show city of residence. An advanced search allows search with DOB.

Criminal Name Search: Access: Mail, in person, online. Both court and visitors may perform in person name searches. Search fee: $10.00 per name. Fee is for written search request. Required to search: name, years to search, DOB; also helpful: address. Criminal records computerized from 1990, on index books from 1985. Mail turnaround time 1-2 days. Criminal PAT goes back to same as civil. Access criminal index on the state system at http://publicsearch.ndcourts.gov/default.aspx. Index goes back to 11/1993. Includes Mandan Municipal Court. Search by name and case number, result may show city of residence. Online results show name only. An advanced search allows search with DOB.

Mountrail County

Mountrail County District Court PO Box 69, Stanley, ND 58784; 701-628-2915; fax: 701-628-2276; 8AM-4:30PM (CST). *Felony, Misdemeanor, Civil, Eviction, Small Claims, Probate.*

General Information: Probate is a separate index at this same address. Probate fax is same as main fax number. No adoption, sealed, juvenile, mental health, expunged records released. No fee to fax documents. Court makes copy: $.25 per page. Certification fee: $10.00 per document includes copy fee. Payee: Clerk of District Court. Personal checks and major credit cards accepted. Prepayment required.

Civil Name Search: Access: Mail, in person, fax, phone, online. Both court and visitors may perform in person name searches. Search fee: $10.00 per name. Required to search: name, years to search; also helpful: address. Civil index on docket books from 1909; on computer back to 1998. Mail turnaround time 1-2 days. Civil PAT goes back to 1998. Online access to civil is same as criminal via the statewide court website. Search by name and case number, result may show city of residence. An advanced search allows search with DOB.

Criminal Name Search: Access: Mail, in person, online. Both court and visitors may perform in person name searches. Search fee: $10.00 per name. Fee is for written search. Required to search: name, years to search, DOB. Criminal records indexed in books from 1909; on computer back to 1998. Mail turnaround time 1-2 days. Criminal PAT goes back to same as civil. Results include charges. Access criminal index on the state system at http://publicsearch.ndcourts.gov/default.aspx. Index goes back to 1/1998. Search by name and case number, result may show city of residence. Online results show name only. An advanced search allows search with DOB.

Nelson County

Northeast Central Judicial District Court Nelson County Recorder-Clerk of Court, 210 B Ave W, #203, Lakota, ND 58344-7410; 701-247-2462; fax: 701-247-2412; 8:30AM-N; 1-4:30PM (CST). *Felony, Misdemeanor, Civil, Eviction, Small Claims, Probate.*
www.nelsonco.org/recorder.html

General Information: Probate fax is same as main fax number. No adoption, sealed, juvenile, mental health, expunged or dismissed records released. Will fax documents $3.00 each. Court makes copy: $1.00 per 4-page document; $.25 each add'l. Certification fee: $10.00 includes copies. Payee: Clerk of Courts. Personal checks and major credit cards accepted. Prepayment required. Mail requests: SASE required.

Civil Name Search: Access: Fax, mail, in person, email, online. Both court and visitors may perform in person name searches. Search fee: $10.00 per name. Required to search: name, years to search; also helpful: address. Civil index on docket books from 1883. Mail turnaround time 1-2 days. Civil PAT goes back to 10 years for judgments, 20 if renewed. Results can show year of birth and town. Online access to civil is same as criminal. Search by name and DOB and case type, results may show city of residence.

Criminal Name Search: Access: Fax, mail, in person, email, online. Both court and visitors may perform in person name searches. Search fee: $10.00 per name. Required to search: name, years to search, DOB; also helpful: address, SSN. Criminal records indexed in books from 1883. Mail turnaround time 1-2 days. Criminal PAT goes back to 2002. Results may show year of birth and last 4 digits of SSN. Access criminal index on the state system at http://publicsearch.ndcourts.gov/default.aspx. Index goes

back to 3/2002. Search by name and DOB and case type, results may show city of residence. Online results show name only.

Oliver County

South Central Judicial District Court Box 125, Center, ND 58530; 701-794-8777; fax: 701-794-3476; 8AM-4PM (CST). *Felony, Misdemeanor, Civil, Eviction, Small Claims, Probate.*

General Information: No adoption, sealed, juvenile, mental health, expunged or dismissed records released. Will fax documents $1.00 1st page, $.50 each add'l. Court makes copy: $.25 per page. Certification fee: $10.00 per doc includes copies. Payee: Clerk of Court. Personal checks and major credit cards accepted. Prepayment required. Mail requests: SASE required.

Civil Name Search: Access: Fax, mail, in person, online. Both court and visitors may perform in person name searches. Search fee: $10.00 per name. Required to search: name, years to search; also helpful: address. Civil cases indexed by defendant. Civil index in docket books from 1920s, there no public access terminal. Mail turnaround time 1-2 days. Online access to civil is same as criminal via the statewide court website. Search by name and case number, result may show city of residence. An advanced search allows search with DOB.

Criminal Name Search: Access: Fax, mail, in person, online. Both court and visitors may perform in person name searches. Search fee: $10.00 per name. Required to search: name, years to search, DOB; also helpful: address. Criminal docket on books from 1920s, no public access terminal available. Mail turnaround time 1-2 days. Access criminal index on the state system at http://publicsearch.ndcourts.gov/default.aspx. Index goes back to 4/2003. Search by name and case number, result may show city of residence. Online results show name only. An advanced search allows search with DOB.

Pembina County

Pembina County District Court 301 Dakota St West #10, Cavalier, ND 58220-4100; 701-265-4373; fax: 701-265-4876; 8:30AM-4:30PM (CST). *Felony, Misdemeanor, Civil, Eviction, Small Claims, Probate.*

General Information: Probate fax is same as main fax number. No adoption, sealed, juvenile, mental health, expunged or dismissed records released. Will fax documents to local or toll free line. Court makes copy: $.15 per page. Certification fee: $10.00 per document includes copy fee. Payee: Pembina County Clerk/Recorder. Personal checks and major credit cards accepted. Prepayment required.

Civil Name Search: Access: Fax, mail, in person, online. Both court and visitors may perform in person name searches. Search fee: $10.00 per name. Required to search: name, years to search; also helpful: address, DOB, SSN. Civil index on docket books from 1940; computerized records go back to 1997. Mail turnaround time 1-2 days. Civil PAT goes back to 1997. Online access to civil is same as criminal. Search by name and DOB and case type, results may show city of residence.

Criminal Name Search: Access: Fax, mail, in person, online. Both court and visitors may perform in person name searches. Search fee: $10.00 per name. Required to search: name, years to search, DOB; also helpful: address, SSN. Felony records kept for 21 years, misdemeanor for 7 years; computerized records go back to 1997. Mail turnaround time 1-2 days. Criminal PAT goes back to 1997. Access criminal index on the state system at http://publicsearch.ndcourts.gov/default.aspx. Index goes back to 10/1997. Search by name and DOB and case type, results may show city of residence. Online results show name only.

Pierce County

Northeast Judicial District Court PO Box 258, 240 SE 2nd St, Rugby, ND 58368; 701-776-6161; fax: 701-776-5707; 9AM-5PM (CST). *Felony, Misdemeanor, Civil, Eviction, Small Claims, Probate.*

General Information: Probate fax is same as main fax number. Online identifiers in results same as on public terminal. No adoption, sealed, juvenile, mental health, expunged or dismissed records released. Court makes copy: $.10 per page. Certification fee: $10.00 per document; $5.00 for an add'l copy. Payee: Clerk of Courts. Personal checks accepted, credit cards are not. Prepayment required. Mail requests: SASE helpful.

Civil Name Search: Access: Fax, mail, in person, online. Both court and visitors may perform in person name searches. Search fee: $10.00 per name. Civil records on computer from 1996 (all civil money judgments are on computer), on index books and docket books from early 1900s. Mail turnaround time 1-2 days. Civil PAT goes back to 1997. Online access to civil is same as criminal. Search by name and DOB and case type, results may show city of residence.

Criminal Name Search: Access: Fax, mail, in person, online. Both court and visitors may perform in person name searches. Search fee: $10.00 per name. Required to search: name, years to search, DOB; also helpful: SSN. Criminal records computerized from 1996, on index books and docket books from early 1900s. Note: Results include address. Mail turnaround time 1-2 days. Criminal PAT goes back to 1997. Access criminal index on the state system at http://publicsearch.ndcourts.gov/default.aspx. Index goes back to 11/1997. Search by name and DOB and case type, results may show city of residence. Online results show name only.

Ramsey County

District Court 524 4th Ave NE #4, Devils Lake, ND 58301; 701-662-1309; fax: 701-662-1303; 8AM-N; 1:00PM-5:00PM (CST). *Felony, Misdemeanor, Civil, Eviction, Small Claims, Probate.*

General Information: No adoption, sealed, juvenile, mental health, expunged or dismissed records released. Will fax documents for $.25. Court makes copy: $.10 per page but $1.00 minimum. Certification fee: $10.00 per initial document, $5.00 ea add'l, doc includes copies. Payee: Clerk of Courts. Personal checks accepted. Credit cards accepted. Prepayment required. Mail requests: SASE required.

Civil Name Search: Access: Mail, in person, online. Both court and visitors may perform in person name searches. Search fee: $10.00 per name. Required to search: name; also helpful: years to search. Civil index on cards from 1985, on index books from early 1900s. Mail turnaround time 1-2 days. Civil PAT goes back to 1997. Identifiers shown varies, there is no pattern. Online access to civil is same as criminal. Search by name and DOB and case type, results may show city of residence.

Criminal Name Search: Access: Mail, in person, online. Both court and visitors may perform in person name searches. Search fee: $10.00 per name. Required to search: name; also helpful: years to search, address, DOB, SSN. Criminal records indexed on cards from 1985, on index books from early 1900s. Mail turnaround time 1-2 days. Criminal PAT goes back to same as civil. Identifiers shown varies, there is no pattern. Access criminal index on the state system at http://publicsearch.ndcourts.gov/default.aspx. Index goes back to 10/1997. Online includes Devils Lake Muni Court. Search by name and DOB and case type, results may show city of residence. Online results show name only.

Ransom County

Southeast Judicial District Court PO Box 626, Lisbon, ND 58054; 701-683-6120; criminal phone: 701-683-6142; fax: 701-683-5826; 8:30AM-5PM (CST). *Felony, Misdemeanor, Civil, Eviction, Small Claims, Probate.*

General Information: No adoption, sealed, juvenile, mental health, expunged or dismissed records released. No fee to fax documents. Court makes copy: $.20 per page. Certification fee: $10.00. Payee: Clerk of Court. Personal checks and major credit cards accepted. Prepayment required. Mail requests: SASE required.

Civil Name Search: Access: Fax, mail, in person, online. Both court and visitors may perform in person name searches. Search fee: $10.00 per name for records prior to 2000 or if written request. Required to search: name, years to search; also helpful: address. Civil records computerized from 2000. Mail turnaround time 3-4 days. Civil PAT goes back to 2000. Online access to civil is same as criminal. Search by name and DOB and case type, results may show city of residence.

Criminal Name Search: Access: Fax, mail, in person, online. Both court and visitors may perform in person name searches. Search fee: $10.00 per name for records prior to 2000 or if written request. Required to search: name, years to search, DOB; also helpful: address. Criminal records computerized from 2000. Mail turnaround time 3-4 days. Criminal PAT goes back to 2000. Access criminal index on the state system at http://publicsearch.ndcourts.gov/default.aspx. Index goes back to 1/2000. Search by name and DOB and case type, results may show city of residence. Online results show name only.

Renville County

Northeast Judicial District Court PO Box 68, Mohall, ND 58761; 701-756-6398; fax: 701-756-6494; 9AM-4:30PM (CST). *Felony, Misdemeanor, Civil, Eviction, Small Claims, Probate.*

www.renvillecountynd.org/

General Information: Email questions to jbender@nd.gov. No adoption, sealed, juvenile, mental health, expunged or dismissed records released. Will fax documents $3.00 1st page, $1.00 each add'l. Court makes copy: $.25 per page. Certification fee: $10.00 per doc. Payee: Clerk of Courts. Personal checks and major credit cards accepted. Prepayment required. Mail requests: SASE required.

Civil Name Search: Access: Fax, mail, in person, online. Both court and visitors may perform in person name searches. Search fee: $10.00 per name. Required to search: name, years to search; also helpful: address. Civil index on docket books from 1910. Mail turnaround time 1-2 days. Public use terminal has civil records back to 2001. Identifiers include year of birth and last 4 digits of SSN. Online access to civil is same as criminal. Search by name and DOB and case type, results may show city of residence.

Criminal Name Search: Access: Fax, mail, in person, online. Both court and visitors may perform in person name searches. Search fee: $10.00 per name. Required to search: name, years to search, DOB; also helpful: address. Criminal records computerized from 1/88, on index books from 1910 but not reliable before 1940. Mail turnaround time 1-2 days. Access criminal index on the state system back to 1/2003 at

http://publicsearch.ndcourts.gov/default.aspx. Search by name and DOB and case type, results may show city of residence.

Richland County

Southeast Judicial District Court 418 2nd Ave North, Wahpeton, ND 58074; 701-671-1524; fax: 701-671-4444; 8AM-5PM (CST). *Felony, Misdemeanor, Civil, Eviction, Small Claims, Probate.*

General Information: No adoption, sealed, juvenile, mental health, or expunged records released. Will fax documents to toll-free number, otherwise fax fee is $.25 per page, $1.00 minimum. Court makes copy: $.10 per page; $1.00 minimum. Certification fee: $10.00 per doc. Payee: Clerk of District Court. Personal checks accepted. Visa/MC/Discover cards accepted. Prepayment required. Mail requests: SASE required.

Civil Name Search: Access: Mail, fax, in person, online. Visitors must perform in person searches themselves. Search fee: $10.00 per name. Required to search: name, years to search, plaintiff and defendant names.; also helpful: address. Plaintiff and defendant names required to search. Civil records indexed in books and computer. Mail turnaround time 1-2 days. Civil PAT goes back to 1998. Online access to civil is same as criminal. The site includes separate search for Wahpeton Municipal Court. Search by name and DOB and case type, results may show city of residence.

Criminal Name Search: Access: Mail, fax, in person, online. Visitors must perform in person searches themselves. Search fee: $10.00 per name. Required to search: name, years to search, DOB, SSN; also helpful: address. Criminal docket on books and computer. Mail turnaround time 1-2 days. Criminal PAT goes back to same as civil. Access criminal index on the state system at http://publicsearch.ndcourts.gov/default.aspx. Index goes back to 1/1998. The site includes separate search for Wahpeton Municipal Court. Search by name and DOB and case type, results may show city of residence. Online results show name only.

Rolette County

Northeast Judicial District Court PO Box 460, 201 2nd St NE 2nd Fl, Rolla, ND 58367; 701-477-3816; fax: 701-477-8594; 8AM-5PM (CST). *Felony, Misdemeanor, Civil, Eviction, Small Claims, Probate.*

General Information: No adoption, sealed, juvenile, mental health, expunged or dismissed records released. Will fax documents $5.00 per doc. Court makes copy: $.10 per page; $1.00 minimum. Self serve copy: same. Certification fee: $10.00. Payee: Clerk of Court. Business checks accepted. No credit cards accepted. Prepayment required. Mail requests: SASE required.

Civil Name Search: Access: Fax, mail, in person, online. Both court and visitors may perform in person name searches. Search fee: $10.00 per name. Required to search: name, years to search; also helpful: address. Civil index stored since 1889; computerized since 1999. Mail turnaround time 1-2 days. Civil PAT goes back to 6/1999. Online access to civil is same as criminal. The site includes separate search for Rolla Municipal Court. Search by name and DOB and case type, results may show city of residence.

Criminal Name Search: Access: Fax, mail, in person, online. Both court and visitors may perform in person name searches. Search fee: $10.00 per name. Required to search: name, years to search; also helpful: address, DOB, SSN. Criminal docket index from 1970, computerized since 2000. Prior to 1970, records hard to find and not very accurate. Mail turnaround time 1-2 days. Criminal PAT goes back to 6/1999. Access criminal index on the state system at http://publicsearch.ndcourts.gov/default.aspx. Index goes back to 6/1999. The site includes separate search for Rolla Municipal Court. Search by name and DOB and case type, results may show city of residence. Online results show name only.

Sargent County

Southeast Judicial District Court 355 Main St S #2, Forman, ND 58032-4149; 701-724-6241 X111 or 112; fax: 701-724-6244; 9AM-N, 12:30-4:30PM (CST). *Felony, Misdemeanor, Civil, Eviction, Small Claims, Probate.*

https://mylocalgov.com/sargentcountynd/index.asp

General Information: No adoption, sealed, juvenile, mental health, expunged or dismissed records released. Will fax documents $3.00 1st page, $1.00 each add'l. Court makes copy: $.10 per page. Self serve copy: same. Certification fee: $10.00. Payee: Clerk of Court. Personal checks and major credit cards accepted. Prepayment required.

Civil Name Search: Access: Fax, mail, in person, online. Both court and visitors may perform in person name searches. Search fee: $10.00 per name. Required to search: name, years to search; also helpful: address. Civil cases indexed by defendant. Civil records on books from early 1800s. Note: Judgments may be searched by the public, but not civil case files. Mail turnaround time 1-2 days. Online access to civil is same as criminal. Search by name and DOB and case type, results may show city of residence.

Criminal Name Search: Access: Fax, mail, in person, online. Both court and visitors may perform in person name searches. Search fee: $10.00 per name. Required to search: name, years to search; also helpful-DOB. Criminal docket on books from early 1800s. Mail turnaround time 1-2 days. Access criminal index on the state system at http://publicsearch.ndcourts.gov/default.aspx. Index goes back to 1/2002. Search by name and DOB and case type, results may show city of residence. Online results show name only.

Sheridan County

South Central Judicial District Court PO Box 409, 215 2nd St E, McClusky, ND 58463; 701-363-2207; fax: 701-363-2953; 9AM-N, 1-5PM (CST). *Felony, Misdemeanor, Civil, Eviction, Small Claims, Probate.*

General Information: No adoption, sealed, juvenile, mental health, expunged or dismissed records released. Will fax documents to local or toll-free number. Court makes copy: $.50 per page. Self serve copy: same. Certification fee: $10.00 per doc. Payee: Clerk of District Court. Business checks accepted. No credit cards accepted. Prepayment required.

Civil Name Search: Access: Mail, in person, online. Both court and visitors may perform in person name searches. Search fee: $10.00 per name. Required to search: name, years to search; also helpful: address. Civil index on docket books from 1909. Mail turnaround time 1-2 days. Online access to civil is same as criminal via the statewide court website. Search by name and case number, result may show city of residence. An advanced search allows search with DOB.

Criminal Name Search: Access: Mail, in person, online. Both court and visitors may perform in person name searches. Search fee: $10.00 per name. Required to search: name, years to search, signed release; also helpful: address, DOB, SSN. Criminal records indexed in books from 1909. Mail turnaround time 1-2 days. Access criminal index on the state system at http://publicsearch.ndcourts.gov/default.aspx. Index goes back to 2/2003. Search by name and case number, result may show city of residence. Online results show name only. An advanced search allows search with DOB.

Sioux County

South Central Judicial District Court Box L, 303 2nd Ave, Fort Yates, ND 58538; 701-854-3853; fax: 701-854-3854; 8AM-4PM (CST). *Felony, Misdemeanor, Civil, Eviction, Small Claims, Probate.*

General Information: No adoption, sealed, juvenile, mental health, expunged or dismissed records released. Fee to fax out file $3.00 each. Court makes copy: $1.00 per page. Certification fee: $10.00 per doc includes copies. Payee: Clerk of Court. Personal checks accepted, credit cards are not. Prepayment required. Mail requests: SASE required.

Civil Name Search: Access: Mail, in person, online. Both court and visitors may perform in person name searches. Search fee: $10.00 per name. Required to search: name, years to search; also helpful: address. Civil index on docket books from 1914. Mail turnaround time 1-2 days. Online access to civil is same as criminal via the statewide court website. Search by name and case number, result may show city of residence. An advanced search allows search with DOB.

Criminal Name Search: Access: Mail, in person, online. Both court and visitors may perform in person name searches. Search fee: $10.00 per name. Required to search: name, years to search; also helpful: address, DOB, SSN. Criminal records indexed in books from 1914. Mail turnaround time 1-2 days. Public use terminal has crim records. Access criminal index on the state system at http://publicsearch.ndcourts.gov/default.aspx. Index goes back to 3/2003. Search by name and case number, result may show city of residence. Online results show name only. An advanced search allows search with DOB.

Slope County

Southwest Judicial District Court PO Box JJ, 206 S Main, Amidon, ND 58620; 701-879-6275; fax: 701-879-6278; 8:30AM-4:30PM (MST). *Felony, Misdemeanor, Civil, Eviction, Small Claims, Probate.*

General Information: No adoption, sealed, juvenile, mental health, expunged or dismissed records released. Will fax documents $2.00 up to 10 pages, then $.25 ea add'l page. Court makes copy: $.25 per page. Self serve copy: $.25 per page. Certification fee: $10.00. Payee: Clerk of Court. Personal checks and major credit cards accepted. Prepayment required. Mail requests: SASE required.

Civil Name Search: Access: Fax, mail, in person, online. Only the court performs in person name searches; visitors may not. Search fee: $10.00 per name. Required to search: name, years to search; also helpful: address. Civil index indexed in books back to 1915. Mail turnaround time 1-2 days. Online access to civil is same as criminal via the statewide court website. Search by name and case number, result may show city of residence. An advanced search allows search with DOB.

Criminal Name Search: Access: Fax, mail, in person, online. Only the court performs in person name searches; visitors may not. Search fee: $10.00 per name. Required to search: name, years to search, also helpful: address, DOB. Criminal docket on books back to 1915. Mail turnaround time 1-2 days. Access criminal index on the state system at http://publicsearch.ndcourts.gov/default.aspx. Index goes back to 3/2003. Search by name and case number, result may show city of residence.

Online results show name only. An advanced search allows search with DOB.

Stark County

District Court 51 Third St E #106, Dickinson, ND 58601; 701-227-3184; criminal phone: 701-227-3180; civil phone: 701-227-3182; probate phone: 701-227-3181; fax: 701-227-3185; 8AM-5PM (MST). *Felony, Misdemeanor, Civil, Eviction, Small Claims, Probate.*

General Information: No adoption, sealed, juvenile, mental health, expunged or dismissed records. Will fax documents $.25 per page, $1.00 minimum. Court makes copy: $.10 per page; $1.00 minimum. Certification fee: $10.00. Payee: Clerk of Court. Personal checks and major credit cards accepted. Prepayment required. Mail requests: SASE required.

Civil Name Search: Access: Mail, in person, online. Both court and visitors may perform in person name searches. Search fee: $10.00 per name. Civil records on computer since 1/92, index cards or docket books since 1800s. Mail turnaround time 1-2 days. Civil PAT goes back to 1992. Online access to civil is same as criminal via the statewide court website. Search by name and case number, result may show city of residence. An advanced search allows search with DOB.

Criminal Name Search: Access: Mail, in person, online. Both court and visitors may perform in person name searches. Search fee: $10.00 per name. Required to search: name, years to search, DOB; also helpful: SSN. Criminal records on computer since 1/92, index cards or docket books since 1800s. Mail turnaround time 1-2 days. Criminal PAT goes back to same as civil. Access criminal index on the state system at http://publicsearch.ndcourts.gov/default.aspx. Index goes back to 4/1992. Online includes Dickinson Muni Court. Online results show name only.

Steele County

East Central Judicial District Court PO Box 296, Finley, ND 58230; 701-524-2152; fax: 701-524-1325; 8AM-N; 1-4:30PM (CST). *Felony, Misdemeanor, Civil, Eviction, Small Claims, Probate.*

General Information: No adoption, sealed, juvenile, mental health, expunged or dismissed records released. Will fax documents $5.00 each. Court makes copy: $2.00 per doc. Certification fee: $10.00 per doc. Payee: Clerk of Court. Business checks accepted. No credit cards accepted. Prepayment required. Mail requests: SASE required.

Civil Name Search: Access: Mail, in person, online. Only the court performs in person name searches; visitors may not. Search fee: $10.00 per name. Required to search: name, years to search; also helpful: address. Civil index in docket books from approx 1894. Mail turnaround time 1-2 days. Online access to civil is same as criminal. Search by name and DOB and case type, results may show city of residence.

Criminal Name Search: Access: Mail, in person, online. Only the court performs in person name searches; visitors may not. Search fee: $10.00 per name. Required to search: name, years to search, DOB, signed release; also helpful: address. Criminal docket on books from approx 1894. Mail turnaround time 1-2 days. Access criminal index on the state system at http://publicsearch.ndcourts.gov/default.aspx. Index goes back to 12/2002. Search by name and DOB and case type, results may show city of residence. Online results show name only.

Stutsman County

Southeast Judicial District Court 511 2nd Ave SE, Jamestown, ND 58401; 701-252-9042; 8AM-5PM (CST). *Felony, Misdemeanor, Civil, Eviction, Small Claims, Probate.*

General Information: Another phone number to use is 701-251-6331. No adoption, sealed, juvenile, mental health, expunged or dismissed records released. Will fax documents to local or toll free line. Court makes copy: $.10 per page, minimum charge $1.00. Certification fee: $10.00, if for 2 sets then $15.00. Payee: Clerk of Court. Personal checks and major credit cards accepted. Prepayment required. Mail requests: SASE required.

Civil Name Search: Access: Mail, fax, in person, online. Both court and visitors may perform in person name searches. Search fee: $10.00 per name. Required to search: name, years to search; also helpful: address. Civil records on computer back to 1/87, on index books from 1800s. Mail turnaround time 1-2 days. Civil PAT goes back to at least 1996. Online access to civil is same as criminal. The site includes separate search for Jamestown Municipal Court. Search by name and DOB and case type, results may show city of residence.

Criminal Name Search: Access: Mail, fax, in person, online. Both court and visitors may perform in person name searches. Search fee: $10.00 per name. Required to search: name, years to search, DOB; also helpful: address. Criminal records computerized from 1/96, on index books from 1800s. Mail turnaround time 1-2 days. Criminal PAT goes back to 1996. Access criminal index on the state system at http://publicsearch.ndcourts.gov/default.aspx. Index goes back to 9/1995. The site includes separate search for Jamestown Municipal Court. Search by name and DOB and case type, results may show city of residence. Online results show name only.

Towner County

Northeast Judicial District Court PO Box 517, 315 2nd St, Cando, ND 58324; 701-968-4340 x3; fax: 701-968-4344; 8:30AM-N; 1-5:00PM (CST). *Felony, Misdemeanor, Civil, Eviction, Small Claims, Probate.* www.ndcourts.gov/court/counties/dc_clerk/towner.htm

General Information: Online identifiers in results same as on public terminal. No adoption, sealed, juvenile, mental health, expunged or dismissed records released. Will fax documents $10.00 each. Court makes copy: $1.00 per page. Certification fee: $10.00 per doc. Payee: Clerk of District Court. Personal checks, Visa/MC accepted. Prepayment required. Mail requests: SASE required.

Civil Name Search: Access: Fax, mail, in person, online. Both court and visitors may perform in person name searches. Search fee: $10.00 per name. Required to search: name, years to search; also helpful: address. Civil index on docket books from 1800s, computerized since 1998. Mail turnaround time 1-2 days. Civil PAT goes back to 1998. Online access to civil is same as criminal. Search by name and DOB and case type, results may show city of residence.

Criminal Name Search: Access: Fax, mail, in person, online. Both court and visitors may perform in person name searches. Search fee: $10.00 per name. Required to search: name, years to search; also helpful: address, DOB, SSN. Records computerized since 1998. Mail turnaround time 1-2 days. Criminal PAT goes back to 1998. Access criminal index on the state system at http://publicsearch.ndcourts.gov/default.aspx. Index goes back to 4/2002. Search by name and DOB and case type, results may show city of residence. Online results show name only.

Traill County

East Central Judicial District Court PO Box 805, Hillsboro, ND 58045; 701-636-4454; fax: 701-636-5124; 8AM-4:30PM (CST). *Felony, Misdemeanor, Civil, Eviction, Small Claims, Probate.* www.co.traill.nd.us/

General Information: No adoption, sealed, juvenile, mental health, expunged or dismissed records released. Will fax documents $1.00 per page. Court makes copy: $.10 per page. Certification fee: $10.00 per doc includes copies. Payee: Clerk of Court. Personal checks accepted, credit cards are not. Prepayment required. Mail requests: SASE required.

Civil Name Search: Access: Phone, fax, mail, in person, online. Only the court performs in person name searches; visitors may not. Search fee: $10.00 per name. Required to search: name, years to search; also helpful: address. Civil index on docket books from 1800s. Mail turnaround time 1-2 days. Online access to civil is same as criminal. Search by name and DOB and case type, results may show city of residence.

Criminal Name Search: Access: Phone, fax, mail, in person, online. Only the court performs in person name searches; visitors may not. Search fee: $10.00 per name. Required to search: name, years to search; also helpful: address, DOB, last four digits of SSN. Criminal records indexed in books from 1800s. Mail turnaround time 1-2 days. Access criminal index on the state system at http://publicsearch.ndcourts.gov/default.aspx. Index goes back to 5/2002. Search by name and DOB and case type, results may show city of residence. Online results show name, DOB.

Walsh County

Northeast Judicial District Court Clerk of District Court, 600 Cooper Ave, Grafton, ND 58237; 701-352-0350; fax: 701-352-4466; 8AM-5PM (CST). *Felony, Misdemeanor, Civil, Eviction, Small Claims, Probate.*

General Information: No adoption, sealed, juvenile, mental health, expunged or dismissed records released. Will fax documents to local or toll-free number. Court makes copy: $.10 per page; $1.00 minimum. Certification fee: $10.00, then $5.00 each add'l copy. Payee: Clerk of Court. Personal checks and major credit cards accepted. Prepayment required. Mail requests: SASE required.

Civil Name Search: Access: Mail, in person, online. Both court and visitors may perform in person name searches. Search fee: $10.00 per name. Required to search: name, years to search; also helpful: address, SSN. Civil index on docket books from early 1900s; on computer from 11/97. Mail turnaround time 2-3 days. Civil PAT goes back to 11/1997. Online access to civil is same as criminal. Grafton Municipal Court dockets are also online. Search by name and DOB and case type, results may show city of residence.

Criminal Name Search: Access: Mail, in person, online. Both court and visitors may perform in person name searches. Search fee: $10.00 per name. Required to search: name with middle initial, years to search, DOB; also helpful: address. Criminal records indexed in books from early 1900s; on computer from 11/97. Mail turnaround time 2-3 days. Criminal PAT goes back to same as civil. Access criminal index on the state system at http://publicsearch.ndcourts.gov/default.aspx. Index goes back to 11/1997. Grafton Municipal Court dockets are also online. Search by name and DOB and case type, results may show city of residence. Online results show name only.

Ward County

Northwest Judicial District Court PO Box 5005, Minot, ND 58702-5005; criminal phone: 701-857-6600 x2; civil phone: 701-857-6600 x1; probate phone: 701-857-6600 x1; fax: 701-857-6623; 8AM-4:30PM (CST). *Felony, Misdemeanor, Civil, Eviction, Small Claims, Probate.*

General Information: No adoption, sealed, juvenile, mental health, domestic violence pending, expunged or dismissed records released. Will fax documents for $.25 per page, $1.00 minimum. Court makes copy: $.10 per page, $1.00 minimum. Certification fee: $10.00 per document. If 2nd certification of same document needed then only $5.00 for second. Payee: Clerk of District Court. Business checks accepted. Major credit cards accepted. Prepayment required. Mail requests: SASE required.

Civil Name Search: Access: Mail, in person, online. Both court and visitors may perform in person name searches. Search fee: $10.00 per name and per case type. Civil index on cards from 1990, on index books from late 1880s; computerized records go back to 1994. Mail turnaround time 5 days. Civil PAT goes back to 1994. Online access to civil is same as criminal. Search by name and case number, result may show city of residence. An advanced search allows search with DOB.

Criminal Name Search: Access: Mail, in person, online. Both court and visitors may perform in person name searches. Search fee: $10.00 per name. Required to search: name, years to search; also helpful: address, DOB, SSN. Criminal records indexed on cards from 1990, on index books from late 1880s; computerized records go back to 1994. Mail turnaround time 5 days. Criminal PAT goes back to same as civil. Access criminal index on the state system at http://publicsearch.ndcourts.gov/default.aspx. Index goes back to 1994 but is incomplete back into 1993 back to 10/1992. Online includes recent Minot Muni Court. Search by name and case number, result may show city of residence. Online results show name only. An advanced search allows search with DOB.

Wells County

Southeast Judicial District Court PO Box 155, Fessenden, ND 58438; 701-547-3122; fax: 701-547-3840; 8AM-4PM (CST). *Felony, Misdemeanor, Civil, Eviction, Small Claims, Probate.*

General Information: Probate fax is same as main fax number. No adoption, sealed, juvenile, mental health, expunged or dismissed records released. Will fax documents to local or toll free line. Court makes copy: $.25 per page. Self serve copy: same. Certification fee: $10.00 per doc includes copies. Payee: District Court. Personal checks and major credit cards accepted. Prepayment required. Mail requests: SASE required.

Civil Name Search: Access: Mail, in person, online. Both court and visitors may perform in person name searches. Search fee: $10.00 per name. Required to search: name, years to search; also helpful: address. Civil index on docket books. Mail turnaround time same day. Online access to civil is same as criminal. Search by name and DOB and case type, results may show city of residence.

Criminal Name Search: Access: Mail, in person, online. Only the court performs in person name searches; visitors may not. Search fee: $10.00 per name. Required to search: name, years to search; also helpful: address, DOB, SSN. Criminal records indexed in books from 1980. Mail turnaround time 1-2 days. Access criminal index on the state system at http://publicsearch.ndcourts.gov/default.aspx. Index goes back to 2/2002. Search by name and DOB and case type, results may show city of residence. Online results show name only.

Williams County

Northwest Judicial District Court PO Box 2047, Williston, ND 58802; 701-774-4374 or 701-774-4377; fax: 701-774-4379; 8AM-5PM (CST). *Felony, Misdemeanor, Civil, Eviction, Small Claims, Probate.*

General Information: No adoption, sealed, juvenile, mental health, expunged or dismissed records released. Will fax documents. Court makes copy: $.10 per page; $1.00 minimum. Self serve copy: same. Certification fee: $10.00. Payee: Clerk of Court. Personal checks and major credit cards accepted. Prepayment required. Mail requests: SASE required.

Civil Name Search: Access: Mail, in person, online. Both court and visitors may perform in person name searches. Search fee: $10.00 per name. Required to search: name, years to search; also helpful: address. Civil records computerized since 1/98, on index cards from 1/92, on index books from 1899. Mail turnaround time 1-2 days. Civil PAT goes back to 1998. Online access to civil is same as criminal via the statewide court website. Search by name and case number, result may show city of residence. An advanced search allows search with DOB.

Criminal Name Search: Access: Mail, in person, online. Both court and visitors may perform in person name searches. Search fee: $10.00 per name. Required to search: name, years to search; also helpful: address, DOB, SSN. Criminal records computerized since 1/98, on index cards from 1/92, on index books from 1899. Mail turnaround time 1-2 days. Criminal PAT goes back to 1998. Access criminal index on the state system at http://publicsearch.ndcourts.gov/default.aspx. Index goes back to 1/1998. Online includes Williston Muni Court. Online results show name only.

Ohio

Time Zone:	EST
Capital:	Columbus, Franklin County
# of Counties:	88
State Web:	www.ohio.gov
Court Web:	www.supremecourt.ohio.gov

Administration

Administrative Director, Supreme Court of Ohio, 65 S Front Street, Columbus, OH 43215-3431; 614-387-9000, Fax: 614-387-9419.

The Supreme Court

The Supreme Court of Ohio possesses constitutional and statutory authority to exercise general powers of superintendence over the courts of the state. The primary function of the Court of Appeals is to hear appeals from the Common Pleas, Municipal and County courts. The Court of Appeals has twelve districts. The 10th District Court of Appeals in Franklin County also hears appeals from the Ohio Court of Claims.

Appellate and Supreme Court opinions may be researched from the website.

The Ohio Courts

Court	Type	How Organized	Jurisdiction Highpoints
Common Pleas*	General	88 Courts in 88 Counties	Felony, Gross Misdemeanor, Civil, Probate, Domestic Relations, Juvenile
County*	Limited	35 Courts	Misdemeanor, Civil Actions under $15,000, Eviction, Small Claims
Municipal*	Limited	128 Courts	Misdemeanor, Traffic, Ordinance
Court of Claims		1	Suits against Ohio
Mayor's Court		317	Ordinance

* = profiled in this book

Details on the Court Structure

The **Court of Common Pleas** is the general jurisdiction court with separate divisions including General, Domestic Relations, Juvenile and Probate. Per the Supreme Court web page, the General Division has original jurisdiction in all criminal felony cases and in all civil cases in which the amount in controversy is more than $15,000. However, the Administrative Director's Office advises the Common Pleas can hear civil cases for $501 or more.

County and **Municipal Courts** handle virtually the same subject matter with some minor operational differences. Both have the authority to conduct preliminary hearings in felony cases, both have jurisdiction over traffic and non-traffic misdemeanors and, and have limited civil jurisdiction in which the amount of money in dispute does not exceed $15,000.

Mayor's Courts are not a part of the judicial branch of Ohio government and are not courts of record. A person convicted in a Mayor's Court may appeal the conviction to the Municipal or County court having jurisdiction within the municipal corporation. Ohio and Louisiana are the only two states that allow the mayors of municipal corporations to preside over a court.

The **Court of Claims** has original jurisdiction to hear and determine all civil actions filed against the state of Ohio and its agencies.

Record Searching Facts You Need to Know

Fees and Record Searching Tips

There is no standardization followed for search fee. Most court charge from $.05 to $.25 for copies. Over 80% of the courts profiled herein offer a public access terminal to view a docket index.

Online Access is Widespread at County Level

Quite a few individual Common Pleas, County and Municipal courts offer online access.

The Supreme Court of Ohio is in the process of implementing the Ohio Court Network (OCN). **There is no public access to OCN at this time.** This system will include court case docket information from all courts of record, including criminal, civil and traffic records. The intent is to provide a secure system with access by court personnel, law enforcement and other justice partner agencies. As of July, 29, 2011, 3111 courts are participating at some level, 146 courts representing 50% of the annual case load have loaded their historical cases into the system.

Adams County

Common Pleas Court 110 W Main, Rm 207, West Union, OH 45693; 937-544-2344; probate phone: 937-544-2921; fax: 937-544-8271; 8AM-4PM (EST). *Felony, Civil Actions over $3,000, Probate.* www.adamscountyoh.com/

General Information: Probate fax- 937-544-8911. Will fax documents to local or toll free line. Court makes copy: $.25 per page. Certification fee: $1.00 per page, includes copy. Payee: Clerk of Court. Personal checks accepted, credit cards are not. Prepayment required.

Civil Name Search: Access: In person only. Both court and visitors may perform in person name searches. Search fee: $10.00 per name. Civil records on computer from 4/1993, prior in books, archived from 1910. Civil PAT goes back to 1993.

Criminal Name Search: Access: Mail, in person. Both court and visitors may perform in person name searches. Search fee: $10.00 per name. Required to search: name, years to search, signed release; also helpful: DOB, SSN. Criminal records computerized from 4/93, prior in books, archived from 1910. Mail turnaround time 1 day. Criminal PAT goes back to same as civil.

County Court 110 W Main, Rm 25, West Union, OH 45693; 937-544-2011; fax: 937-544-6157; 8:30AM-4PM (EST). *Misdemeanor, Civil Actions under $15,000, Small Claims.* www.adamscountyoh.com/

General Information: Will fax documents $1.00 per page. Court makes copy: $.25 per page. Self serve copy: $.25 per page. Certification fee: $1.00. Payee: Adams County Court. Business checks accepted. No credit cards accepted. Prepayment required. Mail requests: SASE required.

Civil Name Search: Access: Mail, in person. Both court and visitors may perform in person name searches. Search fee: $10.00 per name. Civil records on computer from 3/93, index from 1958, prior on dockets and microfilm. Mail turnaround time 1-2 days. Civil PAT goes back to 1993.

Criminal Name Search: Access: Mail, in person. Both court and visitors may perform in person name searches. Search fee: $10.00 per name. Required to search: name, years to search; also helpful: SSN. Criminal records computerized from 3/93, index from 1958, prior on dockets and microfilm. Mail turnaround time 1-2 days. Criminal PAT goes back to same as civil. Terminal results may sometimes show SSNs.

Allen County

Common Pleas Court PO Box 1243, 301 N Main, Lima, OH 45802; 419-228-8513; probate phone: 419-223-8501; fax: 419-222-8427; 8AM-4:30PM (EST). *Felony, Civil Actions, Probate, Domestic Relations.* www.allencountyohio.com/commonpleas/ccom.php

General Information: No secret indictment records released. Will fax documents $2.00 plus $1.00 per page. Court makes copy: $.05 per page, $1.00 per page on a docket. Certification fee: $1.00. Payee: Clerk of Court. Personal checks accepted, credit cards are not. Prepayment required. Mail requests: SASE required for mail return of any copies.

Civil Name Search: Access: In person, online. Visitors must perform in person searches themselves. Required to search: name; also helpful: years to search, address. Civil records on computer back to 1986; in books and archived prior. Civil PAT goes back to 1986. PAT includes domestic cases. Access civil records including judgment liens free at http://65.17.134.12/pa/.

Criminal Name Search: Access: In person, online. Visitors must perform in person searches themselves. Required to search: name, years to search; also helpful: address, DOB, SSN. Criminal records computerized from 1986; in books and archived prior. Criminal PAT goes back to same as civil. Online access to index is free at http://65.17.134.12/pa/. Records go back to 12/1/1988. Online results show middle initial, DOB.

Lima Municipal Court PO Box 1529, 109 N Union St, Lima, OH 45802; 419-221-5275; civil phone: 419-221-5250; criminal fax: 419-998-5526; civil fax: 8AM-5PM; 8AM-5PM (EST). *Misdemeanor, Civil Actions under $15,000, Eviction, Small Claims.* www.limamunicipalcourt.org

General Information: Online identifiers in results same as on public terminal. Fee to fax document $.25 per page. Court makes copy: $.25 per page. Certification fee: $2.00. Payee: Clerk of Court. Business checks accepted. Major credit cards accepted. Prepayment required. Mail requests: SASE required.

Civil Name Search: Access: Phone, fax, mail, in person, email, online. Both court and visitors may perform in person name searches. No search fee. Required to search: name, years to search; also helpful: address. Civil records on computer from 4/1990, books and archived prior. Mail turnaround time same day. Civil PAT goes back to 4/1990. Search index information at www.limamunicipalcourt.org, click on Case Inquiry. Direct email search requests to limamuni@wcoil.com

Criminal Name Search: Access: Phone, fax, mail, in person, email, online. Both court and visitors may perform in person name searches. No search fee. Required to search: name, years to search; also helpful: address, DOB, SSN. Criminal records computerized from 4/90, index and dockets prior. Mail turnaround time same day. Criminal PAT goes back to same as civil. Address included in most search results. Search index information at www.limamunicipalcourt.org, click on Case Inquiry. Direct email search requests to limamuni@wcoil.com Online results show middle initial, DOB.

Ashland County

Common Pleas Court 142 W 2nd St, c/o County Clerk of Courts, Ashland, OH 44805; 419-282-4242; probate phone: 419-282-4325; fax: 419-282-4240; 8AM-4PM (EST). *Felony, Civil Actions over $10,000, Probate.* www.ashlandcounty.org/clerkofcourts/

General Information: Probate court is a separate court at the same address. Online identifiers in results same as on public terminal. No sealed records released. Will fax documents $2.00 transmission fee plus $1.00 per page. Court makes copy: $.20 per page. Certification fee: $1.00 per page includes copy fee. Payee: Ashland County Clerk of Courts. Personal checks accepted, credit cards are not. Prepayment required.

Civil Name Search: Access: In person, online. Visitors must perform in person searches themselves. Required to search: name or case number. Civil records on microfilm from 1800s, computerized court records go back to 6/7/1995. Civil PAT goes back to 6/1995. Access records at www.ashlandcountycpcourt.org.

Criminal Name Search: Access: In person, online. Visitors must perform in person searches themselves. Required to search: name or case number. Criminal records on microfilm from 1800s, computerized court records go back to 6/7/1995. Criminal PAT goes back to same as civil. Access records at www.ashlandcountycpcourt.org.

Ashland Municipal Court 1209 E Main St, PO Box 385, Ashland, OH 44805; 419-289-8137; civil phone: 419-281-4890; fax: 419-289-8545; 8AM-5PM (EST). *Misdemeanor, Civil Actions under $15,000, Eviction, Small Claims.* www.ashland-ohio.com/government/ashland-municipal-court

General Information: No non-public record information released. Fee to fax out file $1.00 per page. Court makes copy: $.10 per page. Certification fee: $1.00. Payee: Municipal Court. Personal checks accepted. Visa/MC cards accepted for account holders. Prepayment required. Mail requests: SASE required.

Civil Name Search: Access: Phone, mail, fax, in person. Both court and visitors may perform in person name searches. No search fee. Civil index in docket books from 1952, computerized since 1995. Mail turnaround time 1-3 days. Civil PAT goes back to 10/1994.

Criminal Name Search: Access: Phone, mail, fax, in person. Both court and visitors may perform in person name searches. No search fee. Required to search: name, years to search, SSN. Criminal docket on books from 1952, computerized since 1995. Mail turnaround time 1-3 days. Criminal PAT goes back to 10/1994. Terminal also gives DR and plate numbers.

Ashtabula County

Common Pleas Court 25 W Jefferson St, Jefferson, OH 44047; 440-576-3637; probate phone: 440-576-3451; fax: 440-576-2819; 8AM-4:30PM (EST). *Felony, Civil Actions over $10,000, Probate.* http://courts.co.ashtabula.oh.us/ClerkofCourts.htm

General Information: Probate is a separate office at the same location. Probate fax is 440-576-3633. Online identifiers in results same as on public terminal. No expungments released. Will not fax documents. Court makes copy: $.25 per page. Certification fee: $1.00 per page plus copy fee. Payee: Clerk of Court. Personal checks accepted, credit cards are not. Prepayment required.

Civil Name Search: Access: In person, online. Visitors must perform in person searches themselves. Required to search: name, years to search; also helpful: address. Civil records on computer back to 5/93, in books back to the 1800s. Civil PAT goes back to 5/1993. Access to index is free at http://courts.co.ashtabula.oh.us/pa.htm.

Criminal Name Search: Access: In person, online. Visitors must perform in person searches themselves. Required to search: name, years to search; also helpful: address, DOB. Criminal records computerized from 5/93, in books back to the 1800s. Criminal PAT goes back to same as civil. Access to index is free at http://courts.co.ashtabula.oh.us/pa.htm. Online results show middle initial, DOB.

Ashtabula Municipal Court 110 W 44th St, Ashtabula, OH 44004; criminal phone: 440-992-7112; civil phone: 440-992-7110; fax: 440-998-5786; 8AM-4:30PM (EST). *Misdemeanor, Civil Actions under $15,000, Eviction, Small Claims.* www.ashtabulamunicipalcourt.com/

General Information: Directory- 440-992-7109. Daily dockets are also available on the website. No expunged records released. Will fax specific case files for $1.00 per document. Court makes copy: $.25 per page. Certification fee: $5.00 per document. Payee: Municipal Court. Personal checks, Visa/MC accepted. Prepayment required.

Civil Name Search: Access: In person, online. Visitors must perform in person searches themselves. Civil records on computer from 1992, books back to 1971. Civil PAT goes back to 1988. Online access to civil court cases are free at www.ashtabulamunicourt.com/searchcivildocket.asp.

Criminal Name Search: Access: In person, online. Visitors must perform in person searches themselves. Required to search: name, years to search, DOB, SSN, signed release. Criminal records computerized from 1992, books back to 1971. Criminal PAT goes back to same as civil. Online access to court cases, including traffic, are free at www.ashtabulamunicourt.com/searchdocket.asp. Online results show middle initial, DOB.

County Court Eastern Division 25 W Jefferson St, Jefferson, OH 44047; 440-576-3617; fax: 440-576-3441; 8AM-4:30PM (EST). *Misdemeanor, Civil Actions under $15,000, Eviction, Small Claims.* http://courts.co.ashtabula.oh.us/pa.htm

General Information: Fee to fax document $.50 per page. Court makes copy: $.50 per page. Self serve copy: same. Certification fee: $1.50. Payee: Eastern County Court. Only cashiers checks and money orders accepted. No credit cards accepted for record searches. Prepayment required. Mail requests: SASE helpful.

Civil Name Search: Access: Mail, fax, in person, online. Both court and visitors may perform in person name searches. No search fee. Civil records on computer since 1/9/95; in books back to 1960s. Mail turnaround time 1-2 days. Civil PAT goes back to 1995. Access to records are free at http://courts.co.ashtabula.oh.us/pa.htm.

Criminal Name Search: Access: Mail, fax, in person, online. Both court and visitors may perform in person name searches. No search fee. Required to search: name, years to search, DOB or SSN. Criminal records on computer since 1/9/95; in books back to 1960s. Mail turnaround time 1-2 days. Criminal PAT goes back to same as civil. Access to records are free at http://courts.co.ashtabula.oh.us/pa.htm. Online results show name, DOB.

County Court Western Division 117 W Main St, Geneva, OH 44041; 440-466-1184; fax: 440-466-7171; 8AM-4:30PM (EST). *Misdemeanor, Civil Actions under $15,000, Small Claims.* www.co.ashtabula.oh.us

General Information: No confidential records released. Will fax documents to local or toll-free number. Court makes copy: $.50 per page. Certification fee: $1.50 per page. Payee: Western County Court. Only cashiers checks and money orders accepted. No credit cards accepted for copies or record searches. Prepayment required. Mail requests: SASE required.

Civil Name Search: Access: In person, mail, fax, online. Visitors must perform in person searches themselves. No search fee. Civil records on computer back to 1995; prior records on docket books. Civil PAT goes back to 1995. Access records free at http://courts.co.ashtabula.oh.us/pa.htm.

Criminal Name Search: Access: In person, mail, fax, online. Visitors must perform in person searches themselves. No search fee. Required to search: name, years to search, DOB, SSN, signed release. Criminal records computerized from 1995; prior records on docket books. Mail turnaround time 72 hours. Criminal PAT goes back to 1995. Access records free at http://courts.co.ashtabula.oh.us/pa.htm. Online results show name only.

Athens County

Common Pleas Court 1 South Court St, Athens, OH 45701-2824; 740-592-3242; probate phone: 740-592-3251; fax: 740-592-3282; 8AM-4PM (EST). *Felony, Civil Actions over $10,000, Probate.* http://athenscountygovernment.com/cpc/

General Information: Probate court is a separate court at the same address. Court makes copy: $.05 per page. Self serve copy: $.05 per page. Certification fee: $1.00. Payee: Clerk of Court. Business checks accepted. No credit cards accepted. Prepayment required. Mail requests: SASE required for mail return of any copies.

Civil Name Search: Access: Mail, in person, online. Both court and visitors may perform in person name searches. No search fee. Required to search: name, years to search; also helpful: address. Civil records on computer back to 1/92; prior in books. Civil PAT goes back to 1992. Online access to CP court records are free at http://coc.athenscountygovernment.com/pa/

Criminal Name Search: Access: mail, in person, online. Both court and visitors may perform in person name searches. No search fee. Required to search: name, years to search; also helpful: address, DOB, SSN. Criminal records computerized from 1/92; prior in books. Criminal PAT goes back to same as civil. Online access to CP court records are free at http://coc.athenscountygovernment.com/pa/

Athens Municipal Court City Hall, 8 E Washington St, Athens, OH 45701; 740-592-3328; fax: 740-592-3331; 8AM-4PM (EST). *Misdemeanor, Civil Actions under $15,000, Eviction, Small Claims.* www.ci.athens.oh.us/amc.cfm

General Information: Online identifiers in results same as on public terminal. No expunged or sealed records released. Will not fax documents. Court makes copy: $.05 per page. Certification fee: $1.00 per page plus copy fee. Payee: ACMC. Personal checks accepted. Credit cards accepted. Prepayment required. Mail requests: SASE required.

Civil Name Search: Access: Mail, in person, online. Visitors must perform in person searches themselves. No search fee. Required to search: name, years to search; also helpful: address. Civil records on computer back to 1994, prior in books. Civil PAT goes back to 1994. Search by name or case number at http://docket.webxsol.com/athens/index.html. Records available from 1992.

Criminal Name Search: Access: Mail, in person, online. Visitors must perform in person searches themselves. No search fee. Required to search: name, years to search; also helpful: address, DOB, SSN. Criminal records computerized from 7/1993, prior in books back to 1974. Mail turnaround time 10 days. Criminal PAT goes back to same as civil. Search by name or case number at http://docket.webxsol.com/athens/index.html. Records available from 1992. Online results show middle initial, DOB.

Auglaize County

Common Pleas Court PO Box 409, 209 S Blackhoof St, Wapakoneta, OH 45895; 419-739-6765; probate phone: 419-739-6778; criminal fax: 419-739-6768; civil fax: 8AM-4:30PM; 8AM-4:30PM (EST). *Felony, Civil Actions over $10,000, Probate.* www2.auglaizecounty.org/courts/common-pleas

General Information: Probate court is a separate court at the same address, Ste #103. Probate fax- 419-739-7563 Fee to fax specific case file $2.00 per page plus $.25 each copy fee. Court makes copy: $.25 per page. Certification fee: $2.00 per document plus copy fee. Payee: Clerk of Court. Personal checks accepted, credit cards are not. Prepayment required.

Civil Name Search: Access: In person, online. Visitors must perform in person searches themselves. Required to search: name, years to search; also helpful: address. Civil records on dockets from 1850, computerized since 220/00. Civil PAT goes back to 2/2000. Access civil records back to 2/2000 free at www.auglaizecounty.org/pa/.

Criminal Name Search: Access: In person, online. Visitors must perform in person searches themselves. Required to search: name, years to search; also helpful: address, DOB, SSN. Criminal docket index from 1850, computerized since 2/2000. Criminal PAT goes back to same as civil. Access criminal records back to 2/2000 free at www.auglaizecounty.org/pa/. Online results show name, DOB.

Auglaize County Municipal Court PO Box 409, Wapakoneta, OH 45895; 419-739-6766; criminal phone: 419-739-6766; civil phone: 419-739-6767; fax: 419-739-6768; 8AM-4:30PM (EST). *Misdemeanor, Civil Actions under $15,000, Eviction, Small Claims.*
www2.auglaizecounty.org/courts/municipal
General Information: No records released. Will fax documents $2.00 fax fee plus $.25 per page. Court makes copy: $.25 per page. Certification fee: $2.00 plus copy fee. Payee: Clerk of Court. Personal checks accepted. Visa/MC accepted for criminal and traffic only. Prepayment required.
Civil Name Search: Access: In person, online. Visitors must perform in person searches themselves. Required to search: name, years to search; also helpful: address. Civil records on computer from 4/1994, docket back to 1976. Civil PAT goes back to 1994. Access civil and small claims court records back to 4/1/1994 free at www.auglaizecounty.org/pa/.
Criminal Name Search: Access: In person, online. Visitors must perform in person searches themselves. Required to search: name, years to search, signed release; also helpful: address, DOB, SSN. Criminal records computerized from 10/1993, docket back to 1976. Criminal PAT goes back to 1993. Access criminal and traffic records back to 10/1/1993 free at www.auglaizecounty.org/pa/. DOB shows sometimes.

Belmont County

Common Pleas Court Belmont County Clerk of Courts, 101 W Main St, St Clairsville, OH 43950; 740-695-2121; civil phone: 740-699-2169; probate phone: 740-695-2144; fax: 740-695-5305; 8:30AM-4:30PM (EST). *Felony, Civil Actions over $3,000, Probate.*
www.belmontcountyohio.org/common_pleas.htm
General Information: Probate court is a separate court at the same address. No secret criminal records released. Will fax documents to local or toll free line. Court makes copy: $1.00 per page. Certification fee: $5.00. Payee: Clerk of Court. Personal checks accepted, credit cards are not. Prepayment required. Mail requests: SASE required.
Civil Name Search: Access: Mail, in person. Both court and visitors may perform in person name searches. Search fee: $3.00 per name. Civil records in books, archived from 1896; computerized from 1995. Mail turnaround time 1 day. Civil PAT goes back to 5/1995.
Criminal Name Search: Access: Mail, in person. Both court and visitors may perform in person name searches. Search fee: $3.00 per name. Criminal records in books, archived from 1896; computerized from 1995. Mail turnaround time 1 day. Criminal PAT goes back to 5/1995.

County Court Eastern Division 400 Imperial Plaza, Bellaire, OH 43906; 740-676-4490; fax: 740-671-6100; 8AM-4PM (EST). *Misdemeanor, Civil Actions under $15,000, Small Claims.*
www.belmontcountyohio.org/county_court.htm
General Information: No sealed or confidential records released. Will fax documents to local or toll-free number. No copy fee. Certification fee: $1.00 per page. Payee: Eastern Division. Only cashiers checks and money orders accepted. Visa/MC accepted. Prepayment required. Mail requests: SASE required.
Civil Name Search: Access: Mail, in person. Both court and visitors may perform in person name searches. No search fee. Civil records on computer from 9/1994, books back to 1950s. Note: Mail access for attorneys only. Civil PAT goes back to 1994.
Criminal Name Search: Access: Mail, in person. Both court and visitors may perform in person name searches. No search fee. Required to search: name, years to search; also helpful: DOB, SSN. Criminal records computerized from 9/1994, books back to 1950s. Mail turnaround time 1 day. Criminal PAT goes back to same as civil.

County Court Northern Division 400 Imperial Plaza, Bellaire, OH 43906; 740-676-4490; 8AM-4PM (EST). *Misdemeanor, Civil Actions under $15,000, Small Claims.*
www.belmontcountyohio.org/county_court.htm
General Information: This court was formerly located in Martins Ferry. In June 2010, this court moved to this address which is the same building housing the Eastern Division County Court. Will fax documents for no fee. No copy fee. Self serve copy: same. No certification fee. No personal checks or credit cards accepted. Prepayment required. Mail requests: SASE not required.
Civil Name Search: Access: Mail, fax, in person. Both court and visitors may perform in person name searches. No search fee. Civil records on computer from 6/1994, books back to 1950s. Mail turnaround time 5-7 days. Civil PAT goes back to 1999. Personal identifiers shown on PAT will vary.
Criminal Name Search: Access: Mail, fax, in person. Both court and visitors may perform in person name searches. No search fee. Required to search: name, years to search, DOB; also helpful: SSN, sex, signed release. Criminal records computerized from 6/1994, books back to 1950s. Mail turnaround time 5-7 days. Criminal PAT goes back to same as civil. Personal identifiers shown on PAT will vary.

County Court Western Division 147 W Main St, St Clairsville, OH 43950; 740-695-2875; fax: 740-695-7285; 8AM-4PM (EST). *Misdemeanor, Civil Actions under $15,000, Small Claims.*
www.belmontcountyohio.org/county_court.htm
General Information: Pending case information not released. No fee to fax documents. No copy fee. No certification fee. Payee: Western Division Court. Only cashiers checks and money orders accepted. No credit cards accepted. Prepayment required. Mail requests: SASE required.
Civil Name Search: Access: Fax, mail, in person. Both court and visitors may perform in person name searches. No search fee. Required to search: name, years to search, address. Civil records on computer from 1994, books back to 1950s. Mail turnaround time 2 days. Civil PAT goes back to 1994.
Criminal Name Search: Access: Fax, mail, in person. Both court and visitors may perform in person name searches. No search fee. Required to search: name, years to search, address, DOB, SSN. Criminal records computerized from 1994, books back to 1950s. Mail turnaround time 1 week. Criminal PAT goes back to same as civil.

Brown County

Common Pleas Court 101 S Main, Georgetown, OH 45121; 937-378-3100; fax: 937-378-1753; 8AM-4PM (EST). *Felony, Civil Actions over $3,000, Domestic.* www.browncountyclerkofcourts.org
General Information: No criminal expungment records released. Will fax documents $1.00 per page. Court makes copy: $.10 per page. Self serve copy: same. Certification fee: $1.00 per certification plus copy fee. Payee: Clerk of Court. Personal checks accepted, credit cards are not. Prepayment required. Mail requests: SASE required.
Civil Name Search: Access: Mail, fax, in person, online. Visitors must perform in person searches themselves. No search fee. Required to search: name, years to search; also helpful: address. Civil records on computer since 1995, in books back to 1860s. Civil PAT goes back to 1995. Search court records free at www.browncountyclerkofcourts.org/Search/.
Criminal Name Search: Access: Mail, fax, in person, online. Visitors must perform in person searches themselves. No search fee. Required to search: name, years to search; also helpful: address, DOB, SSN. Criminal records on computer since 1995, in books back to 1860s. Criminal PAT goes back to same as civil. Search court records free at www.browncountyclerkofcourts.org/Search/. Online results show name only.

County Municipal Court 770 Mount Orab Pike, Georgetown, OH 45121; 937-378-6358; fax: 937-378-2462; 8AM-4PM M-F (EST). *Misdemeanor, Civil Actions under $15,000, Eviction, Small Claims.*
www.browncountycourt.org
General Information: Online identifiers in results same as on public terminal. Will not fax documents. Court makes copy: $.10 per page. No certification fee. Payee: Brown County Municipal Court. Only cashiers checks and money orders accepted. Major credit cards accepted in person only with 3% surcharge. Prepayment required. Mail requests: SASE required.
Civil Name Search: Access: Mail, in person, online. Both court and visitors may perform in person name searches. No search fee. Civil records in books back to 1958, computerized since 1995. Mail turnaround time 3 days. Civil PAT goes back to 1995. Access to records are free at www.browncountycourt.org/search.html. Online criminal search results do not include address and DOB.
Criminal Name Search: Access: Mail, in person, online. Both court and visitors may perform in person name searches. No search fee. Required to search: name, years to search, DOB; also helpful: SSN. Criminal records in books back to 1958, computerized since 1995. Mail turnaround time 3 days. Criminal PAT goes back to 1995. Access to records are free at www.browncountycourt.org/search.html. Online criminal search results include address and DOB. Online results show name, DOB, address.

Probate and Juvenile Court 510 E State St, PO Box 379, Georgetown, OH 45121; probate phone: 937-378-6549; fax: 937-378-4729; 7:30AM-N 12:30PM 4PM (EST). *Probate.*
www.browncountyohio.gov/index.php?option=com_content&view=article&id=12&Itemid=14

Butler County

Common Pleas Court 315 High St, General Division, Gov't Services Ctr, 5th Fl, Hamilton, OH 45011; 513-887-3278; fax: 513-887-3966; 8:30AM-4:30PM (EST). *Felony, Civil Actions over $3,000.*
www.butlercountyclerk.org
General Information: Government Service Center phone number is 513-887-3288. Probate Court is a separate entry at the County. Online identifiers in results same as on public terminal. Court makes copy: $.25 per page. Certification fee: $2.00. Cert fee includes copy fee, fee is per page. Payee: Butler County Clerk of Court. Personal checks accepted. Major credit cards accepted in person only. Prepayment required.

Civil Name Search: Access: Online, in person. Visitors must perform in person searches themselves. Civil records on computer from 1988, records go back to 1987. Civil PAT goes back to 4/1988. Online access to County Clerk of Courts records are free at www.butlercountyclerk.org/pa/pa.urd/pamw6500-display. Search by name, dates, or case number and type. FYI - Online access to Probate records is free at http://66.117.197.22/index.cfm?page=courtRecords. Search the Estate or Guardianship databases.

Criminal Name Search: Access: Online, in person. Visitors must perform in person searches themselves. Required to search: name, years to search, DOB; also helpful: SSN. Criminal records computerized from 1988, prior in books. Criminal PAT goes back to same as civil. Online access to County Clerk of Courts records are free at www.butlercountyclerk.org/pa/pa.urd/pamw6500-display. Search by name, dates, or case number and type. Online results show name, DOB.

County Court Area #1 118 W High, Oxford, OH 45056; 513-523-4748; fax: 513-523-4737; 8AM-5PM (EST). *Misdemeanor, Civil Actions under $15,000, Small Claims.* www.butlercountyohio.org/areacourts/

General Information: No sealed records released. Will not fax documents. No copy fee. No certification fee. Payee: Area 1 Court. No personal checks or credit cards accepted. Prepayment required. Mail requests: SASE required.

Civil Name Search: Access: Phone, mail, in person, online. Both court and visitors may perform in person name searches. No search fee. Civil records on index back to 1983. Mail turnaround time 3 days. Civil PAT goes back to 1993. Click on the Court Records Search link at www.butlercountyclerk.org/.

Criminal Name Search: Access: Mail, in person, phone, online. Both court and visitors may perform in person name searches. No search fee. Required to search: name, years to search, DOB. Criminal records on index back to 1983. Mail turnaround time 1-5 days. Criminal PAT goes back to same as civil. Click on the Court Records Search link at www.butlercountyclerk.org/.

County Court Area #2 Butler County Courthouse, 101 High St, 1st Fl, Hamilton, OH 45011; 513-887-3459; fax: 513-887-3568; 8AM-5PM (EST). *Misdemeanor, Civil Actions under $15,000, Small Claims.* www.butlercountyohio.org/areacourts/

General Information: Probate is a separate index located on Courthouse 2nd Fl. No sealed records released. No copy fee. Self serve copy: $.25 per page. No certification fee. Payee: Area II Court. Only cashiers checks and money orders accepted. No credit cards accepted. Prepayment required. Mail requests: SASE required.

Civil Name Search: Access: Phone, in person, online. Visitors must perform in person searches themselves. No search fee. Civil records on computer from 1993, books back to 1983. Civil PAT goes back to 1993. Click on the Court Records Search link at www.butlercountyclerk.org/.

Criminal Name Search: Access: Phone, mail, in person, online. Visitors must perform in person searches themselves. No search fee. Criminal records computerized from 1993, books back to 1983. Mail turnaround time 2 days. Criminal PAT goes back to same as civil. Results include case number. Click on the Court Records Search link at www.butlercountyclerk.org/.

County Court Area #3 9577 Beckett Rd #300, West Chester, OH 45069; 513-867-5070; fax: 513-777-0558; 8AM-5PM (EST). *Misdemeanor, Civil Actions under $15,000, Small Claims.* www.butlercountyohio.org/areacourts/

General Information: Will not fax documents. Court makes copy: $.25 per page. Certification fee: $1.00. Payee: Area #3 Court. Personal checks accepted. Prepayment required. Mail requests: SASE required.

Civil Name Search: Access: Mail, in person, online. Both court and visitors may perform in person name searches. No search fee. Civil records on computer from 1993, books back to 1983. Mail turnaround time 2-3 days. Click on the Court Records Search link at www.butlercountyclerk.org/.

Criminal Name Search: Access: Mail, in person. Both court and visitors may perform in person name searches. No search fee. Criminal records computerized from 1993, books back to 1983. Mail turnaround time 1-2 weeks. Click on the Court Records Search link at www.butlercountyclerk.org/.

Fairfield Municipal Court 675 Niles Rd, Fairfield, OH 45014; 513-425-7802; fax: 513-867-6001; 8:30AM-4:30PM (EST). *Misdemeanor, Civil Actions under $15,000, Small Claims.* www.fairfield-city.org/municipalcourt/index.cfm

General Information: Online identifiers in results same as on public terminal. No sealed records released. Will fax documents to local or toll free line. Court makes copy: $.05 per page; copies included in search fee. Certification fee: $5.00 for certificate of disposition. Payee: City of Fairfield. No personal checks accepted. Credit cards accepted in person only. Prepayment required. Mail requests: SASE required.

Civil Name Search: Access: Mail, in person, online. Both court and visitors may perform in person name searches. Search fee: $10.00. Civil records on computer from 1993, books back to 1983. Mail turnaround time 3 days. Civil PAT goes back to 1988. Search records online back to 1988 free at www.fairfield-city.org/courtrecords/municipal-court-records.cfm.

Criminal Name Search: Access: Mail, in person, online. Both court and visitors may perform in person name searches. Search fee: $10.00. Criminal records computerized from 1993, books back to 1983. Mail turnaround time is 3 days. Criminal PAT goes back to 1988. Search records online back to 1988 free at www.fairfield-city.org/courtrecords/municipal-court-records.cfm. Online results show middle initial, DOB.

Hamilton Municipal Court 345 High St, 2nd Fl, Hamilton, OH 45011; 513-785-7300; fax: 513-785-7315; 8AM-5PM (EST). *Misdemeanor, Civil Actions under $15,000, Small Claims.* www.hamiltonmunicipalcourt.org

General Information: Online identifiers in results same as on public terminal. No sealed records released. Will fax documents to local or toll free line. Court makes copy: $.05 per page. Certification fee: None; $5.00 for certificate of disposition. Payee: City of Hamilton. Personal checks accepted. Credit cards accepted. Prepayment required.

Civil Name Search: Access: Mail, in person, online. Both court and visitors may perform in person name searches. No search fee. Civil records on computer from 1993, books back to 1983. Mail turnaround time 3 days. Civil PAT goes back to 1992. Search record access free at http://hamiltonmunicipalcourt.org/connect/court/.

Criminal Name Search: Access: Mail, in person, online. Both court and visitors may perform in person name searches. No search fee. Criminal records computerized from 1993, books back to 1983. Mail turnaround time is 3 days. Criminal PAT goes back to same as civil. Search records free at http://hamiltonmunicipalcourt.org/connect/court/. Online results show middle initial, DOB.

Middletown Municipal Court 1 Donham Plaza, Middletown, OH 45042; criminal phone: 513-425-7810; civil phone: 513-425-7816; fax: 513-425-7846; 8AM-N, 1-5PM (EST). *Misdemeanor, Civil Actions under $15,000, Small Claims.* www.cityofmiddletown.org/court/

General Information: If you mail in a search request, they may just mail back the searchable website so that you can search online. No sealed records released. Will fax documents to local or toll free line. Court makes copy: $.05 per page. Certification fee: $3.00 per doc. Payee: Middletown Municipal Court. No personal checks or credit cards accepted. Prepayment required.

Civil Name Search: Access: Mail, In person, online. Both court and visitors may perform in person name searches. No search fee. Civil records on computer from 1993, books back to 1983. Mail turnaround time 2-3 days. Civil PAT goes back to 1993. Index to the civil docket is at http://court.cityofmiddletown.org/connection/court/index.xsp.

Criminal Name Search: Access: In person, online. Both court and visitors may perform in person name searches. No search fee. Records computerized from 1993, books back to 1983. Criminal PAT goes to 1993. Search criminal and traffic records back to early 1990s free at http://court.cityofmiddletown.org/connection/court/index.xsp. Online records go back to 1990.

Probate Court 101 High St, 2nd Fl, Courthouse, Hamilton, OH 45011; 513-887-3294; 8AM-4:30PM (EST). *Probate.* www.butlercountyprobatecourt.org/

General Information: Access to "Estate Lookup, Guardianship Lookup or Civil Commitments Search" found at www.butlercountyprobatecourt.org/index.cfm?page=courtRecords. Click on one of these found at bottom of page.

Carroll County

Common Pleas Court PO Box 367, 119 S Lisbon St, Carrollton, OH 44615; 330-627-4886; probate phone: 330-627-2323; fax: 330-627-0985; 8AM-4PM (EST). *Felony, Civil Actions over $15,000, Probate.* www.carrollcountyohio.net/courts/commonpleascourt.html

General Information: Probate court is a separate court at the same street address, #202. They do not have PO Box. Probate Fax #: 330-627-6004. Will fax specific case file $2.00 for 1st page plus $1.00 each add'l page. Court makes copy: $.05 per page. Certification fee: $1.00 per document plus copy fee. Payee: Clerk of Court. Personal checks accepted in person with photo ID. No credit cards accepted. Prepayment required.

Civil Name Search: Access: In person only. Visitors must perform in person searches themselves. Civil records in books back to 1900s. Note: Clerk will assist visitors to find case numbers. Civil PAT goes back to 3/2000.

Criminal Name Search: Access: In person only. Visitors must perform in person searches themselves. Required to search: name, years to search; also helpful: DOB, SSN. Criminal records in books back to 1900s. Note: Clerk will assist visitors to find case numbers. Criminal PAT goes back to same as civil.

Municipal Court 119 S Lisbon St, #301, Carrollton, OH 44615; 330-627-5049; fax: 330-627-3662; 8AM-4PM (EST). *Misdemeanor, Civil Actions under $15,000, Small Claims, Evictions.*
www.carrollcountyohio.net/courts/municipalcourt.html
General Information: No confidential records released. Will not fax documents. Court makes copy: $.25 per page. Certification fee: $2.00. Payee: Carroll County Municipal Court. Personal checks accepted. Major credit cards accepted. Prepayment required.
Civil Name Search: Access: In person only. Visitors must perform in person searches themselves. Civil records in books from 1958; on computer since 11/95. Civil PAT goes back to 1995.
Criminal Name Search: Access: In person only. Visitors must perform in person searches themselves. Required to search: name, years to search, DOB. Criminal records in books from 1958; on computer since 11/95. Criminal PAT goes back to same as civil.

Champaign County

Common Pleas Court 200 N Main St, Urbana, OH 43078; 937-484-1047; probate phone: 937-484-1028; fax: 937-484-5325; 8AM-4PM (EST). *Felony, Civil Actions over $10,000, Probate.*
General Information: Probate court is a separate court at the same address, 3rd Fl. All records are public. Will fax documents $1.00 per page fee. Court makes copy: $.25 per page. Certification fee: $1.00 per certification plus copy fee. Payee: Clerk of Court. Personal checks over $10.00 not accepted. No credit cards accepted. Prepayment required. Mail requests: SASE required.
Civil Name Search: Access: Phone, mail, in person. Visitors must perform in person searches themselves. No search fee. Civil records on computer from 6/92, books back to late 1800s. Note: Will only do phone or mail searches with a case number. Even in this situation, requesters are limited to 10 files per month if acting as a retriever. Civil PAT goes back to 1992.
Criminal Name Search: Access: Phone, mail, in person. Visitors must perform in person searches themselves. No search fee. Required to search: name, years to search, DOB, SSN, signed release. Criminal records computerized from 6/92, books back to late 1800s. Note: Court will only do mail or phone searches with a case number. Even in this situation, requesters are limited to 10 files per month if acting as a retriever. Criminal PAT goes back to same as civil.

Champaign County Municipal Court PO Box 85, 101 E Main St, Courthouse, Urbana, OH 43078; 937-653-7376; fax: 937-652-4333; 8AM-4PM (EST). *Misdemeanor, Civil Actions under $15,000, Eviction, Small Claims, Traffic.*
www.champaigncountymunicipalcourt.com
General Information: No sealed records released. Will not fax documents. Court makes copy: $.25 per page. Certification fee: $2.50 per page includes copies. Payee: Municipal Court. Cashiers checks and money orders accepted. Major credit cards accepted plus $5.00 processing fee. Prepayment required. Mail requests: SASE required.
Civil Name Search: Access: Mail, in person, online. Both court and visitors may perform in person name searches. No search fee. Civil records on computer from 6/1993, books back to late 1800s. Mail turnaround time 7-10 days. Civil PAT goes back to 1992. Access court records back to 1992 free at www.champaigncountymunicipalcourt.com/Docket.aspx includes civil, criminal and traffic.
Criminal Name Search: Access: Mail, in person, online. Both court and visitors may perform in person name searches. No search fee. Required to search: name, years to search; also helpful: DOB, SSN. Criminal records computerized from 6/1993, books back to late 1800s. Mail turnaround time 7-10 days. Criminal PAT goes back to 1992. Online access to criminal is the same as civil. Online results show middle initial, DOB, address.

Clark County

Common Pleas Court 101 N Limestone St, Rm 210, PO Box 1008, Springfield, OH 45502; 937-521-1680; 937-521-1693 (Domestic); fax: 937-328-2436; 8AM-4:30PM (EST). *Felony, Civil Actions over $10,000.*
www.clarkcountyohio.gov/courts/index.htm
General Information: Online identifiers in results same as on public terminal. Will fax out specific case files for $2.00 plus copy fee. Court makes copy: $.25 per page. Certification fee: $1.00 plus copy fee. Payee: Clerk of Court. Business checks accepted. No credit cards accepted. Prepayment required.
Civil Name Search: Access: In person, online. Visitors must perform in person searches themselves. Civil cases indexed by defendant. Civil records on computer back to 1990, prior in index books. Civil PAT goes back to 1990. Online access to clerk's record index is free at www.clarkcountyohio.gov/Clerk/index.htm.
Criminal Name Search: Access: In person, online. Visitors must perform in person searches themselves. Criminal records computerized from 1990, prior in index books. Note: Last four numbers of DOB not

viewable and must be confirmed by court personnel. Criminal PAT goes back to same as civil. Online access to clerk's record index is free at www.clarkcountyohio.gov/Clerk/index.htm. The Sheriff's most wanted list, criminal incident, and crash reports are at www.clarkcountysheriff.com. Online results show name, DOB.

Clark County Municipal Court 50 E Columbia St, Springfield, OH 45502; 937-328-3700; criminal phone: 937-328-3726; civil phone: 937-328-3715; fax: 937-328-3779; 8AM-5PM (EST). *Misdemeanor, Civil Actions under $15,000, Eviction, Small Claims.*
www.clerkofcourts.municipal.co.clark.oh.us/
General Information: Will fax documents in emergency only. Court makes copy: $.50 per page. Self serve copy: none. Certification fee: $2.00 includes copy fee. Payee: Clerk of Court. No personal checks. Major credit cards accepted. Prepayment required. Mail requests: SASE requested.
Civil Name Search: Access: Phone, mail, in person, online. Both court and visitors may perform in person name searches. No search fee. Civil records on computer since 5/90; prior records go back to 1997. Mail turnaround time 2-3 days. Civil PAT goes back to 5/1990. Terminal results may show business name and SSN. Online access to case information is free at www.clerkofcourts.municipal.co.clark.oh.us/. Images available back to 4/15/06. Name searching on "New Cases;" other types require a case number. Online records go back to 3/90.
Criminal Name Search: Access: Mail, in person, online. Both court and visitors may perform in person name searches. No search fee. Required to search: name, years to search; also helpful: DOB, SSN. Criminal records on computer since 3/90; prior records go back to 1998. Mail turnaround time 2-3 days. Criminal PAT goes back to 3/1990. Online access to case information is free at www.clerkofcourts.municipal.co.clark.oh.us/. Images available back to 4/15/06. Name searching on "New Cases;" other types require a case number. Online records go back to 3/90.

Probate Court 50 E Columbia St, 5th Fl, Springfield, OH 45502; probate phone: 937-521-1845; fax: 937-328-2589; 8AM-4:30PM (EST). *Probate.*
www.probate.clarkcountyohio.gov/
General Information: Record search site at www.probate.clarkcountyohio.gov/search.shtml.

Clermont County

Common Pleas Court 270 Main St, Batavia, OH 45103; criminal phone: 513-732-7339; civil phone: 513-732-7560; fax: 513-732-7050; 8AM-4:30PM (EST). *Felony, Civil Actions over $15,000.*
www.clermontclerk.org/Case_Access.htm
General Information: Will fax documents $2.00 fee plus $.10 per page. Court makes copy: $.10 per page. Certification fee: $1.00 per page. Payee: Clerk of Court. Business checks accepted. No credit cards accepted. Prepayment required.
Civil Name Search: Access: In person, online. Visitors must perform in person searches themselves. Required to search: name, years to search; also helpful: address. Civil records on computer from 1987, some on microfiche from 1920s, index books from 1959. Civil PAT goes back to 1987. Online access to civil records is the same as criminal, see following.
Criminal Name Search: Access: In person, online. Visitors must perform in person searches themselves. Required to search: name, years to search, DOB; also helpful: address, SSN. Criminal records computerized from 1987, some on microfiche from 1920s, index books from 1959. Note: Clerk refers criminal record requests to the Sheriff (513-732-7500) who will do searches for $20.00 per name. Criminal PAT goes back to same as civil. Online access to court records is free at www.clermontclerk.org/Case_Access.htm. Online records go back to 1/1987. Includes later Municipal Court records. Online results show middle initial.

Clermont County Municipal Court 4430 State Rt 222, Batavia, OH 45103; criminal phone: 513-732-7290; civil phone: 513-732-7292; criminal fax: 513-732-7831; civil fax: 8AM-4:30PM; 8AM-4:30PM (EST). *Misdemeanor, Civil Actions under $15,000, Eviction, Small Claims.*
www.clermontclerk.org
General Information: Court makes copy: $.25 per page. Certification fee: $4.00 per doc plus copy fee. Payee: Clerk of Court. Only cashiers checks and money orders accepted. No credit cards accepted. Prepayment required. Mail requests: SASE required.
Civil Name Search: Access: Mail, in person, online. Visitors must perform in person searches themselves. No search fee. Computerized records from 5/96, civil records in books and microfiche from 1959, docket books back to 1800s. Civil PAT goes back to 1996. Access to court records is the same as criminal, see following.
Criminal Name Search: Access: Mail, in person, online. Visitors must perform in person searches themselves. No search fee. Required to search: name, years to search, DOB; also helpful: SSN. Computerized records back to 5/96, criminal records in books and microfiche from 1957, docket books back to 1800s. Criminal PAT goes back to 5/1/1996. Access to court

records is free at www.clermontclerk.org/Case_Access.htm. Online records go back to 5/1/1996. Online results show middle initial, DOB, address.

Probate Court 2370 Clermont Center Dr., Batavia, OH 45103; probate phone: 513-732-7243; fax: 513-732-8183; 8AM-4PM (EST). *Probate.* http://probatejuvenile.clermontcountyohio.gov/probate.aspx

Clinton County

Common Pleas Court 46 S South St, Wilmington, OH 45177; 937-382-2316; probate phone: 937-382-2280; fax: 937-383-3455; 8AM-4PM (EST). *Felony, Civil Actions, Probate.* http://co.clinton.oh.us/courts/
General Information: Probate court is a separate court at the same address, 2nd Fl. Probate fax- 937-383-1158; Probate hours 8AM-4:30PM. No confidential records released. Will fax out documents $.40 per page. Court makes copy: $.10 per page. Certification fee: $1.00. Payee: Clerk of Court. Personal checks accepted, credit cards are not. Prepayment required. Mail requests: SASE required.
Civil Name Search: Access: Fax, mail, in person. Both court and visitors may perform in person name searches. No search fee. Required to search: name, years to search; also helpful: address. Civil records on computer since 1995; prior in books back to 1810. Mail turnaround time 1 week. Civil PAT goes back to 1995.
Criminal Name Search: Access: Mail, in person. Both court and visitors may perform in person name searches. Search fee: $5.00 per name. Required to search: name, years to search, DOB, SSN; also helpful: address. Criminal records on computer since 1995; prior in books back to 1810. Mail turnaround time 1 week. Criminal PAT goes back to same as civil.

Clinton County Municipal Court 69 N South St, PO Box 71, Wilmington, OH 45177; 937-382-8985; fax: 937-383-0130; 8AM-4PM (EST). *Misdemeanor, Civil Actions under $15,000, Eviction, Small Claims.* www.clintonmunicourt.org
General Information: Will fax documents to local or toll free line. Court makes copy: $1.00 per page 1st 5; $.25 per page each add'l. No certification fee. Payee: Clerk of Court. Only cashiers checks and money orders accepted. No credit cards accepted. Prepayment required. Mail requests: SASE required.
Civil Name Search: Access: Fax, mail, in person, online. Both court and visitors may perform in person name searches. No search fee. Required to search: name, years to search, SSN. Civil records in books from 1960; computerized records go back to 1995. Mail turnaround time 1 day. Civil PAT goes back to 1994. Search court records online at www.clintonmunicourt.org/search.html.
Criminal Name Search: Access: Fax, mail, in person, online. Both court and visitors may perform in person name searches. No search fee. Required to search: name, years to search, DOB; also helpful: SSN. Criminal records in books from 1960; computerized records go back to 1995. Mail turnaround time 1 day. Criminal PAT goes back to same as civil. Search court records online at www.clintonmunicourt.org/search.html.

Columbiana County

Common Pleas Court 105 S Market St, Lisbon, OH 44432; 330-424-7777; fax: 330-424-3960; 8AM-4PM (EST). *Felony, Civil Actions over $15,000.* www.ccclerk.org
General Information: Online identifiers in results same as on public terminal. No secret indictment records released. Will not fax documents. Court makes copy: $.05 per page. Self serve copy: same. Certification fee: $1.00 per page. Payee: Clerk of Court. Personal checks accepted. Major credit cards accepted. Prepayment required. Mail requests: SASE or postage required for return of any copies.
Civil Name Search: Access: In person, online. Visitors must perform in person searches themselves. Required to search: name, years to search; also helpful: address. Civil records on computer since 1993; prior in books from 1968, archived back to 1800s. Civil PAT goes back to 3/1993. Access all county court index and docket records free at www.ccclerk.org/case_access.htm. Includes probate.
Criminal Name Search: Access: In person, online. Visitors must perform in person searches themselves. Required to search: name, years to search, DOB; also helpful: address, SSN. Criminal records on computer since 1993; prior in books from 1968, archived back to 1800s. Criminal PAT goes back to same as civil. Access all county court index and docket records free at www.ccclerk.org/case_access.htm. Online results show middle initial, DOB.

East Liverpool Municipal Court 126 W 6th St, East Liverpool, OH 43920; 330-385-5151; fax: 330-385-1566; 8AM-4PM (EST). *Misdemeanor, Civil Actions under $15,000, Eviction, Small Claims.* www.ccclerk.org/
General Information: No expungment records released. No fee to fax documents. Court makes copy: $.10 per page. Certification fee: $1.00 each includes copy fee. Copy fee may also apply if more than 4 pages. Payee: East Liverpool Municipal Court. No business or personal checks, Visa/MC accepted. Prepayment required. Mail requests: SASE required.
Civil Name Search: Access: Phone, fax, mail, in person, online. Both court and visitors may perform in person name searches. No search fee. Civil records in books from 1968, archived back to 1800s, computerized since 11/92. Mail turnaround time 1-2 days. Civil PAT goes back to 1992. Access all county court index and docket records free at www.ccclerk.org/case_access.htm.
Criminal Name Search: Access: Phone, fax, mail, in person, online. Both court and visitors may perform in person name searches. No search fee. Required to search: name, years to search, signed release; also helpful: DOB, SSN. Criminal records in books from 1968, archived back to 1800s, computerized since 11/92. Mail turnaround time 1-2 days. Criminal PAT goes back to same as civil. Access all county court index and docket records free at www.ccclerk.org/case_access.htm. Online results show middle initial, DOB.

Municipal Court 38832 Saltwell, Lisbon, OH 44432; 330-424-5326; fax: 330-424-6658; 8AM-4PM (EST). *Misdemeanor, Civil Actions under $15,000, Small Claims.* www.ccclerk.org/the_courts.htm
General Information: This court is formerly known as the Southwest Area Court. In Sept. 2005, the Northwest Muni Court in Salem and the Eastern Area Muni Court in East Palestine were merged with this court. No expungment records released. Will fax documents $2.00 1st page, $1.00 each add'l. Court makes copy: $.05 per page. Self serve copy: same. Certification fee: $1.00 per page. Payee: Columbiana County Municipal Court. Personal or cashiers checks and money orders accepted. Major credit cards accepted. Prepayment required. Mail requests: SASE required for mail return of any copies.
Civil Name Search: Access: In person, online. Visitors must perform in person searches themselves. No search fee. Civil records in books back to 1958; on computer back to 1994. Note: Court will search for records if prior to 1994. Civil PAT goes back to 1994. Access all county court index and docket records free at www.ccclerk.org/case_access.htm.
Criminal Name Search: Access: In person, online. Visitors must perform in person searches themselves. Required to search: name, years to search; also helpful: DOB, SSN. Criminal records in books back to 1958; on computer back to 1994. Note: Court will search for records if prior to 1994. Criminal PAT goes back to same as civil. Access all county court index and docket records free at www.ccclerk.org/case_access.htm. Online results show middle initial, DOB.

Probate Court 105 S Market St, Lisbon, OH 44432; 330-424-9516; 8AM-4PM. *Probate.* www.ccclerk.org/probate_fees.htm

Coshocton County

Common Pleas Court 318 Main St, Coshocton, OH 43812; 740-622-1456; fax: 740-295-0020; 8AM-4PM (EST). *Felony, Civil Actions over $10,000.* www.coshoctoncounty.net
General Information: No expunged records released. Will not fax documents. Court makes copy: $.25 per page. Self serve copy: same. Certification fee: $1.00 per page plus copy fee. Payee: Clerk of Court. Personal checks accepted, credit cards are not. Prepayment required. Mail requests: SASE not required.
Civil Name Search: Access: Mail, in person. Both court and visitors may perform in person name searches. No search fee. Civil records in books, microfilm back to 1985, archived back to 1800s; on computer back to 1998. Mail turnaround time 2 days. Civil PAT goes back to 1998. Results include name and case number.
Criminal Name Search: Access: Mail, in person. Both court and visitors may perform in person name searches. No search fee. Required to search: name, years to search, DOB; also helpful: SSN. Criminal records in books, microfilm back to 1985, archived back to 1800s; on computer back to 1998. Mail turnaround time 2 days. Criminal PAT goes back to same as civil. Results include name and case number.

Coshocton Municipal Court 760 Chestnut St, Coshocton, OH 43812; 740-622-2871; fax: 740-623-5928; 8AM-4:30PM M-W F; 8AM-N TH (EST). *Misdemeanor, Civil Actions under $15,000, Eviction, Small Claims.* www.coshoctonmunicipalcourt.com
General Information: Online identifiers in results same as on public terminal. No expunged records released. No fee to fax documents. Court makes copy: $1.00 per page. Certification fee: $5.00. Payee: Clerk of Court. Personal checks accepted. Visa/MC accepted via internet only. Prepayment required. Mail requests: SASE requested.
Civil Name Search: Access: Phone, fax, mail, in person, online. Both court and visitors may perform in person name searches. No search fee. Civil records on computer from 1989, books back to 1952. Mail turnaround time same day. Civil PAT goes back to 1989. Online access to civil records is at the website. Search by name, case number, attorney, date.

Criminal Name Search: Access: Phone, fax, mail, in person, online. Both court and visitors may perform in person name searches. No search fee. Required to search: name, years to search; also helpful: DOB, SSN. Criminal records computerized from 1989, books back to 1952. Mail turnaround time same day. Criminal PAT goes back to same as civil. Terminal results also include last known address. Online access to criminal records is the same as civil. Search by name, attorney, citation or case number. Online results show middle initial, DOB.

Probate and Juvenile Court 426 Main St, Coshocton, OH 43812; 740-622-1837; fax: 740-623-6514; 8AM-4PM (EST). *Probate.*
www.coshoctoncounty.net/agency/probate/
General Information: Reach Juvenile Court at 740-622-8969.

Crawford County

Common Pleas Court 112 E Mansfield St, #204, Bucyrus, OH 44820; 419-562-5771; probate phone: 419-562-8891; fax: 419-562-8011; 8:30AM-4:30PM (EST). *Felony, Civil Actions over $3,000, Probate.*
www.crawfordcocpcourt.org/
General Information: The number to the clerk's office is 491-562-2766. Probate court is a separate court at the same address, Suite #101. Probate fax-419-563-1920. No divorce investigations. Will fax documents for no fee. Court makes copy: $.10 per page. Certification fee: $1.00 per page includes copy fee. Payee: Clerk of Court. Personal checks accepted, credit cards are not. Prepayment required. Mail requests: SASE required.
Civil Name Search: Access: Phone, mail, in person, online. Both court and visitors may perform in person name searches. No search fee. Civil records on computer back to 1990, some on microfiche and index books from 1800s. Mail turnaround time usually same day. Civil PAT goes back to 2/1990. Online access to Common Pleas court records is free at www.crawford-co.org/Clerk/default.html and click on "Internet Inquiry."
Criminal Name Search: Access: Mail, in person, online. Both court and visitors may perform in person name searches. No search fee. Criminal records computerized from 1990, some on microfiche and index books from 1800s. Mail turnaround time 1-2 days. Criminal PAT goes back to same as civil. Online access to criminal cases is the same as civil. Online results show middle initial, DOB.

Crawford County Municipal Court PO Box 550, 112 E Mansfield, Courthouse, Bucyrus, OH 44820; 419-562-2731; criminal phone: x3; civil phone: x6; fax: 419-562-7064; 8AM-4:30PM (EST). *Misdemeanor, Civil Actions under $15,000, Eviction, Small Claims.*
General Information: No counseling report records released. Will fax back documents. Court makes copy: $.10 per page. Certification fee: $2.00 per cert plus copy fee. Payee: Crawford County Municipal Court. No personal checks or credit cards accepted. Prepayment required. Mail requests: SASE not required.
Civil Name Search: Access: Phone, fax, mail, in person. Both court and visitors may perform in person name searches. No search fee. Civil records in books back to 1978. Note: Phone search requests must be kept to one name. Mail turnaround time within 1 week. Civil PAT goes to 1996.
Criminal Name Search: Access: Mail, fax, in person. Both court and visitors may perform in person name searches. No search fee. Required to search: name, years to search, DOB. Criminal records in books back to 1978; on computer back to 1996. Note: Court prefers a fax search request. Mail turnaround time within 1 week. Criminal PAT goes back to 1996.

Crawford County Municipal Court East Div 301 Harding Way E, Galion, OH 44833; 419-468-6819; fax: 419-468-6828; 8AM-5PM (EST). *Misdemeanor, Civil Actions under $15,000, Eviction, Small Claims.*
General Information: Will fax back documents. Court makes copy: $.10 per page. Certification fee: $3.00 plus copy fee. Payee: Municipal Court. Only cashiers checks and money orders accepted. No credit cards accepted. Prepayment required. Mail requests: SASE required.
Civil Name Search: Access: Mail, fax, in person. Both court and visitors may perform in person name searches. No search fee. Civil records in books back to 1800s. Mail turnaround time 2-3 days. Civil PAT goes back to 1996.
Criminal Name Search: Access: Mail, fax, in person. Both court and visitors may perform in person name searches. No search fee. Required to search: name, years to search, DOB, SSN, signed release. Criminal records in books back to 1800s. Mail turnaround time 2-3 days. Criminal PAT goes back to same as civil.

Cuyahoga County

Common Pleas Court - General Division 1200 Ontario St, Cleveland, OH 44113; 216-443-8560; criminal phone: 216-443-7985; civil phone: 216-443-7960; fax: 216-443-5424; 8:30AM-4:30PM (EST). *Felony, Civil Actions over $10,000.* http://cp.cuyahogacounty.us/internet/index.aspx
General Information: No expungements or sealed records released. Will not fax documents. Court makes copy: $.10 per page. This office is unable to provide change. Certification fee: $1.00 per page includes copy fee. Payee:

Clerk of Court. Business checks accepted, personal checks not accepted. No credit cards accepted. Prepayment required. Mail requests: SASE required.
Civil Name Search: Access: Phone, mail, in person, online. Both court and visitors may perform in person name searches. No search fee. Required to search: name, years to search; also helpful: address. Civil index and dockets from 1968, archived from 1800s; computerized since 1975. Note: Phone requests to 216-443-7966. Address mail requests to Gerald Fuerst, 1st Fl, Index Dept. Mail turnaround time 4-5 days. Civil PAT goes back to 1970. Online access to Common Please civil courts; click on Civil Case Dockets at http://cpdocket.cp.cuyahogacounty.us/TOS.aspx. Access Probate index at http://probate.cuyahogacounty.us/pa/.
Criminal Name Search: Access: In person, online. Visitors must perform in person searches themselves. Required to search: name, years to search; also helpful: address, DOB, SSN. Criminal records on index and dockets from 1968, archived from 1800s; computerized since 1972. Note: Criminal Dept on 2nd Floor. Any phone requests must have case number or DOB. Criminal PAT goes back to same as civil. Online access to criminal records dockets is free at http://cpdocket.cp.cuyahogacounty.us/TOS.aspx. Online results show name, DOB.

Cleveland Municipal Court - Criminal Division 1200 Ontario St, Level 3, Cleveland, OH 44113; 216-664-6911, 664-4790; fax: 216-664-4299; 8AM-10PM (EST). *Misdemeanor.*
http://clevelandmunicipalcourt.org/home.html
General Information: No adoption or juvenile records released. Will fax documents. Court makes copy: $.25 per page if multiple copies. Certification fee: $5.00 plus copy fee. Payee: Cleveland Municipal Clerk of Court. Personal checks, Visa/MC accepted. Prepayment required.
Criminal Name Search: Access: In person, online. Both court and visitors may perform in person name searches. No search fee. Required to search: name, years to search, DOB, SSN, signed release. Criminal records on computer since 1992, on books to 1982, archived prior. Note: Court recommends mail requests for criminal background checks be sent to Cleveland Police Dept, Attn- Criminal Records - Gracie, 1300 Ontario St, Cleveland 44113. For info, phone 216-623-5336. Fee is a nickel per name, do not send cash. Public use terminal has crim records. Public access terminals are available on the 2nd Fl - 8AM-4PM, M-F. See http://clevelandmunicipalcourt.org/cvdisclaimer.html for docket information. The data is incomplete and should not be relied upon for a full background search. There are limited personal identifiers to view as well.

Bedford Municipal Court 165 Center Rd, Bedford, OH 44146; 440-232-3420; fax: 440-232-2510; 8:30AM-4:30PM M-F (EST). *Misdemeanor, Civil Actions under $15,000, Eviction, Small Claims.*
www.bedfordmuni.org/
General Information: Online identifiers in results same as on public terminal. No sealed records released. No fee to fax documents. Court makes copy: $.05 per page. Certification fee: $2.00. Payee: Bedford Municipal Court. Personal checks, Visa/MC accepted. Prepayment required. Mail requests: SASE required.
Civil Name Search: Access: Fax, mail, in person, online. Both court and visitors may perform in person name searches. No search fee. Civil records on computer from 1990 docket books and index from 1970s, prior archived. Note: Personal identifiers are suppressed, but court personnel will help with common name searches. Mail turnaround time 3 days. Civil PAT goes back to 1990. Access index to court records at www.bedfordmuni.org/info.asp?pageId=5. Click on Case Information.
Criminal Name Search: Access: Fax, mail, in person, online. Both court and visitors may perform in person name searches. No search fee. Criminal records computerized from 1990, docket books and index from 1970s, prior archived. Note: Personal identifiers are suppressed, but court personnel will help with common name searches. Mail turnaround time 3 days. Criminal PAT goes back to 1990. Terminal results may include DR number. Access index to court records at www.bedfordmuni.org/info.asp?pageId=5. Click on Case Information. Online results show middle initial, DOB, address.

Berea Municipal Court 11 Berea Commons, Berea, OH 44017; 440-826-5860; criminal phone: 440-826-5860; civil phone: 440-826-5860; fax: 440-891-3387; 8AM-4:30PM (EST). *Misdemeanor, Civil Actions under $15,000, Eviction, Small Claims.*
www.bereamunicourt.org/
General Information: Traffic fax is same number as criminal fax at 440-234-2768. No probation records released. No fee to fax documents. Court makes copy: $1.00 per page. Certification fee: $5.00 per doc. Payee: Berea Municipal Court. Personal checks accepted. Credit cards accepted. Prepayment required. Mail requests: SASE required.
Civil Name Search: Access: Mail, in person, online. Both court and visitors may perform in person name searches. No search fee. Civil records

on computer back to 1991, prior in books. Mail turnaround time 7-10 days. Civil PAT available. Search docket information at www.bereamunicourt.org/info.asp?pageId=5.

Criminal Name Search: Access: Mail, in person, online. Both court and visitors may perform in person name searches. Search fee: $5.00 per name. Required to search: name, years to search; also helpful: address, DOB, SSN. Criminal records computerized from 1991, prior in books. Mail turnaround time 1 week-10 days. Criminal PAT available. Includes traffic infractions. Search docket info at www.bereamunicourt.org/info.asp?pageId=5. Online results show middle initial, DOB, address.

Cleveland Heights Municipal Court 40 Severance Cir, Cleveland Heights, OH 44118; 216-291-4901; fax: 216-291-2459; 8:30AM-5PM (EST). *Misdemeanor, Civil Actions under $15,000, Eviction, Small Claims.* www.clevelandheightscourt.com

General Information: Limited name searching is offered in person, the court refers the public to the web page. No expungments or search warrant records released. Will not fax documents. Court makes copy: $.10 per page. Certification fee: $2.00. Payee: Municipal Court. Personal checks accepted. Credit cards accepted in person only. Prepayment required.

Civil Name Search: Access: In person, online. Only the court performs in person name searches; visitors may not. Required to search: name, years to search; also helpful: address. Civil records on computer from 1990, prior in books to 1980. Search Muni civil (to $15,000) or misdemeanor docket records from the home page. Search by name or case number.

Criminal Name Search: Access: In person, online. Only the court performs in person name searches; visitors may not. Required to search: name, years to search; also helpful: address, DOB, SSN. Criminal records computerized from 1990, prior in books to 1980s. Search Muni civil (to $15,000) or misdemeanor docket records from the home page. Search by name or case number. Online results show middle initial.

Cleveland Municipal Court - Civil Division 1200 Ontario St, Cleveland, OH 44113; 216-664-4870, 216-664-4790; civil phone: small claims- x5; eviction- x4; general- x8; 8AM-4PM (EST). *Civil Actions under $15,000, Eviction, Small Claims.* http://clevelandmunicipalcourt.org/home.html

General Information: Jurisdiction also includes Village of Bratenahl. Court plans to have online access to case information. Court makes copy: $.25 per page. Certification fee: $1.00 per page plus copy fee. Payee: Municipal Court. Personal checks accepted, credit cards are not. Prepayment required.

Civil Name Search: Access: In person, online. Both court and visitors may perform in person name searches. No search fee. Required to search: name, years to search; also helpful: address. Civil records on computer from 1988, docket books and index from 1950s, prior archived. Public use terminal has civil records back to 1990. See http://clevelandmunicipalcourt.org/cvdisclaimer.html for docket information. Note the data is reportedly incomplete and there are limited personal identifiers to view.

East Cleveland Municipal Court 14340 Euclid Ave, East Cleveland, OH 44112; 216-681-2220; fax: 216-681-2217; 8:30AM-4:30PM (EST). *Misdemeanor, Civil Actions under $15,000, Eviction, Small Claims.* www.eccourt.com/

General Information: Will fax documents no add'l fee. Court makes copy: $1.00 per page. Certification fee: $10.00 plus copy fee. Payee: Municipal Court. Personal checks accepted. VISA,MC, Discover credit cards accepted; may add $3.00 cc fee. Prepayment required.

Civil Name Search: Access: In person, online. Only the court performs in person name searches; visitors may not. No search fee. Civil records go back to 1979; on computer from 2000, docket books and index from 1950s, prior archived. Note: Daily dockets also available at the website. Non-official court record data can be access for free at http://caseinfo.eccourt.com/.

Criminal Name Search: Access: In person, online. Only the court performs in person name searches; visitors may not. No search fee. Required to search: name, years to search, DOB, SSN. Criminal records computerized from 1997, docket books and index from 1950s, prior archived. Note: Address mail requests to Police Record Room. Daily dockets also available at the website. Non-official court record data can be accessed for free at http://caseinfo.eccourt.com/.

Euclid Municipal Court 555 E 222 St, Euclid, OH 44123-2099; 216-289-2888; fax: 216-289-8254; 8:30AM-4:30PM (EST). *Misdemeanor, Civil Actions under $15,000, Eviction, Small Claims.* www.cityofeuclid.com/community/court

General Information: Email questions to btercek@ci.euclid.oh.us. Online identifiers in results same as on public terminal. No expunged records released. Will not fax documents. Court makes copy: $.05 per page. Certification fee: $5.00 but normally included in search fee. Payee: Municipal

Court. Personal checks accepted. Credit cards accepted except for civil filings. Prepayment required. Mail requests: SASE required.

Civil Name Search: Access: Mail, in person, online. Both court and visitors may perform in person name searches. Search fee: $5.00 per name. Civil records on computer from 2004, docket books and index from 1950s, prior archived. Mail turnaround time 1 week. Civil PAT goes back to 2004. Docket index and daily docket lists of civil cases available at www.cityofeuclid.com/community/court/HearingDocketsandCaseInformation

Criminal Name Search: Access: Mail, in person, online. Both court and visitors may perform in person name searches. Search fee: $5.00 per name. Required to search: name, years to search, DOB; also helpful: address, SSN. Criminal records computerized from 1995, docket books and index from 1950s, prior archived. Mail turnaround time 1 week. Criminal PAT goes back to 1995. Docket index and daily docket lists of misdemeanor and traffic cases are available at www.cityofeuclid.com/community/court/HearingDocketsandCaseInformation

Garfield Heights Municipal Court 5555 Turney Rd, Garfield Heights, OH 44125; 216-475-1900; fax: 216-475-3087; 8:30AM-4:30PM (EST). *Misdemeanor, Civil Actions under $15,000, Eviction, Small Claims.* www.ghmc.org

General Information: No expunged records released. Court makes copy: $.05 per page. Certification fee: $1.00 per page. Cert fee includes copies. Payee: Municipal Court. Personal checks, Visa/MC accepted. Prepayment required. Mail requests: SASE required.

Civil Name Search: Access: Phone, mail, in person, online. Both court and visitors may perform in person name searches. No search fee. Required to search: name, years to search; also helpful: address. Civil records on computer from 11/91, docket books and index from 1996, prior archived. Note: Phone access depends on age of case. Mail turnaround time 2 weeks. Civil PAT goes back to 1999. Online access is limited to dockets; search by name, date or case number at http://docket.ghmc.org.

Criminal Name Search: Access: Phone, mail, in person, online. Both court and visitors may perform in person name searches. No search fee. Required to search: name, years to search, DOB; also helpful: address, SSN, signed release. Criminal records computerized from 1996, docket books and index from 1995, prior archived. Mail turnaround time 2 weeks. Criminal PAT goes back to same as civil. Online access is limited to dockets; search by name, date or case number at http://docket.ghmc.org.

Lakewood Municipal Court 12650 Detroit Ave, Lakewood, OH 44107; 216-529-6700; fax: 216-529-7687; 8AM-5PM (EST). *Misdemeanor, Civil Actions under $15,000, Eviction, Small Claims.* www.lakewoodcourtoh.com

General Information: No confidential records released. No fee to fax documents locally only. Court makes copy: $.10 per page. Certification fee: $3.00. Payee: Municipal Court. Personal checks accepted. Credit cards accepted. Prepayment required. Mail requests: SASE required.

Civil Name Search: Access: Phone, fax, mail, in person, online. Both court and visitors may perform in person name searches. No search fee. Required to search: name, years to search; also helpful: address. Civil records on computer from 1987, prior in books. Mail turnaround time 1 week. View weekly dockets only at www.lakewoodcourtoh.com/casesearch.html.

Criminal Name Search: Access: Fax, mail, in person, online. Both court and visitors may perform in person name searches. No search fee. Required to search: name, years to search, DOB; also helpful: address, SSN. Criminal records on computer since 1983, prior in books. Mail turnaround time 1 week. Search weekly dockets only at www.lakewoodcourtoh.com/casesearch.html.

Lyndhurst Municipal Court 5301 Mayfield Rd, Lyndhurst, OH 44124; 440-461-6500; fax: 440-442-1910; 8AM-4PM (EST). *Misdemeanor, Civil Actions under $15,000, Eviction, Small Claims.* www.lyndhurstmunicipalcourt.org/

General Information: Online identifiers in results same as on public terminal. None. Will not fax out documents. Court makes copy: $.05 per page. Certification fee: $3.00 per doc. Payee: Municipal Court. Personal checks, Visa/MC accepted. Mail requests: SASE not required.

Civil Name Search: Access: Mail, in person, online. Only the court performs in person name searches; visitors may not. No search fee. Required to search: name, years to search; also helpful: address. Civil records on computer from 1993, prior in books. Mail turnaround time 1 week. Access court records free at www.lyndhurstmunicipalcourt.org/info.asp?pageId=5.

Criminal Name Search: Access: Mail, in person, online. Only the court performs in person name searches; visitors may not. No search fee. Required to search: name, years to search, signed release; also helpful: address, DOB. Criminal records computerized from 1993, prior in books. Mail turnaround time 1 week. Access court records free at www.lyndhurstmunicipalcourt.org/info.asp?pageId=5. Online results show middle initial, DOB.

Parma Municipal Court 5555 Powers Blvd, Parma, OH 44125; 440-887-7400; criminal phone: 440-887-7400 x1; civil phone: 440-887-7400 x3; criminal fax: 440-887-7481; civil fax: 8:30AM-5PM; 8:30AM-5PM (EST). *Misdemeanor, Civil Actions under $15,000, Eviction, Small Claims.* www.parmamunicourt.org/

General Information: The court blocks the SSN from appearing on search results. Will not fax documents. Court makes copy: $.05 per page. Certification fee: $1.00 for a crim document; $5.00 for a civil document. Payee: Parma Municipal Court. Personal checks accepted. Visa/MC/Discover/AmEx accepted in person only. Prepayment required. Mail requests: SASE required.

Civil Name Search: Access: Phone, mail, in person, online. Both court and visitors may perform in person name searches. No search fee. Required to search: name, years to search; also helpful: address. Civil records on computer from 1993, prior in books to 1977. Mail turnaround time up to 1 week. Public use terminal has civil records back to 1993. Access to the court dockets index is available free at www.parmamunicourt.org/info.asp?pageId=5.

Criminal Name Search: Access: Phone, fax, mail, in person, online. Both court and visitors may perform in person name searches. No search fee. Required to search: name, years to search, DOB; also helpful: address, SSN. Criminal records computerized from 1993, prior in books to 1992. Mail turnaround time up to 1 week. Access to criminal docket is the same as civil, see above.

Rocky River Municipal Court 21012 Hilliard Blvd, Rocky River, OH 44116; 440-333-0066; fax: 440-356-5613; 8:30AM-4:30PM (EST). *Misdemeanor, Civil Actions under $15,000, Eviction, Small Claims.* www.rrcourt.net

General Information: Online identifiers in results same as on public terminal. Will fax documents to toll free line. Court makes copy: $.05 per page. Certification fee: $10.00. Payee: Rocky River Municipal Court. Personal checks, Visa/MC accepted. Prepayment required. Mail requests: SASE required.

Civil Name Search: Access: Phone, fax, mail, in person, online. Visitors must perform in person searches themselves. No search fee. Civil records on computer from 1988, prior in books to 1977. Civil PAT goes back to 1/1988. Public access to record index at https://rrcourt.net/pa/pa.htm.

Criminal Name Search: Access: Phone, fax, mail, in person, online. Visitors must perform in person searches themselves. No search fee. Required to search: name, years to search, DOB. Criminal records computerized from 1987, prior in books to 1977. Mail turnaround time 2 days. Criminal PAT goes back to 6/1987. Access record index free at https://rrcourt.net/pa/pa.htm. Online results show DOB, address.

Shaker Heights Municipal Court 3355 Lee Rd, Shaker Heights, OH 44120; 216-491-1300; fax: 216-491-1314; 8:30AM-4:30PM (EST). *Misdemeanor, Civil Actions under $15,000, Eviction, Small Claims.* www.shakerheightscourt.org/home/

General Information: Criminal Clerk open until 6:30PM on Mondays. No medical or LEADS print-out records released. Will not fax out documents. Court makes copy: $.05 per page. Certification fee: $10.00 per document. Payee: Shaker Heights Municipal Court. Personal checks accepted. Visa, MC, Amex accepted in person only. Prepayment required. Mail requests: SASE required.

Civil Name Search: Access: Mail, fax, in person, online. Both court and visitors may perform in person name searches. No search fee. Required to search: name, years to search; also helpful: address. Civil records on computer from 6/86, prior in books for at least 25 years. Mail turnaround time 2 days. Search case records and dockets at www.shakerheightscourt.org/home/.

Criminal Name Search: Access: Phone, fax, mail, in person, online. Both court and visitors may perform in person name searches. Search fee: None, however certified complete dockets are $10.00. Required to search: name, years to search, DOB and SSN. Criminal records computerized from 06/86, prior in books. For records prior to 1986 provide month & year to search. Mail turnaround time 2 days. Search case records and dockets at www.shakerheightscourt.org/home/. Online results show middle initial, DOB, address.

South Euclid Municipal Court 1349 S Green Rd, South Euclid, OH 44121; 216-381-2880; fax: 216-381-1195; 8AM-4:30PM (EST). *Misdemeanor, Civil Actions under $15,000, Eviction, Small Claims.* www.southeuclidcourt.com/

General Information: Will fax documents to local or toll free line. Court makes copy: $.10 per copy. Certification fee: $1.00 per page, includes copies but if over 10 pages, add $.10 per page. Payee: Clerk of Court, South Euclid Municipal Court. Personal checks accepted. Major credit cards accepted in person only. Prepayment required. Mail requests: SASE required.

Civil Name Search: Access: Phone, fax, mail, in person. Both court and visitors may perform in person name searches. No search fee. Required to search: name, years to search; also helpful: address. Civil records on computer back to 10/97; prior in docket books to 1960s. Mail turnaround time up to 1 week. Civil PAT goes back to 10/1997.

Criminal Name Search: Access: Mail, in person. Both court and visitors may perform in person name searches. No search fee. Required to search: name, years to search, DOB, SSN; also helpful: address. Criminal records computerized from 10/97; prior in docket books to 1960s. Mail turnaround time up to 1 week. Criminal PAT goes back to same as civil.

Probate Court 1 Lakeside Ave, Cleveland, OH 44113; 216-443-8764/8765; *Probate.* http://probate.cuyahogacounty.us/home.htm
General Information: Docket and index searches at http://probate.cuyahogacounty.us/pa/.

Darke County

Common Pleas Court 504 S Broadway, Greenville, OH 45331; 937-547-7335; fax: 937-547-7305; 8AM-4:30PM (EST). *Felony, Civil Actions over $15,000.*

General Information: No secret indictment records released. Will fax out documents. Court makes copy: $.25 per page. Self serve copy: same. Certification fee: $1.00. Payee: Clerk of Court. Business checks accepted. Prepayment required. Mail requests: SASE required.

Civil Name Search: Access: Mail, in person. Both court and visitors may perform in person name searches. Search fee: $5.00 per name. Civil records in books to 1832, on microfiche from 1940s, computerized since 1993. Mail turnaround time 1-2 days. Civil PAT goes back to 1993.

Criminal Name Search: Access: Mail, in person. Both court and visitors may perform in person name searches. Search fee: $5.00 per name. Criminal records in books to 1832, on microfiche from 1940s, computerized since 1987. Mail turnaround time 1-2 days. Criminal PAT goes to 1988.

County Municipal Court Courthouse, 504 S Broadway, Ste 7, Greenville, OH 45331-1990; 937-547-7340; fax: 937-547-7378; 8AM-4:30PM (EST). *Misdemeanor, Civil Actions under $15,000, Small Claims.*

General Information: No sealed or confidential records released. Will fax documents for a fee. Court makes copy: $.25 per page. Certification fee: $5.00 includes copy fee. Payee: County Municipal Court. Cashiers checks and money orders accepted. Visa/MC accepted. Prepayment required. Mail requests: SASE required.

Civil Name Search: Access: Mail, in person. Both court and visitors may perform in person name searches. Search fee: None; limit of 5 search requests per month for commercial requesters. Civil records in books since 1959, computerized since 1996. Mail turnaround time 1 week. Civil PAT goes back to 1996.

Criminal Name Search: Access: Mail, in person. Both court and visitors may perform in person name searches. Search fee: None; limit of 5 search requests per month for commercial requesters. Required to search: name, years to search, DOB; also helpful: SSN. Criminal records in books since 1959. Mail turnaround time 1 week. Criminal PAT goes back to same as civil.

Probate Court 300 Garst Ave, Greenville, OH 45331; 937-547-7350; fax: 937-547-1945 ;. *Probate.* www.lucas-co-probate-ct.org/Darke.htm

Defiance County

Common Pleas Court 221 Clinton St, 3rd Fl, Defiance, OH 43512; 419-782-1936; probate phone: 419-782-4181; fax: 419-782-2437; 8:30AM-4:30PM (EST). *Felony, Civil Actions over $10,000, Probate.* www.defiance-county.com/commonpleas/index.php

General Information: Common Pleas Court records managed by Clerk of Courts. Probate court is a separate court at the same address, 3rd Fl. Probate Fax: 419-782-2437. Will fax documents $2.00 1st page, $1.00 each add'l. Court makes copy: $.25 per page. Self serve copy: same. Certification fee: $1.00 per pleading, plus copy fee. Payee: Clerk of Court. Personal checks accepted, credit cards are not. Prepayment required.

Civil Name Search: Access: Phone, fax, mail, in person. Visitors must perform in person searches themselves. No search fee. Required to search: name, years to search; also helpful: address. Civil Records on computer since 1995. Most recent records are kept here. Civil PAT goes back to 1995. DOB does not always appear.

Criminal Name Search: Access: Phone, fax, mail, in person. Visitors must perform in person searches themselves. No search fee. Required to search: name, years to search; also helpful: address, DOB, SSN. Criminal records on computer since 1995; prior records on docket books. Criminal PAT goes back to same as civil. DOB does not always appear.

Defiance Municipal Court 665 Perry St, Defiance, OH 43512; 419-782-5756; criminal phone: 419-782-5756; civil phone: 419-782-4092; fax: 419-782-2018; 7AM-5PM (EST). *Misdemeanor, Civil Actions under $15,000, Eviction, Small Claims.* www.defiancemunicipalcourt.com/
General Information: No confidential records released. Will fax documents. Court makes copy: 1-19 sheets no charge; if 20 then $1.00 plus $.05 per page ea add'l. Certification fee: $1.00 per page. Payee: Municipal Court. Personal checks accepted. Visa/MC/Discover accepted. Prepayment required. Mail requests: SASE required.
Civil Name Search: Access: Fax, mail, in person. Both court and visitors may perform in person name searches. Search fee: None, but will place document on computer disc for $1.00 or provide a computer printout for $.10. Required to search: name, years to search; also helpful: DOB, SSN, address. Civil records on computer from 12/89, prior in books to 1958. Mail turnaround time approx. 5 days. Civil PAT goes back to 10/1989. Public terminal available M,W,F 8AM-4PM.
Criminal Name Search: Access: Fax, Mail, in person. Both court and visitors may perform in person name searches. Search fee: None, but will place document on computer disc for $1.00 or provide a computer printout for $.10. Required to search: name, years to search; also helpful: address, DOB, SSN. Criminal records computerized from 10/89, prior in books to 1958. Mail turnaround time approx. 5 days. Criminal PAT goes back to same as civil. Public terminal available M,W,F 8AM-4PM.

Delaware County

Common Pleas Court 91 N Sandusky St, Delaware, OH 43015; 740-833-2500; probate phone: 740-833-2680; fax: 740-833-2499; 8:30AM-4:30PM (EST). *Felony, Civil Actions over $15,000, Domestic, Probate.* www.delawarecountyclerk.org
General Information: Probate court is separate at 140 N Sandusky Street. No grand jury proceedings or expungment records released. Will fax documents $1.00 per page. Court makes copy: $.10 per page. Certification fee: $1.00. Payee: Clerk of Court. Personal checks and major credit cards accepted. Prepayment required. Mail requests: SASE required.
Civil Name Search: Access: Mail, in person, online. Both court and visitors may perform in person name searches. No search fee. Required to search: name, years to search; also helpful: address. Civil records on computer from 1992, prior books go back to 1800s. Mail turnaround time 1-2 days. Civil PAT goes back to 1992. Access to court records is free at www.delawarecountyclerk.org. Probate court index from 1852 to 1920 is free at www.midohio.net/dchsdcgs/probate.html.
Criminal Name Search: Access: Mail, in person, online. Both court and visitors may perform in person name searches. No search fee. Required to search: name, years to search, DOB; also helpful: address, SSN. Criminal records computerized from 1992, prior books go back to 1800s. Mail turnaround time 1-2 days. Criminal PAT goes back to same as civil. Access to court records is free at www.delawarecountyclerk.org. Search the sheriff's county database of sex offenders, deadbeat parents, and most wanted list for free at www.delawarecountysheriff.com.

Delaware Municipal Court 70 N Union St, Delaware, OH 43015; 740-203-1550; criminal phone: 740-203-1570; civil phone: 740-203-1560; fax: 740-203-1599; 8AM-4:30PM (EST). *Misdemeanor, Civil Actions under $15,000, Eviction, Small Claims.* www.delawareohio.net/MunicipalCourt/CourtHome/default.aspx
General Information: Online identifiers in results same as on public terminal. No assessment results or probation records released. Will fax back documents. Court makes copy: $.05 per page. Certification fee: $3.00. Payee: Clerk of Court. No personal checks accepted. Major credit cards accepted. Prepayment required. Mail requests: SASE required.
Civil Name Search: Access: Phone, mail, in person, online. Both court and visitors may perform in person name searches. No search fee. Civil records on computer from 1992, prior in books. Mail turnaround time 1-2 weeks. Civil PAT goes back to 1992. Municipal courts records are at www.delawareohio.net/MunicipalCourt/CourtHome/default.aspx
Criminal Name Search: Access: Phone, mail, in person, online. Both court and visitors may perform in person name searches. No search fee. Required to search: name, years to search, DOB; also helpful: SSN. Criminal records computerized from 1992, prior in books. Mail turnaround time 1-2 weeks. Criminal PAT goes back to same as civil. Misdemeanor and traffic case records are free at www.delawareohio.net/MunicipalCourt/CourtHome/default.aspx.

Erie County

Common Pleas Court 323 Columbus Ave, 1st Fl, Sandusky, OH 44870; 419-627-7705; probate phone: 419-627-7750; fax: 419-627-7709; 8AM-4PM M-TH; 8AM-5PM F (EST). *Felony, Civil Actions over $10,000, Probate.* www.eriecounty.oh.gov/popular-links/clerk-of-courts/

General Information: Probate court is a separate court at the same address, 2nd Fl. Passports and expungments not released. Will fax documents $2.00 fax fee plus $1.00 per page. Court makes copy: $.25 per page. Certification fee: $1.00 for 1st page, $.25 each add'l. Payee: Clerk of Court. Personal checks accepted, money order preferred. No credit cards accepted. Prepayment required.
Civil Name Search: Access: In person only. Visitors must perform in person searches themselves. Civil records on books back to 1889. Note: Court will email docket copies - if docket number given. Civil PAT goes back to 1998.
Criminal Name Search: Access: In person only. Visitors must perform in person searches themselves. Required to search: name, years to search, DOB, SSN, signed release. Criminal docket on books; computerized records since 2000. Note: Court will email docket copies - if docket number given. Criminal PAT goes back to 2000.

Erie County Municipal Court 150 W Mason Rd, Milan, OH 44846; 419-499-4689; fax: 419-499-3300; 8AM-4PM (EST). *Misdemeanor, Civil Actions under $15,000, Small Claims.*
General Information: No sealed records released. Will not fax documents. Court makes copy: $.10 per page. No certification fee. Payee: Erie County Municipal Court. No checks accepted. No credit cards accepted for record searches. Prepayment required. Mail requests: SASE required.
Civil Name Search: Access: Mail, in person. Only the court performs in person name searches; visitors may not. No search fee. Required to search: name, years to search; also helpful: address. Civil records on computer back to 1990, microfiche back to 1982. Mail turnaround time 3-4 days.
Criminal Name Search: Access: Mail, in person. Only the court performs in person name searches; visitors may not. No search fee. Required to search: name, years to search; also helpful: address, DOB. Criminal records computerized from 1990, microfiche back to 1982. Mail turnaround time 3-4 days.

Sandusky Municipal Court 222 Meigs St, Sandusky, OH 44870; 419-627-5921; criminal phone: 419-627-5975; civil phone: 419-627-5924; fax: 419-627-5950; 7AM-4PM (EST). *Misdemeanor, Civil Actions under $15,000, Eviction, Small Claims.* www.sanduskymunicipalcourt.org/
General Information: No pending, juvenile crimes of violence records, or expunged records released. Will fax documents $.10 per page. Court makes copy: $.10 per page. Certification fee: $4.00. Payee: Sandusky Municipal Court. No personal checks accepted. Credit cards accepted, $5.00 service fee. Prepayment required. Mail requests: SASE requested.
Civil Name Search: Access: Phone, fax, mail, in person, online. Both court and visitors may perform in person name searches. No search fee. Required to search: name, years to search; also helpful: case number. Civil records on computer from 1987, prior in books. Mail turnaround time 3-4 days. Civil PAT goes back to 1991. Access Muni court records free at www.sanduskymunicipalcourt.org/search.shtml.
Criminal Name Search: Access: Phone, fax, mail, in person, online. Both court and visitors may perform in person name searches. No search fee. Required to search: name, years to search, DOB; also helpful: SSN, case number. Criminal records computerized from 1987, prior in books. Mail turnaround time 3-4 days. Criminal PAT goes back to same as civil. Access Muni court records free at www.sanduskymunicipalcourt.org/search.shtml. Online results show middle initial, DOB.

Vermilion Municipal Court 687 Decatur St, Vermilion, OH 44089-1152; 440-204-2430; fax: 440-204-2431; 8AM-4PM (EST). *Misdemeanor, Civil Actions under $15,000, Eviction, Small Claims.* www.vermilionmunicipalcourt.org
General Information: This court handles cases from both Erie and Lorain counties including townships of Vermilion, Florence and Brownhelm, and the city of Vermilion. They will search both civil and criminal indexes if requested. Online identifiers in results same as on public terminal. no addresses, victim info or confidential report records released without approval from prosecutors office. No fee to fax documents, unless large page numbers. No copy fee. No certification fee. Payee: Vermilion Municipal Court. Personal checks accepted. Credit cards accepted. Prepayment required. Mail requests: SASE required.
Civil Name Search: Access: Mail, fax, in person, online. Both court and visitors may perform in person name searches. No search fee. Required to search: name, years to search; also helpful: address. Civil records on computer since late 1991, indexed in books since 1966. Civil PAT goes back to 1991. Results include name of plaintiff and defendant. Online access to Municipal court records at www.vermilionmunicipalcourt.org/search.shtml.
Criminal Name Search: Access: Fax, mail, in person, online. Both court and visitors may perform in person name searches. No search fee. Required to search: name, years to search; also helpful: SSN. Criminal records on computer since late 1991, indexed in books since 1966. Note: Results include plaintiff's name and defendant's name for civil records,

name for criminal records. Mail 2-7 days. Criminal PAT goes back to same as civil. Online access to municipal court records is at www.vermilionmunicipalcourt.org/search.shtml Online results show name only.

Fairfield County

Common Pleas Court PO Box 370, 224 E Main, Clerk's Office, Lancaster, OH 43130-0370; 740-652-7360; probate phone: 740-652-7464; fax: 740-652-7488; 8AM-4PM (EST). *Felony, Civil Actions over $10,000, Probate, Domestic.* www.fairfieldcountyclerk.com

General Information: Probate court is a separate court at the same address, Room 303. No adoption or juvenile records released. Will fax documents $2.00 1st page, $1.00 each add'l. Court makes copy: $.05 per page; first 20 copies are free. Certification fee: $5.00 per doc plus copy fee. Payee: Clerk of Court. Personal checks accepted. Visa/MC accepted in person only. Prepayment required. Prepayment of copies is not required.

Civil Name Search: Access: In person, online. Visitors must perform in person searches themselves. Required to search: name, years to search; also helpful: address. Civil records on computer from 10/93, in books to 1970, prior archived to 1800s. Civil PAT goes back to 10/1993. Online access to County Clerk's court records database is free at www.fairfieldcountyclerk.com/Search/.

Criminal Name Search: Access: In person, online. Visitors must perform in person searches themselves. Required to search: name, years to search; also helpful: address, DOB. Criminal records computerized from 10/93, in books to 1970, prior archived to 1800s. Criminal PAT goes back to same as civil. Online access to County Clerk's court records database is free at www.fairfieldcountyclerk.com/Search/. Online results show middle initial, DOB.

Fairfield County Municipal Court PO Box 2390, Lancaster, OH 43130; 740-687-6621; fax: 740-681-5014; 8AM-4PM (EST). *Misdemeanor, Civil Actions under $15,000, Eviction, Small Claims.* www.fcmcourt.org

General Information: Will fax documents to local or toll free line. No copy fee. Certification fee: $1.00. Payee: Fairfield County Municipal Court. Personal checks accepted. Credit cards accepted. Prepayment required. Mail requests: SASE required.

Civil Name Search: Access: Mail, in person, online. Both court and visitors may perform in person name searches. No search fee. Civil records on computer from 1990, prior in books. Mail turnaround time 2 days. Civil PAT goes back to 10/1989. Search civil case info online at http://12.49.195.19/cvsearch.shtml.

Criminal Name Search: Access: Mail, in person, online. Both court and visitors may perform in person name searches. No search fee. Criminal records computerized from 1989, prior in books. Mail turnaround time 2 days. Criminal PAT goes back to same as civil. Search criminal and traffic at http://12.49.195.19/trsearch.shtml.

Fayette County

Common Pleas Court 110 E Court St, Washington Court House, OH 43160; 740-335-6371; probate phone: 740-335-0640; fax: 740-333-3522; 9AM-4PM (EST). *Felony, Civil Actions over $10,000, Probate, Domestic.* www.fayette-co-oh.com/Commplea/index.html

General Information: Probate court is a separate court at the same address. No records released. Fee to fax out file $1.00 per page, plus $2.00 for cover page. Court makes copy: $.25 per page. Self serve copy: same. Certification fee: $1.00 per cert. Payee: Clerk of Court. Personal checks accepted, credit cards are not. Prepayment required. Mail requests: SASE required.

Civil Name Search: Access: Mail, in person, online. Visitors must perform in person searches themselves. No search fee. Civil records on computer from 1992, prior in books to 1800s. Civil PAT goes back to 1/1992. Search docket information free at http://cp.onlinedockets.com/fayettecp/case_dockets/search.aspx .

Criminal Name Search: Access: Mail, in person, online. Visitors must perform in person searches themselves. No search fee. Required to search: name, years to search, DOB, SSN. Criminal records computerized from 1992, prior in books to 1800s. Mail turnaround time varies. Criminal PAT goes back to same as civil. Search docket info free at http://cp.onlinedockets.com/fayettecp/case_dockets/search.aspx Online results show middle initial.

Municipal Court Washington Courthouse, 119 N Main St, Washington Court House, OH 43160; 740-636-2350; fax: 740-636-2359; 8AM-4PM (EST). *Misdemeanor, Civil Actions under $15,000, Eviction, Small Claims.* www.ci.washington-court-house.oh.us/

General Information: Online identifiers in results same as on public terminal. No records protected by the privacy act released. Will not fax documents. No copy fee. Certification fee: $5.00 per document includes copies. Payee: Clerk of Court. Personal checks accepted. Credit cards accepted. Prepayment required. Mail requests: SASE not required.

Civil Name Search: Access: Mail, in person, online. Both court and visitors may perform in person name searches. No search fee. Civil records on computer from 1990, prior in books to 1950s. Mail turnaround time 1 week. Civil PAT goes back to 1990. Search record index free at http://70.62.185.171/search.shtml.

Criminal Name Search: Access: Mail, in person, online. Both court and visitors may perform in person name searches. No search fee. Required to search: name, years to search, DOB; also helpful: SSN. Criminal records computerized from 1990, prior in books to 1950s. Mail turnaround time 1 week. Criminal PAT goes back to same as civil. Search record index free at http://70.62.185.171/search.shtml. Online results show name only.

Franklin County

Common Pleas Court 345 S High St, Fl 1B, Clerk of the Court of Common Pleas, Columbus, OH 43215-6311; 614-525-3453; criminal phone: 614-525-3650; civil phone: 614-525-3621; criminal fax: 614-525-4480; civil fax: 8AM-5PM; 8AM-5PM (EST). *Felony, Civil Actions over $15,000.* www.fccourts.org/gen/WebFront.nsf//wp/Home?open

General Information: Franklin County Clerk of Courts is the official record keeper for Common Pleas Court. To contact the Clerk's Office by phone, call 614-525-3600. Online identifiers in results same as on public terminal. No sealed or expunged records released. Will fax out documents for fee. Court makes copy: $.10 per page. Self serve copy: none. Certification fee: $1.00 per page plus copy fee. Payee: Franklin County Clerk of Courts. Only cashiers checks and money orders accepted. No credit cards accepted. Prepayment required.

Civil Name Search: Access: Online, in person. Visitors must perform in person searches themselves. Civil records date to 1820. Civil PAT goes back to 1978. Access records 3AM-11PM at http://fcdcfcjs.co.franklin.oh.us/CaseInformationOnline/ and includes domestic relations cases. The searchable online record index for court records often does not provide identifiers for civil and domestic case searches.

Criminal Name Search: Access: Online, in person. Both court and visitors may perform in person name searches. No search fee. Criminal records available from 1935. Criminal PAT goes back to 1980. Access records at http://fcdcfcjs.co.franklin.oh.us/CaseInformationOnline/ form 3AM-11PM. Most online index lists show the DOB, but not all. Online results show middle initial.

Franklin County Municipal Court - Criminal Division 375 S High St, 2nd Fl, Columbus, OH 43215; criminal phone: 614-645-8186; fax: 614-645-6036; 24 hours a day (EST). *Misdemeanor, Traffic.* www.fmcclerk.com

General Information: No sealed or expunged records released. Court makes copy: $.05 per page. Payee: Franklin County Municipal Court. Personal checks accepted by mail only. Visa/MC accepted. Prepayment required. Mail requests: SASE required.

Criminal Name Search: Access: Mail, online, in person. Both court and visitors may perform in person name searches. No search fee. Required to search: name, years to search; also helpful: DOB, SSN. Criminal records go back to 1987; on computer back to 1992. Mail turnaround time 7 days, usually less. Public use terminal has crim records back to 1992. Background check companies may use the computers located on the 4th Floor in Room 4B for all background checks. Criminal and traffic records from the Clerk of Court Courtview database free online at www.fmcclerk.com/pa/pa.php. Search by name, dates, ticket, address or case numbers.

Franklin County Municipal Court - Civil Division 375 S High St, 3rd Fl, Columbus, OH 43215; 614-645-7220; civil phone: 614-645-8161-file room; fax: 614-645-6919; 8AM-5PM (EST). *Civil Actions under $15,000, Eviction, Small Claims.* www.fmcclerk.com

General Information: Online identifiers in results same as on public terminal. No sealed or expunged records released. Will not fax out documents. Court makes copy: $.05 each. Certification fee: $1.00 per page copy fee included. Payee: Franklin County Municipal Court. Personal checks accepted. Credit cards accepted. Prepayment required. Mail requests: SASE required.

Civil Name Search: Access: Phone, fax, mail, online, in person. Both court and visitors may perform in person name searches. No search fee. Required to search: name only. Civil records on computer from 1992, prior in books to 1974. Mail turnaround time 2-3 days. Public use terminal has civil records back to 1992. Records from the Clerk of Court CourtView database free online at www.fmcclerk.com/pa/pa.php. Search by name or case number. There is a beta test of a new system at www.fmcclerk.com/case/.

Probate Court 373 S High St, 22nd Fl, Columbus, OH 43215-6311; 614-525-3894; probate phone: 614-462-3894; fax: 614-525-7422; 8AM-4:30PM (EST). *Probate.* www.franklincountyohio.gov/probate/

General Information: Search general, marriage and psychiatric indexes at www.franklincountyohio.gov/probate/case-search.cfm. Email to probateinfo@franklincountyohio.gov.

Fulton County

Common Pleas Court 210 S Fulton St, Wauseon, OH 43567; 419-337-9230; probate phone: 419-337-9242; fax: 419-337-9199; 8:30AM-4:30PM (EST). *Felony, Civil Actions, Probate, Domestic.*
www.fultoncountyoh.com
General Information: Probate court is a separate court at the same address, Rm 105. Will fax documents $2.00 plus $1.00 per page. Court makes copy: $.25 per page first 25 pages, $.12 next 75 pages, $.06 thereafter. Certification fee: $1.00 per page. Payee: Paul MacDonald Clerk of Court. Personal checks accepted, credit cards are not. Prepayment required.
Civil Name Search: Access: In person, online. Visitors must perform in person searches themselves. Civil records on computer from 9/88, prior in books to 1968, archived to 1800s. Civil PAT goes back to 9/1988. Access an index of civil case records at www.fultoncountyoh.com/pa/.
Criminal Name Search: Access: In person, online. Visitors must perform in person searches themselves. Criminal records computerized from 9/88, prior in books to 1968, archived to 1800s. Criminal PAT goes back to same as civil. Access the criminal record index at www.fultoncountyoh.com/pa/.

County Court Eastern District 204 S Main St, Swanton, OH 43558; 419-826-5636; fax: 419-825-3324; 8:30AM-4:30PM (EST). *Misdemeanor, Civil Actions under $15,000, Small Claims.*
www.fultoncountyoh.com/
General Information: No pending case records released. Will fax documents for no fee. Court makes copy: No copy fee but must supply own paper for copies. No certification fee. No Personal checks, Visa/MC accepted. Mail requests: SASE required.
Civil Name Search: Access: Mail, fax, in person, online. Both court and visitors may perform in person name searches. No search fee. Civil records on computer from 1988, prior in books. Mail turnaround time less than 2 weeks. Access court records back to 1995 free at www.fultoncountyoh.com/pa/.
Criminal Name Search: Access: Mail, in person, online. Only the court performs in person name searches; visitors may not. No search fee. Required to search: name, years to search, DOB; signed release requested. Criminal records computerized from 1988, prior in books. Mail turnaround time under 2 weeks. Access court records back to 1995 free at www.fultoncountyoh.com/pa/.

County Court Western District 224 S Fulton St, Wauseon, OH 43567; 419-337-9212; fax: 419-337-9286; 8:30AM-4:30PM (EST). *Misdemeanor, Civil Actions under $15,000, Small Claims.*
www.fultoncountyoh.com
General Information: In-person searchers should call first; be aware Tuesdays are busy and hard to get on computer to search. Probate as at a separate court, separate building. Online identifiers in results same as on public terminal. No pending case records released. Will fax documents for no fee. Court makes copy: $.10 per page. Certification fee: $1.00 includes copies. Payee: County Court Western District. No personal checks. Visa/MC accepted. Prepayment required. Mail requests: SASE required.
Civil Name Search: Access: Mail, in person, online. Visitors must perform in person searches themselves. No search fee. Civil records on computer from 1989, prior in books. Mail turnaround time 2-3 days. Civil PAT goes back to 1989. Access court records back to 1995 free at www.fultoncountyoh.com/pa/.
Criminal Name Search: Access: Mail, in person, online. Visitors must perform in person searches themselves. No search fee. Required to search: name, years to search, DOB; also helpful: SSN. Criminal records on computer after Oct. 1988, indexed by name and DOB. Mail turnaround time 2-3 days. Criminal PAT goes back to Oct. 1988. Access court records back to 1995 free at www.fultoncountyoh.com/pa/ Online results show middle initial, DOB.

Gallia County

Common Pleas Court - Gallia County Courthouse 18 Locust St, Rm 1290, Gallipolis, OH 45631-1290; 740-446-4612 x223; probate phone: 740-446-4612 x289; fax: 740-441-2932; 8:30AM-4PM (EST). *Felony, Civil Actions over $10,000, Probate.*
www.gallianet.net/Gallia/clerk_of_courts.htm
General Information: Email questions to clerkofcourts@gallianet.net. Probate court is a separate court at the same address, Rm 1293. Email probate to gshrader@gallianet.net. No records released. Will fax copies for $1.00 per page if pre-paid. Court makes copy: $.25 per page. Certification fee: $1.00. Payee: Clerk of Court. Personal checks accepted. Prepayment required.
Civil Name Search: Access: In person, online. Visitors must perform in person searches themselves. Civil records on computer from 7/91, in books

to 1968, archived to 1800s. Civil PAT goes back to 7/1991. Search the index at http://66.76.210.47/pa/pa.urd/pamw6500.display. Use the various option after name search is completed to find case details. Access this site also via the court's home page.
Criminal Name Search: Access: In person, online. Visitors must perform in person searches themselves. Criminal records computerized from 7/91, in books to 1968, archived to 1800s. Criminal PAT goes back to same as civil. Search the index at http://66.76.210.47/pa/pa.urd/pamw6500.display. Access this site also via the court's home page. DOB will show for criminal cases.

Gallipolis Municipal Court 518 2nd Ave, Gallipolis, OH 45631; 740-446-9400; fax: 740-441-6028; 7:30AM-4PM (EST). *Misdemeanor, Civil Actions under $15,000, Eviction, Small Claims.*
www.gallianet.net/Gallipolis/municipal_court.htm
General Information: No expunged records released. Will not fax documents. Court fee: $.10 per page. Certification fee: $2.00. Payee: Municipal Court. Personal checks accepted. Major credit cards accepted. Prepayment required. Mail requests: SASE required.
Civil Name Search: Access: Phone, mail, in person, online. Both court and visitors may perform in person name searches. No search fee. Required to search: name, years to search; also helpful: address. Civil records on computer from 8/93, prior in books. Mail turnaround time 1 week. Civil PAT goes back to 1993. Search the record index at http://66.76.210.48/searchMC.shtml. Results show address.
Criminal Name Search: Access: Phone, mail, in person, online. Both court and visitors may perform in person name searches. No search fee. Required to search: name, years to search; also helpful: address, DOB, SSN. Criminal records computerized from 8/93, prior in books. Mail turnaround time 1 week. Criminal PAT goes back to 1993. Search the record index at http://66.76.210.48/searchMC.shtml. Results show address and DOB.

Geauga County

Common Pleas Court Clerk of Court, 100 Short Court, Ste 300, Chardon, OH 44024; 440-279-1960; fax: 440-286-2127; 8AM-4:30PM (EST). *Felony, Civil Actions over $10,000.* www.geaugacourts.com
General Information: no sealed records released. Will not fax documents. Court makes copy: $.05 per page. Certification fee: $1.00 per page. Cert fee includes copies. Payee: Clerk of Court. Personal checks accepted. Major credit cards accepted in person only. Prepayment required. Mail requests: SASE required for mail return of any copies.
Civil Name Search: Access: In person, online. Visitors must perform in person searches themselves. Civil records on computer from 1990, in books from 1968, prior archived. Note: Will not and do not index or search over the phone. Civil PAT goes back to 1990. Search court record index free from the home page. Click on type of court then court records. Online records go back to 1990. Includes domestic cases.
Criminal Name Search: Access: In person, online. Visitors must perform in person searches themselves. Criminal records computerized from 1990, in books from 1968, prior archived. Note: Will not and do not index or search over the phone. Criminal PAT goes back to same as civil. Search court record index free from the home page. Click on type of court then court records. Includes traffic.

Chardon Municipal Court 111 Water St, Chardon, OH 44024; 440-286-2670/2684; criminal phone: 440-286-2670; civil phone: 440-286-2684; fax: 440-286-2679; 8AM-4:30PM (EST). *Misdemeanor, Civil Actions under $15,000, Eviction, Small Claims.* www.geaugacourts.org/
General Information: No expunged records released. Will fax documents to local or toll free line. Court makes copy: $.05 per page. Certification fee: $1.50 per request plus copy fee. Payee: Chardon Municipal Court. Personal checks, Visa/MC accepted. Prepayment required. Mail requests: SASE required.
Civil Name Search: Access: Mail, in person, online. Both court and visitors may perform in person name searches. No search fee. Required to search: name, years to search; also helpful: address. Civil records on computer from 1990, prior in books. Mail turnaround time 2-4 days. Civil PAT goes back to 1990. Public terminal available 8AM-4:30PM. Search court record index free at www.auditor.co.geauga.oh.us/pa/. Or, at main county website, click on type of court then court records.
Criminal Name Search: Access: Mail, in person, online. Both court and visitors may perform in person name searches. No search fee. Required to search: name, years to search; also helpful: address, DOB, SSN. Criminal records computerized from 1988, prior in books to 1965. Mail turnaround time 2-4 days. Criminal PAT goes back to same as civil. Public terminal available 8AM-4:30PM. Online access same as civil. Online results show middle initial, DOB.

Probate and Juvenile Court 231 Main St, #200, Courthouse Annex, 2nd Fl, Chardon, OH 44024; 440-279-1830; 8AM-4:30PM (EST). *Probate.*
www.co.geauga.oh.us/commonpleas/Probate.aspx

General Information: Access to cases at http://co.geauga.oh.us/common_pleas/JVPRWebpages/Courtintro.asp.

Greene County

Common Pleas Court 45 N Detroit St, Xenia, OH 45385; 937-562-5290; probate phone: 937-562-5280; fax: 937-562-5309; 8AM-4:30PM (EST). *Felony, Civil Actions over $15,000, Probate.* www.greene.oh.us/COC/clerk.htm

General Information: Probate court is a separate court at the same address, closes at 4PM. No sealed records released. Will fax out specific case files for $2.00 per page, if prepaid. Court makes copy: $.05 per page. Certification fee: $1.00 per page includes copy fee. Payee: Clerk of Court. Personal checks accepted. Major credit cards accepted; convenience fee is added. Prepayment required. Mail requests: SASE required for mail return of any copies.

Civil Name Search: Access: In person, online. Visitors must perform in person searches themselves. Civil records on computer from 1982, prior in books and on microfiche. Civil PAT goes back to 1982. Online access to clerk of court records is free at www.co.greene.oh.us/pa/pa.htm. Search by name or case number. Also, search probate cases free at www.co.greene.oh.us/Probate/search/case_search.asp.

Criminal Name Search: Access: In person, online. Visitors must perform in person searches themselves. Required to search: name, years to search; also helpful: DOB, case number. Criminal records computerized from 1982, prior in books and on microfiche. Criminal PAT goes back to same as civil. Online access to clerk of court records is free at www.co.greene.oh.us/pa/pa.htm. Search by name or case number. Also, search probate cases free at www.co.greene.oh.us/Probate/search/case_search.asp. Online results show middle initial, DOB.

Fairborn Municipal Court 1148 Kauffman Ave, Fairborn, OH 45324; criminal phone: 937-754-3040; civil phone: 937-754-3044; fax: 937-879-4422; 7:30AM-4PM (EST). *Misdemeanor, Civil Actions under $20,000, Eviction, Small Claims.* www.fairbornmunicipalcourt.us/

General Information: No sealed or expunged records released. Will not fax documents. Court makes copy: $.10 per page. Certification fee: $2.00. Payee: Municipal Court. Personal checks accepted. Visa/MC/Discover accepted in person only. Prepayment required. Mail requests: SASE required.

Civil Name Search: Access: Mail, in person, online. Only the court performs in person name searches; visitors may not. No search fee. Required to search: name, years to search; also helpful: address. Civil records on computer from 1991, records go back to 1976. Mail turnaround time 1 week. Website offers free online access to civil, misdemeanor and traffic records from home page.

Criminal Name Search: Access: Mail, in person, online. Only the court performs in person name searches; visitors may not. No search fee. Required to search: name, years to search, SSN; also helpful: address, DOB. Criminal records computerized from mid 1991, records go back to 1976. Mail turnaround time 1 week. Online access same as civil for traffic and misdemeanor.

Xenia Municipal Court 101 N Detroit, Xenia, OH 45385; 937-376-7294; 376-7297 (Civil Clerk); fax: 937-376-7288; 8AM-4:30PM M,T,W; 8AM-4PM TH,F (EST). *Misdemeanor, Civil Actions under $15,000, Eviction, Small Claims.*
www.ci.xenia.oh.us/index.php?page=municipal-court

General Information: Online identifiers in results same as on public terminal. No search warrant records released. No fee to fax documents. Court makes copy: $.10 per page. Certification fee: $2.00 includes copies. Payee: Municipal Court. Business checks accepted. Visa/MC accepted. Prepayment required. Mail requests: SASE required.

Civil Name Search: Access: Mail, in person, online. Both court and visitors may perform in person name searches. Search fee: $10.00 per name. Required to search: name, years to search; also helpful: address. Civil records on computer from 1994, prior in books to 1966. Mail turnaround time 2-3 days. Civil PAT goes back to 1/1994. Online access to Municipal Court records free at www.ci.xenia.oh.us/index.php?page=public-access.

Criminal Name Search: Access: Mail, in person, online. Both court and visitors may perform in person name searches. Search fee: $10.00 per name. Required to search: name, years to search; also helpful: address, DOB, SSN. Criminal records computerized from 1994, prior in books to 1966. Mail turnaround time 2-3 days. Criminal PAT goes back to same as civil. Access to criminal records is the same as civil. Online results show name, DOB.

Guernsey County

Common Pleas Court 801 E Wheeling Ave D-300, Cambridge, OH 43725; 740-432-9230; probate phone: 740-432-9262; fax: 740-432-7807; 8:30AM-4PM (EST). *Felony, Civil Actions over $10,000, Probate.* www.guernseycounty.org/agencies/clerkofcourts.asp

General Information: Probate court is a separate court at the same address, #D-203. Online identifiers in results same as on public terminal. No expunged records released. Will fax documents $1.00 per page. Court makes copy: $.25 per page. Certification fee: $2.00. Payee: Clerk of Court. Personal checks accepted. Major credit cards accepted. Prepayment required. Mail requests: SASE required for mail return of any copies.

Civil Name Search: Access: In person, online. Visitors must perform in person searches themselves. Civil records on computer from 1990, prior in books, archived to 1800s. Civil PAT goes back to 1990. Access case index data free at http://74.218.3.68/pa/. Judge calendars also available online.

Criminal Name Search: Access: In person, online. Visitors must perform in person searches themselves. Required to search: name, years to search, DOB. Criminal records computerized from 1990, prior in books, archived to 1800s. Criminal PAT goes back to 1990. Access case index data free at http://74.218.3.68/pa/. Judge calendars also available online.

Cambridge Municipal Court 150 Highland Ave, Ste1, Cambridge, OH 43725; 740-439-5585; fax: 740-439-5666; 8:30AM-4:30PM (EST). *Misdemeanor, Civil Actions under $15,000, Eviction, Small Claims.* www.cambridgeoh.org/court.htm

General Information: Email is cambcrtclerk@cambridgemunicipalcourt.com. No confidential records released. Will fax documents for $5.00 fee. Court makes copy: no charge first 10 pages, then $.10 per page. Certification fee: $2.00. Payee: Cambridge Municipal Court. Personal checks, Visa/MC accepted. Prepayment required. Mail requests: SASE required.

Civil Name Search: Access: Mail, fax, in person, online. Both court and visitors may perform in person name searches. No search fee. Required to search: name, years to search; also helpful: address. Civil records on computer from 1988, prior in books. Note: Fax civil court requests to 740-439-9405. Mail turnaround time 3-5 days. Civil PAT available. Access Muni Court records free at http://webconnect03.civicacmi.com/cambridge/court/.

Criminal Name Search: Access: Mail, in person, fax, online. Both court and visitors may perform in person name searches. No search fee. Required to search: name, years to search, DOB, SSN; also helpful: address. Criminal records computerized from 1988, prior in books. Mail turnaround time 3-5 days. Criminal PAT available. Access criminal and traffic index online- same as civil above.

Hamilton County

Common Pleas Court 1000 Main St, Rm 315, Cincinnati, OH 45202; criminal phone: 513-946-5675; civil phone: 513-946-5635; probate phone: 513-946-3598; fax: 513-946-5670; 8AM-4PM (EST). *Felony, Civil Actions over $10,000, Probate.* www.courtclerk.org

General Information: Fax number is for felony dept. only. Probate court at 230 N 9th St. Criminal histories not released. Felony Dept will fax documents no fee unless a large number of pages. Court makes copy: 1st 10 pages free, then $.10 per page. Certification fee: $1.00 per pleading. Payee: Clerk of Court. Personal checks accepted. MC/Discover/AmEx credit cards accepted, no Visa. Prepayment required. Mail requests: SASE required.

Civil Name Search: Access: Mail, fax, in person, online. Both court and visitors may perform in person name searches. No search fee. Civil records indexed on computer since 1960s, prior in books and files. Mail turnaround time 2-3 days. Civil PAT goes back to 1999. Records and calendars from the court clerk are free at the website. Online civil index goes back to 1991. Also, search probate records free at www.probatect.org/case_search/casesearch.asp.

Criminal Name Search: Access: Mail, fax, online, in person. Both court and visitors may perform in person name searches. No search fee. Required to search: name, years to search, signed release; also helpful: DOB, SSN. Criminal records indexed on computer since 1960s, prior in books and files. Mail turnaround time 2-3 days. Criminal PAT goes back to 1989. Online access to criminal records is the same as civil. Online criminal index goes back to 1986. Also, there is a subscription service for document access but this appears to be for attorneys only.

Hamilton County Municipal Court - Criminal 1000 Sycamore St #112, Cincinnati, OH 45202; 513-946-6029/6040; 8AM-4PM (EST). *Misdemeanor.* www.courtclerk.org

General Information: Will fax documents for add'l $.10 per page. Court makes copy: $.10 per page. Certification fee: $5.00. Payee: Clerk of Courts. Personal checks accepted. MC, Discover, AMEX accepted, surcharge added. Prepayment required.

Criminal Name Search: Access: In person only. Visitors must perform in person searches themselves. Required to search: name, years to search, DOB; also helpful: SSN. Criminal records computerized from 2000, prior on microfiche back to 1973. Note: Court clerk records are no longer online. Public use terminal has crim records back to 1999.

Hamilton County Municipal Court - Civil 1000 Main St, Rm 115, Cincinnati, OH 45202; 513-946-5700; fax: 513-946-5710; 8AM-4PM (EST). *Civil Actions under $15,000, Eviction, Small Claims.* www.courtclerk.org
General Information: No expungment records released. No fee to fax documents. Court makes copy: $.10 per page; $5.00 for docket sheet. Certification fee: $5.00; exemplification is $10.00. Payee: Clerk of Courts. Personal checks accepted. Visa/MC, Amex and Discover accepted. Prepayment required.
Civil Name Search: Access: Fax, mail, online, in person. Both court and visitors may perform in person name searches. No search fee. Required to search: name; also helpful: years to search. Civil records on computer from 1989, prior on microfilm. Mail turnaround time 5 days. Public use terminal has civil records back to 1989. Case history data from the court clerk is free at the website or www.courtclerk.org/queries.aps.

Probate Court 230 E 9th St, Rm 10150, William Howard Taft Center, Cincinnati, OH 45202; probate phone: 513-946-3600; fax: 513-946-3565 (records); 8AM-4PM (EST). *Probate.* www.probatect.org/
General Information: Access to cases at www.probatect.org/case_search/index.htm.

Hancock County

Common Pleas Court 300 S Main St, Findlay, OH 45840; 419-424-7037/7008; fax: 419-424-7801; 8:30AM-4:30PM (EST). *Felony, Civil Actions over $10,000.* www.co.hancock.oh.us/commonpleas/
General Information: Online identifiers in results same as on public terminal. No home investigations, medical records released. Will not fax documents. Court makes copy: $.25 per page. Certification fee: $1.00 per page plus copy fee. Payee: Clerk of Court. Personal checks accepted, credit cards are not. Prepayment required. Mail requests: SASE required.
Civil Name Search: Access: Mail, in person, online. Both court and visitors may perform in person name searches. Search fee: $15.00 per name. Civil records on computer from 1985, microfiche from 1974, dockets archived to 1800s. Mail turnaround time 10 days. Civil PAT goes back to 1985. Search records online back to 1985 at http://pa.co.hancock.oh.us/.
Criminal Name Search: Access: Mail, in person, online. Both court and visitors may perform in person name searches. Search fee: $15.00 per name. Criminal records computerized from 1985, microfiche from 1974, dockets archived to 1800s. Mail turnaround time 8-10 days. Criminal PAT goes back to same as civil. Search records online back to 1985 at http://pa.co.hancock.oh.us/. Online results show name, DOB.

Findlay Municipal Court PO Box 826, Findlay, OH 45839; 419-424-7805; criminal phone: 419-424-7141; civil phone: 419-424-7143; fax: 419-424-7803; 7:30AM-5:30 PM M,W,TH; 7:30AM-6:30PM Tu; 8AM-12 F (EST). *Misdemeanor, Civil Actions under $15,000, Eviction, Small Claims, Traffic.* www.ci.findlay.oh.us/municourt/
General Information: Will not fax documents. Court makes copy: $.10 per page. Self serve copy: same. Certification fee: $1.00. Payee: Findlay Municipal Court. Hancock County resident's checks accepted. No credit cards accepted for searches or copies. Prepayment required. Mail requests: SASE required.
Civil Name Search: Access: Mail, in person, online. Both court and visitors may perform in person name searches. Search fee: $2.00 per name/SSN. Civil records on computer from 1984. Physical records kept since 1996, but a number of pre-2005 records were destroyed in a flood. Mail turnaround time 24 hours. Civil PAT goes back to 1984. Online access from www.ci.findlay.oh.us/municourt/searchcivildocket.asp?pageId=71.
Criminal Name Search: Access: Mail, in person, online. Both court and visitors may perform in person name searches. Search fee: $2.00 per name/SSN. Required to search: name, years to search, DOB, SSN. Criminal records computerized from 1984. Physical records kept since 1996, but a number of pre-2005 records were destroyed in a flood. Mail turnaround time 24 hours. Criminal PAT goes back to same as civil. Online access same as civil.

Probate Court 308 Dorney Plaza, Findlay, OH 45840-3302; probate phone: 419-424-7079; fax: 419-424-7899; 8:30AM-4:30PM (EST). *Probate.* http://probate.co.hancock.oh.us/
General Information: Record searches go to http://probate.co.hancock.oh.us/search.shtml.

Hardin County

Common Pleas Court 1 Courthouse Sq, #310, Kenton, OH 43326; 419-674-2278; probate phone: 419-674-2230; fax: 419-674-2273; 8:30AM-4PM (EST). *Felony, Civil Actions over $15,000.* www.hardincourts.com/
General Information: Probate court is actually a separate court at the same address, but in Suite 200. Will fax documents $2.00 1st page, $1.00 each add'l. Court makes copy: $.25 per page. Certification fee: $1.00 per page.

Payee: Clerk of Court. Business checks accepted. Major credit cards accepted. Prepayment required. Mail requests: SASE required.
Civil Name Search: Access: Mail, in person, online. Both court and visitors may perform in person name searches. Search fee: $5.00 per name. Required to search: full name, years to search, SSN, DOB, reason for request. Current records on computer as of 10/94. Overall records go back to 1885. Mail turnaround time 2-4 days. Civil PAT goes back to 10/1994. Online access to the civil docket is available at www.hardincourts.com/CLSite/search.dis.shtml.
Criminal Name Search: Access: Mail, fax, in person, online. Both court and visitors may perform in person name searches. Search fee: $5.00 per name. Required to search: full name, years to search, SSN, DOB, reason for request. Current records on computer as of 10/94. Overall records go back to 1885. Mail turnaround time 2-4 days. Criminal PAT goes back to same as civil. Online access to the criminal docket is offered at www.hardincourts.com/CLSite/search.dis.shtml.

Hardin County Municipal Court PO Box 250, 111 W Franklin, Kenton, OH 43326; 419-674-4362; fax: 419-674-4096; 8:30AM-4PM (EST). *Misdemeanor, Civil Actions under $15,000, Eviction, Small Claims.* http://hardincourts.com/
General Information: Will fax documents to local or toll-free number. Court makes copy: $.25 per page. Certification fee: $2.00 per page includes copies. Payee: Hardin County Municipal Court. Business checks accepted. Major credit cards accepted; $5.00 usage fee added per transaction. Prepayment required. Mail requests: SASE required.
Civil Name Search: Access: Mail, in person. Both court and visitors may perform in person name searches. Search fee: $5.00. Civil records on computer since 1989, prior on books. Mail turnaround time 1-2 days. Civil PAT goes back to 1989.
Criminal Name Search: Access: Mail, in person. Both court and visitors may perform in person name searches. Search fee: $5.00. Required to search: name, years to search; also helpful: SSN. Criminal records on computer since 1989, prior on books. Mail turnaround time 1-2 days. Criminal PAT goes back to same as civil.

Harrison County

Common Pleas Court 100 W Market St, Cadiz, OH 43907; 740-942-8863; probate phone: 740-942-8868; fax: 740-942-4693; 8:30AM-4:30PM (EST). *Felony, Civil Actions over $15,000, Domestic, Probate.* www.harrisoncountyohio.org/
General Information: Probate court is a separate court at the same address. Probate fax- 740-942-8483. No secret records released. Will fax documents $.25 per page. Court makes copy: $.25 per page. Certification fee: $1.00. Payee: Clerk of Court. No personal checks or credit cards accepted. Prepayment required. Mail requests: SASE required for civil.
Civil Name Search: Access: Phone, fax, mail, in person. Both court and visitors may perform in person name searches. No search fee. Required to search: name, years to search; also helpful: address. Civil records on computer since 2006, in books back to 1800s. Civil PAT goes back to 2006.
Criminal Name Search: Access: In person only. Both court and visitors may perform in person name searches. No search fee. Required to search: name, years to search; also helpful: address, DOB, SSN. Criminal records on computer since 2006, in books back to 1800s. Criminal PAT goes back to same as civil.

Harrison County Court Courthouse, 100 W Market St, Cadiz, OH 43907; 740-942-2865; fax: 740-942-3541; 8AM-4:30PM (EST). *Misdemeanor, Civil Actions under $15,000, Small Claims.*
General Information: No victim information or SSNs released. Will fax specific case file. Court makes copy: $.05 per page. Certification fee: $6.00 per document. Payee: Harrison County Court. Personal or cashier checks and money orders accepted. No credit cards accepted. Prepayment required.
Civil Name Search: Access: In person only. Visitors must perform in person searches themselves. Civil records in books; on computer back to 2/2000. Civil PAT goes back to 2/2000.
Criminal Name Search: Access: In person only. Visitors must perform in person searches themselves. Required to search: name, years to search, DOB; SSN helpful. Criminal records in books; on computer back to 2/2000. Criminal PAT goes back to same as civil.

Henry County

Common Pleas Court 660 N Perry St #302, Napoleon, OH 43545; 419-592-5926; criminal phone: 419-592-5886; civil phone: 419-592-5886; probate phone: 419-592-7771; criminal fax: 419-592-5888; civil fax: 8:30AM-4:30PM; 8:30AM-4:30PM (EST). *Felony, Civil Actions over $15,000, Probate.* www.henrycountyohio.com/clerk.htm
General Information: Probate court is a separate court at the same address, #301. Probate copies are $1.00 per page. Probate fax- 419-592-7000 No adoption or mental records released. Will fax documents $3.00 1st page, $1.00 each add'l. Court makes copy: $.25 per page first 25 pages; $.12 each

The Guide to County Court Records

up to 75 pages. Certification fee: $1.00 per page. Payee: Henry County Clerk of Courts. No personal checks or credit cards accepted. Prepayment required.

Civil Name Search: Access: Fax, mail, in person. Visitors must perform in person searches themselves. No search fee. Civil records on computer from 10/94, prior in books. Civil PAT goes back to 10/1994.

Criminal Name Search: Access: Fax, mail, in person. Visitors must perform in person searches themselves. No search fee. Criminal records computerized from 10/94, prior in books. Mail turnaround time 3 days. Criminal PAT goes back to 10/1994.

Napoleon Municipal Court PO Box 502, Napoleon, OH 43545; 419-592-2851; fax: 419-592-1805; 8AM-5PM (EST). *Misdemeanor, Civil Actions under $15,000, Eviction, Small Claims.*

General Information: No alcohol treatment records released. Will fax documents for no fee. Court makes copy: $.05 per page. Certification fee: $1.00. Payee: Clerk of Court. Personal checks accepted. Credit cards accepted. Prepayment required. Mail requests: SASE required.

Civil Name Search: Access: Phone, fax, mail, in person. Both court and visitors may perform in person name searches. No search fee. Civil records on computer from 1990, prior in books. Mail turnaround time 1-2 days.

Criminal Name Search: Access: Phone, fax, mail, in person. Both court and visitors may perform in person name searches. No search fee. Required to search: name, years to search, DOB; also helpful: SSN. Criminal records computerized from 1990, prior in books. Mail turnaround time 1-2 days.

Highland County

Common Pleas Court PO Box 821, 105 N High St, Hillsboro, OH 45133; 937-393-9957; probate phone: 937-393-9981; fax: 937-393-9878; 8AM-4:30PM (EST). *Felony, Civil Actions over $10,000, Probate.* www.hccpc.org/

General Information: Probate court is a separate court at the same address. No sealed records released. Will fax documents to local or toll free line. Court makes copy: $.10 per page. Self serve copy: same. Certification fee: $1.00 per page. Payee: Clerk of Court. Personal checks accepted, credit cards are not. Mail requests: SASE required.

Civil Name Search: Access: Mail, fax, in person, online. Both court and visitors may perform in person name searches. No search fee. Required to search: name, years to search; also helpful: address. Civil records in books since 1800s; on computer since 1995. Mail turnaround time usually same day. Civil PAT goes back to 1995. Terminal results may also include address. Search the index online at http://70.61.138.206/eservices/app/home.page.2.

Criminal Name Search: Access: Mail, fax, in person, online. Both court and visitors may perform in person name searches. No search fee. Required to search: name, years to search, DOB, signed release. Criminal records in books since 1800s; on computer since 1986 but name only to 1995. Mail turnaround time same day. Criminal PAT goes back to 1986. Search the index online at http://70.61.138.206/eservices/app/home.page.2.

Hillsboro Municipal Court 130 Homestead Ave, Hillsboro, OH 45133; 937-393-3022; fax: 937-393-0517; 7AM-3:30PM (EST). *Misdemeanor, Civil Actions under $15,000, Eviction, Small Claims.* www.hillsboroohio.net/municipal%20court.html

General Information: No expunged records released. No fee to fax documents local or toll free only. Court makes copy: $.15 per page. Certification fee: $.50 per page. Payee: Hillsboro Municipal Court. No personal checks or credit cards accepted. Prepayment required. Mail requests: SASE required.

Civil Name Search: Access: Phone, fax, mail, in person, online. Only the court performs in person name searches; visitors may not. No search fee. Civil records on computer from 1991, prior in books. Mail turnaround time 1-2 days. Online access is same as criminal, see below.

Criminal Name Search: Access: Phone, fax, mail, in person, online. Only the court performs in person name searches; visitors may not. No search fee. Required to search: name, years to search, DOB, SSN. Criminal records computerized from 1991, prior in books. Mail turnaround time 1-2 days. Online access is free at http://24.123.13.34/.

Hocking County

Common Pleas Court PO Box 108, 1 E Main St, Logan, OH 43138; 740-385-2616; probate phone: 740-385-3022; fax: 740-385-1822; 8:30AM-4PM (EST). *Felony, Civil Actions over $10,000.* www.co.hocking.oh.us/clerk/index.htm

General Information: Probate court is a separate court at the same address, 2nd Fl. No secret records released. Will fax documents $1.00 per page. Court makes copy: $.25 per page, plus $10.00 if extensive/entire case. Self serve copy: $.25 per page. Certification fee: $1.00 per page. Payee: Clerk of Court. Business checks accepted. No credit cards accepted. Prepayment required. Mail requests: SASE required.

Civil Name Search: Access: Fax, mail, in person, online. Both court and visitors may perform in person name searches. No search fee. Required to search: name, years to search; also helpful: address. Civil records on computer since 1996, in books to late 1800s. Mail turnaround time 1-2 days. Civil PAT goes back to 1996. Access the court case index free at www.court.co.hocking.oh.us/cgi-bin/db2www.pgm/cpq.mbr/main.

Criminal Name Search: Access: Fax, mail, in person, online. Both court and visitors may perform in person name searches. No search fee. Required to search: name, years to search; also helpful: address, DOB, SSN. Criminal records date back to 1980 on docket books. Mail turnaround time 1-2 days. Criminal PAT goes back to same as civil. Access the court case index free at www.court.co.hocking.oh.us/cgi-bin/db2www.pgm/cpq.mbr/main. Online results show name only.

Hocking County Municipal Court PO Box 950, 1 E Main St, County Courthouse, 1st Fl, Logan, OH 43138-1278; 740-385-2250; fax: 740-385-3826; 8AM-4PM (EST). *Misdemeanor, Civil Actions under $15,000, Eviction, Small Claims.* www.hockingcountymunicipalcourt.com

General Information: Will fax documents to local or toll-free number. Court makes copy: $.10 per page. Certification fee: $1.00 per page. Payee: Hocking County Municipal Court. Personal checks accepted. Major credit cards accepted. Prepayment required. Mail requests: SASE required.

Civil Name Search: Access: Mail, in person, fax, online. Both court and visitors may perform in person name searches. No search fee. Civil records on computer from 1991, prior in books. Mail turnaround time 1-2 days. Access civil records free at www.hockingcountymunicipalcourt.com/search.shtml. Shows case number, docket entry, charge, case type.

Criminal Name Search: Access: Mail, in person, fax, online. Both court and visitors may perform in person name searches. No search fee. Required to search: name, years to search, DOB, SSN (signed release if for a housing check). Criminal records computerized from 1991 prior in books. Mail turnaround time 1-2 days. Access criminal records free at www.hockingcountymunicipalcourt.com/search.shtml. Shows case number, docket entry, charge, case type. Online results show middle initial.

Holmes County

Common Pleas Court - General Div 1 E Jackson St, #306, Millersburg, OH 44654; 330-674-1876; probate phone: 330-674-5881; fax: 330-674-0289; 8:30AM-4:30PM (EST). *Felony, Civil Actions over $10,000.*

General Information: Probate court is a separate court at the same address, #201. No expunged records released. Fee to fax out file $2.00 1st page, $1.00 each add'l. Court makes copy: $.10 per page. Certification fee: $1.00 per page plus copy fee. Payee: Clerk of Court. Personal checks accepted, credit cards are not. Prepayment required. Mail requests: SASE required.

Civil Name Search: Access: Fax, mail, in person. Both court and visitors may perform in person name searches. Search fee: $5.00 per name. Required to search: name, years to search; also helpful: address. Civil records on computer from 6/30/94, prior in books to 1850. Mail turnaround time 1-2 days. Civil PAT goes back to 1994.

Criminal Name Search: Access: Fax, mail, in person. Both court and visitors may perform in person name searches. Search fee: $5.00 per name. Required to search: name, years to search; also helpful: address, DOB, SSN. Criminal records computerized from 6/30/94, prior in books to 1850. Mail turnaround time 1-2 days. Criminal PAT goes back to same as civil.

Municipal Court 1 E Jackson St, #101, Millersburg, OH 44654; 330-674-4901; fax: 330-674-5514; 8:30AM-4:30PM (EST). *Misdemeanor, Civil Actions under $15,000, Small Claims.*

General Information: The court has separate divisions for Civil and Criminal. Use Room 101 for Civil Div, Room 102 for Criminal Div. No search warrant records released. Will fax documents to local or toll-free number. Court makes copy: $.25 each 1-10 pages; $.10 each add'l. Certification fee: $5.00, same fee for exemplified copies. Payee: Holmes County Court. Personal checks accepted, credit cards are not. Prepayment required. Mail requests: SASE required.

Civil Name Search: Access: Phone, fax, mail, in person. Both court and visitors may perform in person name searches. Search fee: $1.00 per name. Civil records in books going back to 1813; computerized records since 1994. Note: Phone and fax access limited to 1 name. Mail turnaround time 5-10 days. Civil PAT goes back to 1994.

Criminal Name Search: Access: Phone, fax, mail, in person. Both court and visitors may perform in person name searches. Search fee: $1.00 per name. Criminal records in books going back to 1813; computerized records since 1994. Note: Phone and fax access limited to 1 name. Mail turnaround time 5-10 days. Criminal PAT goes back to same as civil.

Huron County

Common Pleas Court Clerk of Courts, 2 E Main St, Rm 207, Norwalk, OH 44857; 419-668-5113; probate phone: 419-668-4838; fax: 419-663-4048; 8AM-4:30PM (EST). *Felony, Civil Actions over $10,000, Probate.* www.huroncountyclerk.com

General Information: Probate court is a separate court at the same address, 1st Fl. No secret records released. Will fax out specific case files for $2.00 each plus $1.00 per page. Court makes copy: $.10 per page. Self serve copy: same. Certification fee: $1.00. Payee: Clerk of Court. Personal checks accepted, credit cards are not. Prepayment required.

Civil Name Search: Access: In person, online. Both court and visitors may perform in person name searches. No search fee. Required to search: name, years to search; also helpful: address. Civil records on computer from 7/1989, prior in books and on microfiche. Civil PAT goes back to 1989. Search court dockets and public records free at the website www.huroncountyclerk.com/html/case_search.html Civil results on internet do not include DOB.

Criminal Name Search: Access: In person, online. Both court and visitors may perform in person name searches. No search fee. Required to search: name, years to search, offense, date of offense; also helpful: address, DOB, SSN. Criminal records on computer since 7/1989, records from 1991 to present in actual files, 1930 to 1991 on microfiche. Criminal PAT goes back to same as civil. Search court dockets and public records free at the website www.huroncountyclerk.com/html/case_search.html. Online results show middle initial, DOB.

Bellevue Municipal Court 3000 Seneca Industrial Pky, Bellevue, OH 44811; 419-483-5880; fax: 419-484-8060; 8:30AM-4:30PM (EST). *Misdemeanor, Civil Actions under $15,000, Eviction, Small Claims, Traffic.*

General Information: Jurisdiction includes City of Bellevue, Sherman, Lyme Township in Huron County, and York township in Sandusky County. Best time of day to perform searches is afternoons. Will fax documents to local or toll free line. Court makes copy: no fee if less than 5 copies, add'l copy fee varies. Certification fee: $1.00. Payee: Bellevue Municipal Court. Only cashiers checks and money orders accepted. No credit cards accepted. Prepayment required. Mail requests: SASE required.

Civil Name Search: Access: Phone, fax, mail, in person. Both court and visitors may perform in person name searches. No search fee. Required to search: name, years to search, also case number if known. Civil records on printed index from 1988, prior in books. Note: Court will only do phone searching if not busy. Mail turnaround time 3-7 days.

Criminal Name Search: Access: Phone, fax, mail, in person. Both court and visitors may perform in person name searches. No search fee. Required to search: name, years to search, DOB; also helpful: SSN. Criminal records computerized from 8/93; paper index goes back further, court will search if/when time available. Use a retriever or abstractor to come in and search back before 8/1993. Mail turnaround time 3-7 days.

Huron Municipal Court 417 Main St, Huron, OH 44839; 419-433-5430; fax: 419-433-5120; 8AM-4PM (EST). *Misdemeanor, Civil Actions under $15,000, Eviction, Small Claims.* www.huronoh.org/huron/court.html

General Information: Fee to fax out file $1.00 per page. Court makes copy: $.05 per page. Certification fee: $2.00 per page. Payee: Municipal Court. No personal checks accepted. Major credit cards accepted. Prepayment required. Mail requests: SASE required.

Civil Name Search: Access: Fax, mail, in person. Both court and visitors may perform in person name searches. No search fee. Required to search: name, years to search; also helpful: address. Civil records on computer back to 1998; prior on docket book to 1976. Mail turnaround time 2-7 days.

Criminal Name Search: Access: Fax, mail, in person. Both court and visitors may perform in person name searches. No search fee. Required to search: name, years to search, DOB, SSN; also helpful: address. Criminal records computerized from 1998, prior on docket books to 1976. Mail turnaround time 2-7 days.

Norwalk Municipal Court 45 N Linwood, Norwalk, OH 44857; 419-663-6750; fax: 419-663-6749; 8:30AM-4:30PM (EST). *Misdemeanor, Civil Actions under $15,000, Eviction, Small Claims.* www.norwalkmunicourt.com

General Information: No SSNs appear on records. Fee to fax out file $1.00 per page. Court makes copy: $.05 per page. Certification fee: $1.00 per page. Payee: Municipal Court. Personal checks accepted, credit cards are not. Prepayment required. Mail requests: SASE required.

Civil Name Search: Access: Fax, mail, in person, online. Both court and visitors may perform in person name searches. No search fee. Required to search: name, years to search; also helpful: address. Civil records on computer from 7/88; prior on docket book to 1976. Mail turnaround time 2-7 days. Civil PAT goes back to 1988. Access records free at www.norwalkmunicourt.com/search.htm.

Criminal Name Search: Access: Fax, mail, in person, online. Both court and visitors may perform in person name searches. No search fee. Required to search: name, years to search, DOB, SSN; also helpful: address. Criminal records computerized from 7/88, prior on docket books to 1976. Mail turnaround time 2-7 days. Criminal PAT goes back to same as civil. Access records free at www.norwalkmunicourt.com/search.htm.

Jackson County

Common Pleas Court 226 Main St, Jackson, OH 45640; 740-286-2006; probate phone: 740-286-1401; fax: 740-286-5186; 8AM-4PM (EST). *Felony, Civil Actions over $10,000, Probate.* www.jcclerk.com/

General Information: Probate court is a separate court at the same address, Suite 6. No juvenile or search warrant record released. Will fax documents $3.00 fee. Court makes copy: $.10 per page. Certification fee: $1.50. Payee: Clerk of Court. Personal checks accepted, credit cards are not. Prepayment required.

Civil Name Search: Access: In person, online. Both court and visitors may perform in person name searches. No search fee. Required to search: name, years to search; also helpful: address. Civil records go back to 1800s, computerized since 6/20/97. Civil PAT goes back to 6/1997. Search the docket by name or case number at http://216.255.18.74/pa/.

Criminal Name Search: Access: In person, online. Both court and visitors may perform in person name searches. Search fee: Searches only performed in emergency situations. Required to search: name, years to search; also helpful: address, DOB, SSN. Criminal records go back to 1/83; computerized since 06/20/97. Criminal PAT goes back to same as civil. Search the docket by name or case number at http://216.255.18.74/pa/.

Jackson County Municipal Court 295 Broadway St, #101, Jackson, OH 45640-1764; 740-286-2718; fax: 740-286-0679; 8AM-4PM (EST). *Misdemeanor, Civil Actions under $15,000, Eviction, Small Claims.* www.jacksoncountymunicipalcourt.com/

General Information: No victim records released. Will fax documents for no fee. Court makes copy: $.10 per page. Certification fee: $5.00. Payee: Clerk of Municipal Court. Cashiers checks and money orders accepted. Visa/MC accepted. Prepayment required.

Civil Name Search: Access: In person, online. Visitors must perform in person searches themselves. Civil records in books readily available for 8-10 years, prior archived. Civil PAT goes back to 1997. Case information includes personal identifiers. Search record index free at www.jacksoncountymunicipalcourt.com/Search/.

Criminal Name Search: Access: In person, online. Visitors must perform in person searches themselves. Required to search: name, years to search, DOB, SSN. Criminal records in books readily available for 8-10 years, prior archived. Criminal PAT goes back to same as civil. Case information includes personal identifiers. Search the record index at www.jacksoncountymunicipalcourt.com/Search/. Online results show middle initial, DOB, address.

Jefferson County

Common Pleas Court PO Box 1326, 301 Market St, Rm 200, Steubenville, OH 43952; 740-283-8583; probate phone: 740-283-8554; 8:30AM-4:30PM (EST). *Felony, Civil Actions over $500, Probate.* www.jeffersoncountyoh.com/

General Information: Probate court is a separate court at the same address, PO Box 549. Online identifiers in results same as on public terminal. No sealed records released. Will not fax documents. Court makes copy: $.10 per page. Certification fee: $1.00 per page, includes copy fee. Payee: Jefferson County Clerk of Courts. Business checks accepted. No credit cards accepted. Prepayment required. Mail requests: SASE required.

Civil Name Search: Access: Mail, in person, online. Both court and visitors may perform in person name searches. No search fee. Civil records on computer back 10 years or so, prior archived. Computerized domestic records go back to 1972. Mail turnaround time 1-3 days. Civil PAT goes back to 1995. Access court index free at http://gov.gbscorp.com/OH.Jefferson.CP/CaseSearch/default.aspx

Criminal Name Search: Access: Mail, in person, online. Both court and visitors may perform in person name searches. No search fee. Required to search: name, years to search, DOB; also helpful-SSN. Criminal records are computerized to 1988, but can go back many years in archives. Mail turnaround time 1-2 days. Criminal PAT goes back to 1988. Online access to criminal is same as civil, see above.

County Court #1 1007 Franklin Ave, Toronto, OH 43964; 740-537-2020; fax: 740-537-1866; 8AM-4PM (EST). *Misdemeanor, Civil Actions under $15,000, Small Claims.* www.jeffersoncountyoh.com/

General Information: All records are public. Will fax documents to local or toll free line. No copy fee. Self serve copy: $.25 per page. No certification fee. Payee: Jefferson County Court #1. Cashiers checks and money orders accepted. Credit cards accepted. Mail requests: SASE required.

Civil Name Search: Access: Mail, in person, online. Both court and visitors may perform in person name searches. Search fee: $5.00 per name. Civil records in books, dating from 1813, computerized records from 6/98. Mail turnaround time 1-2 days. Civil PAT goes back to 6/1998. Search court case index free at www.jeffersoncountyoh.com/CountyCourts/ClerkofCourts/tabid/156/Default.aspx.

Criminal Name Search: Access: Mail, in person, online. Both court and visitors may perform in person name searches. Search fee: $5.00 per name. Required to search: name, years to search, DOB, also helpful: SSN, sex, signed release. Criminal records in books, dating from 1813, computerized records from 6/98. Mail turnaround time 1-2 days. Criminal PAT goes back to same as civil. Terminal results include SSN. Online access to criminal is same as civil, see above.

County Court #2 PO Box 2207, 201 Talbot Dr, Wintersville, OH 43953; 740-264-7644; fax: 740-264-3909; 8AM-4PM (EST). *Misdemeanor, Civil Actions under $15,000, Small Claims.* www.jeffersoncountyoh.com/

General Information: Online identifiers in results same as on public terminal. Will fax documents to local or toll free line. Court makes copy: $.25 per page. Certification fee: $1.00 per page. Payee: County Court #2. Cashiers checks and money orders accepted. Visa/MC accepted plus $1.00 surcharge. Prepayment required. Mail requests: SASE required.

Civil Name Search: Access: Mail, in person, online. Both court and visitors may perform in person name searches. No search fee. Civil records on computer back to 1998; in books from 1950s, prior archived. Mail turnaround time 1-2 days. Civil PAT goes back to 1998. Search court case index free at www.jeffersoncountyoh.com/CountyCourts/ClerkofCourts/tabid/156/Default.aspx.

Criminal Name Search: Access: Mail, in person, online. Both court and visitors may perform in person name searches. Search fee: $5.00 per name. Required to search: name, years to search, DOB or SSN. Criminal records computerized from 1998; in books from 1950s, prior archived. Mail turnaround time 1-2 days. Criminal PAT goes back to same as civil. Online access to criminal is same as civil, see above.

County Court #3 174 Smithfield St, Dillonvale, OH 43917; 740-769-2903; fax: 740-769-7640; 8AM-4PM (EST). *Misdemeanor, Civil Actions under $15,000, Small Claims.* www.jeffersoncountyoh.com/

General Information: Will fax documents $1.00 per page. Court makes copy: $1.00 per page. Certification fee: $1.00. Payee: County Court #3. Cashiers checks and money orders accepted. Credit cards accepted. Prepayment required. Mail requests: SASE required.

Civil Name Search: Access: Mail, fax, in person, online. Both court and visitors may perform in person name searches. Search fee: $5.00. Civil records on computer from 1998, prior manual dockets. Mail turnaround time 1-2 days. Civil PAT goes back to 1998. Search case index free at www.jeffersoncountyoh.com/CountyCourts/ClerkofCourts/tabid/156/Default.aspx.

Criminal Name Search: Access: Mail, in person, online. Both court and visitors may perform in person name searches. Search fee: $5.00. Required to search: name, years to search, DOB; also helpful: SSN. Criminal records computerized from 1998, prior manual dockets. Mail turnaround time 1-2 days. Criminal PAT goes back to 1998. Online access to criminal is same as civil, see above.

Steubenville Municipal Court 123 S 3rd St, Steubenville, OH 43952; 740-283-6000 x2200; fax: 740-283-6167; 8:30AM-4PM (EST). *Misdemeanor, Civil Actions under $15,000, Eviction, Small Claims.* www.cityofsteubenville.us/court/

General Information: Email questions to municipalcourt@cityofsteubenville.us. No expunged records released. Will fax documents to local or toll free line. Court makes copy: $1.00 per page. Certification fee: $2.00. Payee: Steubenville Municipal Court. Only cashiers checks and money orders accepted. Visa/MC accepted. Prepayment required. Mail requests: SASE required.

Civil Name Search: Access: Mail, in person. Both court and visitors may perform in person name searches. No search fee. Required to search: name, years to search; also helpful: address. Civil records on computer from 1991, prior in books. Mail turnaround time 10-14 days. Civil PAT goes back to 1991. Terminal results also include race, sex, hair, eyes.

Criminal Name Search: Access: Mail, in person. Both court and visitors may perform in person name searches. No search fee. Required to search: name, years to search; also helpful: address, DOB, SSN. Criminal records computerized from 1991, prior in books. Mail turnaround time 10-14 days. Criminal PAT goes back to 199. Terminal results also include race, sex, hair, eyes.

Knox County

Common Pleas Court Knox County Clerk of Courts, 117 E High St, #201, Mt Vernon, OH 43050; 740-393-6788; fax: 740-392-3533; 8AM-4PM M-F (EST). *Felony, Civil Actions over $15,000.*

General Information: Probate is a separate office with different address and phone number. If exact case number given, clerk will fax return pages $2.00 1st page, $1.00 each add'l. Court makes copy: $.05 per page. Certification fee: $1.00 plus copy fee. Payee: Knox County Clerk of Courts. Personal checks accepted, credit cards are not. Prepayment required.

Civil Name Search: Access: Online, in person. Visitors must perform in person searches themselves. Civil records on computer since 9/86, on microfilm from 1960, prior archived. Civil PAT goes back to 1986. Search court index, dockets, calendars free online at www.coc.co.knox.oh.us/pa/. Search by name or case number.

Criminal Name Search: Access: Online, in person. Visitors must perform in person searches themselves. Criminal records on computer since 9/86, on microfilm from 1960, prior archived. Criminal PAT goes back to same as civil. Search court index, dockets, calendars free online at www.coc.co.knox.oh.us/pa/. Search by name or case number.

Mount Vernon Municipal Court 5 N Gay St, Mount Vernon, OH 43050; 740-393-9510; fax: 740-393-5349; 8AM-4PM (EST). *Misdemeanor, Civil Actions under $15,000, Eviction, Small Claims.* www.mountvernonmunicipalcourt.org

General Information: Will fax documents. No copy fee. No certification fee. Payee: Mt Vernon Municipal Ct. Personal checks accepted. Credit cards accepted in person. Mail requests: SASE required.

Civil Name Search: Access: Phone, fax, mail, in person, online. Only the court performs in person name searches; visitors may not. No search fee. Civil records on computer from 6/89, prior in books. Note: Results include name, plaintiff, defendant, case number. Mail turnaround time 1 week. Access to the clerk's civil records are free at http://mountvernonmunicipalcourt.org/connection/court/index.xsp.

Criminal Name Search: Access: Phone, fax, mail, in person, online. Only the court performs in person name searches; visitors may not. No search fee. Criminal records computerized from 06/89, prior in books. Note: Results include name, case number, ticket number. Mail turnaround time 1 week. Access to the clerk's criminal and traffic records are free at http://mountvernonmunicipalcourt.org/connection/court/index.xsp.

Probate Court 111 E High St, 1st Fl, Mt Vernon, OH 43050; probate phone: 740-393-6798; fax: 740-393-6832; 8AM-4PM (EST). *Probate, Juvenile.* www.co.knox.oh.us/offices/pj/

Lake County

Common Pleas Court 25 N Park Pl, Painesville, OH 44077; 440-350-2657; probate phone: 440-350-2626; 8AM-4:30PM (EST). *Felony, Civil Actions over $10,000, Probate.* www.lakecountyohio.org

General Information: Probate court is a separate court at the same address. Probate records are available free online. No adoption or juvenile records released. Will not fax documents. Court makes copy: $.08 per page. Certification fee: $1.00 per seal. Payee: Clerk of Court. Business checks accepted. No credit cards accepted. Prepayment required.

Civil Name Search: Access: In person, online. Visitors must perform in person searches themselves. Required to search: name, years to search; also helpful: address. Civil records on computer from 1990, microfilm from 1960, prior archived. Civil PAT goes back to 1990. Online access to court records, dockets, and quick index, including probate records, is free at https://phoenix.lakecountyohio.gov/pa/.

Criminal Name Search: Access: In person, online. Visitors must perform in person searches themselves. Required to search: name, years to search; also helpful: address, DOB. Criminal records computerized from 1990, microfilm from 1960, prior archived. Note: Will accept mail requests for copies if you provide case number. Criminal PAT goes back to same as civil. Online access to court records, dockets, and quick index, including probate records, is free at https://phoenix.lakecountyohio.gov/pa/. Online results show name only.

Mentor Municipal Court 8500 Civic Center Blvd, Mentor, OH 44060-2418; criminal phone: 440-974-5744; civil phone: 440-974-5745; fax: 440-974-5742; 8AM-4PM; W til 6PM (EST). *Misdemeanor, Civil Actions under $15,000, Eviction, Small Claims.* www.mentormunicipalcourt.org/

General Information: Will not fax out case files. Court makes copy: $.25 per page. Certification fee: $1.00 plus copy fee. Payee: Mentor Municipal Court. Cashiers checks and money orders accepted; no personal checks. Major credit cards accepted. Prepayment required.

Civil Name Search: Access: In person, online. Visitors must perform in person searches themselves. Required to search: name. Civil records go back to 1972; on computer back to 11/1995. Record searches at www.mentormunicipalcourt.org/search.shtml. The initial docket list does not show identifiers, but click on the case number to find identifiers.

Criminal Name Search: Access: In person, online. Visitors must perform in person searches themselves. Required to search: name, years to search; also helpful: DOB. Criminal records go back to 1972; on computer back to 11/1995. Note: Prefer all name searches be tried online first. Public access terminals moved out of office. Search records at www.mentormunicipalcourt.org/search.shtml he initial docket list does not show identifiers, but click on the case number to find identifiers.

Painesville Municipal Court PO Box 601, 7 Richmond St, Painesville, OH 44077; 440-392-5900; fax: 440-352-0028; 8AM-4:30PM (EST). *Misdemeanor, Civil Actions under $15,000, Eviction, Small Claims.* www.pmcourt.com

General Information: Probation fax is 440-639-4932. Online identifiers in results same as on public terminal. Will fax documents: local $1.00 per page; long distance $3.00 per page. Court makes copy: $1.00 first page. $.20 each add'l. Certification fee: $2.00 plus $1.00 per page after first. Payee: Municipal Court. Personal checks accepted. Credit cards accepted. Prepayment required. Mail requests: SASE required.

Civil Name Search: Access: Fax, mail, in person, online. Visitors must perform in person searches themselves. No search fee. Required to search: name, years to search; also helpful: address. Civil records on computer from 7/90 (all divisions), prior on books or archived. Civil PAT goes back to 1990. Free online access to index at www.pmcourt.com/search.shtml.

Criminal Name Search: Access: Fax, mail, in person, online. Visitors must perform in person searches themselves. No search fee. Required to search: name, years to search, address; also helpful: DOB, SSN. Criminal records computerized from 7/90 (all divisions), prior on books or archived. Mail turnaround time 1 week. Criminal PAT goes back to 1990. Free online access to index at www.pmcourt.com/search.shtml. Online results show middle initial, DOB.

Willoughby Municipal Court 4000 Erie St, Willoughby, OH 44094; 440-953-4150; criminal phone: 440-953-4150; civil phone: 440-953-4170; fax: 440-953-4149; 7:30AM-4:30 PM, till 7:30PM M (EST). *Misdemeanor, Civil Actions under $15,000, Eviction, Small Claims.* www.willoughbycourt.com

General Information: This court serves these communities: Eastlake, Kirtland, Kirtland Hills, Lakeland Community College, Lakeline, Timberlake, Waite Hill, Wickliffe, Willoughby, Willoughby Hills, and Willowick. Will fax documents $1.00 per page. Court makes copy: $.25 per page. Certification fee: $1.00 per page. Payee: Willoughby Municipal Court. Personal checks accepted. Major credit cards accepted. Prepayment required.

Civil Name Search: Access: Mail, in person, online. Both court and visitors may perform in person name searches. No search fee. Civil cases indexed by defendant. Civil index on docket books since 1960, computerized back to 1986. Mail turnaround time 1-2 days. Civil PAT goes back to 1993. Access the court's case lookup plus schedules free at www.willoughbycourt.com/connection/court/.

Criminal Name Search: Access: Mail, in person, online. Both court and visitors may perform in person name searches. No search fee. Required to search: name; also helpful: DOB, SSN. Criminal records in docket books since 1960, computerized back to 1988. Mail turnaround time 1-2 days. Criminal PAT goes back to 1989. Access the court's case lookup plus warrants and schedules free at www.willoughbycourt.com/connection/court/.

Lawrence County

Common Pleas Court Clerk of the Courts, 111 S 4th St, Ironton, OH 45638; 740-533-4355/4356; fax: 740-533-4383; 8:30AM-4PM (EST). *Felony, Civil Actions.* www.lawrenceclerk.com/

General Information: Online identifiers in results same as on public terminal. Will fax out specific case files. Court makes copy: $.25 per page. No certification fee. Payee: Clerk of Court. Personal checks accepted, credit cards are not. Prepayment required.

Civil Name Search: Access: In person, online. Visitors must perform in person searches themselves. Required to search: name, years to search; also helpful: address. Civil records on computer back to 6/88, prior in books going back to 1800s. Civil PAT goes back to 1988. Online access to civil records is free at www.lawrenceclerk.com/.

Criminal Name Search: Access: In person, online. Visitors must perform in person searches themselves. Required to search: name, years to search; also helpful: address, DOB, SSN. Criminal records computerized from 1/88, prior in books going back to 1800s. Criminal PAT goes back to same as civil. Online access to criminal records is free at www.lawrenceclerk.com/

Ironton Municipal Court PO Box 237, 301 S 3rd St, Ironton, OH 45638; 740-532-3062; fax: 740-533-6088; 8:30AM-4PM (EST). *Misdemeanor, Civil Actions under $15,000, Eviction, Small Claims.*

General Information: Searches of the index books only allowed Wed and Fri. Will fax documents for fee. Court makes copy: $1.00 per page. Certification fee: $1.00 per page plus copy fee. Payee: Municipal Court. No personal checks or credit cards accepted. Prepayment required. Mail requests: SASE required.

Civil Name Search: Access: Mail, in person. Both court and visitors may perform in person name searches. No search fee. Required to search: name, years to search; also helpful: address. Civil records on computer from 7/89, prior in books. Mail turnaround time 1-2 weeks. Civil PAT goes back to 1989.

Criminal Name Search: Access: Mail, in person. Both court and visitors may perform in person name searches. No search fee. Required to search: name, years to search; also helpful: address, DOB, SSN. Criminal records computerized from 7/89, prior in books. Note: Searches of the index books only allowed Wed and Fri. Mail turnaround time 1-2 weeks. Criminal PAT goes back to same as civil.

Lawrence County Municipal Court PO Box 126, Chesapeake, OH 45619; 740-867-3128/3127; fax: 740-867-3547; 8:30AM-4PM (EST). *Misdemeanor, Civil Actions under $15,000, Eviction, Small Claims.* www.lawcomunicourt.com/

General Information: All records public. Will fax documents if search fee prepaid. Court makes copy: $.25 per page. Self serve copy: same. Certification fee: $2.00. Payee: Lawrence County Municipal Court. Personal checks accepted. Visa/MC, Discover accepted on the web only. Prepayment required. Mail requests: SASE required.

Civil Name Search: Access: Phone, fax, mail, in person, online. Both court and visitors may perform in person name searches. Search fee: $10.00 per name. Civil records on computer from 1991. Mail turnaround time 7-10 days. Click on "Record Search" at the web page for a search of the record index.

Criminal Name Search: Access: Phone, fax, mail, in person, online. Both court and visitors may perform in person name searches. Search fee: $10.00 per name. Required to search: name, years to search, DOB; also helpful: SSN. Criminal records computerized from 1991. Mail turnaround time 7-10 days. Click on "Record Search" at the web page for a search of the record index.

Probate Court 1 Veterans Sq, Ironton, OH 45638-1585; 740-533-4343;. *Probate.*

Licking County

Common Pleas Court PO Box 4370, Court SG 2nd Floor, Newark, OH 43058-4370; 740-670-5794; fax: 740-670-5886; 8AM-4:30PM (EST). *Felony, Civil Actions over $15,000.* www.lcounty.com/clerkofcourts/

General Information: Online identifiers in results same as on public terminal. No sealed records released. Will fax documents $2.00 per transmission and $1.00 per page. Court makes copy: $.05 per page. Certification fee: $1.00 per page. Payee: Clerk of Court. Business checks accepted. Major credit cards accepted in person only. Prepayment required.

Civil Name Search: Access: In person, online. Visitors must perform in person searches themselves. Required to search: name, years to search; also helpful: address. Civil records on computer from 1992, prior in books. Civil PAT goes back to 2/1992. County clerk's office offers free Internet access to current records at www.lcounty.com/pa/.

Criminal Name Search: Access: In person, online. Visitors must perform in person searches themselves. Required to search: name, years to search, DOB; also helpful: address n/a; case # search. Criminal records computerized from 1992, prior in books. Criminal PAT goes back to 2/1992. County clerk's office offers free Internet access to current records at www.lcounty.com/pa/.

Licking County Municipal Court 40 W Main St, Newark, OH 43055; criminal phone: 740-670-7800; civil phone: 740-670-7811; fax: 740-345-4250; 8AM-4:30PM (EST). *Misdemeanor, Civil Actions under $15,000, Eviction, Small Claims.* www.lcmunicipalcourt.com

General Information: No sealed records released. Will not fax documents. Court makes copy: $.05 per page. Self serve copy: same. Certification fee: $2.00 per page. Payee: Licking County Municipal Court. Personal checks accepted. Credit cards accepted with $3.50 fee added. Prepayment required. Mail requests: SASE required.

Civil Name Search: Access: Phone, fax, mail, in person, online. Both court and visitors may perform in person name searches. No search fee. Civil records on computer from 1990, prior in books. Mail turnaround time 2-3 days. Civil PAT goes back to 1990. Online access to Municipal Court record docket is free at http://70.61.248.70/connection/court/. Results include addresses.

Criminal Name Search: Access: Phone, fax, mail, in person, online. Both court and visitors may perform in person name searches. No search fee. Criminal records computerized from 1990, prior in books. Mail turnaround time 2-3 days. Criminal PAT goes back to same as civil. Online access to Municipal Court record docket is free at http://70.61.248.70/connection/court/. Results include addresses. Online results show middle initial, DOB.

Probate and Juvenile Court 1 N Park Pl, Newark, OH 43055; 740-670-5624; fax: 740-670-5881; 8:30AM-4:30PM (EST). *Probate.* www.lcounty.com/probate/default.aspx

General Information: Court records search at www.lcounty.com/pa/. Can search by name, case or ticket number.

Logan County

Common Pleas Court 101 S Main St, Rm 18, Bellefontaine, OH 43311-2097; 937-599-7261; criminal phone: 937-599-7256; civil phone: 937-599-7275; probate phone: 937-599-7249; criminal fax: 937-599-7281; civil fax: 8:30AM-4:30PM; 8:30AM-4:30PM (EST). *Felony, Civil Actions over $10,000, Probate.* http://co.logan.oh.us/clerkofcourts/

General Information: Probate court is a separate court at the same address. All records public. Will fax specific case file $2.00 1st page, $1.00 each add'l page. Court makes copy: $.25 per page. Certification fee: $1.00 per page includes copy fee. Payee: Clerk of Court. Only cashiers checks and money orders accepted. No credit cards accepted. Prepayment required.

Civil Name Search: Access: In person, online. Visitors must perform in person searches themselves. Required to search: name, years to search; also helpful: address. Civil records on computer from 6/88, prior in books to 1943. Civil PAT goes back to 6/1988. Search the index free online formthe home page, includes Family court. "Case Status" field may not reflect actual status of case.

Criminal Name Search: Access: In person, online. Visitors must perform in person searches themselves. Required to search: name, years to search, DOB; also helpful: address, SSN. Criminal records computerized from 6/88, prior in books to 1943. Criminal PAT goes back to same as civil. Middle initial will appear on results only if was provided. Online access to the index is from the home page. "Case Status" field may not reflect actual status of case.

Bellefontaine Municipal Court 226 W Columbus Ave, Bellefontaine, OH 43311; 937-599-6127; fax: 937-599-2488; 8AM-4:30PM (EST). *Misdemeanor, Civil Actions under $15,000, Eviction, Small Claims.* www.ci.bellefontaine.oh.us/municipal-court.html

General Information: All records are public. Will fax documents no fee. Court makes copy: $.05 per page. Certification fee: $1.00 per cert. Payee: Bellefontaine Municipal Court. Local checks accepted. Visa/MC accepted for traffic & criminal only. Prepayment required. Mail requests: SASE required.

Civil Name Search: Access: In person, fax, mail. Visitors must perform in person searches themselves. No search fee. Civil records on computer from 1986, prior in books. Civil PAT goes back to 1984.

Criminal Name Search: Access: In person, fax, mail. Visitors must perform in person searches themselves. No search fee. Required to search: name, years to search, DOB, SSN, signed release; also helpful: address. Criminal records computerized from 1986, prior in books. Mail turnaround time 1-2 days. Criminal PAT goes back to same as civil.

Lorain County

Common Pleas Court 225 Court St 1st Fl, Elyria, OH 44035; 440-329-5511; criminal phone: 440-329-5538; civil phone: 440-329-5536; probate phone: 440-329-5175; fax: 440-329-5404; 10AM-4:30PM (EST). *Felony, Civil Actions over $10,000, Probate.* www.loraincounty.com/clerk/

General Information: Probate court is a separate court at the same address, Rm 611. Probate fax- 440-328-2157. Court personnel will not do name searches of records. Online identifiers in results same as on public terminal. No juvenile records released. Will fax documents to local or toll-free number. Court makes copy: $.10 per page. Certification fee: $1.00. Payee: Clerk of Court. Personal checks accepted. Major credit cards accepted. Prepayment required.

Civil Name Search: Access: Online, in person. Visitors must perform in person searches themselves. Civil records on computer from 1988, prior in books archived to 1800s. Some records on microfiche to 1824. Note: Court will not do index searching but they will pull specified records. Civil PAT goes back to 1988. Free access to indices and dockets for common please court cases at http://cp.onlinedockets.com/loraincp/case_dockets/search.aspx. Access probate records at www.loraincounty.com/probate/search.shtml.

Criminal Name Search: Access: Online, in person. Visitors must perform in person searches themselves. Criminal records computerized from 1988, prior in books archived to 1800s. Some records on microfiche to 1960. Note: Court will not do index searching, but they will pull specified records. Criminal PAT goes back to same as civil. Free access to indices and dockets for common please court cases at http://cp.onlinedockets.com/loraincp/case_dockets/search.aspx.

Avon Lake Municipal Court 32855 Walker Rd, Avon Lake, OH 44012; 440-930-4103; fax: 440-930-4128; 8:30AM-4:30PM (EST). *Misdemeanor, Civil Actions under $15,000, Eviction, Small Claims.* www.avonlakecourt.com/

General Information: No non-public records released. Fee to fax out file $3.00 each. Court makes copy: $.10 per page. Certification fee: $1.00 per page. Payee: Avon Lake Municipal Court. Personal checks accepted for record searches. Credit cards accepted in person or on phone. Prepayment required. Mail requests: SASE required if receipt requested.

Civil Name Search: Access: Phone, mail, in person, online. Only the court performs in person name searches; visitors may not. No search fee. Civil records on computer from 5/92, records go back to 1976. Mail turnaround time 1-4 days. Search docket index by name or case number at www.avonlakecourt.com/search.php.

Criminal Name Search: Access: Phone, mail, in person, online. Both court and visitors may perform in person name searches. No search fee. Required to search: name, years to search, DOB; also helpful: SSN. Criminal records computerized from 7/92, records go back to 1976. Mail turnaround time 1-2 days. Search docket index by name, case number or ticket number at www.avonlakecourt.com/search.php. Online results show middle initial, DOB.

Elyria Municipal Court 601 Broad St, Elyria, OH 44035; 440-326-1732; fax: 440-326-1877; 8AM-4:30PM (EST). *Misdemeanor, Civil Actions under $15,000, Eviction, Small Claims.* www.elyriamunicourt.org

General Information: Online identifiers in results same as on public terminal. All records are public. Will not fax out documents. Court makes copy: none; may be a charge after 20 pages. Certification fee: $1.00 per page. Personal checks accepted. Credit cards accepted. Prepayment required. Mail requests: SASE required.

Civil Name Search: Access: Fax, mail, online, in person. Both court and visitors may perform in person name searches. No search fee. Required to search: name, years to search; also helpful: address. Civil records in books to 1956, computer from 1996. Mail turnaround time 5 days. Civil PAT goes back to 1996. Search at the Internet site, also you can request information by email to civil@elyriamunicourt.org.

Criminal Name Search: Access: In person, online. Both court and visitors may perform in person name searches. No search fee. Criminal records in books to 1956, computer from 1996. Criminal PAT goes back to 1992. Search misdemeanor and traffic records back to 1992 at the website, also send email requests to crtr@elyriamunicourt.org. Online results show name, DOB.

Lorain Municipal Court 200 W Erie Ave, Lorain, OH 44052; 440-204-2140; fax: 440-204-2146; 8:30AM-4:30PM (EST). *Misdemeanor, Civil Actions under $15,000, Eviction, Small Claims.* www.lorainmunicourt.org

General Information: Online identifiers in results same as on public terminal. Will not fax documents. Court makes copy: $.25 per page. No certification fee. Payee: Municipal Court. No personal checks accepted. Major credit cards accepted. Prepayment required.

Civil Name Search: Access: In person, online. Visitors must perform in person searches themselves. Required to search: name, years to search; also helpful: address. Civil records in books. Civil PAT goes back to 8/1998. Access municipal court records free at www.lorainmunicourt.org/public/. Search by name, date, case number, driver license number or attorney.

Criminal Name Search: Access: In person, online. Visitors must perform in person searches themselves. Required to search: name, years to search; also helpful: address, DOB, SSN. Criminal records in books. Criminal PAT goes back to same as civil. Access municipal court records free at www.lorainmunicourt.org/public/. Search by name, date, case number, driver license number or attorney. Online results show name, DOB.

Oberlin Municipal Court 85 S Main St, Oberlin, OH 44074; 440-775-1751; fax: 440-775-0619; 8AM-4PM (EST). *Misdemeanor, Civil Actions under $15,000, Eviction, Small Claims.* www.oberlinmunicipalcourt.org

General Information: Will not fax documents. Court makes copy: $.10 per page. No certification fee. Payee: Oberlin Municipal Court. Cashiers check or money orders accepted. Visa/MC accepted. Prepayment required.

Civil Name Search: Access: In person, online. Visitors must perform in person searches themselves. Required to search: name, years to search; also helpful: address. Civil records on computer from 1991, prior in books. Civil PAT goes back to 1991. Access case information free online at www.oberlinmunicipalcourt.org/public.htm.

Criminal Name Search: Access: In person, online. Visitors must perform in person searches themselves. Required to search: name, years to search; also helpful: address, DOB, SSN. Criminal records computerized from 1991, prior in books. Criminal PAT goes back to same as civil. Access case information free online at www.oberlinmunicipalcourt.org/public.htm. Online results show middle initial, DOB, address.

Vermilion Municipal Court *Misdemeanor, Civil Actions under $15,000, Eviction, Small Claims.*
General Information: See Erie County, Vermilion Muni Court. The Erie/Lorain county line is Main street. The Court is located on that street.

Lucas County

Common Pleas Court 700 Adams St, Courthouse, Toledo, OH 43604; 419-213-4483, 4484; criminal phone: 419-213-4480; civil phone: 419-213-4490; probate phone: 419-213-4775; criminal fax: 419-213-4291; civil fax: 8AM-4:45PM; 8AM-4:45PM (EST). *Felony, Civil Actions over $10,000, Probate.*
www.co.lucas.oh.us/index.aspx?nid=83
General Information: File Rm does searches; crim- 419-213-5540, civ- 419-213-4083. Probate court is a separate court at the same address; probate hours are 8:30-4:30. Probate fax- call for fax number. No expunged records released. Will fax documents $3.00 transmittal fee plus copy fees. Court makes copy: $.05 per page. Self serve copy: same. Certification fee: $1.00 per document plus copy fee. Payee: Clerk of Court. Only cashiers checks and money orders accepted. No credit cards accepted. Prepayment required. Mail requests: SASE not required.
Civil Name Search: Access: Fax, mail, in person, online. Both court and visitors may perform in person name searches. No search fee. Civil records computer from 1987, records go back to 1948, prior in books and on film. Civil PAT goes back to 1986. Online access to clerk of courts dockets is free at www.co.lucas.oh.us/index.aspx?NID=99. Online records go back to 9/1997. Search probate records at www.lucas-co-probate-ct.org/.
Criminal Name Search: Access: Fax, mail, in person, online. Both court and visitors may perform in person name searches. Search fee: $5.00 per name. Required to search: name, years to search, DOB, SSN; also helpful: sex, signed release. Criminal records computer from 1987, records go back to 1948, prior in books and on film. Criminal PAT goes back to 1986. Online access to clerk of courts dockets is free at www.co.lucas.oh.us/index.aspx?NID=99. Online record go back to 9/1997. Search sex offenders at www.lucascountysheriff.org/sheriff/disclaimer.asp. Online results show middle initial.

Maumee Municipal Court 400 Conant St, Maumee, OH 43537-3397; criminal phone: 419-897-7136; civil phone: 419-897-7145; fax: 419-897-7129; 8AM-4:30PM (EST). *Misdemeanor, Civil Actions $15,000 and under, Eviction, Small Claims.* www.maumee.org/municipal/default.htm
General Information: Email questions to court@maumee.org. Will fax documents for no fee. Court makes copy: No copy fee up to 20 pages; $.05 per page over 20. Certification fee: $1.00 per page up to 20 pages includes copy fee. Payee: Maumee Municipal Court. Personal checks accepted. Credit cards not accepted for phone orders. Prepayment required. Mail requests: SASE helpful.
Civil Name Search: Access: Phone, fax, mail, in person, online. Only the court performs in person name searches; visitors may not. No search fee. Required to search: name; also helpful: years to search. Civil records in docket books since 1964, on computer since 1989. Mail turnaround time 1 week. Online access to web court system database is free at www.maumee.org/municipal/caseinfo.htm. Online includes civil, criminal, traffic.
Criminal Name Search: Access: Phone, fax, mail, in person, online. Only the court performs in person name searches; visitors may not. No search fee. Required to search: name, years to search, DOB; also helpful: SSN. Criminal records in docket books since 1964, on computer since 1987. Mail turnaround time 1 week. Online access to web court system database is free at www.maumee.org/municipal/caseinfo.htm. Online includes civil, criminal, traffic. Online results show middle initial, DOB.

Oregon Municipal Court 5330 Seaman Rd, Oregon, OH 43616; criminal phone: 419-698-7173; civil phone: 419-698-7008; fax: 419-698-7013; 8:30AM-4:30PM (EST). *Misdemeanor, Civil Actions under $15,000, Eviction, Small Claims, Traffic.*
www.oregonohio.org/View_Court_Records.html
General Information: No fee to fax document; must be local call. Court makes copy: $.10 per page. Certification fee: $2.50 for 1st page, $.10 each add'l. Payee: Oregon Municipal Court. Personal checks accepted. Major credit cards accepted for criminal records only. Prepayment required. Mail requests: SASE required.
Civil Name Search: Access: Phone, fax, mail, in person, email, online. Both court and visitors may perform in person name searches. No search fee. Civil records on books since 1960, computerized since 1989. Mail turnaround time 1-2 days. Direct email civil search requests to court@ci.oregon.oh.us. Search court cases and schedules free at www.oregonohio.org/View_Court_Records.html.

Criminal Name Search: Access: Phone, fax, mail, in person, online. Both court and visitors may perform in person name searches. No search fee. Required to search: name, years to search; also helpful: DOB, SSN. Criminal docket on books since 1960, computerized since 1989. Mail turnaround time 1-2 days. Search court cases and schedules free at www.oregonohio.org/View_Court_Records.html.

Sidney Municipal Court 201 W Poplar St, Sidney, OH 45365; 937-498-0011; fax: 937-498-8179; 8AM-4:15PM (EST). *Misdemeanor, Civil Actions under $15,000, Eviction, Small Claims.*
http://sidneyoh.com/court/court.htm
General Information: Above address is mailing address; court is located at 110 W Court St. Will fax documents to local or toll free line. Court makes copy: $.10 per page. Certification fee: $1.00 per page. Payee: Clerk of Court. Business checks accepted. No credit cards accepted. Prepayment required.
Civil Name Search: Access: Fax, mail, in person. Visitors must perform in person searches themselves. No search fee. Civil records on books since 1964, computerized since 1987. Public use terminal available, records go back to 1992.
Criminal Name Search: Access: Fax, mail, in person. Visitors must perform in person searches themselves. No search fee. Required to search: name, years to search, DOB, SSN. Criminal docket on books since 1964, computerized since 1992. Mail turnaround time 1 week. Public use terminal available, crim records go back to same as civil.

Sylvania Municipal Court 6700 Monroe St, Sylvania, OH 43560-1995; 419-885-8975; criminal phone: 419-885-8975; civil phone: 419-885-8985; fax: 419-885-8987; 8AM-4:15PM (EST). *Misdemeanor, Civil Actions under $15,000, Eviction, Small Claims.* www.sylvaniacourt.com
General Information: Online identifiers in results same as on public terminal. Will fax documents to local or toll free line. Court makes copy: $.10 per page. Certification fee: $2.00 per page. Payee: Clerk of Court. Business checks accepted. Visa/MC accepted. Prepayment required. Mail requests: SASE not required.
Civil Name Search: Access: Fax, mail, in person, online. Visitors must perform in person searches themselves. No search fee. Civil records on books since 1964, computerized since 1987. Civil PAT goes back to 1987. Online access free at http://courtsvr.sylvaniacourt.com/.
Criminal Name Search: Access: Fax, mail, in person, online. Visitors must perform in person searches themselves. No search fee. Required to search: name, years to search, DOB, SSN. Criminal docket on books since 1964, computerized since 1987. Mail turnaround time 1 week. Criminal PAT goes back to 1987. Online access free at http://courtsvr.sylvaniacourt.com/.

Toledo Municipal Court 555 N Erie St, Toledo, OH 43604; 419-936-3650; criminal phone: 419-936-3650; civil phone: 419-936-3650; criminal fax: 419-245-1801; civil fax: 8AM-4:30PM; 8AM-4:30PM (EST). *Misdemeanor, Civil Actions under $15,000, Eviction, Small Claims.*
www.toledomunicipalcourt.org
General Information: The Criminal Division is open 7:30AM-5:30PM. Online identifiers in results same as on public terminal. No sealed records released. Will not fax documents. Court makes copy: $.20 per page. Self serve copy: same. Certification fee: $6.00. Payee: Toledo Municipal Court. Personal checks accepted. Will accept Visa/MC for criminal records. Prepayment required. Mail requests: SASE required.
Civil Name Search: Access: Mail, fax, in person, email, online. Both court and visitors may perform in person name searches. No search fee. Civil cases indexed by defendant. Civil records on computer back to 1985 prior in books since 1960s. Mail turnaround time 3 to 5 days. Public use terminal has civil records back to 1985. Case dockets are online at www.tmc-clerk.com/case/default.asp. Direct email requests to tmc-clerk@noris.org
Criminal Name Search: Access: Mail, fax, in person, email, online. Both court and visitors may perform in person name searches. No search fee. Required to search: name, years to search, DOB, SSN; also helpful: address. Criminal records computerized from 1980, prior in books since 1960s. Note: Have either date of birth or SSN to request a search. Mail turnaround time 3 to 5 days. Daily dockets are online at www.tmc-clerk.com/case/default.asp. Direct email requests to tmc-clerk@noris.org.

Madison County

Common Pleas Court PO Box 557, 1 N Main St, London, OH 43140; 740-852-9776; probate phone: 740-852-0756; fax: 740-845-1778; 8AM-4PM (EST). *Felony, Civil Actions over $10,000, Probate.*
www.co.madison.oh.us/10206.html
General Information: Probate court is a separate court at the same address, Rm 205. Probate Fax: 740-852-7134. No secret indictment records released. Will fax documents for fee; 10 page limit. Court makes copy: $.25 per page. No certification fee. Payee: Clerk of Court. Personal checks accepted, credit cards are not. Prepayment required.

Civil Name Search: Access: In person, online. Visitors must perform in person searches themselves. Civil records in books since 1981. Civil PAT goes back to 2/2001. Search probate records (but no civil records) at http://12.32.69.179/Search/.

Criminal Name Search: Access: In person only. Visitors must perform in person searches themselves. Required to search: name, years to search; also helpful: address, DOB, SSN. Criminal records in books since 1981. Criminal PAT goes back to same as civil.

Madison County Municipal Court PO Box 646, 1 N Main St, London, OH 43140; 740-852-1669; fax: 740-852-0812; 8AM-4PM (EST). *Misdemeanor, Civil Actions under $15,000, Eviction, Small Claims.* www.madisonmunict.com/

General Information: No probation records released. Will not fax out documents. Court makes copy: $.25 per page. Certification fee: $1.00 per cert. Payee: Madison County Municipal Court. Only cashiers checks and money orders accepted. Prepayment required. Mail requests: SASE required.

Civil Name Search: Access: Phone, fax, mail, in person, online. Both court and visitors may perform in person name searches. No search fee. Civil records on computer from 1989, prior in books indexed from 1958. Mail turnaround time up to 1 week. Civil PAT goes back to 1985. Access civil case record free at www.madisonmunict.com/search.shtml. Shows case number, docket entry, charge, case type.

Criminal Name Search: Access: Phone, fax, mail, in person, online. Both court and visitors may perform in person name searches. No search fee. Required to search: name, years to search, DOB, SSN. Criminal records computerized from 1989, prior in books indexed from 1958. Mail turnaround time up to 1 week. Criminal PAT goes back to same as civil. Access criminal case record free at www.madisonmunict.com/search.shtml. Shows case number, docket entry, charge, case type. Includes traffic. Online results show middle initial, DOB, address.

Mahoning County

Common Pleas Court 120 Market St, 2nd Fl, Youngstown, OH 44503; 330-740-2104; probate phone: 330-740-2310; fax: 330-740-2105; 8AM-4:30PM (EST). *Felony, Civil Actions over $15,000, Probate.* www.mahoningcountyoh.gov/tabid/810/default.aspx

General Information: Probate court is a separate court at the same address, 1st Fl, fax-330-740-2325. Online identifiers in results same as on public terminal. No secret indictment records released. Will not fax out documents. Court makes copy: $.10 per page. Certification fee: $1.00 per cert. Payee: Clerk of Court. Personal checks accepted, credit cards are not. Prepayment required. Mail requests: SASE required for criminal.

Civil Name Search: Access: In person, online. Visitors must perform in person searches themselves. Required to search: name, years to search; also helpful: address. Civil records on computer from 1989, prior in books indexed from 1946. Civil PAT goes back to 1989. For online access, see criminal section. Judgments can be printed off the internet.

Criminal Name Search: Access: Mail, fax, in person, online. Both court and visitors may perform in person name searches. No search fee. Required to search: name, years to search; also helpful: address, DOB, SSN. Criminal records computerized from 1989, prior in books indexed from 1946. Mail turnaround time 2 weeks. Criminal PAT goes back to same as civil. Access integrated justice system cases back to 1995 free at http://courts.mahoningcountyoh.gov/. Attorney searching also available. Online results show middle initial, DOB.

Campbell Municipal Court 351 Tenney Ave, Campbell, OH 44405; 330-755-2165; fax: 330-750-3058; 8AM-4PM (EST). *Misdemeanor, Civil Actions under $15,000, Eviction, Small Claims.*

General Information: No sealed records released. Will fax documents to police agencies only. Court makes copy: $.50 per page. Certification fee: $20.00 includes copies. Payee: Campbell Municipal Court. Only cashiers checks and money orders accepted. No credit cards accepted. Prepayment required. Mail requests: SASE required.

Civil Name Search: Access: Fax, mail, in person. Only the court performs in person name searches; visitors may not. No search fee. Civil records in books from 1950s; on computer back to July 1999. Note: Mail and fax access limited to short searches. Mail turnaround time depends on workload.

Criminal Name Search: Access: Fax, mail, in person. Only the court performs in person name searches; visitors may not. No search fee. Required to search: name, years to search; also helpful: DOB, SSN, signed release. Criminal records in books from 1950s; on computer back to July 1999. Mail turnaround time depends on workload.

County Court #2 127 Boardman Canfield Rd, Boardman, OH 44512; 330-726-5546; fax: 330-740-2035; 8:30AM-4PM (EST). *Misdemeanor, Civil Actions under $15,000, Small Claims.* www.mahoningcountyoh.gov/tabid/810/default.aspx

General Information: Expunged records are not released. Will not fax documents. Court makes copy: $.10 per page. Certification fee: $1.00 per cert. Payee: County Court #2. Personal checks accepted, credit cards are not. Prepayment required. Mail requests: SASE required for mail return of any copies.

Civil Name Search: Access: In person, online. Visitors must perform in person searches themselves. Civil records in books and dockets from 1960; on computer back to 1995. Civil PAT goes back to 1995. For online access, see criminal section.

Criminal Name Search: Access: In person, online. Visitors must perform in person searches themselves. Required to search: name, years to search, DOB, SSN, signed release. Criminal records in books and dockets from 1960; on computer back to 1995. Note: Court will not perform party names searches for in-person requesters. Criminal PAT goes back to 1995. Access integrated justice system cases back to 1995 free at http://courts.mahoningcountyoh.gov/. Attorney searching also available.

County Court #3 605 E Ohio Ave, Sebring, OH 44672; 330-938-9873; fax: 330-938-6518; 8:30AM-4PM (EST). *Misdemeanor, Civil Actions under $15,000, Small Claims.* www.mahoningcountyoh.gov/tabid/810/default.aspx

General Information: No expunged records released. Court makes copy: $.10 per page. Certification fee: $1.00 per cert. Payee: Mahoning County Court #3. Personal checks accepted, credit cards are not. Prepayment required. Mail requests: SASE required.

Civil Name Search: Access: In person, online. Visitors must perform in person searches themselves. Civil records in books from 1958; on computer back to 8/95. Note: Court personnel will not perform name searches. The public can use the docket books to search names. Mail turnaround time 1 week. For online access, see criminal section

Criminal Name Search: Access: Mail, in person, online. Only the court performs in person name searches; visitors may not. Search fee: $5.00. Required to search: name, years to search, DOB; also helpful: SSN. Criminal records in books from 1989; on computer back to 8/95. Mail turnaround time 1 week. Access integrated justice system cases back to 1995 free at http://courts.mahoningcountyoh.gov/. Attorney searching also available.

County Court #4 6000 Mahoning Ave, Austintown, OH 44515-2288; 330-740-2001; fax: 330-740-2036; 8:30AM-4PM (EST). *Misdemeanor, Civil Actions under $15,000, Small Claims.* www.mahoningcountyoh.gov/tabid/810/default.aspx

General Information: Online identifiers in results same as on public terminal. No expunged records released. Will not fax out documents. Court makes copy: $.10 per page. Certification fee: $1.00 per page. Payee: County Court #4. Personal checks accepted, credit cards are not. Prepayment required. Mail requests: SASE required.

Civil Name Search: Access: Fax, mail, in person, online. Both court and visitors may perform in person name searches. No search fee. Civil records in books from the 1940s, on microfiche recent; computerized records since 1996. Note: Phone, fax and mail access limited to out of town requests. Mail turnaround time varies. Civil PAT goes back to 1996. For online access, see criminal section.

Criminal Name Search: Access: Fax, mail, in person, online. Both court and visitors may perform in person name searches. No search fee. Required to search: name, years to search, DOB, SSN, signed release. Criminal records in books from the 1940s, on microfiche rec; computerized records since 1996. Mail turnaround time varies. Criminal PAT goes back to same as civil. Access integrated justice system cases back to 1995 free at http://courts.mahoningcountyoh.gov/. Attorney searching also available. Online results show middle initial, DOB.

County Court #5 72 N Broad St, Canfield, OH 44406; 330-533-3643; fax: 330-740-2034; 8:30AM-4PM (EST). *Misdemeanor, Civil Actions under $15,000, Small Claims.* www.mahoningcountyoh.gov/tabid/810/default.aspx

General Information: No LEADS printout records released. Will fax documents $2.00 1st page, $1.00 each add'l. Court makes copy: $.10 per page. Certification fee: $1.00 per page plus copy fee. Payee: County Court #5. Only cashiers checks and money orders accepted. No credit cards accepted. Prepayment required. Mail requests: SASE required for criminal.

Civil Name Search: Access: In person, online. Visitors must perform in person searches themselves. Required to search: name, years to search; also helpful: address. Civil records on computer since 1995; overall records go back to 1991. Civil PAT goes back to 1995. For online access, see criminal section.

Criminal Name Search: Access: Fax, mail, in person, online. Both court and visitors may perform in person name searches. Search fee: $5.00 per name. Fee includes certification. Required to search: name, years to search; also helpful: DOB, SSN. Criminal records on computer since 1995; overall records go back to 1991. Mail turnaround time 5-7 days. Criminal PAT goes back to same as civil. Access integrated justice system cases back to

1995 free at http://courts.mahoningcountyoh.gov/. Attorney searching also available.

Struthers Municipal Court 6 Elm St, Struthers, OH 44471; 330-755-1800; criminal phone: x114; civil phone: x113; fax: 330-755-2790; 8AM-4PM; Public access only- T & Th (EST). *Misdemeanor, Civil Actions under $15,000, Eviction, Small Claims.* www.cityofstruthers.com/court.aspx

General Information: Alternative website is www.strutherscourt.com/. This court services several surrounding jurisdictions- Lowellville, Poland Village, Poland Township, New Middletown, and Springfield Township No pending case records released. Will fax documents no fee. Court makes copy: $.25 per page. Self serve copy: same. Certification fee: $10.00. Payee: Municipal Court. Only cashiers checks and money orders accepted. No credit cards accepted. Prepayment required. Mail requests: SASE required.

Civil Name Search: Access: Mail, in person, online. Both court and visitors may perform in person name searches. No search fee. Civil records in books since 1965; on computer since 1996. Mail turnaround time 2-3 days. Civil PAT goes back to 1996. Public terminal up on Tuesdays and Thursdays. Access court records at http://74.219.105.102/searchMC.shtml - records go back to 1996.

Criminal Name Search: Access: Mail, in person, online. Both court and visitors may perform in person name searches. No search fee. Required to search: name, years to search; also helpful: SSN, DOB, signed release. Criminal records in books since 1965; on computer since 1996. Mail turnaround time 2-3 days. Criminal PAT goes back to same as civil. Public terminal up on Tuesdays and Thursdays. Terminal results include SSN. Access court records at http://74.219.105.102/searchMC.shtml - records go back to 1996. Online results show middle initial.

Youngstown Municipal Court 26 S Phelps St, Youngstown, OH 44503; criminal phone: 330-742-8860; fax: 330-742-8786; 8AM-4PM (EST). *Misdemeanor, Civil Actions under $15,000, Eviction, Small Claims, Traffic.* www.youngstownmuniclerk.com/

General Information: The Court handles most traffic, criminal and civil cases that occur within the boundaries of the City of Youngstown. Will fax documents to local or toll free line. Court makes copy: $.10 per page. Certification fee: $1.00. Fee is $5.00 for Certification of Judgment. Payee: Municipal Court. Cashiers checks and money orders accepted. Visa cards accepted. Mail requests: SASE required.

Civil Name Search: Access: Fax, mail, in person, online. Civil records in books since 1970; on computer since 1998. Mail turnaround time 1-2 days. Civil PAT goes back to 1998. Access cases record data back to 1998 free at www.youngstownmunicipalcourt.com/eservices/app/home.page.2. Search by name, case number, attorney or ticket number.

Criminal Name Search: Access: Fax, mail, in person, online. Both court and visitors may perform in person name searches. No search fee. Required to search: name, years to search, DOB; also helpful: SSN. Criminal records go back to 1966; kept available since 1994 on docket books, microfiche; also on computer since 1998. Mail turnaround time 1 day. Criminal PAT goes back to 1998. Access cases record data back to 1998 free at www.youngstownmunicipalcourt.com/eservices/app/home.page.2. Search by name, case number, attorney or ticket number. Online results show middle initial.

Marion County

Common Pleas Court 100 N Main St, Marion, OH 43301-1823; 740-223-4270; fax: 740-223-4279; 8:30AM-4:30PM (EST). *Felony, Civil Actions over $10,000.* http://mcoprx.co.marion.oh.us/

General Information: No sealed, expunged records released. Fee to fax out file $2.00 per transmission and $1.00 per page. Court makes copy: $.10 per page. Self serve copy: same. Certification fee: $1.00. Payee: Marion County Clerk of Courts. Personal checks accepted. Major credit cards accepted, in person only. Prepayment required. Mail requests: SASE required.

Civil Name Search: Access: Mail, in person, online. Visitors must perform in person searches themselves. Search fee: None - you supply case number in mail requests. Civil records on computer from 1991, prior in books since 1886. Mail turnaround time 3-5 days. Civil PAT goes back to 1991. Court record access free at http://courtrecords.co.marion.oh.us/pa/.

Criminal Name Search: Access: Mail, in person, online. Visitors must perform in person searches themselves. No search fee. Required to search: name, years to search; also helpful: DOB, SSN. Criminal records computerized from 1991, prior in books since 1886. Note: Mail requests accepted if you have the case number and request a specific document. Mail turnaround time 3-5 days. Criminal PAT goes back to same as civil. Court record access free at http://courtrecords.co.marion.oh.us/pa/.

Marion Municipal Court 233 W Center St, Marion, OH 43302-0326; 740-387-0439; criminal phone: 740-382-4031; civil phone: 740-383-6103; fax: 740-382-5274; 8:30AM-4:30PM (EST). *Misdemeanor, Civil Actions under $15,000, Eviction, Small Claims.* www.marionmunicipalcourt.org

General Information: Will fax out documents no fee. Court makes copy: $.10 per page. Certification fee: $5.00. Payee: Municipal Court. Cashiers checks and money orders accepted. Credit cards accepted. Prepayment required. Mail requests: SASE required for criminal.

Civil Name Search: Access: In person, online. Visitors must perform in person searches themselves. Civil records on computer since 1995. Public use terminal available, records go back to 1994. Online case searching available at www.marionmunicipalcourt.org/search.shtml.

Criminal Name Search: Access: Mail, in person, online. Both court and visitors may perform in person name searches. No search fee. Required to search: name, years to search; also helpful: DOB, SSN. Criminal records computerized from 1986, prior in books. Mail turnaround time 7 days. Public use terminal available, crim records go back to 1994. Online case searching available at www.marionmunicipalcourt.org/search.shtml.

Probate Court 222 W Center St, Marion, OH 43302; probate phone: 740-223-4260; fax: 740-223-4269; 8:30AM-4:30PM. *Probate.*

Medina County

Common Pleas Court 93 Public Sq, Rm 129, Medina, OH 44256; 330-725-9722; criminal phone: 330-725-9721; civil phone: 330-725-9722; probate phone: 330-725-9703; fax: 330-764-8454; 8AM-4:30PM (EST). *Felony, Civil Actions over $10,000, Probate.* www.clerk.medinaco.org/

General Information: Probate court is a separate court at the same address. Probate records not managed by the CP clerk. Will not fax documents. Court makes copy: $.25 per page. Certification fee: $1.00 per page plus copy fee; Authentication-Certificate of Record-$5.00. Payee: Clerk of Court. Personal checks accepted. Prepayment required. Mail requests: SASE required.

Civil Name Search: Access: Mail, in person, online. Both court and visitors may perform in person name searches. No search fee. Civil records on computer from 10/92, in books to early 1960s, prior archived. Mail turnaround time 1-2 days. Civil PAT goes back to 1992. Online access is the same as criminal, see below.

Criminal Name Search: Access: Mail, in person, online. Both court and visitors may perform in person name searches. No search fee. Criminal records computerized from 10/92, in books to early 1960s, prior archived. Mail turnaround time 1-2 days. Criminal PAT goes back to 1992. Search court documents, motion dockets, sexual predator judgments and court notices at the web page.

Medina Municipal Court 135 N Elmwood, Medina, OH 44256; 330-723-3287; fax: 330-225-1108; 8AM-4:30PM (EST). *Misdemeanor, Civil Actions under $15,000, Eviction, Small Claims.* www.medinamunicipalcourt.org

General Information: No expunged records released. Court makes copy: $.10 per page. Certification fee: $1.50. Payee: Medina Municipal Court. Personal checks accepted. Visa/MC accepted for criminal and traffic records only. Prepayment required. Mail requests: SASE required.

Civil Name Search: Access: Mail, in person, online. Both court and visitors may perform in person name searches. No search fee. Civil records on computer from 1986, prior in books. Mail turnaround time 7-14 days. Civil PAT goes back to 1987. Access the online Civil Case Lookup free from home page or go direct to http://24.144.216.42/connection/court/index.xsp.

Criminal Name Search: Access: Mail, online, in person. Visitors must perform in person searches themselves. No search fee. Required to search: name, years to search; also helpful: address, DOB, SSN. Criminal records computerized from 1986, prior in books. Mail turnaround time 7-14 days. Criminal PAT goes back to same as civil. Access the online Criminal and Traffic Case Lookup free from home page or go direct to http://24.144.216.42/connection/court/index.xsp. Online results show name only.

Wadsworth Municipal Court 120 Maple St, Wadsworth, OH 44281-1825; 330-335-1596; fax: 330-335-2723; 8AM-4PM (EST). *Misdemeanor, Civil Actions under $15,000, Eviction, Small Claims.* www.wadsworthmunicipalcourt.com/main.htm

General Information: Covers City of Wadsworth and Villages of Gloria Glens, Lodi, Seville, Westfield Center, also Townships of Guilford, Harrisville, Homer, Sharon, Wadsworth, and Westfield. No search warrant records released. No fee to fax documents locally only. Court makes copy: $.05 per page after first 25 pages. Certification fee: $1.00. Payee: Wadsworth Municipal Court. Personal checks accepted. Credit cards accepted. Prepayment required. Mail requests: SASE required.

Civil Name Search: Access: Fax, mail, in person, online. Both court and visitors may perform in person name searches. No search fee. Civil records on computer from 3/90, prior in books. Mail turnaround time 2-4 days. Civil PAT goes back to 1990. Access civil case lookups and queries free at www.wadsworthmunicipalcourt.com/index.php?folder=1&page=45.

Criminal Name Search: Access: Fax, mail, in person, online. Both court and visitors may perform in person name searches. No search fee. Required to search: name, years to search; also helpful: address, DOB, SSN.

Criminal records computerized from 3/90, prior in books. Mail turnaround time up to 1 week. Criminal PAT goes back to same as civil. Online access to criminal case and traffic lookups and case queries is the same as civil, see above.

Meigs County

Common Pleas Court Clerk, PO Box 151, Pomeroy, OH 45769; 740-992-5290; fax: 740-992-4429; 8:30AM-4:30PM (EST). *Felony, Civil Actions over $3,000.*

General Information: Court may offer online access to court records in 2011. No secret records released. Will fax specific doc to local or toll-free number. Court makes copy: $.25 per page. Certification fee: $1.00. Payee: Clerk of Court. Personal checks accepted, credit cards are not. Prepayment required.

Civil Name Search: Access: In person only. Visitors must perform in person searches themselves. Required to search: name, years to search; also helpful: address. Civil records on computer since 1996, in books to 1800s. Note: Will assist in person searchers. Civil PAT goes back to 1996.

Criminal Name Search: Access: In person only. Visitors must perform in person searches themselves. Required to search: name, years to search, DOB; also helpful: address, SSN. Criminal records on computer since 1996, in books to 1800s. Note: Court will assist in person searchers. Criminal PAT goes back to same as civil.

Meigs County Court 100 E 2nd St, Rm 304, Pomeroy, OH 45769; 740-992-2279; fax: 740-992-4570; 8:30AM-4:30PM (EST). *Misdemeanor, Civil Actions under $15,000, Small Claims.*

General Information: No sealed records released. Will not fax out case files. Court makes copy: $.25 per page. Certification fee: $2.00 includes copy fee. Payee: Meigs County Court. Personal checks accepted, credit cards are not. Prepayment required.

Civil Name Search: Access: Fax, in person, online. Only the court performs in person name searches; visitors may not. Civil records on computer from 8/90, prior in docket books. Note: Phone access limited to records from 1990 to present. Access civil records free at http://docket.webxsol.com/meigs/index.html.

Criminal Name Search: Access: Fax, in person, online. Only the court performs in person name searches; visitors may not. No search fee. Required to search: name, years to search, DOB, SSN, signed release. Criminal records computerized from 8/90, prior in docket books. Note: Phone access limited to records from 1990 to present. Access criminal records free at http://docket.webxsol.com/meigs/index.html.

Probate Court 100 E 2nd St, Pomeroy, OH 45769-1030; probate phone: 740-992-3096; fax: 740-992-6727; 8:30AM-4:30PM. *Probate.* www.meigsprobatejuvenilecourt.org/

Mercer County

Common Pleas Court 101 N Main St, Rm 205, PO Box 28, Celina, OH 45822; 419-586-6461; probate phone: 419-586-8779; fax: 419-586-5826; 8:30AM-4PM (EST). *Felony, Civil Actions over $10,000, Probate.* www.mercercountyohio.org/clerk/

General Information: Probate court is a separate court at the same address, Rm 307. Probate fax- 419-586-4506. Email questions to clerk@mercercountyohio.org. No juvenile or sealed records released. Will fax specific document for $3.00 for 1st page; $1.00 for each add'l page. Court makes copy: $.25 per page. Certification fee: $1.00. Payee: Clerk of Court. Personal checks accepted, credit cards are not. Prepayment required.

Civil Name Search: Access: In person, online. Visitors must perform in person searches themselves. Required to search: name, years to search; also helpful: address. Civil records on computer back to 1997, microfiche up to and including 1985, prior in books. Civil PAT goes back to 1997. Online access for the public available from the home page.

Criminal Name Search: Access: In person, online. Visitors must perform in person searches themselves. Required to search: name, years to search; also helpful: address, DOB, SSN. Criminal records computerized from 1997, microfiche up to and including 1985, prior in books. Criminal PAT goes back to same as civil. Online access available for the public from the home page.

Celina Municipal Court PO Box 362, Celina, OH 45822; 419-586-6491; fax: 419-586-4735; 8AM-4:30PM (EST). *Misdemeanor, Civil Actions under $15,000, Eviction, Small Claims.*

General Information: No confidential information released. Will fax documents for $.25 per fax plus $.05 per page. Court makes copy: $.05 per page. Self serve copy: $.25 per page for copies that are not public record. Certification fee: $1.00 per page. Payee: Municipal Court. In-state Personal checks, Visa/MC accepted. Prepayment required. Mail requests: SASE required.

Civil Name Search: Access: Fax, mail, in person. Both court and visitors may perform in person name searches. No search fee. Required to search: name, years to search; also helpful: address. Civil records on computer from

1990, prior in books. Mail turnaround time 2-3 days. Civil PAT goes back to 1990.

Criminal Name Search: Access: Fax, mail, in person. Both court and visitors may perform in person name searches. No search fee. Required to search: name, years to search; also helpful: address, DOB, SSN. Criminal records are on computer since 1989, prior found in books and files. Mail turnaround time 2-3 days. Criminal PAT goes back to 1989. One may search using SSN, but results do not include SSN.

Miami County

Common Pleas Court & Court of Appeals Safety Bldg, 201 W Main St, 3rd Fl, Troy, OH 45373; 937-440-6010; probate phone: 937-440-6050; fax: 937-440-6011; 8AM-4PM (EST). *Felony, Civil Actions over $10,000, Probate.*

General Information: Probate court is a separate court at the same address, 2nd Fl. Probate fax- 937-440-3529 No expunged or sealed records released. Will fax documents $1.00 each. Court makes copy: $.25 per page. Certification fee: $1.00 plus copy fee. Payee: Miami County Clerk of Courts. Personal checks accepted, credit cards are not. Prepayment required. Mail requests: SASE required.

Civil Name Search: Access: Fax, mail, in person. Both court and visitors may perform in person name searches. Search fee: $5.00 per name. Required to search: name, years to search; also helpful: address. Civil records in books for past 30 years, prior are archived; on computer since 1984. Mail turnaround time 1-2 days. Civil PAT goes back to 1989.

Criminal Name Search: Access: Fax, mail, in person. Both court and visitors may perform in person name searches. Search fee: $5.00 per name. Required to search: name, years to search, DOB, SSN; also helpful: address. Criminal records in books for past 30 years, prior are archived; on computer since 1984. Mail turnaround time 1-2 days. Criminal PAT goes back to same as civil.

Miami County Municipal Court 201 W Main St, Courthouse, Troy, OH 45373; 937-440-3918; criminal phone: 937-440-3910; civil phone: 937-440-3919; criminal fax: 937-440-3911; civil fax: 8AM-4PM; 8AM-4PM (EST). *Misdemeanor, Civil Actions under $15,000, Eviction, Small Claims.* www.co.miami.oh.us/muni/index.htm

General Information: If the SSN is not provided by the party doing the search, the court personnel will mask the SSN before providing copies. Online identifiers in results same as on public terminal. No search warrant records released. Will fax documents for no fee. Court makes copy: $.05 per page. Self serve copy: none. Certification fee: $2.00 per page. Payee: Municipal Court. Local Personal checks accepted, credit cards are not. Prepayment required. Mail requests: SASE required.

Civil Name Search: Access: Mail, in person, online. Both court and visitors may perform in person name searches. Search fee: $5.00 per name. Civil records in books go back 25 years; on computer back to 11/89. Mail turnaround time 2-3 days. Civil PAT goes back to 11/1989. Online access to records is free at www.co.miami.oh.us/pa/index.htm.

Criminal Name Search: Access: Mail, in person, online. Both court and visitors may perform in person name searches. Search fee: $5.00 per name. Required to search: name, years to search; also helpful: address. Criminal records computerized from 1985, prior in books. Mail turnaround time 2-3 days. Criminal PAT goes back to 1986. Online access to records is free at www.co.miami.oh.us/pa/index.htm. Online results show middle initial, DOB.

Monroe County

Common Pleas Court 101 N Main St, Rm 26, Woodsfield, OH 43793; 740-472-0761; probate phone: 740-472-1654; fax: 740-472-2549; 8:30AM-4:30PM (EST). *Felony, Civil Actions over $3,000, Probate.*

General Information: Probate court is a separate court at the same address, Rm 39. No secret indictment records released. Fee to fax out file $2.00 per page. Court makes copy: $.25 per page. Certification fee: $1.00 per page plus copy fee. Payee: Clerk of Court. Personal checks accepted, credit cards are not. Prepayment required. Mail requests: SASE required for criminal.

Civil Name Search: Access: In person only. Visitors must perform in person searches themselves. Required to search: name, years to search; also helpful: address. Civil records in books since 1800; computerized records from 11/18/02 to present. Civil PAT goes back to 11/2002.

Criminal Name Search: Access: Mail, fax, in person. Both court and visitors may perform in person name searches. Search fee: $2.00 per name. Clerk of Courts will search more than one name but will charge $2.00 per name. Required to search: name, years to search; also helpful: address, DOB, SSN. Criminal records in books since 1800; computerized records from 11/18/02 to present. Note: The court will not do party names searches for in-person requesters. Mail turnaround time 3 days. Criminal PAT goes back to same as civil. Terminal results include SSN.

County Court 101 N Main St, Rm 12, Woodsfield, OH 43793; 740-472-5181; fax: 740-472-2526; 9AM-N, 1-4:30PM (EST). *Misdemeanor, Civil Actions under $15,000, Small Claims, Evictions.*
www.monroecountyohio.com/County%20Court.html
General Information: No copy fee. Certification fee: $1.00 per page. Payee: Monroe County Court. No personal checks or credit cards accepted. Prepayment required. Mail requests: SASE required.
Civil Name Search: Access: Phone, mail, in person. Both court and visitors may perform in person name searches. No search fee. Civil records in books, indexed back to 1950; on computer back to 8/1999. Mail turnaround time 1-2 days. Civil PAT goes back to 1999.
Criminal Name Search: Access: Phone, mail, in person. Both court and visitors may perform in person name searches. No search fee. Criminal records in books, indexed back to 1979; on computer back to 1999. Mail turnaround time 1-2 days. Criminal PAT goes back to same as civil.

Montgomery County

Common Pleas Court 41 N Perry St, County Clerk of Courts, Dayton, OH 45422; 937-496-7602 (records); criminal phone: 937-225-4536; civil phone: 937-225-4512; probate phone: 937-225-4640; criminal fax: 937-496-7581; civil fax: 8:30AM-4:30PM; 8:30AM-4:30PM (EST). *Felony, Civil Actions over $10,000, Probate.*
www.clerk.co.montgomery.oh.us/
General Information: Probate court is a separate court at the same address (PO Box 972). Domestic Relations phone- 937-4225-4562, same address, Room 104. Online identifiers in results same as on public terminal. No sealed records released. Will fax documents to local or toll-free number. Court makes copy: $.10 per page. Self serve copy: same. Certification fee: $1.00 plus copy fees. Cert fee includes copies. Payee: Clerk of Court. Personal checks accepted, credit cards are not. Prepayment required.
Civil Name Search: Access: Mail, in person, online. Both court and visitors may perform in person name searches. No search fee. Required to search: name, years to search; also helpful: address. Civil records on computer from 1974, prior in books. Note: Address mail requests to "Montgomery County Clerk of Court Civil Records." Mail turnaround time 2 weeks. Civil PAT goes back to 1997. Results may include address if on originating documents. Online access to the Courts countywide PRO system is free at www.clerk.co.montgomery.oh.us/legal/records.cfm. Access probate court-related records free at www.mcohio.org/government/probate/prodcfm/case_search_main.cfm.
Criminal Name Search: Access: In person, online. Visitors must perform in person searches themselves. Required to search: name, years to search; also helpful: address, DOB, SSN. Criminal records computerized from 1997s, prior in books. Criminal PAT goes back to 1997. Results may include address if on originating documents. Online access to the Courts countywide PRO system is free at www.clerk.co.montgomery.oh.us/legal/records.cfm. Online results show middle initial.

Dayton Municipal Court - Criminal Division 301 W 3rd St, Rm 331, Dayton, OH 45402; 937-333-4315; criminal fax: 937-333-4490; civil fax: 8AM-4:30PM; 8AM-4:30PM (EST). *Misdemeanor.*
www.daytonmunicipalcourt.org
General Information: Online identifiers in results same as on public terminal. All records are public. Will not fax documents. Court makes copy: $.25 per page. No certification fee. Payee: Dayton Municipal Court. Personal checks accepted. Credit cards accepted. Prepayment required.
Criminal Name Search: Access: Phone, in person, online. Visitors must perform in person searches themselves. No search fee. Required to search: name, years to search, DOB; also helpful: address, SSN, signed release. Criminal records computerized from 1992, prior in books. Note: Court is known to allow very limited phone access. Public use terminal has crim records back to 1992. Online access to municipal court records is free at www.daytonmunicipalcourt.org/scripts/rgw.dll/Docket; includes traffic and civil. Online results show name, DOB.

Municipal Court - Eastern District 6111 Taylorsville Rd, Huber Heights, OH 45424; 937-496-7231; civil phone: 937-225-5824; fax: 937-496-7236; 8Am-4PM M-W,F; N-7PM Th (EST). *Misdemeanor, Civil Actions under $15,000, Small Claims under $3,000.*
http://mccountycourts.org/Courts/Index.aspx?COURTID=2
General Information: No confidential, forensic evaluation or medical records released. No fee to fax documents. Court makes copy: $.25 per page. Certification fee: $1.00 per cert. Payee: Municipal Court, Eastern Division. Business checks accepted. Major credit cards accepted. Prepayment required. Mail requests: SASE required.
Civil Name Search: Access: Phone, fax, mail, in person, online. Both court and visitors may perform in person name searches. No search fee. Required to search: name, years to search; also helpful: address. Civil records on computer from 1992, prior in books back to 1974. Mail turnaround time

2-7 days. Search countywide records online at www.clerk.co.montgomery.oh.us/.
Criminal Name Search: Access: Phone, fax, mail, in person, online. Both court and visitors may perform in person name searches. No search fee. Required to search: name, years to search; also helpful: address, DOB, SSN. Criminal records computerized from 1992, prior in books back to 1974. Mail turnaround time 2-7 days. Search countywide records online at www.clerk.co.montgomery.oh.us/.

Municipal Court, Western Division 195 S Clayton Rd, New Lebanon, OH 45345-9601; 937-687-9099; fax: 937-687-7119; 8AM-4PM T-TH; 10AM-6PM M; 9AM-4PM F (EST). *Misdemeanor, Civil Actions under $15,000, Small Claims.*
www.clerk.co.montgomery.oh.us
General Information: No medical, PSI report or LEADS print-out records released. Will fax documents to local or toll-free number. Court makes copy: $.10 per page. Certification fee: $1.00. Payee: Clerk of Courts. Personal checks accepted. Credit cards accepted. Prepayment required. Mail requests: SASE required.
Civil Name Search: Access: Mail, in person, online. Both court and visitors may perform in person name searches. No search fee. Civil records on computer from 2/92, prior in books, Archives 937-225-6366. Mail turnaround time 2-3 days. Results include company name, case number. Search countywide records online at www.clerk.co.montgomery.oh.us/.
Criminal Name Search: Access: Mail, in person, online. Both court and visitors may perform in person name searches. No search fee. Required to search: name, years to search; also helpful: SSN. Criminal records computerized from 2/92, prior in books, Archives 937-225-6366. Mail turnaround time 2-3 days. Results include company name, case number. Search countywide records online at www.clerk.co.montgomery.oh.us/.

Dayton Municipal Court - Civil Division 301 W 3rd St, PO Box 10700, Dayton, OH 45402-0968; 937-333-4471; fax: 937-333-4468; 8AM-4:30PM (EST). *Civil Actions under $15,000, Eviction, Small Claims.*
www.daytonmunicipalcourt.com/
General Information: No expunged case records released. Will fax documents to local or toll-free number. Court makes copy: $.25 per page. Certification fee: $1.00. Payee: Clerk of Court. Personal checks, Visa/MC accepted. Prepayment required. Mail requests: SASE required.
Civil Name Search: Access: Phone, fax, mail, in person, online. Both court and visitors may perform in person name searches. No search fee. Required to search: name, years to search; also helpful: address. Civil records on computer back to 1998, prior in books to 1977. Mail turnaround time 2-3 days. Public use terminal has civil records back to 1998. Online access to civil Municipal court records free at www.daytonwejis.com/PA/CvSearch.cfm.

Kettering Municipal Court 2325 Wilmington Pike, Kettering, OH 45420; 937-296-2461; fax: 937-534-7017; 8:30AM-4:30PM (EST). *Misdemeanor, Civil Actions under $15,000, Eviction, Small Claims.*
www.ketteringmunicipalcourt.com
General Information: No expungment records released. Will fax documents to local or toll free line. Court makes copy: $.05 per page. Certification fee: $2.50 per page. Payee: Kettering Municipal Court. Personal and business checks accepted. Credit cards accepted. Prepayment required. Mail requests: SASE required.
Civil Name Search: Access: Phone, mail, fax, in person, online. Both court and visitors may perform in person name searches. No search fee. Civil records on computer from 1988, prior in books. Civil PAT goes back to 1988. Access case lookups free from a vendor at http://caselookup.ketteringmunicipalcourt.com/connection/court/. There is a strong disclaimer that the court does not warrant the accuracy of the data.
Criminal Name Search: Access: Phone, mail, fax, in person, online. Both court and visitors may perform in person name searches. No search fee. Required to search: name, years to search, DOB; also helpful: SSN. Criminal records computerized from 1988, prior in books. Criminal PAT goes back to 1988. Online access same as civil, see above.

Miamisburg Municipal Court 10 N 1st St, Miamisburg, OH 45342; 937-866-2203; fax: 937-866-0135; 8AM-4PM (EST). *Misdemeanor, Civil Actions under $15,000, Eviction, Small Claims.*
www.miamisburgcourts.com
General Information: No police reports, search warrants with no returns records released. Will fax documents to local or toll free line. Court makes copy: $.05 per page. Certification fee: $1.00; $10.00 for exemplified copy of judgment. Payee: Miamisburg Municipal Court. Personal checks, Visa/MC accepted. Prepayment required. Mail requests: SASE required.
Civil Name Search: Access: Mail, in person, online. Visitors must perform in person searches themselves. No search fee. Required to search: name, years to search; also helpful: address. Civil records on computer from 1988, prior in books. Note: Call in advance to schedule in person

searching. Mail request requires SASE. Access case lookup options and case schedules for free at http://64.56.106.117/connection/court/.

Criminal Name Search: Access: Mail, in person, online. Only the court performs in person name searches; visitors may not. No search fee. Required to search: name, years to search; also helpful: address, DOB, SSN. Criminal records computerized from 1988, prior in books. Note: Call in advance to schedule in person searching. Mail request requires SASE. Mail turnaround time 1-2 weeks. Access case lookup options and case schedules for free at http://64.56.106.117/connection/court/.

Oakwood Municipal Court 30 Park Ave, Dayton, OH 45419; 937-293-3058; fax: 937-297-2939; 8AM-4:30PM (EST). *Misdemeanor, Civil Actions under $15,000, Eviction, Small Claims.*

General Information: No sealed, expunged or confidential records released. Will fax documents to local or toll free line. Court makes copy: $.10 per page. Certification fee: $.50. Payee: City of Oakwood. Local checks accepted. No credit cards accepted. Mail requests: SASE required.

Civil Name Search: Access: Mail, in person, fax. Only the court performs in person name searches; visitors may not. No search fee. Required to search: name, years to search; also helpful: address. Civil records in books since 1980s. Mail turnaround time 1-2 weeks.

Criminal Name Search: Access: Mail, in person, phone. Only the court performs in person name searches; visitors may not. No search fee. Required to search: name, years to search; also helpful: address, DOB, SSN. Criminal records in books since 1990s. Note: Address mail search requests to the Police Records Section. Will do phone verifications on a single name. Mail turnaround time 1-2 weeks.

Vandalia Municipal Court PO Box 429, 245 James Bohanan Dr, Justice Ctr, 2nd Fl, Vandalia, OH 45377; 937-898-3996; fax: 937-898-6648; 8AM-4PM (EST). *Misdemeanor, Civil Actions under $15,000, Eviction, Small Claims.* www.vandaliacourt.com

General Information: No medical, psychological reports or domestic violence report records released. Will fax documents to local or toll-free number. Court makes copy: $1.00 per page. No certification fee. Payee: Clerk of Court. Business checks accepted. Major credit cards accepted. Prepayment required. Mail requests: SASE required.

Civil Name Search: Access: Phone, fax, mail, in person, online. Both court and visitors may perform in person name searches. Search fee: $1.00 per page for complete print out from clerk's computer. Civil records on computer from 1986. Mail turnaround time 7 days. Civil PAT goes back to 1986. Search records, including traffic, at http://docket.vandaliacourt.com/.

Criminal Name Search: Access: Fax, mail, in person, online. Both court and visitors may perform in person name searches. Search fee: $.10 per page for complete print out from clerk's computer. Required to search: name, years to search, DOB, SSN. Criminal records computerized from 1986. Mail turnaround time 7 days. Criminal PAT available. Search records, including traffic, at http://docket.vandaliacourt.com/.

Dayton Municipal Court - Traffic Division PO Box 10700, 301 W 3rd St, Dayton, OH 45402; 937-333-4313; fax: 937-333-7558; 8AM-4:30PM (EST). *Misdemeanor, Traffic.* www.daytonmunicipalcourt.org

General Information: It is difficult for the court to provide case information prior to 1995. Search dockets free online at www.daytonmunicipalcourt.org/scripts/rgw.dll/Docket.

Morgan County

Common Pleas Court 19 E Main St, McConnelsville, OH 43756; 740-962-4752; probate phone: 740-962-2861; fax: 740-962-4522; 8AM-4PM M-F (EST). *Felony, Civil Actions over $3,000, Probate.*

General Information: Above number is for Clerk. The Common Pleas Court can be reached at 740-962-3371. Court services closed on Fridays. Probate court is a separate court at the same address. No secret indictment records released. Will not fax documents. No copy fee. Certification fee: $1.00 per page. Payee: Clerk of Court. Personal checks accepted, credit cards are not. Prepayment required. Mail requests: SASE required.

Civil Name Search: Access: Mail, in person. Visitors must perform in person searches themselves. Search fee: $2.00 per name. Required to search: name, years to search; also helpful: address. Civil records in books, some back to 1850. Mail turnaround time 1-3 days. Civil PAT goes back to 2001.

Criminal Name Search: Access: Mail, in person. Both court and visitors may perform in person name searches. Search fee: $2.00 per name. Required to search: name, years to search; also helpful: address, DOB, SSN. Criminal records in books, some back to 1850. Mail turnaround time 1-3 days. Criminal PAT goes back to same as civil.

Morgan County Court 37 E Main St, 2nd Fl, McConnelsville, OH 43756; 740-962-4031; fax: 740-962-2895; 8AM-4PM (EST). *Misdemeanor, Civil Actions under $15,000, Small Claims Under $3,000.*

General Information: The court does not have a web page, but for more information about this county visit www.morgancounty-oh.gov. No fee to fax

documents. Court makes copy: $.10 per page. Self serve copy: same. Certification fee: $1.00. Payee: Morgan County Court. Personal checks accepted. Major credit cards accepted. Prepayment required. Mail requests: SASE required.

Civil Name Search: Access: Fax, mail, in person. Both court and visitors may perform in person name searches. No search fee. Civil records in books from 1950, computerized since 12/02. Mail turnaround time 1-2 days. Civil PAT goes back to 12/2002.

Criminal Name Search: Access: Fax, mail, in person. Both court and visitors may perform in person name searches. No search fee. Required to search: name, years to search, DOB; also helpful: SSN. Criminal records in books from 1950, computerized since 12/02. Mail turnaround time 1-2 days. Criminal PAT goes back to same as civil.

Morrow County

Common Pleas Court 48 E High St, Courthouse, Mount Gilead, OH 43338; 419-947-2085; probate phone: 419-947-5575; fax: 419-947-5421; 8AM-4PM (EST). *Felony, Civil Actions over $3,000, Probate.* http://morrowcommonpleas.com/

General Information: Today's docket available at the website. Probate court is a separate court at the same address. Will fax documents $1.00 per page. Court makes copy: $.35 per page. Self serve copy: same. Certification fee: $1.00 per doc. Payee: Clerk of Court. Personal checks accepted with proper ID. Visa/MC accepted. Prepayment required. Mail requests: SASE required.

Civil Name Search: Access: Phone, fax, mail, in person. Both court and visitors may perform in person name searches. No search fee. Required to search: name, years to search; also helpful: address. Civil records in books from 1960, computerized since 1/02. Mail turnaround time 1 day. Civil PAT goes back to 2002.

Criminal Name Search: Access: Phone, fax, mail, in person. Both court and visitors may perform in person name searches. No search fee. Required to search: name, years to search; also helpful: address, DOB, SSN. Criminal records in books from 1960, computerized since 1/02. Mail turnaround time 5-7 days. Criminal PAT goes back to same as civil.

Municipal Court 48 E High St, Rm A, Mount Gilead, OH 43338; 419-947-5045; civil phone: x237 or x238; fax: 419-946-4070; 7AM-5PM (EST). *Misdemeanor, Civil Actions under $15,000, Small Claims.* www.morrowcountymunict.org/

General Information: No confidential records released. Will fax documents for free. Court makes copy: $1.00 per page. Certification fee: $2.00 per cert. Payee: Morrow County Municipal Court. No Personal checks, Visa/MC accepted. Prepayment required. Mail requests: SASE required for mail return of any copies.

Civil Name Search: Access: Phone, fax, mail, in person. Both court and visitors may perform in person name searches. No search fee. Civil records on computer back to 1997, indexed on books from 1970s, archived from 1960s. Mail turnaround time 1-2 days. Court calendars for the week ahead available www.morrowcountymunict.org/. Site to soon have improved case index searching.

Criminal Name Search: Access: Phone, fax, mail, in person, online. Both court and visitors may perform in person name searches. No search fee. Required to search: name, years to search, DOB, SSN. Criminal records on computer since 1990, indexed on books from 1970s, archived from 1960s. Mail turnaround time 1-2 days. Search upcoming or historical criminal and traffic case records at www.morrowcountymunict.org/.

Muskingum County

Common Pleas Court 401 Main St, Zanesville, OH 43701; 740-455-7104; probate phone: 740-455-7113; fax: 740-455-8245; 8:30AM-4:30PM (EST). *Felony, Civil Actions, Probate.* www.muskingumcounty.org/clerkofcourts.shtm

General Information: As of 1/1/2001, there is no dollar limit on civil actions; prior, the civil action minimum was $15,000. Probate court is a separate court at the same address. Ask court's permission before faxing to court. No grand jury records released. Will not fax documents. Court makes copy: $.10 per page. Self serve copy: same. Certification fee: $1.00 per page include copy fee. Payee: Clerk of Court. Personal checks accepted. Major credit cards accepted. Prepayment required. Mail requests: SASE required.

Civil Name Search: Access: Mail, in person, online. Visitors must perform in person searches themselves. No search fee. Required to search: name, years to search; also helpful: address. Civil records in original files back to 1800s. Mail turnaround time 2 weeks. Civil PAT goes back to 10/17/1994. DOB and address will appear in results only if available. Online access to court records is available at http://clerkofcourts.muskingumcounty.org/PA/. Records indexed back to 1994.

Criminal Name Search: Access: Mail, in person, online. Visitors must perform in person searches themselves. No search fee. Required to search: name, years to search, DOB; also helpful: address, SSN. Criminal docket on books to 1960, original files back to 1800s. Mail turnaround time 2 weeks. Criminal PAT goes back to same as civil. DOB and address will appear in results if they are available. Online access to criminal index is same as civil, above. Online results show name, DOB, address.

County Court 27 N 5th St, Zanesville, OH 43701; 740-455-7138; fax: 740-455-7157; 8AM-4PM (EST). *Misdemeanor, Civil Actions under $15,000, Small Claims.* www.muskingumcountycourt.org
General Information: Online identifiers in results same as on public terminal. No expunged records released. No fee to fax documents. Fax available in emergency only. Court makes copy: $.25 per page. Certification fee: $1.00 per page includes copy fee. Payee: Muskingum County Clerk. Personal checks accepted. Credit cards accepted. Prepayment required. Mail requests: SASE required.
Civil Name Search: Access: Fax, mail, in person, online. Both court and visitors may perform in person name searches. No search fee. Required to search: name, years to search; also helpful: address. Civil records in books from 1958; on computer back to 1995. Mail turnaround time up to 1 week. Civil PAT goes back to 1995. Access to county court records is free at www.muskingumcountycourt.org/sear.html.
Criminal Name Search: Access: Fax, mail, in person, online. Both court and visitors may perform in person name searches. No search fee. Required to search: name, years to search, DOB; also helpful: address, SSN. Criminal records in books from 1958; on computer back to 1995. Mail turnaround time up to 1 week. Criminal PAT goes back to same as civil. Access to county court records is free at www.muskingumcountycourt.org/sear.html. Online results show middle initial, DOB.

Zanesville Municipal Court PO Box 566, 332 South St, Zanesville, OH 43702; 740-454-3269; fax: 740-455-0739; 9:30AM-4:30PM M,T,W,F; 9:30AM-N TH (EST). *Misdemeanor, Civil Actions under $15,000, Eviction, Small Claims.*
www.coz.org/municipal_court.cfm
General Information: Will fax documents no fee. No copy fee. Certification fee: $1.00 per page include copies. Payee: Zanesville Municipal Court. Personal checks accepted. Visa/MC accepted for traffic and criminal only. Prepayment required. Mail requests: SASE required.
Civil Name Search: Access: Mail, in person, online. Only the court performs in person name searches; visitors may not. No search fee. Required to search: name, years to search; also helpful: address. Civil records on computer since 1993. Note: In person searches only available for one or two names. Otherwise, searchers are directed to the webpage. Mail turnaround time 3-5 days. Online access free at http://74.219.84.227/searchMC.shtml
Criminal Name Search: Access: Mail, in person, fax, online. Only the court performs in person name searches; visitors may not. No search fee. Required to search: name, years to search; also helpful: address, DOB, SSN. Criminal records on computer since 1993. Note: In person searches only available for one or two names. Otherwise, researchers are directed to the webpage. Mail turnaround time 3-5 days. Online access is free at http://74.219.84.227/searchMC.shtml and includes traffic and civil searching. Online results show middle initial, DOB.

Noble County

Common Pleas Court 300 Courthouse Sq, Caldwell, OH 43724; 740-732-4408; fax: 740-732-5604; 8AM-4PM M-W; 8AM-N Th; 8AM-6PM F (EST). *Felony, Civil Actions over $3,000.*
General Information: Probate court is a separate court at the same building at 270 Courthouse Sq. No sealed records released. No fee to fax documents. Court makes copy: $.25 per page. Self serve copy: same. Certification fee: $1.00 per page. Payee: Clerk of Court. Personal checks accepted, credit cards are not. Prepayment required. Will bill all court rule copies. Mail requests: SASE required.
Civil Name Search: Access: Phone, fax, mail, in person. Both court and visitors may perform in person name searches. Search fee: $2.00 per name. Required to search: name, years to search; also helpful: address. Civil records in books, archived back to mid-1800s. Recent civil records are computerized. Mail turnaround time 1-2 days. Civil PAT goes back to 7/1997.
Criminal Name Search: Access: Phone, fax, mail, in person. Both court and visitors may perform in person name searches. Search fee: $2.00 per name. Required to search: name, years to search; also helpful: address, DOB, SSN. Criminal records in books, archived back to 1800s. Mail turnaround time 1-2 days. Criminal PAT goes back to same as civil.

Noble County Court 100 Courthouse, Caldwell, OH 43724; 740-732-5795; fax: 740-732-1435; 8:30AM-4PM M-W,F; 8:30AM-N TH (EST). *Misdemeanor, Civil Actions under $15,000, Small Claims.*

General Information: Will fax out documents at no charge. Court makes copy: $.25 per page. Self serve copy: same. Certification fee: $5.00 per document. Payee: County Court. Only cashiers checks and money orders accepted. No credit cards accepted. Mail requests: SASE required.
Civil Name Search: Access: Phone, fax, mail, in person. Both court and visitors may perform in person name searches. No search fee. Civil records in books since 1960, on computer back to 2002. Mail turnaround time same day. Civil PAT goes back to 2002.
Criminal Name Search: Access: Fax, mail, in person. Both court and visitors may perform in person name searches. No search fee. Required to search: name, years to search, DOB; also helpful- SSN, signed release. Criminal records in books since 1960; on computer back to 2002. Mail turnaround time same day. Criminal PAT goes back to same as civil. Terminal results include SSN.

Ottawa County

Common Pleas Court Clerk of Courts, 315 Madison St, Rm 304, Port Clinton, OH 43452; 419-734-6755 (General Division); probate phone: 419-734-6830; fax: 419-734-6875; 8:30AM-4:30PM (EST). *Felony, Civil Actions over $10,000, Probate Appeals.*
www.ottawacocpcourt.com
General Information: Probate court is a separate court at the same address, Rm 306. No sealed records released. Will fax documents for $2.00 fax transmittal fee plus $1.00 per page. Court makes copy: $.15 per page. Certification fee: $1.00. Payee: Clerk of Courts. Personal checks accepted, credit cards are not. Prepayment required. Mail requests: SASE required.
Civil Name Search: Access: Mail, online. Visitors must perform in person searches themselves. No search fee. Required to search: name, years to search; also helpful: address. Civil records on computer from 8/89, prior in books to 1842. Civil PAT goes back to 8/1989. Record search and dockets free at http://96.11.124.244/search.shtml.
Criminal Name Search: Access: Mail, online. Visitors must perform in person searches themselves. No search fee. Criminal records computerized from 8/89, prior in books to 1842. Criminal PAT goes back to same as civil. Record search and dockets free at http://96.11.124.244/search.shtml.

Ottawa County Municipal Court 1860 E Perry St, Port Clinton, OH 43452; 419-734-4143; fax: 419-732-2862; 8:30AM-4:30PM M,T,TH; 7AM-4:30 PM W,F (EST). *Misdemeanor, Civil Actions under $15,000, Eviction, Small Claims.*
www.ottawacountymunicipalcourt.com
General Information: Online identifiers in results same as on public terminal. No sealed records released. Will not fax documents. Court makes copy: $.10 per page. Certification fee: $3.00. Payee: Ottawa County Municipal Court. Only cashiers checks and money orders accepted. No credit cards accepted. Prepayment required.
Civil Name Search: Access: In person, online. Visitors must perform in person searches themselves. Required to search: name, years to search; also helpful: address. Civil records on computer from 1989, prior in books. Civil PAT goes back to 1989. Search record index is at www.ottawacountymunicipalcourt.com/search.php. Includes small claims.
Criminal Name Search: Access: In person, online. Visitors must perform in person searches themselves. Required to search: name, years to search, DOB; also helpful: address, SSN. Criminal records computerized from 1989, prior in books. Criminal PAT goes back to same as civil. Search records at www.ottawacountymunicipalcourt.com/search.php. Includes traffic. Online results show name, DOB.

Paulding County

Common Pleas Court 115 N Williams St, Rm 104, Paulding, OH 45879; 419-399-8210; probate phone: 419-399-8256; fax: 419-399-8248; 8AM-4PM (EST). *Felony, Civil Actions over $3,000, Probate.*
General Information: Probate court is a separate court at the same address, #202. Probate fax- 419-399-8261. This court will not perform name searches for the public. Will fax documents $2.00 fax fee plus $1.00 per page. Court makes copy: $.10 per page. Self serve copy: $.10 per page. Certification fee: $1.00 plus copy fee. Payee: Clerk of Court. Personal checks accepted, credit cards are not. Prepayment required. Mail requests: SASE not required.
Civil Name Search: Access: In person only. Visitors must perform in person searches themselves. Civil records in books, archived from 1800s. Mail turnaround time same day. Civil PAT goes back to 12/2/2002.
Criminal Name Search: Access: In person only. Visitors must perform in person searches themselves. Required to search: name, years to search; also helpful: address, DOB. Criminal records in books, archived from 1800s. Criminal PAT goes back to same as civil.

County Court 201 E Caroline St, #2, Paulding, OH 45879; 419-399-2792; fax: 419-399-3421; 8AM-4:30PM M-Th (EST). *Misdemeanor, Civil Actions under $15,000, Small Claims.*
www.pauldingcountycourt.com
General Information: No fee to fax documents. Court makes copy: $.50 per page. Certification fee: $2.00. Payee: Paulding County Court. No personal checks. Visa/MC accepted. Prepayment required. Mail requests: SASE required.
Civil Name Search: Access: Fax, mail, in person, online. Both court and visitors may perform in person name searches. Search fee: $5.00 per name. Required to search: name, years to search; also helpful: address. Civil records in books since 1985; computerized records since 1997. Mail turnaround time 2-4 days. Civil PAT goes back to 1997. Access to civil records is free at www.pauldingcountycourt.com/Search/index.shtml.
Criminal Name Search: Access: Fax, mail, in person, online. Both court and visitors may perform in person name searches. Search fee: $5.00 per name. Required to search: name, years to search; also helpful: address, DOB, SSN. Criminal records in books since 1985; computerized records since 1997. Mail turnaround time 2-4 days. Criminal PAT goes back to same as civil. Access to criminal records is free at www.pauldingcountycourt.com/Search/index.shtml.

Perry County

Common Pleas Court PO Box 67, 105 N Main St, New Lexington, OH 43764; 740-342-1022; probate phone: 740-342-1493 X2; fax: 740-342-5527; 8AM-4PM (EST). *Felony, Civil Actions over $3,000, Probate.*
General Information: Probate court is a separate court at the same address, PO Box 167. Probate Fax: 740-342-5524. Will fax documents $2.00 1st page, $1.00 ea add'l page. Court makes copy: $.10 per page. Certification fee: $1.00 per cert. Payee: Clerk of Court. Personal checks accepted, credit cards are not. Prepayment required.
Civil Name Search: Access: In person only. Visitors must perform in person searches themselves. Required to search: name, years to search; also helpful: address. Civil records on computer since 3/96, in case files prior, indexed from 1940. Civil PAT goes back to 1996.
Criminal Name Search: Access: In person only. Visitors must perform in person searches themselves. Required to search: name, years to search; also helpful: address, DOB, SSN. Criminal records on computer since 3/96, in case files prior, indexed from 1940. Criminal PAT goes back to same as civil.

Perry County Court PO Box 207, 105 N Main St, New Lexington, OH 43764-0207; 740-342-3156; fax: 740-342-2188; 8:30AM-4:30PM M,W,F; 8AM-4:30PM T,TH (EST). *Misdemeanor, Civil Actions under $15,000, Small Claims.* www.perrycountycourt.com
General Information: All records are public. Will not fax documents. Court makes copy: $1.00 per page. Self serve copy: same. Certification fee: $1.00. Payee: Perry County Court. Personal checks accepted, credit cards are not. Prepayment required.
Civil Name Search: Access: In person, online. Visitors must perform in person searches themselves. Civil records in books 10 to 12 years, computerized since 4/97. Civil PAT goes back to 1997. Access court record index free at www.perrycountycourt.com/Search/.
Criminal Name Search: Access: In person, online. Visitors must perform in person searches themselves. Required to search: name, years to search, DOB, SSN, signed release. Criminal records in books 10 to 12 years, computerized since 4/97. Criminal PAT goes back to same as civil. Online access to criminal records is same as civil.

Pickaway County

Common Pleas Court County Courthouse, 207 S Court St, Circleville, OH 43113; 740-474-5231; probate phone: 740-474-3117; fax: 740-477-3976; 8AM-4PM (EST). *Felony, Civil Actions over $10,000, Probate.*
www.pickawaycountycpcourt.org
General Information: Probate court is a separate court at the same address. Will not fax documents. Court makes copy: $.25 per page. Certification fee: $1.00 per doc plus copy fee. Payee: Clerk of Court. No personal checks or credit cards accepted. Prepayment required. Mail requests: SASE required.
Civil Name Search: Access: Mail, in person, online. Both court and visitors may perform in person name searches. No search fee. Required to search: name, years to search; also helpful: address. Civil cases indexed by defendant. Civil records on computer back to 1988, indexed to 1940s, archived from 1800s. Mail turnaround time 2-3 days. Civil PAT goes back to 1988. Search docket information at www.pickawaycountycpcourt.org.
Criminal Name Search: Access: Mail, in person, online. Both court and visitors may perform in person name searches. No search fee. Required to search: name, years to search; also helpful: address. Criminal records computerized from 1988, indexed to 1940s, archived from 1800s. Mail turnaround time 2-3 days. Criminal PAT goes back to same as civil. Search docket info at www.pickawaycountycpcourt.org. Online results show middle initial.

Circleville Municipal Court PO Box 128, Circleville, OH 43113; 740-474-3171; fax: 740-477-8291; 8AM-4PM (EST). *Misdemeanor, Civil Actions under $15,000, Eviction, Small Claims.*
www.circlevillecourt.com
General Information: No warrant records released. Will fax documents to local or toll-free number. Court makes copy: $.50 per page. No certification fee. Payee: Circleville Municipal Court. Personal checks accepted. Credit cards accepted. Prepayment required. Mail requests: SASE required.
Civil Name Search: Access: Phone, fax, mail, in person, online. Both court and visitors may perform in person name searches. No search fee. Civil records on computer from 1989, prior in books. Mail turnaround time 1-2 days. Civil PAT goes back to 1992. Search online at www.circlevillecourt.com/AccessCourtRecords.asp.
Criminal Name Search: Access: Phone, fax, mail, in person, online. Both court and visitors may perform in person name searches. No search fee. Required to search: name, years to search; also helpful: SSN. Criminal records computerized from 1987, prior in books back to 1983. Mail turnaround time 1-2 days. Criminal PAT goes back to 1990. Search at www.circlevillecourt.com/AccessCourtRecords.asp.

Pike County

Common Pleas Court 100 E 2nd St, 2nd Fl, Waverly, OH 45690; 740-947-2715; criminal phone: x103; fax: 740-947-1729; 8:30AM-4PM (EST). *Felony, Civil Actions over $15,000.*
General Information: No grand jury secret indictment records released. Will fax out documents $2.00 1st page, $1.00 each add'l page. Court makes copy: $.25 per page. Certification fee: $1.00 per cert. Payee: Clerk of Court. Personal checks accepted, credit cards are not. Prepayment required.
Civil Name Search: Access: In person only. Visitors must perform in person searches themselves. Required to search: name, years to search; also helpful: address. Civil records in books back to 1815; on computer back to 1999. Mail turnaround time is 1-3 days Civil PAT goes back to 11/1999.
Criminal Name Search: Access: In person only. Visitors must perform in person searches themselves. Required to search: name, years to search; also helpful: address, DOB, SSN. Criminal records in books back to 1815; on computer back to 1999. Mail turnaround time is 1-3 days. Criminal PAT goes back to same as civil.

Pike County Court 230 Waverly Plaza, #900, Waverly, OH 45690; criminal phone: 740-947-4003; fax: 740-947-7644; 8:30AM-4PM (EST). *Misdemeanor, Civil Actions under $15,000, Small Claims.*
www.pikecountycourt.org/
General Information: No sealed or expunged records released. Will fax documents to local or toll free line. No copy fee. Self serve copy: none. No certification fee. Payee: Pike County Court. Personal checks accepted, credit cards are not. Prepayment required. Mail requests: SASE required.
Civil Name Search: Access: Phone, fax, mail, in person, online. Both court and visitors may perform in person name searches. No search fee. Civil records in books indexed to 1958, computerized since 1996. Mail turnaround time 1 week. Civil PAT goes back to 12/1996. Search the index by name or case number or date at www.pikecountycourt.org/search.shtml. Results give full identifiers.
Criminal Name Search: Access: Phone, fax, mail, in person. Both court and visitors may perform in person name searches. No search fee. Criminal records in books indexed to 1958, computerized since 1996. Mail turnaround time 1 week. Criminal PAT goes back to 12/1996. Search the index by name or case number or date at www.pikecountycourt.org/search.shtml. Results give full identifiers. Includes traffic.

Probate Court 230 Waverly Plaza, #600, Waverly, OH 45690-1386; probate phone: 740-947-2560; fax: 740-941-3086; 7:30AM-4:00PM. *Probate.*

Portage County

Common Pleas Court PO Box 1035, 203 W Main St, Ravenna, OH 44266; 330-297-3644; probate phone: 330-297-3870; fax: 330-297-4554; 8AM-4PM (EST). *Felony, Civil Actions over $15,000.*
www.co.portage.oh.us/clerkofcourts.htm
General Information: Probate court is a separate court at the same address, PO Box 936. Online identifiers in results same as on public terminal. Will fax out specific case files for $1.00 per page. Court makes copy: $.10 per page. Certification fee: $1.00 per page includes copy fee. Payee: Clerk of Court. Personal checks, Visa/MC accepted. Prepayment required. Monthly accounts available.
Civil Name Search: Access: In person, online. Visitors must perform in person searches themselves. Required to search: name, years to search; also helpful: address. Civil records on computer back to 11/1991; Judgment line index back to 1/1982. Civil PAT goes back to 11/1991 for cases, to 1977 for index. For online records from 1977 forward, go to www.co.portage.oh.us/courtsearch.htm. Case number provided.

Criminal Name Search: Access: In person, online. Visitors must perform in person searches themselves. Required to search: name, years to search; also helpful: address, DOB. Criminal records index on computer back to 1977, older cases on microfilm. Criminal PAT goes back to same as civil. Results also includes charge, disposition. For index from 1977 forward or images 06/2005 forward, go to www.co.portage.oh.us/courtsearch.htm. Direct questions about online access to Kathy Gray at 330-297-3648. Online results show middle initial.

Portage County Municipal Court - Ravenna PO Box 958, 203 W Main, Ravenna, OH 44266; criminal phone: 330-297-3639; civil phone: 330-297-3635; criminal fax: 330-297-3526; civil fax: 8AM-4PM; 8AM-4PM (EST). *Misdemeanor, Civil Actions under $15,000, Eviction, Small Claims.* www.co.portage.oh.us

General Information: No records released. Will fax documents $2.00 1st page, $1.00 each add'l page. Court makes copy: $.10 per page. Certification fee: $1.00 per page. Payee: Municipal Court. Personal checks accepted. Visa/MC accepted, 4% surcharge added. Prepayment required. Mail requests: SASE required.

Civil Name Search: Access: Mail, in person, online. Visitors must perform in person searches themselves. Search fee: $5.00. Required to search: name, years to search; also helpful: address. Civil records on computer from 1992. Mail turnaround time 2 days. Civil PAT goes back to 1991. Search records back to 1992 free at www.co.portage.oh.us/courtsearch.htm.

Criminal Name Search: Access: Mail, in person, online. Visitors must perform in person searches themselves. Search fee: $5.00 if time involved or multiple names given. Required to search: name, years to search; also helpful: address, DOB. Criminal records computerized from 1992. Mail turnaround time 2 days. Criminal PAT goes back to same as civil. Results also include charges, disposition. Search records back to 1992 free at www.co.portage.oh.us/courtsearch.htm. Direct questions about online access to Cindy W. at 330-297-5654. Online results show middle initial.

Portage Municipal Court - Kent Branch 214 S Water, Kent, OH 44240; criminal phone: 330-678-9100; civil phone: 330-678-9170; fax: 330-677-9944; 8AM-4PM (EST). *Misdemeanor, Civil Actions under $15,000, Eviction, Small Claims.* www.co.portage.oh.us

General Information: No expunged records released. Will not fax out documents. Will charge for incoming faxes. Court makes copy: $.10 per page. Self serve copy: same. Certification fee: $1.00. Payee: Portage County Municipal Court. Personal checks accepted. Credit cards not accepted for copies or searches. Prepayment required.

Civil Name Search: Access: In person, online. Both court and visitors may perform in person name searches. No search fee. Required to search: name, years to search; also helpful: address. Civil records on computer from 1992, prior in books. Civil PAT goes back to 1992. Online records from 1992 forward at www.co.portage.oh.us/.

Criminal Name Search: Access: In person, online. Both court and visitors may perform in person name searches. No search fee. Required to search: name, years to search; also helpful: address, DOB, SSN. Criminal records computerized from 1992, prior in books. Criminal PAT goes back to same as civil. Records from 1992 forward at www.co.portage.oh.us/. Direct questions about online access to Robyn Godfrey at 330-296-2530.

Probate & Juvenile Court 203 W Main St, PO Box 936, Ravenna, OH 44266; probate phone: 330-297-3870; fax: 330-298-1100; 8AM-4PM (EST). *Probate.* www.co.portage.oh.us/juvenileprobate.htm

Preble County

Common Pleas Court 101 E Main, 3rd Fl, Eaton, OH 45320; 937-456-8165; probate phone: 937-456-8136; fax: 937-456-9548; 8AM-4:30PM (EST). *Felony, Civil, Probate.* www.preblecountyohio.net/

General Information: No secret records released. Will fax documents $.50 per page. Court makes copy: $.50 per page. Certification fee: $1.00 per page. Payee: Clerk of Court. Personal checks accepted, credit cards are not. Prepayment required. Mail requests: SASE required for criminal.

Civil Name Search: Access: In person, online. Visitors must perform in person searches themselves. Required to search: name, years to search; also helpful: address. Civil records on computer from 11/89, prior in books indexed to 1840s. Civil PAT goes back to 11/1989. Access to court records and calendars free at www.preblecountyohio.net/.

Criminal Name Search: Access: Mail, in person, online. Both court and visitors may perform in person name searches. Search fee: $3.00 per name. Required to search: name, years to search; also helpful: address, DOB, SSN. Criminal records computerized from 11/89, prior in books indexed to 1840s. Mail turnaround time 1 day. Criminal PAT goes back to same as civil.

Access to court records and calendars free at www.preblecountyohio.net/.

Eaton Municipal Court 1199 Preble Dr, Eaton, OH 45320; 937-456-4941/6204; fax: 937-456-4685; 8AM-4:30PM (EST). *Misdemeanor, Civil Actions under $15,000, Eviction, Small Claims.* www.eatonmunicipalcourt.com

General Information: Online identifiers in results same as on public terminal. No driving records released. Court makes copy: $.25 per page. Self serve copy: same. Certification fee: $1.00. Payee: Eaton Municipal Court. Personal checks accepted. Credit cards accepted. Prepayment required. Mail requests: SASE required.

Civil Name Search: Access: Mail, in person, online. Both court and visitors may perform in person name searches. No search fee. Civil records on computer from 1989, prior in books indexed to 1959. Mail turnaround time 1 week. Civil PAT goes back to 1989. Search by name or case number free at www.eatonmunicipalcourt.com/docket/index.html. Records go back to 1989.

Criminal Name Search: Access: Mail, in person, online. Both court and visitors may perform in person name searches. No search fee. Required to search: name, years to search; also helpful: SSN. Criminal records computerized from 1989, prior in books indexed to 1959. Mail turnaround time 1 week. Criminal PAT goes back to same as civil. Search by name or case number free at www.eatonmunicipalcourt.com/docket/index.html. Computerized records begin in 1992 for online civil, criminal and traffic cases. Online results show middle initial, DOB.

Putnam County

Common Pleas Court 245 E Main, Rm 301, Ottawa, OH 45875; 419-523-3110; probate phone: 419-523-3012; fax: 419-523-5284; 8:30AM-4:30PM (EST). *Felony, Civil Actions over $10,000, Probate, Domestic.* www.putnamcountyohio.gov/

General Information: Probate court is a separate court at the same address, Rm 204. Probate fax- 419-523-9291. No sealed records released. Will fax documents $3.00 per transmission plus $1.00 per page. Court makes copy: $.25 per page. Certification fee: $1.00 per certification plus copy fee. Payee: Clerk of Court. Putnam County personal checks accepted only. Visa/MC accepted. Prepayment required. Mail requests: SASE not required.

Civil Name Search: Access: Fax, mail, in person, online. Both court and visitors may perform in person name searches. Search fee: $10.00 per name. Civil records on computer from 1992 indexed on docket books back to 1800s. Mail turnaround time 1-4 days. Civil PAT goes back to 1992. Online access is free at www.putnamcountycourtsohio.com/.

Criminal Name Search: Access: Fax, mail, in person, online. Both court and visitors may perform in person name searches. Search fee: $10.00 per name. Required to search: name, years to search; also helpful: address, DOB, SSN. Criminal records computerized from 1992 indexed on docket books back to 1800s. Mail turnaround time 1-4 days. Criminal PAT goes back to same as civil. Online access is free at www.putnamcountycourtsohio.com/. Online results show middle initial, DOB, address.

Putnam County Municipal Court 245 E Main, Rm 303, Ottawa, OH 45875; 419-523-3110; fax: 419-523-5284; 8:30AM-4:30PM (EST). *Misdemeanor, Civil Actions under $15,000, Small Claims, Landlord Tenant.* www.putnamcountyohio.gov/

General Information: Will fax documents $3.00 plus $1.00 per page. Court makes copy: $.25 per page. Certification fee: $1.00 per page. Payee: Clerk of Court. Cashiers checks and money orders accepted. Visa/MC accepted. Prepayment required. Mail requests: SASE required.

Civil Name Search: Access: Mail, fax, in person, online. Both court and visitors may perform in person name searches. Search fee: $10.00 per name. Civil records go back to 1800s; computerized records go back to 1992. Note: Court will perform searches when certification is required; you must request this using the courts request form. Mail turnaround time 48 hours. Civil PAT goes back to 1992. Online access is free at www.putnamcountycourtsohio.com/.

Criminal Name Search: Access: Mail, in person, online. Both court and visitors may perform in person name searches. Search fee: $10.00 per name. Criminal records go back to 1826; computerized records go back to 1992. Note: Court will perform searches when certification is required; you must request this using the courts request form. Mail turnaround time 48 hours. Criminal PAT goes back to same as civil. Online access is free at www.putnamcountycourtsohio.com/. Online results show middle initial, DOB, address.

Richland County

Common Pleas Court 50 Park Ave E, Mansfield, OH 44902; 419-774-5543/5690/8969; fax: 419-774-5547; 9AM-4PM (EST). *Felony, Civil Actions over $10,000, Domestic Relations, Probate.*
www.richlandcountyoh.us/coc.htm
General Information: Probate and Juvenile are separate courts, separate records, and each Court has its own Clerk. Common Pleas is on the 3rd floor, Probate on the 2nd. No sealed records released. Will fax documents for $2.00 plus $1.00 per page. Court makes copy: $.05 per page (first 25 are free). Certification fee: $1.00 per page. Payee: Clerk of Court. Personal checks accepted, credit cards are not. Prepayment required.
Civil Name Search: Access: Mail, fax, in person, online. Both court and visitors may perform in person name searches. No search fee. Required to search: name, years to search; also helpful: address. Civil records on computer from 1989, prior in books and on microfiche to 1960. Mail turnaround time 13 days or less. Civil PAT goes back to 1989. Access to civil records is at www.richlandcountyoh.us/courtv.htm.
Criminal Name Search: Access: Mail, in person, online. Both court and visitors may perform in person name searches. No search fee. Required to search: name, years to search, DOB, SSN, signed release; also helpful: address. Criminal records computerized from 1992, prior in books and on microfiche to 1960. Mail turnaround time 13 days or less. Criminal PAT goes back to 1992. Access to criminal dockets at www.richlandcountyoh.us/courtv.htm.

Mansfield Municipal Court PO Box 1228, Mansfield, OH 44901; 419-755-9633; criminal phone: 419-755-9634; civil phone: 419-755-9637; criminal fax: 419-755-9894; civil fax: 8AM-4PM; 8AM-4PM (EST). *Misdemeanor, Civil Actions under $15,000, Eviction, Small Claims.*
www.ci.mansfield.oh.us/
General Information: Online identifiers in results same as on public terminal. No lead print out records released. No fee to fax documents. Court makes copy: $.05 per page. Certification fee: $1.00 per page plus copy fee. Payee: Clerk of Court or Mansfield Municipal Court. Personal checks accepted except for warrants and forfeitures. Visa/MC accepted. Prepayment required. Mail requests: SASE required.
Civil Name Search: Access: Phone, fax, mail, in person, online. Both court and visitors may perform in person name searches. No search fee. Required to search: name, years to search; also helpful: address. Overall records go back to 1940. Note: Phone and fax access limited to short searches. Mail turnaround time 2-3 days. Civil PAT goes back to 1990. Online access at http://docket.webxsol.com/mansfield/index.html for records from 1992 forward.
Criminal Name Search: Access: Phone, fax, mail, in person, online. Both court and visitors may perform in person name searches. No search fee. Required to search: name, years to search; also helpful: address, DOB, SSN. Criminal records computerized from 1989. Overall records go back to 1940. Mail turnaround time 2-3 days. Criminal PAT goes back to 10/1989. Online access at http://docket.webxsol.com/mansfield/index.html for records from 1992 forward. Online results show middle initial, DOB.

Ross County

Common Pleas Court County Courthouse, 2 N Paint St, #B, Chillicothe, OH 45601; 740-702-3010; probate phone: 740-774-1179; fax: 740-702-3018; 8AM-4PM (EST). *Felony, Civil Actions over $10,000, Probate.*
www.co.ross.oh.us/ClerkOfCourts/
General Information: Probate court is a separate court at the same address. No secret indictment records released. Will fax documents to local or toll free line. Court makes copy: $.05 per page. Certification fee: $1.00. Payee: Clerk of Court. Personal checks accepted, credit cards are not. Prepayment required.
Civil Name Search: Access: In person, online. Both court and visitors may perform in person name searches. No search fee. Required to search: name, years to search; also helpful: address. Civil records on computer from 1989, prior in books to 1800s. Civil PAT goes back to 11/1989. Search records back to 11/89 at www.co.ross.oh.us/ClerkOfCourts/.
Criminal Name Search: Access: In person, online. Both court and visitors may perform in person name searches. No search fee. Required to search: name, years to search; also helpful: address, DOB, SSN. Criminal records computerized from 1989, prior in books to 1800s. Criminal PAT goes back to same as civil. Search records back to 11/89 at www.co.ross.oh.us/ClerkOfCourts/.

Chillicothe Municipal Court 26 S Paint St, Chillicothe, OH 45601; 740-773-3515; fax: 740-774-1101; 7:30AM-4:30PM (EST). *Misdemeanor, Civil Actions under $15,000, Eviction, Small Claims.*
www.chillicothemunicipalcourt.org
General Information: Online identifiers in results same as on public terminal. No confidential records released. Will not fax documents. Court makes copy: $.05 per page. Self serve copy: same. Certification fee: $1.00

per page. Payee: Municipal Court. Business checks accepted. Visa/MC accepted. Prepayment required. Mail requests: SASE required.
Civil Name Search: Access: Mail, in person, online. Both court and visitors may perform in person name searches. No search fee. Required to search: name, also helpful: address. Civil records on computer from 6/93, prior in books. Mail turnaround time 10 days. Civil PAT goes back to 6/1993. Search docket information at http://216.201.21.130/Search/.
Criminal Name Search: Access: Mail, in person, online. Both court and visitors may perform in person name searches. No search fee. Required to search: name only. Criminal records computerized from 6/93, prior in books. Mail turnaround time 10 days. Criminal PAT goes back to same as civil. Search docket info at http://216.201.21.130/Search/. Online results show name only.

Sandusky County

Common Pleas Court 100 N Park Ave, #320, Fremont, OH 43420; 419-334-6161/6163; probate phone: 419-334-6211; fax: 419-334-6164; 8AM-4:30PM (EST). *Felony, Civil Actions over $3,000, Probate.*
www.sandusky-county.org
General Information: Probate court is a separate court at the same address, Suite 224. Probate fax- 419-334-6210 No search warrant records released. Will fax documents $2.00 1st page, $1.00 ea add'l page. Court makes copy: $.10 per page. Certification fee: $1.00 per page plus copy fee. Payee: Clerk of Court. Personal checks accepted, credit cards are not. Prepayment required.
Civil Name Search: Access: In person, online. Visitors must perform in person searches themselves. Required to search: name, years to search; also helpful: address. Civil records on computer from 1988, prior in books to 1800s. Civil PAT goes back to 1988. Access the civil dockets at www.sandusky-county.org/Clerk/Disclaimer/All/default.asp. Search by name or case number.
Criminal Name Search: Access: In person, online. Both court and visitors may perform in person name searches. Required to search: name, years to search; also helpful: address, DOB, SSN. Criminal records computerized from 1988, prior in books to 1800s. Note: Court will assist with onsite research. This is only one public access terminal. Criminal PAT goes back to same as civil. Access misdemeanor traffic and criminal data free at www.sandusky-county.org/Clerk/Disclaimer/All/default.asp.

County Court #1 PO Box 267, 847 E McPherson Hwy, Clyde, OH 43410; 419-547-0915; fax: 419-547-9198; 8AM-4:30PM (EST). *Misdemeanor, Civil Actions under $15,000, Small Claims.*
www.sandusky-county.org
General Information: No fee to fax documents to toll-free number. Court makes copy: $.10 per page. Self serve copy: same. Certification fee: $1.00 per document. Cert fee includes copies. Payee: Sandusky County Court. Only in-state personal checks accepted. Credit cards accepted, there is $3.00 fee. Prepayment required. Mail requests: SASE required.
Civil Name Search: Access: Fax, mail, in person, online. Only the court performs in person name searches; visitors may not. No search fee. Required to search: name, years to search; also helpful: address. Civil records on computer from 1998, prior in books for 25 years. Mail turnaround time 2-3 days. Access civil docket online at www.sandusky-county.org/Clerk/Disclaimer/All/default.asp.
Criminal Name Search: Access: Fax, mail, in person, online. Only the court performs in person name searches; visitors may not. No search fee. Required to search: name, years to search, DOB, SSN; also helpful: address. Criminal records computerized from 1998, prior in books for 25 years. Mail turnaround time 5-7 days. Access misdemeanor traffic and criminal data free at www.sandusky-county.org/Clerk/Clerk_of_Courts/sccoc/search.php.

County Court #2 215 W Main St, Woodville, OH 43469; 419-849-3961; fax: 419-849-3932; 8AM-4:30PM (EST). *Misdemeanor, Civil Actions under $15,000, Small Claims.*
www.sandusky-county.org
General Information: No confidential records released. Will fax document $2.00 for 1st page, $1.00 each add'l. Court makes copy: $.10 per page. Certification fee: $1.00 per page. Payee: Sandusky County Court. Personal checks, Visa/MC accepted. Prepayment required. Mail requests: SASE required.
Civil Name Search: Access: Phone, fax, mail, in person, online. Both court and visitors may perform in person name searches. No search fee. Required to search: name, years to search; also helpful: address. Civil records go back to 1983; on computer back to 1998. Note: Court prefers requests by fax, not phone. Mail turnaround time 2-3 days. Access the civil dockets at www.sandusky-county.org/Clerk/Disclaimer/All/default.asp
Criminal Name Search: Access: Phone, fax, mail, in person, online. Both court and visitors may perform in person name searches. No search fee. Required to search: name, years to search, DOB, SSN. Criminal records go back to 1995; on computer back to 1998. Note: Court prefers requests by fax, not phone. Mail turnaround time 5-7 days. Access misdemeanor

traffic and criminal data free at www.sandusky-county.org/Clerk/Disclaimer/All/default.asp.

Fremont Municipal Court PO Box 886, Fremont, OH 43420-0071; 419-332-1579; fax: 419-332-1570; 8AM-4:30PM (EST). *Misdemeanor, Civil Actions under $15,000, Eviction, Small Claims.*

General Information: The court does not have a web page, but the county does at www.sandusky-county.org. No fee to fax documents locally only. Court makes copy: $.10 per page. Certification fee: $1.00 per page. Cert fee includes copy fee. Payee: Fremont Municipal Court. Cashiers checks and money orders accepted. Visa/MC accepted for criminal and traffic only; $2.00 processing fee applies. Prepayment required.

Civil Name Search: Access: Fax, mail, in person. Both court and visitors may perform in person name searches. No search fee. Civil records in books from 1960, computerized since 1992. Mail turnaround time 2 days. Civil PAT goes back to 1992.

Criminal Name Search: Access: Fax, mail, in person. Both court and visitors may perform in person name searches. No search fee. Required to search: name, years to search; also helpful: DOB, SSN. Criminal records in books from 1960, computerized since 1992. Mail turnaround time 2 days. Criminal PAT goes back to 1992.

Scioto County

Common Pleas Court 602 7th St, Rm 205, Portsmouth, OH 45662; 740-355-8226; probate phone: 740-355-8360; fax: 740-354-2057; 8AM-4:30PM (EST). *Felony, Civil Actions over $15,000.*

www.sciotocountycpcourt.org

General Information: Probate court is a separate court/agency at the same address, Rm 201. No sealed or secret records released. Will fax out specific case files for $1.00 per page. Court makes copy: $1.00 per page. Certification fee: $1.00 per page. Payee: Clerk of Court. No personal checks or credit cards accepted. Prepayment required. Mail requests: SASE required for mail return of any copies.

Civil Name Search: Access: In person, online. Both court and visitors may perform in person name searches. No search fee. Required to search: name, years to search; also helpful: address. Civil records on computer from 1986, dockets to 1800s. Civil PAT goes back to 1/1986. Online access to civil records back to 1/1986 is free at www.sciotocountycpcourt.org/search.htm. Search by court calendar, quick index, general index or docket sheet.

Criminal Name Search: Access: In person, online. Both court and visitors may perform in person name searches. No search fee. Required to search: name, years to search; also helpful: address, DOB. Criminal records computerized from 1986, dockets to 1800s. Criminal PAT goes back to same as civil. Online access to civil records back to 1/1986 is free at www.sciotocountycpcourt.org/search.htm. Search by court calendar, quick index, general index or docket sheet. Online results show name only.

Portsmouth Municipal Court 728 2nd St, Portsmouth, OH 45662; 740-354-3283; fax: 740-353-6645; 8AM-4PM (EST). *Misdemeanor, Civil Actions under $15,000, Eviction, Small Claims.*

www.pmcourt.org

General Information: Online identifiers in results same as on public terminal. No competency hearing, protection order records released. No fee to fax documents. Court makes copy: $.50 per page. Certification fee: $1.00 per page. Payee: Portsmouth Municipal Court. Personal checks accepted, credit cards are not. Prepayment required. Mail requests: SASE required.

Civil Name Search: Access: Fax, mail, in person, online. Both court and visitors may perform in person name searches. Search fee: No fee for computer records search 1989 forward. Mail turnaround time 2-3 days; older records up to 2 weeks. Civil PAT goes back to 11/1989. Access is free at www.pmcourt.org/disc.html.

Criminal Name Search: Access: Fax, mail, in person, online. Both court and visitors may perform in person name searches. Search fee: $20.00 per name if search includes years prior to 1989. No fee for computer records search 1989 forward. Required to search: name, years to search, SSN. Criminal records go back to 1985; on computer back to 1995. Mail turnaround time 2-3 days; older records up to 2 weeks. Criminal PAT goes back to same as civil. Access criminal records online free at www.pmcourt.org/disc.html. Online results show middle initial.

Seneca County

Common Pleas Court 117 E Market, Tiffin, OH 44883; 419-447-0671; fax: 419-443-7919; 8:30AM-4:30PM (EST). *Felony, Civil Actions over $10,000.* www.senecaco.org/clerk/default.html

General Information: Online identifiers in results same as on public terminal. No sealed records released. Will fax out specific case files for $2.00 per transmission. Court makes copy: $.10 per page. Self serve copy: same. Certification fee: $1.00 per document plus copy fee. Payee: Clerk of Court.

Personal checks accepted, credit cards are not. Prepayment required. Mail requests: SASE required for mail return of any copies.

Civil Name Search: Access: In person, online. Both court and visitors may perform in person name searches. No search fee. Required to search: name, years to search; also helpful: address. Civil records on computer from 1/93, prior in books to 1900s, archived to 1800s. Civil PAT goes back to 1/1993. Public terminal located in the Recorder's Office; docket sheets can be printed out for $.10 per page in clerk's office. Search dockets online at www.senecaco.org/clerk/default.html. Click on Internet Inquiry.

Criminal Name Search: Access: In person, online. Both court and visitors may perform in person name searches. No search fee. Required to search: name, years to search, SSN, date of offense. Criminal records computerized from 1/93, prior in books to 1900s, archived to 1800s. Criminal PAT goes back to same as civil. Public terminal located in the Recorder's Office; docket sheets can be printed out for $.10 per page in clerk's office. Search dockets online at www.senecaco.org/clerk/default.html. Click on Internet Inquiry. Online results show middle initial, DOB.

Fostoria Municipal Court PO Box 985, Fostoria, OH 44830; 419-435-8139; fax: 419-435-1150; 8:30AM-5PM (EST). *Misdemeanor, Civil Actions under $15,000, Eviction, Small Claims.*

www.fostoriamunicipalcourt.com/

General Information: No fee if faxed to local or toll free number. Court makes copy: $.10 per page. Certification fee: $1.00 per page includes copies. Payee: Fostoria Municipal Court. Personal checks accepted. No credit cards accepted for record searching. Prepayment required. Mail requests: SASE required.

Civil Name Search: Access: Phone, fax, mail, in person, online. Both court and visitors may perform in person name searches. No search fee. Civil records computerized since 1987. Mail turnaround time 1-2 days. Civil PAT goes back to 1987. Search the index by name or case number at www.fostoriamunicipalcourt.com/search.shtml. The DOB is generally not shown for civil records.

Criminal Name Search: Access: Phone, fax, mail, in person, online. Both court and visitors may perform in person name searches. No search fee. Required to search: name, years to search; also helpful: SSN. Criminal records computerized since 1987. Mail turnaround time 1-2 days. Criminal PAT goes back to 1987. Search the index by name, ticket number, or case number at www.fostoriamunicipalcourt.com/search.shtml. The DOB generally does show for criminal records and traffic tickets. Online results show middle initial, DOB, address.

Tiffin Municipal Court PO Box 694, Tiffin, OH 44883; 419-448-5412; criminal phone: 419-448-5411; civil phone: 419-448-5418; fax: 419-448-5419; 8:30AM-4:30PM (EST). *Misdemeanor, Civil Actions under $15,000, Eviction, Small Claims.*

www.tiffinmunicipalcourt.org/

General Information: No expunged records released. Fee to fax document $.25 per page. Court makes copy: $.05 per page. Self serve copy: same. Certification fee: $1.00. Payee: Municipal Court. Personal checks accepted, credit cards are not. Prepayment required. Mail requests: SASE required.

Civil Name Search: Access: Fax, mail, in person, online. Both court and visitors may perform in person name searches. No search fee. Required to search: name, years to search; also helpful: address. Civil records on computer from 8/90, prior in books. Mail turnaround time 3 days. Civil PAT goes back to 8/1990. Access records free at www.tiffinmunicipalcourt.org/search.shtml.

Criminal Name Search: Access: Fax, mail, in person, online. Both court and visitors may perform in person name searches. No search fee. Required to search: name, years to search, DOB, SSN, signed release; also helpful: address. Criminal records computerized from 8/90, prior in books. Mail turnaround time 3 days. Criminal PAT goes back to same as civil. Access records free at www.tiffinmunicipalcourt.org/search.shtml.

Probate Court 108 Jefferson St, Tiffin, OH 44883-2898; probate phone: 419-447-3121; 8:30A-4:30P. *Probate.*

Shelby County

Common Pleas Court PO Box 947, 100 E Court St, 3rd Fl, Sidney, OH 45365; 937-498-7808; probate phone: 937-498-7265; fax: 937-498-7824; 8:30AM-4PM (EST). *Felony, Civil Actions over $10,000, Probate.*

http://co.shelby.oh.us/CommonPleasCourt/index.asp

General Information: Probate court is a separate court at the same street address, PO Box 4187. No grand jury tapes released, no SSNs shown. Fee to fax out file $3.00 plus $3.00 per page. Court makes copy: $.10 per page. Certification fee: $1.00 per page; $4.00 for exemplification. Payee: Shelby County Clerk of Courts. Personal checks accepted, credit cards are not. Prepayment required. Mail requests: SASE required.

Civil Name Search: Access: Fax, mail, in person. Both court and visitors may perform in person name searches. Search fee: $1.00 per name.

Required to search: name, years to search; also helpful: address. Civil records on computer from 1987, on indexes from 1819. Mail turnaround time 5 days. Civil PAT goes back to 1987.

Criminal Name Search: Access: Mail, in person. Both court and visitors may perform in person name searches. Search fee: $1.00 per name. Required to search: name, years to search DOB, SSN; also helpful: address. Criminal records computerized from 1987, on indexes from 1819. Mail turnaround time 5 days. Criminal PAT goes back to same as civil.

Sidney Municipal Court 201 W Poplar, Sidney, OH 45365; 937-498-0011; fax: 937-498-8179; 8AM-4:15PM (EST). *Misdemeanor, Civil Actions under $15,000, Eviction, Small Claims.*
www.sidneyoh.com

General Information: Send mail requests to the address above; phone and in person searches are made at the court at 110 W Court St. Confidential and probation records are not released. Will fax documents to toll-free number no charge. Court makes copy: $.10 per page. Certification fee: $1.00 per page. Cert fee includes copies. Payee: Municipal Court. No personal checks or credit cards accepted. Prepayment required. Mail requests: SASE required.

Civil Name Search: Access: Phone, fax, mail, in person. Both court and visitors may perform in person name searches. No search fee. Civil records on computer from 1988; prior on books to 1958. Mail turnaround time 4 days. Civil PAT goes back to 1993.

Criminal Name Search: Access: Phone, fax, mail, in person. Both court and visitors may perform in person name searches. No search fee. Required to search: name, years to search; also helpful: address, DOB, SSN. Criminal records computerized from 1988; prior on books to 1958. Mail turnaround time 4 days. Criminal PAT goes back to same as civil.

Stark County

Common Pleas Court - Civil Division PO Box 21160, 101 Market Ave N, Courthouse, Canton, OH 44701; 330-451-7795; fax: 330-451-7853; 10:30AM-4:30PM (EST). *Civil Actions over $15,000.*
www.starkclerk.org

General Information: Online identifiers in results same as on public terminal. No sealed records released. Fee to fax out file $2.00 1st page, $1.00 each add'l. Court makes copy: $.10 per page. Certification fee: $1.00 per page. Payee: Clerk of Court. Personal checks and Visa/MC accepted if in person, $4.00 fee. Prepayment required. Mail requests: SASE required.

Civil Name Search: Access: Phone, fax, mail, in person, online. Both court and visitors may perform in person name searches. No search fee. Civil records on computer from 1985, prior in books from 1940s. Mail turnaround time up to 1 week. Public use terminal has civil records back to 1985. Online access to the county online case docket database is free at www.starkcourt.org/docket/index.html. Search by name or case number.

Common Pleas Court - Criminal Division PO Box 21160, County Clerk of Courts, Canton, OH 44701-1160; 330-451-7929; fax: 330-451-7066; 10:30AM-4:30PM (EST). *Felony.*
www.starkclerk.org

General Information: No secret indictments, expungment records released. Will fax documents. Court makes copy: $.10 per page. Certification fee: $1.00 per page includes copy fee. Payee: Clerk of Courts. Personal checks accepted, credit cards are not. Prepayment required. Mail requests: SASE required.

Criminal Name Search: Access: Mail, in person, online. Both court and visitors may perform in person name searches. No search fee. Required to search: name, years to search, DOB, SSN. Criminal records computerized from 1985, prior in books to 1940s. Mail turnaround time up to 2 weeks. Public use terminal has crim records back to 1985. PAT results may also show full middle name. Online access to county case docket database is free at www.starkcourt.org/docket/index.html. Search by name, case number. Will accept requests by email at crim.clerk@co.stark.oh.us Online results show middle initial.

Alliance Municipal Court 470 E Market St, Rm 16, Alliance, OH 44601; 330-823-6600; criminal fax: 330-829-2230; civil fax: 8:30AM-4:30PM; 8:30AM-4:30PM (EST). *Misdemeanor, Civil Actions under $15,000, Eviction, Small Claims.*
www.alliancecourt.org/

General Information: Jurisdiction includes Alliance, Lexington, Marlboro, Washington, Paris, Minerva, Limaville, and Roberstville. No fee to fax documents. Court makes copy: $.25 per page. Certification fee: $3.00 per page. Payee: Alliance Municipal Court. Personal checks accepted, credit cards are not. Prepayment required. Mail requests: SASE required.

Civil Name Search: Access: Fax, mail, in person, online. Both court and visitors may perform in person name searches. No search fee. Required to search: name. Civil records go back to 1993. Mail turnaround time 1 day. Search the Online Case Docket of the Alliance Court at www.starkcountycjis.org/cjis2/docket/main.html

Criminal Name Search: Access: Fax, mail, in person, online. Both court and visitors may perform in person name searches. No search fee. Required to search: name, years to search; also helpful: DOB. computerized since 1993. Mail turnaround time 1 day. Search the Online Case Docket of the Alliance Court at www.starkcountycjis.org/cjis2/docket/main.html includes traffic and misdemeanor records. Online results show middle initial, DOB.

Canton Municipal Court 218 Cleveland Ave SW, PO Box 24218, Canton, OH 44701-4218; 330-489-3203; criminal phone: 330-489-3207; civil phone: 330-489-3203; criminal fax: 330-489-3372; civil fax: 8AM-4:30PM; 8AM-4:30PM (EST). *Misdemeanor, Civil Actions under $15,000, Eviction, Small Claims.*
www.cantoncourt.org

General Information: Jurisdiction includes Canton, North Canton, Louisville, Lake, Plain, Nimishillen, Osnaburg, Pike, Sandy, Hartville, East Canton, Myers Lake, East Sparta, Waynesburg, and Magnolia. No sealed records released. No fee to fax documents. Court makes copy: $.25 per page. Self serve copy: same. Certification fee: $1.00 per page. Payee: Municipal Court. Personal checks accepted. Visa/MC/Discover cards accepted; $4.00 usage fee. Prepayment required. Mail requests: SASE required.

Civil Name Search: Access: Phone, fax, mail, in person, online. Both court and visitors may perform in person name searches. No search fee. Civil records on computer from 1991, prior in books to 1928. Mail turnaround time 1-2 days. Civil PAT goes back to 1990. Search docket information at www.cantoncourt.org/docket.html.

Criminal Name Search: Access: Phone, fax, mail, in person, online. Both court and visitors may perform in person name searches. No search fee. Required to search: name, years to search; also helpful: DOB, SSN. Criminal records computerized from 1986, books to 1928. Mail turnaround time 1-2 days. Criminal PAT goes back to 1996. Search docket info at www.cantoncourt.org/docket.html. Includes traffic.

Massillon Municipal Court PO Box 1040, Massillon, OH 44648; 330-830-2591; criminal phone: 330-830-1732; civil phone: 330-830-1731; fax: 330-830-3648; 8:30AM-4:30PM (EST). *Misdemeanor, Civil Actions under $15,000, Eviction, Small Claims.*
www.massilloncourt.org

General Information: Jurisdiction includes Massillon, Canal Fulton, Bethlehem, Jackson, Lawrence, Perry, Sugarcreek, Tuscarawas, Beach City, Brewster, Hills and Dales, Navarre, and Wilmot. Online identifiers in results same as on public terminal. No fee to fax documents. Court makes copy: $.05 per page. Certification fee: $2.00 per page. Payee: Massillon Clerk of Court. Personal checks accepted. Major credit cards accepted. Prepayment required. Mail requests: SASE required.

Civil Name Search: Access: Fax, mail, in person, online. Both court and visitors may perform in person name searches. No search fee. Required to search: name. Civil index in docket books from 1986, computerized since 1991. Mail turnaround time 1 week. Civil PAT goes back to 1991. Search the Online Case Docket of the Massillon Court at www.massilloncourt.org.

Criminal Name Search: Access: Fax, mail, in person, online. Both court and visitors may perform in person name searches. No search fee. Required to search: name, years to search; also helpful: DOB, SSN. computerized since 1991. Note: Traffic can be reached at 330-830-1732. Mail turnaround time 1 week. Criminal PAT goes back to same as civil. Search the Online Case Docket of the Massillon Court at the website, includes traffic and misdemeanor records. Online results show name only.

Probate Court 110 Central Plaza S, #501, Canton, OH 44702-1413; probate phone: 330-451-7752; fax: 330-451-7040; 8:30AM-4:30PM. *Probate.*
www.probate.co.stark.oh.us/

General Information: Case searches at www.probate.co.stark.oh.us/search/search.html. Search by name or case number. Complete indices of Probate Court except marriage indices. Marriage indices only current from 4/23/86.

Summit County

Common Pleas Court 209 S High St, Akron, OH 44308; 330-643-2211, 330-643-2201-Divorce; criminal phone: 330-643-2282; civil phone: 330-643-2217; probate phone: 330-643-2330; criminal fax: 330-643-7772; civil fax: 9:30AM-4:15PM; 9:30AM-4:15PM (EST). *Felony, Civil Actions over $10,000, Probate.*
www.cpclerk.co.summit.oh.us/welcome.asp

General Information: For faster service, mail requests to Clerk at 53 University Ave, Akron 44308. Probate court is a separate court at the same address. Online identifiers in results same as on public terminal. No secret indictment records released. Will not fax documents. Court makes copy: $.05 per page. Certification fee: $1.00 per page. Payee: Clerk of Court. Only cashiers checks and money orders accepted. Major credit cards accepted. Prepayment required. Mail requests: SASE required.

Civil Name Search: Access: Mail, fax, in person, online, email. Both court and visitors may perform in person name searches. No search fee. Civil records on computer from 1982, prior in books, some microfiche. Mail turnaround time 1 week. Civil PAT goes back to 1982. Access to county clerk of courts records is free at www.cpclerk.co.summit.oh.us. Click on "Record Search." Access to probate records at http://summitohioprobate.com/pa/pa.urd/pamw6500*display.

Criminal Name Search: Access: Mail, fax, in person, online, email. Both court and visitors may perform in person name searches. Search fee: $2.00 per name. Required to search: name, years to search, DOB; also helpful: SSN. Criminal records computerized from 1982, prior in books, some microfiche. Mail turnaround time 1 week. Criminal PAT goes back to same as civil. Access to county clerk of courts records is free at www.cpclerk.co.summit.oh.us. Click on "Record Search."

Akron Municipal Court 217 S High St, Rm 837, Akron, OH 44308; criminal phone: 330-375-2570; civil phone: 330-375-2920; criminal fax: 330-375-2024; civil fax: 8AM-4:30PM; 8AM-4:30PM (EST). *Misdemeanor, Civil Actions under $15,000, Eviction, Small Claims.* http://courts.ci.akron.oh.us

General Information: No sealed records released. Will fax out documents. Court makes copy: first 10 pages free; $.10 each add'l. Certification fee: $1.00 per page. Payee: Akron Municipal Court. No personal checks or credit cards accepted. Prepayment required. Mail requests: SASE required.

Civil Name Search: Access: Fax, mail, in person, online. Both court and visitors may perform in person name searches. No search fee. Civil records on computer from 1988, prior in books to 1975. Mail turnaround time up to 1 week. Civil PAT goes back to 1988. Online access to court records and schedules is free at http://courts.ci.akron.oh.us/disclaimer.htm.

Criminal Name Search: Access: Fax, mail, in person, online. Both court and visitors may perform in person name searches. No search fee. Required to search: name, years to search, DOB, SSN. Criminal records computerized from 1988, prior in books to 1960. Mail turnaround time up to 1 week. Criminal PAT goes back to same as civil. Online access to court records and schedules is free at http://courts.ci.akron.oh.us/disclaimer.htm. Online results show name, DOB, address.

Barberton Municipal Court Municipal Bldg, 576 W Park Ave, Barberton, OH 44203-2584; 330-753-2261; criminal phone: 330-861-7188; civil phone: 330-861-7192; fax: 330-848-6779; 8AM-4:30PM (civ); Crim/traffic to 8PM (EST). *Misdemeanor, Civil Actions under $15,000, Eviction, Small Claims.* www.cityofbarberton.com/clerkofcourts/doc_home.html

General Information: Criminal desk closes at noon. No fee to fax documents. Court makes copy: $.10 per page. Certification fee: $1.00 per page. Payee: Barberton Municipal Court. Personal checks accepted. Credit cards accepted. Prepayment required.

Civil Name Search: Access: Phone, fax, mail, in person, online. Both court and visitors may perform in person name searches. No search fee. Civil records computerized since 1995. Mail turnaround time 1 week. Civil PAT goes back to 1995. Online records for Barberton, Green, Norton, Franklin, Clinton, Copley and Coventry are free at http://24.123.45.19/.

Criminal Name Search: Access: Phone, fax, mail, in person, online. Both court and visitors may perform in person name searches. No search fee. Required to search: name, years to search; also helpful: DOB, SSN. Criminal records computerized since 1995. Mail turnaround time 1 week. Criminal PAT goes back to same as civil. Online records for Barberton, Green, Norton, Franklin, Clinton, Copley and Coventry are free at http://24.123.45.19/.

Stow Municipal Court 4400 Courthouse Dr, Stow, OH 44224; 330-564-4200/4118; fax: 330-564-4130; 8AM-12; 1PM-4:30PM (EST). *Misdemeanor, Civil Actions under $15,000, Eviction, Small Claims.* www.stowmunicourt.com.

General Information: Formerly Cuyahoga Falls Municipal Court; relocated Winter 2008-9. Serves Boston Hghts, Boston Twp, Cuyahoga Falls, Hudson, Macedonia, Unroe Falls, Northfield, Peninsula, Reminderville, Sagamore Hills, Silver Lk, Stow, Tallmadge, Twinsburg. Will not fax documents. Court makes copy: $.05 per page. Certification fee: $1.00 per page includes copy. Payee: Cuyahoga Falls Municipal Court. Business checks accepted. No credit cards accepted. Prepayment required. Mail requests: SASE required.

Civil Name Search: Access: Phone, mail, in person, online. Both court and visitors may perform in person name searches. No search fee. Civil cases indexed by defendant, plaintiff, or case number. Civil records indexed back to 1954. Mail turnaround time 1 week. Civil PAT goes back to 1992. Court docket information is free at www.stowmunicourt.com/docket.htm.

Criminal Name Search: Access: Phone, mail, in person, online. Both court and visitors may perform in person name searches. No search fee. Required to search: name or case number. Criminal records indexed back to 1954, archived 1980. Note: Results include case number's. Mail turnaround time 1 week. Criminal PAT goes back to same as civil. Can only look at dockets, no case file images. Court docket information is free at www.stowmunicourt.com/docket.htm Online results show name, DOB.

Trumbull County

Common Pleas Court 161 High St, NW, Warren, OH 44481; 330-675-2557; criminal phone: 330-675-3058; civil phone: 330-675-2557; probate phone: 330-675-2521; fax: 330-675-2563; 8:30AM-4:30PM (EST). *Felony, Civil Actions, Probate.* http://clerk.co.trumbull.oh.us/

General Information: Probate court is a separate court at the same address, 1st Fl. Probate fax number- 330-675-3024. No secret or sealed records released. Will not fax documents nor accept fax filings. Court makes copy: $.05 per page. Self serve copy: same. Certification fee: $1.00 per page plus copy fee. Payee: Clerk of Court. Business checks accepted. No credit cards accepted. Prepayment required. Mail requests: SASE required.

Civil Name Search: Access: Phone, mail, in person, online. Both court and visitors may perform in person name searches. Search fee: $5.00 per name. Civil records indexed in books from 1977, archived from 1800s; on computer back to 5/96. Mail turnaround time 1 week. Civil PAT goes back to 5/1996. Online access to court records is free at http://courts.co.trumbull.oh.us/pa.urd/pamw6500.display. Records go back to May, 1996. Includes divorce. Online access to probate court records is free at www.trumbullprobate.org/paccessfront.htm.

Criminal Name Search: Access: Mail, in person, online. Both court and visitors may perform in person name searches. Search fee: $5.00 per name. Required to search: name, years to search, DOB, SSN, signed release. Criminal records indexed in books from 1977, archived from 1800s; on computer back to 5/96. Mail turnaround time 1 week. Criminal PAT goes back to same as civil. Online access to criminal records is at http://courts.co.trumbull.oh.us/pa.urd/pamw6500.display.

Girard Municipal Court City Hall, 100 N Market St, #A, Girard, OH 44420-2559; criminal phone: 330-545-0069; civil phone: 330-545-3177; fax: 330-545-7045; 8AM-4PM (EST). *Misdemeanor, Civil Actions under $15,000, Eviction, Small Claims.*

General Information: Traffic records-330-545-3049. No fee to fax documents. Court makes copy: 1st 10 pages free; each add'l page $.10. Certification fee: $10.00 per document includes copy fee. Payee: Girard Municipal Court. No personal checks or credit cards accepted. Prepayment required. Mail requests: SASE required.

Civil Name Search: Access: Phone, fax, mail, in person, online. Both court and visitors may perform in person name searches. No search fee. Civil records on books since 1990, computerized since 10/96. Mail turnaround time 1 week. Civil PAT goes back to 9/1996. Access available at www.girardmunicipalcourt.com. Click on public access.

Criminal Name Search: Access: Phone, fax, mail, in person, online. Both court and visitors may perform in person name searches. No search fee. Required to search: name, years to search; also helpful: DOB, SSN. Criminal docket on books since 1990, computerized since 10/96. Mail turnaround time 1 week. Criminal PAT goes back to same as civil. Access available at www.girardmunicipalcourt.com. Click on public access.

Newton Falls Municipal Court 19 N Canal St, Newton Falls, OH 44444-1302; 330-872-0302; criminal phone: 330-872-0232; civil phone: 330-872-0232; fax: 330-872-3899; 8AM-4PM (EST). *Misdemeanor, Civil Actions under $15,000, Eviction, Small Claims, Traffic.* www.newtonfallscourt.com

General Information: Will fax documents $2.50 if long distance, must be pre-paid. Court makes copy: $.10 per page. Certification fee: $1.00 per page. Payee: Newton Falls Municipal Court. No personal or business checks accepted; cashiers check or certified funds needed. Credit cards accepted, small use fee charged. Prepayment required. Mail requests: SASE required.

Civil Name Search: Access: Mail, in person, online. Only the court performs in person name searches; visitors may not. No search fee. Civil records in books since 1970, computerized since 1992. Mail turnaround time varies, but usually 1 week or less. Search record index free at www.newtonfallscourt.com/Search/.

Criminal Name Search: Access: Mail, in person, online. Only the court performs in person name searches; visitors may not. No search fee. Required to search: name, years to search, DOB or SSN. Criminal records in books since 1970, computerized since 1992. Mail turnaround time varies, usually 1 week or less. Search record index free at www.newtonfallscourt.com/Search/. Online results include violation, hearing info and disposition. Online results show name, DOB, address.

Niles Municipal Court 15 E State St, Niles, OH 44446-5051; 330-652-5863; fax: 330-544-9025; 8AM-4PM (EST). *Misdemeanor, Civil Actions under $15,000, Eviction, Small Claims.*

General Information: No fee to fax documents locally only. Court makes copy: $.25 per page. No certification fee. Payee: Niles Municipal Court. Cashiers checks and money orders accepted. Major credit cards accepted. Prepayment required.

Civil Name Search: Access: Phone, fax, mail, in person. Both court and visitors may perform in person name searches. No search fee. Civil records on computer since 10/96, in books since 1990, in storage from 1950. Mail turnaround times will vary. Civil PAT goes back to 1997.

Criminal Name Search: Access: Phone, fax, mail, in person. Both court and visitors may perform in person name searches. No search fee. Required to search: name, years to search; also helpful: DOB, SSN. Criminal records on computer since 10/96, in books since 1990, in storage from 1950. Mail turnaround time varies. Criminal PAT goes back to same as civil.

Trumbull County Court Central 180 N Mecca St, Cortland, OH 44410; 330-675-2280; fax: 330-675-2290; 8AM-4PM (EST). *Misdemeanor, Civil Actions under $15,000, Eviction, Small Claims.*

General Information: Statements and lead reports restricted. No fee to fax documents locally only. Court makes copy: $.25 per page. Self serve copy: same. Certification fee: None reported. Payee: Trumbull County Court Central. Personal checks accepted. Credit cards accepted in person only. Prepayment required.

Civil Name Search: Access: Phone, fax, mail, in person. Both court and visitors may perform in person name searches. No search fee. Records available since 1983. Mail turnaround time 1-2 days. Civil PAT goes back to 1993.

Criminal Name Search: Access: Phone, fax, mail, in person. Both court and visitors may perform in person name searches. No search fee. Required to search: name, years to search; also helpful: DOB, SSN. Same record keeping as civil. Mail turnaround time 1-2 days. Criminal PAT goes back to same as civil.

Trumbull County Court East 7130 Brookwood Dr, Brookfield, OH 44403; 330-448-1726; fax: 330-448-6310; 8:30AM-4:30PM (EST). *Misdemeanor, Civil under $15,000, Eviction, Small Claims.*

General Information: No fee to fax documents locally only. Court makes copy: $.05 per page. Self serve copy: same. Certification fee: $1.00 per page, if "non-copies" are used, then $2.00 per page. Payee: Trumbull County Court East. Personal checks accepted, credit cards are not. Prepayment required. Mail requests: SASE required if copies to be returned by mail.

Civil Name Search: Access: Phone, fax, mail, in person. Both court and visitors may perform in person name searches. No search fee. Civil records go back to 1994. Mail turnaround time 1-2 days. Civil PAT goes back to 1994.

Criminal Name Search: Access: Phone, fax, mail, in person. Both court and visitors may perform in person name searches. No search fee. Required to search: name, years to search; also helpful: DOB, SSN. Criminal Records in docket books since 1990, computerized since 1994. Mail turnaround time 1-2 days. Criminal PAT goes back to 1994. Results can include SSN and/or address if available.

Warren Municipal Court PO Box 1550, 141 South St SE, Warren, OH 44482; 330-841-2525; criminal phone: 330-841-2525 x105-110; civil phone: 330-841-2525 x112-115; fax: 330-841-2760; 8AM-4PM (EST). *Misdemeanor, Civil Actions under $15,000, Eviction, Small Claims.* www.warren.org/courts.htm

General Information: No open case records released. No fee to fax documents. Court makes copy: $.05 per page. Certification fee: $1.00 per document. Payee: Warren Municipal Court. Personal checks accepted. Credit cards accepted. Prepayment required. Mail requests: SASE required.

Civil Name Search: Access: Fax, mail, in person, online. Both court and visitors may perform in person name searches. No search fee. Required to search: name, years to search; also helpful: address. Civil records on computer since 1995; prior in books to 1978. Mail turnaround time 1-5 days. Civil PAT goes back to 1995. Public cannot print copies from public access terminal. Access to the docket is free at http://records.warrenmuni.us/warren/search.do. There is a 24 hour delay after filings and actions until the record is posted.

Criminal Name Search: Access: Fax, mail, in person, online. Both court and visitors may perform in person name searches. No search fee. Required to search: name, years to search, DOB, SSN, signed release; also helpful: address. Criminal records on computer since 1995; prior in books to 1978. Mail turnaround time 1-5 days. Criminal PAT goes back to same as civil. Public cannot print copies from public access terminal. Access to the docket is free at http://records.warrenmuni.us/warren/search.do. There is a 24 hour delay after filings and actions until the record is posted. Includes traffic cases. Online results show middle initial, DOB.

Tuscarawas County

Common Pleas Court PO Box 628, 125 E High Ave, New Philadelphia, OH 44663; 330-365-3243; fax: 330-343-4682; 8AM-4:30PM (EST). *Felony, Civil Actions over $15,000.* www.co.tuscarawas.oh.us

General Information: Will fax out specific case documents for $2.00 transmission fee plus $1.00 per page. Court makes copy: $.10 per page. Certification fee: $1.00 per page. Payee: Clerk of Court. Personal checks accepted. Credit cards accepted. Prepayment required. Mail requests: SASE required for mail return of any copies.

Civil Name Search: Access: In person, online. Visitors must perform in person searches themselves. Required to search: name, years to search; also helpful: address. Civil records on computer from 1987, prior in books to 1808, archived prior. Civil PAT goes back to 1987. Results include redacted images. Search dockets online at www.co.tuscarawas.oh.us/PA/pa.urd/pamw6500.display.

Criminal Name Search: Access: In person, online. Visitors must perform in person searches themselves. Required to search: name, years to search; also helpful: address, DOB, SSN. Criminal records go back to 1868, Criminal records computerized from 1987, prior in books to 1808, archived prior. Criminal PAT goes back to same as civil. Results include redacted images. Search dockets online at www.co.tuscarawas.oh.us/PA/pa.urd/pamw6500.display. Can view docket only, no images may be printed. Online results show middle initial, DOB.

County Court 336 E 3rd St, Uhrichsville, OH 44683; 740-922-4795; fax: 740-922-7020; 8AM-4:30PM (EST). *Misdemeanor, Civil Actions under $15,000, Small Claims.* www.tusccourtsouthern.com/

General Information: Probation Office phone: 740-922-3653 & 922-4360 or 866-798-3653. Probation Office hours: 8AM-4:30PM. Online identifiers in results same as on public terminal. No sealed records released. No fee to fax documents locally only. Court makes copy: $.10 per page. No certification fee. Payee: Tuscarawas County Court. Personal checks accepted. Credit cards accepted in person or on website. Prepayment required. Mail requests: SASE required.

Civil Name Search: Access: Fax, mail, in person, online. Both court and visitors may perform in person name searches. No search fee. Civil records go back to 1970's, civil records on computer from 2/94, prior in books. Mail turnaround time 1-2 days. Civil PAT goes back to 1994. Search records free at http://66.219.135.176/

Criminal Name Search: Access: Fax, mail, in person, online. Both court and visitors may perform in person name searches. No search fee. Required to search: name, years to search, DOB. Criminal records computerized from 2/94, prior in books. Mail turnaround time 1-2 days. Criminal PAT goes back to same as civil. Search records free at http://66.219.135.176/. Warrants are also available on the court website. Online results show middle initial, DOB.

New Philadelphia Municipal Court 166 E High Ave, New Philadelphia, OH 44663; 330-343-6797; criminal phone: 330-343-6797; civil phone: x231; fax: 330-364-6885; 8AM-4:30PM (EST). *Misdemeanor, Civil Actions under $15,000, Eviction, Small Claims.* www.npmunicipalcourt.org

General Information: The New Philadelphia Municipal Court has territorial jurisdiction within the municipal corporations of New Philadelphia and Dover, and the villages of Baltic, Bolivar, Midvale, Mineral City, Roswell, Stonecreek, Strasburg, Sugarcreek, and Zoar. Will not fax documents. Court makes copy: $.25 per page. Certification fee: $1.00 per page. Payee: Municipal Court. Personal checks accepted. Visa/MC accepted in person only. Prepayment required.

Civil Name Search: Access: In person, online. Visitors must perform in person searches themselves. Civil records on computer back to 4/91, prior in books to 1976. Civil PAT goes back to 4/1991. Search the docket index form the home page.

Criminal Name Search: Access: In person, online. Visitors must perform in person searches themselves. Required to search: name, SSN. Criminal records computerized from 4/91, prior in books to 1976. Criminal PAT goes back to 4/1991. Search the docket index form the home page.

Probate Court 101 E High Ave, Rm 103, New Philadelphia, OH 44663-2636; probate phone: 330-365-3266; fax: 330-364-3190; 8AM-4:30PM (EST). *Probate.* www.co.tuscarawas.oh.us/Probate/Probate.htm

Union County

Common Pleas Court County Courthouse, Clerk of Courts, 215 W 5th St, Marysville, OH 43040; criminal phone: 937-645-3140; civil phone: 937-645-3006; probate phone: 937-645-3029; fax: 937-645-3162; 8:30AM-4PM (EST). *Felony, Civil Actions over $10,000.* www.co.union.oh.us/GD/Templates/Pages/UC/UCDetail.aspx?page=416

General Information: Probate court is a separate court at the same address. Probate fax is 937-645-3160. Will fax out specific pleadings for $3.00 per fax. Court makes copy: $.10 per page. Certification fee: $1.00 per page. Payee: Clerk of Court. Only cashiers checks and money orders accepted. No credit cards accepted. Prepayment required. Mail requests: SASE required for mail return of any copies.

Civil Name Search: Access: In person, online. Visitors must perform in person searches themselves. Required to search: name, years to search; also helpful: address. Civil records on computer from 1990, records go back to 1850. Civil PAT goes back to 1990. Online access to the court clerk's public records and index is free the home page. Records go back to 1/1990, older records added as accessed. Images go back to 1/2002.

Criminal Name Search: Access: In person, online. Visitors must perform in person searches themselves. Required to search: name, years to search, DOB, also helpful: address. Criminal records computerized from 1990, records go back to 1850. Criminal PAT goes back to same as civil. Online access to court clerk's public record and index is free www.co.union.oh.us/GD/Templates/Pages/UC/UCCrumbTrail.aspx?page=1009. Records go back to 1/1990, older records added as accessed. Images go back to 1/2002.

Marysville Municipal Court City Hall Bldg, 125 E 6th St, Marysville, OH 43040; 937-644-9102; civil phone: x1003; fax: 937-644-1228; 8AM-4PM (EST). *Misdemeanor, Civil Actions under $15,000, Eviction, Small Claims.*

http://municourt.co.union.oh.us/

General Information: If faxing a request for a background check, no more than 2 individuals will be search per request. No probation records released. No fee to fax documents. Court makes copy: $.10 per page after 1st 10 copies free. No certification fee. Payee: Marysville Municipal Court. Personal checks accepted, credit cards are not. Prepayment required. Mail requests: SASE required.

Civil Name Search: Access: Fax, mail, in person. Both court and visitors may perform in person name searches. No search fee. Civil records on computer from 1989, prior on microfilm. Mail turnaround time 1-2 days. Civil PAT goes back to 1989.

Criminal Name Search: Access: Fax, mail, in person. Both court and visitors may perform in person name searches. No search fee. Required to search: name, years to search, SSN. Criminal records computerized from 1989, prior on microfilm. Mail turnaround time 1-2 days. Criminal PAT goes back to same as civil.

Van Wert County

Common Pleas Court 305 Courthouse, 121 E Main St, Van Wert, OH 45891; 419-238-6935; criminal phone: 419-238-1022; civil phone: 419-238-1022; fax: 419-238-4760; 8AM-4PM (EST). *Felony, Civil Actions, Probate.*

www.vwcommonpleas.org

General Information: Fax number for Common Pleas Clerk is 419-238-4760. All records public. Will not fax documents. Court makes copy: $.25 per page. Certification fee: $1.00; $5.00 for exemplification. Payee: Clerk of Court. Personal checks accepted, credit cards are not. Prepayment required.

Civil Name Search: Access: In person only. Visitors must perform in person searches themselves. Some early records on microfiche, have docket books and files, indexed on computer since 5/98. Civil PAT goes back to 5/1998. Court calendars available online.

Criminal Name Search: Access: In person only. Visitors must perform in person searches themselves. Required to search: name, years to search; also helpful: address, DOB, SSN. Some early years on microfiche, have docket books and files, indexed on computer since 5/98. Criminal PAT goes back to same as civil. Court calendar available online.

Van Wert Municipal Court 124 S Market, Van Wert, OH 45891; 419-238-5767; fax: 419-238-5865; 8AM-4PM (EST). *Misdemeanor, Civil Actions under $15,000, Eviction, Small Claims.*

http://vanwert.org/gov/court/index.htm

General Information: Fee to fax out file $1.00 per page. Court makes copy: $.10 per page. Certification fee: $1.00. Payee: Municipal Court. Personal checks, Visa/MC accepted. Prepayment required. Mail requests: SASE required.

Civil Name Search: Access: Mail, in person. Both court and visitors may perform in person name searches. No search fee. Civil records on computer from 1989. Mail turnaround time 1-2 days. Civil PAT goes back to 1988.

Criminal Name Search: Access: Mail, in person. Both court and visitors may perform in person name searches. No search fee. Required to search: name, years to search; also helpful: SSN. Criminal records computerized from 1989. Mail turnaround time 1-2 days. Criminal PAT goes back to same as civil.

Probate Court 108 E Main St, Annex, Van Wert, OH 45891; probate phone: 419-238-0027; 8AM-4PM. *Probate.*

www.lucas-co-probate-ct.org/Van%20Wert.htm

Vinton County

Common Pleas Court County Courthouse, 100 E Main St, McArthur, OH 45651; 740-596-3001; probate phone: 740-596-5480; fax: 740-596-9611; 8:30AM-4PM (EST). *Felony, Civil Actions over $3,000, Probate.*

General Information: Probate court is a separate court at the same address. No sealed records released. Will fax documents to local or toll-free number. Court makes copy: $.25 per page. Certification fee: $2.00. Payee: Vinton County Clerk of Court. Personal checks accepted, credit cards are not. Prepayment required.

Civil Name Search: Access: In person only. Visitors must perform in person searches themselves. Civil records in books since 1850. Note: Will not mail search requests. Civil PAT goes back to 1/1998.

Criminal Name Search: Access: In person only. Visitors must perform in person searches themselves. Required to search: name, years to search; also helpful: DOB, SSN. Criminal records in books since 1850. Note: Will not mail search requests. Criminal PAT goes back to same as civil.

Vinton County Court County Courthouse, 100 E Main St, McArthur, OH 45651; 740-596-5000; fax: 740-596-9721; 8:30AM-4PM (EST). *Misdemeanor, Civil Actions under $15,000, Small Claims $3,000.*

General Information: Will not fax out case files. Court makes copy: $.10 per page. Self serve copy: $.10 per page. No certification fee. Payee: Vinton County Court. No personal checks or credit cards accepted. Prepayment required.

Civil Name Search: Access: In person only. Both court and visitors may perform in person name searches. No search fee. Civil records in books from 1980s, archived from 1800s. Civil PAT goes back to 9/1999.

Criminal Name Search: Access: In person only. Both court and visitors may perform in person name searches. No search fee. Required to search: name, years to search, DOB; SSN helpful. Criminal records in books from 1980s, archived from 1800s. Criminal PAT goes back to 9/1999.

Warren County

Common Pleas Court PO Box 238, 500 Justice Dr, Lebanon, OH 45036; 513-695-1120; fax: 513-695-2965; 8:30AM-4:30PM (EST). *Felony, Civil Actions over $3,000.*

www.co.warren.oh.us/clerkofcourt/

General Information: Online identifiers in results same as on public terminal. Will fax documents $2.00 per fax plus $1.00 per page. Court makes copy: $.05 per page. Certification fee: $1.00 per page; exemplification- $5.00 per doc. Payee: Clerk of Court. Personal checks accepted, credit cards are not. Prepayment required. Mail requests: SASE required.

Civil Name Search: Access: Phone, mail, in person, online. Both court and visitors may perform in person name searches. Search fee: $4.00 per name. Civil records on computer from 1974, archived from 1850. Mail turnaround time 1-4 days. Civil PAT goes back to 1974. Access to court records is free at www.co.warren.oh.us/clerkofcourt/search/index.htm. Index goes back to 1980.

Criminal Name Search: Access: Mail, in person, online. Both court and visitors may perform in person name searches. Search fee: $4.00 per name. Required to search: name, years to search, DOB, signed release; also helpful: SSN. Criminal records computerized from 1974, archived from 1850. Mail turnaround time 1-4 days. Criminal PAT goes back to same as civil. Access to court records is free at www.co.warren.oh.us/clerkofcourt/search/index.htm. Index goes back to 1980. Online results show middle initial.

Lebanon Municipal Court City Bldg, 50 S Broadway, Lebanon, OH 45036-1777; 513-933-7210; fax: 513-933-7212; 8AM-4PM (EST). *Misdemeanor, Civil Actions, Eviction, Small Claims.*

http://court.lebanonohio.gov/

General Information: No fee to fax documents locally only. Court makes copy: $.25 per page; first 6 pages free. No certification fee. No personal checks or credit cards accepted.

Civil Name Search: Access: Fax, mail, in person, online. Both court and visitors may perform in person name searches. No search fee. Civil records on books since 1956, computerized since 1990. Mail turnaround time 2 days. Civil PAT goes back to 1989. Search by name or case number at http://court.lebanonohio.gov/search.shtml. Results show address.

Criminal Name Search: Access: Fax, mail, in person, online. Both court and visitors may perform in person name searches. No search fee. Required to search: name, years to search; also helpful: DOB, SSN. Criminal docket on books since 1956, computerized since 1990. Mail turnaround time 2 days. Criminal PAT goes back to same as civil. Search by name or case number at http://court.lebanonohio.gov/search.shtml. Results show DOB and address.

County Court 550 Justice Dr, Lebanon, OH 45036; criminal phone: 513-695-1370; civil phone: 513-695-1372; fax: 513-695-2990; 8AM-4:30PM (EST). *Misdemeanor, Civil Actions under $15,000, Small Claims under $3000.*

www.co.warren.oh.us/countycourt/

General Information: Will fax documents of 5 pgs or less. Court makes copy: $.05 per page. No certification fee. Payee: Warren County Court. Personal checks accepted. Visa/MC accepted for criminal only. Prepayment required. Mail requests: SASE required.

Civil Name Search: Access: Mail, in person, online. Both court and visitors may perform in person name searches. No search fee. Required to search: name, years to search; also helpful: address. Civil records on computer from 1990. Note: No in person searches on Tuesdays thru Thursdays. Civil PAT goes back to 1990. PAT located at 500 Justice Dr. Search court records on the CourtView system free at http://countycourt.co.warren.oh.us/pa/. Online records go back to 1990; no DOBs on civil results.

Criminal Name Search: Access: Phone, mail, in person, online. Both court and visitors may perform in person name searches. No search fee. Required to search: name, years to search, DOB; also helpful: SSN, address. Criminal records computerized from 1990, prior in books. Note: No in person searches on Tuesdays or Thursdays. Mail turnaround time 1-2 weeks. Criminal PAT goes back to 1990. PAT located at 500 Justice Dr. Note the DOB may not show on all docket look-ups. Search court records on the CourtView system free at http://countycourt.co.warren.oh.us/pa/. Online records go back to 1990. Online results show name, DOB.

Franklin Municipal Court 1 Benjamin Franklin Way, Franklin, OH 45005; 937-746-2858; fax: 937-743-7751; 8:30AM-5PM (EST). *Misdemeanor, Civil Actions under $15,000, Eviction, Small Claims.* www.franklinohio.org/pages/courtmain.asp

General Information: Will fax documents. Court makes copy: $.25 per page. Certification fee: $.25 per document plus copy fee. Payee: Franklin Municipal Court. Personal checks accepted. Credit cards accepted in person only. Prepayment required. Mail requests: SASE required to mail back any docs.

Civil Name Search: Access: Phone, mail, in person. Both court and visitors may perform in person name searches. No search fee. Civil records on computer back to 1990. Mail turnaround time 1-2 days.

Criminal Name Search: Access: Phone, mail, in person. Both court and visitors may perform in person name searches. No search fee. Required to search: name, years to search, signed release; also helpful: DOB, SSN. Criminal records computerized from 1990. Mail turnaround time 1-2 days.

Mason Municipal Court 5950 S Mason Montgomery Rd, Mason, OH 45040-3712; 513-398-7901; fax: 513-459-8085; 7:30AM-4PM (EST). *Misdemeanor, Civil Actions under $15,000, Eviction, Small Claims.* www.masonmunicipalcourt.org

General Information: No fee to fax documents locally only. Court makes copy: n/a. Self serve copy: $.05 per page. Certification fee: $3.00 per page. Payee: Mason Municipal Court. Cashiers checks and money orders accepted. Credit card okay for in person criminal searching only. Prepayment required. Mail requests: SASE required.

Civil Name Search: Access: Phone, fax, mail, in person, online. Both court and visitors may perform in person name searches. No search fee. Civil records in docket books since 1985, computerized since 1988. Mail turnaround time 1-2 weeks. Online access to court records is free at http://courtconnect.masonmunicipalcourt.org/connection/court/.

Criminal Name Search: Access: Phone, fax, mail, in person, online. Both court and visitors may perform in person name searches. No search fee. Required to search: name, years to search; also helpful: SSN. Criminal records in docket books since 1985, computerized since 1988. Mail turnaround time 1-2 weeks. Online access to court records is free at http://courtconnect.masonmunicipalcourt.org/connection/court/. Online results show middle initial.

Probate and Juvenile Court 570 Justice Dr, Lebanon, OH 45036-2361; probate phone: 513-695-1180/1181; fax: 513-695-2945 ;. *Probate.* www.co.warren.oh.us/probate_juvenile/

Washington County

Common Pleas Court 205 Putnam St, Marietta, OH 45750; 740-373-6623 x366, x398; probate phone: x254; fax: 740-374-3758; 8AM-4:15PM (EST). *Felony, Civil Actions over $15,000, Probate.* www.washingtongov.org

General Information: This court will not perform a name search. Probate court is a separate court at the same address, in Annex on 3rd Fl. No sealed, expunged records released. Will fax or transmit document for $2.00 plus $1.00 per page. Court makes copy: $.10 per page. Certification fee: $1.00 per page. Exemplification fee is $2.00 plus $1.00 per page. Payee: Clerk of Court. Personal checks accepted. Credit cards accepted. Prepayment required.

Civil Name Search: Access: In person only. Visitors must perform in person searches themselves. Civil records on computer since 1985, microfilm 1977-1984, index in books from 1795. Civil PAT goes back to 1985. 2 public terminals.

Criminal Name Search: Access: In person only. Visitors must perform in person searches themselves. Criminal records on computer since 1985, microfilm 1977-1984, index in books back to 1795. Criminal PAT goes back to same as civil.

Marietta Municipal Court PO Box 615, 301 Putnam, Marietta, OH 45750; 740-373-4474; fax: 740-373-2547; 8AM-4:30PM (EST). *Misdemeanor, Civil Actions under $15,000, Eviction, Small Claims.* www.mariettacourt.com

General Information: Will not fax documents. Court makes copy: $.05 per page. Certification fee: $1.50. Payee: Municipal Court. Personal checks accepted. Major credit cards accepted. Prepayment required. Mail requests: SASE required.

Civil Name Search: Access: Mail, in person, online. Only the court performs in person name searches; visitors may not. No search fee. Civil records on computer from 11/91, prior in books. Mail turnaround time 1 week. Online access to from 1992 of court dockets is free at www.mariettacourt.com/search.shtml.

Criminal Name Search: Access: Mail, in person, online. Both court and visitors may perform in person name searches. No search fee. Criminal records computerized from 11/91, prior in books back to 1975. Mail turnaround time 1 week. Online access to from 1992 of court dockets is free at www.mariettacourt.com/search.shtml. Online results show middle initial, DOB.

Wayne County

Common Pleas Court PO Box 507, 107 W Liberty St, Wooster, OH 44691; 330-287-5590; probate phone: 330-287-5575; fax: 330-287-5416; 8AM-4:30PM (EST). *Felony, Civil Actions over $15,000, Probate.* www.wayneohio.org/

General Information: Probate court is a separate court at the same address, 2nd Fl. No grand jury indictment records released. Will not fax documents. Court makes copy: $.10 per page. Certification fee: $3.00. Payee: Clerk of Court. Personal checks, Visa/MC accepted. Prepayment required. Mail requests: SASE required.

Civil Name Search: Access: Mail, in person, online. Visitors must perform in person searches themselves. No search fee. Civil records on computer since 1995, in books to 1800s. Note: No name searches are performed by mail. Civil PAT goes back to 1995. Online access same as criminal, see below, probate index included.

Criminal Name Search: Access: Mail, in person, online. Visitors must perform in person searches themselves. No search fee. Criminal records on computer since 1995, in books to 1800s. Mail turnaround time 1 week. Criminal PAT goes back to same as civil. Online access free at www.waynecourts.org/disclaimer.

Wayne County Municipal Court Clerk 215 N Grant St, Wooster, OH 44691-4817; 330-287-5650; criminal phone: 330-287-5651; civil phone: 330-287-5658; fax: 330-263-4043; 8AM-4:30PM (EST). *Misdemeanor, Civil Actions under $15,000, Eviction, Small Claims.* www.waynecourts.org/

General Information: Will fax out specific case files. Court makes copy: $.10 per page. Certification fee: $1.00 per page and includes copy fee. Payee: Wayne County Municipal Court. In state personal checks accepted. Major credit cards accepted. Prepayment required.

Civil Name Search: Access: In person, online. Visitors must perform in person searches themselves. Civil records on computer back to 9/94; in books from 1975. Civil PAT goes back to 9/1994 countywide. Online access is same as criminal, see below.

Criminal Name Search: Access: In person, online. Visitors must perform in person searches themselves. Required to search: name, years to search, offense, date of offense. Criminal records computerized from 9/94; in books from 1975. Criminal PAT goes back to same as civil. Online access free at www.waynecourts.org/disclaimer. Online results show middle initial, DOB.

Williams County

Common Pleas Court 1 Courthouse Sq, Clerk of Court of Common Pleas, Bryan, OH 43506; 419-636-1551; probate phone: 419-636-1548; fax: 419-636-7877; 8:30AM-4:30PM (EST). *Felony, Civil Actions over $10,000, Domestic, Probate.* www.co.williams.oh.us/

General Information: Probate court is a separate court at the same address, 2nd Fl. No expunged records released. Will fax documents $2.00 1st pg, $1.00 each add'l, once copy charges paid;. Court makes copy: $.10 per page. Self serve copy: same. Certification fee: $1.00 per page. Payee: Clerk of Court. Personal checks accepted. Credit cards accepted. Prepayment required. Mail requests: SASE required.

Civil Name Search: Access: Phone, fax, mail, in person. Both court and visitors may perform in person name searches. No search fee. Civil records

on computer from 1988, records go back to 1840. Mail turnaround time 1-2 days. Civil PAT goes back to 4/1988.
Criminal Name Search: Access: Mail, in person. Both court and visitors may perform in person name searches. No search fee. Criminal records computerized from 1988, records go back to 1840. Mail turnaround time 1-2 days. Criminal PAT goes back to same as civil.

Bryan Municipal Court PO Box 546, 1399 E High St, Bryan, OH 43506; 419-636-6939; fax: 419-636-3417; 8:30AM-4:30PM (EST). *Misdemeanor, Civil Actions under $15,000, Eviction, Small Claims.* www.bryanmunicipalcourt.com
General Information: Will fax documents $2.00. No copy fee. Certification fee: $2.00 per page. Payee: Bryan Municipal Court. Personal checks accepted. Credit cards accepted. Prepayment required. Mail requests: SASE requested.
Civil Name Search: Access: Fax, mail, in person, online. Both court and visitors may perform in person name searches. No search fee. Civil records on computer from 1988, prior in books to 1966, indexed prior. Mail turnaround time 5 days. Civil PAT goes back to 1988. Muni Ct data available free at http://casesearch.bryanmunicipalcourt.com/.
Criminal Name Search: Access: Fax, mail, in person, online. Both court and visitors may perform in person name searches. No search fee. Required to search: name, years to search, DOB; also helpful: SSN. Criminal records computerized from 1988, prior in books to 1966, indexed prior. Mail turnaround time 5 days. Criminal PAT goes back to same as civil. Muni Ct data available free at http://casesearch.bryanmunicipalcourt.com/.

Wood County

Common Pleas Court 1 Courthouse Sq, Bowling Green, OH 43402; 419-354-9280; probate phone: 419-354-9231; fax: 419-354-9241; 8:30AM-4:30PM (EST). *Felony, Civil Actions over $15,000, Probate, Domestic Relation.*
http://clerkofcourt.co.wood.oh.us/
General Information: Probate court is a separate court at the same address. Probate fax is 419-354-9357. Search probate records online at the county website. No adoption commitment, parental rights, juvenile, mental illness records released. Fee to fax back is $2.00 plus $1.00 per page. Many documents can be returned via email. Court makes copy: $.06 per page first 25 pages. Certification fee: $1.00. Payee: Wood County Clerk of Courts. Business checks accepted. No credit cards accepted. Prepayment required.
Civil Name Search: Access: In person, online. Both court and visitors may perform in person name searches. Search fee: $2.00. Civil records on computer from 7/90, in books and on microfilm from 1800s, docket books, journals and microfilm back to 1800s. Civil PAT goes back to 7/1990. Access court index free at https://pub.clerkofcourt.co.wood.oh.us/pa/.
Criminal Name Search: Access: In person, online. Both court and visitors may perform in person name searches. Search fee: $2.00. Criminal records computerized from 7/90, in books and on microfilm from 1980, docket books, journals and microfilm back to 1800s. Criminal PAT goes back to 1/1960. Access court index free at https://pub.clerkofcourt.co.wood.oh.us/pa/.

Bowling Green Municipal Court 711 S Dunbridge Rd, Bowling Green, OH 43402; 419-352-5263; fax: 419-352-9407; 8:30AM-4:30PM (EST). *Misdemeanor, Civil Actions under $15,000, Eviction, Small Claims.* www.bgcourt.org
General Information: No fee to fax documents locally only. Court makes copy: $.05 per page. Certification fee: $1.00 per page. Payee: Bowling Green Municipal Court. Personal checks accepted. Credit cards accepted. Mail requests: SASE required.
Civil Name Search: Access: Phone, fax, mail, in person, online. Both court and visitors may perform in person name searches. No search fee. Civil records on computer from 1988. Mail turnaround time 3 days. Civil PAT goes back to 1988. Access is free to civil records at http://bgcourtweb.bgohio.org/connection/court/.
Criminal Name Search: Access: Phone, fax, mail, in person, online. Both court and visitors may perform in person name searches. No search fee. Required to search: name, years to search, DOB; also helpful: SSN. Criminal records computerized from 1988. Mail turnaround time 3 days. Criminal PAT goes back to 1988. Terminal results may include DL or vehicle number. Free access to criminal and traffic records from

http://bgcourtweb.bgohio.org/connection/court/. Online results show middle initial, DOB.

Perrysburg Municipal Court 300 Walnut St, Perrysburg, OH 43551; criminal phone: 419-872-7900; civil phone: 419-872-7910; fax: 419-872-7905; 8AM-4:30PM M, W-F; 8AM-6:30PM T (EST). *Misdemeanor, Civil Actions under $15,000, Eviction, Small Claims.*
www.perrysburgcourt.com
General Information: No expunged records released. Fee to fax out file $5.00 each. Court makes copy: $.10 per page. Self serve copy: same. Certification fee: $5.00 per cert. Payee: Municipal Court. Personal checks not accepted for searches or copies. No credit cards accepted for copies or searches. Prepayment required. Mail requests: SASE required.
Civil Name Search: Access: Mail, fax, online, in person. Only the court performs in person name searches; visitors may not. Search fee: $3.00 per name. Fee is $15.00 to look in closed, stored files. Required to search: name, years to search; also helpful: address. Civil records on computer from 1989, prior in books to 1982, archived from 1972. Mail turnaround time 2 days. Online access to court records is free at www.perrysburgcourt.com/disc.html.
Criminal Name Search: Access: Mail, fax, online, in person. Only the court performs in person name searches; visitors may not. Search fee: $3.00 per name. Fee is $15.00 to look in closed, stored files. Required to search: name, years to search; also helpful: DOB, SSN. Criminal records computerized from 1989, prior in books to 1982, archived from 1972. Mail turnaround time 2 days. Online access to court records is free at www.perrysburgcourt.com/disc.html.

Wyandot County

Common Pleas Court 109 S Sandusky Ave, Rm 31, Upper Sandusky, OH 43351; 419-294-1432; probate phone: 419-294-2302; fax: 419-294-6414; 8:30AM-4:30PM (EST). *Felony, Civil Actions over $10,000, Probate.*
www.co.wyandot.oh.us/clerk/index.html
General Information: Probate court is a separate court at the same address, Rm 23. Will fax documents $2.00 1st page, $1.00 ea add'l. Court makes copy: $.10 per page. Self serve copy: same. Certification fee: $1.00 per page. Payee: Clerk of Court. Personal checks accepted, credit cards are not. Prepayment required. Mail requests: SASE required.
Civil Name Search: Access: In person, online. Visitors must perform in person searches themselves. Civil records on computer from 1990, prior in books from late 1800s. Civil PAT goes back to 1/1990. Click on "Common Pleas Inquiry" from web page to view record index.
Criminal Name Search: Access: Fax, mail, in person, phone, online. Both court and visitors may perform in person name searches. No search fee. Required to search: name, years to search; also helpful: SSN. Criminal records computerized from 1990, prior in books from late 1800s. Mail turnaround time 1-2 days. Criminal PAT goes back to same as civil. Click on "Common Pleas Inquiry" at web page to view record index.

Upper Sandusky Municipal Court 119 N 7th St, Upper Sandusky, OH 43351; 419-294-3354/3809; fax: 419-209-0474; 8AM-4:30PM (EST). *Misdemeanor, Civil Actions under $15,000, Eviction, Small Claims.*
https://www.uppermunicourt.com/
General Information: The Court handles Traffic, Criminal, Civil, and Small Claims cases in Wyandot County including the City of Upper Sandusky and the Villages of Carey, Nevada, Wharton, Kirby and Sycamore. No sealed records released. Will fax documents to local or toll-free number. Court makes copy: $1.00 per page.The $.50 per page self-serve copy fee includes certification. Certification fee: $2.00 per page includes copy fee. Payee: Upper Sandusky. Personal checks accepted; proper ID required. Major credit cards accepted. Prepayment required. Mail requests: SASE required.
Civil Name Search: Access: Mail, in person. Only the court performs in person name searches; visitors may not. No search fee. Civil records on computer from 5/90, prior in books. Mail turnaround time 1-2 days. A free search is provided at https://www.uppermunicourt.com/search.shtml.
Criminal Name Search: Access: Mail, in person. Only the court performs in person name searches; visitors may not. No search fee. Required to search: name, DOB, SSN. Criminal records computerized from 5/90, prior in books. Mail turnaround time 1-2 days. A free search is provided at https://www.uppermunicourt.com/search.shtml.

Oklahoma

Time Zone:	CST
Capital:	Oklahoma City, Oklahoma County
# of Counties:	77
State Web:	**www.ok.gov**
Court Web:	**www.oscn.net**

Administration   Administrative Director of Courts, 1915 N Stiles #305, Oklahoma City, OK, 73105; 405-521-2450, Fax: 405-521-6815.

The Supreme Court and Appellate Courts   Oklahoma is unique – it has two courts of last resort. The Supreme Court determines all issues of a civil nature; the Oklahoma Court of Criminal Appeals decides all criminal matters. There is also an intermediate appeals court – the Court of Civil Appeals. See www.ok.gov/redirect.php?link_id=345 for online access to opinions.

The Oklahoma Courts

Court	Type	How Organized	Jurisdiction Highpoints
District*	General	77 Courts in 26 Districts	Felony, Misdemeanor, Civil, Small Claims, Estate, Domestic Relations, Juvenile, Probate
Municipal*	Limited	2 Courts of Record	Traffic, Ordinance
Municipal	Limited	340 Courts NOT of Record	Traffic, Ordinance

* = profiled in this book

Details on the Court Structure   The **District Court** is the trial court and hears all cases except traffic and ordinance matters. There are 77 District Courts in 26 judicial districts. The Court in Creek County has three Divisions, the Court in Seminole County has two Divisions.

Cities with populations in excess of 200,000 (Oklahoma City and Tulsa) have a criminal **Municipal Courts of Record**. Cities with less than 200,000 do not have such courts.

There is also a **Oklahoma Workers' Compensation Court**.

Record Searching Facts You Need to Know

Fees and Record Searching Tips Online Access is Extensive   Over 75% of the courts charge $5.00 for a name search, $1.00 for first copy and $.50 each add'l. Over 90% of the courts offer a public access terminal to look up dockets.

There are two sites that provide access to trial court records.

The Oklahoma District Court Records site at www1.odcr.com/search.php offers both free and an advanced subscription search service. This service is nearly statewide - all counties except Cimarron participate. The advanced subscription permits searching by DOB, address, and provides email notification and a tracking service. Please note most the record from counties in this system date back at least seven years. **Some courts update monthly, but most are daily.** Images of the public court documents are available by subscription, but only to members of the Oklahoma Bar Association in good standing.

Case information is available in bulk form for downloading to computer. For information, call the Administrative Director of Courts, 405-521-2450.

Also, free Internet access to docket information is available for District Courts in 13 counties and all Appellate courts at www.oscn.net. Both civil and criminal docket information is available for the counties involved. The participating counties, referred to as the OCIS Counties, are: Adair, Canadian, Cleveland, Comanche, Ellis, Garfield, Logan, Oklahoma, Payne, Pushmataha, Roger Mills, Rogers, and Tulsa. Also search the Oklahoma Supreme Court Network from this website.

Adair County

15th Judicial District Court PO Box 426, 220 W Division St, Stilwell, OK 74960; 918-696-7633; fax: 918-696-5365; 8AM-4:30PM (CST). *Felony, Misdemeanor, Civil, Eviction, Small Claims, Probate.* www.oscn.net/applications/oscn/start.asp?viewType=COUNTYINFO&county=ADAIR

General Information: No juvenile, mental health or guardianship records released. Will fax documents to local or toll free line. Court makes copy: $1.00 first page, $.50 each add'l. Certification fee: $.50 per page. Payee: Adair County Court Clerk. Personal checks accepted. Major credit cards accepted in person only. Prepayment required. Mail requests: SASE required.

Civil Name Search: Access: Phone, fax, mail, in person, online. Both court and visitors may perform in person name searches. Search fee: $5.00 per name. Fee is for 7 year search. Civil records archived since 1907. Mail turnaround time 1 day. Civil PAT available. Online access to court dockets is free at www.oscn.net/applications/oscn/casesearch.asp. Not all cases prior to 1/2006 will appear online, only cases with docs filed after 1/2006 will appear online. City and rarely phone may appear on online record. Civil shows name and town only. Also both free and advanced pay search service at www1.odcr.com/search.php.

Criminal Name Search: Access: Phone, fax, mail, in person, online. Both court and visitors may perform in person name searches. Search fee: $5.00 per name. Fee is for 7 year search. Required to search: name, years to search, DOB; also helpful: SSN. Criminal records archived since 1907. Mail turnaround time 1 day. Criminal PAT available. Online access to criminal court dockets is same as civil at both sites. Online results show middle initial.

Alfalfa County

4th Judicial District Court County Courthouse, 300 S Grand, Cherokee, OK 73728; 580-596-3523; fax: 580-596-2556; 8:30AM-4:30PM (CST). *Felony, Misdemeanor, Civil, Eviction, Small Claims, Probate.* www.oscn.net

General Information: Online identifiers in results same as on public terminal. No confidential or guardianship records released. Fee to fax out file $4.00 per page; $2.00 each add'l. Court makes copy: $1.00 first page, $.50 each add'l. Certification fee: $.50 per instrument plus copy fee. Payee: Court Clerk. Only cashiers checks and money orders accepted. Major credit cards accepted in person only. Mail requests: SASE required.

Civil Name Search: Access: Mail, in person, online. Both court and visitors may perform in person name searches. Search fee: $5.00 per name. Civil records archived to 1907; on computer back to 1998. Mail turnaround time immediate. Civil PAT goes back to 1998. Both free and advanced pay search service from 8/1998 at www1.odcr.com/search.php; updated monthly. Address or city and sometimes phone may appear on online record.

Criminal Name Search: Access: Mail, in person, online. Both court and visitors may perform in person name searches. Search fee: $5.00 per name. Criminal records archived to 1907; on computer back to 1998. Mail turnaround time 1 day. Criminal PAT goes back to same as civil. Both free and advanced pay search service from 8/1998 at www1.odcr.com/search.php; updated monthly. Address or city and sometimes phone may appear on online record. Online results show middle initial.

Atoka County

25th Judicial District Court 200 E Court St, Atoka, OK 74525; 580-889-3565; 8:30AM-4:30PM (CST). *Felony, Misdemeanor, Civil, Eviction, Small Claims, Probate.* www.oscn.net

General Information: Online identifiers in results same as on public terminal. No adoption, mental health or juvenile records released. Will not fax documents. Court makes copy: $1.00 first page, $.50 each add'l. Certification fee: $.50 per doc. Payee: Court Clerk. No personal checks accepted. Major credit cards accepted in person. Prepayment required. Mail requests: SASE required.

Civil Name Search: Access: Mail, in person, online. Both court and visitors may perform in person name searches. Search fee: $5.00 per name. Civil records on computer back to 1998; prior on books. Mail turnaround time 1-2 days. Civil PAT goes back to 1998. Both free and advanced pay search service from 1/1998 at www1.odcr.com/search.php; updated monthly. City and rarely phone may appear on online record. Civil shows name and town only.

Criminal Name Search: Access: Mail, in person, online. Both court and visitors may perform in person name searches. Search fee: $5.00 per name. Required to search: name, years to search, DOB or SSN. Criminal docket on books from 1920; on computer back to 1998. Mail turnaround time 1-2 days. Criminal PAT goes back to same as civil. Both free and advanced pay search service from 1/1998 at www1.odcr.com/search.php; updated daily. Online results show middle initial.

Beaver County

1st Judicial District Court PO Box 237 (111 W 2nd), Beaver, OK 73932; 580-625-3191; fax: 580-625-2247; 9AM-5PM (CST). *Felony, Misdemeanor, Civil, Eviction, Small Claims, Probate.* www.oscn.net

General Information: Online identifiers in results same as on public terminal. No adoption, mental health or juvenile records released. Will not fax documents. Court makes copy: $1.00 first page, $.50 each add'l. Certification fee: $.50. Payee: Court Clerk. Personal checks accepted. Major credit cards accepted in person only. Prepayment required. Mail requests: SASE required.

Civil Name Search: Access: Phone, mail, in person, online. Both court and visitors may perform in person name searches. Search fee: $5.00. Civil records on microfilm and archives from late 1800s, computerized back to 1997. Mail turnaround time 3 days. Civil PAT goes back to 1997. Both free and advanced pay search service from 6/1/1997 at www1.odcr.com/search.php; updated daily. City and rarely phone may appear on online record. Civil shows name and town only.

Criminal Name Search: Access: Mail, in person, online. Both court and visitors may perform in person name searches. Search fee: $5.00. Criminal records on microfilm and archives from late 1800s, computerized back to 1997. Mail turnaround time 3-4 days. Criminal PAT goes back to same as civil. Both free and advanced pay search service from 6/1/1997 at www1.odcr.com/search.php; updated daily.

Beckham County

2nd Judicial District Court 104 S 3rd, PO Box 520, Sayre, OK 73662; 580-928-3330; fax: 580-928-9278; 9AM-5PM (CST). *Felony, Misdemeanor, Civil, Eviction, Small Claims, Probate.* www.beckham.okcounties.org/

General Information: Online identifiers in results same as on public terminal. No juvenile, adoption or expunged records released. Fee to fax out file $5.00. Court makes copy: $1.00 first page, $.50 each add'l. Self serve copy: same. Certification fee: $.50 per page or $5.00 for a three-way certification. Payee: Court clerk. Personal checks accepted if local. Credit cards accepted if in person. Prepayment required. Mail requests: SASE required.

Civil Name Search: Access: Fax, mail, in person, online. Both court and visitors may perform in person name searches. Search fee: $5.00 per name. Civil records on microfiche back to 1907; on computer back to 1997. Mail turnaround time 2 weeks. Civil PAT goes back to 1996. Both free and advanced pay search service from 1/2000 at www1.odcr.com/search.php; updated daily. City and rarely phone may appear on online record. Civil shows name and town only.

Criminal Name Search: Access: Fax, mail, in person, online. Both court and visitors may perform in person name searches. Search fee: $5.00 per name. Criminal records on microfiche from 1907; on computer back to 1997. Mail turnaround time 2 weeks. Criminal PAT goes back to same as civil. Both free and advanced pay search service from 1/2000 at www1.odcr.com/search.php; updated daily. Online results show middle initial.

Blaine County

4th Judicial District Court 212 N Weigle St, Watonga, OK 73772; 580-623-5970; fax: 580-623-4781; 8AM-4PM (CST). *Felony, Misdemeanor, Civil, Eviction, Small Claims, Probate.* www.oscn.net

General Information: Online identifiers in results same as on public terminal. No juvenile or expunged records released. Will fax back documents; 1-5 pgs $5.00; 6-10 pgs $10.00. Court makes copy: $1.00 first page, $.50 each add'l. Certification fee: $.50 per page. Payee: Court Clerk. Personal checks accepted. Major credit cards accepted in person only. Prepayment required. Mail requests: SASE required.

Civil Name Search: Access: Fax, mail, in person, online. Both court and visitors may perform in person name searches. Search fee: $5.00 per name. Civil records archived from 1900; on computer back to 1998. Mail turnaround time 7-10 days. Civil PAT goes back to 7/1998. Both free and advanced pay search service from 8/1998 at www1.odcr.com/search.php; updated daily. City and rarely phone may appear on online record. Civil shows name and town only.

Criminal Name Search: Access: Fax, mail, in person, online. Both court and visitors may perform in person name searches. Search fee: $5.00 per name. Criminal records archived from 1900; on computer back to 1998. Mail turnaround time 7-10 days. Criminal PAT goes back to same as civil. Both free and advanced pay search service from 8/1998 at www1.odcr.com/search.php; updated daily. Online results show middle initial.

Bryan County

19th Judicial District Court Courthouse 3rd Fl, 402 W Evergreen St, Durant, OK 74701; 580-924-1446; fax: 580-931-0577; 8AM-5PM (CST). *Felony, Misdemeanor, Civil, Eviction, Small Claims, Probate.* www.oscn.net

General Information: Online identifiers in results same as on public terminal. No juvenile, mental health or adoption records released. Will fax documents for fee. Court makes copy: $1.00 first page, $.50 each add'l. Certification fee: $.50 per page. Payee: Bryan County Court Clerk. Only cashiers checks and money orders accepted. No credit cards accepted. Prepayment required. Mail requests: SASE required.

Civil Name Search: Access: Mail, in person, online. Both court and visitors may perform in person name searches. Search fee: $5.00 per name. Required to search: name, years to search, DOB. Civil records archived from 1907; on computer back to 1994. Mail turnaround time 2 days. Civil PAT goes back to 1994. Both free and advanced pay search service from 7/1994 at www1.odcr.com/search.php; updated daily. City and rarely phone may appear on online record. Civil shows name and town only.

Criminal Name Search: Access: Mail, in person, online. Both court and visitors may perform in person name searches. Search fee: $5.00 per name. Required to search: name, DOB, SSN, signed release. Criminal records archived from 1907; on computer back to 1994. Mail turnaround time 2 days. Criminal PAT goes back to same as civil. Both free and advanced pay search service from 7/1/1994 at www1.odcr.com/search.php; updated daily. Online results show middle initial.

Caddo County

6th Judicial District Court PO Box 10, 201 W Oklahoma Ave, Anadarko, OK 73005; 405-247-3393; fax: 405-247-4127; 8:30AM-4:30PM (CST). *Felony, Misdemeanor, Civil, Eviction, Small Claims, Probate.* www.oscn.net

General Information: Online identifiers in results same as on public terminal. No adoption, mental health, juvenile, and some guardianship records released. Will fax documents to local or toll-free number. Court makes copy: $1.00 1st page, $.50 each add'l page. Certification fee: $.50 per instrument. Payee: Court Clerk. No foreign checks accepted. No credit cards accepted. Prepayment required. Mail requests: SASE helpful.

Civil Name Search: Access: Mail, in person, online. Both court and visitors may perform in person name searches. Search fee: $10.00 per hour. Civil records on computer since 1997; prior on docket books to 1901. Mail turnaround time 1 week. Public use terminal available. Both free and advanced pay search service from 1/1997 at www1.odcr.com/search.php; updated monthly. City and rarely phone may appear on online record. Civil shows name and town only.

Criminal Name Search: Access: Mail, in person, online. Both court and visitors may perform in person name searches. Search fee: $10.00 per hour. Criminal records on computer since 1997, prior on docket books to 1901. Mail turnaround time 1 week. Public use terminal available. Both free and advanced pay search service from 1/1997 at www1.odcr.com/search.php; updated monthly. Online results show middle initial.

Canadian County

26th Judicial District Court PO Box 730, 301 N Choctaw St, El Reno, OK 73036; 405-295-6172; criminal phone: 405-295-6165; civil phone: 405-295-6168; probate phone: 405-295-6160; 8AM-4:30PM (CST). *Felony, Misdemeanor, Civil, Eviction, Small Claims, Probate.* www.oscn.net

General Information: Online identifiers in results same as on public terminal. No expunged criminal cases, juvenile, adoption, confidential portion of guardianship records released. Will not fax documents. Court makes copy: $1.00 first page, $.50 each add'l. Certification fee: $.50 per page. Payee: Court Clerk. Personal checks accepted, credit cards are not. Prepayment required.

Civil Name Search: Access: Mail, in person, online. Both court and visitors may perform in person name searches. Search fee: $5.00 per name. Civil records on computer back to 1993, archived from 1907. Mail turnaround time 2-3 days. Civil PAT goes back to 1993. Online access to court dockets is free at www.oscn.net/applications/oscn/casesearch.asp. Dockets go back to 3/1993. Online record includes physical description, phone. Also both free and advanced pay search service at www1.odcr.com/search.php.

Criminal Name Search: Access: Mail, online, in person. Both court and visitors may perform in person name searches. Search fee: $5.00 per name. Required to search: name, years to search, DOB or SSN. Criminal records computerized from 1993, archived from 1907. Mail turnaround time 2-3

days. Criminal PAT goes back to same as civil. Online access to criminal dockets is same as civil.

Carter County

20th Judicial District Court PO Box 37, Court Clerk, First & B Southwest, Court Clerk, Ardmore, OK 73402; 580-223-5253; 8AM-N, 1-5PM (CST). *Felony, Misdemeanor, Civil, Eviction, Small Claims, Probate.* www.brightok.net/cartercounty/courtclerk.html

General Information: Online identifiers in results same as on public terminal. No juvenile, mental health, or adoption records released. The copy room is filled with Elvis memorabilia. Court makes copy: $1.00 first page, $.50 each add'l. Self serve copy: same. Certification fee: $.50 per page. Payee: Carter County Court Clerk. Personal checks accepted. Prepayment required. Mail requests: SASE required.

Civil Name Search: Access: Mail, in person, online. Both court and visitors may perform in person name searches. Search fee: $5.00 per name. Civil records archived from 1907; on computer back to 1997. Mail turnaround time 1 week. Civil PAT goes back to 1997. Both free and advanced pay search service from 1/1997 at www1.odcr.com/search.php; updated real time. City and rarely phone may appear on online record. Civil shows name and town only.

Criminal Name Search: Access: Mail, in person, online. Both court and visitors may perform in person name searches. Search fee: $5.00 per name. Criminal records archived from 1907; on computer back to 1997. Mail turnaround time 1 week. Criminal PAT goes back to same as civil. Both free and advanced pay search service from 1/1997 at www1.odcr.com/search.php; updated real time. Online results show middle initial.

Cherokee County

15th Judicial District Court 213 W Delaware, Rm 302, Tahlequah, OK 74464; 918-456-0691; fax: 918-458-6587; 8AM-4:30PM (CST). *Felony, Misdemeanor, Civil, Eviction, Small Claims, Probate.* www.oscn.net

General Information: Online identifiers in results same as on public terminal. No juvenile, adoption, guardianship, or mental health released. Will fax documents $5.00 per name. Court makes copy: $1.00 first page, $.50 each add'l. Certification fee: $.50 per page. Payee: Court Clerk. No personal checks or credit cards accepted. Prepayment required. Mail requests: SASE required.

Civil Name Search: Access: Phone, mail, in person, online. Both court and visitors may perform in person name searches. Search fee: $5.00 per name. Civil records stored from 1907 (civil, probate, vital); computerized since 1997. Mail turnaround time 1-2 days. Civil PAT goes back to 1997. Both free and advanced pay search service from 1/1997 at www1.odcr.com/search.php; updated daily. City and rarely phone may appear on online record. Civil shows name and town only.

Criminal Name Search: Access: Phone, mail, in person, online. Both court and visitors may perform in person name searches. Search fee: $5.00 per name. Required to search: name, years to search, DOB. Criminal records kept from 1907. Mail turnaround time 1-2 days. Criminal PAT goes back to same as civil. Both free and advanced pay search service from 1/1997 at www1.odcr.com/search.php; updated daily.

Choctaw County

17th Judicial District Court 300 E Duke, Hugo, OK 74743; 580-326-7554 & 7555; fax: 580-326-0291; 8AM-4PM (CST). *Felony, Misdemeanor, Civil, Eviction, Small Claims, Probate.* www.oscn.net

General Information: Probate fax is same as main fax number. Online identifiers in results same as on public terminal. No juvenile, adoption, guardianship, wills or expunged records released. Will fax documents $7.50 fee. Court makes copy: $1.00 first page, $.50 each add'l. Self serve copy: same. Certification fee: $.50 document plus copy fee. Payee: Court Clerk. Personal checks accepted, credit cards are not. Prepayment required. Mail requests: SASE required.

Civil Name Search: Access: Phone, fax, mail, in person, online. Both court and visitors may perform in person name searches. Search fee: $10.00 per name. Civil records archived from 1907. Mail turnaround time 1 day. Civil PAT available. Both free and advanced pay search service from 8/2002 at www1.odcr.com/search.php; updated daily. City and rarely phone may appear on online record. Civil shows name and town only.

Criminal Name Search: Access: Phone, fax, mail, in person, online. Both court and visitors may perform in person name searches. Search fee: $10.00 per name. Required to search: name, years to search, DOB. Criminal records archived from 1907. Mail turnaround time 1 day. Criminal PAT available. Both free and advanced pay search service from 8/2002 at www1.odcr.com/search.php; updated daily.

Cimarron County

1st Judicial District Court PO Box 788, Boise City, OK 73933; 580-544-2221; fax: 580-544-2006; 9AM-N,1-5PM (CST). *Felony, Misdemeanor, Civil, Eviction, Small Claims, Probate.* www.oscn.net

General Information: All records searches must include a written request and can be obtained by calling Court Clerks office. No juvenile, adoption or mental health records released. Will fax documents to local or toll-free number. Court makes copy: $1.00 first page, $.50 each add'l. Certification fee: $.50 per page. Payee: Court Clerk. Personal checks accepted, credit cards are not. Prepayment required. Mail requests: SASE required, $10.00 mailing fee if no SASE enclosed.

Civil Name Search: Access: Mail, fax, in person. Both court and visitors may perform in person name searches. Search fee: $7.00 per quarter hour search fee. Civil records archived from 1907; on computer back to 8/2001. Mail turnaround time varies. Civil PAT goes back to 2002.

Criminal Name Search: Access: Mail, fax, in person. Both court and visitors may perform in person name searches. Search fee: $7.00 per quarter hour search fee. Criminal records archived from 1907. Mail turnaround time varies. Criminal PAT goes back to 2002.

Cleveland County

21st Judicial District Court 200 S Peters, Norman, OK 73069; 405-321-6402; 8AM-5PM (CST). *Felony, Misdemeanor, Civil, Eviction, Small Claims, Probate.* www.oscn.net

General Information: Probate index and its doc index is also available online. Online identifiers in results same as on public terminal. No juvenile, adoption, or guardianship records released. No expunged, sealed records released. Will not fax documents. Court makes copy: $1.00 first page, $.50 each add'l. Certification fee: $.50 per cert. Payee: Court Clerk. Personal checks, Visa/MC accepted. Prepayment required. Mail requests: SASE required.

Civil Name Search: Access: Mail, in person, online. Both court and visitors may perform in person name searches. No search fee. Civil records on computer from 1989, on microfiche from 1800s, archived since 1970. Mail turnaround time 7-10 days. Civil PAT goes back to 1989. Online access to court cases is free at www.oscn.net/applications/oscn/casesearch.asp. Dockets go back to 1/1989. Online record includes physical description, phone. Also both free and advanced pay search service at www1.odcr.com/search.php.

Criminal Name Search: Access: Mail, in person, online. Both court and visitors may perform in person name searches. No search fee. Criminal records computerized from 1989, on microfiche from 1800s. Mail turnaround time 7-10 days. Criminal PAT goes back to 1989. Online access to court dockets is free at www.oscn.net/applications/oscn/casesearch.asp. Dockets go back to 1/1999. Also both free and advanced pay search service at www1.odcr.com/search.php.

Coal County

25th Judicial District Court 4 N Main St, Coalgate, OK 74538; 580-927-2281; fax: 580-927-2339; 8AM-4PM (CST). *Felony, Misdemeanor, Civil, Eviction, Small Claims, Probate.* www.oscn.net/applications/oscn/start.asp?viewType=COUNTYINFO&county=COAL

General Information: Online identifiers in results same as on public terminal. No juvenile, adoption, mental health, guardianship, wills or expunged records released. Will not fax documents. Court makes copy: $1.00 first page, $.50 each add'l. Certification fee: $.50 per page. Certification included in copy fee. Payee: Court Clerk. Only cashiers checks and money orders accepted. No credit cards accepted. Prepayment required. Mail requests: SASE required.

Civil Name Search: Access: Mail, in person, online. Both court and visitors may perform in person name searches. Search fee: $10.00 per name. Civil records archived since 1907; computerized back to 1999. Mail turnaround time 2-3 days. Civil PAT goes back to 1999. Both free and advanced pay search service from 6/1999 at www1.odcr.com/search.php; updated daily. City and rarely phone may appear on online record. Civil shows name and town only.

Criminal Name Search: Access: Mail, in person, online. Both court and visitors may perform in person name searches. Search fee: $10.00 per name. Criminal records archived since 1907; computerized back to 1999. Mail turnaround time 2-3 days. Criminal PAT goes back to 1999. Both free and advanced pay search service from 6/1999 at www1.odcr.com/search.php. Online results show middle initial.

Comanche County

5th Judicial District Court 315 SW 5th St, Rm 504, Lawton, OK 73501-4390; criminal phone: 580-355-4017; civil phone: 580-581-4565; 8AM-5PM (CST). *Felony, Misdemeanor, Civil, Eviction, Small Claims, Probate.* www.oscn.net

General Information: Traffic and marriage licenses also handled here. Small claims, licenses, Juvenile phone is 580-250-5093 No juvenile, mental health, adoption or some probate records released. Will not fax documents. Court makes copy: $1.00 1st page, $.50 each add'l. Certification fee: $.50 per page includes copy fee. Payee: District Court Clerk. Cashiers check, money

order, or business check accepted. No credit cards accepted. Prepayment required. Mail requests: SASE required.

Civil Name Search: Access: Phone, mail, online, in person. Only the court performs in person name searches; visitors may not. Search fee: $10.00 per name. Civil records on computer from 8/88, prior in books to 1901. Mail turnaround time 1 day. Online access to court dockets is free at www.oscn.net/applications/oscn/casesearch.asp. Dockets go back to 8/1988. City and rarely phone may appear on online record. Civil shows name and town only. Also both free and advanced pay search service at www1.odcr.com/search.php. Call 580-581-4565.

Criminal Name Search: Access: Mail, online, in person. Only the court performs in person name searches; visitors may not. Search fee: $10.00 per name. Required to search: name, years to search; also helpful: DOB, SSN. Criminal records computerized from 8/88, prior in books to 1901. Mail turnaround time 1 day. Online access to court dockets is same as civil. Call 580-581-4565 for the subscription account. Online results show middle initial.

Cotton County

5th Judicial District Court 301 N Broadway, Walters, OK 73572; 580-875-3029; fax: 580-875-2288; 8AM-4PM (CST). *Felony, Misdemeanor, Civil, Eviction, Small Claims, Probate.* www.oscn.net

General Information: Online identifiers in results same as on public terminal. No adoption, juvenile, and some guardianship records released. Will fax documents if $5.00 search fee paid. Court makes copy: $1.00 first page, $.50 each add'l. Certification fee: $5.00 per doc. Payee: Court Clerk. Personal checks accepted. Major credit cards accepted in person only. Prepayment required. Mail requests: SASE not required.

Civil Name Search: Access: Mail, in person, online. Both court and visitors may perform in person name searches. Search fee: $5.00 per name. Civil records archived from 1912; computerized back to 1997. Mail turnaround time 2 days. Civil PAT goes back to 1997. Both free and advanced pay search service from 1/1997 at www1.odcr.com/search.php; updated daily. City and rarely phone may appear on online record. Civil shows name and town only.

Criminal Name Search: Access: Mail, in person, online. Both court and visitors may perform in person name searches. Search fee: $5.00 per name. Required to search: name, years to search, DOB. Criminal records archived from 1912; computerized back to 1997. Mail turnaround time 2 days. Criminal PAT goes back to same as civil. Both free and advanced pay search service from 1/1997 at www1.odcr.com/search.php; updated every 15 minutes. Online results show middle initial.

Craig County

12th Judicial District Court 210 W Delaware, Ste 201, Vinita, OK 74301; 918-256-6451; 8:30AM-4:30PM (CST). *Felony, Misdemeanor, Civil, Eviction, Small Claims, Probate.* www.oscn.net

General Information: Online identifiers in results same as on public terminal. No mental, guardianship, adoption, or juvenile records released. Will not fax documents. Court makes copy: $1.00 first page, $.50 each add'l. Self serve copy: same. Certification fee: $.50 per page includes copy fee. Payee: Court Clerk. Personal checks accepted. Major credit cards accepted in person only. Prepayment required. Mail requests: SASE required.

Civil Name Search: Access: Mail, in person, online. Both court and visitors may perform in person name searches. Search fee: $5.00 per name. Civil records on microfilm from 1902; on computer since 4/97. Mail turnaround time 1-3 days. Civil PAT goes back to 1985. Both free and advanced pay search service from 4/1/1997 at www1.odcr.com/search.php; updated daily. City and rarely phone may appear on online record. Civil shows name and town only.

Criminal Name Search: Access: Mail, in person, online. Both court and visitors may perform in person name searches. Search fee: $5.00 per name. Required to search: name, years to search; also helpful: SSN, DOB, sex. Criminal records on microfilm from 1902; on computer since 4/97. Mail turnaround time 1-3 days. Criminal PAT goes back to same as civil. Both free and advanced pay search service from 4/1/1997 at www1.odcr.com/search.php; updated daily. Online results show middle initial.

Creek County

24th Judicial District Court - Sapulpa 222 E Dewey Ave, #201, Sapulpa, OK 74066; 918-227-2525; fax: 918-227-5030; 8AM-5PM (CST). *Felony, Misdemeanor, Civil, Eviction, Small Claims, Probate.* www.creekcountyonline.com/court_clerk.htm

General Information: All 3 courts in this county should be searched, there is not overall countywide database. Probate fax is same as main fax number. Online identifiers in results same as on public terminal. No juvenile, mental health, or adoption records released. Will not fax documents. Court makes copy: $1.00 first page, $.50 each add'l. Certification fee: $.50 per document; Exemplification fee $5.00. Payee: Creek County Court Clerk.

Personal checks accepted. Major credit cards accepted in person. Prepayment required.

Civil Name Search: Access: In person, online. Visitors must perform in person searches themselves. Required to search: name, years to search; also helpful: address. Computerized records back to 1998, civil records on docket books and files back to 1907. Civil PAT goes back to 1907. Both free and advanced pay search service from 3/1998 at www1.odcr.com/search.php; updated daily. City and rarely phone may appear on online record. Civil shows name and town only.

Criminal Name Search: Access: In person, online. Visitors must perform in person searches themselves. Required to search: name, years to search; also helpful: address, DOB, SSN. Criminal docket on books and files. They go back "many years, no exact date known". Criminal PAT goes back to 1998. Both free and advanced pay search service from 3/1998 at www1.odcr.com/search.php; updated daily. Online results show middle initial.

24th Judicial District Court - Bristow PO Box 1055, 110 W 7th St, Bristow, OK 74010; 918-367-5537; fax: 918-367-5055; 8AM-5PM (CST). *Felony, Misdemeanor, Civil, Eviction, Small Claims, Probate.*
www.oscn.net

General Information: All three courts in this county should be searched, there is not overall countywide database. Online identifiers in results same as on public terminal. No juvenile, mental health, or adoption records released. Will not fax out documents. Court makes copy: $1.00 first page, $.50 each add'l. Certification fee: $.50 per doc. Payee: Creek County Court Clerk. Personal checks accepted. Visa/MC accepted in person. Prepayment required.

Civil Name Search: Access: In person, mail, online. Both court and visitors may perform in person name searches. No search fee. Required to search: name, years to search; also helpful: address. Computerized records back to 1998, civil records on docket books and files back to 1907. Mail turnaround time 0--2 days. Civil PAT available. Both free and advanced pay search service from 10/25/1999 at www1.odcr.com/search.php; updated daily. City and rarely phone may appear on online record. Civil shows name and town only.

Criminal Name Search: Access: In person, mail, online. Both court and visitors may perform in person name searches. No search fee. Required to search: name, years to search; also helpful: address, DOB, SSN. Criminal docket on books and files. They go back "many years, no exact date known". Mail turnaround time 0-2 days. Criminal PAT available. Both free and advanced pay search service from 10/25/1999 at www.odcr.com; updated daily.

24th Judicial District Court - Drumright PO Box 1118, Drumright, OK 74030; 918-352-2575; fax: 918-352-2617; 8AM-5PM (CST). *Felony, Misdemeanor, Civil, Eviction, Small Claims, Probate.*
www.oscn.net

General Information: All three courts in this county should be searched, there is not overall countywide database. This is understaffed and will not perform research. Online identifiers in results same as on public terminal. No juvenile, mental health, or adoption records released. Will fax documents to local or toll-free number. Court makes copy: $1.00 first page, $.50 each add'l. Certification fee: $.50 per page. Payee: Creek County Court Clerk. Personal checks accepted, credit cards are not. Prepayment required. Mail requests: SASE required for return of any documents.

Civil Name Search: Access: In person, mail, online. Visitors must perform in person searches themselves. No search fee. Required to search: name, years to search; also helpful: address. Civil index on docket books and files back at least 20 years. Civil PAT goes back to 1984. Both free and advanced pay search service from 11/15/2004 at www1.odcr.com/search.php; updated daily. City and rarely phone may appear on online record. Civil shows name and town only.

Criminal Name Search: Access: In person, online. Visitors must perform in person searches themselves. Required to search: name, years to search; also helpful: address, DOB, SSN. Criminal docket on books and files. Felony records to 1971, misdemeanors to 07/92. Criminal PAT goes back to 1971. Both free and advanced pay search service from 11/15/2004 at www.odcr.com; updated daily. Online results show middle initial.

Custer County

2nd Judicial District Court PO Box D, 675 B St, Arapaho, OK 73620; 580-323-3233; fax: 580-331-1121; 8AM-4PM (CST). *Felony, Misdemeanor, Civil, Eviction, Small Claims, Probate.*
www.oscn.net

General Information: Probate fax is same as main fax number. Online identifiers in results same as on public terminal. No adoption, juvenile, or mental records released. Will fax out specific case files to local or toll free line. Court makes copy: $1.00 first page, $.50 each add'l. Certification fee: $.50 per page plus copy fee. Payee: Court Clerk. Personal checks accepted. Major credit cards accepted in person only. Prepayment required. Mail requests: SASE not required.

Civil Name Search: Access: In person, online. Visitors must perform in person searches themselves. Required to search: name, years to search; also helpful: address. Civil records go back to 1900's; records on computer go back to 1/95. Civil PAT goes back to 1995. Both free and advanced pay search service from 8/1/2001 at www1.odcr.com/search.php; updated daily. City and rarely phone may appear on online record. Civil shows name and town only.

Criminal Name Search: Access: Mail, in person, online. Both court and visitors may perform in person name searches. Search fee: $5.00 per name. Required to search: name, years to search; also helpful: DOB, SSN. Criminal records go back to 1900's; records on computer go back to 1/95. Mail turnaround time 2-3 days. Criminal PAT goes back to same as civil. Both free and advanced pay search service from 8/1/2001 at www1.odcr.com/search.php; updated daily. Online results show middle initial.

Delaware County

13th Judicial District Court Box 407, (Whitehead & Krause St), Jay, OK 74346; 918-253-4420; fax: 918-253-5739; 8AM-N, 1-4:30PM (CST). *Felony, Misdemeanor, Civil, Eviction, Small Claims, Probate.*
www.oscn.net

General Information: Online identifiers in results same as on public terminal. No juvenile, adoption, guardianship or search warrant records released. Will not fax out documents. Court makes copy: $1.00 1st page, $.50 each add'l. Self serve copy: $1.00 1st page, $.50 each add'l. Certification fee: $.50 per page. Payee: Delaware County Court Clerk. Business checks accepted. Credit cards accepted only accepted in person. Prepayment required. Mail requests: SASE requested.

Civil Name Search: Access: Mail, in person, online. Both court and visitors may perform in person name searches. Search fee: $5.00 per name. Civil records on computer since 1996 and on microfilm from 1913. Mail turnaround time 1-2 weeks. Civil PAT goes back to 1996. Both free and advanced pay search service from 6/1/1991 at www1.odcr.com/search.php; updated daily. City and rarely phone may appear on online record. Civil shows name and town only.

Criminal Name Search: Access: Mail, in person, online. Both court and visitors may perform in person name searches. Search fee: $5.00 per name. Required to search: name, years to search; also helpful: DOB, SSN. Criminal records on computer since 1991. Mail turnaround time 1-2 weeks. Criminal PAT goes back to 1991. Both free and advanced pay search service from 6/1/1991 at www1.odcr.com/search.php; updated daily. Online results show middle initial.

Dewey County

4th Judicial District Court Box 278 (Broadway & Ruble), Taloga, OK 73667; 580-328-5521; fax: 580-328-5658; 8AM-4PM (CST). *Felony, Misdemeanor, Civil, Small Claims, Probate.*
www.oscn.net

General Information: Online identifiers in results same as on public terminal. No expunged, adoption, mental, guardianship, juvenile records released. Will fax documents to local or toll-free number. Court makes copy: $1.00 first page, $.50 each add'l. Certification fee: $.50 per document. Payee: Dewey County Court Clerk. Personal checks accepted, credit cards are not. Prepayment required. Mail requests: SASE requested.

Civil Name Search: Access: Mail, in person, online. Both court and visitors may perform in person name searches. No search fee. Civil records archived from late 1800s, computerized records go back to 1995. Note: All requests must be in writing. Mail turnaround time usually same day. Civil PAT goes back to 1995. Both free and advanced pay search service at www1.odcr.com/search.php. City and rarely phone may appear on online record. Civil shows name and town only.

Criminal Name Search: Access: Mail, in person, online. Both court and visitors may perform in person name searches. No search fee. Required to search: name, years to search; also helpful: SSN. Criminal records archived from late 1800s, computerized records go back to 1995. Note: All requests must be in writing. Mail turnaround time 2 days. Criminal PAT goes back to same as civil. Both free and advanced pay search service from 3/1988 at www.odcr.com. Updated daily. Online results show middle initial.

Ellis County

2nd Judicial District Court PO Box 217, 100 S Washington St, Arnett, OK 73832; 580-885-7255; 8:30AM-4:30PM (CST). *Felony, Misdemeanor, Civil, Eviction, Small Claims, Probate.*
www.oscn.net

General Information: Probate is a separate index at this same address. No expunged records released. Will not fax out documents. Court makes copy: $1.00 first page, $.50 each add'l. Certification fee: $.50 per cert plus copy fee. Payee: Ellis County Court Clerk. Personal checks accepted, credit cards are not. Prepayment required. Mail requests: SASE required.

Civil Name Search: Access: Phone, mail, in person, online. Both court and visitors may perform in person name searches. No search fee. Civil

index in docket books from 1900. Mail turnaround time 1 day. Online access to court dockets is free at www.oscn.net/applications/oscn/casesearch.asp. Both free and advanced pay search service from 6/1995 at www1.odcr.com/search.php; updated real time. Online record includes physical description, phone.
Criminal Name Search: Access: Mail, in person, online. Both court and visitors may perform in person name searches. Search fee: $5.00 per name. Required to search: name, years to search; also helpful: SSN. Criminal docket on books from 1900. Mail turnaround time 1 day. Online access to court dockets is free at www.oscn.net/applications/oscn/casesearch.asp. Both free and advanced pay search service from 6/1995 at www1.odcr.com/search.php; updated real time. Online record includes physical description, phone.

Garfield County
4th Judicial District Court 114 W Broadway, Enid, OK 73701-4024; 580-237-0232; 8AM-4:30PM (CST). *Felony, Misdemeanor, Civil, Eviction, Small Claims, Probate.*
www.oscn.net
General Information: Online identifiers in results same as on public terminal. No juvenile, mental health, or adoption records released. Court makes copy: $1.00 first page, $.50 each add'l. Certification fee: $.50 per page. Payee: Court Clerk. Personal checks, Visa/MC accepted. Prepayment required. Mail requests: SASE required.
Civil Name Search: Access: Mail, in person, online, online. Both court and visitors may perform in person name searches. Search fee: $5.00 per name. Civil records on computer from 3-89, on microfiche from 1893. Mail turnaround time 3 days. Civil PAT goes back to 1989. Online access to court dockets is free at www.oscn.net/applications/oscn/casesearch.asp. Dockets go back to 3/1989. Online record includes physical description, phone. Also both free and advanced pay search service at www1.odcr.com/search.php.
Criminal Name Search: Access: Mail, online, in person, online. Both court and visitors may perform in person name searches. Search fee: $5.00 per name. Required to search: name, years to search, SSN. Criminal records computerized from 1989, on microfiche from 1893. Criminal PAT goes back to same as civil. Online access to criminal dockets is same as civil.

Garvin County
21st Judicial District Court PO Box 239, 201 W Grant, Pauls Valley, OK 73075; 405-238-5596; fax: 405-238-1138; 8:30AM-4:30PM (CST). *Felony, Misdemeanor, Civil, Eviction, Small Claims, Probate.*
www.oscn.net
General Information: Online identifiers in results same as on public terminal. No juvenile, adoption or guardianship released. Will fax documents to local or toll free line. Court makes copy: $1.00 first page, $.50 each add'l. Certification fee: $.50 per page. Payee: Garvin County Court Clerk. Only cashiers checks and money orders accepted. Major credit cards accepted in person. Prepayment required. Mail requests: SASE required.
Civil Name Search: Access: Mail, in person, online. Both court and visitors may perform in person name searches. Search fee: $10.00 per name. Civil records on computer since 1994, docket books from 1907. Mail turnaround time 1 day. Civil PAT goes back to 1994. Both free and advanced pay search service from 6/1995 at www1.odcr.com/search.php; updated real time. City and rarely phone may appear on online record. Civil shows name and town only.
Criminal Name Search: Access: Mail, in person, online. Both court and visitors may perform in person name searches. Search fee: $10.00 per name. SASE enclosed. Required to search: name, years to search; also helpful: SSN, DOB. Criminal records on computer since 1994, docket books from 1907. Mail turnaround time 1 day. Criminal PAT goes back to same as civil. Both free and advanced pay search service from 6/1/1995 to present free at www.odcr.com; updated daily. Online results show middle initial.

Grady County
6th Judicial District Court PO Box 605, 326 W Choctaw Ave, Chickasha, OK 73023; 405-224-7446; 8AM-4:30PM (CST). *Felony, Misdemeanor, Civil, Eviction, Small Claims, Probate.*
www.oscn.net
General Information: Online identifiers in results same as on public terminal. No juvenile, adoption, guardianship or mental health records released. Will not fax documents. Court makes copy: $1.00 first page, $.50 each add'l. Certification fee: $.50 per page. Payee: Court Clerk. No personal checks accepted. Visa/MC/AmEx cards accepted in person only. Prepayment required.
Civil Name Search: Access: In person, online. Visitors must perform in person searches themselves. Civil records on microfiche from 1982, archived from 1907. Civil PAT goes back to 1997. Both free and advanced pay search service from 8/1997 at www1.odcr.com/search.php; updated daily. City and rarely phone may appear on online record. Civil shows name and town only.

Criminal Name Search: Access: In person, online. Visitors must perform in person searches themselves. Required to search: name, years to search; also helpful: address, DOB, SSN. Criminal records on microfiche from 1982, archived from 1907. Criminal PAT goes back to same as civil. Both free and advanced pay search service from 8/1997 at www1.odcr.com/search.php; updated daily. Online results show middle initial.

Grant County
4th Judicial District Court 112 E Guthrie, Medford, OK 73759; 580-395-2828; 8AM-4:30PM (CST). *Felony, Misdemeanor, Civil, Eviction, Small Claims, Probate.*
www.oscn.net
General Information: No juvenile, adoption, mental health, guardianship or wills released. Court makes copy: $1.00 first page, $.50 each add'l. Certification fee: $.50 per page. Payee: Court Clerk. No out of state Personal checks accepted, credit cards are not. Prepayment required. Mail requests: SASE required.
Civil Name Search: Access: Mail, in person, online. Both court and visitors may perform in person name searches. Search fee: $5.00 per name. Civil records archived from 1893, in books since 1898. Mail turnaround time 1-3 days. Civil PAT goes back to 1997. Both free and advanced pay search service from 9/1997 at www1.odcr.com/search.php; updated daily.
Criminal Name Search: Access: Mail, in person, online. Both court and visitors may perform in person name searches. Search fee: $5.00 per name. Required to search: name, years to search; also helpful: SSN. Criminal records archived from 1893, in books since 1898. Mail turnaround time 1-3 days. Criminal PAT goes back to same as civil. Both free and advanced pay search service from 9/1997 at www1.odcr.com/search.php; updated daily.

Greer County
3rd Judicial District Court PO Box 216 (Courthouse Sq), Mangum, OK 73554; 580-782-3665; fax: 580-782-4026; 8AM-4PM (CST). *Felony, Misdemeanor, Civil, Eviction, Small Claims, Probate.* www.oscn.net
General Information: Online identifiers in results same as on public terminal. No juvenile, mental health, adoption or guardianship records released. Fee to fax document $1.00 each. Court makes copy: $1.00 first page, $.50 each add'l. Certification fee: $.50 per page. Payee: Court Clerk. Only cash, cashiers checks or money orders accepted. No credit cards accepted. Prepayment required. Mail requests: SASE required.
Civil Name Search: Access: Mail, in person, online. Both court and visitors may perform in person name searches. Search fee: $5.00 per name. Civil index in docket books from 1901; on computer back to 1997. Mail turnaround time 1-2 days. Civil PAT goes back to 1997. Both free and advanced pay search service from 8/2002 at www1.odcr.com/search.php; updated daily. City and rarely phone may appear on online record. Civil shows name and town only.
Criminal Name Search: Access: Mail, in person, online. Both court and visitors may perform in person name searches. Search fee: $5.00 per name. Required to search: name, years to search, DOB; also helpful: SSN. Criminal docket on books from 1901; on computer back to 1997. Mail turnaround time 1-2 days. Criminal PAT goes back to same as civil. Both free and advanced pay search service from 8/2002 at www1.odcr.com/search.php; updated daily. Online results show middle initial.

Harmon County
3rd Judicial District Court 114 W Hollis, Hollis, OK 73550; 580-688-3617; fax: 580-688-2900; 8AM-4PM (CST). *Felony, Misdemeanor, Civil, Eviction, Small Claims, Probate.*
www.oscn.net
General Information: Probate fax is same as main fax number. Online identifiers in results same as on public terminal. No juvenile, adoption, mental health, or guardianship records released. Will fax documents if prepaid or you provide proof of payment, facsimile of check, etc. Court makes copy: $1.00 first page, $.50 each add'l. Self serve copy: same. Certification fee: $.50 per page. Payee: Harmon County Court Clerk. Personal checks accepted, credit cards are not. Prepayment required. Mail requests: SASE requested.
Civil Name Search: Access: Mail, fax, in person, online. Both court and visitors may perform in person name searches. Search fee: $5.00 per name. Civil index in docket books from 1909; on computer since 1999. Mail turnaround time 1-2 days. Civil PAT goes back to 1999. Both free and advanced pay search service from 1/2003 at www1.odcr.com/search.php; updated daily. City and rarely phone may appear on online record. Civil shows name and town only.
Criminal Name Search: Access: Mail, fax, in person, online. Both court and visitors may perform in person name searches. Search fee: $5.00 per name. Required to search: name, years to search; also helpful: DOB, SSN, sex. Criminal docket on books from 1909; on computer since 1999. Mail turnaround time 1-2 days. Criminal PAT goes back to 1999. Both free

and advanced pay search service from 1/2003 at www1.odcr.com/search.php; updated daily. Online results show middle initial.

Harper County

1st Judicial District Court Box 347 (311 SE 1st St), Buffalo, OK 73834; 580-735-2010; fax: 580-735-2787; 8AM-4PM (CST). *Felony, Misdemeanor, Civil, Eviction, Small Claims, Probate.* www.oscn.net

General Information: No adoption, juvenile, conservatorship, mental health, guardianship, or expunged records released. Will fax documents for fee, call. Court makes copy: $1.00 1st page, $.50 each add'l. Certification fee: $.50 per page plus copy fee. Payee: Harper County Court Clerk. Only cashier's check or money order accepted. No credit cards accepted. Prepayment required. Mail requests: SASE requested.

Civil Name Search: Access: Mail, in person, online. Both court and visitors may perform in person name searches. Search fee: $5.00 per name. Civil index in docket books from 1907. Note: No phoned in search requests accepted. Mail turnaround time 3 or 4 days. Access to court dockets is reportedly free at www.oscn.net/applications/oscn/casesearch.asp. Also, both free and advanced pay search service from 1/2000 at www1.odcr.com/search.php; updated daily. City and rarely phone may appear on online record. Civil shows name and town only.

Criminal Name Search: Access: Mail, in person, online. Both court and visitors may perform in person name searches. Search fee: $5.00 per name. Criminal docket on books from 1907. Note: No phoned in search requests accepted. Mail turnaround time 3 or 4 days. Access to court dockets is reportedly free at www.oscn.net/applications/oscn/casesearch.asp. Also, Both free and advanced pay search service from 1/2000 at www1.odcr.com/search.php; updated daily. Online results show middle initial.

Haskell County

16th Judicial District Court 202 E Main, Stigler, OK 74462; 918-967-3323; fax: 918-967-2819; 8AM-4:30PM (CST). *Felony, Misdemeanor, Civil, Eviction, Small Claims, Probate.* www.oscn.net

General Information: Online identifiers in results same as on public terminal. No juvenile, probate guardianship, adoption or mental health records released. Will not fax documents. Court makes copy: $1.00 first page, $.50 each add'l. Certification fee: $.50 per document. Payee: Haskell County Court Clerk. Personal checks accepted. Major credit cards accepted in person only. Prepayment required. Mail requests: SASE required.

Civil Name Search: Access: Phone, mail, in person, online. Both court and visitors may perform in person name searches. Search fee: $5.00. Civil records archived from 1907, they are in the process of placing files on microfiche starting with 1994; computerized since 1997. Mail turnaround time 2 weeks. Civil PAT goes back to 1997. Both free and advanced pay search service from 11/1/1997 at www1.odcr.com/search.php; updated daily. City and rarely phone may appear on online record. Civil shows name and town only.

Criminal Name Search: Access: Phone, mail, in person, online. Both court and visitors may perform in person name searches. Search fee: $5.00. Required to search: name, years to search; also helpful: SSN. Criminal records archived from 1907, they are in the process of placing files on microfiche starting with 1994; computerized since 1997. Mail turnaround time 2 weeks. Criminal PAT goes back to same as civil. Both free and advanced pay search service from at www.odcr.com. Online results show middle initial.

Hughes County

22nd Judicial District Court 200 N Broadway, PO Box 32, Holdenville, OK 74848; 405-379-3384; 8AM-4:30PM (CST). *Felony, Misdemeanor, Civil, Eviction, Small Claims, Probate.* www.oscn.net

General Information: Probate is a separate index at this same address. Online identifiers in results same as on public terminal. No juvenile or adoption records released. Court makes copy: $1.00 first page, $.50 each add'l. Self serve copy: same. Certification fee: $.50 per cert. Payee: Hughes County Court Clerk. Personal checks accepted, credit cards are not. Prepayment required. Mail requests: SASE required.

Civil Name Search: Access: Mail, in person, online. Both court and visitors may perform in person name searches. Search fee: $5.00 per name. Civil records archived from 1907, computerized records go back to 1998. Mail turnaround time 2 days. Civil PAT goes back to 1998. Both free and advanced pay search service from 12/1998 at www1.odcr.com/search.php; updated daily. City and rarely phone may appear on online record. Civil shows name and town only.

Criminal Name Search: Access: Mail, in person, online. Both court and visitors may perform in person name searches. Search fee: $5.00 per name. Required to search: name, years to search; also helpful: SSN. Criminal records archived from 1907. Mail turnaround time 2 days. Criminal PAT goes back to 1998. Both free and advanced pay search service from

12/1998 at www1.odcr.com/search.php; updated daily. Online results show middle initial.

Jackson County

3rd Judicial District Court PO Box 616, 101 N Main, Rm 303, County Courthouse, Altus, OK 73522; 580-482-0448; 8AM-4PM (CST). *Felony, Misdemeanor, Civil, Eviction, Small Claims, Probate.* www.jacksoncountyok.com/court.htm

General Information: Online identifiers in results same as on public terminal. No adoption, juvenile, mental health, or guardianship records released. Court makes copy: $1.00 first page, $.50 each add'l. Self serve copy: $1.00 per page. Certification fee: $.50 per page. Payee: Jackson County Court Clerk. Business checks accepted; no personal checks. Major credit cards accepted in person. Prepayment required. Mail requests: SASE required.

Civil Name Search: Access: Mail, in person, online. Both court and visitors may perform in person name searches. Search fee: $5.00 per name. Civil records archived from early 1900; computerized records since 7/97. Mail turnaround time 3-4 days. Civil PAT goes back to 1997. Both free and advanced pay search service from 7/1997 at www1.odcr.com/search.php; updated daily. City and rarely phone may appear on online record. Civil shows name and town only.

Criminal Name Search: Access: Mail, in person, online. Both court and visitors may perform in person name searches. Search fee: $5.00 per name. Required to search: name, years to search; also helpful: SSN. Criminal records archived from early 1900; computerized records since 7/97. Mail turnaround time 3-4 days. Criminal PAT goes back to same as civil. Both free and advanced pay search service from 7/1997 at www1.odcr.com/search.php; updated daily. Online results show middle initial.

Jefferson County

5th Judicial District Court 220 N Main, Rm 302, Waurika, OK 73573; 580-228-2961; fax: 580-228-2185; 8AM-4PM (CST). *Felony, Misdemeanor, Civil, Eviction, Small Claims, Probate.* www.oscn.net

General Information: Online identifiers in results same as on public terminal. No juvenile, adoption or guardianship records released. Will fax documents to local or toll-free number. Court makes copy: $1.00 first page, $.50 each add'l. Certification fee: $.50 per page. Payee: Court Clerk. Personal checks accepted. Credit cards accepted. Prepayment required. Mail requests: SASE required.

Civil Name Search: Access: Mail, in person, online. Both court and visitors may perform in person name searches. Search fee: $5.00 per name. Required to search: name, years to search, DOB or SSN. Civil index in docket books from 1907; on computer since 10/1997. Mail turnaround time 1 week. Civil PAT goes back to 10/1997. Only personal identifiers submitted at time of filing appear on terminal. Both free and advanced pay search service from 1/1998 at www1.odcr.com/search.php; updated daily. City and rarely phone may appear on online record. Civil shows name and town only.

Criminal Name Search: Access: Mail, in person, online. Both court and visitors may perform in person name searches. Search fee: $5.00 per name. Required to search: name, years to search, DOB; also helpful: SSN. Criminal docket on books from 1907; on computer since 10/1997. Mail turnaround time 1 week. Criminal PAT goes back to 10/1997. Only personal identifiers submitted at time of filing appear on terminal. Both free and advanced pay search service from 1/1998 at www1.odcr.com/search.php; updated daily. Online results show middle initial.

Johnston County

20th Judicial District Court 403 W Main, #201, Tishomingo, OK 73460; 580-371-3281; 8:30AM-4:30PM (CST). *Felony, Misdemeanor, Civil, Eviction, Small Claims, Probate.* www.oscn.net

General Information: Online identifiers in results same as on public terminal. No juvenile or mental health records released. Will not fax documents. Court makes copy: $1.00 first page, $.50 each add'l. Certification fee: $.50 per page. Payee: Court. Personal checks accepted. Major credit cards accepted in person. Prepayment required. Mail requests: SASE required.

Civil Name Search: Access: Phone, mail, in person, online. Both court and visitors may perform in person name searches. Search fee: $5.00 per name. Civil index in docket books from 1907; on computer back to 1997. Note: All requests must be in writing. Mail turnaround time 2 days. Public use terminal available, records go back to 1997. DOB or SSN may appear on PAT results. Both free and advanced pay search service from 1/1997 at www1.odcr.com/search.php; updated daily. City and rarely phone may appear on online record. Civil shows name and town only.

Criminal Name Search: Access: Mail, in person, online. Both court and visitors may perform in person name searches. Search fee: $5.00 per name. Required to search: name, years to search; also helpful: DOB, SSN. Criminal docket on books from 1907; on computer back to 1997. Note: All requests must be in writing. Mail turnaround time 2 days. Public use terminal available, crim records go back to 1997. DOB and SSN do not always appear in results. Both free and advanced pay search service from 1/1997 at www1.odcr.com/search.php; updated daily. Online results show middle initial.

Kay County

8th Judicial District Court Box 428, Newkirk, OK 74647; 580-362-3350; 8AM-4:30PM (CST). *Felony, Misdemeanor, Civil, Eviction, Small Claims, Probate.* www.courthouse.kay.ok.us/home.html

General Information: This courthouse holds the closed case files for the satellite courts in Ponca City (580-762-2148) and Blackwell (580-363-2080). Online identifiers in results same as on public terminal. No juvenile, adoption, mental health, or sealed records released. Will not fax documents. Court makes copy: $1.00 first page, $.50 each add'l. Certification fee: $.50 per page plus copy fee. Payee: Kay County Court Clerk. No personal checks accepted. Major credit cards accepted in person only. Prepayment required.

Civil Name Search: Access: Mail, in person, online. Both court and visitors may perform in person name searches. Search fee: $5.00 per name. Civil records on microfiche and original records; computerized records since 1995. Mail turnaround time 1 day. Civil PAT goes back to 1995. Both free and advanced pay search service from 5/1/1995 at www1.odcr.com/search.php; updated daily. Blackwell and Ponca City online goes back to 1/1997. City and rarely phone may appear on online record. Civil shows name and town only.

Criminal Name Search: Access: Mail, in person, online. Both court and visitors may perform in person name searches. Search fee: $5.00 per name per index. Required to search: name, years to search; also helpful: DOB, SSN. Criminal records on microfiche and original records; computerized records since 1995. Mail turnaround time 1 day. Criminal PAT goes back to same as civil. Both free and advanced pay search service from 5/1/1995 at www1.odcr.com/search.php; updated daily. Blackwell and Ponca City online goes back to 1/1997. Online results show middle initial.

Kingfisher County

4th Judicial District Court Box 328, 101 S Main St, Kingfisher, OK 73750; 405-375-3813; 8AM-4:30PM (CST). *Felony, Misdemeanor, Civil, Eviction, Small Claims, Probate.* www.oscn.net

General Information: Online identifiers in results same as on public terminal. No juvenile, mental or guardianship records released. Will not fax documents. Court makes copy: $1.00 first page, $.50 each add'l. Certification fee: $.50 per page. Payee: Court Clerk. Personal checks accepted, credit cards are not. Prepayment required.

Civil Name Search: Access: Phone, mail, in person, online. Both court and visitors may perform in person name searches. Search fee: $5.00. Civil records archived from 1900, computerized since 1998. Mail turnaround time 1-2 days. Civil PAT goes back to 1998. Both free and advanced pay search service from 10/1/1997 at www1.odcr.com/search.php; updated daily. City and rarely phone may appear on online record. Civil shows name and town only.

Criminal Name Search: Access: Mail, in person, online. Both court and visitors may perform in person name searches. Search fee: $5.00. Required to search: name, years to search; also helpful: SSN. Criminal records archived from 1900, computerized since 1998. Mail turnaround time 1-2 days. Criminal PAT goes back to same as civil. Both free and advanced pay search service from 10/1/1997 at www1.odcr.com/search.php; updated daily. Online results show middle initial.

Kiowa County

3rd Judicial District Court Box 854 (316 S Main St), Hobart, OK 73651; 580-726-5125; probate phone: 580-726-5125; fax: 580-726-2340; 8AM-4PM (CST). *Felony, Misdemeanor, Civil, Eviction, Small Claims, Probate, Divorce, Traffic.* www.oscn.net

General Information: Online identifiers in results same as on public terminal. No juvenile or adoptions records released. Will not fax out documents. Court makes copy: $1.00 first page, $.50 each add'l. Certification fee: $.50 per page. Payee: Court Clerk. Only cashiers checks and money orders accepted. Major credit cards accepted but only in person. Prepayment required. Mail requests: SASE required.

Civil Name Search: Access: Phone, mail, in person, online. Both court and visitors may perform in person name searches. Search fee: $5.00 per name. Civil records archived from 1900, computerized records from1996. Mail turnaround time 1-2 days. Civil PAT goes back to 1992. Both free and advanced pay search service from 1/1996 at www1.odcr.com/search.php; updated daily. City and rarely phone may appear on online record. Civil shows name and town only.

Criminal Name Search: Access: Phone, mail, in person, online. Both court and visitors may perform in person name searches. Search fee: $5.00 per name. Required to search: name, years to search; also helpful: SSN. Criminal records archived from 1900, computerized records from 1996. Mail turnaround time 1-2 days. Criminal PAT goes back to same as civil. Both free and advanced pay search service from 1/1996 at

www1.odcr.com/search.php; updated daily. Online results show middle initial.

Latimer County

16th Judicial District Court 109 N Central, Rm 200, Wilburton, OK 74578; 918-465-2011; 8AM-4:30PM (CST). *Felony, Misdemeanor, Civil, Eviction, Small Claims, Probate.* www.oscn.net

General Information: Online identifiers in results same as on public terminal. No guardianship, adoption or juvenile records released. Will not fax documents. Court makes copy: $1.00 first page, $.50 each add'l. Certification fee: $.50 per page. Payee: Latimer County Court Clerk. Personal checks not accepted, business checks accepted from law firms and major companies. Major credit cards accepted in person. Prepayment required. Will bill search fee to law firms. Mail requests: SASE required.

Civil Name Search: Access: Phone, mail, in person, online. Both court and visitors may perform in person name searches. Search fee: $5.00 per name. Civil records in original files from 1907, computerized from 1999. Mail turnaround time 2 days. Civil PAT goes back to 1999. Both free and advanced pay search service from 11/1999 at www1.odcr.com/search.php; updated 2:00 PM each day (view only). City and rarely phone may appear on online record. Civil shows name and town only.

Criminal Name Search: Access: Mail, in person, online. Both court and visitors may perform in person name searches. Search fee: $5.00 per name. Required to search: name, years to search; also helpful: DOB, SSN. Criminal records in original files from 1907, computerized from 1999. Mail turnaround time 2 days. Criminal PAT goes back to 1999. Both free and advanced pay search service from 11/1999 at www1.odcr.com/search.php; updated 2:00 PM each day (view only). Online results show middle initial.

Le Flore County

16th Judicial District Court PO Box 688, 100 S Broadway, Poteau, OK 74953; 918-647-3181; 8AM-4:30PM (CST). *Felony, Misdemeanor, Civil, Eviction, Small Claims, Probate.* www.oscn.net

General Information: Online identifiers in results same as on public terminal. No juvenile, adoptions, mental health or guardian records released. Will not fax documents. Court makes copy: $1.00 first page, $.50 each add'l. Certification fee: $.50 per page. Payee: Court Clerk. Personal checks accepted, credit cards are not. Prepayment required. Mail requests: SASE required.

Civil Name Search: Access: Mail, in person, online. Both court and visitors may perform in person name searches. Search fee: $5.00 per name. Civil records on computer since 7/1997; prior records archived since 1904 in files and books. Mail turnaround time 1 week. Civil PAT goes back to 1997. Both free and advanced pay search service from 7/1/1997 at www1.odcr.com/search.php; updated daily. City and rarely phone may appear on online record. Civil shows name and town only.

Criminal Name Search: Access: Mail, in person, online. Both court and visitors may perform in person name searches. Search fee: $5.00 per name. Required to search: name, years to search; also helpful: SSN. Criminal records on computer since 7/1997; prior records archived since 1904 in files and books. Mail turnaround time 1 week. Criminal PAT goes back to 1997. Both free and advanced pay search service from 7/1/1997 at www1.odcr.com/search.php; updated daily. Online results show middle initial.

Lincoln County

23rd Judicial District Court PO Box 307 (811 Manvel Ave), Chandler, OK 74834; 405-258-1309; fax: 405-258-3067; 8:30AM-4:30PM (CST). *Felony, Misdemeanor, Civil, Eviction, Small Claims, Probate.* www.oscn.net

General Information: Online identifiers in results same as on public terminal. No juvenile, adoption or guardianship records released. Will not fax documents. Court makes copy: $1.00 first page, $.50 each add'l. Certification fee: $.50. Payee: Court Clerk. Personal checks accepted. Major credit cards accepted in person. Prepayment required. Mail requests: SASE required.

Civil Name Search: Access: Mail, in person, online. Both court and visitors may perform in person name searches. Search fee: $5.00 per name. Civil records archived since 1891. Mail turnaround time can take 30 days or more. Record searching is a low priority. Civil PAT goes back to 7/1994. Both free and advanced pay search service from 7/1/1994 at www1.odcr.com/search.php; updated daily. City and rarely phone may appear on online record. Civil shows name and town only.

Criminal Name Search: Access: Mail, in person, online. Both court and visitors may perform in person name searches. Search fee: $5.00 per name. Required to search: name, years to search, DOB, signed release; also helpful: SSN. Criminal records archived since 1891. Mail turnaround time can take 30 days or more; record searching is a low priority. Criminal PAT goes back to same as civil. Both free and advanced pay search service from

7/1/1994 at www1.odcr.com/search.php; updated daily. Online results show middle initial.

Logan County

9th Judicial District Court 301 E Harrison, Rm 201, Guthrie, OK 73044; 405-282-0123; 8AM-4:30PM (CST). *Felony, Misdemeanor, Civil, Eviction, Small Claims, Probate.* www.oscn.net

General Information: Online identifiers in results same as on public terminal. No juvenile, mental health, guardianship or adoption records released. Will not fax documents. Court makes copy: $1.00 first page, $.50 each add'l. Certification fee: $.50 per page includes copy fee. Payee: Court Clerk. No personal checks. Visa/MC accepted. Prepayment required. Mail requests: SASE requested.

Civil Name Search: Access: Mail, in person, online. Both court and visitors may perform in person name searches. Search fee: $5.00 per name. Civil records on microfiche from 1907. Mail turnaround time 7-10 days. Civil PAT goes back to 2003. Search court dockets free at www.oscn.net/applications/oscn/casesearch.asp. Also both free and advanced pay search service at www1.odcr.com/search.php. Online record includes physical description, phone.

Criminal Name Search: Access: Mail, in person, online. Both court and visitors may perform in person name searches. Search fee: $5.00 per name. Required to search: name, years to search; also helpful: SSN, DOB. Criminal records on microfiche from 1907. Mail turnaround time 7-10 days. Criminal PAT goes back to same as civil. Search court dockets free at www.oscn.net/applications/oscn/casesearch.asp. Also both free and advanced pay search service at www1.odcr.com/search.php. Online record includes physical description, phone.

Love County

20th Judicial District Court 405 W Main, #201, Marietta, OK 73448; 580-276-2235; 8AM-4:30PM (CST). *Felony, Misdemeanor, Civil, Eviction, Small Claims, Probate.* www.oscn.net

General Information: Online identifiers in results same as on public terminal. No juvenile or adoptions records released. Will not fax out documents. Court makes copy: $1.00 first page, $.50 each add'l. Self serve copy: same. Certification fee: $.50. Payee: Court Clerk. Only cashiers checks and money orders accepted. Major credit cards accepted. Prepayment required. Mail requests: SASE required.

Civil Name Search: Access: Mail, in person, online. Both court and visitors may perform in person name searches. Search fee: $5.00 per name. Civil index in docket books from 1907, computer records back to 1997. Mail turnaround time 1-2 days. Civil PAT goes back to 4/1997. Both free and advanced pay search service from 4/1997 at www1.odcr.com/search.php; updated daily. City and rarely phone may appear on online record. Civil shows name and town only.

Criminal Name Search: Access: Mail, in person, online. Both court and visitors may perform in person name searches. Search fee: $5.00 per name. Required to search: name, years to search; also helpful: DOB, SSN. Criminal docket on books from 1907, computer records back to 1997. Mail turnaround time 1-2 days. Criminal PAT goes back to same as civil. Both free and advanced pay search service from 4/1997 at www1.odcr.com/search.php; updated daily. Online results show middle initial.

Major County

4th Judicial District Court 500 E Broadway, Fairview, OK 73737; 580-227-4690; fax: 580-227-1275; 8:30AM-4:30PM (CST). *Felony, Misdemeanor, Civil, Small Claims, Probate.* www.oscn.net

General Information: Online identifiers in results same as on public terminal. No juvenile, adoptions, guardianships or mental court records released. Will fax documents for $3.00 first page and $1.00 ea add'l. Court makes copy: $1.00 first page, $.50 each add'l. Certification fee: $.50 per page. Payee: Court Clerk. Personal checks accepted. Major credit cards accepted except by phone. Prepayment required. Will bill attorneys or firms with previous credit paid. Mail requests: SASE required.

Civil Name Search: Access: Phone, fax, mail, in person, online. Both court and visitors may perform in person name searches. Search fee: $5.00 per name. Fee is per book. Civil index in docket books from 1907, on microfiche from 1970, on computer back to 1997. Mail turnaround time 3 days. Civil PAT goes back to 1997. Both free and advanced pay search service from 1/1/1998 at www1.odcr.com/search.php; updated monthly. City and rarely phone may appear on online record. Civil shows name and town only.

Criminal Name Search: Access: Phone, fax, mail, in person, online. Both court and visitors may perform in person name searches. Search fee: $5.00 per name. Fee is per book. Required to search: name, years to search, DOB; also helpful: SSN. Criminal docket on books from 1907, on microfiche from 1970; on computer back to 1997. Mail turnaround time 3 days. Criminal PAT goes back to same as civil. Both free and advanced pay search

service from 1/1/1998 at www1.odcr.com/search.php; updated monthly. Online results show middle initial.

Marshall County

20th Judicial District Court PO Box 58, 1 County Court St, Madill, OK 73446; 580-795-3278; 8:30AM-5PM (CST). *Felony, Misdemeanor, Civil, Eviction, Small Claims, Probate.* www.oscn.net

General Information: Online identifiers in results same as on public terminal. No juvenile, adoptions, mental health or guardianship records released. Court makes copy: $1.00 first page, $.50 each add'l. Certification fee: $.50 per page. Payee: Court Clerk. Personal checks accepted. Visa/MC accepted in person only. Prepayment required. Mail requests: SASE required.

Civil Name Search: Access: In person, online. Both court and visitors may perform in person name searches. Search fee: $5.00 per name. Civil index in docket books from 1907; computerized since 1997. Civil PAT goes back to 1997. Both free and advanced pay search service from 1/1/1998 at www1.odcr.com/search.php; updated daily. City and rarely phone may appear on online record. Civil shows name and town only.

Criminal Name Search: Access: Mail, in person, online. Both court and visitors may perform in person name searches. Search fee: $5.00 per name. Required to search: name, years to search, DOB, SSN, signed release. Criminal docket on books from 1907; computerized since 1997. Mail turnaround time 3 days. Criminal PAT goes back to same as civil. Both free and advanced pay search service from 1/1/1998 at www1.odcr.com/search.php; updated daily. Online results show middle initial.

Mayes County

12th Judicial District Court 1 Court Pl Ste 200, County Court Clerk, Pryor, OK 74361; criminal phone: 918-825-0133; civil phone: 918-825-2185; fax: 918-825-4415; 9AM-5PM (CST). *Felony, Misdemeanor, Civil, Eviction, Small Claims, Probate.* http://mayes.okcounties.org/

General Information: Online identifiers in results same as on public terminal. No mental, adoption, most juvenile, and some reports in guardianship records not released. Will not fax documents. Court makes copy: $1.00 first page, $.50 each add'l. Certification fee: $.50 per page. Payee: Clerk of Court. Personal checks accepted. Major credit cards accepted in person only. Prepayment required. Mail requests: SASE required.

Civil Name Search: Access: Phone, mail, in person, online. Both court and visitors may perform in person name searches. Search fee: $1.00 per name per year payable to employee doing research after hours. Civil records archived from 1907 on microfilm, computerized since 1998. Mail turnaround time 1 week. Civil PAT goes back to 7/1998. Both free and advanced pay search service from 7/1/1998 at www1.odcr.com/search.php; updated daily. City and rarely phone may appear on online record. Civil shows name and town only.

Criminal Name Search: Access: Phone, mail, in person, online. Both court and visitors may perform in person name searches. Search fee: $1.00 per name per year. Required to search: name, years to search; also helpful: DOB. Criminal records archived from 1907 on microfile, computerized since 1998. Mail turnaround time 1 week. Criminal PAT goes back to same as civil. Both free and advanced pay search service from 1/1/1998 at www1.odcr.com/search.php; updated daily. Online results show middle initial.

McClain County

21st Judicial District Court 121 N 2nd, Rm 231, Purcell, OK 73080; 405-527-3221; 8AM-4:30PM (CST). *Felony, Misdemeanor, Civil, Eviction, Small Claims, Probate.* www.oscn.net

General Information: Probate is a separate index at this same address. Online identifiers in results same as on public terminal. No adoption, mental health or juvenile records released. Will not fax documents. Court makes copy: $1.00 1st page, $.50 each add'l. Certification fee: $.50 per document plus copy fee. Payee: Court Clerk. Personal checks accepted. Prepayment required. Mail requests: SASE required.

Civil Name Search: Access: Mail, in person, online. Both court and visitors may perform in person name searches. Search fee: $10.00 per name. Civil index on docket books and cards from 1907, computerized since 1/97. Mail turnaround time 2 days. Civil PAT goes back to 1997. Both free and advanced pay search service from 1/1997 at www1.odcr.com/search.php; updated daily. City and rarely phone may appear on online record. Civil shows name and town only.

Criminal Name Search: Access: Mail, in person, online. Both court and visitors may perform in person name searches. Search fee: $10.00 per name. Required to search: name, years to search; also helpful: DOB, SSN. Criminal records kept in individual docket files. Mail turnaround time 2 days. Criminal PAT goes back to same as civil. Both free and advanced pay search service from 1/1997 at www1.odcr.com/search.php; updated daily. Online results show middle initial.

McCurtain County

17th Judicial District Court Box 1378, 108 N Central Ave, Idabel, OK 74745; 580-286-3693; fax: 580-286-7095; 8AM-4PM (CST). *Felony, Misdemeanor, Civil, Eviction, Small Claims, Probate.* www.oscn.net

General Information: Annex is at 580-286-4950. Online identifiers in results same as on public terminal. No adoption, guardianship or juvenile records released. Court makes copy: $1.00 1st page, $.50 each add'l. Certification fee: $.50 per page. Payee: Court Clerk. Personal checks accepted if local. Major credit cards accepted. Prepayment required. Mail requests: SASE required.

Civil Name Search: Access: Mail, in person, online. Both court and visitors may perform in person name searches. Search fee: $5.00 per name. Civil index in docket books from 1907; on computer back to 1998. Mail turnaround time 1 day. Civil PAT goes back to 1998. Both free and advanced pay search service from 6/1/1998 at www1.odcr.com/search.php; updated daily. City and rarely phone may appear on online record. Civil shows name and town only.

Criminal Name Search: Access: Mail, in person, online. Both court and visitors may perform in person name searches. Search fee: $5.00. Required to search: name, years to search; also helpful: SSN. Criminal docket on books from 1907; on computer back to 1998. Mail turnaround time 1 day. Criminal PAT goes back to same as civil. Both free and advanced pay search service from 6/1/1998 at www1.odcr.com/search.php; updated daily. Online results show middle initial.

McIntosh County

18th Judicial District Court Box 426, 110 N 1st St, Eufaula, OK 74432; 918-689-2282; fax: 918-689-2995; 8AM-4PM (CST). *Felony, Misdemeanor, Civil, Eviction, Small Claims, Probate, Traffic.* www.oscn.net

General Information: Online identifiers in results same as on public terminal. No adoption, mental health, guardianship or juvenile records released. Will not fax documents. Court makes copy: $1.00 first page, $.50 each add'l. Certification fee: $.50 per page. Payee: Court Clerk. Only cashiers check or money order accepted. Major credit cards accepted. Prepayment required. Mail requests: SASE required.

Civil Name Search: Access: Mail, in person, online. Both court and visitors may perform in person name searches. Search fee: $5.00 per name. Civil records on microfilm since 1907; computerized back to May 1996. Mail turnaround time 3 days. Civil PAT goes back to 5/1996. Both free and advanced pay search service from 5/1996 at www1.odcr.com/search.php; updated daily. City and rarely phone may appear on online record. Civil shows name and town only.

Criminal Name Search: Access: Mail, in person, online. Both court and visitors may perform in person name searches. Search fee: $5.00 per name. Required to search: name, years to search; also helpful: SSN, DOB. Criminal records on microfilm since 1947; computerized back to May 1996. Mail turnaround time 3 days. Criminal PAT goes back to same as civil. Both free and advanced pay search service from 5/1996 at www1.odcr.com/search.php; updated daily. Online results show middle initial.

Murray County

20th Judicial District Court Box 578, 10th & Wyandotte St, Sulphur, OK 73086; 580-622-3223; 8AM-4:30PM (CST). *Felony, Misdemeanor, Civil, Eviction, Small Claims, Probate.* www.oscn.net

General Information: Online identifiers in results same as on public terminal. No mental health, guardianship, juvenile or adoption records released. Will not fax documents. Court makes copy: $1.00 first page, $.50 each add'l. Certification fee: $.50. Payee: Murray County Court Clerk. Personal checks accepted. Major credit cards accepted. Prepayment required. Mail requests: SASE required.

Civil Name Search: Access: Mail, in person, online. Both court and visitors may perform in person name searches. Search fee: $5.00 per name. Required to search: name, years to search; also helpful: DOB. Civil index in docket books from 1907, from 1973 back records are on microfilm; computerized back to 1997. Mail turnaround time 2 days, immediate if easily accessible. Civil PAT goes back to 9/1997. Both free and advanced pay search service from 1/1/1998 at www1.odcr.com/search.php; updated monthly. City and rarely phone may appear on online record. Civil shows name and town only.

Criminal Name Search: Access: Mail, in person, online. Both court and visitors may perform in person name searches. Search fee: $5.00 per name. Required to search: name, years to search; also helpful: SSN, DOB. Criminal docket on books from 1907, from 1973 back records are on microfilm; computerized back to 1997. Mail turnaround time 2 days, immediate if easily accessible. Criminal PAT goes back to same as civil. Both free and advanced pay search service from 1/1/1998 at www1.odcr.com/search.php; updated monthly. Online results show middle initial.

Muskogee County

15th Judicial District Court PO Box 1350, 220 State St, Muskogee, OK 74402; 918-682-7873; fax: 918-684-1696; 8AM-4:30PM (CST). *Felony, Misdemeanor, Civil, Divorce, Small Claims, Probate.* www.oscn.net

General Information: Search fee includes both civil and criminal indexes and probate. Probate is separate index at this same address. Probate fax is same as main fax number. Online identifiers in results same as on public terminal. No adoption, mental health, guardianship or juvenile records released. Will not fax out documents. Court makes copy: $1.00 1st page, $.50 each add'l. Certification fee: $.50 per page. Payee: Court Clerk. Personal checks accepted. Visa/MC accepted but not over the phone. Prepayment required. Mail requests: SASE required.

Civil Name Search: Access: Mail, in person, online. Both court and visitors may perform in person name searches. Search fee: $10.00 per name. Civil index in docket books from 1907. Mail turnaround time 2-3 days. Civil PAT goes back to 2003. Both free and advanced pay search service from 1/3/2003 at www1.odcr.com/search.php; updated daily. City and rarely phone may appear on online record. Civil shows name and town only.

Criminal Name Search: Access: Mail, in person, online. Both court and visitors may perform in person name searches. Search fee: $10.00 per name. Required to search: name, years to search, DOB; also helpful: SSN. Criminal docket on books from 1907. Mail turnaround time 2-3 days. Criminal PAT goes back to same as civil. Both free and advanced pay search service from 1/3/2003 at www1.odcr.com/search.php; updated daily. Online results show middle initial.

Noble County

8th Judicial District Court 300 Courthouse Dr, x14, Perry, OK 73077; 580-336-5187; 8AM-4:30PM (CST). *Felony, Misdemeanor, Civil, Eviction, Small Claims, Probate.* www.oscn.net

General Information: Probate is separate index at this same address. Online identifiers in results same as on public terminal. No adoption, mental health, guardianship or juvenile records released. Will not fax documents. Court makes copy: $1.00 1st page, $.50 each add'l. Certification fee: $.50 per instrument plus copy fee. Payee: Noble County Court Clerk. Personal checks accepted. Major credit cards accepted in person only. Prepayment required. Mail requests: SASE appreciated.

Civil Name Search: Access: Mail, in person, online. Both court and visitors may perform in person name searches. Search fee: $5.00 per name. Civil records on microfiche from 1893; computerized back to 1997 (complete years). Mail turnaround time 1 day. Civil PAT goes back to 1997. Both free and advanced pay search service from 1/1997 at www1.odcr.com/search.php; updated daily. City and rarely phone may appear on online record. Civil shows name and town only.

Criminal Name Search: Access: Mail, in person, online. Both court and visitors may perform in person name searches. Search fee: $5.00 per name. Required to search: name, years to search, DOB; also helpful: address, SSN. Criminal records on microfiche from 1893; computerized back to 1997 (complete years). Mail turnaround time 1 day. Criminal PAT goes back to same as civil. Both free and advanced pay search service from 1/1997 at www1.odcr.com/search.php; updated daily. Online results show middle initial.

Nowata County

11th Judicial District Court 229 N Maple St, Nowata, OK 74048; 918-273-0808; 8:30AM-4:30PM (CST). *Felony, Misdemeanor, Civil, Eviction, Small Claims, Probate.* www.oscn.net

General Information: Probate is separate index. Online identifiers in results same as on public terminal. No adoption, mental health, guardianship or juvenile records released. Will fax documents to local or toll free line. Court makes copy: $1.00 first page, $.50 each add'l. Certification fee: $.50 per page plus copy fee. Payee: Court Clerk. Personal checks accepted. Prepayment required. Mail requests: SASE requested.

Civil Name Search: Access: Mail, in person, online. Both court and visitors may perform in person name searches. Search fee: $5.00 per name. Civil index in docket books from 1907; on computer since 1998. Mail turnaround time 1 day. Civil PAT goes back to 1998. Both free and advanced pay search service from 7/1/1998 at www1.odcr.com/search.php; updated monthly. City and rarely phone may appear on online record. Civil shows name and town only.

Criminal Name Search: Access: Mail, in person, online. Both court and visitors may perform in person name searches. Search fee: $5.00 per name. Required to search: name, years to search; also helpful: SSN. Criminal docket on books from 1907; on computer since 1998. Mail turnaround time 1 day. Criminal PAT goes back to same as civil. Both free and advanced pay search service from 7/1/1998 at www1.odcr.com/search.php; updated monthly. Online results show middle initial.

Okfuskee County

24th Judicial District Court PO Box 30, 209 N 3rd Street, Okemah, OK 74859; 918-623-0525; fax: 918-623-2687; 8:30AM-4:30PM (CST). *Felony, Misdemeanor, Civil, Eviction, Small Claims, Probate.* www.oscn.net

General Information: Online identifiers in results same as on public terminal. No adoption, mental health, guardianship or juvenile released. Will fax documents to local or toll free line. Court makes copy: $1.00 first page, $.50 each add'l. Certification fee: $.50 per document. Payee: Court Clerk. Personal checks accepted, credit cards are not. Prepayment required. Mail requests: SASE required.

Civil Name Search: Access: Mail, in person, online. Both court and visitors may perform in person name searches. Search fee: $5.00 per name. Civil records in files and docket books from 1907, computerized since 1996. Note: All marriage licenses accessible on the Internet site. Mail turnaround time 3 days. Civil PAT goes back to 1996. Both free and advanced pay search service from 1/1997 at www1.odcr.com/search.php; updated daily. City and rarely phone may appear on online record. Civil shows name and town only.

Criminal Name Search: Access: Mail, in person, online. Both court and visitors may perform in person name searches. Search fee: $5.00 per name. Required to search: name, years to search; also helpful: SSN. Criminal records in files and docket books from 1907, computerized since 1996. Mail turnaround time 3 days. Criminal PAT goes back to 1990. Both free and advanced pay search service from 1/1997 at www1.odcr.com/search.php; updated monthly. Online results show middle initial.

Oklahoma County

District Court 320 Robert S Kerr St, Rm 409, Oklahoma City, OK 73102; 405-713-1705; criminal phone: 405-713-1712; civil phone: 405-713-1727; probate phone: 405-713-1727; fax: 405-713-1722; 8AM-5PM (CST). *Felony, Misdemeanor, Civil, Eviction, Small Claims, Probate.* www.oscn.net

General Information: Small claims: 405-713-1738. Online identifiers in results same as on public terminal. No juvenile, sealed, or expunged records released. Will not fax documents. Court makes copy: $1.00 1st page, $.50 each add'l. Certification fee: $.50 per doc. Payee: District Court Clerk. Personal checks accepted. Major credit cards accepted. Prepayment required. Mail requests: SASE required.

Civil Name Search: Access: Mail, in person, online. Both court and visitors may perform in person name searches. Search fee: Lengthy searches are $5.00 per half hour, otherwise no search fee. Civil records on microfiche from 1980, prior archived. Mail turnaround time 5-10 days. Civil PAT goes back to 1984. Online access to court dockets is free at www.oscn.net/applications/oscn/casesearch.asp. Civil dockets go back to 12/1984. Online record includes physical description, phone. Also both free and advanced pay search service at www1.odcr.com/search.php.

Criminal Name Search: Access: Mail, online, in person. Both court and visitors may perform in person name searches. Search fee: Lengthy searches $5.00 per half hour; commercial purpose searches: $25.00. Required to search: name, years to search, DOB; also helpful: SSN. Criminal records on microfiche from 1980, prior archived. Mail turnaround time 5-10 days. Criminal PAT goes back to same as civil. Online access to criminal dockets is same as civil. Criminal dockets go back to 9/1988 on OSCN. The sheriff's current inmates and warrants list is free at www.oklahomacounty.org/cosheriff/.

Okmulgee County

24th Judicial District Court 314 W 7th, Okmulgee, OK 74447; 918-756-3042; fax: 918-758-1237; 8AM-4:30PM (CST). *Felony, Misdemeanor, Civil, Eviction, Small Claims, Probate.* www.oscn.net

General Information: The Henryetta Branch closed April 2011, all their records are now located here. Online identifiers in results same as on public terminal. No juvenile, mental health, adoption or guardianship records released. Court makes copy: $1.00 first page, $.50 each add'l. Certification fee: $.50 per page. Payee: Court Clerk. Business checks accepted. No credit cards accepted. Prepayment required. Mail requests: SASE requested.

Civil Name Search: Access: Phone, mail, in person, online. Both court and visitors may perform in person name searches. Search fee: $5.00 per name. Civil records on microfiche from 1986, archived from 1907, computerized since 1997. Mail turnaround time 1-2 days. Civil PAT goes back to 1997. Both free and advanced pay search service from 1/1998 at www1.odcr.com/search.php; updated daily. City and rarely phone may appear on online record. Civil shows name and town only.

Criminal Name Search: Access: Phone, mail, in person, online. Both court and visitors may perform in person name searches. Search fee: $5.00 per name. Required to search: name, years to search; also helpful: SSN. Criminal records on microfiche from 1986, archived from 1907, computerized since 1997. Mail turnaround time 1-2 days. Criminal PAT goes back to same as civil. Both free and advanced pay search service

from 1/1998 at www1.odcr.com/search.php; updated daily. Online results show middle initial.

Osage County

10th Judicial District Court County Courthouse, 600 Grandview Rm 304, Pawhuska, OK 74056; 918-287-4104; 8:30AM-5PM (CST). *Felony, Misdemeanor, Civil, Eviction, Small Claims, Probate, Divorce.* www.oscn.net

General Information: Search fee covers a civil and criminal combined. Online identifiers in results same as on public terminal. No juvenile or adoption records released. Will not fax documents. Court makes copy: $1.00 1st page, $.50 each add'l. Certification fee: $.50 per instrument. Payee: Court Clerk. Only cashiers checks and money orders accepted. Credit cards accepted in person. Prepayment required. Mail requests: SASE required.

Civil Name Search: Access: Mail, in person, online. Both court and visitors may perform in person name searches. Search fee: $5.00 per name. Required to search: name, years to search; also helpful: address. Civil records archived from 1969. Mail turnaround time 1-2 days. Civil PAT goes back to 1996. Both free and advanced pay search service from 1/1996 at www1.odcr.com/search.php; updated daily. Civil shows name and town only.

Criminal Name Search: Access: Mail, in person, online. Both court and visitors may perform in person name searches. Search fee: $5.00 per name. Required to search: name, years to search; also helpful: address. Criminal records archived from 1969. Mail turnaround time 1-2 days. Criminal PAT goes back to 1995. Both free and advanced pay search service from 1/1996 at www1.odcr.com/search.php; updated daily. Online results show middle initial.

Ottawa County

13th Judicial District Court 102 E Central Ave, #203, Miami, OK 74354; 918-542-2801; fax: 918-542-8482; 9:00AM-5:00PM (CST). *Felony, Misdemeanor, Civil, Eviction, Small Claims, Probate.* www.oscn.net

General Information: Also, a good web page to use is www.odcr.com. Online identifiers in results same as on public terminal. No juvenile, mental health, adoption or guardianship records released. Will not fax documents. Court makes copy: $1.00 first page, $.50 each add'l. Self serve copy: same. Certification fee: $.50 per document. Payee: Clerk of Court. Money orders accepted. No credit cards accepted. Prepayment required. Mail requests: SASE required.

Civil Name Search: Access: Phone, mail, in person, online. Both court and visitors may perform in person name searches. Search fee: $5.00 per name. Civil index on docket books or cards from 1907, recent records computerized. Mail turnaround time 1-2 days. Civil PAT goes back to 1997. Both free and advanced pay search service from 9/1/1997 at www1.odcr.com/search.php; updated daily. City and rarely phone may appear on online record. Civil shows name and town only.

Criminal Name Search: Access: Mail, in person, online. Both court and visitors may perform in person name searches. Search fee: $5.00. Required to search: name, years to search; also helpful: SSN. Criminal docket on books or cards from 1907, recent records computerized. Mail turnaround time 1-2 days. Criminal PAT goes back to same as civil. Both free and advanced pay search service from 9/1/1997 at www1.odcr.com/search.php; updated daily. Online results show middle initial.

Pawnee County

14th Judicial District Court Courthouse, 500 Harrison St, Pawnee, OK 74058; 918-762-2547; 8AM-4:30PM (CST). *Felony, Misdemeanor, Civil, Eviction, Small Claims, Probate.* www.oscn.net

General Information: Online identifiers in results same as on public terminal. No sealed records released. Will not fax documents. Court makes copy: $1.00 first page, $.50 each add'l. Certification fee: $.50 per page. Payee: Court Clerk. Personal checks accepted, credit cards are not. Prepayment required. Mail requests: SASE required.

Civil Name Search: Access: Mail, in person, online. Both court and visitors may perform in person name searches. Search fee: $5.00. Civil records on docket sheets to 1975, computerized from 1997. Mail turnaround time 1-3 days. Civil PAT goes back to 1997. Both free and advanced pay search service from 1/1997 at www1.odcr.com/search.php; updated daily. Marriage license index also available. City and rarely phone may appear on online record. Civil shows name and town only.

Criminal Name Search: Access: Mail, in person, online. Both court and visitors may perform in person name searches. Search fee: $5.00. Required to search: name, years to search; also helpful: SSN. Criminal records on docket sheets to 1975, computerized from 1997. Mail turnaround time 1-3 days. Criminal PAT goes back to same as civil. Both free and advanced pay search service from 1/1997 at www1.odcr.com/search.php; updated daily. Online results show middle initial.

Payne County

9th Judicial District Court 606 S Husband, Rm 206, Stillwater, OK 74074; 405-372-4774; 8AM-5PM (CST). *Felony, Misdemeanor, Civil, Eviction, Small Claims, Probate.* www.oscn.net

General Information: Online identifiers in results same as on public terminal. No sealed records, juveniles or adoption records released. Will not fax documents. Court makes copy: $1.00 first page, $.50 each add'l. Certification fee: $1.50 per page. Payee: Clerk of Court. Personal checks accepted, credit cards are not. Prepayment required. Mail requests: SASE required.

Civil Name Search: Access: Mail, in person, online. Both court and visitors may perform in person name searches. Search fee: $5.00 plus $1.00 per name per year. Civil index in docket books from late 1800s, as of 1994 on computer. Mail turnaround time 2 days. Civil PAT goes back to 1994. Online access to court dockets is free at www.oscn.net/applications/oscn/casesearch.asp. Dockets go back to 1/1994. Online record includes physical description, phone. Also both free and advanced pay search service at www1.odcr.com/search.php.

Criminal Name Search: Access: Mail, online, in person. Both court and visitors may perform in person name searches. Search fee: $5.00 plus $1.00 per name per year. Required to search: name, years to search, DOB, SSN, signed release. Criminal docket on books from late 1800s, as of 1994 on computer. Mail turnaround time 2 days. Criminal PAT goes back to same as civil. Terminal criminal results may also show SSN. Online access to criminal dockets is same as civil.

Pittsburg County

18th Judicial District Court PO Box 460, 122 E Carl Albert Pky, McAlester, OK 74502; 918-423-4859; 8AM-5PM (CST). *Felony, Misdemeanor, Civil, Eviction, Small Claims, Probate.* www.oscn.net

General Information: Online identifiers in results same as on public terminal. No juvenile, adoptions, mental health or guardianship records released. Will not fax documents. Court makes copy: $1.00 first page, $.50 each add'l. Self serve copy: same. Certification fee: $.50 per page. Payee: Court Clerk. Personal checks accepted. Major credit cards accepted. Prepayment required. Mail requests: SASE required.

Civil Name Search: Access: Mail, in person, online. Both court and visitors may perform in person name searches. Search fee: $5.00 per name. Civil records on microfiche since 1907; on computer since 1997. Mail turnaround time 1-2 days. Civil PAT goes back to 1997. Both free and advanced pay search service from 7/1/1997 at www1.odcr.com/search.php; updated monthly. City and rarely phone may appear on online record. Civil shows name and town only.

Criminal Name Search: Access: Mail, in person, online. Both court and visitors may perform in person name searches. Search fee: $5.00 per name for 10 yr misdemeanor search; add $5.00 to include felonies. Required to search: name, years to search, DOB. Criminal records on microfiche since 1907; on computer since 1997. Mail turnaround time 1-2 days. Criminal PAT goes back to 1997. Both free and advanced pay search service from 7/1/1997 at www1.odcr.com/search.php; updated every 15 minutes.

Pontotoc County

22nd Judicial District Court Box 427, Ada, OK 74820; 580-332-5763; fax: 580-332-5766; 8AM-N; 1-5PM (CST). *Felony, Misdemeanor, Civil, Eviction, Small Claims, Probate.* www.oscn.net

General Information: Online identifiers in results same as on public terminal. No juvenile, adoptions, mental health or guardianship records released. Will fax documents to local or toll-free number if not certified. Court makes copy: $1.00 first page, $.50 each add'l. Certification fee: $.50 per page. Payee: Clerk of Court. Personal checks accepted if in-state. Major credit cards accepted. Prepayment required. Mail requests: SASE required.

Civil Name Search: Access: Mail, in person, online. Both court and visitors may perform in person name searches. Search fee: $5.00 per name. Civil records on book index from 1907; on computer back to 1997. Mail turnaround time 2 days. Civil PAT goes back to 1997. Both free and advanced pay search service from 1/1997 at www1.odcr.com/search.php; updated monthly. City and rarely phone may appear on online record. Civil shows name and town only.

Criminal Name Search: Access: Mail, in person, online. Both court and visitors may perform in person name searches. Search fee: $5.00 per name. Required to search: name, years to search; also helpful: DOB, SSN. Criminal records on card index from 1907; on computer back to 1997. Mail turnaround time 2 days. Criminal PAT goes back to 1987. Both free and advanced pay search service from 1/1997 at www1.odcr.com/search.php; updated monthly. Online results show middle initial.

Pottawatomie County

23rd Judicial District Court 325 N Broadway, Shawnee, OK 74801; 405-273-3624; fax: 405-878-5525; 8:30AM-5PM (CST). *Felony, Misdemeanor, Civil, Eviction, Small Claims, Probate.* www.oscn.net

General Information: Online identifiers in results same as on public terminal. No juvenile, adoptions, mental health or guardianship records released. Will fax documents $1.00 per page. Court makes copy: $1.00 first page, $.50 each add'l. Certification fee: $.50 per page. Payee: Court Clerk. Personal checks accepted, credit cards are not. Prepayment required. Mail requests: SASE requested.

Civil Name Search: Access: Mail, in person, online. Both court and visitors may perform in person name searches. Search fee: $5.00 per name. Civil records on computer from 7/97; prior records on book of names from 1906. Mail turnaround time 2 weeks or less. Civil PAT goes back to 7/1997. Both free and advanced pay search service from 7/1/1997 at www1.odcr.com/search.php; updated daily. City and rarely phone may appear on online record. Civil shows name and town only.

Criminal Name Search: Access: Mail, in person, online. Both court and visitors may perform in person name searches. Search fee: $5.00 per name. Required to search: name, years to search; also helpful: SSN. Criminal records computerized from 7/97; prior records on book of names from 1897. Mail turnaround time 2 weeks or less. Criminal PAT goes back to 1997. Both free and advanced pay search service from 7/1/1997 at www1.odcr.com/search.php; updated daily. Online results show middle initial.

Pushmataha County

17th Judicial District Court Pushmataha County Courthouse, 302 SW B, Antlers, OK 74523; 580-298-2274; fax: 580-298-3696; 8AM-4:30PM (CST). *Felony, Misdemeanor, Civil, Eviction, Small Claims, Probate.* www.oscn.net

General Information: No juvenile or adoption records released. Court makes copy: $1.00 first page, $.50 each add'l. Certification fee: $.50 per page includes copy fee. Payee: Court Clerk. Personal checks accepted. Major credit cards accepted at counter only. Prepayment required. Mail requests: SASE required.

Civil Name Search: Access: Mail, in person, online. Both court and visitors may perform in person name searches. Search fee: $5.00 per name. Civil records on docket book from 1907. Mail turnaround time 1 day. Online access to court dockets is free at www.oscn.net/applications/oscn/casesearch.asp. Online record includes physical description, phone. Also both free and advanced pay search service at www1.odcr.com/search.php.

Criminal Name Search: Access: Mail, in person, online. Both court and visitors may perform in person name searches. Search fee: $5.00 per name. Required to search: name, years to search; also helpful: SSN. Criminal records on docket book from 1907, online from 2004. Mail turnaround time 1 day. Online access to court dockets is same as civil.

Roger Mills County

2nd Judicial District Court PO Box 409, 480 L.L. Males Ave & Broadway St, Cheyenne, OK 73628; 580-497-3361; fax: 580-497-2167; 8AM-4:30PM (CST). *Felony, Misdemeanor, Civil, Eviction, Small Claims, Probate.* www.oscn.net

General Information: Probate fax is same as main fax number. No adoption, juvenile, mental health or guardianship records released. Will fax documents $1.00 per page. Court makes copy: $1.00 first page, $.50 each add'l. Certification fee: $.50 per certification plus copy fee. Payee: Court Clerk. Personal checks accepted. Major credit cards accepted in person. Mail requests: SASE required.

Civil Name Search: Access: Phone, mail, in person, online. Both court and visitors may perform in person name searches. Search fee: None unless 2 or more, then $5.00. Civil records on computer since 2004, in books since 1893. Mail turnaround time 1 day. Online access to court dockets is free at www.oscn.net/applications/oscn/casesearch.asp. No fee to view records. Online record includes physical description, phone. Also both free and advanced pay search service at www1.odcr.com/search.php.

Criminal Name Search: Access: Phone, mail, fax, in person, online. Both court and visitors may perform in person name searches. Search fee: None unless 2 or more, then $5.00. Required to search: name, years to search, DOB; also helpful: SSN. Criminal records on computer since 2004, in books since 1893. Mail turnaround time 1 day. Online access is the same as civil.

Rogers County

Rogers County District Court Box 839 (219 S Missouri), Claremore, OK 74018; 918-341-5711; 8AM-4:30PM (CST). *Felony, Misdemeanor, Civil, Eviction, Small Claims, Probate.* www.oscn

General Information: Online identifiers in results same as on public terminal. No juvenile or adoption records released. Will not fax documents. Court makes copy: $1.00 first page, $.50 each add'l. Certification fee: $.50 per page. Payee: Court Clerk. Personal checks accepted. Major credit cards accepted if in person. Prepayment required. Mail requests: SASE required.

Civil Name Search: Access: Phone, mail, online, in person. Both court and visitors may perform in person name searches. Search fee: None, but phone and mail requests require case number. Civil records in card index since 1907, some computerized. Mail turnaround time 1 day. Civil PAT goes back to 7/1997. Online access to court dockets is free at www.oscn.net/applications/oscn/casesearch.asp. Dockets go back to 7/1997, includes physical description, phone.

Criminal Name Search: Access: Phone, mail, online, in person. Both court and visitors may perform in person name searches. Search fee: None, but phone and mail requests require case number. Required to search: name, years to search, DOB; also helpful: SSN. Criminal records on card index since 1907, some computerized. Mail turnaround time 1 day. Criminal PAT goes back to same as civil. Online access to criminal dockets is the same as civil.

Seminole County

22nd Judicial District Court - Seminole Branch Box 1320, 401 N Main St, Seminole, OK 74868; 405-382-3424; fax: 405-382-9440; 8AM-N, 1PM-4PM (CST). *Civil, Small Claims, Probate.* www.oscn.net

General Information: Criminal records are now maintained at Seminole County Court Clerk, PO Box 130, Wewoka, OK, 405-257-6236. Court makes copy: $1.00 first page, $.50 each add'l. Certification fee: $.50 per page. Payee: Court Clerk. Only cashiers checks and money orders accepted. No credit cards accepted. Prepayment required. Mail requests: SASE required.

Civil Name Search: Access: Phone, fax, mail, in person. Only the court performs in person name searches; visitors may not. Search fee: $5.00 per name. Civil index on cards from 1931, probate from 1969; on computer back to 1995. Mail turnaround time 1 to 2 days.

22nd Judicial District Court - Wewoka Branch PO Box 130, 120 S Wewoka Ave, Wewoka, OK 74884; 405-257-6236; fax: 405-257-2631; 8AM-4PM (CST). *Felony, Misdemeanor, Civil, Eviction, Small Claims, Probate.* www.oscn.net

General Information: Probate records in separate books, but on same computer system. Online identifiers in results same as on public terminal. No juvenile or adoption records released. Will fax documents to toll-free number. Court makes copy: $1.00 first page, $.50 each add'l. Self serve copy: same. Certification fee: $.50 per page plus copy fee. Payee: Court Clerk. Personal checks accepted. Major credit cards accepted in person only. Prepayment required. Mail requests: SASE required.

Civil Name Search: Access: Mail, in person, online. Both court and visitors may perform in person name searches. Search fee: $5.00 per name. Civil records indexed on computer since 1995; prior records on books to 1907. Mail turnaround time 1 day. Civil PAT goes back to 1995. Public terminal includes probate. Both free and advanced pay search service from 1/1995 at www1.odcr.com/search.php; updated daily. City and rarely phone may appear on online record. Civil shows name and town only.

Criminal Name Search: Access: Mail, in person, online. Both court and visitors may perform in person name searches. Search fee: $5.00 per name. Required to search: name, years to search; also helpful: SSN. Criminal records indexed on computer since 1995; prior records on books to 1908. Mail turnaround time 1 day. Criminal PAT goes back to same as civil. Both free and advanced pay search service from 1/1995 at www1.odcr.com/search.php; updated daily. Results show middle initial.

Sequoyah County

15th Judicial District Court 120 E Chickasaw, Sallisaw, OK 74955; 918-775-4411; fax: 918-775-1223; 8AM-4PM (CST). *Felony, Misdemeanor, Civil, Eviction, Small Claims, Probate.* www.oscn.net

General Information: Probate is a separate office at this same address. Probate fax is same as main fax number. Online identifiers in results same as on public terminal. No juvenile, adoptions, mental health or guardianship records released. Will fax documents to toll-free or local number. Court makes copy: $1.00 first page, $.50 each add'l. Self serve copy: same. Certification fee: $5.00 each. Payee: Court Clerk. Personal checks accepted, credit cards are not. Prepayment required. Will bill mail requests. Mail requests: SASE required.

Civil Name Search: Access: Mail, in person, online. Both court and visitors may perform in person name searches. Search fee: $5.00 per name. Civil records in files and dockets from 1907; on computer back to 1997. Mail turnaround time 1 week. Civil PAT goes back to 1997. Both free and advanced pay search service from 7/1/1997 at www1.odcr.com/search.php; updated daily. City and rarely phone may appear on online record. Civil shows name and town only.

Criminal Name Search: Access: Phone, mail, in person, online. Both court and visitors may perform in person name searches. Search fee: $5.00 per name. Required to search: name, years to search; also helpful: SSN. Some Criminal records computerized from 1997, prior in files and dockets. Mail turnaround time 1 week. Criminal PAT goes back to same as civil. Both free and advanced pay search service from 7/1/1997 at www1.odcr.com/search.php; updated daily. Online results show middle initial.

Stephens County

5th Judicial District Court 101 S 11th St, Rm 301, Duncan, OK 73533; 580-470-2000; 8:30AM-4:30PM (CST). *Felony, Misdemeanor, Civil, Eviction, Small Claims, Probate.* www.oscn.net

General Information: Online identifiers in results same as on public terminal. No juvenile, adoptions, mental health or guardianship records released. Will not fax documents. Court makes copy: $1.00 first page, $.50 each add'l. Certification fee: $.50 per page. Payee: Stephens County Court Clerk. No personal checks. No credit cards accepted. Prepayment required. Mail requests: SASE required.

Civil Name Search: Access: Mail, in person, online. Both court and visitors may perform in person name searches. Search fee: $5.00 per name (per court). Civil records on computer from 10/95; prior records on docket books from 1907. Mail turnaround time 1 day. Civil PAT goes back to 1996. Both free and advanced pay search service from 1/1996 at www1.odcr.com/search.php; updated daily. City and rarely phone may appear on online record. Civil shows name and town only.

Criminal Name Search: Access: Mail, in person, online. Both court and visitors may perform in person name searches. Search fee: $5.00 per name (per court). Required to search: name, years to search; also helpful: address, DOB, SSN. Criminal records computerized from 10/95; prior records on docket books from 1907. Mail turnaround time 1 day. Criminal PAT goes back to same as civil. Both free and advanced pay search service from 1/1996 at www1.odcr.com/search.php; updated daily. Online results show middle initial.

Texas County

1st Judicial District Court Box 1081, 319 N Main St, Guymon, OK 73942; 580-338-3003; fax: 580-338-3819; 9AM-5PM (CST). *Felony, Misdemeanor, Civil, Eviction, Small Claims, Probate.* www.oscn.net

General Information: Online identifiers in results same as on public terminal. No juvenile, adoptions, mental health or guardianship records released. Will fax documents. Court makes copy: $1.00 1st page, $.50 ea add'l. Self serve copy: same. Certification fee: $.50 per page. Payee: Court Clerk. Personal checks accepted. Credit cards accepted in person only. Prepayment required. Mail requests: SASE required.

Civil Name Search: Access: Mail, fax, in person, online. Both court and visitors may perform in person name searches. No search fee. Fax requests must be on letterhead. Civil records on microfiche from 1976, archived prior, computerized since 3/95. Mail turnaround time 5 days; 1 day for phone. Civil PAT goes back to 5/1995. Both free and advanced pay search service from 1/15/1995 at www1.odcr.com/search.php; updated daily. City and rarely phone may appear on online record. Civil shows name and town only.

Criminal Name Search: Access: Mail, fax, in person, online. Both court and visitors may perform in person name searches. No search fee. Required to search: name, years to search; also helpful: SSN. Fax requests must be on letterhead. Criminal records on microfiche from 1976, archived prior, computerized since 3/95. Mail turnaround time 5 days; 1 day for phone requests. Criminal PAT goes back to same as civil. Both free and advanced pay search service from 1/15/1995 at www1.odcr.com/search.php; updated daily. Online results show middle initial.

Tillman County

3rd Judicial District Court Box 116, 201 N Main, Frederick, OK 73542; 580-335-3023; criminal phone: 580-335-5536; civil phone: 580-335-5536; fax: 580-335-5613; 8AM-4PM (CST). *Felony, Misdemeanor, Civil, Eviction, Small Claims, Probate.* www.oscn.net

General Information: Online identifiers in results same as on public terminal. No expunged records released. Will fax documents to local or toll-free number. Court makes copy: $1.00 first page, $.50 each add'l. Certification fee: $.50. Payee: District Court. Business checks accepted. No credit cards accepted. Prepayment required., but bill law firms. Mail requests: SASE required.

Civil Name Search: Access: Mail, in person, online. Both court and visitors may perform in person name searches. Search fee: $5.00 per name. Civil index in docket books from 1907; on computer back to 1998. Mail turnaround time 1 day. Civil PAT goes back to 1998. Both free and advanced pay search service from 1/1998 at www1.odcr.com/search.php; updated hourly. City and rarely phone may appear on online record. Civil shows name and town only.

Criminal Name Search: Access: Mail, in person, online. Both court and visitors may perform in person name searches. Search fee: $5.00 per name. Required to search: name, years to search, DOB; also helpful: SSN. Criminal docket on books from 1907; on computer back to 1998. Mail turnaround time 1 day. Criminal PAT goes back to same as civil. Both free and advanced pay search service from 1/1998 at www1.odcr.com/search.php; updated hourly. Online results show middle initial.

Tulsa County

14th Judicial District Court 500 S Denver Ave, Tulsa, OK 74103-3832; 918-596-5000; criminal phone: 918-596-5471; civil phone: 918-596-5436; probate phone: 918-596-5440; fax: 918-596-5402; 8:30AM-5PM (CST). *Felony, Misdemeanor, Civil, Eviction, Small Claims, Probate.* www.oscn.net

General Information: Online identifiers in results same as on public terminal. No juvenile, adoption or guardianship records released. Court makes copy: $1.00 first page, $.50 each add'l. Certification fee: $.50 per cert plus copy fee. Payee: Court Clerk. Personal checks accepted. Major credit cards accepted in person. Prepayment required. Mail requests: SASE required.

Civil Name Search: Access: Mail, in person, online. Both court and visitors may perform in person name searches. Search fee: $5.00 per name. Civil records on computer from 1984, on microfiche from 1907, archived from 1907. Mail turnaround time 1 week. Civil PAT goes back to 1984. Online access to court dockets is free at www.oscn.net/applications/oscn/casesearch.asp. Civil dockets go back to 10/1984. Online record includes physical description, phone. Also both free and advanced pay search service at www1.odcr.com/search.php.

Criminal Name Search: Access: Online, in person. Both court and visitors may perform in person name searches. No search fee. Required to search: name, years to search; also helpful: SSN. Criminal records computerized from 1984, on microfiche from 1907, archived from 1907. Note: For a county criminal search, contact Records Dept at Sheriff's Office, downstairs- 918-596-5670. Fee is $7.50; request should include name, dates, DOB, signed release and also SSN. Criminal PAT goes back to same as civil. Online access to criminal dockets is same as civil. Criminal dockets go back to 1/1988.

Wagoner County

15th Judicial District Court 307 E Cherokee St, PO Box 249, Wagoner, OK 74467-4705; 918-485-4508; fax: 918-485-5836; 8AM-4:30PM (CST). *Felony, Misdemeanor, Civil, Eviction, Small Claims, Probate.* www.oscn.net

General Information: Online identifiers in results same as on public terminal. No juvenile, mental health, adoption or guardianship records released. Will not fax documents. Court makes copy: $1.00 first page, $.50 each add'l. Certification fee: $.50 per page. Payee: Court Clerk. Personal checks accepted, credit cards are not. Prepayment required. Mail requests: SASE required.

Civil Name Search: Access: Mail, in person, online. Both court and visitors may perform in person name searches. Search fee: $5.00 per name. Civil index in docket books from 1980; on computer back to 1997. Mail turnaround time 1-5 days Civil PAT goes back to 1990. Both free and advanced pay search service from 1/1990 at www1.odcr.com/search.php; updated monthly. City and rarely phone may appear on online record. Civil shows name and town only.

Criminal Name Search: Access: Mail, in person, online. Both court and visitors may perform in person name searches. Search fee: $5.00 per name if assisted. Required to search: name, years to search; also helpful: SSN. Criminal records are in files and dockets back to 1907; on computer back to 1997. Mail turnaround time 1-5 days. Criminal PAT goes back to same as civil. Results may also show DL number. Both free and advanced pay search service from 1/1990 at www1.odcr.com/search.php; updated monthly. Online results show middle initial.

Washington County

11th Judicial District Court 420 S Johnstone, Rm 101, Bartlesville, OK 74003; 918-337-2870; fax: 918-337-2897; 8AM-5PM (CST). *Felony, Misdemeanor, Civil, Eviction, Small Claims, Probate.* www.oscn.net

General Information: Online identifiers in results same as on public terminal. No juvenile, mental health, adoption or guardianship records released. Will fax documents to local or toll free line. Court makes copy: $1.00 first page, $.50 each add'l. Certification fee: $.50 per page. Payee: Court Clerk. Personal checks accepted, credit cards are not. Prepayment required.

Civil Name Search: Access: Fax, mail, in person, online. Both court and visitors may perform in person name searches. Search fee: $5.00 per name. Civil index in docket books from 1907; computerized records since 1997. Mail turnaround time 2-4 days. Civil PAT goes back to 1998. Both free and advanced pay search service from 1/1999 at www1.odcr.com/search.php; updated daily. City and rarely phone may appear on online record. Civil shows name and town only.

Criminal Name Search: Access: Fax, mail, in person, online. Both court and visitors may perform in person name searches. Search fee: $5.00 per name. Required to search: name, years to search, signed release; also helpful: DOB, SSN. Criminal docket on books from 1907; computerized records since 1997. Mail turnaround time 2-4 days. Criminal PAT goes back to 1998. Both free and advanced pay search service from 1/1999 at

www1.odcr.com/search.php; updated daily. Online results show middle initial.

Washita County

2nd Judicial District Court Box 397 (111 E Main St), 3rd Floor, Cordell, OK 73632; 580-832-3836; fax: 580-832-4123; 8AM-4PM (CST). *Felony, Misdemeanor, Civil, Small Claims, Probate.* www.oscn.net

General Information: Online identifiers in results same as on public terminal. No juvenile, mental health, adoption or guardianship records released. Will fax documents $1.00 per page. Court makes copy: $1.00 first page, $.50 each add'l. Certification fee: $.50 per doc or $5.00 authenticated certificate. Payee: Court Clerk. Personal checks accepted. Major credit cards accepted in person only. Prepayment required. Mail requests: SASE required.

Civil Name Search: Access: Mail, in person, online. Both court and visitors may perform in person name searches. Search fee: $5.00 per name. Civil records on computer since 1998; prior records on microfiche from 1980s & on docket books from 1892. Mail turnaround time same day. Civil PAT goes back to 1998. Both free and advanced pay search service from 10/1/1997 at www1.odcr.com/search.php; updated daily. City and rarely phone may appear on online record. Civil shows name and town only.

Criminal Name Search: Access: Mail, in person, online. Both court and visitors may perform in person name searches. Search fee: $5.00 per name. Required to search: name, years to search; also helpful: DOB, SSN, aliases. Criminal records on computer since 1998; prior records on microfiche from 1980s & on docket books from 1892. Mail turnaround time same day. Criminal PAT goes back to same as civil. Both free and advanced pay search service from 10/1/1997 at www1.odcr.com/search.php; updated daily. Online results also show address. Online results show middle initial.

Woods County

4th Judicial District Court Box 924, 407 Government St, Alva, OK 73717; 580-327-3119; fax: 580-327-6237; 8AM-5PM (CST). *Felony, Misdemeanor, Civil, Eviction, Small Claims, Probate.* www.oscn.net

General Information: Online identifiers in results same as on public terminal. No juvenile, mental health, adoption or guardianship records released. Will not fax documents. Court makes copy: $1.00 first page, $.50 each add'l. Certification fee: $.50 per page plus copy fee. Payee: Clerk of Court. Personal checks accepted, credit cards are not. Prepayment required. Mail requests: SASE required.

Civil Name Search: Access: Mail, in person, online. Both court and visitors may perform in person name searches. Search fee: $5.00 per name. Civil index in docket books from 1890. Mail turnaround time 2 days. Civil PAT goes back to 2002. Both free and advanced pay search service from 7/2002 at www1.odcr.com/search.php; updated monthly. City and rarely phone may appear on online record. Civil shows name and town only.

Criminal Name Search: Access: Mail, in person, online. Both court and visitors may perform in person name searches. Search fee: $5.00 per name. Criminal records on computer since 1987, on dockets and cards from 1890s. Mail turnaround time 2 days. Criminal PAT goes back to same as civil. Both free and advanced pay search service from 7/2002 at www1.odcr.com/search.php; updated monthly. Online results show middle initial.

Woodward County

4th Judicial District Court 1600 Main St, Woodward, OK 73801; 580-256-3413; fax: 580-254-6807; 9AM-5PM (CST). *Felony, Misdemeanor, Civil, Small Claims, Probate, Divorce.* www.oscn.net

General Information: Online identifiers in results same as on public terminal. No mental, juvenile, adoption, guardianship records released. Will not fax documents. Court makes copy: $1.00 first page, $.50 each add'l. Self serve copy: same. Certification fee: $.50 per page. $5.00 for whole file plus copy fee. Payee: Jenny Hopkins, Court Clerk. Personal checks accepted. Major credit cards accepted in person only. Prepayment required. Mail requests: SASE required.

Civil Name Search: Access: Mail, in person, online. Both court and visitors may perform in person name searches. Search fee: $5.00 per name. Civil index in docket books from 1890, on microfiche from 1989; on computer from 1997. Mail turnaround time 1-2 days unless older cases found. Civil PAT goes back to 1997. Both free and advanced pay search service from 2/1997 at www1.odcr.com/search.php; updated daily. City and rarely phone may appear on online record. Civil shows name and town only.

Criminal Name Search: Access: Mail, in person, online. Both court and visitors may perform in person name searches. Search fee: $5.00 per name. Required to search: name, years to search; also helpful: DOB. Criminal docket on books from 1890, on microfiche from 1989; on computer from 1997. Mail turnaround time 1-2 days unless older cases found. Criminal PAT goes back to same as civil. Both free and advanced pay search service from 2/1/1997 to present free at www.odcr.com; updated daily. Online results show middle initial.

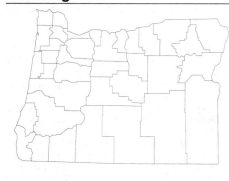

Oregon

Time Zone:	PST
Capital:	Salem, Marion County
# of Counties:	36
State Web:	www.oregon.gov
Court Web:	http://courts.oregon.gov/OJD

Administration

Court Administrator, Supreme Court Building, 1163 State St, Salem, OR, 97301-2563; 503-986-5500, Fax: 503-986-5503.

The Supreme and Appellate Courts

The Supreme Court is the court of last resort. With the exception of a limited number of appeals that go directly to the Supreme Court (i.e. notably death penalty cases, ballot title cases, lawyer discipline matters, and tax court cases) the Court of Appeals receives appeals or judicial reviews from Oregon's trial courts and administrative agencies.

Supreme and Appellate court opinions are found at www.publications.ojd.state.or.us/.

The Oregon Courts

Court	Type	How Organized	Jurisdiction Highpoints
Circuit*	General	36 Courts in 27 Districts	Felony, Misdemeanor, Civil, Small Claims, Juvenile, Traffic, Eviction, Domestic Relations, Estate
County*	Special	7 Courts in 7 Counties	Probate. Some have Juvenile
Justice	Limited	37 Courts	Misdemeanor, Small Claims, Traffic, Ordinance, Juvenile
Municipal	Municipal	127 Courts	Misdemeanor, Traffic, Ordinance
Tax	Special	1 Court	Tax

* = profiled in this book

Details on the Court Structure

Circuit Courts have original jurisdiction in all civil and criminal matters within the state, including probate, juvenile, and some traffic matters, as well as civil and criminal jury trials. The Small Claims limit is $5,000. The Clerk of Court is the record custodian.

The majority of **Municipal Court** cases involve traffic and ordinance matters.

Probate filing is a function of the Circuit Court; however, each county has a **Register in Probate** who maintains and manages the probate, guardianship, and mental health records.

The **Oregon Tax Court** has exclusive jurisdiction to hear tax appeals including personal income tax, property tax, corporate excise tax, timber tax, local budget law and property tax limitations. There are 2 divisions: Magistrate Division and Regular Division.

Record Searching Facts You Need to Know

Fees and Record Searching Tips

Most Circuit Courts with computerized records have public access terminals using the OJIN system (see below). Most records offices close from Noon to 1PM Oregon time for lunch. No staff is available during that period.

The copy fee is generally $.25 per page, the certification fee is $5.00. The courts are permitted to charge $2.00 for the first page and $1.00 for ea add'l page for both incoming and outgoing faxes, but many courts choose not to fax.

The web page for the Tax Court is http://courts.oregon.gov/Tax/index.page.

Online Access is for All Circuit Courts

OJIN is the acronym for the online program provides court case information from Circuit Courts in all 36 counties in the state. It allows one to search for civil, small claims, tax, domestic, and criminal cases. The search mechanism allows single county or statewide searching for either civil or criminal cases. Note OJIN does not provide records from Municipal or County Courts. Also Circuit cases that are confidential and protected statutorily are not available to the public. There is a one-time setup fee of $295.00 plus a monthly usage fee per user based on the type of search, if printed, and time of day. The minimum monthly usage is $10.00. Note that OJIN information is provided in real time from the Oregon Judicial Department database. Although OJIN provides a disclaimer statement (*The information does not constitute the official record. The official record of the court is located at the court site where the case was filed.*), OJIN displays the same data as displayed on public access terminals at the courts. The onsite terminals use OJIN.

See http://courts.oregon.gov/OJD/OnlineServices/OJIN/getstarted.page? or call 800-858-9658.

Baker County

Circuit Court 1995 3rd St, #220, Baker City, OR 97814; 541-523-6305; fax: 541-523-9738; 8AM-N, 1-5PM (PST). *Felony, Misdemeanor, Civil, Probate, Divorce.* http://courts.oregon.gov/Baker/

General Information: Probate fax is same as main fax number. Online identifiers in results same as on public terminal. No adoption, mental, juvenile or sealed records released. Fee to fax out file $2.00 1st page; $1.00 each add'l. Court makes copy: $.25 per page. Certification fee: $5.00 per document plus copy fee. Payee: State of Oregon. Personal checks accepted. Credit cards accepted in person or phone. Prepayment required. Mail requests: SASE required.

Civil Name Search: Access: Phone, fax, mail, in person, online. Both court and visitors may perform in person name searches. No search fee. Civil records on computer from 1987, archives back to 1865. Mail turnaround time 10 days. Civil PAT goes back to 1987. Index online at the state's OJIN system, call 800-858-9658 for information.

Criminal Name Search: Access: Phone, fax, mail, in person, online. Both court and visitors may perform in person name searches. No search fee. Criminal records computerized from 1987, archives back to 1865. Mail turnaround time 10 days. Criminal PAT goes back to same as civil. Index online at the state's OJIN system, call 800-858-9658 for information. Online results show middle initial, DOB.

Benton County

Circuit Court Box 1870, 120 NW 4th St, Corvallis, OR 97339; 541-766-6828; probate phone: 541-766-6825; fax: 541-766-6028; 8AM-N, 1-5PM (PST). *Felony, Misdemeanor, Civil, Eviction, Small Claims, Probate, Divorce.* http://courts.oregon.gov/Benton/

General Information: No adoption, juvenile, sealed by judge, expunged, mental health records released. Will not fax documents. Court makes copy: $.25 per page. Certification fee: $5.00; Exemplification certificates (3 part cert) $10.00 for cert plus $.25 for each page copied. Payee: State of Oregon. Personal checks accepted. Major credit cards and debit cards accepted. Prepayment required. Mail requests: SASE required.

Civil Name Search: Access: Phone, mail, online, in person. Both court and visitors may perform in person name searches. Search fee: None, unless request extensive. Required to search: name, years to search; also helpful: address. Civil cases indexed by defendant, plaintiff, case number. Civil records on computer from 1993, archives and microfiche back to the 1900s. Mail turnaround time up to 1 week. Civil PAT goes back to 1988. Public terminal located outside Rm 106. Results include address if entered. Index online at the state's OJIN system, call 800-858-9658 for information.

Criminal Name Search: Access: Phone, mail, online, in person. Both court and visitors may perform in person name searches. Search fee: None, unless request extensive. Required to search: name, years to search, DOB, offense; also helpful: address, SSN, case number. Criminal records computerized from 1993, archives and microfiche back to the 1900s. Mail turnaround time up to 1 week. Criminal PAT goes back to same as civil. Public terminal located outside Rm 106. Results include address if entered. Online access to criminal records is the same as civil. Criminal index goes back to 1985. Online results show middle initial, DOB.

Clackamas County

Circuit Court 807 Main St, Oregon City, OR 97045; 503-655-8447; criminal phone: 503-655-8643; civil phone: 503-655-8447; probate phone: 503-655-8623; 8AM-5PM (PST). *Felony, Misdemeanor, Civil, Eviction, Small Claims, Probate, Divorce.* http://courts.oregon.gov/Clackamas/

General Information: Records Management: 503-655-8447 No adoption, juvenile, sealed by judge, expunged, mental health records released. Will not fax out nor accept faxes. Court makes copy: $.25 per page. Certification fee: $5.00 per document plus copy fee; exemplification fee $10.00 per document plus copy fee. Payee: State of Oregon. Personal checks accepted. Credit cards

only accepted in person and over phone. Prepayment required. Mail requests: SASE required.

Civil Name Search: Access: Mail, in person, online. Both court and visitors may perform in person name searches. Search fee: $15.00 per hour after first 10 minutes. Required to search: name, years to search, DOB, type of document. Civil records on computer from 1986, microfilm indexing available 1985 and older, all case types. Mail turnaround time 4-6 weeks. Civil PAT goes back to 1986. Identifiers shown on terminal is inconsistent. Index online at the state's OJIN system, call 800-858-9658 for information.

Criminal Name Search: Access: Mail, in person, online. Both court and visitors may perform in person name searches. Search fee: $15.00 per hour after first 10 minutes. Required to search: name, years to search, DOB. Criminal records computerized from 1986, microfilm indexing available 1985 and older. Mail turnaround time 4-6 weeks. Criminal PAT available. Index remotely online on the statewide OJIN system, call 800-858-9658 for information.

Clatsop County

Circuit Court Box 835, Astoria, OR 97103; 503-325-8555; fax: 503-325-8677; 8AM-5PM (PST). *Felony, Misdemeanor, Civil, Eviction, Small Claims, Probate, Divorce, Traffic.* http://courts.oregon.gov/Clatsop/

General Information: Probate fax- 503-325-9300 No adoption, juvenile, sealed by judge, expunged, or mental health records released. Fee to fax out file $5.00 1st page; $1.00 each add'l. Court makes copy: $.25 per page. Certification fee: $5.00 per certification plus copy fee. Payee: Clatsop County Circuit Court. Personal checks accepted. Credit cards accepted. Prepayment required. Mail requests: SASE required.

Civil Name Search: Access: Phone, mail, online, in person. Both court and visitors may perform in person name searches. No search fee. Civil records on computer from 1987, archives back to 1935. Mail turnaround time 2 weeks. Civil PAT goes back to 1987. Terminal results may show year of birth. Index online at the state's OJIN system, call 800-858-9658 for information.

Criminal Name Search: Access: Phone, mail, online, in person. Both court and visitors may perform in person name searches. No search fee. Required to search: name, years to search, DOB. Criminal records computerized from 1987, archives back to 1935. Mail turnaround time 2 weeks. Criminal PAT goes back to same as civil. Terminal results may show year of birth. Online access to criminal records is same as civil.

Columbia County

Circuit Court Columbia County Courthouse, 230 Strand St, St. Helens, OR 97051; 503-397-2327; fax: 503-397-3226; 8:30AM-4:45PM (PST). *Felony, Misdemeanor, Civil, Eviction, Small Claims, Probate, Divorce.* http://courts.oregon.gov/Columbia/

General Information: No adoption, juvenile, sealed by Judge, expunged, mental health records released. Will fax documents $2.00 1st page, $1.00 each add'l. Court makes copy: $.25 per page. Certification fee: $5.00 plus copy fee; exemplified copy fee $10.00 plus copy fee. Payee: State of Oregon. Personal checks, Visa/MC accepted. Prepayment required. Mail requests: SASE required.

Civil Name Search: Access: Mail, fax, online, in person. Both court and visitors may perform in person name searches. Search fee: Depends upon size and complexity of search. Required to search: name, years to search; also helpful: SSN, DOB, address. Civil records on computer from 9/1987, archives back to 1900. Mail turnaround time 5-7 days. Civil PAT goes back to 1987. Index online at the state's OJIN system, call 800-858-9658 for information.

Criminal Name Search: Access: Mail, fax, online, in person. Both court and visitors may perform in person name searches. Search fee: Depends upon size and complexity of search. Required to search: name, years to search, DOB; also helpful: address, SSN, signed release. Criminal records computerized from 9/1987, archives back to 1900. Mail turnaround time 5-7 days. Criminal PAT goes back to 1987. Index online at the state's OJIN system, call 800-858-9658 for information.

Coos County

Circuit Court Courthouse, Coquille, OR 97423; 541-396-3121; criminal phone: X402; civil phone: X401; probate phone: 541-756-2020x556; fax: 541-396-3456; 8AM-N,1-5PM (PST). *Felony, Misdemeanor, Civil, Eviction, Small Claims, Probate, Divorce.* http://courts.oregon.gov/Coos/

General Information: Eviction, Small Claims and Probate records are available at 541-756-2020 ext 556. Probate fax- 541-756-1727. Circuit Court Annex at 1975 McPherson, North Bend, OR 97459. Online identifiers in results same as on public terminal. No adoption, juvenile, sealed by Judge, expunged, paternity or mental health records released. Will fax documents for a fee. Copy fee is $.25 per page.Certification fee: $5.00; exemplified copy- $10.00. Payee: State Courts. Personal checks and credit cards accepted. Prepayment required. Mail requests: SASE required.

Civil Name Search: Access: Phone, mail, online, in person. Both court and visitors may perform in person name searches. No search fee. Required to search: name, years to search; also helpful: address. Civil records on computer from 1987, archives back to 1800. Mail turnaround time 1-2 days. Civil PAT goes back to 1987. Index online at the state's OJIN system, call 800-858-9658 for information.

Criminal Name Search: Access: Phone, mail, online, in person. Both court and visitors may perform in person name searches. No search fee. Required to search: name, years to search, DOB; also helpful: address, SSN. Criminal records computerized from 1987, archives back to 1800. Mail turnaround time 1-2 days. Criminal PAT goes back to 1987. Index online at the state's OJIN system, call 800-858-9658 for information.

Crook County

Circuit Court Crook County Courthouse, 300 NE 3rd St, Prineville, OR 97754; 541-447-6541; fax: 541-447-5116; 8AM-Noon; 1PM-5PM (PST). *Felony, Misdemeanor, Civil, Eviction, Small Claims, Probate, Divorce.* http://courts.oregon.gov/Crook/

General Information: Online identifiers in results same as on public terminal. No adoption, juvenile, sealed by Judge, expunged, paternity or mental health records released. Will fax documents $2.00 1st page, $1.00 ea add'l. This also applies to incoming faxes. Court makes copy: $.25 per page. Certification fee: $5.00 per doc plus copy fee; $10.00 plus copy fee for exemplification. Payee: State of Oregon. Personal checks accepted. Credit cards accepted. Prepayment required. Mail requests: SASE required.

Civil Name Search: Access: Mail, in person, online. Both court and visitors may perform in person name searches. No search fee. Required to search: name, years to search; also helpful: address. Civil records on computer from 1986, microfiche from 1907, archives from 1907. Mail turnaround time 2-30 days. Public use terminal available, records go back to 1987. Index online at the state's OJIN system, call 800-858-9658 for information.

Criminal Name Search: Access: Mail, in person, online. Both court and visitors may perform in person name searches. No search fee. Required to search: name, years to search, DOB; also helpful: address, SSN. Criminal records computerized from 1986, microfiche from 1907, archives from 1907. Mail turnaround time 2-30 days. Public use terminal available, crim records go back to 1987. Index online at the state's OJIN system, call 800-858-9658 for information.

Curry County

Circuit Court PO Box 810, 29821 Ellensburg Ave., Gold Beach, OR 97444; 541-247-4511; 8AM-N, 1-5PM M,T,W,F; 8AM-N, 1:30-5PM TH (PST). *Felony, Misdemeanor, Civil, Eviction, Small Claims, Probate, Divorce.* http://courts.oregon.gov/Coos/

General Information: No adoption, sealed by Judge, expunged, paternity or mental health records released. Will not fax documents. Court makes copy: $.25 per page. Certification fee: $5.00 per doc plus copy fee for add'l pages. Payee: State Courts. Personal checks accepted. Credit cards accepted. Prepayment required. Mail requests: SASE required; add postage if SASE not enclosed.

Civil Name Search: Access: Phone, mail, online, in person. Both court and visitors may perform in person name searches. No search fee. Required to search: name, years to search; also helpful: address. Civil records on computer from 1987, archives back to 1891. Mail turnaround time 1-2 days. Civil PAT goes back to 1987. Index online at the state's OJIN system, call 800-858-9658 for information.

Criminal Name Search: Access: Phone, mail, online, in person. Both court and visitors may perform in person name searches. No search fee. Required to search: name, years to search, DOB; also helpful: address, SSN. Criminal records computerized from 1987, archives back to 1891. Mail turnaround time 1-2 days. Criminal PAT goes back to same as civil. Index online at the state's OJIN system, call 800-858-9658 for information.

Deschutes County

Circuit Court 1100 NW Bond, Bend, OR 97701; 541-388-5300; criminal phone: x5, 2100, 2040; civil phone: x6, 2090; probate phone: x8, 2080; 8AM-5PM (PST). *Felony, Misdemeanor, Civil, Eviction, Small Claims, Probate, Divorce.* http://courts.oregon.gov/Deschutes/

General Information: All public record requests must be made in writing. No adoption, juvenile, sealed by Judge, expunged, mental health records released. Will not fax documents. Court makes copy: $.25 per page. Certification fee: $5.00 per doc. Payee: State of Oregon. Personal checks accepted. Major credit cards accepted in person. Prepayment required. Mail requests: SASE required.

Civil Name Search: Access: Mail, online, in person. Visitors must perform in person searches themselves. No search fee. Civil records on computer from 9/87, books from 1976, archived from 1916 on microfiche. Mail turnaround time 30 days. Civil PAT goes back to 7/1986. Index online at the state's OJIN system, call 800-858-9658 for information. Also, current calendars are free at www.ojd.state.or.us/des/calendar.nsf/.

Criminal Name Search: Access: Mail, online, in person. Visitors must perform in person searches themselves. No search fee. Required to search: name, years to search, DOB. Criminal records computerized from 9/87, books from 1976, archived from 1916 on microfiche. Mail turnaround time 3-5 days. Criminal PAT goes back to 7/1986. Criminal Index available remotely online on the statewide OJIN system, call 800-858-9658. Records from 07/86 forward. Also, current calendars are free at www.ojd.state.or.us/des/calendar.nsf/.

Douglas County

Circuit Court 1036 SE Douglas Ave, Rm 201, Roseburg, OR 97470; 541-957-2471; fax: 541-957-2462; 8AM-5PM (PST). *Felony, Misdemeanor, Civil, Eviction, Small Claims, Probate, Divorce.* http://courts.oregon.gov/Douglas/

General Information: No adoption, juvenile, sealed by Judge, expunged or mental health records released. Court makes copy: $.25 per page in person, otherwise $5.00. Certification fee: $5.00. Payee: Oregon Judicial Department. Personal checks accepted. Credit cards accepted in person and by phone. Prepayment required. Mail requests: SASE required.

Civil Name Search: Access: Phone, mail, online, in person. Both court and visitors may perform in person name searches. No search fee. Civil records on computer back to 10/1987, microfiche from 1974 (district) 1962 (circuit), archived from 1910. Note: Contact court for copy request form. Mail turnaround time at 2-6 weeks. Civil PAT goes back to 10/1987. Index online at the state's OJIN system, call 800-858-9658 for information.

Criminal Name Search: Access: Phone, mail, online, in person. Both court and visitors may perform in person name searches. No search fee. Required to search: name, years to search, DOB. Criminal records computerized from 10/1987, microfiche from 1974 (district) 1962 (circuit), archived from 1910. Note: Will scan documents and send as PDF via email, if paid in advance. Contact court for copy request form. Mail turnaround time 2-6 weeks. Criminal PAT goes back to same as civil. Terminal results include SSN. Index online at the state's OJIN system, call 800-858-9658 for information.

Gilliam County

Circuit Court Box 622, Condon, OR 97823; 541-384-3572; fax: 541-384-2170; 1-5PM (PST). *Felony, Misdemeanor, Civil, Divorce.* http://courts.oregon.gov/Gilliam/

General Information: No adoption, juvenile, sealed by Judge, expunged, mental health records released. Will fax documents for an add'l fee. Court makes copy: $.25 per page.Add'l postage may be required if copy weight exceeds 1 oz. Certification fee: $5.00 1st page, $1.00 each add'l page. Payee: State of Oregon. Personal checks, Visa/MC accepted. Prepayment required. Mail requests: SASE required.

Civil Name Search: Access: Phone, mail, online, in person. Only the court performs in person name searches; visitors may not. No search fee. Civil records on computer from 1989, index cards back to 1800s. Mail turnaround time 1-2 days. Index online at the state's OJIN system, call 800-858-9658 for information.

Criminal Name Search: Access: Phone, mail, online, in person. Only the court performs in person name searches; visitors may not. No search fee. Required to search: name, years to search; also helpful: DOB. Criminal records computerized from 1989, index cards back to 1800s. Mail turnaround time 1-2 days. Online access to criminal records is same as civil.

County Court PO Box 427, 221 S Oregon, Condon, OR 97823; 541-384-2311/3303; fax: 541-384-2166; 7;30AM-5:30PM M-W; till 5PM Th (PST). *Probate, Juvenile.* www.co.gilliam.or.us/departments/county_court/index.html

General Information: Probate index is NOT online on the OJIN system.

Grant County

Circuit Court PO Box 159, 201 S Humbolt St, Canyon City, OR 97820; 541-575-1438; fax: 541-575-2165; 8AM-N, 1-5PM (PST). *Felony, Misdemeanor, Civil, Divorce.* http://courts.oregon.gov/Grant/

General Information: No adoption, juvenile, sealed by Judge, expunged, mental health records released. Will not fax documents. Court makes copy: $.25 per page. Certification fee: $5.00 per document plus copy fee. Payee: Grant County Circuit Court. Personal checks accepted. Major credit cards accepted in person only. Prepayment required. Mail requests: SASE required.

Civil Name Search: Access: Mail, in person, online. Only the court performs in person name searches; visitors may not. No search fee. Civil records on computer from 1987, microfiche from 1950-1965, archives back to 1880 in Salem. Mail turnaround time 3-5 days. Index online at the state's OJIN system, call 800-858-9658 for information.

Criminal Name Search: Access: Mail, online, in person. Only the court performs in person name searches; visitors may not. No search fee. Criminal records computerized from 1987, microfiche from 1950-1965, archives back to 1880. Mail turnaround time 3-5 days. Index online at the state's OJIN system, call 800-858-9658 for information.

County Court 201 S Humbolt St, #290, Canyon City, OR 97820-6186; 541-575-1675; fax: 541-575-2248; 8AM-5PM (PST). *Probate.*

General Information: Probate index is NOT online on the OJIN system.

Harney County

Circuit Court 450 N Buena Vista #16, Burns, OR 97720; 541-573-5207; fax: 541-573-5715; 8AM-N; 1PM-5PM (PST). *Felony, Misdemeanor, Civil, Divorce.* http://courts.oregon.gov/Harney/

General Information: In this county, misdemeanor records are located at the Justice Court. Call 541-573-2346. The court is located in the same building. No adoption, juvenile, sealed by Judge, expunged, paternity or mental health records released. Will fax documents $2.00 1st page, $1.00 each add'l. Court makes copy: $.25 per page. Certification fee: $5.00. Payee: Harney Circuit Court. Personal checks accepted. Credit cards accepted. Prepayment required. Mail requests: SASE required.

Civil Name Search: Access: Phone, fax, mail, online, in person. Both court and visitors may perform in person name searches. No search fee. Civil records on computer from 1988, microfiche from 1970-1979, archives back to 1880. Mail turnaround time 5 days. Civil PAT goes back to 1988. Terminal results irregularly include DOB, SSN, address. Index online at the state's OJIN system, call 800-858-9658 for information.

Criminal Name Search: Access: Phone, fax, mail, online, in person. Both court and visitors may perform in person name searches. No search fee. Criminal records computerized from 1988, microfiche from 1970-1979, archives back to 1880. Mail turnaround time 1-2 days. Criminal PAT goes back to same as civil. Terminal results do not include DOB, SSN, address. Index online at the state's OJIN system, call 800-858-9658 for information.

County Court 450 N Buena Vista Ave, Burns, OR 97720-1518; 541-573-6641; fax: 541-573-8370; 8:30AM-N, 1-5PM (PST). *Probate.* www.co.harney.or.us/countycourt.html

General Information: Probate index is NOT online on the OJIN system.

Hood River County

Circuit Court 309 State St, Hood River, OR 97031; 541-386-3535; fax: 541-386-3465; 8AM-N, 1-5PM (PST). *Felony, Misdemeanor, Civil, Eviction, Small Claims, Probate, Divorce.* http://courts.oregon.gov/Hood_River/

General Information: No adoption, juvenile, sealed by Judge, expunged, paternity or mental health records released. Will fax documents for $2.00 first page, $1.00 ea addl. Fees are for incoming or outgoing. Court makes copy: $.25 per page. Certification fee: $5.00 per doc plus copy fee. Payee: Hood River Circuit Court. Personal checks accepted. Major credit cards accepted. Prepayment required. Mail requests: SASE required.

Civil Name Search: Access: Phone, fax, mail, online, in person. Both court and visitors may perform in person name searches. No search fee. Civil records on computer from 1989, docket books from 1950. Mail turnaround time 14 days. Civil PAT goes back to 1988. Index online at the state's OJIN system, call 800-858-9658 for information.

Criminal Name Search: Access: Phone, fax, mail, online, in person. Both court and visitors may perform in person name searches. No search fee. Required to search: name, years to search, DOB. Criminal records computerized from 1989, docket books from 1950. Mail turnaround time 14 days. Criminal PAT goes back to same as civil. Index online at the state's OJIN system, call 800-858-9658 for information.

Jackson County

Circuit Court 100 S Oakdale, Medford, OR 97501; 541-776-7171; criminal phone: x583; civil phone: x582; probate phone: x584; fax: 541-776-7057; 8AM-5PM (PST). *Felony, Misdemeanor, Civil Actions, Eviction, Small Claims, Probate, Divorce.* http://courts.oregon.gov/Jackson/

General Information: For record requests pre-1999, dial x132 for James; for newer records, call Records at x0. Probate fax is same as main fax number. Online identifiers in results same as on public terminal. No adoption, juvenile, sealed by Judge, expunged, mental health records released. Will fax documents; $2.00 for 1st page, $1.00 each add'l. Court makes copy: $.25 per page. Certification fee: $5.00 per document, $10.00 if for exemplification. Payee: Jackson County Courts. Personal checks accepted. Major credit cards accepted. Prepayment required. Mail requests: SASE required.

Civil Name Search: Access: Mail, fax, online, in person. Visitors must perform in person searches themselves. No search fee. Civil records on computer from 1988, prior records on docket books and microfilm. Civil PAT goes back to late 1980s. Public access terminal uses the statewide OJIN system. Index online at the state's OJIN system, call 800-858-9658 for information.

Criminal Name Search: Access: Mail, fax, online, in person. Visitors must perform in person searches themselves. No search fee. Required to search: name, years to search, DOB. Criminal records computerized from 1988, prior records on docket books and microfilm. Mail turnaround time up to 3 weeks depending on volume. Criminal PAT goes back to same as civil. Public access terminal uses the statewide OJIN system. Index online at the state's OJIN system, call 800-858-9658 for information.

Jefferson County

Circuit Court 75 SE C St, #C, Madras, OR 97741-1750; 541-475-3317; fax: 541-475-3421; 8AM-Noon; 1PM-5PM (PST). *Felony, Misdemeanor, Civil, Eviction, Small Claims, Probate, Divorce.* http://courts.oregon.gov/Crook/

General Information: Online identifiers in results same as on public terminal. No adoption, juvenile, sealed by Judge, expunged, mental health records released. Will fax documents $2.00 1st page, $1.00 ea add'l. Copy fee is $.25 per page.Certification fee: $5.00 per doc plus copy fee; $10.00 exemplification fee plus copy fee. Payee: State of Oregon. Personal checks accepted. Credit cards accepted. Prepayment required. Mail requests: SASE required.

Civil Name Search: Access: Mail, online, in person. Both court and visitors may perform in person name searches. No search fee. Civil records on computer from 10/1986, archives from 1916-1986. Mail turnaround time 2-3 weeks. Civil PAT goes back to 10/1986. Index online at the state's OJIN system, call 800-858-9658 for information.

Criminal Name Search: Access: Mail, fax, online, in person. Both court and visitors may perform in person name searches. No search fee. Required to search: name, years to search, DOB. Criminal records computerized from 10/1986, archives from 1916-1986. Mail turnaround time 2-3 weeks. Criminal PAT goes back to same as civil. Index online at the state's OJIN system, call 800-858-9658 for information.

Josephine County

Circuit Court Josephine County Courthouse, 500 NW 6th St, Dept 17, Grants Pass, OR 97526; 541-476-2309; fax: 541-471-2079; 8AM-5PM (PST). *Felony, Misdemeanor, Civil, Eviction, Small Claims, Probate, Divorce.* http://courts.oregon.gov/Josephine/

General Information: No adoption, juvenile, sealed by Judge, expunged, mental health records released. No fee to fax out. Court makes copy: $.25 per page. Certification fee: $5.00 per doc plus copy fee. Payee: Josephine County Court. Personal checks accepted. Credit cards accepted. Prepayment required. Mail requests: SASE required.

Civil Name Search: Access: Fax, mail, online, in person. Visitors must perform in person searches themselves. No search fee. Civil records on computer from 1987, microfilm prior to 1980, archives from 1920, index books. Mail turnaround time 8-10 days. Civil PAT goes back to 1987. Public terminal located on 2nd Fl Law Library. Index online at the state's OJIN system, call 800-858-9658 for information.

Criminal Name Search: Access: Fax, mail, online, in person. Visitors must perform in person searches themselves. No search fee. Required to search: name, years to search, DOB. Criminal records computerized from 1987, microfilm prior to 1980, archives from 1920, index books. Mail turnaround time 5 days. Criminal PAT goes back to same as civil. Public terminal located on 2nd Fl Law Library. Index online at the state's OJIN system, call 800-858-9658 for information. Online results show name, DOB.

Klamath County

Circuit Court 316 Main St, Klamath Falls, OR 97601; 541-883-5503; criminal phone: x232; civil phone: x222; probate phone: x222; fax: 541-882-6109; 8AM-5PM M-TH, 8:30AM-5:30PM Fri (PST). *Felony, Misdemeanor, Civil, Eviction, Small Claims, Probate, Divorce.* http://courts.oregon.gov/Klamath/

General Information: No adoption, juvenile, sealed by Judge, expunged, paternity or mental health records released. Fee to fax out file $2.00 1st page and $1.00 each add'l page. Court makes copy: $.25 per page. Certification fee: $5.00 per doc plus copy fee. Payee: Klamath County Circuit Court. No Personal checks, Visa/MC accepted. Prepayment required. Mail requests: SASE required.

Civil Name Search: Access: Mail, fax, in person, online. Both court and visitors may perform in person name searches. No search fee. Civil records on computer from 1988, microfiche from 1940-1980. Mail turnaround time 2 weeks. Civil PAT goes back to 1989. Index online at the state's OJIN system, call 800-858-9658 for information.

Criminal Name Search: Access: Mail, fax, in person, online. Both court and visitors may perform in person name searches. No search fee. Criminal records computerized from 1988, felony cases on microfiche from 1940-1980. Mail turnaround time 2 weeks. Criminal PAT goes back to same as civil. Index online at the state's OJIN system, call 800-858-9658 for information.

Lake County

Circuit Court 513 Center St, Lakeview, OR 97630; 541-947-6051; probate phone: 541-947-6051; fax: 541-947-3724; 8AM-N, 1-5PM (PST). *Felony, Misdemeanor, Civil, Eviction, Small Claims, Probate, Divorce.* http://courts.oregon.gov/Lake/

General Information: Probate fax is same as main fax number. No adoption, juvenile, sealed by Judge, expunged or mental health records released. Will fax $2.00 1st page, $1.00 each add'l only if local and prepaid. Court makes copy: $.25 per page. Certification fee: $5.00. Payee: Lake County Circuit Court. Personal checks, Visa/MC accepted. Prepayment required. Mail requests: SASE required.

Civil Name Search: Access: Mail, in person, online. Both court and visitors may perform in person name searches. Search fee: None; if pre-1988- $7.50 per name. Civil records on computer from 1988, index cards prior. Mail turnaround time 2 weeks. Civil PAT goes back to 1988. Index online at the state's OJIN system, call 800-858-9658 for information.

Criminal Name Search: Access: Mail, online, in person. Both court and visitors may perform in person name searches. Search fee: None; if pre-1988- $7.50 per name. Criminal records computerized from 1988, index cards prior. Mail turnaround time 2 weeks. Criminal PAT goes back to same as civil. Index online at the state's OJIN system, call 800-858-9658 for information.

Lane County

Circuit Court 125 E 8th Ave, Eugene, OR 97401; 541-682-4020; 8AM-5PM (PST). *Felony, Misdemeanor, Civil, Eviction, Small Claims, Probate, Divorce.* http://courts.oregon.gov/Lane/

General Information: No adoption, juvenile, sealed by Judge, expunged, mental health records released. Will not fax documents. Court makes copy: $.25 per page. Certification fee: $5.00 per doc plus copy fee. Payee: Lane County Courts. Personal checks accepted. Visa/MC accepted via phone only. Prepayment required.

Civil Name Search: Access: Online, in person. Visitors must perform in person searches themselves. Civil records on computer from 1983, index books prior. Civil PAT goes back to 1983. Index online at the state's OJIN system, call 800-858-9658 for information.

Criminal Name Search: Access: Online, in person. Visitors must perform in person searches themselves. Criminal records computerized from 1983, index books prior. Criminal PAT goes back to 1982. Index online at the state's OJIN system, call 800-858-9658 for information. Online results show middle initial.

Lincoln County

Circuit Court PO Box 100, 225 W Olive St, Newport, OR 97365; 541-265-4236; criminal phone: x1; civil phone: x3; fax: 541-265-7561; 8AM-N, 1-5PM (PST). *Felony, Misdemeanor, Civil, Eviction, Small Claims, Probate, Divorce.* http://courts.oregon.gov/Lincoln/

General Information: No adoption, sealed by Judge, expunged, or mental health records released. Will fax documents $2.00 1st page, $1.00 each add'l. Court makes copy: $.25 per page. Certification fee: $5.00 first page only or $10 per doc. Payee: State of Oregon. Personal checks, Visa/MC accepted; with $.50 minimum. Prepayment required. Mail requests: SASE required.

Civil Name Search: Access: Mail, fax, online, in person. Both court and visitors may perform in person name searches. No search fee. Required to search: name. Civil records on computer from 2/88, archives back to 1893, prior to 1988, years to search must be specified. Mail turnaround time 3 days. Civil PAT goes back to 2/1988. Public access terminal found on 3rd Fl. Index online at the state's OJIN system, call 800-858-9658 for information.

Criminal Name Search: Access: Mail, fax, online, in person. Both court and visitors may perform in person name searches. No search fee. Criminal records computerized from 2/88, archives back to 1893, prior to 1988, years to search must be specified. Mail turnaround time 1 week. Criminal PAT goes back to same as civil. Index online at the state's OJIN system, call 800-858-9658 for information.

Linn County

Circuit Court PO Box 1749, 300 Fourth St SW, #107, Albany, OR 97321; criminal phone: 541-967-3841; civil phone: 541-967-3845; probate phone: 541-967-3845; fax: 541-928-8725; 8AM-5PM (PST). *Felony, Misdemeanor, Civil, Eviction, Small Claims, Probate, Divorce.* http://courts.oregon.gov/Linn/

General Information: Public access terminal found in Room 107. Phone for copies/archives- 541-812-8770 No adoption, juvenile, sealed by judge, expunged, paternity or mental health records released. Will fax documents $2.00 1st page, $1.00 ea addl. Court makes copy: $.25 per file plus copy fee. Certification fee: $5.00 per file plus copy fee. Payee: State of Oregon. Personal checks accepted. Visa/MC accepted in person. Prepayment required. Mail requests: SASE required.

Civil Name Search: Access: Mail, in person, online. Both court and visitors may perform in person name searches. No search fee. Civil records on computer from 6/1987, archives back to 1863. Mail turnaround time 5-10 days. Civil PAT goes back to 6/1987. Results show year birth only in DOB. Index online at the state's OJIN system, call 800-858-9658 for information.

Criminal Name Search: Access: Mail, online, in person. Both court and visitors may perform in person name searches. No search fee. Required to search: name, years to search, DOB. Criminal records computerized from 6/1987, archives back to 1863. Mail turnaround time 5-10 days. Criminal PAT goes back to 6/1987. Results show year of birth only in DOB. Index online at the state's OJIN system, call 800-858-9658 for information.

Malheur County

Circuit Court PO Box 670, Vale, OR 97918-0670; 541-473-5171; fax: 541-473-2213; 8AM-N, 1-5PM (MST). *Felony, Misdemeanor, Civil, Eviction, Small Claims.* http://courts.oregon.gov/Malheur/

General Information: Physical Address: Oregon Judicial Department, Malheur County Circuit Court, 251 B St W, Vale, OR 97918. No adoption, juvenile, sealed by Judge, expunged, mental health records released. Fee to fax out file $2.00 1st page, $1.00 ea add'l. Incoming fax fee: $2.00 1st page, $1.00 2nd page. Copy fee is $.25 per page. Certification fee: $5.00. Payee: State Courts. Personal checks, Visa/MC accepted. Prepayment required. Mail requests: SASE requested.

Civil Name Search: Access: Mail, in person, online. Both court and visitors may perform in person name searches. Search fee: No fee. Civil records on computer from 7/1988, archived from 1887. Mail turnaround time 2 weeks minimum. Civil PAT goes back to 1988. Index online at the state's OJIN system, call 800-858-9658 for information.

Criminal Name Search: Access: Mail, online, in person. Both court and visitors may perform in person name searches. No search fee. Required to search: name, years to search, DOB. Criminal records computerized from 7/1988, archived from 1887. Mail turnaround time 2 weeks. Criminal PAT goes back to 1988. Index online at the state's OJIN system, call 800-858-9658 for information. Online results show middle initial, DOB.

County Court 251 B St West #4, Vale, OR 97918; 541-473-5124; probate phone: 541-473-5151 for files; fax: 541-473-5523; 8:30AM-5PM (MST). *Probate.*

General Information: Probate index is NOT online on the OJIN system.

Marion County

Circuit Court PO Box 12869, 100 High St NE, Salem, OR 97309; 503-588-5101; fax: 503-373-4360; 8AM-5PM (PST). *Felony, Misdemeanor, Civil, Eviction, Small Claims, Probate, Divorce.* http://courts.oregon.gov/Marion/

General Information: No adoption, juvenile, sealed by Judge, expunged, paternity or mental health records released. Will fax documents $2.00 1st page; $1.00 each add'l page. Court makes copy: $.25 per page. Certification fee: $5.00. Payee: State of Oregon. Personal checks, Visa/MC accepted. Prepayment required. Mail requests: SASE required.

Civil Name Search: Access: Mail, in person, online. Both court and visitors may perform in person name searches. No search fee. Civil records on computer from 10/1986, prior on microfiche/microfilm. Mail turnaround time minimum 5 days. Civil PAT goes back to 1986. Index online at the state's OJIN system, call 800-858-9658 for information.

Criminal Name Search: Access: Mail, online, in person. Both court and visitors may perform in person name searches. No search fee. Required to search: name, years to search; also helpful: DOB. Criminal records computerized from 10/1986, prior on microfiche/microfilm. Mail turnaround time minimum 5 days. Criminal PAT goes back to same as civil. Index online at the state's OJIN system, call 800-858-9658 for information.

Morrow County

Circuit Court PO Box 609, 100 Court St, Heppner, OR 97836; 541-676-5264; fax: 541-676-9902; 8AM-N, 1-4:30PM (PST). *Felony, Misdemeanor, Civil, Eviction, Small Claims, Probate, Divorce.* www.morrowcountyoregon.com/

General Information: Search includes both indexes. There is a County Court in Morrow that handles only juvenile cases. No adoption, juvenile, sealed by Judge, expunged, paternity or mental health records released. Will fax documents $2.00 1st page, $1.00 each add'l. Court makes copy: $.25 per page. Certification fee: $5.00 per doc plus copy fee. Payee: Circuit Court. Personal checks, Visa/MC accepted. Prepayment required. Mail requests: SASE required.

Civil Name Search: Access: Phone, fax, mail, in person, online. Both court and visitors may perform in person name searches. Search fee: $2.25 per 15 minutes, per name. Civil records on computer from 1987, archives back to 1940, index cards, docket books by case #. Mail turnaround time 1-3 days. Index online at the state's OJIN system, call 800-858-9658 for information.

Criminal Name Search: Access: Phone, fax, mail, online, in person. Both court and visitors may perform in person name searches. Search fee: $2.25 per 15 minutes, per name. Required to search: name, years to search, DOB. Criminal records computerized from 1987, archives back to 1940, index cards, docket books by case #. Mail turnaround time 1-3 days. Index online at the state's OJIN system, call 800-858-9658 for information.

County Court PO Box 327, 701 Adams, Rm 204, Heppner, OR 97830; 541-763-2400; fax: 541-763-2026; 8:30AM-4PM (PST). *Probate, Juvenile.*

General Information: Probate index is NOT online on the OJIN system.

Multnomah County

Circuit Court 1021 SW 4th Ave, Rm 131, Portland, OR 97204; 503-988-3003; 8AM-5PM (PST). *Felony, Misdemeanor, Civil, Probate, Divorce.* www.courts.oregon.gov/Multnomah/

General Information: No adoption, juvenile, sealed by Judge, expunged or mental health records released. Will fax documents for $2.00 first page, $1.00 ea add'l. Court makes copy: $.25 per page. Certification fee: $5.00. Payee: State of Oregon. Personal checks accepted. Major credit cards accepted. Prepayment required. Mail requests: SASE required.

Civil Name Search: Access: Mail, in person, online. Both court and visitors may perform in person name searches. No search fee. Civil records on computer from 1988, microfiche, index books, docket books back to 1857. Mail turnaround time 4-5 days. Civil PAT goes back to 1988. Index online at the state's OJIN system, call 800-858-9658 for information.

Criminal Name Search: Access: Mail, online, in person. Both court and visitors may perform in person name searches. No search fee. Required to search: name, years to search; also helpful: DOB. Criminal records computerized from 1988, microfiche, index books, docket books back to 1857. Mail turnaround time 4-5 days. Criminal PAT goes back to same as civil. Index online at the state's OJIN system, call 800-858-9658 for information.

Circuit Court - Civil Division 1021 SW 4th Ave, Rm 210, Portland, OR 97204; 503-988-3022; criminal phone: 503-988-3235; civil phone: 503-988-3022 x3; probate phone: 503-988-3022 x4; fax: 503-988-3425; 8AM-5PM (PST). *Civil Actions, Eviction, Small Claims.* http://courts.oregon.gov/Multnomah/

General Information: Records room is #131. No adoption, juvenile, sealed by Judge, expunged, paternity or mental health records released. Will not fax documents. Court makes copy: $.25 per page. Certification fee: $5.00 per document; exemplified-$10.00 plus copy fee. Payee: State of Oregon. Personal checks, Visa/MC accepted. Prepayment required. Mail requests: SASE required.

Civil Name Search: Access: Mail, in person, online. Both court and visitors may perform in person name searches. No search fee. Civil records on computer from 1988, microfiche 1984-1988, docket cards by case and year. Note: Some search limitations may apply. Mail turnaround time 5 days. Public use terminal has civil records back to 1988. Index online at the state's OJIN system, call 800-858-9658 for information.

Polk County

Circuit Court Polk County Courthouse, Rm 301, 850 Main St, Dallas, OR 97338; 503-623-3154; criminal phone: 503-831-1778; criminal fax: 503-623-6614; civil fax: 8AM-5PM; 8AM-5PM (PST). *Felony, Misdemeanor, Civil, Eviction, Small Claims, Probate, Divorce, Family.* http://courts.oregon.gov/Polk/

General Information: 2nd fax- 503-623-6614, Probate is a separate index at this same address. No adoption, juvenile, sealed by Judge, expunged, mental health records released. Will fax documents for $2.00 first page, $1.00 ea add'l. Copy fee is $.25 per page. Certification fee: $5.00. Payee: State of Oregon. Personal checks accepted. Credit cards accepted for in person and phone requests only. Prepayment required. Mail requests: SASE required.

Civil Name Search: Access: Phone, fax, mail, online, in person. Both court and visitors may perform in person name searches. No search fee. Civil records on computer from 1985, microfilm, archives from 1969 (District) back to 1800s (Circuit). Mail turnaround time 2 weeks. Civil

PAT goes back to 1985. Index online at the state's OJIN system, call 800-858-9658 for information.

Criminal Name Search: Access: Phone, fax, mail, online, in person. Both court and visitors may perform in person name searches. No search fee. Required to search: name, years to search, DOB; also helpful: SSN. Criminal records computerized from 1985, microfilm, archives from 1969 (District) back to 1800s (Circuit). Mail turnaround time 2 weeks. Criminal PAT goes back to same as civil. Index online at the state's OJIN system, call 800-858-9658 for information. Online results show middle initial, DOB.

Sherman County

Circuit Court PO Box 402, Moro, OR 97039; 541-565-3650; fax: 541-565-3249; 1-5PM (PST). *Felony, Misdemeanor, Civil, Divorce.*

General Information: No adoption, juvenile, sealed by Judge, expunged, paternity or mental health records released. Will fax documents $2.00 1st page, $1.00 each add'l. Copy fee is $.25 per page. Certification fee: $5.00 per document plus copy fee. Payee: Sherman County Circuit Court. Personal checks accepted. Credit cards accepted. Prepayment required. Mail requests: SASE required.

Civil Name Search: Access: Phone, mail, online, in person. Both court and visitors may perform in person name searches. No search fee. Civil records on computer from 1992, microfiche up to 1987, index books, judgment docket books. Mail turnaround time 2-5 days. Index online at the state's OJIN system, call 800-858-9658 for information.

Criminal Name Search: Access: Phone, mail, online, in person. Both court and visitors may perform in person name searches. No search fee. Required to search: name, years to search, DOB. Criminal records computerized from 1992, microfiche up to 1987, index books, judgment docket books. Mail turnaround time 2-5 days. Index online at the state's OJIN system, call 800-858-9658 for information.

County Court PO Box 365, 500 Court St, Moro, OR 97039; 541-565-3606; fax: 541-565-3771; 8AM-5PM (PST). *Probate, Juvenile.* www.sherman-county.com

General Information: Probate index is NOT online on the statewide OJIN system. County Court phone number is 541-565-3416. probate may also be filed in the Circuit Court.

Tillamook County

Circuit Court 201 Laurel Ave, Tillamook, OR 97141; 503-842-2596; fax: 503-842-2597; 8AM-N; 1PM-5PM (PST). *Felony, Misdemeanor, Civil, Eviction, Small Claims, Probate, Divorce.* http://courts.oregon.gov/Tillamook/

General Information: Probate fax is same as main fax number. No adoption, juvenile, sealed by Judge, expunged, paternity or mental health records released. Will fax documents $2.00 1st page; $1.00 each add'l. Court makes copy: $.25 per page. Certification fee: $5.00. Payee: Tillamook Circuit Court. Personal checks, Visa/MC accepted. Prepayment required. Mail requests: SASE required.

Civil Name Search: Access: Mail, fax, online, in person. Both court and visitors may perform in person name searches. Search fee: None, unless massive searching needed. Civil records on computer from 1987, prior on case files. Mail turnaround time- call for estimate. Civil PAT goes back to 1987. Index online at the state's OJIN system, call 800-858-9658 for information.

Criminal Name Search: Access: Mail, fax, online, in person. Both court and visitors may perform in person name searches. Search fee: None, unless massive searching needed. Criminal records computerized from 1987, prior on case files. Mail turnaround time 2-3 days. Criminal PAT goes back to same as civil. Index online at the state's OJIN system, call 800-858-9658 for information. Online results show name, DOB.

Umatilla County

Circuit Court PO Box 1307, 216 SE 4th St, Pendleton, OR 97801; 541-278-0341; criminal phone: x254; civil phone: x236; fax: 541-276-9030; 8AM-4:30PM (PST). *Felony, Misdemeanor, Civil, Eviction, Small Claims, Probate, Divorce.* http://courts.oregon.gov/Umatilla/index.page?

General Information: No adoption, juvenile, sealed by Judge, expunged, paternity or mental health records released. Will not fax documents. Court makes copy: $.25 per page. Certification fee: $5.00 per document. Payee: Trial Court Administrator. Personal checks, Visa/MC accepted. Prepayment required. Mail requests: SASE required.

Civil Name Search: Access: Mail, in person, online. Both court and visitors may perform in person name searches. Search fee: $12.65 per hour. Civil records on computer from 11/86, microfiche, index card, docket books. Mail turnaround time 1-3 weeks. Civil PAT goes back to 1985. Public access terminal found in Rm 209. Index online at the state's OJIN system, call 800-858-9658 for information.

Criminal Name Search: Access: Mail, online, in person. Both court and visitors may perform in person name searches. Search fee: $12.65 per hour. Criminal records computerized from 11/86, microfiche, index card, docket books. Mail turnaround time 1-3 weeks. Criminal PAT goes back to same as civil. Public access terminal found in Room 209. Index online at the state's OJIN system, call 800-858-9658 for information. Online results show name, DOB.

Union County

Circuit Court 1008 K Ave, La Grande, OR 97850; 541-962-9500; fax: 541-963-0444; 8AM-N, 1-5PM (PST). *Felony, Misdemeanor, Civil, Eviction, Small Claims, Probate, Divorce.* http://courts.oregon.gov/Union/
General Information: Faxed search requests must be pre-approved, fee charged. Search details other than case number and type are considered a 'detailed search' and may incur copy costs. Limited weekly calendars available at the website. Court at 1007 S 4th St. No adoption, juvenile, sealed by Judge, expunged, paternity or mental health records released. Will fax documents $2.00 1st page, $1.00 ea add'l. Court makes copy: $.25 per page. Certification fee: $5.00 per doc plus copy fee; exemplified copies are $10.00 each. Payee: Circuit Court. Personal checks accepted. Credit cards accepted. Prepayment required. Mail requests: SASE required.
Civil Name Search: Access: Mail, in person, online. Both court and visitors may perform in person name searches. No search fee. Civil records on computer from 1986, archives back to 1865, on ledger books/docket books. Note: Email questions to union.county@ojd.state.or.us. Mail turnaround time 1-2 weeks. Civil PAT goes back to 1986. Index online at the state's OJIN system, call 800-858-9658 for information.
Criminal Name Search: Access: Mail, fax, online, in person. Both court and visitors may perform in person name searches. No search fee. Required to search: name, years to search, DOB. Criminal records computerized from 1986, archives back to 1800s on ledger books/docket books. Note: Email questions to union.county@ojd.state.or.us. Mail turnaround time 1-2 weeks. Criminal PAT goes back to 1986. Index online at the state's OJIN system, call 800-858-9658 for information. Online results show middle initial, DOB.

Wallowa County

Circuit Court 101 S River St, Rm 204, Enterprise, OR 97828; 541-426-4991; fax: 541-426-4992; 8AM-N; 1-5PM (PST). *Felony, Misdemeanor, Civil, Eviction, Small Claims, Probate, Divorce.*
http://courts.oregon.gov/Wallowa/
General Information: No adoption, juvenile, sealed, expunged, paternity or mental health records released. Faxed documents in or out are $2.00 1st pg, $1.00 each add'l. Copy fee: $.25 per page. Certification fee: $5.00. Payee: Circuit Court. Personal checks and credit cards accepted. Prepayment required. Copy fees may be billed. Mail requests: SASE required.
Civil Name Search: Access: Phone, mail, online, in person. Both court and visitors may perform in person name searches. No search fee. Civil records on computer from 1987, prior on docket books. Mail turnaround time 1 week. Index online at the state's OJIN system, call 800-858-9658 for information.
Criminal Name Search: Access: Phone, mail, online, in person. Both court and visitors may perform in person name searches. No search fee. Criminal records computerized from 1987, prior on docket books. Mail turnaround time 1 week. Index online at the state's OJIN system, call 800-858-9658 for information.

Wasco County

Circuit Court PO Box 1400, The Dalles, OR 97058-1400; 541-506-2700; 8AM-N,1-5PM (PST). *Felony, Misdemeanor, Civil, Eviction, Small Claims, Probate, Divorce.* http://courts.oregon.gov/Wasco/
General Information: No adoption, juvenile, sealed by Judge, expunged, paternity or mental health records released. Will not fax out documents. Copy fee is $.25 per page.Certification fee: $5.00. Payee: Wasco County Circuit Court. Personal checks accepted. Credit cards accepted. Prepayment required. Mail requests: SASE required.
Civil Name Search: Access: Phone, fax, mail, online, in person. Both court and visitors may perform in person name searches. No search fee. Civil records on computer from 1989, prior records in docket books by case # and year back to 1900s. Mail turnaround time 2-3 days. Civil PAT goes back to 1989. Index online at the state's OJIN system, call 800-858-9658 for information.
Criminal Name Search: Access: Phone, fax, mail, online, in person. Both court and visitors may perform in person name searches. No search fee. Required to search: name, years to search, DOB. Criminal records computerized from 1989, prior records in docket books by case # and year back to 1900s. Note: Record requests must be in writing. Mail turnaround time 2-3 days. Criminal PAT goes back to same as civil. Index online at the state's OJIN system, call 800-858-9658 for information.

Washington County

Circuit Court 150 N 1st, Hillsboro, OR 97124; 503-846-8888 x8266 (civ) x8252 (crim); probate phone: 503-846-2366; fax: 503-846-2935; 8AM-5PM (PST). *Felony, Misdemeanor, Civil, Eviction, Small Claims, Probate, Divorce.* http://courts.oregon.gov/Washington/

General Information: Probate fax- 503-846-8289 Online identifiers in results same as on public terminal. No adoption, juvenile, sealed by Judge, expunged, paternity or mental health records released. Will fax documents $2.00 1st page, $1.00 ea add'l. Court makes copy: $.25 per page. Certification fee: $5.00; $10.00 if for exemplification. Payee: State of Oregon. Personal checks, Visa/MC accepted. Prepayment required.
Civil Name Search: Access: Phone, mail, online, in person. Both court and visitors may perform in person name searches. No search fee. Civil records on computer from 1982, prior on docket books. Mail turnaround time 2-5 days. Civil PAT goes back to 1983. Index online at the state's OJIN system, call 800-858-9658 for information.
Criminal Name Search: Access: Phone, mail, online, in person. Both court and visitors may perform in person name searches. No search fee. Required to search: name, years to search, DOB. Criminal records computerized from 1982, prior on docket books. Mail turnaround time 2-5 days. Criminal PAT goes back to same as civil. Index online at the state's OJIN system, call 800-858-9658 for information. Online results show middle initial, DOB.

Wheeler County

Circuit Court PO Box 308, Fossil, OR 97830; 541-763-2541; fax: 541-763-2543; 8:30AM-11:30AM (PST). *Felony, Misdemeanor, Civil, Divorce.* http://courts.oregon.gov/Wheeler/
General Information: This court will only hear and misdemeanor charges if tried with a felony case, Otherwise, misdemeanors are found at the local Justice Court level. No adoption, juvenile, sealed by Judge, expunged, paternity or mental health records released. Will fax documents to local or toll free line, otherwise extra fee incurred. Court makes copy: $.25 per page. Self serve copy: same.If postage to return results is over $.44, then add'l postage fees will apply. Certification fee: $5.00 per certification plus copy fee. Payee: State of Oregon. Personal checks, Visa/MC accepted. Prepayment required. Mail requests: SASE required.
Civil Name Search: Access: Phone, mail, online, in person. Both court and visitors may perform in person name searches. No search fee. Civil cases indexed by defendant. Civil records on computer from 1989, docket books by case # and yr. Mail turnaround time 1 week. Index online at the state's OJIN system, call 800-858-9658 for information.
Criminal Name Search: Access: Phone, mail, online, in person. Only the court performs in person name searches; visitors may not. No search fee. Required to search: name, years to search, DOB. Criminal records computerized from 1989, docket books by case # and yr. Mail turnaround time 1 week. Index online at the state's OJIN system, call 800-858-9658 for information.

County Court - Clerks Office PO Box 327, 701 Adams, Rm 204, Fossil, OR 97830; 541-763-2400; fax: 541-763-2026; 8:30AM-4PM (PST). *Probate, Juvenile.* www.wheelercounty-oregon.com/clerknrecords.html
General Information: Probate index is NOT online on the OJIN system.

Yamhill County

Circuit Court 535 NE 5th, McMinnville, OR 97128; 503-434-7530; probate phone: 502-434-7493; fax: 503-472-5805; 8AM-N, 1-4PM (PST). *Felony, Misdemeanor, Civil, Eviction, Small Claims, Probate, Divorce.* http://courts.oregon.gov/Yamhill/
General Information: Online identifiers in results same as on public terminal. No adoption, juvenile, sealed by Judge, expunged or mental health records released. Will fax documents $2.00 1st page, $1.00 ea add'l. Court makes copy: $.25 per page. Certification fee: $5.00; Exemplification fee- $10.00 plus copy fee. Payee: Trial Court. Two party, payroll checks not accepted. Visa/MC accepted. Prepayment required. Mail requests: SASE requested.
Civil Name Search: Access: Mail, in person, online. Both court and visitors may perform in person name searches. None, but court may charge fee if search is lengthy. Civil records on computer from 1981, microfiche, archives back to 1900s, docket books by case # and yr. Mail turnaround time 1-7 days. Civil PAT goes back to 1987. Note that civil results do not show a DOB. Index online at the state's OJIN system, call 800-858-9658 for information. Current dockets online only at main website.
Criminal Name Search: Access: Mail, online, in person. Both court and visitors may perform in person name searches. Search fee: None, but court may charge fee if search is lengthy. Required to search: name, years to search, DOB. Criminal records computerized from 1987, microfiche (10 yrs Dist, unlimited Circuit), archives back to 1900s, docket books by case # and yr. Mail turnaround time 1-7 days. Criminal PAT goes back to same as civil. Online access to criminal records is the same as civil. Current dockets online only. Also, search sheriff's inmates and most wanted lists free at www.co.yamhill.or.us/sheriff/index.asp. Online results show middle initial, DOB.

Pennsylvania

Time Zone:	EST
Capital:	Harrisburg, Dauphin County
# of Counties:	67
State Web:	www.pa.gov
Court Web:	www.pacourts.us

Administration

Administrative Office of Pennsylvania Courts, PO Box 229, Mechanicsburg, PA, 17055; 717-795-2097, Fax: 717-795-2013.

The Supreme Court and Appellate Courts

The Supreme Court of Pennsylvania is the highest court in the Commonwealth and is the oldest appellate court in the nation, dating to 1684. The Supreme Court can take up any case in any court in Pennsylvania if it considers an issue of immediate public importance to be at stake. When it does this, the court exercises one of two powers known as the "King's Bench" power or the power of "extraordinary jurisdiction." View opinions and dockets from www.courts.state.pa.us/T/SupremeCourt/.

The Appellate Court level has two courts - the Commonwealth Court and the Superior Court. The Commonwealth Court also acts as a court of original jurisdiction, or a trial court, when lawsuits are filed by or against the Commonwealth. View opinions and docket at www.courts.state.pa.us/T/Commonwealth/default.htm

The Pennsylvania Courts

Court	Type	How Organized	Jurisdiction Highpoints
Common Pleas*	General	17Courts in 9 Districts	Felony, Misdemeanor, Civil, Probate
Philadelphia Municipal	Limited	1 Court	Felony, Misdemeanor, Civil over $10,000, Eviction, Small Claims
Pittsburgh Municipal	Limited	1 Court	Felony Misdemeanor, Civil, Eviction, Small Claims
Magisterial District	Limited	546 Courts (Judges)	Civil under $8,000, Eviction, Misdemeanor, Certain Traffic, Ordinance
Register of Wills	Special	67	Probate

* = profiled in this book

Details on the Court Structure

The **Courts of Common Pleas** are the general trial courts, with jurisdiction over both civil and criminal matters and appellate jurisdiction over matters disposed of by the special courts. Note that the **civil records clerk** of the Court of Common Pleas is called the **Prothonotary**. The Prothonotary is elected by the county and is not a state employee. But Allegheny County (Pittsburgh) civil records are an exception - in 2008, a Dept. of Court Records Civil/Family Division was created and civil records were removed from the Prothonotary Office. The Superior Court is a Court of Appeals. Probate is handled by the Register of Wills.

The **Philadelphia Municipal Court** is a Court of Record and hears felony cases. Philadelphia also has its own Traffic Court. The **Pittsburgh Municipal Court** is not a court of record, but does have criminal, traffic, and non-traffic divisions.

The **Magisterial District Justice Courts**, which are designated as "special courts," also handle civil cases up to $8,000. These courts are in all counties except Philadelphia. Small claims cases are usually handled by the Magisterial District Justice Courts; however, all small claims are recorded with the other civil records through the Prothonotary Section of the Court of Common Pleas, which then holds the records. Thus it is not necessary to check with each Magisterial District Court, but rather to check with the county Prothonotary.

Record Searching Facts You Need to Know

Fees and Record Searching Tips

Fees vary widely among jurisdictions and change often. The copy fee for records in Magisterial Courts is mandated not to exceed $.25.

Many courts will not conduct searches due to a lack of personnel or, if they do search, turnaround time may be excessively lengthy. Many courts offer public access terminals for in-person searches.

Online Access is Fairly Widespread

The web page at http://ujsportal.pacourts.us/ provides *The Public Web Docket Sheets* access to search, view and print the docket sheets for Pennsylvania's Appellate Courts, Criminal Courts of Common Pleas, Magisterial District Courts and the Philadelphia Municipal Court. In addition, a Court Summary Information report is available for Criminal Courts of Common Pleas and Philadelphia Municipal Court cases. **A word of caution** – professional researchers indicate certain discrepancies: the UJS dockets may lack sentencing information, have incomplete gradings, no mention of violation of probations, and alias' are not always listed. Also noted is at times incomplete terms of probation and amended charges were not displayed on the UJS system.

Other search services available from this web page includes access to court calendars and an eServices – a specialized access system only available to users with a secure login. Approval for this service must be granted by a county clerk of court or district court administrator – access it is not available to the general public.

30 PA counties use the Infocon County Access System to provide a commercial direct dial-up access to county public records, most provide court record information. There is a $25.00 base set-up fee plus a minimum $25.00 per month with a $1.10 fee per minute. For information, call Infocon at 814-472-6066 or visit www.infoconcountyaccess.com.

A vendor at www.landex.com/remote provides access to the index and to some file images for Register of Will records from twelve counties. Fees are involved. Participating counties include: Blair, Bradford, Clearfield, Columbia, Luzerne, Monroe, Northumberland, Perry, Sullivan, Susquehanna, Tioga, and York.

Adams County

Court of Common Pleas - Civil 117 Baltimore St, Rm 104, Gettysburg, PA 17325; 717-334-6781 x360; fax: 717-334-0532; 8AM-4:30PM (EST). *Civil, Eviction.*

General Information: No mental health, sealed records released. Will not fax documents. Copy fee: $.25 per page. Certification fee: $5.50 per doc includes copies. Payee: Prothonotary. Personal checks accepted, credit cards are not. Prepayment required.

Civil Name Search: Access: In person only. Visitors must perform in person searches themselves. Civil records on computer from 1988, some microfiche (dates unsure), on index from 1800s. Public use terminal has civil records back to 1988. Not all terminal results include address.

Court of Common Pleas - Criminal 117 Baltimore St, #103, Gettysburg, PA 17325; 717-337-9806; fax: 717-334-9333; 8AM-4:30PM (EST). *Felony, Misdemeanor.* www.adamscounty.us/

General Information: Historical records are located at the PA Historical Museum Commission. Online identifiers in results same as on public terminal. No juvenile records released. Will fax documents for fee. Court makes copy: $.50 per page. Self serve copy: same. Certification fee: $9.50 per cert plus copy fee. Payee: Clerk of Courts. Personal checks accepted; no third party checks. No credit cards accepted. Prepayment required. Mail requests: SASE required.

Criminal Name Search: Access: Mail, in person, online. Both court and visitors may perform in person name searches. Search fee: $9.50 per name. Required to search: name, years to search, DOB. Criminal records on computer since 1986; some not all on microfiche since 1974, some on microfilm to 1800s. Mail turnaround time 5 days. Public use terminal has crim records back to 1986. Search dockets online free at http://ujsportal.pacourts.us/DocketSheets/CP.aspx back to 1986. Online results show name, DOB.

Register of Wills 117 Baltimore St Rm 102, Gettysburg, PA 17325-2398; 717-337-9826; fax: 717-334-1758; 8AM-4:30PM (EST). *Probate.* www.adamscounty.us

Allegheny County

Court of Common Pleas - Civil 414 Grant St, 1st Fl, City County Bldg, Pittsburgh, PA 15219; 412-350-4200;; 8:30AM-4:30PM (EST). *Civil.* www.alleghenycounty.us/civil/index.aspx

General Information: The clerk of civil court records was the Prothonotary. However, all civil court records for the county are combined and administered by the Dept. of Court Records - Civil/Family Division. No juvenile records released. Will not fax documents. Will not accept fax papers, must have original papers. Court makes copy: $1.00 per page. Self serve copy: $.50 per page. Certification fee: $10.00 per doc. Payee: Allegheny County. Business checks accepted. No credit cards accepted. Prepayment required. Businesses may set up a draw down account. Mail requests: SASE required.

Civil Name Search: Access: Mail, in person, online. Both court and visitors may perform in person name searches. Search fee: $25.00 per name. Civil records archived from 1700s; on computer since 1/1/95. Mail turnaround time 10 days. Public use terminal has civil records back to 1/1995. Public terminal also offers Family Court records. Search civil cases after registration at https://dcr.alleghenycounty.us/. Credit card payment or drawn down account; fee is $.15 per search during office hours, $.10 if not. Search civil opinions at www.alleghenycourts.us/search/default.aspx?source=opinions_civil.

Court of Common Pleas - Criminal 436 Grant St, Rm 114, Pittsburgh, PA 15219; 412-350-5322; fax: 412-350-3842; 8:30AM-4:30PM (EST). *Felony, Misdemeanor.* www.alleghenycounty.us/crim/index.aspx

General Information: On January 7, 2008, the Department of Court Records combined the offices of the Prothonotary, Clerk of Courts and Register of Wills. Online identifiers in results same as on public terminal. All records public. Will not fax out documents except to government agencies. Court makes copy: n/a. Self serve copy: $.50 per page. Certification fee: $10.00 per doc includes copies. Payee: Dept of Court Records. No business or personal checks. No credit cards accepted. Prepayment required. Mail requests: SASE required.

Criminal Name Search: Access: Mail, in person, online. Both court and visitors may perform in person name searches. Search fee: $25.00 per name. Required to search: name, years to search, DOB, SSN. Criminal records on files, microfilm back to 1800s; on computer since. Mail turnaround time 2-7 days. Public use terminal has crim records back to 1974. Access to Common Pleas criminal records is free at http://ujsportal.pacourts.us/DocketSheets/CP.aspx back to 1974. Online results show middle initial, DOB, address.

Pittsburgh Municipal Court 660 First Ave, PIttsburgh, PA 15219; 412-350-6710; criminal phone: 412-350-6715;; 8AM-4:15PM (EST). *Misdemeanor, Traffic, Ordinance.*
www.alleghenycounty.us/courtrec/
General Information: There are three Divisions: Criminal, Non-Criminal, and Traffic. The phone number for Traffic is 412-350-6712.

Register of Wills 414 Grant St, City County Bldg, First floor, Dept of Court Records. Wills/Orphans Ct, PIttsburgh, PA 15219; 412-350-4184; fax: 412-350-3028; 8:30AM-4:30PM (EST). *Probate.*
www.alleghenycounty.us/courtrec/
General Information: On January 7, 2008, the Department of Court Records combined the offices of the Prothonotary, Clerk of Courts and Register of Wills.

Armstrong County

Court of Common Pleas - Civil 500 E Market St, Kittanning, PA 16201; 724-548-3251; fax: 724-548-3351; 8AM-4:30PM (EST). *Civil, Eviction.* www.co.armstrong.pa.us/departments/elected-officials/proth-coc
General Information: No juvenile, civil commitment records released. Will not fax documents. Court makes copy: $.50 per page onsite, $10.00 if mailed. Certification fee: $3.00 1st page; $1.00 each add'l. Payee: Prothonotary. No out-of-state checks accepted. No credit cards accepted. Prepayment required.
Civil Name Search: Access: Online, in person. Both court and visitors may perform in person name searches. No search fee. Civil records on files, microfiche since 1930; on computer since 9/94. Public use terminal has civil records back to 9/1994. Online access is by subscription from private company-Infocon at www.infoconcountyaccess.com, 814-472-6066. See note in court summary section for fees. Images are not available; only the index.

Court of Common Pleas - Criminal 500 Market St, Kittanning, PA 16201; 724-548-3252; ; 8AM-4:30PM (EST). *Felony, Misdemeanor.*
www.co.armstrong.pa.us/departments/elected-officials/proth-coc
General Information: No juvenile or mental health records released. Will not fax documents. Court makes copy: $.50 per page, $1.00 if by mail. Self serve copy: $.50 per page. Certification fee: $5.00 first page. Payee: Clerk of Courts. Personal checks accepted if in-state. No credit cards accepted. Prepayment required. Mail requests: SASE required.
Criminal Name Search: Access: Mail, online, in person. Both court and visitors may perform in person name searches. Search fee: $10.00 per name. Required to search: name, years to search; also helpful: DOB, SSN. Criminal records in card file from early 1930; on computer since 1994. Mail turnaround time 3 days. Public use terminal has crim records back to 1994. Search dockets online free at http://ujsportal.pacourts.us/DocketSheets/CP.aspx back to 1994. Also, see note at beginning of section. Online results show name, DOB.

Register of Wills 500 Market St, #102, Armstrong County Courthouse, Kittanning, PA 16201; 724-548-3220; fax: 724-548-3236; 8:30AM-4:30PM (EST). *Probate.*
www.co.armstrong.pa.us/departments/elected-officials/reg-rec
General Information: Online access available by subscription from private company-Infocon at www.infoconcountyaccess.com, 814-472-6066. See note at beginning of section. Images are available.

Beaver County

Court of Common Pleas - Civil Beaver County Courthouse, 810 3rd St, Beaver, PA 15009; 724-770-4570; fax: 724-728-3360; 8:30AM-4:30PM (EST). *Civil, Eviction.*
www.beavercountypa.gov/ElectedOffical/Prothonotary/MeetYourProthonotary.aspx
General Information: No sealed records released. Will not fax documents. Court makes copy: $.50 per page. Certification fee: $5.25 per cert includes copies. Payee: Prothonotary. Personal checks accepted, credit cards are not. Prepayment required.
Civil Name Search: Access: In person, online. Both court and visitors may perform in person name searches. No search fee. Civil records go back to 1800; on computer back to 1995. Public use terminal has civil records back to 1995. Online access to civil records is by subscription from private company-Infocon at www.infoconcountyaccess.com, 814-472-6066. A link is at the court's home page. Also at the court's home page is a link to naturalization records.

Court of Common Pleas - Criminal Beaver County Courthouse, 810 3rd St, Beaver, PA 15009; 724-770-4588; fax: 724-728-8853; 8AM-4:30PM (EST). *Felony, Misdemeanor.*
www.beavercountycourts.org/index.htm
General Information: Online identifiers in results same as on public terminal. Records sealed by court order not released. Fee to fax out file $1.75 per page. Court makes copy: $.50 per page. Certification fee: $12.00. Payee:

Clerk of Courts Office. Personal checks accepted. Credit cards accepted in person. Prepayment required. Mail requests: SASE required.
Criminal Name Search: Access: Fax, mail, in person, online. Both court and visitors may perform in person name searches. Search fee: $24.00 per name. Required to search: name, years to search; also helpful: DOB, SSN. Criminal records computerized from 1973, on microfiche since 1802. Mail turnaround time 1 week. Public use terminal has crim records. Terminal results also gives city/town of residence. Search dockets online free at http://ujsportal.pacourts.us/DocketSheets/CP.aspx back to 1958. Images are Online access available by subscription from private company-Infocon at www.infoconcountyaccess.com, 814-472-6066. Online results show middle initial, DOB.

Register of Wills Beaver County Courthouse, 810 3rd St, Beaver, PA 15009; 724-770-4549/4550; fax: 724-728-9810; 8:30AM-4:30PM (EST). *Probate.*
www.beavercountypa.gov/ElectedOfficals/RegisterOfWills/RegisterHome.aspx
General Information: Online access is by subscription from private company-Infocon at www.infoconcountyaccess.com, 814-472-6066. See note in court summary section for fees. Images are not available; only the index.

Bedford County

Court of Common Pleas - Criminal/Civil Bedford County Courthouse, Bedford, PA 15522; 814-623-4833; fax: 814-623-4831; 8:30AM-4:30PM (EST). *Felony, Misdemeanor, Civil, Eviction.*
General Information: No sex related or juvenile records released. Will fax documents to local or toll free line, if prepaid. Court makes copy: $.50 per page. Self serve copy: $.25 per page. Certification fee: $4.50 includes copies. Payee: Prothonotary of Bedford County. Personal checks accepted, credit cards are not. Prepayment required. Mail requests: SASE required.
Civil Name Search: Access: Mail, in person, online. Both court and visitors may perform in person name searches. Search fee: $22.00 per name. Civil records on file from late 1700s. Mail turnaround time 2 weeks. Civil PAT goes back to 5/1998. Online access is by subscription from private company-Infocon at www.infoconcountyaccess.com, 814-472-6066. See note in court summary section. Images are available.
Criminal Name Search: Access: Mail, online, in person. Both court and visitors may perform in person name searches. Search fee: $22.00 per name. Required to search: name, years to search, DOB. Criminal records on file from late 1905. Mail turnaround time 2 weeks. Criminal PAT goes back to same as civil. Also, search dockets online free at http://ujsportal.pacourts.us/DocketSheets/CP.aspx back to 1981. Also, access is by subscription from private company-Infocon at www.infoconcountyaccess.com, 814-472-6066. See note at beginning of section. Online results show name, DOB.

Register of Wills 200 S Juliana St, Bedford, PA 15522; 814-623-4836; fax: 814-624-0488; 8:30AM-4:30PM (EST). *Probate, Ordinance.*
General Information: Online access available by subscription from private company-Infocon at www.infoconcountyaccess.com, 814-472-6066. See note at beginning of section. Images are available.

Berks County

Court of Common Pleas - Civil Prothonotary, 633 Court St, 2nd Fl, Reading, PA 19601; 610-478-6970; fax: 610-478-6969; 8AM-4PM (EST). *Civil, Eviction.*
www.co.berks.pa.us/prothonotary/site/default.asp
General Information: Passports available up to 3:30PM. No mental, sealed records released. Will fax documents $7.50 1st page, $1.25 each add'l; for emergency only. Court makes copy: $5.00 1st page; $1.25 each add'l. Self serve copy: $.50 per page printed from computer. Certification fee: $7.45 1st page; $1.85 each add'l. Payee: Prothonotary. No personal checks or credit cards accepted. Prepayment required. Mail requests: SASE required for civil.
Civil Name Search: Access: Mail, in person, online. Both court and visitors may perform in person name searches. Search fee: None, but you must provide the case number in mail requests. Civil records partially on microfiche, on manual index files from 1752. Mail access limited to docket information only. Images available for 2000 to present. Mail turnaround time 1-2 days. Public use terminal has civil records back to 1996. The Prothonotary has a remote system to access dockets from 2002 forward. Subscription fee is $300 per year. For information, call 610-478-6970.

Court of Common Pleas - Criminal 4th Fl, 633 Court St, Reading, PA 19601; 610-478-6550; fax: 610-478-6593; 8AM-5PM (EST). *Felony, Misdemeanor.*
www.co.berks.pa.us/courts/site/default.asp
General Information: No juvenile records released. Will not fax documents. Court makes copy: $.25 per page first 10, $1.00 each add'l. Certification fee: $8.00. Payee: Berks County Clerk of Courts. Only cash, cashiers checks and money orders accepted. Credit cards accepted for payments on criminal cases only. Prepayment required. Mail requests: SASE required.

Criminal Name Search: Access: In person, online. Visitors must perform in person searches themselves. Required to search: name, years to search; also helpful: DOB, SSN. Criminal records computerized from 1985 in files from 1992, prior archived. Note: Will not do name lists by mail. Public use terminal has crim records back to 1985. Search dockets online free at http://ujsportal.pacourts.us/DocketSheets/CP.aspx back to 1967. Online results show name, DOB.

Register of Wills 633 Court St, 2nd Fl, Reading, PA 19601; 610-478-6600; fax: 610-478-6251; 8AM-5PM (EST). *Probate.* www.co.berks.pa.us/rwills/site/default.asp

Blair County

Court of Common Pleas - Criminal/Civil 423 Allegheny St, #144, Hollidaysburg, PA 16648; 814-693-3080; criminal phone: 814-693-3080; fax: 814-317-1600; 8AM-4PM (EST). *Felony, Misdemeanor, Civil, Eviction.*

General Information: No adoption records released. Will fax documents for $1.00 per page. Court makes copy: $.50 per page. Self serve copy: same. Certification fee: $7.00 per cert. Payee: Blair County Prothonotary. Personal checks accepted, credit cards are not. Prepayment required. Mail requests: SASE required for criminal.

Civil Name Search: Access: In person, online. Visitors must perform in person searches themselves. Civil records on computer from 1989, on index books from 1846 to 1989. Civil PAT goes back to 1989. Online access is by subscription from private company-Infocon at www.infoconcountyaccess.com, 814-472-6066. See note in court summary section. Images are not available.

Criminal Name Search: Access: Mail, online, in person. Both court and visitors may perform in person name searches. Search fee: $10.00 per name. Required to search: name, years to search, DOB; also helpful: SSN. Criminal records computerized from 1989, on index books from 1846 to 1989. Mail turnaround time is 3-5 days. Criminal PAT goes back to same as civil. Search criminal dockets free at http://ujsportal.pacourts.us/DocketSheets/CP.aspx back to 1989. Also, access is by subscription from private company-Infocon at www.infoconcountyaccess.com, 814-472-6066. See note at beginning of section. Online results show name, DOB.

Register of Wills 423 Allegheny St, #145, Hollidaysburg, PA 16648-2022; 814-693-3095; fax: 814-693-3093; 8AM-4PM (counter closes at 3:45) (EST). *Probate.* www.blaircountyrecorder.com/

General Information: Online access to the index from 5/1/2005 forward is by subscription from private company at www.landex.com. See note in court summary section for fees.

Bradford County

Court of Common Pleas - Criminal/Civil 301 Main St, Towanda, PA 18848; 570-265-1707; fax: 570-265-1788; 8AM-5PM (EST). *Felony, Misdemeanor, Civil, Eviction.* www.bradfordcountypa.org/Courts/

General Information: Search fee includes both civil and criminal indexes Will not fax documents. Court makes copy: $1.00 per page. Self serve copy: $.25 per page. Certification fee: $5.00 Civil. $8.00 for most criminal record files. Payee: Prothonotary. Personal checks accepted, credit cards are not. Prepayment required. Mail requests: SASE required.

Civil Name Search: Access: Mail, in person. Both court and visitors may perform in person name searches. Search fee: $9.00 per name. Civil records on computer from 1986, on microfiche from mid 1800s, archived from mid-1940s. Mail turnaround time 1-2 days. Civil PAT goes back to 1986. DOB and other identifiers may appear on the record, but not in index search results.

Criminal Name Search: Access: Mail, in person, online. Both court and visitors may perform in person name searches. Search fee: $9.00 per name. Required to search: name, years to search, DOB. Criminal records computerized from 1986, on microfiche from mid 1800s, archived from mid-1940s. Mail turnaround time 7 days. Criminal PAT goes back to same as civil. DOB and other identifiers may appear on the record, but not in index search results. Search dockets online free at http://ujsportal.pacourts.us/DocketSheets/CP.aspx back to 1984.

Register of Wills 301 Main St., Towanda, PA 18848; 570-265-1702; fax: 570-265-1721; 8AM-5PM (EST). *Probate.* www.bradfordcountypa.org/Courts/

General Information: Access to 'estates' images back to approximately 1997 is by subscription at www.landex.com/remote/. Fee is $.20 per minute

Bucks County

Court of Common Pleas - Civil 55 E Court St, Courthouse, Doylestown, PA 18901; 215-348-6191; fax: 215-348-6184; 8AM-4:15PM (EST). *Civil, Eviction.* www.buckscounty.org/courts/CourtInfo/CommonPleas.aspx

General Information: No mental, sealed records released. Court makes copy: $.25 per page. Self serve copy: $.25 per page. Certification fee: $5.00 plus $1.60 each add'l page, certifications are for documents filed in their office, with the original document in the files. Payee: Prothonotary. Personal checks accepted, credit cards are not. Prepayment required.

Civil Name Search: Access: Online, in person. Visitors must perform in person searches themselves. Civil records on computer back to 1980, prior on dockets. Public use terminal has civil records back to 1980. Civil docket available at http://ujsportal.pacourts.us/.

Court of Common Pleas - Criminal 55 E Court St, Bucks County Courthouse, Doylestown, PA 18901; 215-348-6389; fax: 215-348-6740; 8AM-4:30PM (EST). *Felony, Misdemeanor.* www.buckscounty.org/courts/

General Information: No sealed, juvenile or mental records released. Will not fax documents. Court makes copy: $.30 per page. Self serve copy: same.The fee is $1.50 per page for a copy from microfilm or microfiche. Certification fee: $9.00. Payee: Clerk of Courts Criminal Division. Personal checks accepted. Credit cards accepted. Prepayment required. Mail requests: SASE required.

Criminal Name Search: Access: Mail, online, in person. Both court and visitors may perform in person name searches. Search fee: $16.50 per name. Required to search: name, years to search, DOB. Criminal records computerized from 1980, some records on microfiche, on card index from 1932 to 1979. Mail turnaround time 5 days or less. Public use terminal has crim records back to 1980. Access criminal court records free at http://ujsportal.pacourts.us/DocketSheets/CP.aspx back to 1984. Online results show name, DOB.

Register of Wills Bucks County Courthouse, 55 E Court St., 3rd Fl, Doylestown, PA 18901; 215-348-6265; fax: 215-348-6156; 8AM-4:30PM (EST). *Probate.* www.buckscounty.org

General Information: Email questions to registerofwills@co.bucks.pa.us. The clerk is also Clerk of the Orphans' Court.

Butler County

Court of Common Pleas - Civil PO Box 1208, 124 W Diamond, Butler County Courthouse, Butler, PA 16001-1208; 724-284-5214; ; 8:30AM-4:30PM (EST). *Civil, Eviction.* www.co.butler.pa.us

General Information: No mental records released. Will not fax documents. Court makes copy: $.25 per page criminal; civil- $.50 per page; $1.00 for film copies. Certification fee: $5.00 per document plus copy fee. Payee: Prothonotary. Personal checks accepted, credit cards are not. Prepayment required.

Civil Name Search: Access: Phone, mail, online, in person. Visitors must perform in person searches themselves. No search fee. Civil records on computer from 4/1/93, prior on docket books back to 1800. Public use terminal has civil records back to 4/1/1993. Online access is by subscription from a private company - Infocon at www.infoconcountyaccess.com, 814-472-6066. See note in court summary section. Images are available.

Court of Common Pleas - Criminal PO Box 1208, 124 W Diamond St, County Courthouse, Butler, PA 16003-1208; 724-284-5233; fax: 724-284-5244; 8:30AM-4:30PM (EST). *Felony, Misdemeanor.* www.co.butler.pa.us/

General Information: Online identifiers in results same as on public terminal. No mental, sealed, juvenile (16 & under) victim records released. Will fax back to gov't agencies only. Court makes copy: $.50 per page; $1.00 for computer printout. Certification fee: $8.50 per page. Payee: Clerk of Courts. Personal checks accepted. Credit cards accepted in person with ID. Prepayment required. Mail requests: SASE required.

Criminal Name Search: Access: Mail, online, in person. Both court and visitors may perform in person name searches. Search fee: $17.50 per name. Required to search: name, DOB; also helpful: years to search. Original records in office for 10 years. Computerized from 1988 to present, prior in Russell Index. Mail turnaround time 1-2 days. Public use terminal has crim records back to 1987. Search dockets online free at http://ujsportal.pacourts.us/DocketSheets/CP.aspx back to 1988 for complete index. Also, online access to the index is by subscription from private company-Infocon at www.infoconcountyaccess.com, 814-472-6066. See note in court summary section for fees. Online results show middle initial, DOB.

Register of Wills PO Box 1208, 124 W Diamond St, Butler County Courthouse, Butler, PA 16003-1208; 724-284-5348; fax: 724-284-5278; 8:30AM-4PM (EST). *Probate.*

General Information: Online access available by subscription from private company-Infocon at www.infoconcountyaccess.com until early to mid 2009. Then search index is free at http://counties.recordfusion.com/index.jsp. Also, see note at beginning of section.

Cambria County

Court of Common Pleas - Civil 200 S Center St, Ebensburg, PA 15931; 814-472-1638; fax: 814-472-5632; 9AM-4PM (EST). *Civil, Eviction.* www.co.cambria.pa.us/Pages/Prothonotary.aspx
General Information: Small claims cases are handled by district judges. No divorce or mental records released. Fee to fax out file $1.00 per page. Court makes copy: $.25 per page. Self serve copy: same. Certification fee: $3.00 includes copies. Payee: Prothonotary. Personal checks accepted, credit cards are not. Prepayment required. Mail requests: SASE required for civil.
Civil Name Search: Access: Phone, mail, fax, in person, online. Both court and visitors may perform in person name searches. No search fee. Civil records on computer from 1/1/94, prior on dockets from 1800s. Mail turnaround time usually 1 day. Public use terminal has civil records back to 1/1994. Access to civil index is available by subscription at Infocon.com; Signup online or get details at 814-472-6066. Images are not available.

Court of Common Pleas - Criminal 200 S Center St, County Courthouse, Ebensburg, PA 15931; 814-472-1540; fax: 814-472-0761; 9AM-4PM (EST). *Felony, Misdemeanor.*
www.co.cambria.pa.us/Pages/ClerkofCourts.aspx
General Information: No sealed or child victim records released. Will fax documents to local or toll free number; all fees prepaid. Court makes copy: $.50 per page. Certification fee: $10.75 per doc includes copies. Payee: Clerk of Court. Third party checks not accepted. No credit cards accepted. Prepayment required.
Criminal Name Search: Access: Mail, fax, in person, online. Only the court performs in person name searches; visitors may not. Search fee: $5.75 per name. Required to search: name, years to search, DOB; also helpful: SSN. Criminal conviction records are computerized, indexed from 1800s. Mail turnaround time 5-7 days. Search dockets online free at http://ujsportal.pacourts.us/DocketSheets/CP.aspx back to 1990. Online results include city, state, and ZIP, and year of birth (not full DOB).

Register of Wills 200 S Center St, Ebensburg, PA 15931; 814-472-1440; fax: 814-472-0762; 9AM-4PM (EST). *Probate, Orphans' Court, Vitial Records.* www.co.cambria.pa.us/Pages/RegisterofWills.aspx
General Information: Online access is by subscription from private company-Infocon at www.infoconcountyaccess.com, 814-472-6066. See note in court summary section for fees. Images are available.

Cameron County

Court of Common Pleas - Civil Cameron County Courthouse, 20th E 5th St, Emporium, PA 15834; 814-486-3349; fax: 814-486-0464; 8:30AM-4PM (EST). *Civil, Eviction, Divorce.* www.co.elk.pa.us/judicial/
General Information: No adoption, military discharge records released. Will fax documents to local or toll-free number. Court makes copy: $.50 per page. Certification fee: $10.00 per doc includes copies. Payee: Prothonotary. No personal checks or credit cards accepted. Prepayment required. Will bill fees with prior permission from clerk. Mail requests: SASE required.
Civil Name Search: Access: Phone, mail, in person. Both court and visitors may perform in person name searches. No search fee. Civil records on computer from 1985, archived from 1860 to present. Mail turnaround time same day. Public use terminal has civil records back to 1985.

Court of Common Pleas - Criminal 20 E 5th St, Emporium, PA 15834; criminal phone: 814-486-9330; fax: 814-486-0464; 8:30AM-4PM (EST). *Felony, Misdemeanor.* www.co.elk.pa.us/judicial/
General Information: Online identifiers in results same as on public terminal. No juvenile, mental health records released. Will not fax documents. Court makes copy: $.50 per page. Self serve copy: $.50 per page. Certification fee: $10.00 includes copies. Cert fee includes copies. Payee: Clerk of Court. No personal checks or credit cards accepted. Prepayment required. Mail requests: SASE required.
Criminal Name Search: Access: Phone, fax, mail, in person, online. Both court and visitors may perform in person name searches. Search fee: $10.00. Required to search: name, years to search; also helpful: address, DOB, SSN. Criminal records archived from 1860. Mail turnaround time same day. Public use terminal has crim records back to 4/2004. Search dockets online free at http://ujsportal.pacourts.us/DocketSheets/CP.aspx back to 1991. Online results show name, DOB.

Register of Wills Cameron County Courthouse, 20 E 5th St, Emporium, PA 15834; 814-486-3355; fax: 814-486-0464; 8:30AM-4PM (EST). *Probate.*

Carbon County

Court of Common Pleas - Civil PO Box 130, Courthouse, Jim Thorpe, PA 18229; 570-325-2481; fax: 570-325-8047; 8:30AM-4:30PM (EST). *Civil, Small Claims, Eviction.*
www.carboncourts.com
General Information: Small Claims and Evictions are found at the local magistrate court and can be reached by 570-325-2751. There are 4 magistrate courts in Carbon County. No abuse, mental health records released. Will fax documents $1.00 per page. Court makes copy: $1.00 per page. Self serve copy: $.25 per page. Certification fee: $10.50 per cert. Payee: Prothonotary of Carbon County. Personal checks accepted, credit cards are not. Prepayment required.
Civil Name Search: Access: In person, online. Visitors must perform in person searches themselves. Required to search: name. Civil records on computer from 1/84, financing statements from 1/87, on microfiche from 1/84, prior archived. Public use terminal has civil records back to 1984. Online access to the clerk of courts docket records is free at www.carboncourts.com/pubacc.htm. Registration required.

Court of Common Pleas - Criminal County Courthouse, PO Box 107, Jim Thorpe, PA 18229; 570-325-3637; fax: 570-325-5705; 8:30AM-4:30PM (EST). *Felony, Misdemeanor.*
www.carboncourts.com
General Information: No juvenile, mental health records released. Will not fax documents. Court makes copy: none. No certification fee. Payee: Clerk of Courts Carbon County. Personal checks accepted, credit cards are not. Prepayment required. Mail requests: SASE required.
Criminal Name Search: Access: Phone, mail, in person, online. Only the court performs in person name searches; visitors may not. No search fee. Required to search: name, years to search, DOB; also helpful: SSN. Criminal records computerized from 1973, on microfiche from 1800. Mail turnaround time 1 day. Online access to clerk of courts docket records is free at www.carboncourts.com/pubacc.htm. Registration required. Also, search dockets online free at http://ujsportal.pacourts.us/DocketSheets/CP.aspx back to 1986. Online results show middle initial, DOB.

Register of Wills PO Box 286, 4 Broadway, Jim Thorpe, PA 18229; 570-325-2261; fax: 570-325-5098; 8:30AM-4:30PM (EST). *Probate.*
General Information: Docket information is available free online at www.carboncourts.com/pubacc.htm. Registration required.

Centre County

Court of Common Pleas - Criminal/Civil 102 S Allegheny St, Centre County Courthouse - Prothonotary, Bellefonte, PA 16823; 814-355-6796; ; 8:30AM-5PM (EST). *Felony, Misdemeanor, Civil, Eviction.*
www.co.centre.pa.us/271.asp
General Information: Evictions are with the local Magistrate Ct. No sex related, juvenile, mental records released. Will not fax documents. Court makes copy: $.50 per page. Self serve copy: same. Certification fee: $4.00 1st page, $2.00 ea add'l. Payee: Clerk of Court. Personal checks accepted, credit cards are not. Prepayment required. Mail requests: SASE required for criminal.
Civil Name Search: Access: In person only. Visitors must perform in person searches themselves. Required to search: name, years to search, DOB. Civil records on computer from 7-1-94, on docket books from 1986, on microfiche and archived from 1800 to 1992. Civil PAT goes back to 7/1994.
Criminal Name Search: Access: Mail, in person, online. Both court and visitors may perform in person name searches. Search fee: $7.00 per name. Required to search: name, years to search, DOB. Criminal records computerized from 7-1-94, on card files and docket books from 1986, on microfiche and archived from 1800 to 1992. Mail turnaround time 3-5 days. Criminal PAT goes back to same as civil. Search dockets online free at http://ujsportal.pacourts.us/DocketSheets/CP.aspx back to 1979. Online results show name, DOB.

Register of Wills Willowbank Office Bldg, 414 Holmes Ave, #2, Bellefonte, PA 16823; 814-355-6724, 355-6760; fax: 814-355-8685; 8:30AM-5PM (EST). *Probate, Orphan's Court.*
www.co.centre.pa.us/224.asp
General Information: Some records may be available online; call for current information. This court also holds estate, marriage, birth and death records.

Chester County

Court of Common Pleas - Civil PO Box 2748, 201 W Market St, West Chester, PA 19382; 610-344-6300; criminal phone: 610-344-6135; ; 8:30AM-4:30PM (EST). *Civil, Eviction.*
http://dsf.chesco.org/courts/site/default.asp
General Information: No sealed records released. Will not fax documents. Court makes copy: $1.00 per page criminal; civil- $1.30 1st page; $.60 each add'l. Certification fee: $6.35. Payee: Prothonotary. Business checks accepted. No credit cards accepted. Prepayment required.
Civil Name Search: Access: Online, in person. Visitors must perform in person searches themselves. Civil records on dockets from 1985 to present, on microfiche from 1981 to 1984, archived from 1700s. Public use terminal has civil records back to 1990. Internet access to county records

including court records requires a sign-up and credit card payment. Application fee: $50. There is a $10.00 per month minimum (no charge for no activity); and $.10 each transaction beyond 100. Sign-up and/or logon at http://epin.chesco.org/. Also, a court case list is free at http://dsf.chesco.org/courts/site/default.asp and click on "Miscellaneous List."

Court of Common Pleas - Criminal PO Box 2746, 201 W Market St, #1400, West Chester, PA 19382; 610-344-6135; fax: 610-344-6605; 8:30AM-4:30PM (EST). *Felony, Misdemeanor.*
http://dsf.chesco.org/courts/site/default.asp
General Information: No juvenile records released. Will not fax documents. Court makes copy: $1.00 per page. Self serve copy: same. Certification fee: $9.00. Payee: Clerk of Courts. Business checks accepted. No credit cards accepted. Prepayment required.
Criminal Name Search: Access: Mail, online, in person. Both court and visitors may perform in person name searches. Search fee: $19.00 per name. Required to search: name, years to search; also helpful: DOB. Criminal records on computer and microfiche from mid-70s, archived from the 1700s. Mail turnaround time 1 day, usually. Public use terminal has crim records back to mid-1970's. Search criminal dockets online free at http://ujsportal.pacourts.us/DocketSheets/CP.aspx back 20 to 25 years Online results show name, DOB.

Register of Wills PO Box 2746, 201 W Market St #2200, West Chester, PA 19380; 610-344-6335; fax: 610-344-6218; 8:30AM-4:30PM (EST). *Probate.* http://dsf.chesco.org/wills/cwp/browse.asp?a=3
General Information: The records go back to 1924 for Register of Wills and Orphans' Court. Marriage Licenses go back to 1930. Records are either in paper or microfilm form. Email record requests to rwills@chesco.org.

Clarion County

Court of Common Pleas - Civil 421 Main St, Ste 25, Clarion County Courthouse,, Clarion, PA 16214; 814-226-1119; fax: 814-227-2501; 8:30AM-4:30PM (EST). *Civil, Eviction.* www.co.clarion.pa.us/
General Information: Online identifiers in results same as on public terminal. No juvenile, mental health records released. Will fax documents $3.00 1st page, $1.00 ea add'l. Court makes copy: $.50 per page. Self serve copy: same. Certification fee: $8.00. Payee: Prothonotary. Personal checks accepted, credit cards are not. Prepayment required. Mail requests: SASE required.
Civil Name Search: Access: Phone, fax, mail, online, in person. Visitors must perform in person searches themselves. Search fee: $10.00 per name. Civil records on computer from 1995, older dockets from 1800s. Note: Will do limited name searches if only back to 1995. Mail turnaround time 2-3 days. Public use terminal has civil records back to 1995. Online access is by subscription from private company-Infocon at www.infoconcountyaccess.com, 814-472-6066. See note in court summary section. Images are not available.

Court of Common Pleas - Criminal 421 Main St, Ste 25, Clarion, PA 16214; 814-226-1119; fax: 814-227-2501; 8:30AM-4:30PM (EST). *Felony, Misdemeanor.*
General Information: Online identifiers in results same as on public terminal. No juvenile, mental health records released. Will fax documents $3.00. Court makes copy: $.50 per page. Certification fee: $8.00 per cert plus copy fee. Payee: Clerk of Court. Personal checks accepted, credit cards are not. Prepayment required. Mail requests: SASE required.
Criminal Name Search: Access: Fax, mail, online, in person. Both court and visitors may perform in person name searches. Search fee: $10.00 per name. Required to search: name, years to search, DOB. Criminal records computerized from 1990, microfiche 1976-1985, on docket books from 1800s. Mail turnaround time same day. Public use terminal has crim records back to 6/1990. Search dockets online free at http://ujsportal.pacourts.us/DocketSheets/CP.aspx back to 1983. Online results show name, DOB.

Register of Wills Clarion County Courthouse, 421 Main St, Ste 24, Clarion, PA 16214; 814-226-4000 X3501; fax: 814-226-1117; 8:30AM-4:30PM (EST). *Probate.* www.co.clarion.pa.us/
General Information: Online access available by subscription from private company-Infocon at www.infoconcountyaccess.com, 814-472-6066. See note at beginning of section. Images are available.

Clearfield County

Court of Common Pleas - Criminal/Civil PO Box 549, 1 N 2nd St, Clearfield, PA 16830; 814-765-2641; criminal phone: x1336; civil phone: x1330; fax: 814-765-7659; 8:30AM-4PM (EST). *Felony, Misdemeanor, Civil, Eviction.* www.clearfieldco.org
General Information: Online identifiers in results same as on public terminal. No juvenile, sealed or mental health records released. Will not fax documents. Court makes copy: $.25 per page; $1.00 minimum. Self serve copy: $.25 per page. Certification fee: $1.50. Payee: Prothonotary. Personal

checks accepted, credit cards are not. Prepayment required. Mail requests: SASE required.
Civil Name Search: Access: Mail, in person. Both court and visitors may perform in person name searches. Search fee: $7.00 per name, 5-years search. Required to search: name, years to search; also helpful: address. Civil records indexed (Russell System) on dockets from 1822; on computer back to 11/00. Mail turnaround time same day. Civil PAT goes back to 11/2000. Terminal results show address when available.
Criminal Name Search: Access: Mail, in person, online. Both court and visitors may perform in person name searches. Search fee: $7.00 per name, 5-year search. Required to search: name, years to search, address, DOB, SSN, signed release. Criminal records indexed (Russell System) on dockets from 1822; on computer back to 1/95. Mail turnaround time 2 days. Criminal PAT goes back to 1990. Search dockets online free at http://ujsportal.pacourts.us/DocketSheets/CP.aspx back to 1990. Online results show middle initial, DOB.

Register of Wills & Clerk of Orphans Court PO Box 361, 1 N 2nd St, Clearfield, PA 16830; 814-765-2641 X1351; fax: 814-765-6089; 8:30AM-4PM (EST). *Probate.*
www.clearfieldco.org/registerofwills.htm
General Information: Estates are on file from 1832 to the present. Estates are indexed on the computer from 1990 to the present. Estates are scanned on the computer from 12-1-98 to the present. Access to data is by subscription at www.landex.com/remote/.

Clinton County

Court of Common Pleas - Criminal/Civil 230 E Water St, Lock Haven, PA 17745; 570-893-4007; fax: 570-893-4288; 8AM-5PM M, T,TH,F; 8AM-12:30PM W (EST). *Felony, Misdemeanor, Civil, Eviction.* www.clintoncountypa.com/departments/court_services/prothonotary/
General Information: No sealed, mental health or minor victim abuse cases records released. Will not fax documents. Court makes copy: $.50 per page. Certification fee: Civil is $5.00 first page, $1.50 ea add'l. Criminal is $5.75 first page. $1.50 ea add'l. Payee: Clerk of Court or Prothonotary. Personal checks accepted, credit cards are not. Prepayment required.
Civil Name Search: Access: Online, in person. Visitors must perform in person searches themselves. Civil records on computer from 1992, on files from 1839. Civil PAT goes back to 1992. Online access is by subscription from private company-Infocon at www.infoconcountyaccess.com, 814-472-6066. See note in court summary section for fees. Images are available.
Criminal Name Search: Access: Online, in person. Visitors must perform in person searches themselves. Required to search: name, years to search, DOB, SSN, signed release. Criminal records computerized from 1992, on files from 1839. Criminal PAT goes back to same as civil. Internet access to court records is by subscription from a private company-Infocon at www.ic-access.com, 814-472-6066. See note at beginning of section. Also, search dockets online free at http://ujsportal.pacourts.us/DocketSheets/CP.aspx back to 1992. Online results show name, DOB.

Register of Wills & Recorder of Deeds PO Box 943, 230 E Water St, Lock Haven, PA 17745; 570-893-4010; fax: 570-893-4273; 8:30AM-5PM M,T,TH,F; 8AM-12:30PM W (EST). *Probate.*
www.clintoncountypa.com
General Information: Online access available by subscription from private company-Infocon at www.infoconcountyaccess.com, 814-472-6066. See note at beginning of section. Images are available.

Columbia County

Court of Common Pleas - Criminal/Civil PO Box 380, Bloomsburg, PA 17815; 570-389-5614; fax: 570-389-5620; 8AM-4:30PM (EST). *Felony, Misdemeanor, Civil, Eviction.*
http://columbiapa.org/courts/
General Information: Opinions for civil and criminal cases on the website. Fax to "Attention Barb." No juvenile, adoption, mental health petition or OAPSA records released. May fax documents for fee. Court makes copy: $.50 per page. Self serve copy: same. Certification fee: $4.00 plus copy fee. Payee: Prothonotary or Clerk of Court. No personal checks or credit cards accepted. Prepayment required. Mail requests: SASE required for criminal.
Civil Name Search: Access: In person only. Visitors must perform in person searches themselves. Civil records on computer to 1992, on microfiche from 1814. Civil PAT goes back to 1992.
Criminal Name Search: Access: Mail, fax, in person, online. Both court and visitors may perform in person name searches. Search fee: $20.00 per name. Required to search: name, years to search; also helpful: DOB. Criminal records on computer to 1992, on microfiche from 1814. Note: Fax requests only accepted from government agencies. Mail turnaround time same or next day. Criminal PAT goes back to same as civil. Search dockets online free at http://ujsportal.pacourts.us/DocketSheets/CP.aspx back to 1991. Online results show name, DOB.

Register of Wills 35 W Main St, Bloomsburg, PA 17815; 570-389-5632; fax: 570-389-5636; 8AM-4:30PM (EST). *Probate.*
www.columbiapa.org/registerrecorder/index.php
General Information: Access to data is by subscription at www.landex.com/remote/.

Crawford County

Court of Common Pleas - Civil Crawford County Courthouse, 903 Diamond Pk, Meadville, PA 16335; 814-333-7324; criminal phone: 814-333-7442; fax: 814-337-5416; 8:30AM-4:30PM (EST). *Civil, Eviction.*
General Information: No mental health, sealed records released. Will fax documents $1.60 per page. Court makes copy: $.80 per page; docket copy $1.75 per page. Self serve copy: $.80 per page. Certification fee: $1.75. Payee: Prothonotary Crawford County. Personal checks accepted with ID. Prepayment required. Mail requests: SASE required.
Civil Name Search: Access: Mail, in person. Both court and visitors may perform in person name searches. Search fee: $8.00 per name. Civil records on dockets from 1800s. Mail turnaround time 3 days. Public use terminal has civil records back to 10/1999.

Court of Common Pleas - Criminal Crawford County Courthouse, 903 Diamond Pk, Meadville, PA 16335; 814-333-7442; fax: 814-333-7489; 8:30AM-4:30PM (EST). *Felony, Misdemeanor.*
www.crawfordcountypa.net
General Information: No juvenile records released. Will not fax documents. Court makes copy: $1.00 per page. Certification fee: $6.00 per cert plus copy fee. Payee: Clerk of Courts. Personal checks accepted, credit cards are not. Prepayment required. Mail requests: SASE required.
Criminal Name Search: Access: Mail, in person, online. Both court and visitors may perform in person name searches. Search fee: $15.00 to search up to 5 names. Required to search: name, years to search, signed release; also helpful: DOB & SSN. Criminal records computerized since 2000, on microfiche from 1984, on dockets from 1914, archived from 1880s. Mail turnaround time 7-14 days. Public use terminal has crim records back to 2000. Clerk will verify identifiers on PAT results. Search dockets online free at http://ujsportal.pacourts.us/DocketSheets/CP.aspx back to 1981. Online results show name, DOB.

Register of Wills 903 Diamond Pk, Crawford County Courthouse, Meadville, PA 16335; 814-373-2537; fax: 814-337-5296; 8:30AM-4:30PM (EST). *Probate.* www.crawfordcountypa.net

Cumberland County

Court of Common Pleas - Civil Cumberland County Courthouse, Rm 100, One Courthouse Sq, Carlisle, PA 17013-3387; 717-240-6195; fax: 717-240-6573; 8AM-4:30PM (EST). *Civil, Eviction.*
www.ccpa.net/index.asp?nid=121
General Information: No mental health records released. Will not fax out case files. Court makes copy: $.50 per page. Self serve copy: same. Certification fee: $5.00 1st page; $1.00 each add'l. Payee: Office of Prothonotary. No personal checks accepted, attorney checks are accepted. No credit cards accepted. Prepayment required.
Civil Name Search: Access: In person, online. Visitors must perform in person searches themselves. Required to search: name, years to search; also helpful: address. Civil records on computer from 1994, on microfiche from 1966-2000, on dockets from 1800s. Note: Selected opinions free at http://records.ccpa.net/weblink_public/Browse.aspx?dbid=8. Public use terminal has civil records back to 1994. Online access available by subscription from private company-Infocon at www.infoconcountyaccess.com, 814-472-6066. See note at beginning of section. Images are available. Also, searchable civil records by docket # at www.ccpa.net/index.aspx?nid=2657.

Court of Common Pleas - Criminal Cumberland County Courthouse, 1 Courthouse Sq, Rm 205, Carlisle, PA 17013-3387; 717-240-6250; fax: 717-240-6571; 8AM-4:30PM (EST). *Felony, Misdemeanor.*
www.ccpa.net/index.asp?nid=1129
General Information: Online identifiers in results same as on public terminal. No juvenile records released (Including any case with a juvenile as the victim). Will fax documents as part of search fee. Court makes copy: $.50 per page. No certification fee. Payee: Clerk of Courts. Personal checks accepted, credit cards are not. Prepayment required. Mail requests: SASE required.
Criminal Name Search: Access: Mail, in person, online. Both court and visitors may perform in person name searches. Search fee: $19.00 per name. Criminal records computerized from 1993, in files from 1976, archived from 1800s. Mail turnaround time same day. Public use terminal has crim records back to 1993. Search results include address but only city, state, ZIP. Search dockets online free at http://ujsportal.pacourts.us/DocketSheets/CP.aspx back to 1994. Also, you may also search at www.ccpa.net/index.asp?NID=2743 and select Criminal Records and Documents. First acquire username and password

from Clerk of Courts Office. Selected opinions free at http://records.ccpa.net/weblink_judges/Browse.aspx?dbid=3. Online results show middle initial, DOB, address.

Register of Wills Cumberland County Courthouse, Rm 102, 1 Courthouse Sq, Carlisle, PA 17013; 717-240-6345; fax: 717-240-7797; 8AM-4:30PM (EST). *Probate.* www.ccpa.net/index.asp?nid=125

Dauphin County

Court of Common Pleas - Civil 101 Market Street, Rm 101, Harrisburg, PA 17101; criminal phone: 717-780-6530; civil phone: 717-780-6520;; 8AM-4:30PM (EST). *Civil, Eviction.*
www.dauphincounty.org/court-departments/
General Information: No mental health released. Will not fax documents. Court makes copy: $.25 per page. Self serve copy: same. Certification fee: $5.75 1st pg; $1.75 each add'l. Payee: Dauphin County Prothonotary. Business checks accepted; no personal checks. No credit cards accepted. Prepayment required. Mail requests: SASE required.
Civil Name Search: Access: Phone, mail, in person, online. Both court and visitors may perform in person name searches. Search fee: $11.50 per name. Fee is per 5 years searched. Civil judgments on microfilm and dockets from 1970s, archived from 1700s; on computer back to 11/2001. Mail turnaround time 1 day. Public use terminal has civil records back to 1983. Access civil cases back to 11/2001, suits (1992-10/31/2001) and judgments back to 1983 free at www.dauphinc.org/onlineservices/public/header.asp.

Court of Common Pleas - Criminal Court Clerk's Office, 101 Market Street, Harrisburg, PA 17101; 717-780-6530; fax: 717-780-6463; 8AM-4:30PM (EST). *Felony, Misdemeanor.*
www.dauphincounty.org/court-departments/
General Information: Online identifiers in results same as on public terminal. No juvenile, mental records released. Will not fax documents. Court makes copy: $.50 per page. Certification fee: $10.00 per cert includes 4 copy pages; add copy fee for each add'l page. Payee: Clerk of Court. Business checks accepted. No personal checks. No credit cards accepted. Prepayment required. Mail requests: SASE not required.
Criminal Name Search: Access: Mail, in person, online. Both court and visitors may perform in person name searches. Search fee: $23.00 per name. Required to search: name, years to search; also helpful: DOB, SSN. Criminal records on dockets and computer from 1950, archived from 1700s. Mail turnaround time 1 week. Public use terminal has crim records back to 2002. Results show offender city, state, zip. Search dockets free at http://ujsportal.pacourts.us/DocketSheets/CP.aspx back to 1971. Online results show name, DOB.

Register of Wills 101 Market Sts, Rm 103, Harrisburg, PA 17101; 717-780-6500; fax: 717-780-6474; 8AM-4:30PM (EST). *Probate.*
www.dauphincounty.org/publicly-elected-officials/register-of-wills/

Delaware County

Court of Common Pleas - Criminal/Civil 201 W Front St, Media, PA 19063; 610-891-4370; criminal fax: 610-891-7257; civil fax: 8:30AM-4:30PM; 8:30AM-4:30PM (EST). *Felony, Misdemeanor, Civil, Eviction, Domestic* .www.co.delaware.pa.us
General Information: No juvenile, mental health records released. Court makes copy: $1.00 per page. Certification fee: $5.95 civil doc, $8.50 criminal doc, plus copy fee. Payee: Office of Judicial Support. Attorney business checks only accepted. No credit cards accepted. Prepayment required. Mail requests: SASE required for criminal.
Civil Name Search: Access: Online, in person. Visitors must perform in person searches themselves. Civil records on computer from early 1990, on card file from 1920s, archived from 1800s. Public use terminal has civil records back to 1990. Online access to court civil records free (may begin charging in near future) at http://w01.co.delaware.pa.us/pa/publicaccess.asp. Search online by document type, document number, etc.
Criminal Name Search: Access: Mail, in person, online. Visitors must perform in person searches themselves. No search fee. Required to search: name, years to search; also helpful: DOB, SSN. Criminal records computerized from late 1970s, prior on files. Mail turnaround time 1-3 days. Search dockets online free at http://ujsportal.pacourts.us/DocketSheets/CP.aspx back to 1974.

Register of Wills Delaware County Courthouse, 201 W Front St, Media, PA 19063; 610-891-4400; fax: 610-891-4812; 8:30AM-4:30PM (EST). *Probate.* www.co.delaware.pa.us/registerofwills/

Elk County

Court of Common Pleas - Criminal/Civil PO Box 237, Ridgway, PA 15853; 814-776-5344; fax: 814-776-5303; 8:30AM-4PM (EST). *Felony, Misdemeanor, Civil, Eviction.*
www.co.elk.pa.us/Municipalities/prothonotary.html

General Information: No mental health or juvenile records released. Will not fax documents. Court makes copy: $.50 per page. Certification fee: $5.25 for civil; $9.25 for criminal. Payee: Elk County Prothonotary. Personal checks accepted, credit cards are not. Prepayment required. Mail requests: SASE requested.

Civil Name Search: Access: Phone, fax, mail, in person. Both court and visitors may perform in person name searches. Search fee: $9.00 per name. Civil records on dockets from 1843, on computer back to 1998. Mail turnaround time 1 day. Civil PAT goes back to 1998.

Criminal Name Search: Access: Phone, fax, mail, in person, online. Both court and visitors may perform in person name searches. Search fee: $10.00 per name. Required to search: name, years to search, DOB. Criminal docket index from 1843, on computer back to 1998. Mail turnaround time 1 day. Criminal PAT goes back to same as civil. Search dockets online free at http://ujsportal.pacourts.us/DocketSheets/CP.aspx back to 1998. Online results show name, DOB.

Register of Wills PO Box 314, 240 Main St, Ridgway, PA 15853; 814-776-5349; fax: 814-776-5382; 8:30AM-4PM (EST). *Probate.* www.co.elk.pa.us/registerrecorder.html

Erie County

Court of Common Pleas - Civil Erie County Courthouse, 140 W 6th St, Erie, PA 16501; 814-451-6080; civil phone: 814-451-6250; probate phone: 814-451-6260; fax: 814-451-7400; 8AM-4:30PM (EST). *Civil, Eviction.* www.eriecountygov.org/

General Information: No sealed records released. Will fax documents to local or toll free line. Court makes copy: $.25 per page. Self serve copy: same. Certification fee: $5.00. Payee: Prothonotary. Personal checks accepted, credit cards are not. Prepayment required. Mail requests: SASE required.

Civil Name Search: Access: Mail, in person, online. Both court and visitors may perform in person name searches. Search fee: $10.00. Civil records on computer from 1992, on dockets from 1971, on microfilm/microfiche from 1800s. Mail turnaround time same day. Public use terminal has civil records back to 1992. Online access is by subscription from private company-Infocon at www.infoconcountyaccess.com, 814-472-6066. See note in court summary section. Images are available.

Court of Common Pleas - Criminal Erie County Courthouse, 140 W 6th St, Rm 103, Erie, PA 16501; 814-451-6221; fax: 814-451-6492; 8AM-4:30PM (EST). *Felony, Misdemeanor.* www.eriecountygov.org/default.aspx?id=courts

General Information: No juvenile records released. Will fax documents to local or toll free line. Court makes copy: $.25 per page. No certification fee. Payee: Clerk of Courts. Personal checks accepted, credit cards are not. Prepayment required. Mail requests: SASE not required.

Criminal Name Search: Access: Mail, online, in person. Both court and visitors may perform in person name searches. Search fee: $10.00 per name. Required to search: name, years to search, DOB. Criminal records go back to 1950; records computerized back to 1992. Mail turnaround time 1 week. Public use terminal has crim records back to 1992. Search dockets online free at http://ujsportal.pacourts.us/DocketSheets/CP.aspx back to 1992. Online results show name, DOB.

Register of Wills Erie County Courthouse, 140 W 6th St, Erie, PA 16501; 814-451-6260; fax: 814-451-7010; 8AM-4:30PM (EST). *Probate, Orphans' Court.* http://eriecountygov.org/default.aspx?id=rw

General Information: Online access available by subscription from private company-Infocon at www.infoconcountyaccess.com, 814-472-6066. See note at beginning of section. Images are available.

Fayette County

Court of Common Pleas - Civil 61 E Main St, Uniontown, PA 15401; 724-430-1272; civil phone: 724-430-1272; fax: 724-430-4555; 8AM-4:30PM (EST). *Civil, Eviction.*

General Information: No mental records released. Will not fax documents. Court makes copy: $.25 per page. Self serve copy: same. Certification fee: $12.00 per document includes copy fee. Payee: Prothonotary. Personal checks accepted, credit cards are not. Prepayment required. Mail requests: SASE required.

Civil Name Search: Access: Mail, in person, online. Both court and visitors may perform in person name searches. Search fee: $5.00 per name. Civil records on computer from 1999, archived from 1700s. Mail turnaround time 2 weeks. Public use terminal has civil records back to 1999. Internet access to court records is by subscription from a private company-Infocon at www.ic-access.com, 814-472-6066. See note at beginning of section. Images are available.

Court of Common Pleas - Criminal 61 E Main St, 3rd Fl, Uniontown, PA 15401; 724-430-1230; fax: 724-430-1001; 8AM-4:30PM (EST). *Felony, Misdemeanor.* www.co.fayette.pa.us/CourtAdmin/Pages/default.aspx

General Information: No sex related or juvenile records released. Will fax documents $1.50 each. Court makes copy: $.25 per page. Certification fee: $10.00. Payee: Clerk of Courts. No personal checks or credit cards accepted. Prepayment required. Mail requests: SASE not required.

Criminal Name Search: Access: Mail, fax, in person, online. Both court and visitors may perform in person name searches. Search fee: $10.00 for 5-year search; $10.00 for 5-yr. plus. Required to search: name, years to search, DOB; also helpful: SSN. Criminal records computerized from 1993, on files from 1800s. Mail turnaround time 3-5 days. Search dockets online free at http://ujsportal.pacourts.us/DocketSheets/CP.aspx back to 1975. Online results show name, DOB.

Register of Wills 61 E Main St, #1D, Uniontown, PA 15401; 724-430-1206; fax: 724-430-1275; 8AM-N, 1-4:30PM (EST). *Probate.*

General Information: Online access available by subscription from private company-Infocon at www.infoconcountyaccess.com, 814-472-6066. Images are not available. Index back to 12/31/08. Also see www.landex.com/ for records 1999 forward.

Forest County

Court of Common Pleas 526 Elm St, #2, County Courthouse, Tionesta, PA 16353; 814-755-3526; fax: 814-755-8837; 9AM-4PM (EST). *Felony, Misdemeanor, Civil, Eviction, Probate.* www.warrenforestcourt.org/

General Information: Computerized records includes the Register of Wills. Probate records are separate index at same address. Probate fax is same as main fax number. Online identifiers in results same as on public terminal. No adoption records released. Will fax documents $4.00 per document, under 6 pages. Court makes copy: $2.00 per docket. Self serve copy: $.25 per page. Certification fee: $3.00. Payee: Clerk of Courts. Personal checks accepted. Major credit cards accepted. Prepayment required. Mail requests: SASE required.

Civil Name Search: Access: In person, online. Visitors must perform in person searches themselves. Computerized records from 2002, civil records on dockets since 1995, archived from 1857. Mail turnaround time same day. Civil PAT goes back to 2002. Online access available by subscription from private company-Infocon at www.infoconcountyaccess.com, 814-472-6066. See note at beginning of section. Images are available from 2006.

Criminal Name Search: Access: In person, online. Visitors must perform in person searches themselves. Required to search: name, years to search; also helpful: DOB, SSN. Computerized records from 1995, archived from 1995. Mail turnaround time same day. Criminal PAT goes back to 1995. Terminal results include SSN. Search dockets online free at http://ujsportal.pacourts.us/DocketSheets/CP.aspx back to 1995. Online results show name, DOB.

Franklin County

Court of Common Pleas - Civil 157 Lincoln Way E, Chambersburg, PA 17201; 717-261-3858; fax: 717-264-6772; 8:30AM-4:30PM (EST). *Civil, Eviction.*

General Information: No mental records released. Will fax out specific case files for $1.00 per page. Court makes copy: $.50 per page. Certification fee: $5.00 per document plus copy fee for add'l pages. Payee: Prothonotary. Personal checks accepted, credit cards are not. Prepayment required.

Civil Name Search: Access: In person, online. Visitors must perform in person searches themselves. Civil records on file from 1985; on computer back to 4/1/1999. Public use terminal has civil records back to 11/1998. Public terminal also offers access to liens, division records, custody, protection from abuse and judgment histories from 1981-1990. Access index by subscription from private company-Infocon at www.infoconcountyaccess.com, 814-472-6066. See note at beginning of section. Images are not available.

Court of Common Pleas - Criminal 157 Lincoln Way E, Chambersburg, PA 17201; 717-261-3805; fax: 717-261-3896; 8:30AM-4:30PM (EST). *Felony, Misdemeanor.*

General Information: Online identifiers in results same as on public terminal. No juvenile records released. Will fax documents. Court makes copy: $.25 per page. Self serve copy: same. Certification fee: $8.00 per document plus copy fee. Payee: Clerk of Courts. Personal checks accepted, credit cards are not. Prepayment required. Mail requests: SASE requested.

Criminal Name Search: Access: Mail, in person, online. Both court and visitors may perform in person name searches. Search fee: $15.00 per name. Required to search: name, years to search, DOB. Computerized back to 1995; criminal records on files for 50 years, archived from 1800s. Mail turnaround time same day. Public use terminal has crim records back to 1995. Search dockets online free at http://ujsportal.pacourts.us/DocketSheets/CP.aspx back to 1995. Online results show middle initial, DOB.

Register of Wills 157 Lincoln Way E, Chambersburg, PA 17201; 717-261-3872; fax: 717-709-7211; 8:30AM-4:30PM (EST). *Probate.*

General Information: Online access available by subscription from private company-Infocon at www.infoconcountyaccess.com, 814-472-6066. See note at beginning of section. Images are not available.

Fulton County

Court of Common Pleas - Criminal/Civil Fulton County Courthouse, 201 N 2nd St, McConnellsburg, PA 17233; 717-485-4212; fax: 717-485-5568; 8:30AM-4:30PM (EST). *Felony, Misdemeanor, Civil, Eviction.* www.co.fulton.pa.us/court-common-pleas.php

General Information: Send faxes to Attention-Court of Common Pleas. No juvenile, adoption records released. Will fax documents $5.00 per doc. Court makes copy: $.50 per page. Certification fee: $7.50 per doc includes copy fee. Payee: Prothonotary. Personal checks accepted, credit cards are not. Prepayment required. Mail requests: SASE required for criminal.

Civil Name Search: Access: In person only. Visitors must perform in person searches themselves. Civil records on docket index from 1850s; on computer back to 1999. Civil PAT goes back to 1999. Online access available by subscription from private company-Infocon at www.infoconcountyaccess.com, 814-472-6066. See note at beginning of section. Images are available. Images not available.

Criminal Name Search: Access: Mail, in person, online. Visitors must perform in person searches themselves. Search fee: $10.00 per name. Criminal records on docket index from 1850s; on computer back to 1994. Mail turnaround time 3-5 days. Criminal PAT goes back to 1996. Search dockets online free at http://ujsportal.pacourts.us/DocketSheets/CP.aspx back to 1994.

Register of Wills 201 N 2nd St, McConnellsburg, PA 17233; 717-485-4212; fax: 717-485-5568; 8:30AM-4:30PM (EST). *Probate.* www.co.fulton.pa.us/index.php

Greene County

Court of Common Pleas - Civil Greene County Courthouse 1st Fl, 10 E High St, Rm 105, Waynesburg, PA 15370; 724-852-5288; civil phone: 724-852-5289; probate phone: 724-852-5283; fax: 724-852-5353; 8:30AM-4:30PM (EST). *Civil, Eviction.* www.co.greene.pa.us/secured/gc2/depts/lo/PROTH/proth.htm

General Information: No mental health records released. Will not fax documents. Court makes copy: $.50 per page. Self serve copy: same. Certification fee: $18.00 per record plus copy fee. Payee: Prothonotary. Personal checks accepted, credit cards are not. Prepayment required. Mail requests: SASE required.

Civil Name Search: Access: Mail, in person. Visitors must perform in person searches themselves. Search fee: None; if numerous, then $.50 per name. Civil records go back to 1797; on computer back to 1996. Mail turnaround time 1 week. Public use terminal has civil records back to 1996.

Court of Common Pleas - Criminal Greene County Courthouse 1st Fl, 10 E High St, Rm 105, Waynesburg, PA 15370; 724-852-5281; fax: 724-852-5316; 8:30AM-4:30PM (EST). *Felony, Misdemeanor.* www.co.greene.pa.us/secured/gc2/depts/lo/coc/coc.htm

General Information: No juvenile, adoption records released. Fee to fax out file $2.00 1st page; $1.00 each add'l. Court makes copy: $.50 per page. Self serve copy: $.50 per page. Certification fee: $8.00 per document. Payee: Clerk of Courts. Personal checks accepted, credit cards are not. Prepayment required. Mail requests: SASE required.

Criminal Name Search: Access: Mail, in person, online. Both court and visitors may perform in person name searches. Search fee: $10.00 per name. Required to search: name, years to search, DOB, signed release; also helpful: SSN. Criminal records indexed in books from 1940s, on computer since 1996. Mail turnaround time same day. Public use terminal has crim records back to 1996. Public terminal has limited number of cases only. Search dockets online free at http://ujsportal.pacourts.us/DocketSheets/CP.aspx back to 1996. Online results show middle initial, DOB.

Register of Wills Greene County Courthouse #100, 10 E High St, Waynesburg, PA 15370; 724-852-5284; fax: 724-852-5316; 8:30AM-4:30PM (EST). *Probate.* www.co.greene.pa.us/secured/gc2/depts/lo/rr/rr.htm

Huntingdon County

Court of Common Pleas - Criminal/Civil PO Box 39, Courthouse, Huntingdon, PA 16652; 814-643-1610; fax: 814-643-4271; 8:30AM-4:30PM (EST). *Felony, Misdemeanor, Civil, Eviction.*

General Information: No juvenile records released. Will fax documents $1.00 per page. Court makes copy: $.25 per page. Certification fee: $4.50 per cert includes copies. Payee: Prothonotary. Personal checks accepted, credit cards are not. Prepayment required.

Civil Name Search: Access: In person, mail, online. Both court and visitors may perform in person name searches. No search fee. Required to search: name, years to search; also helpful: address. Civil records on computer from 8/03/92, on dockets from 1788. Civil PAT goes back to 8/1992. Online access is by subscription from private company-Infocon at www.infoconcountyaccess.com, 814-472-6066. See note in court summary section. Images not shown.

Criminal Name Search: Access: In person, mail, online. Visitors must perform in person searches themselves. No search fee. Required to search: name, years to search; also helpful: DOB, SSN. Criminal records computerized from 8/03/92, on dockets from 1788. Mail turnaround time 1 day. Criminal PAT goes back to same as civil. Search dockets online free at http://ujsportal.pacourts.us/DocketSheets/CP.aspx back to 1992. Online results show name, DOB.

Register of Wills Courthouse, 223 Penn St, Huntingdon, PA 16652; 814-643-2740; fax: 814-643-1790; 8:30AM-4:30PM (EST). *Probate.*

General Information: When faxing, put "Attn: Register's Office."

Indiana County

Court of Common Pleas - Criminal/Civil County Courthouse, 825 Philadelphia St, Indiana, PA 15701; 724-465-3855/3858; fax: 724-465-3968; 8AM-4PM (EST). *Felony, Misdemeanor, Civil, Eviction.* www.countyofindiana.org/courts

General Information: No juvenile, commitment records released. Will fax documents $.25 per page. Court makes copy: $.25 per page. Certification fee: $3.25 for divorce decrees. Payee: Clerk of Court or Prothonotary. Personal checks accepted, credit cards are not. Prepayment required. Mail requests: SASE required.

Civil Name Search: Access: Mail, in person, online. Both court and visitors may perform in person name searches. Search fee: $7.50 per name. Will not conduct judgment searches. Civil records on computer from 1994, prior on index files to1806. Mail turnaround time same day. Civil PAT goes back to 1994. Online access is by subscription from private company-Infocon at www.infoconcountyaccess.com, 814-472-6066. See note in court summary section. Images not shown.

Criminal Name Search: Access: Mail, in person, online. Both court and visitors may perform in person name searches. Search fee: $10.75 per name. Required to search: name, years to search, DOB, signed release. Criminal records computerized from 1994, prior on index files to 1806. Mail turnaround time same day. Criminal PAT goes back to same as civil. Search dockets online free at http://ujsportal.pacourts.us/DocketSheets/CP.aspx back to 1975. Online results show name, DOB.

Register of Wills County Courthouse, 825 Philadelphia St, Indiana, PA 15701; 724-465-3860; fax: 724-465-3863; 8AM-4PM (EST). *Probate.*

Jefferson County

Court of Common Pleas - Criminal/Civil Courthouse, 200 Main St, Brookville, PA 15825; 814-849-1606; fax: 814-849-1625; 8:30AM-4:30PM (EST). *Felony, Misdemeanor, Civil, Eviction.*

General Information: No juvenile, mental health, records released, including criminal cases with a minor as a victim. Will fax documents $3.00 1st page; $1.00 ea add'l page. Court makes copy: $.50 per page. Self serve copy: same. Certification fee: $1.50 per page. Payee: Clerk of Courts. Personal checks accepted, credit cards are not. Prepayment required. Mail requests: SASE required.

Civil Name Search: Access: Mail, in person, online. Both court and visitors may perform in person name searches. Search fee: $10.00 per name. Civil records on computer back to 1987; all incoming records microfilmed, records since 1823 on microfilm. Mail turnaround time 2 days. Civil PAT goes back to 1987. Online access is by subscription from private company-Infocon at www.infoconcountyaccess.com, 814-472-6066. See note in court summary section. Images not shown.

Criminal Name Search: Access: Mail, in person, online. Both court and visitors may perform in person name searches. Search fee: $10.00 per name. Required to search: name, years to search, DOB; also helpful: SSN. Criminal records computerized from 1987; all incoming records microfilmed, records since 1947 on microfilm. Mail turnaround time 2 days. Criminal PAT goes back to same as civil. Search dockets online free at http://ujsportal.pacourts.us/DocketSheets/CP.aspx back to 1973. Online results show name, DOB.

Register of Wills Jefferson County Courthouse, 200 Main St, Brookville, PA 15825; 814-849-1610; fax: 814-849-1677; 8:30AM-4:30PM (EST). *Probate.*

General Information: $10.00 search fee; $1.00 per page copy fee. Online access is by subscription from private company-Infocon at www.infoconcountyaccess.com, 814-472-6066. See note in court summary section.

Juniata County

Court of Common Pleas - Criminal/Civil Juniata County Courthouse, Mifflintown, PA 17059; 717-436-7715; fax: 717-436-7734; 8AM-4:30PM (EST). *Felony, Misdemeanor, Civil, Eviction.*
www.co.juniata.pa.us/

General Information: This court will not do name searches. Online identifiers in results same as on public terminal. No juvenile records released. Will fax documents. Court makes copy: $.50 per page. Certification fee: $2.25 per page plus copy fee. Payee: Prothonotary or Clerk of Courts. Personal checks accepted, credit cards are not. Prepayment required.

Civil Name Search: Access: In person only. Visitors must perform in person searches themselves. Civil records on computer go back to 1993, on dockets from 1864. Civil PAT goes back to 1993.

Criminal Name Search: Access: In person, online. Visitors must perform in person searches themselves. Criminal records on computer go back to 1993, on dockets from 1894. Criminal PAT goes back to same as civil. Search dockets online free at http://ujsportal.pacourts.us/DocketSheets/CP.aspx back to 1975. Online results show name, DOB.

Register of Wills County Courthouse, 1 N Main St, PO Box 68, Mifflintown, PA 17059; 717-436-7709; fax: 717-436-7756; 8AM-4:30PM M-F, 8AM-N Wed (June-Sept) (EST). *Probate.*
www.co.juniata.pa.us/register.php

General Information: Online access available by subscription from private company-Infocon at www.infoconcountyaccess.com, 814-472-6066. See note at beginning of section. Images not shown.

Lackawanna County

Court of Common Pleas - Civil Clerk of Judicial Records, 436 Spruce St, Brooks Bldg, Scranton, PA 18503-1551; 570-963-6723; fax: 570-963-6387; 9AM-4PM (EST). *Civil, Eviction.*
www.lackawannacounty.org/viewDepartment.aspx?DeptID=40

General Information: No juvenile records released. Will not fax documents. Court makes copy: $.25 per page; $1.00 for mail requesters first copy, $.25 each add'l. Self serve copy: same. Certification fee: $4.75. Payee: Clerk of Judicial Records. Business checks accepted. Major credit cards accepted. Prepayment required.

Civil Name Search: Access: In person only. Visitors must perform in person searches themselves. Civil records computerized since 9/95, dockets from 1920s, archived from 1800s. Case number is required. Note: No civil searches performed by court but exceptions made. Public use terminal has civil records back to 1995.

Court of Common Pleas - Criminal Lackawanna County Courthouse, Scranton, PA 18503; 570-963-6759; fax: 570-963-6459; 9AM-4PM (EST). *Felony, Misdemeanor.*
www.lackawannacounty.org/viewDepartment.aspx?DeptID=40

General Information: Online identifiers in results same as on public terminal. No juvenile records released. Will fax documents to local or toll free line. Court makes copy: $.25 per page. Certification fee: $8.00 per doc includes copies. Payee: Clerk of Judicial Records. Business checks accepted. Visa/MC in person only accepted. Prepayment required. Mail requests: SASE required.

Criminal Name Search: Access: Mail, in person, online. Both court and visitors may perform in person name searches. Search fee: $10.00 per name. Required to search: name, years to search, DOB. Criminal records computerized since 10/95, on dockets from 1983, archived from 1941, indexed by defendant only. Mail turnaround time 1-2 days. Public use terminal has crim records back to 1995. Results include LKA. Search dockets online free at http://ujsportal.pacourts.us/DocketSheets/CP.aspx back to 1982. Online results show name, DOB.

Register of Wills Scranton Electric Bldg, 507 Linden St, #400, Scranton, PA 18503; 570-963-6702; fax: 570-963-6377; 9AM-4PM (EST). *Probate.*
www.lackawannacounty.org/viewDepartment.aspx?DeptID=35

Lancaster County

Court of Common Pleas - Civil 50 N Duke St, PO Box 83480, Lancaster, PA 17608-3480; 717-299-8282; fax: 717-293-7210; 8:30AM-5PM (EST). *Civil, Eviction.*
www.co.lancaster.pa.us/courts/site/default.asp

General Information: Names and dates naturalization records released. Will fax documents $2.00 1st page, $1.00 each add'l. Fee higher for out of state faxing. Court makes copy: $.25 per page. Certification fee: $5.00 per document plus copy fee. Payee: Prothonotary. Personal checks accepted, credit cards are not. Prepayment required. Mail requests: SASE required.

Civil Name Search: Access: Online, in person. Visitors must perform in person searches themselves. Required to search: name, years to search; also helpful: address. Civil records on computer from 7/87, in files from 1987, judgments on dockets from 1800s, others archived from 1800s. Public use

terminal has civil records back to 7/1987. Access to the Prothonotary's civil court records is free at http://gisweb1.co.lancaster.pa.us/bannerwebimg/. Also, historical court case schedules are free at www.co.lancaster.pa.us, click on "Court Calendar Archives." Includes Register, Treasurer, and other courthouse record data. Results include addresses. Call Kathy Harris at 717-299-8252 for info.

Court of Common Pleas - Criminal Clerk of Courts, 50 N Duke St, Lancaster, PA 17602; 717-299-8275; fax: 717-295-3686; 8:30AM-5PM (EST). *Felony, Misdemeanor.*
www.co.lancaster.pa.us/courts/site/default.asp

General Information: Online identifiers in results same as on public terminal. No juvenile records released. Will not fax documents. Court makes copy: $.25 per page. Certification fee: $8.75 per doc. Payee: Clerk of Courts. Only cashiers checks and money orders accepted. No credit cards accepted. Prepayment required. Mail requests: SASE required.

Criminal Name Search: Access: Mail, in person, online. Both court and visitors may perform in person name searches. Search fee: $21.50 per name. Required to search: name, years to search, and SSN, DOB or case docket number. Criminal records computerized from 1988, paper back to 1983, archived from 1901, indexes to 1729. Mail turnaround time 2 days. Public use terminal has crim records back to 1988. Search dockets online free at http://ujsportal.pacourts.us/DocketSheets/CP.aspx back to 1977. Online results show name, DOB.

Register of Wills 50 N Duke St., Lancaster, PA 17602; 717-299-8243; fax: 717-295-5914; 8:30AM-5PM (EST). *Probate.*
www.co.lancaster.pa.us/lanco/cwp/view.asp?a=562&q=588899&lancoNav=| &lancoNav_GID=1003

General Information: Access probate back to 1933 and marriage records back to 1948 free at http://paperless.co.lancaster.pa.us/viewerportal.

Lawrence County

Court of Common Pleas - Criminal/Civil 430 Court St, New Castle, PA 16101-3593; 724-656-2126; criminal phone: 724-656-2188; civil phone: 724-656-1960; fax: 724-656-1988; 8AM-4PM (EST). *Felony, Misdemeanor, Civil, Eviction.*
www.co.lawrence.pa.us

General Information: 2nd fax number- 724-656-2479 No adoption, juvenile, impounded, or juvenile sex crime victim records released. Will fax documents: local $1.00 plus $.50 per pg; long distance $5.00 plus $.90 per pg. Court makes copy: $.50 per page.If copies are mailed,: $3.25 per case, or if individual pages then $1.50 first page and $.50 ea addl. Microfilm copies are $1.80 ea. Certification fee: $1.50 per page. Payee: Prothonotary. Business checks accepted. No credit cards accepted. Prepayment required. Mail requests: SASE requested.

Civil Name Search: Access: Fax, mail, online, in person. Both court and visitors may perform in person name searches. Search fee: $10.00 per name. Civil records on computer from 1994, on Russell Index from 1885. Mail turnaround time ASAP. Civil PAT goes back to 1987. Online access is by subscription from private company-Infocon at www.infoconcountyaccess.com, 814-472-6066. See note in court summary section. Images shown.

Criminal Name Search: Access: Fax, mail, online, in person. Both court and visitors may perform in person name searches. Search fee: $17.75 per name. Required to search: name, years to search, signed release; also helpful: DOB, SSN. Criminal records computerized from 1994, on Russell Index from 1885. Mail turnaround time ASAP. Criminal PAT goes back to 1994. Internet access to court records is by subscription from a private company-Infocon at www.ic-access.com, 814-472-6066. See note at beginning of section. Also, search dockets online free at http://ujsportal.pacourts.us/DocketSheets/CP.aspx back to 1968. Online results show name, DOB.

Register of Wills 430 Court St, New Castle, PA 16101-3593; 724-656-2159; fax: 724-656-1966; 8AM-4PM (EST). *Probate.*
www.co.lawrence.pa.us/rr/index.html

Lebanon County

Court of Common Pleas - Civil Municipal Bldg, Rm 104, 400 S 8th St, Lebanon, PA 17042; 717-228-4418; fax: 717-228-4467; 8:30AM-4:30PM (EST). *Civil, Eviction; Family-Divorce, Custody.*
http://lebcounty.org/Prothonotary/Pages/Home.aspx

General Information: No mental health records released. Will fax documents $.50 per page. Court makes copy: $.50 per page. Certification fee: $11.00 per cert plus copy fee (for a year period going forward). Payee: Prothonotary. Personal checks accepted, credit cards are not. Prepayment required.

Civil Name Search: Access: In person only. Visitors must perform in person searches themselves. Required to search: name, years to search; also helpful: address. Civil records on computer from 1985, on files from 1883. Public use terminal has civil records back to 1985.

Court of Common Pleas - Criminal Municipal Bldg, Rm 102, 400 S 8th St, Lebanon, PA 17042; 717-274-2801 X2118; fax: 717-228-4467; 8:30AM-4:30PM (EST). *Felony, Misdemeanor.*
http://lebcounty.org/Pages/default.aspx
General Information: No juvenile records released. Will fax documents to local or toll-free number if pre-paid. Court makes copy: $.50 per page. Certification fee: $10.00 per doc includes copy fee. Payee: Clerk of Court. Personal checks accepted, credit cards are not. Prepayment required. Mail requests: SASE required.
Criminal Name Search: Access: In person, online. Both court and visitors may perform in person name searches. No search fee. Criminal records computerized from 1986, indexed from 1800s. Note: Action number required for phone access. Mail turnaround time varies. Public use terminal has crim records back to 1986. Search dockets online free at http://ujsportal.pacourts.us/DocketSheets/CP.aspx back to 1967. Online results show name, DOB.

Register of Wills Municipal Bldg, Rm 105, 400 S 8th St, Lebanon, PA 17042; 717-228-4415; fax: 717-228-4460; 8:30AM-4:30PM (EST). *Probate.*
General Information: Search fee is $5.00 per name.

Lehigh County

Court of Common Pleas - Civil 455 W Hamilton St, Allentown, PA 18101-1614; 610-782-3148; criminal fax: 610-770-3840; civil fax: 8AM-4PM; 8AM-4PM (EST). *Civil, Eviction.*
www.lccpa.org
General Information: Probate fax- 610-782-3932. Clerk of records at www.lehighcounty.org/Departments/ClerkofJudicialRecords/tabid/327/Default.aspx. Online identifiers in results same as on public terminal. No sealed, confidential, or impounded records released. Will not fax documents. Court makes copy: $.50 per page; docket printout $3.00. Self serve copy: $.25 per page. Certification fee: $5.00. Payee: Clerk of Judicial Records. Personal checks accepted. Credit cards accepted. Prepayment required.
Civil Name Search: Access: In person, online. Visitors must perform in person searches themselves. Civil records on computer since 1985, on microfilm from 1812. Note: Court will not conduct name searches. Mail turnaround time 2 days. Public use terminal has civil records. Terminal results include litigant names. Access to the county online system requires $300.00 annual usage fee. Search by name or case number. Call Lehigh Cty Fiscal Office at 610-782-3112 for more information.

Court of Common Pleas - Criminal Clerk of Judicial Records, 455 W Hamilton St, Allentown, PA 18101-1614; 610-782-3077; fax: 610-770-6797; 8AM-4:30PM (EST). *Felony, Misdemeanor.*
www.lccpa.org
General Information: Online identifiers in results same as on public terminal. No juvenile or impounded records released. Will fax documents if search prepaid. Court makes copy: $.50 per page. Self serve copy: $.25 per page. Certification fee: $9.85 per doc. Payee: County of Lehigh. Personal checks accepted, credit cards are not. Prepayment required. Mail requests: SASE required.
Criminal Name Search: Access: Online, in person. Visitors must perform in person searches themselves. Required to search: name, years to search, DOB; SSN helpful. Criminal records computerized from 1990, on alpha index from 1962 to 1990, on microfilm from 1812. No DOB on records 1962-1989. Note: Court personnel will not perform name searches for the public. Mail turnaround time 1 week. Public use terminal has crim records back to 1990. Search dockets online free at http://ujsportal.pacourts.us/DocketSheets/CP.aspx back to 1990. Also, free online access is available for Calendars & Schedules. Online results show name, DOB.

Register of Wills 455 W Hamilton, Rm 121, Allentown, PA 18101-1614; 610-782-3170; ; 8AM-4PM (EST). *Probate.*
www.lccpa.org/
General Information: Online access to Wills: call Lehigh Cty Computer Svcs Dept at 610-782-3286 for info.

Luzerne County

Court of Common Pleas - Civil 200 N River St, Office of the Prothonotary, Wilkes Barre, PA 18711-1001; 570-825-1745; fax: 570-825-1757; 9AM-4:30PM (EST). *Civil, Eviction.*
www.luzernecounty.org/county/row_offices/prothonotary
General Information: No mental, sealed records released. Fee to fax out file $2.25 per page. Court makes copy: $2.25 per page. Self serve copy: $.25 per page. Certification fee: $7.00 1st page; $3.50 each add'l. Payee: Prothonotary. No personal checks accepted. Visa, MC, AmEx accepted. Prepayment required. Mail requests: SASE required.

Civil Name Search: Access: Phone, mail, in person. Both court and visitors may perform in person name searches. Search fee: $19.50 per name for 5 years, $3.50 each add'l year. Required to search: name, years to search, address. Civil records partially on microfiche and archives, on dockets from 1935. Mail turnaround time 5 days. Public use terminal has civil records back to 3/2005.

Court of Common Pleas - Criminal 200 N River St, Wilkes Barre, PA 18711; 570-825-1555; fax: 570-820-6303; 8AM-4:30PM (EST). *Felony, Misdemeanor.*
www.luzernecountycourts.com/
General Information: Note that the phone numbers given above are direct to the records section. The county home page is www.luzernecounty.org. No "M" number (confidential custody case) records released. No fee to fax documents. Court makes copy: $.35 per page, but copies may be included in search fee. Certification fee: $7.00 per doc. Payee: Clerk of Courts. No personal checks or credit cards accepted. Prepayment required. Mail requests: SASE not required.
Criminal Name Search: Access: Fax, mail, in person, online. Only the court performs in person name searches; visitors may not. Search fee: $15.00 for information requested up to 45 pages printed, each add'l $.35 per page. If microfilm then $15.00 covers first 10 pages then $1.50 ea addl. Data prior to 1966 is $30.00. Required to search: name, years to search, DOB or SSN. Criminal records on docket sheets 1989 to present, Onbase 1997 to present, microfilm 1996 and prior. Mail turnaround time 1-2 days. Public use terminal has crim records. Search dockets online free at http://ujsportal.pacourts.us/DocketSheets/CP.aspx back to 1989. Online results show middle initial, DOB.

Register of Wills 20 N Pennsylvania Ave, #231, Penn Place Annex, Wilkes Barre, PA 18701; 570-825-1668, 408-825-8241; fax: 570-826-0869; 9AM-4:30PM (closed 12-1) (EST). *Probate.*
General Information: Access to data is by subscription at www.landex.com/remote/.

Lycoming County

Court of Common Pleas - Criminal/Civil 48 W 3rd St, Williamsport, PA 17701; 570-327-2251; fax: 570-327-2505; 8:30AM-5PM (EST). *Felony, Misdemeanor, Civil, Eviction. Small Claims.*
www.lyco.org/
General Information: No juvenile, cases involving minors, mental records released. Will not fax documents. Court makes copy: $.50 per page. Self serve copy: $.50 per page. Certification fee: $7.75 per cert includes copies. Payee: Prothonotary. Personal checks accepted, credit cards are not. Prepayment required.
Civil Name Search: Access: In person only. Visitors must perform in person searches themselves. Required to search: name, years to search; also helpful: address. Civil records on computer from 1983, on dockets from 1795. Civil PAT goes back to 1983. Clerk will verify personal identifiers of PAT results.
Criminal Name Search: Access: In person, online. Visitors must perform in person searches themselves. Required to search: name, years to search, DOB; also helpful: address. Criminal records computerized from 1910. Criminal PAT goes back to 1910. Clerk will verify personal identifiers of PAT results. Search dockets online free at http://ujsportal.pacourts.us/DocketSheets/CP.aspx back to 1968. Online results show middle initial, DOB.

Register of Wills Lycoming Co Courthouse, 48 W 3rd St, Williamsport, PA 17701; 570-327-2263, 327-2258; fax: 570-327-6790; 8:30AM-5PM (EST). *Probate.*

McKean County

Court of Common Pleas - Criminal/Civil PO Box 273, Smethport, PA 16749; 814-887-3270; fax: 814-887-3219; 8:30AM-4:30PM (EST). *Felony, Misdemeanor, Civil, Eviction.*
General Information: No sex related, juvenile, mental health records released. Will fax documents $2.00 per page. Court makes copy: $.50 per page. Computer printout $1.00 per page. Self serve copy: $.50 per page. Certification fee: $10.00. Payee: Prothonotary or Clerk of Courts. Personal checks accepted. Credit cards accepted for subscription and on-going services only. Prepayment required. Mail requests: SASE required.
Civil Name Search: Access: Phone, fax, mail, in person, online. Both court and visitors may perform in person name searches. Search fee: $15.00 per name. Civil records on computer since 1994, on microfiche from 1952 to 1962, on dockets from 1872. Mail turnaround time same day. Civil PAT goes back to 1994. Online access is by subscription from private company-Infocon at www.infoconcountyaccess.com, 814-472-6066. Monthly usage fee and per minute fees apply.
Criminal Name Search: Access: Mail, in person, online. Both court and visitors may perform in person name searches. Search fee: $15.00 per name. Required to search: name, years to search, DOB. Criminal records on computer since 1994, on dockets from 1872. Mail turnaround time same

day. Criminal PAT goes back to same as civil. Search dockets online free at http://ujsportal.pacourts.us/DocketSheets/CP.aspx back to 1994. One-time non-refundable account setup is $25.00. Access rate charged per minute plus monthly usage fee. Online results show name, DOB.

Register of Wills PO Box 202, 500 W Main St, Smethport, PA 16749-0202; 814-887-3260; fax: 814-887-3255; 8:30AM-4:30PM (EST). *Probate.* www.mckeancountypa.org/Departments/Register_Wills_Clerk_Orphans/Index.aspx

Mercer County

Court of Common Pleas - Civil 105 Mercer County Courthouse, Mercer, PA 16137; 724-662-3800; fax: 724-662-2021; 8:30AM-4:30PM (EST). *Civil, Eviction.* www.mcc.co.mercer.pa.us
General Information: Daily court schedule at www.mcc.co.mercer.pa.us/Court_Schedule/Default.htm. No mental, sealed records released. Will not fax records, unless prior arrangement with Prothonotary. Court makes copy: $.25 per page. Certification fee: $4.50 per cert. Payee: Prothonotary or Clerk of Courts. Personal checks accepted, credit cards are not. Prepayment required.
Civil Name Search: Access: In person, online. Visitors must perform in person searches themselves. Civil records on computer since 1994; prior records on dockets from 1930s, archived from 1700s. Include SSN and DOB in your search. Public use terminal has civil records back to 1994. Online access is by subscription from private company-Infocon at www.infoconcountyaccess.com, 814-472-6066. See note in court summary section. Images not shown.

Court of Common Pleas - Criminal 112 Mercer County Courthouse, Mercer, PA 16137; 724-662-3800; criminal phone: X2248; fax: 724-662-1604; 8:30AM-4:30PM (EST). *Felony, Misdemeanor.* www.mcc.co.mercer.pa.us
General Information: Daily court schedule at www.mcc.co.mercer.pa.us/Court_Schedule/Default.htm. Online identifiers in results same as on public terminal. No juvenile records released. Fee to fax document $1.00 1st page, $.25 ea add'l. Court makes copy: $.25 per page. Certification fee: $9.00. Payee: Clerk of Courts. Personal checks accepted. Major credit cards accepted. Prepayment required. Mail requests: SASE required.
Criminal Name Search: Access: Mail, in person, online. Both court and visitors may perform in person name searches. Search fee: $10.00 per name. Required to search: name, years to search; also helpful: DOB, SSN. Criminal records on computer since 1993, indexed since 1920, on files from 1980. Mail turnaround time 2-4 days. Public use terminal has crim records back to 1993. Search dockets online free at http://ujsportal.pacourts.us/DocketSheets/CP.aspx back to Mercer. Online results show name, DOB.

Register of Wills 112 Mercer County Courthouse, Mercer, PA 16137; 724-662-3800 x2253, x2246; fax: 724-662-1604; 8:30AM-4:30PM (EST). *Probate.*

Mifflin County

Court of Common Pleas - Criminal/Civil Clerk of Courts/Prothonotary, 20 N Wayne St, Lewistown, PA 17044; 717-248-8146; fax: 717-248-5275; 8AM-4:30PM (EST). *Felony, Misdemeanor, Civil, Eviction.* www.co.mifflin.pa.us/CourtOffice/Pages/CRT_main_pg.aspx
General Information: This agency will not perform name searches. Online identifiers in results same as on public terminal. No juvenile, mental health records released. Will not fax out documents. Court makes copy: $.25 per page. Certification fee: $4.50. Payee: Prothonotary/Clerk of Courts. No personal checks or credit cards accepted. Prepayment required. Mail requests: SASE required for mail return of any copies.
Civil Name Search: Access: In person, online. Visitors must perform in person searches themselves. Civil records on computer from 1993, on microfiche from 1968-1990, prior on books. Civil PAT goes back to 1993. Online access is by subscription from private company-Infocon at www.infoconcountyaccess.com, 814-472-6066. See note in court summary section. Images not shown. Court calendar available at main website.
Criminal Name Search: Access: In person, online. Visitors must perform in person searches themselves. Criminal records computerized from 1993, on microfiche from 1969-1990, prior on books. Criminal PAT goes back to 2005. Court calendar at main website. Search dockets online free at http://ujsportal.pacourts.us/DocketSheets/CP.aspx back to 1986. Online results show middle initial.

Register of Wills 20 N Wayne St., Lewistown, PA 17044; 717-242-1449; fax: 717-248-2503; 8AM-4:30PM (EST). *Probate.* http://co.mifflin.pa.us/Probation/Pages/PRB_main_pg.aspx

General Information: Online access available by subscription from private company-Infocon at www.infoconcountyaccess.com, 814-472-6066. Some images not shown, but not all.

Monroe County

Court of Common Pleas - Civil Monroe County Courthouse - Prothonotary, 610 Monroe St, Stroudsburg, PA 18360; 570-517-3988; ; 8:30AM-4:30PM (EST). *Civil, Eviction.*
General Information: Passport info 570-517-3370. No juvenile records released. Will not fax documents. Court makes copy: $1.00 per page. Self serve copy: $.25 per page. Certification fee: $4.00 plus copy fee. Payee: Monroe County Prothonotary. Only cashiers checks and money orders accepted. No credit cards accepted. Prepayment required.
Civil Name Search: Access: In person, online. Visitors must perform in person searches themselves. Required to search: name, years to search; also helpful: DOB, SSN, signed release. Civil records indexed on computer 1995 to present, prior in dockets, books. Public use terminal has civil records back to 1995. Online access is by subscription from private company-Infocon at www.infoconcountyaccess.com, 814-472-6066. See note in court summary section. Images not shown.

Court of Common Pleas - Criminal Monroe County Courthouse, Rm 312, 7th and Monroe Sts, Stroudsburg, PA 18360-2190; 570-517-3385; criminal phone: 570-517-3339; fax: 570-517-3949; 8:30AM-4:30PM (EST). *Felony, Misdemeanor.*
General Information: The court will no longer do name searches for the public. No sex related, juvenile, adoption records released. Will not fax documents. Court makes copy: $1.00 per page. Self serve copy: $.25 per page. Certification fee: $5.00 per doc plus copy fee. Payee: Clerk of Court. Only cashiers checks and money orders accepted. No credit cards accepted. Prepayment required. Mail requests: SASE required.
Criminal Name Search: Access: In person, online. Visitors must perform in person searches themselves. Required to search: name, years to search; also helpful: address, DOB, SSN. Criminal records on computer since 1995; prior on dockets. Mail turnaround time 1 day. Public use terminal has crim records back to 1995. Search dockets online free at http://ujsportal.pacourts.us/DocketSheets/CP.aspx back to 1972. Online results show name, DOB.

Register of Wills Monroe County Courthouse, 7th & Monroe Sts, Stroudsburg, PA 18360; 570-517-3359; fax: 570-517-3873; 8:30AM-4:30PM (EST). *Probate.* www.co.monroe.pa.us/planning_records/cwp/view.asp?a=1549&Q=605594&planning_recordsNav=|34352|
General Information: Access wills records online at www.landex.com/remote/. Fee is $.20 per minute and $.50 per fax page. Wills go back to 11/1836.

Montgomery County

Court of Common Pleas - Civil PO Box 311, 400 Swede St, Norristown, PA 19404-0311; 610-278-3360; fax: 610-278-5994; 8:30AM-4:15PM (EST). *Civil, Eviction.* http://prothy.montcopa.org/prothy/site/default.asp
General Information: Landlord/tenant actions are found at the local District Court level. See www.courts.montcopa.org/courts/cwp/view,a,1434,q,65381.asp. No mental health, divorce, sealed records released. Will not fax documents. Court makes copy: $.25 per page. Certification fee: $5.00 per cert includes copies. Payee: Prothonotary. No personal checks or credit cards accepted. Prepayment required.
Civil Name Search: Access: Mail, in person, online. Visitors must perform in person searches themselves. Search fee: $8.25 per name. Civil records on computer from 4/82, on microfilm from 1800s. Public use terminal has civil records back to 1992. Search court and other record indices free from Prothonotary at http://webapp.montcopa.org/PSI/. This includes active and purged civil cases, also active probate cases, also calendars.

Court of Common Pleas - Criminal PO Box 311, Main & Swede St, Norristown, PA 19404-0311; 610-278-3346; fax: 610-278-5188; 8:30AM-4:15PM (EST). *Felony, Misdemeanor.* www.courts.montcopa.org/courts/site/default.asp
General Information: The Court Administration Office can be reached at 610-278-3224. No impounded, sealed records released. Will not fax documents. Court makes copy: $1.00 per page, $2.00 per page from microfiche. Certification fee: $9.25 per cert. Payee: Clerk of Courts. Attorney firm checks accepted; no personal checks. Accepts Visa/MC/Discover cards. Prepayment required. Mail requests: SASE required.
Criminal Name Search: Access: Mail, online, in person. Both court and visitors may perform in person name searches. Search fee: $18.50 per name. Required to search: name, years to search, DOB, signed release. Criminal records computerized from 10/84, prior archived and on microfiche. Mail turnaround time 2-5 days. Public use terminal has crim records

back to 1984. Terminal gives only DOB year. Search dockets online free at http://ujsportal.pacourts.us/DocketSheets/CP.aspx back to 1979. Results shows year of birth only. Online results show middle initial.

Register of Wills One Montgomery Plaza, 4th Fl, Norristown, PA 19401; 610-278-3400; fax: 610-278-3240; 8:30AM-4:15PM (EST). *Probate, Orphan's Court.* http://rwoc.montcopa.org/rwoc/site/default.asp?
General Information: Search active cases at www.montcopa.org/registerofwillsorphanscourt/rwocviewer/. Office probates wills and processes intestate estates (estates without wills). The Office is also agent for the Commonwealth in the collection of inheritance taxes.

Montour County

Court of Common Pleas - Criminal/Civil Montour County Courthouse, 29 Mill St, Danville, PA 17821; 570-271-3010; fax: 570-271-3089; 9AM-4PM (EST). *Felony, Misdemeanor, Civil, Eviction.* www.montourco.org/Pages/Prothonotary.aspx
General Information: Online identifiers in results same as on public terminal. No sex related, juvenile or adoption records released. Will fax documents $5.00 fee. Court makes copy: $.50 per page. Certification fee: $5.00. Payee: Prothonotary. Personal checks accepted, credit cards are not. Prepayment required. Mail requests: SASE required.
Civil Name Search: Access: Phone, fax, mail, in person, online. Both court and visitors may perform in person name searches. Search fee: $20.00 per name. Civil records on books since 1991, on microfiche since 1939, on computer back to 1995. Actual files kept for 20 years. Mail turnaround time 1-2 days. Civil PAT goes back to 1996. Online access is by subscription from private company-Infocon at www.infoconcountyaccess.com, 814-472-6066. See note in court summary section. Images not shown.
Criminal Name Search: Access: Phone, fax, mail, in person, online. Both court and visitors may perform in person name searches. Search fee: $20.00 per name. Required to search: name, years to search, DOB. Criminal docket on books since 1991, on microfiche since 1939, on computer back to 1995. Mail turnaround time 1-2 days. Criminal PAT goes back to same as civil. Online access is by subscription from private company-Infocon at www.infoconcountyaccess.com, 814-472-6066. See note in court summary section. Images not shown. Record date back to 8/25/2005, no images. Search dockets online free at http://ujsportal.pacourts.us/DocketSheets/CP.aspx back to 1992. Online results show middle initial, DOB.

Register of Wills 29 Mill St, Danville, PA 17821; 570-271-3012; fax: 570-271-3071; 9AM-4PM (EST). *Probate.* www.montourco.org/Pages/default.aspx
General Information: Will index 1850 to present at www.montourco.org/RegisterRecorder/Pages/WillIndex1850toPresent.aspx. Online access available by subscription from private company-Infocon at www.infoconcountyaccess.com, 814-472-6066.

Northampton County

Court of Common Pleas - Civil Gov't Center, 669 Washington St, Lower Level, Easton, PA 18042-7498; 610-559-3060; fax: 610-559-3710; 8:30AM-4:30PM (EST). *Civil, Eviction.* www.nccpa.org
General Information: No impounded or PFA abuse records released. Will not fax documents. Court makes copy: $1.00 per page; $1.25 if mailed. Self serve copy: $.25 per page. Certification fee: $5.75. Payee: Clerk of Court-Civil or Prothonotary's Office. Business or certified checks accepted; no personal checks. No credit cards accepted. Prepayment required.
Civil Name Search: Access: In person only. Visitors must perform in person searches themselves. Required to search: name, years to search; also helpful: address. Civil records on computer since 1/85 (Civil) and 2/90 (Judgments). Public use terminal has civil records back to 1985. Search calendars and schedules for free at www.nccpa.org/schedule.html. Opinions and judgments may be available.

Court of Common Pleas - Criminal 669 Washington St, Easton, PA 18042-7494; 610-559-3000 X3046; fax: 610-252-4391; 8:30AM-4:30PM (EST). *Felony, Misdemeanor.* www.nccpa.org
General Information: Online identifiers in results same as on public terminal. No juvenile, expunged records released. Will fax documents to local or toll-free number. Court makes copy: $.50 per page. Certification fee: $9.00. Payee: Criminal Division. Business checks accepted, no personal checks. Visa/MC accepted in person only. Prepayment required. Mail requests: SASE not required.
Criminal Name Search: Access: Mail, in person, online. Both court and visitors may perform in person name searches. Search fee: $10.00 per name. Required to search: name, years to search, DOB; also helpful: SSN. Criminal records computerized from 1984, on files from 1800s. Mail turnaround time 5 days. Public use terminal has crim records back to 1984. Search calendars and schedules for free online at

www.nccpa.org/schedule.html. Opinions to be available soon. Also, search dockets online free at http://ujsportal.pacourts.us/DocketSheets/CP.aspx back to 1995. Online results show middle initial, DOB.

Register of Wills Governnment Ctr, 669 Washington St, Easton, PA 18042; 610-559-3094; fax: 610-559-3735; 8:30AM-4:30PM (EST). *Probate.*
www.northamptoncounty.org/northampton/cwp/view.asp?a=1521&q=620168

Northumberland County

Court of Common Pleas - Civil County Courthouse, 201 Market St, Rm #7, Sunbury, PA 17801-3468; 570-988-4151; fax: 570-988-4581; 9AM-5PM M; 9AM-4:30PM T-F (EST). *Civil, Liens, Judgments, Executions, Old Naturalizations.*
General Information: No adult abuse, involuntary treatment records released. Court makes copy: $.25 per page in person; $1.10 1st page, $.25 each add'l for mail. Certification fee: $4.25 1st page, $1.10 each add'l page. Payee: Northumberland County Prothonotary. Cash, money orders or attorney checks only. No credit cards accepted. Prepayment required. Mail requests: SASE required.
Civil Name Search: Access: Mail, in person. Both court and visitors may perform in person name searches. Search fee: $7.50 per name. Civil records on file from 1772 to present; on computer back to 1998. Mail turnaround time 4-5 days. Public use terminal has civil records back to 1998.

Court of Common Pleas - Criminal County Courthouse, 201 Market St, Rm 7, Sunbury, PA 17801-3468; 570-988-4148; criminal phone: 570-988-4149; fax: 570-988-4581; 9AM-5PM M; 9AM-4:30PM T-F (EST). *Felony, Misdemeanor.*
General Information: No juvenile records released. Will not fax documents. Court makes copy: By mail: $1.10 for first page, $.25 each add'l. In person: $.25. Certification fee: $4.25 1st page, $1.10 each add'l page. Payee: Clerk of Courts Office. No personal checks or credit cards accepted. Prepayment required. Mail requests: SASE required.
Criminal Name Search: Access: Mail, in person, online. Both court and visitors may perform in person name searches. Search fee: $10.00 per name. Required to search: name, years to search, DOB; also helpful: SSN. Criminal records indexed in office from 1945, on dockets from 1776, archived from 1776 to 1945, on computer back to 1998. Mail turnaround time 1-2 days. Public use terminal has crim records back to 1998. Terminal results do not always show DOB or SSN. Search dockets online free at http://ujsportal.pacourts.us/DocketSheets/CP.aspx back to 1998. Online results show name, DOB.

Register of Wills 201 Market St, #6, County Courthouse, Sunbury, PA 17801; 570-988-4143; 570-988-4140; fax: 570-988-4141; 9AM-4:30PM (EST). *Probate.*

Perry County

Court of Common Pleas - Criminal/Civil PO Box 325, New Bloomfield, PA 17068; 717-582-2131; criminal phone: 717-582-2131 X2241; civil phone: 717-582-2131 X2240; fax: 717-582-5167; 8AM-4PM (EST). *Felony, Misdemeanor, Civil, Eviction.*
www.perryco.org/Dept/Courts/Prothonotary_ClerkOfCourts/Pages/Prothonotaryand ClerkOfCourts.aspx
General Information: Access estate records index back to 1987 via www.landex.com/remote/. Registration and password required. Recorded judgments are on the County Recorder web page. No juvenile records released. Will fax documents $3.00. Court makes copy: $.25 per page. Self serve copy: same. Certification fee: $7.95 per document includes copy fee. Payee: Prothonotary or Clerk of Courts. Personal checks accepted, credit cards are not. Prepayment required. Will bill to attorneys and abstract companies upon approval. Mail requests: SASE required for criminal search requests.
Civil Name Search: Access: In person only. Visitors must perform in person searches themselves. Civil records on dockets from 1800s. Civil PAT goes back to 1995. Recorded judgments are on the County Recorder web page.
Criminal Name Search: Access: Phone, fax, mail, in person, online. Both court and visitors may perform in person name searches. Search fee: $10.00 per name. Required to search: name, years to search; also helpful: DOB, SSN. Criminal docket index from 1950. Mail turnaround time 1 week; phone turnaround immediate. Criminal PAT goes back to 1994; 1973-1993 being added. Search dockets online free at http://ujsportal.pacourts.us/DocketSheets/CP.aspx back to 1975. Online results show name, DOB.

Register of Wills PO Box 223, 2 E Main St, New Bloomfield, PA 17068; 717-582-2131; fax: 717-582-5149; 8AM-4PM (EST). *Probate.*
www.perryco.org/Dept/RegisterAndRecorder/Pages/RegisterAndRecorder.aspx
General Information: Access to data is by subscription at www.landex.com/remote/.

Philadelphia County

Court of Common Pleas - Civil First Judicial District of PA Prothonotary, Rm 284, City Hall, Philadelphia, PA 19107; 215-686-6653; fax: 215-567-7380; 9AM-5PM (EST). *Civil Actions Above $10,000.* http://courts.phila.gov

General Information: Has separate search unit (215-686-6656/8859), record unit (215-686-6661), and cert unit (215-686-6665). Get case number from web or search unit (Rm 262), then get case files from record unit (Record Rm 264), then certify at Rm 269. No mental health, divorce, abuse, adoption records released. Will not fax out documents. Court makes copy: $.50 per page. Self serve copy: $.50 per page. Certification fee: $41.58 per doc. Payee: Prothonotary. Business checks accepted; no personal checks. Credit cards accepted. Prepayment required. Mail requests: SASE required.

Civil Name Search: Access: Mail, in person, online. Both court and visitors may perform in person name searches. No search fee. Civil records on computer from 1/82 to present, archived on files from 1700s to 1982. Note: Docket number required in any mail request. Current records unit phone- 215-686-6661, Rm 268. Mail turnaround time 1-5 days. Public use terminal has civil records back to 1982. Public Terminal in Rm #262. Supply personal info in request to help court match record to name. Access to 1st Judicial District Civil Trial records is free at www.courts.phila.gov/casesearch/. Search by name, judgment and docket info.

Municipal Criminal Trial Division Information Services, 1301 Filbert St, #310, Philadelphia, PA 19107; 215-683-7505; fax: 215-683-7507; 8AM-5PM (EST). *Felony, Misdemeanor.* http://courts.phila.gov

General Information: The clerk also holds closed records of misdemeanors for the Municipal Court Misdemeanor Division. Online identifiers in results same as on public terminal. No sealed, grand jury, mental records released. Will not fax documents. Court makes copy: $.25 per page. Self serve copy: $.25 per page. Fee is $3.00 per doc for printouts from the computer. Certification fee: $12.50 per doc. Payee: Clerk of Quarter Sessions. Business checks accepted; no personal. No credit cards accepted. Prepayment required. Mail requests: SASE required.

Criminal Name Search: Access: Mail, fax, in person, online. Both court and visitors may perform in person name searches. Search fee: $3.00 per name. Required to search: name, years to search, DOB; also helpful: address, race, sex. Criminal records on computer and microfiche from 1969, archived from 1800s; has case records back to late 1980s. Mail turnaround time 2-3 weeks. Public use terminal has crim records back to 1969. Search dockets online free at www.courts.phila.gov/casesearch/ back to 1968. Online results show name, DOB.

Municipal Court - Civil 34 S 11th St, Judgments & Petitions, Philadelphia, PA 19107; 215-686-7950, 7989; fax: 215-686-7575; 9AM-4PM (EST). *Civil Actions under $10,000, Eviction, Small Claims.* http://fjd.phila.gov

General Information: Info here is for the Municipal Court which has Active cases only; inactive cases with the Prothonotary ofc. Will not fax documents. Court makes copy: $.50 per page. Self serve copy: same. Certification fee: $29.70. Payee: Municipal Court. Cashiers checks and money orders accepted. Major credit cards accepted in person only. Prepayment required. Mail requests: SASE required.

Civil Name Search: Access: Phone, mail, in person, online. Only the court performs in person name searches; visitors may not. No search fee. Required to search: name, years to search; also helpful- address. Civil records on computer from 1969. Note: Court will search 1 or 2 names over the phone only - it is best to have a case number. Mail turnaround time 1-2 days. Prothonotary in Rm #262 where you may find a public access terminal. Access Muni court dockets online free at http://fjdclaims.phila.gov/phmuni/login.do or you may register for a username and password.

Municipal Court - Misdemeanor 1301 Filbert St, #310, Criminal Justice Ctr, Philadelphia, PA 19107; 215-683-7518; fax: 215 683-7208; 8:30AM-5PM (EST). *Misdemeanor (less than 5 years), Felony Hearings.* http://courts.phila.gov./municipal/criminal/

General Information: All closed misdemeanor cases held by Clerk of Quarter Sessions - see separate listing. Info Desk phone- 215-683-7004. Online identifiers in results same as on public terminal. Will not fax documents. Court makes copy: $.25 per page for active cases. Self serve copies available in the attorney review rm. Get copies of closed Muni misdemeanor records at the Clerk of Quarter Sessions Court. Certification fee: $10.00 per doc. No personal checks accepted. Major credit cards accepted. Prepayment required.

Criminal Name Search: Access: In person, online. Both court and visitors may perform in person name searches. Required to search: name, years to search, address, DOB, signed release. Criminal records computerized from 1969. Note: Access disposed cases at Clerk of Quarter Sessions. Public use terminal has crim records back to open cases only. Public terminal located at 2nd Fl Information Counter, or in #310. Access

docket info free at http://ujsportal.pacourts.us/DocketSheets/MC.aspx. Online results show middle initial, DOB.

Register of Wills City Hall, Rm 180, Broad and Markets Sts, Philadelphia, PA 19107; 215-686-6250; fax: 215-686-6268; 8:30AM-5PM (EST). *Probate.* http://secureprod.phila.gov/wills/default.aspx

General Information: Search marriage records free back to 1995 at http://secureprod.phila.gov/wills/marriagesearch.aspx. For marriage records call 215-686-2234.

Pike County

Court of Common Pleas 412 Broad St, Milford, PA 18337; 570-296-7231; fax: 570-296-1931; 8:30AM-4:30PM (EST). *Felony, Misdemeanor, Civil, Eviction.* www.pikepa.org

General Information: No juvenile, adoption, sealed records released. Will not fax documents. Court makes copy: $.50 per page; $5.00 for docket entries. Self serve copy: $.50 per page. Certification fee: $5.25 per page. Payee: Prothonotary. Personal checks not exceeding $10.00 accepted. No credit cards accepted. Prepayment required. Mail requests: SASE required.

Civil Name Search: Access: Phone, mail, online, in person. Both court and visitors may perform in person name searches. Search fee: $5.00 per name. Civil records on files for 100 yrs, computerized since 1995. Note: The court will only do searches from 01/95 forward. Mail turnaround time varies. Civil PAT goes back to 1995. Online access is by subscription from private company-Infocon at www.infoconcountyaccess.com, 814-472-6066. See note in court summary section. Images shown.

Criminal Name Search: Access: Phone, mail, online, in person. Both court and visitors may perform in person name searches. Search fee: $5.00 per name. Criminal records on files for 100 yrs, computerized since 1995. Note: The court will only do searches from 01/95 forward. Mail turnaround time varies. Criminal PAT goes back to same as civil. Internet access to court records is by subscription from a private company-Infocon at www.infoconcountyaccess.com, 814-472-6066. See note at beginning of section. Images shown. Also, search dockets online free at http://ujsportal.pacourts.us/DocketSheets/CP.aspx back to 1993. Online results show middle initial, DOB.

Register of Wills Administration Building, 506 Broad St, Milford, PA 18337; 570-296-3508; fax: 570-296-3514; 8:30AM-4:30PM (EST). *Probate.* www.pikepa.org/regwill.html

General Information: Online access available by subscription from private company-Infocon at www.infoconcountyaccess.com, 814-472-6066. See note at beginning of section. Images not shown.

Potter County

Court of Common Pleas 1 E 2nd St, Rm 23, Coudersport, PA 16915; 814-274-9740; fax: 814-274-3361; 8:30AM-4:30PM (EST). *Felony, Misdemeanor, Civil, Eviction.*

General Information: No juvenile records released. Will fax documents at no charge, but only a limited number of pages. Court makes copy: $.50 per page. Self serve copy: $.25 per page. Certification fee: $5.00; Exemplification fee-$24.00. Payee: Prothonotary & Clerk of Courts. Personal checks accepted, credit cards are not. Prepayment required. Mail requests: SASE required.

Civil Name Search: Access: Phone, fax, mail, in person, online. Both court and visitors may perform in person name searches. No search fee. Civil records on dockets from early 1833 to 11/97; on computer since 11/97. Mail turnaround time 2 weeks, phone turnaround immediate unless a lengthy search. Civil PAT goes back to 11/1997. Online access is by subscription from private company-Infocon at www.infoconcountyaccess.com, 814-472-6066. See note in court summary section. Images shown.

Criminal Name Search: Access: Phone, fax, mail, in person, online. Both court and visitors may perform in person name searches. No search fee. Required to search: name, years to search, DOB. Criminal records on card index from 1983 to 6/27/97; on computer since 6/27/97; archived since 1839. Mail turnaround time 2 weeks; phone turnaround immediate unless a lengthy search. Criminal PAT goes back to 6/27/1997. Search dockets online free at http://ujsportal.pacourts.us/DocketSheets/CP.aspx back to 1992. Online results show name, DOB.

Register of Wills 1 N Main St, Coudersport, PA 16915; 814-274-8370; fax: 814-274-3360; 8:30AM-4:30PM (EST). *Probate.*

General Information: Online access available by subscription from private company-Landex at www.landex.com, 717-274-5890. Index back to 1997; images to 2003. See note at beginning of section.

Schuylkill County

Court of Common Pleas - Civil 401 N 2nd St, Pottsville, PA 17901-2528; 570-628-1270; fax: 570-628-1261; 8:30AM-4:30PM (EST). *Civil, Eviction.* www.co.schuylkill.pa.us

General Information: Online identifiers in results same as on public terminal. No master reports or sealed records released. Will not fax documents. Court makes copy: $.25 per page. Self serve copy: same. Certification fee: $7.00 per page. Payee: Prothonotary. Personal checks accepted, credit cards are not. Prepayment required. Mail requests: SASE requested.

Civil Name Search: Access: Mail, in person, online. Both court and visitors may perform in person name searches. Search fee: $12.00 per name. Civil records (suits) on computer from 1989, judgments on computer from 1999 and on dockets from 1800s. Mail turnaround time 1 day. Public use terminal has civil records back to 1989. Judgments on public terminal go back to 1999. Access civil court records and judgments free at www.co.schuylkill.pa.us/info/Civil/Inquiry/Search.csp.

Court of Common Pleas - Criminal 401 N 2nd St, Pottsville, PA 17901; 570-628-1133; fax: 570-628-1169; 8:30AM-4:30PM (EST). *Felony, Misdemeanor.* www.co.schuylkill.pa.us

General Information: No juvenile records released. No fee to fax documents. Court makes copy: $.25 per page. Certification fee: $10.00 per doc plus copy fee. Payee: Clerk of Courts. Business checks accepted. No credit cards accepted. Prepayment required. Mail requests: SASE not required.

Criminal Name Search: Access: Fax, mail, in person, online. Both court and visitors may perform in person name searches. Search fee: $11.50 per name. Required to search: name, years to search, DOB; also helpful: SSN. Criminal records computerized from 4/88, on dockets from 1800s. Mail turnaround time same day. Public use terminal has crim records back to 1988. Search dockets online free at http://ujsportal.pacourts.us/DocketSheets/CP.aspx back to 1974. Online results show name, DOB.

Register of Wills Courthouse 401 N 2nd St, Pottsville, PA 17901-2520; 570-628-1377; fax: 570-628-1384; 8:30AM-4:30PM (EST). *Probate.* www.co.schuylkill.pa.us/Offices/RegisterOfWills/index.asp

General Information: For a marriage index for free go to www.co.schuylkill.pa.us/Offices/RegisterOfWills/index.asp. Also at this court is birth and death records from 1893-1905.

Snyder County

Court of Common Pleas - Criminal/Civil PO Box 217, 9 W Market St, Snyder County Courthouse, Middleburg, PA 17842; 570-837-4202; fax: 570-837-4275; 8:30AM-4:30PM (EST). *Felony, Misdemeanor, Civil, Eviction.* www.snydercounty.org/Pages/default.aspx

General Information: No juvenile records released. Will fax documents to local or toll-free number for $2.00 first page and $1.00 ea add'l. Court makes copy: $.35 per page. Self serve copy: same. Certification fee: $6.00 per cert plus copy fee. Payee: Prothonotary or Clerk of Courts. No out-of-state personal checks. No credit cards accepted. Prepayment required. Mail requests: SASE required.

Civil Name Search: Access: Mail, in person. Both court and visitors may perform in person name searches. No search fee. Civil records on dockets from 1855, some on microfilm, computerized since 2001. Mail turnaround time 2 days. Civil PAT goes back to 5/2001.

Criminal Name Search: Access: Mail, in person, online. Both court and visitors may perform in person name searches. No search fee. Criminal docket index from 1855, some on microfilm, computerized since 2001. Mail turnaround time 2 days. Criminal PAT goes back to same as civil. Search dockets online free at http://ujsportal.pacourts.us/DocketSheets/CP.aspx back to 1970. Online results show name, DOB.

Register of Wills County Courthouse, 9 W Market St, PO Box 217, Middleburg, PA 17842; 570-837-4224; fax: 570-837-4299; 8:30AM-4PM (EST). *Probate.* www.snydercounty.org/Pages/default.aspx

Somerset County

Court of Common Pleas - Civil 111 E Union St, #165, Somerset, PA 15501; 814-445-1428; fax: 814-444-9270; 8:30AM-4PM (EST). *Civil, Eviction, Divorce.* www.co.somerset.pa.us

General Information: No commitment records released. Will fax documents to local or toll-free number. Court makes copy: $.25 per page. Self serve copy: same. No certification fee. Payee: Prothonotary of Somerset Co. Business checks accepted. No credit cards accepted. Prepayment required.

Civil Name Search: Access: In person only. Both court and visitors may perform in person name searches. No search fee. Civil records on computer from 1/92, on microfiche from 1920 to 1999, on dockets (Russell System for all other years prior to 1992. Public use terminal has civil records back to 1992. Court calendars (no names) and daily schedules free at www.co.somerset.pa.us. Also, judgments may appear on the Landex system at www.landex.com/remote/ - registration and password required. Court calendars free at www.co.somerset.pa.us/courtcalendar/ but no name searching.

Court of Common Pleas - Criminal 111 E Union St, #110, Somerset, PA 15501; 814-445-1435; fax: 814-444-5851; 8:30AM-4PM (EST). *Felony, Misdemeanor.* www.co.somerset.pa.us

General Information: When faxing, send to the attention of the Clerk of Courts. No impounded records released. Will fax documents to local or toll-free number. Court makes copy: $.25 per page. Certification fee: $1.00. Payee: Clerk of Courts. Personal checks accepted, credit cards are not. Will bill copy fees. Mail requests: SASE not required.

Criminal Name Search: Access: Phone, mail, in person, online. Both court and visitors may perform in person name searches. Search fee: $5.00 per name. Required to search: name, years to search, DOB; also helpful: SSN. Criminal records on microfilm from 1920, archive dates uncertain, computerized since 1996. Mail turnaround time same day; phone turnaround immediate. Public use terminal has crim records back to 1996. Search dockets online free at http://ujsportal.pacourts.us/DocketSheets/CP.aspx back to 1990. Court calendars free at www.co.somerset.pa.us/courtcalendar/ but no name searching. Online results show name, DOB.

Register of Wills 111 E Union St, #145, Somerset, PA 15501-1416; 814-445-1548; fax: 814-445-1542; 8:30AM-4PM (EST). *Probate.* www.co.somerset.pa.us/county.asp?deptnum=71

Sullivan County

Court of Common Pleas - Criminal/Civil Sullivan County Courthouse, 245 Muncy Street, Laporte, PA 18626; 570-946-7351; probate phone: 570-946-7351; fax: 570-946-7105; 8:30AM-4PM (EST). *Felony, Misdemeanor, Civil, Eviction, Probate.* www.sullivancounty-pa.org/

General Information: The Register of Wills has access to data is by subscription at www.landex.com/remote/. No juvenile records released. Will fax documents $3.00 per page. Court makes copy: $2.00 per page. Self serve copy: $.25 per page. Certification fee: $3.00 for the first 4 pages, $.25 ea add'l. Payee: Prothonotary or Clerk of Courts. Personal checks accepted, credit cards are not. Prepayment required.

Civil Name Search: Access: In person only. Visitors must perform in person searches themselves. Civil records on dockets from 1847 to present and on computer from 8/2000. Civil PAT goes back to 8/7/2000.

Criminal Name Search: Access: In person, online. Visitors must perform in person searches themselves. Required to search: name, years to search; also helpful: SSN. Criminal docket index from 1847 to present and on computer from 8/2000. Criminal PAT goes back to same as civil. search dockets online free at http://ujsportal.pacourts.us/DocketSheets/CP.aspx back to 1999. Online results show name, DOB.

Susquehanna County

Court of Common Pleas - Civil Susquehanna Courthouse, PO Box 218, Montrose, PA 18801; 570-278-4600 x121;; 8:30AM-4:30PM (EST). *Civil, Eviction.*

General Information: No juvenile records released. Will not fax documents. Court makes copy: $.25 per page. Self serve copy: same. Certification fee: $4.50 per cert. Payee: Prothonotary. Personal checks accepted, credit cards are not. Prepayment required. Mail requests: SASE required.

Civil Name Search: Access: In person, online. Visitors must perform in person searches themselves. Civil records on dockets from 1800s. Note: Court personnel will not perform names searches for the public. Mail turnaround time usually same day. Public use terminal has civil records back to 8/1996. Online access is by subscription from private company-Infocon at www.infoconcountyaccess.com, 814-472-6066. See note in court summary section. Images not shown.

Court of Common Pleas - Criminal PO Box 218, 11 Maple St, Susquehanna Courthouse, Montrose, PA 18801; 570-278-4600 x321, x320, x323; fax: 570-278-4191; 8:30AM-4:30PM (EST). *Felony, Misdemeanor.* www.susquehannacountyclerkofcourts.com/

General Information: No juvenile records released. Will not fax out documents. Court makes copy: $.25 per page. Certification fee: $4.50 per cert. Cert and copy fees may be increased early 2009. Payee: Clerk of Courts. Personal checks accepted, credit cards are not. Prepayment required. Mail requests: SASE required.

Criminal Name Search: Access: Mail, in person, online. Both court and visitors may perform in person name searches. Search fee: $5.00 per name per 5 years. Required to search: name, years to search, DOB, SSN. Criminal docket index from 1800s, archived from 1971, computerized since 8/96. Mail turnaround time 1-2 days. Public use terminal has crim records back to 1996. Clerk will verify personal identifiers of public terminal result. Search dockets free at http://ujsportal.pacourts.us/DocketSheets/CP.aspx back to 1996. Online results show middle initial, DOB.

Register of Wills PO Box 218, 105 Maple St, County Courthouse, Montrose, PA 18801; 570-278-4600 X113; fax: 570-278-2963; 8:30AM-4:30PM (EST). *Probate.*
www.susqco.com/subsites/gov/pages/regrec/regrechome.htm
General Information: Access to data is by subscription at www.landex.com/remote/.

Tioga County

Court of Common Pleas - Criminal/Civil 116 Main St, Wellsboro, PA 16901; 570-724-9281; fax: 570-724-2986; 9AM-4:30PM (EST). *Felony, Misdemeanor, Civil, Eviction.*
www.tiogacountypa.us/Departments/Prothonotary_Clerk_of_Courts/Pages/Prothonotary.aspx
General Information: No mental health, juvenile, abuse (14 or younger) records released. Will not fax documents. Court makes copy: $.25 per page. Self serve copy: same. Certification fee: $5.00. Payee: Tioga County Prothonotary. Personal checks accepted, credit cards are not. Prepayment required. Mail requests: SASE required for criminal.
Civil Name Search: Access: In person only. Visitors must perform in person searches themselves. Required to search: name. Civil records on dockets from 1827; computerized records since 1997. Civil PAT goes back to 1997.
Criminal Name Search: Access: Mail, in person, online. Both court and visitors may perform in person name searches. Search fee: $5.00 per name and $1.00 for each file found. Required to search: name, years to search, signed release. Criminal docket index from 1827; computerized records since 1965. Mail turnaround time same day when possible. Criminal PAT goes back to 1965. Search dockets online free statewide at http://ujsportal.pacourts.us/DocketSheets/CP.aspx back to 1975. Online results show name, DOB.

Register of Wills 116 Main St, Wellsboro, PA 16901; 570-724-9260; ; 9AM-4:30PM (EST). *Probate.*
General Information: Online access to wills is available through a private company at www.landex.com/remote/. Fee is $.20 per minute and $.50 per fax page. Images and wills go back to 2/1999.

Union County

Court of Common Pleas - Criminal/Civil 103 S 2nd St, Lewisburg, PA 17837; 570-524-8751; fax: 570-524-8628; 8:30AM-4:30PM (EST). *Felony, Misdemeanor, Civil, Eviction.*
www.unionco.org
General Information: Online identifiers in results same as on public terminal. No juvenile records released. Will not fax documents. Court makes copy: $.25 per page. Self serve copy: same. Certification fee: $6.50 per cert; $20.00 for exemplification. Payee: Prothonotary or Clerk of Courts. Personal checks or money order accepted. No credit cards accepted. Prepayment required. Mail requests: SASE required.
Civil Name Search: Access: Phone, mail, in person. Visitors must perform in person searches themselves. No search fee. Civil records on computer from 1988, on microfiche (orphans court 1813 to 1988, marriage 1885 to 2001), on dockets from 1800s to 1988. Mail turnaround time same day schedule permitting. Civil PAT goes back to 1988.
Criminal Name Search: Access: Phone, mail, in person, online. Visitors must perform in person searches themselves. No search fee. Criminal records computerized from 1988, on dockets from 1800s to 1988. Mail turnaround time same day if possible. Criminal PAT goes back to same as civil. Search dockets online free at http://ujsportal.pacourts.us/DocketSheets/CP.aspx back to 1988. Online results show name, DOB.

Register of Wills 103 S 2nd St, Lewisburg, PA 17837-1996; 570-524-8761; ; 8:30AM-4:30PM (EST). *Probate.*
www.unioncountypa.org/residents/government/courts/wills/default.asp

Venango County

Court of Common Pleas - Criminal/Civil Venango County Courthouse, 1168 Liberty St, Franklin, PA 16323; 814-432-9577; criminal phone: 814-432-9574; civil phone: 814-432-9577; fax: 814-432-9579; 8:30AM-4:30PM (EST). *Felony, Misdemeanor, Civil, Eviction.*
www.co.venango.pa.us
General Information: Online identifiers in results same as on public terminal. No juvenile records released. Fee to fax out file $1.00 per page. Court makes copy: $.50 per page. Self serve copy: same. Certification fee: $7.50 per case plus copy fee. Payee: Clerk of Courts. Personal checks accepted, credit cards are not. Prepayment required. Mail requests: SASE required.
Civil Name Search: Access: Mail, in person. Both court and visitors may perform in person name searches. Search fee: $7.00 per name. Civil records on computer from 1993, on dockets from 1800s on microfiche. Mail turnaround time same day. Civil PAT goes back to 1993.

Criminal Name Search: Access: Mail, in person, online. Both court and visitors may perform in person name searches. Search fee: $7.00 per name. Required to search: name, years to search, DOB; also helpful: SSN. Criminal records computerized from 1993, on dockets from 1800s. Mail turnaround time same as civil. Criminal PAT goes back to same as civil. Search dockets online free at http://ujsportal.pacourts.us/DocketSheets/CP.aspx back to 1975. Online results show name, DOB.

Register of Wills/Recorder of Deeds PO Box 831, 1168 Liberty St, Franklin, PA 16323; 814-432-9539; probate phone: 814-432-9538; fax: 814-432-9569; 8:30AM-4:30PM (EST). *Probate, Estate.*
General Information: Clerk also holds recorded land records.

Warren County

Court of Common Pleas - Criminal/Civil 204 4th Ave, Warren, PA 16365; 814-728-3440; fax: 814-728-3459; 8:30AM-4:30PM (EST). *Felony, Misdemeanor, Civil, Eviction.*
www.warrenforestcourt.org/
General Information: Search fee includes civil and criminal indexes if you ask for both. Also, Hickory Street Annex is located at 333 Hickory. No juvenile records released. No fee to fax back documents. Court makes copy: $.25 per page. Certification fee: $4.00 per cert. Payee: Prothonotary or Clerk of Courts. Business checks accepted. No credit cards accepted. Prepayment required. Mail requests: SASE required.
Civil Name Search: Access: Fax, mail, in person. Both court and visitors may perform in person name searches. Search fee: $20.00 per name. Civil records on computer from 2000, on dockets from 1800s. Mail turnaround time 2 days. Civil PAT goes back to 2000.
Criminal Name Search: Access: Fax, mail, in person, online. Both court and visitors may perform in person name searches. Search fee: $20.00 per name. Required to search: name, years to search; also helpful: DOB. Criminal records computerized from 2000, on dockets from 1800s. Mail turnaround time 2 days. Criminal PAT goes back to same as civil. Search dockets online free at http://ujsportal.pacourts.us/DocketSheets/CP.aspx back to 1999. Online results show name, DOB.

Register of Wills 204 4th Ave, Courthouse, Warren, PA 16365; 814-728-3430; fax: 814-728-3476; 8:30AM-4:30PM (EST). *Probate.*

Washington County

Court of Common Pleas - Civil 1 S Main St, #1001, Washington, PA 15301; 724-228-6770; fax: 724-229-5913; 9AM-4:30PM (EST). *Civil.*
www.co.washington.pa.us
General Information: Court personnel will not perform name searches except if for a change of name filing. But personnel will give assistance on how to do the search. Will not fax documents. Court makes copy: $1.50 per page. Self serve copy: $.25 per page. Certification fee: $4.50. Payee: Prothonotary. Only cashiers checks and money orders accepted. Checks from attorneys accepted. No credit cards accepted. Prepayment required.
Civil Name Search: Access: In person, online. Visitors must perform in person searches themselves. Civil records on computer from 1988, prior on dockets to 1800s. Public use terminal has civil records back to 1988. Access to Prothonotary civil records including also orphans court is by subscription; enroll form at www.co.washington.pa.us/downloadpage.aspx?menuDept=28. Also, records available on Common Pleas Ct database at www.co.washington.pa.us/wccourtdocuments/code/login.asp. Registration, username, and password required.

Court of Common Pleas - Criminal Courthouse, #1005, 1 S Main St, Washington, PA 15301; 724-228-6787; fax: 724-250-4658; 9AM-4:30PM (EST). *Felony, Misdemeanor, Eviction.*
www.co.washington.pa.us
General Information: Online identifiers in results same as on public terminal. No juvenile records released. Will not fax documents. Court makes copy: $.25 per page. Self serve copy: same. Certification fee: $10.50. Payee: Clerk of Courts. Personal checks accepted. Major credit cards accepted. In person only. Prepayment required. Mail requests: SASE required.
Criminal Name Search: Access: Mail, in person, online. Both court and visitors may perform in person name searches. Search fee: $10.50 per name. Required to search: name, years to search, DOB; also helpful: address, SSN. Criminal records on computer since 10/87, prior on dockets, archived from 1785. Mail turnaround time over 1 week. Public use terminal has crim records back to 1987. Search dockets online free at http://ujsportal.pacourts.us/DocketSheets/CP.aspx back to 1987. Also, records available on Common Pleas Ct database at www.co.washington.pa.us/wccourtdocuments/code/login.asp. Registration, username, and password required. Online results show middle initial, DOB.

Register of Wills 1 S Main St, #1002, Courthouse, Washington, PA 15301; 724-228-6775; fax: 724-250-4821; 9AM-4:30PM (EST). *Probate.*
www.washingtoncourts.us/pages/roRegisterOfWills.aspx

General Information: Wills available on Common Pleas Ct database at www.co.washington.pa.us/wccourtdocuments/code/login.asp. Registration, username, and password required.

Wayne County

Court of Common Pleas - Criminal/Civil 925 Court St, Honesdale, PA 18431; 570-253-5970 X1210; fax: 570-253-0687; 8:30AM-4:30PM (EST). *Felony, Misdemeanor, Civil, Eviction.*

General Information: Juvenile records not released. Will not fax documents. Court makes copy: $.50 per page. Self serve copy: same. No certification fee. Payee: Wayne County Prothonotary. Personal checks accepted, credit cards are not. Prepayment required.

Civil Name Search: Access: In person only. Visitors must perform in person searches themselves. Civil records on daily docket entries, computerized since 1996. Civil PAT goes back to 1996.

Criminal Name Search: Access: In person, online. Visitors must perform in person searches themselves. Criminal records on daily docket entries, computerized since 1996. Criminal PAT goes back to same as civil. Search dockets online free at http://ujsportal.pacourts.us/DocketSheets/CP.aspx back to 1995. Online results show name, DOB.

Register of Wills 925 Court St, Honesdale, PA 18431; 570-253-5970; probate phone: x4040;; 8:30AM-4:30PM (EST). *Probate.*

Westmoreland County

Court of Common Pleas - Civil 2 N Main St,, Rm 501, Courthouse Sq, Greensburg, PA 15601; 724-830-3502; fax: 724-830-3517; 8:30AM-4PM (EST). *Civil, Eviction.* www.co.westmoreland.pa.us/westmoreland/cwp/view.asp?a=1425&q=620994&westmorelandNav=|33740|

General Information: Online identifiers in results same as on public terminal. No mental health records released. Will fax documents for $3.00 1st page, $1.00 each add'l. Court makes copy: $.50 per page. Computer printout $1.00 per page. Certification fee: $6.00 per cert plus copy fee. Payee: Prothonotary. Business checks accepted; no personal checks. No credit cards accepted. Prepayment required.

Civil Name Search: Access: Online, in person. Visitors must perform in person searches themselves. Civil records on computer from 9/85, on dockets from 1700s. Public use terminal has civil records back to 1985. Access civil court dockets back to 1985 free at http://westmorelandweb400.us:8088/EGSPublicAccess.htm. Also, search Register of Wills and marriages free back to 1986. Access to full remote online system has $100 setup (no set-up if accessed via Internet) plus $20 monthly minimum. System includes civil, criminal, Prothonotary indexes and recorder data. For info, call 724-830-3874, or click on "e-services" at website.

Court of Common Pleas - Criminal 2 N. main Street, Greensburg, PA 15601-1168; 724-830-3732; fax: 724-850-3979; 8:30AM-4PM (EST). *Felony, Misdemeanor.* www.co.westmoreland.pa.us/westmoreland/cwp/view.asp?a=1425&q=620987&westmorelandNav=|33740|

General Information: No juvenile records released. Will fax documents $10.00 per doc. Court makes copy: $1.00 per page. Self serve copy: same. Certification fee: $10.00per cert. Payee: Clerk of Courts. Attorney's checks accepted. Major credit cards accepted. Prepayment required. Mail requests: SASE not required.

Criminal Name Search: Access: Fax, mail, online, in person. Both court and visitors may perform in person name searches. Search fee: $20.00 per name. Required to search: name, years to search, signed release; also helpful: DOB, SSN. Criminal records computerized from 1941, on microfiche from 1793 to 1950, archived from 1773. Mail turnaround time 7-10 working days. Public use terminal has crim records back to 1941. Search dockets online free at http://ujsportal.pacourts.us/DocketSheets/CP.aspx back to 1971. Online results show name, DOB.

Register of Wills 2 N Main St, #301, Greensburg, PA 15601; 724-830-3177; fax: 724-850-3976; 8:30AM-4PM (EST). *Probate.* www.co.westmoreland.pa.us/westmoreland/cwp/view.asp?a=1453&Q=576845&westmorelandNav=|33740|

General Information: Search estate indices free back to 1986 at http://westmorelandweb400.us:8088/EGSPublicAccess.htm; marriage index online back to 1885. Fuller data requires registration and fees. Office has births/deaths 1893-1905. Estates start 1773.

Wyoming County

Court of Common Pleas - Criminal/Civil Wyoming County Courthouse, Tunkhannock, PA 18657; 570-836-3200 X232-234; fax: 570-996-0193; 8:30AM-4PM (EST). *Felony, Misdemeanor, Civil, Eviction.*

General Information: No juvenile records released. Will not fax documents. Court makes copy: $.25 per page. Self serve copy: same.

Certification fee: $10.00. Payee: Prothonotary or Clerk of Courts. Personal checks accepted, credit cards are not. Prepayment required.

Civil Name Search: Access: In person only. Visitors must perform in person searches themselves. Civil records on dockets from 1800s. Civil PAT goes back to 1996.

Criminal Name Search: Access: In person, online. Visitors must perform in person searches themselves. Required to search: name, years to search; also helpful: DOB. Criminal docket index from 1800s. Criminal PAT goes back to same as civil. Search dockets online free at http://ujsportal.pacourts.us/DocketSheets/CP.aspx back to 1995. Online results show name, DOB.

Register of Wills Wyoming County Courthouse, 1 Courthouse Sq, Tunkhannock, PA 18657; 570-836-3200; fax: 570-996-5053; 8:30AM-4PM (EST). *Probate.*

General Information: Also, 570-996-2237.

York County

Court of Common Pleas - Civil York County Courthouse, 45 N George St, York, PA 17401; 717-771-9611; fax: 717-771-3252; 8:30AM-4:30PM (EST). *Civil.*

General Information: No mental health records released. Will not fax documents. Court makes copy: $1.00 per page. Self serve copy: $.50 per page. Certification fee: $6.00 per page. Payee: Prothonotary. Only cashiers checks and money orders accepted. No credit cards accepted. Prepayment required.

Civil Name Search: Access: In person only. Visitors must perform in person searches themselves. Civil records on computer from mid-1988, on dockets from 1800s, archived from mid-1700s. Public use terminal has civil records back to mid-1988.

Court of Common Pleas - Criminal 45 N George St, York County Courthouse, York, PA 17401; 717-771-9612; fax: 717-771-9096; 8:15AM-4:30PM (EST). *Felony, Misdemeanor.* www.york-county.org/departments/courts/YCCOC/index.htm

General Information: Direct search requests to the attention of Beth Ruth. Online identifiers in results same as on public terminal. No sex crime, juvenile records released. Will fax back documents - must be prepaid and pre-approved. Court makes copy: $.55 per page. Self serve copy: $.25 per page. Self serve copier is in law library. Certification fee: $10.00 per doc includes some copies; $.55 each for add'l pages. Payee: Clerk of Courts. Personal checks accepted. MC/Discover cards accepted. Prepayment required. Mail requests: SASE required.

Criminal Name Search: Access: Fax, mail, online, in person. Both court and visitors may perform in person name searches. Search fee: $11.00 per name. Required to search: name, approximate date to search. Criminal records computerized from 1986, on dockets from 1942, archived from 1700s. Mail turnaround time 1-2 weeks. Public use terminal has crim records back to 1986. Several public terminals available. Search dockets online free at http://ujsportal.pacourts.us/DocketSheets/CP.aspx back to 1969. Online results show middle initial, DOB.

Register of Wills York County Judicial Center, 45 N George St, York, PA 17401; 717-771-9263; fax: 717-771-4678; 8AM-4:15PM (EST). *Probate.* www.york-county.org/departments/courts/wills.htm

General Information: Access to data is by subscription at www.landex.com/remote/.

Rhode Island

Time Zone:	EST
Capital:	Providence, Providence County
# of Counties:	5
State Web:	www.ri.gov
Court Web:	www.courts.ri.us

Administration

Court Administrator, Supreme Court, 250 Benefit St, Providence, RI, 02903; 401-222-3266, Fax: 401-222-4224.

The Supreme Court

The Rhode Island Supreme Court is the court of last resort and has absolute appellate jurisdiction over questions of law and equity, supervisory powers over other state courts.

The Rhode Island Courts

Court	Type	How Organized	Jurisdiction Highpoints
Superior*	General	4 Courts in 4 Divisions	Felony, Civil
District*	Limited	4 Courts in 6 Divisions	Misdemeanor, Civil, Small Claims, Eviction
Municipal	Limited	16 Courts	Misdemeanor, Traffic, Ordinance
Family	Limited	4 Courts	Domestic, Juvenile, Divorce
Traffic Tribunal	Special		Traffic

* = profiled in this book

Details on the Court Structure

The **Superior Court** has original jurisdiction in all felony proceedings, in civil cases where the amount in controversy exceeds $10,000, and in equity matters. The court has concurrent jurisdiction with the District Court in civil matters when the amount in controversy is between $5,000 and $10,000.

The **District Court** has exclusive jurisdiction of all civil actions at law wherein the amount in controversy is under $5,000.

Rhode Island has five counties but only four Superior/District Court Locations— 2nd-Newport, 3rd-Kent, 4th-Washington, and 6th-Providence/Bristol Districts. Bristol and Providence counties are completely merged at the Providence location.. For questions regarding the Superior Courts, telephone 401-222-2622. For questions regarding the District Courts, telephone 401-458-5201.

Probate is handled by the Town Clerk at the 39 cities and towns, not at the courts. The contact information is shown herein. The **Traffic Tribunal** has original jurisdiction over civil traffic offenses committed in Rhode Island, including breathalyzer refusals.

Record Searching Facts You Need to Know

Fees and Record Searching Tips

The copy fee has been set at $.15 per page; one District Court refuses to make copies – you must do yourself. Most courts will not perform a name search. All courts permit the public to do its own in-person searching of Supreme, District, Superior, and Family Court cases. Throughput dates of the records indices vary.

Online Access is Moderate

The Rhode Island Judiciary offers free access to an index of county criminal cases statewide at http://courtconnect.courts.state.ri.us. The year of birth is shown on results. The site provides a strong disclaimer that the search is provided only as an informational service and should not be relied upon as an official record of the court. The disclaimer also states that the court employees will not confirm case content referenced for the Web service by telephone. There is no statewide access to the other types of court records.

Bristol County

Superior & District Courts Former Bristol civil and criminal cases are handled by the Providence County courts.

Barrington Town Hall 283 County Road, Barrington, RI 02806; 401-247-1900 x4; fax: 401-247-3765; 8:30AM-4:30PM (EST). *Probate.* http://72.46.3.26/probatejudge.php

Bristol Town Hall 10 Court St, Bristol, RI 02809; 401-253-7000; fax: 401-253-2647; 8:30AM-4PM (EST). *Probate.* www.bristolri.us/

Warren Town Hall 514 Main St, Warren, RI 02885; 401-245-7340; fax: 401-245-7421; 9AM-4PM (EST). *Probate.*

Kent County

Superior Court 222 Quaker Ln, 4th Fl, Noel Judicial Complex, Warwick, RI 02886; 401-822-6900; civil phone: 401-822-6906; fax: 401-822-6905; 8:30AM-4:00PM (EST). *Felony, Civil Actions over $5,000, Family.* www.courts.ri.gov/courts/superiorcourt/default.aspx

General Information: The Family Court Division can be reached at 401-822-6725. The Superior Court has concurrent jurisdiction with the District Court on civil matters between $5,000 and $10,000. Online identifiers in results same as on public terminal. No adoption, confidential or sealed records released. Copy fee is $.20. Certification fee: $3.00 per page. Exemplified copies: $9.00 each plus cert fee. Payee: Clerk of Superior Court. Personal checks accepted, credit cards are not. Prepayment required.

Civil Name Search: Access: In person only. Visitors must perform in person searches themselves. Civil records on computer from 1987. Civil PAT goes back to 1997.

Criminal Name Search: Access: In person, online. Visitors must perform in person searches themselves. Required to search: name, years to search, signed release; also helpful: DOB. Criminal records computerized from 1987. Criminal PAT goes back to 1987. Terminal results show year of birth only. Access criminal records free at http://courtconnect.courts.state.ri.us as an informational service only; should not be relied upon as official court record. Online results include middle initial and aliases, but only birth year of DOB.

3rd Division District Court 222 Quaker Ln, 2nd Fl, Warwick, RI 02886-0107; 401-822-6750 or 401-822-6760; fax: 401-822-6755; 8:30AM-4:30PM, till 4PM in Summer (EST). *Misdemeanor, Civil Actions under $10,000, Eviction, Small Claims.* www.courts.ri.gov

General Information: Online identifiers in results same as on public terminal. No mental or sealed records released. Will not fax documents. Court makes copy: Court will not make copies. Self serve copy: $.15 per page. Certification fee: $9.00 per page. Payee: 3rd District Court. No Personal checks, Visa/MC accepted. Prepayment required.

Civil Name Search: Access: In person only. Visitors must perform in person searches themselves. Civil records 1995-2008 on index cards. Archives stored at RI Judicial Records Ctr, 1 Hill St, Pawtucket, RI 02860, 401-277-3249. Records destroyed after 10 years, but remain in computer.

Criminal Name Search: Access: In person, online. Visitors must perform in person searches themselves. Required to search: name, years to search, DOB, signed release. Criminal records 1995-1997 on index cards. Archives at RI Judicial Records Ctr. Records destroyed after 10 years, but remain in computer. Public use terminal has crim records. Terminal results show year of birth only. Access criminal records free at http://courtconnect.courts.state.ri.us as an informational service only; should not be relied upon as official court record. Online results include middle initial and aliases, but only birth year of DOB.

Coventry Town Hall 1670 Flat River Rd, Coventry, RI 02816; 401-822-9173; fax: 401-822-9132; 8:30AM-4:30PM (EST). *Probate.*

East Greenwich Town Hall PO Box 111, 125 Main St, East Greenwich, RI 02818; 401-886-8607; 8604; fax: 401-886-8625; 8:30AM-4:30PM (EST). *Probate.* www.eastgreenwichri.com/matriarch/

Warwick City Hall 3275 Post Rd, Warwick, RI 02886; 401-738-2000 (x6213); fax: 401-732-7640; 8:30AM-4:30PM (EST). *Probate.*

West Greenwich Town Hall 280 Victory Hwy, West Greenwich, RI 02817; 401-392-3800; ; 8:30AM-4PM (EST). *Probate.* www.wgtownri.org/departments/townclerk/probate.php

West Warwick Town Hall 1170 Main St, West Warwick, RI 02893-4829; 401-822-9201; fax: 401-822-9266; 8:30AM-4:30PM; 8:30AM-4PM June 1st-Labor Day (EST). *Probate.* www.westwarwickri.org/

Newport County

Superior Court Florence K Murray Judicial Complex, 45 Washington Sq, Newport, RI 02840; 401-841-8330; fax: 401-846-1673; 8:30AM-4:30PM (July and August till 4PM) (EST). *Felony, Civil over $5,000, Family.*

General Information: The Family Court Division can be reached at 401-841-8340. The Superior Court has concurrent jurisdiction with the District

Court on civil matters between $5,000 and $10,000. Online identifiers in results same as on public terminal. No child molestation or sexual assault records released. Will not fax documents. Court makes copy: $.15 per page. Certification fee: $3.00 per page. Payee: Clerk Superior Court. Personal checks accepted, credit cards are not. Prepayment required. Mail requests: SASE required.

Civil Name Search: Access: Mail, in person. Both court and visitors may perform in person name searches. Search fee: $15.00 per hour for search and review for all searches over 30 minutes. Civil records on computer from 1989. Prior records archived at Rhode Island Records Center. Mail turnaround time 1 day. Civil PAT goes back to mid 1980's.

Criminal Name Search: Access: Mail, fax, in person, online. Both court and visitors may perform in person name searches. Search fee: $15.00 per hour for search and review. Required to search: name, years to search, DOB. Criminal records computerized from 1983, index from 1968. Prior records archived at Records Center. Mail turnaround time 1 day. Criminal PAT goes back to early 1980's. Terminal results show year of birth only. Access criminal records free at http://courtconnect.courts.state.ri.us as an informational service only; should not be relied upon as official court record. Online results cannot be relied on nor accurate for background checking or employment screening and is discouraged. Online results include middle initial and aliases, but only birth year of DOB.

2nd District Court 45 Washington Sq, Newport, RI 02840; 401-841-8350;; 8:30AM-4:30PM (til 4PM-summer) (EST). *Misdemeanor, Civil Actions under $10,000, Eviction, Small Claims.*

General Information: Online identifiers in results same as on public terminal. No juvenile, family court, sealed, expunged or ordered by judge or adoption records released. Will not fax documents. Court makes copy: $.15 per page. Self serve copy: same. Certification fee: none. Payee: 2nd District Court. No Personal checks, Visa/MC accepted. Prepayment required.

Civil Name Search: Access: In person only. Visitors must perform in person searches themselves. Civil index on cards for past 3 years, prior archived at Pawtucket Judicial Records Center. Civil PAT goes to 1999.

Criminal Name Search: Access: In person, online. Visitors must perform in person searches themselves. Required to search: name. Overall records from 1999-2002. Computerized records from 1999-2004. Criminal PAT goes back to 1999. Clerk will assist. Terminal results show year of birth only. Access criminal records free at http://courtconnect.courts.state.ri.us as an informational service only; should not be relied upon as official court record. Online results include middle initial and aliases, but only birth year of DOB.

Jamestown Town Hall 93 Narragansett Ave, Jamestown, RI 02835; 401-423-7200; fax: 401-423-7230; 8AM-4:30PM (EST). *Probate.*

General Information: Court held on first Wed. of every month at 2PM.

Little Compton Probate Court 40 Commons, PO Box 226, Little Compton, RI 02837; 401-635-4400; fax: 401-635-2470; 8AM-4PM (EST). *Probate.*

Middletown Town Hall 350 E Main Rd, Middletown, RI 02842; 401-847-0009; fax: 401-845-0406; 8AM-4PM (EST). *Probate, Traffic, Ordinance.* www.middletownri.com/

Newport City Hall 43 Broadway, Newport, RI 02840; 401-845-5349; fax: 401-849-8757; 8:30AM-4:30PM (EST). *Probate.* www.cityofnewport.com/departments/city-clerk/probate.cfm

Portsmouth Town Hall 2200 E Main Rd, Portsmouth, RI 02871; 401-683-2101; 8:30AM-4:30PM (EST). *Probate.* www.portsmouthri.com/clerk/#probate

Tiverton Town Hall 343 Highland Rd, Tiverton, RI 02878; 401-625-6703; fax: 401-625-6705; 8:30AM-4PM (EST). *Probate.*

Providence County

Providence/Bristol Superior Court 250 Benefit St, Providence, RI 02903; 401-222-3250;; 8:30AM-4:30PM (EST). *Felony, Civil Actions over $5,000.*

General Information: All civil and criminal cases for Bristol County are handled here. The Family Court Division can be reached at 401-45802200. The Superior Court has concurrent jurisdiction with the District Court on civil matters between $5,000 and $10,000. Online identifiers in results same as on public terminal. No adoption, confidential or sealed records released. Will not fax documents. Copy fee is $.20. Certification fee: $3.00 per page. Payee: Providence Superior Court. Personal checks accepted, credit cards are not. Prepayment required.

Civil Name Search: Access: Phone, mail, in person. Both court and visitors may perform in person name searches. Search fee: None; only one name may be requested over phone. Civil records on computer since 1983. Mail turnaround time 7-10 days by mail. Civil PAT goes back to 1992.

Criminal Name Search: Access: In person, online. Both court and visitors may perform in person name searches. Required to search: name, years to search, DOB. Criminal records on computer since 1983. Criminal

PAT goes back to same as civil. Terminal results show year of birth only. Access criminal records free at http://courtconnect.courts.state.ri.us as an informational service only; should not be relied upon as official court record. Online results cannot be relied on nor accurate for background checking or employment screening and is discouraged. Online results include middle initial and aliases, but only birth year of DOB.

6th Division District Court 1 Dorrance Plaza, 2nd Fl, Judicial Complex, Providence, RI 02903; 401-458-5400; criminal: x1; civil: x2;; 8:30AM-4PM (EST). *Misdemeanor, Civil Actions under $10,000, Eviction, Small Claims.*
General Information: Online identifiers in results same as on public terminal. No adoption, confidential or sealed records released. Court makes copy: $.15 per page. Certification fee: $1.50 per doc. Payee: 6th Division District Court. No personal checks accepted. Credit cards accepted in person only. Prepayment required. Mail requests: SASE required.
Civil Name Search: Access: Mail, in person. Both court and visitors may perform in person name searches. No search fee. Civil records on card files 2006 to 2007; on computer in 2008. Mail turnaround time varies. Civil PAT goes back to 2008.
Criminal Name Search: Access: Mail, in person, online. Both court and visitors may perform in person name searches. No search fee. Criminal records for misdemeanor on computer from 1989; records at court only 2 years. Mail turnaround time varies. Criminal PAT goes back to 1992. Terminal results show year of birth only. Access criminal records free at http://courtconnect.courts.state.ri.us as an informational service only; should not be relied upon as official court record. Online results include middle initial and aliases, but only birth year of DOB.

Burrillville Town Hall 105 Harrisville Main St, Harrisville, RI 02830; 401-568-4300 x114 or x110; fax: 401-568-0490; 8:30AM-4:30PM M-W; 8:30AM-7:00PM TH; 8:30AM-12:30PM F (EST). *Probate.* www.burrillville.org/Public_Documents/BurrillvilleRI_Clerk/probate

Central Falls City Hall City Clerk's Office, 580 Broad St, Central Falls, RI 02863; 401-727-7400; fax: 401-727-7406; 8:30AM-4:30PM; summer til 3:30PM (EST). *Probate.* www.centralfallsri.us

Cranston City Hall 869 Park Ave, Cranston, RI 02910; 401-461-1000 X3197; probate phone: 401-780-3197; fax: 401-780-3165; 8:30AM-4:30PM (EST). *Probate.* www.cranstonri.com/generalpage.php?page=20

Cumberland Town Hall PO Box 7, 45 Broad St, Cumberland, RI 02864; 401-728-2400; probate phone: x137; fax: 401-724-1103; 8:30AM-4:30PM; Summer- 9AM-4PM (EST). *Probate, Traffic.* www.cumberlandri.org/municipal.htm

East Providence City Hall 145 Taunton Ave, East Providence, RI 02914; 401-435-7595; fax: 401-435-4630; 8AM-4PM (EST). *Probate.*

Foster Town Hall 181 Howard Hill Rd, Foster, RI 02825; 401-392-9200; fax: 401-702-5010; 8:30AM-5:30PM M-Th (EST). *Probate.*
General Information: Court is closed on Fridays.

Glocester Town Hall PO Box B, 1145 Putnam Pike, Chepachet, RI 02814; 401-568-6206; fax: 401-568-5850; 8AM-4:30PM (EST). *Probate.* www.glocesterri.org

Johnston Town Hall 1385 Hartford Ave, Johnston, RI 02919; 401-351-6618; fax: 401-553-8835; 8:30AM-4:30PM (EST). *Probate.*

Lincoln Town Hall PO Box 100, 100 Old River Rd, Lincoln, RI 02865; 401-333-8450; fax: 401-333-3648; 9AM-4:30PM (EST). *Probate.*

North Providence Town Hall 2000 Smith St, North Providence, RI 02911; 401-232-0900; fax: 401-233-1409; 8:30AM-4:30PM (EST). *Probate.*

North Smithfield 575 Smithfield Rd, Municipal Annex, North Smithfield, RI 02896; 401-767-2200 x326; fax: 401-356-4057; 8AM-4PM M,T,W; 8AM-7PM TH; 8AM-N F (EST). *Probate.* www.nsmithfieldri.org/

Pawtucket City Hall 137 Roosevelt Ave, Pawtucket, RI 02860; 401-728-0500 x259 or x223; fax: 401-728-8932; 8:30AM-4:30PM (EST). *Probate.* www.pawtucketri.com/

Providence Probate Court 25 Dorrance St, Providence, RI 02903; 401-421-7740; fax: 401-861-6208; 8:30AM-4:00PM (EST). *Probate.* http://cityof.providenceri.com/probate-court

Scituate Town Hall 195 Danielson Pike, PO Box 328, North Scituate, RI 02857; 401-647-2822; fax: 401-647-7220; 8:30AM-4PM (EST). *Probate.*

Smithfield Town Hall 64 Farnum Pike, Smithfield, RI 02917; 401-233-1000 x111; probate phone: 401-233-1000 X114; fax: 401-232-7244; 8:30AM-4:30PM (EST). *Probate.* www.smithfieldri.com/

Woonsocket City Hall 169 Main St, Woonsocket, RI 02895; 401-762-6400; 401-767-9248; fax: 401-765-0022; 8:30AM-4PM (EST). *Probate.*

Washington County

Superior Court 4800 Towerhill Rd #173, Wakefield, RI 02879; 401-782-4121; fax: 401-782-4190; 8:30AM-4:30PM (EST). *Felony, Civil Actions over $5,000, Family.*
General Information: The Family Court Division can be reached at 401-782-4111. The Superior Court has concurrent jurisdiction with the District Court on civil matters between $5,000 and $10,000. Online identifiers in results same as on public terminal. No confidential or sealed records released. Will fax documents to local or toll free line. Court makes copy: $.15 per page. Self serve copy: same. Certification fee: $3.00 per page. Payee: Washington Superior Court. Personal checks accepted, credit cards are not. Prepayment required. Mail requests: SASE required.
Civil Name Search: Access: Phone, mail, in person. Both court and visitors may perform in person name searches. No search fee. Civil records on computer from 1984, on index prior to 1984. Archived at Record Center, 401-721-2640. Note: Phone requests taken only after 3PM. Mail turnaround time 1 week. Civil PAT goes back to 1984.
Criminal Name Search: Access: Mail, in person, online. Both court and visitors may perform in person name searches. No search fee. Required to search: name, years to search; also helpful: DOB. Criminal records computerized from 1984, on index prior to 1984. Archived at Record Center, 401-721-2640. Mail turnaround time 1 week. Criminal PAT goes back to same as civil. Terminal results show year of birth only. Access criminal records free at http://courtconnect.courts.state.ri.us as an informational service only; should not be relied upon as official court record. Online results cannot be relied on nor accurate for background checking or employment screening and is discouraged. Online results include middle initial and aliases, but only birth year of DOB.

4th District Court 4800 Towerhill Rd, #123, McGrath Judicial Center, Wakefield, RI 02879; 401-782-4131; criminal phone: x2; civil phone: x1; ; 8:30AM-4:30PM (til 4PM in Summer) (EST). *Misdemeanor, Civil Actions under $10,000, Eviction, Small Claims.*
General Information: Online identifiers in results same as on public terminal. No family court records released. Will not fax documents. Court makes copy: $.15 per page. Certification fee: $3.00 per cert. Payee: Fourth District Court. No Personal checks, Visa/MC accepted. Prepayment required.
Civil Name Search: Access: In person, mail. Both court and visitors may perform in person name searches. No search fee. Civil index on cards, computer. Hard copies back to 11/2008 only. Small claims indexed by plaintiff only. Note: Will do search based on mail request but it's best to call to confirm first. Civil PAT goes back to 11/2008.
Criminal Name Search: Access: In person, mail, online. Both court and visitors may perform in person name searches. No search fee. Required to search: name, years to search, DOB. Criminal records available on computer beginning in 1996. Note: Will do search based on mail request but it's best to call to confirm first. Criminal PAT goes back to 1996. Terminal results show year of birth only. Access criminal records free at on the statewide system at http://courtconnect.courts.state.ri.us. Records back to 1996. Online results include aliases, but only birth year. The site is an informational service only and should not be relied upon as official court record. Online results show middle initial.

North Kingstown Town Hall 80 Boston Neck Rd, North Kingstown, RI 02852-5762; 401-268-1552; probate phone: 401-294-3331 x122; fax: 401-294-2437; 8:30AM-4:30PM (EST). *Probate.* www.northkingstown.org/departments/town-clerk/probate-court

Charlestown Town Hall 4540 S County Tr, Charlestown, RI 02813; 401-364-1200; fax: 401-364-1238; 8:30AM-4:30PM (EST). *Probate.*

Exeter Town Hall 675 Ten Rod Rd, Exeter, RI 02822; 401-294-3891 (295-7500); fax: 401-295-1248; 9AM-4PM (EST). *Probate.* www.town.exeter.ri.us
General Information: Court held 4th Monday monthly at 2:00 PM.

Hopkinton Town Hall 1 Town House Rd, Hopkinton, RI 02833; 401-377-7777; fax: 401-377-7788; 8:30AM-4:30PM or by appointment (EST). *Probate.*

Narragansett Town Hall 25 5th Ave, Town Clerk Office, Narragansett, RI 02882; 401-782-0621; 401-782-0622; fax: 401-783-9637; 8:30AM-4:30PM (EST). *Probate.* www.narragansettri.gov/index.aspx?nid=311

New Shoreham Town Hall 16 Old Town Rd, PO Drawer 220, Block Island, RI 02807; 401-466-3200; fax: 401-466-3219; 9AM-3PM (EST). *Probate.*

Richmond Town Hall 5 Richmond Townhouse Rd, Wyoming, RI 02898; 401-539-9000 x9; fax: 401-539-1089; 9AM-4PM (EST). *Probate.*

South Kingstown Town 180 High St, Wakefield, RI 02879; 401-789-9331 x1235; fax: 401-788-9792; 8:30AM-4:30PM (EST). *Probate.*

Westerly Municipal and Probate 45 Broad St, Westerly Town Hall, Westerly, RI 02891; 401-348-2535; fax: 401-348-2318; 8:30AM-4:30PM (EST). *Probate, Misdemeanor, Traffic, Ordinance.*

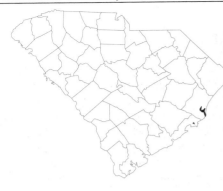

South Carolina

Time Zone:	**EST**
Capital:	**Columbia, Richland County**
# of Counties:	**46**
State Web:	**www.sc.gov**
Court Web:	**www.sccourts.org**

Administration

Court Administration, 1015 Sumter St, 2nd Fl, Columbia, SC, 29201; 803-734-1800, Fax: 803-734-1355.

The Supreme Court and Appellate Court

The Supreme Court is the court of last resort. The Court of Appeals was created to hear most types of appeals from the circuit court and the family court. Exceptions are when the appeal falls within any of the seven classes of exclusive jurisdiction listed under the Supreme Court. Opinions from the Supreme Court and Court of Appeals are viewable from the web page at www.sccourts.org.

The South Carolina Courts

Court	Type	How Organized	Jurisdiction Highpoints
Circuit*	General	46 courts in 16 circuits	Felony, Misdemeanor, Civil, Small Claims, Family, Probate, Juvenile, Traffic, Eviction, Domestic Relations, Environmental
Magistrate (Summary)	Limited	161 courts	Misdemeanor, Civil under $7,500, Ordinance
Municipal	Municipal	206 courts	Misdemeanor, Ordinance
Probate	Special	46 courts	Probate, Estate, marriage
Family	Special	46 courts	Juvenile, Domestic

* = profiled in this book

Details on the Court Structure

The **Circuit Court** is the state's court of general jurisdiction. It has a civil court called the **Court of Common Pleas**, and a criminal court called the **Court of General Sessions**. In addition to its general trial jurisdiction, the Circuit Court has limited appellate jurisdiction over appeals from the Probate Court, Magistrate's Court, and Municipal Court. Masters-In-Equity have jurisdiction in matters referred to them by the Circuit Courts.

Magistrate Courts (also known as **Summary Courts**) generally have criminal trial jurisdiction over all offenses subject to the penalty of a fine, as set by statute, but generally, not exceeding $500.00 or imprisonment not exceeding 30 days, or both. In addition, they are responsible for setting bail, conducting preliminary hearings, and issuing arrest and search warrants. Magistrates have civil jurisdiction when the amount does not exceed $7,500.

Municipal Courts have jurisdiction over cases arising under ordinances of the municipality, and over all offenses which are subject to a fine not exceeding $500.00 or imprisonment not exceeding 30 days, or both, and which occur within the municipality. In addition Municipal Courts may hear cases transferred from General Sessions when the penalty for which does not exceed one year imprisonment or a fine of $5,000, or both.

Probate Courts have jurisdiction over marriage licenses, estates, guardianships of incompetents, conservatorships of estates of minors and incompetents, minor settlements under $25,000 and involuntary commitments to institutions for mentally ill and/or chemically dependent persons.

The **Family Court** has exclusive jurisdiction over all matters involving domestic or family relationships.

Record Searching Facts You Need to Know

Fees and Record Searching Tips

Most South Carolina courts will not conduct searches. However, if a name and case number are provided, many will pull and copy the record. For courts that do searches, the fees vary widely as they are set individually by county. Prepayment is required unless otherwise noted.

If requesting a record in writing, it is recommended that the phrase "Request that General Session, Common Pleas, and Family Court records be searched" be included in the request.

Online Access is by County, but Statewide

The web page at www.sccourts.org/caseSearch/ gives individual county links for a case record search. All counties participate. But the search is available on a per-county look-up; there is no statewide single search. The search is the same search shown at the court location using the on-site public access terminal.

Many of these county online search sites give users an initial choice between searching for records from a Circuit Court or Summary Court. It is worth noting that a number of local record researchers indicate that not all Summary (Magistrate) Courts' records are online. Also, searchers indicate there are instances when Summary records may be missing cases, sentence details, probation updates/violations.

Abbeville County

Circuit Court PO Box 99, Court Sq, Rm 103, Abbeville, SC 29620; 864-366-5312 x55; fax: 864-366-9188; 8AM-5PM (EST). *Felony, Misdemeanor, Civil Actions over $7,500.*
www.abbevillecountysc.com/clerkcourt.aspx
General Information: No adoption, juvenile, sealed or expunged records released. Will not fax documents. Court makes copy: $.50 per page. Certification fee: $1.00 per page. Payee: Clerk of Court. Personal checks accepted, credit cards are not. Prepayment required.
Civil Name Search: Access: In person, online. Visitors must perform in person searches themselves. Civil records on card index from 1870. Civil PAT available. Public access terminals are located in the records room. Online access to the index for both the Circuit and Summary courts at http://publicindex.sccourts.org/abbeville/publicindex/.
Criminal Name Search: Access: In person, online. Visitors must perform in person searches themselves. Required to search: name, years to search; SSN helpful. Criminal records on card index from 1870. Criminal PAT available. Public access terminals are located in the records room. Online access to the index for both the Circuit and Summary courts at http://publicindex.sccourts.org/abbeville/publicindex/.

Abbeville Magistrate Court PO Drawer 1156, 21 Old Calhoun Falls Rd, Abbeville, SC 29620; 864-446-6500; fax: 864-446-6555; 8:30AM-5PM (EST). *Misdemeanor, Civil Actions under $7,500, Eviction, Small Claims, Traffic.* www.abbevillecountysc.com/magistrate.aspx
General Information: Email questions to abvmagadm@wctel.net.

Probate Court PO Box 70, 102 Court Sq, #102, Abbeville, SC 29620; 864-366-5312 x62; fax: 864-366-4023; 8:30AM-5PM (EST). *Probate.* www.abbevillecountysc.com

Aiken County

Circuit Court PO Box 583, 109 Park Ave SE, 2nd Fl (29801), Aiken, SC 29802; 803-642-1715; fax: 803-642-1718; 8:30AM-5PM (EST). *Felony, Misdemeanor, Civil Actions over $7,500.*
www.aikencountysc.gov/DspOfc.cfm?qOfcID=COCCV
General Information: No adoption, juvenile, sealed or expunged records released. Will not fax out case files. Court makes copy: $.25 per page. Self serve copy: same. Certification fee: $1.00. Payee: Clerk of Court. Only cashiers checks and money orders accepted. No credit cards accepted. Prepayment required.
Civil Name Search: Access: In person, online. Both court and visitors may perform in person name searches. No search fee. Civil records on computer from 1988; on microfiche, archives and index books from 1800s. Civil PAT goes back to 1988. http://courts.aikencountysc.gov/scjd55702/publicindex/publicindexdefault.aspx. Online records may be missing cases, sentence details, probation updates/violations. The following information is available: Judgments from 1998 to present, Lis Pendens from 2002 to present, Common Pleas from 1990 to present.
Criminal Name Search: Access: In person, online. Both court and visitors may perform in person name searches. Search fee: Court may charge a search fee. Required to search: name, years to search, DOB; SSN helpful. Criminal records computerized from 1990; on microfiche, archives and index books from 1800s. Criminal PAT goes back to same as civil. Access the record index for the General Sessions from 1990 to present at

http://courts.aikencountysc.gov/scjd55702/publicindex/publicindexdefault.aspx.

Aiken Magistrate Court 1680 Richland Ave W, #70, Aiken, SC 29801; 803-642-1744/1747; fax: 803-642-1749; 9AM-5PM (EST). *Misdemeanor, Civil Actions under $7,500, Eviction, Small Claims.*
General Information: Online records (www.sccourts.org/caseSearch/) may be missing cases, sentence details, and probation updates/violations.

Graniteville Magistrate Summary Court 50 Canal St, #14, Graniteville, SC 29829; 803-663-6634; fax: 803-663-6638; 9AM-5PM (EST). *Civil Actions under $7,500, Misdemeanor, Eviction, Small Claims.* www.aikencountysc.gov/Sgovernment.cfm
General Information: Misdemeanor records accessed same as civil. Online records (www.sccourts.org/caseSearch/) may be missing cases, sentence details, and probation updates/violations.

Langley Magistrate Court PO Box 769, 129 Langley Dam Rd, Langley, SC 29834; 803-593-5171/5172; fax: 803-593-8402; 9AM-5PM (EST). *Misdemeanor, Civil Actions under $7,500, Eviction, Small Claims.*
General Information: Online records (www.sccourts.org/caseSearch/) may be missing cases, sentence details, and probation updates/violations.

Monetta Magistrate Court 5697 Columbia Hwy N, PO Box 190, Monetta, SC 29105; 803-685-7125; fax: 803-685-7988; 8:30AM-12:30PM; 1:30-4:30PM (EST). *Misdemeanor, Civil Actions under $7,500, Eviction, Small Claims.*
General Information: Online records (www.sccourts.org/caseSearch/) may be missing cases, also sentence details, probation updates/violations.

New Ellenton Magistrate Court PO Box 40, 1680 Richmond Ave W #70, Aiken, SC 29801; 803-652-3609; fax: 803-642-1749; 8:30AM-5PM (EST). *Misdemeanor, Civil Actions under $7,500, Eviction, Small Claims.*
General Information: The New Ellington Court is now located in Aiken. Record index online at www.sccourts.org/caseSearch/.

North Augusta Magistrate Court PO Box 6493, North Augusta, SC 29861; 803-202-3580/3581; fax: 803-202-3583; 9AM-5PM (EST). *Misdemeanor, Civil Actions under $7,500, Eviction, Small Claims.*
General Information: Physical address: 537 Edgefield Rd, Belvedere, SC 29841. Online records (www.sccourts.org/caseSearch/) may be missing cases, sentence details, and probation updates/violations.

Probate Court PO Box 1576, Aiken, SC 29802-1576; 803-642-2001; fax: 803-642-2007; 8:30AM-5PM (EST). *Probate.*
www.aikencountysc.gov/DspDept.cfm?qDeptID=PBC

Allendale County

Circuit Court PO Box 126, 292 Barnwell Hwy, Allendale, SC 29810; 803-584-2737; fax: 803-584-7046; 9AM-5PM (EST). *Felony, Misdemeanor, Civil Actions over $7,500.*
General Information: No adoption, juvenile, sealed or expunged records released. Will fax documents $1.00 per page fee. Court makes copy: $.50 per page. Certification fee: $2.00. Payee: Clerk of Court. Personal checks accepted, credit cards are not. Prepayment required. Mail requests: SASE required.
Civil Name Search: Access: Phone, fax, mail, in person, online. Both court and visitors may perform in person name searches. Search fee: $5.00 per name. Civil records on computer 1988, card index from 1919. Mail turnaround time 2 days. Civil PAT goes back to 1987. Terminal results

also show SSNs. Search the index at http://publicindex.sccourts.org/allendale/publicindex/.

Criminal Name Search: Access: Phone, fax, mail, in person, online. Both court and visitors may perform in person name searches. Search fee: $5.00 per name. Required to search: name, years to search, DOB, signed release; also helpful: SSN. Criminal records kept on computer for 3 years. Mail turnaround time 2 days. Criminal PAT goes back to same as civil. Terminal results include SSN. Search the index at http://publicindex.sccourts.org/allendale/publicindex/.

Allendale Magistrate Court 160 Law Enforcement Court, Fairfax, SC 29827; 803-584-3755; fax: 803-584-7980; 9AM-5PM (EST). *Misdemeanor, Civil Actions under $7,500, Eviction, Small Claims.*
General Information: Now combined with Fairfax Court; address and phone given above. Online records (www.sccourts.org/caseSearch/) may be missing cases, sentence details, and probation updates/violations.

Fairfax Magistrate Court 160 Law Enforcement Court, PO Box 516, Fairfax, SC 29827; 803-584-3755; fax: 803-584-7980; 9-5PM (EST). *Misdemeanor, Civil Actions under $7,500, Eviction, Small Claims, Traffic.*
General Information: Online records (www.sccourts.org/caseSearch/) may be missing cases, sentence details, and probation updates/violations.

Probate Court PO Box 603, Courthouse Complex, 292 Barnwell Hiway, Allendale, SC 29810; 803-584-3157; fax: 803-584-7082; 9AM-5PM (EST). *Probate.*

Anderson County

Circuit Court PO Box 8002, 100 S Main St, Courthouse, Anderson, SC 29622; 864-260-4053; fax: 864-260-4715; 8:30AM-5PM (EST). *Felony, Misdemeanor, Civil Actions over $7,500.*
www.judicial.state.sc.us/index.cfm
General Information: Online identifiers in results same as on public terminal. No adoption, juvenile, sealed or expunged records released. Will not fax documents. Court makes copy: $.50 per page. No certification fee. Payee: Clerk of Court. No personal checks or credit cards accepted. Prepayment required.
Civil Name Search: Access: In person, online. Visitors must perform in person searches themselves. Civil records on computer back to 1994, prior on cards. Note: Mail searches available to state agencies only. Civil PAT goes back to 1993. Access the record index at www.andersoncountysc.org/web/scjdweb/publicindex/.
Criminal Name Search: Access: In person, online. Visitors must perform in person searches themselves. Required to search: name, years to search, DOB, SSN, signed release. Criminal records computerized from 1994, prior on cards. Criminal PAT goes back to 1992. Terminal results may include SSN. Access to criminal case details is the same as civil.

Anderson Magistrate Court 2404 N Main St., PO Box 8002, Anderson, SC 29621; 864-260-4156/4055; fax: 864-260-4144; 8:30AM-5PM (EST). *Misdemeanor, Civil Actions under $7,500, Eviction, Small Claims, Traffic.* www.andersoncountysc.org/web/magistrates_00.asp
General Information: Search records online at www.andersoncountysc.org/web/scjdweb/publicindex/. Online records may be missing cases, sentence details, probation updates/violations.

Honea Path Magistrate Court PO Box 505, 204-B South Main Street, Honea Path, SC 29654; 864-369-0015; 8AM-2PM M,T,TH; (EST). *Misdemeanor, Civil Actions under $7,500, Eviction, Small Claims.* www.andersoncountysc.org/web/magistrates_00.asp
General Information: Search records online at www.andersoncountysc.org/web/scjdweb/publicindex/. Online records may be missing cases, sentence details, probation updates/violations.

Iva/Starr Magistrate Court 622-A E. Front Street, PO Box 863, Iva, SC 29655; 864-348-6657; fax: 864-348-6647; 8AM-3:30PM M-W (EST). *Misdemeanor, Civil Actions under $7,500, Eviction, Small Claims.*

Pelzer Magistrate Court PO Box 824, 26 Main St, Pelzer, SC 29669; 864-947-5225; 9AM-4PM M,T, 11AM-3PM W, 9AM-1PM TH, Closed Fri (EST). *Civil Actions under $7,500, Eviction, Small Claims, Misdemeanor.* www.andersoncountysc.org/web/magistrates_00.asp
General Information: Search records online at www.andersoncountysc.org/web/scjdweb/publicindex/. Online records may be missing cases, sentence details, probation updates/violations.

Pendleton Magistrate Court PO Box 76, 100 E Queen St, Pendleton, SC 29670; 864-646-6701; fax: 864-646-6704; 8AM-4PM T W; 8AM-2PM TH (EST). *Misdemeanor, Civil Actions under $7,500, Eviction, Small Claims.* www.andersoncountysc.org/web/magistrates_00.asp
General Information: Search records online at www.andersoncountysc.org/web/scjdweb/publicindex/. Online records may be missing cases, sentence details, probation updates/violations.

Piedmont/Powdersville Magistrate Court PO Box 51312, Piedmont, SC 29673; 864-269-5947; fax: 864-269-5952; 9AM-5PM; M, Tu Wed (EST). *Misdemeanor, Civil Actions under $7,500, Eviction, Small Claims.* www.andersoncountysc.org/web/magistrates_00.asp
General Information: Search records online at www.andersoncountysc.org/web/scjdweb/publicindex/. Online records may be missing cases, sentence details, probation updates/violations.

Starr Magistrate Court Starr Magistrate Court closed 2006; records assumed to be at Anderson Magistrate Court. Starr also held records for Iva Magistrate Court which also has been closed.

Williamston Magistrate Court 12 W Main St, PO Box 125, Williamston, SC 29697-0125; 864-847-8580; 9AM-4PM T, W, TH (EST). *Misdemeanor, Civil Actions under $7,500, Eviction, Small Claims.* www.andersoncountysc.org/web/magistrates_00.asp
General Information: Search records online at www.andersoncountysc.org/web/scjdweb/publicindex/. Fax number is same as voice, call first before trying to fax.

Probate Court PO Box 8002, 100 S Main St, Anderson, SC 29622; 864-260-4049; fax: 864-260-4811; 8:30AM-5PM (EST). *Probate.* www.andersoncountysc.org/web/probate_00.asp
General Information: Access to the county probate court, marriage, estate, and guardian/conservatorship records is available free at http://acpass.andersoncountysc.org/Probate_Main.htm

Bamberg County

Circuit Court PO Box 150, 2559 Main Highway, Bamberg, SC 29003; 803-245-3025; fax: 803-245-3088; 9AM-5PM (EST). *Felony, Misdemeanor, Civil Actions over $7,500.*
General Information: No adoption, juvenile, sealed or expunged records released. Will not fax documents. Court makes copy: $.25 per page. Self serve copy: same. Certification fee: $5.00 per cert. Payee: Clerk of Court. No personal checks or credit cards accepted. Prepayment required. Mail requests: SASE required.
Civil Name Search: Access: Mail, fax, in person, online. Both court and visitors may perform in person name searches. Search fee: $5.00 per name. Civil index on docket books, files back to 1890. Mail turnaround time 1-2 days. Free access to the Circuit and Summary Courts' record index at http://publicindex.sccourts.org/bamberg/publicindex/.
Criminal Name Search: Access: Mail, fax, in person, online. Both court and visitors may perform in person name searches. Search fee: $5.00 per name. Required to search: name, years to search, DOB; also helpful: SSN. Criminal records indexed in books, files back to 1890. Mail turnaround time 1-2 days. Free access to the Circuit and Summary Courts' record index at http://publicindex.sccourts.org/bamberg/publicindex/.

Bamberg Magistrate Court PO Box 187, 2873 Main Hwy, Bamberg, SC 29003; 803-245-3016; fax: 803-245-3085; 9AM-5PM (EST). *Misdemeanor, Civil Actions under $7,500, Eviction, Small Claims.*

Probate Court PO Box 180, 2959 Main Hwy, Rm 103, Bamberg, SC 29003; 803-245-3008; fax: 803-245-3195; 9AM-5PM (EST). *Probate.*

Barnwell County

Circuit Court PO Box 723, 141 Main St, Barnwell, SC 29812; 803-541-1020; fax: 803-541-1025; 9AM-5PM (EST). *Felony, Misdemeanor, Civil Actions over $7,500.*
General Information: Records location is 141 Main St, Barnwell, SC, 29812. No adoption, juvenile, sealed or expunged records released. Will not fax documents. Court makes copy: $.50 per page. Self serve copy: same. Certification fee: $1.00. Payee: Clerk of Court. Business checks accepted. No credit cards or personal checks accepted. Prepayment required.
Civil Name Search: Access: In person, online. Visitors must perform in person searches themselves. Civil cases indexed by defendant. Civil records on computer from 1988. Civil PAT available. Record docket online at http://publicindex.sccourts.org/barnwell/publicindex/. Includes General Sessions records.
Criminal Name Search: Access: In person, online. Visitors must perform in person searches themselves. Required to search: name, years to search, DOB, SSN. Criminal records computerized from 1988. Criminal PAT available. Record docket online at http://publicindex.sccourts.org/barnwell/publicindex/.

Barnwell Magistrate Court PO Box 1205, 599 Joey Zorn Blvd, Barnwell, SC 29812; 803-541-1035; fax: 803-541-1055; 9AM-N, 1-5PM (EST). *Misdemeanor, Civil Actions under $7,500, Eviction, Small Claims.*

Blackville Magistrate Court 5997 N Lartigue St, Blackville, SC 29817; 803-284-2765; fax: 803-284-9107; 8AM-5PM M,T,Th,F; 8AM-N W (EST). *Misdemeanor, Civil Actions under $7,500, Eviction, Small Claims.*

Williston Magistrate Court PO Box 485, 12445 Main St, Williston, SC 29853; 803-266-3700; fax: 803-266-5496; 9AM-5PM (EST). *Misdemeanor, Civil Actions under $7,500, Eviction, Small Claims.*

Probate Court 57 Wall St, Barnwell County Courthouse, Rm 108, Barnwell, SC 29812; 803-541-1032; fax: 803-541-1012; 9AM-5PM (EST). *Probate.*

General Information: Record docket online at http://publicindex.sccourts.org/barnwell/publicindex/.

Beaufort County

Circuit Court PO Drawer 1128, 102 Ribaut Rd, Rm 208, Beaufort, SC 29901; criminal phone: 843-255-5057; civil phone: 843-255-5050; probate phone: 843-255-5850; fax: 843-255-9412; 8AM-4PM (EST). *Felony, Misdemeanor, Civil Actions over $7,500.* www.bcgov.net/

General Information: No adoption, juvenile, sealed or expunged records released. Will not fax documents. Court makes copy: $.50 per page. Self serve copy: same. Certification fee: $1.00. Payee: Clerk of Court. No personal checks or credit cards accepted. Prepayment required.

Civil Name Search: Access: Mail, in person, online. Both court and visitors may perform in person name searches. Search fee: $25.00 per name. Civil records on computer back to 1997; prior in index books to 1936. Mail turnaround time 1 week Civil PAT goes back to 1997. Access to public case index and court dockets for free go to www.beaufortcourt.org.

Criminal Name Search: Access: In person, online. Visitors must perform in person searches themselves. Required to search: name, years to search, DOB; also helpful: SSN. Criminal records computerized from 1990; prior in index books. Note: Court personnel will not perform name searches of the criminal index. Mail turnaround time is 1 week. Criminal PAT goes back to 1985. Access to public case index and court dockets for free go to www.beaufortcourt.org.

Beaufort Magistrate Court PO Box 2207, 100 Ribaut Rd, Beaufort, SC 29901-2207; 843-255-5700; criminal fax: 843-255-9427; civil fax: 8AM-4PM (EST); 8AM-4PM (EST). *Misdemeanor, Civil Actions under $7,500, Eviction, Small Claims, Traffic.*

General Information: This court holds records for the St Helena Island Magistrate Court which is now closed. Access court records and dockets free at www.beaufortcourt.org/publicindex/.

Bluffton Magistrate Court PO Box 840, 4819 Bluffton Pky, Bluffton, SC 29910; 843-757-1500 X6; fax: 843-757-9510; 8AM-4PM (EST). *Misdemeanor, Civil Actions under $7,500, Eviction, Small Claims.*

General Information: Access records free at www.beaufortcourt.org/publicindex/. Search dockets at www.beaufortcourt.org/onlinedocket/.

Hilton Head Magistrate Court - Closed - See Bluffton Magistrate Court for Records *Misdemeanor, Civil Actions under $7,500, Eviction, Small Claims.*

Lobeco Magistrate Court PO Box 845, 1860 Trask Pky, Lobeco, SC 29931-0845; 843-846-3902; 2PM-6P W only (EST). *Misdemeanor, Civil Actions under $7,500, Eviction, Small Claims.*

General Information: Access records free at www.beaufortcourt.org/publicindex/. Search dockets free at www.beaufortcourt.org/onlinedocket/.

St Helena Island Magistrate Court - Closed .See Beaufort Municipal Court *Misdemeanor, Civil Actions under $7,500, Eviction, Small Claims.*

Probate Court PO Box 1083, 102 Ribaut Rd, Beaufort, SC 29901-1083; 843-255-5850; fax: 843-255-9447; 8AM-5PM (EST). *Probate.* www.sccourts.org/probate/index.cfm?countyno=7

Berkeley County

Circuit Court PO Box 219, 300 California Ave, Moncks Corner, SC 29461; 843-719-4400; fax: 843-719-4511; 9AM-5PM (EST). *Felony, Misdemeanor, Civil Actions over $7,500.* www.berkeleycountysc.gov/

General Information: No adoption, juvenile, sealed or expunged records released. Will not fax documents. Court makes copy: $.35 per page. Certification fee: 1st cert free; $1.00 per doc each add'l. Payee: Berkeley County Clerk of Court. Personal checks accepted, credit cards are not. Prepayment required.

Civil Name Search: Access: In person, online. Visitors must perform in person searches themselves. Civil records on computer from early 1980s, prior on books. Civil PAT goes back to 1984. A case index search is offered at http://courts.berkeleycountysc.gov/publicindex/.

Criminal Name Search: Access: In person, online. Visitors must perform in person searches themselves. Required to search: name, years to search, DOB, SSN. Criminal records computerized from early 1980s, prior on books. Criminal PAT goes back to 1982. A case index search is offered at http://courts.berkeleycountysc.gov/publicindex/.

Central Summary Court 223 N Live Oak Dr, Moncks Corner, SC 29461; 843-719-4050 or 723-3800 X4050; fax: 843-719-4534; 9AM-5PM (EST). *Misdemeanor, Civil Actions under $7,500, Eviction, Small Claims, Ordinance.* www.berkeleycountysc.gov/dept/magistrate/

General Information: Formerly Moncks Corner Magistrate Court. Online records (www.sccourts.org/caseSearch/) may be missing cases, also sentence details, probation updates/violations.

Goose Creek Magistrate Court 303-B Goose Creek Blvd, Goose Creek, SC 29445; 843-553-7080; fax: 843-553-7074; 9AM-5PM (EST). *Misdemeanor, Civil Actions under $7,500, Eviction, Small Claims.* www.berkeleycountysc.gov/dept/magistrate/

General Information: The former Summerville Magistrate Court merged with this court. Note there is also a Summerville Magistrate Court in Dorchester county. Small Claims phone number- 843-553-6099.

St Stephen Magistrate Court 1158 S Main St, St Stephen, SC 29479; 843-567-7400; fax: 843-567-3102; 9AM-5PM (EST). *Misdemeanor, Civil Actions under $7,500, Eviction.* www.berkeleycountysc.gov/dept/magistrate/

General Information: Online records (www.sccourts.org/caseSearch/) may be missing cases, also sentence details, probation updates/violations.

Probate Court 300 B California Ave, Moncks Corner, SC 29461; 843-719-4519; fax: 843-719-4527; 9AM-5PM (EST). *Probate.* www.berkeleycountysc.gov/dept/probate/

General Information: This court also holds marriage license and guardian/conservator records.

Calhoun County

Circuit Court PO Box 709, 902 S FR Huff Dr, St Matthews, SC 29135-0709; 803-874-3524; fax: 803-874-1942; 9AM-5PM (EST). *Felony, Misdemeanor, Civil Actions over $7,500.*

General Information: No adoption, juvenile, sealed or expunged records released. Will not fax out case files. Court makes copy: $.25 per page. Self serve copy: $.25 per page. No certification fee. Payee: Clerk of Court. Personal checks accepted, credit cards are not. Prepayment required.

Civil Name Search: Access: In person, online. Visitors must perform in person searches themselves. Civil records on computer from 1984, prior on index books from 1908. Civil PAT goes back to 1962. Search the index at http://publicindex.sccourts.org/calhoun/publicindex/.

Criminal Name Search: Access: In person, online. Both court and visitors may perform in person name searches. No search fee. Required to search: name, years to search, DOB. Criminal records computerized from 1984, prior on index books from 1908. Criminal PAT goes back to 1973. Search the index at http://publicindex.sccourts.org/calhoun/publicindex/.

Cameron Magistrate Court PO Box 663, 204 Boyce Lawton Dr, Cameron, SC 29030; 803-823-2266; fax: 803-823-2288; 9-5PM Tuesday (EST). *Misdemeanor, Civil Actions under $7,500, Eviction, Small Claims, Traffic.*

General Information: Online records (http://publicindex.sccourts.org/calhoun/publicindex/) may missing cases, also sentence details, probation updates/violations.

Cameron Magistrate Court PO Box 663, 204 Boyce Lawton Dr, Cameron, SC 29030; 803-823-2266; fax: 803-823-2288; 1-5PM T,TH (EST). *Misdemeanor, Civil Actions under $7,500, Eviction, Small Claims.*

General Information: This court is also a Municipal Court. Online records (www.sccourts.org/caseSearch/) may be missing cases, also sentence details, probation updates/violations.

St Matthews Magistrate Court 1623 Bridge St W, PO Box 191, St Matthews, SC 29135; 803-874-1112; fax: 803-874-1111; 9AM-4PM (EST). *Misdemeanor, Civil Actions under $7,500, Eviction, Small Claims.*

General Information: Online records (www.sccourts.org/caseSearch/) may be missing cases, also sentence details, probation updates/violations.

Probate Court 902 Huff Dr., St Matthews, SC 29135; 803-874-3514; fax: 803-874-1942; 9AM-5PM (EST). *Probate.*

Charleston County

Circuit Court 100 Broad St, #106, Charleston, SC 29401-2210; 843-958-5000; criminal phone: x3; civil phone: x2; fax: 843-958-5020; 8:30AM-5PM (EST). *Felony, Misdemeanor, Civil Actions over $7,500.* www3.charlestoncounty.org

General Information: No adoption, juvenile, sealed or expunged records released. No fee to fax documents. Court makes copy: $.50 per page. Self serve copy: same. Certification fee: $1.00 per doc. Payee: Clerk of Court. Business checks accepted. No credit cards accepted. Prepayment required.

Civil Name Search: Access: Online, in person. Visitors must perform in person searches themselves. Civil records on computer from 1988, all prior dates indexed in books on microfilm. General Session records available on computer from 4/92, prior in books. Civil PAT goes back to 1975. Civil case details 1988 forward, also judgments and lis pendens are free at www3.charlestoncounty.org/connect. Online document images go back to 1/1/1999. Also accessible via www.sccourts.org/casesearch/.

Criminal Name Search: Access: Mail, online, in person. Both court and visitors may perform in person name searches. Search fee: $25.00 per name, includes copy fee. Required to search: name, years to search, DOB; also helpful: SSN. Criminal records computerized from 4/92, prior on books and microfilm from 1918. Criminal PAT goes back to 1992. Access to criminal case details from 04/92 forward free at www3.charlestoncounty.org/connect. Search by name or case number. Also accessible via www.sccourts.org/casesearch/. Online results show middle initial, DOB, address.

Small Claims Court - North 4045 Bridgeview Dr, Charleston, SC 29405; 843-202-6650; fax: 843-202-6620; 8:30AM-4:30PM (EST). *Small Claims.* www3.charlestoncounty.org/docs/Magistrates/index.html

Charleston Magistrate Court 995 Morrison Dr, Charleston, SC 29402; 843-724-6720; fax: 843-724-6785; 8:30AM-4:30PM (EST). *Small Claims, Evictions.* www.charlestoncounty.org

General Information: Access civil, judgment, criminal and traffic records at www3.charlestoncounty.org/connect.

East Cooper Magistrate Court 1189 Sweet Grass Gasket Pky, PO Box 584, Mt Pleasant, SC 29466; 843-856-1205; fax: 843-856-1204; 8:30AM-4:30PM (EST). *Misdemeanor, Civil Actions under $7,500, Eviction.* www3.charlestoncounty.org/docs/CoC/index.html

General Information: Access civil, judgment, criminal and traffic records at www3.charlestoncounty.org/connect. Mailing address is PO Box 584, ZIP 29422

Edisto Island Magistrate Court See Ravenel Magistrate Court, SC;. *Misdemeanor, Civil Actions under $7,500, Eviction, Traffic.* www3.charlestoncounty.org

General Information: The court on Edisto Island is closed; jurisdiction and case files reside with the Ravenel Magistrate Court.

James Island Magistrate Court 615 Riverland Dr, James Island, SC 29412; 843-795-1140; fax: 843-406-2753; 8:30AM-12:30PM, 1:30-4:30PM M-TH; 8AM-N F (EST). *Misdemeanor, Civil Actions under $7,500, Eviction.* www3.charlestoncounty.org/docs/CoC/index.html

General Information: Access civil, judgment, criminal and traffic records at www3.charlestoncounty.org/connect.

Johns Island/Wadmalaw Magistrate Court 1527 Main Rd, #100, Johns Island, SC 29455; 843-559-1218; fax: 843-559-2378; 8:30AM-12:30PM, 1:30-4:30PM (EST). *Misdemeanor, Civil Actions under $7,500, Eviction.* www3.charlestoncounty.org

General Information: Access civil, judgment, criminal and traffic records at www3.charlestoncounty.org/connect.

Magistrate Court - North Area 3 7272 Cross County Rd, North Charleston, SC 29418; 843-767-2743; fax: 843-760-6887; 8:30AM-4:30PM (EST). *Misdemeanor, Civil Actions under $7,500, Eviction.* www3.charlestoncounty.org

General Information: Access civil, judgment, criminal and traffic records at www3.charlestoncounty.org/connect.

Magistrate Court- North Area 1 4045 Bridge View Dr., PO Box 70235, North Charleston, SC 29415; 843-202-6650/6610; fax: 843-202-6652; 8:30AM-4:30PM (EST). *Misdemeanor, Civil Actions under $7,500, Small Claims.* www3.charlestoncounty.org

General Information: Access civil, judgment, criminal and traffic records at www3.charlestoncounty.org/connect.

Magistrate Court-North Charleston 2 2145 Melbourne Ave #100, North Charleston, SC 29405; 843-745-2215; fax: 843-745-2334; 8:30AM-1PM, 2-4:30PM (EST). *Misdemeanor, Civil Actions under $7,500, Eviction, Small Claims.* www3.charlestoncounty.org

General Information: Access civil, judgment, criminal and traffic records at http://jcmsweb.charlestoncounty.org/publicindex/PISearch.aspx.

McClellanville Magistrate Court PO Box 7, 10009 Hwy 17 N, McClellanville, SC 29458; 843-887-3334; fax: 843-887-3901; 9AM-N, 1-4PM M & TH (EST). *Misdemeanor, Civil Actions under $7,500, Eviction, Small Claims.* www3.charlestoncounty.org

General Information: Access civil, judgment, criminal and traffic records at www3.charlestoncounty.org/connect.

Ravenel Magistrate Court 5962 Hwy 165, #200, Ravenel, SC 29470-5514; 843-889-8332; fax: 843-889-9202; 8:30AM-4:30PM (EST). *Misdemeanor, Civil Actions under $7,500, Eviction.* www3.charlestoncounty.org

General Information: Holds case files for closed court on Edisto Is. Access civil, judgment, criminal, traffic recs at www3.charlestoncounty.org/connect.

West Ashley Magistrate Court 1720 Sam Rittenberg Blvd, Unit 11, Charleston, SC 29407; 843-766-6531; fax: 843-571-4751; 8:30AM-4:30PM M-F (EST). *Civil Actions under $7,500, Eviction.* www3.charlestoncounty.org

General Information: Access civil, judgment, criminal and traffic records at www3.charlestoncounty.org/connect. Also, free court records are found at http://jcmsweb.charlestoncounty.org/publicindex/.

Probate Court 84 Broad St, 3rd Fl, Charleston, SC 29401; 843-958-5030, 958-5180; fax: 843-958-5044; 8:30AM-5PM (EST). *Probate.* www.charlestoncounty.org

General Information: Access to Estate and Wills records is available free at www3.charlestoncounty.org/surfer/group2?ref=Conserv.

Cherokee County

Circuit Court PO Drawer 2289, 125 E Floyd-Baker Blvd, Gaffney, SC 29342; 864-487-2571; civil phone: 864-487-2533; probate phone: 864-487-2588; fax: 864-487-2754; 8:30AM-5PM (EST). *Felony, Misdemeanor, Civil Actions over $7,500.*

General Information: No adoption, juvenile, sealed or expunged records released. Will fax documents $5.00 per fax. Court makes copy: $.50 per page. Self serve copy: same. Certification fee: $1.00. Payee: Clerk of Court. Business checks accepted. No credit cards accepted for copy fees. Prepayment required.

Civil Name Search: Access: In person, online. Visitors must perform in person searches themselves. Civil records go back to 1897; computerized records go back to 1994. Civil PAT goes back to 1991. Civil case details online at http://publicindex.sccourts.org/cherokee/publicindex/.

Criminal Name Search: Access: In person, online. Visitors must perform in person searches themselves. Criminal records computerized from 1994, prior on books. Criminal PAT goes back to same as civil. Access case details online at http://publicindex.sccourts.org/cherokee/publicindex/.

Blacksburg Magistrate Court 101 S John St #A, PO Box 427, Blacksburg, SC 29702; 864-839-2492; fax: 864-839-3415; 8:30AM-5PM (EST). *Misdemeanor, Civil Actions under $7,500, Eviction, Small Claims.*

General Information: Access court records online at http://publicindex.sccourts.org/cherokee/publicindex/.

Cherokee County Magistrate Court PO Box 336, 312 E Frederick St, Gaffney, SC 29342-0336; 864-487-2533/2501; criminal phone: 864-487-2533; civil phone: 864-487-2502; fax: 864-902-8425; 8:30AM-5PM M-F (EST). *Misdemeanors, Civil Actions under $7,500, Eviction, Small Claims.* www.cherokeemagistrate.com

General Information: Access court records online at http://publicindex.sccourts.org/cherokee/publicindex/. Online records may be missing cases, sentence details, probation updates/violations.

Probate Court PO Box 22, 1434 N Limestone St, Peachtree Ctr, Gaffney, SC 29342; 864-487-2583; fax: 864-902-8426; 9AM-4:30PM (EST). *Probate, Marriage.* www.cherokeecountyprobate.com

General Information: Marriage license phone-864-487-2589.

Chester County

Circuit Court PO Drawer 580, 140 Main St, Chester, SC 29706; 803-385-2605; fax: 803-581-7975; 8:30AM-5PM (EST). *Felony, Misdemeanor, Civil Actions over $7,500.* www.chestersc.org

General Information: No adoption, juvenile, sealed or expunged records released. Will not fax documents. Court makes copy: $.50 per 11x17 page; $.25 per letter page. Self serve copy: same. Certification fee: $1.00 per doc plus copy fee. Payee: Clerk of Court. Personal checks accepted, credit cards are not. Prepayment required.

Civil Name Search: Access: In person, online. Visitors must perform in person searches themselves. Required to search: name, years to search, address. Civil records on computer from 1989, microfiche from 1927. Civil PAT goes back to 1992. Results may include identifiers entered originally. Search the index at http://publicindex.sccourts.org/chester/publicindex/.

Criminal Name Search: Access: In person, online. Visitors must perform in person searches themselves. Required to search: name, years to search, DOB, signed release; also helpful: SSN. Criminal records computerized from 1994, docket books prior. Criminal PAT goes back to only a partial index. Search the index at http://publicindex.sccourts.org/chester/publicindex/.

Chester Magistrate Court 2740 Dawson Dr, Chester, SC 29706; 803-581-5136; 581-3040; fax: 803-581-3033; 8:30AM-5PM (EST). *Misdemeanor.*

General Information: Online records (www.sccourts.org/caseSearch/ and then click on Chester) may be missing cases, also sentence details, probation updates/violations.

Probate Court PO Drawer 580, 1476 J A Cochran Bypass, Chester, SC 29706; 803-385-2604; fax: 803-581-5180; 8:30AM-5PM (EST). *Probate.* www.chestercounty.org/departments/probate_court.html

General Information: Records go back to late 1780s. The clerk also handles guardianship, conservatorship, and marriage records.

Chesterfield County

Circuit Court PO Box 529, Chesterfield, SC 29709; 843-623-2574; probate phone: 843-623-2376; fax: 843-623-6944; 8:30AM-5PM (EST). *Felony, Misdemeanor, Civil Actions over $7,500.*

General Information: No adoption, juvenile, sealed or expunged records released. Will fax documents $5.00. Court makes copy: $2.00 per document and $.25 per page after 1st 4 pages. Self serve copy: $.25 per page. No certification fee. Payee: Clerk of Court. Personal checks accepted, credit cards are not. Prepayment required. Mail requests: SASE required.

Civil Name Search: Access: Mail, in person. Both court and visitors may perform in person name searches. Search fee: $5.00 per name. Civil records on computer back to 1986, prior on docket books. Mail turnaround time 3 days.

Criminal Name Search: Access: Mail, in person. Both court and visitors may perform in person name searches. Search fee: $5.00 per name. Required to search: name, years to search, DOB, SSN. Criminal records computerized from 1986, prior on docket books. Mail turnaround time 3 days.

Cheraw Magistrate Court Closed - This court and judge have retired.

Chesterfield II Magistrate Court Magistrate has retired; court records now at Chesterfield, address and phone given above.

Chesterfield Magistrate Court 115 Green St, Chesterfield, SC 29741; 843-623-9009; fax: 843-623-3459; 9AM-4:30PM (EST). *Misdemeanor, Civil Actions under $7,500, Eviction, Small Claims,.*

McBee Magistrate Court Closed *2008. Records now located at Chesterfield Magistrate Ct.*

Pageland Magistrate Court 310 W McGregor St, PO Box 133, Pageland, SC 29728; 843-672-5685; fax: 843-672-9501; 10AM-3PM (EST). *Misdemeanor, Civil Actions under $7,500, Eviction, Small Claims.*

General Information: This location houses the Patrick court as well.

Patrick Magistrate Court c/o Chesterfield Magistrate Court, 115 Green St, Chesterfield, SC 29741; 843-498-6398; fax: 843-623-3459; pAM-4:30PM (EST). *Misdemeanor, Civil Actions under $7,500, Eviction, Small Claims.*

Probate Court County Courthouse, 200 W Main St, Chesterfield, SC 29709; 843-623-2376; fax: 843-623-9886; 8:30AM-5PM (EST). *Probate.*

Clarendon County

Circuit Court PO Box 136, Manning, SC 29102; 803-435-4443; criminal phone: x309; fax: 803-435-4844; 8:30AM-5PM (EST). *Felony, Misdemeanor, Civil Actions over $7,500.*

General Information: No adoption, juvenile, sealed or expunged records released. Will fax documents to local or toll-free number. Court makes copy: $.25 per page. Certification fee: $2.00 plus copy fees. Payee: Clerk of Court. Personal checks accepted, credit cards are not. Prepayment required. Mail requests: SASE required.

Civil Name Search: Access: Mail, in person, online. Visitors must perform in person searches themselves. No search fee. Civil records on computer from 1988, index books from 1865. Mail turnaround time 5 days. Civil PAT goes back to 1988. Civil case details free on state system at http://publicindex.sccourts.org/clarendon/publicindex/.

Criminal Name Search: Access: Mail, in person, fax, online. Visitors must perform in person searches themselves. No search fee. Criminal records computerized from 1983, index books from 1865. Mail turnaround time 5 days. Criminal PAT goes back to same as civil. Terminal results include SSN. Access case details free on state system at http://publicindex.sccourts.org/clarendon/publicindex/.

Manning Magistrate/Summary Court 102 S Mill St, PO Box 371, Manning, SC 29102; 803-435-2670; fax: 803-435-0885; 8:30AM-5PM (EST). *Misdemeanor, Civil Actions under $7,500, Eviction, Small Claims.* www.clarendoncounty.sc.gov/

General Information: Access court records free on state system at http://publicindex.sccourts.org/clarendon/publicindex/. Results include address but may be missing cases, sentence details, probation updates/violations.

Summerton Municipal Court 10 W Main St, PO Box 279, Summerton, SC 29148; 803-485-2525 x20; fax: 803-485-2914; 8AM-5PM (EST). *Misdemeanor, Civil Actions under $7,500, Eviction, Small Claims.*

General Information: Access certain records free at http://publicindex.sccourts.org/clarendon/publicindex/. Results include address but may be missing some cases. Email courtclerk@sc.rr.com.

Probate Court PO Box 307, 3 W Keitt Street, Manning, SC 29102; 803-435-8774; fax: 803-435-8698; 8:30AM-5PM (EST). *Probate.*

Colleton County

Circuit Court PO Box 620, 101 Hampton St, Walterboro, SC 29488; 843-549-5791; fax: 843-549-2875; 8AM-5PM (EST). *Felony, Misdemeanor, Civil Actions over $7,500.* www.colletoncounty.org/secondary.aspx?pageID=162

General Information: No adoption, juvenile, PTI, sealed or expunged records released. Extra $2.00 fee to receive and fax documents. Court makes copy: $.50 per page. Self serve copy: $.25 per page. Certification fee: $1.00. Payee: Clerk of Court. Business checks accepted, but not personal checks. No credit cards accepted. Prepayment required. Mail requests: SASE not required.

Civil Name Search: Access: Phone, fax, mail, in person, online. Both court and visitors may perform in person name searches. Search fee: $5.00 per name. Civil records on computer from 1986, on index books from 1865. Mail turnaround time 2 days. Civil PAT goes back to 1998. Online access to the index is at http://publicindex.sccourts.org/colleton/publicindex/.

Criminal Name Search: Access: Phone, fax, mail, in person, online. Both court and visitors may perform in person name searches. Search fee: $5.00 per name. Required to search: name, years to search; also helpful: SSN, DOB. Criminal records computerized from 1986, on index books from 1865. Mail turnaround time 2 days. Criminal PAT goes back to 1985-6. Online access at http://publicindex.sccourts.org/colleton/publicindex/.

Magistrate Court 40 Klein St, PO Box 1732, Walterboro, SC 29488; 843-549-1122; fax: 843-549-9010; 8AM-5PM (EST). *Misdemeanor, Civil Actions under $7,500, Eviction, Small Claims.* www.colletoncounty.org/secondary.aspx?pageID=137

General Information: All magistrate courts were combined, all records are located here. Online records at www.sccourts.org/caseSearch/ may be missing cases, also sentence details, probation updates/violations.

Probate Court PO Box 1036, 188 N Walter St, Walterboro, SC 29488-0031; 843-549-7216; fax: 843-549-5571; 8AM-5PM (EST). *Probate.* www.colletoncounty.org/secondary.aspx?pageID=146

General Information: This court also issues marriage licenses. Records date back to 07/01/1911.

Darlington County

Circuit Court PO Box 1177, Darlington, SC 29540; 843-398-4339; fax: 843-393-6871; 8:30AM-5PM (EST). *Felony, Misdemeanor, Civil Actions over $7,500.* www.darcosc.com/ClerkofCourt/

General Information: No adoption, juvenile, sealed or expunged records released. Will not fax out documents. Court makes copy: $1.00 per page if court make copy. Self serve copy: $.25 per page. No certification fee. Payee: Clerk of Court. Business checks accepted; no personal checks. No credit cards accepted. Prepayment required.

Civil Name Search: Access: In person. Visitors must perform in person searches themselves. Civil records on computer from 1989, on index books from 1805. Civil PAT goes back to 1989.

Criminal Name Search: Access: In person. Visitors must perform in person searches themselves. Required to search: name, years to search; also helpful: DOB, SSN. Criminal records computerized from 1989, on index books from 1805. Note: Court will give disposition & sentence over phone if case number given. Criminal PAT goes back to same as civil.

Darlington Magistrate Court 115 Camp Rd, Darlington, SC 29532; 843-398-4340; fax: 843-398-4458; 8:30AM-5PM (EST). *Misdemeanor, Civil Actions under $7,500, Eviction, Small Claims.*

Hartsville Magistrate Court 404 S 4th St, PO Box 1765, Hartsville, SC 29550; 843-332-9661; fax: 843-332-7212; 8:30AM-5PM (EST). *Misdemeanor, Civil Actions under $7,500, Eviction, Small Claims.*

Lamar Magistrate Court 103 Warren Ave, PO Box 38, Lamar, SC 29069; 843-326-5441; fax: 843-326-1543; 8AM-6PM T,W,TH (EST). *Misdemeanor, Traffic.* www.darcosc.com/Magistrate/

General Information: Does not handle civil cases.

Probate Court #1 Public Sq, Courthouse, Rm 208, Darlington, SC 29532; 843-398-4310; fax: 843-398-4076; 8:30AM-5PM (EST). *Probate.* www.darcosc.com/probatecourt/

Dillon County

Circuit Court PO Drawer 1220, 301 W Main St, Dillon, SC 29536; 843-774-1425; fax: 843-841-3706; 8:30AM-5PM (EST). *Felony, Misdemeanor, Civil Actions over $7,500.*

General Information: No adoption, juvenile, sealed or expunged records released. Will fax documents to local or toll free line. Court makes copy: $.50 per page. Self serve copy: same. No certification fee. Payee: Clerk of Court.

Personal checks accepted, credit cards are not. Prepayment required. Mail requests: SASE required.

Civil Name Search: Access: Mail, in person, online. Visitors must perform in person searches themselves. Search fee: $10.00 per name. Civil records on computer from 1990, on docket books prior. Note: Public can search index books for free. Court will assist. Mail turnaround time 1 day. Access online index at http://publicindex.sccourts.org/dillon/publicindex/. However, judgments of the Circuit Court only go back to Feb 2010.

Criminal Name Search: Access: Mail, in person, online. Both court and visitors may perform in person name searches. Search fee: $10.00 per name. Required to search: name, years to search; also helpful: DOB, SSN. Criminal records computerized from 1990, on docket books prior. Note: Public can search index books for free. Mail turnaround time 1 day. Access online index at http://publicindex.sccourts.org/dillon/publicindex/.

Dillon Magistrate Court 200 S 5th Ave, PO Box 1016, Dillon, SC 29536; 843-774-1407; fax: 843-774-1453; 8:30AM-5PM (EST). *Misdemeanor, Civil Actions under $7,500, Eviction, Small Claims.*
General Information: Access online index at http://publicindex.sccourts.org/dillon/publicindex/.

Lake View Municipal Court PO Box 824, 205 N Main St, Lake View, SC 29563; 843-759-9656; fax: 843-759-0177; 9:30AM-Noon M,W,TH,F; 9:30AM-4PM T (EST). *Misdemeanor, Ordinance.*

Probate Court PO 189, Dillon, SC 29536-0189; 843-774-1423; fax: 843-841-3732; 8:30AM-4:30PM (EST). *Probate.*
General Information: Mail to PO Box 189 with 29536-0189 as ZIP.

Dorchester County

Circuit Court 5200 Jim Bildton Blvd, St George, SC 29477; 843-563-0160; criminal phone: x2; civil phone: 843-563-0113; fax: 843-563-0178; 8:30AM-5PM (EST). *Felony, Misdemeanor, Civil Actions over $7,500, Small Claims.* www.dorchestercounty.net/
General Information: No adoption, juvenile, sealed or expunged records released. Will not fax out case files. Court makes copy: $.50 per page. Self serve copy: same. No certification fee. Payee: Clerk of Court. Personal checks, Visa/MC accepted. Prepayment required.
Civil Name Search: Access: In person, online. Visitors must perform in person searches themselves. Civil index on docket books back to 1950s, on computer since 1994. Civil PAT goes back to 1994. Civil case details free at http://webapp.dorchestercounty.net/SCJDWeb/PublicIndex/.
Criminal Name Search: Access: In person, online. Visitors must perform in person searches themselves. Required to search: name, years to search, DOB, signed release; SSN helpful. Criminal records indexed in books back to 1950s, on computer since 1994. Criminal PAT goes back to 1987. Access case details free at http://webapp.dorchestercounty.net/SCJDWeb/PublicIndex/.

St George Magistrate Court 5200 East Jim Bilton Blvd, St. George, SC 29477; 843-563-0130; fax: 843-563-0123; 8:30AM-5PM (EST). *Misdemeanor, Civil Actions under $7,500, Eviction, Small Claims.* www.dorchestercounty.net/
General Information: Access court records free at www.dorchestercounty.net/scjdweb/publicindex/. Online records may be missing cases, sentence details, probation updates/violations.

Summerville Magistrate Court 212 Deming Way, Box 10, Summerville, SC 29483; 843-832-0370; fax: 843-832-0371; 8:30AM-5PM (EST). *Misdemeanor, Civil Actions under $7,500, Eviction, Small Claims.* www.dorchestercounty.net/
General Information: Access court records free at www.dorchestercounty.net/scjdweb/publicindex/. Online records may be missing cases, sentence details, probation updates/violations.

Probate Court 5200 E Jim Bilton Blvd, St George, SC 29477; 843-832-0136; fax: 843-832-0222; 8:30AM-5PM (EST). *Probate.* www.dorchestercounty.net/Probate.htm

Edgefield County

Circuit Court PO Box 34, 129 Courthouse Sq, Edgefield, SC 29824; 803-637-4082; fax: 803-637-4117; 8:30AM-5PM (EST). *Felony, Misdemeanor, Civil Actions over $7,500.*
www.edgefieldcounty.sc.gov/
General Information: No adoption, juvenile, sealed or expunged records released. Will not fax documents. Court makes copy: $.50 per page. Self serve copy: same. Certification fee: $1.00 per doc plus copy fee. Payee: Clerk of Court. Business checks accepted. No credit cards accepted. Prepayment required. Mail requests: SASE required.
Civil Name Search: Access: Mail, in person, online. Both court and visitors may perform in person name searches. Search fee: $5.00 per name. Civil records archived from 1839; on computer back to 1980. Mail turnaround time 1 day. Civil PAT goes back to 1980. Civil case details free at http://publicindex.sccourts.org/edgefield/publicindex/. Also search pending cases free at http://publicindex.sccourts.org/edgefield/courtrosters/PendingCases.aspx.

Criminal Name Search: Access: Mail, in person, online. Both court and visitors may perform in person name searches. Search fee: $5.00 per name. Required to search: name, years to search, DOB; also helpful: SSN. Criminal records archived from 1839; on computer back to 1980. Mail turnaround time 1 day. Criminal PAT goes back to 1980. Access to criminal case details is the same as civil.

Edgefield Magistrate Court 215 Jeter St, PO Box 664, Edgefield, SC 29824; criminal phone: 803-637-4052/4059; civil phone: 803-637-4090; fax: 803-637-4101; 8:30AM-5PM (EST). *Misdemeanor, Civil Actions under $7,500, Eviction, Small Claims.*
General Information: Access court records free at http://publicindex.sccourts.org/edgefield/publicindex/. Online records may be missing cases, sentence details, probation updates/violations.

Probate Court 129 Courthouse Square, #212, PO Box 45, Edgefield, SC 29824; 803-637-4076; fax: 803-637-7157; 8:30AM-5PM (EST). *Probate.*

Fairfield County

Circuit Court PO Drawer 299, 101 S Congress, Courthouse, Winnsboro, SC 29180; 803-712-6526; fax: 803-712-1506; 9AM-5PM (EST). *Felony, Misdemeanor, Civil Actions over $7,500.*
General Information: No adoption, juvenile, sealed or expunged records released. Will not fax documents. Court makes copy: $.50 per page for ledger size; $.25 per page for letter or legal size. Self serve copy: $.25 per page. Certification fee: $1.00 per doc. Payee: Clerk of Court. Personal checks accepted, credit cards are not. Prepayment required.
Civil Name Search: Access: In person, online. Visitors must perform in person searches themselves. Civil index on docket books. Note: The court provides an index, but will not do record searching for you. A case index search if found at http://publicindex.sccourts.org/fairfield/publicindex/.
Criminal Name Search: Access: In person, online. Visitors must perform in person searches themselves. Required to search: name, years to search, DOB. Criminal docket on books. Public use terminal has crim records back to 2000, but this is case dispositions mostly. A case index search if found at http://publicindex.sccourts.org/fairfield/publicindex/.

Winnsboro Magistrate Court 115-B S Congress St, Winnsboro, SC 29180; 803-635-4525; fax: 803-635-5717; 912:30PM; 1:30PM-5PM (EST). *Misdemeanor, Civil Actions under $7,500, Eviction, Small Claims.* www.fairfieldsc.com/secondary.aspx?pageID=197
General Information: Online records (www.sccourts.org/caseSearch/) may be missing cases, also sentence details, probation updates/violations.

Probate Court PO Box 385, Courthouse, Congress St, Winnsboro, SC 29180; 803-712-6519; fax: 803-712-6939; 9AM-5PM (EST). *Probate.* www.fairfieldsc.com/

Florence County

Circuit Court PO Drawer E, 180 N Irby St, City County Complex, Florence, SC 29501; 843-665-3031; criminal phone: x3; civil phone: x2; fax: 843-665-3097; 8:30AM-5PM (EST). *Felony, Misdemeanor, Civil Actions over $7,500.*
http://florenceco.org/elected-offices/clerk-of-court/
General Information: No adoption, juvenile, sealed or expunged records released. Will not fax documents. Court makes copy: $1.00 per page. Self serve copy: $.25 per page. No certification fee. Payee: Clerk of Court. No personal checks or credit cards accepted. Prepayment required.
Civil Name Search: Access: In person, online. Both court and visitors may perform in person name searches. Search fee: $5.00 per name. Civil records on computer from 1984, on microfiche and docket books from 1900s. Civil PAT goes back to 1998. Search judgments back to 1994 at www.sccourts.org/caseSearch/.
Criminal Name Search: Access: In person, online. Visitors must perform in person searches themselves. Required to search: name, years to search, DOB; also helpful: SSN. Criminal records computerized from 1984, on microfiche and docket books from 1898. Criminal PAT goes back to same as civil. Access crim records from 1995 forward at www.sccourts.org/caseSearch/.

Florence Magistrate Court 180 N Irby St, MSC-W, 120 Courthouse Sq, Florence, SC 29501; 843-665-0031; fax: 843-661-7800; 8:30AM-5PM (EST). *Misdemeanor, Civil Actions under $7,500, Eviction, Small Claims.* http://florenceco.org/offices/magistrate/
General Information: Online records at www.sccourts.org/caseSearch/ may be missing cases, also sentence details, probation updates/violations.

Johnsonville Magistrate Court PO Box 904, 117 W Broadway St, Johnsonville, SC 29555; 843-380-9211; fax: 843-380-9411; 9AM-5PM M &W; Till 1PM F (EST). *Misdemeanor, Civil Actions up to $7,500, Eviction, Small Claims, Traffic.* http://florenceco.org/offices/magistrate/
General Information: Online records (www.sccourts.org/caseSearch/) may be missing cases, also sentence details, probation updates/violations.

Lake City Magistrate Court PO Box 39, 345 S Ron McNair Blvd, Lake City, SC 29560; 843-394-5461; fax: 843-394-3865; 8:30AM-5PM (EST). *Misdemeanor, Civil Actions under $7,500, Eviction, Small Claims.* http://florenceco.org/offices/magistrate/
General Information: Online records (www.sccourts.org/caseSearch/) may be missing cases, also sentence details, probation updates/violations.

Olanta Magistrate Court PO Box 362, 220 E Main St, Olanta, SC 29114; 843-396-9056; fax: 843-396-9406; 8:30AM-5PM T,W; 8:30AM-4PM Th (EST). *Misdemeanor, Civil Actions under $7,500, Eviction, Small Claims.* http://florenceco.org/offices/magistrate/
General Information: Online records (www.sccourts.org/caseSearch/) may be missing cases, also sentence details, probation updates/violations. Closed Monday and Friday.

Pamplico Magistrate Court PO Box 367, 124 3rd Ave E, Pamplico, SC 29583; 843-493-0072; fax: 843-493-5391; 8:30AM-5PM M-TH (EST). *Civil Actions under $7,500, Misdemeanor, Eviction, Small Claims, Traffic.* http://florenceco.org/offices/magistrate/
General Information: Online records (www.sccourts.org/caseSearch/) may be missing cases, also sentence details, probation updates/violations.

Timmonsville Magistrate Court PO Box 190, 307 Smith St, Timmonsville, SC 29161; 843-346-7472; fax: 843-346-0660; 8:30AM-5PM (EST). *Misdemeanor, Civil Actions under $7,500, Eviction, Small Claims.*
General Information: Online records (www.sccourts.org/caseSearch/) may be missing cases, also sentence details, probation updates/violations.

Probate Court 180 N Irby St, Box L, Florence, SC 29501; 843-665-3085; fax: 843-665-3068; 8:30AM-5PM (EST). *Probate.* http://florenceco.org/elected-offices/probate/

Georgetown County

Circuit Court PO Box 479, 401 Cleland St, Georgetown, SC 29442; 843-545-3041; fax: 843-545-3003; 8:30AM-5PM (EST). *Felony, Misdemeanor, Civil Actions over $7,500.*
General Information: No adoption, juvenile, sealed or expunged records released. Will not fax documents. Court makes copy: n/a. Self serve copy: $.25 per page. Certification fee: $1.00 per doc. Payee: Clerk of Court. In-state business checks accepted. No personal checks accepted. Visa/MC accepted plus $1.45 transaction fee. Prepayment required.
Civil Name Search: Access: In person, online. Visitors must perform in person searches themselves. Civil docket indexed from 1926. Civil PAT goes back to 2000. Access Common Pleas court dockets free at http://secure.georgetowncountysc.org/courtrosters/. Access Common Pleas records back to 7/2000 free at http://secure.georgetowncountysc.org/publicindex/ but Online records may be missing cases, sentence details, probation updates/violations. Also, access Common Pleas case details free at Extended Index Search at www.georgetowncountysc.org/commonpleas/.
Criminal Name Search: Access: In person, online. Visitors must perform in person searches themselves. Required to search: name, years to search, DOB; SSN helpful. Criminal records indexed from 1926, computerized since 2001. Criminal PAT goes back to same as civil. Online access to Common Pleas Court records are the same as civil; see civil. Online results show middle initial, DOB, address.

Andrews Magistrate Court 110 N Morgan Ave, Andrews, SC 29510; 843-545-3631; fax: 843-264-5177; 8:30AM-4:30PM (EST). *Misdemeanor, Civil Actions under $7,500, Eviction, Small Claims.*
General Information: Access court records free at http://secure.georgetowncountysc.org/publicindex/. Online records may be missing cases, sentence details, probation updates/violations.

Georgetown Magistrate Court 333 Cleland St, Georgetown, SC 29442; 843-545-3381; criminal phone: 843-545-3380; fax: 843-545-3394; 8:30AM-12; 1PM-5PM (EST). *Misdemeanor, Civil Actions under $7,500, Eviction, Small Claims.* www.georgetowncountysc.org/magistrate/default.html
General Information: Access court records free at http://secure.georgetowncountysc.org/publicindex/. Online records may be missing cases, sentence details, probation updates/violations.

Murrells Inlet Magistrate Court 4450 Murrells Inlet Rd, PO Box 859, Murrells Inlet, SC 29576; 843-545-3635; fax: 843-651-6685; 8AM-4:30PM (EST). *Misdemeanor, Civil Actions under $7,500, Eviction, Small Claims.*

General Information: Access court records free at http://secure.georgetowncountysc.org/publicindex/. Online records may be missing cases, sentence details, probation updates/violations.

Pawleys Island Magistrate Court 291 Parkersville Rd, PO Box 1830, Pawleys Island, SC 29585; 843-545-3633; fax: 843-545-3640; 8:30AM-4:30PM (EST). *Misdemeanor, Civil Actions under $7,500, Eviction, Small Claims.*
General Information: Access court records free at http://secure.georgetowncountysc.org/publicindex/. Online records may be missing cases, sentence details, probation updates/violations.

Pleasant Hill Magistrate Court 9174 Pleasant Hill Dr, Hemingway, SC 29554; 843-558-9711; fax: 843-558-5827; 8:30AM-N, 1PM-5 (EST). *Misdemeanor, Civil Actions under $7,500, Eviction, Small Claims,.*
General Information: Access court records free at http://secure.georgetowncountysc.org/publicindex/. Online records may be missing cases, sentence details, probation updates/violations.

Probate Court PO Box 421270, 401 Cleland Street, Room # 140, Georgetown, SC 29442; 843-545-3274; fax: 843-545-3512; 8:30AM-5PM (EST). *Probate.* www.georgetowncountysc.org/probate/

Greenville County

Circuit Court 305 E North St, Rm 227, Greenville, SC 29601; 864-467-8551; 8:30AM-5PM (EST). *Felony, Misdemeanor, Civil Actions over $7,500.* www.greenvillecounty.org
General Information: Online identifiers in results same as on public terminal. No adoption, juvenile, sealed or expunged records released. Will not fax documents. Court makes copy: Court will not make copies. Self serve copy: $.25 per page. Certification fee: $1.00. Payee: Clerk of Court. Only cashiers checks and money orders accepted. No credit cards accepted. Prepayment required.
Civil Name Search: Access: In person, online. Visitors must perform in person searches themselves. Civil records on computer from 1985, on docket books from 1900s. Civil PAT goes to 1982. Family Court and civil index at www.greenvillecounty.org/scjd/publicindex23.asp..
Criminal Name Search: Access: In person, online. Visitors must perform in person searches themselves. Criminal records computerized from 1985, on docket books from 1900s. Criminal PAT goes back to same as civil. Access case details free at www.greenvillecounty.org/scjd/publicindex/disclaim23.asp. Online results show middle initial, DOB, address.

Bates Magistrate Summary Magistrate Court 114 N Poinsett Hwy, Travelers Rest, SC 29690; 864-834-6910; fax: 864-834-6911; 9AM-5PM (EST). *Misdemeanor, Civil Actions under $7,500, Eviction, Small Claims.* www.greenvillecounty.org/Magistrate_Courts/Bates.asp
General Information: Formerly known as Travelers Rest Magistrate Court. Nearby courts are Cleveland, Highlands, and Greer. Access court records free at www.greenvillecounty.org/scjd/publicindex/disclaim23.asp. Records go back to 1988 but may be missing data.

Chick Springs Summary Magistrate Court 2810 Wade Hampton Blvd, Taylor, SC 29687; 864-244-2922, 864-467-5312; fax: 864-268-1333; 8:30AM-5PM (EST). *Misdemeanor, Civil Actions under $7,500, Eviction, Small Claims.* www.greenvillecounty.org/Magistrate_Courts/
General Information: Access court records free at www.greenvillecounty.org/scjd/publicindex/disclaim23.asp. Records go back to 1988.

Cleveland Summary Magistrate Court 3208 Geer Highway, Marietta, SC 29661; 864-834-3671; 9AM-5PM (EST). *Misdemeanor, Civil Actions under $7,500, Eviction, Small Claims.* www.greenvillecounty.org/Magistrate_Courts/Bates.asp
General Information: Formerly known as Travelers Rest Magistrate Court. Nearby courts are Cleveland, Highlands, and Greer. Access court records free at www.greenvillecounty.org/scjd/publicindex/disclaim23.asp. Records go back to 1988 but may be missing data.

Fairview/Austin Summary Magistrate Court 205 N Maple, #4, Simpsonville, SC 29681; 864-963-3457; fax: 864-963-0029; 8:30AM-5PM (EST). *Misdemeanor, Civil Actions under $7,500, Eviction, Small Claims.* www.greenvillecounty.org/Magistrate_Courts
General Information: Formerly Simpsonville Magistrate Court. Access court records free at www.greenvillecounty.org/scjd/publicindex/disclaim23.asp. Records go back to 1988 but may be missing data.

Gantt Summary Court 1103 White Horse Rd, Greenville, SC 29605; 864-277-4429; fax: 864-277-4376; 8:30AM-12:30 PM; 1:30PM--5PM (EST). *Misdemeanor, Civil Actions under $7,500, Eviction, Small Claims.* www.greenvillecounty.org/Magistrate_Courts/
General Information: Access court records free at www.greenvillecounty.org/scjd/publicindex/disclaim23.asp. Records go back

to 1988. Online records may be missing cases, sentence details, probation updates/violations.

Greenville Bond Court #1 & #2 4 McGhee St, LEC Rm 116A, Greenville, SC 29601; 864-467-5312-City #1, 864-467-5302-City #2; fax: 864-467-5105; 8:30AM-4:30PM (EST). *Misdemeanor, Civil Actions under $7,500, Eviction, Small Claims.*
www.greenvillecounty.org/Magistrate_Courts/
General Information: Access court records free at www.greenvillecounty.org/scjd/publicindex/disclaim23.asp. Records go back to 1988. Online records may be missing cases, sentence details, probation updates/violations.

Greer Summary Magistrate Court 100 S Main St Ste A, Greer, SC 29650; 864-877-7464; fax: 864-834-6911; 9AM-5PM (EST). *Misdemeanor, Civil Actions under $7,500, Eviction, Small Claims.*
www.greenvillecounty.org/Magistrate_Courts/Greer.asp
General Information: Formerly known as Travelers Rest Magistrate Court. Nearby courts are Cleveland, Highlands, and Greer. Access court records free at www.greenvillecounty.org/scjd/publicindex/disclaim23.asp. Records go back to 1988 but may be missing data.

Highlands Magistrate Summary Court 6 Bailey Mill Rd, Travelers Rest, SC 29690-8790; 864-895-0478; 9AM-5PM (EST). *Misdemeanor, Civil Actions under $7,500, Eviction, Small Claims.*
www.greenvillecounty.org/Magistrate_Courts/Highlands.asp
General Information: Formerly known as Travelers Rest Magistrate Court. Nearby courts are Cleveland, Highlands, and Greer. Access court records free at www.greenvillecounty.org/scjd/publicindex/disclaim23.asp. Records go back to 1988 but may be missing data.

South Greenville Summary Magistrate Court 8150 Augusta Rd, Piedmont, SC 29673; 864-277-9555; fax: 864-277-8345; 8:30AM-5PM (EST). *Misdemeanor, Civil Actions under $7,500, Eviction, Small Claims.*
www.greenvillecounty.org/Magistrate_Courts/
General Information: Formerly known as Piedmont Magistrate Court. Access court records free at www.greenvillecounty.org/scjd/publicindex/disclaim23.asp. Records go back to 1988 but may be missing data.

West Greenville Summary Magistrate Court 6247 White Horse Rd, Greenville, SC 29611; 864-294-4810; fax: 864-294-4801; 8:30AM-5PM (EST). *Misdemeanor, Civil Actions under $7,500, Eviction, Small Claims.* www.greenvillecounty.org/Magistrate_Courts/
General Information: Access court records free at www.greenvillecounty.org/scjd/publicindex/disclaim23.asp. Records go back to 1988. Online records may be missing cases, sentence details, probation updates/violations.

Probate Court 301 University Ridge, #1200, Greenville, SC 29601; 864-467-7170; fax: 864-467-7198; 8:30AM-5PM (EST). *Probate.*
www.greenvillecounty.org/probate/
General Information: Search probate records free online at www.greenvillecounty.org/ProbateSearch/default.asp. Also http://greenvillecounty.org/mlsearch/default.asp is for marriage licenses. And www.greenvillecounty.org/historical_records/default.asp.

Greenwood County

Circuit Court Courthouse, Rm 114, 528 Monument St, Greenwood, SC 29646; 864-943-8089; criminal phone: 864-942-8612; civil phone: 864-943-8089; fax: 864-942-8693; 8:30AM-5PM (EST). *Felony, Misdemeanor, Civil Actions over $7,500.*
General Information: No adoption, juvenile, sealed or expunged records released. Will not fax documents. Court makes copy: $.25 per page. Self serve copy: same. Certification fee: $2.00 per doc plus copy fee. Payee: Clerk of Court. Business and Personal checks accepted, credit cards are not. Prepayment required.
Civil Name Search: Access: In person, online. Visitors must perform in person searches themselves. Civil index in docket books from 1897; on computer back to 2000. Civil PAT goes back to 2000. Online access to the docket index is at www.sccourts.org/caseSearch/.
Criminal Name Search: Access: In person, online. Visitors must perform in person searches themselves. Required to search: name, years to search, DOB; also helpful: SSN. Criminal records on alpha index from 1897; on computer back to 2000. Criminal PAT goes back to 1988. Online access to the docket index is at www.sccourts.org/caseSearch/.

Greenwood County Magistrate Court 528 Monument Street, Rm 100, Greenwood, SC 29646; 864-942-8655; fax: 864-942-8663; 8:30AM-5PM (EST). *Misdemeanor, Civil Actions under $7,500, Eviction, Small Claims.* www.co.greenwood.sc.us
General Information: Online records (www.sccourts.org/caseSearch/) may be missing cases, also sentence details, probation updates/violations.

Probate Court PO Box 1210, 528 Monument St, Greenwood, SC 29648; 864-942-8625; fax: 864-942-8620; 8:30AM-5PM (EST). *Probate.*
www.greenwoodsc.gov/probatecourt.aspx
General Information: To search online, at the webpage, click on Estate Records Search or go to http://gis.greenwoodsc.gov/Probate/default.aspx.

Hampton County

Circuit Court PO Box 7, 1 Elm St, Courthouse Sq, Hampton, SC 29924; 803-914-2250; fax: 803-914-2258; 8AM-5PM (EST). *Felony, Civil Actions over $7,500.*
General Information: No adoption, juvenile, sealed or expunged records released. Will fax documents $1.00 per page. Court makes copy: $.50 per page. Self serve copy: $.50 per page. Certification fee: $1.00 per cert. Payee: Clerk of Court. Personal checks accepted, credit cards are not. Prepayment required. Mail requests: SASE required.
Civil Name Search: Access: Fax, mail, in person, online. Visitors must perform in person searches themselves. Search fee: $2.00 per name. Civil index on docket books, archived from 1878. Search the index free at http://publicindex.sccourts.org/hampton/publicindex/.
Criminal Name Search: Access: Fax, mail, in person, online. Visitors must perform in person searches themselves. Search fee: $2.00 per name. Required to search: name, years to search, DOB; also helpful: SSN. Criminal docket on books, archived from 1878. Search the index free at http://publicindex.sccourts.org/hampton/publicindex/.

Estill Magistrate Court PO Box 969, 125 Railroad St. SE, Estill, SC 29918; 803-625-3232; fax: 803-625-2148; 2PM-5PM M-F (EST). *Misdemeanor, Civil Actions under $7,500, Eviction, Small Claims.*
General Information: Online records (www.sccourts.org/caseSearch/) may be missing cases, also sentence details, probation updates/violations.

Varnville Magistrate Court Law Enforcement Ctr, 411 Cemetery Rd, PO Box 1299, Varnville, SC 29944; 803-914-2230; fax: 803-914-2239; 8:30AM-4:30PM (EST). *Misdemeanor, Civil Actions under $7,500, Eviction, Small Claims.*
General Information: Online records (www.sccourts.org/caseSearch/) may be missing cases, also sentence details, probation updates/violations.

Probate Court 1 Elm St, Courthouse Sq, Hampton, SC 29924; 803-914-2172; fax: 803-914-2183; 8AM-5PM (EST). *Probate.*
www.hamptoncountysc.org/index.aspx?nid=25
General Information: Probate office is located in the new building. For mailing, use PO 601, same ZIP.

Horry County

Circuit Court PO Box 677, 1301 2nd Ave, Conway, SC 29526; 843-915-5080; fax: 843-915-6081; 8AM-5PM (EST). *Felony, Misdemeanor, Civil Actions over $7,500.*
General Information: No adoption, juvenile, sealed or expunged records released. Court makes copy: $.25 per page. Self serve copy: $.25 per page. Certification fee: $1.00 per page plus copy fee. Payee: Clerk of Court. Business checks accepted. No credit cards accepted. Prepayment required. Mail requests: SASE helpful.
Civil Name Search: Access: In person, online. Both court and visitors may perform in person name searches. Civil records on computer from 1987, on alpha index from 1920s. Civil PAT available. Public terminal located in Law Library. Civil case details free at www.horrycounty.org/SCJDWEB/onlinedocket/.
Criminal Name Search: Access: Phone, fax, mail, n person, online. Both court and visitors may perform in person name searches. Search fee: $3.00 per name. Required to search: name, years to search, DOB, signed release. Criminal records computerized from 1987, on alpha index from 1920s. Mail turnaround time 2 days. Criminal PAT available. Criminal docket access online is same as civil. Online results show middle initial, DOB, address.

Little River Magistrate Court 107 Highway 57 N, Little River, SC 29566; 843-915-5292; fax: 843-915-6292; 8AM-5PM (EST). *Civil Actions under $7,500, Eviction, Small Claims, Misdemeanors.*
General Information: Access court records free at www.horrycounty.org/publicindex/. Online records may be missing cases, sentence details, probation updates/violations.

Aynor Magistrate Court 640 9th Ave, Aynor, SC 29511; 843-358-5508; fax: 843-358-0704; 8AM-5PM (EST). *Misdemeanor, Civil Actions under $7,500, Eviction, Small Claims.*
General Information: Access court records free at www.horrycounty.org/publicindex/. Online records may be missing cases, sentence details, probation updates/violations.

Conway Magistrate Court 1201 3rd Ave., Conway, SC 29528; 843-915-5290; fax: 843-915-6290; 8AM-5PM (EST). *Misdemeanor, Civil Actions under $7,500, Eviction, Small Claims.*
General Information: Access court records free at www.horrycounty.org/publicindex/. Online records may be missing cases, sentence details, probation updates/violations.

Conway Magistrate Court 1201 3rd Ave, 2nd Fl, Conway, SC 29526; 843-915-5290; fax: 843-915-6290; 8AM-5PM (EST). *Misdemeanor, Civil Actions under $7,500, Eviction, Small Claims.*
General Information: Access court records free at www.horrycounty.org/publicindex/. Online records may be missing cases, sentence details, probation updates/violations.

Green Sea Magistrate Court 5527 Hwy #9, PO Box 153, Green Sea, SC 29545; 843-915-5294; fax: 843-915-6293; 8AM-5PM (EST). *Misdemeanor, Civil Actions under $7,500, Eviction, Small Claims.*

Loris Magistrate Court 3817 Walnut St, Loris, SC 29569; 843-756-7918/6674; fax: 843-756-1355; 8AM-5PM (EST). *Misdemeanor, Civil Actions under $7,500, Eviction, Small Claims.*
General Information: Access court records free at www.horrycounty.org/publicindex/. Online records may be missing cases, sentence details, probation updates/violations.

Myrtle Beach Magistrate Court 1201 21st Ave N, Myrtle Beach, SC 29577; 843-915-5293; fax: 843-444-6131; 8AM-5PM (EST). *Misdemeanor, Civil Actions under $7,500, Eviction, Small Claims.*
General Information: Access court records free at www.horrycounty.org/publicindex/. Online records may be missing cases, sentence details, probation updates/violations.

South Strand Magistrate Court 9630 Scipio Ln, Myrtle Beach, SC 29588-7568; 843-915-5291; fax: 843-915-6291; 8AM-5PM (EST). *Misdemeanor, Civil Actions under $7,500, Eviction, Small Claims, Ordinance.*
General Information: Access court records free at www.horrycounty.org/publicindex/. Online records may be missing cases, sentence details, probation updates/violations.

Probate Court PO Box 288, 1301 2nd Ave, 2nd Fl, Right Wing, Conway, SC 29528; 843-915-5370; fax: 843-915-6370; 8AM-5PM (EST). *Probate.* www.horrycounty.org/probatecourt/index.asp

Jasper County

Circuit Court PO Box 248, Ridgeland, SC 29936; 843-726-7710; fax: 843-726-7711; 9AM-5PM (EST). *Felony, Misdemeanor, Civil Actions over $7,500.* www.jaspercourt.org/
General Information: No adoption, juvenile, sealed or expunged records released. Fee to fax specific case file $2.00 per page. Court makes copy: $1.00 per page. Self serve copy: same. Certification fee: $1.00. Payee: Clerk of Court. No personal checks. Major credit cards accepted. Prepayment required.
Civil Name Search: Access: In person, online. Visitors must perform in person searches themselves. Civil records on computer back to 1999; prior on books to 1912. Civil PAT goes back to 1993. Civil case details and dockets free at http://publicindex.sccourts.org/Jasper/publicindex/.
Criminal Name Search: Access: In person, online. Visitors must perform in person searches themselves. Required to search: name, years to search, DOB; SSN helpful, signed release. Criminal records computerized from 1999; prior on books to 1912. Note: The court refers requests for criminal name searches to the state agency (SLED). Criminal PAT goes back to same as civil. Access court records and dockets free at http://publicindex.sccourts.org/Jasper/publicindex/. Online results show middle initial, DOB, address.

Hardeeville Magistrate Court 21 Martin St, PO Box 1169, Hardeeville, SC 29927; 843-784-2628; fax: 843-784-3245; 9AM-5PM (EST). *Misdemeanor, Civil Actions under $7,500, Eviction, Small Claims.*
General Information: Access court records free at www.jaspercourt.org/publicindex. Online results include address and DOB may be missing cases, sentence details, probation updates/violations.

Pineland Magistrate Court *Closed - See Ridgeland Magistrate Court.*

Ridgeland Magistrate Court PO Box 748, 967 W Adams St, Ridgeland, SC 29936; 843-726-7933; fax: 843-726-4191; 9AM-N; 1-5PM (EST). *Misdemeanor, Civil Actions under $7,500, Eviction, Small Claims.*
General Information: Access court records free at www.jaspercourt.org/publicindex/. Online results include address and DOB but may be missing cases, sentence details, probation updates/violations.

Probate Court PO Box 1028, 265 Russell St, Ridgeland, SC 29936; 843-726-7718; fax: 843-726-5173; 9AM-5PM (EST). *Probate.* www.jaspercountysc.org/secondary.aspx?pageID=43
General Information: Access court records free at www.jaspercourt.org/publicindex/. Online results include address and DOB.

Kershaw County

Circuit Court County Courthouse, Rm 313, PO Box 1557, Camden, SC 29021; 803-425-7223; fax: 803-425-1505; 8:30AM-5PM (EST). *Felony, Misdemeanor, Civil Actions over $7,500.*
General Information: No adoption, juvenile, sealed or expunged records released. Will not fax documents. Court makes copy: $.50 per page. Self serve copy: same. Certification fee: $1.00 per document plus copy fee. Payee: Clerk of Court. Personal checks accepted. Major credit cards accepted in person only. Prepayment required. Mail requests: SASE required.
Civil Name Search: Access: Mail, in person, online. Visitors must perform in person searches themselves. Search fee: $20.00. Civil records archived from 1797, computerized records from 1994. Mail turnaround time 1 day. Civil PAT goes back to 1994. Online access to the docket index is at www.sccourts.org/caseSearch/.
Criminal Name Search: Access: Mail, in person, online. Visitors must perform in person searches themselves. Search fee: $20.00. Required to search: name, years to search, DOB; also helpful: SSN. Criminal records archived from 1880, computerized records from 1994. Mail turnaround time 1 day. Criminal PAT goes back to same as civil. Terminal results include SSN. Online access to the docket index is at www.sccourts.org/caseSearch/. Online results show middle initial, DOB, address.

Bethune Magistrate Court **Closed** formerly located at 202 N Main St, Bethune.

Camden Magistrate Court PO Box 1528, 1121 Broad St, County Courthouse, #202, Camden, SC 29020; 803-425-1500 x5382; fax: 803-425-6044; 8:30AM-5PM (EST). *Misdemeanor, Civil Actions under $7,500, Eviction, Small Claims, Traffic.*
General Information: Online records at http://publicindex.sccourts.org/kershaw/publicindex.

Probate Court 1121 Broad St, Camden, SC 29020; 803-425-7223; fax: 803-425-1505; 8:30AM-5PM (EST). *Probate.*
General Information: Mailing address: PO Box 1557, ZIP is 29021.

Lancaster County

Circuit Court PO Box 1809, 100 N main, Lancaster, SC 29721; 803-285-1581; fax: 803-416-9388; 8:30AM-5PM (EST). *Felony, Misdemeanor, Civil Actions over $7,500.*
General Information: The court is moving to a different location late in 2011. Phone numbers will remain the same. At that time the court may provide a public terminal for use. No adoption, juvenile, sealed or expunged records released. Will not fax documents. Court makes copy: $.25 per page. Self serve copy: same. Certification fee: $2.00. Payee: Clerk of Court. Personal checks accepted. No credit cards accepted for research or copies. Prepayment required.
Civil Name Search: Access: In person, online. Visitors must perform in person searches themselves. Civil records on computer from 1987, microfiche from 1937, alpha index from 1764. Note: This court will not perform name searches for the public. Online access to the docket index is at www.sccourts.org/caseSearch/.
Criminal Name Search: Access: In person, online. Visitors must perform in person searches themselves. Required to search: name, years to search, DOB; SSN helpful. Criminal records computerized from 1987. Note: This court will not perform name searches for the public. Online access to the docket index is at www.sccourts.org/caseSearch/.

Lancaster Magistrate Court 761 Lancaster Bypass East, Lancaster, SC 29720; 803-283-3983; fax: 803-416-9407; 8:30AM-5PM (EST). *Misdemeanor, Civil Actions under $7,500, Eviction, Small Claims, Traffic.* www.sccourts.org/magistrateCourt/magistrates.cfm?countyno=29

Probate Court PO Box 1809, 101 N Main St Rm 121 (29720), Lancaster, SC 29721; 803-283-3379; fax: 803-283-3370; 8:30AM-5PM (EST). *Probate.*
http://mylancastersc.org/index.asp?Type=B_BASIC&SEC={24B1DCB2-E909-4DFA-AB05-9710F48BB93C}

Laurens County

Circuit Court PO Box 287, 100 Hillcrest Sq, Laurens, SC 29360; 864-984-3538; fax: 864-984-7023; 9AM-5PM (EST). *Felony, Misdemeanor, Civil Actions over $7,500.*
General Information: No adoption, juvenile, sealed or expunged records released. Will not fax documents. Court makes copy: $.50 per page. Self serve copy: $.50 per page. Certification fee: $1.00 per page. Payee: Clerk of Court. No personal checks or credit cards accepted. Prepayment required.
Civil Name Search: Access: In person, online. Both court and visitors may perform in person name searches. Civil index on docket books back to 1800s; on computer back to 1980. Civil PAT goes back to 1987. Online access to the docket index for the Circuit and Summary Courts at http://publicindex.sccourts.org/laurens/publicindex/.
Criminal Name Search: Access: In person, online. Both court and visitors may perform in person name searches. Required to search: name, years to search, DOB; also helpful: SSN. Criminal records indexed in books back to 1950s; on computer back to 1980. Criminal PAT goes back to 1987. Online access to the docket index is at http://publicindex.sccourts.org/laurens/publicindex/.

Clinton Magistrate Court 203 W Pitts St, Clinton, SC 29325; 864-833-5879; fax: 864-833-7502; 8AM-5PM M, T; 8AM-N W; 8AM-10AM F (EST). *Misdemeanor, Civil Actions under $7,500, Eviction, Small Claims.*
General Information: Online records (www.sccourts.org/caseSearch/) may be missing cases, also sentence details, probation updates/violations.

Gray Court Magistrate Court PO Box 438, 329 Main St, Gray Court, SC 29645; 864-876-4390 X3; 9AM-5PM,M,T,W; 9AM-2PM Th (EST). *Misdemeanor, Civil Actions under $7,500, Eviction, Small Claims.*
General Information: Online records (www.sccourts.org/caseSearch/) may be missing cases, also sentence details, probation updates/violations.

Laurens Magistrate Court PO Box 925, 100 Hillcrest Square, Laurens, SC 29360; 864-683-4485; 9AM-5PM (EST). *Misdemeanor, Civil Actions under $7,500, Eviction, Small Claims.*
General Information: Online records (www.sccourts.org/caseSearch/) may be missing cases, also sentence details, probation updates/violations.

Probate Court PO Box 194, Laurens, SC 29360-194; 864-984-7315; fax: 864-984-3779; 9AM-5PM (EST). *Probate.* www.sccourts.org/probate/index.cfm?countyno=30

Lee County

Circuit Court PO Box 387, Bishopville, SC 29010; 803-484-5341; fax: 803-484-1632; 9AM-5PM (EST). *Felony, Misdemeanor, Civil Actions over $7,500.*
General Information: No adoption, juvenile, sealed or expunged records released. Will not fax documents. Court makes copy: $.50 per page, $1.00 minimum. Self serve copy: $.50 per page. Certification fee: $1.00 per page includes copy fee. Payee: Clerk of Court. Business checks accepted. No credit cards accepted. Prepayment required. Mail requests: SASE required.
Civil Name Search: Access: Mail, in person. Both court and visitors may perform in person name searches. Search fee: $5.00 per name. Civil records on computer from 1991, on archives from 1900s. Mail turnaround time 2 days. Civil PAT goes back to 1985.
Criminal Name Search: Access: Mail, in person. Both court and visitors may perform in person name searches. Search fee: $2.00 per name. Required to search: name, years to search, DOB; also helpful: SSN. Criminal records computerized from 1991, on archives from 1900s. Mail turnaround time 2 days. Criminal PAT goes back to same as civil.

Bishopville Magistrate Court 115 Gregg St, PO Box 2, Bishopsville, SC 29010; 803-484-6463; fax: 803-484-5163; 9AM-5-PM (EST). *Misdemeanor, Civil Actions under $7,500, Eviction, Small Claims, Traffic.*

Probate Court PO Box 24, 123 S Main St, Bishopville, SC 29010; 803-484-5341 X338, X339, X361; fax: 803-484-6881; 9AM-5PM (EST). *Probate.* www.sccourts.org/probate/index.cfm?countyno=31

Lexington County

Circuit Court Lexington County Judicial Ctr, Rm 107, 205 E Main St, Lexington, SC 29072; 803-785-8212; criminal phone: 803-785-8223; civil phone: 803-785-8252; probate phone: 803-785-8324; fax: 803-785-8603; 8AM-5PM (EST). *Felony, High Misdemeanor, Civil Actions over $7,500.* www.lex-co.com/Departments/ClerkOfCourt/Index.html
General Information: No adoption, juvenile, sealed or expunged records released. Will fax documents $.25 per page. Court makes copy: $.25 per page; included in search fee. Self serve copy: $.25 per page. Certification fee: $1.00 per cert plus copy fee. Payee: County of Lexington. Personal checks accepted, credit cards are not. Prepayment required. Mail requests: SASE required.
Civil Name Search: Access: Mail, in person, online. Both court and visitors may perform in person name searches. Search fee: $3.00 per name. Civil docket indexed from 1936. Mail turnaround time 3 days. Civil PAT goes back to 1984. Search record index free at http://cms.lex-co.com/scjdweb/publicindex/.
Criminal Name Search: Access: Fax, mail, in person, online. Both court and visitors may perform in person name searches. Search fee: $3.00 per name. Required to search: name, years to search, DOB, SSN. Criminal records on computer since 1983. Mail turnaround time 3 days. Criminal PAT goes back to 1983. Search the record index at http://cms.lex-co.com/scjdweb/publicindex/. Online results show middle initial, DOB, address.

Batesburg Leesville Magistrate Court 231 W Church St, Batesburg, SC 29006; 803-359-8330; criminal phone: 803-785-8330; civil phone: 803-332-0204; fax: 803-332-0357; 8AM-4:30PM (EST). *Misdemeanor, Civil Actions under $7,500, Eviction, Small Claims.* www.lex-co.com/Departments/MagistrateCourt/ALC.html

Cayce-West Columbia Magistrate Court 650 Knox Abbott Dr, Cayce, SC 29033; 803-796-7100; fax: 803-796-7635; 8AM-4:30PM (EST). *Misdemeanor, Civil Actions under $7,500, Eviction, Small Claims.* www.lex-co.com/Departments/MagistrateCourt/ALC.html

Irmo Magistrate Court 111 Lincreek, Columbia, SC 29212; 803-781-7584; fax: 803-749-4050; 8AM-4:30PM (EST). *Misdemeanor, Civil Actions under $7,500, Eviction, Small Claims.* www.lex-co.com/Departments/MagistrateCourt/ALC.html

Lexington Magistrate Court 139 E Main St, Ste B, Magistrate's Office, Lexington, SC 29072; 803-785-8221; fax: 803-785-8155; 8AM-5PM (EST). *Misdemeanor, Civil Actions under $7,500, Eviction, Small Claims.* www.lex-co.com/Departments/MagistrateCourt/ALC.html

Swansea Magistrate Court 500 Charlie Rast Rd, PO Box 457, Swansea, SC 29160; 803-785-3616; fax: 803-785-4078; 8:30AM-4:30PM (EST). *Misdemeanor, Civil Actions under $7,500, Eviction, Small Claims.* www.lex-co.com/Departments/MagistrateCourt/Index.html

Probate Court 205 E Main St, Suite 134, Lexington, SC 29072; 803-785-8324; 8AM-5PM (EST). *Probate.* www.lex-co.com/Departments/probatecourt/Index.html

Marion County

Circuit Court 100 W Court St, Marion, SC 29571; 843-423-8240; fax: 843-423-8242; 8:30AM-5PM (EST). *Felony, Misdemeanor, Civil Actions over $7,500.*
General Information: No adoption, juvenile, sealed or expunged records released. Will not fax documents. Court makes copy: $.25 per page. Self serve copy: $.25 per page. Certification fee: $1.00 per cert. Payee: Circuit Court Clerk. No personal checks or credit cards accepted. Prepayment required.
Civil Name Search: Access: In person, online. Visitors must perform in person name searches themselves. Civil records on computer since 1988; prior records on index cards from 1800s. Civil PAT goes back to 1980s. A free name index search is at http://publicindex.sccourts.org/marion/publicindex/. Online records may be missing cases, sentence details, probation updates/violations.
Criminal Name Search: Access: In person, online. Visitors must perform in person searches themselves. Required to search: name, years to search, DOB. Criminal records on computer since 1988; prior records on index cards from 1800s. Criminal PAT goes back to 1980s. A free name index search is at http://publicindex.sccourts.org/marion/publicindex/. Online records may be missing cases, sentence details, probation updates/violations.

Gresham Magistrate Court 2715 Hwy 76 E., #B, Mullins, SC 25974; 843-423-8208; fax: 843-423-8394; 8:30AM-5PM (EST). *Misdemeanor, Civil Actions under $7,500, Eviction, Small Claims.*
General Information: Online records (www.sccourts.org/caseSearch/) may be missing cases, also sentence details, probation updates/violations.

Marion/Mullins Magistrate Court 2715 E Hwy 76, #B, Mullins, SC 29574-6015; 843-423-8208; fax: 843-423-8394; 8:30AM-5PM (EST). *Misdemeanor, Civil Actions under $7,500, Eviction, Small Claims.*
General Information: Online records (www.sccourts.org/caseSearch/) may be missing cases, also sentence details, probation updates/violations.

Probate Court PO Box 583, 100 W Court St Rm 202, Marion, SC 29571; 843-423-8244; fax: 843-431-5026; 8:30AM-5PM (EST). *Probate, Estate, Guardianship, Conservatorship, Marriage.*

Marlboro County

Circuit Court PO Drawer 996, 105 Main St, Bennettsville, SC 29512; 843-479-5613; fax: 843-479-5640; 8:30AM-5PM (EST). *Felony, Misdemeanor, Civil Actions over $7,500.*
General Information: No adoption, juvenile, sealed or expunged records released. Will not fax documents. Court makes copy: $3.00 per set. Self serve copy: $.25 per page. Certification fee: $3.00,per document, add $.25 per page. Payee: Clerk of Court. In-state Personal checks accepted, credit cards are not. Prepayment required. Mail requests: SASE required.
Civil Name Search: Access: Mail, in person, online. Visitors must perform in person searches themselves. Search fee: $5.00 per name. Civil records on computer from 1985, on index from 1786. Mail turnaround time 1 day. Civil PAT goes back to 1985. Free access to the docket index at http://publicindex.sccourts.org/marlboro/publicindex/. Includes search for civil judgments.
Criminal Name Search: Access: Mail, in person, online. Visitors must perform in person searches themselves. Search fee: $5.00 per name. Required to search: name, years to search, DOB; also helpful: SSN. Criminal records computerized from 1985, on index from 1786. Mail turnaround time 1 day. Criminal PAT available. Free access to the docket index at http://publicindex.sccourts.org/marlboro/publicindex/. Search by name or case number.

Bennettsville Magistrate Court PO Box 418, Bennettsville, SC 29512; 843-479-5620; fax: 843-479-5646; 8:30AM-4:30PM M-TH; Civil 4-5PM (EST). *Misdemeanor, Civil Actions under $7,500, Eviction, Small Claims.*

Marlboro County Summary Court PO Box 418, 249 Throop St, Bennettsville, SC 29512; 843-479-5620; fax: 843-479-5646; 8:30AM-4:30PM (EST). *Civil Actions under $7,500, Eviction, Small Claims.*
General Information: Same searching and fees as at Circuit Court.

Probate Court PO Box 455, 105 E Main St, Bennettsville, SC 29512; 843-479-5610; fax: 843-479-5668; 8:30AM-5PM (EST). *Probate.*
www.sccourts.org/probate/index.cfm?countyno=34

McCormick County

Circuit Court 133 S Mine St, Rm 102, McCormick, SC 29835; 864-852-2195; probate phone: 864-852-2630; fax: 864-852-0071; 9AM-5PM (EST). *Felony, Misdemeanor, Civil Actions over $7,500.*
General Information: No adoption, juvenile, sealed or expunged records released. Will not fax out case files. Court makes copy: criminal court $.50 per page. Self serve copy: $.50 per page. Certification fee: $1.00 per page. Payee: Clerk of Court. Personal checks accepted, credit cards are not. Prepayment required.
Civil Name Search: Access: In person, online. Visitors must perform in person searches themselves. Civil index on docket books from 1916. A free index search is at http://publicindex.sccourts.org/mccormick/publicindex/.
Criminal Name Search: Access: In person, online. Visitors must perform in person searches themselves. Required to search: name, years to search, DOB; SSN helpful. Criminal records indexed in books from 1916. A free index search is at http://publicindex.sccourts.org/mccormick/publicindex/.

McCormick Magistrate Court 211 W Augusta Ext., PO Box 1116, McCormick, SC 29835; 864-852-2316; fax: 864-852-2582; 8AM-N, 1-4PM (EST). *Misdemeanor, Civil Actions under $7,500, Eviction, Small Claims.*
General Information: Online records (www.sccourts.org/caseSearch/) may be missing cases, also sentence details, probation updates/violations. Payments can be made online.

Probate Court 133 S Mine St, #101, McCormick, SC 29835; 864-852-2630; fax: 864-852-0071; 9AM-5PM (EST). *Probate.*

Newberry County

Circuit Court PO Drawer 10, 1226 College St, Newberry, SC 29108; 803-321-2110; fax: 803-321-2111; 8:30AM-5PM (EST). *Felony, Misdemeanor, Civil Actions over $7,500.*
www.newberrycounty.net/clerk/index.html
General Information: No adoption, juvenile, sealed, PTI or expunged records released. Will fax documents $2.00 per page. Court makes copy: $.20 per page. Certification fee: $1.00 per page. Payee: Clerk of Court. Only cashiers checks and money orders accepted. No credit cards accepted. Prepayment required.
Civil Name Search: Access: In person, online. Visitors must perform in person searches themselves. Civil records on computer from 1983, docket books from 1776. Civil PAT goes back to 1989. Access the docket index from the Circuit and Summary Courts at http://publicindex.sccourts.org/newberry/publicindex/.
Criminal Name Search: Access: In person, online. Visitors must perform in person searches themselves. Required to search: name, years to search, DOB; SSN helpful. Criminal records computerized from 1983, docket books from 1776. Criminal PAT goes back to same as civil. Access the docket index from the Circuit and Summary Courts at http://publicindex.sccourts.org/newberry/publicindex/.

Little Mountain Magistrate Court PO Box 100, 824 Main St, Little Mountain, SC 29075; 803-345-1040; fax: 803-945-7222; 2PM-5PM T,W (EST). *Misdemeanor, Civil Actions under $7,500, Eviction, Small Claims.*
www.newberrycounty.net/magistrate/mountain.htm

Newberry Magistrate Court 3239 Louis Rich Rd, Newberry, SC 29108; criminal phone: 803-321-2144; civil phone: 803-321-2145; probate phone: 803-321-2118; fax: 803-321-2172; 8:30AM-5PM (EST). *Misdemeanor, Civil Actions under $7,500, Eviction, Small Claims, Traffic.*
www.newberrycounty.net/
General Information: Probate fax is same as main fax number.

Peak Magistrate Court 441 Church St, Peak, SC 29122; 803-345-5052; 8:30AM-4:30PM (EST). *Misdemeanor, Civil Actions under $7,500, Eviction, Small Claims.*
www.newberrycounty.net/magistrate/peak.htm

Whitmire Magistrate Court 313 Main St, Whitmire, SC 29178; 803-694-5756 or 321-2144; fax: 803-694-5756; 8:30AM-4:30PM (EST). *Misdemeanor, Civil Actions under $7,500, Eviction, Small Claims.*
www.newberrycounty.net/magistrate/whitmire.htm

Probate Court PO Box 442, 1309 College St, Newberry, SC 29108; 803-321-2118; fax: 803-321-2119; 8:30AM-5PM (EST). *Probate.*
www.newberrycounty.net
General Information: Records here include marriage. Guardianship, and conservatorship.

Oconee County

Circuit Court PO Box 678, 205 W Main St, Walhalla, SC 29691; 864-638-4280; fax: 864-638-4282; 8:30AM-5PM (EST). *Felony, Misdemeanor, Civil Actions over $7,500.*
www.oconeesc.com/
General Information: No adoption, juvenile, sealed or expunged records released. Will not fax documents. Court makes copy: $1.00 first page, $.50 each add'l. Self serve copy: $.50 per page. No certification fee. Payee: Clerk of Court. No personal checks accepted. Major credit or debit cards accepted if in person. Prepayment required.
Civil Name Search: Access: In person, online. Visitors must perform in person searches themselves. Civil index on cards from 1868; on computer back to 1994. Civil PAT goes back to 1996. Search the index free at http://publicindex.sccourts.org/oconee/publicindex/.
Criminal Name Search: Access: In person, online. Visitors must perform in person searches themselves. Required to search: name, years to search; also helpful: DOB, SSN, signed release. Criminal records indexed on cards from 1868; on computer back to 1994. Criminal PAT goes back to same as civil. Search the index free at http://publicindex.sccourts.org/oconee/publicindex/.

Walhalla Magistrate (Summary) Court 208 Booker Dr, Walhalla, SC 29691; 864-638-4125; fax: 864-638-4229; 8:30AM-5PM M-F (EST). *Misdemeanor, Civil Actions under $7,500, Eviction, Small Claims, Traffic.*
General Information: Also known as Oconee County Summary Court. Online records (www.sccourts.org/caseSearch/) may be missing cases, also sentence details, probation updates/violations. Will not fax documents. Court makes copy: Criminal court copy $.50 per page. Payee: Oconee County Summary Court. Personal checks accepted. Major credit cards accepted. Prepayment required.
Civil Name Search: Access: Mail, in person, online. Only the court performs in person name searches; visitors may not. Search fee: Fee determined by amount of clerk's time taken. Required to search: name. Indexed by defendant. Small claims and civil in same index. Evictions destroyed annually; complaints after 10 years; claim/delivery records after 3 years. Mail turnaround time 5-7 days. The index is searchable at http://publicindex.sccourts.org/oconee/publicindex/.
Criminal Name Search: Access: Mail, in person, online. Only the court performs in person name searches; visitors may not. Search fee: Fee determined by amount of clerk's time taken. The index is searchable at http://publicindex.sccourts.org/oconee/publicindex/.

County Summary Court CLOSED See Walhalla Magistrate Court.

Westminster Magistrate Court 106 E Windsor St, Westminster, SC 29693; 864-647-5998; fax: 864-647-4844; 8:30-4:30PM (EST). *Misdemeanor, Civil Actions under $7,500, Eviction, Small Claims, Traffic.*
General Information: Same fees and search rules as at Walhalla Ct and Seneca Ct. Online records (www.sccourts.org/caseSearch/) may be missing cases.

Probate Court PO Box 471, 415 S Pine St, Walhalla, SC 29691; 864-638-4275; fax: 864-638-4278; 8:30AM-5PM (EST). *Probate.*
www.oconeesc.com/Departments/KZ/ProbateCourt.aspx

Orangeburg County

Circuit Court PO Box 9000, 101 Docket Av, Orangeburg, SC 29116; 803-533-6260; criminal phone: 803-533-6262; civil phone: 803-533-6219; fax: 803-534-3848; 8:30AM-5PM (EST). *Felony, Misdemeanor, Civil Actions over $7,500.* www.orangeburgcounty.org/
General Information: No adoption, juvenile, sealed or expunged records released. Will not fax documents. Court makes copy: $.50 per page. Self serve copy: $.50 per page. Certification fee: $2.00. Payee: Clerk of Court. Personal checks accepted, credit cards are not. Prepayment required.
Civil Name Search: Access: In person, online. Visitors must perform in person searches themselves. Civil index on cards from 1924. Civil PAT goes back to 1998. Online access to the docket index is at www.sccourts.org/caseSearch/.
Criminal Name Search: Access: In person, online. Visitors must perform in person searches themselves. Required to search: name, years to search, DOB; SSN helpful. Criminal records indexed on cards from 1924. Criminal PAT goes back to 1998. Online access to the docket index is at www.sccourts.org/caseSearch/.

Bowman Magistrate Court *Misdemeanor, Civil Actions under $7,500, Eviction, Small Claims.*

General Information: Direct records search requests to Holly Hill Magistrate Court. Search index online free at www.orangeburgcounty.org/scjdweb/publicindex/.

Branchville Magistrate Court PO Box 85, 7644 Freedom Rd, Branchville, SC 29432; 803-274-8000; fax: 803-274-8760; 8:30AM-5PM (EST). *Misdemeanor, Civil Actions under $7,500, Eviction, Small Claims.*
General Information: Direct records search requests to Orangeburg County Magistrate Court. Search index online free at www.orangeburgcounty.org/scjdweb/publicindex/.

Elloree Magistrate Court *Misdemeanor, Civil Actions under $7,500, Eviction, Small Claims.*
General Information: Direct record searches to Holly Hill Magistrate Ct. Search index free at www.orangeburgcounty.org/scjdweb/publicindex/ but may be missing cases, also sentence details, probation updates/violations.

Eutawville Magistrate Court *Misdemeanor, Civil Actions under $7,500, Eviction, Small Claims.*
General Information: Direct record searches to Holly Hill Magistrate Court. Search index online free at www.orangeburgcounty.org/scjdweb/publicindex/.

Holly Hill Magistrate Court - Eastern PO Box 154, 7324 Old State Rd, Hwy 176, Holly Hill, SC 29059; 803-496-9533; fax: 803-496-5661; 8:30AM-5PM (EST). *Misdemeanor, Civil Actions under $7,500, Eviction, Small Claims.*
www.orangeburgcounty.org/
General Information: Also holds records for Magistrate courts in Elloree, Bowman, and Eutawville. Search index online free at www.orangeburgcounty.org/scjdweb/publicindex/.

Neeses Magistrate Court - Western 6357 Savannah Highway, PO Box 387, North, SC 29107; 803-247-2011; fax: 803-247-2058; 8:30AM-5PM (EST). *Misdemeanor, Civil Actions under $7,500, Eviction, Small Claims.*
General Information: Also holds records for Magistrate courts in North, Springfield, and Norway. Neeses was a new court location in 2007. Search index online free at www.orangeburgcounty.org/scjdweb/publicindex/.

Norway Magistrate Court. *Misdemeanor, Civil Actions under $7,500, Eviction, Small Claims.*
General Information: Direct records search requests to Neeses Magistrate Court. Search index online free at www.orangeburgcounty.org/scjdweb/publicindex/.

Orangeburg Central Region Magistrate Court PO Box 9000, 1540 Ellis Ave NE, Orangeburg, SC 29116; 803-533-5880/5879; fax: 803-516-4011; 8:30AM-5PM (EST). *Misdemeanor, Civil Actions under $7,500, Eviction, Small Claims.*
General Information: Also holds records for Branchville Magistrate Court. Search index online free at www.orangeburgcounty.org/scjdweb/publicindex/.

Orangeburg Magistrate Court PO Box 9000, 1540 Ellis Ave, Orangeburg, SC 29116; 803-533-5843; fax: 803-516-4011; 8:30AM-5PM (EST). *Misdemeanor, Civil Actions under $7,500, Eviction, Small Claims.*
General Information: Search index online free at www.orangeburgcounty.org/scjdweb/publicindex/. Online records may be missing cases, sentence details, probation updates/violations.

Springfield and North Magistrate Courts. *Misdemeanor, Civil Actions under $7,500, Eviction, Small Claims.*
General Information: Direct records search requests to Neeses Magistrate Court. Search index online free at www.orangeburgcounty.org/scjdweb/publicindex/.

Probate Court PO Drawer 9000, 190 Gibson St, Orangeburg, SC 29116-9000; 803-533-6280; fax: 803-533-6279; 8:30AM-5PM (EST). *Probate.*
www.sccourts.org/probate/index.cfm?countyno=38

Pickens County

Circuit Court PO Box 215, 214 E Main St, Pickens, SC 29671; 864-898-5857; criminal phone: 864-898-5864; civil phone: 864-898-5862; fax: 864-898-5863; 8:30AM-5PM (EST). *Felony, Misdemeanor, Civil Actions over $7,500.* www.co.pickens.sc.us
General Information: Online identifiers in results same as on public terminal. No adoption, juvenile, sealed or expunged records released. Will not fax documents. Court makes copy: $.25 per page. Certification fee: $1.00. Payee: Clerk of Court. Personal checks accepted, credit cards are not. Prepayment required.
Civil Name Search: Access: In person, online. Both court and visitors may perform in person name searches. No search fee. Civil records on computer from 1990, on index from 1970. Civil PAT goes back to 1990. Civil case details free at www.greenvillecounty.org/scjd/publicindex/.
Criminal Name Search: Access: In person, online. Both court and visitors may perform in person name searches. No search fee. Required to

search: name, years to search, DOB; also helpful: SSN. Criminal records computerized from 1990, on index from 1970. Criminal PAT goes back to same as civil. Access case details free at www.greenvillecounty.org/scjd/publicindex/. Online results show name, DOB.

Clemson Magistrate Court 115-B Commons Way, Central, SC 29630; 864-639-8084; fax: 864-639-0701; 8:30AM-4:30PM (EST). *Misdemeanor, Civil Actions under $7,500, Eviction, Small Claims.*
General Information: Access court records free at www.greenvillecounty.org/scjd/publicindex/. Online records may be missing cases, sentence details, probation updates/violations.

Easley Magistrate Court 135 Folger Ave, Easley, SC 29640; 864-850-7076; fax: 864-850-7075; 8:30AM-4:30PM (EST). *Misdemeanor, Civil Actions under $7,500, Eviction, Small Claims.*
General Information: Access court records free at www.greenvillecounty.org/scjd/publicindex/. Online records may be missing cases, sentence details, probation updates/violations.

Liberty Magistrate Court 147-B Kay Holcombe Rd, Liberty, SC 29657; 864-843-5821; fax: 864-843-5824; 8:30AM-5PM (EST). *Misdemeanor, Civil Actions under $7,500, Eviction, Small Claims.*
General Information: Access court records free at www.greenvillecounty.org/scjd/publicindex/. Online records may be missing cases, sentence details, probation updates/violations.

Pickens Magistrate Court 216-A, Law Enforcement Ctr Rd, Pickens, SC 29671; 864-898-5551/5552; fax: 864-898-5546; 8:30AM-4:30PM (EST). *Misdemeanor, Civil Actions under $7,500, Eviction, Small Claims.*
www.co.pickens.sc.us/Magistrate/default.aspx
General Information: Access court records free at www.greenvillecounty.org/scjd/publicindex/. Online records may be missing cases, sentence details, probation updates/violations.

Probate Court 222 McDaniel Ave, #B-16, Pickens, SC 29671; 864-898-5903; fax: 864-898-5924; 8AM-5PM (EST). *Probate.*
www.co.pickens.sc.us/Probate/default.aspx

Richland County

Circuit Court Clerk of Court, 1701 Main St, Ste 205, Columbia, SC 29201; 803-576-1950; fax: 803-576-1785; 8:30AM-5PM (EST). *Felony, Misdemeanor, Civil Actions over $7,500.*
www.richlandonline.com/departments/clerkofcourt/
General Information: Mail address is PO Box 2766, Zip 29202-2766. No adoption, juvenile, sealed or expunged records released. Will fax to gov't agencies only. Court makes copy: $.25 per page. Certification fee: $1.00. Payee: Richland County Clerk. No personal checks or credit cards accepted. Prepayment required. Mail requests: SASE required for civil.
Civil Name Search: Access: Mail, in person, online. Both court and visitors may perform in person name searches. Search fee: $5.00 per name. Civil records on computer from 1990. Many prior records indexed to 1920's. Civil PAT goes back to 1987. Limited civil case details free at www4.rcgov.us/publicindex/default.aspx. Online court records at www.richlandonline.com/departments/clerkofcourt/courtroster.asp; search by date.
Criminal Name Search: Access: In person, online. Visitors must perform in person searches themselves. Required to search: name, years to search; also helpful: DOB, SSN. Criminal records on index to 1920's, computerized since 1987. Criminal PAT goes back to same as civil. Limited access case details free at www4.rcgov.us/publicindex/default.aspx. Online court records at www.richlandonline.com/departments/clerkofcourt/courtroster.asp; search by date. Online results show middle initial, DOB, address.

Central Magistrate Court 1400 Huger St, PO Box 192, Columbia, SC 29201; 803-576-2300; fax: 803-576-2326; 8:30AM-5PM (EST). *Misdemeanor, Criminal Domestic Violence, Felony Prelims, Civil Actions under $7,500, Traffic.*
General Information: Access court records free at www4.rcgov.us/publicindex/default.aspx. Online court records may be missing cases, sentence details, and probation updates/violations.

Columbia Magistrate Court 1515 Richland St, Columbia, SC 29201; 803-576-2510; fax: 803-576-2519; 8:30AM-5PM (EST). *Misdemeanor, Civil Actions under $7,500, Eviction, Small Claims.*
General Information: Access court records free at www4.rcgov.us/publicindex/default.aspx. Online court records may be missing cases, sentence details, and probation updates/violations.

Dentsville Magistrate Court 2500 Decker Blvd, #B-1, Box 10, Columbia, SC 29206; 803-576-2560; fax: 803-576-2569; 8:30AM-5PM (EST). *Misdemeanor, Civil Actions under $7,500, Eviction, Small Claims.*
www.rcgov.us/departments/Magistrate/index.asp

General Information: Access court records free at www4.rcgov.us/publicindex/default.aspx. Online court records may be missing cases, sentence details, and probation updates/violations.

Dutch Fork Magistrate Court 1019 Beatty Rd, Columbia, SC 29210-4630; 803-576-2540; fax: 803-576-2545; 8AM-4:30PM (EST). *Misdemeanor, Civil Actions under $7,500, Small Claims, Eviction.*
General Information: Access court records free at www4.rcgov.us/publicindex/default.aspx. Online court records may be missing cases, sentence details, and probation updates/violations.

Eastover Magistrate Court PO Box 762, 4501 E Main St, Eastover, SC 29044; 803-576-2580; fax: 803-576-2589; 8:30AM-5PM (EST). *Misdemeanor, Civil Actions under $7,500, Eviction, Small Claims.* www.richlandonline.com/departments/magistrate/index.asp
General Information: Access court records free at www4.rcgov.us/publicindex/default.aspx. Online court records may be missing cases, sentence details, and probation updates/violations.

Hopkins Magistrate Court 6108 Cabin Creek Rd, PO Box 70, Hopkins, SC 29061; 803-576-2530; fax: 803-576-2535; 8AM-4:30PM (EST). *Misdemeanor, Civil Actions under $7,500, Eviction, Small Claims.*
General Information: Access court records free at www4.rcgov.us/publicindex/default.aspx. Online court records may be missing cases, sentence details, and probation updates/violations.

Lykesland Magistrate Court 1403 Caroline Rd, Columbia, SC 29209; 803-576-2500; fax: 803-576-2504; 8:30AM-5PM (EST). *Misdemeanor, Civil Actions under $7,500, Eviction, Small Claims.*
General Information: Access court records free at www4.rcgov.us/publicindex/default.aspx. Online court records may be missing cases, sentence details, and probation updates/violations.

Olympia Magistrate Court 1601 B Shop Rd, Columbia, SC 29201; 803-576-2550; fax: 803-576-2555; 8:30AM-5PM (EST). *Misdemeanor, Civil Actions under $7,500, Eviction, Small Claims.* www.richlandonline.com/departments/magistrate/index.asp
General Information: Access court records free at www4.rcgov.us/publicindex/default.aspx. Online court records may be missing cases, sentence details, and probation updates/violations.

Pontiac Magistrate Court 10509 Two Notch Rd, #D, Elgin, SC 29045; 803-576-2520; fax: 803-576-2522; 8:30AM-5PM (EST). *Misdemeanor, Civil Actions under $7,500, Eviction, Small Claims.* www.richlandonline.com/departments/magistrate/index.asp
General Information: Access court records free at www4.rcgov.us/publicindex/default.aspx. Online court records may be missing cases, sentence details, and probation updates/violations.

Upper Township Magistrate Court 4919 Rhett St, Columbia, SC 29203; 803-576-2570; fax: 803-576-2579; 8:30AM-5PM (EST). *Misdemeanor, Civil Actions under $7,500, Eviction, Small Claims.* www.rcgov.us/departments/Magistrate/index.asp
General Information: Access court records free at www4.rcgov.us/publicindex/default.aspx. Online court records may be missing cases, sentence details, and probation updates/violations.

Waverly Magistrate Court 2712 Middleburg Dr, #106, Columbia, SC 29204; 803-576-2590; fax: 803-576-2599; 8AM-4:30PM (EST). *Misdemeanor, Civil Actions under $7,500, Eviction, Small Claims.* www.rcgov.us/departments/Magistrate/index.asp
General Information: Access court records free at www4.rcgov.us/publicindex/default.aspx. Online court records may be missing cases, sentence details, and probation updates/violations.

Probate Court 1701 Main St, #207, Columbia, SC 29201; 803-576-1961; fax: 803-576-1993; 8:30AM-5PM (EST). *Probate.* www.richlandonline.com/departments/probate/index.asp
General Information: Access county estate records back to 1983 free at www.richlandonline.com/services/estatesinquiry2.asp.

Saluda County

Circuit Court County Courthouse, 100 E Church St, #6, Saluda, SC 29138; 864-445-4500; fax: 864-445-3772; 8:30AM-5PM (EST). *Felony, Misdemeanor, Civil Actions over $7,500.*
General Information: No adoption, juvenile, sealed or expunged records released. Will not fax documents. Court makes copy: $.25 per page. Self serve copy: same. Certification fee: $1.00. Payee: Clerk of Court. Personal checks accepted, credit cards are not. Prepayment required. Mail requests: SASE required for mail return of any copies.
Civil Name Search: Access: In person, online. Both court and visitors may perform in person name searches. No search fee. Required to search: name, years to search, address. Civil records on computer from 1995, on index from 1897. Civil PAT goes back to 1995. Search the case record index at http://publicindex.sccourts.org/saluda/publicindex/. Includes access to civil judgments.

Criminal Name Search: Access: In person. Both court and visitors may perform in person name searches. No search fee. Required to search: name, years to search, address, DOB, signed release; also helpful: SSN. Criminal records computerized from 1995, on index from 1897. Note: Request must be in writing, even though in person and not mail requests are accepted. Criminal PAT goes back to same as civil. Search the case record index at http://publicindex.sccourts.org/saluda/publicindex/. Search by name or case number.

Saluda Magistrate Court 108 S Rudolph St, Courthouse Annex, Saluda, SC 29138; 864-445-4500; criminal phone: x2236; fax: 864-445-3684; 8AM-4:30PM (EST). *Misdemeanor, Civil Actions under $7,500, Eviction, Small Claims.* www.judicial.state.sc.us/magistrateCourt/

Probate Court 100 E Church St #4, Saluda, SC 29138; 864-445-4500 x2220; fax: 864-445-9726; 8:30AM-5PM (EST). *Probate.*

Spartanburg County

Circuit Court County Courthouse, 180 Magnolia St, Ste 500, Spartanburg, SC 29306; 864-596-2591; fax: 864-596-2239; 8:30AM-5PM (EST). *Felony, Misdemeanor, Civil Actions over $7,500.* www.spartanburgcounty.org/govt/depts/coc/index.htm
General Information: No adoption, juvenile, sealed or expunged records released. Will not fax documents. Court makes copy: $1.00 per page. Certification fee: $1.00 per cert plus copy fee. Payee: Clerk of Court. Personal checks accepted. Prepayment required.
Civil Name Search: Access: In person, online. Visitors must perform in person searches themselves. Civil records on computer from 1975, on microfiche from 1960, on alpha index from 1800s. Public use terminal has civil records back to 1970. Civil case details free at http://192.146.148.40/publicindex/.
Criminal Name Search: Access: In person, online. Visitors must perform in person searches themselves. Required to search: name, years to search, DOB, SSN, signed release. Criminal records computerized from 1975, on microfiche from 1960, on alpha index from 1800s. Note: The public may search the index. Access case details free at http://192.146.148.40/publicindex/.

Chesnee Magistrate Court 201 W Cherokee St, Chesnee, SC 29323; 864-461-3402; fax: 864-461-3404; 3:30-9PM T: 12-9PM TH (EST). *Misdemeanor, Civil Actions under $7,500, Eviction, Small Claims.*
General Information: Access court records free at http://192.146.148.40/publicindex/. Online records may be missing cases, sentence details, probation updates/violations.

Inman Magistrate Court 20 S Main St, Inman, SC 29349; 864-472-4447/6247; fax: 864-596-3622; 8AM-8PM M; 8AM-11AM T (EST). *Misdemeanor, Civil Actions under $7,500, Eviction, Small Claims.*
General Information: Access court records free at http://192.146.148.40/publicindex/. Online records may be missing cases, sentence details, probation updates/violations.

Landrum Magistrate Court 104 E Tucker St, Landrum, SC 29356; 864-457-7245; fax: 864-457-7245; 8AM-6PM T; 9AM-1PM W (EST). *Misdemeanor, Civil Actions under $7,500, Eviction, Small Claims.*
General Information: Access court records free at http://192.146.148.40/publicindex/. Online records may be missing cases, sentence details, probation updates/violations.

Pacolet Magistrate Court 980 Sunny Acres Rd, PO Box 416, Pacolet Mills, SC 29373; 864-474-0344/3391; fax: 864-474-4444; 6PM-10PM M & W; 6PM-19PM TH (EST). *Misdemeanor, Civil Actions under $7,500, Eviction, Small Claims.*
General Information: Access court records free at http://192.146.148.40/publicindex/. Online records may be missing cases, sentence details, probation updates/violations.

Reidville Magistrate Court 162 Leonard Rd, PO Box 124, Reidville, SC 29375; 864-433-9223; 9AM-6PM M; 6PM-9PM T (EST). *Misdemeanor, Civil Actions under $7,500, Eviction, Small Claims.*
General Information: Access court records free at http://192.146.148.40/publicindex/. Online records may be missing cases, sentence details, probation updates/violations.

Spartanburg Magistrate Court County Courthouse, Rm 105, 180 Magnolia St, Spartanburg, SC 29306-2392; 864-596-2564; fax: 864-596-3622; 8:30AM-5PM (EST). *Misdemeanor, Civil Actions under $7,500, Eviction, Small Claims.* www.spartanburgmagistrates.com/
General Information: Access court records free at http://192.146.148.40/publicindex/. Online records may be missing cases, sentence details, probation updates/violations.

Probate Court 180 Magnolia St, Rm 302, Spartanburg, SC 29306-2392; 864-596-2556; fax: 864-596-2011; 8:30AM-5PM (EST). *Probate.*

Sumter County

Circuit Court 141 N Main, Sumter, SC 29150; 803-436-2227; criminal phone: 803-436-2264/65; civil phone: 803-436-2231/2228; fax: 803-436-2223; 8:30AM-5PM (EST). *Felony, Misdemeanor, Civil Actions over $7,500.*
www.sumtercountysc.org
General Information: No adoption, juvenile, sealed or expunged records released. Will not fax documents. Court makes copy: $.25 per page. Self serve copy: same. Certification fee: $5.00. Payee: Sumter County Treasurer. Business checks accepted. No credit cards accepted. Prepayment required. Mail requests: SASE required.
Civil Name Search: Access: Mail, in person, online. Both court and visitors may perform in person name searches. Search fee: $10.00 per name. Required to search: name, years to search; also helpful: address. Civil records on computer from 1987, microfiche and books from 1900s. Mail turnaround time 2 days. Civil PAT goes back to 1986. Civil record index is at www.sumtercountysc.org/judicialsearch.htm. Family court case details online at the website.
Criminal Name Search: Access: Mail, in person, online. Both court and visitors may perform in person name searches. Search fee: $10.00 per name. Required to search: name, years to search, DOB, SSN, signed release; also helpful: address. Criminal records in books. Mail turnaround time 2 days. Criminal PAT goes back to 1986. Access criminal record index is at www.sumtercountysc.org/judicialsearch.htm. Online results show middle initial, DOB, address.

Mayesville Magistrate Court PO Box 236, Town Hall, Mayesville, SC 29104; 803-436-2280; 3rd Thur Eve (EST). *Misdemeanor, Civil Actions under $7,500, Eviction, Small Claims.*
General Information: Hours may change. Access courts records free at www.sumtercountysc.org/publicindex/. The phone number here is for the main magistrate court; ask for Judge Gibson.

Sumter Magistrate Court 115 N Harvin St, PO Box 1428, Sumter, SC 29151; 803-436-2280; fax: 803-436-2789; 8:30AM-5PM (EST). *Misdemeanor, Civil Actions under $7,500, Eviction, Small Claims.*
www.sumtercountysc.org/departments/summarycourt.htm
General Information: Access courts records free at www.sumtercountysc.org/publicindex/ or www.sumtercountysc.org/CourtDocketsum/. This court also holds traffic, preliminary hearings, warrants and bond records.

Probate Court 141 N Main, Rm 111, Sumter, SC 29150; 803-436-2166; fax: 803-436-2407; 8:30AM-5PM (EST). *Probate.*
www.sumtercountysc.org/departments/probate.htm
General Information: Court is also responsible for issuance of marriage licenses.

Union County

Circuit Court PO Box 703, 210 W Main St, Union, SC 29379; 864-429-1630; fax: 864-429-1715; 9AM-5PM (EST). *Felony, Misdemeanor, Civil Actions over $7,500.* www.countyofunion.org
General Information: The court will mail or fax specific case documents, if case number provided. Fees involved. No adoption, juvenile, sealed or expunged records released. Will fax documents for fee. Fee depends on amount of pages faxed. Court makes copy: $.50 per page. Self serve copy: same. Certification fee: $1.00 per doc. Payee: Clerk of Court. Personal checks accepted, credit cards are not. Prepayment required.
Civil Name Search: Access: In person, online. Visitors must perform in person searches themselves. All records on computer. Civil PAT goes back to 1981. Terminal results also show SSNs. Search the case index free at http://publicindex.sccourts.org/union/publicindex/. Also includes search of civil judgments.
Criminal Name Search: Access: In person, online. Visitors must perform in person searches themselves. Required to search: name, years to search; SSN helpful, DOB. Criminal records on computer. Criminal PAT goes back to same as civil. Terminal results include SSN. Search the case index free at http://publicindex.sccourts.org/union/publicindex/. Search by name or case number.

Union Magistrate Court 210 W Main St, Union, SC 29379; 864-429-1648; fax: 864-429-1685; 9AM-5PM (EST). *Misdemeanor, Civil Actions under $7,500, Eviction, Small Claims.* www.countyofunion.org/
General Information: This is the only Magistrate court bldg in county.

Probate Court PO Box 447, 210 W Main St, Union, SC 29379; 864-429-1625; fax: 864-427-1198; 9AM-5PM (EST). *Probate.*
www.countyofunion.org/

Williamsburg County

Circuit Court 125 W Main St, Kingstree, SC 29556; 843-355-9321 X552; fax: 843-355-9319; 8AM-5PM (EST). *Felony, Misdemeanor, Civil Actions over $7,500.*

General Information: No adoption, juvenile, sealed or expunged records released. Will not fax documents. Court makes copy: $.25 per page. Certification fee: $3.00 per doc. Payee: Clerk of Court. Personal checks, Visa/MC accepted. Prepayment required.
Civil Name Search: Access: In person, online. Both court and visitors may perform in person name searches. Civil records on books, archived from 1980-1989, indexed from 1806; computerized records since 1993. Civil PAT goes back to 1994. Search record index free at http://publicindex.sccourts.org/williamsburg/publicindex/. Online records may include missing/incorrect IDs, wrong charge codes, and be missing some cases, also sentence details, probation updates/violations.
Criminal Name Search: Access: In person, online. Both court and visitors may perform in person name searches. Required to search: name, years to search, DOB. Criminal docket on books, archived from 1980-1989, indexed from 1806; computerized records since 1993. Note: An office staffer is available after-hours for hire to perform searches. Criminal PAT goes back to 1994. Online access same as civil.

Hemingway Magistrate Court 206 E Broad St, Hemingway, SC 29554; 843-558-4145; 9AM-Noon, M & T (EST). *Misdemeanor, Civil Actions under $7,500, Eviction, Small Claims.*
www.williamsburgcounty.sc.gov/

Nesmith Magistrate Court , *Court is closed; Nesmith cases now heard in Kingstree.*

Williamsburg County Magistrate Court 209 Short St, Kingstree, SC 29556; 843-355-9565; fax: 843-355-6444; 8AM-5PM (EST). *Civil Actions under $7,500, Eviction, Small Claims, Ordinance.*
www.williamsburgsc.com/magistrate.html

Probate Court PO Box 1005, 125 W Main, Kingstree, SC 29556; 843-355-9321 x558; 8AM-5PM (EST). *Probate.*
www.williamsburgcounty.sc.gov/

York County

Circuit Court PO Box 649, 1675 - 1G York Hwy, York, SC 29745; 803-684-8506; criminal phone: 803-628-3036; civil phone: 803-684-8507; probate phone: 803-684-8513; criminal fax: 803-628-3133; civil fax: 8AM-5PM; 8AM-5PM (EST). *Felony, Misdemeanor, Civil Actions over $7,500.*
www.yorkcountygov.com/Default.aspx?TabID=182
General Information: Civil court located at 2 S Congress St. Due to courthouse renovations all Common Pleas (civil) files dated 2000 and older are stored off premises. No adoption, juvenile, sealed or expunged records released. Will not fax documents. Court makes copy: $.40 per page. Self serve copy: available for civil only. Certification fee: $1.00 per page. Payee: Clerk of Court. No personal checks or credit cards accepted. Prepayment required. Mail requests: SASE required.
Civil Name Search: Access: Mail, in person, online. Both court and visitors may perform in person name searches. Search fee: $5.00 per name. Civil records on computer from 1982, in books from 1932. Mail turnaround time 1 day. Civil PAT goes back to 6/1982. Civil case details free at http://judicial.yorkcountygov.com/scjdpublicindex/.
Criminal Name Search: Access: Mail, in person, online. Both court and visitors may perform in person name searches. Search fee: $5.00 per name back 10 years only. Required to search: name, years to search, DOB; also helpful: SSN. Criminal records computerized from 2005, in books from 1932. Mail turnaround time 1 day. Criminal PAT goes back to 1983. Access case details free at http://judicial.yorkcountygov.com/scjdpublicindex/. Online records at http://judicial.yorkcountygov.com/courtdocket/. Online results show middle initial, DOB, address.

Bullock Creek Magistrate Court 5800 Wylie Ave, Hickory Grove, SC 29717; 803-925-2815; 9AM-N, T ,3-5PM W, TH, Fri (EST). *Misdemeanor, Civil Actions under $7,500, Eviction, Small Claims.*
www.yorkcountygov.com/Departments/DepartmentsFP/Magistrate.aspx
General Information: Search Summary Ct records free at http://judicial.yorkcountygov.com/scjdpublicindex/. Online records may be missing cases, sentence details, probation updates/violations.

Clover Magistrate Court 201 S Main St, Clover, SC 29710; 803-222-9404; fax: 803-222-3653; 8AM-5PM (EST). *Misdemeanor, Civil Actions under $7,500, Eviction, Small Claims.*
www.yorkcountygov.com/Departments/DepartmentsFP/Magistrate.aspx
General Information: Search Summary Ct records free at http://judicial.yorkcountygov.com/scjdpublicindex/. Online records may be missing cases, sentence details, probation updates/violations.

Fort Mill Magistrate Court 114 Springs St, Fort Mill, SC 29715; 803-547-5572/5573; fax: 803-547-6344; 8AM-5PM (EST). *Misdemeanor, Civil Actions under $7,500, Eviction, Small Claims.*
www.yorkcountygov.com/Departments/DepartmentsFP/Magistrate.aspx

General Information: Search Summary Ct records free at http://judicial.yorkcountygov.com/scjdpublicindex/. Online records may be missing cases, sentence details, probation updates/violations.

Rock Hill Magistrate Court 529 S Cherry Rd, Rock Hill, SC 29730; 803-909-7600; fax: 803-909-7606; 9AM-5:30PM (EST). *Misdemeanor, Civil Actions under $7,500, Eviction, Small Claims.*

www.yorkcountygov.com/Departments/DepartmentsFP/Magistrate.aspx

General Information: Search Summary Ct records free at http://judicial.yorkcountygov.com/scjdpublicindex/. Online records may be missing cases, sentence details, probation updates/violations.

York Magistrate Court 1675 York Hwy, York, SC 29745; 803-628-3029; fax: 803-628-3225; 8AM-5PM (EST). *Misdemeanor, Civil Actions under $7,500, Eviction, Small Claims, Traffic.*

www.yorkcountygov.com/Departments/DepartmentsFP/Magistrate.aspx

General Information: Search Summary Ct records free at http://judicial.yorkcountygov.com/scjdpublicindex/. Online records may be missing cases, sentence details, probation updates/violations.

Probate Court PO Box 219, 1 E Liberty St, York, SC 29745; 803-684-8513; fax: 803-684-8536; 8AM-5PM (EST). *Probate, Marriage. Estate, Guardianship.*

www.yorkcountygov.com/Departments/DepartmentsFP/ProbateCourt.aspx

General Information: Email questions to probate@yorkcountygov.com.

Common Abbreviations Found in Text

- DL   Driver's license
- PAT   Public use access terminal
- SASE   Self-addressed, stamped envelope
- SSN   Social Security Number

South Dakota

Time Zone: **CST & MST***

* South Dakota's eighteen western-most counties are MST: They are: Bennett, Butte, Corson, Custer, Dewey, Fall River, Haakon, Harding, Jackson, Lawrence, Meade, Mellette, Pennington, Perkins, Shannon, Stanley, Todd, Ziebach,

Capital: **Pierre, Hughes County**

# of Counties: **66**

State Web: **www.sd.gov**

Court Web: **www.sdjudicial.com**

Administration

State Court Administrator, State Capitol Building, 500 E Capitol Ave, Pierre, SD, 57501; 605-773-3474, Fax: 605-773-8437.

The Supreme Court

The Supreme Court has the responsibility of administering the statewide unified court system which includes the Circuit and Magistrate Courts. There is not a Court of Appeals in South Dakota. The Supreme Court calendar, opinions, rules and archived oral arguments may be searched from the judicial website.

The South Dakota Courts

Court	Type	How Organized	Jurisdiction Highpoints
Circuit*	General	64Courts in 7 Circuits Districts	Felony, Misdemeanor, Civil Actions, Probate
Magistrate*	Limited	64 Courts	Misdemeanor, Civil Actions under $12,000, Eviction, Small Claims, Ordinance
Tribal Courts	Special	By Tribe	Criminal, Civil, Disputes, Family

* = profiled in this book

Details on the Court Structure

The **Circuit Courts** are the general trial courts of the Unified Judicial System. These courts have original jurisdiction in all civil and criminal cases.

Magistrate Courts operate under the authority and supervision of the Circuit Courts, and assist in processing preliminary hearings for felony cases, hear minor criminal cases, municipal ordinance violations, and hear uncontested civil and small claims cases under $12,000. Circuit Courts also have jurisdiction over appeals from **Magistrate Court** decisions.

There are 66 counties, but 63 courts. Circuit cases for Buffalo County are handled at the Brule County Circuit Court. Circuit cases for Shannon County are handled by the Fall River County Circuit Court. Circuit cases for Todd County are handled by the Tripp County Circuit Court. The state re-aligned their circuits from 8 to 7 effective June, 2000.

Record Searching Facts You Need to Know

Fees and Record Searching Tips

Most South Dakota courts do not allow the public to perform a name search in person. Searches must be performed by the clerk, usually for a mandated $15.00 per name fee for either criminal (01/01/1989 to present) or civil (01/01/2001 to present).

Most courts charge $.20 per page for a copy. Most clerks' offices require record requests in writing, even if in person. Written requests may be forwarded to the central location (see below). The state's Record Search Request Form should be used, download the form at http://ujs.sd.gov/Uploads/downloads/prcdr/rsrf.pdf. Clerks are not required to respond to telephone requests. A search done at the local court will only be for a countywide search. See below for statewide request procedures.

Centralized Mail Request Center for Statewide Criminal Record Searches - The state asks that all mail requests be directed to the processing center at: Union County Clerk of Court, 209 East Main, Ste 230, Elk Point, SD 57025. 605-356-2132, fax 605-356-3687. However – the state will periodically change designated county for the processing center. Be sure to call first.

Commercial Account for Ongoing Requesters for All Record Types - The State Court Administrator's Office provides a service for ongoing requesters who have multiple searches for criminal, civil and probate records. To set up a commercial account, write or fax to Jill Gusso, Director, Public Information, State Court Administrator's Office, 500 East Capitol Ave, Pierre, SD 57501, 605-773-4874, fax is 605-773-8437. Her email is jill.gusso@ujs.state.sd.us.

Neither processing system above contains information from the Tribal Courts.

Online Access is Limited to Civil Records

A web search for all active money judgments and inactive civil money judgments from 04/19/2004 forward is offered by the SD Court Administrator's Office. This service includes a search of both the Circuit and Magistrate Courts. Charges for searches using a credit/debit card are $4.00 per name or date range search. There is an additional $1.00 charge to access the judgment docket. The system works off a pre-paid deposit using a credit card, so the system deducts from your balance. Users may also obtain unlimited access to system, including bulk downloading of civil money judgment information, by subscribing on a monthly or yearly basis. Contact the State Court Administrator's Office, Attn: Jill Gusso, 500 E. Capitol Avenue, Pierre, SD 57501. Note that this service is only for end-users; the agreement with the agency disallows any resale of the data. For more information see https://apps.sd.gov/applications/judgmentquery/login.aspx.

This online system does not provide probate or criminal information. There is no online access to criminal records.

Aurora County

Circuit Court PO Box 366, 401 N Main St, Plankinton, SD 57368-0366; 605-942-7165; fax: 605-942-7170; 8AM-N, 1-5PM (CST). *Felony, Misdemeanor, Civil, Eviction, Small Claims, Domestic, Probate.*
http://ujs.sd.gov/cc/FirstCircuit/Default.aspx
General Information: Note that civil cases for amounts up to $12,000 may be held at the Magistrate Court, but all money judgments can be accessed as described below. No juvenile, sealed, adoption or mental health records released. Will fax documents $1.00 per page, $5.00 minimum. Court makes copy: $.20 per page. Certification fee: $2.00 per page. Payee: Aurora County Clerk of Court. Business and personal checks accepted. Major credit cards accepted. Prepayment required. Mail requests: SASE required.
Civil Name Search: Access: Fax, mail, in person, online. Only the court performs in person name searches; visitors may not. Search fee: $15.00 per name. Required to search: name, years to search; also helpful: address. Civil records on manual index since 1879, some computerized since 1988. Mail turnaround time for document requests 1-4 days. **For details on commercial access and online access to civil records see the profile at front or back of this chapter.**
Criminal Name Search: Access: Fax, mail, in person. Only the court performs in person name searches; visitors may not. Search fee: $15.00 per name. Required to search: name, years to search, DOB; also helpful: address, SSN or DL#. Criminal records are computerized since 7/89 on a statewide system. Note: This court forwards all mail requests for criminal record searches to the County Clerk in Union County. This office suggests to mail the original request to that county clerk. In person request will only receive a countywide search. Mail turnaround time for document requests 1-2 days.

Beadle County

Circuit Court PO Box 1358, 450 3rd St SW, Huron, SD 57350-1358; 605-353-7165; fax: 605-353-0118; 8AM-5PM (CST). *Felony, Misdemeanor, Civil, Eviction, Small Claims, Domestic, Probate.*
www.sdjudicial.com/cc/ThirdCircuit/Default.aspx
General Information: Searching party must complete form requesting examination of file; clerk will redact any data of a confidential or personal nature. Probate fax is same as main fax number. No juvenile, sealed, adoption, or mental health records released. Will not fax out documents. Court makes copy: $.20 per page. Certification fee: $2.00 per cert. Payee: Beadle County Clerk of Court. Personal checks accepted. Out of state checks not accepted. Major credit cards accepted. Prepayment required.
Civil Name Search: Access: Mail, in person, online. Only the court performs in person name searches; visitors may not. Search fee: $15.00

per name. Civil records on computer from 1990 (limited), cards from 1900. Not for public use. Note: Will email specific case file documents. Mail turnaround time for document requests 1-4 days. **For details on commercial access and online access to civil records see the profile at front or back of this chapter.**
Criminal Name Search: Access: Mail, in person. Only the court performs in person name searches; visitors may not. Search fee: $15.00 per name. Required to search: name, years to search, DOB; also helpful: address, SSN or DL#. Criminal records are computerized since 7/89 on a statewide system. Note: This court forwards all mail requests for criminal record searches to the County Clerk in Union County. This office suggests to mail the original request to that county clerk. In person request will only receive a countywide search. Mail turnaround time for document requests up to 2 weeks.

Bennett County

Circuit Court PO Box 281, Martin, SD 57551-0281; 605-685-6969; fax: 605-685-1075; 8AM-Noon: 12:30PM-4:30PM (MST). *Felony, Misdemeanor, Civil, Eviction, Small Claims, Domestic, Probate.*
http://ujs.sd.gov/contactinfo/cccontacts.aspx
General Information: Probate a separate index at this same address. No juvenile, sealed, or mental health records released. Will fax documents $1.00 per page, $5.00 minimum. Court makes copy: $.20 per page. Certification fee: $2.00 includes copy. Payee: Bennett County Clerk of Courts. Business checks accepted. Major credit cards accepted. Prepayment required. Mail requests: SASE required.
Civil Name Search: Access: Mail, in person, online. Only the court performs in person name searches; visitors may not. Search fee: $15.00 per name. Required to search: name, years to search; also helpful: address. Civil docket indexed from 1912. Mail turnaround time for document requests 48 hours. **For details on commercial access and online access to civil records see the profile at front or back of this chapter.**
Criminal Name Search: Access: Mail, in person. Only the court performs in person name searches; visitors may not. Search fee: $15.00 per name. Required to search: name, years to search, DOB; also helpful: address, SSN or DL#. Criminal records are computerized since 7/89 on a statewide system, searchable since 1912. Note: This court forwards all mail requests for criminal record searches to the County Clerk in Union County. This office suggests to mail the original request to that county clerk. In person request will only receive a countywide search. Mail turnaround time for document requests 48 hours.

Bon Homme County

Circuit Court PO Box 6, Tyndall, SD 57066-0006; 605-589-4215; fax: 605-589-4245; 8AM-4:30PM (CST). *Felony, Misdemeanor, Civil, Eviction, Small Claims, Domestic, Probate.*
www.sdjudicial.com/cc/FirstCircuit/Default.aspx

General Information: Public is allowed to search in person. No juvenile, sealed, or mental health records released. Will fax documents $1.00 per page, $5.00 minimum. Court makes copy: $.20 per page. Self serve copy: $.10 per page. Certification fee: $2.00 per cert. Cert fee includes copies. Payee: Bon Homme County Clerk of Court. Personal checks accepted. Major credit cards accepted. Prepayment required. Mail requests: SASE required.

Civil Name Search: Access: Fax, mail, in person, online. Both court and visitors may perform in person name searches. Search fee: $15.00 per name. Required to search: name, years to search; also helpful: address. Civil records on alpha index books from 1877, computerized since 1996. Note: Requests should be in writing. Mail turnaround time for document requests 3 days to 1 week. **For details on commercial access and online access to civil records see the profile at front or back of this chapter.**

Criminal Name Search: Access: Mail, in person. Both court and visitors may perform in person name searches. Search fee: $15.00 per name. Required to search: name, years to search, DOB; also helpful: address, SSN or DL#. Criminal records are computerized since 7/89 on a statewide system. Note: This court forwards all mail requests for criminal record searches to the County Clerk in Union County. This office suggests to mail the original request to that county clerk. In person request will only receive a countywide search. Mail turnaround time for document requests 3 days to 1 week.

Brookings County

Circuit Court 314 6th Ave, Ste 6, Brookings, SD 57006-2085; 605-688-4200; fax: 605-688-4952; 8AM-5PM (CST). *Felony, Misdemeanor, Civil, Eviction, Small Claims, Domestic, Probate.*
www.sdjudicial.com/cc/ThirdCircuit/Default.aspx

General Information: Note that civil cases for amounts up to $12,000 may be held at the Magistrate Court, but all money judgments can be accessed as described below. No juvenile, sealed, or mental health records released. Will fax documents $1.00 per page, $5.00 minimum. Court makes copy: $.20 per page. Self serve copy: same. Certification fee: $2.00 per document. Payee: Brookings County Clerk of Court. Only cashiers checks and money orders accepted. Major credit cards accepted. Prepayment required. Mail requests: SASE required.

Civil Name Search: Access: Mail, in person, online. Both court and visitors may perform in person name searches. Search fee: $15.00 per name. Required to search: name, years to search; also helpful: address. Civil records on alpha index books from 1900s. Mail turnaround time for document requests 3 days. **For details on commercial access and online access to civil records see the profile at front or back of this chapter.**

Criminal Name Search: Access: Mail, in person. Only the court performs in person name searches; visitors may not. Search fee: $15.00 per name. Required to search: name, years to search, DOB; also helpful: address, SSN or DL#. Criminal records on computer since 7/1989 on a statewide system. Note: This court forwards all mail requests for criminal record searches to the County Clerk in Union County. This office suggests to mail the original request to that county clerk. In person request will only receive a countywide search. Mail turnaround time for document requests 3 days.

Brown County

Circuit Court 101 1st Ave SE, Aberdeen, SD 57401-4203; 605-626-2451; fax: 605-626-2491; 8AM-5PM (CST). *Felony, Misdemeanor, Civil, Eviction, Small Claims, Domestic, Probate.*
http://ujs.sd.gov/cc/FifthCircuit/Default.aspx

General Information: Note that civil cases for amounts up to $12,000 may be held at the Magistrate Court, but all money judgments can be accessed as described below. No juvenile, sealed, or mental health records released. Will fax documents $1.00 per page, $5.00 minimum. Court makes copy: $.20 per page. Certification fee: $2.00 per cert. Payee: Brown County Clerk of Court. Personal checks accepted. Major credit cards accepted. Prepayment required. Mail requests: SASE required.

Civil Name Search: Access: Mail, in person, online. Only the court performs in person name searches; visitors may not. Search fee: $15.00 per name. Required to search: name, years to search; also helpful: address. Civil records on registers from 1975 (misdemeanor), registers from 1900s (civil). Mail turnaround time for document requests 1-3 days. **For details on commercial access and online access to civil records see the profile at front or back of this chapter.**

Criminal Name Search: Access: Mail, in person. Only the court performs in person name searches; visitors may not. Search fee: $15.00

per name. Required to search: name, years to search, DOB; also helpful: address, SSN or DL#. Criminal records on computer since 7/1989 on a statewide system, on registers back to 1900. Note: This court forwards all mail requests for criminal record searches to the County Clerk in Union County. This office suggests to mail the original request to that county clerk. In person request will only receive a countywide search. Mail turnaround time for document requests 1-3 days.

Brule County

Circuit Court 300 S Courtland, Ste #111, Chamberlain, SD 57325-1599; 605-734-4580; fax: 605-734-4582; 8AM-N, 1-5PM (CST). *Felony, Misdemeanor, Civil, Eviction, Small Claims, Domestic, Probate.*
www.sdjudicial.com/cc/FirstCircuit/Default.aspx

General Information: Records from the Buffalo County Circuit Court are housed here. No juvenile, sealed, or mental health records released. Will fax documents $1.00 per page, $5.00 minimum. Court makes copy: $.20 per page. Certification fee: $2.00 per doc plus copy fee. Payee: Brule County Clerk of Court. Personal checks accepted. Major credit cards accepted. Prepayment required. Mail requests: SASE required.

Civil Name Search: Access: Mail, in person, online. Only the court performs in person name searches; visitors may not. Search fee: $15.00 per name. Required to search: name, years to search; also helpful: address. Civil index on docket books or docket books from 1880. Mail turnaround time for document requests 1-4 days. **For details on commercial access and online access to civil records see the profile at front or back of this chapter.**

Criminal Name Search: Access: Mail, fax, in person. Only the court performs in person name searches; visitors may not. Search fee: $15.00 per name. Required to search: name, years to search, DOB; also helpful: address, SSN or DL#. Criminal records on computer since 7/1989 on a statewide system, on manual system back to 1880. Note: This court forwards all mail requests for criminal record searches to the County Clerk in Union County. This office suggests to mail the original request to that county clerk. In person request will only receive a countywide search. Mail turnaround time for document requests 3-5 days.

Buffalo County

Circuit Court 300 S Courtland, Ste #111, Chamberlain, SD 57325; 605-734-4580; fax: 605-734-4582; 9AM-5PM (CST). *Felony, Misdemeanor, Civil, Eviction, Small Claims, Domestic, Probate.*
www.sdjudicial.com/cc/FirstCircuit/Default.aspx

General Information: The Brule County Clerk services Buffalo County. Address and phone information displayed here is for Brule County.

Butte County

Circuit Court PO Box 250, 839 5th Ave, Belle Fourche, SD 57717; 605-892-2516; fax: 605-892-2836; 8AM-N, 1-5PM (MST). *Felony, Misdemeanor, Civil, Eviction, Small Claims, Domestic, Probate.*
www.sdjudicial.com/cc/FourthCircuit/Default.aspx

General Information: Note that civil cases for amounts up to $12,000 may be held at the Magistrate Court, but all money judgments can be accessed as described below. No juvenile, sealed, or mental health records released. Will fax documents $1.00 per page, $5.00 minimum. Court makes copy: $.20 per page. Certification fee: $2.00 per cert. Payee: Butte County Clerk of Court. Personal checks accepted. Major credit cards accepted. Prepayment required. Mail requests: SASE required.

Civil Name Search: Access: Mail, in person, online. Only the court performs in person name searches; visitors may not. Search fee: $15.00 per name. Required to search: name, years to search; also helpful: DOB, address. All data on alpha index from 1900s. Mail turnaround time for document requests 1-4 days. **For details on commercial access and online access to civil records see the profile at front or back of this chapter.**

Criminal Name Search: Access: Mail, in person. Only the court performs in person name searches; visitors may not. Search fee: $15.00 per name. Required to search: name, years to search, DOB; also helpful: address, SSN or DL#. Criminal records on computer since 7/89 on a statewide system. Note: This court forwards all mail requests for criminal record searches to the County Clerk in Union County. This office suggests to mail the original request to that county clerk. In person request will only receive a countywide search. Mail turnaround time for document requests varies.

Campbell County

Circuit Court PO Box 146, 111 2nd St, Mound City, SD 57646; 605-955-3536; fax: 605-955-5303; 8AM-N T-W-F (CST). *Felony, Misdemeanor, Civil, Eviction, Small Claims, Domestic, Probate.*
http://ujs.sd.gov/cc/FifthCircuit/Default.aspx

General Information: Note that civil cases for amounts up to $12,000 may be held at the Magistrate Court, but all money judgments can be accessed as described below. No juvenile, sealed, or mental health records released. Will fax documents $1.00 per page, $5.00 minimum. Court makes copy: $.20 per page. Certification fee: $2.00 per cert plus copy fee. Payee: Campbell County Clerk of Court. Cashiers checks and money orders accepted. Major credit cards accepted. Prepayment required. Mail requests: SASE required.

Civil Name Search: Access: Mail, in person, online. Only the court performs in person name searches; visitors may not. Search fee: $15.00 per name. Required to search: name, years to search; also helpful: address. All data on alpha index latter 1900s, archived from 1800s. Mail turnaround time for document requests 1-4 days. **For details on commercial access and online access to civil records see the profile at front or back of this chapter.**

Criminal Name Search: Access: Mail, in person. Only the court performs in person name searches; visitors may not. Search fee: $15.00 per name. Required to search: name, years to search, DOB; also helpful: address, SSN or DL#. Although records are computerized at the state level, this office has records and indices on paper. Note: This court forwards all mail requests for criminal record searches to the County Clerk in Union County. This office suggests to mail the original request to that county clerk. In person request will only receive a countywide search. Mail turnaround time for document requests varies. To search on computer, you may go to Edmunds Circuit Ct.

Charles Mix County

Circuit Court PO Box 640, Main St Courthouse, Lake Andes, SD 57356; 605-487-7511; fax: 605-487-7547; 8AM-4:30PM (CST). *Felony, Misdemeanor, Civil, Eviction, Small Claims, Domestic, Probate.*
www.sdjudicial.com/cc/FirstCircuit/Default.aspx

General Information: Note that civil cases for amounts up to $12,000 may be held at the Magistrate Court, but all money judgments can be accessed as described below. No juvenile, sealed, or mental health records released. Will fax documents $1.00 per page, $5.00 minimum. Court makes copy: $.20 per page. Certification fee: $2.00 per doc. Payee: Charles Mix County Clerk of Court. Personal check accepted with SSN or DL#. Major credit cards accepted. Prepayment required. Mail requests: SASE required.

Civil Name Search: Access: Mail, in person, online. Only the court performs in person name searches; visitors may not. Search fee: $15.00 per name. Required to search: name, years to search; also helpful: address. Civil records on alpha index books from 1917. Mail turnaround time for document requests 1-4 days. **For details on commercial access and online access to civil records see the profile at front or back of this chapter.**

Criminal Name Search: Access: Mail, in person. Only the court performs in person name searches; visitors may not. Search fee: $15.00 per name. Required to search: name, years to search, DOB; also helpful: address, SSN or DL#. Criminal records on computer since 7/89 on a statewide system located in Douglas County. Note: This court forwards all mail requests for criminal record searches to the County Clerk in Union County. This office suggests to mail the original request to that county clerk. In person request will only receive a countywide search. Mail turnaround time for document requests 2-5 days.

Clark County

Circuit Court PO Box 294, Attn: Clerk of Courts, Clark, SD 57225; 605-532-5851; fax: 605-532-4257; 8AM-N, 1-5PM (CST). *Felony, Misdemeanor, Civil, Eviction, Small Claims, Domestic, Probate.*
www.sdjudicial.com/cc/ThirdCircuit/Default.aspx

General Information: Note that civil cases for amounts up to $12,000 may be held at the Magistrate Court, but all money judgments can be accessed as described below. No juvenile, sealed, or mental health records released. Will fax documents $1.00 per page, $5.00 minimum. Court makes copy: $.20 per page. Certification fee: $2.00 per cert. Payee: Clark County Clerk of Court. Personal checks accepted. Major credit cards accepted. Prepayment required. Mail requests: SASE not required.

Civil Name Search: Access: Mail, in person, online. Only the court performs in person name searches; visitors may not. Search fee: $15.00 per name. Required to search: name, years to search; also helpful: address, DOB. All records on books from 1800s. Mail turnaround time for document requests 1-4 days. **For details on commercial access and online access to civil records see the profile at front or back of this chapter.**

Criminal Name Search: Access: Mail, in person. Only the court performs in person name searches; visitors may not. Search fee: $15.00 per name. Required to search: name, years to search, DOB; also helpful: address, SSN or DL#. Criminal records on computer since 1994 on a statewide system. Note: This court forwards all mail requests for criminal record searches to the County Clerk in Union County. This office suggests to mail the original request to that county clerk. In person request will only receive a countywide search. Mail turnaround time for document requests 1-4 days.

Clay County

Circuit Court PO Box 377, Vermillion, SD 57069; 605-677-6756; fax: 605-677-8885; 8AM-5PM (CST). *Felony, Misdemeanor, Civil, Eviction, Small Claims, Domestic, Probate.*
www.sdjudicial.com/cc/FirstCircuit/Default.aspx

General Information: Note that civil cases for amounts up to $12,000 may be held at the Magistrate Court, but all money judgments can be accessed as described below. No juvenile, sealed, or mental health records released. Will fax documents for $1.00 per page, minimum fee $10.00. Court makes copy: $.20 per page. Self serve copy: same. Certification fee: $2.00 per doc. Payee: Clay County Clerk of Court. Personal checks accepted. Major credit cards accepted. Prepayment required. Mail requests: SASE required.

Civil Name Search: Access: Mail, in person, online. Only the court performs in person name searches; visitors may not. Search fee: $15.00 per name. Required to search: name, years to search; also helpful: address. Civil records on computer from 1993, on microfilm to 1920, and archived from 1800s. Mail turnaround time for document requests 2-4 days. **For details on commercial access and online access to civil records see the profile at front or back of this chapter.**

Criminal Name Search: Access: Mail, in person. Only the court performs in person name searches; visitors may not. Search fee: $15.00 per name. Required to search: name, years to search, DOB; also helpful: address, SSN or DL#. Criminal records computerized from 1989, on microfilm to 1920, and archived from 1800s. Note: This court forwards all mail requests for criminal record searches to the County Clerk in Union County. This office suggests to mail the original request to that county clerk. In person request will only receive a countywide search. Mail turnaround time for document requests 2-4 days.

Codington County

Circuit Court Clerk of Court, PO Box 1054, Watertown, SD 57201; 605-882-5095; fax: 605-882-5384; 8AM-5PM (CST). *Felony, Misdemeanor, Civil, Eviction, Small Claims, Domestic, Probate.*
www.sdjudicial.com/cc/ThirdCircuit/Default.aspx

General Information: Note that civil cases for amounts up to $12,000 may be held at the Magistrate Court, but all money judgments can be accessed as described below. No juvenile, sealed, or mental health records released. Fax fee of $10.00 in or $5.00 out PLUS $1.00 per page. Court makes copy: $.20 per page. Certification fee: $2.00 per document. Payee: Codington County Clerk of Court. Business checks accepted. Major credit cards accepted. Prepayment required. Mail requests: SASE required.

Civil Name Search: Access: Mail, in person, online. Only the court performs in person name searches; visitors may not. Search fee: $15.00 per name (includes copies, unless copying entire file). Required to search: name, DOB, years to search. Civil records on computer from 1991. Record index here to 1911, prior at State Archives. Mail turnaround time for document requests 1-4 days. **For details on commercial access and online access to civil records see the profile at front or back of this chapter.**

Criminal Name Search: Access: Mail, in person. Only the court performs in person name searches; visitors may not. Search fee: $15.00 per name (includes copies, unless copying entire file). Required to search: name, years to search, DOB; also helpful: address, SSN or DL#. Criminal records on computer since 7/89 on a statewide system. Record index here to 1911, prior at State Archives. Note: This court forwards all mail requests for criminal record searches to the County Clerk in Union County. This office suggests to mail the original request to that county clerk. In person request will only receive a countywide search. Mail turnaround time for document requests 2 days.

Corson County

Circuit Court PO Box 175, 111 2nd Ave E, McIntosh, SD 57641; 605-273-4201; fax: 605-273-4597; 9:30AM-2:30PM (MST). *Felony, Misdemeanor, Civil, Eviction, Small Claims, Domestic, Probate.*
www.sdjudicial.com/cc/FourthCircuit/Default.aspx

General Information: Probate fax is same as main fax number. No juvenile, sealed, adoption or mental health records released. Will fax documents $1.00 per page, $5.00 minimum. Court makes copy: $.20 per page. Self serve copy: same. Certification fee: $2.00 per cert plus copy fee. Payee: Corson County Clerk of Court. Major credit cards accepted. Prepayment required. Mail requests: SASE not required.

Civil Name Search: Access: Mail, in person, online. Only the court performs in person name searches; visitors may not. Search fee: $15.00 per name. Required to search: name, years to search; also helpful: address. All data on alpha index from 1940s. Mail turnaround time for document requests 1-4 days. **For details on commercial access and online access to civil records see the profile at front or back of this chapter.**

Criminal Name Search: Access: Mail, fax, in person. Only the court performs in person name searches; visitors may not. Search fee: $15.00 per name. Required to search: name, years to search, DOB; also helpful:

address, SSN or DL#. Criminal records computerized from 1989. Note: This court forwards all mail requests for criminal record searches to the County Clerk in Union County. This office suggests to mail the original request to that county clerk. In person request will only receive a countywide search. Mail turnaround time for document requests 1 day.

Custer County

Circuit Court 420 Mt Rushmore Rd, #6, Custer, SD 57730; 605-673-4816; fax: 605-673-3416; 8AM-N, 1-4:45PM (MST). *Felony, Misdemeanor, Civil, Eviction, Small Claims, Domestic, Probate.*
www.sdjudicial.com/cc/SeventhCircuit/Default.aspx
General Information: Note that civil cases for amounts up to $12,000 may be held at the Magistrate Court, but all money judgments can be accessed as described below. No juvenile, sealed, or mental health records released. Will fax documents for $1.00 per page, minimum fee $10.00. Court makes copy: $.25 per page. Certification fee: $2.00 per doc. Payee: Custer County Clerk of Court. Personal checks accepted. Major credit cards accepted. Prepayment required. Mail requests: SASE required.
Civil Name Search: Access: Mail, in person, online. Only the court performs in person name searches; visitors may not. Search fee: $15.00 per name. Required to search: name, years to search, SSN; also helpful: address. Probate on microfiche from 1915, all other data on docket books and index cards from 1960s. Mail turnaround time for document requests 1-4 days. **For details on commercial access and online access to civil records see the profile at front or back of this chapter.**
Criminal Name Search: Access: Mail, in person. Only the court performs in person name searches; visitors may not. Search fee: $15.00 per name. Required to search: name, years to search, DOB; also helpful: address, SSN or DL#. Criminal records on computer since 7/89 on a statewide system. Note: This court forwards all mail requests for criminal record searches to the County Clerk in Union County. This office suggests to mail the original request to that county clerk. In person request will only receive a countywide search. Mail turnaround time for document requests 2 days.

Davison County

Circuit Court PO Box 927, 200 E Fourth Ave, Mitchell, SD 57301; 605-995-8105; fax: 605-995-8112; 8AM-5PM (CST). *Felony, Misdemeanor, Civil, Eviction, Small Claims, Domestic, Probate.*
www.sdjudicial.com/cc/FirstCircuit/Default.aspx
General Information: Note that civil cases for amounts up to $12,000 may be held at the Magistrate Court, but all money judgments can be accessed as described below. No juvenile, sealed, or mental health records released. Will fax documents $1.00 per page, $5.00 minimum. Court makes copy: $.20 per page. Certification fee: $2.00 per doc. Payee: Davison County Clerk of Court. Personal checks accepted. Out of state checks not accepted. Major credit cards accepted. Prepayment required. Mail requests: SASE required.
Civil Name Search: Access: Mail, in person, online. Only the court performs in person name searches; visitors may not. Search fee: $15.00 per name. Required to search: name, years to search; also helpful: address. Civil cases indexed by defendant. All data on alpha index from 1930s or 1940s. Mail turnaround time for document requests 1-4 days. **For details on commercial access and online access to civil records see the profile at front or back of this chapter.**
Criminal Name Search: Access: Mail, in person. Only the court performs in person name searches; visitors may not. Search fee: $15.00 per name. Required to search: name, years to search, DOB; also helpful: address, SSN or DL#. Criminal records are computerized since 7/89 on a statewide system. Note: This court forwards all mail requests for criminal record searches to the County Clerk in Union County. This office suggests to mail the original request to that county clerk. In person request will only receive a countywide search. Mail turnaround time for document requests 1 week.

Day County

Circuit Court 711 W 1st St #201, Webster, SD 57274-1362; 605-345-3771; fax: 605-345-3818; 8AM-5PM (CST). *Felony, Misdemeanor, Civil, Eviction, Small Claims, Domestic, Probate.*
http://ujs.sd.gov/cc/FifthCircuit/Default.aspx
General Information: Mail requests managed by the Edmonds County Clerk of Courts No juvenile, sealed, or mental health records released. Will fax documents $1.00 per page, $5.00 minimum. Court makes copy: $.20 per page. Certification fee: $2.00 per doc. Payee: Day County Clerk of Court. Personal checks accepted. Major credit cards accepted. Prepayment required.
Civil Name Search: Access: In person, online. Only the court performs in person name searches; visitors may not. Search fee: $15.00 per name. Required to search: name, years to search; also helpful: address. Civil cases indexed by defendant. Civil index in docket books from 1800s. Mail turnaround time for document requests 1-4 days. **For details on**

commercial access and online access to civil records see the profile at front or back of this chapter.
Criminal Name Search: Access: In person only. Only the court performs in person name searches; visitors may not. Search fee: $15.00 per name. Required to search: name, years to search, DOB; also helpful: address, SSN or DL#. Criminal records on computer since 1982 on a statewide system. Note: This court forwards all mail requests for criminal record searches to the County Clerk in Union County. This office suggests to mail the original request to that county clerk. In person request will only receive a countywide search.

Deuel County

Circuit Court 408 Fourth St W, Clear Lake, SD 57226; 605-874-2120; fax: 605-874-2916; 8AM-12: 1PM-5PM (CST). *Felony, Misdemeanor, Civil, Eviction, Small Claims, Domestic, Probate.*
www.sdjudicial.com/cc/ThirdCircuit/Default.aspx
General Information: Note that civil cases for amounts up to $12,000 may be held at the Magistrate Court, but all money judgments can be accessed as described below. No juvenile, sealed, or mental health records released. Will fax documents for $1.00 per page with $5.00 minimum. Court makes copy: $.20 per page. Self serve copy: same. Certification fee: $2.00 per doc includes copy fee. Payee: Deuel County Clerk of Court. Personal checks accepted. Major credit cards accepted. Prepayment required. Mail requests: SASE required.
Civil Name Search: Access: Mail, in person, online. Only the court performs in person name searches; visitors may not. Search fee: $15.00 per name. Required to search: name, years to search; also helpful: address. Civil index on docket books. Mail turnaround time for document requests 1-2 days. **For details on commercial access and online access to civil records see the profile at front or back of this chapter.**
Criminal Name Search: Access: Mail, in person. Only the court performs in person name searches; visitors may not. Search fee: $15.00 per name. Required to search: name, years to search, DOB; also helpful: address, SSN or DL#. Criminal records on computer since 7/89 on a statewide system. Note: This court forwards all mail requests for criminal record searches to the County Clerk in Union County. This office suggests to mail the original request to that county clerk. In person request will only receive a countywide search. Mail turnaround time for document requests 1-2 days.

Dewey County

Circuit Court PO Box 96, C St, County Courthouse, Timber Lake, SD 57656; 605-865-3566; fax: 605-865-3641; 9:30AM-2:30PM (MST). *Felony, Misdemeanor, Civil, Eviction, Small Claims, Domestic, Probate.*
www.sdjudicial.com/cc/FourthCircuit/Default.aspx
General Information: Note that civil cases for amounts up to $12,000 may be held at the Magistrate Court, but all money judgments can be accessed as described below. No juvenile, adoption, sealed, or mental health records released. Will fax documents $1.00 per page, $5.00 minimum. Court makes copy: $.25 per page. Certification fee: $2.00 per doc. Payee: Dewey County Clerk of Court. Personal checks accepted. Major credit cards accepted. Prepayment required. Mail requests: SASE required.
Civil Name Search: Access: Mail, in person, online. Only the court performs in person name searches; visitors may not. Search fee: $15.00 per name. Required to search: name, years to search; also helpful: address. All data on alpha index and docket books from 1900s; computerized back to 1999. Mail turnaround time for document requests 1-4 days. **For details on commercial access and online access to civil records see the profile at front or back of this chapter.**
Criminal Name Search: Access: Mail, in person. Only the court performs in person name searches; visitors may not. Search fee: $15.00 per name. Required to search: name, years to search, DOB; also helpful: address, SSN or DL#. Criminal records data on alpha index and docket books from 1900s; computerized back to 1999. Note: This court forwards all mail requests for criminal record searches to the County Clerk in Union County. This office suggests to mail the original request to that county clerk. In person request will only receive a countywide search. Mail turnaround time for document requests 2 days to 1 week.

Cheyenne River Sioux Tribe Judicial Dept PO Box 120, Eagle Butte, SD 57625 Pine Ridge, SD 57770; criminal: 605-964-2996; civil 605-064-6002 (MST). *Felony, Misdemeanor, Civil, Marriage, Divorce, Domestic, Probate.*
www.sioux.org/English/tribal_council.php
General Information: The Enrollment Records Dept is at PO Box 325, Eagle Butte, SD 57625; 605-964-6612/6613; fax is 605-964-6614.

Douglas County

Circuit Court Clerk of Court, PO Box 36, Armour, SD 57313-0036; 605-724-2585; fax: 605-724-2508; 8AM-3PM M,T,TH (CST). *Felony, Misdemeanor, Civil, Eviction, Small Claims, Domestic, Probate.*
www.sdjudicial.com/cc/FirstCircuit/Default.aspx

General Information: Note that civil cases for amounts up to $12,000 may be held at the Magistrate Court, but all money judgments can be accessed as described below. No juvenile, sealed, or mental health records released. Will fax documents $1.00 per page, $5.00 minimum. Court makes copy: $.20 per page. Self serve copy: same. Certification fee: $2.00 per cert. Payee: Douglas County Clerk of Court. Personal checks accepted. Major credit cards accepted. Prepayment required. Mail requests: SASE required.

Civil Name Search: Access: Mail, in person, online. Only the court performs in person name searches; visitors may not. Search fee: $15.00 per name. Required to search: name, years to search; also helpful: address. Civil cases indexed by defendant. Civil index in docket books from late 1800s. Mail turnaround time for document requests 1-4 days. **For details on commercial access and online access to civil records see the profile at front or back of this chapter.**

Criminal Name Search: Access: Fax, mail, in person. Only the court performs in person name searches; visitors may not. Search fee: $15.00 per name. Required to search: name, years to search, DOB; also helpful: address, SSN or DL#. Criminal records are computerized since 7/89 on a statewide system. Note: This court forwards all mail requests for criminal record searches to the County Clerk in Union County. This office suggests to mail the original request to that county clerk. In person request will only receive a countywide search. Mail turnaround time for document requests 1 week.

Edmunds County

Circuit Court PO Box 384, Ipswich, SD 57451; 605-426-6671; fax: 605-426-6323; 8AM-N, 1-5PM (CST). *Felony, Misdemeanor, Civil, Eviction, Small Claims, Domestic, Probate.*
http://ujs.sd.gov/cc/FifthCircuit/Default.aspx

General Information: Probate fax is same as main fax number. No juvenile, sealed or mental health records released. Will fax documents $1.00 per page, $5.00 minimum. Court makes copy: $.20 per page. Self serve copy: same. Certification fee: $2.00 per cert. Payee: Edmunds County Clerk of Court. Personal checks accepted. Major credit cards accepted. Prepayment required. Mail requests: SASE required.

Civil Name Search: Access: Fax, mail, in person, online. Only the court performs in person name searches; visitors may not. Search fee: $15.00 per name. Required to search: name, years to search; also helpful: address. Civil index in docket books from late 1800s. Note: Can pull from statewide index from 2003 to present. Active money judgment go back 20 years. Mail turnaround time for document requests 1-4 days. **For details on commercial access and online access to civil records see the profile at front or back of this chapter.**

Criminal Name Search: Access: Fax, mail, in person. Only the court performs in person name searches; visitors may not. Search fee: $15.00 per name. Required to search: name, years to search, DOB; also helpful: address, SSN or DL#. Criminal records on computer since 7/89; prior records on docket books. Note: This court forwards all mail requests for criminal record searches to the County Clerk in Union County. This office suggests to mail the original request to that county clerk. In person request will only receive a countywide search. Mail turnaround time for document requests 24-48 hours.

Fall River County

Circuit Court 906 N River St, Hot Springs, SD 57747; 605-745-5131; fax: 605-745-5688; 8AM-5PM (MST). *Felony, Misdemeanor, Civil, Eviction, Small Claims, Domestic, Probate.*
www.sdjudicial.com/cc/SeventhCircuit/Default.aspx

General Information: Also handles cases for Shannon County. Specify which county in any search request, records are not co-mingled. No juvenile, sealed, adoption, or mental health records released. Will fax documents $1.00 per page, $5.00 minimum. Court makes copy: $.20 per page. Certification fee: $2.00 per doc. Payee: Clerk of Court. Personal checks accepted. Major credit cards accepted. Prepayment required. Mail requests: SASE required.

Civil Name Search: Access: Mail, in person, online. Only the court performs in person name searches; visitors may not. Search fee: $15.00 per name. Required to search: name, years to search; also helpful: DOB. Civil records on computer from 1992, files from 1889 archived off site. Mail turnaround time for document requests 1-4 days. **For details on commercial access and online access to civil records see the profile at front or back of this chapter.**

Criminal Name Search: Access: Mail, in person. Only the court performs in person name searches; visitors may not. Search fee: $15.00 per name. Required to search: name, years to search, DOB; also helpful: address, SSN or DL#. Criminal records on computer since 7/89 on a statewide system. Note: This court forwards all mail requests for criminal record searches to the County Clerk in Union County. This office suggests to mail the original request to that county clerk. In person request will only receive a countywide search. Mail turnaround time for document requests 1-2 weeks.

Faulk County

Circuit Court PO Box 357, Faulkton, SD 57438-0357; 605-598-6223; fax: 605-598-6252; 1:00-5:00PM (CST). *Felony, Misdemeanor, Civil, Eviction, Small Claims, Domestic, Probate.*
http://ujs.sd.gov/cc/FifthCircuit/Default.aspx

General Information: Note that civil cases for amounts up to $12,000 may be held at the Magistrate Court, but all money judgments can be accessed as described below. No juvenile, sealed, adoption, or mental health records released. Will fax documents $1.00 per page, $5.00 minimum. Court makes copy: $.20 per page. Certification fee: $2.00 per cert. Payee: Faulk County Clerk of Court. Personal checks accepted. Major credit cards accepted. Prepayment required. Mail requests: SASE required.

Civil Name Search: Access: Mail, in person, online. Both court and visitors may perform in person name searches. Search fee: $15.00 per name. Required to search: name, years to search; also helpful: address. Civil cases indexed by defendant. Civil index in docket books from 1900s. Mail turnaround time for document requests 1-4 days. **For details on commercial access and online access to civil records see the profile at front or back of this chapter.**

Criminal Name Search: Access: Mail, in person. Both court and visitors may perform in person name searches. Search fee: $15.00 per name. Required to search: name, years to search, DOB; also helpful: address, SSN or DL#. Criminal records are computerized since 7/89 on a statewide system. Note: This court forwards all mail requests for criminal record searches to the County Clerk in Union County. This office suggests to mail the original request to that county clerk. In person request will only receive a countywide search. Mail turnaround time for document requests 1-2 days.

Grant County

Circuit Court PO Box 509, 210 E 5th Ave, Milbank, SD 57252; 605-432-5482; fax: 605-432-5328; 8AM-N, 1-5PM (CST). *Felony, Misdemeanor, Civil, Eviction, Small Claims, Domestic, Probate.*
www.sdjudicial.com/cc/ThirdCircuit/Default.aspx

General Information: Note that civil cases for amounts up to $12,000 may be held at the Magistrate Court, but all money judgments can be accessed as described below. No juvenile, sealed, adoption or mental health records released. Will fax documents $1.00 per page, $5.00 minimum. Court makes copy: $.20 per page. Certification fee: $2.00 per doc. Payee: Grant County Clerk of Court. Personal checks accepted. Major credit cards accepted. Prepayment required. Mail requests: SASE required.

Civil Name Search: Access: Mail, in person, online. Only the court performs in person name searches; visitors may not. Search fee: $15.00 per name. Required to search: name, years to search; also helpful: address. Civil records on computer from 1995, docket books from 1800s. Mail turnaround time for document requests 1-4 days. **For details on commercial access and online access to civil records see the profile at front or back of this chapter.**

Criminal Name Search: Access: Mail, in person. Only the court performs in person name searches; visitors may not. Search fee: $15.00 per name. Required to search: name, years to search, DOB; also helpful: address, SSN or DL#. Criminal records on computer since 7/89 on a statewide system. Note: This court forwards all mail requests for criminal record searches to the County Clerk in Union County. This office suggests to mail the original request to that county clerk. In person request will only receive a countywide search. Mail turnaround time for document requests 1 week by mail; immediate by phone if on computer.

Gregory County

Circuit Court PO Box 430, Burke, SD 57523-0430; 605-775-2665; fax: 605-775-2965; 8AM-N, 1-5PM (CST). *Felony, Misdemeanor, Civil, Eviction, Small Claims, Domestic, Probate.*
http://ujs.sd.gov/contactinfo/cccontacts.aspx

General Information: Probate is a separate index at this same address. No juvenile, sealed, or mental health records released. Will fax documents $1.00 per page, $5.00 minimum. Court makes copy: $.20 per page. Certification fee: $2.00 plus copy fee. Payee: Gregory County Clerk of Court. Cashiers checks and money orders accepted. No credit cards accepted. Prepayment required. Mail requests: SASE required.

Civil Name Search: Access: Mail, in person, online. Only the court performs in person name searches; visitors may not. Search fee: $15.00 per name. Required to search: name, years to search; also helpful: address. Civil index in docket books from late 1800s, computerized since 1999. Mail turnaround time for document requests 1-4 days. **For details on**

commercial access and online access to civil records see the profile at front or back of this chapter.

Criminal Name Search: Access: Mail, in person. Only the court performs in person name searches; visitors may not. Search fee: $15.00 per name. Required to search: name, years to search, DOB; also helpful: address, SSN or DL#. Criminal records computerized from 7/89 on a statewide system. Note: This court forwards all mail requests for criminal record searches to the County Clerk in Union County. This office suggests to mail the original request to that county clerk. In person request will only receive a countywide search. Mail turnaround time for document requests 1 week.

Haakon County

Circuit Court PO Box 70, Philip, SD 57567; 605-859-2627; fax: 605-859-2257; 8AM-N (MST). *Felony, Misdemeanor, Civil, Eviction, Small Claims, Domestic, Probate.*

http://ujs.sd.gov/contactinfo/cccontacts.aspx

General Information: Probate fax is same as main fax number. No juvenile, sealed, or mental health records released. Will not fax out documents. Court makes copy: $.20 per page. Certification fee: $2.00 includes copy fee. Payee: Haakon County Clerk of Court. Local checks accepted only. No credit cards accepted. Prepayment required. Mail requests: SASE required.

Civil Name Search: Access: Mail, in person, online. Only the court performs in person name searches; visitors may not. Search fee: $15.00 per name. Required to search: name, years to search; also helpful: address. Civil records on register from 1915. Mail turnaround time for document requests 1-4 days. **For details on commercial access and online access to civil records see the profile at front or back of this chapter.**

Criminal Name Search: Access: Mail, in person. Only the court performs in person name searches; visitors may not. Search fee: $15.00 per name. Required to search: name, years to search, DOB; also helpful: address, SSN or DL#. Criminal records are computerized since 7/89 on a statewide system. Note: This court forwards all mail requests for criminal record searches to the County Clerk in Union County. This office suggests to mail the original request to that county clerk. In person request will only receive a countywide search. Mail turnaround time for document requests 1 day.

Hamlin County

Circuit Court PO Box 256, Hayti, SD 57241; 605-783-3751; fax: 605-783-2157; 9:30AM-4PM (CST). *Felony, Misdemeanor, Civil, Eviction, Small Claims, Domestic, Probate.*

www.sdjudicial.com/cc/ThirdCircuit/Default.aspx

General Information: Probate fax is same as main fax number. No juvenile, sealed, or mental health records released. Will fax documents $1.00 per page, $5.00 minimum. Court makes copy: $.20 per page. Self serve copy: same. Certification fee: $2.00 per cert. Payee: Hamlin County Clerk of Court. Personal checks accepted. Major credit cards accepted. Prepayment required. Mail requests: SASE required.

Civil Name Search: Access: Mail, in person, online. Both court and visitors may perform in person name searches. Search fee: $15.00 per name. Required to search: name, years to search; also helpful: address. Civil index in docket books from 1800s. Mail turnaround time for document requests 1-4 days. **For details on commercial access and online access to civil records see the profile at front or back of this chapter.**

Criminal Name Search: Access: Mail, in person. Both court and visitors may perform in person name searches. Search fee: $15.00 per name. Required to search: name, years to search, DOB; also helpful: address, SSN or DL#. Criminal records on computer since 7/89 on a statewide system. Note: This court forwards all mail requests for criminal record searches to the County Clerk in Union County. This office suggests to mail the original request to that county clerk. In person request will only receive a countywide search. Mail turnaround time for document requests 1 day.

Hand County

Circuit Court 415 West 1st Ave. #11, Miller, SD 57362; 605-853-3337; fax: 605-853-3779; 8AM-5PM (CST). *Felony, Misdemeanor, Civil, Eviction, Small Claims, Domestic, Probate.*

www.sdjudicial.com/cc/ThirdCircuit/Default.aspx

General Information: Probate fax is same as main fax number. No juvenile, sealed, or mental health records released. Will fax documents $1.00 per page, $5.00 minimum. Court makes copy: $.20 per page. Self serve copy: same. Certification fee: $2.00 includes copy fees. Payee: Hand County Clerk of Court. Business checks accepted. Major credit cards accepted. Prepayment required. Mail requests: SASE required.

Civil Name Search: Access: Mail, in person, online. Only the court performs in person name searches; visitors may not. Search fee: $15.00 per name. Required to search: name, years to search; also helpful: address. Civil cases indexed by defendant. All data on alpha index and docket books from late 1800s. Mail turnaround time for document requests 1-4 days.

For details on commercial access and online access to civil records see the profile at front or back of this chapter.

Criminal Name Search: Access: Fax, mail, in person. Only the court performs in person name searches; visitors may not. Search fee: $15.00 per name. Required to search: name, years to search, DOB; also helpful: address, SSN or DL#. Criminal records on computer since 7/89 on a statewide system. Note: This court forwards all mail requests for criminal record searches to the County Clerk in Union County. This office suggests to mail the original request to that county clerk. In person request will only receive a countywide search. Mail turnaround time for document requests 1 day.

Hanson County

Circuit Court PO Box 127, 720 Fifth St, Alexandria, SD 57311; 605-239-4446; fax: same number - call first; 8AM-4:30PM; Closed- N-12:30PM (CST). *Felony, Misdemeanor, Civil, Eviction, Small Claims, Domestic, Probate.*

www.sdjudicial.com/cc/FirstCircuit/Default.aspx

General Information: Probate fax is same as main fax number. No juvenile, sealed, adoption or mental health records released. Will fax documents $1.00 per page, $5.00 minimum. Court makes copy: $.20 per page. Self serve copy: same. Certification fee: $2.00 per doc includes copy fee. Payee: Hanson County Clerk of Court. Personal checks accepted. Major credit cards accepted. Prepayment required. Mail requests: SASE required.

Civil Name Search: Access: Mail, in person, online. Only the court performs in person name searches; visitors may not. Search fee: $15.00 per name. Required to search: name, years to search; also helpful: address. Civil index in docket books from 1902; on computer back to 2000. Mail turnaround time for document requests 1-4 days. **For details on commercial access and online access to civil records see the profile at front or back of this chapter.**

Criminal Name Search: Access: Mail, in person. Only the court performs in person name searches; visitors may not. Search fee: $15.00 per name. Required to search: name, years to search, DOB; also helpful: address, SSN or DL#. Criminal records computerized since 7/89 on a statewide system. Note: This court forwards all mail requests for criminal record searches to the County Clerk in Union County. This office suggests to mail the original request to that county clerk. In person request will only receive a countywide search. Mail turnaround time for document requests varies.

Harding County

Circuit Court PO Box 534, Buffalo, SD 57720; 605-375-3351; fax: 605-375-3432; 9AM-N, 1-4PM (MST). *Felony, Misdemeanor, Civil, Eviction, Small Claims, Domestic, Probate.*

www.sdjudicial.com/cc/FourthCircuit/Default.aspx

General Information: This court is a designated search center for South Dakota court records. For eviction information the court says to contact Harding County Sheriff, PO Box 293, Buffalo SD 57720. No juvenile, sealed, or mental health records released. Will fax documents $1.00 per page, $5.00 minimum. Court makes copy: $.20 per page. Certification fee: $2.00 plus copy fee. Payee: Harding County Clerk of Court. Personal checks accepted. Major credit cards accepted. Prepayment required. Mail requests: SASE required.

Civil Name Search: Access: Mail, in person, online. Only the court performs in person name searches; visitors may not. Search fee: $15.00 per name. Required to search: name, years to search, DOB; also helpful: address. Civil cases indexed by defendant. Civil records in archives from 1909 to 1920, index books from 1920. Case files available here from 01/2006 forward. Mail turnaround time for document requests 1-2 days. **For details on commercial access and online access to civil records see the profile at front or back of this chapter.**

Criminal Name Search: Access: Fax, mail, in person. Only the court performs in person name searches; visitors may not. Search fee: $15.00 per name. Required to search: name, years to search, DOB; also helpful: address, SSN or DL#. Criminal records are computerized since 7/89 on a statewide system. Note: This court forwards all mail requests for criminal record searches to the County Clerk in Union County. This office suggests to mail the original request to that county clerk. In person request will only receive a countywide search. Mail turnaround time for document requests 1 week.

Hughes County

Circuit Court 104 E Capital, Pierre, SD 57501; 605-773-3713; fax: 605-773-3875; 8AM-5PM (CST). *Felony, Misdemeanor, Civil, Eviction, Small Claims, Domestic, Probate.*

http://ujs.sd.gov/contactinfo/cccontacts.aspx

General Information: Note that civil cases for amounts up to $12,000 may be held at the Magistrate Court, but all money judgments can be accessed as described below. No juvenile, sealed, adoption or mental health records released. Will fax documents for $1.00 per page with $5.00 minimum. Court makes copy: $.20 per page. Certification fee: $2.00 per cert. Payee: Hughes County Clerk of Court. Personal checks accepted. Major credit cards accepted. Prepayment required. Mail requests: SASE required.

Civil Name Search: Access: Mail, in person, online. Only the court performs in person name searches; visitors may not. Search fee: $15.00 per name. Required to search: name, years to search; also helpful: address. Civil records on microfiche from 1948 to 1973. From 1974 forward have hard copy file, starting 1991 index and docketing on computer. Mail turnaround time for document requests approx. 2 days. **For details on commercial access and online access to civil records see the profile at front or back of this chapter.**

Criminal Name Search: Access: Mail, in person. Only the court performs in person name searches; visitors may not. Search fee: $15.00 per name. Required to search: name, years to search, DOB; also helpful: address, SSN or DL#. Criminal records on computer since 1988 on a statewide system. Note: This court forwards all mail requests for criminal record searches to the County Clerk in Union County. This office suggests to mail the original request to that county clerk. In person request will only receive a countywide search. Mail turnaround time for document requests approx. 2 days.

Hutchinson County

Circuit Court 140 Euclid, Rm 36, Olivet, SD 57052-2103; 605-387-4215; fax: 605-387-4208; 8AM-4:30PM M-TH; Closed F (CST). *Felony, Misdemeanor, Civil, Eviction, Small Claims, Domestic, Probate.*
www.sdjudicial.com/cc/FirstCircuit/Hutchinson.aspx

General Information: Note that civil cases for amounts up to $12,000 may be held at the Magistrate Court, but all money judgments can be accessed as described below. No juvenile, sealed, adoption or mental health records released. Will fax documents $1.00 per page, $5.00 minimum. Court makes copy: $.20 per page. Certification fee: $2.00 per cert. Payee: Hutchinson County Clerk of Court. Business checks accepted. Major credit cards accepted. Prepayment required. Mail requests: SASE required.

Civil Name Search: Access: Fax, mail, in person, online. Only the court performs in person name searches; visitors may not. Search fee: $15.00 per name. Required to search: name, years to search; also helpful: address. Civil index on docket books and index cards from 1800s, on computer since 1994. Mail turnaround time for document requests 1-4 days. **For details on commercial access and online access to civil records see the profile at front or back of this chapter.**

Criminal Name Search: Access: Fax, mail, in person. Only the court performs in person name searches; visitors may not. Search fee: $15.00 per name. Required to search: name, years to search, DOB; also helpful: address, SSN or DL#. Older records on docket books and index cards, records since 7/89 are computerized on a statewide system. Note: This court forwards all mail requests for criminal record searches to the County Clerk in Union County. This office suggests to mail the original request to that county clerk. In person request will only receive a countywide search. Mail turnaround time for document requests 1 day.

Hyde County

Circuit Court PO Box 306, Highmore, SD 57345; 605-852-2512; fax: 605-852-2767; 8AM-N (CST). *Felony, Misdemeanor, Civil, Eviction, Small Claims, Domestic, Probate.*
http://ujs.sd.gov/contactinfo/cccontacts.aspx

General Information: Probate fax is same as main fax number. No juvenile, sealed, or mental health records released. Will fax documents $1.00 per page, $5.00 minimum. Court makes copy: $.20 per page. Self serve copy: same. Certification fee: $2.00 per cert includes copies. Payee: Hyde County Clerk of Courts. Personal checks accepted, credit cards are not. Prepayment required. Mail requests: SASE required.

Civil Name Search: Access: Fax, mail, in person, online. Only the court performs in person name searches; visitors may not. Search fee: $15.00 per name. Required to search: name, years to search; also helpful: address. Civil index in docket books from 1920s, computerized from 2000. Mail turnaround time for document requests 1-4 days. **For details on commercial access and online access to civil records see the profile at front or back of this chapter.**

Criminal Name Search: Access: Fax, mail, in person. Only the court performs in person name searches; visitors may not. Search fee: $15.00 per name. Required to search: name, years to search, DOB; also helpful: address, SSN or DL#. Criminal records are computerized since 7/89 on a statewide system. Note: This court forwards all mail requests for criminal record searches to the County Clerk in Union County. This office suggests to mail the original request to that county clerk. In person request will only receive a countywide search. Mail turnaround time for document requests 1-3 days.

Jackson County

Circuit Court PO Box 128, Kadoka, SD 57543; 605-837-2122; fax: 605-837-2120; 8AM-N, 1-5PM (MST). *Felony, Misdemeanor, Civil, Eviction, Small Claims, Domestic, Probate.*
http://ujs.sd.gov/contactinfo/cccontacts.aspx

General Information: Note that civil cases for amounts up to $12,000 may be held at the Magistrate Court, but all money judgments can be accessed as described below. No juvenile, sealed, or mental health records released. Will fax documents $1.00 per page, $5.00 minimum. Court makes copy: $.20 per page. Self serve copy: same. Certification fee: $2.00 per cert. Payee: Jackson County Clerk of Court. Personal checks accepted. Major credit cards accepted. Prepayment required. Mail requests: SASE required.

Civil Name Search: Access: Mail, in person, online. Only the court performs in person name searches; visitors may not. Search fee: $15.00 per name. Required to search: name, years to search; also helpful: address. Civil cases indexed by defendant. Civil records on "Register of Action" from 1915; on computer back to 1993. Mail turnaround time for document requests 1-4 days. **For details on commercial access and online access to civil records see the profile at front or back of this chapter.**

Criminal Name Search: Access: Mail, in person. Only the court performs in person name searches; visitors may not. Search fee: $15.00 per name. Required to search: name, years to search, DOB; also helpful: address, SSN or DL#. Criminal records computerized from 7/89 on a statewide system; other records go back to 1920. Note: This court forwards all mail requests for criminal record searches to the County Clerk in Union County. This office suggests to mail to this court for a statewide search. Mail turnaround time for document requests 1-2 days.

Jerauld County

Circuit Court PO Box 435, 203 S Wallace St, Wessington Springs, SD 57382; 605-539-1202; fax: 605-539-1203; 8AM-Noon, 1PM-5PM (CST). *Felony, Misdemeanor, Civil, Eviction, Small Claims, Domestic, Probate.*
www.sdjudicial.com/cc/ThirdCircuit/Default.aspx

General Information: Note that civil cases for amounts up to $12,000 may be held at the Magistrate Court, but all money judgments can be accessed as described below. No juvenile, sealed, or mental health records released. Will fax documents $1.00 per page, $5.00 minimum. Court makes copy: $.25 per page. Certification fee: $2.00 per doc. Payee: Jerauld County Clerk of Court. Personal checks accepted. Major credit cards accepted. Prepayment required. Mail requests: SASE required.

Civil Name Search: Access: Mail, in person, online. Only the court performs in person name searches; visitors may not. Search fee: $15.00 per name. Required to search: name, years to search; also helpful: address. Civil cases indexed by defendant. Civil index in docket books from 1900s, computerized from 2006. Mail turnaround time for document requests 1-4 days. **For details on commercial access and online access to civil records see the profile at front or back of this chapter.**

Criminal Name Search: Access: Mail, in person. Only the court performs in person name searches; visitors may not. Search fee: $15.00 per name. Required to search: name, years to search, DOB; also helpful: address, SSN or DL#. Criminal records are computerized since 1989 on a statewide system. Note: This court forwards all mail requests for criminal record searches to the County Clerk in Union County. This office suggests to mail the original request to that county clerk. In person request will only receive a countywide search. Mail turnaround time for document requests 2 days.

Jones County

Circuit Court PO Box 448, 310 Main St, Murdo, SD 57559; 605-669-2361; fax: 605-669-2641; 8AM-Noon (CST). *Felony, Misdemeanor, Civil, Eviction, Small Claims, Domestic, Probate.*
http://ujs.sd.gov/contactinfo/cccontacts.aspx

General Information: Criminal cases and records at Potter County. No juvenile, sealed, or mental health records released. Will fax documents $1.00 per page, $5.00 minimum. Court makes copy: $.20 per page. Certification fee: $2.00 per doc. Payee: Jones County Clerk of Court (civil cases); Potter County Clerk of Court (criminal cases). Business checks accepted. Major credit cards accepted. Prepayment required. Mail requests: SASE required.

Civil Name Search: Access: Mail, in person, online. Only the court performs in person name searches; visitors may not. Search fee: $15.00 per name. Required to search: name, years to search; also helpful: address. Civil index in docket books from 1919. Mail turnaround time for document requests 1-4 days. **For details on commercial access and online access to civil records see the profile at front or back of this chapter.**

Criminal Name Search: Access: Mail, in person. Only the court performs in person name searches; visitors may not. Search fee: $15.00 per name. Required to search: name, years to search, DOB; also helpful: address, SSN or DL#. Criminal records are computerized since 7/89 on a statewide system. Records on books go back to 1917. Note: This court forwards all mail requests for criminal record searches to the County

Clerk in Union County. This office suggests to mail the original request to that county clerk. In person request will only receive a countywide search. Mail turnaround time for document requests 3 days to 1 week.

Kingsbury County

Circuit Court PO Box 176, De Smet, SD 57231-0176; 605-854-3811; fax: 605-854-9080; 8AM-N, 1-5PM (CST). *Felony, Misdemeanor, Civil, Eviction, Small Claims, Domestic, Probate.*
www.sdjudicial.com/cc/ThirdCircuit/Default.aspx

General Information: Probate is a separate index at this same address. Probate fax is same as main fax number. No juvenile, sealed, adoption or mental health records released. Will fax documents $1.00 per page, $5.00 minimum. Court makes copy: $.20 per page. Certification fee: $2.00 per cert includes copy fee. Payee: Kingsbury County Clerk of Court. Personal checks accepted. Major credit cards accepted. Prepayment required. Mail requests: SASE required.

Civil Name Search: Access: Mail, in person, online. Only the court performs in person name searches; visitors may not. Search fee: $15.00 per name. Required to search: name, years to search; also helpful: address plus DOB. Civil records on computer printed index from 1978 and bound books from 1890. Mail turnaround time for document requests 1-4 days. **For details on commercial access and online access to civil records see the profile at front or back of this chapter.**

Criminal Name Search: Access: Mail, in person. Only the court performs in person name searches; visitors may not. Search fee: $15.00 per name. Required to search: name, years to search, DOB; also helpful: address, SSN or DL#. Criminal records on computer since 7/89 on a statewide system. Note: This court forwards all mail requests for criminal record searches to the County Clerk in Union County. This office suggests to mail the original request to that county clerk. In person request will only receive a countywide search. Mail turnaround time for document requests same day.

Lake County

Circuit Court 200 E Center St, Madison, SD 57042; 605-256-5644; fax: 605-256-5012; 8AM-N, 1-5PM (CST). *Felony, Misdemeanor, Civil, Eviction, Small Claims, Domestic, Probate.*
www.sdjudicial.com/cc/ThirdCircuit/Default.aspx

General Information: Note that civil cases for amounts up to $12,000 may be held at the Magistrate Court, but all money judgments can be accessed as described below. No juvenile, sealed, or mental health records released. Will fax documents $1.00 per page, $5.00 minimum. Court makes copy: $.20 per page. Certification fee: $2.00 per doc. Payee: Lake County Clerk of Court. Personal checks accepted. Major credit cards accepted. Prepayment required. Mail requests: SASE required.

Civil Name Search: Access: Mail, in person, online. Both court and visitors may perform in person name searches. Search fee: $15.00 per name. Required to search: name, years to search; also helpful: address. Civil cases indexed by defendant. Civil records on computer from 1989, docket books from 1800s. Mail turnaround time for document requests 1-4 days. **For details on commercial access and online access to civil records see the profile at front or back of this chapter.**

Criminal Name Search: Access: Mail, in person. Both court and visitors may perform in person name searches. Search fee: $15.00 per name. Required to search: name, years to search, DOB; also helpful: address, SSN or DL#. Criminal records on computer since 1989 on a statewide system; prior records on docket books since 1800s. Note: This court forwards all mail requests for criminal record searches to the County Clerk in Union County. This office suggests to mail the original request to that county clerk. In person request will only receive a countywide search. Mail turnaround time for document requests 1 day. Also, see note at beginning of section for locations of the 2 state-recommended mail processing centers.

Lawrence County

Circuit Court PO Box 626, 78 Sherman St, Deadwood, SD 57732; 605-578-2040; fax: 605-578-1571; 8AM-N, 1-5PM (MST). *Felony, Misdemeanor, Civil, Eviction, Small Claims, Domestic, Probate.*
www.sdjudicial.com/cc/FourthCircuit/Default.aspx

General Information: Note that civil cases for amounts up to $12,000 may be held at the Magistrate Court, but all money judgments can be accessed as described below. No juvenile, sealed, or mental health records released. Will fax documents $1.00 per page, $5.00 minimum. Court makes copy: $.20 per page. Certification fee: $2.00 per doc. Payee: Lawrence County Clerk of Court. Personal checks accepted. Major credit cards accepted. Prepayment required. Mail requests: SASE required.

Civil Name Search: Access: Mail, in person, online. Only the court performs in person name searches; visitors may not. Search fee: $15.00 per name. Required to search: name, years to search; also helpful: address. Civil records on computer from 1989 and index books from 1800s. Mail

turnaround time for document requests 1-4 days. **For details on commercial access and online access to civil records see the profile at front or back of this chapter.**

Criminal Name Search: Access: Mail, in person. Only the court performs in person name searches; visitors may not. Search fee: $15.00 per name. Required to search: name, years to search, DOB; also helpful: address, SSN or DL#. Criminal records on computer since 7/89 on a statewide system. Note: This court forwards all mail requests for criminal record searches to the County Clerk in Union County. This office suggests to mail the original request to that county clerk. In person request will only receive a countywide search. Mail turnaround time for document requests 1-3 days.

Lincoln County

Circuit Court Clerk of Courts, 104 N Main St, Canton, SD 57013; 605-987-5891; fax: 605-987-9088; 8AM-5PM (CST). *Felony, Misdemeanor, Civil, Eviction, Small Claims, Domestic, Probate.*
www.sdjudicial.com/cc/SecondCircuit/Default.aspx

General Information: Note that civil cases for amounts up to $12,000 may be held at the Magistrate Court, but all money judgments can be accessed as described below. No juvenile, sealed, adoption or mental health records released. Will fax documents $1.00 per page, $5.00 minimum. Court makes copy: $.20 per page. Certification fee: $2.00 per doc. Payee: Lincoln County Clerk of Court. Personal checks accepted. Major credit cards accepted. Prepayment required. Mail requests: SASE required.

Civil Name Search: Access: Mail, in person, online. Only the court performs in person name searches; visitors may not. Search fee: $15.00 per name. Required to search: name, years to search; also helpful: address. Civil index in docket books from 1900s. Visitor may search written index pre-1993; only the court searches computer records 1994 forward. Mail turnaround time for document requests 3 days, longer for probate. **For details on commercial access and online access to civil records see the profile at front or back of this chapter.**

Criminal Name Search: Access: Mail, in person. Only the court performs in person name searches; visitors may not. Search fee: $15.00 per name. Required to search: name, years to search, DOB; also helpful: address, SSN or DL#. Criminal records on computer since 7/89 on a statewide system. Note: This court forwards all mail requests for criminal record searches to the County Clerk in Union County. This office suggests to mail the original request to that county clerk. In person request will only receive a countywide search. Mail turnaround time for document requests 3 days, longer for probate.

Lyman County

Circuit Court PO Box 235, 300 S Main, Courthouse, Kennebec, SD 57544; 605-869-2277; fax: 605-869-2177; 9AM-4PM M-TH (CST). *Felony, Misdemeanor, Civil, Eviction, Small Claims, Domestic, Probate.*
http://ujs.sd.gov/contactinfo/cccontacts.aspx

General Information: The public may search the docket books. No juvenile, sealed, or mental health records released. Will fax documents $1.00 per page, $5.00 minimum. Court makes copy: $.20 per page. Certification fee: $2.00 per cert. Payee: Lyman County Clerk of Court. Personal checks accepted. Major credit cards accepted. Prepayment required. Mail requests: SASE required.

Civil Name Search: Access: Mail, in person, online. Both court and visitors may perform in person name searches. Search fee: $15.00 per name. Required to search: name, years to search; also helpful: address. Civil index in docket books from 1900s; on computer back approx. one year. Mail turnaround time for document requests 1-4 days. **For details on commercial access and online access to civil records see the profile at front or back of this chapter.**

Criminal Name Search: Access: Mail, in person. Both court and visitors may perform in person name searches. Search fee: $15.00 per name. Required to search: name, years to search, DOB; also helpful: address, SSN or DL#. Criminal records on computer since 7/89 on a statewide system. Note: This court forwards all mail requests for criminal record searches to the County Clerk in Union County. This office suggests to mail the original request to that county clerk. In person request will only receive a countywide search. Mail turnaround time for document requests 1 week.

Lower Brule Sioux Tribe, 605-473-5528 (Courthouse)
www.lbst.org/newsite/home.htm

Marshall County

Circuit Court PO Box 130, Britton, SD 57430; 605-448-5213; fax: 605-448-5201; 8AM-N, 1-5PM M-TH (CST). *Felony, Misdemeanor, Civil, Eviction, Small Claims, Domestic, Probate.*
http://ujs.sd.gov/cc/FifthCircuit/Marshall.aspx

General Information: Note that civil cases for amounts up to $12,000 may be held at the Magistrate Court, but all money judgments can be accessed as described below. No juvenile, sealed, or mental health records released. Will fax documents $1.00 per page, $5.00 minimum. Court makes copy: $.20 per page. Certification fee: $2.00 per cert. Payee: Marshall County Clerk of Court. Personal checks accepted. Major credit cards accepted. Prepayment required. Mail requests: SASE required.

Civil Name Search: Access: Mail, in person, online. Only the court performs in person name searches; visitors may not. Search fee: $15.00 per name. Required to search: name, years to search; also helpful: address. Civil index in docket books from 1800s. Mail turnaround time for document requests 1-4 days. **For details on commercial access and online access to civil records see the profile at front or back of this chapter.**

Criminal Name Search: Access: Mail, in person. Only the court performs in person name searches; visitors may not. Search fee: $15.00 per name. Required to search: name, years to search, DOB; also helpful: address, SSN or DL#. Criminal records are computerized since 7/89 on a statewide system. Note: This court forwards all mail requests for criminal record searches to the County Clerk in Union County. This office suggests to mail the original request to that county clerk. In person request will only receive a countywide search. Mail turnaround time for document requests 1 week.

McCook County

Circuit Court PO Box 504, Salem, SD 57058; 605-425-2781; fax: 605-425-3144; 8AM-12:30; 1-4:30PM (CST). *Felony, Misdemeanor, Civil, Eviction, Small Claims, Domestic, Probate.*

www.sdjudicial.com/cc/FirstCircuit/Default.aspx

General Information: Note that civil cases for amounts up to $12,000 may be held at the Magistrate Court, but all money judgments can be accessed as described below. No juvenile, sealed, or mental health records released. Will fax documents $1.00 per page, $5.00 minimum. Court makes copy: $.20 per page. Certification fee: $2.00 per cert. Payee: McCook County Clerk of Court. Personal checks accepted. Major credit cards accepted. Prepayment required. Mail requests: SASE required.

Civil Name Search: Access: Mail, in person, online. Only the court performs in person name searches; visitors may not. Search fee: $15.00 per name. Required to search: name, years to search; also helpful: address, DOB, SSN. Civil records in index and docket books from late 1800s, computerized form 1989. Mail turnaround time for document requests 1-4 days. **For details on commercial access and online access to civil records see the profile at front or back of this chapter.**

Criminal Name Search: Access: Mail, in person. Only the court performs in person name searches; visitors may not. Search fee: $15.00 per name. Required to search: name, years to search, DOB; also helpful: address, SSN or DL#. Criminal records are computerized since 7/89 on a statewide system. Note: This court forwards all mail requests for criminal record searches to the County Clerk in Union County. This office suggests to mail the original request to that county clerk. In person request will only receive a countywide search. Mail turnaround time for document requests 1 day.

McPherson County

Circuit Court PO Box 248, Leola, SD 57456; 605-439-3361; fax: 605-439-3297; 8AM-N (CST). *Felony, Misdemeanor, Civil, Eviction, Small Claims, Domestic, Probate.*

http://ujs.sd.gov/cc/FifthCircuit/Default.aspx

General Information: The pubic may view the Register of Action books. No juvenile, sealed, adoption or mental health records released. Will fax documents $1.00 per page, $5.00 minimum. Court makes copy: $.25 per page. Self serve copy: same. Certification fee: $2.00 per cert. Payee: McPherson County Clerk of Court. Personal checks accepted. Major credit cards accepted. Prepayment required. Mail requests: SASE required.

Civil Name Search: Access: Mail, in person, online. Both court and visitors may perform in person name searches. Search fee: $15.00 per name. Required to search: name, years to search; also helpful: address. Civil records on register of action from 1880s, records are not computerized. Note: When searching in person there is no fee if case number is known. Mail turnaround time for document requests 1-4 days. **For details on commercial access and online access to civil records see the profile at front or back of this chapter.**

Criminal Name Search: Access: Mail, in person. Both court and visitors may perform in person name searches. Search fee: $15.00 per name. Required to search: name, years to search, DOB; also helpful: address, SSN or DL#. Criminal records on register of action from 1910, records are not computerized. Note: This court forwards all mail requests for criminal record searches to the County Clerk in Union County. This office suggests to mail the original request to that county clerk. In person request will only receive a countywide search. Mail turnaround time for document requests 1 day to 1 week.

Meade County

Circuit Court PO Box 939, 1425 Sherman St, Sturgis, SD 57785; 605-347-4411; fax: 605-347-3526; 8AM-N, 1-5PM (MST). *Felony, Misdemeanor, Civil, Eviction, Small Claims, Domestic, Probate.*

www.sdjudicial.com/cc/FourthCircuit/Default.aspx

General Information: Note that civil cases for amounts up to $12,000 may be held at the Magistrate Court, but all money judgments can be accessed as described below. No juvenile, sealed, or mental health records released. Will fax documents $1.00 per page, $5.00 minimum. Court makes copy: $.20 per page. Certification fee: $2.00 per doc. Payee: Meade County Clerk of Courts. Personal checks (instate only) accepted. Major credit cards accepted. Prepayment required. Mail requests: SASE required.

Civil Name Search: Access: Mail, in person, online. Only the court performs in person name searches; visitors may not. Search fee: $15.00 per name. Required to search: name, years to search; also helpful: address. Civil index on cards and docket books from 1800s, computerized form 1990. Mail turnaround time for document requests 1-4 days. **For details on commercial access and online access to civil records see the profile at front or back of this chapter.**

Criminal Name Search: Access: Mail, in person. Only the court performs in person name searches; visitors may not. Search fee: $15.00 per name. Required to search: name, years to search, DOB; also helpful: address, SSN or DL#. Criminal records on computer since 7/89 on a statewide system. Note: This court forwards all mail requests for criminal record searches to the County Clerk in Union County. This office suggests to mail the original request to that county clerk. In person request will only receive a countywide search. Mail turnaround time for document requests 1 day to 2 weeks.

Mellette County

Circuit Court PO Box 257, White River, SD 57579; 605-259-3230; fax: 605-259-3030; 8AM-N (CST). *Felony, Misdemeanor, Civil, Eviction, Small Claims, Domestic, Probate.*

http://ujs.sd.gov/contactinfo/cccontacts.aspx

General Information: Note that civil cases for amounts up to $12,000 may be held at the Magistrate Court, but all money judgments can be accessed as described below. No juvenile, sealed, or mental health records released. Will fax documents $1.00 per page, $5.00 minimum. Court makes copy: $.20 per page. Certification fee: $2.00 per cert. Payee: Mellette County Clerk of Court. Personal checks accepted, credit cards are not. Prepayment required. Mail requests: SASE required.

Civil Name Search: Access: Phone, mail, in person, online. Only the court performs in person name searches; visitors may not. Search fee: $15.00 per name. Required to search: name, years to search; also helpful: address. Civil cases indexed by defendant. Civil index on cards and docket books from 1900s. Mail turnaround time for document requests 3 days; probate up to 1 month. **For details on commercial access and online access to civil records see the profile at front or back of this chapter.**

Criminal Name Search: Access: Mail, in person. Only the court performs in person name searches; visitors may not. Search fee: $15.00 per name. Required to search: name, years to search, DOB; also helpful: address, SSN or DL#. Criminal records are computerized since 7/89 on a statewide system. Note: This court forwards all mail requests for criminal record searches to the County Clerk in Union County. This office suggests to mail the original request to that county clerk. In person request will only receive a countywide search. Mail turnaround time for document requests 3 days; probate up to 1 month.

Miner County

Circuit Court PO Box 265, Howard, SD 57349; 605-772-4612; fax: 605-772-4412; 8AM-N; 1-5PM (CST). *Felony, Misdemeanor, Civil, Eviction, Small Claims, Domestic, Probate.*

www.sdjudicial.com/cc/ThirdCircuit/Default.aspx

General Information: Probate fax is same as main fax number. No juvenile, sealed, dismissed or mental health records released. Will fax documents $1.00 per page, $5.00 minimum. Court makes copy: $.20 per page criminal; Civil- $1.00 per page. Certification fee: $2.00 per page. Cert fee includes copies. Payee: Miner County Clerk of Court. Personal checks accepted. Major credit cards accepted. Prepayment required. Mail requests: SASE required.

Civil Name Search: Access: Mail, in person, online. Only the court performs in person name searches; visitors may not. Search fee: $15.00 per name plus copy fees. Civil index in docket books from 1900's, computerized since 1990. Mail turnaround time for document requests 1-4 days. **For details on commercial access and online access to civil records see the profile at front or back of this chapter.**

Criminal Name Search: Access: Fax, mail, in person. Only the court performs in person name searches; visitors may not. Search fee: $15.00 per name. Required to search: name, years to search, DOB; also helpful: address, SSN or DL#. Criminal records are computerized since 1989. Note:

This court forwards all mail requests for criminal record searches to the County Clerk in Union County. This office suggests to mail the original request to that county clerk. In person request will only receive a countywide search. Mail turnaround time for document requests 2 days.

Minnehaha County

Circuit Court 425 N Dakota Ave, Sioux Falls, SD 57104; 605-367-5920; fax: 605-367-5916; 8AM-5PM (CST). *Felony, Misdemeanor, Civil, Eviction, Small Claims, Domestic, Probate.*
www.sdjudicial.com/cc/SecondCircuit/Default.aspx

General Information: Please use their request form when requesting a search. No juvenile, sealed, dismissed or mental health records released. Will fax documents $1.00 per page, $5.00 minimum. Court makes copy: $.20 per page. Certification fee: $2.00 per doc. Payee: Minnehaha County Clerk of Court. Personal checks accepted. Major credit cards accepted. Prepayment required. Mail requests: SASE required.

Civil Name Search: Access: Mail, in person, online. Only the court performs in person name searches; visitors may not. Search fee: $15.00 per name. Required to search: name, years to search; also helpful: address. Civil records on computer from 1989, docket books from 1800s. Mail turnaround time for document requests 1-4 days. **For details on commercial access and online access to civil records see the profile at front or back of this chapter.**

Criminal Name Search: Access: Mail, in person. Only the court performs in person name searches; visitors may not. Search fee: $15.00 per name. Required to search: name, years to search, DOB; also helpful: address, SSN or DL#. Criminal records on computer since 7/89. Note: This court forwards all mail requests for criminal record searches to the County Clerk in Union County. This office suggests to mail the original request to that county clerk. In person request will only receive a countywide search. Mail turnaround time for document requests 2 weeks.

Moody County

Circuit Court 101 E Pipestone, P O Box 226, Flandreau, SD 57028; 605-997-3181; fax: 605-997-3861; 8AM-12: 1PM-5PM (CST). *Felony, Misdemeanor, Civil, Eviction, Small Claims, Domestic, Probate.*
www.sdjudicial.com/cc/ThirdCircuit/Moody.aspx

General Information: Probate records are in a separate index at this address. Probate fax is same as main fax number. No juvenile, sealed, adoption or mental health records released. Will fax documents $1.00 per page, $5.00 minimum. Court makes copy: $.20 per page. Certification fee: $2.00 per page includes copy fee. Payee: Moody County Clerk of Court. Personal checks accepted. Major credit cards accepted. Prepayment required. Mail requests: SASE required.

Civil Name Search: Access: Mail, in person, online. Only the court performs in person name searches; visitors may not. Search fee: $15.00 per name. Required to search: name, years to search; also helpful: address. Civil records on computer from 1992 and docket books from 1800s. Mail turnaround time for document requests 1-4 days. **For details on commercial access and online access to civil records see the profile at front or back of this chapter.**

Criminal Name Search: Access: Mail, in person. Only the court performs in person name searches; visitors may not. Search fee: $15.00 per name. Required to search: name, years to search, DOB; also helpful: address, SSN or DL#. Criminal records on computer since 7/89 on a statewide index. Note: This court forwards all mail requests for criminal record searches to the County Clerk in Union County. This office suggests to mail the original request to that county clerk. In person request will only receive a countywide search. Mail turnaround time for document requests 2-3 days.

Flandreau Santee Sioux Tribal Court, PO Box 283, 603 W Broad Ave, Flandreau, SD 57028; 605-997-3593 X2
www.fsst.org/

Pennington County

Circuit Court PO Box 230, Rapid City, SD 57709; 602-394-2575; criminal phone: 605-394-2570; civil phone: 605-394-2575; probate phone: 605-394-2575; fax: 605-394-2590; 8AM-5PM (MST). *Felony, Misdemeanor, Civil, Eviction, Small Claims, Domestic, Probate.*
www.sdjudicial.com/cc/SeventhCircuit/Default.aspx

General Information: Note that civil cases for amounts up to $12,000 may be held at the Magistrate Court, but all money judgments can be accessed as described below. No juvenile, sealed, or mental health records released. Will not fax documents. Court makes copy: $.20 per page. Certification fee: $2.00 per cert. Payee: Clerk of the Court. Personal checks accepted. Major credit cards accepted. Prepayment required. Mail requests: SASE required.

Civil Name Search: Access: Mail, in person, online. Only the court performs in person name searches; visitors may not. Search fee: $15.00 per name. Required to search: name, years to search; also helpful: address. Civil records on computer from 1991, cards and docket books from 1930.

Mail turnaround time for document requests 1-4 days. **For details on commercial access and online access to civil records see the profile at front or back of this chapter.**

Criminal Name Search: Access: Mail, in person. Only the court performs in person name searches; visitors may not. Search fee: $15.00 per name. Required to search: name, years to search, DOB; also helpful: address, SSN or DL#. Criminal records computerized to 1989, on other media form 1950. Note: This court forwards all mail requests for criminal record searches to the County Clerk in Union County. This office suggests to mail the original request to that county clerk. In person request will only receive a countywide search. Mail turnaround time for document requests 2 weeks.

Perkins County

Circuit Court PO Box 426, 101 Main St, Bison, SD 57620-0426; 605-244-5626; fax: 605-244-7110; 9AM-N, 1-4PM (MST). *Felony, Misdemeanor, Civil, Eviction, Small Claims, Domestic, Probate.*
www.sdjudicial.com/cc/FourthCircuit/Default.aspx

General Information: Note that civil cases for amounts up to $12,000 may be held at the Magistrate Court, but all money judgments can be accessed as described below. No juvenile, sealed or mental health records released. Will fax documents $1.00 per page, $5.00 minimum. Court makes copy: $.20 per page. Self serve copy: same. Certification fee: $2.00 per cert. Payee: Perkins County Clerk of Courts. Only cashiers checks and money orders accepted. Major credit cards accepted. Prepayment required. Mail requests: SASE requested.

Civil Name Search: Access: Mail, in person, online. Only the court performs in person name searches; visitors may not. Search fee: $15.00 per name. Civil index in docket books from 1908; on computer back to 1999. Mail turnaround time for document requests 1-4 days. **For details on commercial access and online access to civil records see the profile at front or back of this chapter.**

Criminal Name Search: Access: Mail, in person. Only the court performs in person name searches; visitors may not. Search fee: $15.00 per name. Required to search: name, years to search, DOB; also helpful: address, SSN or DL#. Criminal records are computerized back to 7/89 on a statewide system. Note: This court forwards all mail requests for criminal record searches to the County Clerk in Union County. This office suggests to mail the original request to that county clerk. In person request will only receive a countywide search. Mail turnaround time for document requests varies.

Potter County

Circuit Court PO Box 67, 201 S Exene St, Gettysburg, SD 57442; 605-765-9472; fax: 605-765-9670; 7:30AM-N, 12:30-5PM M-TH; 7:30AM-N F (CST). *Felony, Misdemeanor, Civil, Eviction, Small Claims, Domestic, Probate.*
http://ujs.sd.gov/contactinfo/cccontacts.aspx

General Information: Note that civil cases for amounts up to $12,000 may be held at the Magistrate Court, but all money judgments can be accessed as described below. No juvenile, sealed, adoption or mental health records released. Will not fax out documents. Court makes copy: $.20 per page. Certification fee: $2.00 per doc. Payee: Potter County Clerk of Court. Personal checks accepted. Major credit cards accepted. Prepayment required. Mail requests: SASE required.

Civil Name Search: Access: Mail, in person, online. Only the court performs in person name searches; visitors may not. Search fee: $15.00 per name. Required to search: name, years to search; also helpful: address. Civil index on cards and docket books from 1889. Note: Requests should be in writing. Mail turnaround time for document requests 1-4 days. **For details on commercial access and online access to civil records see the profile at front or back of this chapter.**

Criminal Name Search: Access: Mail, in person. Only the court performs in person name searches; visitors may not. Search fee: $15.00 per name. Required to search: name, years to search, DOB; also helpful: address, SSN or DL#. Criminal records are indexed on computer since 7/89 on a statewide system. Note: This court forwards all mail requests for criminal record searches to the County Clerk in Union County. This office suggests to mail the original request to that county clerk. In person request will only receive a countywide search. Mail turnaround time for document requests 1-2 days.

Roberts County

Circuit Court 411 2nd Ave E, Sisseton, SD 57262-1403; 605-698-3395; fax: 605-698-7894; 8AM-5PM (CST). *Felony, Misdemeanor, Civil, Eviction, Small Claims, Domestic, Probate.*
http://ujs.sd.gov/cc/FifthCircuit/Default.aspx

General Information: Note that civil cases for amounts up to $12,000 may be held at the Magistrate Court, but all money judgments can be accessed as described below. No juvenile, sealed, adoption or mental health records released. Will fax documents $1.00 per page, $5.00 minimum. Court makes copy: $.20 per page. Certification fee: $2.00 includes copy fee. Payee: Roberts County Clerk of Court (or, Edmunds City Clerk, if a criminal search). Personal checks accepted. Major credit cards accepted. Prepayment required. Mail requests: SASE required.

Civil Name Search: Access: Mail, in person, online. Only the court performs in person name searches; visitors may not. Search fee: $15.00 per name. Required to search: name, years to search; also helpful: address. Civil records on computer from 1992, microfilm from 1920 to 1993 and original files from 1994. Note: Searches performed on a time available basis. Mail turnaround time for document requests 1-4 days. **For details on commercial access and online access to civil records see the profile at front or back of this chapter.**

Criminal Name Search: Access: Mail, in person. Only the court performs in person name searches; visitors may not. Search fee: $15.00 per name. Required to search: name, years to search, DOB; also helpful: address, SSN or DL#. Criminal records on computer since 1988 on a state wide system. Note: This court forwards all mail requests for criminal record searches to the County Clerk in Union County. This office suggests to mail the original request to that county clerk. In person request will only receive a countywide search. Mail turnaround time for document requests 2-3 days.

Sanborn County

Circuit Court PO Box 56, 604 W 6th St, Woonsocket, SD 57385; 605-796-4515; fax: 605-796-4502; 9AM-4:30PM (CST). *Felony, Misdemeanor, Civil, Eviction, Small Claims, Domestic, Probate.*
www.sdjudicial.com/cc/ThirdCircuit/Default.aspx

General Information: Note that civil cases for amounts up to $12,000 may be held at the Magistrate Court, but all money judgments can be accessed as described below. No juvenile, sealed, or mental health records released. Will fax documents $1.00 per page, $5.00 minimum. Court makes copy: $.20 per page. Certification fee: $2.00 per cert. Payee: Sanborn County Clerk of Courts. Personal checks accepted; no two party checks. Major credit cards accepted. Prepayment required. Mail requests: SASE required.

Civil Name Search: Access: Mail, in person, online. Both court and visitors may perform in person name searches. Search fee: $15.00 per name. Required to search: name, years to search; also helpful: address. Civil index in docket books from 1890s, computerized since 2005. Mail turnaround time for document requests 1-4 days. **For details on commercial access and online access to civil records see the profile at front or back of this chapter.**

Criminal Name Search: Access: Mail, in person. Both court and visitors may perform in person name searches. Search fee: $15.00 per name. Required to search: name, years to search, DOB; also helpful: address, SSN or DL#. Criminal records are computerized since 1989 on a statewide system. Note: This court forwards all mail requests for criminal record searches to the County Clerk in Union County. This office suggests to mail the original request to that county clerk. In person request will only receive a countywide search. Mail turnaround time for document requests 1 week.

Shannon County

Circuit Court C/O Fall River Circuit Court, 906 N River St, Hot Springs, SD 57747; 605-745-5131; ; 8AM-5PM (MST). *Felony, Misdemeanor, Civil, Eviction, Small Claims, Domestic, Probate.*
www.sdjudicial.com/cc/SeventhCircuit/Default.aspx

General Information: Note that cases, proceedings, and records for the Shannon County Circuit Court are handled by the Fall River Circuit Court. Records are not co-mingled. Be specific in your request. Tribal court handles Tribal matters - 605-867-5131. No juvenile, sealed, adoption, or mental health records released. Will fax documents $1.00 per page, $5.00 minimum. Court makes copy: $.20 per page. Certification fee: $2.00 per doc plus copy fee. Payee: Shannon County Clerk of Court. Personal checks accepted. Major credit cards accepted. Prepayment required. Mail requests: SASE required.

Civil Name Search: Access: Mail, in person, online. Only the court performs in person name searches; visitors may not. Search fee: $15.00 per name. Required to search: name, years to search; also helpful: address, DOB, SSN. Civil records on computer from 1992, older files archived off site to 1889. Mail turnaround time for document requests 1-4 days. **For details on commercial access and online access to civil records see the profile at front or back of this chapter.**

Criminal Name Search: Access: Mail, in person. Only the court performs in person name searches; visitors may not. Search fee: $15.00 per name. Required to search: name, years to search, DOB; also helpful: address, SSN or DL#. Criminal records on computer since 7/89 on a statewide system. Note: This court forwards all mail requests for criminal record searches to the County Clerk in Union County. This office suggests to mail the original request to that county clerk. In person request will only receive a countywide search. Mail turnaround time for document requests 1-2 weeks.

Oglala Sioux Tribe Court Administration PO Box 280, Pine Ridge, SD 57770; 605-867-5151 MST). *Felony, Misdemeanor, Civil, Marriage, Divorce, Domestic, Probate.*
http://www.oglalalakotanation.org/OLN/Tribal_Programs_Court_Administration.html

General Information: The Oglala Sioux Tribal Court provides justice to enrolled members of the Tribe whom reside within the boundaries of the Pine Ridge Indian Reservation.

Spink County

Circuit Court 210 E 7th Ave, Redfield, SD 57469; 605-472-4535; fax: 605-472-4352; 8AM-12: 1PM-5PM (CST). *Felony, Misdemeanor, Civil, Eviction, Small Claims, Domestic, Probate.*
http://ujs.sd.gov/cc/FifthCircuit/Default.aspx

General Information: Probate fax is same as main fax number. No juvenile, sealed, or mental health records released. Will fax documents $1.00 per page, $5.00 minimum. Court makes copy: $.20 per page. Certification fee: $2.00 per doc includes copy fee. Payee: Spink County Clerk of Court. Personal checks accepted. Major credit cards accepted. Prepayment required. Mail requests: SASE required.

Civil Name Search: Access: Phone, fax, mail, in person, online. Only the court performs in person name searches; visitors may not. Search fee: $15.00 per name. Required to search: name, years to search; also helpful: address. Civil index in docket books from 1882. Mail turnaround time for document requests 1-4 days. **For details on commercial access and online access to civil records see the profile at front or back of this chapter.**

Criminal Name Search: Access: Phone, fax, mail, in person. Only the court performs in person name searches; visitors may not. Search fee: $15.00 per name. Required to search: name, years to search, DOB; also helpful: address, SSN or DL#. Criminal records on computer since 1988 on a statewide system. Note: This court forwards all mail requests for criminal record searches to the County Clerk in Union County. This office suggests to mail the original request to that county clerk. In person request will only receive a countywide search. Mail turnaround time for document requests 1 day.

Stanley County

Circuit Court PO Box 758, E. 2nd Ave Courthouse, #8, Fort Pierre, SD 57532; 605-223-7735; fax: 605-223-7738; 8AM-5PM (CST). *Felony, Misdemeanor, Civil, Eviction, Small Claims, Domestic, Probate.*
http://ujs.sd.gov/contactinfo/cccontacts.aspx

General Information: Note that civil cases for amounts up to $12,000 may be held at the Magistrate Court, but all money judgments can be accessed as described below. No juvenile, sealed, or mental health records released. Will fax documents $1.00 per page, $5.00 minimum. Court makes copy: $.20 per page. Certification fee: $2.00 per cert. Payee: Stanley County Clerk of Court. Personal checks accepted. Major credit cards accepted. Prepayment required. Mail requests: SASE required.

Civil Name Search: Access: Fax, mail, in person, online. Both court and visitors may perform in person name searches. Search fee: $15.00 per name. Required to search: name, years to search; also helpful: address. Civil index in docket books from 1973, can search back to 1892. Note: Requests should be in writing. Mail turnaround time for document requests 1-4 days. **For details on commercial access and online access to civil records see the profile at front or back of this chapter.**

Criminal Name Search: Access: Fax, mail, in person. Both court and visitors may perform in person name searches. Search fee: $15.00 per name. Required to search: name, years to search, DOB; also helpful: address, SSN or DL#. Criminal records on computer since 1989 on a statewide system, records can be search locally to 1892. Note: This court forwards all mail requests for criminal record searches to the County Clerk in Union County. This office suggests to mail the original request to that county clerk. In person request will only receive a countywide search. Mail turnaround time for document requests 1-2 days.

Sully County

Circuit Court PO Box 188, Onida, SD 57564; 605-258-2535; fax: 605-258-2270; 8AM-N (CST). *Felony, Misdemeanor, Civil, Eviction, Small Claims, Domestic, Probate.*
http://ujs.sd.gov/contactinfo/cccontacts.aspx

General Information: Note that civil cases for amounts up to $12,000 may be held at the Magistrate Court, but all money judgments can be accessed as described below. No juvenile, sealed, or mental health records released. Will fax documents $1.00 per page, $5.00 minimum. Court makes copy: $.25 per page plus tax $.02. Self serve copy: same. Certification fee: $2.00 per cert. Payee: Sully County Clerk of Court. Personal checks accepted, credit cards are not. Prepayment required. Mail requests: SASE required.

Civil Name Search: Access: Mail, in person, online. Both court and visitors may perform in person name searches. Search fee: $15.00 per

name. Required to search: name, years to search; also helpful: address. Civil index in docket books from 1900s. Note: The public may search the docket books. Mail turnaround time for document requests 1-4 days. **For details on commercial access and online access to civil records see the profile at front or back of this chapter.**
Criminal Name Search: Access: Mail, in person. Both court and visitors may perform in person name searches. Search fee: $15.00 per name. Required to search: name, years to search, DOB; also helpful: address, SSN or DL#. Criminal records on computer since 7/89 on statewide system; local computer back to 2000. Note: This court forwards all mail requests for criminal record searches to the County Clerk in Union County. This office suggests to mail the original request to that county clerk. In person request will only receive a countywide search. Mail turnaround time for document requests 1-2 days.

Todd County

Circuit Court PO Box 311, 200 E 3rd St, Winner, SD 57580; 605-842-2266; fax: 605-842-2267; 8AM-5PM (MST). *Felony, Misdemeanor, Civil, Eviction, Small Claims, Domestic, Probate.*
http://ujs.sd.gov/contactinfo/cccontacts.aspx
General Information: Court records are maintained by Tripp County - contact information is shown for Tripp.

Rosebud Sioux Tribal Court, Courthouse, PO Box 129, Rosebud, SD 57570; 605-747-2278 (both civil and criminal), 605-747-2832 Fax. 8AM-5PM. (MST)
www.rosebudsiouxtribe-nsn.gov/

Tripp County

Circuit Court PO Box 311, 200 E 3rd St, Winner, SD 57580; 605-842-2266; fax: 605-842-2267; 8AM-5PM (CST). *Felony, Misdemeanor, Civil, Eviction, Small Claims, Domestic, Probate.*
http://ujs.sd.gov/contactinfo/cccontacts.aspx
General Information: This court also maintains records for Todd County. No juvenile, sealed, or mental health records released. Will fax documents $1.00 per page, $5.00 minimum. Court makes copy: $.25 per page criminal; civil- $.20 per page. Certification fee: $2.00 per doc. Payee: Tripp County Clerk of Court. Personal checks accepted. Major credit cards accepted. Prepayment required. Mail requests: SASE required.
Civil Name Search: Access: Mail, in person, online. Only the court performs in person name searches; visitors may not. Search fee: $15.00 per name. Required to search: name, years to search; also helpful: address. Civil index in docket books from 1920s. Note: Requests should be in writing. Mail turnaround time for document requests 1-4 days. **For details on commercial access and online access to civil records see the profile at front or back of this chapter.**
Criminal Name Search: Access: Mail, in person. Only the court performs in person name searches; visitors may not. Search fee: $15.00 per name. Required to search: name, years to search, DOB; also helpful: address, SSN or DL#. Criminal records on computer since 1989 on statewide system. Note: This court forwards all mail requests for criminal record searches to the County Clerk in Union County. This office suggests to mail the original request to that county clerk. In person request will only receive a countywide search. Mail turnaround time for document requests 2 days.

Turner County

Circuit Court PO Box 446, Parker, SD 57053; 605-297-3115; fax: 605-297-2115; 8:30AM-5PM (CST). *Felony, Misdemeanor, Civil, Eviction, Small Claims, Domestic, Probate.*
www.sdjudicial.com/cc/FirstCircuit/Default.aspx
General Information: Note that civil cases for amounts up to $12,000 may be held at the Magistrate Court, but all money judgments can be accessed as described below. No juvenile, sealed, or mental health records released. Will fax documents $1.00 per page, $5.00 minimum. Court makes copy: $.20 per page. Certification fee: $2.00 plus copy fee. Payee: Turner County Clerk of Courts. Personal checks accepted. Major credit cards accepted. Prepayment required. Mail requests: SASE required.
Civil Name Search: Access: Mail, in person, online. Only the court performs in person name searches; visitors may not. Search fee: $15.00 per name. Required to search: name, years to search; also helpful: address, DOB, and drivers license number. Civil index on cards and docket books from 1900s. Mail turnaround time for document requests 1-4 days. **For details on commercial access and online access to civil records see the profile at front or back of this chapter.**
Criminal Name Search: Access: Mail, in person. Both court and visitors may perform in person name searches. Search fee: $15.00 per name. Required to search: name, years to search, DOB; also helpful: address, SSN or DL#. Criminal records on computer since 7/89 on a statewide system. Note: This court forwards all mail requests for criminal record searches to the County Clerk in Union County. This office suggests to mail the

original request to that county clerk. In person request will only receive a countywide search. Mail turnaround time for document requests 2 days.

Union County

Circuit Court 209 E Main St #230, Elk Point, SD 57025; 605-356-2132; fax: 605-356-3687; 8AM-5PM (CST). *Felony, Misdemeanor, Civil, Eviction, Small Claims, Domestic, Probate.*
www.sdjudicial.com/cc/FirstCircuit/Default.aspx
General Information: Note that civil cases for amounts up to $12,000 may be held at the Magistrate Court, but all money judgments can be accessed as described below. No juvenile, sealed, or mental health records released. Will fax documents $1.00 per page, $5.00 minimum. Court makes copy: $.20 per page. Certification fee: $2.00 per name. Payee: Union County Clerk of Court. Personal checks accepted. Major credit cards accepted. Prepayment required. Mail requests: SASE required.
Civil Name Search: Access: Fax, mail, in person, online. Only the court performs in person name searches; visitors may not. Search fee: $15.00 per name. Required to search: name, years to search; also helpful: address. Civil records on computer from 1990, docket books from 1900s. Mail turnaround time for document requests 1-4 days. **For details on commercial access and online access to civil records see the profile at front or back of this chapter.**
Criminal Name Search: Access: Fax, mail, in person. Only the court performs in person name searches; visitors may not. Search fee: $15.00 per name. Required to search: name, years to search, DOB; also helpful: address, SSN or DL#. Criminal records on computer since 1988 on a statewide system, on docket books from 1900s. Note: A statewide search will be performed. Mail turnaround time for document requests 1-2 days.

Walworth County

Circuit Court PO Box 328, Selby, SD 57472; 605-649-7311; fax: 605-649-7624; 8AM-5PM (CST). *Felony, Misdemeanor, Civil, Eviction, Small Claims, Domestic, Probate.*
http://ujs.sd.gov/cc/FifthCircuit/Default.aspx
General Information: Note that civil cases for amounts up to $12,000 may be held at the Magistrate Court, but all money judgments can be accessed as described below. No juvenile, sealed, or mental health records released. Will fax documents $1.00 per page, $5.00 minimum. Court makes copy: $.20 per page. Certification fee: $2.00 per doc. Payee: Walworth County Clerk of Court. Personal checks accepted. Major credit cards accepted. Prepayment required. Mail requests: SASE required.
Civil Name Search: Access: Mail, in person, online. Only the court performs in person name searches; visitors may not. Search fee: $15.00 per name. Required to search: name, years to search; also helpful: address. Civil index on cards and docket books from 1900s, computerized since 1993. Mail turnaround time for document requests 1-4 days. **For details on commercial access and online access to civil records see the profile at front or back of this chapter.**
Criminal Name Search: Access: Mail, in person. Only the court performs in person name searches; visitors may not. Search fee: $15.00 per name. Required to search: name, years to search, DOB; also helpful: address, SSN or DL#. Criminal records on computer since 7/89 in a statewide system. Note: This court forwards all mail requests for criminal record searches to the County Clerk in Union County. This office suggests to mail the original request to that county clerk. In person request will only receive a countywide search. Mail turnaround time for document requests 1-2 days.

Yankton County

Circuit Court Clerk of Courts, 410 Walnut St, Yankton, SD 57078; 605-668-3080; fax: 605-668-5411; 8AM-5PM (CST). *Felony, Misdemeanor, Civil, Eviction, Small Claims, Domestic, Probate.*
www.sdjudicial.com/cc/FirstCircuit/Default.aspx
General Information: Probate is a separate index at this same address. Probate fax is same as main fax number. No juvenile, sealed, or mental health records released. Will fax documents $1.00 per page, $5.00 minimum. Court makes copy: $.20 per page. Certification fee: $2.00 per doc plus copy fee. Payee: Yankton County Clerk of Court. Personal checks accepted. Major credit cards accepted. Prepayment required. Mail requests: SASE required.
Civil Name Search: Access: Mail, in person, online. Only the court performs in person name searches; visitors may not. Search fee: $15.00 per name. Required to search: name, years to search; also helpful: address, DOB, SSN. Civil records on computer from 1991, docket books from 1900s. Note: Visitors only have access to the book index. Mail turnaround time for document requests 1-4 days. **For details on commercial access and online access to civil records see the profile at front or back of this chapter.**
Criminal Name Search: Access: Mail, in person. Only the court performs in person name searches; visitors may not. Search fee: $15.00 per name. Must be a state authorized account. Required to search: name,

years to search, DOB; also helpful: address, SSN or DL#. Criminal records on computer since 7/89 on a statewide system, Class II offenses not accessible on computer to public. Note: This court forwards all mail requests for criminal record searches to the County Clerk in Union County. This office suggests to mail the original request to that county clerk. In person request will only receive a countywide search. Mail turnaround time for document requests 1 week.

Ziebach County

Circuit Court PO Box 306, Dupree, SD 57623; 605-365-5159; fax: 605-365-5652; 9:30AM-N, 1-2:30PM (MST). *Felony, Misdemeanor, Civil, Eviction, Small Claims, Domestic, Probate.*

www.sdjudicial.com/cc/FourthCircuit/Default.aspx

General Information: Probate is a separate index at this same address. No juvenile, sealed, adoption or mental health records released. Will fax documents $1.00 per page, $5.00 minimum. Court makes copy: $.20 per page. Certification fee: $2.00 per doc includes copies. Payee: Ziebach Clerk of Court. Personal checks accepted. Major credit cards accepted. Prepayment required. Mail requests: SASE required.

Civil Name Search: Access: Mail, in person, online. Only the court performs in person name searches; visitors may not. Search fee: $15.00 per name. Required to search: name, years to search; also helpful: address. Civil cases indexed by defendant. Civil index on docket books from 1900s. Mail turnaround time for document requests 1-2 days. **For details on commercial access and online access to civil records see the profile at front or back of this chapter.**

Criminal Name Search: Access: Mail, in person. Only the court performs in person name searches; visitors may not. Search fee: $15.00 per name. Required to search: name, years to search, DOB; also helpful: address, SSN or DL#. Criminal records indexed in books from 1900s. Note: This court forwards all mail requests for criminal record searches to the County Clerk in Union County. This office suggests to mail the original request to that county clerk. In person request will only receive a countywide search. Mail turnaround time for document requests 1-2 days.

About Online Access to Civil Records

A web search for all active money judgments and inactive civil money judgments from 04/19/2004 forward is offered by the SD Court Administrator's Office. This service includes a search from both the Circuit and Magistrate Courts. Charges for searches using a credit/debit card are $4.00 per name or date range search. There is an additional $1.00 charge to access the judgment docket. The system works off a pre-paid deposit using a credit card, so the system deducts from your balance.

Users may also obtain unlimited access to system, including bulk downloading of civil money judgment information, by subscribing on a monthly or yearly basis. Contact the State Court Administrator's Office, Attn: Jill Gusso, 500 E. Capitol Avenue, Pierre, SD 57501. Note that this service is only for end-users; the agreement with the agency disallows any resale of the data. For more information see https://apps.sd.gov/applications/judgmentquery/login.aspx.

Note this online system does not provide probate or criminal information.

Tennessee

Time Zone: **CST & EST***

* Tennessee's thirty Eastern-most counties are EST: They are: Anderson, Blount, Bradley, Campbell, Carter, Claiborne, Cocke, Grainger, Greene, Hamblen, Hamilton, Hancock, Hawkins, Jefferson, Johnson, Knox, Loudon, McMinn, Meigs, Monroe, Morgan, Polk, Rhea, Roane, Scott, Sevier, Sullivan, Unicoi, Union, Washington.

Capital: **Nashville, Davidson County**

# of Counties: **95**

State Web: **www.tennessee.gov**

Court Web: **www.tncourts.gov**

Administration

Administrative Office of the Courts, 511 Union St, Nashville City Center, #600, Nashville, TN, 37219; 615-741-2687, Fax: 615-741-6285.

The Supreme Court and Appellate Courts

The Tennessee Supreme Court is the state's court of last resort. The Court of Appeals hears appeals in civil—or non-criminal—cases from trial courts and certain state boards and commissions. The Court of Criminal Appeals hears trial court appeals in felony and misdemeanor cases, as well as post-conviction petitions.

The Tennessee Courts

Court	Type	How Organized	Jurisdiction Highpoints
Circuit*	General	95 Courts	Felony, Misdemeanor, Civil
Chancery*	General	67 Courts	Civil, Eviction, Small Claims
General Sessions*	Limited	100 Courts	Misdemeanor, Civil, Small Claims, Juvenile, Domestic, Traffic, Ordinance
Criminal*	General	13	Felony, Misdemeanor
Municipal	Limited	300	Ordinance
Probate	Special	1 in Shelby County	Probate
Juvenile & Family	Special	17 (plus 81 in General Sessions)	Juvenile, Domestic

* = profiled in this book

Details on the Court Structure

Circuit Courts hear civil and criminal cases and appeals of decisions from City, Juvenile, Municipal and General Sessions Courts. The jurisdiction of Circuit Courts often overlaps with that of the Chancery Courts.

Criminal cases are tried in Circuit Court except in districts with separate **Criminal Courts** established by the General Assembly. Criminal Courts exist in 13 of the 31 districts.

Chancery Courts handle a variety of issues including lawsuits, contract disputes, application for injunctions and name changes. A number of matters, such as divorces, adoptions, and workers' compensation, can be heard in either Chancery or Circuit court.

General Sessions Court jurisdiction varies from county to county based on state laws and private acts. But every county is served by this court of limited jurisdiction, which hears both civil and criminal cases. Combining of Circuit Court and General Sessions Courts in a county often occurs.

Each **Juvenile & Family Court**, with the exception of Bristol and Johnson City, is county-based and administered with at least one juvenile court located in each of the state's 95 counties. There are 98 courts, but 17 are designated "Private Act" Juvenile Courts while the remaining 81 are General Sessions Courts with juvenile jurisdiction.

Record Searching Facts You Need to Know

Fees and Record Searching Tips
Fees vary widely, for example the fee for a criminal name search will vary from $5.00 to $25.00, or no fee at all. Over two-thirds of the general jurisdiction courts offer public access terminals to view docket indices.

Online Access is Limited
Only a half a dozen counties offer online access to court records. There is no statewide access system other than the access to Supreme and Appellate Court data.

Anderson County

7th District Circuit & General Sessions Court 100 N Main St, Rm 301, Clinton, TN 37716; 865-457-5400; criminal phone: 865-463-6822; civil phone: 865-463-6821; fax: 865-259-2345; 8AM-4:30PM (EST). *Felony, Misdemeanor, Civil, Eviction, Small Claims.* www.andersoncountycircuitcourtclerk.com/

General Information: The current docket list is found at www.anderson.mytncourts.com/01201dlydocketshort.pdf. Historical data is not available online. No juvenile records released. Will not fax out case files. Court makes copy: $.50 per page. Self serve copy: $.25 per page. Certification fee: $5.00 per cert. Payee: Circuit Court Clerk or General Sessions Clerk. Personal checks accepted. Visa, M/C, AMEX accepted by phone to 1-866-347-1902 or online only. Prepayment required.

Civil Name Search: Access: In person only. Visitors must perform in person searches themselves. Civil records on computer from 1988, archived from 1947. Civil PAT goes back to 1988.

Criminal Name Search: Access: In person only. Visitors must perform in person searches themselves. Required to search: name, years to search, DOB, SSN. Criminal records computerized from 1988, archived from 1947. Criminal PAT goes back to 1992. Court dockets schedule available at the website.

Chancery Court Anderson County Courthouse, PO Box 501, Clinton, TN 37717; 865-457-5400; probate phone: 865-457-6207; fax: 865-457-6267; 8:30AM-4:30PM (EST). *Civil, Probate.*

General Information: The current docket list is found at www.anderson.mytncourts.com/01201dlydocketshort.pdf. Historical data is not available online. No adoption or mental health records released. Will not fax documents. Court makes copy: $.50 per page. Self serve copy: $.25 per page. Certification fee: $5.00 per cert. Payee: Clerk and Master. Personal checks accepted, credit cards are not. Prepayment required. Mail requests: SASE not required.

Civil Name Search: Access: Phone, mail, in person. Visitors must perform in person searches themselves. No search fee. Civil records on computer 1992 to present, prior records on another system.

Bedford County

17th District Circuit & General Sessions Court 1 Public Sq, #200, Shelbyville, TN 37160; 931-684-3223; fax: 931-684-4141; 8AM-4PM (CST). *Felony, Misdemeanor, Civil, Eviction, Small Claims.*

General Information: No juvenile, adoptions, mental health, expunged or sealed records released. Court makes copy: $.50 per page. Self serve copy: same. Certification fee: $2.00 per cert. Payee: Thomas Smith, Clerk. No personal checks or credit cards accepted. Prepayment required.

Civil Name Search: Access: Fax, in person. Both court and visitors may perform in person name searches. Search fee: $5.00 per name. Civil records on archives and books from 1934; computerized records since 1994. Civil PAT goes back to 10 years.

Criminal Name Search: Access: Fax, in person. Both court and visitors may perform in person name searches. Search fee: $5.00 per name. Required to search: name, years to search, DOB; SSN helpful. Criminal records on archives and books from 1934; computerized records since 1994. Criminal PAT goes back to 10 years.

Chancery Court Chancery Court, 1 Public Sq, #302, Shelbyville, TN 37160; 931-684-1672; fax: 931-680-0144; 8AM-4PM (CST). *Civil, Probate.*

General Information: No adoption records released. Will not fax documents. Court makes copy: $.50 per page. Certification fee: $5.00 per cert. Payee: Clerk and Master. Personal checks accepted, credit cards are not. Prepayment required.

Civil Name Search: Access: In person only. Visitors must perform in person searches themselves. Civil records on books from 9/82 (probate), prior records back to 1800s filed in county clerk's office.

Benton County

24th District Circuit 1 E Court Sq, Rm 207, Camden, TN 38320; 731-584-6711; fax: 731-584-2181; 8AM-4PM M-TH; 8AM-5PM F (CST). *Felony, Misdemeanor, Civil, Eviction, Small Claims.*

General Information: Sessions court is in Rm 210. Records Room phone is 731-584-6165. No juvenile records released without judge approval. Will not fax documents. Court makes copy: $1.00 per page. Certification fee: $5.00 per cert. Payee: Circuit Court Clerk or General Session. Business checks accepted. No credit cards accepted. Prepayment required.

Civil Name Search: Access: In person only. Both court and visitors may perform in person name searches. Civil records computerized since 1995. Public can only use docket books to search, older records archived to 1800s. Civil PAT goes back to 1996.

Criminal Name Search: Access: In person only. Both court and visitors may perform in person name searches. Criminal records computerized since 1995. Public can only use docket books to search, older records archived to 1800s. Criminal PAT goes back to 1996.

Chancery Court 1 E Court Sq, Courthouse Rm 206, Camden, TN 38320; 731-584-4435; fax: 731-584-1407; 8AM-4PM M-TH; 8AM-5PM F (CST). *Civil, Probate.*

General Information: No adoption or sealed records released. Will fax documents to local or toll-free number. Court makes copy: $.50 per page. Certification fee: $5.00 per cert. Payee: Clerk & Master. Personal checks accepted, credit cards are not. Prepayment required.

Civil Name Search: Access: In person only. Only the court performs in person name searches; visitors may not. Civil records on computer back to 1994; in books since 1880. Note: Will search probate records for $10.00.

Bledsoe County

12th District Circuit & General Sessions Court PO Box 455, Pikeville, TN 37367; 423-447-6488; fax: 423-447-2534; 8AM-4PM (CST). *Felony, Misdemeanor, Civil, Eviction, Small Claims.*

General Information: No juvenile records released. Will fax documents no fee. Court makes copy: $.50 per page. Self serve copy: same. Certification fee: $5.00. Payee: Circuit Court. Checks and money orders accepted. No credit cards accepted. Prepayment required.

Civil Name Search: Access: In person only. Visitors must perform in person searches themselves. Civil cases indexed by plaintiff. Civil records archived from 1920 in books. Note: Books available for public to search.

Criminal Name Search: Access: In person only. Visitors must perform in person searches themselves. Required to search: name, years to search, DOB. Criminal records archived from 1920 in books. Note: Books available for public to search.

Chancery Court PO Box 389, Pikeville, TN 37367; 423-447-2484; 8AM-4PM M,T,W,F; 8AM-N TH (CST). *Civil, Probate.*

General Information: No juvenile or adoption records released. Will fax documents $2.00 per page. Court makes copy: $.50 per page. Self serve copy: $.25 per page. Certification fee: $5.00 per cert. Payee: Bledsoe County Clerk and Master. Personal checks accepted, credit cards are not. Prepayment required.

Civil Name Search: Access: Phone, mail, in person. Both court and visitors may perform in person name searches. No search fee. Civil records on books since 1856. Mail turnaround time 3 days.

Blount County

5th District General Sessions Court 926 E Lamar Alexander Pky, Maryville, TN 37804-6201; 865-273-5450; criminal phone: 865-273-5400; fax: 865-273-5411; 7:30AM-4:30PM (EST). *Misdemeanor, Civil, Eviction, Small Claims.* www.blountccc.com/generalsessions.aspx

General Information: The court encourages the public to use the public access terminals. No juvenile records released. Will fax documents. Court makes copy: $.50 per page. Any job requiring over one hour of copying is charged differently. Self serve copy: same. Certification fee: $5.50 per document, exemplification fee is $11.00. Payee: Circuit Court Clerk or General Session. Business checks accepted. Credit cards accepted for orders via the internet and at window (no Visa credit cards in person). Prepayment required. Mail requests: SASE required.

Civil Name Search: Access: Mail, in person. Both court and visitors may perform in person name searches. Search fee: $15.00 per name if extensive. Required to search: name, years to search, identifiers. Civil records in books back to 1991; on computer back to 1997, prior archived not on site. Mail turnaround time 6-10 days. Civil PAT goes back to 1997.

Criminal Name Search: Access: Mail, in person. Both court and visitors may perform in person name searches. Search fee: $15.00 per name if extensive. Required to search: name, years to search, identifiers. Criminal records in books back to 1991; on computer back to 1997, prior archived not on site. Mail turnaround time 6-10 days. Criminal PAT goes to 1997.

Circuit Court 926 E Lamar Alexander Pky, 1st Fl, Maryville, TN 37804; 865-273-5400; probate phone: 865-273-5800; fax: 865-273-5411; 8AM-4:30PM (EST). *Felony, Misdemeanor, Civil.*
www.blountcc.com/circuitcourt.aspx

General Information: No juvenile records or SSNs released. Will fax documents $.50 per page. Court makes copy: $.50 per page. Self serve copy: same. Certification fee: $5.50 per cert; $11.00 for exemplification. Payee: Circuit Court Clerk. No personal checks accepted; business checks and attorney checks are accepted. Major credit cards accepted in person except VISA. Prepayment required. Mail requests: SASE required.

Civil Name Search: Access: Mail, in person. Both court and visitors may perform in person name searches. Search fee: $15.00 per name. Required to search: name, years to search, identifiers. Civil cases indexed by defendant. Civil records on books. Civil PAT goes back to 8 years.

Criminal Name Search: Access: Mail, in person. Visitors must perform in person searches themselves. Search fee: $15.00 per name. Required to search: name, years to search, identifiers. Criminal docket on books. Criminal PAT goes back to 10 years. Online results show middle initial.

County Clerk 345 Court St., Maryville, TN 37804; 865-273-5800; fax: 865-273-5815; 8AM-4:30PM (EST). *Probate.*

Bradley County

10th District Circuit & General Sessions Court - Civil Courthouse, Rm 205, 155 N Ocoee St, Cleveland, TN 37311-5068; 423-728-7220; fax: 423-476-0488; 8:30AM-4:30PM M-TH, 8:30AM-5PM F (EST). *Civil, Eviction, Small Claims.*

General Information: No juvenile records released. Fee to fax out file $1.00 per page. Court makes copy: $.50 per page. Self serve copy: $.50 per page. Certification fee: $5.00 per cert. Payee: Circuit Court Clerk or General Session. Personal checks accepted, credit cards are not. Prepayment required. Mail requests: SASE required.

Civil Name Search: Access: Mail, in person. Both court and visitors may perform in person name searches. Search fee: $25.00 per name. Civil records archived from 1990, on computer from 1990. Mail turnaround time 10 days. Public use terminal has civil records back to 1990.

10th District Circuit & General Sessions Court - Criminal 2230 Blythe Ave, County Justice Center, Cleveland, TN; 423-728-7215 circuit; 423-728-7053 Sessions; fax: 423-476-0487; 8:30AM-4:30PM M-TH, 8:30AM-5PM F (EST). *Felony, Misdemeanor.*
www.bradleyco.net/circuitcourtclerkhome.aspx

General Information: Civil is at old courthouse as of May, 2004, see separate listing. No juvenile records released. Fee to fax out file $1.00 per page. Court makes copy: $.50 per page. Certification fee: $5.00 per page. Payee: Circuit Court Clerk or General Session. No personal checks accepted. No credit or debit cards accepted. Prepayment required.

Criminal Name Search: Access: Mail, in person. Both court and visitors may perform in person name searches. Search fee: $25.00 per name; $5.00 for basic background check for record. Required to search: name, years to search, signed release. Criminal records archived from 1990, on computer from 1990. Mail turnaround time 10 days. Public use terminal has crim records back 10 years.

Chancery Court 155 N Ocoee St, Rm 203, Cleveland, TN 37311; 423-728-7205; probate phone: 423-728-7208; fax: 423-339-0723; 8:30AM-4:30PM M-TH, 8:30AM-5PM F (EST). *Civil, Probate.*

General Information: No adoption records released. Will fax documents $1.00 per page. Court makes copy: $.50 per page. Certification fee: $5.00 per cert plus copy fee. Payee: Clerk and Master. Personal checks accepted, credit cards are not. Prepayment required.

Civil Name Search: Access: Phone, mail, fax, n person. Only the court performs in person name searches; visitors may not. No search fee. Civil records filed in books back to 1861, on computer back to 2003. Mail turnaround time 3-5 days

Campbell County

8th District Circuit & General Sessions Court PO Box 26, 570 Main St, Jacksboro, TN 37757; 423-562-2624; fax: 423-563-0342; 8AM-4:30PM (EST). *Felony, Misdemeanor, Civil, Eviction, Small Claims.*
www.campbellcocircuitcourt.com/

General Information: No juvenile, adoption and judicial hospitalization records released. Will not fax documents. Court makes copy: $.50 per page. Certification fee: $5.00. Payee: Circuit Court Clerk or General Session. Business checks accepted. Visa/MC accepted. Prepayment required.

Civil Name Search: Access: Mail, in person. Only the court performs in person name searches; visitors may not. No search fee. Civil records on computer since 1991. On microfiche from 1987 and archived, since court started, at La Follett Library, La Follett, TN 37766. Mail turnaround time depends on type of search.

Criminal Name Search: Access: Mail, in person. Only the court performs in person name searches; visitors may not. No search fee. Required to search: name, years to search, DOB, SSN. Criminal records on computer since 1991. On microfiche from 1987 and archived, since court started, at La Follette Library, La Follette, TN 3776. Mail turnaround time depends on type of search.

Chancery Court PO Box 182 (570 Main St, #110), Jacksboro, TN 37757; 423-562-3496; fax: 423-562-9732; 8AM-4:30PM (EST). *Civil, Probate.*

General Information: No adoption records released. Fee to fax document $1.00 1st page, $.50 ea add'l. Court makes copy: $.50 per page. Certification fee: $5.00. Payee: Clerk and Master. Business checks accepted. No credit cards accepted. Prepayment required. Mail requests: SASE preferred.

Civil Name Search: Access: In person, mail. Visitors must perform in person searches themselves. No search fee. Civil records filed in books, microfiche available at LaFollette Library since 1842. Mail time 1-2 days.

Cannon County

16th District Circuit & General Sessions Court County Courthouse Public Sq, Woodbury, TN 37190; 615-563-4461; fax: 615-563-6391; 8AM-4PM M,T,TH,F; 8AM-N W (CST). *Felony, Misdemeanor, Civil, Eviction, Small Claims.*

General Information: No juvenile records released. Court makes copy: $.50 per page. Self serve copy: same. Certification fee: $5.00. Payee: Circuit Court Clerk or General Session. Personal checks accepted, credit cards are not. Prepayment required.

Civil Name Search: Access: In person only. Visitors must perform in person searches themselves. Civil records archived on books from 1980s, computerized since 10/2003. Civil PAT goes back to 12/2003.

Criminal Name Search: Access: In person only. Visitors must perform in person searches themselves. Required to search: name, years to search, DOB. Criminal records archived on books from 1980s, computerized since 12/2003. Criminal PAT goes back to same as civil.

County Court 1 County Courthouse Public Square, 200 W Main St, Woodbury, TN 37190; 615-563-4278; fax: 615-563-1289; 8AM-4PM M,T,TH,F; 8AM-N Sat (CST). *Probate.*

Carroll County

24th District Circuit & General Sessions Court 99 Court Sq, #103, Huntingdon, TN 38344; 731-986-1932; criminal phone: 731-986-1927; civil phone: 731-986-1929 (Circuit), 731-986-1926 (Gen Sess); fax: 731-986-1930; 8AM-4PM (CST). *Felony, Misdemeanor, Civil, Eviction, Small Claims.*

General Information: Will not fax out case files. Court makes copy: $.50 per page. No copies by mail. Self serve copy: same. Certification fee: $5.00 per record plus copy fee. Payee: Circuit Court Clerk or General Session. Only cashiers checks and money orders accepted. No credit cards accepted. Prepayment required.

Civil Name Search: Access: In person only. Only the court performs in person name searches; visitors may not. Search fee: $5.00 per name. Civil records archived from 1924; on computer from 1989.

Criminal Name Search: Access: In person only. Only the court performs in person name searches; visitors may not. Search fee: $5.00 per name. Required to search: name, years to search, DOB. Criminal records archived from 1925; on computer from 1989.

Chancery Court 99 Court Sq, #105, Huntingdon, TN 38344; 731-986-1920; fax: 731-986-6051; 8AM-4PM (CST). *Civil, Probate.*

General Information: No adoption or sealed documents released. Will fax documents $2.00 per page. Court makes copy: $1.00 per page. Self serve copy: same. Certification fee: $5.00 per cert. Payee: Clerk and Master. Checks, money orders and cashiers checks accepted. No credit cards accepted. Prepayment required. Mail requests: SASE or $.52 postage required.

Civil Name Search: Access: Mail, in person. Both court and visitors may perform in person name searches. Search fee: $10.00. Civil records on computer since 6/88, records go back to 1822. Mail turnaround time 5 days.

Carter County

1st District Circuit & General Sessions Court Carter County Justice Ctr, 900 E Elk Ave, Elizabethton, TN 37643; 423-542-1835; civil phone: 423-542-1825; fax: 423-542-3742; 8AM-4:30PM (EST). *Felony, Misdemeanor, Civil, Eviction, Small Claims.*
www.cartercountytn.gov/government/officials/circuitcourtclerk.html

General Information: No juvenile, psychiatric or expunged records released. Will not fax documents. Court makes copy: $1.00 per page. Self serve copy: $1.00 per page. Certification fee: $7.00 per cert. Payee: Circuit Court Clerk or General Session. Personal checks accepted. Visa/MC, Discover accepted. Prepayment required.

Civil Name Search: Access: Mail, in person. Visitors must perform in person searches themselves. Search fee: $15.00 per name. Civil records archived from 1800s (partial lost in fire), on computer from 2/92. Mail turnaround time 1 week. Civil PAT goes back to 1992.

Criminal Name Search: Access: Mail, in person. Visitors must perform in person searches themselves. Search fee: $15.00 per name. Criminal records archived from 1800s (partial lost in fire), on computer from 4-92. Criminal PAT goes back to 1996. Terminal results include SSN.

Chancery Court 801 E Elk Ave., Clerk & Masters Office, Elizabethton, TN 37643; 423-542-1812; fax: 423-547-1504; 8AM-4:30PM (EST). *Probate.* www.cartercountytn.gov/government/officials/clerkandmaster.html

Cheatham County

23rd District Circuit Court 100 Public Sq, Rm 225, Ashland City, TN 37015; 615-792-3272; fax: 615-792-3203; 8AM-4PM (CST). *Felony, Misdemeanor, Civil Actions over $15,000.*

General Information: Circuit Court is Rm 225, General Sessions is Rm 223 (615-792-4866); they must be searched separately. Circuit court handles felony, civil actions over $15,000 (concurrent $15,000 to $25,000 with General Session), some misdemeanors. No juvenile records released. Will not fax documents. Court makes copy: $.15 per page. Certification fee: $5.00. Payee: Circuit Court Clerk. No personal checks or credit cards accepted. Prepayment required. Mail requests: SASE required.

Civil Name Search: Access: Mail, in person. Both court and visitors may perform in person name searches. Search fee: $5.00 per name. Civil records archived on books from 1946 in office, since court started in storage and on computer from 1990. Mail turnaround time 2-3 days. Public use terminal available.

Criminal Name Search: Access: Mail, in person. Both court and visitors may perform in person name searches. Search fee: $5.00 per name. Required to search: name, years to search, and DOB or SSN or Driver's License No. Criminal records archived on books from 1946 in office, since court started in storage and on computer from 1990. Mail turnaround time 2-3 days. Public use terminal available.

Chancery Court Clerk & Master, #106, 100 Public Square, Ashland City, TN 37015; 615-792-4620; fax: 615-792-6059; 8AM-4PM (CST). *Civil, Probate.*

General Information: No adoption records released. Will not fax documents. Court makes copy: $.50 per page. Certification fee: $5.00. Payee: Chancery Court. No personal checks accepted. Prepayment required.

Civil Name Search: Access: In person only. Visitors must perform in person searches themselves. Civil records on computer 5 years, kept on books back to 1800s.

General Sessions 100 Public Sq, Rm 223, Ashland City, TN 37015; 615-792-4866; fax: 615-792-3203; 8AM-4PM (CST). *Misdemeanor, Civil under $25,000, Eviction, Small Claims.*

General Information: No juvenile records released. Will not fax documents. Court makes copy: $.15 per page. Self serve copy: same. Certification fee: $5.00. Payee: General Sessions Clerk. No personal checks accepted. No credit cards accepted debit cards accepted in-person only. Prepayment required. Mail requests: SASE required.

Civil Name Search: Access: Mail, in person. Both court and visitors may perform in person name searches. Search fee: $5.00 per name. Civil records archived on books from 1946 in office, since court started in storage and on computer from 1990. Mail turnaround time 2-3 days. Public use terminal available.

Criminal Name Search: Access: Mail, in person. Both court and visitors may perform in person name searches. Search fee: $5.00 per name. Required to search: name, (DOB, SSN or Drivers License #), and years to search. Criminal records archived on books from 1946 in office, since court started in storage and on computer from 1990. Mail turnaround time 2-3 days. Public use terminal available.

Chester County

26th District Circuit & General Sessions Court 333 Eric Bell Dr, #D, Henderson, TN 38340; 731-989-2454; fax: 731-989-9184; 8AM-4PM (CST). *Felony, Misdemeanor, Civil, Eviction, Small Claims.*

General Information: Search fee includes all court indexes, if you ask. No juvenile records released. Will not fax documents. Court makes copy: $1.00 per page. Certification fee: $5.00. Payee: Circuit Court, or General Sessions Clerk. No personal checks or credit cards accepted. Prepayment required.

Civil Name Search: Access: Mail, in person. Both court and visitors may perform in person name searches. Search fee: $20.00. Civil records in books and archived from 1892. Mail turnaround time 2 days. Civil PAT goes back to 1998.

Criminal Name Search: Access: Mail, in person. Both court and visitors may perform in person name searches. Search fee: $20.00 per name. Required to search: name, years to search, DOB. Criminal records in books and archived from 1892. Mail turnaround time 2 days. Criminal PAT available.

Chancery Court Clerk & Master, 333 Eric Bell Dr #C, Henderson, TN 38340; 731-989-7171; fax: 731-989-7176; 8AM-4PM (CST). *Civil, Probate, Juvenile.*

General Information: No adoption or sealed records released. Will fax out for fee of $5.00 per copy. Court makes copy: $1.00 p page. Self serve copy: $.50 per page. Certification fee: $5.00. Payee: Clerk and Master. Personal checks accepted, credit cards are not. Prepayment required.

Civil Name Search: Access: Mail, in person. Visitors must perform in person searches themselves. Search fee: $5.00 per name. Civil records on books. Note: Older files are stored off-site. Mail turnaround time 2 days. Public use terminal has civil records back to 10/2003.

Claiborne County

8th District Criminal, Circuit & General Sessions Court 415 Straight Creek Rd, #5, New Tazewell, TN 37825; criminal phone: 423-626-3334; civil phone: 423-626-3334; fax: 423-526-2703; 8:30AM-4:30PM M-TH, 8:30AM-4:30PM F (EST). *Felony, Misdemeanor, Civil, Eviction, Small Claims.*

General Information: For a complete civil record search, both courts in this county should be contacted. No adoption records released. Fee to fax document $.50 per page. Court makes copy: Included in search fee. Self serve copy: $.50 per page. Certification fee: $5.00. Payee: Circuit Court Clerk or General Sessions. Business checks or in state Personal checks, Visa/MC accepted. Prepayment required. Mail requests: SASE required.

Civil Name Search: Access: Mail, fax, in person. Both court and visitors may perform in person name searches. Search fee: $10.00 per name. Civil records archived since 1932; on computer back to 1986. Mail turnaround time 2-3 days. Civil PAT goes back to 1988.

Criminal Name Search: Access: Mail, fax, in person. Both court and visitors may perform in person name searches. Search fee: $10.00 per name. Criminal records archived since 1932; on computer back to 1986. Mail turnaround time 2-3 days. Criminal PAT goes back to same as civil.

Chancery Court 1740 Main St, Tazewell, TN 37879; 423-626-3284; fax: 423-626-3604; 8:30AM-N, 1-4PM (EST). *Civil, Probate.*

General Information: For a complete civil record search, both courts in this county should be contacted. No adoption records released. Will fax documents $.50 per page. Court makes copy: $.50 per page. Certification fee: $5.00 per document; exemplification- $15.00. Payee: Clerk and Master. Personal checks accepted, credit cards are not. Prepayment required.

Civil Name Search: Access: Mail, in person. Both court and visitors may perform in person name searches. No search fee. Civil records kept on books back to 1932; computerized since 1997. Mail turnaround time 1-2 days. Public use terminal has civil records back to 1976.

Clay County

13th District Circuit & General Sessions Court PO Box 749, Celina, TN 38551; 931-243-2557; fax: 931-243-2556; 7:30AM-5PM M,T,TH,F; 8AM-N W,Sat (CST). *Felony, Misdemeanor, Civil, Eviction, Small Claims.*

General Information: No juvenile records released. Will fax back $1.00 per page. Court makes copy: $.50 per page. Self serve copy: same. Certification fee: $5.00. Payee: Circuit Court, or General Sessions Clerk. No personal checks accepted. Major credit cards accepted. Prepayment required. Mail requests: SASE required for mail return of any copies.

Civil Name Search: Access: In person only. Both court and visitors may perform in person name searches. No search fee. Civil cases indexed by plaintiff, defendant. Civil records archived from early 1900s, on computer back to 2000. Note: The court will search the computer back to 2000 for visitors. Civil PAT goes back to 2000.

Criminal Name Search: Access: In person only. Both court and visitors may perform in person name searches. No search fee. Criminal records archived from early 1900s, on computer back to 2000. Note: The court will search the computer back to 2000 for visitors. Criminal PAT goes back to 2000.

Chancery Court PO Box 332, 100 Courthouse Sq, Celina, TN 38551; 931-243-3145; fax: 931-243-3157; 7:30 AM-4PM M,T,TH; 8AM-10AM W; 7AM-3:30PM F (CST). *Civil, Probate.*

General Information: No juvenile records released. Will not fax documents. Court makes copy: $.50 per page. Certification fee: $5.00 per doc plus copy fee. Payee: Chancery Court Clerk. Personal checks and business checks accepted. No credit cards accepted. Prepayment required.

Civil Name Search: Access: Mail, in person. Both court and visitors may perform in person name searches. No search fee. Civil records on books. Mail turnaround time 1 week.

Cocke County

4th District Circuit Court 111 Court Ave, Rm 201, Newport, TN 37821; 423-623-6124; fax: 423-625-3889; 8:30AM-5PM (EST). *Felony, Misdemeanor, Civil Actions over $15,000.*

General Information: Current criminal dockets at posted at www.cocke.mytncourts.com/15201dlydocket.pdf. No divorce or sealed records released. Will fax documents to local or toll free line. Court makes copy: $.50 per page. Certification fee: $5.00. Payee: Circuit Court. Personal checks accepted, credit cards are not. Prepayment required. Mail requests: SASE required.

Civil Name Search: Access: Mail, in person. Only the court performs in person name searches; visitors may not. Search fee: $3.00 per name. Civil records archived from late 1800s. Mail turnaround time ASAP.

Criminal Name Search: Access: Mail, in person. Only the court performs in person name searches; visitors may not. Search fee: $3.00 per name. Required to search: name, years to search, DOB. Criminal records archived from late 1800s. Mail turnaround time ASAP.

Chancery Court Courthouse Annex, 360 E Main St, #103, Newport, TN 37821; 423-623-3321; fax: 423-625-3642; 8AM-4:30PM (EST). *Civil, Probate.*

General Information: No sealed records released. Will fax documents to local or toll free line. Court makes copy: $.50 per page. Self serve copy: same. Certification fee: $5.00 plus copy fee. Payee: Chancery Court, Clerk and Master. Personal checks accepted, credit cards are not. Prepayment required. Mail requests: SASE required.

Civil Name Search: Access: Phone, mail, in person. Only the court performs in person name searches; visitors may not. No search fee. Civil records on computer since 1984, on books from 1930, archived to 1876. Mail turnaround time 1 week.

General Sessions Court 111 Court Ave, Newport, TN 37821; 423-623-8619; fax: 423-623-9808; 8AM-4PM (EST). *Misdemeanor, Civil Actions under $25,000, Eviction, Small Claims.*

General Information: Will fax documents, if prepaid. Court makes copy: $.25 per page. Certification fee: $6.00. Payee: General Sessions Court. Business checks accepted. No credit cards accepted. Prepayment required. Mail requests: SASE required.

Civil Name Search: Access: Mail, in person. Both court and visitors may perform in person name searches. Search fee: $3.00 per name. Civil records on books at least 10 years. Mail turnaround time varies. Civil PAT goes back to 2000.

Criminal Name Search: Access: Mail, in person. Both court and visitors may perform in person name searches. Search fee: $3.00 per name. DOB, SSN. Criminal docket on books at least 10 years. Mail turnaround time varies. Criminal PAT goes back to 2001. Court computer terminal search results may have incorrect identifiers and nicknames are common.

Coffee County

14th District Circuit & General Sessions Court PO Box 629, 300 Hillsboro Blvd, Manchester, TN 37349; 931-723-5110; fax: 931-723-5116; 8AM-4:30PM (CST). *Felony, Misdemeanor, Civil, Eviction, Small Claims.*

General Information: No juvenile record released. Will not fax documents. Court makes copy: $.50 per page. Certification fee: $3.50 per doc. Payee: General Sessions Clerk. Local personal checks accepted. Visa/MC cards accepted; 4% usage fee charged. Prepayment required. Mail requests: SASE required.

Civil Name Search: Access: Mail, in person. Both court and visitors may perform in person name searches. Search fee: $5.00 per name per year per court. Civil records archived from late 1800s, indexed chronologically by court date. Mail turnaround time 1 week. Civil PAT goes back to 1996.

Criminal Name Search: Access: Mail, in person. Both court and visitors may perform in person name searches. Search fee: $5.00 per name per year, per court. Required to search: name, years to search, DOB; also helpful: SSN. Criminal records archived from late 1800s, indexed chronologically by court date. Mail turnaround time 1 week. Criminal PAT goes back to 1995.

Chancery Court 300 Hillsboro Blvd, Manchester, TN 37355; 931-723-5132; fax: 931-723-5116; 8AM-4:30PM (CST). *Civil, Probate.*

General Information: No juvenile or adoption records released. Will not fax documents. Court makes copy: $.50 per page. Certification fee: $5.00 per doc. Payee: Chancery Court. Personal checks accepted, credit cards are not. Prepayment required. Mail requests: SASE helpful.

Civil Name Search: Access: Mail, in person. Both court and visitors may perform in person name searches. No search fee. Civil records on books after 1980, before 1980 filed in County Clerk's Office. Mail turnaround time 1-2 days. Public use terminal has civil records back to 1989.

Crockett County

Circuit & General Sessions Court 1 S Bell St, #6, Courthouse, Alamo, TN 38001; 731-696-5462; fax: 731-696-2605; 8AM-4PM (CST). *Felony, Misdemeanor, Civil, Eviction, Small Claims.*

General Information: No adoption or mental records released. Will fax documents if fees prepaid. Court makes copy: $1.00 per page. Self serve copy: same. Certification fee: $6.00 per cert. Payee: Circuit Court, or General Sessions Clerk. Business checks accepted. No credit cards accepted. Prepayment required. Mail requests: SASE requested.

Civil Name Search: Access: Mail, fax, in person. Both court and visitors may perform in person name searches. Search fee: $10.00 per name. Civil records archived since court started, records prior to 1986 on docket books. Note: All requests must be in writing. Will only accept fax requests if prepaid. Mail turnaround time 1-2 days. Civil PAT goes back to 1992. Terminal results do not always include address.

Criminal Name Search: Access: Mail, fax, in person. Both court and visitors may perform in person name searches. Search fee: $10.00 per name. Required to search: name, years to search, DOB; also helpful: SSN, sex. Criminal docket on books, on computer from 1993. Note: All requests must be in writing. Will only accept fax requests if prepaid. Mail turnaround time 1-2 days. Criminal PAT goes back to 1991. Address may be included in terminal search results.

Chancery Court 1 S Bells St, #5, Alamo, TN 38001; 731-696-5458; fax: 731-696-3028; 8AM-4PM (CST). *Civil, Probate.*

General Information: The public can look through rule dockets which are indexed on a terminal. No adoption records released. Will fax documents $10.00. Court makes copy: $.50 per page. Certification fee: $5.00 per cert, plus $.50 per page. Payee: Chancery Court Clerk. Personal checks accepted, credit cards are not. Prepayment required. Mail requests: SASE required.

Civil Name Search: Access: Mail, in person. Both court and visitors may perform in person name searches. No search fee. Civil records on books back to 1872. Mail turnaround time 1-3 days.

Cumberland County

13th District Circuit & General Sessions Court 60 Justice Center Dr, Ste 300, Crossville, TN 38555; 931-484-6647; fax: 931-456-5013; 8AM-4PM (CST). *Felony, Misdemeanor, Civil, Eviction, Small Claims.*

General Information: Above phone number is for General Sessions; Circuit can be reached at 931-484-5852. No sealed records released. Court makes copy: none. No certification fee. Payee: Cumberland County Court. No personal checks or credit cards accepted. Prepayment required.

Civil Name Search: Access: In person only. Visitors must perform in person searches themselves. Civil records archived on books from 1940s approx.; on computer back to 1996. Civil PAT goes back to 1996.

Criminal Name Search: Access: In person only. Visitors must perform in person searches themselves. Required to search: name, years to search, DOB; SSN helpful. Criminal records archived on books from 1940s approx.; on computer back to 1996. Criminal PAT goes back to same as civil.

Chancery Court 60 Justice Center Dr, #336, Crossville, TN 38555; 931-484-4731; fax: 931-456-4007; 8AM-4PM (CST). *Civil, Probate.*

General Information: No juvenile, adoption records released. Will not fax documents. Court makes copy: $.50 per page. Certification fee: $5.00 per doc, if large file then $7.00. Payee: Clerk and Master. Business checks accepted. No credit cards accepted. Prepayment required. Mail requests: SASE requested.

Civil Name Search: Access: Mail, in person. Only the court performs in person name searches; visitors may not. No search fee. Civil records on computer since 1991, on books since 1900s. Mail turnaround time 2 days.

Davidson County

20th District Criminal Court 408 2nd Ave N, #2120, Justice A Birch Bldg, Nashville, TN 37201; 615-862-5601; 8AM-4:30PM (CST). *Felony, Misdemeanor.*

http://ccc.nashville.gov/portal/page/portal/ccc/home/

General Information: No records unauthorized by statutes released. Will not fax documents. Court makes copy: $.50 per page. Certification fee: $5.00 per cert. Payee: Criminal Court Clerk. Personal checks accepted but not for record checks. Only Visa credit cards accepted. Prepayment required. Mail requests: SASE required.

Criminal Name Search: Access: Mail, online, in person. Both court and visitors may perform in person name searches. Search fee: $5.00 per name. Required to search: name, years to search (if over 10 years old), DOB, also helpful: SSN, race. Mail turnaround time 2-3 days. Public use terminal has crim records back to 1980. Access Davidson County Criminal Court Clerk database at http://ccc.nashville.gov/portal/page/portal/ccc/caseSearch/caseSearchPublic/caseSearchPublicForms. Online results show middle initial, DOB, address.

Circuit Court PO Box 196303, One Public Sq, Rm 302 Historic Courthouse, Nashville, TN 37201; 615-862-5181; fax: 615-862-5191; 8AM-4:30PM (CST). *Civil.* www.nashville.gov/circuit/

General Information: Online identifiers in results same as on public terminal. No juvenile or adoption records released. Will not fax documents. Court makes copy: $.50 per page. Certification fee: $5.00 per doc plus $.50 per page, includes copies. Payee: Circuit Court Clerk. No personal checks or credit cards accepted. Prepayment required. Mail requests: SASE required.

Civil Name Search: Access: Mail, fax, in person, phone, online. Both court and visitors may perform in person name searches. No search fee.Domestic records go back to 1947. Civil records archived on books from 1800s, on computer since 1975. Mail turnaround time 2-3 days. Public use terminal has civil records back to 1974. 3 terminals available. Addresses appear on search results rarely. Access filed cases online on CaseLink at www.nashville.gov/circuit/caselink/; $35.00 per month fee required plus username, password. Email Caselink@Nashville.Gov for signup or add'l info. The type of case information accessible through CaseLink is: style of the case (plaintiff vs. defendant), pleadings filed, court dates, judgments, addresses, representing attorneys, service of process, and history of payments.

General Sessions Court 408 2nd Ave N, #2110, PO Box 196304, Nashville, TN 37219-6304; 615-862-5195; fax: 615-862-5924; 8AM-4:30PM (CST). *Civil Actions under $25,000, Eviction, Small Claims.* http://circuitclerk.nashville.gov/sessions/

General Information: There is no "Small Claims" court, these type of cases are handled by the General Sessions Civil Division. Online identifiers in results same as on public terminal. No juvenile records released. Will fax documents for fee. Court makes copy: $.50 per page. Certification fee: $5.50 per page. Payee: General Sessions Court Clerk. No personal checks or credit cards accepted. Prepayment required.

Civil Name Search: Access: Mail, in person, online. Both court and visitors may perform in person name searches. No search fee. Records indexed on computer since 1990. Public use terminal has civil records back to 1990. Access filed cases online on CaseLink at http://caselink.nashville.gov/; $35.00 per month fee required, plus username and password. Email Caselink@Nashville.Gov for signup or add'l info. The type of case information accessible through CaseLink is: style of the case (plaintiff vs. defendant), pleadings filed, court dates, judgments, addresses, representing attorneys, service of process, and history of payments.

Probate Court 1 Public Sq, Rm 303, PO Box 196300 (37219), Nashville, TN 37201; 615-862-5980; fax: 615-862-5987; 8AM-4:30PM (CST). *Probate.* http://circuitclerk.nashville.gov/probate/

General Information: Regular address is; 105 Metro Courthouse; temporarily away. Records online on CaseLink. See http://circuitclerk.nashville.gov/caselink/.

De Kalb County

13th District Circuit & General Sessions Court 1 Public Sq, Rm 303, Smithville, TN 37166; 615-597-5711; fax: 615-597-9919; 8AM-4:30PM M-TH; 8AM-5PM F (CST). *Felony, Misdemeanor, Civil, Eviction, Small Claims.*

General Information: No juvenile records released. Will fax specific case file $1.00 per page. Court makes copy: $.50 per page. Self serve copy: same. Certification fee: $5.00 per cert. Payee: Circuit Court, or General Sessions Clerk. Personal checks, Visa/MC accepted. Prepayment required. Mail requests: SASE required.

Civil Name Search: Access: Mail, fax, In person. Both court and visitors may perform in person name searches. No search fee. Civil records archived in office last 10 years. Prior to 1982, records are not very accurate because of fire. Public use terminal available, records go back to 2000.

Criminal Name Search: Access: Mail, fax, in person. Visitors must perform in person searches themselves. No search fee. Required to search: name, years to search, DOB; SSN helpful. Criminal records archived in office last 10 years. Prior to 1982, records are not very accurate because of fire. Public use terminal available, crim records go back to 2000.

Chancery Court 1 Public Square, Rm 302, Smithville, TN 37166; 615-597-4360; fax: 615-597-3441; 8AM-4PM (CST). *Civil, Probate.*

General Information: No adoption, juvenile records released. Will fax documents $5.00 plus $1.00 per page. Court makes copy: $.50 per page. Self serve copy: same. Certification fee: $5.00 per cert. Payee: Clerk and Master. Personal checks accepted, credit cards are not. Prepayment required.

Civil Name Search: Access: In person only. Visitors must perform in person searches themselves. Civil records on books thru 06/00, computerized as of 6/00. Public use terminal has civil records back to 6/2000.

Decatur County

24th District Circuit & General Sessions Court PO Box 488, 22 Main St, Decaturville, TN 38329; 731-852-3125; fax: 731-852-4172; 8AM-4PM M,T,TH,F; 8AM-Noon W,Sat (CST). *Felony, Misdemeanor, Civil, Eviction, Small Claims.*

General Information: No adoption records released. Will not fax documents. Court makes copy: $.50 per page. Certification fee: $5.00 per doc. Payee: Circuit Court. Business checks accepted, no personal checks. Visa/MC accepted. Prepayment required.

Civil Name Search: Access: In person only. Visitors must perform in person searches themselves. Civil records archived on books from 1927; computerized since 1996. Civil PAT goes back to 8/1996.

Criminal Name Search: Access: In person only. Visitors must perform in person searches themselves. Required to search: name, years to search, DOB, SSN, signed release. Criminal records archived on books from 1927; computerized since 1996. Criminal PAT goes back to same as civil.

Chancery Court Clerk & Master, Decaturville, TN 38329; 731-852-3422; fax: 731-852-3422; 9M-4PM M,T,TH,F; 9AM-N Wed (CST). *Civil, Probate.* www.dcchancery.com/

General Information: No adoption records released. Will fax out documents. Court makes copy: $.50 per page. Certification fee: $5.00. Payee: Elizabeth Carpenter, Clerk and Master. Personal checks accepted, credit cards are not. Prepayment required.

Civil Name Search: Access: In person only. Visitors must perform in person searches themselves. Civil cases indexed by plaintiff. Probate records in books since 1869 for probate, civil records in books since 1958.

Dickson County

23rd District Circuit Court Court Square, PO Box 70, Charlotte, TN 37036; 615-789-7010; fax: 615-789-7018; 8AM-4PM (CST). *Felony, Misdemeanor, Civil Actions over $25,000.*

General Information: No adoption records released. Will fax documents $6.00 plus $.50 per page. Court makes copy: $.50 per page. Self serve copy: same. Certification fee: $5.00 plus copy fee. Payee: Circuit Court Clerk. No personal checks. Major credit cards accepted. Prepayment required. Mail requests: SASE required.

Civil Name Search: Access: Phone, fax, mail, in person. Both court and visitors may perform in person name searches. Search fee: $6.00 per name. Civil records archived from 1800s, on computer from 1986, some records back to 1974. Mail turnaround time 1 day.

Criminal Name Search: Access: Phone, fax, mail, in person. Both court and visitors may perform in person name searches. Search fee: $6.00 per name. Required to search: name, years to search; also helpful: DOB. Criminal records archived from 1800s, on computer from 1986, some records back to 1974. Mail turnaround time 1 day.

General Sessions PO Box 217, Charlotte, TN 37036; 615-789-5414; fax: 615-789-3456; 8AM-4PM (CST). *Civil Actions under $25,000, Eviction, Small Claims.* www.dicksoncounty.net/government/courts/general_sessions/index.html

General Information: No sealed or expunged records released. Will fax documents $4.00 in state or $6.00 out of state fee. Court makes copy: $.50 per page. Self serve copy: same. Certification fee: $5.00. Payee: General Sessions. No personal checks accepted. No credit cards accepted, but debit cards are. Prepayment required. Mail requests: SASE required.

Civil Name Search: Access: Phone, mail, in person. Both court and visitors may perform in person name searches. Search fee: $6.00 per case. Civil dockets archived (records sent to archives after 10 years as applicable) since court began, on computer from 8/1991. Mail turnaround time 2-3 days. Public use terminal has civil records back to 1991. Public terminal includes Dues.

County Court Court Square, 4000 Hwy 48 N, #1, Charlotte, TN 37036; 615-789-0250; fax: 615-789-0295; 8AM-4PM (CST). *Probate.*

Dyer County

29th District Circuit & General Sessions Court PO Box 1360, 1 Veteran Sq, Courthouse, Dyersburg, TN 38025; 731-286-7809; fax: 731-288-7728; 8:30AM-4:30PM (CST). *Felony, Misdemeanor, Civil, Eviction, Small Claims.*

General Information: Public may search books. Search fee includes both civil and criminal indexes, if asked for. No juvenile records released. Will fax documents but only if not busy. Court makes copy: None. No certification fee. Payee: Circuit Court, or General Sessions Clerk. No personal checks. No credit cards accepted. Prepayment required. Mail requests: SASE required.

Civil Name Search: Access: Mail, fax, in person. Both court and visitors may perform in person name searches. Search fee: $25.00 per name. Civil records archived since 1992, computerized. Mail turnaround time 2 weeks. Civil PAT goes back to 1992. Terminal results may include DOB, address.

Criminal Name Search: Access: Mail, fax, in person. Both court and visitors may perform in person name searches. Search fee: $25.00 per name. Required to search: name, years to search, DOB, SSN. Criminal records archived since 1992, computerized. Mail turnaround time 2 weeks. Criminal PAT goes back to same as civil. Terminal results may include DOB, address, and/or SSN.

Chancery Court PO Box 1360, Dyersburg, TN 38024; 731-286-7818; fax: 731-288-7706; 8:30AM-4:30PM (CST). *Civil, Probate.*

General Information: No adoption, juvenile records released. Will fax documents to local or toll-free number. Court makes copy: $.50 per page. Certification fee: $5.50. Payee: Chancery Court Clerk. Personal checks accepted, credit cards are not. Prepayment required. Mail requests: SASE requested.

Civil Name Search: Access: Mail, in person. Both court and visitors may perform in person name searches. No search fee. Mail turnaround time 1 week. Public use terminal has civil records back to 2001.

Fayette County

25th District Circuit & General Sessions Court PO Box 670, Somerville, TN 38068; 901-465-5205; fax: 901-465-5215; 8:30AM-4:30PM (CST). *Felony, Misdemeanor, Civil, Eviction, Small Claims.*

General Information: No adoption or sealed records released. Court makes copy: $.50 per page. Certification fee: $5.00 per cert. Payee: Circuit Court, or General Sessions Clerk. Personal checks accepted. Major credit cards accepted via phone; only debit cards in person or online. Prepayment required.

Civil Name Search: Access: In person only. Visitors must perform in person searches themselves. Civil records on computer since 1991, prior records archived since court began, some older records destroyed by fire. Civil PAT goes back to 1990.

Criminal Name Search: Access: In person only. Visitors must perform in person searches themselves. Required to search: name, years to search, DOB, SSN. Criminal records on computer since 1991, prior records archived since court began, some older records destroyed by fire. Criminal PAT goes back to same as civil.

Chancery Court PO Drawer 220, 16775 Highway 64 #210, Somerville, TN 38068; 901-465-5220; fax: 901-465-5217; 9AM-5PM (CST). *Civil, Probate.*

General Information: No adoption records released. Will fax specific case file copies. Court makes copy: $.50 per page. Certification fee: $5.00 per document plus copy fee per page. Payee: Clerk and Master. Personal checks accepted, credit cards are not. Prepayment required.

Civil Name Search: Access: In person only. Visitors must perform in person searches themselves. Civil records on computer since 10/92; on books. Public use terminal has civil records back to 1992.

Fentress County

8th District Circuit & General Sessions Court PO Box 699, Jamestown, TN 38556; 931-879-7919; fax: 931-879-3014; 8AM-4PM M-F (CST). *Felony, Misdemeanor, Civil, Eviction, Small Claims.*

General Information: Will not fax documents. Court makes copy: $.50 per page. Certification fee: $20.00 per doc. Payee: Circuit Court Clerk or General Session. Personal checks accepted, credit cards are not. Prepayment required. Mail requests: SASE required.

Civil Name Search: Access: Mail, in person. Both court and visitors may perform in person name searches. Search fee: $25.00 per name. Civil records archived from 1800s, readily available for 20 years. Mail turnaround time 5 days. Civil PAT available.

Criminal Name Search: Access: Mail, in person, fax. Both court and visitors may perform in person name searches. Search fee: $25.00 per name. Required to search: name, years to search, DOB, SSN. Criminal records archived from 1800s, readily available for 20 years. Mail turnaround time 5 days. Criminal PAT available.

Chancery Court PO Box 66, Jamestown, TN 38556; 931-879-8615; fax: 931-879-4236; 9AM-4PM M,T,TH,F; 9AM-N Wed (CST). *Civil, Probate.*

General Information: No sealed or adoption records released. Will fax documents $1.50 per page. Court makes copy: $.50 per page. Certification fee: $5.00. Payee: Clerk and Master. Personal checks accepted, credit cards are not. Prepayment required.

Civil Name Search: Access: Mail, in person. Both court and visitors may perform in person name searches. Search fee: $20.00. Civil records in books. Mail turnaround time 1-5 days.

Franklin County

12th District Circuit Court & General Sessions 360 Wilton Circle, Winchester, TN 37398; 931-967-2923; fax: 931-962-1479; 8AM-4:30PM (CST). *Felony, Misdemeanor, Civil, Eviction, Small Claims.*
http://franklincountycircuitcourtclerk.org/

General Information: The Circuit Court is at Room 57. The General Sessions room is at 164. No juvenile records released. Will fax documents. Court makes copy: $.25 per page. Certification fee: $5.00 per cert includes copy fee. Payee: Circuit Court Clerk or General Session. Business checks accepted. No credit cards accepted. Prepayment required.

Civil Name Search: Access: Mail, in person. Both court and visitors may perform in person name searches. Search fee: $10.00 per name. Civil records archived on docket books from 1940s, on computer since mid 1991. Note: Historical records are not online, but recent dockets are shown on the web. Mail turnaround time 1 week. Civil PAT goes back to mid-1991.

Criminal Name Search: Access: Mail, in person, online. Both court and visitors may perform in person name searches. Search fee: $10.00 per name. Required to search: name, years to search, DOB; also helpful: SSN. Criminal records archived on docket books from 1940s, on computer since mid 1991. Note: Historical records are not online, but recent dockets are shown on the web. Mail turnaround time 1 week. Criminal PAT goes back to same as civil.

County Court 360 Wilton Circle, #157, Winchester, TN 37398; 931-967-2089; fax: 931-967-9965. *Probate.*
http://franklincountycircuitcourtclerk.org/PROBATE.html

Gibson County

28th District Circuit & General Sessions Court 295 N College, PO Box 147, Trenton, TN 38382; 731-855-7615; fax: 731-855-7676; 8AM-4:30PM (CST). *Felony, Misdemeanor, Civil, Eviction, Small Claims.*

General Information: No adoption or expunged records released. $5.00 fee to fax back documents. Court makes copy: $.50 per page. Self serve copy: same. Certification fee: $5.00 per cert. Payee: Circuit Court Clerk. Business checks accepted. In-state checks accepted. Major credit cards accepted online. Prepayment required. Mail requests: SASE requested.

Civil Name Search: Access: Fax, mail, in person. Both court and visitors may perform in person name searches. Search fee: $5.00 per name. Required to search: name, years to search; also helpful: address. Civil records archived in vault mid 1800s, in office since 1982. On computer since 1990. Mail turnaround time 1-3 days. Civil PAT goes back to 1992.

Criminal Name Search: Access: Fax, mail, in person. Both court and visitors may perform in person name searches. Search fee: $5.00 per name. Required to search: name, years to search and either the DOB or the SSN. Criminal records archived in vault mid 1800s, in office since 1982. On computer since 1990. Mail turnaround time 1-3 days. Criminal PAT goes back to 1990.

Chancery Court Clerk & Master, PO Box 290, Trenton, TN 38382; 731-855-7639; fax: 731-855-7655; 8AM-4:30PM (CST). *Civil, Probate.*

General Information: No adoption, commitment records released. Will fax documents $5.00 fee plus $1.00 per page. Will invoice. Court makes copy: $.50 per page. Self serve copy: $.50 per page. Certification fee: $5.00 per cert. Payee: Clerk & Master. No personal checks or credit cards accepted. Prepayment required.

Civil Name Search: Access: In person only. Both court and visitors may perform in person name searches. Search fee: Office will want to know purpose of the search before naming a fee, if any. Probate records in this office since 9/82, prior records filed in County Clerk's office, computerized records go back to 1967. Public use terminal has civil records back to 1958. Results include plaintiffs and defendants.

Giles County

22nd District Circuit & General Sessions Court PO Box 678, #1 Public Sq, Pulaski, TN 38478; 931-363-5311; fax: 931-424-4790; 8AM-4PM (CST). *Felony, Misdemeanor, Civil, Eviction, Small Claims.*

General Information: No juvenile records released without signed release. Will fax documents $5.00 per doc. Court makes copy: $.50 per page from file; $1.00 per page from computer. Self serve copy: same. Certification fee: $5.50 per doc. Payee: Circuit Court Clerk. No personal checks accepted. Major credit cards accepted. Prepayment required. Mail requests: SASE required.

Civil Name Search: Access: mail, fax, in person. Both court and visitors may perform in person name searches. No search fee. Civil records on computer from 1/90, remaining records filed in docket books. Mail turnaround time 1 week. Civil PAT goes back to 1990.

Criminal Name Search: Access: Phone, mail, fax, in person. Both court and visitors may perform in person name searches. No search fee. Required to search: name, years to search, DOB; also helpful: SSN. Criminal records computerized from 1/90, remaining records filed in docket books. Mail turnaround time 1 week. Criminal PAT goes back to same as civil.

Chancery Court PO Box 678, 1 Public Sq, Pulaski, TN 38478; 931-363-2620; fax: 931-363-2106; 8AM-4PM (CST). *Probate.*

General Information: Also oversees divorce, delinquent taxes and some civil.

Grainger County

4th District Circuit & General Sessions Court PO Box 157, 270 Justice Ctr Dr, Rutledge, TN 37861; 865-828-3605 Circuit; 805-828-4436 Sessions; fax: 865-828-3339; 8:30AM-4:30PM M,T,TH,F (W & Sat 8:30AM-N) (EST). *Felony, Misdemeanor, Civil, Eviction, Small Claims.*

General Information: No sealed records released. Will fax documents to local or toll-free number. Court makes copy: $.50 per page. Self serve copy: same. Certification fee: $6.00. Payee: Circuit Court Clerk. Business checks accepted. No credit cards accepted. Prepayment required.

Civil Name Search: Access: In person only. Visitors must perform in person searches themselves. Civil records archived from 1977 in office. Note: Court will assist public, but will not do the search. Civil PAT goes back to 11/2001.

Criminal Name Search: Access: In person only. Visitors must perform in person searches themselves. Required to search: name, years to search, DOB, SSN. Criminal records archived from 1977 in office. Note: Court will assist public, but will not do the search. Criminal PAT goes back to same as civil. Results include driver license number.

Chancery Court Clerk & Master, PO Box 160, Rutledge, TN 37861; 865-828-4436; fax: 865-828-8714; 8:30AM-4:30PM M,T,TH,F, 8:30AM-N W (EST). *Civil, Probate.*

General Information: No adoption records released. Will fax documents to local or toll free line. Court makes copy: $.50 per page. Self serve copy: same. Certification fee: $4.00. Payee: Clerk & Master. Personal checks accepted, credit cards are not. Prepayment required. Mail requests: SASE requested.

Civil Name Search: Access: Phone, fax, mail, in person. Both court and visitors may perform in person name searches. No search fee. Civil records on books. Mail turnaround time varies.

Greene County

3rd District Circuit & General Sessions Court 101 S Main, County Courthouse, Greeneville, TN 37743; 423-798-1760;; 8AM-4:30PM (EST). *Felony, Misdemeanor, Civil, Eviction, Small Claims.*

General Information: No adoption records released. Will not fax documents. Court makes copy: $.50 per page. Certification fee: $5.00. Payee: Circuit Court Clerk. Personal checks accepted. Major credit cards accepted. Prepayment required.

Civil Name Search: Access: In person only. Visitors must perform in person searches themselves. Civil records archived since court started, on computer from end of 1990. Civil PAT goes back to 10/1990.

Criminal Name Search: Access: In person only. Visitors must perform in person searches themselves. Criminal records archived since court started, on computer from end of 1990. Criminal PAT goes to 10/1990.

County Court 101 S Main St #104, County Courthouse Annex, Greeneville, TN 37743; 423-798-1742; fax: 423-798-1743; 8AM-4:30PM (EST). *Probate.*

Grundy County

12th District Circuit & General Sessions Court PO Box 161, Altamont, TN 37301; 931-692-3368; fax: 931-692-2414; 8AM-4PM M-TH; 8AM-5PM F (CST). *Felony, Misdemeanor, Civil, Eviction, Small Claims.*

General Information: The court has no records from 12/1985 to May 3, 1990. No juvenile records released. Fee to fax out file $4.00 each. Court makes copy: $.50 per page. Certification fee: $5.00. Payee: Circuit Court Clerk. In-state Personal checks accepted, credit cards are not. Prepayment required. Mail requests: SASE required.

Civil Name Search: Access: Mail, fax, in person. Both court and visitors may perform in person name searches. Search fee: $5.00 per name. Fee is per court. Civil records on computer since 1993, prior records in books to 1990. No records from 12/85 to 5/3/1990, previous on microfiche since 1868. Note: Onsite searches may need to be picked up later, up to 3 days. Mail turnaround time 5 days.

Criminal Name Search: Access: Mail, fax, in person. Both court and visitors may perform in person name searches. Search fee: $5.00 per name. Fee is per court. Required to search: name, years to search, DOB; also helpful: SSN. Criminal records on computer since 1993, prior records in books to 1990. No records from 12/85 to 5/3/1990, previous on microfiche since 1868. Note: Onsite searches may need to be picked up later, up to 3 days. Mail turnaround time 5 days.

Chancery Court PO Box 174, Altamont, TN 37301; 931-692-3455; fax: 931-692-4125; 8AM-4PM M-TH; 8AM-5PM F (CST). *Civil, Probate.*

General Information: No adoption records released. Will fax documents to local or toll free line. Court makes copy: $.50 per page. Certification fee: $6.00. Payee: Clerk & Master. Personal checks accepted, credit cards are not. Prepayment required. Mail requests: SASE requested.

Civil Name Search: Access: Phone, mail, in person. Only the court performs in person name searches; visitors may not. Search fee: $5.00 per name. Civil records on computer since 1993, on books back to 1990. Mail turnaround time 5 days.

Hamblen County

3rd District Circuit & General Sessions Court 510 Allison St, Morristown, TN 37814; 423-586-5640; fax: 423-585-2764; 8AM-4PM (EST). *Felony, Misdemeanor, Civil, Eviction, Small Claims.*

General Information: No adoption records released. Will fax documents for $5.00 per doc plus $1.00 per page. Court makes copy: $.50 per page. Self serve copy: same. Certification fee: $5.00 per doc plus copy fee. Payee: Circuit Court Clerk or General Sessions. No personal checks or credit cards accepted. Prepayment required. Mail requests: SASE required.

Civil Name Search: Access: Mail, in person. Both court and visitors may perform in person name searches. Search fee: $5.00 per name. Civil records archived from early 1900s, on computer from 1989. Mail turnaround time 3 days. Civil PAT goes back to 1989.

Criminal Name Search: Access: Mail, in person. Both court and visitors may perform in person name searches. Search fee: $5.00 per name. Required to search: name, years to search, DOB; also helpful: SSN. Criminal records archived from early 1900s, on computer from 1989. Mail turnaround time 3 days. Criminal PAT goes back to same as civil.

Chancery Court 511 W 2nd North St, Morristown, TN 37814; 423-586-9112; fax: 423-318-2510; 8AM-4PM M-TH; 8AM-4:30PM F (EST). *Civil, Probate.*

General Information: No adoption records released. Will fax documents $1.00 per page. Court makes copy: $.50 per page. Self serve copy: same. Certification fee: $5.00 per doc plus copy fee. Payee: Clerk & Master. Personal checks, Visa/MC accepted. Prepayment required.

Civil Name Search: Access: Phone, fax, mail, in person. Both court and visitors may perform in person name searches. No search fee. Civil records on computer from 1979; prior on books back to 1870's. Mail turnaround time 3-5 days. Public use terminal has civil records back to 1979.

Hamilton County

11th District Civil Court Rm 500, Courthouse, 625 Georgia Ave, Chattanooga, TN 37402; 423-209-6700; fax: 423-209-6701; 8AM-4PM (EST). *Civil Actions over $15,000.* www.hamiltontn.gov/courts/

General Information: No adoption or judicial hospitalization records released. Will not fax out documents. Court makes copy: $.50 per page. Certification fee: $5.00, Acts of Congress Certification-$10.00. Payee: Circuit Court Clerk. Personal checks accepted, credit cards are not. Prepayment required. Mail requests: SASE required.

Civil Name Search: Access: Phone, fax, mail, in person, online. Both court and visitors may perform in person name searches. No search fee. Civil records archived from 1921, on computer back to 7/89. Court minutes are on microfiche thru 1997, from 1997 forward on digital images. Mail turnaround time 1 week. Public use terminal has civil records back to 1989. Online access to current court dockets are free at www.hamiltontn.gov/courts/Default.aspx

Chancery Court Chancery Court, Clerk & Master, 625 Georgia Ave, Rm 300, Chattanooga, TN 37402; 423-209-6600; fax: 423-209-6601; 8AM-4PM (EST). *Civil, Probate.* www.hamiltontn.gov/courts/Default.aspx

General Information: No mental health, adoption records released. Local fax fee $1.00 plus $.50 per page; long distance $2.00 plus $.50 per page not to exceed 10 pages. Court makes copy: $.50 per page. Certification fee: $5.00 plus $.50 per page. Payee: Hamilton County Clerk and Master. Personal checks accepted. Major credit cards accepted. Prepayment required. Mail requests: SASE required.

Civil Name Search: Access: Phone, mail, in person, online. Both court and visitors may perform in person name searches. No search fee. Civil index on cards from 1919, on dockets and microfilm; on computer 1995-present. Mail turnaround time 2-3 days. Public use terminal has civil records. Chancery motion dockets are online at www.hamiltontn.gov/courts/Chancery/dockets/default.aspx

11th District Criminal Court 600 Market St, Rm 102, Chattanooga, TN 37402; 423-209-7500; fax: 423-209-7501; 8AM-4PM (EST). *Felony, Misdemeanor.* www.hamiltontn.gov/courts

General Information: No juvenile records released. Will not fax documents. Court makes copy: $.50 per page. Certification fee: $5.00. Payee: Criminal Court Clerk. Only cashiers checks and money orders accepted. No credit cards accepted. Prepayment required. Mail requests: SASE helpful.

Criminal Name Search: Access: Mail, in person, online. Both court and visitors may perform in person name searches. Search fee: $10.00 per name. Required to search: name, years to search, DOB, signed release; also helpful: SSN. Criminal records on computer since 1990, prior records in books. Mail turnaround time 1 week. Public use terminal has crim records back to 1990. Search disposition records and court dates free at http://cjuscriminal.hamiltontn.gov/AppFolder/CC_Web_Calendar.aspx

and records go back to 1989. Also, online access to current court dockets is free at web page.

11th District General Sessions Court Civil Division, 600 Market St, Rm 111, Chattanooga, TN 37402; 423-209-7630; fax: 423-209-7631; 8AM-4PM (EST). *Civil Actions under $25,000, Eviction, Small Claims.* www.hamiltontn.gov/courts/sessions/

General Information: No mental health records released. Will not fax documents. Court makes copy: $.50 per page. Certification fee: $4.00. Payee: Sessions Court Clerk. Personal checks accepted, credit cards are not. Prepayment required.

Civil Name Search: Access: Phone, mail, in person, online. Both court and visitors may perform in person name searches. No search fee. Civil records archived on docket books, on computer from 6/1985. Mail turnaround time 3-4 days. Public use terminal has civil records back to 1985. Online access to current (7 days) court dockets is free on the web. Search dispositions and calendars free at http://cjusgeneralsessions.hamiltontn.gov/appfolder/GS_Web_Calendar.aspx

Hancock County

3rd District Circuit & General Sessions Court PO Box 347, Sneedville, TN 37869; 423-733-2954; fax: 423-733-2119; 8AM-4PM M,T,TH,F; 8AM-N W,Sat (EST). *Felony, Misdemeanor, Civil, Eviction, Small Claims, Juvenile.*

General Information: Office does not have resources for employment-related searches; suggests using a retriever. Note that some records were destroyed by fire and are not available. No juvenile records released. Will fax documents. Court makes copy: $.50 per page. Self serve copy: same. Certification fee: $5.00 per doc. Payee: Circuit Court Clerk. Personal checks accepted, credit cards are not. Prepayment required. Mail requests: SASE required.

Civil Name Search: Access: Mail, in person. Both court and visitors may perform in person name searches. Search fee: $4.00 per name. Civil cases indexed by plaintiff. Civil records archived on books from 1934. Mail turnaround time 5-10 days. Civil PAT goes back to July 2010. To search older records, you must view the books.

Criminal Name Search: Access: Mail, in person. Both court and visitors may perform in person name searches. Search fee: $4.00 per name. Criminal records archived on books from 1934. Mail turnaround time 5-10 days. Criminal PAT goes back to July 2010. To search older records, you must view the books.

Chancery Court PO Box 347, 1237 Main St, Sneedville, TN 37869; 423-733-4524; fax: 423-733-2762; 8:30AM-N, 1PM-4PM (EST). *Civil, Probate.*

General Information: No adoption records released. Will fax documents $1.00 per page. Court makes copy: $.50 per page. Self serve copy: same. Certification fee: $5.00. Payee: Clerk & Master. Personal checks accepted, credit cards are not. Prepayment required. Mail requests: SASE requested.

Civil Name Search: Access: Mail, in person. Only the court performs in person name searches; visitors may not. No search fee. Civil records on books and microfilm back to 1850's. Mail turnaround time 2 days.

Hardeman County

25th District Circuit & General Sessions Court 505 S Main, Ste A, Courthouse, Bolivar, TN 38008; 731-658-6524; fax: 731-658-4584; 8:30AM-4:30PM M-TH, 8AM-5PM Fri (CST). *Felony, Misdemeanor, Civil, Eviction, Small Claims.*

General Information: No juvenile records released. Will not fax out case files. Court makes copy: $.50 per page. Certification fee: $5.00 per cert. Payee: Circuit Court Clerk. Cashiers checks and money orders accepted. Hardeman county personal checks accepted, credit cards are not. Prepayment required.

Civil Name Search: Access: In person only. Visitors must perform in person searches themselves. Civil records on computer since 12/92, archived General Sessions from 1960 and Circuit from 1800s. Public use terminal available.

Criminal Name Search: Access: In person only. Visitors must perform in person searches themselves. Required to search: name, years to search, DOB, SSN, signed release. Criminal records on computer since 12/92, archived General Sessions from 1960 and Circuit from 1800s. Public use terminal available.

Chancery Court PO Box 45, Bolivar, TN 38008; 731-658-3142; fax: 731-658-4580; 8:30AM-4:30PM M-TH, 8:30AM-5PM F (CST). *Civil, Probate.*

General Information: No mental health, adoption records released. Fee to fax out file $1.00 per page. Court makes copy: $.50 per page, add'l fee for postage. Certification fee: $5.00 for the seal plus $.50 per page. Payee: Chancery Court Clerk. Business checks accepted. No credit cards accepted. Prepayment required. Mail requests: SASE requested.

Civil Name Search: Access: Phone, mail, fax, in person. Both court and visitors may perform in person name searches. No search fee. Civil records on books back to 1825; computerized back to 1975. Mail turnaround time 1 day. Public use terminal has civil records back to 1975.

Hardin County

24th District Circuit & General Sessions Court 465 Main St, Savannah, TN 38372; 731-925-3583; fax: 731-926-2955; 8AM-4:30PM M,T,TH,F; 8AM-N W (CST). *Felony, Misdemeanor, Civil, Eviction, Small Claims.*

General Information: No juvenile records released. Will not fax documents. Court makes copy: $.50 per page. Certification fee: $5.00 plus copy fee. Payee: Circuit Court Clerk. Hardin county Personal checks accepted, credit cards are not. Prepayment required.

Civil Name Search: Access: In person only. Visitors must perform in person searches themselves. Civil records archived on books and on microfiche from 1800s, on computer from 1996. Civil PAT goes back to 1996.

Criminal Name Search: Access: In person only. Visitors must perform in person searches themselves. Criminal records archived on books and on microfiche from 1800s, on computer from 1996. Criminal PAT goes back to same as civil.

Clerk and Master Office 465 Main St, Savannah, TN 38372; 731-925-8166; fax: 731-925-0255; 8AM-4:30PM M,T,TH,F; 8AM-N W (CST). *Probate.*

General Information: Clerk and Master became managers of probate records in 2004; formerly, records were with County Court clerk.

Hawkins County

3rd District Circuit & General Sessions Court 115 Justice Center Dr, Ste 1237, Rogersville, TN 37857; 423-272-3397; fax: 423-272-9646; 8AM-4PM (EST). *Felony, Misdemeanor, Civil, Eviction, Small Claims.*

General Information: Records prior to 1950 are kept off-site and are monitored by a genealogical group. No juvenile records released. Will not fax documents. Court makes copy: $.50 per page. Certification fee: $5.00 per cert. Payee: Circuit Court Clerk. No Personal checks, Visa/MC accepted.

Civil Name Search: Access: In person only. Visitors must perform in person searches themselves. Civil records archived on books from 1800s. Civil PAT goes back to 1995.

Criminal Name Search: Access: In person only. Visitors must perform in person searches themselves. Criminal records archived on books from 1800s. Criminal PAT goes back to same as civil.

Chancery Court Clerk and Master's Office, 150 E Washington St, Rogersville, TN 37857; 423-272-8150; fax: 423-272-7347; 8AM-4PM (EST). *Civil, Probate.*

General Information: No adoption records released. Will fax documents $5.00 plus $1.00 per page. Many documents are too large to fax. Court makes copy: $.50 per page. Certification fee: $5.00 per document. Payee: Hawkins County Clerk and Master. Personal checks accepted, credit cards are not. Prepayment required.

Civil Name Search: Access: In person, mail. Visitors must perform in person searches themselves. Search fee: No fee, except for genealogy. Civil index on docket books from 1927 to present. Mail turnaround time 5-10 days

Haywood County

28th District Circuit & General Sessions Court 100 S Dupree, Brownsville, TN 38012; 731-772-1112; fax: 731-772-8139; 8:30AM-5PM (CST). *Felony, Misdemeanor, Civil, Eviction, Small Claims.*

General Information: No juvenile records released. Court makes copy: $.50 per page. Self serve copy: same. Certification fee: $5.00. Payee: Circuit Court Clerk. In-county personal checks accepted. Money orders preferred. Major credit cards accepted. Prepayment required. Mail requests: SASE required.

Civil Name Search: Access: Phone, mail, in person. Visitors must perform in person searches themselves. No search fee. Civil records on computer since 8/1991. General Sessions archived since 1960's; Circuit Court archived since 1800s. Civil PAT goes back to 8/1991.

Criminal Name Search: Access: Phone, mail, in person. Visitors must perform in person searches themselves. No search fee. Required to search: name, years to search, DOB; also helpful: SSN. General Sessions criminal back to 08/1991; Circuit criminal back to 01/1992 on computer. Mail turnaround time depends on search complexity. Criminal PAT goes back to 8/1991.

Chancery Court 1 N Washington, Brownsville, TN 38012; 731-772-0122; fax: 731-772-3197; 8:30AM-5PM (CST). *Civil, Probate.* www.haywoodcountybrownsville.com/HaywoodCounty/ChanceryCourt.aspx

General Information: The office is not computerized. No adoption or sealed records released. Will fax documents $10.00. Court makes copy: $.50 per page. Self serve copy: same. Certification fee: $5.00 plus copy fee;

exemplification $15.00 plus copy fee. Payee: Chancery Court. Personal checks accepted, credit cards are not. Prepayment required.

Civil Name Search: Access: In person only. Visitors must perform in person searches themselves. Probate records on books since 9/82; other records go back to 1800s.

Henderson County

26th District Circuit & General Sessions Court 170 Justice Center Dr, Lexington, TN 38351; 731-968-2031; fax: 731-967-9441; 8AM-4:30PM (CST). *Felony, Misdemeanor, Civil, Eviction, Small Claims.*

General Information: No sealed indictment records released. Will fax documents $10.00 each. Court makes copy: $1.00 per page. Self serve copy: same. Certification fee: $5.00 per doc. Payee: General Sessions Court Clerk. No personal checks or credit cards accepted. Prepayment required.

Civil Name Search: Access: In person only. Visitors must perform in person searches themselves. Civil records on cards or books, archived from 1800s; on computer back 5 years. Civil PAT goes back to 1994.

Criminal Name Search: Access: In person only. Visitors must perform in person searches themselves. Required to search: name, years to search, DOB; also helpful- SSN. Criminal records on cards or books, archived from 1800s; on computer back 5 years. Criminal PAT goes back to same as civil.

Chancery Court 17 Monroe, Rm 2, 2nd Fl, Lexington, TN 38351; 731-968-2801; fax: 731-967-5380; 8AM-4:30PM (CST). *Civil, Probate.* www.hcchancery.com/

General Information: No confidential adoption records released. Fee to fax out file $.50 per page. Court makes copy: $.50 per page. Certification fee: $5.00. Payee: Chancery Court. No personal or business checks accepted. No credit cards accepted. Prepayment required. Mail requests: SASE required.

Civil Name Search: Access: Phone, mail, fax, in person. Only the court performs in person name searches; visitors may not. No search fee. Civil records on computer back to 1989; prior in books to 1895. Mail turnaround time depends on search length.

Henry County

24th District Circuit & General Sessions Court PO Box 429, Paris, TN 38242; 731-642-0461; probate phone: 731-642-2310; fax: 731-642-1244; 8AM-4:30PM (CST). *Felony, Misdemeanor, Civil, Eviction, Small Claims, Probate, Juvenile.*

General Information: The General Sessions Court records date 1995 to present. No juvenile records released. Will fax documents only if account is set up; requests must be prepaid. Court makes copy: $.50 per page. Self serve copy: same. Certification fee: $5.00 per cert plus copy fee. Payee: Circuit Court Clerk or General Sessions Court Clerk. Personal checks accepted, credit cards are not. Proof of payment such as account set-up to be paid monthly or fax copy of individual payment check accepted. Mail requests: SASE required.

Civil Name Search: Access: Fax, mail, in person. Both court and visitors may perform in person name searches. Search fee: $5.00. Civil records archived from 1820s (you search) or 1900s (they search); General Sessions on computer from 1991. Mail turnaround time 2-3 days. Will fax same day. Civil PAT goes back to 1991 for General Sessions; 2002 for Circuit. Terminal results may also include SSNs.

Criminal Name Search: Access: Fax, mail, in person. Both court and visitors may perform in person name searches. Search fee: $5.00. Required to search: name, years to search; also helpful: SSN, DOB. Criminal records archived from 1820s to 1939, (you search) or 1940 present (they search); General Sessions on computer from 1991. Mail turnaround time 2-3 days. Will fax same day. Criminal PAT goes back to same as civil. Terminal results may also include SSNs.

Hickman County

21st District Circuit & General Sessions Court 104 College Ave, #204, Centerville, TN 37033; 931-729-2211; probate phone: 931-729-2522; fax: 931-729-6141; 8AM-4PM (CST). *Felony, Misdemeanor, Civil, Eviction, Small Claims.*

General Information: Court will search criminal and civil all for one fee, if requested. No juvenile records released. Will fax documents if copy of check faxed in. Court makes copy: $.50 per page. Certification fee: $5.00 per doc. Payee: Circuit Court Clerk. No personal checks or credit cards accepted. Prepayment required.

Civil Name Search: Access: Mail, fax, in person. Both court and visitors may perform in person name searches. Search fee: $10.00 per name. Civil records on computer since 1993, prior records on books to 1849.

Criminal Name Search: Access: Mail, fax, in person. Both court and visitors may perform in person name searches. Search fee: $10.00 per name. Criminal records on computer since 1993, prior records on books to 1849.

Chancery Court 104 College Ave, #202, Centerville, TN 37033; 931-729-2522; fax: 931-729-3726; 8AM-4PM (CST). *Civil, Probate.*

General Information: No confidential or adoption records released. Will fax documents $2.00 per page. Court makes copy: $.50 per page. Certification fee: $5.00. Payee: Clerk & Master. Personal checks accepted, credit cards are not. Prepayment required. Mail requests: SASE requested.

Civil Name Search: Access: Mail, in person. Both court and visitors may perform in person name searches. No search fee. Civil records on books since 1865; computerized records since 2001. Mail turnaround time 1 week.

Houston County

23rd District Circuit & General Sessions Court PO Box 414, Erin, TN 37061; 931-289-4673; fax: 931-289-5182; 8AM-N, 1-4:30PM (CST). *Felony, Misdemeanor, Civil, Eviction, Small Claims.*

General Information: No juvenile records released. Will not fax documents. Court makes copy: $.50 per page. Certification fee: $5.00. Payee: Circuit Court Clerk. No personal checks or credit cards accepted. Prepayment required.

Civil Name Search: Access: Mail, in person. Visitors must perform in person searches themselves. Search fee: $10.00 per name. Civil records archived from 1930s in books.

Criminal Name Search: Access: Mail, in person. Visitors must perform in person searches themselves. Search fee: $10.00 per person. Required to search: name, years to search, DOB; SSN helpful. Criminal records archived from 1930s in books.

Chancery Court PO Box 332, 4725 E Main, Erin, TN 37061; 931-289-3870; fax: 931-289-5679; 8AM-4PM (CST). *Civil, Probate.*

General Information: No adoption records released. Court makes copy: $.50 per page. Self serve copy: same. Certification fee: $5.00. Payee: Clerk & Master. Personal checks accepted, credit cards are not. Prepayment required. Mail requests: SASE required.

Civil Name Search: Access: Mail, in person. Both court and visitors may perform in person name searches. No search fee. Civil records on books. Note: All requests must be in writing. Mail turnaround time 2 days. Public use terminal has civil records back to 09/01/2009.

Humphreys County

23rd District Circuit & General Sessions Court Courthouse, Rm 106, Waverly, TN 37185; 931-296-2461; fax: 931-296-1651; 8AM-4:30PM (CST). *Felony, Misdemeanor, Civil, Eviction, Small Claims.*

General Information: No expunged records released. Will fax documents to local or toll-free number. Court makes copy: $.50 per page. Certification fee: $5.00 seal; plus $1.00 per page. Payee: Circuit Court. Business checks accepted. No credit cards accepted. Prepayment required. Mail requests: SASE required.

Civil Name Search: Access: Fax, mail. Only the court performs in person name searches; visitors may not. Search fee: $1.00 per name per year minimum 7 years. If more than 15 years, flat $25.00 fee. Civil records on computer back to 1989. Mail turnaround time 10 days.

Criminal Name Search: Access: Fax, mail, in person. Only the court performs in person name searches; visitors may not. Search fee: $1.00 per name per year minimum 7 years. If more than 15 years, flat $25.00 fee. Required to search: name, years to search, DOB, SSN, signed release. Criminal records computerized from 1989. Mail turnaround time 10 days.

County Court Clerk, Rm 2 Rawlings Bldg., 102 Thompson St, Waverly, TN 37185; 931-296-7671, 931-296-6503; fax: 931-296-0823; 8AM-4:30PM (CST). *Probate.*

Jackson County

15th District Circuit & General Sessions Court PO Box 205, Gainesboro, TN 38562; 931-268-9314; fax: 931-268-4555; 8AM-4PM M,T,TH,F; 8AM-12 W (CST). *Felony, Misdemeanor, Civil, Eviction, Small Claims.* www.jacksonco.com/circuit-court-clerk.htm

General Information: No juvenile records released. Will not fax documents. Court makes copy: $.50 per page. Certification fee: $5.00 per doc. Payee: Circuit Court Clerk. Business checks accepted. No credit cards accepted. Prepayment required. Mail requests: SASE required.

Civil Name Search: Access: Fax, mail, in person. Both court and visitors may perform in person name searches. Search fee: $5.00 per name. Civil records archived from 1900s in books, computerized since 2000. Mail turnaround time 1 week. Civil PAT goes back to 2000.

Criminal Name Search: Access: Fax, mail, in person. Both court and visitors may perform in person name searches. Search fee: $5.00 per name. Required to search: name, years to search, DOB; also helpful: SSN. Criminal records archived from 1900s in books, computerized since 2000. Mail turnaround time 1 week. Criminal PAT goes back to same as civil.

Chancery Court PO Box 342, 101 E Hull Ave, Gainesboro, TN 38562-0342; 931-268-9516; fax: 931-268-9512; 8AM-4PM M,T,TH,F; 8AM-12PM Wed (CST). *Probate.* www.jacksonco.com/clerkandmaster/index.html

Jefferson County

4th District Circuit & General Sessions Court PO Box 671, 765 Justice Center Dr, Dandridge, TN 37725; 865-397-2786; fax: 865-397-4894; 8AM-4PM (EST). *Felony, Misdemeanor, Civil, Eviction, Small Claims.* www.jeffersoncountytn.gov/

General Information: Current dockets are posted at http://jefferson.mytncourts.com/. No adoption or juvenile records released. Will not fax documents. Court makes copy: $.50 per page. Certification fee: $5.00. Payee: Circuit Court Clerk. Only cashiers checks and money orders accepted. No credit cards accepted. Prepayment required.

Civil Name Search: Access: In person only. Visitors must perform in person searches themselves. Civil records archived from early 1900s on books. Civil PAT goes back to mid 1990's. Records are not online, but a PDF list of the daily docket schedule for at least 7 days appears at www.jefferson.mytncourts.com/.

Criminal Name Search: Access: In person, only. Visitors must perform in person searches themselves. Required to search: name, years to search, DOB, SSN, signed release. Criminal records archived from early 1900s on books. Criminal PAT available. Public record goes back to 2005. Records are not online, but a PDF list of the daily docket schedule for at least 7 days appears at www.jefferson.mytncourts.com/45201dlydocket.pdf. Online results show middle initial.

County Court PO Box 710, 214 W Main St, Dandridge, TN 37725; 865-397-2935; fax: 865-397-3839; 8AM-4:30PM M-F, 8AM-11PM Sat (EST). *Probate.* www.jeffersoncountytn.gov

General Information: Current dockets are posted at http://jefferson.mytncourts.com/.

Johnson County

1st District Circuit & General Sessions Court PO Box 73, 222 W Main St, Mountain City, TN 37683; 423-727-9012; fax: 423-727-3963; 8:30AM-5PM (EST). *Felony, Misdemeanor, Civil, Eviction, Small Claims.*

General Information: No adoption, expunged or juvenile records released. Will fax documents $10.00 per name. Court makes copy: none. Certification fee: None, but $2.00 if done by the Clerk and Master's Office. Payee: Circuit Court Clerk. Only cashiers checks and money orders accepted. No credit cards accepted. Prepayment required. Mail requests: SASE required.

Civil Name Search: Access: Phone, mail, in person. Both court and visitors may perform in person name searches. Search fee: $10.00 per name. Civil records in docket books, sessions 1976, criminal & circuit 1800s. Mail turnaround time 2-3 days. Civil PAT goes back to 2000. Terminal results also show SSNs.

Criminal Name Search: Access: Phone, mail, in person. Both court and visitors may perform in person name searches. Search fee: $10.00 per name. Required to search: name, years to search, DOB. Criminal records in docket books, sessions 1976, criminal & circuit 1800s. Mail turnaround time 2-3 days. Criminal PAT goes back to same as civil. Terminal results include SSN.

Chancery Court PO Box 196, Mountain City, TN 37683; 423-727-7853; fax: 423-727-7012; 8:30AM-N; 1-5PM (EST). *Civil, Probate.*

General Information: No adoption records released. Will not fax documents. Court makes copy: $2.00 to copy complete file, no fee for individual pages. No certification fee. Payee: Clerk & Master. Only cashiers checks and money orders accepted. No credit cards accepted. Prepayment required. Mail requests: SASE required.

Civil Name Search: Access: Mail, in person. Only the court performs in person name searches; visitors may not. No search fee. Civil records on books and files. Mail turnaround time same day.

Knox County

6th District Criminal Court 400 W Main St, Rm 149, Knoxville, TN 37902; 865-215-2492; criminal phone: 865-215-2375 Gen Sessions; fax: 865-215-4291; 8AM-4:30PM (EST). *Felony, Misdemeanor.* www.knoxcounty.org/criminalcourt/index.php

General Information: No sealed records released. Will not fax documents. Court makes copy: $2.00 per page. Certification fee: $2.00 per page. Payee: Criminal Court Clerk. Personal checks accepted. Major credit cards accepted. Prepayment required. Mail requests: SASE not required.

Criminal Name Search: Access: Fax, mail, in person. Both court and visitors may perform in person name searches. Search fee: $10.00 per name. Required to search: name, years to search, DOB; also helpful: address, SSN, signed release. Criminal records computerized from 1980; on books from 1962. Mail turnaround time 48 hours. Public use terminal has crim records back to mid-1980s.

Chancery Court 400 W Main St, Rm 125, Knoxville, TN 37902; 865-215-2555 (Chancery); probate phone: 865-215-2389; fax: 865-215-2920; 8AM-4:30PM (EST). *Civil, Probate.* www.knoxcounty.org

General Information: No commitment or adoption records released. Will fax documents $1.00 per page. Court makes copy: $1.00 per page. Certification fee: $2.00. Payee: Chancery or Probate Court. Personal checks accepted, credit cards are not. Prepayment required. Mail requests: SASE requested.

Civil Name Search: Access: Phone, fax, mail, in person. Visitors must perform in person searches themselves. No search fee. Civil records on computer since 1978, prior records on books. Mail turnaround time 1-2 days. Public use terminal has civil records back to 1999.

Circuit Court 400 Main Ave, Rm M-30, PO Box 379, Knoxville, TN 37901; 865-215-2400; fax: 865-215-4251; 8AM-4:30PM (EST). *Civil Actions over $25,000.* www.knoxcounty.org/circuit/index.php

General Information: No adoption or sealed records released. Court makes copy: $1.00 per page. Self serve copy: same. Certification fee: $3.00, exemplification fee- $10/50. Payee: Circuit Court Clerk. Personal checks accepted. Credit cards accepted. Prepayment required. Mail requests: SASE required.

Civil Name Search: Access: Phone, fax, mail, in person, online. Both court and visitors may perform in person name searches. Search fee: $5.00 per name. Civil records on computer from 1986, prior records archived and on microfilm. Mail turnaround time 2-3 days. Public use terminal has civil records back to mid-1980s. Current dockets are found at www.knoxcounty.org/circuit/docket.php. There is no access to historical documents.

General Sessions Court 300 Main Ave, Rm 318, PO Box 379, Knoxville, TN 37901; 865-215-2518; fax: 865-215-4296; 8AM-4:30PM (EST). *Civil Actions under $25,000, Eviction, Small Claims.* www.knoxcounty.org/circuit/

General Information: Historical dockets are not online, but info on current dockets can be viewed from the web page. No juvenile or adoption records released. Will not fax out documents. Court makes copy: $1.50 per page. Certification fee: $3.50; $10.50 for exemplification. Payee: General Sessions Court. Personal checks accepted with DOB, DL#, phone. Visa/MC accepted. Prepayment required. personal checks accepted only if an address is shown on the check.

Civil Name Search: Access: Mail, in person. Both court and visitors may perform in person name searches. Search fee: $5.00 per name. Civil records on books and computer. Mail turnaround time 1 week. Public use terminal has civil records back to 2000.

Lake County

29th District Circuit & General Sessions Court 229 Church St, PO Box 11, Tiptonville, TN 38079; 731-253-7137; fax: 731-253-8930; 8AM-4PM (CST). *Felony, Misdemeanor, Civil, Eviction, Small Claims.*

General Information: No sealed records released. Will not fax out documents to the public. Court makes copy: $.50 per page. Certification fee: $5.00. Payee: Circuit Court Clerk. Only cash and money order accepted. No credit cards accepted. Prepayment required.

Civil Name Search: Access: In person only. Visitors must perform in person searches themselves. Civil records archived on books in office up to 30 yrs, vault records before 1960; General Sessions computerized records go back to 1997. Note: Public must look-up records on docket books.

Criminal Name Search: Access: In person only. Visitors must perform in person searches themselves. Required to search: name, years to search, DOB; SSN helpful. Criminal records archived on books in office up to 30 yrs, vault records before 1960. Note: Public must look-up records on docket books.

Chancery Court 229 Church St, Box 12, Tiptonville, TN 38079; 731-253-8926; fax: 731-253-9815; 8:30AM-4PM (CST). *Probate.*

Lauderdale County

25th District Circuit Court PO Box 509, 675 Hwy 51 S, Lauderdale County Justice Ctr, Ripley, TN 38063; 731-635-0101; criminal phone: 731-635-2572; civil phone: 731-635-2572; fax: 731-221-8663; 8AM-4:30PM (CST). *Felony, Misdemeanor, Civil Actions over $25,000.*

General Information: No sealed or adoption records released. Will fax documents $1.00 per page. Court makes copy: $.50 per page. Self serve copy: same. Certification fee: $5.00 per case. Payee: Circuit Court Clerk. Personal checks accepted in county. No credit cards accepted. Prepayment required. Mail requests: SASE required.

Civil Name Search: Access: Phone, mail, in person. Both court and visitors may perform in person name searches. Search fee: $10.00 per name. Civil records archived on books from 1800s; on computer back to 1992. Mail turnaround time 2-3 days. Civil PAT goes back to 1992.

Criminal Name Search: Access: Mail, in person. Both court and visitors may perform in person name searches. Search fee: $10.00 per name. Required to search: name, years to search; also helpful: DOB, SSN. Criminal records archived on books from 1800s; on computer back to 1992. Mail turnaround time 2-3 days. Criminal PAT goes back to same as civil.

General Sessions Court PO Box 509, Ripley, TN 38063; 731-635-2572; fax: 731-221-8663; 8AM-4:30PM M,T,TH,F; 8AM-N W (CST). *Civil Actions under $25,000, Eviction, Small Claims.*

General Information: Located at 675 Highway 51 South. No confidential records released. Will fax documents $.50 per page. Court makes copy: $5.00 per case. Self serve copy: same. Certification fee: $10.00 per case. Payee: General Sessions. Business checks accepted. No credit cards accepted. Prepayment required. Mail requests: SASE required.

Civil Name Search: Access: Mail, in person. Both court and visitors may perform in person name searches. Search fee: $10.00 per name. Civil records on computer since 1992, records prior to 1984 on docket books. Mail turnaround time 2-3 days. Public use terminal has civil records back to 1992.

County Court Courthouse, 100 Court Sq, Ripley, TN 38063; 731-635-2561; fax: 731-635-4301; 8AM-4:30PM (CST). *Probate.*

General Information: email questions to lsummar@1ctngov.com

Lawrence County

22nd District Circuit & General Sessions Court 240 W Gaines, NBU #12,, Lawrenceburg, TN 38464; 931-762-4398; fax: 931-766-4471; 8AM-4:30PM (CST). *Felony, Misdemeanor, Civil, Eviction, Small Claims, Probate.* www.lawcotn.org/departments/circuit-county-clerk/

General Information: No expunged records released. Will fax specific case file $1.00 per page, maximum 20 pages. Court makes copy: $.50 per page. Certification fee: $5.00 per cert. Payee: Circuit Court Clerk. Only cashiers checks and money orders accepted. No credit cards accepted. Prepayment required.

Civil Name Search: Access: In person only. Visitors must perform in person searches themselves. Civil records archived on books since court started in 1940s. Civil PAT goes back to 1994.

Criminal Name Search: Access: In person only. Visitors must perform in person searches themselves. Required to search: name, years to search, DOB, SSN. Criminal records archived on books since court started in 1940s. Criminal PAT goes back to same as civil.

Lewis County

21st District Circuit & General Sessions Court Courthouse, 110 Park Ave N, Rm 201, Hohenwald, TN 38462; 931-796-3724; fax: 931-796-6021; 8AM-4:30PM (CST). *Felony, Misdemeanor, Civil, Eviction, Small Claims.*

General Information: No juvenile, adoption records released. Will not fax out case files. Court makes copy: $.50 per page. Self serve copy: same. Certification fee: $5.00 per doc plus copy fee. Payee: Circuit Court Clerk. Personal checks accepted, credit cards are not. Prepayment required.

Civil Name Search: Access: In person only. Visitors must perform in person searches themselves. Civil records archived 15 years in office, 1800s in vault. Civil PAT goes back to 1995.

Criminal Name Search: Access: In person only. Visitors must perform in person searches themselves. Required to search: name, years to search; SSN helpful. Criminal records archived 15 years in office, 1800s in vault. Criminal PAT goes back to 1995.

Chancery Court Lewis County Courthouse, 110 Park Ave N, Rm 208, Hohenwald, TN 38462; 931-796-3734/931-796-6016; fax: 931-796-6017; 8AM-4:30PM (CST). *Civil, Probate.*

General Information: No adoption records released. Will fax documents $5.00 fee + $1.00 per page up to $10.00. Court makes copy: $.50 per page. Certification fee: $5.00 plus copy fee for add'l pages. Payee: Clerk & Master. Personal checks accepted, credit cards are not. Prepayment required.

Civil Name Search: Access: In person only. Visitors must perform in person searches themselves. Civil records on computer since 10/94, prior records indexed on computer by name or case number. Public use terminal has civil records back to 1995.

Lincoln County

17th District Circuit & General Sessions Court 112 Main Ave S, Rm 203, Fayetteville, TN 37334; 931-433-2334 Circuit; 931-433-1482 Sessions; fax: 931-438-1577; 8AM-4PM (CST). *Felony, Misdemeanor, Civil, Eviction, Small Claims.*

General Information: No probation records released. Will fax documents $2.00 per page. Court makes copy: $.50 per page. Certification fee: $5.00 per cert. Payee: Circuit Court Clerk. No business checks accepted. Visa/MC and debit cards accepted. Prepayment required. Mail requests: SASE required.

Civil Name Search: Access: Phone, fax, mail, in person. Both court and visitors may perform in person name searches. Search fee: $5.00 per name. Fee is for 5 years. Add $1.00 for each add'l year. Civil records archived on books since court started; files go back 10 years; on computer back to 1995. Mail turnaround time 1-2 days. Civil PAT goes back to 1995.

Criminal Name Search: Access: Phone, fax, mail, in person. Both court and visitors may perform in person name searches. Search fee: $5.00 per name. Fee is for 5 years. Add $1.00 for each add'l year. Required to search:

name, years to search, DOB, SSN, signed release. Criminal records archived on books since court started; files go back 10 years; on computer back to 1995. Mail turnaround time 1-2 days. Criminal PAT goes back to 1995.

Chancery Court 112 Main Ave, Rm B109, Fayetteville, TN 37334; 931-433-1482; fax: 931-433-9313; 8AM-12: 12:30PM-4PM (CST). *Civil, Probate.*

General Information: No adoption, divorce records released. Will fax documents for $.50 per page. Court makes copy: $.50 per page. Certification fee: $5.00 per cert. Payee: Clerk & Master. Personal checks accepted, credit cards are not. Prepayment required.

Civil Name Search: Access: In person only. Visitors must perform in person searches themselves. Civil records archived on books.

Loudon County

9th District Criminal & Circuit Court PO Box 280, Loudon, TN 37774; 865-458-2042; fax: 865-458-2043; 8AM-4:30PM (EST). *Felony, Civil.* www.loudoncounty.com/ccc.htm

General Information: No juvenile, adoption records released. Will fax documents for no fee. Court makes copy: $.50 per page. Certification fee: $5.00 per document. Payee: Circuit Court. Personal checks accepted. Major credit cards accepted. Prepayment required. Mail requests: SASE requested.

Civil Name Search: Access: Phone, fax, mail, in person. Both court and visitors may perform in person name searches. Search fee: $5.00 per name. Civil records archived from 1870 on books, on computer from 8/1994. Mail turnaround time 2-4 days.

Criminal Name Search: Access: Phone, fax, mail, in person. Both court and visitors may perform in person name searches. Search fee: $5.00 per name. Criminal records archived from 1800s on books, on computer from 8/1994. Mail turnaround time 2-4 days.

General Sessions Court 12680 Hwy 11 W, #3, Lenoir City, TN 37771; 865-986-3505; fax: 865-986-7355; 8AM-5PM (EST). *Misdemeanor, Eviction, Small Claims, Probate.* www.loudoncounty.com/ccc.htm

General Information: No juvenile, adoption records released. Will fax documents, except for Last Will & Testaments, for $5.00 fee. Court makes copy: $.50 per page. Certification fee: $5.00. Payee: General Sessions Court. Cashiers check, money orders or cash accepted. Major credit cards accepted. Prepayment required. Mail requests: SASE requested.

Civil Name Search: Access: Phone, fax, mail, in person. Both court and visitors may perform in person name searches. Search fee: $5.00 per name. Civil records archived from 1960 on books, on computer from 11/94. Note: Probate records archived form 11/01/1870, computerized 1986 forward. Court performed probate record search is $10.00. Mail turnaround time 2-4 days. Civil PAT goes back to 11/94.

Criminal Name Search: Access: Phone, fax, mail, in person. Both court and visitors may perform in person name searches. Search fee: $5.00 per name. Criminal records archived from 1960 on books, on computer from 11/94. Mail turnaround time 2-4 days. Criminal PAT goes back to 11/94.

Macon County

15th District Circuit & General Sessions Court Court Clerk, 904 Hwy 52 Bypass, E, Lafayette, TN 37083; 615-666-2354; probate phone: 615-666-2000; fax: 615-666-3001; 8AM-4PM M-TH; 8AM-4PM F (CST). *Felony, Misdemeanor, Civil, Eviction, Small Claims, Probate.* Www.maconcircuitcourt.com

General Information: Probate located at 906 Hwy 52 Bypass E with Chancery Court; hours are 8AM-4PM. Probate fax- 615-666-8943. Court is closed for lunch noon-1PM on Wed. No juvenile or adoption records released. Will not fax out case files. Court makes copy: $.50 per page. Self serve copy: same. Certification fee: $5.00 per certification. Payee: Circuit Court Clerk. Personal checks accepted only if from this county. Visa/MC accepted. Prepayment required.

Civil Name Search: Access: In person only. Visitors must perform in person searches themselves. Civil records archived in office from 1975, rest in records room from 1960; on computer since 1997. Civil PAT goes back to 1997.

Criminal Name Search: Access: In person only. Visitors must perform in person searches themselves. Required to search: name, years to search, DOB; SSN helpful. Criminal records archived in office from 1975, rest in records room from 1960, on computer since1997. Criminal PAT goes back to same as civil.

Madison County

26th Judicial District Circuit Court Circuit Court, 515 S Liberty St, #200, Jackson, TN 38301; 731-423-6035; fax: 731-988-3007; 8AM-4PM (CST). *Felony, Misdemeanor, Civil Actions over $25,000.* www.co.madison.tn.us

General Information: Misdemeanor cases here are usually accompanied by felonies. Court has a list of document retrievers who may search for you.

No sealed records released. Will not fax out case files. Court makes copy: n/a. Self serve copy: $.50 per page. Certification fee: $5.00 per document. Payee: Circuit Court Clerk. Cashiers checks and money orders accepted. Major credit cards accepted online only. Prepayment required.

Civil Name Search: Access: In person only. Visitors must perform in person searches themselves. Civil records archived on books in office from 1963; on computer back to 1995, older records in archives. Civil PAT goes back to 1995.

Criminal Name Search: Access: In person only. Visitors must perform in person searches themselves. Required to search: name, years to search; also helpful: DOB, SSN. Criminal records computerized since 1995, on books from 1965, older records in archives. Criminal PAT goes back to same as civil. Terminal results also include gender, race, and sometimes DL or middle initial.

General Sessions Court 515 S Liberty St, Jackson, TN 38301; criminal phone: 731-423-6128; civil phone: 731-423-6016; fax: 731-265-5398; 8AM-4PM (CST). *Misdemeanor, Civil Actions under $25,000, Eviction, Small Claims.*
www.co.madison.tn.us/index.aspx?nid=151
General Information: Will fax out docs for $5.00 fee. Court makes copy: $.50 per page. Certification fee: $5.00 per cert. Payee: General Sessions Court. Only cashiers checks and money orders accepted. Credit cards accepted at www.paymentchek.com/tn/madisonco. Prepayment required. Mail requests: SASE required.
Civil Name Search: Access: Mail, in person. Visitors must perform in person searches themselves. No search fee. Civil records computerized since 1/98, archived on books in office from 1982, rest stored elsewhere from 1950s. Note: No telephone searches!! Civil PAT goes back to 1994.
Criminal Name Search: Access: Mail, in person. Visitors must perform in person searches themselves. No search fee. Required to search: name; case number helpful. Records stored since 1950s, computerized since 1/98. Criminal PAT goes back to 1998.

Probate Division - General Sessions Division II 110 Irby St, #102, Jackson, TN 38301; 731-988-3025; fax: 731-988-3807; 8:30AM-N, 1-4:30PM (CST). *Probate.*

Marion County

12th District Circuit & General Sessions Court PO Box 789, Courthouse Sq, Jasper, TN 37347; 423-942-2134; fax: 423-942-4160; 8AM-4PM (CST). *Felony, Misdemeanor, Civil, Eviction, Small Claims.*
General Information: No adoption records released. Will fax documents to local or toll free line. Court makes copy: $.50 per page. Self serve copy: $.50 per page. Certification fee: $3.00. Payee: Circuit Court Clerk. Personal checks accepted, credit cards are not. Prepayment required.
Civil Name Search: Access: Phone, mail, in person. Both court and visitors may perform in person name searches. Search fee: $3.00 per name. Civil records on computer from 1988, prior records archived on books and microfiche since 1922. Mail turnaround time 1 week.
Criminal Name Search: Access: Phone, mail, in person. Both court and visitors may perform in person name searches. Search fee: $3.00 per name. Required to search: name, years to search, DOB; also helpful: SSN. Criminal records computerized from 1988, prior records archived on books and microfiche since 1922. Mail turnaround time 1 week.

Chancery Court PO Box 789, One Courthouse Square, Jasper, TN 37347; 423-942-2601; fax: 423-942-0291; 8AM-4PM (CST). *Civil, Probate.*
General Information: No adoption records released. Will not fax documents. Court makes copy: $.50 per page. Certification fee: $5.00. Payee: Clerk and Master. Personal checks accepted, credit cards are not. Prepayment required. Mail requests: SASE requested.
Civil Name Search: Access: Mail, in person. Both court and visitors may perform in person name searches. No search fee. Civil records on computer since 3/94, prior records on books. Mail turnaround time 1-3 days. Public use terminal has civil records back to 3/1994.

Marshall County

17th District Circuit & General Sessions Court 302 Marshall County Courthouse, Lewisburg, TN 37091; 931-359-0536; fax: 931-359-2993; 8AM-4PM (CST). *Felony, Misdemeanor, Civil, Eviction, Small Claims.*
General Information: No adoption records released. Will fax specific doc to local or toll-free number. Court makes copy: $.50 per page. Self serve copy: same. Certification fee: $5.00 per document plus copy fee. Payee: Circuit & General Sessions Court Clerk. No personal checks or credit cards accepted. Prepayment required. Mail requests: SASE required.
Civil Name Search: Access: Mail, in person. Both court and visitors may perform in person name searches. Search fee: $10.00 per name. Civil cases indexed by plaintiff. Civil records archived on books; also on computer back to 2000. Civil PAT goes back to 2000.

Criminal Name Search: Access: Mail, in person. Both court and visitors may perform in person name searches. Search fee: $10.00 per name. Required to search: name, years to search; also helpful: DOB, SSN. Criminal records go back to 1987; on computer back to 2000. Criminal PAT goes back to same as civil.

Chancery Court 201 Marshall County Courthouse, Lewisburg, TN 37091; 931-359-2181; fax: 931-359-0524; 8AM-4PM (CST). *Probate, Domestic.*
General Information: Probate is handled by the Clerk & Master.

Maury County

Circuit & General Sessions Pt I Court Maury County Courthouse, 41 Public Square, Columbia, TN 38401; 931-381-3690; criminal phone: 931-375-1103; civil phone: 931-375-1110; criminal fax: 931-375-1114; civil fax: 8AM-4PM; 8AM-4PM (CST). *Felony, Misdemeanor, Civil, Eviction, Small Claims.* www.maurycounty-tn.gov/Circuit/circuit.htm
General Information: The General Sessions Court handles civil actions under $25,000 and criminal/traffic citations. The case index at both General Sessions Courts can be accessed from either court location. No juvenile records released. Will fax documents $1.00 per page. Court makes copy: $.50 per page. Self serve copy: same. Certification fee: $5.00 per cert. Payee: Circuit Court Clerk. Only cashiers check or money order accepted. Credit and Debit cards accepted in person or on web only. Prepayment required.
Civil Name Search: Access: Fax, mail, in person. Visitors must perform in person searches themselves. No search fee. Civil records on books since 1984; on computer back to 1989. Civil PAT goes back to 1989.
Criminal Name Search: Access: In person only. Visitors must perform in person searches themselves. Required to search: name, years to search; also helpful: DOB, SSN. Criminal records computerized from 1989; others go back to early 1900s. Criminal PAT goes back to same as civil.

General Sessions Part II Court Courthouse, 115 N Main St, Mt Pleasant, TN 38479; 931-379-3340; fax: 931-379-4864; 8AM-4PM (CST). *Misdemeanor, Civil under $25,000, Eviction, Small Claims.* www.maurycounty-tn.gov/Circuit/circuit.htm
General Information: The case index at both General Sessions Courts can be accessed from either court location. No juvenile records released. Will fax documents $1.00 per page. Court makes copy: $.50 per page. Self serve copy: same. Certification fee: $5.00 per cert. Payee: Circuit Court Clerk. Only cashiers check or money order accepted. Credit and Debit cards accepted in person or on web only. Prepayment required.
Civil Name Search: Access: Fax, mail, in person. Visitors must perform in person searches themselves. No search fee. Closed case files are kept for 10 years.
Criminal Name Search: Access: In person only. Visitors must perform in person searches themselves. Required to search: name, years to search; also helpful: DOB, SSN. Closed case files are kept for 10 years.

Probate And Chancery Court Maury County Courthouse, Clerk & Masters Office, 41 Public Square, Columbia, TN 38401; 931-375-1300; fax: 931-375-1319; 8AM-4PM (CST). *Probate.*
General Information: Records on computer go back to 1991.

McMinn County

10th District Circuit & General Sessions Court 6 E Madison Ave, #301, Athens, TN 37303-3666; 423-745-1923; criminal phone: 423-745-1924; civil phone: 423-745-1924; probate phone: 423-745-1281; fax: 423-744-1642; 8:30AM-4PM (EST). *Felony, Misdemeanor, Civil, Eviction, Small Claims, Probate.*
General Information: Probate records handled by Chancery Court after 07/04; prior in Circuit Court. No juvenile, adoption records released. Will fax documents. Court makes copy: $.50 per page. Self serve copy: same. Certification fee: $5.00 per cert plus $2.00 per page. Payee: Circuit Court Clerk. Business checks accepted. No credit cards accepted. Prepayment required.
Civil Name Search: Access: Phone, fax, mail, in person. Both court and visitors may perform in person name searches. No search fee. Required to search: name, years to search; also helpful: address. Civil records archived approximately 20 years; computerized back to 1996. Visitor must search using books. Note: Phone searches limited to three names. Mail turnaround time 24-48 hours. Public use terminal has civil records.
Criminal Name Search: Access: Phone, fax, mail, in person. Only the court performs in person name searches; visitors may not. No search fee. Required to search: name, years to search, DOB, SSN; also helpful: address. Criminal records archived approximately 20 years; computerized back to 1996. Mail turnaround time 24-48 hours.

McNairy County

25th District Circuit & General Sessions Court 300 Industrial Park Dr, Selmer, TN 38375; 731-645-1016/1015; fax: 731-645-1003;

8AM-4:30PM M,T,TH,F; 8AM-N W (CST). *Felony, Misdemeanor, Civil, Eviction, Small Claims.*

General Information: No juvenile records released. Will fax documents to local or toll-free number. Court makes copy: $.25 per page. Self serve copy: $.50 per page. Certification fee: $6.00 per cert. Payee: Circuit Court Clerk. Company checks accepted, personal checks are not. Major credit cards accepted. Prepayment required.

Civil Name Search: Access: Mail, in person. Both court and visitors may perform in person name searches. Search fee: $20.00 per name. Civil records archived on docket books since 1966; computerized records since 2/95. Mail turnaround time 1-2 days. Civil PAT goes back to 1995.

Criminal Name Search: Access: Mail, in person. Both court and visitors may perform in person name searches. Search fee: $20.00 per name. Required to search: name, years to search, DOB, SSN. Criminal records archived on docket books since 1966; computerized records since 2/95. Mail turnaround time 1-2 days. Criminal PAT goes back to same as civil.

Chancery Court Chancery Court, Clerk & Master, Courthouse, Rm 205, Selmer, TN 38375; 731-645-5446; fax: 731-646-1165; 8AM-4PM; closed W (CST). *Civil, Probate.*

General Information: Will fax documents, $5.00 surcharge. Court makes copy: $.50 per page. Self serve copy: $.50 per page. Certification fee: $5.00. Payee: Clerk & Master. No personal checks or credit cards accepted. Prepayment required.

Civil Name Search: Access: In person only. Visitors must perform in person searches themselves. Civil records on books. Public use terminal has civil records back to 1998.

Meigs County

9th District Circuit & General Sessions Court PO Box 205, Decatur, TN 37322; 423-334-5821 Circuit; 423-334-5821 Sessions; fax: 423-334-7201; 8:30AM-5P; till Noon W (EST). *Felony, Misdemeanor, Civil, Eviction, Small Claims.*

www.meigscountytn.com/

General Information: Daily/weekly dockets are available in PDF from the web page. Historical dockets are not available. No juvenile records released. Will not fax documents. Court makes copy: $.50 per page. Certification fee: $5.00 per cert. Payee: Circuit Court Clerk. Personal checks accepted, credit cards are not. Prepayment required.

Civil Name Search: Access: Mail, in person. Both court and visitors may perform in person name searches. Search fee: None; Fee does apply to search of archived records. Civil records archived in office from 1930s, records in storage go further. Mail turnaround time 1 week. Civil PAT goes back to 2004.

Criminal Name Search: Access: In person only. Both court and visitors may perform in person name searches. Search fee: None; but fee does apply to search of archived records. Criminal records archived in office from 1930s, records in storage go further. Criminal PAT goes back to 2004.

Chancery Court PO Box 5, 17214 State Hwy 58 N, Decatur, TN 37322; 423-334-5243; 8:30AM-4:30PM M,T,TH,F; 8:30AM-12 W (EST). *Civil, Probate.*

General Information: No adoption records released. Will fax documents $.25 per page for 3 pages or less. Court makes copy: $.50 per page. Certification fee: $5.00 per cert plus copy fee. Cert fee includes copies. Payee: Meigs County Chancery Court. Personal checks accepted, credit cards are not. Prepayment required.

Civil Name Search: Access: In person only. Visitors must perform in person searches themselves. Civil records on dockets before 1940.

Monroe County

10th District Circuit Courts 105 College St South, #3, Madisonville, TN 37354; 423-442-2396; fax: 423-442-9538; 8AM-4:30PM (EST). *Felony, Misdemeanor, Civil.*

www.monroegovernment.org

General Information: This court does name record searches for the General Sessions Court. No juvenile records released. Will fax documents $2.00 per page. Court makes copy: $.50 per page. Certification fee: $5.00. Payee: Circuit Court Clerk. Personal checks accepted, credit cards are not. Prepayment required. Mail requests: SASE not required.

Civil Name Search: Access: Mail, in person. Both court and visitors may perform in person name searches. Search fee: $10.00 per name. Civil records on computer since 1991, records on books in office for 10 years, unspecified prior to then. Mail turnaround time 2 days. Civil PAT goes back to 1991. Public terminal also holds records for General Sessions Court.

Criminal Name Search: Access: Mail, in person. Both court and visitors may perform in person name searches. Search fee: $10.00 per name. Criminal records on computer since 1991, records on books in office for 10 years, unspecified prior to then. Mail turnaround time 2 days. Criminal

PAT goes back to 1992. Public terminal also holds misdemeanor records for General Sessions Court.

Chancery Court 105 College St South, #2, Madisonville, TN 37354; 423-442-2644; civil phone: 423-442-5940; probate phone: 423-442-4573; fax: 423-420-0048; 8:30AM-4:30PM till 4PM W (EST). *Civil, Probate.*

www.monroegovernment.org/

General Information: No adoption, sealed records released. Will fax documents to local or toll free line. Court makes copy: $.50 per page. Certification fee: $5.00. Payee: Chancery Court. Personal checks accepted, credit cards are not. Prepayment required. Mail requests: SASE requested.

Civil Name Search: Access: Mail, in person. Only the court performs in person name searches; visitors may not. No search fee. Civil cases indexed by plaintiff and defendant. Civil records on computer since 05/92, prior records on books. Mail turnaround time 2-3 days.

General Sessions Court 310 Tellico St South, #1, Madisonville, TN 37354-1391; 423-442-9537; fax: 423-420-9091; 7:30AM-4:30PM; 7:30AM-4PM W (EST). *Civil under $25,000, Eviction, Small Claims.*

General Information: No juvenile records released. Will fax documents $2.00 per page. Court makes copy: $.50 per page. Self serve copy: same. Certification fee: $5.00 per cert. Payee: Circuit Court Clerk. No personal checks or credit cards accepted. Prepayment required.

Civil Name Search: Access: Mail, in person. Both court and visitors may perform in person name searches. Search fee: $10.00 per name. Civil records on computer since 1991, records on books in this office for 3 years, otherwise in offsite storage. Note: All name searches must be performed at the Circuit Clerk's office. They have a public access terminal there. All mail requests are also forwarded to the Circuit Clerks Office. Mail turnaround time 2 days. Public use terminal has civil records back to 1991. Public terminal located at General Sessions Clerk's office.

Montgomery County

Montgomery County Circuit & General Sessions Court 2 Millennium Plaza, #115, Clarksville, TN 37040; 931-648-5700; fax: 931-648-5729; 8AM-4:30PM (CST). *Felony, Misdemeanor, Civil, Evictions, Small Claims.*

www.montgomerycountytn.org/county/index.htm

General Information: One representative handles all the archives for both civil and criminal records. No juvenile records released. Will not fax documents. Court makes copy: $.50 per page. Certification fee: $5.00 per doc plus copy fee. Payee: Circuit Court (Criminal) or General Sessions Court (civil). Business checks accepted. Major credit cards accepted. Prepayment required. Mail requests: SASE required.

Civil Name Search: Access: Mail, fax, in person. Visitors must perform in person searches themselves. No search fee. Civil records on computer back to 11/1999, archived on books in office from 1970s, on microfiche from 1950s. Mail turnaround time 24-48 hours up to 7 days. Civil PAT goes back to 11/1999.

Criminal Name Search: Access: Mail, fax, in person. Both court and visitors may perform in person name searches. Search fee: $10.00. Required to search: name, years to search, DOB; also helpful-signed release, SSN. Criminal records computerized from 1985; prior records archived on books from 1970s, on microfiche from 1950s. Mail turnaround time generally 24-48 hours or up to 7 days. Criminal PAT goes back to 1985.

County Court County Courts Center/Clerk & Master, 2 Millennium Plaza, #101, Clarksville, TN 37040; 931-648-5703; fax: 931-648-5759; 8AM-4:30PM (CST). *Civil, Probate.*

www.montgomerycountytn.org/county/index.htm

General Information: Probate fax is same as main fax number. No adoption or sealed records released. Will fax documents for fee. Court makes copy: $.50 per page. Certification fee: $5.00 per doc. Payee: Court Clerk. Attorney checks accepted. Major credit cards and debit cards accepted, small service fee added. Prepayment required.

Civil Name Search: Access: Mail, fax, in person. Both court and visitors may perform in person name searches. No search fee. Civil records on books, microfilm, or computer. Note: Will add service fee to use fax. Public use terminal has civil records back to 1995.

Moore County

17th District Circuit & General Sessions Court PO Box 206, 196 Main St, Courthouse, Lynchburg, TN 37352; 931-759-7208;; 8AM-N, 1-4:30PM M,Tu,W,F; 8AM-N Sat (CST). *Felony, Misdemeanor, Civil, Eviction, Small Claims.*

General Information: No juvenile records released. Will fax documents to local or toll-free number. Court makes copy: $.50 per page. Certification fee: $5.00 per doc plus copy fee. Payee: Circuit Court Clerk. Only cashiers checks and money orders accepted. Prepayment required. Mail requests: SASE required.

Civil Name Search: Access: In person only. Visitors must perform in person searches themselves. Search fee: $5.00 per name if and when they have personnel to do so in future. Civil records archived to 1862, on docket books and microfiche from 1862 to 1980s. Mail turnaround time 7-10 days.

Criminal Name Search: Access: In person only. Visitors must perform in person searches themselves. Search fee: $5.00 per name if and when they have personnel to do so in future. Criminal records archived to 1862, on docket books and microfiche from 1862 to 1980s. Mail turnaround time 7-10 days.

Chancery Court PO Box 206, 196 Main St, Courthouse, Lynchburg, TN 37352; 931-759-7028; fax: 931-759-5610; 8AM-N, 1-4:30PM M,W,F; 8AM-N Sat (CST). *Civil, Probate.*

General Information: No adoption or sealed records released. Will not fax documents. Court makes copy: $.50 per page. Self serve copy: same. Certification fee: $5.00 per document. Payee: Clerk and Master. Only cashiers checks and money orders accepted. Prepayment required.

Civil Name Search: Access: In person only. Visitors must perform in person searches themselves. Civil cases indexed by plaintiff. Civil records on books.

Morgan County

9th District Circuit & General Sessions Court PO Box 163, 415 N Kingston, Wartburg, TN 37887; 423-346-3503; fax: 423-346-5947; 8AM-4PM (EST). *Felony, Misdemeanor, Civil, Eviction, Small Claims.*

General Information: No sealed records released. Court makes copy: $.50 per page. Certification fee: $5.00 per cert. Payee: Circuit Court Clerk. Only cashiers checks and money orders accepted. No credit cards accepted. Prepayment required.

Civil Name Search: Access: In person only. Visitors must perform in person searches themselves. Civil records archived on books from 1855.

Criminal Name Search: Access: In person only. Visitors must perform in person searches themselves. Required to search: name, years to search; also helpful: DOB, SSN. Criminal records archived on books from 1855; computerized since 2/01.

Chancery Court PO Box 789, Wartburg, TN 37887; 423-346-3881; fax: 423-346-4217; 8AM-4PM (EST). *Civil, Probate.*

General Information: Probate is separate index at same address. Probate fax is same as main fax number. No adoption or conservatorship records released. Will fax documents to local or toll free line. Court makes copy: $.50 per page. Certification fee: $5.00 per cert. Payee: Clerk & Master. Personal checks accepted, credit cards are not. Prepayment required. Mail requests: SASE required.

Civil Name Search: Access: Phone, mail, in person. Both court and visitors may perform in person name searches. No search fee. Civil records in books since 1883, on microfiche since 1939 at state archives. Mail turnaround time 1-8 days.

Obion County

27th District Circuit Court 7 Bill Burnett Cir, Union City, TN 38261; 731-885-1372; fax: 731-885-7922; 8:30AM-4:30PM (CST). *Felony, Misdemeanor, Civil Actions over $25,000.*

General Information: No adoption records released. Will fax documents to local or toll-free number. Court makes copy: $.50 per page. Certification fee: $5.00. Payee: Circuit Court. Business checks accepted. No credit cards accepted for record searches. Prepayment required. Mail requests: SASE required.

Civil Name Search: Access: Mail, in person. Both court and visitors may perform in person name searches. Search fee: $5.00 per name. Civil records archived on books from 1969, civil on books from 1974, rest are located elsewhere. Mail turnaround time 2 days. Civil PAT goes back to 12/1993.

Criminal Name Search: Access: Mail, in person. Both court and visitors may perform in person name searches. Search fee: $5.00. Required to search: name, years to search, DOB, SSN. Criminal records for archived on books from 1969. Mail turnaround time 2 days. Criminal PAT goes back to 12/1993.

Chancery Court PO Box 187, Union City, TN 38281; 731-885-2562; fax: 731-885-7922; 8:30AM-4:30PM (CST). *Civil, Probate.*

General Information: No adoption or sealed records released. Will fax documents $3.00 each plus copy fee. Court makes copy: $.50 per page. Certification fee: $5.00. Payee: Clerk and Master. Personal checks accepted, credit cards are not. Prepayment required.

Civil Name Search: Access: Phone, mail, in person. Both court and visitors may perform in person name searches. Search fee: $5.00 per name. Civil records (probate) from 9/82 on books in Chancery office, prior records back to 1800s on index books in County Clerk's office. Mail turnaround time 2 days. Public use terminal has civil records. beginning 06/01/2009, only the name is shown on PAT.

General Sessions Court 9 Bill Burnett Cir, Union City, TN 38281-0236; 731-885-1811; fax: 731-885-7922; 8:30AM-4:30PM (CST). *Civil Actions under $25,000, Eviction, Small Claims.*

General Information: No juvenile or adoption records released. Will fax documents to local or toll-free number. Court makes copy: $.50 per page. Certification fee: $5.00. Payee: Circuit Court Clerk. Personal checks accepted. No credit cards accepted for copies or searches. Prepayment required. Mail requests: SASE required.

Civil Name Search: Access: Mail, in person. Both court and visitors may perform in person name searches. Search fee: $5.00 per name, 5 years or less; $10.00 over 5 years. Required to search: name. Civil records kept in office for last 10 years, computerized since 1994. Mail turnaround time 2 days. Public use terminal has civil records to 1994.

Overton County

13th District Circuit & General Sessions Court Overton County Justice Center, 1000 John T Poindexter Dr, Livingston, TN 38570; 931-823-2312; fax: 931-823-9728; 8AM-4:30PM (CST). *Felony, Misdemeanor, Civil, Eviction, Small Claims.*

General Information: No juvenile records released. Will not fax documents. Court makes copy: $.50 per page. Certification fee: $5.00 per page. Payee: Circuit Court Clerk. Local business checks accepted. Major credit cards accepted. Prepayment required. Mail requests: SASE required.

Civil Name Search: Access: Mail, in person. Both court and visitors may perform in person name searches. No search fee. Civil records archived on books from late 1800s; computerized records since 1996. Mail turnaround time 3-5 days.

Criminal Name Search: Access: Mail, in person. Both court and visitors may perform in person name searches. No search fee. Required to search: name, years to search, DOB, SSN, signed release. Criminal records archived on books from late 1800s; computerized records since 1996. Mail turnaround time 3-5 days.

County Court 100 Court Square, Livingston, TN 38570; 931-823-2536; fax: 931-823-7631; 8AM-4PM (CST). *Probate.*

Perry County

21st District Circuit & General Sessions Court PO Box 91, 121 main, Linden, TN 37096; 931-589-2218; fax: 931-589-2350; 8AM-4PM (CST). *Felony, Misdemeanor, Civil, Eviction, Small Claims.*

General Information: No adoption records released. Court makes copy: $.50 per page. Self serve copy: same. Certification fee: $5.00. Payee: Circuit Court Clerk. Personal checks accepted only if local. No credit cards accepted. Prepayment required. Mail requests: SASE required.

Civil Name Search: Access: Mail, in person. Both court and visitors may perform in person name searches. No search fee. Civil records archived on books from 1941, on microfiche (limited) at library. Mail turnaround time 2-3 days.

Criminal Name Search: Access: Mail, in person. Both court and visitors may perform in person name searches. No search fee. Required to search: name, years to search, DOB, SSN. Criminal records archived on books from 1941, on microfiche (limited) at library. Mail turnaround time 2-3 days.

Chancery Court PO Box 251, Linden, TN 37096; 931-589-2217; fax: 931-589-6369; 8AM-4PM (CST). *Civil, Probate.*

General Information: No adoption records released. Will not fax documents. Court makes copy: $.50 per page. Self serve copy: same. Certification fee: $5.00. Payee: Clerk and Master. Local checks accepted. No credit cards accepted. Prepayment required.

Civil Name Search: Access: In person only. Both court and visitors may perform in person name searches. No search fee. Civil records (probate) on books from 1982, prior records in County Clerks office. Public use terminal has civil records back to 2002.

Pickett County

13th District Circuit & General Sessions Court PO Box 188, 1 Courthouse Sq, Byrdstown, TN 38549; 931-864-3958; fax: 931-864-6885; 8AM-4PM, except W 8-11AM (CST). *Felony, Misdemeanor, Civil, Eviction, Small Claims.*

General Information: No adoption or juvenile records released. Will not fax documents. Court makes copy: $.50 per page. No certification fee. Payee: Circuit Court Clerk. Personal checks accepted, credit cards are not. Prepayment required.

Civil Name Search: Access: Mail, in person. Both court and visitors may perform in person name searches. Search fee: $10.00 per name. Civil cases indexed by defendant. Civil records archived on books but not specific. Mail turnaround time 3-4 days. Civil PAT goes back to 2000.

Criminal Name Search: Access: Mail, in person. Both court and visitors may perform in person name searches. Search fee: $10.00 per name. Required to search: name, years to search; also helpful: SSN. Criminal records computerized since 2000, older records within books. Mail turnaround time 3-4 days. Criminal PAT goes back to 2000.

County Court 1 Courthouse Sq, Ste 201, Byrdstown, TN 38549; 931-864-3879; fax: 931-864-7087; 8AM-4PM M T,TH,F, 8-11AM W,S (CST). *Probate.*

Polk County

10th District Circuit & General Sessions Court PO Box 256, Benton, TN 37307; 423-338-4524; fax: 423-338-8611; 8:30AM-4:30PM (EST). *Felony, Misdemeanor, Civil, Eviction, Small Claims.*
General Information: No juvenile records released. Will fax documents $5.00 per name. Court makes copy: $.50 per page. Self serve copy: same. Certification fee: $7.50 per cert. Payee: Circuit Court Clerk. Personal checks accepted, credit cards are not. Prepayment required. Mail requests: SASE requested.
Civil Name Search: Access: Mail, fax, in person. Both court and visitors may perform in person name searches. Search fee: $5.00 per name. Civil records archived from 1936, computerized since 2000. Mail turnaround time 1 day. Civil PAT goes back to 2000.
Criminal Name Search: Access: Mail, fax, in person. Both court and visitors may perform in person name searches. Search fee: $5.00 per name. Required to search: name, years to search, DOB, SSN. Criminal records archived from 1936, computerized since 2000. Mail turnaround time 3 days. Criminal PAT goes back to same as civil.

Chancery Court PO Box 689, Benton, TN 37307; 423-338-4522; fax: 423-338-4553; 8:30AM-4:30PM (EST). *Civil, Probate.*
General Information: No adoption records released. Will fax documents to local or toll free line. Court makes copy: $.50 per page. Certification fee: $5.00 per cert plus all copies fees. Payee: Chancery Court. Personal checks accepted, credit cards are not. Prepayment required.
Civil Name Search: Access: Mail, in person. Both court and visitors may perform in person name searches. Search fee: Fee varies by document. Civil records on books up to 1800s, computerized since 10/00. Mail turnaround time 2 days.

Putnam County

13th District Circuit & General Sessions Court 421 E Spring St, 1C-49A, Cookeville, TN 38501; 931-528-1508; fax: 931-526-2004; 8AM-4PM (CST). *Felony, Misdemeanor, Civil, Eviction, Small Claims, Probate.* www.dockets.putnamco.org
General Information: Current docket information available at the website. As of July 1, 2008 this office handles the Juvenile and Probate Courts. No juvenile or adoption records released. Will fax out documents. Court makes copy: $.50 per page. Self serve copy: same. Certification fee: $5.00. Payee: Circuit Court Clerk. Business checks accepted, no personal checks. Visa/MC/AmEx/Discover accepted through VitalChek. Prepayment required.
Civil Name Search: Access: In person, online. Visitors must perform in person searches themselves. Civil records archived in office from 1980s, unknown before then; computerized records since 1995. Civil PAT goes back to 1995, countywide for probate. PAT results may also include a DOB. Current docket information available at the website. There is no historical data.
Criminal Name Search: Access: In person, online. Visitors must perform in person searches themselves. Required to search: name, years to search; also helpful: SSN. Criminal records computerized since 1995. Criminal PAT goes back to 1995. PAT results may also include a DOB. Current docket information available at the website. There is no historical data.

Probate & Juvenile Court 421 E Spring St, Rm 1C, #49A, Cookeville, TN 38501; 931-528-1508; fax: 931-526-2004; 8AM-4:00PM (CST). *Probate.* www.putnamcountytn.gov/

Rhea County

12th District Circuit & General Sessions Court 1475 Market St, Rm 102, Dayton, TN 37321; 423-775-7805; criminal phone: 423-775-7818; probate phone: 423-775-7806; fax: 423-775-7895; 8AM-4:30PM (EST). *Felony, Misdemeanor, Civil, Eviction, Small Claims, Probate.*
General Information: Probate located at the Rhea County Clerk and Master's Office. Probate fax- 423-775-4046 No adoption records released. Will not fax documents. Court makes copy: $.50 per page. Certification fee: $5.00 per doc. Payee: Circuit Court Clerk. Local personal checks accepted; no out of state checks. No credit cards accepted. Prepayment required. Mail requests: SASE required.
Civil Name Search: Access: Phone, mail, in person. Visitors must perform in person searches themselves. No search fee. Civil records in docket books and on computer. Note: Phone and mail search requests are performed on computer back to 7/2002 only. Civil PAT available.
Criminal Name Search: Access: Phone, mail, in person. Both court and visitors may perform in person name searches. No search fee. Required to search: name, years to search; also helpful: DOB, SSN. Criminal records in docket books and on computer. Note: Phone and mail search requests are performed on computer back to 7/2002 only. Criminal PAT available.

Roane County

9th District Circuit & General Sessions Court 200 E Rare St, #16 (Sessions), #11 (Circuit), Kingston, TN 37763; 865-376-2390; fax: 865-717-4141; 8:30AM-6PM M; 8:30AM-4:30PM T-F (EST). *Felony, Misdemeanor, Civil, Eviction, Small Claims.*
General Information: General Sessions phone is 865-376-5584, their records are separate from Circuit Court records. No adoption, expunged records released. Will fax documents. Court makes copy: $.50 per page. Self serve copy: same. Certification fee: $5.00. Payee: Circuit Court Clerk. Business checks accepted. No credit cards accepted. Prepayment required. Mail requests: SASE required.
Civil Name Search: Access: Mail, fax, in person. Both court and visitors may perform in person name searches. Search fee: $5.00 per name. Civil records archived since court started, General Sessions and Circuit are on computer since 1991. Mail turnaround time 2-3 days. Civil PAT goes back to 1990.
Criminal Name Search: Access: Mail, fax, in person. Both court and visitors may perform in person name searches. Search fee: $5.00 per name. Required to search: name, years to search, DOB; also helpful, SSN, signed release. Criminal records archived since court started, General Sessions and Circuit are on computer since 1991. Mail turnaround time 2-3 days. Criminal PAT goes back to same as civil.

Chancery Court 200 E Race Dt, #12, Kingston, TN 37763; 865-376-2487; fax: 865-376-1228; 8:30AM-6PM M, 8:30AM-4:30PM T-F (EST). *Civil, Probate.*
General Information: No adoption records released. Fee to fax out file $1.00 per page. Court makes copy: $.50 per page. Certification fee: $5.00; Exemplification fee- $20.00. Payee: Clerk and Master. Personal checks accepted, credit cards are not. Prepayment required. Mail requests: SASE not required.
Civil Name Search: Access: Phone, mail, in person. Both court and visitors may perform in person name searches. Search fee: $5.00. Civil records on books; on computer since 7/95. Tax records on computer since 1982. Note: Searches made by employees are on the computer, searches made by visitor by books. Mail turnaround time same day.

Robertson County

County Circuit Court Robertson County Courthouse, Rm 109, Springfield, TN 37172; 615-384-7864; fax: 615-384-0246; 8AM-4:30PM (CST). *Felony, Misdemeanor.*
General Information: No sealed records released. Will fax documents to local or toll-free number. Court makes copy: $.50 per page. Self serve copy: same. Certification fee: $5.00 plus $.50 per page. Payee: Circuit Court Clerk. No personal checks. Credit cards accepted by phone. In person will take debit. Prepayment required. Mail requests: SASE required.
Civil Name Search: Access: Phone, fax, mail, in person. Both court and visitors may perform in person name searches. Search fee: $5.00 per name. Civil records archived in office from 2003, archived from 1800s located elsewhere. Mail turnaround time 15 days. Civil PAT goes back to 1994.
Criminal Name Search: Access: Phone, fax, mail, in person. Both court and visitors may perform in person name searches. Search fee: $5.00 per name. Required to search: name, years to search; also helpful: DOB, SSN. Criminal records archived in office from 2003, archived from 1800s located elsewhere. Mail turnaround time 15 days. Criminal PAT goes back to same as civil.

Chancery Court 501 Main St, Rm 103, County Courthouse, Springfield, TN 37172; 615-384-5650; fax: 615-382-3128; 8AM-4:30PM (CST). *Civil, Probate.*
General Information: No adoption records released. Will not fax out documents. Court makes copy: $.50 per page. Self serve copy: same. Certification fee: $5.00 plus copy fee. Payee: Clerk & Master. Personal checks accepted. Prepayment required. Mail requests: SASE required.
Civil Name Search: Access: Mail, in person. Visitors must perform in person searches themselves. Search fee: $5.00. Probate records in books since 1982, computerized from 9/94 to present, all Chancery records on books. Mail turnaround time 1-2 days.

General Sessions Court 529 S Brown St., Springfield, TN 37172-2941; 615-382-2324; fax: 615-382-3113; 8AM-4:30PM (CST). *Misdemeanor, Civil Actions under $25,000, Eviction, Small Claims, Traffic.*
General Information: No sealed records released. Will not fax out documents to the public. Court makes copy: $.50 per page. Self serve copy: same. Certification fee: $5.00 per doc plus copy fee. Payee: General Sessions Court Clerk. No personal checks. Major credit cards accepted. Prepayment required. Mail requests: SASE required.
Civil Name Search: Access: Fax, mail, in person. Both court and visitors may perform in person name searches. Search fee: $5.00 per name. Civil records archived in office from 2000, archived from 1800s located elsewhere. Mail turnaround time 7 days. Civil PAT goes back to 1994.

Criminal Name Search: Access: Fax, mail, in person. Both court and visitors may perform in person name searches. Search fee: $5.00 per name. Required to search: name, years to search; also helpful: DOB, SSN. Criminal records archived in office from 2000, archived from 1800s located elsewhere. Mail turnaround time 7 days. Criminal PAT goes back to same as civil.

Rutherford County

16th District Circuit Court Judicial Bldg, Rm 201, Murfreesboro, TN 37130; criminal phone: 615-898-7812; civil phone: 615-898-7820; criminal fax: 615-217-7119; civil fax: 8AM-4:15PM; 8AM-4:15PM (CST). *Felony, Misdemeanor, Civil Actions over $15,000.*
General Information: No expunged, sealed criminal records released. Will not fax documents. Court makes copy: $.50 per page. Self serve copy: $.50 per page. Certification fee: $4.00 plus $.50 per page. Payee: Circuit Court Clerk. Personal checks accepted, credit cards are not. Prepayment required.
Civil Name Search: Access: In person only. Visitors must perform in person searches themselves. Civil on computer since 1986. Civil PAT goes back to 1986.
Criminal Name Search: Access: In person only. Visitors must perform in person searches themselves. Required to search: name, years to search, DOB, signed release; SSN helpful. Criminal on computer since 1990. Criminal PAT goes back to 1990.

General Sessions Court Judicial Bldg, Rm 101, 220 N Public Sq, Murfreesboro, TN 37130; 615-898-7831; fax: 615-898-7835; 8AM-4:15PM (CST). *Civil Actions under $25,000, Eviction, Small Claims.*
General Information: No juvenile records released. Will fax documents. Court makes copy: $.50 per page. Self serve copy: $.50 per page. Certification fee: $5.00. Payee: General Sessions Court. No personal checks or credit cards accepted. Prepayment required.
Civil Name Search: Access: In person only. Visitors must perform in person searches themselves. Required to search: name, years to search, DOB, SSN. Civil records go back to 1948; on computer from 1986. Public use terminal has civil records back to 1986.

County Court County Clerk, 319 N Maple St, Ste 121, Murfreesboro, TN 37130; 615-898-7798; fax: 615-217-6597; 8AM-4PM M-TH; 8AM-5PM F (CST). *Probate, Guardianship.*
www.rutherfordcountytn.gov

Scott County

Circuit & General Sessions Court PO Box 330, Huntsville, TN 37756; 423-663-2440; fax: 423-663-2595; 8AM-4:30PM (EST). *Felony, Misdemeanor, Civil, Eviction, Small Claims, Probate.*
General Information: Probate is a separate index at this same address. Probate fax is same as main fax number. No juvenile records released. Will fax documents to local or toll free line. Court makes copy: $.50 per page. Self serve copy: same. Certification fee: $5.00 per seal plus copy fee. Payee: Circuit Court Clerk. Personal checks accepted, credit cards are not. Prepayment required. Mail requests: SASE required.
Civil Name Search: Access: Phone, mail, in person. Both court and visitors may perform in person name searches. Search fee: $10.00 per name per year. Civil records archived in docket books but not specified, on computer from 1991. Mail turnaround time same week.
Criminal Name Search: Access: Phone, mail, in person. Both court and visitors may perform in person name searches. Search fee: $10.00 per name per year. Fee varies according to info requested. Required to search: name, years to search, DOB; also helpful: SSN. Criminal records archived in docket books but not specified, on computer from 1991. Mail turnaround time same week.

Sequatchie County

12th District Circuit & General Sessions Court 351 Fredonia Rd, Ste B, Dunlap, TN 37327; 423-949-2618; fax: 423-949-2902; 8AM-4PM (CST). *Felony, Misdemeanor, Civil, Eviction, Small Claims.*
General Information: No adoption records released. Will fax documents $1.00 per page. Court makes copy: $.50 per page. Certification fee: $5.00. Payee: Circuit Court Clerk. Personal checks, Visa/MC accepted. Prepayment required. Mail requests: SASE required.
Civil Name Search: Access: Phone, fax, mail, in person. Both court and visitors may perform in person name searches. No search fee. Civil records archived on books but not specified. Mail turnaround time 1 week.
Criminal Name Search: Access: Phone, fax, mail, in person. Both court and visitors may perform in person name searches. No search fee. Required to search: name, years to search, DOB; also helpful: SSN. Criminal records not computerized. Mail turnaround time 1 week.

Chancery Court PO Box 1651, 22 Cherry St, Dunlap, TN 37327; 423-949-3670; fax: 423-949-2570; 8AM-4PM (CST). *Civil, Probate.*
General Information: No sealed or adoption records released. Will fax documents $1.00 per page. Court makes copy: $.50 per page. Certification fee: $5.00 per cert. Payee: Clerk and Master. Personal checks accepted, credit cards are not. Prepayment required.
Civil Name Search: Access: In person only. Only the court performs in person name searches; visitors may not. Civil records on books, but court is process of computerizing more data.

Sevier County

4th District Circuit Court 125 Court Ave, #204E, Sevierville, TN 37862; 865-453-5536; criminal phone: x2; civil phone: x1; fax: 865-774-3620; 8AM-4:30PM M-TH, 8AM-5PM F (EST). *Felony, Misdemeanor, Civil Actions over $15,000.*
General Information: No expunged records released. Will fax documents $1.00 per page. Court makes copy: $.50 per page. Self serve copy: same. Certification fee: $5.00 per cert. Payee: Circuit Court or General Sessions Clerk. No personal checks or credit cards accepted. Prepayment required. Mail requests: SASE required.
Civil Name Search: Access: Fax, mail, in person. Both court and visitors may perform in person name searches. Search fee: $10.00 per name. Civil records computerized back to 1993. Records before 1980s are archived. Mail turnaround time 1 week. Civil PAT goes back to 1993.
Criminal Name Search: Access: Fax, mail, in person. Both court and visitors may perform in person name searches. Search fee: $10.00 per name. Criminal records computerized back to 1993. Mail turnaround time 1 week. Criminal PAT goes back to same as civil.

General Sessions Court 125 Court Ave, #107E, Sevierville, TN 37862; 865-453-6116; criminal phone: 865-453-6116; civil phone: 865-429-5671; criminal fax: 865-774-3842; civil fax: 8AM-4:30PM M-TH, 8AM-5PM F; 8AM-4:30PM M-TH, 8AM-5PM F (EST). *Misdemeanor, Civil Actions under $25,000, Eviction, Small Claims.*
General Information: No expunged records released. Will fax documents $1.00 per page. Court makes copy: $.50 per page. Self serve copy: $1.00 per case. Certification fee: $5.00. Payee: General Sessions Clerk. No personal checks. Money order or cash only. No credit cards accepted. Prepayment required. Mail requests: SASE not required.
Civil Name Search: Access: Phone, fax, mail. Both court and visitors may perform in person name searches. No search fee. Civil records computerized back to 1995. Records before 1980s difficult to locate. Mail turnaround time 1 week. Civil PAT goes back to 6/1995.
Criminal Name Search: Access: Fax, mail. Both court and visitors may perform in person name searches. No search fee. Required to search: name, years to search; also helpful: date of arrest. Criminal records computerized back to 1995; index back to 1973. Mail turnaround time 1 week. Criminal PAT goes back to 6/1995.

County Clerk 125 Court Ave, #202 East, Sevierville, TN 37862; 865-453-5502; fax: 865-453-6830; 8AM-4:30PM M-Th, 8AM-5PM F (EST). *Probate.*

Shelby County

Circuit Court 140 Adams Ave, Rm 324, Memphis, TN 38103; 901-545-4710; fax: 901-545-4723; 8AM-4:30PM (CST). *Civil Actions over $25,000.*
http://circuitcourt.shelbycountytn.gov/
General Information: The East Office is no longer open. Online identifiers in results same as on public terminal. No juvenile or adoption records released. Will fax documents $1.00 per page. Court makes copy: $.50 per page. Self serve copy: same. Certification fee: $5.00 per cert. Payee: Circuit Court Clerk. Personal checks accepted, credit cards are not. Prepayment required.
Civil Name Search: Access: Fax, mail, in person, online. Both court and visitors may perform in person name searches. Search fee: $5.00 per name. Required to search: name; also helpful: years to search. Civil records archived from early 1900s, on computer from 1991, on microfiche from 1980. Mail turnaround time 5-8 days. Public use terminal has civil records back to 1994. Search clerk's circuit court records for free at the website or at http://circuitdata.shelbycountytn.gov/crweb/ck_public_qry_main.cp_main_idx.

30th District Criminal Court Office of the Criminal Court, 201 Poplar Ave, Rm 401, Memphis, TN 38103; 901-545-5040; fax: 901-545-3679; 8AM-4:30PM (CST). *Felony.*
www.shelbycountytn.gov/index.aspx?nid=224
General Information: No expunged or sealed records released. Fee to fax out file $4.00 if out of town, $3.00 if in-town. Court makes copy: $.50 per page. Certification fee: $5.00 per cert. Payee: Criminal Court Clerk. Business checks accepted. Visa/MC accepted in person only. Prepayment required.
Criminal Name Search: Access: Fax, mail, in person, online. Both court and visitors may perform in person name searches. Search fee: $5.00 per name. Required to search: name, years to search, DOB, SSN. Criminal records on computer as far back as 1989, prior records archived. Mail turnaround time 3 days. Public use terminal has crim records back to

1989 but may not be complete. Search the criminal court records for free at http://jssi.shelbycountytn.gov/. Online results show middle initial, DOB.

Chancery Court 140 Adams, Rm 308, Memphis, TN 38103; 901-545-4002; fax: 901-545-2588; 8AM-4:30PM (CST). *Civil Actions under $25,000, Equity Cases (also, lower Circuit Court Civil issues).*
http://chancerycourt.shelbycountytn.gov/
General Information: No juvenile or adoption records released. Will not fax documents. Court makes copy: $.50 per page. Certification fee: $5.00 per cert. Payee: Chancery Court Clerk. No personal checks or credit cards accepted. Prepayment required. Mail requests: SASE requested.
Civil Name Search: Access: Mail, fax, in person, online. Only the court performs in person name searches; visitors may not. Search fee: $5.00 per name. Civil records go back to 1972. Mail turnaround time 1 week. Public use terminal has civil records. Search court records for free at http://chancerydata.shelbycountytn.gov/chweb/ck_public_qry_main.cp_main_idx.

General Sessions - Civil 140 Adams, Rm 106, Memphis, TN 38103; 901-545-4031; fax: 901-545-2515; 8AM-4:30PM (CST). *Civil Actions under $25,000, Eviction, Small Claims.*
http://gs4.shelbycountytn.gov/gscvinq/gscv_civilhome
General Information: There are two Satellite Offices: 1075 Station Rd, Room #115 West, Memphis 38134, 901-379-7052; and 3768 S Hickory Ridge Mall, Ste 514, Memphis 38115, 901-545-4220. Online identifiers in results same as on public terminal. No mental commitment records released. Will not fax documents. Court makes copy: $.50 per page. Self serve copy: same. Certification fee: $5.00 per cert. Payee: General Sessions Court Clerk. Personal checks accepted. Major credit cards accepted. Prepayment required.
Civil Name Search: Access: In person, online. Visitors must perform in person searches themselves. Civil records archived 10 years in office, some microfiche and on computer from 1982. No paper indexes. Note: Note-Soundex does not always work. Public use terminal has civil records back to 10-20 years, depending on case type. Search case history for free at http://gs4.shelbycountytn.gov/gscvinq/gscv_caseinquirieshome.

General Sessions - Criminal 201 Poplar, Rm LL 81, Memphis, TN 38103; criminal phone: 901-545-5100; fax: 901-545-3655; 8AM-4:30PM (CST). *Misdemeanor.*
http://gs4.shelbycountytn.gov/gscvinq/gscr_criminaldivision
General Information: No mental records released. Court makes copy: $.50 per page. No certification fee. Payee: General Sessions Court. Personal checks accepted. Major credit cards accepted. Prepayment required. Mail requests: SASE not required.
Criminal Name Search: Access: Mail, in person, online. Both court and visitors may perform in person name searches. Search fee: $10.00 per name. Use of public access terminal is now free. Required to search: name, years to search, DOB; also helpful: SSN. Criminal records on computer since 1982, prior records archived since court started. Mail turnaround time 2-5 days. Public use terminal has crim records back to 1982. Search criminal court records free at http://jssi.shelbycountytn.gov/. Online results show middle initial, DOB, address.

Probate Court 140 Adams Ave, Rm 124, Memphis, TN 38103; 901-545-4040; fax: 901-545-4746; 7AM-5PM (CST). *Probate.*
http://probate.shelbycountytn.gov/
General Information: Probate court records and dockets are free at http://probatedata.shelbycountytn.gov/. Search online by name or case number. Email to chris.thomas@shelbycountytn.gov.

Smith County

15th District Circuit & General Sessions Court 322 Justice Drive, Carthage, TN 37030; 615-735-0500 (Gen Sess.); 615-735-8260 (Circuit Ct); fax: 615-735-8261; 8AM-4PM (CST). *Felony, Misdemeanor, Civil, Eviction, Small Claims.*
General Information: No juvenile records released. Will not fax documents. Court makes copy: $.50 per page. Certification fee: $6.00. Payee: Circuit Court Clerk. Only cashiers checks and money orders accepted. Major credit cards accepted. Prepayment required.
Civil Name Search: Access: Mail, in person. Visitors must perform in person searches themselves. No search fee. Civil records on computer from 3/92, prior records archived on books, questionable to dates. Mail turnaround time 1-2 days.
Criminal Name Search: Access: Phone, mail, in person. Visitors must perform in person searches themselves. No search fee. Criminal records computerized from 3/92, prior records archived on books, questionable to dates. Mail turnaround time 1-2 days.

Chancery Court 322 Justice Dr, Ste 105, Carthage, TN 37030; 615-735-2092; fax: 615-735-8431; 8AM-4PM (CST). *Civil, Probate.*

General Information: No adoption records released. Fee to fax out file $1.00 per page. Court makes copy: $1.00 per page if mailed, $.50 if in person. Self serve copy: $.50 per page. Certification fee: $5.00 per doc plus copy fee. Payee: Clerk and Master. Personal checks accepted, credit cards are not. Prepayment required. Mail requests: SASE requested.
Civil Name Search: Access: Fax, mail, in person. Only the court performs in person name searches; visitors may not. No search fee. Civil records on books back to 1825. Mail turnaround time 1 day.

Stewart County

23rd District Circuit & General Sessions Court PO Box 193, Dover, TN 37058; 931-232-7042/232-8474; fax: 931-232-3115; 8AM-4:30PM (CST). *Felony, Misdemeanor, Civil, Eviction, Small Claims.*
General Information: The PO Box for the General Sessions Court is PO 398. No expunged records released. Will not fax out documents. Court makes copy: $.50 per page. Certification fee: $5.00 per doc, includes copy fee for first page. Payee: Circuit Court. No personal checks or credit cards accepted. Prepayment required.
Civil Name Search: Access: In person only. Visitors must perform in person searches themselves. Civil cases indexed by plaintiff. Civil records archived on books from 1800s, on computer through 8/1993.
Criminal Name Search: Access: In person only. Visitors must perform in person searches themselves. Criminal records archived on books from 1800s, on computer through 8/1993.

Chancery Court PO Box 102, Dover, TN 37058; 931-232-5665; fax: 931-232-0049; 8AM-4:30PM (CST). *Civil, Probate.*
General Information: No adoption records released. Will fax documents $1.00 per page. Court makes copy: $.50 per page. Certification fee: $5.00. Payee: Clerk and Master. Personal checks accepted, credit cards are not. Prepayment required. Mail requests: SASE required.
Civil Name Search: Access: Mail, in person. Only the court performs in person name searches; visitors may not. No search fee. Civil records on books to 1865; computerized since 1994. Mail turnaround time 1 week.

Sullivan County

Bristol Circuit Court - Civil Division Courthouse, Rm 131, 801 Anderson St, Bristol, TN 37620; 423-989-4354; fax: 423-968-1138; 8AM-5PM (EST). *Civil.*
www.sullivancounty.org/sessionscourt.htm
General Information: Current daily dockets are posted at http://sullivan.mytncourts.com/. No adoption or sealed records released. Will not fax documents. Court makes copy: $.50 per page. Certification fee: $5.50 for seal plus copy fee. Payee: Circuit Court Clerk. No personal checks accepted.
Civil Name Search: Access: In person only. Visitors must perform in person searches themselves. Civil records archived from 1930s (minute books, unsure of docket books), on computer from 1986. Public use terminal has civil records back to 1986.

Chancery Court PO Box 327, Blountville, TN 37617; 423-323-6483; fax: 423-279-3280; 8AM-5PM (EST). *Civil, Probate.*
www.sullivancounty.org/chancerycourt.htm
General Information: Current daily dockets are posted at http://sullivan.mytncourts.com/. No adoption records released. Will fax documents $.50 per page. Court makes copy: $.50 per page. Self serve copy: same. Certification fee: $5.00; Exemplification- $10.00. Payee: Chancery Court. No personal checks or credit cards accepted. Prepayment required.
Civil Name Search: Access: Mail, in person. Both court and visitors may perform in person name searches. No search fee. Civil records on books back to 1867; computerized records go back to 1996. Public use terminal has civil records back to 1984.

Kingsport Circuit Court - Civil Division 225 W Center St, Kingsport, TN 37660; 423-224-1724; fax: 423-246-1924; 8AM-5PM (EST). *Civil Actions over $25,000.*
www.sullivancounty.org/circuitcourt.htm
General Information: Current daily dockets are posted at http://sullivan.mytncourts.com/. No juvenile, adoption records released. Will fax documents to local or toll-free number. Court makes copy: $.50 per page. Certification fee: $5.00 per cert. Payee: Circuit Court Clerk. No personal checks accepted, money orders preferred. No credit cards accepted. Prepayment required. Mail requests: SASE requested.
Civil Name Search: Access: Phone, fax, mail, in person. Both court and visitors may perform in person name searches. No search fee. Civil records archived from 1920s, on computer from 1985. Mail turnaround time 2-3 days. Public use terminal has civil records back to 1985.

2nd District Circuit Court PO Box 585, 140 Blountville Bypass, Blountville, TN 37617; 423-279-2752; fax: 423-323-3741; 8AM-5PM (EST). *Felony, Misdemeanor.*
www.sullivancounty.org/circuitcourt.htm

General Information: Find civil records in Bristol 423-989-4354, or at Kingsport, 423-224-1724. Current daily dockets are posted at http://sullivan.mytncourts.com/. No juvenile records released. Will not fax documents. Court makes copy: $.50 per page. Certification fee: $5.50 per cert. Payee: Circuit Court Clerk. No personal checks accepted.

Criminal Name Search: Access: In person only. Visitors must perform in person searches themselves. Required to search: name, years to search, DOB; SSN helpful. Criminal records on computer since 12/83; prior records archived since the 1800s. Public use terminal has crim records back to 1984.

Bristol General Sessions Court Courthouse, 801 Anderson St, Rm 131, Bristol, TN 37620; 423-989-4352; criminal phone: 423-652-1030; fax: 423-968-1138; 8AM-5PM (EST). *Civil Actions under $25,000, Eviction, Small Claims.*
www.sullivancounty.org/

General Information: Current daily dockets are posted at http://sullivan.mytncourts.com/. No juvenile records released. Will not fax documents. Court makes copy: $.50 per page. Certification fee: $5.00 per cert plus copy. Payee: Circuit Court Clerk. No personal checks accepted. Visa/MC accepted, add 5% usage fee; for use of debit card, add $2.50. Prepayment required.

Civil Name Search: Access: In person only. Visitors must perform in person searches themselves. Civil records archived since court started (stored in Blountville), on computer from 1986. Public use terminal has civil records back to 1986.

Kingsport General Sessions 200 Shelby St, Kingsport, TN 37660; 423-224-1711; fax: 423-224-1766; 8AM-5PM (EST). *Misdemeanor, Civil Actions under $15,000, Eviction, Small Claims.*
www.sullivancounty.org/sessionscourt.htm

General Information: Current daily dockets are posted at http://sullivan.mytncourts.com/. No juvenile records released. Will fax out documents. Court makes copy: $.50 per page. Certification fee: $5.00 per cert. Payee: General Sessions Clerk. No personal checks accepted. Major credit cards accepted. Prepayment required.

Civil Name Search: Access: In person only. Visitors must perform in person searches themselves. Civil records archived in office from 1973, on computer from 1981. Mail Current daily dockets are posted at http://sullivan.mytncourts.com/. Civil PAT goes back to 1981.

Criminal Name Search: Access: In person only. Visitors must perform in person searches themselves. Required to search: name, years to search; SSN helpful. Criminal records archived in office from 1973, on computer from 1981. Criminal PAT goes back to same as civil.

Sumner County

18th District Circuit & General Sessions Court Public Sq, PO Box 549, Gallatin, TN 37066; 615-452-4367; criminal phone: 615-451-3209- Circuit Crim.; civil phone: 615-452-4310 Sessions Civ/Crim; fax: 615-451-6027; 8AM-4:30PM (CST). *Felony, Misdemeanor, Civil, Eviction, Small Claims.*

General Information: General Sessions phone is 615-452-4310. No juvenile, adoption records released. Will not fax documents. Court makes copy: $.50 per page. Certification fee: $5.00. Payee: Circuit Court Clerk. Only cashiers checks and money orders accepted. No credit cards accepted. Prepayment required.

Civil Name Search: Access: In person only. Visitors must perform in person searches themselves. Search fee: Court will only assist. no fee. Civil records archived on books in office from 1981.

Criminal Name Search: Access: In person only. Visitors must perform in person searches themselves. Search fee: Court will only assist. no fee. Criminal records archived on index books in office from 1958; computerized back to 1997. Public use terminal has crim records back to 1997.

Chancery Court Rm 400, Sumner County Courthouse, Gallatin, TN 37066; 615-452-4282; fax: 615-451-6031; 8AM-4:30PM (CST). *Civil, Probate.*

General Information: No juvenile or adoption records released. Will fax documents $1.00 per page. Court makes copy: $.50 per page. Certification fee: $5.00 plus $.50 per page. Payee: Clerk and Master. Only money orders, cash, or business checks accepted. No credit cards accepted. Prepayment required.

Civil Name Search: Access: Phone, fax, mail, in person. Both court and visitors may perform in person name searches. Search fee: $35.00 charge if search takes 1 hour. Civil records go back to 1983. Mail turnaround time 1-2 days.

Tipton County

25th District Circuit & General Sessions Court 1801 S College, Rm 102, Covington, TN 38019; 901-475-3310; fax: 901-475-3318; 8AM-5PM (CST). *Felony, Misdemeanor, Civil, Eviction, Small Claims.*

General Information: No juvenile or adoption records released. Will not fax documents. Court makes copy: $.50 per page. Self serve copy: $.50 per page. Certification fee: $5.00. Payee: Circuit Court Clerk or General Sessions. Business checks, cash or money orders accepted. Debit cards accepted in office. Prepayment required. Mail requests: SASE requested.

Civil Name Search: Access: In person. Visitors must perform in person searches themselves. Civil records no computer info prior to 7/1991, prior records on docket books and are archived. Note: Court will not perform name search. Civil PAT goes back to 1992.

Criminal Name Search: Access: In person. Both court and visitors may perform in person name searches. Required to search: name, years to search, DOB; also helpful: SSN. Criminal records computerized from 7/1992, prior records on docket books. Note: Court will not perform name search. Criminal PAT goes back to 7/1992.

Chancery Court Tipton County Justice Ctr, 1801 S College, #110, Covington, TN 38019; 901-476-0209; fax: 901-476-0246; 8AM-5PM (CST). *Civil, Probate.*

General Information: No adoption records released. Court makes copy: $.50 per page. Self serve copy: same. Certification fee: $4.00 plus $2.00 per page. Payee: Tipton County Chancery Court. Personal checks accepted, credit cards are not. Prepayment required. Mail requests: SASE required.

Civil Name Search: Access: Phone, fax, mail, in person. Both court and visitors may perform in person name searches. Search fee: $5.00. Civil records on books since 1800s, on computer since 1991. Mail turnaround time ASAP. Public use terminal has civil records.

Trousdale County

15th District Circuit & General Sessions Court 200 E Main St, Rm 5, Hartsville, TN 37074; 615-374-3411; criminal fax: 615-374-1130; civil fax: 8AM-4:30PM; 8AM-4:30PM (CST). *Felony, Misdemeanor, Civil, Eviction, Small Claims.*

General Information: No juvenile or adoption records released. Will fax specific case file for prepaid fee. Court makes copy: $.50 per page. Certification fee: $5.00 plus $.50 per page. Payee: Circuit Court Clerk. Only cashiers checks and money orders accepted. No credit cards accepted. Prepayment required.

Civil Name Search: Access: In person only. Visitors must perform in person searches themselves. Civil records archived on books since 1927.

Criminal Name Search: Access: In person only. Visitors must perform in person searches themselves. Criminal records archived on books since 1940.

Chancery Court Courthouse Rm 1, 200 E Main St, Hartsville, TN 37074; 615-374-2996; fax: 615-374-1100; 8AM-4:30PM (CST). *Civil, Probate.*

General Information: No adoption or sealed records released. Will fax documents. Court makes copy: $.50 per page. Certification fee: $5.00 plus $.50 per page. Payee: Clerk and Master. Personal checks accepted, credit cards are not. Prepayment required.

Civil Name Search: Access: In person only. Visitors must perform in person searches themselves. Civil records searchable since 1905. Probate on book since 9/80, prior records in County Clerks office.

Unicoi County

1st District Circuit & General Sessions Court PO Box 2000, 100 N Main St, Erwin, TN 37650; 423-743-3541; fax: 423-743-1118; 9AM-5PM (EST). *Felony, Misdemeanor, Civil, Eviction, Small Claims.*

General Information: No adoption records released. Will fax documents to local or toll free line. Court makes copy: $.50 per page. Certification fee: $5.00 per cert; exemplification fee is $6.00. Payee: Circuit Court Clerk. Personal checks accepted. Major credit cards accepted. Prepayment required.

Civil Name Search: Access: Mail, in person. Only the court performs in person name searches; visitors may not. Search fee: $10.00 per name. Civil records archived on books from 1932 (felonies) and 1961 (misdemeanors); only general sessions is on computer back to late 1996. Mail turnaround time 2 days.

Criminal Name Search: Access: Mail, in person. Only the court performs in person name searches; visitors may not. Search fee: $10.00 per name. Required to search: name, years to search, DOB. Criminal records archived on books from 1932 (felonies) and 1961 (misdemeanors); only general sessions is on computer back to late 1996. Mail turnaround time 2 days.

Probate Court PO Box 2000, 100 N Maine Ave, Erwin, TN 37650; 423-743-3541; fax: 423-743-1118; 9AM-5PM M-F (EST). *Probate.*

Union County

Union Circuit & General Sessions Court 901 E Main St, #220, Maynardville, TN 37807; 865-992-5493; fax: 865-992-8099; 8AM-4PM M-F; 8AM-N Sat (EST). *Felony, Misdemeanor, Civil, Eviction, Small Claims.*
www.unioncountytn.com/barbara_williams/circuitcourtclerk.htm

General Information: No sealed records released. Will fax documents. Court makes copy: $.50 per page. Self serve copy: same. Certification fee: $5.00 includes copy fee. Payee: Circuit Court Clerk. No personal checks accepted. Money orders or cash only. No credit cards accepted. Prepayment required.

Civil Name Search: Access: In person only. Visitors must perform in person searches themselves. Civil records archived on books from 1969. Civil PAT goes back to 1987 civil; Circuit civil back to 2000.

Criminal Name Search: Access: In person only. Visitors must perform in person searches themselves. Required to search: name, years to search, DOB, SSN. Criminal records archived on books from 1969. Criminal PAT goes back to 1994; General Sessions criminal back to 1994.

Chancery Court 901 Main St, #215, Maynardville, TN 37807; 865-992-5942; fax: 865-992-9338; 8AM-4PM (EST). *Civil, Probate.*

General Information: Probate is a separate index at this same address. No adoption records released. Fee to fax out file $1.00 per page. Court makes copy: $.50 per page. Self serve copy: same. Certification fee: $5.00 per document plus copies. Payee: Union County Clerk and Master. Personal checks accepted, credit cards are not. Prepayment required.

Civil Name Search: Access: Phone, mail, in person. Both court and visitors may perform in person name searches. No search fee. Civil cases indexed by plaintiff, cross indexed by defendant. Civil records on books back to 1969. Mail turnaround time 1 week.

Van Buren County

31st District Circuit & General Sessions Court PO Box 126, 179 Veteran's Sq, Spencer, TN 38585; 931-946-2153; fax: 931-946-2190; 8AM-5PM (CST). *Felony, Misdemeanor, Civil, Eviction, Small Claims, Probate.*

General Information: Search fee includes both civil and criminal indexes, if asked for. Probate records from office of Clerk & Master. No juvenile records released. Will fax documents to local or toll free line. Court makes copy: $.50 per page. Certification fee: $3.00 per cert. plus copy fee. Payee: Circuit Court Clerk. No personal checks or credit cards accepted. Prepayment required. Mail requests: SASE required.

Civil Name Search: Access: Mail, in person. Both court and visitors may perform in person name searches. Search fee: $10.00 per name. Civil cases indexed by defendant. Civil records archived on books, date unspecified. Mail turnaround time 2 weeks.

Criminal Name Search: Access: Mail, in person. Both court and visitors may perform in person name searches. Search fee: $10.00 per name. Required to search: name, years to search, DOB; also helpful: SSN. Criminal records archived on books, date unspecified. Mail turnaround time 2 weeks.

Warren County

31st District Circuit & General Sessions Court 111 Court Sq, PO Box 639, McMinnville, TN 37111; 931-473-2373; fax: 931-473-3726; 8AM-4:30PM M-TH; 8AM-5PM F (CST). *Felony, Misdemeanor, Civil, Eviction, Small Claims.*

General Information: No adoption or juvenile records released. Will not fax out documents. Court makes copy: $1.00 per page. Certification fee: $2.00. Payee: Circuit Court Clerk. Personal checks accepted, credit cards are not. Prepayment required. Mail requests: SASE required.

Civil Name Search: Access: In person. Both court and visitors may perform in person name searches. Civil records on computer since 1988 (General Sessions), archived in office from 1939 (Circuit). Civil PAT goes back to 1996.

Criminal Name Search: Access: In person. Both court and visitors may perform in person name searches. Required to search: name, years to search, DOB, SSN, offense, date of offense. Criminal records on computer since 1988 (General Sessions), archived in office from 1939 (Circuit). Criminal PAT goes back to same as civil.

Chancery Court PO Box 639, McMinnville, TN 37111; 931-473-2364; fax: 931-473-3232; 8AM-4:30PM M-TH, 8AM-5PM F (CST). *Civil, Probate.*

www.warrencountytn.gov/court/chancery.asp

General Information: No adoption records released. Will fax out documents $.50 per page. Court makes copy: $.50 per page. Certification fee: $5.00. Payee: Clerk and Master. Personal checks accepted, credit cards are not. Prepayment required. Mail requests: SASE required.

Civil Name Search: Access: Mail, in person. Both court and visitors may perform in person name searches. No search fee. Civil records on books. Mail turnaround time 1 week.

Washington County

1st District Circuit & General Sessions Court 108 W Jackson, Ste 2167, Jonesborough, TN 37659; 423-788-1475; fax: 423-753-0142; 8AM-5PM (EST). *Felony, Misdemeanor, Civil, Eviction, Small Claims.*
www.washingtoncountytn.org/law_justice

General Information: Felonies are tried in the Criminal Court. All criminal records for county are found here in Jonesborough. Johnson City civil records are found in Johnson City. Access current dockets at http://washington.mytncourts.com/. No sealed, juvenile, adoption records released. Will not fax documents. Court makes copy: $.50 per page. Certification fee: $5.00. Payee: Circuit Court Clerk. Personal checks accepted. Major credit cards accepted, surcharge added. Prepayment required.

Civil Name Search: Access: In person only. Both court and visitors may perform in person name searches. No search fee. Civil records archived from 1800s, on computer from 1989. Civil PAT goes back to 1989.

Criminal Name Search: Access: In person only. Both court and visitors may perform in person name searches. No search fee. Criminal records archived from 1800s, on computer from 1989. Criminal PAT goes back to same as civil.

Johnson City Law Court - Civil 108 W Jackson, PO Box 219, Jonesborough, TN 37659; 423-753-1621; fax: 423-753-1647; 8AM-5PM (EST). *Civil Actions over $15,000.*
www.washingtoncountytn.com/

General Information: Access criminal records at the Jonesborough Court. Access current dockets at http://washington.mytncourts.com/. No sealed records released. Will not fax documents. Court makes copy: $.50 per page. Certification fee: $5.00 per doc. Payee: Circuit Court Clerk. No personal or out-of-state checks accepted. Visa/MC accepted. Prepayment required.

Civil Name Search: Access: In person only. Visitors must perform in person searches themselves. Civil records on computer from 1988. Public use terminal has civil records back to 1988.

General Sessions 108 W Jackson Blvd, Ste 1210, Jonesborough, TN 37659; 423-788-1425; civil phone: 423-788-1481; fax: 423-788-0138; 8AM-5PM (EST). *Civil Actions under $15,000, Eviction, Small Claims.*

General Information: Court will only search for a record if provided a case number. Access criminal records at the Jonesborough Court. Access current dockets at http://washington.mytncourts.com/. No sealed records released. Court makes copy: $.50 per page. Self serve copy: same. Certification fee: $5.00 per cert. Payee: Circuit Court Clerk. In state checks accepted. No credit cards accepted. Prepayment required.

Civil Name Search: Access: In person only. Visitors must perform in person searches themselves. Civil records archived since court started, computerized since 1989. Public use terminal has civil records back to 1989.

Probate Court 108 W Jackson, Ste 2109, Jonesborough, TN 37659; 423-753-1623; fax: 423-753-0190; 8:30AM-5PM (EST). *Probate.*

Wayne County

22nd District Circuit & General Sessions Court PO Box 869, 100 Court Circle #302, Waynesboro, TN 38485; 931-722-5519; fax: 931-722-9949; 8AM-4PM M,T,TH,F; 8AM-N Wed,Sat (CST). *Felony, Misdemeanor, Civil, Eviction, Small Claims.*

General Information: No juvenile or adoption records released. Will fax documents. Court makes copy: $.50 per page. Certification fee: $5.00. Payee: Circuit Court Clerk. Personal checks accepted, credit cards are not. Prepayment required.

Civil Name Search: Access: Phone, mail, in person. Both court and visitors may perform in person name searches. No search fee. Civil records archived on books from 1900s. Mail turnaround time 7-10 days. Civil PAT goes back to 1997.

Criminal Name Search: Access: Mail, in person. Both court and visitors may perform in person name searches. Search fee: $5.00 per name. Required to search: name, years to search, DOB, SSN. Criminal records archived on books from 1900s. Mail turnaround time 7-10 days. Criminal PAT goes back to 1997.

Chancery Court PO Box 101, Waynesboro, TN 38485; 931-722-5517; fax: 931-722-5758; 8AM-4:30PM (CST). *Civil, Probate.*

General Information: No adoption records released. Will fax documents to local or toll free line. Court makes copy: $.50 per page. Certification fee: $5.00 minimum or $.50 per page. Payee: Clerk and Master. Personal checks accepted, credit cards are not. Prepayment required. Mail requests: SASE requested.

Civil Name Search: Access: Mail, in person. Both court and visitors may perform in person name searches. No search fee. Civil records on books; computerized since 12/92. Mail turnaround time 2 days.

Weakley County

27th District Circuit & General Sessions Court 116 W Main St - Courthouse, 2nd Fl, Rm 203, Dresden, TN 38225; 731-364-3455; fax: 731-364-6765; 8AM-4:30PM (CST). *Felony, Misdemeanor, Civil, Eviction, Small Claims.*
www.weakleycountytn.gov/circuitcourtclerk.html

General Information: No adoption or sealed records released. Will not fax documents. Court makes copy: $.50 per page. Self serve copy: same. Certification fee: $5.00 per cert. Payee: Circuit Court Clerk. No personal checks accepted. Credit cards accepted. Prepayment required.

Civil Name Search: Access: In person only. Visitors must perform in person searches themselves. Civil records archived on since court started, on books; computerized since 1997. Civil PAT goes back to 1997.

Criminal Name Search: Access: In person only. Visitors must perform in person searches themselves. Required to search: name, years to search, DOB; SSN helpful. Criminal records archived on since court started, on books; computerized since 1997. Criminal PAT goes back to 1997.

Chancery Court PO Box 197, 116 W Main St #301, Dresden, TN 38225; 731-364-3454; fax: 731-364-5247; 8AM-4:30PM (CST). *Civil, Probate.*
www.weakleycountytn.gov/clerkandmaster.html

General Information: Court will not do searches for genealogy. No adoption or sealed records released. Will fax documents $1.00 per page, prepaid. Court makes copy: $.15 per page. Self serve copy: $.15 per page. Certification fee: $5.00. Payee: Clerk and Master. Personal checks accepted, credit cards are not. Prepayment required.

Civil Name Search: Access: Mail, in person. Both court and visitors may perform in person name searches. Search fee: None unless research requires 1 hour or more, then $20.00 per hour. Civil records on computer since 1982, prior records indexed from 1927; Probate to 1800s. Mail turnaround time 1 week.

White County

13th District Circuit & General Sessions Court 111 Depot St, #1, Sparta, TN 38583; 931-836-3205; fax: 931-836-3526; 8AM-5PM (CST). *Felony, Misdemeanor, Civil, Eviction, Small Claims.*
www.whiteccc.com/

General Information: No juvenile, adoption records released. Will fax documents $1.00 per page. Court makes copy: $.50 per page. Self serve copy: $.50 per page. Certification fee: $5.00 per cert. Payee: Circuit Court Clerk. No personal checks or credit cards accepted. Prepayment required.

Civil Name Search: Access: In person, online. Visitors must perform in person searches themselves. Civil records archived since court started, some are offsite, computerized since 1996. Civil PAT goes back to mid-1996. Current case dockets available free at www.whiteccc.com/ but no historical data.

Criminal Name Search: Access: In person, online. Visitors must perform in person searches themselves. Criminal records archived since court started, some are offsite; computerized records since 1996. Criminal PAT available. Current case dockets available free at www.whiteccc.com/ but no historical data.

Chancery Court White County Courthouse, Rm 303, Sparta, TN 38583; 931-836-3787; fax: 931-836-2124; 8AM-4PM (CST). *Civil, Probate.*

General Information: No adoption records released. Will fax documents if prepaid. Court makes copy: $.50 per page. Self serve copy: same. Certification fee: $5.00. Payee: Clerk and Master. Personal checks accepted, credit cards are not. Prepayment required. Mail requests: SASE required.

Civil Name Search: Access: Phone, in person. Visitors must perform in person searches themselves. No search fee. Overall records go back to 1842.

Williamson County

21st District Circuit & General Sessions Court 135 4th Ave, Rm 203, Franklin, TN 37064; 615-790-5454; fax: 615-790-5411; 8AM-4:30PM (CST). *Felony, Misdemeanor, Civil, Eviction, Small Claims.*
www.williamsoncounty-tn.gov/index.asp?nid=243

General Information: Fax for the Gen Sessions court- 615-790-5626. Will fax documents to local or toll-free number. Court makes copy: $.50 per page. Certification fee: $5.00 per doc. Payee: Circuit Court Clerk. Personal checks accepted. Visa/MC/AmEx cards accepted; add 5% usage fee. Prepayment required.

Civil Name Search: Access: In person only. Visitors must perform in person searches themselves. Civil records archived on books from 1810, on computer from 1992. Civil PAT goes back to 1992.

Criminal Name Search: Access: In person only. Visitors must perform in person searches themselves. Required to search: name, years to search; also helpful: DOB, SSN. Criminal records archived on books from 1810, on computer from 1992. Criminal PAT goes back to same as civil.

Chancery Court Clerk & Master, PO Box 1666, 135 4th Ave S Rm 236, Franklin, TN 37065; 615-790-5428; fax: 615-790-5626; 8AM-4:30PM (CST). *Civil, Probate.*
www.williamsonchancery.org/

General Information: No adoption, sealed records released. Will not fax documents. Court makes copy: $.50 per page. Certification fee: $5.00 per document. Payee: Clerk and Master. Local checks accepted. Major credit cards accepted, service fee charged. Prepayment required. Mail requests: SASE requested.

Civil Name Search: Access: Phone, mail, in person. Both court and visitors may perform in person name searches. No search fee. Civil records on computer since 1991, prior records on books since 1800s (no probate on computer). Mail 1-2 weeks. Public use terminal has civil records back to 1991.

Wilson County

15th District Circuit Court PO Box 518, 134 S College St, Lebanon, TN 37088-0518; 615-444-2042; fax: 615-449-3420; 8AM-4PM M-TH; 8AM-5PM F (CST). *Felony, Civil Actions over $25,000.*

General Information: No adoption, juvenile records released. Will not fax documents. Court makes copy: $.50 per page. Certification fee: $5.00 per cert. Payee: Circuit Court Clerk. Business checks accepted. No credit cards accepted. Prepayment required.

Civil Name Search: Access: In person, mail. Visitors must perform in person searches themselves. Search fee: none if SASE supplied. Civil records on computer from 1991, on microfiche from 1940s. Civil PAT goes back to 1990.

Criminal Name Search: Access: In person only. Visitors must perform in person searches themselves. Required to search: name, years to search, DOB. Criminal records archived in office from 1982, indexed on computer from 1991, on microfiche from 1940s. Criminal PAT goes back to same as civil.

General Sessions Court 115 E High St, Lebanon, TN 37088; 615-444-2045; fax: 615-443-1186; 8AM-4PM (CST). *Misdemeanor, Civil Actions under $25,000, Eviction, Small Claims.*

General Information: No adoption, juvenile records released. Will not fax documents. Court makes copy: $.50 per page. Certification fee: $5.00 per cert. Payee: Circuit Court Clerk. Personal checks accepted, credit cards are not. Prepayment required.

Civil Name Search: Access: In person only. Visitors must perform in person searches themselves. Civil records archived in office from 1982, on computer from 1990, on microfiche from 1940s. Civil PAT goes back to 1991.

Criminal Name Search: Access: In person only. Visitors must perform in person searches themselves. Required to search: name, years to search, DOB. Criminal records computerized from 1990. Criminal PAT goes back to 1991.

Probate Court PO Box 1557, 134 S College St, Lebanon, TN 37088; 615-444-2835; fax: 615-443-6191; 8AM-4PM (CST). *Probate, Civil Actions.*
www.wilsoncountytn.com/courts.htm

General Information: Probate is now Clerk & Master.

Texas

Time Zone:	**CST & MST***

* Texas' two western-most counties are MST:
They are: El Paso and Hudspeth,

Capital:	**Austin, Travis County**
# of Counties:	**254**
State Web:	**www.texasonline.com**
Court Web:	**www.courts.state.tx.us**

Administration Office of Court Administration, PO Box 12066, Austin, TX, 78711; 512-463-1625, Fax: 512-463-1648.

The Appellate Courts The Supreme Court has the final appellate jurisdiction in civil cases and juvenile cases. The Court of Criminal Appeals has the final appellate jurisdiction in criminal cases. The 14 Courts of Appeals hear intermediate appeals from trial courts with their respective districts.

Case records of the Supreme Court can be searched at www.supreme.courts.state.tx.us. Appellate Court case information is searchable free at the website of each Appellate Court, reached online from www.courts.state.tx.us/courts/coa.asp. Court of Criminal Appeals opinions are found at www.cca.courts.state.tx.us.

The Texas Courts

Court	Type	How Organized	Jurisdiction Highpoints
District*	General	456 Courts in 456 Districts BUT Record Keeping is by County	Felony, Civil, Divorce, Juvenile, Contested Probate
County Constitutional*	Limited	254 Courts in 254 Counties	Misdemeanors, Civil Actions under $10,000, Uncontested Probate, Juvenile
County Courts at Law		233 Courts	Misdemeanor, Civil up to $100,000 or more
Justice of the Peace	Limited	819 Courts	Misdemeanor, Civil under $10,000, Small Claims, Ordinance
Municipal*	Limited	920 Courts in 920 Cities	Misdemeanor, Traffic, Ordinance
Probate	Limited	18 Courts in Counties	Probate

* = profiled in this book

Details on the Court Structure Generally, Texas **District Courts** have general civil jurisdiction and exclusive felony jurisdiction, along with typical variations such as contested probate and divorce. There are 360 Districts fully within one county and 96 Districts within more than one county. There can be multiple Districts and multiple District Courts in one courthouse. But the record keeping is organized by county and there is only one searchable database per courthouse. Therefore the profiles of the District Courts are herein organized by county.

The **County Court** structure consists of two forms of courts - **Constitutional** and **At Law**. The Constitutional upper civil claim limit is $10,000 while the At Law upper limit is $100,000 and some jurisdictions are higher. County Courts have original jurisdiction for misdemeanors with fines greater than $500 or jail sentences. Within the county the District Court or County Court can handles **evictions.** In 69 counties, one individual serves as both the District Clerk and County Clerk.

Justice Courts handle misdemeanors where the fine is less than $500 and no jail sentences.

Probate is handled in **Probate Court** in the ten largest counties and in the County Court elsewhere. The County Clerk is responsible for these records in every county.

A PDF file of the addresses and phone numbers of the 920 **Municipal Courts** is found at www.courts.state.tx.us/pubs/JudicialDirectory/MNCourts.pdf.

Record Searching Facts You Need to Know

Fees and Record Searching Tips

Often, a record search is automatically combined for two courts, for example a District Court with a County Court, or both County Courts. Most District Courts charge $5.00 to do a name search, but nearly 15% charge $10.00. Most courts charge $1.00 for a copy, a few charge between $.25 and $.50. Over half of the courts provide public access terminals for the public to view docket indices.

Online Access is By Court or County, is not Statewide

There is no statewide portal of case records. However, at press time over 25% of the courts offer online access. At least 133 local county courts provide online access to civil records and at least 127 to criminal records. 63 of the civil courts and 83 of the criminal courts use a designated vendor – www.idocket.com.

Anderson County

District Court 500 N Church St, #18, Palestine, TX 75801; 903-723-7412; fax: 903-723-7491; 8AM-N, 1-5PM (CST). *Felony, Civil, Family.* www.co.anderson.tx.us

General Information: The court also holds Family Cases. No juvenile or adoption records released. Will not fax documents. Court makes copy: $1.00 per page. Certification fee: $1.00 per page. Payee: Anderson County District Clerk. Personal checks accepted, credit cards are not. Prepayment required. Mail requests: SASE required.

Civil Name Search: Access: Phone, mail, in person. Both court and visitors may perform in person name searches. Search fee: $5.00 per name. Civil records on computer from 1984; prior on card index back to 1946. Mail turnaround time 2-4 days. Civil PAT goes back to 1984.

Criminal Name Search: Access: Mail, in person. Both court and visitors may perform in person name searches. Search fee: $5.00 per name. Required to search: name, years to search, DOB, SSN. Criminal records computerized from 1984; prior on index. Mail turnaround time 2-4 days. Criminal PAT goes back to same as civil.

County Court Anderson County Clerk, 500 N Church, Rm 10, Palestine, TX 75801; 903-723-7432; probate phone: 903-723-7432; fax: 903-723-4625; 8AM-5PM (CST). *Misdemeanor, Civil, Probate.* www.co.anderson.tx.us/

General Information: Probate fax is same as main fax number. Records dealing with mental matters are restricted. Will fax documents for fee. Call first. Court makes copy: $1.00 per page. Self serve copy: same. Certification fee: $5.00. Payee: County Clerk. Personal checks accepted, credit cards are not. Prepayment required. Mail requests: SASE required.

Civil Name Search: Access: Mail, in person. Both court and visitors may perform in person name searches. Search fee: $5.00 per name. Civil records on computer from 1982. Mail turnaround time 10 days. Civil PAT goes back to 1982.

Criminal Name Search: Access: Mail, in person. Both court and visitors may perform in person name searches. Search fee: $5.00 per name. Required to search: name, years to search, DOB. Criminal records computerized from 1969. Mail turnaround time up to 10 days. Criminal PAT goes back to 1969. Terminal results include SSN.

Andrews County

District Court 201 N Main St Rm 102, Andrews, TX 79714-6517; 432-524-1417; 8AM-5PM (CST). *Felony, Civil.*

General Information: No juvenile, mental, sealed, terminations or adoption records released. Will not fax documents. Court makes copy: $1.00 first page, $.50 each add'l. Certification fee: $2.00. Payee: District Clerk. Personal checks accepted, credit cards are not. Prepayment required. Mail requests: SASE required.

Civil Name Search: Access: Mail, in person. Only the court performs in person name searches; visitors may not. Search fee: $5.00 per name. Civil records computerized since 1975. Mail turnaround time 1 day.

Criminal Name Search: Access: Mail, in person. Only the court performs in person name searches; visitors may not. Search fee: $5.00 per name. Required to search: name, years to search, DOB; also helpful: SSN. Criminal records computerized back to 1910. Mail turnaround time 1 day.

County Court PO Box 727, Andrews, TX 79714; 432-524-1426; fax: 432-524-1464; 8AM-5PM (CST). *Misdemeanor, Civil, Probate.*

General Information: Probate in a separate, manual index at this same address No juvenile, mental, sealed records released. Will not fax documents. Court makes copy: $1.00 per page. Certification fee: $5.00 per document plus copy fee. Payee: Kenda Heckler County Clerk. Personal checks accepted if in state. No credit cards accepted. Prepayment required. Mail requests: SASE not required.

Civil Name Search: Access: Phone, mail, in person. Both court and visitors may perform in person name searches. Search fee: $10.00 per name. Civil records on computer since 1980; prior records in manual index. Mail turnaround time 1 day.

Criminal Name Search: Access: Phone, mail, in person. Only the court performs in person name searches; visitors may not. Search fee: $10.00 per name. Required to search: name, years to search, DOB or SSN; also helpful: sex. Criminal records in manual index. Mail turnaround time 1 day.

Angelina County

District Court PO Box 908, Lufkin, TX 75902; 936-634-4312; fax: 936-634-5915; 8AM-5PM (CST). *Felony, Civil.* www.angelinacounty.net

General Information: No juvenile, mental, sealed, or adoption records released. Will fax documents $5.00 fee. Court makes copy: $1.00 per page. Certification fee: $2.00 per document. Payee: District Clerk. No personal checks. No credit cards accepted. Prepayment required. Mail requests: SASE required.

Civil Name Search: Access: Mail, in person. Both court and visitors may perform in person name searches. Search fee: $5.00 per name. Civil records on computer from 1996, on index books from 1800s. Note: Must state whether search is on plaintiff or defendant. Mail turnaround time 2-3 days. Civil PAT goes back to 1986. Terminal results also show SSNs.

Criminal Name Search: Access: Mail, in person. Both court and visitors may perform in person name searches. Search fee: $5.00 per name. Required to search: name, years to search, DOB; also helpful: SSN. Criminal records computerized from 1984, on index books from 1800s. Mail turnaround time 2-3 days. Criminal PAT goes back to 1986. Terminal results include SSN.

County Court PO Box 908, 215 E Lufkin Ave, Lufkin, TX 75902; 936-634-8339; fax: 936-634-8460; 8AM-5PM (CST). *Misdemeanor, Civil, Probate.* www.angelinacounty.net

General Information: No mental or sealed records released. These records are not filed in our office. Will not fax documents. Court makes copy: $1.00 per page. Certification fee: $5.00. Payee: County Clerk. Business checks accepted. No credit cards accepted. Prepayment required. Mail requests: SASE required.

Civil Name Search: Access: Mail, in person, online. Both court and visitors may perform in person name searches. Search fee: $5.00 per name plus 10-year period. Civil records go back to 1893; computerized records go back to 8/1995. Mail turnaround time 1-2 days. Online access to dockets is through www.idocket.com; registration and password required. Civil cases from 11/30/96; probate from 1/31/95.

Criminal Name Search: Access: Mail, in person, online. Both court and visitors may perform in person name searches. Search fee: $5.00 per name plus 10-year period. Will search back to 1984,. Required to search: name, years to search; also helpful: DOB. Criminal records go back to 1893; computerized records go back to 1983. Mail turnaround time 1-2 days.

Online access to misdemeanor dockets is through www.idocket.com; registration and password required. Misdemeanor cases from 12/31/83.

Aransas County

District Court 301 N Live Oak, Rockport, TX 78382; 361-790-0128; fax: 361-790-5211; 8AM-5PM (CST). *Felony, Civil.*
www.aransascountytx.gov/districtclerk/

General Information: Online identifiers in results same as on public terminal. No juvenile, mental, sealed, or adoption records released. Will not fax documents. Court makes copy: $1.00 per page. Self serve copy: same. Certification fee: $1.00 per document plus copy fee. Payee: District Clerk. Personal checks accepted. Discover CC accepted. Prepayment required. Mail requests: SASE required.

Civil Name Search: Access: Mail, in person, online. Both court and visitors may perform in person name searches. Search fee: $5.00 per name. Civil records in index books from 1800s, computerized since 1999. Mail turnaround time 1-2 days. Civil PAT goes back to 2000. Online case access at www.idocket.com; registration and password required. Civil and family law records (no probate) go back to 01/01/2001. One free name search permitted a day, otherwise subscription required.

Criminal Name Search: Access: Mail, in person, online. Both court and visitors may perform in person name searches. Search fee: $5.00 per name. Criminal docket on books from 1800s, computerized since 1999. Mail turnaround time 1-2 days. Criminal PAT goes back to 1965. Online index to 01/01/1960 at www.idocket.com; registration and password required. One free name search permitted a day, otherwise subscription required.

County Court at Law 301 N Live Oak St, Aransa County Courthouse, Rockport, TX 78382; 361-790-0122; fax: 361-790-0119; 8AM-4:30PM (CST). *Misdemeanor, Civil, Probate.*
www.aransascountytx.gov/clerk/

General Information: The court will not respond to search requests by telephone. No mental or sealed records released; we do not have juvenile or adoption records in our office. Will fax documents to local or toll free line. Court makes copy: $1.00 per page. Certification fee: $5.00 per doc. Payee: County Clerk. In-state personal checks accepted with ID. No credit cards accepted. Prepayment required. Mail requests: SASE required.

Civil Name Search: Access: Mail, in person, online. Both court and visitors may perform in person name searches. Search fee: $10.00 per name. Civil records in index books from 1947, computerized records go back to 1995. Mail turnaround time 2 days. Civil PAT goes back to 1995. Address appears on terminal if available. Online case access at www.idocket.com; registration and password required. Civil and family law records, probate, go back to 01/01/2001. One free name search permitted a day, otherwise subscription required.

Criminal Name Search: Access: Mail, in person, online. Both court and visitors may perform in person name searches. Search fee: $10.00 per name. Required to search: name, years to search, DOB. Criminal docket on books from 1947; computerized records go back to 1992. Mail turnaround time 2 days. Criminal PAT goes back to 1992. Online index to 01/01/1960 at www.idocket.com; registration and password required. One free name search permitted a day, otherwise subscription required.

Archer County

District Court PO Box 815, Archer City, TX 76351; 940-574-4615; fax: 940-574-2432; 8:30AM-5PM (CST). *Felony, Civil.*
General Information: No juvenile, mental, sealed, or adoption records released. Will fax documents after search fee is paid. Court makes copy: $1.00 per page. Self serve copy: same. Certification fee: $1.00 per doc plus copy fee. Payee: District Clerk. Personal checks accepted, credit cards are not. Prepayment required. Mail requests: SASE helpful.

Civil Name Search: Access: Mail, in person. Both court and visitors may perform in person name searches. Search fee: $5.00 per name. Fee is per index searched. Civil records in index books from 1900s. Mail turnaround time 2-3 days.

Criminal Name Search: Access: Mail, in person. Both court and visitors may perform in person name searches. Search fee: $5.00 per name. Fee is per index searched. Criminal docket on books from 1900s. Mail turnaround time 2-3 days.

County Court PO Box 427, Archer City, TX 76351; 940-574-4302; fax: 940-574-2876; 8:30AM-5PM (CST). *Misdemeanor, Civil, Probate.*
General Information: Probate is a separate index at this same address. Probate fax is same as main fax number. No juvenile, mental, sealed, or adoption records released. Will fax documents $2.00 per page. Court makes copy: $1.00 per page. Self serve copy: same. Certification fee: $5.00 per doc plus copy fee. Payee: County Clerk. Personal checks accepted. Major credit cards accepted. Prepayment required. Mail requests: SASE required.

Civil Name Search: Access: Phone, mail, in person. Both court and visitors may perform in person name searches. Search fee: $5.00 per name.

Fee is per index searched. Civil records in index books from 1900s. Mail turnaround time 1 day. Civil PAT goes back to 2007.

Criminal Name Search: Access: Phone, mail, in person. Both court and visitors may perform in person name searches. Search fee: $5.00 per name. Fee is per index searched. Criminal docket on books from 1900s. Mail turnaround time 1 day. Criminal PAT goes back to 2006.

Armstrong County

District & County Court PO Box 309, 100 Trice St., Claude, TX 79019; 806-226-2081; fax: 806-226-5301; 8AM-N, 1-5PM (CST). *Felony, Misdemeanor, Civil, Probate.*
www.co.armstrong.tx.us/ips/cms/districtcourt/

General Information: Probate is a separate index at this same address. Probate fax is same as main fax number. No juvenile, mental, sealed, or adoption records released. Will fax documents $1.00 per fax. Court makes copy: $1.00 per page. Self serve copy: same. Certification fee: $5.00 per cert plus copy fee. Payee: County Clerk. Personal checks accepted, credit cards are not. Prepayment required. Mail requests: SASE required.

Civil Name Search: Access: Mail, in person. Both court and visitors may perform in person name searches. Search fee: $5.00 per name. Civil records in index books from 1800s. Mail turnaround time 1-2 days.

Criminal Name Search: Access: Mail, in person. Both court and visitors may perform in person name searches. Search fee: $5.00 per name. Criminal docket on books from 1800s; computerized back to 1992. Mail turnaround time 1-2 days. Public use terminal has crim records back to 1912.

Atascosa County

District Court Courthouse Circle, #4-B, Jourdanton, TX 78026; 830-769-3011; fax: 830-769-1332; 8AM-N, 1-4:30PM (CST). *Felony, Civil.*
www.81st-218thdistrictcourt.org/

General Information: No juvenile, mental, sealed, or adoption records released. Fee to fax out file $2.00 per page. Court makes copy: $1.00 per page. Self serve copy: same. Certification fee: $1.00. Payee: District Clerk. Personal checks accepted, credit cards are not. Prepayment required. Mail requests: SASE required.

Civil Name Search: Access: Mail, in person. Both court and visitors may perform in person name searches. Search fee: $5.00 per name, separate search plaintiff or defendant. Required to search: name, years to search; also helpful: address. Civil records in index books from 1857.

Criminal Name Search: Access: Mail, in person. Both court and visitors may perform in person name searches. Search fee: $5.00 per name. Required to search: name, years to search; also helpful: DOB, SSN. Criminal docket on books from 1857.

County Court #1 Courthouse Circle, #102, Jourdanton, TX 78026; 830-767-2511; fax: 830-769-1021; 8AM-4:30PM (CST). *Misdemeanor, Civil, Probate.*
General Information: No juvenile, mental, sealed, or adoption records released. Will fax documents $1.50 per page. Court makes copy: $1.00 per page. Certification fee: $5.00. Payee: County Clerk. Personal checks accepted, credit cards are not. Prepayment required. Mail requests: SASE required for civil.

Civil Name Search: Access: Mail, in person. Both court and visitors may perform in person name searches. No search fee. Civil records in index books from 1900s; on computer back to 2000. Mail turnaround time 1 week. Civil PAT goes back to 2000. Add'l scanned documents may contain add'l identifiers.

Criminal Name Search: Access: In person only. Visitors must perform in person searches themselves. Criminal docket on books from 1900s; on computer back to 2000. Criminal PAT goes back to 2000. Add'l scanned documents may contain add'l identifiers.

Austin County

District Court 1 E Main, Bellville, TX 77418-1598; 979-865-5911 x2255; fax: 979-865-8350; 8AM-N, 1-5PM (CST). *Felony, Civil.*
www.austincounty.com/dclerk.html

General Information: The 155 District website is www.cvtv.net/~tx155district/. Daily dockets available. No juvenile, mental, sealed, or adoption records released. Fee to fax out file $2.00 each. Court makes copy: $1.00 per page. Self serve copy: same. Certification fee: Included in copy fee; will certify only if document is complete. Payee: District Clerk. Personal checks accepted, credit cards are not. Prepayment required. Mail requests: SASE required.

Civil Name Search: Access: Mail, in person. Both court and visitors may perform in person name searches. Search fee: $5.00 per name. Civil records in index books from 1843; on computer back to 1995. Mail turnaround time 1 day. Civil PAT goes back to 1995. Terminal results also show SSNs.

Criminal Name Search: Access: Mail, in person. Both court and visitors may perform in person name searches. Search fee: $5.00 per name. Required to search: name, years to search; also helpful: DOB, SSN. Criminal docket on books from 1843; on computer back to 1996. Mail turnaround time 1 day. Criminal PAT goes back to 1996. Terminal results include SSN.

County Court at Law 1 E Main, Bellville, TX 77418; 979-865-5911; criminal phone: x2233; civil phone: x2234; probate phone: x2234; fax: 979-865-0336; 8AM-5PM (CST). *Misdemeanor, Civil, Probate.*

General Information: Probate fax is same as main fax number. No juvenile, mental, sealed, or adoption records released. Will fax documents $2.00 per page. Court makes copy: $1.00 per page. Self serve copy: same. Certification fee: $5.00 per document plus copy fee. Payee: Carrie Gregor, County Clerk. Personal checks accepted, credit cards are not. Prepayment required. Mail requests: SASE not required.

Civil Name Search: Access: Mail, in person. Both court and visitors may perform in person name searches. Search fee: $5.00 per name. Civil records on computer from 1983, index books from 1843. Mail turnaround time 2-3 days. Civil PAT goes back to 1983.

Criminal Name Search: Access: Mail, in person. Both court and visitors may perform in person name searches. Search fee: $5.00 per name. Required to search: name, years to search, DOB; also helpful: SSN. Criminal records computerized from 1/85; index books from 1876. Mail turnaround time 2-3 days. Criminal PAT goes back to 1985. PAT results may include SSN and DL number.

Bailey County

District Court 300 S 1st St, Muleshoe, TX 79347; 806-272-3165; fax: 806-272-3124; 8AM-5PM (CST). *Felony, Civil.*

General Information: No juvenile, mental, sealed, or adoption records released. Will fax documents $1.00 per page. Court makes copy: $1.00 per page. Self serve copy: same. Certification fee: $1.00 per page. Payee: District Clerk. Personal checks accepted, credit cards are not. Prepayment required. Mail requests: SASE required.

Civil Name Search: Access: Phone, mail, fax, in person, online. Both court and visitors may perform in person name searches. Search fee: $5.00 per name. Civil records in index books, archived from 1925, computerized back to 1995. Mail turnaround time 1 day. Online access is through www.idocket.com; registration and password required. Records go back to 12/31/1995. One free name search permitted a day, otherwise subscription required.

Criminal Name Search: Access: Phone, mail, in person, online. Both court and visitors may perform in person name searches. Search fee: $5.00 per name. Criminal index in books, archived from 1925, computerized back to 1995. Mail turnaround time 1 day. Online access is through www.idocket.com; registration and password required. Records go back to 12/31/1995. One free name search permitted a day, otherwise subscription required.

County Court 300 S 1st St, #200, Muleshoe, TX 79347; 806-272-3044; fax: 806-272-3538; 8:30AM-N, 1-5PM (CST). *Misdemeanor, Civil, Probate.*

General Information: Probate has a separate index. Probate fax is same as main fax number. No juvenile, mental, sealed, or adoption records released. Will fax documents. Court makes copy: $1.00 per page. Self serve copy: same. Certification fee: $5.00 per document. Payee: County Clerk. Personal checks accepted, credit cards are not. Prepayment required. Mail requests: SASE required.

Civil Name Search: Access: Mail, in person, online. Both court and visitors may perform in person name searches. Search fee: $10.00 per name. Civil records in index books, archived from 1925. Mail turnaround time 10 days. Online access is through www.idocket.com; registration and password required. Civil records go back to 12/31/1995 and 13/31/96 for probate. One free name search permitted a day, otherwise subscription required.

Criminal Name Search: Access: Mail, in person, online. Both court and visitors may perform in person name searches. Search fee: $10.00 per name. Criminal index in books, archived from 1925. Mail turnaround time 10 days. Online access is through www.idocket.com; registration and password required. Records go back to 12/31/1996. One free name search permitted a day, otherwise subscription required.

Bandera County

District Court PO Box 2688, 3360 State Highway 173N, Bandera, TX 78003; 830-796-4606; fax: 830-796-8499; 7:30AM-4:30PM (CST). *Felony, Civil, Probate.*

www.banderacounty.org/departments/district_clerk.htm

General Information: Online identifiers in results same as on public terminal. No juvenile, mental or sealed records released. Fee to fax out file $2.00 1st page, $1.00 each add'l. Court makes copy: $1.00 per page certified; non-certified is $1.00 1st pg, $.25 each add'l pg per doc. Certification fee: $5.00. Payee: Bandera County District Clerk. Personal checks accepted. Major credit cards accepted. Prepayment required. Mail requests: SASE required.

Civil Name Search: Access: Phone, fax, mail, in person, online. Both court and visitors may perform in person name searches. Search fee: $5.00 per name plus $5.00 per record or document. Required to search: name, years to search; also helpful: address. Civil records on computer back to 1988, index books from 1857. Mail turnaround time 2 days. Civil PAT goes back to 1990. Civil case information is free at www.idocket.com. Registration and password required. Records go back to 12/31/1990. One free name search permitted a day, otherwise subscription required.

Criminal Name Search: Access: Fax, mail, in person, online. Both court and visitors may perform in person name searches. Search fee: $5.00 per name plus $5.00 per record or document. Required to search: name, years to search, signed release; also helpful: address, DOB, SSN. Criminal records computerized from 1988, index books from 1857. Mail turnaround time 2 days. Criminal PAT goes back to same as civil. Felony record index access is through www.idocket.com; registration and password required; records go back to 12/31/1990. One free name search permitted a day, otherwise subscription required. Online results show middle initial, DOB.

County Court PO Box 823, 500 Main St, Bandera, TX 78003; 830-796-3332; fax: 830-796-8323; 8AM-4:30PM (CST). *Misdemeanor, Civil, Eviction, Probate.*

www.banderacounty.org/departments/county_clerk.htm

General Information: No juvenile, mental or sealed records released. Fee to fax out file $2.00 1st page, $1.00 each add'l. Court makes copy: $1.00 per page. Certification fee: $5.00 per document plus copy fee. Payee: Bandera County Clerk. Personal checks accepted. Major credit cards accepted. Prepayment required. Mail requests: SASE required.

Civil Name Search: Access: Fax, mail, in person, online. Both court and visitors may perform in person name searches. Search fee: $5.00 per name. Required to search: name, years to search; also helpful: address. Civil records on computer back to 1994, index books back to 1857. Mail turnaround time 2 days. Public use terminal available, records go back to 1994. Online access to dockets is through www.idocket.com; registration and password required. Civil cases from 1/1994; probate from 1/1991. One free name search permitted a day, otherwise subscription required.

Criminal Name Search: Access: Fax, mail, in person, online. Both court and visitors may perform in person name searches. Search fee: $5.00 per name. Required to search: name, years to search, signed release; also helpful: address, DOB, SSN. Criminal records computerized from 1990, index books back to 1857. Mail turnaround time 2 days. Public use terminal available, crim records go back to 1990. Online access to dockets is through www.idocket.com; registration and password required. Misdemeanor cases from 1/1992. One free name search permitted a day, otherwise subscription required. Online results show name, DOB.

Bastrop County

District Court PO Box 770, Bastrop, TX 78602; 512-332-7244; fax: 512-332-7249; 8AM-5PM (CST). *Felony, Civil.*

www.co.bastrop.tx.us/site/content/districtclerk

General Information: No juvenile, mental, sealed, or adoption records released. Court makes copy: $.50 per page. Self serve copy: same. Certification fee: $1.00 per page. Payee: District Clerk. Personal checks accepted. Major credit cards accepted. Prepayment required. Mail requests: SASE required.

Civil Name Search: Access: Mail, in person, fax, online. Both court and visitors may perform in person name searches. Search fee: $5.00 per name. Civil records on microfilm from 1986, archived from early 1800s. Mail turnaround time 1 day. Civil PAT goes back to 1996. Search online docket at www.co.bastrop.tx.us:8080/default.aspx.

Criminal Name Search: Access: Mail, in person, fax, online. Both court and visitors may perform in person name searches. Search fee: $5.00 per name. Required to search: name, years to search, signed release. Criminal records on computer since 1989; prior on microfilm from 1986, archived from early 1800s. Mail turnaround time 1 day. Criminal PAT goes back to 1989. Search online docket at www.co.bastrop.tx.us:8080/default.aspx.

County Court PO Box 577, Bastrop, TX 78602; 512-332-7234; fax: 512-332-7241; 8AM-5:PM (CST). *Misdemeanor, Probate.*

www.co.bastrop.tx.us/site/content/countyclerk

General Information: No juvenile, mental, sealed, or adoption records released. Fee to fax out file $5.00. Court makes copy: $1.00 per page. Certification fee: $5.00, if exemplification then $7.00 per case. Payee: Bastrop County Clerk. Personal checks accepted, include DL number and DOB on back. Credit cards accepted; $3.00 convenience fee will be added. Prepayment required. Mail requests: SASE required.

Criminal Name Search: Access: Mail, in person, online. Both court and visitors may perform in person name searches. Search fee: $5.00 per name. Required to search: name, years to search, DOB, SSN. Criminal records on computer since 1986, prior on index books. Mail turnaround time 1-2 days. Public use terminal has crim records back to 1986, countywide. Search online docket at www.co.bastrop.tx.us:8080/default.aspx.

Baylor County

District & County Court 101 S Washington St, #C, Seymour, TX 76380-2566; 940-889-3322; fax: 940-889-4300; 8:30AM-5PM (CST). *Felony, Misdemeanor, Civil, Probate.*

General Information: No juvenile, mental, sealed, or adoption records released. Will not fax documents. Court makes copy: $1.00 per page. Certification fee: $3.00 felony, $6.00 misdemeanor County Court certification. Payee: Baylor County Clerk. Personal checks accepted, credit cards are not. Prepayment required. Mail requests: SASE required.

Civil Name Search: Access: Phone, mail, in person. Both court and visitors may perform in person name searches. Search fee: $10.00 per name. Civil records in books from 1900s. Mail turnaround time 1-2 days.

Criminal Name Search: Access: Phone, mail, in person. Both court and visitors may perform in person name searches. Search fee: $10.00 per name. Criminal records in books from 1900s. Mail turnaround time 1-2 days.

Bee County

District Court PO Box 666, 105 Corpus Christi, Beeville, TX 78104-0666; 361-362-3242; fax: 361-362-3282; 8AM-5PM (CST). *Felony, Civil.* www.co.bee.tx.us/ips/cms/districtcourt/

General Information: No juvenile, mental, sealed, or adoption records released. Will fax documents. Court makes copy: $1.00 per page. Certification fee: $5.00. Payee: District Clerk. No personal checks accepted, will accept business checks, money orders and cashiers checks. Visa/MC accepted. Prepayment required. Mail requests: SASE required.

Civil Name Search: Access: Mail, in person, online. Both court and visitors may perform in person name searches. Search fee: $5.00 per name. Civil index on docket books from 1856, computerized since 2000. Mail turnaround time 1-5 days. Civil PAT goes back to 2000. Online access is at www.idocket.com; registration and password required. A fee service; only one free name search per day. Records may go back to 12/31/1987.

Criminal Name Search: Access: Mail, in person, online. Both court and visitors may perform in person name searches. Search fee: $5.00 per name. Required to search: name, years to search, signed release. Criminal records indexed in books from 1856, computerized since 2000. Mail turnaround time 1-5 days. Criminal PAT goes back to same as civil. Felony case record access at www.idocket.com; registration and password required. A fee service; only one free name search a day. Records may go back to 12/31/1994.

County Court 105 W Corpus Christi St, Rm 108, Beeville, TX 78102; 361-362-3245; fax: 361-362-3247; 8AM-N, 1-5PM (CST). *Misdemeanor, Civil, Probate.*

General Information: Probate fax is same as main fax number. Fee to fax out file $2.00 per page. Court makes copy: $1.00 per page. Certification fee: $2.00 per page includes copy fee. Add $5.00 for certificate. Payee: County Clerk. Personal checks accepted, credit cards are not. Prepayment required. Mail requests: SASE required.

Civil Name Search: Access: Mail, in person. Both court and visitors may perform in person name searches. Search fee: $5.00 per name. Civil index on docket books from 1900. Mail turnaround time 10 days.

Criminal Name Search: Access: Mail, in person. Both court and visitors may perform in person name searches. Search fee: $6.00 per name. Required to search: name, years to search, DOB; also helpful: SSN. Criminal records indexed in books from 1900. Mail turnaround time 10 days.

Bell County

District Court PO Box 909, 1201 Huey Rd, Belton, TX 76513; 254-933-5197; criminal phone: 254-933-5957; civil phone: 254-933-5191; criminal fax: 254-933-5199; civil fax: 8AM-5PM; 8AM-5PM (CST). *Felony, Civil.* www.bellcountytx.com/districtcourts/index.htm

General Information: The fax for the civil section is 254-933-5292. The above number goes to the criminal section. Address correspondence to the District Clerk. No juvenile, mental, sealed, or adoption records released. Will fax documents for $5.00 first page, $1.00 each add'l page. Court makes copy: $.50 per page. Self serve copy: same. Certification fee: $1.00 per page. Payee: District Clerk, Bell County. No personal checks accepted. Major credit cards accepted in person with ID. Prepayment required. Mail requests: SASE required.

Civil Name Search: Access: Mail, in person, online. Both court and visitors may perform in person name searches. Search fee: $5.00 per name. Civil records on computer back to 1987, alpha index from 1982, chrono from 1800. Mail turnaround time 1-2 days. Civil PAT goes back to 1987. Access the current civil docket data at www.bellcountytx.com/districtcourts/dctcor_civil_docket.htm. The data is in PDF format.

Criminal Name Search: Access: Mail, in person, online. Both court and visitors may perform in person name searches. Search fee: $5.00 per name. Required to search: name, years to search, DOB; also helpful, SSN, signed release, cause number. Criminal records computerized from 1987, alpha index from 1982, chrono from 1800. Mail turnaround time 1-2 days. Criminal PAT goes back to same as civil. the current criminal docket and calendar is found at www.bellcountytx.com/districtcourts/dctcor_criminal_docket.htm.

County Court 1201 Huey Rd, Bell County Clerk's Office, PO Box 480, Belton, TX 76513; 254-933-5160; criminal phone: 254-933-5170; civil phone: 254-933-5174; probate phone: 254-933-5167; fax: 254-933-5176; 8AM-5PM (CST). *Misdemeanor, Civil, Probate.* www.co.bell.tx.us/countyclerk/index.htm

General Information: No juvenile, mental, sealed, or adoption records released. Will not fax documents. Court makes copy: $1.00 per page. Self serve copy: same. Certification fee: $1.00. Payee: County Clerk. Local checks accepted only. Major credit cards accepted if in person. Prepayment required. Mail requests: SASE not required.

Civil Name Search: Access: Mail, in person. Both court and visitors may perform in person name searches. Search fee: $5.00 per name. Civil records on computer back to 9/1989. Mail turnaround time 5 days. Civil PAT goes back to 1989.

Criminal Name Search: Access: Mail, in person. Both court and visitors may perform in person name searches. Search fee: $5.00 per name. Required to search: name, years to search, DOB, SSN. Criminal records computerized from 1986. Mail turnaround time 5 days. Criminal PAT goes back to 1986, countywide.

Bexar County

District Court - Central Records Paul Elizondo Tower, Basement, 101 W Nueva, San Antonio, TX 78205; 210-335-2113; criminal phone: 210-335-2591; civil phone: 210-335-2653; criminal fax: 210-335-3956; civil fax: 8AM-5PM; 8AM-5PM (CST). *Felony, Civil.* http://gov.bexar.org/dc/

General Information: No juvenile, mental, sealed, or adoption records released. Will not fax documents. Court makes copy: $.75 per page. Self serve copy: same. Certification fee: $1.00 per page. Cert fee includes copy fee. Payee: District Clerk. Only cashiers checks, money orders accepted. Discover cards accepted. Prepayment required. Mail requests: SASE required.

Civil Name Search: Access: Mail, fax, online, in person. Both court and visitors may perform in person name searches. Search fee: $5.00 per name. Civil records on computer from 1982-present, chrono index from 1837. Note: For fax requests, call court clerk to request form, or find form on website, then submit form with payment with Discover Card. Mail turnaround time up to 10 days. Civil PAT goes back to 1982. Access to the remote online system back to 1980 requires $100 setup fee, plus a $25 monthly fee, plus inquiry fees. Call BCIT for info at 210-335-0202. Also, search civil litigants free at https://apps.bexar.org/dklitsearch/search.aspx. Civil and family law record access at www.idocket.com; registration and password required. A fee service; only one free name search a day. Records go back to 01/01/1980.

Criminal Name Search: Access: Mail, fax, online, in person. Both court and visitors may perform in person name searches. Search fee: $5.00 per name. Required to search: name, years to search, signed release, DOB; also helpful- SSN, DR number. Criminal records computerized from 1974, chrono index from 1837. Note: For fax requests, call criminal department clerk to request form or find it online, then submit form with payment with Discover Card. Mail turnaround time up to 10 days. Criminal PAT goes back to 1974. Terminal results also show sex, race. Felony case record access at www.idocket.com; registration and password required. A fee service; only one free name search a day. Access to the remote online system back to 1980 requires $100 setup fee, plus a $25 monthly fee, plus inquiry fees. Call BCIT for info at 210-335-0202.

County Court - Civil Central Filing Department 100 Dolorosa, San Antonio, TX 78205-3083; 210-335-2231; fax: 210-335-2097; 8AM-5PM (CST). *Civil.* www.bexar.org/judges/countycourts.html

General Information: There are twelve hearing locations in this county where open cases are held. All closed cases are forwarded here. No mental, sealed records released. Will not fax documents. Court makes copy: $1.00 per page. Certification fee: $5.00. Payee: County Clerk. Personal checks accepted with proper ID, DL. No credit cards accepted. Prepayment required. Mail requests: SASE required.

Civil Name Search: Access: Mail, in person. Both court and visitors may perform in person name searches. Search fee: $5.00 per name. Fee is for 10 year search. Civil records on computer go back 10 years, index books prior. Open and closed records maintained. Mail turnaround time 5-7 days. Public use terminal has civil records back to 1980.

County Court - Criminal 100 Dolorosa, Rm 104, San Antonio, TX 78205-3083; 210-335-2238; fax: 210-335-3938; 8AM-5PM (CST). *Misdemeanor.*

http://gov.bexar.org/dc/Criminal.html

General Information: The fax is reserved for use only for governmental agencies. No sealed records released. Will fax documents $1.00 per page. Court makes copy: $1.00 per page. Certification fee: $5.00 per document. Payee: Bexar County Clerk. Personal checks accepted, credit cards are not. Prepayment required. Mail requests: SASE not required.

Criminal Name Search: Access: Mail, online, in person. Both court and visitors may perform in person name searches. Search fee: $5.00 per name. Fee is per 10 year period. $1.00 for each add'l year. Required to search: name, years to search, DOB, signed release; also helpful: SSN. Criminal records on computer since 1983, alpha index since 1983, on card index from 1909, records go back to 1899. Note: This court requires an $11.00 search and cert fee for a background check with a certified letter. Mail turnaround time 2-3 days. Public use terminal has crim records back to 1983. Access to the criminal online system requires $100 setup fee, plus a $25 monthly fee, plus inquiry fees. Call Alma Flores at 210-335-0202 for more information.

Probate Courts #1 and #2 100 Dolorosa St Ste 108, San Antonio, TX 78205; 210-335-2546; probate phone: 210-335-2241- Admin; fax: 210-335-2029; 8AM-5PM (CST). *Probate.*

www.co.bexar.tx.us/pcourt/probatecourts.htm

Blanco County

County Court PO Box 65, Johnson City, TX 78636; 830-868-7357; fax: 830-868-4158; 8AM-4:30PM (CST). *Misdemeanor, Civil, Probate.*

General Information: Probate is separate index at this same address. No juvenile, mental, sealed, or adoption records released. Will fax back documents. Court makes copy: $1.00 per page. Self serve copy: same. Certification fee: $5.00 per document plus copy fee. Payee: County Clerk. Personal checks accepted, credit cards are not. Prepayment required. Mail requests: SASE required.

Civil Name Search: Access: Mail, in person. Both court and visitors may perform in person name searches. Search fee: $5.00 per name. Civil records on computer from 1994, index books back to 1876. Mail turnaround time 2 days. Civil PAT goes back to 1994.

Criminal Name Search: Access: Mail, in person. Both court and visitors may perform in person name searches. Search fee: $5.00 per name. Required to search: name, years to search, DOB, SSN. Criminal records computerized from 1994, index books back to 1876. Mail turnaround time 1 day. Criminal PAT goes back to same as civil.

District Court PO Box 382, Johnson City, TX 78636; 830-868-0973; fax: 830-868-2084; 8AM-4:30PM (CST). *Felony, Civil, Probate.*

http://dcourt.org

General Information: Probate fax is same as main fax number. No juvenile, mental, sealed, or adoption records released. Will not fax documents. Court makes copy: $1.00 first page, $.25 ea add'l. Certification fee: $1.00 per certification plus $1.00 page for copy fee. Payee: District Clerk. Personal checks accepted, credit cards are not. Prepayment required. Mail requests: SASE required.

Civil Name Search: Access: Mail, in person. Both court and visitors may perform in person name searches. Search fee: $5.00 per name. Civil records on computer from 1994, index books back to 1876. Mail turnaround time 1 day. Civil PAT goes back to 1992. Results also give case type, dates.

Criminal Name Search: Access: Mail, in person. Both court and visitors may perform in person name searches. Search fee: $5.00 per name. Required to search: name, years to search, DOB, SSN. Criminal records computerized from 1994, index books back to 1876. Mail turnaround time 1 day. Criminal PAT goes back to 1992. Also gives arrest and disposition dates, offense.

Borden County

District & County Court PO Box 124, Gail, TX 79738; 806-756-4312; fax: 806-756-4324; 8AM-5PM (CST). *Felony, Misdemeanor, Civil, Probate.*

General Information: Probate fax is same as main fax number. No juvenile, mental, sealed, or adoption records released. Fee to fax out file $1.00 per page. Court makes copy: $1.00 per page. Certification fee: $5.00 per cert plus copy fee. Payee: District Clerk. Personal checks accepted, credit cards are not. Prepayment required. Mail requests: SASE required.

Civil Name Search: Access: Mail, in person. Both court and visitors may perform in person name searches. Search fee: $5.00 per name. Civil records in index books, archived from 1900. Mail turnaround time 1 week.

Criminal Name Search: Access: Mail, in person. Both court and visitors may perform in person name searches. Search fee: $5.00 per name. Criminal index in books, archived from 1900. Mail turnaround time 1 week.

Bosque County

District Court PO Box 674 (Main & Morgan St), Meridian, TX 76665; 254-435-2334; 8AM-5PM (CST). *Felony, Civil.*

General Information: In person searches are conducted by viewing index books. No juvenile, mental, sealed, or adoption records released. Will not fax documents. Court makes copy: $1.00 per page. Self serve copy: same. Certification fee: $1.00 per doc. Payee: District Clerk. Personal checks accepted, credit cards are not. Prepayment required. Mail requests: SASE required.

Civil Name Search: Access: Mail, in person. Both court and visitors may perform in person name searches. Search fee: $5.00 per name. Some civil records on computer from 1994, files/books from 1870s. Mail turnaround time 1 day.

Criminal Name Search: Access: Mail, in person. Both court and visitors may perform in person name searches. Search fee: $5.00 per name. Required to search: name, years to search, DOB or SSN. Some computerized records from 1994, criminal records on books/files from 1856. Mail turnaround time 1 day.

County Court PO Box 617, Meridian, TX 76665; 254-435-2201; fax: 254-435-2152; 8AM-5PM (CST). *Misdemeanor, Civil, Probate.*

General Information: No juvenile, mental, sealed, or adoption records released. Will not fax documents. Court makes copy: $1.00 per page. Self serve copy: $1.00 per page. Certification fee: $5.00. Payee: County Clerk. In state personal checks accepted for civil records. Major credit cards accepted. Prepayment required. Mail requests: SASE required.

Civil Name Search: Access: Mail, in person. Both court and visitors may perform in person name searches. Search fee: $5.00 per name. Civil records in index books from 1854; on computer back to 1997. Mail turnaround time 1-2 days.

Criminal Name Search: Access: Mail, in person. Only the court performs in person name searches; visitors may not. Search fee: $5.00 per name. Required to search: name, years to search, DOB, SSN. Criminal docket on books from 1854; on computer back to 1997. Mail turnaround time 1-2 days.

Bowie County

District & County Court at Law 710 James Bowie Dr, PO Box 248, New Boston, TX 75570; 903-628-6750; criminal phone: 903-628-6766; civil phone: 903-628-6751; probate phone: 903-628-6743; fax: 903-628-6761; 8AM-5PM (CST). *Felony, Misdemeanor, Civil, Probate.*

www.co.bowie.tx.us

General Information: Probate records are at this address in the County Clerk's office. No juvenile, mental, sealed, or adoption records released. Will fax documents $5.00 each. Court makes copy: $1.00 per page. Certification fee: $1.00. Payee: District Clerk. Personal checks, Visa/MC accepted. Prepayment required. Mail requests: SASE required.

Civil Name Search: Access: Mail, in person. Both court and visitors may perform in person name searches. Search fee: $5.00 per name. Civil records on computer from 1988, chrono index from 1800s. Mail turnaround time 3 days. Civil PAT available.

Criminal Name Search: Access: Mail, in person. Both court and visitors may perform in person name searches. Search fee: $5.00 per name. Required to search: name, years to search, DOB. Criminal records computerized from 1988, chrono index from 1800s. Mail turnaround time 3 days. Criminal PAT available.

Brazoria County

District Court Clerk's Office, 111 E Locust St, #500, Angleton, TX 77515-4678; 979-864-1316; fax: 979-864-1770; 8AM-5PM (CST). *Felony, Civil, Family.*

www.brazoria-county.com/dclerk/

General Information: Online identifiers in results same as on public terminal. No juvenile, mental, sealed, or adoption records released. Will fax documents $10.00 each. Court makes copy: $1.00 per page. Self serve copy: same. Certification fee: $1.00. Payee: District Clerk. No personal checks accepted. Credit cards accepted. Prepayment required. Mail requests: SASE required.

Civil Name Search: Access: Phone, mail, in person, online. Both court and visitors may perform in person name searches. Search fee: $5.00 per name. Fee is per 10 year period. Civil records on computer from 1987, index chrono from 1900, prior alpha. Mail turnaround time 1-2 days. Civil PAT goes back to 1987. Access civil record docket free at their Judicial Record Search site at http://records.brazoria-county.com/.

Criminal Name Search: Access: Phone, mail, in person, online. Both court and visitors may perform in person name searches. Search fee: $5.00 per name. Fee is per 10 year period. Required to search: name, years to search, DOB, signed release; also helpful: SSN. Criminal records computerized from 1986, index chrono from 1900, prior alpha. Mail turnaround time 1-2 days. Criminal PAT goes back to same as civil.

Drivers' License number may show up on the public terminal and online results. Access criminal record docket free at same site mentioned for civil; Sheriff bond and jail records also available. Online results show middle initial, DOB.

County Court 111 E Locust, #200, Angleton, TX 77515; criminal phone: 979-864-1380; civil phone: 979-864-1385; fax: 979-864-1020; 8AM-4:30PM (CST). *Misdemeanor, Civil.*
www.brazoria-county.com
General Information: Online identifiers in results same as on public terminal. No juvenile, mental, sealed records released. Will not fax documents. Court makes copy: $1.00 per page. Certification fee: $5.00 per document. Payee: Joyce Hudman, County Clerk. Personal checks accepted, credit cards are not. Prepayment required. Mail requests: SASE required.
Civil Name Search: Access: Fax, mail, in person, online. Both court and visitors may perform in person name searches. Search fee: $5.00 per name. Civil records on computer from 1984; prior on books or microfiche back to 1800s. Note: Fee must be prepaid before faxing in a search request. Mail turnaround time 2 days. Civil PAT goes back to 1/1986. Results include name and case number. Access civil record docket free at http://records.brazoria-county.com/. Also, access index and docs back to 1/1/1986 at www.idocket.com; registration and password required. This is a fee service; only one free name search per day.
Criminal Name Search: Access: Fax, mail, in person, online. Both court and visitors may perform in person name searches. Search fee: $5.00 per name. Required to search: name, years to search, DOB. Criminal records computerized from 1986; prior on books or microfiche back to 1800s. Note: Results include name and case number. Mail turnaround time 2 days. Criminal PAT goes back to same as civil. Results include name and case number. Access criminal court and county inmate and bond records free at http://records.brazoria-county.com. Also, access index and docs back to 1/1/1986 at www.idocket.com; registration and password required. This is a fee service, unless more than one name searched a day.

Probate Court County Clerk, 111 E Locust, #200, Angleton, TX 77515; 979-864-1367; fax: 979-864-1031; 8AM-5PM (CST). *Probate, Guardianship.* www.brazoria-county.com
General Information: Access probate records free at http://records.brazoria-county.com/. For a fee you can go to http://idocket.com/homepage2.htm for court records. Must have an User ID and Password.

Brazos County

District Court 300 E 26th St, #216, Bryan, TX 77803; 979-361-4230; fax: 979-361-0197; 8AM-5PM (CST). *Felony, Misdemeanors C, Civil.*
www.co.brazos.tx.us/courts/
General Information: No juvenile, mental, sealed, or adoption records released. Will fax documents to toll free number. Court makes copy: $.50 per page. Certification fee: $1.00 per page. Payee: District Clerk. Personal checks accepted, credit cards are not. Prepayment required. Mail requests: SASE required.
Civil Name Search: Access: Mail, in person, online. Both court and visitors may perform in person name searches. Search fee: $5.00 per name. Civil records on computer, index chromo from 1800s. Mail turnaround time 10 days. Civil PAT available. Civil case index and hearing index available at http://justiceweb.co.brazos.tx.us/judicialsearch/.
Criminal Name Search: Access: Mail, in person, online. Both court and visitors may perform in person name searches. Search fee: $5.00 per name. Required to search: name, years to search; also helpful: DOB, SSN, cause number. Criminal records on computer, index chrono from 1800s. Mail turnaround time 10 days. Criminal PAT available. Criminal case index and hearing index available at http://justiceweb.co.brazos.tx.us/judicialsearch/. Online results show middle initial, DOB.

County Court 300 E 26th St, #120, Bryan, TX 77803; 979-361-4128; criminal phone: 979-361-4132; fax: 979-361-4125; 8AM-5PM (CST). *Misdemeanor, Civil under $500, Probate.*
www.co.brazos.tx.us/courts/countyCourts.php
General Information: County Clerk holds misdemeanor records prior to 1986 only. Newer cases are filed at the District Clerks Office. The current docket may be viewed at the web page, sorted by Judge. No juvenile, mental, sealed, or adoption records released. Will fax documents $1.00 per page to a local or toll-free line, $2.00 to fax back long distance. Court makes copy: $1.00 per page. Certification fee: $5.00. Payee: County Clerk or District Clerk. Only cashiers checks and money orders accepted. No credit cards accepted. Prepayment required. Mail requests: SASE required.
Civil Name Search: Access: Mail, in person, online. Both court and visitors may perform in person name searches. Search fee: $5.00 per name. Civil records on computer from 1986, index chrono from 1958. Mail turnaround time 2-3 days. Civil PAT goes back to 1986. Current dockets available at web page.

Criminal Name Search: Access: Mail, in person, online. Both court and visitors may perform in person name searches. Search fee: $5.00 per name. Required to search: name, years to search, DOB. Criminal records computerized from 1986, index chrono from 1958. Mail turnaround time 2-3 days. Criminal PAT goes back to same as civil. Current dockets available at web page.

Brewster County

District Court PO Box 1024, Alpine, TX 79831; 432-837-6216; fax: 432-837-6217; 9AM-12, 1-5PM (CST). *Felony, Civil.*
General Information: Adoptions and Expungments if court ordered. No fee to fax documents to local number. Court makes copy: $1.00 per page. Certification fee: $1.00 per page plus copy fee. Payee: District Clerk. Personal checks accepted. Prepayment required.
Civil Name Search: Access: Phone, fax, mail, in person. Both court and visitors may perform in person name searches. Search fee: $8.00. Required to search: name; also helpful: years to search. Civil records are computerized since 1994, indexed from 1899. Mail turnaround time 2-3 days.
Criminal Name Search: Access: Phone, fax, mail, in person. Both court and visitors may perform in person name searches. Search fee: $8.00. Required to search: name, DOB; also helpful: years to search. Criminal records are computerized since 1994, indexed from 1899. Mail turnaround time 2-3 days.

County Court PO Box 119 (201 W Ave. E), Alpine, TX 79831; 432-837-3366; fax: 432-837-6217; 8:30AM-N, 1PM-5PM (CST). *Misdemeanor, Civil, Probate.*
General Information: No juvenile, mental, sealed, or adoption records released. Fee to fax out file $2.00 per page. Court makes copy: $1.00 per page. Self serve copy: same. Certification fee: $5.00. Payee: County Clerk. Personal checks accepted, credit cards are not. Prepayment required. Mail requests: SASE not required.
Civil Name Search: Access: Mail, fax, in person. Both court and visitors may perform in person name searches. Search fee: $10.00 per name. Civil records in index books from 1950s; computerized since 1995. Mail turnaround time 1 week. Civil PAT goes back to 1994.
Criminal Name Search: Access: Mail, fax, in person. Both court and visitors may perform in person name searches. Search fee: $10.00 per name. Required to search: name, years to search, DOB, signed release; also helpful: SSN. Criminal docket on books from 1920s, computerized since 1994. Mail turnaround time 1 week. Criminal PAT goes back to same as civil.

Briscoe County

District & County Court PO Box 555, Silverton, TX 79257; 806-823-2134; fax: 806-823-2076; 8AM-5PM (CST). *Felony, Misdemeanor, Civil, Probate.*
General Information: No juvenile, mental, sealed, or adoption records released. Will fax documents $5.00 per name if prepaid or copy of check faxed in. Court makes copy: $1.00 per page. Certification fee: $5.00. Payee: District or County Clerk. Personal checks accepted. Visa/MC/Discover/AmEx accepted. Prepayment required. Mail requests: SASE required.
Civil Name Search: Access: Fax, mail, in person. Both court and visitors may perform in person name searches. Search fee: $5.00 per name. Civil records in index books from 1892. Mail turnaround time 1 day.
Criminal Name Search: Access: Fax, mail, in person. Both court and visitors may perform in person name searches. Search fee: $5.00 per name. Required to search: name, years to search, DOB. Criminal docket on books from 1892. Mail turnaround time 1 day.

Brooks County

District Court PO Box 534, Falfurrias, TX 78355; 361-325-5604; criminal phone: x22; civil phone: x19; fax: 361-325-5679; 8AM-5PM (CST). *Felony, Civil.*
General Information: No juvenile, mental, sealed, or adoption records released. Fee to fax out file $1.00 per page. Court makes copy: $1.00 per page. Self serve copy: $.25 per page. Certification fee: $2.00 per document. Payee: District Clerk. Business checks accepted. Major credit cards accepted. Prepayment required. Mail requests: SASE required.
Civil Name Search: Access: Phone, fax, mail, online, in person. Both court and visitors may perform in person name searches. Search fee: $10.00 per name. Required to search: name, years to search; also helpful: address. Civil records on computer back to 1992, index books since 1920. Mail turnaround time 1 week. Civil PAT goes back to 1993. Civil case index and doc online at www.idocket.com. Records go back to 12/31/1993. One free name search permitted a day, otherwise subscription required.
Criminal Name Search: Access: Phone, fax, mail, online, in person. Both court and visitors may perform in person name searches. Search fee: $10.00 per name. Required to search: name, years to search, DOB, SSN; also helpful: address. Criminal records computerized from 1992, index books

since 1920, microfiche since 1939. Mail turnaround time 1 week. Criminal PAT available. Criminal case index and docs online through www.idocket.com; registration and password required. Records go back to 12/31/1993. One free name search permitted a day, otherwise subscription required. Online results show middle initial.

County Court PO Box 427, 100 E Miller, Falfurrias, TX 78355; 361-325-5604 x9; fax: 361-325-4944; 8AM-N, 1-5PM (CST). *Misdemeanor, Civil Actions Less Than $5,000, Probate.*

General Information: This court recommends that civil be cases be filed in District Court, thus there are very few civil records here. The search fee includes both the civil and criminal indexes if you ask for both. No juvenile, mental, sealed, or adoption records released. Will fax documents $5.00 per doc. Court makes copy: $1.00 per page. Self serve copy: same. Certification fee: $5.00 per cert plus copy fees. Payee: County Clerk. Personal checks accepted, credit cards are not. Prepayment required. Mail requests: SASE required.

Civil Name Search: Access: Phone, fax, mail, in person. Both court and visitors may perform in person name searches. Search fee: $10.00 per name. Civil cases indexed by plaintiff. Civil records in index books since 1911. Mail turnaround time 1-2 days.

Criminal Name Search: Access: Phone, fax, mail, in person, online. Both court and visitors may perform in person name searches. Search fee: $10.00 per name. Required to search: name, years to search, DOB. Criminal docket on books from 1911. Mail turnaround time 1-2 days. Access misdemeanor case info back to 12/31/94 at www.idocket.com; registration and password required. This is a fee service; only one free name search per day.

Brown County

District Court 200 S Broadway, Brownwood, TX 76801; 325-646-5514; 8AM-5PM (CST). *Felony, Civil.*

General Information: No juvenile, mental, sealed, or adoption records released. Will not fax documents. Court makes copy: $1.00 per page. Self serve copy: $.50 per page. Certification fee: $1.00 per page. Payee: District Clerk. Business checks accepted. No credit cards accepted. Prepayment required. Mail requests: SASE required.

Civil Name Search: Access: Mail, in person. Both court and visitors may perform in person name searches. Search fee: $5.00 per case found. Civil records on computer since 1995; prior records on books to 1930s. Mail turnaround time 2-3 days. Civil PAT goes back to 1995.

Criminal Name Search: Access: In person. Both court and visitors may perform in person name searches. Search fee: $5.00 per case found. Criminal records on computer since 1995; prior records on books to 1930s. Criminal PAT goes back to same as civil. Terminal results include SSN.

County Court 200 S Broadway, Rm 101, Brownwood, TX 76801; 325-643-2594; 8:30AM-5PM (CST). *Misdemeanor, Civil, Probate.*

www.browncountytx.org/ips/cms

General Information: No juvenile, mental, sealed records released. Will not fax documents. Court makes copy: $1.00 per page. Self serve copy: $.25 per page. Certification fee: $5.00. Payee: Brown County Clerk. Personal checks accepted, credit cards are not. Prepayment required. Mail requests: SASE not required.

Civil Name Search: Access: Mail, in person. Both court and visitors may perform in person name searches. Search fee: $5.00 per name. Civil records on computer from 1987 on microfiche from 1900s. Mail turnaround time 1-2 days. Civil PAT goes back to 1987.

Criminal Name Search: Access: Mail, in person. Both court and visitors may perform in person name searches. Search fee: $5.00 per name. Required to search: name, years to search; also helpful: DOB, SSN. Criminal records computerized from 1987, on microfiche from 1900s. Mail turnaround time 1-2 days. Criminal PAT goes back to same as civil.

Burleson County

District Court 100 W Buck, #303, Caldwell, TX 77836; 979-567-2336; 8AM-N, 1-5PM (CST). *Felony, Civil.*

General Information: No juvenile, mental, sealed, or adoption records released. Will not fax out documents. Court makes copy: $1.00 per page. Certification fee: $1.00. Payee: District Clerk. Personal checks accepted with proper ID. No credit cards accepted. Prepayment required. Mail requests: SASE or toll-free phone number required.

Civil Name Search: Access: Mail, in person. Both court and visitors may perform in person name searches. Search fee: $10.00 per name. Civil records on microfilm from 1980, index books prior. Mail turnaround time 1-5 days.

Criminal Name Search: Access: Mail, in person. Both court and visitors may perform in person name searches. Search fee: $10.00 per name. Criminal records on microfilm from 1980, index books prior. Mail turnaround time 1-5 days.

County Court 100 W Buck, #203, Caldwell, TX 77836; 979-567-2329; fax: 979-567-2376; 8AM-5PM (CST). *Misdemeanor, Civil, Probate.*

General Information: No juvenile, mental, or sealed records released. Fee to fax out file $1.00 per page. Court makes copy: $1.00 per page. Certification fee: $5.00. Payee: Burleson County Clerk. Personal checks accepted; cashiers check or money order is faster return. Major credit cards accepted online. Prepayment required. Mail requests: SASE required.

Civil Name Search: Access: Phone, mail, fax, in person. Both court and visitors may perform in person name searches. Search fee: $10.00 per name, per case. Civil records indexed in book to 1990, records archived to 1900s. Mail turnaround time 2-4 days.

Criminal Name Search: Access: Mail, fax, in person. Both court and visitors may perform in person name searches. Search fee: $10.00 per name, per case. Required to search: name, years to search, DOB, SSN. Criminal records indexed to 1990 in books, records archived to 1900s. Mail turnaround time 2-4 days.

Burnet County

District Court 1701 E Polk St, Ste 90, Burnet, TX 78611-2757; 512-756-5450; fax: 512-756-5023; 8:30AM-5PM (CST). *Felony, Civil, Family.*

www.burnetcountytexas.org/

General Information: Also see http://dcourt.org. Marriages, Misdemeanors, Probate and JP Civil Cases are handled by the County Clerk. No juvenile, mental, sealed, or adoption records released. Will fax documents $2.00 per page long distance and $1.00 if local number. Court makes copy: $1.00 per page. Certification fee: $2.00 per doc plus copy fee; exemplification fee is $5.00. Certification included in copy fee. Personal checks not accepted. Major credit cards accepted. Prepayment required. Mail requests: SASE required.

Civil Name Search: Access: Mail, in person, online. Both court and visitors may perform in person name searches. Search fee: $5.00 per name. Civil records on computer from 1991, index books from 1856. Note: Signup for email notifications of civil dockets at www.dcourt.org/_attys/dockets.htm. Mail turnaround time 3 days. Civil PAT goes back to 1990. For online access go to www.burnetcountytexas.org/default.aspx?name=dclerk.home and click on Burnet County Online Court Records Search. Login Required: user id - visitor, password - visitor.

Criminal Name Search: Access: Mail, in person. Both court and visitors may perform in person name searches. Search fee: $5.00 per name. Required to search: name, years to search; also helpful: DOB, SSN. Criminal records computerized from 1990, index book from 1856. Mail turnaround time 3 days. Criminal PAT goes back to same as civil. Terminal results include SSN if on the file. Signup for email notifications of criminal dockets at www.dcourt.org/_attys/dockets.htm. Online access to the criminal record docket index same as civil. The site also offers "Law Enforcement" records which includes a wide variety of incident types.

County Court 220 S Pierce, Burnet, TX 78611; 512-756-5403; criminal phone: 512-756-5407; civil phone: 512-756-5481; probate phone: 512-756-5408; fax: 512-756-5410; 9AM-5PM (CST). *Misdemeanor, Civil, Probate.*

General Information: Probate fax is same as main fax number. No juvenile, mental, sealed, or adoption records released. Will fax documents $3.00 per page. Court makes copy: $1.00 per page. Self serve copy: same. Certification fee: $5.00 per document plus copy fee. Payee: County Clerk. Personal checks accepted. Major credit cards accepted. Prepayment required. Mail requests: SASE required.

Civil Name Search: Access: Fax, mail, in person, online. Both court and visitors may perform in person name searches. Search fee: $10.00 per name. Civil records on computer from 1989, on microfiche from 1852. Mail turnaround time 2 days. Civil PAT goes back to 1989. Results include name and case number. No images. Search civil, family and probate cases at http://pubody.burnetcountytexas.org/CaseManagement/PublicAccess/login.aspx. Use "visitor" as both user ID and password.

Criminal Name Search: Access: Fax, mail, in person, online. Both court and visitors may perform in person name searches. Search fee: $10.00 per name. Required to search: name, years to search, offense, date of offense. Criminal records computerized from 1989, on microfiche from 1852. Mail turnaround time 2 days. Criminal PAT goes back to same as civil. Results include name and case number. No images. Search criminal cases free at http://pubody.burnetcountytexas.org/CaseManagement/PublicAccess/login.aspx. Use "visitor" as both user ID and password. The site also offers "Law Enforcement" records which includes a variety of incident types.

Caldwell County

District Court 201 E San Antonio St, Lockhart, TX 78644; 512-398-1806; fax: 512-398-1805; 8:30AM-N, 1-5PM (CST). *Felony, Civil.*

www.co.caldwell.tx.us/ips/cms

General Information: No juvenile, mental, sealed, or adoption records released. Will fax documents to local or toll free line. Court makes copy: $1.00 per page. Certification fee: $1.00. Payee: District Clerk. Personal checks accepted. Credit cards accepted. Prepayment required. Mail requests: SASE required.

Civil Name Search: Access: Phone, fax, mail, in person. Both court and visitors may perform in person name searches. Search fee: $5.00 per name. Civil records on computer since 1988, index books from 1846. Mail turnaround time 1-3 days. Civil PAT goes back to 1988.

Criminal Name Search: Access: Phone, fax, mail, in person. Both court and visitors may perform in person name searches. Search fee: $5.00 per name. Required to search: name, years to search; also helpful: DOB, SSN. Criminal records on computer since 1988, index books from 1846. Mail turnaround time 1-3 days. Criminal PAT goes back to same as civil.

County Court PO Box 906, Lockhart, TX 78644; 512-398-1804; criminal phone: 512-398-1824; fax: 512-398-1816; 8:30AM-5PM (CST). *Misdemeanor, Civil, Probate.*

General Information: Probate is a separate index at this same address. No juvenile, mental, sealed, or adoption records released. Will not fax documents. Court makes copy: $1.00 per page. Certification fee: $5.00 per document plus copy fee. Payee: Caldwell County Clerk. Personal checks accepted, credit cards are not. Prepayment required. Mail requests: SASE not required.

Civil Name Search: Access: Mail, in person. Both court and visitors may perform in person name searches. Search fee: $5.00 per name. Civil records in index books since 1967. Mail turnaround time 2-4 days. Civil PAT available.

Criminal Name Search: Access: Mail, in person. Both court and visitors may perform in person name searches. Search fee: $5.00 per name. Required to search: name, years to search, DOB, offense, date of offense. Criminal docket on books from 1967. Mail turnaround time 2-4 days. Criminal PAT available.

Calhoun County

District Court District Clerk, 211 S Ann Courthouse, Port Lavaca, TX 77979; 361-553-4630; fax: 361-553-4637; 8AM-N, 1-5PM (CST). *Felony, Civil.*

General Information: Search requests must be in writing. No mental, sealed, or adoption records released. Will not fax documents. Court makes copy: $1.00 per page. Self serve copy: same. Certification fee: $1.00 per page plus copy fee. Payee: District Clerk. No personal checks or credit cards accepted. Prepayment required. Mail requests: SASE required.

Civil Name Search: Access: Fax, mail, in person, online. Both court and visitors may perform in person name searches. Search fee: $5.00 per name. Civil records in index books from 1852. Mail turnaround time 3-5 days. Access case records including probate at www.idocket.com; registration and password required. A fee service; only one free name search per day. Records go back to 01/01/1998.

Criminal Name Search: Access: Fax, mail, in person, online. Both court and visitors may perform in person name searches. Search fee: $5.00 per name. Required to search: name, years to search, signed release; also helpful: DOB. Criminal docket on books from 1852. Mail turnaround time 3-5 days. Same online access as civil. Records go back to 01/01/1999.

County Court At Law 211 S Ann, Port Lavaca, TX 77979; 361-553-4411; criminal phone: 361-553-4412; civil phone: 361-553-4415; probate phone: 361-553-4418; fax: 361-553-4420; 8AM-5PM (CST). *Misdemeanor, Civil, Probate.*

General Information: Established 11/1986. No juvenile, mental, sealed, or adoption records released. Will not fax documents. Court makes copy: $1.00 per page. Certification fee: $5.00. Payee: County Clerk. Personal checks accepted, credit cards are not. Prepayment required. Mail requests: SASE required.

Civil Name Search: Access: Phone, mail, in person, online. Both court and visitors may perform in person name searches. Search fee: $5.00 per name. Civil records in index books from 11/1986; indexed on computer back to 2000. Mail turnaround time 1-2 days. Civil PAT goes back to 6/2005. Access index and images online at http://idocket.com/homepage2.htm. Registration required. One free name search permitted a day, otherwise subscription required. Records go back to 01/01/2006.

Criminal Name Search: Access: Phone, mail, in person, online. Both court and visitors may perform in person name searches. Search fee: $5.00 per name. Criminal docket on books from 11/1986; indexed on computer back to 1993. Mail turnaround time 1-2 days. Criminal PAT goes back to 01/1993. Access index and images online at http://idocket.com/homepage2.htm. Registration required. One free name search permitted a day, otherwise subscription required. Records go back to 01/01/1992.

Callahan County

District Court 100 W 4th St, #300, Baird, TX 79504-5396; 325-854-5825; fax: 325-854-5826; 8AM-5PM (CST). *Felony, Civil.*
www.callahancounty.org/

General Information: No juvenile, mental, sealed, or adoption records released. Will fax documents to local or toll-free number. Court makes copy: $1.00 per page. Certification fee: $1.00. Payee: District Clerk. Personal checks accepted, credit cards are not. Prepayment required. Mail requests: SASE required.

Civil Name Search: Access: Mail, in person. Both court and visitors may perform in person name searches. Search fee: $5.00 per name. Civil records in index books since 1879. Mail turnaround time 1-2 days.

Criminal Name Search: Access: Mail, in person. Both court and visitors may perform in person name searches. Search fee: $5.00 per name. Criminal docket on books from 1879. Mail turnaround time 1-2 days.

County Court 100 W 4th St, #104, Baird, TX 79504-5300; 325-854-5815; fax: 325-854-5816; 8AM-N, 1-5PM (CST). *Misdemeanor, Civil, Probate.*
www.callahancounty.org/

General Information: No juvenile, mental, sealed, or adoption records released. Fee to fax out file $1.00 per page. Court makes copy: $1.00 per page. Self serve copy: same. Certification fee: $5.00 per document. Payee: County Clerk. Personal checks accepted, credit cards are not. Prepayment required. Mail requests: SASE required.

Civil Name Search: Access: Mail, in person. Both court and visitors may perform in person name searches. Search fee: $6.00 per name. Civil records go back to 1877; computerized records go back to 1992. Mail turnaround time 1-2 days. Civil PAT available.

Criminal Name Search: Access: Phone, fax, mail, in person. Both court and visitors may perform in person name searches. Search fee: $6.00 per name. Criminal records go back to 1877; computerized records go to 1992. Mail turnaround time 1-2 days. Criminal PAT available.

Cameron County

District Court 974 E Harrison St, Brownsville, TX 78520; criminal phone: 956-544-0839; civil phone: 956-544-0838; fax: 956-548-9591; 8AM-5PM (CST). *Felony, Civil.*

General Information: No juvenile, mental, sealed, or adoption records released. Will fax documents to local or toll-free number. Court makes copy: $1.00 per page. No certification fee. Payee: Cameron County District Clerk. Personal checks accepted. Visa/MC/Discover credit cards accepted. Prepayment required. Mail requests: SASE required.

Civil Name Search: Access: Mail, fax, in person, online. Both court and visitors may perform in person name searches. Search fee: $5.00 per name per index. Civil records on computer from 1989. Mail turnaround time 1 week. On cases prior to 1990 turnaround can be more than 1 week. Civil PAT goes back to 1989. Results include name and case number. Online access to cases is at www.idocket.com; registration and password required. A fee service; only one free name search per day.

Criminal Name Search: Access: Mail, fax, in person, online. Both court and visitors may perform in person name searches. Search fee: $5.00 per name per index. Required to search: name, years to search, DOB, SSN, signed release, offense. Criminal records on computer since 1989. Mail turnaround time 1 week; cases prior to 1990 turnaround can be more than 1 week. Criminal PAT goes back to 1990. Felony records access is at www.idocket.com; registration and password required. This is a fee service, unless only one name search a day. Records may go back to 12/31/1988.

County Court No. 1, 2 & 3 PO Box 2178, 974 E Harrison, Brownsville, TX 78522-2178; criminal phone: 956-544-0848; civil phone: 956-544-0867; probate phone: 956-544-0867; criminal fax: 956-544-0894; civil fax: 8AM-5PM; 8AM-5PM (CST). *Misdemeanor, Civil, Probate.*
www.co.cameron.tx.us/courts_at_law/index.htm

General Information: Probate fax is same as main fax number. No juvenile, mental, sealed, or adoption records released. Will fax documents for $4.75 1st page and $2.75 ea addl. Court makes copy: $1.00 per page. Self serve copy: same. Certification fee: $5.00 per document plus copy fee. Payee: Joe G Rivera, County Clerk. No personal checks. No credit cards accepted. Prepayment required. Mail requests: SASE required.

Civil Name Search: Access: Mail, in person, online. Both court and visitors may perform in person name searches. Search fee: $5.00 per name. Civil records on optical imaging since 1994, on computer from 1987, index books from 1912. Mail turnaround time 1-2 days. Civil PAT goes back to 1993. Access case records back to 12/01/93 including probate at www.idocket.com; registration and password required. A fee service; only one free name search per day.

Criminal Name Search: Access: Mail, in person, online. Both court and visitors may perform in person name searches. Search fee: $5.00 per name. Required to search: name, years to search, DOB. Criminal records on optical imaging since 1994, on computer from 1987, index books from 1912. Mail turnaround time 1-2 days. Criminal PAT goes back to 1987. Criminal online access same as civil, see above.

Camp County

District Court 126 Church St, Rm 204, Pittsburg, TX 75686; 903-856-3221; fax: 903-856-0560; 8AM-N, 1-4:45PM (CST). *Felony, Civil.*

General Information: No juvenile, mental, sealed, or adoption records released. Fee to fax document $.25 per page. Court makes copy: $1.00 per page. Self serve copy: same. Certification fee: $5.00 per doc. Payee: District Clerk. Personal checks accepted, credit cards are not. Prepayment required. Mail requests: SASE required.

Civil Name Search: Access: Mail, fax, in person. Both court and visitors may perform in person name searches. Search fee: $5.00 per name. Civil records in index books from 1874; computerized since 1995. Mail turnaround time 1 week.

Criminal Name Search: Access: Mail, fax, in person. Both court and visitors may perform in person name searches. Search fee: $5.00 per name. Required to search: name, years to search, signed release. Criminal docket on books from 1874; computerized since 1993. Mail turnaround time 1 week.

County Court 126 Church St, Rm 102, Pittsburg, TX 75686; 903-856-2731; probate phone: 903-856-2731; fax: 903-856-6112; 8AM-N, 1-5PM (CST). *Misdemeanor, Civil, Probate.*

General Information: No juvenile, mental, sealed, or adoption records released. Will fax documents $1.00 per page. Court makes copy: $1.00 per page. Self serve copy: same. Certification fee: $5.00. Payee: Camp County Clerk. Personal checks accepted, credit cards are not. Prepayment required. Mail requests: SASE required.

Civil Name Search: Access: Fax, mail, in person. Both court and visitors may perform in person name searches. Search fee: $10.00 per name. Civil records in index books from 1960; computerized since 1999. Note: Fax access is only allowed if fees prepaid. Mail turnaround time 1 day.

Criminal Name Search: Access: Fax, mail, in person. Both court and visitors may perform in person name searches. Search fee: $10.00 per name. Required to search: name, years to search, signed release, offense. Criminal docket on books from 1960; computerized since 1999. Mail turnaround time 1 day.

Carson County

District & County Court PO Box 487, 501 Main St, Panhandle, TX 79068; 806-537-3873; fax: 806-537-3623; 8AM-N, 1-5PM (CST). *Felony, Misdemeanor, Civil, Probate.*

General Information: This court will not perform criminal record searches but welcomes researchers. Probate is a separate index at this same address. Probate fax is same as main fax number. No juvenile, mental, sealed, or adoption records released. Will fax documents if fees prepaid. Court makes copy: $1.00 per page. Certification fee: $5.00 per document plus copy fee. Payee: Carson County Clerk. Personal checks accepted. Major credit cards accepted. Prepayment required. Mail requests: SASE required for civil.

Civil Name Search: Access: Mail, fax, in person. Both court and visitors may perform in person name searches. Search fee: $5.00 per name. Civil/Real Property records on computer from 1981, index books from 1800s. Mail turnaround time 1 day or less.

Criminal Name Search: Access: In person only. Visitors must perform in person searches themselves. Criminal records are not computerized.

Cass County

District Court PO Box 510, Linden, TX 75563; 903-756-7514; fax: 903-756-5253; 8AM-5PM (CST). *Felony, Civil.*
www.co.cass.tx.us/ips/cms

General Information: No juvenile, mental, sealed, or adoption records released. Fee to fax document $.25 per minute; minimum $3.00. Court makes copy: $1.00 per page. Certification fee: n/a. Payee: District Clerk. Personal checks accepted. Major credit cards accepted. Prepayment required. Mail requests: SASE required.

Civil Name Search: Access: Mail, in person. Both court and visitors may perform in person name searches. Search fee: $5.00 per name. Civil records on computer from 1947, index books from 1900s. Mail turnaround time 1 day. Civil PAT goes back to 1947.

Criminal Name Search: Access: Mail, in person. Both court and visitors may perform in person name searches. Search fee: $5.00 per name. Criminal records computerized from 1985, index books from 1900s. Mail turnaround time 1 day. Criminal PAT goes back to 1979.

County Court PO Box 449, 604 Highway 8 North, Linden, TX 75563; 903-756-5071; fax: 903-756-8057; 8AM-5PM (CST). *Misdemeanor, Probate.*

General Information: Probate is a separate index at same address. Probate fax is same as main fax number. No juvenile, mental, sealed, or adoption records released. Will not fax documents. Court makes copy: $1.00 per page. Certification fee: $5.00 per doc plus copy fee. Payee: County Clerk. Personal

checks accepted, credit cards are not. Prepayment required. Mail requests: SASE required.

Criminal Name Search: Access: Mail, in person. Both court and visitors may perform in person name searches. Search fee: $5.00 per name. Criminal docket on books from 1983, computerized since 1999. Mail turnaround time 1 day.

Castro County

District & County Court 100 E Bedford, Rm 101, Dimmitt, TX 79027; 806-647-3338; fax: 806-647-5438; 8AM-5PM (CST). *Felony, Misdemeanor, Civil, Probate.* www.242ndcourt.com

General Information: Monthly schedules and daily docket available free at website. No juvenile, mental, sealed, or adoption records released. Will fax documents $3.00 plus $1.00 per page. Court makes copy: $1.00 per page. Self serve copy: same. Certification fee: $5.00 per doc in county court, $1.00 in district per page. Payee: County or District Court Clerk. Personal checks accepted, credit cards are not. Prepayment required. Mail requests: SASE required.

Civil Name Search: Access: Mail, in person. Both court and visitors may perform in person name searches. Search fee: $5.00 per name. Civil index in books. Mail turnaround time 1 day.

Criminal Name Search: Access: Mail, in person. Both court and visitors may perform in person name searches. Search fee: $5.00 per name. Required to search: name, years to search; also helpful: DOB, SSN. Criminal index in books; computerized records since 2000. Mail turnaround time 1 day.

Chambers County

District Clerk Drawer NN, Anahuac, TX 77514; 409-267-2400; fax: 409-267-8209; 8AM-N 1PM-5PM (CST). *Felony, Civil, family.* www.co.chambers.tx.us/District%20Clerk/districtclerk.html

General Information: No juvenile, mental, sealed, or adoption records released. Will not fax documents. Court makes copy: $1.00 per page. Self serve copy: same. Certification fee: $5.00. Payee: Chambers County. Personal checks accepted. Major credit cards accepted. Prepayment required. Mail requests: SASE required.

Civil Name Search: Access: Mail, in person, online. Both court and visitors may perform in person name searches. Search fee: $5.00 per name. Civil records on computer back to 1800s. Mail turnaround time 1 day. Civil PAT available. Search online after registering free for login and password at www.chambersonline.net/districtclerk/

Criminal Name Search: Access: Mail, in person, online. Both court and visitors may perform in person name searches. Search fee: $5.00 per name. Required to search: name, years to search, DOB, SSN. Criminal records computerized from 1940s. Mail turnaround time 1 day. Criminal PAT available. Online access same as civil, see above.

County Court PO Box 728, Anahuac, TX 77514; 409-267-2418; criminal phone: 409-267-2417; civil phone: 409-267-2422; probate phone: 409-267-2422; criminal fax: 409-267-8405; civil fax: 8AM-5PM; 8AM-5PM (CST). *Misdemeanor, Civil, Probate.* www.co.chambers.tx.us

General Information: Probate fax is same as the civil fax number. No juvenile or mental records released. Will fax documents $1.00 per page if local; long-distance fee $1.50 per page. Court makes copy: $1.00 per page. Certification fee: $5.00 per document plus copy fee. Payee: Chambers County Clerk. Personal checks, Visa/MC accepted. Prepayment required. Mail requests: SASE not required.

Civil Name Search: Access: Mail, in person. Both court and visitors may perform in person name searches. Search fee: $5.00 per name per 10 years searched. Required to search: name, years to search; also helpful: address. Civil records on computer from 1990, index books in office from 1905. Mail turnaround time 2-3 days. Civil PAT available.

Criminal Name Search: Access: Mail, in person. Both court and visitors may perform in person name searches. Search fee: $5.00 per name. Required to search: name, years to search, DOB, offense; also helpful: address. Criminal records computerized from 1990, index books in office from 1905. Mail turnaround time 2-3 days. Criminal PAT available.

Cherokee County

District Court Drawer C, Rusk, TX 75785; 903-683-4533; criminal phone: 903-683-6908; civil phone: 903-683-5945/5883; fax: 903-683-2971; 8AM-N, 1-5PM (CST). *Felony, Civil.*
http://co.cherokee.tx.us/ips/cms

General Information: No juvenile, sealed, or adoption records released. Will fax documents to local or toll-free number. Court makes copy: $1.00 per page. Certification fee: $1.00 per page. Payee: District Clerk. Personal checks accepted. No credit cards accepted except online. Prepayment required. Mail requests: SASE required.

Civil Name Search: Access: Mail, fax, in person, online. Both court and visitors may perform in person name searches. Search fee: $5.00 per name. Civil records on computer from 1992, index books from 1848. Mail turnaround time 1-2 days. Civil PAT goes back to 1992. Case record access at www.idocket.com; registration and password required. A fee service; only one free name search a day. Records may go back to 01/01/92.

Criminal Name Search: Access: Mail, fax, in person, online. Both court and visitors may perform in person name searches. Search fee: $5.00 per name. Criminal records computerized from 1992, index books from 1848. Mail turnaround time 1-2 days. Criminal PAT goes back to 1992. Case record access at www.idocket.com; registration and password required. A fee service; only one free name search a day. Records may go back to 01/01/92.

County Court Cherokee County Clerk, PO Box 420, 502 N Main, Rusk, TX 75785; 903-683-2350; fax: 903-683-5931; 8AM-5PM (CST). *Misdemeanor, Civil, Probate.*

General Information: Probate fax is same as main fax number. No juvenile, mental, sealed, or adoption records released. Will not fax documents. Court makes copy: $1.00 per page. Certification fee: $5.00 per document plus copy fee. Payee: County Clerk. Personal checks accepted, credit cards are not. Prepayment required. Mail requests: SASE required.

Civil Name Search: Access: Mail, in person. Both court and visitors may perform in person name searches. Search fee: $5.00 per name. Civil records on computer back to 1987, index books from 1846. Mail turnaround time 2-4 days.

Criminal Name Search: Access: Mail, in person. Both court and visitors may perform in person name searches. Search fee: $10.00 per name. Criminal records computerized from 1984, index books from 1920s. Mail turnaround time 2-4 days.

Childress County

District & County Court Courthouse, Box 4, Childress, TX 79201; 940-937-6143; fax: 940-937-3708; 8:30AM-N, 1-5PM (CST). *Felony, Misdemeanor, Civil, Probate.*

General Information: Probate fax is same as main fax number. No juvenile, mental, sealed, or adoption records released. Will fax documents. Court makes copy: $1.00 per page. Self serve copy: same. Certification fee: $1.00 per cert. County Court cert fee is $5.00 per document plus copy fee. Payee: District or County Clerk. Personal checks accepted, credit cards are not. Prepayment required. Mail requests: SASE not required.

Civil Name Search: Access: Mail, in person. Both court and visitors may perform in person name searches. Search fee: $5.00 per name. Civil records on computer from 1995, index books from 1920. Mail turnaround time 1 day.

Criminal Name Search: Access: Mail, in person. Both court and visitors may perform in person name searches. Search fee: $5.00 per name. Required to search: name, years to search, DOB. Criminal records computerized from 1995, index books from 1920. Mail turnaround time 1 day.

Clay County

District Clerk PO Box 568, Henrietta, TX 76365; 940-538-4561; fax: 940-538-4431; 8AM-N, 1-5PM (CST). *Felony, Civil.* www.97thdistrictcourt.com/id2.html

General Information: No juvenile, mental, sealed, or adoption records released. Will fax certain documents to local or toll-free number. Call first. Court makes copy: $1.00 per page. Self serve copy: $.25 per page. Certification fee: $1.00 per page includes copy fee. Payee: District Clerk. Personal checks accepted, credit cards are not. Prepayment required. Mail requests: SASE not required.

Civil Name Search: Access: Mail, in person. Both court and visitors may perform in person name searches. Search fee: $5.00 per name. Civil records in index books from 1873. Mail turnaround time 1-2 days.

Criminal Name Search: Access: Mail, in person. Both court and visitors may perform in person name searches. Search fee: $5.00 per name. Criminal docket on books from 1873. Mail turnaround time 1-2 days.

County Court PO Box 548, Henrietta, TX 76365; 940-538-4631; fax: 940-264-4160; 8AM-N, 1-5PM (CST). *Misdemeanor, Civil, Probate.*

General Information: Probate is a separate index at this same address. No juvenile, mental, sealed, or adoption records released. Will fax documents for $5.00 per instrument. Court makes copy: $1.00 per page. Self serve copy: same. Certification fee: $5.00 per document plus copy fee. Payee: County Clerk. Personal checks accepted, credit cards are not. Prepayment required. Mail requests: SASE required.

Civil Name Search: Access: Mail, in person. Both court and visitors may perform in person name searches. Search fee: $5.00 per name per 10 years. Civil records in index books from 1873, records go back to 1910; no computerized records. Mail turnaround time 2-4 days.

Criminal Name Search: Access: Mail, in person. Both court and visitors may perform in person name searches. Search fee: $5.00 per name per 10 years. Criminal docket on books from 1873, records go back to 1910; no computerized records. Mail turnaround time 2-4 days.

Cochran County

District & County Court County Courthouse, Rm 102, Morton, TX 79346; 806-266-5450; fax: 806-266-9027; 8AM-5PM (CST). *Felony, Misdemeanor, Civil, Probate.*

General Information: Probate fax is same as main fax number. No juvenile, mental, sealed, or adoption records released. Will fax documents to 800 number free; otherwise fax fee $5.00 plus copy fee. Court makes copy: $1.00 per page. Self serve copy: same. Certification fee: $5.00 per document plus copy fee. Payee: District or County Clerk. Personal checks accepted, credit cards are not. Prepayment required. Mail requests: SASE required.

Civil Name Search: Access: Phone, fax, mail, in person, online. Only the court performs in person name searches; visitors may not. Search fee: $5.00 per name. Civil records in index books go back to 1925. Mail turnaround time 1 day. Email address for search requests is cclerk@door.net.

Criminal Name Search: Access: Fax, mail, in person, online. Only the court performs in person name searches; visitors may not. Search fee: $5.00 per name. Required to search: name, years to search, DOB; also helpful: sex. Criminal docket on books go back to 1925. Mail turnaround time 1 day. Email address for search requests is cclerk@door.net.

Coke County

District & County Court 13 E 7th, Robert Lee, TX 76945; 325-453-2631; fax: 325-453-2650; 8AM-5PM M-TH; 8AM-1PM F (CST). *Felony, Misdemeanor, Civil, Probate.*

General Information: Probate fax is same as main fax number. No juvenile, mental, sealed, or adoption records released. Will fax documents $2.00 per page. Court makes copy: $1.00 per page. Self serve copy: same. Certification fee: $5.00 for County Court; $1.00 for District Court. Payee: Coke County Clerk. Personal checks accepted. Major credit cards accepted. Prepayment required. Mail requests: SASE not required.

Civil Name Search: Access: Mail, in person. Both court and visitors may perform in person name searches. Search fee: $10.00 per name. Civil records in index books since 1889, computerized since 1993. Mail turnaround time 2 days.

Criminal Name Search: Access: Mail, in person. Both court and visitors may perform in person name searches. Search fee: $10.00 per name. Criminal docket on books from 1889. Mail turnaround time 2 days.

Coleman County

District Court 100 Liveaok St, Ste 201, Coleman, TX 76834; 325-625-2568; 8AM-4:30PM (CST). *Felony, Civil.*

General Information: No juvenile, mental, sealed, or adoption records released. Will not fax documents. Court makes copy: $1.00 per page. Certification fee: $1.00. Payee: District Clerk. Personal checks accepted. Prepayment required. Mail requests: SASE required.

Civil Name Search: Access: Mail, in person. Both court and visitors may perform in person name searches. Search fee: $5.00 per name. Civil records in index books since 1934; earlier records not indexed. Mail turnaround time up to 5 days.

Criminal Name Search: Access: Mail, in person. Both court and visitors may perform in person name searches. Search fee: $5.00 per name. Required to search: name, years to search; also helpful are DOB. Criminal docket on books from 1931; earlier records not indexed. Mail turnaround time up to 5 days.

County Court 100 W Liveoak, #105, Coleman, TX 76834; 325-625-2889; fax: 325-625-2889; 8AM-4:45 M-TH; 8AM-4:30PM F (CST). *Misdemeanor, Civil, Probate.* www.co.coleman.tx.us/ips/cms

General Information: No juvenile, mental, sealed, or adoption records released. Will fax documents if paid by a credit card. Court makes copy: $1.00 per page. Certification fee: $5.00. Payee: County Clerk. Personal checks accepted. Major credit cards accepted. Prepayment required. Mail requests: SASE required.

Civil Name Search: Access: Mail, in person. Both court and visitors may perform in person name searches. Search fee: $5.00 per name. Civil records in index books from 1971. Mail turnaround time 1-2 days.

Criminal Name Search: Access: Mail, in person. Both court and visitors may perform in person name searches. Search fee: $5.00 per name. Criminal docket on books from 1977, archived from 1900s. Note: Requests must be in writing on compnay letterhead. Mail turnaround time 1-2 days.

Collin County

District Clerk PO Box 578, McKinney, TX 75070; criminal phone: 972-548-4430; civil phone: 972-548-4320; criminal fax: 972-548-4764; civil fax: 8AM-4:30PM; 8AM-4:30PM (CST). *Felony, Civil.* www.co.collin.tx.us/district_courts/index.jsp

General Information: Online identifiers in results same as on public terminal. No juvenile, mental, sealed, or adoption records released. Will return items by fax, if subscriber. Court makes copy: $1.00 per page. No certification fee. Payee: District Clerk. Personal checks accepted, credit cards are not. Prepayment required. Mail requests: SASE required.

Civil Name Search: Access: Mail, fax, online, in person. Both court and visitors may perform in person name searches. Search fee: $5.00 per name. Civil records on computer and microfiche from 1986 (some records are on computer through the 1970s), index books from 1846. Note: Fax service only to ongoing subscriber. Mail turnaround time 2-3 days. Civil PAT goes back to 1986. Name and case look up is at http://apps.collincountytx.gov/cccasesearch/. Search case schedules for free at www.co.collin.tx.us/ShowScheduleSearchServlet. There is also a commercial system call Lisa Zoski at 972-548-4503 for subscription info.

Criminal Name Search: Access: Mail, fax, online, in person. Both court and visitors may perform in person name searches. Search fee: $5.00 per name. Required to search: name, years to search, DOB. Criminal records on computer and microfiche from 1986 (some records are on computer through the 1970s), index books from 1846. Note: Fax service only to ongoing subscriber. Mail turnaround time 2-3 days. Criminal PAT goes back to same as civil. Name and case look up is at http://apps.collincountytx.gov/cccasesearch/. Search case schedules for free at www.co.collin.tx.us/ShowScheduleSearchServlet. Online results show middle initial, DOB.

County Court At Law 1800 N Graves, #110, McKinney, TX 75069; criminal phone: 972-548-6420; civil phone: 972-548-6423; probate phone: 972-548-6465; fax: 972-548-6433; 8AM-4:30PM (CST). *Misdemeanor, Civil, Probate.*
www.collincountytexas.gov
General Information: Probate is in #115; and has its own public access terminal. Probate search fee is $5.00. Probate fax is 972-548-6468. No juvenile, mental, sealed, or adoption records released. Will not fax documents. Court makes copy: $1.00 per page. Certification fee: $5.00. Payee: County Clerk. Personal checks accepted with valid ID. No credit cards accepted for research or copies. Prepayment required. Mail requests: SASE required.

Civil Name Search: Access: Mail, in person, online. Both court and visitors may perform in person name searches. Search fee: $5.00 per name. Civil records on computer and microfiche from 1975. Mail turnaround time 2-4 days. Civil PAT goes back to 1970s. Online access is free at http://apps.collincountytx.gov/cccasesearch/.

Criminal Name Search: Access: Mail, online, in person. Both court and visitors may perform in person name searches. Search fee: $5.00 per name. Required to search: name, DOB. Criminal records computerized since 1975. Mail turnaround time 2-4 days. Criminal PAT goes back to same as civil. Online access to misdemeanor records back to year 2000 is the same as civil.

Collingsworth County

District & County Court County Courthouse, Rm 3, 800 W Ave, Box 10, Wellington, TX 79095; 806-447-2408; fax: 806-447-2409; 9AM-5PM (CST). *Felony, Misdemeanor, Civil, Probate.*
General Information: No juvenile, mental health, sealed, or adoption records released. Will fax documents $1.50 per page. Court makes copy: $1.00 per page. Self serve copy: same. Certification fee: $5.00. Payee: Collingsworth County Clerk. Personal checks accepted. Prepayment required. Mail requests: SASE required.
Civil Name Search: Access: Phone, fax, mail, in person. Both court and visitors may perform in person name searches. Search fee: $10.00 per name. Civil index on docket books from 1800s. Mail turnaround time 2 days.
Criminal Name Search: Access: Mail, in person. Both court and visitors may perform in person name searches. Search fee: $10.00 per name. Required to search: name, years to search, DOB. Criminal records indexed in books from 1800s. Mail turnaround time 2 days.

Colorado County

District Court County Courthouse, Rm 210E, 400 Spring St, Columbus, TX 78934; 979-732-2536; fax: 979-732-2591; 8AM-N, 1-5PM (CST). *Felony, Civil.*
General Information: Civil and criminal indexes are usually considered separate searches. No juvenile, mental, sealed, or adoption records released. Will not fax documents. Court makes copy: $1.00 per page. Certification fee: No fee to certify. Payee: District Clerk. Personal checks accepted, credit cards are not. Prepayment required. Mail requests: SASE required.
Civil Name Search: Access: Mail, in person. Both court and visitors may perform in person name searches. Search fee: $5.00 per name. Civil records in index books from 1837. Mail turnaround time 1-3 days.
Criminal Name Search: Access: Mail, in person. Both court and visitors may perform in person name searches. Search fee: $5.00 per name. Criminal docket on books from 1837. Mail turnaround time 1-3 days.

County Court 400 Spring St #103, County Courthouse, Columbus, TX 78934; 979-732-2155; fax: 979-732-8852; 8AM-5PM (CST). *Misdemeanor, Civil, Probate.*
General Information: No juvenile, mental, sealed, or adoption records released. Will fax documents $5.00 plus $1.00 per page. Court makes copy: $1.00 per page. Certification fee: $5.00. Payee: County Clerk. Personal checks accepted. Major credit cards accepted. Prepayment required. Mail requests: SASE requested.
Civil Name Search: Access: Mail, in person. Both court and visitors may perform in person name searches. Search fee: $10.00 per name. Civil records in index books from 1850, computerized since 1996. Mail turnaround time 1-2 days.
Criminal Name Search: Access: Mail, in person. Both court and visitors may perform in person name searches. Search fee: $10.00 per name. Criminal docket on books from 1850, computerized since 1996. Mail turnaround time 1-2 days.

Comal County

County Court at Law 199 Main Plaza, New Braunfels, TX 78130; 830-221-1240; criminal phone: x1149; civil phone: x1144 or 1148; probate phone: x1141 or 1153; fax: 830-608-2021; 8AM-4:30PM (CST). *Misdemeanor, Civil, Probate.*
www.comalcounty.net
General Information: No juvenile, mental, sealed or adoption records released. Will fax documents for $5.00, must be paid upfront. Court makes copy: $1.00 per page. Self serve copy: same. Certification fee: $5.00. Payee: County Court at Law. Cashiers checks and money orders accepted. Credit cards accepted. Prepayment required.
Civil Name Search: Access: Phone, fax, mail, in person, online. Both court and visitors may perform in person name searches. Search fee: $5.00 per name. Civil records go back to 1977. Mail turnaround time 1 week. Civil PAT goes back to 1989. Online access county judicial records free at www.co.comal.tx.us/recordsearch.htm. Search by either party name.
Criminal Name Search: Access: Phone, fax, mail, in person, online. Both court and visitors may perform in person name searches. Search fee: $5.00 per name. Required to search: name, years to search; also helpful: address, DOB. Criminal records go back to 1977. Mail turnaround time 1 week. Criminal PAT goes back to 1977. Online access county criminal judicial records free at www.co.comal.tx.us/recordsearch.htm.

District Court Clerk's Office, 150 N Seguin, #304, New Braunfels, TX 78130-5161; 830-221-1250; fax: 830-608-2006; 8AM-5PM (CST). *Felony, Civil.*
www.co.comal.tx.us/DC.htm
General Information: No juvenile, sealed, or adoption records released. Will fax documents $5.00 per page. Fee is for incoming or outgoing faxes. Court makes copy: $1.00 first page, $.25 each add'l. Certification fee: $1.00 per page. Cert fee includes copies. Payee: District Clerk. Personal checks accepted. Credit cards accepted in person. Prepayment required. Mail requests: SASE required.
Civil Name Search: Access: Fax, mail, in person, online. Both court and visitors may perform in person name searches. Search fee: $5.00 per name. Civil records on computer from 1984, index books from 1846. Mail turnaround time 10 days. Civil PAT goes back to 1985. Online access county judicial records free at www.co.comal.tx.us/recordsearch.htm. Search by either party name.
Criminal Name Search: Access: Fax, mail, in person, online. Both court and visitors may perform in person name searches. Search fee: $5.00 per name. Required to search: name, years to search, DOB; also helpful: SSN, sex. Criminal records computerized from 1984, index books from 1846. Mail turnaround time 10 days. Criminal PAT goes back to same as civil, is countywide. Online access county criminal judicial records free at www.co.comal.tx.us/recordsearch.htm. Data includes date filed, disposed, offense, warrant status and attorney. Online results show name, DOB.

Comanche County

District Court County Courthouse, PO Box 206, Comanche, TX 76442; 325-356-2342; fax: 325-356-2150; 8:30AM-N, 1-5PM (CST). *Felony, Civil.*
General Information: No juvenile, mental, sealed, or adoption records released. Will not fax documents. Court makes copy: $1.00 per page. Certification fee: Free with copy fee. Payee: District Clerk. Personal checks accepted. No credit or debit cards accepted. Prepayment required. Mail requests: SASE required.
Civil Name Search: Access: Mail, in person. Only the court performs in person name searches; visitors may not. Search fee: $5.00 per name. Civil records on computer from 2007, index books from 1876. Mail turnaround time 1 day.
Criminal Name Search: Access: Mail, in person. Only the court performs in person name searches; visitors may not. Search fee: $5.00 per

name. Criminal records computerized from 1990, index books from 1876. Mail turnaround time 1 day.

County Court County Courthouse, Comanche, TX 76442; 325-356-2655; fax: 325-356-5764; 8:30AM-5PM (CST). *Misdemeanor, Civil, Probate.*

General Information: No juvenile, mental, sealed, or adoption records released. Will fax documents $1.50 per fax. Court makes copy: $1.00 per page. Certification fee: $5.00. Payee: County Clerk. Personal checks accepted, credit cards are not. Prepayment required. Mail requests: SASE required.

Civil Name Search: Access: Mail, in person. Both court and visitors may perform in person name searches. Search fee: $5.00 per name. Civil records in index books from 1856. Mail turnaround time 1 day.

Criminal Name Search: Access: Mail, in person. Both court and visitors may perform in person name searches. Search fee: $5.00 per name. Criminal docket on books from 1856. Mail turnaround time 1 day.

Concho County

District & County Court PO Box 98, 152 N. Roberts, Paint Rock, TX 76866; 325-732-4322; fax: 325-732-2040; 8:30AM-5PM (CST). *Felony, Misdemeanor, Civil, Probate.*
www.co.concho.tx.us/ips/cms/districtcourt/

General Information: Probate is in a separate index at this address. Probate fax is same as main fax number. No juvenile, mental, sealed, or adoption records released. Will not fax documents. Court makes copy: $1.00 per page. Certification fee: $5.00 for County Court; $1.00 for District. Payee: District or County Clerk. Personal checks accepted. Major credit cards accepted. Prepayment required. Mail requests: SASE required.

Civil Name Search: Access: Mail, in person. Both court and visitors may perform in person name searches. Search fee: $5.00 per name. Civil records in index books from 1879; computerized back to 1994. Mail turnaround time 1 day.

Criminal Name Search: Access: Mail, in person. Only the court performs in person name searches; visitors may not. Search fee: $5.00 per name. Required to search: name, years to search, DOB; also helpful: SSN. Criminal docket on books from 1879; computerized back to 1994. Mail turnaround time 1 day.

Cooke County

District Court 100 S Dixon, County Courthouse, Gainesville, TX 76240; 940-668-5450; fax: 940-668-5476; 8AM-N, 1-5PM (CST). *Felony, Civil.*

General Information: No juvenile, mental, sealed, or adoption records released. Will fax documents. Court makes copy: $1.00 per page. Self serve copy: same. Certification fee: $5.00 per document plus $1.00 per page. Payee: District Clerk. Only cashiers checks and money orders accepted. Visa/MC accepted. Prepayment required. Mail requests: SASE required.

Civil Name Search: Access: Mail, in person. Both court and visitors may perform in person name searches. Search fee: $5.00 per name. Civil records on microfiche from late 1900s, index books from 1800s. Note: Must request specifically if you wish to search back more than 10 years. Mail turnaround time varies.

Criminal Name Search: Access: Mail, in person. Both court and visitors may perform in person name searches. Search fee: $5.00 per name. Criminal records on microfiche from late 1900s, index books from 1800s. Mail turnaround time varies.

County Court County Courthouse Annex, 112 S Dixon St, Rm 116, Gainesville, TX 76240; 940-668-5422/5437; fax: 940-668-5486; 8AM-12; 1-5PM (CST). *Misdemeanor, Civil, Probate.*
www.co.cooke.tx.us/ips/cms

General Information: No juvenile, mental, sealed, or adoption records released. Will fax out files to toll free lines or when prepaid. Court makes copy: $1.00 per page. Self serve copy: same. Certification fee: $5.00 per instrument. Payee: Cooke County Clerk. Personal checks accepted. Major credit cards accepted. Prepayment required. Mail requests: SASE not required.

Civil Name Search: Access: Mail, in person. Both court and visitors may perform in person name searches. Search fee: $5.00 per name. Civil records in index books and original papers from late 1850s. Mail turnaround time 1 day. Civil PAT goes back to 1999.

Criminal Name Search: Access: Mail, in person. Both court and visitors may perform in person name searches. Search fee: $5.00 per name. Required to search: name, years to search, DOB. Criminal records go back to 1969. Mail turnaround time 1 day. Criminal PAT goes back to 1986. PAT may also show DL#.

Coryell County

District Court PO Box 4, Courthouse 2nd Fl, Gatesville, TX 76528; 254-865-5911; fax: 254-865-5064; 8AM-5PM (CST). *Felony, Civil.*
www.coryellcounty.org/district_clerk.html

General Information: No juvenile, sealed, or adoption records released. Fee to fax out file $1.50 per page. Court makes copy: $1.00 per page. No certification fee. Payee: District Clerk. Personal checks accepted from Coryell County residents only. Money order, cashiers check accepted for others. Major credit cards accepted. Prepayment required. Mail requests: SASE required.

Civil Name Search: Access: Fax, mail, in person, online. Both court and visitors may perform in person name searches. Search fee: $5.00 per name. Civil records in index books from 1854; computerized back to 2000. Mail turnaround time 1 day. Civil PAT goes back to 1999. Case record access at www.idocket.com; registration and password required. A fee service; only one free name search a day. Records may go back to 01/01/99.

Criminal Name Search: Access: Fax, mail, in person, online. Both court and visitors may perform in person name searches. Search fee: $5.00 per name. Required to search: name, years to search, DOB, SSN. Criminal docket on books from 1854; computerized back to 2000. Mail turnaround time 1 day. Criminal PAT goes back to same as civil. Case record access at www.idocket.com; registration and password required. A fee service; only one free name search a day. Records may go back to 01/01/99.

County Court PO Box 237, Gatesville, TX 76528; 254-865-5911 x235; fax: 254-865-8631; 8AM-N, 1-5PM (CST). *Misdemeanor, Civil, Probate.*
www.coryellcounty.org

General Information: No juvenile, mental, sealed, or adoption records released. Will fax documents $1.00 per page. Out of county fax is $5.00 plus $1.00 per page. Court makes copy: $1.00 per page. Self serve copy: same. Certification fee: $5.00 per doc plus copy fee. Payee: County Clerk. Business checks accepted. Personal checks must be in county. Visa/MC accepted. Prepayment required. Will mail only when a $10.00 search fee is paid in advance of search (10 year only). Mail requests: SASE required.

Civil Name Search: Access: Mail, in person, online. Visitors must perform in person searches themselves. Search fee: $10.00 per name per 10 years. Civil records on computer back to 1993, index books from 1846. Mail turnaround time 1-5 days. Civil PAT goes back to 1993. Case record access at www.idocket.com; registration and password required. A fee service; only one free name search a day. Records may go back to 01/01/94.

Criminal Name Search: Access: Mail, in person. Visitors must perform in person searches themselves. Search fee: $10.00 per name per 10 years. Required to search: name, years to search, DOB, SSN. Criminal records computerized from 1993; index books from 1846. Mail turnaround time 1-5 days. Criminal PAT goes back to same as civil. Case record access at www.idocket.com; registration and password required. A fee service; only one free name search a day. Records may go back to 01/01/94.

Cottle County

District & County Court PO Box 717, Paducah, TX 79248; 806-492-3823; fax: 806-492-2625; 9AM-5PM; closed Fri (CST). *Felony, Misdemeanor, Civil, Probate.*
www.co.cottle.tx.us/ips/cms/districtcourt/districtClerk.html

General Information: No juvenile, mental, sealed, or adoption records released. Will not fax documents. Court makes copy: $1.00 per page. Self serve copy: No self serve copier but personal scanners are allowed. Certification fee: $1.00 in District Court; $5.00 for County Court. Payee: Cottle County Clerk. Personal checks accepted, credit cards are not. Prepayment required. Mail requests: SASE required.

Civil Name Search: Access: Mail, in person. Both court and visitors may perform in person name searches. Search fee: $5.00 per name. Civil records in index books from 1892. Mail turnaround time 2-3 days.

Criminal Name Search: Access: Mail, in person. Both court and visitors may perform in person name searches. Search fee: $5.00 per name. Criminal docket on books from 1892. Mail turnaround time 2-3 days.

Crane County

District & County Court PO Box 578, Crane, TX 79731; 432-558-3581; fax: 432-558-1148; 8AM-N, 1-5PM (CST). *Felony, Misdemeanor, Civil, Probate.* www.co.crane.tx.us/ips/cms/districtcourt/

General Information: Probate is a separate index at this same address. No juvenile, mental, sealed or adoption records released. Court makes copy: $1.00 per page. Certification fee: $5.00 per doc County Court; $1.00 per doc in Dist Court. Payee: District or County Clerk. Only cashiers checks and money orders accepted. No credit cards accepted. Prepayment required. Mail requests: SASE requested.

Civil Name Search: Access: Mail, in person. Visitors must perform in person searches themselves. Search fee: $5.00 per name per 10 years searched. Limited civil records on computer from 1990; index books from 1927. Mail turnaround time 2-5 days. Civil PAT goes back to 1990.

Criminal Name Search: Access: Mail, in person. Both court and visitors may perform in person name searches. Search fee: $5.00 per name per 10 years searched. Required to search: name, years to search, offense. Limited

Criminal records computerized from 1990; index books from 1927. Mail turnaround time 2-5 days. Criminal PAT goes back to same as civil.

Crockett County

District & County Court PO Drawer C, Ozona, TX 76943; 325-392-2022; fax: 325-392-3742; 8AM-5PM (CST). *Felony, Misdemeanor, Civil, Probate.* www.co.crockett.tx.us/ips/cms

General Information: No juvenile, mental, sealed, or adoption records released. Fee to fax out file $2.00 per page. Court makes copy: $1.00 per page. Self serve copy: same. Certification fee: $5.00 per document plus copy fee. Payee: District or County Clerk. Personal checks accepted, credit cards are not. Prepayment required. Mail requests: SASE not required.

Civil Name Search: Access: Mail, in person. Both court and visitors may perform in person name searches. Search fee: $10.00 per name. Civil records on computer from 1982, index books from 1800s. Mail turnaround time 1 week.

Criminal Name Search: Access: Mail, in person. Both court and visitors may perform in person name searches. Search fee: $10.00 per name. Required to search: name, years to search, DOB, SSN, signed release. Criminal records computerized from 1982, index books from 1800s. Mail turnaround time 1 week.

Crosby County

District Court 201 W Aspen St, #207, Crosbyton, TX 79322-2500; 806-675-2071; fax: 806-675-2433; 8AM-N, 1-5PM (CST). *Felony, Civil.*

General Information: No juvenile, mental, sealed, or adoption records released. Will fax documents to local or toll free numbers only and at $1.00 per page. Court makes copy: $1.00 per page. Certification fee: $5.00. Payee: District Clerk. Personal checks accepted, credit cards are not. Prepayment required. Mail requests: SASE required.

Civil Name Search: Access: Phone, fax, mail, in person. Both court and visitors may perform in person name searches. Search fee: $5.00 per name. Civil records in index books from 1896. Mail turnaround time 1 day.

Criminal Name Search: Access: Phone, fax, mail, in person. Both court and visitors may perform in person name searches. Search fee: $5.00 per name. Criminal docket on books from 1896. Mail turnaround time 1 day.

County Court 201 W Aspen St, #102, Crosbyton, TX 79322-2500; 806-675-2334; 8AM-N, 1-5PM (CST). *Misdemeanor, Civil, Probate.* www.co.crosby.tx.us/ips/cms

General Information: Search fees are per index. Probate is a separate index at this same address. No juvenile, mental, sealed, or adoption records released. Will fax documents $1.00 per page. Court makes copy: $1.00 per page. Certification fee: $5.00 per doc plus copy fee. Payee: County Clerk. Personal checks accepted, credit cards are not. Prepayment required. Mail requests: SASE required.

Civil Name Search: Access: Mail, in person. Both court and visitors may perform in person name searches. Search fee: $5.00 per name. Civil records on microfiche from 1990, index books from 1886. Mail turnaround time 1 day.

Criminal Name Search: Access: Mail, in person. Both court and visitors may perform in person name searches. Search fee: $5.00 per name. Criminal records on microfiche from 1990, index books from 1886, computerized from Aug 2006 forward. Mail turnaround time 1 day.

Culberson County

District & County Court PO Box 158, 300 La Caverna, Van Horn, TX 79855; 432-283-2058; 8AM-N; 1PM-5PM (CST). *Felony, Misdemeanor, Civil, Probate.*

General Information: All search requests must be in writing. No juvenile, mental, sealed, or adoption records released. Fee to fax out file $1.00 per page. Court makes copy: $1.00 per page. Certification fee: $5.00. Payee: District or County Clerk. Personal checks accepted. Prepayment required. Mail requests: SASE required.

Civil Name Search: Access: Mail, in person. Both court and visitors may perform in person name searches. Search fee: $10.00 per name. Civil records in index books since 1911. Mail turnaround time 2 days.

Criminal Name Search: Access: Phone, mail, in person. Both court and visitors may perform in person name searches. Search fee: $10.00 per name. Required to search: name, years to search, signed release. Criminal docket on books from 1911. Mail turnaround time 2 days.

Dallam County

District & County Court PO Box 1352, Dalhart, TX 79022; 806-244-4751; fax: 806-244-3751; 8AM-5PM (CST). *Felony, Misdemeanor, Civil, Probate.* www.dallam.org/

General Information: No juvenile, mental, sealed, or adoption records released. Fee to fax out file $5.00 1st page, $1.00 each add'l. Court makes copy: $1.00 per page. Certification fee: $5.00. Payee: Dallam County Clerk. Personal checks accepted. Major credit cards accepted. Prepayment required. Mail requests: SASE required.

Civil Name Search: Access: Fax, mail, in person. Both court and visitors may perform in person name searches. Search fee: $5.00 per name. Civil records in index books from 1800s; computerized since 1991. Mail turnaround time 1 day. Public use terminal available.

Criminal Name Search: Access: Fax, mail, in person. Both court and visitors may perform in person name searches. Search fee: $5.00 per name. Criminal docket on books from 1800s; computerized since 1991. Mail turnaround time 1 day. Public use terminal available.

Dallas County

County Court - Civil 600 Commerce St, #101, Dallas, TX 75202; 214-653-7131; civil phone: 214-653-7442, 653-7096; fax: 214-653-7779; 8AM-4:30PM (CST). *Civil.* www.dallascounty.org

General Information: No civil claims limit as of 05/23/97. No juvenile, mental, sealed, or adoption records released. Will not fax documents. Court makes copy: $1.00 per page.If over 25 pages, copies must be provided on CD. Certification fee: $5.00 per doc plus copy fee; same fee to exemplify. Payee: County Clerk. No personal checks or credit cards accepted. Prepayment required. Mail requests: SASE required or $2.00 fee charged.

Civil Name Search: Access: Phone, mail, in person, online. Both court and visitors may perform in person name searches. Search fee: $5.00 per name per 10 years. There is a $2.00 document retrieval fee and a $3.00 computer resource fee for electronic copies. Civil records on computer from 1964, index books from 1800s. Mail turnaround time 1 day. Public use terminal has civil records back to 1964. Search civil judgment index at www.dallascounty.org/applications/english/record-search/rec-search_intro.php. No fee unless a record is viewed.

District Court - Civil 600 Commerce St, Dallas, TX 75202-4606; 214-653-7421; fax: 214-653-6634; 8AM-6:00PM (CST). *Civil.* www.dallascounty.com/forms/lstCourts.asp?division=cvd

General Information: Online identifiers in results same as on public terminal. No sealed records released. Will not fax documents. Court makes copy: $1.00 per page. Certification fee: $1.00 per page. Payee: District Clerk. Only cashiers checks and money orders accepted. Major credit cards accepted. Prepayment required.

Civil Name Search: Access: Mail, in person, online. Both court and visitors may perform in person name searches. Search fee: $5.00 per name. Required to search: name, case number. Civil records on computer since 1967; on dockets back to 1940; records prior to 1940 are maintained by Texas Historical Div. of the Dallas Public Lib. Public use terminal has civil records but viewable records are limited to family court documents and civil court efilings. Search district civil and family case index free at www.dallascounty.org/applications/english/record-search/rec-search_intro.php. Cases go back to early 1960s.

District Court - Criminal 133 N River Front Blvd, LB12, Attn: District Clerk, Dallas, TX 75207-4313; 214-653-5950, 214-653-5969 records dept; fax: 214-653-5986; 8AM-4:30PM (CST). *Felony.* www.dallascounty.org

General Information: Online identifiers in results same as on public terminal. No juvenile, mental, sealed, or adoption records released. Will not fax documents. Court makes copy: $1.00 per page. Certification fee: $1.00 per page. Payee: District Clerk. Only cashiers checks and money orders accepted. Major credit cards accepted. Prepayment required. Mail requests: SASE required.

Criminal Name Search: Access: Mail, online, in person. Both court and visitors may perform in person name searches. Search fee: $5.00 per name. Required to search: name, years to search, DOB. Criminal records computerized from 1972, on microfiche from 1979. Mail turnaround time 1-2 days. Public use terminal has crim records back to 1972. PAT terminal in law library but may also be at court. Not all records show DOB but most show race and gender. Name search free at www.dallascounty.org/applications/english/record-search/rec-search_intro.php and free results exhaustive, but there is a small fee to view a document using a credit card for payment. Online results show middle initial.

County Court - Misdemeanor 133 N Riverfront Blvd, Dallas, TX 75207-4313; 214-653-5740; fax: 214-653-5778; 8AM-4:30PM (CST). *Misdemeanor.* www.dallascounty.org

General Information: No juvenile, mental, sealed, or adoption records released. Court makes copy: $1.00 per page. Certification fee: $5.00 per jacket. Payee: County Clerk. Only cashiers checks and money orders accepted or cash if in person. No credit cards accepted. Prepayment required. Mail requests: SASE required.

Criminal Name Search: Access: Mail, online, in person. Both court and visitors may perform in person name searches. Search fee: $5.00 per name, misdemeanors only. Required to search: name, DOB. Criminal records computerized from 1975. Physical records go back to only 1993. For older searches call 214-653-5763, same fees apply. Mail turnaround time 10-11 days. Public use terminal has crim records back to 1975. PAT terminal in law library but may also be at court. Name search free at www.dallascounty.org/applications/english/record-search/rec-search_intro.php. Criminal index includes DOB. There is no fee unless a record is viewed but most records info is viewed for free. Not all records have DOBs but most show race and gender. Online results show middle initial.

Criminal District Courts 1-5 133 N Industrial Blvd, LB12, Attn: District Clerk, Records Department, Dallas, TX 75207; 214-653-5950; fax: 214-653-5986; 8AM-4:30PM (CST). *Felony.*
www.dallascounty.org
General Information: Same records as the main Dallas Criminal Court, see that profile.

Probate Court 509 Main St, 2nd Floor, Records Bldg,, Dallas, TX 75202-3500; 214-653-6166; 8AM-4:30PM (CST). *Probate.*
www.dallascourts.com/forms/lstCourts.asp?division=pro
General Information: There are three probate courts, above number is for Court 3. Search the probate index at http://courts.dallascounty.org/default.aspx. There is no fee unless a record is viewed.

Dawson County

District Court Drawer 1268, Lamesa, TX 79331; 806-872-7373; fax: 806-872-9513; 8:30AM-5PM (CST). *Felony, Civil.*
General Information: No juvenile, mental, sealed, or adoption records released. Will fax documents $1.00 per page. Court makes copy: $1.00 per page. Certification fee: $1.00 per page, but no fee if they make copies. Payee: Dawson County District Clerk. Personal checks accepted, credit cards are not. Prepayment required. Mail requests: SASE not required.
Civil Name Search: Access: Mail, in person. Both court and visitors may perform in person name searches. Search fee: $5.00 per name. Civil records in index books/files from 1905; computerized records since 1995. Mail turnaround time 1 day.
Criminal Name Search: Access: Mail, in person. Both court and visitors may perform in person name searches. Search fee: $5.00 per name. Required to search: name, years to search, signed release. Criminal index in books/files from 1900s; computerized records since 1995. Mail turnaround time 1 day.

County Court Drawer 1268, Lamesa, TX 79331; 806-872-3778; fax: 806-872-2473; 8:30AM-N;1-5PM (CST). *Misdemeanor, Civil, Probate.*
General Information: Probate fax is same as main fax number. No juvenile, mental or sealed records released. Fee to fax out file $5.00 each plus $1.00 per page. Court makes copy: $1.00 per page. Self serve copy: same. Certification fee: $5.00 per document plus copy fee. Payee: County Clerk. Personal checks accepted. AMEX, Discover, MasterCard accepted. Prepayment required. Mail requests: SASE required.
Civil Name Search: Access: Fax, mail, in person. Both court and visitors may perform in person name searches. Search fee: $5.00 per name. Civil records in index files since 1906, on computer back to 1992. Note: Fees must be prepaid before fax access is allowed. Mail turnaround time 1 day. Civil PAT goes back to 1992.
Criminal Name Search: Access: Mail, fax, in person. Both court and visitors may perform in person name searches. Search fee: $5.00 per name. Required to search: name, years to search, DOB; also helpful-signed release, offense, date of offense. Criminal records in index files since 1906; on computer back to 1986. Note: Fees must be prepaid before fax access is allowed. Mail turnaround time 1 day. Criminal PAT goes back to 1982.

De Witt County

District Court PO Box 845, 307 N Gonzales, Cuero, TX 77954; 361-275-0931; fax: 361-275-0934; 8AM-5PM (CST). *Felony, Civil.*
www.co.dewitt.tx.us/ips/cms/districtcourt/
General Information: No juvenile, mental, sealed, or adoption records released. Will not fax documents. Court makes copy: $1.00 per page. Certification fee: $1.00 per doc. Payee: DeWitt County District Clerk. Personal checks accepted, credit cards are not. Prepayment required. Mail requests: SASE required.
Civil Name Search: Access: Mail, in person. Both court and visitors may perform in person name searches. Search fee: $5.00 per name. Mail turnaround time 1 week. Public use terminal available, records go back to 2/1999.
Criminal Name Search: Access: Mail, in person. Both court and visitors may perform in person name searches. Search fee: $5.00 per name. Required to search: name, years to search, DOB, SSN, signed release. Criminal records maintained on computer back to 1999, books back to 1890. Mail turnaround time 1 week. Public use terminal available, crim records go back to 2/1999.

County Court 307 N Gonzales, Cuero, TX 77954; 361-275-0864; fax: 361-275-0866; 8AM-5PM (CST). *Misdemeanor, Probate.*
General Information: Probate is in a separate index at this same address. Probate fax is same as main fax number. No juvenile, mental, sealed, or adoption records released. Fee to fax out file $1.00 per page, pre-paid only. Court makes copy: $1.00 per page. Certification fee: $5.00 per document. Payee: DeWitt County Clerk. Personal checks accepted, credit cards are not. Prepayment required. Mail requests: SASE not required.
Criminal Name Search: Access: Mail, in person. Both court and visitors may perform in person name searches. Search fee: $5.00 per name. Required to search: name, years to search; also helpful: DOB, SSN. Criminal records go back to 1960s; on computer back to 1998.

Deaf Smith County

District Court 235 E 3rd St, Rm 304, Hereford, TX 79045; 806-364-3901; fax: 806-363-7007; 8AM-N, 1PM-5PM (CST). *Felony, Civil.*
General Information: No juvenile, mental, sealed, or adoption records released. Fee to fax out file $2.00 per page. Court makes copy: $1.00 per page. Certification fee: $1.00. Payee: District Clerk. Personal checks accepted, credit cards are not. Prepayment required. Mail requests: SASE required.
Civil Name Search: Access: Fax, mail, in person. Both court and visitors may perform in person name searches. Search fee: $5.00 per name. Required to search: name, years to search, DOB, SSN. Civil records on computer from 2/1993; prior on microfiche from 5/15/1981. Mail turnaround time 3 days. Civil PAT goes back to 2/1993.
Criminal Name Search: Access: Fax, mail, in person. Both court and visitors may perform in person name searches. Search fee: $5.00 per name. Required to search: name, years to search; also helpful: DOB, SSN, case number. Criminal records computerized from 2/1993; prior on microfiche from 5/15/1981. Mail turnaround time 3 days. Criminal PAT goes back to same as civil. Aliases may also be included in PAT search results.

County Court Deaf Smith Courthouse, 235 E 3rd, Rm 203, Hereford, TX 79045; 806-363-7077; fax: 806-363-7023; 8AM-5PM (CST). *Misdemeanor, Civil, Probate.*
General Information: No juvenile, mental, sealed, or adoption records released. Will fax documents $2.00 plus $1.00 copy fee for each page faxed. Court makes copy: $1.00 per page. Self serve copy: same. Certification fee: $5.00 per document plus copy fee. Payee: County Clerk. Personal checks accepted. Major credit cards accepted; 5% usage fee added. Prepayment required. Mail requests: SASE not required.
Civil Name Search: Access: Mail, in person. Both court and visitors may perform in person name searches. Search fee: $5.00 per name. Required to search: name, years to search, DOB. Civil records on computer from 1989, microfiche from 1981, index books from early 1900s. Mail turnaround time 1 day. Civil PAT goes back to 1989.
Criminal Name Search: Access: Mail, in person. Both court and visitors may perform in person name searches. Search fee: $5.00 per name. Required to search: name, years to search; DOB and SSN helpful. Criminal records computerized from 1993, microfiche from 1981, index books from early 1900s. Note: Records also available on CD-ROM special order, usually $22.00 minimum. Mail turnaround time 1 day, usually. Criminal PAT goes back to 1993. Terminal results include SSN.

Delta County

District & County Court 200 W Dallas Ave, Cooper, TX 75432; 903-395-4400 x222; fax: 903-395-4260; 8AM-5PM (CST). *Felony, Misdemeanor, Civil, Probate.*
General Information: Probate is a separate index at this same address. Probate fax is same as main fax number. No juvenile, mental, sealed, or adoption records released. Fee to fax out file $2.00 per page. Court makes copy: $1.00 per page. Self serve copy: same. Certification fee: $5.00 per doc plus copy fee. Payee: County or District Clerk. Personal checks accepted. Major credit cards accepted. Prepayment required. Mail requests: SASE required.
Civil Name Search: Access: Phone, mail, in person. Both court and visitors may perform in person name searches. Search fee: $5.00 per name per court. Civil records in index books from late 1800s. Note: Phone searches must be pre-paid. Mail turnaround time 1 day. Public use terminal has civil records back to - record index not complete.
Criminal Name Search: Access: Phone, mail, in person. Both court and visitors may perform in person name searches. Search fee: $5.00 per name per court. Required to search: name, years to search, DOB. Criminal docket on books from late 1800s. Note: Phone searches must be prepaid. Mail turnaround time 1 day.

Denton County

District Court PO Box 2146, 1450 E. McKinney St, Denton, TX 76202; criminal phone: 940-349-2210; civil phone: 940-349-2200; criminal fax: 940-349-2211; civil fax: 8AM-4:30PM; 8AM-4:30PM (CST). *Felony, Civil.* http://dentoncounty.com/dept/main.asp?Dept=26

General Information: No juvenile, mental, sealed, expunctions or adoption records released. Fee to fax out file $1.00 per page. Court makes copy: $1.00 per page. Certification fee: $1.00 per document. No personal checks accepted. Use of credit card requires a 5% surcharge. Prepayment required. Mail requests: SASE required.

Civil Name Search: Access: Phone, mail, fax, online, in person. Only the court performs in person name searches; visitors may not. Search fee: $5.00 per name. Civil records on computer from 1990, archived from 1936. Mail turnaround time 1-2 weeks. Search civil records free at http://justice.dentoncounty.com. Search by name or cause number.

Criminal Name Search: Access: Mail, fax, online, in person. Only the court performs in person name searches; visitors may not. Search fee: $5.00 per name. Required to search: name, years to search, DOB. Criminal records computerized from 1990, archived from 1936. Mail turnaround time 1-2 weeks. Criminal searches are free at http://justice.dentoncounty.com. Records go back to 1990 forward. Access also includes sheriff bond and jail records.

County Court PO Box 2187, Attn: County Clerk, 1450 McKinney, Denton, TX 76202-2187; 940-349-2012; criminal phone: 940-349-2014; civil phone: 940-349-2016; probate phone: 940-349-2036; criminal fax: 940-349-5215; civil fax: 8AM-5PM, W til 4:30PM; 8AM-5PM, W til 4:30PM (CST). *Misdemeanor, Civil, Probate.* http://dentoncounty.com/deptall.asp

General Information: No juvenile, mental, sealed, or adoption records released. Will fax documents for fee. Court makes copy: $.25 per page. Certification fee: $5.00 per doc. Payee: Denton County Clerk. Cashiers checks and money orders accepted. Visa/MC/AMEX/Discover accepted. Prepayment required. Mail requests: SASE required.

Civil Name Search: Access: Mail, fax, in person, online. Both court and visitors may perform in person name searches. Search fee: $5.00 per name. Add $1.00 per year prior to 1989. Civil records on computer back to 1990. Note: An order form is on the web, order via fax or mail. Mail turnaround time 1-2 weeks. Civil PAT goes back to 1990. Public terminal in Law Library. Online access civil court records free at http://justice.dentoncounty.com/CivilSearch/civfrmd.htm.

Criminal Name Search: Access: Mail, fax, in person, online. Both court and visitors may perform in person name searches. Search fee: $5.00 per name. Add $1.00 per year over first 5. Required to search: name, years to search, DOB. Criminal records computerized from 1990. Note: An order form is on the web, order via fax or mail. Mail turnaround time 1-2 weeks. Criminal PAT goes back to 1990. Public terminal in Law Library. Online access county criminal records free at http://justice.dentoncounty.com/CrimSearch/crimfrmd.htm. Jail, bond, and parole records are also available at http://justice.dentoncounty.com. Search for registered sex offenders by ZIP Code at http://sheriff.dentoncounty.com/sex_offenders/default.htm.

Dickens County

District & County Court PO Box 120, Dickens, TX 79229; 806-623-5531; fax: 806-623-5240; 8AM-5PM (CST). *Felony, Misdemeanor, Civil, Probate.* www.co.dickens.tx.us/ips/cms/districtcourt/

General Information: No juvenile, mental, sealed or adoption records released. Will fax documents $1.00 per page. Court makes copy: $1.00 per page. Self serve copy: same. Certification fee: $5.00. Payee: District Court. Personal checks accepted, credit cards are not. Prepayment required. Mail requests: SASE required.

Civil Name Search: Access: Mail, fax, phone, in person. Both court and visitors may perform in person name searches. Search fee: $5.00 per name. Required to search: name, years to search, DOB, SSN and signed release. Civil records in index books since late 1891. Mail turnaround time 1-2 days.

Criminal Name Search: Access: Mail, fax, phone, in person. Both court and visitors may perform in person name searches. Search fee: $5.00 per name. Required to search: name, years to search; also helpful: DOB, SSN and signed release. Criminal docket on books from late 1891. Mail turnaround time 1-2 days.

Dimmit County

District Court 103 N 5th St, Carrizo Springs, TX 78834; 830-876-4243 x111, x112; criminal phone: 830-876-4280; fax: 830-876-4200; 8AM-N; 1PM-5PM (CST). *Felony, Civil.*

General Information: Probate is in the county clerk office. No juvenile, mental, sealed, or adoption records released. Will not fax documents. Court makes copy: $1.00 per page. Self serve copy: same. Certification fee: $5.00

per doc. Payee: District Clerk. Personal checks accepted, credit cards are not. Prepayment required. Mail requests: SASE required.

Civil Name Search: Access: Mail, in person. Both court and visitors may perform in person name searches. Search fee: $10.00 per name. Required to search: name, years to search; also helpful: address. Civil records in index books, archived from 1922. Mail turnaround time 2-3 days.

Criminal Name Search: Access: Mail, in person. Both court and visitors may perform in person name searches. Search fee: $10.00 per name. Required to search: name, years to search; also helpful: DOB, SSN. Criminal index in books, archived from 1936. Mail turnaround time 2-3 days.

County Court 103 N 5th, # 2A, Carrizo Springs, TX 78834; 830-876-4238/9; fax: 830-876-4205; 8AM-N, 1PM-5PM M, F; 8AM-5PM T, W, TH (CST). *Misdemeanor, Civil, Probate.*

General Information: Probate is a separate index. Probate fax is same as main fax number. No juvenile, mental, sealed, or adoption records released. Fee to fax out file $1.50 1st page; $1.00 each add'l. Court makes copy: $1.00 per page. Self serve copy: same. Certification fee: $5.00 per certification plus copy fee. Payee: County Clerk. Personal checks accepted, credit cards are not. Prepayment required. Mail requests: SASE required.

Civil Name Search: Access: Fax, mail, in person. Both court and visitors may perform in person name searches. Search fee: $10.00 per name. Civil records on microfiche from 1992, index books prior, computerized from 7/03. Mail turnaround time 1 day.

Criminal Name Search: Access: Fax, mail, in person. Both court and visitors may perform in person name searches. Search fee: $10.00 per name. Required to search: name, years to search, signed release, DOB; also helpful: sex, SSN. Paper records since 1930. Mail turnaround time 1 day.

Donley County

District & County Court PO Drawer U, Clarendon, TX 79226; 806-874-3436; fax: 806-874-3351; 8AM-N, 1-5PM (CST). *Felony, Misdemeanor, Civil, Probate.*

General Information: No juvenile, mental, sealed, or adoption records released. Will not fax documents. Court makes copy: $1.00 per page. Self serve copy: same. Certification fee: $5.00. Payee: County Clerk. Personal checks accepted, credit cards are not. Prepayment required. Mail requests: SASE required.

Civil Name Search: Access: Mail, in person. Both court and visitors may perform in person name searches. Search fee: $5.00 per name. Civil records on computer from 1991, index books from 1890s. Mail turnaround time 1 day. Civil PAT goes back to 1994.

Criminal Name Search: Access: Mail, in person. Both court and visitors may perform in person name searches. Search fee: $5.00 per name. Required to search: name, years to search, DOB, signed release, aliases; also helpful: SSN. Criminal records computerized from 1991, index books from 1890s. Mail turnaround time 1 day. Criminal PAT goes back to same as civil.

Duval County

District Court PO Drawer 428, 400 E Gravis, San Diego, TX 78384; 361-279-3322 x239; criminal phone: 361-279-6284; civil phone: 361-279-6240; 8AM-5PM (CST). *Felony, Civil.*

General Information: No sealed, or adoption records released. Will not fax documents. Court makes copy: $1.00 per page. Certification fee: $5.00. Payee: District Clerk. Personal checks accepted, credit cards are not. Prepayment required. Mail requests: SASE required.

Civil Name Search: Access: Mail, in person. Both court and visitors may perform in person name searches. Search fee: $15.00 per name. Civil index on docket books from 1900s. Mail turnaround time 1-2 days.

Criminal Name Search: Access: Phone, mail, in person. Both court and visitors may perform in person name searches. Search fee: $15.00 per name. Criminal records not computerized, indexed in books since 1900's. Mail turnaround time 1-2 days.

County Court PO Box 248, San Diego, TX 78384; 361-279-6249/6272; fax: 361-279-3159; 8AM-5PM (CST). *Misdemeanor, Civil, Probate.*

General Information: No juvenile, mental, sealed, or adoption records released. Will not fax documents. Court makes copy: $1.00 per page. Certification fee: $5.00. Payee: County Clerk. Personal checks accepted, credit cards are not. Prepayment required. Mail requests: SASE required.

Civil Name Search: Access: Mail, in person. Both court and visitors may perform in person name searches. Search fee: $10.00 per name. Civil records in index books from 1800s, records go back to the early 1900's. Mail turnaround time 2 days.

Criminal Name Search: Access: Mail, in person. Both court and visitors may perform in person name searches. Search fee: $10.00 per name. Required to search: name, years to search, offense, date of offense. Criminal docket on books from 1800s. Mail turnaround time 2 days.

Eastland County

District Court 100 W Main St, #206, Eastland, TX 76448; 254-629-2664; fax: 254-629-6070; 8AM-5PM (CST). *Felony, Civil.*
www.eastlandcountytexas.com/dist-clerk/index.html
General Information: No juvenile, mental, sealed, or adoption records released. Will fax documents to toll free line. Court makes copy: $1.00 per page. Certification fee: $5.00 per document. Payee: District Clerk. Personal checks accepted. Credit cards accepted. Prepayment required. Mail requests: SASE required.
Civil Name Search: Access: Mail, in person. Both court and visitors may perform in person name searches. Search fee: $5.00. Civil records on computer from 1930. Mail turnaround time 1 day. Civil PAT available.
Criminal Name Search: Access: Mail, in person. Both court and visitors may perform in person name searches. Search fee: $5.00. Criminal records computerized from 1976, archived from 1875. Mail turnaround time 1 day. Criminal PAT available.

County Court PO Box 110, Eastland, TX 76448; 254-629-1583; fax: 254-629-8125; 8AM-5PM (CST). *Misdemeanor, Probate.*
General Information: No civil records after 1977; criminal and probate records only thereafter. No juvenile, mental, sealed, or adoption records released. Will fax documents $5.00 fee. Court makes copy: $1.00 per page. Certification fee: $5.00 per cert plus copy fee. Payee: Eastland County Clerk. Personal checks accepted; checks must include phone number & DL number. No credit cards accepted. Prepayment required. Mail requests: SASE not required.
Criminal Name Search: Access: Mail, in person. Both court and visitors may perform in person name searches. Search fee: $5.00 per name. Required to search: name, years to search, DOB; also helpful: SSN. Signed release required if subject is a minor. Criminal docket on books and on computer from 1987; name searches only. Mail turnaround time 1-2 days. Public use terminal has crim records back to 1987; terminal also provides access to probate records from earliest date available.

Ector County

District Court County Courthouse, 300 N Grant, Rm 301, Odessa, TX 79761; 432-498-4290; fax: 432-498-4292; 8AM-5PM (CST). *Felony, Civil.*
General Information: No juvenile, mental, sealed, or adoption records released. Will fax documents $2.00 per page. Court makes copy: $.25 per page. Certification fee: $1.00 per page includes copy fee. Payee: Ector County District Clerk. Business checks accepted. No credit cards accepted. Prepayment required. Mail requests: SASE required.
Civil Name Search: Access: Phone, fax, mail, in person. Both court and visitors may perform in person name searches. Search fee: $5.00 per name. Civil records on computer from 1989, index books from 1880. Mail turnaround time 2 weeks. Civil PAT goes back to 1989.
Criminal Name Search: Access: Phone, mail, in person. Both court and visitors may perform in person name searches. Search fee: $5.00 per name. Criminal records computerized from 1989, index books from 1880. Mail turnaround time 2 weeks. Criminal PAT goes back to same as civil.

County Court PO Box 707, 300 N Grant St, Rm 111, Odessa, TX 79760; 432-498-4130; fax: 432-498-4177; 8AM-4:30PM (CST). *Misdemeanor, Civil, Probate.*
General Information: No juvenile, mental, sealed, or adoption records released. Fee to fax out file $2.00 each. Court makes copy: $1.00 per page. Certification fee: $5.00 per doc plus copy fee. Payee: County Clerk. Personal checks accepted. Credit cards accepted. Prepayment required. Mail requests: SASE requested.
Civil Name Search: Access: Mail, in person. Both court and visitors may perform in person name searches. Search fee: $10.00 per name per ten years. Civil records on computer from 1992, index books from 1900s. Mail turnaround time 5 days. Civil PAT goes back to 1992. Results on public terminal may show DR.
Criminal Name Search: Access: Mail, in person. Both court and visitors may perform in person name searches. Search fee: $10.00 per name per ten years. Required to search: name, years to search; also helpful: DOB, SSN, DL#. Criminal records computerized from 1989, index books from 1900s. Mail turnaround time 5 days. Criminal PAT goes back to 1989. Results on public terminal may show DR.

Edwards County

District & County Court PO Box 184, Rocksprings, TX 78880; 830-683-2235; fax: 830-683-5376; 8AM-N, 1-5PM (CST). *Felony, Misdemeanor, Civil, Probate.*
General Information: The court plans to install public access terminals in the near future. No juvenile, mental, sealed, or adoption records released. Fee to fax out file $5.00. Court makes copy: $1.00 per page. Certification fee: $5.00. Payee: Edwards County Clerk. Personal checks accepted, credit cards are not. Prepayment required. Mail requests: SASE required.

Civil Name Search: Access: Phone, fax, mail, in person. Both court and visitors may perform in person name searches. Search fee: $10.00 per name. Real Property on computer from 2003, index books from 1885. Mail turnaround time 1 day or less. Public use terminal has civil records. The public terminal shows OPRs only.
Criminal Name Search: Access: Phone, fax, mail, in person. Both court and visitors may perform in person name searches. Search fee: $10.00 per name. Index books from 1960. Mail turnaround time 1 day.

El Paso County

District Court 500 E San Antonio, Rm 103, El Paso, TX 79901; 915-546-2021; criminal phone: 915-834-8255; civil phone: 915-834-8256; fax: 915-546-8139; 8AM-5PM (MST). *Felony, Civil.*
www.epcounty.com/districtclerk/
General Information: No fee to request a name search of indexes, however a $10 charge per individual if a certified document stating the presence or absence of felony charges against that individual is requested. Each 10 year period prior to 1986 carries an add'l $5 charge. No juvenile, mental, sealed, or adoption records released. Will fax documents $10.00 plus $.50 per page. Court makes copy: $.50 per page. Self serve copy: same. Certification fee: $1.00 per page with maximum $5.00. Payee: District Clerk. Business checks accepted. Major credit cards accepted for mail or phone searches. Prepayment required. Mail requests: SASE required.
Civil Name Search: Access: Mail, in person, online, fax, phone. Both court and visitors may perform in person name searches. Search fee: See above statement regarding fees. Civil records on computer from 1986, microfiche from 1971, index books from 1800s. Mail turnaround time 1-3 days. Civil PAT goes back to 1986. All records disposed or active on public access terminal. Online access to civil court records is free at www.epcounty.com/publicsearch/CivilRecords/CivilRecSearchForm.aspx. Also, access index and images at www.idocket.com; registration and password required; online civil records go back to 12/31/1986.
Criminal Name Search: Access: Mail, in person, online, fax, phone. Both court and visitors may perform in person name searches. Search fee: See above statement regarding fees. Required to search: name, years to search, DOB, signed release; also helpful: sex. Criminal records computerized from 1986, microfiche from 1971, index books from 1800s. Mail turnaround time 1-3 days. Criminal PAT goes back to same as civil. All records disposed or active on public access terminal. Online access to criminal court active records is free at www.epcounty.com/publicsearch/CriminalRecords/CriminalRecordSearchForm.aspx. Also, online access index and images at www.idocket.com; registration and password required; online records go back to 12/31/1986.

County Court 500 E San Antonio St, Rm 105, El Paso, TX 79901; 915-546-2072; fax: 915-546-2012; 8AM-5:30PM (MST). *Misdemeanor, Civil.*
www.co.el-paso.tx.us
General Information: Online identifiers in results same as on public terminal. No juvenile, mental, sealed, or adoption records released. Will not fax documents. Court makes copy: $.50 per page; if by mail $2.00 per page. Certification fee: $5.00 per document plus copy fee. Payee: County Clerk. No personal checks or credit cards accepted. Prepayment required. Mail requests: SASE required.
Civil Name Search: Access: Mail, fax, in person, online. Both court and visitors may perform in person name searches. Search fee: $6.00 per name. Civil records on computer from 1989, on microfiche and archived from 1952. Mail turnaround time up to 1 week. Civil PAT goes back to 1989. Online access to civil court records is free at www.co.el-paso.tx.us/JIMSSearch/CivilRecordsearch.asp. Also, search vital records and recordings. Also, access index and images at www.idocket.com; registration and password required. Civil records go back to 12/31/1986, probate to 12/31/1989.
Criminal Name Search: Access: Phone, mail, fax, in person, online. Both court and visitors may perform in person name searches. Search fee: $6.00 per name. Required to search: name, years to search, DOB, SSN. Criminal records computerized since 1989. Mail turnaround time up to 1 week. Criminal PAT goes back to same as civil. Online access to misdemeanor criminal records is the same as civil at www.co.el-paso.tx.us/JIMSSearch/CriminalRecordsearch.asp and also at www.idocket.com with signup, see civil above.

Probate Courts El Paso County Courthouse, 500 E San Antonio, Rm 703/803, El Paso, TX 79901; 915-546-2161; fax: 915-875-8527; 8AM-Noon,1-5PM (MST). *Probate.*
General Information: There are two courts - #1 and #2. This court is also responsible for the Child Welfare Docket. Access probate records through www.idocket.com; registration and password required. Records go back to 12/31/1989.

Ellis County

District Court 109 S Jackson 2nd Floor, Waxahachie, TX 75165; 972-825-5091; fax: 972-825-5010; 8AM-4:30PM (CST). *Felony, Civil.*
www.co.ellis.tx.us/index.aspx?nid=79
General Information: No juvenile, mental, sealed, or adoption records released. Will not fax documents. Court makes copy: $.50 per page. Certification fee: $1.00 per page. Payee: District Clerk's Office. Only cashiers checks and money orders accepted. Visa/MC accepted. Prepayment required. Mail requests: SASE required.
Civil Name Search: Access: Mail, in person. Both court and visitors may perform in person name searches. Search fee: $5.00 per name. Civil records on computer from 1992, index books from 1800s. Mail turnaround time 1 week. Civil PAT goes back to 1992. Terminal results also show SSNs.
Criminal Name Search: Access: Mail, in person. Both court and visitors may perform in person name searches. Search fee: $5.00 per name. Required to search: name, years to search, DOB, offense. Criminal records computerized from 1992, index books from 1800s. Mail turnaround time 1 week. Criminal PAT goes back to same as civil. Terminal results include SSN.

County Court PO Box 250, Waxahachie, TX 75168; 972-825-5066; civil phone: 972-825-5255; fax: 972-825-5256; 8AM-4:30PM (CST). *Misdemeanor, Civil, Probate.*
www.co.ellis.tx.us
General Information: Probate fax is same as main fax number. No juvenile, mental, sealed, or adoption records released. Will not fax documents. Court makes copy: $1.00 per page. Self serve copy: same. Certification fee: $5.00 per document plus copy fee. Payee: Ellis County Clerk. Personal checks with ID accepted. Credit cards accepted. Prepayment required. Mail requests: SASE required.
Civil Name Search: Access: Mail, in person. Both court and visitors may perform in person name searches. Search fee: $5.00 per name. Fee is per 5 year period. Civil records on computer go back to 1995. Prior to computer records go back to 1969. Mail turnaround time 1-5 days. Civil PAT goes back to 1992.
Criminal Name Search: Access: Mail, in person. Both court and visitors may perform in person name searches. Search fee: $5.00 per name. Fee is per 5 year period. Required to search: name, years to search, DOB, SSN. Criminal records on computer since 1992, index books from 1959. Mail turnaround time 1-5 days. Criminal PAT goes back to same as civil.

Erath County

District Court 112 W College St, Stephenville, TX 76401; 254-965-1486; fax: 254-965-7156; 8AM-5PM (CST). *Felony, Civil.*
http://co.erath.tx.us/districtclerk.html
General Information: No juvenile, mental, sealed, or adoption records released. Fee to fax out file $1.00 per page. Court makes copy: $1.00 per page. Certification fee: $5.00 per doc. Payee: District Clerk. Personal checks accepted. Major credit cards accepted. Prepayment required. Mail requests: SASE required.
Civil Name Search: Access: Mail, in person, online. Both court and visitors may perform in person name searches. Search fee: $5.00 per name. Fee is per name per search. Limited civil records on computer last 10 years, in person must be done using docket books. Mail turnaround time 1-2 days. Civil PAT goes back to 5 years. Access to District Clerk records requires registration, login and password; signup online at www.erathcountyonline.net/districtclerk/
Criminal Name Search: Access: Mail, in person, online. Both court and visitors may perform in person name searches. Search fee: $5.00 per name. Required to search: name, years to search, DOB; also helpful: SSN. Limited criminal records on computer last 10 years, in person must be done using docket books. Mail turnaround time 1-2 days. Criminal PAT goes back to same as civil. Access to District Clerk records requires registration, login and password; signup online at www.erathcountyonline.net/districtclerk/

County Court Erath County Courthouse, 100 W Washington, Stephenville, TX 76401; 254-965-1482; criminal phone: 254-965-1407; civil phone: 254-965-1428; probate phone: 254-965-1428; fax: 254-965-5732; 8AM-4PM (CST). *Misdemeanor, Civil, Probate.*
General Information: Probate is a separate index at this same address. Probate fax is same as main fax number. No juvenile, mental, sealed, or adoption records released. Will fax documents $1.75 fee for the 1st page and $.75 for each additional page. Court makes copy: $1.00 per page. Self serve copy: same. Certification fee: $5.00 per document plus copy fee. Payee: County Clerk. Personal checks accepted, credit cards are not. Prepayment required. Mail requests: SASE required.
Civil Name Search: Access: Mail, in person, online. Both court and visitors may perform in person name searches. Search fee: $5.00 per name. Civil records on computer back to 1993, index books since 1970. Mail turnaround time 1 week. Civil PAT goes back to 1993. Access to County

Court records requires registration, login and password; signup online at www.erathcountyonline.net/countyclerk/.
Criminal Name Search: Access: Mail, in person, online. Both court and visitors may perform in person name searches. Search fee: $10.00 per name. Required to search: name, years to search, DOB. Criminal records computerized from 1993, index books from 1960. Mail turnaround time 1 week. Criminal PAT goes back to same as civil. Results include name and case number. Access to County Court records requires registration, login and password; signup online at www.erathcountyonline.net/countyclerk/.

Falls County

District Court PO Box 229, 125 Bridge St, Rm 301, Marlin, TX 76661; 254-883-1419; fax: 254-804-0190; 8AM-N, 1-5 PM (CST). *Felony, Civil.*
General Information: Mail to Attn: District Clerk. No juvenile, mental, sealed, child support or adoption records released. Faxes in or out are $1.00 per page. Court makes copy: $1.00 per page. No certification fee. Payee: District Clerk. Personal checks accepted, credit cards are not. Prepayment required. Mail requests: SASE required.
Civil Name Search: Access: Mail, in person. Both court and visitors may perform in person name searches. Search fee: $5.00 per name. Overall records go back to 1850's. Computerized records go back to 1998. Mail turnaround time 1-5 days. Civil PAT goes back to 1997.
Criminal Name Search: Access: Mail, in person. Both court and visitors may perform in person name searches. Search fee: $5.00 per name. Required to search: name, years to search; also helpful: DOB. Criminal index in books. Mail turnaround time 1-5 days. Criminal PAT goes back to same.

County Court PO Box 458, Marlin, TX 76661; 254-883-1408; fax: 254-883-1406; 8AM-5PM (CST). *Misdemeanor, Civil, Probate.*
General Information: No juvenile, mental, sealed, or adoption records released. Will not fax documents. Court makes copy: $1.00 per page. Certification fee: $5.00 per instrument. Payee: County Clerk. Local personal and business checks accepted. No credit cards accepted. Prepayment required. Mail requests: SASE required.
Civil Name Search: Access: Phone, mail, in person. Both court and visitors may perform in person name searches. Search fee: $5.00 per name. Civil records in index books from 1985. Note: Court allows phone search only if fee prepaid. Mail turnaround time 1 day.
Criminal Name Search: Access: Phone, mail, in person. Both court and visitors may perform in person name searches. Search fee: $5.00 per name. Required to search: name, years to search, DOB, SSN. Criminal docket on books from 1985. Note: Phone search only if fee is prepaid. Mail turnaround time 1 day.

Fannin County

District Court 101 E Sam Rayburn Dr, #201, Bonham, TX 75418; 903-583-7459; fax: 903-640-1826; 8AM-5PM (CST). *Felony, Civil, Family.*
www.co.fannin.tx.us/ips/cms/departments/districtClerk.html
General Information: No juvenile, mental, sealed, or adoption records released. Will not fax documents. Court makes copy: $1.00 per page. Self serve copy: same. Certification fee: $1.00. Payee: District Clerk, Fannin County. Personal checks accepted, credit cards are not. Prepayment required. Mail requests: SASE required.
Civil Name Search: Access: Fax, mail, in person, online. Both court and visitors may perform in person name searches. Search fee: $5.00 per name. Civil records in index books, archived from 1865. Mail turnaround time 10 days. Civil PAT available. Access to civil, probate and family court dockets at http://71.97.114.198/default.aspx.
Criminal Name Search: Access: Fax, mail, Online. Both court and visitors may perform in person name searches. Search fee: $5.00 per name. Required to search: name, years to search, address, DOB, SSN. Criminal records computerized from 1975, archived from 1865. Mail turnaround time 5 days. Criminal PAT available. Online access to criminal docket records at http://71.97.114.198/default.aspx. Online results show middle initial.

County Court County Courthouse, 101 E Sam Rayburn Ste 102, Bonham, TX 75418; 903-583-7486; criminal phone: 903-583-8502; civil phone: 903-640-2008; probate phone: 903-640-2008; fax: 903-583-9598; 8AM-5PM (CST). *Misdemeanor, Civil, Probate.*
www.co.fannin.tx.us/ips/cms
General Information: Address requests to Ste 103 for criminal and Ste 106 for civil or probate. No juvenile, mental, sealed, or adoption records released. Will not fax documents. Court makes copy: $1.00 per page. Certification fee: $5.00. Payee: County Clerk. No personal checks or credit cards accepted. Prepayment required. Mail requests: SASE required.
Civil Name Search: Access: Mail, in person, online. Both court and visitors may perform in person name searches. Search fee: $10.00 per name. Civil index in books. Mail turnaround time 1-10 days. Public use terminal has civil records. Access to civil, probate and family court dockets at http://71.97.114.198/default.aspx.

Criminal Name Search: Access: Mail, in person, online. Only the court performs in person name searches; visitors may not. Search fee: $10.00 per name. Required to search: name, years to search, DOB; also helpful-SSN. Criminal records computerized from 1979; prior on index books. Mail turnaround time 1-10 days. Online access to criminal docket records at http://71.97.114.198/default.aspx.

Fayette County

District Court Fayette County Courthouse, 151 N Washington, La Grange, TX 78945; 979-968-3548; fax: 979-968-2618; 8AM-5PM (CST). *Felony, Civil over $5,000.*
www.155discttx.com/index.html
General Information: No juvenile, mental, sealed, or adoption records released. Will fax documents $5.00 per page. Court makes copy: $1.00 per page. Certification fee: $2.00. Payee: Fayette County District Clerk. Personal checks accepted, credit cards are not. Prepayment required. Mail requests: SASE required.
Civil Name Search: Access: Mail, in person. Both court and visitors may perform in person name searches. Search fee: $5.00 per name. Civil records in index books, on computer since 1990. Mail turnaround time 2-3 days. Civil PAT goes back to 1990.
Criminal Name Search: Access: Mail, in person. Both court and visitors may perform in person name searches. Search fee: $5.00 per name. Criminal index in books, on computer since 1990. Mail turnaround time 2-3 days. Criminal PAT goes back to 1987.

County Court PO Box 59, 246 W Colorado, La Grange, TX 78945; 979-968-3251; fax: 979-968-8531; 8AM-5PM (CST). *Misdemeanor, Civil under $10,000, Probate.*
www.co.fayette.tx.us
General Information: Copy fees are doubled if copies mailed or faxed. No juvenile, mental, sealed, or adoption records released. Will fax documents for double the copy fee, prepaid. Court makes copy: $1.00 per page. Certification fee: $5.00. Payee: County Clerk. Personal checks accepted. Major credit cards accepted with 4% fee, via a system. Prepayment required. All documents mailed must be pre-paid, including double the copy fee. Mail requests: SASE not required.
Civil Name Search: Access: Mail, in person. Both court and visitors may perform in person name searches. Search fee: $5.00 per name. Civil records in index books, archived from July 1876. Mail turnaround time 1 day. Public use terminal has civil records back to 4/15/1998.
Criminal Name Search: Access: Mail, in person. Both court and visitors may perform in person name searches. Search fee: $5.00 per name. Criminal records computerized from 1980, index books prior. Mail turnaround time 1 day.

Fisher County

District Court PO Box 88, Roby, TX 79543; 325-776-2279; fax: 325-776-3253; 8AM-5PM (CST). *Felony, Civil.*
General Information: No juvenile, mental, sealed, or adoption records released. Fee to fax out file $1.00 per page. Court makes copy: $1.00 per page. Self serve copy: same. Certification fee: $1.00 per page. Payee: District Clerk. Business checks accepted. No credit cards accepted. Prepayment required. Mail requests: SASE required.
Civil Name Search: Access: Mail, in person. Both court and visitors may perform in person name searches. Search fee: $5.00 per name. Required to search: name, years to search; also helpful: address. Civil records in index books from 1886. Mail turnaround time 1-2 days.
Criminal Name Search: Access: Mail, in person. Both court and visitors may perform in person name searches. Search fee: $5.00 per name. Required to search: name, years to search, signed release; also helpful: address, DOB. Criminal docket on books from 1886. Mail turnaround time 1-2 days.

County Court Box 368, Roby, TX 79543-0368; 325-776-2401; fax: 325-776-3274; 8:30AM-4:30PM (CST). *Misdemeanor, Civil, Probate.*
General Information: No juvenile, mental, sealed, or adoption records released. Will not fax documents. Court makes copy: n/a. Self serve copy: $1.00 per page. Certification fee: $5.00 per document. Payee: Fisher County Clerk. Personal checks accepted, credit cards are not. Prepayment required. Mail requests: SASE required.
Civil Name Search: Access: Mail, in person. Both court and visitors may perform in person name searches. Search fee: $5.00 per name, must have year. Civil records on computer from 1994 index books from 1880. Mail turnaround time 1 day. Civil PAT available.
Criminal Name Search: Access: Mail, in person. Both court and visitors may perform in person name searches. Search fee: $5.00 per name, must have year. Required to search: name, years to search, signed release, offense. Criminal records computerized from 1994, index books from 1886. Mail turnaround time 1 day. Criminal PAT available.

Floyd County

District Court 105 S. Main St, Rm 207, Floydada, TX 79235; 806-983-4923; fax: 806-983-4938; 8:30AM-N, 1-4:45PM (CST). *Felony, Civil.*
General Information: No juvenile, mental, sealed, or adoption records released. Will fax out documents for $1.50 per page. Court makes copy: $1.00 per page. Certification fee: $1.00. Payee: District Clerk. Personal checks accepted, credit cards are not. Prepayment required. Mail requests: SASE required.
Civil Name Search: Access: Mail, in person. Both court and visitors may perform in person name searches. Search fee: $5.00 per name. Civil records in index books from early 1891. Mail turnaround time 1 day.
Criminal Name Search: Access: Mail, in person. Both court and visitors may perform in person name searches. Search fee: $5.00 per name. Criminal docket on books from early 1891. Mail turnaround time 1 day.

County Court Courthouse, Rm 101, Main St, Floydada, TX 79235; 806-983-4900; fax: 806-983-4921; 8:30AM-N, 1-5PM (CST). *Misdemeanor, Civil, Probate.*
General Information: No juvenile, mental, sealed, or adoption records released. Will fax documents $1.00 fee plus $1.00 per page. Court makes copy: $1.00 per page. Self serve copy: same. Certification fee: $5.00. Payee: County Clerk. Personal checks accepted, credit cards are not. Prepayment required. Mail requests: SASE not required.
Civil Name Search: Access: Phone, mail, in person. Both court and visitors may perform in person name searches. Search fee: $5.00 per name. Civil records in index books from 1890. Mail turnaround time 2-4 days.
Criminal Name Search: Access: Phone, mail, in person. Both court and visitors may perform in person name searches. Search fee: $5.00 per name. Required to search: name, years to search, DOB. Criminal docket on books from 1890. Mail turnaround time 1-5 days.

Foard County

District & County Court PO Box 539, Crowell, TX 79227; 940-684-1365; fax: 940-684-1918; 9AM-4:30PM (CST). *Felony, Misdemeanor, Civil, Probate.*
General Information: No juvenile, mental, sealed, or adoption records released. Fee to fax out file $2.50 1st page, $.25 per page each add'l. Court makes copy: $1.00 per page. Self serve copy: same. Certification fee: $5.00. Payee: Foard County Clerk. Personal checks accepted, credit cards are not. Prepayment required. Mail requests: SASE required.
Civil Name Search: Access: Mail, in person. Both court and visitors may perform in person name searches. Search fee: $10.00 per name. Civil records go back to 1908, civil records in index books from 1910; on computer from 1989. Mail turnaround time varies.
Criminal Name Search: Access: Mail, in person. Both court and visitors may perform in person name searches. Search fee: $10.00 per name. Required to search: name, years to search, DOB. Criminal records go back to 1908, Criminal index in books from 1910; on computer from 1989. Mail turnaround time varies.

Fort Bend County

District Court 301 Jackson, Richmond, TX 77469; 281-633-7632; fax: 281-341-4519; 8AM-5PM (CST). *Felony, Civil, Family.*
www.co.fort-bend.tx.us
General Information: Physical court location is Fort Bend County Justice Center, 1422 Eugene Heimann Circle, Richmond, TX 77469. Online identifiers in results same as on public terminal. No juvenile, mental, sealed, termination or adoption records released. Court makes copy: $1.00 per page. Certification fee: Included in copy fee. Certification fee or Exemplification fee is $5.00 per doc plus copy fee. Payee: District Clerk. No out of state personal checks accepted. Credit cards accepted, but a convenience fee is added. Prepayment required. Mail requests: SASE required.
Civil Name Search: Access: Phone, mail, online, in person. Visitors must perform in person searches themselves. Search fee: $5.00 per name. Civil records on computer from 1991, index books from early 1900s. Mail turnaround time approx. 3 days. Civil PAT goes back to 1991. Search civil, probate and divorce index at http://tylerpaw.co.fort-bend.tx.us/default.aspx. Partial DOBs shown.
Criminal Name Search: Access: Mail, online, in person. Visitors must perform in person searches themselves. Search fee: $5.00 per name. Required to search: name, years to search, DOB, SSN. Criminal records computerized from 1981, index books from early 1900s. Mail turnaround time approx. 5 days. Criminal PAT goes back to 1981. Search criminal records free at www.co.fort-bend.tx.us/getSitePage.asp?sitePage=5608. Partial DOBs shown. Online results show middle initial.

County Court Attn: Clerk, 1422 Eugene Heimann Cir, Richmond, TX 77469; 281-341-8652; criminal fax: 281-341-8681; civil fax: 8AM-4PM; 8AM-4PM (CST). *Misdemeanor, Civil, Probate.*
www.co.fort-bend.tx.us

General Information: Formerly located at 301 Jackson St, #101. Probate fax- 281-341-4520. Online identifiers in results same as on public terminal. No juvenile, mental, sealed, or adoption records released. Fee to fax out file $1.00 per page, plus $1.00 fee if local or $2.00 long distance for each 5 pages. Court makes copy: $1.00 per page. Certification fee: $5.00 per document plus copy fee. Payee: Ft Bend County Clerk. Personal checks accepted. Credit cards accepted. Prepayment required. Mail requests: SASE not required.

Civil Name Search: Access: Mail, in person, online. Both court and visitors may perform in person name searches. Search fee: $10.00 per name. Search fee is for each type record to be searched. Civil records on computer from 1984, also 1984-present optical imaged. Mail turnaround time 1-2 days. Civil PAT goes back to 1984. Search civil, probate and divorce index at http://tylerpaw.co.fort-bend.tx.us/default.aspx. Partial DOBs shown.

Criminal Name Search: Access: Mail, online, in person. Both court and visitors may perform in person name searches. Search fee: $10.00 per name. A search fee for each type record to be searched required. Required to search: name, years to search, DOB. Criminal records computerized from 1983, also 1983 to present optical imaged. Mail turnaround time 1-2 days. Criminal PAT available. Online access to misdemeanor and felony index is at http://tylerpaw.co.fort-bend.tx.us/default.aspx. Searches records from 1982 forward. Online results show middle initial.

Franklin County

District Court PO Box 750, Mount Vernon, TX 75457; 903-537-8337; fax: 903-537-8338; 8AM-5PM (CST). *Felony, Civil.*

General Information: No juvenile, mental, sealed, or adoption records released. Will fax documents $1.00 per page. Court makes copy: $1.00 per page. Self serve copy: same. Payee: District Clerk. Personal checks accepted, credit cards are not. Prepayment required. Mail requests: SASE required.

Civil Name Search: Access: Mail, in person. Both court and visitors may perform in person name searches. Search fee: $5.00 per name. Civil records on computer from 1987, index books from 1800s. Mail turnaround time 1 day. Civil PAT available.

Criminal Name Search: Access: Mail, in person. Both court and visitors may perform in person name searches. Search fee: $5.00 per name. Required to search: name, years to search; also helpful: DOB, SSN. Criminal records computerized from 1987, index books from 1800s. Mail turnaround time 1 day. Criminal PAT available. Online results show name only.

County Court 200 N Kaufman St, Mount Vernon, TX 75457; 903-537-2342 x2; fax: 903-537-2962; 8AM-N, 1-5PM (CST). *Misdemeanor, Civil, Probate.*

www.franklincountyclerk.net/

General Information: No juvenile, mental, sealed, or adoption records released. Fee to fax out file $1.00 per page. Court makes copy: $1.00 per page. Self serve copy: same. Certification fee: $5.00 per document. Payee: County Clerk. No out-of-state personal checks accepted include DL and phone on check. No credit cards accepted. Prepayment required. Mail requests: SASE required.

Civil Name Search: Access: Mail, fax, in person. Both court and visitors may perform in person name searches. Search fee: $5.00 per name. Civil records on computer from 1993. Mail turnaround time 1 week. Civil PAT goes back to 1993.

Criminal Name Search: Access: Mail, fax, in person, online. Both court and visitors may perform in person name searches. Search fee: $5.00 per name. Required to search: name, years to search, DOB and SSN. Criminal records computerized from 1993. Mail turnaround time 1 week. Criminal PAT goes back to same as civil. Online access is by subscription at https://countygovernmentrecords.com/texas/web/. Registration and user agreement required, or pay by credit card per search.

Freestone County

District Court PO Box 722, 118 Commerce St, Fairfield, TX 75840; 903-389-2534; fax: 903-389-8421; 8AM-5PM (CST). *Felony, Civil.*

General Information: No juvenile, mental, sealed, or adoption records released. Will not fax documents. Court makes copy: $1.00 per page. Certification fee: $1.00 per page. Payee: District Clerk. Personal checks accepted, credit cards are not. Prepayment required. Mail requests: SASE not required.

Civil Name Search: Access: Mail, in person. Both court and visitors may perform in person name searches. Search fee: $5.00 per name. Civil records in index books from 1830s. Mail turnaround time 1 day.

Criminal Name Search: Access: Mail, in person. Both court and visitors may perform in person name searches. Search fee: $5.00 per name. Criminal docket on books from 1830s. Mail turnaround time 1 day.

County Court PO Box 1010, Fairfield, TX 75840; 903-389-2635; fax: 903-389-6956; 8AM-5PM M-TH; 8AM-4:30PM Fri (CST). *Misdemeanor, Civil, Probate.*

General Information: In person researchers may use the docket books to do name searches. No juvenile, mental, sealed, or adoption records released. Will not fax documents. Court makes copy: $1.00 per page. Certification fee: $5.00 per document. Payee: Freestone County Clerk. Personal checks accepted, credit cards are not. Prepayment required. Mail requests: SASE not required.

Civil Name Search: Access: In person only. Visitors must perform in person searches themselves. Civil records in index books from 1967, judgments from 1851.

Criminal Name Search: Access: Mail, in person. Visitors must perform in person searches themselves. Search fee: $5.00 per name, 10-year search. Criminal docket on books from 1967. Mail turnaround time 2 days.

Frio County

District Court 500 E San Antonio, Box 8, Pearsall, TX 78061; 830-334-8073; fax: 830-334-0047; 8AM-5PM (CST). *Felony, Civil.*

www.81st-218thdistrictcourt.org/

General Information: No juvenile, mental, sealed, or adoption records released. Will not fax out documents. Court makes copy: $1.00 per page. Self serve copy: same. Certification fee: $1.00 per page includes copy fee. Payee: District Clerk. Business checks accepted. No credit cards accepted. Prepayment required. Mail requests: SASE required.

Civil Name Search: Access: Mail, in person. Both court and visitors may perform in person name searches. Search fee: $10.00 per name. Required to search: name, years to search; also helpful: address. Civil records in index books from 1948. Mail turnaround time 2-3 days.

Criminal Name Search: Access: Mail, in person. Both court and visitors may perform in person name searches. Search fee: $10.00 per name. Required to search: name, years to search, DOB; also helpful: address. Criminal docket on books from 1950. Mail turnaround time 2-3 days.

County Court 500 E San Antonio St, #6, Pearsall, TX 78061; 830-334-2214; fax: 830-334-0021; 8AM-N, 1-5PM (CST). *Misdemeanor, Civil, Probate.*

General Information: Probate fax is same as main fax number. No juvenile, mental, sealed, or adoption records released. Will fax documents $2.00 per page; $1.00 if faxing to a toll-free number. Court makes copy: $1.00 per page. Self serve copy: same. Certification fee: $5.00 per certificate plus copy fee. Payee: County Clerk. Personal checks accepted, credit cards are not. Prepayment required. Mail requests: SASE required.

Civil Name Search: Access: Fax, mail, in person. Both court and visitors may perform in person name searches. Search fee: $10.00 per name. Civil records go back to 1800s, civil records in index books from 1876, on computer back to 2005. Mail turnaround time 2-4 days. Civil PAT goes back to 2005.

Criminal Name Search: Access: Fax, mail, in person. Both court and visitors may perform in person name searches. Search fee: $10.00 per name. Criminal records go back to 1800s, Criminal index in books from 1876; no computerized records. Mail turnaround time 2-4 days. Criminal PAT goes back to 2005.

Gaines County

District Court 101 S Main, Rm 213, Seminole, TX 79360; 432-758-4013; fax: 432-758-4036; 8AM-N, 1-5PM (CST). *Felony, Civil.*

General Information: No juvenile, mental, sealed, or adoption records released. Will fax documents to local or toll free line. Court makes copy: $1.00 per page. Self serve copy: same. Certification fee: $5.00 per certification plus copy fee. Payee: District Clerk. Personal checks accepted, credit cards are not. Prepayment required. Mail requests: SASE required.

Civil Name Search: Access: Phone, mail, in person. Only the court performs in person name searches; visitors may not. Search fee: $5.00 per name. Civil records on computer from 1980, index books from 1900s. Mail turnaround time 1 day.

Criminal Name Search: Access: Phone, mail, in person. Only the court performs in person name searches; visitors may not. Search fee: $5.00 per name. Criminal records computerized from 1980, index books from 1900s. Mail turnaround time 1 day.

County Court 101 S Main, Rm 107, Seminole, TX 79360; 432-758-4003; fax: 432-758-1442; 8AM-5PM (CST). *Misdemeanor, Civil, Probate.*

General Information: No juvenile, mental, sealed, or adoption records released. Will fax documents $1.00 per page plus $3.00 per call. Court makes copy: $1.00 per page. Self serve copy: same. Certification fee: $5.00. Payee: County Clerk. Personal checks accepted. Major credit cards accepted. Prepayment required. Mail requests: SASE required.

Civil Name Search: Access: Mail, in person. Both court and visitors may perform in person name searches. Search fee: $5.00 per name. Civil records available from 1900s, computerized since 1991. Note: Probate records may be accessed with same criteria as civil records. Mail turnaround time 1 day. Civil PAT goes back to 1991.

Criminal Name Search: Access: Mail, in person. Both court and visitors may perform in person name searches. Search fee: $5.00 per name. Criminal records available from 1900s, computerized since 1991. Mail turnaround time 1 day. Criminal PAT goes back to same as civil.

Galveston County

District Court 600 59th St #4001, Galveston, TX 77551-2388; 409-766-2424/2690; criminal phone: 409-770-5233; civil phone: 409-766-2441; fax: 409-766-2292; 8AM-5PM (CST). *Felony, Civil.*
www.co.galveston.tx.us/District_Clerk/

General Information: No juvenile, mental, sealed, or adoption records released. Will fax documents long distance for $5.00 fax fee plus $1.50 per page. Local fax- $1.50 per page. Court makes copy: $1.00 per page; over 15 pages is $.25 each add'l. Certification fee: $1.50 per page plus the copy fee; exemplified copes are $5.00 plus $1.00 per page. Payee: District Clerk. Personal checks accepted if under $50.00. Credit cards accepted. Prepayment required. Mail requests: SASE required.

Civil Name Search: Access: Fax, mail, in person, online. Both court and visitors may perform in person name searches. Search fee: $5.00 per name per book. Civil records on computer from 1984, on microfiche from 1982, archived from 1849. Note: Fax access is only allowed with prepaid accounts or credit card payment. Mail turnaround time 2-5 days. Civil PAT goes back to 1984. Online access to judge's daily calendars is free at www2.co.galveston.tx.us/District_Clerk/courts.htm.

Criminal Name Search: Access: Fax, mail, in person. Both court and visitors may perform in person name searches. Search fee: $5.00 per name per book. Required to search: name, years to search, DOB. Criminal records computerized from 1984, on microfiche from 1982, archived from 1849. Note: There is a $1.50 per page for incoming faxes. Mail turnaround time 2-5 days. Criminal PAT available. Online access to Judge's daily calendars is free at www2.co.galveston.tx.us/District_Clerk/courts.htm.

County Court PO Box 17253, Galveston, TX 77552-7253; 409-766-2200; criminal phone: 409-766-2390; civil phone: 409-766-2203; probate phone: 409-766-2202; fax: 409-765-3160; 8AM-5PM (CST). *Misdemeanor, Civil, Probate.*
www2.co.galveston.tx.us/County_Clerk/

General Information: No juvenile, mental, sealed, or adoption records released. Will not fax documents. Court makes copy: $1.00 per page. Certification fee: $5.00 per document plus copy fee. Payee: County Clerk. Personal checks accepted. Major credit cards accepted. Prepayment required. Mail requests: SASE required.

Civil Name Search: Access: Mail, in person, online. Both court and visitors may perform in person name searches. Search fee: $5.00 per name. Required to search: name, years to search; DOB or SSN helpful. Civil records on computer from 1984, index books from 1947. Mail turnaround time 1-2 days. Civil PAT goes back to 1984. Online access is at http://ccweb.co.galveston.tx.us/. Generally records go back to 1995.

Criminal Name Search: Access: Mail, in person, online. Both court and visitors may perform in person name searches. Search fee: $5.00 per name. Required to search: name, years to search, DOB; also helpful: SSN. Criminal records computerized from 1984, index books from 1947. Mail turnaround time 1-2 days. Criminal PAT goes back to 1984. Online access is at http://ccweb.co.galveston.tx.us/. Index search is free. Generally records go back to 1995. Online results show middle initial.

Garza County

District & County Court PO Box 366, Post, TX 79356; 806-495-4430; fax: 806-495-4431; 8AM-N,1-5PM (CST). *Felony, Misdemeanor, Civil, Probate.* www.garzacounty.net/id26.html

General Information: No juvenile records released. Fee to fax out file $3.00 1st page $1.00 ea add'l. Court makes copy: $1.00 per page. Certification fee: $5.00. Payee: District or County Clerk. Personal checks accepted, credit cards are not. Prepayment required. Mail requests: SASE not required.

Civil Name Search: Access: Mail, in person. Both court and visitors may perform in person name searches. Search fee: $5.00 per name. Civil index on docket books. Mail turnaround time 2-3 days. Civil PAT goes back to 2000.

Criminal Name Search: Access: Mail, in person. Both court and visitors may perform in person name searches. Search fee: $5.00 per name. Required to search: name, years to search, DOB. Criminal records indexed in books. Mail turnaround time 2-3 days. Criminal PAT goes back to 2000.

Gillespie County

District Court 101 W Main, Rm 204, Fredericksburg, TX 78624; 830-997-6517; fax: 830-992-2613; 8AM-4:30PM (CST). *Felony, Civil.*

General Information: No juvenile, mental, sealed, or adoption records released. Will fax documents if only a page or 2. Court makes copy: $.25 per page. Certification fee: $1.00 per page includes copy fee. Payee: Gillespie

County District Clerk. Personal checks accepted, credit cards are not. Prepayment required. Mail requests: SASE required.

Civil Name Search: Access: Mail, in person. Both court and visitors may perform in person name searches. Search fee: $5.00 per name. Civil records in index books from 1800s. Index #1 from 1800s-1927, Index #2 from 1927-1988, Index #3 from 1989-2008, Index #4 2009 to present. Mail turnaround time 1-2 days.

Criminal Name Search: Access: Mail, in person. Both court and visitors may perform in person name searches. Search fee: $5.00 per name. Required to search: name, years to search; also helpful: DOB, SSN. Criminal docket on books from 1800s. Index #1 from 1800s-1927, Index #2 from 1927-1988, Index #3 from 1989-2008, Index #4 2009 to present. Mail turnaround time 1-2 days.

County Court 101 W Main, #13, Fredericksburg, TX 78624; 830-997-6515; fax: 830-997-9958; 8AM-4PM (CST). *Misdemeanor, Civil, Probate.*

General Information: Probate fax is same as main fax number. No juvenile, mental, sealed, or adoption record released. Will fax documents for no add'l fee once payment of copies received. Court makes copy: $1.00 per page. Certification fee: $10.00 per document plus copy fee. Payee: Mary Lynn Rusche County Clerk. No out-of-town personal checks accepted, credit cards are not. Prepayment required. Mail requests: SASE required.

Civil Name Search: Access: Mail, in person. Both court and visitors may perform in person name searches. Search fee: $5.00 per name. Required to search: name, years to search; also helpful: address. Civil records on computer from 1988, on microfiche from 1990, index books from 1900s. Mail turnaround time 1-2 days. Public use terminal has civil records.

Criminal Name Search: Access: Mail, in person. Both court and visitors may perform in person name searches. Search fee: $5.00 per name. Required to search: name, years to search, aliases; also helpful: DOB, SSN. Criminal records (not at public viewing) on computer from 1988, on microfiche from 1990, index books from 1900s. Mail turnaround time 1-2 days.

Glasscock County

District & County Court PO Box 190, 117 E Currie, Garden City, TX 79739; 432-354-2371; fax: 432-354-2616; 8:30AM-4PM (CST). *Felony, Misdemeanor, Civil, Probate.*

General Information: No juvenile, mental, or adoption records released. Will fax documents $2.00 per page. Court makes copy: $1.00 per page. Certification fee: $5.00 per document plus copy fee. Payee: District or County Clerk. Personal checks accepted. Prepayment required. Mail requests: SASE required.

Civil Name Search: Access: Mail, in person. Both court and visitors may perform in person name searches. Search fee: $10.00 per name. Civil records in index books from 1893.

Criminal Name Search: Access: Mail, in person. Both court and visitors may perform in person name searches. Search fee: $10.00 per name. Required to search: name, years to search, DOB. Criminal docket on books from 1893.

Goliad County

District & County Court PO Box 50 (127 N Courthouse Sq), Goliad, TX 77963; 361-645-3294; fax: 361-645-3858; 8AM-5PM, closed 1 hour at noon (CST). *Felony, Misdemeanor, Civil, Probate.*
www.co.goliad.tx.us/ips/cms/districtcourt/

General Information: Probate fax is same as main fax number. In-person searchers must use docket books. No juvenile, mental, sealed, or adoption records released. Fee to fax out file $2.00 per page includes copy fee. Court makes copy: $1.00 per page. Certification fee: $5.00 for County Court; $1.00 per doc in District Court plus copy fee. Payee: Goliad County/District Clerk. Personal checks accepted. No credit cards accepted at this time. Prepayment required. Mail requests: SASE not required.

Civil Name Search: Access: Mail, in person. Both court and visitors may perform in person name searches. Search fee: $10.00 per name. Fee is per court. Required to search: name, years to search; also helpful: address. Civil records on computer since 1983 (real property only), on microfiche and index books from 1870. Mail turnaround time 1-2 days.

Criminal Name Search: Access: Mail, in person. Both court and visitors may perform in person name searches. Search fee: $10.00 per name. Fee is per court. Required to search: name, years to search; also helpful: address, DOB, SSN, offense. Criminal docket on books and folders from 1870. Mail turnaround time 1-2 days.

Gonzales County

District Court 414 St Joseph #300, Gonzales, TX 78629; 830-672-2326; fax: 830-672-9313; 8AM-5PM (CST). *Felony, Civil.*

General Information: No juvenile, mental, sealed, or adoption records released. Fee to fax out file $1.00 per page. Court makes copy: $1.00 per page. Self serve copy: same. No certification fee. Payee: District Clerk.

Personal checks accepted, credit cards are not. Prepayment required. Mail requests: SASE not required.

Civil Name Search: Access: Phone, fax, mail, in person. Both court and visitors may perform in person name searches. Search fee: $5.00 per name. Required to search: name, years to search; also helpful: address. Civil records on computer from 1991, index books from 1800s. Mail turnaround time 1-2 days.

Criminal Name Search: Access: Phone, fax, mail, in person. Both court and visitors may perform in person name searches. Search fee: $5.00 per name. Required to search: name, years to search; also helpful: address, DOB, SSN. Criminal records computerized from 1991, index books from 1800s. Mail turnaround time 1-2 days.

County Court PO Box 77, Gonzales, TX 78629; 830-672-2801; fax: 830-672-2636; 8AM-5PM (CST). *Misdemeanor, Civil, Probate.*

General Information: Probate fax is same as main fax number. No mental or drug dependant commitment records released. Fee to fax out file $5.00. Court makes copy: $1.00 per page. Self serve copy: same. Certification fee: $5.00 per instrument. Payee: County Clerk. Personal checks accepted, credit cards are not. Prepayment required. Mail requests: SASE required.

Civil Name Search: Access: Fax, mail, in person. Both court and visitors may perform in person name searches. Search fee: $5.00 per name. Required to search: name, years to search, DOB. Civil records on computer since 1993, original jackets since 1975, index books from 1900s. Mail turnaround time 1-2 days.

Criminal Name Search: Access: Mail, in person. Both court and visitors may perform in person name searches. Search fee: $5.00 per name. Required to search: name, years to search, DOB, offense, date of offense. Criminal records on computer since 1993, original jackets, index books from 1900s. Mail turnaround time 1-2 days.

Gray County

District Court PO Box 1139, Pampa, TX 79066-1139; 806-669-8010; fax: 806-669-8053; 8:30AM-5PM (CST). *Felony, Civil.*

General Information: No juvenile, mental, sealed, or adoption records released. Will fax documents $1.00 per page. Court makes copy: $.50 per page.$1.00 per page to mail copies. Certification fee: $1.00 per page. Payee: District Clerk. Personal checks accepted, credit cards are not. Prepayment required. Mail requests: SASE required.

Civil Name Search: Access: Fax, mail, in person. Both court and visitors may perform in person name searches. Search fee: $5.00 per name. Required to search: name, years to search, DOB. Civil records on computer from 1940, index books from 1910. Note: All requests must be in writing. Mail turnaround time 1-2 days. Civil PAT goes back to 1930.

Criminal Name Search: Access: Fax, mail, in person. Both court and visitors may perform in person name searches. Search fee: $5.00 per name. Required to search: name, years to search; also helpful: DOB. Criminal records go back to 1930; Criminal records computerized from 1965. Note: All requests must be in writing. Mail turnaround time 1-2 days. Criminal PAT goes back to 1930.

County & Probate Court PO Box 1902, Pampa, TX 79066-1902; 806-669-8004; fax: 806-669-8054; 8:30AM-5PM (CST). *Misdemeanor, Civil, Probate.*

General Information: No juvenile, mental, sealed, or adoption records released. They will not release any records with the SSN on it. Will fax documents $2.50 1st page, $1.00 each add'l. Court makes copy: $1.00 per page. Self serve copy: same. Certification fee: $5.00. Payee: Susan Winborne, County Clerk. Personal checks accepted. Major credit cards accepted. Prepayment required. Mail requests: SASE required.

Civil Name Search: Access: Phone, fax, mail, in person. Both court and visitors may perform in person name searches. Search fee: $10.00 per name. Fee is per index. Civil records on type written indices from 1900s. Mail turnaround time 1-2 days. Civil PAT goes back to 4/19/02.

Criminal Name Search: Access: Phone, fax, mail, in person. Both court and visitors may perform in person name searches. Search fee: $10.00 per name. Fee is per index. Required to search: name, years to search, DOB. Criminal records on type written indices from 1900s. Mail turnaround time 1-2 days. Criminal PAT goes back to 1983.

Grayson County

District Court 200 S Crockett, Rm 120-A, Sherman, TX 75090; 903-813-4352; fax: 903-870-0609; 8AM-5PM (CST). *Felony, Civil, Family.*

www.co.grayson.tx.us

General Information: No juvenile, mental, sealed, expunction or adoption records released. Will only fax uncertified documents. Court makes copy: $1.00 per page. Certification fee: n/a. Payee: District Clerk. Personal checks accepted. Major credit cards accepted. Prepayment required. Mail requests: SASE required.

Civil Name Search: Access: Mail, fax, in person, online. Both court and visitors may perform in person name searches. Search fee: $5.00 per name. Civil records on computer from 1988, microfilm since 1939, index books

since 1900s. Mail turnaround time 1-2 days. Civil PAT goes back to 1989. Access to judicial records is free at http://24.117.89.66:3007/default.aspx.

Criminal Name Search: Access: Mail, fax, in person, online. Both court and visitors may perform in person name searches. Search fee: $5.00 per name. Required to search: name, years to search, DOB; also helpful: SSN. Criminal records on computer since 1988, microfilm since 1939, index books since 1900s. Mail turnaround time 1-2 days. Criminal PAT goes back to 1983. Access to judicial records is free at http://24.117.89.66:3007/default.aspx.

County Court 200 S Crockett, Sherman, TX 75090; 903-813-4336; civil phone: 903-813-4335; probate phone: 903-813-4241; fax: 903-892-8300; 8AM-12; 1PM5PM (CST). *Misdemeanor, Civil, Probate.*

www.co.grayson.tx.us/courtsmain.htm

General Information: Criminal Clerk #2 is at 903-813-4334 Online identifiers in results same as on public terminal. No juvenile, mental, sealed, or adoption records released. Court makes copy: $1.00 per page. Certification fee: $5.00. Payee: Grayson County Clerk. Personal checks accepted, credit cards are not. Prepayment required. Mail requests: SASE required.

Civil Name Search: Access: Mail, in person, online. Both court and visitors may perform in person name searches. Search fee: $10.00 per name per 10 years. Civil records on computer since 1992, index books since 1952. Mail turnaround time 3-4 days. Civil PAT goes back to 1982. Online access to civil and probate records free at http://24.117.89.66:3007/default.aspx.

Criminal Name Search: Access: In person, online. Both court and visitors may perform in person name searches. Search fee: $10.00 per name per 10 years. Required to search: name, years to search, also helpful: DOB, SSN. Criminal records computerized from 1982. Criminal PAT goes back to same as civil. Online access to civil and probate records free at http://24.117.89.66:3007/default.aspx. Online results show middle initial, DOB.

Gregg County

District Court PO Box 711, Longview, TX 75606; criminal phone: 903-236-8459; civil phone: 903-237-2663; fax: 903-236-8474; 8AM-5PM (CST). *Felony, Civil.*

www.co.gregg.tx.us/government/courts.asp

General Information: No juvenile, mental, sealed, or adoption records released. Will fax documents $1.00 per page. Court makes copy: $1.00 per page. Certification fee: $2.00 per page. Payee: District Clerk. Only cashiers checks and money orders accepted. No credit cards accepted. Prepayment required. Mail requests: SASE required.

Civil Name Search: Access: Phone, fax, mail, in person, online. Both court and visitors may perform in person name searches. Search fee: $5.00 per name. Civil records on computer back to 1981, index books from 1873. Mail turnaround time 1-2 days. Public use terminal available, records go back to 1981. Online access to county judicial records is free at www.co.gregg.tx.us/judsrch.htm. Search by name, cause number, status.

Criminal Name Search: Access: Phone, fax, mail, in person, online. Both court and visitors may perform in person name searches. Search fee: $5.00 per name. Criminal records computerized from 1977, index books from 1873. Mail turnaround time 1-2 days. Public use terminal available, crim records go back to 1977. Online access to criminal records is the same as civil, also includes jail and bond search. Online results show name, DOB.

County Court 101 E Methvin, #200, Longview, TX 75606; 903-236-8430; fax: 903-237-2574; 8AM-5PM (CST). *Misdemeanor, Civil, Probate.*

www.co.gregg.tx.us/government/county_courts/countyclerk.asp

General Information: No juvenile, mental, sealed, or adoption records released. Fee to fax out file $1.00 per page. Court makes copy: $1.00 per page. Self serve copy: same. Certification fee: $5.00 per cert. Payee: Gregg County Clerk. Only in-state Personal checks accepted, credit cards are not. Prepayment required. Mail requests: SASE required.

Civil Name Search: Access: Mail, in person, online. Both court and visitors may perform in person name searches. Search fee: $5.00 per name. Civil records on computer from 1983, index books after 1962. Mail turnaround time 1 week. Civil PAT goes back to 1876. Public terminal probate index goes back to 1908. Online access to county judicial records is free at www.co.gregg.tx.us/judsrch.htm. Search by name, cause number, or status.

Criminal Name Search: Access: Mail, in person, online. Both court and visitors may perform in person name searches. Search fee: $5.00 per name. Required to search: name, years to search, DOB or SSN. Criminal records computerized from 1983, index books after 1932. Mail turnaround time 1 week. Criminal PAT goes back to 1983. Online access to criminal records is the same as civil. Jail and bond search also available.

Grimes County

District Court PO Box 234, Anderson, TX 77830; 936-873-2111; fax: 936-873-2514; 8AM-4:30PM, closed noon hour (CST). *Felony, Civil.* www.co.grimes.tx.us/ips/cms

General Information: No juvenile, mental, sealed, or adoption records released. Will fax documents $1.00 per page. Court makes copy: $1.00 per page. Certification fee: $1.00. Payee: District Clerk. Personal checks accepted. Visa/MC/AmEx accepted on the Official Payments System. Prepayment required. Mail requests: SASE not required.

Civil Name Search: Access: Phone, fax, mail, in person. Both court and visitors may perform in person name searches. Search fee: $5.00 per name. Civil records on computer from 1990, index books from 1800s. Mail turnaround time 1-2 days. Civil PAT goes back to 20 years.

Criminal Name Search: Access: Phone, fax, mail, in person. Both court and visitors may perform in person name searches. Search fee: $5.00 per name. Required to search: name, years to search, DOB, SSN. Criminal records computerized from 1990, index books from 1800s. Mail turnaround time 1-2 days. Criminal PAT goes back to 20 years.

County Court PO Box 209, 101 S Main, Anderson, TX 77830; 936-873-4409; fax: 936-873-3308; 8AM-N, 1-4:30PM (CST). *Misdemeanor, Civil, Probate.*

www.co.grimes.tx.us/ips/cms/countycourt/

General Information: The court calendar is offered online, but the historical dockets are not. No juvenile, mental, sealed, or adoption records released. Will not fax documents. Court makes copy: $1.00 per page. Certification fee: $5.00 plus copy fee. Payee: County Clerk. Personal checks accepted, credit cards are not. Prepayment required. Mail requests: SASE required.

Civil Name Search: Access: Mail, in person. Only the court performs in person name searches; visitors may not. Search fee: $5.00 per name. Civil records in index books from 1850. Mail turnaround time 1-2 days.

Criminal Name Search: Access: Mail, in person. Only the court performs in person name searches; visitors may not. Search fee: $5.00 per name. Required to search: name, years to search, offense, date of offense. Criminal docket on books from 1850. Mail turnaround time 1-2 days.

Guadalupe County

District Court 101 E Court St, #308, Seguin, TX 78155; 830-303-4188; criminal phone: 830.303.8877; civil phone: x262; fax: 830-379-1943; 8AM-4:30PM (CST). *Felony, Civil.*

www.co.guadalupe.tx.us/guadalupe2010/home.php?content=dist_Clerk

General Information: Will look up case record if case number is known. No juvenile, mental, sealed, or adoption records released. Will fax out specific case files for $5.00 fee plus $1.00 per page after 1st page. Court makes copy: $1.00 per page. Certification fee: $1.00 per page and includes copy fee. Payee: District Clerk. Checks accepted for civil only. Criminal payments- cash, money orders and cashiers checks. Credit cards accepted. Prepayment required.

Civil Name Search: Access: In person, online. Visitors must perform in person searches themselves. Search fee: $5.00 per name. Civil records on computer from 1987, index books from 1846. Access to court records and hearings is available free at www.co.guadalupe.tx.us/judicialsearch/judsrch.asp. The calendar is searchable from the home page.

Criminal Name Search: Access: In person, online. Visitors must perform in person searches themselves. Search fee: $5.00 per name. Required to search: name, years to search, DOB; also helpful: SSN. Criminal records computerized from 1985, index books from 1846. Access to court records and hearings is available free at www.co.guadalupe.tx.us/judicialsearch/judsrch.asp. Search sheriff's jail and bond records also. Dockets go back to 12/31/1991. Online results show middle initial, DOB.

County Court 211 W. Court St, Seguin, TX 78155; 830-303-8861; probate phone: 830-303-4188 x237; fax: 830-401-0300; 8AM-4:30PM (CST). *Misdemeanor, Civil, Probate.*

www.co.guadalupe.tx.us/

General Information: There are three courts here, County Court of Law #1, County Court of Law #2, and the County Court. Online identifiers in results same as on public terminal. No juvenile, mental, sealed, or adoption records released. Will not fax documents. Court makes copy: $1.00 per page. Certification fee: $5.00 per doc plus $1.00 per page. Payee: County Clerk. Personal checks not accepted for records. Major credit cards accepted as of June 2011. Prepayment required. Mail requests: SASE required.

Civil Name Search: Access: Mail, in person, online. Visitors must perform in person searches themselves. Search fee: $10.00 per name per year. Civil records on computer from 1988, index books from 1968. Mail turnaround time 5 days. Civil PAT goes back to 1988. County Court of Law #2 has a separate index on the terminal, the other two courts are

combined. All three courts will be on one index in early 2012. Access to court records and hearings is available free at www.co.guadalupe.tx.us/judicialsearch/judsrch.asp.

Criminal Name Search: Access: Mail, in person, online. Visitors must perform in person searches themselves. Search fee: $10.00 per name per year. Required to search: name, years to search, DOB; also helpful: SSN. Criminal records computerized from 1988, index books from 1968. Mail turnaround time 5 days. Criminal PAT goes back to same as civil. County Court of Law #2 has a separate index on the terminal, the other two courts are combined. All three courts will be on one index in early 2012. Access to court records and hearings is available free at www.co.guadalupe.tx.us/judicialsearch/judsrch.asp. Also search sheriff's jail and bond records.

Hale County

District Court 225 Broadway, #4, Plainview, TX 79072-8050; 806-291-5226; fax: 806-291-5206; 8AM-N; 1-5PM (CST). *Felony, Civil.* www.242ndcourt.com

General Information: Monthly schedules and daily docket available free at website. No juvenile, mental, sealed, or adoption records released. Will fax documents $2.00 each. Court makes copy: $1.00 per page. Self serve copy: same. Certification fee: $1.00 each. Payee: District Clerk. Personal checks accepted. Credit cards accepted. Prepayment required. Mail requests: SASE required.

Civil Name Search: Access: Phone, fax, mail, in person, online. Both court and visitors may perform in person name searches. Search fee: $5.00 per name. Civil records on computer back to 1990; index cards from 1975; prior back to 1897. Mail turnaround time 1-2 days. Civil PAT goes back to 1990. Access docket data from 01/1990 online at www.idocket.com; registration and password required. A fee service; only one free name search per day.

Criminal Name Search: Access: Phone, fax, mail, in person, online. Both court and visitors may perform in person name searches. Search fee: $5.00 per name. Required to search: name, years to search, SSN; also helpful: DOB. Criminal records computerized from 1990, index cards from 1975; prior back to 1897. Mail turnaround time 1-2 days. Criminal PAT goes back to same as civil. Access docket data from 01/1990 online at www.idocket.com; registration and password required. A fee service; only one free name search per day.

County Court 500 Broadway, #140, Plainview, TX 79072-8030; 806-291-5261; criminal phone: 806-291-5218; civil phone: 806-291-5261; probate phone: 806-291-5261; fax: 806-291-9810; 8AM-N, 1-5PM (CST). *Misdemeanor, Civil, Probate.*

General Information: Probate records are in a separate index. Probate fax is same as main fax number. No juvenile, mental, sealed, or adoption records released. Will fax documents for copy fee plus $1.00 for long distance call. Court makes copy: $1.00 per page. Self serve copy: same. Certification fee: $5.00 per document. Payee: County Clerk. Personal checks, Visa/MC accepted. Prepayment required. Mail requests: SASE required.

Civil Name Search: Access: Mail, fax, in person, online. Both court and visitors may perform in person name searches. Search fee: $5.00 per name. Required to search: name, years to search, address. Civil records in index books from 1928; on computer back to 1995. Mail turnaround time same day if before 3PM. Civil PAT goes back to 1995. Clerk guarantees accuracy of computer records from 1995 forward on access terminal, which includes SSNs. Online access is through www.idocket.com; registration and password required. Civil and probate data back to 01/1991. One free name search permitted a day, otherwise subscription required.

Criminal Name Search: Access: Mail, fax, in person, online. Both court and visitors may perform in person name searches. Search fee: $5.00 per name. Required to search: name, years to search, DOB. Criminal docket on books from 1928; on computer back to 1995, limited records back to 1990. Mail turnaround time 1-2 days. Criminal PAT goes back to same as civil. Clerk guarantees accuracy of computer records from 1995 forward on access terminal. SSNs appear in results. Online access to misdemeanor docket from 01/91 forward is through www.idocket.com; registration and password required. One free name search permitted a day, otherwise subscription required.

Hall County

District & County Court County Courthouse, 512 Main St, #8, Memphis, TX 79245; 806-259-2627; fax: 806-259-5078; 8:30AM-N; 1-5PM (CST). *Felony, Misdemeanor, Civil, Probate.*

General Information: No juvenile, mental, sealed, or adoption records released. Will fax documents to local or toll free line. Court makes copy: $1.00 per page. Self serve copy: $.25 per page. Certification fee: $5.00. Payee: Hall County Clerk. Personal checks accepted, credit cards are not. Prepayment required. Mail requests: SASE required.

Civil Name Search: Access: Mail, in person. Both court and visitors may perform in person name searches. Search fee: $5.00 per name. Civil records on computer from 1992, index books from 1890. Mail turnaround time 1-2 days.

Criminal Name Search: Access: Mail, in person. Both court and visitors may perform in person name searches. Search fee: $5.00 per name. Required to search: name, years to search, offense. Criminal records computerized from 1992, index books from 1890. Mail turnaround time 1-2 days.

Hamilton County

District Court County Courthouse, Hamilton, TX 76531; 254-386-3417; fax: 254-386-8610; 8AM-5PM M-TH; 8AM-4:30PM F (CST). *Felony, Civil.*

www.hamiltoncountytx.org/HCDC.htm

General Information: No juvenile, mental, sealed, or adoption records released. No fee to fax documents. Court makes copy: $1.00 per page. Self serve copy: same. Certification fee: $2.00 per document. Payee: District Clerk. Personal checks accepted. Prepayment required. Mail requests: SASE required.

Civil Name Search: Access: Fax, mail, in person. Both court and visitors may perform in person name searches. Search fee: $5.00 per name. Civil records since 1985 in index books, computerized since 1999. Mail turnaround time 2-4 days.

Criminal Name Search: Access: Fax, mail, in person. Both court and visitors may perform in person name searches. Search fee: $5.00 per name. Criminal docket on books from 1985, computerized since 1999. Mail turnaround time 2-4 days.

County Court 102 North Rice, County Courthouse, Hamilton, TX 76531; 254-386-3518; fax: 254-386-8727; 8AM-5PM (CST). *Misdemeanor, Civil, Probate.*

General Information: Probate fax is same as main fax number. No juvenile, mental, sealed, or adoption records released. Will fax documents for fee. Court makes copy: $1.00 per page. Self serve copy: same. Certification fee: $1.00 per page. Payee: County Clerk. Personal checks accepted. Major credit cards accepted. Prepayment required. Mail requests: SASE required.

Civil Name Search: Access: Mail, fax, in person. Both court and visitors may perform in person name searches. Search fee: $5.00 per name. Civil records in index books; on computer since. Mail turnaround time 1-2 days.

Criminal Name Search: Access: Mail, fax, in person. Both court and visitors may perform in person name searches. Search fee: $5.00 per name. Required to search: name, years to search, DOB or SSN. Criminal index in books; on computer since. Mail turnaround time 1-2 days.

Hansford County

District & County Court 15 NW Court, Spearman, TX 79081; 806-659-4110; fax: 806-659-4168; 8AM-5PM (CST). *Felony, Misdemeanor, Civil, Probate.*

General Information: No juvenile, mental, sealed, or adoption records released. Will fax documents $3.00 unless you provide toll-free number. Court makes copy: $1.00 per page. Certification fee: $2.00 in District Court; $5.00 in County Court plus copy fee. Payee: District/County Clerk. Personal checks accepted, credit cards are not. Prepayment required. Mail requests: SASE required.

Civil Name Search: Access: Phone, fax, mail, in person. Both court and visitors may perform in person name searches. Search fee: $5.00 per name per court. Civil records on computer from 1/92, index books from 1900s. Mail turnaround time ASAP. Civil PAT goes back to 1992.

Criminal Name Search: Access: Phone, fax, mail, in person. Both court and visitors may perform in person name searches. Search fee: $5.00 per name per court. Required to search: name, years to search; also helpful: DOB, SSN. Criminal records on computer since 6/92, archived from 1900s. Mail turnaround time 1-2 days. Criminal PAT goes back to same as civil.

Hardeman County

District & County Court PO Box 30, Quanah, TX 79252; 940-663-2901; fax: 940-663-5161; 8:30AM-5PM (CST). *Felony, Misdemeanor, Civil, Probate.*

General Information: Probate is separate index at this same address. Probate fax- 940-663-5161 No juvenile, mental, sealed, or adoption records released. Will not fax documents. Court makes copy: $1.00 per page. Self serve copy: same. Certification fee: $5.00 per cert plus copy fee. Payee: District Clerk. Personal checks accepted, credit cards are not. Prepayment required. Mail requests: SASE required.

Civil Name Search: Access: Mail, in person. Both court and visitors may perform in person name searches. Search fee: $10.00 per name. Civil records in index books from 1900s. Mail turnaround time 1-2 days. Civil PAT goes back to 2006.

Criminal Name Search: Access: Mail, in person. Both court and visitors may perform in person name searches. Search fee: $10.00 per name. Criminal docket on books from 1920. Mail turnaround time 1-2 days. Criminal PAT goes back to 2006.

Hardin County

District Court PO Box 2997, 300 Monroe, Kountze, TX 77625; 409-246-5150; fax: 409-246-5288; 8AM-5PM (CST). *Felony, Civil.*

www.co.hardin.tx.us/ips/cms/districtcourt/

General Information: No juvenile, mental, sealed, or adoption records released. Fee to fax out file $1.00 per page. Court makes copy: $1.00 per page. Certification fee: $2.00 per doc. Payee: District Clerk. Business checks accepted. No credit cards accepted. Prepayment required. Mail requests: SASE required.

Civil Name Search: Access: Mail, in person. Both court and visitors may perform in person name searches. Search fee: $5.00 per name. Civil records in index books since 1920, computerized since 1997. Mail turnaround time 1-2 days.

Criminal Name Search: Access: Mail, in person. Both court and visitors may perform in person name searches. Search fee: $5.00 per name. Required to search: name, years to search, DOB; also helpful: SSN, sex. Criminal docket on books from 1920, computerized since 1997. Mail turnaround time 1-2 days.

County Court PO Box 38, 300 Monroe, Kountze, TX 77625; 409-246-5185; fax: 409-246-3208; 8AM-5PM (CST). *Misdemeanor, Civil, Probate.*

www.co.hardin.tx.us/ips/cms/countyoffices/countyClerk.html

General Information: No juvenile, mental, sealed, or adoption records released. Will not fax documents. Court makes copy: $1.00 per page. Self serve copy: same. Certification fee: $5.00 per doc plus $1.00 per copy. Payee: Hardin County Clerk. Personal checks accepted, credit cards are not. Prepayment required. Mail requests: SASE not required.

Civil Name Search: Access: Mail, in person, phone. Both court and visitors may perform in person name searches. Search fee: $5.00 per name. Civil records in index books since 1850; on computer back to 1999. Mail turnaround time 1-2 days. Civil PAT available.

Criminal Name Search: Access: Mail, in person, phone. Both court and visitors may perform in person name searches. Search fee: $5.00 per name. Criminal records on computer since 1992, index books from 1850. Mail turnaround time 1-2 days. Criminal PAT available.

Harris County

District Court 201 Caroline, Suite 420, PO Box 4651, Houston, TX 77210-4651; 713-755-7300; criminal phone: 713-755-5711 x1; civil phone: 713-755-5711 x2; criminal fax: 713-368-3946; civil fax: 8AM-5PM; 8AM-5PM (CST). *Felony, Misdemeanor, Civil over $100,000.*

www.hcdistrictclerk.com/Common/Default.aspx

General Information: Criminal customer service-1201 Franklin, 3rd Fl, #3138. Civil clerk at main address. Dist Clerk's Record Ctr at 1301 Franklin, 1st Fl. No juvenile or sealed records released. Will fax out docs; requires credit card prepayment. Court makes copy: $1.00 per page. Certification fee: $1.00, called Exemplification Fee. Please specify if you wish your search result certified or uncertified. Payee: Harris County District Clerk. Business check accepted from attorney with TX Bar Card, corporate or company check with Harris Co. address. Major credit cards accepted. Prepayment required. Mail requests: SASE required.

Civil Name Search: Access: Phone, mail, fax, online, in person. Both court and visitors may perform in person name searches. Search fee: $5.00 per search, with up to 3 names per search. Civil records on computer from 1969. Note: Free phone search requests are limited to one name only. Fax Express forms available online, click on forms, general forms Civil PAT goes back to 1968. First, an online case lookup service is free at www.cclerk.hctx.net/applications/websearch/Civil.aspx. Online records go back to 10/1989. A docket search is at www.hcdistrictclerk.com/Edocs/Public/Search.aspx?dockettab=1. Qualified subscribers may access records for a fee at http://home.jims.hctx.net/WebServices.aspx. Search civil dockets free at http://apps.jims.hctx.net/courts/.

Criminal Name Search: Access: Phone, mail, fax, online, in person. Both court and visitors may perform in person name searches. Search fee: $5.00 per name. Required to search: name, years to search, DOB. Criminal records on computer since 1976. Note: Free phone search requests are limited to one name only. Fax Express forms available online, click on forms, general forms. Criminal PAT goes back to 1985. Online criminal index case lookup is the same as civil. To become a subscriber, visit www.hcdistrictclerk.com/common/e-services/pros_subscriber.aspx.

County Court PO Box 1525, 201 Caroline, 3rd Fl, Houston, TX 77251-1525; 713-755-6421; fax: 713-755-4710; 8AM-4:30PM (CST). *Civil under $100,000.*

www.cclerk.hctx.net

General Information: The Information Department (for record information) telephone is 713-755-6405, located at County Civil Courthouse, 210 Caroline, 3rd Fl. Small claims and evictions are handled by county Justice of Peace Courts; usually there are two per precinct. Will fax documents $1.00 per page. Court makes copy: $1.00 per page. Certification fee: $5.00. Payee: Harris County Clerk. Business checks and personal checks accepted in person with ID. Credit cards accepted. Prepayment required. Mail requests: SASE required.

Civil Name Search: Access: Phone, mail, online, in person. Both court and visitors may perform in person name searches. Search fee: $5.00 for mail requests. Civil records on computer and microfiche from 1963. Mail turnaround time 24-48 hours. Public use terminal has civil records back to 1977. Public terminal also includes Probate records. Online access is free at www.cclerk.hctx.net. System includes civil data search and county civil settings inquiry and other county clerk functions. For further information, visit the website or call 713-755-6421. Also, civil case online access back to 12/31/1997 at www.idocket.com; registration and password required. A fee service; only one free name search a day.

Probate Dept Harris County Clerk's Office, 201 Caroline ST, #800, Houston, TX 77002; 713-755-6425; fax: 713-755-5468; 8AM-4:30PM (CST). *Probate.*
www.co.harris.tx.us/probate/
General Information: Dockets are available free at www.cclerk.hctx.net/applications/websearch/Probate.aspx. Records go back to 1837.

Harrison County

District Court 200 W Houston St #234, Marshall, TX 75671; 903-935-8409; fax: 903-927-1918; 8AM-5PM (CST). *Felony, Civil.*
www.co.harrison.tx.us
General Information: No juvenile, mental, sealed, or adoption records released. Will not fax documents. Court makes copy: $1.00 per page. Self serve copy: $.50 per page. Certification fee: $1.00 per page. Payee: Harrison County District Clerk. Personal checks, Visa/MC accepted. Prepayment required. Mail requests: SASE required.
Civil Name Search: Access: Mail, in person, online. Both court and visitors may perform in person name searches. Search fee: $5.00 per name. Required to search: name, years to search; also helpful: address. Civil records on computer from 1988, index books from 1845. Mail turnaround time 1-2 days. Civil PAT goes back to 1987. Terminal results also show SSNs. Current docket information is available at the web page. Click on 71st District Court, then on Criminal Docket Information.
Criminal Name Search: Access: Mail, in person, online. Both court and visitors may perform in person name searches. Search fee: $5.00 per name. Required to search: name, years to search, DOB; also helpful: address, SSN. Criminal records computerized from 1988, index books from 1845. Note: Although Mail turnaround time 1-2 days. Criminal PAT goes back to same as civil. Terminal results include SSN. Current docket information is available at the web page. Click on 71st District Court, then on Criminal Docket Information.

County Court PO Box 1365, Marshall, TX 75671; 903-935-8403; fax: 903-935-4877; 8AM-5PM (CST). *Misdemeanor, Civil, Probate.*
General Information: Probate is a separate index at this same address. No juvenile, mental, sealed, birth, death or adoption records released. Fee to fax out file $4.00 plus copy fee. Court makes copy: $1.00 per page. Self serve copy: same. Certification fee: $5.00 per document plus copy fee. Payee: County Clerk. No personal checks accepted. Credit cards accepted. Prepayment required. Mail requests: SASE not required.
Civil Name Search: Access: Mail, in person. Both court and visitors may perform in person name searches. Search fee: $5.00 per name. Civil records in docket books from 1800; on computer back to 2001. Mail turnaround time 10 days. Civil PAT goes back to 2002.
Criminal Name Search: Access: Mail, in person. Both court and visitors may perform in person name searches. Search fee: $5.00 per name. Required to search: name, years to search, DOB. Criminal records in docket books from 1800; on computer back to 2001. Mail turnaround time 10 days. Criminal PAT goes back to 2002.

Hartley County

District & County Court PO Box Q, Channing, TX 79018; 806-235-3582; fax: 806-235-2316; 8:30AM-N, 1-5PM (CST). *Felony, Misdemeanor, Civil, Probate.*
www.co.hartley.tx.us/ips/cms
General Information: Probate is a separate index at this same address No juvenile, mental, sealed, or adoption records released. Will fax documents if prepaid. Court makes copy: $1.00 per page County Ct; $1.00 for District Ct. Certification fee: $5.00 per cert plus copy fee for county; $1.00 per page includes copies for district. Payee: Hartley County Clerk. Personal checks accepted. Credit card payments must be made via OfficialPaymentCorporation.com. Prepayment required. Mail requests: SASE required.
Civil Name Search: Access: Mail, in person. Both court and visitors may perform in person name searches. Search fee: $5.00 per name. Charge is for each book searched. Civil records on computer from 1994, index books from

1890. Mail turnaround time 1-2 days. Civil PAT goes back to 1994. Results include case style, dates, parties, status.
Criminal Name Search: Access: Mail, in person. Both court and visitors may perform in person name searches. Search fee: $5.00 per name, per book searched (misdemeanor or felony). Required to search: name, years to search, DOB. Criminal records computerized from 1994, index books from 1890. Mail turnaround time 1-2 days. Criminal PAT goes back to same as civil. Results include style of case.

Haskell County

District Court PO Box 27, 1 Ave D, 2nd Fl, Haskell, TX 79521; 940-864-2030; fax: 940-864-5616; 8:30AM-N, 1-5PM M-TH; 8:30AM-4:30PM F (CST). *Felony, Civil.*
General Information: No juvenile, mental, sealed, or adoption records released. Will fax documents $2.00 per page. Court makes copy: $1.00 per page. Payee: District Clerk. Business checks accepted. In-state checks accepted. No credit cards accepted. Prepayment required. Mail requests: SASE required.
Civil Name Search: Access: Mail, in person. Both court and visitors may perform in person name searches. Search fee: $5.00 per name. Civil records on computer from 1992, index books from 1896. Mail turnaround time 1-2 days.
Criminal Name Search: Access: Mail, in person. Both court and visitors may perform in person name searches. Search fee: $5.00 per name. Required to search: name, years to search, signed release. Criminal records computerized from 1992, index books from 1896. Mail turnaround time 1-2 days.

County Court PO Box 725, Haskell, TX 79521; 940-864-2451; fax: 940-864-6164; 8:30AM-N, 1-5PM M-TH; 8:30AM-N, 1PM-4:30PM F (CST). *Misdemeanor, Civil, Probate.*
General Information: No juvenile, mental, sealed, or adoption records released. Will fax documents $2.00 per page. Court makes copy: $1.00 per page. Self serve copy: same. Certification fee: $5.00. Payee: County Clerk. Personal checks accepted, credit cards are not. Prepayment required. Mail requests: SASE helpful.
Civil Name Search: Access: Phone, fax, mail, in person. Both court and visitors may perform in person name searches. Search fee: $5.00 per name. Civil records in index books from 1903; computerized records since 1994. Mail turnaround time 1-2 days.
Criminal Name Search: Access: Fax, mail, in person. Both court and visitors may perform in person name searches. Search fee: $5.00 per name. Criminal docket on books from 19; computerized records since 1994. Mail turnaround time 1-2 days.

Hays County

District Court 110 E Martin Luther King, #123, San Marcos, TX 78666; 512-393-7660; fax: 512-393-7674; 8AM-5PM (CST). *Felony, Civil.*
www.co.hays.tx.us/index.php/justice-system-courts/district-clerk/
General Information: No sealed or adoption records released. Court makes copy: $.50 per page. Certification fee: $1.00 per page. Payee: District Clerk. Personal checks accepted. Credit cards accepted. Prepayment required. Mail requests: SASE required.
Civil Name Search: Access: Phone, mail, in person, online. Both court and visitors may perform in person name searches. Search fee: $5.00 per name. Civil records on computer from 1987, index books from 1890s. Mail turnaround time 1-5 days. Civil PAT goes back to 1989. Search by name, case number or attorney from home page or at www.co.hays.tx.us/index.php/justice-system-courts/district-clerk/records-search/. Also, online access is through www.idocket.com; registration and password required. Case records go back to 12/31/1986. One free name search permitted a day, otherwise subscription required.
Criminal Name Search: Access: Phone, mail, in person, online. Both court and visitors may perform in person name searches. Search fee: $5.00 per name. Required to search: name, years to search; also helpful: DOB, SSN. Criminal records computerized from 1987, index books from 1890s. Mail turnaround time 1-5 days. Criminal PAT goes back to same as civil. Online access same as civil.

County Court 137 N Guadalupe St, San Marcos, TX 78666; 512-393-7330; fax: 512-393-7337; 8AM-4:30PM (CST). *Misdemeanor, Civil, Probate.*
www.co.hays.tx.us
General Information: No juvenile, mental, sealed, or adoption records released. Will fax documents if all fees paid. Court makes copy: $1.00 per page. Certification fee: $5.00 per document plus copy fee. Payee: Hays County Clerk. Personal checks accepted. Major credit cards accepted. Prepayment required. Mail requests: SASE not required.
Civil Name Search: Access: Mail, in person, online. Both court and visitors may perform in person name searches. Search fee: $10.00 per name. Civil records on computer from 1988, index books from 1848. Note: www.co.hays.tx.us/ Mail turnaround time 1-2 weeks. Civil PAT goes

back to 1987. Search the docket index free from the home page, click on Public Record Search. Search by name or case number. Includes civil, family and probate cases. Index includes DOB, address on docket. Online access is through www.idocket.com; registration and password required. Includes probate. Case records from 01/88. One free name search permitted a day, otherwise subscription required. Includes DOB

Criminal Name Search: Access: Mail, in person, online. Both court and visitors may perform in person name searches. Search fee: $10.00 per name. Required to search: name, years to search, DOB. Criminal records computerized from 1987, index books from 1848. Mail turnaround time 1-2 weeks. Criminal PAT goes back to same as civil. Search the docket index free from the home page, click on Public Record Search. Search by name or case number. Index includes DOB, address on docket. Misdemeanor records online access is through www.idocket.com; registration and password required. Case records go back to 12/31/1987. One free name search permitted a day, otherwise subscription required.

Hemphill County

District & County Court PO Box 867, 400 Main St, Canadian, TX 79014; 806-323-6212; 8AM-N. 1-5PM (CST). *Felony, Misdemeanor, Civil, Probate.*

General Information: Probate is a separate index at this same address. No juvenile, mental, sealed, or adoption records released. Will not fax documents. Court makes copy: $1.00 per page. Self serve copy: $.50 per page. Certification fee: $5.00 per page. Payee: Hemphill County Clerk. Personal checks accepted, credit cards are not. Prepayment required. Mail requests: SASE required.

Civil Name Search: Access: Mail, in person. Both court and visitors may perform in person name searches. Search fee: $10.00 per name per index. Civil records indexed from 1890s, in storage. Mail turnaround time 1-2 weeks.

Criminal Name Search: Access: Mail, in person. Both court and visitors may perform in person name searches. Search fee: $10.00 per name per index. Required to search: name, years to search, DOB. Criminal records indexed from 1890s, in storage. Mail turnaround time 1-2 weeks.

Henderson County

District Court District Clerk Henderson County, 100 E Tyler, Rm 203, Athens, TX 75751; criminal phone: 903-675-6117; civil phone: 903-675-6115; fax: 903-677-7274; 7:30AM-N, 1PM-4:30PM (CST). *Felony, Civil.*
www.co.henderson.tx.us/ips/cms/districtcourt/districtClerk.html

General Information: This office accepts no fax over 5 pages. No juvenile, mental, sealed, or adoption records released. Will fax documents to local or toll-free number, 4 pages maximum. Court makes copy: $1.00 per page. No certification fee. Payee: District Clerk. Personal checks accepted. Major credit cards accepted. Prepayment required. Mail requests: SASE required.

Civil Name Search: Access: Mail, in person, online. Both court and visitors may perform in person name searches. Search fee: $5.00 per name. Civil records on computer from 1987, index books from 1849. Mail turnaround time 1-2 days. Civil PAT goes back to 1987. Search the index at www.co.henderson.tx.us/ips/cms/JudicialRecordsSearch.html.

Criminal Name Search: Access: Mail, in person, online. Both court and visitors may perform in person name searches. Search fee: $5.00 per name. Required to search: name, years to search, DOB; also helpful: SSN. Criminal records computerized from 1984, index books from 1849. Mail turnaround time 1-2 days. Criminal PAT goes back to 1984. Search the index at www.co.henderson.tx.us/ips/cms/JudicialRecordsSearch.html.

County Court PO Box 632, 100 E Tyler, Athens, TX 75751; 903-675-6140; criminal phone: 903-677-4022; civil phone: 903-675-6144; probate phone: 903-677-7206; fax: 903-675-6105; 8AM-5PM (CST). *Misdemeanor, Civil, Probate.*
www.co.henderson.tx.us/ips/cms/countyoffices/countyClerk.html

General Information: No juvenile, mental, sealed, or adoption records released. Fee to fax out file $5.00 per page. Court makes copy: $1.00 per page. Self serve copy: same. Certification fee: $5.00 per document. Payee: County Clerk. Personal checks accepted, credit cards are not. Prepayment required. Mail requests: SASE required.

Civil Name Search: Access: Phone, mail, fax, in person, online. Both court and visitors may perform in person name searches. Search fee: $5.00 per name. Civil records on computer back to 1984, index books from 1960s. Note: Docket calendars available on the website. Mail turnaround time 1-2 weeks. Civil PAT goes back to 1984. Search the index at www.co.henderson.tx.us/ips/cms/JudicialRecordsSearch.html.

Criminal Name Search: Access: Mail, fax, in person, online. Both court and visitors may perform in person name searches. Search fee: $5.00 per name. Required to search: name, years to search, DOB, SSN. Criminal records computerized from 1984, index books from 1960s. Note: Docket calendars available on the website. Mail turnaround time 1-2 weeks. Criminal PAT goes back to same as civil. Search the index at www.co.henderson.tx.us/ips/cms/JudicialRecordsSearch.html.

Hidalgo County

District Court PO Box 87, 100 N Closner, Edinburg, TX 78540; 956-318-2200; fax: 956-318-2251; 7:30AM-5:30PM (CST). *Felony, Civil.*
www.co.hidalgo.tx.us/index.aspx?nid=192

General Information: Extension numbers for the various clerks are: 92nd-x6204, 93rd- x6206, 139th- x6208, 206th- 6210, 275th- 6212, 332nd- x6215, 370th- x6217, 389th- x6219; 398th- x6221. Dial 0 for main clerk switchboard. No juvenile, mental, sealed, or adoption records released. Will fax documents for $1.00 per page. Court makes copy: $1.00 per page. Certification fee: $1.00 per page plus copy fee. Payee: District Clerk. Business checks accepted. Visa/MC, Discover accepted. Prepayment required. Mail requests: SASE required.

Civil Name Search: Access: Mail, in person, online. Only the court performs in person name searches; visitors may not. Search fee: $5.00 per name. Civil records on computer from 1987. Mail turnaround time 1-2 days. Online case access is through www.idocket.com; registration and password required. Records go back to 12/31/1986. One free name search permitted a day, otherwise subscription required. Interestingly, the court claims it is not providing data to Idocket, but the District Courts located in this county show on the Idocket menu.

Criminal Name Search: Access: Mail, in person, online. Only the court performs in person name searches; visitors may not. Search fee: $5.00 per name. Required to search: name, years to search, DOB. Criminal records computerized from 1987. Mail turnaround time 1-2 days. Online case access is through www.idocket.com; registration and password required. Records go back to 12/31/1986. One free name search permitted a day, otherwise subscription required. Interestingly, the court claims it is not providing data to Idocket, but the District Courts located in this county show on the Idocket menu.

County Court PO Box 58, Hidalgo County Clerk, Edinburg, TX 78540; 956-318-2100; fax: 956-318-2105; 7:30AM-5:30PM (CST). *Misdemeanor, Civil, Probate.*
https://gov.propertyinfo.com/TX-Hidalgo/

General Information: No juvenile, mental, sealed, or adoption records released. Will not fax documents. Court makes copy: $1.00 per page. Self serve copy: same. Certification fee: $5.00 per doc plus copy fee. Payee: County Clerk. Business checks accepted. Credit cards accepted. Prepayment required. Mail requests: SASE required.

Civil Name Search: Access: Mail, in person, online. Both court and visitors may perform in person name searches. Search fee: $5.00 per name. Civil records on computer from 1986, index books before 1986. Mail turnaround time 1-2 days. Civil PAT goes back to 1986. Online case access is through www.idocket.com; registration and password required. Civil and probate records go back to 12/31/1986. One free name search permitted a day, otherwise subscription required.

Criminal Name Search: Access: Mail, in person, online. Both court and visitors may perform in person name searches. Search fee: $5.00 per name. Criminal records computerized from 1986, index books before 1986. Mail turnaround time 1-2 days. Criminal PAT goes back to same as civil. Misdemeanor case records access is through www.idocket.com; registration and password required. Records go back to 12/31/1991. One free name search permitted a day, otherwise subscription required.

Hill County

District Court & County Court at Law PO Box 634, Hillsboro, TX 76645; 254-582-4042; fax: 254-582-4035; 8AM-5PM (CST). *Felony, Misdemeanor, Civil.*
www.co.hill.tx.us/ips/cms/districtcourt/districtClerk.html

General Information: Online identifiers in results same as on public terminal. No juvenile, mental, sealed, or adoption records released. Will fax documents $1.00 per page. Court makes copy: $1.00 per page. Certification fee: $1.00. Payee: District Clerk. Personal checks accepted in person. Visa/MC accepted in person or online; DL number required. Prepayment required. Mail requests: SASE required.

Civil Name Search: Access: Mail, in person, online. Both court and visitors may perform in person name searches. Search fee: $5.00 per name. Civil records on optical imaging from 9/1993, on computer from 1991, microfilm from 1930s to 1950s, index books from 1900s. Mail turnaround time 1-2 days. Civil PAT goes back to 1990. Online case access is through www.idocket.com. One search a day is free; subscription required for more. Records go back to 12/31/1990.

Criminal Name Search: Access: Mail, in person, online. Both court and visitors may perform in person name searches. Search fee: $5.00 per name. Required to search: name, years to search; also helpful: DOB, SSN. Criminal records on optical imaging from 9/1993, on computer from 1989, microfilm from 1930s to 1950s, index books from 1900s. Mail turnaround time 1-2 days. Criminal PAT goes back to same as civil. Criminal case access is through www.idocket.com; registration and password required. Records go back to 12/31/1990. One free name search permitted a day, otherwise subscription required. Online results show name only.

County Court PO Box 398, 1 Courthouse Sq, Hillsboro, TX 76645; 254-582-4030; probate phone: 254-582-4030; fax: 254-582-4003; 8AM-5PM (CST). *Probate.*

Hockley County

District Court 802 Houston St, #316, Levelland, TX 79336; 806-894-8527; fax: 806-894-3891; 9AM-5PM (CST). *Felony, Civil.*

General Information: Probate cases are held by the County Clerk - 806-894-3185. No juvenile, mental, sealed, or adoption records released. Will fax documents $1.00 per page. Court makes copy: $1.00 per page. Certification fee: $2.00. Payee: District Clerk. Only cashiers checks and money orders accepted. Major credit cards accepted. Prepayment required. Mail requests: SASE required.

Civil Name Search: Access: Phone, mail, in person, online. Both court and visitors may perform in person name searches. Search fee: $5.00 per name. Civil records on computer from 1990, archived from 1922. Note: Pay for copies or searches online at www.paytexas.com; ID is 1163294. Mail turnaround time 1-2 days. Civil PAT goes back to 1990. One may search the docket index online at www.hockleycountyonline.net/districtclerk/. There is no fee, but access requires a password. Search civil or probate by name or case number. Online results do not give identifiers.

Criminal Name Search: Access: Phone, mail, in person, online. Both court and visitors may perform in person name searches. Search fee: $5.00 per name. Criminal records computerized from 1990, archived from 1922. Note: Pay for copies or searches online at www.paytexas.com; ID is 1163294. Mail turnaround time 1-2 days. Criminal PAT goes back to 25 years. One may search the criminal docket index online at www.hockleycountyonline.net/districtclerk/. There is no fee, but access requires a password. Online results give DOB.

County Court County Courthouse, 802 Houston St, #213, Levelland, TX 79336; 806-894-3185; 9AM-5PM (CST). *Misdemeanor, Civil, Probate.* www.co.hockley.tx.us/ips/cms/countyoffices/countyClerk.html

General Information: View court activity and dockets available by date at www.co.hockley.tx.us/ips/cms/Court_Dockets/. No juvenile, mental, sealed, or adoption records released. Will not fax documents. Court makes copy: $1.00 per page. Self serve copy: $1.00 per page. Certification fee: $5.00 per document. Payee: Hockley County Clerk. Only cashiers checks and money orders accepted. No credit cards accepted. Prepayment required. Mail requests: SASE required.

Civil Name Search: Access: Mail, in person. Both court and visitors may perform in person name searches. Search fee: $5.00. Civil records on computer from 1990, index books from 1960. Mail turnaround time 1-2 days. Civil PAT goes back to 1990.

Criminal Name Search: Access: Mail, in person. Both court and visitors may perform in person name searches. Search fee: $5.00 per name. Required to search: name, years to search; also helpful: DOB. Criminal records computerized from 1990, index books from 1960. Mail turnaround time 1-2 days. Criminal PAT goes back to 1986. Terminal results may also show DL, SS and SID numbers.

Hood County

District Court County Justice Center, 1200 W Pearl St, Granbury, TX 76048; 817-579-3236; fax: 817-579-3239; 8AM-5PM (CST). *Felony, Civil.* www.co.hood.tx.us/index.aspx?nid=218

General Information: No juvenile, mental, sealed, or adoption records released. Will not fax documents. Court makes copy: $1.00 per page. Certification fee: $1.00 per page includes copy fee. Payee: District Clerk. Personal checks accepted, credit cards are not. Prepayment required. Mail requests: SASE required.

Civil Name Search: Access: Mail, in person. Both court and visitors may perform in person name searches. Search fee: $5.00 per name. Civil records on computer and microfiche from 1983, index books before 1983. Mail turnaround time 1-2 days.

Criminal Name Search: Access: Mail, in person. Both court and visitors may perform in person name searches. Search fee: $5.00 per name. Required to search: name, years to search, DOB, SSN, signed release. Criminal records on computer and microfiche from 1983, index books before 1983. Mail turnaround time 1-2 days.

County Court PO Box 339, 1200 Pearl St, Granbury, TX 76048; 817-579-3222 x1; criminal phone: x1; civil phone: x2; probate phone: x3; fax: 817-408-3459; 8AM-5PM (CST). *Misdemeanor, Civil, Probate.*

General Information: No juvenile, mental, sealed, or adoption records released. Will fax documents if prepaid. Court makes copy: $1.00 per page. Self serve copy: same. Certification fee: $5.00 per doc. Payee: Hood County Clerk. Personal checks accepted. Visa/MC accepted in person only. Prepayment required. Mail requests: SASE required.

Civil Name Search: Access: Mail, in person. Both court and visitors may perform in person name searches. Search fee: $5.00 per name. Civil index in books. Mail turnaround time 1 day.

Criminal Name Search: Access: Mail, in person. Both court and visitors may perform in person name searches. Search fee: $5.00 per name. Required to search: name, years to search; also helpful: DOB. Criminal records on computer and microfiche from 1982, index books before 1982. Mail turnaround time 1 day.

Hopkins County

District Court 118 Church St, Sulphur Springs, TX 75483; 903-438-4083; civil phone: 903-438-4084; 8AM-5PM (CST). *Felony, Civil.*

General Information: No juvenile, mental, sealed, or adoption records released. Will not fax documents. Court makes copy: $1.00 per page. Certification fee: $2.00 per doc. Payee: District Clerk. Personal checks accepted, credit cards are not. Prepayment required. Mail requests: SASE required.

Civil Name Search: Access: Mail, in person. Both court and visitors may perform in person name searches. Search fee: $5.00 per name. Civil records on computer from 1994, index books from 1840. Mail turnaround time 2 days. Civil PAT goes back to 1970s.

Criminal Name Search: Access: Mail, in person. Both court and visitors may perform in person name searches. Search fee: $5.00 per name. Criminal records computerized from 1987, index books from 1840. Mail turnaround time 2 days. Criminal PAT goes back to 1970s.

County Court 128 Jefferson St, #C, Sulphur Springs, TX 75482; 903-438-4074; probate phone: 903-438-4074; fax: 903-438-4110; 8AM-5PM (CST). *Misdemeanor, Civil, Probate.* www.hopkinscountytx.org/

General Information: Probate index is here; Probate Court at 118 Church St at the County Courthouse. Probate records fax is same as main fax number. No juvenile, mental, or sealed records released. Will fax documents $2.00 per page plus copy fee per page. Court makes copy: $1.00 per page. Self serve copy: same. Certification fee: $5.00 per document plus copy fee. Payee: County Clerk. In-state personal checks accepted. No out-of-state checks. Major credit cards accepted. Prepayment required. Mail requests: SASE required.

Civil Name Search: Access: Mail, in person, online. Both court and visitors may perform in person name searches. Search fee: $5.00 per name. Civil records on computer since 1992, index books from 1950. Mail turnaround time 1-2 days. Civil PAT goes back to 1992. Search county court index free after registering for login and password at www.hopkinscountyonline.net/countyclerk/.

Criminal Name Search: Access: Mail, in person, online. Both court and visitors may perform in person name searches. Search fee: $5.00 per name. Required to search: name, years to search; also helpful-DOB, SSN, signed release. Criminal records computerized from 1985, index books from 1950. Mail turnaround time 1-2 days. Criminal PAT goes back to 1985. Terminal results may include DL number. Online access is the same as civil, see above.

Houston County

District Court PO Box 1186, Houston County Courthouse, 401 E Houston, Crockett, TX 75835; 936-544-3255 x228; criminal phone: x229; civil phone: x235; fax: 936-544-9523; 8AM-4:30PM (CST). *Felony, Civil, Family.* www.co.houston.tx.us/ips/cms/districtcourt/districtClerk.html

General Information: No juvenile, mental, sealed, or adoption records released. Will fax documents $3.50 1st page, $.50 each add'l. Court makes copy: $1.00 per page. No certification fee. Payee: Houston County. Personal checks accepted, credit cards are not. Prepayment required. Mail requests: SASE not required.

Civil Name Search: Access: Fax, mail, in person. Both court and visitors may perform in person name searches. Search fee: $5.00 per name. Civil cases indexed by plaintiff. Civil records on computer from 12/93, index books since 1800s. Mail turnaround time 1-2 days. Civil PAT goes back to 10-11 years.

Criminal Name Search: Access: Fax, mail, in person. Both court and visitors may perform in person name searches. Search fee: $5.00 per name. Required to search: name, years to search, signed release; also helpful: DOB, SSN. Criminal records on computer since 12/93, index books since 1800s. Mail turnaround time 1-2 days. Criminal PAT goes back to same as civil.

County Court PO Box 370, Crockett, TX 75835; 936-544-3255; criminal phone: x241; civil phone: x239; probate phone: x239 or x241; fax: 936-544-1954; 8AM-4:30PM (CST). *Misdemeanor, Civil, Probate.* www.co.houston.tx.us/ips/cms/countyoffices/countyClerk.html

General Information: Probate fax is same as main fax number. No juvenile, mental, sealed, or adoption records released. Will fax documents to local or toll-free number $1.00 per document. Court makes copy: $1.00 per page. Self serve copy: same. Certification fee: $5.00 per document. Payee: Houston County Clerk. Personal checks accepted, credit cards are not. Prepayment required. Mail requests: SASE not required.

Civil Name Search: Access: Mail, in person. Both court and visitors may perform in person name searches. Search fee: $5.00 per name. Civil records on computer since 2000, microfiche since 1983, index books since 1881 (probate). Mail turnaround time 1-2 days. Civil PAT goes back to 1999.

Criminal Name Search: Access: Mail, in person. Both court and visitors may perform in person name searches. Search fee: $5.00 per name. Criminal records on computer since 2000, index books since 1881. Mail turnaround time 1-2 days. Criminal PAT goes back to same as civil.

Howard County

District Court PO Box 2138, Big Spring, TX 79721; 432-264-2223; fax: 432-264-2256; 8AM-5PM (CST). *Felony, Civil.*

General Information: No juvenile, mental, sealed or adoption records released. Fee to fax out file $1.00 per page. Court makes copy: $1.00 per page. Certification fee: $1.00 per page. Payee: District Clerk. Personal checks accepted, credit cards are not. Prepayment required. Mail requests: SASE required.

Civil Name Search: Access: Mail, in person, online. Both court and visitors may perform in person name searches. Search fee: $5.00 per name. Civil records on computer from 1990, index books from 1881. Mail turnaround time 1-2 days. Online case access is available by subscription at www.idocket.com including civil (no probate) back to 10/01/1951. One free name search permitted a day, otherwise subscription required.

Criminal Name Search: Access: Mail, in person, online. Both court and visitors may perform in person name searches. Search fee: $5.00 per name. Criminal records computerized from 1990, index books from 1881. Mail turnaround time 1-2 days. Online case access is available by subscription at www.idocket.com including felony back to 10/01/1990. One free name search permitted a day, otherwise subscription required.

County Court PO Box 1468, Big Spring, TX 79721; 432-264-2213; fax: 432-264-2215; 8AM-5PM (CST). *Misdemeanor, Civil, Probate.*

General Information: No juvenile, mental, sealed, or adoption records released. Will fax documents $5.00 per doc. Court makes copy: $1.00 per page. Certification fee: $5.00. Payee: County Clerk. Business checks accepted. Credit card payments can only be made through officialpayments.com. Prepayment required. Mail requests: SASE not required.

Civil Name Search: Access: Phone, mail, in person. Both court and visitors may perform in person name searches. Search fee: $5.00 per name. Civil records in index books since 1881. Mail turnaround time 1-2 days.

Criminal Name Search: Access: Phone, mail, in person. Both court and visitors may perform in person name searches. Search fee: $5.00 per name. Criminal docket on books from 1881. Mail turnaround time 1-2 days.

Hudspeth County

District & County Court PO Drawer 58, 109 W Millican St, Sierra Blanca, TX 79851; 915-369-2301; fax: 915-369-0055; 8AM-5PM (MST). *Felony, Misdemeanor, Civil, Probate.*

General Information: Search fee covers both courts, both civil and criminal. No juvenile, mental, sealed, or adoption records released. Will fax documents $1.00 per page. Court makes copy: $1.00 per page. Self serve copy: same. Certification fee: $5.00 per doc. Payee: District/County Clerk. Personal checks accepted, credit cards are not. Prepayment required. Mail requests: SASE required.

Civil Name Search: Access: Phone, mail, in person. Both court and visitors may perform in person name searches. Search fee: $5.00 per name. Civil records in index books from 1900s; on computer since 1988. Mail turnaround time 1-2 days. Civil PAT goes back to 10 years.

Criminal Name Search: Access: Phone, mail, in person. Both court and visitors may perform in person name searches. Search fee: $5.00 per name. Required to search: name, years to search, DOB. Criminal docket on books from 1900s; on computer since 1998. Mail turnaround time 1-2 days. Criminal PAT goes back to same as civil.

Hunt County

District Court Court Clerk, PO Box 1437, Greenville, TX 75403; 903-408-4172; 8AM-5PM (CST). *Felony, Civil.*

www.huntcounty.net/

General Information: No juvenile, sealed, or adoption records released. Will not fax documents. Court makes copy: $1.00 per page. Self serve copy: same. Certification fee: $1.00. Payee: District Clerk. Personal checks accepted, credit cards are not. Prepayment required. Mail requests: SASE required.

Civil Name Search: Access: Mail, in person. Both court and visitors may perform in person name searches. Search fee: $5.00 per name. Civil records on computer from 1992, microfiche from 1973, index books from 1900s. Mail turnaround time 10 days. Civil PAT goes back to 1992.

Criminal Name Search: Access: Mail, in person. Both court and visitors may perform in person name searches. Search fee: $5.00 per name. Required to search: name, years to search, DOB. Criminal records computerized from 1992, microfilm from 1973, index books from 1900s. Mail turnaround time 10 days. Criminal PAT goes back to 1992.

County Court #1 and #2 PO Box 1316, Greenville, TX 75403-1316; 903-408-4130; fax: 903-408-4287; 8AM-4:30PM (CST). *Misdemeanor, Civil, Probate.*

General Information: No juvenile, mental, sealed, or adoption records released. Will not fax documents. Court makes copy: $1.00 per page. Self serve copy: same. Certification fee: $5.00. Payee: County Clerk. Personal checks accepted, credit cards are not. Prepayment required. Mail requests: SASE required.

Civil Name Search: Access: Mail, in person. Both court and visitors may perform in person name searches. Search fee: $5.00 per name. Civil records on computer since 1986, index books from 1940; on microfilm prior to 1986. Mail turnaround time 1-2 days. Civil PAT goes back to 1986.

Criminal Name Search: Access: Mail, in person. Both court and visitors may perform in person name searches. Search fee: $5.00 per name. Required to search: name, years to search, DOB. Criminal records on computer since 1986, index books from 1940; on microfilm prior to 1986. Mail turnaround time 1-2 days. Criminal PAT goes back to 1987. Terminal results may show DL number.

Hutchinson County

District Court PO Box 580, 206 W 1st Ave, Stinnett, TX 79083; 806-878-4017; fax: 806-878-4042; 9AM-5PM (CST). *Felony, Civil.*

General Information: No juvenile, mental, sealed, or adoption records released. Fee to fax out file $1.00 per page. Court makes copy: $1.00 1st page, $.25 each add'l. Certification fee: $1.00 per page. Payee: District Clerk. Personal checks accepted. Major credit cards accepted. Prepayment required. Mail requests: SASE required.

Civil Name Search: Access: Mail, in person, online. Both court and visitors may perform in person name searches. Search fee: $5.00 per name. Civil records on computer from 1990, docket books from 1920. Mail turnaround time 3 to 5 days. Civil PAT goes back to 3/1990. Online case access is available by subscription at www.idocket.com including civil (no probate) back to 1/1/1990. One free name search permitted a day, otherwise subscription required.

Criminal Name Search: Access: Mail, in person, online. Both court and visitors may perform in person name searches. Search fee: $5.00 per name. Required to search: name, years to search, signed release; also helpful: DOB, SSN. Criminal records computerized from 1989, docket books from 1920. Mail turnaround time 2 days. Criminal PAT goes back to 3/1990. Includes DR number. Online case access is available by subscription at www.idocket.com including criminal back to 1/1/1989. One free name search permitted a day, otherwise subscription required. Online results show middle initial.

County Court PO Box 1186, County Clerk, Stinnett, TX 79083; 806-878-4002; fax: 806-878-3497; 9AM-5PM (CST). *Misdemeanor, Civil, Probate.* www.co.hutchinson.tx.us/ips/cms/countyoffices/countyClerk.html

General Information: No juvenile, mental, sealed, or adoption records released. Will not fax documents. Court makes copy: $1.00 per page. Certification fee: $5.00. Payee: Hutchinson County Clerk. Business & Personal checks accepted, credit cards are not. Prepayment required. Mail requests: SASE not required.

Civil Name Search: Access: Mail, in person. Both court and visitors may perform in person name searches. Search fee: $5.00 per name. Civil records in index books from 1900s. Mail turnaround time 2 days.

Criminal Name Search: Access: Mail, in person. Both court and visitors may perform in person name searches. Search fee: $5.00 per name. Criminal records on computer since 1990, index books from 1900s. Mail turnaround time 2 days.

Irion County

District & County Court PO Box 736, 209 N Parkview, Mertzon, TX 76941-0736; 325-835-2421; fax: 325-835-7941; 8AM-N, 1:15PM-5PM (CST). *Felony, Misdemeanor, Civil, Probate.*

General Information: No juvenile, mental, or sealed records released. Will fax documents $1.00 per page if long distance, $.50 per page if local. Court makes copy: $1.00 per page. Certification fee: $5.00 per doc. Payee: District/County Clerk. Personal checks accepted. Major credit cards accepted, small fee added. Prepayment required. Mail requests: SASE requested.

Civil Name Search: Access: Mail, in person. Both court and visitors may perform in person name searches. Search fee: $5.00 per name. Fee is per court. Civil records in index books from 1889. Mail turnaround time 1-2 days.

Criminal Name Search: Access: Mail, in person. Both court and visitors may perform in person name searches. Search fee: $5.00 per name. Fee is per court. Required to search: name, years to search; also helpful: DOB, DL.

Criminal records indexed in books from 1886. Mail turnaround time 1-2 days.

Jack County

District Court 100 Main St, Ste 310, Jacksboro, TX 76458; 940-567-2141; fax: 940-567-2696; 8AM-12; 1PM-5PM (CST). *Felony, Civil.*

General Information: No juvenile, mental, sealed, or adoption records released. Court makes copy: $.50 per page. Self serve copy: same. Certification fee: $1.00 per page. Payee: Jack County District Clerk. No personal checks or credit cards accepted. Prepayment required. Mail requests: SASE required.

Civil Name Search: Access: Mail, in person. Both court and visitors may perform in person name searches. Search fee: $10.00 per name. Civil records in index books from 1857. Note: Even in person must be in writing if court to perform. Mail turnaround time 2 days.

Criminal Name Search: Access: Mail, in person. Both court and visitors may perform in person name searches. Search fee: $10.00 per name. Criminal docket on books from 1857. Note: Even in person must be in writing if court to perform. Mail turnaround time 2 days.

County Court 100 Main, Jacksboro, TX 76458; 940-567-2111; fax: 940-567-6441; 8AM-5PM (CST). *Misdemeanor, Civil, Probate.*

General Information: No juvenile, mental, sealed, or adoption records released. Will fax documents $1.00 per page. Court makes copy: $1.00 per page. Self serve copy: same. Certification fee: $5.00. Payee: Jack County Clerk. Personal checks accepted. Credit cards accepted. Prepayment required. Mail requests: SASE required.

Civil Name Search: Access: Mail, in person, online. Both court and visitors may perform in person name searches. Search fee: $5.00 per name. Civil records in index books from 1856, computerized since 2005. Mail turnaround time 1-2 days. Online case access is available by subscription at www.idocket.com including civil and probate back to 1/2000. One free name search permitted a day, otherwise subscription required.

Criminal Name Search: Access: Phone, mail, in person, online. Both court and visitors may perform in person name searches. Search fee: $5.00 per name. Criminal docket on books from 1856, computerized since 2002. Mail turnaround time 1-2 days. Public use terminal has crim records. Online misdemeanor case access is available by subscription at www.idocket.com including criminal back to 1/1999. One free name search permitted a day, otherwise subscription required.

Jackson County

District Court 115 W Main, Rm 203, Edna, TX 77957; 361-782-3812; fax: 361-782-3056; 8AM-5PM (CST). *Felony, Civil.*
www.co.jackson.tx.us/ips/cms/districtcourt/districtClerk.html

General Information: No sealed, or adoption records released. Will fax documents for $5.00 fee. Court makes copy: $1.00 per page. Certification fee: $1.00 plus copy fee. Payee: District Clerk. Personal checks accepted. Major credit cards accepted. Prepayment required. Mail requests: SASE required.

Civil Name Search: Access: Phone, mail, in person. Both court and visitors may perform in person name searches. Search fee: $5.00 per name. Civil records in index books from 1850. Mail turnaround time 1 day.

Criminal Name Search: Access: Mail, in person. Both court and visitors may perform in person name searches. Search fee: $5.00 per name. Criminal records on microfiche from 1981, index books from 1850. Mail turnaround time 1-2 days.

County Court 115 W Main, Rm 101, Edna, TX 77957; 361-782-3563; fax: 361-782-3132; 8AM-4PM (CST). *Misdemeanor, Civil, Probate.*

General Information: Probate is separate index at this same address. No juvenile, mental, sealed, or adoption records released. Fee to fax out file $4.25 for the 1st page, $2.25 per page thereafter. Court makes copy: $1.00 per page. Certification fee: $5.00 per document plus copy fee. Payee: County Clerk. Personal checks accepted. Credit cards accepted. Prepayment required. Mail requests: SASE not required.

Civil Name Search: Access: Mail, in person. Both court and visitors may perform in person name searches. Search fee: $5.00 per name. Civil records in index books from 1900s.

Criminal Name Search: Access: Mail, in person. Both court and visitors may perform in person name searches. Search fee: $5.00 per name. Required to search: name, years to search, DOB, offense, date of offense. Criminal docket on books from 1900s. Mail turnaround time 1-2 days.

Jasper County

District Court 121 N Austin, Room 202, PO Box 2088, Jasper, TX 75951; 409-384-2721; fax: 409-383-7501; 8AM-4:30PM (CST). *Felony, Civil, Family.*

General Information: No juvenile, mental, sealed, or adoption records released. Will fax documents for $1.00 per page. Court makes copy: $1.00 per page. Self serve copy: same. Certification fee: $5.00. Payee: District Clerk/Court. Personal checks accepted. Prepayment required. Mail requests: SASE required.

Civil Name Search: Access: Mail, in person. Both court and visitors may perform in person name searches. Search fee: $5.00 per name. Civil records on computer since 1991, index books and microfilm since 1850s. Mail turnaround time 1-2 days. Civil PAT goes back to 1991.

Criminal Name Search: Access: Mail, in person. Both court and visitors may perform in person name searches. Search fee: $5.00 per name. Criminal records on computer since 12/96; index books and microfilm since 1850s. Mail turnaround time 1-2 days. Criminal PAT goes back to 1996.

County Court PO Box 2070, 121 N Austin St, Rm 103, Courthouse, Jasper, TX 75951; 409-384-2632; criminal phone: 409-384-5078; civil phone: 409-384-2632; probate phone: 409-384-2632; fax: 409-384-7198; 8AM-4:30PM (CST). *Misdemeanor, Civil, Probate.*

General Information: Probate fax is same as main fax number. No juvenile, mental, sealed, or adoption records released. Fee to fax out file $3.00 per page. Court makes copy: $1.00 per page. Certification fee: $5.00 per document plus copy fee. Payee: Debbie Newman County Clerk. Personal checks require drivers license. Major credit cards accepted online at www.officialpayments.com. Prepayment required. Mail requests: SASE not required.

Civil Name Search: Access: Mail, fax, in person. Both court and visitors may perform in person name searches. Search fee: $10.00 per name. Civil records in index books; on computer back to 1987. Mail turnaround time 1 day. Civil PAT goes back to 1996. Terminal results also show SSNs.

Criminal Name Search: Access: Mail, fax, in person. Both court and visitors may perform in person name searches. Search fee: $10.00 per name. Required to search: name, years to search, DOB; also helpful: SSN. Criminal index in books; on computer back to 1987. Mail turnaround time 1 day. Criminal PAT goes back to 1990. Terminal results include SSN.

Jeff Davis County

District & County Court PO Box 398, Fort Davis, TX 79734; 432-426-3251; fax: 432-426-3760; 9AM-N, 1-5PM (CST). *Felony, Misdemeanor, Civil, Probate.*

General Information: Probate fax is same as main fax number. No juvenile, mental, sealed, or adoption records released. Will fax documents to local or toll free line. Court makes copy: $1.00 per page. Certification fee: $5.00 per certification plus copy fee. Payee: County Clerk. No personal checks or credit cards accepted. Prepayment required. Mail requests: SASE helpful.

Civil Name Search: Access: Mail, in person. Both court and visitors may perform in person name searches. Search fee: $5.00 per name. Civil index in books. Mail turnaround time 2 days.

Criminal Name Search: Access: Mail, in person, fax. Both court and visitors may perform in person name searches. Search fee: $5.00 per name. Criminal index in books. Mail turnaround time 2 days.

Jefferson County

District Court 1001 Pearl St, Pearl St Courthouse, Beaumont, TX 77701; 409-835-8580; criminal phone: 409-835-8583; civil phone: 409-835-8580; fax: 409-835-8527; 8AM-5PM (CST). *Felony, Civil.*
www.co.jefferson.tx.us/dclerk/dc_home.htm

General Information: No juvenile, mental, sealed, or adoption records released. Will fax documents local for $3.00 1st page, $1.00 each add'l. Long distance 1st page is $5.00. A similar fee applies to fax send to them. Court makes copy: $1.00 per page. Self serve copy: same. Certification fee: $5.00 per instrument; search results are not certified unless done by the court itself. Payee: District Clerk. Only cashiers checks and money orders accepted. No credit cards accepted. Prepayment required. Mail requests: SASE required.

Civil Name Search: Access: Mail, in person, online. Both court and visitors may perform in person name searches. Search fee: $10.00 per name. Civil records on computer and index books since 1940s. Mail turnaround time 2-4 days. Civil PAT goes back to 1945. Public terminal has civil, family, and E-file on selected cases. Online access to the civil records index at www.co.jefferson.tx.us/dclerk/civil_index/main.htm. Search by year by defendant or plaintiff by year 1985 to present. Index goes back to 1995; images back to 12/1998. There is also a Domestic Index.

Criminal Name Search: Access: Mail, online, in person. Both court and visitors may perform in person name searches. Search fee: $10.00 per name. Required to search: name, years to search; also helpful: DOB, SSN. Criminal records on computer and index books since 1940s. Mail turnaround time 2-4 days. Criminal PAT goes back to 1936. Online access to criminal records index is at www.co.jefferson.tx.us/dclerk/criminal_index/main.htm. Search by name by year 1981 to present. Online results show middle initial.

County Court PO Box 1151, Beaumont, TX 77704; 409-835-8475; fax: 409-839-2394; 8AM-4:30PM (CST). *Misdemeanor, Civil, Probate.*
www.co.jefferson.tx.us/cclerk/clerk.htm

General Information: Search probate records back to 1988 free at http://jeffersontxclerk.manatron.com/. Images go back to 1998. Probate records in a separate index. Probate fax is same as main fax number. Will answer phone until 5PM. No juvenile, mental, sealed, or adoption records released. Will fax documents $2.50 1st page, $.25 each add'l. Court makes copy: $1.00 per page. Certification fee: $5.00 per cause number. Payee: County Clerk. Personal checks accepted. Major credit cards accepted plus $2.50 transaction fee. Prepayment required. Mail requests: SASE not required.

Civil Name Search: Access: Mail, in person, online. Both court and visitors may perform in person name searches. Search fee: $10.00 per name. Civil records on computer since 11/1/95, index books to 1836. Mail turnaround time 1 day. Civil PAT goes back to 11/1/1995 for index; 12/14/1998 for images. Public terminal probate index goes back to 10/1988. Search county clerk's civil index free at http://jeffersontxclerk.manatron.com. Index goes back to 1995; images back to 12/1998. $1.00 per page to obtain online docs, plus a $2.50 processing fee. Court reports it is adding additional records in 2011.

Criminal Name Search: Access: Mail, in person, online. Both court and visitors may perform in person name searches. Search fee: $10.00 per name. Required to search: name, years to search, DOB. Criminal records on computer since 1-1-82, index books to 1836. Mail turnaround time 1 day. Criminal PAT goes back to 1/1983 for index; 12/14/1998 for images. Access to Class A&B and C Misdemeanor that are appealed indexes back to 1982 are free at http://jeffersontxclerk.manatron.com/. $1.00 per page to obtain online docs with a $2.50 processing fee. Add'l criminal records being added. Online results show name only.

Jim Hogg County

District & County Court PO Box 878, Hebbronville, TX 78361; 361-527-4031; fax: 361-527-5843; 9AM-5PM (CST). *Felony, Misdemeanor, Civil, Probate.*

General Information: Probate records are in a separate index. Probate fax is same as main fax number. No juvenile, mental, sealed, or adoption records released. Fee to fax out file $3.00 per page. Court makes copy: $1.00 per page. Self serve copy: same. Certification fee: $5.00 per document. Payee: District Clerk. No personal checks or credit cards accepted. Prepayment required. Mail requests: SASE required for civil.

Civil Name Search: Access: Mail, fax, in person. Both court and visitors may perform in person name searches. Search fee: $15.00 per name. Civil index in books.

Criminal Name Search: Access: In person only. Only the court performs in person name searches; visitors may not. Search fee: $15.00 per name. Criminal index in books.

Jim Wells County

District Court PO Box 2219, Alice, TX 78333; 361-668-5717; fax: 361-668-5732; 8AM-N, 1-5PM (CST). *Felony, Civil.*
www.co.jim-wells.tx.us/ips/cms/districtcourt/districtClerk.html

General Information: Fax filings are not accepted. No juvenile, mental, sealed, or adoption records released. Will fax documents $2.00 1st page, $1.00 ea add'l. Court makes copy: $1.00 per page. Certification fee: $2.00. Payee: District Clerk. Personal checks cashier's checks or money orders only accepted. Prepayment required. Mail requests: SASE required.

Civil Name Search: Access: Mail, in person. Both court and visitors may perform in person name searches. Search fee: $5.00 per name. Civil records on computer since 1992, index books since 1912. Mail turnaround time 2 days.

Criminal Name Search: Access: Mail, in person, online. Both court and visitors may perform in person name searches. Search fee: $5.00 per name. Required to search: name, years to search; also helpful: SSN, DOB. Criminal records on computer since 1992, index books since 1912. Mail turnaround time 2 days. Online case access is available by subscription at www.idocket.com including felony back to 05/05/1982. One free name search permitted a day, otherwise subscription required.

County Court PO Box 1459, 200 N Almond St, Alice, TX 78333; 361-668-5702; 8AM-N, 1-5PM (CST). *Misdemeanor, Civil, Probate.*

General Information: No juvenile, mental, sealed, or adoption records released. Will not fax documents. Court makes copy: $1.00 per page. Certification fee: $5.00 per doc plus copy fee. Payee: County Clerk. Personal checks accepted, credit cards are not. Prepayment required. Mail requests: SASE not required.

Civil Name Search: Access: Mail, in person. Both court and visitors may perform in person name searches. Search fee: $10.00 per name. Civil records in index books from 1911. Mail turnaround time 1 day.

Criminal Name Search: Access: Phone, mail, in person. Both court and visitors may perform in person name searches. Search fee: $10.00 per name. Required to search: name, years to search, address, DOB. Criminal records on computer since 1992, index books from 1911. Mail turnaround time 1 day. Public use terminal has crim records. Online results show name, DOB.

Johnson County

District Court PO Box 495, Cleburne, TX 76033-0495; 817-556-6839; fax: 817-556-6120; 8AM-5PM (CST). *Felony, Civil, Domestic.*
www.johnsoncountytx.org

General Information: Court also holds local misdemeanor records prior to 1985. No juvenile, mental, sealed, or adoption records released without a court order on file. Fee to fax out or to email file $2.00 per page. Court makes copy: $1.00 per page. Self serve copy: same. Certification fee: $1.00 per document include copy fee. Payee: District Clerk. Business checks and money orders accepted. Major credit cards accepted in person. Prepayment required. Mail requests: SASE required.

Civil Name Search: Access: Fax, mail, in person, online. Both court and visitors may perform in person name searches. Search fee: $5.00 per name. Required to search: name; also helpful: years to search. Civil records on computer from mid-1989, index and minute books back to 1800s. Mail turnaround time 4-10 days. Civil PAT goes back to mid-1989. Access index and images online at www.idocket.com; registration and password required. A fee service; only one free name search per day. Records go back to 11/10/1989. Images available. Also search at http://ira.johnsoncountytx.org/.

Criminal Name Search: Access: Fax, mail, in person, online. Both court and visitors may perform in person name searches. Search fee: $5.00 per name. Required to search: name; also helpful: years to search, aliases. Criminal records computerized from mid-1989, index and minute books back to 1800s. Mail turnaround time 4-10 days. Criminal PAT goes back to same as civil. Access index and images online at www.idocket.com; registration and password required. A fee service; only one free name search per day. Records go back to 11/10/1989. Images available. Also search at http://ira.johnsoncountytx.org/

County Court Guinn Justice Center, 204 S Buffalo Ave #407, Cleburne, TX 76033-0662; 817-556-6323; criminal phone: ext 1326; civil phone: ext 1311; probate phone: ext 1310; fax: 817-556-6170; 8AM-N, 1-4:30PM (CST). *Misdemeanor, Civil, Probate, family Law.*
www.johnsoncountytx.org

General Information: No juvenile, mental, sealed, or adoption records released. Will not fax documents. Court makes copy: $1.00 per page. Certification fee: $5.00. Payee: County Clerk. Business checks accepted. No personal checks accepted. Credit cards accepted. Prepayment required. Mail requests: SASE required.

Civil Name Search: Access: Mail, in person, online. Both court and visitors may perform in person name searches. Search fee: $5.00 per name. Civil records on computer since 1985. Note: Only searches made by court will be certified. Mail turnaround time 2-3 days. Civil PAT goes back to 1985. Access index and images online at http://idocket.com/homepage2.htm. Registration required. Civil records back to 12/31/85, probate to 01/01/1918. One free name search permitted a day, otherwise subscription required. Also search at http://ira.johnsoncountytx.org/.

Criminal Name Search: Access: Mail, in person, online. Both court and visitors may perform in person name searches. Search fee: $5.00 per name. Required to search: name, years to search, and DOB or SSN or DL#. Criminal records on computer since 1988, index books since 1985. Note: Only searches made by court will be certified. Mail turnaround time 1-2 days. Criminal PAT goes back to 1988. Results include name and case number, some images available. Access misdemeanor index and images online at http://idocket.com/homepage2.htm. Registration required. Records back to 12/31/88. One free name search permitted a day, otherwise subscription required. Also search at http://ira.johnsoncountytx.org/.

Jones County

District & County Court PO Box 308, 12th and Commercial Sts, Anson, TX 79501; 325-823-3731; fax: 325-823-3289; 8AM-5PM (CST). *Felony, Misdemeanor, Civil.*

General Information: No juvenile, mental, sealed, or adoption records released. Will fax documents to local or toll free line. Court makes copy: $1.00 per page. Self serve copy: same. Certification fee: $1.00. Payee: lacey Hansen, District Clerk. Personal checks accepted; deposit accounts can be setup. No credit cards accepted. Prepayment required. Mail requests: SASE required.

Civil Name Search: Access: Mail, in person. Both court and visitors may perform in person name searches. Search fee: $5.00 per name. Civil records on computer since 1990, index books since 1881. Mail turnaround time same day.

Criminal Name Search: Access: Mail, in person. Both court and visitors may perform in person name searches. Search fee: $5.00 per name. Required to search: name, years to search, DOB. Criminal records on computer since 1986, index books since 1881. Mail turnaround time same day.

Karnes County

District Court County Courthouse, 101 N Panna Maria Ave, Karnes City, TX 78118-2930; 830-780-2562; fax: 830-780-3227; 8AM-N, 1-5PM (CST). *Felony, Civil.*
www.81st-218thdistrictcourt.org/
General Information: No juvenile, mental, sealed, or adoption records released. Will fax documents $.25 per page. Court makes copy: $1.00 per page. Certification fee: $5.00 plus copy fee. Payee: District Clerk. Personal checks accepted, credit cards are not. Prepayment required. Mail requests: SASE required.
Civil Name Search: Access: Mail, in person. Both court and visitors may perform in person name searches. Search fee: $5.00 per name. Civil records in index books from 1858. Mail turnaround time 1-2 days.
Criminal Name Search: Access: Mail, in person. Both court and visitors may perform in person name searches. Search fee: $5.00 per name. Required to search: name, years to search, DOB, SSN or other identifiers. Criminal docket on books from 1906. Mail turnaround time 1-2 days.

County Court 101 N Panna Maria Ave, #9 Courthouse, Karnes City, TX 78118-2929; 830-780-3938; fax: 830-780-4576; 8AM-5PM (CST). *Misdemeanor, Civil, Probate.*
General Information: Probate fax is same as main fax number. No juvenile, mental, sealed, or adoption records released. Fee to fax out file $2.00 per page. Court makes copy: $1.00 per page. Self serve copy: same. Certification fee: $5.00 per doc plus copy fee. Payee: Alva Jonas, County Clerk. Personal checks accepted. Credit cards accepted. Prepayment required. Mail requests: SASE required.
Civil Name Search: Access: Mail, in person. Both court and visitors may perform in person name searches. Search fee: $10.00 per name. Civil records in index books from 1920, no computerization. Mail turnaround time 2 days. Civil PAT goes back to 2005.
Criminal Name Search: Access: Mail, in person. Both court and visitors may perform in person name searches. Search fee: $10.00 per name. Criminal docket on books from 1900, computerized since 1991. Mail turnaround time 2 days. Criminal PAT goes back to 1992.

Kaufman County

District Court County Courthouse, 100 W Mulberry St, Kaufman, TX 75142; 972-932-0274; 8AM-5PM (CST). *Felony, Civil, Family.*
www.kaufmancounty.net/dc.html
General Information: No sealed, or adoption records released. Will not fax documents. Court makes copy: $1.00 per page. Self serve copy: same. Certification fee: $1.00 per doc. Payee: Kaufman District Clerk. Personal checks accepted, credit cards are not. Prepayment required. Mail requests: SASE required.
Civil Name Search: Access: Mail, in person, online. Both court and visitors may perform in person name searches. Search fee: $5.00 per name. Civil records on computer or books from 1849. Mail turnaround time up to 1 week. Civil PAT goes back to 1849. Access court record index for civil and family free at http://12.14.175.23/default.aspx. Online court records do not always show all identifiers.
Criminal Name Search: Access: Mail, in person, online. Both court and visitors may perform in person name searches. Search fee: $5.00 per name. Criminal records on computer or books from 1849. Mail turnaround time up to 1 week. Criminal PAT goes back to same as civil. Access criminal court record index free at http://12.14.175.23/default.aspx. Online court records do not always show complete dispositions.

County Court County Courthouse, Kaufman, TX 75142; 972-932-4331 x1101; criminal fax: 972-962-8018; civil fax: 8AM-4:30PM; 8AM-4:30PM (CST). *Misdemeanor, Civil, Probate.*
www.kaufmancountyclerk.com/
General Information: Probate fax- 972-932-0659 Online identifiers in results same as on public terminal. No juvenile, mental, sealed, or adoption records released. Will fax documents $3.00 each. Court makes copy: $1.00 per page. Self serve copy: same. Certification fee: $5.00 first page; $1.00 each add'l page, plus copy fee. Payee: County Clerk. Personal checks accepted. Major credit cards accepted. Prepayment required. Mail requests: SASE required.
Civil Name Search: Access: Mail, in person, online. Both court and visitors may perform in person name searches. Search fee: $5.00 per name; probate is $10.00 per name. Civil records on computer from 1985, index books to 1959. Mail turnaround time 10 days. Civil PAT goes back to 1985. Access court record index for civil and probate free at http://12.14.175.23/default.aspx. Online court records do not always show all identifiers.
Criminal Name Search: Access: Mail, in person, online. Both court and visitors may perform in person name searches. Search fee: $5.00 per name. Criminal records computerized from 1985, index books to 1870. Mail turnaround time 10 days. Criminal PAT goes back to same as civil. Access criminal court record index free at http://12.14.175.23/default.aspx. Online court records do not always show complete dispositions. Online results show middle initial.

Kendall County

District Court - 216th Judicial District 201 E. San Antonio, #201, Boerne, TX 78006; 830-249-9343; fax: 830-249-1763; 8AM-N, 1-5PM (CST). *Felony, Civil.*
General Information: No juvenile, mental, sealed, or adoption records released. Will not fax documents. Court makes copy: $.50 per page. Certification fee: $1.00 per page. Payee: District Clerk. Personal checks accepted, credit cards are not. Prepayment required. Mail requests: SASE required.
Civil Name Search: Access: Mail, in person. Both court and visitors may perform in person name searches. Search fee: $5.00 per name. Civil index in docket books from early 1900s. Mail turnaround time 1-2 days.
Criminal Name Search: Access: Mail, in person. Both court and visitors may perform in person name searches. Search fee: $5.00 per name. Required to search: name, DOB, years to search, signed release; also helpful: SSN. Criminal docket on books back to early 1900s. Mail turnaround time 2-4 days.

County Court 201 E San Antonio, #127, Boerne, TX 78006; 830-249-9343; fax: 830-249-3472; 8AM-5PM (CST). *Misdemeanor, Probate.*
General Information: No juvenile, mental, sealed, or adoption records released. No fee to fax documents. Court makes copy: $1.00 per page. Self serve copy: same. Certification fee: $5.00. Payee: County Clerk. Personal checks accepted, credit cards are not. Prepayment required. Mail requests: SASE required.
Criminal Name Search: Access: Mail, in person. Both court and visitors may perform in person name searches. Search fee: $5.00 per name. Criminal docket on books from 1860s. Mail turnaround time 2-4 days.

Kenedy County

District & County Court PO Box 227, Sarita, TX 78385; 361-294-5220; fax: 361-294-5218; 8:30AM-N, 1:30PM-4:30PM (CST). *Felony, Misdemeanor, Civil, Probate.*
General Information: No juvenile, mental, sealed, or adoption records released. Will fax documents $5.00 1st page, $2.00 ea add'l. Court makes copy: $1.00 per page. Certification fee: $5.00 per doc. Payee: District/County Clerk. Personal checks accepted, credit cards are not. Prepayment required. Mail requests: SASE not required.
Civil Name Search: Access: Phone, fax, mail, in person. Both court and visitors may perform in person name searches. Search fee: $5.00 per name. Civil records on microfilm since 1991, minute books since 1921. Mail turnaround time 5 days.
Criminal Name Search: Access: Phone, fax, mail, in person. Both court and visitors may perform in person name searches. Search fee: $5.00 per name. Criminal records on microfilm since 1991, minute books since 1921. Mail turnaround time 5 days.

Kent County

District & County Court PO Box 9, Jayton, TX 79528; 806-237-3881; fax: 806-237-2632; 8:30AM-N, 1-5PM (CST). *Felony, Misdemeanor, Civil, Probate.*
General Information: Probate fax is same as main fax number. No juvenile, mental, sealed, or adoption records released. Will not fax documents. Court makes copy: $1.00 per page. Self serve copy: same. Certification fee: $5.00 per document plus copy fee. Payee: County Clerk. Personal checks accepted, credit cards are not. Prepayment required. Mail requests: SASE required.
Civil Name Search: Access: Mail, in person. Visitors must perform in person searches themselves. Search fee: $5.00 per name. Civil index in books. Mail turnaround time ASAP.
Criminal Name Search: Access: Mail, in person. Visitors must perform in person searches themselves. Search fee: $5.00 per name. Criminal index in books. Mail turnaround time ASAP.

Kerr County

District Court 700 Main St, Courthouse, Kerrville, TX 78028; 830-792-2281; fax: 830-792-2289; 8AM-5PM (CST). *Felony, Civil.*
www.co.kerr.tx.us/dclerk/districtclerk.html
General Information: No juvenile, mental, sealed, or adoption records released. Fee to fax out file $1.00 per page. Court makes copy: $1.00 1st page; $.25 each add'l. Self serve copy: same. Certification fee: $1.00 per page. Payee: District Clerk. Personal checks accepted. Credit cards accepted. Prepayment required. Mail requests: SASE required.
Civil Name Search: Access: Mail, in person, online. Both court and visitors may perform in person name searches. Search fee: $5.00 per name. Civil records on computer from late 1991, index books prior to 1991. Mail turnaround time 2-4 days. Civil PAT goes back to early 1990s. Search all

court indexes also jail and bond indexes free at http://public.co.kerr.tx.us/CaseManagement/PublicAccess/default.aspx.
Criminal Name Search: Access: Mail, in person, Online. Both court and visitors may perform in person name searches. Search fee: $5.00 per name. Criminal records computerized from late 1990, index books prior. Mail turnaround time 2-4 days. Criminal PAT goes back to same as civil. Online access is the same as civil.

County Court & County Court at Law 700 Main St, #122, Kerrville, TX 78028-5389; 830-792-2262; probate phone: 830-792-2261; fax: 830-792-2274; 8:30AM-5PM (CST). *Misdemeanor, Probate.* www.co.kerr.tx.us/

General Information: Probate fax is same as main fax number. All other civil cases in District Court, upstairs. See www.texasonline.com/efiling for E-filing of probate cases. No juvenile, mental, sealed, or adoption records released. Fee to fax out file $1.00 per page. Court makes copy: $1.00 per page. Self serve copy: $.10 per page. Certification fee: $5.00 per document plus copy fee. Payee: Kerr County Clerk. Only cashiers checks and money orders accepted. Major credit cards accepted. Prepayment required. Mail requests: SASE not required.
Civil Name Search: Access: Mail, fax, in person, online. Both court and visitors may perform in person name searches. Search fee: $5.00 per name. Civil records on computer since 1988, microfiche since 1985, index books prior to 1985. Mail turnaround time 3 days. Civil PAT goes back to 1986. For online access, see criminal section, below.
Criminal Name Search: Access: Mail, fax, in person, online. Both court and visitors may perform in person name searches. Search fee: $5.00 per name. Required to search: name, years to search, DOB; also helpful: SSN. Criminal records on computer since 1985, index books prior to 1918. Mail turnaround time 3 days. Criminal PAT goes back to 1986. Terminal results include SSN. Search court records, jail and bond records free at http://public.co.kerr.tx.us/CaseManagement/PublicAccess/default.aspx.

Kimble County

District & County Court 501 Main St, Junction, TX 76849; 325-446-3353; fax: 325-446-2986; 8AM-N, 1-5PM (CST). *Felony, Misdemeanor, Civil, Probate.* www.co.kimble.tx.us/ips/cms
General Information: Probate records are in a separate index. Probate fax is same as main fax number. No juvenile, mental, sealed, or adoption records released. Will fax documents to local or toll free line, fee is $5.00. Court makes copy: $1.00 per page. Certification fee: $5.00. Payee: Kimble County/District Clerk. Instate personal checks accepted. No out of state checks accepted. No credit cards accepted. Prepayment required. Mail requests: SASE required for criminal.
Civil Name Search: Access: In person only. Visitors must perform in person searches themselves. Civil records in index books (records are micro-filmed for security only).
Criminal Name Search: Access: Mail, in person. Both court and visitors may perform in person name searches. Search fee: $5.00 per name. Required to search: name, years to search, DOB. Criminal docket on books (records are micro-filmed for security only). Note: The clerk will search back 7 years. Request for criminal search must be in writing and can be faxed if you have prearranged for payment. Mail turnaround time 3-4 days.

King County

District & County Court PO Box 135, Guthrie, TX 79236; 806-596-4412; criminal phone: 806-596-4412; civil phone: 806-596-4412; probate phone: 806-596-4412; fax: 806-596-4664; 9AM-N, 1-5PM (CST). *Felony, Misdemeanor, Civil, Probate.*
General Information: No juvenile, mental, sealed, or adoption records released. Will fax documents $1.00 per page. Court makes copy: $1.00 per page. Self serve copy: same. Certification fee: $5.00. Payee: District Clerk or King County Clerk. Personal checks accepted, credit cards are not. Prepayment required. Mail requests: SASE required.
Civil Name Search: Access: Mail, in person. Both court and visitors may perform in person name searches. Search fee: $5.00 per name. Civil index in books. Mail turnaround time 2-4 days.
Criminal Name Search: Access: Mail, in person. Both court and visitors may perform in person name searches. Search fee: $5.00 per name. Required to search: name, years to search, DOB. Criminal index in books. Mail turnaround time 2-4 days.

Kinney County

District & County Court PO Drawer 9, 501 S Ann St, Brackettville, TX 78832; 830-563-2521; fax: 830-563-2644; 8AM-5PM (CST). *Felony, Misdemeanor, Civil, Probate.*
General Information: No juvenile, mental, sealed, or adoption records released. Will fax documents $3.00 1st page; $2.00 ea add'l. Court makes copy: $1.00 per page. Self serve copy: same. Certification fee: $5.00 in

County or District Court. Payee: County & District Clerk. Personal checks accepted, credit cards are not. Prepayment required. Mail requests: SASE required.
Civil Name Search: Access: Phone, fax, mail, in person. Both court and visitors may perform in person name searches. Search fee: $10.00 per name. Civil records in index books from late 1800s; computerized back to 1996. Mail turnaround time 1 week.
Criminal Name Search: Access: Phone, fax, mail, in person. Both court and visitors may perform in person name searches. Search fee: $10.00 per name. Required to search: name, years to search, DOB. Criminal docket on books from late 1800s; computerized records back to 1996. Mail turnaround time 1 week.

Kleberg County

District & County Court at Law PO Box 312, Kingsville, TX 78364-0312; 361-595-8561; fax: 361-595-8525; 8AM-N, 1-5 PM (CST). *Felony, Civil.*
General Information: Online identifiers in results same as on public terminal. No sealed or adoption records released. Will fax documents $5.00 per every 10 pages. Will not accept incoming faxes. Court makes copy: $1.00 1st page, $.25 each add'l. Certification fee: $1.00 per page. Payee: District Clerk. Local personal checks accepted only. No credit cards accepted. Prepayment required. Mail requests: SASE required.
Civil Name Search: Access: Phone, fax, mail, in person, online. Both court and visitors may perform in person name searches. Search fee: $5.00 per name. Civil records in index books since 1916. Computerized records go back to 1992. Mail turnaround time 1-2 days. Civil PAT goes back to 1992. Online access is at www.idocket.com; registration and password required. A fee service, only one free name search per day. Records go back to 1/1992.
Criminal Name Search: Access: Phone, fax, mail, in person, online. Both court and visitors may perform in person name searches. Search fee: $5.00 per name. Required to search: name, years to search; also helpful: DOB. Criminal docket on books from 1913. Computerized records go to 1995. Mail turnaround time 1-2 days. Criminal PAT goes back to 1995. Online case access is at www.idocket.com; registration and password required. A fee service; only one free name search per day. Records go back to 12/31/1995. Online results show middle initial.

County Court - Criminal PO Box 1327, Kingsville, TX 78364; 361-595-8548; fax: 361-593-1355; 8AM-5PM (CST). *Misdemeanor, Probate.* www.co.kleberg.tx.us/courtatlaw.html
General Information: Court also handles civil cases dealing with occupational licenses and bond forfeitures. Online identifiers in results same as on public terminal. No juvenile or mental records released. Will not fax documents. Court makes copy: $1.00 per page. Certification fee: $5.00. Payee: Kleberg County Clerk. Business checks accepted. Major credit cards accepted. Prepayment required. Mail requests: SASE requested.
Criminal Name Search: Access: Phone, mail, in person, online. Both court and visitors may perform in person name searches. Search fee: $10.00 per name. Required to search: name, years to search, DOB. Criminal records on computer since 1989, index books since 1913. Note: Hard copy records prior to 1987 have been destroyed. Mail turnaround time 3 to 5 days. Public use terminal has crim records back to 1983. Online case access at www.idocket.com; registration and password required. A fee service; only one free name search per day. Records go back to 1/1/1983. Online results show middle initial, DOB.

Knox County

District & County Court PO Box 196, Benjamin, TX 79505; 940-459-2441; fax: 940-459-2005; 8AM-5PM (CST). *Felony, Misdemeanor, Civil, Probate.*
General Information: Probate is separate index at this same address. Probate fax is same as main fax number. No SSNs, juvenile, mental, sealed, or adoption records released. Fee to fax out file $1.00 per page. Court makes copy: $1.00 per page. Self serve copy: same. Certification fee: $5.00 per document plus copy fee. Payee: District/County Clerk. Personal checks accepted, credit cards are not. Prepayment required. Mail requests: SASE required.
Civil Name Search: Access: Mail, in person. Both court and visitors may perform in person name searches. Search fee: $5.00 per name. Civil index in books. Mail turnaround time same day.
Criminal Name Search: Access: Mail, in person. Both court and visitors may perform in person name searches. Search fee: $5.00 for a misdemeanor search; $5.00 for a felony search. Required to search: name, years to search, DOB, SSN, signed release. Criminal docket on books back to 1885. Mail turnaround time 1 day.

La Salle County

District & County Courts Courthouse Square, #107, Cotulla, TX 78014; 830-879-4432; fax: 830-879-2933; 8AM-5PM (CST). *Misdemeanor, Civil, Probate.*
www.81st-218thdistrictcourt.org/
General Information: Probate fax is same as main fax number. No juvenile, mental, sealed, or adoption records released. Will fax documents $1.00 per page. Court makes copy: $1.00 per page. Self serve copy: same. Certification fee: $5.00 per document. Payee: District & County Clerk. Personal checks accepted, credit cards are not. Prepayment required. Mail requests: SASE not required.
Civil Name Search: Access: Phone, mail, in person. Both court and visitors may perform in person name searches. Search fee: $5.00 per name. Civil records on computer since 1994, prior on index books. Mail turnaround time 1-2 days.
Criminal Name Search: Access: Mail, in person. Both court and visitors may perform in person name searches. Search fee: $5.00 per name. Criminal records on computer since 1994, prior on index books. Mail turnaround time 1-2 days.

Lamar County

District Court 119 N Main, Rm 405, Paris, TX 75460; 903-737-2427; fax: 903-785-4905; 8AM-5PM (CST). *Felony, Civil.*
www.co.lamar.tx.us
General Information: No juvenile, mental, sealed, or adoption records released. Court makes copy: $1.00 per page. Self serve copy: same. No certification fee. Payee: District Clerk. Personal checks accepted. Prepayment required. Mail requests: SASE required.
Civil Name Search: Access: Mail, in person, online. Both court and visitors may perform in person name searches. Search fee: $5.00 per name. Civil records on computer since 1/1994, index books prior to 1994. Mail turnaround time 1-2 days. Civil PAT goes back to 1994. Access to county judicial records is free at www.co.lamar.tx.us/. Search by either party name.
Criminal Name Search: Access: Mail, in person, online. Both court and visitors may perform in person name searches. Search fee: $5.00 per name. Criminal records on computer since 1/1994, index books prior to 1994. Mail turnaround time 1-2 days. Criminal PAT goes back to 1987. Access to county judicial records is free online at www.co.lamar.tx.us. Search by defendant name.

County Court 119 N Main, Paris, TX 75460; 903-737-2420; fax: 903-782-1111; 8AM-12; 1PM-5PM (CST). *Misdemeanor, Civil, Probate.*
www.co.lamar.tx.us
General Information: No juvenile, mental, sealed, or adoption records released. Will not fax documents. Court makes copy: $1.00 per page. Self serve copy: same. Certification fee: $5.00 per document plus copy fee. Payee: County Clerk. Business checks accepted; will accept local personal checks. No credit cards accepted. Prepayment required. Mail requests: SASE not required.
Civil Name Search: Access: Phone, fax, mail, in person, online. Both court and visitors may perform in person name searches. Search fee: $10.00 per name. Civil records in index books since 1913; on computer back to 1998. Mail turnaround time 2-3 days. Access to county judicial records is free at http://68.89.102.225/. Search by either party name.
Criminal Name Search: Access: Phone, fax, mail, in person, online. Both court and visitors may perform in person name searches. Search fee: $5.00 per name. Required to search: name, years to search, DOB; SSN or drivers license number also required. Criminal records computerized from 1988, index books since 1913. Mail turnaround time 2-3 days. Access to county judicial records is free online at www.co.lamar.tx.us. Search by defendant name.

Lamb County

District Court 100 6th Dr, Rm 212, Courthouse, Littlefield, TX 79339; 806-385-4222; fax: 806-385-3554; 8:30AM-5PM (CST). *Felony, Civil.*
General Information: Search fee includes both civil and criminal indexes if you ask for both. No juvenile, mental, sealed, or adoption records released. Will fax documents to local or toll free line. Court makes copy: $1.00 per page. Self serve copy: same. No certification fee To certify, indicate that "it needs to be certified". Payee: District Court. Personal checks accepted, credit cards are not. Prepayment required. Mail requests: SASE required.
Civil Name Search: Access: Mail, in person. Both court and visitors may perform in person name searches. Search fee: $5.00 per name. Civil records on computer since 1987; on index books back to 1940. Mail turnaround time 2-3 days.
Criminal Name Search: Access: Mail, in person. Both court and visitors may perform in person name searches. Search fee: $5.00 per name. Required to search: name, years to search; also helpful: DOB, SSN. Criminal

docket on books to 1940s; on computer since 1987. Mail turnaround time 2-3 days.

County Court County Courthouse, Rm 103, Littlefield, TX 79339-3366; 806-385-4222 X214; fax: 806-385-6485; 8:30AM-N, 1-5PM (CST). *Misdemeanor, Civil, Probate.*
www.co.lamb.tx.us
General Information: No juvenile, mental, sealed, or adoption records released. Court makes copy: $1.00 per page. Certification fee: $5.00 per document plus copy fee. Payee: Lamb County Clerk. Personal checks accepted. Major credit cards accepted online only; $5.95 usage charge added. Prepayment required. Mail requests: SASE not required.
Civil Name Search: Access: Mail, in person. Both court and visitors may perform in person name searches. Search fee: $5.00 per name. Civil index in books. Mail turnaround time 1-7 working days.
Criminal Name Search: Access: Mail, in person. Both court and visitors may perform in person name searches. Search fee: $5.00 per name. Required to search: name, years to search; also helpful: DOB, SSN. Criminal index in books. Mail turnaround time 1-7 working days.

Lampasas County

District Court PO Box 327, Lampasas, TX 76550; 512-556-8271 X240; fax: 512-556-9463; 8AM-5PM (CST). *Felony, Civil.*
General Information: No juvenile, mental, sealed, or adoption records released. Fee to fax out file $1.00 per page. Court makes copy: $1.00 per page. Self serve copy: same. Certification fee: $2.00 per document plus copy fee. Payee: District Clerk. Business checks accepted. No credit cards accepted. Prepayment required. Mail requests: SASE required.
Civil Name Search: Access: Mail, in person. Both court and visitors may perform in person name searches. Search fee: $5.00 per name. Civil records in index books, computerized since 1997. Mail turnaround time 2-4 days.
Criminal Name Search: Access: Mail, in person. Both court and visitors may perform in person name searches. Search fee: $5.00 per name. Criminal index in books; on computer for 5 years. Mail turnaround time 2-4 days.

County Court PO Box 347, 409 S Pecan, Lampasas, TX 76550; 512-556-8271 x202; 8AM-5PM (CST). *Misdemeanor, Civil, Probate.*
General Information: Probate is separate index at this same address. No juvenile, mental, sealed, or adoption records released. Will not fax documents. Court makes copy: $1.00 per page. Self serve copy: same. Certification fee: $5.00 per document plus copy fee. Payee: County Clerk. Personal checks must be in state. No credit cards accepted. Prepayment required. Mail requests: SASE requested.
Civil Name Search: Access: Mail, in person. Both court and visitors may perform in person name searches. Search fee: $5.00 per name. Civil index in books. Mail turnaround time 1-2 days.
Criminal Name Search: Access: Mail, in person. Both court and visitors may perform in person name searches. Search fee: $5.00 per name. Required to search: name, years to search; also helpful: DOB, SSN. Criminal index in books. Mail turnaround time 1-2 days.

Lavaca County

District Court PO Box 306, Hallettsville, TX 77964; 361-798-2351; fax: 361-798-5674; 8AM-N, 1-5PM (CST). *Felony, Civil.*
General Information: No juvenile, Department of Human Services, adoptions and expunction records released. Will fax documents to local or toll free line. Court makes copy: $1.00 per page. Self serve copy: same. Certification fee: $2.00. Payee: Lavaca County District Clerk. Personal checks accepted, credit cards are not. Prepayment required. Mail requests: SASE required.
Civil Name Search: Access: Phone, mail, in person. Both court and visitors may perform in person name searches. Search fee: $5.00 per name. Civil records in index books from 1847. Mail turnaround time same day.
Criminal Name Search: Access: Mail, in person. Both court and visitors may perform in person name searches. Search fee: $5.00 per name. Criminal docket on books from 1847. Mail turnaround time same day.

County Court PO Box 326, Courthouse, Hallettsville, TX 77964; 361-798-3612; fax: 361-798-1610; 8AM-5PM (CST). *Misdemeanor, Civil, Probate.*
General Information: No mental health or sealed records released. Will fax out documents $2.00 per page fee. Court makes copy: $1.00 per page. Certification fee: $5.00 per document. Payee: County Clerk. Personal checks accepted. Visa/MC accepted at www.certifiedpayments.net. Prepayment required. Mail requests: SASE not required.
Civil Name Search: Access: Mail, in person. Both court and visitors may perform in person name searches. Search fee: $5.00 per name. Required to search: name, years to search, DOB; also helpful: address, SSN, DL#. Civil records on computer go back to late 1993; earlier in index books. Mail turnaround time same day as received. Civil PAT goes back to 12/1993.

Criminal Name Search: Access: Mail, in person. Both court and visitors may perform in person name searches. Search fee: $5.00 per name. Required to search: name, years to search; also helpful: address, DOB, DL#, SSN. Records on computer go back to late 1993; earlier in index books. Mail turnaround time same day as received. Criminal PAT goes back to same as civil.

Lee County

District Court PO Box 176, Giddings, TX 78942; 979-542-2947; fax: 979-542-2444; 8AM-N, 1-5PM (CST). *Felony, Civil.* www.co.lee.tx.us/ips/cms/districtcourt/

General Information: No juvenile or adoption records released. Will fax documents to local or toll free line. Court makes copy: $1.00 per page. Self serve copy: same. Certification fee: $2.00 per cert plus copy fee. Payee: District Clerk, Lee County. Personal checks accepted. Major credit cards accepted. Prepayment required. Mail requests: SASE required.

Civil Name Search: Access: Mail, in person. Both court and visitors may perform in person name searches. Search fee: $5.00 per name. Civil index on docket books from 1800s. Mail turnaround time 1-2 days.

Criminal Name Search: Access: Mail, in person. Both court and visitors may perform in person name searches. Search fee: $5.00 per name. Required to search: name, years to search; also helpful: DOB, SSN. Criminal records on computer since 1989. Mail turnaround time 1-2 days.

County Court PO Box 419, Giddings, TX 78942; 979-542-3684; fax: 979-542-2623; 8AM-5PM (CST). *Misdemeanor, Civil, Probate.*

General Information: Probate fax is same as main fax number. No juvenile, mental, sealed or adoption records released. Will fax documents to local or toll free line. Court makes copy: $1.00 per page. Certification fee: $5.00. Payee: County Clerk. Personal checks accepted. Credit cards accepted. Prepayment required. Mail requests: SASE required.

Civil Name Search: Access: Mail, in person. Both court and visitors may perform in person name searches. Search fee: $5.00 per name. Civil records in index books since 1874 (beginning 1995 on computer). Mail turnaround time 1-3 days.

Criminal Name Search: Access: Mail, in person. Both court and visitors may perform in person name searches. Search fee: $5.00 per name. Criminal records on computer since 1992, index books since 1874. Mail turnaround time 1-3 days.

Leon County

District Court PO Box 39, 139 E Main St, Centerville, TX 75833; 903-536-2227; 8AM-5PM (CST). *Felony, Civil.* www.co.leon.tx.us

General Information: Fax available by permission only; call ahead. No juvenile, mental, sealed, or adoption records released. Will not fax documents. Court makes copy: $1.00 per page. Certification fee: $1.00. Payee: Leon County District Clerk. Personal checks accepted if DOB and DL shown on check. No credit cards accepted. Prepayment required. Mail requests: SASE required.

Civil Name Search: Access: Mail, in person. Both court and visitors may perform in person name searches. Search fee: $5.00 per name. Civil records in index books. Mail turnaround time 2-10 days.

Criminal Name Search: Access: Mail, in person. Both court and visitors may perform in person name searches. Search fee: $5.00 per name. Criminal index in books. Mail turnaround time 2-10 days.

County Court PO Box 98, 115 N Casf St, Centerville, TX 75833; 903-536-2352; 8AM-5PM (CST). *Misdemeanor, Civil, Probate.*

General Information: No juvenile, mental, sealed records released. Will not fax documents. Court makes copy: $1.00 per page. Certification fee: $5.00 per doc. Payee: Leon County Clerk. Business checks accepted. Personal checks accepted in person only. No credit cards accepted. Prepayment required. Mail requests: SASE required.

Civil Name Search: Access: Mail, in person. Both court and visitors may perform in person name searches. Search fee: $5.00 per name. Civil index in books. Mail turnaround time 1-3 days.

Criminal Name Search: Access: Mail, in person. Both court and visitors may perform in person name searches. Search fee: $5.00 per name. Required to search: name, years to search, signed release. Criminal records only 1950 to present. Mail turnaround time 1-3 days.

Liberty County

District Court PO Box 10145, 1923 Sam Houston, #115, Liberty, TX 77575; 936-336-4600 x4; criminal phone: 936-336-4682; civil phone: 936-336-4683; 8AM-N, 1-5PM (CST). *Felony, Civil.* www.co.liberty.tx.us/dclerk.html

General Information: No juvenile, mental, sealed, or adoption records released. Will not fax documents. Court makes copy: $1.00 per page. Certification fee: No fee to certify. Payee: District Clerk. Personal checks

accepted. Major credit cards accepted. Prepayment required. Mail requests: SASE required.

Civil Name Search: Access: Mail, in person, online. Both court and visitors may perform in person name searches. Search fee: $5.00 per name. Civil records on computer since 1993, index books prior. Mail turnaround time 2-4 days. Civil PAT goes back to 1875. A docket name search is offered at http://libertycountyonline.net/districtclerk/search.faces. Probate records available as well.

Criminal Name Search: Access: Mail, in person, online. Both court and visitors may perform in person name searches. Search fee: $5.00 per name. Criminal records on computer since 1993, index books prior. Mail turnaround time 2-4 days. Criminal PAT goes back to 1894. A docket name search is offered at http://libertycountyonline.net/districtclerk/search.faces. Online results show name only.

County Court and County Court at Law PO Box 369, 1923 Sam Houston #209, Liberty, TX 77575; 936-336-4670; fax: 936-334-8174; 8AM-5PM (CST). *Misdemeanor, Civil, Probate.* www.co.liberty.tx.us/ips/cms/countyoffices/countyCourtAtLaw.html

General Information: No juvenile, mental, sealed, or adoption records released. Will fax documents to local or toll-free number. Court makes copy: $1.00 per page. Certification fee: $5.00 per doc plus copy fee. Payee: County Clerk. Business and personal checks accepted. Major credit cards accepted with 5% or $5.95 surcharge. Prepayment required. Mail requests: SASE required.

Civil Name Search: Access: Mail, in person. Both court and visitors may perform in person name searches. Search fee: $5.00 per name. Civil records in index books; later on computer. Mail turnaround time 2-4 days. Civil PAT goes back to 1995.

Criminal Name Search: Access: Mail, in person. Both court and visitors may perform in person name searches. Search fee: $5.00 per name. Required to search: name, years to search, DOB, SSN, signed release. Criminal index in books; later on computer. Mail turnaround time 2-4 days. Criminal PAT goes back to same as civil.

Limestone County

District Court PO Box 230, Groesbeck, TX 76642; 254-729-3206; fax: 254-729-2960; 8AM-5PM (CST). *Felony, Civil.*

General Information: No juvenile, mental, sealed, or adoption records released. Will fax documents $1.00 1st page, $.25 each add'l. Court makes copy: $1.00 per page. Self serve copy: $.50 per page. Certification fee: $2.00 per cert. Payee: District Clerk. Personal checks accepted, credit cards are not. Prepayment required. Mail requests: SASE required.

Civil Name Search: Access: Mail, in person. Both court and visitors may perform in person name searches. Search fee: $5.00 per name. Civil records on computer since 9/1990, index books since 1883. Mail turnaround time 1 week. Civil PAT goes back to 1991.

Criminal Name Search: Access: Mail, in person. Both court and visitors may perform in person name searches. Search fee: $5.00 per name. Required to search: name, years to search, DOB; also helpful: SSN. Criminal records on computer since 9/1990, index books since 1911. Mail turnaround time 1 week. Criminal PAT goes back to same as civil.

County Court PO Box 350, Groesbeck, TX 76642; 254-729-5504; fax: 254-729-2951; 8AM-5PM (CST). *Misdemeanor, Civil, Probate.* www.co.limestone.tx.us/ips/cms

General Information: No juvenile, mental, sealed, or adoption records released. Fee to fax out file $2.00 per page. Court makes copy: $1.00 per page. Certification fee: $5.00. Payee: Limestone County Clerk. Personal checks accepted. Major credit cards accepted. Prepayment required. Mail requests: SASE not required.

Civil Name Search: Access: Mail, in person. Both court and visitors may perform in person name searches. Search fee: $5.00 per name. Civil records in index books to early 1900s, computerized since 1985. Mail turnaround time 2 days. Public use terminal available.

Criminal Name Search: Access: Mail, in person. Both court and visitors may perform in person name searches. Search fee: $5.00 per name. Required to search: name, years to search; also helpful: DOB, SSN, signed release. Criminal docket on books to 1900s, computerized since 1985. Mail turnaround time 2 days. Public use terminal available.

Lipscomb County

District & County Court PO Box 70, Lipscomb, TX 79056; 806-862-3091; fax: 806-862-3004; 8:30AM-N, 1-5PM (CST). *Felony, Misdemeanor, Civil, Probate.*

General Information: No juvenile, mental, sealed, or adoption records released. Will fax documents $1.00 1st page, $.50 each add'l. Court makes copy: $1.00 per page. Self serve copy: same. Certification fee: $5.00 in County Court; $1.00 in District. Payee: County Clerk. Personal checks accepted, credit cards are not. Prepayment required. Mail requests: SASE required.

Civil Name Search: Access: Fax, mail, in person. Both court and visitors may perform in person name searches. Search fee: $10.00 per name. Required to search: name. Civil records in index books since 1887; on computer back to 1999. Mail turnaround time 2 days.

Criminal Name Search: Access: Fax, mail, in person. Both court and visitors may perform in person name searches. Search fee: $5.00 per name. Required to search: name; also helpful: DOB. Criminal docket on books from 1887; on computer back to 1999. Mail turnaround time 2 days.

Live Oak County

District Court PO Drawer 440, George West, TX 78022; 361-449-2733 X1047; fax: 361-449-2992; 8AM-5PM (CST). *Felony, Civil.*

General Information: No juvenile, mental, sealed, or adoption records released. Will fax documents $1.00 per page. Court makes copy: $1.00 per page. Self serve copy: same. Certification fee: $1.00. Payee: District Clerk. Personal checks accepted, credit cards are not. Prepayment required. Mail requests: SASE required.

Civil Name Search: Access: Phone, fax, mail, in person. Both court and visitors may perform in person name searches. Search fee: $10.00 per name. Civil records in index books and microfiche since 1850s. Mail turnaround time 1-2 days.

Criminal Name Search: Access: Phone, fax, mail, in person. Both court and visitors may perform in person name searches. Search fee: $10.00 per name. Required to search: name, years to search, DOB; also helpful: SSN. Criminal docket on books and microfiche since 1850s. Mail turnaround time 1-2 days.

County Court PO Box 280, George West, TX 78022; 361-449-2733; criminal phone: x1029; civil phone: x1003; probate phone: x1003; 9AM-4PM (CST). *Misdemeanor, Civil, Probate.*

General Information: No juvenile, mental, sealed, or adoption records released. No fax machine. Court makes copy: $1.00 per page. Certification fee: $5.00. Payee: County Clerk. Personal checks accepted. Major credit cards accepted. Prepayment required. Mail requests: SASE not required.

Civil Name Search: Access: Mail, in person. Both court and visitors may perform in person name searches. Search fee: $10.00 per name. Civil index in books. Mail turnaround time 1-2 days.

Criminal Name Search: Access: Mail, in person. Both court and visitors may perform in person name searches. Search fee: $10.00 per name. Criminal index in books. Mail turnaround time 1-2 days.

Llano County

District Clerk 832 Ford St, Llano, TX 78643-0877; 325-247-5036; fax: 325-248-0492; 7:30AM-4:30PM (CST). *Felony, Civil.*

http://dcourt.org

General Information: Signup for email notifications of civil and criminal dockets at www.dcourt.org/_attys/dockets.htm. No juvenile, mental, sealed, or adoption records released. Will fax documents to local or toll free line. Court makes copy: $1.00 per page. Self serve copy: same. Certification fee: $1.00 per page. Payee: Llano County District Clerk. Personal checks accepted, credit cards are not. Prepayment required. Mail requests: SASE required.

Civil Name Search: Access: Mail, in person. Both court and visitors may perform in person name searches. Search fee: $5.00 per name. Fee is per 5 year period. Civil index in docket books from 1900, computerized back to 1940. Mail turnaround time 1-3 days. Civil PAT goes back to 1995.

Criminal Name Search: Access: Mail, in person. Both court and visitors may perform in person name searches. Search fee: $5.00 per name. Fee is per 5 year period. Criminal docket on books back to 1900, computerized back to 1983. Mail turnaround time 1-3 days. Criminal PAT goes back to 1983.

County Court PO Box 40, Llano, TX 78643-0040; 325-247-4455; fax: 325-247-2406; 8AM-4:30PM (CST). *Misdemeanor, Civil, Probate.*

General Information: No juvenile, mental, sealed, or adoption records released. Will fax documents to local or toll free line if prepaid. Court makes copy: $1.00 per page. Self serve copy: same. Certification fee: $5.00. Payee: County Clerk. Personal checks accepted. Major credit cards accepted. Prepayment required. Mail requests: SASE not required.

Civil Name Search: Access: Phone, mail, in person. Both court and visitors may perform in person name searches. Search fee: $5.00 per name. Civil records on computer since 1985, index books prior. Mail turnaround time 2-4 days. Civil PAT goes back to 1985.

Criminal Name Search: Access: Phone, mail, in person. Both court and visitors may perform in person name searches. Search fee: $5.00 per name. Required to search: name, years to search; also helpful: DOB. Criminal records on computer since 1985, index books prior. Mail turnaround time 2-4 days. Criminal PAT goes back to same as civil.

Loving County

District & County Court PO Box 194, Mentone, TX 79754; 432-377-2441; fax: 432-377-2701; 9AM-5PM (CST). *Felony, Misdemeanor, Civil, Probate.*

General Information: No juvenile, mental, sealed, or adoption records released. Fee to fax out file $1.50 per page. Court makes copy: $1.00 per page. Certification fee: $5.00 per doc. Payee: Loving County Clerk. Personal checks accepted, credit cards are not. Prepayment required. Mail requests: SASE not required.

Civil Name Search: Access: Mail, in person. Both court and visitors may perform in person name searches. Search fee: $5.00 per name. Civil records in index books from 1935. Mail turnaround time 2 days.

Criminal Name Search: Access: Mail, in person. Both court and visitors may perform in person name searches. Search fee: $5.00 per name. Criminal docket on books from 1935; computerized back to 1987. Mail turnaround time 2 days.

Lubbock County

District Court PO Box 10536 (904 Broadway #105), Lubbock, TX 79408-3536; 806-775-1623; fax: 806-775-1382; 8AM-5PM (CST). *Felony, Civil.*

www.co.lubbock.tx.us/department/?fDD=11-0

General Information: No juvenile, sealed, or adoption records released. Will fax documents $5.00 plus $1.00 per page copy fee. Court makes copy: $1.00 per page. Certification fee: $1.00 per document. Payee: District Clerk. Money order or cashiers checks accepted. Visa/MC accepted by phone or mail only. Prepayment required. Mail requests: SASE required.

Civil Name Search: Access: Fax, mail, in person. Both court and visitors may perform in person name searches. Search fee: $5.00 per name. Civil records on computer back to 1979, in index books to 1908. Mail turnaround time 2 business days. Civil PAT goes back to 1979.

Criminal Name Search: Access: Fax, mail, in person. Both court and visitors may perform in person name searches. Search fee: $5.00 per name. Required to search: name, years to search, DOB; also helpful: SSN, signed release. Criminal records computerized from 1979, in index books to 1908. Mail turnaround time 2 business days. Criminal PAT goes back to same as civil. The court offers a subscription service to criminal records. The application is found at www.co.lubbock.tx.us/egov/docs/1294749845_585784.pdf. Access excludes images prior to May 2007.

County Courts Courthouse, Rm 207, PO Box 10536, Lubbock, TX 79408; criminal phone: 806-775-1044; civil phone: 806-775-1047; probate phone: 806-775-1053; 8:30AM-5PM (CST). *Misdemeanor, Civil, Probate.*

www.co.lubbock.tx.us/judiciary/

General Information: The County Clerk's office is the custodian of records for the three County Courts at Law. All cases are filed and processed which exceed $200 but not more than $100,000. No mental or sealed records released. Court makes copy: $1.00 per page. Certification fee: $5.00 per doc plus copy fee. Payee: County Clerk. Personal checks accepted; include copy of your DL# and your phone. No credit cards accepted. Prepayment required. Mail requests: SASE required.

Civil Name Search: Access: Mail, in person. Both court and visitors may perform in person name searches. Search fee: $10.00 per name. Fee is for each 10 year period. Civil records on computer back to 1994, index books prior. Civil PAT goes back to 1994.

Criminal Name Search: Access: Mail, in person, online. Both court and visitors may perform in person name searches. Search fee: $10.00 per name. Required to search: name, years to search; DOB helpful. Criminal records computerized from 1987, index books prior. Mail turnaround time 3-5 days. Criminal PAT goes back to 1987. The court offers a subscription service to records. The application is found at www.co.lubbock.tx.us/egov/docs/1294749845_585784.pdf. Interestingly the application asks the subscriber to check which the user group he/she belongs to, but left out the biggest user group of criminal records. Online results show name, DOB.

Lynn County

District Court PO Box 939, Tahoka, TX 79373; 806-561-4274; fax: 806-561-4151; 8:30AM-5PM (CST). *Felony, Civil.*

General Information: No juvenile, mental, sealed, or adoption records released. Will fax documents $2.00 per page. Court makes copy: $1.00 per page. Certification fee: $1.00 per page. Payee: District Clerk. Personal checks accepted, credit cards are not. Prepayment required. Mail requests: SASE required.

Civil Name Search: Access: Fax, mail, in person. Both court and visitors may perform in person name searches. Search fee: $5.00 per name. Civil records on computer from 1997, index books from 1916. Mail turnaround time 2 days.

Criminal Name Search: Access: Fax, mail, in person. Both court and visitors may perform in person name searches. Search fee: $5.00 per name.

Criminal records computerized from 1997, index books from 1916. Mail turnaround time 2 days.

County Court PO Box 937, 1501 S 1st, Tahoka, TX 79373; 806-561-4750; fax: 806-561-4988; 8:30AM-5PM (CST). *Misdemeanor, Civil, Probate.*

General Information: No juvenile, mental, sealed, or adoption records released. Fee to fax out file $2.00 per page. Court makes copy: $1.00 per page. Certification fee: $5.00. Payee: Lynn County Clerk. Personal checks accepted. Major credit cards accepted. Prepayment required. Mail requests: SASE required.

Civil Name Search: Access: Mail, in person. Both court and visitors may perform in person name searches. Search fee: $5.00. Civil records in index books from 1903; on computer back to 1997. Mail turnaround time same day. Civil PAT goes back to 1997.

Criminal Name Search: Access: Mail, in person. Both court and visitors may perform in person name searches. Search fee: $5.00. Criminal docket on books from 1903; on computer back to 1997. Mail turnaround time same day. Criminal PAT goes back to same as civil.

Madison County

District Court 101 W Main, Rm 226, Madisonville, TX 77864; 936-348-9203; 8AM-N, 1-5PM (CST). *Felony, Civil.*

General Information: No juvenile, mental, sealed, or adoption records released. Will not fax documents. Court makes copy: $1.00 per page. Self serve copy: same. No certification fee. Payee: District Clerk. Personal checks accepted. No credit cards accepted for research. Prepayment required. Mail requests: SASE required.

Civil Name Search: Access: Mail, in person. Both court and visitors may perform in person name searches. Search fee: $5.00 per name. Civil records in index books to 1935, in archives to 1873. Mail turnaround time 1 day.

Criminal Name Search: Access: Mail, in person. Both court and visitors may perform in person name searches. Search fee: $5.00 per name. Criminal docket on books to 1835. Mail turnaround time 1 day.

County Court 101 W Main, Rm 102, Madisonville, TX 77864; 936-348-2638; fax: 936-348-5858; 8AM-4:30PM (CST). *A & B Misdemeanors, Civil, Probate.*

www.co.madison.tx.us/ips/cms/countyoffices/countyClerk.html

General Information: Probate fax is same as main fax number. No juvenile, mental, sealed, or adoption records released. Fee to fax out file $1.00 per page. Court makes copy: $1.00 per page. Certification fee: $5.00 per document plus copy fee. Payee: Madison County Clerk. Personal checks accepted. Visa/MC/Discover/AmEx cards accepted. Prepayment required. Mail requests: SASE required.

Civil Name Search: Access: Mail, in person. Both court and visitors may perform in person name searches. Search fee: $10.00 per name. Civil records on computer from 1/00; index books back to 1970. Mail turnaround time as soon as fees are paid. Public use terminal available, records go back to 2000.

Criminal Name Search: Access: Mail, in person. Both court and visitors may perform in person name searches. Search fee: $10.00 per name. Required to search: name, years to search, DOB. Criminal records computerized from 1982; records go back to early 1900's (not indexed). Mail turnaround time 1 day. Public use terminal available, crim records go back to 1985.

Marion County

District Court PO Box 628, Jefferson, TX 75657; 903-665-2441/2013; fax: 903-665-2102; 8AM-5PM (CST). *Felony, Civil.*

www.co.marion.tx.us/ips/cms/districtcourt/

General Information: No juvenile, mental, sealed, or adoption records released. Will not fax documents. Court makes copy: $1.00 per page. Certification fee: $1.00. Payee: District Clerk. Personal checks accepted, credit cards are not. Prepayment required. Mail requests: SASE required.

Civil Name Search: Access: Mail, in person. Both court and visitors may perform in person name searches. Search fee: $5.00 per name. Civil records on computer from 1997, index books up to 1996. Mail turnaround time 1 week. Civil PAT goes back to 1997.

Criminal Name Search: Access: Mail, in person. Both court and visitors may perform in person name searches. Search fee: $5.00 per name. Criminal records computerized from 1997, index books up to 1996. Mail turnaround time 1 week. Criminal PAT goes back to 1997. Terminal results may also show SSN, DL numbers.

County Court 102 W Austin St, #206, Jefferson, TX 75657; 903-665-3971; fax: 903-665-8732; 8AM-N, 1-5PM (CST). *Misdemeanor, Probate.*

General Information: No juvenile, mental, sealed, or adoption records released. Will not fax documents. Court makes copy: $1.00 per page. Self serve copy: same. Certification fee: $5.00. Payee: County Clerk. Personal checks accepted, credit cards are not. Prepayment required. Mail requests: SASE required.

Criminal Name Search: Access: Phone, mail, in person. Only the court performs in person name searches; visitors may not. No search fee. Criminal docket on books from 1966; computerized back to 1997. Mail turnaround time 2-4 days.

Martin County

District & County Court PO Box 906, Stanton, TX 79782; 432-756-3412; fax: 432-607-2212; 8AM-N, 1-5PM (CST). *Felony, Misdemeanor, Civil, Probate.*

General Information: No juvenile, mental, sealed, or adoption records released. Fee to fax out file $2.00. Will return searches to a toll-free line. Court makes copy: $1.00 per page. Certification fee: $5.00. Payee: County/District Clerk. Personal checks accepted, credit cards are not. Prepayment required. Mail requests: SASE required.

Civil Name Search: Access: Mail, in person. Both court and visitors may perform in person name searches. Search fee: $5.00 per name. Civil records in index books to 1900. Mail turnaround time 2-4 days.

Criminal Name Search: Access: Mail, in person. Both court and visitors may perform in person name searches. Search fee: $5.00 per name. Criminal docket on books to 1900, computerized since 1980. Mail turnaround time 2-4 days.

Mason County

District & County Court PO Box 702, Mason, TX 76856; 325-347-5253; fax: 325-347-6868; 8AM-N, 1-4PM (CST). *Felony, Misdemeanor, Civil, Probate.*

General Information: Search fee includes a search in both county and district courts. Probate fax is same as main fax number. No juvenile, mental, sealed, or adoption records released. Will fax documents for no add'l fee. Court makes copy: $1.00 per page. Self serve copy: same. Certification fee: $5.00 per doc County Ct; $1.00 per cert for District Ct. Payee: County/District Clerk. Personal checks accepted, credit cards are not. Prepayment required. Mail requests: SASE required.

Civil Name Search: Access: Mail, in person. Both court and visitors may perform in person name searches. Search fee: $10.00 per name. Civil records in index books to 1858; on computer back to 1993. Mail turnaround time 2 days.

Criminal Name Search: Access: Mail, in person. Both court and visitors may perform in person name searches. Search fee: $10.00 per name. Required to search: name, years to search; also helpful: DOB, SSN. Criminal records go back to 1877; on computer back to 1993. Mail turnaround time 2 days.

Matagorda County

District Court 1700 7th St, Rm 307, Bay City, TX 77414-5092; 979-244-7621; 8AM-N, 1-5PM (CST). *Felony, Civil.*

www.co.matagorda.tx.us

General Information: No juvenile, sealed, or adoption records released. Will not fax documents. Court makes copy: $1.00 per page. Certification fee: $2.00. Payee: District Clerk. Personal checks accepted, credit cards are not. Prepayment required. Mail requests: SASE required.

Civil Name Search: Access: Mail, in person. Both court and visitors may perform in person name searches. Search fee: $5.00 per name. Civil index in docket books from 1910; computerized back to 1994. Mail turnaround time 1-2 days. Civil PAT goes back to 1994.

Criminal Name Search: Access: Mail, in person. Both court and visitors may perform in person name searches. Search fee: $5.00 per name. Required to search: name, years to search, DOB. Criminal docket on books back to 1910; computerized back to 1994. Mail turnaround time 1-2 days. Criminal PAT goes back to same as civil.

County Court 1700 7th St, Rm 202, Bay City, TX 77414-5094; 979-244-7680; criminal phone: 979-244-7682; civil phone: 979-244-7683; probate phone: 979-244-7685; fax: 979-244-7688; 8AM-5PM (CST). *Misdemeanor, Civil, Probate.*

www.co.matagorda.tx.us/ips/cms

General Information: Probate is a separate index at this address. Probate fax is same as main fax number. No juvenile, mental, sealed, or adoption records released. Fee to fax out file $2.00 per page. Court makes copy: $1.00 per page. Self serve copy: same. Certification fee: $5.00 per document. Payee: County Clerk. Provide ID then Personal checks, Visa/MC accepted. Prepayment required. Mail requests: SASE required.

Civil Name Search: Access: Mail, in person. Both court and visitors may perform in person name searches. Search fee: $10.00 per name. Civil records on computer from 1994, index books prior. Mail turnaround time 1-10 days. Civil PAT goes back to 1987.

Criminal Name Search: Access: Mail, in person. Both court and visitors may perform in person name searches. Search fee: $10.00 per name. Required to search: name, years to search, DOB; also helpful: SSN, DL number. Criminal records computerized from 1994, index books prior. Mail turnaround time 1-10 days. Criminal PAT goes back to same as civil.

Maverick County

District Court 500 Quarry St, #5, Eagle Pass, TX 78853; 830-773-2629; fax: 830-773-4439; 8AM-5PM (CST). *Felony, Civil.*

General Information: No juvenile, mental, sealed, or adoption records released. Fee to fax back $1.00 per page. Court makes copy: $1.00 per page. Self serve copy: same. Certification fee: $5.00. Payee: District Clerk. No personal checks. No credit cards accepted. Prepayment required. Mail requests: SASE required.

Civil Name Search: Access: Mail, in person, online. Both court and visitors may perform in person name searches. Search fee: $5.00 per name. Civil records in index books; recent records computerized. Mail turnaround time 1 week. Civil PAT goes back to 1996. Access cases online back to 11/1994 at www.idocket.com; registration and password required. A fee service; only one free name search per day.

Criminal Name Search: Access: Mail, in person, online. Both court and visitors may perform in person name searches. Search fee: $5.00 per name. Criminal index in books; recent records computerized. Mail turnaround time 2-4 days. Criminal PAT goes back to 1996. Access felony cases back to 8/1/1995 at www.idocket.com; registration and password required. A fee service; only one free name search per day.

County Court 500 Quarry St, #2, Eagle Pass, TX 78853; 830-773-2829 x228; fax: 830-752-4479; 8AM-5PM (CST). *Misdemeanor, Civil, Probate.* www.co.maverick.tx.us/ips/cms

General Information: No juvenile, mental, sealed, or adoption records released. Fee to fax out file $1.00 per page. Court makes copy: $1.00 per page. Certification fee: $5.00 per cert plus copy fee. Payee: County Clerk. Personal checks accepted. MC/Visa credit cards accepted but there is a usage fee charged. Prepayment required. Mail requests: SASE required.

Civil Name Search: Access: Mail, in person, online. Both court and visitors may perform in person name searches. Search fee: $10.00 per name. Civil records on index books. Mail turnaround time 1-2 days. Access cases online back to 1/2006 at www.idocket.com; registration and password required. A fee service; only one free name search per day.

Criminal Name Search: Access: Mail, in person, online. Both court and visitors may perform in person name searches. Search fee: $10.00 per name. Required to search: name, years to search, DOB, SSN. Criminal records indexed in books. Mail turnaround time 1-2 days. Access misdemeanor cases back to 1/1999 at www.idocket.com; registration and password required. A fee service; only one free name search per day.

McCulloch County

District Court 199 County Courthouse, Rm 103, Brady, TX 76825; 325-597-0733 X1; fax: 325-597-0606; 8:30AM-5PM (CST). *Felony, Civil.*

General Information: No juvenile, mental, sealed, or adoption records released. Will fax documents $2.00 per page. Court makes copy: $1.00 per page. Certification fee: $1.00 plus copy fee. Payee: District Clerk. Personal checks accepted, credit cards are not. Prepayment required. Mail requests: SASE required.

Civil Name Search: Access: Mail, fax, in person, online. Both court and visitors may perform in person name searches. Search fee: $5.00 per name. Civil index in docket books from 1900s. Mail turnaround time 2-4 days. Civil PAT goes back to 1995. Access civil cases at www.idocket.com. Records go back to 12/31/1995. One free name search permitted a day, otherwise subscription required.

Criminal Name Search: Access: Mail, fax, in person, online. Both court and visitors may perform in person name searches. Search fee: $5.00 per name. Required to search: name, years to search; also helpful: DOB, SSN. Criminal docket on books back to 1990; on computer back to 1995. Mail turnaround time 2-4 days. Criminal PAT goes back to same as civil. Access felony cases online through www.idocket.com; registration and password required. Records go back to 12/31/1995. One free name search permitted a day, otherwise subscription required. Online results show middle initial, DOB.

County Court County Courthouse, 199 Courthouse Square, Brady, TX 76825; 325-597-0733; fax: 325-597-0606; 8AM-Noon; 1-5PM (CST). *Misdemeanor, Civil, Probate.* www.co.mcculloch.tx.us/ips/cms

General Information: No juvenile, mental, sealed, or adoption records released. Court makes copy: $1.00 per page. Certification fee: $1.00 per doc plus $1.00 per page. Payee: County Clerk. Personal checks accepted, credit cards are not. Prepayment required. Mail requests: SASE required.

Civil Name Search: Access: Mail, in person, online. Both court and visitors may perform in person name searches. Search fee: $5.00 per name. Civil records in index books since early 1900's, computerized since 10/95. Mail turnaround time 7-10 days. Online case access is through www.idocket.com; registration and password required. Records go back to 12/31/1996; includes probate. One free name search permitted a day, otherwise subscription required.

Criminal Name Search: Access: Mail, in person, online. Both court and visitors may perform in person name searches. Search fee: $5.00 per name. Criminal docket on books from 1900's, computerized since 10/95. Mail turnaround time 7-10 days. Online misdemeanor case access is through www.idocket.com; registration and password required. Records go back to 12/31/1996. One free name search permitted a day, otherwise subscription required.

McLennan County

District Court PO Box 2451, 501 Washington Ave, 300 Courthouse Annex, Waco, TX 76703; criminal phone: 254-757-5054; civil phone: 254-757-5057; fax: 254-757-5060; 8AM-5PM (CST). *Felony, Civil.* www.co.mclennan.tx.us/distclerk/index.aspx

General Information: No juvenile, mental, sealed, or adoption records released. Will fax documents to local or toll-free number for $3.00 1st page, $1.00 ea add'l. If long distance then $5.00 1st page $2.00 ea add'l. The court will charge $1.00 per page when receiving a fax. Court makes copy: $1.00 per page. Certification fee: $3.00 per doc. Payee: Karen C Matkin, District Clerk. Personal checks, Visa/MC accepted. Prepayment required. Mail requests: SASE required.

Civil Name Search: Access: Fax, mail, in person, online. Both court and visitors may perform in person name searches. Search fee: $5.00 per name. Civil records on computer since 1955, index books from 1850. Mail turnaround time 3 days. Civil PAT goes back to 1959. Online index and image access is through http://idocket.com/homepage2.htm; registration, password and fees required. Records go back to 1/1955; no probate. One free name search permitted a day, otherwise subscription required.

Criminal Name Search: Access: Mail, fax, in person, online. Both court and visitors may perform in person name searches. Search fee: $5.00 per name. Criminal records on computer since 1959, index books from 1850. Mail turnaround time 3 days. Criminal PAT goes back to same as civil. Online index and image access is through www.idocket.com; registration and password required. Felony records go back to 1/1981. One free name search permitted a day, otherwise subscription required.

County Clerk's Office PO Box 1727, 215 N. 5th St., Rm 223-A, Waco, TX 76703; 254-757-5140; criminal phone: 254-757-5185; civil phone: 254-757-5189; probate phone: 254-757-5186; fax: 254-757-5146; 8AM-5PM (CST). *Misdemeanor, Civil, Probate.* www.co.mclennan.tx.us/cclerk/index.aspx

General Information: No mental or sealed records released. Court makes copy: $1.00 per page. Certification fee: $5.00. Payee: County Clerk. Business checks accepted. Major credit cards accepted. Prepayment required. Mail requests: SASE required.

Civil Name Search: Access: Mail, in person. Both court and visitors may perform in person name searches. Search fee: $5.00 per name. Civil index in docket books from 1876 computerized since 2000. Probate to 1850, computerized since 1967. Mail turnaround time 1-3 days. Civil PAT goes back to 2000. Terminal results may include last 4 digits of DL, SSN, and/or CC's.

Criminal Name Search: Access: Mail, in person. Both court and visitors may perform in person name searches. Search fee: $5.00 per name. Required to search: name, years to search; also helpful: DOB, SSN. Criminal records on computer since 1993; in index books to 1935. Mail turnaround time 2-4 days. Criminal PAT goes back to 1993. Same as civil terminal.

McMullen County

District & County Court PO Box 235, Tilden, TX 78072; 361-274-3215; fax: 361-274-3858; 8AM-4PM (CST). *Felony, Misdemeanor, Civil, Probate.*

General Information: No juvenile, mental, sealed, or adoption records released. Will fax documents $3.00 1st page, $1.00 each add'l, must be pre-paid. Court makes copy: $1.00 per page. Certification fee: $5.00. Payee: County Clerk. Personal checks accepted. Prepayment required. Mail requests: SASE required.

Civil Name Search: Access: Mail, in person. Both court and visitors may perform in person name searches. Search fee: $5.00 per name. Civil records in index books from 1918. Mail turnaround time 2-4 days.

Criminal Name Search: Access: Mail, in person. Both court and visitors may perform in person name searches. Search fee: $10.00 per name. Criminal docket on books from 1918. Mail turnaround time 2-4 days.

Medina County

District Court County Courthouse, Rm 209, 1100 16th St, Hondo, TX 78861; criminal phone: 830-741-6070; civil phone: 830-741-6070; 8AM-5PM (CST). *Felony, Civil, Family.*

General Information: No juvenile, mental, sealed, or adoption records released. Will not fax documents. Court makes copy: $1.00 first page; $.25 each add'l. Certification fee: $1.00 per page. Payee: Medina County District Clerk. No personal or out-of-state checks accepted. No credit cards accepted. Prepayment required. Mail requests: SASE required.

Civil Name Search: Access: Phone, mail, in person, online. Both court and visitors may perform in person name searches. Search fee: $5.00 per name. Civil records on computer since 1990, index books since 1849. Mail turnaround time 2-3 days. Civil PAT goes back to 1990. Online index and image access is through http://idocket.com/homepage2.htm; registration, password and fees required. Records go back to 01/01/1990; no probate. One free name search permitted a day, otherwise subscription required.

Criminal Name Search: Access: Mail, in person, online. Both court and visitors may perform in person name searches. Search fee: $5.00 per name. Required to search: name, years to search, DOB, SSN. Criminal records on computer since 1990, index books since 1849. Mail turnaround time 2-3 days. Criminal PAT goes back to same as civil. Online index and image access is through http://idocket.com/homepage2.htm; registration, password and fees required. Records go back to 01/01/1990. One free name search permitted a day, otherwise subscription required.

County Court at Law Medina County Clerk, 1100 16th St, Rm 109, Hondo, TX 78861; 830-741-6040; fax: 830-741-6015; 8AM-N, 1-5PM (CST). *Misdemeanor, Civil, Probate.*

General Information: No juvenile, mental, or sealed records released. Will fax documents $3.00 plus $1.00 per page. Court makes copy: $1.00 per page. Self serve copy: same. Certification fee: $5.00 plus $1.00 per page per document. Payee: County Clerk. Personal checks accepted. Major credit cards accepted only for criminal fees. Prepayment required. Mail requests: SASE helpful.

Civil Name Search: Access: Phone, mail, in person. Both court and visitors may perform in person name searches. Search fee: $5.00 per name. Civil records on computer since late 1993, index books prior to 1881. Mail turnaround time 5 days.

Criminal Name Search: Access: Phone, mail, in person. Both court and visitors may perform in person name searches. No search fee. Required to search: name, years to search; also helpful: address, DOB, SSN. Criminal records on computer since late 1985, index books prior to 1953. Mail turnaround time 1-2 days.

Menard County

District & County Court PO Box 1038, 206 E San Saba Ave, Menard, TX 76859; 325-396-4682; fax: 325-396-2047; 8AM-N, 1-5PM M-TH; 8AM-N, 104PM F (CST). *Felony, Misdemeanor, Civil, Probate.*

General Information: No juvenile, mental, sealed, or adoption records released. Will fax documents $1.00 per page. Court makes copy: $1.00 per page. Certification fee: $5.00 per doc plus copy fee. Payee: District/County Clerk. Personal checks accepted, credit cards are not. Prepayment required. Mail requests: SASE required.

Civil Name Search: Access: Fax, mail, in person. Both court and visitors may perform in person name searches. Search fee: $10.00 per name. Civil index in docket books from 1900s. Mail turnaround time 2-4 days.

Criminal Name Search: Access: Mail, in person. Both court and visitors may perform in person name searches. Search fee: $10.00 per name. Criminal docket on books back to 1900s. Mail turnaround time 2-4 days.

Midland County

District Court 500 N Loraine Ste 300, Midland, TX 79701; 432-688-4500; criminal phone: x4; civil phone: x3; fax: 432-688-4934; 8AM-5PM (CST). *Felony, Civil.*

www.co.midland.tx.us/DC/default.asp

General Information: No juvenile, mental, sealed, or adoption records released. Fee to fax out file $1.00 per page, but it must be prepaid. Court makes copy: $1.00 per page. No certification fee. Payee: District Clerk. Business checks accepted; no personal checks. No credit cards accepted. Prepayment required. Mail requests: SASE required.

Civil Name Search: Access: Mail, in person, online. Both court and visitors may perform in person name searches. Search fee: $5.00 per name. Civil records on computer back to 1965, index books prior. Mail turnaround time 2 days. Civil PAT goes back to 1965. Online access to district clerk database is at www.co.midland.tx.us/DC/Database/search.asp. Registration and password required; Fee is $120 per year plus $.10 per image. Contact the clerk for access restrictions.

Criminal Name Search: Access: Mail, in person, online. Both court and visitors may perform in person name searches. Search fee: $5.00 per name. Criminal records computerized from 1940, index books prior. Mail turnaround time 2 days. Criminal PAT goes back to 1940. Online access to district clerk database is at www.co.midland.tx.us/DC/Database/search.asp. Registration and password required; Fee is $120 per year plus $.10 per image. Contact the clerk for access restrictions.

County Court PO Box 1350, Midland, TX 79702-1350; 432-688-4402; civil phone: 432-688-4405; probate phone: 432-688-4480; fax: 432-688-4926; 8AM-5PM (CST). *Misdemeanor, Civil, Probate.*

www.co.midland.tx.us/CC/default.asp

General Information: Probate fax is same as main fax number. Online identifiers in results same as on public terminal. No juvenile, mental, sealed, or adoption records released. Will fax documents $2.00 plus copy fee. Court makes copy: $1.00 per page. Certification fee: $5.00 per cert plus copy fee. Payee: County Clerk. Cashiers checks and money orders accepted; no personal checks. Credit cards accepted at www.officialpayments.com. Prepayment required. Mail requests: SASE not required.

Civil Name Search: Access: Mail, in person, online. Both court and visitors may perform in person name searches. Search fee: $5.00 per name. Required to search: name; also helpful: years to search, address. Civil records on computer since 1987, index books since 1885. Probate records on computer since 1885. Mail turnaround time 1-2 days. Civil PAT goes back to 1989. Online access to the County Clerk database is free at www.co.midland.tx.us/CC/Database/default.asp.

Criminal Name Search: Access: Mail, in person, online. Both court and visitors may perform in person name searches. Search fee: $5.00 per name. Required to search: name; also helpful: years to search, address, DOB, SSN. Criminal records on computer since 1970, index books since 1885. Mail turnaround time 1-2 days. Criminal PAT goes back to 1970. Online access to the County Clerk database is free at www.co.midland.tx.us/CC/Database/default.asp. Online results show middle initial, DOB.

Milam County

District Court 102 S Fannin Ave #5, Cameron, TX 76520; 254-697-7052; 8AM-5PM (CST). *Felony, Civil.*

General Information: No juvenile, mental, sealed, or adoption records released. Will not fax documents. Court makes copy: $1.00 per page. Certification fee: $1.00 per doc. Payee: District Clerk. Only cashiers checks, money orders and Personal checks accepted, credit cards are not. Prepayment required. Mail requests: SASE required.

Civil Name Search: Access: Mail, in person. Both court and visitors may perform in person name searches. Search fee: $5.00 per name. Civil records on microfilm and index books. Mail turnaround time same day. Civil PAT available.

Criminal Name Search: Access: Mail, in person. Both court and visitors may perform in person name searches. Search fee: $5.00 per name. Criminal records on microfilm and index books. Mail turnaround time same day. Criminal PAT goes back to various years, irregular results.

County Court 107 W Main St, Cameron, TX 76520; 254-697-7049; fax: 254-697-7055; 8AM-5PM (CST). *Misdemeanor, Civil, Probate.*

General Information: Probate fax is same as main fax number. No juvenile, mental, sealed, or adoption records released. Fee to fax out file $2.00 plus $1.00 per page. Court makes copy: $1.00 per page. Self serve copy: same. Certification fee: $5.00 per document. Payee: Milam County Clerk. Personal checks accepted, credit cards are not. Prepayment required. Mail requests: SASE not required.

Civil Name Search: Access: Mail, in person. Both court and visitors may perform in person name searches. Search fee: $5.00 per name. Civil records in books go back to 1874, computerized since 1992. Mail turnaround time 1-2 days. Civil PAT goes back to 1992.

Criminal Name Search: Access: Mail, in person. Both court and visitors may perform in person name searches. Search fee: $5.00 per name. Required to search: name, years to search, signed release, SSN. Criminal records in books go back to 1874, computerized since 1992. Mail turnaround time 1-2 days. Criminal PAT goes back to same as civil.

Mills County

District & County Court PO Box 646, Goldthwaite, TX 76844; 325-648-2711; fax: 325-648-3251; 8AM-N, 1-5PM (CST). *Felony, Misdemeanor, Civil, Probate.*

General Information: Probate fax is same as main fax number. No juvenile, mental, sealed, or adoption records released. Will not fax documents. Court makes copy: $1.00 per page. Self serve copy: same. Certification fee: $5.00 per cert plus copy fee. Payee: County-District Clerk. Personal checks accepted, credit cards are not. Prepayment required. Mail requests: SASE requested.

Civil Name Search: Access: Fax, mail, in person. Both court and visitors may perform in person name searches. Search fee: $5.00 per search. Required to search: name, years to search; also helpful: cause number. Civil records in index books since 1887; no computerized records. Mail turnaround time 1-2 days.

Criminal Name Search: Access: Mail, fax, in person. Both court and visitors may perform in person name searches. Search fee: $5.00 per search for felony or misdemeanor. Required to search: name, years to search, DOB, signed release; also helpful: cause number. Criminal docket on books from 1887; no computerized records. Mail turnaround time 1-2 days.

Mitchell County

District Court County Courthouse, 349 Oak St, Rm 302, Colorado City, TX 79512; 325-728-5918; 9AM-4PM (CST). *Felony, Civil.*

General Information: No juvenile, mental, sealed, or adoption records released. Will not fax documents. Court makes copy: $.35 per page. Certification fee: $1.00 per document. Payee: District Clerk. No personal checks. No credit cards accepted. Prepayment required. Mail requests: SASE required.

Civil Name Search: Access: Mail, in person. Both court and visitors may perform in person name searches. Search fee: $5.00 per name. Civil index in books. Mail turnaround time 1 day.

Criminal Name Search: Access: Mail, in person. Only the court performs in person name searches; visitors may not. Search fee: $5.00 per name. Criminal index in books. Mail turnaround time 1 day.

County Court 349 Oak St, Rm 103, Colorado City, TX 79512; 325-728-3481; fax: 325-728-5322; 8AM-N, 1-5PM (CST). *Misdemeanor, Civil, Probate.*

General Information: Probate fax is same as main fax number. No juvenile, mental, sealed, or adoption, commitment records released. Will fax documents long distance for $3.00 for 1st page, $1.00 per add'l page. Fax to local or toll-free number for $2.00 for 1st page and $1.00 per add'l page. Court makes copy: $1.00 per page. Self serve copy: same. Certification fee: $5.00 per cert plus copy fee. Payee: Mitchell County Clerk. No out of state personal checks. Money orders accepted. Credit cards accepted with 4% fee added. Prepayment required.

Civil Name Search: Access: Fax, mail, in person, online. Both court and visitors may perform in person name searches. Search fee: $5.00 per name. Civil index in docket books from 1882; on computer from 4/1984 to present. Mail turnaround time 2-4 days. Civil PAT goes back to 4/1984. Access to dockets is free at www.edoctecinc.com, data is within 24 hours of being current.

Criminal Name Search: Access: Mail, in person, online. Both court and visitors may perform in person name searches. Search fee: $5.00 per name. Required to search: name, years to search; also helpful: DOB. Criminal docket on books back to 1948; on computer from 5/1973 to present. Mail turnaround time 2-4 days. Criminal PAT goes back to 5/1973. Online access to criminal dockets is same as civil. Online results show middle initial.

Montague County

District Clerk PO Box 155, Montague, TX 76251; 940-894-2571; fax: 940-894-2077; 8AM-5PM (CST). *Felony, Civil.* www.97thdistrictcourt.com/

General Information: Physical address is 101 E Franklin, same ZIP. No juvenile, mental, sealed, or adoption records released. Will not fax documents. Court makes copy: $1.00 per page. No certification fee. Payee: District Clerk. No personal checks. Major credit cards accepted. Prepayment required. Mail requests: SASE required.

Civil Name Search: Access: Mail, in person. Both court and visitors may perform in person name searches. Search fee: $5.00 per name. Civil records on computer and index books. Mail turnaround time 2-4 days.

Criminal Name Search: Access: Mail, in person. Both court and visitors may perform in person name searches. Search fee: $5.00 per name. Criminal records on computer and index books. Mail turnaround time 2-4 days.

County Court PO Box 77, Montague, TX 76251; 940-894-2461; fax: 940-894-6601; 8AM-4:45PM (CST). *Misdemeanor, Civil, Probate.* www.co.montague.tx.us/ips/cms/countyoffices/countyClerk.html

General Information: No juvenile, mental, sealed, or adoption records released. Will fax documents $2.75 1st page, $.75 each add'l page. Court makes copy: $1.00 per page. Self serve copy: same. Certification fee: $5.00. Payee: County Clerk. Personal checks accepted. Major credit cards accepted. Prepayment required. Mail requests: SASE required.

Civil Name Search: Access: Mail, in person. Both court and visitors may perform in person name searches. Search fee: $10.00 per 10 years per name. Civil records on computer since 1993, index books prior. Mail turnaround time 1-2 days. Public use terminal available.

Criminal Name Search: Access: Mail, in person. Both court and visitors may perform in person name searches. Search fee: $5.00 per 10 years per name. Required to search: name, years to search, DOB. Criminal records on computer since 1993, index books prior. Mail turnaround time 1-2 days. Public use terminal available, crim records go back to 1993.

Montgomery County

District Court PO Box 2985, 301 N Main, Conroe, TX 77305; 936-539-7855; criminal fax: 936-539-7829; civil fax: 8AM-5PM; 8AM-4PM 1st Wed of month; 8AM-5PM; 8AM-4PM 1st Wed of month (CST). *Felony, Civil.*

www.co.montgomery.tx.us/departments_d-k/--district_courts/index.html

General Information: Probate is a separate index at this Annex with County Clerk. A 14-day docket list is shown at www.co.montgomery.tx.us/dcourts/dockets/ALL.COURT.DOCKET.TXT. No juvenile, mental, sealed, or adoption records released. Will not fax documents. Court makes copy: $1.00 per page. No certification fee. Payee: Barbara Adamick, District Clerk. No personal checks. Visa/MC accepted. Prepayment required. Mail requests: SASE required.

Civil Name Search: Access: Mail, in person. Both court and visitors may perform in person name searches. Search fee: $5.00 per name. Civil records in index books since 1900, on computer since 1990. Mail turnaround time 3-6 days. Civil PAT goes back to 1990. Terminal results also show SSNs.

Criminal Name Search: Access: Mail, in person. Both court and visitors may perform in person name searches. Search fee: $5.00 per name. Criminal docket on books from 1900, on computer since 1990. Mail turnaround time 3-6 days. Criminal PAT goes back to same as civil.

County Court PO Box 959, 210 W Davis (77301), Conroe, TX 77305; 936-539-7885; probate phone: 936-539-7892; fax: 936-760-6990; 8AM-5PM (CST). *Misdemeanor, Civil, Probate.* www.mctx.org/dept/departments_c/county_clerk/index.html

General Information: There is also a South County Annex (Mon,Wed,Fri) and an East County Annex (Tues,Thur). No mental or sealed records released. Will fax documents for $2.00 per page. Court makes copy: $1.00 per page. Certification fee: $5.00 plus $1.00 per page. Payee: County Clerk. Personal checks accepted with ID. No credit cards accepted. Prepayment required. Mail requests: SASE required.

Civil Name Search: Access: Mail, in person, online. Visitors must perform in person searches themselves. Search fee: $5.00 per name. Civil records on computer since 1971, and index books. Mail turnaround time 2-5 days. Civil PAT goes back to 1971. Search the civil docket and probate docket online at http://ccinternet.mctx.org/php/menu/menu-public.php. 14-day daily dockets free at the main website.

Criminal Name Search: Access: Mail, in person, online. Visitors must perform in person searches themselves. Search fee: $5.00 per name. Required to search: name, years to search, DOB and SSN. Criminal records on computer since 1985, and index books. Mail turnaround time 2-5 days. Criminal PAT goes back to 1985. Search the county clerk's misdemeanor records free at http://ccinternet.mctx.org/php/menu/menu-public.php. Online search results also give physical features. Also, 14-day daily dockets free at the main website. Access misdemeanor cases online at www.idocket.com; registration and password required. A fee service. Records go back to 12/31/1989. Online results show name, DOB, address.

Moore County

District Court 715 Dumas Ave, #109, Dumas, TX 79029; 806-935-4218; fax: 806-935-6325; 8:30AM-5PM (CST). *Felony, Civil.*

General Information: No juvenile, mental, sealed, or adoption records released. Will fax documents for $2.00. Court makes copy: $1.00 per page. Certification fee: $1.00 per page. Payee: District Clerk. Personal checks, Visa/MC accepted. Prepayment required. Mail requests: SASE required.

Civil Name Search: Access: Mail, in person. Both court and visitors may perform in person name searches. Search fee: $5.00 per name. Civil docket books and original files from 1990; computerized since 2006. Mail turnaround time 1 day. Civil PAT goes back to 2006.

Criminal Name Search: Access: Mail, in person. Both court and visitors may perform in person name searches. Search fee: $5.00 per name. Required to search: name, years to search, DOB; also helpful: SSN. Criminal records docket books and original files from 1990; computerized since 2006. But some records are computerized far back as 1900s. Mail turnaround time 1 day. Criminal PAT goes back to same as civil.

County Court 715 Dumas Ave, Rm 107, Dumas, TX 79029; 806-935-6164/2009; fax: 806-935-9004; 8:30AM-5PM (CST). *Misdemeanor, Civil, Probate.*

General Information: No juvenile, mental, sealed, or adoption records released. Fee to fax out file $5.00 plus $1.00 per page. Court makes copy: $1.00 per page. Self serve copy: same. Certification fee: $5.00. Payee: Moore County Clerk. Business checks accepted. Major credit cards accepted. Prepayment required. Mail requests: SASE required.

Civil Name Search: Access: Mail, in person. Both court and visitors may perform in person name searches. Search fee: $5.00 per name. Civil records on computer back to 1996, in index books prior. Mail turnaround time 24 hours. Civil PAT goes back to 1986.

Criminal Name Search: Access: Mail, fax, in person. Both court and visitors may perform in person name searches. Search fee: $5.00 per name. Required to search: name, years to search, signed release, DOB or SSN. Criminal records computerized from 1987, in index books prior. Mail turnaround time 24 hours. Criminal PAT goes back to 1986.

Morris County

District Court 500 Broadnax, Daingerfield, TX 75638; 903-645-2321; fax: 903-645-3433; 8AM-5PM (CST). *Felony, Civil.*

General Information: No juvenile, mental, sealed, or adoption records released. Will not fax documents. Court makes copy: $1.00 per page. Certification fee: $1.00. Payee: Morris County District Clerk. Personal checks accepted, credit cards are not. Prepayment required. Mail requests: SASE required.

Civil Name Search: Access: Mail, in person. Both court and visitors may perform in person name searches. Search fee: $5.00 per name. Civil records in index books and file folders from 1930s, computerized since 2000. Mail turnaround time 1 day.

Criminal Name Search: Access: Mail, in person. Both court and visitors may perform in person name searches. Search fee: $5.00 per name. Required to search: name, years to search, DOB. Criminal docket on books and file folders from 1930s, computerized since 2000. Mail turnaround time 1 day.

County Court 500 Broadnax, Ste D, Daingerfield, TX 75638; 903-645-3911; probate phone: 903-645-3911; fax: 903-645-4026; 8AM-N, 1-5PM (CST). *Misdemeanor, Probate.*

General Information: Probate fax is same as main fax number. No juvenile, mental, sealed, or adoption records released. Will fax documents $3.00 fee. Court makes copy: $1.00 per page. Certification fee: $5.00. Payee: County Clerk. Personal checks accepted. Credit cards accepted. Prepayment required. Mail requests: SASE requested.

Criminal Name Search: Access: Mail, in person. Both court and visitors may perform in person name searches. Search fee: $5.00 per name. Required to search: name, DOB, years to search. Criminal record on index books, computerized since 1999. Mail turnaround time 1 day.

Motley County

District & County Court PO Box 660, Matador, TX 79244; 806-347-2621; fax: 806-347-2220; 9AM-N, 1-5PM (CST). *Felony, Misdemeanor, Civil, Probate.*

General Information: No juvenile, mental, sealed or adoption records released. Will fax documents to local or toll free number. Court makes copy: $1.00 per page. Certification fee: $5.00 per instrument plus copy fee. Payee: Motley County Clerk. Personal checks accepted, credit cards are not. Prepayment required. Mail requests: SASE required.

Civil Name Search: Access: Mail, fax, in person. Both court and visitors may perform in person name searches. Search fee: $10.00 per name. Required to search: name, years to search, address. Civil records in docket books, archived from 1891. Mail turnaround time 1-2 days.

Criminal Name Search: Access: Mail, fax, in person. Only the court performs in person name searches; visitors may not. Search fee: $10.00 per name. Required to search: name, years to search, DOB. Criminal records in docket books, archived from 1891. Mail turnaround time 1-2 days.

Nacogdoches County

District Court 101 W Main, Rm #120, Nacogdoches, TX 75961; 936-560-7730; criminal phone: 936-560-7740; civil phone: 936-560-7729; fax: 936-560-7839; 8AM-5PM (CST). *Felony, Civil.*

General Information: No juvenile, mental, sealed, or adoption records released. Will fax documents to local or toll free line. Court makes copy: $1.00 per page. No certification fee. Payee: District Clerk. Business checks accepted. No credit cards accepted. Prepayment required. Mail requests: SASE required.

Civil Name Search: Access: In person, online. Both court and visitors may perform in person name searches. No search fee. Civil records on computer from 1987, index books prior. Civil PAT goes back to 1987. Online case access is available by subscription at www.idocket.com including civil and family back to 12/31/1986. One free name search permitted a day, otherwise subscription required.

Criminal Name Search: Access: Mail, in person, online. Both court and visitors may perform in person name searches. Search fee: $5.00 per name. Required to search: name, years to search, signed release. Criminal records computerized from 1987, index books prior. Mail turnaround time 5-6 days. Criminal PAT goes back to same as civil. Online case access is available by subscription at www.idocket.com; online records go back to 12/31/1986. One free name search permitted a day, otherwise subscription required. Online results show name only.

County Court County Clerk, 101 W Main, Rm 110, Nacogdoches, TX 75961; 936-560-7733; fax: 936-559-5926; 8AM-5PM (CST). *Misdemeanor, Civil, Probate.* www.co.nacogdoches.tx.us

General Information: The County Clerk is the Clerk for County Court at Law, except for Juvenile, Family Law, including Divorce & Adoption (for these cases see the District Clerk). Online identifiers in results same as on public terminal. No sealed released. Will fax documents to local or toll free line. Court makes copy: $1.00 per page. Self serve copy: same. Certification

fee: $5.00. Exemplification- add $2.00. Payee: County Clerk. Personal checks accepted, credit cards are not. Prepayment required. Mail requests: SASE required.

Civil Name Search: Access: Mail, in person, online. Both court and visitors may perform in person name searches. Search fee: $5.00 per name. Civil records on computer since 6/1986, index books prior. Mail turnaround time 2-4 days. Civil PAT goes back to 1986. Online case access is available by subscription at www.idocket.com including civil and probate back to 12/31/1986. One free name search permitted a day, otherwise subscription required.

Criminal Name Search: Access: Mail, in person, online. Both court and visitors may perform in person name searches. Search fee: $5.00 per name. Criminal records on computer since 1986, index books prior. Mail turnaround time 2-4 days. Criminal PAT goes back to same as civil. Online case access is available by subscription at www.idocket.com; online records go back to 12/31/1986. One free name search permitted a day, otherwise subscription required.

Navarro County

District Court PO Box 1439, Corsicana, TX 75151; 903-654-3040; fax: 903-654-3088; 8AM-5PM (CST). *Felony, Civil.* www.co.navarro.tx.us/ips/cms/districtcourt/

General Information: No juvenile, sealed, or adoption records released. Will fax documents $5.00 1st page, $1.00 each add'l. Court makes copy: $1.00 first page, $.25 each add'l. Certification fee: $1.00 per page. Payee: District Clerk. Personal checks accepted. Credit cards accepted. Prepayment required. Mail requests: SASE required.

Civil Name Search: Access: Phone, fax, mail, online, in person. Both court and visitors may perform in person name searches. Search fee: $5.00 per name. Civil records on computer since 1990, index books and microfiche since 1900s. Mail turnaround time 1-2 days. Civil PAT goes back to 1990. Online civil case access is through www.idocket.com. Records go back to 12/31/1990. One free name search permitted a day, otherwise subscription required.

Criminal Name Search: Access: Phone, fax, mail, in person, online. Both court and visitors may perform in person name searches. Search fee: $5.00 per name. Criminal records on computer since 1990, index books and microfiche since 1900s. Mail turnaround time 1-2 days. Criminal PAT goes back to same as civil. Online criminal case access is through www.idocket.com; registration and password required. Records go back to 12/31/1990. One free name search permitted a day, otherwise subscription required.

County Court PO Box 423, 300 W 3rd Ave Ste 101, Corsicana, TX 75151; 903-654-3035; fax: 903-872-7329; 8AM-5PM (til 4PM for instruments) (CST). *Misdemeanor, Civil, Probate.* www.co.navarro.tx.us/ips/cms

General Information: No mental, sealed records released. Will not fax documents. Court makes copy: $1.00 per page. Self serve copy: same. Certification fee: $5.00. Payee: County Clerk. Personal checks accepted. Credit cards accepted. Prepayment required. Mail requests: SASE requested.

Civil Name Search: Access: Mail, in person. Both court and visitors may perform in person name searches. Search fee: $5.00 per name. Fee is for 10 year period. Civil records in index books to 1960's; on computer back to 1990. Mail turnaround time 2-4 days. Civil PAT goes back to 1990.

Criminal Name Search: Access: Mail, in person. Both court and visitors may perform in person name searches. Search fee: $5.00 per name. Fee is for 10 year period. Required to search: name, years to search, DOB or SSN. Criminal docket on books to 1930's; on computer back to 1999. Mail turnaround time 2-4 days. Criminal PAT goes back to 1999.

Newton County

District Court PO Box 535, Newton, TX 75966; 409-379-3951; fax: 409-379-9087; 8AM-4:30PM (CST). *Felony, Civil.*

General Information: No juvenile, mental, sealed, or adoption records released. Will fax documents $2.00 per page. Court makes copy: $1.00 per page. Certification fee: $2.00. Payee: District Clerk. Personal checks accepted, credit cards are not. Prepayment required. Mail requests: SASE required.

Civil Name Search: Access: Mail, in person. Both court and visitors may perform in person name searches. Search fee: $5.00 per name. Civil index in books. Mail turnaround time same day.

Criminal Name Search: Access: Mail, in person. Both court and visitors may perform in person name searches. Search fee: $5.00 per name. Criminal index in books. Mail turnaround time same day.

County Court PO Box 484, Newton, TX 75966; 409-379-5341; fax: 409-379-9049; 8AM-4:30PM (CST). *Misdemeanor, Civil, Probate.*

General Information: No juvenile, mental, sealed, or adoption records released. Fee to fax document $.50 per page. Court makes copy: $1.00 per page. Certification fee: $5.00. Payee: County Clerk. Personal checks accepted, credit cards are not. Prepayment required. Mail requests: SASE not required.

Civil Name Search: Access: Mail, in person. Both court and visitors may perform in person name searches. Search fee: $5.00 per name. Civil index on docket books from 1953. Mail turnaround time 1-2 days.

Criminal Name Search: Access: Mail, in person. Both court and visitors may perform in person name searches. Search fee: $5.00 per name. Criminal records indexed in books from 1953. Mail turnaround time 1-2 days.

Nolan County

District Court 100 E 3rd, #200A, Sweetwater, TX 79556; 325-235-2111; 8:30AM-N, 1-5PM (CST). *Felony, Civil.*

General Information: No juvenile, mental, sealed, or adoption records released. Will not fax documents. Court makes copy: $1.00 first page, $.50 each add'l. Certification fee: $1.00 per page. Payee: District Clerk. Personal checks accepted, credit cards are not. Prepayment required. Mail requests: SASE required.

Civil Name Search: Access: Mail, in person. Both court and visitors may perform in person name searches. Search fee: $5.00 per name. Civil index in docket books from 1800s; records are computerized a few years back. Mail turnaround time same day.

Criminal Name Search: Access: Mail, in person. Only the court performs in person name searches; visitors may not. Search fee: $5.00 per name. Criminal docket on books back to 1900, records are computerized 7 years or more. Note: Include which years to search. If requester provides a toll-free number, the court will call with results if asked. Mail turnaround time same day.

County Court 100 E 3rd St, #108, Sweetwater, TX 79556-4546; 325-235-2462; 8:30AM-5PM (CST). *Misdemeanor, Civil, Probate.*

General Information: Direct faxes to "Attn County Clerk;" no fax search requests accepted without payment. No juvenile, mental, sealed, or adoption records released. Will fax out documents $2.00 per doc. Court makes copy: $1.00 per page. Certification fee: $5.00 per doc plus. Payee: County Clerk. Personal checks accepted. Major credit cards accepted. Prepayment required. Mail requests: SASE required.

Civil Name Search: Access: Mail, in person. Both court and visitors may perform in person name searches. Search fee: $5.00 per name, same fee for probate search. Civil records in index books, computerized since 1999. Mail turnaround time same day. Civil PAT goes back to 1982.

Criminal Name Search: Access: In person. Visitors must perform in person searches themselves. Criminal index in books, computerized since 1999. Criminal PAT goes back to same as civil.

Nueces County

District & County Court PO Box 2987, Corpus Christi, TX 78403-2987; 361-888-0450; criminal phone: 361-888-0495; fax: 361-888-0571; 8AM-5PM (CST). *Felony, Misdemeanor, Civil, Probate.*
www.co.nueces.tx.us/districtclerk/

General Information: Records are combined at this location. No juvenile, mental, sealed, or adoption records released. Will fax documents to local or toll-free number, fee is $5.00 1st page then $2.50 ea add'l. Incoming faxes incur a $2.00 1st page then $1.00 ea add'l. Court makes copy: $1.00 per page. Certification fee: $5.00. Payee: District Clerk. In county personal checks accepted, credit cards are not. Prepayment required. Mail requests: SASE required.

Civil Name Search: Access: Mail, in person, online. Both court and visitors may perform in person name searches. Search fee: $5.00 per name. Civil records on computer since 1980, index books prior. Mail turnaround time 2-4 days. Civil PAT goes back to 1980. Online access to civil District & County Court records are free at www.co.nueces.tx.us/districtclerk/. Click on Civil/Criminal Case Search, register, then search by name, company, or cause number.

Criminal Name Search: Access: Mail, in person, online. Both court and visitors may perform in person name searches. Search fee: $5.00 per name. Criminal records on computer since 1980, index books prior. Mail turnaround time 2-4 days. Criminal PAT goes back to same as civil. Terminal results include SSN. Online access to criminal District & County Court records are free at www.co.nueces.tx.us/districtclerk/. Click on Civil/Criminal Case Search, register, then search by name, SID number, or cause number. Online results show middle initial, DOB.

Ochiltree County

District Court 511 S Main, Perryton, TX 79070; 806-435-8054; fax: 806-435-8058; 8:30AM-5PM (CST). *Felony, Civil.*

General Information: No juvenile, mental, sealed, or adoption records released. Will fax documents $1.00 per page. Court makes copy: $1.00 per page. Certification fee: $1.00. Payee: District Clerk. Personal checks accepted, credit cards are not. Prepayment required. Mail requests: SASE required.

Civil Name Search: Access: Fax, mail, in person, online. Both court and visitors may perform in person name searches. Search fee: $5.00 per name. Civil records in index books; on computer back to 1948. Mail turnaround time 7 days. Online index and image access is through http://idocket.com/homepage2.htm; registration, password and fees required. Civil and Family records go back to 01/01/1948. One free name search permitted a day, otherwise subscription required.

Criminal Name Search: Access: Fax, mail, in person, online. Only the court performs in person name searches; visitors may not. Search fee: $5.00 per name. Criminal index in books; on computer back to 1995. Mail turnaround time 7 days. Online index and image access is through http://idocket.com/homepage2.htm; registration, password and fees required. Records go back to 01/01/2002. One free name search permitted a day, otherwise subscription required.

County Court 511 S Main St, Perryton, TX 79070; 806-435-8039; fax: 806-435-2081; 8:30AM-N, 1-5PM (CST). *Misdemeanor, Civil, Probate.*

General Information: Probate fax is same as main fax number. There is a public access terminal here to view the probate index. No juvenile, mental, sealed, or adoption records released. Will fax documents $2.00 per page. Court makes copy: $1.00 per page. Certification fee: $5.00 per cert plus copy fee. Payee: Ochiltree County Clerk. Personal checks accepted, credit cards are not. Prepayment required. Mail requests: SASE requested.

Civil Name Search: Access: Fax, mail, in person, online. Visitors must perform in person searches themselves. Search fee: $5.00 per name. Civil index in books. Mail turnaround time same day. Online index and image access is through http://idocket.com/homepage2.htm; registration, password and fees required. Records go back to 01/01/1992, probate to 01/01/1996. One free name search permitted a day, otherwise subscription required.

Criminal Name Search: Access: Fax, mail, in person, online. Visitors must perform in person searches themselves. Search fee: $5.00 per name. Criminal index in books. Mail turnaround time usually mailed same day as received. Online index and image access is through http://idocket.com/homepage2.htm; registration, password and fees required. Records go back to 01/01/1983. One free name search permitted a day, otherwise subscription required.

Oldham County

District & County Court PO Box 360, Vega, TX 79092; 806-267-2667; 8:30AM-N, 1-5PM (CST). *Felony, Misdemeanor, Civil, Probate.*

General Information: No juvenile, mental, sealed, or adoption records released. Will not fax documents. Court makes copy: $1.00 per page. Certification fee: $5.00 per doc. Payee: Oldham County/District Clerk. Personal checks accepted, credit cards are not. Prepayment required. Mail requests: SASE required.

Civil Name Search: Access: Mail, in person, online. Both court and visitors may perform in person name searches. Search fee: $5.00 per name. Civil index in books. Mail turnaround time 2-4 days. Online case access is through www.idocket.com; registration and password required. Records go back to 3/1998, probate to 2/1996. Civil County cases to 3/1/1998, civil District cases to 03/01/1994. One free name search permitted a day, otherwise subscription required.

Criminal Name Search: Access: Mail, in person, online. Both court and visitors may perform in person name searches. Search fee: $5.00 per name. Criminal index in books. Mail turnaround time 2-4 days. Online case access is through www.idocket.com; registration and password required. Misdemeanor records go back to 1/1993, felony to 1/1992. One free name search permitted a day, otherwise subscription required.

Orange County

District Court 801 W Division Ave, Orange, TX 77630; 409-883-7740; fax: 409-882-7083; 8AM-5PM (CST). *Felony, Civil.*
www.co.orange.tx.us/

General Information: No juvenile, mental, sealed, or adoption records released. Court makes copy: $1.00 per page. Self serve copy: $.50 per page. Certification fee: $1.00. Payee: District Clerk. Only cashiers checks and money orders accepted. No credit cards accepted. Prepayment required. Mail requests: SASE required.

Civil Name Search: Access: Mail, in person. Both court and visitors may perform in person name searches. Search fee: $5.00 per name. Civil records on computer since 1986, index books prior. Mail turnaround time 2-4 days. Civil PAT goes back to 1986.

Criminal Name Search: Access: Mail, in person, fax. Both court and visitors may perform in person name searches. Search fee: $5.00 per name. Criminal records computerized since 1986. Mail turnaround time 2-4 days. Criminal PAT goes back to same as civil.

County Court 123 S 6th St, Orange, TX 77630; 409-882-7055; fax: 409-882-7012; 8AM-5PM (CST). *Misdemeanor, Civil, Probate.*
www.co.orange.tx.us

General Information: No juvenile, mental, sealed,. Will not fax out documents. Court makes copy: $1.00 per page. Self serve copy: $.50 per page. Certification fee: $5.00; exemplified is $6.00 plus $1.00 per page in file. Payee: Karen Jo Vance, County Clerk. Personal checks accepted, credit cards are not. Prepayment required.

Civil Name Search: Access: Mail, in person, online. Both court and visitors may perform in person name searches. Search fee: $5.00. Civil records back to 1852; on computer back to 1982. Most records older than 2005 are probably on microfilm. Mail turnaround time 7-10 days. Civil PAT goes back to 1982. View court documents online. Go to home page, click on Departments, then click on county clerk. Please read instructions. No name searching, must have case number to access the record. All probate is online. Scanned cycle is online.

Criminal Name Search: Access: Mail, in person, online. Both court and visitors may perform in person name searches. Search fee: $5.00. Criminal records back to 1852 and computerized. Mail turnaround time 7-10 days. Criminal PAT goes back to 1897. Search misdemeanor warrants free at www.co.orange.tx.us/Misdomeanor%20Warrants.htm. Also, search misdemeanor records to 2005 by case number online as described for civil records.

Palo Pinto County

District Court PO Box 189, 520 Oak St, Palo Pinto, TX 76484-0189; 940-659-1279; 8AM-4:30PM (CST). *Felony, Civil.*

General Information: No juvenile, mental, sealed, or adoption records released. Will not fax documents. Court makes copy: $1.00 per page. Certification fee: Included in copy fee but you must request certification. Payee: District Clerk. Personal checks accepted, credit cards are not. Prepayment required. Mail requests: SASE required.

Civil Name Search: Access: Mail, in person. Both court and visitors may perform in person name searches. Search fee: $5.00 per name. Civil records on computer since 1993, index books prior. Mail turnaround time 1-2 days. Civil PAT goes back to 1890.

Criminal Name Search: Access: Mail, in person. Both court and visitors may perform in person name searches. Search fee: $5.00 per name. Criminal records on computer since 1993, index books prior. Mail turnaround time 1-2 days. Criminal PAT goes back to same as civil.

County Court PO Box 219, Palo Pinto, TX 76484; 940-659-1277; criminal phone: 940-659-1218; civil phone: 940-659-1220; probate phone: 940-659-1220; fax: 940-659-2289; 8:30AM-4:30PM (CST). *Misdemeanor, Civil, Probate.*

www.co.palo-pinto.tx.us/ips/cms/countyoffices/countyClerk.html

General Information: Probate in separate index at this same address. Probate fax is same as main fax number. No juvenile, mental, sealed records released. Will not fax documents. Court makes copy: $1.00 per page. Self serve copy: same. Certification fee: $5.00 per instrument plus copy fee. Payee: County Clerk. Personal checks accepted, credit cards are not. Prepayment required. Mail requests: SASE not required.

Civil Name Search: Access: Mail, in person, phone. Both court and visitors may perform in person name searches. Search fee: $5.00 per name. Civil records on computer back to 1998 index books from 1857. Mail turnaround time next day.

Criminal Name Search: Access: Mail, in person. Both court and visitors may perform in person name searches. Search fee: $5.00 per name. Required to search: name, years to search, DOB; also helpful: SSN. Criminal records computerized from 1986; index books from 1857. Mail turnaround time next day.

Panola County

District Court & County Court at law 110 S Sycamore St, #227, Carthage, TX 75633; 903-693-0306; fax: 903-693-6914; 8AM-5PM (CST). *Felony, Civil.*

www.co.panola.tx.us/ips/cms/districtcourt/

General Information: No sealed, or adoption records released. Fee to fax out file $1.00 per page. Court makes copy: $1.00 per page. Certification fee: none. Exemplified copy- $5.00. Payee: District Clerk. Personal checks accepted, credit cards are not. Prepayment required. Mail requests: SASE required.

Civil Name Search: Access: Mail, in person, online. Both court and visitors may perform in person name searches. Search fee: $5.00 per name. Civil records in index books from 1865; computerized back to mid-April 1994. Mail turnaround time 3 days. Civil PAT goes back to 04/1994. Access to civil records is free at www.panolacountyjudicial.com/.

Criminal Name Search: Access: Mail, in person, online. Both court and visitors may perform in person name searches. Search fee: $5.00 per name. Required to search: name, years to search, DOB. Criminal docket on books from 1900's; computerized back to mid-1994. Mail turnaround time 3 days. Criminal PAT goes back to same as civil. Access to criminal records is free at www.panolacountyjudicial.com/.

County Court 110 S Sycamore St, Room 201, Carthage, TX 75633; 903-693-0302; fax: 903-693-0328; 8AM-5PM (CST). *Misdemeanor, Civil, Probate.*

General Information: Probate is a separate index at this same address. No juvenile, mental, sealed, or adoption records released. Will fax documents $1.00 per 10 pages. Court makes copy: $1.00 per page. Self serve copy: same. Certification fee: $5.00 per document plus copy fee. Payee: County Clerk. Personal checks require ID. No credit cards accepted. Prepayment required. Mail requests: SASE not required.

Civil Name Search: Access: Mail, in person. Both court and visitors may perform in person name searches. Search fee: $5.00 per name. Civil records in index books; computerized since 1996. Mail turnaround time 2-4 days. Civil PAT available. Clerk will verify personal identifiers you provide.

Criminal Name Search: Access: Mail, in person, fax. Both court and visitors may perform in person name searches. Search fee: $5.00 per name. Required to search: name, years to search, DOB. Criminal index in books; computerized since 1996. Mail turnaround time 2-4 days. Criminal PAT available. Clerk will verify personal identifiers you provide.

Parker County

District Court PO Box 2050, 117 Ft. Worth Highway, Weatherford, TX 76086; criminal phone: 817-598-6194; civil phone: 817-598-6114; 8AM--5PM (CST). *Felony, Civil.*

www.parkercountytx.com

General Information: Online identifiers in results same as on public terminal. No juvenile, mental, sealed, or adoption records released. Will not fax documents. Court makes copy: $1.00 per page. Certification fee: Cert fee included in copy fee. Payee: District Clerk. Personal checks accepted with valid DR number. Prepayment required. Mail requests: SASE required.

Civil Name Search: Access: Mail, in person, online. Both court and visitors may perform in person name searches. Search fee: $5.00 per name. Required to search: name, years to search, and/or cause number. Civil index in books from 1800s, computerized since 2003. Mail turnaround time same day. Civil PAT available. Results also include both party names, case style, atty. Access to court records is free at www.parkercountytx.com. Online civil records go back to 1/2003. Civil results include party names, case type, atty.

Criminal Name Search: Access: Mail, in person, online. Both court and visitors may perform in person name searches. Search fee: $5.00 per name. Required to search: name, years to search, DOB, and/or cause number; also helpful: SSN. Criminal index in books; on computer back to 7/1988. Mail turnaround time same day. Criminal PAT available. Results also include arty, offense, disposition. Access to criminal records and sheriff inmates and bonds search is free at www.parkercountytx.com. Online criminal records go back to 7/88. Online results include atty, offense, disposition.

County Court Parker County Clerk - Court Division, 1 Courthouse Sq, Weatherford, TX 76086-0819; 817-594-1632; 8AM-N, 1-5PM (CST). *Misdemeanor.*

www.parkercountytx.com

General Information: There are two District Courts (43rd & 415th) and two County Courts-at-Law at this location. The County Court records are co-mingled, but not with District Court records. No juvenile, mental, sealed, or adoption records released. Will not fax documents. Court makes copy: $1.00 per page. Certification fee: $5.00 per cert. Payee: County Clerk. Personal checks accepted, credit cards are not. Prepayment required. Mail requests: SASE required.

Civil Name Search: Access: Phone, mail, in person, online. Both court and visitors may perform in person name searches. Search fee: $5.00 per name. Civil records in index books; on computer since 8/1985. Mail turnaround time 1-2 days. Civil PAT goes back to 2003. Online access to civil is same as criminal, see below.

Criminal Name Search: Access: Phone, mail, in person, online. Both court and visitors may perform in person name searches. Search fee: $5.00 per name. Required to search: name, years to search, DOB; signed release. Criminal records on computer since 8/1985, index books and archived since 1900s. Mail turnaround time 1-2 days. Criminal PAT goes back to 1985. Online access is free at www.parkercountytx.com. Search the sheriff bond and jail lists here also.

Probate Court 1112 Santa Fe Dr, Weatherford, TX 76086; 817-594-6018; fax: 817-598-6147; 8AM-12; 1PM-5PM (CST). *Probate.*

Parmer County

District Court PO Box 195, Farwell, TX 79325-0195; 806-481-3419; fax: 806-481-9416; 8:30AM-N, 1-5PM (CST). *Felony, Civil.*

General Information: No juvenile, mental, sealed, or adoption records released. Will fax documents $1.00 per page. Court makes copy: $1.00 per page. No certification fee. Payee: District Clerk. Personal checks accepted, credit cards are not. Prepayment required. Mail requests: SASE required.

Civil Name Search: Access: Fax, mail, in person, online. Both court and visitors may perform in person name searches. Search fee: $5.00 per name.

Civil records in index books since 1917. Mail turnaround time 1 day. Online case access is through www.idocket.com; registration and password required. Records go back to 12/31/1995. One free name search permitted a day, otherwise subscription required.

Criminal Name Search: Access: Fax, mail, in person, online. Both court and visitors may perform in person name searches. Search fee: $5.00 per name. Criminal docket on books from 1917. Mail turnaround time 1 day. Online case access is through www.idocket.com; registration and password required. Records go back to 12/31/1995. One free name search permitted a day, otherwise subscription required. Online results show name only.

County Court PO Box 356, Farwell, TX 79325; 806-481-3691; fax: 806-481-9154; 8:30AM-N; 1-5PM (CST). *Misdemeanor, Civil, Probate.*

General Information: Probate fax is same as main fax number. No juvenile, mental, sealed, or adoption records released. Will fax documents $1.50 per page. Court makes copy: $1.00 per page. Certification fee: $5.00. Payee: County Clerk. Personal checks accepted, credit cards are not. Prepayment required. Mail requests: SASE required.

Civil Name Search: Access: Mail, in person. Both court and visitors may perform in person name searches. Search fee: $5.00 per name. Civil records in index books to 1920, computerized since 1996. Mail turnaround time 2-4 days. Civil PAT goes back to 1996.

Criminal Name Search: Access: Mail, in person. Both court and visitors may perform in person name searches. Search fee: $5.00 per name. Criminal docket on books to 1920, computerized since 1996. Mail turnaround time 2-4 days. Criminal PAT goes back to same as civil.

Pecos County

District Court 400 S Nelson, Fort Stockton, TX 79735; 432-336-3503; fax: 432-336-6437; 8AM-5PM (CST). *Felony, Civil.*

General Information: No juvenile, mental, sealed, or adoption records released. Fee to fax out file $1.00 per page. Court makes copy: $1.00 per page. Certification fee: $1.00. Payee: District Clerk. Personal checks accepted, credit cards are not. Prepayment required. Mail requests: SASE required.

Civil Name Search: Access: Mail, in person. Both court and visitors may perform in person name searches. Search fee: $5.00 per name. Required to search: name, years to search, SSN. Civil records on computer since 1996, index books prior to the 1920's. Note: A ten-year search is performed. Mail turnaround time 10 days.

Criminal Name Search: Access: Mail, in person. Both court and visitors may perform in person name searches. Search fee: $5.00 per name. Required to search: name, years to search, DOB, signed release; also helpful-address, SSN. Criminal records on computer since 1996, index books prior to 1924. Mail turnaround time 10 days.

County Court 103 W Callaghan, Fort Stockton, TX 79735; 432-336-7555; fax: 432-336-7557; 8AM-5PM (CST). *Misdemeanor, Civil, Probate.*

General Information: No juvenile, mental, or sealed records released. Will fax documents $5.00 plus $1.00 per page. Court makes copy: $1.00 per page. Certification fee: $5.00. Payee: County Clerk. Personal checks accepted, credit cards are not. Prepayment required. Mail requests: SASE required.

Civil Name Search: Access: Mail, in person. Both court and visitors may perform in person name searches. Search fee: $5.00 per name. Civil records index books to 1955. Mail turnaround time same day (if file not in basement).

Criminal Name Search: Access: Mail, in person. Both court and visitors may perform in person name searches. Search fee: $5.00 per name. Criminal records computerized from 1989 and index books to 1955. Mail turnaround time same day.

Polk County

District Court 101 W Church, #205, Livingston, TX 77351; 936-327-6814; fax: 936-327-6851; 8AM-5PM (CST). *Felony, Civil.*

General Information: No juvenile, mental, sealed, or adoption records released. Will fax documents for $1.00 per page. Court makes copy: $1.00 per page. Certification fee: $2.00 per doc plus copy fee. Payee: District Clerk. No personal checks or credit cards accepted. Prepayment required. Mail requests: SASE required.

Civil Name Search: Access: Mail, in person. Both court and visitors may perform in person name searches. Search fee: $10.00 per name per 10 year period. Civil records in index books, computerized since 1996. Note: Search fee for civil with criminal indexes is $15.00 per name. Mail turnaround time 2-4 days. Civil PAT goes back to mid-1996.

Criminal Name Search: Access: Mail, in person. Both court and visitors may perform in person name searches. Search fee: $5.00 per name per 10 year period. Required to search: name, years to search; also helpful: DOB. Criminal index in books, computerized since 1996. Mail turnaround time 2-4 days. Criminal PAT goes back to mid-1996.

County Court PO Box 2119, Livingston, TX 77351; 936-327-6804; criminal phone: 936-327-6805; civil phone: 936-327-6804; probate phone: 936-327-6804; fax: 936-327-6874; 8AM-5PM (CST). *Misdemeanor, Civil, Probate.*

General Information: Probate is a separate index at this same address. Probate fax is same as main fax number. No mental records released. Fee to fax out file $2.00 each plus $1.00 per page. Court makes copy: $1.00 per page. Self serve copy: same. Certification fee: $5.00 per document plus copy fee. Payee: County Clerk. Personal checks accepted for civil only. Major credit cards accepted. Prepayment required. Mail requests: SASE required.

Civil Name Search: Access: Mail, in person, online. Both court and visitors may perform in person name searches. Search fee: $5.00 per name. Civil records in index books, on computer since 1988, available since 1846. Mail turnaround time 2-4 days. Civil PAT goes back to 1846. Civil case information is free at www.idocket.com. Registration and password required. One free name search permitted a day, otherwise subscription required.

Criminal Name Search: Access: Mail, in person, online. Both court and visitors may perform in person name searches. Search fee: $5.00 per name. Required to search: name, years to search; also helpful: DOB, SSN. Criminal index in books; on computer back to 1989. Mail turnaround time 2-4 days. Criminal PAT goes back to 1989. Terminal results include SSN. Criminal case information is free at www.idocket.com. Registration and password required. One free name search permitted a day, otherwise subscription required.

Potter County

District Court PO Box 9570, Amarillo, TX 79105-9570; 806-379-2300; criminal phone: 806-379-2311; civil phone: 806-379-2307; fax: 806-372-5061; 7:30AM-5:30PM (CST). *Felony, Civil.* www.co.potter.tx.us/districtclerk/

General Information: Online identifiers in results same as on public terminal. No juvenile, mental, sealed, or adoption records released. Will fax documents $1.00 per page. Court makes copy: $.50 per page. Self serve copy: same. Certification fee: $1.00 per page. Payee: District Clerk. Business checks accepted; no personal checks. Will accept credit cards for certified payments, call for instructions. Prepayment required. Mail requests: SASE required.

Civil Name Search: Access: Fax, mail, online, in person. Both court and visitors may perform in person name searches. Search fee: $5.00 per name. Civil records on computer since 9/87, index books prior. Mail turnaround time less than 10 days. Civil PAT goes back to 1988. Civil index and images back to 1988 online at www.idocket.com. One free name search permitted a day, otherwise subscription required.

Criminal Name Search: Access: Fax, mail, online, in person. Both court and visitors may perform in person name searches. Search fee: $5.00 per name. Criminal records on computer since 9/87, index books prior. Mail turnaround time 2-4 days. Criminal PAT goes back to same as civil. Felony cases online at www.idocket.com. Felonies go back to 1/1989. One free name search permitted a day, otherwise subscription required.

County Court & County Courts at Law 1 & 2 PO Box 9638, 500 S Fillmore St, Amarillo, TX 79105; 806-379-2285; criminal phone: 806-379-2283; probate phone: 806-379-2280; fax: 806-379-2296; 8AM-5PM (CST). *Misdemeanor, Probate (Civil under $5,000 Lmt'd).* www.co.potter.tx.us/countyclerk/index.html

General Information: Limited civil records filed here, most are with the District Clerk. Any civil after 1987 are with the District Clerk. Probate records on a separate index at this address. No juvenile, mental or sealed records released. Will fax documents for fee. Court makes copy: $1.00 per page. Self serve copy: same. Certification fee: $5.00 per doc; Exemplification- $7.00; Certification of Fact- $5.00. Payee: Potter County Clerk. Personal checks accepted. Major credit cards accepted; add 3% surcharge. Prepayment required. Mail requests: SASE required.

Civil Name Search: Access: Mail, in person, online. Both court and visitors may perform in person name searches. Search fee: None, but must pay the certificate of fact fee. Required to search: exact name, years to search. Civil records on in books and microfiche to 1987, probate from early 1800s. Mail turnaround time 1-2 days. Civil PAT goes back to 1987. Online case access is through www.idocket.com; registration and password required. Records go back to 9/1/1987, probate back to 1/1886. One free name search permitted a day, otherwise subscription required.

Criminal Name Search: Access: Mail, in person, online. Both court and visitors may perform in person name searches. Search fee: None, but must pay the certificate of fact fee. Required to search: exact name, years to search, DOB, offense. Criminal records on computer since 1889. Mail turnaround time 1-2 days. Criminal PAT goes back to early 1990s. Misdemeanor cases online at www.idocket.com. Misdemeanors go back to 1/1991. One free name search permitted a day, otherwise subscription required. Online results show name only.

Presidio County

District & County Court PO Box 789, 320 N Highland, Marfa, TX 79843; 432-729-4812; Dist.-729-3857; fax: 432-729-4313; 8AM-N, 1-4PM (CST). *Felony, Misdemeanor, Civil, Probate.*
General Information: Probate is a separate index as this same address. Probate fax is same as main fax number. No juvenile, mental, sealed, or adoption records released. Will fax documents $3.00 each. Court makes copy: $1.00 per page. Self serve copy: same. Certification fee: $5.00 per document plus copy fee. Payee: District Clerk. Personal checks accepted, credit cards are not. Prepayment required. Mail requests: SASE required.
Civil Name Search: Access: Mail, in person. Both court and visitors may perform in person name searches. Search fee: $6.00 per name. Civil index in docket books from 1800s. Note: Requests must be in writing. Mail turnaround time 2-4 days. Civil PAT goes back to 1800s.
Criminal Name Search: Access: Mail, in person. Both court and visitors may perform in person name searches. Search fee: $6.00 per name. Criminal docket on books back to 1800s. Note: Search requests must be in writing. Mail turnaround time 2-4 days. Criminal PAT goes back to same.

Rains County

District Court PO Box 187, 220 W Quitman St, Emory, TX 75440; 903-473-5000 x101; fax: 903-473-5008; 8AM-5PM (CST). *Felony, Civil.*
General Information: No juvenile, mental, sealed, or adoption records released. Will fax documents to local or toll-free number. Court makes copy: $1.00 per page. Self serve copy: same. No certification fee. Payee: Rains County District Clerk. Personal checks accepted if proper ID provided; DL, DOB. No credit cards accepted. Prepayment required. Mail requests: SASE required.
Civil Name Search: Access: Mail, fax, in person. Both court and visitors may perform in person name searches. Search fee: $5.00 per name. Required to search: name. Civil records on computer back to 1990, index books back to 1903. Mail turnaround time same day. Civil PAT available. Weekly dockets ahead up to 2 weeks available online.
Criminal Name Search: Access: Mail, fax, in person. Both court and visitors may perform in person name searches. Search fee: $5.00 per name. Required to search: name; also helpful: DOB. Criminal records computerized from 1990, index books back to 1880. Mail turnaround time same day. Criminal PAT available. Terminal to be available Summer '08. Weekly dockets ahead up to 2 weeks available online.

County Court PO Box 1150, 220 W Quitman St, Emory, TX 75440; 903-473-5000 x103; criminal phone: x106; probate phone: x105; fax: 903-473-5086; 8AM-5PM (CST). *Misdemeanor, Civil, Probate.*
General Information: No juvenile, mental, sealed, or adoption records released. Will not fax out documents. Court makes copy: $1.00 per page. Self serve copy: same. Certification fee: $5.00 per cert. Payee: Rains County Clerk. Personal checks accepted, credit cards are not. Prepayment required. Mail requests: SASE required.
Civil Name Search: Access: Mail, In person. Visitors must perform in person searches themselves. Search fee: $5.00 per name. Required to search: name. Civil records on paper indices in 10 year increments back to 1989, index books prior to 1903. Mail turnaround time 2-3 days.
Criminal Name Search: Access: Mail, in person. Visitors must perform in person searches themselves. Search fee: $5.00 per name. Required to search: name; also helpful: DOB. Criminal records on paper indices in 10 year increments back to 1989, index books prior to 1880. Mail turnaround time 2-3 days.

Randall County

District Courts 2309 Russell Long Blvd, #101, PO Box 660, Canyon, TX 79015; 806-468-5505; fax: 806-468-5509; 8AM-5PM (CST). *Felony, Civil.*
www.randallcounty.org/cclerk/
General Information: No juvenile, mental, sealed, or adoption records released. Fee to fax out file $5.00 1st pg; $1.00 each add'l. Court makes copy: $1.00 per page. Self serve copy: same. Certification fee: $1.00 per page includes copy fee. Payee: District Clerk. Personal checks accepted. No credit cards accepted for record searching or copies. Prepayment required. Mail requests: SASE not required.
Civil Name Search: Access: Fax, mail, online, in person. Both court and visitors may perform in person name searches. Search fee: $5.00 per name. Civil records on computer since 1984. Mail turnaround time 1-2 days. Civil PAT goes back to 1983. Civil case information at www.idocket.com. Records from 12/31/84. Subscription required.
Criminal Name Search: Access: Fax, mail, online, in person. Both court and visitors may perform in person name searches. Search fee: $5.00 per name. Criminal records on computer since 1985; prior in docket books. Mail turnaround time 1-2 days. Criminal PAT goes back to 1985. Felony cases online at Idocket at http://idocket.com/counties.htm. Is a fee service. Felony records go back to 1/1992. Subscription required.

County Court PO Box 660, Canyon, TX 79015; 806-468-5505; criminal phone: x4132; civil phone: 806-468-5548; fax: 806-468-5509; 8AM-5PM (CST). *Misdemeanor, Civil, Probate.*
www.randallcounty.org/cclerk
General Information: Probate is separate index at this same address. No juvenile, mental, sealed, or adoption records released. Fee to fax out file $1.00 per page, $5.00 fee add'l if call is long distance. Court makes copy: $1.00 per page. Self serve copy: same. Certification fee: $5.00 per document plus copy fee. Payee: Randall County Clerk. Personal checks accepted. Major credit cards accepted but not over the phone. Court charges a 2.5% credit card fee. Prepayment required. Mail requests: SASE required.
Civil Name Search: Access: Mail, fax, in person, email, online. Both court and visitors may perform in person name searches. Search fee: $10.00 per name. Required to search: name, years to search, SASE. Civil records in index books 1900 to present. Mail turnaround time 2-4 days. Civil PAT goes back to 1999. Most records have name only, but a few have some personal identifiers. Civil case information at www.idocket.com. Records go back to 1/2000; probate back to 9/11/1969. One free name search permitted a day, otherwise subscription required. Direct email records requests to countyclerk@randallcounty.org.
Criminal Name Search: Access: Mail, fax, in person, online, email. Both court and visitors may perform in person name searches. Search fee: $10.00 per name. Required to search: name, years to search; also helpful: DOB. Criminal records on computer since 1984; prior records in index books. Mail turnaround time 2-4 days. Criminal PAT goes back to 1991. Misdemeanor cases online at Idocket at http://idocket.com/counties.htm. Is a fee service. Misd. records go back to 1/1985. One free name search permitted a day, otherwise subscription required. Direct email records requests to countyclerk@randallcounty.org.

Reagan County

District & County Court PO Box 100, 3rd St at Plaza, Big Lake, TX 76932; 325-884-2442; fax: 325-884-1503; 8:30AM-5PM M-TH, 8:30AM-4PM F (CST). *Felony, Misdemeanor, Civil, Probate.*
General Information: No juvenile, mental, sealed, or adoption records released. Will fax documents $2.00; no fee to a toll-free number. Court makes copy: $1.00 per page. Certification fee: $5.00 per doc plus copy fee. Payee: County/District Clerk. Personal checks not accepted if out-of-state. No credit cards accepted. Prepayment required. Mail requests: SASE required.
Civil Name Search: Access: Mail, in person. Both court and visitors may perform in person name searches. Search fee: $5.00 per name. Civil records in index books to 1903. Mail turnaround time same day. Civil PAT available.
Criminal Name Search: Access: Mail, in person. Both court and visitors may perform in person name searches. Search fee: $5.00 per name. Criminal docket on books to 1903. Mail turnaround time same day. Criminal PAT available.

Real County

District & County Court PO Box 750, Leakey, TX 78873; 830-232-5202; fax: 830-232-6888; 8AM-5PM (CST). *Felony, Misdemeanor, Civil, Probate.*
General Information: No juvenile, mental, sealed, or adoption records released. Will fax documents for fee. Fee varies. Court makes copy: $1.00 per page. Certification fee: $5.00 per document. Payee: District/County Court. Personal checks accepted. No credit cards accepted for searches or copies. Prepayment required. Mail requests: SASE required.
Civil Name Search: Access: Mail, in person. Both court and visitors may perform in person name searches. Search fee: $5.00 per name. Civil index in books.
Criminal Name Search: Access: In person only. Visitors must perform in person searches themselves. Required to search: name, years to search, DOB. Criminal index in books.

Red River County

District Court 400 N Walnut, Clarksville, TX 75426; 903-427-3761; fax: 903-427-1201; 8:30AM-N, 1-5PM (CST). *Felony, Civil.*
General Information: No juvenile, mental, sealed, or adoption records released. Will fax documents to local or toll free line. Court makes copy: $1.00 per page. Certification fee: $1.00 per page includes copies. Payee: District Clerk. Personal checks accepted, credit cards are not. Prepayment required. Mail requests: SASE required.
Civil Name Search: Access: Mail, in person. Both court and visitors may perform in person name searches. Search fee: $5.00 per name. Civil records in index books and on microfilm to 1800s. Mail turnaround time same day. Civil PAT goes back to 2002.
Criminal Name Search: Access: Mail, in person. Both court and visitors may perform in person name searches. Search fee: $5.00 per name.

Criminal docket on books and on microfilm to 1800s. Mail turnaround time same day. Criminal PAT goes back to same as civil.

County Court 200 N Walnut, Clarksville, TX 75426; 903-427-2401; fax: 903-427-3589; 8AM-5PM (CST). *Misdemeanor, Probate.*

General Information: No mental, sealed, or adoption records released. Will not fax out documents. Court makes copy: $1.00 per page. Self serve copy: same. Certification fee: $5.00 per instrument. Payee: County Clerk. Personal checks accepted. Major credit cards accepted. Prepayment required. Mail requests: SASE not required.

Criminal Name Search: Access: Mail, in person. Both court and visitors may perform in person name searches. Search fee: $5.00 per name. Required to search: name, years to search, SSN. Criminal records on computer (name only) since 1980, in index books since 1960s. Mail turnaround time 1-2 days. Public use terminal has crim records back to 1980. Results may also show DL number.

Reeves County

District Court PO Box 848, Pecos, TX 79772; 432-445-2714; fax: 432-445-7455; 8AM-N, 1-5PM (CST). *Felony, Civil.*

General Information: Probate records handled by County Clerk. No juvenile, mental, sealed, or adoption records released. Will not fax documents. Court makes copy: $1.00 per page. Self serve copy: same. Certification fee: $1.00 per page. Payee: District Clerk Reeves County. Personal checks accepted, credit cards are not. Prepayment required. Mail requests: SASE required.

Civil Name Search: Access: Phone, mail, in person. Both court and visitors may perform in person name searches. Search fee: $5.00 per name. Civil records on computer since 1/91, index books prior. Mail turnaround time 2 days.

Criminal Name Search: Access: Mail, in person. Both court and visitors may perform in person name searches. Search fee: $5.00 per name. Criminal records computerized from 1/90, index books prior. Mail turnaround time 2-4 days.

County Court PO Box 867, Pecos, TX 79772; 432-445-5467; fax: 432-445-3997; 8AM-5PM (CST). *Misdemeanor, Civil, Probate.*

General Information: Probate is a separate index at this same address. Probate fax is same as main fax number. No juvenile, mental, sealed, or adoption records released. Will fax documents $.50 per page. Court makes copy: $1.00 per page. Certification fee: $5.00 per cert includes copy fee. Payee: Reeves County Clerk. Personal checks accepted, credit cards are not. Prepayment required. Mail requests: SASE required.

Civil Name Search: Access: Mail, in person. Both court and visitors may perform in person name searches. Search fee: $10.00 per name. Required to search: name, years to search; also helpful: address. Civil records on computer go back 10 years, index books prior. Mail turnaround time 1-3 days. Civil PAT goes back to 1993.

Criminal Name Search: Access: Mail, in person. Both court and visitors may perform in person name searches. Search fee: $10.00 per name. Required to search: name, years to search, DOB; also helpful: address. Criminal records on computer go back 10 years; index books prior. Mail turnaround time 5 days. Criminal PAT goes back to 1993.

Refugio County

District Court PO Box 736, Refugio, TX 78377; 361-526-2721; 8AM-N, 1-5PM (CST). *Felony, Civil.*

General Information: No juvenile, mental, sealed, or adoption records released. Will not fax documents. Court makes copy: $1.00 per page. Certification fee: $1.00 per seal. Payee: District Clerk. Personal checks accepted, credit cards are not. Prepayment required. Mail requests: SASE required.

Civil Name Search: Access: Mail, in person, online. Both court and visitors may perform in person name searches. Search fee: $5.00 per name. Civil records on computer back to 1992, index books back to 1879. Mail turnaround time 2-4 days. Access cases back to 1/1994 at www.idocket.com; registration and password required. A fee service; only one free name search per day.

Criminal Name Search: Access: Mail, in person. Both court and visitors may perform in person name searches. Search fee: $5.00 per name. Required to search: name, years to search, date of birth; also helpful-SSN, signed release. Criminal records computerized from 1992, index books back to 1879. Note: The felony record index is not online, but the misdemeanor index kept by the County court is. Mail turnaround time 2-4 days.

County Court PO Box 704, Refugio, TX 78377; 361-526-2233 x306; fax: 361-526-1325; 8AM-N, 1-4PM (CST). *Misdemeanor, Civil, Probate.*

General Information: No juvenile, mental, sealed, or adoption records released. Will not fax documents. Court makes copy: $1.00 per page. Certification fee: $5.00 per document plus copy fee. Payee: Ruby Garcia, County Clerk. Personal checks accepted, credit cards are not. Prepayment required. Mail requests: SASE not required.

Civil Name Search: Access: Mail, in person, online. Both court and visitors may perform in person name searches. Search fee: $10.00 per name. Civil records in index books, began computerization in 2003. Mail turnaround time 5-10 days. Access cases back to 1/1994 at www.idocket.com; registration and password required. A fee service; only one free name search per day.

Criminal Name Search: Access: Mail, in person, online. Both court and visitors may perform in person name searches. Search fee: $10.00 per name. Criminal records on computer since 1992, index books prior. Mail turnaround time 5-10 days. Access misdemeanor cases back to 1/1991 at www.idocket.com; registration and password required. A fee service; only one free name search per day.

Roberts County

District & County Court PO Box 477, Miami, TX 79059; 806-868-2341; fax: 806-868-3381; 8AM-N, 1-5PM (CST). *Felony, Misdemeanor, Civil, Probate.*

General Information: No juvenile, mental, sealed, or adoption records released. Will fax documents $3.00 1st page; $1.00 each add'l. Court makes copy: $1.00 per page. Include postage with copy fee. Certification fee: $5.00 per doc in County Court; $1.00 per page in District Court. Payee: Roberts County. Personal checks accepted, credit cards are not. Prepayment required. Mail requests: SASE required.

Civil Name Search: Access: Mail, in person. Both court and visitors may perform in person name searches. Search fee: $5.00 per name. Civil index in books. Note: Written search requests only. Mail turnaround time 2-4 days.

Criminal Name Search: Access: Mail, in person. Both court and visitors may perform in person name searches. Search fee: $5.00 per name. Required to search: name, years to search, DOB, SSN. Criminal index in books. Note: Written search requests only. Mail turnaround time 2-4 days.

Robertson County

District Court PO Box 250, Franklin, TX 77856; 979-828-3636; 8AM-5PM (CST). *Felony, Civil.*
www.co.robertson.tx.us

General Information: No juvenile, sealed, or adoption records released. Will not fax documents. Court makes copy: $1.00 per page. Self serve copy: same. Certification fee: $1.00 per page plus copy fee. Payee: Robertson County District Clerk. No personal checks accepted. Cash or money orders only. No credit cards accepted. Prepayment required. Mail requests: SASE required.

Civil Name Search: Access: Mail, in person. Both court and visitors may perform in person name searches. Search fee: $5.00 per name. Required to search: name, years to search, SSN. Civil records on computer since 1987 and index books. Mail turnaround time 1-2 days. Civil PAT available.

Criminal Name Search: Access: Mail, in person. Both court and visitors may perform in person name searches. Search fee: $5.00 per name. Required to search: name, years to search, DOB; also helpful: SSN. Criminal records on computer since 1987 and index books. Mail turnaround time 1-2 days. Criminal PAT available.

County Court PO Box 1029, Franklin, TX 77856; 979-828-4130; fax: 979-828-1260; 8AM-5PM (CST). *Misdemeanor, Civil, Probate.*

General Information: No juvenile, mental, sealed, or adoption records released. Will not fax documents. Court makes copy: $1.00 per page. Certification fee: $5.00. Payee: Robertson County Clerk. Personal checks accepted, credit cards are not. Prepayment required. Mail requests: SASE not required.

Civil Name Search: Access: Mail, fax, in person. Both court and visitors may perform in person name searches. Search fee: $5.00 per name. Civil records on computer back from 1990 to present, index books from 1985 to present. Mail turnaround time same day.

Criminal Name Search: Access: Mail, fax, in person. Both court and visitors may perform in person name searches. Search fee: $5.00 per name. Required to search: name, years to search, DOB. Criminal records computerized from 1986 to present, index books from 1918. Mail turnaround time same day.

Rockwall County

District Court 1101 Ridge Rd, #209, Rockwall, TX 75087; 972-204-6610; fax: 972-204-6609; 8AM-5PM (CST). *Felony, Civil.*
www.rockwallcountytexas.com

General Information: No juvenile, mental, sealed, or adoption records released. Will not fax documents. Court makes copy: $1.00 per page. Certification fee: $1.00 per page. Payee: District Clerk. Personal checks accepted, credit cards are not. Prepayment required. Mail requests: SASE required.

Civil Name Search: Access: Mail, in person, online. Both court and visitors may perform in person name searches. Search fee: $5.00 per name.

Fee is per 5 year period. Civil records on computer back to 1994, index books prior. Mail turnaround time 2-4 days. Civil PAT goes back to 1994. Online access is same as criminal, see below.

Criminal Name Search: Access: Mail, in person, online. Both court and visitors may perform in person name searches. Search fee: $5.00 per name. Required to search: name, years to search, DOB. Criminal records computerized from 1980, index books prior. Mail turnaround time 2-4 days. Criminal PAT goes back to 1981. Online access is free at http://trueauto.rockwallcountytexas.com/judicialsearch/. Search sheriff bond and jail lists too. Online court records only go back 7 years; some dismissals/deferred cases are not online.

County Court at Law 1101 Ridge Rd, #101, Attn- County Clerk, Rockwall, TX 75087; 972-204-6410; fax: 972-204-6419; 8AM-5PM (CST). *Misdemeanor, Civil, Probate.*
www.rockwallcountytexas.com/index.asp?nid=77

General Information: Online identifiers in results same as on public terminal. No juvenile, mental, sealed, or adoption records released. Fee to fax out file $5.00 each. Court makes copy: $1.00 per page. Self serve copy: same. Certification fee: $5.00. Payee: County Clerk. Personal checks accepted. Major credit cards accepted, with 4% surcharge. Prepayment required. Mail requests: SASE required.

Civil Name Search: Access: Phone, mail, in person, online. Both court and visitors may perform in person name searches. Search fee: $5.00 per name. Civil records on computer back to 1987 and in index books from 1800s. Mail turnaround time 2-4 days. Civil PAT goes back to 1987. Online access is same as criminal, see below.

Criminal Name Search: Access: Phone, mail, in person, online. Both court and visitors may perform in person name searches. Search fee: $5.00 per name. Criminal records computerized from 1987 and in index books from 1800s. Mail turnaround time 2-4 days. Criminal PAT goes back to same as civil. Online access is free at http://trueauto.rockwallcountytexas.com/judicialsearch/. Search sheriff bond and jail lists too. Online court records only go back 7 years; some dismissals/deferred cases are not online. Online results show name, DOB.

Runnels County

District Court PO Box 166, Ballinger, TX 76821; 325-365-2638; fax: 325-365-9229; 8:30AM-5PM (CST). *Felony, Civil.*

General Information: No juvenile, mental, sealed or adoption records released. Will fax documents $1.00 per page. Court makes copy: $1.00 per page. Self serve copy: same. Certification fee: $1.00 per cert plus copy fee. Payee: District Clerk. Personal checks accepted, credit cards are not. Prepayment required. Mail requests: SASE not required.

Civil Name Search: Access: Phone, fax, mail, in person. Both court and visitors may perform in person name searches. Search fee: $5.00 per name. Required to search: name; also helpful: years to search. Civil records in index books since 1882. Mail turnaround time 1-2 days. Public use terminal available.

Criminal Name Search: Access: Phone, fax, mail, in person. Both court and visitors may perform in person name searches. Search fee: $5.00 per name. Required to search: name; also helpful: years to search, DOB, SSN. Criminal docket on books from 1882. Mail turnaround time 1-2 days. Public use terminal available.

County Court PO Box 189, Ballinger, TX 76821; 325-365-2720; fax: 325-365-3408; 8:30AM-N, 1-5PM (CST). *Misdemeanor, Civil, Probate.*

General Information: Probate fax is same as main fax number. No juvenile or mental records released. Will fax documents to toll-free number. Court makes copy: $1.00 per page. Self serve copy: $.50 per page. Certification fee: $5.00. Payee: County Clerk, Runnels County. Personal checks accepted, credit cards are not. Prepayment required. Mail requests: SASE not required.

Civil Name Search: Access: Phone, mail, in person. Both court and visitors may perform in person name searches. Search fee: $5.00. Civil records in docket books with alphabetical index and file jacket by number; computerized since 1992. Mail turnaround time 1-2 days. Civil PAT available.

Criminal Name Search: Access: Phone, mail, in person. Both court and visitors may perform in person name searches. Search fee: $5.00. Required to search: name, years to search; also helpful: DOB. Criminal records in docket books with alphabetical index and file jacket by number; computerized since 1992. Mail turnaround time 1-2 days. Criminal PAT available.

Rusk County

District Court PO Box 1687, 115 N Main St #301, Henderson, TX 75653; 903-657-0353; fax: 903-657-1914; 8AM-5PM (CST). *Felony, Civil.*

General Information: No juvenile, mental, sealed, or adoption records released. Will not fax documents. Court makes copy: $1.00 per page.

Certification fee: $1.00 per page includes copy fee. Payee: District Clerk. No personal checks or credit cards accepted. Prepayment required. Mail requests: SASE required.

Civil Name Search: Access: Mail, in person. Both court and visitors may perform in person name searches. Search fee: $5.00 per name. Civil records in index books; on computer back to 1990. Mail turnaround time 2-4 days. Civil PAT goes back to 1990.

Criminal Name Search: Access: Mail, in person. Both court and visitors may perform in person name searches. Search fee: $5.00 per name. Required to search: name, years to search, DOB, SSN, signed release. Criminal index in books; on computer back to 1990. Mail turnaround time 2-4 days. Criminal PAT goes back to same as civil.

County Court at Law PO Box 758, 115 N Main St #206, Henderson, TX 75653-; 903-657-0330; fax: 903-657-0062; 8AM-5PM (CST). *Misdemeanor, Civil, Contested Probate.*

General Information: Misdemeanor & probate records are at County Clerk. No juvenile, mental, sealed, or adoption records released. Will not fax documents. Court makes copy: $1.00 per page. Certification fee: $5.00 per doc plus copy fee. Payee: County Clerk. Business checks accepted. No credit cards accepted. Prepayment required. Mail requests: SASE required.

Civil Name Search: Access: Mail, in person. Both court and visitors may perform in person name searches. Search fee: $5.00 per name. Civil index in books. Mail turnaround time 2-4 days. Civil PAT goes back to 1997 countywide.

Criminal Name Search: Access: Mail, in person. Both court and visitors may perform in person name searches. Search fee: $5.00 per name. Required to search: name, years to search, DOB, SSN. Criminal records computerized. Mail turnaround time 2-4 days. Criminal PAT goes back to 1997. Terminal results may include DL or ID number.

Sabine County

District Court PO Box 850, Hemphill, TX 75948; 409-787-2912; fax: 409-787-2623; 8AM-4:00PM (CST). *Felony, Civil.*

General Information: No juvenile, mental, sealed, or adoption records released. Will not fax documents. Court makes copy: $1.00 per page. Self serve copy: same. No certification fee. Payee: District Clerk. Personal checks accepted, credit cards are not. Prepayment required. Mail requests: SASE required.

Civil Name Search: Access: Mail, in person. Both court and visitors may perform in person name searches. Search fee: $10.00 per name. Civil records on computer since 1992. Overall records go back to 1900. Mail turnaround time 1-2 days.

Criminal Name Search: Access: Mail, in person. Both court and visitors may perform in person name searches. Search fee: $10.00 per name. Criminal records on computer since 1990. Overall records go back to 1900. Mail turnaround time 1-2 days.

County Court PO Drawer 580, Hemphill, TX 75948-0580; 409-787-2889; fax: 409-787-3795; 8AM-4PM (CST). *Misdemeanor, Probate.*

General Information: No juvenile, mental, sealed, or adoption records released. Will not fax documents. Court makes copy: $1.00 per page. Self serve copy: same. Certification fee: $5.00. Payee: Sabine County Clerk. Business checks accepted. No credit cards accepted. Prepayment required. Mail requests: SASE required.

Civil Name Search: Access: Mail, in person. Both court and visitors may perform in person name searches. Search fee: $10.00 per name. Criminal records on computer since 1992, index books prior. Note: Court will search 10 years, no further. Mail turnaround time 2 days.

San Augustine County

District Court County Courthouse, Rm 202, San Augustine, TX 75972; 936-275-2231; fax: 936-275-2389; 8AM-4PM (CST). *Felony, Civil.*

General Information: No juvenile, mental, sealed, or adoption records released. Will fax documents to local or toll free line. Court makes copy: $1.00 per page. Self serve copy: same. No certification fee. Payee: District Clerk. Personal checks accepted, credit cards are not. Prepayment required. Mail requests: SASE required.

Civil Name Search: Access: Phone, mail, in person. Both court and visitors may perform in person name searches. Search fee: $5.00 per name. Civil cases indexed by plaintiff. Civil index in books. Mail turnaround time 2-4 days.

Criminal Name Search: Access: Phone, mail, in person. Only the court performs in person name searches; visitors may not. Search fee: $5.00 per name. Criminal index in books. Mail turnaround time 2-4 days.

County Court 223 N Harrison St, San Augustine, TX 75972; 936-275-2452; fax: 936-275-263; 8AM-4PM M-TH; 8AM-3PM Fri (CST). *Misdemeanor, Probate.*

General Information: No juvenile, mental, sealed, or adoption records released. Will not fax out documents. Court makes copy: $1.00 per page. Self serve copy: same. Copies must be paid for in advance. Certification fee:

$5.00. Payee: County Clerk. Personal checks accepted, credit cards are not. Prepayment required. Mail requests: SASE required.

Criminal Name Search: Access: Phone, mail, in person. Both court and visitors may perform in person name searches. Search fee: $10.00 per name. Required to search: name, years to search; also helpful: address, DOB, SSN. Criminal records go back to 1984; on computer since 1990. Mail turnaround time 2-3 days.

San Jacinto County

District Court 1 State Hwy 150, Rm 4, Coldspring, TX 77331; 936-653-2909; fax: 936-653-4659; 8AM-N, 1-5PM (CST). *Felony, Civil.*

General Information: No juvenile, mental, sealed, or adoption records released. Will fax documents $1.00 per page. Court makes copy: $1.00 per page. Certification fee: $5.00. Payee: District Clerk. Personal checks accepted, credit cards are not. Prepayment required. Mail requests: SASE required.

Civil Name Search: Access: Mail, in person. Both court and visitors may perform in person name searches. Search fee: $5.00 per name. Civil cases indexed by plaintiff. Civil records in index books. Mail turnaround time 2-4 days. Civil PAT goes back to 1999. Not all records show personal identifiers; SSNs sometimes appear.

Criminal Name Search: Access: Mail, in person. Both court and visitors may perform in person name searches. Search fee: $5.00 per name. Criminal records on computer since 1999, indexed in books. Mail turnaround time 2-4 days. Criminal PAT goes back to same as civil. Not all records show personal identifiers, some show SSN.

County Court 1 State Hwy 150, Rm 2, Coldspring, TX 77331; 936-653-2324; fax: 936-653-8312; 8AM-4:30PM (CST). *Misdemeanor, Civil, Probate.*

www.co.san-jacinto.tx.us/ips/cms/countyoffices/countyClerk.html

General Information: No juvenile, mental, sealed, or adoption records released. Will fax documents $3.00 fee. Court makes copy: $1.00 per page. Certification fee: $5.00 per doc. Payee: County Clerk. Personal checks accepted. Only cashiers checks and money orders accepted for criminal searches. No credit cards accepted. Prepayment required. Mail requests: SASE required.

Civil Name Search: Access: Mail, in person. Both court and visitors may perform in person name searches. Search fee: $11.00 per name. Civil records in index books and on computer. Mail turnaround time 1 week. Civil PAT goes back to 1995.

Criminal Name Search: Access: Mail, in person. Both court and visitors may perform in person name searches. Search fee: $11.00 per name. Required to search: name, years to search; also helpful: address, DOB, SSN. Criminal index in books. Mail turnaround time 1 week. Criminal PAT goes back to 1997.

San Patricio County

District Court PO Box 1084, Sinton, TX 78387; 361-364-9377; fax: 361-364-9477; 8AM-5PM (CST). *Felony, Civil.*

www.co.san-patricio.tx.us/ips/cms/districtcourt/districtClerk.html

General Information: No juvenile, mental, sealed, or adoption records released. Will fax documents for $2.00 per page long distance, $1.00 per page local. Court makes copy: $1.00 per page. Certification fee: $1.00 per document. Payee: District Clerk. Business checks accepted. Credit cards accepted. Prepayment required. Mail requests: SASE required.

Civil Name Search: Access: Mail, fax, in person, online. Both court and visitors may perform in person name searches. Search fee: $5.00 per name. Civil records in index books from 1800s; computerized from 1993 forward. Mail turnaround time 2-4 days. Civil PAT goes back to 1993. Access civil cases online back to 11/1992 at www.idocket.com; registration and password required. One free name search permitted a day, otherwise subscription required.

Criminal Name Search: Access: Mail, fax, in person, online. Both court and visitors may perform in person name searches. Search fee: $5.00 per name. Criminal docket on books from 1800s; computerized from 1993 forward. Mail turnaround time 2-4 days. Criminal PAT goes back to same as civil. Online access to felony cases back to 1/1994 at www.idocket.com; registration and password required. One free name search permitted a day, otherwise subscription required.

County Court PO Box 578, Sinton, TX 78387; 361-364-9350; fax: 361-364-9450; 8AM-5PM (CST). *Misdemeanor, Civil, Probate.*

www.co.san-patricio.tx.us

General Information: No mental, or sealed records released. Will not fax documents. Court makes copy: $1.00 per page. Certification fee: $5.00. Payee: County Clerk. Personal checks accepted for civil and probate only. Visa, MC, Discover accepted. Prepayment required. Mail requests: SASE required.

Civil Name Search: Access: Mail, in person, online. Both court and visitors may perform in person name searches. Search fee: $5.00 per name.

Required to search: name, years to search; also helpful: address. Civil records in index books and microfilm, some as far back as 1824; computerized back to 1997. Mail turnaround time 2-3 days. Public use terminal has civil records back to 1998. Access civil cases including probate online back to 1/1997 at www.idocket.com; registration and password required. One free name search permitted a day, otherwise subscription required.

Criminal Name Search: Access: Mail, in person, online. Both court and visitors may perform in person name searches. Search fee: $5.00 per name. Required to search: name, years to search; also helpful: address, DOB, SSN, anything. Criminal docket on books and microfilm; computerized back to 1997. Mail turnaround time 2-3 days. Online access to Misd. cases back to 1/1994 at www.idocket.com; registration and password required. One free name search permitted a day, otherwise subscription required.

San Saba County

District & County Court County Courthouse, 500 E Wallace, #202, San Saba, TX 76877; 325-372-3375; 8AM-N, 1-4:30PM (CST). *Felony, Misdemeanor, Civil, Probate.*

http://dcourt.org

General Information: No juvenile, mental, sealed, or adoption records released. Will not fax documents. Court makes copy: $1.00 per page. Certification fee: $5.00. Payee: District/County Clerk. Personal checks accepted, credit cards are not. Prepayment required. Mail requests: SASE required.

Civil Name Search: Access: Phone, mail, in person. Both court and visitors may perform in person name searches. Search fee: $10.00 per name. Civil index in books. Mail turnaround time 2-3 days.

Criminal Name Search: Access: Mail, in person. Both court and visitors may perform in person name searches. Search fee: $10.00 per name. Required to search: name, years to search; also helpful: DOB. Criminal index in books. Mail turnaround time 2-3 days.

Schleicher County

District & County Court PO Drawer 580, Courthouse Sq, Eldorado, TX 76936; 325-853-2833; fax: 325-853-2768; 9AM-N, 1-5PM (CST). *Felony, Misdemeanor, Civil, Probate.*

General Information: No juvenile, mental, sealed, or adoption records released. Will fax documents $2.00 per page, must be paid before search. Court makes copy: $1.00 per page. Self serve copy: same. Certification fee: $5.00 per doc plus copy fee. Payee: District/County Clerk. Personal checks accepted. Major credit cards accepted. Prepayment required. Mail requests: SASE required.

Civil Name Search: Access: Mail, in person. Both court and visitors may perform in person name searches. Search fee: $10.00 per name. Civil index in books. Mail turnaround time 1 day in order received. Civil PAT goes back to 01/09.

Criminal Name Search: Access: Mail, in person. Both court and visitors may perform in person name searches. Search fee: $10.00 per name. Criminal index in books. Mail turnaround time 1 day in order received. Criminal PAT goes back to 01/09.

Scurry County

District Court 1806 25th St, #402, County District Clerk Office, Snyder, TX 79549; 325-573-5641; fax: 325-573-1081; 8:15AM-N, 1-5PM (CST). *Felony, Civil.*

General Information: No juvenile, mental, sealed, or adoption records released. Fee to fax out file $1.00 per page. Court makes copy: $1.00 first page, $.25 each add'l per doc. Certification fee: $1.00 per page. Cert fee includes copies. Payee: District Clerk. Personal checks accepted, credit cards are not. Prepayment required. Mail requests: SASE required.

Civil Name Search: Access: Mail, in person. Both court and visitors may perform in person name searches. Search fee: $5.00 per name. Civil records go back to 1890; computerized records since 1994. Note: All requests must be in writing. Mail turnaround time 1-2 days.

Criminal Name Search: Access: Mail, in person. Both court and visitors may perform in person name searches. Search fee: $5.00 per name. Required to search: name, years to search, address, DOB, SSN, sex. Criminal records go back to 1890; computerized records since 1994. Note: All requests must be in writing. Mail turnaround time 1-2 days.

County Court County Courthouse, 1806 25th St, #300, Snyder, TX 79549; 325-573-5332; fax: 325-573-7396; 8:30AM-5PM (CST). *Misdemeanor, Civil, Probate.*

General Information: No mental or sealed records released. Fee to fax out file $1.00 per page. Court makes copy: $1.00 per page. Certification fee: $5.00. Payee: County Clerk Scurry County. Personal checks accepted. Major credit cards accepted. Prepayment required. Mail requests: SASE not required.

Civil Name Search: Access: Mail, in person. Both court and visitors may perform in person name searches. Search fee: $10.00 per name. Civil records in index books since 1900s; on computer back to 1996. Mail turnaround time 1-2 days.

Criminal Name Search: Access: Mail, in person. Both court and visitors may perform in person name searches. Search fee: $5.00 per name. Fee includes copies. Required to search: name, years to search; also helpful: address, DOB, SSN. Criminal docket on books from 1900s; on computer back to 1996. Note: Written request always required. Mail turnaround time 1-2 days.

Shackelford County

District & County Court PO Box 247, Albany, TX 76430; 325-762-2232 x100; fax: 325-762-3756; 8:30AM-N, 1-5PM (CST). *Felony, Misdemeanor, Civil, Probate.*

www.shackelfordcountytexas.com/Co-Dist-Clerk.html

General Information: No juvenile, mental, sealed, or adoption records released. Will fax back if payment received or by credit card. Court makes copy: $1.00 per page. Certification fee: $5.00 per document District Ct; $1.00 if County Ct. Payee: Clerk, Shackelford County. Personal checks, Visa/MC accepted. Prepayment required. Mail requests: SASE required.

Civil Name Search: Access: Mail, in person. Both court and visitors may perform in person name searches. Search fee: $5.00 per name. Fee is per court. Civil records on computer since 1987, index books since 1867. Note: In person searchers must use docket books. Mail turnaround time 2-5 days after receipt. Civil PAT available.

Criminal Name Search: Access: Mail, in person. Both court and visitors may perform in person name searches. Search fee: $5.00 per name. Fee is per court. Criminal records on computer since 1987, index books since 1867. Note: In person searchers must use docket books. Mail turnaround time 2-5 days after received. Criminal PAT available.

Shelby County

District Court PO Drawer 1953, Clerk's Office, 200 S Augustine St, Ste. B, Center, TX 75935; 936-598-4164; 8AM-4:30PM (CST). *Felony, Civil.*

General Information: No juvenile, mental, sealed, or adoption records released. Will not fax documents. Court makes copy: $1.00 per page. Certification fee: $1.00 per doc. Payee: District Clerk. Personal checks accepted, credit cards are not. Prepayment required. Mail requests: SASE required.

Civil Name Search: Access: Mail, in person. Both court and visitors may perform in person name searches. Search fee: $5.00 per name. Civil records in index books; on computer back to 2000. Mail turnaround time 2-3 days.

Criminal Name Search: Access: Mail, in person. Both court and visitors may perform in person name searches. Search fee: $5.00 per name. Required to search: name, years to search, signed release. Criminal index in books; on computer back to 2000. Mail turnaround time 2-3 days.

County Court PO Box 1987, Center, TX 75935; 936-598-6361; fax: 936-598-3701; 8AM-4:30PM (CST). *Misdemeanor, Civil, Probate.*

http://cc.co.shelby.tx.us/

General Information: Probate records in a separate index at this same address. Probate fax is same as main fax number. No juvenile, mental, sealed, or adoption records released. Will fax documents for fee. Court makes copy: $1.00 per page. Certification fee: $5.00 per certification. Payee: Shelby County Clerk. Personal checks accepted. Major credit cards accepted. Prepayment required. Mail requests: SASE required.

Civil Name Search: Access: Mail, in person, online. Both court and visitors may perform in person name searches. Search fee: $10.00 per name. Civil & probate records in index books back to 1882; on computer back to 1990. Mail turnaround time 1-2 days. Civil PAT goes back to 1993. Access court index free at http://cc.co.shelby.tx.us/.

Criminal Name Search: Access: Mail, in person, online. Both court and visitors may perform in person name searches. Search fee: $5.00 per name. Required to search: name, years to search, SSN, DOB; also helpful: signed release. Criminal docket on books back to 1920; on computer back to 1990. Note: All requests must be in writing. Mail turnaround time 1-2 days. Criminal PAT goes back to 1993. Terminal results may also show DL#. Access court records free at http://cc.co.shelby.tx.us/.

Sherman County

District & County Court PO Box 270, 701 N 3rd St, Stratford, TX 79084; 806-366-2371; fax: 806-366-5670; 8AM-N, 1-5PM (CST). *Felony, Misdemeanor, Civil, Probate.*

General Information: Probate fax is same as main fax number. No juvenile, mental, sealed, or adoption records released. Will fax documents $5.00 1st page, $1.00 each add'l. Court makes copy: $1.00 per page. Self serve copy: same. Certification fee: $5.00 per document, plus copy fee. Payee: Sherman County Clerk. Personal checks accepted, credit cards are not. Prepayment required. Mail requests: SASE required.

Civil Name Search: Access: Mail, fax, in person. Both court and visitors may perform in person name searches. Search fee: $5.00 per name, per 5 years, per record, per court. Civil cases indexed by plaintiff. Civil records to

1930. Note: Fax search requests must be prepaid. Mail turnaround time 2-3days.

Criminal Name Search: Access: Mail, fax, in person. Only the court performs in person name searches; visitors may not. Search fee: $5.00 per name, per 5 years, per record, per court. Criminal records to 1947. Note: Fax search requests must be prepaid. Mail turnaround time 2-3 days.

Smith County

District Court PO Box 1077, Attn: District Clerk, Tyler, TX 75710; 903-590-590-1660/1672; fax: 903-590-1661; 8AM-5PM (CST). *Felony, Civil.* www.smith-county.com/

General Information: No juvenile, mental, sealed, or adoption records released. Will not fax documents. Court makes copy: $1.00 per page. Certification fee: $1.00 per doc. Payee: District Clerk. Cashiers checks and money orders accepted. No credit cards accepted. Prepayment required. Mail requests: SASE required.

Civil Name Search: Access: Mail, in person, online. Both court and visitors may perform in person name searches. Search fee: $5.00 per name. Civil index in books. Mail turnaround time 2-3 days. Civil PAT goes back to 1999. Access court indexes and sheriff's jail and bond data free at http://judicial.smith-county.com/judsrch.asp.

Criminal Name Search: Access: Mail, in person, online. Both court and visitors may perform in person name searches. Search fee: $5.00 per name. Criminal docket on books to 1846, computerized since 1/99. Mail turnaround time 2-3 days. Criminal PAT goes back to 1999. Name and cause number needed. Online access to criminal is same as civil above. Results give full range of identifiers.

County Court at Law 1, 2, 3 PO Box 1018, 200 E Ferguson, #300, Tyler, TX 75710; 903-590-4670; criminal phone: 903-590-4681; civil phone: 903-590-4673; probate phone: 903-590-4677; fax: 903-590-4689; 8AM-5PM (CST). *Misdemeanor, Civil, Probate.* www.smith-county.com/

General Information: There are three Courts at Law at this location. No juvenile, mental, sealed, or adoption records released. Will fax documents $1.00 per page. Court makes copy: $1.00 per page. Certification fee: $5.00 per certificate. Payee: Smith County Clerk. No personal checks accepted, money orders or cashier's checks accepted. No credit cards accepted. Prepayment required. Mail requests: SASE required.

Civil Name Search: Access: Mail, in person, online. Both court and visitors may perform in person name searches. Search fee: $5.00 per name. Civil index in books. Mail turnaround time 2-4 days. Civil PAT goes back to 1997. Probates records on public access terminal back to 1992. Access court and probate indexes and sheriff's jail and bond data free at http://judicial.smith-county.com/judsrch.asp.

Criminal Name Search: Access: Mail, in person, online. Both court and visitors may perform in person name searches. Search fee: $5.00 per name. Required to search: name, years to search; also helpful: DOB, SSN, middle initial. Criminal index in books. Mail turnaround time 2-4 days. Criminal PAT goes back to 1995. Online access to criminal is same as civil above. Online results show middle initial, DOB, address.

Somervell County

District & County Court PO Box 1098, Glen Rose, TX 76043; 254-897-4427; fax: 254-897-3233; 8AM-5PM (CST). *Felony, Misdemeanor, Civil, Probate.*

General Information: Evictions are handled by Justice of the Peace, POB 237, Glen Rose, TX 76043, 254-897-2120. No juvenile, mental, sealed, or adoption records released. Fee to fax out file $1.00 per page. Court makes copy: $1.00 per page. Self serve copy: same. Certification fee: $5.00. Payee: County/District Clerk. Personal checks accepted, credit cards are not. Prepayment required. Mail requests: SASE preferred.

Civil Name Search: Access: Mail, in person. Visitors must perform in person searches themselves. Search fee: $5.00 per name. Required to search: name, years to search; also helpful: address. Civil records on microfilm since 1980, index books since 1875. Mail turnaround time same day.

Criminal Name Search: Access: Mail, in person. Visitors must perform in person searches themselves. Search fee: $5.00 per name. Required to search: name, years to search, DOB, SSN, signed release; also helpful: address. Criminal records on microfilm since 1980, index books since 1875. Mail turnaround time same day.

Starr County

District & County Court Starr County Courthouse, Rm 304, 401 N Britton Ave, Rio Grande City, TX 78582; 956-716-4800, ext 8482.; probate phone: 956-487-8032; fax: 956-487-8493; 8AM-5PM (CST). *Felony, Misdemeanor, Civil, Probate.*

www.co.starr.tx.us/ips/cms/districtcourt/

General Information: The civil court also here handles civil county court cases. Probate is handled by the County Clerk at this address is room 201. No adoption records released. Will fax documents $5.00 1st page; $1.00 each add'l. Court makes copy: $1.00 per page. Certification fee: $5.00 per document. Payee: District Clerk. Personal checks accepted, credit cards are not. Prepayment required. Mail requests: SASE required.

Civil Name Search: Access: Phone, fax, mail, in person, online. Both court and visitors may perform in person name searches. Search fee: $7.00 per name. Civil index on docket books from 1920s, computerized since 9/07. Mail turnaround time 2 days. Access index and images online at www.idocket.com; registration and password required. A fee service; only one free name search per day. Records go back to 01/2003. Probate is not online.

Criminal Name Search: Access: Phone, fax, mail, in person, online. Both court and visitors may perform in person name searches. Search fee: $7.00 per name. Required to search: name, years to search, SSN; also helpful: DOB. Criminal records on computer since 9/07, in docket books to 1800s. Mail turnaround time 2 days. Public use terminal has crim records back to 2006. Access felony index and images online at www.idocket.com; registration and password required. A fee service; only one free name search per day. Felony records go back to 1/2003, misdemeanors to 12/31/1996.

County Court Starr County Courthouse, Rm 201, 401 N Britton Ave, Rio Grande City, TX 78582; 956-487-8032; fax: 956-487-8674; 8AM-5PM (CST). *Misdemeanor.*

General Information: See District & County Court for civil county court cases. No juvenile, mental, sealed, or adoption records released. Fee to fax out file $1.00 per page. Court makes copy: $1.00 per page. Certification fee: $5.00 per doc. Payee: County Clerk. Personal checks accepted, credit cards are not. Prepayment required. Mail requests: SASE requested.

Criminal Name Search: Access: Mail, in person, online. Both court and visitors may perform in person name searches. Search fee: $10.00 per name. Required to search: name, years to search; also helpful: SSN, DOB. Criminal records on computer since 1997, in index books since 1984, archived prior. Mail turnaround time 2-4 days. Online access is at www.idocket.com; registration and password required. A fee service; only one free name search per day. Records go back to 12/31/96.

Stephens County

District Court 200 W Walker, Breckenridge, TX 76424; 254-559-3151; fax: 254-559-8127; 8:30AM-5PM (CST). *Felony, Civil, Misdemeanor.*

General Information: No juvenile, mental, sealed, or adoption records released. Will fax documents $1.00 per page; available to local and 800 numbers only. Court makes copy: $1.00 per page. Certification fee: $1.00. Payee: District Clerk. Personal checks accepted, credit cards are not. Prepayment required. Mail requests: SASE required.

Civil Name Search: Access: Fax, mail, in person. Both court and visitors may perform in person name searches. Search fee: $5.00 per name. Civil records in index books, archived from 1900; on computer back to 1995. Mail turnaround time same day.

Criminal Name Search: Access: Fax, mail, in person. Both court and visitors may perform in person name searches. Search fee: $5.00 per name. Required to search: name, years to search, DOB. Criminal index in books, archived from 1900; on computer back to 1995. Mail turnaround time same day.

County Clerk 200 W Walker, Stephens County Courthouse, Breckenridge, TX 76424; 254-559-3700; fax: 254-559-5892; 8:30AM-N, 1-5PM (CST). *Probate.*

Sterling County

District & County Court PO Box 55, Sterling City, TX 76951; 325-378-5191; fax: 325-378-3111; 8AM-4PM M-TH; 8AM-2PM F (CST). *Felony, Misdemeanor, Civil, Probate.*

General Information: Probate is a separate index at this same address. No juvenile, mental, sealed, or adoption records released. Fee to fax out file $1.00 per page. Court makes copy: $1.00 per page. Certification fee: $5.00 per document plus copy fee. Payee: Sterling County/District Clerk. In-state personal checks accepted only. No credit cards accepted. Prepayment required. Mail requests: SASE helpful.

Civil Name Search: Access: Mail, in person. Both court and visitors may perform in person name searches. Search fee: $5.00 per name. Required to search: name, years to search; also helpful: address. Civil records in index books from 1900s. Mail turnaround time 1-2 days.

Criminal Name Search: Access: Mail, in person. Both court and visitors may perform in person name searches. Search fee: $5.00 per name. Required to search: name, years to search; also helpful: DOB, SSN. Criminal docket on books from 1900s. Mail turnaround time 1-2 days.

Stonewall County

District & County Court PO Drawer P, Aspermont, TX 79502; 940-989-2272; fax: 940-989-2715; 8AM-N, 1-4:30PM (CST). *Felony, Misdemeanor, Civil, Probate.*

General Information: No juvenile, mental, sealed, or adoption records released. Will fax documents $2.00 per page. Court makes copy: $1.00 per page. Self serve copy: same. Certification fee: $5.00. Payee: County Clerk. Personal checks accepted, credit cards are not. Prepayment required. Mail requests: SASE required.

Civil Name Search: Access: Phone, mail, in person. Both court and visitors may perform in person name searches. Search fee: $5.00 per name. Civil records in index books to 1900's. Mail turnaround time 2 days.

Criminal Name Search: Access: Phone, mail, in person. Both court and visitors may perform in person name searches. Search fee: $5.00 per name. Criminal docket on books to 1900's. Mail turnaround time 2 days.

Sutton County

District & County Court 300 E Oak, #3, Sonora, TX 76950; 325-387-3815; fax: 325-387-6028; 8:30AM-4:30PM (CST). *Felony, Misdemeanor, Civil, Probate.*

General Information: No juvenile, mental, sealed, or adoption records released. Will fax documents to local or toll free line, after copy fee paid. Court makes copy: $1.00 per page. Self serve copy: same. Certification fee: $5.00 plus copy fee. Payee: Sutton County Clerk. Personal checks accepted, credit cards are not. Prepayment required. Mail requests: SASE required.

Civil Name Search: Access: Phone, mail, in person. Both court and visitors may perform in person name searches. Search fee: $10.00 per name. Civil records on computer back to 1992, index books prior. Mail turnaround time 2-4 days.

Criminal Name Search: Access: Mail, in person. Both court and visitors may perform in person name searches. Search fee: $10.00 per name. Criminal records computerized since 1995, index books prior to 1890. Mail turnaround time 2-4 days.

Swisher County

64th and 242nd District Court & County Court 119 S Maxwell, County Courthouse, Tulia, TX 79088; 806-995-4396; fax: 806-995-4121; 7:30AM-5:30PM M-Th, 8AM-4PM Fri (CST). *Felony, Misdemeanor, Civil, Probate.*

www.co.swisher.tx.us/ips/cms/districtcourt/districtClerk.html

General Information: Probate is a separate index at this same address. Probate fax is same as main fax number. Web address is only for 242nd District Court. The 64th District Court does not have a web page. No juvenile, mental, sealed, or adoption records released. Fee to fax out file $3.00 per page plus $1.00 ea add'l. Court makes copy: $1.00 per page. Self serve copy: $.50 per page. Certification fee: $1.00 per page. Payee: County/District Clerk. Personal checks accepted. Will accept credit cards for email or fax requests and at the counter. Prepayment required. Mail requests: SASE requested.

Civil Name Search: Access: Mail, fax, in person, email. Both court and visitors may perform in person name searches. Search fee: $5.00 per name. Civil records on computer since 1992, index books prior. Note: Direct email search requests to brenda.hudson@swisher-tx.net. Mail turnaround time 1 day. Only daily docket and monthly calendar for 242nd Court are online.

Criminal Name Search: Access: Mail, fax, in person, email. Both court and visitors may perform in person name searches. Search fee: $5.00 per name. Required to search: name, years to search, DOB and SSN. Criminal records on computer since 1992, index books prior to early 1900's. Note: Direct email search requests to brenda.hudson@swisher-tx.net. Mail turnaround time 1-2 days. Only daily docket and monthly calendar for 242nd Court are online.

Tarrant County

District Court 401 W Belknap, County District Clerk's Office, Fort Worth, TX 76196-0402; 817-884-1574 (884-1265 Family Division); criminal phone: 817-884-1342; civil phone: 817-884-1240; 8AM-5PM (CST). *Felony, Civil, Family.*

www.tarrantcounty.com/ecourts/site/default.asp

General Information: No juvenile, mental, sealed, or adoption records released. Will not fax documents. Court makes copy: $.35 per page. Certification fee: $1.00 per page. Payee: District Clerk. Business checks accepted. Major credit cards accepted. Prepayment required. Mail requests: SASE not required.

Civil Name Search: Access: Mail, in person, online. Both court and visitors may perform in person name searches. Search fee: $5.00 per name if the office does the search. Required to search: full name and DOB. Civil records on computer since 1989, file jackets prior to 1989; records go back to 1800s. Mail turnaround time 1-3 days. Civil PAT goes back to 1975. Access to the remote online system requires a $50 setup fee and $35.00 monthly with add'l month prepaid; for 1 to 5 users; fees increase with more users. Call 817-884-1345 for info and signup. Index records are available for free at http://cc.co.tarrant.tx.us/CivilCourts/ccl/default.asp.

Criminal Name Search: Access: Mail, online, in person. Both court and visitors may perform in person name searches. Search fee: $5.00 per name if the office does the search. Required to search: full name, years to search, DOB; also helpful: SSN. Criminal records computerized from 1975, microfilm since 1970, index books and case files since 1800s. Mail turnaround time 1-3 days. Criminal PAT goes back to same as civil. Access to the remote online system requires $50 setup fee and $35.00 monthly with add'l month prepaid; for 1 to 5 users; fees increase with more users. Call 817-884-1345 for info and signup. Index records are available for free at http://cc.co.tarrant.tx.us/CivilCourts/ccl/default.asp. Online results show middle initial, DOB, address.

County Court - Criminal 401 W Belknap, County Clerk's Office, Fort Worth, TX 76196-0402; 817-884-1195; criminal phone: 817-884-1066; fax: 817-884-3409; 7:30AM-4:30PM (CST). *Misdemeanor.*
www.tarrantcounty.com/ecourts/site/default.asp
General Information: Small Claims, Evictions, and low-level civil cases are handled by JP/Municipal Courts. No juvenile, mental, sealed, or adoption records released. Will not fax documents. Court makes copy: $1.00 per page. Certification fee: $5.00 per case plus copy fee. Payee: County Clerk. Only money orders or cashier's checks accepted. No credit cards accepted. Prepayment required. Mail requests: SASE required.
Criminal Name Search: Access: Mail, online, in person. Both court and visitors may perform in person name searches. Search fee: $5.00 per name. Required to search: name, years to search, DOB. Criminal records on computer back 25 years. Mail turnaround time 1-3 days. Public use terminal has crim records back to 25 years. Access to the remote online system requires $50 setup fee and $35.00 monthly with add'l month prepaid; this is for 1 to 5 users. Fees increase with more users. The District Court records are on this system also. Call 817-884-1345 for more information. Online results show middle initial, DOB, address.

Probate Court#1 100 W Weatherford St, Rm 260A, Fort Worth, TX 76196; 817-884-1200; probate phone: 817-884-1254; fax: 817-884-3178; 8AM-4:30PM (CST). *Probate.*
www.tarrantcounty.com/ecourts/site/default.asp
General Information: Search probate records by name or case number at http://cc.co.tarrant.tx.us/CivilCourts/Probate/default.asp or http://cc.co.tarrant.tx.us/CivilCourts/Probate/default.asp?eprobatecourtsNav=|

Taylor County

District Court 300 Oak St, #400, Abilene, TX 79602; 325-674-1316; 8AM-N, 1-5PM (CST). *Felony, Civil.*
www.taylorcountytexas.org/
General Information: No juvenile, mental, sealed, or adoption records released. Will not fax documents. Court makes copy: $1.00 per page. Certification fee: $1.00. Payee: Taylor County District Clerk. Business checks accepted. No credit cards accepted. Prepayment required. Mail requests: SASE required.
Civil Name Search: Access: Mail, in person, online. Both court and visitors may perform in person name searches. Search fee: $5.00 per name. Civil records on computer since 1994; prior records in index books to 1885. Mail turnaround time 5 days. Civil PAT goes back to 1994. Search Taylor County Case/Court records free online at http://69.39.36.76/default.aspx.
Criminal Name Search: Access: Mail, in person, online. Both court and visitors may perform in person name searches. Search fee: $5.00 per name. Required to search: name, years to search, DOB; also helpful: SSN. Criminal records on computer since 1982; prior records in index books to 1885. Mail turnaround time 5 days. Criminal PAT goes back to 1982. Search Taylor County Case/Court records free online at http://69.39.36.76/default.aspx.

County Court 300 Oak St, #100, Abilene, TX 79602; 325-674-1202; fax: 325-674-1279; 8AM-5PM (CST). *Misdemeanor, Civil, Probate.*
www.taylorcountytexas.org/county.html
General Information: Court will search both indexes for price of one, if requested. No juvenile, mental, sealed, or adoption records released. Fee to fax out file $1.00 per page; $2.00 per doc if faxed to a toll-free number. Court makes copy: $1.00 per page. Certification fee: $5.00 per doc. Payee: County Clerk. No personal checks accepted. Major credit cards accepted. Prepayment required. Mail requests: SASE required.
Civil Name Search: Access: Mail, in person, online. Both court and visitors may perform in person name searches. Search fee: $5.00 per name per 10 years searched. Probate searches are $5.00, years not applicable. Civil records on computer less than ten years, index books prior. Mail turnaround time 2-4 days. Civil PAT goes back to 1981. Public access terminal has probate back to 1888. Results include name and case number. Search Taylor County Case/Court records free online at http://69.39.36.76/default.aspx.
Criminal Name Search: Access: Mail, in person, online. Both court and visitors may perform in person name searches. Search fee: $5.00 per name per 10 years searched. Required to search: name, years to search, DOB; also helpful: address, SSN. Criminal records computerized from 1980; overall

records go back to 1949. Mail turnaround time 2-4 days. Criminal PAT goes back to same as civil. Search Taylor County Case/Court records free online at http://69.39.36.76/default.aspx.

Terrell County

District & County Court PO Drawer 410, Sanderson, TX 79848; 432-345-2391; fax: 432-345-2740; 9AM-N, 1-5PM (CST). *Felony, Misdemeanor, Civil, Probate.*
General Information: No juvenile, mental, sealed, or adoption records released. Will not fax documents. Court makes copy: $1.00 per page. Certification fee: $5.00. Payee: County Clerk. Personal checks accepted, credit cards are not. Prepayment required.
Civil Name Search: Access: Mail, in person. Both court and visitors may perform in person name searches. Search fee: $10.00 per name. Civil index in books. Note: All requests must be in writing. Mail turnaround time 2-4 days. Civil PAT goes back to 1994.
Criminal Name Search: Access: Mail, in person. Both court and visitors may perform in person name searches. Search fee: $10.00 per name. Criminal index in books. Note: All requests must be in writing. Mail turnaround time 2-4 days. Criminal PAT goes back to same as civil.

Terry County

District Court 500 W Main, Rm 209E, Brownfield, TX 79316; 806-637-4202; fax: 806-637-1333; 8:30AM-5PM (CST). *Felony, Civil.*
General Information: No juvenile, mental, sealed, or adoption records released. Will fax documents to local or toll free line. Court makes copy: $1.00 per page. Certification fee: $1.00 per document plus copy fee. Payee: District Clerk. Personal checks accepted. Major credit cards accepted. Prepayment required. Mail requests: SASE required.
Civil Name Search: Access: Mail, in person. Both court and visitors may perform in person name searches. Search fee: $5.00 per name. Civil records in index books and on computer. Mail turnaround time same day. Civil PAT goes back to 7 years.
Criminal Name Search: Access: Mail, in person. Both court and visitors may perform in person name searches. Search fee: $5.00 per name. Required to search: name, years to search, DOB; also helpful: SSN. Criminal docket on books and on computer. Mail turnaround time same day. Criminal PAT goes back to 7 years.

County Court 500 W Main, Rm 105, Brownfield, TX 79316-4398; 806-637-8551; fax: 806-637-4874; 8:30AM-5PM (CST). *Misdemeanor, Civil, Probate.*
General Information: No juvenile, mental, sealed, or adoption records released. Fee to fax out file $1.00 plus $1.00 per page. Court makes copy: $1.00 per page. Certification fee: $5.00. Payee: County Clerk. Personal checks accepted, credit cards are not. Prepayment required. Mail requests: SASE required.
Civil Name Search: Access: Mail, in person. Both court and visitors may perform in person name searches. Search fee: $10.00 per name. Civil records in index books to 1904, computerized since 1981. Mail turnaround time 2-3 days. Civil PAT goes back to 1994.
Criminal Name Search: Access: Mail, in person. Both court and visitors may perform in person name searches. Search fee: $10.00 per name. Required to search: name, years to search; also helpful: address, DOB, SSN. Criminal docket on books back to 1904, computerized since 1981. Mail turnaround time 1-2 days. Criminal PAT goes back to 1994.

Throckmorton County

District & County Court PO Box 309, Throckmorton, TX 76483; 940-849-2501; fax: 940-849-3032; 8AM-N, 1-4:30PM M,TH; 8AM-N F (CST). *Felony, Misdemeanor, Civil, Probate.*
General Information: No juvenile, mental, sealed, or adoption records released. Will fax documents $2.00 per page. Court makes copy: $1.00 per page. Self serve copy: same. Certification fee: $5.00. Payee: County/District Clerk. Personal checks accepted; $35.00 is charged if it is returned to court. No credit cards accepted. Prepayment required. Mail requests: SASE required.
Civil Name Search: Access: Mail, in person. Both court and visitors may perform in person name searches. Search fee: $10.00 per name. Civil records in index books; computerized records go back to 1990. Mail turnaround time 1 week. Civil PAT goes back to 1990.
Criminal Name Search: Access: Mail, in person. Both court and visitors may perform in person name searches. Search fee: $10.00 per name. Criminal index in books; computerized records go back to 1990. Mail turnaround time 2-4 days. Criminal PAT goes back to 1990.

Titus County

District Court 105 W 1st St, PO Box 492, Mount Pleasant, TX 75455; criminal phone: 903-577-6721; civil phone: 903-577-6720; fax: 903-577-6719; 8AM-5PM (CST). *Felony, Civil.*
www.co.titus.tx.us/district_clerk/district_clerk.htm

General Information: No juvenile, mental, sealed, or adoption records released. Will not fax documents. Court makes copy: $1.00 per page. Self serve copy: same. Certification fee: No charge. Payee: District Clerk. Personal checks accepted, credit cards are not. Prepayment required. Mail requests: SASE required.

Civil Name Search: Access: Phone, mail, in person. Both court and visitors may perform in person name searches. Search fee: $5.00 per name. Civil records in index books from 1895; computerized back to 1992. Mail turnaround time 2-3 days. Civil PAT goes back to 10 years. Results include name and case number.

Criminal Name Search: Access: Phone, mail, in person. Both court and visitors may perform in person name searches. Search fee: $5.00 per name. Criminal docket on books from 1895; computerized back to 1992. Mail turnaround time 2-3 days. Criminal PAT goes back to same as civil.

County Court 100 W 1st St, #204, Mount Pleasant, TX 75455; 903-577-6796; fax: 903-572-5078; 8AM-4:45PM (CST). *Misdemeanor, Civil, Probate.*

www.co.titus.tx.us/

General Information: No juvenile, mental, sealed, or adoption records released. Will not fax documents. Court makes copy: $1.00 per page. Self serve copy: same. Certification fee: $6.00. Payee: County Clerk. Business checks accepted. Major credit cards accepted. Prepayment required. Mail requests: SASE required.

Civil Name Search: Access: Mail, in person, online. Both court and visitors may perform in person name searches. Search fee: $10.00 per name. Required to search: name, years to search; also helpful: address. Civil records on computer since 1/1982, index books since 1895. Mail turnaround time 7-10 days. Civil PAT goes back to 1982. Access to court records from www.tituscountyonline.net/countyclerk/. Must be registered. Also gives vital record index. Also gives vital record index from home page, click on County Clerk then Index Search.

Criminal Name Search: Access: Mail, in person, online. Both court and visitors may perform in person name searches. Search fee: $10.00 per name. Required to search: name, years to search; also helpful: address, DOB, SSN. Criminal records on computer since 1/1996, index books since 1930. Mail turnaround time 1 week to 10 days. Criminal PAT goes back to 1996. Access to court records from www.tituscountyonline.net/countyclerk/. Must be registered.

Tom Green County

District Court County Courthouse, 112 W Beauregard, San Angelo, TX 76903; 325-659-6579; fax: 325-659-3241; 8AM-5PM (CST). *Felony, Civil.*

www.co.tom-green.tx.us/distclrk/

General Information: No juvenile, mental, sealed, or adoption records released. Fee to fax out file $1.50 per page. Court makes copy: $1.00 per page. Self serve copy: $.25 per page. No certification fee. Payee: District Clerk. Business checks accepted. Visa/MC accepted. Prepayment required. Mail requests: SASE required.

Civil Name Search: Access: Mail, in person, online. Both court and visitors may perform in person name searches. Search fee: $5.00 per name per 5 years searched. Required to search: name, years to search; also helpful. Civil records in index books from 1900s; on computer back to 1993. Mail turnaround time 1 week. Civil PAT goes back to 1994. Online access to civil case records back to 1994 is online at http://odysseypa.co.tom-green.tx.us/. Search by name, case number. Also, online case access back to 4/4/1992 at www.idocket.com; registration and password required.

Criminal Name Search: Access: Mail, in person, online. Both court and visitors may perform in person name searches. Search fee: $5.00 per name per 5 years searched. Required to search: name, years to search, DOB. Criminal docket on books from 1900s; on computer back to 1993. Mail turnaround time 1 week. Criminal PAT goes back to same as civil. Online access to criminal case records back to 1994 at http://odysseypa.co.tom-green.tx.us/. Search by name, case number. Also, online felony case access back to 10/1/1991 at www.idocket.com; registration and password required.

County Court 124 W Beauregard, San Angelo, TX 76903; 325-659-6551; criminal phone: 325-659-6555; civil phone: 325-659-6554; fax: 325-659-3251; 7:45AM-4:30PM (CST). *Misdemeanor, Civil, Probate.*

http://justice.co.tom-green.tx.us

General Information: No juvenile, mental, sealed, or adoption records released. Will fax documents to local or toll free line. Court makes copy: $1.00 per page. Self serve copy: same. Certification fee: $5.00. Payee: County Clerk. Only local personal checks accepted for record searching. Major credit cards accepted. Prepayment required. Certified payments may be made online. Mail requests: SASE required.

Civil Name Search: Access: Mail, in person, online. Both court and visitors may perform in person name searches. Search fee: $5.00 per name. Required to search: name, years to search; also helpful: address. Civil records

on computer from 1994, index books prior. Mail turnaround time same day. Civil PAT goes back to 1994. Online access to civil records is free at http://odysseypa.co.tom-green.tx.us/default.aspx.

Criminal Name Search: Access: Mail, in person, online. Both court and visitors may perform in person name searches. Search fee: $5.00 per name. Required to search: name, years to search, DOB; also helpful: address, SSN. Criminal records on computer since 1994, index books prior. Mail turnaround time same day. Criminal PAT goes back to same as civil. Online access to criminal records is the same as civil. Website also includes sheriff's jail and bond records.

Travis County

District & County Courts Blackwell-Thurman Criminal Justice Center, 509 W. 11th St, Austin, TX 78701; 512-854-9244; fax: 512-854-4464; 8AM-5PM (CST). *Felony, Misdemeanor.*

General Information: The Criminal Courts of Travis County consist of seven District Courts, six County Courts at Law, and one Drug Court that hear criminal cases in Travis County. No juvenile, mental, sealed, or adoption records released (all felony cases are public record). Will not fax documents. Court makes copy: $1.00 per page. Self serve copy: $.20 per page. Certification fee: $5.00 per document. Payee: District Clerk. Personal checks accepted. VISA, MC, Amex, Discover cards accepted, there is a surcharge of $3.00 or 3%, which ever is greater. Prepayment required. Mail requests: SASE required.

Criminal Name Search: Access: Fax, mail, in person, online. Both court and visitors may perform in person name searches. Search fee: $5.00; $10.00 if prior to 1981. Required to search: name, years to search, DOB. Felony records on computer since 1988, index books prior to 1988; misdemeanor records on computer since 1981; prior records on microfilm to 1845. Mail turnaround time 2-3 days, usually. Public use terminal has crim records back to 1988. Online case access is through www.idocket.com; registration and password required. Records date back to 11/01/2004. One free name search permitted a day, otherwise subscription required. Current docket information is available at www.co.travis.tx.us/courts/files/dockets/dockets_criminal.asp.

District & County Courts 1000 Guadalupe St, Heman Marion Sweatt Travis County Courthouse, Austin, TX 78701; 512-854-2484; fax: 512-854-9174; 8AM-5PM (CST). *Civil, Probate.*

www.co.travis.tx.us/courts/civil/default.asp

General Information: The Travis County Civil Court system is comprised of ten District Courts, three Associate Courts and two County Courts at Law. No juvenile, mental, sealed, or adoption records released. Will fax documents $1.00 per page. Court makes copy: $.50 per page. Self serve copy: $.25 per page. Certification fee: $1.00 per cert plus $1.00 per page. Payee: Travis County Clerk. Personal checks accepted. Major credit cards accepted. Prepayment required. Mail requests: SASE not required.

Civil Name Search: Access: Phone, mail, in person, online. Both court and visitors may perform in person name searches. Search fee: $5.00 per name per 10 years, $1.00 each additional year. Civil records on computer since 6/86, microfilm 1845 to 1986, probate from 1/1992 forward. Mail turnaround time 2-5 days. Civil PAT goes back to 6/1986. Current docket information is available at www.co.travis.tx.us/courts/files/dockets/dockets_Civil.asp. Online case access is through www.idocket.com; registration and password required. Records date back to 12/01/2005 for civil and family law. One free name search permitted a day, otherwise subscription required.

Trinity County

District Court PO Box 549, Groveton, TX 75845; 936-642-1118; fax: 936-642-0002; 8:30AM-N, 1PM-4:30PM (CST). *Felony, Civil.*

General Information: No juvenile, mental, sealed, or adoption records released. Will not fax documents. Court makes copy: $1.00 per page. Self serve copy: same. Certification fee: $1.00 per page. Payee: District Clerk. Personal checks accepted. Prepayment required.

Civil Name Search: Access: Mail, in person. Both court and visitors may perform in person name searches. Search fee: $5.00 per name. Civil records on computer since 1980, index books prior. Mail turnaround time 1 day.

Criminal Name Search: Access: Mail, in person. Both court and visitors may perform in person name searches. Search fee: $5.00 per name. Criminal records on computer since 1980, index books prior. Mail turnaround time 1 day.

County Court PO Box 456, 109 S Main St, Groveton, TX 75845; 936-642-1208; fax: 936-642-3004; 8AM-5PM (CST). *Misdemeanor, Civil, Probate.*

www.co.trinity.tx.us/ips/cms/County_Court/

General Information: Probate fax is same as main fax number. No juvenile, mental, sealed, or adoption records released. Fee to fax out file $2.00 per page; $5.00 if large amount. Court makes copy: $1.00 per page. Self serve copy: same. Certification fee: $5.00 1st page, $1.00 each add'l.

Payee: County Clerk. Personal checks accepted, credit cards are not. Prepayment required. Mail requests: SASE required.

Civil Name Search: Access: Mail, in person, online. Both court and visitors may perform in person name searches. Search fee: $10.00 per name. Required to search: name, years to search; also helpful: address. Civil index in docket books from 1982. Date of birth helpful for searching. Mail turnaround time 1 day. Online case access is through www.idocket.com; registration and password required. One free name search permitted a day, otherwise subscription required.

Criminal Name Search: Access: Mail, in person, online. Both court and visitors may perform in person name searches. Search fee: $5.00 per name. Required to search: name, years to search, SSN; also helpful: address, DOB, sex. Criminal docket on books back to 1982. Mail turnaround time 1 day. Online case access is through www.idocket.com; registration and password required. One free name search permitted a day, otherwise subscription required.

Tyler County

District Court 203 Courthouse, 100 W Bluff, Woodville, TX 75979; 409-283-2162; 8AM-N, 1-4:30PM (CST). *Felony, Civil.*

General Information: No juvenile, mental, sealed, or adoption records released. Will not fax documents. Court makes copy: $1.00 per page. Self serve copy: same. No certification fee. Payee: District Clerk. Business checks accepted. No credit cards accepted. Prepayment required. Mail requests: SASE required.

Civil Name Search: Access: Mail, in person. Both court and visitors may perform in person name searches. Search fee: $5.00 per name. Civil index in books. Mail turnaround time same day.

Criminal Name Search: Access: Mail, in person. Both court and visitors may perform in person name searches. Search fee: $5.00. Criminal index in books. Mail turnaround time same day.

County Court County Courthouse, 116 S Charlton, Woodville, TX 75979; 409-283-2281; fax: 409-283-8049; 8AM-4:30PM (CST). *Misdemeanor, Civil, Probate.*

General Information: No juvenile, mental, sealed or adoption records released. Will fax documents $3.00 per page. Court makes copy: $1.00 per page. Self serve copy: same. Certification fee: $5.00. Payee: County Clerk. Personal checks accepted, credit cards are not. Prepayment required. Mail requests: SASE not required.

Civil Name Search: Access: Phone, mail, in person. Both court and visitors may perform in person name searches. Search fee: $5.00 per name. Civil records on computer back to 1989, microfilm since 1973, index books from 1800s. Mail turnaround time 3-5 days. Civil PAT goes back to 1989.

Criminal Name Search: Access: Mail, in person. Both court and visitors may perform in person name searches. Search fee: $5.00 per name. Required to search: name, years to search; also helpful: address, DOB, SSN. Criminal records computerized from 1989, microfilm since 1973, index books from 1800s. Mail turnaround time 3-5 days. Criminal PAT goes back to same as civil.

Upshur County

District Court 405 N Titus, Gilmer, TX 75644; 903-843-5031; fax: 903-843-3540; 8AM-4:30PM M-TH; 8AM-4PM Fri (CST). *Felony, Civil, Probate.* www.countyofupshur.com

General Information: The County Clerk actually handles the Probate matters, call 903-843-4015. No juvenile, mental, sealed or adoption records released. Will not fax documents. Court makes copy: $1.00 per page. Certification fee: $1.00 per document plus copy fee. Payee: District Clerk. No personal checks or credit cards accepted. Prepayment required. Mail requests: SASE required.

Civil Name Search: Access: Mail, in person, online. Both court and visitors may perform in person name searches. Search fee: $5.00 per name. Civil records in index books to 1800s. Mail turnaround time same day. Civil PAT goes back to 1975. Results include name and case number. Access court records and hearings free at www.countyofupshur.com/judicialsearch/.

Criminal Name Search: Access: Mail, in person, online. Both court and visitors may perform in person name searches. Search fee: $5.00 per name. Criminal docket on books to 1800s. Note: Results include name and case number. Mail turnaround time same day. Criminal PAT goes back to 1992. Access court records and hearings free at www.countyofupshur.com/judicialsearch/.

County Court PO Box 730, Courthouse Sq, Hwy 154 West, Gilmer, TX 75644; 903-843-4015; fax: 903-843-5492; 8AM-4:30PM (CST). *Misdemeanor, Civil, Probate.* www.countyofupshur.com/

General Information: Online identifiers in results same as on public terminal. No juvenile, mental, sealed or adoption records released. Will fax documents $1.00 per page, prepaid. Court makes copy: $1.00 per page. Self serve copy: $1.00 per page. Certification fee: $5.00 per doc. Payee: County

Clerk. Personal checks accepted, credit cards are not. Prepayment required. Mail requests: SASE required.

Civil Name Search: Access: Mail, in person, online. Both court and visitors may perform in person name searches. Search fee: $5.00 per name per 10 year period. Civil records in index books to 1936; on computer 1993 to present. Mail turnaround time same day. Civil PAT goes back to 1993. Access court records and hearings free at www.countyofupshur.com/judicialsearch/.

Criminal Name Search: Access: Mail, in person, online. Both court and visitors may perform in person name searches. Search fee: $5.00 per name per 10 year period. Required to search: name, years to search, DOB, offense, signed release. Criminal docket on books to 1936; on computer 1993 to present. Mail turnaround time same day. Criminal PAT goes back to same as civil. Access court records and hearings free at www.countyofupshur.com/judicialsearch/. Online results show middle initial.

Upton County

District & County Court PO Box 465, Rankin, TX 79778; 432-693-2861; fax: 432-693-2129; 8AM-5PM (CST). *Felony, Misdemeanor, Civil, Probate.*

www.co.upton.tx.us

General Information: Probate fax is same as main fax number. No juvenile, mental, sealed, or adoption records released. Fee to fax out file $2.00 per page. Court makes copy: $1.00 per page. Certification fee: $5.00 per document. Payee: District/County Clerk. Personal checks accepted, credit cards are not. Prepayment required. Mail requests: SASE required.

Civil Name Search: Access: Fax, mail, in person. Both court and visitors may perform in person name searches. Search fee: $5.00 per name. Civil records on computer back to 1987; in index books to 1910. Mail turnaround time 1-2 days.

Criminal Name Search: Access: Fax, mail, in person. Both court and visitors may perform in person name searches. Search fee: $5.00 per name. Required to search: name, years to search, signed release; also helpful: address, DOB. Criminal records computerized from 1987; in index books to 1910. Mail turnaround time 1-2 days.

Uvalde County

District Court County Courthouse, #15, Uvalde, TX 78801; 830-278-3918; 8AM-5PM (CST). *Felony, Civil.* www.uvaldecounty.com/

General Information: No juvenile, mental, sealed, or adoption records released. Will not fax documents. Court makes copy: $.75 per page. Certification fee: $1.00 per page plus copy fee. Payee: District Clerk. No personal checks or credit cards accepted. Prepayment required. Mail requests: SASE required.

Civil Name Search: Access: Phone, mail, in person. Both court and visitors may perform in person name searches. Search fee: $5.00 per name. Civil index in books. Mail turnaround time 2-3 days.

Criminal Name Search: Access: Mail, in person. Both court and visitors may perform in person name searches. Search fee: $5.00 per name. Required to search: name, years to search, DOB, SSN. Criminal index in books. Mail turnaround time 2-3 days.

County Clerk PO Box 284, 100 Getty St, Uvalde, TX 78802; 830-278-6614; fax: 830-278-8692; 8AM-4:30PM (CST). *Misdemeanor, Civil, Probate.*

www.uvaldecounty.com/

General Information: No juvenile, mental, sealed, or adoption records released. Will not fax out documents. Court makes copy: $1.00 per page. Certification fee: $5.00 per page plus copy fee. Payee: Romana Esquivel Hobbs, Uvalde County Clerk. Personal checks accepted, credit cards are not. Prepayment required. Mail requests: SASE not required.

Civil Name Search: Access: Mail, in person. Both court and visitors may perform in person name searches. Search fee: $10.00 per name; 10 year search. Civil records in index books from 1856, computerized records from 1997. Mail turnaround time 1-2 days. Civil PAT goes back to 1997.

Criminal Name Search: Access: In person. Visitors must perform in person searches themselves. Required to search: name, years to search, DOB, SSN. Criminal docket on books from 1856, computerized records from 1997. Criminal PAT goes back to 6/1997.

Val Verde County

District Court PO Box 1544, 100 E Broadway, 1st Fl, Del Rio, TX 78841; 830-774-7538; criminal phone: 830-774-7539; fax: 830-774-7643; 8AM-4:30PM (CST). *Felony, Civil.*

www.valverdecounty.org/District_Clerk.html

General Information: No juvenile, mental, sealed, or adoption records released. Will not fax documents. Court makes copy: $.50 per page. Certification fee: $1.00 per page includes copy fee. Payee: District Clerk. Business and local checks accepted. No credit cards accepted. Prepayment required. Mail requests: SASE required.

Civil Name Search: Access: Mail, in person, online. Both court and visitors may perform in person name searches. Search fee: $5.00 per name. Civil records on computer since 1990, index books prior. Mail turnaround time 2-5 days. Civil PAT goes back to 1989. Public terminal results may contain DOB, SSN, address if included at time of filing. Access civil cases except probate at www.idocket.com; registration and password required. A fee service; only one free name search per day. Records go back to 12/31/89.

Criminal Name Search: Access: Mail, in person, online. Both court and visitors may perform in person name searches. Search fee: $5.00 per name. Criminal records on computer since 1990, index books prior. Mail turnaround time 2-5 days. Criminal PAT goes back to 1993. Public terminal criminal results may contain DOB, address and more. Access felonies at www.idocket.com; registration and password required. A fee service; only one free name search per day. Felonies go back to 12/31/93.

County Court PO Box 1267, 400 Pecan St, Del Rio, TX 78841-1267; 830-774-7564; fax: 830-774-7608; 8AM-N, 1-4:30PM (CST). *Misdemeanor, Civil, Probate.*
www.valverdecounty.org/

General Information: Municipal Court is responsible for the judicial enforcement of all Class C misdemeanors, i.e. traffic cases and ordinance violation cases which occur within the city of Del Rio. See www.cityofdelrio.com/index.aspx?nid=67. No juvenile, mental, sealed, or adoption records released. Will fax documents for fee $1.00 per page. Court makes copy: $1.00 per page. Self serve copy: same. Certification fee: $5.00 per doc plus copy fee. Payee: County Clerk. Personal checks accepted, credit cards are not. Prepayment required. Mail requests: SASE required.

Civil Name Search: Access: Mail, in person. Both court and visitors may perform in person name searches. Search fee: $10.00 per name. Civil index in docket books from 1885, computerized since 1999. Mail turnaround time 1-2 days.

Criminal Name Search: Access: Mail, in person. Both court and visitors may perform in person name searches. Search fee: $10.00 per name. Required to search: name, years to search; also helpful: address, DOB, SSN. Criminal index in books, computerized since 1999. Mail turnaround time 1-2 days.

Van Zandt County

District Court 121 E Dallas St, Rm 302, Canton, TX 75103; 903-567-6576; fax: 903-567-1283; 8AM-5PM (CST). *Felony, Civil.*
www.vanzandtcounty.org/ips/cms/districtcourt/

General Information: No juvenile, mental, sealed, or adoption records released. Will fax documents $1.00 per page. Court makes copy: $1.00 per page. Certification fee: $1.00. Payee: District Clerk. Personal checks accepted. Prepayment required. Mail requests: SASE required.

Civil Name Search: Access: Phone, fax, mail, in person. Both court and visitors may perform in person name searches. Search fee: $5.00 per name. Civil index in docket books from 1800s; on computer back to 1980. Mail turnaround time 2-4 days. Civil PAT goes back to 1980.

Criminal Name Search: Access: Mail, fax, in person. Both court and visitors may perform in person name searches. Search fee: $5.00 per name. Required to search: name, years to search, DOB. Criminal docket on books back to 1800s; on computer back to 1980. Mail turnaround time 2-4 days. Criminal PAT goes back to same as civil.

County Court 121 E Dallas St, #202, Canton, TX 75103; 903-567-6503; fax: 903-567-6722; 8AM-4:30PM (CST). *Misdemeanor, Civil, Probate.*
www.vanzandtcounty.org/ips/cms/countyoffices/countyClerk.html

General Information: Probate fax is same as main fax number. No juvenile, mental, sealed, or adoption records released. Fee to fax out file $3.00 each plus $1 per page. Court makes copy: $1.00 per page. Certification fee: $6.00 1st page; $2.00 each add'l. Payee: County Clerk. Personal checks accepted. Major credit cards and debit cards accepted. Prepayment required. Mail requests: SASE not required.

Civil Name Search: Access: Mail, in person. Both court and visitors may perform in person name searches. Search fee: $5.00 per name. Civil records on computer back to 1993. Mail turnaround time 2-4 days. Civil PAT available.

Criminal Name Search: Access: Mail, in person. Both court and visitors may perform in person name searches. Search fee: $5.00 per name. Required to search: name, years to search; also helpful: address, DOB, SSN. Criminal records computerized from 1987. Mail turnaround time 2-4 days. Criminal PAT available.

Victoria County

District Court PO Box 2238, 115 N. Bridge St, 3rd Fl, Victoria, TX 77902; 361-575-0581; fax: 361-572-5682; 8AM-5PM (CST). *Felony, Civil.*
www.vctx.org/

General Information: Online identifiers in results same as on public terminal. No juvenile, mental, sealed, or adoption records released. No fee for local fax; Long distance fax fee $5.00 plus $1.00 per pg. Court makes copy: $1.00 per page. Certification fee: $1.00 per document plus copy fee. Payee: District Clerk. Personal checks accepted, credit cards are not. Prepayment required. Mail requests: SASE required.

Civil Name Search: Access: Mail, in person, online. Both court and visitors may perform in person name searches. Search fee: $5.00 per name. Civil records on computer since 1838. Mail turnaround time 1-2 days. Civil PAT goes back to 1838. Terminal index also includes other branch courts. Online index and images at www.idocket.com; registration and password required. Records go back to 12/31/1993. One free name search permitted a day, otherwise subscription required. Images available.

Criminal Name Search: Access: Mail, in person, online. Both court and visitors may perform in person name searches. Search fee: $5.00 per name. Required to search: name, years to search, DOB. Criminal records on computer since 1838. Note: Civil online results include middle initial, criminal online results include DOB, SSN, middle initial. Mail turnaround time 1-2 days. Criminal PAT goes back to same as civil. Terminal index also includes other branch courts. Terminal results include SSN. Access felony index and images at www.idocket.com; registration and password required. Records go back to 12/31/1993. One free name search permitted a day, otherwise subscription required.

County Court 115 N Bridge, Rm 110, Victoria, TX 77901; 361-575-1478; fax: 361-575-6276; 8AM-5PM (CST). *Misdemeanor, Civil, Probate.*
www.vctx.org

General Information: Probate fax is same as main fax number. No juvenile, mental, sealed, birth, death or adoption records released. Will fax documents $3.50 each or $3.50 plus $1.50 per page to non-toll-free number. Court makes copy: $1.00 per page. Self serve copy: same. Certification fee: $5.00 per document plus copy fee; $15.00 if exemplified. Payee: Victoria County Clerk. Personal checks, Visa/MC accepted. Prepayment required. Mail requests: SASE required.

Civil Name Search: Access: Phone, mail, in person, online. Both court and visitors may perform in person name searches. Search fee: $10.00 per name. Civil records on Cox index back to 1838; on computer back to 1991. Mail turnaround time 1 day. Civil PAT goes back to 1991. Results include case type. Online case access at www.idocket.com; registration and password required. Civil records go back to 12/31/1991; probate to 6/31//1991. One free name search permitted a day, otherwise subscription required.

Criminal Name Search: Access: Phone, fax, mail, in person, online. Both court and visitors may perform in person name searches. Search fee: $10.00 per name. Required to search: name, years to search; also helpful: address, DOB, SSN. Criminal records on Cox index back to 1838; on computer back to 1989. Mail turnaround time 1 day. Criminal PAT goes back to 1989. Results include case type. Access Misd. cases online at www.idocket.com; registration and password required. Records go back to 12/31/1989. One free name search permitted a day, otherwise subscription required. Online results show name only.

Walker County

District Court 1100 University Ave, Rm 209, Huntsville, TX 77340; 936-436-4972; fax: 936-436-4973; 8AM-N, 1-5PM, Fri til 4:45PM (CST). *Felony, Civil.*
www.co.walker.tx.us/department/?fDD=9-0

General Information: No juvenile, mental, sealed, abortion or adoption records released. Will fax documents to local or toll free line. Court makes copy: $1.00 per page. No certification fee. Payee: District Clerk. Business checks accepted. No credit cards accepted. Prepayment required. Mail requests: SASE required.

Civil Name Search: Access: Mail, in person. Both court and visitors may perform in person name searches. Search fee: $5.00 per name. Civil index on docket books. Mail turnaround time 1-2 days.

Criminal Name Search: Access: Mail, in person. Both court and visitors may perform in person name searches. Search fee: $5.00 per name. Criminal records indexed in books. Mail turnaround time 1-2 days.

County Court PO Box 210, Huntsville, TX 77342-0210; 936-436-4922; criminal fax: 936-436-4962; civil fax: 8AM-4:45PM; 8AM-4:45PM (CST). *Misdemeanor, Civil, Probate.*
www.co.walker.tx.us/department/index.php?fDD=5-0

General Information: Civil and Probate fax- 936-436-4928 No juvenile, mental, sealed, or adoption records released. Will not fax documents. Court makes copy: $1.00 per page. Certification fee: $5.00 per document plus copy fee. Payee: County Clerk. Personal checks accepted. Major credit cards accepted. Prepayment required. Mail requests: SASE required.

Civil Name Search: Access: Mail, in person. Both court and visitors may perform in person name searches. Search fee: $5.00 per name. Civil index in books. Note: This office will not search probate records. Mail turnaround time 3-5 days.

Criminal Name Search: Access: Mail, in person. Both court and visitors may perform in person name searches. Search fee: $5.00 per name. Required to search: name, years to search; also helpful: address, DOB, SSN. Criminal docket on books to 1977, computerized since 1998. Mail turnaround time 3-5 days. Public use terminal has crim records back to 1991; records back to 9/1977 being added.

Waller County

District Court 836 Austin St, Rm 318, Hempstead, TX 77445; 979-826-7735; fax: 979-826-7738; 8AM-N, 1-5PM (CST). *Felony, Civil.*
http://ww2.co.waller.tx.us/district_clerk.html
General Information: No juvenile, mental, sealed, or adoption records released. Will not fax documents. Court makes copy: $1.00 per page. Certification fee: $1.00. Payee: District Clerk. Personal checks accepted, credit cards are not. Prepayment required. Mail requests: SASE required.
Civil Name Search: Access: Mail, in person, online. Both court and visitors may perform in person name searches. Search fee: $5.00 per name. Required to search: name, years to search, DOB, SSN. Civil records on index books to 1866, computerized in 2000. Mail turnaround time 2 days. Civil PAT goes back to 01/2000. Online case access at www.idocket.com; registration and password required. Civil records (no probate) go back to 01/01/2000. One free name search permitted a day, otherwise subscription required.
Criminal Name Search: Access: Mail, in person. Both court and visitors may perform in person name searches. Search fee: $5.00 per name. Required to search: name, years to search, DOB. Criminal records on computer since 01/98, archived to early 1900s. Mail turnaround time 2 days. Criminal PAT goes back to 1/1998. Online case access at www.idocket.com; registration and password required. Felony records (no misdemeanor) go back to 01/01/1998. One free name search permitted a day, otherwise subscription required.

County Court 836 Austin St, Rm 217, Hempstead, TX 77445; 979-826-7711; fax: 979-826-7771; 8AM-5PM (CST). *Misdemeanor, Civil, Probate.*
General Information: No juvenile, mental, sealed, or adoption records released. Court makes copy: $1.00 per page. Certification fee: $5.00. Payee: Waller County Clerk. No personal checks accepted for copies. No credit cards accepted. Prepayment required. Mail requests: SASE required.
Civil Name Search: Access: Mail, in person. Both court and visitors may perform in person name searches. Search fee: $5.00 per name. Civil records in index books; on computer back to 1994. Mail turnaround time same day if possible. Civil PAT goes back to 1994.
Criminal Name Search: Access: Mail, in person. Both court and visitors may perform in person name searches. Search fee: $5.00 per name. Required to search: name, years to search, signed release; also helpful: DOB, SSN. Criminal index in books; on computer back to 1994. Mail turnaround time 2-3 days. Criminal PAT goes back to same as civil.

Ward County

District Court PO Box 440, Monahans, TX 79756; 432-943-2751; fax: 432-943-3810; 8AM-N-1-5PM (CST). *Felony, Civil.*
General Information: No juvenile, mental, sealed, or adoption records released. Will fax documents $2.00 per page, if prepaid. Court makes copy: $.50 per page. Certification fee: $1.00 per page; Exemplification fee- $5.00. Payee: District Clerk. Business checks accepted. No credit cards accepted. Prepayment required. Mail requests: SASE required.
Civil Name Search: Access: Mail, in person. Both court and visitors may perform in person name searches. Search fee: $5.00 per name. Civil records on computer since 1980, index books prior. Mail turnaround time 1-2 days.
Criminal Name Search: Access: Mail, in person. Both court and visitors may perform in person name searches. Search fee: $5.00 per name. Criminal docket on books, computerized since 1980. Mail turnaround time 1-2 days.

County Court 400 S Allen, #101, c/o Ward County Clerk, Monahans, TX 79756; 432-943-3294; fax: 432-943-6054; 8AM-5PM (CST). *Misdemeanor, Civil, Probate.*
General Information: No juvenile, mental, sealed, or adoption records released. Fee to fax out file $3.00 per page, prepaid. Court makes copy: $1.00 per page. Certification fee: $5.00. Payee: County Clerk. No personal checks or credit cards accepted. Prepayment required. Mail requests: SASE required.
Civil Name Search: Access: Mail, in person. Both court and visitors may perform in person name searches. Search fee: $5.00 per name. Civil records in index books; computerized records go back 10 years. Note: In person requests must be accompanied by written request. Mail turnaround time 1-2 days.
Criminal Name Search: Access: Mail, in person. Both court and visitors may perform in person name searches. Search fee: $5.00 per name. Required to search: name, years to search, DOB, signed release; also helpful: address, SSN. Criminal index in books; computerized records go back 10

years. Note: In person requests must be accompanied by a written request. Mail turnaround time 1-2 days.

Washington County

District Court 100 E Main, #304, Brenham, TX 77833-3753; 979-277-6200; 8AM-5PM (CST). *Felony, Civil.*
General Information: No juvenile, sealed, or adoption records released. Court makes copy: $.50 per page. Self serve copy: same. Certification fee: $1.00 per page. Payee: District Clerk. Personal checks accepted, credit cards are not. Prepayment required. Mail requests: SASE not required.
Civil Name Search: Access: Mail, in person, online. Both court and visitors may perform in person name searches. Search fee: $5.00 per name. Civil records in index books since 1800s; on computer back to 1988. Mail turnaround time 3-5 days. Civil PAT goes back to 1988. Online case access at www.idocket.com. Dockets from 12/30/1988. One search a day is free; subscription required for more.
Criminal Name Search: Access: Mail, in person, online. Both court and visitors may perform in person name searches. Search fee: $5.00 per name. Required to search: name, years to search; also helpful: DOB. Criminal docket on books from 1800s; on computer back to 1988. Mail turnaround time 3-5 days. Criminal PAT goes back to same as civil. Access felony cases at www.idocket.com. Dockets from 12/30/1988. One search a day is free; subscription required for more.

County Court 100 E Main, #102, Brenham, TX 77833; 979-277-6200; fax: 979-277-6278; 8AM-5PM (CST). *Misdemeanor, Civil, Probate.*
General Information: No juvenile, mental, sealed, or adoption records released. Fee to fax out file $1.00 per page prepaid. Court makes copy: $1.00 per page. Certification fee: $5.00 per instrument. Payee: Washington County Clerk. Personal checks accepted. Visa/MC/AmEx accepted. Prepayment required. Mail requests: SASE required.
Civil Name Search: Access: Mail, in person, online. Both court and visitors may perform in person name searches. Search fee: $5.00 per name. Civil records in index books from 1868; computerized back to 1985. Note: In person request must be accompanied by a written request. Mail turnaround time 1-2 days. Civil PAT goes back to 1985. Online case access at www.idocket.com; registration and password required. Civil records go back to 12/31/85; probate to 12/31/68. One free name search permitted a day, otherwise subscription required.
Criminal Name Search: Access: Mail, in person, online. Both court and visitors may perform in person name searches. Search fee: $5.00 per name. Required to search: name, years to search; also helpful: address, DOB. Criminal docket on books from 1870; computerized back to 1992. Note: In person request must be accompanied by a written request. Mail turnaround time 1-2 days. Criminal PAT goes back to 1990. Access Misd. cases at www.idocket.com; registration and password required. Misdemeanor records back to 12/31/1985. One free name search permitted a day, otherwise subscription required. Online results show middle initial, DOB.

Webb County

District Court PO Box 667, 1110 Victoria #203, Laredo, TX 78042-0667; 956-523-4268; fax: 956-523-5063; 8AM-5PM (CST). *Felony, Civil.*
www.webbcountytx.gov
General Information: Add'l fax number- 956-523-5121. No juvenile, mental, sealed, or adoption records released. Will fax documents $5.00 plus add'l $1.00 per page. Court makes copy: $1.00 per page. Certification fee: $1.00 per page includes copy fee. Payee: District Clerk. Personal checks accepted, credit cards are not. Prepayment required. Mail requests: SASE required.
Civil Name Search: Access: Phone, mail, fax, in person, online. Both court and visitors may perform in person name searches. Search fee: $5.00 per name. Required to search: name, years to search, address; also helpful: DOB, SSN. Civil records on computer back to 11//1/1988, index books prior. Mail turnaround time 1 week. Civil PAT goes back to 1988. Online case access at www.idocket.com; registration and password required. Civil records (no probate) go back to 12/31/1988. One free name search permitted a day, otherwise subscription required.
Criminal Name Search: Access: Mail, fax, in person, online. Both court and visitors may perform in person name searches. Search fee: $5.00 per name. Required to search: name, years to search, DOB or SSN, signed release. Criminal records computerized from 11/1/1988, index books prior. Mail turnaround time 1 week. Criminal PAT goes back to same as civil. Results may show DL and partial SSN. Online felony cases at www.idocket.com; registration and password required. Felonies go back to 12/31/1988. One free name search permitted a day, otherwise subscription required.

The Guide to County Court Records

County Court 1110 Victoria, #201, Laredo, TX 78040; 956-523-4266; criminal phone: 956-523-4261; civil phone: 956-523-4259; probate phone: 956-523-4257; fax: 956-523-5035; 8AM-5PM (CST). *Misdemeanor, Civil under $5,000, Probate.*
www.webbcountytx.gov/
General Information: Court does not have public access terminal but staff will assist you with searches on their computers. Any records before 1975 can be found at the District Clerk's Office. No juvenile, mental, sealed, or adoption records released. Will fax documents $4.00 1st page; $.50 each add'l page; half that fee per page for incoming faxes. Court makes copy: $1.00 per page. Self serve copy: same. Certification fee: $5.00. Payee: County Clerk. Personal checks accepted, credit cards are not. Prepayment required. Mail requests: SASE required.
Civil Name Search: Access: Mail, in person. Both court and visitors may perform in person name searches. Search fee: $10.00 per name. Civil records on computer since 1988, index books prior to 1800s. Mail turnaround time 2-3 days. Civil PAT goes back to 1989.
Criminal Name Search: Access: Mail, in person, online. Both court and visitors may perform in person name searches. Search fee: $10.00 per name. Required to search: name, years to search, DOB; also helpful: address, SSN. Criminal records on computer since 1975, index books prior to 10/75. Mail turnaround time 2-3 days. Criminal PAT goes back to 1989. The online search is for traffic warrants only. See www.webbcountytx.gov/warrant-lookup/Search.aspx.

Wharton County

District Court PO Drawer 391, Wharton, TX 77488; 979-532-5542; fax: 979-532-1299; 8AM-N, 1-4:30PM (CST). *Felony, Civil.*
www.329th.com/
General Information: No juvenile, mental, or adoption records released. Will fax documents $5.00 plus add'l $1.00 per page. Court makes copy: $1.00 per page. Self serve copy: $1.00 per page. Certification fee: $2.00 per document plus copy fee. Payee: District Clerk of Wharton. Personal checks accepted, credit cards are not. Prepayment required. Mail requests: SASE required.
Civil Name Search: Access: Mail, fax, in person. Both court and visitors may perform in person name searches. Search fee: $5.00 per name. Civil records on computer since 1989, index books prior to 1848. Mail turnaround time same day. Civil PAT goes back to 1989.
Criminal Name Search: Access: Mail, fax, in person. Both court and visitors may perform in person name searches. Search fee: $5.00 per name. Criminal records on computer since 1989, index books prior to 1932. Mail turnaround time same day. Criminal PAT goes back to 1989. DL may also appear on terminal.

County Court PO Box 69, Wharton, TX 77488; 979-532-2381; fax: 979-532-8426; 8AM-5PM (CST). *Misdemeanor, Civil, Probate.*
General Information: No juvenile, mental, sealed, or adoption records released. Fee to fax out file $2.00 plus $1.00 per page, prepaid. Court makes copy: $1.00 per page. Self serve copy: same. Certification fee: $5.00 plus copy fee. Payee: County Clerk. Business checks accepted; personal checks accepted only if local resident with ID. No credit cards accepted. Prepayment required. Mail requests: SASE required.
Civil Name Search: Access: Mail, in person, online. Both court and visitors may perform in person name searches. Search fee: $5.00 per name per 10 years searched. Civil records on computer since 1991, index books since 1978, prior indexes in storage back to 1893. Mail turnaround time 1-2 days. Civil PAT goes back to 1991. Access case records including probate at www.idocket.com; registration and password required. A fee service; only one free name search per day.
Criminal Name Search: Access: Mail, in person, online. Both court and visitors may perform in person name searches. Search fee: $5.00 per name per 10 years searched. Required to search: name, years to search, DOB, signed release; also helpful: address, SSN, copy of ID. Criminal records on computer since 1991, index books since 1978, prior indexes in storage to 1893. Mail turnaround time 1-2 days. Criminal PAT goes back to 1991. Cases older than 2005 do not include the DOB, only 2005 and later. Terminal results may include DL#. Online access same as civil.

Wheeler County

District Court PO Box 528, Wheeler, TX 79096; 806-826-5931; fax: 806-826-5503; 8AM-5PM (CST). *Felony, Civil.*
General Information: No juvenile, mental, sealed, or adoption records released. Will fax documents $2.00 per page. Court makes copy: $1.00 per page. Self serve copy: same. Certification fee: $1.00. Payee: District Clerk. Personal checks accepted. Prepayment required. Mail requests: SASE not required.
Civil Name Search: Access: Phone, mail, in person. Both court and visitors may perform in person name searches. Search fee: $5.00 per name. Civil index in books. Mail turnaround time 2-3 days.

Criminal Name Search: Access: Phone, mail, in person. Both court and visitors may perform in person name searches. Search fee: $5.00 per name. Criminal index in books. Mail turnaround time 2-3 days.

County Court PO Box 465, 401 Main St, Wheeler, TX 79096; 806-826-5544; fax: 806-826-3282; 8AM-5PM (CST). *Misdemeanor, Civil, Probate.*
General Information: No juvenile, mental, sealed, or adoption records released. Will fax documents $2.00 per page. Court makes copy: $1.00 per page. Certification fee: $5.00 per doc plus copy fee. Payee: Wheeler County Clerk. Business checks accepted. No credit cards accepted. Prepayment required. Mail requests: SASE required.
Civil Name Search: Access: Mail, in person. Both court and visitors may perform in person name searches. Search fee: $10.00 per name. Civil index in docket books from 1800s. Mail turnaround time 1 day.
Criminal Name Search: Access: Mail, in person. Both court and visitors may perform in person name searches. Search fee: $10.00 per name. Required to search: name, years to search; also helpful: DOB, SSN. Criminal index in books. Mail turnaround time 1 day.

Wichita County

District Court 900 7th St, #303, Wichita Falls, TX 76301; criminal phone: 940-766-8187; civil phone: 940-766-8190; 8AM-5PM (CST). *Felony, Civil.*
www.co.wichita.tx.us/district_clerk.htm
General Information: No juvenile, mental, sealed, or adoption records released. Will not fax documents. Court makes copy: $1.00 per page. Self serve copy: same. Certification fee: $1.00, $500 for exemplification. Payee: District Clerk. Personal checks accepted, credit cards are not. Prepayment required. Mail requests: SASE required.
Civil Name Search: Access: Phone, mail, in person. Both court and visitors may perform in person name searches. Search fee: $5.00 per name. Civil records on computer since 1800s. Note: Phone searches must be prepaid. Mail turnaround time 2-3 days. Civil PAT goes back to 1800s.
Criminal Name Search: Access: Phone, mail, in person. Both court and visitors may perform in person name searches. Search fee: $5.00 per name. Criminal records on computer since 1800s, some older record dockets are computerized. Note: Phone searches must be prepaid. Mail turnaround time 2-3 days. Criminal PAT goes back to same as civil.

County Court PO Box 1679, Wichita Falls, TX 76307; criminal phone: 940-766-8173; probate phone: 940-766-8172; fax: 940-716-8554; 8AM-5PM (CST). *Misdemeanor, Probate.*
General Information: No juvenile, mental, sealed, or adoption records released. Mental can be released with an order from the judge. Will fax to toll-free numbers only. Court makes copy: $1.00 per page. Self serve copy: same. Certification fee: $5.00 per document. Payee: Wichita County Clerk. No personal checks or credit cards accepted. Prepayment required. Mail requests: SASE required.
Criminal Name Search: Access: Phone, mail, in person. Both court and visitors may perform in person name searches. Search fee: $10.00 per name searched. Required to search: name, years to search; also helpful: DOB, SSN. Criminal records on computer or printed index from 1980 to present. Mail turnaround time 1 week or less. Public use terminal has crim records back to 1980. Terminal results sometimes include.

Wilbarger County

District Court 1700 Wilbarger, Rm 33, Vernon, TX 76384; 940-553-3411; fax: 940-553-2316; 8AM-5PM (CST). *Felony, Civil.*
www.co.wilbarger.tx.us/DistrictClerk2.htm
General Information: No juvenile, mental, sealed, or adoption records released. Will return results by fax or phone if an 800 number is provided. Will fax documents to toll-free number. Court makes copy: $1.00 per page. Self serve copy: same. Certification fee: $5.00 per document. Payee: District Clerk. Business checks accepted. No credit cards accepted. Prepayment required. Mail requests: SASE required.
Civil Name Search: Access: Mail, in person. Both court and visitors may perform in person name searches. Search fee: $5.00 per name. Civil records go back to 1800s; computerized records go back 10 years. Mail turnaround time 2-3 days.
Criminal Name Search: Access: Mail, in person. Both court and visitors may perform in person name searches. Search fee: $5.00 per name. Required to search: name, years to search, DOB. Criminal records go back to 1800s; computerized records go back 10 years. Mail turnaround time 2-3 days.

County Court 1700 Wilbarger, Rm 15, Vernon, TX 76384; 940-552-5486; fax: 940-553-1202; 8AM-5PM (CST). *Misdemeanor, Civil, Probate.*

General Information: Probate is a separate index at this same address. No juvenile, mental, sealed, or adoption records released. Fee to fax out file is $5.00 plus $1.00 per page. Court makes copy: $1.00 per page. Self serve copy: same. Certification fee: $5.00 per document plus copy fee. Payee: County Clerk. Personal checks accepted, credit cards are not. Prepayment required. Mail requests: SASE not required.

Civil Name Search: Access: Mail, in person. Both court and visitors may perform in person name searches. Search fee: $5.00 per 7 year search. Civil cases indexed by Plaintiff. Civil records go back to 1887; no computerized records. Mail turnaround time same day.

Criminal Name Search: Access: Mail, in person. Both court and visitors may perform in person name searches. Search fee: $5.00 per 7 year search. Required to search: name, years to search; also helpful: address, DOB, SSN. Criminal records go back to 1887; computerized records go back to 1999. Mail turnaround time same day.

Willacy County

District Court County Courthouse, Raymondville, TX 78580; 956-689-2532; fax: 956-689-5713; 8AM-5PM (CST). *Felony, Civil.*

General Information: No juvenile, mental, sealed, or adoption records released. Will fax documents $2.00 per page. Court makes copy: $1.00 per page. Self serve copy: same. No certification fee. Payee: District Clerk. Personal checks accepted, credit cards are not. Prepayment required. Mail requests: SASE required.

Civil Name Search: Access: Mail, in person, phone, online. Both court and visitors may perform in person name searches. Search fee: $5.00 per name. Civil index in books. Mail turnaround time 2-3 days. Civil PAT goes back to 1990. Access cases back to 01/01/1990 at www.idocket.com; registration and password required. A fee service; only one free name search per day.

Criminal Name Search: Access: Mail, in person, online. Both court and visitors may perform in person name searches. Search fee: $5.00 per name. Criminal index in books. Mail turnaround time 2-3 days. Criminal PAT goes back to 1974. Access cases back to 01/01/1989 at www.idocket.com; registration and password required. A fee service; only one free name search per day.

County Court 576 W Main, Raymondville, TX 78580; 956-689-2710; fax: 956-689-9849; 8AM-N, 1-5PM (CST). *Misdemeanor, Civil, Probate.*

General Information: No juvenile, mental, sealed, or adoption records released. Will not fax documents. Court makes copy: $1.00 per page. Self serve copy: same. Certification fee: $5.00. Payee: County Clerk. No personal checks or credit cards accepted. Prepayment required. Mail requests: SASE required.

Civil Name Search: Access: Mail, in person, online. Both court and visitors may perform in person name searches. Search fee: $10.00 per name, ten year search only. Required to search: name, years to search; also helpful: address. Civil records go back to 1920's. Mail turnaround time 2-3 days. Access civil and family law case index back to 01/01/1989 at www.idocket.com; registration and password required. A fee service; only one free name search per day.

Criminal Name Search: Access: Mail, in person. Both court and visitors may perform in person name searches. Search fee: $10.00 per name. Required to search: name, years to search; also helpful: address, DOB, SSN. Criminal records go back to 1921, computerized since 1990. Note: Misdemeanor records are not available online. Mail turnaround time 2-3 days.

Williamson County

District Court PO Box 24, 405 Martin Luther Ste 135, Georgetown, TX 78626; 512-943-1212; fax: 512-943-1222; 8AM-5PM (CST). *Felony, Civil.*

www.wilco.org/default.aspx?tabid=448

General Information: No juvenile, mental, sealed, or adoption records released. Will not fax documents. Court makes copy: $1.00 1st page; $.25 each add'l. Certification fee: $1.00 certified per page. Payee: District Clerk. Personal checks accepted, credit cards are not. Prepayment required. Mail requests: SASE required.

Civil Name Search: Access: Mail, in person, Online. Both court and visitors may perform in person name searches. Search fee: $5.00 per name. Civil records on computer since 1989, index books prior. Mail turnaround time 2-3 days. Civil PAT goes back to 1989. Search the civil docket index at http://judicialrecords.wilco.org/. Search by case number, party, or attorney.

Criminal Name Search: Access: Mail, in person. Both court and visitors may perform in person name searches. Search fee: $5.00 per name. Required to search: name, years to search, DOB, signed release; also helpful: SSN. Criminal records on computer since 1989, index books prior. Mail turnaround time 2-3 days. Criminal PAT goes back to same as civil. Sheriff bond and inmate data is free at http://judicialsearch.wilco.org. There is no access to the docket index. Online results show name only.

County Court 405 Martin Luther King St, PO Box 14, Georgetown, TX 78626; criminal phone: 512-943-1150; civil phone: 512-943-1140; probate phone: 512-943-1140; criminal fax: 512-943-1445; civil fax: 8AM-5PM; 8AM-5PM (CST). *Misdemeanor, Civil, Probate.*

www.wilcogov.org/

General Information: No juvenile, mental, sealed, or adoption records released. Fee to fax out file $1.00 per page to local numbers only. Court makes copy: $1.00 per page. Certification fee: $5.00 per case plus copy fee. Payee: County Clerk. Personal checks accepted. Credit cards accepted. Prepayment required. Mail requests: SASE required.

Civil Name Search: Access: Mail, in person, online. Both court and visitors may perform in person name searches. Search fee: $10.00 per name. Civil records on computer since 1985, index books since 1848.GA. Mail turnaround time 2 days. Civil PAT goes back to 1985. Access to limited civil case records is free at http://judicialrecords.wilco.org/default.aspx. Also various court records available for free at https://deed.wilco.org/. JP Court #1 records are free at www.edoctecinc.com but there may be a 2 week to 1 month lag time.

Criminal Name Search: Access: Mail, in person, online. Both court and visitors may perform in person name searches. Search fee: $10.00 per name. Required to search: name, years to search; also helpful: DOB, SSN. Criminal records on computer since 1983. Overall records go back to 1800. Mail turnaround time 2 days. Criminal PAT goes back to 1983. Access to a criminal case records from 1983 is free at http://judicialrecords.wilco.org/default.aspx. Sheriff bond and inmate data is also available. Also various court records available for free at https://deed.wilco.org/. Results include DOB. Online results show middle initial.

Wilson County

District Court PO Box 812, 1420 3rd St 2nd Fl, Floresville, TX 78114; 830-393-7322; fax: 830-393-7319; 8AM-N, 1-5PM (CST). *Felony, Civil.*

www.81st-218thdistrictcourt.org/

General Information: Request must be in writing if court personnel are to do search. No juvenile, mental, sealed, or adoption records released. Will fax documents to local or toll free line. Court makes copy: $.50 per page. Self serve copy: same. Certification fee: $1.00 per page. Payee: District Clerk. Personal checks accepted w/ proper ID. No credit cards accepted. Prepayment required. Mail requests: SASE required.

Civil Name Search: Access: Fax, mail, in person. Both court and visitors may perform in person name searches. Search fee: $5.00 per name. Civil records go back to 1960. Mail turnaround time 2-3 days.

Criminal Name Search: Access: Fax, mail, in person. Both court and visitors may perform in person name searches. Search fee: $5.00 per name. Required to search: name, years to search; also helpful: DOB. Criminal records go back to 1975. Mail turnaround time 2 days.

County Court PO Box 27, Floresville, TX 78114; 830-393-7308; fax: 830-393-7334; 8AM-5PM (CST). *Misdemeanor, Civil, Probate.*

General Information: Will not fax documents. Court makes copy: $1.00 per page. Self serve copy: same. Certification fee: $5.00. Payee: Eva S Martinez, County Clerk. Personal checks accepted, credit cards are not. Prepayment required. Mail requests: SASE not required.

Civil Name Search: Access: Phone, mail, fax, in person. Both court and visitors may perform in person name searches. No search fee. Civil records available from 1862. Mail turnaround time same day.

Criminal Name Search: Access: Phone, mail, fax, in person. Both court and visitors may perform in person name searches. No search fee. Required to search: name, years to search, DOB. Criminal records stored since 1917, computerized since 11/2002. Mail turnaround time same day.

Winkler County

District Court PO Box 1065, Kermit, TX 79745; 432-586-3359; 8AM-12; 1PM-5PM (CST). *Felony, Civil.*

General Information: No juvenile, mental, sealed, or adoption records released. Will not fax documents. Court makes copy: $1.00 per page. No certification fee. Payee: District Clerk. Personal checks accepted, credit cards are not. Prepayment required. Mail requests: SASE required.

Civil Name Search: Access: Phone, mail, in person. Both court and visitors may perform in person name searches. Search fee: $5.00 per name. Civil records on computer since 1991, index books prior. Mail turnaround time 3-4 days.

Criminal Name Search: Access: Mail, in person. Both court and visitors may perform in person name searches. Search fee: $5.00 per name. Required to search: name, years to search, DOB, SSN. Criminal records on computer since 1991, index books prior. Mail turnaround time 3-4 days.

County Court PO Box 1007, 100 E Winkler St, Kermit, TX 79745; 432-586-3401; 8AM-5PM (CST). *Misdemeanor, Civil, Probate.*

General Information: No juvenile, mental, sealed, or adoption records released. Will not fax documents. Court makes copy: $1.00 per page.

Certification fee: $5.00. Payee: County Clerk. Business checks accepted. No credit cards accepted. Prepayment required. Mail requests: SASE required.

Civil Name Search: Access: Mail, in person. Visitors must perform in person searches themselves. Search fee: $5.00 per name. All civil records in index books. Mail turnaround time 2-3 days.

Criminal Name Search: Access: Mail, in person. Visitors must perform in person searches themselves. Search fee: $5.00 per name. Required to search: name, years to search; also helpful: address, DOB, SSN. Criminal records computerized from 1991; prior in index books. Mail turnaround time 2-3 days.

Wise County

District Court PO Box 308, Decatur, TX 76234; 940-627-5535; fax: 940-627-0705; 8AM-5PM (CST). *Felony, Civil.*

General Information: No juvenile, mental, sealed, or adoption records released. Will fax documents. Court makes copy: $1.00 per page. Certification fee: $1.00 per doc. Payee: Wise County District Clerk. Personal checks accepted, credit cards are not. Prepayment required. Mail requests: SASE required.

Civil Name Search: Access: Mail, in person. Both court and visitors may perform in person name searches. Search fee: $5.00 per name. Civil records in index books since 1895, computerized since 1999. Mail turnaround time same day. Civil PAT goes back to 1999.

Criminal Name Search: Access: Mail, in person. Both court and visitors may perform in person name searches. Search fee: $5.00 per name. Required to search: name, years to search; also helpful-DOB, SSN. Criminal records in docket books to 1896, computerized since 1999. Mail turnaround time same day. Criminal PAT goes back to 1999.

County Court at Law PO Box 359, Decatur, TX 76234; 940-627-3351; fax: 940-627-3790; 8AM-5PM (CST). *Misdemeanor, Civil, Probate.*

General Information: Physical address is 200 N Trinity, same ZIP. No mental health or sealed records released. Will not fax out documents. Court makes copy: $1.00 per page. Certification fee: $5.00. Payee: Wise County Clerk. Personal checks accepted, credit cards are not. Prepayment required. Mail requests: SASE required.

Civil Name Search: Access: Mail, in person. Both court and visitors may perform in person name searches. Search fee: $10.00 per name. Civil records in index books since sovereignty; on computer back to 1998. Mail turnaround time 1 day. Civil PAT goes back to 1998.

Criminal Name Search: Access: Mail, in person. Both court and visitors may perform in person name searches. Search fee: $10.00 per name. Required to search: name, years to search; also helpful: DOB, SSN. Criminal docket on books from sovereignty; on computer back to 1997. Mail turnaround time 1 day. Criminal PAT goes back to 1997.

Wood County

District Court PO Box 1707, Quitman, TX 75783; 903-763-2361; fax: 903-763-1511; 8AM-5PM (CST). *Felony, Civil.*

http://judicial.co.wood.tx.us

General Information: No juvenile, mental, sealed, or adoption records released. Will not fax documents. Court makes copy: $1.00 per page. Certification fee: $1.00 per document. Payee: District Clerk. Personal checks accepted, credit cards are not. Prepayment required. Mail requests: SASE required.

Civil Name Search: Access: Mail, fax, in person, online. Both court and visitors may perform in person name searches. Search fee: $5.00 per name. Civil records on computer since 1990, microfilm since 1981, index books since 1890. Mail turnaround time 2-3 days. Civil PAT goes back to 1980. Search civil case index at http://judicial.co.wood.tx.us/CivilSearch/civfrmd.asp.

Criminal Name Search: Access: Mail, fax, in person, online. Both court and visitors may perform in person name searches. Search fee: $5.00 per name. Required to search: name, years to search; also helpful: DOB, SSN. Criminal records on computer since 1990, microfilm since 1981, index books since 1890. Mail turnaround time 2-3 days. Criminal PAT goes back to same as civil. Other identifiers include gender, race, height and weight. Search criminal case index at http://judicial.co.wood.tx.us/CrimSearch/crimfrmd.asp. Online results show middle initial, DOB.

County Court PO Box 1796, Quitman, TX 75783; 903-763-2711; fax: 903-763-5641; 8AM-4PM (CST). *Misdemeanor, Civil, Probate.*

www.co.wood.tx.us/ips/cms

General Information: Probate is a separate index at this same address. No mental or sealed records released. Will fax documents $2.00 per page. Court makes copy: $1.00 per page. Certification fee: $5.00 per document plus copy fee. Payee: Wood County Clerk. Personal checks accepted, if proper ID. No credit cards accepted. Prepayment required. Mail requests: SASE required.

Civil Name Search: Access: Mail, in person, online. Both court and visitors may perform in person name searches. Search fee: $5.00 per name. Civil records on computer since 1980; index books since early 1900s. Mail turnaround time same day. Civil PAT goes back to 1980. Search all courts free at http://judicial.co.wood.tx.us/.

Criminal Name Search: Access: Mail, in person, online. Both court and visitors may perform in person name searches. Search fee: $5.00 per name. Required to search: name, years to search; also helpful DOB, SSN, signed release, DL#. Criminal records computerized from 1986; index books from 1965, archived to 1900. Mail turnaround time same day. Criminal PAT goes back to same as civil. Search all courts and Sheriff bond and inmate lists free at http://judicial.co.wood.tx.us/. Online results show name, DOB.

Yoakum County

District Court PO Box 899, Plains, TX 79355; 806-456-7491 x297; fax: 806-456-8767; 8AM-5PM (CST). *Felony, Civil.*

www.co.yoakum.tx.us/ips/cms/districtcourt/districtClerk.html

General Information: No juvenile, mental, sealed, or adoption records released. Will not fax documents. Court makes copy: $1.00 1st page, $.25 each add'l. Certification fee: $1.00 per page. Thee is no fee for copies made form microfilm or other electronic methods used by court. Payee: District Clerk. No personal checks or credit cards accepted. Prepayment required. Mail requests: SASE required.

Civil Name Search: Access: Fax, mail, in person, online. Both court and visitors may perform in person name searches. Search fee: $5.00 per name. Civil records on computer since 1980, index books since 1907. Mail turnaround time same day. Civil PAT goes back to 1980. Results include case type. Access civil cases except probate at www.idocket.com; registration and password required. A fee service; only one free name search per day. Civil and Family Law cases go back to 12/31/1980.

Criminal Name Search: Access: Fax, mail, in person, online. Both court and visitors may perform in person name searches. Search fee: $5.00 per name. Required to search: name, years to search, DOB; also helpful: SSN. Criminal records on computer since 1980, index books since 1910. Mail turnaround time same day. Criminal PAT goes back to same as civil. Results include offense. Access civil cases except probate at www.idocket.com; registration and password required. A fee service; only one free name search per day. Felony case information goes back to 12/31/1980.

County Court PO Box 309, Cowboy Way and Avenue G, Plains, TX 79355; 806-456-7491; fax: 806-456-2258; 8AM-5PM (CST). *Misdemeanor, Civil, Probate.*

General Information: No juvenile or mental records released. Will fax documents $2.00 per fax plus $1.00 per page, prepaid. Court makes copy: $1.00 per page. Certification fee: $5.00 per document plus copy fee. Payee: County Clerk, Yoakum County. Personal checks accepted. Major credit cards accepted. Prepayment required. Mail requests: SASE not required.

Civil Name Search: Access: Phone, mail, in person. Both court and visitors may perform in person name searches. Search fee: $5.00 per name. Required to search: name, years to search; also helpful: address. Civil records in minutes books and microfilm since 9/1986; on computer back to 1/1986. Mail turnaround time same day. Civil PAT goes back to 9/1986.

Criminal Name Search: Access: Mail, in person. Both court and visitors may perform in person name searches. Search fee: $5.00 per name. Required to search: name, years to search, DOB; also helpful: address, SSN. Criminal minutes books and microfilm since 9/1986; on computer back to 1/1986. Mail turnaround time same day. Criminal PAT goes back to same as civil.

Young County

District Court 516 4th St, Rm 201, Courthouse, Graham, TX 76450; 940-549-0029; fax: 940-549-4874; 8:30AM-N, 1-5PM (CST). *Felony, Civil.*

www.co.young.tx.us/ips/cms/index.html

General Information: No juvenile, mental, sealed, or adoption records released. No fee to fax documents. Court makes copy: $1.00 first page, $.50 each add'l. Certification fee: $1.00 per page. Payee: District Clerk. Personal checks accepted. Major credit cards accepted. Prepayment required. Mail requests: SASE required.

Civil Name Search: Access: Mail, in person, online. Both court and visitors may perform in person name searches. Search fee: $5.00 per name. Civil records on computer since 1989, index books prior. Note: Search fee must be prepaid before fax access is allowed. Mail turnaround time 1-2 days. Civil PAT goes back to 1989. Access civil cases except probate at www.idocket.com; registration and password required. A fee service; only one free name search per day. Civil cases go back to 3/1/1998.

Criminal Name Search: Access: Mail, in person, online. Both court and visitors may perform in person name searches. Search fee: $5.00 per name. Required to search: name, years to search; also helpful: DOB, SSN. Criminal records on computer since 1989, index books prior. Mail turnaround time 1-2 days. Criminal PAT goes back to 1989. Access felony cases at www.idocket.com; registration and password required. A fee service; only one free name search per day. Records go back to 3/1/1998.

County Court 516 4th St, Rm 104, Graham, TX 76450; 940-549-8432; fax: 940-521-0305; 8:30AM-N, 1-5PM (CST). *Misdemeanor, Civil, Probate, Juvenile.*

General Information: No juvenile, mental, sealed, or adoption records released. Fee to fax out file $2.00 plus $1.00 per page copy fee. Court makes copy: $1.00 per page. Self serve copy: same. Certification fee: $5.00. Payee: County Clerk. Personal checks accepted, credit cards are not. Prepayment required. Mail requests: SASE not required.

Civil Name Search: Access: Mail, in person. Both court and visitors may perform in person name searches. Search fee: $5.00 per name. Civil records on computer since 1991, index books prior to 1800s. Mail turnaround time same day. Civil PAT goes back to 1991.

Criminal Name Search: Access: Mail, in person. Both court and visitors may perform in person name searches. Search fee: $5.00 per name. Criminal records on computer since 1991, index books prior to 1800s. Mail turnaround time same day. Criminal PAT goes back to same as civil.

Zapata County

District Court PO Box 788, Clerk's Office, Zapata, TX 78076; 956-765-9930; fax: 956-765-9931; 8AM-N, 1-5PM (CST). *Felony, Civil.*

General Information: No juvenile, mental, sealed, or adoption records released. Will fax documents up to 10 pages to local or toll-free number. Court makes copy: $1.00 per page. Self serve copy: same. Certification fee: $5.00 per document plus copy fee. Payee: District Clerk/County Clerk. Personal checks accepted, credit cards are not. Prepayment required. Mail requests: SASE required.

Civil Name Search: Access: Mail, in person. Both court and visitors may perform in person name searches. Search fee: $5.00 per name. Civil cases indexed by plaintiff. Civil index is computerized. Mail turnaround time 1-3 days. Civil PAT goes back to 15 years.

Criminal Name Search: Access: Mail, in person. Both court and visitors may perform in person name searches. Search fee: $5.00 per name. Criminal index is computerized. Mail turnaround time 1-3 days. Criminal PAT goes back to 15 years.

County Court PO Box 789, Zapata, TX 78076; 956-765-9915; fax: 956-765-9933; 8AM-5PM (CST). *Misdemeanor, Civil, Probate.*

General Information: Probate fax is same as main fax number. No juvenile, mental, sealed, or adoption records released. Will fax documents $4.00 for 1st page, $1.00 each add'l. Court makes copy: $1.00 per page. Self serve copy: same. Certification fee: $5.00 per doc plus copy fee. Payee: County Clerk. Personal checks accepted, credit cards are not. Prepayment required. Mail requests: SASE not required.

Civil Name Search: Access: Mail, in person. Both court and visitors may perform in person name searches. Search fee: $5.00 per name. Civil cases indexed by plaintiff only. Civil records in index books since 1800s, computerized records back to 1990. Mail turnaround time 1-2 days.

Criminal Name Search: Access: Mail, in person. Both court and visitors may perform in person name searches. Search fee: $5.00 per name. Required to search: name, years to search, DOB, SSN. Criminal docket on books from 1800s, computerized records back to 1930. Mail turnaround time 1-2 days.

Zavala County

District Court PO Box 704, Crystal City, TX 78839; 830-374-3456; fax: 830-374-2632; 8AM-N, 1-5PM (CST). *Felony, Civil.*

General Information: No juvenile, mental, sealed, or adoption records released. Will fax back documents for no fee. Court makes copy: $1.00 per page. Self serve copy: same. No certification fee. Payee: Zavala District Clerk. Personal checks accepted, credit cards are not. Prepayment required. Mail requests: SASE required.

Civil Name Search: Access: Phone, mail, in person. Both court and visitors may perform in person name searches. Search fee: $10.00 per name. Civil records in index books from 1900s. Mail turnaround time 1-2 days.

Criminal Name Search: Access: Phone, mail, in person. Both court and visitors may perform in person name searches. Search fee: $10.00 per name. Criminal docket on books from 1900s. Mail turnaround time 1-2 days.

County Court Zavala County Courthouse, 200 E Uvalde, Crystal City, TX 78839; 830-374-2331; fax: 830-374-5955; 8AM-5PM (CST). *Misdemeanor, Civil, Probate.*

General Information: Probate fax is same as main fax number. No juvenile, mental, sealed, or adoption records released. Will fax documents $8.00 1st page, $2.00 ea add'l. Court makes copy: $1.00 per page. Self serve copy: same. Certification fee: $5.00. Payee: Zavala County Clerk. Personal checks accepted, credit cards are not. Prepayment required. Mail requests: SASE required.

Civil Name Search: Access: Mail, in person. Both court and visitors may perform in person name searches. Search fee: $10.00 per name. Civil records in index books from 1880s. Mail turnaround time 1-2 days. Civil PAT goes back to 1988.

Criminal Name Search: Access: Mail, in person. Both court and visitors may perform in person name searches. Search fee: $10.00 per name. Required to search: name, years to search, DOB. Criminal docket on books from 1880s. Mail turnaround time 1-2 days. Criminal PAT goes back to 1988.

Common Abbreviations Found in Text

- DL Driver's license
- PAT Public use access terminal
- SASE Self-addressed, stamped envelope
- SSN Social Security Number

Utah

Time Zone:	**MST**
Capital:	**Salt Lake City, Salt Lake County**
# of Counties:	**29**
State Web:	**www.utah.gov**
Court Web:	**www.utcourts.us**

Administration

Court Administrator, 450 S State St, Salt Lake City, UT, 84114; 801-578-3800, Fax: 801-578-3859.

The Supreme and Appellate Courts

The Supreme Court is the court of last resort in Utah. The Court has appellate jurisdiction to hear first degree and capital felony convictions from the District Court and civil judgments other than domestic cases. The Court of Appeals hears all appeals from the Juvenile and District Courts, except those from the small claims department of a District Court and those mentioned above. Opinions, dockets and calendars are viewable at www.utcourts.gov/courts/sup/

The Utah Courts

Court	Type	How Organized	Jurisdiction Highpoints
District*	General	29 Courts in 8 Districts	Felony, Misdemeanor, Civil, Domestic, Eviction. Probate
Justice*	Limited	134 Courts by Township	B & C Misdemeanor, Small Claims, Ordinance, Traffic
Juvenile*	Limited	29 Courts	Juvenile

* = profiled in this book

Details on the Court Structure

The **District Court** has original jurisdiction for all civil cases, all criminal felonies, certain misdemeanors, domestic relations cases such as divorces, child custody and support, adoption, and probate.

Justice Courts, established by counties and municipalities, deal with class B and C misdemeanors, violations of ordinances, small claims, and infractions committed within their territorial jurisdiction.

Record Searching Facts You Need to Know

Fees and Record Searching Tips

Most District Courts charge $15.00 per hour to do a name search, but some provide the first 15-20 minutes free. Most courts charge $.25 for a copy and $4.00 for certification.

Most courts provide a public access terminal that provides the same data shown on the XChange – see below.

The Salt Lake District Court has an automated information phone line that provides court appearance look-ups, outstanding fine balance look-ups, and judgment/divorce decree lookups. Call 801-238-7830.

Online Access is Statewide

Case information from all Utah District Court locations and 43 Justice Courts is available online through XChange. Recently the case information from Justice Courts became available on this system, although the data throughput dates may vary. Fees include a $25.00 registration fee and $30.00 per month fee which includes 200 searches. Each additional search is billed at $.10 per search. The search provides a summary of the docket index; case files and copies are not available. Information about XChange and the subscription agreement can be found at www.utcourts.gov/records or call 801-578-3850.

Beaver County

5th Judicial District Court PO Box 1683, 2270 South 525 West, Beaver, UT 84713; 435-438-5309; fax: 435-438-5395; 8AM-5PM (MST). *Felony, Misdemeanor, Civil, Eviction, Probate, Domestic.* http://utcourts.gov/

General Information: No adoption, juvenile, sealed records released. Fee to fax out file $5.00 minimum, $.50 each page over 10. Court makes copy: $.25 per page. Certification fee: $4.00 plus $.50 per page includes copies; exemplification fee is $6.00 plus $.50 per page. Payee: 5th District Court. Personal checks, Visa/MC accepted. Prepayment required. Mail requests: SASE required or postage must be included.

Civil Name Search: Access: Fax, mail, in person, online. Both court and visitors may perform in person name searches. Search fee: No fee for name search unless extensive, then $15.00 per hour fee. Civil records on computer back to 1997. Mail turnaround time 2-7 days. Civil PAT goes back to 1997. Online access through XChange, see www.utcourts.gov/records/. Also, see state introduction.

Criminal Name Search: Access: Fax, mail, in person, online. Both court and visitors may perform in person name searches. Search fee: No fee for name search unless extensive, then $15.00 per hour fee. Required to search: name, years to search, DOB. Criminal records computerized from 1997. Mail turnaround time 2-7 days. Criminal PAT goes back to 1997. Online access through XChange, see www.utcourts.gov/records/. Also, see state introduction.

Beaver County Justice Court 600 W 2160 S, PO Box 387, Beaver, UT 84713; 435-438-6470; fax: 435-438-5348; *Misdemeanor (B & C), Small Claims, Infractions, Traffic.*

Beaver County Justice Court (Milford) PO Box 922, Milford, UT 84751; 435-387-5571; fax: 435-387-2524; 8:30AM-3PM M 9AM-3PM T,W 9AM-5:30PM Th 9AM-Noon F (MST). *Misdemeanor (B & C), Small Claims, Infractions, Traffic.*

Beaver County/Minersville Justice Court PO Box 268, Minersville, UT 84752; 435-386-2586; fax: 435-386-2586; 9AM-10AM M,T,TH,F; 3PM-5PM W (MST). *Misdemeanor (B & C), Small Claims, Infractions, Traffic.*

Box Elder County

1st District Court PO Box 873, 43 N Main St, Brigham City, UT 84302; 435-734-4600; fax: 435-734-4610; 8AM-5PM (MST). *Felony, Misdemeanor, Civil, Eviction, Small Claims, Probate.* http://utcourts.gov/

General Information: No adoption, sealed records released. Fee to fax out file $5.00 up to 10 pages, then $.50 per add'l page. Court makes copy: $.25 per page. Certification fee: $4.00 plus $.50 per page; Exemplification fee-$6.00 plus $.50 per page. Payee: 1st District Court. Personal checks, Visa/MC accepted. Prepayment required. Mail requests: SASE required.

Civil Name Search: Access: Phone, fax, mail, online, in person. Both court and visitors may perform in person name searches. Search fee: None, but after 30 minutes a minimum $22 per hour fee applies. Required to search: name, years to search; helpful- case number. Civil records on computer from 3/87, books, microfiche, archived from 1856. Mail turnaround time 3-4 days Civil PAT goes back to 3/1987. Identifiers, particularly SSNs, do not appear on all records. Online access through XChange, see www.utcourts.gov/records/. Also, see state introduction.

Criminal Name Search: Access: Phone, fax, mail, online, in person. Both court and visitors may perform in person name searches. Search fee: None, but after 30 minutes a minimum $22 per hour fee applies. Required to search: name, years to search; also helpful: DOB, SSN. Criminal records computerized from 3/87, books, microfiche, archived from 1856. Mail turnaround time 3-4 days. Criminal PAT goes back to same as civil. Identifiers do not show on all records. Online access through XChange, see www.utcourts.gov/records/. Also, see state introduction.

Box Elder County Justice Court 81 N Main St, #103, Brigham City, UT 84302-4904; 435-734-3390; fax: 435-734-3376; 8AM-5PM (MST). *Misdemeanor (B & C), Small Claims, Infractions, Traffic.*

Garland Justice Court 72 N Main, PO Box 129, Garland, UT 84312; 435-257-8352; fax: 435-257-8352; *Misdemeanor (B & C), Small Claims, Infractions, Traffic.*

Mantua Justice Court 409 N Main, Mantua, UT 84324; 435-723-7054; fax: 435-723-8427; 9AM-1PM (MST). *Misdemeanor (B & C), Small Claims, Infractions, Traffic.*

Tremonton Justice Court 102 S Tremont St, Tremonton, UT 84337; 435-257-9509; fax: 435-257-9513; 9AM-5PM M-F (MST). *Misdemeanor (B & C), Small Claims, Infractions, Traffic.*

Willard Justice Court PO Box 593, Willard, UT 84340; 435-723-2634; fax: 435-723-6164; 9AM-7PM M 9AM-5PM T-F (MST). *Misdemeanor (B & C), Small Claims, Infractions, Traffic.*

Cache County

1st District Court 135 N 100 W, Logan, UT 84321; 435-750-1300; fax: 435-750-1355; 8AM-5PM (MST). *Felony, Misdemeanor, Civil, Eviction, Small Claims, Probate.* http://utcourts.gov/

General Information: No sealed records released. Fee to fax out file $5.00 for up to 10 pages then $.50 ea add'l. Court makes copy: $.25 per page. Certification fee: $4.00 plus $.50 per page. Payee: 1st Judicial District. Personal checks accepted. Credit cards accepted. Prepayment required. Mail requests: SASE required.

Civil Name Search: Access: Phone, mail, online, in person. Both court and visitors may perform in person name searches. Search fee: $15.00 per hour. Civil records on computer from 11/87, archived from 1983, microfiche in Salt Lake City. Mail turnaround time 10 days. Civil PAT goes back to 1987. Online access through XChange, see www.utcourts.gov/records/. Also see state introduction.

Criminal Name Search: Access: Phone, mail, online, in person. Both court and visitors may perform in person name searches. Search fee: $15.00 per hour. Required to search: name, years to search; also helpful: DOB, SSN. Criminal records computerized from 11-87, archived from 1983, microfiche in Salt Lake City. Mail turnaround time 2 weeks. Criminal PAT goes back to same as civil. Online access through XChange, see www.utcourts.gov/records/. Also see state introduction. Online results show middle initial, DOB.

Clarkston Justice Court PO Box 371, Clarkston, UT 84305; 435-563-9090; fax: 435-563-9196; *Misdemeanor (B & C), Small Claims, Infractions, Traffic.*

Hyrum Justice Court 83 W Main, Hyrum, UT 84319; 435-245-0114; fax: 435-245-4470; 1PM-5PM M-F (MST). *Misdemeanor (B & C), Small Claims, Infractions, Traffic.* www.hyrumcity.com/

Lewiston Justice Court 29 S Main, PO Box 36, Lewiston, UT 84320; 435-258-2141; fax: 435-258-3621; 9AM-5PM M,W 9AM-1PM T,Th, F (MST). *Misdemeanor (B & C), Small Claims, Infractions, Traffic.*

Logan Justice Court 446 N 100 W, Logan, UT 84321; 435-716-9540 ext 2; fax: 435-716-9559; 8AM-5PM M,T, Th, F 8AM-6PM W (MST). *Misdemeanor (B & C), Small Claims, Infractions, Traffic.* www.loganutah.org/Administration/Justice%20Courts/index.cfm

Newton/Amalga Justice Court 51 S Center St, PO Box 146, Newton, UT 84327; 435-563-9283; 9:30AM-11:30AM (MST). *Misdemeanor (B & C), Small Claims, Infractions, Traffic.*

Nibley Justice Court 625 W 3200 N, Nibley, UT 84321; 435-752-0431; fax: 435-753-1510; 10AM-2PM (MST). *Misdemeanor (B & C), Small Claims, Infractions, Traffic.*
General Information: Address will change 01/2012.

North Logan/Hyde Park Justice Court 113 E Center, PO Box 489, Hyde Park, UT 84318; 435-563-6923; fax: 435-563-9029; 8AM-5PM (MST). *Misdemeanor (B & C), Small Claims, Infractions, Traffic.*

Providence Justice Court 15 S Main, Providence, UT 84332; 435-752-9441 ext 18; fax: 435-753-1586; 7:30AM-5:30PM M-Th Fri by appt. (MST). *Misdemeanor (B & C), Small Claims, Infractions, Traffic.*

Richmond Justice Court 6 W Main, PO Box 9, Richmond, UT 84333; 435-932-0341; fax: 435-258-3604; leave message (MST). *Misdemeanor (B & C), Small Claims, Infractions, Traffic.*

Smithfield Justice Court 96 S Main, PO Box 96, Smithfield, UT 84335; 435-792-7987; fax: 435-563-6227; 9AM - 5PM M-F (MST). *Misdemeanor (B & C), Small Claims, Infractions, Traffic.*

Wellsville Justice Court 75 E Main, PO Box 6, Wellsville, UT 84339; 435-245-3686; fax: 435-245-7958; 9AM-5PM M-th; 9AM-12 F (MST). *Misdemeanor (B & C), Small Claims, Infractions, Traffic.*

Carbon County

7th District Court 149 E 100 S, Price, UT 84501; 435-636-3400; fax: 435-637-7349; 8AM-5PM (MST). *Felony, Misdemeanor, Civil, Eviction, Probate.* https://www.utcourts.gov/directory/courthouse.cgi?county=4

General Information: Misdemeanor records are Class A. No sealed records released. Fee to fax out file $5.00 1st 10 pages, $.50 each add'l page. Court makes copy: $.25 per page. Certification fee: $4.00 plus $.50 per page includes copies. Payee: 7th District Court. Personal checks, Visa/MC accepted. Prepayment required. Mail requests: SASE required.

Civil Name Search: Access: Phone, mail, online, in person. Both court and visitors may perform in person name searches. Search fee: $15.00 per hour. Civil records on computer from 1988, on microfiche from 1985, archived prior to 1988. Mail turnaround time 48 hours. Civil PAT goes back to 1987. Online access through XChange, see www.utcourts.gov/records/. Also see state introduction.

Criminal Name Search: Access: Phone, mail, online, in person. Both court and visitors may perform in person name searches. Search fee: $15.00 per hour. Required to search: name, years to search, DOB; also helpful: SSN. Criminal records computerized from 1988, on microfiche from 1985, archived prior to 1988. Mail turnaround time 48 hours. Criminal PAT goes back to same as civil. Online access through XChange, see www.utcourts.gov/records/. Also see state introduction.

Carbon County Justice Court 120 E Main St, County Bldg, Price, UT 84501; 435-636-3289; fax: 435-636-3209; 8AM-5PM (MST). *Misdemeanor (B & C), Small Claims, Infractions, Traffic.*

East Carbon City Justice Court 101 W Geneva Dr, PO Box 70, East Carbon, UT 84520; 435-888-6613; fax: 435-888-4448; 1PM-5PM M-F 3rd Thurs 9:30AM-5PM (MST). *Misdemeanor (B & C), Small Claims, Infractions, Traffic.*

Helper Justice Court PO Box 221, Helper, UT 84526; 435-472-3039; fax: 435-472-0498; *Misdemeanor (B & C), Small Claims, Infractions, Traffic.*

Wellington Justice Court PO Box 559, Wellington, UT 84542; 435-637-5353; fax: 435-637-1586; 8AM-5PM (MST). *Misdemeanor (B & C), Small Claims, Infractions, Traffic.*

Daggett County

8th District Court PO Box 400, 95 N 1st W, Manila, UT 84046; 435-784-3154; fax: 435-784-3335; 8AM-N, 1-5PM (MST). *Felony, Misdemeanor, Civil, Eviction, Probate.*
http://utcourts.gov/

General Information: Faxed in search requests require prior approval. Any phone search requests will only be on clerk's computer. No sealed records released. Will fax back file $5.00 each up to 10 pages, $.50 per add'l page. Court makes copy: $.25 per page. Self serve copy: same. Certification fee: $6.00 per doc plus copy fee. Payee: Daggett County. Personal checks accepted, credit cards are not. Prepayment required. Mail requests: SASE required.

Civil Name Search: Access: Phone, fax, mail, in person, online. Both court and visitors may perform in person name searches. Search fee: $15.00 per hour, 1st 15 minutes no charge. Civil records archived from 1918; on computer at least 5 years. Mail turnaround time 10 days. Online access through XChange, see www.utcourts.gov/records/. Also see state introduction.

Criminal Name Search: Access: Fax, mail, in person, online. Both court and visitors may perform in person name searches. Search fee: $15.00 per hour, 1st 15 minutes no charge. Required to search: name, years to search, DOB; signature and record request form required. Criminal records archived from 1918; on computer at least 5 years. Mail turnaround time 10 days. Online access through XChange, see www.utcourts.gov/records/. Also see state introduction. Online results show name, DOB.

Daggett County Justice Court (Dutch John) PO Box 304, Dutch John, UT 84023; 435-885-3183; fax: 435-885-3274; *Misdemeanor (B & C), Small Claims, Infractions, Traffic.*

Daggett County Justice Court (Manila) Courthouse, PO Box 219, Manila, UT 84046; 435-784-3216; fax: 435-784-3335; 9AM-N (MST). *Misdemeanor (B & C), Small Claims, Infractions, Traffic.*

Davis County

2nd District Court PO Box 769, Farmington, UT 84025; 801-447-3800; fax: 801-447-3881; 8AM-5PM (MST). *Felony, Civil, Probate.*
http://utcourts.gov/

General Information: Probate fax is same as main fax number. No adoption, criminal pre-sentence investigation records released. Will fax documents $5.00. Court makes copy: $.25 per page. Certification fee: $4.00 per document plus $.50 per page. Payee: 2nd District Court. Personal checks, Visa/MC accepted. Prepayment required. Mail requests: SASE required.

Civil Name Search: Access: Phone, mail, online, in person. Both court and visitors may perform in person name searches. Search fee: $15.00 per hour. First 15 minutes no charge. Civil records on computer back to 1982, prior on microfiche and archived to 1896. Mail turnaround time 2-3 days. Civil PAT goes back to 1982. Online access through XChange, see www.utcourts.gov/records/. Also see state introduction.

Criminal Name Search: Access: Phone, mail, online, in person. Both court and visitors may perform in person name searches. Search fee: $15.00 per hour. First 15 minutes no charge. Required to search: name, years to search, DOB; also helpful: SSN. Criminal records computerized from 1989, prior on microfiche and archived to 1896. Mail turnaround time 2-3 days. Criminal PAT goes back to 1990. Online access through XChange, see www.utcourts.gov/records/. Also see state introduction. Online results show middle initial, DOB.

2nd District Court - Bountiful Department 805 S Main, Bountiful, UT 84010; 801-397-7008; criminal phone: 801-397-7007; civil phone: 801-397-7004; fax: 801-397-7010; 8AM-5PM (MST). *Felony, Misdemeanor, Civil, Eviction, Small Claims, Probate.*
http://utcourts.gov/

General Information: Small Claims x2; Traffic at x1. Will fax documents $5.00 1st 10 pages, then $.25 each add'l page. Court makes copy: $.25 per page. Certification fee: $4.00 plus $.50 per page. Payee: Second District Court. Personal checks, Visa/MC accepted. Prepayment required. Mail requests: SASE required.

Civil Name Search: Access: Phone, online, in person. Both court and visitors may perform in person name searches. No search fee. Required to search: name, years to search; also helpful: address. Civil records on computer since 10/86. Civil PAT available. Online access through XChange, see www.utcourts.gov/records/. Also see state introduction.

Criminal Name Search: Access: Phone, mail, online, in person. Both court and visitors may perform in person name searches. No search fee. Required to search: name, years to search; helpful- DOB. Criminal records on computer since 10/86. Mail turnaround time 1 week. Criminal PAT available. Online access through XChange, see www.utcourts.gov/records/. Also see state introduction.

2nd District Court - Layton Department 425 Wasatch Dr, Layton, UT 84041; 801-444-4300; fax: 801-546-8224; 8AM-5PM (MST). *Misdemeanor, Civil, Eviction, Domestic, Probate, Traffic.*
http://utcourts.gov/

General Information: No confidential records, probation reports, sealed records released. Will fax documents $5.00 per page. Court makes copy: $.25 per page. Certification fee: $4.00 plus $.50 per add'l page includes copy fee. Payee: 2nd District Court. Personal checks, Visa/MC accepted. Prepayment required. Mail requests: SASE requested.

Civil Name Search: Access: Mail, in person, online. Visitors must perform in person searches themselves. Search fee: None, for first 20 minutes. Civil records on computer from 1988, archived from start of court. Computer index alpha and case number, archives by alpha from 1982, prior to 1982 n. Civil PAT goes back to 1988. Online access through XChange, see www.utcourts.gov/records/. Also see state introduction.

Criminal Name Search: Access: Mail, online, in person. Both court and visitors may perform in person name searches. Search fee: None, for first 20 minutes. Required to search: name, years to search; also helpful: DOB, SSN. Criminal records computerized from 1988, archived from start of court. Computer index alpha and case number, archives by alpha from 1982, prior to 198. Mail turnaround time 1 day. Criminal PAT goes back to same as civil. Online access through XChange, see www.utcourts.gov/records/. Also see state introduction.

Centerville Justice Court 250 N Main, Centerville, UT 84014-1824; 801-295-8344; fax: 801-294-0459; *Misdemeanor (B & C), Small Claims, Infractions, Traffic.*

Clearfield Justice Court 55 S State, Clearfield, UT 84015; 801-525-2760; fax: 801-525-2867; 8AM05PM (MST). *Misdemeanor (B & C), Small Claims, Infractions, Traffic.*
www.clearfieldcity.org/

Clinton Justice Court 2267 N 1500 W, Clinton, UT 84015; 801-614-0760; fax: 801-614-0772; 8AM-5PM (MST). *Misdemeanor (B & C), Small Claims, Infractions, Traffic.*
www.clintoncity.net/

Davis County Justice Court 800 W State St, PO Box 618, Farmington, UT 84025; 801-451-4488; fax: 801-451-4481; *Misdemeanor (B & C), Small Claims, Infractions, Traffic.*

North Salt Lake Justice Court 10 E Center St, North Salt Lake, UT 84054; 801-335-8640; fax: 801-335-8649; 7AM-5:30PM M-Th (MST). *Misdemeanor (B & C), Small Claims, Infractions, Traffic.*
www.nslcity.org/court.main.html

South Weber Justice Court 1600 E South Weber Dr, South Weber, UT 84405; 801-479-3177; fax: 801-479-0066; 7AM-5PM M-Th; 7AM-11AM F (MST). *Misdemeanor (B & C), Small Claims, Infractions, Traffic.*
www.southwebercity.com/justicecourt.main.html

Sunset Justice Court 200 W 1300 N, Sunset, UT 84015; 801-825-3303; fax: 801-614-9198; 9AM-5PM M-F (MST). *Misdemeanor (B & C), Small Claims, Infractions, Traffic.*

Syracuse Justice Court 1979 W 1900 S, Syracuse, UT 84705; 801-825-1477; fax: 801-825-3001; 8AM-5PM (MST). *Misdemeanor (B & C), Small Claims, Infractions, Traffic.*

Woods Cross Justice Court 1555 S 800 W, Woods Cross, UT 84087; 801-292-4421; fax: 801-292-2225; 8AM-5PM (MST). *Misdemeanor (B & C), Small Claims, Infractions, Traffic.*

General Information: The Court Administrator's hours are 7:30AM-3:30PM.

Duchesne County

8th District Court PO Box 990, Duchesne, UT 84021; 435-738-2753; fax: 435-738-2754; 8AM-5PM (MST). *Felony, Misdemeanor, Civil, Eviction, Small Claims, Probate.*
http://utcourts.gov/
General Information: Probate fax is same as main fax number. No confidential records released. Fee to fax out file $5.00 for 10 pages or less; $.50 each add'l over 10 pages. Court makes copy: $.25 per page. Certification fee: $4.00 per doc plus $.50 per page. Payee: 8th District Court. Personal checks and money orders accepted. Visa/MC accepted. Prepayment required. Mail requests: SASE required.
Civil Name Search: Access: Phone, mail, fax, online, in person. Both court and visitors may perform in person name searches. Search fee: $15.00 per hour. First 15 minutes no charge. Civil records on computer back to 6/1993, civil on microfiche back to 1912. Mail turnaround time 1-5 days. Civil PAT goes back to 6/1993. Online access through XChange, see www.utcourts.gov/records/.
Criminal Name Search: Access: Phone, mail, fax, online, in person. Both court and visitors may perform in person name searches. Search fee: $15.00 per hour. First 15 minutes no charge. Criminal records computerized from 1993; index books back to 1912. Mail turnaround time 1-5 days. Criminal PAT goes back to same as civil. Criminal records access through XChange. For information contact Jolene Cox 578-3831. Also, see state introduction.

8th District Court - Roosevelt Department PO Box 1286, 255 S State St, Roosevelt, UT 84066; 435-722-0235; fax: 435-722-0236; 8AM-5PM (MST). *Felony, Misdemeanor, Civil, Eviction, Probate.*
http://utcourts.gov/
General Information: No confidential, sealed, expunged or juvenile records released. Will fax documents $5.00 plus $.50 each add'l page. Court makes copy: $.25 per page. Certification fee: $4.00 plus $.50 per page includes copies. Payee: 8th District. Personal checks, Visa/MC accepted. Prepayment required. Mail requests: SASE required.
Civil Name Search: Access: Mail, fax, online, in person. Both court and visitors may perform in person name searches. Search fee: $15.00 per hour, first 15 minutes no charge. Civil records on computer since 1993. Mail turnaround time 2-5 days. Civil PAT goes back to 1991. Online access through XChange, see www.utcourts.gov/records/. Also see state introduction.
Criminal Name Search: Access: Mail, fax, online, in person. Both court and visitors may perform in person name searches. Search fee: $15.00 per hour, first 15 minutes no charge. Required to search: name, years to search; also helpful: DOB. Criminal records on computer since 1994. Mail turnaround time 2-5 days. Criminal PAT goes back to same as civil. Online access through XChange, see www.utcourts.gov/records/. Also see state introduction.

Duchesne Justice Court (East Precinct) 270 N 500 W, Roosevelt, UT 84066; 435-722-3354; fax: 435-738-0115; *Misdemeanor (B & C), Small Claims, Infractions, Traffic.*

Duchesne Justice Court (West Precinct) PO Box 15, Duchesne, UT 84021; 435-738-0109; fax: 435-738-0115; 8:30AM -1:30PM M-F (MST). *Misdemeanor (B & C), Small Claims, Infractions, Traffic.*
www.duchesnegov.net/legal/justicecriminaljustice.html

Emery County

7th District Court PO Box 635, 1850 N 560 W, Castle Dale, UT 84513; 435-381-2619; fax: 435-381-5625; 8AM-5PM (MST). *Felony, Misdemeanor, Civil, Eviction, Probate.*
http://utcourts.gov/
General Information: Phone for hearing impaired is 800-992-0172. No adoption, sealed records released. Will fax documents $5.00 1st page, $.50 each add'l. Court makes copy: $.25 per page. Certification fee: $4.00 plus $.50 per page includes copy fee; Exemplification fee $6.00 plus $.50 per page. Payee: 7th District Court. Personal checks, Visa/MC accepted. Prepayment required. Mail requests: SASE required.
Civil Name Search: Access: Phone, fax, mail, in person, online. Both court and visitors may perform in person name searches. No search fee. Civil records on computer from 1997, older on microfilm and archived. Mail turnaround time 1 week. Civil PAT goes back to 1997. Online access through XChange, see www.utcourts.gov/records/. Also see state introduction.
Criminal Name Search: Access: Phone, fax, mail, in person, online. Both court and visitors may perform in person name searches. No search fee. Required to search: name, years to search, DOB. Criminal records computerized from 1997, older on microfilm and archived. Mail turnaround time 1 week. Criminal PAT goes back to same as civil. Online access

through XChange, see www.utcourts.gov/records/. Also see state introduction.

Emery County/Castle Dale Justice Court PO Box 555, Castle Dale, UT 84513; 435-381-5194; fax: 435-381-5196; *Misdemeanor (B & C), Small Claims, Infractions, Traffic.*
Emery County/Green River Justice Court 48 Farrer St, PO Box 328, Green River, UT 84525; 435-564-3204; fax: 435-564-8322; *Misdemeanor (B & C), Small Claims, Infractions, Traffic.*

Garfield County

6th District Court PO Box 77, 55 S Main, Panguitch, UT 84759; 435-676-1104; fax: 435-676-8629; 8AM-5:30PM M-TH (MST). *Felony, Misdemeanor, Civil, Eviction, Small Claims, Probate.*
http://utcourts.gov/
General Information: No adoption records released. Fee to fax out file $1.00 for 1st page, $.50 each add'l. Court makes copy: $.25 per page. Self serve copy: $.10 per page. Certification fee: $4.00 plus $.50 per page. Payee: 6th District Court. Personal checks accepted, credit cards are not. Prepayment required. Mail requests: SASE not required.
Civil Name Search: Access: Phone, fax, mail, in person, online. Only the court performs in person name searches; visitors may not. Search fee: $15.00 per hour. Civil records archived for 100 years; on computer back to 2000. Mail turnaround time 1 day. Online access through XChange, see www.utcourts.gov/records/. Also see state introduction.
Criminal Name Search: Access: Fax, mail, in person, online. Only the court performs in person name searches; visitors may not. Search fee: $15.00 per hour. Criminal records archived for 100 years; on computer back to 2000. Mail turnaround time 1 day. Online access through XChange, see www.utcourts.gov/records/. Also see state introduction.

Escalante Justice Court 56 N 100 W, PO Box 189, Escalante, UT 84726; 435-826-4644; fax: 435-826-4642; 8AM-4PM M-F (MST). *Misdemeanor (B & C), Small Claims, Infractions, Traffic.*
Garfield County Justice Court 55 S Main, PO Box 77, Panguitch, UT 84759; 435-676-8826 ext 3; fax: 435-676-8239; 8AM-5:30 M-Th (MST). *Misdemeanor (B & C), Small Claims, Infractions, Traffic.*
Panguitch Justice Court PO Box 77, Panguitch, UT 84759; 435-676-1115; fax: 435-676-8239; 8AM-5:30 M-Th (MST). *Misdemeanor (B & C), Small Claims, Infractions, Traffic.*

Grand County

7th District Court 125 E Center St, Moab, UT 84532; 435-259-1349; fax: 435-259-4081; 8AM-5PM (MST). *Felony, Misdemeanor, Civil, Eviction, Probate, Domestic.*
http://utcourts.gov/
General Information: Phone search requests are limited one or two index names, less if clerk doesn't emphasize. No adoption, expunged records released. Will fax documents $5.00 flat rate for 1-10 pages, then $.50 each after 10. Court makes copy: $.25 per page. Certification fee: $4.00 plus $.50 per page. Payee: 7th District Court. Personal checks, Visa/MC accepted. Prepayment required. Mail requests: SASE required.
Civil Name Search: Access: Phone, mail, online, in person. Both court and visitors may perform in person name searches. Search fee: None for 1st 20 minutes; $15.00 per hour thereafter. District records on computer from Spring 1990, Circuit from spring 1989, archived since court started. Mail turnaround time 5 days. Civil PAT goes back to 1990. Online access through XChange, see www.utcourts.gov/records/. Also see state introduction.
Criminal Name Search: Access: Phone, mail, online, in person. Both court and visitors may perform in person name searches. Search fee: None for 1st 20 minutes; $15.00 per hour thereafter. Required to search: name, years to search; also helpful: DOB, SSN. District records on computer from spring 1990, Circuit from spring 1989, archived since court started. Mail turnaround time 1-5 days. Criminal PAT goes back to same as civil. Online access through XChange, see www.utcourts.gov/records/. Also see state introduction. Online results show middle initial, DOB.

Grand County Justice Court 125 E Center St, Moab, UT 84532; 435-259-1334; fax: 435-259-3070; 8AM-4:30PM M-F (MST). *Misdemeanor (B & C), Small Claims, Infractions, Traffic.*

Iron County

Fifth District Court 40 N 100 E, Cedar City, UT 84720; 435-867-3250; fax: 435-867-3212; 8AM-5PM (MST). *Felony, Misdemeanor, Civil, Eviction, Probate, Domestic.*
http://utcourts.gov/
General Information: Hearing location also in Parowan, but records held here. Probate fax is same as main fax number. No sealed records released. Will fax documents $5.00 up to 10 pages. Court makes copy: $.25 per page. Certification fee: $4.00 per doc plus $.50 per page; exemplification- $6.00 plus $.50 per page. Payee: 5th District Court. Personal checks accepted.

Major credit cards accepted. Prepayment required. Mail requests: SASE required.

Civil Name Search: Access: Mail, phone, in person, online. Both court and visitors may perform in person name searches. Search fee: varies. Required to search: name. District records on computer from 4/89, former Circuit Court records on computer from 1987, archived from 1900. Mail turnaround time 2-3 days. Civil PAT goes back to 1987. Online access through XChange, see www.utcourts.gov/records/. Also see state introduction.

Criminal Name Search: Access: Mail, phone, online, in person. Both court and visitors may perform in person name searches. Search fee: varies. Required to search: name, years to search, DOB, SSN. District records on computer from 4/89, former Circuit Court records on computer from 1987, archived from 1900. Mail turnaround time 2-3 days. Criminal PAT goes back to 1987. Online access through XChange, see www.utcourts.gov/records/. Also see state introduction.

Iron County Justice Court 82 N 100 E #101, Cedar City, UT 84720; 435-865-5335; fax: 435-865-5349; 8:30-5PM M-F (MST). *Misdemeanor (B & C), Small Claims, Infractions, Traffic.*

Parowan City Justice Court PO Box 1118, Parowan, UT 84761; 435-477-3940; fax: 435-477-8896; 8:30AM-4PM M-F (MST). *Misdemeanor (B & C), Small Claims, Infractions, Traffic.*

Juab County

4th District Court 160 N. Main, PO Box 249, Nephi, UT 84648; 435-623-0901; fax: 435-623-0922; 8AM-5PM (MST). *Felony, Misdemeanor, Civil, Eviction, Probate.*
http://utcourts.gov/

General Information: Probate fax is same as main fax number. Online identifiers in results same as on public terminal. All records must be viewed in this office. Will fax documents for $5.00 up to 10 pages, then $.50 ea add'l. Court makes copy: $.25 per page. Certification fee: $4.00 plus $.50 per page includes copies. Payee: 4th District Court. Personal checks, Visa/MC accepted. Prepayment required. Mail requests: SASE required.

Civil Name Search: Access: Phone, mail, online, in person. Both court and visitors may perform in person name searches. Search fee: $15.00 per hour. First 15 minutes are no charge. Civil records on computer from 11/94, archived since court started. Mail turnaround time 1 week. Civil PAT goes back to 11/1994. Online access through XChange, see www.utcourts.gov/records/. Also see state introduction.

Criminal Name Search: Access: Phone, mail, online, in person. Both court and visitors may perform in person name searches. Search fee: $15.00 per hour. First 15 minutes are no charge. Criminal records computerized from 11/94, archived since court started. Mail turnaround time 1 week. Criminal PAT goes back to same as civil. Online access through XChange, see www.utcourts.gov/records/. Also see state introduction. Online results show name only.

Juab County Justice Court (Nephi Precinct Court) 146 N Main, Nephi, UT 84648; 435-623-3440; fax: 435-623-5937; 8:30AM-5PM (MST). *Misdemeanor (B & C), Small Claims, Infractions, Traffic.*

Levan Justice Court PO Box 40, Levan, UT 84639; 435-623-1959; fax: 435-623-2730; 9AM-12 M-TH (MST). *Misdemeanor (B & C), Small Claims, Infractions, Traffic.*

Nephi City Justice Court 42 E 200 N, Nephi, UT 84648; 435-623-1263; fax: 435-623-0309; 3PM -5PM T-F (MST). *Misdemeanor (B & C), Small Claims, Infractions, Traffic.*

Kane County

6th District Court 76 N Main, Kanab, UT 84741; 435-644-2458; fax: 435-644-4939; 8AM-5PM (MST). *Felony, Misdemeanor, Civil, Eviction, Probate.*
http://kane.utah.gov/deptinfo.cfm?ID=11

General Information: No sealed, expunged records released. Fee to fax document $5.00 first 10 pages then $.50 ea add'l page. Court makes copy: $.25 per page. Self serve copy: same. Certification fee: $4.00 per doc plus $.50 per page. Payee: Sixth District Court. Personal checks accepted, credit cards are not. Prepayment required. Mail requests: SASE required.

Civil Name Search: Access: Phone, fax, mail, in person, online. Only the court performs in person name searches; visitors may not. Search fee: First 15 minutes of search is free, thereafter $25.00 per hour. Civil records on computer from 1985, archived since court started. Mail turnaround time 2-3 days. Online access through XChange, see www.utcourts.gov/records/. Also see state introduction.

Criminal Name Search: Access: Phone, fax, mail, in person, online. Only the court performs in person name searches; visitors may not. Search fee: First 15 minutes of search is free, thereafter $25.00 per hour. Criminal records computerized from 1985, archived since court started. Mail turnaround time 2-3 days. Online access through XChange, see www.utcourts.gov/records/. Also see state introduction.

Big Water Justice Court PO Box 410182, Big Water, UT 84741-2182; 435-675-3923; *Misdemeanor (B & C), Small Claims, Infractions, Traffic.*

Kanab City Justice Court PO Box 128, Kanab, UT 84741; 435-644-5797; fax: 435-644-3223; 8AM-5PM M-F (MST). *Misdemeanor (B & C), Small Claims, Infractions, Traffic.*

Kane County Justice Court 76 N Main, Kanab, UT 84741; 435-644-2351; fax: 435-644-2052; 8AM-5PM M-F (MST). *Misdemeanor (B & C), Small Claims, Infractions, Traffic.*

Orderville Justice Court PO Box 165, Orderville, UT 84758; 435-648-2534; fax: 435-648-2535; 9AM-5PM (MST). *Misdemeanor (B & C), Small Claims, Infractions, Traffic.*

Millard County

4th District Court 765 S Hwy 99, #6, Fillmore, UT 84631; 435-743-6223; fax: 435-743-6923; 8AM-5PM (MST). *Felony, Misdemeanor, Civil, Eviction, Small Claims, Probate.*
http://utcourts.gov/

General Information: No pre-sentence, expunged or sealed records released. Will not fax documents. Court makes copy: $.25 per page. Certification fee: $4.00 plus $.50 per page. Payee: 4th District Court. Business checks accepted. No credit cards accepted. Prepayment required. Mail requests: SASE required.

Civil Name Search: Access: Phone, mail, online, in person. Both court and visitors may perform in person name searches. No search fee. Civil records on computer from 1988, archived from 1896. Mail turnaround time 1 day. Civil PAT goes back to 1988. Online access through XChange, see www.utcourts.gov/records/. Also see state introduction.

Criminal Name Search: Access: Phone, mail, online, in person. Both court and visitors may perform in person name searches. No search fee. Criminal records computerized from 1988, archived from 1896. Mail turnaround time 1 day. Criminal PAT goes back to same as civil. Online access through XChange, see www.utcourts.gov/records/. Also see state introduction. Online results show middle initial, DOB.

Delta City Justice Court 76 N 200 W, Delta, UT 84624; 435-864-2759; fax: 435-864-4313; 7AM-6PM M,T (MST). *Misdemeanor (B & C), Small Claims, Infractions, Traffic.*

Fillmore City Justice Court 75 W Center St, Fillmore, UT 84631; 435-743-5425; fax: 435-743-5195; 8AM-5PM (MST). *Misdemeanor (B & C), Small Claims, Infractions, Traffic.*
www.fillmorecity.org/justicecourt.html

Millard County Justice Court (East Courtroom) 765 S Hwy 99 #2, Fillmore, UT 84631; 435-743-6952; fax: 435-743-4325; 8:30AM-5PM M-F (MST). *Misdemeanor (B & C), Small Claims, Infractions, Traffic.*

Millard County Justice Court (West Courtroom) 71 S 200 W, PO Box 854, Delta, UT 84624; 435-864-1403; fax: 435-864-1404; 7AM-5:45PM M-TH (MST). *Misdemeanor (B & C), Small Claims, Infractions, Traffic.*

Morgan County

2nd District Court PO Box 886, 48 W yound St, Morgan, UT 84050; 801-845-4020; fax: 801-829-6176; 8AM-5PM (MST). *Felony, Misdemeanor, Civil, Eviction, Small Claims, Probate.*
http://utcourts.gov/

General Information: No sealed records released. Will fax documents $5.00 fee. Court makes copy: $.25 per page. Certification fee: $4.00 plus $.50 per page. Payee: Morgan District. Personal checks, Visa/MC accepted. Prepayment required. Mail requests: SASE requested.

Civil Name Search: Access: Phone, fax, mail, online, in person. Both court and visitors may perform in person name searches. Search fee: $25.00 per name, if extensive. Civil records on computer since 1992; on microfiche, books, archived from 1862. Mail turnaround time several days. Civil PAT goes back to 1992. Online access through XChange, see www.utcourts.gov/records/. Also see state introduction. Extensive (special) search requests must be in writing.

Criminal Name Search: Access: Phone, fax, mail, online, in person. Both court and visitors may perform in person name searches. Search fee: $25.00 per name, if extensive. Required to search: name, years to search, DOB; also helpful: SSN. Criminal records on computer since 1992, prior in books. Mail turnaround time several days. Criminal PAT goes back to same as civil. Online access through XChange, see www.utcourts.gov/records/. Also see state introduction. Extensive (special) search requests must be in writing.

Morgan City Justice Court 90 W Young St, PO 1085, Morgan, UT 84050; 801-829-3461; fax: 801-829-6684; 7AM-6PM M-Th (MST). *Misdemeanor (B & C), Small Claims, Infractions, Traffic.*

Morgan County Justice Court 48 W Young St, PO Box 786, Morgan, UT 84050; 801-845-4021; fax: 801-845-6008; 8:30AM-5PM (MST). *Misdemeanor (B & C), Small Claims, Infractions, Traffic.*

Piute County

6th District Court PO Box 99, 550 N Main St, Junction, UT 84740; 435-577-2840; fax: 435-577-2433; 9AM-N, 1-5PM (MST). *Felony, Misdemeanor, Civil, Eviction, Small Claims, Probate.*
http://utcourts.gov/
General Information: No sealed records released. Will fax out documents in emergency for $.50 per page. Court makes copy: $.25 per page. Certification fee: $4.00 plus $.50 per page. Payee: Piute County District Court. Personal checks accepted, credit cards are not. Mail requests: SASE required.
Civil Name Search: Access: Mail, in person, online. Both court and visitors may perform in person name searches. No search fee. Civil records archived from 1889. Mail turnaround time 2-3 days. Online access through XChange, see www.utcourts.gov/records/. Also see state introduction.
Criminal Name Search: Access: Mail, in person, online. Both court and visitors may perform in person name searches. No search fee. Criminal records archived from 1889. Mail turnaround time 2-3 days. Online access through XChange, see www.utcourts.gov/records/. Also see state introduction.

Piute County Justice Court County Courthouse, PO Box 99, Junction, UT 84740; 435-577-2840; fax: 435-577-2433; *Misdemeanor (B & C), Small Claims, Infractions, Traffic.*

Rich County

1st District Court PO Box 218, Randolph, UT 84064; 435-793-2415; fax: 435-793-2410; 9AM-5PM (MST). *Felony, Misdemeanor, Civil, Eviction, Probate.*
http://utcourts.gov/
General Information: Probate fax is same as main fax number. No sealed records released. Will fax documents to local or toll free line. Court makes copy: $.25 per page. Self serve copy: same. Certification fee: $4.00 per page plus copy fee. Payee: Rich County. Personal checks accepted, credit cards are not. Prepayment required. Mail requests: SASE required.
Civil Name Search: Access: Phone, fax, mail, in person, online. Both court and visitors may perform in person name searches. Search fee: $10.00 per hour. Required to search: name, years to search; also helpful: address. Civil records ago back to 1896; computerized records since 2000. Mail turnaround time 2-3 days. Online access through XChange, see www.utcourts.gov/records/. Also see state introduction.
Criminal Name Search: Access: Phone, fax, mail, in person, online. Both court and visitors may perform in person name searches. Search fee: $10.00 per hour. Required to search: name, years to search; also helpful: address, DOB, SSN. Criminal records go back to 1896; computerized records since 2000. Mail turnaround time 2-3 days. Online access through XChange, see www.utcourts.gov/records/. Also see state introduction.

Rich Justice Court PO Box 218, Randolph, UT 84064; 435-793-2415; fax: 435-793-2410; Open 21 hours per week. Times not indicated (MST). *Misdemeanor (B & C), Small Claims, Infractions, Traffic.*

Salt Lake County

3rd District Court - Salt Lake Dept. PO Box 1860, 450 S State St, Salt Lake City, UT 84111; 801-238-7300; criminal phone: x3 or 238-7321; civil phone: x5 or 238-7480; probate phone: 801-238-7164; fax: 801-238-7404; 8AM-5PM (MST). *Felony, Misdemeanor, Civil, Eviction, Small Claims, Probate.*
http://utcourts.gov/
General Information: Probate fax- 801-238-7396. No confidential records released. Will fax documents $5.00 up to 10 pages; $.50 per each add'l page. Court makes copy: $.25 per page. Certification fee: $4.00 per doc plus $.50 per page; exemplification- $6.00 per doc and $.50 per page. Payee: 3rd District Court. Personal checks, Visa/MC accepted. Prepayment required.
Civil Name Search: Access: Phone, mail, in person, online. Both court and visitors may perform in person name searches. Search fee: First 15 minutes no charge, then $15.00 per hour. Civil records on computer from 1985, archived after 1969. Note: Clerk will answer phone requests for a few names only; can search W Jordan Div also. Mail turnaround time 2-3 days. Civil PAT goes back to 1985. Terminal results may also show SSNs. Online access through XChange, see www.utcourts.gov/records/. Also see state introduction.
Criminal Name Search: Access: Mail, fax, online, in person. Both court and visitors may perform in person name searches. Search fee: First 15 minutes no charge, then $15.00 per hour. Required to search: name, years to search, DOB; also helpful: SSN. Criminal records computerized from 1986, archived after satisfaction or dismissal, destroyed prior to 1985. Note: Once search completed, court will phone you for payment options. Mail turnaround time 2-3 days. Criminal PAT goes back to 1988. Online access through XChange, see www.utcourts.gov/records/. Also see state introduction. Online results show middle initial, DOB.

3rd District Court - West Jordan Department 8080 S Redwood Rd, Ste 1701, West Jordan, UT 84088; 801-233-9700; criminal fax: 801-233-9727; civil fax: 8AM-5PM; 8AM-5PM (MST). *Felony, Misdemeanor, Civil, Eviction, Domestic, Probate.*
http://utcourts.gov/
General Information: Now combined with old Sandy Division; formerly known as the West Valley Dept. No sealed records released. Will fax documents $5.00 1st 10 pages; $.50 ea add'l page. Court makes copy: $.25 per page. Certification fee: $4.00 plus $.50 per page. Payee: 3rd District Court. Personal checks, Visa/MC accepted. Prepayment required. Mail requests: SASE required.
Civil Name Search: Access: Mail, in person, online. Both court and visitors may perform in person name searches. Search fee: First 15 minutes no charge, then $15.00 per hour. Civil records on computer since 1986, archived from 1983. Mail turnaround time 1 week. Civil PAT goes back to 1986. Online access through XChange for a fee, see www.utcourts.gov/records/. Also see state introduction.
Criminal Name Search: Access: Mail, online, in person. Both court and visitors may perform in person name searches. Search fee: First 15 minutes no charge, then $15.00 per hour. Criminal records on computer since 1986, archived from 1983. Mail turnaround time 1 week. Criminal PAT goes back to same as civil. Online access through XChange for a fee, see www.utcourts.gov/records/. Also see state introduction.

3rd District Court - Sandy Department , West Jordan, UT 84088; *Felony, Misdemeanor, Civil, Eviction, Small Claims.*
http://utcourts.gov/
General Information: Now combined with the old West Valley Dept. to form the new West Jordan Dept.

Alta Justice Court PO Box 8016, Alta, UT 84092; 801-363-5105; fax: 801-742-1006; 8AM-5PM (MST). *Misdemeanor (B & C), Small Claims, Infractions, Traffic.*

Bluffdale Justice Court 14175 S 1700 W, Bluffdale, UT 84065; 801-446-9219; fax: 801-446-6332; 8:30 AM-5PM M,W,F; til 2PM T,TH (MST). *Misdemeanor (B & C), Small Claims, Infractions, Traffic.*

Draper Justice Court 1020 E Pioneer Rd, Draper, UT 84020-9628; 801-576-6544; fax: 801-576-6343; 8AM-5PM M-F (MST). *Misdemeanor (B & C), Small Claims, Infractions, Traffic.*

Herriman City Justice Court 13011 S Pioneer St, Herriman, UT 84096; 801-446-5323; fax: 801-446-5324; 8AM-5PM (MST). *Misdemeanor (B & C), Small Claims, Infractions, Traffic.*
www.herrimancity.net/

Holladay Justice Court 4580 S 2300 E, Holladay, UT 84117; 801-273-9731; fax: 801-527-2497; 8AM-5PM M-F (MST). *Misdemeanor (B & C), Small Claims, Infractions, Traffic.*

Midvale Justice Court 655 W Center St, Midvale, UT 84047; 801-255-4234; fax: 801-567-1696; 8AM-6PM M-F (MST). *Misdemeanor (B & C), Small Claims, Infractions, Traffic.*
www.midvalecity.org/mp.aspx?p=9

Murray City Justice Court 688 E Vine St, Murray, UT 84107; 801-284-4280; fax: 801-284-4285; 8AM-5 PM M-F (MST). *Misdemeanor (B & C), Small Claims, Infractions, Traffic.*
www.murray.utah.gov/index.aspx?NID=83

Riverton Justice Court 12830 S 1700 W, PO Box 429, Riverton, UT 84065; 801-208-3131; fax: 801-446-4274; 8AM-6PM M-TH; 8AM-5PM F (MST). *Misdemeanor (B & C), Small Claims, Infractions, Traffic.*

Salt Lake City Justice Court 333 S 200 E, Salt Lake City, UT 84111; 801-535-6300; fax: 801-535-6302; 7:30AM-5PM (MST). *Misdemeanor (B & C), Small Claims, Infractions, Traffic.*
www.slcgov.com/courts/

Salt Lake County Justice Court 2001 S State Rm 4200, Salt Lake City, UT 84190; 801-468-3430; fax: 801-468-3483; 8AM-5PM M-F (MST). *Misdemeanor (B & C), Small Claims, Infractions, Traffic.*

Sandy City Justice Court 210 W Sego Lily Dr, Sandy, UT 84070; 801-568-7160; fax: 801-568-7166; 8:45AM-5PM M-F (MST). *Misdemeanor (B & C), Small Claims, Infractions, Traffic.*

South Jordan Justice Court 1600 W Towne Center Dr, South Jordan, UT 84095; 801-254-6381; fax: 801-253-5219; 8AM -5PM M-F Closed 3rd Friday 2-3:30 (MST). *Misdemeanor (B & C), Small Claims, Infractions, Traffic.*
www.southjordancity.org/court.asp

South Salt Lake Justice Court 220 E Morris Ave (2430 S), South Salt Lake, UT 84115; 801-483-6072; fax: 801-464-6786; 8AM-5PM M-F (MST). *Misdemeanor (B & C), Small Claims, Infractions, Traffic.*

Taylorsville Justice Court 2600 W Taylorsville Blvd, Taylorsville, UT 84118; 801-963-0268; fax: 801-963-0576; 8AM-5PM M-F (MST). *Misdemeanor (B & C), Small Claims, Infractions, Traffic.*
www.utcourts.gov

West Jordan Justice Court 8040 S Redwood Rd, West Jordan, UT 84088; 801-256-2290 ext1; fax: 801-256-2283; 8AM-5PM M-F (MST). *Misdemeanor (B & C), Small Claims, Infractions, Traffic.*

West Valley Justice Court 3590 S 2700 W, West Valley, UT 84119; 801-963-3590; fax: 801-963-3589; 8AM-6PM (MST). *Misdemeanor (B & C), Small Claims, Infractions, Traffic.*

San Juan County

7th District Court PO Box 68, Monticello, UT 84535; 435-587-2122; fax: 435-587-2372; 8AM-5PM (MST). *Felony, Misdemeanor, Civil, Eviction, Probate.*
http://utcourts.gov/

General Information: No juvenile records released. Fee to fax out file $5.00 up to 10 pages; $.50 for each add'l page. Court makes copy: $.25 per page. Certification fee: $4.00 plus $.50 per page. Payee: 7th District Court. Personal checks accepted. Visa/MC accepted in person and by phone. Prepayment required. Mail requests: SASE required or postage.

Civil Name Search: Access: Phone, mail, fax, online, in person. Both court and visitors may perform in person name searches. Search fee: $15.00 per hour. Civil records on computer since 1991; on index books from 1919 to 1991. Mail turnaround time 1 week. Civil PAT goes back to 1991. Results include last 4 digits of SSN. Online access through XChange, see www.utcourts.gov/records/. Also see state introduction.

Criminal Name Search: Access: Mail, fax, online, in person. Both court and visitors may perform in person name searches. Search fee: $15.00 per hour. Criminal records on computer since 1991; on index books from 1919 to 1991. Note: Results include last 4 digits on SSN. Mail turnaround time 1 week. Criminal PAT goes back to same as civil. Results include last 4 digits of SSN. Online access through XChange, see www.utcourts.gov/records/. Also see state introduction. Online results show middle initial, DOB.

Blanding Justice Court 167 E 500 N, Blanding, UT 84511; 435-678-2334; fax: 435-678-1507; 7:30-5:30 M-Th (MST). *Misdemeanor (B & C), Small Claims, Infractions, Traffic.*

Monticello Justice Court PO Box 1158, Monticello, UT 84535; 435-587-2399; fax: 435-587-2272; 8AM-5PM (MST). *Misdemeanor (B & C), Small Claims, Infractions, Traffic.*

San Juan County Justice Court 297 S Main St, PO Box 833, Monticello, UT 84535; 435-587-2544; fax: 435-587-2171; 8AM-5PM (MST). *Misdemeanor (B & C), Small Claims, Infractions, Traffic.*

Sanpete County

6th District Court 160 N Main, Manti, UT 84642; 435-835-2121; 8AM-5PM (MST). *Felony, Misdemeanor, Civil, Eviction, Small Claims, Probate.*
http://utcourts.gov/

General Information: No criminal, expunged, or sealed records released. Will fax documents $5.00 fee; add $.50 per page over 10. Court makes copy: $.25 per page. Certification fee: $4.00 plus $.50 per page; exemplification fee is $6.00 plus $.50 per page. Payee: 6th District Court. Personal checks accepted. Major credit cards accepted. Prepayment required. Mail requests: SASE requested.

Civil Name Search: Access: Phone, fax, mail, in person, online. Both court and visitors may perform in person name searches. Search fee: $15.00 per hour after first 15 minutes free. Civil records on computer from 1998. Mail turnaround time 10 days. Civil PAT goes back to 9/1998. Online access through XChange, see www.utcourts.gov/records/. Also see state introduction.

Criminal Name Search: Access: Phone, fax, mail, in person, online. Both court and visitors may perform in person name searches. Search fee: $15.00 per hour. Required to search: name, years to search; also helpful: DOB. Criminal records computerized from 1998. Mail turnaround time 10 days. Criminal PAT goes back to 9/1998. Online access through XChange, see www.utcourts.gov/records/. Also see state introduction.

Ephraim Justice Court 5 S Main St, Ephraim, UT 84627; 435-283-4631; fax: 435-283-4867; 9AM-4PM M-W (MST). *Misdemeanor (B & C), Small Claims, Infractions, Traffic.*

Fairview Justice Court 85 S State, PO Box 97, Fairview, UT 84629; 435-427-3858; fax: 435-427-3275; 8AM-3PM (MST). *Misdemeanor (B & C), Small Claims, Infractions, Traffic.*

Fountain Green Justice Court PO Box 97, Fountain Green, UT 84632; 435-445-3453; fax: 435-445-3375; 9AM-2PM M-F (MST). *Misdemeanor (B & C), Small Claims, Infractions, Traffic.*

Gunnison Justice Court 38 W Center, PO Box 790, Gunnison, UT 84634; 435-528-5494; fax: 435-528-7958; 10AM-Noon M-F (MST). *Misdemeanor (B & C), Small Claims, Infractions, Traffic.*

Manti Justice Court 50 S Main St, Manti, UT 84642; 435-835-4631; fax: 435-835-2632; *Misdemeanor (B & C), Small Claims, Infractions, Traffic.*

Moroni City Justice Court 80 S 200 W, PO Box 870, Moroni, UT 84646-0010; 435-436-8359 ext 3; fax: 435-436-8178; 10AM-2PM M-F (MST). *Misdemeanor (B & C), Small Claims, Infractions, Traffic.*

Mount Pleasant Justice Court 115 W Main St, Mt Pleasant, UT 84647; 435-462-2456 x106; fax: 435-462-2581; N-4PM (MST). *Misdemeanor (B & C), Small Claims, Infractions, Traffic.*

Sanpete County Justice Court 160 N Main, PO Box 146, Manti, UT 84642; 435-835-2103; fax: 435-835-2106; 9AM-3PM (MST). *Misdemeanor (B & C), Small Claims, Infractions, Traffic.*

Spring City Justice Court 150 E Center, PO Box 189, Spring City, UT 84662; 435-462-2244; fax: 435-462-2654; 10 hours weekly - varies (MST). *Misdemeanor (B & C), Small Claims, Infractions, Traffic.*

Sevier County

6th District Court 895 E 300 N, Richfield, UT 84701-2345; 435-896-2700; fax: 435-896-8047; 8AM-5PM (MST). *Felony, Misdemeanor, Civil, Eviction, Probate.*
http://utcourts.gov/

General Information: No sealed records released. Will fax documents $5.00 1st 10 pages, $.50 each add'l. Court makes copy: $.25 per page. Self serve copy: computer access terminal copies $.25 each. Certification fee: $4.00 plus $.50 per page includes copies; Exemplifications fee- $6.00. Payee: 6th District Court. Personal checks, Visa/MC accepted. Prepayment required. Mail requests: SASE required.

Civil Name Search: Access: Phone, fax, mail, online, in person. Both court and visitors may perform in person name searches. Search fee: $15.00 per hour. For search requiring 15 minutes or less, no charge. Circuit records on computer from 1989, District on computer from 1991. Mail turnaround time 2-3 days. Civil PAT goes back to 1992. Online access through XChange, see www.utcourts.gov/records/. Also see state introduction.

Criminal Name Search: Access: Fax, mail, online, in person. Both court and visitors may perform in person name searches. Search fee: $15.00 per hour minimum. For search requiring 15 minutes or less, no charge. Required to search: name, years to search, DOB, SSN. Circuit records on computer from 1989, District on computer from 1991. Mail turnaround time 2-3 days. Criminal PAT goes back to same as civil. Online access through XChange, see www.utcourts.gov/records/. Also see state introduction. Online results show middle initial, DOB.

Aurora Justice Court 240 N 200 W, PO Box 477, Aurora, UT 84620; 435-529-7643; fax: 435-529-3808; 9AM-12 (MST). *Misdemeanor (B & C), Small Claims, Infractions, Traffic.*

Salina Justice Court 90 W Main St, PO Box 69, Salina, UT 84654; 435-529-3651; fax: 435-529-1235; 10AM-5:30PM M-TH (MST). *Misdemeanor (B & C), Small Claims, Infractions, Traffic.*

Sevier County Justice Court 250 N Main #124, Richfield, UT 84701; 435-893-0461; fax: 435-896-8888; 8AM-5PM (MST). *Misdemeanor (B & C), Small Claims, Infractions, Traffic.*

Summit County

3rd District Court 6300 N Silver Creek, Park City, UT 84098; 435-615-4300; fax: 435-658-1067; 8AM-5PM. *Felony, Misdemeanor, Civil, Small Claims, Evictions, Probate.*
http://utcourts.gov/

General Information: Will fax documents $5.00 1st 1-10 pages, then $.50 per page. Court makes copy: $.25 per page. Certification fee: $4.00 plus $.50 per page. Payee: 3rd District Court. Personal checks accepted. Major credit cards accepted. Prepayment required. Mail requests: SASE required.

Civil Name Search: Access: Mail, in person, online. Both court and visitors may perform in person name searches. Search fee: $15.00 per hour, first 15 minutes free. Required to search: name, years to search; also helpful: DOB. By plaintiff and defendant. All indexes on computer back to 1993, records archived back to 1900's. Mail turnaround time 2 days. Civil PAT goes back to 9/1993. The last 4 digits of the SSN may appear on the terminal. Online access through XChange, see www.utcourts.gov/records/. Also see state introduction.

Criminal Name Search: Access: Mail, online, in person. Both court and visitors may perform in person name searches. Search fee: $15.00 per hour. First 15 minutes no charge. Required to search: name, years to search; also helpful: DOB. Criminal records on computer since 1993. Mail turnaround time 2 days. Criminal PAT goes back to same as civil. The last 4 digits of the SSN may appear on the terminal. Online access through XChange, see www.utcourts.gov/records/. Also see state introduction.

Summit County Justice Court 6300 N Silver Creek Dr, Park City, UT 84098; 435-615-3800; fax: 435-615-3810; 8AM-5PM. *Misdemeanor (B & C), Small Claims, Infractions, Traffic.*

Tooele County

3rd District Court 74 South 100 East, #14, Tooele, UT 84074; 435-833-8000; fax: 435-833-8058; 8AM-5PM (MST). *Felony, Misdemeanor, Civil, Eviction, Small Claims, Probate.*
www.utcourts.gov/courts/dist/distsites/3rd/tooele.html
General Information: No adoption records released. Will fax documents $5.00 for 10 pages; $.50 each add'l. Court makes copy: $.25 per page. Self serve copy: same. Certification fee: $4.00 plus $.50 per page; exemplifications $6.00 plus $.50 per page. Payee: 3rd District Court. Personal checks accepted. Credit cards accepted. Prepayment required. Mail requests: SASE required.
Civil Name Search: Access: Fax, mail, online, in person. Both court and visitors may perform in person name searches. Search fee: $15.00 per hour. First 20 minutes no charge. Civil records on computer from 1982, archived since court started. Mail turnaround time 2-3 days. Civil PAT goes back to 1982. Online access through XChange, see www.utcourts.gov/records/. Also see state introduction. Fees involved.
Criminal Name Search: Access: Fax, mail, online, in person. Both court and visitors may perform in person name searches. Search fee: $15.00 per hour. First 20 minutes no charge. Required to search: name, years to search; also helpful: SSN. Criminal records computerized from 1989, archived since court started. Mail turnaround time 2-3 days. Criminal PAT goes back to 1989. Online access through XChange, see www.utcourts.gov/records/. Also see state introduction. Fees involved

Grantsville Justice Court 429 E Main, Grantsville, UT 84029; 435-884-6271; fax: 435-884-0237; 9AM - 5PM M-F (MST). *Misdemeanor (B & C), Small Claims, Infractions, Traffic.*

Stockton Justice Court PO Box 240, Stockton, UT 84071; 435-882-3877; fax: 435-833-9031; 9AM-4PM M,T,TH,F; 9AM-10AM W (MST). *Misdemeanor (B & C), Small Claims, Infractions, Traffic.*

Tooele Valley Justice Court 74 S 100 E #12, Tooele, UT 84074; 435-843-3230; fax: 435-843-4702; 8AM-4:30 M-F (MST). *Misdemeanor (B & C), Small Claims, Infractions, Traffic.*

Wendover City Justice Court 920 East Blvd, PO Box 665, Wendover, UT 84043; 435-665-7000; fax: 435-665-7070; *Misdemeanor (B & C), Small Claims, Infractions, Traffic.*

Uintah County

8th District Court 920 E Hwy 40, Vernal, UT 84078; 435-781-9300; fax: 435-789-0564; 8AM-5PM (MST). *Felony, Misdemeanor, Civil, Eviction, Probate.*
http://utcourts.gov/
General Information: Online identifiers in results same as on public terminal. No sealed records released. Will fax documents to local or toll free line. Court makes copy: $.25 per page. Certification fee: $4.00 plus $.50 per page. Payee: 8th District Court. Personal checks accepted. Credit cards accepted. Prepayment required. Mail requests: SASE required.
Civil Name Search: Access: Mail, in person, online. Both court and visitors may perform in person name searches. Search fee: $15.00 per hour. First 20 minutes no charge. Circuit records on computer from 1987, everything else from 1989, archived since court started. Mail turnaround time 2-3 days. Civil PAT goes back to 1987. Online access through XChange, see www.utcourts.gov/records/. Also see state introduction.
Criminal Name Search: Access: Mail, online, in person. Both court and visitors may perform in person name searches. Search fee: $15.00 per hour. First 20 minutes no charge. Circuit records on computer from 1987, everything else from 1989, archived since court started. Mail turnaround time 2-3 days. Criminal PAT goes back to same as civil. Online access through XChange, see www.utcourts.gov/records/. Also see state introduction. Online results show middle initial, DOB.

Naples Justice Court 1420 E 2850 S, Naples, UT 84078; 435-789-9292; fax: 435-789-9458; 9AM-5PM M-F (MST). *Misdemeanor (B & C), Small Claims, Infractions, Traffic.*

Uintah County Justice Court 641 E 300 S #100, Vernal, UT 84078; 435-781-5338; fax: 435-781-6726; 8AM-5PM M-F (MST). *Misdemeanor (B & C), Small Claims, Infractions, Traffic.*

Vernal Justice Court 374 E Main St, Vernal, UT 84078; 435-789-7137; fax: 435-789-1753; 8AM-5PM M-F (MST). *Misdemeanor (B & C), Small Claims, Infractions, Traffic.*

Utah County

4th District Court 125 N 100 W, Provo, UT 84601; 801-429-1000; fax: 801-429-1033; 8AM-5PM (MST). *Felony, Misdemeanor, Civil, Eviction, Small Claims, Probate.*
http://utcourts.gov/
General Information: The court is organized by "Judge Teams" rather than civil or criminal. Online identifiers in results same as on public terminal. No sealed records released. Will fax documents $5.00 up to 10 pages, then $.50 per page. Court makes copy: $.25 per page. Certification fee: $4.00 plus $.50 per page. Payee: 4th District Court. Personal checks, Visa/MC accepted. Prepayment required. Mail requests: SASE required.
Civil Name Search: Access: Phone, mail, fax, in person, online. Both court and visitors may perform in person name searches. Search fee: $15.00 per hour or based on search. Civil and probate on computer from 1986, judgments, tax liens, and divorce decrees on microfiche from 1900 to 1975, archived from 1900s. Mail turnaround time 7-10 days. Civil PAT goes back to 1986. Online access through XChange, see www.utcourts.gov/records/. Also see state introduction.
Criminal Name Search: Access: Phone, mail, fax, in person, online. Both court and visitors may perform in person name searches. Search fee: $15.00 per hour or based on search. Required to search: name, years to search; also helpful: DOB. Felony on computer from 1989; archived from 1900s. Mail turnaround time 7-10 days. Criminal PAT goes back to 1989. Online access through XChange, see www.utcourts.gov/records/. Also see state introduction. Online results show middle initial, DOB.

4th District Court - Orem Department 97 E Center, Orem, UT 84057; 801-764-5860; criminal phone: 801-764-5865; civil phone: 801-764-5864; fax: 801-226-5244; 8AM-5PM (MST). *Misdemeanor, Civil, Eviction, Small Claims.*
http://utcourts.gov/
General Information: No sealed, expunged or confidential records released. Will fax documents to local or toll-free number. Court makes copy: $.25 per page. Certification fee: $4.00 plus $.50 per page. Payee: 4th District Court. Personal checks accepted. Credit cards accepted. Prepayment required.
Civil Name Search: Access: Mail, in person, online. Both court and visitors may perform in person name searches. Search fee: $15.00 per hour. First 20 minutes no charge. Civil records on computer since 1988. Mail turnaround time 5-7 days. Civil PAT goes back to 1988. Online access through XChange, see www.utcourts.gov/records/. Also see state introduction.
Criminal Name Search: Access: Mail, online, in person. Both court and visitors may perform in person name searches. Search fee: $15.00 per hour. First 20 minutes no charge. Required to search: name, years to search; also helpful: DOB. Criminal records on computer since 1988. Mail turnaround time 5-7 days. Criminal PAT goes back to same as civil. Online access through XChange, see www.utcourts.gov/records/. Also see state introduction.

4th District Court - Spanish Forks Department 775 W Center, Spanish Forks, UT 84660; 801-804-4800; fax: 801-804-4699; 8AM-5PM (MST). *Misdemeanor, Civil, Eviction, Small Claims.*
http://utcourts.gov/
General Information: No sealed, expunged or confidential records released. No fee to fax documents. Fax requires prior arrangement. Court makes copy: $.25 per page. Self serve copy: same. Certification fee: $4.00 plus $.50 per page. Payee: 4th District Court. Personal checks accepted. Credit cards accepted. Prepayment required.
Civil Name Search: Access: Phone, fax, mail, online, in person. Both court and visitors may perform in person name searches. Search fee: $15.00 per hour. First 15 minutes no charge. Civil records stored from 1978, on computer since 1987. Mail turnaround time 5-7 days. Civil PAT goes back to 1987. Online access through XChange, see www.utcourts.gov/records/. Also see state introduction.
Criminal Name Search: Access: Phone, fax, mail, online, in person. Both court and visitors may perform in person name searches. Search fee: $15.00 per hour. First 15 minutes no charge. Required to search: name, years to search; also helpful: DOB. Criminal records stored from 1978, on computer since 1987. Mail turnaround time 5-7 days. Criminal PAT goes back to same as civil. Online access through XChange, see www.utcourts.gov/records/. Also see state introduction.

4th District Court - American Fork Department 75 E 80 N, #202, American Fork, UT 84003; 801-756-9654; fax: 801-763-0153; 8AM-5PM (MST). *Felony, Misdemeanor, Civil, Eviction, Domestic.*
http://utcourts.gov/
General Information: Online identifiers in results same as on public terminal. No sealed, expunged or confidential records released. Will fax documents $5.00 per fax plus $.50 per page after 10 pages. Court makes copy: $.25 per page. Certification fee: $4.00 plus $.50 per page. Payee: 4th

District Court. Personal checks, Visa/MC accepted. Prepayment required. Mail requests: SASE required.

Civil Name Search: Access: Mail, in person, online. Both court and visitors may perform in person name searches. Search fee: $15.00 per hour. First 15 minutes no charge. Civil records on computer since 1988. Mail turnaround time 5-7 days. Civil PAT goes back to 5/1988. Online access through XChange, see www.utcourts.gov/records/. Also see state introduction.

Criminal Name Search: Access: Mail, online, in person. Both court and visitors may perform in person name searches. Search fee: $15.00 per hour. First 15 minutes no charge. Required to search: name, years to search; also helpful: DOB. Criminal records stored since 1988. Mail turnaround time 5-7 days. Criminal PAT goes back to same as civil. Online access through XChange, see www.utcourts.gov/records/. Also see state introduction. Online results show middle initial, DOB.

Alpine Justice Court 5400 W Civic Center Dr #4, Highland, UT 84003; 801-756-5751; fax: 801-756-6903; 7:30AM-6:30PM M-Th & 8:30-11:30AM F (MST). *Misdemeanor (B & C), Small Claims, Infractions, Traffic.*

City of Orem Justice Court 97 E Center, Orem, UT 84057; 801-724-3900; fax: 801-724-3934; 8AM-5PM (MST). *Misdemeanor (B & C), Small Claims, Infractions, Traffic.*
www.orem.org/

Genola Justice Court 275 W Main, Santaquin, UT 84655; 801-754-5376; fax: 801-754-1699; 9AM-5PM M-TH; 9AM-1PM F (MST). *Misdemeanor (B & C), Small Claims, Infractions, Traffic.*

Goshen Justice Court 275 W Main, Santaquin, UT 84655; 801-754-5376; fax: 801-754-1699; 9AM-5PM M-TH; 9AM-1PM F (MST). *Misdemeanor (B & C), Small Claims, Infractions, Traffic.*

Highland Justice Court 5400 W Civic Center Dr #4, Highland, UT 84003; 801-756-5751 ext 2; fax: 801-756-6903; 7:30AM-6:00PM M-Th 8:30AM-11:30AM F (MST). *Misdemeanor (B & C), Small Claims, Infractions, Traffic.*

Lehi City Justice Court 154 N Center, Lehi, UT 84043; 801-768-7160; fax: 801-768-8405; 8AM-5PM (MST). *Misdemeanor (B & C), Small Claims, Infractions, Traffic.*
www.lehi-ut.gov/

Lindon City Justice Court 100 N State St, Lindon, UT 84042; 801-785-1971; fax: 801-785-4336; 8AM-5PM M-F (MST). *Misdemeanor (B & C), Small Claims, Infractions, Traffic.*

Mapleton Justice Court 125 W 400 N, Mapleton, UT 84664; 801-489-7445; fax: 801-489-5657; 8:30AM-5PM M,T,TH,F; 8AM-10AM W (MST). *Misdemeanor (B & C), Small Claims, Infractions, Traffic.*

Payson Justice Court 439 W Utah Ave, Payson, UT 84651; 801-465-5210; fax: 801-465-5223; 7:30AM-6PM M-TH; 9AM-11AM F (MST). *Misdemeanor (B & C), Small Claims, Infractions, Traffic.*

Pleasant Grove Justice Court 70 S 100 E, Public Safety Bldg, Pleasant Grove, UT 84062; 801-785-9461; fax: 801-785-8304; 7:30AM-4:30PM M-Th 8:00-11:30AM F (MST). *Misdemeanor (B & C), Small Claims, Infractions, Traffic.*

Provo City Justice Court 310 W Center St, Provo, UT 84601; 801-852-6878; fax: 801-494-1091; 8AM-5PM (MST). *Misdemeanor (B & C), Small Claims, Infractions, Traffic.*

Santaquin Justice Court 275 W Main, Santaquin, UT 84655; 801-754-5376; fax: 801-754-1699; 9AM-5PM M-TH; 9AM-1PM F (MST). *Misdemeanor (B & C), Small Claims, Infractions, Traffic.*
www.santaquin.org/

Saratoga Springs Justice Court 1307 N Commerce Dr #200, Saratoga Springs, UT 84045; 801-766-6508; fax: 801-766-9794; 8AM-6PM M-TH; 8AM-5PM F (MST). *Misdemeanor (B & C), Small Claims, Infractions, Traffic.*
www.saratogaspringscity.com/

Springville Justice Court 110 S Main, Springville, UT 84663; 801-489-2707; fax: 801-491-7815; 8AM-5PM M-F (MST). *Misdemeanor (B & C), Small Claims, Infractions, Traffic.*
General Information: justicecourt@springville.org

Utah County Justice Court 151 S University Ave #3300, Provo, UT 84601; 801-851-7200; fax: 801-851-7201; 8AM-4PM M-F (MST). *Misdemeanor (B & C), Small Claims, Infractions, Traffic.*

Wasatch County

4th District Court 1361 S Hwy 40, PO Box 730, Heber City, UT 84032; 435-654-4676; fax: 435-654-5281; 8AM-5PM (MST). *Felony, Misdemeanor, Civil, Eviction, Probate, Domestic.*
http://utcourts.gov/

General Information: Small claims are handled at one of two Justice Courts. Heber City Justice Court- 435-654-1662, Wasatch County Justice Court- 435-654-2679. Probate fax is same as main fax number. No adoption records released. Will fax documents for $5.00 for up to 10 pages then $.50 per page ea add'l. Court makes copy: $.25 per page. Certification fee: $4.00 plus $.50 per page. Payee: 4th District Court. Personal checks accepted. Credit cards accepted. Prepayment required. Mail requests: SASE required.

Civil Name Search: Access: Phone, fax, mail, online, in person. Only the court performs in person name searches; visitors may not. No search fee. Civil records on computer since 1/95; on books prior; records archived since court started. Mail turnaround time 1-2 days. Online access through XChange, see www.utcourts.gov/records/. Also see state introduction.

Criminal Name Search: Access: Phone, fax, mail, online, in person. Only the court performs in person name searches; visitors may not. No search fee. Required to search: name, years to search; also helpful: DOB, signed release. Criminal records on computer since 1/95; records archived since court started. Mail turnaround time 1-2 days. Online access through XChange, see www.utcourts.gov/records/. Also see state introduction.

Heber City Justice Court 75 N Main St, Heber City, UT 84032; 435-654-1662; fax: 435-654-6494; 7:30AM-5PM M-Th 8:00-Noon Friday (MST). *Misdemeanor (B & C), Small Claims, Infractions, Traffic.*
www.ci.heber.ut.us/justice_court.htm

Wasatch County Justice Court 1361 S Hwy 40, PO Box 730, Heber City, UT 84032; 435-654-2679; fax: 435-654-5048; 8AM-5PM (MST). *Misdemeanor (B & C), Small Claims, Infractions, Traffic.*

Washington County

5th District Court 206 W Tabernacle, St. George, UT 84770; 435-986-5700 or 5701; fax: 435-986-5723; 8AM-5PM (MST). *Felony, Misdemeanor, Civil, Eviction, Probate.*
http://utcourts.gov/

General Information: Small Claims are found at the Justice Court at this location at 435-986-5700. Online identifiers in results same as on public terminal. No mental health, sealed, private, or adoption records released. Fee to fax out file extra $.25 per page; minimum $5.00 charge. Court makes copy: $.25 per page. Certification fee: $4.00 plus $.50 per page; exemplification fee- $6.00 per doc plus $.50 per page. Payee: 5th District Court. Personal checks accepted. Credit cards accepted. Prepayment required. Mail requests: SASE required.

Civil Name Search: Access: Mail, fax, online, in person. Both court and visitors may perform in person name searches. Search fee: None; fee will apply if search exceeds 15 minutes. Required to search: name. District Court records on computer from 4/1990; Circuit Court on computer from 1987. Mail turnaround time 8-10 days. Public use terminal available. Online access through XChange, see www.utcourts.gov/records/. Also see state introduction.

Criminal Name Search: Access: Mail, online, in person, fax. Both court and visitors may perform in person name searches. Search fee: None; fee will apply if search exceeds 15 minutes. District Court records on computer from 4/1990; Circuit Court on computer from 1987. Mail turnaround time 10 days. Public use terminal available. Online access through XChange, see www.utcourts.gov/records/. Also see state introduction. Online results show middle initial, DOB.

Enterprise Justice Court PO Box 340, Enterprise, UT 84725; 435-878-2221; fax: 435-878-2311; 8AM - 4:30 M-F (MST). *Misdemeanor (B & C), Small Claims, Infractions, Traffic.*

Hildale Justice Court 320 E Newel Ave, PO Box 840490, Hildale, UT 84784-0490; 435-874-2323; fax: 435-874-2603; 8AM-6PM M-TH (MST). *Misdemeanor (B & C), Small Claims, Infractions, Traffic.*

Hurricane Justice Court 80 S 700 W, Hurricane, UT 84737; 435-635-4072 ext. 102; fax: 435-635-5066; 8Am - 5PM M-Th 8AM-3PM F (MST). *Misdemeanor (B & C), Small Claims, Infractions, Traffic.*
www.cityofhurricane.com/categories/departments/justice/

Santa Clara Justice Court 2603 Santa Clara Dr, Santa Clara, UT 84765; 435-673-6712; fax: 435-628-7338; 8AM-5PM (MST). *Misdemeanor (B & C), Small Claims, Infractions, Traffic.*

Washington City Justice Court 111 N 100 E, Washington City, UT 84780; 435-656-6350; fax: 435-656-6372; 8AM-5PM (MST). *Misdemeanor (B & C), Small Claims, Infractions, Traffic.*
http://new.washingtoncity.org/government/index.php?sub=Court

Washington County Justice Court 87 N 200 E 3rd Fl, St George, UT 84770-3401; 435-634-5728; fax: 435-656-3003; 8AM-5PM (MST). *Misdemeanor (B & C), Small Claims, Infractions, Traffic.*
www.washco.utah.gov/justicecourt/

Wayne County

6th District Court PO Box 189, 18 S Main, Loa, UT 84747; 435-836-1301; fax: 435-836-2479; 9AM-5PM (MST). *Felony, Misdemeanor, Civil, Eviction, Small Claims, Probate.*
http://utcourts.gov/

General Information: No sealed records released. Fee to fax out file $1.00 per page. Court makes copy: $.25 per page. Certification fee: $4.00 plus $.50 per page. Payee: 6th District Court. Personal checks accepted, credit cards are not. Prepayment required. Mail requests: SASE required.

Civil Name Search: Access: Phone, mail, fax, in person, online. Both court and visitors may perform in person name searches. Search fee: $15.00 per hour. Civil records archived since court started; computerized from 10/2000. Mail turnaround time 2-3 days. Online access through XChange, see www.utcourts.gov/records/. Also see state introduction.

Criminal Name Search: Access: Phone, mail, fax, in person, online. Both court and visitors may perform in person name searches. Search fee: $15.00 per hour. Required to search: name, years to search; also helpful: SSN. Criminal records archived since court started; computerized from 10/2000. Mail turnaround time 2-3 days. Online access through XChange, see www.utcourts.gov/records/. Also see state introduction.

Wayne County Justice Court PO Box 327, Loa, UT 84747; 435-836-1320; fax: 435-836-2479; 9AM - 5PM M,T (MST). *Misdemeanor (B & C), Small Claims, Infractions, Traffic.*
General Information: Call for appt.

Weber County

2nd District Court 2525 Grant Ave, Ogden, UT 84401; 801-395-1079; probate phone: 801-395-1058; fax: 801-395-1182; 8AM-5PM (MST). *Felony, Misdemeanor, Civil, Eviction, Small Claims, Probate.*
http://utcourts.gov/

General Information: Until 12/02, there was a District Court also in Roy. However, this court is now a Justice Court with records are held in Ogden. Online identifiers in results same as on public terminal. No adoption, involuntary commitments, expunged criminal records released. Will fax documents $5.00 includes up to 10 pages; add $.50 per page over 10. Court makes copy: $.25 per page. Certification fee: $4.00 plus $.50 per page. Payee: Ogden District Court. Personal checks, Visa/MC accepted. Prepayment required. Mail requests: SASE required.

Civil Name Search: Access: Phone, mail, online, in person. Both court and visitors may perform in person name searches. Search fee: $15.00 per hour. First 15 minutes no charge. Civil records on computer the past 20 years, microfilm prior to that. Records prior to 1950 at state archives. Mail turnaround time 2-9 days. Civil PAT goes back to 1987. Online access through XChange, see www.utcourts.gov/records/. Also see state introduction. An automated court information line allows phone access to court dates, fine balances, and judgment/divorce decrees (case or citation number required) at 888-824-2678.

Criminal Name Search: Access: Phone, mail, online, in person. Both court and visitors may perform in person name searches. Search fee: $15.00 per hour. First 15 minutes no charge. Required to search: name, years to search, DOB; last four digits of SSN helpful. Criminal records on computer the past 20 years, microfilm prior to that. Records prior to 1950 at state archives. Mail turnaround time 2-9 days. Criminal PAT goes back to same as civil. Online access through XChange, see www.utcourts.gov/records/. Also see state introduction. Online results show middle initial, DOB.

Farr West Justice Court 1896 N 1800 W, Farr West, UT 84404; 801-731-4187; fax: 801-731-7732; 8:30AM-4 M-Th 8:30-Noon F (MST). *Misdemeanor (B & C), Small Claims, Infractions, Traffic.*

Harrisville Justice Court 363 W Independence Blvd, Harrisville, UT 84404; 801-782-4100; fax: 801-782-1449; 8AM-5PM M-th; 8AM-12 F (MST). *Misdemeanor (B & C), Small Claims, Infractions, Traffic.*
www.cityofharrisville.com/services/court

North Ogden Justice Court 515 E 2600 N, North Ogden, UT 84414; 801-737-2203; fax: 801-782-6958; 10AM-2PM M; 9AM-5:30PM T-F (MST). *Misdemeanor (B & C), Small Claims, Infractions, Traffic.*

Ogden Justice Court 310 26th St, Ogden, UT 84401; 801-629-8569 (main); 629-8560 (small claims); fax: 801-393-6629; *Misdemeanor (B & C), Small Claims, Infractions, Traffic.*

Plain City Justice Court 4160 W 2200 N, Plain City, UT 84404; 801-731-4908; fax: 801-731-8619; *Misdemeanor (B & C), Small Claims, Infractions, Traffic.*

Pleasant View Justice Court 520 W Elberta Dr, Pleasant View, UT 84414; 801-782-6741; fax: 801-782-0539; 8AM-5PM M-Th (MST). *Misdemeanor (B & C), Small Claims, Infractions, Traffic.*
General Information: Court is held Tuesday nights.

Riverdale Justice Court 4600 S Weber River Rd, Riverdale, UT 84414; 801-394-9314; fax: 801-394-0036; 8AM-5PM M-F (MST). *Misdemeanor (B & C), Small Claims, Infractions, Traffic.*

Roy Justice Court 5051 S 1900 W, Roy, UT 84067; 801-774-1051; fax: 801-774-1060; 8AM-5PM M-F (MST). *Misdemeanor (B & C), Small Claims, Infractions, Traffic.*

South Ogden Justice Court 3950 Adams Ave, South Egden, UT 84403; 801-622-2700; fax: 801-622-2718; 8AM-5PM (MST). *Misdemeanor (B & C), Small Claims, Infractions, Traffic.*
www.southogdencity.com/

Uintah Justice Court 2191 E 6550 S, Uintah, UT 84405; 801-479-4130; fax: 801-476-7269; 9AM-5PM M-Th 9AM-1PM F (MST). *Misdemeanor (B & C), Small Claims, Infractions, Traffic.*
www.co.uintah.ut.us/justicecourt/faq.php

Washington Terrace Justice Court 5249 S 400 E, Washington, UT 84405; 801-393-8951; fax: 801-627-1872; 2:30 & 4:30 W (MST). *Misdemeanor (B & C), Small Claims, Infractions, Traffic.*

Vermont

Time Zone:	**EST**
Capital:	**Montpelier, Washington County**
# of Counties:	**14**
State Web:	**http://vermont.gov/portal**
Court Web:	**www.vermontjudiciary.org**

Administration — Court Administrator's Office, 111 State St (mailing address is 109 State St), Montpelier, VT 05609; 802-828-3278, Fax: 802-828-3457

The Supreme Court — The Supreme Court is the court of last resort and has appellate jurisdiction. Opinions from the Supreme Court are viewable from the web page, click on *Legal Information*.

The Vermont Trial Courts

Court	Type	How Organized	Jurisdiction Highpoints
Superior*	General	14 courts in 14 counties 5 Divisions per Court	Felony, Misdemeanor, Civil, Small Claims, Family, Probate, Juvenile, Traffic, Eviction, Domestic Relations, Environmental

* = profiled in this book

Details on the Trial Court Structure — The Superior Court has five Divisions: **Criminal, Civil, Family, Probate**, and **Environmental**. The Civil Division of the Superior Court hears predominantly civil, tort, real estate, and small claims cases. On rare occasion it hears criminal cases, but the Criminal Division of the Superior Court hears predominantly criminal cases, but will also hear some civil suspension cases, fish and wildlife violations, and appeals from the Judicial Bureau. Specialty courts include Probate Division Courts and Family Division Courts. The Environmental Division hears municipal land use enforcement cases and enforcement actions brought by states natural resources agencies.

In Vermont, the **Judicial Bureau** has jurisdiction over traffic, municipal ordinances, and Fish and Game violations, minors in possession, and hazing.

Record Searching Facts You Need to Know

Fees and Record Searching Tips — The statewide search, certification, and copy fees set by the legislature are as follows: search fee- $30.00 per name; certification fee- $5.00 per document plus copy fee; copy fee- $.25 per page with a $1.00 minimum. Be aware that some courts vary slightly from this schedule.

Online Access is Widespread — Vermont Courts Online provides access to civil and small claim cases and court calendar information from 12 of the county Superior Courts. Access is not offered for Chittenden (which has its own system) and Franklin. Go to https://secure.vermont.gov/vtcdas/user. Records are in real-time mode. There is a $12.50 activation fee plus a fee of $.50 per case for look-up after the 1st 5 cases.

A great source of Vermont legal decisions including those made by Judiciary Boards is found at http://libraries.vermont.gov/law.

See Probate locations at www.vermontjudiciary.org/courts/probate/probateinfo/index.htm.

Addison County

Superior Court Civil Division 7 Mahady Ct, Middlebury, VT 05753; 802-388-7741; fax: 802-388-4621; 8AM-4:30PM (EST). *Civil, Eviction, Small Claims, Probate.* www.vermontjudiciary.org

General Information: No sealed or unserved records released. Will not fax documents. Court makes copy: $.25 per page, $1.00 minimum. Certification fee: $5.00 per doc plus copy fee. Payee: Addison Superior Court. Personal checks accepted, credit cards are not. Prepayment required.

Civil Name Search: Access: Fax, mail, in person, online. Only the court performs in person name searches; visitors may not. No search fee. Civil index on cards and recording books, computerized since 1995. Mail turnaround time 2-3 days. **For information on civil online access see the section at the front or rear of this chapter.**

Superior Court Criminal Division 7 Mahady Ct, Middlebury, VT 05753; 802-388-4237; fax: 802-388-4643; 8AM-4:30PM (EST). *Felony, Misdemeanor.* www.vermontjudiciary.org/GTC/criminal/default.aspx

General Information: No adoption, juvenile, sealed, or expunged records released. Will not fax documents. Court makes copy: $.25 per page, $1.00 minimum. Certification fee: $5.00 per doc plus copy fee. Payee: Addison Superior Court. Personal checks accepted, credit cards are not. Prepayment required.

Criminal Name Search: Access: Mail, in person. Only the court performs in person name searches; visitors may not. Search fee: $30.00 per name. Required to search: name, years to search, DOB. Criminal records on computer since mid 1991; prior on dockets and index cards. Mail turnaround time up to 1 week. Click on Calendars by Date and County at https://secure.vermont.gov/vtcdas/user.

Probate Division 7 Mahady Ct, Middlebury, VT 05753; 802-388-2612; fax: 802-388-4621; 8AM-4:30PM (EST). *Probate.* http://vermontjudiciary.org/GTC/probate/default.aspx

Bennington County

Superior Court Civil Division 207 South St, Bennington, VT 05201-2247; 802-447-2700; fax: 802-447-2703; 8AM-4:30PM (EST). *Civil, Eviction, Small Claims.* http://vermontjudiciary.org/default.aspx

General Information: No deposition, adoption, juvenile, sealed or expunged records released. Will not fax documents. Court makes copy: $.25 per page, $1.00 minimum. Self serve copy: $.10 per page. Certification fee: $5.00 per doc plus copy fee. Payee: Bennington County. Personal checks accepted, credit cards are not. Prepayment required.

Civil Name Search: Access: Fax, phone, mail, in person, online. Both court and visitors may perform in person name searches. No search fee. Civil records on computer from 1997, index from 1968. Mail turnaround time 2-3 days. **For information on civil online access see the section at the front or rear of this chapter.**

Superior Court Criminal Division 150 Veterans Memorial Dr, Bennington, VT 05201; 802-447-2727; fax: 802-447-2750; 7:45AM-4:30PM (EST). *Felony, Misdemeanor.* www.vermontjudiciary.org

General Information: No sealed, diversion case records released. Will fax documents to toll free line. Court makes copy: $.25 per page. $1.00 minimum. Certification fee: $5.00 per doc plus copy fee. Payee: Vermont Superior Court. Personal checks accepted, credit cards are not. Prepayment required. Mail requests: SASE requested.

Criminal Name Search: Access: Mail, in person. Both court and visitors may perform in person name searches. Search fee: $30.00 per name includes copy of docket sheet. Required to search: name, years to search, DOB. Criminal records indexed on computer form 1990, prior on cards, docket books. Mail turnaround time varies. Public use terminal has crim records back to 1990. Click on Calendars by Date and County at https://secure.vermont.gov/vtcdas/user.

Probate Division - Bennington District 207 South St, PO Box 65, Bennington, VT 05201; 802-447-2705; fax: 802-447-2703; 8AM-N, 1-4pm (EST). *Probate.* http://vermontjudiciary.org/GTC/probate/default.aspx

General Information: Fax to "Attention Probate Court."

Probate Division - Manchester District PO Box 446, 3588 Main St, Manchester, VT 05254; 802-362-1410; ; 8AM-N, 1-4:20PM (EST). *Probate.* http://vermontjudiciary.org/GTC/probate/default.aspx

General Information: This court will move into the Bennington location in the first quarter of 2011.

Caledonia County

Superior Court Civil Division 1126 Main St, #1, St Johnsbury, VT 05819; 802-748-6600; fax: 802-748-6603; 8AM-4:30PM (EST). *Civil, Eviction, Small Claims.* www.vermontjudiciary.org

General Information: No adoption, juvenile, sealed or expunged records released. Will fax documents $2.00 per page. Court makes copy: $.25 per page, $1.00 minimum. Certification fee: $5.00 per doc plus copy fee. Payee: Caledonia Superior Court. Personal checks accepted, credit cards are not. Prepayment required. Mail requests: SASE requested.

Civil Name Search: Access: Phone, mail, in person, online. Only the court performs in person name searches; visitors may not. No search fee. Civil records on computer from 1992, in archives before 1985, index from 1985, all other records on index cards. Mail turnaround time 1 week. **For information on civil online access see the section at the front or rear of this chapter.**

Superior Court Criminal Division 1126 Main St, #1, St Johnsbury, VT 05819; 802-748-6600; fax: 802-748-6603; 8AM-4:30PM (EST). *Felony, Misdemeanor.* http://vermontjudiciary.org/default.aspx

General Information: No adoption, juvenile, sealed or expunged records released. Will fax documents $2.00 per page. Court makes copy: $.25 per page; $1.00 minimum. Certification fee: $5.00 per doc plus copy fee. Payee:

VT Superior Court. Personal checks accepted, credit cards are not. Prepayment required. Mail requests: SASE required.

Criminal Name Search: Access: Fax, mail, in person. Only the court performs in person name searches; visitors may not. Search fee: $30.00 per name. Required to search: name, years to search, DOB. Criminal records on computer since 1991, prior on index cards to 1950. Mail turnaround time less than 1 week. Click on Calendars by Date and County at https://secure.vermont.gov/vtcdas/user.

Probate Division 1126 Main St, Ste 3, St Johnsbury, VT 05819; 802-748-6605; fax: 802-748-6603; 8AM-4:30PM (EST). *Probate.* http://vermontjudiciary.org/GTC/probate/default.aspx

Chittenden County

Superior Court Civil Division PO Box 187, 175 Main St, Burlington, VT 05402; 802-863-3467; ; 8AM-4:30PM (EST). *Civil, Eviction, Small Claims.* www.chittendensuperiorcourt.com/index.htm

General Information: No adoption, juvenile, sealed or expunged records released. Will not fax documents. Court makes copy: $.25 per page, $1.00 minimum. Certification fee: $5.00 per doc plus copy fee. Payee: Superior Court. Personal checks accepted, credit cards are not. Prepayment required.

Civil Name Search: Access: Phone, mail, in person. Only the court performs in person name searches; visitors may not. No search fee. Civil records on computer back to 1983, small claims since 1996, prior records on books from 1800s. Mail turnaround time 1 week. Access case information free at www.chittendensuperiorcourt.com/index.htm and click on Cases. Calendars also online.

Superior Court Criminal Division 32 Cherry St, #300, Burlington, VT 05401; 802-651-1950; fax: 802-651-1759; 8AM-4:30PM (EST). *Felony, Misdemeanor.* www.vermontjudiciary.org

General Information: No adoption, juvenile, sealed or expunged records released. Will not fax out documents. Court makes copy: $.25 per page, $1.00 minimum. Certification fee: $5.00 per doc plus copy fee. Payee: Vermont Superior Court. Personal checks accepted, credit cards are not. Prepayment required. Mail requests: SASE required.

Criminal Name Search: Access: Mail, in person. Both court and visitors may perform in person name searches. Search fee: $30.00 per name. Required to search: name, years to search; also helpful: DOB. Criminal records on new computer from 6/90, on old computer from 6/85 to 6/90, books by alpha name from 12/69 to 1980, on index cards from 1970. Mail turnaround time 1-2 days. Public use terminal has crim records back to 6/1990. Click on Calendars by Date and County at https://secure.vermont.gov/vtcdas/user.

Probate Division PO Box 511, 175 Main St, Burlington, VT 05402; 802-651-1518; ; 8AM-4:30PM; till 4PM F (EST). *Probate.* http://vermontjudiciary.org/GTC/probate/default.aspx

Essex County

Superior Court Box 75, Guildhall, VT 05905; 802-676-3910; fax: 802-676-3463; 8AM-4:30PM (EST). *Felony, Misdemeanor, Civil, Eviction, Small Claims.* www.vermontjudiciary.org

General Information: No adoption, juvenile, sealed or expunged records released. Will fax documents $1.00 per page. Court makes copy: $.25 per page, $1.00 minimum. Certification fee: $5.00 per doc plus copy fee. Payee: Superior Court. Only cashiers checks and money orders accepted. No credit cards accepted. Prepayment required. Mail requests: SASE required.

Civil Name Search: Access: Phone, fax, mail, in person, online. Only the court performs in person name searches; visitors may not. No search fee. Civil records indexed from 1974; on computer from 5/94. Note: Will not accept phone requests for more than 2 names. Mail turnaround time 1 week. **For information on civil online access see the section at the front or rear of this chapter.**

Criminal Name Search: Access: Mail, in person. Only the court performs in person name searches; visitors may not. Search fee: $30.00 per name. Required to search: name, years to search, DOB. Criminal records indexed from 1974; on computer from 5/94. Mail turnaround time 1 week. Click on Calendars by Date and County at https://secure.vermont.gov/vtcdas/user.

Probate Division PO Box 426, 49 Mill St Ext., Island Pond, VT 05846; 802-723-4770; fax: 802-723-4770; 8:30AM-N, 1-3:30PM (EST). *Probate.* http://vermontjudiciary.org/GTC/probate/default.aspx

Franklin County

Superior Court Civil Division 17 Church St, St Albans, VT 05478; 802-524-3863; fax: 802-524-7996; 8AM-4:30PM (EST). *Civil, Eviction, Small Claims.* www.vermontjudiciary.org

General Information: No adoption, juvenile, sealed or expunged records released. Will not fax documents. Court makes copy: $.25 per page, $1.00 minimum. Certification fee: $5.00 per doc plus copy fee. Payee: Superior

Court Civil Division. Personal checks accepted, credit cards are not. Prepayment required. Mail requests: SASE requested.

Civil Name Search: Access: Mail, in person. Only the court performs in person name searches; visitors may not. No search fee. Required to search: name, years to search; or by docket number. Civil records on computer since 1996; prior on index cards from 1840. Mail turnaround time 1 week.

Superior Court Criminal Division 36 Lake St, St Albans, VT 05478; 802-524-7997; fax: 802-524-7946; 8AM-4:30PM (EST). *Felony, Misdemeanor, Probate.* http://vermontjudiciary.org/default.aspx

General Information: No adoption, juvenile, sealed or expunged records released. Fee to fax document $1.00 each plus $.25 per page. Court makes copy: $.25 per page, $1.00 minimum. Certification fee: $5.00 per doc plus copy fee. Payee: Vermont Superior Court. Personal checks accepted, credit cards are not. Prepayment required. Mail requests: SASE required.

Criminal Name Search: Access: Mail, in person. Both court and visitors may perform in person name searches. Search fee: $30.00 per name. Required to search: name, years to search; also helpful: DOB, SSN. Criminal records on computer since 1990. Note: Court will perform in person searches only if time permits. Mail turnaround time 7-10 days. Public use terminal has crim records back to 1990. Click on Calendars by Date and County at https://secure.vermont.gov/vtcdas/user.

Probate Division 17 Church St, St Albans, VT 05478; 802-524-7948; 8AM-N, 1-4:30PM (EST). *Probate, Marriage.* http://vermontjudiciary.org/GTC/probate/default.aspx

Grand Isle County

Superior Court PO Box 7, North Hero, VT 05474; 802-372-8350; fax: 802-372-3221; 8AM-4:30PM (EST). *Felony, Misdemeanor, Civil, Eviction, Small Claims.* www.vermontjudiciary.org

General Information: No adoption, juvenile, sealed or expunged records released. Will not fax documents. Court makes copy: $.25 per page, $1.00 minimum. Self serve copy: $.25 per page. Certification fee: $5.00 per doc plus copy fee. Payee: Grand Isle Superior or District Court. Personal checks accepted, credit cards are not. Prepayment required.

Civil Name Search: Access: Phone, fax, mail, in person, online. Both court and visitors may perform in person name searches. No search fee. Civil records on computer from 1990, on index 1940, in-house from 1970. Mail turnaround time 1-2 days. **For information on civil online access see the section at the front or rear of this chapter.**

Criminal Name Search: Access: Fax, mail, in person. Both court and visitors may perform in person name searches. Search fee: $30.00 per name. Required to search: name, years to search; also helpful: DOB, SSN. Criminal records computerized from 1990, on index from 1940, in-house from 1979. Note: Fax requests not processed until payment received; court suggest just to mail in your request. Mail turnaround time 1-2 days. Click on Calendars by Date and County at https://secure.vermont.gov/vtcdas/user.

Probate Division PO Box 7, 3677 US Route 2, North Hero, VT 05474; 802-372-8350; fax: 802-372-3221; 8AM-12; 12:30PM-4:30PM (EST). *Probate.* http://vermontjudiciary.org/GTC/probate/default.aspx

Lamoille County

Superior Court Civil Division Box 490, 154 Main St, Hyde Park, VT 05655; 802-888-2207; 8AM-Noon; 12:30-4:30PM (EST). *Civil, Eviction, Small Claims.* www.vermontjudiciary.org

General Information: No adoption, juvenile, sealed or expunged records released. Will not fax documents. Court makes copy: $.25 per page, $1.00 minimum. Certification fee: $5.00 per doc plus copy fee. Payee: Lamoille Superior Court. Personal checks accepted, credit cards are not. Prepayment required. Mail requests: SASE required.

Civil Name Search: Access: Mail, in person, online. Only the court performs in person name searches; visitors may not. No search fee. Civil records on computer from 1989, index from 1970s. Mail turnaround time 1 week or more. Public use terminal has civil records back to 1994. **For information on civil online access see the section at the front or rear of this chapter.**

Superior Court Criminal Division PO Box 570, Hyde Park, VT 05655; 802-888-3887; fax: 802-888-2591; 8AM-4:30PM (EST). *Felony, Misdemeanor.* www.vermontjudiciary.org

General Information: No adoption, juvenile, sealed or expunged records released. Will fax documents to toll free or local line only. Court makes copy: $.25 per page; $1.00 minimum. Certification fee: $5.00 per doc plus copy fee. Payee: Vermont District Court. Personal checks accepted. Planning to accept credit cards. Prepayment required. Mail requests: SASE required.

Criminal Name Search: Access: Mail, in person. Only the court performs in person name searches; visitors may not. Search fee: $30.00 per name. Required to search: name, DOB; also helpful: years to search. Criminal records on computer since 6/88; prior on index cards. Mail

turnaround time 3 days if record on-site; 1 week if off-site. Click on Calendars by Date and County at https://secure.vermont.gov/vtcdas/user.

Probate Division PO Box 570, 154 Main St, Hyde Park, VT 05655-0102; 802-888-3306; fax: 802-888-0669; 8AM-Noon, 12:30-4:30PM (EST). *Probate.* http://vermontjudiciary.org/GTC/probate/default.aspx

Orange County

Superior Court 5 Court St, Chelsea, VT 05038-9746; 802-685-4610; fax: 802-685-3173; 8AM-4:30PM (EST). *Felony, Misdemeanor, Civil, Eviction, Small Claims.* www.vermontjudiciary.org

General Information: No adoption, juvenile, sealed or expunged records released. Fee to fax out file $1.00 per page. Court makes copy: $.25 per page, $1.00 minimum. Certification fee: $5.00 per doc plus copy fee. Payee: Superior Court. Personal checks accepted, credit cards are not. Prepayment required.

Civil Name Search: Access: Fax, mail, in person, online. Only the court performs in person name searches; visitors may not. No search fee. Required to search: name, years to search; also helpful: address. Civil records on computer from 7/94, on index from 1967. Mail turnaround time 1 week. **For information on civil online access see the section at the front or rear of this chapter.**

Criminal Name Search: Access: Phone, fax, mail, in person. Only the court performs in person name searches; visitors may not. Search fee: $30.00 per name. Required to search: name, years to search, DOB; also helpful: address. Criminal records computerized from 1990, on index from 1967. Mail turnaround time 1 week. Click on Calendars by Date and County at https://secure.vermont.gov/vtcdas/user.

Probate Division 5 Court St, County Courthouse, Chelsea, VT 05038-9746; 802-685-4610; fax: 802-685-3173; 8AM-4:30PM (EST). *Probate.* http://vermontjudiciary.org/GTC/probate/default.aspx

General Information: The Bradford and Randolph Districts were consolidated into this one probate court as of June 1, 1994.

Orleans County

Superior Court Civil Division 247 Main St, #1, Newport, VT 05855-1203; 802-334-3344; fax: 802-334-4429; 8AM-4:30PM M,W,TH,F; 12:30-4:30PM T (EST). *Civil, Eviction, Small Claims.* www.vermontjudiciary.org

General Information: No juvenile records released. Will not fax documents. Court makes copy: $.25 per page, $1.00 minimum. Certification fee: $5.00 per doc plus copy fee. Payee: Orleans Superior Court. Personal checks accepted, credit cards are not. Prepayment required. Mail requests: SASE required.

Civil Name Search: Access: Phone, fax, mail, in person, online. Only the court performs in person name searches; visitors may not. No search fee. Required to search: name; also helpful: years to search. Civil records on computer since 1994; prior records on index from 1800s. Mail turnaround time 1 week or so. **For information on civil online access see the section at the front or rear of this chapter.**

Superior Court Criminal Division 217 Main St, #4, Newport, VT 05855; 802-334-3325; ; 8AM-4:30PM (EST). *Felony, Misdemeanor.* www.vermontjudiciary.org

General Information: No adoption, juvenile, sealed or expunged records released. Will fax documents to toll-free number only. Court makes copy: $.25 per page, $1.00 minimum; add $6.00 if copies retrieved from public records. Self serve copy: $.25 per page. Certification fee: $5.00 per doc plus copy fee. Payee: Superior Court of Vermont. Personal checks accepted, credit cards are not. Prepayment required. Mail requests: SASE required.

Criminal Name Search: Access: Mail. Only the court performs in person name searches; visitors may not. Search fee: $30.00 per name. Required to search: name, years to search, DOB. Criminal records on computer since 1/91; prior on index cards back to 1971. Mail turnaround time 1 week. Click on Calendars by Date and County at https://secure.vermont.gov/vtcdas/user.

Probate Division 247 Main St, Newport, VT 05855; 802-334-3366; fax: 802-334-3385; 8AM-N 1PM-4PM (EST). *Probate.* http://vermontjudiciary.org/GTC/probate/default.aspx

Rutland County

Superior Court Civil Division 83 Center St, Rutland, VT 05701; 802-775-4394; fax: 802-775-2291; 8AM-4:30PM (EST). *Civil, Eviction, Small Claims, Probate.* www.vermontjudiciary.org

General Information: No adoption, juvenile, sealed or expunged records released. Will fax documents to local or toll free line. Court makes copy: $.25 per page; $1.00 minimum. Certification fee: $5.00 per cert plus copy fee. Payee: Rutland Superior Court. Personal checks accepted, credit cards are not. Prepayment required. Mail requests: SASE required.

Civil Name Search: Access: Mail, in person, online. Only the court performs in person name searches; visitors may not. Search fee: None; a fee may apply for more sophisticated searches. Civil records on computer from 1987, on index from late 1700s. Mail turnaround time 1 week. **For information on civil online access see the section at the front or rear of this chapter.**

Superior Court Criminal Division 9 Merchants Row, Rutland, VT 05701-2886; 802-786-5880; 8AM-4:30PM (EST). *Felony, Misdemeanor.* http://vermontjudiciary.org/default.aspx

General Information: No sealed, expunged records released. Court makes copy: $.25 per page. $1.00 minimum. Certification fee: $5.00 per doc plus copy fee. Payee: Superior Court of Vermont. Personal checks accepted. No credit cards accepted for searches or copy fees. Prepayment required. Mail requests: SASE required.

Criminal Name Search: Access: Phone, mail, in person. Both court and visitors may perform in person name searches. Search fee: $30.00 per name. Required to search: name, years to search, DOB. Criminal records computerized from mid 1991. Mail turnaround time 1 week. Public use terminal has crim records back to 1991. Click on Calendars by Date and County at https://secure.vermont.gov/vtcdas/user.

Probate Court - Fair Haven District This court closed effective Feb 1, 2011, see below .

Probate Court - Rutland District 82 Center St, Rutland, VT 05701; 802-775-0114; fax: 802-775-1671; 8AM-4:30PM (EST). *Probate.* http://vermontjudiciary.org/GTC/probate/default.aspx

General Information: Effective Feb 2011 the Fair Haven probate court closed, all records were transferred here.

Washington County

Superior Court Civil Division 65 State St, Montpelier, VT 05602-3594; 802-828-2091; 8AM-4:30PM (EST). *Civil, Eviction, Small Claims* www.vermontjudiciary.org

General Information: No adoption, juvenile or expunged records released. Will fax documents $1.00 per page, but only if an emergency. Court makes copy: $.25 per page, $1.00 minimum. Certification fee: $5.00 per doc plus copy fee. Payee: Washington County Superior Court. Personal checks accepted, credit cards are not. Prepayment required. Mail requests: SASE requested.

Civil Name Search: Access: Phone, mail, in person, online. Only the court performs in person name searches; visitors may not. No search fee. Required to search: name, years to search; also helpful: address. Civil records on computer from 1993, archives from 1900s. Mail turnaround time 1-2 days. **For information on civil online access see the section at the front or rear of this chapter.**

Superior Court Criminal Division 255 N Main, Ste, Barre, VT 05641; 802-479-4252; 8AM-4:30PM (EST). *Felony, Misdemeanor.* www.vermontjudiciary.org

General Information: No adoption, juvenile, sealed or expunged records released. Court makes copy: $.25 per page. $1.00 minimum. Certification fee: $5.00 per doc plus copy fee. Payee: Washington Superior Court. Personal checks accepted, credit cards are not. Prepayment required. Mail requests: SASE requested.

Criminal Name Search: Access: Mail, in person. Only the court performs in person name searches; visitors may not. Search fee: $30.00 per name. Required to search: name, years to search; also helpful: DOB. Criminal records on computer since 1989; prior records in index from 1970s. Mail turnaround time 3-5 days. Click on Calendars by Date and County at https://secure.vermont.gov/vtcdas/user.

Probate Division 10 Elm St, #2, Montpelier, VT 05602; 802-828-3405; 8AM-4:30PM (EST). *Probate.* http://vermontjudiciary.org/GTC/probate/default.aspx

Windham County

Superior Court Civil Division Box 207, 7 Court St, Newfane, VT 05345; 802-365-7979; fax: 802-365-4360; 8AM-4:30PM (EST). *Civil, Eviction, Small Claims.* http://vermontjudiciary.org/default.aspx

General Information: No adoption, juvenile, sealed or expunged records released. No fee to fax documents. Court makes copy: $.25 per page, $1.00 minimum. Certification fee: $5.00 per doc plus copy fee. Payee: Windham Superior Court. Personal checks accepted, credit cards are not. Prepayment required. Mail requests: SASE required.

Civil Name Search: Access: Phone, fax, mail, in person, online. Both court and visitors may perform in person name searches. No search fee. Civil records on computer from 1994, on index from 1919. Fax access available only in emergency. Mail turnaround time 1-2 days. **For information on civil online access see the section at the front or rear of this chapter.**

Superior Court Criminal Division 30 Putney Rd, 2nd Floor, Brattleboro, VT 05301; 802-257-2800; 8AM-4:30PM (EST). *Felony, Misdemeanor, Civil Suspension.* www.vermontjudiciary.org

General Information: This court also has records of "civil suspensions" of driver licenses. No adoption, juvenile, sealed or expunged records released. Fee to fax document $.25 per page. Court makes copy: $.25 per page, $1.00 minimum if recent case.Copies form archives are $6.00 plus $.25 per page; if taken from microfiche then $10.00 plus $.550 per page. Certification fee: $5.00 per doc plus copy fee. Payee: Superior Court. Personal checks accepted, credit cards are not. Prepayment required. Mail requests: SASE requested.

Criminal Name Search: Access: Mail, in person. Both court and visitors may perform in person name searches. Search fee: $30.00 per name. Required to search: name, years to search; also helpful: address, DOB, SSN. Criminal record go back to 1969s; computer since 1990; prior on index cards and docket books. Mail turnaround time 5-7 days. Public use terminal has crim records back to 1991. Click on Calendars by Date and County at https://secure.vermont.gov/vtcdas/user.

Probate Court - Marlboro District 80 Flat St, #104, Brattleboro, VT 05301; 802-257-2898; fax: 802-251-2139; 8AM-N, 1-4:30PM (EST). *Probate.* http://vermontjudiciary.org/default.aspx

Probate Court - Westminster District PO Box 47, 39 Square, Bellows Falls, VT 05101-0047; 802-463-3019; fax: 802-463-0144; 8AM-N,1-4:30PM (EST). *Probate.* http://vermontjudiciary.org/GTC/probate/default.aspx

Windsor County

Superior Court Civil Division 12 The Green, Woodstock, VT 05091; 802-457-2121; fax: 802-457-3446; 8AM-4:30PM (EST). *Civil, Eviction, Small Claims.* www.vermontjudiciary.org

General Information: No sealed or expunged records released. Court makes copy: $.25 per page, $1.00 minimum. Certification fee: $5.00 per doc plus copy fee. Payee: Windsor County Clerk or Windsor Superior Court. Personal checks accepted, credit cards are not. Prepayment required. Mail requests: SASE required.

Civil Name Search: Access: Phone, mail, in person, online. Only the court performs in person name searches; visitors may not. Search fee: Up to $10.00. Civil records available since on computer 1990. Note: The court hopes to have a public access terminal installed by early 2012. Mail turnaround time 3-4 days **For information on civil online access see the section at the front or rear of this chapter.**

Superior Court Criminal Division Windsor Criminal and Family Division, 82 Railroad Row, White River Junction, VT 05001-1962; 802-295-8865; fax: 802-295-8897; 8AM-4:30PM (EST). *Felony, Misdemeanor.* www.vermontjudiciary.org/default.aspx

General Information: No adoption, juvenile, sealed or expunged records released. Will fax documents to local or toll-free number. Court makes copy: $.25 per page, $1.00 minimum. Certification fee: $5.00 per doc plus copy fee. Payee: Vermont Superior Court. Personal checks accepted, credit cards are not. Prepayment required. Mail requests: SASE requested.

Criminal Name Search: Access: Mail, in person. Only the court performs in person name searches; visitors may not. Search fee: $30.00 per name. Required to search: name, years to search; also helpful: DOB, SSN. Criminal records computerized from 1990, index from 1968. Note: Record request forms available, please use. Mail turnaround time 7 days. Click on Calendars by Date and County at https://secure.vermont.gov/vtcdas/user.

Probate Division 62 Pleasant St, Woodstock, VT 05091; 802-457-1503; fax: 802-457-5203; 8AM-N, 1-4:30PM (EST). *Probate.* http://vermontjudiciary.org/GTC/probate/default.aspx

General Information: Effective Jan 20, 2011, the Probate Court located in North Springfield closed and all files and open cases were transferred to this location.

About Online Access to Civil Records

Vermont Courts Online provides access to civil and small claim cases and court calendar information from 12 of the county Superior Courts. Access is not offered for Chittenden (which has its own system) and Franklin.

Go to https://secure.vermont.gov/vtcdas/user. Records are in real-time mode. There is a $12.50 activation fee plus a fee of $.50 per case for look-up after the 1st 5 cases.

Virginia

Time Zone:	EST
Capital:	Richmond City (County)
# of Counties:	95
State Web:	www.virginia.gov
Court Web:	www.courts.state.va.us

Administration

Executive Secretary, Administrative Office of Courts, 100 N. Ninth Street, 3rd Fl, Supreme Court Building, Richmond, Virginia, 23219; 804-786-6455, Fax: 804-786-4542.

The Supreme and Appellate Courts

The Supreme Court reviews decisions of the Circuit Courts, the Court of Appeals when such appeals have been allowed, decisions from the State Corporation Commission, and certain disciplinary actions of the Virginia State Bar regarding attorneys. Virginia's intermediate appellate court, the Court of Appeals, reviews decisions of the Circuit Courts in domestic relations matters, traffic infractions and criminal cases (except death penalty cases), appeals from administrative agencies, and decisions of the Virginia Workers' Compensation Commission. Opinions are available from the home page.

The Virginia Courts

Court	Type	How Organized	Jurisdiction Highpoints
Circuit*	General	120 Courts in 31 Circuits	Felony, Civil, Estate, Domestic, Probate
General District*	Limited	132 Courts in 32 Circuits	Misdemeanor, Civil Actions under $25,000, Eviction, Small Claims, Domestic, Juvenile, Eviction
Magistrate	Limited	Local, in all Districts	Traffic, Ordinance, Minor Misdemeanor

* = profiled in this book

Details on the Court Structure

The **Circuit Court** handles felonies, all civil cases with claims of more than $25,000 but it shares authority with the General District court to hear matters involving claims between $4,500 and $25,000. The Circuit Court also handles family matters including divorce. There is a Circuit Court in each city and county in Virginia.

The **General District Court** decides all offenses involving ordinances laws, and by-laws of the county or city where it is located and all misdemeanors under state law, and small claims ($4,500 or less). A misdemeanor is any charge that carries a penalty of no more than one year in jail or a fine of up to $2,500, or both. Please note that a District can comprise a county or a city.

As stated, records of civil action from $4,500 to $25,000 can be at either the Circuit Court or District Court as either can have jurisdiction. Thus it is necessary to check both record locations as there is no concurrent database or index.

Fifteen independent cities share the Clerk of Circuit Court with the county (but have separate District Courts) - Bedford, Covington (Alleghany County), Emporia (Greenville County), Fairfax, Falls Church (Arlington or Fairfax County), Franklin (Southhampton County), Galax (Carroll County), Harrisonburg (Rockingham County), Lexington (Rockbridge County), Manassas and Manassas Park (Prince William County), Norton (Wise County), Poquoson (York County), South Boston (Halifax County), and Williamsburg (James City County).

Magistrate Offices issue various types of processes such as arrest warrants, summonses, bonds, search warrants, subpoenas, and certain civil warrants. Magistrates may also conduct bail hearings.

Record Searching Facts You Need to Know

Fees and Record Searching Tips

In most Circuit Courts the certification fee is $2.00 per document plus copy fee which is usually $.50 per page. The General District Court fees are more varied by location.

Charles City and James City are counties, not cities. The City of Franklin is not in Franklin County, but is its own separate jurisdiction. The City of Richmond is not in Richmond County, but is its own separate jurisdiction. The City of Roanoke is not in Roanoke County, but is its own separate jurisdiction.

Online Access is Nearly Statewide

There is one online system for the Circuit Courts Court case records, one for the District Courts, and finally a pay system for recorded documents at the Circuit Courts. The reason this third system in mentioned is that it can included civil judgments. Each court type and each county or county equivalent must be searched separately.

1) At http://wasdmz2.courts.state.va.us/CJISWeb/circuit.html the case docket index may be searched for all of the Circuit Courts except Alexandria, City of Charlottesville, Chesterfield, Fairfax, Greene, Henrico and King and Queen counties.

2) All General District Courts except Clifton Forge City are searchable at a different site, see http://epwsgdp1.courts.state.va.us/gdcourts/captchaVerification.do?landing=landing page.

The two free online systems usually include partial DOBs in criminal results; civil results sometimes include addresses.

3) The Records Management System provides the Secure Remote Access System at https://risweb.courts.state.va.us/index.html for participating recording offices at the Circuit Court level. This is a subscription system. Records available include deeds, marriage licenses, judgments, and wills for selected counties. This is limited to participating Circuit Court recording section. Each local Circuit Court Clerk's office must be contacted for requirements, fees, and log-in.

Accomack County

2nd Circuit Court PO Box 126, 23316 Courthouse Ave, Accomac, VA 23301; 757-787-5776; probate phone: 757-787-5778; fax: 757-787-1849; 9AM-5PM (EST). *Felony, Civil Actions over $4,500, Probate.* www.courts.state.va.us/courts/circuit.html

General Information: No juvenile, sealed, probate, tax return or adoption records released. Fee to fax out file $2.00 1st page, $.50 each add'l. Court makes copy: $.50 per page. Self serve copy: same. Certification fee: $2.00. Payee: Samuel H Cooper Jr, Clerk of Court. Personal checks, Visa/MC accepted. Prepayment required. Mail requests: SASE required.

Civil Name Search: Access: Fax, mail, online, in person. Both court and visitors may perform in person name searches. No search fee. Civil records on microfiche and archived from 1663; on computer back to 1998. Mail turnaround time 1-2 days. **See details about online access at front or rear of this chapter.**

Criminal Name Search: Access: Fax, mail, online, in person. Both court and visitors may perform in person name searches. No search fee. Required to search: name, years to search, DOB; also helpful: SSN. Criminal records on microfiche and archived from 1663; on computer back to 1994. Note: Results include full name Mail turnaround time 1-2 days. Search free by name or case number at www.courts.state.va.us/. Results show address of subject and the day and month of birth, but not year.

2A General District Court PO Box 276, 23371 Front St, Accomac, VA 23301; 757-787-0923; criminal phone: x117; civil phone: x123; fax: 757-787-5619; 8:30AM-4:30PM (EST). *Misdemeanor, Civil Actions under $25,000, Eviction, Small Claims.* www.courts.state.va.us

General Information: No juvenile, sealed, adoption records released. Will not fax documents. Court makes copy: no fee if less than 5 pages. No certification fee. Payee: Accomack District Court. Personal checks accepted. Credit cards accepted. Prepayment required. Mail requests: SASE required.

Civil Name Search: Access: Phone, mail, online, in person. Both court and visitors may perform in person name searches. No search fee. Civil cases indexed by defendant. Civil records retained ten years. Mail turnaround time 1-3 days. Civil PAT goes back to 1996. **See details about online access at front or rear of this chapter.**

Criminal Name Search: Access: Phone, mail, online, in person. Both court and visitors may perform in person name searches. No search fee. Required to search: name, years to search, DOB; also helpful: SSN. Criminal records retained ten years. Mail turnaround time 1-3 days. Criminal PAT

goes back to same as civil. Search free by name or case number at http://epwsgdp1.courts.state.va.us/gdcourts/captchaVerification.do?landing=landing. Results show address of subject and the day and month of birth, but not year. Online results show middle initial.

Albemarle County

16th Circuit & District Court 501 E Jefferson St, Charlottesville, VA 22902; criminal phone: 434-972-4086; civil phone: 434-972-4085; fax: 434-972-4071; 8:30AM-4:30PM (EST). *Felony, Misdemeanor, Civil, Eviction, Probate.* www.courts.state.va.us/courts/circuit.html

General Information: Circuit and District Court have to be searched separately. Phone for District Court Clerk- 434-972-4167, Fax- 434-972-4092. District Court is Suite 138. Circuit court records on 2nd Fl, Circuit Clerk on 3rd. No juvenile, sealed records released. Will not fax documents. Court makes copy: $.50 per page. Certification fee: $2.00. Payee: Albemarle Clerk of Court. Personal checks accepted, credit cards are not. Prepayment required.

Civil Name Search: Access: Mail, in person, online. Both court and visitors may perform in person name searches. Search fee: $5.00 per name. Civil records on microfiche from 1980 to present and archived from 1700s to 1990. Mail turnaround time 7-10 days. Public use terminal has civil records back to 2001. **See details about online access at front or rear of this chapter.**

Criminal Name Search: Access: Mail, online, in person. Both court and visitors may perform in person name searches. Search fee: $5.00 per name. Criminal records on microfiche from 1980 to present and archived from 1700s to 1990. Mail turnaround time 7-10 days. **See details about online access at front or rear of this chapter.** District court search online free at http://epwsgdp1.courts.state.va.us/gdcourts/.

Alexandria City

18th Circuit Court 520 King St, #307, Alexandria, VA 22314; 703-746-4044; 9AM-5PM (EST). *Felony, Civil Actions over $4,500, Probate.* www.alexandriava.gov/clerkofcourt/

General Information: No juvenile, sealed, adoption or expunged records released. Will not fax documents. Court makes copy: $.50 per page. Self serve copy: same. Certification fee: $2.00. Payee: Clerk of Court. Only cashiers checks and money orders accepted. No credit cards accepted. Prepayment required.

Civil Name Search: Access: In person, online. Visitors must perform in person searches themselves. Civil records on computer from 1983 to present, microfiche from 1970s to present. Civil PAT goes back to 1983. Images are available. There is limited free online access to civil docket information from 1/01/1983, and a subscription service ($500 per year or $50 per month) to full data including images. Visit https://cheyenne.alexandriava.gov/ajis/index.php.

Criminal Name Search: Access: In person, online. Visitors must perform in person searches themselves. Required to search: name, years to search; also helpful: DOB. Criminal records on computer since 7/87. Criminal PAT goes back to 1987. Images are available. Online access to criminal records available back to 7/01/1987. Visit https://cheyenne.alexandriava.gov/ajis/index.php. Online results show middle initial.

18th General District Court PO Box 320489, 520 King St, #201, Alexandria, VA 22320; 703-746-4041; criminal phone: 703-746-4030; civil phone: 703-746-4021; 8AM-4PM (EST). *Misdemeanor, Civil Actions under $25,000, Eviction, Small Claims.* www.courts.state.va.us/

General Information: Will not fax documents. Court makes copy: $1.00 each first 2 pages, $.50 each add'l. No certification fee. Payee: District Court. Visa/MC accepted.

Civil Name Search: Access: Online, in person. Both court and visitors may perform in person name searches. No search fee. Civil cases indexed by defendant. Civil records on computer for 10 years to present. Civil PAT available. SSNs may appear as an identifier on some records. **See details about online access at front or rear of this chapter.** Also, search Clerk's system at https://secure.alexandriava.gov/ajis/index.php. Extended data is available in a subscription format.

Criminal Name Search: Access: Online, in person. Visitors must perform in person searches themselves. Required to search: name. Criminal records computerized for 10 years to present. Criminal PAT available. SSNs may also appear as an identifier on some records. Online access same as civil. Online results show middle initial.

Alleghany County

25th Circuit Court PO Box 670, 266 W Main St, Covington, VA 24426; 540-965-1730; fax: 540-965-1732; 8:30AM-5PM (EST). *Felony, Civil Actions over $4,500, Probate.* www.courts.state.va.us/

General Information: No juvenile, adoption or sealed records released. Will not fax documents. Court makes copy: $.50 per page. Self serve copy: same. Certification fee: $2.00 per doc plus copy fee. Payee: Clerk of Court. Personal checks discouraged. No credit cards accepted. Prepayment required.

Civil Name Search: Access: In person, online. Visitors must perform in person searches themselves. Required to search: name. Civil cases indexed by plaintiff. Civil records available from 1822, all on microfilm. **See details about online access at front or rear of this chapter.**

Criminal Name Search: Access: In person, online. Required to search: name. Criminal records available from 1822, all on microfilm. **See details about online access at front or rear of this chapter.**

25th General District Court PO Box 139, 266 W Main St, Covington, VA 24426; 540-965-1720; fax: 540-965-1722; 9AM-5PM (EST). *Misdemeanor, Civil Actions under $25,000, Eviction, Small Claims.* www.courts.state.va.us

General Information: No juvenile, sealed records released. Will fax back documents. Court makes copy: $.50 per page. No certification fee. Payee: Court. Personal checks, Visa/MC accepted. Prepayment required.

Civil Name Search: Access: Online, in person. Visitors must perform in person searches themselves. Civil records on computer from 1/90, prior on index cards. Civil PAT goes back to 10 years. **See details about online access at front or rear of this chapter.**

Criminal Name Search: Access: Online, in person. Visitors must perform in person searches themselves. Required to search: name, years to search; also helpful: DOB, SSN. Criminal records computerized from 1/90, prior on index cards. Criminal PAT goes back to 10 years. **See details about online access at front or rear of this chapter.**

Amelia County

11th Circuit Court PO Box 237, 16441 Court St, Amelia, VA 23068; 804-561-2128; fax: 804-561-6364; 8:30AM-4:30PM (EST). *Felony, Civil Actions over $4,500, Probate.* www.courts.state.va.us

General Information: No juvenile, sealed records released. Will not fax documents. Court makes copy: $.50 per page. Self serve copy: same. Certification fee: $2.00 plus copy fee. Payee: Amelia County Circuit Court. Personal checks accepted, credit cards are not. Prepayment required. Mail requests: SASE required.

Civil Name Search: Access: Mail, in person, online. Both court and visitors may perform in person name searches. No search fee. Civil records on microfiche 1735 to present, indexed on books. Note: In person searchers must use the index books to research names. Court will search per phone request if not busy and if a simple look-up. Mail turnaround time 3-5 days. **See details about online access at front or rear of this chapter.**

Criminal Name Search: Access: Mail, online, in person. Both court and visitors may perform in person name searches. No search fee. Required to search: name, years to search, DOB; also helpful: SSN. Criminal records on microfiche 1735 to present, indexed on books. Note: In person searchers must use the index books to research names. Court will search per phone request if not busy and if a simple look-up. Mail turnaround time 3-5 days. **See details about online access at front or rear of this chapter.**

11th General District Court PO Box 24, Amelia, VA 23002; 804-561-2456; fax: 804-561-6956; 8:30AM-4:30PM (EST). *Misdemeanor, Civil Actions under $25,000, Eviction, Small Claims.* www.courts.state.va.us

General Information: Online identifiers in results same as on public terminal. No juvenile, sealed records released. Will not fax documents. Court makes copy: $1.00 1st 2 pages, $.50 each add'l. No certification fee. Payee: Amelia District Court. Personal checks, Visa/MC accepted. Prepayment required. Mail requests: SASE required for mail return of any copies.

Civil Name Search: Access: Online, in person. Visitors must perform in person searches themselves. Civil records on computer since 12/20/92. Civil PAT available. **See details about online access at front or rear of this chapter.**

Criminal Name Search: Access: Online, in person. Visitors must perform in person searches themselves. Required to search: name, years to search, DOB; also helpful: SSN. Criminal records on computer since 12/20/92. Criminal PAT available. Search free by name or case number at http://epwsgdp1.courts.state.va.us/gdcourts/captchaVerification.do?landing=landing. Results show address of subject and the day and month of birth, but not year. Online results show middle initial.

Amherst County

24th Circuit Court PO Box 462, Amherst, VA 24521; 434-946-9321; fax: 434-946-9323; 8AM-5PM (EST). *Felony, Civil Actions over $4,500, Probate.* www.courts.state.va.us/courts/circuit.html

General Information: No juvenile, sealed or adoption records released. Will not fax documents. Court makes copy: $.50 per page. Self serve copy: same. Certification fee: $2.00. Payee: Clerk of Circuit Court. Personal checks accepted, credit cards are not. Prepayment required.

Civil Name Search: Access: In person, online. Visitors must perform in person searches themselves. Civil index on docket books from 1761; on computer back to 1997. Civil PAT goes back to 1998. **See details about online access at front or rear of this chapter.** Also, remote online access to court case indexes may also be via LOPAS; call 804-786-5511 to apply.

Criminal Name Search: Access: In person, online. Visitors must perform in person searches themselves. Required to search: name, years to search, date of offense. Criminal records indexed in books back to 1761; on computer back to 1997. Criminal PAT goes back to same as civil. **See details about online access at front or rear of this chapter.**

24th General District Court PO Box 513, Amherst, VA 24521; 434-946-9351; fax: 434-946-9359; 8AM-4PM (EST). *Misdemeanor, Civil Actions under $25,000, Eviction, Small Claims.* www.courts.state.va.us

General Information: Has handled misdemeanor cases since 1985. No sealed records released. Will fax documents. Court makes copy: $1.00 per page. No certification fee. Payee: Clerk of Court. Personal checks accepted. Credit cards accepted. Prepayment required. Mail requests: SASE required for mail return of any copies.

Civil Name Search: Access: Mail, fax, online, in person. Both court and visitors may perform in person name searches. Search fee: $10.00. Civil records on computer 10 years prior. Mail turnaround time 48 hours. Civil PAT goes back to 10 years. **See details about online access at front or rear of this chapter.**

Criminal Name Search: Access: Mail, online, in person. Both court and visitors may perform in person name searches. Search fee: $10.00. Required to search: name, years to search, DOB, SSN. Criminal records on computer 10 years prior. Mail turnaround time 48 hours. Criminal PAT goes back to same as civil. **See details about online access at front or rear of this chapter.**

Appomattox County

10th Circuit Court PO Box 672, 297 Court St, Ste B, Appomattox, VA 24522; 434-352-5275; fax: 434-352-2781; 8:30AM-4:30PM (EST). *Felony, Civil Actions over $4,500, Probate.* www.courts.state.va.us/courts/circuit.html

General Information: No juvenile, sealed records released. Will not fax documents. Court makes copy: $.50 per page. No certification fee. Payee: Clerk of Circuit Court. Personal checks accepted, credit cards are not. Prepayment required.

Civil Name Search: Access: In person, online. Visitors must perform in person searches themselves. Civil records on books from 1892 to present;

on computer since 1997. Civil PAT goes back to 7/1997. **See details about online access at front or rear of this chapter.**

Criminal Name Search: Access: In person, online. Visitors must perform in person searches themselves. Criminal docket on books from 1892 to present; on computer since 1997. Criminal PAT goes back to same as civil. **See details about online access at front or rear of this chapter.**

10th General District Court PO Box 187, 297 Court St, Appomattox, VA 24522; 434-352-5540; fax: 434-352-0717; 8:30AM-4:30PM (EST). *Misdemeanor, Civil Actions under $25,000, Eviction, Small Claims.* www.courts.state.va.us/

General Information: Online identifiers in results same as on public terminal. No juvenile, sealed records released. No fee to fax documents. Court makes copy: $1.00 1st page; $.50 each add'l. No certification fee. Payee: General District Court. Personal checks accepted. Credit cards accepted. Prepayment required. Mail requests: SASE required.

Civil Name Search: Access: Fax, mail, online, in person. Both court and visitors may perform in person name searches. No search fee. Civil records on computer back ten years. Mail turnaround time 1-5 days. Civil PAT goes back to ten years. Results include name and case number. **See details about online access at front or rear of this chapter.**

Criminal Name Search: Access: Fax, mail, online, in person. Both court and visitors may perform in person name searches. No search fee. Required to search: name, years to search; also helpful: SSN. Criminal records computerized from ten years. Note: Results include address and case number. Mail turnaround time 1-5 days. Criminal PAT goes back to ten years. **See details about online access at front or rear of this chapter.**

Arlington County

17th Circuit Court 1425 N Courthouse Rd, Arlington, VA 22201; 703-228-7010; criminal phone: 703-228-4399; civil phone: 703-228-7010; probate phone: 703-228-4376; 8AM-4PM (EST). *Felony, Civil Actions over $4,500, Probate.* www.courts.state.va.us/courts/circuit.html

General Information: No juvenile, adoption or sealed records released. Will not fax documents. Court makes copy: $.50 per page. Certification fee: $2.00. Payee: Clerk of Court. Personal checks accepted. Prepayment required.

Civil Name Search: Access: In person, online. Visitors must perform in person searches themselves. Civil records on computer from 1987; prior on books from mid-1930 to present. Civil PAT goes back to 1987. **See details about online access at front or rear of this chapter.**

Criminal Name Search: Access: In person, online. Visitors must perform in person searches themselves. Criminal records computerized from 1987; prior on books from mid-1930 to present. Criminal PAT goes back to same as civil. **See details about online access at front or rear of this chapter.**

17th General District Court 1425 N Courthouse Rd, Rm 2400, Arlington, VA 22201; 703-228-7900; fax: 703-228-4593; 8AM-4PM (EST). *Misdemeanor, Civil Actions under $25,000, Eviction, Small Claims.* www.courts.state.va.us/

General Information: No juvenile, sealed records released. Will not fax documents. Court makes copy: $1.00 first page, $.50 each add'l. No certification fee. Payee: Clerk of Court. Personal checks accepted, credit cards are not. Prepayment required.

Civil Name Search: Access: Phone, mail, online, in person. Both court and visitors may perform in person name searches. No search fee. Required to search: name, years to search, case number. Civil cases indexed by defendant. Civil records on computer back 10 years, books from early 1970s. Note: Phone access limited to 4 requests. Mail turnaround time 5 days. Civil PAT goes back to 10 years. **See details about online access at front or rear of this chapter.**

Criminal Name Search: Access: Phone, mail, online, in person. Both court and visitors may perform in person name searches. No search fee. Required to search: name, years to search, DOB. Criminal records on computer back 10 years. Note: Phone access limited to 4 requests. Mail turnaround time 5 days. Criminal PAT goes back to same as civil. **See details about online access at front or rear of this chapter.**

Augusta County

25th Circuit Court PO Box 689, Staunton, VA 24402-0689; 540-245-5321; fax: 540-245-5318; 8:30AM-5PM (EST). *Felony, Civil Actions over $4,500, Probate.* www.courts.state.va.us/courts/circuit.html

General Information: Court prefers that searches be done in person. Mail access is limited; they will only search back to 1987. Phone available for very short search only. No juvenile, adoption or sealed records released. Will not fax documents. Court makes copy: $.50 per page. Self serve copy: same. Certification fee: $2.00. Payee: Clerk, Augusta County Circuit Court.

Personal checks accepted, credit cards are not. Prepayment required. Mail requests: SASE required.

Civil Name Search: Access: Mail, in person, online. Both court and visitors may perform in person name searches. No search fee. Civil records on computer from 1987 to present, books from 1745 to 1986. Mail turnaround time 1-2 days. Civil PAT goes back to 1987. **See details about online access at front or rear of this chapter.**

Criminal Name Search: Access: Mail, in person, online. Both court and visitors may perform in person name searches. No search fee. Required to search: name, years to search; also helpful: DOB, SSN. Criminal records go back to 1987 felonies only. Mail turnaround time 1-2 days. Criminal PAT available. **See details about online access at front or rear of this chapter.**

25th General District Court 6 E Johnson St, 2nd Fl, Staunton, VA 24401; 540-245-5300; fax: 540-245-5365; 8:30AM-4:30PM (EST). *Misdemeanor, Civil Actions under $25,000, Eviction, Small Claims.* www.courts.state.va.us/courts/gd/Augusta/home.html

General Information: This court also handles traffic infractions. Online identifiers in results same as on public terminal. Will not fax documents. Court makes copy: $.50 per page. No certification fee. Payee: Augusta General District Court. Personal checks, Visa/MC accepted. Prepayment required. Mail requests: SASE requested.

Civil Name Search: Access: Mail, in person, online. Both court and visitors may perform in person name searches. No search fee. Civil records kept for 10 years on computer. Mail turnaround time 5-7 days. Civil PAT goes back to 10 years. **See details about online access at front or rear of this chapter.** Results show name and sometimes address.

Criminal Name Search: Access: Mail, online, in person. Both court and visitors may perform in person name searches. No search fee. Criminal records kept for 10 years on computer, then destroyed. Mail turnaround time 5-7 days. Criminal PAT goes back to same as civil. **See details about online access at front or rear of this chapter.**

Bath County

25th Circuit Court PO Box 180, 65 Courthouse Hill Rd, Warm Springs, VA 24484; 540-839-7226; probate phone: 540-839-7226; fax: 540-839-7248; 8:30AM-4:30PM (EST). *Felony, Civil Actions over $4,500, Probate.* www.courts.state.va.us/courts/circuit.html

General Information: Probate fax- 540-839-7248 No juvenile, sealed or adoption records released. Will not fax documents. Court makes copy: $.50 per page. Self serve copy: same. Certification fee: $2.00. Payee: Bath County Circuit Court. Personal checks accepted, credit cards are not. Prepayment required.

Civil Name Search: Access: Mail, in person, online. Visitors must perform in person searches themselves. No search fee. Civil records on books from 1791 to present. Mail turnaround time 3-4 days. Search free by name only or by case number at www.courts.state.va.us/. Results show address of subject and the day and month of birth, but not year.

Criminal Name Search: Access: In person, online. Visitors must perform in person searches themselves. Required to search: name, years to search; also helpful: DOB. Criminal docket on books from 1791 to present. Search free by name only or by case number at www.courts.state.va.us/. Results show address of subject and the day and month of birth, but not year. Online results show middle initial.

25th General District Court PO Box 96, Warm Springs, VA 24484; 540-839-7241; fax: 540-839-7242; 8:30AM-4:30PM (EST). *Misdemeanor, Civil Actions under $25,000, Eviction, Small Claims.* www.courts.state.va.us/

General Information: No juvenile, sealed records released. Will fax documents $.50 per page. Court makes copy: $.50 per page. No certification fee. Payee: Bath County Combined Court. Personal checks accepted. Credit cards accepted. Prepayment required. Mail requests: SASE requested.

Civil Name Search: Access: Phone, fax, mail, online, in person. Both court and visitors may perform in person name searches. No search fee. Civil records on files 10 years to present, Prior records in Circuit Court. Mail turnaround time 2 days; will give immediate response on phone if not an extensive search. **See details about online access at front or rear of this chapter.**

Criminal Name Search: Access: Phone, fax, mail, online, in person. Both court and visitors may perform in person name searches. No search fee. Required to search: name, years to search, DOB; also helpful: SSN. Criminal records on files back 10 years, Prior records in Circuit Court. Mail turnaround time 2 days; immediate response by phone if not extensive search. Search free by name or case number at http://epwsgdp1.courts.state.va.us/gdcourts/captchaVerification.do?landing=landing. Results show address of subject and the day and month of birth, but not year. Online results show middle initial.

Bedford County

County Circuit Court 123 E Main St, #201, Bedford, VA 24523; 540-586-7632; fax: 540-586-6197; 8:30AM-5PM, registers close at 4:30PM (EST). *Felony, Civil Actions over $4,500, Probate.*
www.courts.state.va.us/courts/circuit.html
General Information: Online identifiers in results same as on public terminal. No juvenile, sealed records released. Will not fax documents. Court makes copy: $.50 per page. Self serve copy: $.50 per page. Certification fee: $2.00 plus copy fee. Payee: Bedford Clerk of Court. Personal checks accepted, credit cards are not. Prepayment required.
Civil Name Search: Access: In person, online. Visitors must perform in person searches themselves. Civil records on computer from 1998, index books. Civil PAT goes back to 1998. **See details about online access at front or rear of this chapter.**
Criminal Name Search: Access: In person, online. Visitors must perform in person searches themselves. Required to search: name, years to search, DOB. Criminal records computerized from 1988, index books. Criminal PAT goes back to 1999. **See details about online access at front or rear of this chapter.**

24th General District Court 123 E Main St, #202, Bedford, VA 24523; 540-586-7637; fax: 540-586-7684; 8AM-4PM (EST). *Misdemeanor, Civil Actions under $25,000, Eviction, Small Claims, Traffic.*
www.courts.state.va.us/
General Information: Online identifiers in results same as on public terminal. No sealed records released. Will not fax documents. Court makes copy: $1.00 1st 2 pages, $.50 each add'l. No certification fee. Payee: Bedford General District Court. Personal checks accepted. Credit cards accepted. Prepayment required. Mail requests: SASE required.
Civil Name Search: Access: In person, online. Visitors must perform in person searches themselves. Required to search: name. Civil cases indexed by defendant. Civil records on computer for ten years. Note: The court will not perform name searches. Civil PAT goes back to 10 years. **See details about online access at front or rear of this chapter.**
Criminal Name Search: Access: Online, in person. Visitors must perform in person searches themselves. Search fee: n/a. Required to search: name. Criminal records on computer for ten years. Note: The court will not perform name searches. Criminal PAT goes back to same as civil. **See details about online access at front or rear of this chapter.**

Bedford City
Circuit & District Courts - See Bedford County

Bland County

27th Circuit Court PO Box 295, Bland, VA 24315; 276-688-4562; fax: 276-688-2438; 8AM-6PM (EST). *Felony, Civil Actions over $4,500, Probate.* www.courts.state.va.us/courts/circuit.html
General Information: No juvenile, sealed or adoption records released. Will fax documents $1.00 per page. Court makes copy: $.50 per page. Self serve copy: same. Certification fee: $2.00. Payee: Clerk of Court. Personal checks accepted, credit cards are not. Prepayment required. Mail requests: SASE required.
Civil Name Search: Access: Phone, fax, mail, in person, online. Both court and visitors may perform in person name searches. Search fee: $10.00 per name. Civil records on books from 1861 to present. Mail turnaround time 2 days. Civil PAT goes back to 1993. **See details about online access at front or rear of this chapter.**
Criminal Name Search: Access: Phone, fax, mail, in person, online. Both court and visitors may perform in person name searches. Search fee: $10.00 per name. Required to search: name, years to search, signed release; also helpful: SSN. Criminal docket on books from 1861 to present. Mail turnaround time 2 days. Criminal PAT goes back to 1993. **See details about online access at front or rear of this chapter.**

27th General District Court PO Box 157, 612 Main St, Ste 106, Bland, VA 24315; 276-688-4433; fax: 276-688-4789; 8AM-4:30PM (EST). *Misdemeanor, Civil Actions under $25,000, Eviction, Small Claims.*
www.bland.org/government/generaldistrictcourt.html
General Information: No juvenile, sealed or adoption records released. Will fax documents to local or toll-free number. Court makes copy: $1.00 1st 2 pages, $.50 each add'l. No certification fee. Payee: General District Court. Personal checks accepted. Credit cards accepted. Mail requests: SASE required.
Civil Name Search: Access: Phone, fax, mail, online, in person. Both court and visitors may perform in person name searches. No search fee. Civil cases indexed by defendant. Civil records on computer from 4/23/95. Mail turnaround time 1-2 days. Civil PAT goes back to 1995. **See details about online access at front or rear of this chapter.**
Criminal Name Search: Access: Phone, fax, mail, online, in person. Both court and visitors may perform in person name searches. No search fee. Required to search: name, years to search; also helpful: DOB, SSN. Criminal

records computerized from 4/23/92. Note: Phone access limited to specific cases only. Mail turnaround time 1-2 days. Criminal PAT goes back to 1996. **See details about online access at front or rear of this chapter.**

Botetourt County

25th Circuit Court PO Box 219, 1 W Main St, Courthouse, Fincastle, VA 24090; 540-473-8274; fax: 540-473-8209; 8:30AM-4:30PM (EST). *Felony, Civil Actions over $4,500, Probate.*
www.courts.state.va.us/courts/circuit/Botetourt/home.html
General Information: Specify index to search; civil, criminal, or both. No juvenile, sealed or adoption records released. Will not fax documents. Court makes copy: $.50 per page. Certification fee: $2.00. Payee: Clerk of Court. Personal checks accepted, credit cards are not. Prepayment required. Mail requests: SASE required.
Civil Name Search: Access: Mail, in person, online. Both court and visitors may perform in person name searches. No search fee. Civil records on computer 7/1/91 to present, books back to 1770. Mail turnaround time same day. Civil PAT goes back to 1991. **See details about online access at front or rear of this chapter.**
Criminal Name Search: Access: Mail, online, in person. Both court and visitors may perform in person name searches. No search fee. Required to search: name, years to search, DOB, SSN. Criminal records on computer 7/1/91 to present, books back to 1770. Mail turnaround time same day. Criminal PAT goes back to 1991. **See details about online access at front or rear of this chapter.**

25th General District Court PO Box 858, Fincastle, VA 24090-0858; 540-473-8244; fax: 540-473-8344; 8AM-4PM (EST). *Misdemeanor, Civil Actions under $25,000, Eviction, Small Claims.*
www.courts.state.va.us
General Information: No juvenile, sealed records released. Will not fax documents. Court makes copy: $.50 per page. Self serve copy: $.10 per page. No certification fee. Payee: General District Court. Personal checks accepted; checks requiring verification calls not accepted. Credit cards accepted. Prepayment required. Mail requests: SASE required.
Civil Name Search: Access: Mail, in person, online. Both court and visitors may perform in person name searches. No search fee. Civil records on computer 10 years. Mail turnaround time 3-4 days. Civil PAT goes back to 10 years. **See details about online access at front or rear of this chapter.**
Criminal Name Search: Access: Mail, online, in person. Both court and visitors may perform in person name searches. No search fee. Criminal records computerized for 10 years. Mail turnaround time 3-4 days. Criminal PAT goes back to same as civil. **See details about online access at front or rear of this chapter.**

Bristol City

28th Circuit Court 497 Cumberland St, Bristol, VA 24201; 276-645-7321; fax: 276-821-6097; 9AM-5PM (EST). *Felony, Civil Actions over $4,500, Probate.* www.courts.state.va.us/courts/circuit.html
General Information: Online identifiers in results same as on public terminal. No juvenile, sealed or adoption records released. Will not fax documents. Court makes copy: $.50 per page. Self serve copy: $.50 per page. Certification fee: $2.00 per doc plus copy fee; Exemplification fee-$2.50. Payee: Clerk of Circuit Court. Personal checks accepted, credit cards are not. Prepayment required. Mail requests: SASE required.
Civil Name Search: Access: Mail, in person, online. Visitors must perform in person searches themselves. Search fee: $5.00 per name. Civil records indexed from 1890 to present; on computer back to 1994. Civil PAT goes back to 1994. Only month and day of DOB appears, plus sex, race. **See details about online access at front or rear of this chapter.**
Criminal Name Search: Access: Mail, in person, online. Visitors must perform in person searches themselves. Search fee: $5.00 per name. Criminal records indexed from 1890 to present; on computer back to 1994. Criminal PAT goes back to same as civil. Only month and day of DOB appears, plus sex, race. **See details about online access at front or rear of this chapter.**

28th General District Court 497 Cumberland St, Courthouse Rm 208, Bristol, VA 24201; 276-645-7341; fax: 276-645-7342; 8:30AM-4:30PM (EST). *Misdemeanor, Civil Actions under $25,000, Eviction, Small Claims.*
www.courts.state.va.us/courts/circuit/Bristol/home.html
General Information: No juvenile, sealed records released. Will not fax documents. Court makes copy: None. No certification fee. Payee: General District Court. Personal checks, Visa/MC accepted. Prepayment required.
Civil Name Search: Access: Online, in person. Both court and visitors may perform in person name searches. No search fee. Civil records on computer from 1997, card file 1983 to 1988. **See details about online access at front or rear of this chapter.**
Criminal Name Search: Access: Online, in person. Visitors must perform in person searches themselves. Required to search: name, years to

search, DOB, SSN. Criminal records computerized from 1997, card file 1983 to 1988. Note: Results include name and case number. **See details about online access at front or rear of this chapter.**

Brunswick County

6th Circuit Court 216 N Main St, Lawrenceville, VA 23868; 434-848-2215; fax: 434-848-4307; 8:30AM-5PM (EST). *Felony, Civil, Probate.* www.courts.state.va.us/courts/circuit.html

General Information: No juvenile, sealed or adoption records released. Will not fax documents. Court makes copy: $.50 per page. Certification fee: $2.00. Payee: Clerk of Court. Personal checks accepted, credit cards are not. Prepayment required.

Civil Name Search: Access: In person, online. Visitors must perform in person searches themselves. Civil records in books back to 1732; on computer since 1992 (office use only). Search free by name only or by case number at www.courts.state.va.us/. Results show address of subject and the day and month of birth, but not year. **See details about online access at front or rear of this chapter.**

Criminal Name Search: Access: In person, online. Visitors must perform in person searches themselves. Criminal records in books back to 1732; on computer back to 1992 (office use only). Access record images via http://208.210.219.102/cgi-bin/p/rms.cgi; registration and password required. Search free by name only or by case number at www.courts.state.va.us/. Results show address of subject and the day and month of birth, but not year.

6th General District Court 202 Main St N, Albertis S. Harrison Jr. Courthouse, Lawrenceville, VA 23868-0066; 434-848-2315/8376; fax: 434-848-2550; 8AM-4PM (EST). *Misdemeanor, Civil Actions under $25,000, Eviction, Small Claims.* www.courts.state.va.us/courts/combined/Brunswick/home.html

General Information: Online identifiers in results same as on public terminal. No juvenile, sealed records released. Will not fax documents. Court makes copy: $1.00 per page. No certification fee. Payee: Brunswick G D Court. Personal checks accepted. Visa/MC accepted in person only. Prepayment required. Mail requests: SASE required.

Civil Name Search: Access: Mail, in person, online. Both court and visitors may perform in person name searches. No search fee. Civil records computerized since 1988, records go back 11 years. Note: Court will search time permitting. Mail turnaround time 1-2 days. Civil PAT goes back to 11 years. **See details about online access at front or rear of this chapter.**

Criminal Name Search: Access: Mail, in person, online. Both court and visitors may perform in person name searches. No search fee. Required to search: name, years to search, DOB; also helpful: SSN, signed release. Criminal records computerized since 1991; records go back 10 years. Note: Court will perform in person searches only if time permits. Mail turnaround time 1-2 days. Criminal PAT goes back to same as civil. **See details about online access at front or rear of this chapter.**

Buchanan County

29th Circuit Court PO Box 929, Grundy, VA 24614; 276-935-6567; criminal phone: 276-935-6575; civil phone: 276-935-6575; fax: 276-935-7086; 8:30AM-5PM (EST). *Felony, Misdemeanor, Civil Actions over $4,500, Probate.* www.courts.state.va.us/courts/circuit.html

General Information: This court has records of Misdemeanors under appeal. See the 29th Judicial District Court for originating Misdemeanor records. Online identifiers in results same as on public terminal. No juvenile, sealed records released. Will fax documents to local or toll-free number. Court makes copy: $.50 per page. Self serve copy: same. Certification fee: $2.00. Payee: Clerk of Circuit Court. Personal checks accepted if in state. Visa/MC accepted. Prepayment not required unless extensive copies needed. Mail requests: SASE not required.

Civil Name Search: Access: Phone, mail, online, in person. Both court and visitors may perform in person name searches. No search fee. Required to search: name, years to search; also helpful: address. Civil records on computer back to 1991, in books back to 1923. Mail turnaround time 1 week. Civil PAT goes back to 1991. Only month and day of DOB appears, plus sex, race. Search free by name or case number at www.courts.state.va.us/.

Criminal Name Search: Access: Online, in person. Visitors must perform in person searches themselves. Required to search: name, years to search, DOB; also helpful: address, SSN. Criminal records computerized from 1991; in books back to 1928. Criminal PAT goes back to 1991. Only month and day of DOB appears, plus sex, race. S **See details about online access at front or rear of this chapter.**

29th General District Court PO Box 654, Grundy, VA 24614; 276-935-6526; fax: 276-935-5479; 8AM-4PM (EST). *Misdemeanor, Civil Actions under $25,000, Eviction, Small Claims, Traffic.* www.courts.state.va.us/

General Information: Also search the Circuit Court for appealed Misdemeanor records. Online identifiers in results same as on public terminal. Will fax to toll-free or local numbers only. Court makes copy: $1.00 first two pages, $.50 ea addl. No certification fee. Payee: General District Court. Personal checks, Visa/MC accepted. Prepayment required. Mail requests: SASE required.

Civil Name Search: Access: Fax, mail, in person, phone, online. Both court and visitors may perform in person name searches. No search fee. Required to search: name; also helpful: years to search. Civil records are indexed for 10 years, computerized back to 1993. Mail turnaround time 1 week. Civil PAT available. **See details about online access at front or rear of this chapter.**

Criminal Name Search: Access: Fax, mail, in person, online. Both court and visitors may perform in person name searches. No search fee. Required to search: name; also helpful: years to search. Criminal Records computerized back to 1993. Criminal PAT available. **See details about online access at front or rear of this chapter.**

Buckingham County

10th Circuit Court PO Box 107, Rte 60, Buckingham, VA 23921; 434-969-4734; fax: 434-969-2043; 8:30AM-4:30PM (EST). *Felony, Civil Actions over $4,500, Probate.* www.courts.state.va.us/courts/circuit.html

General Information: No juvenile, sealed or adoption records released. Will fax documents $2.00 per page. Court makes copy: $.50 per page. Self serve copy: same. Certification fee: $2.00. Payee: Clerk of Court. Personal checks accepted, credit cards are not. Mail requests: SASE required.

Civil Name Search: Access: Mail, in person, online. Both court and visitors may perform in person name searches. No search fee. Civil records on books from 1869 to present, computerized since 2001. Civil PAT goes back to 1990. **See details about online access at front or rear of this chapter.**

Criminal Name Search: Access: In person, online. Both court and visitors may perform in person name searches. No search fee. Required to search: name, years to search; also helpful: DOB. Criminal docket on books from 1869 to present, computerized since 2001. Criminal PAT goes back to 1990. Search free by name only or by case number at www.courts.state.va.us/. Results show address of subject and the day and month of birth, but not year. Online results show middle initial.

Buckingham General District Court PO Box 127, Courthouse, Buckingham, VA 23921; 434-969-4755; fax: 434-969-1762; 8:30AM-4:30PM (EST). *Misdemeanor, Civil Actions under $25,000, Eviction, Small Claims.* www.courts.state.va.us/courts/combined/buckingham/home.html

General Information: No juvenile, sealed records released. Will not fax documents. Court makes copy: none. No certification fee. Payee: Buckingham. Personal checks, Visa/MC accepted. Prepayment required.

Civil Name Search: Access: Mail, in person, online, fax. Only the court performs in person name searches; visitors may not. No search fee. Civil cases indexed by defendant. Civil records on computer or hard copy from 1993, prior records on index cards. Mail turnaround time 2 weeks. **See details about online access at front or rear of this chapter.**

Criminal Name Search: Access: Mail, online, in person, fax. Only the court performs in person name searches; visitors may not. No search fee. Required to search: name, years to search, DOB, SSN, signed release. Criminal records on computer or hard copy from 1993, prior on index cards. Mail turnaround time 2 weeks. **See details about online access at front or rear of this chapter.**

Buena Vista City

25th Circuit & District Court 2039 Sycamore Ave, Buena Vista, VA 24416; 540-261-8627; fax: 540-261-8625; 8:30AM-5PM (EST). *Felony, Misdemeanor, Civil, Eviction, Probate.* www.courts.state.va.us/courts/Buena_Vista/home.html

General Information: Probate fax is same as main fax number. Online identifiers in results same as on public terminal. No juvenile, sealed records released. Will not fax documents. Court makes copy: $.50 per page. Self serve copy: same. Certification fee: $2.00 per cert plus copy fee. Payee: Buena Vista Circuit Court. Personal checks accepted, credit cards are not. Prepayment required. Mail requests: SASE required.

Civil Name Search: Access: Mail, in person, online. Both court and visitors may perform in person name searches. No search fee. Civil records on manual records 1892 to present, computerized since 1996. Mail turnaround time 1 day. Public use terminal has civil records back to 1/1993. **See details about online access at front or rear of this chapter.**

Criminal Name Search: Access: Mail, online, in person. Both court and visitors may perform in person name searches. No search fee. Criminal records on manual records 1892 to present, computerized since 1996. Mail turnaround time 1 day. **See details about online access at front or rear of this chapter.**

Campbell County

24th Circuit Court 732 Village Hwy, PO Box 7, Rustburg, VA 24588; 434-592-9517; criminal phone: 434-592-9614; civil phone: 434-592-9610; probate phone: 434-592-9517; fax: 434-332-9598; 8:30AM-4:30PM (EST). *Felony, Civil Actions over $4,500, Probate.*
www.courts.state.va.us/courts/circuit.html
General Information: Requests not accepted by fax. No juvenile, sealed or adoption records released. Will not fax documents. Court makes copy: $.50 per page. Self serve copy: same. Certification fee: $2.00 per cert plus copy fee. Payee: Clerk of Court. Personal checks accepted, credit cards are not. Prepayment required. Mail requests: SASE required.
Civil Name Search: Access: In person, online. Visitors must perform in person searches themselves. Civil index on docket books. Mail turnaround time 5 days. Civil PAT goes back to 1994-95. **See details about online access at front or rear of this chapter.**
Criminal Name Search: Access: Online, in person. Visitors must perform in person searches themselves. Required to search: name, years to search; also helpful: DOB. Criminal records indexed in books. Mail turnaround time 5 days. Criminal PAT goes back to same as civil. **See details about online access at front or rear of this chapter.**

24th General District Court PO Box 97, 732 Village Hwy, Rustburg, VA 24588; 434-332-9546; fax: 434-332-9694; 8AM-4PM (EST). *Misdemeanor, Civil Actions under $25,000, Eviction, Small Claims.*
www.courts.state.va.us/courts/gd/Campbell/home.html
General Information: Online identifiers in results same as on public terminal. Will fax documents if copy fee is prepaid. Court makes copy: $1.00 1st 2 pages, $.50 each add'l. No certification fee. Payee: Clerk of Court. Personal checks accepted. Credit cards accepted in person. Prepayment required.
Civil Name Search: Access: Online, in person. Visitors must perform in person searches themselves. Civil records on computer for 10 years. Public use terminal available, records go back to 10 years. **See details about online access at front or rear of this chapter.**
Criminal Name Search: Access: Online, in person. Visitors must perform in person searches themselves. Criminal records on computer for 10 years. Public use terminal available, crim records go back to 10 years. **See details about online access at front or rear of this chapter.**

Caroline County

15th Circuit Court 112 Courthouse Ln, #A, PO Box 309, Bowling Green, VA 22427-0309; 804-633-5800; criminal phone: 804-633-1093; civil phone: 804-633-1094; probate phone: 804-633-1091; fax: 804-633-0519; 8:30AM-4PM (EST). *Felony, Civil Actions over $4,500, Probate.*
www.courts.state.va.us/courts/circuit.html
General Information: No juvenile, sealed, adoption records released. Will not fax documents. Court makes copy: $.50 per page. Self serve copy: same. Certification fee: $2.50. Payee: Clerk of Court. Personal checks accepted. Credit cards accepted for payment of fines and costs only. Not accepted over the phone. Prepayment required. Mail requests: SASE required for mail return of any copies.
Civil Name Search: Access: In person, online. Visitors must perform in person searches themselves. Civil records on books from early 1900s to present. Civil PAT goes back to 1991. **See details about online access at front or rear of this chapter.**
Criminal Name Search: Access: In person, online. Visitors must perform in person searches themselves. Required to search: name, years to search; also helpful: DOB. Criminal docket on books from early 1900s to present, computerized since 1896. Criminal PAT goes back to same as civil. Search free by name only or by case number at www.courts.state.va.us/. Results show address of subject and the day and month of birth, but not year. Online results show middle initial.

15th General District Court PO Box 511, 111 Ennis St, Bowling Green, VA 22427; 804-633-5720; fax: 804-633-3033; 8AM-4PM (EST). *Misdemeanor, Civil Actions under $25,000, Eviction, Small Claims.*
www.courts.state.va.us/
General Information: Will not fax documents. Court makes copy: $1.00 first page, $.50 ea add'l. No certification fee. Payee: Caroline General District Court. Personal checks, Visa/MC accepted.
Civil Name Search: Access: Online, in person. Both court and visitors may perform in person name searches. No search fee. Civil records on computer from 1/92. Note: At the court's discretion, usually for high volume, you may have to fill out a research request form before they'll search. Civil PAT goes back to 10 years. **See details about online access at front or rear of this chapter.**
Criminal Name Search: Access: Online, in person. Both court and visitors may perform in person name searches. No search fee. Required to search: name, years to search, SSN. Criminal records on computer back 10 years. Records older than 10 years are destroyed/expunged/purged. Note: At the court's discretion, usually for high volume, you may have to fill out a

research request form before they'll search. Criminal PAT goes back to 10 years. **See details about online access at front or rear of this chapter.**

Carroll County

27th Circuit Court PO Box 218, 605 Pine St, #A230, Hillsville, VA 24343; 276-730-3070; fax: 276-730-3071; 8AM-5PM (EST). *Felony, Civil Actions over $4,500, Probate.*
www.courts.state.va.us/courts/circuit.html
General Information: No juvenile, sealed, adoption records released. Will fax documents $2.50 per page. Court makes copy: $.50 per page. Self serve copy: same. Certification fee: $2.00. Payee: Clerk of Court. Personal checks, Visa/MC accepted. Prepayment required. Mail requests: SASE required.
Civil Name Search: Access: Mail, in person, online. Both court and visitors may perform in person name searches. Search fee: $5.00 per name. Required to search: name, years to search, also helpful: SSN. Civil records on books from 1842 to present, on computer back to 1991. Mail turnaround time 3 days. **See details about online access at front or rear of this chapter.**
Criminal Name Search: Access: Mail, in person, online. Both court and visitors may perform in person name searches. Search fee: $5.00 per name. Required to search: name, years to search; also helpful: SSN. Criminal docket on books from 1842 to present; on computer back to 1991. Mail turnaround time 3 days. **See details about online access at front or rear of this chapter.**

Carroll Combined District Court PO Box 698, 605 Pine St, Hillsville, VA 24343; 276-730-3050; fax: 276-730-3054; 8AM-4PM (EST). *Misdemeanor, Civil Actions under $25,000, Eviction, Small Claims.*
www.courts.state.va.us
General Information: No juvenile, sealed records released. Will not fax documents. Court makes copy: none. No certification fee. Payee: Carroll County. Personal checks, Visa/MC accepted. Prepayment required.
Civil Name Search: Access: In person, online. Visitors must perform in person searches themselves. Civil records on books from 1800s, on computer from 1988; no plaintiff index prior to computerization. Civil PAT goes back to 1996. **See details about online access at front or rear of this chapter.**
Criminal Name Search: Access: In person, online. Visitors must perform in person searches themselves. Required to search: name, years to search, DOB. Criminal docket on books from 1800s, on computer 10 years. Criminal PAT goes back to same as civil. **See details about online access at front or rear of this chapter.**

Charles City County

9th Circuit Court PO Box 86, 10780 Courthouse Rd,, Charles City, VA 23030-0086; 804-652-2105; fax: 804-829-5647; 8:30AM-4:30PM, stop recording at 4PM (EST). *Felony, Civil Actions over $4,500, Probate.*
www.courts.state.va.us/courts/circuit/Charles_City/home.html
General Information: No juvenile, sealed records released. Will not fax out documents. Court makes copy: $.50 per page. Self serve copy: same. Certification fee: $2.00. Payee: Clerk of Circuit Court. Personal checks accepted, credit cards are not. Prepayment required.
Civil Name Search: Access: In person only, online. Visitors must perform in person name searches themselves. No search fee. Civil records on computer from 2000, on books from 1789-2000. Civil PAT goes back to 2000. **See details about online access at front or rear of this chapter.**
Criminal Name Search: Access: In person, online. Visitors must perform in person searches themselves. Required to search: name, years to search, DOB. Criminal records computerized from 2000, on books from 1789-2000. Criminal PAT goes back to same as civil. **See details about online access at front or rear of this chapter.**

9th General District Court PO Box 57, Charles City Courthouse, 10780 Courthouse Rd, Charles City, VA 23030; 804-652-2188; fax: 804-829-6390; 8:30AM-4:30PM (EST). *Misdemeanor, Civil Actions under $25,000, Eviction, Small Claims.*
www.courts.state.va.us/courts/combined/Charles_City/home.html
General Information: No juvenile, sealed records released. Will not fax documents. Court makes copy: $.50 per page but $1.00 minimum. No certification fee. Payee: Charles City County District Court. Personal checks accepted. No credit cards accepted for copy fees. Prepayment required. Mail requests: SASE required.
Civil Name Search: Access: Mail, in person, online. Both court and visitors may perform in person name searches. No search fee. Civil records on computer back 10 years. Mail turnaround time 3 days. Civil PAT goes back to 10 years. **See details about online access at front or rear of this chapter.**
Criminal Name Search: Access: Mail, online, in person. Both court and visitors may perform in person name searches. No search fee. Required to search: name, years to search, DOB, SSN. Criminal records computerized for

10 years, then deleted. Mail turnaround time 3 days. Criminal PAT goes back to 10 years. **See details about online access at front or rear of this chapter.**

Charlotte County

10th Circuit Court PO Box 38, 125 David Bruce Ave, Charlotte Courthouse, VA 23923; 434-542-5147; fax: 434-542-4336; 8:30AM-4:30PM (EST). *Felony, Civil Actions over $4,500, Probate.* www.courts.state.va.us/courts/circuit/Charlotte/home.html

General Information: No juvenile, sealed records released. Will not fax documents. Court makes copy: $.50 per page. Certification fee: $3.00. Payee: Clerk of Circuit Court. Personal checks accepted, credit cards are not. Prepayment required.

Civil Name Search: Access: In person, online. Visitors must perform in person searches themselves. Civil records on books from 1765, in folders by case number. **See details about online access at front or rear of this chapter.**

Criminal Name Search: Access: In person, online. Visitors must perform in person searches themselves. Required to search: name, years to search, DOB. Criminal docket on books from 1765, in folders by case number. Search free by name only or by case number at www.courts.state.va.us/. Results show address of subject and the day and month of birth, but not year. Online results show middle initial.

Charlotte General District Court PO Box 127, 111 Legrand Ave, Charlotte Courthouse, VA 23923; 434-542-5600; fax: 434-542-5902; 8:30AM-4:30PM (EST). *Misdemeanor, Civil Actions under $25,000, Eviction, Small Claims.* www.courts.state.va.us/courts/gd/Charlotte/home.html

General Information: No juvenile, sealed records released. Will not fax documents. Court makes copy: $.50 per page. Self serve copy: same. No certification fee. Payee: Clerk of General District Court. Personal checks, Visa/MC accepted. Prepayment required.

Civil Name Search: Access: Online, in person. Visitors must perform in person searches themselves. Civil records on computer back to 5/97. Civil PAT goes back to 10 years. **See details about online access at front or rear of this chapter.**

Criminal Name Search: Access: Online, in person. Visitors must perform in person searches themselves. Required to search: name, years to search, DOB; also helpful-SSN, signed release. Criminal records computerized from 5/97. Criminal PAT goes back to 10 years. **See details about online access at front or rear of this chapter.**

Charlottesville City

16th Circuit Court 315 E High St, Charlottesville, VA 22902; 434-970-3766; 8:30AM-4:30PM (EST). *Felony, Civil Actions over $4,500, Probate.* www.courts.state.va.us/courts/circuit/Charlottesville/home.html

General Information: No juvenile, sealed or adoption records released. Will not fax documents. Court makes copy: $.50 per page. Certification fee: $2.00 per doc. Payee: Charlottesville Circuit Court Clerk's Office. No out of state checks accepted. No credit cards accepted. Prepayment required.

Civil Name Search: Access: In person. Visitors must perform in person searches themselves. Civil records on books from 1888 to present. Note: The court will not perform a name search.

Criminal Name Search: Access: In person. Visitors must perform in person searches themselves. Required to search: name, years to search; also helpful: DOB. Criminal docket on books from 1888 to present. Note: The court will not perform a name search.

Charlottesville General District Court PO Box 2677, 606 E Market St, Charlottesville, VA 22902-2677; 434-970-3388; criminal phone: 434-970-3366; civil phone: 434-970-3391; fax: 434-970-3387; 8:30AM-4:30PM (EST). *Misdemeanor, Civil Actions under $25,000, Eviction, Small Claims.* www.courts.state.va.us/courts/gd/Charlottesville/home.html

General Information: Traffic phone- 434-970-3386. Online identifiers in results same as on public terminal. No juvenile, sealed, confidential records released. Will fax documents to local or toll-free number. Court makes copy: $1.00 first page, $.50 each add'l. Self serve copy: $.50 per page. Certification fee: Included in copy fee. Payee: General District Court. Personal checks, Visa/MC accepted. Prepayment required. Mail requests: SASE required.

Civil Name Search: Access: Mail, in person, online. Both court and visitors may perform in person name searches. No search fee. Civil records kept for 10 years. Mail turnaround time 3 days. Civil PAT goes back to 10 years. **See details about online access at front or rear of this chapter.**

Criminal Name Search: Access: Mail, online, in person. Both court and visitors may perform in person name searches. No search fee. Required to search: name, years to search; also helpful: DOB, SSN. Criminal records kept for 10 years. Mail turnaround time 3 days. Criminal PAT goes back to same as civil. **See details about online access at front or rear of this chapter.**

Chesapeake County

1st Circuit Court 307 Albemarle Dr, #300A, Chesapeake, VA 23322-5579; 757-382-3000; fax: 757-382-3034; 8AM-4PM (EST). *Felony, Civil Actions over $4,500, Probate.* www.courts.state.va.us/courts/circuit.html

General Information: No juvenile, sealed records released. Will not fax out documents. Court makes copy: $.50 per page. Certification fee: $2.00. Payee: Clerk of Circuit Court. Personal checks, Visa/MC accepted. Mail requests: SASE required.

Civil Name Search: Access: Mail, online, in person. Visitors must perform in person searches themselves. No search fee. Civil records on books from 1637, on computer from 1989. Mail turnaround time 1 week. Civil PAT goes back to 1989. **See details about online access at front or rear of this chapter.**

Criminal Name Search: Access: Mail, online, in person. Visitors must perform in person searches themselves. No search fee. Required to search: name, years to search, DOB; also helpful: SSN, sex, signed release. Criminal docket on books from 1800s; on computer from 1989. Mail turnaround time 1 week. Criminal PAT goes back to same as civil. **See details about online access at front or rear of this chapter.**

Chesapeake City

1st General District Court 307 Albemarle Dr, #100, Chesapeake, VA 23322; 757-382-3100; criminal phone: 757-382-3134; civil phone: 757-382-3143; criminal fax: 757-382-3171; civil fax: 8AM-4PM; 8AM-4PM (EST). *Misdemeanor, Civil Actions under $25,000, Eviction, Small Claims, Traffic.* www.courts.state.va.us/

General Information: Indicate division (civil, criminal or traffic) in address. Traffic phone is 757-382-3119. Online identifiers in results same as on public terminal. No juvenile, sealed records released. Will not fax documents. Court makes copy: $1.00 per copy. Certification fee: none. Payee: General District Court. Personal checks, Visa/MC accepted. Prepayment required.

Civil Name Search: Access: Mail, in person, online. Both court and visitors may perform in person name searches. Search fee: Varies according to research needed, would not give figures. Civil records on computer back to 1990; prior on books. Mail turnaround time up to 4 weeks. Civil PAT goes back to 1990. **See details about online access at front or rear of this chapter.**

Criminal Name Search: Access: Mail, online, in person. Both court and visitors may perform in person name searches. Search fee: Varies according to research needed, would not give figures. Required to search: name, years to search, DOB; also helpful: SSN. Criminal records computerized from 1990; prior on books. Mail turnaround time 2-14 days. Criminal PAT goes back to same as civil. Partial addresses are sometimes shown. **See details about online access at front or rear of this chapter.**

Chesterfield County

12th Circuit Court 9500 Courthouse Rd, PO Box 125, Chesterfield, VA 23832; 804-748-1241; fax: 804-796-5625; 9AM-4PM (EST). *Felony, Civil Actions over $4,500, Probate.* www.chesterfield.gov/content2.aspx?id=2902

General Information: No juvenile, adoption, sealed records released. Will not fax documents. Court makes copy: $.50 per page. Certification fee: $2.00. Payee: Chesterfield Circuit Court. Personal checks accepted, credit cards are not. Prepayment required. Mail requests: SASE required.

Civil Name Search: Access: Mail, in person, online. Both court and visitors may perform in person name searches. No search fee. Civil records on computer go back to 1989; prior on index books. Mail turnaround time 1-2 days. Civil PAT goes back to 1989. Remote online access to court case indexes is via LOPAS. This is a limited system and the program is not taking on new clients.

Criminal Name Search: Access: Mail, in person, online. Both court and visitors may perform in person name searches. No search fee. Required to search: name, years to search; also helpful: DOB, SSN, charge. Criminal records on computer go back to 1989, prior on index books. Mail turnaround time 1 week. Criminal PAT goes back to 1989. Remote online access to court case indexes is via LOPAS. This is a limited system and the program is not taking on new clients.

12th General District Court PO Box 144, 9500 Courthouse Rd, Chesterfield, VA 23832; 804-748-1231; fax: 804-748-1757; 8AM-4PM (EST). *Misdemeanor, Civil Actions under $25,000, Eviction, Small Claims.* www.courts.state.va.us/courts/gd/Chesterfield/home.html

General Information: No sealed records released. Will not fax documents. Court makes copy: $1.00 first page, $.50 ea addl. Certification fee: $2.00. Payee: Court. Personal checks, Visa/MC accepted. Prepayment required.

Civil Name Search: Access: Mail, in person, online. Both court and visitors may perform in person name searches. No search fee. Civil records on computer from 1990 to present. Mail turnaround time 2 days. Civil PAT available. **See details about online access at front or rear of this chapter.**

Criminal Name Search: Access: Mail, online, in person. Both court and visitors may perform in person name searches. No search fee. Required to search: name, years to search, DOB, SSN. Criminal records computerized from 1990 to present. Note: Results include name and address. Mail turnaround time 5 days. Criminal PAT available. **See details about online access at front or rear of this chapter.**

Clarke County

26th Circuit Court PO Box 189, 102 N. Church Street, Berryville, VA 22611; 540-955-5116; fax: 540-955-0284; 9AM-5PM (EST). *Felony, Civil Actions over $4,500, Probate.*

www.courts.state.va.us/courts/circuit.html

General Information: No juvenile, sealed or adoption records released. No criminal records by mail. Fee to fax document $.50 per page. Court makes copy: $.50 per page. Self serve copy: same. No certification fee. Payee: Clerk of Court. Personal checks accepted. Prepayment required.

Civil Name Search: Access: In person, online. Visitors must perform in person searches themselves. Civil records on books from 1920s. **See details about online access at front or rear of this chapter.**

Criminal Name Search: Access: In person, online. Visitors must perform in person searches themselves. Required to search: name, years to search, signed release. Criminal docket on books from 1920s. **See details about online access at front or rear of this chapter.**

General District Court PO Box 612, 104 N Church St, Berryville, VA 22611; 540-955-5128; fax: 540-955-1195; 8:30AM-4:30PM (EST). *Misdemeanor, Civil Actions under $25,000, Eviction, Small Claims.*

www.courts.state.va.us

General Information: The court does not have a web page, but the county site is www.clarkecounty.gov/. Also, see www.courts.state.va.us. Online identifiers in results same as on public terminal. Will not fax documents. Court makes copy: $.50 per page. Self serve copy: same. No certification fee. Payee: Clarke County General District Court. Personal checks require name and address. No credit cards accepted for copies or record searches. Mail requests: SASE required for mail return of any copies.

Civil Name Search: Access: Online, in person. Visitors must perform in person searches themselves. Civil records on computer back 10 years. Civil PAT goes back to 10 years. **See details about online access at front or rear of this chapter.**

Criminal Name Search: Access: Online, in person. Visitors must perform in person searches themselves. Required to search: name, years to search, DOB, date of conviction, charge; also helpful: docket number, defendant's name. Criminal records on computer back 10 years. Criminal PAT goes back to 10 years. **See details about online access at front or rear of this chapter.**

Clifton Forge Cityy

25th Circuit Court Closed -This court closed 7/1/01 and was combined with the Alleghany County Circuit Court.

25th General District Court Closed - As of 7/1/2001, the Clifton Forge Court combined with the Alleghany County District Court to form the 25th Combined District Court.

Colonial Heights City County

12th Circuit Court PO Box 3401, 401 Temple Ave, Colonial Heights, VA 23834; 804-520-9364; fax: 804-524-8726; 8:30AM-5PM (EST). *Felony, Civil Actions over $4,500, Probate.*

www.courts.state.va.us/courts/circuit.html

General Information: No juvenile, sealed or adoption records released. Court makes copy: $.50 per page. Self serve copy: same. Certification fee: $2.00 per document plus copy fee. Payee: Clerk of Circuit Court. Personal checks accepted. No credit cards accepted except for criminal payments. Prepayment required. Mail requests: SASE required.

Civil Name Search: Access: Mail, in person, online. Both court and visitors may perform in person name searches. Search fee: $5.00 per name. Civil records on books from 1961, on computer from 1990. Mail turnaround time 2 days. **See details about online access at front or rear of this chapter.**

Criminal Name Search: Access: Mail, in person, online. Both court and visitors may perform in person name searches. Search fee: $5.00 per name. Required to search: name, years to search; also helpful: DOB, SSN. Criminal docket on books from 1961, on computer from 1990. Mail turnaround time 2 days. **See details about online access at front or rear of this chapter.**

12th General District Court PO Box 3401, 401 Temple Ave, Colonial Heights, VA 23834; 804-520-9346 (ext 0); fax: 804-520-9370; 8AM-4PM (EST). *Misdemeanor, Civil Actions under $25,000, Eviction, Small Claims.*

www.courts.state.va.us/

General Information: No juvenile, sealed records released. Will not fax documents. Court makes copy: $.50 per page. No certification fee. Payee: Colonial Heights Combined Court. Personal checks, Visa/MC accepted. Prepayment required. Mail requests: SASE requested.

Civil Name Search: Access: Mail, fax, online, in person. Both court and visitors may perform in person name searches. No search fee. Civil records on computer for 10 years. Mail turnaround time 1 week. Civil PAT goes back to 10 years. Results include name and case number, but only a partial SSN. **See details about online access at front or rear of this chapter.**

Criminal Name Search: Access: Mail, fax, online, in person. Both court and visitors may perform in person name searches. No search fee. Required to search: name, years to search, DOB, SSN. Criminal records on computer for 10 years. Mail turnaround time 1 week. Criminal PAT goes back to 10 years. **See details about online access at front or rear of this chapter.**

Covington City
Circuit & District Courts - See Alleghany County Courts.

Craig County

25th Circuit Court 182 Main St, #4, New Castle, VA 24127-0185; 540-864-6141; fax: 540-864-7471; 9AM-5PM (EST). *Felony, Civil Actions over $4,500, Probate.*

www.courts.state.va.us/courts/circuit.html

General Information: No juvenile, sealed or adoption records released. Will not fax documents. Court makes copy: $.50 per page. Self serve copy: same. Certification fee: $2.00. Payee: Clerk of Court. Personal checks accepted, credit cards are not. Prepayment required.

Civil Name Search: Access: Online, in person. Visitors must perform in person searches themselves. Civil cases indexed by defendant. Civil records on books from mid 1800s. Civil PAT goes back to 1984. **See details about online access at front or rear of this chapter.**

Criminal Name Search: Access: Online, in person. Visitors must perform in person searches themselves. Required to search: name, years to search; also helpful: SSN. Criminal docket on books from mid 1800s. Criminal PAT goes back to 1984. **See details about online access at front or rear of this chapter.**

25th General District Court Craig County General District Court, PO Box 232, New Castle, VA 24127; 540-864-5989; fax: 540-864-7385; 8:30AM-4:30PM (EST). *Misdemeanor, Civil Actions under $25,000, Eviction, Small Claims.* www.courts.state.va.us

General Information: No juvenile, sealed records released. Will not fax documents. Court makes copy: $.50 per page. No certification fee. Payee: Craig County District Court. Personal checks accepted. Credit cards accepted. Prepayment required. Mail requests: SASE required.

Civil Name Search: Access: Mail, in person, online. Visitors must perform in person searches themselves. No search fee. Civil records in files 10 years back. Mail turnaround time 2-3 days. Civil PAT goes back to 10 years. **See details about online access at front or rear of this chapter.**

Criminal Name Search: Access: Mail, online, in person. Visitors must perform in person searches themselves. No search fee. Required to search: name, years to search; also helpful: SSN. Criminal records in files 10 years back. Note: Lengthy searches must be performed in person. Mail turnaround time is 2-3 days. Criminal PAT goes back to same as civil. **See details about online access at front or rear of this chapter.**

Culpeper County

16th Circuit Court 135 W Cameron St, Culpeper, VA 22701-3097; 540-727-3438; fax: 540-727-3475; 8:30AM-4:30PM (EST). *Felony, Civil Actions over $4,500, Probate.*

www.courts.state.va.us/courts/circuit/Culpeper/home.html

General Information: No juvenile, sealed records released. Will not fax documents. Court makes copy: $.50 per page. Self serve copy: $.50 per page. Certification fee: $2.00. Payee: Clerk of Court. No personal checks. No credit cards accepted. Prepayment required.

Civil Name Search: Access: In person, online. Visitors must perform in person searches themselves. Civil records on computer from 1991, docket books from 1800s. Note: Court will assist with in person searches. Civil PAT goes back to 1991. **See details about online access at front or rear of this chapter.**

Criminal Name Search: Access: In person, online. Visitors must perform in person searches themselves. Required to search: name, years to search, signed release. Criminal records computerized from 1991, docket books from 1800s. Note: Court will assist with in person searches. Criminal PAT goes back to same as civil. **See details about online access at front or rear of this chapter.**

16th General District Court 135 W Cameron St, Culpeper, VA 22701; 540-727-3417; fax: 540-727-3474; 8:30AM-4:30PM (EST). *Misdemeanor, Civil Actions under $25,000, Eviction, Small Claims.* www.courts.state.va.us

General Information: No juvenile, sealed records released. Will not fax documents. Court makes copy: $1.00 1st 2 pages, $.50 each add'l. No certification fee. Payee: General District Court. Personal checks, Visa/MC accepted. Prepayment required. Mail requests: SASE required.

Civil Name Search: Access: Mail, in person, online. Both court and visitors may perform in person name searches. No search fee. Civil records on computerized. Mail turnaround time 5-10 days. Civil PAT goes back to back 10 years. **See details about online access at front or rear of this chapter.**

Criminal Name Search: Access: Mail, online, in person. Both court and visitors may perform in person name searches. No search fee. Criminal records computerized. Mail turnaround time 5-10 days. Criminal PAT goes back to same as civil. **See details about online access at front or rear of this chapter.**

Cumberland County

10th Circuit Court PO Box 8, 1 Courthouse Circle, Cumberland, VA 23040; 804-492-4442; fax: 804-492-4876; 8:30AM-4:30PM (EST). *Felony, Civil Actions over $4,500, Probate.* www.courts.state.va.us/courts/circuit.html

General Information: No juvenile, sealed records released. Will fax documents $1.00 per page. Court makes copy: $.50 per page. Self serve copy: same. No certification fee. Payee: Clerk of Circuit Court. Personal checks accepted, credit cards are not. Prepayment required.

Civil Name Search: Access: Online, in person. Visitors must perform in person searches themselves. Civil records computerized from 1/2001. Note: Phone access only for simple requests. Public use terminal available. **See details about online access at front or rear of this chapter.**

Criminal Name Search: Access: Online, in person. Visitors must perform in person searches themselves. Criminal records computerized from 1/2001. Public use terminal available. Online access to criminal records is same as civil. Online results show middle initial.

10th General District Court PO Box 24, Cumberland, VA 23040; 804-492-4848; fax: 804-492-9455; 8:30AM-4:30PM (EST). *Misdemeanor, Civil Actions under $25,000, Eviction, Small Claims, Traffic.* www.courts.state.va.us/

General Information: No juvenile, sealed records released. Will not fax documents. Court makes copy: $1.00 per page. No certification fee. Payee: Clerk of District Court. Personal checks accepted. Credit cards accepted. Prepayment required. Mail requests: SASE required.

Civil Name Search: Access: Phone, fax, mail, online, in person. Only the court performs in person name searches; visitors may not. No search fee. Civil records are purged/expunged after 10 years. Mail turnaround time 2 days. **See details about online access at front or rear of this chapter.**

Criminal Name Search: Access: Phone, fax, mail, online, in person. Only the court performs in person name searches; visitors may not. No search fee. Required to search: name, years to search; also helpful: DOB, SSN, sex. Criminal records are purged/expunged after 10 years. Mail turnaround time 2 days. **See details about online access at front or rear of this chapter.**

Danville City

22nd Circuit Court PO Box 3300, 401 Patton St, Danville, VA 24543; 434-799-5168; fax: 434-799-6502; 9AM-4PM (EST). *Felony, Civil Actions over $4,500, Probate.* www.danville-va.gov/index.aspx?nid=496

General Information: No juvenile, sealed or adoption records released. Will not fax documents. Court makes copy: $.50 per page. Self serve copy: same. Certification fee: $2.00. Payee: Gerald A Gibson, Clerk. Personal checks accepted, credit cards are not. Prepayment required.

Civil Name Search: Access: In person, online. Visitors must perform in person searches themselves. Civil records in index books from 1841, judgments on computer since 1990. Civil PAT goes back to 1988. **See details about online access at front or rear of this chapter.** Also, search daily docket from the web page.

Criminal Name Search: Access: In person, online. Visitors must perform in person searches themselves. Criminal docket on books from 1841. Criminal records computerized from 1988. Criminal PAT goes back to same as civil. **See details about online access at front or rear of this chapter.**

22nd General District Court PO Box 3300, Danville, VA 24543; 434-799-5179; fax: 434-797-8814; 8:30AM-4:30PM (EST). *Misdemeanor, Civil Actions under $25,000, Eviction, Small Claims, Traffic.* www.courts.state.va.us/

General Information: Online identifiers in results same as on public terminal. No juvenile, sealed records released. Court makes copy: $1.00 1st 2 pages, $.50 each add'l. No certification fee. Payee: General District Court. Personal checks accepted. Credit cards accepted. Prepayment required. Mail requests: SASE required.

Civil Name Search: Access: Mail, in person, online. Both court and visitors may perform in person name searches. No search fee. Civil records go back 10 years on computer. Mail turnaround time 2 days. Civil PAT goes back to 10 years. **See details about online access at front or rear of this chapter.**

Criminal Name Search: Access: Mail, online, in person. Both court and visitors may perform in person name searches. No search fee. Criminal records go back 10 years; on computer back to 1999. Mail turnaround time 2 days. Criminal PAT goes back to same as civil. **See details about online access at front or rear of this chapter.**

Dickenson County

29th Circuit Court PO Box 190, 293 Clintwood Main St, Clintwood, VA 24228; 276-926-1616; fax: 276-926-6465; 8AM-4:30PM (EST). *Felony, Civil Actions over $4,500, Probate.* www.courts.state.va.us/courts/circuit.html

General Information: Online identifiers in results same as on public terminal. No juvenile, sealed, adoption, confidential records released. Will not fax documents. Court makes copy: $.50 per page. Self serve copy: same. Certification fee: $2.50 plus copy fee. Payee: Richard W. Edwards, Clerk of Circuit Court. No personal checks. Major credit cards accepted. Prepayment required. Mail requests: SASE requested.

Civil Name Search: Access: Mail, in person, online. Both court and visitors may perform in person name searches. No search fee. Civil records on computer from 2001, index book from 1880. Mail turnaround time 1 week. Civil PAT goes back to 2001. Only month and day of DOB appears, plus sex, race. **See details about online access at front or rear of this chapter.**

Criminal Name Search: Access: Mail, online, in person. Both court and visitors may perform in person name searches. No search fee. Required to search: name, years to search, DOB; also helpful: SSN. Criminal records computerized from 1989, index book from 1880. Note: Results include name, address and case number. Mail turnaround time 1 week. Criminal PAT goes back to same as civil. Only month and day of DOB appears, plus sex, race. **See details about online access at front or rear of this chapter.**

29th General District Court PO Box 128, Clintwood, VA 24228; 276-926-1630; fax: 276-926-4815; 8:30AM-4:30PM (EST). *Misdemeanor, Civil Actions under $25,000, Eviction, Small Claims.* www.courts.state.va.us/

General Information: Online identifiers in results same as on public terminal. No juvenile, sealed records released. Will fax documents. Court makes copy: $.10 per page. No certification fee. Payee: Dickenson Combined Court or General District Court. Personal checks accepted. Credit cards accepted. Prepayment required. Mail requests: SASE requested.

Civil Name Search: Access: Phone, mail, in person, online. Both court and visitors may perform in person name searches. No search fee. Civil cases indexed by defendant. Civil records on computer back 10 years. Mail turnaround time 1 week. Civil PAT goes back to 10 years. **See details about online access at front or rear of this chapter.**

Criminal Name Search: Access: Phone, mail, in person, online. Both court and visitors may perform in person name searches. No search fee. Criminal records on computer back 10 years. Mail turnaround time 1 week. Criminal PAT goes back to 10 years. **See details about online access at front or rear of this chapter.**

Dinwiddie County

11th Circuit Court PO Box 63, Dinwiddie, VA 23841; 804-469-4540; fax: 804-469-5386; 8:30AM-4:30PM (EST). *Felony, Civil Actions over $4,500, Probate.* www.courts.state.va.us/courts/circuit.html

General Information: Probate is separate index at this same address. No juvenile, sealed or expunged records released. Will not fax documents. Court makes copy: $.50 per page. Self serve copy: same. Certification fee: $2.00 plus copy fee. Payee: Clerk of Court. Personal checks accepted. Visa/MC accepted for criminal payments only accepted. Prepayment required. Mail requests: SASE requested.

Civil Name Search: Access: Mail, in person, online. Both court and visitors may perform in person name searches. No search fee. Required to search: name, years to search; also helpful: address. Civil index on cards from 1833; deeds on computer since 1989. Mail turnaround time 3 days. Civil PAT goes back to 1997. **See details about online access at front or rear of this chapter.**

Criminal Name Search: Access: Mail, online, in person. Both court and visitors may perform in person name searches. No search fee. Required to search: name, years to search; also helpful: DOB, SSN. Criminal records indexed on cards from 1833; deeds on computer since 1989. Mail turnaround time 3 days. Criminal PAT goes back to 1997. **See details about online access at front or rear of this chapter.**

11th General District Court PO Box 280, Dinwiddie, VA 23841; 804-469-4533; fax: 804-469-5383; 8:30AM-4:30PM (EST). *Misdemeanor, Civil Actions under $25,000, Eviction, Small Claims, Traffic.*
www.courts.state.va.us

General Information: No juvenile, sealed records released. Will not fax documents. Court makes copy: $.50 per page. Payee: District Court. Personal checks accepted. Credit cards accepted. Prepayment required. Mail requests: SASE required.

Civil Name Search: Access: Mail, in person, online. Both court and visitors may perform in person name searches. No search fee. Civil records go back 10 years. Mail turnaround time 3 days. Civil PAT goes back to 10 years. **See details about online access at front or rear of this chapter.**

Criminal Name Search: Access: Mail, online, in person. Both court and visitors may perform in person name searches. No search fee. Criminal records computerized from 1989. Mail turnaround time 3 days. Criminal PAT goes back to 10 years. Search free by name or case number at http://epwsgdp1.courts.state.va.us/gdcourts/captchaVerification.do?landing=landing. Results show address of subject and the day and month of birth, but not year. Online results show middle initial.

Emporia City

6th General District Court See Greenville County, Greensville-Emporia Combined Court.

Circuit Court - See Greensville County See Greensville County.

Essex County

15th Circuit Court PO Box 445, 305 Prince St, Tappahannock, VA 22560; 804-443-3541; fax: 804-445-1216; 8:30AM-4:30PM (EST). *Felony, Civil Actions over $4,500, Probate.*
www.courts.state.va.us/courts/circuit.html

General Information: No juvenile, sealed records released. Will fax documents $.50 per page. Court makes copy: $.50 per page. Self serve copy: same. Certification fee: $2.00 plus copy fee. Payee: Clerk of Court. Personal checks accepted. Prepayment required.

Civil Name Search: Access: In person, online. Visitors must perform in person searches themselves. Civil records on books from 1656; deed index on computer back to 2006. **See details about online access at front or rear of this chapter.**

Criminal Name Search: Access: In person, online. Visitors must perform in person searches themselves. Criminal docket on books from 1656. Public use terminal has crim records. **See details about online access at front or rear of this chapter.**

15th General District Court PO Box 66, 300 Prince St, Tappahannock, VA 22560; 804-443-3744; fax: 804-443-4122; 8AM-4PM (EST). *Misdemeanor, Civil Actions under $25,000, Eviction, Small Claims.*
www.courts.state.va.us

General Information: No juvenile, sealed records released. Will not fax documents. Court makes copy: $1.00 per page. No certification fee. Payee: Court. Personal checks, Visa/MC accepted. Prepayment required.

Civil Name Search: Access: Online, in person. Both court and visitors may perform in person name searches. No search fee. Civil records on computer from 5/92. Civil PAT goes back to 10 years. **See details about online access at front or rear of this chapter.**

Criminal Name Search: Access: Online, in person. Visitors must perform in person searches themselves. Required to search: name, years to search, DOB, SSN. Criminal records computerized from 5/92. Criminal PAT goes back to same as civil. **See details about online access at front or rear of this chapter.**

Fairfax County

19th Circuit Court 4110 Chain Bridge Rd, Fairfax, VA 22030; 703-691-7320; criminal phone: 703-246-2228; civil phone: 703-691-7320 x3-1-1; fax: 703-273-6564; 8AM-4PM (EST). *Felony, Civil Actions over $4,500, Probate.*
www.fairfaxcounty.gov/courts/circuit/

General Information: Online identifiers in results same as on public terminal. No juvenile, sealed records released. Will not fax documents. Court makes copy: $.50 per page.Separate fees for electronically generated docs. Certification fee: $2.00 per doc, paper or electronic. Payee: Fairfax Circuit Court. No personal checks. Visa/MC accepted; add 4% usage fee. Prepayment required.

Civil Name Search: Access: In person, online. Visitors must perform in person searches themselves. Civil records computerized from 1979; index books for prior years; scanned back to 1700s. Civil PAT goes back to 1979. Only month and day of DOB appears, plus sex, race. Access to current court case indexes is via CPAN subscription; call 703-246-2366 IT Dept. or see www.fairfaxcounty.gov/courts/circuit/cpan.htm to apply. Fee is

$50.00 per month per user. Also, daily and Friday's Motion dockets are available free at www.fairfaxcounty.gov/circuitcourtdocket/.

Criminal Name Search: Access: Mail, In person, online. Visitors must perform in person searches themselves. No search fee. Required to search: name, years to search, DOB; also helpful: SSN. Criminal records computerized from 1979. Criminal PAT goes back to same as civil. Only month and day of DOB appears, plus sex, race. Online access to criminal same as civil, see above. Online results show middle initial.

19th General District Court PO Box 10157, 4110 Chain Bridge Rd, Fairfax, VA 22038; criminal phone: 703-246-3305; civil phone: 703-246-3012; fax: 703-591-2349; 8AM-4PM (EST). *Misdemeanor, Civil Actions under $25,000, Eviction, Small Claims.*
www.fairfaxcounty.gov/courts/gendist/

General Information: Traffic Division- 703-246-3764. Also has branches in Herndon and Vienna. No juvenile, sealed records released. Will not fax documents as a general rule. Court makes copy: $.50 per page. Self serve copy: same. No certification fee. Payee: Fairfax General District Court. Personal checks, Visa/MC accepted. Prepayment required.

Civil Name Search: Access: In person, online. Visitors must perform in person searches themselves. Civil indexes for 10 years; onsite records held only 3 years before archiving; on computer back 10 years. Civil PAT goes back to 10 years. **See details about online access at front or rear of this chapter.**

Criminal Name Search: Access: In person, online. Both court and visitors may perform in person name searches. No search fee. Required to search: name, years to search; also helpful: DOB, SSN, offense. Criminal & traffic records on computer for 10 years; onsite records held only 3 years before archiving. Criminal PAT goes back to 10 years. **See details about online access at front or rear of this chapter.**

Fairfax City

19th General District Court 10455 Armstrong St, #101, Fairfax, VA 22030; 703-385-7866; fax: 703-352-3195; 8:30AM-4:30PM (EST). *Misdemeanor, Traffic.*
www.courts.state.va.us/courts/gd/Fairfax_City/home.html

General Information: Find Circuit Court cases and General District civil cases for this city in Fairfax County. No juvenile or sealed records released. Will not fax documents. Court makes copy: $1.00 for first 2 pages, $.50 each add'l. No certification fee. Payee: General District Court. Personal checks, Visa/MC accepted. Prepayment required. Mail requests: SASE requested.

Criminal Name Search: Access: Mail, in person, online. Both court and visitors may perform in person name searches. No search fee. Required to search: name, years to search; also helpful: SSN. Criminal records on computer and index from 1996. Mail turnaround time same day. Public use terminal has crim records back to 1998. **See details about online access at front or rear of this chapter.**

Circuit Court - See Fairfax County

Falls Church City

17th General District Courts Combined Falls Church District, 300 Park Ave, Falls Church, VA 22046-3305; 703-248-5096 (GDC); civil phone: 703-248-5098; fax: 703-241-1407; 8AM-4PM (EST). *Misdemeanor, Civil Actions under $25,000, Eviction, Small Claims.*
www.fallschurchva.gov

General Information: Small claims phone is 703-248-5157; juvenile and domestic relations is 703-248-5099. No juvenile or sealed records released. No fee to fax documents. Court makes copy: $1.00 1st page; $.50 each add'l. No certification fee. Payee: Falls Church District Court. Personal checks, Visa/MC accepted. Prepayment required.

Civil Name Search: Access: Fax, online. Only the court performs in person name searches; visitors may not. No search fee. Civil records on computer back to 1997. **See details about online access at front or rear of this chapter.**

Criminal Name Search: Access: Fax, online, in person. Only the court performs in person name searches; visitors may not. No search fee. Required to search: name, years to search; also helpful: DOB, SSN. Criminal records computerized from 1997. **See details about online access at front or rear of this chapter.**

Circuit Court - See Arlington County

Fauquier County

Circuit Court 29 Ashby St 1st Fl, Circuit Clerk Office, Warrenton, VA 20186-3298; 540-422-8100; 8AM-4:30PM (EST). *Felony, Civil Actions over $4,500, Probate.*
www.fauquiercounty.gov/government/departments/circuitcourt/

General Information: No juvenile, sealed, adoption records released. Will not fax documents. Court makes copy: $.50 per page. Self serve copy: same. Self serve copier requires $10.00 purchase of encoder device. Certification fee: $2.00 per doc. Payee: Clerk of Fauquier Circuit Court. Personal checks accepted. No credit or debit cards accepted. Prepayment required.

Civil Name Search: Access: Mail, in person, online. Visitors must perform in person searches themselves. Search fee: $5.00 per name. Civil records on computer back to 1988. Mail turnaround time 1-5 days. Civil PAT goes back to 1988. Search free by name or case number at www.courts.state.va.us/. DOB not shown, middle initial does.

Criminal Name Search: Access: Mail, in person, online. Visitors must perform in person searches themselves. Search fee: $5.00 per name. Criminal records computerized from 1988. Note: Court recommends you contact the VA State Police. Mail turnaround time 1-5 days. Criminal PAT goes back to same as civil. **See details about online access at front or rear of this chapter.**

20th General District Court 6 Court St, Warrenton, VA 20186; 540-422-8035; fax: 540-422-8033; 8:30AM-4:30PM (EST). *Misdemeanor, Civil Actions under $25,000, Eviction, Small Claims.* www.courts.state.va.us

General Information: Online identifiers in results same as on public terminal. No juvenile, sealed records released. Will not fax documents. Court makes copy: $1.00 1st 2 pages, $.50 each add'l. No certification fee. Payee: General District Court. Personal checks accepted. Credit cards accepted. Prepayment required. Mail requests: SASE required for mail return of any copies.

Civil Name Search: Access: Online, in person. Visitors must perform in person searches themselves. Civil records on computerized back 10 years. Civil PAT goes back to 10 years. **See details about online access at front or rear of this chapter.**

Criminal Name Search: Access: Online, in person. Visitors must perform in person searches themselves. Criminal records computerized back 10 years, criminal records only go back 10 years. Note: In the rare instances when the court performs a search, there is no fee. Criminal PAT goes back to same as civil. **See details about online access at front or rear of this chapter.**

Floyd County

27th Circuit Court 100 E Main St, #200, Floyd, VA 24091; 540-745-9330; fax: 540-745-9303; 8:30AM-4:30PM, 8:30AM-N Sat (EST). *Felony, Civil Actions over $4,500, Probate.* www.floydcova.org/departments/circuit_court.shtml

General Information: Closed on Saturdays if it is a holiday. Online identifiers in results same as on public terminal. No juvenile, sealed records released. Will not fax documents. Court makes copy: $.50 per page. Certification fee: $2.00 per cert plus copy fee. Payee: Clerk of Circuit Court. Personal checks accepted, credit cards are not. Prepayment required.

Civil Name Search: Access: In person, online. Visitors must perform in person searches themselves. Civil records on files from 1831. Civil PAT goes back to 1996. Only month and day of DOB appears, plus sex, race. **See details about online access at front or rear of this chapter.**

Criminal Name Search: Access: In person, online. Visitors must perform in person searches themselves. Required to search: name, years to search; also helpful: DOB, SSN. Criminal records on files from 1831. Criminal PAT goes back to 1996. Only month and day of DOB appears, plus sex, race. **See details about online access at front or rear of this chapter.**

27th General Combined District Court 100 E Main St, #208, Floyd, VA 24091-2101; 540-745-9327; fax: 540-745-9329; 8AM-4:30PM (EST). *Misdemeanor, Civil Actions under $25,000, Eviction, Small Claims.* www.courts.state.va.us

General Information: No juvenile, sealed records released. Will not fax documents. Court makes copy: $.50 per page. Certification fee: None reported. Payee: Clerk of District Court. Personal checks accepted, credit cards are not. Prepayment required.

Civil Name Search: Access: In person, online. Visitors must perform in person searches themselves. Civil records computerized since 1993. Note: Phone search results may be of limited content. Civil PAT goes back to 1996. **See details about online access at front or rear of this chapter.**

Criminal Name Search: Access: In person, online. Visitors must perform in person searches themselves. Required to search: name, years to search, DOB. Criminal records computerized since 1993. Note: Phone search results may be of limited content. Criminal PAT goes back to 1996. **See details about online access at front or rear of this chapter.**

Fluvanna County

16th Circuit Court PO Box 550, Palmyra, VA 22963; 434-591-1970; fax: 434-591-1971; 8AM-4:30PM (EST). *Felony, Civil Actions over $4,500, Probate.* www.courts.state.va.us/courts/circuit.html

General Information: No juvenile or sealed records released. Fee to fax out file $2.00 each. Court makes copy: $.50 per page. Certification fee: $2.00.

Payee: Clerk of Circuit Court. Personal checks accepted, credit cards are not. Prepayment required. Mail requests: SASE required.

Civil Name Search: Access: Mail, in person, online. Both court and visitors may perform in person name searches. Search fee: $5.00 per name. Civil index on docket books from 1777; computerized back to 1985. Mail turnaround time same 1-2 days. Civil PAT available. **See details about online access at front or rear of this chapter.**

Criminal Name Search: Access: Mail, in person, online. Both court and visitors may perform in person name searches. Search fee: $5.00 per name. Required to search: name, years to search, DOB; also helpful: SSN. Criminal records indexed in books from 1777; computerized back to 1985. Mail turnaround time 1-2 days. Criminal PAT available. **See details about online access at front or rear of this chapter.**

16th General District Court PO Box 417, 72 Main St #B, County Courthouse, Palmyra, VA 22963; 434-591-1980; fax: 434-591-1981; 8:30AM-4PM (EST). *Misdemeanor, Civil Actions under $25,000, Eviction, Small Claims.* www.courts.state.va.us/courts/combined/Fluvanna/home.html

General Information: For fax, dial, wait for answer, then press 4. Online identifiers in results same as on public terminal. No juvenile records released. Will not fax documents. Court makes copy: $.50 per page. No certification fee. Payee: Fluvanna District Court. Personal checks accepted, credit cards are not. Prepayment required.

Civil Name Search: Access: Online, in person. Visitors must perform in person searches themselves. Civil records on computer since 12/91, on books since 1984. Civil PAT goes back to 10 years. **See details about online access at front or rear of this chapter.**

Criminal Name Search: Access: Online, in person. Visitors must perform in person searches themselves. Required to search: name, years to search; also helpful: DOB, SSN. Criminal records on computer since 12/91, on books since 1984. Criminal PAT goes back to same as civil. **See details about online access at front or rear of this chapter.**

Franklin County

22nd Judicial Circuit Court PO Box 567, 275 S Main St, #212, Rocky Mount, VA 24151; 540-483-3065; fax: 540-483-3042; 8:30AM-5PM (EST). *Felony, Civil Actions over $4,500, Probate.* www.courts.state.va.us/courts/circuit/Franklin/home.html

General Information: Note that Franklin City is not the same as Franklin County. Only Franklin County information is given here. Contact the Sheriff's office at 540-483-3000 for record searches. Online identifiers in results same as on public terminal. No juvenile records released. Will fax documents $.50 per page. Court makes copy: $.50 per page. Self serve copy: $.50 per page. Certification fee: $2.00 per page. Payee: Court. Personal checks accepted, credit cards are not. Prepayment required. Mail requests: SASE required for mail return of any copies.

Civil Name Search: Access: In person, online. Visitors must perform in person searches themselves. Required to search: name. Civil PAT goes back to 1986. Only month and day of DOB appears, plus sex, race. **See details about online access at front or rear of this chapter.**

Criminal Name Search: Access: In person, online. Visitors must perform in person searches themselves. Criminal records file on computer. Criminal PAT goes back to same as civil. Only month and day of DOB appears, plus sex, race. **See details about online access at front or rear of this chapter.**

22nd General District Court PO Box 569, 275 S Main St, #111, Rocky Mount, VA 24151; 540-483-3060; fax: 540-483-3036; 8:30AM-4:30PM (EST). *Misdemeanor, Civil Actions under $25,000, Eviction, Small Claims.* www.courts.state.va.us/courts/gd/Franklin_County/home.html

General Information: Contact the Sheriff's office at 540-483-3000 for criminal record searches. Online identifiers in results same as on public terminal. Will not fax documents. Court makes copy: n/a. No certification fee. Personal checks, Visa/MC accepted. Prepayment required.

Civil Name Search: Access: Online, in person. Visitors must perform in person searches themselves. Civil records file on computer for 10 years. Civil PAT goes back to 10 years. **See details about online access at front or rear of this chapter.**

Criminal Name Search: Access: Online, in person. Visitors must perform in person searches themselves. Criminal records file on computer for 10 years. Criminal PAT goes back to 10 years. **See details about online access at front or rear of this chapter.**

Franklin City

5th Judicial General District Combined 1020 Pretlow St, Franklin, VA 23851; 757-562-1158; fax: 757-562-1156; 8AM-4PM (EST). *Misdemeanor, Civil Actions under $25,000, Eviction, Traffic.* www.courts.state.va.us/courts/combined/Franklin_City/home.html

General Information: Southampton County serves as the Circuit Court for City of Franklin. No juvenile records released. Will not fax documents. Court makes copy: $1.00 1st page; $.50 each add'l. No certification fee. Payee: Clerk of the District Court. Personal checks, Visa/MC accepted. Prepayment required.

Civil Name Search: Access: Mail, in person, online. Both court and visitors may perform in person name searches. No search fee. Civil cases indexed by plaintiff. Civil records on computer since 1990. Mail turnaround time 5 days. Civil PAT goes back to 1990. **See details about online access at front or rear of this chapter.**

Criminal Name Search: Access: Mail, online, in person. Both court and visitors may perform in person name searches. No search fee. Required to search: name, years to search; also helpful: SSN. Criminal records on computer since 1990. Mail turnaround time 5 days. Criminal PAT goes back to same as civil. **See details about online access at front or rear of this chapter.**

Circuit Court - See Southampton County Circuit Court

Frederick County

Circuit Court 5 N Kent St, Winchester, VA 22601; 540-667-5770; probate phone: 540-665-5659; fax: 540-545-8711; 9AM-5PM (EST). *Felony, Misdemeanor, Civil, Probate.* www.winfredclerk.com

General Information: No juvenile, sealed or adoption records released. Will not fax documents. Court makes copy: $.50 per page. Certification fee: $3.00. Payee: Clerk of Circuit Court. No personal checks or credit cards accepted. Prepayment required. Mail requests: SASE required.

Civil Name Search: Access: Mail, in person, online. Both court and visitors may perform in person name searches. No search fee. Civil records on books from 1970s. Note: Mail access limited to simple requests. Mail turnaround time 1-2 days. Civil PAT goes back to 1985. **See details about online access at front or rear of this chapter.**

Criminal Name Search: Access: In person, online. Visitors must perform in person searches themselves. Criminal docket on books from 1970s. Criminal PAT goes back to same as civil. **See details about online access at front or rear of this chapter.**

26th General District Court 5 N Kent St, Judicial Center, Winchester, VA 22601; 540-722-7208; fax: 540-722-1063; 8AM-4PM (EST). *Misdemeanor, Civil Actions up to $25,000.*

www.courts.state.va.us/courts/gd/Frederick~Winchester/home.html

General Information: Will not fax documents. Court makes copy: $.50 per page. Payee: Frederick District Court. Personal checks, Visa/MC accepted. Prepayment required.

Civil Name Search: Access: In person, online. Visitors must perform in person searches themselves. Civil records go back to 1987. Civil PAT goes back to 10 years. **See details about online access at front or rear of this chapter.**

Criminal Name Search: Access: In person, online. Visitors must perform in person searches themselves. Criminal records go back to 1987. Criminal PAT goes back to same as civil. **See details about online access at front or rear of this chapter.**

Fredericksburg City County

15th Circuit Court PO Box 359, 601 Caroline St. 2nd Fl, Fredericksburg, VA 22404-0359; 540-372-1066; 8:30AM-4PM (EST). *Felony, Civil Actions over $4,500, Probate.*

www.courts.state.va.us/courts/circuit/fredericksburg/home.html

General Information: No juvenile, probate tax returns, sealed or adoption records released. Will not fax documents. Court makes copy: $.50 per page. Self serve copy: same. Certification fee: $2.00 per doc plus copy fee. Payee: Clerk of Circuit Court. Personal checks accepted. Major credit cards accepted, there is a 4% surcharge. Prepayment required.

Civil Name Search: Access: In person, online. Visitors must perform in person searches themselves. Civil index on docket books from 1765; computerized records since 1987. Civil PAT goes back to 1987. **See details about online access at front or rear of this chapter.**

Criminal Name Search: Access: In person, online. Visitors must perform in person searches themselves. Required to search: name, years to search, DOB. Criminal records indexed in books from 1765; computerized index since 1987. Criminal PAT goes back to same as civil. The month and day of the DOB appears, not the year. **See details about online access at front or rear of this chapter.**

15th General District Court PO Box 180, 615 Princess Ann St, Fredericksburg, VA 22404; criminal phone: 540-372-1043; civil phone: 540-372-1044; criminal fax: 540-372-1228; civil fax: 8AM-4PM; 8AM-4PM (EST). *Misdemeanor, Civil Actions under $25,000, Eviction, Small Claims.* www.courts.state.va.us/

General Information: Online identifiers in results same as on public terminal. No sealed records released. Will fax out documents. Court makes copy: $1.00 1st 2 pages, $.50 each add'l. Payee: Fredericksburg District Court. Personal checks accepted. Major credit cards accepted for criminal only. Prepayment required. Mail requests: SASE required.

Civil Name Search: Access: Mail, fax, online, in person. Both court and visitors may perform in person name searches. No search fee. Civil records on computer the past 10 years, prior on index books. Mail turnaround time 5-7 days. Civil PAT goes back to 10 years. **See details about online access at front or rear of this chapter.**

Criminal Name Search: Access: Mail, fax, online, in person. Both court and visitors may perform in person name searches. No search fee. Required to search: name, years to search, DOB, SSN. Criminal records on computer the past 10 years, prior on index books. Mail turnaround time 5-7 days. Criminal PAT goes back to 10 years. **See details about online access at front or rear of this chapter.**

Galax City County

27th General District Court 353 N Main St, Ste 214, Galax, VA 24333-0214; 276-236-8731; fax: 276-236-2754; 8AM-4:30PM (EST). *Misdemeanor, Civil Actions under $25,000, Eviction, Small Claims.* www.courts.state.va.us/

General Information: Circuit Court jurisdiction for this city can be in Carroll County or Grayson County depending on side of the city the offense occurred. No juvenile, sealed records released. Will not fax documents. Court makes copy: $1.00 first 2 pages, then $.50 ea addl. No certification fee. Payee: Galax Combined Court. Personal checks accepted. Credit cards accepted. Prepayment required.

Civil Name Search: Access: Mail, fax, online, in person. Both court and visitors may perform in person name searches. No search fee. Civil records on computer ten years. Mail turnaround time 1-5 days. Public use terminal available, records go back to 10 years. **See details about online access at front or rear of this chapter.**

Criminal Name Search: Access: Mail, fax, online, in person. Both court and visitors may perform in person name searches. No search fee. Criminal records on computer ten years. Mail turnaround time 1-5 days. Public use terminal available, crim records go back to 10 years. **See details about online access at front or rear of this chapter.**

Circuit Court For Galax City area Circuit Court records, see Carroll County for Hillsville area and Grayson County for Independence area.

Giles County

27th Circuit Court 501 Wenonah Ave, PO Box 502, Pearisburg, VA 24134; 540-921-1722; fax: 540-921-3825; 8:30AM-5PM (EST). *Felony, Civil Actions over $4,500, Probate.*

www.gilescounty.org/clerk-of-court/index.htm

General Information: No juvenile, sealed records released. Will not fax documents. Court makes copy: $.50 per page. Self serve copy: same. Certification fee: $3.00. Payee: Giles County Circuit Court. Personal checks accepted, credit cards are not. Prepayment required. Mail requests: SASE required if copies to be mailed back.

Civil Name Search: Access: Mail, in person, online. Visitors must perform in person searches themselves. No search fee. Civil records go back to 1994. Mail turnaround time 1-2 days. **See details about online access at front or rear of this chapter.**

Criminal Name Search: Access: In person, online. Visitors must perform in person searches themselves. Required to search: name, years to search, DOB; SSN helpful. Criminal records go back to 1994. **See details about online access at front or rear of this chapter.**

27th General District Court 120 N Main St, #1, Pearisburg, VA 24134; 540-921-3533; fax: 540-921-3752; 8:30AM-4:30PM (EST). *Misdemeanor, Civil Actions under $25,000, Eviction, Small Claims.* www.courts.state.va.us/courts/combined/Giles/home.html

General Information: Online identifiers in results same as on public terminal. No juvenile, sealed records released. Will not fax out documents. Court makes copy: $1.00 first page, $.50 each add'l. No certification fee. Payee: General District Court. Personal checks, Visa/MC accepted.

Civil Name Search: Access: Fax, mail, online, in person. Both court and visitors may perform in person name searches. No search fee. Civil records on computer since 1990. Mail turnaround time 3-7 days. Civil PAT goes back to 1990. Terminal results also show SSNs. **See details about online access at front or rear of this chapter.**

Criminal Name Search: Access: Fax, mail, online, in person. Both court and visitors may perform in person name searches. No search fee. Required to search: name, years to search; also helpful: SSN. Criminal records on computer since 1990. Mail turnaround time 3-7 days. Criminal PAT goes back to same as civil. **See details about online access at front or rear of this chapter.**

Gloucester County

9th Circuit Court 7400 Justice Dr #327, Gloucester, VA 23061-0570; 804-693-2502; fax: 804-693-2186; 8AM-4:30PM (EST). *Felony, Civil Actions over $4,500, Probate.*
www.courts.state.va.us/courts/circuit/gloucester/home.html
General Information: No juvenile, sealed or adoption records released. Will not fax documents. Court makes copy: $.50 per page. Self serve copy: same. Certification fee: $2.00; $2.50 if judge's signature required. Payee: Clerk of Circuit Court. Personal checks accepted. Major credit cards accepted. Prepayment required.
Civil Name Search: Access: Online, in person. Both court and visitors may perform in person name searches. No search fee. Civil index on docket books from 1862; on computer since 1990. Civil PAT goes back to 1994. **See details about online access at front or rear of this chapter.**
Criminal Name Search: Access: Online, in person. Visitors must perform in person searches themselves. Required to search: name, years to search, DOB. Criminal records indexed in books from 1862; on computer since 1990. Criminal PAT goes back to same as civil. **See details about online access at front or rear of this chapter.**

9th General District Court PO Box 873, 7400 Justice Dr, Rm 102, Gloucester, VA 23061; 804-693-4860; fax: 804-693-6669; 8AM-4:30PM (EST). *Misdemeanor, Civil Actions under $25,000, Eviction, Small Claims.*
www.courts.state.va.us/courts/gd/gloucester/home.html
General Information: No juvenile, sealed records released. No fee to fax documents. Court makes copy: $.50 per page. No certification fee. Payee: Gloucester District Court. Personal checks accepted. Credit cards accepted. Prepayment required. Mail requests: SASE requested.
Civil Name Search: Access: Fax, mail, online, in person. Both court and visitors may perform in person name searches. No search fee. Civil index on docket books from 1985; computerized back to 1992. Mail turnaround time 1 week. Civil PAT goes back to 10 years. **See details about online access at front or rear of this chapter.**
Criminal Name Search: Access: Fax, mail, online, in person. Both court and visitors may perform in person name searches. No search fee. Required to search: name, years to search; also helpful: DOB, SSN. Criminal records indexed in books for 10 years; computerized back to 1992. Mail turnaround time 1 week. Criminal PAT goes back to same as civil. **See details about online access at front or rear of this chapter.**

Goochland County

16th Circuit Court PO Box 196, 2938 River Rd W, Bldg B, Goochland, VA 23063; 804-556-5353; fax: 804-556-4962; 8:30AM-5PM (EST). *Felony, Civil Actions over $4,500, Probate.*
www.courts.state.va.us/courts/circuit.html
General Information: Online identifiers in results same as on public terminal. No juvenile, sealed or adoption records released. Will not fax documents. Court makes copy: $.50 per page. Certification fee: $2.00. Payee: Clerk of Circuit Court. Personal checks accepted. Visa/MC accepted for criminal cases only. Prepayment required.
Civil Name Search: Access: Online, in person. Visitors must perform in person searches themselves. Civil index on docket books from 1850. Public use terminal has civil records back to 2001. Results include name and case number. **See details about online access at front or rear of this chapter.**
Criminal Name Search: Access: Online, in person. Visitors must perform in person searches themselves. Criminal records indexed in books from 1850. Note: Results include name and case number. **See details about online access at front or rear of this chapter..**

General District Court PO Box 47, 2938 River Rd, Goochland, VA 23063; 804-556-5309; fax: 804-556-4494; 8:30AM-4:30PM (EST). *Misdemeanor, Civil Actions under $25,000, Eviction, Small Claims.*
www.courts.state.va.us/
General Information: No juvenile records released. Court makes copy: none. No certification fee. Personal checks accepted. Credit cards accepted. Prepayment required.
Civil Name Search: Access: Online, in person. Visitors must perform in person searches themselves. Civil index on docket books and computer back ten years. Civil PAT goes back to ten years. **See details about online access at front or rear of this chapter.**
Criminal Name Search: Access: Online, in person. Visitors must perform in person searches themselves. Required to search: name, years to search, DOB. Criminal records indexed in books and computer back ten years. Criminal PAT goes back to same as civil. **See details about online access at front or rear of this chapter.**

Grayson County

27th Circuit Court PO Box 130, Independence, VA 24348; 276-773-2231; fax: 276-773-3338; 8AM-5PM (EST). *Felony, Civil Actions over $4,500, Probate.*
www.courts.state.va.us/courts/circuit.html
General Information: Probate is a separate index at this address. Probate fax is same as main fax number. No juvenile, sealed or adoption records released. Will fax documents $.50 per page. Court makes copy: $.50 per page. Self serve copy: same. Certification fee: $2.00 per instrument. Payee: Clerk of Circuit Court. Personal checks accepted, credit cards are not. Prepayment required. Mail requests: SASE requested.
Civil Name Search: Access: Mail, in person, online. Both court and visitors may perform in person name searches. No search fee. Civil index on docket books since 1793. Mail turnaround time 2-3 days. Civil PAT goes back to 2001. **See details about online access at front or rear of this chapter.**
Criminal Name Search: Access: Mail, online, in person. Visitors must perform in person searches themselves. No search fee. Required to search: name, years to search, DOB. Criminal records indexed in books since 1793. Mail turnaround time 2-3 days. Criminal PAT goes back to same as civil. **See details about online access at front or rear of this chapter.**

27th General District Court PO Box 217, 129 Davis St, Independence, VA 24348; 276-773-2011; fax: 276-773-3174; 8AM-5PM (EST). *Misdemeanor, Civil Actions under $25,000, Eviction, Small Claims.*
www.courts.state.va.us
General Information: Online identifiers in results same as on public terminal. No juvenile, sealed records released. Will fax documents to local or toll free line. Court makes copy: $.50 per page. No certification fee. Payee: Grayson District Court..
Civil Name Search: Access: In person, online. Visitors must perform in person searches themselves. Civil cases indexed by defendant. Civil records on computer for 10 years. Mail turnaround time 1 week. Civil PAT goes back to 10 years. **See details about online access at front or rear of this chapter.**
Criminal Name Search: Access: online, in person. Required to search: name, years to search; also helpful: DOB, SSN. Criminal records computerized from 1997. Note: Results include name and address. Mail turnaround time 1 week. Criminal PAT goes back to same as civil. **See details about online access at front or rear of this chapter.**

Greene County

16th Circuit Court PO Box 386, 22 Court Street, Stanardsville, VA 22973; 434-985-5208; fax: 434-985-6723; 8:15AM-4:30PM (EST). *Felony, Civil Actions over $4,500, Probate.*
www.courts.state.va.us/courts/circuit.html
General Information: Probate is a separate index at this same address. Probate fax is same as main fax number. No juvenile, sealed or adoption records released. Will not fax documents. Court makes copy: $.50 per page. Self serve copy: same. Certification fee: $2.00 per instrument plus copy fee. Payee: Clerk of Circuit Court or Greene County Circuit. Personal checks accepted, credit cards are not. Prepayment required. Mail requests: SASE required.
Civil Name Search: Access: Mail, in person, online. Visitors must perform in person searches themselves. Civil index on docket books from 1838. Remote online access to court case indexes is via LOPAS. This is a limited system and the program is not taking on new clients.
Criminal Name Search: Access: In person. Visitors must perform in person searches themselves. Criminal records indexed in books from 1838. Mail turnaround time 7-10 days.

16th General District Court PO Box 245, 85 Stanard St, Stanardsville, VA 22973; 434-985-5224; fax: 434-985-1448; 8:30AM-4PM (EST). *Misdemeanor, Civil Actions under $25,000, Eviction, Small Claims.*
www.courts.state.va.us/
General Information: No juvenile, sealed records released. No fee to fax documents. Court makes copy: $.50 per page. No certification fee. Payee: Clerk of General District Court or Greene County Combined Court. Personal checks accepted. Credit cards accepted. Prepayment required. Mail requests: SASE required.
Civil Name Search: Access: Fax, mail, online, in person. Both court and visitors may perform in person name searches. No search fee. Civil data retained 10 years on computer, older data is archived. Civil PAT goes back to 10 years. **See details about online access at front or rear of this chapter.**
Criminal Name Search: Access: In person, online. Visitors must perform in person searches themselves. Required to search: name, years to search, DOB; also helpful: SSN. Criminal data retained 10 years on computer, older data is archived. Note: Results include name and address. Criminal PAT goes back to same as civil. **See details about online access at front or rear of this chapter.**

Greensville County

6th Circuit Court PO Box 631, 337 S Main St, Emporia, VA 23847; 434-348-4215; fax: 434-348-4020; 9AM-5PM; 9AM-N W (EST). *Felony, Civil Actions over $4,500, Probate.*
www.courts.state.va.us/courts/circuit.html

General Information: No juvenile, sealed records released. Will not fax documents. Court makes copy: $.50 per page. Certification fee: $2.00. Payee: Clerk of Circuit Court. Business checks accepted. No credit cards accepted. Prepayment required.

Civil Name Search: Access: In person, online. Visitors must perform in person searches themselves. Civil index on docket books from 1781; on computer since 1989. Civil PAT goes back to 1989. **See details about online access at front or rear of this chapter.**

Criminal Name Search: Access: In person, online. Visitors must perform in person searches themselves. Criminal records indexed in books from 1781; on computer since 1989. Note: Court does not conduct criminal searches. Criminal PAT goes back to same as civil. **See details about online access at front or rear of this chapter.**

Greensville/Emporia Combined Court 315 S Main St, Emporia, VA 23847; 434-634-5400; fax: 434-634-0049; 8AM-4PM (EST). *Misdemeanor, Civil Actions under $25,000, Eviction, Small Claims.*
www.courts.state.va.us/courts/combined/emporia/home.html

General Information: Holds records for the former Emporia City General District Court. No juvenile, sealed records released. Will not fax documents. Court makes copy: $.50 per page. No certification fee. Payee: Clerk of General District Court. Personal checks, Visa/MC accepted.

Civil Name Search: Access: Online, in person. Visitors must perform in person searches themselves. Civil index on docket books from 1800s; on computer back 10 years. Civil PAT goes back to 10 years. **See details about online access at front or rear of this chapter..**

Criminal Name Search: Access: Online, in person. Visitors must perform in person searches themselves. Required to search: name, years to search, DOB; also helpful: SSN. Criminal records indexed in books from 1800s; on computer back 10 years. Criminal PAT goes back to same as civil. **See details about online access at front or rear of this chapter.**

Halifax County

10th Circuit Court PO Box 729, 8 S. Main, Halifax, VA 24558; 434-476-6211; fax: 434-476-2890; 8:30AM-4:30PM (EST). *Felony, Civil Actions over $4,500, Probate.* www.courts.state.va.us/courts/circuit.html

General Information: No juvenile, sealed records released. Will fax documents $.50 per page plus search fee per telephone call. Court makes copy: $.50 per page. Self serve copy: same. Certification fee: $2.00 per document. Payee: Circuit Court. Personal checks accepted, credit cards are not. Prepayment required. Mail requests: SASE required for criminal.

Civil Name Search: Access: Online, in person. Visitors must perform in person searches themselves. Civil records on computer from 1988, on index books from 1752. Civil PAT goes back to 1989. **See details about online access at front or rear of this chapter.**

Criminal Name Search: Access: Mail, online, in person. Both court and visitors may perform in person name searches. Search fee: No search fee, copy and certification fees can be charged. Criminal records computerized from 1988, on index books from 1752. Mail turnaround time 1-5 days. Criminal PAT goes back to same as civil. **See details about online access at front or rear of this chapter.**

10th General District Court PO Box 458, 8 S Main St, Courthouse Sq, Halifax, VA 24558; 434-476-3385; fax: 434-476-3387; 8:30AM-4:30PM (EST). *Misdemeanor, Civil Actions under $25,000, Eviction, Small Claims.*
www.courts.state.va.us

General Information: No juvenile, sealed records released. Fax back fee only charged for large number of pages. Court makes copy: $.50 per page. Self serve copy: same. No certification fee. Payee: General District Court. Personal checks, Visa/MC accepted. Prepayment required.

Civil Name Search: Access: Fax, mail, online, in person. Both court and visitors may perform in person name searches. No search fee. Required to search: name, years to search, address. Civil records on computer from 1993. Mail turnaround time within 7 days. Civil PAT goes back to 10 years. **See details about online access at front or rear of this chapter.** Results show city and state of subject and the day and month of birth, but not year.

Criminal Name Search: Access: Fax, mail, online, in person. Both court and visitors may perform in person name searches. No search fee. Required to search: name. Criminal records computerized from 1993. Mail turnaround time within 7 days. Criminal PAT goes back to same as civil. **See details about online access at front or rear of this chapter.**

Hampton City

8th Circuit Court PO Box 40, 101 King's Way, Hampton, VA 23669-0040; 757-727-6105; fax: 757-728-3505; 8:30AM-4PM (EST). *Felony, Civil Actions over $4,500, Probate*
www.courts.state.va.us/courts/circuit.html

General Information: No pre-sentence, criminal correspondence, chancery, judges notes or medical records released. Will fax documents. Court makes copy: $.50 per page. Self serve copy: same. Certification fee: $2.00. Payee: Clerk of Court. No out of state checks accepted. No credit cards accepted. Prepayment required. Mail requests: SASE required.

Civil Name Search: Access: Phone, mail, fax, in person, online. Both court and visitors may perform in person name searches. Search fee: $10.00 per name. Computerized records back to 1995, civil records on index books since 1834. Mail turnaround time 5-10 days. Civil PAT goes to 1995. **See details about online access at front or rear of this chapter.**

Criminal Name Search: Access: Mail, online, in person, online. Both court and visitors may perform in person name searches. Search fee: $10.00 per name. Computerized records back to 1995, criminal records on index books since1949. Mail turnaround time 3 days. Criminal PAT goes back to same as civil. **See details about online access at front or rear of this chapter.**

8th General District Court PO Box 70, 236 King St, Courthouse, Hampton, VA 23669-0070; criminal phone: 757-727-6260; civil phone: 757-727-6480; fax: 757-727-6035; 8AM-4PM (EST). *Misdemeanor, Civil Actions under $25,000, Eviction, Small Claims, Traffic.*
www.courts.state.va.us/

General Information: No sealed records released. Will not fax documents. Court makes copy: $1.00 for 1st and 2nd copy, $.50 each add'l copy. Certification fee: $7.00 per certification. Payee: Hampton District Court. Personal checks accepted. Credit Cards accepted for fines only. Prepayment required.

Civil Name Search: Access: Online, in person. Visitors must perform in person searches themselves. Required to search: name. Civil index on computer for 10 years. Note: Mail access limited to specific case and two names. Civil PAT goes back to 10 years. **See details about online access at front or rear of this chapter.**

Criminal Name Search: Access: Online, in person. Visitors must perform in person searches themselves. Required to search: name. Criminal records indexed on computer for 10 years. Criminal PAT goes back to same as civil. **See details about online access at front or rear of this chapter.**

Hanover County

15th Circuit Court 7507 Library Dr, PO Box 39, Hanover, VA 23069; 804-365-6151; criminal phone: 804-365-3137; civil phone: 804-365-6148; probate phone: 804-365-6478; fax: 804-365-6278; 8AM-4:30PM (EST). *Felony, Civil Actions over $4,500, Probate.*
www.co.hanover.va.us/circuitct/default.htm

General Information: No juvenile, sealed records released. Will not fax documents. Court makes copy: $.50 per page. Certification fee: $2.00 per cert. Payee: Clerk of Circuit Court. Personal checks accepted, credit cards are not. Prepayment required.

Civil Name Search: Access: Online, in person. Visitors must perform in person searches themselves. Required to search: name, years to search; helpful- case number. Civil records index in books, older records date from 1865. Civil PAT goes back to 1990. Sometimes, however, the middle initial is shown. **See details about online access at front or rear of this chapter.**

Criminal Name Search: Access: Online, in person. Visitors must perform in person searches themselves. Required to search: name, years to search; helpful- case number. Criminal records index in books, older records date from 09/01/1966. Criminal PAT goes back to 1990. The month and day will show, but not the whole DOB. **See details about online access at front or rear of this chapter..**

15th General District Court PO Box 176, County Courthouse, Hanover, VA 23069; 804-365-6191; civil phone: 804-365-6457; criminal fax: 804-365-6290; civil fax: 8AM-4PM; 8AM-4PM (EST). *Misdemeanor, Civil Actions under $25,000, Eviction, Small Claims.*
www.courts.state.va.us/

General Information: Will not fax documents. Court makes copy: $1.00 per page 1st 2 pages, $.50 each add'l up to 10 pages. No certification fee. Only cash accepted for the copy fee. No credit cards accepted for copies or record searches.

Civil Name Search: Access: Online, in person. Visitors must perform in person searches themselves. Civil records on computer back 10 years. Civil PAT goes back to 10 years. **See details about online access at front or rear of this chapter.**

Criminal Name Search: Access: Online, in person. Visitors must perform in person searches themselves. Required to search: name, years to

search, DOB; also helpful: SSN. Criminal records on computer back 10 years. Criminal PAT goes back to same as civil. Day and moth shown, not year on DOB; name & address only on inactive cases. **See details about online access at front or rear of this chapter.**

Harrisonburg City
Circuit & District Courts - See Rockingham County

Henrico County

14th Circuit Court PO Box 90775, Henrico, VA 23273-7032; 804-501-4202; criminal phone: 804-501-5448; civil phone: 804-501-5422; probate phone: 804-501-4316; fax: 804-501-5214; 8AM-4:30PM (EST). *Felony, Civil Actions over $4,500, Probate.* www.co.henrico.va.us/clerk/
General Information: No juvenile, judges notes, adoption sealed records released. Will not fax documents. Court makes copy: $.50 per page. Self serve copy: same. Certification fee: $2.00 per document. Payee: Clerk of Circuit Court. Personal checks accepted, credit cards are not. Prepayment required. Mail requests: SASE required for mail return of any copies.
Civil Name Search: Access: In person, online. Visitors must perform in person searches themselves. Civil records on computer from 11/88, on index cards from 1850. Civil PAT goes back to 11/1988. Remote online access to court case indexes is via LOPAS. This is a limited system and the program is not taking on new clients.
Criminal Name Search: Access: In person, online. Visitors must perform in person searches themselves. Criminal records computerized from 11/88, on index cards from 1850. Criminal PAT goes back to 1989. Results include partial data of birth. Remote online access to court case indexes is via LOPAS. This is a limited system and the program is not taking on new clients. Online results show middle initial.

14th General District Court PO Box 90775, Henrico, VA 23273; criminal phone: 804-501-4723; civil phone: 804-501-4727; criminal fax: 804-501-7388; civil fax: 8AM-4PM; 8AM-4PM (EST). *Misdemeanor, Civil Actions under $25,000, Eviction, Small Claims.* www.co.henrico.va.us/gendistcourt/
General Information: No juvenile, sealed records released. Will not fax documents. Court makes copy: $1.00 minimum for 1st 2 pages, $.50 ea add'l; Civil- $1.00 per page. No certification fee. Payee: Clerk of General District Court. Personal checks accepted. Visa/MC accepted but not over the phone. Prepayment required.
Civil Name Search: Access: Online, in person. Visitors must perform in person searches themselves. Civil cases indexed by defendant. Civil records on computer back to 2001. Civil PAT goes back to 2001. **See details about online access at front or rear of this chapter.**
Criminal Name Search: Access: Online, in person. Visitors must perform in person searches themselves. Required to search: name, years to search, DOB. Criminal records computerized from 2001. Criminal PAT goes back to same as civil. **See details about online access at front or rear of this chapter.**

Henry County

Circuit Court 3160 Kings Mountain Rd, #B, Martinsville, VA 24112; 276-634-4880; criminal phone: 276-634-4889 or 276-634-4885; civil phone: 276-634-4884; probate phone: 276-634-4883; 9AM-5PM (EST). *Felony, Civil Actions over $4,500, Probate.*
www.courts.state.va.us/courts/circuit/Henry/home.html
General Information: Online identifiers in results same as on public terminal. No juvenile, expungments, sealed or adoption records released. Will not fax documents. Court makes copy: $.50 per page. Self serve copy: same. Certification fee: $2.00. Payee: Clerk of Circuit Court. Personal checks accepted, credit cards are not. Prepayment required.
Civil Name Search: Access: Online, in person. Visitors must perform in person searches themselves. Civil records on computer since 4/92, index back to 1777. Civil PAT goes back to 1992. Only month and day of DOB appears, plus sex, race. Search free by name or case number at www.courts.state.va.us/.
Criminal Name Search: Access: Online, in person. Visitors must perform in person searches themselves. Required to search: name, years to search, DOB; also helpful: SSN. Criminal records computerized since 7/92, index back to 1777. Criminal PAT goes back to same as civil. Only month and day of DOB appears, plus sex, race. Online access to criminal records is same as civil. Results show day and month of birth, gender, and race. Online results show middle initial.

21st General District Court 3160 King's Mountain Rd #A, Martinsville, VA 24112; 276-634-4815; fax: 276-634-4825; 9AM-5PM (EST). *Misdemeanor, Civil Actions under $25,000, Eviction, Small Claims.* www.courts.state.va.us/courts/gd/Henry/home.html
General Information: No sealed records released. Will not fax documents. Court makes copy: $.50 per page. No certification fee. Payee: Henry County

General District Court. Personal checks accepted. VISA MC credit cards accepted. Prepayment required.
Civil Name Search: Access: Online, in person. Visitors must perform in person searches themselves. Required to search: name, years to search; also helpful: address. Civil records on computer for 10 years. Civil PAT goes back to 10 years. **See details about online access at front or rear of this chapter.**
Criminal Name Search: Access: Online, in person. Visitors must perform in person searches themselves. Required to search: name, years to search, DOB; also helpful: address, SSN. Criminal records computerized for 10 years. Criminal PAT goes back to same as civil. **See details about online access at front or rear of this chapter.**

Highland County

25th Circuit Court PO Box 190, 165 W Main St, Monterey, VA 24465; 540-468-2447; fax: 540-468-3447; 8:30AM-4:30PM (EST). *Felony, Civil Actions over $4,500, Probate.*
www.courts.state.va.us/courts/circuit.html
General Information: No juvenile, sealed records released. Will fax documents $2.00 plus $.50 per page. Court makes copy: $.50 per page. Self serve copy: same. Certification fee: $2.00. Payee: Clerk of Circuit Court. Personal checks accepted, credit cards are not. Prepayment required.
Civil Name Search: Access: Mail, in person, online. Both court and visitors may perform in person name searches. No search fee. Civil index on docket books from 1868. Mail turnaround time up to 1 week. **See details about online access at front or rear of this chapter.**
Criminal Name Search: Access: Mail, online, in person. Both court and visitors may perform in person name searches. No search fee. Criminal records indexed in books from 1868. Mail turnaround time up to 1 week. Online access to criminal records is same as civil. Online results show middle initial.

25th General District Court PO Box 88, Highland County Courthouse, 165 W Main St, Monterey, VA 24465; 540-468-2445; fax: 540-468-3449; 8:30AM-5PM (EST). *Misdemeanor, Civil Actions under $25,000, Eviction, Small Claims.*
www.courts.state.va.us/
General Information: No juvenile, sealed records released. Will fax back documents. Court makes copy: $1.00 first 2 pages; $.50 each add'l. No certification fee. Payee: General District Court. Personal checks, Visa/MC accepted. Prepayment required. Mail requests: SASE requested.
Civil Name Search: Access: Fax, mail, online, in person. Both court and visitors may perform in person name searches. No search fee. Civil index on docket books for 11 years; computerized to present. Mail turnaround time 2-3 days. **See details about online access at front or rear of this chapter.**
Criminal Name Search: Access: Fax, mail, online, in person. Both court and visitors may perform in person name searches. No search fee. Required to search: name, years to search; also helpful: DOB, SSN, signed release. Criminal records indexed in books for 11 years; computerized to present. Mail turnaround time 2-3 days. **See details about online access at front or rear of this chapter.**

Hopewell City

6th Circuit Court 100 E Broadway, PO Box 310, 2nd Fl, Rm 251, Hopewell, VA 23860; 804-541-2239; fax: 804-541-2438; 8:30AM-4PM (EST). *Felony, Civil Actions over $4,500, Probate.*
www.courts.state.va.us/courts/circuit.html
General Information: Online identifiers in results same as on public terminal. No juvenile, sealed records released. Will not fax documents. Court makes copy: $.50 per page. Self serve copy: same. Certification fee: $2.00. Payee: Clerk of Circuit Court. Personal checks accepted, credit cards are not. Prepayment required. Mail requests: SASE required for mail return of any copies.
Civil Name Search: Access: In person, online. Visitors must perform in person searches themselves. Civil index on docket books since 1916. Civil PAT goes back to 1990. Only month and day of DOB appears, plus sex, race. **See details about online access at front or rear of this chapter.**
Criminal Name Search: Access: Online, in person. Visitors must perform in person searches themselves. Required to search: name, years to search, DOB. Criminal records indexed in books since 1916. Criminal PAT goes back to same as civil. Only month and day of DOB appears, plus sex, race. **See details about online access at front or rear of this chapter.**

Hopewell General District Court 100 E Broadway, Hopewell, VA 23860; 804-541-2257; fax: 804-541-2364; 8:30AM-4:30PM (EST). *Misdemeanor, Civil Actions under $25,000, Eviction, Small Claims.*
www.courts.state.va.us/courts/combined/Hopewell/home.html
General Information: No juvenile, sealed or domestic relations records released. Will not fax documents. Court makes copy: $1.00 per page 1st 2

pages, then $.50 each. No certification fee. Payee: Clerk of General District Court. Personal checks accepted. Credit cards accepted. Prepayment required. Mail requests: SASE requested.

Civil Name Search: Access: Mail, in person, online. Both court and visitors may perform in person name searches. No search fee. Civil records on computer from 1988, older case records archived. Mail turnaround time 3-5 days. Civil PAT goes back to 1988. Search free by name or case number at http://epwsgdp1.courts.state.va.us/gdcourts/captchaVerification.do?landing=landing. Results show subject's day and month of birth, but not year.

Criminal Name Search: Access: Mail, online, in person. Both court and visitors may perform in person name searches. No search fee. Required to search: name, years to search, DOB; also helpful: SSN. Criminal records computerized from 1988, older case records are archived. Mail turnaround time 3-5 days. Criminal PAT goes back to same as civil. Search free by name or case number at http://epwsgdp1.courts.state.va.us/gdcourts/captchaVerification.do?landing=landing. Results show subject's day and month of birth, but not year. Online results show middle initial.

Isle of Wight County

5th Circuit Court 17000 Josiah Parker Circle, PO Box 110, Isle of Wight, VA 23397; 757-365-6233; fax: 757-357-0884; 9AM-5PM (EST). *Felony, Civil Actions over $4,500, Probate.*
www.courts.state.va.us/courts/circuit.html

General Information: Online identifiers in results same as on public terminal. No juvenile, adoption, or sealed records released. Will not fax documents. Court makes copy: $.50 per page. Certification fee: $2.00. Payee: Clerk of Circuit Court. Personal checks accepted, credit cards are not. Prepayment required. Mail requests: SASE required for mail return of any copies.

Civil Name Search: Access: Online, in person. Visitors must perform in person searches themselves. Civil index on docket books from 1800s; on computer back to 1988. Note: Court will only search the computer indices for you to determine is a name exists. Civil PAT goes back to 1988. Only month and day of DOB appears, plus sex, race. **See details about online access at front or rear of this chapter.**

Criminal Name Search: Access: Online, in person. Visitors must perform in person searches themselves. Required to search: name, years to search, DOB. Criminal records indexed in books from 1800s; on computer back to 1988. Note: Court will only search the computer indices for you to determine is a name exists. Criminal PAT goes back to same as civil. Only month and day of DOB appears, plus sex, race. Online access to criminal records is same as civil. Online results show middle initial.

5th General District Court PO Box 122, 17110 Monument Circle, Courthouse, Isle of Wight, VA 23397; 757-365-6244; fax: 757-365-6246; 8AM-4PM (EST). *Misdemeanor, Civil Actions under $25,000, Eviction, Small Claims.* www.courts.state.va.us/

General Information: The Clerk can be reached at 757-365-6244. Juvenile and sealed records not released. Court makes copy: None. Certification fee: $1.00. Payee: Clerk of GDC. Personal checks, Visa/MC accepted. Prepayment required.

Civil Name Search: Access: Online, in person. Visitors must perform in person searches themselves. Civil index on docket books back to 1800s; on computer back 10 years. Civil PAT goes back to 10 years. **See details about online access at front or rear of this chapter.**

Criminal Name Search: Access: Online, in person. Visitors must perform in person searches themselves. Criminal records indexed in books back to 1800s; on computer back 10 years. Criminal PAT goes back to same as civil. Records purged after 10 years. **See details about online access at front or rear of this chapter.**

James City County

Williamsburg-James City Circuit Court 5201 Monticello Ave #6, Williamsburg, VA 23188-8218; 757-564-2242; fax: 757-564-2329; 8:30AM-4:30PM, systems close at 4PM (EST). *Felony, Civil Actions over $4,500, Probate.* www.courts.state.va.us/courts/circuit.html

General Information: Court will assist - and tell if a name exists - but not perform searches. No juvenile, sealed, adoption records released. Fee to fax out file $1.00 per page. Court makes copy: $.50 per page. Self serve copy: same. Certification fee: $2.00. Payee: Clerk of Circuit Court. No personal checks. No credit cards accepted. Prepayment required.

Civil Name Search: Access: Phone, in person, online. Visitors must perform in person searches themselves. Search fee: $10.00 per name. Civil records on computer since 1987, archived from 1970, prior on index books. Note: Phone access very limited. Civil PAT goes back to 1987. **See details about online access at front or rear of this chapter.**

Criminal Name Search: Access: Phone, in person, online. Visitors must perform in person searches themselves. Search fee: $10.00 per name. Required to search: name, years to search, DOB; also helpful: SSN. Criminal

records on computer since 1987, archived from 1970, prior on index books. Note: Phone access very limited. Criminal PAT goes back to same as civil. **See details about online access at front or rear of this chapter.**

County General District Court James City County Courthouse, 5201 Monticello Ave, #2, Williamsburg, VA 23188-8218; 757-564-2400; fax: 757-564-2410; 7:30AM-4PM (EST). *Misdemeanor, Civil Actions under $25,000, Eviction, Small Claims.*
www.courts.state.va.us/

General Information: Online identifiers in results same as on public terminal. No juvenile, sealed records released. Will fax documents; fee depends on the documents needing to be faxed. Court makes copy: copy fee if extensive searching or copies needed. No certification fee. Payee: General District Court. Personal checks, Visa/MC accepted. Prepayment required. Mail requests: SASE not required.

Civil Name Search: Access: Fax, mail, in person, online. Both court and visitors may perform in person name searches. No search fee. Civil records index books go back 10 years, on computer back 10 years. Mail turnaround time 10 days. Civil PAT goes back to 10 years. Search free at http://epwsgdp1.courts.state.va.us/gdcourts/captchaVerification.do?landing=landing. Results show name and DOB month/day.

Criminal Name Search: Access: Fax, mail, in person, online. Both court and visitors may perform in person name searches. No search fee. Required to search: name, years to search, DOB; also helpful: SSN. Criminal records index books go back 10 years, on computer back 10 years. Mail turnaround time 10 days. Criminal PAT goes back to 10 years. **See details about online access at front or rear of this chapter.**

King and Queen County

9th Circuit Court PO Box 67, 234 Allen's Circle, King & Queen Court House, VA 23085; 804-785-5984; fax: 804-785-5698; 9AM-5PM (EST). *Felony, Civil Actions over $4,500, Probate.*
www.courts.state.va.us/courts/circuit.html

General Information: No juvenile, sealed or adoption records released. Will fax documents $1.00 per page. Court makes copy: $.50 per page. Certification fee: $2.00. Payee: Clerk of Circuit Court. Personal checks accepted, credit cards are not. Prepayment required.

Civil Name Search: Access: In person, online. Visitors must perform in person searches themselves. Civil cases indexed by plaintiff. Civil records archived from 1864, computerized since 1995 for index, images back to 2005. Civil PAT goes back to 08/01/2995. Remote online access to court case indexes is via LOPAS. This is a limited system and the program is not taking on new clients.

Criminal Name Search: Access: Online, in person. Visitors must perform in person searches themselves. Criminal records archived from 1864, computerized since 1995 for index, images back to 08/01/2005. Criminal PAT goes back to same as civil. Remote online access to court case indexes is via LOPAS. This is a limited system and the program is not taking on new clients. Online results show middle initial, DOB.

King & Queen General District Court PO Box 86, 242 Allen's Circle, Ste F, King & Queen Courthouse, VA 23085-0086; 804-785-5982; fax: 804-785-5694; 8:30AM-4:30PM (EST). *Misdemeanor, Civil Actions under $25,000, Eviction.*
www.kingandqueenco.net/html/Govt/gendist.html

General Information: The General District Court also holds preliminary hearings in felony cases. Online identifiers in results same as on public terminal. No fee to fax documents. Court makes copy: $1.00 first page, $.50 each add'l. No certification fee. Payee: General District Court. Personal checks, Visa/MC accepted. Prepayment required. Mail requests: SASE required.

Civil Name Search: Access: Fax, mail, online, in person. Both court and visitors may perform in person name searches. No search fee. Civil records on computer back to 2000. Mail turnaround time 1-5 days. Civil PAT goes back to 2000. **See details about online access at front or rear of this chapter.**

Criminal Name Search: Access: Fax, mail, online, in person. Both court and visitors may perform in person name searches. No search fee. Required to search: name, years to search, DOB; also helpful: SSN, signed release. Criminal records computerized from 2000. Mail turnaround time 1-5 days. Criminal PAT goes back to same as civil. **See details about online access at front or rear of this chapter.**

King George County

15th Circuit Court 9483 Kings Highway, #3, King George, VA 22485; 540-775-3322; fax: 540-775-5466; 8:30AM-4:30PM (EST). *Felony, Civil Actions over $4,500, Probate.*
www.courts.state.va.us/courts/circuit/King_George/home.html

General Information: No sealed records released. Will not fax documents. Court makes copy: $.50 per page. Self serve copy: same. Certification fee:

$2.00. Payee: Clerk of Circuit court. Personal checks accepted, credit cards are not. Prepayment required. Mail requests: SASE required.

Civil Name Search: Access: Mail, in person, online. Both court and visitors may perform in person name searches. Search fee: $10.00 per name. Civil index on docket books from 1800s; computerized records since 1990. Mail turnaround time 30 days. Civil PAT goes back to 1990. **See details about online access at front or rear of this chapter.**

Criminal Name Search: Access: Mail, in person, online. Both court and visitors may perform in person name searches. Search fee: $10.00 per name. Criminal records indexed in books from 1800s; computerized records since 1990. Mail turnaround time 30 days. Criminal PAT goes back to same as civil. **See details about online access at front or rear of this chapter.**

15th General District Combined Court PO Box 279, County Courthouse, 9483 Kings Hwy, King George, VA 22485; 540-775-3573; 8AM-4PM (EST). *Misdemeanor, Civil Actions under $25,000, Eviction, Small Claims.*

www.courts.state.va.us/courts/combined/king_george/home.html

General Information: No juvenile, sealed records released. Will not fax documents. Court makes copy: $1.00 per page 1st 2 pages, $.50 each add'l. No certification fee. Payee: Clerk of General District Court. Personal checks, Visa/MC accepted. Prepayment required. Mail requests: SASE required.

Civil Name Search: Access: Mail, in person, online. Both court and visitors may perform in person name searches. No search fee. Civil index on docket books from early 1900s; computerized records since 1992. Mail turnaround time 1-5 days. Civil PAT goes back to 1992. O **See details about online access at front or rear of this chapter.**

Criminal Name Search: Access: Mail, in person, online. Both court and visitors may perform in person name searches. No search fee. Required to search: name, years to search, DOB; also helpful: SSN. Criminal records indexed in books from early 1900s; computerized records since 1992. Mail turnaround time 1-5 days. Criminal PAT goes back to same as civil. **See details about online access at front or rear of this chapter.**

King William County

9th Circuit Court 351 Courthouse Ln, PO Box 216, King William, VA 23086; 804-769-4936; criminal phone: 804-769-4938; civil phone: 804-769-4936; probate phone: 804-769-4936; fax: 804-769-4991; 8:30AM-4:30PM (EST). *Felony, Civil Actions over $4,500, Probate.*

www.courts.state.va.us/courts/circuit.html

General Information: Probate fax is same as main fax number. Online identifiers in results same as on public terminal. No juvenile, sealed records released. Will fax documents to local or toll free line. Court makes copy: $.50 per page. Self serve copy: same. Certification fee: $2.00 per instrument plus copy fee. Payee: Clerk of Circuit Court. Personal checks accepted, credit cards are not. Prepayment required. Mail requests: SASE required.

Civil Name Search: Access: Mail, in person, online. Both court and visitors may perform in person name searches. No search fee. Civil index on docket books from 1885. Mail turnaround time 1 week. Civil PAT goes back to 1999. Only month and day of DOB appears, plus sex, race. **See details about online access at front or rear of this chapter.**

Criminal Name Search: Access: Mail, in person, online. Both court and visitors may perform in person name searches. No search fee. Required to search: name, years to search, DOB; also helpful: SSN. Criminal records indexed in books from 1885, computerized records from 1999. Mail turnaround time 1 week. Criminal PAT goes back to same as civil. Only month and day of DOB appears, plus sex, race. **See details about online access at front or rear of this chapter.**

King William General District Court PO Box 5, 351 Courthouse Lane, King William, VA 23086; 804-769-4948; fax: 804-769-4971; 8:30AM-4:30PM (EST). *Misdemeanor, Civil Actions under $25,000, Eviction, Small Claims.*

www.kingwilliamcounty.us/GD_Court.htm

General Information: Online identifiers in results same as on public terminal. No juvenile, sealed records released. No fee to fax documents. Court makes copy: $1.00 first 2 pages, $.50 each add'l. Self serve copy: same. No certification fee. Payee: General District Court. Personal checks accepted. Credit cards accepted. Prepayment required. Mail requests: SASE requested.

Civil Name Search: Access: Fax, mail, online, in person. Both court and visitors may perform in person name searches. No search fee. Civil records on computer since 2001. Mail turnaround time 1-3 days. Civil PAT goes back to 2001. **See details about online access at front or rear of this chapter.**

Criminal Name Search: Access: Fax, mail, online, in person. Both court and visitors may perform in person name searches. No search fee. Required to search: name, years to search, DOB; also helpful: signed release, SSN. Criminal records computerized from 2001. Mail turnaround time 1-3

days. Criminal PAT goes back to 2001. **See details about online access at front or rear of this chapter.**

Lancaster County

15th Circuit Court PO Box 99, Courthouse Bldg, 8265 Mary Ball Rd, Lancaster, VA 22503; 804-462-5611; fax: 804-462-9978; 8:30AM-4:30PM (EST). *Felony, Civil Actions over $4,500, Probate.*

www.courts.state.va.us/courts/circuit.html

General Information: No juvenile, sealed records released. Will not fax documents. Court makes copy: $.50 per page. Certification fee: $2.00. Payee: Clerk of Circuit Court. Personal checks accepted. Out of state checks not accepted. No credit cards accepted. Prepayment required. Mail requests: SASE required.

Civil Name Search: Access: Mail, in person, online. Only the court performs in person name searches; visitors may not. No search fee. Civil index on docket books from 1845. Mail turnaround time same day. **See details about online access at front or rear of this chapter.**

Criminal Name Search: Access: Mail, online, in person. Both court and visitors may perform in person name searches. No search fee. Criminal records indexed in books from 1845. Mail turnaround time same day. **See details about online access at front or rear of this chapter.**

15th General District Court PO Box 129, 8265 Mary Ball Rd #121, Lancaster, VA 22503; 804-462-0012; fax: 804-462-0371; 8AM-N; 1-4:30PM (EST). *Misdemeanor, Civil Actions under $25,000, Eviction, Small Claims.* www.courts.state.va.us/

General Information: No sealed records released. Will not fax documents. Court makes copy: $1.00 1st page; $1.00 2nd page, $.50 each add'l. No certification fee. Payee: Clerk of General District Court. Personal checks accepted. Visa/MC accepted but no debit cards. Prepayment required. Mail requests: SASE helpful.

Civil Name Search: Access: Mail, in person, online. Both court and visitors may perform in person name searches. No search fee. Civil cases indexed by defendant. Civil records kept for 10 years. Mail turnaround time 2-3 days. Civil PAT goes back to 10 years. Terminal only shows DOB if submitted, and not the year. **See details about online access at front or rear of this chapter.**

Criminal Name Search: Access: Mail, online, in person. Both court and visitors may perform in person name searches. No search fee. Required to search: name, years to search, DOB. Criminal records computerized from 11/93. Hard copies kept 10 years. Mail turnaround time 2-3 days. Criminal PAT goes back to same as civil. Terminal does not show the DOB year. Traffic records go back 10 years. **See details about online access at front or rear of this chapter.**

Lee County

30th Circuit Court PO Box 326, Jonesville, VA 24263; 276-346-7763; fax: 276-346-3440; 8:30AM-5PM (EST). *Felony, Civil Actions over $4,500, Probate.* www.courts.state.va.us/courts/circuit/Lee/home.html

General Information: No juvenile, sealed records released. Will fax documents to local or toll free line. Court makes copy: $.50 per page. Self serve copy: same. Certification fee: $2.00. Payee: Clerk of Circuit Court. Personal checks accepted, credit cards are not. Prepayment required. Mail requests: SASE required.

Civil Name Search: Access: Phone, fax, mail, online, in person. Both court and visitors may perform in person name searches. No search fee. Civil index on docket books from 1800s. Note: Phone & fax access limited to short searches. Mail turnaround time 1-3 days. Civil PAT goes back to 1988. **See details about online access at front or rear of this chapter.**

Criminal Name Search: Access: Phone, fax, mail, online, in person. Both court and visitors may perform in person name searches. No search fee. Required to search: name, years to search, DOB; also helpful: SSN. Criminal records indexed in books from 1800s. Mail turnaround time 1-3 days. Criminal PAT goes back to same as civil. **See details about online access at front or rear of this chapter.**

30th General District Court PO Box 306, Main St Courthouse, #108, Jonesville, VA 24263; 276-346-7729; fax: 276-346-7701; 8AM-4:30PM (EST). *Misdemeanor, Civil Actions under $25,000, Eviction, Small Claims.* www.courts.state.va.us/

General Information: No juvenile, sealed records released. Will fax back documents. Court makes copy: $1.00 first page, $.50 each add'l. No certification fee. Payee: Clerk of General District Court. Personal checks, Visa/MC accepted. Prepayment required. Mail requests: SASE helpful.

Civil Name Search: Access: Mail, in person, online. Both court and visitors may perform in person name searches. No search fee. Civil index on docket books from 1800s, on computer from 11/7/90. Mail turnaround time 1-2 days. Civil PAT goes back to 1990. **See details about online access at front or rear of this chapter.**

Criminal Name Search: Access: Mail, online, in person, fax. Both court and visitors may perform in person name searches. No search fee.

Criminal records indexed in books from 1800s, on computer from 11/7/90. Mail turnaround time 1-2 days. Criminal PAT goes back to same as civil. **See details about online access at front or rear of this chapter.**

Lexington City County
Circuit & District Courts - See Rockbridge County

Loudoun County

20th Circuit Court PO Box 550, Leesburg, VA 20178; 703-777-0270; probate phone: 703-777-0272; fax: 703-777-0376; 8:30AM-4:00PM (EST). *Felony, Civil Actions over $4,500, Probate.* www.loudoun.gov/Default.aspx?tabid=798

General Information: Probate fax- 703-737-8096. Online identifiers in results same as on public terminal. No juvenile, sealed or adoption records released. Will not fax documents. Court makes copy: $.50 per page. Certification fee: $2.00 per doc plus copy fee. Payee: Clerk of Circuit Court. Business checks accepted. Personal checks accepted if in state. No credit cards accepted. Prepayment required.

Civil Name Search: Access: Phone, online, in person. Both court and visitors may perform in person name searches. No search fee. Civil records on computer since 1995; prior on index books from 1700s. Note: Phone access limited to simple requests. Civil PAT goes back to 1987. Only month and day of DOB appears, plus sex, race. **See details about online access at front or rear of this chapter.** Also, docket lists are free at www.loudoun.gov/Default.aspx?tabid=318&fmpath=/Dockets.

Criminal Name Search: Access: Online, in person. Both court and visitors may perform in person name searches. No search fee. Required to search: name, years to search, DOB; also helpful: SSN. Criminal records on computer since 1995; prior on index books from 1700s. Criminal PAT goes back to same as civil. Only month and day of DOB appears, plus sex, race. **See details about online access at front or rear of this chapter.** Also, docket lists are online free at www.loudoun.gov/Default.aspx?tabid=318&fmpath=/Dockets.

20th General District Court 18 E Market St, Leesburg, VA 20176; 703-777-0310; fax: 703-771-5284; 8AM-4PM (EST). *Misdemeanor, Civil Actions under $25,000, Eviction.* www.courts.state.va.us/courts/gd/Loudoun/home.html

General Information: Will not fax documents. Court makes copy: $.50 per page. Certification fee: $.50. Payee: General District Court. Personal checks accepted. Credit cards accepted. Prepayment required. Mail requests: SASE required.

Civil Name Search: Access: Mail, fax, online, in person. Both court and visitors may perform in person name searches. No search fee. Civil records on computer back 10 years. Mail turnaround time 5 days. Civil PAT goes back to 10 years. **See details about online access at front or rear of this chapter.**

Criminal Name Search: Access: Mail, fax, online, in person. Both court and visitors may perform in person name searches. No search fee. Criminal records on computer back 10 years. Mail turnaround time 5 days. Criminal PAT goes back to same as civil. **See details about online access at front or rear of this chapter.**

Louisa County

16th Circuit Court PO Box 37, 100 W Main St, Louisa, VA 23093; 540-967-5312; fax: 540-967-2705; 8:30AM-5PM (EST). *Felony, Civil Actions over $4,500, Probate.* www.courts.state.va.us/courts/circuit/Louisa/home.html

General Information: No juvenile, sealed records released. Will not fax documents. Court makes copy: $.50 per page. Self serve copy: same. Certification fee: $2.00. Payee: Clerk of Circuit Court. Personal checks accepted. Prepayment required.

Civil Name Search: Access: Online, in person. Visitors must perform in person searches themselves. Civil records archived from 1742; on computer back to 1989. Civil PAT available. **See details about online access at front or rear of this chapter.**

Criminal Name Search: Access: Online, in person. Both court and visitors may perform in person name searches. No search fee. Required to search: name, years to search, DOB or SSN. Criminal records archived from 1742; on computer back to 1989. Criminal PAT available. **See details about online access at front or rear of this chapter.**

16th General District Court PO Box 524, Louisa, VA 23093; 540-967-5330; fax: 540-967-2369; 8:30AM-4:30PM (EST). *Misdemeanor, Civil Actions under $25,000, Eviction, Small Claims.* www.courts.state.va.us/

General Information: No juvenile, sealed records released. Will not fax documents. Court makes copy: $1.00 first page, $.50 each add'l. Payee: Louisa District Court. Personal checks accepted. Major credit cards accepted. Prepayment required.

Civil Name Search: Access: Online, in person. Visitors must perform in person searches themselves. Civil records on computer for 10 years. Civil PAT goes back to 10 years. **See details about online access at front or rear of this chapter.**

Criminal Name Search: Access: Online, in person. Visitors must perform in person searches themselves. Criminal records computerized for 10 years. Criminal PAT goes back to same as civil. **See details about online access at front or rear of this chapter.**

Lunenburg County

10th Circuit Court 11435 Courthouse Rd, Lunenburg, VA 23952; 434-696-2230 or 2132; fax: 434-696-3931; 8:30AM-5PM (EST). *Felony, Civil Actions over $4,500, Probate.* www.courts.state.va.us/courts/circuit.html

General Information: No juvenile, sealed records released. No fee to fax documents. Court makes copy: $.50 per page. Certification fee: $2.00 per page. Payee: Clerk of Circuit Court. Personal checks accepted, credit cards are not. Prepayment required.

Civil Name Search: Access: Online, in person. Visitors must perform in person searches themselves. Civil index on docket books from 1700s; computerized records since 2002. Civil PAT goes back to 2000. **See details about online access at front or rear of this chapter.**

Criminal Name Search: Access: In person, online. Visitors must perform in person searches themselves. Criminal records indexed in books from 1700s; computerized records since 2002. Criminal PAT goes back to 2001. **See details about online access at front or rear of this chapter.**

10th General District Court 160 Courthouse Sq, #201, Lunenburg, VA 23952; 434-696-5508; fax: 434-696-3665; 8:30AM-4:30PM (EST). *Misdemeanor, Civil Actions under $25,000, Eviction, Small Claims.* www.courts.state.va.us

General Information: Online identifiers in results same as on public terminal. No juvenile records released. Will not fax documents. Court makes copy: $.50 per page. No certification fee. Payee: Lunenburg District Court. Personal checks accepted. Major credit cards accepted. Mail requests: SASE required.

Civil Name Search: Access: Mail, in person, online. Both court and visitors may perform in person name searches. No search fee. Civil records computerized for ten year; original on index books and cards from 1991, prior to 1985 at Circuit Court. Mail turnaround time 3 days. Civil PAT goes back to 1995. **See details about online access at front or rear of this chapter.**

Criminal Name Search: Access: Mail, online, in person. Both court and visitors may perform in person name searches. No search fee. Required to search: name, years to search, DOB, SSN. Criminal records computerized for 10 years. Mail turnaround time 3 days. Criminal PAT goes back to same as civil. **See details about online access at front or rear of this chapter.**

Lynchburg City

24th Circuit Court 900 Court St, PO Box 4, Lynchburg, VA 24505-0004; 434-455-2620; fax: 434-847-1864; 8:15AM-4:45PM (EST). *Felony, Civil Actions over $4,500, Probate.* www.courts.state.va.us/courts/circuit.html

General Information: Court also hears misdemeanor appeals. No juvenile, sealed records released. Court makes copy: $.50 per page. Self serve copy: same. Certification fee: $2.00. Payee: Clerk of Circuit Court. Personal checks accepted. Major credit cards accepted. Prepayment required.

Civil Name Search: Access: In person, online. Both court and visitors may perform in person name searches. No search fee. Civil index on docket books from 1800s, on computer since 1993. Civil PAT goes back to 2000. **See details about online access at front or rear of this chapter.**

Criminal Name Search: Access: In person, online. Both court and visitors may perform in person name searches. No search fee. Required to search: name, years to search; also helpful: DOB, SSN. Criminal records indexed in books from 1800s, on computer since 1987. Criminal PAT goes back to 2001. **See details about online access at front or rear of this chapter.**

24th General District Court - Civil Division 905 Court St, Public Safety Bldg, Lynchburg, VA 24504; civil phone: 434-455-2640; fax: 434-847-1779; 8AM-4PM (EST). *Civil Actions under $25,000, Eviction, Small Claims.* www.courts.state.va.us

General Information: No juvenile, sealed records released. Will not fax documents. Court makes copy: $1.00 first 2 pages, $.50 each add'l. No certification fee. Payee: Lynchburg General District Court. Personal checks accepted, credit cards are not. Prepayment required.

Civil Name Search: Access: Online, in person. Both court and visitors may perform in person name searches. No search fee. On computer 10 years. Public use terminal has civil records back to 10 years. Public terminal also has traffic cases. DOB or SSN not shown. **See details about online access at front or rear of this chapter.**

24th General District Court - Criminal Division 905 Court St, Public Safety Bldg, Lynchburg, VA 24504; 434-455-2630; fax: 434-847-1779; 8AM-4PM (EST). *Misdemeanor.*
www.courts.state.va.us
General Information: No juvenile, sealed records released. Will not fax documents. Court makes copy: $1.00 for first 2 pages, $.50 each add'l. No certification fee. Payee: Lynchburg General District Court. Personal checks, Visa/MC accepted. Prepayment required.
Criminal Name Search: Access: Online, in person. Visitors must perform in person searches themselves. Criminal records indexed in books and computer go back 10 years. Note: Mail access limited to specific cases only; no name searches. Public use terminal has crim records back to 10 years. **See details about online access at front or rear of this chapter.**

Madison County

16th Circuit Court PO Box 220, 1 Main St, Madison, VA 22727; 540-948-6888; fax: 540-948-3759; 8:30AM-4:30PM (EST). *Felony, Civil Actions over $4,500, Probate.*
www.courts.state.va.us/courts/circuit.html
General Information: No juvenile, sealed records released. Will not fax documents. Court makes copy: $.50 per page. Self serve copy: $.50 per page. Certification fee: $2.00. Payee: Clerk of Circuit Court. Personal checks accepted, credit cards are not. Prepayment required. Mail requests: SASE required.
Civil Name Search: Access: Mail, in person, online. Visitors must perform in person searches themselves. No search fee. Civil index on docket books from 1792, on computer since 1989. Mail turnaround time 1 week. **See details about online access at front or rear of this chapter.**
Criminal Name Search: Access: Mail, online, in person. Visitors must perform in person searches themselves. No search fee. Required to search: name, years to search, DOB; also helpful: SSN. Criminal records indexed in books from 1792, on computer since 1989. Mail turnaround time 1 week. Search free by name or case number at www.courts.state.va.us/. Results show address of subject but not DOB. Online results show middle initial.

16th General District Court 2 Main St, PO Box 470, Madison, VA 22727; 540-948-4657; fax: 540-948-5649; 8:30AM-4:30PM (EST). *Misdemeanor, Civil Actions under $25,000, Eviction, Small Claims.*
www.courts.state.va.us
General Information: The court does not provide a counter service for name searches. No juvenile, sealed or pre-trial records released. No fee to fax documents. Court makes copy: $1.00 first page, $.50 ea addl. No certification fee. Payee: Madison Combined Court. Personal checks, Visa/MC accepted. Prepayment required. Mail requests: SASE required.
Civil Name Search: Access: Phone, fax, mail, online. Only the court performs in person name searches; visitors may not. No search fee. Civil index on docket books and computer back to 2001. Mail turnaround time 3-4 days. **See details about online access at front or rear of this chapter.**
Criminal Name Search: Access: Phone, fax, mail, online. Only the court performs in person name searches; visitors may not. No search fee. Required to search: name, years to search, DOB; also helpful: address, SSN. Criminal records indexed in books and computer back to 1999. Mail turnaround time 3-4 days. **See details about online access at front or rear of this chapter.**

Manassas City
Circuit & District Courts - See Prince William County

Manassas Park City
Circuit & District Courts - See Prince William County

Martinsville City

21st Circuit Court PO Box 1206, Martinsville, VA 24114-1206; 276-403-5106; fax: 276-403-5232; 9AM-5PM (EST). *Felony, Civil Actions over $4,500, Probate.*
www.martinsville-va.gov/Circuit-Court-Clerk.html
General Information: Online identifiers in results same as on public terminal. No juvenile, sealed records released. Will fax documents for $1.00 per request. Court makes copy: $.50 per page. Self serve copy: same. Certification fee: $2.00. Payee: Clerk of Circuit Court. Personal checks, Visa/MC accepted. Prepayment required.
Civil Name Search: Access: Online, in person, mail. Visitors must perform in person searches themselves. Search fee: $1.00. Civil records on computer since 1988, on index books from 1942. Civil PAT goes back to 2002. **See details about online access at front or rear of this chapter.**
Criminal Name Search: Access: Online, in person, mail. Visitors must perform in person searches themselves. Search fee: $1.00. Required to search: name, years to search; also helpful: DOB, SSN. Criminal records on computer since 1988, on index books from 1942. Criminal PAT goes back to same as civil. **See details about online access at front or rear of this chapter.**

21st General District Court PO Box 1402, 55 W Church St, Martinsville, VA 24112; 276-403-5125; fax: 276-403-5114; 9AM-5PM (EST). *Misdemeanor, Civil Actions under $25,000, Eviction, Small Claims.*
www.courts.state.va.us/courts/gd/Martinsville/home.html
General Information: No sealed or expunged records released. Will not fax documents. Court makes copy: $.50 per page. No certification fee. Payee: Martinsville General Dist Ct. Personal checks, Visa/MC accepted. Prepayment required.
Civil Name Search: Access: Online, in person. Visitors must perform in person searches themselves. Civil records on computer back 10 years. Note: Public terminals available in County General District Court, 3160 Kings Mountain Rd, Martinsville, VA. **See details about online access at front or rear of this chapter.**
Criminal Name Search: Access: Online, in person. Visitors must perform in person searches themselves. Criminal records computerized for 10 years. Note: Public terminals available in County General District Court, 3160 Kings Mountain Rd, Martinsville, VA. **See details about online access at front or rear of this chapter.**

Mathews County

9th Circuit Court PO Box 463, Mathews, VA 23109; 804-725-2550; 8AM-4PM (EST). *Felony, Civil Actions over $4,500, Probate.*
www.courts.state.va.us/courts/circuit/Mathews/home.html
General Information: No juvenile, sealed records released. Will not fax documents. Court makes copy: $.50 per page. Certification fee: $2.00. Payee: Clerk of Circuit Court. Personal checks accepted, credit cards are not. Prepayment required.
Civil Name Search: Access: In person, online. Visitors must perform in person searches themselves. Civil index on docket books from 1800s. Public use terminal has civil records back to 7/1/2006. **See details about online access at front or rear of this chapter.**
Criminal Name Search: Access: In person, online. Visitors must perform in person searches themselves. Required to search: name, years to search; also helpful: DOB, SSN. Criminal records indexed in books from 1800s. Online access same as civil.

9th General District Court PO Box 169, Saluda, VA 23149; 804-758-4312; fax: 804-758-4343; 8:30AM-4PM (EST). *Misdemeanor, Civil Actions under $25,000, Eviction, Small Claims.*
www.courts.state.va.us/
General Information: The physical location is 10622 Buckley Hall Rd, Liberty Square, Mathews VA. No juvenile, sealed records released. Will not fax documents. Court makes copy: n/a. No certification fee. Payee: Clerk of General District Court. Personal checks, Visa/MC accepted. Prepayment required. Mail requests: SASE required.
Civil Name Search: Access: Mail, in person, online. Only the court performs in person name searches; visitors may not. No search fee. Civil cases indexed by defendant. Civil records on computer 10 years back. Mail turnaround time 7-10 days. **See details about online access at front or rear of this chapter.**
Criminal Name Search: Access: Mail, online, in person. Only the court performs in person name searches; visitors may not. No search fee. Required to search: name, years to search, DOB, date of offense; also helpful: SSN. Criminal records on computer 10 years back. Mail turnaround time 7-10 days. **See details about online access at front or rear of this chapter.**

Mecklenburg County

10th Circuit Court 393 Washington St, Courthouse, Boydton, VA 23917; 434-738-6191 x4220; civil phone: x4215; fax: 434-738-6861; 8:30AM-5PM (EST). *Felony, Civil Actions over $4,500, Probate.*
www.courts.state.va.us/courts/circuit/Mecklenburg/home.html
General Information: No juvenile, adoption, and sealed or direct indictments records released. Will fax specific case file data $1.00 per page to local or toll-free numbers, but only for ongoing accounts. Court makes copy: n/a. Self serve copy: $.50 per page. Certification fee: $2.00. Payee: Clerk of Circuit Court. Personal checks accepted, credit cards are not. Prepayment required.
Civil Name Search: Access: Online, in person. Visitors must perform in person searches themselves. Civil index on docket books from 1800s, on computer from 1988. Civil PAT goes back to 1988. **See details about online access at front or rear of this chapter.**
Criminal Name Search: Access: Online, in person. Visitors must perform in person searches themselves. Criminal records indexed in books from 1800s, on computer from 1988. Criminal PAT goes back to same as civil. **See details about online access at front or rear of this chapter.**

10th General District Court PO Box 306, 911 Madison St, Boydton, VA 23917; 434-738-6260; fax: 434-738-0761; 8:30AM-4:30PM (EST). *Misdemeanor, Civil Actions under $25,000, Eviction, Small Claims.*
www.courts.state.va.us/courts/gd/Mecklenburg/home.html

General Information: Online identifiers in results same as on public terminal. Sealed, and adoption records not released. Will fax documents $1.00 per page. Court makes copy: $.50 per page. No certification fee. Payee: Clerk of General District Court. Personal checks accepted. Credit cards accepted. Prepayment required. Mail requests: SASE required.

Civil Name Search: Access: Fax, mail, online, in person. Both court and visitors may perform in person name searches. Search fee: $5.00. Civil records on computer back 10 years. Mail turnaround time 2 days. Civil PAT goes back to 10 years. **See details about online access at front or rear of this chapter.**

Criminal Name Search: Access: Fax, mail, online, in person. Both court and visitors may perform in person name searches. Search fee: $5.00. Required to search: name, years to search; also helpful: DOB, SSN. Criminal records on computer ten years. Mail turnaround time 2 days. Criminal PAT goes back to 10 years. **See details about online access at front or rear of this chapter.**

Middlesex County

9th Circuit Court PO Box 158, 73 Bowden St, Saluda, VA 23149; 804-758-5317; fax: 804-758-8637; 8:30AM-4:30PM (EST). *Felony, Civil Actions over $4,500, Probate.* www.courts.state.va.us/courts/circuit.html

General Information: No juvenile, sealed records released. Will fax documents to local number only. Court makes copy: $.50 per page. Self serve copy: same. Certification fee: $2.00 per doc. Payee: Clerk of Circuit Court. Personal checks accepted, credit cards are not. Prepayment required.

Civil Name Search: Access: In person, online. Visitors must perform in person searches themselves. Civil index on docket books from 1672; on computer back to 1992. **See details about online access at front or rear of this chapter.**

Criminal Name Search: Access: In person, online. Visitors must perform in person searches themselves. Required to search: name, years to search, DOB, SSN. Criminal records indexed in books from 1674; on computer back to 1992. Public use terminal has crim records back to 2006. Online access same as civil. Online results show middle initial.

9th General District Court PO Box 169, 73 Bowden St, Saluda, VA 23149; 804-758-4312; fax: 804-758-4343; 8:30AM-4:30PM (EST). *Misdemeanor, Civil Actions under $25,000, Eviction, Small Claims.* www.courts.state.va.us/

General Information: No juvenile, sealed records released. Will not fax documents. Court makes copy: $1.00 per page. No certification fee. Payee: Clerk of General District Court. Personal checks, Visa/MC accepted. Prepayment required. Mail requests: SASE required.

Civil Name Search: Access: Mail, in person, online. Both court and visitors may perform in person name searches. No search fee. Civil cases indexed by defendant. Civil records held 10 years, computerized since 1997. Mail turnaround time 7-10 days. **See details about online access at front or rear of this chapter.**

Criminal Name Search: Access: Mail, online, in person. Only the court performs in person name searches; visitors may not. No search fee. Criminal records held 10 years, computerized since 1997. Mail turnaround time 7-10 days. **See details about online access at front or rear of this chapter.**

Montgomery County

27th Circuit Court 1 E. Main St. # B-5, Christiansburg, VA 24068; 540-382-5760; probate phone: 540-382-3384; fax: 540-382-6937; 8:30AM-4:30PM (EST). *Felony, Civil Actions over $4,500, Probate.* www.courts.state.va.us/courts/circuit.html

General Information: Search requests must be in writing and prepaid, and include SASE for return; call first to learn the copy fee. No juvenile, sealed records released. Will not fax documents. Court makes copy: $.50 per page. Self serve copy: same. Certification fee: $2.00 per doc. Payee: Clerk of Circuit Court. Personal checks, Visa/MC accepted. Prepayment required. Mail requests: SASE required.

Civil Name Search: Access: Phone, mail, online, in person. Both court and visitors may perform in person name searches. No search fee. Civil index on docket books from 1800s, on computer from 1/94. Note: Phone and mail access limited to cases filed 7/1993-to-present. Civil PAT goes back to 1994. **See details about online access at front or rear of this chapter.**

Criminal Name Search: Access: Online, in person. Visitors must perform in person searches themselves. Required to search: name, years to search; also helpful: DOB, SSN. Criminal records on computer since 9/93, prior in books. Criminal PAT goes back to 6/1993. **See details about online access at front or rear of this chapter.**

27th General District Court Montgomery County Courthouse, 1 E Main St, #201, Christiansburg, VA 24073; 540-382-5735; criminal phone: 540-394-2086; civil phone: 540-394-2085; fax: 540-382-6988; 8:30AM-4:30PM (EST). *Misdemeanor, Civil Actions under $25,000, Eviction, Small Claims.* www.courts.state.va.us

General Information: No juvenile records released. Will fax documents to local or toll-free number. Court makes copy: $.50 per page. No certification fee. Payee: Clerk General District Court. Personal checks accepted. Major credit cards accepted. Prepayment required. Mail requests: SASE required for mail return of any copies.

Civil Name Search: Access: Online, in person. Only the court performs in person name searches; visitors may not. Civil records on computerized records go back ten years. **See details about online access at front or rear of this chapter.** Separate searches required for Blacksburg or Christiansburg.

Criminal Name Search: Access: In person, online. Only the court performs in person name searches; visitors may not. Computerized records go back ten years. **See details about online access at front or rear of this chapter.** Separate searches required for Blacksburg or Christiansburg.

Nelson County

24th Circuit Court PO Box 10, Lovingston, VA 22949; 434-263-7020; fax: 434-263-7027; 8AM-5PM (EST). *Felony, Civil Actions over $4,500, Probate.* www.courts.state.va.us/courts/circuit.html

General Information: No juvenile, sealed records released. Will fax documents $1.00 1st page, $.50 ea add'l. Court makes copy: $.50 per page. Certification fee: $2.50. Payee: Clerk of Circuit Court. Personal checks accepted, credit cards are not. Prepayment required. Mail requests: SASE required for mail return of any copies.

Civil Name Search: Access: Online, in person. Visitors must perform in person searches themselves. Civil index on docket books from 1800s, deeds on computer from 7/93. **See details about online access at front or rear of this chapter.**

Criminal Name Search: Access: Online, in person. Visitors must perform in person searches themselves. Required to search: name, years to search; also helpful- DOB, SSN. Criminal records indexed in books from 1800s, deeds on computer from 7/93. **See details about online access at front or rear of this chapter.**

24th General District Court PO Box 514, 84 Courthouse Sq, County Courthouse, Lovingston, VA 22949; 434-263-7040; fax: 434-263-7033; 8AM-4PM (EST). *Misdemeanor, Civil Actions under $25,000, Eviction, Small Claims.* www.courts.state.va.us/

General Information: No sealed records released. No fee to fax documents. Court makes copy: $.50 per page. No certification fee. Payee: Clerk of General District Court. Personal checks accepted, credit cards are not. Prepayment required. Mail requests: SASE required.

Civil Name Search: Access: Fax, mail, online, in person. Both court and visitors may perform in person name searches. No search fee. Civil records on computer for 10 years. Mail turnaround time 3-4 days. **See details about online access at front or rear of this chapter.**

Criminal Name Search: Access: Fax, mail, online, in person. Both court and visitors may perform in person name searches. No search fee. Criminal records on computer for 10 years. Mail turnaround time 3-4 days. **See details about online access at front or rear of this chapter.**

New Kent County

9th Circuit Court PO Box 98, 12001 Court House Circle, New Kent, VA 23124; 804-966-9520; fax: 804-966-9528; 8:30AM-4:30PM (EST). *Felony, Civil Actions over $4,500, Probate.* www.courts.state.va.us/courts/circuit.html

General Information: No juvenile, sealed, adoption records released. Court makes copy: $.50 per page. Self serve copy: $.50 per page. Certification fee: $2.00. Payee: Circuit Court. Personal checks accepted, credit cards are not. Prepayment required.

Civil Name Search: Access: Online, in person. Visitors must perform in person searches themselves. Civil index on docket books from 1865, some on cards; computerized back to 1974; Chancery to 1976. Civil PAT goes back to 1990. **See details about online access at front or rear of this chapter.**

Criminal Name Search: Access: Online, in person. Visitors must perform in person searches themselves. Required to search: name, years to search, DOB, SSN. Criminal records indexed in books from 1923, some on cards; computerized back to 1985. Criminal PAT goes back to same as civil. **See details about online access at front or rear of this chapter.**

General District Court PO Box 127, 12001 Courthouse Circle, New Kent, VA 23124; 804-966-9530; fax: 804-966-9535; 8:30AM-4:30PM (EST). *Misdemeanor, Civil Actions under $25,000, Eviction, Small Claims, Traffic.*

www.courts.state.va.us/

General Information: In person requests are not processed on demand; SASE must be included for mail return within 10 days. No juvenile, sealed records released. Court makes copy: $1.00 first page, $.50 ea add'l. No certification fee. Payee: New Kent General District Court. Personal checks accepted. Credit cards accepted. Prepayment required. Mail requests: SASE required.

Civil Name Search: Access: Mail, in person, online. Only the court performs in person name searches; visitors may not. No search fee. Civil records go back 10 years. Mail turnaround time 10 days. **See details about online access at front or rear of this chapter.**

Criminal Name Search: Access: In person, online. Only the court performs in person name searches; visitors may not. No search fee. Required to search: name, years to search; also helpful: DOB and signed release. Criminal records go back 10 years. Note: Provide case number and SASE and written mail request and clerk will process. The sheriff's department or Commonwealth attorney are both alternative sources for criminal records. **See details about online access at front or rear of this chapter.**

Newport News City

7th Circuit Court 2500 Washington Ave, Newport News, VA 23607; 757-926-8561; fax: 757-926-8531; 8AM-4:30PM (EST). *Felony, Civil Actions over $4,500, Probate.*

www.courts.state.va.us/courts/circuit/Newport_News/home.html

General Information: No adoption, juvenile, sealed records released. Will not fax documents. Court makes copy: $.50 per page. Certification fee: $2.00. Payee: Clerk of Circuit Court. In state Personal checks, Visa/MC accepted. Prepayment required. Mail requests: SASE required for civil.

Civil Name Search: Access: Mail, in person, online. Both court and visitors may perform in person name searches. No search fee. Civil records on computer from 1987, prior on index books. Note: Mail access only available for old records. Mail turnaround time 1-2 days. Civil PAT goes back to 1987. **See details about online access at front or rear of this chapter.**

Criminal Name Search: Access: In person, online. Visitors must perform in person searches themselves. Criminal records computerized from 1987, on index books from 1985 to 1987, prior on judgment books. Note: The court requests that the public use the web page for name searches. Criminal PAT goes back to same as civil. **See details about online access at front or rear of this chapter.**

7th General District Court 2500 Washington Ave, Newport News, VA 23607; criminal phone: 757-926-8811; civil phone: 757-926-3520; fax: 757-926-8496; 7:30AM-4PM (EST). *Misdemeanor, Civil Actions under $25,000, Eviction, Small Claims.*

www.courts.state.va.us/

General Information: Online identifiers in results same as on public terminal. No juvenile, sealed records released. Court makes copy: $.50 per page. No certification fee. Payee: General District Court. Personal checks, Visa/MC accepted. Prepayment required.

Civil Name Search: Access: Phone, fax, mail, in person, online. Visitors must perform in person searches themselves. No search fee. Civil records go back to 10 years. Civil PAT goes back to 10 years. Partial, not full, DOB may appear. **See details about online access at front or rear of this chapter.**

Criminal Name Search: Access: Phone, fax, mail, online, in person. Both court and visitors may perform in person name searches. No search fee. Criminal records on computer back 10 years. Mail turnaround time varies. Criminal PAT goes back to same as civil. Partial, not full, DOB may appear. **See details about online access at front or rear of this chapter.** Traffic is a separate search. Online results show middle initial.

Norfolk City

4th Circuit Court 100 St Paul's Blvd, Norfolk, VA 23510; 757-664-4380; criminal phone: 757-664-4384; civil phone: 757-664-4387; probate phone: 757-664-4385; fax: 757-664-4581; 8:45AM-4:45PM (EST). *Felony, Civil Actions over $4,500, Probate.* www.icourt.info/

General Information: No juvenile, sealed records released. Will not fax documents. Court makes copy: $.50 per page. Certification fee: $2.00. Payee: Clerk of Circuit Court. Personal checks, Visa/MC accepted. Prepayment required.

Civil Name Search: Access: In person, online. Both court and visitors may perform in person name searches. Search fee: $10.00 if years to search prior to 1996, none if later. Civil records on computer back to 1996, docket books back to 1800s. S **See details about online access at front or rear of this chapter.** Also access record images via

http://208.210.219.102/cgi-bin/p/rms.cgi; registration and password required. Also, the Clerk of Circuit court subscription online system contains judgment records, wills, marriages, recorded documents etc. at www.norfolk.gov/Circuit_Court/remoteaccess.asp. Fee is $50 per month. Judgments, Wills, Marriages, etc back to 1993.

Criminal Name Search: Access: In person, online. Both court and visitors may perform in person name searches. Search fee: $10.00 if years to search prior to 1996, none if later. Required to search: name, years to search, DOB, SSN, signed release. Criminal records go back to 1972; on computer back to 1996, docket books back to 1800s. Online same as civil.

4th General District Court 811 E City Hall Ave, Norfolk, VA 23510; 757-664-4910; criminal phone: 757-664-4915/6; civil phone: 757-664-4913/4; 8AM-4:30PM (EST). *Misdemeanor, Civil Actions under $25,000, Eviction, Small Claims.*

www.courts.state.va.us/courts/gd/norfolk/home.html

General Information: No juvenile, sealed, or adoption records released. Court makes copy: $1.00 per page. Certification fee: none. Payee: Norfolk General District Court. Personal checks, Visa/MC accepted. Prepayment required.

Civil Name Search: Access: Mail, in person, online. Visitors must perform in person searches themselves. Search fee: $10.00 per name. Civil records in files, on computer back 10 years. Mail turnaround time 1-2 weeks. Civil PAT goes back to 1998. **See details about online access at front or rear of this chapter.**

Criminal Name Search: Access: Mail, online, in person. Visitors must perform in person searches themselves. Search fee: $10.00 per name. Criminal records in files, on computer back 10 years. Mail turnaround time 1-2 weeks. Criminal PAT goes back to 1998. **See details about online access at front or rear of this chapter.**

Northampton County

2nd Circuit Court PO Box 36, 5229 The Hornes, Eastville, VA 23347-0036; 757-678-0465; fax: 757-678-5410; 9AM-4:30PM (EST). *Felony, Civil Actions over $4,500, Probate.*

www.courts.state.va.us/courts/circuit.html

General Information: Court claims to have the oldest continuous records in the USA. Probate fax is same as main fax number. No juvenile, sealed records released. Will fax documents $1.00 per page. Court makes copy: $.50 per page. Self serve copy: same. Certification fee: $2.00 per instrument plus copy fee. Payee: Clerk of Circuit Court. Personal checks, Visa/MC accepted. Prepayment required. Mail requests: SASE required.

Civil Name Search: Access: Phone, fax, mail, online, in person. Both court and visitors may perform in person name searches. No search fee. Civil index on docket books from 1632; on computer back to 1993. Mail turnaround time 1 week. Civil PAT goes back to 7/1997. **See details about online access at front or rear of this chapter.**

Criminal Name Search: Access: Phone, mail, online, in person. Both court and visitors may perform in person name searches. No search fee. Required to search: name, years to search, DOB. Criminal records indexed in books from 1632; on computer back to 1993, some previous. Mail turnaround time 1 week. Criminal PAT goes back to same as civil. Online access to criminal index is same as civil. Online results show middle initial.

Northampton General District Court PO Box 1289, Eastville, VA 23347; 757-678-0466; 8:30AM-4:30PM (EST). *Misdemeanor, Civil Actions under $25,000, Eviction, Small Claims, Traffic.*

www.courts.state.va.us

General Information: Online identifiers in results same as on public terminal. Will not fax documents. Court makes copy: $1.00 first page, $.50 ea addl. No certification fee. Payee: General District Court. Personal checks accepted. No credit cards accepted for records or copies. Prepayment required. Mail requests: SASE required.

Civil Name Search: Access: Mail, in person, online. Both court and visitors may perform in person name searches. No search fee. Civil records on computer since 1990. Mail turnaround time 1-2 days. Civil PAT goes back to 1999. Results show address of subject and the day and month of birth, but not year. **See details about online access at front or rear of this chapter.**

Criminal Name Search: Access: Mail, online, in person. Both court and visitors may perform in person name searches. No search fee. Required to search: name, years to search, DOB or SSN. Criminal records on computer since 1990. Mail turnaround time 1-2 days. Criminal PAT goes back to 1999. Results show address of subject and the day and month of birth, but not year. **See details about online access at front or rear of this chapter.**

Northumberland County

15th Circuit Court PO Box 217, 39 Judicial Place, Heathsville, VA 22473; 804-580-3700; fax: 804-580-2261; 8:30AM-4:45PM (EST). *Felony, Civil Actions over $4,500, Probate.* www.courts.state.va.us/courts/circuit.html

General Information: No juvenile, sealed records released. Court makes copy: $.50 per page. Self serve copy: same. Certification fee: $2.00. Payee: Clerk of Circuit Court. Personal checks accepted, credit cards are not. Mail requests: SASE required.

Civil Name Search: Access: Mail, in person, online. Both court and visitors may perform in person name searches. No search fee. Civil index on docket books from 1650. Mail turnaround time 1-2 days. **See details about online access at front or rear of this chapter.**

Criminal Name Search: Access: Mail, online, in person. Both court and visitors may perform in person name searches. No search fee. Required to search: name, years to search, DOB. Criminal records indexed in books from 1650. Mail turnaround time 1-2 days. **See details about online access at front or rear of this chapter.**

Northumberland General District Court PO Box 114, 39 Judicial Pl, Northumberland Courthouse, Heathsville, VA 22473; 804-580-4323; fax: 804-580-6702; 8AM-4:30PM (EST). *Misdemeanor, Civil Actions under $25,000, Eviction, Small Claims.* www.courts.state.va.us

General Information: No juvenile, sealed records released. Will fax documents to local or toll-free number. Court makes copy: $.50 per page. No certification fee. Payee: Northumberland General District Court. Personal checks, Visa/MC accepted. Prepayment required. Mail requests: SASE required for mail return of any copies.

Civil Name Search: Access: Online, in person. Both court and visitors may perform in person name searches. No search fee. Civil records on computer back 10 years. Civil PAT goes back to 10 years. **See details about online access at front or rear of this chapter.**

Criminal Name Search: Access: Online, in person. Both court and visitors may perform in person name searches. No search fee. Required to search: name, years to search, DOB; also helpful: SSN. Criminal records on computer back 10 years. Criminal PAT goes back to same as civil. Terminal results show DOB as birth month and day only. **See details about online access at front or rear of this chapter.**

Norton City
Circuit & District Courts - See Wise County

Nottoway County

11th Circuit Court 328 W Courthouse Rd, Nottoway, VA 23955; 434-645-9043; fax: 434-645-2201; 8:30AM-4:30PM, stop recording at 4PM (EST). *Felony, Civil Actions over $4,500, Probate.* www.courts.state.va.us/

General Information: No juvenile, sealed records released. Will not fax documents. Court makes copy: $.50 per page. Self serve copy: same. Certification fee: $2.00. Payee: Clerk's Office. Personal checks accepted, credit cards are not. Prepayment required. Mail requests: SASE required for civil.

Civil Name Search: Access: Mail, in person, online. Both court and visitors may perform in person name searches. Search fee: $10.00 per hour. Civil index on docket books from late 1700s; on computer back to 2000. Civil PAT goes back to 2000. **See details about online access at front or rear of this chapter.**

Criminal Name Search: Access: In person, online. Visitors must perform in person searches themselves. Required to search: name, years to search; also helpful: DOB, SSN. Criminal records indexed in books from late 1700s; on computer back to 2000. Criminal PAT goes back to same as civil. **See details about online access at front or rear of this chapter.**

11th General District Court PO Box 25, 328 W Courthouse Rd, Nottoway, VA 23955; 434-645-9312; fax: 434-645-8584; 8AM-4:15PM (EST). *Misdemeanor, Civil Actions under $25,000, Eviction, Small Claims.* www.courts.state.va.us

General Information: No juvenile records released. Will not fax documents. Court makes copy: $1.00 first page, $.50 each add'l. No certification fee. Payee: Nottoway District Court. Personal checks, Visa/MC accepted. Prepayment required. Mail requests: SASE required.

Civil Name Search: Access: Mail, in person, online. Both court and visitors may perform in person name searches. No search fee. Civil index on computer the past 10 years. Mail turnaround time 10 days. **See details about online access at front or rear of this chapter.**

Criminal Name Search: Access: Mail, online, in person. Both court and visitors may perform in person name searches. No search fee. Required to search: name, years to search; also helpful: DOB, SSN. Criminal records on computer the past 10 years. Mail turnaround time 10 days. **See details about online access at front or rear of this chapter.**

Orange County

16th Circuit Court PO Box 230, Orange, VA 22960; 540-672-4030; fax: 540-672-2939; 8AM-5PM (EST). *Felony, Civil Actions over $4,500, Probate.* www.courts.state.va.us/courts/circuit.html

General Information: Probate fax is same as main fax number. No juvenile, sealed records released. Will not fax out documents. Court makes copy: $.50 per page. No certification fee. Payee: Clerk of Circuit Court. Personal checks accepted, credit cards are not. Prepayment required.

Civil Name Search: Access: Online, in person. Visitors must perform in person searches themselves. Civil records on computer since 1989, in index books from 1734 for deeds, from 1853 for births, from 1912 for marriages. Note: Court staff will not perform name searches. Civil PAT goes back to 2000. Search free by name or case number at www.courts.state.va.us/. Results may show few identifiers.

Criminal Name Search: Access: Phone, fax, mail, online, in person. Visitors must perform in person searches themselves. Required to search: name, years to search, DOB; also helpful: SSN. Criminal records on computer since 1989, in index books from 1734. Note: Court staff will not perform name searches. Mail turnaround time 1 week-10 days. Criminal PAT goes back to same as civil. **See details about online access at front or rear of this chapter.**

16th General District Court Orange County Courthouse,, PO Box 821, Orange, VA 22960; 540-672-3150; 8:30AM-4:30PM (EST). *Misdemeanor, Civil Actions under $25,000, Eviction, Small Claims.* www.courts.state.va.us

General Information: Online identifiers in results same as on public terminal. No juvenile, sealed records released. Will not fax documents. Court makes copy: $1.00 first page, $.50 each add'l. Certification fee: No charge. Payee: Clerk of District Court. In state checks accepted. Visa/MC accepted. Prepayment required.

Civil Name Search: Access: Mail, in person, online. Both court and visitors may perform in person name searches. No search fee. Civil index on docket books from 1800s, on computer from 1990. Mail turnaround time 1-2 days. Civil PAT goes back to Terminal shows the online system. **See details about online access at front or rear of this chapter.**

Criminal Name Search: Access: Mail, online, in person. Both court and visitors may perform in person name searches. No search fee. Required to search: name, years to search, DOB; also helpful: SSN. Criminal records indexed in books from 1800s, on computer from 1990. Mail turnaround time 1-2 days. Criminal PAT available. **See details about online access at front or rear of this chapter.**

Page County

26th Circuit Court 116 S Court St, #A, Luray, VA 22835; 540-743-4064; fax: 540-743-2338; 9AM-5PM (EST). *Felony, Civil Actions over $4,500, Probate.* www.courts.state.va.us/courts/circuit.html

General Information: Online identifiers in results same as on public terminal. No juvenile, sealed records released. Will fax documents after payment. Court makes copy: $.50 per page. Self serve copy: same. Certification fee: $2.00. Payee: Ron Wilson, Clerk. No 2-party checks accepted. No credit cards accepted. Prepayment required.

Civil Name Search: Access: Online, in person. Visitors must perform in person searches themselves. Civil index on docket books from 1831. Computerized records go back to 1995. Civil PAT goes back to 1995. Terminal also shows month and day of birth, but not year. **See details about online access at front or rear of this chapter.**

Criminal Name Search: Access: Online, in person. Visitors must perform in person searches themselves. Required to search: name, years to search, DOB; also helpful: SSN. Criminal records indexed in books from 1831. Computerized records go back to 1995. Criminal PAT goes back to same as civil. Only month and day of DOB appears, plus sex, race. **See details about online access at front or rear of this chapter.**

26th General District Court 116 S Court St, Luray, VA 22835; 540-743-5705; fax: 540-743-5334; 8AM-4:00PM (EST). *Misdemeanor, Civil Actions under $25,000, Eviction, Small Claims.* www.pagecounty.virginia.gov/

General Information: Online identifiers in results same as on public terminal. No sealed records released. Will fax documents to local or toll-free number. Court makes copy: $.50 per page. Self serve copy: same. Certification fee: $2.00 per page. Payee: District Court. Personal checks, Visa/MC accepted. Prepayment required. Mail requests: SASE requested.

Civil Name Search: Access: Mail, in person, online. Both court and visitors may perform in person name searches. No search fee. Civil records on computer go back 10 years. Mail turnaround time 7-10 days. Civil PAT goes back to 10 years. **See details about online access at front or rear of this chapter.**

Criminal Name Search: Access: Mail, online, in person. Both court and visitors may perform in person name searches. No search fee. Required to search: name, years to search; also helpful: DOB. Criminal records on computer go back 10 years. Mail turnaround time 7-10 days. Criminal PAT goes back to same as civil. **See details about online access at front or rear of this chapter.**

Patrick County

21st Circuit Court PO Box 148, Main St Courthouse, Stuart, VA 24171; 276-694-7213; fax: 276-694-6943; 9AM-5PM (EST). *Felony, Civil Actions over $4,500, Probate.* www.courts.state.va.us/courts/circuit.html
General Information: Records available in office from 4/7/02 to present for both civil and criminal. No juvenile, sealed records released. Will not fax documents. Court makes copy: $.50 per page. Self serve copy: same. Certification fee: $2.00. Payee: Clerk of Circuit Court. Personal checks accepted, credit cards are not. Prepayment required.
Civil Name Search: Access: In person, online. Visitors must perform in person searches themselves. Civil cases indexed by plaintiff. Civil index on docket books from 1791. **See details about online access at front or rear of this chapter.**
Criminal Name Search: Access: Online, in person. Visitors must perform in person searches themselves. Required to search: name, years to search; also helpful: DOB, SSN. Criminal records indexed in books from 1791. **See details about online access at front or rear of this chapter.**

21st General District Court PO Box 149, 106 Rucker St, #319, Stuart, VA 24171; 276-694-7258; fax: 276-694-5614; 8:30AM-5PM (EST). *Misdemeanor, Civil Actions under $25,000, Eviction, Small Claims.* www.courts.state.va.us/courts/gd/Patrick/home.html
General Information: The public access terminal is not in operation. Online identifiers in results same as on public terminal. No juvenile, sealed records released. Will not fax documents. Court makes copy: $.50 per page. No certification fee. Payee: Court. Personal checks, Visa/MC accepted. Mail requests: SASE requested.
Civil Name Search: Access: Mail, fax, online, in person. Only the court performs in person name searches; visitors may not. No search fee. Civil records go back on computer from 2000. Mail turnaround time 1 week. **See details about online access at front or rear of this chapter.**
Criminal Name Search: Access: Mail, online, in person. Only the court performs in person name searches; visitors may not. No search fee. Required to search: name, years to search, DOB; also helpful: SSN. Criminal records go back on computer from 2000. Mail turnaround time 1 week. **See details about online access at front or rear of this chapter.**

Petersburg City

11th Circuit Court 7 Courthouse Ave, Petersburg, VA 23803; 804-733-2367; fax: 804-732-5548; 8AM-4PM (EST). *Felony, Civil Actions over $4,500, Probate.* www.courts.state.va.us/courts/circuit.html
General Information: No juvenile, sealed or adoption records released. Will not fax documents. Court makes copy: $.50 per page. Self serve copy: same. Certification fee: $2.00. Payee: Petersburg Circuit Court Clerk. Personal checks accepted. Out of state checks not accepted. No credit cards accepted. Prepayment required. Mail requests: SASE required for mail return of any copies.
Civil Name Search: Access: In person, online. Visitors must perform in person searches themselves. Civil index on docket books back to 1784; on computer back to 1988. Public use terminal has civil records back to 10/88. **See details about online access at front or rear of this chapter.**
Criminal Name Search: Access: In person, online. Visitors must perform in person searches themselves. Required to search: name, years to search; also helpful: DOB, SSN. Criminal records go back to 1970; on computer back to 1996. **See details about online access at front or rear of this chapter.**

11th General District Court 35 E Tabb St, Petersburg, VA 23803; 804-733-2374; criminal phone: X4152; civil phone: X4153; fax: 804-733-2375; 8AM-4PM (EST). *Misdemeanor, Civil Actions under $25,000, Eviction, Small Claims.* www.courts.state.va.us/courts/gd/Petersburg/home.html
General Information: When faxing, put to attention of civil or criminal. No sealed records released. Will fax out documents. Court makes copy: $1.00 first 2 pages. $.50 each add'l. No certification fee. Payee: General District Court. In state Personal checks, Visa/MC accepted. Prepayment required. Mail requests: SASE required.
Civil Name Search: Access: Mail, in person, online. Both court and visitors may perform in person name searches. No search fee. Civil index on docket books back to 1999, computerized back 10 years. Mail turnaround time 1 week. Civil PAT goes back to 10 years. Public terminal available M,W,TH,F after 1PM. Results show partial address. **See details about online access at front or rear of this chapter.**
Criminal Name Search: Access: Mail, online, in person. Both court and visitors may perform in person name searches. No search fee. Required to search: name, years to search, DOB; also helpful: SSN. Criminal records

indexed on books for 10 years; on computer back ten years. Mail turnaround time 1 week. Criminal PAT goes back to 10 years. Public terminal available M,W,TH,F after 1PM. Results show partial address. **See details about online access at front or rear of this chapter.**

Pittsylvania County

22nd Circuit Court PO Box 31, 3 N Main St, Chatham, VA 24531; 434-432-7887; probate phone: 434-432-7892; fax: 434-432-7913; 8:30AM-5PM (EST). *Felony, Civil Actions over $4,500, Probate.* www.courts.state.va.us/courts/circuit.html
General Information: No juvenile, sealed records released. Will not fax documents. Court makes copy: $.50 per page. Self serve copy: same. If documents mailed, add $1.00 per page if SASE not included. Certification fee: $2.00. Payee: Clerk of Circuit Court. Personal checks accepted, credit cards are not. Prepayment required.
Civil Name Search: Access: In person, online. Visitors must perform in person searches themselves. No search fee. Civil index on docket books back to 1767; computerized records since 1995. Civil PAT goes back to 1995. **See details about online access at front or rear of this chapter.**
Criminal Name Search: Access: In person, online. Visitors must perform in person searches themselves. No search fee. Required to search: name, years to search, DOB, SSN. Criminal records indexed in books back to 1767; computerized records since 1995. Criminal PAT goes back to 1995. **See details about online access at front or rear of this chapter.**

22nd General District Court PO Box 695, Courthouse Annex, 11 Bank St Ste 201, Chatham, VA 24531; 434-432-7880; fax: 434-432-7915; 8:30AM-4:30PM (EST). *Misdemeanor, Civil Actions under $25,000, Eviction, Small Claims, Traffic.* www.courts.state.va.us/courts/gd/Pittsylvania/home.html
General Information: No juvenile records released. Will not fax documents. Court makes copy: $.50 per page. No certification fee. Payee: General District Court. Personal checks accepted. Major credit cards accepted. Prepayment required.
Civil Name Search: Access: Online, in person. Visitors must perform in person searches themselves. Civil records on computer for 10 years. Civil PAT goes back to 10 years. **See details about online access at front or rear of this chapter.**
Criminal Name Search: Access: Online, in person. Visitors must perform in person searches themselves. Criminal records on computer for 10 years. Criminal PAT goes back to 10 years. **See details about online access at front or rear of this chapter.**

Poquoson City
Circuit & District Courts - See York County

Portsmouth City

Circuit Court PO Drawer 1217, 601 Crawford St, Portsmouth, VA 23705; 757-393-8671; criminal phone: x5143; civil phone: x5129; probate phone: x5127; fax: 757-399-4826; 8:30AM-4:30PM (EST). *Felony, Civil Actions over $4,500, Probate.* www.courts.state.va.us/courts/circuit.html
General Information: No juvenile, sealed records released. Will not fax documents. Court makes copy: $.50 per page. Self serve copy: same. Certification fee: $2.00. Payee: Cynthia P Morrison, Clerk. Business checks accepted. No credit cards accepted. Prepayment required.
Civil Name Search: Access: Mail, in person, online. Visitors must perform in person searches themselves. Search fee: $10.00 per name. Civil records on computer back to 6/1987, prior on index books back to 1858. Note: Phone access limited to simple requests. Mail turnaround time 2 weeks. Civil PAT goes back to 2002. **See details about online access at front or rear of this chapter.**
Criminal Name Search: Access: Mail, online, in person. Both court and visitors may perform in person name searches. Search fee: $10.00 per name. Required to search: name, years to search, DOB; also helpful: SSN. Criminal records computerized from 2002, prior indexed on books back to 1858. Mail turnaround time 72 hours for records before 2000. Criminal PAT goes back to same as civil. **See details about online access at front or rear of this chapter.**

General District Court PO Box 129, Portsmouth, VA 23705; criminal phone: 757-393-8681; civil phone: 757-393-8624; criminal fax: 757-393-8634; civil fax: 8:30AM-4:30PM; 8:30AM-4:30PM (EST). *Misdemeanor, Civil Actions under $25,000, Eviction, Small Claims.* www.courts.state.va.us/
General Information: Traffic Division: 757-393-8506. Juvenile, sealed records not released. Will not fax documents. Court makes copy: $1.00 1st copy, $.50 each add'l copy. No certification fee. Payee: General District Court. Personal checks accepted. Credit cards accepted. Prepayment required. Mail requests: SASE required for criminal.
Civil Name Search: Access: Online, in person. Visitors must perform in person searches themselves. Civil records on computer from 1999. Civil

PAT goes back to 2000. **See details about online access at front or rear of this chapter.**

Criminal Name Search: Access: Mail, fax, online, in person. Visitors must perform in person searches themselves. Search fee: None, will charge the copy fee. Required to search: name, years to search; also helpful: DOB, SSN. Criminal records on computer and case (paper files) maintained for 10 years. Mail turnaround time within 14 days. Criminal PAT goes back to same as civil. **See details about online access at front or rear of this chapter.**

Powhatan County

11th Circuit Court PO Box 37, Powhatan, VA 23139-0037; 804-598-5660; fax: 804-598-5608; 8:30AM-5PM (EST). *Felony, Civil Actions over $4,500, Probate.*
www.courts.state.va.us/courts/circuit.html
General Information: Probate records are in a separate index. Probate fax is same as main fax number. Online identifiers in results same as on public terminal. No juvenile, sealed records released. Will not fax documents. Court makes copy: $.50 per page. Self serve copy: same. Certification fee: $2.00 per document. Payee: Clerk of Court. Personal checks accepted, credit cards are not. Prepayment required.
Civil Name Search: Access: In person, online. Visitors must perform in person searches themselves. Civil index on docket books from 1777, on computer from 1993. Civil PAT goes back to 1993. **See details about online access at front or rear of this chapter.**
Criminal Name Search: Access: In person, online. Visitors must perform in person searches themselves. Required to search: name, years to search, signed release; also helpful: SSN. Criminal records indexed in books from 1777, on computer from 1993. Criminal PAT goes back to same as civil. **See details about online access at front or rear of this chapter.**

11th General District Court Courthouse, 3880 Old Buckingham Rd, Powhatan, VA 23139; 804-598-5665; fax: 804-598-5648; 8:30AM-4:30PM (EST). *Misdemeanor, Civil Actions under $25,000, Eviction, Small Claims.*
www.courts.state.va.us
General Information: No juvenile, sealed records released. Will fax documents to local or toll-free number. Court makes copy: $.50 per page. No certification fee. Payee: Powhatan District Court. Personal checks accepted. Credit cards accepted. Prepayment required.
Civil Name Search: Access: Phone, fax, mail, online, in person. Only the court performs in person name searches; visitors may not. No search fee. Civil cases indexed by plaintiff, defendant. 10 years. Mail turnaround time 1 week. **See details about online access at front or rear of this chapter.**
Criminal Name Search: Access: Phone, fax, mail, online, in person. Only the court performs in person name searches; visitors may not. No search fee. Required to search: name, years to search, DOB; also helpful: SSN. 10 years. Mail turnaround time 1 week. **See details about online access at front or rear of this chapter.**

Prince Edward County

Circuit Court PO Box 304, North Main St, Farmville, VA 23901-0304; 434-392-5145; fax: 434-392-3913; 8:30AM-4:30PM (EST). *Felony, Civil Actions over $4,500, Probate.*
www.courts.state.va.us/courts/circuit/Prince_Edward/home.html
General Information: No juvenile, sealed records released. Will not fax documents. Court makes copy: $.50 per page; court may charge for the time to make copies. Self serve copy: $.50 per page. Certification fee: $2.00. Payee: Clerk of Circuit Court. Personal checks, Visa/MC accepted. Prepayment required.
Civil Name Search: Access: Online, in person. Visitors must perform in person searches themselves. Civil records on computer from 1990, books from 1930s. Civil PAT goes back to 1990. 5 public access terminals available. **See details about online access at front or rear of this chapter.**
Criminal Name Search: Access: Online, in person. Visitors must perform in person searches themselves. Required to search: name, years to search, DOB; also helpful: SSN. Criminal records computerized from 1990, books from 1930s. Criminal PAT goes back to same as civil. 5 public access terminals available. **See details about online access at front or rear of this chapter.**

General District Court PO Box 41, Farmville, VA 23901-0041; 434-392-4024; fax: 434-392-3800; 8:30AM-4:30PM (EST). *Misdemeanor, Civil Actions under $25,000, Eviction, Small Claims.*
www.courts.state.va.us/
General Information: No juvenile, sealed records released. Will fax documents $1.00 per page. Court makes copy: $1.00 per page. Self serve copy: same. No certification fee. Payee: Clerk of District Court. Personal checks, Visa/MC accepted. Prepayment required. Mail requests: SASE required.

Civil Name Search: Access: Phone, mail, online, in person. Visitors must perform in person searches themselves. No search fee. Required to search: name, years to search; also helpful: address. Civil records on computer go back 10 years. Civil PAT goes back to 10 years. **See details about online access at front or rear of this chapter.**
Criminal Name Search: Access: Mail, online, in person. Visitors must perform in person searches themselves. No search fee. Required to search: name, years to search; also helpful: DOB, SSN. Criminal records on computer go back 10 years. Mail turnaround time 1 week. Criminal PAT goes back to same as civil. **See details about online access at front or rear of this chapter.**

Prince George County

Circuit Court PO Box 98, 6601 Courts Dr, Prince George, VA 23875; 804-733-2640; fax: 804-861-5721; 8:30AM-5PM (EST). *Felony, Civil Actions over $4,500, Probate.*
www.courts.state.va.us/courts/circuit.html
General Information: No juvenile or sealed records released. Will not fax documents. Court makes copy: $.50 per page. Self serve copy: same. Certification fee: $2.00. Payee: Clerk of the Circuit Court. Personal checks accepted, credit cards are not. Prepayment required.
Civil Name Search: Access: Online, in person. Visitors must perform in person searches themselves. Civil index on docket books since 1930s, computerized since 4/96. Civil PAT goes back to 1996. **See details about online access at front or rear of this chapter.**
Criminal Name Search: Access: Online, in person. Visitors must perform in person searches themselves. Required to search: name, years to search, DOB; also helpful: SSN. Criminal records indexed in books since 1930s, computerized since 1/90. Criminal PAT goes back to 1990. **See details about online access at front or rear of this chapter.**

6th General District Court PO Box 187, 6601 Courts Dr, Prince George, VA 23875; 804-733-2783; fax: 804-733-2678; 8:30AM-4:30PM (EST). *Misdemeanor, Civil Actions under $25,000, Eviction, Small Claims.*
www.courts.state.va.us/courts/combined/Prince_George/home.html
General Information: No juvenile records released. Will not fax out documents. Court makes copy: $1.00 each first 2 pages. $.50 each add'l. No certification fee. Payee: Prince George Combined Court. Personal checks accepted, credit cards are not.
Civil Name Search: Access: Online, in person. Visitors must perform in person searches themselves. Civil records on computer for 10 years. Civil PAT goes back to 10 years. **See details about online access at front or rear of this chapter.**
Criminal Name Search: Access: Online, in person. Visitors must perform in person searches themselves. Required to search: name, years to search; also helpful: SSN. Criminal records on computer for 10 years. Criminal PAT goes back to same as civil. **See details about online access at front or rear of this chapter.**

Prince William County

31st Circuit Court 9311 Lee Ave, Rm 306, Judicial Center, Manassas, VA 20110; 703-792-6015; criminal phone: 703-792-6025; civil phone: 703-792-6029; probate phone: 703-792-5587; criminal fax: 703-792-4721; civil fax: 8:30AM-5PM; 8:30AM-5PM (EST). *Felony, Civil Actions over $4,500, Probate.* www.pwcgov.org/default.aspx?topic=04005200251
General Information: Also hears Misdemeanor appeals. No juvenile or adoption records released. Will not fax documents. Court makes copy: $.50 per page. Certification fee: $2.00 per document plus copy fee. Payee: Clerk of Circuit Court. Personal checks accepted. Visa/MC accepted in near future. Prepayment required.
Civil Name Search: Access: In person, online. Visitors must perform in person searches themselves. Civil records on computer since 1989; prior on microfiche or books to 1939. Civil PAT goes back to 1989. **See details about online access at front or rear of this chapter.**
Criminal Name Search: Access: Mail, in person, online. Visitors must perform in person searches themselves. Required to search: name, years to search, DOB. Criminal records on computer since 1989; prior on microfiche or books to 1939. Mail turnaround time 1 week. Criminal PAT goes back to same as civil. **See details about online access at front or rear of this chapter..**

31st General District Court 9311 Lee Ave, Manassas, VA 20110; criminal phone: 703-792-6141; civil phone: 703-792-6149; criminal fax: 703-792-6121; civil fax: 8AM-4PM; 8AM-4PM (EST). *Misdemeanor, Civil Actions under $25,000, Eviction, Small Claims.*
www.courts.state.va.us/courts/gd/Prince_William/home.html
General Information: Online identifiers in results same as on public terminal. No juvenile or sealed records released. Court makes copy: $1.00 first 2 pages. $.50 each add'l. No certification fee. Payee: Clerk G.D.C. Personal checks accepted. Visa/MC accepted for traffic only. Prepayment required. Mail requests: SASE required.

Civil Name Search: Access: Mail, fax, online, in person. Both court and visitors may perform in person name searches. No search fee. Civil records on computer go back 10 years. Mail turnaround time 10 days. Civil PAT goes back to 10 years. **See details about online access at front or rear of this chapter.**
Criminal Name Search: Access: Mail, fax, online, in person. Both court and visitors may perform in person name searches. No search fee. Criminal records on computer go back 10 years. Mail turnaround time 10 days. Criminal PAT goes back to same as civil. **See details about online access at front or rear of this chapter.**

Pulaski County

Circuit Court 45 3rd St NW, #101, Pulaski, VA 24301; 540-980-7825; fax: 540-980-7835; 8:30AM-4:30PM (EST). *Felony, Civil Actions over $4,500, Probate.*
www.courts.state.va.us/courts/circuit/pulaski/home.html
General Information: Online identifiers in results same as on public terminal. No juvenile, sealed records released. Will fax documents $1.00 per page. Court makes copy: $1.00 per page. Self serve copy: $.50 per page. Certification fee: $1.00. Payee: Clerk of Court. Personal checks accepted, credit cards are not. Prepayment required. Mail requests: SASE required for mail return of any copies.
Civil Name Search: Access: Online, in person. Visitors must perform in person searches themselves. Civil index on docket books from 1839, online since 1998. Civil PAT goes back to 1998. Only month and day of DOB appears, plus sex, race. Online access to court records is $300 annual fee http://records.pulaskicircuitcourt.com/icris/splash.jsp. Registration required; search by name, document type or number. **Also see details about online access at front or rear of this chapter..**
Criminal Name Search: Access: Online, in person. Visitors must perform in person searches themselves. Required to search: name, years to search, DOB; also helpful: SSN. Criminal records indexed in books from 1839, online since 1998. Note: This agency will perform no record checks and refer all requests to the State Police. Results include file number. Criminal PAT goes back to same as civil. Only month and day of DOB appears, plus sex, race. Online access to court records is $300 annual fee http://records.pulaskicircuitcourt.com/icris/splash.jsp. Registration required; search by name, document type or number. **Also see details about online access at front or rear of this chapter.**

27th General District Court 45 3rd St NW, #102, Pulaski, VA 24301; 540-980-7470; fax: 540-980-7792; 8:30AM-4:30PM (EST). *Misdemeanor, Civil Actions under $25,000, Eviction, Small Claims.*
www.courts.state.va.us/courts/gd/Pulaski/home.html
General Information: No juvenile, sealed records released. Will not fax documents. Court makes copy: n/a. No certification fee. Payee: Clerk of General District Court. Personal checks accepted. Credit cards accepted. Prepayment required.
Civil Name Search: Access: Online, in person. Visitors must perform in person searches themselves. Civil records on computer since 1996. Civil PAT goes back to 10 years. **See details about online access at front or rear of this chapter.**
Criminal Name Search: Access: Online, in person. Visitors must perform in person searches themselves. Required to search: name, years to search, DOB; also helpful: SSN. Criminal records on computer 10 years. Criminal PAT goes back to same as civil. **See details about online access at front or rear of this chapter.**

Radford City

27th Circuit Court 619 2nd St, Radford, VA 24141; 540-731-3610; fax: 540-731-3612; 8:30AM-5PM; no transaction- 4:30PM (EST). *Felony, Civil Actions over $4,500, Probate.*
www.courts.state.va.us/courts/circuit.html
General Information: Online identifiers in results same as on public terminal. No juvenile, sealed or adoption records released. Will fax documents no add'l fee. Court makes copy: $.50 per page. Self serve copy: same. Certification fee: $2.00. Payee: Radford Circuit Court. Personal checks accepted. Major credit cards accepted. Prepayment required. Mail requests: SASE required.
Civil Name Search: Access: Fax, mail, online, in person. Both court and visitors may perform in person name searches. No search fee. Civil records on books from 1892; on computer back to 6/2000. Mail turnaround time same day. Civil PAT goes back to 1996. Only month and day of DOB appears, plus sex, race. **See details about online access at front or rear of this chapter.**
Criminal Name Search: Access: Fax, mail, online, in person. Both court and visitors may perform in person name searches. No search fee. Required to search: name, years to search, DOB, signed release; also helpful: SSN. Criminal docket on books from 1892; on computer back to 6/2000. Mail turnaround time same day. Criminal PAT goes back to 1996. Only

month and day of DOB appears, plus sex, race. **See details about online access at front or rear of this chapter.**

27th General District Court 619 2nd St, Radford, VA 24141; 540-731-3609; fax: 540-731-3692; 8:30AM-4:30PM (EST). *Misdemeanor, Civil Actions under $25,000, Eviction, Small Claims.*
www.courts.state.va.us/courts/combined/Radford/home.html
General Information: Online identifiers in results same as on public terminal. No juvenile, sealed records released. Will fax documents $.50 per page. Court makes copy: $.50 per page. Self serve copy: same. No certification fee. Payee: District Court. Personal checks, Visa/MC accepted. Prepayment required.
Civil Name Search: Access: Mail, in person, online. Both court and visitors may perform in person name searches. Search fee: A search fee may be required. Civil records go back 10 years. Mail turnaround time 7 days or longer. Civil PAT goes back to 10 years. **See details about online access at front or rear of this chapter.**
Criminal Name Search: Access: Fax, mail, online, in person. Both court and visitors may perform in person name searches. Search fee: None, unless it is a lengthy search. Required to search: name, years to search, DOB, SSN, signed release. Criminal records on computer 10 years. Mail turnaround time 7 days or longer. Criminal PAT goes back to same as civil. Terminal results include a partial address. **See details about online access at front or rear of this chapter.** Online results show middle initial, DOB.

Rappahannock County

20th Circuit Court PO Box 517, 238 Gay St, Washington, VA 22747; 540-675-5350; 8:30AM-4:30PM (EST). *Felony, Civil Actions over $4,500, Probate.* www.courts.state.va.us/courts/circuit.html
General Information: No juvenile, sealed records released. Court makes copy: $.50 per page. Self serve copy: same. Certification fee: $2.50 per document. Payee: Clerk of the Circuit Court. Personal checks accepted, credit cards are not. Prepayment required. Mail requests: SASE required.
Civil Name Search: Access: Mail, in person, online. Visitors must perform in person searches themselves. No search fee. Civil records computerized since 1995, on index cards from 1833, early records archived. Note: Mail access limited to specific cases only. Court will only do searches as time permits. Civil PAT goes back to 1995. **See details about online access at front or rear of this chapter.**
Criminal Name Search: Access: Mail, online, in person. Visitors must perform in person searches themselves. Search fee: Searches performed only as time permits. Required to search: name, years to search; also helpful: DOB, SSN. Criminal records computerized since 1995, on index cards from 1833, early records archived. Note: Mail access limited to specific cases only. Mail turnaround time 1-2 days. Criminal PAT goes back to same as civil. **See details about online access at front or rear of this chapter.**

20th District Combined Court PO Box 206, 250 Gay St, Washington, VA 22747; 540-675-5356; fax: 540-675-5357; 8AM-4PM M-F (EST). *Misdemeanor, Civil Actions under $25,000, Eviction, Small Claims.*
www.courts.state.va.us/
General Information: No juvenile, sealed records released. Will not fax documents. Court makes copy: $1.00 per page. No certification fee. Payee: Clerk of General District Court. Personal checks accepted. Credit cards accepted. Prepayment required. Mail requests: SASE requested.
Civil Name Search: Access: Mail, in person, online. Both court and visitors may perform in person name searches. No search fee. Civil records on computer back to 1994, on index cards back to 1990, prior in Circuit Court. Note: Court staff will only do name searches if time permitting. Do not count on regularity. Mail turnaround time up to 2 weeks. **See details about online access at front or rear of this chapter.**
Criminal Name Search: Access: Mail, online, in person. Both court and visitors may perform in person name searches. No search fee. Required to search: name, years to search, DOB; also helpful: SSN, signed release. Criminal records computerized from 1994, index cards back to 1985, prior in Circuit Court. Note: Court staff will only do name searches if time permitting. Do not count on regularity. Mail turnaround time up to 2 weeks. **See details about online access at front or rear of this chapter.**

Richmond County

15th Circuit Court PO Box 1000, 101 Court Cir,, Warsaw, VA 22572; 804-333-3781; fax: 804-333-5396; 9AM-5PM (EST). *Felony, Civil Actions over $4,500, Probate.*
www.courts.state.va.us/courts/circuit.html
General Information: Do not confuse Richmond County (here) with Richmond City. Probate fax is same as main fax number. No juvenile, sealed records released. Will fax documents to local or toll free line. Court makes copy: $.50 per page; $1.00 per page if genealogy records. Self serve copy: same. Certification fee: $2.00 per document. Payee: Clerk of Circuit Court.

Personal checks accepted, credit cards are not. Prepayment required. Mail requests: SASE required.

Civil Name Search: Access: Phone, mail, in person, online. Both court and visitors may perform in person name searches. No search fee. Required to search: name, years to search; also helpful: address, SSN. Civil records archived from 1692. Mail turnaround time same day. Civil PAT goes back to 2000. **See details about online access at front or rear of this chapter.**

Criminal Name Search: Access: Mail, in person, online. Both court and visitors may perform in person name searches. No search fee. Required to search: name, years to search, DOB; also helpful: address. Criminal records archived from 1692, computerized since 1994. Mail turnaround time same day. Criminal PAT goes back to 2000. **See details about online access at front or rear of this chapter.**

15th General District Court PO Box 1000, County Courthouse,, 201 Court Circle, Warsaw, VA 22572; 804-333-4616; fax: 804-333-3741; 8AM-4:30PM (EST). *Misdemeanor, Civil Actions under $25,000, Eviction, Small Claims.* www.courts.state.va.us/

General Information: No juvenile, sealed records released. Will not fax documents. Court makes copy: $.50 per page. No certification fee. Personal checks, Visa/MC accepted. Mail requests: SASE requested.

Civil Name Search: Access: Mail, in person, online. Both court and visitors may perform in person name searches. No search fee. Civil records archived 10 years back; on computer from 1994. Mail turnaround time 2 days. Civil PAT goes back to 10 years. **See details about online access at front or rear of this chapter.**

Criminal Name Search: Access: Mail, online, in person. Both court and visitors may perform in person name searches. No search fee. Required to search: name, years to search; also helpful: DOB, SSN. Criminal records archived 10 years back; on computer from 1994. Mail turnaround time 2 days. Criminal PAT goes back to same as civil. **See details about online access at front or rear of this chapter.**

Richmond City

13th Circuit Court John Marshall Courts Bldg, 400 N 9th St, Richmond, VA 23219; 804-646-6505; criminal phone: 804-646-6553; civil phone: 804-646-6536; fax: 804-646-6562; 8:45AM-4:45PM (EST). *Felony, Civil Actions over $4,500, Probate.*
www.courts.state.va.us/courts/circuit/Richmond/home.html

General Information: This court now holds records from the Manchester Division Courthouse which has been closed 4/9/07. No juvenile, sealed records released. Will not fax documents. Court makes copy: $.50 per page. Certification fee: $2.00 per cert. Payee: Bevill M Dean, Clerk. Personal checks accepted. Major credit cards accepted. Prepayment required.

Civil Name Search: Access: Mail, fax, online, in person. Visitors must perform in person searches themselves. No search fee. Civil records on computer from 1989. On microfilm from 1980, on card index from 1970s, on index books from 1800s. Mail turnaround time 1-5 days Civil PAT goes back to 1987. **See details about online access at front or rear of this chapter.**

Criminal Name Search: Access: Mail, fax, online, in person. Visitors must perform in person searches themselves. No search fee. Required to search: name, years to search; also helpful: DOB, SSN. Criminal records computerized from 1987. On microfilm from 1980, on card index from 1970s, on index books from 1782. Mail turnaround time is 1-5 days. Criminal PAT goes back to same as civil. **See details about online access at front or rear of this chapter.**

13th General District Court - Manchester Division II 920 Hall St, Richmond, VA 23224; 804-646-8990; fax: 804-646-0387; 8AM-4PM (EST). *Misdemeanor, Traffic.*
www.courts.state.va.us/

General Information: No juvenile, sealed records released. Will not fax documents. Court makes copy: $1.00 per page. Payee: Clerk of General District Court. Personal checks, Visa/MC accepted. Prepayment required.

Criminal Name Search: Access: Mail, online, in person. Both court and visitors may perform in person name searches. No search fee. Required to search: name, years to search, DOB; also helpful: SSN. Criminal records computerized from 1986, records prior to 1980 destroyed. Mail turnaround time 1-5 days. Public use terminal has crim records back to 1986. **See details about online access at front or rear of this chapter.**

13th Jud Dist - General District Court - Civil Division 400 N 9th St, Rm 203, Richmond, VA 23219; 804-646-6461; fax: 804-646-8758; 8AM-4PM (EST). *Civil Actions up to $25,000, Eviction, Small Claims.*
www.courts.state.va.us/

General Information: Online identifiers in results same as on public terminal. No juvenile, sealed records released. Will not fax out documents. Court makes copy: $.50 per page. Certification fee: $3.00 for first 6 pages then $.50 ea add'l page. Payee: Clerk of General District Court, Civil

Division. Business checks accepted. Visa/MC accepted. Prepayment required. Mail requests: SASE required.

Civil Name Search: Access: Phone, mail, online, in person. Both court and visitors may perform in person name searches. No search fee. Required to search: name. Civil records computerized since 1994. Civil judgment files are purged after 10 years. Mail turnaround time 1-2 days. Public use terminal has civil records back to 10 years. **ee details about online access at front or rear of this chapter.**

13th Circuit Court Manchester - Div 2 Court closed - see Richmond City 13th Circuit Court - Division I.

Roanoke County

23rd Circuit Court PO Box 1126, 305 E Main St, Salem, VA 24153-1126; 540-387-6205; fax: 540-387-6145; 8:30AM-4:30PM (EST). *Felony, Civil Actions over $4,500, Probate.*
www.roanokecountyva.gov

General Information: No juvenile, sealed records released. Will not fax documents. Court makes copy: $.50 per page. Certification fee: $2.00. Payee: Clerk of Circuit Court. Personal checks accepted, credit cards are not. Prepayment required.

Civil Name Search: Access: Online, in person. Visitors must perform in person searches themselves. Civil records on computer from 1986, on index books from 1838 to 1986, prior records to Botetourt County. Civil PAT goes back to 1986. Public terminal at the Roanoke County Courthouse. **See details about online access at front or rear of this chapter.**

Criminal Name Search: Access: Online, in person. Visitors must perform in person name searches themselves. Required to search: name, years to search, DOB; also helpful: SSN. Criminal records computerized from 1986, on index books from 1838 to 1986, prior records to Botetourt County. Criminal PAT goes back to same as civil. Public terminal at the City of Salem Courthouse. **See details about online access at front or rear of this chapter.**

23rd General District Court PO Box 997, Salem, VA 24153; 540-387-6168; fax: 540-387-6066; 8:15AM-4:15PM (EST). *Misdemeanor, Civil Actions under $25,000, Eviction, Small Claims.*
www.courts.state.va.us/courts/gd/Roanoke_County/home.html

General Information: The court provides no means to do a name search of the criminal docket other than online. No sealed records released. Will fax documents to local numbers only. Court makes copy: $.50 per page. No certification fee. Payee: General. Personal checks, Visa/MC accepted. Prepayment required. Mail requests: SASE required.

Civil Name Search: Access: Mail, in person, online. Both court and visitors may perform in person name searches. No search fee. Required to search: name, years to search, written request for staff to research. Computerized records the past 10 years, on index cards from 1980. Prior at Circuit Court or Archives. Mail turnaround time 5 days. **See details about online access at front or rear of this chapter.**

Criminal Name Search: Access: online only. Both court and visitors may perform in person name searches. Required to search: name, years to search, DOB, written request for staff to research; also helpful: SSN. Computerized records the past 10 years, on index cards from 1980. Prior at Circuit Court or Archives. Mail turnaround time 5 days. **See details about online access at front or rear of this chapter.**

Roanoke City

23rd Circuit Court PO Box 2610, Roanoke, VA 24010-2610; criminal phone: 540-853-6723; civil phone: 540-853-6702; probate phone: 540-853-6712; criminal fax: 540-853-1024; civil fax: 8:15AM-4:45PM; 8:15AM-4:45PM (EST). *Felony, Civil Actions over $4,500, Probate.*
www.roanokeva.gov/85256A8D0062AF37/CurrentBaseLink/N254MHW7086JCRTEN

General Information: No juvenile, sealed records released. Will not fax documents. Court makes copy: $.50 per page. Self serve copy: same. Certification fee: $2.00. Payee: Clerk of Circuit Court. Personal checks accepted. Visa/MC accepted - 4% surcharge. Prepayment required.

Civil Name Search: Access: Mail, in person, online. Visitors must perform in person searches themselves. No search fee. Civil records on computer from 1986, on microfiche from 1884. Mail turnaround time 1 week Civil PAT goes back to late 1986 (index). **See details about online access at front or rear of this chapter.**

Criminal Name Search: Access: Mail, online, in person. Visitors must perform in person searches themselves. No search fee. Required to search: name, years to search, DOB; also helpful: SSN. Criminal records computerized from 1985, criminal on index books from 1800s. Mail turnaround time is 1 week. Criminal PAT goes back to 1986 (index). No document images. **See details about online access at front or rear of this chapter.**

General District Court 315 W Church Ave, 2nd Fl, Roanoke, VA 24016-5007; criminal phone: 540-853-2361; civil phone: 540-853-2364; criminal fax: 540-853-2487; civil fax: 8AM-4PM; 8AM-4PM (EST). *Misdemeanor, Civil Actions under $25,000, Eviction, Small Claims, Traffic.* www.courts.state.va.us

General Information: Per state law, the court cannot release DOB and SSN. No juvenile records released. Will not fax documents. Court makes copy: $1.00 per page. No certification fee. Payee: General District Court. Business checks accepted. Prepayment required. Mail requests: SASE required for civil.

Civil Name Search: Access: Mail, in person, online. Both court and visitors may perform in person name searches. Search fee: $1.00 per name. Required to search: name, date to search, case number. Civil records on computer for past 10 years. Mail turnaround time 1 week. **See details about online access at front or rear of this chapter.**

Criminal Name Search: Access: In person, online. Visitors must perform in person searches themselves. Required to search: name, date to search, case number, DOB; also helpful: SSN. Criminal records on computer for past 10 years. **See details about online access at front or rear of this chapter.**

Rockbridge County

25th Circuit Court 20 S Randolph St, #101, Lexington, VA 24450; 540-463-2232; fax: 540-463-3850; 8:30AM-4:30PM (EST). *Felony, Civil Actions over $4,500, Probate.* www.courts.state.va.us/courts/circuit.html

General Information: No juvenile, sealed records released. Will not fax documents. Court makes copy: $.50 per page. Self serve copy: same. Certification fee: $2.00. Payee: Clerk of Circuit Court. Personal checks accepted, credit cards are not. Prepayment required.

Civil Name Search: Access: Online, in person. Both court and visitors may perform in person name searches. No search fee. Civil records on computer from 1985, index books from 1778. Civil PAT goes back to 1985. **See details about online access at front or rear of this chapter.**

Criminal Name Search: Access: Online, in person. Visitors must perform in person searches themselves. No search fee. Required to search: name, years to search, DOB. Criminal records computerized from 1985, index books from 1778. Criminal records easily obtained from the late 1960s; earlier records are not. Criminal PAT goes back to same as civil. **See details about online access at front or rear of this chapter.**

General District Court 20 S Randolph St, Ste 200, Lexington, VA 24450; 540-463-3631; fax: 540-463-4213; 8:30AM-4:30PM (EST). *Misdemeanor, Civil Actions under $25,000, Eviction, Small Claims.* www.courts.state.va.us

General Information: No juvenile, sealed records released. Will not fax documents. Court makes copy: $1.00 each first 2 pages; $.50 each add'l. No certification fee. Payee: District Court. Personal checks accepted, credit cards are not. Prepayment required. Mail requests: SASE required.

Civil Name Search: Access: Mail, in person, online. Both court and visitors may perform in person name searches. No search fee. Civil records on computer from 1989, on index cards from 1985 to 1989, prior to 1985 at Circuit Court. Records destroyed after 10 years. Mail turnaround time 5-7 days. Civil PAT goes back to 10 years. **See details about online access at front or rear of this chapter.**

Criminal Name Search: Access: Mail, online, in person. Both court and visitors may perform in person name searches. No search fee. Required to search: name, years to search, DOB; also helpful: SSN. Criminal records computerized from late 1989, on index cards from 1985 to 1989, prior to 1985 at Circuit Court. Mail turnaround time 5-7 days. Criminal PAT goes back to same as civil. **See details about online access at front or rear of this chapter.**

Rockingham County

26th Circuit Court Courthouse, 80 Court Sq, Harrisonburg, VA 22802; 540-564-3111; criminal phone: 540-564-3118; civil phone: 540-564-3114; fax: 540-564-3127; 9AM-5PM (EST). *Felony, Civil Actions over $4,500, Probate.* www.courts.state.va.us/courts/circuit.html

General Information: No juvenile, sealed records released. Will fax documents for fee. Court makes copy: $.50 per page. Certification fee: $2.00. Payee: Clerk of Circuit Court. Personal checks accepted. Major credit cards accepted, 4% surcharge.

Civil Name Search: Access: Online, in person, mail. Both court and visitors may perform in person name searches. No search fee. Civil index on cards from the beginning of the county. Civil PAT goes back to 1995. **See details about online access at front or rear of this chapter.**

Criminal Name Search: Access: Online, in person, mail. Visitors must perform in person searches themselves. No search fee. Criminal records indexed on cards from the beginning of the county. Criminal PAT goes back to 1992. **See details about online access at front or rear of this chapter.**

26th General District Court 53 Court Sq, Rm 132, Harrisonburg, VA 22801; criminal phone: 540-564-3130; civil phone: 540-564-3135; fax: 540-564-3096; 8AM-4PM (EST). *Misdemeanor, Civil Actions under $25,000, Eviction, Small Claims.* www.courts.state.va.us/

General Information: Civil and criminal searches are separate. Online identifiers in results same as on public terminal. No juvenile, sealed, adoption records released. Will not fax documents. Court makes copy: $.50 per page. Certification fee: included in copy fee. Payee: General District Court. Personal checks accepted. Credit cards accepted. Prepayment required. Mail requests: SASE required.

Civil Name Search: Access: Phone, mail, online, in person. Both court and visitors may perform in person name searches. Search fee: $3.50 per name. Civil records on computer the past 10 years, on index cards from 1978, prior at Circuit Court. Mail turnaround time up to 1 week. Civil PAT goes back to 10 years. **See details about online access at front or rear of this chapter.**

Criminal Name Search: Access: Phone, mail, online, in person. Both court and visitors may perform in person name searches. Search fee: $3.50 per name. Required to search: name, years to search, DOB; also helpful: SSN. Criminal records computerized from the past 10 years, on index cards from 1985, prior at Circuit Court. Mail turnaround time up to 1 week. Criminal PAT goes back to same as civil. **See details about online access at front or rear of this chapter.**

Russell County

29th Circuit Court PO Box 435, 53 E Main St, Lebanon, VA 24266; 276-889-8023; fax: 276-889-8003; 8:30AM-4:30PM (EST). *Felony, Civil Actions over $4,500, Probate.* www.courts.state.va.us/courts/circuit.html

General Information: Probate fax is same as main fax number. No juvenile, sealed records released. Will not fax documents. Court makes copy: $.50 per page. Self serve copy: same. No certification fee. Payee: Clerk of Circuit Court. Personal checks, Visa/MC accepted. Prepayment required. Mail requests: SASE required for mail return of any copies.

Civil Name Search: Access: Mail, in person, online. Both court and visitors may perform in person name searches. No search fee. Required to search: signed release, name, years to search. Civil records on computer from 1990, archived from 1809. Mail turnaround time 2-3 weeks. Civil PAT goes back to 2000. **See details about online access at front or rear of this chapter.**

Criminal Name Search: Access: Online, in person. Both court and visitors may perform in person name searches. No search fee. Required to search: signed release, name, years to search. Criminal records computerized from 1990, archived from 1809. Criminal PAT goes back to same as civil. **See details about online access at front or rear of this chapter.**

29th General District Court Russell County Courthouse, PO Box 65, Lebanon, VA 24266; 276-889-8051; fax: 276-889-8091; 8:30AM-4:30PM (EST). *Misdemeanor, Civil Actions under $25,000, Eviction, Small Claims.* www.courts.state.va.us

General Information: Online identifiers in results same as on public terminal. No juvenile, sealed records released. No fee to fax documents. Court makes copy: none. No certification fee. Payee: Court. Personal checks accepted. Major credit cards accepted. Mail requests: SASE required.

Civil Name Search: Access: Phone, fax, mail, online, in person. No search fee. Required to search: name. Civil records on computer for past 10 years. Mail turnaround time 2-5 days. Civil PAT goes back to for past 10 years. **See details about online access at front or rear of this chapter.**

Criminal Name Search: Access: Phone, fax, mail, online, in person. Both court and visitors may perform in person name searches. No search fee. Required to search: name, DOB; also helpful: SSN. Criminal records on computer for past 10 years. Mail turnaround time 2-5 days. Criminal PAT goes back to for past 10 years. **See details about online access at front or rear of this chapter.**

Salem City

23rd Circuit Court 2 E Calhoun St, Salem, VA 24153; 540-375-3067; fax: 540-375-4039; 8AM-4:30PM (EST). *Felony, Civil Actions over $4,500, Probate.* www.courts.state.va.us/courts/circuit.html

General Information: Online identifiers in results same as on public terminal. No juvenile, sealed or adoption records released. Will not fax documents. Court makes copy: $.50 per page. Certification fee: $2.00. Payee: Clerk of Circuit Court. Personal checks accepted, credit cards are not. Prepayment required.

Civil Name Search: Access: Online, in person. Both court and visitors may perform in person name searches. No search fee. Civil records on computer from 1985, on index books from 1968, prior at Roanoke Circuit Court. Civil PAT goes back to 10 years. Only month and day of DOB appears, plus sex, race. **See details about online access at front or rear of this chapter.**

Criminal Name Search: Access: Online, in person. Visitors must perform in person searches themselves. Required to search: name, years to

search, DOB; also helpful: SSN. Criminal records computerized from 1985, on index books from 1968, prior at Roanoke Circuit Court. Criminal PAT goes back to same as civil. Only month and day of DOB appears, plus sex, race. **See details about online access at front or rear of this chapter.**

23rd General District Court 2 E Calhoun St, Salem, VA 24153; 540-375-3044; fax: 540-375-4024; 8AM-4PM (EST). *Misdemeanor, Civil Actions under $25,000, Eviction, Small Claims.* www.courts.state.va.us
General Information: No juvenile, sealed records released. Will not fax documents. Court makes copy: $1.00 per page 1st 2 pages; $.50 each add'l. Certification fee: $1.00 per page. Payee: General District Court. Personal checks accepted. Credit cards accepted. Prepayment required. Mail requests: SASE required for mail return of any copies.
Civil Name Search: Access: Online, in person. Visitors must perform in person searches themselves. Civil records on computer for 10 years, prior records at City of Salem Circuit Court. Civil PAT goes back to 10 years. **See details about online access at front or rear of this chapter.**
Criminal Name Search: Access: Online, in person. Visitors must perform in person searches themselves. Required to search: name, years to search, DOB, SSN. Criminal records on computer for 10 years, prior records at City of Salem Circuit Court. Criminal PAT goes back to same as civil. **See details about online access at front or rear of this chapter.**

Scott County

Circuit Court 202 W Jackson St, #102, Gate City, VA 24251; 276-386-3801; fax: 276-386-2430; 8:30AM-5PM (EST). *Felony, Civil Actions over $4,500, Probate.* www.courts.state.va.us/courts/circuit.html
General Information: No juvenile, sealed records released. Fee to fax out file $4.00 per page. Court makes copy: $.50 per page. Self serve copy: same. Certification fee: $2.00. Payee: Mark A "Bo" Taylor, Clerk. Personal checks, Visa/MC accepted. Prepayment required. Mail requests: SASE required.
Civil Name Search: Access: Phone, mail, online, in person. Both court and visitors may perform in person name searches. No search fee. Civil index on docket books back to 1815; on computer back to 1999. Mail turnaround time 3-4 days. Civil PAT goes back to 1815. **See details about online access at front or rear of this chapter.**
Criminal Name Search: Access: Mail, online, in person. Both court and visitors may perform in person name searches. No search fee. Required to search: name, years to search, DOB; also helpful: SSN. Criminal records indexed in books back to 1815; on computer back to 1999. Mail turnaround time 3-4 days. Criminal PAT goes back to 1815. **See details about online access at front or rear of this chapter.**

30th General District Court 202 W Jackson St, Ste 302, Gate City, VA 24251; 276-386-7341; fax: 276-386-2840; 8AM-4:30PM (EST). *Misdemeanor, Civil Actions under $25,000, Eviction, Small Claims.* www.courts.state.va.us
General Information: No juvenile, sealed records released. Will fax back documents. Court makes copy: $1.00 per page. No certification fee. Payee: General District Court. Personal checks, Visa/MC accepted. Prepayment required. Mail requests: SASE required.
Civil Name Search: Access: Mail, in person, online. Only the court performs in person name searches; visitors may not. No search fee. Civil cases indexed by plaintiff. Civil index on docket books, on computer from 1999. Mail turnaround time up to 1-2 days. **See details about online access at front or rear of this chapter.**
Criminal Name Search: Access: Mail, online, in person. Only the court performs in person name searches; visitors may not. No search fee. Required to search: name, years to search, DOB; also helpful: SSN. Criminal records indexed in books, on computer from 1999. Mail turnaround time 1-2 days. **See details about online access at front or rear of this chapter.**

Shenandoah County

26th Circuit Court 112 S Main St, PO Box 406, Woodstock, VA 22664; 540-459-6150; fax: 540-459-6155; 9AM-5PM (EST). *Felony, Civil Actions over $4,500, Probate.* www.courts.state.va.us/courts/circuit.html
General Information: No juvenile, sealed records released. Will not fax documents. Court makes copy: $.50 per page. Certification fee: $2.00 per doc plus copy fee. Payee: Clerk of Circuit Court. Personal checks accepted. Credit cards accepted for amounts of $25 or more. Prepayment required. Mail requests: SASE required for civil.
Civil Name Search: Access: Mail, in person, online. Both court and visitors may perform in person name searches. No search fee. Civil records on computer from 1996, on index cards from 1772. Note: Mail access limited to specific cases only, or a single name search. **See details about online access at front or rear of this chapter.**
Criminal Name Search: Access: In person, online. Visitors must perform in person searches themselves. Required to search: name, years to search, DOB; also helpful: SSN. Criminal records computerized from 1996, on index cards from 1772. **See details about online access at front or rear of this chapter.**

26th General District Court 215 Mill Rd Ste 128, Woodstock, VA 22664; 540-459-6130; fax: 540-459-7279; 8:30AM-4:00PM (EST). *Misdemeanor, Civil Actions under $25,000, Eviction, Small Claims.* www.courts.state.va.us/
General Information: No sealed or adoption records relapsed. Court makes copy: $1.00 minimum 1st 2 pages, $.50 each add'l. No certification fee. Payee: General District Court. Personal checks accepted. Major credit cards accepted only for online functions. Prepayment required.
Civil Name Search: Access: Mail, in person, online. Visitors must perform in person searches themselves. No search fee. Civil records on computer from 1999, prior at Circuit Court. Civil PAT goes back to 1999. Terminal results show day and month only, no year on DOB. **See details about online access at front or rear of this chapter.**
Criminal Name Search: Access: Online, in person. Visitors must perform in person searches themselves. Required to search: name, years to search, DOB; also helpful: SSN. Criminal records computerized from 1995, prior at Circuit Court. Note: This agency will not do criminal record checks and refer all requesters to the State Police or the online system. Criminal PAT goes back to same as civil. **See details about online access at front or rear of this chapter.**

Smyth County

County Circuit Court 109 W Main St, #144, Marion, VA 24354-2510; 276-782-4044; fax: 276-782-4045; 9AM-5PM (EST). *Felony, Civil Actions over $4,500, Probate.*
www.courts.state.va.us/courts/circuit/smyth/home.html
General Information: Probate is in a separate index at this address. Probate fax is same as main fax number. No juvenile, sealed or adoption records released. Fee to fax out file $1.25 per page. Court makes copy: $.50 per page. Self serve copy: same. Certification fee: $2.00. Payee: Clerk of Circuit Court. Personal checks accepted, credit cards are not. Prepayment required. Mail requests: SASE requested.
Civil Name Search: Access: Online, in person. Visitors must perform in person searches themselves. Civil index from 1832, most are computerized since 1/90. Note: The court will not perform name searches for the public. Civil PAT goes back to 07/2008. **See details about online access at front or rear of this chapter.**
Criminal Name Search: Access: Online, in person. Visitors must perform in person searches themselves. Required to search: name, years to search; also helpful: DOB. Criminal records indexed from 1832, most are computerized since 1/90. Note: The court will not perform name searches for the public. Criminal PAT goes back to 10/2007. **See details about online access at front or rear of this chapter.**

28th General District Court Smyth County Courthouse, Rm 231, 109 W Main St, Marion, VA 24354; 276-782-4047; fax: 276-782-4048; 8:30AM-4:30PM (EST). *Misdemeanor, Civil Actions under $25,000, Eviction, Small Claims.*
www.courts.state.va.us/courts/gd/smyth/home.html
General Information: No juvenile, sealed records released. Will not fax documents. Court makes copy: $.50 per page. Certification fee: none. Payee: General District Court. Personal checks accepted, credit cards are not. Prepayment required.
Civil Name Search: Access: Phone, mail, online, in person. Both court and visitors may perform in person name searches. No search fee. Required to search: name, years to search; also helpful: address. Civil records on computer back to 7/90. Mail turnaround time 1-2 days. Civil PAT goes back to 7/1990. **See details about online access at front or rear of this chapter.**
Criminal Name Search: Access: Phone, mail, online, in person. Both court and visitors may perform in person name searches. No search fee. Required to search: name, years to search, DOB; also helpful: SSN. Criminal records computerized from 7/90. Mail turnaround time 1-2 days. Criminal PAT goes back to same as civil. **See details about online access at front or rear of this chapter.**

South Boston City
Circuit & District Courts - See Halifax County

Southampton County

5th Circuit Court PO Box 190, Courtland, VA 23837; 757-653-2200; fax: 757-653-2547; 8:30AM-5PM (EST). *Felony, Civil Actions over $4,500, Probate.* www.courts.state.va.us/courts/circuit.html
General Information: No juvenile, sealed, adoption records released. Will not fax documents. Court makes copy: $.50 per page. Certification fee: $2.00 per document. Payee: Clerk of Circuit Court. Personal checks accepted. Major credit cards accepted, 3% fee added. Prepayment required. Mail requests: SASE required.
Civil Name Search: Access: Mail, in person, online. Both court and visitors may perform in person name searches. Search fee: $5.00 per name.

Civil cases indexed by plaintiff. Civil index on docket books from 1749; on computer back to 1990. Note: Will not certify searches. Mail turnaround time 1-5 days. Civil PAT goes back to current cases only. **See details about online access at front or rear of this chapter.**

Criminal Name Search: Access: Mail, online, in person. Both court and visitors may perform in person name searches. Search fee: $5.00. Criminal records indexed in books from 1749; on computer back to 1990. Note: Will not certify searches. Mail turnaround time 1-5 days. Criminal PAT goes back to current cases only. **See details about online access at front or rear of this chapter.**

5th General District Court PO Box 347, 22350 Main St, Courtland, VA 23837; 757-653-2673; fax: 757-653-2656; 8:30AM-4:30PM (EST). *Misdemeanor, Civil Actions under $25,000, Eviction, Small Claims.* www.courts.state.va.us

General Information: Online identifiers in results same as on public terminal. No juvenile, sealed, adoption records released. Fee to fax out file $2.00 each. Court makes copy: $.50 per page. No certification fee. Payee: Clerk of General District Court. Personal checks, Visa/MC accepted. Prepayment required. Mail requests: SASE required.

Civil Name Search: Access: Mail, in person, online. Both court and visitors may perform in person name searches. No search fee. Civil cases indexed by defendant. Civil records on computer, 1985 and prior records at Circuit Court. Mail turnaround time 1-5 days. Civil PAT goes back to 10 years. **See details about online access at front or rear of this chapter.**

Criminal Name Search: Access: Mail, online, in person. Both court and visitors may perform in person name searches. No search fee. Required to search: name, years to search, DOB; also helpful: SSN. Criminal records on computer, 1985 and prior records at Circuit Court. Mail turnaround time 1-5 days. Criminal PAT goes back to same as civil. **See details about online access at front or rear of this chapter.**

Spotsylvania County

15th Circuit Court PO Box 96, 9115 Courthouse Rd, Spotsylvania, VA 22553; 540-507-7600; criminal phone: 540-507-7618; civil phone: 540-507-7614; fax: 540-582-2169; 8AM-4:30PM (EST). *Felony, Civil Actions over $4,500, Probate.* www.courts.state.va.us/courts/circuit.html

General Information: No juvenile, sealed, adoption records released. Will not fax documents. Court makes copy: $.50 per page. Self serve copy: same. Certification fee: $2.00. Payee: Clerk of Circuit Court. Personal checks accepted. Visa/MC accepted for fines and fees. Prepayment required. Mail requests: SASE required for mail return of any copies.

Civil Name Search: Access: Online, in person. Visitors must perform in person searches themselves. Civil records on computer from 1993, on index books from late 1700s. Note: Mail access limited to specific case only. Civil PAT goes back to 1996. **See details about online access at front or rear of this chapter.**

Criminal Name Search: Access: Online, in person. Visitors must perform in person searches themselves. Required to search: name, years to search, DOB, SSN. Criminal records computerized from 1993, on index books from late 1700s. Criminal PAT available. PAT will show only month and day for DOB. Online access same as civil. Online results show middle initial.

15th General District Court PO Box 339, 9111 Courthouse Rd, Spotsylvania, VA 22553; 540-507-7680; fax: 540-582-7288; 8AM-4PM (EST). *Misdemeanor, Civil Actions under $25,000, Eviction, Small Claims.* www.courts.state.va.us/courts/gd/spotsylvania/home.html

General Information: Online identifiers in results same as on public terminal. No juvenile, sealed records released. Will not fax documents. Court makes copy: $1.00 1st page, $.50 each add'l. Certification fee: $1.00 per cert plus copy fee. Payee: Clerk of General District Court. Personal checks accepted. Major credit cards accepted. Prepayment required.

Civil Name Search: Access: Mail, in person, online. Visitors must perform in person searches themselves. No search fee. Civil records go back 10 years; on computer back to 1988. Mail turnaround time 5 days. Civil PAT goes back to 10 years. **See details about online access at front or rear of this chapter..**

Criminal Name Search: Access: Mail, online, in person. Visitors must perform in person searches themselves. No search fee. Criminal records go back 10 years; on computer back to 1988. Mail turnaround time 5 days. Criminal PAT goes back to same as civil. **See details about online access at front or rear of this chapter..**

Stafford County

15th Circuit Court PO Box 69, 1300 Courthouse Rd, Stafford, VA 22554; 540-658-8750; criminal phone: 540-658-8753; civil phone: 540-658-4220; probate phone: 540-658-4176; fax: 540-658-4653; 8AM-4PM (EST). *Felony, Civil Actions over $4,500, Probate.* www.co.stafford.va.us/index.aspx?NID=760

General Information: No juvenile, sealed records released. Will not fax documents. Court makes copy: $.50 per page. Self serve copy: same. Certification fee: $2.00 per cert. Payee: Clerk of Circuit Court. Personal checks, Visa/MC accepted. Prepayment required.

Civil Name Search: Access: Mail, in person, online. Both court and visitors may perform in person name searches. No search fee. Civil records in index books from 1699, back on computer to 1992. Mail turnaround time 2-3 weeks. Civil PAT goes back to 1993. **See details about online access at front or rear of this chapter.**

Criminal Name Search: Access: Mail, online, in person. Both court and visitors may perform in person name searches. No search fee. Required to search: name, years to search, DOB; also helpful: SSN. Criminal docket on books from 1699, back on computer to 1992. Mail turnaround time 2-3 weeks. Criminal PAT goes back to same as civil. **See details about online access at front or rear of this chapter.**

15th General District Court PO Box 940, 1300 Courthouse Rd, Judicial Ctr, Stafford, VA 22555; 540-658-8763; criminal phone: 540-658-8935; civil phone: 540-658-4641; fax: 540-658-4834; 8AM-4PM (EST). *Misdemeanor, Civil Actions under $25,000, Eviction, Small Claims.* www.courts.state.va.us/courts/gd/stafford/home.html

General Information: No sealed records released. Will fax documents to local or toll-free number. Court makes copy: $1.00 1st page, $.50 each add'l. No certification fee. Payee: Clerk of General District Court. Personal checks, Visa/MC accepted. Prepayment required. Mail requests: SASE requested.

Civil Name Search: Access: Phone, fax, mail, online, in person. Both court and visitors may perform in person name searches. No search fee. Civil records on computer since 1986, prior at Circuit Court. Mail turnaround time 2-7 days. Civil PAT goes back to 1995. Terminal results also show SSNs. **See details about online access at front or rear of this chapter.**

Criminal Name Search: Access: Phone, fax, mail, online, in person. Both court and visitors may perform in person name searches. No search fee. Criminal records on computer since 1986, prior at Circuit Court. Mail turnaround time 2-7 days. Criminal PAT goes back to same as civil. Terminal results include SSN. **See details about online access at front or rear of this chapter.**

Staunton City

25th Circuit Court 113 E Beverly Street, Staunton, VA 24901; 540-332-3874; fax: 540-332-3970; 8:30AM-5PM (EST). *Felony, Civil Actions over $4,500, Probate.* www.courts.state.va.us/courts/circuit.html

General Information: No juvenile, sealed or adoption records released. Fee to fax document $1.00 per page. Court makes copy: $.50 per page. Self serve copy: same. Certification fee: $2.00. Payee: Clerk of Circuit Court. Personal checks accepted, credit cards are not. Prepayment required. Mail requests: SASE required for mail return of any copies.

Civil Name Search: Access: Mail, in person, online. Both court and visitors may perform in person name searches. No search fee. Civil index on docket books since 1802; on computer back to 1988. Mail turnaround time 1 week. Civil PAT goes back to 1988. **See details about online access at front or rear of this chapter.**

Criminal Name Search: Access: Online, in person. Both court and visitors may perform in person name searches. No search fee. Criminal records indexed in books since 1802; on computer back to 1988. Criminal PAT goes back to same as civil. **See details about online access at front or rear of this chapter.**

Staunton General District Court 113 E Beverly St, Staunton, VA 24401-4390; 540-332-3878; fax: 540-332-3985; 8:30AM-4:30PM (EST). *Misdemeanor, Civil Actions under $25,000, Eviction, Small Claims.* www.courts.state.va.us

General Information: Online identifiers in results same as on public terminal. Will not fax documents. Court makes copy: $.50 per page. No certification fee. Payee: Staunton General District Court. Personal checks accepted. Credit cards accepted for criminal, civil and traffic cases only. Prepayment required. Mail requests: SASE required.

Civil Name Search: Access: Mail, in person, online. Both court and visitors may perform in person name searches. No search fee. Required to search: name, years to search; also helpful: address. Civil records on computer back 10 years. Mail turnaround time 1-5 days. Civil PAT goes back to 10 years. **See details about online access at front or rear of this chapter.** Common name searches may need to have case files reviewed. Records maintained 10 years.

Criminal Name Search: Access: Mail, online, in person. Both court and visitors may perform in person name searches. No search fee. Required to search: name, years to search, DOB. Criminal records on computer back 10 years. Mail turnaround time 1-5 days. Criminal PAT goes back to 10 years. **See details about online access at front or rear of this**

chapter.Results show DOB month and day, sex, race; records maintained 10 years. Online results show middle initial.

Suffolk City

Suffolk 5th Circuit Court PO Box 1604, 150 N Main St, Suffolk, VA 23439-1604; 757-514-7800; fax: 757-514-7103; 8:30AM-5PM (EST). *Felony, Civil Actions over $4,500, Probate.* www.courts.state.va.us/courts/circuit.html

General Information: Online identifiers in results same as on public terminal. No juvenile, sealed, adoption records released. Will not fax documents. Court makes copy: $.50 per page. Certification fee: $2.00. Payee: Clerk of Circuit Court. Personal checks, Visa/MC accepted. Prepayment required.

Civil Name Search: Access: Online, in person. Visitors must perform in person searches themselves. Civil records on computer from 1989, on index books from 1866. Civil PAT goes back to 1996. Only month and day of DOB appears, plus sex, race. **See details about online access at front or rear of this chapter.** Remote online access to court case indexes is also via LOPAS. This is a limited system and the program is not taking on new clients.

Criminal Name Search: Access: Online, in person. Visitors must perform in person searches themselves. Criminal records computerized from 1989, on index books from 1866. Criminal PAT goes back to same as civil. Only month and day of DOB appears, plus sex, race. **See details about online access at front or rear of this chapter.** Remote online access to court case indexes is also via LOPAS. This is a limited system and the program is not taking on new clients.

5th General District Court 150 N Main St, Suffolk, VA 23434; 757-514-4822; fax: 757-514-7783; 8AM-4PM (EST). *Misdemeanor, Civil Actions up to $25,000, Eviction, Small Claims.* www.courts.state.va.us

General Information: Online identifiers in results same as on public terminal. No juvenile, sealed, adoptions records released. Will not fax documents. Court makes copy: $.50 per page. No certification fee. Payee: Suffolk General District Court. Personal checks accepted. Credit cards accepted. Prepayment required. Mail requests: SASE required.

Civil Name Search: Access: Mail, in person, online. Both court and visitors may perform in person name searches. No search fee. Civil records on computer for 10 years, prior on index cards. Records destroyed after 10 years. Mail turnaround time 1 week. Civil PAT goes back to 10 years. **See details about online access at front or rear of this chapter.**

Criminal Name Search: Access: Online, mail, in person. Visitors must perform in person searches themselves. No search fee. Required to search: name, years to search, DOB; also helpful: SSN. Criminal records computerized for ten years, prior on index cards. Mail turnaround time 1 week. Criminal PAT goes back to same as civil. **See details about online access at front or rear of this chapter.**

Surry County

Circuit Court 28 Colonial Trail East, Surry, VA 23883; 757-294-3161; fax: 757-294-0471; 9AM-5PM (EST). *Felony, Civil Actions over $4,500, Probate.* www.courts.state.va.us/courts/circuit.html

General Information: Probate fax is same as main fax number. Juvenile, sealed records not released. Will not fax documents. Court makes copy: n/a. Self serve copy: $.50 per page. Certification fee: $2.00 per document. Payee: Circuit Clerk. Business checks accepted.

Civil Name Search: Access: In person, online. Visitors must perform in person searches themselves. Civil records on cards. Civil PAT goes back to 2000. **See details about online access at front or rear of this chapter.** There is a subscription service for access to lien judgment documents at www.surryvacocc.org/Opening.asp. The fee is $50 per month paid quarterly.

Criminal Name Search: Access: In person, online. Visitors must perform in person searches themselves. Required to search: name, years to search, DOB; also helpful: SSN. Criminal records on cards. Criminal PAT goes back to 2000. **See details about online access at front or rear of this chapter.**

6th General District Court PO Box 332, 45 School St, Gov't Ctr, Surry, VA 23883; 757-294-5201; fax: 757-294-0312; 8:30AM-4:30PM (EST). *Misdemeanor, Civil Actions under $25,000, Eviction, Small Claims.* www.courts.state.va.us/courts/combined/surry/home.html

General Information: No juvenile, sealed, adoption records released. Will not fax documents. Court makes copy: none. Certification fee: $2.00 first 2 pages; add copy fee for each add'l page. Payee: General District Court. No personal checks or credit cards accepted. Prepayment required.

Civil Name Search: Access: Online, in person. Visitors must perform in person searches themselves. Civil records on computer since 11/93, on books from 1985, prior at Circuit Court. Civil PAT goes back to 1997. **See details about online access at front or rear of this chapter.**

Criminal Name Search: Access: Online, in person. Visitors must perform in person searches themselves. Required to search: name, years to search, DOB; also helpful: SSN. Criminal records on computer since 11/93, on books from 1985, prior at Circuit Court. Criminal PAT goes back to same as civil. **See details about online access at front or rear of this chapter.**

Sussex County

6th Circuit Court PO Box 1337, Sussex, VA 23884; 434-246-1017; probate phone: 434-246-1012; fax: 434-246-2203; 9AM-5PM (EST). *Felony, Civil Actions over $4,500, Probate.* www.courts.state.va.us/courts/circuit.html

General Information: No juvenile, sealed, adoption, or confidential records released. Fee to fax out file $1.00 per page. Court makes copy: $.50 per page. Self serve copy: same. Certification fee: $2.00. Payee: Clerk of Circuit Court. Personal checks accepted, credit cards are not. Prepayment required.

Civil Name Search: Access: Mail, in person, online. Only the court performs in person name searches; visitors may not. Search fee: $5.00. Civil index on docket books from 1950. Mail turnaround time 1-2 days. **See details about online access at front or rear of this chapter.**

Criminal Name Search: Access: Mail, online, in person. Only the court performs in person name searches; visitors may not. Search fee: $5.00. Required to search: name, years to search, DOB, SSN, signed release. Criminal records indexed in books from 1754; on computer back to 1991. Mail turnaround time 1-2 days. **See details about online access at front or rear of this chapter.**

Sussex 6th Judicial District Court Sussex County Courthouse, 15098 Courthouse Rd, Ste 735, PO Box 1315, Sussex, VA 23884; 434-246-1096; criminal phone: 434-246-1033; civil phone: 434-246-1029; fax: 434-246-6604; 8:30AM-4:30PM, payments stop at 4PM (EST). *Misdemeanor, Civil Actions under $25,000, Eviction, Small Claims.* www.courts.state.va.us/

General Information: Online identifiers in results same as on public terminal. No juvenile, sealed, adoption records released. Will not fax out documents. Court makes copy: $1.00 minimum 1st 2 pages, $.50 each add'l. No certification fee. Payee: Sussex District Court. Personal checks accepted. Credit cards accepted. Prepayment required.

Civil Name Search: Access: Online, in person. Visitors must perform in person searches themselves. Civil records on computer from 9/88, on index cards from 1985, prior in Circuit Court. Civil PAT goes back to 1998. **See details about online access at front or rear of this chapter.**

Criminal Name Search: Access: Online, in person. Visitors must perform in person searches themselves. Required to search: name, years to search, DOB; also helpful: SSN. Criminal records computerized from 9/88, on index cards from 1985, prior in Circuit Court. Criminal PAT goes back to 1998. **See details about online access at front or rear of this chapter.**

Tazewell County

29th Circuit Court 101 E main St #202, Tazewell, VA 24651; 276-988-1222; civil phone: 276-988-1266; probate phone: 276-988-1227; fax: 276-988-7501; 8AM-4:30PM (EST). *Felony, Civil Actions over $4,500, Probate.* www.courts.state.va.us/courts/circuit.html

General Information: Probate fax is same as main fax number. No juvenile, sealed records released. Will fax documents to local or toll free line for $1.00; if long distance then $2.50. Court makes copy: $.50 per page. Self serve copy: same. Certification fee: $2.00. Payee: Clerk of Circuit Court. Personal checks accepted. Credit cards accepted. Prepayment required. Mail requests: SASE required.

Civil Name Search: Access: Mail, in person, online. Both court and visitors may perform in person name searches. No search fee. Civil index on cards from 1800s. Mail turnaround time 1-3 days. Civil PAT goes back to 1991. **See details about online access at front or rear of this chapter.**

Criminal Name Search: Access: Mail, online, in person. Both court and visitors may perform in person name searches. No search fee. Required to search: name, years to search, signed release. Criminal records computerized from 1992. Mail turnaround time 1-3 days. Criminal PAT goes back to same as civil. **See details about online access at front or rear of this chapter.**

29th General District Court 104 Court St, #3, Tazewell, VA 24651; 276-988-9057; fax: 276-988-6202; 8:30AM-4:30PM (EST). *Misdemeanor, Civil Actions under $25,000, Eviction, Small Claims.* www.courts.state.va.us/

General Information: No sealed records released. Will not fax out documents. Court makes copy: $.50 per page. Self serve copy: same. No certification fee. Payee: Clerk of General District Court. Personal checks accepted. Credit cards accepted. Prepayment required. Mail requests: SASE required.

Civil Name Search: Access: Mail, fax, online, in person. Both court and visitors may perform in person name searches. No search fee. Civil records on computer back to 2000, prior records to 1985 at Circuit Court. Mail turnaround time 7 days. Civil PAT goes back to 2001. Terminal results show month and day but not year on DOB. **See details about online access at front or rear of this chapter.**

Criminal Name Search: Access: Mail, fax, online, in person. Both court and visitors may perform in person name searches. No search fee. Required to search: name, years to search, DOB; also helpful: SSN, signed release. Criminal records computerized from 2000, prior records to 1985 at Circuit Court. Mail turnaround time 7 days. Criminal PAT goes back to 2001. Terminal results show month and day but not year on DOB. **See details about online access at front or rear of this chapter.**

Virginia Beach City

2nd Circuit Court 2425 Nimmo Pky, Bldg 10B, Virginia Beach, VA 23456-9017; 757-385-4181; criminal phone: 757-385-4186; civil phone: 757-385-4186; probate phone: 757-385-8831; 8:30AM-4PM (EST). *Felony, Civil Actions over $4,500, Probate.*

www.vbgov.com/vgn.aspx?dept_list=d47c7e192ca49010VgnVCM1000008 70b640aRCRD&x=11&y=9

General Information: Probate is a separate index at this same address Online identifiers in results same as on public terminal. No juvenile, sealed, presentencing probation report, judges notes or adoption records released. Will not fax documents. Court makes copy: $.50 per page. Certification fee: $2.00 per document plus copy fee. Payee: Clerk of Circuit Court. Personal checks accepted, credit cards are not. Prepayment required.

Civil Name Search: Access: Online, in person. Visitors must perform in person searches themselves. Civil records on computer from 1986, on files from 1960s. Civil PAT goes back to late 1986. Only month and day of DOB appears, plus sex, race. **See details about online access at front or rear of this chapter.**

Criminal Name Search: Access: Online, in person. Visitors must perform in person searches themselves. Required to search: name, years to search, DOB; also helpful: SSN. Criminal records computerized from 1986, on files from 1960s. Criminal PAT goes back to same as civil. Only month and day of DOB appears, plus sex, race. **See details about online access at front or rear of this chapter.**

2nd General District Court 2425 Nimmo Pky, Judicial Center, Bldg 10, Virginia Beach, VA 23456-9057; 757-385-8531; criminal phone: x2; civil phone: x3; fax: 757-385-5672; 8AM-4PM (EST). *Misdemeanors, Civil Actions under $25,000, Eviction, Small Claims.*

www.courts.state.va.us/

General Information: No juvenile, sealed, adoption or mental records released. No fee to fax documents. Court makes copy: $1.00 1st page, $.50 each add'l. No certification fee. Payee: General District Court. Personal checks, Visa/MC accepted. Prepayment required. Mail requests: SASE required.

Civil Name Search: Access: Mail, in person, online. Visitors must perform in person searches themselves. No search fee. Civil records on computer from 2000. Note: Civil cases retained 10 years. Civil PAT goes back to 2000. **See details about online access at front or rear of this chapter.**

Criminal Name Search: Access: Mail, online, in person. Visitors must perform in person searches themselves. No search fee. Required to search: name, years to search, DOB; also helpful: SSN. Criminal records on computer back ten years, then destroyed. Mail turnaround time 3-4 weeks. Criminal PAT goes back to 10 years. **See details about online access at front or rear of this chapter.** Traffic records also shown.

Warren County

Circuit Court 1 E Main St, Front Royal, VA 22630; 540-635-2435; fax: 540-636-3274; 9AM-5PM (EST). *Felony, Civil, Probate.*

www.courts.state.va.us/courts/circuit/warren/home.html

General Information: Probate fax is same as main fax number. Online identifiers in results same as on public terminal. No juvenile, sealed, adoption records released. Will fax documents to local or toll-free line. Court makes copy: $.50 per page. Self serve copy: same. Certification fee: $2.00. Payee: Jennifer R Sims Clerk. Personal checks accepted. Major credit cards accepted, 3% fee is added. Prepayment required. Mail requests: SASE required.

Civil Name Search: Access: Mail, in person, online. Both court and visitors may perform in person name searches. No search fee. Civil records on archives from 1836; on computer since 1986. Mail turnaround time 1 week. Civil PAT goes back to 1986. Results show hearing dates and disposition. **See details about online access at front or rear of this chapter.**

Criminal Name Search: Access: Mail, online, in person. Both court and visitors may perform in person name searches. No search fee. Required to search: name, years to search, DOB; also helpful: SSN. Criminal records on archives from 1836; on computer since 1986. Mail turnaround time 1 week. Criminal PAT goes back to same as civil. Only month and day of DOB appears, plus sex, race. **See details about online access at front or rear of this chapter.**

26th General District Court 1 E Main St, Front Royal, VA 22630; 540-635-2335; fax: 540-636-8233; 8:15AM-4:15PM (EST). *Misdemeanor, Civil Actions under $25,000, Eviction, Small Claims.*

www.courts.state.va.us/courts/gd/Warren/home.html

General Information: Online identifiers in results same as on public terminal. Will fax out documents. Court makes copy: $.50 per page. No certification fee. Payee: General District Court. Personal checks, Visa/MC accepted. Prepayment required. Mail requests: SASE required.

Civil Name Search: Access: Mail, fax, online, in person. Both court and visitors may perform in person name searches. No search fee. Civil cases indexed by defendant. Civil records on computer from 1989. Mail turnaround time 2-3 days. Civil PAT goes back to 1989. **See details about online access at front or rear of this chapter.**

Criminal Name Search: Access: Mail, fax, online, in person. Both court and visitors may perform in person name searches. No search fee. Criminal records in archives, on computer from 1989. Mail turnaround time 2-3 days. Criminal PAT goes back to same as civil. **See details about online access at front or rear of this chapter.**

Washington County

Circuit Court PO Box 289, 189 E Main St, Courthouse, Abingdon, VA 24212-0289; 276-676-6224/6226; fax: 276-676-6218; 8AM-5PM (EST). *Felony, Civil Actions over $4,500, Probate.*

www.courts.state.va.us/courts/circuit/Washington/home.html

General Information: No juvenile, sealed or adoption records released. Will fax documents to local or toll free line. Court makes copy: $.50 per page. Self serve copy: same. Certification fee: $2.00. Payee: Clerk, Circuit Court. Personal checks accepted, credit cards are not. Prepayment required.

Civil Name Search: Access: In person, online. Both court and visitors may perform in person name searches. Search fee: If search is performed, fee is determined by time involved. Required to search: name, years to search within 5 year. Civil records on archives from 1777, on computer from 1991. Civil PAT goes back to 1990. **See details about online access at front or rear of this chapter.**

Criminal Name Search: Access: In person, online. Visitors must perform in person searches themselves. Criminal records on archives from 1777, on computer from 1991. Criminal PAT goes back to same as civil. **See details about online access at front or rear of this chapter.**

28th General District Court 191 E Main St, Abingdon, VA 24210; 276-676-6281; fax: 276-676-3136; 8:30AM-4:30PM (EST). *Misdemeanor, Civil Actions under $25,000, Eviction, Small Claims.*

www.courts.state.va.us/

General Information: No sealed records released. Will not fax documents. Court makes copy: $1.00 first 2 pages, $.50 each add'l. No certification fee. Payee: General District Court. Personal checks accepted. VISA and MC cards accepted. Prepayment required. Mail requests: SASE required.

Civil Name Search: Access: Mail, in person, online. Both court and visitors may perform in person name searches. No search fee. Civil records on archives from 1777, on computer from 1997. Mail turnaround time 5 days. Civil PAT goes back to 10 years. **See details about online access at front or rear of this chapter.**

Criminal Name Search: Access: Mail, online, in person. Both court and visitors may perform in person name searches. No search fee. Criminal records on archives from 1777, on computer from 1997. Mail turnaround time 5 days. Criminal PAT goes back to same as civil. **See details about online access at front or rear of this chapter.**

Waynesboro City

25th Circuit Court 250 S Wayne Ave, PO Box 910, Waynesboro, VA 22980; 540-942-6616; fax: 540-942-6774; 8:30AM-5PM (EST). *Felony, Civil Actions over $4,500, Probate.*

www.courts.state.va.us/courts/circuit.html

General Information: No juvenile, sealed, adoptions released. Will not fax documents. Court makes copy: $.50 per page. Self serve copy: same. Certification fee: $2.00. Payee: Nicole A Briggs, Clerk. Personal checks accepted, credit cards are not. Prepayment required. Mail requests: SASE required for mail return of any copies.

Civil Name Search: Access: Online, in person. Visitors must perform in person searches themselves. Civil records on computer from 11/88 (some), all on index books from 5/48. Civil PAT goes back to 1988. **See details about online access at front or rear of this chapter.**

Criminal Name Search: Access: Online, in person. Visitors must perform in person searches themselves. Required to search: name, years to search, DOB; also helpful: SSN. Criminal records computerized from 11/88 (some), all on index books from 5/48. Criminal PAT goes back to same as civil. **See details about online access at front or rear of this chapter.**

25th General District Court - Waynesboro 250 S Wayne Ave #100, 237 Market Ave, Waynesboro, VA 22980; 540-942-6636; fax: 540-942-6666; 8:30AM-4:30PM (EST). *Misdemeanor, Civil Actions under $25,000, Eviction, Small Claims.*

www.courts.state.va.us/courts/gd/Waynesboro/home.html

General Information: Will not fax documents. Court makes copy: $.50 per page. Self serve copy: same. No certification fee. Payee: General District Court. Personal checks, Visa/MC accepted. Mail requests: SASE required for mail return of any copies.

Civil Name Search: Access: Mail, fax, online, in person. Visitors must perform in person searches themselves. No search fee. Civil records on computer 10 years. Mail turnaround time 1-2 days. Civil PAT goes back to 10 years. **See details about online access at front or rear of this chapter.**

Criminal Name Search: Access: Mail, fax, online, in person. Visitors must perform in person searches themselves. No search fee. Criminal records on computer for 10 years. Mail turnaround time up to 1 week. Criminal PAT goes back to same as civil. **See details about online access at front or rear of this chapter.**

Westmoreland County

15th Circuit Court PO Box 307, Montross, VA 22520; 804-493-0108; fax: 804-493-0393; 9AM-5PM (EST). *Felony, Civil Actions over $4,500, Probate.*

www.courts.state.va.us/courts/circuit.html

General Information: Probate index is separate. In person name searches are done using the docket books. No juvenile, sealed, adoption records released. Will not fax documents. Court makes copy: $.50 per page. Self serve copy: same. Certification fee: $3.00 includes copy fee. Payee: Clerk of Circuit Court. No personal checks or credit cards accepted. Prepayment required. Will bill copy fees. Mail requests: SASE required for mail return of any copies.

Civil Name Search: Access: In person, online. Visitors must perform in person searches themselves. Civil index on docket books from 1977. **See details about online access at front or rear of this chapter.**

Criminal Name Search: Access: In person, online. Visitors must perform in person searches themselves. Required to search: name, years to search, DOB; also helpful: SSN. Criminal records indexed in books from 1977. Search free by name only or by case number at www.courts.state.va.us/. Results show address of subject and the day and month of birth, but not year. Online results show middle initial.

15th General District Court PO Box 688, Montross, VA 22520; 804-493-0105; fax: 804-493-0104; 8AM-4:30PM (EST). *Misdemeanor, Civil Actions under $25,000, Small Claims.*

www.courts.state.va.us

General Information: All records public. Will not fax documents. Court makes copy: $1.00 first page, $.50 each add'l. No certification fee. Payee: General District Court. Personal checks accepted. Attorney checks accepted. Visa/MC accepted. Prepayment required. Mail requests: SASE required.

Civil Name Search: Access: Mail, in person, online. Both court and visitors may perform in person name searches. No search fee. Required to search: name, years to search, case number. Civil records on computer back 10 years. Mail turnaround time 1 week. Civil PAT goes back to 10 years. **See details about online access at front or rear of this chapter.**

Criminal Name Search: Access: Mail, online, in person. Both court and visitors may perform in person name searches. No search fee. Required to search: name, years to search; also helpful: DOB, SSN, date of offense. Criminal records on computer back 10 years. Mail turnaround time 1 week. Criminal PAT goes back to same as civil. **See details about online access at front or rear of this chapter.**

Williamsburg City

Circuit & District Courts - See James City

Winchester City

26th Circuit Court 5 N Kent St, Winchester, VA 22601; 540-667-5770; fax: 540-667-6638; 9AM-5PM (EST). *Felony, Civil Actions over $4,500, Probate.*

www.winfredclerk.com

General Information: The Winchester Court and the Frederick County Court Clerks are housed in the same judicial center. No juvenile, sealed, adoption records released. Will not fax out documents. Court makes copy: $.50 per page. Self serve copy: same. Certification fee: $2.00 plus copy fee.

Payee: Clerk of Circuit Court. Personal checks accepted, credit cards are not. Prepayment required. Mail requests: SASE required for criminal.

Civil Name Search: Access: Online, in person. Visitors must perform in person searches themselves. Civil records on computer from 1985 to present, on index books from 1790. Civil PAT goes back to 1985. **See details about online access at front or rear of this chapter.**

Criminal Name Search: Access: Mail, online, in person. Both court and visitors may perform in person name searches. No search fee. Required to search: name, years to search; also helpful: DOB, SSN. Criminal records computerized from 1985 to present, on index books from 1790. Note: Results include hearing date, status. Mail turnaround time same day. Criminal PAT goes back to 1985. Results include hearing date, status. **See details about online access at front or rear of this chapter.**

26th General District Court 5 N Kent St, Winchester, VA 22601; 540-722-7208; fax: 540-722-1063; 8AM-4PM (EST). *Misdemeanor, Civil Actions under $25,000, Eviction, Small Claims.*

www.courts.state.va.us

General Information: No sealed records released. Will fax documents for no fee. Court makes copy: $.50 per page. No certification fee. Payee: Clerk of General District Court. Personal checks accepted, credit cards are not. Prepayment required.

Civil Name Search: Access: Online, in person. Visitors must perform in person searches themselves. Civil records on computer from 1992, on index cards from 1985 to 1987, prior at Circuit Court. Civil PAT goes back to 10 years. **See details about online access at front or rear of this chapter.**

Criminal Name Search: Access: Online, in person. Visitors must perform in person searches themselves. Required to search: name, years to search, DOB, SSN, signed release. Criminal records computerized from 1992, on index cards from 1985 to 1987, prior at Circuit Court. Note: Forms for criminal searches available from State Police. Criminal PAT goes back to same as civil. **See details about online access at front or rear of this chapter.**

Wise County

30th Circuit Court PO Box 1248, 206 E Main St, Rm 245, Wise, VA 24293-1248; 276-328-6111; 328-4324; fax: 276-328-0039; 8:30AM-4:30PM (EST). *Felony, Civil Actions over $4,500, Probate.*

www.courts.state.va.us/courts/circuit/wise/home.html

General Information: No juvenile, sealed or adoption records released. Will not fax documents. Court makes copy: $.50 per page. Self serve copy: same. Certification fee: $2.00 plus copy fee. Payee: Clerk of Circuit Court. Personal checks accepted. Visa/MC accepted; 3% usage fee added. Prepayment required.

Civil Name Search: Access: Mail, online, in person. Both court and visitors may perform in person name searches. Search fee: $10.00 per name. Required to search: name, years to search; also helpful: address. Civil records on archives from 1856. Mail turnaround time 2-3 days. Civil PAT goes back to 1856. Search free by name only or by case number at www.courts.state.va.us/. Results show address of subject and the day and month of birth, but not year. Also, access court indexes and images via www.courtbar.org. Records go back to June, 2000.

Criminal Name Search: Access: Mail, online, in person. Both court and visitors may perform in person name searches. No search fee. Required to search: name, years to search, DOB; also helpful: SSN. Criminal records on archives from 1856. Mail turnaround time 2-3 days. Criminal PAT goes back to same as civil. Search free by name only or by case number at www.courts.state.va.us/. Results show address of subject and the day and month of birth, but not year. Online results show middle initial.

30th General District Court PO Box 829, 206 E Main St, Wise County Courthouse, Wise, VA 24293; 276-328-3426; fax: 276-328-4576; 8AM-4PM (EST). *Misdemeanor, Civil Actions under $25,000, Eviction, Small Claims.*

www.courts.state.va.us/courts/gd/Wise~Norton/home.html

General Information: Online identifiers in results same as on public terminal. No juvenile, sealed records released. Will not fax documents. Court makes copy: $.50 per page. No certification fee. Payee: General District Court. Personal checks, Visa/MC accepted. Prepayment required. Mail requests: SASE required.

Civil Name Search: Access: Phone, mail, online, in person. Both court and visitors may perform in person name searches. No search fee. Civil records on computer back 10 years. Mail turnaround time 5 days. Civil PAT goes back to 10 years. **See details about online access at front or rear of this chapter.**

Criminal Name Search: Access: Phone, mail, online, in person. Both court and visitors may perform in person name searches. No search fee. Required to search: name, years to search; also helpful: DOB, SSN. Criminal records on computer back 10 years. Mail turnaround time 5 days. Criminal PAT goes back to same as civil. **See details about online access at front or rear of this chapter.**

Wythe County

27th Circuit Court 225 S 4th St, Rm 105, Wytheville, VA 24382; 276-223-6050; fax: 276-223-6057; 8:30AM-5PM (EST). *Felony, Civil Actions over $4,500, Probate.*

www.courts.state.va.us/courts/circuit.html

General Information: Online identifiers in results same as on public terminal. No juvenile, sealed, adoption records released. Will fax documents to local or toll-free number. Court makes copy: $.50 per page. Self serve copy: same. Certification fee: none. Payee: Clerk of Circuit Court. Personal checks accepted. Major credit cards accepted, 2% surcharge added. Prepayment required.

Civil Name Search: Access: In person, online. Both court and visitors may perform in person name searches. No search fee. Civil records on computer from 1989, on index cards/books from 1950s (some back to 1790s). Civil PAT goes back to 1/17/95. Only month and day of DOB appears, plus sex, race. **See details about online access at front or rear of this chapter.**

Criminal Name Search: Access: In person, online. Both court and visitors may perform in person name searches. No search fee. Required to search: name, years to search; also helpful: DOB, SSN. Criminal records computerized from 1989, on index cards/books from 1950s (some back to 1790s). Criminal PAT goes back to same as civil. Only month and day of DOB appears, plus sex, race. **See details about online access at front or rear of this chapter.**

Wythe General District Court 245 S 4th St, #205, Wytheville, VA 24382-2595; 276-223-6079; fax: 276-223-6087; 8AM-4:30PM (EST). *Misdemeanor, Civil Actions under $25,000, Eviction, Small Claims.*

www.courts.state.va.us

General Information: Will fax documents. Court makes copy: $.50 per page. Self serve copy: same. No certification fee. Payee: General District Court. Personal checks accepted. Credit cards accepted. Prepayment required. Mail requests: SASE required for mail return of any docs.

Civil Name Search: Access: Mail, fax, in person, online. Visitors must perform in person searches themselves. No search fee. Fee is only applied to requests for excessive amounts of information. Civil records maintained on computer for 10 years. Mail turnaround time 5 days. Civil PAT goes back to 10 years. **See details about online access at front or rear of this chapter.**

Criminal Name Search: Access: Online, in person. Visitors must perform in person searches themselves. Required to search: name, years to search; also helpful: DOB, SSN. Criminal records maintained on computer for 10 years. Criminal PAT goes back to same as civil. **See details about online access at front or rear of this chapter.**

York County

9th Circuit Court PO Box 371, Yorktown, VA 23690; 757-890-3350; criminal phone: 757-890-4104; civil phone: 757-890-4105; probate phone: 757-890-4106; fax: 757-890-3364; 8:15AM-4:45PM (EST). *Felony, Civil Actions over $4,500, Probate.*

www.yorkcounty.gov/Default.aspx?alias=www.yorkcounty.gov/circuitcourt

General Information: Also includes City of Poquoson. Probate is separate index at this same address. No juvenile, sealed, adoption records released. Will not fax documents. Court makes copy: $.50 per page. Self serve copy: same. Certification fee: $2.00 plus copy fee. Payee: Clerk of Circuit Court. Personal checks accepted. Major credit cards accepted. Prepayment required.

Civil Name Search: Access: Online, in person. Visitors must perform in person searches themselves. Civil index on docket books back to 2/1950, computerized since 1986. Civil PAT goes back to 1986. **See details about online access at front or rear of this chapter.**

Criminal Name Search: Access: Online, in person. Visitors must perform in person searches themselves. Criminal records indexed in books back to 2/1950, computerized since 1986. Criminal PAT goes back to same as civil. **See details about online access at front or rear of this chapter.**

9th General District Court York County GDC, PO Box 316, Yorktown, VA 23690-0316; 757-890-3450; fax: 757-890-3459; 8:30AM-4:30PM (EST). *Misdemeanor, Civil Actions under $25,000, Eviction, Small Claims.*

www.yorkcounty.gov/Default.aspx?alias=www.yorkcounty.gov/districtcourt

General Information: Online identifiers in results same as on public terminal. No juvenile, sealed, adoption records released. Will fax documents $1.00 1st page, $.50 each add'l. Court makes copy: None. Certification fee: $1.00 first page, $.50 each add'l. Payee: York County General District Court. Personal checks, Visa/MC accepted. Prepayment required. Mail requests: SASE required.

Civil Name Search: Access: Fax, mail, online, in person. Both court and visitors may perform in person name searches. No search fee. Civil records on computer back to 1997; prior to 1985 at Circuit Court. Mail turnaround time 5 days. Civil PAT goes back to 10 years. **See details about online access at front or rear of this chapter.**

Criminal Name Search: Access: Fax, mail, online, in person. Both court and visitors may perform in person name searches. No search fee. Required to search: name, years to search, DOB, SSN. Criminal records computerized from 1997; prior to 1985 at Circuit Court. Mail turnaround time 5 days. Criminal PAT goes back to 10 years. **See details about online access at front or rear of this chapter.**

About Online Access in Virginia

There is one online system for the Circuit Courts Court case records, one for the District Courts, and finally a pay system for recorded documents at the Circuit Courts. The reason this third system in mentioned is that it can included civil judgments. Each court type and each county or county equivalent must be searched separately.

1. At   http://wasdmz2.courts.state.va.us/CJISWeb/circuit.html the case docket index may be searched for all of the Circuit Courts except Alexandria, City of Charlottesville, Chesterfield, Fairfax, Greene, Henrico and King and Queen counties.

2. All General District Courts except Clifton Forge City are searchable on a different web, see http://epwsgdp1.courts.state.va.us/gdcourts/captchaVerification.do?landing=landing page.

   (The two free online systems usually include partial DOBs in criminal results; civil results sometimes include addresses.)

3. The Records Management System provides the Secure Remote Access System for participating recording offices at the Circuit Court level. at https://risweb.courts.state.va.us/index.html This is a subscription system. Records available include deeds, marriage licenses, judgments, and wills for selected counties. This is limited to participating Circuit Court recording section. Each local Circuit Court Clerk's office must be contacted for requirements, fees, and log-in.

Washington

Time Zone:	**PST**
Capital:	**Olympia, Thurston County**
# of Counties:	**39**
State Web:	**http://access.wa.gov**
Court Web:	**www.courts.wa.gov**

Administration Court Administrator, Temple of Justice, PO Box 41174, Olympia, WA, 98504; 360-753-3365, Fax: 360-586-8869.

The Supreme and Appellate Courts The Supreme Court is the state's court of last resort. Most cases come from the state Court of Appeals, though certain cases can be appealed directly from Superior Court. Opinions and decisions are accessible from the web page.

The Washington Courts

Court	Type	How Organized	Jurisdiction Highpoints
Superior*	General	39 Courts in 30 Districts	Felony, Misdemeanor, Civil over $50,000, Domestic, Estate, Probate, Juvenile
District*	Limited	49 Courts in 39 Counties	Misdemeanor, Civil Actions $75,000 or less, Eviction, Small Claims ($5,000)
Municipal*	Limited	127 Courts	Misdemeanor, Traffic, Ordinance

* = profiled in this book

Details on the Court Structure **Superior Court** is the court of general jurisdiction, and has exclusive jurisdiction for felony matters, real property rights, domestic relations, estate, mental illness, juvenile, and civil cases over $50,000. The Superior Courts also hear appeals from courts of limited jurisdiction.

District Courts have concurrent jurisdiction with superior courts over misdemeanor and gross misdemeanor violations, and civil cases under $75,000. District Courts have exclusive jurisdiction over small claims and infractions. Criminal jurisdiction over misdemeanors, gross misdemeanors, and criminal traffic cases. The maximum penalty for gross misdemeanors is one year in jail and a $5,000 fine. The maximum penalty for misdemeanors is 90 days in jail and a $1,000 fine.

Municipal Courts have concurrent jurisdiction with Superior Courts over misdemeanor and gross misdemeanor violations and have exclusive jurisdiction over infractions. Cities electing not to establish a Municipal Court may contract with the District Court for services. Many Municipal Courts combine their record keeping with a District Court housed in the same building.

Record Searching Facts You Need to Know

Fees and Record Searching Tips District Courts retain civil records for ten years from date of final disposition, then the records are destroyed. District Courts retain criminal records forever.

A July 2005 law mandated the filing, copy and certification fees for Superior and District Courts. In the Superior Court the fee for an uncertified copy is $.50 and $.25 for an electronic computer printout; for a certified copy the fee is $5.00 for the first page and $1.00 for each additional page. District Courts often charge $5.00 for certification of a document plus any copy fees.

An SASE is required in most courts that respond to written search requests.

Online Access is Statewide

For detailed case docket data, the AOC provides the Judicial Information System's subscription service called **JIS-Link**. JIS-Link, provides access to all counties and court levels. One may search a single county or statewide for criminal searches; however, searching for civil records is by single county only. The subscription includes access to SCOMIS (the case management system) and ACORDS (appellate courts data). It is important to note that when a SCOMIS case number is found in the JIS application, detail level of the case may need to be viewed within the appropriate SCOMIS court display.

Fees include a one-time $100.00 per site, a transaction fee of $.065. There is a $6.00 per month minimum charge. Visit www.courts.wa.gov/jislink or call 360-357-3365.

There is also a limited, free look-up of docket information at http://dw.courts.wa.gov/. Search by name or case number. The search is by Municipal and District cases or by Superior cases or by Appellate cases.

Worth mentioning is a new online resource provided by a vendor is ClerkePass found at www.clerkepass.com. A certified document from participating Superior Courts can be ordered on online. Name searching is not offered. Fees are involved.

Adams County

Superior Court PO Box 187, 210 W Broadway, Ritzville, WA 99169-0187; 509-659-3257; fax: 509-659-0118; 8:30AM-N, 1-4:30PM (PST). *Felony, Civil, Eviction, Probate.*
www.co.adams.wa.us/departments/superior.asp
General Information: Probate fax is same as main fax number. No sealed, adoption, paternity, mental health, sex offenders (victims) records released. Will fax documents $5.00 first page, $1.00 ea add'l. Court makes copy: $.50 per page. Certification fee: $5.00 plus $1.00 each add'l page. Cert fee includes copies. Payee: Adams County Clerk. Business checks accepted. No credit cards accepted. Prepayment required. Mail requests: SASE required.
Civil Name Search: Access: Phone, fax, mail, online, in person. Both court and visitors may perform in person name searches. Search fee: $30.00 per hour. Required to search: name, years to search; also helpful: address. Civil records on computer from 1985, archived from 1900s. Note: A microfiche index is available to the public, but it is no longer updated. Mail turnaround time 1-4 weeks. Civil PAT goes back to 1990 or so. Index online from JIS-Link; see www.courts.wa.gov/jislink/ (also, see state introduction for subscription service.). Also, search name index back to 1989 and calendars free at http://dw.courts.wa.gov/index.cfm.
Criminal Name Search: Access: Phone, fax, mail, online, in person. Both court and visitors may perform in person name searches. Search fee: $30.00 per hour. Required to search: name, years to search; also helpful: address, DOB, SSN. Criminal records computerized from 1985, archived from 1900s. Note: A microfiche index is available to the public, but it is no longer updated by the state. Mail turnaround time 4 weeks. Criminal PAT goes back to 1990 or so. Online access to criminal indexes is the same as civil.

Othello District Court 425 E Main St, Othello, WA 99344; 509-488-3935; fax: 509-488-3480; 8:30AM-4:30PM (PST). *Misdemeanor, Civil Actions under $75,001, Small Claims.*
www.co.adams.wa.us/departments/court.asp
General Information: Record searches are often referred to Washington State Patrol 360-705-5100. No sealed, juvenile, adoption, paternity, mental health, sex offenders (victims) or (sometimes) DUI records released. No fee to fax documents. Court makes copy: $2.50 for 1st page, $1.00 each add'l. Self serve copy: $.50 per page. Certification fee: $5.00 plus $.50 per page. Payee: Othello District Court. Personal checks accepted. Prepayment required. Mail requests: SASE required.
Civil Name Search: Access: Phone, fax, mail, online, in person. Only the court performs in person name searches; visitors may not. No search fee. Required to search: name, years to search; also helpful: address, signed release. Civil records on computer for 10 years, prior on index cards. Mail turnaround time 7-10 days. Index online from JIS-Link; see www.courts.wa.gov/jislink/ (also, see state introduction for subscription service.). Also, search name index back to 1989 and calendars free at http://dw.courts.wa.gov/index.cfm.
Criminal Name Search: Access: Phone, fax, mail, online, in person. Only the court performs in person name searches; visitors may not. No search fee. Required to search: name, years to search, signed release; also helpful: address, DOB, SSN. Criminal records on computer for 10 years, prior on index cards. Mail turnaround time 7-10 days. Online access to criminal indexes is the same as civil.

Ritzville District Court 210 W Broadway, Ritzville, WA 99169; 509-659-1002; fax: 509-659-0118; 8:30AM-N, 1-4:30PM (PST). *Misdemeanor, Civil Actions under $75,001, Small Claims.*
www.co.adams.wa.us/departments/court_ritzville.asp
General Information: No sealed, juvenile, adoption, paternity, mental health, sex offenders (victims) or (sometimes) DUI records released. Will fax documents $5.00 1st page, $1.00 each add'l. Court makes copy: $1.00 per page. Certification fee: $5.00 1st page, $1.00 ea add'l. Payee: Ritzville District Court. Personal checks accepted. Visa/MC/AmEx accepted. Prepayment required. Mail requests: SASE required.
Civil Name Search: Access: Fax, mail, online, in person. Only the court performs in person name searches; visitors may not. Search fee: $20.00 per hour. Required to search: name, years to search; also helpful: address. Civil records on computer from 10/90. Mail turnaround time 5 days. Index online from JIS-Link; see www.courts.wa.gov/jislink/ (also, see state introduction for subscription service.). Also, search name index back to 1989 and calendars free at http://dw.courts.wa.gov/index.cfm.
Criminal Name Search: Access: Fax, mail, online, in person. Only the court performs in person name searches; visitors may not. Search fee: $20.00 per hour. Required to search: name, years to search, DOB; also helpful: address, SSN. Criminal records computerized from 10/90. Mail turnaround time 5 days. Online access to criminal indexes is the same as civil.

Othello Municipal Court See Othello District Court
Ritzville Municipal Court See Ritzville District Court

Asotin County

Superior Court PO Box 159, Asotin, WA 99402-0159; 509-243-2081; fax: 509-243-4978; 8AM-5PM (PST). *Felony, Civil, Eviction, Probate, Domestic, Juvenile.*
General Information: No sealed, juvenile, adoption, paternity, mental health, sex offenders (victims) or (sometimes) DUI records released. Will not fax documents. Court makes copy: $.50 per page. Certification fee: $5.00 1st page, $1.00 ea add'l. Cert fee includes copies. Payee: Asotin County Clerk. Personal checks accepted, credit cards are not. Prepayment required. Mail requests: SASE required.
Civil Name Search: Access: Phone, fax, mail, online, in person. Only the court performs in person name searches; visitors may not. Search fee: None; but may charge $10.00 per hour for extensive search. Required to search: name, years to search; also helpful: address. Civil records on computer from mid 1985, on microfiche from 1970s, archived from 1895. Mail turnaround time 1-5 days. Index online from JIS-Link; see www.courts.wa.gov/jislink/ (also, see state introduction for subscription service.). Also, search name index back to 1989 and calendars free at http://dw.courts.wa.gov/index.cfm.
Criminal Name Search: Access: Phone, fax, mail, online, in person. Only the court performs in person name searches; visitors may not. Search fee: None; but may charge $10.00 per hour for extensive search. Required to search: name, years to search, DOB; also helpful: address, SSN. Criminal records computerized from mid 1985, on microfiche from 1970s, archived from 1895. Mail turnaround time 1 day. Online access to criminal indexes is the same as civil.

District Court PO Box 429, 135 2nd St, Asotin, WA 99402-0429; 509-243-2027; fax: 509-243-2091; 8AM-5PM (PST). *Misdemeanor, Civil Actions under $75,001, Small Claims.*
www.co.asotin.wa.us/
General Information: Also has records for Municipal courts in Asotin and Clarkston. This court hold Gross Misdemeanors. No sealed, juvenile, adoption, paternity, mental health, sex offenders (victims) or (sometimes) DUI records released. No fee to fax documents. Court makes copy: $1.00 per page. Certification fee: $12.00. Payee: Asotin County District Court. Personal

checks accepted. Major credit cards accepted. Prepayment required. Mail requests: SASE required.

Civil Name Search: Access: Fax, mail, online, in person. Only the court performs in person name searches; visitors may not. Search fee: $6.00 per name. Required to search: name, years to search; also helpful: address. Civil records on computer since 1993; prior records on log books. Mail turnaround time up to 2 weeks. Index online from JIS-Link; see www.courts.wa.gov/jislink/ (also, see state introduction for subscription service.). Also, search name index back to 1989 and calendars free at http://dw.courts.wa.gov/index.cfm.

Criminal Name Search: Access: Fax, mail, online, in person. Only the court performs in person name searches; visitors may not. Search fee: $6.00 per name. Required to search: name, years to search; also helpful: address, DOB, SSN. Criminal records computerized from 1993. Mail turnaround time up to 2 weeks. Online access to criminal indexes is the same as civil.

Asotin Municipal Court See District Court

Clarkson Municipal Court See District Court

Benton County

Superior Court Benton County Clerk, 7122 W Okanagan Pl, Bldg A, Kennewick, WA 99336-; 509-735-8388; fax: 509-736-3892; 8AM-N, 1-4PM (PST). *Felony, Civil, Probate, Domestic.*

www.co.benton.wa.us/pView.aspx?id=828&catid=45

General Information: Archive files are located in Kennewick and Prosser. Call 509-735-8388 or 509-786-5624 for assistance. No sealed, dependency, adoption, paternity, mental health, sex offenders (victims). Will fax documents $3.00 1st page, $1.00 each add'l. Court makes copy: $.50 per page. Certification fee: $5.00 plus $1.00 per page after first. Payee: Benton County Clerk. No personal checks accepted. Major credit cards accepted. Prepayment required. Mail requests: SASE required.

Civil Name Search: Access: Mail, in person, online. Both court and visitors may perform in person name searches. Search fee: $30.00 per hour or portion thereof. Required to search: name, years to search; also helpful: address. Civil records on computer from 1979, pre-1979 on index books. Mail turnaround time 5-10 working days. Civil PAT goes back to 1979. Index online from JIS-Link; see www.courts.wa.gov/jislink/ (also, see state introduction for subscription service.). Also, search name index back to 1989 and calendars free at http://dw.courts.wa.gov/index.cfm.

Criminal Name Search: Access: Mail, in person, online. Both court and visitors may perform in person name searches. Search fee: $30.00 per hour or portion thereof. Required to search: name, years to search; also helpful: address, DOB, SSN. Criminal records computerized from 1979, pre-1979 on index books. Mail turnaround time 5-10 days. Criminal PAT goes back to 1979. Online access to criminal indexes is the same as civil.

District Court 7122 W Okanogan Pl, Bldg A, County Justice Center, Kennewick, WA 99336; 509-735-8476; fax: 509-736-3069; 8AM-N 1PM-4PM (PST). *Misdemeanor, Civil Actions under $75,000, Small Claims, Traffic.*

www.co.benton.wa.us/pView.aspx?id=705&catid=45

General Information: Telephone for the Prosser Courthouse is 509-786-5480, 509-786-5484 (fax). No sealed, juvenile, adoption, paternity, mental health, sex offenders (victims) or (sometimes) DUI records released. Will not fax out documents. Court makes copy: first 50 copies free, then $.15 each. Certification fee: $5.00 per doc plus copy fee. Payee: Benton County District Court. Personal checks accepted, credit cards are not. Prepayment required. Mail requests: SASE requested.

Civil Name Search: Access: Mail, fax, online, in person. Both court and visitors may perform in person name searches. Search fee: $10.00 per name. Required to search: name, years to search; also helpful: address. Civil records on computer for 10 years, data archived to at least 07/91. Mail turnaround time 14 days. Civil PAT goes back to 10 years. Index online from JIS-Link; see www.courts.wa.gov/jislink/ (also, see state introduction for subscription service.). Also, search name index back to 1989 and calendars free at http://dw.courts.wa.gov/index.cfm.

Criminal Name Search: Access: Mail, fax, online, in person. Both court and visitors may perform in person name searches. Search fee: $10.00 per name. Required to search: name, years to search, DOB, signed release; also helpful: address, SSN. Criminal records computerized for 10 years, stored from 1988. Note: Request must be in writing, with payment. Mail turnaround time 14 days. Criminal PAT goes back to same as civil. Online access to criminal indexes is the same as civil.

Kennewick Municipal Court See District Court

Prosser Municipal Court See District Court

Richland Municipal Court See District Court

West Richland Municipal Court See District Court

Chelan County

Superior Court PO Box 3025, 350 Orondo, Wenatchee, WA 98807-3025; 509-667-6380; fax: 509-667-6611; 9AM-5PM (PST). *Felony, Civil, Eviction, Probate, Domestic.*

www.co.chelan.wa.us/scc/scc_main.htm

General Information: No sealed, juvenile, adoption, paternity, mental health, sex victim records released. Will fax documents $3.00 1st page, $1.00 each add'l. Clerk will also email back copies for a add'l fee. Court makes copy: $.50 per page; if ordered online $.25 each plus convenience fee. Self serve copy: same. Certification fee: $5.00 1st page, $1.00 ea add'l; convenience fee added if purchased online. Cert fee includes copies. Payee: Chelan County Clerk. Personal checks accepted. Major credit cards accepted. Prepayment required. Mail requests: SASE required.

Civil Name Search: Access: Phone, fax, mail, online, in person. Both court and visitors may perform in person name searches. Search fee: $30.00 per hour. Civil docket records on computer back to 1900. Mail turnaround time 1 day. Civil PAT goes back to 1900. Civil dockets and case files form 1900 forward are at www.courts.wa.gov/jis/jis_superior/. Index online from JIS-Link; see www.courts.wa.gov/jislink/. Must purchase to view. Also, see state introduction for subscription svc. Search name index back to 1900 and calendars free at http://dw.courts.wa.gov/index.cfm. Also order a document for a fee (no name searching) at www.clerkepass.com.

Criminal Name Search: Access: Phone, fax, mail, online, in person. Both court and visitors may perform in person name searches. Search fee: $30.00 per hour. Required to search: full name, years to search; also helpful: address, DOB. Criminal records computerized from 1900. Mail turnaround time 1 day. Criminal PAT goes back to same as civil. Online access to criminal indexes is the same as civil for 1900 to present. Must purchase document to view.

Chelan County District Court PO Box 2686, 350 Orondo, Courthouse 4th Fl, Wenatchee, WA 98807; 509-667-6600; fax: 509-667-6456; 8:30AM-4:30PM (PST). *Misdemeanor, Civil Actions under $75,001, Small Claims.*

www.co.chelan.wa.us/dcc/dcc_main.htm

General Information: Online identifiers in results same as on public terminal. No sealed, domestic violence victim info, alcohol/probation evaluation records released. Court makes copy: $.50 per page. Certification fee: $5.00 plus $1.00 each page after 1st. Payee: Chelan County District Court. Personal checks, Visa/MC accepted. Prepayment required. Mail requests: SASE required.

Civil Name Search: Access: Fax, mail, online, in person. Both court and visitors may perform in person name searches. Search fee: $15.00 per name. Required to search: name; also helpful: years to search, address. Civil records on computer from 1984. Records destroyed 5 years from closure. Mail turnaround time 1 week. Civil PAT goes back to 10 years. Index online from JIS-Link; see www.courts.wa.gov/jislink/ (also, see state introduction for subscription service.). Also, search name index back to 1989 and calendars free at http://dw.courts.wa.gov/index.cfm.

Criminal Name Search: Access: Fax, mail, online, in person. Both court and visitors may perform in person name searches. Search fee: $15.00 per name. Required to search: name, DOB, signed release; also helpful: years to search, address, SSN, aliases. Criminal records on computer. Criminal paper files may be destroyed 5 years after close of case, infractions destroyed 3 years after close. Mail turnaround time 1 week. Criminal PAT goes back to 5 years. Online access to criminal indexes is the same as civil. Online results show middle initial.

Cashmere & Leavenworth Municipal Court See District Court

Clallam County

Superior Court 223 E 4th St, #9, Port Angeles, WA 98362-3098; 360-417-2508; fax: 360-417-2495; 9AM-4:30PM (PST). *Felony, Civil, Eviction, Probate.*

www.clallam.net/scourt

General Information: No sealed, juvenile, adoption, paternity, mental health, sex offenders (victims) records released. Will not fax out documents. Court makes copy: $.50 per page. Self serve copy: same. Certification fee: $5.00 plus $1.00 per page after first. Payee: Clerk. Business checks accepted. Major credit cards accepted. Prepayment required. Mail requests: SASE required.

Civil Name Search: Access: Phone, mail, in person. Both court and visitors may perform in person name searches. No search fee. Required to search: name, years to search; also helpful: address. Civil records on computer from 10/83, on microfiche from 1914, some records on index cards. Mail turnaround time minimum 1 week. Civil PAT goes back to 10/13/83. Index online from JIS-Link; see www.courts.wa.gov/jislink/ (also, see state introduction for subscription service.).

Criminal Name Search: Access: Phone, mail, online, in person. Both court and visitors may perform in person name searches. No search fee.

Required to search: name, years to search; also helpful: address, DOB. Criminal records computerized from 10/83, on microfiche from 1914, some records on index cards. Mail turnaround time minimum 1 week. Criminal PAT goes back to same as civil. Results include driver's license. Online access to criminal indexes is the same as civil.

District Court 1 223 E 4th St, Ste 10, Port Angeles, WA 98362; 360-417-2560; fax: 360-417-2403; 9AM-12; 1PM-4:30PM (PST). *Misdemeanor, Civil Actions under $75,001, Small Claims.*
www.clallam.net/Departments/html/dept_dc1.htm
General Information: District 1 Court also has jurisdiction on Civil Anti-Harassment Petitions and Orders. No sealed, juvenile, adoption, paternity, mental health, sex offenders (victims) or (sometimes) DUI records released. Will not fax documents. Court makes copy: $.15 per page. Self serve copy: free. Certification fee: $5.00 per doc. Payee: Clallam County District Court 1. Personal checks accepted. Prepayment required.
Civil Name Search: Access: Mail, fax, online, in person. Visitors must perform in person searches themselves. No search fee. Required to search: name, years to search; also helpful: address. Civil records on computer from 1986. Mail turnaround time 1-2 days. Civil PAT goes back to 1990. Index online from JIS-Link; see www.courts.wa.gov/jislink/ (also, see state introduction for subscription service.). Also, search name index back to 1989 and calendars free at http://dw.courts.wa.gov/index.cfm.
Criminal Name Search: Access: Mail, fax, online, in person. Visitors must perform in person searches themselves. No search fee. Required to search: name, years to search, DOB, signed release; also helpful: address, SSN, nationality. Criminal records computerized from 1986. Mail turnaround time up to 1 week. Criminal PAT goes back to same as civil. Online access to criminal indexes is the same as civil. Online results show middle initial, DOB.

District Court II 502 E Division St, Forks, WA 98331; 360-374-6383; fax: 360-374-2100; 8:30AM-4:30PM (PST). *Misdemeanor, Civil Actions under $75,001, Small Claims.*
www.clallam.net/Courts/html/court_district_2.htm
General Information: Clallam County District Court II serves the West End of Clallam County, including Forks, Neah Bay, Clallam Bay, Sekiu and LaPush. No sealed, juvenile, adoption, paternity, mental health, sex offenders (victims) or (sometimes) DUI records released. Fee to fax out file $5.00 1st page, $1.00 each add'l page. Court makes copy: $.15 per page. Certification fee: $5.00. Cert fee includes copies. Payee: Clallam County District II Court. Personal checks, Visa/MC accepted. Prepayment required. Mail requests: SASE required or provide postage.
Civil Name Search: Access: Mail, in person, online. Only the court performs in person name searches; visitors may not. No search fee. Required to search: name, years to search; also helpful: address. Limited civil records go back to 1997. Mail turnaround time 2 weeks. Index online from JIS-Link; see www.courts.wa.gov/jislink/ (also, see state introduction for subscription service.). Also, search name index back to 1989 and calendars free at http://dw.courts.wa.gov/index.cfm.
Criminal Name Search: Access: Mail, online, in person. Only the court performs in person name searches; visitors may not. No search fee. Required to search: name, years to search DOB; also helpful: address, SSN. Criminal records kept 10 years, infractions 5 years. Mail turnaround time 2 weeks. Online access to criminal indexes is the same as civil.

Hoh Tribal Court PO Box 2196, 2482 Lower Hoh Rd, Forks, WA 98331; 360-374-3167/7772; fax: 360-374-6549 ;. *Misdemeanor, Civil.*
http://hohtribe-nsn.org/justice.html
General Information: Felony actions are sent to the federal court. The records from this court are not on the JIS state system.

Jamestown S'Klallam Tribal Court (NICS) 1033 Old Blyn Hwy, Sequim, WA 98382; 360-683-1109; fax: 360-681-4611; 8AM-5PM only (PST). *Misdemeanor, Civil.*
www.jamestowntribe.org
General Information: Felony actions are sent to the federal court. The records from this court are not on the JIS state system.

Lower Elwha Tribal Court 4821 Dry Creek Rd, Port Angeles, WA 98363; 360-452-6759 x311; fax: 360-452-9560; 8AM-4:30PM (PST). *Misdemeanor, Civil.*
General Information: Felony actions are sent to the federal court. The records from this court are not on the JIS state system.

Makah Tribal Court PO Box 117, 81 Resort Dr, Neah Bay, WA 98357-0117; 360-645-3302; fax: 360-645-2760; 8AM-5PM (PST). *Misdemeanor, Civil.*
General Information: Felony actions are sent to the federal court. The records from this court are not on the JIS state system.

Port Angeles Municipal Court See District Court 1

Quileute Tribal Court PO Box 69, 21 Quileute Nation St, La Push, WA 98350-0069; 360-374-4305; fax: 360-374-5275; 8AM-4PM (PST). *Misdemeanor, Civil.*
General Information: Felony actions are sent to the federal court. The records from this court are not on the JIS state system.

Sequim Municipal Court See District Court 1

Clark County

Superior Court PO Box 5000, Attn: County Clerk, 1200 Franklin St, Vancouver, WA 98666-5000; 360-397-2049 Court Admin.; criminal phone: 360-397-2295; civil phone: 360-397-2292; fax: 360-397-6099; 8:30AM-4:30PM (PST). *Felony, Civil, Eviction, Probate.*
www.clark.wa.gov/courts/superior/index.html
General Information: No sealed, juvenile, adoption, paternity, mental health, sex offenders (victims). Will not fax documents. Court makes copy: $.50 per page. Self serve copy: same.The fee for electronic or emailed documents is $.25 per page. Certification fee: $5.00 1st page, $1.00 ea add'l. Payee: County Clerk. Only cashiers checks, money orders and attorney checks accepted. No credit cards accepted. Prepayment required.
Civil Name Search: Access: Phone, mail, online, in person, email. Both court and visitors may perform in person name searches. Search fee: $20.00 per hour if extensive. Civil records on computer back to 1979 indexed, on microfiche from 1960, and index books prior to 1979. Mail turnaround time 1-3 days. Civil PAT goes back to 1979. Index online from JIS-Link; see www.courts.wa.gov/jislink/ (also, see state introduction for subscription service.). Also, search name index back to 1989 and calendars free at http://dw.courts.wa.gov/index.cfm. Also, daily dockets are at www.clark.wa.gov/courts/superior/docket.html. Also order a document for a fee (no name searching) at www.clerkepass.com.
Criminal Name Search: Access: Phone, mail, online, in person, email. Both court and visitors may perform in person name searches. Search fee: $20.00 per hour if extensive. Required to search: name, years to search, DOB; also helpful: address, signed release (if for employment). Criminal records computerized from 1979, prior to 1988 on microfilm. Mail turnaround time 1-3 days. Criminal PAT goes back to 1975. Online access to criminal indexes is the same as civil.

District Court PO Box 9806, 1200 Franklin St, Vancouver, WA 98666-8806; criminal phone: 360-397-2424; civil phone: 360-397-2060; fax: 360-397-6044; 8AM-4:30PM (PST). *Misdemeanor, Civil Actions under $75,001, Small Claims.*
www.clark.wa.gov/courts/district/index.html
General Information: No sealed, juvenile, adoption, paternity, mental health, sex offenders (victims) or (sometimes) DUI records released. $3.00 fee to fax documents. Court makes copy: $.50 per page. Certification fee: $5.00 per doc plus $1.00 per copy page certified. Payee: Clark County District Court. No personal checks accepted. Credit cards accepted. Prepayment required. Mail requests: SASE required.
Civil Name Search: Access: Fax, mail, online, in person. Only the court performs in person name searches; visitors may not. Search fee: $20.00 minimum. Required to search: name, years to search; also helpful: address. Civil records on computer for approximately 5 years. Mail turnaround time 1 week. Index online from JIS-Link; see www.courts.wa.gov/jislink/ (also, see state introduction for subscription service.). Also, search name index back to 1989 and calendars free at http://dw.courts.wa.gov/index.cfm. Also, daily dockets are at www.clark.wa.gov/courts/district/docket.html
Criminal Name Search: Access: Fax, mail, online, in person. Only the court performs in person name searches; visitors may not. Search fee: $20.00 minimum. Required to search: name, DOB, signed release; also helpful: years to search, address. Criminal records on computer for approximately 5 years. Mail turnaround time 1 week. Online access to criminal indexes is the same as civil. Also, daily dockets are at www.clark.wa.gov/courts/district/docket.html.

Battle Ground Municipal Court 109 SW 1st St #272, Battle Ground, WA 98604-2818; 360-342-5150; fax: 360-342-5159; 8AM-5PM (PST). *Misdemeanor, Infraction.*
www.cityofbg.org/departments/court.php
General Information: Index online from JIS-Link; see www.courts.wa.gov/jislink/ (also, see state introduction for subscription service.). Also, search name index back to 1989 and calendars free at http://dw.courts.wa.gov/index.cfm.

Camas-Washougal Municipal Court 89 C St, Washougal, WA 98671-2142; 360-397-2125; fax: 360-833-0818; 8AM-4:30PM (PST). *Misdemeanor.*
General Information: Index online from JIS-Link; see www.courts.wa.gov/jislink/ (also, see state introduction for subscription service.). Also, search name index back to 1989 and calendars free at http://dw.courts.wa.gov/index.cfm.

LaCenter Municipal Court See Battle Ground Municipal Court

Ridgefield Municipal Court See Battle Ground Municipal Court

Vancouver Municipal Court See Clark County District Court

Yacolt Municipal Court See Clark County District Court

Columbia County

Superior Court 341 E Main St, Ste 2, Dayton, WA 99328; 509-382-4321; fax: 509-382-4830; 8:30AM-N, 1-4:30PM (PST). *Felony, Civil ocer $25,000, Eviction, Probate.*

www.columbiaco.com/index.aspx?nid=25

General Information: No sealed, juvenile, adoption, paternity, mental health, sex offenders (victims). Will not fax documents. Court makes copy: $.50 per page. Self serve copy: same. Certification fee: $5.00 plus $1.00 per page after first. Cert fee includes copies. Payee: Columbia County Clerk. Personal checks accepted, credit cards are not. Prepayment required. Mail requests: SASE required.

Civil Name Search: Access: Phone, fax, mail, online, in person. Only the court performs in person name searches; visitors may not. Search fee: $20.00 per hour. Civil records on computer from 1987, some records on index cards and books, archived from 1900s. Mail turnaround time 1 week. Index online from JIS-Link; see www.courts.wa.gov/jislink/ (also, see state introduction for subscription service.). Also, search name index back to 1989 and calendars free at http://dw.courts.wa.gov/index.cfm.

Criminal Name Search: Access: Phone, fax, mail, online, in person. Only the court performs in person name searches; visitors may not. Search fee: $20.00 per hour. Criminal records computerized from 1987, some records on index cards and books, archived from 1900s. Mail turnaround time 1 week. Online access to criminal indexes is the same as civil.

District Court PO Box 31, 341 E Main St, Dayton, WA 99328-0031; 509-382-4812; fax: 509-382-2490; 8:30AM-4:30PM (PST). *Misdemeanor, Civil Actions under $75,000, Small Claims.*

www.columbiaco.com/index.aspx?nid=70

General Information: Will fax documents to local or toll-free number. Court makes copy: $.50 per page. Certification fee: $5.00 1st page, $1.00 ea add'l. Cert fee includes copies. Payee: District Court. Personal checks accepted, credit cards are not. Prepayment required. Mail requests: SASE required.

Civil Name Search: Access: Mail, in person, online. Only the court performs in person name searches; visitors may not. No search fee. Required to search: name, years to search; also helpful: address. Civil cases indexed by plaintiff. Civil records on computer since 5/96; prior on index books. Mail turnaround time 7-10 days. Index online from JIS-Link; see www.courts.wa.gov/jislink/ (also, see state introduction for subscription service.). Also, search name index back to 1989 and calendars free at http://dw.courts.wa.gov/index.cfm.

Criminal Name Search: Access: Mail, online, in person. Only the court performs in person name searches; visitors may not. Search fee: Fee may be charged if more than 1 case. Required to search: name, years to search, DOB, signed release; also helpful: address. Criminal records computerized from 1996, on books prior. Mail turnaround time 7-10 days. Online access to criminal indexes is the same as civil.

Dayton Municipal Court PO Box 31, 341 E Main St, Dayton, WA 99328-0031; 509-382-4812; fax: 509-382-2490; 8:30AM-N, 1-4:30PM (PST). *Misdemeanor, Civil.*

www.columbiaco.com/index.aspx?nid=70

General Information: See Columbia District Court, this address, same phones.

Cowlitz County

Superior Court 312 SW 1st Ave Rm 233, Kelso, WA 98626-1724; 360-577-3016; criminal phone: 360-577-3017; civil phone: 360-577-3016 x2115; fax: 360-577-2323; 8:30AM-4;30PM (PST). *Felony, Civil, Probate.*

www.co.cowlitz.wa.us/clerk/

General Information: Online identifiers in results same as on public terminal. No sealed, juvenile, adoption, paternity, mental health records released. Certain civil and domestic cases may be sealed. Will not fax documents. Court makes copy: $.50 per page. Certification fee: $5.00 1st page, $1.00 each add'l page; exemplification fee $9.00 1st page, $1.00 each add'l page. Payee: Cowlitz County Superior Court Clerk. No personal checks accepted. Checks from law firms accepted. No credit cards accepted for record searches. Prepayment required. Mail requests: SASE required.

Civil Name Search: Access: Phone, mail, online, in person. Both court and visitors may perform in person name searches. Search fee: $30.00 per hour. Civil records on computer back to 1982; on microfilm through 1992. Note: Public must search records prior to 1982. Mail turnaround time 1-2 days. Civil PAT goes back to 6/1982. Index online from JIS-Link; see www.courts.wa.gov/jislink/ (also, see state introduction for subscription service.). Also, search name index back to 1989 and calendars free at http://dw.courts.wa.gov/index.cfm.

Criminal Name Search: Access: Phone, mail, online, in person. Both court and visitors may perform in person name searches. Search fee: $30.00 per hour. Criminal records computerized from 1982, on microfilm through 1992. Mail turnaround time 1-2 days. Criminal PAT goes back to same as civil. Online access to criminal indexes is the same as civil. Online results show middle initial.

District Court 312 SW 1st Ave, Rm 207, Kelso, WA 98626-1724; 360-577-3073; fax: 360-577-3132; 8:30AM-5PM (PST). *Misdemeanor, Civil Actions under $75,000, Small Claims.*

www.co.cowlitz.wa.us/districtcourt/

General Information: Will fax (and email) documents. Court makes copy: $.50 per page; $.25 for computer printout. Certification fee: $5.00 first page and $1.00 ea add'l. Payee: District Court. Personal checks accepted. Credit cards accepted. Prepayment required.

Civil Name Search: Access: Phone, fax, mail, online, in person. Only the court performs in person name searches; visitors may not. Search fee: Only copy fee charged unless extensive searching, then $20.00 per hour. Required to search: name, DOB, years to search; also helpful: address. Civil index back to 1999. Mail turnaround time 2 weeks. Index online from JIS-Link; see www.courts.wa.gov/jislink/ (also, see state introduction for subscription service.). Also, search name index back to 1989 and calendars free at http://dw.courts.wa.gov/index.cfm.

Criminal Name Search: Access: Mail, fax, online, in person. Only the court performs in person name searches; visitors may not. Search fee: Only copy fee charged unless extensive searching, then $20.00 per hour. Required to search: name, years to search, DOB; also helpful: address, SSN. Criminal records are stored based on case type, will go back at least 7 years. Mail turnaround time 2 weeks. Online access to criminal indexes is the same as civil.

Castle Rock Municipal Court

General Information: Court Closed 10/2004, contracted with county for court services; see District Court

Kalama Municipal Court See District Court

Kelso Municipal Court See District Court

Longview Municipal Court See District Court

Woodland Municipal Court See District Court

Douglas County

Superior Court PO Box 516, Waterville, WA 98858-0516; 509-745-8529; fax: 509-745-8027; 8AM-5PM (PST). *Felony, Civil, Eviction, Probate.*

www.douglascountywa.net

General Information: Address and phone here is for the County Clerk, who holds the records. Superior Ct Admin is reached at 509-745-9063. No sealed, juvenile, adoption, paternity, mental health, sex offenders (victims). Will fax documents $5.00 1st page, $1.00 each add'l. Court makes copy: $.50 per page. Self serve copy: same. Certification fee: $5.00 1st page, $1.00 ea add'l. Cert fee includes copies. Payee: Douglas County Clerk. Business checks accepted. No credit cards accepted. Prepayment required. Mail requests: SASE required for civil.

Civil Name Search: Access: Phone, fax, mail, online, in person. Both court and visitors may perform in person name searches. Search fee: $30.00 per hour. Required to search: name, years to search; also helpful: address. Civil records on computer from 1985, archived and on microfiche from 1883, some records on index books. Mail turnaround time 1 week. Civil PAT goes back to 1985. Index online from JIS-Link; see www.courts.wa.gov/jislink/ (also, see state introduction for subscription service.). Also, search name index back to 1985 and calendars free at http://dw.courts.wa.gov/index.cfm. Also order a document for a fee (no name searching) at www.clerkepass.com.

Criminal Name Search: Access: In person, online. Both court and visitors may perform in person name searches. Search fee: $30.00 per hour. Required to search: name, years to search, DOB; also helpful: address, SSN. Criminal records computerized from 1985, archived and on microfiche from 1883, some records on index books. Criminal PAT goes back to same as civil. Online access to criminal indexes is the same as civil. Also order a document for a fee (no name searching) at www.clerkepass.com.

District Court - Bridgeport PO Box 730, 1206 Columbia Ave, Bridgeport, WA 98813-0730; 509-686-2034; fax: 509-686-0532; 9AM-4PM (PST). *Misdemeanor, Small Claims.*

www.douglascountywa.net/departments/districtcourt/default.asp

General Information: This is a rural branch. If record not found in this court, your request forwarded to East Wenatchee court (main court). No sealed, juvenile, adoption, paternity, mental health, sex offenders (victims) or (sometimes) DUI records released. Will fax documents to local or toll free line. Court makes copy: $.15 per page. Certification fee: $5.00 1st page, $1.00 ea add'l. Cert fee includes copies. Payee: Douglas County District

Court Bridgeport. Personal checks accepted. No credit cards accepted for record searches. Prepayment required. Mail requests: SASE required.

Civil Name Search: Access: Fax, mail, online, in person. Only the court performs in person name searches; visitors may not. Search fee: $10.00 per name. Required to search: name, years to search; also helpful: address. Civil cases indexed by defendant. Civil records on computer back to 2/95. Note: Please use the court's "Request for Information" form. Mail turnaround time 10 days. Index online from JIS-Link; see www.courts.wa.gov/jislink/ (also, see state introduction for subscription service.). Also, search name index back to 1989 and calendars free at http://dw.courts.wa.gov/index.cfm.

Criminal Name Search: Access: Fax, mail, online, in person. Only the court performs in person name searches; visitors may not. Search fee: $10.00 per name. Required to search: name, years to search; also helpful: address, DOB, SSN. Criminal records computerized from 2/95. Note: Please use the court's "Request for Information" form. Mail turnaround time 10 days. Online access to criminal indexes is the same as civil.

District Court - East Wenatchee 110 2nd St NE #100, East Wenatchee, WA 98802; 509-884-3536; fax: 509-884-5973; 9AM-4PM (PST). *Misdemeanor, Civil Actions under $75,001, Small Claims.*
www.douglascountywa.net/departments/districtcourt/default.asp

General Information: If record not found in this court, request forwarded to Bridgeport Branch (North) County District Court. No sealed, juvenile, adoption, paternity, mental health, sex offenders (victims), Alcohol records, treatment reports released. Will fax documents $1.00 1st page, $1.00 each add'l. Local faxing only. Court makes copy: $.50 per page. Self serve copy: same. Certification fee: $5.00; $10.00 for notarized. Payee: Douglas District Court. Personal checks, Visa/MC accepted. Prepayment required. For credit card payment you will need to call 800-272-9829 with the jurisdiction #5665, after contacting the court for the costs of records. Mail requests: SASE required.

Civil Name Search: Access: Fax, mail, online, in person. Both court and visitors may perform in person name searches. Search fee: $10.00. Required to search: name, years to search; also helpful: address. Civil cases go back to close date plus 3 years. Note: Record request forms are on the court webpage. Mail turnaround time 1 week. Civil PAT goes back to 2003. Index online from JIS-Link; see www.courts.wa.gov/jislink/ (also, see state introduction for subscription service.). Also, search name index back to 1989 and calendars free at http://dw.courts.wa.gov/index.cfm.

Criminal Name Search: Access: Fax, mail, online, in person. Both court and visitors may perform in person name searches. Search fee: $10.00. Required to search: Full name, address, DOB, SSN. Criminal records computerized from 1992. Mail turnaround time 1 week. Criminal PAT goes back to beginning of 2006. Online access to criminal indexes is the same as civil.

Bridgeport Municipal Court See Bridgeport District Court

East Wenatchee Municipal Court 271 9th St NE, East Wenatchee, WA 98802-4438; 509-884-0680; fax: 509-886-4501; 8:30AM-4:30PM (PST). *Misdemeanor, Traffic.*
http://east-wenatchee.com/municipal-court_319.html
General Information: Index online from JIS-Link; see www.courts.wa.gov/jislink/ (also, see state introduction for subscription service.). Also, search name index back to 1989 and calendars free at http://dw.courts.wa.gov/index.cfm.

Rock Island Municipal Court See East Wenatchee District Court

Waterville Municipal Court See East Wenatchee District Court

Ferry County

Superior Court 350 E Delaware, #4, Republic, WA 99166; 509-775-5245; 8AM-4PM (PST). *Felony, Civil, Probate.*
General Information: Depending on the civil case type, a civil case may be found here or in District Court. Here, you can ask that a civil and criminal search be combined under a single search fee. Online identifiers in results same as on public terminal. No sealed, adoption, paternity, mental health or sex offenders (victims). Will fax documents for $.50 per page. Court makes copy: $1.00 for 1st page, $.50 ea add'l. Self serve copy: $.25 per page. Certification fee: $5.00 per cert. Add $5.00 if exemplification needed. Payee: Ferry County Clerk. Personal checks accepted, credit cards are not. Prepayment required. Mail requests: SASE required.
Civil Name Search: Access: Phone, mail, online, in person. Both court and visitors may perform in person name searches. Search fee: $30.00 per hour. Required to search: name, years to search; also helpful: address. Civil records on computer back to 1987; other records go back to 1900. Mail turnaround time 1-4 days. Civil PAT goes back to 1987. Access on public terminal is limited - call for availability. Index online from JIS-Link; see www.courts.wa.gov/jislink/ (also, see state introduction for subscription service.). Also, search name index back to 1989 and calendars free at http://dw.courts.wa.gov/index.cfm.

Criminal Name Search: Access: Phone, mail, online, in person. Both court and visitors may perform in person name searches. Search fee: $30.00 per hour. Required to search: name, years to search; also helpful: address, DOB. Criminal records computerized from 1987; other records go back to 1900. Mail turnaround time 1-4 days. Criminal PAT available. Access on public terminal is limited - call for availability. Online access to criminal indexes is the same as civil.

District Court 350 E Delaware, #6, Republic, WA 99166-9747; 509-775-5225 X 2504; fax: 509-775-5221; 8AM-4PM (PST). *Misdemeanor, Civil Actions under $75,001, Small Claims.*
www.ferry-county.com
General Information: Depending on the civil case type, a civil case may be found here or in Superior Court. No sealed, juvenile, adoption, paternity, mental health, sex offenders (victims) or (sometimes) DUI records released. No fee to fax documents. Court makes copy: $1.00 1st page, $.50 each add'l. Certification fee: $5.00 per cert. Payee: Ferry County District Court. Personal checks accepted, credit cards are not. Prepayment required. Mail requests: SASE required.
Civil Name Search: Access: Fax, mail, online, in person. Only the court performs in person name searches; visitors may not. No search fee. Required to search: name, years to search; also helpful: address. Civil cases indexed by case number. Civil records on computer back to 1995; others back to 1995. Mail turnaround time 1 week. Index online from JIS-Link; see www.courts.wa.gov/jislink/ (also, see state introduction for subscription service.). Also, search name index back to 1989 and calendars free at http://dw.courts.wa.gov/index.cfm.
Criminal Name Search: Access: Mail, fax, online, in person. Only the court performs in person name searches; visitors may not. No search fee. Required to search: name, years to search, DOB; also helpful: address, SSN, signed release. Criminal records computerized from 1995; others back to 1995. Mail turnaround time 1 week. Online access to criminal indexes is the same as civil.

Franklin County

Superior Court 1016 N 4th Ave, 3rd Fl, Rm 306, Pasco, WA 99301; 509-545-3525; 8:30AM-N, 1-4PM (PST). *Felony, Civil, Eviction, Probate, Domestic, Juvenile.*
www.co.franklin.wa.us/clerk/
General Information: No sealed, juvenile, adoption, paternity, mental health, sex offenders (victims). Fee to fax out file $3.00 1st page, $1.00 each add'l. Court makes copy: $.50 per page; electronic- $.25. Certification fee: $5.00 1st page, $1.00 ea add'l. Exemplified- $7.00 and $2. each add'l. Cert fee includes copies. Payee: Franklin County Superior Court Clerk. Business checks accepted; no personal checks. Visa/MC/AmEx accepted. Prepayment required. Mail requests: SASE required.
Civil Name Search: Access: Mail, in person, online, email. Only the court performs in person name searches; visitors may not. Search fee: $30.00 per hour. Required to search: name, years to search; also helpful: DOB. Civil records on computer from 10/83, on index books, archived from 1900s. Mail turnaround time 1 week. Index online from JIS-Link; see www.courts.wa.gov/jislink/ (also, see state introduction for subscription service.). Also, search name index back to 1989 and calendars free at http://dw.courts.wa.gov/index.cfm. Also, search Superior court records free at http://dw.courts.wa.gov/. Direct email requests to civil court at mkillian@co.franklin.wa.us/clerk. Also order a document for a fee (no name searching) at www.clerkepass.com.
Criminal Name Search: Access: Mail, online, in person, email. Only the court performs in person name searches; visitors may not. Search fee: $30.00 per hour. Required to search: name, years to search, DOB; also helpful: address, SSN. Criminal records computerized from 7/83, on index books, archived from 1900s. Mail turnaround time 1 week. Online access to criminal indexes is the same as civil. Direct email requests to clerkrecords@co.franklin.wa.us. Also, criminal record index found at http://dw.courts.wa.gov/.

District Court 1016 N 4th St, Pasco, WA 99301; 509-545-3593; civil phone: 509-546-5810; fax: 509-545-3588; 8:30AM-5PM (PST). *Misdemeanor, Civil Actions under $75,000, Small Claims.*
www.co.franklin.wa.us/district_court/
General Information: No sealed, juvenile, adoption, paternity, mental health, sex offenders (victims) or (sometimes) DUI records released. Will fax documents for no fee. Court makes copy: first 35 free then $.15 per page. Certification fee: $5.00 per cert plus copy fee. Payee: Franklin District Court. Personal checks accepted. Major credit cards accepted. Prepayment required. Mail requests: SASE required.
Civil Name Search: Access: Mail, in person, online, fax. Only the court performs in person name searches; visitors may not. Search fee: $10.00 per name. Required to search: name, years to search; also helpful: address. Civil records on computer from 1993, prior on index cards. Mail turnaround time 7 days. Index online from JIS-Link; see www.courts.wa.gov/jislink/

(also, see state introduction for subscription service.). Also, search name index back to 1989 and calendars free at http://dw.courts.wa.gov/index.cfm.

Criminal Name Search: Access: Mail, online, in person, fax. Only the court performs in person name searches; visitors may not. Search fee: $10.00 per name. Required to search: name, years to search, DOB. Criminal records computerized from 1987. Mail turnaround time 7 days. Online access to criminal indexes is the same as civil.

Connell Municipal Court 1016 N 4th St, Pasco, WA 99326-0187; 509-545-3593; fax: 509-545-3588; 9AM-5PM (PST). *Misdemeanor.*
www.cityofconnell.com/city_municipalcourt.html
General Information: This court moved from Connell and is now housed in the same location as the District Court in Pasco.

Kahlotus Municipal Court 130 E Weston St, Kahlotus, WA 99335-0100; 509-282-3372; 8AM-4:30PM (PST). *Misdemeanor.*
General Information: Index online from JIS-Link; see www.courts.wa.gov/jislink/ (also, see state introduction for subscription service.). Also, search name index back to 1989 and calendars free at http://dw.courts.wa.gov/index.cfm.

Pasco Municipal Court 1016 N 4th, Pasco, WA 99301-3706; 509-545-3491; fax: 509-543-2912; 8:30AM-12:30PM, 1:30-4PM (PST). *Misdemeanor.*
www.pasco-wa.gov/
General Information: Index online from JIS-Link; see www.courts.wa.gov/jislink/ (also, see state introduction for subscription service.). Also, search name index back to 1989 and calendars free at http://dw.courts.wa.gov/index.cfm.

Garfield County

Superior Court PO Box 915, Pomeroy, WA 99347-0915; 509-843-3731; fax: 509-843-1224; 8:30AM-N, 1-5PM (PST). *Felony, Civil, Eviction, Probate.*
General Information: No sealed, juvenile, adoption, paternity, mental health, sex offenders (victims). Will fax documents $.50 per page. Court makes copy: $.50 per page. Self serve copy: same. Certification fee: $5.00 plus $1.00 per page after first. Cert fee includes copies. Payee: Garfield County Clerk. Personal checks accepted. Major credit cards accepted. Prepayment required. Mail requests: SASE requested.
Civil Name Search: Access: Phone, fax, mail, online, in person. Only the court performs in person name searches; visitors may not. Search fee: $30.00 per hour. Required to search: name, years to search; also helpful: address. Civil index on docket books, on computer back to 1993. Mail turnaround time 1 week. Index online from JIS-Link; see www.courts.wa.gov/jislink/ (also, see state introduction for subscription service.). Also, search name index back to 1989 and calendars free at http://dw.courts.wa.gov/index.cfm.
Criminal Name Search: Access: Fax, mail, online, in person, email. Only the court performs in person name searches; visitors may not. Search fee: $30.00 per hour. Required to search: name, years to search, DOB; also helpful: address, SSN. Criminal docket on books, on computer back to 1993. Mail turnaround time 1 week. Online access to criminal indexes is the same as civil. Also, you may direct email record requests to superiorcourt@co.garfield.wa.us.

District Court PO Box 817, Pomeroy, WA 99347-0817; 509-843-1002; fax: 509-843-3815; 8:30AM-5PM (PST). *Misdemeanor, Civil Actions under $75,001, Small Claims.*
www.co.garfield.wa.us/district-court/county-district-court
General Information: No sealed, juvenile, adoption, mental health, sex offenders (victims) or (sometimes) DUI records released. Court makes copy: $.25 per page. Certification fee: $5.00 plus copy fee. Payee: Garfield County District Court. Personal checks accepted. Money order and cash accepted. Visa/MC and debit cards accepted. Prepayment required.
Civil Name Search: Access: Mail, fax, online. Only the court performs in person name searches; visitors may not. No search fee. Required to search: name, years to search; also helpful: address. Civil cases indexed by defendant. Civil index on cards. Note: Written request required. Mail turnaround time 2 days. Index online from JIS-Link; see www.courts.wa.gov/jislink/ (also, see state introduction for subscription service.). Also, search name index back to 1989 and calendars free at http://dw.courts.wa.gov/index.cfm.
Criminal Name Search: Access: Mail, fax. Only the court performs in person name searches; visitors may not. No search fee. Required to search: name, years to search, DOB; also helpful: address, SSN. Criminal records indexed on cards. Note: Written request required. Mail turnaround time 2 days. Online access to criminal indexes is the same as civil.

Grant County

Superior Court PO Box 37, 35 C St NW, Ephrata, WA 98823-0037; 509-754-2011 x430; fax: 509-754-6568; 8AM-4:30PM (PST). *Felony, Civil, Eviction, Probate, Juvenile, Domestic.*
www.grantcountyweb.us/clerk/index.htm
General Information: Search fee includes search of all public indices including both civil and criminal. No sealed, juvenile, adoption, paternity, mental health, sex offenders (victims) records released. Will not fax documents, but they can email page copies back for $.25 per page. Court makes copy: $.50 per page. Certification fee: $5.00 plus $1.00 per page after first. Cert fee includes copies. Payee: Grant County Clerk's Office. Business and personal checks accepted. Major credit cards accepted except VISA. Prepayment required. Mail requests: SASE required.
Civil Name Search: Access: Mail, in person, online. Only the court performs in person name searches; visitors may not. Search fee: $15.00 per 1/2 hour. Required to search: name, years to search; also helpful: address. Civil records on computer from 1982, and some on index cards, archived from 1909. Mail turnaround time 2 weeks. Index online from JIS-Link; see www.courts.wa.gov/jislink/ (also, see state introduction for subscription service.). Also, search name index back to 1982 free at http://dw.courts.wa.gov/index.cfm. The county participates at www.clerkepass.com; order a document for a fee, no name searching.
Criminal Name Search: Access: Mail, online, in person. Only the court performs in person name searches; visitors may not. Search fee: $15.00 per 1/2 hour. Required to search: name, years to search; also helpful: address, DOB, SSN. Criminal records computerized from 1982, and some on index cards, archived from 1909. Note: The search fee includes a search of all public indices. Mail turnaround time 2 weeks. Index online from JIS-Link; see www.courts.wa.gov/jislink/ (also, see state introduction for subscription service.). Also, search name index back to 1982 free at http://dw.courts.wa.gov/index.cfm.

District Court PO Box 37, Ephrata, WA 98823-0037; 509-754-2011 X628; criminal phone: x389; civil phone: x435; fax: 509-754-6099; 8AM-5PM (PST). *Misdemeanor, Civil Actions under $75,001, Small Claims.*
www.courts.wa.gov/court_dir/orgs/273.html
General Information: No sealed, probation, juvenile, adoption, paternity, mental health, sex offenders (victims) or (sometimes) DUI records released. Will fax documents per copy fee rates. Court makes copy: $2.00 1st page, $1.00 each add'l. Certification fee: $5.00 per page plus copy fee. Payee: Grant County District Court. Personal checks accepted, credit cards are not. Prepayment required. Mail requests: SASE not required.
Civil Name Search: Access: Mail, in person, online. Both court and visitors may perform in person name searches. Search fee: $20.00 per hour, $.50 per page. Required to search: name, years to search; also helpful: address. Civil indexed on computer per state retention schedule - 3 years. Mail turnaround time 30 days or more. Civil PAT goes back to 1989. Index online from JIS-Link; see www.courts.wa.gov/jislink/ (also, see state introduction for subscription service.). Also, search name index back to 1989 and calendars free at http://dw.courts.wa.gov/index.cfm.
Criminal Name Search: Access: Mail, online, in person. Both court and visitors may perform in person name searches. Search fee: $20.00 per name. Required to search: name, years to search, DOB; also helpful: address, SSN. Criminal indexed on computer per state retention schedule - 3 years. Mail turnaround time up to 30 days. Criminal PAT goes back to 1989. Online access to criminal indexes is the same as civil.

Coulee City Municipal Court PO Box 398, 501 W Main, Coulee City, WA 99115-0398; 509-632-5331; fax: 509-632-5125; 9AM-5PM (PST). *Traffic, Ordinance.*
www.courts.wa.gov/court_dir/orgs/273.html

Ephrata Municipal Court 121 Alder St SW, Ephrata, WA 98823; 509-754-4601 x110; fax: 509-754-0912; 7:30AM-4:30PM (PST). *Municipal Infractions.*
www.courts.wa.gov/court_dir/orgs/273.html
General Information: Index online from JIS-Link; see www.courts.wa.gov/jislink/ (also, see state introduction for subscription service.). Also, search name index back to 1989 and calendars free at http://dw.courts.wa.gov/index.cfm.

George Municipal Court PO Box 5277, 102 Richmond Ave, George, WA 98824; 509-785-5081; fax: 509-785-4880; 8AM-N M,T,W (PST). *Misdemeanor, Ordinance.*
www.courts.wa.gov/court_dir/orgs/273.html
General Information: Actual records available at the Grant County main court. Index online from JIS-Link; see www.courts.wa.gov/jislink/ (see state intro for subscription service.). Also, search name index back to 1989 and calendars free at http://dw.courts.wa.gov/index.cfm.

Grand Coulee Municipal Court PO Box 180, 306 Midway Ave, Grand Coulee, WA 99133-0180; 509-633-1150; fax: 509-633-1370; 8AM-5PM (PST). *Misdemeanor, Traffic.*
www.courts.wa.gov/court_dir/orgs/273.html

Moses Lake Municipal Court PO Box 1579, Moses Lake, WA 98837-0244; 509-764-3701; fax: 509-764-3739; 9AM-5PM (PST). *Misdemeanor, Ordinance.*
www.courts.wa.gov/court_dir/orgs/273.html
General Information: Index online from JIS-Link; see www.courts.wa.gov/jislink/ (also, see state introduction for subscription service.). Also, search name index back to 1989 and calendars free at http://dw.courts.wa.gov/index.cfm.

Quincy Municipal Court PO Box 338, 104 B St SW, Quincy, WA 98848-0338; 509-787-3523; fax: 509-787-1284; 9AM-5PM (PST). *Ordinance.*
www.courts.wa.gov/court_dir/orgs/273.html
General Information: Index online from JIS-Link; see www.courts.wa.gov/jislink/ (also, see state introduction for subscription service.). Also, search name index back to 1989 and calendars free at http://dw.courts.wa.gov/index.cfm.

Royal City Municipal Court PO Box 1239, 445 Camelia St NE, Royal City, WA 99357-1239; 509-346-2263; fax: 509-346-2040; 8AM-5PM (PST). *Misdemeanor.*
www.courts.wa.gov/court_dir/orgs/273.html

Warden Municipal Court PO Box 428, 201 S Ash Ave, Warden, WA 98857; 509-349-2326; fax: 509-349-2027; 9AM-5PM (PST). *Misdemeanor.*
www.courts.wa.gov/court_dir/orgs/273.html
General Information: Index online from JIS-Link; see www.courts.wa.gov/jislink/ (also, see state introduction for subscription service.). Also, search name index back to 1989 and calendars free at http://dw.courts.wa.gov/index.cfm.

Grays Harbor County

Superior Court 102 W Broadway, Rm 203, Montesano, WA 98563-3606; 360-249-3842; fax: 360-249-6381; 8AM-5PM (closed 12-1); Wed opens at 8;30 (PST). *Felony, Civil, Eviction, Probate.*
www.co.grays-harbor.wa.us/info/clerk/
General Information: A document request form is at the web page. No sealed, juvenile, adoption, paternity, mental health, sex offenders (victims). Will not fax out documents. Court makes copy: $.50 per page; $.25 if sent by email. Certification fee: $5.00 1st page, $1.00 ea add'l. Cert fee includes copies. Payee: Grays Harbor County Clerk. Business checks accepted, no personal checks. Visa/MC/AmEx/Discover cards accepted. Prepayment required. Mail requests: SASE required.
Civil Name Search: Access: Mail, online, in person. Both court and visitors may perform in person name searches. Search fee: $30.00 per name. No fee for records after 1990. Required to search: name, years to search; also helpful: address. Civil records on computer from 12/1980, on microfiche from 1856. Mail turnaround time 5 days. Civil PAT goes back to 12/1980. Index online from JIS-Link; see www.courts.wa.gov/jislink/ (also, see state introduction for subscription service.). Also, search name index back to 1989 and calendars free at http://dw.courts.wa.gov/index.cfm.
Criminal Name Search: Access: Phone, fax, mail, online, in person. Both court and visitors may perform in person name searches. Search fee: $30.00 per name. No fee for records after 1990. Required to search: name, years to search; also helpful: address, DOB, SSN. Criminal records computerized from 12/1980, on microfiche from 1856. Mail turnaround time 5 days or less. Criminal PAT goes back to 12/1980. Online access to criminal indexes is the same as civil. Online results show name only.

District Court No 1 102 W Broadway, Rm 202, Montesano, WA 98563; 360-249-3441; fax: 360-249-6382; 8AM-N, 1-5PM (PST). *Misdemeanor.*
www.co.grays-harbor.wa.us/info/judicial/
General Information: All civil filings and hearings are held in the District Court Dept 2 in Aberdeen. No sealed, juvenile, adoption, paternity, mental health, sex offenders (victims) records released. Will fax documents $.25 per page. Court makes copy: $.50 per page. Self serve copy: same. Certification fee: $5.00. Payee: Grays Harbor District Court #1. Personal checks accepted. Credit cards accepted. Prepayment required. Mail requests: SASE required.
Criminal Name Search: Access: Phone, fax, mail, online, in person. Only the court performs in person name searches; visitors may not. Search fee: None normally. Required to search: name, years to search, DOB; also helpful: address, SSN. Criminal records computerized from 4/91, on index cards. Mail turnaround time 1 week. Index online from JIS-Link; see www.courts.wa.gov/jislink/. Also see state introduction for subscription service. Also, search name index back to 1991 and calendars free at

http://dw.courts.wa.gov/index.cfm. Personal identifiers on results may include driver's license number.

District Court No 2 2109 Sumner Ave, Aberdeen, WA 98520-0035; 360-532-7061; fax: 360-532-7704; 8AM-N, 1-5PM (PST). *Civil Actions under $75,001, Small Claims.*
www.co.grays-harbor.wa.us
General Information: This court no longer handles criminal cases. No sealed, juvenile, adoption, paternity, mental health, sex offenders (victims) or (sometimes) DUI records released. No fee to fax documents. Court makes copy: $.50 per page. Certification fee: $5.00 plus copy fee. Payee: Grays Harbor District Court #2. Personal checks accepted. Credit cards accepted. Prepayment required. Mail requests: SASE required.
Civil Name Search: Access: Fax, mail, online, in person. Only the court performs in person name searches; visitors may not. No search fee. Required to search: name, years to search; also helpful: address. Civil records on computer from 4/91, on index cards. Mail turnaround time 1 week. Index online from JIS-Link; see www.courts.wa.gov/jislink/ (also, see state introduction for subscription service.). Also, search name index back to 1989 and calendars free at http://dw.courts.wa.gov/index.cfm.

Aberdeen Municipal Court 210 E Market St, Aberdeen, WA 98520-5242; 360-533-5411; fax: 360-537-3247; 8AM-N, 1-5PM (PST). *Misdemeanor, GrossMisdemeanors, Traffic.*
http://aberdeeninfo.com/court/
General Information: Index online from JIS-Link; see www.courts.wa.gov/jislink/ (also, see state introduction for subscription service.). Also, search name index back to 1989 and calendars free at http://dw.courts.wa.gov/index.cfm.

Chehalis Tribal Court PO Box 536, 30 Neidermann Rd, Oakville, WA 98568; 360-273-5911; fax: 360-273-7242; 8AM-5PM (PST). *Misdemeanor, Civil.*
General Information: Felony actions are sent to the federal court. The records from this court are not on the JIS state system.

Cosmopolis Municipal Court PO Box 478, 1312 First St, Cosmopolis, WA 98537-0478; 360-532-9264; fax: 360-532-9273; 8AM-4PM (PST). *Misdemeanor.*
General Information: Index online from JIS-Link; see www.courts.wa.gov/jislink/ (also, see state introduction for subscription service.). Also, search name index back to 1989 and calendars free at http://dw.courts.wa.gov/index.cfm.

Elma Municipal Court PO Box 2013, 108 N 2nd St, Elma, WA 98541-2013; 360-482-2603; fax: 360-482-0103; 8AM-4PM (PST). *Misdemeanor.*
www.cityofelma.com
General Information: Index online from JIS-Link; see www.courts.wa.gov/jislink/ (also, see state introduction for subscription service.). Also, search name index back to 1989 and calendars free at http://dw.courts.wa.gov/index.cfm.

Hoquiam Municipal Court 609 8th St, Hoquiam, WA 98550-3522; 360-637-6035; fax: 360-533-3602; 8:30AM-5PM (PST). *Misdemeanor.*
www.cityofhoquiam.com
General Information: Index online from JIS-Link; see www.courts.wa.gov/jislink/ (also, see state introduction for subscription service.). Also, search name index back to 1989 and calendars free at http://dw.courts.wa.gov/index.cfm.

McCleary Municipal Court 100 S 3rd St, McCleary, WA 98557-9652; 360-495-3790; fax: 360-495-3097; 8AM-4:30PM (PST). *Misdemeanor.*
General Information: Index online from JIS-Link; see www.courts.wa.gov/jislink/ (also, see state introduction for subscription service.). Also, search name index back to 1989 and calendars free at http://dw.courts.wa.gov/index.cfm.

Montesano Municipal Court 112 N Main St, Second Floor, Montesano, WA 98563-3707; 360-249-4245; fax: 360-249-6225; 8AM-5PM (PST). *Misdemeanor.*
www.montesano.us/index.aspx?nid=563
General Information: Index online from JIS-Link; see www.courts.wa.gov/jislink/ (also, see state introduction for subscription service.). Also, search name index back to 1989 and calendars free at http://dw.courts.wa.gov/index.cfm.

Oakville Municipal Court PO Box D, 204 E Main, Oakville, WA 98568-0078; 360-273-5531; 360-249-4245; fax: 360-273-5120; 5:30P 2nd & 4th M (PST). *Misdemeanor.*
General Information: Index online from JIS-Link; see www.courts.wa.gov/jislink/ (also, see state introduction for subscription service.). Also, search name index back to 1989 and calendars free at http://dw.courts.wa.gov/index.cfm.

Ocean Shores Municipal Court PO Box 909, 710 Point Brown Ave NE, Ocean Shores, WA 98569-0909; 360-289-2486; fax: 360-289-2022; 8AM-4PM (PST). *Misdemeanor.*

General Information: Index online from JIS-Link; see www.courts.wa.gov/jislink/ (see state introduction for subscription service.). Also, search name index back to 1989 & calendars free at http://dw.courts.wa.gov/index.cfm. Also do Gross Misdemeanor/Infractions in this court.

Quinault Tribal Court PO Box 99, Taholah, WA 98587; 360-276-8211; fax: 360-276-4606; 8AM-4:30PM (PST). *Misdemeanor, Civil, Small Claims, Eviction, Probate.*
General Information: Felony actions are sent to the federal court. The records from this court are not on the JIS state system.

Westport Municipal Court PO Box 1208, 506 N Montesano St, Westport, WA 98595-1208; 360-268-0125; fax: 360-268-1363; 7:30AM-5PM (PST). *Misdemeanor.*
www.ci.westport.wa.us/
General Information: Will fax documents no fee. Court makes copy: $.10 per page. No certification fee. Payee: Westport Municipal Ct. Personal checks accepted, credit cards are not. Prepayment required.
Criminal Name Search: Access: Mail, fax, in person, email, online. Only the court performs in person name searches; visitors may not. No search fee. Required to search: name, DOB, SSN, years to search. criminal records go back 5 years hard copies, on computer back to late 1980s. Mail turnaround time same day. Index online from JIS-Link; see www.courts.wa.gov/jislink/ (also, see state introduction for subscription service.). Also, search name index back to 1989 and calendars free at http://dw.courts.wa.gov/index.cfm. Also, you may direct email criminal record requests to judy.stiles@mail.courts.wa.gov.

Island County

Superior Court PO Box 5000, 101 NE 6th St, 1st Fl, Coupeville, WA 98239-5000; 360-679-7359 x6; 8AM-4:30PM (PST). *Felony, Civil, Eviction, Probate.*
www.islandcounty.net/clerk/
General Information: No access to sealed, dependency, truancy, adoption, paternity, mental health, sex offenders (victims). Will not fax documents. Court makes copy: $.50 per page. Self serve copy: $.15 per page. Certification fee: $5.00 first page; $1.00 each add'l; exemplification- $9.00. Payee: Island county Clerk. No credit cards accepted. Prepayment required. Mail requests: SASE required.
Civil Name Search: Access: Phone, mail, in person, online. Both court and visitors may perform in person name searches. Search fee: $30.00 per hour. Civil records on computer from 7/1984, microfiche from 1889. Archived in Bellingham, WA. Note: Physical records older than 5 years not currently active may be located at the Offsite County Storage facility; call clerk. Mail turnaround time 1 week. Civil PAT goes back to 1984. Index online from JIS-Link; see www.courts.wa.gov/jislink/ (also, see state introduction for subscription service.). Also, search name index back to 1989 and calendars free at http://dw.courts.wa.gov/index.cfm. Also, registered users and guests may request and pay for documents online at https://www.clerkpass.com/Island/ - case details and fees required.
Criminal Name Search: Access: Phone, mail, in person, online. Both court and visitors may perform in person name searches. Search fee: $30.00 per hour. Criminal records computerized from 7/1984, microfiche from 1889. Archived in Bellingham, WA. Note: Physical records older than 5 years not currently active may be located at the Offsite County Storage facility; call clerk. Mail turnaround time 1 week. Criminal PAT goes back to 1984. Online access to criminal indexes is the same as civil.

District Court 800 S 8th Ave, Oak Harbor, WA 98277; 360-675-5988; fax: 360-675-8231; 8AM-4:30PM (PST). *Misdemeanor, Civil Actions under $75,001, Small Claims.*
General Information: Records requests are done as time permits. Is bottom of priority list. No sealed, juvenile, adoption, paternity, mental health, sex offenders (victims) or (sometimes) DUI records released. Will fax documents $1.00 per page. Court makes copy: $.50 per page; $1.00 if electronic docket. Certification fee: $5.00. Payee: Island District Court. Personal checks accepted, credit cards are not. Prepayment required. Mail requests: SASE required.
Civil Name Search: Access: Fax, mail, online, in person. Only the court performs in person name searches; visitors may not. No search fee. Required to search: name, years to search; also helpful: address. Civil cases indexed by defendant. Civil records on computer from 1991, on index by alpha. Mail turnaround time 1-7 days. Index online from JIS-Link; see www.courts.wa.gov/jislink/ (also, see state introduction for subscription service.). Also, search name index back to 1989 and calendars free at http://dw.courts.wa.gov/index.cfm.
Criminal Name Search: Access: Fax, mail, online, in person. Only the court performs in person name searches; visitors may not. No search fee. Required to search: name, years to search, DOB; also helpful: address, SSN. Criminal records computerized from 1991, on index by alpha. Mail turnaround time 1-7 days. Online access to criminal indexes is the same as civil.

Coupeville Municipal Court See District Court
Langely Municipal Court See District Court.
Oak Harbor Municipal Court See District Court

Jefferson County

Superior Court PO Box 1220, Port Townsend, WA 98368-0920; 360-385-9125 clerk; 385-9360 Ct; fax: 360-385-5672; 8AM-5PM (PST). *Felony, Civil, Eviction, Probate, Domestic.*
www.co.jefferson.wa.us/supcourt/
General Information: No sealed, juvenile, adoption, paternity, mental health records released. Will not fax out results. Will email digitized records at $.25 per page prepaid. Court makes copy: $.50 per page. Self serve copy: $.15 per page; $.25 per digital page. Certification fee: $5.00 plus $1.00 per page after first. Cert fee includes copies. Payee: County Clerk. Personal checks accepted but not out of state checks. Major credit cards accepted online at the Superior Court Payment tab at www.co.jefferson.wa.us/supcourt/default.asp. Prepayment required. Mail requests: SASE required.
Civil Name Search: Access: Phone, mail, online, in person. Both court and visitors may perform in person name searches. Search fee: $20.00 per hour. Civil records on computer from 1983, on microfiche from 1890s. Archive in Bellingham, WA. Mail turnaround time 2 days. Civil PAT goes back to 1988. Results include name of parties. Index online from JIS-Link; see www.courts.wa.gov/jislink/ (also, see state introduction for subscription service.). Also, search name index back to 1989 and calendars free at http://dw.courts.wa.gov/index.cfm. Also order a document for a fee (no name searching) at www.clerkpass.com.
Criminal Name Search: Access: Phone, mail, online, in person. Both court and visitors may perform in person name searches. Search fee: $20.00 per hour. Required to search: name, years to search; also helpful: DOB. Criminal records computerized from 1983, on microfiche from 1890s. Archive in Bellingham, WA. Mail turnaround time 2 days. Criminal PAT goes back to 1983. Results include names of parties. Online access to criminal indexes is the same as civil. Also order a document for a fee (no name searching) at www.clerkpass.com. Online results show name only.

District Court PO Box 1220, Port Townsend, WA 98368-0920; 360-385-9135; criminal phone: 360-385-9135; civil phone: 360-385-9135; fax: 360-385-9367; 8:30AM-4:30PM (PST). *Misdemeanor, Civil Actions under $75,000, Small Claims.*
www.co.jefferson.wa.us
General Information: No sealed, juvenile, adoption, paternity, mental health, sex offenders (victims) records released. Will fax documents $3.00 1st page, $1.00 ea add'l. Court makes copy: $.15 per page. Certification fee: $6.00 per document plus copy fee. Payee: Jefferson County District Court. Personal checks accepted. Visa/MC/AmEx cards accepted. Prepayment required. Mail requests: SASE required.
Civil Name Search: Access: Phone, fax, mail, online, in person. Only the court performs in person name searches; visitors may not. No search fee. Required to search: name, years to search; also helpful: address. Civil cases indexed by defendant. Civil records on DISCIS computer from 1993, on computer from '90-'93, on log books prior to 1990. Physical files kept 10 years from disposition per ret. Mail turnaround time 1 week. Index online from JIS-Link; see www.courts.wa.gov/jislink/ (also, see state introduction for subscription service.). Also, search name index back to 1989 and calendars free at http://dw.courts.wa.gov/index.cfm.
Criminal Name Search: Access: Phone, mail, online, in person. Only the court performs in person name searches; visitors may not. Search fee: Call first, can be by the hour. Required to search: name, DOB; also helpful: years to search, address. Criminal records on DISCIS computer from 1993, on computer from '90-'93, on log books prior to 1990. Physical files kept 3 years from disposition per. Mail turnaround time 1 week. Online access to criminal indexes is the same as civil.

Port Townsend Municipal Court See District Court

King County

Superior Court 516 3rd Ave, E-609, Seattle, WA 98104-2386; 206-296-9300, 800-325-6165 in state, 800-325-6165 x69300 out of state; fax: 206-296-0986; 8:30AM-4:30PM (PST). *Felony, Civil, Eviction, Probate, Family.*
www.kingcounty.gov/courts/Clerk.aspx
General Information: Phone wait can be lengthy but they will answer. Separate search fees for civil and criminal. Records from Superior Court at Maleng Justice Center also accessible here. Online identifiers in results same as on public terminal. No sealed, juvenile, dependency, adoption, paternity (except for final judgments), mental health, sex offenders (victims)

records released. Will not fax back documents. Research and copy requests not accepted. Court makes copy: $.50 per page. Self serve copy: $.15 if from paper, $.25 per page if microfilm or scanned. Certification fee: $5.00 plus $1.00 per page after first includes copies. Payee: King County Superior Court Clerk. Personal checks accepted if in state, or from attorney firm or business. No credit or debit cards accepted. Prepayment required. Mail requests: SASE required, otherwise $3.00 fee charged.

Civil Name Search: Access: Mail, in person, online. Both court and visitors may perform in person name searches. Search fee: $30.00 per hour. No search fee if you have case number. Required to search: name, years to search, case type, your phone. Civil records on computer since 1979; older records on microfilm back to 1800s. Cases initiated after 2000 are scanned. Mail turnaround time 2 weeks. Civil PAT goes back to 07/1979. Search on PC or for older records on microfilm. Index online from JIS-Link; see www.courts.wa.gov/jislink/ (also, see state intro for subscription service.). Also, search civil, criminal and probate name indices for case numbers back to 1989 and calendars free at http://dw.courts.wa.gov/index.cfm. Also, with registration, search county superior court civil, criminal and probate cases filed after 11/1/2004 at https://dja-ecreweb.metrokc.gov/ecronline. Fee of $.15 per page to view, print, or download documents; for info- 206-205-1600.

Criminal Name Search: Access: Mail, online, in person. Both court and visitors may perform in person name searches. Search fee: $30.00 per hour. No search fee if you have case number. Required to search: name, years to search, case type, your phone. Criminal records on computer since 1979; older records on microfilm back to 1800s. Cases initiated after 2000 are scanned. Mail turnaround time 2 weeks. Criminal PAT goes back to 07/1979. Search on PC or for older records on microfilm. Online access to criminal indexes is the same as civil. Online results show middle initial.

Superior Court - Kent Maleng Justice Center, 401 4th Ave N, Room 2C, Kent, WA 98032; 206-296-9300, 800-325-6165 in state, 800-325-6165 x69300 out of state; fax: 206-296-0986; 9AM-12:15PM, 1:15PM-4:30PM (PST). *Felony, Civil, Eviction, Probate, Family.*
www.kingcounty.gov/courts/Clerk.aspx

General Information: Phone wait can be lengthy but they will answer. Separate search fees for civil and criminal. Records from Superior Court at Seattle King County Courthouse also accessible here. Both courts use this phone #. Online identifiers in results same as on public terminal. No sealed, juvenile, dependency, adoption, paternity (except for final judgments), mental health, sex offenders (victims) records released. Will not fax back documents. Research and copy requests not accepted. Court makes copy: $.50 per page. Self serve copy: $.15 if from paper, $.25 per page if microfilm or scanned. Certification fee: $5.00 plus $1.00 per page after first includes copies. Payee: King County Superior Court Clerk. Personal checks accepted if in state, or from attorney firm or business. No credit or debit cards accepted. Prepayment required. Mail requests: SASE required, otherwise $3.00 fee charged.

Civil Name Search: Access: Mail, in person, online. Both court and visitors may perform in person name searches. Search fee: $30.00 per hour. No search fee if you have case number. Required to search: name, years to search, case type, your phone. Civil records on computer since 1979; older records on microfilm back to 1800s. Cases initiated after 2000 are scanned. Mail turnaround time 2 weeks. Civil PAT goes back to 07/1979. Search on PC or for older records on microfilm. Index online from JIS-Link; see www.courts.wa.gov/jislink/ (also, see state intro for subscription service.). Also, search civil, criminal and probate name indices for case numbers back to 1989 and calendars free at http://dw.courts.wa.gov/index.cfm. Also, with registration, search county superior court civil, criminal and probate cases filed after 11/1/2004 at https://dja-ecreweb.metrokc.gov/ecronline. Fee of $.10 per page to view, print, or download documents; for info- 206-205-1600.

Criminal Name Search: Access: Mail, online, in person. Both court and visitors may perform in person name searches. Search fee: $30.00 per hour. No search fee if you have case number. Required to search: name, years to search, case type, your phone. Criminal records on computer since 1979; older records on microfilm back to 1800s. Cases initiated after 2000 are scanned. Mail turnaround time 2 weeks. Criminal PAT goes back to 07/1979. Search on PC or for older records on microfilm. Online access to criminal indexes is the same as civil. Also, access inmate information at http://ingress.kingcounty.gov/inmatelookup/. Online results show middle initial.

Muckleshoot Tribal Court (NICS) 39015 172nd Ave SE, Auburn, WA 98092-9763; 253-939-3311; 8AM-N. 1PM-5PM (PST). *Civil, Ordinance, Family.*
www.muckleshoot.nsn.us/services/tribal-court.aspx

General Information: Felony actions are sent to the federal court. The records from this court are not on the JIS state system. Will fax back documents no fee. Court makes copy: $.25 per page. No certification fee.

Payee: Muckleshoot Tribal Court. Personal checks accepted, credit cards are not. Prepayment required. Mail requests: SASE required.

Civil Name Search: Access: Mail, fax, in person, email. Only the court performs in person name searches; visitors may not. Search fee: $5.00 per name. Required to search: name, DOB, years to search. Civil records go back to 1997, some older. Note: Court actually prefers email requests. Direct email search requests to marcellina.delatorre@muckleshoot.nsn.us. Mail turnaround time 30 days.

Criminal Name Search: Access: Mail, fax, in person, email, online. Only the court performs in person name searches; visitors may not. No search fee. Required to search: name, DOB, years to search. Criminal records go back to 1980. Mail turnaround time 30 days. Index online from JIS-Link; see www.courts.wa.gov/jislink/ (also, see state introduction for subscription service.). Also, search name index back to 1989 and calendars free at http://dw.courts.wa.gov/index.cfm. Court actually prefers email requests. Direct email search requests to marcellina.delatorre@muckleshoot.nsn.us.

District Court East Division - Issaquah 5415 220th Ave SE, Issaquah, WA 98029-6839; 206-205-9200, 800-325-6165 x59200; fax: 206-296-0591; 8:30AM-4:30PM (PST). *Misdemeanor, Civil Actions under $75,000, Small Claims.*
www.kingcounty.gov/courts/districtCourt.aspx

General Information: Area: Issaquah, Sammamish, High Pt, Preston, Fall City, Snoqualmie, North Bend, Cedar Falls, Tokul, Alpental, Bellevue, Eastgate, Factoria, Mercer Is, Clyde Hill, Beaux Arts, Newcastle, Redmond, Kirkland, Woodinville, Bothell, Duvall, Carnation, Juanita. No sealed, juvenile, sex offenders (victims) or (sometimes) DUI records released. Will fax documents to local or toll-free number. Court makes copy: $.50 per page; $.25 per page from computer. Certification fee: $5.00 per doc includes copy fee. Payee: King County District Court. Personal checks accepted. No credit cards accepted in person. Prepayment required. Mail requests: SASE required.

Civil Name Search: Access: Mail, in person, online. Both court and visitors may perform in person name searches. No search fee. Required to search: name, years to search; also helpful: address. Civil records on computer back 10 years. Mail turnaround time 1-5 days. Civil PAT goes back to 1995. Add'l identifiers may be in case file. Any District public terminal has all district courts. Index online from JIS-Link; see www.courts.wa.gov/jislink/ (also, see state introduction for subscription service.). Also, search name index back to 1989 and calendars free at http://dw.courts.wa.gov/index.cfm.

Criminal Name Search: Access: Mail, online, in person. Both court and visitors may perform in person name searches. No search fee. Required to search: name, years to search, DOB, signed release; also helpful: address. Criminal records on computer back 5 years. Note: Mail requests are not generally recommended. Mail turnaround time 1-5 days. Criminal PAT goes back to same as civil. Add'l identifiers may be in case file. Any District public terminal has all district courts. Online access to criminal indexes is the same as civil. Online results show middle initial, DOB.

District Court South Division - Burien 601 SW 149th St, Burien, WA 98166-1935; 206-205-9200, 800-325-6165 x59200; fax: 206-296-0124; 8:30AM-4:30PM (PST). *Misdemeanor, Civil Actions under $75,000, Small Claims.*
www.kingcounty.gov/courts/districtCourt.aspx

General Information: Formerly Southwest Division, name change 12/2002. In 2003 merged with the Renton court. No sealed, juvenile, adoption, paternity, mental health, sex offenders (and victims) or DUI records sometimes released. Will not fax out documents. Court makes copy: $.50 per page; $.25 per page from computer. Self serve copy: same. Certification fee: $5.00 per doc plus $1.00 per page. Payee: King County District Court. No personal checks accepted. No credit cards accepted in person. Prepayment required.

Civil Name Search: Access: Mail, in person, online. Both court and visitors may perform in person name searches. No search fee. Required to search: name, years to search; also helpful: address. Civil records on computer back 5 years. Mail turnaround time 1 day. Civil PAT goes back to 1995. Any District public terminal has all district courts. Index online from JIS-Link; see www.courts.wa.gov/jislink/ (also, see state introduction for subscription service.). Also, search name index back to 1989 and calendars free at http://dw.courts.wa.gov/index.cfm.

Criminal Name Search: Access: Mail, online, in person. Both court and visitors may perform in person name searches. No search fee. Required to search: name, years to search; also helpful: address, DOB, SSN. Criminal records computerized from 1987. Mail turnaround time 1 day. Criminal PAT goes back to same as civil. Online access to criminal indexes is the same as civil.

District Court South Division - Kent 1210 Central Ave S, Kent, WA 98032-7426; 206-205-9200, 800-325-6165 x59200; fax: 206-296-0588; 8:30AM-4:30PM (PST). *Misdemeanor, Civil Actions under $75,000, Small Claims.*

www.kingcounty.gov/courts/districtCourt.aspx

General Information: Civil Area: Enumclaw, Kent, Auburn, Black Diamond, Maple Valley, Covington, Algona, Pacific, Ravensdale, Hobart, Federal Way, Burien, Des Moines, Normandy Pk, Vashon Is, SeaTac, Renton, Tukwila. In 2003 Federal Way Div merged operations with Kent. No sealed, juvenile, adoption, paternity, mental health, sex offenders (victims) or (sometimes) DUI records released. Will fax documents $.15 per page fee. Court makes copy: $.25 per page from computer. Certification fee: $5.00 per doc includes copy fee. Payee: King County District Court. Personal checks accepted. No credit cards accepted in person. Prepayment required. Mail requests: SASE required.

Civil Name Search: Access: Mail, in person, online. Both court and visitors may perform in person name searches. No search fee. Required to search: name, years to search; also helpful: address. Civil records on computer 5 years back. Mail turnaround time 1 day. Civil PAT goes back to 1995. Any District public terminal has all district courts. Index online from JIS-Link; see www.courts.wa.gov/jislink/ (also, see state introduction for subscription service.). Also, search name index back to 1989 and calendars free at http://dw.courts.wa.gov/index.cfm.

Criminal Name Search: Access: Mail, online, in person. Both court and visitors may perform in person name searches. No search fee. Required to search: name, years to search, DOB; also helpful: address. Criminal records on computer 5 years back. Mail turnaround time 1 day. Criminal PAT goes back to same as civil. Online access to criminal indexes is the same as civil.

District Court West Division - Seattle 516 3rd Ave, #E-327, Courthouse, Seattle, WA 98104-3273; 206-205-9200, 800-325-6165 x59200; fax: 206-296-0910; 8:30AM-4:30PM (PST). *Misdemeanor, Infractions, Civil Actions under $75,000, Small Claims.*

www.kingcounty.gov/courts/districtCourt.aspx

General Information: The boundaries of Seattle District Court are identical to the City of Seattle's boundary. No sealed, juvenile, adoption, paternity, mental health, sex offenders (victims), treatment plans or (sometimes) DUI records released. Will not fax documents. Court makes copy: $.50 per page; $.25 per page from computer. Certification fee: $5.00 per doc includes copy fee. Payee: King County District Court, Seattle. Personal checks accepted. No credit cards accepted in person. Prepayment required. Mail requests: SASE required.

Civil Name Search: Access: Fax, mail, online, in person. Visitors must perform in person searches themselves. No search fee. Required to search: name, years to search; also helpful: address. Civil records on computer from back 10 years. Mail turnaround time 10 days. Civil PAT goes back to 1995. Public terminal 90% of info available to public, other 10% can only be searched by staff. Any District public terminal has all district courts. Index online from JIS-Link; see www.courts.wa.gov/jislink/ (also, see state introduction for subscription service.). Also, search name index back to 1989 and calendars free at http://dw.courts.wa.gov/index.cfm.

Criminal Name Search: Access: Fax, mail, online, in person. Both court and visitors may perform in person name searches. No search fee. Required to search: name, years to search, DOB, signed release; also helpful: address, SSN. Criminal records computerized from back 10 years. Mail turnaround time 10 days. Criminal PAT goes back to same as civil. Any District public terminal has all district courts. Online access to criminal indexes is the same as civil.

District Court West Division - Shoreline 18050 Meridian Ave N, Shoreline, WA 98133-4642; 206-205-9200, 206-296-3679; 800-325-6165 x59200; fax: 206-296-0594; 8:30AM-4:30PM (PST). *Misdemeanor, Civil Actions under $75,000, Small Claims.*

www.kingcounty.gov/courts/districtCourt.aspx

General Information: Civil Filings for: Shoreline, Kenmore, Lake Forest Park should be filed in Seattle Facility. No sealed, juvenile, adoption, paternity, mental health, sex offenders (victims) or (sometimes) DUI records released. Will only fax back documents for critical situations. Court makes copy: $.50 per page; $.25 per page from computer. Certification fee: $5.00 per doc includes copy fee. Payee: King County District Court. Personal checks accepted. No credit cards accepted in person. Prepayment required. Mail requests: SASE required.

Civil Name Search: Access: Fax, mail, online, in person. Both court and visitors may perform in person name searches. No search fee. Required to search: name, years to search; also helpful: address. Civil records on computer from 1985. Mail turnaround time 1 week. Civil PAT goes back to 1995. Any District public terminal has all district courts. Index online from JIS-Link; see www.courts.wa.gov/jislink/ (also, see state

introduction for subscription service.). Also, search name index back to 1989 and calendars free at http://dw.courts.wa.gov/index.cfm.

Criminal Name Search: Access: Fax, mail, online, in person. Both court and visitors may perform in person name searches. No search fee. Required to search: name, years to search; also helpful: address, DOB, SSN. Criminal records computerized from 1987. Note: Please limit criminal requests to 5 and use their request form. Mail turnaround time 1 week. Criminal PAT goes back to same as civil. Online access to criminal indexes is the same as civil. Online results show middle initial, DOB.

District Court East Division - Redmond 8601 160th Ave NE, Redmond, WA 98052-3548; 206-205-9200, 206-296-3667; 800-325-6165 x59200; 8:30AM-4:30PM (PST). *Misdemeanor.*

www.kingcounty.gov/courts/districtCourt.aspx

General Information: In 2003, the East Division formed a civil court in the Issaquah Courthouse. All civil and small claims actions which previously were filed in the Redmond Courthouse are now filed and heard in Issaquah. No sealed, juvenile, adoption, paternity, mental health, sex offenders (victims) or (sometimes) DUI records released. Will not fax out documents. Court makes copy: $.50 per page; $.25 per page from computer. Certification fee: $5.00 per doc includes copy fee. Payee: King County District Court. Personal checks accepted. No credit cards accepted in person. Prepayment required.

Criminal Name Search: Access: Mail, online, in person. Both court and visitors may perform in person name searches. No search fee. Required to search: name, years to search, DOB; also helpful: address. Criminal records on computer back 5 years. Mail turnaround time 1-2 weeks. Public use terminal has crim records back to 1995. Index online from JIS-Link; see www.courts.wa.gov/jislink/ (also, see state introduction for subscription service.). Also, search name index back to 1989 and calendars free at http://dw.courts.wa.gov/index.cfm.

District Court East Division - Bellevue 585 112th Ave SE, Bellevue, WA 98004; 206-205-9200; 800-325-6165 x59200; 8:30AM-4:30PM (PST). *Misdemeanor.*

www.kingcounty.gov/courts/districtCourt.aspx

General Information: Closed as of 01/01/2009. Bellevue area civil cases are now filed and handled in the Issaquah facility.

Algona Municipal Court See Auburn Municipal Court.

Auburn Municipal Court 340 E Main St #101, Auburn, WA 98002-5548; 253-931-3076; fax: 253-804-5011; 8AM-4PM (PST). *Misdemeanor.*

www.auburnwa.gov/government/municipal_court.asp

General Information: Index online from JIS-Link; see www.courts.wa.gov/jislink/ (also, see state introduction for subscription service.). Also, search name index back to 1989 and calendars free at http://dw.courts.wa.gov/index.cfm.

Bellevue Municipal Court See East Division, KCDC

Black Diamond Municipal Court PO Box 599, 25510 Lawson St, Black Diamond, WA 98010-0599; 360-886-7784; fax: 360-886-5354; 8:30AM-5PM (PST). *Misdemeanor.*

General Information: Index online from JIS-Link; see www.courts.wa.gov/jislink/ (also, see state introduction for subscription service.). Also, search name index back to 1989 and calendars free at http://dw.courts.wa.gov/index.cfm.

Bothell Municipal Court 10116 NE 183rd St, Bothell, WA 98011-3416; 425-487-5587; fax: 425-488-3052; 8AM-5PM (PST). *Misdemeanor.*

www.ci.bothell.wa.us/CityServices/MunicipalCourt.ashx

General Information: Index online from JIS-Link; see www.courts.wa.gov/jislink/ (also, see state introduction for subscription service.). Also, search name index back to 1989 and calendars free at http://dw.courts.wa.gov/index.cfm.

Burien Municipal Court See South Division, KCDC

Carnation Municipal Court See East Division, KCDC

Clyde Hill Municipal Court See Kirkland Municipal Court

Covington Municipal Court See South Division, KCDC

Des Moines Municipal Court 21630 11th Ave S #C, Des Moines, WA 98198-6317; 206-878-4597; fax: 206-870-4387; 8AM-4:30PM (PST). *Misdemeanor.*

www.desmoineswa.gov/dept/court/court.html

General Information: Index online from JIS-Link; see www.courts.wa.gov/jislink/ (also, see state introduction for subscription service.). Also, search name index back to 1989 and calendars free at http://dw.courts.wa.gov/index.cfm.

Duvall Municipal Court See East Division, KCDC

Enumclaw Municipal Court 1339 Griffin Ave, Enumclaw, WA 98022-3011; 360-825-7771; fax: 360-802-0107; 8AM-5PM (PST). *Misdemeanor, Civil.*

www.cityofenumclaw.net/index.asp

General Information: Includes Maple Valley Court. Index online from JIS-Link; see www.courts.wa.gov/jislink/ (also, see state introduction for subscription service.). Also, search name index back to 1989 and calendars free at http://dw.courts.wa.gov/index.cfm.

Federal Way Municipal Court 33325 8th Ave S, Federal Way, WA 98003; 253-835-3000; fax: 253-835-3020; 8:30AM-4:30PM (PST). *Misdemeanor.*
www.cityoffederalway.com/index.aspx?nid=196
General Information: Index online from JIS-Link; see www.courts.wa.gov/jislink/ (also, see state introduction for subscription service.). Also, search name index back to 1989 and calendars free at http://dw.courts.wa.gov/index.cfm.

Hunts Point Municipal Court See Kirkland Municipal Court

Issaquah Municipal Court PO Box 7005, 135 E Sunset Way, Issaquah, WA 98027; 425-837-3170; fax: 425-837-3178; 8:30AM-4:30PM (PST). *Misdemeanor.*
www.ci.issaquah.wa.us/SectionIndex.asp?SectionID=27
General Information: Index online from JIS-Link; see www.courts.wa.gov/jislink/ (also, see state introduction for subscription service.). Also, search name index back to 1989 and calendars free at http://dw.courts.wa.gov/index.cfm.

Kenmore Municipal Court See East Division, KCDC

Kent Municipal Court 1220 S Central, Kent, WA 98032-7426; 253-856-5730 x5; fax: 253-856-6730; 8:30AM-4:30PM (open 7AM on W) (PST). *Misdemeanor.*
www.ci.kent.wa.us/content.aspx?id=1268
General Information: Index online from JIS-Link; see www.courts.wa.gov/jislink/ (also, see state introduction for subscription service.). Also, search name index back to 1989 and calendars free at http://dw.courts.wa.gov/index.cfm.

Kirkland Municipal Court 11515 NE 118th St, Kirkland, WA 98033; 425-587-3160; fax: 425-587-3161; 8:30AM-4:30PM (PST). *Misdemeanor.*
www.kirklandwa.gov/depart/Municipal_Court.htm
General Information: Index online from JIS-Link; see www.courts.wa.gov/jislink/ (also, see state introduction for subscription service.). Also, search name index back to 1989 and calendars free at http://dw.courts.wa.gov/index.cfm.

Lake Forest Park Municipal Court 17425 Ballinger Way NE, Lake Forest Park, WA 98155-5556; 206-364-7711; fax: 206-364-7712; 9AM-5PM (PST). *Misdemeanor, Civil Infractions.*
www.cityoflfp.com/city/court.html

Maple Valley Municipal Court 1339 Griffin Ave, Enumclaw, WA 98022-3011; 360-825-7771; fax: 360-802-0107; 9AM-5PM (PST). *Misdemeanor.*
www.cityofenumclaw.net
General Information: Includes Enumclaw Muni Ct. Index online from JIS-Link; see www.courts.wa.gov/jislink/ (also, see state introduction for subscription service.). Also, search name index back to 1989 & calendars free at http://dw.courts.wa.gov/index.cfm.

Medina Municipal Court See Kirkland Municipal Court

Mercer Island Municipal Court 9611 SE 36th St, Mercer Island, WA 98040-3732; 206-275-7604; fax: 206-275-7980; 9AM-4 M-TH (closed F) (PST). *Misdemeanor.*
General Information: Index online from JIS-Link; see www.courts.wa.gov/jislink/ (also, see state introduction for subscription service.). Also, search name index back to 1989 and calendars free at http://dw.courts.wa.gov/index.cfm.

Newcastle Municipal Court See Mercer Island Municipal Court

Normandy Park Municipal Court See Des Moines Municipal Court

North Bend Municipal Court See East Division, KCDC

Pacific & Algona Municipal Court 100 3rd Ave SE, Pacific, WA 98047-1349; 253-929-1140; fax: 253-929-1195; 8AM-5PM (PST). *Misdemeanor.*
http://cityofpacific.com/courts.html
General Information: Algona location closed, case files here. Office "window" is 8:30AM to 4:30PM.

Redmond Municipal Court See East Division, KCDC

Renton Municipal Court 1055 S Grady Way, Renton, WA 98057; 425-430-6550; fax: 425-430-6544; 8AM-5PM (PST). *Misdemeanor.*
http://rentonwa.gov/living/default.aspx?id=1942

Sammamish Municipal Court See East Division, KCDC

SeaTac Municipal Court 4800 S 188th St, SeaTac, WA 98188; 206-973-4610; fax: 206-973-4629; 8:30AM-5PM (PST). *Misdemeanor, Civil Limited, Traffic.*
www.ci.seatac.wa.us/index.aspx?page=130
General Information: The Judge is authorized by the Revised Code of Washington to preside over civil infractions, traffic infractions, criminal misdemeanor and gross misdemeanor violations, and civil orders for protection.

Seattle Municipal Court PO Box 34987, 600 5th Ave, Seattle, WA 98124-4987; 206-684-5600; fax: 206-684-8115; 8AM-5PM (PST). *Misdemeanor.*
www.seattle.gov/courts/
General Information: Search Seattle Muni Court records free at http://web1.seattle.gov/courts/cpi/.

Shoreline Municipal Court See East Division, KCDC

Skykomish Municipal Court See East Division, KCDC

Snoqualmie Municipal Court See East Division, KCDC

Tukwila Municipal Court 6200 Southcenter Blvd, Tukwila, WA 98188-2544; 206-433-1840; fax: 206-433-7160; 8:30AM-4:30PM (PST). *Misdemeanor.*
www.ci.tukwila.wa.us/mayor/court.html
General Information: Search dockets with subscription to the judicial system at www.courts.wa.gov/jislink/index.cfm.

Woodinville Municipal Court See East Division, KCDC

Yarrow Point Municipal Court See Kirkland Municipal Court

Kitsap County

Superior Court 614 Division St, MS34, County Clerk, Port Orchard, WA 98366-4699; 360-337-7164; fax: 360-337-4927; 8AM-12:15PM 1PM-4:30PM M-TH; 8AM-12:15PM F (PST). *Felony, Civil, Eviction, Probate.*
www.kitsapgov.com/clerk/
General Information: Online identifiers in results same as on public terminal. No dependencies, adoption or mental illness records released. Will fax documents for $5.00 1st page and $1.00 ea add'l. Additional $10 imposed per requested copies per each 25 pages. Court makes copy: $.50 per page; $.25 if from image media, $.50 if microfiche. Self serve copy: $.15 per page.There is an add'l $5.00 handling fee if copies requested by mail, includes postage. Certification fee: $5.00 1st page, $1.00 ea add'l. Payee: Kitsap County Clerk. No personal checks accepted. Major credit cards accepted. Pay online at www.officialpayments.com. Jurisdiction code 5624. Prepayment required. Mail requests: SASE not required.
Civil Name Search: Access: Mail, in person, online. Both court and visitors may perform in person name searches. Search fee: $30.00 per certified copy. Civil records on computer from 1978, on microfiche and archived from 1857. Mail turnaround time 2 weeks. Civil PAT goes back to 1978. Index online from JIS-Link; see www.courts.wa.gov/jislink/ (also, see state introduction for subscription service.). Also, search name index back to 1978 and calendars free at http://dw.courts.wa.gov/index.cfm. Also order a document for a fee (no name searching) at www.clerkepass.com.
Criminal Name Search: Access: Mail, online, in person. Both court and visitors may perform in person name searches. Search fee: $30.00 per certified copy. Required to search: name, years to search; also helpful: address, DOB, SSN. Criminal records computerized from 1978, on microfiche and archived from 1857. Mail turnaround time 2 weeks. Criminal PAT goes back to same as civil. Online access to criminal indexes is the same as civil. Also order a document for a fee (no name searching) at www.clerkepass.com. Online results show middle initial.

District Court 614 Division St, MS 25, Port Orchard, WA 98366-4614; criminal phone: 360-337-7109; civil phone: 360-337-7109; criminal fax: 360-337-4865; civil fax: 8AM-12:15PM, 1:15-4:30PM; 8AM-12:15PM, 1:15-4:30PM (PST). *Misdemeanor, Civil Actions under $75,001, Small Claims.*
www.kitsapgov.com/dc/
General Information: No fee to fax documents. Court makes copy: $.50 per page. Certification fee: $5.00 first page, 41.00 ea add'l. Payee: Kitsap County District Court. Personal checks accepted, credit cards are not. Prepayment required.
Civil Name Search: Access: Phone, fax, mail, online, in person. Only the court performs in person name searches; visitors may not. Search fee: $30.00 per hour. Civil records on computer from 1/95, prior in archives. Mail turnaround time 3 days. Index online from JIS-Link; see www.courts.wa.gov/jislink/ (also, see state introduction for subscription service.). Also, search name index back to 1989 and calendars free at http://dw.courts.wa.gov/index.cfm.
Criminal Name Search: Access: Phone, fax, mail, online, in person. Only the court performs in person name searches; visitors may not. Search fee:

$30.00 per hour. Required to search: name, years to search; also helpful: DOB. Criminal records computerized from 1/95, prior in archives. Mail turnaround time 3 days. Online access to criminal indexes is the same as civil.

Bainbridge Island Municipal Court PO Box 151, 10255 NE Valley Rd, Bainbridge Is, Rolling Bay, WA 98061-0151; 206-842-5641; fax: 206-842-0316; 8AM-4PM (PST). *Misdemeanor.*

www.ci.bainbridge-isl.wa.us/municipal_court.aspx

General Information: Index online from JIS-Link; see www.courts.wa.gov/jislink/ (also, see state introduction for subscription service.). Also, search name index back to 1989 and calendars free at http://dw.courts.wa.gov/index.cfm.

Bremerton Municipal Court 550 Park Ave, Bremerton, WA 98337-1875; 360-473-5260; fax: 360-473-5262; 8AM-5PM (PST). *Misdemeanor.*

www.ci.bremerton.wa.us/display.php?id=53

General Information: Index online from JIS-Link; see www.courts.wa.gov/jislink/ (also, see state introduction for subscription service.). Also, search name index back to 1989 and calendars free at http://dw.courts.wa.gov/index.cfm.

Port Gamble S'Kallam Tribal Court (NICS) 31912 Little Boston Rd NE, Kingston, WA 98346-9700; 360-633-1890; fax: 360-297-6306; 8AM-4:30PM (PST). *Misdemeanor, Civil Actions under $3,000, Eviction.*

www.pgst.nsn.us/

General Information: Felony actions are sent to the federal court. The records from this court are not on the JIS state system.

Port Orchard Municipal Court 216 Prospect St, Port Orchard, WA 98366-5326; 360-876-1701; fax: 360-895-3071; 8AM-4:30PM (PST). *Misdemeanor.*

www.cityofportorchard.us/municipal-court

General Information: Index online from JIS-Link; see www.courts.wa.gov/jislink/ (also, see state introduction for subscription service.). Also, search name index back to 1989 and calendars free at http://dw.courts.wa.gov/index.cfm.

Poulsbo Municipal Court 200 NE Moe St, Poulsbo, WA 98370; 360-779-9846; fax: 360-779-1584; 8AM-12:15PM, 1:15-4:30PM (PST). *Misdemeanor.*

www.cityofpoulsbo.com/municipal/municipal.htm

General Information: Index online from JIS-Link; see www.courts.wa.gov/jislink/ (also, see state introduction for subscription service.). Also, search name index back to 1989 and calendars free at http://dw.courts.wa.gov/index.cfm.

Suquamish Tribal Court PO Box 1209, 18490 Suquamish Way #105, Suquamish, WA 98392-1209; 360-394-8521; fax: 360-598-5333; 8AM-4:30PM (PST). *Felony, Misdemeanor, Civil, Small Claims, Eviction.*

General Information: Felony actions are sent to the federal court. The records from this court are not on the JIS state system.

Kittitas County

Superior Court 205 W 5th, Rm 210, Ellensburg, WA 98926; 509-962-7531; fax: 509-962-7667; 9AM-N, 1-5PM (PST). *Felony, Misdemeanor, Civil, Eviction, Probate.*

www.co.kittitas.wa.us/clerk/

General Information: No dependencies, adoption, and mental illness records released. No fee to fax documents. Fax available in emergency only. Court makes copy: $.50 per page. Certification fee: $5.00 first page; $1.00 each add'l. Electronic certification available through Clerk's Epass. Payee: Kittitas County Clerk. Personal checks accepted. Major credit cards accepted through Ncourt. Prepayment required.

Civil Name Search: Access: Phone, fax, mail, online, in person. Only the court performs in person name searches; visitors may not. Search fee: $10.00 per name. Required to search: name, years to search; also helpful: address. Civil records on computer from 9/1982, on microfiche and archived from 1890. Some records on index cards. Mail turnaround time 2 days. Index online from JIS-Link; see www.courts.wa.gov/jislink/ (also, see state introduction for subscription service.). Also, search name index back to 1989 and calendars free at http://dw.courts.wa.gov/index.cfm.

Criminal Name Search: Access: Phone, fax, mail, online, in person. Only the court performs in person name searches; visitors may not. Search fee: $10.00 per name. Required to search: name, years to search; also helpful: address, DOB, SSN. Criminal records computerized from 9/1982, on microfiche and archived from 1890. Some records on index cards. Mail turnaround time 2 days. Online access to criminal indexes is the same as civil.

District Court Lower Kittitas 205 W 5th, Rm 180, Ellensburg, WA 98926; 509-962-7511; fax: 509-962-7575; 9AM-5PM (PST). *Misdemeanor, Civil Actions under $75,001, Small Claims.*

General Information: Since 01/01/09 holds case files from former Kittitas Municipal Court. No dependencies, adoption, and mental illness records

released. Will fax documents to local or toll free line. Court makes copy: $.50 per page. Certification fee: $5.00 includes copy fee. Payee: Lower Kittitas County District Court. Personal checks accepted, credit cards are not. Prepayment required. Mail requests: SASE required.

Civil Name Search: Access: Mail, in person, online. Only the court performs in person name searches; visitors may not. No search fee. Required to search: name, years to search, DOB. Civil records on computer from 8/97, archived back 10 years. Records retained for 10 years. Mail turnaround time 5 days. Index online from JIS-Link; see www.courts.wa.gov/jislink/ (also, see state introduction for subscription service.). Also, search name index back to 1989 and calendars free at http://dw.courts.wa.gov/index.cfm.

Criminal Name Search: Access: Fax, mail, online, in person. Only the court performs in person name searches; visitors may not. No search fee. Required to search: name, years to search, DOB. Criminal records computerized from 8/97. Mail turnaround time 5 days. Online access to criminal indexes is the same as civil.

District Court Upper Kittitas 700 E 1st, Cle Elum, WA 98922; 509-674-5533; fax: 509-674-4209; 9AM-5PM (PST). *Misdemeanor, Civil Actions under $75,001, Small Claims.*

General Information: No dependencies, adoption, and mental illness records released. Fee to fax out file $1.00 per page. Court makes copy: $.15 per page. Certification fee: $5.00. Payee: UKCDC. Personal checks accepted. Credit cards accepted. Prepayment required.

Civil Name Search: Access: Mail, in person, online. Only the court performs in person name searches; visitors may not. No search fee. Civil records on computer since 8/91; prior records archived from 1890, some on index cards. Records retained for 10 years. Mail turnaround time 1 week. Index online from JIS-Link; see www.courts.wa.gov/jislink/ (also, see state introduction for subscription service.). Also, search name index back to 1989 and calendars free at http://dw.courts.wa.gov/index.cfm.

Criminal Name Search: Access: Fax, mail, online, in person. Only the court performs in person name searches; visitors may not. No search fee. Required to search: name, years to search, DOB, signed release; also helpful: SSN. Criminal records computerized from 1997; prior records archived from 1890, some on index cards. Records retained for 5 years. Mail turnaround time 1 week. Online access to criminal indexes is the same as civil.

Cle Elum Municipal Court 700 E 1st St, Cle Elum, WA 98922-1251; 509-674-5533; fax: 509-674-4209; 7AM-5PM M-TH; 8AM-5PM Fri (PST). *Misdemeanor.*

General Information: Index online from JIS-Link; see www.courts.wa.gov/jislink/ (also, see state introduction for subscription service.). Also, search name index back to 1989 and calendars free at http://dw.courts.wa.gov/index.cfm.

Ellensburg Municipal Court See Lower Kittitas District Court

Kittitas Municipal Court See District Court Lower Kittitas

Roslyn Municipal Court 700 E 1st St, Cle Elum, WA 98922-1251; 509-674-5533; fax: 509-674-4209; 7AM-5PM (PST). *Misdemeanor.*

General Information: Index online from JIS-Link; see www.courts.wa.gov/jislink/ (also, see state introduction for subscription service.). Also, search name index back to 1989 and calendars free at http://dw.courts.wa.gov/index.cfm.

Klickitat County

Superior Court County Clerk, 205 S Columbus, MS CH-O3, Goldendale, WA 98620; 509-773-5744;; 9AM-5PM (PST). *Felony, Civil, Eviction, Probate.*

www.klickitatcounty.org/

General Information: No dependencies, adoption, and mental illness records released. Will not fax documents. Court makes copy: $.50 per page. Certification fee: $5.00 plus $1.00 per page after first. Payee: Klickitat County Clerk. No personal checks accepted. No credit cards accepted for searches and copies. Prepayment required. Mail requests: SASE required.

Civil Name Search: Access: Phone, mail, online, in person. Only the court performs in person name searches; visitors may not. Search fee: $30.00 per hour. Required to search: name, years to search; also helpful: address. Civil index on computer from 9/87, prior on books. Mail turnaround time 1-2 weeks or sooner. Index online from JIS-Link; see www.courts.wa.gov/jislink/ (also, see state introduction for subscription service.). Also, search name index back to 1989 and calendars free at http://dw.courts.wa.gov/index.cfm. Also order a document for a fee (no name searching) at www.clerkepass.com.

Criminal Name Search: Access: Phone, mail, online, in person. Only the court performs in person name searches; visitors may not. Search fee: $30.00 per hour. Required to search: name, years to search; also helpful: address, DOB, SSN. Criminal index computer from 9/87; prior on books back to 1886. Mail turnaround time 1-2 weeks or sooner. Online access to criminal indexes is the same as civil. Also order a document for a fee (no name searching) at www.clerkepass.com.

East District Court 205 S Columbus, MS-CH11, Goldendale, WA 98620-9290; 509-773-4670; fax: 509-773-4653; 8AM-N, 1-5pm (PST). *Misdemeanor, Civil Actions under $75,001, Small Claims.* www.klickitatcounty.org/

General Information: No dependencies, adoption, and mental illness records released. Will fax documents to local or toll free line. Court makes copy: 1st 10 pages free, each add'l page $.15. Certification fee: $5.00. Payee: East District Court. Personal checks accepted. Major credit cards accepted. Mail requests: SASE required.

Civil Name Search: Access: Phone, mail, fax, in person, online. Both court and visitors may perform in person name searches. No search fee. Civil records on computer from 4/93, on index cards prior. Retained for 10 years. Mail turnaround time 1 week. Index online from JIS-Link; see www.courts.wa.gov/jislink/ (also, see state introduction for subscription service.). Also, search name index back to 1989 and calendars free at http://dw.courts.wa.gov/index.cfm.

Criminal Name Search: Access: Phone, mail, fax, in person, online. Both court and visitors may perform in person name searches. No search fee. Required to search: name, years to search, DOB. Criminal records computerized from 4/93, on index cards prior. Retained for 10 years. Mail turnaround time 1 week. Online access to criminal indexes is the same as civil.

West District Court PO Box 435, White Salmon, WA 98672-0435; 509-493-1190; fax: 509-493-4469; 8AM-12; 1PM-5PM (PST). *Misdemeanor, Civil Actions under $75,001, Small Claims.* www.klickitatcounty.org/WDistrictCourt/

General Information: No dependencies, adoption, sealed and mental illness records released. Will not fax documents. Court makes copy: $1.00 per page. Certification fee: $6.00 per doc plus copy fee. Cert fee includes copies. Payee: West District Court. Personal checks accepted, credit cards are not. Prepayment required. Mail requests: SASE required.

Civil Name Search: Access: Mail, in person, online. Only the court performs in person name searches; visitors may not. No search fee. Civil records on computer from 5/93, on docket books. Mail turnaround time 3-5 days. Index online from JIS-Link; see www.courts.wa.gov/jislink/ (also, see state introduction for subscription service.). Also, search name index back to 1989 and calendars free at http://dw.courts.wa.gov/index.cfm.

Criminal Name Search: Access: Mail, in person, online. Only the court performs in person name searches; visitors may not. No search fee. Required to search: name, years to search, DOB; also helpful: address. Criminal records computerized from 5/93, on docket books. Mail turnaround time 3-5 days. Online access to criminal indexes is the same as civil.

Bingen Municipal Court See West District Court

Goldendale Municipal Court See East District Court

White Salmon Municipal Court See West District Court

Lewis County

Superior Court 345 W Main St, County Clerk's Office, MS:CLK 01, Chehalis, WA 98532-1900; 360-740-2704; criminal phone: 360-740-1395; civil phone: 360-740-2756; probate phone: 360-740-2776; fax: 360-748-1639; 8AM-5PM (PST). *Felony, Misdemeanor, Civil, Eviction, Probate, Domestic.* http://lewiscountywa.gov/clerk

General Information: Online identifiers in results same as on public terminal. No dependencies, adoption, paternity, and mental illness records released. Fee to fax out file $1.00 per page. Court makes copy: $.50 per page. Certification fee: $5.00 1st page, $1.00 ea add'l. Cert fee includes copies. Payee: Lewis County Clerk. Personal checks accepted. Visa/MC accepted through Point & Pay Inc. Prepayment required. Mail requests: SASE required.

Civil Name Search: Access: Phone, mail, online, in person. Both court and visitors may perform in person name searches. Search fee: No charge unless extensive research required. Required to search: name, years to search; also helpful: address. Civil records on computer from 1983, archived from 1900s. Mail turnaround time up to 7 days. Civil PAT goes back to 1983. Index online from JIS-Link; see www.courts.wa.gov/jislink/ (also, see state introduction for subscription service.). Also, search name index back to 1989 and calendars free at http://dw.courts.wa.gov/index.cfm.

Criminal Name Search: Access: Phone, mail, online, in person. Both court and visitors may perform in person name searches. Search fee: No charge unless extensive research required. Required to search: name, years to search; also helpful: address, DOB, SSN. Criminal records computerized from 1983, archived from 1900s. Mail turnaround time up to 7 days. Criminal PAT goes back to same as civil. Online access to criminal indexes is the same as civil. Online results show name only.

District Court PO Box 600, Chehalis, WA 98532-0600; 360-740-1203; fax: 360-740-2779; 8AM-5PM (PST). *Misdemeanor, Civil Actions under $45,000, Small Claims.*

General Information: No dependencies, adoption, and mental illness records released. No fee to fax documents. Court makes copy: $.25 per page. Certification fee: $5.00 per doc. Payee: Lewis County District Court. Personal checks accepted, credit cards are not. Prepayment required. Mail requests: SASE required.

Civil Name Search: Access: Fax, mail, online, in person. Both court and visitors may perform in person name searches. No search fee. Civil records on computer from 1983. Records retained 10 years. Mail turnaround time 1 week. Index online from JIS-Link; see www.courts.wa.gov/jislink/ (also, see state introduction for subscription service.). Also, search name index back to 1989 and calendars free at http://dw.courts.wa.gov/index.cfm.

Criminal Name Search: Access: Fax, mail, online, in person. Only the court performs in person name searches; visitors may not. No search fee. Required to search: name, years to search, DOB, sex, signed release; also helpful: address, SSN. Criminal records on computer since 1981. Records retained for 5 years after court closure. Mail turnaround time 1 week. Online access to criminal indexes is the same as civil.

Centralia Municipal Court PO Box 609, 118 W Maple St, Centralia, WA 98531-0609; 360-330-7667; fax: 360-330-7668; 8AM-5PM (PST). *Misdemeanor.* www.cityofcentralia.com/SectionIndex.asp?SectionID=10

General Information: Index online from JIS-Link; see www.courts.wa.gov/jislink/ (also, see state introduction for subscription service.). Also, search name index back to 1989 and calendars free at http://dw.courts.wa.gov/index.cfm.

Chehalis Municipal Court 350 N Market Blvd, Rm 105, Chehalis, WA 98532-0871; 360-345-1025; fax: 360-345-1050; 8AM-5PM (PST). *Misdemeanor, Gross Misdemeanor, City Ordinances.* http://ci.chehalis.wa.us/municipalcourt

General Information: Index online from JIS-Link; see www.courts.wa.gov/jislink/ (also, see state introduction for subscription service.). Also, search name index back to 1989 & calendars free at http://dw.courts.wa.gov/index.cfm.

Morton Municipal Court See District Court

Mossyrock Municipal Court See District Court

Napavine Municipal Court PO Box 179, 407 Birch Ave SW, Napavine, WA 98565-0810; 360-262-9231; fax: 360-262-9885; 8AM-5PM M-TH (PST). *Misdemeanor, Ordinance.* www.cityofnapavine.com/municipalcourt.html

General Information: Index online from JIS-Link; see www.courts.wa.gov/jislink/ (also, see state introduction for subscription service.). Also, search name index back to 1989 and calendars free at http://dw.courts.wa.gov/index.cfm.

Pe Ell Municipal Court See District Court

Toledo Municipal Court See District Court

Vader Municipal Court See Winlock Municipal Court

Winlock Municipal Court PO Box 777, 323 NE 1st St, Winlock, WA 98596-0777; 360-785-3811; fax: 360-785-4378; 9AM-4:30PM (PST). *Misdemeanor, Traffic, Infractions.* www.winlockwa.govoffice2.com/

General Information: Index online from JIS-Link; see www.courts.wa.gov/jislink/ (also, see state introduction for subscription service.). Also, search name index back to 1989 and calendars free at http://dw.courts.wa.gov/index.cfm.

Lincoln County

Superior Court Box 68, Davenport, WA 99122-0068; 509-725-1401; fax: 509-725-1150; 9AM-4PM (PST). *Felony, Misdemeanor, Civil, Eviction, Probate.*

General Information: Probate is in a separate index. Probate fax is same as main fax number. No dependencies, adoption, and mental illness records released. Will not fax documents. Court makes copy: $.50 per page. Certification fee: $5.00 1st page; $1.00 each add'l page. Payee: Lincoln County Clerk. Business checks accepted. Prepayment required. Mail requests: SASE required.

Civil Name Search: Access: Mail, in person, online. Both court and visitors may perform in person name searches. Search fee: $30.00 per hour. Required to search: name, years to search; also helpful: address. Civil records on computer and microfiche from 11/82, archived from 1903. Mail turnaround time 4 days. Civil PAT goes back to 11/1982. Index online from JIS-Link; see www.courts.wa.gov/jislink/ (also, see state introduction for subscription service.). Also, search name index back to 1989 and calendars free at http://dw.courts.wa.gov/index.cfm.

Criminal Name Search: Access: Mail, online, in person, phone. Both court and visitors may perform in person name searches. Search fee: $30.00 per hour. Required to search: name, years to search; also helpful: address, DOB, SSN. Criminal records on computer and microfiche from

11/82, archived from 1903. Mail turnaround time 4 days. Criminal PAT goes back to same as civil. Online access to criminal indexes is the same as civil.

District Court PO Box 329, Davenport, WA 99122-0329; 509-725-2281; fax: 509-725-6481; 9AM-4PM (PST). *Misdemeanor, Civil Actions under $75,000, Small Claims.*
www.co.lincoln.wa.us
General Information: This is a small office with limited time allowable for searches. No dependencies, adoption, and mental illness records released. Will fax documents to local or toll-free number. Court makes copy: $.50 per page. Certification fee: $6.00 per doc plus copy fee. Cert fee includes copies. Payee: Lincoln County District Court. Business checks accepted. Major credit cards accepted. Prepayment required. Mail requests: SASE required.
Civil Name Search: Access: Mail, fax, online, in person. Both court and visitors may perform in person name searches. Search fee: $25.00 per hour. Civil cases indexed by defendant. Civil records on computer back to 6/93, in books from 1985. Mail turnaround time 1 week. Civil PAT goes back to 1990. Index online from JIS-Link; see www.courts.wa.gov/jislink/ (also, see state introduction for subscription service.). Also, search name index back to 1989 and calendars free at http://dw.courts.wa.gov/index.cfm.
Criminal Name Search: Access: Mail, fax, online, in person, phone. Both court and visitors may perform in person name searches. Search fee: $25.00 per hour. Required to search: name, years to search, DOB. Criminal records computerized from 6/93; hard copy files back to 1990. Mail turnaround time 1 week. Criminal PAT goes back to same as civil. Online access to criminal indexes is the same as civil.

Almira Municipal Court See District Court

Davenport Municipal Court See District Court

Harrington Municipal Court See District Court

Odessa Municipal Court See District Court

Reardan Municipal Court See District Court

Spraque Municipal Court See District Court

Wilbur Municipal Court See District Court

Mason County

Superior Court PO Box 340, 419 N 4th St, Shelton, WA 98584; 360-427-9670 x346; 8:30AM-5PM (PST). *Felony, Civil Actions Above $25,000, Eviction, Probate.*
www.co.mason.wa.us/clerk/index.php
General Information: No dependencies, adoption, and mental illness records released. Will not fax documents. Court makes copy: $.50 per page. Certification fee: $5.00 per document plus copy fee. Payee: Mason County Clerk. Local attorney checks accepted. No personal checks or credit cards accepted. Prepayment required. Mail requests: SASE required.
Civil Name Search: Access: Mail, in person, online. Both court and visitors may perform in person name searches. Search fee: $30.00 per hour. Required to search: name, years to search; also helpful: address. Civil records on computer from 1982; on microfiche and archived from 1890; on index or docket books prior to 1982. Mail turnaround time 1 week. Civil PAT goes back to 10 years or more. Index online from JIS-Link; see www.courts.wa.gov/jislink/ (also, see state introduction for subscription service.). Also, search name index back to 1989 and calendars free at http://dw.courts.wa.gov/index.cfm. Also order a document for a fee (no name searching) at www.clerkepass.com.
Criminal Name Search: Access: Mail, online, in person. Both court and visitors may perform in person name searches. Search fee: $30.00 per hour. Required to search: name, years to search; also helpful: address, DOB. Criminal records computerized from 1982; on microfiche and archived from 1890; on index or docket books prior to 1982. Mail turnaround time 1 week. Criminal PAT goes back to 10 years or more. Online access to criminal indexes is the same as civil. Also order a document for a fee (no name searching) at www.clerkepass.com.

District Court PO Box "O", Shelton, WA 98584-0090; 360-427-9670; criminal phone: X339; civil phone: X343; fax: 360-427-7776; 8:30AM-5PM (PST). *Misdemeanor, Civil Actions under $75,001, Small Claims.*
www.co.mason.wa.us/district_court/index.php
General Information: Court makes copy: $.50 per page. Certification fee: $5.00 1st page plus copy fee for add'l pages. Payee: Mason County District Court. Personal checks, Visa/MC accepted. Prepayment required. Mail requests: SASE required.
Civil Name Search: Access: Mail, in person, online. Only the court performs in person name searches; visitors may not. Search fee: $20.00 per name. Fee is for extensive searching. Required to search: name, years to search; also helpful: address. Civil records on computer from 12/92. Mail turnaround time 1 week. Index online from JIS-Link; see www.courts.wa.gov/jislink/ (also, see state introduction for subscription

service.). Also, search name index back to 1989 and calendars free at http://dw.courts.wa.gov/index.cfm.
Criminal Name Search: Access: Mail, in person, online. Only the court performs in person name searches; visitors may not. Search fee: Will charge $20.00 for extensive search. Required to search: name, years to search, DOB, signed release; also helpful: address, SSN. Criminal records computerized from 12/92, prior on index book. Mail turnaround time 1 week. Online access to criminal indexes is the same as civil.

Shelton Municipal Court 525 W Cota St, Civic Center, Shelton, WA 98584-2239; 360-426-9772; fax: 360-426-3301; 8AM-5PM (PST). *Misdemeanor.*
www.ci.shelton.wa.us/municipal_court/index.php
General Information: Index online from JIS-Link; see www.courts.wa.gov/jislink/ (also, see state introduction for subscription service.). Also, search name index back to 1989 and calendars free at http://dw.courts.wa.gov/index.cfm.

Skokomish Tribal Court (NICS) 80 N Tribal Center Rd, Shelton, WA 98584-9748; 360-426-4740; fax: 360-877-6672; 8AM-4PM (PST). *Misdemeanor, Civil.*
www.skokomish.org/frame.htm
General Information: Felony actions are sent to the federal court. The records from this court are not on the JIS state system.

Squaxin Island Tribal Court 70 SE Squaxin Ln, Shelton, WA 98584; 360-432-3828; fax: 360-462-1181; 8AM-4PM (PST). *Misdemeanor, Civil, Family.*
www.squaxinisland.org/government/departments/
General Information: Felony actions are sent to the federal court. The records from this court are not on the JIS state system.

Okanogan County

Superior Court PO Box 72, 149 N 3rd, Okanogan, WA 98840; 509-422-7275; probate phone: 509-422-7275; fax: 509-422-7277; 8:30AM-5PM (PST). *Felony, Misdemeanor, Civil, Eviction, Probate.*
www.okanogancounty.org/superior_court.htm
General Information: Probate fax is same as main fax number. No dependencies, adoption, and mental illness records released. Will not fax documents. Court makes copy: $.50 per page. Self serve copy: same. Certification fee: $5.00 plus $1.00 per page after first. Cert fee includes copies. Payee: Okanogan County Clerk. Personal checks accepted, credit cards are not. Prepayment required. Mail requests: SASE required.
Civil Name Search: Access: Phone, fax, mail, online, in person. Only the court performs in person name searches; visitors may not. Search fee: $20.00 per hour. Required to search: name, years to search; also helpful: address. Civil records on computer from 1984, on hand-written indexes from 1895. Mail turnaround time 1-7 days. Index online from JIS-Link; see www.courts.wa.gov/jislink/ (also, see state introduction for subscription service.). Also, search name index back to 1989 and calendars free at http://dw.courts.wa.gov/index.cfm.
Criminal Name Search: Access: Phone, fax, mail, online, in person. Only the court performs in person name searches; visitors may not. Search fee: $20.00 per hour. Criminal records computerized from 1984, on hand-written indexes from 1895. Mail turnaround time 1-7 days. Online access to criminal indexes is the same as civil.

District Court PO Box 980, 149 N 3rd Ave, Rm 306, Okanogan, WA 98840-0980; 509-422-7170; fax: 509-422-7174; 8:00AM-5PM, closed for lunch hour on 3rd Fri each month (PST). *Misdemeanor, Civil Actions under $75,000, Small Claims.*
www.okanogancounty.org/DC/index.htm
General Information: Daily court calendar is at www.okanogancounty.org/DC/calendar2.htm. No alcohol related evaluations, mental illness records released. Will fax documents $1.00 1st page, $.50 each add'l. Court makes copy: $.50 per page. Certification fee: $5.00 per cert includes copy fee. Payee: Okanogan County District Court. Personal checks, Visa/MC accepted. Prepayment required. Mail requests: SASE requested.
Civil Name Search: Access: Phone, fax, mail, in person, online. Both court and visitors may perform in person name searches. Search fee: $20 per hour in 1/2 hour increments. Civil records on computer for 10 years. Records files maintained 10 years if judgment, otherwise 3 years. Mail turnaround time 7 days. Civil PAT goes back to 3/1996. Index online from JIS-Link; see www.courts.wa.gov/jislink/ (also, see state introduction for subscription service.). Also, search name index back to 1989 and calendars free at http://dw.courts.wa.gov/index.cfm.
Criminal Name Search: Access: Phone, fax, mail, in person, online. Both court and visitors may perform in person name searches. Search fee: $20 per hour in 1/2 hour increments. Required to search: name, years to search, DOB. Criminal records on computer for 10 years. Mail turnaround time 7 days. Criminal PAT goes back to same as civil. Online access to criminal indexes is the same as civil.

Brewster Municipal Court PO Box 1074, 105 S 3rd St, Brewster, WA 98812-1074; 509-689-2756; fax: 509-689-3096; 8AM-4PM (PST). *Misdemeanor, Ordinance, Traffic.*
General Information: Index online from JIS-Link; see www.courts.wa.gov/jislink/ (also, see state introduction for subscription service.). Also, search name index back to 1989 and calendars free at http://dw.courts.wa.gov/index.cfm.

Colville Confederated Tribal Court PO Box 150, 2 Joe Moses Rd, Nespelem, WA 99155-0150; 509-634-2500; fax: 509-634-2511; 7:30AM-4PM (PST). *Misdemeanor, Civil, Tribal Law.*
www.colvilletribes.com/tribal_courts.php
General Information: Felony actions are sent to the federal court. The records from this court are not on the JIS state system.

Coulee Dam Municipal Court See District Court

Okanogan Municipal Court See District Court

Omak Municipal Court PO Box 72, 2 N Ash, Omak, WA 98841-0072; 509-826-2971; fax: 509-826-6531; 8AM-5PM (PST). *Misdemeanor, Traffic.*
www.omakcity.com/municipal.html
General Information: Index online from JIS-Link; see www.courts.wa.gov/jislink/ (also, see state introduction for subscription service.). Also, search name index back to 1989 and calendars free at http://dw.courts.wa.gov/index.cfm.

Orville Municipal Court See District Court

Pateros Municipal Court See Brewster Municipal Court

Riverside Municipal Court See District Court.

Tonasket Municipal Court PO Box 487, 209 S Whitcomb Ave, Tonasket, WA 98855-0487; 509-486-2132; fax: 509-486-1831; 8AM-4:30PM (PST). *Misdemeanor.*
www.tonasketcity.org/

Twisp Municipal Court PO Box 278, 118 Glover St, Twisp, WA 98856-0278; 509-997-6112; fax: 509-997-1096; 9AM-5PM M-TH; 9AM-N F (PST). *Ordinance, Traffic.*
www.townoftwisp.com

Winthrop Municipal Court PO Box 459, 206 Riverside Ave, Winthrop, WA 98862-0459; 509-996-2320; fax: 509-996-9221; 8AM-4PM (PST). *Misdemeanor.*
General Information: Index online from JIS-Link; see www.courts.wa.gov/jislink/ (also, see state introduction for subscription service.). Also, search name index back to 1989 and calendars free at http://dw.courts.wa.gov/index.cfm.

Pacific County

Superior Court PO Box 67, 300 Memorial Drive, South Bend, WA 98586; 360-875-9320; 8:30AM-4:30PM (PST). *Felony, Civil, Eviction, Probate.*
www.co.pacific.wa.us/courts/clerk/index.htm
General Information: If you know the docket number you can order copies by phone. No dependencies, adoption, and mental illness records released. Will not fax documents. Court makes copy: $.50 per page in person; if a specific page is requested by phone then $1.00.Microfilm copy is an additional $1.00 per page copy fee. Certification fee: $5.00 1st page, $1.00 each add'l page. Payee: Pacific County Clerk. Personal checks accepted, credit cards are not. Prepayment required. Mail requests: SASE required.
Civil Name Search: Access: Phone, mail, online, in person. Only the court performs in person name searches; visitors may not. Search fee: $30.00 per hour. Civil records on computer from 2/84, archived from 1887, some on docket books. Mail turnaround time varies. Index online from JIS-Link; see www.courts.wa.gov/jislink/ (also, see state introduction for subscription service.). Also, search name index back to 1989 and calendars free at http://dw.courts.wa.gov/index.cfm. Also order a document for a fee (no name searching) at www.clerkepass.com.
Criminal Name Search: Access: Mail, online, in person. Only the court performs in person name searches; visitors may not. Search fee: None, but $30.00 per hour if searching before 1984. Criminal records computerized from 2/84, archived from 1887, some on docket books. Mail turnaround time varies. Online access to criminal indexes is the same as civil. Also order a document for a fee (no name searching) at www.clerkepass.com.

District Court North Box 134, South Bend, WA 98586-0134; 360-875-9354; 9AM-5PM (PST). *Misdemeanor, Civil Actions under $75,001, Small Claims.*
General Information: No dependencies, MVRs, defendant case histories, adoption, and mental illness records released. Will not fax documents. Court makes copy: $1.00 first page, $.50 each add'l. Certification fee: $5.00, and $.50 each add'l. Payee: North District Court. Personal checks accepted, credit cards are not. Prepayment required. Mail requests: SASE required.

Civil Name Search: Access: Phone, fax, mail, online, in person. Only the court performs in person name searches; visitors may not. No search fee. Required to search: name, years to search; also helpful: address. Civil records on computer back to 3/93, prior on index cards. Depending on disposition date, civil records retained 3 years after disposition. Mail turnaround time 1-6 weeks. Index online from JIS-Link; see www.courts.wa.gov/jislink/ (also, see state introduction for subscription service.). Also, search name index back to 1989 and calendars free at http://dw.courts.wa.gov/index.cfm.
Criminal Name Search: Access: Phone, mail, in person, online. Only the court performs in person name searches; visitors may not. No search fee. Required to search: name, DOB. Criminal Records retained on hard copy three years after disposition, on computer back to 3/93. Mail turnaround time 1-6 weeks. Online access to criminal indexes is the same as civil.

District Court South 7013 Sandridge Rd, Long Beach, WA 98631; 360-642-9417; fax: 360-642-9416; 7:30AM-4PM (PST). *Misdemeanor, Civil Actions under $75,001, Small Claims.*
www.co.pacific.wa.us/courts/sdc/
General Information: No dependencies, adoption, and mental illness records released. No fee to fax documents. Court makes copy: $1.00 first page, $.50 each add'l. Certification fee: $5.00 per doc plus copy fee. Payee: South District Court. Personal checks accepted. Credit cards accepted. Prepayment required. Mail requests: SASE required.
Civil Name Search: Access: Phone, fax, mail, online, in person. Only the court performs in person name searches; visitors may not. No search fee. Required to search: name, years to search; also helpful: address. Civil records on computer for current and open cases. Records retained for 10 years. Mail turnaround time 1 week. Index online from JIS-Link; see www.courts.wa.gov/jislink/ (also, see state introduction for subscription service.). Also, search name index back to 1989 and calendars free at http://dw.courts.wa.gov/index.cfm.
Criminal Name Search: Access: Fax, mail, online, in person. Only the court performs in person name searches; visitors may not. No search fee. Required to search: name; also helpful: years to search, address, DOB, SSN. Criminal records on computer for current and open cases. Records retained for 10 years. Mail turnaround time 1 week. Online access to criminal indexes is the same as civil.

Shoalwater Bay Tribal Court (NICS) PO Box 130, 2373 Old Tokeland Rd, Tokeland, WA 98590; 360-267-8172, 267-6766 x2100; fax: 360-267-3306; 8:30AM-4:30PM (PST). *Felony, Misdemeanor, Civil., Indian Child Welfare, Traffic.*
www.shoalwaterbay-nsn.gov/
General Information: Felony actions are sent to the federal court. The records from this court are not on the JIS state system.

Ilwaco / Long Beach Municipal Court PO Box 310, 115 Bolstad Ave W, Long Beach, WA 98631-0310; 360-642-8845; fax: 360-642-8841; 8AM-5PM (PST). *Misdemeanor, Ordinance.*
General Information: Index online from JIS-Link; see www.courts.wa.gov/jislink/ (also, see state introduction for subscription service.). Also, search name index back to 1989 and calendars free at http://dw.courts.wa.gov/index.cfm.

Raymond Municipal Court 230 2nd St, Raymond, WA 98577-2406; 360-942-4102; fax: 360-942-4137; 7:30AM-4PM (PST). *Misdemeanor, Infraction, City Ordinance.*
General Information: Index online from JIS-Link; see www.courts.wa.gov/jislink/ (also, see state introduction for subscription service.). Also, search name index back to 1989 and calendars free at http://dw.courts.wa.gov/index.cfm.

South Bend Municipal Court 1102 W 1st St, South Bend, WA 98586; 360-875-5571; fax: 360-875-4009; 8AM-4PM (PST). *Misdemeanor.*
General Information: Index online from JIS-Link; see www.courts.wa.gov/jislink/ (also, see state introduction for subscription service.). Also, search name index back to 1989 and calendars free at http://dw.courts.wa.gov/index.cfm.

Pend Oreille County

Superior Court PO Box 5020, 229 S Garden Ave, Newport, WA 99156-5020; 509-447-2435; fax: 509-447-2734; 8AM-4:30PM (PST). *Felony, Civil, Eviction, Probate.*
www.pendoreilleco.org/county/superior.asp
General Information: Probate fax is same as main fax number. No dependencies, adoption, and mental illness records released. Fee to fax out file $3.00 1st page, $1.00 each add'l. Court makes copy: $.50 per page. Certification fee: $5.00 first page, $1.00 ea add'l. Payee: Pend Oreille County Clerk. Personal checks accepted. Major credit cards accepted. Prepayment required. Mail requests: SASE required.
Civil Name Search: Access: Mail, in person, online. Both court and visitors may perform in person name searches. Search fee: $20.00 per hour. Required to search: name, years to search; also helpful: address. Civil

records on computer and microfiche from 9/82, archived from 1911, on docket books prior to 9/82. Mail turnaround time same day. Index online from JIS-Link; see www.courts.wa.gov/jislink/ (also, see state introduction for subscription service.). Also, search name index back to 1989 and calendars free at http://dw.courts.wa.gov/index.cfm. Also order a document for a fee (no name searching) at www.clerkepass.com.

Criminal Name Search: Access: Phone, mail, in person, online. Both court and visitors may perform in person name searches. No search fee. Required to search: name, years to search; also helpful: address, DOB, SSN. Criminal records on computer and microfiche from 9/82, archived from 1911, on docket books prior to 9/82. Mail turnaround time same day. Online access to criminal indexes is the same as civil. Also order a document for a fee (no name searching) at www.clerkepass.com.

District Court PO Box 5030, 229 S Garden Ave, Newport, WA 99156-5030; 509-447-4110; civil phone: 800-359-1506; fax: 509-447-5724; 8AM-4:30PM (PST). *Misdemeanor, Civil Actions under $75,000, Small Claims.*

www.pendoreilleco.org/county/court.asp

General Information: No dependencies, adoption, and mental illness records released. No fee to fax documents. Court makes copy: $.25 per page. Self serve copy: $.25 per page. Certification fee: $5.00 per doc plus copy fee. Payee: Pend Oreille County District Court. Personal checks accepted, credit cards are not. Prepayment required. Mail requests: SASE required.

Civil Name Search: Access: Phone, fax, mail, online, in person. Both court and visitors may perform in person name searches. No search fee. Required to search: name, years to search; also helpful: address. Civil records on DISCIS computer from 10/92. Records retained for 10 years. Mail turnaround time 10 days. DOB not available for civil defendants. Index online from JIS-Link; see www.courts.wa.gov/jislink/ (also, see state introduction for subscription service.). Also, search name index back to 1989 and calendars free at http://dw.courts.wa.gov/index.cfm.

Criminal Name Search: Access: Fax, mail, online, in person. Both court and visitors may perform in person name searches. No search fee. Required to search: name, DOB; also helpful: years to search, address. Criminal records on DISCIS computer from 10/92. Records retained for 5 years. Mail turnaround time 10 days. Online access to criminal indexes is the same as civil.

Cusick Municipal Court See District Court

Ione Municipal Court See District Court

Kalispel Tribal Court PO Box 96, 22 Camas Flat Rd, Cusick, Usk, WA 99180-0096; 509-445-1664; fax: 509-445-4039; 7AM-5PM M-TH (PST). *Misdemeanor, Civil, Family Law, Criminal.*

http://kalispeltribe.com/tribal-court/

General Information: Felony actions are sent to the federal court. The records from this court are not on the JIS state system.

Metaline Falls Municipal Court See District Court

Metaline Municipal Court See District Court

Newport Municipal Court See District Court

Pierce County

Superior Court 930 Tacoma Ave S, Rm 110, Tacoma, WA 98402; 253-798-7455; probate phone: 253-798-7461; fax: 253-798-3428; 8:30AM-4:30PM (PST). *Felony, Civil, Eviction, Probate.*

www.co.pierce.wa.us/pc/abtus/ourorg/clerk/home.htm

General Information: No sealed, juvenile, adoption, paternity, mental health, sex offenders (victims) or (sometimes) DUI records released. Will fax documents; $5.00 minimum. Court makes copy: $.50 per page. Self serve copy: same. Certification fee: $5.00 plus $1.00 per page after first. Cert fee includes copies. Payee: Pierce County Clerk. Business checks accepted, no personal. No credit cards accepted. Prepayment required. Mail requests: SASE required.

Civil Name Search: Access: Fax, mail, online, in person. Both court and visitors may perform in person name searches. Search fee: $30.00 per hour. Required to search: name, years to search; also helpful: address. Civil records on computer from 5/81. Mail turnaround time 2-5 days. Civil PAT goes back to 1983. Calendars and Courts records are online at www.co.pierce.wa.us/cfapps/linx/search.cfm. Also, Index online from JIS-Link; see www.courts.wa.gov/jislink/ (also, see state introduction for subscription service.). Also, search name index back to 1989 and calendars free at http://dw.courts.wa.gov/index.cfm.

Criminal Name Search: Access: Fax, mail, online, in person. Both court and visitors may perform in person name searches. Search fee: $30.00 per hour. Required to search: name, years to search, DOB; also helpful: address. Criminal records computerized from 5/81, archived from 1890. Mail turnaround time 2-5 days. Criminal PAT goes back to same as civil. Online access to criminal indexes is the same as civil.

District Court - Criminal 930 Tacoma Ave S, Rm 601, Tacoma, WA 98402-2175; 253-798-7487, 253-798-7487 auto info line; fax: 253-798-3428; 8:30AM-4:30PM (PST). *Misdemeanor.*

www.co.pierce.wa.us/pc/abtus/ourorg/distct/abtusdst.htm

General Information: The District Court #3 in Eatonville was closed 1/13/03, all open misdemeanors were transferred to this court. No sealed, juvenile, adoption, paternity, mental health, sex offenders (victims) or some DUI records released. Will fax out documents. Court makes copy: No charge if 3 or less, if 4 to 7 then $1.00, if 8 to 11 $2,.00, etc. Certification fee: $5.00 per document. Payee: Pierce County District Court. No personal checks or credit cards accepted. Mail requests: SASE required.

Criminal Name Search: Access: Mail, fax, in person, online. Only the court performs in person name searches; visitors may not. No search fee. Required to search: name, years to search, DOB. Criminal records computerized from 8/1990. Mail turnaround time 3-4 weeks. Criminal Index online from JIS-Link; see www.courts.wa.gov/jislink/ (also, see state introduction for subscription service.). Also, search name index back to 1989 and calendars free at http://dw.courts.wa.gov/index.cfm. Online results show name, DOB.

District Court - Civil Infractions Division 1902 96th St S, Tacoma, WA 98444; 253-798-7487; fax: 253-798-6310; 9AM-N 1:30PM-4:30PM (PST). *Civil Actions under $75,001, Small Claims, Traffic.*

www.co.pierce.wa.us/pc/abtus/ourorg/distct/abtusdst.htm

General Information: District Court #3 in Eatonville, #2 in Gig Harbor, and #4 in Buckley were closed 1/13/03; all civil records were transferred to this court. No sealed, juvenile, adoption, paternity, mental health, sex offenders (victims) or some DUI records released. Will not fax documents. Court makes copy: $1.00 for 1st page, $.50 each add'l. Certification fee: $5.00 plus $1.00 each add'l page. Payee: Pierce County District Court. Personal checks accepted. Credit cards accepted. Prepayment required. Mail requests: SASE required for mail return of any copies.

Civil Name Search: Access: Online, in person. Both court and visitors may perform in person name searches. No search fee. Required to search: full name, years to search, DOB; also helpful: address, date of arrest/charge. Civil records on computer back to 1990; Records go back 5 years. Index online from JIS-Link; see www.courts.wa.gov/jislink/ (also, see state introduction for subscription service.). Also, search name index back to 1989 and calendars free at http://dw.courts.wa.gov/index.cfm. Pending cases in person searches only.

District Court #2 This court - formerly in Gig Harbor - is closed and records are now houses at the main court in Tacoma.

District Court #3 , , WA; . *Misdemeanor, Civil Actions under $75,001, Small Claims.*

General Information: This court was closed on 01/10/03. All records have been transferred to the Pierce County District Court in Tacoma.

Bonney Lake Municipal Court 9002 Main St E, Ste 100, Bonney Lake, WA 98391-0944; 253-862-6606; fax: 253-862-3053; 8:30AM-5PM (PST). *Misdemeanor.*

www.ci.bonney-lake.wa.us

General Information: Index online from JIS-Link; see www.courts.wa.gov/jislink/ (see state introduction for subscription service.). Also, search name index back to 1989 & calendars free at http://dw.courts.wa.gov/index.cfm. South Prairie Municipal Court records at this court.

Buckley Municipal Court PO Box 1452, 811 Main St, Buckley, WA 98321-1452; 360-829-2118; fax: 360-829-9363; 8:30AM-4PM M,W,F (PST). *Misdemeanor.*

General Information: Index online from JIS-Link; see www.courts.wa.gov/jislink/ (also, see state introduction for subscription service.). Also, search name index back to 1989 and calendars free at http://dw.courts.wa.gov/index.cfm.

District Court #4 This court was closed on 1/10/03. All records have been transferred to the Pierce County District Court in Tacoma.

DuPont Municipal Court See Pierce County District Court

Eatonville Municipal Court PO Box 309, 201 Center St W, Eatonville, WA 98328-0309; 360-832-3361; fax: 360-832-3977; 9AM-5PM (PST). *Misdemeanor.*

General Information: Index online from JIS-Link; see www.courts.wa.gov/jislink/ (also, see state introduction for subscription service.). Also, search name index back to 1989 and calendars free at http://dw.courts.wa.gov/index.cfm.

Fife Municipal Court 3737 Pacific Hwy E, Fife, WA 98424-1135; 253-922-6635; fax: 253-926-5435; 8:30AM-4:30PM (PST). *Misdemeanor.*

http://cityoffife.org/?p=city_departments&a=municipal_court

General Information: Index online from JIS-Link; see www.courts.wa.gov/jislink/ (also, see state introduction for subscription service.). Also, search name index back to 1989 and calendars free at http://dw.courts.wa.gov/index.cfm.

Fircrest Municipal Court 115 Ramsdell St, Fircrest, WA 98466-6912; 253-564-8922; fax: 253-564-3645; 8AM-4PM (PST). *Misdemeanor.*
www.cityoffircrest.net/
General Information: Index online from JIS-Link; see www.courts.wa.gov/jislink/ (also, see state introduction for subscription service.). Also, search name index back to 1989 and calendars free at http://dw.courts.wa.gov/index.cfm.

Gig Harbor Municipal Court 3510 Grandview St, Gig Harbor, WA 98335-1214; 253-851-7808; fax: 253-853-5483; 8AM-5PM (PST). *Misdemeanor, Traffic.*
www.cityofgigharbor.net/page.php?id=36
General Information: Index online from JIS-Link; see www.courts.wa.gov/jislink/ (also, see state introduction for subscription service.). Also, search name index back to 1989 and calendars free at http://dw.courts.wa.gov/index.cfm.

Lakewood Municipal Court 6000 Main St SW, Lakewood, WA 98499-5027; 253-512-2258; fax: 253-512-2267; 8:30AM-5PM (PST). *Misdemeanor.*
www.cityoflakewood.us/index.php?option=com_content&task=view&id=53&Itemid=97
General Information: Index online from JIS-Link; see www.courts.wa.gov/jislink/ (also, see state introduction for subscription service.). Also, search name index back to 1989 and calendars free at http://dw.courts.wa.gov/index.cfm.

Milton Municipal Court 1000 Laurel St, Milton, WA 98354-8850; 253-922-7625; fax: 253-248-1999; 8AM-5PM (PST). *Misdemeanor.*
www.cityofmilton.net/page.php?id=93
General Information: Index online from JIS-Link; see www.courts.wa.gov/jislink/ (also, see state introduction for subscription service.). Also, search name index back to 1989 and calendars free at http://dw.courts.wa.gov/index.cfm.

Orting Municipal Court PO Box 489, 401 Washington Ave S, Orting, WA 98360-0489; 360-893-3160; fax: 360-893-3129; 9AM-5PM (PST). *Misdemeanor.*
General Information: Index online from JIS-Link; see www.courts.wa.gov/jislink/ (also, see state introduction for subscription service.). Also, search name index back to 1989 and calendars free at http://dw.courts.wa.gov/index.cfm.

Puyallup Municipal Court 929 E Main Ste 120, Puyallup, WA 98372-3116; 253-841-5450; fax: 253-770-3365; 8:30AM-N, 1-5PM (window closes at 4:30) (PST). *Misdemeanor.*
www.cityofpuyallup.org/government/municipal-court/
General Information: Index online from JIS-Link; see www.courts.wa.gov/jislink/ (also, see state introduction for subscription service.). Also, search name index back to 1989 and calendars free at http://dw.courts.wa.gov/index.cfm.

Puyallup Tribal Court 1638 E 29th St, Tacoma, WA 98404-4903; 253-680-5586; fax: 253-680-5599; 8AM-5PM (PST). *Misdemeanor, Civil.*
General Information: Felony actions are sent to the federal court. The records from this court are not on the JIS state system.

Roy Municipal Court PO Box 700, 216 McNaught St, Roy, WA 98580-0700; 253-843-0463; fax: 253-843-0279; 8:30AM-4:30PM (PST). *Misdemeanor, Ordinance.*
General Information: Index online from JIS-Link; see www.courts.wa.gov/jislink/ (also, see state introduction for subscription service.). Also, search name index back to 1989 and calendars free at http://dw.courts.wa.gov/index.cfm.

Ruston Municipal Court 5117 N Winifred St, Ruston, WA 98407-6597; 253-759-8545; fax: 253-752-3754; 9AM-N M, 9AM-4PM T-F (PST). *Misdemeanor.*
General Information: Index online from JIS-Link; see www.courts.wa.gov/jislink/ (also, see state introduction for subscription service.). Also, search name index back to 1989 and calendars free at http://dw.courts.wa.gov/index.cfm.

South Prairie Municipal Court This court is closed. Records are now located at Bonney Lake Municipal Court (address and phone numbers above).

Steilacoom Municipal Court 1030 Roe St, Steilacoom, WA 98388-4010; 253-581-1910; fax: 253-582-0651; 8AM-N (PST). *Misdemeanor, Civil Actions.*
General Information: Index online from JIS-Link; see www.courts.wa.gov/jislink/ (also, see state introduction for subscription service.). Also, search name index back to 1989 and calendars free at http://dw.courts.wa.gov/index.cfm. Hearing held at 1717 Lafayette.

Sumner Municipal Court 1104 Maple St, Ste 100, Sumner, WA 98390-1407; 253-863-7635; fax: 253-299-5629; 8AM-4:30PM (PST). *Misdemeanor.*
www.ci.sumner.wa.us/Government/Municipal_Court.htm
General Information: Index online from JIS-Link; see www.courts.wa.gov/jislink/ (also, see state introduction for subscription service.). Also, search name index back to 1989 and calendars free at http://dw.courts.wa.gov/index.cfm.

Tacoma Municipal Court 930 Tacoma Ave S Rm 841, Tacoma, WA 98402-2181; 253-591-5357; fax: 253-573-2511; 8:30AM-4:30PM (PST). *Misdemeanor.*
www.cityoftacoma.org/Page.aspx?hid=1557
General Information: Index online from JIS-Link; see www.courts.wa.gov/jislink/ (also, see state introduction for subscription service.). Also, search name index back to 1989 and calendars free at http://dw.courts.wa.gov/index.cfm.

Wilkeson Municipal Court PO Box 409, 540 Church St, Wilkeson, WA 98396-9800; 360-829-0171; fax: 360-829-0898; 9AM-4PM TH (PST). *Misdemeanor.*
General Information: Index online from JIS-Link; see www.courts.wa.gov/jislink/ (also, see state introduction for subscription service.). Also, search name index back to 1989 and calendars free at http://dw.courts.wa.gov/index.cfm.

San Juan County

Superior Court 350 Court St, #7, Friday Harbor, WA 98250; 360-378-2163; fax: 360-378-3967; 8AM-5PM (PST). *Felony, Civil, Eviction, Probate.*
www.co.san-juan.wa.us/clerk/default.aspx
General Information: No dependencies, adoption, and mental illness records released. Will fax documents $5.00 1st page, $1.00 each add'l. Court makes copy: $.50 per page. Certification fee: $5.00 plus $1.00 each add'l page. Cert fee includes copies. Payee: San Juan County Clerk. Personal checks accepted. No credit cards accepted for record searches. Prepayment required. Mail requests: SASE required.
Civil Name Search: Access: Phone, fax, mail, online, in person. Both court and visitors may perform in person name searches. No search fee. Required to search: name, years to search; also helpful: case number. Civil records on computer back to 1987, on digitized format and archived from 1890s. Mail turnaround time 3 days. Civil PAT goes back to 1987. Index online from JIS-Link; see www.courts.wa.gov/jislink/ (also, see state introduction for subscription service.). Also, search name index back to 1987 and calendars free at http://dw.courts.wa.gov/index.cfm.
Criminal Name Search: Access: Phone, fax, mail, online, in person. Both court and visitors may perform in person name searches. No search fee. Required to search: name, years to search, DOB; also helpful: address, SSN, case number. Criminal records computerized from 1987, digitized and archived from 1890s. Mail turnaround time 3 days. Criminal PAT goes back to same as civil. Online access to criminal indexes is the same as civil.

District Court PO Box 127, 350 Court Sq, Friday Harbor, WA 98250-0127; 360-378-4017; fax: 360-378-4099; 8:30AM-4:30PM (PST). *Misdemeanor, Civil Actions under $75,001, Small Claims.*
www.co.san-juan.wa.us/distcourt/default.aspx
General Information: No dependencies, adoption, confidential social files and mental illness records released. Will fax documents to local or toll-free number. Court makes copy: $.25 per page. Certification fee: $5.00. Payee: San Juan County District Court. Personal checks accepted. Credit cards accepted at OfficialPayments.com or 1-877-876-7619. Provide them with your case # or ticket #. Prepayment required. Mail requests: SASE required.
Civil Name Search: Access: Mail, in person, online. Both court and visitors may perform in person name searches. Search fee: None; but $20.00 if an archive search. Required to search: full legal name, DOB, years to search; also helpful: address. Civil records on computer from 1990, on index cards prior. Records retained for 10 years. Mail turnaround time 1-3 days. Civil PAT available. Index online from JIS-Link; see www.courts.wa.gov/jislink/ (also, see state introduction for subscription service.). Also, search name index back to 1989 and calendars free at http://dw.courts.wa.gov/index.cfm.
Criminal Name Search: Access: Mail, in person, fax, online. Both court and visitors may perform in person name searches. Search fee: None; but $20.00 if an archive search. Required to search: full legal name, DOB, years to search, signed release; also helpful: address, DOB, SSN. Criminal records computerized from 1990, log book prior. Retained 5 years. Mail turnaround time 1-3 days. Criminal PAT available. Online access to criminal indexes is the same as civil.

Friday Harbor Municipal Court See District Court

Skagit County

Superior Court 205 W Kincaid, #103, Mount Vernon, WA 98273; 360-336-9440; 8:30AM-4:30PM (PST). *Felony, Civil, Eviction, Probate, Domestic, Juvenile.*

www.skagitcounty.net/Common/asp/default.asp?d=Clerk&c=General&p=main.htm

General Information: No dependencies, adoption, and mental illness, juvenile offender prior to 07/01/78 records released. Will not fax documents. Court makes copy: $.25 per page. Certification fee: $5.00 for first cert page, $1.00 each add'l. Payee: Skagit County Clerk. Only cashiers checks and money orders accepted. Major credit cards accepted. Prepayment required. Mail requests: SASE required.

Civil Name Search: Access: Mail, in person, online. Both court and visitors may perform in person name searches. Search fee: $30.00 per hour. Civil records on computer from 10/81, scanned or on microfilm and archived from 1878. Note: The court provides access to the docket index, but not on a terminal. Mail turnaround time 5 days. Index online from JIS-Link; see www.courts.wa.gov/jislink/ (also, see state introduction for subscription service.). Also, search name index back to 1989 and calendars free at http://dw.courts.wa.gov/index.cfm. Also order a document for a fee (no name searching) at www.clerkepass.com.

Criminal Name Search: Access: Mail, in person, online. Both court and visitors may perform in person name searches. Search fee: $30.00 per hour. Criminal records computerized from 10/81, scanned or on microfilm and archived from 1878. Note: The court provides access to the docket index, but not on a terminal. Mail turnaround time 5 days. Online access to criminal indexes is the same as civil. Also order a document for a fee (no name searching) at www.clerkepass.com.

District Court PO Box 340, 600 S 3rd St, Mount Vernon, WA 98273-0340; 360-336-9319; fax: 360-336-9318; 8:30AM-4:30PM (PST). *Misdemeanor, Civil Actions under $75,001, Small Claims.*

General Information: No dependencies, alcohol, adoption, and mental illness records released. Will not fax out documents. Court makes copy: $.25 per page. Certification fee: $5.00 1st page, $1.00 ea add'l. Payee: District Court, Skagit County. Personal checks accepted, credit cards are not. Prepayment required. Mail requests: SASE required or $.50 per page postage return.

Civil Name Search: Access: Fax, mail, online, in person. Both court and visitors may perform in person name searches. No search fee. If court must search archives, $5.00 fee for 1-5 cases, $20 for 6 or more. Required to search: name, years to search; also helpful: address. Civil records on computer from 1986, archived for 12 years. Open records retained for 10 years. Note: Mail search requires a special form. Mail turnaround time 3-4 days. Civil PAT goes back to 1987. Index online from JIS-Link; see www.courts.wa.gov/jislink/ (also, see state introduction for subscription service.). Also, search name index back to 1989 and calendars free at http://dw.courts.wa.gov/index.cfm.

Criminal Name Search: Access: Fax, mail, online, in person. Both court and visitors may perform in person name searches. No search fee.If court must search archives, $5.00 fee for 1-5 cases, $20 for 6 or more. Required to search: name, years to search, DOB; also helpful: SSN. Criminal records prior to 1995 only retained for 5 years. Mail turnaround time 3-4 days. Criminal PAT goes back to same as civil. Online access to criminal indexes is the same as civil.

Anacortes Municipal Court 1218 24th St, Anacortes, WA 98221-2565; 360-293-1913; fax: 360-293-4224; 8:30AM-4:30PM (PST). *Misdemeanor.*

www.cityofanacortes.org/Legal/court.htm

General Information: Index online from JIS-Link; see www.courts.wa.gov/jislink/ (also, see state introduction for subscription service.). Also, search name index back to 1989 and calendars free at http://dw.courts.wa.gov/index.cfm.

Burlington Municipal Court 311 Cedar #A, Burlington, WA 98233-2803; 360-755-0492; fax: 360-755-2391; 8AM-5PM (PST). *Misdemeanor & Gross Misdemeanors.*

www.ci.burlington.wa.us/page.asp_Q_navigationid_E_303

General Information: Index online from JIS-Link; see www.courts.wa.gov/jislink/ (also, see state introduction for subscription service.). Also, search name index back to 1989 and calendars free at http://dw.courts.wa.gov/index.cfm.

LaConner Municipal Court See Skagit County District Court

Mount Vernon Municipal Court 1805 Continental Pl, Mount Vernon, WA 98273-5625; 360-336-6205; fax: 360-336-6254; 8AM-5PM (PST). *Misdemeanor. Ordinance, Traffic.*

www.ci.mount-vernon.wa.us/page.asp_Q_navigationid_E_237

General Information: Index online from JIS-Link; see www.courts.wa.gov/jislink/ (also, see state introduction for subscription

service.). Also, search name index back to 1989 and calendars free at http://dw.courts.wa.gov/index.cfm.

Sedro-Woolley Municipal Court 325 Metcalf St, Sedro-Woolley, WA 98284; 360-855-0366; fax: 360-855-1526; N-4:30PM; 8AM-4:30PM Thu (PST). *Misdemeanor.*

General Information: Index online from JIS-Link; see www.courts.wa.gov/jislink/ (also, see state introduction for subscription service.). Also, search name index back to 1989 and calendars free at http://dw.courts.wa.gov/index.cfm.

Swinomish Tribal Court 17337 Reservation Rd, LaConner, WA 98257-0755; 360-466-7217; fax: 360-466-1506; 8:30AM-5PM (PST). *Misdemeanor, Civil.*

www.swinomish.org

General Information: All requests must include reason for search. This office does not always answer the telephone. Felony actions are sent to the federal court. The records from the civil court are not on the JIS state system. Will fax documents for no fee. Court makes copy: $.05 per page. No certification fee. Personal checks accepted, credit cards are not. Prepayment required.

Civil Name Search: Access: Mail, fax, in person. Only the court performs in person name searches; visitors may not. No search fee. Required to search: name; also helpful- at least one: DOB, SSN, years to search. Civil records go back to 1990, on computer back to 1995. Mail turnaround time varies.

Criminal Name Search: Access: Mail, fax, in person, online. Only the court performs in person name searches; visitors may not. No search fee. Required to search: name; also helpful- at least one: DOB, SSN, years to search. Criminal records go back to 1990. Mail turnaround time varies. Index online from JIS-Link; see www.courts.wa.gov/jislink/ (also, see state introduction for subscription service.). Also, search name index back to 1989 and calendars free at http://dw.courts.wa.gov/index.cfm. Online results show name only.

Upper Skagit Tribal Court 25944 Community Plaza Way, Sedro Woolley, WA 98284; 360-854-7080; fax: 360-854-7085; 8:30AM-4PM (PST). *Misdemeanor, Civil.*

General Information: Felony actions are sent to the federal court. The records from this court are not on the JIS state system.

Skamania County

Superior Court Attn: County Clerk, 240 Vancouver Ave, Rm 33, Stevenson, WA 98648; 509-427-3770; fax: 509-427-3777; 8:30AM-5PM (PST). *Felony, Civil, Eviction, Probate.*

www.courts.wa.gov/court_dir/orgs/289.html

General Information: Also, can use PO Box 790. The fee for digital record copies is $.25 per image and $20.00 per CD. No dependencies, adoption, and mental illness records released. Will not fax documents. Court makes copy: $.50 per page. Certification fee: $5.00 1st page, $1.00 each add'l. Payee: Skamania County Clerk. Personal checks accepted. No credit cards accepted for record searches. Prepayment required. Mail requests: SASE required.

Civil Name Search: Access: Phone, mail, online, in person. Both court and visitors may perform in person name searches. Search fee: $30.00 per hour. Required to search: name, years to search; also helpful: address. Civil records on computer from 1984, on microfiche and archived from 1900. Mail turnaround time 2 days. Civil PAT goes back to 10/2006. Index online from JIS-Link; see www.courts.wa.gov/jislink/ (also, see state introduction for subscription service.). Also, search name index back to 1985 and calendars free at http://dw.courts.wa.gov/index.cfm. Also order a document for a fee (no name searching) at www.clerkepass.com.

Criminal Name Search: Access: Phone, mail, online, in person. Both court and visitors may perform in person name searches. Search fee: $30.00 per hour. Required to search: name, years to search; also helpful: address, DOB. Criminal records computerized from 1984, on microfiche and archived from 1900. Mail turnaround time 2 days. Criminal PAT available. Online access to criminal indexes is the same as civil. Also order a document for a fee (no name searching) at www.clerkepass.com. Online results show middle initial, DOB.

District Court PO Box 790, Stevenson, WA 98648; 509-427-3780; fax: 509-427-3777; 8:30AM-5PM (PST). *Misdemeanor, Civil Actions under $75,000, Small Claims.*

General Information: No dependencies, adoption, and mental illness records released. No fee to fax documents. Court makes copy: $.1 per page. Certification fee: $5.00 per document; exemplification is $20 per document. Payee: Skamania County District Court. Personal checks accepted. Credit cards accepted via automat. Prepayment required. Mail requests: SASE required.

Civil Name Search: Access: Phone, fax, mail, online, in person. Both court and visitors may perform in person name searches. Search fee: $40.00 per hour. Required to search: name, years to search; also helpful:

address, DOB, signed release. Civil records retained per state requirements. Mail turnaround time 7 days. Public use terminal available. Index online from JIS-Link; see www.courts.wa.gov/jislink/ (also, see state introduction for subscription service.). Also, search name index back 10 years and calendars free at http://dw.courts.wa.gov/index.cfm.

Criminal Name Search: Access: Phone, fax, mail, online, in person. Both court and visitors may perform in person name searches. Search fee: $40.00 per hour. Required to search: name, years to search; also helpful: address, DOB, signed release. Criminal records retained per state requirements. Mail turnaround time 7 days. Public use terminal available. Online access to criminal indexes is the same as civil. Online results show middle initial, DOB, address.

North Bonneville Municipal Court PO Box 7, City Hall, 214 CBD Mall, Cascade Dr, North Bonneville, WA 98639-0007; 509-427-8182; fax: 509-427-7214; 8AM-5PM (PST). *Misdemeanor.*

General Information: Index online from JIS-Link; see www.courts.wa.gov/jislink/ (also, see state introduction for subscription service.). Also, search name index back to 1989 and calendars free at http://dw.courts.wa.gov/index.cfm.

Stevenson Municipal Court PO Box 371, 7121 E Loop Rd, Stevenson, WA 98648-0371; 509-427-5970; fax: 509-427-8202; 8AM-5PM (PST). *Misdemeanor.*

General Information: Index online from JIS-Link; see www.courts.wa.gov/jislink/ (also, see state introduction for subscription service.). Also, search name index back to 1989 and calendars free at http://dw.courts.wa.gov/index.cfm.

Snohomish County

Superior Court 3000 Rockefeller, MS 605, Everett, WA 98201; 425-388-3466; 8:30-12; 12:45PM-4:30PM (PST). *Felony, Civil Actions, Eviction, Probate, Divorce.*

www1.co.snohomish.wa.us/Departments/Clerk/

General Information: No sealed, juvenile, adoption, paternity, mental health, sex offenders (victims). Court makes copy: $.25 per page. Self serve copy: same. Certification fee: $5.00 plus $1.00 per page after first. Payee: County Clerk or Snohomish County Clerk's Office. Business checks accepted; no personal checks. Credit and debit cards accepted in person only. Prepayment required. Mail requests: SASE required.

Civil Name Search: Access: Phone, mail, online, in person. Both court and visitors may perform in person name searches. Search fee: $30.00 per hour, one hr min. Civil records on computer from 1978, prior on database index. Mail turnaround time 1 week. Civil PAT goes back to 1978. Index online from JIS-Link; see www.courts.wa.gov/jislink/ (also, see state introduction for subscription service.). Also, search name index back to 1989 and calendars free at http://dw.courts.wa.gov/index.cfm.

Criminal Name Search: Access: Phone, mail, online, in person. Both court and visitors may perform in person name searches. Search fee: $30.00 per hour, one hr min. Criminal records computerized from 1978, prior on database index. Mail turnaround time 1 week. Criminal PAT goes back to same as civil. Online access to criminal index is same as civil.

Cascade Division District Court 415 E Burke St, Arlington, WA 98223; 360-435-7700; fax: 360-435-0873; 8:30AM-11:50AM:12:50-4:30PM (PST). *Misdemeanor, Civil Actions under $75,001, Small Claims.*

General Information: No sealed, mental health, sex offenders (victims) or some DUI records released. Will not fax documents. Court makes copy: $.50 per page. Certification fee: $5.00 first page, $1.00 ea add'l. An exemplification is an additional $2.00 per seal. Payee: Cascade Division. Personal checks, Visa/MC accepted. Prepayment required.

Civil Name Search: Access: Mail, in person, online. Both court and visitors may perform in person name searches. Search fee: $5.00 per name. Required to search: name, years to search; also helpful: address. Civil records on computer from 1985. Mail turnaround time 1 week. Index online from JIS-Link; see www.courts.wa.gov/jislink/ (also, see state introduction for subscription service.). Also, search name index back to 1989 and calendars free at http://dw.courts.wa.gov/index.cfm.

Criminal Name Search: Access: Mail, online, in person. Both court and visitors may perform in person name searches. Search fee: $5.00 per name. Required to search: name, years to search, DOB; also helpful: address, SSN. Criminal records computerized from 1987. Mail turnaround time 1 week. Online access to criminal indexes is the same as civil.

Everett Division District Court 3000 Rockefeller Ave, MS 508, County Courthouse 3rd Floor, Everett, WA 98201; 425-388-3331; civil phone: 425-388-3595; fax: 425-388-3565; 8:30AM-4:30PM (PST). *Misdemeanor, Civil Actions under $75,001, Small Claims.*

www1.co.snohomish.wa.us/

General Information: Limited DUI records released. No fee to fax documents. Court makes copy: $.25 per page. Certification fee: $5.00. Payee: Everett District Court. Personal checks, Visa/MC accepted. Prepayment required. Mail requests: SASE required.

Civil Name Search: Access: Fax, mail, online, in person. Both court and visitors may perform in person name searches. No search fee. Required to search: complete name, years to search; also helpful: address. Civil records on computer back to 1998, on paper or microfilm from 1977, but this changes as records are purged. Mail turnaround time 2-3 days. Civil PAT goes back to 10 years. Index online from JIS-Link; see www.courts.wa.gov/jislink/ (also, see state introduction for subscription service.). Also, search name index back to 1989 and calendars free at http://dw.courts.wa.gov/index.cfm.

Criminal Name Search: Access: Fax, mail, online, in person. Both court and visitors may perform in person name searches. No search fee. Required to search: complete name, years to search, DOB; also helpful: address, SSN. Criminal records computerized from 1986. Mail turnaround time 1 week. Criminal PAT goes back to 1998. Online access to criminal indexes is the same as civil.

Evergreen Division District Court 14414 179th Ave SE, Monroe, WA 98272-0625; 360-805-6776; fax: 360-805-6755; 8:30AM-4:30PM (PST). *Misdemeanor, Civil Actions under $75,000, Small Claims.*

www1.co.snohomish.wa.us/Departments/District_Court/

General Information: No sealed, juvenile, adoption, paternity, mental health, sex offenders (victims) or some DUI records released. Will fax documents for no fee. Court makes copy: $.25 per page. Certification fee: $5.00 per page plus copy fee. Payee: Snohomish County District Court. Personal checks accepted. Credit cards accepted. Prepayment required. Mail requests: SASE requested.

Civil Name Search: Access: Mail, in person, online. Both court and visitors may perform in person name searches. No search fee. Required to search: name, years to search; also helpful: address. Civil records on computer back 10 years; file retained until closure. Mail turnaround time 1 week. Public use terminal available. Index online from JIS-Link; see www.courts.wa.gov/jislink/ (also, see state introduction for subscription service.). Also, search name index back to 1989 and calendars free at http://dw.courts.wa.gov/index.cfm.

Criminal Name Search: Access: Mail, in person, online. Both court and visitors may perform in person name searches. No search fee. Required to search: name, years to search; also helpful: address, DOB. Criminal records on computer archived 3 years after closure by state. Mail turnaround time 1 week. Public use terminal available. Online access to criminal indexes is the same as civil.

South Division District Court 20520 68th Ave W, Lynnwood, WA 98036-7406; 425-774-8803; fax: 425-744-6820; 8:30-11:50AM, 12:50-4:30PM (PST). *Misdemeanor, Civil Actions under $75,001, Small Claims.*

www1.co.snohomish.wa.us/Departments/District_Court/

General Information: No sealed, juvenile, adoption, paternity, mental health, sex offenders (victims) or some DUI records released. Will not fax documents. Court makes copy: $.50 per page. Self serve copy: same. Certification fee: $5.00 first page, $1.00 ea add'l. Payee: SCDC South Division. Personal checks accepted. Prepayment required. Mail requests: SASE requested.

Civil Name Search: Access: Mail, in person, online. Both court and visitors may perform in person name searches. No search fee. Civil cases indexed by case number. Civil records on computer since 1987. Mail turnaround time 2-4 days. Civil PAT available. Index online from JIS-Link; see www.courts.wa.gov/jislink/ (also, see state introduction for subscription service.). Also, search name index back to 1989 and calendars free at http://dw.courts.wa.gov/index.cfm.

Criminal Name Search: Access: Mail, online, in person. Both court and visitors may perform in person name searches. No search fee. Criminal records on computer since 1989. Mail turnaround time 5-10 days. Criminal PAT available. Online access to criminal indexes is the same as civil. Online results show name, DOB.

Arlington Municipal Court See Cascade Division District Court

Brier Municipal Court See South Division District Court

Darrington Municipal Court See Cascade Division District Court

Edmonds Municipal Court 250 5th Ave N, Edmonds, WA 98020-3146; 425-771-0210; fax: 425-771-0269; 8:30AM-4:30PM (PST). *Misdemeanor.*

www.ci.edmonds.wa.us/muni_court.stm

General Information: Index online from JIS-Link; see www.courts.wa.gov/jislink/ (also, see state introduction for subscription service.). Also, search name index back to 1989 and calendars free at http://dw.courts.wa.gov/index.cfm.

Everett Municipal Court 3028 Wetmore Ave, Everett, WA 98201-4018; 425-257-8778; fax: 425-257-8678; 8AM-5PM (PST). *Misdemeanor.*

www.everettwa.org/default.aspx?ID=49

General Information: Index online from JIS-Link; see www.courts.wa.gov/jislink/ (also, see state introduction for subscription service.). Also, search name index back to 1989 and calendars free at http://dw.courts.wa.gov/index.cfm.

Gold Bar Municipal Court See Evergreen Division District Court

Granite Falls Municipal Court See Cascade Division District Court

Index Municipal Court See Evergreen Division District Court

Lake Stevens Municipal Court See Marysville Municipal Court

Lynnwood Municipal Court 19321 44th Ave W, Lynnwood, WA 98036; 425-670-5100; fax: 425-774-7039; 8:30AM-4:30PM (PST). *Misdemeanor, Gross Misdemeanor, Infraction.* www.ci.lynnwood.wa.us/Content/CityHall.aspx?id=153
General Information: Index online from JIS-Link; see www.courts.wa.gov/jislink/ (also, see state introduction for subscription service). Also, search name index back to 1990 and calendars free at http://dw.courts.wa.gov/index.cfm.

Marysville Municipal Court 1015 State Ave, Marysville, WA 98270; 360-363-8050; fax: 360-657-2960; 8AM-4:30PM (PST). *Misdemeanor.* http://marysvillewa.gov/
General Information: Index online from JIS-Link; see www.courts.wa.gov/jislink/ (also, see state introduction for subscription service.). Also, search name index back to 1989 and calendars free at http://dw.courts.wa.gov/index.cfm.

Mill Creek Municipal Court See South Division District Court

Monroe Municipal Court See Evergreen Division District Court

Mountlake Terrace Municipal Court See South Division District Court

Mukilteo Municipal Court See Everett Division District Court

Northwest Intertribal Court System (NICS) 20818 44th Ave W #120, Lynnwood, WA 98036; 425-774-5808; fax: 425-744-7704; 8AM-4:30PM (PST). *Misdemeanor, Civil.* www.nics.ws/
General Information: Felony actions are sent to the federal court. The records from this court are not on the JIS state system.

Sauk-Suiattle Tribal Court (NICS) 5318 Chief Brown Ln, Darrington, WA 98241-9420; 360-436-1400; fax: 360-436-0242; 8:30AM-4:30PM (PST). *Misdemeanor, Civil.* www.sauk-suiattle.com
General Information: Felony actions are sent to the federal court. The records from this court are not on the JIS state system.

Snohomish Municipal Court See Evergreen Division District Court

Stanwood Municipal Court See Cascade Division District Court

Stillaguamish Tribal Court PO Box 3067, Arlington, WA 98223; 360-474-8562; fax: 360-474-9458 *Misdemeanor, Civil.* www.stillaguamish.com/courtsjustice.asp
General Information: Felony actions are sent to the federal court. The records from this court are not on the JIS state system.

Sultan Municipal Court
General Information: See Evergreen Division District Court

Tulalip Tribal Court 6103 31st Ave NE, Tulalip, WA 98271; 360-716-4773; 8AM-4:30PM (PST). *Misdemeanor, Civil, Small Claims, Eviction.* www.tulaliptribes-nsn.gov/Home/Government/Departments/TribalCourt.aspx
General Information: Felony actions are sent to the federal court. The records from this court are not on the JIS state system.

Woodway Municipal Court See South Division District Court

Spokane County

Superior Court Spokane County Clerk, 1116 W Broadway, #300, Spokane, WA 99260-0090; 509-477-2211; 8:30AM-12; 1PM-4PM (PST). *Felony, Civil, Eviction, Probate, Domestic, Adoption.* www.spokanecounty.org/clerk/content.aspx?c=1812
General Information: No sealed, juvenile dependency, adoption, paternity, mental health records released. Will not fax documents. Court makes copy: $.50 per page. Certification fee: $5.00 1st page of ea doc, plus $1.00 ea add'l. Payee: Spokane County Clerk. Personal checks accepted, credit cards are not. Prepayment required. Mail requests: SASE required.
Civil Name Search: Access: Phone, mail, online, in person. Both court and visitors may perform in person name searches. Search fee: $30.00 per hour. Civil records on computer from 1973, archives back to 1800s, docket books prior to computer. Mail turnaround time 1-4 days. Civil PAT goes back to 1973. Index online from JIS-Link; see www.courts.wa.gov/jislink/ (also, see state introduction for subscription service.). Also, search name index back to 1989 and calendars free at http://dw.courts.wa.gov/index.cfm.

Criminal Name Search: Access: Phone, mail, online, in person. Both court and visitors may perform in person name searches. Search fee: $30.00 per hour. Required to search: name, years to search; also helpful: DOB. Criminal records computerized from 1973, archives back to 1800s, docket books prior to computer. Mail turnaround time 1-4 days. Criminal PAT goes back to same as civil. Online access to criminal indexes is the same as civil.

District Court 1100 W Mallon, Spokane, WA 99260; 509-477-4770; criminal fax: 509-477-6445; civil fax: 8:30AM-4PM; 8:30AM-4PM (PST). *Misdemeanor, Civil Actions under $75,001.* www.spokanecounty.org/districtcourt/content.aspx?c=1551
General Information: Physical address- 721 N Jefferson. Records flagged as confidential are restricted from the public view. Will fax documents to local or toll-free number. Court makes copy: $1.00 per page. Certification fee: $5.00 per cert includes copy fee. Payee: Spokane County District Court. Business checks accepted. Personal checks accepted for civil records only. No credit cards accepted. Prepayment required. Mail requests: SASE required.
Civil Name Search: Access: Phone, mail, online, in person. Only the court performs in person name searches; visitors may not. No search fee. Required to search: name, years to search; also helpful: address. Civil records on computer go back 10 years. Mail turnaround time 1 week. Index online from JIS-Link; see www.courts.wa.gov/jislink/ (also, see state introduction for subscription service.). Also, search name index back to 1989 and calendars free at http://dw.courts.wa.gov/index.cfm.
Criminal Name Search: Access: Phone, mail, online, in person. Only the court performs in person name searches; visitors may not. No search fee. Required to search: name, years to search, signed release; also helpful: address, DOB. Criminal records are computer since 1984, but searches are only done for five years time. Mail turnaround time 1 week. Online access to criminal indexes is the same as civil. Online results show middle initial, DOB.

Airway Heights Municipal Court 13120 W 13th Ave, 2nd Fl, Airway Heights, WA 99001; 509-244-2773; fax: 509-244-1852; 8:30AM-4:30PM (PST). *Misdemeanor.* www.cawh.org/municipal_court.asp
General Information: Mail address is 1208 S Lundstrom. Index online from JIS-Link; see www.courts.wa.gov/jislink/. Also, search name index back to 1989 and calendars free at http://dw.courts.wa.gov/index.cfm.

Cheney Municipal Court 611 2nd St, Cheney, WA 99004; 509-498-9231; fax: 509-498-9332; 8AM-5PM (PST). *Misdemeanor, Civil.* www.cityofcheney.org/index.php?section=judicial-branch
General Information: Will fax documents no fee with proof of ID. Court makes copy: 1st 10 pages free; $.15 per page beyond 10. No certification fee. Payee: Cheney Municipal Court. Personal checks, Visa/MC accepted.
Civil Name Search: Access: Mail, fax, in person, email. Only the court performs in person name searches; visitors may not. No search fee. Required to search: name, DOB. Note: Direct email record requests to tcooper@cityofcheney.org.
Criminal Name Search: Access: Mail, fax, in person, email, online. Only the court performs in person name searches; visitors may not. No search fee. Required to search: name, DOB. Mail turnaround time 5 working days. Index online from JIS-Link; see www.courts.wa.gov/jislink/. Also, see state introduction for subscription service. Also, search name index back to 1989 and calendars free at http://dw.courts.wa.gov/index.cfm. Also, you may direct email record requests to tcooper@cityofcheney.org. Online results show middle initial, DOB.

Deer Park Municipal Court This court closed 12/31/2010. Records are at the Spokane District Court.

Medical Lake Municipal Court PO Box 369, 124 S Lefevre St, Medical Lake, WA 99022-0369; 509-565-5000; fax: 509-565-5008; 8AM-5PM (PST). *Misdemeanor.* www.medical-lake.org/
General Information: Will not fax documents. Court makes copy: $.15 per page. Payee: Medical Lake Municipal Court. Personal checks accepted, credit cards are not. Prepayment required. Mail requests: SASE not required.
Criminal Name Search: Access: Mail, fax, in person, online. Only the court performs in person name searches; visitors may not. Search fee: varies. Required to search: name, DOB, SSN. Criminal record hard copies go back 3 years after disposition; computer records are archived. Mail turnaround time 5 days. Index online from JIS-Link; see www.courts.wa.gov/jislink/ (also, see state introduction for subscription service.). Also, search name index back to 1989 and calendars free at http://dw.courts.wa.gov/index.cfm.

Spokane Municipal Court 1100 W Mallon Ave, Public Safety Bldg, Spokane, WA 99260-0150; 509-625-4400; fax: 509-625-4442; 8AM-5PM (PST). *Misdemeanor.*

General Information: Index online from JIS-Link; see www.courts.wa.gov/jislink/ (also, see state introduction for subscription service.). Also, search name index back to 1989 and calendars free at http://dw.courts.wa.gov/index.cfm.

Stevens County

Superior Court 215 S Oak, Rm 206, Colville, WA 99114; 509-684-7575; 8:30AM-N, 1:30-4PM (PST). *Felony, Civil, Eviction, Probate.*

General Information: No sealed, juvenile, adoption, paternity, mental health, sex offenders (victims). Will not fax documents. Court makes copy: $.50 per page. Certification fee: $5.00 1st page, $1.00 ea add'l. Payee: Stevens County Clerk. Personal checks accepted; put case number on check. No credit cards accepted for research. Prepayment required. Mail requests: SASE required.

Civil Name Search: Access: Phone, mail, online, in person. Only the court performs in person name searches; visitors may not. Search fee: $20.00 per hour. Required to search: name, years to search; also helpful: address. Civil records on computer from 10-82, microfiche from 1889-1982, archives 1889, index cards prior to 1982. Mail turnaround time same day. Index online from JIS-Link; see www.courts.wa.gov/jislink/ (also, see state introduction for subscription service.). Also, search name index back to 1989 and calendars free at http://dw.courts.wa.gov/index.cfm. Also order a document for a fee (no name searching) at www.clerkepass.com.

Criminal Name Search: Access: Mail, online, in person. Only the court performs in person name searches; visitors may not. Search fee: $30.00 per hour. Required to search: name, years to search, DOB; also helpful: address, SSN. Criminal records computerized from 10-82, microfiche from 1889-1982, archives 1889, index cards prior to 1982. Mail turnaround time same day. Online access to criminal indexes is the same as civil. Also order a document for a fee (no name searching) at www.clerkepass.com. Online results show name only.

District Court 215 S Oak, Rm 213, Colville, WA 99114; 509-684-5249; fax: 509-684-7571; 8AM-3:30PM M-W; 9AM-3:30PM TH,F (PST). *Misdemeanor, Civil Actions under $75,000, Small Claims.*
www.co.stevens.wa.us/distcourt/departments.htm

General Information: No sealed, juvenile, adoption, paternity, mental health, sex offenders (victims) or some DUI records released. Fee to fax out file $3.00 first page and $1.00 ea addl. Court makes copy: $.50 per page. Certification fee: $5.00 includes copy fee first page, then $1.00 ea addl. Payee: Stevens County District Court. Business checks accepted. No credit cards accepted. Prepayment required.

Civil Name Search: Access: Mail, in person, online. Only the court performs in person name searches; visitors may not. Search fee: $5.00. Required to search: name, years to search; also helpful: address. Civil cases indexed by defendant. Civil records on computer from 1/93, some prior on docket books to 1988. Note: Faxes accepted with prior approval, $3.00 first page, $1.00 ea addl. Mail turnaround time 1 week. Index online from JIS-Link; see www.courts.wa.gov/jislink/ (also, see state introduction for subscription service.). Also, search name index back to 1989 and calendars free at http://dw.courts.wa.gov/index.cfm.

Criminal Name Search: Access: Fax, mail, online, in person. Only the court performs in person name searches; visitors may not. Search fee: $5.00. Required to search: name, years to search, DOB; also helpful: address, signed request. Criminal records computerized from 7/93, some prior on docket books to 1988. Note: Faxes accepted with prior approval, $3.00 first page, $1.00 ea addl. Mail turnaround time 1 week. Online access to criminal indexes is the same as civil. Online results show middle initial.

Chewelah Municipal Court See District Court

Colville Municipal Court See District Court.

Kettle Falls Municipal Court See District Court

Northport Municipal Court See District Court

Spokane Tribal Court PO Box 225, Agency Sq Rd, Bldg 258, Wellpinit, WA 99040-0225; 509-258-7717; fax: 509-258-9223; 8AM-4:30PM (PST). *Misdemeanor, Civil.*

General Information: Felony actions are sent to the federal court. The records from this court are not on the JIS state system.

Springdale Municipal Court See District Court

Thurston County

Superior Court Thurston County Clerk, 2000 Lakeridge Dr SW, Bldg 2, Olympia, WA 98502; 360-786-5430; fax: 360-753-4033; 8AM-5PM - closed one hour 12-1 (PST). *Felony, Misdemeanor, Civil, Eviction.*
www.co.thurston.wa.us/clerk/

General Information: Email questions to county_clerk@co.thurston.wa.us. No sealed, juvenile, adoption, paternity, mental health, sex offenders (victims). Will fax documents $5.00 1st page, $1.00 ea add'l. Court makes copy: $.50 per page; add $5.00 if purchased from web page. Self serve copy: $.50 per page. Certification fee: $5.00 first page, $1.00 each add'l, inclusive of all copy fees. Payee: Thurston County Clerk. Checks accepted. Visa/MC accepted. Prepayment required. Mail requests: SASE required.

Civil Name Search: Access: Phone, mail, in person, email, online. Both court and visitors may perform in person name searches. Search fee: $30.00 per hour. Required to search: name, years to search; also helpful: address. Civil records on computer from 1978. Special arrangements necessary to view historical records. Mail turnaround time 2-3 days. Civil PAT goes back to 1978. The terminal shows scanned images, no files are pulled for viewing. Index online from JIS-Link; see www.courts.wa.gov/jislink/ (also, see state introduction for subscription service.). Also, search name index back to 1989 and calendars free at http://dw.courts.wa.gov/index.cfm. Also, you may search for a case by a party's name or case number at www.co.thurston.wa.us/clerk/caseno.htm. Purchase copies for $.25 per page plus convenience fee of $5.00.

Criminal Name Search: Access: Phone, mail, in person, email, online. Both court and visitors may perform in person name searches. Search fee: $30.00 per hour. Required to search: name, years to search, DOB, signed release; also helpful: address, SSN. Criminal records computerized from 1978. Special arrangements necessary to view historical records. Mail turnaround time 2-3 days. Criminal PAT goes back to 1978. The terminal shows scanned images, no files are pulled for viewing. Online access to criminal indexes is the same as described for civil. Request and purchase certified copies for $.25 per page plus convenience fee of $5.00.

District Court 2000 Lakeridge Dr SW, Bldg 3, Olympia, WA 98502; 360-786-5450; fax: 360-754-3359; 8:30AM-4PM (PST). *Misdemeanor, Civil Actions under $75,001, Small Claims, Traffic.*
www.co.thurston.wa.us/distcrt/

General Information: Daily court calendars are available at www.co.thurston.wa.us/distcrt/courtcalendars.htm. No sealed, juvenile, adoption, paternity, mental health, sex offenders (victims) or some DUI records released. Will fax documents for $1.00 per page. Court makes copy: $.75 per page. Certification fee: $5.00 first page, $1.00 ea add'l. Payee: Thurston County District Court. Personal checks accepted, credit cards are not. Prepayment required.

Civil Name Search: Access: Online, in person. Visitors must perform in person searches themselves. Required to search: name, years to search; also helpful: address. Civil records on computer from 1983. Civil PAT goes back to 1990. Index online from JIS-Link; see www.courts.wa.gov/jislink/ (also, see state introduction for subscription service.). Also, search name index back to 1989 and calendars free at http://dw.courts.wa.gov/index.cfm.

Criminal Name Search: Access: Online, in person. Visitors must perform in person searches themselves. Required to search: name, years to search; also helpful: address, DOB, SSN. Criminal records computerized from 1988. Criminal PAT goes back to same as civil. Online access to criminal indexes is the same as civil. Online results show name only.

Superior Court Family and Juvenile Courthouse, 2801 32nd Ave, SW, Tumwater, WA 98512; 360-709-3260; criminal phone: 360-786-5430;; 8AM-5PM (PST). *Probate, Domestic, Juvenile.*
www.co.thurston.wa.us/clerk/

General Information: Web access available, fees involved.

Bucoda Municipal Court See Tenino Municipal Court

Lacey Municipal Court See Thurston County District Court

Nisqually Tribal Court 4820 She-Nah-Num Dr SE, Olympia, WA 98513-9105; 360-456-5221; fax: 360-456-5280; 8AM-5PM (PST). *Misdemeanor, Civil.*

General Information: Felony actions are sent to the federal court. The records from this court are not on the JIS state system.

Olympia Municipal Court 909 8th Ave SE, Olympia, WA 98501; 360-753-8312; fax: 360-753-8775; 8AM-4PM (phone hours: 1AM-12, 1PM-3:30PM) (PST). *Misdemeanor.*
http://olympiawa.gov/city-government/municipal-court.aspx

General Information: Index online from JIS-Link; see www.courts.wa.gov/jislink/ (also, see state introduction for subscription service.). Also, search name index back to 1989 and calendars free at http://dw.courts.wa.gov/index.cfm.

Rainier Municipal Court See Tenino Municipal Court

Tenino Municipal Court 149 Hodgden St S, PO Box 4019, Tenino, WA 98589-4019; 360-264-4157; fax: 360-264-5772; 8AM-4PM (PST). *Misdemeanor.*
www.ci.tenino.wa.us/

General Information: Index online from JIS-Link; see www.courts.wa.gov/jislink/ (also, see state introduction for subscription service.). Also, search name index back to 1989 and calendars free at http://dw.courts.wa.gov/index.cfm.

Tumwater Municipal Court 555 Israel Rd SW, Tumwater, WA 98501-6515; 360-754-4190; fax: 360-754-4138; 8AM-5PM (PST). *Misdemeanor.*
General Information: Index online from JIS-Link; see www.courts.wa.gov/jislink/ (also, see state introduction for subscription service.). Also, search name index back to 1989 and calendars free at http://dw.courts.wa.gov/index.cfm.

Yelm Municipal Court 206 McKenzie Ave SE, Yelm, WA 98597; 360-458-3242; fax: 360-458-3566; 8AM-5PM (PST). *Misdemeanor, Civil Infractions, Ordinance.*
www.ci.yelm.wa.us/default.asp?dept=court
General Information: Index online from JIS-Link; see www.courts.wa.gov/jislink/ (also, see state introduction for subscription service.). Also, search name index back to 1989 and calendars free at http://dw.courts.wa.gov/index.cfm.

Wahkiakum County

Superior Court PO Box 116, Cathlamet, WA 98612; 360-795-3558; fax: 360-795-8813; 8AM-4PM (PST). *Felony, Misdemeanor, Civil, Eviction, Probate.*
www.co.wahkiakum.wa.us/
General Information: No sealed, juvenile, adoption, paternity, mental health, sex offender victims. Fee to fax document $.50 per page. Court makes copy: $.50 per page. Will email copies of $.25 per page. Certification fee: $5.00 for 1st page, $1.00 ea add'l. Cert fee includes copies. Payee: County Clerk. Personal checks accepted. No credit cards accepted for record searching. Prepayment required. Mail requests: SASE required.
Civil Name Search: Access: Fax, mail, online, in person. Both court and visitors may perform in person name searches. Search fee: $20.00 per hour. Civil records on computer 1850s. Mail turnaround time 1 day. Index online from JIS-Link; see www.courts.wa.gov/jislink/ (also, see state introduction for subscription service.). Also, search name index back to 1989 and calendars free at http://dw.courts.wa.gov/index.cfm.
Criminal Name Search: Access: Fax, mail, online, in person. Both court and visitors may perform in person name searches. Search fee: $20.00 per hour. Required to search: name, years to search; also helpful: address, DOB. Criminal records computerized from 1850s. Mail turnaround time 1 day. Online access to criminal indexes is the same as civil.

District Court PO Box 144, Cathlamet, WA 98612; 360-795-3461; fax: 360-795-6506; 8AM-4PM (PST). *Misdemeanor, Civil Actions under $75,001, Small Claims.*
www.co.wahkiakum.wa.us/
General Information: No sealed, juvenile, adoption, paternity, mental health, sex offenders (victims) or some DUI records released. No fee to fax documents. Court makes copy: $.25 per page. Certification fee: $5.00. Payee: Wahkiakum District Court. Personal checks accepted. No credit cards accepted for searches. Prepayment required. Mail requests: SASE required.
Civil Name Search: Access: Phone, fax, mail, online, in person. Only the court performs in person name searches; visitors may not. No search fee. Required to search: name, years to search; also helpful: address. Civil records on computer from 1997, index cards back to 1980, archived prior. Mail turnaround time 2 days. Index online from JIS-Link; see www.courts.wa.gov/jislink/ (also, see state introduction for subscription service.). Also, search name index back to 1989 and calendars free at http://dw.courts.wa.gov/index.cfm.
Criminal Name Search: Access: Phone, fax, mail, online, in person. Only the court performs in person name searches; visitors may not. No search fee. Required to search: name, years to search; also helpful: DOB. Criminal records computerized from 1997, index cards back to 1990, archived prior. Mail turnaround time 2 days. Online access to criminal indexes is the same as civil.

Cathlamet Municipal Court PO Box 68, 100 Main St, Cathlamet, WA 98612-0068; 360-795-3203; fax: 360-795-8500; 9AM-4:30PM (PST). *Misdemeanor.*
General Information: Index online from JIS-Link; see www.courts.wa.gov/jislink/ (also, see state introduction for subscription service.). Also, search name index back to 1989 and calendars free at http://dw.courts.wa.gov/index.cfm.

Walla Walla County

Superior Court PO Box 836, Walla Walla, WA 99362; 509-524-2780; fax: 509-524-2779; 9AM-12: 1PM-5PM (PST). *Felony, Civil, Eviction, Probate, Dissolution.*
www.co.walla-walla.wa.us/
General Information: No sealed, juvenile, adoption, paternity, mental health, sex offenders (victims). Will not fax documents. Court makes copy: $.50 per page. Certification fee: $5.00 1st page, $1.00 ea add'l. Cert fee includes copies. Payee: Walla Walla County Clerk; only cashiers checks and money orders accepted. No credit cards accepted. Prepayment required. Mail requests: SASE required.

Civil Name Search: Access: Phone, mail, in person. Only the court performs in person name searches; visitors may not. Search fee: $30.00 per hour. Required to search: name, years to search; also helpful: DOB. Civil records on computer from 7/81, prior in docket books. Mail turnaround time 2 days.
Criminal Name Search: Access: Phone, mail, in person. Only the court performs in person name searches; visitors may not. Search fee: $30.00 per hour. Required to search: name, years to search, DOB; also helpful: address, SSN. Criminal records computerized from 7/81, prior in docket books. Mail turnaround time 2 days.

District Court 317 W Rose St, Walla Walla, WA 99362; 509-524-2760; fax: 509-524-2775; 9AM-4PM (PST). *Misdemeanor, Civil Actions $75,000 or less, Small Claims.*
www.co.walla-walla.wa.us/
General Information: No sealed, juvenile, adoption, paternity, mental health, sex offenders (victims) or some DUI records released. Will fax documents for no add'l fee. Court makes copy: $1.00 first page, $.50 each add'l. Self serve copy: same. Certification fee: $5.00 per document; add copy fee for add'l pages. Payee: Walla Walla District Court. Personal checks accepted, credit cards are not. Prepayment required. Mail requests: SASE required.
Civil Name Search: Access: Mail, in person, online. Only the court performs in person name searches; visitors may not. Search fee: $20.00 per name. Required to search: full name, DOB years to search. Civil records on computer from 7/87. Mail turnaround time 1-3 days. Index online from JIS-Link; see www.courts.wa.gov/jislink/ (also, see state introduction for subscription service.). Also, search name index back to 1989 and calendars free at http://dw.courts.wa.gov/index.cfm.
Criminal Name Search: Access: Mail, online, in person. Only the court performs in person name searches; visitors may not. Search fee: $20.00 per name. Required to search: full name, DOB years to search, signed release; also helpful: address, SSN. Criminal records computerized from 7/87, on index books. Records retained for 10 years. Mail turnaround time 1-3 days. Online access to criminal indexes is the same as civil.

Burbank Municipal Court www.co.walla-walla.wa.us/ See District Court

College Place Municipal Court 625 S College Ave, College Place, WA 99324-1516; 509-529-1200 x16; fax: 509-525-5352; 8AM-5PM M-TH; 8AM-5PM F (PST). *Misdemeanor.*
www.ci.college-place.wa.us/page/MunicipalCourt
General Information: Index online from JIS-Link; www.courts.wa.gov/jislink/index.cfm (also, see state introduction for subscription service.). Also, search name index back to 1989 and calendars free at http://dw.courts.wa.gov/index.cfm.

Prescott Municipal Court Court closed after 2007. See Walla Walla County District Court.

Waitsburg Municipal Court See District Court

Walla Walla Municipal Court See District Court

Whatcom County

Superior Court 311 Grand Ave #301, Bellingham, WA 98225; 360-676-6777; criminal phone: x50013; civil phone: x50014; fax: 360-676-6693; 8:30AM-4:30PM (PST). *Felony, Civil, Eviction, Probate.*
www.whatcomcounty.us/superior/
General Information: No sealed, juvenile, adoption, paternity, mental health, sex offenders (victims). Court makes copy: $.50 per page, microfilm $.50 per page. Self serve copy: $.15 per page. Certification fee: $5.00 1st page, $1.00 ea add'l. Cert fee includes copies. Payee: Whatcom County Clerk. Only cashiers checks and money orders accepted. No credit cards accepted. Prepayment required. Mail requests: SASE required.
Civil Name Search: Access: Phone, fax, mail, online, in person. Both court and visitors may perform in person name searches. Search fee: No search fee if record is on computer. Required to search: name, years to search; also helpful: address. Civil records on computer from 1980, archives back to 1800s, microfilm. Mail turnaround time up to 1 week. Civil PAT goes back to 1/2005. Index online from JIS-Link; see www.courts.wa.gov/jislink/ (also, see state introduction for subscription service.). Also, search name index back to 1989 and calendars free at http://dw.courts.wa.gov/index.cfm.
Criminal Name Search: Access: Phone, fax, mail, online, in person. Both court and visitors may perform in person name searches. Search fee: $30.00 per hour. Required to search: name, years to search; also helpful: address, DOB, SSN. Criminal records computerized from 1980, archives back to 1800s, microfilm. Mail turnaround time up to 1 week. Criminal PAT goes back to same as civil. Online access to criminal indexes is the same as civil. Online results show name, DOB.

District Court 311 Grand Ave, #401, Bellingham, WA 98225; 360-676-6770; fax: 360-676-7685; 8AM-4:30PM (PST). *Misdemeanor, Civil Actions under $75,001, Small Claims.*
www.whatcomcounty.us/
General Information: No sealed, juvenile, adoption, paternity, mental health, sex offenders (victims) or some DUI records released. Court makes copy: $.15 per page. Certification fee: $5.00 per cert includes copy fee. Payee: Whatcom District Court. Personal checks accepted, credit cards are not. Prepayment required.
Civil Name Search: Access: Fax, mail, online, in person. Only the court performs in person name searches; visitors may not. No search fee. Required to search: name, years to search; also helpful: address. Civil records on computer since 1984. Mail turnaround time 2 days. Index online from JIS-Link; see www.courts.wa.gov/jislink/ (also, see state introduction for subscription service.). Also, search name index back to 1989 and calendars free at http://dw.courts.wa.gov/index.cfm.
Criminal Name Search: Access: Fax, mail, online, in person. Only the court performs in person name searches; visitors may not. No search fee. Required to search: name, years to search; also helpful: address, DOB. Criminal records on computer 10 years back, archived since 1984. Mail turnaround time 2 days. Online access to criminal indexes is the same as civil. Online results show middle initial.

Bellingham Municipal Court 2014 C St, Bellingham, WA 98225-4019; 360-778-8150; fax: 360-778-8151; 9AM-N, 1-4PM (PST). *Misdemeanor.*
www.cob.org/government/court/index.aspx
General Information: Index online from JIS-Link; see www.courts.wa.gov/jislink/ (also, see state introduction for subscription service.). Also, search name index back to 1989 and calendars free at http://dw.courts.wa.gov/index.cfm.

Blaine Municipal Court 344 H St, Blaine, WA 98230-4109; 360-332-8311; fax: 360-332-8330; 8AM-5PM (PST). *Misdemeanor.*
www.ci.blaine.wa.us/index.aspx?nid=166
General Information: Index online from JIS-Link; see www.courts.wa.gov/jislink/ (also, see state introduction for subscription service.). Also, search name index back to 1989 and calendars free at http://dw.courts.wa.gov/index.cfm.

Drug Court 311 Grand Ave, Bellingham, WA 98225-4038; 360-676-6754; fax: 360-676-7634; 8AM-5PM (PST). *Misdemeanor.*
General Information: In the District court Complex. Index online from JIS-Link; see www.courts.wa.gov/jislink/ (also, see state introduction for subscription service.). Also, search name index back to 1989 and calendars free at http://dw.courts.wa.gov/index.cfm.

Everson-Nooksack Municipal Court PO Box 315, 111 W Main St, Everson, WA 98247-0315; 360-966-3411; fax: 360-966-3466; 9AM-5PM (PST). *Misdemeanor.*
General Information: Index online from JIS-Link; see www.courts.wa.gov/jislink/ (also, see state introduction for subscription service.). Also, search name index back to 1989 and calendars free at http://dw.courts.wa.gov/index.cfm.

Ferndale Municipal Court PO Box 291, 2095 Main St, City Hall, Ferndale, WA 98248-0291; 360-384-2827; fax: 360-383-0938; 9AM-5PM (PST). *Misdemeanor, Traffic.*
www.ferndalecourts.org/
General Information: Index online from JIS-Link; see www.courts.wa.gov/jislink/ (also, see state introduction for subscription service.). Also, search name index back to 1989 and calendars free at http://dw.courts.wa.gov/index.cfm.

Lummi Tribal Court 2616 Kwina Rd, Bellingham, WA 98226-9291; 360-384-2305; fax: 360-312-1734; 8AM-4:30PM (PST). *Misdemeanor, Civil.* www.lummi-nsn.org/
General Information: Class B felony cases have been tried here since 11/2009. Other felony actions are sent to the federal court. The records from this court are not on the JIS state system.

Lynden Municipal Court 300 4th Street, Lynden, WA 98264-1918; 360-354-4270; fax: 360-318-0301; 8AM-5PM (PST). *Misdemeanor, Gross Misdemeanors.*
www.lyndenwa.org
General Information: Index online from JIS-Link; see www.courts.wa.gov/jislink/ (also, see state introduction for subscription service.). Also, search name index back to 1989 and calendars free at http://dw.courts.wa.gov/index.cfm.

Nooksack Tribal Court PO Box 157, 5016 Deming Rd, Deming, WA 98244; 360-592-4158; criminal phone: x1010; civil phone: x1009;; 8:30AM-5PM (PST). *Misdemeanor, Civil Actions under $3,000, Eviction (Tribal Housing).*
www.nooksack-tribe.org/court_clerk.htm

General Information: Felony actions are sent to the federal court. The records from this court are not on the JIS state system.

Sumas Municipal Court PO Box 9, 433 Cherry St, Sumas, WA 98295-0009; 360-988-5711; fax: 360-988-8855; 8AM-5PM (PST). *Misdemeanor.*
General Information: Index online from JIS-Link; see www.courts.wa.gov/jislink/ (also, see state introduction for subscription service.). Also, search name index back to 1989 and calendars free at http://dw.courts.wa.gov/index.cfm.

Whitman County

Superior Court Whitman County Clerk, PO Box 390, Colfax, WA 99111; 509-397-6240; fax: 509-397-3546; 9AM-5PM (PST). *Felony, Civil, Eviction, Probate.*
www.whitmancounty.org/
General Information: No sealed, juvenile, adoption, paternity, mental health, sex offenders (victims). Will fax documents $5.00 1st page, $1.00 each add'l. Court makes copy: $.50 per page. Certification fee: $5.00 plus $1.00 per page; exemplified copies are $9.00 plus $1.00 per page. Payee: Whitman County Clerk. Personal checks accepted, credit cards are not. Prepayment required. Mail requests: SASE required.
Civil Name Search: Access: Phone, fax, mail, online, in person. Only the court performs in person name searches; visitors may not. Search fee: $30.00 per hour. Required to search: name, years to search; also helpful: address. Civil records on computer from 1985, archives back to 1887. Mail turnaround time 1 week. Index online from JIS-Link; see www.courts.wa.gov/jislink/ (also, see state introduction for subscription service.). Also, search name index back to 1989 and calendars free at http://dw.courts.wa.gov/index.cfm.
Criminal Name Search: Access: Phone, fax, mail, online, in person. Only the court performs in person name searches; visitors may not. Search fee: $30.00 per hour. Required to search: name, years to search, signed release; also helpful: address, DOB, SSN. Criminal records computerized from 1985, archives back to 1887. Mail turnaround time 1 week. Online access to criminal indexes is the same as civil. Online results show name only.

District Court 400 N Main St, PO Box 230, Colfax, WA 99111; 509-397-6260; fax: 509-397-5584; 8AM-5PM; Public Hours: 9AM-4:30PM (PST). *Misdemeanor, Civil Actions under $75,001, Small Claims.*
www.whitmancounty.org/
General Information: No sealed, juvenile, adoption, paternity, mental health, sex offenders (victims) or some DUI records released. Fee to fax out file $2.00. Court makes copy: $.15 per page. Certification fee: $5.00. Payee: Whitman County. Personal checks, Visa/MC accepted. Prepayment required. Mail requests: SASE required.
Civil Name Search: Access: Phone, fax, mail, online, in person. Only the court performs in person name searches; visitors may not. Search fee: $8.00. Required to search: name, years to search; also helpful: address. Civil records on DISCIS computer system from 7/91, prior on index log. Mail turnaround time 2 weeks. Index online from JIS-Link; see www.courts.wa.gov/jislink/ (also, see state introduction for subscription service.). Also, search name index back to 1989 and calendars free at http://dw.courts.wa.gov/index.cfm.
Criminal Name Search: Access: Phone, fax, mail, online, in person. Only the court performs in person name searches; visitors may not. Search fee: $8.00. Required to search: name, years to search, DOB; also helpful: address, SSN. Criminal records on DISCIS computer system from 7/91, no index available for prior years. Mail turnaround time 2 weeks. Online access to criminal indexes is the same as civil.

District Court 325 SE Paradise St, Pullman, WA 99163; 509-332-2065; fax: 509-338-3318; 8AM-5PM (PST). *Misdemeanor, Civil Actions under $75,001, Small Claims.*
www.courts.wa.gov/court_dir/orgs/297.html
General Information: No sealed, juvenile, adoption, paternity, mental health, sex offenders (victims) or some DUI records released. No fee to fax documents. Court makes copy: $.15 per page. Certification fee: $5.00. Payee: Whitman District Court. Personal checks, Visa/MC accepted. Prepayment required. Mail requests: SASE required.
Civil Name Search: Access: Fax, mail, online, in person. Only the court performs in person name searches; visitors may not. Search fee: $8.00 per name. Required to search: name, years to search; also helpful: address. Civil records on DISCIS computer system from 7/91; records prior to this date destroyed. Mail turnaround time 2 weeks. Index online from JIS-Link; see www.courts.wa.gov/jislink/ (also, see state introduction for subscription service.). Also, search name index back to 1989 and calendars free at http://dw.courts.wa.gov/index.cfm.
Criminal Name Search: Access: Fax, mail, online, in person. Only the court performs in person name searches; visitors may not. Search fee: $8.00 per name. Required to search: name, years to search; also helpful: address, DOB, SSN. Criminal records on DISCIS computer system from

7/91; records prior to this date destroyed. Mail turnaround time 2 weeks. Online access to criminal indexes is the same as civil.

Albion Municipal Court . *Misdemeanor.*
General Information: See District Court. Index online from JIS-Link; see www.courts.wa.gov/jislink/ (also, see state introduction for subscription service.). Also, search name index back to 1989 and calendars free at http://dw.courts.wa.gov/index.cfm.

Colfax Municipal Court PO Box 229, 400 N Mills St, Colfax, WA 99111-0229; 509-397-3861; fax: 509-397-3044; 8AM-5PM (PST). *Misdemeanor.*
General Information: Index online from JIS-Link; see www.courts.wa.gov/jislink/ (also, see state introduction for subscription service.). Also, search name index back to 1989 and calendars free at http://dw.courts.wa.gov/index.cfm.

Colton Municipal Court PO Box 157, 706 Broadway, Colton, WA 99113-0157; 509-229-3887; fax: 509-229-3294; 9AM-N, 1-3PM M-TH, Closed F (PST). *Traffic.*
General Information: Traffic court records only at this time. Index online from JIS-Link; see www.courts.wa.gov/jislink/. Also, search name index back to 1989 and calendars free at http://dw.courts.wa.gov/index.cfm.

Uniontown Municipal Court PO Box 87, City Hall, 110 S Montgomery St, Uniontown, WA 99179-0087; 509-229-3805; fax: 509-229-3748; 9AM-5PM (PST). *Misdemeanor.*
General Information: Index online from JIS-Link; see www.courts.wa.gov/jislink/ (also, see state introduction for subscription service.). Also, search name index back to 1989 and calendars free at http://dw.courts.wa.gov/index.cfm.

Yakima County

Superior Court Yakima County Clerk, 128 N 2nd St, Rm 323, Yakima, WA 98901; 509-574-1430; probate phone: 509-574-1430;; 8:30AM-4:30PM (PST). *Felony, Civil, Domestic Relations, Probate.*
www.yakimacounty.us/superiorcourt/
General Information: Divorce records can also be obtained from this agency. No sealed, juvenile, adoption, paternity, mental health, sex offenders (victims). Will not fax documents. Court makes copy: $.50 per page. Microfilm copies $.25 per page. Self serve copy: $.50 per page. Certification fee: $5.00 plus $1.00 per page after first. Payee: Yakima County Clerk. Business checks accepted; no personal checks. Prepayment required. Mail requests: SASE required.
Civil Name Search: Access: Phone, mail, in person, online. Both court and visitors may perform in person name searches. Search fee: $30.00 per hour. Civil records on computer from 1978, archives back to 1890s. Mail turnaround time varies. Civil PAT available. Index online from JIS-Link; see www.courts.wa.gov/jislink/ (also, see state introduction for subscription service.). Also, search name index back to 1989 and calendars free at http://dw.courts.wa.gov/index.cfm.
Criminal Name Search: Access: Phone, mail, in person, online. Both court and visitors may perform in person name searches. Search fee: $30.00 per hour. Criminal records computerized from 1978, archives back to 1890s. Mail turnaround time varies. Criminal PAT available. Online access to criminal indexes is the same as civil.

District Court 128 N 2nd St, Rm 217, Yakima, WA 98901-2631; 509-574-1800; fax: 509-574-1831; 8:30AM-4:30PM (PST). *Misdemeanor, Civil Actions under $75,001, Small Claims.*
www.yakimacounty.us/DistrictCourt/Default.htm
General Information: No sealed or some DUI records released. No fee to fax documents. Court makes copy: $1.00 per page 1st page, $.50 ea add'l. Certification fee: $5.00 per doc plus copy fee. Payee: Yakima County District Court. Personal checks, Visa/MC accepted. Prepayment required. Mail requests: SASE requested.
Civil Name Search: Access: Fax, mail, online. Only the court performs in person name searches; visitors may not. No search fee. Required to search: name, years to search; also helpful: address. Civil record indexed on computer; paper files kept 3 years once settled, 10 years max. Note: Search requests to the court must be in writing; you must use their form. Mail turnaround time 2 days. Index online from JIS-Link; see www.courts.wa.gov/jislink/ (also, see state introduction for subscription service.). Also, search name index back to 1989 and calendars free at http://dw.courts.wa.gov/index.cfm.
Criminal Name Search: Access: Fax, mail, online. Only the court performs in person name searches; visitors may not. No search fee. Required to search: name, years to search, DOB; also helpful: address, case number, DRL, SSN. Criminal records computerized from 1984, generally. Note: Search requests to the court must be in writing. Must use their form. Mail turnaround time 2 days. Online access to criminal indexes is the same as civil.

Grandview Municipal Court See Yakima County District Court

Granger Municipal Court PO Box 1100, 102 Main St, Granger, WA 98932-1100; 509-854-1725; fax: 509-854-2103; 9AM-5PM (PST). *Misdemeanor.*
General Information: Index online from JIS-Link; see www.courts.wa.gov/jislink/ (also, see state introduction for subscription service.). Also, search name index back to 1989 and calendars free at http://dw.courts.wa.gov/index.cfm.

Moxee City Municipal Court PO Box 249, 255 W Seattle, Moxee City, WA 98936-0249; 509-575-8851; fax: 509-575-8852; 8AM-5PM M-F (PST). *Misdemeanor, Traffic.*
General Information: Index online from JIS-Link; see www.courts.wa.gov/jislink/ (also, see state introduction for subscription service.). Also, search name index back to 1989 and calendars free at http://dw.courts.wa.gov/index.cfm.

Selah Municipal Court 115 W Naches Ave, Selah, WA 98942-1323; 509-698-7329; fax: 509-698-7338; 8AM-5PM M-Tues; 8AM-12 W, TH, F (PST). *Misdemeanor, Infractions.*
www.ci.selah.wa.us/inner/court.html
General Information: Index online from JIS-Link; see www.courts.wa.gov/jislink/ (also, see state introduction for subscription service.). Also, search name index back to 1989 and calendars free at http://dw.courts.wa.gov/index.cfm.

Sunnyside Municipal Court 401 Homer St, Sunnyside, WA 98944-1354; 509-839-4427; fax: 509-836-6272; 7:30AM-6PM M-TH (PST). *Misdemeanor, Traffic.*
General Information: Will fax documents for no fee. Court makes copy: none. No certification fee. Payee: Sunnyside Municipal Ct. Personal checks accepted, credit cards are not. Prepayment required. Mail requests: SASE required.
Criminal Name Search: Access: Mail, fax, in person, email, online. Visitors must perform in person searches themselves. No search fee. Required to search: name, DOB, SSN. Criminal records go back to- varies. Mail turnaround time 1 day. Index online from JIS-Link; see www.courts.wa.gov/jislink/ Also, see state introduction for subscription service. Also, search name index back to 1989 and calendars free at http://dw.courts.wa.gov/index.cfm. Also, you may direct criminal record requests to dmendoza@ci.sunnyside.wa.us. Online results show middle initial, DOB, address.

Tieton Municipal Court See Yakima County District Court

Toppenish Municipal Court 21 W 1st Ave, Toppenish, WA 98948-1524; 509-865-5959; fax: 509-865-3864; 7:30AM-6PM M-Th (PST). *Misdemeanor.*
General Information: Index online from JIS-Link; see www.courts.wa.gov/jislink/ (also, see state introduction for subscription service.). Also, search name index back to 1989 and calendars free at http://dw.courts.wa.gov/index.cfm.

Union Gap Municipal Court PO Box 3008, Union Gap, WA 98903-0008; 509-576-8911; fax: 509-249-9298; 7AM-5:45PM M-Th (closed F) (PST). *Misdemeanor.*
General Information: Index online from JIS-Link; see www.courts.wa.gov/jislink/ (also, see state introduction for subscription service.). Also, search name index back to 1989 and calendars free at http://dw.courts.wa.gov/index.cfm.

Wapato Municipal Court 205 S Simcoe Ave, Wapato, WA 98951-1352; 509-877-6269; fax: 509-877-4589; 8AM-5PM (PST). *Misdemeanor.*
www.wapato-city.org/
General Information: Index online from JIS-Link; see www.courts.wa.gov/jislink/ (also, see state introduction for subscription service.). Also, search name index back to 1989 and calendars free at http://dw.courts.wa.gov/index.cfm.

Yakama Tribal Court PO Box 151, Toppenish, WA 98948-0151; 509-865-5121; fax: 509-865-4954; 8AM-5PM (PST). *Misdemeanor, Civil.*
www.yakamanation-nsn.gov/index.php
General Information: Felony actions are sent to the federal court. The records from this court are not on the JIS state system.

Yakima Municipal Court 200 S 3rd St, Yakima, WA 98901-2830; 509-575-3050; fax: 509-575-3020; 8AM-4PM (PST). *Misdemeanor, Traffic.*
General Information: Index online from JIS-Link; see www.courts.wa.gov/jislink/ (also, see state introduction for subscription service.). Also, search name index back to 1989 and calendars free at http://dw.courts.wa.gov/index.cfm.

Zillah Municipal Court PO Box 388, 111 7th St, Zillah, WA 98953-0388; 509-829-3543; fax: 509-829-5605; 8AM-5PM (PST). *Misdemeanor.*
General Information: Index online from JIS-Link; see www.courts.wa.gov/jislink/ (also, see state introduction for subscription service.). Also, search name index back to 1989 and calendars free at http://dw.courts.wa.gov/index.cfm.

West Virginia

Time Zone:	**EST**
Capital:	**Charleston, Kanawha County**
# of Counties:	**55**
State Web:	**www.wv.gov**
Court Web:	**www.state.wv.us/wvsca**

Administration

Administrative Office, Supreme Court of Appeals, 1900 Kanawha Blvd, Bldg 1, Rm E 100, State Capitol, Charleston, WV, 25305; 304-558-0145, Fax: 304-558-1212

The Supreme Court

The Supreme Court of Appeals is West Virginia's highest court and the court of last resort. West Virginia is one of only 11 states with a single appellate court. Supreme Court of Appeals Opinions and Calendar are available at the web page.

The West Virginia Courts

Court	Type	How Organized	Jurisdiction Highpoints
Circuit*	General	55 Courts in 31 Circuits	Felony, Misdemeanor, Civil $300, Juvenile, Probate
Magistrate*	Limited	55 Courts in 55 Counties	Misdemeanor, Civil Actions under $5,000, Eviction, Traffic, Small Claims
Family		55 Courts in 27 Circuits	Family, Divorce, Child Custody
Municipal	Limited	122 Courts	Traffic, Ordinance

* = profiled in this book

Details on the Court Structure

The trial courts of general jurisdiction are the **Circuit Courts** which handle civil cases at law over $300 or more or in equity, felonies and misdemeanor and appeals from the Family Courts and Magistrate Court cases. Probate is handled by the Circuit Court.

The **Magistrate Courts**, which are akin to small claims courts, issue arrest and search warrants, hear misdemeanor cases, conduct preliminary examinations in felony cases, and hear civil cases with $5,000 or less in dispute. Magistrates also issue emergency protective orders in cases involving domestic violence.

Family Courts hear cases involving divorce, annulment, separate maintenance, family support, paternity, child custody, and visitation. Family Court judges also conduct final hearings in domestic violence cases.

Municipal Courts are administered locally and are constitutionally limited to those cases involving ordinance violations.

Record Searching Facts You Need to Know

Fees and Record Searching Tips

There is a statewide requirement that search turnaround times not exceed five business days. However, most courts do far better than that limit. The search fees range from $5.00 to $25.00. The copy fee is set by statute at $.75 per copy. Release of public information is governed by WV Code Sec.29B-1-1 et seq. Find court forms at www.wvcourtnet.org/public.asp.

Online Access is Limited

23 Circuit Courts show accessible record dockets at www.swcg-inc.com/page.cfm/circuit-courts/circuit-express. No images are available. There is a $125 sign-up fee and a monthly flat fee of $ 38.00 plus connect charge of $ 1.00 a minute. Records are available from 02/1997. Search by name or case number. The case summary is shown, no identifiers are provided. The WV Supreme Court prohibits court-related websites from displaying

personal identifiers.

Barbour County

Circuit Court 8 N Main St, Philippi, WV 26416; 304-457-3454; fax: 304-457-2790; 8:30AM-4:30PM (EST). *Felony, Civil Actions over $5,000, Probate.*

General Information: Probate is handled by the County Clerk at this address. No sealed, juvenile, adoptions, mental health, expunged records released. No fee to fax documents if one or two pages only. Court makes copy: $.75 per page. Certification fee: $1.00 per cert plus copy fee. Payee: Barbour County Circuit Clerk. Personal checks accepted, credit cards are not. Prepayment required. Mail requests: SASE requested.

Civil Name Search: Access: Phone, fax, mail, in person. Both court and visitors may perform in person name searches. No search fee. Civil records some on microfiche from 1843 to 1980s, on index cards back to 1862, on dockets back to 1960. Mail turnaround time 1 day. Civil PAT goes back to 2001.

Criminal Name Search: Access: Phone, fax, mail, in person. Both court and visitors may perform in person name searches. No search fee. Computerized records to 2000, paper/microfilm to 1960. Mail turnaround time 1 day. Criminal PAT goes back to same as civil.

Magistrate Court PO Box 541, Philippi, WV 26416; 304-457-3676; fax: 304-457-4999; 8:30AM-4:30PM (EST). *Misdemeanor, Civil Actions under $5,000, Eviction, Small Claims.*

General Information: All mail requests must be on letterhead. Will fax documents 2.00 per page. Court makes copy: $.25 per page. Court will bill for copies, but no further searches until paid in full. Certification fee: $.50 per page. Payee: Barbour County Magistrate Clerk. No personal checks accepted. Major credit cards accepted. Prepayment required. Mail requests: SASE required.

Civil Name Search: Access: Mail, in person. Both court and visitors may perform in person name searches. Search fee: $25.00 per name. Required to search: Name, DOB, SSN, and any other personal identifiers. Records go back 10 years, computerized since 1997. Mail turnaround time varies. Civil PAT goes back to 7 years. Records may be purged from public terminal, so records are not the full index.

Criminal Name Search: Access: Mail, in person. Visitors must perform in person searches themselves. Search fee: $25.00 per name. Records go back 10 years, computerized since 1997. Mail turnaround time varies. Criminal PAT goes back to 7 years. Records may be purged from public terminal, so records are not the full index.

Berkeley County

Circuit Court 380 W South St, #2200, Attn: Circuit Court Clerk, Martinsburg, WV 25401; 304-264-1918; criminal phone: x4; civil phone: x3; fax: 304-262-3139; 9AM-5PM (EST). *Felony, Civil Actions over $5,000, Probate.*

General Information: Fiduciary Records Clerk handles probate; address 100 W King St, Rm 2, Martinsburg, 25401. No sealed, juvenile, adoptions, mental health, guardianship records released. Will fax specific case file $2.00 per page if prepaid. Court makes copy: $1.00 per page. No certification fee. Payee: Clerk of Circuit Court. Business checks accepted; no personal checks. No credit cards accepted. Prepayment required.

Civil Name Search: Access: In person only. Visitors must perform in person searches themselves. Civil records on computer from 1/1990, on index books from 1863. Civil PAT goes back to 1990.

Criminal Name Search: Access: In person only. Visitors must perform in person searches themselves. Required to search: name, years to search; also helpful: DOB, SSN. Criminal records computerized from 1/1990, on index books from 1800s. Criminal PAT goes back to same as civil.

Magistrate Court Berkeley County Judicial Center, 380 W South St, #3100, Martinsburg, WV 25401; 304-264-1957; fax: 304-267-1373; 9AM-4PM (EST). *Misdemeanor, Civil Actions under $5,000, Eviction, Small Claims.*

General Information: Will fax documents $2.00 per page. Court makes copy: $.25 per page. Certification fee: $.50 per page. Payee: Berkeley County Magistrate Court. No personal checks accepted. Major credit cards accepted. Prepayment required.

Civil Name Search: Access: In person only. Both court and visitors may perform in person name searches. Search fee: $25.00 per name. Records stored since 2000. Civil PAT goes back to 1997.

Criminal Name Search: Access: In person only. Both court and visitors may perform in person name searches. Search fee: $25.00 per name if the court has to do search. Required to search: name, years to search; also helpful: address, DOB, SSN. Records stored since 2000. Criminal PAT goes back to same as civil. Terminal results include SSN.

Boone County

Circuit Court 200 State St, Madison, WV 25130; 304-369-3925; probate phone: 304-369-7337; fax: 304-369-7326; 8AM-4PM (EST). *Felony, Civil Actions over $5,000, Probate.*

General Information: Probate is handled by County Clerk, 200 State St, Madison, WV 25130. No sealed, guardianship, juvenile, adoptions, mental health, expunged records released. Fee to fax out file $5.00; 30 pg limit. Court makes copy: $1.00 per page. No certification fee. Payee: Circuit Clerk. Business checks accepted; no personal checks. No credit cards accepted. Prepayment required. Mail requests: SASE requested.

Civil Name Search: Access: Phone, fax, mail, in person. Both court and visitors may perform in person name searches. No search fee. Civil records on computer from 1984 to present, on index books 1956 to present, on dockets back to 1900. Mail turnaround time 1 day. Civil PAT goes back to 1984. Only the last 4 numbers of SSN appear on results.

Criminal Name Search: Access: Phone, fax, mail, in person. Both court and visitors may perform in person name searches. No search fee. Required to search: name, years to search, signed release. Criminal records computerized from 1984 to present, on index books 1956 to present, on dockets back to 1864. Mail turnaround time 1 day. Criminal PAT goes back to same as civil.

Magistrate Court 200 State St., Madison, WV 25130; 304-369-7364; fax: 304-369-1932; 8AM-4PM (EST). *Misdemeanor, Civil Actions under $5,000, Eviction, Small Claims.*

General Information: Will fax documents $2.00 per page. Court makes copy: $.25 per page. Self serve copy: same. No certification fee . No personal checks accepted. Major credit cards accepted. Prepayment required.

Civil Name Search: Access: In person. Both court and visitors may perform in person name searches. Search fee: $25.00 per search. Civil records go back to 1977; computerized since 1996. Civil PAT goes back to 1996.

Criminal Name Search: Access: Mail, in person. Visitors must perform in person searches themselves. Search fee: $25.00 per name. Required to search: name, years to search; also helpful: DOB, SSN. Criminal records go back to 1977; computerized records since 1996. Criminal PAT goes back to same as civil.

Braxton County

Circuit Court 300 Main St, Sutton, WV 26601; 304-765-2837; probate phone: 304-765-2833; fax: 304-765-2947; 8AM-4PM (EST). *Felony, Civil Actions over $5,000, Probate.*

General Information: Probate is located across the hall in the same building. No adoption, juvenile, mental hygiene records released. Will fax documents $2.00 per page. Court makes copy: $.75 per page. No certification fee. Payee: JW Morris, Clerk. Personal checks accepted, credit cards are not. Prepayment required. Mail requests: SASE required.

Civil Name Search: Access: Mail, fax, in person, email. Both court and visitors may perform in person name searches. No search fee. Civil records on microfiche 1806 to 1910, on dockets back to 1810; on computer back to 1993. Note: If a search is done by this office, a notarized release sign by subject is required. Mail turnaround time 2-3 days. Civil PAT goes back to 1993.

Criminal Name Search: Access: Mail, fax, in person. Both court and visitors may perform in person name searches. No search fee. Required to search: name, years to search, notarized signed release. Criminal records on microfiche 1806 to 1910, on dockets back to 1810. Note: If a search is done by this office, a notarized release sign by subject is required. Mail turnaround time 2-3 days. Criminal PAT goes back to 1987.

Magistrate Court 307 Main St, Sutton, WV 26601; 304-765-7362; fax: 304-765-2612; 8:30AM-4PM (EST). *Misdemeanor, Civil Actions under $5,000, Eviction, Small Claims.*

General Information: Fee to fax out file $2.00 per page. Court makes copy: $.50 per page. Self serve copy: same. Certification fee: included as part of copy fee. Payee: Braxton County Magistrate Court. Personal checks accepted. Major credit cards accepted; no debit cards. Prepayment required. Mail requests: SASE not required.

Civil Name Search: Access: Mail, in person. Visitors must perform in person searches themselves. Search fee: $25.00 per name. Records go back 10 years; on computer back to 1999. Mail turnaround time up to 10 days. Civil PAT goes back to 1999.

Criminal Name Search: Access: Mail, in person. Visitors must perform in person searches themselves. Search fee: $25.00 per name. Required to search: name, years to search, DOB; also helpful: address, SSN, signed release. Paper go back to 1998, except minor traffic which are destroyed and stored electronically; on computer back to at least 1999. Note: Court will not perform criminal record searches and suggests researchers contact State Police, 304-746-2180. Mail turnaround time up to 10 days. Criminal PAT goes back to same as civil.

Brooke County

Circuit Court Brooke County Courthouse, PO Box 474, Wellsburg, WV 26070; 304-737-3662; probate phone: 304-737-3661; fax: 304-737-0352; 9AM-5PM (EST). *Felony, Civil Actions over $5,000, Probate.*

General Information: Probate is handled by County Clerk, 632 Main St, Courthouse, Wellsburg, WV 26070. No divorce, juvenile, mental hygiene, adoption records released. Will fax documents $2.00 per page. Court makes copy: $.75 per page. Self serve copy: same. Certification fee: $.50 per page. Payee: Brooke County Circuit Clerk. Personal checks accepted, credit cards are not. Prepayment required. Mail requests: SASE required.

Civil Name Search: Access: Mail, in person. Both court and visitors may perform in person name searches. Search fee: $5.00 per name. Required to search: name; also helpful: years to search. Civil records on dockets and files from prior to 1960 to present, in boxes back to 1800s; computerized records since 1997. Mail turnaround time same day, longer if in archives.

Criminal Name Search: Access: Mail, in person. Both court and visitors may perform in person name searches. Search fee: $5.00 per name. Required to search: name; also helpful: years to search, DOB, SSN. Criminal records on dockets and files from prior to 1960 to present, in boxes back to 1800s; computerized records since 1997. Mail turnaround time same day, longer if in archives.

Magistrate Court 744 Charles St, #4, Wellsburg, WV 26070; 304-737-1321; fax: 304-737-1509; 8:30AM-4:30PM (EST). *Misdemeanor, Civil Actions under $5,000, Eviction, Small Claims.*

General Information: Will fax documents $2.00 per page. Court makes copy: $.25 per page. Certification fee: $.50 per seal plus copy fee. No personal checks or 3rd party checks accepted. Visa/MC accepted. Prepayment required.

Civil Name Search: Access: Mail, in person. Visitors must perform in person searches themselves. Search fee: $25.00 per name. Civil records go back to 1977; computerized back to 1996. Civil PAT goes back to 1996.

Criminal Name Search: Access: Mail, in person. Visitors must perform in person searches themselves. Search fee: $25.00 per name. Required to search: name; also helpful: DOB, SSN, signed release. Criminal records go back to 1977; computerized back to 1996. Criminal PAT goes back to same as civil.

Cabell County

Circuit Court PO Box 0545, 750 Fifth Ave, Huntington, WV 25710-0545; 304-526-8622; fax: 304-526-8699; 8:30AM-4:30PM (EST). *Felony, Civil Actions over $5,000, Probate.*

General Information: Probate is separate office. No sealed, juvenile, adoptions, mental health, guardianship records released. Will fax documents $2.00 per page. Court makes copy: $.75 per page. Self serve copy: same. No certification fee. Payee: Clerk of Circuit Court. Business checks accepted. No credit cards accepted. Prepayment required. Mail requests: SASE required.

Civil Name Search: Access: Fax, mail, in person. Both court and visitors may perform in person name searches. Search fee: $5.00 per name. Civil records on computer from 1990 to present. On index books back to 1854. Mail turnaround time 1 day. Civil PAT goes back to 1990.

Criminal Name Search: Access: Fax, mail, in person. Both court and visitors may perform in person name searches. Search fee: $5.00 per name. Required to search: name, years to search; also helpful: address, DOB, SSN. Criminal records computerized from 1990 to present. On index books back to 1854. Mail turnaround time 1 day. Criminal PAT goes back to same as civil.

Magistrate Court 750 5th Ave, Basement, Rm B 113 Courthouse, Huntington, WV 25701; 304-526-8642; fax: 304-526-8646; 8:30AM-4:30PM (EST). *Misdemeanor, Civil Actions under $5,000, Eviction, Small Claims.*

General Information: Will fax specific case file $2.00 per page. Court makes copy: $.25 per page. Certification fee: $.50 per page. Cert fee includes copy fee. Payee: Magistrate Court Clerk. Personal checks, Visa/MC accepted. Prepayment required. Mail requests: SASE not required.

Civil Name Search: Access: Main, in person. Visitors must perform in person searches themselves. Search fee: $25.00 per name. Required to search: name. Records go back to 1997; on computer back to 1991. Mail turnaround time 1-2 days. Civil PAT goes back to 1991.

Criminal Name Search: Access: Mail, in person. Visitors must perform in person searches themselves. Search fee: $25.00 per name. Required to search: name. Records go back to 1998; on computer back to 1991. Mail turnaround time 1-2 days. Criminal PAT goes back to same as civil.

Calhoun County

Circuit Court PO Box 266, Grantsville, WV 26147; 304-354-6910; probate phone: 304-354-6725; fax: 304-354-6910; 8:30AM-4PM (EST). *Felony, Civil Actions over $5,000, Probate.*

General Information: Probate is located with the County Clerk office. Probate fax- 304-354-6725 No adoption, juvenile, divorce, domestic relations, guardianship/conservatorship records released. Will fax documents $3.00 1st page, $.50 each add'l. Court makes copy: $.75 per page. Self serve copy: same. Certification fee: $1.00 per page plus copy fee. Payee: Circuit Clerk. Personal checks accepted, credit cards are not. Prepayment required. Mail requests: SASE helpful.

Civil Name Search: Access: Phone, fax, mail, in person, online. Both court and visitors may perform in person name searches. No search fee. Civil index on docket books from 1800s. Mail turnaround time same day received. **Online access is available via a designated vendor. See the front or back of this chapter for details.**

Criminal Name Search: Access: Phone, fax, mail, in person, online. Both court and visitors may perform in person name searches. No search fee. Required to search: name, years to search; also helpful: DOB, SSN. Criminal docket index from 1900s. Mail turnaround time same day received. **Online access is available via a designated vendor. See the front or back of this chapter for details.**

Magistrate Court PO Box 186, 363 Main St. #103, Grantsville, WV 26147; 304-354-6698; civil phone: 304-354-6844; fax: 304-354-9041; 8:30AM-N; 1-4PM (EST). *Misdemeanor, Civil Actions under $5,000, Eviction, Small Claims, Citation.*

General Information: Domestic violence records restricted. Will fax out documents $2.00 per page. Court makes copy: $.25 per page. Certification fee: $.50 per page plus copy fee. Payee: Calhoun Magistrate Court. Personal checks, Visa/MC accepted. Prepayment required. Mail requests: SASE helpful.

Civil Name Search: Access: Phone, fax, mail, in person. Both court and visitors may perform in person name searches. Search fee: $25.00 per name. Civil records computerized since 1999. Mail turnaround time 1 week. Civil PAT goes back to 1999.

Criminal Name Search: Access: In person, fax, mail, phone. Both court and visitors may perform in person name searches. Search fee: $25.00 per name. Required to search: name; also helpful: years to search, DOB, SSN, alias or maiden name. Criminal records computerized since 1999. Mail turnaround time 1 week. Criminal PAT goes back to same as civil.

Clay County

Circuit Court PO Box 129, Clay, WV 25043; 304-587-4256; probate phone: 304-587-4269; fax: 304-587-4346; 8AM-4PM (EST). *Felony, Civil Actions over $5,000, Probate.*

General Information: Probate fax is same as main fax number. No juvenile, guardianship, conservatorship or mental health records released. Fee to fax document $.75 per page. Court makes copy: $.75 per page. Self serve copy: same. No certification fee. Payee: Clerk of the Circuit Court. Personal checks accepted, credit cards are not. Prepayment required. Mail requests: SASE required for criminal.

Civil Name Search: Access: In person only. Both court and visitors may perform in person name searches. No search fee. Required to search: name, years to search, address. Civil index on docket books and index books back to 1962, computerized back to 1998. Civil PAT goes back to 1970s.

Criminal Name Search: Access: Phone, fax, mail, in person. Both court and visitors may perform in person name searches. No search fee. Required to search: name, years to search, address, DOB, SSN. Criminal docket on books and index books back to 1962, computerized back to 1998. Note: Court will do name only searches if time allows. Mail turnaround time approx. 3 days. Criminal PAT goes back to 1980s.

Magistrate Court PO Box 393, 225 Main St, Clay, WV 25043; 304-587-2131; fax: 304-587-2727; 8AM-4PM (EST). *Misdemeanor, Civil Actions under $5,000, Eviction, Small Claims.*

General Information: Will fax documents to local or toll-free number. Court makes copy: $.25 per page. Self serve copy: same. Certification fee: $.50 per page. Payee: Court. Personal checks accepted. Major credit cards accepted. Prepayment required. Mail requests: SASE not required.

Civil Name Search: Access: Mail, in person. Both court and visitors may perform in person name searches. Search fee: $25.00 per name. Paper civil records go back to 1999; computerized since 2000. Mail turnaround time 5 days. Civil PAT goes back to 2000.

Criminal Name Search: Access: Mail, in person. Both court and visitors may perform in person name searches. Search fee: $25.00 per name. Required to search: name, offense; also helpful: years to search, DOB, SSN. paper criminal records go back to 1999; computerized since 2000. Mail turnaround time 5 days. Criminal PAT goes back to same as civil.

Doddridge County

Circuit Court 118 E. Court St, Rm 104, West Union, WV 26456; 304-873-2331; probate phone: 304-873-2631; fax: 304-873-2260; 8:30AM-4PM (EST). *Felony, Civil Actions over $5,000, Probate.*

General Information: Probate is handled by the County Clerk's office, located in same building. No juvenile, adoption, mental, domestic records released. Will fax documents to local or toll free number. Court makes copy: $.75 per page. Self serve copy: same. No certification fee. Payee: Clerk of

Circuit Court. Personal checks accepted, credit cards are not. Prepayment required. Mail requests: SASE required.

Civil Name Search: Access: Phone, mail, in person, online. Both court and visitors may perform in person name searches. No search fee. Civil index on docket books 1960 to present, archived from 1845 to 1960; computerized records go back to 1999. Mail turnaround time 1-5 days. **Online access is available via a designated vendor. See the front or back of this chapter for details.**

Criminal Name Search: Access: Phone, mail, fax, in person, online. Both court and visitors may perform in person name searches. No search fee. Criminal docket on books and files from 1845; computerized records go back to 1999. Mail turnaround time 1-5 days. **Online access is available via a designated vendor. See the front or back of this chapter for details.**

Magistrate Court PO Box 207, West Union, WV 26456; 304-873-2694; fax: 304-873-2643; 8AM-4PM (EST). *Misdemeanor, Civil Actions under $5,000, Eviction, Small Claims.*

General Information: Will fax documents. Court makes copy: $.25 per page. Self serve copy: same. Certification fee: $.50 per page plus copy fee. Payee: Magistrate Court. Checks accepted. Major credit cards accepted. Prepayment required. Mail requests: SASE requested.

Civil Name Search: Access: In person, mail. Both court and visitors may perform in person name searches. Search fee: $25.00 per name. Required to search: name, DOB, years to search; also helpful-signed release, SSN. Civil records go back to 1977; on computer back to 1999. Records from 1994 back are at Archives. Mail turnaround time 5 days. Civil PAT goes back to 1999.

Criminal Name Search: Access: In person, mail, fax. Both court and visitors may perform in person name searches. Search fee: $25.00 per name. Required to search: name, years to search DOB, SSN, signed release; also helpful: offense. Criminal records go back to 1977; on computer back to 1999. Records from 1994 back are at Archives. Mail turnaround time 5 days. Criminal PAT goes back to same as civil.

Fayette County

Circuit Court 100 N Court St, Fayetteville, WV 25840; criminal phone: 304-574-4303/4250; civil phone: 304-574-4249; probate phone: 304-574-4226; fax: 304-574-4314; 8AM-4PM (EST). *Felony, Civil Actions over $5,000, Probate.*

General Information: Searches done only for governmental or law enforcement agencies by mail or fax. Probate is handled by County Clerk, PO Box 569, Fayetteville, WV 25840. No divorce, adoption, mental, juvenile records released. Will fax documents to local or toll-free number. Court makes copy: $.75 per page. Self serve copy: same. Certification fee: $5.00 per doc plus copy fee. Payee: Circuit Clerk of Fayette County. No personal checks or credit cards accepted. Prepayment required. Mail requests: SASE not required.

Civil Name Search: Access: In person, online. Both court and visitors may perform in person name searches. No search fee. Required to search: name; also helpful: years to search. Civil records on computer since 1995; prior records on file 1832 to present. Mail turnaround time 1 week. Civil PAT goes back to 1995. **Online access is available via a designated vendor. See the front or back of this chapter for details.**

Criminal Name Search: Access: In person, online. Visitors must perform in person searches themselves. No search fee. Required to search: name, years to search; also helpful: DOB, SSN. Criminal records on computer since 1995; prior records on file 1832 to present. Mail turnaround time 1 week. Criminal PAT goes back to same as civil. **Online access is available via a designated vendor. See the front or back of this chapter for details.**

Magistrate Court 100 Church St, Fayetteville, WV 25840; 304-574-4279; fax: 304-574-2458; 8AM-4PM (EST). *Misdemeanor, Civil Actions under $5,000, Eviction, Small Claims.*

General Information: Domestic Violence Petitions are restricted from the public. Will fax search-specific case file for $2.00 per page. Court makes copy: $.25 per page. Certification fee: $.50 per page plus copy fee. Payee: Magistrate Court. Personal checks accepted. Credit cards accepted. Prepayment required. Mail requests: SASE required for mail return of any copies.

Civil Name Search: Access: Mail, in person. Visitors must perform in person searches themselves. Search fee: $25.00 per name. Required to search: name. Civil records on computer back to 1997, records in-house since 1997. Civil PAT goes back to 1997.

Criminal Name Search: Access: Mail, in person. Visitors must perform in person searches themselves. Search fee: $25.00 per name. Criminal records computerized from part of 1997, records in-house since 1997. Mail turnaround time- processed same day. Criminal PAT goes back to same as civil.

Gilmer County

Circuit Court Gilmer County Courthouse, 10 Howard St, Glenville, WV 26351; 304-462-7641; probate phone: 304-462-7241; fax: 304-462-7038; 8AM-4PM (EST). *Felony, Civil Actions over $5,000, Probate.*

General Information: Probate index is separate and located in the County Clerk's office, downstairs. Probate fax is 304-462-8855. No juvenile, mental, confidential records released. Fee to fax out file $1.50 per page, $3.00 minimum. Court makes copy: $.75 per page. Certification fee: Copy fee includes certification. Payee: Circuit Clerk. Personal checks accepted, credit cards are not. Mail requests: SASE not required.

Civil Name Search: Access: Phone, mail, fax, in person. Both court and visitors may perform in person name searches. No search fee. Civil records on dockets and files from 1845 to present; computerized back to 1999. Mail turnaround time 1 day. Civil PAT goes back to 1999.

Criminal Name Search: Access: Phone, mail, fax, in person. Both court and visitors may perform in person name searches. No search fee. Criminal records on dockets and files from 1845 to present; computerized back to 1999. Mail turnaround time 1 day. Criminal PAT goes back to same as civil. Terminal results include SSN.

Magistrate Court Courthouse Annex, 201N Court St, Glenville, WV 26351; 304-462-7812; fax: 304-462-8582; 8AM-4PM (EST). *Misdemeanor, Civil Actions under $5,000, Eviction, Small Claims.*

General Information: Fee to fax out file $2.00 per page. Court makes copy: $.25 per page. Certification fee: $.50 per page plus copy fee. Payee: Gilmer County Magistrate Court. Certified and personal checks accepted. Major credit cards accepted. Prepayment required.

Civil Name Search: Access: Mail, in person. Both court and visitors may perform in person name searches. Search fee: $25.00 per search. Required to search: name, DOB, years to search, other names used; also helpful-case number, address, signed release. Civil records on computer back to 2000; other records back to 1997. Mail turnaround time 1-5 days. Civil PAT goes back to 2000.

Criminal Name Search: Access: Mail, in person. Both court and visitors may perform in person name searches. Search fee: $25.00 per search. Required to search: name, years to search; also helpful: DOB, SSN. Criminal records computerized from 07/00. Mail turnaround time 1-5 days. Criminal PAT goes back to same as civil.

Grant County

Circuit Court 5 Highland Ave, Petersburg, WV 26847; 304-257-4545; fax: 304-257-2593; 8:30AM-4:30PM (EST). *Felony, Civil Actions over $5,000, Probate.*
www.state.wv.us/wvsca/circuits/21st.htm

General Information: Send fax to "Attention Circuit Court." No juvenile, guardianship, adoptions, mental, domestic violence order records released. Fee to fax out file $1.50 1st page, $.75 each add'l page. Court makes copy: $.75 per page. Self serve copy: same. Certification fee: $1.50. Payee: Circuit Clerk. Business checks or in state Personal checks accepted, credit cards are not. Prepayment required. Mail requests: SASE required.

Civil Name Search: Access: Fax, mail, in person, online. Both court and visitors may perform in person name searches. No search fee. Required to search: name, years to search; also helpful: address. Computerized records from 1999, on books from 1983, archived back to 1866. Mail turnaround time 1-2 days. Civil PAT goes back to 1999. Terminal may be down. **Online access is available via a designated vendor. See the front or back of this chapter for details.**

Criminal Name Search: Access: Fax, mail, in person, online. Both court and visitors may perform in person name searches. No search fee. Required to search: name, years to search, DOB, SSN; also helpful: address. Computerized records from 1999, on books to 1988, archived back to 1866. Mail turnaround time 1-2 days. Criminal PAT goes back to same as civil. Terminal may be down. **Online access is available via a designated vendor. See the front or back of this chapter for details.** Online results show middle initial.

Magistrate Court 4 North Main St, Petersburg, WV 26847; 304-257-1289/4637; fax: 304-257-9501; 8:30AM-4:30PM (EST). *Misdemeanor, Civil Actions under $5,000, Eviction, Small Claims.*

General Information: Domestic Violence Petitions restricted. Court makes copy: $.25 per page. Self serve copy: same. Certification fee: $.50 per page. Payee: Grant County Magistrate Court. Personal checks accepted. Credit cards accepted. Prepayment required. Mail requests: SASE not required.

Civil Name Search: Access: Fax, mail, in person. Both court and visitors may perform in person name searches. Search fee: $25.00 per name. Required to search: Include DOB and SSN. Records on computer back to 1994; prior records go back to 1977. Mail turnaround time 2 days. Civil PAT goes back to 1994.

Criminal Name Search: Access: Fax, mail, in person. Both court and visitors may perform in person name searches. Search fee: $25.00 per name. Required to search: name, years to search, DOB, SSN. Records on computer back to 1994; prior back to 1977. Mail turnaround time 1-2 days. Criminal PAT goes back to same as civil.

Greenbrier County

Circuit Court PO Drawer 751, Lewisburg, WV 24901; 304-647-6626; fax: 304-647-6666; 8:30AM-4:30PM (EST). *Felony, Civil Actions over $5,000, Probate.*

General Information: No juvenile, adoptions, mental health records released. Fee to fax out file $2.50 per page. Court makes copy: $.75 per page. Self serve copy: same. Certification fee: $5.00 per doc (authenticated copies). Payee: Clerk of Circuit Court. Personal checks accepted, credit cards are not. Prepayment required.

Civil Name Search: Access: Mail, in person. Both court and visitors may perform in person name searches. No search fee. Civil records indexed by general and docket books from 1800s; computerized back to 1994. Mail turnaround time 1-2 days.

Criminal Name Search: Access: Mail, in person. Both court and visitors may perform in person name searches. No search fee. Required to search: name, years to search; also helpful: DOB, SSN, signed release. Criminal records indexed by general and docket books from 1800s; computerized back to 1995. Note: No information given over the telephone on criminal matters except to authorized personnel. Mail turnaround time 1-2 days.

Magistrate Court 203 Green Ln, Lewisburg, WV 24901; 304-647-6632; fax: 304-647-6668; 8:30AM-4:30PM (EST). *Misdemeanor, Civil Actions under $5,000, Eviction, Small Claims.*

General Information: The court sends the requester of record searches to WV State for record searches. Phone # of WV State Police is 304-746-2179. Fee to fax out file $2.00 per page. Court makes copy: $.25 per page. Self serve copy: same. Certification fee: $.50 plus copy fee. Payee: Greenbrier County Magistrate Court. Personal checks, Visa/MC accepted. Prepayment required.

Civil Name Search: Access: Phone, fax, mail, in person. Visitors must perform in person searches themselves. No search fee. Civil records on computer back 10 years, active civil indefinitely. Mail turnaround time 1-2 days. Public use terminal available.

Criminal Name Search: Access: Phone, fax, mail, in person. Both court and visitors may perform in person name searches. Search fee: $25.00. Required to search: name, years to search; also helpful: DOB, SSN. Criminal records computerized for 10 years, older dockets to 1977. Note: Requests for a background check must be in writing on letterhead. Contact the office for results in three days. If results are to be mailed, include postage or SASE plus the copy fee. Mail turnaround time 1-2 days. Public use terminal available, crim records go back to same as civil. Not all results show DOB, sometimes SSN.

Hampshire County

Circuit Court PO Box 343, 50 S Hight Street, Romney, WV 26757; 304-822-5022; probate phone: 304-822-5112; fax: 304-822-8257; 8AM-5PM (EST). *Felony, Civil Actions over $5,000, Probate.*

General Information: Probate handled by County Clerk, PO Box 806, Romney, WV 26757. No juvenile, divorce or adoption records released. Court makes copy: $1.00 per page. No certification fee. Payee: Clerk of Circuit Court. Personal checks accepted, credit cards are not. Prepayment required. Mail requests: SASE required.

Civil Name Search: Access: Fax, mail, in person. Both court and visitors may perform in person name searches. Search fee: $10.00 per name. Civil records on index files from 1957 to present, on index cards in storage 1885 to 1957. Mail turnaround time 1 week.

Criminal Name Search: Access: Fax, mail, in person. Both court and visitors may perform in person name searches. Search fee: $10.00 per name. Criminal records on index files from 1957 to present, on index cards in storage 1885 to 1957. Mail turnaround time 1 week.

Magistrate Court PO Box 881, 50 S High Street. Ste 3, Romney, WV 26757; 304-822-4311; fax: 304-822-3981; 8AM-4PM (EST). *Misdemeanor, Civil Actions under $5,000, Eviction, Small Claims.*

General Information: Domestic violence records are restricted from public view, unless in final order from Circuit Court. Will fax to toll-free numbers no charge. Court makes copy: $.25 per page. Self serve copy: $.25 per page. Certification fee: $.50 per page. Payee: Magistrate Court Clerk. Personal checks accepted. Major credit cards accepted. Prepayment required. Mail requests: SASE not required.

Civil Name Search: Access: Fax, mail, in person. Both court and visitors may perform in person name searches. Search fee: $25.00 per name prepaid. Required to search: name; also helpful-DOB, SSN, years to search, signed release, other names used. Civil records go back to 1977; on computer back to 1995. Mail turnaround time 15 days. Civil PAT goes back to 1995.

Criminal Name Search: Access: Fax, mail, in person. Both court and visitors may perform in person name searches. Search fee: $25.00 per name prepaid. Required to search: name, years to search; also helpful: DOB,

SSN. Criminal records go back to 1977; on computer back to 1995. Mail turnaround time 15 days. Criminal PAT goes back to same as civil.

Hancock County

Circuit Court PO Box 428, New Cumberland, WV 26047; 304-564-3311; probate phone: x279; fax: 304-564-5014; 8:30AM-4:30PM (EST). *Felony, Civil Actions over $5,000, Probate.*

General Information: Probate is handled by County Clerk, address is PO Box 367. No adoption, juvenile, mental hygiene released. Fee to fax out file $2.00 per page. Court makes copy: $.75 per page. Certification fee: $1.50. Payee: Clerk of Circuit Court. Personal checks accepted, credit cards are not. Prepayment required. Mail requests: SASE required.

Civil Name Search: Access: Fax, mail, in person, online. Both court and visitors may perform in person name searches. Search fee: $5.00 per name. Required to search: name, years to search; also helpful: address. Civil records on computer since 1972, record books go back further. Mail turnaround time same day. Civil PAT goes back to 1972. **Online access is available via a designated vendor. See the front or back of this chapter for details.**

Criminal Name Search: Access: Fax, mail, in person, online. Both court and visitors may perform in person name searches. Search fee: $5.00 per name. Required to search: name, years to search, signed release; also helpful: address, DOB, SSN. Criminal records on computer since 1972, , files kept for 75 years. Mail turnaround time same day. Criminal PAT goes back to same as civil. **Online access is available via a designated vendor. See the front or back of this chapter for details.**

Magistrate Court 106 Court St, New Cumberland, WV 26047; 304-564-3355; fax: 304-564-3852; 8:30AM-4:30PM (EST). *Misdemeanor, Civil Actions under $5,000, Eviction, Small Claims.*

General Information: Alternative fax number is 304-564-5357. Information on search warrants is restricted. Will fax documents $2.00 per page. Court makes copy: $.25 per page. Certification fee: $.50 per page. Personal checks accepted, credit cards are not. Prepayment required.

Civil Name Search: Access: Mail, in person. Both court and visitors may perform in person name searches. Search fee: $25.00 per name. Required to search: Name, and years to search: records only go back 10 years. Civil records on computer since 1996, older records have been destroyed. Note: Phone, fax or mail access is limited, call ahead for turnaround time. Mail turnaround time 1-2 days. Civil PAT goes back to 1996.

Criminal Name Search: Access: Mail, in person. Both court and visitors may perform in person name searches. Search fee: $25.00 per name. Required to search: name, years to search; also helpful: DOB, SSN. Criminal records on computer since 1996, older records have been destroyed. Note: Phone, fax and mail access limited, but available. Mail turnaround time 1-2 days. Criminal PAT goes back to same as civil.

Hardy County

Circuit Court 204 Washington St, Rm 237, Moorefield, WV 26836; 304-530-0230; fax: 304-530-0231; 9AM-4PM (EST). *Felony, Civil Actions over $5,000, Probate.*

General Information: No juvenile, mental, domestic records released. Will not fax out case files. Court makes copy: $.75 per page. Self serve copy: same. Certification fee: $1.00. Payee: Clerk of Circuit Court. Personal checks accepted. Prepayment required.

Civil Name Search: Access: Mail, fax, in person, online. Both court and visitors may perform in person name searches. No search fee. Civil index on docket books back to 1960 (chromo index in front of book). Computerized records go back to 1995. **Online access is available via a designated vendor. See the front or back of this chapter for details.**

Criminal Name Search: Access: Mail, fax, in person, online. Both court and visitors may perform in person name searches. No search fee. Required to search: name, years to search, DOB; SSN helpful. Criminal docket on books back to 1960 (chrono index in front of book). Computerized records go back to 1995. **Online access is available via a designated vendor. See the front or back of this chapter for details.**

Magistrate Court 204 Washington St, Moorefield, WV 26836; 304-530-0212; fax: 304-530-0213; 8:30AM-4:30PM (EST). *Misdemeanor, Civil Actions under $5,000, Eviction, Small Claims.*

General Information: Will fax documents $2.00 per page. Court makes copy: $.25 per page. Self serve copy: same. Certification fee: $.50 per page. Payee: Hardy County Magistrate Court. Personal checks accepted. Major credit cards accepted. Prepayment required. Mail requests: SASE helpful.

Civil Name Search: Access: Fax, mail, in person. Both court and visitors may perform in person name searches. Search fee: $25.00 per name. Civil records on computer back to 1990; others back to 1977. Mail turnaround time 10 days, 5 days if records on computer. Civil PAT goes back to 1990.

Criminal Name Search: Access: Fax, mail, in person. Both court and visitors may perform in person name searches. Search fee: $25.00 per name. Required to search: name, years to search; also helpful: DOB, SSN. Criminal records computerized from 1990; others back to 1977. Mail turnaround time 10 days, 5 if record on computer. Criminal PAT goes back to same as civil.

Harrison County

Circuit Court 301 W. Main, Ste 301, Clarksburg, WV 26301-2967; 304-624-8640; probate phone: 304-624-8673; fax: 304-624-8710; 8:30AM-4:30PM (EST). *Felony, Civil Actions over $5,000, Probate.*
General Information: Probate is handled by County Clerk, 301 W Main St, Courthouse, Clarksburg, WV 26301. No adoption, juvenile, guardianship, mental health records released. Court makes copy: $.75 per page. No certification fee. Payee: Harrison County Circuit Clerk. Only cashiers checks and money orders accepted. No credit cards accepted. Prepayment required.
Civil Name Search: Access: In person only. Visitors must perform in person searches themselves. Civil records on computer from 1990 to present. On index books back to mid-1800s. Civil PAT goes back to 1990.
Criminal Name Search: Access: In person only. Visitors must perform in person searches themselves. Required to search: name, years to search; also helpful: DOB, SSN (not available for search). Criminal records computerized from 1990 to present. On index books back to mid-1800s. Criminal PAT goes back to same as civil.

Magistrate Court 306 Washington Ave, Rm 222, Clarksburg, WV 26301; 304-624-8645; fax: 304-624-8740; 8AM-4PM (EST). *Misdemeanor, Civil Actions under $5,000, Eviction, Small Claims.*
General Information: No domestic violence records released except to defendant or plaintiff with ID. Court makes copy: $.25 per page. Certification fee: $.50 per page. Payee: Magistrate Court. Personal checks accepted. Major credit cards accepted. Prepayment required.
Civil Name Search: Access: Fax, mail, in person. Both court and visitors may perform in person name searches. Search fee: $25.00 per name. Civil records computerized since 9/97, paper to 01/99. Mail turnaround time 5 days. Civil PAT goes back to 1997.
Criminal Name Search: Access: Fax, mail, in person. Both court and visitors may perform in person name searches. Search fee: $25.00 per name. Required to search: name, years to search; also helpful: DOB, SSN. Criminal records go back 9/97. Mail turnaround time 5 days. Criminal PAT goes back to 1997.

Jackson County

Circuit Court PO Box 427, 100 Court St, Ripley, WV 25271; 304-373-2210; probate phone: 304-373-2251; fax: 304-372-6237; 8:30AM-N, 1PM-4:30PM (EST). *Felony, Civil Actions over $5,000, Probate.*
General Information: Probate is a separate index; probate mailing address is PO Box 800. Probate fax- 304-373-0245 No juvenile, mental, adoption, domestic records released. Will fax documents $2.00 per page. Court makes copy: $1.00 per page. No certification fee. Payee: Clerk of Circuit Court. Only cashiers checks and money orders accepted. No credit cards accepted. Prepayment required. Mail requests: SASE required.
Civil Name Search: Access: Phone, mail, in person, online. Both court and visitors may perform in person name searches. No search fee. Civil index on docket books back to 1800s. Computerized records back to 1999. Mail turnaround time 1-2 days. Civil PAT goes back to 1999. Terminal results may include SSN. **Online access is available via a designated vendor. See the front or back of this chapter for details.**
Criminal Name Search: Access: Phone, mail, in person, online. Both court and visitors may perform in person name searches. No search fee. Required to search: name, years to search; also helpful: DOB, SSN. Criminal records indexed in books back to 1800s. Computerized records back to 1999. Mail turnaround time 1-2 days. Criminal PAT goes back to 1999. Terminal results may include SSN. No sexual cases on public access terminals. **Online access is available via a designated vendor. See the front or back of this chapter for details.**

Magistrate Court PO Box 368, Ripley, WV 25271; 304-373-2313; fax: 304-372-7155; 8:30AM-4:30PM (EST). *Misdemeanor, Civil Actions under $5,000, Eviction, Small Claims, Traffic.*
General Information: Will fax documents to local or toll-free number. Court makes copy: $.25 per page. Self serve copy: same. Certification fee: $.50 per page. Payee: Jackson County Magistrate Court. Personal checks accepted. Major credit cards accepted. Prepayment required. Mail requests: SASE not required.
Civil Name Search: Access: Mail, in person. Visitors must perform in person searches themselves. Search fee: $25.00 per name. Records available for 10 years or unless active. Mail turnaround time 1-3 days. Civil PAT goes back to 10 years.
Criminal Name Search: Access: Mail, in person. Visitors must perform in person searches themselves. Search fee: $25.00 per name. Required to search: name, years to search; also helpful: DOB, SSN. Records available for 10 years or unless active. Mail turnaround time 1-3 days. Criminal PAT goes back to same as civil.

Jefferson County

Circuit Court PO Box 1234, 119 N George St, Ste 100, Charles Town, WV 25414; 304-728-3231; fax: 304-728-3398; 9AM-5PM (EST). *Felony, Civil Actions over $5,000.*
www.jeffcowvcircuitclerk.com/index.html
General Information: No juvenile, guardianship, adoption, or mental health records released. Will fax specific case file to local or toll-free number, if all prepaid. Court makes copy: $.75 per page. Certification fee: $.50 per page; triple seal $3.00. Payee: Circuit Clerk. No personal checks accepted, money orders and cashiers checks accepted. Major credit cards accepted. Prepayment required.
Civil Name Search: Access: In person. Visitors must perform in person searches themselves. Civil records on computer back to 1940s; index books 1960 to 1985. 1960-1800s in storage. Civil PAT goes back to 1940s. Daily Circuit Ct dockets free at www.jeffcowvcircuitclerk.com/Circuit_Court_Docket.pdf.
Criminal Name Search: Access: In person. Visitors must perform in person searches themselves. Criminal records computerized from 1940s; index books 1960 to 1985. 1960-1800s in storage. Criminal PAT goes back to 1940s. Daily Circuit Ct dockets free at www.jeffcowvcircuitclerk.com/Circuit_Court_Docket.pdf.

Magistrate Court PO Box 607, 110 N George St, Charles Town, WV 25414; 304-728-3233; fax: 304-728-3235; 7:30AM-4:30PM (EST). *Misdemeanor, Civil Actions under $5,000, Eviction, Small Claims.*
www.jeffersoncountywv.org/
General Information: Will fax documents to local or toll-free number. Court makes copy: $.25 per page. Self serve copy: same. Certification fee: $.50 per page. Payee: Magistrate Clerk. Personal checks accepted. Major credit cards accepted. Prepayment required.
Civil Name Search: Access: Fax, mail, in person. Both court and visitors may perform in person name searches. Search fee: $25.00 per name. Civil records held 10 years or if active. Civil PAT goes back to 1996.
Criminal Name Search: Access: Fax, mail, in person. Both court and visitors may perform in person name searches. Search fee: $25.00 per name. Required to search: name, years to search, DOB; also helpful: SSN, signed release. Criminal records held 10 years or if active. Mail turnaround time is 5 days. Criminal PAT goes back to same as civil.

Kanawha County

Circuit Court PO Box 2351, 111 Court St, Charleston, WV 25328; 304-357-0440; probate phone: 304-357-0125; fax: 304-357-0473; 8AM-5PM (EST). *Felony, Civil Actions over $5,000, Probate.*
www.state.wv.us/wvsca/circuits/13th.htm
General Information: Probate is handled by County Clerk, 409 Virginia St E, Charleston, WV 25301. No juvenile, neglect, adoption, domestic, guardianship, mental health or conservatorship records released. Will fax documents for $2.00 per page. Court makes copy: $.75 per page. Certification fee: $.50 per page. Payee: Kanawha Circuit Clerk. No personal or business checks accepted. Visa/MC accepted. Prepayment required.
Civil Name Search: Access: In person, online. Visitors must perform in person searches themselves. Required to search: name, years to search; also helpful: address. Civil records on computer from 7/1989 to present. On microfiche back to 1800s. Civil PAT goes back to 1989. **Online access is available via a designated vendor. See the front or back of this chapter for details.**
Criminal Name Search: Access: In person, online. Visitors must perform in person searches themselves. Required to search: name, years to search; also helpful: address, DOB, SSN. Criminal records computerized from 7/1989 to present. On microfiche back to 1800s. Criminal PAT goes back to same as civil. **Online access is available via a designated vendor. See the front or back of this chapter for details.**

Magistrate Court 111 Court St, Charleston, WV 25333; 304-357-0400; fax: 304-357-0431; 8:30AM-5PM (EST). *Misdemeanor, Civil Actions under $5,000, Eviction, Small Claims.*
www.state.wv.us/wvsca/
General Information: Will fax documents to local or toll free line. Court makes copy: $.25 per page. Certification fee: $.50 per page. Payee: Kanawha Magistrate Court. Personal checks accepted. Major credit cards accepted. Prepayment required. Mail requests: SASE required.
Civil Name Search: Access: Mail, in person. Both court and visitors may perform in person name searches. Search fee: $25.00. Civil records go back to 1982; computerized records since 1996. Mail turnaround time 14 days. Civil PAT goes back to 2000.
Criminal Name Search: Access: Fax, mail, in person. Both court and visitors may perform in person name searches. Search fee: $25.00 per search. Required to search: name, years to search; also helpful: DOB, SSN. Criminal records go back to 1982; computerized records since 1991. Mail turnaround time 14 days. Criminal PAT goes back to 1998. Terminal results do not include SSN.

Lewis County

Circuit Court PO Box 69, Weston, WV 26452; 304-269-8210; probate phone: 304-269-8215; fax: 304-269-8249; 8:30AM-4:30PM (EST). *Felony, Civil Actions over $5,000, Probate.*

General Information: Probate fax- 304-269-8202 No adoption, juvenile, domestic records released. Fee to fax out file $2.00 per page, $10.00 if for a criminal name search. Court makes copy: $.75 per page. Certification fee: $1.00 per case plus copy fee. Payee: Clerk of Circuit Court. Business checks accepted. No credit cards accepted. Prepayment required. Mail requests: SASE not required.

Civil Name Search: Access: Phone, fax, mail, in person. Only the court performs in person name searches; visitors may not. No search fee. Civil index on docket books 1977 to 1992; on computer back to 1984. No index for chancery books back to 1800s. Mail turnaround time 2 days.

Criminal Name Search: Access: Phone, fax, mail, in person. Only the court performs in person name searches; visitors may not. Search fee: None unless faxed, then $10.00 fee. Required to search: name, years to search; also helpful: SSN. Criminal records indexed in books 1977 to 1992; on computer back to 1984. No index for chancery books back to 1800s. Mail turnaround time 2 days.

Magistrate Court 111 Court St, PO Box 260, Weston, WV 26452; 304-269-8230; fax: 304-269-8239; 8:30AM-N, 1-4:30PM (EST). *Misdemeanor, Civil Actions under $5,000, Eviction, Small Claims.*

General Information: Juvenile and domestic violence records restricted. Will fax documents $2.00 per sheet. Court makes copy: $.25 per page. Self serve copy: same. Certification fee: $.50 per page plus copy fee. Payee: Lewis County Magistrate Court. Personal checks accepted. Major credit cards accepted. Prepayment required. Mail requests: SASE required.

Civil Name Search: Access: In person, mail, fax. Both court and visitors may perform in person name searches. No search fee. Required to search: name, DOB, SSN, years to search. Civil records computerized since 1991, indexed since 1977. Mail turnaround time 5 days. Civil PAT goes back to 1997.

Criminal Name Search: Access: In person, mail, fax. Both court and visitors may perform in person name searches. Search fee: $25.00 per name. Required to search: name, years to search; also helpful: DOB, SSN. Criminal records computerized since 1992. Mail turnaround time 5 days. Criminal PAT goes back to 1992.

Lincoln County

Circuit Court PO Box 338, 8000 Court Av, #205, Hamlin, WV 25523; 304-824-7887 x239; probate phone: x233; fax: 304-824-2011; 9AM-4:30PM (EST). *Felony, Civil Actions over $5,000, Probate.*
www.lincolncountywv.org/

General Information: Probate mailing address is PO Box 497; direct records requests to the county clerk at x233. No juvenile, adoption, guardianship, drug court, divorce or mental hygiene records released. Will fax back documents for $5.00 per fax. Court makes copy: $1.50 1st page, $1.00 each add'l. No certification fee. No personal checks or credit cards accepted. Prepayment required.

Civil Name Search: Access: In person only. Both court and visitors may perform in person name searches. No search fee. Civil records computerized since 1991, on index books 1971 to present, on docket books back to 1909.

Criminal Name Search: Access: In person only. Only the court performs in person name searches; visitors may not. No search fee. Required to search: name, years to search, DOB, SSN; also helpful: address. Criminal records computerized since 1998, on index books 1971 to present, on docket books back to 1909.

Magistrate Court PO Box 573, 8000 Court Ave, Hamlin, WV 25523; 304-824-5001 x235; fax: 304-824-5280; 9AM-4PM (EST). *Misdemeanor, Civil Actions under $5,000, Eviction, Small Claims.*

General Information: Searches performed by court only on second and fourth Thursday of each month. Will fax out documents $2.00 per page. Court makes copy: $.50 per page criminal; civil- $.25 per page. Self serve copy: same. Payee: Magistrate Court. Personal checks accepted. Prepayment required. Mail requests: SASE requested.

Civil Name Search: Access: Mail, in person. Both court and visitors may perform in person name searches. Search fee: $25.00 per name. Required to search: name, DOB, SSN. Mail turnaround time 1-14 days. Civil PAT goes back to 1998.

Criminal Name Search: Access: Mail, in person. Both court and visitors may perform in person name searches. Search fee: $25.00 per name. Required to search: name, years to search; also helpful: DOB, SSN. Mail turnaround time 1-14 days. Criminal PAT goes back to same as civil.

Logan County

Circuit Court Logan County Courthouse, Rm 311, Logan, WV 25601; 304-792-8550; criminal phone: 304-792-8562/3; fax: 304-792-8589; 8:30AM-4:30PM (EST). *Felony, Civil Actions over $5,000, Probate.*

General Information: No adoption, juvenile, domestic records released. Fee to fax out file $1.00 per page. Court makes copy: $.75 per page. Certification fee: $1.50 plus $.50 per page after first 2. Payee: Clerk of Circuit Court. Only cashiers checks and money orders accepted. No credit cards accepted. Prepayment required. Will bill to attorneys. Mail requests: SASE not required.

Civil Name Search: Access: In person, online. Only the court performs in person name searches; visitors may not. No search fee. Civil index on docket books back to 1800s, on computer from 1995. **Online access is available via a designated vendor. See the front or back of this chapter for details.**

Criminal Name Search: Access: Mail, fax, in person, online. Only the court performs in person name searches; visitors may not. Search fee: $25.00 per name. Required to search: name, years to search, SSN. Criminal records indexed in books back to 1800s, on computer from 1995. Mail turnaround time 1-2 days. **Online access is available via a designated vendor. See the front or back of this chapter for details.**

Logan Magistrate Court Logan County Courthouse, 300 Stratton St, Logan, WV 25601; 304-792-8651; fax: 304-752-0790; 8:30AM-N; 1-4:30PM (EST). *Misdemeanor, Civil Actions under $5,000, Eviction, Small Claims.*

General Information: Domestic violence petitions are restricted from view. Will fax back doc $2.00 per page paid up front. Court makes copy: $.25 per page. Certification fee: $.50 per page. Payee: Logan Magistrate Court. Personal checks, Visa/MC accepted. Prepayment required. Prepayment required for copies. Mail requests: SASE requested.

Civil Name Search: Access: Mail, in person. Both court and visitors may perform in person name searches. Search fee: $25.00 per name. Records are computerized since 1999. Mail turnaround time 5 days. Civil PAT goes back to 1999.

Criminal Name Search: Access: Mail, in person. Both court and visitors may perform in person name searches. Search fee: $25.00 per name. Required to search: name, years to search; also helpful: address, DOB, SSN. Records go back to 1999. Mail turnaround time 5 days. Criminal PAT available.

Marion County

Circuit Court 217 Adams St, #211, Fairmont, WV 26554; 304-367-5360; fax: 304-367-5374; 8:30AM-4:30PM (EST). *Felony, Civil Actions over $3,000.*

General Information: No adoption, juvenile, mental or guardianship records released. Will fax back documents, no fee. Court makes copy: $.75 per page. Certification fee: $.50 per page. Payee: Clerk of Circuit Court. Business checks accepted, no personal checks. No credit cards accepted. Prepayment required. Mail requests: SASE requested.

Civil Name Search: Access: Phone, fax, mail, in person. Both court and visitors may perform in person name searches. No search fee. Civil records on computer from 1/1988 to present. On docket books from 1849 to 1988. Mail turnaround time 2-3 days. Civil PAT goes back to 1988.

Criminal Name Search: Access: In person, mail, fax. Visitors must perform in person searches themselves. No search fee. Required to search: name, years to search; also helpful: DOB, SSN. Criminal records computerized from 1/1988 to present. On docket books from 1849 to 1988. Note: The court refers all written requests to the Dept of Public Safety. Mail turnaround time 2-3 days. Criminal PAT goes back to same as civil.

Magistrate Court 200 Jackson St, Fairmont, WV 26554; 304-367-5330; fax: 304-367-5336; 8:30AM-4:30PM M-T-W-F; 8:30AM-7PM TH (EST). *Misdemeanor, Felony Pre-lims, Civil Actions under $5,000, Eviction, Small Claims.*

General Information: No record checks performed between 11:30AM and 1:30PM. Will fax documents for $2.00, pre-payment required. Court makes copy: $.25 per page. Self serve copy: same. Certification fee: $.50 per page. Payee: Marion County Magistrate Clerk. Personal checks accepted. Credit cards accepted. Prepayment required. Mail requests: SASE requested.

Civil Name Search: Access: Mail, in person. Both court and visitors may perform in person name searches. Search fee: $25.00 per name. Civil records go back to 1998; computerized since 1998. Mail turnaround time 5-15 days. Civil PAT goes back to 1996.

Criminal Name Search: Access: Mail, in person. Both court and visitors may perform in person name searches. Search fee: $25.00 per name. Required to search: name, years to search; also helpful: DOB, SSN. Criminal records go back to 1998; computerized since 1996. Mail turnaround time 5-15 days; ASAP for phone requests, as time permits. Criminal PAT goes back to same as civil.

Marshall County

Circuit Court Marshall County Courthouse, 7th St, Moundsville, WV 26041; 304-845-2130; fax: 304-845-3948; 8:30AM-4:30PM M-TH; 8:30AM-5:30PM F (EST). *Felony, Civil Actions over $5,000.*

General Information: No juvenile, mental, adoption, sealed, conservatorship, guardianship or divorce records released. Fee to fax out file $2.00 per page. Court makes copy: $.75 per page. Self serve copy: $.25 per page. Certification fee: $1.00. Payee: Clerk of Circuit Court. Personal checks accepted, credit cards are not. Prepayment required. Will bill to attorneys. Mail requests: SASE not required.

Civil Name Search: Access: Fax, mail, in person, online. Both court and visitors may perform in person name searches. No search fee. Civil records on computer since 1/98; prior records on index books and in files from 1836 to present. Mail turnaround time 1-2 days. **Online access is available via a designated vendor. See the front or back of this chapter for details.**

Criminal Name Search: Access: Fax, mail, in person, online. Both court and visitors may perform in person name searches. No search fee. Required to search: name, years to search; also helpful: DOB, SSN. Criminal records on computer since 1/98; prior records on index books and in files from 1836 to present. Mail turnaround time 1-2 days. **Online access is available via a designated vendor. See the front or back of this chapter for details.**

Mason County

Circuit Court Mason County Courthouse, Point Pleasant, WV 25550; 304-675-4400; fax: 304-675-7419; 8:30AM-4:30PM (EST). *Felony, Civil Actions over $5,000, Probate.*

General Information: No juvenile records released and only final orders of divorces. Will fax documents $2.00 per page. Court makes copy: $.75 per page. Self serve copy: same. No certification fee. Payee: Circuit Court Clerk. Personal checks accepted, credit cards are not. Prepayment required.

Civil Name Search: Access: In person, online. Visitors must perform in person searches themselves. Civil records on computer from 1994. No time limit on open cases. Index books with data back to 1800s. Civil PAT goes back to 1994. Results also include SSN. **Online access is available via a designated vendor. See the front or back of this chapter for details.**

Criminal Name Search: Access: In person, online. Visitors must perform in person searches themselves. Criminal records computerized from 1994. No time limit on open cases. Index books with data back to 1800s. Note: Results also include address. Criminal PAT goes back to same as civil. **Online access is available via a designated vendor. See the front or back of this chapter for details.** Online results show middle initial, DOB.

Magistrate Court 200 6th St, 3rd Fl, Point Pleasant, WV 25550; 304-675-6840; fax: 304-675-5949; 8:30AM-4:30PM (EST). *Misdemeanor, Civil Actions under $5,000, Eviction, Small Claims.*

General Information: Magistrates offices- Ross 304-675-6400 and Roush 304-675-6636. Will fax documents $2.00 per page. Court makes copy: $.25 per page. Self serve copy: same. Certification fee: $.50 per page. Payee: Court. Personal checks accepted. Major credit cards accepted. Prepayment required. Mail requests: SASE required.

Civil Name Search: Access: Mail, in person. Both court and visitors may perform in person name searches. Search fee: $25.00. Civil records hardcopy go back ten years; computerized since 1998. Mail turnaround time 3-4 days. Civil PAT goes back to 1998.

Criminal Name Search: Access: Mail, in person. Both court and visitors may perform in person name searches. Search fee: $25.00. Criminal records hardcopy go back ten years; computerized since 1998. Mail turnaround time 3-4 days. Criminal PAT goes back to same as civil.

McDowell County

Circuit Court 9 Wyoming St, Ste 201, Welch, WV 24801; 304-436-8535; probate phone: 304-436-8544; fax: 304-436-6994; 9AM-5PM (EST). *Felony, Civil Actions over $5,000, Probate.*

General Information: Probate is handled by County Clerk, 90 Wyoming St, #109, Welch, WV 24801. Online identifiers in results same as on public terminal. No sealed, juvenile, adoption, mental health, guardianship records released. Will fax documents $2.00 per page. Court makes copy: $.75 per page. Certification fee: $.75 per page. Payee: Clerk of Circuit Court. Business checks accepted. No credit cards accepted. Prepayment required. Mail requests: SASE required.

Civil Name Search: Access: Mail, in person, online. Both court and visitors may perform in person name searches. No search fee. Civil index on docket books back to 1800s; on computer back to 1999. Mail turnaround time 1 week. Civil PAT goes back to 1998. **Online access is available via a designated vendor. See the front or back of this chapter for details.**

Criminal Name Search: Access: Mail, in person, online. Both court and visitors may perform in person name searches. No search fee. Required to search: name, years to search; also helpful: DOB, SSN. Criminal records indexed in books back to 1800s; on computer back to 1999. Mail turnaround time 1 week. Criminal PAT goes back to same as civil. **Online access is available via a designated vendor. See the front or back of this chapter for details.** Online results show name only.

Magistrate Court PO Box 447, Welch, WV 24801; 304-436-8588; fax: 304-436-8575; 9AM-5PM (EST). *Misdemeanor, Civil Actions under $5,000, Eviction, Small Claims.*

General Information: Fee to fax out file $2.00 per page. Court makes copy: $.25 per page. Certification fee: $.50 per page. Payee: Magistrate Court. No personal checks accepted. Credit cards accepted. Prepayment required. Mail requests: SASE required.

Civil Name Search: Access: Mail, fax, in person. Visitors must perform in person searches themselves. Search fee: $25.00 per name. Records on computer go back to 1997. Mail turnaround time 5 days. Civil PAT goes back to 1998.

Criminal Name Search: Access: Mail, fax, in person. Both court and visitors may perform in person name searches. Search fee: $25.00 per name. Required to search: name, years to search, DOB, SSN. Records on computer go back to 1997. Records on criminal now go back to 1997. Mail turnaround time 5 days. Criminal PAT goes back to same as civil.

Mercer County

Circuit Court 1501 Main St, Ste. 111, Princeton, WV 24740; 304-487-8323/8371; criminal phone: 304-487-8410/304-487-8372; civil phone: 304-487-8369; fax: 304-425-1598; 8:30AM-4:30PM (EST). *Felony, Civil Actions over $5,000.*

General Information: Probate court is a separate office. No juvenile, adoption, mental health, guardianship or conservatorship records released. Will fax documents $2.00 per page. Court makes copy: $.75 per page. Certification fee: $.50 per page. Payee: Circuit Court Clerk. Business checks accepted. Prepayment required. Mail requests: SASE required.

Civil Name Search: Access: Phone, fax, mail, in person, online. Both court and visitors may perform in person name searches. No search fee. Civil records on computer from 10/1989 to present. On index books from 1930-1989 (Cott System). On index cards back to 1890s. Mail turnaround time 4-5 days. Civil PAT goes back to 10/1989. **Online access is available via a designated vendor. See the front or back of this chapter for details.**

Criminal Name Search: Access: Fax, mail, in person, online. Both court and visitors may perform in person name searches. No search fee. Required to search: name, years to search; also helpful: DOB, SSN. Criminal records computerized from 10/1989 to present. On index books from 1930-1989 (Cott System). On index cards back to 1890s. Mail turnaround time 4-5 days. Criminal PAT goes back to same as civil. You must pull the file to properly identify the subject of a name search. **Online access is available via a designated vendor. See the front or back of this chapter for details.**

Magistrate Court 120 Scott St #103, Princeton, WV 24740; 304-431-7115; criminal phone: 304-431-7122; civil phone: 304-431-7121; fax: 304-425-6106; 8:30AM-4:30PM (EST). *Misdemeanor, Civil Actions under $5,000, Eviction, Small Claims, Traffic.*

General Information: Will fax documents $2.00 per page. Court makes copy: $.25 per page. Certification fee: $.50 per page plus copy fee. Payee: Mercer County Magistrate Court. Cashiers checks and money orders accepted. Visa/MC accepted. Prepayment required. Mail requests: SASE required for criminal.

Civil Name Search: Access: In person, mail, fax. Both court and visitors may perform in person name searches. Search fee: $25.00 per name. Required to search: name, years to search; also helpful: address, DOB. Civil records held 10 years or if active. Mail turnaround time 1-2 days. Civil PAT goes back to 1994.

Criminal Name Search: Access: In person, mail, fax. Both court and visitors may perform in person name searches. Search fee: $25.00 per name. Required to search: name, years to search; also helpful: address, DOB. Criminal records held 10 years or if active. Mail turnaround time 1-2 days. Criminal PAT goes back to same as civil.

Mineral County

Circuit Court 150 Armstrong St, Keyser, WV 26726; 304-788-1562; probate phone: 304-788-3924; fax: 304-788-4109; 8:30AM-5PM (EST). *Felony, Civil Actions over $5,000, Probate.*
www.mineralcountywv.com/circuitclerk/index.asp

General Information: Probate court is a separate office at the same address, 2nd Fl. Probate fax is same as main fax number. No juvenile, adoption, divorce, mental hygiene, conservatorship or guardianship records released. Will fax documents, no fee. Court makes copy: $.75 per page. Self serve copy: same. No certification fee. Payee: Clerk of Circuit Court. Personal checks accepted, credit cards are not. Prepayment required. Mail requests: SASE requested.

Civil Name Search: Access: Fax, mail, in person, online. Both court and visitors may perform in person name searches. Search fee: $5.00 per name. Civil records on computer 1/1991 to present, on dockets from 1920s. Note: Fax access not guaranteed. Mail turnaround time 2-4 days. **Online access is available via a designated vendor. See the front or back of this chapter for details.**

Criminal Name Search: Access: Fax, mail, in person, online. Both court and visitors may perform in person name searches. Search fee: $5.00 per name. Required to search: name, years to search; also helpful: DOB, SSN. Criminal records on computer 1/1991 to present, on dockets from 1920s. Note: Fax access not guaranteed. Mail turnaround time 2-4 days. **Online access is available via a designated vendor. See the front or back of this chapter for details.**

Magistrate Court 105 West St, Keyser, WV 26726; 304-788-2625; fax: 304-788-9835; 8:30AM-4:30PM (EST). *Misdemeanor, Civil Actions under $5,000, Eviction, Small Claims.*

General Information: Will fax documents $2.00 per page. Court makes copy: $.25 per page. Certification fee: $.50 per page. Payee: Magistrate Court. Personal checks accepted. Major credit cards accepted. Prepayment required. Mail requests: SASE requested.

Civil Name Search: Access: Mail, in person. Both court and visitors may perform in person name searches. Search fee: $25.00 per name. Civil records on computer back to 1991. Mail turnaround time as time permits. Civil PAT goes back to 1991.

Criminal Name Search: Access: Mail, in person. Both court and visitors may perform in person name searches. Search fee: $25.00 per name. Required to search: name, years to search; also helpful: DOB, SSN. Records on computer back to 1991. Mail turnaround time as time permits. Criminal PAT goes back to same as civil.

Mingo County

Circuit Court PO Box 435, 75 E 2nd Ave, Rm 232, Williamson, WV 25661; 304-235-0320; probate phone: 304-235-0330; fax: 304-235-0326; 8:30AM-N, 1-4:30PM (EST). *Felony, Civil Actions over $5,000, Probate.*

General Information: Probate is handled by County Clerk, 75 E 2nd Ave, Williamson, WV 25661. No adoption, mental hygiene, juvenile records released. Will fax documents to local or toll-free number. Court makes copy: $.75 per page. Self serve copy: same. Certification fee: $2.00. Payee: Mingo County Circuit Clerk. No credit cards accepted. Prepayment required. Mail requests: SASE required.

Civil Name Search: Access: In person only. Both court and visitors may perform in person name searches. No search fee. Civil records on computer from 1/91 to present, civil on index books back to 1960, chancery books back to 1800s (written or in person only). Civil PAT goes back to 1991.

Criminal Name Search: Access: Mail, in person. Both court and visitors may perform in person name searches. Search fee: $10.00 per name. Required to search: name, years to search; also helpful: DOB. Criminal records on computer since 1/91, Index books back to 1955. Mail turnaround time 1-2 weeks. Criminal PAT goes back to same as civil.

Magistrate Court PO Box 986, Williamson, WV 25661; 304-235-2445; fax: 304-235-3179; 8:30AM-4:30PM (EST). *Misdemeanor, Civil Actions under $5,000, Eviction, Small Claims.*

General Information: Will not fax out documents. Court makes copy: $.25 per page. Certification fee: $.50 per page. Payee: Magistrate Court. Personal checks accepted. Visa/MC, Discover accepted. Prepayment required.

Civil Name Search: Access: Phone, mail, fax, in person. Both court and visitors may perform in person name searches. Search fee: $25 per name. Required to search: name, years to search; also helpful: DOB. Civil records go back to 1977; on computer back to 1998. Mail turnaround time 1 week. Civil PAT goes back to 1998. Public terminal located only in Court Clerk's office.

Criminal Name Search: Access: Mail, fax, in person. Both court and visitors may perform in person name searches. Search fee: $25.00 per name. Required to search: name, years to search; also helpful: DOB, SSN. Criminal records go back to 1977; on computer back to 1998. Mail turnaround time 1 week, sooner for phone requests. Criminal PAT goes back to same as civil. Public terminal located only in Court Clerk's office.

Monongalia County

17th Circuit Court County Courthouse, 243 High St, Rm 110, Morgantown, WV 26505; 304-291-7240; fax: 304-291-7273; 8:30AM-7PM M; 8:30AM-5PM T-F (EST). *Felony, Civil Actions over $5,000, Probate.*

General Information: A disclaimer for the Clerk must be included by mail requesters. No juvenile, divorce, mental hygiene, adoption, guardianship, conservatorship or domestic records released. Fee to fax out file $1.00 per page. Court makes copy: $.75 per page. Self serve copy: same. Certification fee: $.75 per page. Payee: Circuit Clerk. Business checks accepted. No credit cards accepted. Prepayment required. Mail requests: SASE required.

Civil Name Search: Access: Mail, in person. Both court and visitors may perform in person name searches. Search fee: $5.00 per name. Civil records on computer from 1/90 to present, on index book separated by plaintiff and defendant back to 1865. Mail turnaround time 1 day. Civil PAT goes back to 1990.

Criminal Name Search: Access: Mail, in person. Both court and visitors may perform in person name searches. Search fee: $5.00 per name. Required to search: name, years to search; also helpful: DOB, SSN. Criminal records computerized from 1/90 to present, on index book separated by plaintiff and defendant back to 1865. Note: Court plans to have records online in the future. Mail turnaround time 1 day. Criminal PAT goes back to 1994.

Magistrate Court 265 Spruce St, Morgantown, WV 26505; 304-291-7296; fax: 304-284-7313; 8AM-12; 1PM-7PM (EST). *Misdemeanor, Civil Actions under $5,000, Eviction, Small Claims.*

General Information: Will not fax documents. Court makes copy: $.25 per page. Self serve copy: same. Certification fee: $.50 per page. Payee: Magistrate Court. Personal checks accepted. Major credit cards accepted. Prepayment required.

Civil Name Search: Access: Mail, fax, in person. Both court and visitors may perform in person name searches. Search fee: $25.00. Records on computer back to 1999; prior in books back 10 years. Mail turnaround time 10-14 days. Civil PAT goes back to 2000.

Criminal Name Search: Access: Mail, fax, in person. Both court and visitors may perform in person name searches. Search fee: $25.00 per name. Required to search: name, years to search; also helpful: DOB, SSN, signed release. Records on computer go back to 1999; prior in books back 10 years only. Mail turnaround time 10-14 days. Criminal PAT goes back to same as civil.

Monroe County

Circuit Court PO Box 350, Union, WV 24983-0350; 304-772-3017; probate phone: 304-772-3096; fax: 304-772-4497; 8AM-4PM (EST). *Felony, Civil Actions over $5,000, Probate.*

www.monroecountywv.net/Circuit_Clerk/index.html

General Information: Probate is with the County Clerk, PO Box 350, Union, WV 24983. No juvenile, adoption, divorce records released. Will fax documents to local or toll free line. Court makes copy: $.75 per page. Include postage with copy fee. Certification fee: $1.00 per document. Payee: Clerk of Circuit Court. Personal checks accepted, credit cards are not. Prepayment required. Mail requests: SASE requested.

Civil Name Search: Access: Phone, mail, in person. Both court and visitors may perform in person name searches. No search fee. Civil index on docket books 1799 to present; on computer back to 2000. Mail turnaround time 1 week.

Criminal Name Search: Access: Phone, mail, in person. Both court and visitors may perform in person name searches. No search fee. Required to search: name, years to search; also helpful: DOB, SSN. Criminal records indexed in books 1799 to present; on computer back to 2000. Mail turnaround time 1 week.

Magistrate Court PO Box 4, Union, WV 24983; 304-772-3321; fax: 304-772-4557; 8:30AM-4:30PM (EST). *Misdemeanor, Civil Actions under $5,000, Eviction, Small Claims.*

www.monroecountywv.net/Magistrate/

General Information: Will fax documents $2.00. Court makes copy: $.25 per page. Self serve copy: same. Certification fee: $.50 per page plus copy fee. Payee: Monroe County Magistrate Court. Personal checks accepted. Credit cards accepted. Mail requests: SASE required.

Civil Name Search: Access: Mail, in person. Both court and visitors may perform in person name searches. Search fee: $25.00 per name. Required to search: name, DOB, SSN. Civil records go back to 1998; computerized records since mid 2001. Mail turnaround time 1-2 days. Civil PAT goes back to mid 2001.

Criminal Name Search: Access: Mail, in person, fax. Both court and visitors may perform in person name searches. Search fee: $25.00 per name. Required to search: name, years to search; also helpful: DOB, SSN. Misdemeanor records go back to 1998; computerized felony records since 2005. Mail turnaround time 1-2 days. Criminal PAT goes back to same as civil.

Morgan County

Circuit Court 77 Fairfax St, Rm 302, Berkeley Springs, WV 25411-1501; 304-258-8554; probate phone: 304-258-8547; fax: 304-258-7319; 9AM-5PM M-F (EST). *Felony, Civil Actions over $5,000.*

http://morgancountywv.gov/#

General Information: Probate is County Clerk's office located at the same address in 102. Due to courthouse fire 8/10/06, Circuit court records temporarily at 77 Fairfax St. No juvenile, adoption, mental health, divorce records released. Will not fax documents. Court makes copy: $.75 per page. Self serve copy: same. No certification fee. Payee: Kimberly J Jackson,

Circuit Clerk. Only cashiers checks and money orders accepted. No credit cards accepted. Prepayment required. Will bill to attorneys.

Civil Name Search: Access: In person only. Visitors must perform in person searches themselves. Civil records on computer back to 1/93, index cards back to 1960; in person searching only on index books back to 1800s. Civil PAT available.

Criminal Name Search: Access: In person only. Visitors must perform in person searches themselves. Required to search: name, years to search; also helpful-DOB, SSN, signed release. Criminal records computerized from 1/93, index cards back to 1960. Criminal PAT available.

Magistrate Court 111 Fairfax St, Berkeley Springs, WV 25411; 304-258-8631; fax: 304-258-8639; 9AM-4:30PM (EST). *Misdemeanor, Civil Actions under $5,000, Eviction, Small Claims.*

General Information: Will not fax documents. Court makes copy: $.25 per page. Certification fee: $.50 per page. Payee: Magistrate Court. Only cashiers checks and money orders accepted. Major credit cards accepted in person only. Prepayment required.

Civil Name Search: Access: Mail, in person. Visitors must perform in person searches themselves. Search fee: $25.00 per request. Civil records go back 10 years from last action; records computerized since 1998. Public use terminal available, records go back to 6/1998.

Criminal Name Search: Access: Mail, in person. Visitors must perform in person searches themselves. Search fee: $25.00 per request. Required to search: name, years to search; also helpful: DOB, SSN. Criminal records go back 10 years from last action; records computerized since 1998. Note: Phone, fax and mail access limited. Public use terminal available, crim records go back to 06/1998.

Nicholas County

Circuit Court 700 Main St #5, Summersville, WV 26651; 304-872-7810; probate phone: 304-872-7820; fax: 304-872-7863; 8:30AM-4:30PM (EST). *Felony, Civil Actions over $5,000, Probate.*

General Information: Probate is handled by County Clerk, 700 Main St, #2, Summersville, WV 26651. No juvenile, adoption, mental, guardianship records released. Will fax documents $2.00 per page. Court makes copy: $.75 per page. Self serve copy: same. No certification fee. Payee: Circuit Clerk. Personal checks accepted, credit cards are not. Prepayment required. Mail requests: SASE required.

Civil Name Search: Access: Mail, in person, online. Both court and visitors may perform in person name searches. No search fee. Civil records on computer since 1994; prior records on index cards from 1976 to 1994 on dockets back to 1818. Mail turnaround time 1 week. **Online access is available via a designated vendor. See the front or back of this chapter for details.**

Criminal Name Search: Access: Mail, in person, online. Both court and visitors may perform in person name searches. No search fee. Required to search: name, years to search; also helpful: DOB, SSN. Criminal records on computer since 06/1994; prior records on index cards from 1976 to 1994 on dockets back to 1818. Mail turnaround time 1 week. **Online access is available via a designated vendor. See the front or back of this chapter for details.**

Magistrate Court 511 Church St, #206, 2nd Fl, Summersville, WV 26651; 304-872-7829; fax: 304-872-7888; 8:30AM-4:30PM (EST). *Misdemeanor, Civil Actions under $5,000, Eviction, Small Claims.*

General Information: Domestic records restricted. Will fax documents for $2.00 per page. Court makes copy: $.25 per page. Certification fee: $.50 per page. Payee: Magistrate Court. Personal checks accepted. Major credit cards accepted. Prepayment required. Mail requests: SASE not required.

Civil Name Search: Access: Mail, in person. Visitors must perform in person searches themselves. Search fee: $25.00 per name. Civil records on computer back to 10/90, cases available since 1994. Note: Request must be in writing. Civil PAT goes back to 10/1990.

Criminal Name Search: Access: Mail, in person. Visitors must perform in person searches themselves. Search fee: $25.00 per name. Required to search: name, years to search; also helpful: DOB, SSN. Criminal records computerized from 1990, cases available since 1994. Note: Request must be in writing. Criminal PAT goes back to same as civil.

Ohio County

Circuit Court 1500 Chapline St, City & County Bldg, Rm 403, Wheeling, WV 26003; 304-234-3611; probate phone: 304-234-3656; fax: 304-232-0550; 8:30AM-5PM (EST). *Felony, Civil Actions over $5,000, Probate.*

General Information: Probate records are with the county clerk at this address, Rm 205. No domestic, juvenile, mental, adoption records released. Fee to fax out file $2.00 per page. Court makes copy: $.75 per page. Certification fee: $1.50 per document for triple seal, includes copies. Payee: Ohio County Circuit Court. Business checks accepted. No credit cards accepted. Prepayment required. Mail requests: SASE required.

Civil Name Search: Access: Fax, mail, in person, online. Both court and visitors may perform in person name searches. Search fee: $5.00 per name.

Civil records on computer from 10/1986 to present, on index books back to 1800s. Mail turnaround time up to 48 hours. Civil PAT goes back to 1986. **Online access is available via a designated vendor. See the front or back of this chapter for details.**

Criminal Name Search: Access: Fax, mail, in person, online. Both court and visitors may perform in person name searches. Search fee: $5.00 per name. Required to search: name, years to search; also helpful: DOB, SSN. Criminal records computerized, older records on index books back to 1800s. Mail turnaround time 1 week for accounts only. Criminal PAT goes back to 1986. **Online access is available via a designated vendor. See the front or back of this chapter for details.** Online results show middle initial.

Magistrate Court Courthouse Annex, 26 15th St, Wheeling, WV 26003; 304-234-3709; fax: 304-234-6439; 8:30AM-4:30PM (EST). *Misdemeanor, Civil Actions under $5,000, Eviction, Small Claims.*

General Information: Will fax documents for $2.00 per page, paid in advance. Court makes copy: $.25 per page. Self serve copy: same. Certification fee: $.50 per page. Payee: Court. Personal checks accepted with proper identification. Major credit cards accepted. Mail requests: SASE requested.

Civil Name Search: Access: Mail, fax, in person. Both court and visitors may perform in person name searches. Search fee: $25.00 per name. Paper record kept 10 years, but there may be some case history sheets older. Court will only search back 10 years. Mail turnaround time 1 week. Public use terminal available, records go back to 1999.

Criminal Name Search: Access: Mail, fax, in person. Both court and visitors may perform in person name searches. Search fee: $25.00 per name. Required to search: name, years to search; also helpful: DOB. Paper record kept 10 years, but there may be some case history sheets older. Court will only search back 10 years. Mail turnaround time 1 week. Public use terminal available, crim records go back to 1999.

Pendleton County

Circuit Court PO Box 846, 100 S Main St, Franklin, WV 26807; 304-358-7067; fax: 304-358-2152; 8:30AM-4:30PM (EST). *Felony, Civil Actions over $5,000, Probate.*

General Information: Probate is at different number. No juvenile, divorce records released. Will fax documents $2.00 per page. Court makes copy: $.75 per page. Self serve copy: same. No certification fee. Payee: Pendleton County Circuit Clerk. Local checks accepted. No credit cards accepted. Prepayment required. Mail requests: SASE required.

Civil Name Search: Access: Phone, fax, mail, in person, online. Both court and visitors may perform in person name searches. No search fee. Civil index on docket books back to 1800s. Mail turnaround time 2-3 days. **Online access is available via a designated vendor. See the front or back of this chapter for details.**

Criminal Name Search: Access: Phone, fax, mail, in person, online. Both court and visitors may perform in person name searches. No search fee. Required to search: name, years to search; also helpful: DOB, SSN. Criminal records indexed in books back to 1800s. Mail turnaround time 2-3 days. **Online access is available via a designated vendor. See the front or back of this chapter for details.**y

Magistrate Court PO Box 637, Franklin, WV 26807; 304-358-2343/2344; fax: 304-358-3870; 8:30AM-4:30PM (EST). *Misdemeanor, Civil Actions under $5,000, Eviction, Small Claims.*

General Information: Will fax documents to local or toll free line. Court makes copy: $.25 per page. Certification fee: $.50 per page plus copy fee. Payee: Magistrate Court. Personal checks accepted. Major credit cards accepted. Prepayment required. Mail requests: SASE not required.

Civil Name Search: Access: Mail, in person. Both court and visitors may perform in person name searches. Search fee: $25.00 per name. Civil records computerized since 1993. Note: No fee if public uses terminal. Mail turnaround time 5-10 days. Civil PAT goes back to 1993.

Criminal Name Search: Access: Mail, in person. Both court and visitors may perform in person name searches. Search fee: $25.00 per name. Records computerized since 1993. Note: No fee if public uses terminal. Mail turnaround time 5-10 days. Criminal PAT goes back to same as civil.

Pleasants County

Circuit Court 301 Court Ln, Rm 201, St. Mary's, WV 26170; 304-684-3513; probate phone: 304-684-3542; fax: 304-684-3514; 8:30AM-4:30PM (EST). *Felony, Civil Actions over $5,000, Probate.*

General Information: Probate is handled by County Clerk, 301 Court Ln, Rm 101, St Mary's, WV 26170. No domestic, marriage, adoption, juvenile or mental health records released. Will fax documents to local or toll-free number. Court makes copy: $.75 per page. Certification fee: $.50 per page. Payee: Circuit Clerk. Personal checks accepted, credit cards are not. Prepayment required.

Civil Name Search: Access: In person only. Visitors must perform in person searches themselves. Civil records on computer from 1/1960 to present, on index cards from 1960 to present, on index books back to 1800s. Civil PAT goes back to 1960.

Criminal Name Search: Access: In person only. Visitors must perform in person searches themselves. Criminal records computerized from 1/1960 to present, on index cards from 1960 to present, on index books back to 1800s. Criminal PAT available.

Magistrate Court 301 Court Ln, Rm B-6, St Mary's, WV 26170; 304-684-7197; fax: 304-684-3882; 8:30AM-4:30PM (EST). *Misdemeanor, Civil Actions under $5,000, Eviction, Small Claims.*

General Information: Domestic violence records restricted. Fee to fax files is $2.00 per page. Court makes copy: $.25 per page. Self serve copy: $.25 per page. Certification fee: $.50 per page. Payee: Pleasants County Magistrate Court. Personal checks accepted. Credit cards accepted. Prepayment required. Mail requests: SASE required.

Civil Name Search: Access: Mail, in person. Both court and visitors may perform in person name searches. Search fee: $25.00 per name. Required to search: name, years to search; also helpful: DOB or SSN. Records go back to 1977, on computer since mid-2000. Civil PAT goes back to 2000.

Criminal Name Search: Access: Mail, in person. Both court and visitors may perform in person name searches. Search fee: $25.00 per name. Required to search: name, years to search; also helpful: DOB, SSN. Records go back to 1977, on computer since mid-2000. Criminal PAT goes back to 2000.

Pocahontas County

Circuit Court 900-C 10th Ave, Marlinton, WV 24954; 304-799-4604; fax: 304-799-0833; 8:30AM-4:30PM (EST). *Felony, Civil Actions over $5,000.*

General Information: No juvenile, domestic cases involving finances, adoption, guardianship records released. Will fax documents $2.00 per page. Court makes copy: $.75 per page. Self serve copy: same. No certification fee. Payee: Clerk of Circuit Court. Personal checks accepted, credit cards are not. Prepayment required. Mail requests: SASE not required.

Civil Name Search: Access: Phone, mail, in person, online. Both court and visitors may perform in person name searches. No search fee. Required to search: name, years to search; also helpful: address. Civil index on docket books from 1948 to present, order books back to 1800s. Computerized from 1995 to present. Mail turnaround time same day. Civil PAT goes back to 10 years. **Online access is available via a designated vendor. See the front or back of this chapter for details.**

Criminal Name Search: Access: Phone, mail, in person, online. Both court and visitors may perform in person name searches. No search fee. Required to search: name, years to search; also helpful: DOB, SSN. Criminal records indexed in books from 1948 to present, order books back to 1800s. Computerized records from 1995 to present. Mail turnaround time same day. Criminal PAT goes back to 10 years. **Online access is available via a designated vendor. See the front or back of this chapter for details.**

Magistrate Court 900 10th Ave, Marlinton, WV 24954; 304-799-6603; fax: 304-799-5430; 9AM-4:30PM (EST). *Misdemeanor, Civil Actions under $5,000, Eviction, Small Claims.*

General Information: No Domestic cases released except for final orders. Will fax documents $2.00 per page. Court makes copy: $.25 per page. Self serve copy: same. Certification fee: $.75 per page plus copy fee. Payee: Pocahontas Co Magistrate Court. Personal checks, Visa/MC accepted. Prepayment required. Mail requests: SASE required.

Civil Name Search: Access: Mail, in person. Both court and visitors may perform in person name searches. Search fee: $25.00 per name. Required to search: name. Records stored since 1977, computerized since 10-14-99; actual record destroyed after 10 years. Mail turnaround time at clerk's convenience. Civil PAT goes back to 1999 for most. Results include name of defendant and case number.

Criminal Name Search: Access: Mail, in person. Both court and visitors may perform in person name searches. Search fee: $25.00 per name. Required to search: name, years to search; also helpful: DOB, SSN. Records stored since 1977, computerized since 10-14-99; actual record is destroyed after 10 years except DUIs. Mail turnaround time at clerk's convenience. Criminal PAT goes back to same as civil. Results include name of defendant and case number.

Preston County

Circuit Court 101 W Main St, Rm 301, Kingwood, WV 26537; 304-329-0047; probate phone: 304-329-0070; fax: 304-329-1417; 9AM-5PM M-F (EST). *Felony, Misdemeanor, Civil Actions over $5,000, Probate.*

General Information: Probate is handled by County Clerk, 106 W Main St, Rm 103, Kingwood, WV 26537. No juvenile, adoption, domestic, mental hygiene records released. Fee to fax out file $2.00 per page. Court makes copy: $.75 per page. No certification fee. Payee: Betsy Castle, Circuit Clerk.

Personal checks accepted, credit cards are not. Prepayment required. Mail requests: SASE required.

Civil Name Search: Access: Phone, fax, mail, in person. Only the court performs in person name searches; visitors may not. No search fee. Civil records on computer from 1/80 to present, on index books 1965 to 1980, chancery file from 1869 to 1965. Mail turnaround time 1 week.

Criminal Name Search: Access: Phone, fax, mail, in person. Only the court performs in person name searches; visitors may not. No search fee. Required to search: name, years to search, DOB, SSN. Criminal docket on books from 1869 to 1979, records on computer since 1979. Mail turnaround time 1 week.

Magistrate Court 101 W Main St #201, Kingwood, WV 26537; 304-329-2764; fax: 304-329-0855; 8:30AM-4:30PM (EST). *Misdemeanor, Civil Actions under $5,000, Eviction, Small Claims.*

General Information: Physical address is 101 W Main St. Will fax documents for $2.00 per page. Court makes copy: $.25 per page. Self serve copy: same. Certification fee: $.50 per page. Payee: Court. Personal checks, Visa/MC accepted. Prepayment required. Mail requests: SASE requested.

Civil Name Search: Access: Fax, mail, in person. Both court and visitors may perform in person name searches. Search fee: $25.00. Civil records go back to 1977; computerized records since 1987. Mail turnaround time 1 week. Civil PAT goes back to 1989.

Criminal Name Search: Access: Fax, mail, in person. Both court and visitors may perform in person name searches. Search fee: $25.00. Required to search: name, years to search; also helpful: DOB, SSN. Criminal records go back to 1977; computerized records since 1987. Mail turnaround time 1 week. Criminal PAT goes back to same as civil.

Putnam County

Circuit Court Putnam County Judicial Bldg, 3389 Winfield Rd, Winfield, WV 25213; 304-586-0203; fax: 304-586-0221; 8:30AM-4:30PM (EST). *Felony, Civil Actions over $5,000, Probate.*

General Information: No divorce records released. Court makes copy: $.75 per page. No certification fee. Payee: Circuit Clerk. Business checks accepted. No credit cards accepted. Prepayment required. Mail requests: SASE required for mail return of any copies.

Civil Name Search: Access: In person, online. Both court and visitors may perform in person name searches. No search fee. Civil records on computer from 1989 to present, on index books back to 1800s. Public use terminal available. **Online access is available via a designated vendor. See the front or back of this chapter for details.**

Criminal Name Search: Access: In person, online. Visitors must perform in person searches themselves. Required to search: name, years to search; also helpful: DOB, SSN. Criminal records computerized from 1982 to present. Public use terminal available. **Online access is available via a designated vendor. See the front or back of this chapter for details.** Online results show middle initial.

Magistrate Court 3389 Winfield Rd, Winfield, WV 25213; 304-586-0234; fax: 304-586-0267; 8:30AM-4:30PM (EST). *Misdemeanor, Civil Actions under $5,000, Eviction, Small Claims.*

General Information: Will fax documents $2.00 per page. Court makes copy: $.25 per page. Self serve copy: same. Certification fee: $.50 per page. Payee: Magistrate Court. Personal checks accepted. Major credit cards accepted. Prepayment required.

Civil Name Search: Access: Mail, in person. Both court and visitors may perform in person name searches. Search fee: $25.00. Required to search: name, DOB. Records are computerized since 1996, overall records kept since 1977. Mail turnaround time 1 week. Civil PAT goes back to 1996.

Criminal Name Search: Access: Mail, in person. Both court and visitors may perform in person name searches. Search fee: $25.00. Required to search: name, years to search; also helpful: DOB. Records stored since 1977. Mail turnaround time 1 week. Criminal PAT goes back to 1996.

Raleigh County

Circuit Court 215 Main St, Beckley, WV 25801; 304-255-9135; probate phone: 304-255-9123; fax: 304-255-9353; 8:30AM-4:30PM (EST). *Felony, Civil Actions over $5,000, Probate.*

www.raleighcounty.com/Default.aspx?id=15

General Information: Probate is handled by County Clerk, 215 Main St, Courthouse, Beckley, WV 25801. No divorce, juvenile, adoption records released. Fee to fax out file $2.00 per page. Court makes copy: $.75 per page. Self serve copy: same. No certification fee. Payee: Clerk of Circuit Court. Business checks accepted. No credit cards accepted. Prepayment required. Will bill to attorneys. Mail requests: SASE required for criminal.

Civil Name Search: Access: In person, online. Visitors must perform in person searches themselves. Civil records on master index books from 1977; on computer back to 1997; on dockets back to 1800s. Civil PAT goes back to 1997. **Online access is available via a designated vendor. See the front or back of this chapter for details.**

Criminal Name Search: Access: Phone, mail, in person. Both court and visitors may perform in person name searches. No search fee. Required to search: name, years to search; also helpful: DOB, SSN. Criminal records on master index books from 1977; on computer back to 1997; on dockets back to 1800s. Criminal PAT goes back to 1997. **Online access is available via a designated vendor. See the front or back of this chapter for details.**

Magistrate Court 115 W Prince St, #A, Beckley, WV 25801; 304-255-9197; fax: 304-255-3701; 8AM-4PM (EST). *Misdemeanor, Civil Actions under $5,000, Eviction, Small Claims.*

General Information: Will fax specific case file $2.00 per page. Court makes copy: $.25 per page. Self serve copy: same. Certification fee: $.50 per page includes copy fee. Payee: Magistrate Court. Personal checks accepted. Credit cards accepted. Prepayment required. Mail requests: SASE not required.

Civil Name Search: Access: Mail, in person. Both court and visitors may perform in person name searches. Search fee: $25.00 per name. Required to search: name. Civil records go back to 1991, are computerized. Older records have been destroyed. Mail turnaround time 5-7 days. Civil PAT goes back to 1991. Also, middle initial may appear in PAT results.

Criminal Name Search: Access: Mail, in person. Both court and visitors may perform in person name searches. Search fee: $25.00 per name. Required to search: name, years to search; also helpful: DOB, SSN, offense, date of offense. Criminal records go back to 1992. Mail turnaround time 5-7 days. Criminal PAT goes back to 1992. Also, middle initial may appear in PAT results.

Randolph County

Circuit Court Courthouse, 2 Randolph Ave, Elkins, WV 26241; 304-636-2765; fax: 304-637-3700; 8AM-4:30PM (EST). *Felony, Civil Actions over $5,000.*

General Information: Probate records are with the County Clerk - 304-636-0543. No juvenile, adoption, mental health, or guardianship records released. Will fax documents $2.00 per page. Court makes copy: $1.00 per page. Self serve copy: same. No certification fee. Payee: Circuit Clerk. Personal checks accepted. Prepayment required.

Civil Name Search: Access: Fax, mail, in person. Visitors must perform in person searches themselves. No search fee. Civil records on computer from 1/91 to present. On index books back to late 1800s. Note: If the record request is for a background check, then request can only be in person. Civil PAT goes back to 1991.

Criminal Name Search: Access: Fax, mail, in person. Visitors must perform in person searches themselves. No search fee. Criminal records computerized from 1/91 to present. On index books back to late 1800s. Note: If the record request is for a background check, then request can only be in person. Criminal PAT goes back to same as civil.

Magistrate Court #11 Randolph Ave, Elkins, WV 26241; 304-636-5885; fax: 304-636-2510; 8AM-4:30PM (EST). *Misdemeanor, Civil Actions under $5,000, Eviction, Small Claims.*

General Information: Domestic case info is restricted. Will fax documents $2.00 per page prepaid. Court makes copy: $.25 per page. Self serve copy: same. Certification fee: $.50 per page plus copy fee. Payee: Randolph County Magistrate Court. Personal checks accepted. Major credit cards accepted. Prepayment required. Mail requests: SASE required for mail return of any copies.

Civil Name Search: Access: Mail, in person. Both court and visitors may perform in person name searches. Search fee: $25.00 per name. Civil records go back to 1977; computerized records since 10/90. Mail turnaround time 3 days. Civil PAT goes back to 1992.

Criminal Name Search: Access: Mail, in person. Both court and visitors may perform in person name searches. Search fee: $25.00 per name. Required to search: name, years to search; also helpful: DOB, SSN. Criminal records go back to 1977; computerized records since 10/90. Mail turnaround time 3 days. Criminal PAT goes back to same as civil.

Ritchie County

Circuit Court 115 E. Main St, Rm 301, Harrisville, WV 26362; 304-643-2164 x229; civil phone: x1; fax: 304-643-2534; 8AM-4PM (EST). *Felony, Civil Actions over $5,000, Probate.*

General Information: Probate office is located at the same address, but in county clerks office. No juvenile, mental health, adoption records released. Will not fax documents. Court makes copy: $.75 per page. Self serve copy: same. No certification fee. Payee: Circuit Clerk. Personal checks accepted, credit cards are not. Prepayment required. Mail requests: SASE requested.

Civil Name Search: Access: Phone, mail, in person. Both court and visitors may perform in person name searches. No search fee. Civil index on cards from 1960 to present. On index books back to mid-1800s; on computer back to 2000. Mail turnaround time 1-2 days. Civil PAT goes back to 2000.

Criminal Name Search: Access: Phone, mail, in person. Both court and visitors may perform in person name searches. No search fee. Required to search: name, years to search; also helpful: DOB, SSN. Criminal records indexed on cards from 1960 to present. On index books back to mid-1800s; on computer back to 2000. Mail turnaround time 1-2 days. Criminal PAT goes back to same as civil.

Magistrate Court 130 N Court St, Harrisville, WV 26362; 304-643-4409; fax: 304-643-2098; 8AM-4PM (EST). *Misdemeanor, Civil Actions under $5,000, Eviction, Small Claims.*

General Information: 2nd fax: 304-643-2311. No domestic violence or juvenile records released. Will fax out documents $2.00 per page. Court makes copy: $.25 per page. Certification fee: $.50 per page. Payee: Ritchie County Magistrate Court. Personal checks accepted. Credit & debit cards accepted. Prepayment required. Mail requests: SASE not required.

Civil Name Search: Access: Phone, fax, mail, in person. Both court and visitors may perform in person name searches. Search fee: $25.00 per name, paid at time of request. Required to search: name, years to search; also helpful: DOB, SSN. Civil records go back 10 yrs; computerized from 1990. Note: Phone, fax or mail access is limited, call ahead for turnaround time. Mail turnaround time 1-2 days, 1-2 hours for phone requests. Civil PAT goes back to 1990.

Criminal Name Search: Access: Fax, mail, in person. Both court and visitors may perform in person name searches. Search fee: $25.00 per name. Required to search: name, years to search; also helpful: DOB, SSN. Criminal records go back 10 yrs; computerized from 1990. Mail turnaround time 1-2 days, 1-2 hours for phone request. Criminal PAT goes back to same as civil.

Roane County

Circuit Court PO Box 122, Spencer, WV 25276; 304-927-2750; fax: 304-927-2164; 8:30AM-N, 1-4PM; 9AM-N 1st Sat of Month (EST). *Felony, Civil Actions over $5,000, Probate.*

General Information: No sealed, juvenile, adoption records released. Will fax documents $1.50 1st page; $1.00 each add'l. Court makes copy: $.75 per page. Certification fee: $.50 per page. Checks only accepted form law firms. No credit cards accepted. Prepayment required. Mail requests: SASE not required.

Civil Name Search: Access: Phone, fax, mail, in person, online. Only the court performs in person name searches; visitors may not. No search fee. Civil index on docket books back to early 1900s; computerized records go back to 1998. Mail turnaround time 1-2 days, less for phone requests. **Online access is available via a designated vendor. See the front or back of this chapter for details.**

Criminal Name Search: Access: Phone, fax, mail, in person, online. Only the court performs in person name searches; visitors may not. No search fee. Required to search: name, years to search; also helpful: DOB, SSN. Criminal records indexed in books back to early 1900s; computerized records go back to 1998. Mail turnaround time 1-2 days, less for phone request. **Online access is available via a designated vendor. See the front or back of this chapter for details.**

Magistrate Court 201 Main St, Spencer, WV 25276; 304-927-4750; fax: 304-927-2754; 8:30AM-4PM (EST). *Misdemeanor, Civil Actions under $5,000, Eviction, Small Claims.*

General Information: Record requests can be directed to 304-746-2180. Will fax documents $2.00 per page. Court makes copy: $.25 per page. Self serve copy: same. Certification fee: $.50 per page. Payee: Roane County Magistrate Court. Personal checks, Visa/MC accepted. Prepayment required. Will bill to attorneys.

Civil Name Search: Access: Mail, in person. Both court and visitors may perform in person name searches. Search fee: $25.00 per name. Records on computer back to 1997; prior records go back to 1976. Civil PAT goes back to 1997.

Criminal Name Search: Access: In person. Both court and visitors may perform in person name searches. Search fee: $25.00 per name. Required to search: name, DOB; also helpful: years to search, SSN. Records on computer back to 1997; prior records go back to 1976. Criminal PAT goes back to same as civil. Terminal results include SSN.

Summers County

Circuit Court PO Box 1058, Hinton, WV 25951; 304-466-7103; criminal phone: 304-746-2177; fax: 304-466-7124; 8:30AM-4:30PM (EST). *Felony, Civil Actions over $5,000, Probate.*

General Information: No juvenile, adoption, child abuse records released. Court makes copy: n/a. Self serve copy: $.75 per page. Certification fee: $1.00. Payee: Clerk of Circuit Court. Personal checks accepted, credit cards are not. Prepayment required.

Civil Name Search: Access: In person only. Both court and visitors may perform in person name searches. No search fee. Civil index on docket books back to late 1800s; computerized records since 1999. Note: Clerk will lookup names on court's terminal for in person searchers.

Criminal Name Search: Access: In person only. Both court and visitors may perform in person name searches. No search fee. Required to search: name, years to search; also helpful: DOB, SSN. Criminal records indexed in books back to 1878, computerized since 1999. Note: Clerk will lookup names on court's terminal for in person searchers.

Magistrate Court PO Box 1059, Hinton, WV 25951; 304-466-7108; fax: 304-466-4912; 8:30AM-4:30PM (EST). *Misdemeanor, Civil Actions under $5,000, Eviction, Small Claims.*

General Information: Probate fax is same as main fax number. Records on domestic violence are restricted. Will fax documents $2.00 per fax. Court makes copy: $.25 per page. Certification fee: $.50 per page plus copy fee. Payee: Magistrate Court. Personal checks accepted. Credit cards accepted. Prepayment required. Mail requests: SASE required.

Civil Name Search: Access: Phone, fax, mail, in person. Both court and visitors may perform in person name searches. Search fee: $25.00. Required to search: name, years to search, other names used; also helpful-address. Civil index on docket books to 1977 and computer back to 1998. Mail turnaround time 1-2 days. Civil PAT goes back to 1998.

Criminal Name Search: Access: Phone, fax, mail, in person. Both court and visitors may perform in person name searches. Search fee: $25.00. Required to search: name, years to search; also helpful: DOB, SSN. Criminal docket on books to 1977, and computer back to 1998. Mail turnaround time 1-2 days. Criminal PAT goes back to same as civil.

Taylor County

Circuit Court 214 W Main St, Rm 104, Grafton, WV 26354; 304-265-2480; fax: 304-265-1404; 8:30AM-N, 1-4:30PM (EST). *Felony, Civil Actions over $5,000, Probate.*

General Information: Probate records held by the County Clerk. No juvenile, adoptions, mental health records released. Fee to fax out file $2.00 per page. Court makes copy: $.75 per page. No certification fee. Payee: Circuit Clerk. Personal checks accepted only from local residents. No credit cards accepted. Prepayment required. Mail requests: SASE required; any add'l fee for postage is 3 times the amount.

Civil Name Search: Access: Phone, mail, in person. Only the court performs in person name searches; visitors may not. No search fee. Civil index on docket books back to 1844, computerized since 1996. Mail turnaround time 2 days.

Criminal Name Search: Access: Phone, mail, in person. Only the court performs in person name searches; visitors may not. No search fee. Required to search: name, years to search; also helpful: DOB, SSN. Criminal records indexed in books back to 1929, computerized since 1996. Mail turnaround time 2 days.

Magistrate Court 214 W Main St, Grafton, WV 26354; 304-265-1322; fax: 304-265-5708; 8:30AM-4:30PM (EST). *Misdemeanor, Civil Actions under $5,000, Eviction, Small Claims.*

General Information: Search fee will include both civil and criminal indexes, if you ask. Will fax documents $2.00 per page, prepaid. Court makes copy: $.25 per page. Self serve copy: same. Certification fee: $.50 per page includes copy fee. Payee: Magistrate Court. Business checks accepted. Major credit cards accepted. Prepayment required. Mail requests: SASE required.

Civil Name Search: Access: Mail, fax, in person. Both court and visitors may perform in person name searches. Search fee: $25.00 per name. Computerized records go back to 1992. Mail turnaround time 1-2 days. Civil PAT goes back to 1992. The public terminal is at the Magistrate window.

Criminal Name Search: Access: Mail, in person. Both court and visitors may perform in person name searches. Search fee: $25.00. Required to search: name, years to search; also helpful: DOB, SSN, signed release. Computerized records go back to 1992. Mail turnaround time 1-2 days. Criminal PAT goes back to 1992. The public terminal is actually the clerk's terminal.

Tucker County

Circuit Court 215 1st St, #2, Parsons, WV 26287; 304-478-2606 ext 202; fax: 304-478-4464; 8AM-4PM (EST). *Felony, Civil Actions over $5,000.*

General Information: No juvenile, guardianship, adoption or mental hygiene records released. Domestic orders only released. Will fax documents for $2.00 per page; no charge for record check to a toll-free line. Court makes copy: $.75 per page. Self serve copy: same. No certification fee. Payee: Circuit Court Clerk. Personal checks accepted; no out of state checks. No credit cards accepted. Prepayment required. Mail requests: SASE required.

Civil Name Search: Access: Mail, in person. Both court and visitors may perform in person name searches. No search fee. Civil index on docket books from 1856 to 1996, 1997 to present on computer. Note: Due to limited staff, the court cannot do extensive civil searches. Court prefers all requests to be in writing. Mail turnaround time 2-5 days.

Criminal Name Search: Access: Mail, in person, fax. Both court and visitors may perform in person name searches. No search fee. Required to search: name, years to search, SSN; also helpful: DOB, case number.

Criminal records indexed in books to 1856 to 1996; 1997 to present on computer. Note: Court prefers all requests to be in writing, may be faxed in. Mail turnaround time 2 days.

Magistrate Court 201 Walnut St, Parsons, WV 26287; 304-478-2665; fax: 304-478-4836; 8:30AM-4:00PM (EST). *Misdemeanor, Civil Actions under $5,000, Eviction, Small Claims.*

General Information: Domestic violence case files not released. Will fax documents to local or toll-free number. Court makes copy: $.25 per page. Self serve copy: same. Certification fee: $.50 per page. Payee: Magistrate Court Tucker County. Personal checks accepted, credit cards are not. Prepayment required.

Civil Name Search: Access: In person only. Both court and visitors may perform in person name searches. No search fee. Civil records go back to 1977; computerized since 8/1999. Civil PAT goes back to 8/1999.

Criminal Name Search: Access: In person only. Both court and visitors may perform in person name searches. Search fee: $25.00 per name. Criminal records go back to 1977; computerized since 8/1999. Criminal PAT goes back to same as civil.

Tyler County

Circuit Court PO Box 8, 129 Main St, Middlebourne, WV 26149; 304-758-4811; fax: 304-758-4008; 8AM-4PM (EST). *Felony, Civil Actions over $5,000.*

General Information: No adoption, juvenile, or domestic records released. Fee to fax out file $2.00 per page. Court makes copy: $1.00 per page. Self serve copy: same. No certification fee. Payee: Tyler County Circuit Clerk. No personal checks or credit cards accepted. Prepayment required. Mail requests: SASE required.

Civil Name Search: Access: Mail, fax, in person. Visitors must perform in person searches themselves. No search fee. Civil index on docket books back to 1800s; computerized back to 1997. Mail turnaround time 1-2 days. Civil PAT available.

Criminal Name Search: Access: Mail, fax, in person. Visitors must perform in person searches themselves. No search fee. Required to search: name, years to search; also helpful: DOB, SSN. Criminal records indexed in books back to 1864; computerized back to 1997. Mail turnaround time 1-2 days. Criminal PAT available.

Magistrate Court PO Box 127, Middlebourne, WV 26149; 304-758-2137; fax: 304-758-2692; 9AM-4PM (EST). *Misdemeanor, Civil Actions under $5,000, Eviction, Small Claims.*

General Information: Domestic records restricted. Will fax documents $2.00 per page, in advance. Court makes copy: $.25 per page. Certification fee: $.50 per page includes copy fee. Payee: Tyler County Magistrate Court. Personal checks accepted. Major credit cards accepted. Prepayment required. Mail requests: SASE required.

Civil Name Search: Access: Mail, in person. Both court and visitors may perform in person name searches. Search fee: $25.00 per name. Required to search: Name, years to search, other names used, address; also helpful- DOB, SSN. Records go back to 1/1/77; on computer back to 1/1/2000, hard copies 10 years. Mail turnaround time 1 week. Civil PAT goes back to 1/2000.

Criminal Name Search: Access: Mail, in person. Both court and visitors may perform in person name searches. Search fee: $25.00 per name. Required to search: name, years to search; also helpful: DOB, SSN. Records go back to 1/1/2000. Mail turnaround time 1 week. Criminal PAT goes back to same as civil.

Upshur County

Circuit Court 38 W. Main St, Rm 304, Upshur County Court House Annex, Buckhannon, WV 26201; 304-472-2370; probate phone: 304-472-1068; fax: 304-472-2168; 8AM-4:30PM (EST). *Felony, Civil Actions over $5,000, Probate.*

www.upshurcounty.org/ctclerk/index.html

General Information: Probate is handled by County Clerk, 40 W Main, Courthouse, Rm 101, Buckhannon, WV 26201. Probate fax- 304-472-1029 No mental health, juvenile, adoption records released. Will fax findings to toll-free numbers. Court makes copy: $.75 per page. Certification fee: $.75 per page. Payee: Circuit Clerk. Business checks accepted. Visa/MC accepted in person. Prepayment required. Mail requests: SASE requested.

Civil Name Search: Access: In person only. Visitors must perform in person searches themselves. Civil index on docket books from 1947 to present, card index 1900 to 1960, on computer from 1900. Civil PAT goes back to 1900.

Criminal Name Search: Access: Fax, mail, in person. Both court and visitors may perform in person name searches. Search fee: $5.00 per name. Required to search: name, years to search; also helpful: DOB, SSN. Criminal records computerized from 1900 to present, on index books 1947 to present, on dockets back to 1800s. Mail turnaround time 1-2 days. Criminal PAT goes back to 1900.

Magistrate Court 38 W Main, Rm 204 Courthouse Annex, Buckhannon, WV 26201; 304-472-2053; fax: 304-472-2061; 8AM-4PM (EST). *Misdemeanor, Civil Actions under $5,000, Eviction, Small Claims.*
General Information: Will fax documents $2.00 per page. Court makes copy: $.25 per page. Self serve copy: same. Certification fee: $.50 per page. Payee: Magistrate Court. Personal checks accepted. Major credit cards accepted. Prepayment required.
Civil Name Search: Access: Mail, in person. Both court and visitors may perform in person name searches. Search fee: $25.00. Civil records computerized back to 1998. Mail turnaround time 1-2 days. Civil PAT goes back to 1998.
Criminal Name Search: Access: Mail, in person. Both court and visitors may perform in person name searches. Search fee: $25.00. Required to search: name; also helpful: DOB, SSN. Criminal records computerized back to 1998. Mail turnaround time 1-2 days. Criminal PAT goes back to 1998.

Wayne County

Circuit Court PO Box 68, Court Street, Wayne, WV 25570; 304-272-6360; civil phone: 304-272-6359; probate phone: 304-272-4372; ; 8AM-4PM M,T,W,F; 8AM-8PM TH (EST). *Felony, Civil Actions over $5,000, Probate.*
www.state.wv.us
General Information: Probate is handled by County Clerk, PO Box 248, Wayne, WV 25570. No juvenile, adoption, mental records released. Will not fax documents. Court makes copy: $.75 per page. Self serve copy: same. No certification fee. Payee: Clerk of Circuit Court. Business checks accepted. No credit cards accepted. Prepayment required. Mail requests: SASE required for civil.
Civil Name Search: Access: Phone, mail, in person. Both court and visitors may perform in person name searches. No search fee. Civil records on computer back to 1993; prior on index books from 1960 to present. Contact Circuit Clerk for books prior to 1900s. Note: The staff will not conduct genealogical searches. Mail turnaround time 1-2 days.
Criminal Name Search: Access: In person only. Visitors must perform in person searches themselves. Required to search: name, years to search, SSN; also helpful: DOB. Criminal records computerized from 1993; prior on index books from 1960 to present. Contact Circuit Clerk for books prior to 1900s.

Magistrate Court PO Box 667, Wayne, WV 25570; 304-272-5648/6388; fax: 304-272-5988; 8AM-N, 1-4PM (EST). *Felony, Misdemeanor, Civil Actions under $5,000, Eviction, Small Claims.*
www.state.wv.us/wvsca/courthouses/wayne.htm
General Information: Will fax documents $2.00 per page. Court makes copy: $.25 per page. Self serve copy: same. Certification fee: $.50 per page. Payee: Wayne County Magistrate Court. Personal checks accepted. Major credit cards accepted. Prepayment required. Mail requests: SASE required.
Civil Name Search: Access: Phone, fax, mail, in person. Both court and visitors may perform in person name searches. Search fee: $25.00 per name. Required to search: name; also helpful: years to search, DOB, SSN. Civil records on computer back to 1996. Mail turnaround time 1-2 days, usually same day for phone requests. Civil PAT goes back to 1996.
Criminal Name Search: Access: Fax, mail, in person. Both court and visitors may perform in person name searches. Search fee: $25.00 per name. Required to search: name; also helpful: years to search, DOB, SSN. Criminal records computerized from 1996. Mail turnaround time 1-2 days; usually same day for phone request. Criminal PAT goes back to same as civil.

Webster County

Circuit Court 2 Court Square, Rm G-4, Webster Springs, WV 26288; 304-847-2421; fax: 304-847-2062; 8:30AM-4PM (EST). *Felony, Civil Actions over $5,000, Probate.*
General Information: No mental health, juvenile, guardianship, adoption, paternity records released. Will fax documents $1.00 per page. Court makes copy: $.75 per page. Certification fee: $.50 per page. Payee: Clerk of Circuit Court. Personal checks accepted, credit cards are not. Prepayment required. Mail requests: SASE requested.
Civil Name Search: Access: Phone, fax, mail, in person. Both court and visitors may perform in person name searches. No search fee. Civil index on cards from 1977 to present, also on computer since 8/99. Mail turnaround time 3-5 days.
Criminal Name Search: Access: Phone, fax, mail, in person. Both court and visitors may perform in person name searches. No search fee. Required to search: name, years to search; also helpful: DOB, SSN. Felony dockets back to 1800s. Criminal records also on computer from 8/99. Mail turnaround time 3-5 days.

Magistrate Court 112 Bell St, #A, Webster Springs, WV 26288; 304-847-2613; fax: 304-847-7747; 8:30AM-4PM (EST). *Misdemeanor, Civil Actions under $5,000, Eviction, Small Claims.*

General Information: The agency recommends that criminal name searches be directed to the Court Repository in Charleston, 304-746-2180. Certain domestic cases are restricted. Will fax documents to local or toll free line. Court makes copy: $.25 per page. Self serve copy: same. Certification fee: $.50 per page. Payee: Magistrate Court Clerk. Personal checks accepted, credit cards are not. Prepayment required. Mail requests: SASE required.
Civil Name Search: Access: Fax, mail, in person. Both court and visitors may perform in person name searches. Search fee: $25.00 per name. Civil cases indexed by both defendant/plaintiff. Civil records go back to 1998; on computer since 2001. Mail turnaround time 7-10 days. Civil PAT goes back to 2000.
Criminal Name Search: Access: Fax, mail, in person. Both court and visitors may perform in person name searches. Search fee: $25.00 per name. Required to search: name, years to search; also helpful: DOB, SSN. Criminal records go back to 1998; on computer since 2001. Mail turnaround time 7-10 days. Criminal PAT goes back to same as civil.

Wetzel County

Circuit Court PO Box 263, New Martinsville, WV 26155; 304-455-8219; fax: 304-455-1069; 9AM-4:30PM; till 4PM only TH; 9AM-N Sat (EST). *Felony, Civil Actions over $5,000.*
General Information: No juvenile, domestic records released. Will fax documents if less than 10 pages. Court makes copy: $.75 per page. No certification fee. Payee: Circuit Clerk. Personal checks accepted, credit cards are not. Prepayment required.
Civil Name Search: Access: In person, online. Visitors must perform in person searches themselves. Civil index on docket books back to mid 1863; computerized back to 1996. Civil PAT goes back to 1996. **Online access is available via a designated vendor. See the front or back of this chapter for details.**
Criminal Name Search: Access: In person, online. Visitors must perform in person searches themselves. Required to search: name. Criminal records indexed in books back to mid 1863; computerized back to 1996. Criminal PAT goes back to same as civil. **Online access is available via a designated vendor. See the front or back of this chapter for details.**

Magistrate Court PO Box 147, New Martinsville, WV 26155; 304-455-5040\5171\2450; fax: 304-455-2859; 8:30AM-4:30PM (EST). *Misdemeanor, Civil Actions under $5,000, Eviction, Small Claims.*
General Information: Will fax documents. Court makes copy: $.25 per page. Payee: Wetzel County Magistrate Court. Personal checks, Visa/MC accepted. Prepayment required. Mail requests: SASE required.
Civil Name Search: Access: mail, fax, in person. Both court and visitors may perform in person name searches. Search fee: $25.00 per name. Required to search: name, DOB, SSN, years to search. Civil records go back to 1995. Mail turnaround time 1-2 days. Civil PAT goes back to 11/1999.
Criminal Name Search: Access: mail, fax, in person. Both court and visitors may perform in person name searches. Search fee: $25.00 per name. Required to search: name, years to search; also helpful: DOB, SSN. Criminal records go back to 1980. Mail turnaround time 1-2 days. Criminal PAT goes back to same as civil.

Wirt County

Circuit Court PO Box 465, Elizabeth, WV 26143; 304-275-6597; probate phone: 304-275-4271; fax: 304-275-3230; 8:30AM-4PM (EST). *Felony, Civil Actions over $5,000, Probate.*
General Information: Probate records located at the county clerk's office. Probate fax- 304-275-3418 No juvenile or adoption records released. No fee to fax documents. Court makes copy: $.10 per page. Certification fee: $.50 per page includes copy fee. Payee: Wirt County Circuit Clerk. Personal checks accepted, credit cards are not. Prepayment required. Mail requests: SASE required for civil.
Civil Name Search: Access: Phone, fax, mail, in person. Both court and visitors may perform in person name searches. No search fee. Civil index on cards from 1848 to present; computerized back to 9/2000.
Criminal Name Search: Access: Fax, in person. Both court and visitors may perform in person name searches. No search fee. Required to search: name, years to search, DOB, SSN. Criminal records indexed on cards from 1848 to present; computerized back to 9/2000.

Magistrate Court PO Box 249, Court St, Elizabeth, WV 26143; 304-275-3641/2; fax: 304-275-4882; 8:30AM-4PM (EST). *Misdemeanor, Civil Actions under $5,000, Eviction, Small Claims.*
General Information: Will fax documents $2.00 per page. Court makes copy: $.25 per page. Certification fee: $.50 per page. Payee: County Magistrate Court. Personal checks, Visa/MC accepted. Prepayment required. Mail requests: SASE required.
Civil Name Search: Access: Mail, in person. Both court and visitors may perform in person name searches. Search fee: $25.00. Civil records go back 10 years; computerized back to 9/2000. Civil PAT goes back to 9/2000.
Criminal Name Search: Access: Main, in person. Both court and visitors may perform in person name searches. Search fee: $25.00. Required to

search: name, years to search; also helpful: address, DOB, SSN. Criminal records go back 10 years; computerized back to 9/2000. Criminal PAT goes back to same as civil.

Wood County

Circuit Court Wood County Judicial, #2 Government Sq, Parkersburg, WV 26101-5353; 304-424-1700; probate phone: 304-424-1850; fax: 304-424-1804; 8:30AM-4:30PM (EST). *Felony, Civil Actions over $5,000, Probate.*

www.woodcountywv.com/

General Information: Probate is handled by County Clerk, PO Box 1474, Parkersburg, WV 26102. No juvenile, domestic, adoption, mental hygiene, guardianship records released. Will fax documents $2.00 per page. Court makes copy: $1.00 per page. Certification fee: None, part of copy fee. Payee: Carole Jones, Clerk. No checks accepted. No credit cards accepted. Prepayment required.

Civil Name Search: Access: Phone, mail, in person. Both court and visitors may perform in person name searches. No search fee. Civil records on computer from 1978 to present, on index books back to 1885. Mail turnaround time approx. 2-3 days. Civil PAT available.

Criminal Name Search: Access: Mail, in person. Both court and visitors may perform in person name searches. No search fee. Required to search: name, years to search, DOB, SSN. Criminal records on computer since 1979; prior records on index back to 1885. Mail turnaround time approx. 2-3 days. Depends on how busy. Criminal PAT available.

Magistrate Court 208 Avery St, Parkersburg, WV 26101; 304-422-3444;; 8:30AM-4:30PM (EST). *Misdemeanor, Civil Actions under $5,000, Eviction, Small Claims.*

General Information: Will fax documents $2.00 per page. Do not fax in record search requests. Court makes copy: $.25 per page. Certification fee: $.50 per page includes copy fee. Payee: Wood County Magistrate Court. Personal checks accepted. Credit cards accepted. Prepayment required. Mail requests: SASE required.

Civil Name Search: Access: Mail, in person. Both court and visitors may perform in person name searches. No search fee. Required to search: name, DOB, SSN, years to search. Civil records go back 10 years. Note: Fax and mail access limited. Mail turnaround time 10 days. Civil PAT goes back to 1996.

Criminal Name Search: Access: Mail, in person. Both court and visitors may perform in person name searches. Search fee: If the court does record search fee is $25.00. Required to search: name, years to search, address; also helpful: DOB, SSN. Criminal records go back 10 years. Note: Fax and mail access limited. Mail turnaround time 10 days. Criminal PAT goes back to same as civil.

Wyoming County

Circuit Court PO Box 190, Pineville, WV 24874; 304-732-8000 X238; fax: 304-732-7262; 8AM-4PM M-TH; 8AM-6PM F (EST). *Felony, Civil Actions over $5,000.*

www.state.wv.us/wvsca/courthouses/Wyoming.htm

General Information: No juvenile, mental hygiene, adoption, or sealed records released. Will not fax documents. Court makes copy: $.75 per page. Certification fee: $.75 but this includes the copy fee. Payee: David Stover, Circuit Clerk. Business checks accepted. No credit cards accepted. Prepayment required. Mail requests: SASE preferred.

Civil Name Search: Access: Phone, mail, in person, online. Both court and visitors may perform in person name searches. No search fee. Civil index on docket books back to 1800s. Note: In-person research may view the docket books. Mail turnaround time 1-2 days, less for phone requests. **Online access is available via a designated vendor. See the front or back of this chapter for details.**

Criminal Name Search: Access: Phone, mail, in person, online. Both court and visitors may perform in person name searches. No search fee. Required to search: name, years to search; also helpful: DOB, SSN. Criminal records indexed in books back to 1800s. Note: In-person research may view the docket books. Mail turnaround time 1-2 days, less for phone request. **Online access is available via a designated vendor. See the front or back of this chapter for details.**

Magistrate Court PO Box 598, Pineville, WV 24874; 304-732-8000 X218; fax: 304-732-7247; 9AM-4PM M-TH, 9AM-6PM Fri (EST). *Misdemeanor, Civil Actions under $5,000, Eviction, Small Claims.*

General Information: Information on search warrants are not released. Fee to fax files is $2.00 per page. Court makes copy: $.25 per page. Self serve copy: same. Certification fee: $.75. Payee: Wyoming County Magistrate Court. Personal checks accepted, credit cards are not. Prepayment required. Mail requests: SASE not required.

Civil Name Search: Access: Mail, in person. Both court and visitors may perform in person name searches. Search fee: $25.00 per name. The search fee includes a search of "citation, criminal and civil.". Civil records computerized back to 1995. Mail turnaround time 1-2 days. Civil PAT goes back to 9/1995.

Criminal Name Search: Access: Mail, in person. Both court and visitors may perform in person name searches. Search fee: $25.00 per name. The search fee includes a search of "citation, criminal and civil.". Required to search: name, years to search; also helpful: DOB, SSN. Criminal records computerized back to 1995. Mail turnaround time 1-2 days. Criminal PAT goes back to same as civil.

About Online Access

23 Circuit Courts show accessible record dockets at www.swcg-inc.com/page.cfm/circuit-courts/circuit-express. No images are available.

There is a $125 sign-up fee and a monthly flat fee of $ 38.00 plus connect charge of $ 1.00 a minute. Records are available from 02/1997. Search by name or case number.

The case summary is shown, no identifiers are provided. The WV Supreme Court prohibits court-related websites from displaying personal identifiers.

Wisconsin

Time Zone:	CST
Capital:	Madison, Dane County
# of Counties:	72
State Web:	www.wisconsin.gov
Court Web:	http://wicourts.gov

Administration

Director of State Courts, Supreme Court, PO Box 1688, Madison, WI, 53701; 608-266-6828, Fax: 608-267-0980.

The Supreme and Appellate Courts

The Supreme Court is the court of last resort. The Court of Appeals had four districts and hears appealed cases from the Circuit Courts. Appellate and Supreme Court opinions are available from the court web page.

The Wisconsin Courts

Court	Type	How Organized	Jurisdiction Highpoints
Circuit*	General	72 Courts in 10 Districts	Felony, Misdemeanor, Civil, Small Claims, Juvenile, Traffic, Eviction, Domestic Relations, Estate
Probate*	Special	72 Courts	Probate, Estate
Municipal	Limited	240 Courts	Traffic, Ordinance, Juvenile

* = profiled in this book

Details on the Court Structure

Circuit Courts have original jurisdiction in all civil and criminal matters within the state, including juvenile, and some traffic matters, as well as civil and criminal jury trials. The Small Claims limit is $5,000. The Clerk of Court is the record custodian.

The majority of **Municipal Court** cases involve traffic and ordinance matters.

Probate filing is a function of the Circuit Court; however, each county has a **Register in Probate** who maintains and manages the probate records, guardianship, and mental health records.

Record Searching Facts You Need to Know

Fees and Record Searching Tips

Public access terminals are available at each court. The statutory fee schedule for the Circuit Courts is as follows: search fee - $5.00 per name; copy fee - $1.25 per page; certification fee - $5.00.

The fee schedule for Probate Courts is as follows: search fee - $4.00 per name; certification fee - $3.00 per document plus copy fee; copy fee - $1.00 per page. Most Registers in Probate are putting pre-1950 records on microfilm and destroying the hard copies. This is done as "time and workloads permit," so microfilm archiving is not uniform across the state.

Online Access is Statewide

The Wisconsin Circuit Court Access (WCCA) is a public access website that provides open record information per state law §§ 19.21-.39. Users may view **Circuit Court** case information at http://wcca.wicourts.gov. Access is free. With the recent addition of Portage county, data is now available from all counties.

Searches can be conducted either statewide or by a specific county. WCCA provides detailed information about circuit cases including criminal, civil and traffic. A docketed civil judgment search is also offered. Data throughput dates vary by county, but in general most counties have participated since the early 1990s.

Search results generally includes the middle initial. The DOB is shown some of the time, and sometimes the DOB is only the month and year. WCCA also offers the ability to generate reports. Due to statutory requirements, WCCA users are not be able to view restricted cases. The probate records are included for all counties.

A Cautionary Note - This database consists of information voluntarily provided by county court staff. There is no mandate that all information must be reported. However, WI has legislated that the WI Department of Justice to be the official record holder of criminal record information. It is advised to check with an attorney if using the WCCA for pre-employment screening purposes.

WCCA offers a data extraction program on a subscription basis. See the web page for details.

Adams County

Circuit Court PO Box 220, 400 Main St, Friendship, WI 53934; 608-339-4208; fax: 608-339-4503; 8AM-4:30PM (CST). *Felony, Misdemeanor, Civil, Eviction, Small Claims.*
www.co.adams.wi.gov/
General Information: Online identifiers in results same as on public terminal. No juvenile, paternity, financial, PSI reports released. Fee to fax out file $1.25 per page. Court makes copy: $1.25 per page. Certification fee: $5.00 plus copy fees. Payee: Clerk of Court. Personal checks accepted, credit cards are not. GPS will facilitate payment by credit card. Prepayment required. Mail requests: SASE required.
Civil Name Search: Access: Mail, in person, online. Both court and visitors may perform in person name searches. Search fee: $5.00 per name; $5.00 per record found. Civil records on computer from 1993, on index cards and books from 1950. Historical societies have previous records and indexes organized back to 1848. Mail turnaround time 1-2 days. Civil PAT goes back to 1993. Civil case lookup free online at http://wcca.wicourts.gov/index.xsl, records go back to July 1992. Online results show DOB most of time; however, sometimes DOB is month and year only on the index.
Criminal Name Search: Access: Mail, online, in person. Both court and visitors may perform in person name searches. Search fee: $5.00 per name; $5.00 per record found. Required to search: name, years to search, DOB. Criminal records computerized from 1993, on index cards and books from 1950. Historical societies have previous records and indexes. Organized 1848. Mail turnaround time 1-2 days. Criminal PAT goes back to same as civil. Access criminal index free at http://wcca.wicourts.gov/index.xsl, records go back to July 1992. Online results show DOB most of time; however, sometimes DOB is month and year only on the index.

Register in Probate PO Box 200, 402 Main St, Friendship, WI 53934; 608-339-4213; fax: 608-339-4596; 8AM-4:30PM (CST). *Probate.*
General Information: Probate records free online at www.wicourts.gov/index.xsl.

Ashland County

Circuit Court Courthouse, 201 W Main St, Rm 307, Ashland, WI 54806; 715-682-7016; fax: 715-682-7919; 8AM-4PM (CST). *Felony, Misdemeanor, Civil, Eviction, Small Claims.*
www.co.ashland.wi.us
General Information: Online identifiers in results same as on public terminal. No juvenile or paternity records released. Will fax documents $1.25 per page. Court makes copy: $1.25 per page. Certification fee: $5.00 per cert plus copy fee. Payee: Clerk of Court. Local or pre-approved checks accepted. Prepayment required. Mail requests: SASE required.
Civil Name Search: Access: Phone, fax, mail, online, in person. Both court and visitors may perform in person name searches. Search fee: $5.00 per name. Civil index on cards and index books concurrently from 1960. Organized 1860. Mail turnaround time 1-2 days. Civil PAT goes back to 1994. Civil case lookup free online at http://wcca.wicourts.gov/index.xsl, records go back to November 1992. Online results show DOB most of time; however, sometimes DOB is month and year only on the index.
Criminal Name Search: Access: Fax, mail, online, in person. Both court and visitors may perform in person name searches. Search fee: $5.00 per name. Required to search: name, years to search, DOB. Criminal records computerized from 1994. Mail turnaround time 1-2 days. Criminal PAT goes back to same as civil. Access criminal index free at http://wcca.wicourts.gov/index.xsl, records go back to November 1992. Online results show DOB most of time; however, sometimes DOB is month and year only on the index.

Register in Probate Courthouse, Rm 203, 201 W Main, Ashland, WI 54806; 715-682-7009; fax: 715-685-9977; 8AM-N, 1-4PM (CST). *Probate, Guardianship, Adoption, Mental Health, Juvenile.*
General Information: Probate records free at http://wcca.wicourts.gov/index.xsl.

Barron County

Circuit Court Barron County Justice Center, 1420 State Hwy 25 N, Barron, WI 54812; 715-537-6265; criminal phone: 715-537-6152; civil phone: 715-537-6271; probate phone: 715-537-6261; fax: 715-537-6269; 8AM-4:30PM (CST). *Felony, Misdemeanor, Civil, Eviction, Small Claims.*
www.barroncountywi.gov
General Information: Online identifiers in results same as on public terminal. No expunged, paternity or sealed records released. Will fax documents $2.00. Court makes copy: $1.25 per page. Certification fee: $5.00 per document plus copy fee. Payee: Clerk of Court. Personal checks accepted. Credit cards accepted. Prepayment required.
Civil Name Search: Access: Main, online, in person. Both court and visitors may perform in person name searches. Search fee: $5.00. Civil records on computer, index cards from 1983. Organized 1859. Civil PAT goes back to mid-1993. Civil case lookup free online at http://wcca.wicourts.gov/index.xsl, records go back to February 1993. Online results show DOB most of time; however, sometimes DOB is month and year only on the index.
Criminal Name Search: Access: Mail, online, in person. Both court and visitors may perform in person name searches. Search fee: $5.00. Criminal records on computer, index cards from 1983. Organized 1859. Criminal PAT goes back to same as civil. Access criminal index free at http://wcca.wicourts.gov/index.xsl, , records go back to February 1993. Online results show DOB most of time; however, sometimes DOB is month and year only on the index.

Register in Probate Barron Justice Ctr, 1420 State Hwy 25 N, Rm 2700, Barron, WI 54812; 715-537-6261; fax: 715-637-6769; 8AM-4:30PM (CST). *Probate.*
www.barroncountywi.gov/
General Information: Probate record index back to 1989-90 free at http://wcca.wicourts.gov/index.xsl.

Bayfield County

Circuit Court 117 E 5th, Washburn, WI 54891; 715-373-6108; fax: 715-373-6153; 8AM-4PM (CST). *Felony, Misdemeanor, Civil, Eviction, Small Claims.*
www.bayfieldcounty.org/clerkofcourts/default.asp
General Information: Online identifiers in results same as on public terminal. No sealed records released. Fee to fax out file $1.25 per page. Court makes copy: $1.25 per page. Self serve copy: same. Certification fee: $5.00. Payee: Clerk of Court. Personal checks accepted, credit cards are not. Prepayment required. Mail requests: SASE required.
Civil Name Search: Access: Mail, in person, online. Both court and visitors may perform in person name searches. Search fee: $5.00 per name. Civil records on computer for all open cases since 1982, on index cards from 1979, index books in archives from 1845 to 1979. Mail turnaround time 1-2 days. Civil PAT goes back to 1993. Civil case lookup free online at http://wcca.wicourts.gov/index.xsl. Online results show DOB most of time; however, sometimes DOB is month and year only on the index.
Criminal Name Search: Access: Mail, online, in person. Both court and visitors may perform in person name searches. Search fee: $5.00 per name. Required to search: name, years to search, DOB. Criminal records on computer since 3/93. Mail turnaround time 1-2 days. Criminal PAT goes back to same as civil. Access criminal index free at http://wcca.wicourts.gov/index.xsl. Online results show DOB most of time; however, sometimes DOB is month and year only on the index.

Register in Probate PO Box 536, 117 E 5th St, Washburn, WI 54891; 715-373-6108; fax: 715-373-6317; 8AM-4PM (CST). *Probate.*
General Information: Probate records free at http://wcca.wicourts.gov/index.xsl.

Brown County

Circuit Court PO Box 23600, 100 S Jefferson St, Courthouse Lower Level, Green Bay, WI 54305-3600; 920-448-4161; probate phone: 920-448-4275; fax: 920-448-4156; 8AM-4:30PM (CST). *Felony, Misdemeanor, Civil, Eviction, Small Claims.*
www.co.brown.wi.us/departments/?department=6b052f1617e8
General Information: Online identifiers in results same as on public terminal. No juvenile or pre-adjudicated paternity records released. Will fax documents $1.25 per page. Court makes copy: $1.25 per page. Certification fee: $5.00. Payee: Brown County Clerk of Circuit Court. Personal checks accepted. Prepayment required. Mail requests: SASE required.
Civil Name Search: Access: Mail, in person, online. Both court and visitors may perform in person name searches. Search fee: $5.00 per name. Civil records on computer since 1990, on microfiche from 1987-1990. Mail turnaround time 10 days. Civil PAT goes back to 1990. Civil case lookup free online at http://wcca.wicourts.gov/index.xsl. Online results show DOB most of time; however, sometimes DOB is month and year only on the index.
Criminal Name Search: Access: Mail, online, in person. Both court and visitors may perform in person name searches. Search fee: $5.00 per name. Required to search: name, years to search, DOB. Criminal records on computer since 1990, on microfiche from 1987-1990, archives from 1962-1990. Crossed on index cards from 1972, index books from 198. Mail turnaround time 10 days. Criminal PAT goes back to 1991. Access criminal index free at http://wcca.wicourts.gov/index.xsl. Online results show DOB most of time; however, sometimes DOB is month and year only on the index.
Register in Probate PO Box 23600, Green Bay, WI 54305-3600; 920-448-4275; fax: 920-448-6208; 8AM-4:30PM (CST). *Probate.*
General Information: Copies are $1.00 per page. Free access to Probate index at http://wcca.wicourts.gov/index.xsl. Physical address: 100 S Jefferson St, Green Bay, MI 54301.

Buffalo County

Circuit Court 407 S 2nd, PO Box 68, Alma, WI 54610; 608-685-6212; fax: 608-685-6211; 8AM-4:30PM (CST). *Felony, Misdemeanor, Civil, Eviction, Small Claims.*
www.buffalocounty.com/Buffalo%20County%20Clerk%20of%20Courts.htm
General Information: Online identifiers in results same as on public terminal. No closed records released. Fee to fax out file $1.25 per page. Court makes copy: $1.25 per page. Certification fee: $5.00 per document plus copy fee. Payee: Buffalo County Clerk of Court. Personal checks accepted, credit cards are not. Prepayment required. Mail requests: SASE required.
Civil Name Search: Access: Phone, fax, mail, online, in person. Both court and visitors may perform in person name searches. Search fee: $5.00 per name. Civil records on computer from 1994, on index cards from 1979. No civil records available before 1962. Mail turnaround time 1 week. Civil PAT goes back to 1994. Civil case lookup free online at http://wcca.wicourts.gov/index.xsl. Online results show DOB most of time; however, sometimes DOB is month and year only on the index.
Criminal Name Search: Access: Phone, fax, mail, online, in person. Both court and visitors may perform in person name searches. Search fee: $5.00 per name. Criminal records computerized from 1994. Felonies retained 50 years; misdemeanors 20 years. Mail turnaround time 1 week. Criminal PAT goes back to same as civil. Access criminal index free at http://wcca.wicourts.gov/index.xsl. Online results show DOB most of time; however, sometimes DOB is month and year only on the index.
Register in Probate 407 S 2nd, PO Box 68, Alma, WI 54610; 608-685-6202; fax: 608-685-6211; 8AM-4:30PM (CST). *Probate.*
General Information: Probate records free at http://wcca.wicourts.gov/index.xsl. You can search probate indexes from 1994-present on the state website.

Burnett County

Circuit Court 7410 County Road K, #115, Siren, WI 54872; 715-349-2147; probate phone: 715-349-2177; fax: 715-349-7659; 8:30AM-4:30PM (CST). *Felony, Misdemeanor, Civil, Eviction, Small Claims.*
www.burnettcounty.com/index.aspx?NID=238
General Information: Online identifiers in results same as on public terminal. No paternity, juvenile, sealed or confidential records released. Will fax documents to local or toll free line. Fees must be prepaid. Court makes copy: $1.25 per page. Certification fee: $5.00 per document plus copy fee.

Payee: Clerk of Courts. Personal checks accepted. Major credit cards accepted. Prepayment required. Mail requests: SASE required.
Civil Name Search: Access: Mail, in person, online. Both court and visitors may perform in person name searches. Search fee: $5.00 per name. Civil records on computer from 10/92, on index books from 1800s. Organized 1856. Mail turnaround time 1-2 days. Civil PAT goes back to 1992. Civil case lookup free online at http://wcca.wicourts.gov/index.xsl. Online results show DOB most of time; however, sometimes DOB is month and year only on the index.
Criminal Name Search: Access: Mail, online, in person. Both court and visitors may perform in person name searches. Search fee: $5.00 per name. Criminal records computerized from 10/92, on index books from 1800s. Organized 1856. Mail turnaround time 1-2 days. Criminal PAT goes back to same as civil. Access criminal index free at http://wcca.wicourts.gov/index.xsl. Online results show DOB most of time; however, sometimes DOB is month and year only on the index.
Register in Probate 7410 County Road K #110, Siren, WI 54872; 715-349-2177; fax: 715-349-7659; 8:30AM-4:30PM (CST). *Probate.*
www.burnettcounty.com/index.aspx?nid=474
General Information: Probate records only free at http://wcca.wicourts.gov/index.xsl. This court also holds Juvenile, Guardianship, Mental Commitments, Adoptions, and Term. of Parental Right.

Calumet County

Circuit Court 206 Court St, Chilton, WI 53014; 920-849-1414; fax: 920-849-1483; 8AM-4:30PM (CST). *Felony, Misdemeanor, Civil, Eviction, Small Claims.*
www.co.calumet.wi.us/
General Information: Online identifiers in results same as on public terminal. No pending juvenile or paternity records released. Will fax documents $1.50 per page. Court makes copy: $1.25 per page. Certification fee: $5.00. Payee: Clerk of Court. Personal checks accepted, credit cards are not. Prepayment required. Mail requests: SASE required.
Civil Name Search: Access: Mail, in person, online. Both court and visitors may perform in person name searches. Search fee: $5.00 per name. Civil records on computer from 1992, index cards from 1978, index books from 1800s. Mail turnaround time 2 days. Civil PAT goes back to 1992. Civil case lookup free online at http://wcca.wicourts.gov/index.xsl. Online results show DOB most of time; however, sometimes DOB is month and year only on the index.
Criminal Name Search: Access: Mail, online, in person. Both court and visitors may perform in person name searches. Search fee: $5.00 per name. Required to search: name, years to search, DOB. Criminal records computerized from 1992, index cards from 1978, index books from 1800s. Mail turnaround time 2 days. Criminal PAT goes back to same as civil. Access criminal index free at http://wcca.wicourts.gov/index.xsl. Online results show DOB most of time; however, sometimes DOB is month and year only on the index.
Register in Probate 206 Court St, Chilton, WI 53014-1198; 920-849-1455; fax: 920-849-1435; 8AM-N, 1-4:30PM (CST). *Probate.*
General Information: Free access to Probate index at http://wcca.wicourts.gov/index.xsl.

Chippewa County

Circuit Court 711 N Bridge St, Chippewa Falls, WI 54729-1879; 715-726-7758; probate phone: 715-726-7737; fax: 715-726-7786; 8AM-4:30PM (CST). *Felony, Misdemeanor, Civil, Eviction, Small Claims.*
www.co.chippewa.wi.us/
General Information: Online identifiers in results same as on public terminal. Paternity records released only to party or attorney of record, or with written court authorization. Fee to fax out file $2.00 1st page, $1.00 each add'l. Court makes copy: $1.25 per page. Certification fee: $5.00. Payee: Chippewa County Clerk of Courts. Personal checks accepted. Pay with credit card via GPS, www.GovPayNow.com, 888-604-7888, Code #1116 - there is a service fee. Prepayment required. Mail requests: SASE required.
Civil Name Search: Access: Mail, fax, online, in person. Both court and visitors may perform in person name searches. Search fee: $5.00 per name. Required to search: name, years to search; also helpful: address, records sought. Civil records on computer from 1990, index cards from 1980, index books from 1900s. Mail turnaround time same as criminal. Civil PAT goes back to 1990. Only the DOB month and year appear on results. Civil case lookup free online at http://wcca.wicourts.gov/index.xsl. Online results show DOB most of time; however, sometimes DOB is month and year only on the index.
Criminal Name Search: Access: Mail, fax, online, in person. Both court and visitors may perform in person name searches. Search fee: $5.00 per name. Required to search: name, years to search, DOB; also helpful: SSN. Criminal records computerized from 1990, index cards from 1979, index books from 1900s. Mail turnaround time 10 days or less; up to 30 days if

pre-1990. Criminal PAT goes back to 1990. Only the DOB month and year appear on results. Access criminal index free at http://wcca.wicourts.gov/index.xsl. Online results show DOB most of time; however, sometimes DOB is month and year only on the index.

Register in Probate 711 N Bridge St, Chippewa Falls, WI 54729; 715-726-7737; fax: 715-738-2626; 8AM-4:30PM (CST). *Probate.* www.co.chippewa.wi.us/index.php?option=com_content&view=article&id=85&Itemid=42
General Information: Probate records free at http://wcca.wicourts.gov/index.xsl.

Clark County

Circuit Court 517 Court St, #405, Neillsville, WI 54456-1971; 715-743-5181; fax: 715-743-5187; 8AM-4:30PM (CST). *Felony, Misdemeanor, Civil, Eviction, Small Claims.*
www.co.clark.wi.us/ClarkCounty/circuit_court.asp
General Information: Online identifiers in results same as on public terminal. No sealed or paternity records released. Will fax documents. Court makes copy: $1.25 per page. Certification fee: $5.00 per doc. Payee: Clerk of Court. Personal checks accepted. Prepayment required. Mail requests: SASE required.
Civil Name Search: Access: Mail, in person, online. Both court and visitors may perform in person name searches. Search fee: $5.00 per name. Civil records on computer from 1994, on index cards from 1981, index books from 1900s. Mail turnaround time 1-2 weeks. Civil PAT goes back to 1993. Civil case lookup free online at http://wcca.wicourts.gov/index.xsl. Online results show DOB most of time; however, sometimes DOB is month and year only on the index.
Criminal Name Search: Access: Mail, online, in person. Both court and visitors may perform in person name searches. Search fee: $5.00 per name. Criminal records computerized from 1994, on index cards from 1981, index books from 1900s. Mail turnaround time 1-2 weeks. Criminal PAT goes back to same as civil. Access criminal index free at http://wcca.wicourts.gov/index.xsl. Online results show DOB most of time; however, sometimes DOB is month and year only on the index.

Register in Probate 517 Court St, Rm 403, Neillsville, WI 54456; 715-743-5172; fax: 715-743-5120; 8AM-4:30PM (CST). *Probate.*
www.co.clark.wi.us/ClarkCounty/
General Information: There is a $4.00 search fee. Also, probate records free online at http://wcca.wicourts.gov/index.xsl.

Columbia County

Circuit Court PO Box 587, Portage, WI 53901; 608-742-9642; criminal phone: 608-742-9643; civil phone: 608-742-9624; probate phone: 608-742-9636; fax: 608-742-9601; 8AM-4:30PM (CST). *Felony, Misdemeanor, Civil, Eviction, Small Claims, Probate.*
General Information: Probate fax is same as main fax number. Online identifiers in results same as on public terminal. No juvenile or paternity records released. Fee to fax out file $1.25 per page. Court makes copy: $1.25 per page. Certification fee: $5.00. Payee: Clerk of Court. Personal checks accepted. Major credit cards accepted. Prepayment required. Mail requests: SASE required.
Civil Name Search: Access: Mail, in person, online. Both court and visitors may perform in person name searches. Search fee: $5.00 per name. Civil records on computer from 1994, on microfiche to 1960s, concurrent index cards/books from 1940s. Mail turnaround time 1-2 weeks. Civil PAT goes back to 1994. Search civil and probate court records free at http://wcca.wicourts.gov/index.xsl. Online results show DOB most of time; however, sometimes DOB is month and year only on the index.
Criminal Name Search: Access: Mail, online, in person. Both court and visitors may perform in person name searches. Search fee: $5.00 per name. Required to search: name, years to search, DOB. Criminal records computerized from 1994, on microfiche to 1960s, concurrent index cards/books from 1940s. Mail turnaround time 1-2 weeks. Criminal PAT goes back to same as civil. Access criminal index free at http://wcca.wicourts.gov/index.xsl. Online results show DOB most of time; however, sometimes DOB is month and year only on the index.

Crawford County

Circuit Court 220 N Beaumont Rd, Prairie Du Chien, WI 53821; 608-326-0211; criminal phone: 608-326-0209; civil phone: 608-326-0210; probate phone: 608-326-0206; fax: 608-326-0288; 8AM-4:30PM (CST). *Felony, Misdemeanor, Civil, Eviction, Small Claims.*
www.crawfordcountywi.org/clerkofcourts/
General Information: Online identifiers in results same as on public terminal. No juvenile, paternity, mental records released. Will not fax documents. Court makes copy: $1.25 per page. Certification fee: $5.00 plus copy fee. Payee: Clerk of Court. Personal checks accepted, credit cards are not. Prepayment required. Mail requests: SASE required.

Civil Name Search: Access: Mail, in person, online. Both court and visitors may perform in person name searches. Search fee: $5.00 per name. Civil records on computer from 1993, on index cards from 1984, index books from 1900. Historical Society has archives. Mail turnaround time 10 working days. Civil PAT goes back to mid-1993. Civil case lookup free online at http://wcca.wicourts.gov/index.xsl. Online results show DOB most of time; however, sometimes DOB is month and year only on the index.
Criminal Name Search: Access: Mail, online, in person. Both court and visitors may perform in person name searches. Search fee: $5.00 per name. Criminal records computerized from 1993, on index cards from 1984, index books from 1900. Historical Society has archives. Mail turnaround time 10 working days. Criminal PAT goes back to same as civil. Access criminal index free at http://wcca.wicourts.gov/index.xsl. Online results show DOB most of time; however, sometimes DOB is month and year only on the index.

Register in Probate 220 N Beaumont Rd, Prairie Du Chien, WI 53821; 608-326-0206; fax: 608-326-0288; 8AM-4:30PM (CST). *Probate.*
General Information: Probate records free at http://wcca.wicourts.gov/index.xsl.

Dane County

Circuit Court Dane County Courthouse, Rm 1000, 215 S Hamilton St, Madison, WI 53703-3285; 608-266-4311; probate phone: 608-266-4331; fax: 608-267-8859; 7:45AM-4:30PM (CST). *Felony, Misdemeanor, Civil, Eviction, Small Claims.*
www.countyofdane.com/court/
General Information: Online identifiers in results same as on public terminal. No "confidential records" released. Will fax documents to local or toll-free number if 20 pages or less. Court makes copy: $1.25 per page. Certification fee: $5.00 per doc plus copy fee; exemplification $15.00 plus copy fee. Payee: Dane County Clerk of Courts. Personal checks accepted. Major credit cards accepted. Prepayment required. If under $5.00, prepayment not required. Mail requests: SASE required.
Civil Name Search: Access: Fax, mail, online, in person. Both court and visitors may perform in person name searches. Search fee: $5.00 per name. Civil record index on computer from 1981 (with some exceptions), on microfiche prior to 1992, plaintiff index books 1848. Mail turnaround time 1-10 business days. Civil PAT goes back to 1990s. Small claims index available back to 1984 on the public terminal. Civil case lookup free online at http://wcca.wicourts.gov/index.xsl. Online results show partial DOB most of time.
Criminal Name Search: Access: Fax, mail, online, in person. Both court and visitors may perform in person name searches. Search fee: $5.00 per name. Required to search: name, years to search, DOB. Criminal record index on computer from 1984, index back to 1848. Mail turnaround time 1-10 business days. Criminal PAT goes back to 1984. Access criminal index free at http://wcca.wicourts.gov/index.xsl. The Dane County Sheriff's Office provides an online request only site for accident reports, incident reports, and other records. See www.danesheriff.com/records.aspx. Online results show middle initial, DOB, address.

Register in Probate 215 S Hamilton St, County Courthouse Rm 1005, Madison, WI 53703-3285; 608-266-4331; fax: 608-267-4152; 7:45AM-4:30PM (CST). *Probate.*
www.countyofdane.com/court/probate.aspx
General Information: Probate records free at http://wcca.wicourts.gov/index.xsl. Older indexes not online. Room 1005 is the physical room. If mailed, use Room 1000.

Dodge County

Circuit Court 210 W Center St, Juneau, WI 53039; 920-386-3570; fax: 920-386-3587; 8AM-4:30PM (CST). *Felony, Misdemeanor, Civil, Eviction, Small Claims.*
www.co.dodge.wi.us/courts/index.html
General Information: Online identifiers in results same as on public terminal. No juvenile or John Doe records released. Fee to fax out file $1.50 per page. Court makes copy: $1.25 per page. Certification fee: $5.00 per doc. Payee: Clerk of Courts. Personal checks accepted, credit cards are not. Prepayment required. Mail requests: SASE required.
Civil Name Search: Access: Mail, online. Both court and visitors may perform in person name searches. Search fee: $5.00 per name. Civil records on computer from 1993, on index cards from 1986, microfiche from 1972, index books from 1950s. Mail turnaround time 1-2 days. Civil PAT goes back to 1993. Civil case lookup free online at http://wcca.wicourts.gov/index.xsl. Online results show DOB month and year only on the index.
Criminal Name Search: Access: Mail, online. Both court and visitors may perform in person name searches. Search fee: $5.00 per name. Required to search: name, years to search, DOB. Criminal records

computerized from 1993, on index cards from 1986, microfiche from 1972, index books from 1950s. Mail turnaround time 1-2 days. Criminal PAT available. Access criminal index free at http://wcca.wicourts.gov/index.xsl. Online results show DOB month and year only on the index. Online results show middle initial, DOB, address.

Register in Probate 210 W Center St, Juneau, WI 53039-1091; 920-386-3550; fax: 920-386-3933; 8AM-4:30PM (CST). *Probate.* www.co.dodge.wi.us/courts/probate.html
General Information: $4.00 search fee; records computerized since 1992. Also, probate records free at http://wcca.wicourts.gov/index.xsl.

Door County

Circuit Court 1205 S Duluth Ave, Sturgeon Bay, WI 54235; 920-746-2205; fax: 920-746-2520; 8AM-4:30PM (CST). *Felony, Misdemeanor, Civil, Eviction, Small Claims.*
General Information: Online identifiers in results same as on public terminal. No financial or paternity records released. Fee to fax out file $3.00 each. Court makes copy: $1.25 per page. Self serve copy: same. Certification fee: $5.00 per document plus copy fee. Payee: Clerk of Court. Personal checks accepted, credit cards are not. Prepayment required. Mail requests: SASE required.
Civil Name Search: Access: Mail, in person, online. Both court and visitors may perform in person name searches. Search fee: $5.00 per file. Civil records on computer from 4/93, on index cards from 1984. Mail turnaround time 2-3 days. Civil PAT goes back to 4/1993. Civil case lookup free online at http://wcca.wicourts.gov/index.xsl. Online results show DOB most of time; however, sometimes DOB is month and year only on the index.
Criminal Name Search: Access: Mail, online, in person. Both court and visitors may perform in person name searches. Search fee: $5.00 per file. Required to search: name, years to search, DOB. Criminal records computerized from 4/93, on index cards from 1984, index books from 1900s. Mail turnaround time 2-3 days. Criminal PAT goes back to 1993. Access criminal index free at http://wcca.wicourts.gov/index.xsl. Online results show DOB most of time; however, sometimes DOB is month and year only on the index.

Register in Probate 1207 S. Duluth Ave, Rm C258, County Justice Center, Sturgeon Bay, WI 54235; 920-746-2482; fax: 920-746-5959; 8AM-4:30PM (CST). *Probate.*
General Information: Probate records free at http://wcca.wicourts.gov/index.xsl.

Douglas County

Circuit Court 1313 Belknap, Superior, WI 54880; criminal phone: 715-395-1240; civil phone: 715-395-1203; fax: 715-395-1581; 8AM-4:30PM (CST). *Felony, Misdemeanor, Civil, Eviction, Small Claims.*
www.douglascountywi.org/index.aspx?nid=167
General Information: Online identifiers in results same as on public terminal. No juvenile or paternity records released. Will fax documents $1.00 per page. Court makes copy: $1.25 per page. Certification fee: $5.00 per document. Payee: Clerk of Courts. Only cashiers checks and money orders accepted. Douglas County Personal checks accepted, credit cards are not. Prepayment required. Mail requests: SASE required.
Civil Name Search: Access: Mail, in person, online. Both court and visitors may perform in person name searches. Search fee: $5.00 per name. Civil records on computer since 1994; prior records on index cards from 1976, index books from 1900s. Mail turnaround time 1-2 weeks. Civil PAT goes back to 1994. Civil case lookup free online at http://wcca.wicourts.gov/index.xsl. Online results show DOB most of time; however, sometimes DOB is month and year only on the index.
Criminal Name Search: Access: Mail, online, in person. Both court and visitors may perform in person name searches. Search fee: $5.00 per name. Required to search: name, years to search; also helpful: DOB. Criminal records on computer since 1994; prior records on index cards from 1976, index books from 1900s. Mail turnaround time 1-2 weeks. Criminal PAT goes back to same as civil. Access criminal index free at http://wcca.wicourts.gov/index.xsl. Online results show DOB most of time; however, sometimes DOB is month and year only on the index.

Register in Probate 1313 Belknap, Ste 304, Superior, WI 54880; 715-395-1220; fax: 715-395-1550; 8AM-4:30PM (CST). *Probate.* www.douglascountywi.org/index.aspx?nid=348
General Information: Probate records free at http://wcca.wicourts.gov/index.xsl. This court also takes care of Guardianship, Mental Commitment, Adoptions

Dunn County

Circuit Court 615 Stokke Parkway, #1500, Menomonie, WI 54751; 715-232-2611; fax: 715-232-6888; 8AM-4:30PM (CST). *Felony, Misdemeanor, Civil, Eviction, Small Claims.*
http://dunncountywi.govoffice2.com/

General Information: Online identifiers in results same as on public terminal. No juvenile, family financial, sealed records released. Will fax documents $.25 per page fee prepaid. Court makes copy: $1.25 per page. Self serve copy: $.25 per page. Certification fee: $5.00 per document. Payee: Clerk of Court. Personal checks accepted. Credit card payment accepted via GPS- 888-604-7888 A, Loc code #2030. Prepayment required. Mail requests: SASE not required.
Civil Name Search: Access: Mail, in person, online. Both court and visitors may perform in person name searches. Search fee: $5.00 per name. Civil records on computer from 1987, index cards from 1977, index books from 1900s, archives from 1970. Mail turnaround time 2-3 days. Civil PAT goes back to 1987. Civil case lookup free online at http://wcca.wicourts.gov/index.xsl. Online results show DOB most of time; however, sometimes DOB is month and year only on the index.
Criminal Name Search: Access: Mail, online, in person. Both court and visitors may perform in person name searches. Search fee: $5.00 per name. Required to search: name, years to search, DOB. Criminal records computerized from 1987, index cards from 1977, index books from 1900s, archives from 1970. Mail turnaround time 2-3 days. Criminal PAT goes back to same as civil. Access criminal index free at http://wcca.wicourts.gov/index.xsl. Online results show DOB most of time; however, sometimes DOB is month and year only on the index.

Register in Probate 615 Stokke Pky, #1300, Menomonie, WI 54751; 715-232-6782; fax: 715-232-6787; 8AM-4:30PM (CST). *Probate.*
General Information: Probate records free at http://wcca.wicourts.gov/index.xsl.

Eau Claire County

Circuit Court 721 Oxford Ave, Eau Claire, WI 54703; 715-839-4816; fax: 715-839-4817; 8AM-4PM (CST). *Felony, Misdemeanor, Civil, Eviction, Small Claims, Traffic.*
www.co.eau-claire.wi.us/CountyDepartments/ClerkOfCourts/index.html
General Information: Online identifiers in results same as on public terminal. No paternity, financial disclosure, expungment or sealed records released. Will fax documents. Court makes copy: $1.25 per page. Self serve copy: $.25 per page. Certification fee: $5.00 per document. Payee: Clerk of Court-Eau Claire County. Personal checks accepted unless you passed a bad check or your DR license is suspended. Major credit cards accepted. Prepayment required. Mail requests: SASE required.
Civil Name Search: Access: Mail, in person, online. Both court and visitors may perform in person name searches. Search fee: $5.00 per name. Civil records on computer from 7/92, on index cards from 1970, index books from 1968. Mail turnaround time 1-10 days. Civil PAT goes back to 7/1992. Civil case lookup free online at http://wcca.wicourts.gov/index.xsl. Online results show DOB most of time; however, sometimes DOB is month and year only on the index.
Criminal Name Search: Access: Mail, online, in person. Both court and visitors may perform in person name searches. Search fee: $5.00 per name. Required to search: name, years to search, DOB. Criminal records computerized from 7/92, on index cards from 1970, index books from 1968. Mail turnaround time 1-10 days. Criminal PAT goes back to same as civil. Access criminal index free at http://wcca.wicourts.gov/index.xsl. Online results show DOB most of time; however, sometimes DOB is month and year only on the index.

Register in Probate 721 Oxford Ave, Rm 2201, Eau Claire, WI 54703; 715-839-4823; fax: 715-831-5835; 8AM-N, 1-5PM (CST). *Probate.* www.co.eau-claire.wi.us/
General Information: Probate records free at http://wcca.wicourts.gov/index.xsl.

Florence County

Circuit Court PO Box 410, Florence, WI 54121; 715-528-3205; fax: 715-528-5470; 8:30AM-4PM (CST). *Felony, Misdemeanor, Civil, Eviction, Small Claims.*
www.florencewisconsin.com/ClerkOfCourts/clerk_of%20 courts.htm
General Information: Online identifiers in results same as on public terminal. No juvenile, mental health, adoption or guardianship records released. Will fax documents to local or toll-free number. Court makes copy: $1.25 per page. Certification fee: $5.00. Payee: Clerk of Courts. Personal checks accepted, credit cards are not. Prepayment required. Mail requests: SASE required.
Civil Name Search: Access: Mail, in person, online. Both court and visitors may perform in person name searches. Search fee: $5.00 per name. Civil records on computer from 1991; prior records on index books from 1900s. Mail turnaround time 2 weeks. Civil PAT goes back to 1994. Civil case lookup free online at http://wcca.wicourts.gov/index.xsl. Online results show DOB most of time; however, sometimes DOB is month and year only on the index.
Criminal Name Search: Access: Mail, online, in person. Both court and visitors may perform in person name searches. Search fee: $5.00 per name.

Criminal records computerized from 1991; prior records on index books from 1900s. Mail turnaround time 2 weeks. Criminal PAT goes back to same as civil. Access criminal index free at http://wcca.wicourts.gov/index.xsl. Online results show DOB most of time; however, sometimes DOB is month and year only on the index.

Register in Probate PO Box 410, 501 Lake Ave, Florence, WI 54121; 715-528-3205; fax: 715-528-5460; 8:30AM-N, 12:30-4PM (CST). *Probate.*
General Information: Probate records free at http://wcca.wicourts.gov/index.xsl.

Fond du Lac County

Circuit Court 160 S Macy, Fond du Lac, WI 54936-1355; 920-929-3040; fax: 920-929-3933; 8AM-4:30PM (CST). *Felony, Misdemeanor, Civil, Eviction, Small Claims.*
General Information: Online identifiers in results same as on public terminal. No juvenile or paternity records released. Fee to fax out $2.00 per document page. Court makes copy: $1.25 per page. Certification fee: $5.00 per doc. Payee: Clerk of Circuit Court. Personal checks accepted, credit cards are not. Prepayment required. Mail requests: SASE required.
Civil Name Search: Access: Mail, in person, online. Both court and visitors may perform in person name searches. Search fee: $5.00 per name. Civil records on computer from 1990, index cards from 1978, microfiche 1836 to 1978, archives prior to 1900s. Old files destroyed and on microfiche. Mail turnaround time 1-2 days. Civil PAT goes back to 1990. Civil case lookup free online at http://wcca.wicourts.gov/index.xsl. Online results show DOB most of time; however, sometimes DOB is month and year only on the index.
Criminal Name Search: Access: Mail, online, in person. Both court and visitors may perform in person name searches. Search fee: $5.00 per name. Required to search: name, years to search, DOB. Criminal records computerized from 1990, index cards from 1978, microfiche 1836 to 1978, archives prior to 1900s. Old files destroyed and on microfiche. Mail turnaround time 1-2 days. Criminal PAT goes back to same as civil. Access criminal index free at http://wcca.wicourts.gov/index.xsl. Online results show DOB most of time; however, sometimes DOB is month and year only on the index.

Register in Probate 160 S Macy St, City-County Government Center, Fond du Lac, WI 54935; 920-929-3084, 906-4743; fax: 920-906-5540; 8AM-4:30PM (CST). *Probate.*
www.fdlco.wi.gov/index.aspx?page=75
General Information: Probate records available at http://wcca.wicourts.gov/index.xsl.

Forest County

Circuit Court 200 E Madison St, Crandon, WI 54520; 715-478-3323; fax: 715-478-3211; 8:30AM-4:30PM (CST). *Felony, Misdemeanor, Civil, Eviction, Small Claims, Traffic.*
General Information: Online identifiers in results same as on public terminal. No juvenile, paternity records released. Fee to fax out file $1.25 per page. Court makes copy: $1.25 per page. Self serve copy: $.10 per page plus tax. Certification fee: $5.00 per document. Payee: Clerk of Court. Personal checks accepted, credit cards are not. Prepayment required. Mail requests: SASE required.
Civil Name Search: Access: Mail, in person, online. Both court and visitors may perform in person name searches. Search fee: $5.00 per name. Civil records on computer from 1994, on index cards from 1979, index books from 1920s. Mail turnaround time 1-2 days. Civil PAT goes back to 1994. Civil case lookup free online at http://wcca.wicourts.gov/index.xsl. Online results show DOB most of time; however, sometimes DOB is month and year only on the index.
Criminal Name Search: Access: Mail, online, in person. Both court and visitors may perform in person name searches. Search fee: $5.00 per name. Required to search: name, years to search, DOB. Criminal records computerized from 1994, on index cards from 1979, index books from 1920s. Mail turnaround time 1-2 days. Criminal PAT goes back to same as civil. Access criminal index free at http://wcca.wicourts.gov/index.xsl. Online results show DOB most of time; however, sometimes DOB is month and year only on the index.

Register in Probate 200 E Madison St, Crandon, WI 54520; 715-478-2418; fax: 715-478-2430; 8:30AM-N,1-4:30PM (CST). *Probate.*
General Information: Probate records free at http://wcca.wicourts.gov/index.xsl.

Grant County

Circuit Court PO Box 110, Lancaster, WI 53813; 608-723-2752; fax: 608-723-7370; 8AM-4:30PM (CST). *Felony, Misdemeanor, Civil, Eviction, Small Claims.*
General Information: Online identifiers in results same as on public terminal. No juvenile, paternity records released. Will fax documents to local

or toll free line. Court makes copy: $1.25 per page. Certification fee: $5.00 per document plus copy fee. Payee: Clerk of Court. Personal checks accepted, credit cards are not. Prepayment required. Mail requests: SASE required.
Civil Name Search: Access: Phone, mail, fax, online, in person. Visitors must perform in person searches themselves. No search fee. Civil records on computer from 10/93, on index books from 1900s. Mail turnaround time 2 weeks. Civil PAT goes back to 10/1993. Civil case lookup free online at http://wcca.wicourts.gov/index.xsl. Online results show DOB most of time; however, sometimes DOB is month and year only on the index.
Criminal Name Search: Access: Phone, mail, fax, online, in person. Visitors must perform in person searches themselves. No search fee. Criminal records computerized from 10/93, on index books from 1900s. Mail turnaround time 2 weeks. Criminal PAT goes back to same as civil. Access criminal index free at http://wcca.wicourts.gov/index.xsl. Online results show DOB most of time; however, sometimes DOB is month and year only on the index.

Register in Probate 130 W Maple St, Rm A360, Lancaster, WI 53813; 608-723-2697; fax: 608-723-7370; 8AM-4:30PM (CST). *Probate.*
General Information: $4.00 search fee, records computerized since 1993. Probate records free at http://wcca.wicourts.gov/index.xsl.

Green County

Circuit Court 2841 Sixth St, Green County Justice Center, Monroe, WI 53566; 608-328-9433; fax: 608-328-9459; 8AM-4:30PM (CST). *Felony, Misdemeanor, Civil, Eviction, Small Claims.*
www.co.green.wi.gov
General Information: Online identifiers in results same as on public terminal. No juvenile, paternity or sealed records released. Will fax documents $1.00 per page. Court makes copy: $1.25 per page. Certification fee: $5.00 per doc plus copy fee. Payee: Clerk of Court. Personal checks accepted, credit cards are not. Prepayment required. Mail requests: SASE required.
Civil Name Search: Access: Mail, in person, online. Both court and visitors may perform in person name searches. Search fee: $5.00 per name. Required to search: name, years to search; also helpful: address. Civil index on cards from 1984, index books from 1900s; computerized back to 1994. Mail turnaround time 1-2 days. Civil PAT goes back to 1994. Civil case lookup free online at http://wcca.wicourts.gov/index.xsl. Online results show DOB most of time; however, sometimes DOB is month and year only on the index.
Criminal Name Search: Access: Mail, online, in person. Both court and visitors may perform in person name searches. Search fee: $5.00 per name. Required to search: name, years to search; also helpful: DOB. Criminal records indexed on cards from 1984, index books from 1900s; computerized back to 1994. Mail turnaround time 1-2 days. Criminal PAT goes back to same as civil. Access criminal index free at http://wcca.wicourts.gov/index.xsl. Online results show DOB most of time; however, sometimes DOB is month and year only on the index.

Register in Probate 2841 6th St, Green County Justice Center, Monroe, WI 53566; 608-328-9567; fax: 608-328-9459; 8AM-N, 1PM-4:30PM (CST). *Probate.*
www.co.green.wi.gov
General Information: Probate records free at http://wcca.wicourts.gov/index.xsl.

Green Lake County

Circuit Court PO Box 3188, 571 County Rd A, Green Lake, WI 54941; 920-294-4142; 8AM-4:30PM (CST). *Felony, Misdemeanor, Civil, Eviction, Small Claims.*
www.co.green-lake.wi.us
General Information: Civil and criminal search treated as one. Online identifiers in results same as on public terminal. No paternity or juvenile ordinance records released. Will not fax documents. Court makes copy: $1.25 per page. Certification fee: $5.00 per doc. Payee: Clerk of Circuit Clerk. Personal checks accepted. Credit cards accepted. Prepayment required. Mail requests: SASE required.
Civil Name Search: Access: Mail, in person, online. Both court and visitors may perform in person name searches. Search fee: $5.00 per name. Civil records on computer from 4/93, on index cards since 1900s. Mail turnaround time 1-3 days. Civil PAT goes back to 1993. Civil case lookup free online at http://wcca.wicourts.gov/index.xsl. Online results show DOB most of time; however, sometimes DOB is month and year only on the index.
Criminal Name Search: Access: Mail, online, in person. Both court and visitors may perform in person name searches. Search fee: $5.00 per name. Criminal records computerized from 4/93, on index cards since 1900s. Mail turnaround time 1-3 days. Criminal PAT goes back to same as civil. Access criminal index free at http://wcca.wicourts.gov/index.xsl. Online results show DOB most of time; however, sometimes DOB is month and year only on the index.

Register in Probate PO Box 3188, 571 County Rd A, Green Lake, WI 54941; 920-294-4044; 8AM-4:30PM (CST). *Probate.*
www.co.green-lake.wi.us
General Information: Probate records free at http://wcca.wicourts.gov/index.xsl.

Iowa County

Circuit Court 222 N Iowa St, Dodgeville, WI 53533; 608-935-0395; probate phone: 608-935-0347; fax: 608-935-0386; 8:30AM-4:30PM (CST). *Felony, Misdemeanor, Civil, Eviction, Small Claims.*
General Information: Online identifiers in results same as on public terminal. No adoption, paternity or mental records released. Fee to fax back-$5.00 plus $1.25 per page. Court makes copy: $1.25 per page. Certification fee: $5.00 per doc. Payee: Clerk of Court. Personal checks accepted, credit cards are not. Prepayment required. Mail requests: SASE required.
Civil Name Search: Access: Mail, in person, online. Both court and visitors may perform in person name searches. Search fee: $5.00 per name. Civil records on computer from 1992, index cards from 1987, archives from 1917, index books from 1829. Mail turnaround time same day. Civil PAT goes back to 1992. Civil case lookup free online at http://wcca.wicourts.gov/index.xsl. Online results show DOB most of time; however, sometimes DOB is month and year only on the index.
Criminal Name Search: Access: Mail, online, in person. Both court and visitors may perform in person name searches. Search fee: $5.00 per name. Required to search: name, years to search, DOB. Criminal records computerized from 1992, index cards from 1987, archives from 1917, index books from 1829. Mail turnaround time same day. Criminal PAT goes back to same as civil. Access criminal index free at http://wcca.wicourts.gov/index.xsl. Online results show DOB most of time; however, sometimes DOB is month and year only on the index.

Register in Probate 222 N Iowa St, Rm 206, Dodgeville, WI 53533; 608-935-0347; fax: 608-935-0386; 8:30AM-N, 12:30-4:30PM (CST). *Probate.*
General Information: Probate records free at http://wcca.wicourts.gov/index.xsl.

Iron County

Circuit Court 300 Taconite St, #207, Hurley, WI 54534; 715-561-4084; fax: 715-561-4054; 8AM-4PM (CST). *Felony, Misdemeanor, Civil, Eviction, Small Claims.*
General Information: Online identifiers in results same as on public terminal. No juvenile or paternity records released. Will fax documents to local or toll free line. Court makes copy: $1.25 per page. Certification fee: $5.00 per doc plus copy fee. Payee: Clerk of Court. Personal checks accepted, credit cards are not. Prepayment required. Mail requests: SASE required.
Civil Name Search: Access: Phone, mail, online, in person. Both court and visitors may perform in person name searches. Search fee: $5.00 per name. Civil index on cards from 1989, index books from 1920. Note: Phone access for title companies only. Mail turnaround time 2-3 days. Civil PAT goes back to 1993. Civil case lookup free online at http://wcca.wicourts.gov/index.xsl. Online results show DOB most of time; however, sometimes DOB is month and year only on the index.
Criminal Name Search: Access: Mail, online, in person. Both court and visitors may perform in person name searches. Search fee: $5.00 per name. Required to search: name, years to search, DOB. Criminal records indexed on cards from 1989, index books from 1920. Mail turnaround time 2-3 days. Criminal PAT goes back to same as civil. Access criminal index free at http://wcca.wicourts.gov/index.xsl. Online results show DOB most of time; however, sometimes DOB is month and year only on the index.

Register in Probate 300 Taconite St, #209, Hurley, WI 54534; 715-561-3434; fax: 715-561-4054; 8AM-4PM (CST). *Probate.*
General Information: Probate records free at http://wcca.wicourts.gov/index.xsl. Also, for simple case searches for free go to http://wcca.wicourts.gov/index.xsl.

Jackson County

Circuit Court 307 Main St, Black River Falls, WI 54615; 715-284-0208; probate phone: 715-284-0213; fax: 715-284-0270; 8AM-4:30PM (CST). *Felony, Misdemeanor, Civil, Eviction, Small Claims, Family, Traffic.*
www.co.jackson.wi.us
General Information: Online identifiers in results same as on public terminal. No juvenile or pre-judgment paternity records released. Will fax documents $3.00, if prepaid. Court makes copy: $1.25 per page. Certification fee: $5.00. Payee: Clerk of Court. Personal checks accepted, credit cards are not. Prepayment required if over $5.00. Mail requests: SASE required.
Civil Name Search: Access: Mail, in person, online. Both court and visitors may perform in person name searches. Search fee: $5.00 per name. Civil records on computer from 6/92, on index cards from 1979, index books to 1980, files and indexes prior to 1980 destroyed. Mail turnaround time 1-4 days. Civil PAT goes back to 1992. Civil case lookup free online at http://wcca.wicourts.gov/index.xsl. Online results show DOB most of time; however, sometimes DOB is month and year only on the index.
Criminal Name Search: Access: Mail, online, in person. Both court and visitors may perform in person name searches. Search fee: $5.00 per name. Required to search: name, years to search, DOB. Criminal records computerized from 6/92. Felonies 1879 to 1929 at State Historical Society. Mail turnaround time 1-4 days. Criminal PAT goes back to same as civil. Access criminal index free at http://wcca.wicourts.gov/index.xsl. Online results show DOB most of time; however, sometimes DOB is month and year only on the index.

Register in Probate 307 Main St, Black River Falls, WI 54615; 715-284-0213 x286; fax: 715-284-0277; 8AM-4:30PM (CST). *Probate.*
General Information: Probate records free at http://wcca.wicourts.gov/index.xsl.

Jefferson County

Circuit Court 320 S Main St, Jefferson, WI 53549; 920-674-7150; fax: 920-674-7425; 8AM-4:30PM (CST). *Felony, Misdemeanor, Civil, Eviction, Small Claims.*
www.jeffersoncountywi.gov/jc/public/jchome.php?page_id=261
General Information: Online identifiers in results same as on public terminal. No juvenile or mental health records released. Will fax documents $1.25 per page. Court makes copy: $1.25 per page. Certification fee: $5.00. Payee: Clerk of Courts. Personal checks accepted. Credit card payments can be made through GPS, 888-604-7888, pay location 2039. Prepayment required. Mail requests: SASE required.
Civil Name Search: Access: Mail, in person, online. Both court and visitors may perform in person name searches. Search fee: $5.00 per name. Civil records on computer from 1992, on index cards from 1979, index books from late 1800s. Mail turnaround time 2-3 days. Civil PAT goes back to 1992. Civil case lookup free online at http://wcca.wicourts.gov/index.xsl. Online results show DOB most of time; however, sometimes DOB is month and year only on the index.
Criminal Name Search: Access: Mail, online, in person. Both court and visitors may perform in person name searches. Search fee: $5.00 per name. Required to search: name, years to search, DOB. Criminal records computerized from 1992, on index cards from 1979, index books from late 1800s. Mail turnaround time 2-3 days. Criminal PAT goes back to same as civil. Access criminal index free at http://wcca.wicourts.gov/index.xsl. Online results show DOB most of time; however, sometimes DOB is month and year only on the index.

Register in Probate 320 S Main St, Jefferson, WI 53549; 920-674-7245; fax: 920-675-0134; 8AM-4:30PM (CST). *Probate.*
General Information: Probate records free at http://wcca.wicourts.gov/index.xsl.

Juneau County

Circuit Court 200 Oak St, County Justice Ctr, Mauston, WI 53948; 608-847-9356; fax: 608-847-9360; 8AM-4:30PM (CST). *Felony, Misdemeanor, Civil, Eviction, Small Claims.*
www.co.juneau.wi.gov/
General Information: Online identifiers in results same as on public terminal. No juvenile, confidential family or paternity records released. Will fax documents $2.00 up to 15 pages. Court makes copy: $1.25 per page. Certification fee: $5.00 per doc. Payee: Juneau County Clerk of Court. Personal checks accepted. Major credit cards accepted. Prepayment required. Mail requests: SASE required.
Civil Name Search: Access: Mail, in person, online. Both court and visitors may perform in person name searches. Search fee: $5.00 per case. Required to search: name, years to search, DOB. Civil records on computer from 1988, index cards from 1977, index books from 1900, microfiche from 1856-1900. Mail turnaround time 1 week. Civil PAT goes back to 1996. Civil case lookup free online at http://wcca.wicourts.gov/index.xsl. Online results show DOB most of time; however, sometimes DOB is month and year only on the index.
Criminal Name Search: Access: Mail, online, in person. Both court and visitors may perform in person name searches. Search fee: $5.00 per case. Required to search: name, years to search, DOB. Criminal records computerized from 1988, index cards from 1977, index books from 1900, microfiche from 1856-1900. Mail turnaround time 1 week. Criminal PAT goes back to 1996. Access criminal index free at http://wcca.wicourts.gov/index.xsl. Criminal background checks available at www.doj.state.wi.us/dles/cib/crimback.asp for a fee.

Register in Probate 200 Oak St, Rm 2300, Mauston, WI 53948; 608-847-9346; fax: 608-847-9349; 8AM-4:30PM (CST). *Probate.*
General Information: Probate records free at http://wcca.wicourts.gov/index.xsl.

Kenosha County

Circuit Court 912 56th St, Kenosha, WI 53140; 262-653-2664; fax: 262-653-2435; 8AM-5PM (CST). *Felony, Misdemeanor, Civil, Eviction, Small Claims.*

www.co.kenosha.wi.us/clerkcourt/index.html

General Information: Online identifiers in results same as on public terminal. No juvenile or paternity records released. Will fax documents for fee - call first. Court makes copy: $1.25 per page. Certification fee: $5.00. Payee: Clerk of Court. Personal checks accepted. Credit cards accepted; a 3% surcharge is added. Prepayment required. Mail requests: SASE required.

Civil Name Search: Access: Mail, in person, online. Both court and visitors may perform in person name searches. Search fee: $5.00 per name. Civil records on computer from 1989, index cards from 1960, microfiche from 1850. Mail turnaround time 1-2 days. Civil PAT goes back to 1995. Civil case lookup free online at http://wcca.wicourts.gov/index.xsl. Online results show DOB most of time; however, sometimes DOB is month and year only on the index.

Criminal Name Search: Access: Mail, online, in person, fax. Both court and visitors may perform in person name searches. Search fee: $5.00 per name. Required to search: name, years to search; also helpful: DOB, SSN. Criminal records computerized from 1989, index cards from 1960, microfiche from 1850. Mail turnaround time 1-2 days. Criminal PAT goes back to same as civil. Access criminal index free at http://wcca.wicourts.gov/index.xsl. Online results show DOB most of time; however, sometimes DOB is month and year only on the index.

Register in Probate Courthouse, Rm LL04, 912 56th St, Kenosha, WI 53140; 262-653-2675; fax: 262-653-2673; 8AM-5PM (CST). *Probate.*

General Information: $4.00 per search, records indexed on computer back to 1992; cards prior. Probate records free at http://wcca.wicourts.gov/index.xsl.

Kewaunee County

Circuit Court 613 Dodge St, Kewaunee, WI 54216; 920-388-7144; criminal phone: 920-388-7145; civil phone: 920-388-7146; fax: 920-388-7049; 8AM-4:30PM (CST). *Felony, Misdemeanor, Civil, Eviction, Small Claims.*

www.kewauneeco.org/

General Information: Online identifiers in results same as on public terminal. No paternity records released. Will fax documents $1.25 per page. Court makes copy: $1.25 per page. Self serve copy: same. Certification fee: $5.00 per document. Payee: Clerk of Circuit Court. Personal checks accepted. Credit cards accepted. Prepayment required. Mail requests: SASE helpful.

Civil Name Search: Access: Phone, mail, online, in person. Both court and visitors may perform in person name searches. Search fee: $5.00 per name. Computerized records from 1993, civil records on index cards from 1950, index books from 1852. Mail turnaround time 1-2 days. Civil PAT goes back to 1993. Civil case lookup free online at http://wcca.wicourts.gov/index.xsl. Online results show DOB most of time; however, sometimes DOB is month and year only on the index.

Criminal Name Search: Access: Phone, mail, online, in person. Both court and visitors may perform in person name searches. Search fee: $5.00 per name. Required to search: name, years to search, DOB. Computerized records from 1993, criminal records on index cards from 1950, index books from 1852. Mail turnaround time 1-2 days. Criminal PAT goes back to same as civil. Access criminal index free at http://wcca.wicourts.gov/index.xsl.

Register in Probate 613 Dodge St, Kewaunee, WI 54216; 920-388-7143; fax: 920-388-0852; 8AM-4:30PM (CST). *Probate.*

www.kewauneeco.org/

General Information: Probate records free at http://wcca.wicourts.gov/index.xsl.

La Crosse County

Circuit Court 333 Vine St, LEC, Rm 1200, La Crosse, WI 54601; 608-785-9590/9573; fax: 608-789-7821; 8:30AM-5PM (CST). *Felony, Misdemeanor, Civil, Eviction, Small Claims.*

www.co.la-crosse.wi.us/departments/court/

General Information: Online identifiers in results same as on public terminal. No juvenile, paternity or finances in family records released. Fee to fax out file $1.25 per page. Court makes copy: $1.25 per page. Certification fee: $5.00 per doc. Payee: Clerk of Courts. Personal checks accepted. Credit cards accepted. Prepayment required. Mail requests: SASE required.

Civil Name Search: Access: Fax, mail, online, in person. Both court and visitors may perform in person name searches. Search fee: $5.00 per name. Civil records on computer from 1993, on index cards from 1983, index books from 1917. Files maintained for 20 years. Mail turnaround time 1-2 days. Civil PAT goes back to 1993. Civil case lookup free online at http://wcca.wicourts.gov/index.xsl. Online results show DOB most of time; however, sometimes DOB is month and year only on the index.

Criminal Name Search: Access: Fax, mail, online, in person. Both court and visitors may perform in person name searches. Search fee: $5.00 per name. Required to search: name, years to search; also helpful: DOB. Criminal records computerized from 1993, on index cards from 1983, index books from 1917. Mail turnaround time 1-2 days. Criminal PAT goes back to 1983. Access criminal index free at http://wcca.wicourts.gov/index.xsl. Retention period 20 years for misdemeanor, felony is 50-75 years.

Register in Probate 333 Vine St, Rm 1201, La Crosse, WI 54601; 608-785-9882; fax: 608-789-7821; 8:30AM-5PM (CST). *Probate.*

General Information: Probate records free at http://wcca.wicourts.gov/index.xsl.

Lafayette County

Circuit Court 626 Main St, Attn: County Clerk of Court, Darlington, WI 53530; 608-776-4832; probate phone: 608-776-4811; fax: 608-776-4845; 8AM-4:30PM (CST). *Felony, Misdemeanor, Civil, Eviction, Small Claims.*

General Information: Online identifiers in results same as on public terminal. No juvenile records released. Will not fax documents. Court makes copy: $1.25 per page. Certification fee: $5.00 per document plus copy fee. Payee: Clerk of Circuit Court. Personal checks accepted, credit cards are not. Prepayment required. Mail requests: SASE required.

Civil Name Search: Access: Mail, in person, online. Both court and visitors may perform in person name searches. Search fee: $5.00 per name. Civil cases indexed by defendant. Civil index on cards from 1973, index books from 1900; computerized back to 1993. Mail turnaround time 2-3 days. Civil PAT goes back to 1993. Civil case lookup free online at http://wcca.wicourts.gov/index.xsl. Online results show DOB most of time; however, sometimes DOB is month and year only on the index.

Criminal Name Search: Access: Mail, online, in person. Both court and visitors may perform in person name searches. Search fee: $5.00 per name. Criminal records indexed on cards from 1973, index books from 1900; computerized back to 1993. Mail turnaround time 2-3 days. Criminal PAT goes back to same as civil. Access criminal index free at http://wcca.wicourts.gov/index.xsl. Online results show DOB most of time; however, sometimes DOB is month and year only on the index.

Register in Probate 626 Main St, Rm 302, Darlington, WI 53530; 608-776-4811; fax: 608-776-4845; 8AM-N, 1-4:30PM (CST). *Probate.*

General Information: Probate records free at http://wcca.wicourts.gov/index.xsl.

Langlade County

Circuit Court 800 Clermont St, Antigo, WI 54409; 715-627-6215; 8:30AM-4:30PM (CST). *Felony, Misdemeanor, Civil, Eviction, Small Claims.*

General Information: Ask that they combine a search of both the civil and criminal indices. Online identifiers in results same as on public terminal. No confidential records released. Will not fax documents. Court makes copy: $1.25 per page. Certification fee: $5.00 per cert plus copy fee. Payee: Clerk of Court. Personal checks accepted if in-state only. No credit cards accepted. Prepayment required. Mail requests: SASE required.

Civil Name Search: Access: Mail, in person, online. Both court and visitors may perform in person name searches. Search fee: $5.00 per name. Civil index on docket books from 1905, computerized since 1993. Mail turnaround time 2-3 days. Civil PAT goes back to 1993. Civil case lookup free online at http://wcca.wicourts.gov/index.xsl. Usually DOB does not show, but sometimes month and year only is shown on the index.

Criminal Name Search: Access: Mail, online, in person. Both court and visitors may perform in person name searches. Search fee: $5.00 per name. DOB is helpful. Criminal records indexed in books from 1905, computerized since 1993. Mail turnaround time 2-3 days. Criminal PAT goes back to same as civil. Access criminal index free at http://wcca.wicourts.gov/index.xsl. Online results show DOB most of time; however, sometimes DOB is month and year only on the index.

Register in Probate 800 Clermont St, Antigo, WI 54409; 715-627-6213; fax: 715-627-6329; 8:30AM-4:30PM (CST). *Probate, Giardianship, Adoption.*

General Information: There is a $4.00 search fee. Probate records free at http://wcca.wicourts.gov/index.xsl.

Lincoln County

Circuit Court 1110 E Main St, Merrill, WI 54452; 715-536-0319; fax: 715-536-0361; 8AM-4:30PM (CST). *Felony, Misdemeanor, Civil, Eviction, Small Claims.*

http://wicourts.gov

General Information: Online identifiers in results same as on public terminal. No paternity or sealed records released. Will fax documents $1.00 per fax; cannot fax certified copies. Court makes copy: $1.25 per page. Certification fee: $5.00 per document plus copy fee. Payee: Clerk of Court.

Local Personal checks accepted, credit cards are not. Prepayment required. Mail requests: SASE required.

Civil Name Search: Access: Mail, in person, online. Both court and visitors may perform in person name searches. Search fee: $5.00 per name. Civil cases indexed by defendant. Civil records on computer from 1990, index cards from 1982, index books from 1900s. Mail turnaround time 1-2 days. Civil PAT goes back to 1990. Civil case lookup free online at http://wcca.wicourts.gov/index.xsl. Online results show DOB most of time; however, sometimes DOB is month and year only on the index.

Criminal Name Search: Access: Mail, online, in person. Both court and visitors may perform in person name searches. Search fee: $5.00 per name. Required to search: name, years to search; also helpful: DOB, SSN. Criminal records computerized from 1990, index cards from 1982, index books from 1900s. Mail turnaround time 1-2 days. Criminal PAT goes back to same as civil. Access criminal index free at http://wcca.wicourts.gov/index.xsl. Online results show DOB most of time; however, sometimes DOB is month and year only on the index.

Register in Probate 1110 E Main St, Merrill, WI 54452; 715-536-0342; fax: 715-539-2762; 8:15AM-N, 1-4:30PM (CST). *Probate.* www.co.lincoln.wi.us/

General Information: Probate records free back to 1986 at http://wcca.wicourts.gov/index.xsl. Older records being added.

Manitowoc County

Circuit Court PO Box 2000, Manitowoc, WI 54221-2000; 920-683-4030; criminal phone: 920-683-4027; civil phone: 920-683-4031; fax: 920-683-2733; 8:30AM-5PM M; 8:30AM-4:30PM T-F (CST). *Felony, Misdemeanor, Civil, Eviction, Small Claims, Traffic.* www.manitowoccounty.org/department/dept_home.asp?ID=4

General Information: Also Family, Paternity and Juvenile case records held here. Online identifiers in results same as on public terminal. No confidential records released. Court makes copy: $1.25 per page. Certification fee: $5.00 per document plus copy fee. Payee: Clerk of Circuit Court. Personal checks accepted. Credit cards accepted by phone, 1-866-480-8552 or online at www.manitowoccounty.org. Prepayment required. Mail requests: SASE requested.

Civil Name Search: Access: Phone, mail, online, in person. Both court and visitors may perform in person name searches. Search fee: $5.00 per name. Civil cases indexed by first named defendant, plaintiff. Civil records on computer from 1993, on index cards from 1962, index books from 1906, Historical Society has prior records. Mail turnaround time 5-7 days. Civil PAT goes back to 1993. Civil case lookup free online at http://wcca.wicourts.gov/index.xsl.

Criminal Name Search: Access: Phone, mail, online, in person. Both court and visitors may perform in person name searches. Search fee: $5.00 per name. Required to search: name, years to search, DOB. Criminal records computerized from 1993, on index cards from 1962, index books from 1906, Historical Society has prior records. Mail turnaround time 5-7 days. Criminal PAT goes back to 1993. Access criminal index free at http://wcca.wicourts.gov/index.xsl.

Register in Probate 1010 S 8th St, Rm 116, Manitowoc, WI 54220; 920-683-4016; fax: 920-683-5182; 8:30AM-4:30PM Tu-F; 8:30AM-5PM M (CST). *Probate.*

http://manitowoc-county.com/department/dept_home.asp?ID=20

General Information: Probate records free at http://wcca.wicourts.gov/index.xsl.

Marathon County

Circuit Court 500 Forest St, Wausau, WI 54403; 715-261-1300; criminal phone: 715-261-1270; civil phone: 715-261-1310; criminal fax: 715-261-1279; civil fax: 8AM-4:30PM; 8AM-4:30PM (CST). *Felony, Misdemeanor, Civil, Eviction, Small Claims, Family.* www.co.marathon.wi.us/dep_detail.asp?dep=9

General Information: Small claims phone is 261-1310; Traffic, 261-1270. Online identifiers in results same as on public terminal. No mental health or juvenile records released. Will fax documents to local or toll-free number. Court makes copy: $1.25 per page. Certification fee: $5.00 per Cert. Payee: Clerk of Court. Personal checks accepted. Major credit cards accepted via GPS. Prepayment required. Mail requests: SASE required.

Civil Name Search: Access: Mail, in person, online. Both court and visitors may perform in person name searches. Search fee: $5.00 per name. Civil records on computer from 1992, on index cards prior to 1992. Note: All requests must be in writing, using their form if possible. Mail turnaround time 1-3 days. Civil PAT goes back to 1991 for all non-confidential records. Civil case lookup free online at http://wcca.wicourts.gov/index.xsl. Online results show DOB most of time; however, sometimes DOB is month and year only on the index.

Criminal Name Search: Access: Mail, online, in person. Both court and visitors may perform in person name searches. Search fee: $5.00 per name. Required to search: name, years to search, DOB. Criminal records computerized from 1992, on index cards prior to 1992. Note: All requests must be in writing, using their form if possible. Mail turnaround time 1-3 days. Criminal PAT goes back to same as civil. Access criminal index free at http://wcca.wicourts.gov/index.xsl. Online results show DOB most of time; however, sometimes DOB is month and year only on the index.

Register in Probate 500 Forest St, Wausau, WI 54403; 715-261-1260; fax: 715-261-1269; 8AM-4:30PM (CST). *Probate.* www.co.marathon.wi.us

General Information: Probate records free at http://wcca.wicourts.gov/index.xsl.

Marinette County

Circuit Court 1926 Hall Ave, Marinette, WI 54143-1717; 715-732-7450; probate phone: 715-732-7475; fax: 715-732-7461; 8:30AM-4:30PM (CST). *Felony, Misdemeanor, Civil, Eviction, Small Claims.* www.wicourts.gov

General Information: Online identifiers in results same as on public terminal. No paternity records released. Will fax documents to local or toll free line. Court makes copy: $1.25 per page. Certification fee: $5.00. Payee: Clerk of Courts. Personal checks accepted, credit cards are not. Prepayment required. Mail requests: SASE required.

Civil Name Search: Access: Mail, in person, online. Both court and visitors may perform in person name searches. Search fee: $5.00 per name. Civil records on computer from 1989, index cards from 1980, index books from 1906, prior records at Historical Society. Mail turnaround time 2-3 days. Civil PAT goes back to 1994. Civil court records 1994 to present are free online at http://wcca.wicourts.gov/index.xsl. Online results show DOB most of time; however, sometimes DOB is month and year only on the index.

Criminal Name Search: Access: Mail, online, in person. Both court and visitors may perform in person name searches. Search fee: $5.00 per name. Required to search: name, years to search, DOB. Criminal records computerized from 1989, index cards from 1980, index books from 1906, prior records at Historical Society. Mail turnaround time 2-3 days. Criminal PAT goes back to same as civil. Access criminal index free at http://wcca.wicourts.gov/index.xsl. Online results show DOB most of time; however, sometimes DOB is month and year only on the index.

Register in Probate 1926 Hall Ave, Marinette, WI 54143-1717; 715-732-7475; fax: 715-732-7461; 8:30AM-4:30PM (CST). *Probate.* www.marinettecounty.com/departments/?department=7d789cb6839e

General Information: Probate records free at http://wcca.wicourts.gov/index.xsl.

Marquette County

Circuit Court 77 W Park St, Rm 200, Montello, WI 53949; 608-297-3100 x3005; fax: 608-297-9188; 8AM-4:30PM (CST). *Felony, Misdemeanor, Civil, Eviction, Small Claims.* www.co.marquette.wi.us/Departments/ClerkCourt/clerkcourt.html

General Information: Courthouse has the largest tree growing in the state. Online identifiers in results same as on public terminal. No adoption, juvenile, paternity, guardianship, mental or termination of parental right records released. Fee to fax out file $1.25 each. Will accept correspondence by fax only with prior authorization by court. Court makes copy: $1.25 per page. Certification fee: $5.00 per doc. Payee: Clerk of Circuit Court. Personal checks accepted, credit cards are not. Prepayment required. Mail requests: SASE requested.

Civil Name Search: Access: Phone, mail, online, in person. Both court and visitors may perform in person name searches. Search fee: $5.00 per name. Civil index on docket books from 1983, prior records at Historical Society; computerized back to 1996. Mail turnaround time 7-10 days. Civil PAT goes back to 1996. Civil case lookup free online at http://wcca.wicourts.gov/index.xsl. Online results show DOB most of time; however, sometimes DOB is month and year only on the index.

Criminal Name Search: Access: Mail, online, in person. Both court and visitors may perform in person name searches. Search fee: $5.00 per name. Required to search: name, years to search, DOB, full name. Criminal records indexed in books from 1900s, prior records at Historical Society; computerized back to 1996. Mail turnaround time 7-10 days. Criminal PAT goes back to same as civil. Access criminal index free at http://wcca.wicourts.gov/index.xsl.

Register in Probate 77 W Park St, PO Box 749, Montello, WI 53949; 608-297-3009; 8AM-4:30PM (CST). *Probate.*

General Information: Probate records free at http://wcca.wicourts.gov/index.xsl.

Menominee County

Circuit Court PO Box 279, W3269 Courthouse Ln, Keshena, WI 54135; 715-799-3313; fax: 715-799-1322; 8AM-4:30PM (CST). *Felony, Misdemeanor, Civil, Eviction, Small Claims.*

General Information: No juvenile, mental, adoption. Will fax documents to local or toll free line. Court makes copy: $1.25 per page. Certification fee: $5.00. Payee: Clerk of Court. Personal checks accepted, credit cards are not. Prepayment required. Mail requests: SASE helpful.

Civil Name Search: Access: Mail, in person, online. Only the court performs in person name searches; visitors may not. Search fee: $5.00 per name. Civil records are indexed by cards, kept in files since 1979, computerized since 1992. Older records are at the Historical Society. Mail turnaround time 3-4 days. Civil case lookup free online at http://wcca.wicourts.gov/index.xsl. Online results show DOB most of time; however, sometimes DOB is month and year only on the index.

Criminal Name Search: Access: Mail, online, in person, fax. Only the court performs in person name searches; visitors may not. Search fee: $5.00 per name. Required to search: name, years to search, DOB. Criminal records are indexed by cards, kept in files since 1979, computerized since 1992. Older records are at the Historical Society. Mail turnaround time 3-4 days. Access criminal index back to 1992 free at http://wcca.wicourts.gov/index.xsl.

Register in Probate 311 N Main St, Rm 203, Shawano, WI 54166; 715-526-8631; fax: 715-526-8622; 8AM-4:30PM (CST). *Probate.* www.co.shawano.wi.us

General Information: Menominee Probate is combined with Shawano County Probate and located there. Tribal probate records only in Keshena (Menominee Tribal Court); Non-tribal records are in Shawano County. Probate records free at http://wcca.wicourts.gov/index.xsl.

Milwaukee County

Circuit Court - Civil 901 N 9th St, Rm G-9, Milwaukee, WI 53233; 414-278-4120; fax: 414-223-1256; 8AM-5PM (CST). *Civil, Eviction, Small Claims.*

http://county.milwaukee.gov/AdministrativeServic11475.htm

General Information: Email questions to cticivil-milwaukee@wicourts.gov. Online identifiers in results same as on public terminal. No paternity records released unless post-judgment. Will not fax documents. Court makes copy: $1.25 per page. Self serve copy: $.25 per page.Copy of a court order is $5.00 per doc. Certification fee: $5.00. Payee: Milwaukee County Clerk of Circuit Court. Personal checks accepted, credit cards are not. Prepayment required. Mail requests: SASE required for civil.

Civil Name Search: Access: Mail, in person, online. Both court and visitors may perform in person name searches. Search fee: $5.00 per name. Required to search: name, years to search; also helpful-DOB. Civil records on computer from 1985, on microfiche from 1949, prior with County Historical Society. Mail turnaround time 1-2 weeks. Public use terminal has civil records back to 1985. Public terminal in Rm 117 of Safety Bldg. Civil case lookup free online at http://wcca.wicourts.gov/index.xsl.

Circuit Court - Criminal Division 821 W State St, Rm 117, Milwaukee, WI 53233; 414-278-4538; fax: 414-223-1262; 8AM-5PM (CST). *Felony, Misdemeanor, Traffic.*

http://county.milwaukee.gov/ClerkofCircuitCourtC210507.htm

General Information: The Milwaukee County Clerk of Circuit Court Criminal Division is responsible for felony, misdemeanor, and traffic cases and county ordinance cases, as well as jury trial requests from 19 municipal courts located in Milwaukee County. Online identifiers in results same as on public terminal. No sealed records released. Will fax out documents for additional $5.00 per doc. Court makes copy: $1.25 per page. Certification fee: $5.00 per doc. Payee: Clerk of Circuit Court. Personal checks accepted, credit cards are not. Prepayment required. However, ongoing approved accounts may be billed. Mail requests: SASE required.

Criminal Name Search: Access: Fax, mail, online, in person. Both court and visitors may perform in person name searches. Search fee: $5.00 per name per case if 0-1 case; $10.00 if 2-5 cases found; $15.00 if more than 5 cases found. Required to search: name, years to search, DOB. Criminal records computerized from 10/86, index books and cards prior. Note: Additional search time needed for older records in storage off-site. Ongoing accounts may be billed. Mail turnaround time 10 days. Public use terminal has crim records back to 1998 but some older records on system. Access criminal index free at http://wcca.wicourts.gov/index.xsl. Also, although not from this court, criminal case records on Milwaukee Municipal Court Case Information System database are free at http://query.municourt.milwaukee.gov/. Search ordinance and traffic violations by case or citation number, or by name.

Register in Probate 901 N 9th St, Rm 207, Milwaukee, WI 53233; 414-278-4444; fax: 414-223-1814; 8AM-4:30PM (CST). *Probate.*

General Information: Probate records free at http://wcca.wicourts.gov/index.xsl.

Monroe County

Circuit Court 112 S Court St, #203, Sparta, WI 54656-1764; 608-269-8745; criminal phone: 608-269-8962; civil phone: 608-269-8748; probate phone: 608-269-8701; fax: 608-269-8781; 8AM-4:30PM (CST). *Felony, Misdemeanor, Civil, Eviction, Small Claims.*

General Information: Online identifiers in results same as on public terminal. No paternity, medical or financial records released. Will fax documents $1.25 per page. Court makes copy: $1.25 per page. Certification fee: $5.00 per document plus copy fee. Payee: Clerk of Court. Local checks accepted. Pay via GPS at 888-604-7888. Prepayment required. Mail requests: SASE required.

Civil Name Search: Access: Fax, mail, online, in person. Both court and visitors may perform in person name searches. Search fee: $5.00 per name. Civil records on computer and cards. Mail turnaround time 1 week. Civil PAT goes back to 1993. Traffic records on public terminal go back to 1996. Civil case lookup free online at http://wcca.wicourts.gov/index.xsl. Online results show DOB most of time; however, sometimes DOB is month and year only on the index.

Criminal Name Search: Access: Fax, mail, online, in person. Both court and visitors may perform in person name searches. Search fee: $5.00 per name. Criminal records on computer and cards. Mail turnaround time 1 week. Criminal PAT goes back to same as civil. Traffic records on public terminal go back to 1996. Access criminal index free at http://wcca.wicourts.gov/index.xsl. Online results show DOB most of time; however, sometimes DOB is month and year only on the index.

Register in Probate 112 S Court, Rm 301, Sparta, WI 54656-1765; 608-269-8701; fax: 608-269-8950; 8AM-4:30PM (CST). *Probate.*

General Information: Probate records free at http://wcca.wicourts.gov/index.xsl.

Oconto County

Circuit Court 301 Washington St, Oconto, WI 54153; 920-834-6855; fax: 920-834-6867; 8AM-4PM (CST). *Felony, Misdemeanor, Civil, Small Claims.*

General Information: Online identifiers in results same as on public terminal. No juvenile or paternity records released. Will fax back documents, but not more than a few pages. Court makes copy: $1.25 per page civil; Regular copy $.25 each. Certification fee: $5.00 per doc. Payee: Oconto County Clerk of Court. Personal checks accepted, credit cards are not. Prepayment required. Mail requests: SASE required.

Civil Name Search: Access: Mail, in person, online. Both court and visitors may perform in person name searches. Search fee: $5.00 per name. Civil records on computer since 1994; prior records on index books from 1930s, Historical Society has earlier records. Mail turnaround time 1-2 days. Civil PAT goes back to 1994. Civil case lookup free online at http://wcca.wicourts.gov/index.xsl. Online results show DOB most of time; however, sometimes DOB is month and year only on the index.

Criminal Name Search: Access: Mail, online, in person. Both court and visitors may perform in person name searches. Search fee: $5.00 per name. Required to search: name, years to search, DOB. Criminal records on computer since 1994; prior records on index books from 1930s; Historical Society has earlier records. Mail turnaround time 1-2 days. Criminal PAT goes back to same as civil. Access criminal index free at http://wcca.wicourts.gov/index.xsl. Online results show DOB most of time; however, sometimes DOB is month and year only on the index.

Register in Probate 301 Washington St, Oconto, WI 54153; 920-834-6839; fax: 920-834-6867; 8AM-4PM (CST). *Probate.*

General Information: Probate records free at http://wcca.wicourts.gov/index.xsl.

Oneida County

Circuit Court PO Box 400, Rhinelander, WI 54501; 715-369-6120; criminal phone: 715-369-6123; civil phone: 715-369-6124; probate phone: 715-369-6159; fax: 715-369-6160; 8AM-4:30PM (CST). *Felony, Misdemeanor, Civil, Eviction, Small Claims.*

General Information: Online identifiers in results same as on public terminal. Will fax documents $1.25 per page. Court makes copy: $1.25 per page. Certification fee: $5.00 per document. Payee: Clerk of Court. Personal checks accepted, credit cards are not. Prepayment required. Mail requests: SASE not required.

Civil Name Search: Access: Mail, in person, online. Both court and visitors may perform in person name searches. Search fee: $5.00 per name. Civil records on computer from 1992, index cards from 1980, index books from 1900s. Mail turnaround time 1 week. Civil PAT goes back to 1992. Civil case lookup free online at http://wcca.wicourts.gov/index.xsl. Online results show DOB most of time; however, sometimes DOB is month and year only on the index.

Criminal Name Search: Access: Mail, online, in person. Both court and visitors may perform in person name searches. Search fee: $5.00 per name. Required to search: name, years to search, DOB. Criminal records computerized from 1992, index cards from 1980, index books from 1900s. Note: Post judgment records are released. Mail turnaround time 1 week. Criminal PAT goes back to same as civil. Access criminal index free at http://wcca.wicourts.gov/index.xsl. Online results show DOB most of time; however, sometimes DOB is month and year only on the index.

Register in Probate PO Box 400, 1 S. Oneida Ave, Rhinelander, WI 54501; 715-369-6159; 8AM-N, 1-4:30PM (CST). *Probate.*
General Information: Probate records free at http://wcca.wicourts.gov/index.xsl.

Outagamie County
Circuit Court 320 S Walnut St, Appleton, WI 54911; 920-832-5131; civil phone: 920-832-5131; fax: 920-832-5115; 8AM-4:30PM (CST). *Felony, Misdemeanor, Civil, Eviction, Small Claims.*
www.co.outagamie.wi.us/clerkcrts/
General Information: Records at 920-832-5130. Online identifiers in results same as on public terminal. No adoption or juvenile records released. Will fax documents $1.25 per page. Court makes copy: $1.25 per page. Self serve copy: same. Certification fee: $5.00 per document plus copy fee. Payee: Clerk of Court. Personal checks, Visa/MC accepted. Prepayment required. Mail requests: SASE required.
Civil Name Search: Access: In person, online, mail. Visitors must perform in person searches themselves. Search fee: $5.00. Civil records on computer from 1983, index books from 1901, some records on microfiche. Mail turnaround time 2-3 days. Civil PAT goes back to 10/1989. Civil case lookup free online at http://wcca.wicourts.gov/index.xsl. Online results show DOB most of time; however, sometimes DOB is month and year only on the index.
Criminal Name Search: Access: Mail, in person, online. Both court and visitors may perform in person name searches. Search fee: $5.00 per name. Required to search: name, years to search, DOB. Criminal records computerized from 10/87, index cards from 1983, index books from 1901, some records on microfiche. Mail turnaround time 2-3 days. Criminal PAT goes back to 1990. Criminal court records free at http://wcca.wicourts.gov/index.xsl. Online results show DOB most of time; however, sometimes DOB is month and year only on the index.
Register in Probate 320 S Walnut St, Appleton, WI 54911; 920-832-5601; fax: 920-832-5115; 8AM-N, 1-5PM (CST). *Probate.*
General Information: Probate records free at http://wcca.wicourts.gov/index.xsl.

Ozaukee County
Circuit Court 1201 S Spring St, Port Washington, WI 53074; 262-284-8409; fax: 262-284-8491; 8AM-5PM (CST). *Felony, Misdemeanor, Civil, Eviction, Small Claims.*
www.co.ozaukee.wi.us/ClerkCourts/Index.htm
General Information: Online identifiers in results same as on public terminal. No paternity records released. Will fax documents $1.25 per page. Court makes copy: $1.25 per page. Self serve copy: same. Certification fee: $5.00. Payee: Clerk of Court. Business checks or in state personal checks accepted. Credit cards accepted. Prepayment required. Mail requests: SASE required.
Civil Name Search: Access: Mail, in person, online. Both court and visitors may perform in person name searches. Search fee: $5.00 per name. Civil records on computer from 1991, index cards from late 1950s. Mail turnaround time 1 week. Civil PAT goes back to 1991. Civil case lookup free online at http://wcca.wicourts.gov/index.xsl. Access is also with the use of county "Remote Access". This data is for inquiries only and includes civil, family, and traffic courts. For info, contact the Technology Resources Dept. at 262-284-8309.
Criminal Name Search: Access: Mail, online, in person. Both court and visitors may perform in person name searches. Search fee: $5.00 per name. Required to search: name, years to search, DOB. Criminal records computerized from 1989. Mail turnaround time 1 week. Criminal PAT goes back to 1987. Access criminal index free at http://wcca.wicourts.gov/index.xsl. Online results show DOB most of time; however, sometimes DOB is month and year only on the index.
Register in Probate PO Box 994, 1201 S Spring St, Port Washington, WI 53074; 262-284-8370; fax: 262-284-8491; 8:30AM-5PM (CST). *Probate.*
General Information: Probate records free at http://wcca.wicourts.gov/index.xsl.

Pepin County
Circuit Court PO Box 39, 740 7th Ave W, Durand, WI 54736; 715-672-8861; 8:30AM-N, 12:30-4:30PM (CST). *Felony, Misdemeanor, Civil, Eviction, Small Claims.*
www.co.pepin.wi.us/cogovt/circuit_court.htm
General Information: No minor or financial divorce records released. Will fax documents to local or toll free line. Court makes copy: $1.25 per page. Certification fee: $5.00 per document plus copy fee. Payee: Clerk of Court.

Personal checks accepted. Credit card payments can be made through GPS, 888-604-7888. Prepayment required. Mail requests: SASE required.
Civil Name Search: Access: Mail, in person, online. Both court and visitors may perform in person name searches. Search fee: $5.00 per name. Civil cases indexed by plaintiff. Civil records on computer from 1995, index books from 1900s. Mail turnaround time 1 week. Civil PAT goes back to 1995. PAT can include middle initial if on compliant. Civil case lookup free online at http://wcca.wicourts.gov/index.xsl. Online results show DOB most of time; however, sometimes DOB is month and year only on the index.
Criminal Name Search: Access: Mail, online, in person. Both court and visitors may perform in person name searches. Search fee: $5.00 per name. Required to search: name, years to search, DOB. Criminal records computerized from 1995, index books from 1900s. Mail turnaround time 1 week. Criminal PAT goes back to same as civil. PAT can include middle initial if on compliant. Access criminal index free at http://wcca.wicourts.gov/index.xsl. Online results show DOB and middle initial most of time; however, sometimes DOB is month and year only on the index.
Register in Probate PO Box 39, 740 7th Ave W, Durand, WI 54736; 715-672-8859/715-672-8868; fax: 715-672-8521; 8:30AM-N, 12:30PM-4:30PM (CST). *Probate.*
General Information: Probate records free at http://wcca.wicourts.gov/index.xsl.

Pierce County
Circuit Court PO Box 129, 414 W Main St, Ellsworth, WI 54011; 715-273-3531 x6400; fax: 715-273-6855; 8AM-5PM (CST). *Felony, Misdemeanor, Civil, Eviction, Small Claims, Family.*
www.co.pierce.wi.us/Circuit%20Court/Circuit_Court_Main.html
General Information: Online identifiers in results same as on public terminal. No sealed records released. Will fax documents $1.25 per page. Court makes copy: $1.25 per page. Certification fee: $5.00. Payee: Clerk of Court. Personal checks accepted. Major credit cards accepted. Prepayment required. Mail requests: SASE required.
Civil Name Search: Access: Mail, in person, online. Both court and visitors may perform in person name searches. Search fee: $5.00 per name per type of case. Civil records are retained 20 years; on computer back to 1994. Archives in River Falls. Mail turnaround time 2-3 days. Civil PAT goes back to 1994. Civil case lookup free online at http://wcca.wicourts.gov/index.xsl. Online results show DOB most of time; however, sometimes DOB is month and year only on the index.
Criminal Name Search: Access: Mail, online, in person. Both court and visitors may perform in person name searches. Search fee: $5.00 per name. Required to search: name, years to search, DOB. Felony records are retained 50-75 years; misdemeanors for 20. Criminal records computerized from 1994. Archives in River Falls. Mail turnaround time 2-3 days. Criminal PAT goes back to same as civil. Access criminal index free at http://wcca.wicourts.gov/index.xsl. Online results show DOB most of time; however, sometimes DOB is month and year only on the index.
Register in Probate 414 W Main, PO Box 97, Ellsworth, WI 54011; 715-273-6752; fax: 715-273-6794; 8AM-5PM (CST). *Probate.*
General Information: Probate records free at http://wicourts.gov. Also at this court are guardianship, mental, adoption and juvenile records.

Polk County
Circuit Court 1005 W Main St, Ste 300, Balsam Lake, WI 54810; 715-485-9299; fax: 715-485-9262; 8:30AM-4:30PM (window closes at 4:25PM) (CST). *Felony, Misdemeanor, Civil, Eviction, Small Claims.*
General Information: Online identifiers in results same as on public terminal. No juvenile, paternity or confidential records released. Will fax documents $1.25 per page. Court makes copy: $1.25 per page. Certification fee: $5.00 per doc. Payee: Clerk of Court. Personal checks accepted, credit cards are not. Prepayment required. Mail requests: SASE required.
Civil Name Search: Access: Mail, in person, online. Both court and visitors may perform in person name searches. Search fee: $5.00 per name per record/file. Civil records go back to 1970s; on computer back to 1992. Mail turnaround time 2-3 days. Civil PAT goes back to 9/1992. Terminal shows DOB month and year only. Civil case lookup free online at http://wcca.wicourts.gov/index.xsl. Online results show DOB most of time; however, sometimes DOB is month and year only on the index.
Criminal Name Search: Access: Mail, online, in person. Both court and visitors may perform in person name searches. Search fee: $5.00 per name. Fee is per record/file. Required to search: name, years to search, DOB. Criminal records go back to 1970s; on computer back to 1992. Mail turnaround time 2-3 days. Criminal PAT goes back to same as civil. Terminal shows DOB month and year only. Access criminal index free at http://wcca.wicourts.gov/index.xsl. Online results show DOB most of time; however, sometimes DOB is month and year only on the index.

Register in Probate 1005 W Main, #500, Balsam Lake, WI 54810; 715-485-9238; fax: 715-485-9275; 8:30AM-4:30PM (CST). *Probate.*
www.co.polk.wi.us
General Information: Probate records free at http://wcca.wicourts.gov/index.xsl. Records available are from 1992 to present.

Portage County

Circuit Court (Branches 1, 2 & 3) 1516 Church St, Stevens Point, WI 54481; 715-346-1364; fax: 715-346-1236; 7:30AM-4:30PM (CST). *Felony, Misdemeanor, Civil, Eviction, Small Claims.*
www.co.portage.wi.us/
General Information: Online identifiers in results same as on public terminal. No expunged records released. Will fax documents to local or toll free line for $5.00 fee. Court makes copy: $1.25 per page. Certification fee: $5.00 per doc. Payee: Clerk of Court. Business checks accepted. Credit cards accepted. Prepayment required. Mail requests: SASE required.
Civil Name Search: Access: Mail, in person, online. Both court and visitors may perform in person name searches. Search fee: $5.00 per name. Civil cases indexed by number, then defendant, plaintiff. Civil records on computer from 6/91, index cards from 1980, index books from 1900s. Mail turnaround time 10 working days. Civil PAT goes back to 1990. Internet access is upon approval. Request in writing to Data Processing Dept, 1462 Strong Ave, Stevens Point 54481. Explain purpose of record requests. Online results show DOB most of time; however, sometimes DOB is month and year only on the index.
Criminal Name Search: Access: Mail, in person, online. Both court and visitors may perform in person name searches. Search fee: $5.00 per name. Required to search: name, years to search, address, DOB, SSN, signed release. Criminal records computerized from 6/91, index cards from 1980, index books from 1900s. Mail turnaround time 10 working days. Criminal PAT goes back to same as civil. Internet access is upon approval. Request in writing to Data Processing Dept, 1462 Strong Ave, Stevens Point 54481. Explain purpose of record requests. Online results show DOB most of time; however, sometimes DOB is month and year only on the index.

Register in Probate 1516 Church St, Stevens Point, WI 54481; 715-346-1362; fax: 715-346-1236; 7:30AM-4:30PM (CST). *Probate.*
General Information: Probate records free at http://wcca.wicourts.gov/index.xsl.

Price County

Circuit Court Courthouse, 126 Cherry St, Phillips, WI 54555; 715-339-2353; fax: 715-339-5114; 8AM-N, 1-4:30PM (CST). *Felony, Misdemeanor, Civil, Eviction, Small Claims, Traffic, Family.*
www.co.price.wi.us/
General Information: Online identifiers in results same as on public terminal. No confidential records per statute or order released. Will fax documents to local or toll free line. Court makes copy: $1.25 per page. Self serve copy: $.25 per page. Certification fee: $5.00 per document. Payee: Clerk of Circuit Court. Personal checks accepted, credit cards are not. Prepayment required. Mail requests: SASE required.
Civil Name Search: Access: Mail, in person, online. Both court and visitors may perform in person name searches. Search fee: $5.00 per name. Civil records on computer from 1997, prior on index books. Mail turnaround time 1-2 days. Civil PAT goes back to 1993. Civil case lookup free online at http://wcca.wicourts.gov/index.xsl. Online results show DOB most of time; however, sometimes DOB is month and year only on the index.
Criminal Name Search: Access: Mail, online, in person. Both court and visitors may perform in person name searches. Search fee: $5.00 per name. Required to search: name, years to search, DOB. Criminal records computerized from 1997, prior on index books. Mail turnaround time 1-2 days. Criminal PAT goes back to same as civil. Access criminal index free at http://wcca.wicourts.gov/index.xsl.

Register in Probate 126 Cherry St, Courthouse Rm 209, Phillips, WI 54555; 715-339-3078; fax: 715-339-3079; 8AM-4:30PM (CST). *Probate.*
General Information: Probate records free at http://wcca.wicourts.gov/index.xsl (information available is case, party names and addresses, information on judgments and court record events.

Racine County

Circuit Court 730 Wisconsin Ave, Racine, WI 53403; 262-636-3333; probate phone: 262-636-3137; fax: 262-636-3341; 8AM-5PM (CST). *Felony, Misdemeanor, Civil, Eviction, Small Claims, Probate, Family.*
www.racineco.com/courts/index.aspx
General Information: Probate fax- 262-636-3870. Online identifiers in results same as on public terminal. No adoption, juvenile, paternity or mental commitment records released. Will fax documents to local or toll free line. Court makes copy: $1.25 per page. Self serve copy: same. Certification

fee: $5.00 per document plus copy fee. Payee: Clerk of Circuit Court. Personal checks accepted. Major credit cards accepted in person, surcharge may apply. Prepayment required. Mail requests: SASE required.
Civil Name Search: Access: Mail, in person, online. Both court and visitors may perform in person name searches. Search fee: $5.00 per name. Required to search: name, years to search, DOB. Civil records on computer from 1990, index cards from 1980; records kept no long than 20 years. Mail turnaround time 2-3 weeks. Civil PAT goes back to 1994. Public terminal on the 8th Fl. Civil case lookup free online at http://wcca.wicourts.gov/index.xsl. Online results show DOB most of time; however, sometimes DOB is month and year only on the index.
Criminal Name Search: Access: Mail, online, in person. Both court and visitors may perform in person name searches. Search fee: $5.00 per name. Required to search: name, years to search, DOB. Criminal records computerized from 1990, index cards from 1970, archives prior to 1970. Mail turnaround time 2-3 weeks. Criminal PAT goes back to 1994. Public terminal on 8th Fl. Access criminal index free at http://wcca.wicourts.gov/index.xsl. Online results show DOB most of time; however, sometimes DOB is month and year only on the index.

Register in Probate 730 Wisconsin Ave, Racine, WI 53403; 262-636-3137; fax: 262-636-3870; 8AM-5PM (CST). *Probate.*
General Information: Probate records free at http://wcca.wicourts.gov/index.xsl.

Richland County

Circuit Court PO Box 655, 181 W Seminary St, Richland Center, WI 53581; 608-647-3956; fax: 608-647-3911; 8:30AM-4:30PM (CST). *Felony, Misdemeanor, Civil, Eviction, Small Claims.*
http://justice.co.richland.wi.us/
General Information: The search fee includes search of both civil and criminal indexes. Online identifiers in results same as on public terminal. No juvenile or paternity records released. Will fax documents to local or toll-free number. Court makes copy: $1.25 per page. Certification fee: $5.00 per doc. Payee: Clerk of Circuit Court. No personal out-of-state checks accepted. No credit cards accepted - may accept in 2009. Prepayment required. Mail requests: SASE required.
Civil Name Search: Access: Mail, in person, online. Both court and visitors may perform in person name searches. Search fee: $5.00 per name. Civil index on cards from 1982, index books from 1972, archives prior to 1972, on computer back to 1993. Mail turnaround time within 2 days unless if older record. Civil PAT goes back to 1993. Civil case lookup free online at http://wcca.wicourts.gov/index.xsl. Online results show DOB most of time; however, sometimes DOB is month and year only on the index.
Criminal Name Search: Access: Mail, online, in person. Both court and visitors may perform in person name searches. Search fee: $5.00 per name. Required to search: name, years to search, DOB. Criminal records indexed on cards from 1982, index books from 1972, archives prior to 1972, on computer back t0 1993. Mail turnaround time 1 week. Criminal PAT goes back to same as civil. Access criminal index free at http://wcca.wicourts.gov/index.xsl. Online results show DOB most of time; however, sometimes DOB is month and year only on the index.

Register in Probate PO Box 427, 181 W Seminary St, Richland Center, WI 53581; 608-647-2626; fax: 608-647-5747; 8:30AM-N, 1-4:30PM (CST). *Probate.*
http://justice.co.richland.wi.us/
General Information: Probate records free at http://wcca.wicourts.gov/index.xsl. This court also holds guardianship, juvenile, mental and adoption records.

Rock County

Circuit Court 51 S Main, Janesville, WI 53545; 608-743-2200; criminal phone: 608-743-2211; civil phone: 608-743-2210; fax: 608-743-2223; 8AM-5PM (CST). *Felony, Misdemeanor, Civil, Eviction, Small Claims.*
www.co.rock.wi.us/index.php/departments/departments-a-f/courts
General Information: Online identifiers in results same as on public terminal. No juvenile, paternity or sealed records released. Will fax documents to local or toll-free number. Court makes copy: $1.25 per page. Certification fee: $5.00. Payee: Clerk of Court. Personal checks accepted. Major credit cards accepted. Prepayment required. Mail requests: SASE required.
Civil Name Search: Access: Mail, in person, online. Both court and visitors may perform in person name searches. Search fee: $5.00 per name. Civil records on computer from 6/93, on index cards from 6/91, index books from 1940, archives prior to 1940. Mail turnaround time 2-3 days. Civil PAT goes back to 1993. Civil case lookup free online at http://wcca.wicourts.gov/index.xsl. Online results show DOB most of time; however, sometimes DOB is month and year only on the index.
Criminal Name Search: Access: Mail, online, in person. Both court and visitors may perform in person name searches. Search fee: $5.00 per name.

Required to search: name, years to search, DOB. Criminal records computerized from 6/93, on index cards from 6/91, index books from 1940, archives prior to 1940. Mail turnaround time 2-3 days. Criminal PAT goes back to same as civil. Access criminal index free at http://wcca.wicourts.gov/index.xsl. Online results show DOB most of time; however, sometimes DOB is month and year only on the index.

Register in Probate 51 S Main, Janesville, WI 53545; 608-757-5635; fax: 608-757-5769; 8AM-5PM (CST). *Probate.*

General Information: Probate records free at http://wcca.wicourts.gov/index.xsl.

Rusk County

Circuit Court 311 Miner Ave E, #L350, Attn: Clerk of Circuit Court, Ladysmith, WI 54848; 715-532-2108; probate phone: 715-532-2147; fax: 715-532-2110; 8AM-4:30PM (CST). *Felony, Misdemeanor, Civil, Small Claims.*

General Information: Probate fax- 715-532-2266 Online identifiers in results same as on public terminal. No juvenile or paternity records released. Will fax documents $1.25 per page. Court makes copy: $1.25 per page. Certification fee: $5.00 per document plus copy fee. Payee: Clerk of Court. Personal checks accepted. Credit card payments accepted via GPS. Prepayment required. Mail requests: SASE required.

Civil Name Search: Access: Mail, phone, fax, in person, online. Both court and visitors may perform in person name searches. Search fee: $5.00 per name. Civil records on computer from 1992, on index cards from 1978, index books from 1901. Note: Phone requests are accepted if the case number is known. Mail turnaround time 5 days. Public use terminal has civil records back to 1992. Civil case lookup free online at http://wcca.wicourts.gov/index.xsl. Online results show DOB most of time; however, sometimes DOB is month and year only on the index.

Criminal Name Search: Access: Mail, online, in person, online. Both court and visitors may perform in person name searches. Search fee: $5.00 per name, no charge for persons performing their own search. Required to search: name, years to search, DOB. Criminal records computerized from 1992, on index cards from 1978, index books from 1901. Note: Phone requests are accepted if the case number is known. Mail turnaround time 5 days. Access criminal index free at http://wcca.wicourts.gov/index.xsl. Online results show DOB most of time; however, sometimes DOB is month and year only on the index.

Register in Probate 311 E Miner Ave, #C-330, Ladysmith, WI 54848; 715-532-2147; fax: 715-532-2266; 8AM-4:30PM (CST). *Probate.*

General Information: Probate records free at http://wcca.wicourts.gov/index.xsl.

Sauk County

Circuit Court 515 Oak St, Baraboo, WI 53913; 608-355-3287; fax: 608-355-3480; 8AM-4:30PM (CST). *Felony, Misdemeanor, Civil, Eviction, Small Claims.*

General Information: Online identifiers in results same as on public terminal. No paternity, juvenile records released. Fee to fax out file $5.28 if one page, $6.33 if 2 pages, $7.39 if 3 pages, $8.44 if 4 pages, $9.50 if 5 pages; call for higher amts. Court makes copy: $1.25 per page. Certification fee: $5.00 per doc. Payee: Clerk of Court. Personal checks, Visa/MC accepted. Prepayment required. Mail requests: SASE required.

Civil Name Search: Access: Mail, in person, online. Both court and visitors may perform in person name searches. Search fee: $5.00 per name per index. Civil records on computer from 1990, index cards from 1980, index books from 1967. Mail turnaround time 2-3 days. Civil PAT goes back to 1993. Civil case lookup free online at http://wcca.wicourts.gov/index.xsl. Online results show DOB most of time; however, sometimes DOB is month and year only on the index.

Criminal Name Search: Access: Mail, online, in person. Both court and visitors may perform in person name searches. Search fee: $5.00 per name per index. Criminal records computerized from 1990, index cards from 1980, index books from 1967. Mail turnaround time 2-3 days. Criminal PAT goes back to same as civil. Access criminal index free at http://wcca.wicourts.gov/index.xsl. Online results show DOB most of time; however, sometimes DOB is month and year only on the index.

Register in Probate 515 Oak St, Baraboo, WI 53913; 608-355-3226; fax: 608-355-4436; 8AM-4:30PM (CST). *Probate.*
www.co.sauk.wi.us/registerinprobatepage/about-register-probate

General Information: The Probate Register handles the administration of all informal probate proceedings, testate and intestate. Probate records free at http://wcca.wicourts.gov/index.xsl.

Sawyer County

Circuit Court 10610 Main Street, Ste 74, Hayward, WI 54843; 715-634-4887; fax: 715-638-3297; 8AM-4PM (CST). *Felony, Misdemeanor, Civil, Eviction, Small Claims.* www.sawyercountygov.org/

General Information: Online identifiers in results same as on public terminal. Will fax documents $1.00 plus $.25 per page. Court makes copy: $1.25 per page. Certification fee: $5.00 per document. Payee: Clerk of Court. Personal checks accepted, credit cards are not. Prepayment required. Mail requests: SASE required.

Civil Name Search: Access: Mail, in person, online. Both court and visitors may perform in person name searches. Search fee: $5.00 per name. Civil index on cards from 7/85, prior on books. Mail turnaround time 3 days. Civil PAT goes back to 4/1993. Civil case lookup free online at http://wcca.wicourts.gov/index.xsl. Online results show DOB most of time; however, sometimes DOB is month and year only on the index.

Criminal Name Search: Access: Mail, online, in person. Both court and visitors may perform in person name searches. Search fee: $5.00 per name. Criminal records indexed on cards from 7/85, prior on books. Mail turnaround time 3 days. Criminal PAT goes back to same as civil. DOB shown in results is month and year only. Access criminal index free at http://wcca.wicourts.gov/index.xsl. Online results show DOB most of time; however, sometimes DOB is month and year only on the index.

Register in Probate PO Box 447, 10610 Main St, Hayward, WI 54843; 715-634-7519; fax: 715-638-3297; 8AM-4PM (CST). *Probate.*

General Information: Probate records free at http://wcca.wicourts.gov/index.xsl.

Shawano County

Circuit Court 311 N Main, Rm 206, Shawano, WI 54166; 715-526-9347; probate phone: 715-526-8631; fax: 715-526-4915; 8AM-4:30PM (CST). *Felony, Misdemeanor, Civil, Eviction, Small Claims.*
www.co.shawano.wi.us

General Information: Online identifiers in results same as on public terminal. No juvenile, closed files or mental records released. Will fax documents $1.25 per page, add $2.50 for long distance. Court makes copy: $1.25 per page. Certification fee: $5.00. Payee: Clerk of Court. Personal checks accepted, credit cards are not. Prepayment required. Mail requests: SASE required.

Civil Name Search: Access: Fax, mail, online, in person. Both court and visitors may perform in person name searches. Search fee: $5.00 per name. Civil records on computer from 1993, on index books from 1930s, prior in archives. Mail turnaround time 10-20 days. Civil PAT goes back to 3/1993. Results show only month and year of birth. Civil case lookup free online at http://wcca.wicourts.gov/index.xsl. Online results show DOB most of time; however, sometimes DOB is month and year only on the index.

Criminal Name Search: Access: Fax, mail, online, in person. Both court and visitors may perform in person name searches. Search fee: $5.00 per name. Required to search: name, years to search, DOB. Criminal records computerized from 1993, on index books from 1930s, prior in archives. Mail turnaround time 10-20 days. Criminal PAT goes back to same as civil. Access criminal index free at http://wcca.wicourts.gov/index.xsl. Online results show DOB most of time; however, sometimes DOB is month and year only on the index.

Register in Probate 311 N Main, Rm 203, Shawano, WI 54166; 715-526-8631; fax: 715-526-8622; 8AM-4:30PM (CST). *Probate.*
www.co.shawano.wi.us

General Information: This is also the location of Menominee County Probate. Tribal probate records are not housed here; tribal records are at Keshena (Menominee Tribal Court). Also, probate records free at http://wcca.wicourts.gov/index.xsl.

Sheboygan County

Circuit Court 615 N 6th St, Sheboygan, WI 53081; 920-459-3068; fax: 920-459-3921; 8AM-5PM (CST). *Felony, Misdemeanor, Civil, Eviction, Small Claims, Family, Traffic, Ordinance.*
www.co.sheboygan.wi.us/html/d_crtclrk.html

General Information: Online identifiers in results same as on public terminal. No juvenile or pre-adjudication paternity records released. Will fax documents for $3.00 prepaid. Court makes copy: $1.25 per page. Certification fee: $5.00 per document. Payee: Clerk of Circuit Court. Personal checks accepted, credit cards are not. Prepayment required. Mail requests: SASE required.

Civil Name Search: Access: Mail, in person, online. Both court and visitors may perform in person name searches. Search fee: $5.00 per case. Required to search: name, years to search; also helpful: address. Civil records on computer since 1992; prior records on index cards from 1960, archives prior to 1971. Mail turnaround time 2-3 days. Civil PAT goes back to 1992. Civil case lookup free online at http://wcca.wicourts.gov/index.xsl. Online results show DOB month and year only on the index.

Criminal Name Search: Access: Mail, online, in person. Both court and visitors may perform in person name searches. Search fee: $5.00 per case. Required to search: name, years to search, DOB; also helpful: address. Criminal records on computer since 1992; prior records on index cards from

1970, index books from 1850s, archives prior to 1971. Mail turnaround time 2-3 days. Criminal PAT goes back to 1992. Access statewide criminal index free at http://wcca.wicourts.gov/index.xsl. Online results show full DOB.

Register in Probate 615 N 6th St, Sheboygan, WI 53081; 920-459-3050, 459-3051; fax: 920-459-0541; 8AM-5PM (CST). *Probate.*
General Information: There is a $4.00 search fee. Probate records free at http://wcca.wicourts.gov/index.xsl.

St. Croix County

Circuit Court 1101 Carmichael Rd, Hudson, WI 54016; 715-386-4630; criminal phone: 715-386-4631; civil phone: 715-386-4633; probate phone: 715-386-4619; fax: 715-381-4396; 8AM-5PM (CST). *Felony, Misdemeanor, Civil, Eviction, Small Claims.*
General Information: Online identifiers in results same as on public terminal. No juvenile forfeitures, paternity, some case specific documents or sealed records released. Will fax documents $1.25 per page. Court makes copy: $1.25 per page. Certification fee: $5.00. Payee: Clerk of Court. Personal checks accepted. Major credit cards accepted. Prepayment required. Mail requests: SASE required.
Civil Name Search: Access: Mail, in person, online. Both court and visitors may perform in person name searches. Search fee: $5.00 per name. Civil records on computer from 10/92, on index cards from 1982, index books from 1965. Mail turnaround time within 10 days. Civil PAT goes back to 1992. Civil case lookup free online at http://wcca.wicourts.gov/index.xsl. Online results show DOB most of time; however DOB is only month and year on the index.
Criminal Name Search: Access: Mail, online, in person. Both court and visitors may perform in person name searches. Search fee: $5.00 per name. Required to search: name, years to search, DOB. Criminal records computerized from 10/92, on index cards from 1982, index books from 1900s. Mail turnaround time 5-10 days. Criminal PAT goes back to same as civil. Access criminal index free at http://wcca.wicourts.gov/index.xsl. Online results show DOB most of time; however, sometimes DOB is month and year only on the index.

Register in Probate 1101 Carmichael Rd, Rm 2242, Hudson, WI 54016; 715-386-4619; fax: 715-381-4318; 8AM-5PM (CST). *Probate.*
General Information: Probate records free at http://wcca.wicourts.gov/index.xsl.

Taylor County

Circuit Court 224 S 2nd St, Medford, WI 54451-1811; 715-748-1425; probate phone: 715-748-1435; fax: 715-748-2465; 8:30AM-4:30PM (CST). *Felony, Misdemeanor, Civil, Eviction, Small Claims, Ordinance, Family, Traffic.*
www.co.taylor.wi.us/departments/circuit/circuit.html
General Information: Online identifiers in results same as on public terminal. No sealed records released. Will fax documents for 42.00 per page. Court makes copy: $1.25 per page. Certification fee: $5.00 per doc plus copy fee. Payee: Clerk of Circuit Court. Personal checks, Visa/MC accepted. Prepayment required. Mail requests: SASE required.
Civil Name Search: Access: Mail, in person, online. Both court and visitors may perform in person name searches. Search fee: $5.00 per name. Civil records on computer from 1989; prior records index books from 1917. Mail turnaround time 1-2 days. Civil PAT goes back to 1989. Civil case lookup free online at http://wcca.wicourts.gov/index.xsl. Online results show DOB most of time; however, sometimes DOB is month and year only on the index.
Criminal Name Search: Access: Mail, online, in person. Both court and visitors may perform in person name searches. Search fee: $5.00 per name. Required to search: name, years to search, DOB. Criminal records computerized from 1989; prior records index books from 1917. Mail turnaround time 1-2 days. Criminal PAT goes back to same as civil. Access criminal index free at http://wcca.wicourts.gov/index.xsl. Online results show DOB most of time; however, sometimes DOB is month and year only on the index.

Register in Probate 224 S 2nd, Medford, WI 54451; 715-748-1435; fax: 715-748-1524; 8:30AM-4:30PM (CST). *Probate.*
www.co.taylor.wi.us
General Information: Probate records free at http://wcca.wicourts.gov/index.xsl.

Trempealeau County

Circuit Court PO Box 67, 36245 Main St, Whitehall, WI 54773; 715-538-2311; fax: 715-538-4400; 8AM-4:30PM (CST). *Felony, Misdemeanor, Civil, Eviction, Small Claims.*
www.tremplocounty.com/clerkofcourt/default.htm
General Information: Online identifiers in results same as on public terminal. No juvenile, paternity or child support records released. Will fax documents $2.00 per page. Court makes copy: $1.25 per page. Certification

fee: $5.00 per doc. Payee: Clerk of Circuit Court. Personal checks accepted via GPS, 888-604-7888. No credit cards accepted. Prepayment required. Mail requests: SASE required.
Civil Name Search: Access: Mail, in person, online. Both court and visitors may perform in person name searches. Search fee: $5.00 per name. Civil records on computer from 1993, on index cards from 1987, index books from 1940, archives prior to 1940. Mail turnaround time 2-3 days. Civil PAT goes back to 1994. Civil case lookup free online at http://wcca.wicourts.gov/index.xsl. Online results show DOB most of time; however, sometimes DOB is month and year only on the index.
Criminal Name Search: Access: Mail, online, in person. Both court and visitors may perform in person name searches. Search fee: $5.00 per name. Required to search: name, years to search, DOB. Criminal records computerized from 1993, on index cards from 1987, index books from 1940, archives prior to 1940. Note: All mail requests must be in writing. Mail turnaround time 2-3 days. Criminal PAT goes back to same as civil. Access criminal index free at http://wcca.wicourts.gov/index.xsl. Online results show DOB most of time; however, sometimes DOB is month and year only on the index.

Register in Probate 36245 Main St, PO Box 67, Whitehall, WI 54773; 715-538-2311 X238; fax: 715-538-4123; 8AM-4:30PM (CST). *Probate.*
www.tremplocounty.com/clerkofcourt/default.htm
General Information: Probate records free at http://wcca.wicourts.gov/index.xsl.

Vernon County

Circuit Court PO Box 426, Viroqua, WI 54665; 608-637-5340; criminal phone: 608-637-5338; civil phone: 608-637-5338; fax: 608-637-5554; 8:30AM-4:30PM (CST). *Felony, Misdemeanor, Civil, Eviction, Small Claims.*
www.vernoncounty.org/courts/index.htm
General Information: Online identifiers in results same as on public terminal. No paternity or juvenile records released. Will fax documents. Court makes copy: $1.25 per page. Self serve copy: same. Certification fee: $5.00 per document plus copy fee. Payee: Clerk of Court. Personal checks accepted. Major credit cards accepted. Prepayment required. Will bill to attorneys credit agencies. Mail requests: SASE required.
Civil Name Search: Access: Phone, fax, mail, online, in person. Both court and visitors may perform in person name searches. Search fee: $5.00 per name. Required to search: name, years to search, DOB. Civil records on computer back to 1993; on index books & cards 1950 to 1992. Mail turnaround time 2-3 days. Civil PAT goes back to 1993. Civil case lookup free online at http://wcca.wicourts.gov/index.xsl. Online results show DOB most of time; however, sometimes DOB is month and year only on the index.
Criminal Name Search: Access: Phone, fax, mail, online, in person. Both court and visitors may perform in person name searches. Search fee: $5.00 per name. Required to search: name, years to search; also helpful: DOB. Criminal records computerized from 1993; on index books & cards 1950 to 1992. Mail turnaround time 2-3 days. Criminal PAT goes back to same as civil. Access criminal index free at http://wcca.wicourts.gov/index.xsl. Online results show DOB most of time; however, sometimes DOB is month and year only on the index.

Register in Probate PO Box 448, 400 Courthouse Sq, Viroqua, WI 54665; 608-637-5347; fax: 608-637-5554; 8:30AM-4:30PM (CST). *Probate.*
www.vernoncounty.org/courts/RIP/regInProb.htm
General Information: Probate records free at http://wcca.wicourts.gov/index.xsl.

Vilas County

Circuit Court 330 Court St, Eagle River, WI 54521; 715-479-3632; criminal phone: 715-479-3633; fax: 715-479-3740; 8AM-4PM (CST). *Felony, Misdemeanor, Civil, Eviction, Small Claims.*
http://co.vilas.wi.us/
General Information: Online identifiers in results same as on public terminal. No paternity records released. Fee to fax out file $1.25 per page. Court makes copy: $1.25 per page. Self serve copy: $.25 per page. Certification fee: $5.00. Payee: Clerk of Circuit Court. Personal checks accepted, credit cards are not. Prepayment required. Mail requests: SASE required.
Civil Name Search: Access: Mail, in person, online. Both court and visitors may perform in person name searches. Search fee: $5.00 per name. Civil records on computer back to 1978, index cards from 1978, index books from 1900s. Mail turnaround time 2 weeks. Civil PAT goes back to 1992. Civil case lookup free online at http://wcca.wicourts.gov/index.xsl. Online results show DOB most of time; however, sometimes DOB is month and year only on the index.
Criminal Name Search: Access: Mail, online, in person. Both court and visitors may perform in person name searches. Search fee: $5.00 per name.

Required to search: name, years to search, DOB. Criminal records computerized from 1992; index cards from 1978, index books from 1900s. Mail turnaround time 2 weeks. Criminal PAT goes back to same as civil. Access criminal index free at http://wcca.wicourts.gov/index.xsl. Online results show DOB most of time; however, sometimes DOB is month and year only on the index.

Register in Probate 330 Court St, Eagle River, WI 54521; 715-479-3642; fax: 715-479-3740; 8AM-4PM (CST). *Probate.*
General Information: Probate records free at http://wcca.wicourts.gov/index.xsl.

Walworth County

Circuit Court PO Box 1001, 1800 County Rd NN, Elkhorn, WI 53121-1001; 262-741-7012; fax: 262-741-7050; 8AM-5PM (CST). *Felony, Misdemeanor, Civil, Eviction, Small Claims.*
www.co.walworth.wi.us
General Information: Online identifiers in results same as on public terminal. No sealed or confidential records released. Will fax documents $1.25 per page. Court makes copy: $1.25 per page. Certification fee: $5.00 per document plus copy fee. Payee: Clerk of Courts. Business checks accepted. Credit cards accepted in person only. Prepayment required. Mail requests: SASE required.
Civil Name Search: Access: Mail, in person, online. Both court and visitors may perform in person name searches. Search fee: $5.00 per name. Required to search: name. Civil records on computer from 1989, older cases on index cards. Mail turnaround time 1-5 days. Civil PAT goes back to 1989. Civil case lookup free online at http://wcca.wicourts.gov/index.xsl. Online results show DOB most of time; however, sometimes DOB is month and year only on the index.
Criminal Name Search: Access: Mail, in person, online. Both court and visitors may perform in person name searches. Search fee: $5.00 per name. Required to search: name, years to search; also helpful- DOB. Criminal records computerized from 1989, older cases on index cards. Mail turnaround time 1-5 days. Criminal PAT goes back to same as civil. Access criminal index free at http://wcca.wicourts.gov/index.xsl. Online results show DOB most of time; however, sometimes DOB is month and year only on the index.
Register in Probate PO Box 1001, 1800 County Rd NN, Elkhorn, WI 53121; 262-741-7014; fax: 262-741-7002; 8AM-5PM (CST). *Probate.*
General Information: Free access to Probate index at http://wcca.wicourts.gov/index.xsl.

Washburn County

Circuit Court PO Box 339, Shell Lake, WI 54871; 715-468-4677; fax: 715-468-4678; 8AM-4:30PM (CST). *Felony, Misdemeanor, Civil, Eviction, Small Claims.*
www.co.washburn.wi.us/
General Information: Online identifiers in results same as on public terminal. No sealed records released. Will fax documents to local or toll free line. Court makes copy: $1.25 per page. Certification fee: $5.00 per document plus copy fee. Payee: Clerk of Court. Personal checks accepted, credit cards are not. Prepayment required. Mail requests: SASE required.
Civil Name Search: Access: Mail, in person, online. Both court and visitors may perform in person name searches. Search fee: $5.00 per name. Civil records on computer since 1993 (civil money judgments back to 1/1/90); on index books from 1883. Mail turnaround time 2-3 days. Civil PAT goes back to 1993. Civil case lookup free online at http://wcca.wicourts.gov/index.xsl. Online results show DOB most of time; however, sometimes DOB is month and year only on the index.
Criminal Name Search: Access: Mail, online, in person. Both court and visitors may perform in person name searches. Search fee: $5.00 per name. Required to search: name, years to search; also helpful: DOB. Criminal records on computer since 1993; on index books from 1883. Mail turnaround time 2-3 days. Criminal PAT goes back to same as civil. Access criminal index free at http://wcca.wicourts.gov/index.xsl. Online results show DOB most of time; however, sometimes DOB is month and year only on the index.
Register in Probate PO Box 316, 10 Fourth Ave, Shell Lake, WI 54871; 715-468-4688; fax: 715-468-4678; 8AM-N, 1-4:30PM (CST). *Probate.*
General Information: Probate records free at http://wcca.wicourts.gov/index.xsl.

Washington County

Circuit Court PO Box 1986, 432 E Washington St, Rm 3151, West Bend, WI 53095-7986; 262-335-4341; fax: 262-335-4776; 8AM-4:30PM (CST). *Felony, Misdemeanor, Civil, Eviction, Small Claims.*
www.co.washington.wi.us/departments.iml?mdl=departments.mdl&ID=COC
General Information: Online identifiers in results same as on public terminal. No paternity records released prior to adjudication. Will fax documents to local or toll free line. Court makes copy: $1.25 per page.

Certification fee: $5.00. Payee: Clerk of Court. Personal checks accepted. Major credit cards accepted if total is for $20 or more. Service fees may be applied. Prepayment required. Mail requests: SASE required.
Civil Name Search: Access: Mail, fax, online, in person. Both court and visitors may perform in person name searches. Search fee: $5.00 per name. Required to search: name, years to search; also helpful: address. Civil records on computer from 1986, index cards from 1976, index books from 1836. Mail turnaround time 2 weeks. Civil PAT goes back to 1986. DOB may appear as month and year only on index. Civil case lookup free online at http://wcca.wicourts.gov/index.xsl. Online results show DOB most of time; however, sometimes DOB is month and year only on the index.
Criminal Name Search: Access: Mail, fax, online, in person. Both court and visitors may perform in person name searches. Search fee: $5.00 per name. Required to search: name, years to search, DOB; also helpful: address. Criminal records computerized from 1986, index cards from 1976, index books from 1836. Mail turnaround time 2 weeks. Criminal PAT goes back to same as civil. DOB may appear as month and year only on index. Access criminal index free at http://wcca.wicourts.gov/index.xsl. Online results show DOB most of time; however, sometimes DOB is month and year only on the index.
Register in Probate PO Box 82, 432 E Washington St, #3135, West Bend, WI 53095; 262-335-4333; fax: 262-306-2224; 8AM-4:30PM (CST). *Probate.*
www.co.washington.wi.us/
General Information: Probate records free at http://wcca.wicourts.gov/index.xsl.

Waukesha County

Circuit Court Clerk PO Box 1627, 515 W Moreland Blvd, Waukesha, WI 53188; criminal phone: 262-548-7484; civil phone: 262-548-7525; criminal fax: 262-896-8228; civil fax: 8AM-4:30PM; 8AM-4:30PM (CST). *Felony, Misdemeanor, Civil, Eviction, Family, Small Claims, Traffic.*
www.waukeshacounty.gov/CourtDivisions.aspx?id=21012
General Information: Online identifiers in results same as on public terminal. No paternity, mental commitment records released. Fee to fax out file 1-5 pages $3.00; 6-10 $10.00. Will fax no more than 10 pages. Court makes copy: $1.25 per page. Certification fee: $5.00 per document plus copy fee. Payee: Clerk of Circuit Court. Personal checks accepted. Accepts credit cards in person only. Prepayment required. Mail requests: SASE required for civil and family records.
Civil Name Search: Access: Mail, in person, online. Both court and visitors may perform in person name searches. Search fee: $5.00 per name. Civil records on computer back to 1994. Mail turnaround time 2-3 days. Civil PAT goes back to 1994. Civil case lookup free online at http://wcca.wicourts.gov/index.xsl. Online results show DOB most of time; however, sometimes DOB is month and year only on the index.
Criminal Name Search: Access: Mail, online, in person. Both court and visitors may perform in person name searches. Search fee: $5.00 per name. Required to search: name, years to search, DOB. Criminal records indexed on computer back to 1989; on microfilm back to 1980; index cards to 1940. Mail turnaround time 2-3 days. Criminal PAT goes back to 1989. Access criminal index free at http://wcca.wicourts.gov/index.xsl. Online results show DOB most of time; however, sometimes DOB is month and year only on the index.
Register in Probate 515 W Moreland Blvd, Rm-C380, Waukesha, WI 53188; 262-548-7468; fax: 262-896-8397; 8AM-4:30PM (CST). *Probate.*
www.waukeshacounty.gov
General Information: Probate record index free at http://wcca.wicourts.gov/index.xsl.

Waupaca County

Circuit Court 811 Harding St, Waupaca, WI 54981; 715-258-6460; fax: 715-258-6497; 8AM-4PM (CST). *Felony, Misdemeanor, Civil, Eviction, Small Claims.*
www.wicourts.gov/
General Information: Online identifiers in results same as on public terminal. No juvenile, JO, paternity excluding past judgments released. Court makes copy: $1.25 per page. Computer document copy fee $.50 per page. Certification fee: $5.00 per document. Payee: Clerk of Court. Business check and personal in-state check accepted. No credit cards accepted. Prepayment required. Mail requests: SASE required.
Civil Name Search: Access: Mail, in person, online. Both court and visitors may perform in person name searches. Search fee: $5.00 per name. Civil records on computer from 1992. Mail turnaround time 3-4 days. Public use terminal available. Civil case lookup free online at http://wcca.wicourts.gov/index.xsl. Online results show DOB most of time; however, sometimes DOB is month and year only on the index.

Criminal Name Search: Access: Mail, online, in person. Both court and visitors may perform in person name searches. Search fee: $5.00 per name. Criminal records computerized from 1992. Mail turnaround time 3-4 days. Public use terminal available. Access criminal index free at http://wcca.wicourts.gov/index.xsl. Online results show DOB most of time; however, sometimes DOB is month and year only on the index.

Register in Probate 811 Harding St, Waupaca, WI 54981; 715-258-6429; probate phone: 715-258-6431 Dep Reg.; fax: 715-258-6440; 8AM-4PM (CST). *Probate.*

http://public3.co.waupaca.wi.us/Departments/Probate/tabid/424/Default.aspx

General Information: Probate records free at http://wcca.wicourts.gov/index.xsl. Copies can be purchased for $1.00 per page.

Waushara County

Circuit Court PO Box 507, Wautoma, WI 54982; 920-787-0441; fax: 920-787-0481; 8AM-4:30PM (CST). *Felony, Misdemeanor, Civil, Eviction, Small Claims.*

www.co.waushara.wi.us/circuit_court.htm

General Information: Online identifiers in results same as on public terminal. Will fax documents if prepaid. Court makes copy: $1.25 per page. Certification fee: $5.00. Payee: Clerk of Court. Personal in-state checks accepted; money orders for out of state requests. Major credit cards accepted, surcharge added. Prepayment required. Mail requests: SASE required.

Civil Name Search: Access: Mail, fax, online, in person. Both court and visitors may perform in person name searches. Search fee: $5.00 per name. fee only if court does search. Civil cases indexed by defendant. Civil records on computer from 1992, index cards to 1978, index books prior. Mail turnaround time 1 day. Civil PAT goes back to 1992. Civil court record index online at http://wcca.wicourts.gov/index.xsl. Note this is not the official index; the only official index is located at the Clerk's office. Online results show DOB most of time; however, sometimes DOB is month and year only on the index.

Criminal Name Search: Access: Mail, fax, online, in person. Both court and visitors may perform in person name searches. Search fee: $5.00 per name. Required to search: name, years to search, DOB. Criminal records computerized from 1993, prior on cards and books. Mail turnaround time 1 day. Criminal PAT goes back to 1993. Access criminal index at http://wcca.wicourts.gov/index.xsl.

Register in Probate PO Box 508, 209 S St. Marie St, County Courthouse, Wautoma, WI 54982; 920-787-0448; fax: 920-787-0481; 8AM-4:30PM (CST). *Probate.*

www.co.waushara.wi.us

General Information: Probate records at http://wcca.wicourts.gov/index.xsl on subscription basis, go to http://wcca.wicourts.gov/index.xsl for more information.

Winnebago County

Circuit Court PO Box 2808, Oshkosh, WI 54903-2808; 920-236-4848; criminal phone: 920-236-4855; civil phone: 920-236-4848; probate phone: 920-236-4833; fax: 920-424-7780; 8AM-4:30PM (CST). *Felony, Misdemeanor, Civil, Eviction, Small Claims.*

www.co.winnebago.wi.us/clerk-courts

General Information: Online identifiers in results same as on public terminal. No juvenile, paternity, financial records released. Fee to fax out file $1.25 per page. Court makes copy: $1.25 per page. Certification fee: $5.00. Payee: Clerk of Courts. Personal checks accepted. No credit cards accepted for copies or searches except online and in person. Prepayment required. Mail requests: SASE not required.

Civil Name Search: Access: Mail, fax, online, in person. Both court and visitors may perform in person name searches. Search fee: $5.00 per name. Civil records are on computer since 1992, prior on books and cards to 1970. Historical Society has records to 1938. Mail turnaround time 1 week. Civil PAT goes back to 1992, countywide. Civil case lookup free online at http://wcca.wicourts.gov/index.xsl. Online results show DOB most of time; however, sometimes DOB is month and year only on the index.

Criminal Name Search: Access: Mail, fax, online, in person. Both court and visitors may perform in person name searches. Search fee: $5.00 per name. Required to search: full name, years to search, DOB. Criminal records are on computer since 1990, prior on books and cards. organized since 1978. Mail turnaround time 1 week. Criminal PAT goes back to 1990, countywide. Access criminal index free at http://wcca.wicourts.gov/index.xsl. Online results show DOB most of time; however, sometimes DOB is month and year only on the index.

Register in Probate 415 Jackson St, Rm 412, Oshkosh, WI 54903-2808; 920-236-4833; fax: 920-424-7536; 8AM-N, 1-4:30PM (CST). *Probate.*

www.co.winnebago.wi.us/probate

General Information: There is a $4.00 search fee, copy fee is $1.00 per page. The state maintains a fee docket index search to probate records at http://wcca.wicourts.gov/index.xsl.

Wood County

Circuit Court PO Box 8095, 400 Market St, Wisconsin Rapids, WI 54494-958095; 715-421-8490; civil phone: 715-421-8807; fax: 715-421-8691; 8AM-4:30PM (CST). *Felony, Misdemeanor, Civil, Eviction, Small Claims.*

www.co.wood.wi.us/Departments/Courts/

General Information: Online identifiers in results same as on public terminal. No paternity or sealed records released. Will` fax out documents for $1.25 per page. Court makes copy: $1.25 per page. Self serve copy: same. Certification fee: $5.00. Payee: Clerk of Court. Personal checks accepted. Credit card paying is managed through a 3rd party vendor. Prepayment required. Mail requests: SASE required.

Civil Name Search: Access: Mail, in person, online. Both court and visitors may perform in person name searches. Search fee: $5.00 per name. Civil records on computer from 1983, microfiche from 1856-1980s. Mail turnaround time within 10 days. Civil PAT goes back to 1983. Civil case lookup free online at http://wcca.wicourts.gov/index.xsl. Online results show DOB most of time; however, sometimes DOB is month and year only on the index.

Criminal Name Search: Access: Mail, online, in person. Both court and visitors may perform in person name searches. Search fee: $5.00 per name. Required to search: name, years to search, DOB. Criminal records computerized from 1980; manual search required for pre-1980 records. Mail turnaround time within 10 days. Criminal PAT goes back to same as civil. Access criminal index free at http://wcca.wicourts.gov/index.xsl. Online results show DOB most of time; however, sometimes DOB is month and year only on the index.

Register in Probate PO Box 8095, 400 Market St, County Courthouse, Wisconsin Rapids, WI 54495-8095; 715-421-8523; fax: 715-421-8896; 8AM-4:30PM (CST). *Probate.*

General Information: Court also holds guardianships, juveniles, mental and adoption records. Probate records free at http://wcca.wicourts.gov/index.xsl.

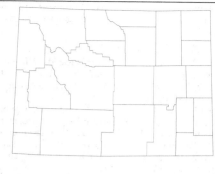

Wyoming

Time Zone: MST

Capital: Cheyenne, Laramie County

# of Counties: 23

State Web: www.wyoming.gov

Court Web: www.courts.state.wy.us

Administration

Court Administrator, 2301 Capitol Av, Supreme Court Bldg, Cheyenne, WY, 82002; 307-777-7583, Fax: 307-777-3447.

The Supreme Court

The Supreme Court of Wyoming, is the court of last resort. There is no intermediate court of appeals. Most cases docketed in the Supreme Court are appeals from District courts. The docket is searchable from the web page.

The Wyoming Courts

Court	Type	How Organized	Jurisdiction Highpoints
District*	General	23Courts in 9 Districts	Felony, Civil Actions. Juvenile, Probate
Circuit*	Limited	27 Courts in 23 Counties	Misdemeanor, Civil Actions under $50,000, Eviction, Small Claims
Municipal	Limited	80 Courts	Misdemeanor, Traffic, Ordinance

* = profiled in this book

Details on the Court Structure

Each county has a **District Court** which oversees felony criminal cases, large civil cases, and juvenile and probate matters.

The **Circuit Court** is of limited jurisdiction and oversee civil cases when the amount sought does not exceed $50,000 (raised from $7,000 effective 07/2011) and small claims to $5,000. Circuit Courts also hear family violence cases and all misdemeanors. Three counties have two Circuit Courts each: Fremont, Park, and Sweetwater. Cases may be filed in either of the two court offices in those counties, and records requests are referred between the two courts. Effective January 1, 2003, all Justice Courts became Circuit Courts and follow Circuit Court rules.

Municipal Courts operate in all incorporated cities and towns; their jurisdiction covers all ordinance violations and has no civil jurisdiction. The Municipal Court judge may assess penalties of up to $750 and/or six months in jail.

Record Searching Facts You Need to Know

Fees and Record Searching Tips

Fees for searching and record copies are set statewide by Rule. For the most part, these guidelines are followed; the search fee is $10.00 per name, the copy fee is $1.00 for the first page and $.50 each add'l, and there is a $2.00 charge for clerks to send or receive a fax. Certification fees vary. Recently all courts had public access terminal installed.

A State Rule effective January 1, 2011 directed redaction of the birth day and birth month and the first 5 digits of an SSN on public record pleadings and exhibits filed at the courts. From this date forward, the courts have two copies of each document – one public that is redacted, and one non-public that contains the full DOB and SSN. It is important to note that some courts have chosen to redact these partial identifiers on all prior cases filed, not just since 01/01/11.

Online Access is Non-Existent

Wyoming's statewide case management system is for internal use only. Planning is underway for a new case management system that will ultimately allow public access.

Albany County

2nd Judicial District Court 525 Grand Ave #305, Laramie, WY 82070; 307-721-2508; fax: 307-721-2520; 8AM-5PM (MST). *Felony, Civil Actions over $50,000, Probate.*
www.co.albany.wy.us/clerk-of-court.aspx

General Information: No sex offenses records released, signed release required for child support cases. Will not fax out documents. Court makes copy: $1.00 first page, $.50 each add'l. No certification fee . Payee: Clerk of District Court. Personal checks accepted, credit cards are not. Prepayment required. Mail requests: SASE required.

Civil Name Search: Access: Phone, mail, in person. Both court and visitors may perform in person name searches. No search fee. Required to search: name; also helpful: years to search. Civil records on computer go back to 1988, prior records on card index to 1890. Note: Call and ask permission first before faxing. Mail turnaround time same day. Civil PAT goes back to 1988 countywide.

Criminal Name Search: Access: Mail, in person. Both court and visitors may perform in person name searches. Search fee: $10.00 per name. Search results can be phoned back to a toll-free number only. Required to search: name, years to search, DOB. Criminal records on computer go back to 1988, prior records on card index to 1890. Note: Effective 01/01/2011 per State Rule, on all new case files the birth day and birth month and the first five digits of an SSN are redacted on court files viewable by the public. Prior records probably will not be redacted. Mail turnaround time same day. Criminal PAT goes back to 1988 countywide.

Albany Circuit Court 525 Grand, Rm 400, County Courthouse, Laramie, WY 82070; 307-742-5747; fax: 307-742-5610; 8AM-5PM (MST). *Misdemeanor, Civil Actions under $50,000, Eviction, Small Claims.*
www.courts.state.wy.us/

General Information: No SSN or family violence records released. Fee to fax files is $2.00 per document. Court makes copy: $1.00 1st page, $.50 each add'l. Certification fee: $5.00 per document. Payee: Albany Circuit Court. In state personal checks accepted. Major credit cards accepted for record searches. Prepayment required. Mail requests: SASE required.

Civil Name Search: Access: Mail, in person. Both court and visitors may perform in person name searches. Search fee: $10.00 per name. Civil records on computer from 1993, prior on docket books to 1984. Note: Effective 01/01/2011 per State Rule, on all new case files the birth day and birth month and the first five digits of an SSN are redacted on court files viewable by the public. Prior records probably will not be redacted. Mail turnaround time same day if possible. Civil PAT available. Statewide access provided, year of birth shown.

Criminal Name Search: Access: Mail, in person, fax. Both court and visitors may perform in person name searches. Search fee: $10.00 per name. Required to search: name, years to search, DOB. Criminal records computerized from 1990, prior on docket books to 1984. Note: A $10.00 "court fee" may be applied to each in person search. Effective 01/01/2011 per State Rule, on all new case files the birth day and birth month and the first five digits of an SSN are redacted on court files viewable by the public. Prior records pr Mail turnaround time same day if possible. Criminal PAT available. Statewide access provided, year of birth shown.

Big Horn County

5th Judicial District Court PO Box 670, Basin, WY 82410; 307-568-2381; fax: 307-568-2791; 8AM-N, 1-5PM (MST). *Felony, Civil Actions over $50,000, Probate.*
www.bighorncountywy.gov/dep-clerk-of-district-court.htm

General Information: Probate fax is same as main fax number. Some confidential records not released. Will fax out files for $2.00. Court makes copy: $1.00 first page, $.50 each add'l. Certification fee: $.50 per page plus copy fee. Payee: Clerk of Court. Business checks accepted. No credit cards accepted. Prepayment required. Mail requests: SASE required.

Civil Name Search: Access: Fax, mail, in person. Both court and visitors may perform in person name searches. Search fee: $10.00 per name. Civil records on computer since 1988, 1907 to present on cards. Note: Effective 01/01/2011 per State Rule, on all new case files the birth day and birth month and the first five digits of an SSN are redacted on court files viewable by the public. Prior records probably will not be redacted. Mail turnaround time 24 hours.

Criminal Name Search: Access: Mail, in person. Both court and visitors may perform in person name searches. Search fee: $10.00 per name. Criminal records on computer 1989, 1907 to present on cards. Note: Effective 01/01/2011 per State Rule, on all new case files the birth day and birth month and the first five digits of an SSN are redacted on court files viewable by the public. Prior records probably will not be redacted. Mail turnaround time 24 hours.

Basin Circuit Court PO Box 749, Basin, WY 82410; 307-568-2367; fax: 307-568-2554; 8AM-5PM (MST). *Misdemeanor, Civil Actions under $50,000, Small Claims.* www.courts.state.wy.us/

General Information: Note that misdemeanor records from the Basin and the Lovell locations are not combined. No sex or juvenile offenses released. Fee to fax files is $2 per document. Court makes copy: $1.00 1st page, $.50 each add'l. Certification fee: $5.00 per document. Payee: Big Horn Cty Circuit Court. Personal checks accepted. Credit cards accepted, surcharge may apply. Prepayment required. Mail requests: SASE required.

Civil Name Search: Access: Fax, mail, in person. Both court and visitors may perform in person name searches. Search fee: $10.00 per name. Required to search: name, years to search; also helpful: address. Civil cases indexed by defendant. Civil records on microfiche for 10 years. Note: Effective 01/01/2011 per State Rule, on all new case files the birth day and birth month and the first five digits of an SSN are redacted on court files viewable by the public. Prior records probably will not be redacted. Mail turnaround time 1 day. Civil PAT available. Statewide access provided, year of birth shown.

Criminal Name Search: Access: Fax, mail, in person. Both court and visitors may perform in person name searches. Search fee: $10.00 per name. Required to search: name, DOB; also helpful: SSN. Criminal records on computer since 1990, microfiche 1985. Note: Effective 01/01/2011 per State Rule, on all new case files the birth day and birth month and the first five digits of an SSN are redacted on court files viewable by the public. Prior records probably will not be redacted. Mail turnaround time 1 day. Criminal PAT available. Statewide access provided, year of birth shown.

Lovell Circuit Court PO Box 595, Lovell, WY 82431; 307-548-7601; fax: 307-548-9691; 8AM-5PM (MST). *Misdemeanor, Civil Actions under $50,000, Small Claims.* www.courts.state.wy.us/

General Information: Note that misdemeanor records from the Basin Circuit Court and this Lovell Court are not combined. No sex or juvenile offenses released. Fee to fax files is $2.00 per document. Court makes copy: $1.00 1st page, $.50 each add'l. Certification fee: $5.00 per document. Payee: Lovell Circuit Court. Personal checks accepted. Credit cards accepted. Prepayment required. Mail requests: SASE not required.

Civil Name Search: Access: Fax, mail, in person. Both court and visitors may perform in person name searches. Search fee: $10.00 per name. Required to search: name, years to search; also helpful: address. Civil cases indexed by defendant. Civil records computerized back to 8/2002. Note: Effective 01/01/2011 per State Rule, on all new case files the birth day and birth month and the first five digits of an SSN are redacted on court files viewable by the public. Prior records probably will not be redacted. Mail turnaround time 1 day. Civil PAT available. Statewide access provided, year of birth shown.

Criminal Name Search: Access: Fax, mail, in person. Both court and visitors may perform in person name searches. Search fee: $10.00 per name. Required to search: name, DOB; also helpful: SSN. Criminal records computerized from 1990. Note: Effective 01/01/2011 per State Rule, on all new case files the birth day and birth month and the first five digits of an SSN are redacted on court files viewable by the public. Prior records probably will not be redacted. Mail turnaround time 1 day. Criminal PAT available. Statewide access provided, year of birth shown.

Campbell County

6th Judicial District Court PO Box 817, 500 S Gillette St, Ste 2600, Gillette, WY 82717; 307-682-3424; fax: 307-687-6209; 8AM-5PM (MST). *Felony, Civil Actions over $50,000, Probate.*
www.courts.state.wy.us/

General Information: Probate fax is same as main fax number. Names of victims in sex cases, confidential records not released. Will fax documents $2.00 per 10 pages. Court makes copy: $1.00 first page, $.50 each add'l. Self serve copy: $.25 per page. Certification fee: $.50 per doc. Payee: Clerk of District Court. Local personal checks accepted; no out of state. No credit cards accepted. Prepayment required. Mail requests: SASE required.

Civil Name Search: Access: Mail, in person. Visitors must perform in person searches themselves. Search fee: $10.00 per name. Civil records archived from 1913; on computer back to 1986. Note: Effective 01/01/2011 per State Rule, on all new case files the birth day and birth month and the first five digits of an SSN are redacted on court files viewable by the public. Prior records probably will not be redacted. Mail turnaround time 1-2 days. Civil PAT goes back to 1999.

Criminal Name Search: Access: Mail, in person. Visitors must perform in person searches themselves. Search fee: $10.00 per name. Criminal records archived from 1913; on computer back to 1985. Note: Effective 01/01/2011 per State Rule, on all new case files the birth day and birth month and the first five digits of an SSN are redacted on court files viewable by the public. Prior records probably will not be redacted. Mail turnaround time 1-2 days. Criminal PAT goes back to 1999.

Campbell Circuit Court 500 S Gillette Ave, #2200, Gillette, WY 82716; 307-682-2190; fax: 307-687-6214; 8AM-5PM (MST). *Misdemeanor, Civil Actions under $50,000, Eviction, Small Claims.*
www.courts.state.wy.us/

General Information: No sex related cases released. Fee to fax files is $2 per document. Court makes copy: $1.00 1st page, $.50 each add'l. Self serve copy: same. Certification fee: $5.00 per document. Payee: Campbell County Circuit Court. Personal checks accepted. Visa/MC, Discover accepted. Prepayment required. Mail requests: SASE requested.

Civil Name Search: Access: Mail, in person. Both court and visitors may perform in person name searches. Search fee: $10.00 per name. Required to search: name, years to search; also helpful: address. Civil records on computer since 1983, archives from 1979. Note: Effective 01/01/2011 per State Rule, on all new case files the birth day and birth month and the first five digits of an SSN are redacted on court files viewable by the public. Prior records probably will not be redacted. Mail turnaround time 2 days. Civil PAT available. Statewide access provided, year of birth shown.

Criminal Name Search: Access: Mail, in person. Both court and visitors may perform in person name searches. Search fee: $10.00 per name. Required to search: name, years to search, DOB; also helpful: address. Criminal records on computer since 1983, archives from 1979. Note: Effective 01/01/2011 per State Rule, on all new case files the birth day and birth month and the first five digits of an SSN are redacted on court files viewable by the public. Prior records probably will not be redacted. Mail turnaround time 1-2 days; longer for cases prior to 2001. Criminal PAT available. Statewide access provided, year of birth shown.

Carbon County

Carbon County District Court Clerk of District Court, PO Box 67, Rawlins, WY 82301; 307-328-2628; fax: 307-328-2629; 8AM-5PM (MST). *Felony, Civil Actions over $50,000, Probate.*
www.courts.state.wy.us/

General Information: The office has a master index with all cases on the index. No juvenile or adoption records released. Fee to fax files depends on number of pages. Court makes copy: $1.00 first page, $.50 each add'l. Self serve copy: same. No certification fee . Payee: Clerk of District Court, Carbon County. Personal checks accepted, credit cards are not. Prepayment required. Mail requests: SASE required.

Civil Name Search: Access: Phone, fax, mail, in person. Both court and visitors may perform in person name searches. Search fee: $10.00 per name. Required to search: name, years to search; also helpful: address. Civil records on file from late 1800s, index cards, docket books, then computer 1997 to present. Note: Public can search on the manual index. Effective 01/01/2011 per State Rule, on all new case files the birth day and birth month and the first five digits of an SSN are redacted on court files viewable by the public. Prior records probably will not be reda Mail turnaround time 4-5 days.

Criminal Name Search: Access: Phone, fax, mail, in person. Both court and visitors may perform in person name searches. Search fee: $10.00 per name. Required to search: name, years to search; also helpful: address, DOB, SSN. Criminal records indexed on cards and docket books; on computer 1997 to present. Note: Public can search on the manual index. Effective 01/01/2011 per State Rule, on all new case files the birth day and birth month and the first five digits of an SSN are redacted on court files viewable by the public. Prior records probably will not be reda Mail turnaround time 4-5 days.

Carbon Circuit Court Attn: Chief Clerk, Courthouse Bldg, 415 W Pine St, Rawlins, WY 82301; 307-324-6655; fax: 307-324-9465; 8AM-5PM (MST). *Misdemeanor, Civil Actions under $50,000, Eviction, Small Claims.* www.courts.state.wy.us/

General Information: Names of victims not released in sex related cases. Will fax out files to a toll-free number. Court makes copy: $1.00 1st page, $.50 each add'l. Certification fee: $5.00 per document. Payee: Circuit Court of Carbon County. Personal checks accepted. Visa/MC accepted, add $8.00 usage fee. Prepayment required. Mail requests: SASE requested.

Civil Name Search: Access: Mail, in person. Both court and visitors may perform in person name searches. Search fee: $10.00 per name. Required to search: name, years to search; also helpful: address. Civil records on computer back to 3/95. Note: Effective 01/01/2011 per State Rule, on all new case files the birth day and birth month and the first five digits of an SSN are redacted on court files viewable by the public. Prior records probably will not be redacted. Mail turnaround time 1 week. Civil PAT available. Statewide access provided, year of birth shown.

Criminal Name Search: Access: Mail, in person. Both court and visitors may perform in person name searches. Search fee: $10.00 per name. Required to search: name, years to search, DOB. Criminal records computerized from 8/87. Note: Effective 01/01/2011 per State Rule, on all new case files the birth day and birth month and the first five digits of an SSN are redacted on court files viewable by the public. Prior records

probably will not be redacted. Mail turnaround time 1 week. Criminal PAT available. Statewide access provided, year of birth shown.

Converse County

8th Judicial District Court Box 189, Douglas, WY 82633; 307-358-3165; fax: 307-358-9783; 8AM-5PM (MST). *Felony, Civil Actions over $50,000, Probate.* www.courts.state.wy.us/

General Information: Probate fax is same as main fax number. No juvenile, adoptions or mental cases released. Will fax out files no add'l fee if 10 pages or less. Court makes copy: $.50 per page. Self serve copy: $.25 per page. Certification fee: $1.00 fee for 1st page and $.50 for the seal; plus copy fee. Add'l fee for copies and postage if mailed. Payee: Clerk of District Court. Personal checks accepted, credit cards are not. Prepayment required. Mail requests: SASE not required.

Civil Name Search: Access: Phone, fax, mail, in person. Both court and visitors may perform in person name searches. Search fee: $10.00 per name or case. Required to search: name, years to search; also helpful: address. Civil records on card file from 1888. Note: Effective 01/01/2011 per State Rule, on all new case files the birth day and birth month and the first five digits of an SSN are redacted on court files viewable by the public. Prior records probably will not be redacted. Mail turnaround time usually same day.

Criminal Name Search: Access: Phone, fax, mail, in person. Both court and visitors may perform in person name searches. Search fee: $10.00 per name or case. Required to search: name, years to search; also helpful: address, DOB, SSN. Criminal records on card file from 1850. Note: Effective 01/01/2011 per State Rule, on all new case files the birth day and birth month and the first five digits of an SSN are redacted on court files viewable by the public. Prior records probably will not be redacted. Mail turnaround time usually same day.

Converse Circuit Court 107 N 5th St, #231, PO Box 45, Douglas, WY 82633; 307-358-2196; fax: 307-358-2501; 8AM-5PM (MST). *Misdemeanor, Civil Actions under $50,000, Eviction, Small Claims.* www.courts.state.wy.us/

General Information: No sealed records released. Fee to fax files is $2.00 per document. Court makes copy: $1.00 1st page, $.50 each add'l. Certification fee: $5.00 per document. Payee: Circuit Court of Converse County. Cashiers checks and money orders accepted. Visa/MC accepted but there is a $5.00 surcharge. Prepayment required. Mail requests: SASE required.

Civil Name Search: Access: Mail, in person. Both court and visitors may perform in person name searches. Search fee: $10.00 per name. Required to search: name, years to search, and DOB or SSN. Civil records on computer from 1994, card file prior. Note: Effective 01/01/2011 per State Rule, on all new case files the birth day and birth month and the first five digits of an SSN are redacted on court files viewable by the public. Prior records probably will not be redacted. Mail turnaround time 1-2 days. Civil PAT goes back to 1994. Statewide access provided, year of birth shown.

Criminal Name Search: Access: Mail, in person. Both court and visitors may perform in person name searches. Search fee: $10.00 per name. Required to search: name, years to search, DOB also helpful: address, SSN. Criminal records computerized from 1990, card file prior. Note: Effective 01/01/2011 per State Rule, on all new case files the birth day and birth month and the first five digits of an SSN are redacted on court files viewable by the public. Prior records probably will not be redacted. Mail turnaround time 1-2 days. Criminal PAT goes back to 1990. Statewide access provided, year of birth shown.

Crook County

6th Judicial District Court Box 904, Sundance, WY 82729; 307-283-2523; fax: 307-283-2996; 8AM-5PM (MST). *Felony, Civil Actions over $50,000, Probate, High Misdemeanor pre-7/1/02.* www.crookcounty.wy.gov/coc.html

General Information: High misdemeanor cases no longer heard by this court, effective 7/1/02; high misdemeanor records prior to that date can be found here. Probate fax is same as main fax number. No sealed records released. Will fax documents to local or toll-free number for no extra fee. Court makes copy: $.50 per page. Self serve copy: same. Certification fee: $1.00 per certification. Payee: Clerk of District Court. Business checks accepted. No credit cards accepted. Prepayment required. Mail requests: SASE required.

Civil Name Search: Access: Mail, in person. Both court and visitors may perform in person name searches. Search fee: $10.00 per name. Required to search: name, years to search; also helpful: address. Civil records on card file from late 1800s; on computer back to 1999. Note: Effective 01/01/2011 per State Rule, on all new case files the birth day and birth month and the first five digits of an SSN are redacted on court files viewable by the public. Prior records will not be redacted. Mail turnaround time usually same day.

Criminal Name Search: Access: Mail, in person. Both court and visitors may perform in person name searches. Search fee: $10.00 per name. Required to search: name, years to search; also helpful: address, DOB, SSN. Criminal records on card file from late 1800s; on computer back to 1999. Note: As of 7/1/02, high misdemeanor cases are no longer heard by this court, however, cases prior to that date will remain here. Mail turnaround time usually same day.

Circuit Court PO Box 650, Sundance, WY 82729; 307-283-2929; fax: 307-283-2931; 8AM-5PM (MST). *Misdemeanor, Civil Actions under $5,000, Small Claims.* www.courts.state.wy.us/

General Information: This former Justice Court became a Circuit Court on 7/1/2002. No sex related cases released. Fee to fax files is $2.00 per document; no charge if $10.00 search fee paid. Court makes copy: $1.00 1st page, $.50 each add'l. Certification fee: $5.00 per document. Payee: Crook County Circuit Court. Personal checks accepted. Major credit cards accepted ($8.00 fee). Prepayment required. Mail requests: SASE required.

Civil Name Search: Access: Mail, fax, in person. Both court and visitors may perform in person name searches. Search fee: $10.00 per name. Required to search: name, years to search; also helpful: address. Civil records on cards, archives back to 1977; on computer back to 1998. Note: Effective 01/01/2011 per State Rule, on all new case files the birth day and birth month and the first five digits of an SSN are redacted on court files viewable by the public. Prior records probably will not be redacted. Mail turnaround time 3-5 days. Civil PAT available. Statewide access provided, year of birth shown.

Criminal Name Search: Access: Mail, fax, in person. Both court and visitors may perform in person name searches. Search fee: $10.00 per name. Required to search: name, years to search, DOB, SSN. Criminal records go back to 1983; on computer back to 6/1980. Note: Effective 01/01/2011 per State Rule, on all new case files the birth day and birth month and the first five digits of an SSN are redacted on court files viewable by the public. Prior records probably will not be redacted. Mail turnaround time 3-5 days. Criminal PAT available. Statewide access provided, year of birth shown.

Fremont County

9th Judicial District Court PO Box 370, 450 N 2nd St, Rm 235, Lander, WY 82520; 307-332-1134; fax: 307-332-1143; 8AM-N, 1-5PM (MST). *Felony, Civil Actions over $50,000, Probate.* www.courts.state.wy.us/

General Information: No juvenile, involuntary hospitalization or adoption records released. Will fax documents $2.00 per page. Court makes copy: $.50 per page. Self serve copy: no fee. No certification fee . Payee: Clerk of District Court. Personal checks accepted, credit cards are not. Mail requests: SASE required.

Civil Name Search: Access: Phone, fax, mail, in person. Both court and visitors may perform in person name searches. Search fee: $10.00 per name. Required to search: name, years to search; also helpful: address. Civil records on computer since 1992, in books since 1991, on microfiche since 1939 and on card file from 1898. Note: Effective 01/01/2011 per State Rule, on all new case files the birth day and birth month and the first five digits of an SSN are redacted on court files viewable by the public. Prior records probably will not be redacted. Mail turnaround time same day. Civil PAT goes back to 1992. Clerk will pull file to match DOB you provide.

Criminal Name Search: Access: Phone, fax, mail, in person. Both court and visitors may perform in person name searches. Search fee: $10.00 per name. Required to search: name, years to search; also helpful: address, DOB, SSN. Criminal records on computer since 1992 (newer system records go back to 2004), in books since 1991, microfiche since 1939 and on card file from 1898. Note: Effective 01/01/2011 per State Rule, on all new case files the birth day and birth month and the first five digits of an SSN are redacted on court files viewable by the public. Prior records probably will not be redacted. Mail turnaround time same day. Criminal PAT goes back to same as civil. Clerk will pull file to match DOB.

Dubois Circuit Court PO Box 952, 712 Meckem, Dubois, WY 82513; 307-455-2920; fax: 307-455-2132; 8AM-2:00PM (MST). *Misdemeanor, Civil Actions under $50,000, Eviction, Small Claims.* www.courts.state.wy.us/

General Information: This is a satellite of the Lander Court. No juvenile, sexual data released. Will fax documents to local or toll-free number. Court makes copy: $1.00 1st page, $.50 each add'l. Certification fee: $10.00 per doc. Payee: Fremont County Circuit Court. Personal checks accepted. VISA cards accepted. Prepayment required. Mail requests: SASE not required.

Civil Name Search: Access: Mail, in person. Both court and visitors may perform in person name searches. Search fee: $10.00 per name. Civil records indexed. Note: Effective 01/01/2011 per State Rule, on all new case files the birth day and birth month and the first five digits of an SSN are redacted on court files viewable by the public. Prior records probably

will not be redacted. Mail turnaround time 4 days. Civil PAT available. Statewide access provided, year of birth shown.

Criminal Name Search: Access: Mail, in person. Both court and visitors may perform in person name searches. Search fee: $10.00 per name. Required to search: name, years to search; also helpful: DOB. Criminal records on computer since 12/98; prior records on indexes. Note: Effective 01/01/2011 per State Rule, on all new case files the birth day and birth month and the first five digits of an SSN are redacted on court files viewable by the public. Prior records probably will not be redacted. Mail turnaround time 4 days. Criminal PAT available. Statewide access provided, year of birth shown.

Lander Circuit Court 450 N 2nd, Rm 230, Lander, WY 82520; 307-332-3239; fax: 307-332-1152; 8AM-5PM (MST). *Misdemeanor, Civil Actions under $50,000, Eviction, Small Claims.* www.courts.state.wy.us/

General Information: This is the main Circuit Court for Fremont County. No juvenile or sexual data released. Fee to fax files is $2.00 per document. Court makes copy: $1.00 1st page, $.50 each add'l. Certification fee: (exemplification) $5.00 per document. Payee: Circuit Court. In state personal checks accepted. Credit cards accepted, minimum $8.00 fee. Prepayment required. Mail requests: SASE required.

Civil Name Search: Access: Phone, fax, mail, in person. Both court and visitors may perform in person name searches. Search fee: $10.00 per name. Required to search: name, years to search; also helpful: address. Civil records on computer from 1998, archive back to 1989. Note: Effective 01/01/2011 per State Rule, on all new case files the birth day and birth month and the first five digits of an SSN are redacted on court files viewable by the public. Prior records probably will not be redacted. Mail turnaround time 2 days. Civil PAT available. Statewide access provided, year of birth shown.

Criminal Name Search: Access: Phone, fax, mail, in person. Both court and visitors may perform in person name searches. Search fee: $10.00 per name. Required to search: name, years to search; also helpful: address, DOB, SSN. Criminal records computerized from 1993, archive back to 1979. Note: Effective 01/01/2011 per State Rule, on all new case files the birth day and birth month and the first five digits of an SSN are redacted on court files viewable by the public. Prior records probably will not be redacted. Mail turnaround time 2 days. Criminal PAT available. Statewide access provided, year of birth shown.

Riverton Circuit Court 818 S Federal Blvd, Riverton, WY 82501; 307-856-7259; fax: 307-857-3635; 8AM-5PM (MST). *Misdemeanor, Civil Actions under $50,000, Eviction, Small Claims.* www.courts.state.wy.us/

General Information: No sex released cases released. Fee to fax files is $2.00 per document. Court makes copy: $1.00 1st page, $.50 each add'l. Certification fee: $5.00 per document. Payee: Fremont County Circuit Court. In state personal checks accepted. Visa/MC/Discover accepted. Prepayment required. Mail requests: SASE required.

Civil Name Search: Access: Mail, in person. Both court and visitors may perform in person name searches. Search fee: $10.00 per name. Civil records are computerized since 1997; prior in books to 1981. Note: Effective 01/01/2011 per State Rule, on all new case files the birth day and birth month and the first five digits of an SSN are redacted on court files viewable by the public. Prior records will be redacted as well. Mail turnaround time 2 days. Civil PAT available. Statewide access provided, year of birth shown.

Criminal Name Search: Access: Mail, in person. Both court and visitors may perform in person name searches. Search fee: $10.00 per name. Required to search: name, years to search, DOB; also helpful: SSN. Criminal records on computer since 1989; prior in books to 1981. Note: Effective 01/01/2011 per State Rule, on all new case files the birth day and birth month and the first five digits of an SSN are redacted on court files viewable by the public. Prior records will be redacted as well. Mail turnaround time 2 days. Criminal PAT available. Statewide access provided, year of birth shown.

Goshen County

8th Judicial District Court PO Box 818, Clerk of District Court, 2125 E "A" St #236, Torrington, WY 82240; 307-532-2155; fax: 307-532-8608; 7:30AM-4PM (MST). *Felony, Civil Actions over $50,000, Probate.* www.courts.state.wy.us/

General Information: No juvenile records released. Will fax results; prefer toll free line. Court makes copy: $1.00 first page, $.50 each add'l. Certification fee: $.50 per page plus copy fee. Payee: Clerk of District Court. In state Personal checks accepted, credit cards are not. Prepayment required. Mail requests: SASE required.

Civil Name Search: Access: Mail, in person. Both court and visitors may perform in person name searches. Search fee: $10.00 per name. Required to search: name, years to search; also helpful: address. Civil records on index file only since 1913. Note: Effective 01/01/2011 per State Rule, on all new case files the birth day and birth month and the first five digits of an SSN are redacted on court files viewable by the public. Prior records probably will not be redacted. Mail turnaround time 2 days.

Criminal Name Search: Access: Mail, in person. Both court and visitors may perform in person name searches. Search fee: $10.00 per name. Required to search: name, years to search; also helpful: address, DOB, SSN. Criminal records on index file only since 1913, on computer back to 2005. Note: Effective 01/01/2011 per State Rule, on all new case files the birth day and birth month and the first five digits of an SSN are redacted on court files viewable by the public. Prior records probably will not be redacted. Mail turnaround time 2 days.

Goshen Circuit Court PO Box 980, Torrington, WY 82240; 307-532-2938; criminal phone: X250; civil phone: X251; fax: 307-532-5101; 7AM-4PM M-F (MST). *Misdemeanor, Civil Actions under $50,000, Eviction, Small Claims.* www.courts.state.wy.us/

General Information: No juvenile records released. Fee to fax files is $2.00 per doc; free if a toll-free number is provided. Court makes copy: $1.00 1st page, $.50 each add'l. Certification fee: $5.00 per document. Payee: Circuit Court 8th Judicial District. No personal checks. No credit cards accepted for record searches. Prepayment required. Mail requests: SASE required.

Civil Name Search: Access: Mail, in person. Both court and visitors may perform in person name searches. Search fee: $10.00 per name; alias separate. Required to search: name, years to search; also helpful: address. Civil cases indexed by case number, defendant. Civil records go back to 1988; on computer back to 3/97, prior archived. Note: Effective 01/01/2011 per State Rule, on all new case files the birth day and birth month and the first five digits of an SSN are redacted on court files viewable by the public. Prior records probably will not be redacted. Mail turnaround time 3-4 days. Civil PAT available. Statewide access provided, year of birth shown.

Criminal Name Search: Access: Mail, in person. Both court and visitors may perform in person name searches. Search fee: $10.00 per name; alias separate. Required to search: name, years to search, DOB; also helpful: address, SSN. Criminal records go back to 10/92; on computer back to 4/89 for disposition data, to 1984 for felonies or high misdemeanors, prior archived. Note: Effective 01/01/2011 per State Rule, on all new case files the birth day and birth month and the first five digits of an SSN are redacted on court files viewable by the public. Prior records probably will not be redacted. Mail turnaround time 3-4 days. Criminal PAT available. Statewide access provided, year of birth shown.

Hot Springs County

5th Judicial District Court 415 Arapahoe St, Thermopolis, WY 82443; 307-864-3323; fax: 307-864-3210; 8AM-5PM (MST). *Felony, Civil Actions over $50,000, Probate.*
www.hscounty.com/Departments/Clerk_of_Court/Default.aspx

General Information: No juvenile, adoption or sexual data released. Will fax out files to a local or toll free line. Court makes copy: $1.00 1st page, $.50 each add'l. Self serve copy: $.50 per page. Certification fee: $.50 per page. Payee: Clerk of District Court. Personal checks accepted, credit cards are not. Prepayment required. Mail requests: SASE required.

Civil Name Search: Access: Mail, in person. Both court and visitors may perform in person name searches. Search fee: $10.00 per name. Required to search: name, years to search; also helpful: address. Civil records on card index back to 1900s. Note: Effective 01/01/2011 per State Rule, on all new case files the birth day and birth month and the first five digits of an SSN are redacted on court files viewable by the public. Prior records probably will not be redacted. Mail turnaround time 1 day.

Criminal Name Search: Access: Mail, in person. Both court and visitors may perform in person name searches. Search fee: $10.00 per name. Required to search: name, years to search, DOB, SSN; also helpful: address. Criminal records on card index back to 1900s. Note: Effective 01/01/2011 per State Rule, on all new case files the birth day and birth month and the first five digits of an SSN are redacted on court files viewable by the public. Prior records probably will not be redacted. Mail turnaround time 1 day.

Hot Springs Circuit Court 417 Arapahoe St, Thermopolis, WY 82443; 307-864-5161; fax: 307-864-2067; 8AM-5PM (MST). *Misdemeanor, Civil Actions under $50,000, Small Claims.* www.courts.state.wy.us/

General Information: No closed case records released. Fee to fax files is $2 per document. Court makes copy: $1.00 1st page, $.50 each add'l. Certification fee: $5.00 per document. Payee: Circuit Court. Business checks accepted. No credit cards accepted. Prepayment required. Mail requests: SASE required.

Civil Name Search: Access: Mail, in person. Both court and visitors may perform in person name searches. Search fee: $10.00 per name. Civil records on computer from 1990, prior in card file. Note: Effective 01/01/2011 per State Rule, on all new case files the birth day and birth month and the first five digits of an SSN are redacted on court files viewable by the public. Prior records probably will not be redacted. Mail

turnaround time 2-3 days. Civil PAT available. Statewide access provided, year of birth shown.

Criminal Name Search: Access: Mail, in person. Both court and visitors may perform in person name searches. Search fee: $10.00 per name. Criminal records computerized from 1990, prior in card file to 1980. Note: Effective 01/01/2011 per State Rule, on all new case files the birth day and birth month and the first five digits of an SSN are redacted on court files viewable by the public. Prior records probably will not be redacted. Mail turnaround time 2-3 days. Criminal PAT available. Statewide access provided, year of birth shown.

Johnson County

4th Judicial District Court 76 N Main St, Buffalo, WY 82834; 307-684-7271; fax: 307-684-5146; 8AM-5PM (MST). *Felony, Civil Actions over $50,000, Probate.*
www.johnsoncountywyoming.org/government/clerk_of_district_court/

General Information: In person searchers may view file cards. No adoption or juvenile records released. Will fax out files for $2.00 plus $1.00 per page. Court makes copy: $1.00 first page; $.50 each add'l page. Self serve copy: same. Certification fee: $.50 per page. Payee: Clerk of District Court. In state Personal checks accepted, credit cards are not. Prepayment required. Mail requests: SASE required.

Civil Name Search: Access: Fax, mail, in person. Both court and visitors may perform in person name searches. Search fee: $10.00 per name. Required to search: name, years to search; also helpful: address. Civil records on computer from 1989, card index since 1892. Note: Effective 01/01/2011 per State Rule, on all new case files the birth day and birth month and the first five digits of an SSN are redacted on court files viewable by the public. Prior records probably will not be redacted. Mail turnaround time 1 week.

Criminal Name Search: Access: Fax, mail, in person. Both court and visitors may perform in person name searches. Search fee: $10.00 per name. Required to search: name, years to search; also helpful: address, DOB, SSN. Criminal records computerized from 1989, card index since 1892. Note: Effective 01/01/2011 per State Rule, on all new case files the birth day and birth month and the first five digits of an SSN are redacted on court files viewable by the public. Prior records probably will not be redacted. Mail turnaround time 1 week.

Circuit Court 76 N Main St, Buffalo, WY 82834-1847; 307-684-5720; fax: 307-684-7308; 8AM-5PM (MST). *Misdemeanor, Civil Actions under $50,000, Small Claims.* www.courts.state.wy.us/

General Information: Formally a Justice Court; became a Circuit Court on 1/03. No sex cases released. Will fax docs for $2.00 each for non-toll free phone numbers. Court makes copy: $1.00 1st page; $.50 each add'l. Certification fee: $5.00 per case. Payee: Circuit Court. Personal checks accepted. Credit cards accepted, $5.00 usage fee. Prepayment required. Mail requests: SASE required.

Civil Name Search: Access: Mail, fax, in person. Both court and visitors may perform in person name searches. Search fee: $10.00 per name. Required to search: name, years to search; also helpful: address. Civil records on computer since 1995; prior records on index cards. Note: Effective 01/01/2011 per State Rule, on all new case files the birth day and birth month and the first five digits of an SSN are redacted on court files viewable by the public. Prior records probably will not be redacted. Mail turnaround time 2 days. Civil PAT goes back to 1995. Statewide access provided, year of birth shown.

Criminal Name Search: Access: Mail, fax, in person. Both court and visitors may perform in person name searches. Search fee: $10.00 per name. Required to search: name, years to search, DOB; also helpful: SSN. Criminal records on computer since 5/90, card index back to 1979. Note: Effective 01/01/2011 per State Rule, on all new case files the birth day and birth month and the first five digits of an SSN are redacted on court files viewable by the public. Prior records probably will not be redacted. Mail turnaround time 2 days. Criminal PAT goes back to 1990. Statewide access provided, year of birth shown.

Laramie County

1st Judicial District Court 309 W 20th St, #3205, PO Box 787, Cheyenne, WY 82003; 307-633-4270; fax: 307-633-4277; 8AM-5PM (MST). *Felony, Misdemeanor, Civil Actions over $50,000, Probate.*
www.laramiecounty.com/_departments/_district_court/index.asp

General Information: No juvenile or paternity records released. No fee to fax results to 800 numbers only. Court makes copy: $1.00 first page, $.50 each add'l. Self serve copy: same. Certification fee: $.50 per page, Exemplification fee- $5.00 plus copy fees. Payee: Laramie County Clerk of District Court. Business checks accepted. Major credit cards accepted. Prepayment required. Mail requests: SASE required.

Civil Name Search: Access: Fax, mail, in person. Both court and visitors may perform in person name searches. Search fee: $10.00 per name. Civil records on card index from 1890; on computer back to mid April 1992. Note:

Effective 01/01/2011 per State Rule, on all new case files the birth day and birth month and the first five digits of an SSN are redacted on court files viewable by the public. Prior records probably will not be redacted. Mail turnaround time 2 days. Civil PAT goes back to 04/1992.

Criminal Name Search: Access: Fax, mail, in person. Both court and visitors may perform in person name searches. Search fee: $10.00 per name. Required to search: name, years to search, DOB, SSN. Criminal records on card index from 1890 to mid April 1992, computerized forward. Note: Effective 01/01/2011 per State Rule, on all new case files the birth day and birth month and the first five digits of an SSN are redacted on court files viewable by the public. Prior records probably will not be redacted. Mail turnaround time 2 days. Criminal PAT goes back to same as civil.

Laramie County Circuit Court 309 W 20th St, Rm 2300, Cheyenne, WY 82001; criminal phone: 307-633-4298; civil phone: 307-633-4326; fax: 307-633-4392; 8AM-5PM (MST). *Misdemeanor, Civil Actions under $50,000, Eviction, Small Claims.*
www.courts.state.wy.us/

General Information: Fee to fax back is $2.00 per doc to non toll-free number; otherwise free. Court makes copy: $1.00 1st page, $.50 each add'l. Certification fee: $5.00 per document. Payee: Laramie County Circuit Court. Business checks and local personal checks only. Visa/MC accepted. Add $8.00 credit card convenience fee for criminal fees if request by phone. Prepayment required. Mail requests: SASE required for mail return.

Civil Name Search: Access: Fax, mail, in person. Both court and visitors may perform in person name searches. Search fee: $10.00 per name. Required to search: name, years to search, DOB; also helpful: address. Civil records on computer from 1992, card index from late 1977. Note: Effective 01/01/2011 per State Rule, on all new case files the birth day and birth month and the first five digits of an SSN are redacted on court files viewable by the public. Prior records probably will not be redacted. Mail turnaround time 48 hours. Civil PAT goes back to 1992. Statewide access provided, year of birth shown.

Criminal Name Search: Access: Fax, mail, in person. Both court and visitors may perform in person name searches. Search fee: $10.00 per name. Required to search: name, years to search; also helpful: address. Criminal records computerized from 1988, card index from late 1977. Note: Effective 01/01/2011 per State Rule, on all new case files the birth day and birth month and the first five digits of an SSN are redacted on court files viewable by the public. Prior records probably will not be redacted. Mail turnaround time 48 hours. Criminal PAT goes back to 1988. Statewide access provided, year of birth shown.

Cheyenne Municipal Court 309 W 20th St, Rm 2100, Cheyenne, WY 82001; 307-633-4422; fax: 307-633-4471; 8AM-5PM (MST). *Misdemeanor, Ordinance.*
www.cheyennecity.org/index.aspx?nid=61

Lincoln County

3rd Judicial District Court PO Drawer 510, Kemmerer, WY 83101; 307-877-3320; criminal phone: 307-877-3320; fax: 307-877-6263; 8AM-5PM (MST). *Felony, Civil Actions over $50,000, Probate.*
www.courts.state.wy.us/

General Information: No juvenile, sexual or PD records released. Will fax out files $5.00 per doc. Court makes copy: $1.00 first page, $.50 each add'l. Self serve copy: same. Certification fee: $2.50. Payee: 3rd Judicial District Court. Personal checks accepted, credit cards are not. Prepayment required. Mail requests: SASE required.

Civil Name Search: Access: Fax, mail, in person. Both court and visitors may perform in person name searches. Search fee: $10.00 per name. Required to search: name; also helpful: years to search, address. Civil cases indexed by defendant. Civil records on card index and computer back to 1916. Note: Effective 01/01/2011 per State Rule, on all new case files the birth day and birth month and the first five digits of an SSN are redacted on court files viewable by the public. Prior records probably will not be redacted. Mail turnaround time same day. Civil PAT goes back to early 1900s.

Criminal Name Search: Access: Fax, mail, in person. Both court and visitors may perform in person name searches. Search fee: $10.00 per name. Required to search: name; also helpful: years to search, address, DOB, SSN. Criminal records on card index and computer back to 1916. Note: Effective 01/01/2011 per State Rule, on all new case files the birth day and birth month and the first five digits of an SSN are redacted on court files viewable by the public. Prior records probably will not be redacted. Mail turnaround time same day. Criminal PAT goes back to early 1900s.

Lincoln Circuit Court PO Box 949, Kemmerer, WY 83101; 307-877-4431; fax: 307-877-4936; 8AM-5PM (MST). *Misdemeanor, Civil Actions under $50,000, Eviction, Small Claims.* www.courts.state.wy.us/

General Information: No sexual or PD records released. Will fax out files to local or toll free line. Court makes copy: $1.00 1st page, $.50 each add'l.

Certification fee: $5.00 per document. Payee: Lincoln Circuit Court. Business checks accepted. Out of state checks not accepted. Visa/MC accepted ($5.00 fee added for using credit cards). Prepayment required. Mail requests: SASE requested.

Civil Name Search: Access: Mail, in person. Both court and visitors may perform in person name searches. Search fee: $10.00 per name or alias. Civil records on computer from 1/90, on card index from 1984, prior data in archives. Note: All search requests must be in writing. Effective 01/01/2011 per State Rule, on all new case files the birth day and birth month and the first five digits of an SSN are redacted on court files viewable by the public. Prior records probably will not be red Mail turnaround time same day. Civil PAT available. Statewide access provided, year of birth shown.

Criminal Name Search: Access: Mail, in person. Both court and visitors may perform in person name searches. Search fee: $10.00 per name or alias. Required to search: name, years to search, DOB; also helpful: SSN. Criminal records computerized from 10/90, card index from 1984, prior in archives. Note: All search requests must be in writing. Effective 01/01/2011 per State Rule, on all new case files the birth day and birth month and the first five digits of an SSN are redacted on court files viewable by the public. Prior records probably will not be red Mail turnaround time same day. Criminal PAT available. Statewide access provided, year of birth shown.

Natrona County

7th Judicial District Court 115 N Center, Ste 100, Casper, WY 82601; 307-235-9243; fax: 307-235-9496; 8AM-5PM (MST). *Felony, Civil Actions over $50,000, Probate.*
www.courts.state.wy.us/

General Information: The 9496 fax number is for record room. No misdemeanor records here unless they were originally felony charges. No adoption, juvenile, paternity, mental health records released. Will fax out files $2.00 fee. No email return. Court makes copy: $1.00 first page, $.50 each add'l. Self serve copy: Make your own copies from microfiche. $.15 per page if non-court document. Certification fee: $.50 per doc; $5.00 to authenticate. Payee: Clerk of District Court. Business checks accepted; no personal checks. No credit cards accepted. Prepayment required. Mail requests: SASE required.

Civil Name Search: Access: Phone, fax, mail, in person. Both court and visitors may perform in person name searches. Search fee: $10.00 per name. Required to search: name, years to search; also helpful: address. Civil records on computer, microfiche from 1891. Note: Effective 01/01/2011 per State Rule, on all new case files the birth day and birth month and the first five digits of an SSN are redacted on court files viewable by the public. Prior records probably will not be redacted. Mail turnaround time same day. Civil PAT goes back to 1891.

Criminal Name Search: Access: Mail, in person. Both court and visitors may perform in person name searches. Search fee: $10.00 per name. Required to search: name, years to search; also helpful: address, DOB, SSN. Criminal records on computer, microfiche from 1891. Note: Effective 01/01/2011 per State Rule, on all new case files the birth day and birth month and the first five digits of an SSN are redacted on court files viewable by the public. Prior records probably will not be redacted. Mail turnaround time same day to 2 days max. Criminal PAT goes back to same as civil. ID verifications can be made with the clerk.

Natrona Circuit Court 115 North Center, Ste 400, Casper, WY 82601; 307-235-9266; fax: 307-235-9331; 8AM-5PM (MST). *Misdemeanor, Civil Actions under $50,000, Eviction, Small Claims.*
www.courts.state.wy.us/

General Information: No sexual, abuse records released. Fee to fax out file $2.00: no fee to fax to 800 numbers. Court makes copy: $1.00 1st page, $.50 each add'l. Certification fee: $5.00 per document. Payee: Natrona Circuit Court. Personal checks accepted. Visa/MC/Discover accepted. Prepayment required. Mail requests: SASE required.

Civil Name Search: Access: Mail, in person. Both court and visitors may perform in person name searches. Search fee: $10.00 per name. Required to search: name, years to search; also helpful: address. Civil records on computer from 1994. Microfiche from 1891 is at Archives in Cheyenne. Note: Effective 01/01/2011 per State Rule, on all new case files the birth day and birth month and the first five digits of an SSN are redacted on court files viewable by the public. Prior records probably will not be redacted. Mail turnaround time 2-5 days. Civil PAT available. Statewide access provided, year of birth shown.

Criminal Name Search: Access: Mail, in person. Both court and visitors may perform in person name searches. Search fee: $10.00 per name. Required to search: name, years to search; also helpful: address, DOB, SSN. Criminal records computerized from 1989. Microfiche from 1891 is at Archives in Cheyenne. Note: All search requests must be in writing. Effective 01/01/2011 per State Rule, on all new case files the birth day and birth month and the first five digits of an SSN are redacted on court files viewable by the public. Prior records probably will not be redacted Mail turnaround time 2-5 days. Criminal PAT available. Statewide access provided, year of birth shown.

Niobrara County

8th Judicial District Court Clerk of District Court, PO Box 1318, Lusk, WY 82225; 307-334-2736; fax: 307-334-2703; 8AM-N, 1-4PM (MST). *Felony, Civil Actions over $50,000, Probate.*
www.courts.state.wy.us/
General Information: Probate fax is same as main fax number. No juvenile or adoption related released, no PD released. Fee to fax files is $1.00 per page. Court makes copy: $1.00 first page, $.50 each add'l. Certification fee: $.50 per page plus copy fee. Payee: Niobrara County Clerk of District Court. Personal checks accepted, credit cards are not. Prepayment required. Mail requests: SASE required.
Civil Name Search: Access: Mail, in person. Visitors must perform in person searches themselves. Search fee: $10.00 per name. Civil records on card index from early 1900s. Note: Effective 01/01/2011 per State Rule, on all new case files the birth day and birth month and the first five digits of an SSN are redacted on court files viewable by the public. Prior records probably will not be redacted. Mail turnaround time 2 days.
Criminal Name Search: Access: Mail, in person. Both court and visitors may perform in person name searches. Search fee: $10.00 per name. Required to search: name, years to search, DOB, SSN. Criminal records on card index from 1913. Note: Effective 01/01/2011 per State Rule, on all new case files the birth day and birth month and the first five digits of an SSN are redacted on court files viewable by the public. Prior records probably will not be redacted. Mail turnaround time 2 days.

Circuit Court PO Box 209, 223 S Main St, Lusk, WY 82225; 307-334-2049; fax: 307-334-3846; 9AM-N, 1-5PM (MST). *Misdemeanor, Civil Actions under $50,000, Small Claims.*
www.courts.state.wy.us/
General Information: This was a Justice Court until 01/03. No juvenile data released. Fee to fax files is $2 per doc. Court makes copy: $1.00 1st page; $.50 each add'l. Certification fee: $5 per document. Payee: Niobrara Circuit Court. Personal checks, Visa/MC accepted. Prepayment required. Mail requests: SASE requested.
Civil Name Search: Access: Mail, in person. Both court and visitors may perform in person name searches. Search fee: $10.00 per name. Required to search: name, years to search; also helpful: address. Civil cases indexed by plaintiff. Civil records on computer back to 2003, also index cards. Note: Effective 01/01/2011 per State Rule, on all new case files the birth day and birth month and the first five digits of an SSN are redacted on court files viewable by the public. Prior records probably will not be redacted. Mail turnaround time 2 days. Civil PAT goes back to 2003. Statewide access provided, year of birth shown.
Criminal Name Search: Access: Mail, in person. Both court and visitors may perform in person name searches. Search fee: $10.00 per name. Required to search: name, years to search, DOB, SSN, signed release; also helpful: address. Criminal records computerized from 1988, prior archived. Note: Effective 01/01/2011 per State Rule, on all new case files the birth day and birth month and the first five digits of an SSN are redacted on court files viewable by the public. Prior records probably will not be redacted. Mail turnaround time 2 days. Criminal PAT goes back to 1998. Statewide access provided, year of birth shown.

Park County

5th Judicial District Court Clerk of District Court, PO Box 1960, 1002 Sheridan Ave, Cody, WY 82414; 307-527-8690; fax: 307-527-8687; 8AM-5PM (MST). *Felony, Civil Actions over $50,000, Probate.*
www.parkcounty.us/districtcourt/districtcourt.html
General Information: Probate fax is same as main fax number. No juvenile, adoptions or PD released. Will fax documents $2.00 fee. Court makes copy: $1.00 first page, $.50 each add'l. Certification fee: $.50 per page; exemplification fee is $5.00. Payee: Clerk of District Court. No personal checks. Prepayment required. Mail requests: SASE preferred.
Civil Name Search: Access: Phone, fax, mail, in person. Only the court performs in person name searches; visitors may not. Search fee: $10.00 per name. Required to search: name, years to search; also helpful: address. Civil records on computer from 1989, card index and files back to 1911. Note: Effective 01/01/2011 per State Rule, on all new case files the birth day and birth month and the first five digits of an SSN are redacted on court files viewable by the public. Prior records probably will not be redacted. Mail turnaround time 6 hours.
Criminal Name Search: Access: Phone, fax, mail, in person. Only the court performs in person name searches; visitors may not. Search fee: $10.00 per name. Required to search: name, years to search; also helpful: DOB, SSN. Criminal records computerized from 1989, card index and files back to 1911. Note: Effective 01/01/2011 per State Rule, on all new case files the birth day and birth month and the first five digits of an SSN are

redacted on court files viewable by the public. Prior records probably will not be redacted. Mail turnaround time 6 hours.

Cody Circuit Court 1002 Sheridan Ave., Cody, WY 82414; 307-527-8590; fax: 307-527-8596; 8AM-5PM (MST). *Misdemeanor, Civil Actions under $50,000, Eviction, Small Claims.*
www.courts.state.wy.us/
General Information: This court has records for the Powell Circuit Court Branch. No sexual or confidential data released. Will fax out files to local or toll free line. Court makes copy: $1.00 1st page, $.50 each add'l. Certification fee: $.50 per document. Payee: Park County Circuit Court. Business checks accepted. Major credit cards accepted. Prepayment required. Mail requests: SASE required.
Civil Name Search: Access: Mail, in person. Both court and visitors may perform in person name searches. Search fee: $10.00 per name. Required to search: name, years to search; also helpful: address. Civil records on computer since 8/95; limited records available prior to 8/95. Note: Effective 01/01/2011 per State Rule, on all new case files the birth day and birth month and the first five digits of an SSN are redacted on court files viewable by the public. Prior records probably will not be redacted. Mail turnaround time 5 days. Civil PAT available. Statewide access provided, year of birth shown.
Criminal Name Search: Access: Mail, in person. Both court and visitors may perform in person name searches. Search fee: $10.00 per name. Required to search: name, years to search, DOB, SSN (one or other is required) also helpful: address,. Criminal records on computer since 1990; limited records available prior to 1990. Note: Effective 01/01/2011 per State Rule, on all new case files the birth day and birth month and the first five digits of an SSN are redacted on court files viewable by the public. Prior records probably will not be redacted. Mail turnaround time 5 days. Criminal PAT available. Statewide access provided, year of birth shown.

Powell Circuit Court 109 W 14th, Powell, WY 82435; 307-754-8890; fax: 307-754-8896; 8AM-N, 1-5PM (MST). *Misdemeanor, Small Claims.*
www.courts.state.wy.us/
General Information: Powell court misdemeanor records are also available at the main Circuit Court in Cody. No sexual, confidential records released. Fee to fax files is $2.00 per document. Court makes copy: $1.00 1st page, $.50 each add'l. Certification fee: $.50 per doc. Payee: Park County Circuit Court. Personal checks, Visa/MC accepted. Prepayment required. Mail requests: SASE required.
Civil Name Search: Access: Mail, in person. Both court and visitors may perform in person name searches. Search fee: $10.00 per name. Civil records on computer from 1995; prior records very poor. Note: Effective 01/01/2011 per State Rule, on all new case files the birth day and birth month and the first five digits of an SSN are redacted on court files viewable by the public. Prior records probably will not be redacted. Mail turnaround time 1 week. Civil PAT available. Statewide access provided, year of birth shown.
Criminal Name Search: Access: Mail, in person. Both court and visitors may perform in person name searches. Search fee: $10.00 per name. Required to search: name, years to search, DOB or SSN. Criminal records computerized from 1990; prior records very poor. Note: Effective 01/01/2011 per State Rule, on all new case files the birth day and birth month and the first five digits of an SSN are redacted on court files viewable by the public. Prior records probably will not be redacted. Mail turnaround time 1 week. Criminal PAT available. Statewide access provided, year of birth shown.

Platte County

8th Judicial District Court PO Box 158, Wheatland, WY 82201; 307-322-3857; fax: 307-322-5402; 8AM-5PM (MST). *Felony, Civil Actions over $50,000, Probate.*
www.courts.state.wy.us/
General Information: No juvenile data released. Will fax out files to local or toll free line. Court makes copy: $1.00 first page, $.50 each add'l. Certification fee: $.50 per page. Payee: Clerk of the Court. Personal checks accepted, credit cards are not. Prepayment required. Mail requests: SASE required.
Civil Name Search: Access: Mail, fax, in person. Both court and visitors may perform in person name searches. Search fee: $10.00 per name. Required to search: name, years to search; also helpful: address. Civil records go back to 1998. Note: Effective 01/01/2011 per State Rule, on all new case files the birth day and birth month and the first five digits of an SSN are redacted on court files viewable by the public. Prior records probably will not be redacted. Mail turnaround time same day.
Criminal Name Search: Access: Mail, fax, in person. Both court and visitors may perform in person name searches. Search fee: $10.00 per name. Required to search: name, years to search; also helpful: address, DOB, SSN. Criminal records go back to 1997. Note: Effective 01/01/2011 per State Rule, on all new case files the birth day and birth month and the

first five digits of an SSN are redacted on court files viewable by the public. Prior records probably will not be redacted. Mail turnaround time same day.

Circuit Court PO Box 306, Wheatland, WY 82201; 307-322-3441; fax: 307-322-1371; 8AM-5PM (MST). *Misdemeanor, Civil Actions under $50,000, Small Claims.*

www.courts.state.wy.us/

General Information: This former Justice Court became a Circuit Court as of 1/2003. No juvenile data released. Fee to fax results included in search fee. Court makes copy: included in search fee. Certification fee: $5.00 per document. Payee: Platte County Circuit Court. Business checks accepted. No credit cards accepted. Prepayment required. Fax requests should include a copy of the check. Mail requests: SASE required.

Civil Name Search: Access: Phone, mail, fax, in person. Both court and visitors may perform in person name searches. Search fee: $10.00 per name. Required to search: name, years to search; also helpful: address. Civil cases indexed by defendant. Civil records on computer since 11/95; on card index since 1976. Note: Fax copy of check, when faxing. Effective 01/01/2011 per State Rule, on all new case files the birth day and birth month and the first five digits of an SSN are redacted on court files viewable by the public. Prior records probably will not be redacted. Mail turnaround time 2 days. Civil PAT available. Statewide access provided, year of birth shown.

Criminal Name Search: Access: Phone, mail, fax, in person. Both court and visitors may perform in person name searches. Search fee: $10.00 per name includes common name variations. Required to search: name, years to search, signed release, DOB; also helpful: address, SSN. Criminal records computerized from 11/92, card index from 1976. Note: When faxing request, include copy of payment check. Effective 01/01/2011 per State Rule, on all new case files the birth day and birth month and the first five digits of an SSN are redacted on court files viewable by the public. Prior records probably will not be redacted. Mail turnaround time 2 days. Criminal PAT available. Statewide access provided, year of birth shown.

Sheridan County

4th Judicial District Court 224 S Main, #B-11, Sheridan, WY 82801; 307-674-2960; fax: 307-674-2589; 8AM-5PM (MST). *Felony, Civil Actions over $50,000, Probate.*

www.sheridancounty.com/info/cdc/overview.php

General Information: No escs related, juvenile or adoption cases released except by judges permission. Fee to fax files is $2.00 per doc. Court makes copy: $1.00 first page, $.50 each add'l. Certification fee: $.50 per doc; exemplification- $5.00 per doc. Payee: Clerk of District Court. Personal checks accepted, credit cards are not. Prepayment required. Mail requests: SASE required.

Civil Name Search: Access: Phone, mail, in person. Both court and visitors may perform in person name searches. Search fee: $10.00. Civil records archived from 1800s; index cards back to 1972. Note: Effective 01/01/2011 per State Rule, on all new case files the birth day and birth month and the first five digits of an SSN are redacted on court files viewable by the public. Prior records probably will not be redacted. Mail turnaround time 24 hours.

Criminal Name Search: Access: Phone, mail, fax, in person. Both court and visitors may perform in person name searches. Search fee: $10.00 per name. Required to search: name, years to search, DOB, SSN. Criminal records archived from late 1800s; index cards back to 1972. Note: Effective 01/01/2011 per State Rule, on all new case files the birth day and birth month and the first five digits of an SSN are redacted on court files viewable by the public. Prior records probably will not be redacted. Mail turnaround time 24 hours.

Circuit Court 224 S Main, #B-7, Sheridan, WY 82801; 307-674-2940; fax: 307-674-2944; 8AM-5PM (MST). *Misdemeanor, Civil Actions under $50,000, Eviction, Small Claims.*

www.courts.state.wy.us/

General Information: Identity of victims not released in sexual assault cases. After fees are paid, will fax documents to toll-free number for estar $2.00 fax fee. Court makes copy: $1.00 1st page, $.50 each add'l. Certification fee: $5.00 per document. Payee: Sheridan Circuit Court. Personal checks accepted. Visa/MC, Discover accepted; an $8.00 fee added if over the phone. Prepayment required. Mail requests: SASE required.

Civil Name Search: Access: Mail, fax, in person. Both court and visitors may perform in person name searches. Search fee: $10.00 per name. Required to search: name, years to search, DOB, SSN; also helpful: address. Civil records on cards from 1983; computerized records go back to 1996. Note: Effective 01/01/2011 per State Rule, on all new case files the birth day and birth month and the first five digits of an SSN are redacted on court files viewable by the public. Prior records probably will not be redacted. Mail turnaround time ASAP. Civil PAT available. Statewide access provided, year of birth shown.

Criminal Name Search: Access: Mail, fax, in person. Both court and visitors may perform in person name searches. Search fee: $10.00 per name. Required to search: name, years to search, DOB, SSN; also helpful: address. Criminal records computerized from 1990, on cards from 1983. Note: Effective 01/01/2011 per State Rule, on all new case files the birth day and birth month and the first five digits of an SSN are redacted on court files viewable by the public. Prior records probably will not be redacted. Mail turnaround time same or next day. Criminal PAT available. Statewide access provided, year of birth shown.

Sublette County

9th Judicial District Court PO Box 764, Pinedale, WY 82941-0764; 307-367-4376; fax: 307-367-6474; 8AM-5PM (MST). *Felony, Civil Actions over $50,000, Probate.*

www.sublettewyo.com/

General Information: Probate fax is same as main fax number. No PD or juvenile records released. Will fax out files for $1.00 per page. Court makes copy: $1.00 first page, $.50 each add'l. Self serve copy: same. No certification fee . Payee: Clerk of District Court. Personal checks accepted, credit cards are not. Prepayment required. Mail requests: SASE required.

Civil Name Search: Access: Mail, in person. Both court and visitors may perform in person name searches. Search fee: $10.00 per name. Required to search: name; also helpful: years to search, address. Civil records on card file from 1923. Note: Effective 01/01/2011 per State Rule, on all new case files the birth day and birth month and the first five digits of an SSN are redacted on court files viewable by the public. Prior records probably will not be redacted. Mail turnaround time same day.

Criminal Name Search: Access: Mail, in person. Both court and visitors may perform in person name searches. Search fee: $10.00 per name. Required to search: name, years to search; also helpful: address, DOB, SSN. Criminal records go back to 1923. Note: Effective 01/01/2011 per State Rule, on all new case files the birth day and birth month and the first five digits of an SSN are redacted on court files viewable by the public. Prior records probably will not be redacted. Mail turnaround time same day.

Sublette Circuit Court PO Box 1796, 40 S Fremont Ave, Pinedale, WY 82941; 307-367-2556; fax: 307-367-2658; 8AM-5PM (MST). *Misdemeanor, Civil Actions under $50,000, Eviction, Small Claims.*

www.courts.state.wy.us/

General Information: Will fax out documents no fee to toll-free number, otherwise $2.00 per fax. Court makes copy: $1.00 1st page, $.50 each add'l. Certification fee: $5.00 per doc. Payee: Circuit Court of Sublette County. Credit cards accepted; $5.00 surcharge if not in person. Prepayment required. Mail requests: SASE not required.

Civil Name Search: Access: Mail, in person. Both court and visitors may perform in person name searches. Search fee: $10.00 per name. Required to search: name, years to search; also helpful: address. Civil records go back 21 years, computerized from 1998. Note: Effective 01/01/2011 per State Rule, on all new case files the birth day and birth month and the first five digits of an SSN are redacted on court files viewable by the public. Prior records probably will not be redacted. Mail turnaround time 2 business days. Civil PAT available. Statewide access provided, year of birth shown.

Criminal Name Search: Access: Mail, in person. Both court and visitors may perform in person name searches. Search fee: $10.00 per name. Required to search: name, years to search, DOB; also helpful: address, SSN. Criminal records computerized from 1993. Note: Effective 01/01/2011 per State Rule, on all new case files the birth day and birth month and the first five digits of an SSN are redacted on court files viewable by the public. Prior records probably will not be redacted. Mail turnaround time 2 business days. Criminal PAT available. Statewide access provided, year of birth shown.

Sweetwater County

3rd Judicial District Court PO Box 430, 80 W Flaming Gorge Way, Ste 255, Green River, WY 82935; 307-872-3820; fax: 307-872-6439; 8AM-5PM (MST). *Felony, Civil Actions over $50,000, Probate.*

www.sweet.wy.us

General Information: No juvenile, paternity, or adoption records released. Will fax back documents for $2.00 fee plus $1.00 per page. Court makes copy: $1.00 first page, $.50 each add'l. Certification fee: 1st page free, $.50 each add'l; exemplification fee is $5.00. Payee: Clerk of District Court. Business checks accepted. No credit cards accepted. Prepayment required. Mail requests: SASE required.

Civil Name Search: Access: Fax, mail, in person. Both court and visitors may perform in person name searches. Search fee: $10.00 per name. Civil records on computer from 1985, on microfiche from 1960, archived from late 1800. Note: Requests must be in writing. Effective 2011 per State Rule, on new case files the birth day and birth month and the first five SSN digits redacted on court files viewable. Prior records probably will not be redacted. Mail turnaround time same day. Civil PAT goes back to 1985. Later records may not have all identifiers, or SSNs.

Criminal Name Search: Access: Fax, mail, in person. Both court and visitors may perform in person name searches. Search fee: $10.00 per name. Criminal records computerized from 1985, on microfiche from 1960, archived from late 1800. Note: Requests must be in writing. Effective 2011 per State Rule, on new case files the birth day and birth month and the first five SSN digits redacted on court files viewable. Prior records probably will not be redacted. Mail turnaround time same day. Criminal PAT goes back to same as civil. Later records may not have all identifiers; most have SSNs.

Green River Circuit Court PO Drawer 1720, 177 N Center St, Green River, WY 82935; criminal phone: 307-872-3800; civil phone: 307-872-3805; fax: 307-872-3973; 8AM-5PM (MST). *Misdemeanor, Civil Actions under $50,000, Eviction, Small Claims.*
www.courts.state.wy.us/

General Information: No sealed, sexual assault records released. Fee to fax files is $2.00 per fax. Court makes copy: $1.00 1st page, $.50 each add'l. Certification fee: $5.00 per document. Payee: Sweetwater County Circuit Court. Business checks accepted. In-state checks only. Visa/MC accepted; add $5.00 transaction fee if request made by phone. Prepayment required. Mail requests: SASE required.

Civil Name Search: Access: Mail, in person. Both court and visitors may perform in person name searches. Search fee: $10.00 per name includes copies. Required to search: name, years to search; helpful- SSN, DOB. Civil records on computer from 1994, in card file from 1981-1994, archived prior to 1981. Note: Requests must be in writing. Effective 01/01/2011 per State Rule, on all new case files the birth day and birth month and the first five digits of an SSN are redacted on court files viewable by the public. Prior records probably will not be redacted. Mail turnaround time same day. Civil PAT available. Statewide access provided, year of birth shown.

Criminal Name Search: Access: Mail, in person. Both court and visitors may perform in person name searches. Search fee: $10.00 per name includes copies. Required to search: name, years to search, DOB; also helpful: SSN. Criminal Records computerized since 1990, on card file from 1981 to 1990. Note: Requests must be in writing. Effective 01/01/2011 per State Rule, on all new case files the birth day and birth month and the first five digits of an SSN are redacted on court files viewable by the public. Prior records probably will not be redacted. Mail turnaround time same day. Criminal PAT available. Statewide access provided, year of birth shown.

Sweetwater Circuit Court PO Box 2028, 731 C St, Rock Springs, WY 82902; 307-922-5220; fax: 307-352-6758; 8AM-5PM (MST). *Misdemeanor, Civil Actions under $50,000, Eviction, Small Claims.*
www.courts.state.wy.us/

General Information: Search fee covers civil and criminal indexes. No sexual assault, sealed records released. Fee to fax files is $2.00 per doc. Court makes copy: $1.00 1st page, $.50 each add'l. Certification fee: $5.00 per doc plus copy fee. Payee: Sweetwater Circuit Court. Business checks accepted. Major credit cards accepted. Prepayment required. Mail requests: SASE required.

Civil Name Search: Access: Fax, mail, in person. Both court and visitors may perform in person name searches. Search fee: $10.00 per name. Required to search: name, years to search; also helpful: address. Civil records on computer from 1995, archived to 1981. Note: Effective 01/01/2011 per State Rule, on all new case files the birth day and birth month and the first five digits of an SSN are redacted on court files viewable by the public. Prior records probably will not be redacted. Mail turnaround time 2 days. Civil PAT available. Statewide access provided, year of birth shown.

Criminal Name Search: Access: Fax, mail, in person. Both court and visitors may perform in person name searches. Search fee: $10.00 per name. Required to search: name, years to search; also helpful: address, DOB, SSN. Criminal records computerized from 1989, archived to 1981. Note: Effective 01/01/2011 per State Rule, on all new case files the birth day and birth month and the first five digits of an SSN are redacted on court files viewable by the public. Prior records probably will not be redacted. Mail turnaround time 2 days. Criminal PAT available. Statewide access provided, year of birth shown.

Teton County

9th Judicial District Court PO Box 4460, Jackson, WY 83001; 307-733-2533; fax: 307-734-1562; 8AM-5PM (MST). *Felony, Civil Actions over $50,000, Probate.*
www.courts.state.wy.us/

General Information: No juvenile or adoption records released. Will fax out files to local or toll free line. Court makes copy: $1.00 first page, $.50 each add'l. Self serve copy: $.15 per page. Certification fee: $.50 per page.

Payee: Clerk of District Court. Personal checks accepted, credit cards are not. Prepayment required. Mail requests: SASE required.

Civil Name Search: Access: Phone, fax, mail, in person. Both court and visitors may perform in person name searches. Search fee: $10.00 per name. Required to search: name, years to search; also helpful: address. Civil records on computer since 1990, card index back to 1920s. Note: Effective 01/01/2011 per State Rule, on all new case files the birth day and birth month and the first five digits of an SSN are redacted on court files viewable by the public. Prior records probably will not be redacted. Mail turnaround time 2 days. Civil PAT goes back to 1995. Sometime the DOB and middle name will show.

Criminal Name Search: Access: Phone, fax, mail, in person. Both court and visitors may perform in person name searches. Search fee: $10.00 per name. Required to search: name, years to search; also helpful: address, DOB, SSN. Criminal records on computer since 1990, card index back to 1920s. Note: Effective 01/01/2011 per State Rule, on all new case files the birth day and birth month and the first five digits of an SSN are redacted on court files viewable by the public. Prior records probably will not be redacted. Mail turnaround time 2 days. Criminal PAT goes back to same as civil. Records prior to 2011 may have some DOBs and middle initials.

Circuit Court PO Box 2906, 180 S King St, Jackson, WY 83001; 307-733-7713; fax: 307-733-8694; 8AM-5PM (MST). *Misdemeanor, Civil Actions under $50,000, Small Claims under $5,000.*
www.courts.state.wy.us/

General Information: This was a Justice Court until 01/03. No juvenile, sexual or PD released. Fee to fax back- $2.00 per doc. Court makes copy: $1.00 1st page, $.50 each add'l. Certification fee: $5.00 per document. Payee: Teton County Circuit Court. Personal checks accepted, credit cards are not. Prepayment required. Mail requests: SASE requested.

Civil Name Search: Access: Mail, in person. Both court and visitors may perform in person name searches. Search fee: $10.00 per name. Required to search: name, years to search; also helpful-DOB, SSN. Civil index on docket books back to 1979. Actual files 5 years. Note: Effective 01/01/2011 per State Rule, on all new case files the birth day and birth month and the first five digits of an SSN are redacted on court files viewable by the public. Prior records probably will not be redacted. Mail turnaround time 3-4 days; may be longer for pre-1992 criminal records. Civil PAT available. Statewide access provided, year of birth shown.

Criminal Name Search: Access: Mail, in person. Both court and visitors may perform in person name searches. Search fee: $10.00 per name. Required to search: name, years to search, DOB, SSN. Criminal records citations on computer from 1991. No citation record older than 5 years. On docket books and card files back to 1979. Note: Effective 01/01/2011 per State Rule, on all new case files the birth day and birth month and the first five digits of an SSN are redacted on court files viewable by the public. Prior records probably will not be redacted. Mail turnaround time 3-4 days; longer for pre-1992 records. Criminal PAT available. Statewide access provided, year of birth shown.

Uinta County

3rd Judicial District Court PO Drawer 1906, Attn: Clerk of District Court, Evanston, WY 82931; 307-783-0456; fax: 307-783-0400; 8AM-5PM (MST). *Felony, Civil Actions over $50,000, Probate.*
www.uintacounty.com

General Information: Signed notarized release necessary on confidential cases. Fee to fax files is $2.00 per doc. Court makes copy: $1.00 first page; $.50 each add'l. Certification fee: $.50 per seal. Payee: Clerk of District Court. Personal checks accepted, credit cards are not. Prepayment required. Mail requests: SASE required.

Civil Name Search: Access: Mail, in person. Both court and visitors may perform in person name searches. Search fee: $10.00 per name. Required to search: name, years to search; also helpful: address. Civil records on microfiche from the late 1800s to early 1990's. Note: Effective 01/01/2011 per State Rule, on all new case files the birth day and birth month and the first five digits of an SSN are redacted on court files viewable by the public. Prior records probably will not be redacted. Mail turnaround time 1 day.

Criminal Name Search: Access: Mail, in person. Both court and visitors may perform in person name searches. Search fee: $10.00 per name. Required to search: name, years to search, DOB, SSN; also helpful: address. Criminal records on microfiche since 1938 to early 1990s. Note: Effective 01/01/2011 per State Rule, on all new case files the birth day and birth month and the first five digits of an SSN are redacted on court files viewable by the public. Prior records probably will not be redacted. Mail turnaround time 1 day.

Uinta Circuit Court 225 9th St, 2nd Fl, Evanston, WY 82931; 307-789-2471; fax: 307-789-5062; 8AM-5PM (MST). *Misdemeanor, Civil Actions under $50,000, Eviction, Small Claims.*
www.courts.state.wy.us/

General Information: No juvenile records released. Fee to fax files is $2.00 per document. Court makes copy: $1.00 1st page, $.50 each add'l. Certification fee: $5.00 per doc plus copy fee. Payee: Uinta County Circuit Court. Out of state checks not accepted. Add $8.00 transaction fee if paying by credit card. Prepayment required. Mail requests: SASE requested.

Civil Name Search: Access: Mail, in person. Both court and visitors may perform in person name searches. Search fee: $10.00 per name. Required to search: name, years to search; also helpful: address, DOB. Civil records on computer from 1994, prior on card index. Note: All requests must be in writing. Court only searches back 10 years. Effective 01/01/2011 per State Rule, on all new case files the birth day and birth month and the first five digits of an SSN are redacted on court files viewable by the public. Prior records probably will not be redacted .Mail turnaround time 3 days. Civil PAT available. Statewide access provided, year of birth shown.

Criminal Name Search: Access: Mail, in person. Both court and visitors may perform in person name searches. Search fee: $10.00 per name. Required to search: name, years to search; also helpful: address, DOB, SSN. Criminal records on computer since 1989, prior on index cards. Note: Requests must be in writing. Court only searches back 10 years. Effective 01/01/2011 per State Rule, on all new case files the birth day and birth month and the first five digits of an SSN are redacted on court files viewable by the public. Prior records probably will not be redacted. Mail turnaround time 3 days. Criminal PAT available. Statewide access provided, year of birth shown.

Washakie County

5th Judicial District Court PO Box 862, Worland, WY 82401; 307-347-4821; fax: 307-347-4325; 8AM-5PM (MST). *Felony, Civil Actions over $50,000, Probate, Juvenile.*
www.courts.state.wy.us/

General Information: No juvenile, sexual or PD released. Will fax out files $2.00 per page. Court makes copy: $1.00 first page, $.50 each add'l. Self serve copy: same. Certification fee: $.50 per document plus copy fee. Payee: Clerk of Court. Personal checks accepted, credit cards are not. Prepayment required. Mail requests: SASE required.

Civil Name Search: Access: Fax, mail, in person. Both court and visitors may perform in person name searches. Search fee: $10.00 per name. Required to search: name; also helpful: years to search, address, DOB. Civil records on computer back to 1985, prior on file index. Note: Effective 01/01/2011 per State Rule, on all new case files the birth day and birth month and the first five digits of an SSN are redacted on court files viewable by the public. Prior records probably will not be redacted. Mail turnaround time same day when possible. Civil PAT goes back to 2005, some older.

Criminal Name Search: Access: Phone, fax, mail, in person. Both court and visitors may perform in person name searches. Search fee: $10.00 per name. Required to search: name, years to search; also helpful: address, DOB, SSN. Criminal records computerized from 1985, prior on file index. Note: Effective 01/01/2011 per State Rule, on all new case files the birth day and birth month and the first five digits of an SSN are redacted on court files viewable by the public. Prior records probably will not be redacted. Mail turnaround time same day if possible. Criminal PAT goes back to 2005, some older.

Circuit Court PO Box 927, 1001 Big Horn Ave, Worland, WY 82401; 307-347-2702; fax: 307-347-8459; 8AM-5PM (MST). *Misdemeanor, Civil Actions under $50,000, Small Claims.*
www.courts.state.wy.us/

General Information: This was a Justice Court until 01/03. No juvenile or PD released; criminal only. Fee to fax files is $2.00 per document. Court makes copy: $1.00 1st page; $.50 each add'l. Certification fee: $5.00 per document. Payee: Circuit Court. Personal checks accepted. Credit cards accepted. Prepayment required. Mail requests: SASE not required.

Civil Name Search: Access: Mail, fax. Both court and visitors may perform in person name searches. Search fee: $10.00 per name. Civil cases indexed by defendant. Civil records on computer since 1998, on card index from late 1970, prior archived. Note: Effective 01/01/2011 per State Rule, on all new case files the birth day and birth month and the first five digits of an SSN are redacted on court files viewable by the public. Prior records probably will not be redacted. Mail turnaround time same day. Civil PAT available. Statewide access provided, year of birth shown.

Criminal Name Search: Access: Mail, fax, in person. Both court and visitors may perform in person name searches. Search fee: $10.00 per name. Required to search: name, years to search, DOB; also helpful: SSN. Criminal records on computer since 1995, on card index from late 1970, prior archived. Note: Effective 01/01/2011 per State Rule, on all new case files the birth day and birth month and the first five digits of an SSN are redacted on court files viewable by the public. Prior records probably will not be redacted. Mail turnaround time same day. Criminal PAT available. Statewide access provided, year of birth shown.

Weston County

6th Judicial District Court 1 W Main, Newcastle, WY 82701; 307-746-4778; fax: 307-746-4778; 8AM-5PM (MST). *Felony, Civil Actions over $50,000, Probate.*
www.courts.state.wy.us/

General Information: Probate fax is same as main fax number. No juvenile, sexual or PD released. Fee to fax files is $2.00 per doc plus copy fee. Court makes copy: $1.00 1st page, $.50 each add'l. Certification fee: $.50 per certification. Payee: Clerk of District Court. Personal checks accepted, credit cards are not. Prepayment required. Mail requests: SASE required.

Civil Name Search: Access: Mail, fax, in person. Both court and visitors may perform in person name searches. Search fee: $10.00 per name. Required to search: name; also helpful: years to search, address. Civil records on card index from 1913; computerized back to 1999. Note: Effective 01/01/2011 per State Rule, on all new case files the birth day and birth month and the first five digits of an SSN are redacted on court files viewable by the public. Prior records probably will not be redacted. Mail turnaround time same day.

Criminal Name Search: Access: Phone, fax, mail, in person. Both court and visitors may perform in person name searches. Search fee: $10.00 per name. Required to search: name; also helpful: years to search, address, DOB, SSN. Criminal records on card index from 1913; computerized back to 1999. Note: Effective 01/01/2011 per State Rule, on all new case files the birth day and birth month and the first five digits of an SSN are redacted on court files viewable by the public. Prior records probably will not be redacted. Mail turnaround time same day.

Circuit Court 6 W Warwick, Newcastle, WY 82701; 307-746-3547; fax: 307-746-3558; 8AM-5PM (MST). *Misdemeanor, Civil Actions under $50,000, Small Claims up to $5000.*
www.courts.state.wy.us/

General Information: This was a Justice Court until 01/03. Fee to fax files is $2.00 per document or no charge if search fee paid. Court makes copy: $1.00 first page; $.50 each add'l. Self serve copy: same. Certification fee: $5.00 per document. Payee: Circuit Court. Business checks accepted. Prepayment required. Mail requests: SASE required.

Civil Name Search: Access: Mail, in person. Both court and visitors may perform in person name searches. Search fee: $10.00 per name. Required to search: name, DOB, years to search; also helpful: address. Civil cases indexed by defendant. Civil records in files back to 1970s; on computer back to 1998. Note: For in person civil searches of closed cases, let court know in advance and they will pull the files for you. Effective 01/01/2011 per State Rule, on all new case files the birth day and birth month and the first five digits of an SSN are redacted on court files viewable by the public. Prior records probably will not be redacted.Mail turnaround time minimum 1 day. Civil PAT available. Statewide access provided, year of birth shown.

Criminal Name Search: Access: Mail, in person. Both court and visitors may perform in person name searches. Search fee: $10.00 per name. Required to search: name, years to search, DOB; also helpful: address, offense, date of offense, SSN. Criminal records in files back to 1970s; on computer back to 1996. Note: Effective 01/01/2011 per State Rule, on all new case files the birth day and birth month and the first five digits of an SSN are redacted on court files viewable by the public. Prior records probably will not be redacted. Mail turnaround time minimum 1 day. Criminal PAT available. Statewide access provided, year of birth shown.

A Checklist to Use Before You Place an Order With a Record Retriever

On-site record retrievers represent a key link in the *information food chain*. If you hire record retriever to search for a court record, you should follow some common sense rules. If you are not clear at the outset what you expect a record retriever to do for you, you may be asking for trouble. Major misunderstandings can be avoided if the expectations between the retriever and the client are clearly understood.

The article below is provided by the Public Record Retriever Network (PRRN), see www.prrn.us. Here are ten aspects of a search we think are essential to review before you hire a retriever for any type of public record.

1. Determine Exactly What Type of Records You Want Searched

You must always be crystal clear about what information you need. Do not give the retriever vague instructions. For example regarding Criminal Searches—

An order to do a "criminal record search," is not an adequate description. Is it for felonies only, for felonies and misdemeanors, or for both? If misdemeanors are desired, should the search include DWIs? Is a federal court search also required?

2. Determine Where Do You Want to Search

Frequently this question is associated with the previous question. Simply make sure to ask if there is more than one location where the information requested might be obtained. Court locations provide a complex example in a number of states and counties. A county may have two courts with the same jurisdictions, but without a combined index to search. Or municipal courts in a county may have overlapping jurisdiction with the state court in the county with respect to misdemeanors. You must determine if you wish the retriever to search all or only part of the county court structure.

Another consideration is which county to search. There are over 8,000 ZIP Codes that cross county lines. Your may wish to independently check which county is correct for the given address or ZIP Code of the subject. When asked, the retriever can perform a more thorough job by searching in highly populous contiguous counties where additional records might be located.

3. Decide the Time Period to Search

When hiring a retriever, you need to give specific instructions on how far back to make the search. Better yet, ask what is the retriever's norm or standard search period for that particular county. Many local jurisdictions have computerized an index to records, but the index may only go back a limited number of years. If the date range of the index does not meet your needs, the retriever will need to perform a separate, manual search of the older records.

4. Know the Subject's Name

You should develop standards to determine if the subject name you give a retriever is adequate for searching.

Individual names such as "George H. Ruth" may be adequate for your purposes, or you may want to ask whether the middle initial is known, especially if the name is common. Also, "G. Herman Ruth" may create real search problems for the retriever if you don't know what the "G" stands for.

You will need to state clearly in your request the names you wish to be searched and any constraints or limitations on search procedures due to the form of the name. A retriever may be expected to find common variations of the subject name, but cannot, nor is responsible to, determine all the weird variations that a keypuncher might inflict on a name.

5. Let the Retriever Know if You Anticipate Records or Hits

Public record searching is not a test. It always helps the retriever to know if you are aware of any records that now exist on the subject. You may say, "That's none of his or her business, the retriever is hired to do the search." That's OK, but you realize that public records can be mis-indexed by the filing officers or court personnel. Most retrievers will extend their search procedures beyond their usual thorough methods if they did not get a hit when one was anticipated.

A major trend is for companies to prescreen a name using a supplemental online resource for a particular jurisdiction. In fairness to the retriever, it is appropriate to inform the retriever when this process is used. Another consideration is when a government office charges a lot for copies, and automatically makes copies for all searches. If you know the subject has multiple cases, you may ask the retriever to advise a more cost-efficient way to search the records without incurring substantial copy charges.

6. Prepare to Ask How the Search Will be Conducted

Who performs that actual search? Some agencies require that the names to be searched for be handed over to the clerk who performs the actual search. Some agencies have computer terminals that a researcher can view in person. The researcher may have to type in each name, or the researcher may review a list of names to see if the subject's name appears. Some agencies index names in other searchable formats such as ledgers, microfiche, or microfilm. Some ways may be official, and some unofficial but provided by the agency.

Therefore, it is incumbent upon you to ask the retriever about the possible search methods and clarify how you wish the search to be performed. If for legal reasons you require an "official" search, one done by the government office itself and certified, make that requirement clear at the outset.

In those jurisdictions where a retriever has the option of searching on a private, third party database rather than on the official database of the agency, the retriever should never conduct a search on the private database without your expressed permission.

7. Know What Documents You Want to Obtain or What Results You Want Reported

Obtaining documents can be quite costly. Perhaps you think you are asking for a list or index of public records on a subject and the retriever hands you copies of 500 UCC filings. Make sure you find out first if you have no choice but to obtain documents as part of a search. The retriever should inform you of the possibility of excessive copy costs in advance of performing the search.

What if the retriever finds an exact name match, but another identifier (like a DOB) does not match? What if the first and last name match as well as the DOB, but the middle initial does not? Do you want to have this information reported to you? A good idea is to ask the retriever what his/her standard procedure is when near matches occur. Keep in mind that there have been lawsuits filed by employers when a close match is not reported that was a positive "hit" on a criminal record.

8. Know Your Deadline

Let the retriever know when you need the results and ask if you have a reasonable time expectation. In those jurisdictions where government personnel must perform the search you need to know if the normal turnaround time does not fit your needs. In those situations, ask if the government agency offers an expedited service for an additional fee or you will need to adjust your expectations.

9. Determine How You Want the Results Given to You

Be clear on how you expect the form of delivery of the search results. Do you want them by fax, by telephone, email, overnight courier, or by regular mail? Ask if there are different fees for different delivery methods.

10. Keep a Written Log of the Request

The nine items summarized above should indicate your complete instructions. If you have an ongoing relationship with a retriever, that retriever should maintain a standard set of client instructions for your orders. If you are working with a new or relatively new retriever, you will lose nothing by being comprehensive with your instructions. Keep a log with the date and time the order was placed, the time and method of expected delivery, and whom you spoke if you placed the order by telephone. Using standard, written procedures will minimize the chances of making a mistake and help insure your instructions are legible and complete.

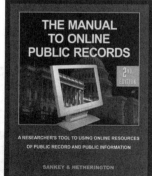